THIS VOLUME IS DEDICATED TO
SYDNEY GREENSTREET
BUTTERFLY MCQUEEN
ART CARNEY
LILLIAN GISH
JACKIE COOPER
THELMA RITTER
and all the great
character people

THE MOTION PICTURE GUIDE

THE MOTION PICTURE GUIDE

N - R

1927 - 1983

Jay Robert Nash
Stanley Ralph Ross

CINEBOOKS, INC.

Chicago, 1986

Publishers of THE COMPLETE FILM RESOURCE CENTER

Publishers: Jay Robert Nash, Stanley Ralph Ross; **Editor-in-Chief:** Jay Robert Nash; **Executive Editor:** Stanley Ralph Ross; **Associate Publisher and Director of Development:** Kenneth H. Petchenik; **Senior Editor-in-Charge:** Jim McCormick; **Senior Editors:** David Tardy, Robert B. Connelly; **Production Editor:** William Leahy; **Associate Editors:** Oksana Lydia Creighton, Jeffrey H. Wallenfeldt, Edie McCormick, Michaela Tuohy, Jeannette Hori, **Contributing Editors:** James J. Mulay (Chief Contributing Editor), Daniel Curran, Michael Theobald, Arnie Bernstein, Phil Pantone, Brian Brock; Andrew Ross, **Assistant Editors:** Debra Schwieder, Susan Fisher, Donna Roth, Marla Kruglik, Kristina Marcy, Sarah von Fremd, Wendy Anderson; **Art Production and Book Design:** Cathy Anetsberger; **Research Staff:** Shelby Payne (Associate Editor and Chief Researcher), William C. Clogston, Tobi Elliott, Carol Pappas, Rosalyn Mathis, Millicent Mathis, Andrea Nash; **Business/Legal:** Judy Anetsberger.

Associate Publishers: Howard Grafman, Lynn Christian, James and Monica Vrettos, Antoinette Mailliard, Brent H. Nettle, Michael Callie, Constance Shea, Barbara Browne Cramer.

Editorial and Sales Offices: CINEBOOKS, 6135 N. Sheridan Road, Chicago; Illinois 60660.

Library of Congress Catalog Card Number: 85-071145
ISBN: 0-933997-00-0 THE MOTION PICTURE GUIDE (10 Vols.)
        0-933997-06-X THE MOTION PICTURE GUIDE, Vol VI (N–R)

Printed in the United States
First Edition
This volume contains 4,327 entries.

1 2 3 4 5 6 7 8 9 10

HOW TO USE INFORMATION IN THIS GUIDE

ALPHABETICAL ORDER

All entries have been arranged alphabetically throughout this and all subsequent volumes. In establishing alphabetical order, all articles (A, An, The) appear after the main title (AFFAIR TO REMEMBER, AN). In the case of foreign films the article precedes the main title (LES MISERABLES appears in the letter L) which makes, we feel, for easier access and uniformity. Contractions are grouped together and these will be followed by non-apostrophized words of the same letters. B.F.'s DAUGHTER is at the beginning of the letter B, not under BF.

TITLES

It is important to know what title you are seeking; use the *complete* title of the film. The film ADVENTURES OF ROBIN HOOD, THE, cannot be found under merely ROBIN HOOD. Many films are known under different titles and we have taken great pains to cross-reference these titles. (AKA, also known as) as well as alternate titles used in Great Britain (GB). In addition to the cross-reference title only entries, AKAs and alternate titles in Great Britain can be found in the title line for each entry. An alphabetically arranged comprehensive list of title changes appears in the Index volume (Vol. X).

RATINGS

We have rated each and every film at critical levels that include acting, directing, script, and technical achievement (or the sad lack of it). We have a *five-star* rating, unlike all other rating systems, to signify a film superbly made on every level, in short, a masterpiece. At the lowest end of the scale is *zero* and we mean it. The ratings are as follows: *zero* (not worth a glance), *(poor), **(fair), ***(good), ****(excellent), *****(masterpiece, and these are few and far between). Half-marks mean almost there but not quite.

YEAR OF RELEASE

We have used in all applicable instances the year of United States release. This sometimes means that a film released abroad may have a different date elsewhere than in these volumes but this is generally the date released in foreign countries, not in the U.S.

FOREIGN COUNTRY PRODUCTION

When possible, we have listed abbreviated names of the foreign countries originating the production of a film. This information will be found within the parenthesis containing the year of release. If no country is listed in this space, it is a U.S. production.

RUNNING TIME

A hotly debated category, we have opted to list the running time a film ran at the time of its initial U.S. release but we will usually mention in the text if the film was drastically cut and give the reasons why. We have attempted to be as accurate as possible by consulting the most reliable sources.

PRODUCING AND DISTRIBUTING COMPANIES

The producing and/or distributing company of every film is listed in abbreviated entries next to the running time in the title line (see abbreviations; for all those firms not abbreviated, the entire firm's name will be present).

COLOR OR BLACK-AND-WHITE

The use of color or black-and-white availability appears as c or bw following the producing/releasing company entry.

CASTS

Whenever possible, we give *the complete cast and the roles played* for each film and this is the case in 95% of all entries, the only encyclopedia to ever offer such comprehensive information in covering the entire field. The names of actors and actresses are in Roman lettering, the names of the roles each played in Italic inside parentheses.

SYNOPSIS

The in-depth synopsis for each entry (when such applies) offers the plot of each film, critical evaluation, anecdotal information on the production and its personnel, awards won when applicable and additional information dealing with the production's impact upon the public, its success or failure at the box office, its social significance, if any. Acting methods, technical innovations, script originality are detailed. We also cite other productions involving an entry's personnel for critical comparisons and to establish the style or genre of expertise of directors, writers, actors and technical people.

REMAKES AND SEQUELS

Information regarding films that have sequels, sequels themselves or direct remakes of films can be found at the very end of each synopsis.

DUBBING AND SUBTITLES

We will generally point out in the synopsis when a foreign film is dubbed in English, mostly when the dubbing is poor. When voices are dubbed, particularly when singers render vocals on songs mimed by stars, we generally point out these facts either in the cast/role listing or inside the synopsis. If a film is in a foreign language and subtitled, we signify the fact in a parenthetical statement at the end of each entry (In Italian, English subtitles).

CREDITS

The credits for the creative and technical personnel of a film are extensive and they include: p (producer, often executive producer); d (director); w (screenwriter, followed by adaptation, if any, and creator of original story, if any, and other sources such as authors for plays, articles, short stories, novels and non-fiction books); ph (cinematographer, followed by camera system and color process when applicable, i.e., Panavision, Technicolor); m (composer of musical score); ed (film editor); md (music director); art d (art director); set d (set decoration); cos (costumes); spec eff (special effects); ch (choreography); m/l (music and lyrics); stunts, makeup, and other credits when merited. When someone receives two or more credits in a single film the credits may be combined (p&d, John Ford) or the last name repeated in subsequent credits shared with another (d, John Ford; w, Ford, Dudley Nichols).

GENRES/SUBJECT

Each film is categorized for easy identification as to genre and/or subject and themes at the left-hand bottom of each entry. (Western, Prison Drama, Spy Drama, Romance, Musical, Comedy, War, Horror, Science-Fiction, Adventure, Biography, Historical Drama, Children's Film, Animated Feature, etc.) More specific subject and theme breakdowns will be found in the Index (Vol. X).

PR AND MPAA RATINGS

The Parental Recommendation provides parents having no knowledge of the style and content of each film with a guide; if a film has excessive violence, sex, strong language, it is so indicated. Otherwise, films specifically designed for young children are also indicated. The Parental Recommendation (**PR**) is to be found at the right-hand bottom of each entry, followed, when applicable, by the **MPAA** rating. The PR ratings are as follows: **AAA** (must for children); **AA** (good for children); **A** (acceptable for children); **C** (cautionary, some objectionable scenes); **O** (completely objectionable for children).

KEY TO ABBREVIATIONS

Foreign Countries:

Arg.	Argentina
Aus.	Australia
Aust.	Austria
Bel.	Belgium
Braz.	Brazil
Brit.	Great Britain (GB when used for alternate title)
Can.	Canada
Chi.	China
Czech.	Czechoslovakia
Den.	Denmark
E. Ger.	East Germany
Fin.	Finland
Fr.	France
Ger.	Germany (includes W. Germany)
Gr.	Greece
Hung.	Hungary
Ital.	Italy
Jap.	Japan
Mex.	Mexico
Neth.	Netherlands
Phil.	Philippines
Pol.	Poland
Rum.	Rumania
S.K.	South Korea
Span.	Spain
Swed.	Sweden

Key to Abbreviations (continued)

Switz.	Switzerland
Thai.	Thailand
USSR	Union of Soviet Socialist Republics
Yugo.	Yugoslavia

Production Companies, Studios and Distributors (U.S. and British)

AA	ALLIED ARTISTS
ABF	Associated British Films
AE	Avco Embassy
AEX	Associated Exhibitors
AH	Anglo-Hollandia
AIP	American International Pictures
AM	American
ANCH	Anchor Film Distributors
ANE	American National Enterprises
AP	Associated Producers
AP&D	Associated Producers & Distributors
ARC	Associated Releasing Corp.
Argosy	Argosy Productions
Arrow	Arrow Films
ART	Artcraft
Astra	Astra Films
AY	Aywon
BA	British Actors
B&C	British and Colonial Kinematograph Co.
BAN	Banner Films
BI	British Instructional
BIFD	B.I.F.D. Films
BIP	British International Pictures
BJP	Buck Jones Productions
BL	British Lion
Blackpool	Blackpool Productions
BLUE	Bluebird
BN	British National
BNF	British and Foreign Film
Boulting	Boulting Brothers (Brit.)
BP	British Photoplay Production
BPP	B.P. Productions
BRIT	Britannia Films
BRO	Broadwest
Bryanston	Bryantston Films (Brit.)
BS	Blue Streak
BUS	Bushey (Brit.)
BUT	Butchers Film Service
BV	Buena Vista (Walt Disney)
CAP	Capital Films
CC	Christie Comedy
CD	Continental Distributing
CHAD	Chadwick Pictures Corporation
CHES	Chesterfield
Cineguild	Cineguild
CL	Clarendon
CLIN	Clinton
COL	COLUMBIA
Colony	Colony Pictures
COM	Commonwealth
COMM	Commodore Pictures
COS	Cosmopolitan (Hearst)
DE	Dependable Exchange
DGP	Dorothy Gish Productions
Disney	Walt Disney Productions
DIST	Distinctive
DM	DeMille Productions
DOUB	Doubleday
EAL	Ealing Studios (Brit.)
ECF	East Coast Films
ECL	Eclectic
ED	Eldorado
EF	Eagle Films
EFF & EFF	E.F.F. & E.F.F. Comedy
EFI	English Films Inc.
EIFC	Export and Import Film Corp.
EL	Eagle-Lion
EM	Embassy Pictures Corp.

EMI	EMI Productions
EP	Enterprise Pictures
EPC	Equity Pictures Corp.
EQ	Equitable
EXCEL	Excellent
FA	Fine Arts
FC	Film Classics
FD	First Division
FN	First National
FOX	20TH CENTURY FOX (and Fox Productions)
FP	Famous Players (and Famous Players Lasky)
FRP	Frontroom Productions
Gainsborough	Gainsborough Productions
GAU	Gaumont (Brit.)
GEN	General
GFD	General Films Distributors
Goldwyn	Samuel Goldwyn Productions
GN	Grand National
GOTH	Gotham
Grafton	Grafton Films (Brit.)
H	Harma
HAE	Harma Associated Distributors
Hammer	Hammer Films (Brit.)
HD	Hagen and Double
HM	Hi Mark
HR	Hal Roach
IA	International Artists
ID	Ideal
IF	Independent Film Distributors (Brit.)
Imperator	Imperator Films (Brit.)
IP	Independent Pictures Corp.
IN	Invincible Films
INSP	Inspirational Pictures (Richard Barthelmess)
IV	Ivan Film
Javelin	Javelin Film Productions (Brit.)
JUR	Jury
KC	Kinema Club
KCB	Kay C. Booking
Knightsbridge	Knightsbridge Productions (Brit.)
Korda	Alexander Korda Productions (Brit.)
Ladd	Ladd Company Productions
LAS	Lasky Productions (Jesse L. Lasky)
LFP	London Films
LIP	London Independent Producers
Lorimar	Lorimar Productions
LUM	Lumis
Majestic	Majestic Films
Mascot	Mascot Films
Mayflowers	Mayflowers Productions (Brit.)
Metro	Metro
MFC	Mission Film Corporation
MG	Metro-Goldwyn
MGM	METRO-GOLDWYN-MAYER
MON	Monogram
MOR	Morante
MS	Mack Sennett
MUT	Mutual
N	National
NG	National General
NGP	National General Pictures (Alexander Korda, Brit.)
NW	New World
Orion	Orion Productions
Ortus	Ortus Productions (Brit.)
PAR	PARAMOUNT
Pascal	Gabriel Pascal Productions (Brit.)
PDC	Producers Distributors Corp.

Key to Abbreviations (continued)

PEER	Peerless	Beta	Beta Films (Ger.)
PWN	Peninsula Studios	CA	Cine-Alliance (Fr.)
PFC	Pacific Film Company	Caddy	Caddy Films (Fr.)
PG	Playgoers	CCFC	Compagnie Commerciale Francais Einematographique (Fr.)
PI	Pacific International	CDD	Cino Del Duca (Ital.)
PIO	Pioneer Film Corp.	CEN	Les Films de Centaur (Fr.)
PM	Pall Mall	CFD	Czecheslovak Film Productions
PP	Pro Patria	CHAM	Champion (Ital.)
PRC	Producers Releasing Corporation	Cinegay	Cinegay Films (Ital.)
PRE	Preferred	Cines	Cines Films (Ital.)
		Cineriz	Cinerez Films (Ital.)
QDC	Quality Distributing Corp.	Citel	Citel Films (Switz.)
		Como	Como Films (Fr.)
RAY	Rayart	CON	Concordia (Fr.)
RAD	Radio Pictures	Corona	Corona Films (Fr.)
RANK	J. Arthur Rank (Brit.)		
RBP	Rex Beach Pictures	D	Documento Films (Ital.)
REA	Real Art	DD	Dino De Laurentiis (Ital.)
REG	Regional Films	Dear	Dear Films (Ital.)
REN	Renown	DIF	Discina International Films (Fr.)
REP	Republic	DPR	Films du Palais-Royal (Fr.)
RF	Regal Films		
RFD	R.F.D. Productions (Brit.)	EX	Excelsa Films (Ital.)
RKO	RKO RADIO PICTURES		
Rogell	Rogell	FDP	Films du Pantheon (Fr.)
Romulus	Romulus Films (Brit.)	Fono	Fono Roma (Ital.)
Royal	Royal	FS	Filmsonor Productions (Fr.)
SB	Samuel Bronston	Gala	Fala Films (Ital.)
SCHUL	B.P. Schulberg Productions	Galatea	Galatea Productions (Ital.)
SEL	Select	Gamma	Gamma Films (Fr.)
SELZ	Selznick International (David O. Selznick)	Gemma	Gemma Cinematografica (Ital.)
SF	Selznick Films	GFD	General Film Distributors, Ltd. (Can.)
SL	Sol Lesser	GP	General Productions (Fr.)
SONO	Sonofilms	Gray	(Gray Films (Fr.)
SP	Seven Pines Productions (Brit.)		
SRP	St. Regis Pictures	IFD	Intercontinental Film Distributors
STER	Sterling		
STOLL	Stoll	Janus	Janus Films (Ger.)
SUN	Sunset	JMR	Macques Mage Releasing (Fr.)
SYN	Syndicate Releasing Co.		
SZ	Sam Zimbalist	LF	Les Louvre Films (Fr.)
		LFM	Les Films Moliere (Fr.)
TC	Two Cities (Brit.)	Lux	Lux Productions (Ital.)
T/C	Trem-Carr		
THI	Thomas H. Ince	Melville	Melville Productions (Fr.)
TIF	Tiffany	Midega	Midega Films (Span.)
TRA	Transatlantic Pictures		
TRU	Truart	NEF	N.E.F. La Nouvelle Edition Francaise (Fr.)
TS	Tiffany/Stahl	NFD	N.F.D. Productions (Ger.)
UA	UNITED ARTISTS	ONCIC	Office National pour le Commerce et L'Industrie Cinematographique (Fr.)
UNIV	UNIVERSAL (AND UNIVERSAL INTERNATIONAL)	Ortus	Ortus Films (Can.)
Venture	Venture Distributors	PAC	Production Artistique Cinematographique (Fr.)
VIT	Vitagraph	Pagnol	Marcel Pagnol Productions (Fr.)
		Parc	Parc Films (Fr.)
WAL	Waldorf	Paris	Paris Films (Fr.)
WB	WARNER BROTHERS (AND WARNER BROTHERS-SEVEN ARTS)	Pathe	Pathe Films (Fr.)
		PECF	Productions et Editions Cinematographique Francais (Fr.)
WEST	Westminster	PF	Parafrench Releasing Co. (Fr.)
WF	Woodfall Productions (Brit.)	PIC	Produzione International Cinematografica (Ital.)
WI	Wisteria	Ponti	Carlo Ponti Productions (Ital.)
WORLD	World		
WSHP	William S. Hart Productions	RAC	Realisation d'Art Cinematographique (Fr.)
		Regina	Regina Films (Fr.)
ZUKOR	Adolph Zukor Productions	Renn	Renn Productions (Fr.)
		SDFS	Societe des Films Sonores Tobis (Fr.)
Foreign		SEDIF	Societe d'Exploitation ed de Distribution de Films (Fr.)
ABSF	AB Svensk Film Industries (Swed.)	SFP	Societe Francais de Production (Fr.)
Action	Action Films (Fr.)	Sigma	Sigma Productions (Fr.)
ADP	Agnes Delahaie Productions (Fr.)	SNE	Societe Nouvelle des Establishments (Fr.)
Agata	Agata Films (Span.)		
Alter	Alter Films (Fr.)	Titanus	Titanus Productions (Ital.)
Arch	Archway Film Distributors	TRC	Transcontinental Films (Fr.)
Argos	Argos Films (Fr.)		
Argui	Argui Films (Fr.)	UDIF	U.D.I.F. Productions (Fr.)
Ariane	Les Films Ariane (Fr.)	UFA	Deutsche Universum-Film AG (Ger.)
Athos	Athos Films (Fr.)	UGC	Union Generale Cinematographique (Fr.)
		Union	Union Films (Ger.)
Belga	Belga Films (Bel.)		
		Vera	Vera Productions (Fr.)

N

N. P.** (1971, Ital.) 106m Zeta-A-Elle c (AKA: N.P.—THE SECRET)
Francesco Rabal (*N.P.*), Ingrid Thulin (*His Wife*), Irene Papas (*Housewife*).

A futuristic fable with a potentially interesting premise about an industrial tycoon who is abducted and brainwashed before he is able to enact a plan to replace human workers with automation. His memory is erased and he is turned into a common laborer, eventually rising to a leader in a worker's rights movement. Unfortunately hampered by Agosti's stale direction.

p, Enrico Zaccaria; d&w, Silvano Agosti; ph, Nicola Dimitri; m, Nicola Piovani; art d, Isabella Genoese.

Science Fiction/Political Drama (PR:A MPAA:NR)

NA SEMI VETRAKH (SEE: HOUSE, ON THE WATER FRONT LINE, THE, 1963)

NABONGA zero (1944) 72m PRC bw (GB: JUNGLE WOMAN; AKA: GORILLA)

Buster Crabbe (*Ray Gorman*), Fifi D'Orsay (*Marie*), Barton MacLane (*Carl Hurst*), Julie London (*Doreen Stockwell*), Bryant Washburn (*Hunter*), Herbert Rawlinson (*Stockwell*), Prince Modupe (*Tobo*), Jackie Newfield (*Doreen, Child*), Nabonga (*The Gorilla*).

London, the daughter of an embezzler, crash lands in the Belgian Congo, and befriends a wounded gorilla. Nabonga, as the gorilla is called, serves as her protector for several years until Crabbe shows up looking for the embezzled cash. London persuades Nabonga that Crabbe is OK, and the big ape helps him fight the villainous MacLane and D'Orsay. This film marked London's screen debut.

p, Sigmund Neufeld; d, Sam Newfield; w, Fred Myton; ph, Robert Cline; m, David Chudnow; ed, Holbrook N. Todd.

Adventure **Cas.** (PR:A MPAA:NR)

NACHTS, WENN DER TEUFEL KAM (SEE: DEVIL STRIKES AT NIGHT, THE, 1959, Ger.)

NACKT UNTER WOLFEN (SEE: NAKED AMONG THE WOLVES, 1967, Ger.)

NADA (SEE: NADA GANG, THE, 1974, Fr./Ital.)

NADA GANG, THE** (1974, Fr./Ital.) 128m Les Films La Boetie-Italian International/New Line c (AKA: NADA)

Fabio Testi (*Diaz*), Mariangela Melato (*Cash*), Maurice Garrel (*Epaulard*), Michel Duchaussoy (*Treufais*), Maurice Aumont (*Goemond*), Didier Kaminka (*Meyer*), Lou Castel (*D'Arcy*), Katia Romanoff (*Anna*), Andre Falcon (*Minister*), Lyle Joyce (*Ambassador*), Viviane Romance (*Gabrielle*), François Perrot (*Chief*).

A partially effective political drama about a terrorist group called Nada which kidnaps an American ambassador in Paris. A sadistic police inspector eventually corners the terrorists in a farm house and everyone involved, including the ambassador, is shot down. One of the better films in director Chabrol's 1970s decline, which is not saying much.

p, Andre Genoves; d, Claude Chabrol; w, Chabrol, Jean-Patrick Manchette (based on the book by Manchette); ph, Jean Rabier (Eastmancolor); ed, Jacques Gaillard.

Drama/Crime (PR:A MPAA:NR)

NADA MAS QUE UNA MUJER*½ (1934) 100m FOX bw

Berta Singerman, Alfredo del Diestro, Juan Torena, Luana Alcaniz, Lucio Villegas, Carmen Rodrigues, Julian Rivero.

Singerman is an artist in the Philippines who has fallen on hard times and is forced to support herself by reciting poetry in sleazy bars. She falls in love with a young American who is temporarily blind after receiving a beating at the hands of some Filipino hooligans. Spanish-language film shot at the same time and on the same sets as PURSUED, an American film, starring Rosemary Ames and Pert Kelton. A pleasant musical diversion for the bilingual. (In Spanish.)

d, Harry Lachman; w, Raymond Van Sickle, John Reinhardt; Spanish dialog, Miguel de Zarraga.

Musical (PR:A MPAA:NR)

NAGANA** (1933) 72m UNIV bw

Tala Birell (*Countess Sandra Lubeska*), Melvyn Douglas (*Dr. Walter Radnor*), Mike Morita (*Dr. Kabayochi*), Onslow Stevens (*Dr. Roy Stark*), Everett Brown (*Nogu*), Dr. Billie McClain (*The King*), William H. Dunn (*Mukovo*), Frank Lackteen (*Ivory Trader*), Noble Johnson (*Head Boatman*).

An attempt to give rise to another Marlene Dietrich was the goal of this picture which starred Birell as a countess in the African jungle tagging along after Douglas, a doctor searching for a cure for Nagana, the native word for sleeping sickness. Douglas and Birell fight native supersittions and crocodiles before surrendering to science and romance. Birell soon sank from sight after a brief movie stint.

d, Ernst L. Frank; w, Dale Van Every, James Light, Don Ryan (based on the story by Lester Cohen); ph, George Robinson.

Adventure (PR:A MPAA:NR)

NAKED ALIBI*** (1954) 85m UNIV bw

Sterling Hayden (*Joseph E. Conroy*), Gloria Grahame (*Marianna*), Gene Barry (*Al Willis*), Marcia Henderson (*Helen Willis*), Casey Adams (*Detective Lt. Parks*), Billy Chapin (*Petey*), Chuck Connors (*Capt. Owen Kincaide*), Don Haggerty (*Matt Matthews*), Stuart Randall (*Chief A. S. Babcock*), Don Garrett (*Tony*), Richard Beach (*Felix*), Tol Avery (*Irish*), Paul Leavitt (*Gerald Frazier*), Fay Roope (*Commissioner F. J. O'Day*), Joseph Mell (*Otto Stoltz*), Bud Wolfe (*Lt. Fitzpatrick*), John Day (*Sgt. Jenkins*), Frank Wilcox (*Goodwin*).

A hard-hitting chase film, NAKED ALIBI stars Hayden as a detective discharged from his duties when he accuses Barry, a pillar of the community, of the murder of three police officers. Hayden persists with his inquiries to prove that he is correct, following Barry to the Mexican border town where his girl friend, Grahame, is a singer. Hayden captures Barry but lets him escape in the hope that the murder weapon will emerge. This results in a wild rooftop chase in which Grahame is killed and Barry falls to the pavement below.

p, Ross Hunter; d, Jerry Hopper; w, Lawrence Roman (based on the story "Cry Copper" by Robert Breen, Cladys Atwater); ph, Russell Metty; m, George Mitchell, James Dempsey; ed, Al Clark; cos, Rosemary Odell; ch, Kenny Williams.

Crime Drama (PR:A MPAA:NR)

NAKED AMONG THE WOLVES*** (1967, Ger.) 100m DEFA/Lopert bw (NACKT UNTER WOLFEN)

Erwin Geschonneck (*Kramer*), Fred Delmare (*Pippig*), Gerry Wolff (*Bockow*), Armin Mueller-Stahl (*Hofel*), Boleslaw Plotnicki (*Janowski*), Krystyn Wojcik (*Kropinski*), Peter Sturm (*Rose*), Viktor Avdiushko (*Bogorski*), Wolfram Handel (*Zweiling*), Fred Ludwig (*Mandrill*), Gerd Ehlers (*Gay*), Erik S. Klein, Herbert Kofer, Heinz Scholz, Zygmunt Malanowicz, Jan Pohan, Leonid Swjetlow, Bruno Apitz, Werner Mohring, Joachim Tomaschewsky, Hermann Eckhardt, Peter-Paul Goest, Gunter Ruger, Angela Brunner, Albert Zahn, Werner Dissel, Christoph Engel, Hans-Helmut Kruger, Joachim Jablouski, Jurgen Strauch, Hans Hardt-Hardtloff, Richard Hilgert, Steffen Klaus, Janusz Roszkowski, Boris Suchow, Klaus Urban.

A powerful film of hope and determination set against the background of Germany's death camps during the last days of WW II. During a transfer of prisoners, a small Jewish boy, Delmare, is saved from the gas chambers by hiding in a suitcase. A young German officer eavesdrops on a group of inmates talking about Delmare and an intense search for the boy is held. When American planes are sighted, the prisoners begin to revolt using their stock of stolen weapons. Although many die, Delmare is fortunate enough to survive the battle and is given his freedom.

p, Hans Mahlich; d, Frank Beyer; w, Willi Schafer, Alfred Hirschmeier (based on a story by Bruno Apitz); ph, Gunter Marszinkowsky (Totalscope); ed, Hildegard Conrad; art d, Alfred Hirschmeier; cos, Gunther Schmidt; makeup, Kurt Tauchmann.

War Drama (PR:C MPAA:NR)

NAKED AND THE DEAD, THE* (1958) 131m RKO-Gregjac/WB c

Aldo Ray (*Croft*), Cliff Robertson (*Hearn*), Raymond Massey (*Gen. Cummings*), Lili St. Cyr (*Lily*), William Campbell (*Brown*), Barbara Nichols (*Mildred*), Richard Jaeckel (*Gallagher*), James Best (*Ridges*), Joey Bishop (*Roth*), Jerry Paris (*Goldstein*), Robert Gist (*Red*), L.Q. Jones (*Wilson*), Casey Adams (*Dalleson*), John Berardino (*Mantelli*), Edward McNally (*Conn*), Greg Roman (*Minetta*), Henry Amargo (*Martinez*).

A dismal film of a talky, overrated novel from Mailer, darling of the New York literati. Perhaps the only motivation for making this posturing mess was the enormous success of the book, which was more notorious for its foul language than credited for its literary achievement. The film follows the WW II exploits of a doomed platoon involved in the taking of a small Pacific island and how its members are killed one by one. The incessant intellectual bantering and heaving of hyperbole between Robertson and his military superior, Massey, is a big waste of time. The acting is terrible, the direction is sluggish and uninspired, and even the production credits are weak. What do come through loud and clear are Mailer's cynical attitudes, which were originally collected in a college white paper that was later thrown en masse into the novel, or so it seems. This is also a brutal, excessively violent film that gratuitously dismembers and shrivels bodies. Its dialog and action are full of hate, bitterness, and resentment. Symbolic of the production and story is the strip-tease by burlesque queen St. Cyr, which the producers threw into the film which, in fact, is probably the best thing about this lowbrow, cross-eyed view of WW II.

p, Paul Gregory; d, Raoul Walsh; w, Denis Sanders, Terry Sanders (based on a novel by Norman Mailer); ph, Joseph LaShelle (WarnerScope, Technicolor); m, Bernard Herrmann; ed, Arthur P. Schmidt; art d, Ted Haworth, William L. Kuehl; md, Herrmann.

War **Cas.** (PR:O MPAA:NR)

NAKED ANGELS* (1969) 83m Favorite/Crown International-Goldstone c

Michael Greene (*Mother*), Jennifer Gan (*Marlene*), Richard Rust (*Fingers*), Art Jenoff, Felicia Guy, Leonard Coates, Tedd King, Bruce Sunkees, Corey Fischer, Sahn Berti, Howard Lester, Joe Kasey, Glenn Lee, Penelope Sprerris, Carol Ries, Pat McChrystle.

Roger Corman acted as executive producer on this cheapie biker flick about an animalistic Los Angeles gang leader (Greene), who seeks revenge on a rival Las Vegas gang, the Hotdoggers. Greene and his pals leaves miles of dust clouds behind them as they zoom through the desert in search of the Hotdoggers' hidden haven. His violent attitude is too much for even his friends (imagine how he treats his enemies), and they kick him out of his own gang. Eventually they have a change of heart, let him back in, and ride off in the hopes of kicking the sand out of the Hotdoggers. With a name as dumb as the Hotdoggers, they deserve to get some sense beaten into them.

p, David R. Dawdy; d&w, Bruce Clark; ph, Robert Eberlein, Bill Kaplan (EastmanColor); ed, Johanna Bryant.

Action **(PR:O MPAA:R)**

NAKED APE, THE* (1973) 85m UNIV c

Johnny Crawford *(Lee)*, Victoria Principal *(Cathy)*, Dennis Olivieri *(Arnie)*. Diana Darrin, Robert Ito, John Hellerman, Marvin Miller, Norman Grabowski, Brett Parker, Helen Horowitz.

Produced by *Playboy* magnate Hugh Hefner, this boring semi-documentary traces man's evolution from the apeman to the present day. Full of metaphors, sexuality, and humor that isn't too rough for the younger set, guaranteeing a PG rating. Stars Victoria Principal who later evolved into a member of TV's "Dallas."

p, Zev Bufman; d&w, Donald Driver (based on the book by Desmond Morris); ph, John Alonzo (Technicolor); m, Jimmy Webb; ed, Michael Economou, Robert L. Wolfe; prod d, Lawrence G. Paull; set d, Nick Romanac; animation, Charles Swenson.

Comedy/Fantasy **(PR:C MPAA:PG)**

NAKED AUTUMN** (1963, Fr.) 98m United bw (LES MAUVAIS COUPS)

Simone Signoret *(Roberte)*, Reginald Kernan *(Milan)*, Alexandra Stewart *(Helene)*, Marcel Pagliero *(Luigi)*, Serge Rousseau *(Duval)*, Serge Sauvion, Marie-Claude Poirier, Dorian Leigh Parker, Nicole Chollet, Marcelle Ranson, Antoine Roblot, Jose Luis de Vilallonga.

The story of a love between two people that begins to wane after 10 wonderful years of marriage. The film stars Kernan as a former race car driver who plans to write his autobiography with his wife, Signoret. They meet Stewart, a young school teacher, through whom Signoret relives her youth, and with whom Kernan falls in love. Kernan decides to return to the race track, but instead of taking one woman with him, he leaves them both.

p, Jean Thuillier; d, Francois Leterrier; w, Roger Vailland, Leterrier; ph, Jean Badal (Dyaliscope); m, Maurice Le Roux; ed, Leonide Azar; art d, Pierre Charbonnier.

Drama **(PR:A MPAA:NR)**

NAKED BRIGADE, THE** (1965, U.S./Gr.) 99m Box Office Attractions-Alfa Studios/UNIV bw (HE GYMNE TAXIARCHIA)

Shirley Eaton *(Diana Forsythe)*, Ken Scott *(Christo)*, Mary Chronopoulou *(Katina)*, John Holland *(Maj. Hamilton)*, Sonia Zoidou *(Athena)*, Eleni Zaferiou *(Sofia)*, Aris Vlachopoulos *(Father Nicholas)*, Patrick Kavanaugh *(Lt. Bentley)*, Clive Russell *(Cpl. Reade)*, Nicholas Papakonstantantinou *(Maj. Heilmann)*, Karl Nurk *(Professor Forsythe)*, Christopher Himaras *(Spyros Karrayiannis)*, Socrates Corres *(Lefteris Karrayiannis)*, Zanino Papadopoulos *(Yannis Karrayiannis)*, Gikas Biniaris *(Stavros Karrayiannis)*, Kostas Balademas *(Manolakakis)*.

In 1941, Eaton arrives on the island of Crete just ahead of the Nazi invasion. She wants to get her archaeologist father, Nurk, off the island and to England before it is too late. The Nazis invade the island soon after and Nurk is killed. Eaton finds refuge with an all-girl force of guerrillas led by Scott. Eaton helps them and Scott offers to get her back to England. After one escape attempt fails, Eaton continues to help the band of freedom fighters and falls in love with Scott. The finale of the film has the girls stripping off their fatigues and swimming underwater to blow up a German munitions ship docked in port. With the important mission over, Scott arranges for a British submarine to take Eaton back to safety. Eaton probably is best known as the painted girl from GOLDFINGER.

p, Albert J. Cohen; d, Maury Dexter; w, Cohen, A. Sanford Wolf (based on a story by Irwin Winehouse, Wolf); ph, Aristedes Karides-Fuchs; m, Theo Fanidi; ed, El Siaskas; art d, Em Zampelas; spec eff, John Samiotis.

War **(PR:A MPAA:NR)**

NAKED CHILDHOOD (SEE: ME, 1970, Fr.)

NAKED CITY, THE**** (1948) 96m UNIV bw

Barry Fitzgerald *(Lt. Dan Muldoon)*, Howard Duff *(Frank Niles)*, Dorothy Hart *(Ruth Morrison)*, Don Taylor *(Jimmy Halloran)*, Ted de Corsia *(Garzah)*, House Jameson *(Dr. Stoneman)*, Anne Sargent *(Mrs. Halloran)*, Adelaide Klein *(Mrs. Batory)*, Grover Burgess *(Mr. Batory)*, Tom Pedi *(Detective Perelli)*, Enid Markey *(Mrs. Hylton)*, Frank Conroy *(Capt. Donahue)*, Mark Hellinger *(Narrator)*, Walter Burke *(Backalis)*, David Opatoshu *(Ben Miller)*, John McQuade *(Constantino)*, Hester Sondergaard *(Nurse)*, Paul Ford *(Henry Fowler)*, Ralph Bunker *(Dr. Hoffman)*, Curt Conway *(Nick)*, Kermit Kegley *(Qualen)*, George Lynn *(Fredericks)*, Arthur O'Connell *(Shaeffer)*, Jean Adair *(Little Old Lady)*, Nicholas Joy *(McCormick)*, Virginia Mullen *(Martha)*, Beverly Bayne *(Mrs. Stoneman)*, Celia Adler *(Proprietor)*, Grace Coppin *(Miss Livingston)*, Robert Harris *(Druggist)*, James Gregory *(Hicks)*, Edwin Jerome *(Publisher)*, Amelia Romano *(Shop Girl)*, Anthony Rivers *(Ed Garzah)*, Bernard Hoffman *(Wrestler)*, Elliott Sullivan *(Trainer)*, Charles P. Thompson *(Ticket Taker)*, G. Pat Collins *(Freed)*, John Marley *(Managing Editor)*, Russ Conway *(Ambulance Doctor)*, Joe Kerr *(Ned Harvey)*, William Cottrell *(Bisbee)*, Mervin Williams *(Clerk)*, John Randolph *(Policeman)*, Cavada Humphrey *(Mother)*, Stevie Harris *(Halloran's Son)*, Al Kelley *(Newsboy)*, Ray [Raymond] Greenleaf *(City Editor)*, Johnny Dale *(Mr. Stillman)*, Judson Laire *(Publisher)*, Joyce Allen *(Shop Girl)*, Sarah Cunningham *(Nurse)*, Ralph Simone *(Old Gentleman)*, Pearl Gaines *(Maid)*, Alexander Campbell *(Policeman)*, Harris Brown *(Janitor)*, Carl Milletaire *(Young Man)*, Kathleen Freeman *(Stout Girl)*, Lee Shumway *(Patrolman)*, Perc Launders *(Police Photographer)*, Earle Gilbert *(Banker)*, Victor Zimmerman, David Kermen, George Sherwood, *(Patrolmen)*, Andre D. Foster *(Jeweler)*, Blanche Obronska *(Mother)*, William Green *(Man)*, Marion Leeds *(Nurse)*, Joseph Karney *(Wrestler)*, Janie Leslie Alexander *(Little Girl)*, Richard W. Shankland *(Blind Man)*, Retta Coleman *(Crippled Girl)*, Mildred Stronger, Carole Selvester, Clifford Sales, Maureen Latorella, Charles Latorella, Denise Doyle, Margaret McAndrew, Marsha McClelland, Bobbie Gusehoff, John Joseph Mulligan, Reggie Jouvain, Judith Suzanne Locker, Norma Jane Marlowe, Diana Pat Marlowe *(Children)*, Harold Crane *(Man)*.

This superlative film set the pattern for a myriad of documentary-type dramas to come. Its producer, Hellinger, patterned the tale after the tabloid newspaper stories he wrote in his youth and he narrates the picture with the same kind of terse but poignant vitality that was the hallmark of his sensational prose. Though basically a crime story—with, oddly, only character actor Fitzgerald as its star—the film is also a love story of the city itself, one where Hellinger embraces soiled urchins and immaculate *grande dames* with equal passion. The story opens with the bathtub murder of a beautiful blonde playgirl. The police are left with no clues. Fitzgerald and his brash young assistant Taylor are assigned the case and spend most of their time running down weak leads that reveal nothing. It is the routine of their lives that is detailed, the various suspects and would-be witnesses who make up much of the story. Fitzgerald, a cop for 30 years, is relentless and states his oft-repeated line: "I haven't had a busy day since yesterday." Taylor, who lives in a modest home and kisses his wife good-bye every morning on his way to headquarters, tries to please his superiors and cover up his lack of experience, but he slowly learns the wily ways of the cop under Fitzgerald's expert tutorship. Their tedious procedures are summed up by narrator Hellinger: "Ask a question, get an answer, ask another." But the dogged Fitzgerald finally gets enough right answers to lead him to playboy Duff, whom the cop traps into admitting that he is broke and killed the blonde for riches, a deed actually performed by de Corsia, a strong-arm goon and friend of Duff. Police take Duff into custody without a struggle but de Corsia, a strutting, egocentric, one-time wrestler, is another matter. He flees for his life, with police hot in pursuit through the streets and on the elevated trains of Manhattan, a spectacular chase that culminates on the high girders of the Brooklyn Bridge, where cops are forced to shoot the killer to death. Shot completely on location in New York City, THE NAKED CITY chronicles the grim urban landscape and depicts its everyday life and citizens, embracing swank Fifth Avenue, Broadway, kids playing hop-skip-and-jump in the streets, straphangers en route to work and back on the crowded subways. Dassin's direction is as taut and telling as the tale he relates with visual punch and panache, much like his other starkly realistic films, BRUTE FORCE (1947), NIGHT AND THE CITY (1950), and THIEVES' HIGHWAY (1949). His association with Hellinger (who also produced BRUTE FORCE) drew heavily from the one-time newspaperman's visual perspective of historical sensationalism, such as Hellinger's THE ROARING TWENTIES, a 1939 crime production starring James Cagney and Humphrey Bogart, which interspersed—among the dramatic scenes—newsreel clips of the excesses of the Jazz Age. Much of the influence for such total on-location shooting stems from films such as THE HOUSE ON 92ND STREET (1945) and CONFESSIONS OF A NAZI SPY (1939). More than 100 location sites were employed in the filming of THE NAKED CITY with the brilliant cameraman Daniels cleverly shooting most of his scenes from inside a van parked along the streets, using a one-way mirror and tinted windows so that passersby were oblivious to the camera's presence. In the late 1950s and early 1960s, a long-running TV series on ABC used this film's title to show the "slice-of-life" type drama the original film typified, and also employed Hellinger's postscript in this, his last feature production, which became a household tagline: "There are eight million stories in the naked city. This has been one of them."

p, Mark Hellinger; d, Jules Dassin; w, Albert Maltz, Malvin Wald (based on a story by Wald); ph, William Daniels; m, Miklos Rozsa, Frank Skinner; ed, Paul Weatherwax; md, Milton Schwartwald; art d, John F. DeCuir; set d, Russell Gausman, Oliver Emert; cos, Grace Houston; makeup, Bud Westmore.

Crime Drama **(PR:C MPAA:NR)**

NAKED DAWN, THE½** (1955) 82m UNIV c

Arthur Kennedy *(Santiago)*, Betta St. John *(Maria)*, Eugene Iglesias *(Manuel)*, Charlita *(Tita)*, Roy Engel *(Guntz)*.

Exploring the way in which greed corrupts, this Edgar G. Ulmer low-budget film shot in Mexico features three characters who are lacking in their convictions. Kennedy hires a simple Mexican farmer, Iglesias, to help him steal money from a train. The prospect of a large amount of money warps Iglesias' morals and the once simple farmer plots Kennedy's death so he can keep all of the money. Iglesias' wife, St. John, is equally confused and tries to persuade Kennedy to hang on to the cash for himself and run away with her. None of the plans sees fruition because the police catch up with Kennedy. In a gun battle, Kennedy is fatally wounded while rescuing Iglesias but stalls the police long enough to ensure the getaway of the couple who are left to begin their lives anew together.

p, James Q. Radford; d, Edgar G. Ulmer; w, Nina and Herman Schneider; ph, Fredrick Gately (Technicolor); m, Herschel Burke Gilbert; ed, Dan Milner; md, Gilbert, art d, Martin Lancer; m/l, "Al Hombre," Gilbert, William Copeland (sung by Charlita).

Crime **(PR:A MPAA:NR)**

NAKED EARTH, THE*½ (1958, Brit.) 96m Foray/FOX bw

Richard Todd *(Danny)*, Juliette Greco *(Maria)*, John Kitzmiller *(David)*, Finlay Currie *(Father Verity)*, Laurence Naismith *(Skin Trader)*, Christopher Rhodes *(Al)*, Orlando Martins *(Tribesman)*, Harold Kasket *(Arab Captain)*, Modesta, Blasio Kiyaga.

A melodramatic adventure picture set in 1895 in Uganda with Todd as a poor Irishman who travels to the Dark Continent to help a friend harvest a tobacco crop.

On his arrival, Todd discovers that his friend was eaten by a crocodile. For some reason (the screenwriters were stuck?), his friend's mistress, Greco, suggests they marry. They work on the tobacco crop with the help of natives, but when they all depart for a ceremonial ritual, the crop cannot be farmed. Todd turns to crocodile hunting and gets enough skins to go back to Ireland and send Greco back to France. When a couple of traders take Todd's skins as their own, three natives are killed trying to get them back. Feeling indebted to the natives, he decides to stay with Greco and learn to adapt to the culture while teaching the natives Western ways.

p, Adrian Worker; d, Vincent Sherman; w, Milton Holmes; ph, Erwin Hillier (Cinemascope); m, Arthur Benjamin; ed, Russell Lloyd; art d, Terence Verity; cos, Felix Evans.

Drama **(PR:A MPAA:NR)**

NAKED EDGE, THE** (1961) 99m Pennebaker-Baroda/UA bw

Gary Cooper *(George Radcliffe)*, Deborah Kerr *(Martha Radcliffe)*, Eric Portman *(Jeremy Clay)*, Diane Cilento *(Mrs. Heath)*, Hermione Gingold *(Lilly Harris)*, Peter Cushing *(Mr. Wrack)*, Michael Wilding *(Morris Brooke)*, Ronald Howard *(Mr. Claridge)*, Ray McAnally *(Donald Heath)*, Sandor Eles *(Manfridi)*, Wilfrid Lawson *(Mr. Pom)*, Helen Cherry *(Miss Osborne)*, Joyce Carey *(Victoria Hicks)*, Diane Clare *(Betty)*, Frederick Leister *(Judge)*, Martin Boddey *(Jason Roote)*, Peter Wayn *(Chauffeur)*.

Cooper's last of 92 films was far from his best. The cancer that was to take his life before the picture was released was already showing on his face. Ehrlich wrote a pretty good little thriller with his book but it was not served well by Anderson's leisurely direction. The executive producer was Marlon Brando's father and it was done through Brando's company. Shot in England at Elstree Studios, it's a bag full of red herrings that eventually begin to smell up the place. Cooper is an American in England, where he testifies against McAnally and says that he saw the man commit robbery and murder. Then, quick as an agent's handshake, Cooper and Wilding, his co-worker at the firm where McAnally also worked, have a few bucks and they buy out a shipping company. What's strange is that McAnally, who has been sentenced to life, insists that he never did anything and the money that was stolen was never found. When Cooper is suddenly rich, he tells his wife, Kerr, that he turned a tidy profit in the stock market and that's what is financing his new business enterprise. Time passes and Cooper is now very rich. A blackmail letter from Portman arrives. He is a one-time lawyer who has been asked to doff the wig and quit the bar. He thinks that Cooper is responsible for the crime which McAnally now serves time for. Kerr was never satisfied with Cooper's explanation of how he got the stake upon which he's built his fortune, so she begins snooping on her own and each clue brings her closer to the belief that Cooper may be guilty. She visits Portman, who says that his theory is based on fact. He claims that he actually saw Cooper kill the man during the robbery. She worries that Cooper will now kill her, so she goes home to quickly bathe and get the heck out of there. In her bath, we see her relax but then watch as a hand picks up a razor and moves in on her. Is it Cooper? Not on her life, pal. It's Portman and he means to slash Kerr to ribbons. Cooper gets there before the nicks are made, whacks Portman, and the man finally admits that he was the killer who murdered the man in the first reel. A few holes in the screenplay that were not there in the book take away from whatever impact this might have made. Cilento is seen briefly as McAnally's wife. She was married to Sean Connery at the time, but later divorced him to marry SLEUTH and FRENZY writer Anthony Shaffer and move to a remote area in Australia.

p, Walter Seltzer, George Glass; d, Michael Anderson; w, Joseph Stefano (based on a novel *First Train to Babylon* by Max Ehrlich); ph, Erwin Hillier; m, William Alwyn; ed, Gordon Pilkington; md, Muir Mathieson; art d, Carmen Dillon; set d, Vernon Dixon; cos, Julie Harris;, makeup, Tony Sforzinio.

Thriller/Mystery **(PR:A-C MPAA:NR)**

NAKED EVIL (SEE: EXORCISM AT MIDNIGHT, 1966, Brit.)

NAKED FLAME, THE** (1970, Can.) 90m Corona/Headliner c

Dennis O'Keefe, Kasey Rogers, Al Ruscio, Linda Bennett, Tracey Roberts, Barton Heyman, Robert Howay.

An outsider marries into a tightly knit sect of Russian Christians called Dukhobors. When a rash of violence coincides with his arrival, the community naturally blames him. One division of the sect likes to romp around in the nude and pass it off as a ritual. Only for indiscriminate audiences. Filmed in 1963, the picture was held from release for seven years.

p&d, Larry Matanski; w, Al Everett Dennis; ph, Paul Ivano (Eastmancolor); art d, Meredith Evans.

Drama **(PR:C MPAA:NR)**

NAKED FURY½** (1959, Brit.) 60m Coenda/BUT bw

Reed de Rouen *(Eddy)*, Kenneth Cope *(Johnny)*, Leigh Madison *(Carol)*, Arthur Lovegrove *(Syd)*, Thomas Eytle *(Steve)*, Alexander Field *(Vic)*, Ann Lynn *(Judy)*, Marianne Brauns *(Joy)*, Katy Cashfield *(Commere)*, Redmond Phillips, Michael Collins, Eric Woodburn, Anne Sharp, Eric Corrie, Geoffrey Denton, Denis Shaw, Vickie Gray, Julie Cavall, Mary Deighan, Sheree Winton, Eve Eden, Jill Burrows, Norma Parnell, Arthur Gross.

Four robbers kill a nightwatchman in the course of a robbery, then flee with his daughter (Madison) as a hostage. While holed up in a dilapidated warehouse, one of the quartet (Cope) falls for the woman. This sets off bickering within the group, with all four men dying at the film's end. Not much, but entertaining for what it is.

p. Guido Coen; d, Charles Saunders; w, Brock Williams (based on a story by Coen); ph, Geofrrey Faithfull.

Crime **(PR:C MPAA:NR)**

NAKED FURY, THE, 1964 (SEE: PLEASURE LOVERS, THE, 1964, Brit.)

NAKED GENERAL, THE½** (1964, Jap.) 92m Toho c (HADAKA NO TAISHO)

Keiju Kobayashi *(Kiyoshi Yamashita)*, Aiko Mimasu *(His Mother)*, Yasuko Nakada *(Girl in a Lunch Shop)*, Daisuke Kato *(Master of an Eating House)*, Kyoko Aoyama *(Girl in an Eating House)*, Eijiro Tono *(Commander)*, Reiko Dan *(Bus Conductor)*.

Film focuses on the life of famed Japanese artist Kiyoshi Yamashita, portrayed by Kobayashi. The film opens during WW II when the poverty stricken Kobayashi proclaims himself to be a pacifist. To avoid conscription, he disrobes in public, a stunt that lands him briefly in a mental institution. The remainder of the film recounts his climb to the top of the art world as his work achieves international recognition. Made in 1958, the movie did not reach the U.S. until six years later.

d, Hiromichi Horikawa; w, Yoko Mizuki; ph, Asaichi Nakai (Tohoscope, Agfacolor); art d, Yasuhide Kato.

Biography/Comedy **(PR:A MPAA:NR)**

NAKED GODDESS, THE (SEE: DEVIL'S HAND, THE, 1961)

NAKED GUN, THE* (1956) 69m Associated Film bw

Willard Parker, Mara Corday, Barton MacLane, Billy House, Veda Ann Borg, Morris Ankrum, Chick Chandler, Bill Phillips, Tom Brown, Timothy Carey, X Brands, Steve Raines, Jim Hayward, Rick Vallin, Elene Di Vinci, Jody McCrea, Tony McCoy, Bill Ward, Merry Ogden, Helen Jay, Doris Simons.

A veteran cast of mediocre actors shine above the lifeless script and invisible direction that THE NAKED GUN has to offer. An insurance man gets tired of his boring existence and sets out to locate a cursed Aztec treasure (which Aztec treasures aren't cursed?) and the girl who is its rightful heir. The title's the best thing about it—and that isn't even that great.

p, Ron Ormond; d, Edward Dew; w, Ormond, Jack Lewis.

Mystery **(PR:A MPAA:NR)**

NAKED HEART, THE*½ (1955, Brit.) 96m Dominant bw (AKA: MARIA CHAPDELAINE)

Michele Morgan *(Maria Chapdelaine)*, Kieron Moore *(Lorenzo Surprenant)*, Francoise Rosay *(Laura Chapdelaine)*, Jack Watling *(Robert Gagnon)*, Philippe Lemaire *(Francois Paradis)*, Nancy Price *(Theresa Suprenant)*, Francis De Wolff *(Papa Suprenant)*, George Woodbridge *(Samuel Chapdelaine)*, Fred Johnson *(Esdras the Bonesetter)*, Dimitri *(Chappie)*, Michael Mulcaster *(Legare)*, Brian Roper *(Tit-Be)*, Catherine Bradshaw *(Alma-Rose)*, George Mulcaster, Rufus Cruickshank, Harry Locke, Ewen Solon, Richard George.

French director Allegret made several English-language films and this may be his worst. Set in Canada, the film tells the story of Maria (Morgan) who returns to her village after five years in a convent. She falls in love with three men—Moore, Lemaire, and Watling—and the remainder of the film depicts her problems in finding Mr. Right. Made in 1950 but not released in the U.S. until 1955, the movie offers little to recommend. Roger Vadim, who would achieve great notoriety the following year as the director of AND GOD CREATED WOMEN, learned his trade from Allegret. He served as an assistant to Allegret from 1947-55 and is credited with writing the dialog for THE NAKED HEART.

p, Nelson Scott; d, Marc Allegret; w, Allegret, Roger Vadim, Hugh Mills, J. McLaren-Ross, C. K. Jaeger (based on the novel *Maria Chapdelaine* by Louis Hemon); ph, Armand Thirard; m, Guy Bernard; ed, Maurice Rootes; cos, Germaine Lecomte, Michael Whittaker.

Drama **(PR:A MPAA:NR)**

NAKED HEARTS*½ (1970, Fr.) 90m Ploquin-Sodor/Altura bw (LES COEURS VERTS)

Gerard Zimmerman *(Zim)*, Marise Maire *(Jacqueline)*, Erick Penet *(Jean-Pierre)*, Francoise Bonneau *(Patricia)*, Arlette Thomas *(Jean-Pierre's Mother)*, Elliott Stein, Nat Lilienstein.

Sometimes touching but rather lackluster tale of juvenile delinquency in Paris, with a plot reminiscent of old James Cagney-Pat O'Brien movies. Zimmerman plays a youngster who is sent to reform school on a minor theft charge. There he meets Penet who is from the same Paris suburb as Zimmerman. The two are released on the same day, and Zimmerman resolves to go straight while Penet continues to pursue less honorable endeavors. Zimmerman gets a job, does well, and meets Bonneau at a local dance. Penet gets arrested for auto theft. Made in 1966. (In French; English subtitles.)

p, Raoul Ploquin; d&w, Edouard Luntz; ph, Jean Badal; m, Serge Gainsbourg, Henri Renaud; ed, Suzanne Sandberg, Colette Kouchner; m/l, "Be-Bop-a-Lula," Gene Vincent, Sheriff Tex Davis.

Drama **(PR:A MPAA:NR)**

NAKED HILLS, THE** (1956) 72m LaSalle/AA c

David Wayne *(Tracy Powell)*, Keenan Wynn *(Sam Wilkins)*, James Barton *(Jimmo McCann)*, Marcia Henderson *(Julie)*, Jim Backus *(Willis Haver)*, Denver Pyle *(Bert Killian)*, Myrna Dell *(Aggie)*, Lewis Russell *(Baxter)*, Frank Fenton *(Harold)*, Fuzzy Knight *(Pitch Man)*, Jim Hayward *(Counter Man)*, Chris Olsen *(Billy, as a Boy)*, Steven Terrell *(Billy as a Young Man)*.

A routine western starring Wayne as a man who never overcomes his gold fever. Beginning in 1849, when a young Wayne leaves his wife and child behind to venture into the hills and pan for gold, this episodic film traces his search through the next 40 years. Meanwhile, Pyle, Wayne's first partner, tries to bed Henderson, but never gets his chance.

p,d&w, Josef Shaftel (based on a story by Helen S. Bilkie); ph, Frederick Gately

(Pathe Color); m, Herschel Burke Gilbert; ed, Gene Fowler, Jr.; md, Gilbert; art d, Rudi Feld; m/l, "Four Seasons," Gilbert, Bob Russell (sung by James Barton).

Western Cas. (PR:A MPAA:NR)

NAKED HOURS, THE*** (1964, Ital.) 92m Atlantica bw (LE ORE NUDE)

Keir Dullea *(Aldo)*, Rossana Podesta *(Carla)*, Philippe Leroy *(Massimo)*, Odardo Spadaro *(Nonno)*.

An insightful study of sexual relationships, featuring a very good performance by Podesta. Her husband, Leroy, is a devotee of group sex, and Podesta indulges his desires. She meets student Dullea and has a one-day affair with him. The story covers only three days in the lives of the characters, but in that framework Vicario manages to offer a perceptive examination of the principals. A good score and fine camerawork enhance the story, which was written by Moravia, who would go on to become one of Italy's foremost novelists and screenwriters.

p&d, Marco Vicario; w, Alberto Moravia, Tonino Guerra, Vicario (based on a story by Moravia); ph, Carlo di Palma; m, Riz Ortolani.

Drama (PR:C MPAA:NR)

NAKED IN THE SUN** (1957) 79m Empire/AA c

James Craig, Lita Milan, Barton MacLane, Robert Wark, Jim Boles, Tony Hunter, Douglas Wilson, Bill Armstrong, Dennis Cross, Peter Dearing, Tony Morris, Mike Crecco.

A slow-moving, based-in-truth western. The story involves the Osceola and Seminole tribes in their fight against an evil slave trader.

p&d, R. John Hugh; w, Frank G. Slaughter, Hugh (based on the novel *The Warrior* by Slaughter); ph, Charles T. O'Rork (Eastmancolor); ed, William A. Slade; md, Laurence Rosenthal; art d, Larry Duren.

Western Cas. (PR:C MPAA:NR)

NAKED ISLAND (SEE: ISLAND, THE, 1962, Jap.)

NAKED JUNGLE, THE*½** (1953) 95m PAR c

Eleanor Parker *(Joanna Leiningen)*, Charlton Heston *(Christopher Leiningen)*, Abraham Sofaer *(Incacha)*, William Conrad *(Commissioner)*, Romo Vincent *(Boat Captain)*, Douglas Fowley *(Medicine Man)*, John Dierkes *(Gruber)*, Leonard Strong *(Kutina)*, Norma Calderon *(Zala)*, John Mansfield *(Foreman)*, Ronald Alan Numkena, Bernie Gozier, Jack Reitzen, Rodd Redwing, Pilar Del Rey, John E. Wood, Jerry Groves, Leon Lontoc, Carlos Rivero.

In the Amazonian jungle at the turn of the century, Heston has carved himself his own plantation empire, so large it takes a day from the time boats coming up the river enter his property until they reach the landing. Arriving at the landing as the movie opens is Parker, a New Orleans woman who has married Heston by proxy and has now come to meet her husband. Heston at first is cruel to her, and when she tries to make a small joke he says, "You have a sense of humor. I don't like humor in a woman." She tries again and again to penetrate his shell, but too many years in the jungle by himself have hardened him. When she lets slip that she has been married before, Heston angrily decides to send her packing. The next evening, before she can leave, Conrad, the province commissioner, comes to dinner. He tells Heston about strange happenings in the jungle, massive animal migrations, and when Heston asks him what he thinks is causing them, Conrad says the dreaded word, "Marabunda." The massive movement of a huge swarm of soldier ants, 20 miles long, two miles wide, traveling six miles a day, devouring everything in their path. Conrad tells Heston that the only intelligent course is to get out of their way, but Heston has fought the jungle too long and too hard to simply walk away from his home now and leave it to a bunch of insects. Parker argues that if Heston sends her away in the face of this threat, the native workers will also flee and Heston won't have a chance of fighting them, an argument that impresses Heston. He begins preparing his plantation for the onslaught, blowing up the bridges and flooding some of the approaches. The ants, though, almost seem guided by a higher intelligence as they cut leaves and build rafts to cross the moats, and build bridges from their own locked-together bodies. Time and again Heston manages to stop the threat from one quarter when the assault is renewed on another. Many of the natives flee in panic and it looks as though Heston is beaten. In a desperate last-ditch effort, he covers himself with grease and makes his way through the swarm to the main dam that holds back the water from which he claimed his plantation. With the ants almost covering his body, Heston plants dynamite charges on the dam and blows it up. The ants are washed away and Heston, with Parker at his side, prepares to rebuild his plantation. Amazing adventure drama with some incredible special effects of billions of ants ravaging the countryside. For some of the closer shots, with ants only covering a few square yards, no special effects were involved, they simply got that many ants. Heston gives a good performance, free of the bombast he often brings to the screen. Parker is impressive as a woman strong enough to stand up to all the abuse her husband can heap upon her, yet still winning his respect and love by the picture's conclusion. Some of the scripting is awkward and obvious, but once the insect attack occurs, dialog becomes unimportant. Of all the movies of people threatened by insects, from the giant ants of THEM (released shortly later in 1954) to the killer bees of THE SWARM (1978), this is probably the best, and certainly the most realistic. Producer Pal was the driving force behind many films which won Oscars for their effects, such as DESTINATION MOON (1950) and THE TIME MACHINE (1960).

p, George Pal; d, Byron Haskin; w, Philip Yordan, Ranald MacDougall (based on the story "Leiningen Versus the Ants" by Carl Stephenson); ph, Ernest Laszlo (Technicolor); m, Daniele Amfitheatrof; ed, Everett Douglas; cos, Edith Head; spec eff, John P. Fulton, Farciot Edouart.

Adventure/Drama (PR:A-C MPAA:NR)

NAKED KISS, THE½** (1964) 92m F&F/AA bw (AKA: THE IRON KISS)

Constance Towers *(Kelly)*, Anthony Eisley *(Griff)*, Michael Dante *(Grant)*, Virginia Grey *(Candy)*, Patsy Kelly *(Mac)*, Betty Bronson *(Miss Josephine)*, Marie Devereux *(Buff)*, Karen Conrad *(Dusty)*, Linda Francis *(Rembrandt)*, Barbara Perry *(Edna)*, Walter Mathews *(Mike)*, Betty Robinson *(Bunny)*, Gerald Michenaud *(Kip)*, Christopher Barry *(Peanuts)*, George Spell *(Tim)*, Patty Robinson *(Angel Face)*, Neyle Morrow *(Officer Sam)*, Monte Mansfield *(Farlunde)*, Fletcher Fist *(Barney)*, Gerald Milton *(Zookie)*, Breena Howard *(Redhead)*, Sally Mills *(Marshmallow)*, Edy Williams *(Hatrack)*, Michael Barrere *(Young Delinquent)*, Patricia Gayle *(Nurse)*, Sheila Mintz *(Receptionist)*, Bill Sampson *(Jerry)*, Charlie *(Charlie)*.

Perhaps director Fuller's grimmest, most disturbing work (in a career filled with grim and disturbing portraits of humanity), THE NAKED KISS details prostitute Towers' vain attempt at leaving her life of sin to enter mainstream society—a society that proves to be more depraved than the world she has fled. The film opens with a pre-credits sequence which sees Towers embroiled in a violent fight with her pimp who is trying to cheat her. During the brutal battle the pimp tries to totally demoralize Towers by pulling her wig off, revealing a bald head which he had shaved (a shocking, monstrous image that Fuller had used before in VERBOTEN! in 1958). Outraged at yet another savage violation, Towers kills her pimp and leaves town. Seeking to reform herself, Towers ventures into the heart of small-town America. Soon after her arrival, Towers has a brief affair with the sheriff, Eisley, who knows about her past and suggests she take up with a new madam, Grey, who operates a brothel on the other side of town. She rejects his suggestion and instead gets herself a job as a nurse caring for crippled children. Her work is highly successful and gains the attention of an appreciative town and a philanthropic millionaire, Dante. Towers falls in love with Dante and soon they speak of marriage. Wanting to be honest with him, Towers tells Dante of her past. After some deliberation, Dante agrees to marry Towers, promising her the home and family she has always yearned for. The engagement is sealed with a kiss, but the embrace shakes Towers. Dante's kiss is one she has felt before—a kiss touched with deep perversion. Ignoring the warning sign, Towers buys a wedding dress and triumphantly returns to Dante's home to show it off. She enters the house and is surprised to hear a recording of the song she used to sing to the children in the hospital. As she nears Dante's bedroom, a little girl runs out of the room and Towers is horrified that she has interrupted her fiance just as he was about to molest a child. Revulsion sweeps through Towers and her outrage once again turns to violence as she beats Dante to death with a telephone. When the town learns of Towers' past it quickly turns against her, branding her a murderer. With Eisley's help, Towers is able to locate the little girl and clear her name. The citizens of the hypocritical community do an immediate about-face and hail Towers as a heroine, but she is too disgusted by them to stay, so she exits "respectable" society. THE NAKED KISS is Fuller's most developed and unrelentingly bleak view of the dark underbelly of American society. While Towers is a prostitute and killer, she is more honorable than the "respectable" citizens because she is sincere and honest in her attempt to reform her life. Towers has a moral code, a line she allows no one to cross. The community, however, worships cosmetics. Towers is hired as a nurse because she looks wholesome. Dante is a respected member of the community because he is rich and benevolent, but in reality he is a child molester—the most reprehensible person on Earth to Fuller, who sees children as symbols of hope for mankind. While Fuller shows that children may dream in a scene where Towers encourages the handicapped children to pretend that they are able to run and play, he holds no such illusions for adults. When Dante courts Towers he fills her head with fantasies of romance in Vienna, but the dream comes to an abrupt end that leads to the reality of his cold, perverse kiss.

p,d&w, Samuel Fuller; ph, Stanley Cortez; m, Paul Dunlap; ed, Jerome Thoms; art d, Eugene Lourie; set d, Victor Gangelin; cos, Act III, Einar H. Bourman, Hazel Allensworth; m/l, "Santa Lucia," sung by John Guarniere; makeup, Harry Thomas.

Drama (PR:O MPAA:NR)

NAKED LOVERS, THE (SEE: NAKED ZOO, THE, 1970)

NAKED MAJA, THE* (1959, Ital./U.S.) 111m Titanus/UA c

Ava Gardner *(Duchess of Alba)*, Anthony Franciosa *(Francisco Goya)*, Amedeo Nazzari *(Prime Minister Manuel Godoy)*, Gino Cervi *(King Carlos IV)*, Lea Padovani *(Queen Maria Luisa)*, Massimo Serato *(Sanchez)*, Carlo Rizzo *(Juanito)*, Renzo Cesana *(Bayeu)*, Ivana Kislinger *(Pepa)*, Audrey MacDonald *(Anita)*, Patrick Crean *(Enrique)*, Tonio Selwart *(Aranda)*, Peter Meersman *(Dr. Peral)*, Enzo Fiermonte *(Navarra)*, Yemiko Fullwood *(Maria de la Luz)*, Carlo Giustini *(Jose)*, Erminio Spalla *(Rojas the Innkeeper)*, John Karlsen *(The Inquisitor)*, Paul Muller *(French Ambassador)*, Renata Mauro, Pina Bottin *(Majas)*, Amru Sani *(The Singer)*, Carmen Mora *(The Ballerina)*, Clayton Hall *(Goya's Assistant)*, Gustavo De Nardo *(The Priest)*, Andre Esterhazi *(Count De Fuentes)*, Amina Pirani Maggi *(Governess Assuncion)*, Leonardo Botta *(Prince Ferdinando)*, Roberta Primavera *(Princess of Portugal)*, Pamela Sharp *(Maria Isabella)*, Alberto Plebani *(Don Antonio)*, Nadia Balabin *(Carlotta Joaquins)*, Giuseppe Giardina *(Luigi of Perma)*, Stella Vitelleschi *(Maria Josefa)*.

Wonderful sets, gorgeous costumes, stunning photography, superior music, and none of it can overcome the dumb script, the inane direction, and the rotten acting by much of the cast. Franciosa is a poor painter, Goya, and he meets Gardner, a duchess, in a local inn. They like each other immediately but she takes an imagined slight at something he's said. Later, Franciosa is made the official painter of the Spanish court, a deliberate move by Queen Padovani to stick it to Gardner, whom she dislikes. Franciosa learns of a plot by prime minister Nazzari to bring in Napoleon's troops and tells the king, Cervi, about it. Meanwhile, Franciosa paints Gardner as a Maja (which means she is a woman of easy virtue), although she never posed for him in the nude. The Inquisitors, those spoilsports, don't much like

Fransciosa's liberal attitude and would like to see him boiled in olive oil (first pressing only) but Cervi gets him off the hook. Gardner gets on the wrong side of Nazzari and he arranges to have her poisoned by a slow and painful bane. She and Franciosa get together just before she dies and the picture mercifully concludes. This bears as much resemblance to real history as Dom DeLuise bears resemblance to a matinee idol. This is a waste of time and one of the scenes is so derivative of Eisenstein's POTEMKIN that it is shocking. (It's the one where the soldiers push the crowd of innocent men, women, and children down a flight of stairs.) It was surprising to see a writer of quality material like Norman Corwin involved with this nonsense.

p, Goffredo Lombardo; d, Henry Koster, Mario Russo; w, Norman Corwin, Giorgio Prosperi (based on a story by Oscar Saul, Talbot Jennings); ph, Giuseppe Rotunno (Technirama, Technicolor); m, Angelo Francesco Lavaginno; art d, Piero Filipponi; set d, Gino Brosio, Emilio D'Andria; cos, Dario Cecchi, Maria Barone; ch, Alberto Lorca; makeup, Euclide Santoli, Franco Freda, Alma Santoli, Alfio Meniconi.

Biography **(PR:A MPAA:NR)**

NAKED NIGHT, THE*** (1956, Swed.) 82m Sandrew/Times bw (GYCKLARNAS AFTON; GB: SAWDUST AND TINSEL; AKA: SUNSET OF A CLOWN)

Harriet Andersson *(Anne)*, Ake Groenberg *(Albert Johansson)*, Hakke Ekman *(Frans)*, Anders Ek *(Teodor Frost)*, Annika Tretow *(Alma Johansson)*, Kiki *(Agda)*, Gudrun Brost *(Alma Frost)*, Gunnar Bjornstrand *(Sjuberg)*, Erik Strandmark *(Jens)*, Ake Fridell *(Officer)*, Curt Lowgren.

Released in Sweden in 1953 (at 95 minutes), this Bergman picture was one of a handful sent to the U.S. after THE SEVENTH SEAL arrived and "Bergmania" struck. It subscribes to all the theories, at the time, of what an "art film" should be, especially a "Swedish art film." It is filled with depressing, humiliating images, intellectual (though superficial) dialog, and psychoanalytic or religious symbolism. What it lacks is what almost all Bergman films lack—subtlety and hope. Groenberg is the owner of a traveling circus who leaves his mistress, Andersson, and tries to reunite with his wife, Tretow. She turns him away, but in the meantime, Andersson lets herself be seduced by Ekman. Groenberg becomes the subject of Ekman's verbal and physical abuse. Groenberg attempts suicide, but lacking the courage to shoot himself, instead fires at a bear. He gives in to his destiny and continues on with Andersson. Hailed by some at the time of its release as Bergman's masterpiece, it was the film that established the "Bergman style" in terms of themes and visuals. This was Nykvist's first assignment as Bergman's cinematographer. (In Swedish; English subtitles.)

p, Rune Waldekranz; d&w, Ingmar Bergman; ph, Sven Nykvist, Hilding Bladh; m, Karl-Birger Blomdahl; ed, Carl-Olof Skeppstedt; art d, Bibi Lindstrom.

Drama **(PR:O MPAA:NR)**

NAKED PARADISE** (1957) 68m AIP c (AKA: THUNDER OVER HAWAII)

Richard Denning *(Duke)*, Beverly Garland *(Max)*, Lisa Monteil *(Keena)*, Leslie Bradley *(Zac)*, Richard Miller *(Mitch)*, Jonathan Haze *(Stony)*.

Film is set in Hawaii where Denning is the captain of a schooner. Bradley is a criminal who charters Denning's boat as his means of escape following a robbery, though Denning has no knowledge of the illegal activities. Garland is Bradley's girl friend, who falls for Denning. A lot of action and some good photography of the Hawaiian sights make this passable fare. Alvin Kaleolani provides some native songs, helping to capture a little island flavor.

p&d, Roger Corman; w, Charles B. Griffith, Mark Hanna; ph, Floyd Crosby (Pathecolor); m, Ronald Stein; ed, Charles Gross, Jr.

Drama **(PR:A MPAA:NR)**

NAKED PREY, THE*½** (1966, U.S./South Africa) 96m Theodora-Sven Persson/PAR c

Cornel Wilde *(Man)*, Gert van den Berg *(2nd Man)*, Ken Gampu *(Warrior Leader)*, Patrick Mynhardt *(Safari Overseer)*, Bella Randels *(Little Girl)*, Jose Sithole, Richard Mashiya, Eric Sabela, Joe Diaminl, Frank Mdhluli, Sandy Nkomo, Fusi Zazayokwe, John Marcus, Horace Gilman *(Warriors)*, Morrison Gampu *(Tribal Chief)*.

In the South African bush near the end of the 19th Century, Wilde is a safari guide leading van den Berg, Mynhardt, and others on an ivory hunting expedition. Despite Wilde's warnings and recommendations, van den Berg offends local tribesmen. In an ambush, the natives kill all but six of the party, who are taken back to the tribesmen's village for ritual torture and execution. One victim is caked with mud, hollow breathing tubes are inserted in his nostrils, then he is put on a spit and roasted alive, screaming all the while. Another is feathered, hobbled, then butchered like a chicken. Van den Berg is staked out with his head at the only opening in a ring of fire that surrounds a deadly cobra. Wilde, presumably because the natives have some respect for him, is offered "The Chance of the Lion." Stripped naked, he is given a head start of a few hundred yards. Then six warriors, each of whom has killed 10 lions, set out to hunt him down. One impetuous warrior runs out in front of the others and hurls his spear, but Wilde dodges it and then uses it to kill the pursuer. Before the others can catch up he has taken the dead man's sandals, loincloth, and water bottle. The chase continues as Wilde evades not only the men hunting him, but natural hazards such as scorpions, spike-covered lizards, and thorns five inches long on the trees. He kills two more of the warriors, then manages to lose the others for a few days by cutting off their chase with a brush fire he sets. From a hiding place he watches a slavery raid on a peaceful village and briefly befriends a young girl who escapes. They travel together for a few days, then part. After more walking over hostile terrain, the remaining hunters begin to draw nearer their prey and Wilde again has to run for his life. Finally he breaks out of the bush into a clearing where a British fort stands. As he dashes across the open ground, the leader of the warriors runs out to make a final attempt to kill him. As he is about to throw his spear, a red-coated soldier marching on duty shoots him dead. As the exhausted Wilde is taken into the stockade he looks back to see the remaining warriors, and hunter and hunted wave their respect for each other, much the same way the Zulu armies salute the British defenders of Rorke's Drift in ZULU (1963). Wilde's fourth directorial outing is easily his best, tightly constructed and dizzyingly fast-paced (fewer than 15 minutes pass between the credits and Wilde's being set out into the bush for the chase). Wilde took the idea from a radio show about fur trappers chased across the American west by hostile Indians and transposed it to South Africa and the Zulus. Production, though inexpensive, was arduous—at one point a lizard latched onto Wilde's leg and had to be killed before it would let go. The unit manager was bitten by a cobra. Five crew members were hospitalized after a swarm of bees attacked. Wilde contracted tick fever, a debilitating malady similar to malaria, but took advantage of his less-than-healthy appearance to look even more exhausted and pressed as the tribesmen pursued him. While shooting in Africa, thieves broke into Wilde's Hollywood home. Using wooden matches to light their way, they stole thousands of dollars worth of jewels, furs, and guns. At another point in the shooting, Wilde shocked a native chief by turning down the chief's generous offer of a 15-year-old girl for a wife. Chief Shwasa, with six wives himself, couldn't understand how Wilde could be happy with only one. The film is almost entirely action—a condition that greatly aids the performance of Wilde, always slightly wooden in speech but exciting in motion—and his direction is ideal for the story. The film was fairly successful both critically and at the box office and is vividly recalled by a generation that saw it on TV at an impressionable age and never forgot it.

p&d, Cornel Wilde; w, Clint Johnston, Donald A. Peters; ph, H.A.R. Thomson (Panavision, Eastmancolor); ed, Roger Cherrill; cos, Freda Thompson; m/l, title song, sung by The Principal Warriors; makeup, Trevor Crole-Rees.

Adventure **Cas.** **(PR:O MPAA:NR)**

NAKED RUNNER, THE* (1967, Brit.) 104m Artanis-Sinatra Enterprises/WB c

Frank Sinatra *(Sam Laker)*, Peter Vaughan *(Martin Slattery)*, Darren Nesbitt *(Col. Hartmann)*, Nadia Gray *(Karen Gisevius)*, Toby Robins *(Ruth)*, Inger Stratton *(Anna)*, Cyril Luckham *(Cabinet Minister)*, Edward Fox *(Ritchie Jackson)*, J. A. B. Dubin-Berhmann *(Joseph)*, Michael Newport *(Patrick Laker)*.

The plot of 1985's TARGET (Gene Hackman, Gayle Hunnicutt) was not unlike this effort and the results were similar: incredulity and boredom. Ever since Brad Dexter saved Sinatra's life when he nearly drowned, he's worked for Ol' Blue Eyes and his job here was to produce this alleged suspense film. Director Furie, who thinks he is Vermeer with a camera, gets in the way of any possible suspense by saying, "look at me, I'm directing!" with every single trick shot in his arsenal of angles. Sinatra is living in London with his teenage son, Newport. The boy's mother is long since dead and father and son are close enough for daddy to want to take sonny along with him on a trip to Germany. Sinatra sees an old familiar face, Vaughan. The two shared many WW II experiences and Vaughan is now employed by British Intelligence. Vaughan informs Sinatra that one of the top Brits has defected to the Red side and must be taken out, and since Sinatra is a marksman, he's being asked to do it. Sinatra tells him to stuff it, so Vaughan asks him for one other favor, for old time's sake: Can he deliver a message in Leipzig to Gray, who had been with the Underground during the war? Sinatra is reluctant but he does owe Gray an unrepaid favor. He arrives in Germany, gives Gray the message, and when he returns to his hotel, he is shocked to learn that Newport has been abducted. Nesbitt, a Commie chief, says that Newport will stay in hiding unless Sinatra does an assassination on a spy who has defected to Denmark. Sinatra agrees in order to save his son's life, but the target for the killing never shows up. Sinatra goes back to Leipzig and is told that Newport has been killed by Nesbitt because he failed to carry out the killing. Angry and filled with vengeance, Sinatra begins to trail Nesbitt, learns his patterns, and sets his high-powered rifle on the road where Nesbitt passes daily. When Nesbitt's car goes by, Sinatra puts the man in his crosshairs and fires. The driver dies. No sooner does he finish the deed than Vaughan and Nesbitt (it wasn't him at all) arrive to tell Sinatra that Newport is, in fact, alive, and the man Sinatra has just murdered was the same defector that Vaughan had asked him to kill in reel one. Filmed in London, Copenhagen, and various other places, THE NAKED RUNNER only walks. . .and fully-clothed, too. Furie had done THE IPCRESS FILE two pictures before and attempted to infuse this with the same techniques. He didn't. That kind of cinematicaca may be all right for one film, but when a director attempts to do it all the time, it's as boring as a night at the in-laws.

p, Brad Dexter; d, Sidney J. Furie; w, Stanley Mann (based on a novel by Francis Clifford); ph, Otto Heller (Techniscope, Technicolor); m, Harry Sukman; ed, Barry Vince; md, Morris Stoloff; art d, Peter Proud, Bill Alexander.

Spy Drama **(PR:A-C MPAA:NR)**

NAKED SET (SEE: NAKED ROAD, THE, 1962)

NAKED SPUR, THE**** (1953) 91m MGM c

James Stewart *(Howard Kemp)*, Janet Leigh *(Lina Patch)*, Robert Ryan *(Ben Vandergroat)*, Ralph Meeker *(Roy Anderson)*, Millard Mitchell *(Jesse Tate)*.

Another superb western from director Anthony Mann, who, along with Budd Boetticher, created an outstanding series of engrossing, thoughtful, and challenging films that helped keep the genre fresh and vital during the 1950s. Stewart is excellent as the obsessed, disillusioned Civil War veteran who returns home to find that he has lost his land. To raise the money needed to regain his land, Stewart decides to become a bounty hunter and enters the Colorado Territory in search of escaped killer Ryan, who has a $5,000 reward on his head. Ryan is accompanied by Leigh, a lonely young woman who wants to escape to California with the killer. While searching for Ryan, Stewart picks up a pair of companions. The first is

Mitchell, a grizzled prospector, the second Meeker, a Union soldier who was dishonorably discharged. The two drifters believe Stewart to be a lawman and they agree to help him capture Ryan. The trio corner Ryan and the girl on a rugged hillside and take them prisoner. Soon after, Mitchell and Meeker learn that Stewart is no lawman and they demand an equal share of the reward. Stewart refuses. Ryan sees that his only means of escape is to divide the three men, so, with Leigh's help, he begins a clever campaign to pit the men against each other. During the seven day trip through dangerous Indian territory back to Abilene, Ryan baits the men by encouraging each to kill the other two and take the reward solo. Leigh, meanwhile, flirts with both Stewart and Meeker, which further erodes the uneasy partnership. Seeking to eliminate his competition, Meeker causes an Indian uprising in the hopes that the redskins will massacre the group. Stewart is wounded in the attack, but they manage to defeat the Indians and push on. As the group nears Abilene, Ryan talks Mitchell into helping him escape. The old prospector does so and Ryan murders him. The crazed killer then sets a trap for Stewart and Meeker. Leigh, who has fallen in love with Stewart, foils Ryan's plot, but not before Meeker and Ryan lie dead. Stewart, by now almost insane with his obsession over the bounty, retrieves Ryan's body and puts it head down over a horse. Leigh, disturbed and disgusted by the whole experience, persuades an unwilling Stewart to abandon the body and go off to California with her. Exhausted and defeated, Stewart finally allows his repressed humanity to surface and rides off with Leigh to start a new life. Mann's protagonists are men who allow their desire for vengeance to consume their inherent qualities of honor and decency. Their quests through rugged landscapes are enlightening journeys of near-religious revelation that see these men finally come to grips with themselves and their lives. The characters in THE NAKED SPUR form a highly volatile family unit that can explode into chaos at any moment. Each of them are in varying degrees of mental unbalance, with Ryan's killer at one extreme and Leigh at the other. When the smoke clears, the unforgiven, unsalveagable die, giving the repentant Stewart a new lease on life. THE NAKED SPUR actually found some support among the Academy of Motion Picture Arts & Sciences (rare for a western—especially a low-budget one) and the screenplay was nominated for an Academy Award.

p, William H. Wright; d, Anthony Mann; w, Sam Rolfe, Harold Jack Bloom; ph, William Mellor (Technicolor); m, Bronislau Kaper; ed, George White; art d, Cedric Gibbons, Malcolm Brown.

Western (PR:A-C MPAA:NR)

NAKED SPUR, 1968 (SEE: HOT SPUR, 1968)

NAKED STREET, THE* (1955) 84m UA bw

Farley Granger (*Nicky Bradna*), Anthony Quinn (*Phil Regal*), Anne Bancroft (*Rosalie Regalzyk*), Peter Graves (*Joe McFarland*), Else Neft (*Mrs. Regalzyk*), Jerry Paris (*Latzi Franks*), Frank Sully (*Nutsy*), John Dennis (*Big Eddie*), Angela Stevens (*Janet*), Joy Terry (*Margie*), G. Pat Collins (*Mr. Hough*), Mario Siletti (*Antonio Cardini*), Whit Bissell (*Attorney Blaker*), Jeanne Cooper (*Evelyn Shriner*), Sara Berner (*Millie*), James Flavin (*Attorney Flanders*), Harry Harvey (*Judge Roder*), Judge Stanley (*Alex Campbell*), Jackie Loughery (*Francis*), Frank Kreig (*Ollie*), Joe Turkel (*Shimmy*), Harry O. Tyler (*Barricks*), Sammie Weiss (*Lennie*).

A solid, fast-paced crime tale starring Quinn as a brutal and powerful gangster who is shocked to learn tht his sister, Bancroft, is pregnant by a small time hood about to be executed. Not wanting his sister to wind up an unwed mother, Quinn pulls every trick in the book to get the father of the baby, Granger, out of the electric chair. The scheme works and Granger soon finds himself married to Bancroft, a situation that does not please him. When the baby is stillborn, Quinn flies into a rage and persecutes Granger. Granger reacts by diving once again into a life of crime, cheating on Bancroft all the while. Outraged, Quinn frames Granger on a murder rap which sends the kid back to the chair. Before he is executed, Granger spills the beans to Graves, a local reporter and former childhood sweetheart of Bancroft. Graves turns the heat on Quinn in the press and soon the pressure from the district attorney causes one of the mob boss' hoods to crack. Armed with enough evidence to put Quinn away, the police move in on the crime boss. Quinn attempts to escape in a chase across the rooftops, but he slips up and falls to his death. Rid of all the unsavory elements in her life, Bancroft rekindles her romance with Graves. While the script for THE NAKED STREET isn't particularly original or clever, the film makes the most of its fine cast. Quinn brings a varied set of emotions to his brutish character, which even allows this cruel mobster to look forward to the day he will become an uncle. Bancroft however, steals the film as the forever manipulated sister who is allowed no choices of her own.

p, Edward Small; d&w, Maxwell Shane (based on a story by Leo Katcher); ph, Floyd Crosby; m, Emil Newman; ed, Grant Whytock; md, Newman; art d, Ted Haworth.

Crime Drama (PR:C MPAA:NR)

NAKED TEMPTATION (SEE: WOMAN AND TEMPTATION, 1967, Arg.)

NAKED TEMPTRESS, THE (SEE: THE NAKED WITCH 1964)

NAKED TRUTH, THE (SEE: YOUR PAST IS SHOWING, 1958, Brit.)

NAKED UNDER LEATHER (SEE: GIRL ON A MOTORCYCLE, 1968, Brit./Fr.)

NAKED WITCH, THE*½ (1964) 60m Alexander/Mishkin c (AKA: THE NAKED TEMPTRESS)

Beth Porter (*Beth*), Robert Burgos (*Stephen*), Bryarly Lee (*Bella*), Lee Forbes (*Deaf-and-Dumb Hunchback*), Maggie Rogers (*Mary*), Esther Travers (*Stephen's Mother*), Vernon Newman (*Robert*), Haal Borske (*Willie*), Josef Bush (*Bud*), Phyllis Newman (*Robert's Mother*), Robert Likala (*Jay*).

Burgos is an incredibly stupid college student who researches witchcraft by digging

up the grave of Porter, a long-dead witch. The crazed girl hops out of her coffin and runs wild, bringing a reign of terror to the community in the same manner she did nearly 200 years earlier. The film serves only as an argument against student aid for younsters who can't prove they'll make good use of it. Filmed in Dallas in 1961, the movie was released in 1964, and re-released in 1967 with an additional 20 minutes.

p, Claude Alexander; d, Andy Milligan; w, Clay Guss, ph, Milligan (Eastmancolor).

Horror (PR:C MPAA:NR)

NAKED WOMAN, THE* (1950, Fr.) 90m Sigma/Cohen bw

Giselle Pascal (*Loulou*), Yves Vincent (*Pierre*), Pierre Magnier (*Le Prince*), Jean Davy (*Rouchard*), Paul Faivre (*Le Pere Louis*), Arthur Allan (*Jacopoulos*), Jean Toulout (*Garsin*), Michele Philippe (*La Princesse*), Paulette Dubost (*Suzon*).

Vincent is a struggling Parisian artist who lives with model Pascal. His works are soon acclaimed and he becomes famous, with success going to his head. He meets and has an affair with the wealthy Phillippe, though he has tied the knot with Pascal. Pascal tries to kill herself, then leaves Vincent for Davy, another artist. Standard love-triangle material given an uninspired treatment. Kelber, who worked with Jean Cocteau, Jean Renoir, and Nicholas Ray, does a commendable job with the photography. (In French; English subtitles).

d, J. Berthomieu; w, S.H. Terac, C. Exbrayat (based on the novel *La Femme Nue* by Henry Bataille); ph, Michel Kelber.

Drama (PR:A MPAA:NR)

NAKED WORLD OF HARRISON MARKS, THE *½ (1967, Brit.) 84m Token/Manson c (AKA: THE DREAM WORLD OF HARRISON MARKS)

Harrison Marks (*Himself/Al Capone/Toulouse-Lautrec/James Bond/Napoleon/Alfie/Count Dracula*), Valentine Dyall, Beryl Christy (*Narrators*), Pamela Green, June Palmer, Chris Williams, Jutka Goz, Annette Johnson, Chris Bromfield, Ken Hayes, Derek Nichols, David Roberts.

This sexploitation fantasy film stars photographer, Harrison Marks, as himself, packaging and distributing feminine beauty. Meanwhile, he dreams that he is Al Capone, Toulouse-Lautrec, James Bond, Napoleon, Alfie, and Dracula and then fears that he has been charged with the prostitution of art.

p&d, George Harrison Marks; w, Marks, Terry Maher, Jim McDonald, William Templeton; ph, Len Harris; m, John Hawksworth; ed, Jim Connock; md, Hawksworth; art d, Tony Roberts.

Fantasy (PR:O MPAA:NR)

NAKED YOUTH*½** (1961, Jap.) Shochiku/New Yorker c (SEISHUN ZANOKU MONOGATARI; AKA: CRUEL STORY OF YOUTH; A STORY OF THE CRUELTIES OF YOUTH)

Yasuke Kawazu (*Kiyoshi Fujii*), Miyuki Kuwano (*Makoto Shinjo*), Yoshiko Kuga (*Yuki Shinjo*), Fumio Watanaba (*Akimoto*), Shinji Tanaka (*Ito*), Shinjiro Matsuzaki (*Terada*), Toshiko Kobayashi (*Teruko Shimonishi*), Jun Hamamura (*Masahiro Shinjo*), Shinko Ujiie, Aki Morishima, Yuki Tominaga, Kei Sate, Asao Sano, Nan Nihonyanagi.

Called by some "the REBEL WITHOUT A CAUSE of Japan," this second feature from Oshima is an energetic, expressionistic venture into an Americanized youth culture. Set apart from traditional Japanese films, in part, by its stark colors and bold, bright neons, it is less concerned with preserving a culture than it is with creating a sensation and is clearly influenced by Godard and American popular music. Kuwano gets through her drab life by picking out men who can drive her home, until one day she chooses a middle-aged pervert who attacks her. Kawazu comes to her aid, knocks the man around, then blackmails him. The young rebels meet again, taking a boat ride on the money they earned the night before. Kawazu makes his move on the still-virginal girl, who slaps his face. Angered and insulted he tosses her into the murky water. Eventually they become lovers, satisfying their growing sexual curiosities. Kuwano soon gives her cigarette-smoking beau the news that he may be a father. Slow to react (he'd rather dance for awhile) he tells her that she can't have the child, later taking her to a dilapidated abortion clinic. They get involved with a group of hoods and wind up in trouble with the police. In the end, overcome by their surroundings (the film was shot in the slum section of Osaka), both die a tragic death at the hands of the hoods. With this picture's release, Oshima quickly rose to the top of the ranks of world film circles, providing a polar opposite to the Japanese mannerisms of directors like Yasujiro Ozu. A beautifully decadent essay on young romanticism, which was followed by the similar THE SUN'S BURIAL. Made in 1960, the film did not gain wide release in the U.S. until 1984, under the title CRUEL STORY OF YOUTH. (In Japanese; English subtitles.)

p, Tomio Ikeda; d&w, Nagisa Oshima; ph, Ko Kawamata (Shochiku Grandscope, Eastmancolor); m, Riichiro Manabe; ed, Keichi Uraoka; art d, Koji Uno.

Drama/Crime (PR:C-O MPAA:NR)

NAKED YOUTH, 1961 (SEE: WILD YOUTH, 1961)

NAKED ZOO, THE zero (1970) 91m Film Artists/R&S c (AKA: THE HALLUCINATORS; THE GROVE; THE NAKED LOVERS)

Rita Hayworth (*Mrs. Golden*), Stephen Oliver (*Terry Shaw*), Ford Rainey (*Mr. Golden*), Fay Spain (*Golden's Daughter*), Fleurette Carter (*Black Woman*), Willie Pastrano, Joe E. Ross, Canned Heat, Steve Alaimo.

Sad to see Hayworth winding down her career in this misguided effort (she would make just one more film before illness forced her retirement). The film is set in Miami where Hayworth lives with Rainey, her crippled millionaire husband. She has an affair with young writer Oliver, and provides him with funds to support his activities, which include hosting LSD parties. Rainey discovers the affair and Oliver kills him in a struggle. Police believe the death was accidental, and Hayworth threatens to tell them otherwise unless Oliver ministers to her needs. He eventually murders her, then has an affair with her daughter, Spain, who kills him at the film's end. The movie had a limited release and so has been seldom seen, a fate it richly deserves. Rock group Canned Heat and 1960s pop singer Steve Alaimo provide some music.

p&d, William Grefe; w, Grefe, Ray Preston (based on a story by Preston)

Drama **(PR:C MPAA:R)**

NAM ANGELS (SEE: LOSERS, THE, 1970)

NAME FOR EVIL, A* (1970) 74m Penthouse/Cinerama c

Robert Culp, Samantha Eggar, Sheila Sullivan, Mike Lane, Reed Sherman, Clarence Miller, Sue Hathaway.

A bizarre and unsuccessful mixture of midlife crisis melodrama and out-and-out horror sees upwardly mobile architect Culp suddenly quit his high-paying job and drag wife Eggar off to the wilds of Canada, where he takes up residence in his great-great- granddaddy's spooky old mansion. Of course the place is haunted, but the ghost happens to be a dashing specter on a white horse and he soon seduces Eggar. Having to compete with a phantom for his wife's affections doesn't suit Culp, so he wanders off into the mountains and into the arms of a willing local lass. Once again one must wonder why actors as talented as Culp and Eggar keep turning up in junk like this.

p, Reed Sherman; d&w, Bernard Girard (based on a novel by Andrew Lytele); m, Dominic Frontiere.

Horror **Cas.** **(PR:C-O MPAA:NR)**

NAME OF THE GAME IS KILL, THE**½ (1968) 88m Fanfare c
(AKA: LOVERS IN LIMBO; THE FEMALE TRAP)

Jack Lord (Symcha Lipa), Susan Strasberg (Mickey Perry), Collin Wilcox (Diz Perry), Tisha Sterling (Nan Perry), T.C. Jones (Mr./Mrs. Perry), Mort Mills (Sheriff Kendall), Marc Desmond (The Doctor).

A real curiosity which Swedish director Hellstrom evidently intended to be a parody of low-budget murder and mayhem films. Set in Jermome, Arizona, the film centers on the bizarre Perry family, headed by Jones, who seems to be Mrs. Perry, but in reality makes himself up to look like his murdered wife. The three Perry daughters are a psychotic Strasberg, a spider-loving Sterling, and the androgynous Wilcox. Lord, a Hungarian refugee, stumbles into the brood when Strasberg picks him up while he is hitchhiking and brings him back to the family gas station. Lord takes a job at the station and then falls in love with Strasberg. Perturbed, the other two sisters try to do him in by tossing him into the incinerator, but the lovers escape and head for California. Apparently Lord didn't stop there as he went from this film to the set of "Hawaii Five-O" as that TV series began its long run. Vilmos Zsigmond (here billed as William) provided the cinematography, as he did for several low-budget projects before stepping up in class in 1971 with Robert Altman's McCABE AND MRS. MILLER.

p, Robert Poore; d, Gunnar Hellstrom; w, Gary Crutcher; ph, William [Vilmos] Zsigmond (Eastmancolor); m, Stu Phillips; ed, Louis Lombardo; md, Phillips; art d, Ray Markham; cos, Sara Anderson; m/l, "Shadows," Phillips, Mike Gordon (sung by The Electric Prunes); makeup, Louis Lane.

Drama **(PR:C MPAA:NR)**

NAME THE WOMAN* (1934) 62m COL bw

Richard Cromwell, Arline Judge, Rita La Roy, Charles Wilson, Thomas Jackson, Bradley Page, Henry Kolker, Purnell Pratt, Crane Wilbur, Eddie Chandler, Wallis Clark, George Humbert, Al Hill, Stanley Fields.

Cromwell stars as a dimwitted rookie reporter who, with the aid of Judge, finds himself hot on the trail of a wanted murderer. He surprises the entire news staff when he uncovers the killer's identity and brings him to justice. Standard crime stuff, which was filmed in 1928 as a silent.

d, Albert Rogell; w, Fred Niblo, Jr., Herbert Asbury; ph, John Stumar; ed, John Rawlins.

Crime/Mystery **(PR:A MPAA:NR)**

NAMELESS (SEE: FRAULEIN DOKTOR, 1969)

NAMONAKU MAZUSHIKU UTSUKUSHIKU (SEE: HAPPINESS OF US ALONE, 1962)

NAMU, THE KILLER WHALE**½ (1966) 86m Tors/UA c

Robert Lansing (Hank Donner), John Anderson (Joe Clausen), Robin Mattson (Lisa Rand), Richard Erdman (Deke), Lee Meriwether (Kate Rand), Joe Higgins (Burt), Michael Shea (Nick), Clara Tarte (Carrie), Edwin Rochelle (Charlie), Namu the Whale.

In the mid-1960s, a killer whale was confined at the Seattle Public Aquarium and its behavior helped to dispel several myths about the species. The whale was named Namu, and it inspired the making of this film, in which it appears as the title character. Lansing plays a marine biologist who is studying whales when a wounded one and his mate swim into a cove. The wounded one dies, and Lansing strings netting across the mouth of the cove so that he might study the survivor. The whale proves to be friendly, but the locals want it destroyed. The whales feed on salmon, and since many of the nearby residents are salmon fisherman, they have little use for Namu and its ilk. The conflict heats up until Lansing finally releases Namu, who swims off and is joined by a new mate. Things did not end so happily for Namu in real life—in trying to escape from the Seattle aquarium, he was caught in netting under a pier and drowned (whales are air-breathing mammals).

p&d, Laslo Benedek; w, Arthur Weiss; ph, Lamar Boren (DeLuxe Color); m, Samuel Matlovsky; ed, Warren Adams; art d, Eddie Imazu; m/l, "The Ballad of Namu the Killer Whale [Live and Let Live]" Tom Glazer (sung by Glazer).

Adventure **(PR:A MPAA:NR)**

NANA**½ (1934) 89m Goldwyn/UA bw (GB: LADY OF THE BOULEVARDS)

Anna Sten (Nana), Phillips Holmes (Lt. George Muffat), Lionel Atwill (Col. Andre Muffat), Richard Bennett (Gaston Greiner), Mae Clarke (Satin), Muriel Kirkland (Mimi), Reginald Owen (Bordenave), Jessie Ralph (Zoe), Lawrence Grant (Grand Duke Alexis), Helen Freeman (Sabine Muffat), Ferdinand Gottschalk (Finot), Hardie Albright (Lt. Gregory), Branch Stevens (Leon), Barry Norton (Louis), Lauri Beatty (Estelle Muffat), Lucille Ball (Chorus Girl), Eily Malyon, Clarence Wilson, Albert Conti, Gino Corrado, Bramwell Fletcher, Wilson Benge, Tom Ricketts, Charles Middleton.

Goldwyn pumped a fortune into this overblown vehicle for his new discovery, Russian actress Sten, but despite its lavish appearance and very real costs, NANA was a miserable failure and Sten went on to become what the industry sneeringly called "Goldwyn's Folly." The Zola story of a famous, beautiful whore was toned down considerably to conform to the newly established Hays censorship office, and, as such, made for a curious, if tepid rags-to-riches tale. Discovered by Bennett, a theatrical impressario, Sten is promoted from street girl to ravishing musical revue entertainer who becomes the rage of 1870s Paris. Every male who meets the beauteous Sten falls under her amorous sway, including a Grand Duke, Grant, and two vying brothers, Holmes and Atwill. In the end, the noble lady commits suicide in order to bring the feuding brothers back together again. (She dies slowly of smallpox in the novel.) Though Arzner's direction, much influenced by Mamoulian and Sternberg, is deft and well-constructed, the main drawback is Sten who is overweight, unconvincing, and a poor imitation of the women Goldwyn envisioned in shaping her screen personality—Garbo and Dietrich. She sings one Rodgers and Hart song, "That's Love," in the same throaty manner as Dietrich, but her Russian accent is so thick that this and all her lines are near-incomprehensible. The Russian-born, Stanislavsky-trained Sten (real name Anjuschka Stenski) had appeared in Pudovkin's STORM OVER ASIA and TEMPEST opposite Emil Jannings. Her English was so bad that it inspired Cole Porter to write a clever and unpublished verse for his tune, "Anything Goes": "If Sam Goldwyn can with great conviction/ Instruct Anna Sten in diction/Then Anna shows/Anything Goes." Goldwyn first saw Sten in a German version of THE BROTHERS KARAMAZOV (DER MORDER DIMITRI KARAMASOFF, 1931), and originally thought to redo this Russian classic with Sten in the leading role but then opted for NANA and brought in his favorite director, George Fitzmaurice. But the production dragged and Fitzmaurice could do nothing with Sten and her interfering husband, Dr. Eugene Frenke. Halfway through the production, Goldwyn looked at the footage and exploded. He fired Fitzmaurice, scrapped all the film shot to date, and hired the expeditious Arzner. Still, Sten never learned English, spoke in rote patterns, and none of the spontaneity she had exhibited in THE BROTHERS KARAMAZOV was present. Goldwyn, who had spent a fortune on the film, decided to throw good money after bad and tried to buy an audience for the film, spending tens of thousands of dollars on publicity. It almost worked. He packed viewers into theaters premiering NANA but audiences soon dwindled and the film fizzled. Goldwyn persisted, putting Sten into two more expensive bombs, WE LIVE AGAIN (1934) and WEDDING NIGHT (1935), but the Russian actress was wholly rejected by American audiences and she went into eclipse.

p, Samuel Goldwyn; d, Dorothy Arzner; w, Willard Mack, Harry Wagstaff Gribble (based on the novel by Emile Zola); ph, Gregg Toland; m, Alfred Newman; ed, Frank Lawrence; art d, Richard Day; cos, Travis Banton, John W. Harkrider, Adrian; m/l, "That's Love," Richard Rodgers, Lorenz Hart.

Drama **(PR:C MPAA:NR)**

NANA*½ (1957, Fr./Ital.) 100m Roitfeld-Cigno/Times c

Martine Carol (Nana), Charles Boyer (Count Muffat), Jacques Castelot (Count Vandeuvres), Paul Frankeur (Bordenave), Noel Roquevert (Steiner), Walter Chiari (Fontan), Jean Debucourt (Napoleon III), Elisa Cegani (Countess Muffat), Marguerite Pierry (Zoe), Pierre Palau (Venot), Dora Doll, Dario Michaelis, Louisella Boni, Jacqueline Plessis, Nerio Bernardi, Jacques Tarride, Germaine Kerjean, Daniel Ceccaldi, Nicole Riche.

An alleged adaptation of the Zola novel features Carol as the luxury-loving slum girl who has a tragic affair with a high government official (Boyer), which leads to the downfall of both characters. Christian-Jacque has filled the movie with his standard high-gloss touches and the film bears little resemblance to Zola's work. (In French; English subtitles.)

d, Christian-Jaque; w, Jean Ferry, Albert Valentin, Henri Jeanson, Christian-Jaque (based on the novel by Emile Zola); ph, Christian Matras (Eastmancolor); m, Georges Van Pary; ed, Jacques Desagneaux.

Drama **Cas.** **(PR:A-C MPAA:NR)**

NANA zero (1983, Ital.) 92m Cannon c

Katya Berger (Nana), Jean-Pierre Aumont (Count Muffat), Mandy Rice-Davis (Countess Sabine), Debra Berger (Satin), Shirin Taylor (Zoe), Yehuda Efroni (Steiner), Paul Mueller (Xavier), Robert Bridges (Fontan), Massimo Serato (Faucherie), Marcus Beresford (Hector), Annier Belle (Renee), Tom Felleghy (Mellier).

A resounding failure, reportedly based ("loosely," the producers say) on Emile Zola's famed novel. All that this fraudulent piece of filmmaking has in common with Zola is the title. Berger is the title character, an opportunistic femme fatale who works her way up the social and financial ladder by first getting support from an amorous banker, then from a government official. The finale has the rungs giving out from under her as she tumbles back to the gutter. Notable only for Morricone's score.

p, Menahem Golan, Yoram Globus; d, Dan Wolman; w, Marc Behm; ph, Armando Nannuzzi; m, Ennio Morricone; prod d, Amadeo Mellone; cos, Ugo Pericoli.

Drama   Cas.   (PR:O MPAA:NR)

NANCY DREW AND THE HIDDEN STAIRCASE**½
(1939) 60m WB bw

Bonita Granville (Nancy Drew), Frankie Thomas (Ted Nickerson), John Litel (Carson Drew), Frank Orth (Capt. Tweedy), Renie Riano (Effie Schneider), Vera Lewis (Floretta Turnbull), Louise Carter (Rosemary Turnbull), William Gould (Daniel Talbert), George Guhl (Smitty), John Ridgely, De Wolf [William] Hopper, Creighton Hale (Reporters), Frank Mayo (Photographer), Fred Tozere (District Attorney Investigator), Don Rowan (Phillips), Dick Elliott (McKeever).

One of the better entries in the Drew series casts Granville in the familiar role of the female sleuth, solving a murder, and helping a children's hospital. A will has bequeathed a mansion to the hospital if two spinsters can spend every night in it for 20 years. Two weeks before the time has expired strange things start happening in the house. Drew and boy friend Thomas get on the case and discover that a gang is trying to drive the old ladies out to acquire the site for a planned racetrack. The cast is solid and the pace is quick. (See NANCY DREW series, Index.)

p, Bryan Foy; d, William Clemens; w, Kenneth Gamet (based on a story by Carolyn Keene); ph, L. William O'Connell; ed, Louis Hesse.

Mystery/Comedy   (PR:AA MPAA:NR)

NANCY DREW—DETECTIVE**
(1938) 60m WB bw

Bonita Granville (Nancy Drew), John Litel (Carson Drew), James Stephenson (Challon), Frankie Thomas (Ted Nickerson), Frank Orth (Inspector Milligan), Renie Riano (Effie Schneider), Helena Phillips Evans (Mary Eldridge), Charles Trowbridge (Hollister), Dick Purcell (Keifer), Ed Keane (Adam Thorne), Brandon Tynan (Dr. Spires), Vera Lewis (Miss Van Deering), Mae Busch (Miss Tyson), Tommy Bupp (Spud Murphy), Lottie Williams (Mrs. Spires).

The movie that started the series based on the popular female sleuth created by Carolyn Keene. The story deals with an eccentric old woman who wants to leave $250,000 to a school. Crooks try to show the old woman is crazy so they can get the money, but Granville proves the woman is sane and the school gets the cash. A pleasant, good-humored romp. (See NANCY DREW series, Index.)

p, Bryan Foy; d, William Clemens, John Langan; w, Kenneth Gamet (based on the story "The Password to Larkspur Lane" by Carolyn Keene); ph, L. William O'Connell; ed, Frank Magee; cos, Milo Anderson.

Mystery/Comedy   (PR:AA MPAA:NR)

NANCY DREW—REPORTER**
(1939) 65m WB-FN bw

Bonita Granville (Nancy Drew), John Litel (Carson Drew), Frank Thomas, Jr. (Ted Nickerson), Mary Lee (Mary), Sheila Bromley (Bonnie Lucas), Larry Williams (Miles Lambert), Betty Amann (Eula Denning), Thomas Jackson (Bostwick), Dickie Jones (Killer Parkins), Olin Howland (Sgt. Entwhistle), Frank Orth (Capt. Tweedy), Charles Halton, Joan Leslie, Florence Halop, Lois Verner, Jack Wagner, Charles Smith.Granville wins a newspaper contest and gets to play reporter. Naturally, she attacks the new task with her customary zeal and in no time she solves a murder, captures the criminals, and clears a suspect's name. Implausible, but entertaining for the youngsters. (See NANCY DREW series, Index.)

p, Bryan Foy; d, William Clemens, John Langan; w, Kenneth Gamet (based on the character created by Carolyn Keene); ph, Arthur Edeson; m, Heinz Roemheld; ed, Frank Dewar.

Mystery/Comedy   (PR:AA MPAA:NR)

NANCY DREW, TROUBLE SHOOTER**½
(1939) 70m WB bw

Bonita Granville (Nancy Drew), Frankie Thomas (Ted Nickerson), John Litel (Carson Drew), Aldrich Bowker (Matt Brandon), Charlotte Wynters (Edna Gregory), Edgar Edwards (Chuck Marley), Renie Riano (Effie Schneider), Roger Imhof (Sheriff Riggs), Erville Alderson (Clinton Griffith), Willie Best (Apollo Johnson), John Harron (Greenhouse Clerk), Cliff Saum (1st Deputy Sheriff), Tom Wilson (2nd Deputy Sheriff).

Gutsy gal sleuth Nancy Drew, again played by Granville, helps her father prove that an old friend is innocent of murder. Dad (Litel) doesn't get much of a chance, however, as Granville out-snoops him and finds the clues that clear the friend's name. (See NANCY DREW series, Index.)

p, Bryan Foy; d, William Clemens; w, Kenneth Gamet (based on the character created by Carolyn Keene); ph, William O'Connell; ed, Doug Gould.

Mystery/Comedy   (PR:AA MPAA:NR)

NANCY GOES TO RIO**½
(1950) 99m MGM c

Jane Powell (Nancy Barklay), Ann Sothern (Frances Elliott), Barry Sullivan (Paul Berten), Carmen Miranda (Marina Rodriguez), Louis Calhern (Gregory Elliott), Scotty Beckett (Scotty Sheldon), Fortunio Bonanova (Ricardo Domingos), Glenn Anders (Arthur Barrett), Nella Walker (Mrs. Harrison), Hans Conried (Alfredo), Frank Fontaine (Masher), Leon Belasco (Prof. Gama), Leonid Kinskey (Ivan Putroff), Danny Scholl (Charles), Ransom Sherman (Dr. Ballard), Sig Arno (Captain of Waiters), Pierre Watkin (Kenneth), Forbes Murray, Bess Flowers (Party Guests).

A remake of IT'S A DATE (1940), which starred Deanna Durbin, NANCY GOES TO RIO features Sothern and Powell as a mother and daughter vying for the same part in a play and the same man—Sullivan. Sothern goes to Rio to ready herself for a part in a new play, and Powell follows, revealing the news that she got the part.

The conflict is intensified with the mistaken belief that Powell is pregnant. In the end, Powell gets the part and Sothern gets Sullivan. The cast is uniformly good, with Calhern supplying some humor as Sothern's father, and it all amounts to pleasant entertainment. Songs include "Time and Time Again" by Earl Brent and Fred Spielman (sung by Powell); "Shine On Harvest Moon" by Jack Norworth, Nora Bayes (sung by Powell, Sothern, Calhern); "Cha Bomm Pa Pa," "Yipsee-I-O" by Ray Gilbert (both sung by Miranda); "Magic is the Moonlight" by Charles Pasquale, Maria Grever (sung by Powell); "Musetta's Waltz" from "La Boheme" by Giacomo Puccini (sung by Powell); "Love is Like This" Jay Gilbert (sung by Powell); "Nancy Goes To Rio" by Georgie Stoll, Brent (sung by Beckett). This was Sothern's last film for MGM, ending a relationship that had started in 1929 when she signed with the studio as a chorus girl named Harriet Lake.

p, Joe Pasternak; d, Robert Z. Leonard; w, Sidney Sheldon (based on a story by Jane Hall, Frederick Kohner, Ralph Block); ph, Ray June (Technicolor); ed, Adrienne Fazan; md, Georgie Stoll; art d, Cedric Gibbons, Jack Martin Smith; cos, Helen Rose.

Musical   (PR:A MPAA:NR)

NANCY STEELE IS MISSING***
(1937) 86m FOX bw

Victor McLaglen (Dannie O'Neill), Walter Connolly (Michael Steele), Peter Lorre (Prof. Sturm), June Lang (Sheila O'Neill/Nancy Steele), Robert Kent (Jimmie Wilson), Shirley Deane (Nancy), John Carradine (Harry Wilkins), Jane Darwell (Mrs. Flaherty), Frank Conroy (Dan Mallon), Granville Bates (Joseph F. X. Flaherty), George Taylor (Gus Crowder), Kane Richmond (Tom), Margaret Fielding (Miss Hunt), DeWitt Jennings (Doctor on Farm), George Humbert (Giuseppi), Robert Murphy, Ed Deering, Frederick Burton, Stanley Andrews, Guy Usher.

Antiwar activist McLaglen kidnaps the baby daughter of munitions magnate Connolly to protest the businessman's involvement in WW I. He renames the girl and leaves her with two life-long friends who know nothing of his crime and assume that the child is his. Meanwhile the press goes wild trying to find the whereabouts of Nancy Steele. Soon after the kidnaping McLaglen is arrested for a fight and is sentenced to two years in prison. While in prison he is unjustly accused of participating in a breakout attempt and his sentence is lengthened to life. As the years roll by Lorre, McLaglen's cellmate, hears the man talk in his sleep and learns the details of the kidnaping. Realizing that the information could be quite valuable to him in the future, Lorre says nothing. Eventually McLaglen is released and he returns home to his "daughter" (Lang), now full grown. Believing McLaglen to be her natural father, Lang accompanies him to New York where he lands a job with Connolly (her real father) as a gardener. When McLaglen learns of a $100,000 reward for the return of Lang, the big man attempts to destroy the only evidence of her identity—the clothes she was wearing when he kidnaped her. Unfortunately Lorre, now out of prison, has tracked McLaglen down and shoots him before he can dispose of the clothes. Lorre takes the clothes and convinces the authorities that another young woman is in fact the missing heiress. McLaglen, whose wounds weren't fatal, recovers and goes after Lorre. Learning that his former cellmate is about to leave the country, McLaglen stops him and forces a full confession, regardless of the fact that the information will send him back to prison for the rest of his life. Secure that Lang, whom he has grown to love as his own, will now reap the benefits of her true parentage, McLaglen nobly faces his fate. While the script of NANCY STEELE IS MISSING may ask the audience to accept more than its fair share of coincidence, the most remarkable aspect of the film is that it got past the Hays Office at all. With the country still stinging from the heart-wrenching kidnaping of the Charles A. Lindbergh child, Hollywood's censor decreed that no films would detail the activities of kidnapers. Not only does NANCY STEELE IS MISSING deal with kidnaping, the kidnaper is shown in a sympathetic light.

p, Nunnally Johnson; d, George Marshall; w, Hal Long, Gene Fowler (based on the story "Ransom" by Charles Francis Coe); ph, Barney McGill; ed, Jack Murray; md, David Buttolph; cos, Gwen Wakeling.

Crime   (PR:A MPAA:NR)

NANNY, THE***
(1965, Brit.) 93m Seven Arts-Hammer/FOX bw

Bette Davis (Nanny), Wendy Craig (Virgie Fane), Jill Bennett (Pen), James Villiers (Bill Fane), William Dix (Joey), Pamela Franklin (Bobby), Jack Watling (Dr. Medman), Alfred Burke (Dr. Wills), Maurice Denham (Dr. Beamaster), Nora Gordon (Mrs. Griggs), Sandra Power (Sarah), Harry Fowler (Milkman), Angharad Aubrey (Susy).

An engaging and disturbing thriller which casts Davis as a well-groomed and proper nanny who, underneath her facade, is really a psychotic killer. When 10-year-old Dix returns from a two-year stay in a home for disturbed children, he reacts coldly to Davis, whom he believes drowned his sister (Aubrey) two years earlier. No one believed his story then, putting the blame on him and having him institutionalized. Still, no one believes him, except for his teenage neighbor Franklin. Dix refuses to eat any food Davis prepares, declines to use the room she prepared for him, and won't talk to her. His mother is hospitalized for food poisoning (after eating one of Davis' special dishes) and when faced with staying alone with Davis, he objects strenuously. Bennett, the boy's aunt, is sent for. She suffers from a heart condition and must keep her heart medicine nearby at all times. Dix runs to Bennett, accusing Davis of trying to drown him in the bathtub. She doesn't believe the tormented boy and sends him to his room. When she checks in on him, however, she finds the nanny preparing to smother him with a pillow. A struggle ensues and Bennett, her pills out of reach, collapses. While she is dying, Davis confesses to the murder of Aubrey. Davis explains that she was giving the two a bath when she received word that her illegitimate daughter, whom she had abandoned years before, was dying after an abortion, and panic-stricken, she left the children unattended, a mistake which resulted in Aubrey's death. Following her confession, Davis returns to Dix's room, to finish him off. While trying to drown him, she has a vision of Aubrey and stops. Tears pouring from her eyes, she packs her bags and leaves. A spotty film which is often frightening, but at times clumsy, though Davis' performance is noteworthy.

p, Jimmy Sangster; d, Seth Holt; w, Sangster (based on the novel by Evelyn Piper); ph, Harry Waxman; m, Richard Rodney Bennett; ed, James Needs; prod d, Edward Carrick; md, Philip Martell; cos, Rosemary Burrows; makeup, Tom Smith.

Horror (PR:O MPAA:NR)

NAPOLEON** (1955, Fr.) 190m Filmsonor-CLM-Francinex/Cinedis c

Jean Pierre Aumont (*Renault de Saint-Jean d'Angely*), Jeanne Boitel (*Mme. de Dino*), Pierre Brasseur (*Barras*), Gianna-Maria Canale (*Pauline Borghese*), Daniel Gelin (*Bonaparte*), Raymond Pellegrin (*Napoleon*), Danielle Darrieux (*Eleonore Denuelle*), Sacha Guitry (*Talleyrand*), Lana Marconi (*Marie Walewska*), Michele Morgan (*Josephine de Beauharnais*), Dany Robin (*Desiree Clary*), Erich von Stroheim (*Beethoven*), Henri Vidal (*Murat*), Orson Welles (*Hudson Lowe*), Pauline Carton (*An Innkeeper*), Jean Chevrier (*Gen. Duroc*), Clement Duhour (*Marshal Ney*), Jacques Dumesnil (*Bernadotte*), O. W. Fisher (*Metternich*), Jean Gabin (*Marshal Lannes*), Cosetta Greco (*Elisa Bacchiochi*), Madeline Lebeau (*Emilie Pellapra*), Jean Marais (*Count de Montholon*), Luis Mariano (*The Singer, Garat*), Armand Mestral (*Marshal Oudinot*), Yves Montand (*Marshal Lefebvre*), Patachou (*Mme. Sans-Gene*), Roger Pigaut (*Caulaincourt*), Micheline Presle (*Hortense de Beauharnais*), Serge Regianni (*Lucien Bonaparte*), Noel Roquevert (*Gen. Cambronne*), Eleonora Rossi-Drago (*Mme. Foures*), Maria Schell (*Marie-Louis d'Autriche*), Maurice Teynac (*Las Cases*).

Guitry's attempt to capture the glory and splendor of Napoleon's reign is largely a failure, despite its star-studded cast and large budget (it was made at a reported cost of $1.8 million, which was at that time a record for a French film). Rather than concentrating on the major events of Napoleon's life and times, Guitry focuses on smaller happenings in the great man's life, as well as his affairs of the heart. The large cast performs competently, with Guitry as statesman Talleyrand getting the best of the script. Hollywood director Eugene Lourie staged the battle scenes and did a commendable job. The movie has a nice look, too, and a satisfactory score, but overall the film's aim exceeds its reach.

d&w, Sacha Guitry; ph, Pierre Montazel (Eastmancolor); m, Jean Francaix; ed, Raymond Lamy.

Biography (PR:A MPAA:NR)

NAPOLEON AND SAMANTHA**½ (1972) 92m Disney/BV c

Michael Douglas (*Danny*), Will Geer (*Grandpa*), Arch Johnson (*Chief of Police*), Johnny Whitaker (*Napoleon Wilson*), Jodie Foster (*Samantha*), Henry Jones (*Mr. Gutteridge*), Major (*Major, the Lion*), Vito Scotti (*The Clown*), John Crawford (*Desk Sergeant*), Mary Wickes (*Clerk*), Ellen Corby (*Gertrude*), Rex Holman (*Mark*), Claude Johnson (*Gary*), John Lupton (*Pete*), John Ortega, Monty Margetts.

The story is set in Oregon where Whitaker lives on a farm with his grandfather, Geer. A little excitement enters their lives when a circus performer persuades them to take in Major, an aging lion. The fun is short-lived, however, as Geer falls ill and dies. Fearing he'll be sent to an orphanage, Whitaker, with the help of Douglas, covers up the death. When the locals start to suspect something is wrong, Whitaker and his friend Foster take off with Major to find Douglas, who lives somewhere in the mountains. The rest of the film recounts their exploits, climaxing with a last-minute rescue from Holman, a dangerous psychotic who has escaped from a mental institution. The basic Disney staples of kids, animals, and nature combine to make this a worthwhile film for the children. The movie marked Foster's screen debut.

p, Winston Hibler; d, Bernard McEveety; w, Stewart Raffill; ph, Monroe P. Askins (Technicolor); m, Buddy Baker; ed, Robert Stafford; art d, John B. Mansbridge, Walter M. Simonds; set d, Emile Kuri; cos, Chuck Keehne, Emily Sundby; makeup, Robert J. Schiffer.

Adventure (PR:AAA MPAA:G)

NARAYAMA-BUSHI-KO (SEE: BALLAD OF NARAYAMA, 1961, Jap.)

NARCO MEN, THE** (1969, Span./Ital.) 95m Pan-Latina/RAF c (PERSECUCION HASTA VALENCIA; IL SAPORE DELLA VENDETTA)

Tom Tryon (*Harry Bell*), Lorenza Guerrieri (*Jill*), Ana Castor (*Sonia*), Jose Bodalo (*Marcos*), Richard Deacon, Mirko Ellis, Jesus Puente, Aurora de Alba, Franco Fantasia, Paul Muller, Jose Maria Prada, Wolfgang Hillinger, Robert Hundar, Carlos Ballesteros, Franco Ressel, Emilio Redondo, Raf Baldassarre, Carlos Mendy, Angel Jordan, Carlos Riera, Luis Gasper, Saturno Carra, Diego Santiesteban, Jose Ignacio Pidal, Francisco Brana, Victor Israel, Hector Quiroga, Angel Menendez.

Tryon is a cynical former INTERPOL agent who was framed for a crime and did a stretch in prison. Bodalo is a criminal who is held responsible by his bosses when a shipment of heroin is stolen, and is told he'll be killed unless he can get the shipment back. He hires Tryon to help, and the trail takes him from Madrid to Barcelona, Rome, Naples, Valencia, and Athens. Along the way, he finds and does away with the woman who framed him and locates the heroin, turning it over to the authorities—leading to the death of Bodalo. More travelog than movie, this may have been the film that drove Tryon from the acting profession. After the movie he took up writing, his most successful work being the novel *The Other* which was turned into a popular film in 1972.

p, Sam X. Abarbanel, Angel Ibarra, Santiago Moncada; d, Julio Coll; w, Howard Berk, Moncada, Sergio Donati, Coll; ph, Oberdan Trojani (Techniscope, Eastmancolor); m, Marcello Giombini; ed, Mercedes Alonso; art d, Eduardo Torre de la Fuente.

Crime (PR:O MPAA:M)

NARCOTICS STORY, THE zero (1958) 75m Police Science/ Harry Stern c (AKA: THE DREADED PERSUASION)

Sharon Strand, Darlene Hendricks, Herbert Crisp, Fred Marratto, Allen Pitt, Patricia Lynn, Bob Hopkins.

Originally produced as a police training film on drug enforcement, this movie had a limited release in 1958. It's a semi-documentary which, in addition to depicting the evils of drug addiction, also serves as something as a primer for aspiring drug users, detailing how drugs are obtained and used. Professional actors portray the alleged real-life film characters, with little dialog utilized since most of the story is told in narration. A curious theatrical release which might serve as a companion piece to REEFER MADNESS (1936).

p&d, Robert W. Larsen; w, Roger E. Garris; ph, Jerry L. May (Eastmancolor); m, Alexander Laszlo; ed, Dave DePate.

Drama (PR:O MPAA:NR)

NARK, THE (SEE: LA BALANCE, 1983, Fr.)

NARROW CORNER, THE*** (1933) 71m WB bw

Douglas Fairbanks, Jr. (*Fred Blake*), Patricia Ellis (*Louise Frith*), Dudley Digges (*Dr. Saunders*), Ralph Bellamy (*Eric*), Arthur Hohl (*Capt. Nichols*), Henry Kolker (*Fred's Father*), Willie Fung (*Ah Kay*), Reginald Owen (*Frith*), William V. Mong (*Swan*), Joseph Swickard (*Dutch Constable*), Sidney Toler, Henry Kolker, Willie Fung.

An engrossing film adaptation of Somerset Maugham's novel featuring an outstanding cast of supporting players. Fairbanks plays a young Englishman who commits a murder in Australia and is sent out to sea by his powerful father, Kolker, in the hopes that the furor over the crime will die down. Kolker entrusts his son to craggy old skipper Hohl, who drinks heavily to numb the pain of the cancer that slowly consumes him. Fairbanks and Hohl become friends, and at one port of call they acquire Digges, an opium-smoking defrocked physician who comes along for the ride. After braving some violent South Seas storms, the trio stop at a tiny island and are invited to dinner by an eccentric British family that lives there. At dinner Fairbanks falls in love with the daughter, Ellis, despite the fact that she is engaged to Bellamy (the eternal doomed fiancee of the 1930s). Seeing that his sweetheart has fallen for the seafaring stranger, Bellamy commits suicide, leaving behind enough evidence to throw suspicion of murder on Fairbanks once again. THE NARROW CORNER is a solid adventure film which contains some surprisingly intense and effective scenes of sea storms while etching a memorable array of characterizations. The wandering misfits (Fairbanks, Hohl, and Digges) are vividly portrayed, each with his own endearing character quirks. Hohl is especially fine as the gruff, drunken, and slowly dying captain. The film was remade in 1936 as ISLE OF FURY, an early Humphrey Bogart vehicle, but the original version remains the better of the two.

p, Hal Wallis; d, Alfred E. Green; w, Robert Presnell (based on a novel by W. Somerset Maugham); ph, Tony Gaudio; ed, Bert Levy.

Adventure (PR:C MPAA:NR)

NARROW MARGIN, THE*** (1952) 71m RKO bw

Charles McGraw (*Walter Brown*), Marie Windsor (*Mrs. Neil*), Jacqueline White (*Ann Sinclair*), Gordon Gebert (*Tommy Sinclair*), Queenie Leonard (*Mrs. Troll*), David Clrake (*Kemp*), Peter Virgo (*Densel*), Don Beddoe (*Gus Forbes*), Paul Maxey (*Jennings*), Harry Harvey (*Train Conductor*), Mike Lally (*Taxi Driver*), Don Dillaway, George Sawaya (*Reporters*), Tony Merrill (*Officer Allen*), Howart Mitchell (*Train Conductor*), Milton Kibbee (*Tenant*), Don Haggerty (*Detective Wilson*), Johnny Lee, Ivan H. Browning, Clarence Hargrave, Edgar Murray (*Waiters*), Napoleon Whiting, Bobbie Johnson (*Redcaps*), Will Lee (*Newsstand Owner*), Franklin Parker (*Telegraph Attendant*), Jasper Weldon (*Porter*).

A competent B movie from RKO which takes place almost entirely on board a train from Chicago to Los Angeles. McGraw is a hard-boiled detective who, with his partner Beddoe, is assigned to escort a racketeer's widow, Windsor, to a West Coast court where she will give testimony before a grand jury. However, three thugs aboard the train are trying to shut her up—permanently. Unfortunately for the gang they do not know what the widow looks like, forcing them to bump off anyone they suspect might be she. Beddoe is quickly killed, angering McGraw, who feels that his partner's life was more worthwhile than Windsor's. McGraw is befriended by White, a rather pleasant woman who is making the trip with her son, Gebert. The gang becomes more threatening and tries to bribe McGraw, as well as physically intimidate him. McGraw holds his ground and remains loyal to Windsor and his badge. Pushed to the limit, the gang kills Windsor. McGraw, however, learns that Windsor was actually a policewoman acting as a decoy on behalf of White, who is really the racketeer's widow. White's true identity was obscured only because the police thought McGraw might buckle under the pressure and supply the gang with crucial information. White safely reaches her destination while McGraw admits his disappointment in himself for wrongly and falsely judging the two women. While far from a masterpiece crime picture, THE NARROW MARGIN is a well-executed programmer which turned a fantastic profit for RKO, considering its meager $230,000 budget. Audiences loved the film—thrilling at the plot twists, the characters, and the trick train photography—and turned it into one of the studio's most profitable B movies.

p, Stanley Rubin; d, Richard Fleischer; w, Earl Fenton (based on a story by Martin Goldsmith, Jack Leonard); ph, George E. Diskant; ed, Robert Swink; art d, Albert S. D'Agostino, Jack Okey; set d, Darrell Silvera, William Stevens.

Crime/Drama Cas. (PR:A MPAA:NR)

NARROWING CIRCLE, THE**½   (1956, Brit.) 66m Fortress/Eros bw

Paul Carpenter (Dave Nelson), Hazel Court (Rosemary Speed), Russell Napier (Sir Henry Dimmock), Trevor Reid (Inspector "Dumb" Crambo), Paula Byrne (Laura Martin), June Ashley (Christy), Ferdy Mayne (Bill Strayte), Basil Dignam (George Pacey), Ronald [Ronnie] Stevens, Mary Jones, Alan Robinson, Hugh Latimer.

Two men who are both up for the same position on a magazine are also after the same woman. One of the rivals is found dead in the other man's apartment, leaving the remaining writer in deep trouble. He can't prove his alibi, so he must take up his own search into the crime. Not a bad film, with some good performances.

p, Frank Bevis; d, Charles Saunders; w, Doreen Montgomery (based on the novel by Julian Symonds); ph, Jonah Jones.

Crime   **(PR:C MPAA:NR)**

NASHVILLE*****   (1975) 159m PAR c

David Arkin (Norman, Chauffeur), Barbara Baxley (Lady Pearl), Ned Beatty (Delbert Reese), Karen Black (Connie White), Ronee Blakley (Barbara Jean), Timothy Brown (Tommy Brown), Keith Carradine (Tom Frank), Geraldine Chaplin (Opal), Robert Doqui (Wade), Shelley Duvall (L. A. Joan), Allen Garfield [Goorwitz] (Barnett), Henry Gibson (Haven Hamilton), Scott Glenn (Pfc. Glenn Kelly), Jeff Goldblum (Tricycle Man), Barbara Harris (Albuquerque), David Hayward (Kenny Fraiser), Michael Murphy (John Triplette), Allan Nicholls (Bill), Dave Peel (Bud Hamilton), Cristina Raines (Mary), Bert Remsen (Star), Lily Tomlin (Linnea Reese), Gwen Welles (Sueleen Gay), Keenan Wynn (Mr. Green), James Dan Calvert (Jimmy Reese), Donna Denton (Donna Reese), Merle Kilgore (Trout, Bar Owner), Carol McGinnis (Jewel), Sheila Bailey, Patti Bryant (Smokey Mountain Laurel), Richard Baskin (Frog, Piano Player), Jonnie Barnett, Vassar Clements, Misty Mountain Boys, Sue Barton, Elliott Gould, Julie Christie (Themselves).

NASHVILLE is Robert Altman's triumph. Would that he could return to the thinking he put into this film instead of some of the misfires he's done since. Perhaps the most complex modern picture ever made, it sprawls over two and one-half hours and never flags as it successfully introduces, defines, and wraps up 24 different characters so wonderfully that we never have the feeling we're watching a Tin Pan Valley soap opera, which, of course, it is. It isn't easy to single out performances because every actor has his or her moment to strut on stage and each one scores. Although apparently a melange of sights and sounds, everything miraculously comes together at the conclusion and we sit there at the finale, limp from having been pushed, dragged, uplifted, and wrung out by Altman's direction and Tewkesbury's script (although it is said that the actors spent a great deal of time improvising on her theme and that much of the dialog was contributed by the players). The music is more a part of NASHVILLE than in most films and even if you do not cotton to country sounds, you'll still enjoy this. Altman cuts back and forth between the characters (in the same way that several prime-time TV shows have taken to doing), but with such aplomb that the narrative is never lost and even the simplest of minds can follow the action, which all takes place on one climactic weekend in the Country Music Capital of America. There's a huge music festival taking place in Nashville, and, at the same time, a political rally is slated to promote the candidacy of the never-seen presidential hopeful Hal Phillip Walker, who leads a new entity known as the Replacement Party. Although Walker's politics are not deeply plumbed, he sounds vaguely like George Wallace did when he was running on his third-party ticket. Walker's aides, Murphy and Beatty, know who his appeal is to and they prevail upon several of the top singers of this kind of music to help. Gibson, playing a veteran performer who appeared to be patterned after Hank Snow, is the gray eminence whom most of the younger performers believe and venerate. Despite his "down home" smile as he sings, Gibson manages to give the audience the subtext of who he really is: a mean, rotten, and self-serving man who would sell his mother for a gold record. Also in the top echelon is Blakley, a nervous young folk singer who has just recovered from a mental breakdown and seems to be teetering on the edge of another. The festival has attracted singers from all over the country, all hoping to have their moment in the sun, be discovered, and take their places in the Pantheon of Pickin' and Grinnin'. Carradine is one of a trio of folk singers. He's skin stretched over lechery and is currently sleeping with partner Nicholl's wife, Raines. That doesn't stop him from spreading his favors with Tomlin, Beatty's wife, and Chaplin, a BBC correspondent who is covering the festival for the listeners in the British Isles. Blakley's first concert is a flop, as she can't handle being in front of a crowd after such a long layoff, and her husband-manager, Garfield, tells the annoyed assemblage that she will give them all a free concert in a couple of days to make up for this one. Blakley's character seems to have been based on the life of Loretta Lynn, which was further delineated by Sissy Spacek in her award-winning performance in the COAL MINER'S DAUGHTER. Beatty comes to Blakley and Garfield and asks her to appear for Walker at the rally and she agrees. Beatty and Murphy stage a small fund-raising stag party and hire waitress Welles to sing. She has a great figure but a voice that only flirts with the melody she attempts, so when it becomes an embarrassment, the men at the stag scream for her to "take it off," and when Beatty tells her that he'll give her a chance to sing at the rally, she does just that—thereby giving the movie an "R" rating for the brief look at her breasts. (Note: The leering men at the stag were actually played by some members of the Nashville Chamber of Commerce who were totally convincing.) After she finishes, Beatty vainly attempts to bed Welles. On the day of the rally, Hayward, whom we've seen flit in and out of the film carrying a violin case, comes to the stage and shoots Gibson and Blakley after their singing has stopped the show. Blakley is carried off by medical aides, and unknown Harris, who's been waiting patiently to get her break, races to the microphone and begins to sing in order to calm down the crowd while Welles stands in the wings for the chance that will not be given. Now. . .that's the basic plot but the touches and the other roles are all worth a mention. Karen Black is one of those second-line singers who open for Johnny Cash and who has never had a record that went higher than number 32 on the C&W charts. Baxley impresses as the owner of a small bar who is cynical until she lets her hair down and talks of her love for the slain Kennedys. Wynn and Duvall appear briefly, but tellingly, as a rich Southerner and his country groupie girl friend. Tim Brown (playing a character not unlike Charlie Pride) is the black singer who has crossed over to become a success in the white world. Glenn is the faithful puppy-dog serviceman who is entranced by Blakley, Goldblum is the local hippie, Arkin is a chauffeur who has seen it all, and Peel is Gibson's son, a boy who does whatever his father asks and hates every minute of it. On top of all that, Gould and Christie come in to do cameos as themselves, two movie stars tub-thumping a new project. Amazingly, this movie was shot for about $2 million in less than 45 days. In order to do that, there was a favored-nations clause among the stars and they all received the same amount of money for their roles. With no special or economic jealousy, they worked closely with each other, and, when not called before the cameras, spent their off-hours honing their scenes and being prepared for the snappy shooting schedule. Tewkesbury and Altman were quite willing to allow the script to be altered by the actors if they felt it could be improved. Made on location in Nashville, the final concert scenes used many cameras and were shot in one day. That morning, there was a rainstorm and since it was the last day of shooting, the moisture could have wreaked havoc, but legend has it that Altman stepped outside, looked up at the gray skies, and shouted, "Stop!" and it did. (This may or may not have had any influence on Altman's later films.) The huge crowd was assembled by the promise of free food and free entertainment at the Parthenon, a replica of the Greek edifice that was built in 1876 as part of Tennessee's Centennial Exposition. Earlier on the final shooting day, some dangerous convicts had escaped from a local jail and the crowd was peppered with real police officers on the off chance that the prisoners might try to get away by using the huge crowd as a shield. Susan Anspach was supposed to play the neurotic singer, but there was some trouble about her contract, and Altman decided to hire Anspach's vocal coach instead. Blakley, who later married German director Wim Wenders and continued her acting career after debuting in NASHVILLE. If we had to pick out stars, they'd be Harris, as a quirky tyro; Garfield as the greedy, grasping husband of Blakley; Tomlin as Beatty's wife, in a carefully controlled dramatic performance; and, most of all, Gibson, as the man who holds it all together. Gibson's career soared when he created the meek poet character which put him on "Laugh-In," but he is an actor of such enormous range that he manages to convince us in this difficult role that he is the man he wants us to believe he is. With all of the above plot, they still managed to get in some fine songs, many of which were written by the actors themselves. Composer Baskin teamed with several to do the bulk of the material. Songs include: "Two Hundred Years," "Keep A'Goin'" (Richard Baskin, Henry Gibson), "One, I Love You," "Let Me Be the One" (Baskin), "The Day I Looked Jesus in the Eye" (Baskin, Robert Altman), "For the Sake of the Children" (Baskin, Richard Reicheg), "I Never Get Enough" (Baskin, Ben Raleigh), "It Don't Worry Me," "I'm Easy" "Honey" (Keith Carradine), "Down to the River," "Tapedeck in His Tractor (The Cowboy Song)," "Bluebird," "My Idaho Home," "Dues" (Ronee Blakley), "Sing a Song" (Joe Raposo), "The Heart of a Gentle Woman" (Dave Peel), "Rose's Cafe" (Allan Nicholls), "Old Man Mississippi" (Juan Grizzle), "Since You've Gone" (Gary Busey), "Trouble in the U.S.A." (Arlene Barnett), "My Baby's Cookin' in Another Man's Pan" (Jonnie Barnett), "Swing Low, Sweet Chariot" (Traditional, arranged by Millie Clements), "Yes, I Do" (Baskin, Lily Tomlin), "Memphis," "I Don't Know If I Found It in You," "Rolling Stone" (Karen Black). Jonnie Barnett, Sue Barton, Vassar Clements and the Misty Mountain Boys also appeared as themselves. This was an ambitious project, a bold idea, and a perfect realization of Altman's dream. Make more of these, Robert, instead of those dreadful exercises like HEALTH, A WEDDING, and QUINTET. Carradine's tune, "I'm Easy," won the Oscar, and the movie, Altman, Tomlin, and Blakley were nominated as well. Gibson was wrongfully overlooked but the Academy must have had a hard time deciding who was a leading performer and who was a supporter in a movie where everyone was a star who supported the others.

p&d, Robert Altman; w, Joan Tewkesbury; ph, Paul Lohmann, (Panavision, Metrocolor); m, Richard Baskin; ed, Sidney Levin, Dennis Hill; md, Baskin; makeup, Tommy Thompson.

Drama   **Cas.**   **(PR:C-O MPAA:R)**

NASHVILLE GIRL   (SEE: NEW GIRL IN TOWN, 1977)

NASHVILLE REBEL**   (1966) 95m AIP c

Waylon Jennings (Arlin Grove), Tex Ritter, Sonny James, Faron Young, Loretta Lynn, Porter Wagoner, Wilburn Brothers, Henny Youngman, Archie Campbell, Cousin Jody (Themselves), Gordon Oas-Heim (Wesley Lang), Mary Frann (Molly Morgan), Ce-Ce Whitney (Margo Powell).

Chock full of some excellent country music singers, this film stars Jennings as an ex-GI who becomes a local sensation with his singin' and a' strummin'. He marries Frann, and has a run-in with a crooked agent, eventually resorting to drink. His wife puts him back on his feet when she cons Ritter into giving Jennings a shot at the Grand Ole Opry. Songs include "Nashville Rebel," "Green River," "Long Way from Home," "Nashville Bum," "Silver Ribbons" (sung by Jennings), "Hillbilly Heaven" (sung by Ritter), "Country Music's Gone to Town" (Wagoner), "Sweet Dream of You" (sung by Young), "Do What You Do, Do Well" (sung by James), "Christmas at the Opry" (sung by Wilburn Brothers, Lynn), "You Ain't Woman Enough" (sung by Lynn).

p, Fred A. Niles; d, Jay Sheridan; w, Ira Kerns, Sheridan (based on a story by Click Weston); ph, John Eisenbach (Techniscope, Technicolor); m, Robert Blanford; ed, James Miller; cos, Mary Ann Curtis.

Musical   **(PR:A MPAA:NR)**

NASILJE NA TRGU   (SEE:SQUARE OF VIOLENCE, 1963, US/Yugo.)

NASTY HABITS*** (1976, Brit.) 92m Bowden/Brut c

Glenda Jackson *(Alexandra)*, Melina Mercouri *(Gertrude)*, Geraldine Page *(Walburga)*, Sandy Dennis *(Winifred)*, Anne Jackson *(Mildred)*, Anne Meara *(Geraldine)*, Susan Penhaligon *(Felicity)*, Edith Evans *(Hildegarde)*, Jerry Stiller *(P.R. Priest)*, Rip Torn *(Maximilian)*, Eli Wallach *(Monsignor)*, Suzanne Stone *(Bathildis)*, Peter Bromilow *(Baudouin)*, Shane Rimmer *(Officer)*, Harry Ditson *(Ambrose)*, Chris Muncke *(Gregory)*, Oliver Maguire *(1st Policeman)*, Alick Hayes *(Abbot)*, Bill Reimbold *(Bishop's Secretary)*, Anthony Forrest *(Thomas)*, Mike Douglas, Bill Jorgensen, Jessica Savitch, Howard K. Smith *(Themselves)*.

Based on a British novel by Muriel Spark, they've transposed the setting to a Philadelphia convent and paralleled the tactics and backstabbing of the Watergate affair to make their point. It's a *roman a clef* with women playing the roles of the real men who almost took the U.S. under. True, it's only one joke and they do it over and over, but Glenda Jackson, as a cloistered Nixon, and Dennis, who looks enough like John Dean to be his sister, play their parts to the hilt, and the lack in the plot is more than made up for by the sharp dialog and excellent ensemble acting. The picture was either hated or loved by those who saw it, and you must make that decision yourself. Evans is the old abbess of the Pennsylvania convent and she is dying (she actually did die shortly after this film was made and it was her last picture in a movie career that only began when she turned 60) and ready to name Glenda Jackson, a rock-ribbed hard-liner, to take over. Jackson and her aides, Page and Anne Jackson, have to get Evans to sign a document of intent. Along comes Penhaligon, a liberal breath of fresh air, who wants to change the nature of the institution. Her interruption is what keeps Evans from signing the document and Evans expires. Now the leadership of the convent must be put to a vote of the members. Mercouri, a jet-setting missionary, arrives for the funeral services but Glenda Jackson wants to get rid of her right away, as she fears her popularity might upset matters. Jackson knows that Penhaligon is getting it on with Forrest, a Jesuit, and she intends to bring that to the light of day. Jackson has the entire convent wired for sound by men posing as plumbers (get it?) and the controls for the electronic eavesdropping are placed in a statue on the grounds. The plan is to purloin Forrest's love letters to Penhaligon and show them around. The missives are in the girl's sewing basket, but all the thieves come up with is a thimble. Penhaligon is alerted to the theft, catches the crooks, locks them in a room, and calls the cops. Page and Anne Jackson try to talk the cops out of it but the news hits the media. Glenda Jackson begins a campaign among the nuns and wins the election, thereby causing Penhaligon to flee the convent and begin public demonstrations in downtown Philadelphia. She decries the convent's corruption, gives out tracts, and the papers and TV pounce on the story. Jackson and the others seek to keep it mum, but the two Jesuit thieves have their collars taken off and say they will spill the beans unless they get some monetary compensation. Jackson, Page, and Anne Jackson get hold of the addled Dennis and ask her to make a cash payment to the two men. Meanwhile, Penhaligon contacts Mike Douglas, does a TV appearance, and demands a federal probe. She knows there are tapes of what's been happening and wants them exposed. Page and Anne Jackson tell Jackson that she must destroy the evidence, but the abbess thinks she can edit them and use them for blackmail. Dennis, dressed in male drag, is arrested in a men's room as she makes another payment to the blackmailers. Jackson goes on TV and announces that she's had to fire her aides, Page, Anne Jackson, and Dennis, for some infractions and she claims that she knew nothing of what was transpiring in the convent (insisting that she wants to make things "perfectly clear" all the while). There is still a demand for the tapes although Jackson says that they are as sacrosanct as anything said in the confessional. Jackson is fired by the powers in Rome and replaced by Meara. As Jackson departs for the Vatican on a plane, she still maintains that she is not guilty of any wrongdoing and mentions that the assembled press "won't have her to kick around anymore." Sure it's belabored, and, yes, we know exactly what's going to happen, but screenwriter Enders has dipped his quill in acid and written a scathing denunciation that is as funny as it is vicious. We would have liked to have seen more of Evans, who, at 88, stole the scenes in which she appeared. Cameo appearances by Douglas, Howard K. Smith, Jessica Savitch, and a local Philly newsman, Bill Jorgenson.

p, Robert Enders; d, Michael Lindsay-Hogg; w, Enders (based on a novel *The Abbess of Crewe* by Muriel Spark); ph, Douglas Slocombe (Panavision, Technicolor); m, John Cameron; ed, Peter Tanner; art d, Robert Jones; set d, Harry Cordwell; makeup, Richard Mills, George Frost, Enrico Cortese.

Satire **(PR:C MPAA:PG)**

NASTY RABBIT, THE** (1964) 85m Fairway International c (AKA: SPIES-A-GO-GO)

Mischa Terr *(Mischa Lowzoff)*, Arch Hall, Jr. *(Britt Hunter)*, Melissa Morgan *(Cecelia)*, William Watters [Arch Hall, Sr.] *(Marshall Malouf/Malcolm McKinley)*, Little Jack Little *(Maxwell Stoppic)*, Ray Vegas *(Gonzales)*, John Akana *(Col. Kobayaski)*, Harold Bizzy *(Heinrich Krueger)*, Sharon Ryker *(Jackie)*, Hal Bokar *(Gavin)*, George Morgan *(Hubert Jackson)*, Leslie [Laszlo] Kovacs *(The Idiot)*, Pat and Lolly Vegas, The Archers *(Themselves)*.

Fairway International, which had achieved some success churning out sex and violence epics for the drive-in crowd, ventured into comedy this time out with unimpressive results. Story features Terr as a Soviet agent assigned to smuggle the title creature into the U.S. The rabbit is contaminated with deadly germs, and Terr is to release it, allowing it to wander the country, causing a lethal epidemic. Terr heads for a Wyoming dude ranch where he disguises himself as a cowboy and battles with the rest of the cast, all of whom are agents of various nations. Eventually, the bunny is rendered harmless by an FBI agent and a Pentagon employee. A funny premise which fails badly in execution. The cinematography is notable, however, handled admirably by Zsigmond and his assistant, Laszlo Kovacs, both of whom would go on to be among the most respected cameramen in the industry. Kovacs, billed as Leslie Kovacs, also has a small part in the film as "The Idiot."

p, Nicholas Merriwether [Arch Hall, Sr.]; d, James Landis; w, Arch Hall, Sr., Jim Crutchfield; ph, William [Vilmos] Zsigmond (Techniscope, Technicolor); ed, Anthony M. Lanza; art d, Don Schneider; m/l, "The Robot Walk," "Jackie," "The Spy Waltz," "The Jackrabbit Shuffle," Pat Vegas, Lolly Vegas (sung by Arch Hall, Jr., Pat Vegas, Lolly Vegas, The Archers); makeup, Rafaelle Harrod.

Comedy/Musical **(PR:A MPAA:NR)**

NATCHEZ TRACE** (1960) 80m Panorama bw

Zachary Scott *(John A. Morrow)*, William Campbell *(Virgil Stewart)*, Marcia Henderson *(Ruth Henning)*, Irene James *(Lolette)*, Kenne Duncan *(William Murrell)*, Ann Kelly *(Flo)*, Jim Reppert *(Sam Goodrich)*, Annette Alexander *(Emily Goodrich)*, Al Scott *(Sheriff Beesom)*, Mario Galento *(Turner)*, Frank Cunningham *(Nobby Simpkins)*, Frank White *(Mr. Henning)*, Robert Booth *(Clanton)*, Tom Moore *(Bo Hunter)*, Roy Haggard, Sr. *(Governor)*, Curtis Dossett *(Maddox)*, Doug Underwood *(Young Captain)*, Cecil Scaife *(Sentry)*, Gloria Adams *(Liza)*, Willie Adams *(Buck)*.

Scott plays a cruel outlaw in 1830s Tennessee who is determined to create his own network of marauders. He accidentally kills Campbell's father-in-law to be, so the righteous man swears revenge. Henderson is a woman in between the two men. She wants Campbell to find her father's killer, but isn't content to let him do all the work and takes a job in the bar owned by Scott's brother. Nothing special.

p, Lloyd Royal, Tom Carray; d, Alan Crosland; w, D. D. Beauchamp, William R. Cox.

Western **(PR:C MPAA:NR)**

NATE AND HAYES½** (1983, U.S./New Zealand 100m PAR c (GB: SAVAGE ISLANDS)

Tommy Lee Jones *(Capt. Bully Hayes)*, Michael O'Keefe *(Nate Williamson)*, Max Phipps *(Ben Pease)*, Jenny Seagrove *(Sophie)*, Grant Tilly *(Count von Rittenberg)*, Peter Rowley *(Louis Beck)*, Bill Johnson *(Rev. Williamson)*, Kate Harcourt *(Mrs. Williamson)*, Reg Ruka *(Moaka)*, Roy Billing *(Auctioneer)*, Bruce Allpress *(Blake)*, David Letch *(Ratbag)*, Prince Tui Teka *(King of Ponape)*, Pudji Waseso *(Fong)*, Peter Vere Jones *(Gunboat Captain)*, Tom Vanderlaan *(Count's Lieutenant)*, Mark Hadlow *(Gun Operator)*, Phillip Gordon *(Timmy)*, Norman Fairley *(Pegleg)*, Warwick Simmons *(Pug)*, Paul Farrel, Frank Taurua, Norman Kessing, Robert Bruce, Timothy Lee, Peter Bell, Peter Diamond, John Rush, Grant Price, Karl Bradley *(Crewmen)*.

Although the title sounds more like a prime time television cop show, NATE AND HAYES is an admirable attempt to recreate the swashbuckling movies of days gone by. Flashbacks tell the tale of a friendship between pirate Jones and missionary O'Keefe, who together search the seas for Phipps (Jones' murderous ex-partner) and Seagrove (O'Keefe's kidnaped wife). The photography shows the New Zealand and Fiji Islands locations to their best advantage, and Jones turns in an impressively athletic performance, but heavy reliance on cliches renders this film only slightly above-average entertainment.

p, Lloyd Phillips, Rob Whitehouse; d, Ferdinand Fairfax; w, John Hughes, David Odell (based on a screen story by Odell and a story by Phillips); ph, Tomy Imi (Rank-Film Lab Color); m, Trevor Jones; ed, John Shirley; prod d, Maurice Cain; art d, Jo Ford, Dan Hennah, Rick Kofoed; cos, Norma Moriceau; spec eff, Peter Dawson.

Adventure/Comedy **Cas.** **(PR:C MPAA:PG)**

NATHALIE½** (1958, Fr.) 100m SNEG-Internationale-Electra/Times bw (AKA: FOXIEST GIRL IN PARIS)

Martine Carol *(Nathalie)*, Michel Piccoli *(Frank Marchal, Policeman)*, Philippe Clay *(Coco, The Giraffe)*, Mischa Auer *(Cyril Boran)*, Lise Delamare *(The Countess de Lancey)*, Aime Clariond *(The Count)*, Louis Seigner *(Inspector Pippart)*, Armande Navarre *(Pivoine)*, Jacques Dufilho *(Simon, the Valet)*, Frederic O'Brady *(The Traveler)*, Gernand Ruzena *(Geo)*, Jess Hahn *(Sam)*.

Director Christian-Jaque casts his wife, Carol, as a sprightly Paris model who is mistakenly accused of theft. This leads to a series of comic misadventures as she gets involved with a couple of rival gangs while attempting to clear her name. Eventually she does, and falls in love with policeman Piccoli in the process. The nicely handled plot complications and Carol's winning performance combine to make this an enjoyable comedy. (In French; English subtitles.)

p&d, Christian-Jaque; w, Pierre Apesteguy, Jean Ferry, Jacques Emmanuel (based on a novel by Franck Marchal); ph, Robert Le Febvre; ed, Jacques Desagneaux; English subtitles, Herman G. Weinberg.

Comedy **(PR:A MPAA:NR)**

NATHALIE, AGENT SECRET** (1960, Fr.) 95m Sirius-SFC/CFDC bw (AKA: ATOMIC AGENT)

Martine Carol *(Nathalie)*, Felix Marten *(Inspector)*, Dany Saval *(Pivoine)*, Dargio Moreno *(Don Jose)*, Jacques Berthier *(Jean)*, Noel Roquevert *(Darbon)*.

A sequel to NATHALIE (1958), this film again features Carol as the engaging Parisian model who has a knack for getting involved with police affairs. This time she stumbles onto a ring of spies who are trying to steal the plans for an atomic motor. Naturally, she proves to be more adept than the police, and thwarts the spies. Though the well-paced action keeps the film moving, it lacks the humor of the first venture. (In French; English subtitles.)

d, Henri Decoin; w, Pierre Apesteguy, Jacques Robert, Henri Jeanson (based on the novel by Franck Marchal); m, George Van Parys; ph, Robert Le Febvre; ed, Claude Durand; set d, Robert Clovel.

Spy Drama **(PR:A MPAA:NR)**

NATHALIE GRANGER* (1972, Fr.) 83m Mouflet Et Cie bw

Lucia Bose *(Isabelle)*, Jeanne Moreau *(Other Woman)*, Gerard Depardieu *(Salesman)*, Luce Garcia-Ville *(Teacher)*, Dionys Mascolo *(Granger)*, Valerie Mascolo *(Nathalie)*, Nathalie Bourgeois *(Laurence)*.

Cinematic minimalism offered by French playwright and novelist Duras. For the most part, Duras simply points her camera and lets it record the words and actions (or inactions) of Bose, her friend Moreau, and a few others who wander into their lives. Moreau spends a lot of time burning branches and Bose expresses some concerns about her daughter Nathalie (Mascolo). A visit from a washing machine salesman proves to be the film's high point—which pretty much sums up all one needs to know about this movie. (In French; English subtitles.)

d&w, Marguerite Duras; ph, Ghislain Cloquet; m, Duras; ed, Nicole Lubtchansky.

Drama **(PR:C MPAA:NR)**

NATHANIEL HAWTHORNE'S "TWICE TOLD TALES" (SEE: TWICE TOLD TALES, 1963)

NATION AFLAME zero (1937) 74m Treasure Pictures/Television bw

Noel Madison *(Sandino)*, Lila Lee *(Mona Burtis)*, Norma Trelvar *(Wynne Adams)*, Douglas Walton *(Tommy Franklin)*, Harry Holman *(Adams)*, Arthur Singley *(Sherman)*, Earl Hodgins *(Wilson)*, Snub Pollard *(Wolfe)*, Si Wills *(Walker)*, Lee Shumway *(Campbell)*, Roger Williams *(Burtis)*, Alan Cavan, Dorothy Kildare, Elaine Deane, Lee Phelps, Carl Stockdale, Montague Shaw.

A poorly made expose of a real-life secret terror organization called the Black Legion, known as the Avenging Angels in the film. Using a lot of stock footage from newsreels, the story depicts the rise of the organization and its shady dealings. Trelvar plays a woman who sacrifices her life in order to stop the group. Madison is the mastermind behind the society.

p, Edward Halperin, Victor Halperin; d, Victor Halperin; w, Oliver Drake (based on a story by Thomas Dixon); ph, Arthur Martinelli; ed, Holbrook N. Todd.

Drama **(PR:A MPAA:NR)**

NATIONAL BARN DANCE** (1944) 76m PAR bw

Jean Heather *(Betty)*, Charles Quigley *(Johnny)*, Robert Benchley *(Mr. Mitcham)*, Mabel Paige *(Mrs. Gates)*, Charles Dingle *(Mr. Gates)*, Luther W. Ossenbrink *(Arkie)*, Pat Buttram, Joe Kelly, Lulu Belle and Scotty, Dinning Sisters, Hoosier Hot Shots.

"National Barn Dance" was for many years a popular radio show that spotlighted the talents of various country musicians, and was produced by WLS radio in Chicago. The film offers a fictionalized account of how the program originated, with Quigley playing a promoter who tries to sell the idea of a radio show to ad agency owner Benchley. Benchley wants something with hillbilly entertainers and Quigley heads south to find them. He discovers Lulu Belle and Scotty, the three Dinning Sisters, the Hoosier Hot Shots, Pat Buttram, and Joe Kelly, and flies them all to Chicago, but Benchley has changed his mind. The performers then pose as Benchley's servants and give him a performance which quickly changes his mind about the show. Songs include "When Pa Was Courtin' Ma" (sung by Lulu Belle and Scotty), "Angels Never Leave Heaven" (sung by Dinning Sisters).

p, Walter MacEwen; d, Hugh Bennett; w, Lee Loeb, Hal Fimberg; ph, Henry Sharp; m, Irvin Talbot; ed, Everett Douglas; art d, Hans Dreier, Walter Hyler; ch, Jack Crosby.

Musical **(PR:A MPAA:NR)**

NATIONAL HEALTH, OR NURSE NORTON'S AFFAIR, THE*** (1973, Brit.) 95m COL c

Lynn Redgrave *(Nurse Sweet/Betty)*, Eleanor Bron *(Sister McFee/Sister Mary)*, Sheila Scott-Wilkinson *(Nurse Powell/Cleo Norton)*, Donald Sinden *(Mr. Carr/Boyd)*, Jim Dale *(Barnet/Neil)*, Neville Aurelius *(Leyland/Monk)*, Colin Blakely *(Loach)*, Clive Swift *(Ash)*, Mervyn Johns *(Rees)*, David Hutcheson *(Mackie)*, Bert Palmer *(Flagg)*, Bob Hoskins *(Foster)*, John Hamill *(Kenny)*, Robert Gillespie *(Tyler)*, Patience Collier *(Lady Visitor)*, Maureen Pryor *(Matron)*, Jumoko Debayo *(Nurse Lake)*, Gillian Barge *(Dr. Bird)*, George Browne *(Chaplain)*, James Hazeldine *(Student Doctor)*, Graham Weston *(Michael)*, Don Hawkins *(Les)*.

The British National Health System is skewered in this comedy set in a rundown London hospital. The hospital is filled with wacky characters, both staff and patients, as the film strives to get all it can from their humorous escapades. The movie also includes a satire-within-a-satire with "Nurse Norton's Affair" providing a send-up of TV hospital soap operas and giving some cast members the chance to play two roles. The movie tries for both comedy and social commentary, but can't quite pull it off, although the competent cast does its best with the material.

p, Ned Sherrin, Terry Glinwood; d, Jack Gold; w, Peter Nichols (based on his play); ph, John Coquillon (Technicolor); m, Carl Davis; ed, Ralph Sheldon; prod d, Ray Simm.

Comedy **(PR:C MPAA:NR)**

NATIONAL LAMPOON'S ANIMAL HOUSE*½** (1978) 109m UNIV c

John Belushi *(John "Bluto" Blutarsky)*, Tim Matheson *(Eric "Otter" Stratton)*, John Vernon *(Dean Vernon Wormer)*, Thomas Hulce *(Larry "Pinto" Kroger)*, Cesare Danova *(Mayor Carmine DePasto)*, Mary Louise Weller *(Mandy Pepperidge)*, Stephen Furst *(Kent "Flounder" Dorfman)*, James Daughton *(Greg Marmalard)*, Bruce McGill *(Daniel Simpson "D-Day" Day)*, Mark Metcalf *(Doug Neidermeyer)*, DeWayne Jessie *(Otis Day)*, Karen Allen *(Katy)*, James Widdoes *(Robert Hoover)*, Martha Smith *(Babs Jensen)*, Sarah Holcomb *(Clorette DePasto)*, Lisa Baur *(Shelly)*, Kevin Bacon *(Chip Diller)*, Peter Riegert *(Donald "Boon" Schoenstein)*, Douglas Kenney *(Stork)*, Christian Miller *(Hardbar)*, Joshua Daniel *(Mothball)*, Bruce Bonnheim *(B.B.)*, Donald Sutherland *(Prof. Dave Jennings)*, Junior *(Trooper)*, Sunny Johnson *(Otter's Co-Ed)*, Verna Bloom *(Marion Wormer)*, Stacy Grooman *(Sissy)*, Stephan Bishop *(Charming Guy with Guitar)*, Eliza Garrett *(Brunella)*, Aseneth Jurgenson *(Beth)*, Katherine Denning *(Noreen)*, Raymone Robinson *(Mean Dude)*, Robert Elliott *(Meaner Dude)*, Reginald H. Farmer *(Meanest Dude)*, Jebidiah R. Dumas *(Huge Dude)*, Priscilla Lauris *(Dean's Secretary)*, Rick Eby *(Omega)*, John Freeman *(Man on Street)*, Sean McCartin *(Lucky Boy)*, Helen Vick *(Sorority Girl)*, Rick Greenough *(Mongol)*, Gary McLarty, Albert M. Mauro, Karen Werner, Fred Hice, Bill Hooker, Clifford Happy, Pam Bebermeyer, Bud Ekins, Jim Halty, R.A. Rondell, Walter Wyatt, Gilbert Combs *(Stunt People)*.

Rude, rough, tasteless, but sometimes funny, this movie was a huge hit with young audiences and grossed more than $80 million as it grossed out the older viewers. Apparently based on the actual college experiences of the screenwriters (specifically Miller's year at Dartmouth), it served to introduce to films the anarchistic talents of Belushi as he played off the fine work by Hulce, Matheson, and others. It takes place in the early 1960s, before the war in the Far East had heated up. Hulce and rotund Furst attempt to join fraternities on their campus but they are turned away and wind up at Delta House, a pigsty, where they are welcomed by the house's chief, Matheson. Dean Vernon is keeping an eye on this particular house because they seem to break every rule, with beer parties and orgies, and the things all the boys have in common are rotten grades and a generally lackluster attitude regarding anything to do with cracking their schoolbooks. Vernon would like to see the place shut down, and begins an unlikely plot to do that with Daughton, the conservative boy who leads a conservative fraternity. In order to "break" the place, Daughton, who also leads the school's ROTC unit, becomes Lou Gossett to Furst's Richard Gere (as seen in AN OFFICER AND A GENTLEMAN) and attempts to take the wind out of the fat boy's sails. To get even for that, Furst takes Daughton's pet horse to Vernon's office late one night and shoots the beast, leaving the animal as a prize for when Vernon arrives in the morning. Daughton's girl friend is the comely Weller, and Belushi is nuts about her, so he sneaks to her sorority house and peeks through a window as she doffs her clothing after coming back from an evening with Daughton, who is a virgin and means to stay that way. At the next school lunch, Belushi begins a "food fight" and the members of the conservative fraternity are hit hard by anything that can be thrown. Vernon thinks he can get the house closed if the boys fail their exams, but Belushi steals the mid-terms and gives them to his fellows. The only trouble is that he stole the wrong exams and the result is that the entire house fails their tests. The boys are depressed and toss a toga party during which Matheson takes the opportunity to seduce Vernon's wife, the nymphomaniacal Bloom. When Vernon finds that booze was offered at the party, that's enough to bring the house up for discipline in front of a committee stacked against it. The house is closed and all members of the frat are tossed out and forbidden to march in the annual parade that traditionally ends the school year. The boys wreak revenge by wrecking the parade, using a number of cars they have altered as attack vehicles, and, in the end, they are all allowed to return to school because Vernon fears any further action from them. The final epilog includes shots of the actors and what they did in later years. Belushi marries Weller and becomes a U.S. Senator, Daughton is killed in Vietnam action, another of the conservative boys becomes an assistant to President Nixon and gets raped in prison, yet another winds up as a Universal Studios tour guide. Although this was the first of these films, it was not the best. REVENGE OF THE NERDS not only had funnier scenes, but also it had more to say. Landis' penchant for crashing cars came to a head with his disastrous movie, THE BLUES BROTHERS, and he still hasn't come close to the fun he managed to engender in this one. In a small role, note composer Stephan Bishop. The costumer was Landis' girl friend but she does a good job despite that. Fans of raunch will love it; people of more sophisticated comedic taste will wonder why it did so well. They tried so hard to be outrageous that it has a tendency to feel forced in many sequences. It was shot on location in Oregon at Eugene and Cottage Grove. Songs: "Animal House," "Dream Girl" (Stephan Bishop, sung by Bishop), "Shout," "Shama Lama Ding Dong," "Louie, Louie" (sung by the Kingsmen), "Money" (sung by Belushi), "Hey Paula" (sung by Paul and Paula), "Wonderful World," "Twistin' the Night Away" (sung by Sam Cooke), "Let's Dance" (sung by Chris Montez), "Who's Sorry Now?" (sung by Connie Francis), "Tossin' and Turnin'" (sung by Bobby Lewis).

p, Matty Simmons, Ivan Reitman; d, John Landis; w, Harold Ramis, Douglas Kenney, Chris Miller; ph, Charles Correll (Panavision, Technicolor); m, Elmer Bernstein; ed, George Folsey, Jr.; art d, John J. Lloyd; set d, Hal Gausman; cos, Deborah Nadoolman; spec eff, Henry Millar; makeup, Lynn Brooks, Gerald Soucie; stunts, Gary R. McLarty; hairstyles, Marilyn Phillips.

Comedy **Cas.** **(PR:C MPAA:R)**

NATIONAL LAMPOON'S CLASS REUNION zero (1982) 84m ABC/FOX c

Gerrit Graham *(Bob Spinnaker)*, Michael Lerner *(Dr. Young)*, Fred McCarren *(Gary Nash)*, Miriam Flynn *(Bunny Packard)*, Stephen Furst *(Hubert Downs)*, Marya Small *(Iris Augen)*, Shelley Smith *(Meredith Modess)*, Zane Buzby *(Delores Salk)*, Jacklyn Zeman *(Jane Washburn)*, Blackie Dammett *(Walter Baylor)*, Barry Diamond *(Chip Hendrix)*, Art Evans *(Carl Clapton)*, Marla Pennington *(Mary Beth McFadden)*, Randolph Powell *(Jeff Barnes)*, Misty Rowe *(Cindy Shears)*, Jim Staahl *(Egon Von Stoker)*, Gary Hibbard *(Fritz Shears)*, Anne Ramsey *(Mrs. Tabazooski)*, Steve Tracy *(Milt Friedman)*, Isabel West *(Gloria Barnes)*, Diane Black, Wendy Goldman, Robin Eurich, Anyavel Glynn, Terry Green, Chris Hubbell, Timothy Phillips, Roger Hamilton Spotts, Chuck Berry.

A very unfunny film released after the even worse NATIONAL LAMPOON AT THE MOVIES and the successful NATIONAL LAMPOON'S ANIMAL HOUSE. The film, which died at the box office, focuses on the 10th reunion of a 1972 high school graduating class. Introducing both comedy and horror-slasher elements into the plot, the combination doesn't work. As the plot unfolds, a murderer is killing off class members, who are such unfunny, dull creatures that no one can blame him.

The killer, alas, turns out to be the class transvestite. Even Chuck Berry, who makes a brief appearance singing a medley of his songs, can't save this one.

p, Matty Simmons; d, Michael Miller; w, John Hughes; ph, Phil Lathrop (Metrocolor); ed, Richard C. Meyer, Ann Mills; prod d, Dean Edward Mitzner; set d, Jack Taylor; cos, Jean Pierre Dorleac; spec eff, Paul Stewart, James Camomile; ch, Rita Graham; m/l, Peter Bernstein, Mark Goldenberg (title song sung by Gary U.S. Bonds); makeup, John Chambers.

Comedy Cas. (PR:O MPAA:R)

NATIONAL LAMPOON'S VACATION** (1983) 98m WB c

Chevy Chase *(Clark Griswold)*, Beverly D'Angelo *(Ellen Griswold)*, Imogene Coca *(Aunt Edna)*, Randy Quaid *(Cousin Eddie)*, Anthony Michael Hall *(Rusty Griswold)*, Dana Barron *(Audrey Griswold)*, Eddie Bracken *(Roy Walley)*, Brian Doyle-Murray *(Kamp Komfort Clerk)*, Miriam Flynn *(Cousin Catherine)*, James Keach *(Motorcycle Cop)*, Eugene Levy *(Car Salesman)*, Frank McRae *(Grover)*, John Candy *(Lasky)*, Christie Brinkley *(Girl in Red Ferrari)*, Jane Krakowski *(Cousin Vicki)*, John Navin *(Cousin Dale)*, Nathan Cook *(Man Giving Directions)*, Christopher Jackson *(Pimp)*, Mickey Jones *(Mechanic)*, John Diehl *(Assistant Mechanic)*, Jeannie Dimter Barton *(Dodge City Cashier)*, Randolph Dreyfuss *(Wyatt Earp)*, Virgil Wyaco II *(Indian)*, Gerry Black *(Davenport)*, James Staley *(Motel Desk Clerk)*, Adelaid Wilder *(Car Hop)*, Tessa Richarde *(Motel Guest)*, Fritz Ford, Eric Stacey, Jr. *(Neighbors)*, Scott Perry *(Swat Leader)*, Dennis Freeman *(Policeman)*, Michael Talbot *(Cowboy)*.

After two successive failures at the box office, National Lampoon hit box office pay dirt with this funny, yet often obvious, comedy. Harold Ramis, star and co-writer of STRIPES and GHOST BUSTERS, keeps this film moving and humorous with his inclusion of comic bit characters. Chase, a man obsessed with taking his family on a cross-country vacation, takes off for an amusement park in California called Wally World. Things go wrong from the beginning: the new car they order for the trip turns out to be a ghastly station wagon that nobody wants. They visit Quaid, D'Angelo's scum cousin, who pitches elderly aunt Coca on them. When Coca dies during the trip, the family straps her to the roof of the car. Meanwhile, Chase has the hots for a mysterious blonde, Brinkley, but finds himself in trouble every time she pops up. When they finally make it to Wally World, they find it's been closed for remodeling. In an obsessed rage, Chase pulls a B.B. gun and forces park guard Candy to admit them. The police arrive, but Chase manages to talk his way out of trouble. The comics in cameo appearances make the film.

p, Matty Simmons; d, Harold Ramis; w, John Hughes; ph, Victor J. Kemper (Technicolor); m, Ralph Burns; ed, Paul Herring; prod d, Jack Collis.

Comedy Cas. (PR:C-O MPAA:R)

NATIONAL VELVET**** (1944) 125m MGM c

Mickey Rooney *(Mi Taylor)*, Donald Crisp *(Mr. Brown)*, Elizabeth Taylor *(Velvet Brown)*, Anne Revere *(Mrs. Brown)*, Angela Lansbury *(Edwina Brown)*, Juanita Quigley *(Malvolia Brown)*, Jackie "Butch" Jenkins *(Donald Brown)*, Reginald Owen *(Farmer Ede)*, Terry Kilburn *(Ted)*, Alec Craig *(Tim)*, Eugene Loring *(Mr. Taski)*, Norma Varden *(Miss Sims)*, Arthur Shields *(Mr. Hallam)*, Dennis Hoey *(Mr. Greenford, the Farmer)*, Aubrey Mather *(Entry Official)*, Frederic Worlock *(Stewart)*, Arthur Treacher *(Man with Umbrella)*, Harry Allen *(Van Driver)*, Billy Bevan *(Constable)*, Barry Macollum *(Townsman)*, Matthew Boulton *(Entry Clerk)*, Leyland Hodgson *(1st Pressman)*, Leonard Carey *(2nd Pressman)*, Colin Campbell *(Cockney)*, Frank Benson *(Englishman)*, Wally Cassell *(Jockey)*, Alec Harford *(Valet)*, William Austin *(Reporter)*, Gerald Oliver Smith *(Cameraman)*, Olaf Hytten *(1st Villager)*, George Kirby *(Second Villager)*, Moyna MacGill *(Woman)*, Donald Curtis *(American)*, Rene Austin, Jane Isbell, Virginia McDowall, Gail Peyton, Iris Kirskey, Bertha Stinchfield, Felicity Bilbrook, Paula Allen, Rhoda Williams, Beverly Billman *(Schoolgirls)*, Stephen Bowson, Howard Taylor, Harold deBecker, Jr., Richard Haydel, Murray Coombs *(Schoolboys)*, Gordon Richards *(Doctor)*, Rose Langdon, William Bailey *(Bookies)*, Eric Wilton *(English Bookie)*, Major Douglas Francis *(Track Official)*.

Rooney's diminutive stature made him a perfect choice to play the ex-jockey in this, one of the most beloved children's films that MGM ever made. In later years, he would do other horse films including THE BLACK STALLION. Don't let his small size fool you, though, as he is acknowledged by his peers as being a giant among actors, a man who can do any role, dramatic or comedic, and make you believe what he is pretending to be. The place is Sussex in England, where the radiant Taylor meets Rooney, who is passing through the tiny village. They get on well with each other and she asks him to come home and share dinner with her family, Revere, Quigley, Lansbury, Jenkins, and Crisp, the patriarch. Crisp likes Rooney and gives him a job in the family business. Taylor loves horses, and sister Lansbury is equally mad about boys. Taylor wins a horse in a raffle and asks Rooney to help her train the animal to run in the famous Grand National, but the entrance fee is too high for the family to afford. Then Revere, who won the Best Supporting Actress Oscar for this role, gives Taylor some money she'd won years before as a result of having swum the English Channel, and the fee is paid. They have a jockey for the race and when he can't do it, Rooney cuts Taylor's hair and she takes the place of the jockey in one of the best horse-racing sequences ever filmed. (It was the incredible editing of this that won Kern an Oscar.) The horse wins the big race but Taylor falls off at the end, and when the doctor examines her and finds that she's a girl, the win is disqualified. Taylor is happy, nevertheless, because she has proved that her horse is a winner. Rooney, who was unsure of his abilities as a trainer and feared riding himself because he once ran a race where a friend died, now has his confidence back and he bids them all farewell, to follow his star. It took until 1977 for the British to allow a woman to race in the Grand National, so life imitated art in this case. Rooney, who could steal a scene from an orangutan, held himself in check and let Taylor have all the moments, the result being that she became a huge star and signed a contract that kept her at MGM for the next 17 years. Rooney went into military service after this film and didn't return to movies until LOVE LAUGHS AT ANDY HARDY, three years later. Taylor was not the first choice for the role, as it had been bandied about since the novel was written 10 years before. Pandro Berman bought it at RKO for Katharine Hepburn, then it was sold to Paramount, then MGM, where Spencer Tracy was penciled in to play the father and Margaret Sullavan was being considered as Velvet. Shirley Temple was also a possibility but that didn't work out. Taylor had already done four films, including LASSIE, COME HOME, but Berman thought she was too frail. With her mother, Sara, watching over her, Taylor went into a severe training program, gained weight, grew a few inches, and won the role. She was able to ride horses well, but the producers hired Australian Jockey Snowy Baker to double for her in the climactic scene. A year later, Bagnold adapted her own novel for a play on the London stage, but the femme star, Tilsa Page, was nowhere near Taylor and that play never went very far. Revere's Academy Award came as a surprise to just about everyone, including Revere. Lansbury had been nominated for her work in THE PICTURE OF DORIAN GRAY, but the odds-on favorite was Ann Blyth for her part in MILDRED PIERCE. Brown, Smith, Gibbons, McCleary, Willis, and Griffiths also were awarded nominations by the Academy. Another attempt at the story was done by Bryan Forbes in 1977. Called INTERNATIONAL VELVET, it starred Tatum O'Neal. It was a flop and cost more money to make (over $5 million) than this one raked in on its first release (a little over $4 million). A warm, loving, and exciting picture that can be seen and appreciated by anyone.

p, Pandro S. Berman; d, Clarence Brown; w, Theodore Reeves, Helen Deutsch (based on the novel by Enid Bagnold); ph, Leonard Smith (Technicolor); m, Herbert Stothart; ed, Robert J. Kern; art d, Cedric Gibbons, Urie McCleary; set d, Edwin B. Willis, Mildred Griffiths; cos, Irene; spec eff, Warren Newcombe.

Drama Cas. (PR:AAA MPAA:NR)

NATIVE LAND½** (1942) 80m Frontier bw

Fred Johnson *(The Farmer)*, Mary George *(His Wife)*, John Rennick *(His Son)*, Amelia Romano *(Slavey)*, Housely Stevens, Louis Grant *(Sharecroppers)*, James Hanney *(Union President)*, Howard da Silva *(Stool Pigeon)*, Art Smith *(Vice President)*, Richard Bishop *(Spy Executive)*, Tom Pedi, Bert Conway *(Members)*, Charles Jordan *(Contact Man)*, Vaughn King *(Wife of President)*, Robert Strauss *(Grocer)*, Dolores Cornell *(Little Girl)*, John Marlieb *(Thug)*, Tom Connors *(Joseph Shoemaker)*, Harry Wilson *(Poulnot)*, Rev. Charles Webber *(Minister)*, Virginia Stevens *(Widow)*, Clancy Cooper *(Speaker)*, Paul Robeson *(Narrator)*.

Based on U.S. Senate Civil Liberties Commission and public documents, this is American propaganda at its finest. Paul Robeson narrates this drama, which is designed to instill patriotism in the little man. Encouraging the American worker to perform at top efficiency while producing munitions, it rightly knocks the Ku Klux Klan, labor spies, and land barons—almost anyone considered a threat to the working man. NATIVE LAND presents a series of violations of the Bill of Rights through re-enactments. One scene depicts an assault on a Michigan farmer who dares to raise his voice at a farmer's association meeting; another shows the murders of two sharecroppers by vigilantes.

Drama (PR:A MPAA:NR)

NATIVE SON½** (1951, U.S., Arg.) 91m Argentina Sono/Classic bw

Richard Wright *(Bigger Thomas)*, Jean Wallace *(Mary Dalton)*, Nicholas Joy *(Mr. Dalton)*, Gloria Madison *(Bessie Mears)*, Charles Cane *(Britten)*, Jean Michael *(Jan Herlons)*, George Rigaud *(Farley)*, George Green *(Panama)*, Willa Pearl Curtiss *(Hannah Thomas)*, Don Dean *(Max)*, Ruth Roberts *(Mrs. Dalton)*, Ned Campbell *(Buckley)*, Charles Simmonds *(Ernie)*, Leslie Straughn *(Buddy Thomas)*, Lidia Alves *(Vera Thomas)*, George Nathanson *(Joe)*, George Roos *(Scoop)*, Lewis MacKenzie *(Stanley)*, Cecile Lezard *(Peggy)*.

A deeply disappointing but nonetheless fascinating film adaptation of black author Richard Wright's 1940 literary masterpiece. Shot on locations as diverse and surprising as Argentina and the South Side of Chicago (where the novel's action takes place), Wright himself plays his main character, Bigger Thomas, a young black whose frustrations with racism explode into violence. Hired as a chauffeur by a rich white family eager to help him out of the slums, Wright soon finds that his main duty is to drive the family's wild daughter Wallace wherever she feels like going. Wallace uses the fact that Wright is intimidated by her to ensure his silence when she goes off to visit her boy friend, Michael, a labor organizer (whose Marxist philosophies are much more apparent in the novel—as were Wright's) whom she has been forbidden to date. Wallace and her beau fill Wright's head with confusing notions of equality between the races and classes. Naturally, Wright's character is a bit suspicious of these two young white people's motives, and he becomes even more confused when it appears that Wallace is making subtle sexual advances toward him. One night, Wright finds himself driving a very drunk Wallace home. Not wanting her to get in trouble, he carries the unconscious girl to her bedroom. Before he can leave, Wallace awakens from her drunken stupor and Wright panics, thinking the girl will scream at the sight of a black man in her bedroom. Before she can utter a sound, Wright tries to muffle the girl's voice and accidentally kills her. Knowing he is doomed to hang for killing a white woman, Wright covers up his crime by disposing of the body in the furnace and then framing her boy friend on a kidnaping charge. This throws off the police for a while, but reporters soon find the body and Wright flees, accompanied by his girl friend, Madison. As the police close in, Wright's anger and paranoia consume him and he murders Madison for fear that she will betray him. Eventually Wright is caught, convicted of murder, and sentenced to death. NATIVE SON is a moving tragedy in which all efforts of understanding between the races are thwarted because of skepticism, misunderstanding, and thoughtlessness. Michael and Wallace want to help Wright, but he does not conform to their idealized conception of the perfect black "victim" of white racial and economic suppression. Wright is indeed a victim, but not one content to let others control his destiny, regardless of their good intentions. While the novel is a powerful and eloquent statement, the film version is less than successful. It is interesting and almost irresistible to watch the author of this great literary work play his own very vivid main character, but Wright is simply too old (he was 42 when the film was in production—Bigger is no older than 21 in the book) and has limited acting ability to be able to bring all the nuances necessary to the role. While the rest of the cast is fine, director Chenal's visual talents are flat and uninteresting, barely disguising the cheapness of the production. The script itself has problems, with the more intense scenes of the novel toned down for the screen, and the left-wing political motivations are practically nonexistent. Wright rejected communism shortly after the publication of his novel, his fertile mind not to be controlled by any man or ideology. NATIVE SON is as important and vital a novel today as the day it was published and Wright's rage screams out for a film version featuring actors and a director who will do it justice.

p, James Prades; d, Pierre Chenal; w, Chenal, Richard Wright (based on the novel by Wright); ph, A.U. Meray; m, John Elhert; ed, George Garate.

Crime/Drama **(PR:C-O MPAA:NR)**

NATSUKASHIKI FUE YA TAIKO (SEE: EYES, THE SEA AND A BALL, 1968)

NATTLEK (SEE: NIGHT GAMES, 1966, Swed.)

NATTVARDSGASTERNA (SEE: WINTER LIGHT, 1963, Swed.)

NATURAL BORN SALESMAN (SEE: EARTHWORM TRACTORS, 1936)

NATURAL ENEMIES*½ (1979) 100m Cinema 5 c

Hal Holbrook *(Paul Steward)*, Louise Fletcher *(Miriam Steward)*, Peter Armstrong *(Tony Steward)*, Beth Berridge *(Sheila Steward)*, Steve Austin *(Alex Steward)*, Jim Pappas *(Man on Train)*, Ellen Barber *(Secretary)*, John Bartholomew *(Astronaut)*, Charles Randall *(Doctor)*, Jose Ferrer *(Harry Rosenthal)*, Lisa Carroll *(The Madam)*, June Berry, Alisha Fontaine, Pat Mauceri, Michele O'Brien, Claire Reilly *(Girls in Brothel)*, Viveca Lindfors *(Dr. Baker)*, Frank Bongiorno *(Cabdriver)*, Harry Daley *(Conductor)*, Patricia Elliott *(Woman on Train)*, Robert Perry *(Newscaster)*.

A plodder that even amphetamines couldn't speed up. Holbrook is a bored publisher who thinks about wiping out his whole family as a way to "start over." Others might turn to drugs or drinking for relief. But Holbrook just sits there and ponders, without ever making a decision. The viewer is left wondering whether he actually pulled it off.

p, John E. Quill; d&w, Jeff Kanew (based on the novel by Julius Horwitz); ph, Richard E. Brooks (TVC Color); m, Don Ellis; ed, Kanew; art d, Hank Aldrich; cos, Peggy Farrell.

Drama **(PR:O MPAA:R)**

NATURE'S MISTAKES (SEE: FREAKS, 1932)

NAUGHTY ARLETTE** (1951, Brit.) 80m Pinnacle/UA bw (GB: THE ROMANTIC AGE,)

Mai Zetterling *(Arlette)*, Hugh Williams *(Arnold Dickson)*, Margot Grahame *(Helen Dickson)*, Petula Clark *(Julie Dickson)*, Carol Marsh *(Patricia)*, Raymond Lovell *(Hedges)*, Paul Dupuis *(Henri Sinclair)*, Margaret Barton *(Bessie)*, Marie Ney *(Miss Hallam)*, Mark Daly *(Withers)*, Judith Furse *(Miss Adams)*, Betty Impey *(Jill)*, Adrienne Corri *(Nora)*, May Hallatt, Dorothy Latta, Jean Anderson, Viola Johnstone, Colette Melville, Brenda Cameron, Margaret Anderson, June Charlier, Christina Forrest, Christine Finn, Ann Smith, Mary Merritt, Betty Leslie Smith, Howard Douglas, Joan Kirkpatrick, Cecily Walper, Charlotte Mitchell, Margaret Ridgway, Walter Horsbrugh, Jacqueline Allerton, Susan Dudley.

While teaching art at a girls' finishing school, Williams is seduced by Zetterling, a French student. The comely young girl is also a friend of Williams' daughter Grahame, which causes some emotional discomfort for the man. Eventually the affair ends, leaving Williams sad, but a better individual. It's not a particularly tasteful theme, nor is the comedy handled with the wit necessary to pull it off. The results are fairly pedestrian and lacking any real style.

p, Edward Dryhurst, Eric l'Epine Smith; d, Edmond T. Greville; w, Dryhurst, Peggy Barwell (based on the novel *Lycee Des Jeaunes Filles* by Serge Weber); ph, Hone Glendinning; m, Charles Williams; ed, Ralph Kemplen; art d, Anthony Mazzei; cos, Eleanor Abbey.

Romance/Comedy **(PR:C-O MPAA:NR)**

NAUGHTY BUT NICE** (1939) 90m WB bw

Ann Sheridan *(Zelda Manion)*, Dick Powell *(Prof. Hardwick)*, Gale Page *(Linda McKay)*, Helen Broderick *(Aunt Martha)*, Allen Jenkins *(Joe Dirk)*, ZaSu Pitts *(Aunt Penelope)*, Ronald Reagan *(Ed Clark)*, Maxie Rosenbloom *(Killer)*, Jerry Colonna *(Allie Gray)*, Vera Lewis *(Aunt Annabella)*, Elizabeth Dunne *(Aunt Henrietta)*, Luis Alberni *(Stanislaus Pysinski)*, Bill Davidson *(Sam Hudson)*, Granville Bates *(Judge)*, Halliwell Hobbes *(Dean Burton)*, Peter Lind Hayes *(Band Leader)*, Bert Hanlon *(Johnny Collins)*, John Ridgely *(Hudson's Assistant)*, Herbert Rawlinson *(Plaintiff's Attorney)*, Selmer Jackson *(Defense Attorney)*, Hobart Cavanaugh *(Piano Tuner)*, Grady Sutton *(Mankton)*, Sally Sage *(Miss Danning)*, Elise Cavanna *(Maid)*, Jack Mower, Wedgwood Nowell, Sidney Bracy *(Professors)*, Ed McWade *(Prof. Trill)*, Bob Sherwood *(Announcer)*, Ernest Wood *(Headwaiter)*, Stuart Holmes *(Capt. Gregory Waddington-Smith)*, Jerry Mandy *(Waiter)*, Daisy Dufford *(Maid)*, Tom Dugan *(Man with Seals)*, Billy Newell *(Arranger)*, Harrison Greene, Garry Owen *(Bartenders)*, Jimmy Conlin *(Pedestrian)*, Cliff Saum *(Man)*, Frank Mayo, William Gould *(Bailiffs)*, John Harron *(Clerk)*, National Jitterbug Champions.

A few laughs, but that's about it in this yarn about Tin Pan Alley. Powell is a small-town composer who goes to New York in search of that elusive big break. He hooks up with a group led by songstress Sheridan. One of his best tunes is stolen and remade into a song titled "Hooray for Spinach," an upbeat number sung by Sheridan. Powell then becomes the object of both Sheridan's and Page's affection. This was Powell's last film for Warner Bros. which, in an ungracious send off, gave him second billing behind Sheridan, the studio's new "Oomph girl." Songs also include "Corn Pickin'," "I Don't Believe in Signs," "Happy About the Whole Thing," "In a Moment of Weakness." (Johnny Mercer, Harry Warren).

p, Sam Bischoff; d, Ray Enright; w, Richard Macaulay, Jerry Wald (based on their story "Always Leave Them Laughing"); ph, Arthur L. Todd; ed, Thomas Richards; md, Leo F. Forbstein; cos, Howard Shoup.

Musical **(PR:A MPAA:NR)**

NAUGHTY CINDERELLA** (1933, Brit.) 56m WB-FN bw

John Stuart *(Michael Wynard)*, Winna Winfried *(Brita Rasmusson)*, Betty Huntley Wright *(Elinore)*, Marion Gerth *(Elsa)*, Marie Wright *(Mrs. Barrow)*, Victor Fairley *(Herr Amsel)*, Catherine Watts *(Clara Field)*.

Winfried meets up with Stuart, her former guardian of years before. He doesn't recognize the woman, so she pretends to be both a society lady and rugged tomboy. Stuart falls for the society personna and the two end up living happily ever after. Not much of a comic romance, and well below the talents of Winfried, a fine and unfortunately poorly used comedienne.

p, Irving Asher; d, John Daumery; w, Randall Faye (based on a story by W. Scott Darling).

Comedy **(PR:A MPAA:NR)**

NAUGHTY FLIRT, THE* (1931) 79m FN-WB bw

Alice White *(Kay Elliott)*, Paul Page *(Alan Ward)*, Myrna Loy *(Linda Gregory)*, Robert Agnew *(Wilbur Fairchild)*, Douglas Gilmore *(Jack Gregory)*, George Irving *(John R. Elliot)*.

Boring, stiff film that casts White as a pampered heiress who has been dating Page. He tells her he finds her selfish ways unsufferable, so she breaks off the romance. Gilmore makes his move, but his mind is not on love, just her money. Loy, as his sister, spurs him on. He had been enjoying the fine life until he lost his money in the stock market crash of 1929. He corrals White to the altar, but right before the "I do's" she realizes her heart belongs to Page. Even though White was a popular screen star in the late 1920s and early 1930s, she lost some points with this one. This was Loy's last film for First National-Warner Bros.

d, Edward Cline; w, Richard Weil, Earl Baldwin (based on a story by Baldwin, from the story "Man Crazy" by Frederick Bowen); ph, Sid Hickox.

Drama **(PR:A MPAA:NR)**

NAUGHTY MARIETTA*½** (1935) 80m MGM bw

Jeanette MacDonald *(Princess Marie de Namours de la Bonfain, "Marietta Franini")*, Nelson Eddy *(Capt. Richard Warrington)*, Frank Morgan *(Governor Gaspard d'Annard)*, Elsa Lanchester *(Mme. d'Annard)*, Douglas Dumbrille *(Prince de Namours de la Bonfain)*, Joseph Cawthorn *(Herr Schuman)*, Cecilia Parker *(Julie)*, Walter Kingsford *(Don Carlos de Braganza)*, Greta Meyer *(Frau Schuman)*, Akim Tamiroff *(Rudolpho, Puppet Master)*, Harold Huber *(Abraham, "Abe")*, Edward Brophy *(Ezekiel Cramer, "Zeke")*, Mary Doran, Jane Mercer, Marjorie Main, Jean Chatburn, Pat Farley, Jane Barnes, Kay English, Linda Parker, *(Casquette Girls)*, Arthur Belasco, Tex Driscoll, Edward Hearn, Edmund Cobb, Charles Dunbar, Ed Brady *(Mercenary Scouts)*, Dr. Edouard Lippe *(Landlord)*, Marietta *(Cocker Spaniel)*, Olive Carey *(Mme. Renavent)*, William Desmond *(Havre Gendarme Chief)*, Cora Sue Collins *(Felice)*, Helen Shipman *(Marietta Franini)*, William Burress *(Bouget the Petshop Keeper)*, Catherine Griffith *(Prunella, Marie's Maid)*, Billy Dooley *(Drunk, Marietta's "Brother")*, Guy Usher *(Ship's Captain)*, Walter Long *(Pirate Captain)*, Harry Cording, Frank Hagney, Constantine Romanoff *(Pirates)*, Henry Roquemore *(Herald)*, Mary Foy *(Duenna)*, James C. Morton *(Barber)*, Louis Mercier *(Dueler)*, Robert McKenzie *(Town Crier)*, Delos Jewkes *(Priest on Dock)*, Zarubi Elmassian *(Voice of Suzette [Peter Potter])*, William Moore *(Jacques, Suitor)*, Harry Tenbrook *(Suitor)*, Ben Hall *(Mama's Boy)*, Ed Keane *(Maj. Cornell)*, Roger Gray *(Sergeant)*, Ralph Brooks, Edward Norris *(Marie's Suitors)*, Richard Powell *(Herald)*, Wilfred Lucas *(Herald at Ball)*, Jack Mower *(Nobleman)*.

Marietta may have been Naughty when she first came onto the Broadway stage, but by the time she reached the screen, she was anything but. MGMagnate Louis B. Mayer loved this operetta and handed it to Stromberg to produce for MacDonald. Mayer's first choice for the male lead was Allan Jones (Jack's father), but he was busy on a tour, so someone else had to be found. At the time, they had a young, blonde baritone under contract whose previous trio of films, BROADWAY TO HOLLYWOOD, DANCING LADY, and STUDENT TOUR had all been tiny parts. When not sitting around the studio, the young man was busy exciting audiences at concerts under the guidance of his vocal coach, Edouard Lippe. Who was the man, you ask? Why, it was Nelson Eddy, who made his first full-fledged debut in this, the first of eight movies he would costar in with MacDonald. The creaky old warhorse was taken out, dusted off, got a new screenplay, several new lyrics by Gus Kahn, and the result was a movie that was nominated as Best Picture of the year and won an Oscar for sound recordist Douglas Shearer. It won little else but the hearts of Americans who began flocking back to see musicals after a bit of a hiatus from the genre. A fortune was spent on the sets which covered many acres of the MGM lot, and more than 1,000 actors and extras were used (a far cry from MY DINNER WITH ANDRE) in the hopes of attracting an audience. It worked and the picture was a box office success. The play only had a brief run of 136 performances and starred Emma Trentini and Orville Harrold, so no one could predict what this one would do, but Mayer, that old softy, loved the project and put all his power behind it, especially since he had failed to have the U.S. swallow Lawrence Tibbett and Grace Moore in a few films and was determined to find the right couple to make this kind of movie. With speed merchant Van Dyke at the helm (he was known as "one-take" Woodie because he moved with unaccustomed alacrity), the film had a neat pace that belied its stage origins. French MacDonald has been pledged to marry Spanish grandee Kingsford, and she is not happy about it, but the thought of her marriage delights her uncle, Dumbrille, who is a prince, and it has also been approved by the King of France. The union is planned for the next week and MacDonald is eager to flee, so she substitutes her maid for herself and takes the girl's place aboard a ship bound for Louisiana. On that ship are a passel of young women who are to marry the lonesome colonists. (If that plot sounds familiar, you must have already read the synopsis of NEW MOON.) Her maid, Shipman, loves a poor boy from Marseilles, but they don't have enough cash to make it work, so MacDonald gives Shipman the needed francs and the girl is thrilled. Then MacDonald gets on the ship amd makes friends with the other girls in a surface fashion. She tries to be pleasant but not get too close to any of them. The ship is raided by pirates and the girls are dragged ashore to do the bidding of these cutthroats. Now Eddy, leading a troop of scouts, comes to the rescue and saves the girls. Need we tell you that MacDonald is soon gaga over Eddy? He appreciates her feelings, but as far as he's concerned, it's "Hi-Diddle-Dee-Dee, A Soldier's Life For Me," and there is no room in that life for a woman. The rescued girls are brought to New Orleans to meet the men they are to marry, but MacDonald doesn't like any of them and tells Morgan, the area's governor, that she is a woman of ill repute. Morgan and his wife, Lanchester, separate MacDonald from the other sweet young things, lest she contaminate their virginity with her presence. MacDonald finds work making marionettes and is soon located by Eddy, who has come to his blonde senses and realizes that he loves this lady. But before he can sing her praises, she's arrested by Morgan's men. Her true persona is now known and Dumbrille and Kingsford have come to Louisiana (with no banjos on their knees) to drag her back to France and, sigh, marriage to a man she doesn't love. There's a huge fete tossed by Morgan, and MacDonald, now that Morgan knows who she is, is the centerpiece. Dumbrille tells her to acquiesce and return or Eddy may be killed in retaliation. Eddy arrives at the party and she doesn't tell him that she's sailing immediately, but he soon learns the truth and pleads with her to elope with him. She agrees and they flee, with the help of Eddy's men, and look forward to a life together, far from this madding crowd. A good film with some fun from Brophy and Huber, but nowhere near as good as some of MacDonald's others, specifically THE MERRY WIDOW, where her comedic talents shone. Someone at MGM must have had a good feeling about the movie as they premiered it in Washington, D.C., in front of 35 U.S. senators, several Supreme Court judges, and the Russian ambassador. We can only presume that the Russian understood it was a fantasy. Songs include: "Italian Street Song" (Victor Herbert, Rida Johnson Young, sung by Jeanette MacDonald, Nelson Eddy, male chorus, reprised by Zarubi Elmassian, Eddy, MacDonald, chorus), "Chansonette," "Antoinette and Anatole" (Herbert, Gus Kahn), "Prayer" (Herbert, Kahn, sung by Delos Jewkes, MacDonald, chorus), "Tramp, Tramp, Tramp" (Herbert, Young, Kahn, sung by Eddy, male chorus), "The Owl and the Bobcat" (Herbert, Kahn, sung by Eddy, male chorus), "Neath the Southern Moon" (Herbert, Young, sung by Eddy), "Mon Ami Pierrot" (traditional French song), "Ship Ahoy" (Herbert, Kahn), "I'm Falling in Love with Someone" (Herbert, Young, sung by Eddy), "Ah, Sweet Mystery of Life" (Herbert, Young, sung by MacDonald, Eddy).

p, Hunt Stromberg; d, W.S. Van Dyke II; w, John Lee Mahin, Frances Goodrich, Albert Hackett (based on the operetta by Victor Herbert, Rida Johnson Young); ph, William Daniels; ed, Blanche Sewell; art d, Cedric Gibbons; cos, Adrian.

Musical   Cas.   (PR:A MPAA:NR)

NAUGHTY NINETIES, THE   (1945) 76m UNIV bw

Bud Abbott (Dexter Broadhurst), Lou Costello (Sebastian Dinwiddie), Alan Curtis (Crawford), Rita Johnson (Bonita Farrell), Henry Travers (Capt. Sam Jackson), Lois Collier (Caroline Jackson), Joe Sawyer (Bailey), Jack Norton (Drunk), Sam McDaniel (Matt), Billy Green (Minstrel), Bud Wolfe, Henry Russell, Joe Kirk, Bud O'Connor, Jack Worth (Croupiers), Lillian Yarbo (Effie), Emmett Vogan (Citizen), Milt Bronson (Gambler), John Hamilton (Sheriff), Ed Gargan (Baxter, Saloon Bartender), Jack Chefe (Waiter), Barbara Pepper (Girl at Golden Cage), The Rainbow Four (Specialty), Ben Johnson, John Indrisano, Donald Kerr, Ruth Lee, Cyril Ring, Gladys Blake, Jack Rice, Jack Overman, Arthur Loft, Carol Hughes, Tom Fadden, Rex Lease, Sarah Selby, Sidney Fields, William Desmond.

A below-par Abbott and Costello film that places them on a river showboat during the 1890s. The story follows the comedians in their efforts to help the captain of the ship, Travers, keep from losing his boat to some shady gamblers. Most of the comic material seems stale. Some of their funnier pieces include the all-time classic "Who's on First?" Songs include "Rolling Down the River," "Uncle Tom's Cabin," "I Can't Get You Out of My Mind" (Jack Brooks, Edgar Fairchild), "On a Sunday Afternoon" (Andrew B. Sterling, Albert von Tilzer), "I'd Leave My Happy Home for You" (Will Heelan, von Tilzer), "Nora Malone" (Junie McCree, von Tilzer), "Ma Blushin' Rosie (John Stromberg, Edgar Smith), "The Showboat's Comin' to Town," "A Blarney from Killarney," "Rosie, My Little Posie," "I Give My Heart to You, Oo-Ooh."

p, Edmund L. Hartmann, John Grant; d, Jean Yarbrough; w, Hartmann, Grant, Edmund Joseph, Hal Fimberg; ph, George Robinson; ed, Arthur Hilton; md, Fairchild; art d, John B. Goodman, Harold H. MacArthur; set d, Russell A. Gausman, Leigh Smith; cos, Vera West; ch, John Boyles.

Musical/Comedy   (PR:AAA MPAA:NR)

NAVAJO*   (1952) 70m Lippert bw

Francis Kee Teller (Son of the Hunter), John Mitchell (Grey Singer), Mrs. Teller (Mother), Billy Draper (Ute Guide), Hall Bartlett (Indian School Counsel), Sammy Ogg (Narrator).

An independently-made western by actor Hall Bartlett's production company, shot almost entirely on a Navajo Indian reservation. The film, which examines the conflicting white and Indian cultures, focuses on Francis Teller, a 7-year-old Navajo boy. He and his mother, grandfather, and sisters live a meager but happy existence on the reservation. The government takes the boy off the reservation, and away from his family, for mandatory schooling. Teller resists all efforts to embrace white culture despite encouragement from Bartlett and Draper that he do so. Sick of fighting the system he hates, Teller takes off into the canyons of Arizona. Draper and Bartlett chase him, but Teller escapes. The two men, no match for Teller, become lost themselves. In a happy-ending twist, Teller ends up saving the two men he was running from. Miller's cinematography is outstanding. Bartlett, who produced the film, is the only professional actor in the cast. This film's portrayal of Indian life is more on the mark than the 1969 film, TELL THEM WILLIE BOY IS HERE.

p, Hall Bartlett; d&w, Norman Foster; ph, Virgil E. Miller; m, Leith Stevens; ed, Lloyd Nosler.

Western   (PR:A MPAA:NR)

NAVAJO JOE   (1967, Ital./Span.) 89m DD-C.B. Films/UA c
(UN DOLLARO A TESTA; JOE, EL IMPLACABLE)

Burt Reynolds (Navajo Joe), Aldo Sambrell [Sam Brell] (Marvin "Vee" Duncan), Nicoletta Machiavelli (Estella), Tanya Lopert (Maria), Fernando Rey (Parson Rattigan), Franca Polesello (Barbara), Lucia Modugno (Geraldine), Pierre Cressoy (Lynne), Nino Imparato (Chuck), Alvaro de Luna (Sancho Ramirez), Valeria Sabel (Honor Blackwood Lynne), Mario Lanfranchi (Mayor Jefferson Clay), Lucio Rosato (Jeffrey Duncan), Simon Arriaga (Monkey), Chris Huerta (El Gordo), Angel Ortiz (El Cojo), Gianni Di Stolfo (Sheriff Elmo Reagan), Angel Alvarez (Oliver Blackwood), Rafael Albaicin, Lorenzo Robledo (Bandits).

Working with his dark looks, Reynolds stars as an Indian in his first spaghetti western, filmed in Spain. Reynolds is a Navajo whose tribe, along with his family, has been killed by outlaw Sambrell. The film focuses on how Reynolds systematically hunts down and kills every member who took part in the massacre. In doing so he helps a beleaguered western town that had been terrorized by Sambrell's gang. Despite his tackling the bad guys alone, the town is unappreciative, fearful of another attack. Final scene has Reynolds doing in Sambrell with his bare hands and riding off into the sunset. Sharp cinematography by Ippoliti helps salvage this below-par production.

p, Ermanno Donati, Luigi Carpentieri; d, Sergio Corbucci; w, Fernando Di Leo, Dean Craig [Mario Pierotti] (based on a story by Ugo Pirro); ph, Silvano Ippoliti; (Techniscope, Technicolor); m, Ennio Morricone; art d, Aurelio Crugnola; makeup, Franco Freda.

Western   (PR:C MPAA:NR)

NAVAJO KID, THE*½   (1946) 59m PRC bw

Bob Steele (Navajo Kid), Syd Saylor (Happy), Edward Cassidy (Sheriff Roy Landon), Caren Marsh (Winifred McMasters), Stanley Blystone (Matt Crandall), Edward Howard (Bo Talley), Charles King, Jr. (Lee Hedges), Bud Osborne (Abe Murdock), Budd Buster (Pinky), Henry Hall (Dr. Cole), Gertrude Glorie, Bert Dillard, Rex Rossi.

Steele again is the star in this run-of-the-mill western production. Instead of a cowboy hat, he dons a feather to play an adopted Indian in search of a killer who murdered his adoptive father. The plot thickens every minute along the way, with one coincidence after another. Steele succeeds in getting revenge, but is arrested by the sheriff. The town's sheriff turns out to be his real father. This was the last starring role for Steele.

p, Arthur Alexander; d&w, Harry Fraser; ph, Jack Greenhalgh; ed, Roy Livingston; md, Lee Zahler; art d, George Montgomery.

Western   (PR:A MPAA:NR)

NAVAJO RUN   (1966) 83m Lorajon/AIP bw

Johnny Seven (Matthew Whitehawk), Warren Kemmerling (Luke Grog), Virginia Vincent (Sarah Grog), Ron Soble (Jesse Grog).

The film doesn't do justice to the story's premise. What on paper should have been fast-paced, exciting, and suspenseful ends up being slow-moving and dull. A half-breed Indian, Seven, shows up at Kemmerling's door after being bitten by a rattlesnake. The rancher wants to help, but his wife, Vincent, wants nothing to do with him. Finally, Kemmerling forces her to nurse him back to health. While there, he makes friends with Kemmerling's brother, who is mute. The rancher sets a trap and invites Seven to go hunting. Forcing him into the woods with no food or water, Seven becomes the object of Kemmerling's hunt, as did 16 others before him. After chasing him down, Kemmerling traps Seven, who grabs a rattlesnake and uses it like a whip to kill the evil and sadistic rancher.

p&d, Johnny Seven; w, Jo Helms; ph, Gregory Sandor; m, William Loose, Emil Cadkin; ed, Lee Gilbert.

Western   (PR:C MPAA:NR)

NAVAJO TRAIL, THE   (1945) 60m MON bw

Johnny Mack Brown, Raymond Hatton, Jennifer Holt, Riley Hill, Edmund Cobb, Charles King, Ray Bennett, Bud Osborne, Tom Quinn, Edward Cassidy, John Carpenter, Jim Hood, Jasper L. Palmer, Earl Crawford, Mary MacLaren.

Trouble brews along the title path in this Monogram western. Leave it to perennial cowboy hero Brown to ride in and save the day. This was just one of eight films for which programmer veteran Bretherton took the direction credit in 1945.

p, Charles J. Bigelow; d, Howard Bretherton; w, Jess Bowers, Adele Buffington (based on a story by Frank Young); ph, Marcel Le Picard; ed, Arthur H. Bell; set d, Vin Taylor.

Western   (PR:A MPAA:NR)

NAVAJO TRAIL RAIDERS** (1949) 60m REP bw

Alan "Rocky" Lane *(Himself)*, Eddy Waller *(Nugget Clark)*, Robert Emmett Keane *(John Blanford)*, Barbara Bestar *(Judy Clark)*, Hal Landon *(Tom Stanley)*, Dick Curtis *(Brad)*, Dennis Moore *(Frank Stanley)*, Ted Adams *(Sheriff Robbins)*, Forrest Taylor *(Sam Brynes)*, Marshall Reed *(Jed)*, Steve Clark *(Larkin)*, Chick Hannon, Black Jack the Horse.

A typical western, plenty of fights, gunslinging, and a little romance for Lane one more time. This time, he has to stop some outlaws who are stopping food and gold shipments to a village called Yellow Creek. He takes off on the Navajo Trail and breaks up a shipment raid. The rest of the time, he tries to capture the gang leader, who turns out to be the editor of the town newspaper. Unlike many westerns put out at the time, this one has no singing, just action to please the youngsters.

p, Gordon Kay; d, R.G. Springsteen; w, M. Coates Webster; ph, John MacBurnie; m, Stanley Wilson; ed, Arthur Roberts; art d, Fred A. Ritter; set d, John McCarthy, Jr., James Redd.

Western **(PR:A MPAA:NR)**

NAVAL ACADEMY*½ (1941) 67m COL bw

Freddie Bartholomew *(Steve Kendall)*, Jimmy Lydon *(Tommy Blake)*, Billy Cook *(Dick Brewster)*, Pierre Watkin *(Capt. Davis)*, Warren Ashe *(Lt. Brackett)*, Douglas Scott *(Jimmy Henderson)*, Warren Lloyd *(Ray Cameron)*, James Butler *(Matt Cooper)*, Joe Brown, Jr. *(Bill Foster)*, David Durand *(Fred Bailey)*, Tommy Bupp *(Joey Martin)*, John Dilson *(John Frazier)*, William Blees *(C.P.O. Caldwell)*.

A group of young men, from different backgrounds, are thrown together at a naval academy. The film follows the agonies and ecstasies they experience while going through the rigors of training. One young man is from a family with a long tradition in the Navy, one is the punk from reform school, and one is just a spoiled brat. Ashe is the officer who has seen this before and lends a strong but helping hand through it all.

p, Wallace MacDonald; d, Eric C. Kenton; w, David Silverstein, Gordon Rigby (based on a story by Robert James Cosgriff); ph, John Stumar; ed, William Lyon.

Drama **(PR:A MPAA:NR)**

NAVY BLUE AND GOLD** (1937) 94m MGM bw

Robert Young *(Roger Ash)*, James Stewart *(John "Truck" Cross)*, Lionel Barrymore *(Capt. "Skinny" Dawes)*, Florence Rice *(Patricia Gates)*, Billie Burke *(Mrs. Alyce Gates)*, Tom Brown *(Richard Arnold Gates, Jr.)*, Samuel S. Hinds *(Richard A. Gates, Sr.)*, Paul Kelly *(Tommy Milton)*, Frank Albertson *(Weeks)*, Barnett Parker *(Albert Graves)*, Minor Watson *(Lt. Milburn)*, Robert Middlemass *(Academy Superintendent)*, Phillip Terry *(Kelly)*, Charles Waldron *(Comdr. Carter)*, Pat Flaherty *(Coach of Southern Institute)*, Matt McHugh *(Heckler)*, Ted Pearson *(Harnet)*, Donald Barry *(Fellow Back)*, Jack Pennick *(Fireman)*, Paul Barrett, William Morgan *(Classmen)*, Edward Hart *(Official)*, Tom Hanlon, John Hiestand *(Commentators)*, Roger Converse *(Size Inspector)*, Donald Douglas *(Lt. North)*, Robert Hoover *(Parr)*, Walter Soderling *(Dr. Ryder)*, Stanley Morner [Dennis Morgan] *(Lieutenant of Marines)*, K.T. Stevens.

Stories about the various service academies have always proved fine fodder for Hollywood's cannons, from all the West Point tales to AN OFFICER AND A GENTLEMAN. In this, the male stars are a tad long in the tooth to play midshipmen at Annapolis, as Young was already 30, Stewart was 27, and Brown, the youngest, was 24. They're all football players and Stewart has registered under another name because his father was once in the navy and had been cashiered due to some infractions. Stewart is the football team's center and Young is the star back, and when Stewart is in a classroom and hears an untrue tale about his late dad, he can't take it any longer, so he stands up and tells the real story to the class and admits that he is the son of that man. For that, he is suspended and his team goes to play The Big Game with Army, but without him. The powers at the Academy think twice about what he did. By admitting everything, he's shown his bravery. Further, he stood up for his father as any true Navy man would do. They find him guilty but grant him reinstatement for the way he's handled himself. The game is already going when Stewart checks into the huddle. The score is tied and Young is handed the ball and follows Stewart's interference until he crosses the goal line, winning a glorious victory for the Blue and Gold. Once across the line, he hands the game ball to Stewart, who is then accorded the high honor of ringing the school bell in honor of another football hero, Barrymore. This is a film about honor and commitment to excellence; would that the film was as excellent as their commitment. The story was old when it was new, but it made little difference to audiences who flocked to see it anyhow.

p, Sam Zimbalist; d, Sam Wood; w, George Bruce (based on a novel by Bruce); ph, John Seitz; m, Edward Ward; ed, Robert J. Kern; art d, Cedric Gibbons, Urie McCleary; set d, Edwin B. Willis; cos, Dolly Tree; spec eff, John Hoffman.

Drama **(PR:A MPAA:NR)**

NAVY BLUES** (1930) 75m MGM bw

William Haines *(Kelly)*, Anita Page *(Alice)*, Karl Dane *(Sven Swanson)*, J.C. Nugent *(Mr. Brown)*, Edyth Chapman *(Mrs. Brown)*, Wade Boteler *(Higgins, CPO)*, Gertrude Sutton *(Hilda)*.

A tearjerker is this sudsy sailor drama. Haines is a sailor who becomes the object of desire for Page at a dance while he is in port. She falls head over heels for him and rushes him over to meet her folks. But her mother despises him immediately and tosses him out. Page follows. The tables turn when he states he is not the marrying type and dumps her. After a change of heart, Haines goes back to Page's home to make up and finds her not there. She hasn't been home since she left with him. After searching for her, he finds her employed in the world's oldest profession in a seedy cafe. Though no longer sweet and innocent, Haines takes her for his bride.

d, Clarence Brown; w, Dale Van Every, J.C. Nugent, Elliott Nugent, W.L. River (based on a story by Raymond L. Schrock); ph, Merritt B. Gerstad; ed, Hugh Wynn; art d, Cedric Gibbons; cos, David Cox.

Drama **(PR:A MPAA:NR)**

NAVY BLUES* (1937) 68m REP bw

Richard Purcell *(Rusty)*, Mary Brian *(Doris)*, Warren Hymer *(Biff)*, Joseph Sawyer *(Chips)*, Edward Woods *(Everett)*, Horace MacMahon *(Gateleg)*, Chester Clute *(Wayne)*, Lucille Gleason *(Mrs. Wayne)*, Ruth Fallows *(Goldie)*, Alonzo Price *(Dr. Crowley)*, Mel Ruick *(Lawson)*, Carleton Young *(Spencer)*.

Below-par spine-tingler devoid of thrills and suspense. Purcell is a rough sailor who goes out with the prim and proper librarian, Brian, on a wager with his sailor buddies. He pretends to be a Naval Academy candidate to impress her but she can tell he is a phony in a minute. "No really," he says, "I'm actually with naval intelligence." This statement gets them in trouble with a group of spies plotting to kill a visiting diplomat. He and Brian are kidnaped, but instead of the cavalry sounding the rescue charge, the Navy is called in and the assassination attempt is foiled at the last minute.

p, Burt Kelly; d, Ralph Staub; w, Gordon Kahn, Eric Taylor (based on a story by Kahn, Taylor); ph, Jack Marta; m, Harry Grey; ed, Murray Seldeen, Roy Livingston; cos, Eloise.

Spy Drama **(PR:A MPAA:NR)**

NAVY BLUES½** (1941) 108m WB bw

Ann Sheridan *(Margie Jordan)*, Jack Oakie *(Cake O'Hara)*, Martha Raye *(Lilibelle)*, Jack Haley *(Powerhouse Bolton)*, Herbert Anderson *(Homer Mathews)*, Jack Carson *(Buttons Johnson)*, Richard Lane *(Rocky Anderson)*, William T. Orr *(Mac)*, Jackie Gleason *(Tubby)*, John Ridgely *(Jersey)*, Howard da Silva *(1st Petty Officer)*, Ray Cooke *(Lucky)*, Richard Travis *(Tex)*, William Hopper *(Ens. Walters)*, Hardie Albright, Frank Wilcox *(Officers)*, Marguerite Chapman, Leslie Brooks, Claire James, Katherine [Kay] Aldridge, Georgia Carroll, Peggy Diggins *(Navy Blues Sextette)*, Ralph Byrd *(Lieutenant)*, Jean Ames, Maris Wrixon, Lucia Carroll *(Girls)*, Tom Dugan *(Hot Dog Stand Proprietor)*, Gaylord Pendleton, Don Rowan, Pat McVeigh, Walter Sande *(Marines)*, Dick Wessel, Victor Zimmerman *(Petty Officers)*, Charles Drake, Emmett Vogan *(Officers)*, Selmer Jackson *(Capt. Willard)*, Harry Strang *(CPO Lane)*, Gig Young, Murray Alper, Lane Allen, Will Morgan, Garland Smith, George O'Hanlon, Arthur Gardner *(Sailors)*.

Despite the solid talents of Sheridan, Haley, Oakie, and Raye, director Bacon (who had helmed the non-Busby Berkeley sections of 42nd STREET in 1933) couldn't lift the weak script of NAVY BLUES off the ground. Oakie and Haley play two dimwitted sailors desperate to snare a superior marksman on their ship for the upcoming gunnery trials. The boys have a lot of money wrapped up in the contest and go to great lengths to keep Iowa-born-and-bred gunner Anderson from wandering off before the big day. To ensure that they won't lose Anderson whose term is up, the gamblers employ the lovely Sheridan to seduce the kid into reenlisting. She does so, but then falls in love with the farm boy. To further muddle the action, Raye, Haley's wife, is in hot pursuit of her husband who has been dodging her efforts to connect. The comedy bits are forced and unimaginative, the musical numbers lack spunk, and the whole production lies there like a dead fish not responding to the cast's efforts to revive it. Director Bacon was capable of much better (KNUTE ROCKNE—ALL AMERICAN, 1940, ACTION IN THE NORTH ATLANTIC, 1943), though cinematography buffs may be interested in the dance sequences photographed by James Wong Howe. Songs: "In Waikiki," "You're a Natural," "Navy Blues," "When Are We Going to Land Abroad?" (Arthur Schwartz, Johnny Mercer).

p, Hal B. Wallis; d, Lloyd Bacon; w, Wald, Richard Macaulay, Arthur T. Horman (based on a story by Horman); ph, Tony Gaudio, James Wong Howe; m, Arthur Schwartz; ed, Rudi Fehr; cos, Howard Shoup; ch, Seymour Felix.

Musical/Comedy **(PR:A MPAA:NR)**

NAVY BORN* (1936) 68m REP bw

William Gargan *(Red Furness)*, Claire Dodd *(Bernice)*, Douglas Fowley *(Bassett)*, George Irving *(Adm. Kingston)*, Dorothy Tree *(Daphne)*, William Newell *(Bill Lyons)*, Addison Randall *(Tex)*, Georgia Caine *(Aunt Minnie)*, Claudia Coleman *(Mrs. Farrington)*, Douglas Wood *(Mr. Strickland)*, Paul Fix, Hooper Atchley, M. Lou Wastal, Larry Steers, Myra Marsh, Charles Marsh, George Guhl, Harry Strang, Elsa Newell, Gladys Gale, Lloyd Whitlock, Billie Van Every, Hal Price, Don Brodie, Earl Montgomery, Lucille Ward.

There is more involved in the plot than this wooden effort can sail on. A boy is orphaned when his parents die in an automobile accident. Gargan is a naval officer who had promised the child's father that he would take care of him if anything should happen. But the boy's relatives do not care too much for the boy growing up under the auspices of the Navy. While this battle is being waged, a gangster spots the child, who looks like the son who had been stolen from him. He snatches the boy and it's up to Gargan and the Navy to get him back. Along the way, the boy's aunt, Dodd, becomes romantically involved with Gargan. Once they bring the boy back to safety they can marry and live as one big, happy family.

p, Nat Levine; d, Nate Watt; w, Marcus Goodrich, Albert DeMond, Olive Cooper, Claire Church (Based on a story by Mildred Cram); ph, Ernest Miller, Jack Marta; ed, Dick Fantl.

Adventure **(PR:A MPAA:NR)**

NAVY BOUND*½ (1951) 61m MON bw

Tom Neal *(Joe Morelli)*, Wendy Waldron *(Lisa)*, Regis Toomey *(Capt. Danning)*, John Abbott *(Pappa Cerrano)*, Murray Alper *(Chris "Warthog" Novak)*, Paul Bryar *(Robert Garrells)*, Harvey Parry *(Sweeney)*, Ric Roman *(Tony)*, John Compton *(Vincent)*, Stephen Harrison *(Pietro)*, Billy Bletcher *(Schott)*, Ray Kemper *(1st Sailor)*, Herb Lytton, Riley Hill.

It just proves that tuna fishing and boxing do not mix at any time. Neal is the Navy boxing champ who must hang up his gloves when the family fishing business encounters money troubles. However, he yearns to return to the ring. A fight is set up with a professional boxer on the rise. If Neal wins, there will be enough money to get the family business onto dry financial land and he will be off the hook so he can return to the Navy. It probably was the tuna fishing industry's biggest loss but the Navy's gain.

p, William F. Broidy; d, Paul Landres; w, Sam Roeca (based on the story by Talbert Joslyn); ph, Harry Neumann; ed, Otho Lovering; art d, Dave Milton.

Drama (PR:A MPAA:NR)

NAVY COMES THROUGH, THE** (1942) 81m RKO bw

Pat O'Brien (Mallory), George Murphy (Sands), Jane Wyatt (Myra), Jackie Cooper (Babe), Carl Esmond (Kroner), Max Baer (Berringer), Desi Arnaz (Tarriba), Ray Collins (Capt. McCall), Lee Bonnell (Kovac), Frank Jenks (Sampter), John Maguire (Bayliss), Frank Fenton (Hodum), Joey Ray (Dennis), Marten Lamont (Navy Doctor), Cyril Ring (1st Officer) Edgar Dearing (Chief Petty Officer), Monte Montague (3rd Mate), Mary Young (Mrs. Duttson), Joe Cunningham (Mr. Duttson), Ralph Dunn (Cop), Helmut Dantine (Young German Seaman), George Melford (Chief Engineer), George Blagoi (Captain of German Submarine).

Almost unrealistic military film that grossed big money during the war years. Cooper, Baer, and Arnaz are sailors on a decrepit old freighter that single-handedly destroys the Nazi war fleet. The sharp captain and his crew sink enemy subs and shoot down German bombers like they are going out of style. Plenty of newsreel footage is intercut within the film to spice up the action and stir up the patriots in the audience. The main story—centering on Murphy and Wyatt—is boy meets girl, boy loses girl, and boy eventually wins girl back.

p, Islin Auster; d, A. Edward Sutherland; w, Roy Chanslor, Earl Baldwin, John Twist, Aeneas MacKenzie (based on the story "Pay to Learn" by Borden Chase); ph, Nicholas Musuraca; ed, Samuel E. Beetley; md, C. Bakaleinikoff; art d, Albert S. D'Agostino, Carroll Clark; cos, Renie; spec eff, Vernon L. Walker.

War (PR:A MPAA:NR)

NAVY HEROES** (1959, Brit.) 93m Group 3-Beaconsfield/BL bw (AKA: THE BLUE PETER)

Kieron Moore (Mike Merriworth), Greta Gynt (Mary Griffith), Sarah Lawson (Gwyneth Thomas), Mervyn Johns (Capt. Snow), John Charlesworth (Andrew Griffin), Harry Fowler (Charlie Barton), Mary Kerridge (Mrs. Snow), Ram Gopal (Dr. Tigara), Russell Napier (Raymond Curtiss), Brian Roper (Tony Mullins), Anthony Newley (Sparrow), Vincent Ball (Digger), Edwin Richfield, William Ingram, Donald McCorkindale, Keith Faulkner, Michael Bennett, Harold Siddons.

Wounded war hero takes on the job of athletic director at a boys' camp, and the experience lifts his spirits and alters his jaded view of the world. Several humorous scenes of camping life and a lively group of youngsters brighten an otherwise routine programmer.

p, Herbert Mason; d, Wolf Rilla; w, Don Sharp, John Pudney; ph, Arthur Grant (Eastmancolor); m, Anthony Hopkins.

Children (PR:A MPAA:NR)

NAVY LARK, THE** (1959, Brit.) 82m FOX bw

Cecil Parker (Comdr. Stanton, R.N.), Ronald Shiner (Chief Petty Officer Banyard), Leslie Phillips (Lt. Pouter, R.N.), Elvi Hale (Leading WREN Heather), Nicholas Phipps (Capt. Povey R.N.), Cardew Robinson (Lt. Binns, R.N.), Gordon Jackson (Leading Seaman Johnson), Harold Kasket (Gaston Higgins), Hattie Jacques (Fortune Teller), Reginald Beckwith (C.N.I.), Kenneth J. Warren (Brown), Wanda Ventham (Mabel), Richard Coleman (Lt. Bates, R.N.), Llewelyn Rees (Adm. Troutbridge), Clive Morton (Rear Admiral), Gordon Harris (Group Captain), Van Boolen (Fred), Gordon Whiting (Commander), Tom Gill (Naval Commander), Walter Hudd (Naval Captain).

The British services again become the foil for this fluffy farce that pokes fun at the British navy. The men on a forgotten naval base enjoy the free and easy life, undisciplined and unwatched by their superiors on a small island. A new captain comes in and decides they are not needed anymore. Then come the laughs as the men try to save their good life and will do almost anything to keep it. They even fake a revolution by the island natives to show they are still needed to protect Britain's holdings.

p, Herbert Wilcox; d, Gordon Parry; w, Sid Colin, Laurie Wyman (based on a BBC radio series by Laurie Wyman); ph, Gordon Dines (CinemaScope); m, James Moody, Tommy Reilly; ed, Basil Warren.

Comedy (PR:A MPAA:NR)

NAVY SECRETS** (1939) 60m MON bw

Fay Wray (Carol), Grant Withers (Steve), Dewey Robinson (Nick), William von Brincken (Conjer), Craig Reynolds (Jimmy), George Sorrell (Slavins), Andre Cheron (Benje), Robert Frazer (Peter), Joseph Crehan (Daly), Duke York (Babe), Arthur Housman (Drunk), Joe Girard (Captain).

A muddled film with a weak plot line that makes it a mystery as to why this film was made. Wray and Withers are federal agents investigating a case of government secret stealing. Problems arise because neither knows that the other is on the case and both consider the other to be their prime suspect. They track down the real crooks at the same time and become more than just partners in work at the end.

p, William Lackey; d, Howard Bretherton; w, Harvey Gates (based on a story by Steve Fisher); ph, Harry Neumann; ed, Russell Schoengarth.

Spy Drama/Mystery (PR:A MPAA:NR)

NAVY SPY zero (1937) 56m GN bw

Conrad Nagel (Alan O'Connor), Eleanor Hunt (Bobbie Reynolds), Judith Allen (Anno Novna), Jack Doyle (Lt. Don Carrington), Phil Dunham (Dr. Matthews), Don Barclay (Bertie), Howard Lang (Barradine), Crauford Kent (Capt. Leeds).

Low-budget espionage film that glorifies Nagel's role as a federal agent. Foreign agents kidnaped a naval officer who has possession of a secret formula. Nagel is called in and the chase is on. Hunt is also an FBI agent and Nagel's girl friend. This film is full of stock footage to fill in the gaps. And there are plenty of gaps to fill.

p, George A. Condor; d&w, Crane Wilbur; ph, Mack Stengler; ed, Tony Martinelli.

Spy Drama/Mystery (PR:A MPAA:NR)

NAVY STEPS OUT, THE (SEE: GIRL, A GUY, AND A GOB, A, 1941)

NAVY VS. THE NIGHT MONSTERS, THE** (1966) 90m REA c (AKA: THE NIGHT CRAWLERS)

Mamie Van Doren (Lt. Nora Hall), Anthony Eisley (Lt. Charles Brown), Pamela Mason (Maria, a Scientist), Billy Gray (Petty Officer Fred Twining), Bobby Van (Ens. Rutherford Chandler), Walter Sande (Dr. Arthur Beecham), Phillip Terry (Spalding), Edward Faulkner, Russ Bender.

One of those films that is so bad you go and see it for the laughs instead of the chills. Eisley is in charge of a South Pacific naval base that must care for a plane from Antarctica filled with ice-age vegetation. The plane crashes and the rescue team, consisting of Eisley and the attractive Van Doren, find the pilot dead, frozen in shock. To save the plant life, Eisley transplants them near some hot springs, and all of a sudden people start disappearing. It is discovered that the trees have been chewing up people and that the trees can walk on their furry roots. The trees multiply and move in on the survivors but Eisley torches and kills them with Molotov cocktails. This is the only film directed by screenwirter Hoey and features Gray, who was Bud on TV's "Father Knows Best."

p, George Edwards; d&w Michael A. Hoey (based on the novel Monster from the Earth's End by Murray Leinster); ph, Stanley Cortez (DeLuxe Color); m, Gordon Zahler; ed, George White; art d, Paul Sylos; spec eff, Edwin Tillman; makeup, Harry Thomas.

Horror **Cas.** (PR:C MPAA:NR)

NAVY WAY, THE* (1944) 74m PAR bw

Robert Lowery (Johnny Jersey), Jean Parker (Ellen Sayre), Bill Henry (Mal Randall), Roscoe Karns (Frankie Gimball), Sharon Douglas (Trudy), Robert Armstrong (Chief Petty Officer Harper), Richard Powers (Steve Appleby), Larry Nunn (Billy Jamison), Mary Treen (Agnes), Joseph Crehan.

Another quickly made war propaganda film. This one concerns naval training and recruits from all walks of life who are tossed together for one concern. Main plot is about Lowery, a prizefighter inducted right before his title shot. Though bitter, he changes through training and his love for Parker. But in another twist to make him a real man, she decides she loves Henry and Lowery accepts it gracefully by asking to be shipped out.

p, William Pine, William Thomas; d, William Berke; w, Maxwell Shane; ph, Fred Jackman, Jr.; m, Willy Stahl; ed, Howard Smith; art d, F. Paul Sylos.

War/Drama (PR:A MPAA:NR)

NAVY WIFE** (1936) 72m FOX bw

Claire Trevor (Vicky Blake), Ralph Bellamy (Dr. Quentin Harden), Jane Darwell (Mrs. Keats), Warren Hymer (Butch), Ben Lyon (Dr. Pete Milford), Kathleen Burke (Serena Morrison), George Irving (Dr. Keats), Anne Howard (Susan Harden), Jonathan Hale (Norton), Ruth Gillette (Mamie), John Kelly (Spike), Susan Fleming (Jenny), Murray Alper (Dr. Barratt).

Hawaiian background footage is more impressive than the story which asks, "Who suffers more—the naval officer or his wife?" Trevor, who has seen much of divorce, is hesitant about falling in love. She softens when Bellamy comes into her life but Trevor thinks he is still in love with his late wife. As the loneliness mounts, she marries him anyway because his crippled daughter needs care and Trevor finds out that he really does love her.

p, Sol M. Wurtzel; d, Allan Dwan; w, Sonya Levien, Edward T. Lowe (based on the novel Beauty's Daughter Kathleen Norris); ph, John Seitz, Rudolph Mate; md, David Buttolph.

Romance/Drama (PR:A MPAA:NR)

NAVY WIFE*½ (1956) 83m AA bw (GB: MOTHER, SIR!)

Joan Bennett (Peg Blain), Gary Merrill (Jack Blain), Judy Nugent (Debby Blain), Maurice Manson (Capt. Arwin), Teru Shimada (Mayor Yoshida), Tom Komuro (Ohara), Shizue Nakamura (Mitsuko), Robert Nichols (Oscar), Carol Veazie (Amelia), John Craven (Dr. Carter), Shirley Yamaguchi (Akashi), Arnold Ishii (Sato), Ziro Tenkai (Goto), Kyoko Kamo (Kimiko), Julia Katayama (Akiko), Karie Shindo (Reiko), Micko Shintani (Tomiko), Rollin Moriyama (Frock-Coated Man), Tauenko Takahashi (Mrs. Yoshida), Dona Jean Okubo (Sister Cecilia), Yoshiko Nilya (Sister Frances), Dick Tyler, Morgan Jones, Jack Bradford (Officers), Michiyo Kamo (Old Woman), Bob Okazaki (Porter), Matsukichi Kamo, John Matautani (Gardeners), Sono Shirai, Mash Kunitomi (Operators), Miyoshi Jingu (Female Attendant), Kimiko Hiroshigi (Woman), Kent Shoji (Small Boy), Karen Yamamoto (Small Girl), Jack Shintani, Kuni Morishima (Workmen), Tomiji Nagao (Man), Jim Yagi (Mr. Okato), Maudie Prickett (Nurse), Phil Arnold (Photographer), Dorothy Furamura (Geisha).

A supposed comedy that falls way short. Japanese wives, known for their obedience, start copying the independent ways of their American counterparts, and that's supposed to be funny. Bennett, who comes to Japan to be with her husband, is the catalyst of all the trouble. She comes in and plays the typical dominant American housewife and the Japanese women try to do the same with their husbands, but with modest results.

p, Walter Wanger; d, Edward L. Bernds; w, Kay Lenard (based on the novel *Mother Sir* by Tats Blain); ph, Wilfrid Cline; m, Hans Salter; ed, Richard Cahoon; m/l, "Mother Sir," Jack Brooks, Salter.

Comedy (PR:A MPAA:NR)

NAZARIN**½ (1968, Mex.) 92m Altura bw

Francisco Rabal (*Don Nazario*), Marga Lopez (*Beatriz*), Rita Macedo (*Andara, Prostitute*), Jesus Fernandez (*Ujo, the Dwarf*), Ignacio Lopez Tarso (*The Sacrilegist*), Luis Aceves Castaneda (*The Parricide*), Ofelia Guilmain (*Chanfa*), Noe Murayama (*El Pinto*), Rosenda Monteros (*La Prieta*), Ada Carrasco, Antonio Bravo, Aurora Molina, David Reynoso, Manuel Arvide, Edmundo Barbero, Raul Dantes, Pilar Pellicer.

A film with never a cheerful moment, its grimness continually pounds on the viewer. Rabal plays a priest who tries to follow the exact life of Christ in turn-of-the-century Mexico. He is completely ridiculed in the village he serves. When he gives shelter to a prostitute, he runs into trouble with the church elders, so he goes on the road to live among and serve the poor. He is accompanied on his travels by Macedo, the prostitute, and Lopez, a woman he talked out of committing suicide. When he returns to his village, those who mocked him now think of him as a saint, and it bothers him immensely. He performs some miracle-like deeds in the village. He gets arrested, is beaten up in prison, and is saved by a church thief. The church elders come in to help but the audience is left wondering about his fate.

p, Manuel Barbachano Ponce; d, Luis Bunuel; w, Julio Alejandro, Bunuel (based on a novel by Benito Perez Galdos); ph, Gabriel Figueroa; m, Rodolfo Halffter; ed, Carlos Savage; art d, Edward Fitzgerald; m/l, "Dios Nunca Muere" Macedonio Alcala; makeup, Armando Meyer.

Religious/Drama (PR:A MPAA:NR)

NAZI AGENT**½ (1942) 82m MGM bw (AKA: SALUTE TO COURAGE)

Conrad Veidt (*Otto Becker/Baron Hugo von Detner*), Ann Ayars (*Kaaren De Relle*), Frank Reicher (*Fritz*), Dorothy Tree (*Miss Harper*), Ivan Simpson (*Prof. Sterling*), William Tannen (*Ludwig*), Martin Kosleck (*Kurt Richten*), Marc Lawrence (*Joe Aiello*), Sidney Blackmer (*Arnold Milbar*), Moroni Olsen (*Brenner*), Pierre Watkin (*Grover McHenry*), Margaret Bert (*Mrs. Dennis*), Barbara Bedford (*Woman*), Mark Daniels, Robert Davis (*Cab Drivers*), Harry B. Stafford (*Elderly Man*), Roper Moore (*Messenger*), Stuart Crawford (*Commentator's Voice*), Hal Cooke (*Clerk*), George Noisom (*Bellboy*), Roland Varno (*Bauer*), William Tannen (*Ludwig the Chauffeur*), William Norton Bailey (*Cigar Clerk*), Tim Ryan, Walter Byron (*Officers*), Tom Stevenson (*Headwaiter*), Christian Rub (*Mohr*), Hermine Sterler (*Mrs. Mohr*), Jeff York (*Keeler*), Jessie Arnold (*Landlady*), Cliff Danielson (*Youth*), James Millican (*Operator*), Philip Van Zandt, George Magrill (*Thugs*), Joe Yule (*Barney*), Bernadene Hayes (*Rosie*), Arthur Belasco, Charles Sherlock (*Detectives*), William Post, Jr. (*Harry's Voice*), Clyde Courtright (*Doorman*), Polly Bailey (*Fat Woman*), Joe Gilbert (*Sub-Radio Man*), Edward Hearn, Jack Daley, Drew Demarest, Wilbur Mack (*Reporters*), Baldy Cooke (*Waiter*), Frank Marlowe, Duke York, Ernie Alexander (*Sailors*), Robert E. Homans, Russell Simpson (*Captains*), Ray Teal (*Officer Graves*), Brick Sullivan (*Radio Operator*), Roy Barcroft (*Chief Petty Officer*).

Another patriotic war film that shows love of country comes first, even between brothers. Veidt is in a dual role, playing an evil Nazi and also a German-born but loyal American. The nasty brother forces his good brother to help some German spies, but the good twin kills the bad one as soon as he can, then pretends he is the Nazi to catch all of the spy ring. Ayars loves them both and good always wins, of course.

p, Irving Asher; d, Jules Dassin; w, Paul Gangelin, John Meehan, Jr. (based on an idea by Lother Mendes); ph, Harry Stradling; ed, Frank E. Hull; cos, Howard Shoup.

Spy/Drama (PR:A MPAA:NR)

NAZI SPY RING (SEE: DAWN EXPRESS, 1942)

NAZI TERROR AT NIGHT (SEE: DEVIL STRIKES AT NIGHT, THE, 1961, W. Ger.)

NEANDERTHAL MAN, THE*½ (1953) 78m UA bw

Robert Shayne (*Dr. Cliff Groves*), Richard Crane (*Dr. Ross Harkness*), Doris Merrick (*Ruth Marshall*), Joyce Terry (*Jan*), Robert Long (*Jim*), Dick Rich (*Sheriff Andrews*), Jean Quinn (*Celia*), Robert Easton, Beverly Garland.

A stiff effort at a horror film. Dupont was brought in to direct because of his reputation as a film critic and filmmaker in Germany. Shayne is a mad scientist who creates a serum that makes people turn into neandertal creatures. He first experiments with his housekeeper, and she turns into an ape-woman. Next is his pet kitten that turns into a sabre-toothed tiger. And then himself. He flounders around in an expressionless mask and is eventually done in by his own work: he is mauled by the tiger. The best part is when it is finally over.

p, Aubrey Wisberg, Jack Pollexfen; d, E.A. Dupont; w, Wisberg, Pollexfen; ph, Stanley Cortez

Horror (PR:A MPAA:NR)

NEAPOLITAN CAROUSEL*** (1961, Ital.) 124m LUX c
(CAROSELLO NAPOLETANO; AKA: NEOPOLITAN CAROUSEL)

Paolo Stoppa (*Salvatore Esposito*), Clelia Matania (*Donna Concetta, His Wife*), Vittoria Barracaracciolo (*Maria*), Jean Quick (*Angela*), Nadia Gray (*"The Spirit of Naples"*), Maria Fiore (*Brigida*), Maria Pia Casilio (*Her Rival, the Hairdresser*),

Antonio (*Their Flame*), Yvette Chauvire (*Donna Margherita*), Folco Lulli (*Don Raffaele*), Sophia Loren (*Sisina*), Giacomo Rondinella (*Luigino*), Alberto Bonucci, Vittorio Caprioli (*Luigino's Pals*), Leonide Massine (*Leonide Punchinello*), Loris Gizzi (*Mr. Gustafson*), Vera Nandi (*Lily Kangy/Singing Voice*), Joan Baron (*French Can-Can Dancer*), Franco Coop, Enrico Viarisio, Guglielmo Barnabo, Galeazzo Benti (*Conquerors*), Beniamino Gigli, Carlo Tagliabue, Mario Cioffi, Marinelli Meli (*Singing Voices*), Antonio Cifariello, Aldo Bufi Landi, Dolores Palumbo, Rosita Segovia, Marjorie Tallchief, Joan Baron, Rosella Hightower, Grand Ballett de Marquis de Cueras, Ballet Africain de Keita Fodeba, Rome Opera Theater Corps de Ballet, Italian State Radio Orchestra of Rome.

An Italian musical extravaganza structured after the Commedia dell'Arte, which boasts performances of ballet, opera, popular song, street dancing, and mime. The musical numbers are linked by a family of street musicians which has traveled from town to town performing for hundreds of years. Stoppa, patriarch of the family, pauses in his wanderings to introduce the various set-pieces that span several centuries. Among them: "The Sailor's Lament," inspired by a Salvatore Rosi painting of the Moorish invasion; a ballet called "Naples Incarnate" which details the courting of a young Neapolitan girl by several men dressed in costumes from different countries; the beginnings of the barter system; a tragic romance between Loren, a model for naughty postcards, and a soldier who is killed during WW I; a performance of the traditional *Michelemma*, the oldest known Italian melody; the invasion of Saracens and the occupation of Naples by the French, Spanish, and Germans is given a ballet interpretation; the dance of the tarantella; and a mass street dance along the streets of Naples concluding the festivities. NEAPOLITAN CAROUSEL, which was released in Europe in 1953 with a 125-minute running time, didn't find an American audience until 1961 after 11 minutes had been cut. The film was a bit of a disappointment for U.S. audiences who had seen Loren in Vittorio De Sica's superb TWO WOMEN four months earlier, and few realized that NEAPOLITAN CAROUSEL was actually shot eight years before when Loren was still a rising star. Nevertheless, the film is a musical feast for the eyes and ears that offers a variety of native Italian dances, songs, and entertainment to the devotee of cultural traditions. (In Italian; English subtitles.)

d, Ettore Giannini; w, Giuseppe Marotta, Giannini, Remigio Del Grosso (based on a story by Giannini); ph, Piero Portalupi (Pathe Color); m, Raffaele Gervasio; ed, Nicolo Lazzari; art d, Mario Chiari; cos, Maria De Matteis; ch, Leonide Massine; English subtitles, Clare Catalano.

Musical (PR:A MPAA:NR)

NEAR THE RAINBOW'S END** (1930) 56m T/C/TIF bw

Bob Steele (*Jim Bledsoe*), Louise Lorraine (*Ruth Wilson*), Lafe McKee (*Tom Bledsoe*), Al Ferguson (*Buck Rankin*), Alfred Hewston (*Tug Wilson*), Hank Bell, Merrill McCormick.

Bob Steele's first talking western is about cattlemen and sheep herders at odds again, but it's the rustlers who are causing the trouble. Steele is from a cattle raising family; he eventually catches bad guy Ferguson and ends the trouble, but not before there are the customary fist fights to provide the action. Steele settles the feuding completely when he weds Lorraine, daughter of a sheep herder, and it's happy trails once again.

p, Trem Carr; d, J.P. McGowan; w, Sally Winters, Charles A. Post; ph, Hap Depew, T.E. Jackson; ed, Charles J. Hunt; set d, E. R. Hickson; m/l, "Ro-Ro-Rolling Along," Murray Mencher, Billy Moll, Harry Richman.

Western (PR:A MPAA:NR)

NEAR THE TRAIL'S END** (1931) 53m T/C/TIF bw

Bob Steele, Marion Shockley, Jay Morley, Si Jenks, Hooper Atchley, Murdock McQuarrie, Henry Rocquemore, Fred Burns, Artie Ortego.

Steele is the new marshal in town and is after some stagecoach bandits. While chasing the bandits, he still has time to woo Shockley. It was to be Steele's last film before he jumped to a more lucrative deal with World Wide.

d, Wallace Fox; w, G.A. Durlam (based on a story by Robert Quigley); ph, Archie Stout.

Western (PR:A MPAA:NR)

NEARLY A NASTY ACCIDENT** (1962, Brit.) 92m Marlow/UNIV bw

Jimmy Edwards (*Group Capt. Kingsley*), Kenneth Connor (*A.C.2 Alexander Wood*), Shirley Eaton (*Cpl. Jean Briggs*), Richard Wattis (*Wagstaffe*), Ronnie Stevens (*Flight Lt. Pocock*), Jon Pertwee (*Gen. Birkenshaw*), Eric Barker (*Minister*), Peter Jones (*Flight Lt. Winters*), Jack Watling (*Flight Lt. Grogan*), Cyril Chamberlain (*Warrant Officer Breech*), John Forrest (*Bunthorpe*), Charlotte Mitchell (*Miss Chamberlain*), Joyce Carey (*Lady Trowborough*), Terry Scott (*Sam Stokes*), Vincent Ball (*Crybwyth Sergeant*), Harold Goodwin (*Aircraft Mechanic*), Joe Baker (*Watkins*), Jack Douglas (*Balmer*), Ian Whittaker (*Railway Transport Officer*), Emrys Leyshon (*Ambulance Driver*).

Connor is a man who is obsessed with repairing things and is fascinated with anything mechanical in this fair and cute British comedy. But mechanical he is not, so his little adventures have devastating effects, like accidentally launched missiles and crashed airplanes. His actions are causing his captain, Edwards, to get a trifle upset because it might cost Edwards the promotion he has been longing for. He tries to have Connor taken out of the service, but Connor innocently disappears and becomes a media figure. Everyone wants him found before he has any more costly accidents. After causing a flood in South Wales and blacking out part of the country, he is finally found and taken back to his base. The air defence minister arrives and Connor comes to his aid to fix something. Edwards panics, dives in to stop Connor, and the result is disastrous for everyone.

p, Bertram Ostrer; d, Don Chaffey; w, Jack Davies, Hugh Woodhouse (based on the play "Touch Wood" by David Stringer, David Carr); ph, Paul Beeson; m, Ken

Jones; ed, Bill Lenny; art d, Charles Bishop; spec eff, Wally Veevers; makeup, Ernest Gasser.

Comedy (PR:A MPAA:NR)

NEARLY EIGHTEEN** (1943) 61m MON bw

Gale Storm (Jane), Rick Vallin (Tony), Bill Henry (Leonard), Luis Alberni (Gus), Ralph Hodges (Tom), Jerry Rush (Dick), George O'Hanlon (Eddie), Bebe Fox (Harriet).

A talented young woman, Storm, wants to be a singer, but at 17 is too young to work the nightclub circuit. So she opts for a prestigious music academy, but is turned down because she is older than 14. What's a talented girl to do? Lie about her age, of course, but instead of pretending she is older, as most would, she chooses a younger age and quickly lines up an affair with a teacher. Has the guy no morals? Finally, her long-awaited birthday arrives and she can sing at the club. Her teacher learns her real age and true love takes off from there with everyone happy and old enough to enjoy it.

p, Lindsley Parsons; d, Arthur Dreifuss; w, George Sayre (based on an original story by Margaret Englander); ph, Mack Stengler; ed, Dick Currier; md, Edward Kay; art d, Dave Milton; m/l, "Smiles for Sale," "Walking on Air."

Drama (PR:A MPAA:NR)

'NEATH BROOKLYN BRIDGE**½ (1942) 61m BAN/MON bw

Leo Gorcey (Muggs McGinnis), Huntz Hall (Glimpy), Bobby Jordan (Danny Lyons), "Sunshine Sammy" Morrison (Scruno), Stanley Clements (Stash), Bobby Stone (Skinny), Ann Gillis (Sylvia), Noah Beery, Jr. (Butch), Marc Lawrence (McGaffey), Gabriel Dell (Skid), David O'Brien (Sgt. Phil Lyons), Jack Raymond (Sniffy), Bud Osborn (Morley), Patsy Moran (Glimpy's Mother), Betty Wells (Bunny), Dewey Robinson (Police Captain), Jack Mulhall (Sgt. Clancy), J. Arthur Young (Skipper), Betty Sinclair (Saleswoman), Snub Pollard (Soup Customer), Leo Gorcey, Huntz Hall (Babies: Slaine, Chowderhead).

An appealing movie with the Bowery Boys in the middle of things again. After her guardian is killed by bar owner Beery, the boys hide Gillis for safety. All evidence seems to point to the boys as the guilty parties in the murder. Beery forces Hall to help with a warehouse robbery, but before it can take place they find a witness to the murder. It is Gillis' grandfather. He is paralyzed and cannot speak but blinks his eyes in Morse code to reveal who did it. Hall goes through with the robbery but, in actuality, brings Beery, the guilty party, to the authorities. (See BOWERY BOYS series, Index.)

p, Sam Katzman, Jack Dietz; d, Wallace Fox; w, Harvey H. Gates; ph, Mack Stengler; ed, Carl Pierson; md, Edward Kay; art d, David Milton

Comedy **Cas.** (PR:A MPAA:NR)

'NEATH THE ARIZONA SKIES** (1934) 57m MON bw

John Wayne (Chris Morrell), Sheila Terry (Clara Moore), Jay Wilsey [Buffalo Bill, Jr.] (Jim Moore), Shirley Ricketts [Shirley Jane Rickey] (Nina), George Hayes (Matt Downing), Yakima Canutt (Sam Black), Jack Rockwell (Vic Byrd), Phil Keefer (Hodges), Frank Hall Crane (Express Agent), Earl Dwire, Weston Edwards, Artie Ortego, Tex Phelps, Eddie Parker.

Wayne rides tall in the saddle in this early western that has him changing clothes to get the bad guys. Wayne is in charge of Ricketts, an Indian girl who is in line for some rich oil property. He is attacked by crooks who are after Ricketts, and he ends up changing clothes with a hunted murderer. A drawn out but exciting fist fight has Wayne and bad guy Canutt exchanging blows in the middle of a river.

p, Paul Malvern; d, Harry Fraser; w, Burl Tuttle (based on a story by Tuttle); ph, Archie Stout; ed, Carl Pierson.

Western **Cas.** (PR:A MPAA:NR)

NEBO ZOVYOT (SEE: BATTLE BEYOND THE SUN, 1963)

NEBRASKAN, THE* (1953) 68m COL c

Phil Carey (Wade Harper), Roberta Haynes (Paris), Wallace Ford (McBride), Richard Webb (Ace Eliot), Lee Van Cleef (Reno), Maurice Jara (Wingfoot), Regis Toomey (Col. Markham), Jay Silverheels (Spotted Bear), Pat Hogan (Yellow Knife), Dennis Weaver (Capt. DeWitt), Boyd "Red" Morgan (Sgt. Phillips).

Even pathetic 3-D visual effects couldn't help this poor western. Indians are after Jara, an Indian aide to Carey, who they think knocked off a tribal elder. A U.S. Army scout has to protect him and they end up with a strange mob in an old house holding off the wild Indians with death in their eyes. Saving grace is the appearance of Van Cleef in his first of many bad-guy roles.

p, Wallace MacDonald; d, Fred F. Sears; w, David Lang, Martin Berkeley (based on a story by Lang); ph, Henry Freulich (3-D, Technicolor); ed, Al Clark, James Sweeney; md, Ross DiMaggio; art d, Robert Peterson.

Western (PR:A MPAA:NR)

NECK AND NECK* (1931) 63m Sono Art-World Wide bw

Glen Tryon (Bill Grant), Vera Reynolds (Norma Rickson), Walter Brennan (Hector), Lafe McKee (Col. Rickson), Carroll Nye (Frank Douglas), Stepin Fetchit (The Hustler), Richard Cramer, Gene Morgan, Lloyd Whitlock.

Low budget meant no laughs in this wooden comedy. Tryon is a small-time gambler who spends more time embellishing his accomplishments than actually doing anything. He has a small run of good luck when he wins a racehorse during a poker game. This enables him to enjoy the life style he has been bragging about for so long. While in high society, he falls for Reynolds, whose father is big in racing circles. Tryon's horse wins the big race, surprising even Tryon in the lackluster finale.

p, George W. Weeks; d, Richard Thorpe; w, Betty Burbridge (based on a story by Burbridge; ph, Jules Cronjager; ed, Viola Roehl.

Comedy (PR:A MPAA:NR)

NECROMANCY* (1972) 82m Cinerama c (AKA: THE WITCHING)

Orson Welles (Mr. Cato), Pamela Franklin (Lori Brandon), Lee Purcell (Priscilla), Michael Ontkean (Frank Brandon), Harvey Jason (Jay), Lisa James (Georgette), Sue Bernard (Nancy), Terry Quinn (Cato's Son).

More than witchcraft would be needed to save this blah horror film that leaves a void when it comes to thrills. Franklin is a housewife whose husband has been transferred to a small town. The town, which has only one industry—making objects used in witchcraft practices—is owned by Welles, whose name they hoped would save this tepid film. Welles wants to bring his son back to life and uses Franklin for that purpose by trading her life for his son's. Better left dead.

p,d&w, Bert I. Gordon; ph, Winton Hoch; m, Fred Karger; ed, John Woelz; art d, Frank Sylos; set d, Robert De Vestel; cos, Bernard Pollack; spec eff, William "Dutch" Vanderbyl; makeup, William Tuttle, Don Schoenfeld.

Horror (PR:C MPAA:PG)

NED KELLY**½ (1970, Brit.) 103m Woodfall/UA c

Mick Jagger (Ned Kelly), Allen Bickford (Dan Kelly), Geoff Gilmour (Steve Hart), Mark McManus (Joe Byrne), Serge Lazareff (Wild Wright), Peter Sumner (Tom Lloyd), Ken Shorter (Aaron Sherritt), James Elliott (Pat O'Donnell), Clarissa Kaye (Mrs. Kelly), Diane Craig (Maggie Kelly), Susan Lloyd (Kate Kelly), Alexi Long (Grace Kelly), Bruce Barry (George King), Janne Wolmsley (Caitlyn), Ken Goodlet (Nicholson), Nigel Lovell (Standish), Martyn Sanderson (Fitzpatrick), Robert Bruning (Sgt. Steele), John Laws (Kennedy), Liam Reynolds (Lonigan), Lindsay Smith (McIntyre), John Gray (Stratton), Reg Gorman (Bracken), John Hopkins (O'Connor), Peter Whittle (Devine), Anne Harvey (Mrs. Devine), Bill Charlton (Richards), Graham Keating (1st Trooper), Ben Blakeney (Tracker), Bill Hunter (Officer), Frank Thring (Judge Barry), Alexander Cann (McInnes), Gerry Duggan (Father O'Hea), John Dease (Whitty), Andrew Sanders (Farrell), Patsy Dance (Mrs. Whitty), Erika Crowne (Mrs. Farrell), Tony Bazell (Mr. Scott), Jessica Noad (Mrs. Scott), Colin Tilley (Bank Clerk), Tim Van Rellim, Patrick McCarville (Sportsmen), Kamahl (Gloster), Ronald Golding (Casement), Gordon McDougall (Tarleton), Clifford Neate (Living), Brian Niland (Mackie), Doreen Warburton (Mrs. Jones), Gary Fisher (Jack Jones), Karin Altman (Jane Jones), David Copping (Mr. Curnow), Penny Stehli (Mrs. Curnow), Francis Yin (Sympathizer), Shirley May Donald (Mrs. Byrne), Mary Marshall (Mrs. Barry), Claire Balmford (Nell Sherritt), Kurt Beimel (Anton Wicks), Moshe Kedem (Baumgarten), Keith Peterson (Referee), Terry Erwin (Chinese), Harry Kelly (Aborigine), Jack Allen (Melbourne), Michael Boddy.

Jagger is a bit miscast, but manages to hold his own in this film based on the life of Ned Kelly, one of Australia's most famous outlaws. Jagger is forced into a life of crime after being sent to prison for a crime he didn't commit. Upon release, Jagger, his brothers, and their stepfather, Barry, become horse thieves and begin a reign of terror. The police pursue the robbers, but several of their number are killed by the gang in an ambush, which only intensifies the manhunt. Cleverly, the governor arrests Jagger's mother for the murder in hopes the gang will come out of hiding. Jagger offers himself to the authorities in exchange for his mother, but the governor refuses. Eventually the gang is cornered in a saloon, but Jagger's brothers commit suicide rather than be taken alive. Jagger is captured, tried, and hanged. When Jagger was first cast for NED KELLY, the producers also wanted his real-life girl friend, Marianne Faithfull, to play Ned Kelly's girl. Unfortunately, Faithfull became ill just before shooting, and she lost the role. Though not a bad film by any means, NED KELLY lacks the punch and energy that would become characteristic of the "new" Australian cinema, perhaps because of its British director, Tony Richardson, who manages to sap the life of almost anything he touches (see THE BORDER or THE LOVED ONE). A better version of the same material appeared in 1976 starring Dennis Hopper in a film called MAD DOG MORGAN.

p, Neil Hartley; d, Tony Richardson; w, Richardson, Ian Jones; ph, Gerry Fisher (Technicolor); m, Shel Silverstein; prod d, Jocelyn Herbert; ed, Charles Rees; art d, Andrew Sanders; cos, Herbert; m/l, "Ned Kelly," "Son of a Scoundrel," "Shadow of the Gallows," "Lonigan's Widow," "Stony Cold Ground," "The Kellys Keep Comin'," "Marchin' in the Evenin'," "Blame It on the Kellys," "Pleasures of a Sunday Afternoon," "Hey Ned," (Shel Silverstein, sung by Waylon Jennings), "She Moved Through the Fair" (sung by Glen Tomasetti), "The Wild Colonial Boy" (sung by Mick Jagger).

Drama/Biography (PR:C MPAA:GP)

NEFERTITE, REGINA DEL NILO (SEE: QUEEN OF THE NILE, 1964)

NEGATIVES** (1968, Brit.) 90m Kettledrum-Narizzano/Continental c

Peter McEnery (Theo), Diane Cilento (Reingard), Glenda Jackson (Vivien), Maurice Denham (Father), Steven Lewis (The Dealer), Norman Rossington (Auctioneer), Billy Russell (Old Man).

Bizarre and very different film that deals with sexual fantasy and death. An unmarried couple, Jackson and McEnery can only satisfy themselves sexually if McEnery dresses up as an early 1900s murderer and Jackson as his wife. By chance, Cilento, a German photographer, gets some pictures during their little ritual, and then moves into the apartment with them. All the time, McEnery's father is dying of cancer. McEnery is always depressed after their little sex game, while Jackson is exhilarated. Cilento starts feeding McEnery the notion that he is a noted WW I flying ace, and McEnery starts slipping deeper and deeper into that role. Jackson wants in on his solitary fantasy, but McEnery responds with violence. As McEnery fights an imaginary foe, Cilento announces that she is leaving. Strange last shot has a bleeding McEnery slumped over in the vintage plane that he has installed on the roof.

p, Judd Bernard; d, Peter Medak; w, Peter Everett, Roger Lowry (based on a novel by Everett); ph, George Minassian (Technicolor); m, Basil Kirchin; ed, Barrie Vince; art d, Ted Tester; set d, Dimity Collins; cos, Clive Evans.

Drama (PR:C MPAA:NR)

NEHEZELETUEK (SEE: THE ROUND UP, 1969, Hung.)

NEIGE (SEE: SNOW, 1982, Fr.)

NEIGHBORS½** (1981) 95m COL c

John Belushi (Earl Keese), Kathryn Walker (Enid Keese), Cathy Moriarty (Ramona), Dan Aykroyd (Vic), Igors Gavon (Chic), Dru-Ann Chukron (His Wife), Tim Kazurinsky (Pa Greavy), Tino Insana (Perry), P. L. Brown, Henry Judd Baker (Police), Lauren-Marie Taylor (Elaine Keese), Dale Two Eagle (Thundersky), Sherman Lloyd, Bert Kittel, J. B. Friend, Bernie Friedman, Edward Kotkin, Michael Manoogian (Firemen).

This is a film that could have been a classic in bizarre comedy but unfortunately lacked the pell-mell pacing to make it work. Belushi and wife Walker are a pair of suburbanites who live a comfortable, if humdrum, life in their own corner of the U.S. Without warning, Aykroyd and his wife Moriarty move in next door, throwing Belushi and Walker's life into semi-controlled chaos. Aykroyd, who dubs himself "Captain Vic," goes out of his way to be neighborly and engages Belushi in an outrageous battle of wit and nerve. Belushi's sedate life style is thrown for a loop by this madman and his wife, as the two try to top each other with bizarre "getting even" stunts. In the end Belushi is a changed man, gleefully destroying his home and riding off in the car with his new neighbors for sites unspecific. Belushi and Aykroyd were cast here against their usual types (for once Aykroyd is the slob and Belushi is Mr. Normal and Sedate) with good effect, playing well against audience expectations of the popular duo. However, Avildsen is hardly a comedy director. Best known for his Oscar-winning ROCKY, he shows little sense of comic set up and delivery, leaving his actors to carry the majority of the film. They do, but considering the strange nature of their ongoing war, strong direction was essential. The result peters out about halfway through the film, with only touches of bizarre flavor encompassing the rest. A box-office disappointment, this would be Belushi's last picture. A few months after its Christmas release he was dead of a drug overdose.

p, Richard D. Zanuck, David Brown; d, John G. Avildsen; w, Larry Gelbart (based on the novel by Thomas Berger); ph, Gerald Hirschfeld (Technicolor); m, Bill Conti; ed, Jane Kurson; prod d, Peter Larkin; cos, John Boxer.

Comedy Cas. (PR:O-C MPAA:R)

NEIGHBORS' WIVES½** (1933) 61m Fanchon Royer bw

Dorothy Mackaill, Tom Moore, Mary Kornman, Vivien Oakland, Cyril Ring, Emerson Treacy, James Gordon, Mabel Van Buren, Paul Weigel.

Melodramatic drivel starring Mackaill, who nobly (but stupidly) becomes embroiled in the personal affairs of her husband's sister, Kornman. Vivacious Kornman has become involved with a "bad" boy and to save the foolish girl from his evil advances (and also to avoid a scandal for her husband, a former cop, now a lawyer) Mackaill goes too far and kills the boy. Husband Moore misinterprets the situation and assumes his wife has been cheating on him and covered up her own indiscretion with the murder. All winds up well after all the skeletons have been sorted out by a sympathetic judge who clears Mackaill's name.

d, Reeves Eason; w, John Francis Natteford.

Crime/Drama (PR:A MPAA:NR)

NEITHER BY DAY NOR BY NIGHT** (1972, U.S./Israel) 87m Motion Pictures International c

Zalman King (Adam), Miriam Berstein-Cohen (Sokolova), Dalia Friedland (Nurse), Edward G. Robinson (Father).

A sensitively told tale starring King as a young American soldier who was blinded in battle and placed in an Israeli hospital to recover. There he meets Berstein-Cohen, an elderly woman, also blind, who believes the young soldier is the lover she lost years ago. The woman's delusions bring back the youth she had nearly forgotten, and the memories give her a renewed purpose in life. Berstein-Cohen's new conviction enables King to deal with his blindness as well, and he even gains enough confidence to begin a romance with his nurse, Friedland. While a bit melodramatic at times, the film is held together by Berstein-Cohen's powerful performance. Robinson is fine in a brief cameo as King's father. (In English.)

p, Mordechai Slonim; d, Steven Hillard Stern; w, Stern, Gisa W. Slonim (based on a play by Abraham Raz); ph, Ammon Salomon (Eastmancolor); m, Vladimir Cosma; ed, Alain Jukabowicz.

Drama (PR:A MPAA:NR)

NEITHER THE SEA NOR THE SAND* (1974, Brit.) 116m Tigon/International Amusement c

Susan Hampshire (Anna Robinson), Michael Petrovitch (Hugh Dabernon), Frank Finlay (George Dabernon), Michael Craze (Collie), Jack Lambert (Dr. Irving), David Garth (Mr. MacKay), Betty Duncan (Mrs. MacKay), Anthony Booth (Delamare).

Strange twist on a passionate love theme has Hampshire as a married housewife visiting the Isle of Jersey to straighten out her life. While there, she meets and falls in love with a lighthouse-keeper, Petrovitch. The two run off to Scotland together where, while they are making love on the beach, Petrovitch dies. But he comes back to life, making for some problems on the part of Hampshire and other friends

as they try to relate to this new state. Picture has tinges of Ingmar Bergman, in both the photography of the barren landscape and in the sparse dialog.

p, Jack Smith, Peter Fetterman; d, Fred Burnley; w, Gordon Honeycombe, Rosemary Davies (based on the novel by Honeycombe); ph, David Muir (Eastmancolor); m, Nachum Heiman; ed, Norman Wanstall; art d, Michael Bastow.

Drama/Fantasy (PR:A MPAA:R)

NELL GWYN** (1935, Brit.) 75m British and Dominions/UA bw

Anna Neagle (Nell Gwyn), Cedric Hardwicke (King Charles II), Jeanne de Casalis (Duchess of Portsmouth), Muriel George (Meg), Miles Malleson (Chiffinch), Esme Percy (Samuel Pepys), Moore Marriott (Robin), Lawrence Anderson (Duke of York), Craighall Sherry (Ben), Helena Pickard (Mrs. Pepys), Dorothy Robinson (Mrs. Knipp), Julie Suedo (Hortense), Hugh E. Wright, Abraham Sofaer.

Set in 17th-Century England, Neagle plays the title character, a cockney dance hall girl who caught the fancy of King Charles II, played by Hardwicke. Having seen her perform a rousing drinking song, Hardwicke brings the uncultured Neagle into his inner circle and makes her his mistress, much to the dismay of his court which is used to more refined visitors. The angriest member of Hardwicke's entourage is de Casalis, his current concubine, who feels threatened by this pretty young girl. With the battle lines drawn, Hardwicke sits back and watches with amusement as his mistresses fight for his attentions. The hostilities between the two women peak when Neagle publicly snubs de Casalis by wearing a ridiculously large and gaudy hat—a direct insult to her rival, whose penchant for loud headgear was a source of constant amusement to the court. Soon it becomes apparent that Neagle has captured Hardwicke's heart for good and she remains his favorite mistress until his death. NELL GWYN was given a lush and historically accurate production by producer/director Wilcox, who was anxious to flaunt the talents of his discovery (and later wife) Neagle, a rising star in England. His gamble with NELL GWYN paid off. The film, which was racy, even ribald at times (Neagle's performance is frank and open, enhanced by revealing costumes that caused a stir), was well received by the public which had come to know Neagle as a shy personality on screen. The shocking change of image in NELL GWYN was exactly what Wilcox was hoping for (he had done the same for Dorothy Gish in his silent version of the same material in 1926). While the British public delighted in Neagle's saucy performance, American censors cringed at the thought of allowing the film into U.S. theaters without substantial changes. To begin with, several shots that revealed too much of Neagle's anatomy were snipped. Then a framing story was added which saw the film open after Hardwicke's death. Neagle is shown as a penniless hag who dies in the gutter, which then dissolves to the original film, making the entire British production a flashback! The film then concludes back in the gutter, just to remind American audiences that an adulterous life doesn't pay. As if that were not enough, the Hays Office forced the studio to shoot an entirely false and historically inaccurate scene which saw King Charles II and Nell getting married, just to satisfy the warped sense of morality prevalent among the industry's paranoid custodians. Despite the cuts and additions, NELL GWYN did reasonably well in America and helped establish Neagle as a box office personality in the U.S., though England would remain the strongest market for the films directed and produced by her soon-to-be husband Wilcox, who would guide Neagle through her greatest roles.

p&d, Herbert Wilcox; w, Miles Malleson (based largely on the diaries of Samuel Pepys); ph, Frederick A. Young; m, Edward German; ed, Melville White; cos, Doris Zinkeisen; m/l, German, Philip Barham.

Historical Drama/Romance (PR:A-C MPAA:NR)

NELLA CITTA L'INFERNO (SEE: AND THE WILD, WILD WOMEN, 1961)

NELLY'S VERSION½** (1983, Brit.) 98m Mithras/Channel Four Television c

Eileen Atkins (Nelly), Anthony Bate (George), Barbara Jefford (Miss Wyckham), Nicholas Ball (Inspector Leach), Brian Deacon (David), Marsha Fitzalan (Susan), Stella Maris (Carmelita), Hugh Fraser (Brush Salesman), Hilton McRae (Vagrant), Susannah York (Narrator).

Atkins plays an amnesiac who fails to recognize any of the people close to her, while a detective tries to persuade her that she may be linked with various crimes. She regains her memory and goes back to her boring life as a housewife. The film is loaded with symbolism, but lacks any real dramatic content. Viewers are left with no real understanding of what lay behind Atkins' memory loss, a loss for the audience as well. Highly structured camera-work places emphasis upon the alienating environment.

p, Penny Clark; d&w, Maurice Hatton; ph, Curtis Clark; m, Michael Nyman; ed, Thomas Scwalm; prod d, Grant Hicks; art d, Pete Nutton.

Drama (PR:A MPAA:NR)

NELSON AFFAIR, THE* (1973, Brit.) 118m UNIV c (GB: BEQUEST TO THE NATION)

Glenda Jackson (Lady Emma Hamilton), Peter Finch (Lord Horatio Nelson), Michael Jayston (Capt. Hardy), Anthony Quayle (Lord Minto), Margaret Leighton (Lady Frances Nelson), Dominic Guard (Master George Matcham, Jr.), Nigel Stock (George Matcham, Sr.), Barbara Leigh-Hunt (Catherine Matcham), Roland Culver (Lord Barham), Pat Heywood (Emily), Clelia Matania (Francesca), John Nolan (Capt. Blackwood), Richard Mathews (Rev. William Nelson), Liz Ashley (Sarah Nelson), Stephen Jack (Major-Domo), Andre Maranne (Adm. Villeneuve).

An endlessly talky version of the famous story that scandalized England nearly two centuries ago, THE NELSON AFFAIR is yet another picture in Hal Wallis' continuing Anglophilia. In the past, he'd made ANNE OF THE THOUSAND DAYS, BECKET, MARY, QUEEN OF SCOTS, THE ADVENTURES OF ROBIN HOOD, ELIZABETH AND ESSEX, and THE CHARGE OF THE LIGHT BRIGADE among others. For a boy born in Chicago just before the turn of the century, that's a lot of British history to cover. It's the summer of 1805 and Finch is returning home after two years on the bounding main where he successfully kept Napoleon's navy at bay. He's long been separated from his wife, Leighton, and now he wants a sabbatical to have a few months off with one-time blacksmith's daughter Jackson, who is now Lady Hamilton. She is staying at Finch's estate in Surrey and her fabled beauty has now faded due to too many trips to the liquor cabinet and years of discontent at Finch's travels. Finch invites his sister, Leigh-Hunt; her husband, Stock; and their young son, Guard; to stay at the home as well. There is bad feeling between Finch's relatives and Leighton, but young Guard likes her and while Leighton is taking the waters at Bath (she has a bad case of rheumatism), he agrees to be her inside spy (he'd done the same thing before in THE GO-BETWEEN, three years earlier). Jackson gets drunk at a party and verbally lashes Jayston, one of Finch's trusted men, then launches into a tirade against the king and queen, and then, for good measure, has some choice epithets to say against Leighton. Guard is shocked and says that he knows Finch has been ignoring some important correspondence from Leighton. Finch is appalled at Jackson's behavior and she pleads for his forgiveness, then says that she understands that he yearns to be at sea, and if that's what will make him happy, he should do it. Finch goes back to active duty and gets ready for a battle against the French. Prior to leaving, he sends a letter to the king asking that Jackson be taken care of with enough money for the rest of her life—on the off chance that he winds up roommates with Davey Jones. There is the huge Battle of Trafalgar (not well shot, with little production value and some stock footage that jars the eyes and it is intercut with the other scenes), and Finch is felled by a bullet, then dies in Jayston's arms. Leighton learns of her husband's death, goes to see Jackson, and tells her what Finch did with his letter to the king. However, since their affair was so blatant, the request is never honored. Jackson loses everything, goes to prison as a debtor twice, and eventually winds up in France, where she dies in poverty 10 years after Finch's demise. Based on a play by Terence Rattigan which starred Zoe Caldwell, Ian Holm, Leueen MacGrath, and Michael Aldridge, this owes much to a better picture, THAT HAMILTON WOMAN, which was made in the early 1940s and starred Vivian Leigh in the title role. Although the latter was far more romantic, it also had a life to it that this did not. Director Jones, who had helmed TV's "The Forsyte Saga," made his movie debut with this feature and it was not an auspicious one. Jackson and Finch had earlier been together in SUNDAY, BLOODY SUNDAY to greater advantage to both. Jackson appeared to be doing an impression of Bette Davis and Finch was trying hard to be a Richard Burton, with a touch of Errol Flynn. Leighton comes off best as the abandoned wife. It's amazing that Jackson did not need a full mouth transplant after having chewed up so much of Stephens and Dixon's lovely scenery. Lots of foul language makes this a nix for the little ones. Locations in Devon, Somerset, Surrey, Berkshire, Bath, Windsor, and other sites. Beautiful to look at and apparently authentically helmed, THE NELSON AFFAIR is that historical picture that we are supposed to like if we have any culture at all, but, try as we may, it's almost impossible.

p, Hal B. Wallis; d, James Cellan Jones; w, Terence Rattigan (based on his play "A Bequest to the Nation"); ph, Gerry Fisher (Panavision, Technicolor); m, Michel Legrand; ed, Anne V. Coates; prod d, Carmen Dillon; art d, Jack Stephens; set d, Vernon Dixon; cos, Margaret Furse; makeup, George Frost; hairstyles, Joan Carpenter.

Historical Drama/Romance   **(PR:C   MPAA:PG)**

NELSON TOUCH, THE   (SEE: CORVETTE K-225, 1943)

NEON PALACE, THE**   (1970, Can.) 100m Acme Idea & Sale Production/Film Canada c

Judy Soroka, Peter Whittal, Steven Sherriff, Jack Woolwich, Harvey Aitken, Billy Edwards, Sweet Daddy Siki.

A nostalgia film that strips away the sentiment to reveal how silly Western culture is when it follows new fads. Picture juxtaposes popular images from the 1950s and 1960s, using comic strips, stock footage, popular songs, radio programs, and commercials to give an impression of how openly the public is manipulated in matters of style while remaining frozen it its attitudes toward different races and cultures.

p,d&w, Peter Rowe; ph, Jim Lewis (Eastmancolor); ed, Lewis, Rome; art d, Michael Bain.

Satire   **(PR:A   MPAA:NR)**

NEPTUNE DISASTER, THE   (SEE: NEPTUNE FACTOR, THE, 1973, Can.)

NEPTUNE FACTOR, THE*½   (1973, Can.) 98m Quadrant-Bellevue-Pathe/FOX c (AKA: AN UNDERWATER ODYSSEY; THE NEPTUNE DISASTER)

Ben Gazzara (Comdr. Adrian Blake), Yvette Mimieux (Leah Jansen), Walter Pidgeon (Dr. Samuel Andrews), Ernest Borgnine (Don "Mack" MacKay), Chris Wiggens (Capt. Williams), Donnelly Rhodes (Bob Cousins), Ed McGibbon (Norton Shepherd), Michael J. Reynolds (Hal Hamilton), David Yorkston (Stephens), Stuart Gillard (Bradley), Mark Walker (Moulton), Kenneth Pogue (Thomas), Frank Perry (Sub Captain), Dan MacDonald (Lt. Hobbs), Leslie Carlson (Briggs), David Renton (Warrant Officer), Joan Gregson (Dobson), Dave Mann (Hawkes), Kay Fujiwara (Anita), Richard Whelan (Radio Officer).

Overly predictable underwater yarn has Gazzara as the skipper of a vessel sent on a rescue mission to save the crew of an underwater laboratory damaged by an earthquake. During their search the crew stumbles into an eerie undersea world where giant fish, atomically mutated to 100 times their normal size, pose a bit of a problem for the ship. Underwater photography is nice, but the story suffers from lack of development and characters who are little more than stereotypes.

p, Sanford Howard; d, Daniel Petrie; w, Jack DeWitt; ph, Harry Makin, Paul Hergermann, Lamar Boren (Panavision, DeLuxe Color); m, William McCauley, Lalo Schifrin; ed, Stan Cole; prod d, Dennis Lynton Clark, Jack McAdam; set d, Ed Watkins.

Science Fiction   **(PR:A   MPAA:G)**

NEPTUNE'S DAUGHTER**½   (1949) 92m MGM c

Esther Williams (Eve Barrett), Red Skelton (Jack Spratt), Ricardo Montalban (Jose O'Rourke), Betty Garrett (Betty Barrett), Keenan Wynn (Joe Backett), Xavier Cugat (Himself), Ted de Corsia (Lukie Luzette), Mike Mazurki (Mac Mozolla), Mel Blanc (Julio), Juan Duval (2nd Groom), George Mann (Tall Wrangler), Frank Mitchell (Little Wrangler), William Lewin (Official), Harold S. Kruger (Coach), Matt Moore (Official), Joi Lansing (Linda), Carl Saxe (Announcer), Danilo Valente (South American Player), Theresa Harris (Matilda), Juan Duval (Voice of Record), Elaine Sterling (Miss Pratt), Henry Sylvester (Headwaiter), Lillian Molieri (Cigarette Girl), Pierre Watkin (Mr. Canford), Clarence Hennecke (Gardner), Dewey Robinson (1st Henchman), Michael Jordon (2nd Henchman), Dick Simmons (Mr. Magoo), Del Henderson (Man), Kay Mansfield (Woman), Heinie Conklin, Roque Ybarra (Grooms), Bette Arlen, Jonnie Pierce, Dorothy Abott, Sue Casey, Diane Gump, Jackie Hammette (Models).

Thin story line has Williams and Wynn as partners in a bathing suit company, with Williams continually fighting off the advances of millionaire playboy Montalban. At the same time, her dim-witted sister, Garrett, is on the make for Skelton, a masseur whom she has mistaken for Montalban. But this only serves as the framework for a showcase of song, dance, and other fanfare, which have all been combined very effectively by director Buzzell. The addition of Skelton's comic routines makes for a steady supply of hilarity. "Baby, It's Cold Outside" (Frank Loesser, sung by Williams and Montalban and reprised by Garrett and Skelton) won the Academy Award for best song. Other numbers include "I Love Those Men" (sung by Garrett) and "My Heart Beats Faster" (Loesser, sung by Williams, Montalban).

p, Jack Cummings; d, Edward Buzzell; w, Dorothy Kingsley, Ray Singer, Dick Chevillat; ph, Charles Rosher (Technicolor); ed, Irving Warburton; md, Georgie Stoll; art d, Cedric Gibbons, Edward Carfagno; set d, Edwin B. Willis, Arthur Krams; cos, Irene; ch, Jack Donahue; makeup, Jack Dawn.

Musical/Comedy   **(PR:A   MPAA:NR)**

NERO'S BIG WEEKEND   (SEE: NERO'S MISTRESS, 1962, Ital.)

NERO'S MISTRESS zero   (1962, Ital.) 86m Titanus-Lux-Vides-Marceau/Art Films c (MIO FIGLIO NERONE; AKA: NERO'S BIG WEEKEND; MY SON NERO)

Gloria Swanson (Agrippina), Alberto Sordi (Nero), Vittorio De Sica (Seneca), Brigitte Bardot (Poppaea).

Swanson plays the tyrannical mother of the Roman emperor in a film intended to be satire but coming off as highly stylized slapstick. However, the picture is worth seeing, if only to catch the amazing show Swanson puts on; she dominates the picture, proving that she is still one of the great actresses. Swanson took part in this production while moonlighting as a reporter for the UPI.

d, Steno; w, (based on a story by Rodolfo Sonego); ph, Mario Bava (CinemaScope, Eastmancolor).

Comedy/Drama   **(PR:C   MPAA:NR)**

NEST, THE**½   (1982, Span.) 97m ELSA/Premier c (EL NIDO)

Hector Alterio (Alejandro), Ana Torrent (Goyita), Luis Politti (Eladio), Agustin Gonzalez (Sargento), Patricia Adriani (Marisa), Maria Luisa Ponte (Amaro), Mercedes Alonso (Mercedes), Luisa Rodrigo (Gumer), Amparo Baro (Fuen), Ovidi Montllor, Mauricia Calvo, Tony, Yiyi, Bernabe, Arantza, Tomas, Juan, Carmen, Fremin, Jaime, Quino, Catalina, Jacobo.

Touching story of the passionate but chaste love an elderly man feels toward a young schoolgirl who shares his love of nature. But their continued meetings become a source of local gossip. Film is weakened by its reluctance to take a stand. Are the townspeople right to be concerned, or aren't they? (In Spanish; English subtitles.)

d&w, Jaime de Arminan; ph, Teodoro Escamilla (Eastmancolor); m, Franz Joseph Haydn; ed, Jose Luis Matesanz; art d, Jean Claude Hoerner; cos, Trini Ardura.

Drama   **Cas.**   **(PR:A   MPAA:NR)**

NEST OF THE CUCKOO BIRDS, THE*   (1965) 88m bw

Bert Williams, Chuck Frankle, Ann Long, Jacky Scalso, Larry Wright.

Williams wrote, produced, directed, and starred in this offbeat film in which he plays a revenue agent wandering through the Everglades in search of moonshiners. His energies soon turn in a different direction when he stops at a small inn presided over by a zany woman taxidermist who likes to stuff things other than animals in her Chapel of the Dead.

p,d&w, Bert Williams; m/l, title song, Peggy Williams (performed by The Four Bits).

Horror/Drama   **(PR:C   MPAA:NR)**

NEST OF VIPERS*½   (1979, Ital.) 105m Mars /PAR c (RITRATTO DI BORGHESIA IN NERO)

Ornella Muti (Elena Mazzarini), Senta Berger (Carla Richter), Christian Borromeo (Mattio Morandi), Capucine (Amalia Mazzarani), Giulina Calandra, Stefano Patrizi, Giancarlo Sbragia, Paolo Bonacelli, Mattia Sbragia, Maria Monti, Eros Pagni, Antonia Cancellieri, Suxanne Creese Bates, Raffaelle Di Mario, Giancarlo Marinangeli, Giovanni Caenazzo.

Familiar theme has Berger as a piano teacher who seduces one of her son's young friends, Borromeo. But the young man becomes captivated by the vivacious Muti, whom he falls in love with and wants to marry. This causes great jealousy in Berger, who is Muti's teacher. The beautiful photography of Venice and the captivating screen presence of both Berger and Muti make this film more memorable than it might have been.

p, Piero La Mantia; d, Tonino Cervi; w, Cervi, Cesare Frugoni, Goffredo Parise (based on the story "The Piano Teacher" by Roger Peyrefitte); ph, Armando Nannuzzi; m, Vincenzo Tempera; ed, Nino Baragli.

Drama **(PR:O MPAA:R)**

NESTING, THE*½ (1981) 104m Nesting/Feature Films c (AKA: PHOBIA)

Robin Groves *(Lauren Cochran)*, Christopher Loomis *(Mark Felton)*, Michael David Lally *(Daniel Griffith)*, John Carradine *(Col. LeBrun)*, Gloria Grahame *(Florinda Costello)*, Bill Rowley *(Frank Beasley)*, David Tabor *(Abner Welles)*, Patrick Farelley *(Dr. Webb)*, Bobo Lewis *(Catherine Beasley)*, June Berry *(Saphire)*, Cecile Lieman *(Helga)*, Ann Varley *(Gwen)*, Ron Levine *(Leland LeBrun)*, Bruce Kronenberg *(Young Abner)*, Jim Nixon *(Young Frank)*, James Saxon *(Earl)*, Cliff Cudney *(Sheriff)*, Jeffrey McLaughlin *(Butler)*, Lee Steele *(Doctor)*, James Hayden, Jerry Hewitt *(GIs)*.

Gory picture in which neurotic mystery writer Groves manages to rid herself of her groundless fear of leaving her townhouse, only to move to a haunted Victorian mansion, a former brothel. She is used by the ghosts to get even with their murderers, but not until she is shown, in slow motion, the original massacre. Direction has a tendency to rely too much on standard "gore" picture techniques. This almost destroys an interesting story which is a departure from the usual plots of horror flicks. Grahame, in what would prove to be her last role, starred as one of the ghosts.

p&d, Armand Weston; w, Weston, Daria Price; ph, Joao Fernandes; m, Jack Malken, Kim Scholes; ed, Jack Foster; spec eff, Matt Vogel.

Horror **(PR:O MPAA:R)**

NET, THE (SEE: PROJECT M7, 1953, Brit.)

NETWORK***** (1976) 120m MGM/UA c

Fay Dunaway *(Diana Christensen)*, William Holden *(Max Schumacher)*, Peter Finch *(Howard Beale)*, Robert Duvall *(Frank Hackett)*, Wesley Addy *(Nelson Chaney)*, Ned Beatty *(Arthur Jensen)*, Arthur Burghardt *(Great Ahmed Kahn)*, Bill Burrows *(TV Director)*, John Carpenter *(George Bosch)*, Jordan Charney *(Harry Hunter)*, Kathy Cronkite *(Mary Ann Gifford)*, Ed Crowley *(Joe Donnelly)*, Jerome Dempsey *(Walter C. Amundsen)*, Conchata Ferrell *(Barbara Schlesinger)*, Gene Gross *(Milton K. Steinman)*, Stanley Grover *(Jack Snowden)*, Cindy Grover *(Caroline Schumacher)*, Darryl Hickman *(Bill Herron)*, Mitchell Jason *(Arthur Zangwill)*, Paul Jenkins *(TV Stage Manager)*, Ken Kercheval *(Merrill Grant)*, Kenneth Kimmins *(Associate Producer)*, Lynn Klugman *(TV Production Assistant)*, Carolyn Krigbaum *(Max's Secretary)*, Zane Lasky *(Audio Man)*, Michael Lombard *(Willie Stein)*, Pirie MacDonald *(Herb Thackeray)*, Russ Petranto *(TV Associate Director)*, Bernard Pollack *(Lou)*, Roy Poole *(Sam Haywood)*, William Prince *(Edward George Ruddy)*, Sasha Von Scherler *(Helen Miggs)*, Lane Smith *(Robert McDonough)*, Theodore Sorel *(Giannini)*, Beatrice Straight *(Louise Schumacher)*, Fred Stuthman *(Mosaic Figure)*, Cameron Thomas *(TV Technical Director)*, Marlene Warfield *(Laureen Hobbs)*, Lydia Wilson *(Hunter's Secretary)*, Lee Richardson *(Narrator)*, Michael Lipton *(Tommy Pellegrino)*.

Peter Finch became the first actor to ever win an Oscar after his death. It was one of four that included Dunaway (Best Actress), Straight (Best Supporting Actress) and Chayefsky (Best Original Screenplay). The film was also nominated as Best Picture, Best Actor (Holden), Best Supporting Actor (Beatty), Best Direction (Lumet), and Best Cinematography (Roizman), and might have captured more statuettes were it not for the incredible popularity of ROCKY that year. Chayefsky had vented his spleen against the medical profession in HOSPITAL a few years before, and took this opportunity to aptly skewer television and all the medium's excesses. There's no question that he used his script to get some personal grudges out and that there is much posturing and railing, but it is done with such brilliance that we can forgive some of the verbal fireworks—some of which seem to be accompanied by an invisible flashing sign that reads "author's message" as the actors strut and fret. It is hard to believe, but absolutely true, that there was, for some years, a woman not unlike Dunaway's rapacious, scheming character, in network television; a woman who could stop in the midst of making love and discuss the ratings of her company's programs. Lawyers and taste prevent us from revealing the name of the woman, but her story is almost duplicated in the screenplay and Hollywood insiders chuckled and chortled as they watched the movie and knew precisely who the woman was. Although no longer a network executive, the malfeasant still functions in the medium and occasionally produces a TV film. Finch is a veteran newsman for the mythical United Broadcasting System and is sent over the mental edge when he is told that he will be fired after a quarter of a century on the air. He can't handle the situation and tells his audience that he intends to commit suicide on his final broadcast the following week. Ratings go straight through the roof and his fan mail comes in by the carload. On the night he plans to put a gun to his head, Finch relents, apologizes to the millions watching (it's his largest audience ever), and stands up like an electronic Messiah to shout "go to your nearest window and yell as loud as you can 'I'm Mad As Hell and I'm Not Going To Take It Anymore!'" And his audience does just that. The words rattle across hill and dale, valley and mountain, in and out of the city's concrete canyons. Dunaway, a programming executive at UBS, knows how to make capital of this, so she signs Finch to a weekly show where he can let it all hang out. This idea is opposed by Holden, the man in charge of network news and an old pal of Finch. He can see that Finch is on the edge of insanity and he can't stand the thought of the news being used to further ratings; it should be sacrosanct and above the Neilsen wars. Dunaway's bosses like the idea and fire Holden for his disagreement. Finch's program, a melange of various items, goes on and is a smash hit, with Finch closing each program like a latter-day Jesus as he regales the audience with the Gospel according to Finch. Dunaway, now a star at the network, has other innovations in mind. She intends doing a show about urban guerrillas, but instead of hiring actors, she wants the terrorists to play themselves. Holden and Dunaway meet again and are soon involved, something that causes Holden to leave his wife, Straight, in one of the most moving (and least gimmicky) scenes in the film as he tells her why he is departing. Holden moves in with the cold Dunaway and finds it impossible to crack her facade. Sure, she sleeps with him and all, but she always holds something in reserve, a place where no one can visit. Holden works on a book about his life in TV as Dunaway's star rises higher and higher. Eventually, Holden gets mad as Hell and can't take Dunaway anymore and returns to Straight. Finch is now out of hand and dealing with subjects that annoy the conglomerateurs who own the network. His tirade about the way America's finances are handled enrages Beatty, the head man, who calls Finch in and gives him a talking-to regarding how little the average Joe means or matters. Finch is mesmerized by Beatty's logic and goes on the air to tell his adoring audience that they don't amount to anything and that their lives are worthless. Suddenly, this champion of the underdog, this defender of the downtrodden, is sneered at and his ratings begin to plummet. Dunaway talks to her immediate boss, Duvall (the hatchet man) and the decision is made to cancel Finch, the hard way. Finch's show serves as lead-in to the Terrorist program and, in order to boost the ratings for the new show, Finch is summarily assassinated. Phew! As weird as some of this movie is (and satire must always extend reality to make the point), there was so much truth to be heard that the Academy voters recognized it and awarded the aforementioned Oscars. There are several superb scenes, including the one where the Communist guerrilla's lawyers hassle with the network's representatives over the ancillary rights and syndication money that will accrue from their show. Every small role is well cast and Jordan Charney, who also appeared in HOSPITAL, is a standout. Darryl Hickman, who actually became a TV network executive, was playing one in this, his first film in 17 years. Kercheval went on to have a large career on TV in "Dallas" and Warfield as the Communist who brings in terrorist Burghardt is superior. For any students considering a career in television, NETWORK is a must-see and will probably send them quickly to medical or dental school.

p, Howard Gottfried; d, Sidney Lumet; w, Paddy Chayefsky; ph, Owen Roizman (Panavision, Metrocolor); m, Elliot Lawrence; ed, Alan Heim; prod d, Philip Rosenberg; set d, Edward Stewart; cos, Theoni V. Aldredge; makeup, John Alese, Lee Harman.

Drama **Cas.** **(PR:C MPAA:R)**

NEUNZIG MINUTEN NACH MITTER NACHT (SEE: TERROR AFTER MIDNIGHT, 1965)

NEUTRAL PORT½** (1941, Brit.) 92m Gainsborough/GFD bw

Will Fyffe *(Capt. Ferguson)*, Leslie Banks *(George Carter, British Consul)*, Yvonne Arnaud *(Rosa Pirenti, Cafe Owner)*, Phyllis Calvert *(Helen Carter)*, Hugh McDermott *(Jim Grey)*, John Salew *(Wilson)*, Cameron Hall *(Charlie Baxter)*, Frederick Valk *(Capt. Traumer)*, Albert Lieven *(Capt. Grosskraft)*, Anthony Holles *(Chief of Police)*, Sigurd Lohde *(German Consul)*, Denis Wyndham *(Terry)*, Jack Raine *(Alf)*, Wally Patch *(Fred)*, Mignon O'Doherty *(Miss Fleming)*, Noel Dainton, Len Sharpe, Ernest Metcalfe, Charles Rolfe, Stuart Lathom, Keith Shepherd, John Rae, Sam Lee, Eric Clavering, Yvonne Andre, Cot d'Ordan, Rowland Douglas, Gerik Schjelderup, Frank Henderson, Hugh Griffith.

Fyffe plays the captain of a ship which is sunk in a neutral port. This fixes his mind on revenge, and he and his crew seize a German supply ship, which he sinks by ramming it into a Nazi sub. Fyffe lands in jail for his escapades, but he is in no way subdued. Direction manages a good blend of comic situations with action and romantic sequences, and the script keeps the tension mounting.

p, Edward Black; d, Marcel Varnel; w, J.B. Williams, T.J. Morrison; ph, Jack Cox, Arthur Crabtree.

War/Drama **(PR:A MPAA:NR)**

NEUTRON CONTRA EL DR. CARONTE* (1962, Mex.) 80m Estudios America/Producciones Corsa bw

Wolf Ruvinskis *(Black Masked Wrestler)*, Julio Aleman *(Dr. Caronte)*, Armando Silvestre, Rosita Aremas, Roberto Ramirez, Rodolfo Landa, Trio Los Diamantes, Los Tres Ases.

Follow-up to NEUTRON EL EMNASCARADO NEGRO, in which the evil doctor Aleman was presumed to be dead. But in this feature he proves very much alive and uses his robots to keep Ruvinskis and Silvestre from obtaining his secret formula for a neutron bomb. He also succeeds in kidnaping Arenas, whom Ruvinskis, as the Black Masked Wrestler, rescues when he turns the robots against Aleman.

p, Emilio Gomez Muriel; d, Federico Curiel; w, Alfredo Ruanova; ph, Fernando Alvarez Garces Colin.

Fantasy **(PR:A MPAA:NR)**

NEUTRON EL ENMASCARADO NEGRO* (1962, Mex.) 80m Estudios America/Producciones Corsa bw

Wolf Ruvinskis *(Black Masked Wrestler)*, Julio Aleman *(Dr. Caronte)*, Armando Silvestre, Rosita Arenas, Roberto Ramirez, Claudio Brook, David Lama, Trio Los Diamantes, Los Tres Ases.

First of three segments about a super-hero type, Ruvinskis, helping to foil evil scientist Aleman's plan to dominate the world. Aleman invents a neutron bomb which will give him absolute power, but Ruvinskis, along with a few friends, is able to stop the mad doctor, at least until the next segment.

p, Emilio Gomez Muriel; d, Federico Curiel; w, Alfredo Ruanova; ph, Fernando Alvarez Garces Colin.

Fantasy (PR:A MPAA:NR)

NEVADA** (1936) 58m PAR bw

Larry "Buster" Crabbe (Nevada), Kathleen Burke (Hettie Ide), Syd Saylor (Cash Burridge), Monte Blue (Clem Dillon), William Duncan (Ben Ide), Richard Carle (Judge Franklidge), Stanley Andrews (Cawthorne), Frank Sheridan (Tom Blaine), Raymond Hatton (Sheriff), Glen [Leif] Erickson (Bill Ide), Jack Kennedy (McTurk), Albert Taylor (Hedge), Murdock MacQuarrie (Watson), Robert E. Homans (Carver), Barney M. Furey (Bystander to Card Game), Henry Roquemore (Bartender), William Desmond (Wilson), Frank Rice (Shorty), O.C. "Dutch" Hendrian (Cawthorne's Henchman), William L. Thorne, Harry Dunkinson (Card Players).

Crabbe plays a gambler who wins a ranch in a poker game and joins a group of ranchers in a large cattle drive. The ranchers are taking a route they hope will keep them out of the hands of rustlers, but several of them distrust Crabbe because they suspect that he's in with the rustlers. In the end Crabbe proves his worth by trapping the real cow thief who turns out to be one of the ranchers. Good photography and well-paced action make this a step above the routine western.

p, Harold Hurley; d, Charles Barton; w, Garnett Weston, Stuart Anthony (based on the novel Nevada by Zane Grey); ph, Archie Stout; ed, Jack Dennis.

Western (PR:A MPAA:NR)

NEVADA**½ (1944) 62m RKO bw

Robert Mitchum (Jim "Nevada" Lacy), Anne Jeffreys (Julie Dexter), Nancy Gates (Hattie Ide), Craig Reynolds (Cash Burridge), Guinn "Big Boy" Williams (Dusty), Richard Martin (Chito Rafferty), Harry Woods (Joe Powell), Edmund Glover (Ed Nelson), Alan Ward (William Brewer), Harry McKim (Marvie Ide), Wheaton Chambers (Dr. Darien), Philip Morris (Ed Nolan), Emmett Lynn (Comstock), Larry Wheat (Ben Ide), Jack Overman (Red Barry), George DeNormand, Sammy Blum (Bartenders), Russell Hopton (Henchman), Mary Halsey, Patti Brill, Margie Stewart, Virginia Belmont, Bryant Washburn, Bert Moorhouse.

This Zane Grey story originally was made as a silent film in 1927, starring Gary Cooper in the role that Mitchum fills in this remake. Mitchum plays a cowpoke out to try his hand at panning for gold, but on the way he is mistaken for the murderer of a homesteader, narrowly escaping being hanged. He then uncovers the real killer, while falling in love with the homesteader's daughter, Gates. The film marked Mitchum's first lead role and created the persona that would identify him for the next 30 years as the tough but laconic hero. Remake of the 1936 version.

p, Herman Schlom, Sig Rogell; d, Edward Killy; w, Norman Houston (based on the story by Zane Grey); ph, Harry Wild; m, Paul Sawtell; ed, Roland Gross; md, C. Bakaleinikoff; art d, Albert D'Agostino, Lucius Croxton; set d, Darrell Silvera, William Stevens; cos, Renie.

Western (PR:A MPAA:NR)

NEVADA BADMEN*½ (1951) 58m Frontier/MON bw

Whip Wilson, Fuzzy Knight, Jim Bannon, Phyllis Coates, I. Stanford Jolley, Marshall Reed, Riley Hill, Lee Roberts, Pierce Lyden, Bill Kennedy, Bud Osborne, Stanley Price, Artie Ortego, Carl Mathews, Kenne Duncan.

Wilson puts his whip to good use, though from the looks of this it would be hard to believe he knows how to crack nuts, much less a whip, as he battles encroaching meanies. The comic antics of stuttering Knight as his saddle partner help keep this from sinking completely out of sight.

p, Vincent M. Fennelly; d, Lewis Collins; w, Joseph O'Donnell; ph, Ernest Miller; ed, Dick Heermance; art d, Dave Milton.

Western (PR:A MPAA:NR)

NEVADA CITY** (1941) 58m REP bw

Roy Rogers, George Hayes, Sally Payne, Fred Kohler, Jr., George Cleveland, Billy Lee, Joseph Crehan, Pierre Watkin, Jack Ingram, Art Mix, Syd Saylor, Hank Bell, Yakima Canutt, Rex Lease, Henry Wills, Bob Woodward, Jack Kirk, Fred Burns, Trigger.

Rogers and Hayes play stagecoach drivers for boss Crehan, when the railroad is starting to make its mark across the desert. A bitter feud develops between Crehan and the owner of the railroad, Cleveland. The feud is actually instigated by a couple of no-gooders out for their own profit. Rogers and Hayes, who have been attempting a reconciliation between the two owners, stop the real criminals and restore peace to all involved.

p&d, Joseph Kane; w, James R. Webb; ph, William Nobles; m, Cy Feuer; ed, Les Orlebeck; md, Feuer.

Western **Cas.** (PR:A MPAA:NR)

NEVADA SMITH***½ (1966) 128m Solar-Embassy/PAR c

Steve McQueen (Nevada Smith/Max Sand), Karl Malden (Tom Fitch), Brian Keith (Jonas Cord), Arthur Kennedy (Bill Bowdre), Suzanne Pleshette (Pilar), Raf Vallone (Father Zaccardi), Janet Margolin (Neesa), Pat Hingle (Big Foot), Howard Da Silva (Warden), Martin Landau (Jesse Coe), Paul Fix (Sheriff Bonnell), Gene Evans (Sam Sand), Josephine Hutchinson (Mrs. Elvira McCanles), John Doucette (Uncle Ben McCanles), Val Avery (Buck Mason), Sheldon Allman (Sheriff), Lyle Bettger (Jack Rudabaugh), Bert Freed (Quince), David McLean (Romero), Steve Mitchell (Buckshot), Merritt Bohn (River Boat Pilot), Sandy Kenyon (Bank Clerk), Ric [Ricardo] Roman (Cipriano), John Lawrence (Hogg), Stanley Adams (Storekeeper), George Mitchell (Paymaster), John Litel (Doctor), Ted de Corsia (Hudson, Bartender).

This is an offbeat sequel to the trashy THE CARPETBAGGERS, presenting McQueen as the title character previously played by Alan Ladd, profiling the cowboy's early years. Here, before becoming a cowboy movie star, McQueen spends his time tracking down the killers of his parents, with the aid of gunsmith and sharpshooter Keith. He finally catches up with villains Kennedy and Landau and dispatches them. Hathaway does a creditable job with the tale and McQueen is outstanding as the incompetent youth who becomes an expert gunman and cowboy. (It is generally agreed that the Nevada Smith role was originally based on movie cowboy Ken Maynard.) The photography by Ballard is outstanding, as is Newman's score. The film is nevertheless overlong, Pleshette's performance embarrassingly overacted, and the episodes presented are somewhat disjointed. Only McQueen's dynamic presence sustains viewer interest. This was a joint venture by McQueen's Solar Productions and Joseph E. Levine's Embassy Pictures, one that unexpectedly met with box-office approval and gleaned well over $5 million in its initial release. The action in NEVADA SMITH is spectacular but the film is overloaded with excessive violence and sex. The location sites are awesome, paticularly the footage shot around Mammoth, Banner Peak, and Mount Ritter in northern California. For the episodes showing McQueen as a prisoner on a chain gang, the production moved to Baton Rouge, Louisiana and McQueen waded through chest-high slime in the bayous of the Atchafalya Basin.

p&d, Henry Hathaway; w, John Michael Hayes (based on a character in The Carpetbaggers by Harold Robbins); ph, Lucien Ballard (Panavision, Eastmancolor); m, Alfred Newman; ed, Frank Bracht; art d, Hal Pereira, Tambi Larsen, Al Roelofs; set d, Robert R. Benton; cos, Frank Beetson, Jr.; spec eff, George C. Thompson, Paul K. Lerpae; makeup, Del Acevedo.

Western (PR:C MPAA:NR)

NEVADAN, THE**½ (1950) 81m COL c (GB: THE MAN FROM NEVADA)

Randolph Scott (Andrew Barkley), Dorothy Malone (Karen Galt), Forrest Tucker (Tom Tanner), Frank Faylen (Jeff), George Macready (Edward Galt), Charles Kemper (Dyke Merrick), Jeff Corey (Bart), Tom Powers (Bill Martin), Jock O'Mahoney (Sandy), Stanley Andrews (Deputy Morgan), James Kirkwood (Tex), Kate Drain Lawson (Mama Lite), Olin Howlin (Rusty), Louis Mason (Duke).

Scott plays an undercover marshal trying to track down Tucker and his $250,000 in gold. Greedy rancher Macready also wants to get his hands on the loot, so Tucker and Scott team up to fight off Macready and his gang. The two then have to face each other. Fine color photography of the outdoor scenery is an added plus to this well-paced action picture.

p, Harry Joe Brown; d, Gordon Douglas; w, George W. George, George F. Slavin, Rowland Brown; ph, Charles Lawton, Jr. (Cinecolor); ed, Richard Fantl; md, Morris Stoloff; art d, George Brooks.

Western (PR:A MPAA:NR)

NEVER A DULL MOMENT** (1943) 60m UNIV bw

Harry Ritz, Al Ritz, Jimmy Ritz (Three Funny Bunnies), Frances Langford (Julie Russell), Stuart Crawford (Dick Manning), Elisabeth Risdon (Mrs. Scuyler Manning), Mary Beth Hughes (Flo), George Zucco (Tony Rocco), Jack LaRue (Joey), Sammy Stein (Romeo), Barbara Brown (Mrs. Vandrake), Douglas Wood (Commodore Barclay), Charles Jordan (Murphy), Franklin Pangborn (Sylvester), Lorin Raker (Reggie), John Sheehan (Bartender), Eddie Dunn (Capt. Fogerty), Ruby Dandridge (Daisy), George Chandler (Businessman), James Eagles (Soda Jerk), Milton Kibbee (Mr. Morgan), Gene O'Donnell (Bandleader), Jan Wiley (Checkroom Girl), Spec O'Donnell (Newsboy), Rogers Dancers, Grace and Igor Poggi.

The Ritz Brothers pose as Chicago gangsters in a nightclub routine, only to discover that they are being used to receive the stolen jewelry of wealthy patrons, via the hands of pickpocket Hughes. The brothers want out, but this is easier said than done. A thin plot line serves mainly as a backdrop for other forms of entertainment, although the Ritz Brothers manage some fine comedy. Songs include: "My Blue Heaven" (George Whiting, Walter Donaldson, sung by Langford); "Sleepytime Gal" (Richard Whiting, Joseph Alden, Ray Egan, Ange Lorenzo, sung by Langford); "Hello," "Yakimboomba" (Eddie Cherkose, David Rose, Jacques Press, sung by the Ritz Brothers); "Once You Find Your Guy" (Cherkose, Rose). (See RITZ BROTHERS series, Index.)

p, Howard Benedict; d, Edward Lilley; w, Mel Ronson, Stanley Roberts (based on the story by Roberts); ph, Charles Van Enger; ed, Paul Landres; art d, John Goodman; cos, Bill Thomas.

Musical/Comedy (PR:A MPAA:NR)

NEVER A DULL MOMENT** (1950) 89m RKO bw

Irene Dunne (Kay), Fred MacMurray (Chris), William Demarest (Mears), Andy Devine (Orvie), Gigi Perreau (Tina), Natalie Wood (Nan), Philip Ober (Jed), Jack Kirkwood (Papa Dude), Ann Doran (Jean), Margaret Gibson (Pokey), Lela Bliss (Mama Dude), Irving Bacon (Tunk Johnson), Virginia Mullen, Victoria Horne, Connie Van, Edna Holland (Women), Gene Evans, Olin Howlin, Paul "Tiny" Newlan (Hunters), Anne O'Neal (Julia Craddock), Chester Conklin (Albert), Ralph Peters (Gabe), Janine Perreau (Little Girl Dude), Jim Hawkins (Chalmers), Jack Jackson (Laddie), Alan Dinehart III (Sonny Boy), Carl Sklover, Art Dupuis, Bob Thom (Vendors), Jacqueline De Wit (Myra Van Elson), George Leigh (Fred Van Elson), Harry Tyler (Klinger), Jo Ann Marlowe (Sister).

This film had nothing to do with 1968's NEVER A DULL MOMENT in content or quality. Dunne is a female songwriter who meets western rancher MacMurray at a rodeo in New York. They fall in love and she goes back to his place where his two daughters, Wood and Perreau, welcome her. An easterner by birth, Dunne tries very hard to adapt herself to this rough life, but she makes every mistake that the writers can dream up, including the accidental death of a prize bull owned by crusty neighbor Demarest, the man upon whom MacMurray depends for his water. MacMurray's foreman, Devine, adds a little humor but most of the film's gags are predictable and, thus, unfunny. The songs were written by the author of the novel upon which the screenplay was based and they are just fair as Dunne sings them in a thin voice. The tunes are "Once You Find Your Guy," "Sagebrush Lullaby," and "The Man With the Big Felt Hat." None of them was memorable, although novelist-songwriter Swift is credited with having written some of the best popular songs of her era, including "Can't We Be Friends?" "Fine and Dandy," and "Forever and a Day."

p, Harriet Parsons; d, George Marshall; w, Lou Breslow, Doris Anderson (based on the novel *Who Could Ask for Anything More* by Kay Swift); ph, Joseph Walker; m, Frederick Hollander; ed, Robert Swink; md, Constantin Bakaleinikoff; art d, Albert S. D'Agostino, Walter E. Keller; m/l, Swift.

Comedy **(PR:A MPAA:NR)**

NEVER A DULL MOMENT*** (1968) 99m Disney/BV c

Dick Van Dyke *(Jack Albany)*, Edward G. Robinson *(Leo Joseph Smooth)*, Dorothy Provine *(Sally Inwood)*, Henry Silva *(Frank Boley)*, Joanna Moore *(Melanie Smooth)*, Tony Bill *(Florian)*, Slim Pickens *(Cowboy Schaeffer)*, Jack Elam *(Ace Williams)*, Ned Glass *(Rinzy Tobreski)*, Ricbard Bakalyan *(Bobby Macoon)*, Mickey Shaughnessy *(Francis)*, Philip Coolidge *(Fingers Felton)*, James Milhollin *(Museum Director)*, Johnny Silver *(Prop Man)*, Anthony Caruso *(Tony Preston)*, Paul Condylis *(Lenny)*, Bob Homel *(2nd TV Actor, "Police Captain Jacoby")*, Dick Winslow *(1st TV Actor)*, Jackie Russell *(Sexy Girl)*, Rex Dominick *(Sam)*, Ken Lynch *(Police Lieutenant)*, Eleanor Audley *(Matron)*, John Cliff *(1st Museum Guard)*, Tyler McVey *(Police Chief Grayson)*, Jerry Paris *(Police Photographer)*, John Dennis *(2nd Museum Guard)*.

The picture lives up to the title as it moves effortlessly through a series of funny incidents on the way to a satisfying conclusion. Van Dyke is a poor actor who has just finished a tiny role on a TV show; he fears that a mugger is on his tail so he ducks into a doorway where Bill, a hoodlum, mistakes him for the hired killer he is supposed to have a rendezvous with. Bill is very tough and Van Dyke attempts to convince him that he's made a mistake, but Bill has an assignment and he means to satisfy it. Bill drives Van Dyke to Robinson's estate. Edward G. is a mob boss with a penchant for art and he intends to steal a priceless painting that has just been purchased by a major museum. Provine works for Robinson as his personal art appreciation teacher, and when Van Dyke tries to tell her that they have the wrong guy, she won't believe him either. Now Elam, the real killer, arrives and Robinson doesn't know which guy is which, so he puts the two of them in a room and figures that the true criminal will emerge victorious. Provine helps Van Dyke win the battle, and when he comes out of the room, the gang welcomes him as a partner. The robbery is about to take place and Van Dyke foils the theft by taking the crooks on a wild art chase through the museum (and through an excellent satire on "pop" art) until Provine can get the cops to arrive and nab the crooks. In the end, Van Dyke is proclaimed a hero and his acting career is assured success, as everyone wants to hire him. Robinson's plot was to get the painting, hold it until after his death, and return it to the museum if they agreed to rename the facility after him. A pleasant way to spend 99 minutes, with more than its share of laughs. After spending several years acting, director Paris had a much better career in TV than he did in films. He also does a cameo as a police photographer.

p, Ron Miller; d, Jerry Paris; w, A.J. Carothers (based on the novel *A Thrill a Minute with Jack Albany* by John Godey); ph, William Snyder (Technicolor); m, Robert F. Brunner; ed, Marsh Hendry; art d, Caroll Clark, John B. Mansbridge; set d, Emile Kuri, Frank R. McKelvy; cos, Bill Thomas; spec eff, Eustace Lycett, Robert A. Mattey; makeup, Gordon Hubbard.

Crime/Comedy **Cas.** **(PR:A MPAA:NR)**

NEVER BACK LOSERS** (1967, Brit.) 61m Merton Park/Schoenfeld bw

Jack Hedley *(Jim Mathews)*, Jacqueline Ellis *(Marion Parker)*, Patrick Magee *(Ben Black)*, Richard Warner *(Crabtree)*, Derek Francis *(R.R. Harris)*, Austin Trevor *(Col. Warburton)*, Harry Locke *(Burnside)*, Larry Martyn *(Clive Parker)*, Howard Pays *(Freddie)*, Hilda Barry *(Mrs. Sanders)*, George Tovey *(Wally Sanders)*, Larry Taylor *(Reilly)*, Harold Goodwin *(Floyd)*, Douglas Bradley-Smith *(Carter)*, Tenniel Evans *(Doctor)*.

Hedley plays an insurance investigator researching the apparent accidental death of a jockey. His uncoverings lead to an illegal gambling organization, as well as the knowledge that the jockey's death was not accidental. He saves the life of another jockey, Martyn, who has been the victim of a couple of accidents.

p, Jack Greenwood; d, Robert Tronson; w, Lukas Heller (based on the novel *The Green Ribbon* by Edgar Wallace); ph, Bert Mason; ed, Derek Holding; md, Bernard Ebbinghouse; art d, Peter Mullins.

Crime/Drama **(PR:A MPAA:NR)**

NEVER CRY WOLF*½** (1983) 91m Amarok/BV c

Charles Martin Smith *(Tyler)*, Brian Dennehy *(Rosie)*, Zachary Ittimangnaq *(Ootek)*, Samson Jorah) *(Mike)*, Hugh Webster *(Drunk)*, Martha Ittimangnaq *(Woman)*, Tom Dahlgren, Walker Stuart *(Hunters)*.

The film captures the haunting story of scientist Smith who is sponsored by a government agency to study the behavior of wolves in the Arctic. New to the wilderness, he packs numerous unneeded items, only to lose a good portion of them during his flight on Dennehy's plane to an uninhabited area of the Arctic. His first night in the wilderness, Smith wonders if he will survive and cannot even tote his own supplies. But a mysterious Eskimo rescues the wanderer and builds him a shelter, only to leave without waiting for thanks. Smith manages to camp opposite a small pack of wolves, building a mutual trust with the head male, who seems to be as interested in studying the ways of Smith as Smith is of him. The scientist also develops some odd experiments of his own, such as eating the mice which have taken over his shelter. The wolves also eat mice, and by relying on the mice to supply all his protein Smith is determining whether the wolves can live on a diet of mice—while also eliminating the pests from his shelter. The ancient Eskimo, Ittamangnaq, eventually reappears to make sure the young white man is all right. The two develop a close friendship, sparked by their mutual interest in wolves. When caribou start their run, the two men follow the wolves during their hunt, discovering that the wolves kill only the sick members of the herd. A group of hunters led by Dennehy, who has become successful transporting gamesmen, nonchalantly kill the healthy caribou. One of the most beautifully photographed wilderness films, matched only by director Ballard's other feature, THE BLACK STALLION, NEVER CRY WOLF captures the changes a man goes through as he makes discoveries about life in the wilds. A warm-hearted, gripping adventure. The film is based on scientist Farley Mowat's actual study of wolves for the Ottawa Wildlife Service.

p, Lewis Allen, Jack Couffer, Joseph Strick; d, Carroll Ballard; w, Curtis Hanson, Sam Hamm, Richard Kletter, C.M. Smith, Eugene Corr, Christina Luescher (based on the book by Farley Mowat); ph, Hiro Narita (Technicolor); m, Mark Isham; ed, Peter Parasheles, Michael Chandler; art d, Graeme Murray; spec eff, John Thomas.

Adventure **Cas.** **(PR:C MPAA:PG)**

NEVER FEAR*** (1950) 81m EL bw

Sally Forrest *(Carol Williams)*, Keefe Brasselle *(Guy Richards)*, Hugh O'Brian *(Len Randall)*, Eve Miller *(Phyllis Townsend)*, Larry Dobkin *(Dr. Middleton)*, Rita Lupino *(Josie)*, Herbert Butterfield *(Walter Williams)*, Kevin O'Morrison *(Red Dawson)*, Stanley Waxman *(Dr. Taylor)*, Jerry Housner *(Mr. Brownlee)*, John Franco *(Carlos)*.

Lupino's directorial debut offers a realistic portrayal of a woman suffering from polio, without lapsing into undo sentiment. Forrest and Brasselle are an up-and-coming dance team and newly engaged until Forrest is stricken with polio. Unable to cope with her fate, she takes to self-pity, desiring only to be left alone. But through the influence of the people around her she realizes that everything is not lost. Even Forrest's brief emotional breakdown when Brasselle finds another partner leads her to a better grasp of the reality of her situation. The tightly woven script, able to inject humor into a depressing subject, remains true to the facts throughout.

p&d, Ida Lupino; w, Lupino, Collier Young; ph, Archie Stout; m, Leith Stevens; ed, William H. Ziegler, Harvey Manger; m/l, John Franco, William Earley.

Drama **(PR:A MPAA:NR)**

NEVER GIVE A SUCKER A BREAK (SEE:NUISANCE, THE, 1933)

NEVER GIVE A SUCKER AN EVEN BREAK*** (1941) 71m UNIV bw (GB:WHAT A MAN)

W.C. Fields *(The Great Man)*, Gloria Jean *(His Niece)*, Leon Errol *(The Rival)*, Billy Lenhart *(Butch)*, Kenneth Brown *(Buddy)*, Anne Nagel *(Mlle. Gorgeous)*, Franklin Pangborn *(The Producer)*, Mona Barrie *(The Producer's Wife)*, Margaret Dumont *(Mrs. Hemogloben)*, Susan Miller *(Ouliotta Delight Hemogloben)*, Charles Lang *(Peter Carson, a Young Engineer)*, Nell O'Day *(Salesgirl)*, Irving Bacon *(Tom, Soda Jerk)*, Claud Allister *(Bitter Englishman)*, Leon Belasco *(Pianist)*, Emil Van Horn *(Gargo, Gorilla)*, Billy Wayne *(Foreman, Stage 6)*, Minerva Urecal *(Mrs. Pastromi, Cleaning Lady)*, Jody Gilbert *(Tiny Waitress)*, William Gould *(Doorman)*, Emmett Vogan *(Steve Roberts, Engineer)*, Jack "Tiny" Lipson *(Huge Turk)*, Dave Willock *(Johnson, Assistant Director)*, Duke York *(Tough Assailant)*, Eddie Bruce *(Cameraman)*, Kay Deslys *(Mrs. Wilson)*, Kathryn Sheldon *(Spinster Passenger)*, Michael Visaroff *(Coachman, Russian Village)*, Irene Colman *(Stewardess)*, Carlotta Monti *(Receptionist)*, Frank Austin *(Diner)*, Frances Morris *(Nurse)*, Jack Roper *(Joe)*, Emma Tansey *(Old Lady)*, Charles McMurphy *(Officer)*, James "Brick" Sullivan *(Fire Truck Driver)*, Charles Lane *(Man)*, Harriet Haddon *(Redhead)*, Marcia Ralston *(Stewardess)*, Bill Wolfe *(Himself)*, Jean Porter *(Passerby)*, Vic Potel *(Mr. Clines, Russian Magistrate)*, Dave Sharpe *(Ubiquitous Stunt Double)*, Prince the Great Dane.

The great W.C. is at his wild antics again, this time spoofing Hollywood and the eccentricities of filmmaking or the insanity of producing films as Fields perceived them. He was later accused of biting the hand that fed him, but W.C. gnawed on anything that moved anyway, while providing one belly laugh after another, and this film is no exception. Fields is shown en route to Esoteric Studios to sell a producer a new script he has written. He stops near the studio and admires a huge billboard advertising his last movie (THE BANK DICK, starring, of course, W.C. Fields), and catches two young boys denigrating his latest film, calling it a "Buptkie." He runs them off, then spots a curvacious cutie and makes a pass at her. The girl's burly boy friend arrives and immediately lands a haymaker on Field's polyp-nosed kisser, driving him over a hedge. Fields requires some refreshment before continuing and drops into a lunchroom for a small snack. A fat, obnoxious waitress, Gilbert, begins to cross off every entree on the menu as Fields mentions the dish, until there's nothing left but eggs. Gilbert carps that Fields is too free with his hands and he tells her that he was "only trying to guess your weight." For his caprice, Fields receives some icewater down the back of his neck, poured unceremoniously by Gilbert. After flirting with the studio receptionist (Monti, Fields' real-life mistress), the comedian is shown into producer Pangborn's office where he relates the tale of his proposed movie. He has little luck in persuading Pangborn of its possiblilities and Fields is then seen meeting with his niece, Gloria Jean, who is in a shooting gallery operated by Errol, father of the two boys who earlier were taunting Fields. Nagel, Gloria Jean's mother, a trapeze artist, is killed in a fall and Fields becomes the young girl's guardian. He and the child immediately leave for Mexico where Fields believes he will become rich by selling wooden nutmegs to Russian immigrants who have established a colony there. While in flight on a plane that offers sleeping berths like that of a train and has an open-air observation deck, Fields drops a bottle of booze and immediately dives after it. He catches up with the bottle in mid-air, screws a cap back on it, and then falls onto a giant mattress. He next meets Russian expatriate Miller and is smitten by her beauty, but before he can properly pitch his woo, Dumont, Miller's mother, appears and is so aggressive that Fields promptly retreats, despite the fact that Dumont and her daughter live in grand luxury in a mountaintop retreat. By the time Fields finds Gloria Jean he learns to his commercial mortification that Errol has beaten him to the punch and cornered the wooden nutmeg business. When Fields learns from engineer Lang just how much money Dumont has, he returns to the man-eating matron but when he again visits Dumont he finds that Errol is already present and is in the ample embrace of the wealthy matron. Thoroughly defeated, Fields is resigned to failure and he withdraws. At that point Fields is shown back in Pangborn's office and it is evident that the whole Mexican adventure is a filming of the very story he has been trying to sell to Pangborn, who thinks the tale so impossible that he has an apoplectic attack before kicking Fields out of his office. The dejected comedian then begins driving home and stops to help an obese woman who tells him she must get to the maternity hospital pronto. He drives madly through downtown Los Angeles, caroming his car off other autos; he even gets entangled in the careening ladder of a fast-moving fire engine but manages to deliver the heavyset woman, and then wrecks his car. Gloria Jean arrives on the crash site to see Fields stagger forth, holding the steering wheel of his car. She smiles adoringly at her uncle and says: "My Uncle Bill...but I still love him." Of course, there is no sense whatever to this utterly plotless film which was Fields' last feature-length movie. Yet the great comedian provides so many crazy scenes and offbeat laughs that it makes little difference. Oddly, this spoof of Hollywood realistically capped Fields' own movie career. The great comedian had pretty much run out his options in Hollywood by the time of NEVER GIVE A SUCKER AN EVEN BREAK and knew that Universal was planning to sidetrack his career in favor of the more slapstick Abbott and Costello, the dynamic duo who would dominate comedy at the studio through the 1940s. In this film Fields thumbs his considerable nose at the industry that was ousting him. Fields had insisted that this film be called THE GREAT MAN but Universal nixed the idea; he had tried to title his previous film the same way but the studio had entitled the film THE BANK DICK. Fields was not happy about the title of NEVER GIVE A SUCKER AN EVEN BREAK, commenting: "It doesn't matter anyway. Their title won't fit on a marquee, so they'll cut it down to 'W.C. Fields—Sucker.' " The title used by Universal was close to one employed by MGM in 1933, NEVER GIVE A SUCKER A BREAK, which was an aka for the official release title of THE NUISANCE, directed by Jack Conway and starring Lee Tracy, Madge Evans, and Frank Morgan. The motto, not to be confused with P.T. Barnum's "there's a sucker born every minute," has been credited to writer-con man Wilson Mizener. Yet Fields himself ad-libbed the line in the play "Poppy" in 1924, and in titles for his silent film IT'S THE OLD ARMY GAME. The two little boys in SUCKER, Lenhart and Brown, goaded Fields off the set and he muttered threats in their direction. Their chaperone loudly demanded that Fields not drink during the production of NEVER GIVE A SUCKER AN EVEN BREAK and the studio hounded the comedian, assigning detectives to follow him about. They cornered him outside his dressing room one day as he was lifting a small bottle of dark-hued liquid to his smiling lips. They yelled in the middle of his swig and Fields sneered and then gave them a wry smile as he removed his hand from the bottle's label, saying: "Just listerine." But Fields did not abandon drinking altogether, even though he proclaimed that he had given up swilling rum and pineapple juice, his favorite libation. He went to straight gin and this caused his feet to swell drastically, he claimed, and he was forced to regularly retreat to his dressing room to soak his feet before propping them up on thick pillows. Fields wrote the script in about four months and it brought a wrathful response from the Hollywood censors at that time, the Breen Office, which labeled the screenplay "vulgar and suggestive" and claimed that Fields made too many references to "drinking and liquor." Out came the scissors, but Fields got revenge of sorts. In one scene in the film he turns directly to the camera and whines: "This scene was supposed to be in a saloon but the censor cut it out. It'll play just as well." Beyond the cameras the comedian kept carping, telling reporters that the censors committed rapine on his script: "Why, those guys won't let me do anything. They find double meaning in commas and semicolons in my scripts. As an example, they made me cut a line out about a drunk. The line reads, 'He's tighter than a dick's hat band.' Now what's wrong with that? They also won't let me look at a girl's legs. I'm just looking, not saying anything, and they censor me." The script was badly tampered with by Universal with a bevy of hack writers assigned to clean up and clarify the screenplay. "They produced the worst script I ever read. I was going to throw it in their faces," Fields stated, "when the director [Cline] told me not to. He said: 'We'll shoot your own script. They won't know the difference.' We did—and they didn't."

d, Edward Cline; w, John T. Neville, Prescott Chaplin (based on a story by Otis Criblecoblis [W.C. Fields]); ph, Charles Van Enger; m, Frank Skinner; ed, Arthur Hilton; md, Charles Previn; art d, Jack Otterson, Richard H. Riedel; set d, R.A. Gausman; cos, Vera West.

Comedy **Cas.** **(PR:A MPAA:NR)**
Cas.

NEVER GIVE AN INCH (SEE: SOMETIMES A GREAT NOTION, 1971)

NEVER LET GO½** (1960, Brit.) 91m Independent Artists/Continental bw

Richard Todd *(John Cummings)*, Peter Sellers *(Lionel Meadows)*, Elizabeth Sellars *(Anne Cummings)*, Adam Faith *(Tommy Towers)*, Carol White *(Jackie)*, Mervyn Johns *(Alfie Barnes, News Vendor)*, Noel Willman *(Inspector Thomas)*, David Lodge *(Cliff)*, Peter Jones *(Alec Berger)*, John Bailey *(MacKinnon)*, Nigel Stock *(Regan)*, John Le Mesurier *(Pennington)*, Charles Houston *(Cyril Spink)*, John Dunbar *(Station Sergeant)*, Cyril Shaps *(Cypriot)*.

After a string of successful forays into comedy, Sellers decided to add a serious, villainous role to his impressive repertoire and came up with this competent but unremarkable effort. Set in the slum area of East London, NEVER LET GO details the activities of Sellers, a brutal, violent gang lord who operates a car-theft ring. Cosmetic salesman Todd becomes involved with Sellers after his car is stolen by the gang. Finding the police no help, Todd becomes determined to retrieve his car. Through contacts, Todd locates Faith, the boy who stole his car. Faith tells him nothing, but Sellers learns of the meeting and beats the young thief for talking. White, Sellers' young mistress, fears her lover and runs off with Faith. Convinced that the only way to be rid of the crime boss' evil influence is to destroy his empire, Faith goes to the police. The police stage a raid on Sellers' warehouse, but find that the cars have been moved to another location. Suspicious, Todd returns to the warehouse that evening and finds his car. Before he can escape, Sellers attacks the salesman and after a brutal beating Todd subdues the crook. The police arrive, arrest Sellers, and Todd finally recovers his car. Aside from the change of pace for Sellers, NEVER LET GO is nothing more than an average crime thriller punctuated by bursts of shocking violence. The film is surprisingly savage and Sellers' character is positively repellent. Guillermin's direction is taut and has some flair, but the script lacks a depth that might have made the characters more than brutal (and brutalized) cutouts.

p, Peter De Sarigny; d, John Guillermin; w, Alun Falconer (based on a story by Guillermin, De Sarigny); ph, Christopher Challis; m, John Barry; ed, Ralph Sheldon; md, Barry; art d, George Provis, cos, Vi Murray, m/l, "Never Let Go," Barry, Lionel Bart; makeup, Trevor Crole-Rees, John Wilcox.

Crime **Cas.** **(PR:C MPAA:NR)**

NEVER LET ME GO** (1953, U.S./Brit.) 69m MGM bw

Clark Gable *(Philip Sutherland)*, Gene Tierney *(Marya Lamarkina)*, Richard Haydn *(Christopher Wellington St. John Denny)*, Bernard Miles *(Joe Brooks)*, Belita *(Valentina Alexandrovna)*, Kenneth More *(Steve Quillan)*, Karel Stepanek *(Commissar)*, Theodore Bikel *(Lieutenant)*, Anna Valentina *(Svetlana Mikhailovna)*, Frederick Valk *(Kuragin)*, Anton Dolin *(Marya's Partner)*, Peter Illing *(N.K.V.D. Man)*, Robert Henderson *(U.S. Ambassador)*, Stanley Maxted *(John Barnes)*, Meinhart Maur *(Lemkov)*, Alexis Chesnakov *(Gen. Zhdanov)*, Anton Diffring, London Festival Ballet.

Love conquers communism in this mildly entertaining but implausible picture that never catches fire, despite the European locations and some important actors. Gable is a newsman in Moscow at the end of the war where he meets and marries Russian ballerina Tierney. They are united by the U.S. ambassador and go off on their honeymoon, where they meet Haydn, a British man, and his new Russian wife, Belita. Haydn is asked to leave Russia by the authorities, but they won't let his wife go with him. Next thing you know, Gable is suffering the same fate. The two men unite and attempt to smuggle their wives out of Mother Russia through the usual means but they are tied up tightly by red tape. They eventually pool their resources to buy a boat, and, with the help of Miles, a British sailor, they make plans to pick their wives up in the Baltic. With further aid from More, a radio broadcaster stationed in Moscow, the wives find out where to be, but only Belita arrives at the jumping-off place. Tierney has been kept in the city to do a ballet in front of an important Soviet army man. Gable comes ashore, robs a Russian of his uniform, gets to the theater, steals his bride away in a feat of bravery, and, after a chase, manages to get her to the ship and freedom. It's more like a "Rambo" adventure than anything else, and if you can believe Stallone as that muscular oaf, then you can surely accept Gable as the one-man assault force who infiltrates Russia to rescue his wife.

p, Clarence Brown; d, Delmer Daves; w, Ronald Millar, George Froeschel (based on the novel *Came the Dawn* by Roger Bax); ph, Robert Krasker; m, Hans May; ed, Frank Clarke; md, May; art d, Alfred Junge.

Adventure/Romance **(PR:A MPAA:NR)**

NEVER LOOK BACK** (1952, Brit.) 73m Hammer/Exclusive bw

Rosamund John *(Anne Maitland, King's Counsel)*, Hugh Sinclair *(Nigel Stuart)*, Guy Middleton *(Guy Ransome)*, Henry Edwards *(Whitcomb)*, Terence Longdon *(Alan)*, John Warwick *(Raynor)*, Brenda de Banzie *(Molly Wheeler)*, Arthur Howard *(Vaughan)*, Bruce Belfrage *(Judge)*, Frances Rowe *(Liz)*, H.S. Hills, Helene Burls, Bill Shine, June Mitchell, Barbara Shaw, David Scase, Norman Somers.

The British court system takes on enough romantic drama to rival a soap opera in this intriguing thriller. Gentle redhead John plays the King's Counsel who takes on the defense of her old flame (Middleton) when he is accused of murdering his latest mistress. In a court battle against the man after her hand in marriage, Sinclair, John frees Middleton of the murder charge only by disclosing her earlier connections with him. Then when it is discovered that Middleton did commit the murder, John's reputation is ruined. But all ends well, with John finally able to marry counsel Sinclair when he is no longer a professional threat.

p, Michael Carreras, James Brennan; d, Francis Searle; w, John Hunter, Guy Morgan, Searle; ph, Reginald Wyer; m, Temple Abady; ed, John Ferris; art d, Alec Gray.

Drama **(PR:A MPAA:NR)**

NEVER LOVE A STRANGER*½ (1958) 91m AA bw

John Drew Barrymore *(Frank Kane)*, Lita Milan *(Julie)*, Robert Bray *("Silk" Fennelli)*, Steve McQueen *(Martin Cabell)*, Salem Ludwig *(Moishe Moscowitz)*, R.G. Armstrong *(Flix)*, Douglas Rodgers *(Brother Bernard)*, Felice Orlandi *(Bert)*, Augusta Merighi *(Mrs. Cazzolina)*, Abe Simon *("Fats" Crown)*, Dolores Vitina *(Frances Kane)*, Walter Burke *(Keough)*, Joseph Leberman *(Price)*, Dort Clark, *(Madigan)*, Robert O'Connell *(Kelly)*, Michael O'Dowd *(Piggy)*, John Dalz *(Father Quinn)*, Mike Enserro *(Tony the Bartender)*, Gino Ardito *(Willy)*, Joseph Costa *(Joe)*.

The story somehow manages to blame Barrymore's plunge into crime on religious beliefs. Barrymore plays an orphaned boy in a Catholic home, where it is discovered that he is of Jewish parentage. Since the law insists that orphans be kept in a home of their own faith, the authorities decide to move him to a different orphanage. Already involved with petty hoodlums, Barrymore views this last form of rejection as a reason to dive deeper into gangland activities. He eventually becomes head of the entire New York-New Jersey syndicate until he is gunned down by police. The script, from Robbins' book, takes a naive approach to subjects such as religion and crime, making the entire story seem unbelievable. Passage of time is not handled in an effective manner, and the cast does little to overcome the inconsistencies in the script and direction.

p, Harold Robbins, Richard Day; d, Robert Stevens; w, Robbins, Day (based on the novel by Robbins); ph, Lee Garmes; m, Raymond Scott; ed, Sidney Katz; md, Jack Shaindlin; art d, Leo Kerz; cos, Ruth Morley; m/l, "Never Love a Stranger," Scott, Lawrence Elow (sung by Dorothy Collins).

Crime   Cas.   **(PR:A MPAA:NR)**

NEVER MENTION MURDER*½   (1964, Brit.) 56m Merton Park/ AE bw

Maxine Audley (*Liz Teasdale*), Dudley Foster (*Philip Teasdale*), Michael Coles (*Tony Sorbo*), Pauline Yates (*Zita Sorbo*), Brian Haines (*Felix Carstairs*), Peter Butterworth (*Porter*), Philip Stone (*Inspector*).

A surgeon gets even with his wife's lover by convincing him that he is in need of a dangerous heart operation. Interesting plot twist was not given its due treatment.

p, Jack Greenwood; d, John Nelson Burton; w, Robert Banks Stewart (based on the story by Edgar Wallace).

Crime/Drama   **(PR:A MPAA:NR)**

NEVER NEVER LAND½**   (1982) 86m Sharp c

Petula Clark, Cathleen Nesbitt, Anne Seymour, Michael J. Shannon, John Castle, Evelyn Laye, Roland Culver, Heather Miller.

Moving and well-acted drama concerning a child left in her own isolated world who resorts to fairy tales as a form of fantasizing friendships. The relationship that develops between her and Nesbitt, a woman suffering from loneliness because of her age, helps to fill holes in both of their lives. Tugs at the heart, and with a lot of grace.

p, Diane Baker; d, Paul Annell; w, Marjorie L. Sigley.

Drama   **(PR:A MPAA:G)**

NEVER ON SUNDAY***   (1960, Gr.) 97m Melina/UA-Lopert bw (POTE TIN KYRIAKI)

Melina Mercouri (*Ilya*), Jules Dassin (*Homer*), Georges Foundas (*Tonio*), Titos Vandis (*Jorgo*), Mitsos Liguisos (*The Captain*), Despo Diamantidou (*Despo*), Dimos Starrenios (*Poubelle*), Dimitri Papamikail (*A Sailor*), Alexis Salomos (*Noface*).

A colorful art-house comedy that broke through and made a ton of money when mass audiences flocked to see it. Filmed for a pittance (under $200,000) in Greece, NEVER ON SUNDAY is the brainchild of Dassin, an American writer-director who ran afoul of the Red-baiters in the 1950s and had to go to Europe to earn a living. He helmed RIFIFI, then went to Greece to do HE WHO MUST DIE; there he met and married Mercouri. The fact that this is the standard "hooker with a heart of gold" story didn't bother anyone, as it was draped in grape leaves which made it look different enough from any predecessor. Dassin not only wrote, produced, and directed, he also costarred as a tweedy American Greco-phile who comes to Piraeus, where he encounters the local peasantry, who are slightly taken aback by his open ways. In his smile, there is a touch of Mr. Hulot, sans the slapstick. Dassin loves Greece and everything about it and soon meets Mercouri, a prostitute with pride in her work who sees nothing immoral about the way she earns her living. She takes on all comers six days a week and reserves Sunday for seeing the great Greek plays, none of which she actually comprehends. For example, she thinks "Oedipus" is a nifty tale of a man who loves and respects his Mama. She feels Medea was a misunderstood woman who was hurt by the men in her life, and she can't believe that Medea actually took her own children's lives, as that happens offstage. Dassin intends to reform Mercouri and his assault on her works is successful at first, as she agrees to lay off for two weeks. But old habits are hard to break, and she eventually goes back on her back again. In the meantime, it is Dassin who has been "reformed," as he comes to realize that Mercouri may well be right. He accepts her profession with a shrug, and he has been altered for the better, in the same way that Anthony Quinn affected the stuffy Alan Bates in ZORBA THE GREEK. Mercouri became a star in this role and later played it as a musical on Broadway in 1967-68, where it was less than enthusiastically welcomed. In the end, Dassin goes home a wiser and happier man. The title song won an Oscar and Dassin's script and direction and Mercouri received nominations. Charming in spots, it wasn't as funny in the U.S. as it must have been in Athens. Most of the dialog is in English with a few speeches in Greek with titles.

p,d&w, Jules Dassin; ph, Jacques Natteau; m, Manos Hadjidakis; ed, Roger Dwyre; cos, Deni Vachlioti; m/l, "Never on Sunday," Hadjidakis.

Comedy/Drama   Cas.   **(PR:O MPAA:NR)**

NEVER PUT IT IN WRITING   (1964) 93m Seven Arts/AA bw

Pat Boone (*Steven Cole*), Milo O'Shea (*Danny O'Toole*), Fidelma Murphy (*Katie O'Connell*), Reginald Beckwith (*Lombardi*), Harry Brogan (*Mr. Breeden*), Nuala Moiselle (*Miss Bull*), John Le Mesurier (*Adams*), Sarah Ballantine (*Adam's Secretary*), John Gardiner (*Security Officer*), Colin Blakely (*Oscar*), Derry Power (*Taxi Driver*), Bill Foley (*Tower Man*), Polly Adams (*Receptionist*), Julia Nelson (*Maid*), Ed Devereaux (*Pringle*), Seamus Healy (*Sorting Office Foreman*), Karal Gardner (*Young Woman*), John Dunbar (*Judge*), Susan Richards (*Judge's Wife*), Liz Lanchbury (*Basil's Girl Friend*), Peter Lamb, Georgina Cookson, Paul Farrell, Sylva Davies, Michael O'Brian, Eddie Golden, Pat Layde, Geoffrey Golden, Philip O'Flynn.

A thin plotline features Boone as an insurance agent in Ireland writing a nasty letter to his employer in London, when he believes he was turned down for a promotion the employer's nephew received. When Boone realizes he is mistaken and actually did get the promotion, he makes a mad rush to London to try to intercept the letter. The film was produced in a competent manner, with Boone giving a standard performance. It was shot on location in Ireland and England.

p, Andrew L. Stone, Virginia Stone; d&w, A. Stone; ph, Martin Curtis; m, Frank Cordell; ed, Noreen Ackland; cos, Norman Hartnell m/l, "Never Put It In Writing," Pat Boone (sung by Boone); stunts, Charlie O'Hara.

Comedy   **(PR:A MPAA:NR)**

NEVER SAY DIE*½   (1939) 80m PAR bw

Martha Raye (*Mickey Hawkins*), Bob Hope (*John Kidley*), Andy Devine (*Henry Munch*), Alan Mowbray (*Prince Smirnov*), Gale Sondergaard (*Juno*), Sig Rumann (*Poppa Ingleborg*), Ernest Cossart (*Jeepers*), Paul Harvey (*Jasper Hawkins*), Frances Arms (*Momma Ingleborg*), Ivan Simpson (*Kretsky*), Monty Woolley (*Dr. Schmidt*), Foy Van Dolsen (*Kretsky's Bodyguard*), Christian Rub (*The Mayor*), Donald Haines (*Julius*), Gustav von Seyffertitz (*Chemist*), Gino Corrado, Albert Dekker, Frank Reicher, Victor Kilian, Hobart Cavanaugh.

Adapted from the William H. Post play, the movie's potential to be a little gem is never fully realized, even with the fine comic talents of Hope. Hope plays a multi-millionaire, who, through a cross-up in the lab, is given a month to live. He escapes marriage to the lusty Sondergaard, only to meet Raye, whose tycoon father insists she marry a certain prince. But Raye's heart belongs to lowly bus driver Devine. Since Hope has only a month to live, he marries Raye, so when he dies and leaves his money to her, she can marry Devine. The pair go on a honeymoon accompanied by Devine. When Hope gets the news about the faulty diagnosis, he finds himself deeply in love with Raye, and she with him. The story drags throughout, with the laughs far too few. Hope is never given a chance to display any of his abilities. Raye, however, gets to sing "The Tra La La and the Oom Pah Pah." The first adaptation of Post's play was filmed as a silent movie in 1924.

p, Paul Jones; d, Elliot Nugent; w, Don Hartman, Frank Butler, Preston Sturges (based on the play by William H. Post); ph, Leo Tover; ed, James Smith; md, Boris Morros; art d, Hans Dreier, Ernst Fegte; set d, A. E. Freudeman; cos, Edith Head; spec eff, Farciot Edouart; m/l, "The Tra La La and the Oom Pah Pah," Ralph Rainger, Leo Robin; makeup, Wally Westmore.

Comedy   **(PR:A MPAA:NR)**

NEVER SAY DIE, 1950   (SEE: DON'T SAY DIE, 1950, Brit.)

NEVER SAY GOODBYE*½   (1946) 97m WB-FN bw

Errol Flynn (*Phil Gayley*), Eleanor Parker (*Ellen Gayley*), Lucile Watson (*Mrs. Hamilton*), S.Z. Sakall (*Luigi, Restaurateur*), Forrest Tucker (*Cpl. Fenwick Lonkowski*), Donald Woods (*Rex DeVallon*), Peggy Knudsen (*Nancy Graham*), Tom D'Andrea (*Jack Gordon*), Hattie McDaniel (*Cozy*), Patti Brady (*Phillippa "Flip" Gayley*), Helen Pender (*Louise*), William Benedict (*Messenger Boy*), Charles Coleman (*Withers*), Arthur Shields (*McCarthy*), Doris Fulton (*Hat Check Girl*), Tom Tyler, Monte Blue (*Policemen*), Sam McDaniel (*Porter*), Roy Gordon (*Detective*), Harry Hays Morgan (*Waiter*).

Errol Flynn is a calendar artist (like Petty or Vargas) and his passion for pulchritude has caused his divorce from Parker. Their daughter, Brandy, spends her time attempting to bring her parents together, and after an hour and a half of every stale joke ever devised, she succeeds. The producers attempted to shore up the levity by hiring some old comedy hands like Sakall, D'Andrea, McDaniel, and Woods, but it didn't help matters much. Flynn gets the chance to warble a few notes of Harry Warren and Al Dubin's "Remember Me?" and also does what appears to be a sensational impression of Bogart, until one learns that Bogie himself looped the words to Flynn's lip movements. There are so many cliches in the picture that to enumerate them would begin a litany of boredom. Ben Barzman, who co-wrote the story with his wife, later became a writing instructor at a California college, thus proving that those who cannot do, teach. Veteran art director Grot is the same man who did the sets for NOAH'S ARK that collapsed on cue and tragically cost the lives of some extras. The sketches attributed to Flynn were done by Zoe Mozert. Co-screenwriter Diamond later became rich and famous when he teamed with Billy Wilder to pen a host of hits, including SOME LIKE IT HOT, THE APARTMENT, ONE TWO THREE, and THE FORTUNE COOKIE.

p, William Jacobs; d, James V. Kern; w, I.A.L. Diamond, Kern, Lewis R. Foster (based on the story "Don't Ever Leave Me" by Ben and Norma Barzman); ph, Arthur Edeson; m, Frederick Hollander; ed, Folmar Blangsted; md, Leo F. Forbstein; art d, Anton Grot; set d, Budd Friend; cos, Leah Rhodes; spec eff, William McGann, Willard Van Enger; makeup, Perc Westmore.

Comedy   **(PR:A MPAA:NR)**

NEVER SAY GOODBYE   (1956) 96m UNIV c

Rock Hudson (*Dr. Michael Parker*), Cornell Borchers (*Lisa Gosting/Dorian Kent*), George Sanders (*Victor*), Ray Collins (*Dr. Bailey*), David Janssen (*Dave Heller*), Shelley Fabares (*Suzy Parker*), Helen Wallace (*Miss Tucker*), John E. Wengraf (*Prof. Zimmelman*), Robert Simon (*Dr. Kenneth Evans*), Raymond Greenleaf (*Dr. Kelly Andrews*), Frank Wilcox (*Dr. Barnes*), Howard Wendell (*Harry*), Casey Adams [Max Showalter] (*Andy Leonard*), Jerry Paris (*Joe Cummings*), Else Neft (*Frau Hempel*), John Banner (*Oskar*), Jeane Wood (*Miss Masters the Nurse*), Ann Loos (*Marie*), Margot Karin (*Luise*), Barbara Bartay (*Hilda*), Gisele Verlaine (*Rosie*), Jill Janssen (*Judy*), Nancy Matthews (*Linda*), Terry Ann Rossworn (*Suzy Parker, Age 2*), Clint Eastwood (*Will*), Gia Scala (*Minnie*), Kurt Katch (*Landlord*), Edward Earle (*Army Maj. Washburn*), Ken Alton (*Russian Sentry*), June McCall (*Ad Lib*), Otto Reichow (*Piano Mover*).

A real tear-jerker features Hudson as a successful doctor who comes across Borchers, the wife and mother to his daughter, whom he had abandoned years before. While a medic during the war he fell in love with and married the German Borchers. In a jealous rage, he walked out on her, taking their young baby with him. Attempts at further communication failed when she was caught behind the Iron Curtain and arrested. When Borchers sees Hudson in the Chicago cafe where she is working for Sanders years later, she runs into the street and is hit by a passing truck. Hudson performs an emergency operation on the woman, creating a reconciliation in the process. Attempts at bringing Borchers together with her 8-year-old daughter prove difficult as the girl does not want to accept the woman as her mother. But the family is reunited in the end. Hudson is his usual bland self, with Sanders adding his unique touch of class. Clint Eastwood has a bit part as a lab assistant to Hudson, his second such role. Eastwood was dropped from his contract with Universal following this film. Borchers made her American film debut with this movie, after winning the British film equivalent of the Oscar for her role in THE DIVIDED HEART. Hudson's house in the movie was the same one seen in Paramount's 1955 release, DESPERATE HOURS, and in the TV series, "Leave It to Beaver" and "Marcus Welby, M.D." Remake of THIS LOVE OF OURS.

p, Albert J. Cohen; d, Jerry Hopper, Douglas Sirk (uncredited); w, Charles Hoffman (based on a screenplay by Bruce Manning, John Klorer, Leonard Lee, from the play "Come Prima Meglio De Prima" by Luigi Pirandello); ph, Maury Gertsman (Technicolor); m, Frank Skinner; ed, Paul Weatherwax; md, Joseph Gershenson; art d, Alexander Golitzen, Robert Boye; cos, Bill Thomas.

Drama **(PR:A MPAA:NR)**

NEVER SAY NEVER AGAIN½** (1983) 137m Woodcote-Taliafilm/WB c

Sean Connery *(James Bond)*, Klaus Maria Brandauer *(Largo)*, Max von Sydow *(Blofeld)*, Barbara Carrera *(Fatima Blush)*, Kim Basinger *(Domino)*, Bernie Casey *(Felix Leiter)*, Alec McCowen *(Q/Algy)*, Edward Fox *(M)*, Pamela Salem *(Miss Moneypenny)*, Rowan Atkinson *(Small-Fawcett)*, Valerie Leon *(Lady in Bahamas)*, Milow Kirek *(Kovacs)*, Pat Roach *(Lippe)*, Anthony Sharp *(Lord Ambrose)*, Prunella Gee *(Patricia)*, Gavan O'Herlihy *(Jack Petachi)*, Ronald Pickup *(Elliot)*, Robert Rietty, Guido Adorni *(Italian Ministers)*, Vincent Marzello *(Culpepper)*, Christopher Reich *(No. 5)*, Billy J. Mitchell *(Capt. Pederson)*, Manning Redwood *(Gen. Miller)*, Anthony Van Laast *(Kurt)*, Saskia Cohen Tanugi *(Nicole)*, Sylvia Marriott, Dan Meaden, Michael Medwin, Lucy Hornak, Derek Deadman, Joanna Dickens, Tony Alleff, Paul Tucker, Brenda Kempner, Jill Meager, John Stephen Hill, Wendy Leach, Roy Bowe.

Connery returns to action after a 12-year absence from the role of the supersleuth. The title itself is a pun on Connery's comment that he would never do a James Bond film again, following his last Bond outing. Basically a remake of THUNDERBALL, the film opens with Bond coming out of retirement as a school teacher to thwart a psychotic Brandauer, who wants to control the world via nuclear missiles. Connery possesses his usual charm and sophistication, with humorous touches in the picture having him switch from martinis to herbal tea to get in shape. The usual female enemy agents, Carrera and Basinger, make their own attempts to get the sleuth out of the way. Brandauer, who received fame in MEPHISTO, makes a great Bond villain, keeping a spark of insanity behind his charming demeanor. The film is devoid of all the technical gadgetry found in later films, making the development of characters more prominent and colorful. This was director Irvin Kershner's first film following the huge success of 1980's THE EMPIRE STRIKES BACK. (See JAMES BOND series, Index.)

p, Jack Schwartzman; d, Irvin Kershner; w, Lorenzo Semple, Jr. (based on a story by Kevin McClory, Jack Whittingham, Ian Fleming); ph, Douglas Slocombe (Panavision, Technicolor); m, Michel Legrand; ed, Robert Lawrence, Ian Crafford; prod d, Philip Harrison, Stephen Grimes; art d, Leslie Dilley, Michael White, Roy Stannard; set d, Peter Howitt; cos, Charles Knode; spec eff, David Dryer, Ian Wingrove; m/l, title song, Legrand, Alan Bergman, Marilyn Bergman (sung by Lani Hall).

Spy/Fantasy **Cas.** **(PR:A MPAA:PG)**

NEVER SO FEW*** (1959) 124m Canterbury/MGM c

Frank Sinatra *(Tom C. Reynolds)*, Gina Lollobrigida *(Carla Vesari)*, Peter Lawford *(Capt. Grey Travis)*, Steve McQueen *(Bill Ringa)*, Richard Johnson *(Capt. Danny de Mortimer)*, Paul Henreid *(Nikko Regas)*, Brian Donlevy *(Gen. Sloane)*, Dean Jones *(Sgt. Jim Norby)*, Charles Bronson *(Sgt. John Danforth)*, Philip Ahn *(Nautaung)*, Robert Bray *(Col. Fred Parkson)*, Kipp Hamilton *(Margaret Fitch)*, John Hoyt *(Col. Reed)*, Whit Bissell *(Capt. Alofson)*, Richard Lupino *(Mike Island)*, Aki Aleong *(Billingsly)*, Maggie Pierce *(Nurse)*, Ross Elliott *(Dr. Barry)*, Leon Lontoc *(Laurel)*.

Sinatra stars as the American leader of a group of British-American regular troops and guerrillas fighting the Japanese in Burma during WW II. Hopelessly outnumbered (600 versus 40,000), Sinatra's men rely on stealth and surprise to combat the enemy. Operations are suspended briefly when Sinatra and another captain, Johnson, are ordered to take a two-week leave in Calcutta to pick up a doctor, Lawford, and medical supplies to be brought back to the troops. Johnson develops malaria and is treated by Lawford, while Sinatra travels around Calcutta with his driver, McQueen. Sinatra meets and falls for Lollobrigida, the mistress of mysterious arms merchant Henreid. The American captain attempts to romance the woman, but she is cool to his advances. Sinatra, Johnson, Lawford, and McQueen return to the front when their leave is over and arrive in time to celebrate Christmas with the troops. Unfortunately, the Japanese launch a surprise attack during the party and Sinatra is wounded. In the hospital, Sinatra is visited by Lollobrigida who has suddenly had a change of heart toward the solider and welcomes his romantic overtures. Eventually Sinatra recovers and rejoins his troops in an attack on a Japanese airfield. The campaign is successful, but the additional support Sinatra was promised never arrives. After the battle the guerrillas are shocked to discover that the reinforcements have been ambushed and slaughtered by Nationalist Chinese troops controlled by a warlord. Outraged, Sinatra leads his men into China seeking reprisal. In a village the soliders have captured, they discover a cache of American supplies and learn that the Chungking government has been outfitting warlord troops to ambush Allied troops, confiscate supplies, and sell them to the Japanese. When Johnson is killed by a wounded Chinese soldier, Sinatra turns savage and orders all the Chinese prisoners executed. During this bloodshed, Sinatra receives belated orders not to attack the village. The angry American sends a wire back to his superiors telling them to go to hell. This action leads to a court-martial hearing for Sinatra. On his way to trial, Sinatra again meets Lollobrigida, who suggests that he plead battle fatigue as a defense. Sinatra rejects the idea, and also declines her offer to have Henreid pull some strings with the Army command. The trial is very tense, but in the end, Sinatra wins his superiors over and the Chungking government is forced to take action against the warlords. Based on a novel by Tom T. Chamales that posed tough questions about the nature of traditional command in guerrilla warfare, screenwriter Kaufman's script skirts some of the more difficult aspects of the story in favor of heroism and romance. Director Sturges did what he could with the material at hand and managed to form a solid war film with the help of an outstanding cast. Aside from Sinatra, who was at the peak of his popularity, Sturges filled his cast with such tried and true performers as Donlevy and relatively new faces such as Bronson and McQueen. McQueen's role was originally intended for Sinatra "Rat Pack" member Sammy Davis, Jr., but Davis and Sinatra had a brief falling out which cost Davis the role. Sturges had been keeping an eye on the young McQueen by watching episodes of "Wanted—Dead or Alive" on television and was impressed with the actor. While McQueen may have won Sturges over, he still had to prove himself to the egotistical and frequently mischievous Sinatra. As McQueen himself stated in his biographer and friend William F. Nolan's book *McQueen*, "One afternoon on location...I was sitting there reading my script...and Frank crept up behind me and slipped a lighted firecracker in one of the loops of my gunbelt. When that thing went off I jumped about three feet straight up. Which naturally delighted Frank. So I grabbed one of the Tommy guns we were using in the film and jammed in a full clip—fifty rounds. Sinatra was walking away laughing it up with his buddies, when I yelled at him, 'Hey, Frank!' He turned around and I let him have it, zap-zap-zap-zap, the whole clip." Blanks fired at close range can be quite painful and the whole set fell quiet while waiting to see what Sinatra's reaction would be. As McQueen stood there staring at Sinatra, the star, "...just started laughing, and it was all over. After that, we got along fine. In fact, we tossed firecrackers at each other all through the picture." While NEVER SO FEW did little to enhance Sinatra's reputation as an actor, it did provide the needed spark for the careers of both McQueen and Bronson. Director Sturges was fond of both actors and teamed them up again in THE MAGNIFICENT SEVEN (1960) and THE GREAT ESCAPE (1963), which were massive hits and catapulted both McQueen and Bronson to stardom.

p, Edmund Grainger; d, John Sturges; w, Millard Kaufman (based on the novel by Tom T. Chamales); ph, William H. Daniels (CinemaScope, Metrocolor), m, Hugo Friedhofer; ed, Ferris Webster; md, Charles Wolcott; art d, Hans Peters, Addison Hehr; set d, Henry Grace, Richard Pefferle; cos, Helen Rose; spec eff, Robert R. Hoag, Lee LeBlanc; makeup, William Tuttle.

War **(PR:C MPAA:NR)**

NEVER STEAL ANYTHING SMALL½** (1959) 94m UNIV c

James Cagney *(Jake MacIllaney)*, Shirley Jones *(Linda Cabot)*, Roger Smith *(Dan Cabot)*, Cara Williams *(Winnipeg)*, Nehemiah Persoff *(Pinelli)*, Royal Dano *(Words Cannon)*, Anthony Caruso *(Lt. Trevis)*, Horace MacMahon *(O.K. Merritt)*, Virginia Vincent *(Ginger)*, Jack Albertson *(Sleep-Out Charlie)*, Robert J. Wilke *(Lennie)*, Herbie Faye *(Hymie)*, Billy M. Green *(Ed)*, John Duke *(Ward)*, Jack Orrison *(Osborne)*, Roland Winters *(Doctor)*, Ingrid Goude *(Model)*, Sanford Seegar *(Fats Ranney)*, Ed "Skipper" McNally *(Thomas)*, Gregg Barton *(Deputy Warden)*, Edwin Parker *(Policeman)*, Jay Jostyn *(Judge)*, John Halloran *(1st Detective)*, Harvey Perry *(2nd Detective)*, Phyllis Rimedy *(Waitress)*, Rebecca Sand *(Coffee Vendor)*.

There was little the great Cagney could ever do wrong in any film but his career did have its share of dubious productions. This is a weird one that misses the mark, although Cagney's sheer dynamic presence still lifts it above the average. He's a waterfront thug, with ambitions to become a union president, who sings and dances on the side. There is little in his nature that is lofty, pure, and idealistic. Cagney is a self-taught, hard-nosed stevedore with eyes for married Jones. To make her his, Cagney tries to frame her lawyer husband, Smith, on a faked charge of corruption and, meanwhile, to gain his own labor-leading ends, practices perjury, bribery, grand larceny, and just about every other crime in the book while his moll-like girl friend Williams tries vainly to reform him. Cagney loses it all in the end but still manages to sing and dance to a few unmemorable tunes: "I'm Sorry, I Want a Ferrari," "I Haven't Got a Thing to Wear," "It Takes Love to Make a Home," "Never Steal Anything Small," and "Helping Out Friends" (Allie Wrubel, Maxwell Anderson). The music is anemic, the lyrics, by Anderson, author of the unproduced musical play "The Devil's Hornpipe" (written with Rouben Mamoulian), are wholly uninspired and everyone except the tireless Cagney appears to want to be somewhere else. Lederer's script is weak, his direction weaker, and the basic premise for the whole thing is unsavory, a typical Rosenberg production. It was the last musical-gangster film attempted by the irrepressible Cagney.

p, Aaron Rosenberg; d, Charles Lederer; w, Lederer (based on the play "The Devil's Hornpipe" by Maxwell Anderson); ph, Harold Lipstein (CinemaScope, Eastmancolor); m, Allie Wrubel; ed, Russ Schoengarth; md, Joseph Gershenson; art d, Alexander Golitzen, Robert Clatworthy; set d, Russell A. Gausman, Ollie Emert; cos, Bill Thomas; spec eff, Clifford Stine; ch, Hermes Pan; makeup, Bud Westmore.

Musical/Crime **(PR:C MPAA:NR)**

NEVER STEAL ANYTHING WET (SEE: CATALINA CAPER, 1967)

NEVER TAKE CANDY FROM A STRANGER***   (1961,
Brit.) 81m Hammer/Sutton-Pathe bw (GB: NEVER TAKE SWEET-
S FROM A STRANGER, AKA: THE MOLESTER)

Gwen Watford (Sally Carter), Patrick Allen (Peter Carter), Felix Aylmer (Clarence Olderberry, Sr.), Niall MacGinnis (Defense Counsel), Alison Leggatt (Martha), Bill Nagy (Clarence Olderberry, Jr.), Macdonald Parke (Judge), Michael Gwynn (Prosecutor), Janina Fay (Jean Carter), Frances Green (Lucille), Estelle Brody (Eunice Kalliduke), James Dyrenforth (Dr. Stevens), Robert Arden (Tom Demarest), Vera Cook (Mrs. Demarest), Bud Knapp (Hammond), Hazel Jennings (Mrs. Olderberry), Cal McCord (Charles Kalliduke), Gaylord Cavallaro (Neal Phillips), Sheila Robins (Miss Jackson), Larry O'Connor (Sam Kingsley), Helen Horton (Sylvia Kingsley), Shirley Butler (Mrs. Nash), Michael Hammond (Sammy Nash), Patricia Marks (Nurse), Peter Carlisle (Usher), Mark Baker (Clerk of the Court), Sonia Fox (Receptionist), John Bloomfield (Foreman of Jury), Charles Maunsell (Janitor), Andre Daker (Olderberry's Chauffeur), Bill Sawyer (Taxi Driver), Jack Lynn (Dr. Montfort), William Abney (State Trooper), Tom Busby (2nd Policeman).

After a series of phenomenally successful horror films, Hammer Films took a chance and produced a serious drama dealing with a grim social problem—child molestation. The resulting film is a sincere, delicately handled work that is quite successful from a social and artistic standpoint, but Hammer could not change its bloody image with the critics overnight, and the film was savaged in the press by writers who assumed that Hammer would exploit the sensitive material. The studio did not, however, and NEVER TAKE CANDY FROM A STRANGER is one of the few films that examines this unsettling and important problem. Allen, his wife Watford, and their young daughter, Faye, move from England to a small town in Canada so that Allen can begin his new job as the high school principal. Also in the town lives Aylmer, a senile old man with severe psychopathic problems and an attraction to little girls. Being one of the few founding fathers of the town left, Aylmer's problems are hidden from the townsfolk who love and respect him. Soon after their arrival, Allen and Watford are shocked to discover that their daughter and another girl, Green, had been enticed to dance naked in front of Aylmer in exchange for candy. The parents take the matter to court, but find extreme hostility from the locals who have been rallied into supporting the old man by his son, Nagy. The defense attorney, MacGinnis, clears Aylmer by berating and confusing little Faye until it appears that she has made up the whole incident. Disgusted by the town's attitude, Allen and his wife pack their bags, but the departure is halted when it is learned that Faye and her girl friend Green have disappeared. A search party is organized and they soon discover Aylmer in the woods standing beside the corpse of Green whom he had just murdered. Panic-stricken that their daughter may have also fallen victim to the sick old man, Allen and Watford are relieved when Faye is found alive nearby, ignorant of the killing. NEVER TAKE CANDY FROM A STRANGER is a powerful, well-balanced film that portrays all its characters with understanding and sensitivity (including the molester), instead of exploiting the viewer's fears, ignorance, or hatred for simple melodramatic effect. Unfortunately, Hammer fans didn't want to see such a serious film from the people that gave them such riveting, nonstop thrills as THE CURSE OF FRANKENSTEIN (1957) and HORROR OF DRACULA (1958) and it soon disappeared from the theaters, never finding an audience.

p, Anthony Hinds; d, Cyril Frankel; w, John Hunter (based on the play "the Pony Cart" by Roger Garis); ph, Freddie Francis; m, Elisabeth Lutyens; ed, James Needs, Alfred Cox; md, John Hollingsworth; art d, Bernard Robinson, Don Mingaye; makeup, Ray Ashton.

Drama   (PR:C-O MPAA:NR)

NEVER TAKE NO FOR AN ANSWER**½   (1952, Brit./
Ital.) 82m Souvaine bw

Vittorio Manunta (Peppino), Denis O'Dea (Father Damico), Guido Celano (Strotti), Nerio Bernardi (Father Superior), Harry Weedon (Monk at Basilica Door), Edward Hitchcock (Old Workman), Frank Coulson (Dr. Bartolo), Eliso della Vedova (Sergeant of Carabiniere), Charles Borelli (Chemist), Giorgio Riganti (Guiseppe), Clelia Matania (Mrs. Strotti), Robert Adamina (Gianni), Ricardo Foti (Monsignor Magana), John Murphy (Father O'Brien), Enzo Fiermonte (Sergeant of Swiss Guards), Dino Nardi (1st Monsignor), Alessandro Tasca (Civilian Clerk), Mino Billi (Weaver), Gorella Gori (Weaver's Wife), John Myhers, Joop van Hulzen, John Le Mesurier, Violetta the Donkey.

The film tells the touching story of an orphaned Italian boy who fends off starvation through work he can find with his pet donkey. He befriends U.S. troops, and after returning to America they send him a parcel with the advice that he never take "no" for an answer. This motto lays the groundwork for the rest of the film as the donkey becomes ill and the boy persists in bringing the animal to the tomb of St. Francis, the patron saint of animals. Although strictly forbidden, the boy insists, until eventually his wish is granted through a meeting with the Pope. Manunta, as the boy, gives a charming performance, proving to be a natural actor.

p, Anthony Havelock-Allan; d, Maurice Cloche, Ralph Smart; w, Paul Gallico, Pauline Gallico, Cloche, Smart (based on the novel The Small Miracle by Paul Gallico); ph, Otto Heller, Robert Day; m, Nino Rota; ed, Peter Graham Scott, Sydney Hayers.

Drama   (PR:A MPAA:NR)

NEVER TAKE SWEETS FROM A STRANGER   (SEE:
NEVER TAKE CANDY FROM A STRANGER, 1960, Brit.)

NEVER THE TWAIN SHALL MEET*½   (1931) 79m MGM bw

Leslie Howard (Dan Pritchard), Conchita Montenegro (Tamea), C. Aubrey Smith (Mr. Pritchard), Karen Morley (Maisie, Dan's Fiancee), Mitchell Lewis (Capt. Larrieau), Hale Hamilton (Mellenger), Clyde Cook (Porter the Beachcomber), Bob Gilbert (Tolongo), Joan Standing (Julia), Eulalie Jensen (Mrs. Craven).

Howard plays a wealthy San Francisco importer who finds himself the guardian of

Polynesian sexpot Montenegro. At first he finds the girl an intrusion to his busy lifestyle, forcing an upset to his usual routine. In no time at all, though, he is so taken by the girl that he takes her back to her South Seas island, adapting the ways of the natives himself. Howard brings a level of satisfaction to his role, with Montenegro doing little other than looking nice. The theme song "Island of Love," is dubbed over Montenegro's voice. The film introduced Howard to MGM's star roster.

d, W.S. Van Dyke; w, Edwin Justus Mayer, Ruth Cummings (based on the novel by Peter B. Kyne); ph, Merritt B. Gerstad; ed, Ben Lewis; m/l, "Islands of Love," Arthur Freed.

Comedy   (PR:A MPAA:NR)

NEVER TO LOVE   (SEE: BILL OF DIVORCEMENT, 1940)

NEVER TOO LATE*½   (1965) 105m Tandem/WB c

Paul Ford (Harry Lambert), Connie Stevens (Kate Clinton), Maureen O'Sullivan (Edith Lambert), Jim Hutton (Charlie Clinton), Jane Wyatt (Grace Kimbrough), Henry Jones (Dr. Kimbrough), Lloyd Nolan (Mayor Crane).

O'Sullivan returned to the screen after a long absence in the role of an aging woman who discovers she's pregnant, much to the consternation of her elderly husband, Ford, and to the surprise of the rest of the town. This leads to numerous family problems, as Ford does not feel up to the responsibility of a child, and daughter Stevens is now forced to cook and clean, something she never had to do before. After a drunken word battle with the town mayor, Nolan, and his wife's departure, Ford decides to resign himself to the fact that he's about to become a father. All the while Stevens tries to become pregnant as well. Pretty childish stuff.

p, Norman Lear; d, Bud Yorkin; w, Sumner Arthur Long (based on his play); ph, Phil Lathrop (Panavision, Technicolor); m, David Rose; ed, William Ziegler; art d, Edward Carrere; set d, Ralph S. Hurst; cos, Sheila O'Brian; m/l, "Never Too Late," Rose, Jay Livingston, Ray Evans (sung by Vic Damone); makeup, Gordon Bau.

Comedy   (PR:A MPAA:NR)

NEVER TROUBLE TROUBLE*½   (1931,
Brit.) 75m Producers' Distributing Corporation bw

Lupino Lane (Oliver Crawford), Renee Clama (Pam Tweet), Jack Hobbs (Jimmie Dawson), Wallace Lupino (Mr. Tweet), Iris Ashley (Gloria Baxter), Dennis Hoey (Stranger), Wally Patch (Bill Hainton), Lola Hunt (Mrs. Hainton), Barry Lupino (Tompkins), George Dewhurst (Inspector Stevens), Tom Shale, Merle Oberon.

This Lane vehicle has the comedian involved with the age-old plot twist about a struggling artist whose life is so miserable he takes out a contract on himself, only to find that things get better all of a sudden. In this case Lane is the recipient of a large inheritance, which makes the man change his mind about wanting to die. At the time the idea was original, but it would be handled much better in later productions. The pretty Oberon made her second screen appearance in a bit role here, before being discovered by Alexander Korda.

p&d, Lupino Lane; w, George Dewhurst (based on a story by Lauri Wylie).

Comedy   (PR:A MPAA:NR)

NEVER TRUST A GAMBLER*½   (1951) 79m COL bw

Dane Clark (Steve Garry), Cathy O'Donnell (Virginia Merrill), Tom Drake (Ed Donovan), Jeff Corey (Lou Brecker), Myrna Dell (Dolores Alden), Rhys Williams (Quentin McCloy), Kathryn Card (Phoebe), Sid Tomack (Emil Gillis), Ruth Warren (Mrs. Gillis), Tom Greenway (Sgt. Wessel).

A predictable plot has Clark as a good-for-nothing gambler who flees San Francisco rather than testify at a murder trial, taking refugee with his former wife, O'Donnell, in Los Angeles. He's actually the real killer, although he's being called to the stand as a witnes only. Problems erupt when Clark accidentally kills a man who has been pestering O'Donnell, than tries to stage it as an auto accident. The police see through the flimsy evidence, and give chase to Clark, who has fled to San Diego using O'Donnell as a hostage. Clark's performance is as standard and predictable as the plotline.

p, Louis B. Appleton, Jr., Monty Shaff; d, Ralph Murphy; w, Jesse L. Lasky, Jr., Jerome Odlum (based on a story by Odlum); ph, Allen Siegler; m, Arthur Morton; ed, Al Clark; md, Morris Stoloff; art d, Victor Greene.

Crime Drama   (PR:A MPAA:NR)

NEVER WAVE AT A WAC***   (1952) 87m Independent Artists/RKO bw
(GB:THE PRIVATE WORE SKIRTS)

Rosalind Russell (Jo McBain), Paul Douglas (Andrew McBain), Marie Wilson (Clara Schneiderman), William Ching (Lt. Col. Schuyler Fairchild), Arleen Whelan (Sgt. Toni Wayne), Leif Erickson (Sgt. Noisy Jackson), Charles Dingle (Sen. Tom Reynolds), Lurene Tuttle (Capt. Murchinson), Hillary Brooke (Phyllis Turnbull), Frieda Inescort (Lily Mae Gorham), Regis Toomey (Gen. Prager), Louise Beavers (Artamesa), Frances Zucco (Prudence Hopewell), Bernadine Simpson (Gussie Gustafson), Jeanne Dean (Mickey Fogarty), Anita Martell (Penny North), Marya Marco (Teresa Tonoku), Francis Morris (Maj. Carturight), Louise Lorimer (Col. Fulbright), Lucia Carroll (Lt. Kohler), Joan Blair (Maj. Thompson), Barbara Woodell (Capt. Smith), Madelon Mitchell (Capt. McGrady), Vince Townsend, Jr. (Henry), Virginia Christine (Lt. Myles), Olan Soule (Lt. Quartermaster), Barbara Jane Smith (Capt. Mallory), Helen Foster (Capt. Finch), Howard Smith (Gen. Prentiss), Allan Frank (Col. Colfax), Jo Gilbert (Civilian Doctor), Frances Helm (Lt. Green), Jane Seymour (Lt. Col Hubbard), Norma Busse (Sergeant Interviewer), Omar Bradley (Himself).

An often-funny film with good performances from everyone concerned, NEVER WAVE AT A WAC came out of the ill-fated Independent Artists Company, a firm begun by one-time RKO topper Floyd Odlum. Russell is the daughter of Dingle, a U.S. senator and the ex-wife of Douglas, a man who dabbles in textiles. She is a

Washington doyenne, like a young Perle Mesta, and enters the WAC because she thinks it might be fun. The expected commission doesn't materialize and she is forced to be a private, like everyone else. Her new beau, Ching, is at the base and she is reasonably happy, despite running into Douglas, who makes her act as a tester for his new fabrics. Wilson is a former burlesque stripteaser who is around to add to the laughs. The reason for her joining was to get away from the lounge lizards who trailed her every move on the outside. Filmed at the Disney studios with locations at the WAC Training Center in Fort Lee, Virginia, NEVER WAVE AT A WAC also boasts the presence of a genuine American hero, Gen. Omar Bradley, who does a short bit as himself. Bradley always liked show business and show people, and his second wife, Kitty, was a screenwriter who took him to every Hollywood party during his final years, when he lived in Beverly Hills. Bradley was part of the "Golden" graduating class at West Point that also included generals Douglas MacArthur and Dwight Eisenhower.

p, Frederick Brisson; d, Norman Z. McLeod; w, Ken Englund (based on a story by Frederick Kohner, Fred Brady); ph, William Daniels; m, Elmer Bernstein; ed, Stanley Johnson; md, Bernstein; art d, William E. Flannery; set d, Howard Bristol; m/l, "WAC Song," Jane Douglass, Camilla Mays Frank.

Comedy   **(PR:A MPAA:NR)**

NEW ADVENTURES OF DR. FU MANCHU, THE   (SEE: RETURN OF DR. FU MANCHU, 1930)

NEW ADVENTURES OF DON JUAN   (SEE: ADVENTURES OF DON JUAN, 1949, Brit.)

NEW ADVENTURES OF GET-RICH-QUICK WALLINGFORD, THE**   (1931) 96m MGM bw (AKA: GET-RICH-QUICK WALLINGFORD)

William Haines (J. Rufus Wallingford), Jimmy Durante (Schnozzle), Ernest Torrence (Blackie Daw), Leila Hyams (Dorothy), Guy Kibbee (McGonigal), Hale Hamilton (Charles Harper), Robert McWade (Mr. Tuttle), Clara Blandick (Mrs. Layton), Walter Walker (Mr. Layton), Henry Armstrong, Lucy Beaumont.

Comedy has Haines and Torrence as a couple of con men, aided by pickpocket Durante. Their pursuit of money and girls makes for a bunch of laughs. Haines goes straight after falling for Hyams and helping her family save their home. This marked the first major appearance for Durante, whose strange blend of humor stole the show, even with a good performance on the part of Haines. This was the first of G.R. Chester's stories to be filmed as a talkie. Previous "adventures" had been movie fodder for silents since 1915.

d, Sam Wood; w, Charles MacArthur (based on "The Wallingford Stories" by George Randolph Chester); ph, Oliver T. Marsh; ed, Frank Sullivan; art d, Cedric Gibbons

Comedy   **(PR:A MPAA:NR)**

NEW ADVENTURES OF TARZAN*½   (1935) 74m Burroughs-Tarzan/ REP bw (AKA: TARZAN AND THE GREEN GODDESS)

Herman Brix [Bruce Bennett] (Tarzan), Ula Holt (Ula Vale), Frank Baker (Maj. Martling, Archaeologist), Dale Walsh (Alice Martling), Harry Ernest (Gordon Hamilton), Don Castello (Raglan), Lewis Sargent (George), Merrill McCormick (Bouchart), Earl Dwire (Renegade), Mrs. Gentry (Queen Maya), Nkima (Jiggs the Monkey).

Originally a 12-part serial that had been edited down to a single feature, the film's production in the Guatemalan jungle would have made a better story than the picture itself. Burroughs formed his own company and took it into the jungles of Guatemala where the crew had to put up with some intolerable conditions. Many got sick from insect and snake bites. Native extras had a hard time acting around Nkima the chimpanzee. And to top it all, in the middle of production, Burroughs fell in love and ran off with his partner's wife. Star Brix, then recently of Olympic fame, was paid a measly $75 a week to accomplish the difficult tricks on his own and to suffer the jungle heat. The results aren't really worth it, as the film is weak in direction and plot development. This is perhaps the only Tarzan movie in which the hero speaks fluent English, as he does in the book. Story revolves around Brix's search for a missing friend, which leads him to the temple of the Lost Goddess, a place filled with priceless gems and guarded by ruthless monster men.

p, Ben S. Cohen, Ashton Dearholt, Edgar Rice Burroughs; d, Edward Kull, W. F. McGaugh; w, Charles F. Royal, Edwin H. Blum (based on the novels by Burroughs); ph, Ernest F. Smith, Kull; ed, Edward Schroeder, Harold Minter; md, Abe Meyer; art d, Charles Clague; spec eff, Ray Mercer, Howard Anderson.

Adventure   **(PR:A MPAA:NR)**

NEW BARBARIANS, THE zero   (1983, Ital.) 91m Deaf International c (I NUOVI BARBARI)

Timothy Brent (Skorpion), Fred Williamson (Nadir), George Eastman, Anna Kanakis, Thomas Moore [Enzo G. Castellari, Enzo Girolami, E. G. Rowland].

Blatant ripoff of THE ROAD WARRIOR, this is an attempt by Castellari to reach the cult film market. Usually, if one tries to make a cult film, one can never hope to succeed. Story takes place in the desert, soon after a nuclear holocaust has rearranged the existing structures. Brent and Williamson are two loners who try to fight off a gang of gay bikers, with a lot of unneeded grotesque violence.

p, Fabrizio De Angelis; d, Enzo G. Castellari [Enzo Girolami, E. G. Rowland, Thomas Moore]; w, Tito Carpi, Castellari; ph, Fausto Zuccoli (Telecolor); m, Claudio Simonetti; ed, Gianfranco Amicucci; prod d, Antonio Visone.

Fantasy   **(PR:O MPAA:NR)**

NEW CENTURIONS, THE**   (1972) 103m COL c (GB: PRECICNT 45: LOS ANGELES POLICE)

George C. Scott (Sgt. Kilvinsky), Stacy Keach (Roy Fehler), Jane Alexander (Dorothy Fehler), Scott Wilson (Gus), Rosalind Cash (Lorrie), Erik Estrada

(Sergio), Clifton James (Whitey), Richard Kalk (Milton), James Sikking (Sgt. Anders), Beverly Hope Atkinson (Alice), Burke Byrnes (Phillips), Mittie Lawrence (Gloria), Isabel Sanford (Wilma), William Atherton (Johnson), Peter De Anda (Gladstone), Ed Lauter (Galloway), Dolph Sweet (Sgt. Runyon), Stefan Gierasch (Landlord), Carol Speed (Martha), Tracee Lyles (Helen), Debbie Fresh (Rebecca Fehler), Michael Lane (Lumberjack), Roger E. Mosley (Truck Driver), Charles H. Gray (Bethel), Read Morgan (Woodrow Gandy), Michael DeLano (Ranatti), Pepe Serna (Young Mexican), Bea Thompkins (Silverpants), Hilly Hicks (Young Black), Adriana Shaw (Drunk Mother).

Real-life cop Wambaugh left the force after he became a best-selling author and we can only figure that this story must have been made up of many of his own experiences. The book was a deserved hit but this adaptation left a lot to be desired, as they pared so much and altered the characters to such an extent that it appears to be a police recruiting picture more than a drama. It shows these men in blue as Knights (there was a mini-series called "The Blue Knight" from another of Wambaugh's books), and reveals little of the corruption that is known to occur. Keach is working toward a law degree and serving as a rookie in the L.A.P.D. He soon leaves the Academy and is placed under the wing of veteran Scott, an old-timer who does not go by the book. One of sergeant Scott's ploys is to round up the hookers, get them drunk on booze, then let them out when they are so bombed that they can't street-walk, only stagger. Scott and Keach get close, and Keach begins to overlook his law studies until his wife, Alexander, starts complaining about it. She doesn't know what Keach sees in police work, a dangerous and low-paying job. These fears are realized when Keach is shot in the line of duty and almost dies from the shotgun blast. Keach comes back to work with Scott who soon retires. (A major error in the film's construction, as Scott is the unifying force of the drama and he is gone about two-thirds of the way through the movie.) Keach is reassigned to the vice squad but hates it and is soon back on a regular beat. Scott can't handle his enforced retirement and takes his own life. At the same time, Alexander dislikes being a cop's wife, so she exits, with daughter Fresh in tow. These two matters shatter Keach and he is now a single man and on his way to becoming what Scott was, lonely and disillusioned. While Keach was recovering from his shotgun wound, he met Cash, a nurse, and he meets her again when her apartment is burglarized. He would like to return, off-duty, but she'll have none of that. Later, he tries to arrest hooker Thompkins, but she races away with Keach holding on to the car door. That results in his being somewhat injured. He goes back to Cash's apartment and she reverts to being a nurse. That propinquity awakens a love in her, and, after a while, she and Keach happily plan to get married. Keach is called upon to handle a minor hassle between a husband and wife and is killed by the hopped-up man when he tries to help. (Cops will tell you that it's the domestic fights that they least like to face.) The picture ends as Keach's life is ebbing, the result of the dumb mistake of not taking the situation seriously. In an excellent cameo, Shaw plays a drunken mother and steals the scene. The lumberjack was played by Mike Lane, who looked a lot smaller than he did when doing the Primo Carnera role in THE HARDER THEY FALL. In small roles, several actors and actresses who went on to achieve some fame, including Atherton (SLAUGHTERHOUSE-FIVE and THE DAY OF THE LOCUST), Estrada ("Chips" TV series), Ed Lauter (MAGIC), and TV's Dolph Sweet and Isabel Sanford. A slick attempt at showing the lives of cops, but it seldom delves beneath the surface and often substitutes gratuitous action for compassion.

p, Irwin Winkler, Robert Chartoff; d, Richard Fleischer; w, Stirling Silliphant (based on the novel by Joseph Wambaugh); ph, Ralph Woolsey (Panavision, Eastmancolor); m, Quincy Jones; ed, Robert C. Jones; prod d, Boris Leven; set d, Harry Reif; cos, Guy Verhille; makeup, Dave Greyson, Del Acevedo.

Police Drama   **Cas.**   **(PR:O MPAA:R)**

NEW EARTH, THE**   (1937, Jap./Ger.) 120m J.O./Towa Shoji bw

Isamu Kosugi, Setsuko Hara, Sessue Hayakawa, Ruth Eveler.

Japanese-German coproduction is a plodding depiction of traditional Japanese culture being threatened by western values. Kosugi plays a young man back from extensive travels in Europe, where he has met a woman he intends to marry. This causes conflict with his foster father, Hayakawa, who reminds Kosugi of his father's wishes that he wed Hara. The young man eventually calls off his marriage to Eveler, who gracefully bows out, and goes through with his marriage to Hara. Picture is filled with beautiful photography of the Japanese landscape, which, though quite nice to look at, does nothing to help move the story along. Film versions in Japanese and English.

d, Dr. Arnold Fanck, Mansaku Itani; w, Fanck; ph, Richard Angst; m, Kosaku Yamada.

Drama   **(PR:A MPAA:NR)**

NEW FACE IN HELL   (SEE: P.J., 1968)

NEW FACES**   (1954) 98m FOX c

Ronny Graham, Eartha Kitt, Robert Clary, Virginia DeLuce, Alice Ghostley, June Carroll, Paul Lynde, Bill Mullikin, Rosemary O'Reilly, Allen Conroy, Jimmy Russell, George Smiley, Polly Ward, Carol Lawrence, Johnny Laverty, Elizabeth Logue, Faith Burwell, Clark Ranger.

A star-studded musical revue with a barely visible plot about an angry creditor from Texas who is determined to close the curtains for good on a Broadway show. The cast, however, is equally determined to keep it open and continues singing, dancing, and joke-telling. Drawn from a 1952 Broadway revue, NEW FACES features an almost nonstop array of tunes including Kitt's smash hits, "C'est Si Bon" (Henri Betti, Jerry Seelen), "Santa Baby" (Joan Javits, Phil Springer, Tony Springer), "Uskadara" (Stella Lee), "Monotonous" (June Carroll, Ronny Graham, Arthur Siegel). Other Songs include: "Bal Petit Bal" (sung by Kitt and Clary), "Boston Beguine" (Sheldon M. Harnick, sung by Ghostley), "I'm In Love with Miss Logan" (Ronny Graham, sung by Clary), "Penny Candy" (June Carroll, Arthur Siegel, sung by Carroll), "Time for Tea" (sung by Ghostley and Carroll). Writer Melvin Brooks later became director Mel Brooks.

p, Edward L. Alperson, Berman Swarttz; d, Harry Horner; w, Ronny Graham, Melvin Brooks, Paul Lynde, Luther Davis, John Cleveland (based on Leonard Sillman's Broadway stage revue "New Faces of 1952"); ph, Lucien Ballard.

Musical(PR:A MPAA:NR)

NEW FACES OF 1937*½　　　　　　(1937) 105m RKO bw

Joe Penner (Seymore Semor), Milton Berle (Wellington Wedge), Parkyakarkus (Parky), Harriet Hilliard (Patricia), William Brady (Jimmy), Jerome Cowan (Robert Hunt), Thelma Leeds (Elaine), Tommy Mack (Judge Hugo Straight), Lorraine Krueger (Suzy), Bert Gordon (Count Mischa Moody), Patricia Wilder (Hunt's Secretary), Richard Lane (Broker), Dudley Clements (Stage Manager), William Corson (Assistant Stage Manager), George Rosener (Doorman), Harry Bernard (Bridge Guard), Dewey Robinson (Joe Guzzola), Lowe, Hite and Stanley, Brian Sisters, Derry Dean, Eddie Rio and Brothers, Seven Loria Brothers, Catherine Brent, Ann Miller, Three Chocolateers, Four Playboys, Dorothy Roberts, Camille Soray, Rene Stone, Diane Toy, Harry C. Bradley, Mary Louise Smith, Betty Johnson, Harriet Brandon, Beatrice Shulte, Juanita Fields, Cynthia Westlake, Mary Frances Gifford.

Just an excuse for another song-and-dance revue with a very thin story line. Cowan plays a crooked producer out to make a deliberate flop, and in this manner pocket all the excess money he has been given by his backers. (The same idea was later used for the story line of Mel Brooks' THE PRODUCERS.) NEW FACES OF 1937 gives the audience a chance to watch numerous auditions, as well as the final show. Songs include: "Our Penthouse on Third Avenue," "Love is Never Out of Season," "It Goes to Your Feet," "If I Didn't Have You," "Take the World Off Your Shoulders," "It's the Doctor's Orders" (Sammy Fain, Lew Brown); "When the Berry Blossoms Bloom" (Joe Penner, Hal Raynor); "The Widow in Lace" (Walter Bullock, Harold Spina); "New Faces" (Charles Henderson); "Peckin'" (Ben Pollack, Harry James, Edward Cherkose).

p, Edward Small; d, Leigh Jason; w, Nat Perrin, Philip G. Epstein, Irving S. Brecher, Harold Kusell, Harry Clark, Howard J. Green, David Freedman (based on the story "Shoestring" by George Bradshaw); ph, J. Roy Hunt; ed, George Crone; md, Roy Webb; spec eff, Vernon L. Walker; ch, Sammy Lee.

Musical　　　　　　　　　　　　(PR:A MPAA:NR)

NEW FRONTIER, THE*½　　　　　　(1935) 59m T/C/REP bw

John Wayne (John Dawson), Muriel Evans (Hanna Lewis), Murdock McQuarrie (Tom Lewis), Alan Cavan (Minister), Mary MacLaren (Minister's Wife), Warner Richmond (Ace Holmes), Al Bridge (Kit), Sam Flint (Milt Dawson), Glenn Strange (Norton), Earl Dwire, Frank Ball, Hooper Atchley, Jack Kirk, Sherry Tansey.

Wayne was just beginning to display the characteristics which would later make him one of the greatest stars of all time. Republic was willing to show the amount of faith they had in the young actor by putting in much more money than customary for this feature. Wayne stars as the sheriff of a small town, where his father had been the previous law officer before being murdered. Wayne's nemesis is the local saloon-keeper, Richmond, whose gang does what it can to keep Wayne busy. Bridge is the leader of a local gang that comes to Wayne's assistance, resulting in the deaths of Richmond and Bridge. Pretty routine stuff.

p, Paul Malvern; d, Carl Pierson; w, Robert Emmett [Tansey]; ph, Gus Peterson; ed, Gerald Roberts.

Western　　　Cas.　　　　(PR:A MPAA:NR)

NEW FRONTIER*½　(1939) 56m REP bw (AKA: FRONTIER HORIZON)

John Wayne (Stony Brooke), Raymond Hatton (Rusty Joslin), Ray Corrigan (Tucson Smith), Phyllis Isley [Jennifer Jones] (Celia), Eddy Waller (Maj. Braddock), Sammy McKim (Stevie), LeRoy Mason (M. C. Gilbert), Harrison Greene (Bill Proctor), Reginald Barlow (Judge Lawson), Burr Caruth (Doc Hall), Dave O'Brien (Jason), Hal Price (Sheriff), Jack Ingram (Harmon), Bud Osborne (Dickson), Charles "Slim" Whitaker (Turner), Bob Burns (Fiddler), Bob Reeves, Frank Ellis, Walt LaRue (Dance Extras), Jody Gilbert (Woman at Dance), Oscar Gahan (Musician), Charles Murphy (Zeke the Mailman), Herman Hack (Jim the Construction-Wagon Driver), George Plues (Henchman), Wilbur Mack (Dodge), Curley Dresden, Cactus Mack, George Chesebro, Bill Wolfe.

This routine western fare has Wayne in his last role as one of "The Three Mesquiteers," prior to achieving stardom in STAGECOACH. The other Mesquiteers were Corrigan and Hatton. Here, the three save a group of settlers from a land-grabbing construction company, which wants to build a dam where the ranchers have settled. The ranchers are given land in a different valley, which they discover is not irrigated. So, Wayne and the boys come back to help make sure the displaced people get a fair deal, which they do. Wayne gives his usual competent performance, the only exception to a perfectly banal picture. Isley, as the feminine lead, was later to receive stardom under the name of Jennifer Jones. (See THREE MESQUITEERS series, Index.)

p, William Berke; d, George Sherman; w, Betty Burbridge, Luci Ward (based on characters created by William Colt MacDonald); ph, Reggie Lanning; m, William Lava; ed, Tony Martinelli.

Western　　　　　　　　　　　(PR:A MPAA:NR)

NEW GIRL IN TOWN**　　　(1977) 90m New World (AKA:
NASHVILLE GIRL; COUNTRY MUSIC DAUGHTER)

Monica Gayle (Jamie), Glenn Corbett (Jeb), Roger Davis (Kelly), Johnny Rodriguez (Himself), Jesse White (C.Y. Ordell), Marcie Barkin (Alice), Shirley Jo Finney (Frisky), Judith Roberts (Fran), Mary S. Harkey (Lois), Jackie Wright (Beauty), Leo Gordon (Burt).

A well-meaning but overly predictable drama in which Gayle plays a would-be

country and western singer who will do anything to get to the top in that competitive business. It's a typical show biz story with a Nashville setting replacing Broadway or Hollywood. Wandering into the country music capital from the farm, Gayle proceeds to sleep with just about anyone who can help her cause. She does manage to attain her dream, but realizes that the sacrifices she has made are not worth it. The Gayle character remains unsympathetic throughout, making her drama one that no one can really care very much about. Popular country music performer Johnny Rodriguez makes an appearance as himself and the soundtrack is full of the requisite country and western songs.

p, Peter J. Oppenheimer; d, Gus Trikonis; w, Oppenheimer; ph, Irv Goodnoff (Metrocolor); m, Kim Richmond; ed, Jerry Cohen; m/l, Rory Bourke, Johnny Wilson, Gene Dobbins, John Wills, Bob Wills.

Drama　　　　　　　　　　　(PR:C-O MPAA:R)

NEW HORIZONS*　　　　　(1939, USSR) 92m Lenfilm/Artkino bw

Boris Chirkov (Maxim), Vera Kibardina (Natasha), M. Zharov (Dymba), N. Uzhvi (Yeudokia), M. Shtraukh (Lenin), M. Gelovani (Joseph Stalin), L. Lyubashevsky (Sverdlov), Y. Tolubeyev (Bugai), A. Chistyakov (Mishchenko), D. Dudnikov (Ropshin), A. Kuznetsov (Turayev).

Pure Soviet propaganda, typical of the Soviet Realism school of this time, the film has Chirkov as the perfect example of a member of the proletariat. He has risen from paltry peasant to become a banker. His wife, Kibardina, is no simple housewife, but the chairman of the Soviet Party in Petrograd. Picture is a follow-up to THE LIFE OF MAXIM, which traced the earlier years of the same character. (In Russian; English subtitles.)

d&w, Gregory Kozintsev, Leonid Trauberg; m, Dmitri Shostakovich.

Drama　　　　　　　　　　　(PR:A MPAA:NR)

NEW HOTEL, THE*½　(1932, Brit.) 50m Producers Distributing Corp. bw

Norman Long, Dan Young, Hal Gordon, Mickey Brantford, Blanche Adele, Alfred Wellesley, Basil Howes, Betty Norton, Hamilton Keene, Kinsley Lark, Ruth Taylor, Bert Weston, Gilly Flower, Lindy Jeune, Frank Adey, Noel Dainton, James Croome, Myno Burnet, Percy Val, Al Davidson and His Band, Barbara Dean's Girls.

A sort of GRAND HOTEL-inspired musical wherein all manner of drama takes place before the opening of a new luxury hotel. Among the story lines crammed into the film's 50 minutes are the trials and tribulations of an alcoholic resident being blackmailed and an evil harlot who strips dimwitted men of their wallets. Needless to say, this extremely cheap production unveiled little in the way of memorable musical numbers.

p&d, Bernard Mainwaring.

Musical　　　　　　　　　　　(PR:A-C MPAA:NR)

NEW HOUSE ON THE LEFT, THE zero　　　　　　(1978,
Brit.) 94m Hallmark/Central Park c (AKA:
SECOND HOUSE FROM THE LEFT)

Kay Beal, Patty Edwards, Norma Knight, Delbert Moss, Richard Davis.

One in a number of slasher movies trying to cash in on the success of THE LAST HOUSE ON THE LEFT, this one is worse than most in that they had to resort to stealing the name as well as the story. The rapes and murders take place on a train this time, and that change of setting is the only element that separates this film from its predecessor.

p&d, Evans Isle.

Horror　　　　　　　　　　　(PR:O MPAA:R)

NEW INTERNS, THE**½　　　　　　(1964) 122m COL bw

Michael Callan (Dr. Alec Considine), Dean Jones (Dr. Lew Worship), Barbara Eden (Laura Rogers), Stefanie Powers (Gloria Worship), Inger Stevens (Nancy Terman), George Segal (Dr. Tony Parelli), Kay Stevens (Didi Loomis), Telly Savalas (Dr. Riccio), George Furth (Dr. Phil Osterman), Ellie Wood (Madeline Osterman), Greg Morris (Clark), Gordon Kee (Chaum), Jimmy Mathers (Freddie), Mike Vandever (Beep), Lee Patrick (Mrs. Hitchcock), Adam Williams (Wolanski), Sue Anne Langdon (Stella), Dawn Wells (Bobbie), Gregory Morton (Dr. Granchard), Michael Fox (Dr. Hellman), Eddie Ryder, Rusty Lane, Alan Reed Jr., Adrianne Ellis, Peter Hobbs, Ken Mayer, Norman Cole, Charles Lane, Marianna Hill, David Winters, Ken Drake.

A followup to the commercially successful THE INTERNS, this film follows the same type of structure and brings in the same leads with Callan, Powers, Savalas, and Stevens. The picture is a fast-paced look at a group of interns struggling through their first year in a real hospital setting. Callan is a girl-crazy intern, returning for his second try at internship after suffering a nervous breakdown the first time. He acts as leader and advisor for the rest of the group, always trying to get his hands on Eden, who eventually forces marriage upon him. Jones, an obstetrician, is married to Powers, but their marriage is threatened when it is discovered that Jones is sterile. Segal, in his first feature role, has grown up in the ghetto and still carries a chip on his shoulder. He's out to make Stevens, who is cold to him after being raped by three ghetto toughs. Several other stories are successfully intermingled with these main ones. The stories lack any resemblance to real hospital situations, but this fault is overlooked because of enjoyable plot distractions. Cast members fit their roles quite well.

p, Robert Cohn; d, John Rich; w, Wilton Schiller (based on characters from the novel The Interns, by Richard Frede); ph, Lucien Ballard; m, Earle Hagen; ed, Gene Milford, Eda Warren; art d, Don Ament; set d, Richard Mansfield; m/l, "Come On, Let Yourself Go," Jan Berry, Artie Kornfeld (sung by The Matadors); makeup, Ben Lane.

Drama　　　　　　　　　　　(PR:C MPAA:NR)

NEW INVISIBLE MAN, THE (SEE: INVISIBLE MAN, THE, 1958, Mex.)

NEW KIND OF LOVE, A*½ (1963) 110m Llenrock/PAR c

Paul Newman *(Steve Sherman)*, Joanne Woodward *(Samantha "Sam" Blake)*, Thelma Ritter *(Lena O'Connor)*, Eva Gabor *(Felicianne Courbeau)*, George Tobias *(Joseph Bergner)*, Marvin Kaplan *(Harry Gorman)*, Robert Clary *(Albert Sardou)*, Jan Moriarty *(Suzanne)*, Joan Staley *(Airline Hostess)*, Robert F. Simon *(Bertram Chalmers)*, Valerie Varda *(Mrs. Chalmers)*, Ted Mapes *(Floor Walker)*, Gladys Roach, Galen Keith Dahle, Minnie C. Logan, Virginia Carr, Jean Argyle, Mildred Shelton, Emily LaRue, Audrey Swanson, Kay Armour, Paul Micale *(Shoppers)*, Marylu Miner, Annabelle George, Pat Jones, Allyn Parsons, Gabrielle, Sondra Teke *(Models)*, Army Archerd *(Onlooker)*, June Smaney, Audrey Betz, Irene Chapman *(Amazons)*, Albert Carrier *(Gendarme)*, Jacqueline May *(French Waitress)*, George Nardelli *(Waiter)*, Lomax Study *(Hansom Cab Driver)*, Gene Ringgold *(Reporter)*, Laurie Mitchell *(Parisienne Poule)*, Patricia Olson *(2nd French Girl)*, Christian Kay *(Model with Pearls)*, Allyson Daniell *(Lingerie Model)*, Sandra Downs *(Stewardess)*, George Nardelli *(Waiter)*, Ralf Harolde *(French Waiter)*, Helen Marler *(Cardin Model)*, Trude Wyler *(Midinette)*, Suzanne Dadolle *(French Columnist)*, Maurice Chevalier, Jimmy Starr, Peter Canon, Vernon Scott *(Themselves)*, Danielle Aubry, Patricia Howard, Judy Garwood, Leno Jo Francen, Anne Ross, Joan Waddell, Vicki Poure, Mabel Smaney, Alphonse Martell, George Bruggeman, Celeste Yarnall, Francine York, Eugene Borden, Francis Ravel, Sue Casey.

Paul Newman can do a lot of things. He can write (HARRY AND SON), he can direct (RACHEL, RACHEL), he can produce, and he can act, but he is a total dud when it comes to comedy, as proven by RALLY ROUND THE FLAG, BOYS (before this) and THE SECRET WAR OF HARRY FRIGG (afterward). So it should come as no surprise that this film fell flatter than Twiggy's bodice. Shavelson (who tripled as writer-producer-director) tried everything to lift it, including having Sinatra sing the 32-year-old title song, but it didn't help this flop, the fifth pairing of Newman and Woodward, vainly attempting to be Paramount's version of Universal's Doris Day and Rock Hudson. Newsman Newman goes to Paris to cover the fashion show (see costume credits) and meets Woodward on the plane. She is with Tobias and Ritter, and all three work for a New York department store. Their job is to steal the fashions and put them out in popular-priced versions. He's drunk and she's somewhat masculine and they don't seem to like each other. After their arrival, Woodward goes to the St. Catherine's Day festival where single women pray to be married. Woodward gets drunk, goes to a local beauty salon, and they outfit her with a glamorous wig to cover her short hair. Meanwhile, lovelorn Ritter disappointedly watches Tobias fall into the clutches of Gabor, the store's local contact. Newman picks up Woodward, doesn't know who she is, and thinks she's a courtesan. She lies about her life as the Parisian Princess of Prostitution and Newman swallows it; he writes up a story and it's an instant circulation booster for his paper. As they fall in love, Newman gets that she's the ugly duckling he met in the first reel. Gabor dumps Tobias, who goes back to Ritter. Newman and Woodward wind up a pair at the finale. Maurice Chevalier does a cameo and sings snatches of "Mimi" and "Louise," but it's all too late and too little to help this tasteless farce. Leith Stevens was nominated for an Oscar for his score. Some sharp lines of dialog, a few too many camera tricks, and a general feeling of going-through-the-motions. Filmed in New York, Paris, and Hollywood.

p,d&w, Melville Shavelson; ph, Daniel L. Fapp (Technicolor); m, Leith Stevens, Erroll Garner; ed, Frank Bracht; art d, Hal Pereira, Arthur Lonergan; set d, Sam Comer, James Payne; cos, Edith Head, Christian Dior, Lanvin-Castille, Pierre Cardin, Yves Saint-Laurent; m/l, "You Brought a New Kind of Love to Me," Sammy Fain, Irving Kahal, Pierre Norman Connor (sung by Frank Sinatra), "Mimi, " Richard Rodgers, Lorenz Hart (sung by Maurice Chevalier), "Louise," Leo Robin, Richard A. Whiting (sung by Chevalier); makeup, Wally Westmore.

Comedy **(PR:A-C MPAA:NR)**

NEW LAND, THE*** (1973, Swed.) 161m Svensk Filmindustri/WB c (NYBYGGARNA; AKA: THE SETTLERS; UNTO A GOOD LAND)

Max von Sydow *(Karl Oskar)*, Liv Ullmann *(Kristina)*, Eddie Axberg *(Robert)*, Hans Alfredson *(Jonas Petter)*, Halvar Bjork *(Anders Mansson)*, Allan Edwall *(Danjel)*, Peter Lindgren *(Samuel Nojd)*, Pierre Lindstedt *(Arvid)*, Oscar Ljung *(Petrus Olausson)*, Karin Nordstrom *(Judit)*, Per Oscarsson *(Pastor Torner)*, Agneta Prytz *(Fina-Kajas)*, Monica Zetterlund *(Ulrika)*, Georg Anaya *(Mario Vallejos)*, Ed Carpenter *(The Doctor)*, Larry Clementson *(Mr. Abbott)*, Tom C. Fouts *(Pastor Jackson)*.

The touching sequel to THE EMIGRANTS follows the struggle of Von Sydow and Ullmann during their first decade in America. The story includes a futile trek to the Southwest to search for gold. Film is a subtle depiction of the hardships people faced as they tried to find a niche for themselves. In this sense the film is representative of an entire era in American history. The story moves slowly at times, but this helps to bring about a greater sense of realism with the focus on changes that the characters undergo. Edited for TV under the title THE IMMIGRANT SAGA.

p, Bengt Forslund; d, Jan Troell; w, Forslund, Troell (based on the novel *The Emigrants* by Vilhelm Moberg); ph, Troell (Technicolor); m, Bengt Ernryd, George Oddner; ed, Troell; art d, P. A. Lundgren; cos, Ulla-Britt Soderlund.

Adventure/Drama **(PR:A MPAA:PG)**

NEW LEAF, A*** (1971) 102m Howard W. Koch-Hillard Elkins/PAR c

Walter Matthau *(Henry Graham)*, Elaine May *(Henrietta Lowell)*, Jack Weston *(Andrew McPherson)*, George Rose *(Harold, Henry Graham's Butler)*, William Redfield *(Beckett)*, James Coco *(Uncle Harry)*, Graham Jarvis *(Bo)*, Doris Roberts *(Mrs. Traggert)*, Rose Arrick *(Gloria Cunliffe)*, Renee Taylor *(Sally Hart)*, Mildred Clinton *(Mrs. Heinrich)*, Marc Gordon *(John)*, Fred Stewart *(Mr. Van Rensaeller)*, David Doyle *(Mel)*, Jess Osuna *(Frank)*, Ida Berlin *(Maid)*, Carol Morley *(Girl at Charity Ball)*.

An often funny film that might have been funnier if anyone ever saw the original version. May, who was tripling as history's first female star-writer-director, attempted to have her credits removed from the picture, as it did not reflect her work after the studio recut it. In her movie, Matthau gets away with murder, disposing of Weston and William Hickey, a blackmailer, who was entirely cut from the movie. Another scene that was cut showed May fantasizing herself as a sexy woman whom men cannot leave alone. The film she handed in ran over 180 minutes and since this one is only 102 minutes, we can only guess what was excised. Nevertheless, and despite her rancor, the picture was delightful and did well with critics and audiences alike. Matthau is a ne'er-do-well who has exhausted the huge trust fund he was left at his father's death. When his attorney, Redfield, tells him that, Matthau is understandably shaken and wonders how he can maintain his high-flying life style, which includes a plush Manhattan town house and a live-in man, Rose. There is only one solution, proposed by Rose, and that is to marry a rich woman. Matthau is against that but soon acquiesces when he sees that it's the only way out. Since he has no money to stay in the swim of things, Matthau borrows several thousand from his hated uncle, Coco, who insists that Matthau pledge everything he owns as collateral for the loan. Matthau strives to find a suitable wife but has no success until he is at a tea with his pal, Jarvis, and meets ungainly and myopic May, a botanist with no sense of style or grace, but who is the heir to a huge fortune. Matthau begins wooing the woman and she agrees to marry him, despite the pleas of her attorney, Weston, who is a crook in his own right. May pays off Coco before the service and they are wed. Once ensconced in her huge estate, Matthau sees why Weston was against the union. The poor, naive May is being bilked by Weston, who is in cahoots with her servants, led by Roberts as the mansion's major domo. Matthau has the servants fired and he takes over her financial dealings. His plan is to kill May when they make her yearly trip to the mountains. She found a unique fern on their honeymoon and named it after her adoring husband, but that doesn't stop him from continuing with his plot to get rid of her. They go off to the mountains and the canoe they are in is overturned. She is not a swimmer and hangs on to a jutting rock as he swims to safety on the shore. He tells her that if she lets go, the rapids will take her to a safe pool below where he'll rescue her. (The truth is, of course, that she'll probably drown once she takes her hands off the rock.) She believes him and is soon being rushed to her death. Then Matthau sees a fern on the shore, the same kind of plant life that she named after him, and he is overcome with guilt about what he's done, so he dives into the rolling water and saves May. They get to the shore and he realizes that he has now put himself into her hands forever. It's a throwback to the screwball comedies of the 1930s and often surpasses many of them in comic invention and wit. Lots of laughs and several excellent observations on greed. There is no music credit as the score of OH DAD, POOR DAD, MAMA'S HUNG YOU IN THE CLOSET AND I'M FEELIN' SO SAD was transferred, almost entirely, to this movie. That score was written by Neal Hefti and worked better here than it did there. It's bizarre and daft and cockeyed but the ending is a bit muddled. Ahthough "G" rated by the MPAA, the motivations of Matthau's character are evil enough to make this questionable for tots.

p, Joe Manduke; d&w, Elaine May (based on the short story "The Green Heart" by Jack Ritchie); ph, Gayne Rescher (Movielab Color); ed, Frederick Steinkamp, Donald Guidice; prod d, Richard Fried; art d, Warren Clymer; set d, Jack Wright; cos, Anthea Sylbert; makeup, Jack Petty, Irving Buchman.

Comedy **(PR:C-O MPAA:G)**

NEW LIFE STYLE, THE*½ (1970, Ger.) 91m CCC-Filmkunst/Dot c (HEISSER SAND AUF SYLT; AKA: JUST TO BE LOVED)

Horst Tappert *(Walter Bergman)*, Renate von Holt *(Renate)*, Alexy Burg *(Alexy)*, Ursula Moot [Mood] *(Uschi)*, Jennifer Stone *(Ava)*, Rocky Graziano, Jake La Motta *(Guest Stars)*, Charlotte Kerr, Babsi Zimmermann, Rolf Eden, Reinhold Timm, Andre Esterhazy, Francis Heym, Jurgen Knop.

Prominent businessman Tappert gets a taste of "free love" and discovers that he can't purge himself of his old moralistic hangups. This attempt to show traditional values in conflict with those of the late 1960s seems trite in retrospect. Savage re-edited this film—originally released in 1968 in West Germany—bringing new actors onto the project, adding several scenes, and cutting others. Among the notable additions to the recut versions were former middleweight boxing champions Rocky Graziano and Jake La Motta.

p, Peter Savage; d, Savage (English sequences), Jerzy Macc; w, Savage (English sequences), Macc, Jurgen Knop; ph, Bob Baldwin (English sequences), Bob Klebig (DeLuxe Color); m, Danny DiMinno, Horace Diaz, Athena Hosey (English version), Maris Musik.

Drama **(PR:O MPAA:NR)**

NEW LOVE*½ (1968, Chile) 100m Sudamericana/Continental c (LA REVOLUCION DE LAS FLORES)

Josephine Guevars, Giovanni Carelli.

A Chilean picture dealing with a group of hippies who go about burning draft cards and passports, symbolically painting the town white, and living "freely" on the beach. Their excesses eventually lead to some hand-slapping by officials, both local and federal. Story has no clear plot line and the movie's only intent seems to be to show off a different type of life style. But this isn't even done well, as the kids who are doing the portraying don't seem very committed. The nice photography of Vina de Mar, a seaside resort town, adds some interest to this otherwise dull picture.

d&w, Alvaro Covacevich; ph, Andres Martorell (Eastmancolor); m, Covacevich.

Drama **(PR:O MPAA:NR)**

NEW MEXICO** (1951) 76m UA c

Lew Ayres (Capt. Hunt), Marilyn Maxwell (Cherry), Robert Hutton (Lt. Vermont), Andy Devine (Sgt. Garrity), Raymond Burr (Pvt. Anderson), Jeff Corey (Coyote), Lloyd Corrigan (Judge Wilcox), Verna Felton (Mrs. Fenway), Ted de Corsia (Acuma, Indian Chief), John Hoyt (Sgt. Harrison), Donald Buka (Pvt. Van Vechton), Robert Osterloh (Pvt. Parsons), Ian MacDonald (Pvt. Daniels), William Tannen (Pvt. Cheever), Arthur Lowe, Jr. (Pvt. Finnegan), Bob Duncan (Cpl. Mack), Jack Kelly (Pvt. Clifton), Allen Matthews (Pvt. Vale), Jack Briggs (Pvt. Lindley), Peter Price (Chia-Kong), Walter Greaza (Col. McComb), Hans Conried (Lincoln), Ralph Volkie (1st Rider), Bud Rae (Stage Driver).

Routine "soldiers versus Indian" action film has Ayres as the captain of a cavalry unit sent to stop an Indian uprising. The Indians, lead by chief de Corsia, are upset over the white man's breaking a treaty de Corsia had signed with President Lincoln. Though Ayres is friends with de Corsia and sympathetic toward his demands, he must still follow orders. The cavalry unit holes up on top of a mesa, is surrounded by Indians, and a murderous battle ensues. The direction handles the action sequences extremely well, putting more than the usual emphasis on the violence and gore of the battle. Maxwell sings "Soldier, Soldier, Won't You Marry Me."

p, Irving Allen, Joseph Justman; d, Irving Reis; w, Max Trell; ph, Jack Greenhalgh, William Snyder (Anscocolor); m, Lucian Maroweck; ed, Louis Sackin.

Western (PR:A MPAA:NR)

NEW MONSTERS, THE (SEE: VIVA ITALIA, 1978, Ital.)

NEW MOON*½ (1930) 78m MGM bw

Lawrence Tibbett (Lt. Michael Petroff), Grace Moore (Princess Tanya Strogoff), Adolphe Menjou (Gov. Boris Brusiloff), Roland Young (Count Strogoff), Gus Shy (Potkin), Emily Fitzroy (Countess Anastia Strogoff).

Screen adaptation of this Romberg-Hammerstein operetta was a costly and lavish production that featured the singing of Moore and Tibbett. Story takes place in Russia where Moore, a princess, and Tibbett, a lieutenant in the army, meet on a boat and fall in love. Problems arise because Moore is to marry the governor Tibbett has been sent to serve under. Menjou, as the governor, solves the conflict between himself and Tibbett by sending the soldier to an outpost known for its rugged treatment of commanding officers. Tibbett proves a worthy soldier, though, and despite being wounded and presumed dead, he manages to come back to romance Moore. The leads, Tibbett and Moore, have wonderful singing voices, but little acting ability. Songs include: "Lover Come Back to Me," "One Kiss," "Stout-Hearted Men," "Wanting You," "Marianne," "Funny Little Sailor Men" (Oscar Hammerstein II, Sigmund Romberg). Following the release of NEW MOON, MGM's Irving Thalberg felt Moore was gaining too much weight to be an effective movie love interest and her contract was allowed to lapse. She went on to Columbia where she enjoyed her greatest successes.

d, Jack Conway; w, Sylvia Thalberg, Frank Butler, Cyril Hume (based on the operetta by Oscar Hammerstein II, Sigmund Romberg, Frank Mandel, Lawrence Schwab); ph, Oliver T. Marsh; ed, Margaret Booth.

Musical (PR:A MPAA:NR)

NEW MOON** (1940) 105m MGM bw

Jeanette MacDonald (Marianne de Beaumanoir), Nelson Eddy (Charles Mission, Duc de Villiers), Mary Boland (Valerie de Rossac), George Zucco (Vicomte de Ribaud), H.B. Warner (Father Michel), Richard "Dick" Purcell (Alexander), Stanley Fields (Tambour), Bunty Cutler (Julie the Maid), Grant Mitchell (Governor of New Orleans), Raymond Walker (Coco), John Miljan (Pierre Brugnon, Overseer), Ivan Simpson (Guizot), George Irving (Ship Captain), Edwin Maxwell (Capt. de Jean), Paul E. Burns (Guard on Ship), Trevor Bardette (Foulette), LeRoy Mason (Grant), William Tannen (Pierre), Cecil Cunningham (Governor's Wife), Claude King (Mons. Dubois), Rafael Storm (De Piron), Winifred Harris (Lady), Buster Keaton (Prisoner, "LuLu"), Robert Warwick (Commissar), Sarah Edwards (Marquise della Rosa), George Lloyd (Quartermaster), Gayne Whitman (Mate), Jean Fenwick (Woman), George Magrill (Guard), Christian J. Frank, Arthur Belasco, Edward Hearn, Nick Copeland, Gino Corrado, Fred Graham, Ralph Dunn, Harry Strang, Ray Teal, Ted Oliver (Bondsmen), Frank Remsden (Man), Ed O'Neil (Lookout), Warren Rock (Mate), Jewell Jordan (Woman), Joe Yule (Maurice), Max Marx (Officer), Alden [Stephen] Chase (Citizen), Jack Perrin (Officer), Claire Rochelle (Drunken Girl), Frank Elliott, Kenneth Gibson, Victor Kendall, Gerald Fielding, Bea Nigro, Hillary Brooke (Guests), Dorothy Granger (Fat Bridesmaid), June Gittelson (Madeline), David Alison (Troubadour), Joe Dominguez (Wounded Bondsman), Florence Shirley (Guest), Forbes Murray (Commandant).

Although filled with fade-in-to-fade-out music, NEW MOON left much to be desired in many departments. It had nothing to do with the Norma Talmadge silent of the same name made in 1919; instead it was the remake of the Lawrence Tibbett-Grace Moore 1930's film, although that one switched the locale from the French Revolution of the late 1700s to the Russian Revolution of the early 1900s, and yet, for some dumb reason, they renamed that picture PARISIAN BELLE when they sold it to television. It borrowed heavily from the plot of 1935's NAUGHTY MARIETTA and audiences sensed that. Eighteen years had passed between the stage versions of "Naughty Marietta" and "New Moon," so the New York critics didn't do their usual carping, but only five years had elapsed 'twixt Eddy and MacDonald's pairing in the former, and the similarities are all too evident. The musical, titled "The New Moon," opened for a road show tryout in Philadelphia at the end of 1927, but soon closed for extensive rewrites. It finally got to Broadway in September, 1928, and stayed for a hefty 509 performances, starring Evelyn Herbert and Robert Halliday in the MacDonald and Eddy roles. It's 1788 and MacDonald has left Paris for New Orleans where she is to take over a vast plantation that has been bequeathed to her by a late uncle. On the same ship is a horde of white slaves who have been sold into servitude. One of them is Eddy, a duke, who posed as an indentured servant in order to escape the wrath of the king

who would like to see his head fall into a wicker basket. MacDonald is the toast of the ship, having smitten King, another passenger, although her aunt, Boland (who lives vicariously through MacDonald), is not impressed by King. The ship's captain asks if MacDonald will sing for the men in the hold and she does, but the men outshout her in their disdain for her song. Eddy and some of the others have been sold to MacDonald's foreman, and when the two meet, she is suitably impressed by his courtly ways. He tells her that he had once been employed by the Duc de Villiers (himself) and can buttle with the best. Eddy's true identity is soon uncovered when evil viscount Zucco arrives. The men decide to make a run for it, and, with MacDonald's help (she is already enamored of Eddy), they free all the other white slaves and go off to the ship that lies at anchor to steal it for their escape. There's a battle and Eddy and his pals win and sail out to sea. Zucco must wait for another ship to take him to France, and when it arrives, MacDonald and Boland board it to return to Paris. The ship, The New Moon, has 100 brides aboard who are to be delivered to Martinique so a stop must be made there before going east on the Atlantic. On their way, the ship is attacked by pirates headed by, you guessed it, Eddy. The women on The New Moon were to be brides of the colonists on Martinique, but they like Eddy's crew and decide to stay with them when the boat lands on an island and Eddy sets up a new nation. MacDonald doesn't betray her affection for Eddy until she notes that the remaining unmarried women all have eyes for his body. Eddy suggests that they get married almost as a joke and she agrees, although their marriage is in name only, for the time being. A French ship is spotted on the horizon and Eddy makes the decision to turn himself in and face madame guillotine, rather than put any of his men in jeopardy. It's here that MacDonald realizes Eddy is a neat guy, besides being a helluva singer, so she decides to stick by him. The ship arrives with the news that the French Revolution has occurred and that Eddy is no longer a fugitive and is now a hero. Eddy and MacDonald clutch each other, look deep into their souls, and the picture ends. Eddy and MacDonald had done a few blockbusters and the MGMoguls thought, "Hey, if we make this much loot with the two, we can double our cash by starring them with others." They were wrong and after MacDonald's BROADWAY SERENADE (with non-singer Lew Ayres) and Eddy's LET FREEDOM RING (costarring Virginia Bruce) and BALALAIKA (with Ilona Massey), they were teamed for this again. Buster Keaton was billed and must have had a larger role because he is barely seen in a crowd here. MacDonald's brother-in-law, Rock, does a bit, as does Mickey Rooney's father, Yule. The many songs have little to do with the plot, which moves along as quickly as a snail with arthritis under Leonard's direction. (There is some talk about Leonard having called in veteran W.S. Van Dyke to help out directing, but we couldn't get corroboration of that.) By the time this picture was made, Eddy was already getting a bit thick in the middle and most of his derring-do was more like derring-don't. Lovely songs in a lame setting. Songs include: "Dance Your Cares Away" (Sigmund Romberg, sung by chorus), "Stranger in Paris" (Romberg, sung by Jeanette MacDonald), "The Way They Do It in Paris" (Romberg, sung by MacDonald, Nelson Eddy, chorus), "Lover Come Back" (Romberg, Oscar Hammerstein II, sung by MacDonald, Eddy, reprise by MacDonald), "Shoes" (Romberg, sung by Eddy), "Softly as in a Morning Sunrise" (Romberg, Hammerstein, sung by Eddy), "One Kiss" (Romberg, Hammerstein, sung by MacDonald), "Troubles of the World," "No More Weeping," "Wailing" (traditional songs, sung by chorus), "Wanting You," (Romberg, Hammerstein, sung by Eddy, MacDonald), "Stout Hearted Men" (Romberg, Hammerstein, sung by Eddy, chorus), "Ombre Ma Fui" (George Frederic Handel), "Marianne" (Romberg, Hammerstein, sung by Eddy, MacDonald, chorus), "The Marseillaise" (Claude Rouget de Lisle, sung by chorus), "Bayou Trouble Tree" (Hebert Stothart, D. Jones). (The songs in which only Romberg is credited are based on melodies from songs he did for the stage version; the lyricist's credit on the new versions in uncertain.)

p&d, Robert Z. Leonard; w, Jacques Deval, Robert Arthur (based on the operetta by Sigmund Romberg, Oscar Hammerstein II, Frank Mandel, Lawrence Schwab, Sigmund Romberg); ph, William Daniels; m, Romberg; ed, Harold F. Kress; md, Herbert Stothart; art d, Cedric Gibbons, Eddie Imazu; set d, Edwin B. Willis; cos, Adrian, Gile Steele; ch, Val Raset; makeup, Jack Dawn.

Musical (PR:A MPAA:NR)

NEW MORALS FOR OLD** (1932) 74m MGM bw

Robert Young (Ralph Thomas), Margaret Perry (Phyllis Thomas), Lewis Stone (Mr. Thomas), Laura Hope Crews (Mrs. Thomas), Myrna Loy (Myra), David Newell (Duff), Jean Hersholt (Hallett), Ruth Selwyn (Estelle), Kathryn Crawford (Zoe), Louise Closser Hale (Mrs. Warburton), Mitchell Lewis (Bodvin, French Artist), Elizabeth Patterson (Aunty Doe), Lillian Harmer (Maid).

Problems between the generations serve as the theme for this screen adaptation of a John Van Druten play, which proved more successful on stage than in film. Young and Perry are the children of Stone and Crews who rebel against their parents' staid conservatism. Young's desire is to be a painter, so he goes to Paris to study under a great artist. When he learns he really has no talent, he returns home for a more traditional life style. While in Paris he manages a quick affair with fellow tenant Loy, which doesn't amount to much. Perry gets herself involved with a married man, who eventually divorces his wife and marries Perry. She then goes about structuring her life in much the same way as her parents. The moral of the story seems to be that no matter how hard they fight it, children will eventually emulate their parents. Performances are all fairly standard, though Stone and Crews are quite believable as the puzzled parents. The film was made during the period in which MGM's Irving Thalberg had vowed to spare no expense to get top writing and production for his films. Britisher Van Druten spent a brief time in Hollywood to assist with the adaptation of his play for the screen, but it didn't seem to help.

d, Charles F. Brabin; w, Zelda Sears, Wanda Tuchock (based on the play "After All" by John Van Druten); ph, John Mescal; ed, William S. Gray.

Drama (PR:A MPAA:NR)

NEW MOVIETONE FOLLIES OF 1930, THE (SEE: FOX MOVIETONE FOLLIES OF 1930, 1930)

NEW ONE-ARMED SWORDSMAN, THE (SEE: TRIPLE IRONS, 1973, Hong Kong)

NEW ORLEANS** (1929) 68m TIF-Tone bw

Ricardo Cortez (*Jim Morley*), William Collier, Jr. (*Billy Slade*), Alma Bennett (*Marie Cartier*).

Collier and Cortez are friends pursuing the same girl, Bennett. The lady has expensive tastes and Cortez successfully woos her with cash stolen from his employer. Jockey Collier sets out to win a big race to get money so that Cortez can replace what he stole, but Bennett takes off with the winnings. Cortez gets a prison term, then the boys renew their friendship. The film was 20 percent dialog, and Bennett, who had been making silent films since 1922, proved to be very appealing as the *femme fatale*. The right role might have brought her to stardom, but it was not to be as she made only a few more films and shorts before retiring in 1930.

d, Reginald Barker; w, John Francis Natteford, Fred Hatton, Fanny Hatton; ph, Harry Jackson; m, Irving Talbot; ed, Robert Kern; m/l, Hugo Reisenfeld, Ted Shapiro, John Raphael.

Drama (PR:A MPAA:NR)

NEW ORLEANS** (1947) 89m UA bw

Dorothy Patrick (*Miralee Smith*), Irene Rich (*Mrs. Smith*), John Alexander (*Col. McArdle*), Arturo de Cordova (*Nick Duquesne*), Billie Holiday (*Endie*), Richard Hageman (*Henri Ferber*), Marjorie Lord (*Grace Volselle*), Shelley Winters (*Secretary*), Louis Armstrong and His All Stars, Kid Ory, Zutty Singleton, Barney Bigard, Bud Scott, Red Callender, Charlie Beale, Woody Herman, Meade Lux Lewis.

The music is the real star of this otherwise ludicrous fictionalized account of the birth and rise of jazz. Forgettable story opens in New Orleans where de Cordova runs a gambling den with Armstrong and his band providing the entertainment. Patrick is a high society lady who falls for de Cordova and Armstrong's music, though her parents disapprove of both. The rest of the movie recounts de Cordova's movements from Chicago to New York, all the while attempting to sell the public on this new music. Naturally he succeeds, even convincing Patrick's parents that jazz is terrific. The insipid plot isn't aided by unconvincing performances from the leads, but Armstrong rises above it all with his music and engaging screen presence. The movie is also notable for the appearance of Holiday. The great blues singer's film career would encompass only this film and a 1935 short entitled "Symphony in Black," though her life would be the subject of LADY SINGS THE BLUES (1972). Musical numbers in NEW ORLEANS include: "Do You Know What It Means to Miss New Orleans" (Edgar De Lange, Louis Alter; performed by Armstrong, his band, Holiday, Herman, Patrick); "Endie" (performed by Armstrong, Herman); "The Blues are Brewin'" (Alter, De Lange; performed by Armstrong, Holiday, Herman); "Where the Blues Were Born in New Orleans" (Bob Carleton, Cliff Dixon; performed by Armstrong); "New Orleans Stomp" (Joe "King" Oliver; performed by Patrick); "West End Blues" (Oliver, Clarence Williams; performed by Armstrong); "Buddy Bolden's Blues" (Jelly Roll Morton; performed by Armstrong); Dippermouth Blues" (Oliver, performed by Armstrong); "Shim-Me-Sha-Wabble," "Basin Street Blues," "Mahogany Hall Stomp" (all by Spencer Williams and performed by Armstrong); "Honky Tonk Train Blues" (performed by Lewis); "Farewell to Storyville" (Williams; performed by Armstrong, Holiday); "Maryland My Maryland" (James Ryder Randall, Walter de Mapes; performed by Armstrong).

p, Jules Levey; d, Arthur Lubin; w, Elliot Paul, Dick Irving Hyland (based on a story by Paul, Herbert, J. Biberman); ph, Lucien Andriot; ed, Bernard W. Burton; md, Nat Finston; art d, Rudi Feld.

Musical (PR:A MPAA:NR)

NEW ORLEANS AFTER DARK** (1958) 69m AA bw

Stacy Harris (*Detective Vic Beaujac*), Louis Sirgo (*Detective John Conroy*), Ellen Moore (*Jean Conroy*), Tommy Pelle (*Pat Conroy*), Wilson Bourg (*Nick Livorno*), Harry Wood (*Carl*), Johnny Aladdin (*Fighter*), Jeanine Thomas (*Sandra*), Leo Zinser (*Caprini*), Kathryn Copponex (*Mary Sherman*), Bob Samuels (*Pete*), Steve Lord (*Blackie*), Louis Gurvich (*Omega*), Frank Fiasconaro (*Solitaire*), Allan Binkley (*Bartender*), Claude Evans (*Frank*), Dottie Lee (*Stripper*), La Vergne Smith (*Herself*), Bill Matthews.

Competent little police programmer shot on location in New Orleans with a story "torn from the files" of the New Orleans Police Department. Harris and Sirgo play two tough detectives who take the viewer on a tour of the seedier side of the city while they pursue various cases. Climax sees the intrepid duo busting a ring of dope peddlers whose nefarious activities had been infecting the city for some time. Popular (at the time) New Orleans nightclub entertainer Smith plays herself in a brief scene.

p, Eric Sayers; d, John Sledge; w, Frank Phares; ph, Willis Winford; ed, John Hemel.

Crime (PR:C MPAA:NR)

NEW ORLEANS UNCENSORED** (1955) 76m COL bw (GB: RIOT ON PIER 6)

Arthur Franz (*Dan Corbett*), Beverly Garland (*Marie Reilly*), Helene Stanton (*Alma Mae*), Michael Ansara (*Zero Saxon*), Stacy Harris (*Scrappy Durant*), William Henry (*Joe Reilly*), Michael Granger (*Jack Petty*), Frankie Ray (*Deuce*), Edwin Stafford Nelson (*Charlie*), Mike Mazurki (*Mike*), Ralph Dupas (*Himself*), Pete Herman (*Himself*), Judge Walter B. Hamlin (*Wayne Brandon*), Al Chittenden (*Himself*), Joseph L. Scheuering, Victor Schiro, Howard L. Dey.

A tale of the New Orleans underworld, told in semi-documentary fashion and casting local citizens in several roles. Franz plays a Navy veteran who comes to the title city to get a job as a dock worker. It isn't long before he discovers all sorts of criminal activities, masterminded by Ansara. When a friend is murdered, Franz goes to police and is persuaded to infiltrate the gang. His efforts succeed in nabbing the criminals and cleaning up the docks. Liberal use of the New Orleans docks and other city sights as film settings provides some authenticity to the movie, but the hackneyed story reduces the picture to standard fare.

p, Sam Katzman; d, William Castle; w, Orville Hampton, Lewis Meltzer (based on the story "Riot On Pier 6" by Hampton); ph, Henry Freulich; ed, Gene Havlick, Al Clark; md, Mischa Bakaleinikoff; art d, Paul Palmentola.

Crime Drama (PR:A MPAA:NR)

NEW TEACHER, THE*½ (1941, USSR) 85m Leningrad Film Studio/ Artkino bw

Boris Chirkov (*Stephan Lautin*), Tamara Makarova (*Agrafena*), Pavel Volkov (*Ivan Lautin*), Vera Pomerant (*Praskovia Lautin*), L. Shapalina (*Maria Lautin*), V. Telegina (*Stepanida Lautin*), M. Ekaterinsky (*Remizov*), Ivan Nazarov (*Uncle Semyon*).

This Soviet picture takes the basic Hollywood "boy-meets-girl" and "rags-to-riches" staples and does nothing new with them. Chirkov plays a high-minded peasant youth who rises above his humble beginnings and also romances, Makarova. He turns her off by making a proposal too quickly, but after spending numerous sleepless nights, she reconsiders and accepts. The film is based on the winning entry from a Soviet writing contest. (In Russian; English subtitles.)

d&w, S. Gerasimov; ph, V. Yakovlev; m, V. Pushkov.

Comedy/Drama (PR:A MPAA:NR)

NEW WINE** (1941) 84m Gloria/UA bw (GB: THE GREAT AWAKENING)

Ilona Massey (*Anna*), Alan Curtis (*Franz Schubert*), Binnie Barnes (*Countess*), Albert Basserman (*Beethoven*), Billy Gilbert (*Poldi*), Sterling Holloway (*Bookkeeper*), Richard Carle (*Hasslinger*), John Qualen (*Clerk*), Barnett Parker (*Duke*), Sig Arno (*Maestro*), Gilbert Emery (*Principal*), Marion Martin (*Mitzi*), Forrest Tucker (*Moritz*), George O'Hanlon (*Peppi*), Maynard Holmes (*Wilhelm*), Erno Verebes (*Karl*), Paul Sutton (*Foreman*), Lou Merrill (*Soldier*), Ann Stewart (*Young Girl at Carnegie Hall*), Kenneth Ferrill (*Young Man*), Lane Allen, Patricia Farr.

A brief segment from the life of the famed composer Franz Schubert is the basis for this film. Curtis, as the composer, flees Vienna to avoid induction into the military. He takes refuge at the estate of Barnes, where he meets and falls in love with Massey, the manager of the estate. They return to Vienna, and Massey concentrates on making sure Curtis receives the recognition he is due, going so far as a meeting with Beethoven (Basserman). Curtis takes a job as a schoolteacher in order to support his future wife, but Massey returns to Hungary to allow the composer to devote himself to his music. The story is intertwined with a performance of a Schubert symphony at Carnegie Hall, where a romance between a young boy and girl in the audience is beginning. There are eight Schubert compositions featured in this picture, making it a worthwhile experience. The direction moves along at a smooth pace, but Massey and Curtis are overly stiff. Basserman provides a good depiction of Beethoven. Massey sings "Ave Maria."

p, William Sekely; d, Reinhold Schunzel; w, Howard Estabrook, Nicholas Jory; m, Franz Schubert; ph, John Mescall; ed, James E. Smith; md, Arthur Guttmann; cos, Rene Hubert.

Drama (PR:A MPAA:NR)

NEW YEAR'S EVIL zero (1980) 90m Cannon c

Roz Kelly (*Diane Sullivan*), Kip Niven (*Richard Sullivan*), Louisa Moritz (*Sally*), Chris Wallace (*Lt. Clayton*), Jed Mills (*Ernie*), Grant Cramer (*Derek Sullivan*), Taafe O'Connell (*Jane*), Jon Greene (*Sgt. Greene*), Anita Crane (*Lisa*), Alice Dhanifu (*Yvonne*), John London (*Floor Manager*), Barry Gibberman (*Hotel Guest*), Teri Copley (*Teenage Girl*), Jennie Anderson (*Nurse Robbie*), Wendy-Sue Rosloff (*Makeup Girl*), John Alderman (*Dr. Reed*), Jerry Chambers (*Clerk*), Mike Mihalich (*Policeman at Hotel*), Jerry Zanitsch, Mark L. Rosen (*Drunks*), Bob Jarvis, Richard E. Kald (*Policemen*), Linda Terito (*Stunt Woman*), Mark de Frani (*Teenage Boy*), Richard Brown (*Swamper*), Julie Kaye Towery (*Space Girl*), Tim Cutt (*Ambulance Attendant (Don Grenough (Punker)*), Ryan Collier, Mark Korngute (*Bar Hustlers*), Celena Allen, Edward Jackson, Bill Blair, Clarisse Kotkin, Roxanne Orbis, Michelle Waxman, Ricky Israel, Cynthia Macarthur, Justin Robin (*Punkers in Car*), Randy Gould, Karen Mills, Jodie Mann, Adrienne Upton (*Phone Girls*), Doug Le Mille, Lyle Pearcy, Jim Amormino, Larry Lindsey (*Clayton's Men*).

Another mad slasher film from the folks at Cannon, this one starring Niven as the guy who hasn't had a very good year and who attempts to vent his frustrations by killing one person per hour on New Year's Eve. Kelly, of TV's "Happy Days," is a disk jockey who is hosting a punk rock party on the murderous day, and Niven keeps calling her to tell her about his latest execution. Climax has Niven crashing the party and unsuccessfully trying to do away with Kelly. A horrid film, made worse by a grating punk rock score.

p, Menahem Golan, Yoram Globus; d, Emmett Alston; w, Leonard Neubauer (based on a story by Alston, Neubauer); m, Laurin Rinder, W. Michael Lewis.

Horror Cas. (PR:O MPAA:R)

NEW YORK (SEE: HALLELUJAH, I'M A BUM 1933)

NEW YORK APPELLE SUPER DRAGON (SEE: SECRET AGENT SUPER DRAGON, 1966)

NEW YORK CONFIDENTIAL** (1955) 87m WB bw

Broderick Crawford (*Charlie Lupo*), Richard Conte (*Nick Magellan*), Marilyn Maxwell (*Iris Palmer*), Anne Bancroft (*Kathy Lupo*), J. Carrol Naish (*Ben Dagajanian*), Onslow Stevens (*Johnny Achilles*), Barry Kelley (*Frawley*), Mike Mazurki (*Arnie*

Wendler), Celia Lovsky *(Mama Lupo)*, Herbert Heyes *(James Marshall)*, Steven Geray *(Morris Franklin)*, Bill Phillips *(Whitey)*, Henry Kulky *(Gino)*, Nestor Paiva *(Martinelli)*, Joe Vitale *(Batista)*, Carl Milletaire *(Sumak)*, William Forrest *(Paul Williamson)*, Ian Keith *(Waluska)*, Charles Evans *(Judge Kincaid)*, Mickey Simpson *(Hartmann)*, Tom Powers *(District Attorney Rossi)*, Lee Trent *(Ferrari)*, Lennie Bremen *(Larry)*, John Doucette *(Shorty)*, Frank Ferguson *(Dr. Ludlow)*, Hope Landin *(Mrs. Wesley)*, Fortunio Bonanova *(Senor)*.

Purportedly approved by the New York City Anti-Crime Committee as a testament to its authenticity, NEW YORK CONFIDENTIAL is, historical accuracy notwithstanding, a fine, solid expose on organized crime. Crawford plays the boss of the New York mob, a powerful member of the "board of directors" of a nationwide criminal empire that has begun dipping its fingers into legitimate business and politics. When a problem arises among the mob rank and file, the powers that be decide to eliminate the troublemaker. Stevens, head of the Chicago chapter, dispatches his best hit man, Conte, to do the job. Conte makes a great impression on Crawford because of the speed and finesse he demonstrate on the hit, so the New York boss makes the young killer his bodyguard. Treating Conte as if he were a son, Crawford swiftly moves the assassin up the ranks and even tries to force a romance between his protege and his daughter, Bancroft. Bancroft despises her father's business and will have nothing to do with it. Meanwhile, the mob's efforts at grabbing a foothold in the oil industry collapse when their man in Washington turns state's evidence. Despite Crawford's protests, the board wants the traitor killed in New York City. Reluctantly Crawford sends three hoods to do the job, and, although they accomplish the task, too many clues are left behind. Angry over the botched job, Crawford orders Conte to kill the hit men. Conte eliminates two of the killers, but the third gets away and spills the beans about Crawford to the police. The crisis explodes in Crawford's face when the syndicate decides that he must take the fall to protect the rest of the crime cartel. His life collapsing around him, Crawford tries to salvage his family and position in the mob by forcing a marriage between Conte and his daughter. Determined not to continue the tradition of murder, crime, and corruption that has plagued the family name, Bancroft commits suicide. Destroyed, Crawford turns against the mob and decides to talk. The mob, however, has anticipated this move and dispatches a hesitant Conte to kill Crawford. Conte swallows any reservations about the job and murders his former boss. Though pleased with his work, the syndicate takes no chances and Conte is killed as well. Fast-paced, grim, and realistic, NEW YORK CONFIDENTIAL is filled with memorable performances from a solid cast of professionals. Crawford brings a brutish eloquence to his role, and Conte is outstanding as the talented newcomer who actually seems to have reservations about his work. Director Rouse was no stranger to the crime genre, having co-written D.O.A. in 1950 and directed THE WELL in 1951, both films which contain fresh twists and approaches to material that had become a bit tired by the 1950s.

p, Clarence Greene; d, Russell Rouse; w, Greene, Rouse (based on a book by Jack Lait, Lee Mortimer); ph, Edward Fitzgerald; m, Joseph Mullendore; ed, Grant Whytock; prod d, Fernando Carrere; set d, Joseph W. Holland; cos, Ernest Newman, Norman Martien; spec eff, Willis Cook; makeup, Harry Thomas.

Crime **(PR:C MPAA:NR)**

NEW YORK, NEW YORK*½** (1977) 155m UA c

Robert De Niro *(Jimmy Doyle)*, Liza Minnelli *(Francine Evans)*, Lionel Stander *(Tony Harwell)*, Mary Kay Place *(Bernice)*, George Memmoli *(Nicky)*, Murray Moston *(Horace Morris)*, Barry Primus *(Paul Wilson)*, Georgie Auld *(Frankie Harte)*, Dick Miller *(Palm Club Owner)*, Lenny Gaines *(Artie Kirks)*, Clarence Clemons *(Cecil Powell)*, Kathi McGinnis *(Ellen Flannery)*, Norman Palmer, Dimitri Logothetis *(Desk Clerks)*, Adam David Winkler *(Jimmy Doyle, Jr.)*, Frank Sivera *(Eddie Di Muzio)*, Diahnne Abbott *(Harlem Club Singer)*, Margo Winkler *(Argumentative Woman)*, Steven Prince *(Record Producer)*, Don Calfa *(Gilbert)*, Bernie Kuby *(Justice of the Peace)*, Selma Archerd *(Wife of Justice of the Peace)*, Bill Baldwin *(Moonlit Terrace Announcer)*, Mary Lindsay *(Hat Check Girl in Meadows)*, Jon Cutler *(Musician in Frankie Harte Band)*, Nicky Blair *(Cab Driver)*, Casey Kasem, Bill McMillan *(Disk Jockeys)*, Jay Salerno *(Bus Driver)*, William Tole *(Tommy Dorsey)*, Sydney Guilaroff *(Hairdresser)*, Peter Savage *(Horace Morris' Assistant)*, Gene Castle *(Dancing Sailor)*, Louie Guss *(Fowler)*, Shera Danese *(Doyle's Girl in Major Chord)*, David Nichols *(Arnold Trench)*, Harry Northup *(Alabama)*, Marty Zagon *(South Bend Ballroom Manager)*, Timothy Blake *(Nurse)*, Betty Cole *(Charwoman)*, De Forest Covan *(Porter)*, Phil Gray *(Trombone Player in Jimmy Doyle's Band)*, Roosevelt Smith *(Bouncer in Major Chord)*, Bruce L. Lucoff *(Cab Driver)*, Bill Phillips Murry *(Harlem Club Waiter)*, Clint Arnold *(Palm Club Trombone Player)*, Richard Alan Berk *(Palm Club Drummer)*, Jack R. Clinton *(Palm Club Bartender)*, Wilfred R. Middlebrooks *(Palm Club Bass Player)*, Jake Vernon Porter *(Palm Club Trumpet Player)*, Nat Pierce *(Palm Club Piano Player)*, Manuel Escobosa *(Fighter in Moonlit Terrace)*, Susan Kay Hunt, Teryn Jenkins *(Moonlit Terrace Girls)*, Mardik Martin *(Well-Wisher in Moonlit Terrace)*, Leslie Summers *(Woman in Black in Moonlit Terrace)*, Brock Michaels *(Man at Table in Moonlit Terrace)*, Booty Reed, Washington Rucker *(Musicians at Hiring Hall)*, David Armstrong, Robert Buckingham, Eddie Garrett, Nico Stevens *(Reporters)*, Peter Fain *(Greeter in Up Club)*, Angelo Lamonea *(Waiter in Up Club)*, Charles A. Tamburro, Wallace McCleskey *(Bouncers in Up Club)*, Ronald Prince *(Dancer in Up Club)*, Robert Petersen *(Photographer)*, Richard Raymond *(Railroad Conductor)*, Hank Robinson *(Francine's Bodyguard)*, Harold Ross *(Cab Driver)*, Eddie Smith *(Man in Bathroom in Harlem Club)*, Joey Forman *(Argumentative Man)*.

A Martin Scorsese film is like eating Chinese food: even when it's just okay, it's still pretty good. This picture was booted around by the same people who thought Francis Coppola's THE COTTON CLUB was going to be a cheery, inane musical. Both Coppola and Scorsese had other things in mind when they made their paeans to musicals past and substituted the banalities of backstage stories with some of the harsher realities of the way it was, or might have been. The picture cost almost $9 million (never recovering the money) and was more than four hours long at the first cut. So much was snipped that it's out of balance in spots. One of the largest slashes was a 12-minute production number (which cost over $300,000 and took two of the 22 weeks used to shoot the film) that featured Larry Kert (the star of Broadway's "West Side Story" who was making his first film appearance). Minnelli's then father-in-law, Jack Haley, Sr., also had a bit that was snipped and the same holds true for Scorsese's former mate, Julia Cameron, who played a band singer. Nepotism seemed to be the rule, rather than the exception, as producer Winkler's relatives took up two of the roles and *Daily Variety* columnist Army Archerd's wife, Selma, also had a bit. It's V-J Day, 1945. (Younger readers should know that this stood for "Victory Over Japan," as opposed to V-E Day, which took place earlier that year and meant "Victory In Europe.") Minnelli is a USO performer at a Manhattan celebration when she sees De Niro, dressed in a Hawaiian shirt and easily spotted among the uniforms. He tries to meet her in the typical "cute-meet" fashion but she resists him, for a while anyhow. They meet again later and he talks her into going with him to a band audition where he hopes to catch on as the orchestra's saxophonist. He finds it a chore to adhere to the band's stodgy tempo and Minnelli steps on stage and leads him into the right mood with her singing. The owner of the club hires them as a pair, but she later gets a call from her agent, Stander, which gives her a band-singer job with Auld's aggregation. She tries to find De Niro to tell him of the change of plans but can't locate the reed man, so she goes south to North Carolina. De Niro soon follows her there and she persuades Auld (a great saxophonist in his own right, he dubbed De Niro's playing) to give De Niro a chance. Their love deepens, and when De Niro discovers that Minnelli has been writing poems about him, he takes her to a justice of the peace, Kuby, where they are married as the JP's wife, Archerd, witnesses the proceedings. They play happily for a while, until Auld decides that the era of Big Band Music is about over, so he gives the group to De Niro. The band does well and De Niro thinks it's his playing that brings in the bucks, but it's really Minnelli's chirping that turns the stiles. Minnelli is expecting and leaves for New York to await the birth of the baby, so De Niro finds another singer, Place, and is soon doing to her what caused Minnelli to exit. After a while, De Niro gives the band to his pianist, Primus, and heads back to the Big Apple to be with Minnelli. She listens to Stander's advice and is soon a hit recording artist who does the kind of white-bread music that De Niro despises, while he contents himself by playing jazz uptown with Clemons, an old friend. They have a son but the marriage breaks up, as De niro feels he must go his way alone. Time goes by and he now runs a very successful club in New York, while she becomes a huge star of motion pictures. He sneaks into the theater to see one of her movies, then goes to a benefit at which she is performing. She sees him in the audience and does a tune they wrote together, and later, with their son, Winkler, they appear to be on the verge of reconciliation. They are going to meet for Chinese food; then she has second thoughts and remembers how it was while they were still married. She doesn't keep the date and De Niro waits patiently for her until he realizes what's happened and senses why she won't be there. He walks away by himself as the picture ends in a very downbeat fashion that is totally true to the nature of the movie and against the grain of those viewers who wanted a happy ending. De Niro has a tough job in the film, as the script calls for him to be vain, selfish, and egotistical. Since he is such a good actor, he totally convinces that he is all of those and more. Minnelli is brilliant, better than her mother ever was, and deserved at least a nomination, but she, and the entire film, were overlooked by the Academy in the sweep of ANNIE HALL. Place, a graduate of Harvey Lembeck's improvisation class, got her first big break in the film, and there was also excellent work by long-time Roger Corman favorite Dick Miller as well as comic Lenny Gaines and rotund George Memmoli (who had previously worked for Scorsese in MEAN STREETS). The huge cast included another Lembeckian, Timothy Blake, as well as deejay Casey Kasem, Tommy Dorsey look-alike Bill Tole, and hairdresser Guilaroff playing what else? a hairdresser. Even the co-author, Martin, took a part. A treat for the ears as well as the eyes, the tunes included: "New York, New York," "There Goes the Ball Game," "Happy Endings, " "But the World Goes 'Round" (John Kander, Fred Ebb, sung by Liza Minnelli), "Night in Tunisia" (Frank Paparelli, Dizzy Gillespie, John Birks), "Opus One" (Sid Garris, Sy Oliver), "Avalon" (Vincent Rose, Al Jolson), "You Brought a New Kind of Love to Me" (Sammy Fain, Irving Kahal, Pierre Norman Connor, sung by Minnelli), "I'm Getting Sentimental Over You" (Ned Washington, George Bassman), "Song of India" (Rimski-Korsakov), "Blue Moon" (Richard Rodgers, Lorenz Hart, sung by Mary Kay Place), "Don't Blame Me" (Jimmy McHugh, Dorothy Fields,), "Once In a While" (Bud Green, Michael Edwards, sung by Minnelli), "Don't Get Around Much Anymore," "Do Nothing Till You Hear from Me" (Duke Ellington, Bob Russell), "You Are My Lucky Star" (Nacio Herb Brown, Arthur Freed, sung by Minnelli), "It's a Wonderful World" (Jan Savitt, Jimmy Weston, Harold Adamson), "Hold Tight" (Leonard Kent, Leonard Ware, Edward Robinson, Willie Spottswood, Jerry Biandow), "Bugle Call Rag" (Elmer Schoebel, Billy Meyers, Jack Pettis), "Don't Be That Way" (Benny Goodman, Mitchell Parish, Edgar Sampson), "For All We Know" (S.M. Lewis, J. Fred Coots, sung by Minnelli), "South America, Take It Away" (Harold Rome, sung by Minnelli), "Taking a Chance on Love" (Vernon Duke, Ted Fettler, John Latouche, sung by Minnelli), "The Man I Love" (George and Ira Gershwin, sung by Minnelli), "Just You, Just Me" (Raymond Klages, Jesse Greer), "Honeysuckle Rose" (Fats Waller, Andy Razaf, sung by Diahnne Abbott), "Flip the Dip," "Game Over" (Georgie Auld), "V-J Stomp," "Hazoy," "Once Again Right Away," "Bobby's Dream" (Ralph Burns). And if we missed any, we're sorry. The 1981 re-release had an additional 10 minutes. This included the "Happy Endings" number.

p, Irwin Winkler, Robert Chartoff; d, Martin Scorsese; w, Earl MacRauch, Mardik Martin (based on a story by MacRauch); ph, Laszlo Kovacs (Panavision, DeLuxe Color); m, Ralph Burns; ed, Irving Lerner, Marcia Lucas, Tom Rolf, B. Lovitt, David Ramirez; md, Burns; prod d, Boris Leven; art d, Harry R. Kemm; set d, Robert Devestel, Robert R. Levitt; cos, Theadora Van Runkle; spec eff, Richard Albain; ch, Ron Field; makeup, Michael Westmore, Christian Smith; hairstyles, Mary Keats, June Miggins, Sydney Guilaroff.

Musical **Cas.** **(PR:C MPAA:PG)**

NEW YORK NIGHTS** (1929) 81m UA bw

Norma Talmadge *(Jill Deverne)*, Gilbert Roland *(Fred Deverne)*, John Wray *(Joe Prividi)*, Lilyan Tashman *(Peggy)*, Mary Doran *(Ruthie Day)*, Roscoe Karns *(Johnny Dolan)*, Landers Stevens *(Gang Chief)*, Stanley Fields *(Hood)*, Jean Harlow.

Norma Talmadge, who had begun a very successful silent film career at the age of 14 in A TALE OF TWO CITIES (1911), here attempted to make the transition to talkies. She plays an actress who is married to Roland, an aspiring composer. Roland's excessive drinking puts a strain on the relationship and eventually leads Talmadge to take up with gangster Wray. Wray tries to get Roland completely out of the picture by pinning a murder charge on him, but the plot fails and Wray is revealed as the real killer. Roland gives up the bottle and is reunited with Talmadge. Though Talmadge is reasonably effective in NEW YORK NIGHTS, her career in talking pictures was short-lived. She would make only one more picture, DU BARRY—WOMAN OF PASSION (1930), before retiring to live off the fortune she had accrued from her silent film career. Jean Harlow appears as an extra in NEW YORK NIGHTS.

p, Joseph M. Schenk; d, Lewis Milestone; w, Jules Furthman (based on the play "Tin Pan Alley" by Hugh Stanislaus Stange); ph, Ray June; ed, Hal Kern; m/l, Al Jolson, Ballard MacDonald, Dave Dryer.

Drama (PR:A MPAA:NR)

NEW YORK TOWN½** (1941) 94m PAR bw

Fred MacMurray *(Victor Ballard)*, Mary Martin *(Alexandra Curtis)*, Akim Tamiroff *(Stefan Janowski)*, Robert Preston *(Paul Bryson, Jr.)*, Lynne Overman *(Sam)*, Eric Blore *(Vyvian)*, Fuzzy Knight *(Gus Nelson)*, Cecil Kellaway *(Shipboard Host)*, Edward McNamara *(Brody the Cop)*, Ken Carpenter *(Master of Ceremonies)*, Oliver Blake *(Bender)*, Sam McDaniel *(Henry)*, Monte Blue *(McAuliffe)*, James Flavin *(Recruiting Sergeant)*, Marshall Ruth *(Spectator in Broadcasting Station)*, Grace Hayle *(Mrs. Bixby)*, Chester Clute *(Mr. Cobbler)*, Frances Morris, Alice Keating *(Nurses)*, Marjorie Deane *(Girl With Oliver)*, Jack Rice *(Oliver)*, Lilyan Irene *(Yvonne)*, George Davis *(Waiter in French Pavilion)*, John Bagni *(The Dip)*, Maynard Holmes *(Scion on Boat)*, Vinton Hayworth, Paul Fierro, Paul McVey *(Men on Boat)*, Ann Doran *(Department Store Demonstrator)*, Milton Kibbee *(Postman)*, Cyril Ring, Harry Bradley *(Spectators)*, Gus Reed *(Businessman)*, Tommy Bond *(Willie)*.

MacMurray plays a young man trying to make a go of it in New York, who meets the down-and-out Martin. He takes her back to the slum apartment he shares with unemployed art professor Tamiroff. The three live amicably until MacMurray persuades Martin to find a rich man to marry. She does, in Preston, all the while being in love with MacMurray, and he with her. The film ends with MacMurray announcing his love for Martin and winning her back from Preston. Story is too hackneyed to offer anything new, but Vidor manages to add a few dramatic touches (e.g., a shot of a dead canary to indicate a suicide). MacMurray is given little to work with, but Martin overcomes the script to give a strong performance. She sings one song, "Yip I Adee I Ay."

p, Anthony Veiller; d, Charles Vidor; w, Jo Swerling, S. Lewis Meltzer (based on a story by Swerling); ph, Charles Schoenbaum; ed, Doane Harrison; art d, Hans Dreier, William Pereira; cos, Edith Head; m/l, Phil Boutelje, Leo Robin, Ralph Rainger, Will Cob, John H. Flynn; makeup, Wally Westmore.

Comedy (PR:A MPAA:NR)

NEWLY RICH*½ (1931) 77m PAR bw (AKA: FORBIDDEN ADVENTURE)

Mitzi Green *(Daisy Tate)*, Edna May Oliver *(Bessie Tate)*, Louise Fazenda *(Maggy Tiffany)*, Jackie Searl *(Tiny Tim Tiffany)*, Bruce Line *(King Max)*, Virginia Hammond *(Queen Sedonia)*, Dell Henderson *(Director)*.

Taurog, McLeod, and Mankiewicz, all soon to become Hollywood heavyweights, working with a Sinclair Lewis story, sounds like a promising venture, but a lightweight comedy is all the collaboration could produce. Oliver and Fazenda are friends who compete with each other through their children, Green and Searl. The youngsters end up in the movies thanks to motherly prompting, and then both families head for London. There the kids meet a young king and he takes off with them on a series of comic episodes. Eventually, the king returns to his subjects and the children head for home. The laughs are limited, but Fazenda and Oliver work well as a comic duo.

d, Norman Taurog; w, Edward Paramore, Jr., Norman McLeod, Joseph L. Mankiewicz (based on the short story "Let's Play King" by Sinclair Lewis); ph, Charles Lang.

Comedy (PR:AA MPAA:NR)

NEWMAN'S LAW** (1974) 98m UNIV c

George Peppard *(Vince Newman)*, Roger Robinson *(Garry)*, Eugene Roche *(Reardon)*, Gordon Pinsent *(Eastman)*, Abe Vigoda *(Dellanzia)*, Louis Zorich *(Falcone)*, Michael Lerner *(Frank Acker)*, Victor Campos *(Jimenez)*, Mel Stewart *(Quist)*, Jack Murdock *(Beutel)*, David Spielberg *(Hinney)*, Theodore Wilson *(Jaycee)*, Pat Anderson *(Sharon)*, Regis J. Cordic *(Clement)*, Marlene Clark *(Edie)*, Kip Niven *(Assistant Coroner)*, Richard Bull *(Immigration Man)*, Howard Platt *(Spink)*, Dick Balduzzi *(Conrad)*, Penelope Gillette *(Matron)*, Kirk Mee *(1st Assistant)*, Don Hammer *(Real Estate Agent)*, Anthony Carbone *(Gino the Policeman)*, Jude Farese *(1st Cop)*, Stack Pierce *(Baines)*, Jac Emil *(Dashiki)*, Donald Newsome *(Ginger)*, Titos Vandis *(Grainie)*, Wilbert Gowdy *(Black Boy)*, Louis J. DiFonzo *(Pants)*, Dea St. Lamont *(Hooker)*.

Standard cop drama has Peppard as a Los Angeles detective who becomes a victim of big city politics, though all along remaining an honest cop. He and his partner, Robinson, while on a routine dope stakeout, uncover a large international drug operation. But the D.A. rips Peppard's testimony to shreds, resulting in Peppard's suspension from the force. Peppard is properly tough and cynical in the lead. Credit directer Heffron with an ability to handle action sequences, as he builds the chase scenes into an eventful climax. He had frequently directed Peppard during the run of the TV series "Banacek." This was his first feature film.

p, Richard Irving; d, Richard Heffron; w, Anthony Wilson; ph, Vilis Lapenieks (Technicolor); m, Robert Prince; ed, John Dumas; art d, Alexander A. Mayer.

Crime Drama (PR:A MPAA:PG)

NEWS HOUNDS** (1947) 68m MON bw

Leo Gorcey *("Slip" Mahoney)*, Huntz Hall *(Sach)*, Bobby Jordan *(Bobby)*, Gabriel Dell *(Gabe)*, Billy Benedict *(Whitey)*, David Gorcey *(Chuck)*, Christine McIntyre *(Jane Ann Connelly)*, Tim Ryan *(John Burke)*, Anthony Caruso *("Dapper Dan" Greco)*, Bill Kennedy *(Mark Morgan)*, Ralph Dunn *(Dutch Miller)*, Nita Bieber *(Mame)*, John Hamilton *(Big Tim Donlin)*, Terry Goodman *(Little Boy)*, Robert Emmett Keane *(Mack Snide, Lawyer)*, Bernard Gorcey *(Louie)*, Buddy Gorman *(Copyboy)*, Russ Whiteman *(Jimmy Gale)*, Emmett Vogan, Jr. *(Johnny Gale)*, John H. Elliott *(Judge)*, Meyer Grace *(Sparring Partner)*, Leo Kaye *(Red Kane)*, Emmett Vogan, Sr. *(Defense Attorney)*, Gene Stutenroth *(Dutch's Henchman)*, Terry Goodman, Meyer Grace.

The Bowery Boys try to make a name for themselves in the world of journalism. Gorcey plays a copyboy out to make it as a reporter and Hall is a photographer for the same paper. Gorcey goes beyond his jurisdiction as he tries to uncover some information on underworld figure Caruso. Acting on a tip from Dell, he and Hall visit the gangster under the premise of being friends of a friend. Gorcey trumps up a story connecting Caruso to a sports fixing racket, and it's published under the name of a sports columnist. The paper is sued by Caruso who denies the charges. But Gorcey produces Hall's photographs, proving the story correct. Film packs a lot of action into a short period of time, but the direction manages to keep it all pretty well paced. Gorcey has his usual sharp tongue, with the rest of the Boys giving competent performances. (See BOWERY BOYS series, Index.)

p, Jan Grippo; d, William Beaudine; w, Edmond Seward, Tim Ryan (based on a story by Seward, Ryan, George Cappy); ph, Marcel Le Picard; ed, William Austin; md, Edward Kay; art d, Dave Milton.

Crime/Drama (PR:A MPAA:NR)

NEWS IS MADE AT NIGHT** (1939) 71m FOX bw

Preston Foster *(Steve Drum)*, Lynn Bari *(Maxine Thomas)*, Russell Gleason *(Albert Hockman)*, George Barbier *(Clanahan)*, Eddie Collins *(Billiard)*, Minor Watson *(Charles Coulton)*, Charles Halton *(Elmer Hinge)*, Paul Harvey *(Inspector Melrose)*, Richard Lane *(Barney Basely)*, Charles Lane *(Rufe Reynolds)*, Betty Compson *(Kitty Truman)*, Paul Fix *(Joe Liddy)*, Paul Guilfoyle *(Bat Randall)*.

The "hard-nosed male editor vs. rebellious female reporter" plot gets competent treatment here, thanks to a strong performance by Foster as the editor. He's obsessed with building circulation and attempts to do so by freeing the innocent and convicting the guilty through his newspaper stories. Bari is the reporter who helps, and the two are constantly at odds, but everyone knows they're truly in love and will end up with each other by the film's end. The story's devoid of credibility, but it all flows rapidly and has nice comic relief provided by the supporting players.

p, Edward Kaufman, d, Alfred Werker; w, John Larkin; ph, Ernest Palmer; ed, Nick De Maggio; md, Samuel Kaylin.

Drama (PR:A MPAA:NR)

NEWSBOY'S HOME*½ (1939) 73m UNIV bw

Jackie Cooper *("Rifle" Edwards)*, Edmund Lowe *(Perry Warner, Editor)*, Wendy Barrie *(Gwen Dutton)*, Edward Norris *(Frankie Barber)*, Samuel S. Hinds *(Howard Price Dutton)*, Irving Pichel *(Tom Davenport)*, Elisha Cook, Jr. *(Danny)*, Harris Berger *(Sailor)*, Hally Chester *(Murphy)*, Charles Duncan *(Monk)*, David Gorcey *(Yap)*, William Benedict *(Trouble)*, Harry Beresford *(O'Dowd)*, Horace MacMahon *(Bartsch)*, George McKay *(Hartley)*, Michael Conroy, Hi Roberts, Bill Cartledge, Billy Graff, Jr., Lee Murray, Lawrence Lathrop *(Newsboys)*, Joseph Crehan *(Sheriff)*, Edwin Stanley *(Bailey)*, Pat Flaherty *(Mulvaney)*, Peter Lynn *(Balky)*, Matty Fain *(Kraft)*, William Gould *(Auctioneer)*, Edward Earle *(FBI Man)*, Edward Gargan *(Policeman)*, Ralph Dunn *(Slugger)*, Jerry Frank, Howard "Red" Christie *(Truck Drivers)*, Frank Sully *(Hartley's Assistant)*, Jimmy O'Gatty *(Mug)*, Russ Powell, Johnny Morris *(Vendors)*, Sydney Greylor *(Slugger)*, Kernan Cripps *(Pressman)*, Jack Egan *(Daniels)*, Eric Efron *(Man)*, Francis Sayles *(Bill)*, Frank O'Connor *(Rewrite Man)*, Heinie Conklin *(Dominic)*, Desmond Gallagher *(Receptionist)*, Eric Wilton *(Butler)*, Anthony Warde *(Blake)*.

"The Little Tough Guys," introduced by Universal the year before in response to the popularity of "The Dead End Kids," here get in the middle of a circulation war between rival newspapers. Cooper leads the gang and he's grateful to "The Globe" because it took him into the title home when his sheriff father was murdered. Barrie has inherited the paper and her mismanagement has brought it to the brink of bankruptcy. Cooper helps her draw readers from the rival "Star" and avenges his dad's death in the process, since the muscle behind the other paper's nasty tactics is none other than the killer of Jackie's father. Inane plot is made a little more palatable by nonstop action, but overall it's old news.

d, Harold Young; w, Gordon Kahn (based on a story by Kahn, Charles Grayson); ph, Milton Krasner; ed, Philip Cahn; md, Charles Previn; art d, Jack Otterson.

Drama (PR:A MPAA:NR)

NEWSFRONT*** (1979, Aus.) 110m Palm Beach Pictures/Roadshow c/bw

Bill Hunter *(Len Maguire)*, Gerard Kennedy *(Frank Maguire)*, Angela Punch *(Fay Maguire)*, Wendy Hughes *(Amy McKenzie)*, Chris Hayward *(Chris Hewett)*, John Ewart *(Charlie)*, Don Crosby *(A. G. Marawood)*, John Dease *(Ken)*, John Clayton

(*Cliff*), Bryan Brown (*Geoff*), Tony Barry (*Greasy*), Drew Forsythe (*Bruce*), Lorna Leslie (*Ellie*), Mark Holden (*Tim*), Chad Morgan (*Country Singer*).

A creative combination of color and black and white photography helps to establish a unique atmosphere for this story of two brothers, Hunter and Kennedy, as newsreel cameramen for competing companies. The story takes place between the years 1949 and 1956, a period of social and political change in Australia, depicted not only in the stories the brothers cover, but in the changes that occur in their own lives. Hunter is unwilling to adapt to changes, preferring to remain at home with his camera recording events. Kennedy is more aggressive, always striving to better himself and eventually leaving for Hollywood as television destroys the newsreel business. Realistic and fictional events are intermingled in a way that moves the narrative in a compelling manner, showing how the changes in the social climate of Australia affect individual lives. For example, strife arises in Hunter's marriage when his wife is distressed by his political views. Hunter gives a powerful performance as a cynical man and maintains a skillful command of the film. This was the feature debut for director Noyce, who proves adept at intermingling narrative and events into a working whole. Technical credits and supporting case are all top-notch.

p, David Elfick; d, Phillip Noyce; w, Noyce, Bob Ellis (based on an idea by Elfick, Phillipe Mora); ph, Vincent Monton (Panavision); m, William Motzing; ed, John Scott; art d, Larry Eastwood; spec eff, Kim Hilder; cos, Norma Moriceau.

Drama **Cas.** **(PR:C MPAA:NR)**

NEXT!* (1971, Ital./Span.) 81m Devon-Copercines/Gemini-Maron c (LO STRANO VIZIO DELLA SIGNORA WARDH; AKA: THE NEXT VICTIM!)

Alberto De Mendoza (*Neil Ward*), Edwige Fenech (*Julie Ward*), Christina Airoldi (*Carol*), George Hilton (*George*), Ivan Rassimov (*Jean*), Manuel Gil, Carlo Alighiero.

Vienna is the setting for this bloody thriller as a razor-wielding madman is raping and slashing his way through the city. Fenech stars as a woman who is almost constantly in danger, with suspicion shifting among her ex-lover (Rassimov), her ex-husband (De Mendoza), and her current lover (Hilton). When the razor killer is himself slain, it appears Fenech is out of danger, but she continues to be the victim of attacks and threats, and apparently dies when she is left unconscious in an apartment with the gas turned on. "Apparently" is the operative word here as nothing in this movie is what it seems to be. Her "death" is just a ruse to identify the culprits and it turns out to be all three men in her life, working together to collect an inheritance. The shocks are plentiful, but the plottings are all pretty transparent and the acting somewhere around competent. The dubbing in English has been poorly done, making some of the allegedly dramatic moments laughable.

p, Luciano Martino, Antonio Crescenzi; d, Sergio Martino; w, Ernesto Gastaldi, Eduardo M. Brochero, Vittorio Caronia (based on a story by Brochero); ph, Emilio Foriscot, Miguel Fernandez-Mila (Eastmancolor); m, Nora Orlandi; ed, Eugenio Alabiso; md, Paolo Ormi; art d, James Perez Cubero, Jose Galicia.

Horror/Mystery **Cas.** **(PR:O MPAA:R)**

NEXT IN LINE (SEE: RIDERS OF THE NORTHLAND, 1943)

NEXT MAN, THE½** (1976) 108m Artists Entertainment/AA c

Sean Connery (*Khalif Abdul-Muhsen*), Cornelia Sharpe (*Nicole Scott*), Albert Paulsen (*Hamid*), Adolfo Celi (*Al Sharif*), Marco St. John (*Justin*), Ted Beniades (*Dedario*), Charles Cioffi (*Fouad*), Salem Ludwig (*Ghassan Kaddara*), Tom Klunis (*Hatim Othman*), Roger Omar Serbagi (*Yassin*), Armand Dahan (*Abdel-Latif Khaldoun*), Charles Randall (*Atif Abbas*), Ian Collier (*Devereaux*), Michael Storm (*Salazar*), Maurice Copeland (*Board Chairman*), George Pravda (*Zolchev*), Alex Jawdokimov (*Russian Chairman*), James Bullett (*Harrison*), Jaime Sanchez (*Rodriguez*), Stephen D. Newman (*Andy Hampses*), Holland Taylor (*TV Interviewer*), Peggy Feury (*Mrs. Scott*), Toru Nagai (*Japanese at Waldorf*), Ryokei Kanokogi (*Japanese Speaker at UN*), Patrick Bedford (*Mr. Scott*), Camill Yarbrough (*UN Reporter*), Martin Bregman, Richard C. Sarafian.

An uneven espionage thriller starring Connery as a UN representative from Saudia Arabia who, to ensure economic stability in the Middle East, attempts to arrange a peace settlement with the Israelis. This political move does not endear Connery in the hearts of Arab terrorists, so they dispatch a frisky female assassin, Sharpe, to eliminate him. Before she can get the handsome diplomat in her sights, they fall in love. The action takes place on locations all over the world (New York, Bavaria, Germany, London, and Morocco), and Chapman's photography of these scenic locations is superb, but passages of the movie seem more a pretty travelog than a necessary part to the forward movement of the narrative. Performances from the two principals are as developed as the frequently convoluted script allows them to be, and there are some fine nude scenes showing beautiful playgirl Sharpe in some arresting and graceful angles.

p, Martin Bregman; d, Richard C. Sarafian; w, Mort Fine, Alan Trustman, David M. Wolf, Sarafian (based on a story by Bregman, Trustman); ph, Michael Chapman (Technicolor); m, Michael Kamen; ed, Aram Avakian, Robert Lovett; prod d, Gene Callahan; set d, Robert Drumheller; cos, Anna Hill Johnstone.

Spy Drama/Romance **(PR:O MPAA:R)**

NEXT OF KIN*½ (1942, Brit.) 84m EAL/UA bw

Mervyn Johns (*Mr. Davis, "No. 23"*), John Chandos (*"No. 16," His Contact*), Nova Pilbeam (*Beppie Leemans*), Reginald Tate (*Maj. Richards*), Stephen Murray (*Mr. Barrett*), Geoffrey Hibbert (*Pvt. John*), Philip Friend (*Lt. Cummins*), Phyllis Stanley (*Miss Clare*), Mary Clare (*"Ma" Webster*), Basil Sydney (*Naval Captain*), Joss Ambler (*Mr. Vernon*), Brefni O'Rorke (*Brigadier*), Alexander Field (*Pvt. Durnford*), David Hutcheson (*Intelligence Officer*), Jack Hawkins (*Brigade Major*), Frederick Leister (*Colonel*), Torin Thatcher (*German General*), Charles Victor (*Seaman*), Richard Norris (*Pvt. Jimmy*), Guy Mas (*Frenchman*), Thora Hird (*A.T.S. Girl*), Basil Radford, Naunton Wayne (*Careless Talkers*), J. Edgar Hoover (*Narrator, Prolog/Epilog*), Johnny Schofield, Frank Allenby.

Originally made by the British Army to warn troops about the dangers of loose talk in wartime. A prolog and epilog delivered by U.S. FBI Director J. Edgar Hoover was added to increase the impact of the film. Propaganda aside, the film stands as a fairly decent war story. Johns plays a German who is sent to England during WW II and picks up vital bits of information from talkative servicemen. Johns' data provide the Germans with the ability to plan for an attack by the British, and, though the British win the battle, casualties are heavy because of the forewarning the Germans had. At the film's end, Johns is seen still busily gathering information in England. Many of the players in the film were in the service at the time it was made, including Johns, Hawkins, Norris, Thatcher, Tate, and Hutcheson. The title is taken from the closing words of British war casualty announcements: ". . .the next of kin have been informed."

p, Michael Balcon; d, Thorold Dickinson; w, Dickinson, Basil Bartlett, Angus McPhail, John Dighton; ph, Ernest Palmer; m, William Walton; ed, Ray Pitt; md, Ernest Irving; art d, Tom Morahan.

War **(PR:A MPAA:NR)**

NEXT OF KIN* (1983, Aus.) 86m SIS Productions-Filmco/Miracle c

Jackie Kerin, John Jarratt, Alex Scott, Gerda Nicolson, Charles McCallum, Bernadette Gibson, Robert Ratti, Vince Deltito, Tommy Dysart, Debra Lawrence, Kristina Marshall, Simon Thorpe, David Allshoru, Alan Rowe, Matt Burns, Daphne Miller, Isobel Harley, Irene Hewitt, Myrtle Woods, Vic Gordon, Peter Lord, Ernest Wilson, John Strahan, Bill Marr, John Bishop, Mitchell Faircloth, Nora Toohey, Sid Krasey.

An Australian entry in the mad slasher field offers a twist: the inhabitants of an old people's home are the victims, rather than the usual teenie boppers. Results are just as predictable as Gibson plays a psychotic old lady out for revenge. Williams tosses in a bunch of quotes from films and literature in an apparent attempt to elevate the proceedings, but it's all to no avail.

p, Robert Le Tet; d, Tony Williams; w, Williams, Michael Heath; ph, Gary Hansen (Eastmancolor); m, Klaus Schulze; ed, Max Lemon; art d, Richard Francis, Nick Hepworth; spec eff, Chris Murray; makeup, E. Fardon.

Horror **(PR:O MPAA:NR)**

NEXT ONE, THE* (1982, U.S./Gr.) 105m Allstar c

Keir Dullea (*Glenn*), Adrienne Barbeau (*Andrea Johnson*), Jeremy Licht (*Tim Johnson*), Peter Hobbs (*Dr. Barnaby Caldwell*).

Pretentious piece of pseudo-religious claptrap about the second coming. When a stranger arrives on a small Greek isle and demonstrates some amazing powers (i.e., bringing the dead back to life; psychic connections with inanimate objects, etc.) the townsfolk begin to wonder if maybe this guy is Him. In the end the stranger wanders off into the sea, leaving the hope that maybe another like him will follow. Pretty ridiculous.

d&w, Nico Mastorakis; ph, Ari Stavrou; m, Stanley Myers; prod d, Paul Acciari.

Science Fiction **(PR:C MPAA:NR)**

NEXT STOP, GREENWICH VILLAGE**** (1976) 111m FOX c

Lenny Baker (*Larry Lapinsky*), Shelley Winters (*Mrs. Lapinsky*), Ellen Greene (*Sarah*), Lois Smith (*Anita*), Christopher Walken (*Robert*), Dori Brenner (*Connie*), Antonio Fargas (*Bernstein*), Lou Jacobi (*Herb*), Mike Kellin (*Mr. Lapinsky*), Michael Egan (*Herbert*), Denise Gallk (*Ellen*), John C. Becher (*Sid Weinberg the Producer*), John Ford Noonan (*Barney*), Helen Hanft (*Herb's Wife*), Rashel Novikoff (*Mrs. Tupperman, Neighbor*), Joe Madden (*Jake the Poet*), Joe Spinnell (*Cop*), Rochelle Oliver (*Abortionist*), Gui Adrisano (*Marco*), Carole Manferdini (*Southern Girl*), Jeff Goldblum (*Clyde the Actor*), Rutanya Alda (*Party Guest*).

Anyone who spent any time in New York's Greenwich Village in the early 1950s will attest to the truth of this wonderful and nostalgic look at that era. It's essentially Mazursky's own story and he manages to capture the time and the people with a loving touch. Mazursky, it is alleged, walked into a session at Brooklyn College and announced he was changing his name. The others there nodded and understood his desire until he said that he was altering it from Irwin Mazursky to Paul Mazursky. Baker is the young man who graduates from Brooklyn College in 1953 and makes the decision to leave his family, Kellin and Winters, and switch boroughs to Manhattan. Winters, the ultimate Jewish mother, is totally against it, but he leaves anyhow and takes up residence in the Village where he takes a job at a health food place, then starts his acting lessons with Egan, a proponent of the "Method." He is soon part of The Scene and his pals include nutty Brenner (who later married Andre Previn and became an important songwriter); Smith, who is always teetering on the brink of suicide; Walken, the WASPish poet who speaks in epigrams; and Fargas, a black homosexual with a Jewish name. (Lest you think that's unique, consider the real-life police chief of Charleston, South Carolina, in 1986, Rubin Greenberg, who is black and a serious Conservative Jew.) The tight-knit group members are symbiotic and help each other when needed, so when Smith tries suicide, they pour coffee into her. Baker's sweetheart, Greene, is expecting and they arrange an abortion. Baker is out of money and due to be tossed out of his apartment and the others stage a "rent party" to raise the cash. (Rent parties were a common occurrence in the Village at that time and there were at least ten going every night.) Baker learns that a major studio wants to cast some juvenile delinquents and he hopes he might get the part. (In real life, Mazursky was in THE BLACKBOARD JUNGLE as "Stoker". It was an MGM picture, although he uses the name of Fox here because this film was produced by that lot.) Winters and Kellin come to see how Baker is living and she is shocked when she learns that Baker and Greene are sleeping together. Before she can faint, Kellin takes Winters home to Brooklyn. The group is saddened to learn that Smith's customary suicide attempt worked this time and they share their grief with each other. Baker gets a chance at the role, then Greene announces that she is going off to Mexico with Walken, Fargas, and Brenner. Baker and Greene make love for the last time and she takes this opportunity to inform him that she is also Walken's lover. An argument erupts as Winters and Kellin enter the apartment surreptitiously. Greene leaves and Baker understands that this part of his life is now finished. Baker bids his pals farewell, goes to his job, and gets the call about the role. He is to report to Hollywood within the week. At the last supper with Winters and Kellin, she reminds him to never forget where he came from. Baker was simply marvelous in the leading role. He went on to play in the Broadway hit musical, "I Love My Wife," before dying of cancer. Mazursky's real acting career began in Stanley Kubrick's first feature, FEAR AND DESIRE, which was followed by THE BLACKBOARD JUNGLE. Co-producer Tony Ray is director Nicholas Ray's son and he later married his father's ex-wife, Gloria Grahame. In a small role, look for Jeff Goldblum, who has since become somewhat of a star with 1985's INTO THE NIGHT. Conti's music is outstanding and evokes the period without parodying it.

p, Paul Mazursky, Tony Ray; d&w, Mazursky; ph, Arthur Ornitz (Panavision, DeLuxe Color); m, Bill Conti; ed, Richard Halsey; prod d, Phil Rosenberg; set d, Ed Stewart; cos, Albert Wolsky; makeup, Bob Jiras.

Comedy/Drama **(PR:C MPAA:R)**

NEXT TIME I MARRY*½

(1938) 64m RKO bw

Lucille Ball *(Nancy Fleming)*, James Ellison *(Tony Anthony)*, Lee Bowman *(Count Georgi)*, Granville Bates *(H. E. Crocker)*, Mantan Moreland *(Tilby)*, Eliot Sullivan *(Red)*, Murray Alper *(Joe)*, Robert E. Homans *(Court Bailiff)*, Dick Elliott *(Justice of the Peace)*, Florence Lake *(Justice of the Peace's Wife)*, Cy Kendall *(Lawyer)*, Ralph Dunn *(Cop)*, Grace Hayle *(Fat Gossip)*, Jack Albertson *(Reporter)*.

Kanin was still learning the ropes as a director (this was his second film) and it showed in this implausible yarn. Ball stars as a woman who stands to inherit $20 million if she'll marry a "real American." Her heart belongs to foreigner Bowman, but she picks Ellison as her husband to qualify for the fortune. Ellison is a ditch-digger and Ball's plan is to head for Reno and a divorce as soon as she gets the money. On the trip to Nevada, Ball and Ellison bicker and battle, all the while becoming closer to one another and finally realizing they are in love. Ball is in good comedic form and she works well with Ellison, but the film suffers from too much action that goes unexplained. A wild ride by trailer to Reno is similar to one that would appear in a film Ball made with her husband, Desi Arnaz, in THE LONG, LONG TRAILER (1954).

p, Cliff Reid; d, Garson Kanin; w, John Twist, Helen Meinardi (based on a story by Thames Williamson); ph, Russell Metty; ed, Jack Hively; md, Roy Webb.

Comedy **(PR:A MPAA:NR)**

NEXT TIME WE LOVE*½

(1936) 87m UNIV bw (GB: NEXT TIME WE LIVE)

Margaret Sullavan *(Cicely Tyler)*, James Stewart *(Christopher Tyler)*, Ray Milland *(Tommy Abbott)*, Grant Mitchell *(Michael Jennings)*, Anna Demetrio *(Mme. Donato)*, Robert McWade *(Frank Carteret)*, Ronnie Cosbey *(Kit at Age 8)*, Florence Roberts *(Mrs. Talbot)*, Christian Rub *(Otto)*, Charles Fallon *(Prof. Dindet)*, Nat Carr *(Assistant Stage Manager)*, Gottlieb Huber *(Swiss Porter)*, Harry C. Bradley *(Desk Clerk)*, Jack Daley, Broderick O'Farrell *(Conductors)*, Buddy Williams *(Porter)*, Dutch Hendrian, Philip Morris, Al Hill, Jack Cheatham *(Taxi Drivers)*, Hattie McDaniel *(Hanna)*, Emmett Vogan *(Bartender)*, Harry Bowe, Jack Mower *(Waiters)*, Donna Mae Roberts *(Cigarette Girl)*, Albert Conti *(Charles)*, George Davis, Ludwig Lowry *(Waiters)*, Tyler Brooke *(Author)*, Leonid Kinskey *(Designer)*, Eddie Phillips *(Ticket Taker)*, John Dilson *(Stage Manager)*, Nat Carr *(Assistant)*, Clark Williams, Clive Morgan *(Leading Men)*, Nan Grey *(Ingenue)*, John King *(Juvenile)*, Tom Manning, King Baggot *(Character Men)*, Daisy Bufford *(Maid)*, Alfred P. James *(Aquarium Attendant)*, Billy Gratton *(Kit at Age 3)*, Jacqueline Smylle *(Susan)*, Arthur Aylesworth *(Secretary)*, Julie Carter *(Sob Sister)*, Don Roberts *(City Editor)*, Paddy O'Flynn *(Reporter)*, Harry Tracy *(Valet)*, Jane Keckley *(Nurse)*, Mika Morita *(Dr. Ito)*, Selmer Jackson *(Dr. Campbell)*, Teru Shimada *(Steward)*, Otto Fries *(Conductor)*, Patsy Green *(Stand-in for Sullavan)*, Hugh Harrison *(Stand-in for Stewart)*, Jack Parker *(Stand-in for Milland)*.

One of the few newspaperman stories where the journalist is not a drunk, a wisecracker, or a fool. Sullavan quits university to marry Stewart, an ambitious newshound. Milland is a wealthy pal who knows Sullavan would like to act, so he arranges an intro to a heavyweight producer and she gets an acting job. Stewart secures the Rome Bureau as an assignment but Sullavan prefers to stay in New York. Once he's gone to Italy, she tells best friend Milland that she's pregnant and Stewart learns of the birth via a letter from their apartment manager. He races back from Rome and pledges to never leave her side again. Becuase he left without notice, he is fired from his good job and has to start at the bottom again as a cub reporter at a local news-gathering company. Milland steps in once more and arranges an acting job for Sullavan. Stewart is morose and Sullavan pleads with his ex-boss to get him another job, even one overseas. Stewart is rehired and must cross the Atlantic right away. Years pass and Sullavan becomes a star and only sees her husband when their schedules coincide, although she continues to love him. Milland now admits he loves Sullavan and asks for her hand—once she can shed Stewart. She travels to Europe to sort things out and soon learns that Stewart is dying of an unspecified ailment he got while on a job in China. They are on a train when she lets that little catch in her throat go and the tears flow as she assures Stewart they will be together until his last breath. A sob story with good performances by all, but overly sentimental. Until the end, Sullavan is so much more interested in her career than in her love for her husband that she doesn't engender much sympathy.

p, Paul Kohner; d, Edward H. Griffith; w, Melville Baker, [uncredited] Preston Sturges (based on the novel *Say Goodbye Again* by Ursula Parrott); ph, Joseph Valentine; m, Franz Waxman; ed, Ted Kent; art d, Charles D. Hall; cos, Vera West; makeup, Jack P. Pierce.

Drama **(PR:A MPAA:NR)**

NEXT TO NO TIME**½

(1960, Brit.) 93m Cornelius/Show c

Kenneth More *(David Webb)*, Betsy Drake *(Georgie Brant)*, Harry Green *(Saul)*, Patrick Barr *(Jerry)*, Maureen Connell *(Mary)*, Bessie Love *(Becky)*, Reginald Beckwith *(Warren)*, John Welsh *(Steve, Bar Steward)*, Howard Marion-Crawford *(Hobbs)*, Clive Morton *(Wallis)*, John Laurie *(Abercrombie)*, Irene Handl *(Mrs. Crowley)*, Raymond Huntley *(Forbes)*, Ferdy Mayne *(Mario)*, Sidney James *(Albert, Cabin Steward)*, Roland Culver *(Sir Godfrey Cowan)*, Sandra Walden *(Hester)*, Barbara Cavan *(Miss Wilkes)*, Paul Whitsun-Jones *(Lord)*, Fred Griffiths *(Customer)*, Sally Travers *(Mother)*, Eleanor Bryan *(Susie)*, Valerie Buckley *(Hester's Girl Friend)*, Russell Waters *(Clerk)*, Anthony Sager *(Ellis)*, Kenneth Evans *(Harry)*, Yvonne Buckingham *(Mario's Girl Friend)*, Arthur Lovegrove, Stanley Escane, Paul Cole, Terry Burton, Fiona Chislett, Maurice Lane, Christopher Sandford, Grace Chang, Anthony Chinn.

Released in the U.S. two years after it was completed, NEXT TO NO TIME is a delightful comedy featuring More as an engineer who must sail to America on the Queen Elizabeth in pursuit of a prospective client for his employer. More's firm wants to sell an automation system to the wealthy Culver and More is assigned the unwanted task of closing the sale. More has limited skills in human relations, but Drake, an American actress on board the ship, and Welsh, the ship's bartender, help him overcome his fears, with an assist from some powerful drinks. More makes the sale and becomes the life of the party in the process. The leads and supporting players are uniformly good, and the story flows smoothly from start to finish. Cornelius, who had begun his directorial career with PASSPORT TO PIMLICO (1949), died before the picture's American release. Though he made only five films during his brief career as a director, he was highly regarded for his deft handling of comedy. His film I AM A CAMERA (1955) served as the basis for the stage musical "Cabaret," which was turned into a film in 1972. He died while working on LAW AND DISORDER (1958) with Charles Crichton finishing the project. This was also the last film for Harry Green, who died shortly after its completion. His acting career started in 1929 with CLOSE HARMONY and included appearances in more than two dozen films.

p, Albert Fennel; d&w, Henry Cornelius (based on a story "The Enchanted Hour" by Paul Gallico); ph, Freddie Francis (Eastmancolor); m, Georges Auric; ed, Peter Hunt.

Comedy **(PR:A MPAA:NR)**

NEXT VOICE YOU HEAR, THE***

(1950) 82m MGM bw

James Whitmore *(Joe Smith, American)*, Nancy Davis *(Mrs. Joe Smith)*, Gary Gray *(Johnny Smith)*, Lillian Bronson *(Aunt Ethel)*, Art Smith *(Mr. Brannan)*, Tom D'Andrea *(Hap Magee)*, Jeff Corey *(Freddie)*, George Chandler *(Traffic Cop)*.

Whitmore and Davis are a married couple very much in love with one another and content with their simple, quiet life. Parents of a son, Gray, the two eagerly await the upcoming birth of their next child. Their contented life style, along with the rest of the world, is shaken one evening when the voice of God emanates from their radio. The world's population at first is skeptical of the strange phenomenon, followed by a growing fear. The Voice returns on broadcast for six evenings, eventually persuading people not to fear His pronouncements. The lives of Whitmore and Davis, along with those of the people of the town, are forever changed as they realize the direction they must now take. Despite a seemingly ludicrous concept, this is a sincere drama handled with care under Wellman's direction. Rather than project a heavy-handed message or any one theology's concept of the Deity, the film concentrates on the effect these broadcasts have on the characters' everyday lives. Whitmore and Davis are genuine as the couple, projecting an honest sense of warmth that adds to the spirit of the picture. Producer Schary's intent with the project was to create a film about God that emphasized His effects on the common man rather than the Biblical spectacles Hollywood was so adept at producing. Schary's one choice as director was Wellman. He had been pleased with the director's skill in both story-telling and the ability to bring in a film under budget when the two had worked together on BATTLEGROUND one year before. Wellman's reputation as a good family man also figured in Schary's decision for him to helm this homespun piece. For his part, Wellman's agreement to do the film had somewhat less noble pretensions. He had a particular dislike for what he felt were message pictures and took on THE NEXT VOICE YOU HEAR for decidedly different reasons. "I knew I could do it in three weeks and they had never made a picture at MGM in three weeks. There was an ego thing in it," he later related. Wellman did much better than expected, finishing the film in just 14 days and $220,000 under the projected $650,000 budget. Despite the rapid work he made it all look professional, projecting a real sense of humanism into the work without ever getting heavy-handed. Because of the low budget the film was a major box-office success. Gossipmonger Hedda Hopper raved about the movie, calling it a film "for every member of the family. In fact, for America." However, in 1956 the ever-vindictive Hopper did a complete turnabout following Schary's ouster from MGM. Coming up with her list of best and worst films in movie history, Hopper called THE NEXT VOICE YOU HEAR the "The First Worst Picture Of All Time." That, to say the least, is hardly a fair critique. This remains a sweet and simple story taking on a weighty subject with respect and reverence, never getting caught up in what could have been a sticky mess of sentimental sap. Though not a great film it certainly is a nice one that never overstates its goals.

p, Dore Schary; d, William A. Wellman; w, Charles Schnee (based on a story by George Sumner Albee); ph, William Mellor; m, David Raksin; ed, John Dunning; art d, Cedric Gibbons, Eddie Imazu; set d, Ralph S. Hurst.

Drama **(PR:AAA MPAA:NR)**

NIAGARA***½   (1953) 92m FOX c

Marilyn Monroe (Rose Loomis), Joseph Cotten (George Loomis), Jean Peters (Polly Cutler), Casey Adams (Ray Cutler), Dennis O'Dea (Inspector Sharkey), Richard Allan (Patrick), Don Wilson (Mr. Kettering), Lurene Tuttle (Mrs. Kettering), Russell Collins (Mr. Qua), Will Wright (Boatman), Lester Matthews (Doctor), Carleton Young (Policeman), Sean McClory (Sam), Minerva Urecal (Landlady), Nina Varela (Wife), Tom Reynolds (Husband), Winfield Hoeny (Straw Boss), Neil Fitzgerald (Customs Officer), Norman McKay (Morris), Gene Wesson (Guide), George Ives (Carillon Tower Guide), Patrick O'Moore (Detective), Arch Johnson, Harry Carey, Jr. (Taxi Drivers), Henry Beckman, Willard Sage (Motorcycle Cops), Bill Foster, Robert Ellis (Young Men), Gloria Gordon (Dancer).

Everyone's honeymoon haven at one time, Niagara Falls, is the deceptive setting for this offbeat but wholly absorbing film noir effort with bowstring tight direction from Hathaway and superb performances from Cotten as a jealous husband and Monroe as a neurotic, cuckolding wife. Newlyweds Peters and Adams arrive at their Niagara honeymoon cottage and meet another couple, Cotten and Monroe. Monroe, from the beginning, complains about her husband being considerably older than she and that he has just been released from a mental institution. Moreover, she flaunts her voluptuous body in tight dresses and skimpy attire. At one point she has a group of young adults play a sensuous tune and begins a suggestive dance. Cotten appears and smashes the record. Monroe is seen later by Peters kissing a young man, Allan, and she learns that the couple plans to murder Cotten. The husband is then reported dead and Monroe goes to the morgue to ostensibly identify his body but it's not Cotten's corpse she sees but lover boy Allan's. Monroe collapses and is later hospitalized. Peters spots Cotten and tells her easygoing husband Adams, who tells Peters that she must be mistaken. Monroe, however, knows the truth and departs the hospital, attempting to escape. When Cotten runs into Peters again, the suspicious young bride flees, thinking he means to kill her, but Cotten prevents her from falling to her death and then tells her that he had to kill Allan out of self-defense. Peters ponders his guilt and can't decide whether or not to tell the police. Cotten sees Monroe and follows her, chasing her up to an observation tower where he strangles her. Peters is later with Adams and friends on a boat picnic. Adams and the friends go to get gas and Peters is left alone on the boat which Cotten, now fleeing the police, gets aboard and navigates down the river, Peters begging him to turn back. The boat is quickly caught in the fast current and is headed for the Falls and watery death. Cotten realizes that the end is near and maneuvers the boat to a large rock where he places Peters just before the boat is sent over the Falls and Cotten to his death. A police helicopter swoops down and plucks Peters to safety. This was Monroe's film all the way, her 18th and the one that promoted her to superstardom. She really doesn't do much more than Theda Bara vamping, jiggling in tight dresses, gushing her words in whispers, and doing that famous bounce-walk, yet the unsophisticated public of the day translated all of that as great acting or something. She is just as neurotic and disturbing to watch as she was in DON'T BOTHER TO KNOCK (1952) playing a kind of mindless but dangerous female, but much more the two-timing schemer here. Cotten is exceptional and Peters is pretty to look at but has nothing more than a supporting role. Adams and just about everyone else is boring. Hathaway does an outstanding job with the on-and-off script and the MacDonald cinematography is breathtaking in many scenes, particularly of the resplendent Falls.

p, Charles Brackett; d, Henry Hathaway; w, Bracket, Walter Reisch, Richard Breen; ph, Joe MacDonald (Technicolor); m, Sol Kaplan; ed, Barbara McLean; md, Lionel Newman; art d, Lyle Wheeler, Maurice Ransford; set d, Stuart Reiss; cos, Dorothy Jeakins; spec eff, Ray Kellogg; m/l, "Kiss," Newman, Haven Gillespie; makeup, Ben Nye.

Crime Drama   **Cas.**   **(PR:C MPAA:NR)**

NICE GIRL?**   (1941) 95m UNIV bw

Deanna Durbin (Jane Dana), Franchot Tone (Richard Calvert), Walter Brennan (Hector Titus, Postman), Robert Stack (Don Webb), Robert Benchley (Oliver Dana), Helen Broderick (Cora Foster, Housekeeper), Ann Gillis (Nancy Dana), Anne Gwynne (Sylvia Dana), Elisabeth Risdon (Martha Peasley), Nana Bryant (Mary Peasley), George Billings (Pinky Greene), Tommy Kelly (Ken Atkins), Marcia Mae Jones (Girl).

Mainly a vehicle for the looks and charms of Durbin, NICE GIRL? attempted to give the budding starlet a more mature role after a string of successes posing her as a teenager. The weak story has Durbin portraying a girl with a crush on Tone, a professor visiting her family in a suburb of New York City. To get the chance to drive Tone home, to New York, Durbin causes him to miss his train. On the drive and in Tone's apartment Durbin attempts several naive advances toward the older man, but each time is met with a mild though pointed rebuff. This sends the girl back to her hometown sweetheart, Stack, but numerous rumors surface about her and Tone. Tone comes back to set everything straight. Durbin gives her role the needed charm, but comes off as being much too innocent, more the fault of the scriptwriters than the actess. The supporting parts, particularly that of Brennan, as a lovesick postman, and Benchley, as the confused father, are the high points in this production. Durbin sings five songs: "Love at Last" (Eddie Cherkose, Jacques Press); "Perhaps" (Aldo Franchetti, Andreas De Segurola); "Beneath the Lights of Home," "Thank You America" (Bernie Grossman, Walter Jurmann); and "The Old Folks at Home" (Stephen Foster).

p, Joe Pasternak; d, William A. Seiter; w, Richard Connell, Gladys Lehman (based on the play by Phyllis Duganne); ph, Joseph Valentine; ed, Bernard W. Burton; md, Charles Previn; cos, Vera West.

Comedy/Drama   **(PR:A MPAA:NR)**

NICE GIRL LIKE ME, A**½   (1969, Brit.) 90m Partisan-Anglo Embassy/
                                                                    AE c

Barbara Ferris (Candida), Harry Andrews (Savage, Caretaker), Gladys Cooper (Aunt Mary), Bill Hinnant (Ed), James Villiers (Freddie), Joyce Carey (Aunt Celia),

Christopher Guinee (Pierre), Fabia Drake (Miss Grimsby, Schoolteacher), Irene Prador (Mme. Dupont), Erik Chitty (Vicar), Totti Truman-Taylor (Miss Charter), John Serret (Museum Attendant), John Clive (Supermarket Shopper), Ann Lancaster (Miss Garland), Shelagh Wilcox (Labor Ward Sister), Susan Whitman (Labor Ward Nurse), Douglas Wilmer (Postnatal Clinic Doctor), Carol Gilles (Marie), Madge Brindley (Pensione 'Mama'), John Gurnsey, Tom Gill (Customs Officers), Barbara Keogh (Maternity Night Nurse), Robert Sidaway (Shopping Line Assistant), Beryl Cook (Bridal Gowns Assistant), Sidney Johnson (Mr. Wright), Bartlett Mullins (Male Basket Weaver), Sylvia Tysick (Supermarket Shopper's Wife), Sarah Golding (1st Schoolgirl), Cunitia Knight (2nd Schoolgirl), Christine Dingle (3rd Schoolgirl), Sorrel Breuning (4th Schoolgirl), Terry Duggan (Radio Cab Driver), Alistair Hunter (Country Hire Car Driver), Carmen Carpoldi (Mrs. Lamplugh), Bill Clancy (Mr. Lamplugh), Elisabeth Gordon (Mrs. Newton), David Armour (Mr. Newton), Nichola Cowper (Valentine at Age 6 Months), Rebecca Bridge (Valentine at Age 12 Months), Angela Jones (Angelina at Age 6 Months), Kate Herman (Angelina at Age 12 Months).

Lighthearted yarn has Ferris as an orphaned girl forced to live with her nagging elderly aunts, Cooper and Carey. She gets away from them under the pretext of going to Paris to study languages, where she has a brief affair with a student, leaving her pregnant. Once back with her aunts she makes up a story that the baby belongs to someone else, and that she is just watching over it. She reveals the truth to her father's caretaker, Andrews. Antsy to get away again, she goes to Venice to continue her "studies," where she has another affair that again leaves her pregnant. This time a young American tourist is the father. On her way back to England, she encounters a desperate Italian mother who sticks an infant in her arms, begging her to watch over the baby. Back home, her aunts note her condition and try to force her to marry her stuffy cousin Villiers. But at the last moment, Ferris admits that she could never marry Villiers, choosing instead to give it a go with Andrews, the man she has really loved all along. Ferris adds the right amount of charm to the whimsical character, with the rest of the cast filling their roles nicely. Story moves at a steady pace, keeping a comic atmosphere throughout—enabling what could lapse into cynicism or mushy romance to remain as pleasant humor.

p, Roy Millichip; d, Desmond Davis; w, Davis, Anne Piper (based on the novel Marry At Leisure by Piper); ph, Gil Taylor, Manny Wynn (Eastmancolor); m, Pat Williams; ed, Ralph Sheldon; art d, Ken Bridgeman; cos, Ruth Myers; m/l, title song, Williams, Hal Shaper (sung by Vikki Carr).

Comedy   **Cas.**   **(PR:C MPAA:NR)**

NICE LITTLE BANK THAT SHOULD BE ROBBED, A*½
                    (1958) 87m FOX bw (GB: HOW TO ROB A BANK)

Tom Ewell (Max Rutgers), Mickey Rooney (Gus Harris), Mickey Shaughnessy (Harold "Rocky" Baker), Dina Merrill (Margie Solitaire), Madge Kennedy (Grace Havens), Frances Bavier (Mrs. Solitaire), Richard Deacon (Mr. Schroeder), Stanley Clements (Fitz), Tom Greenway (Lt. Green).

Charming idea that never quite lived up to its screen potential has Ewell, an auto mechanic, and Rooney, a horse trainer, robbing a bank. They get away with $30,000, which they squander until they buy a racehorse. In order to get the money to train and to enter it in races, they rob another bank. This time they get caught. The horse is claimed by the bank, and goes on to become a big winner.

p, Anthony Muto; d, Henry Levin; w, Sydney Boehm (based on an article by Evan Wylie); ph, Leo Tover (CinemaScope); m, Lionel Newman; ed, Hugh S. Fowler; art d, Lyle R. Wheeler, Walter M. Simonds.

Comedy   **(PR:A MPAA:NR)**

NICE PLATE OF SPINACH, A   (SEE:
             WHAT WOULD YOU SAY TO SOME SPINACH, 1976, Czech.)

NICE WOMAN*   (1932) 72m UNIV bw

Sidney Fox (Bess Girard), Frances Dee (Jerry Girard), Alan Mowbray (Mark Chandler), Lucille Webster Gleason (Mrs. Girard), Russell Gleason (Bill Wells), James Durkin (Mr. Girard), Kenneth Seiling (Jackie Girard), Carmel Myers (Dorothy Drew), Leonard Carey (Butler), Jo Wallace (Miss Ivine), Patsy O'Byrne (Mary), Florence Enright (Maid).

Sappy romance has Fox as a flapper persuaded by her money-seeking mother to ignore her love for Gleason and marry self-made millionaire Mowbray. The story is dull and plodding, with the characterizations unrelated to anything resembling genuine human personalities. A plus can be given to the luscious sets and the photography, but Knopf can't seem to decide if this is a comedy or a drama and the film suffers as a result.

d, Edwin H. Knopf; w, Knopf, Gladys Lehman (based on the play by William A. Grew); ph, Charles Stumar; ed, Robert Carlisle.

Romance   **(PR:A MPAA:NR)**

NICHOLAS AND ALEXANDRA***½   (1971, Brit.) 183m Horizon/
                                                                    COL c

Michael Jayston (Nicholas), Janet Suzman (Alexandra), Roderic Noble (Alexis), Ania Marson (Olga), Lynne Frederick (Tatiana), Candace Glendenning (Marie), Fiona Fullerton (Anastasia), Harry Andrews (Grand Duke Nicholas), Irene Worth (The Queen Mother), Tom Baker (Rasputin), Jack Hawkins (Count Fredericks), Timothy West (Dr. Botkin), Katherine Schofield (Tegleva), Jean-Claude Drouot (Gilliard), John Hallam (Nagorny), Guy Rolfe (Dr. Fedorov), John Wood (Col. Kobylinsky), Laurence Olivier (Count Witte), Eric Porter (Stolypin), Michael Redgrave (Sazonov), Maurice Denham (Kokovtsov), Ralph Truman (Rodzianko), Gordon Gostelow (Guchkov), John McEnery (Kerensky), Michael Bryant (Lenin), Vivian Pickles (Mme. Krupskaya), Brian Cox (Trotsky), James Hazeldine (Stalin), Stephen Greif (Martov), Steven Berkoff (Pankratov), Eric Chapman (Piekhanov), Ian Holm (Yakovlev), Alan Webb (Yurovsky), Leon Lissek (Avadeyev), David

Giles *(Goloshchekin)*, Roy Dotrice *(Gen. Alexeiev)*, Martin Potter *(Prince Yussoupov)*, Richard Warwick *(Grand Duke Dmitry)*, Vernon Dobtcheff *(Dr. Lazovert)*, Alexander Knox *(American Ambassador Root)*, Ralph Neville *(British Ambassador Buchanan)*, Jorge Rigaud *(French Ambassador Paleologue)*, Curt Jurgens *(German Consul Sklarz)*, Julian Glover *(Gapon)*, John Shrapnel *(Petya)*, Diana Quick *(Sonya)*, John Forbes Robertson *(Col. Volkov)*, Alan Dalton *(Flautist)*, Penny Sugg *(Young Opera Singer)*, David Baxter *(Young Bolshevik)*.

The film is almost as overlong as the reign of the Romanovs but it is nevertheless a fascinating look at the last, tragic Russian monarchs. Jayston as the kindly, indecisive Czar Nicholas, and Suzman as his reclusive, fear-haunted Czarina, are excellent in their roles. Their 1894 marriage is fraught with problems from the onset, Suzman being resented by the Russian people since she is a German and despite the fact that she readily accepts her husband's native language and adopts his religion. Moreover, she bears him four daughters which further causes her to be rejected by the Russian masses. When she finally does provide a male heir to the throne, it is learned that the boy is severely afflicted with hemophilia, the dreaded blue-blood disease, and that Suzman, like her grandmother before her, Queen Victoria, is a carrier. As the boy, Noble, grows up, he is in constant danger; any kind of slight fall or bruising might cause internal or external bleeding that might mean his death. Suzman and Jayston live a nightmare life with this discovery and their every move is governed by their fragile son, leaving them in an emotional state that affects governmental decisions and causes them to withdraw from the people almost altogether. Suzman then meets the mystic, profligate monk, Rasputin, played by Baker, and believes he possesses incredible powers that can heal her son. Baker is called to the Imperial Palace when Noble begins bleeding, and, through hypnosis, is able to halt the bleeding. He becomes an overnight mentor to the throne, his power increasing with each attack suffered by Noble, until he is actually governing Russia, despite Jayston's weak efforts to maintain his authority. While Jayston and his family are away on vacation, the Winter Palace in St. Petersburg is approached by thousands of starving peasants, peacefully demonstrating for food. Cossacks panic and fire into the massive crowds, slaughtering hundreds of the czar's most devoted followers, an incident seized by murderous revolutionaries who use this massacre to promote the overthrow of the throne. Bryant (Lenin) and Cox (Trotsky) label Jayston "Bloody Nicholas" and mount a systematic terrorist crusade to unseat the czar. Olivier, Jayston's top political advisor, sees clearly that the country is heading for bloody revolution and pressures the czar into allowing the formation of a Duma (a people's forum), the first concession to a democratic form of government. McEnery, as the spirited Kerensky, lobbies for sweeping reforms and more liberties. But nothing can save the throne. Porter, as the free-thinking premier Stolypin, is assassinated at the Kiev Opera House, then word reaches Jayston that the mad monk, Baker, is practicing widespread perversions among the nobility and is actually attempting to run his government. He attempts to banish the religious fanatic but Suzman, fearing for the life of her son, who is now wholly dependent upon the mystic Baker, defies Jayston and recalls Baker to court to attend her son. Following the declaration of war by Germany against Russia in 1914, Jayston orders the country mobilized and WW I ensues. The army is archaic and ill-equipped and soon suffers tremendous military losses. Jayston, at Suzman's insistence, dismisses Andrews (Grand Duke Nicholas) and assumes the role of commander-in-chief, going into the field to direct his demoralized troops. Meanwhile, Baker attempts to seize control of the government through subterfuge and is murdered by Potter (Prince Yussoupov), the czar's playboy cousin who is banished by an incensed Suzman. While Jayston's troops suffer one ignominious defeat after another, McEnery and other middle ground revolutionaries decree that the Duma is to control Russia and Jayston's abdication is demanded. Surrounded by failure and disaster, Jayston abdicates against Suzman's frantic pleas to hold onto the throne. France, England, and other countries refuse to give the royal family sanctuary for the past sins of its minions, and the Romanovs, along with some faithful servants, are banished to Siberia. The Bolsheviks seize the government in 1917 and Bryant orders the royal family murdered by an execution squad at Ekaterinburg on July 16, 1918; the entire family is taken to a basement room of a deserted house where its members have been held prisoner and all are shot and bayoneted to death. Historically accurate and beautifully mounted with period costumes, sumptuous sets, and lavished with thousands of extras, NICHOLAS AND ALEXANDRA is a feast for the eye but it often drags as director Schaffner (PATTON) attempts to tell too much, encompassing with his greedy cameras more than two decades of tumultuous Russian history with few of the dynamic real-life characters, other than Jayston and Suzman, developed into flesh-and-blood people. Yet, what is profiled is a treat for the history buff. Goldman's script is expectedly unwieldy and his sympathies for the Romanovs are as evident as those of the orginal author, Massie. (Goldman excelled in historical portraits such as THE LION IN WINTER.) The script is nevertheless literate and educational if not entertaining. Baker, as the mad monk Rasputin, plays his role with all the flamboyance and verve embodied in that darkly fascinating creature, but almost all the other characters are wooden caricatures. Producer Spiegel first assigned George Stevens to direct but Stevens bowed out and a string of other directors—Anthony Harvey, Charles Jarrott, Joseph L. Mankiewicz—were taken up, then discarded before Schaffner took over. Mostly in debate was the casting of the film. The subject was wonderfully covered in MGM's RASPUTIN AND THE EMPRESS (1932), starring (in their only film together) the entire Barrymore clan, Ethel, John, and Lionel, the latter as the frenetic and notorious mad monk. Rasputin was also depicted by Harry Baur in the French production, RASPUTIN (1938), by Edmund Purdom in NIGHTS OF RASPUTIN (1960), by Christopher Lee in RASPUTIN THE MAD MONK (1966), and Gert Frobe in I KILLED RASPUTIN (1968). NICHOLAS AND ALEXANDRA was shot on location in Spain and Yugoslavia. Oscars went to Maxsted, Archer, and Parrondo for art direction, to Dixon for set decoration, and to Blake and Castillo for costumes.

p, Sam Spiegel; d, Franklin J. Schaffner; w, James Goldman, Edward Bond (based on a book by Robert K. Massie); ph, Freddie Young (Panavision, Eastmancolor); m, Richard Rodney Bennett; ed, Ernest Walter; prod d, John Box; art d, Jack Maxsted, Ernest Archer, Gil Parrondo; set d, Vernon Dixon; cos, Yvonne Blake, Antonio Castillo; spec eff, Eddie Fowlie; makeup, Neville Smallwood.

Historical Epic Cas. (PR:C MPAA:GP)

NICHOLAS NICKLEBY** (1947, Brit.) 108m EAL/UNIV bw

Cedric Hardwicke *(Ralph Nickleby)*, Stanley Holloway *(Vincent Crummles)*, Alfred Drayton *(Wackford Squeers)*, Cyril Fletcher *(Alfred Mantalini)*, Bernard Miles *(Newman Noggs)*, Derek Bond *(Nicholas Nickleby)*, Sally Ann Howes *(Kate Nickleby)*, Mary Merrall *(Mrs. Nickleby)*, Sybil Thorndike *(Mrs. Squeers)*, Vera Pearce *(Mrs. Crummles)*, Cathleen Nesbitt *(Miss Knagg)*, Athene Seyler *(Miss La Creevy)*, Cecil Ramage *(Sir Mulberry Hawk)*, George Relph *(Mr. Bray)*, Emrys Jones *(Frank Cheerbyle)*, Fay Compton *(Mme. Mantalini)*, Jill Balcon *(Madeleine Bray)*, Aubrey Woods *(Smike)*, James Hayter *(Ned/Charles Cheeryble)*, Vida Hope *(Fanny Squeers)*, Roddy Hughes *(Tim Linkinwater)*, Timothy Bateson *(Lord Verisopht)*, Frederick Burtwell *(Mercury)*, Patricia Hayes *(Phoebe)*, Michael Shepley *(Mr. Gregsnira)*, M.P. Roy Hermitage *(Wackford Squeers, Jr.)*, Una Bart *(Infant Phenomenon)*, June Elvin *(Miss Snevellicci)*, Drucilla Wills *(Mrs. Grudden)*, Laurence Hanray *(Mr. Gride)*, John Salew *(Mr. Lillyvick)*, Arthur Brander *(Mr. Snawley)*, Eliot Makeham *(Postman)*, Dandy Nichols *(Mantalini's Employee)*, John Chandos *(Employment Agent)*, Guy Rolfe, Hattie Jacques.

Following as it did within a year of the release of David Lean's popular and highly regarded GREAT EXPECTATIONS, it was inevitable that this adaptation of a Dickens novel would be compared to the earlier effort. It was, and it came up lacking. Bond is the young man who toils in a boys' school in Yorkshire where he has been apprenticed by his thoroughly reprehensible uncle, played by Hardwicke. Conditions at the school are appalling, and Bond befriends one of the students, Woods, who has been the victim of much of the brutality at the school. They escape, join a traveling theatrical troupe, and enjoy a series of adventures, with Bond meeting and falling in love with Bray. Their relationship is complicated by the fact that Hardwicke has provided testimony which sent Bray's father to debtor's prison in an attempt to force Bray to marry him. Drayton, Hardwicke's henchman, kidnaps Woods and, though he is rescued by Bond, he dies from the abuse and suffering he has been subjected to by Hardwicke. Bond discovers that Woods was Hardwicke's son, and that Hardwicke had abandoned the boy at an early age to acquire a fortune that rightfully belonged to Woods. When Bond reveals his discovery, the shamed Hardwicke kills himself while Bond and Bray find happiness together. Casting couldn't be better and Cavalcanti has created an authentic "Dickensian" mood, but too much story is compressed into the film, making it difficult to follow. The producer's daughter, Jill, made her screen debut here, as did Woods, both coming from the British stage. Neither would make much of a mark in the movie world, however.

p, Michael Balcon; d, Alberto Cavalcanti; w, John Dighton (based on the novel by Charles Dickens); ph, Gordon Dines; m, Lord Berners; ed, Leslie Norman; md, Ernest Irving; art d, Michael Relph; cos, Marion Horn; spec eff, Lionel Banes, Cliff Richardson; makeup, Ernest Taylor.

Drama Cas. (PR:A MPAA:NR)

NICHT VERSOHNT ODER "ES HILFT NUR GEWALT, WO GEWALT HERRSCHT" (SEE: NOT RECONCILED, OR "ONLY VIOLENCE HELPS WHERE IT RULES," 1969)

NICK CARTER IN PRAGUE (SEE: ADELE HASN'T HAD HER SUPPER YET, 1978, Czech.)

NICK CARTER, MASTER DETECTIVE*** (1939) 60m MGM bw

Walter Pidgeon *(Nick Carter/Robert Chalmers)*, Rita Johnson *(Lou Farnsby)*, Henry Hull *(John A. Keller)*, Stanley C. Ridges *(Dr. Frankton)*, Donald Meek *(Bartholomew)*, Addison Richards *(Hiram Streeter)*, Henry Victor *(J. Lester Hammil)*, Milburn Stone *(Dave Krebs)*, Martin Kosleck *(Otto King)*, Frank Faylen *(Pete Foley)*, Sterling Holloway *(Bee-Catcher)*, Wally Maher *(Cliff Parsons)*, Edgar Dearing *(Denny)*, Richard Lane, Lee Phelps *(Airplane Builders)*, Frank Ball *(Peake)*, George Meeker *(Hartley)*, Richard Terry *(Cain)*, Paul Ellis *(Faber)*, Don Castle *(Ed)*, Louis V. Arco *(Captain of Cruiser)*.

MGM purchased more than 1,000 Nick Carter stories and planned to build a series around the sleuth, with this being the first entry. Pidgeon plays the detective who gets on the trail of some spies out to steal the plans for a plane designed by Hull. When not sifting through through clues and chasing the culprits, Pidgeon finds some time to romance Johnson. Meek plays Pidgeon's trusted aide, and he provides some competent comic relief. French-born Tourneur, who would go on to create some highly regarded horror and *noir* films during the 1940s, does a decent job here in only his second U.S. film assignment. An agreeable escapist adventure. (See NICK CARTER series, Index).

p, Lucien Hubbard; d, Jacques Tourneur; w, Bertram Millhauser (based on a story by Millhauser, Harold Buckley); ph, Charles Lawton; ed, Elmo Veron.

Crime (PR:A MPAA:NR)

NICKEL QUEEN, THE** (1971, Aus.) 88m Woomera c

Googie Withers *(Meg Blake)*, John Laws *(Claude Fitzgerald)*, Alfred Sandor *(Benson)*, Ed Devereaux *(Harry Phillips)*, Peter Gwynne *Andy)*, Doreen Warburton *(Mrs. Benson)*, Tom Oliver *(Roy)*, Ross Thompson *(Arthur)*, Joanna McCallum *(Jenny Blake)*.

After an absence of almost 20 years, Withers, a British movie star of the 1940s and 1950s, proved herself to still be a competent actress, adding charm to her role as the owner of a pub in the Australian hinterlands. Things change for her with the discovery of nickel in the area. She stakes a claim, but is bought out by an American company headed by Sandor on the condition that Withers does not sell her shares in the company for a year. This gives Sandor a chance to make some phony reports, enabling him to overvalue his corporate shares. Withers lives it up with her new-found wealth, assisted by gigolo Laws, an ex-hippie. In the end Withers settles down with her long-time admirer Devereaux. Except for Withers, the performances are all pretty routine, as is the script and direction. The excellent photography adds some life. McCallum, Withers' real-life daughter, makes her film debut here as. . .Withers' daughter.

p&d, John McCallum; w, McCallum, Henry C. James, Joy Cavill (based on the story by Henry and Anneke James); m, Sven Libaek; ed, Don Saunders.

Drama **(PR:A MPAA:NR)**

NICKEL RIDE, THE*** (1974) 106m Boardwalk/FOX c

Jason Miller *(Cooper)*, Linda Haynes *(Sarah)*, Victor French *(Paddie)*, John Hillerman *(Carl)*, Bo Hopkins *(Turner)*, Richard Evans *(Bobby)*, Brendan Burns *(Larry)*, Lou Frizzell *(Paulie)*, Jeanne Lange *(Jeannie)*, Bart Burns *(Elias)*, Harvey Gold *(Chester)*, Mark Gordon *(Tonozzi)*, Lee Debroux *(Harry)*.

A depressing but truthful look at a small-time hoodlum in a big-time business. Miller is a two-bit crook who runs his downtown Los Angeles turf like a minor-league Godfather, but he is not long for the territory, as the bosses have decided that he can't handle the situation any longer. They don't like the way he does things and will not tolerate mavericks in the mob. He's attempting to make an agreement for an old warehouse where he can stash some of the syndicate's stolen goods, but the deal is falling through. The bosses sic Hopkins on Miller to keep an eye on him, as they are rankled because he's been unable to make the warehouse deal happen. Evans works for Miller, and when he beats up prizefighter Gordon (who won't go down for the count) and then kills Gordon's manager, Frizzell, the bosses are further angered, even though Miller had nothing to do with Evans' activities. Miller tells Evans he was wrong, but keeps looking over his shoulder at Hopkins and thinks that the man may be there to write "30" on his career. Miller and his lady, Haynes, go off for a weekend in the country where he also hopes to conclude the warehouse business, but it doesn't work out and Miller is rapidly suspecting everyone around him now and becoming increasingly paranoid schizophrenic. His fantasies are very real to him as he imagines Hopkins killing Haynes. To prevent that, he ships Haynes to Nevada and he plans to meet her in Las Vegas the next afternoon. Miller is now convinced that Hopkins is after him, and he goes to his contact in the mob (Hillerman) to complain, but he is assured that it's just his imagination. Fat chance, Miller is preparing to leave for his tryst with Haynes when Hopkins arrives, shoots Miller, and is about to administer the coup de grace. Miller has enough strength to fight back and he crushes the life out of Hopkins' throat, but he has been mortally wounded by the bullet. He's found the following morning, dead on a street bench, and the huge ring of keys that is his mark of authority falls to the ground with a clatter as the film ends. An interesting mixture of reality and fantasy, we are never sure if what we are seeing is what is happening to Miller or what he is thinking. Miller is also a playwright and wrote THAT CHAMPIONSHIP SEASON as well as directing the film. Co-executive producer David Foster is a veteran publicity man who spent many years thumping the tub for various celebrities before teaming with Lawrence Turman (who produced THE GRADUATE) and having great success as a producer.

p&d, Robert Mulligan; w, Eric Roth; ph, Jordan Cronenweth (DeLuxe Color); m, Dave Grusin; ed, O. Nicholas Brown; art d, Larry Paull; set d, Jack Stevens

Drama **(PR:C MPAA:PG)**

NICKELODEON** (1976) 121m COL c

Ryan O'Neal *(Leo Harrigan)*, Burt Reynolds *(Buck Greenway)*, Tatum O'Neal *(Alice Forsyte)*, Brian Keith *(H.H. Cobb)*, Stella Stevens *(Marty Reeves)*, John Ritter *(Franklin Frank)*, Jane Hitchcock *(Kathleen Cooke)*, Harry Carey, Jr. *(Dobie)*, James Best *(Jim)*, George Gaynes *(Reginald Kingsley)*, M. Emmet Walsh *(Logan)*, Jack Perkins, Brion James, Sidney Armus, Joe Warfield, Tamar Cooper, Alan Gibbs, Mathew Anden, Lorenzo Music, Arnold Soboloff, Jeffrey Byron, Priscilla Pointer, Don Calfa, Philip Bruns, Edward Marshall, John Blackwell, E.J. Andre, Christa Lang, Maurice Manson, Louis Guss, Frank Marshall, Andrew Winner, Matilda Calnan, Gustar Unger, Bertil Unger, James O'Connell, Ric Mancini, Mark Dennis, E. Hampton Beagle, Hedgemon Lewis, Bill Riddle, Dino Judd, Jack Verbois, John Chappell, Carleton Ripple, Rita Abrams, Sara Jane Gould, Mary Beth Bell, Miriam Byrd Nethery, Rusty Blitz, Les Josephson, Tom Erhart, Griffin O'Neal, Patricia O'Neal, Morgan Farley, Anna Thea, Elaine Partnow, Joseph G. Medalis, Billy Beck, Roger Hampton, Gordon Hurst, Charles Thomas Murphy, Hamilton Camp, Ted Gehring, Stanley Brock, Vincent Milana, Lee Gordon Moore, John Finnegan, Christian Grey, Robert E. Ball, Chief Elmer Tugsmith, Rude Frimel, Hal Needham, Julie Ann Johnson, Joe Amsler, Ron Stein, Charles Tamburro.

An attempt by director Bogdanovich to capture his great love of early movies in a full-length motion picture. Based on anecdotes Bogdanovitch gleaned from his interviews with John Ford, Howard Hawks, Raoul Walsh, Allan Dwan, and other directors, the picture is a somewhat true account of what the motion picture industry was like before the moguls turned movie-making into a big business. According to NICKELODEON, stars and directors got their starts more through convenience and accessibility than through any great talent or drive to make movies. The results were a haphazard mixture that served as a great form of entertainment for millions. NICKELODEON begins with Reynolds and Ryan O'Neal landing jobs on a production, Reynolds as the leading man and O'Neal, a struggling lawyer, as a director. The first half of the picture is more-or-less a number of slapstick incidents as the untalented filmmakers try to make movies, while O'Neal and Reynolds fight for the affection of leading lady Hitchcock. The tone gets serious as the industry starts to grow, and the players go their separate ways, only to be reunited in a somewhat sappy "happy" ending. Though the fine cast delivers good performances, they are never allowed to show much depth. As an homage to the start of the film industry, this extravaganza is quite a tribute, but as a motion picture it's sadly lacking. Scenes are shown from BIRTH OF A NATION (with a red tint to conform to the color) with Griffith actually taking a bow on the movie theater stage while O'Neal and Reynolds cheer him. This signifies the end of the one-reelers and the beginning of feature films. Reynolds reportedly had a hard time with Tatum O'Neal, later stating: "I like children, but she ain't no kid."

p, Irwin Winkler, Robert Chartoff; d, Peter Bogdanovich; w, Bogdanovich, W. D. Richter; ph, Laszlo Kovacs (Metrocolor); m, Richard Hazard; ed, William Carruth; art d, Richard Berger; set d, Darrell Silvera; cos, Theadora Van Runkle.

Comedy **(PR:C MPAA:PG)**

NIGHT, THE (SEE: LA NOTTE, 1961, Fr./Ital.)

NIGHT AFFAIR** (1961, Fr.) 92m Orex/President bw (LE DESORDRE ET LA NUIT)

Jean Gabin *(Inspector Vallois)*, Danielle Darrieux *(Therese Marken)*, Nadja Tiller *(Lucky)*, Paul Frankeur *(Inspector Chaville)*, Hazel Scott *(Valentine Horse)*, Robert Manuel *(Blasco)*, Robert Berri *(Marquis)*, Roger Hanin *(Simoni)*, Harald Wolff *(Lucky's Father)*, Francois Chaumette *(Commissioner Janin)*, Raoul Saint-Yves, Amy Colin, Edouard Fleming.

Gabin plays a police inspector who's on to the murder of a night club owner, when he falls in love with the drug-addicted mistress (Tiller) of the murdered man. He tries to induce the girl to give him information that will solve the case, and thus keep Tiller from suspicion. But the commissioner wants the case solved, ordering Gabin to lock up Tiller. However, the girl turns up missing, leading Gabin to the home of pharmacist Darrieux, and the real killer.

p, Lucien Viard; d, Gilles Grangier; w, Michel Audiard, Grangier, Jacques Robert; ph, Louis Page; m, Jean Yatove; ed, Jacqueline Douarinou; art d, Robert Bouladoux; set d, Robert Pilat; cos, Irene Pawloff, Nanda Belloni; m/l, Yatove, Henri Contet; makeup, Yvonne Gasperina.

Crime **(PR:A MPAA:NR)**

NIGHT AFTER NIGHT*** (1932) 70m PAR bw

George Raft *(Joe Anton)*, Constance Cummings *(Jerry Healy)*, Wynne Gibson *(Iris Dawn)*, Mae West *(Mandie Triplett)*, Alison Skipworth *(Mrs. Mabel Jellyman)*, Roscoe Karns *(Leo)*, Louis Calhern *(Dick Bolton)*, Bradley Page *(Frankie Guard)*, Al Hill *(Blainey)*, Harry Wallace *(Jerky)*, Dink Templeton *(Patsy)*, Marty Martyn *(Malloy)*, Tom Kennedy *(Tom)*, Gordon Elliott *(Escort)*.

This was Raft's first starring role in films but it was also West's first talking film and the hip-slinging, wisecracking, eye-batting blonde stole the show. Raft is an ambitious low-life with little education and a lot of cash who wants to crash society. He opens a posh nightclub and goes after the carriage trade but he's fearful of his bad manners and gutter diction offending his high society patrons. To correct the situation, Raft hires speech coach Skipworth who tips him on how to speak and even what to talk about. When he spies Park Avenue beauty Cummings, Raft has plenty to say but he learns that Cummings' once wealthy family is now on the rocks, ruined by the Depression. Worse, his hoity-toity club now occupies the very site where her family mansion once stood. Raft arranges for a quiet dinner at his club with Skipworth on hand to chaperone the event. But just as the dinner gets under way in bursts West, one of Raft's uncouth old flames. She bears no ill will toward reformed thug Raft but is only consumed with furthering her own nest egg. West plays havoc with the intimate dinner and throws the very proper Skipworth into a tizzy when she explains the facts of life in no uncertain and very suggestive terms. Meanwhile, Raft's henchman buddy Karns tries to tell him that hoodlums and high society really don't mix and he shouldn't set his sights on Cummings. Then another ex-mistress of Raft's, the raucous Gibson, appears and just about chews up the nightclub until she's subdued. In the end, Karns is proven right; Cummings gives Raft the heave-ho, telling him that she belongs with someone in her own class and intends to marry polo playboy Calhern. At least that's what the audience expects and gets until a turnabout at the last minute by Cummings who realizes Calhern is a snooty cad and Raft is the guy for her. West, though she's only in a supporting role, walks away with all the honors, delivering one sharp wisecrack after another. A hatcheck girl sees her diamonds and shouts: "Goodness!" West's classic retort: "Goodness had nothing to do with it, dearie." West ran roughshod over director Mayo who was then relatively inexperienced, altering his setup shots and doing as she pleased. "She stole everything but the cameras," Raft later quipped. From the first moment on the screen West lets her inimitable presence be known. A doorman stares through a peephole of Raft's club to ask: "Who's dere?" Replies an impatient West: "The fairy princess, ya mug!" Skipworth is also a delight as the matron dithering over West's dubious occupation (although West later reveals that she owns a string of beauty parlors). It's all very sleek and snappy and, when West cavorts before the cameras, it's a riot. Raft and West would not appear together again until 1978 in SEXTETTE. They both died in 1980 within two days of each other, she at 87, he at 85.

p, William LeBaron; d, Archie Mayo; w, Vincent Lawrence, Kathryn Scola, Mae West (based on the novel *Single Night* by Louis Bromfield); ph, Ernest Haller.

Drama **(PR:C MPAA:NR)**

NIGHT AFTER NIGHT AFTER NIGHT*½ (1970 Brit.) 88m Dudley Birch/BUT c

Jack May *(Judge Charles Lomax)*, Justine Lord *(Helena Lomax)*, Gilbert Wynne *(Inspector Bill Rowan)*, Linda Marlowe *(Jenny Rowan)*, Terry Scully *(Carter)*, Donald Sumpter *(Pete Laver)*, Peter Forbes-Robinson *(Powell)*, Jacqueline Clark *(Josie Leach)*, Jack Smethurst *(Chief Inspector)*, April Harlow *(Stripper)*.

A limp attempt to create a psycho-crime drama in which Wynne plays an inspector who is dead set in his opinion that a teenager is guilty of murder. A bit more investigation on his part leads him to the discovery that this youth is innocent and that the real culprit is a well-respected judge. The addition of some sleazy elements does nothing to heighten intrigue.

p, James Mellor; d, Lewis J. Force; w, Dail Ambler.

Crime **(PR:C-O MPAA:NR)**

NIGHT ALARM*½ (1935) 65m Majestic bw

Bruce Cabot, Judith Allen, H. B. Warner, Sam Hardy, Betty Blythe, Fuzzy Knight, Tom Hanlon, Harold Minjir, Harry Holman, John Bleifer.

Cabot is a reporter for a daily that gives town boss Warner a lot of flack, when Warner's daughter, Allen, who wants to try her hand at reporting, takes over Cabot's column. This gives the writer a chance to write a savage attack on the bigwig, causing strife between himself and Allen. But everything is settled when Allen is lost in a blaze at her father's paper factory, and Cabot rescues her. Good playing does little to rescue this poorly paced story.

p, Larry Darmour; d, Spencer Bennett; w, Earle Snell (based on the story by Jack Stanley); ph, James S. Brown, Jr.; ed, Dwight Caldwell.

Drama **(PR:A MPAA:NR)**

NIGHT ALONE½** (1938, Brit.) 75m Welwyn/Pathe bw

Emlyn Williams *(Charles Seaton)*, Leonora Corbett *(Vi)*, Lesley Brook *(Barbara Seaton)*, Cyril Raymond *(Tommy)*, Margot Landa *(Celia)*, Julie Suedo *(Gloria)*, John Turnbull *(Superintendent)*, Wally Patch *(Policeman)*, Basil Cunard, Joseph Cunningham, James Pirrie.

Swiftly moving British farce has Williams and Brook as a devoted couple, spending their first night apart in over seven years. While Brook is off visiting her prickly-tongued sister, Corbett, Williams and a friend go to a local night club to get plastered, and indulge in other forms of galivanting. The loyal husband wakes up in a strange woman's apartment, only to be arrested for the possession of forged banknotes. The only way Williams can prove his innocence is to disclose information which could lead to his wife's discovery of his escapades. Lots of laughs coming from the witty lines of Corbett, and the dual personas of Williams. Could use some tightening in the editing room, but generally moves at a good pace.

p, Warwick Ward; d, Thomas Bentley; w, Victor Kendall, Vernon Clancy (based on the play by Jeffrey Dell); ph, Bryan Langley.

Comedy **(PR:A MPAA:NR)**

NIGHT AMBUSH*** (1958, Brit.) 93m Vega/RANK bw (GB: ILL MET BY MOONLIGHT)

Dirk Bogarde *(Maj. Paddy Leigh-Fermor, "Philidem")*, Marius Goring *(Gen. Karl Kreipe)*, David Oxley *(Capt. Billy Stanley Moss)*, Cyril Cusack *(Sandy)*, Wolfe Morris *(George)*, Laurence Payne *(Manoli)*, Michael Gough *(Andoni Zoidakis)*, Rowland Bartrop *(Micky Akoumianakis)*, Brian Worth *(Stratis Saviolkis)*, Paul Stassino *(Yanni Katsias)*, Adeeb Assaly *(Zahari)*, John Cairney *(Elias)*, George Egeniou *(Charis Zographakis)*, Demitri Andreas *(Nikko)*, Theo Moreas *(Village Priest)*, Takis Frangofinos *(Michali)*, Peter Augustine, Christopher Lee, Christopher Rhodes, David McCallum, John and Phyllis Houseman.

An unlikely pair of heroes, Bogarde and Oxley, kidnap nazi general Goring from the German headquarters on Crete in order to transport him to British-occupied Cairo. Aided by a group of Cretan freedom fighters, they hijack the general's car, then lead their captive through dangerous mountain terrain to a waiting boat, while an immense number of Nazi soldiers look for their missing leader. Loosely based on an actual incident during WW II, the material is handled in an imaginative manner that brings out both the intrigue and the humor in this ordeal. The performances of the three leads add the verve which is vital for the film's success. Foremost among these is Goring as the Nazi general; always overconfident and cocky, he is certain that the two British officers lack the skill with which to carry out such an important mission. Yet, Bogarde and Oxley always come up with some ingenious method with which to thwart their pursuers, never appearing as the unflinching heroes common to so many war films. Goring's last-ditch attempt to alert his soldiers to his whereabouts has him leaving a trail of buttons and medals, which are all picked up by Bogarde and returned to the general after having reached their destination. The score by Theodorakis was his first such credit for an international film.

p,d&w, Michael Powell, Emeric Pressburger (based on the book *Ill Met by Moonlight* by W. Stanley Moss); ph, Christopher Challis (VistaVision); m, Mikis Theodorakis; ed, Arthur Stevens; md, Frederic Lewis; art d, Alex Vetchinsky; spec eff, Bill Warrington.

War **(PR:A MPAA:NR)**

NIGHT AND DAY*½ (1933, Brit.) 77m Gainsborough/GAU bw (GB: JACK'S THE BOY)

Jack Hulbert *(Jack Brown)*, Cicely Courtneidge *(Mrs. Bobday)*, Winifred Shotter *(Ivy)*, Francis Lister *(Jules Martin)*, Peter Gawthorne *(Mr. Brown)*, Ben Field *(Mr. Bobday)*, Charles Farrell *(Martin)*, Ronald Curtis.

A British farce about a boy who becomes a policeman after his father, a Scotland Yard detective, doesn't trust him enough to let him join the Yard. Hulbert appears to be something right out of Mack Sennett in his portrayal of a bumbling cop-detective, chasing some notorious jewel thieves after spoiling the original arrest of the crooks. He is aided by Courtneidge, also the apple of the head crook's eye. Dialog drags a bit, as though it's being read for the stage. Hulbert saves his performance with a lot of likable charm.

p, Michael Balcon; d, Walter Forde; w, W. P. Lipscomb (based on the story by Jack Hulbert, Douglas Furber); ph, Leslie Rowson; m, Vivian Ellis; ed, Ian Dalrymple, John Goldman; m/l, Douglas Furber, Ellis.

Comedy **(PR:A MPAA:NR)**

NIGHT AND DAY*** (1946) 128m WB c

Cary Grant *(Cole Porter)*, Alexis Smith *(Linda Lee Porter)*, Monty Woolley *(Himself)*, Ginny Simms *(Carole Hill)*, Jane Wyman *(Gracie Harris)*, Eve Arden *(Gabrielle)*, Victor Francen *(Anatole Giron)*, Alan Hale *(Leon Dowling)*, Dorothy Malone *(Nancy)*, Tom D'Andrea *(Bernie)*, Selena Royle *(Kate Porter)*, Donald Woods *(Ward Blackburn)*, Henry Stephenson *(Omar Porter)*, Paul Cavanagh *(Bart McClelland)*, Sig Rumann *(Willowsky)*, Carlos Ramirez, Milada Mladova, Estelle Sloan, George Zoritch *(Specialty Dancers)*, Adam, Jayne DiGalano *(Specialty Team)*, Mary Martin *(Herself)*, James Dobbs, John Compton, John Miles, Art Kassel, Paul Garkie, Laddie Rucker *(Students)*, Frank Dae, Boyd Irwin, Sam Flint, Charles Miller *(Professors)*, John Alvin *(Petey)*, Harlan Briggs *(Doorman)*, Harry Seymour *(Clarence the Piano Player)*, Clarence Muse *(Caleb)*, JoAnn Marlowe *(Tina)*, Regina Wallace, Frank Ferguson *(Tina's Parents)*, George Meader *(Minister)*, Virginia Sale *(Minister's Wife)*, Bertha Woolford, Armba Dandridge *(Servants)*, Gregory Muradian *(Small Caroler)*, Lisa Golm, Ernest Golm *(Foreign Couple)*, John Goldsworthy *(Yale Gentleman)*, Gary Owen *(Bartender)*, Crane Whitley *(Commercial Artist)*, Lynne Baggett *(Sexboat)*, Rebel Randall, Arlyne Roberts *(Chorus Girls)*, Paula Drew, Patricia Clark, Jane Harker *(Specialty Trio)*, Creighton Hale, Paul Gustine *(Men in Theater)*, Bob McKenzie *(Hansom Cab Driver)*, Alan Shute, Bill Hind, Eric Wilton *(English Officers)*, Edgar Caldwell, George Volk, Allen Marston *(American Officers)*, Leon Lenoir, Michael Panaieff, Pierre Duval *(French Officers)*, James Dodd *(Red)*, Emile Hilb *(Orchestra Leader)*, Bernard Deroux *(Assistant to Giron)*, George Suzanne, Henry DeSoto *(Waiters)*, Marie Melesch *(Scrub Woman)*, Adrian Doeshou, Rene Mimieux *(Men at Bar)*, Fred Dash, Maurice Brierre, Albert Petit *(French Waiters)*, Frank Marlowe *(Army Driver)*, Rune Hultman *(American Lieutenant), Peter Camlin (French Lieutenant)*, George Riley *(O'Halloran)*, Fern Emmett *(Secretary)*, Ruth Matthews, Betty Blair, Valerie Ardis, Edna Harris, Ellen Lowe, Joan Winfield *(Nurses)*, Dick Erdman, Robert Arthur, Caren Harsh, Patsy Harmon, Dorothy Reisner *(Young Customers)*, Claire Meade, Charles Williams *(Customers)*, Mayo Newhall *(Bearded Man)*, George Nokes *(Wayne Blackburn, Child)*, Gordon Richards *(Coachman)*, Laura Treadwell *(Woman in Theater)*, Frank Miliott *(Man in Theater)*, Howard Freeman *(Producer)*, Bobby Watson *(Director)*, Philip Van Zandt *(Librettist)*, Harry Crocker *(Newspaperman)*, John "Red" Pierson, Herman Bing *("Peaches")*, Chester Clute *(Music Publisher), Joyce Compton, Helen O'Hara, Suzanne Rosser (Chorines)*, Dick Bartell *(Photographer)*, Eddie Kane *(Headwaiter)*, Louis Quince, Marion Gray, Willis Claire, Leota Lorraine *(Couples)*, Rudy Friml *(Orchestra Leader)*, John Vosper *(Man)*, Helen Pender *(Pretty Nurse)*, Eddie Kelly *(Callboy)*, Bill Hardsway, Jack Richardson, Tom McGuire, Ed Biby *(Surgeons)*, Laurie Shermain *(Intern)*, Hobart Cavanaugh, Almira Sessions *(Couple in Hospital Corridor)*, Gene Garrick *(Soldier)*, Jacqueline Milo *(French Girl)*, George Kirby *(Cab Driver)*, Wally Scott *(Chauffeur)*, Colin Kenny *(Doorman)*, Herbert Evans *(Bobby)*, Gladden James, Mike Lally, Dick Earle, J.W. Johnstone *(Doctors)*, Buddy Gorman *(English Page Boy)*, Harold DeBecker *(English Workman)*, Jack Mower *(Livery Chauffeur)*, Elizabeth Valentine *(Matron in Hospital)*, Cyril Ring, Vivien Oakland *(Married Couple)*, Pat Gleason *(Dance Director)*, Don Roy *(Band Leader)*, Hans Herbert *(Headwaiter)*, Ruth Costello, Dorothy Costello *(Twins, Dance Team)*, George Boyce *(Stage Manager)*, Fred Deming *(Guest)*, Bert Moorhouse, Marshall Ruth, Fred Santley *(Yale Alumni, Class of 1916)*, Joe Kirkwood, Jr., Gene Stanley *(Classmates of Cole Porter)*, Henry Hasting *(Black Bartender)*, Nicodemus "Nick" Stewart *(Black Waiter)*.

One of the better biomusicals of the 1940s, NIGHT AND DAY professes to tell the story of Cole Porter but puts more accent on his music than his reclusive life. And that's the way it should be. Untypical is the approach to the composer's life. He was born into wealth and had to struggle little, although he endured physical hardships and endless operations to correct badlegs that would have sent most men into the insane asylum. Contrary to most critical opinion in the past, Grant was not miscast in this role but played the perfectly restrained, distant man that was indeed Porter. He is shown beginning his compositions while at Yale in 1914 where he is loyally supported by professor Woolley who continues to be at Grant's side through thick and thin, cheering him on, encouraging him to produce one important composition after another. He is shown later near the front lines during WW I as an ambulance driver for the French, sitting in a bombed out village, listening to Senegalese troops marching to the trenches, fascinated by their haunting war chant and he begins to compose a tune on the spot but is interrupted and buried by a bomb barrage. He attempts to remember the tune while recovering in the hospital where Smith, a nurse, attends to him. He later puts together out of these memories the powerful "Begin the Beguine." (This part is based on reality; Porter never did get the composition as right as he originally envisioned it and whenever he heard it afterwards he reportedly had deep regrets.) Smith later marries Grant but his musical career takes precedence over everything and Smith walks out on Grant as his successes mount and he becomes a worldwide celebrity in the musical world. Throughout the film Grant's stuffy well-to-do Indiana family rejects him for his chosen profession but finally comes around to paying him the respect he has sought all his life, especially from his aristocratic grandfather, Stephenson, who has a drink with him, congratulates him on his achievements, then dies. Grant is later injured again while horseback riding; his mount is frightened during a thunderstorm and throws him. A series of excruciatingly painful operations is then performed to save Grant's legs, although he is comforted by listening to his music being performed over the airways. In the end, at a Yale reunion, while Grant is walking with the aid of two canes, Smith arrives and the two embrace in the shadows to suggest a happy ending. True, the film does not really get under Porter's skin and reveal the depths of this complex human, nor does it even hint at his homosexuality, but it does provide a grand showcase for Porter's tunes, albeit the film is overlong and the attempt to include almost all of his greatest hits leaves many of these marvelous compositions truncated. It's still pleasant throughout and Woolley is the smiling, witty counterpoint to Oscar Levant in RHAPSODY IN BLUE (the equally obtrusive biopic of George Gershwin). Music includes: "My Heart Belongs to Daddy" (sung to a polite striptease by Martin which she introduced in the 1938 musical on Broadway "Leave It To Me"), "You're the Top" (sung by Grant and Simms in a medley, songs originally introduced on Broadway by Ethel Merman), "Begin the Beguine" (sung by Ramirez, accompanied by the dance team of Mladova and

Zoritch), "I've Got You Under My Skin" (Simms, with Adam and Jayne Di Gatano accompanying), "Just One of Those Things," "I Get a Kick Out of You"(Simms), "Night and Day," "What Is This Thing Called Love," "Do I Love You," "An Old-Fashioned Garden," "Miss Otis Regrets," "Love For Sale," "In the Still of the Night," "Bullfrog," "You Do Something to Me," "Easy to Love," "Let's Do It," "I'm Unlucky at Gambling," "Rosalie," "You've Got That Thing," "Don't Fence Me In," "I'm in Love Again," "Anything Goes," and, by Jack Yellen and Milton Ager, "I Wonder What's Become of Sally."

p, Arthur Schwartz; d, Michael Curtiz; w, Charles Hoffman, Leo Townsend, William Bowers (based on the career of Cole Porter adapted by Jack Moffitt); ph, Peverell Marley, William V. Skall (Technicolor); m, Max Steiner; ed, David Weisbart; md, Leo F. Forbstein; art d, John Hughes; set d, Armor Marlowe; cos, Milo Anderson, Travilla; spec eff, Robert Burks; ch, LeRoy Prinz; makeup, Perc Westmore.

Musical/Biography   Cas.   (PR:A   MPAA:NR)

NIGHT AND THE CITY***½   (1950, Brit.) 95m FOX bw

Richard Widmark (*Harry Fabian*), Gene Tierney (*Mary Bristol*), Googie Withers (*Helen Nosseross*), Hugh Marlowe (*Adam Dunn*), Francis L. Sullivan (*Phil Nosseross*), Herbert Lom (*Kristo*), Stanislaus [Stanley] Zbyszko (*Gregorius*), Mike Mazurki (*Strangler*), Charles Farrell (*Beer*), Ada Reeve (*Molly*), Ken Richmond (*Nikolas*), Elliot Makeham (*Pinkney*), Betty Shale (*Mrs. Pinkney*), Russell Westwood (*Yosh*), James Hayter (*Figler*), Tomy Simpson (*Cozen*), Maureen Delaney (*Anna Siberia*), Thomas Gallagher (*Bagrag*), Edward Chapman, Gibb Mclaughlin, Aubrey Dexter, Derek Blomfield, Kay Kendall.

A dark, brooding, almost clammy production, NIGHT AND THE CITY is terrific *film noir* and Widmark is a riveting standout as a hustling promoter who sinks into the quagmire of his own ambitions and drowns in them. Widmark works for obese Sullivan, owner of a sleazy dive to which the hustler steers suckers on the promise of witnessing some racy shows. But it's all very tame and even proper Tierney sings there, she being a disapproving girl friend of wily Widmark. Tierney keeps after Widmark to get a decent job but the con is in his blood and he is obsessed with developing wildcatting money schemes. He overhears famed wrestler Zbyszko talking to his protege Richmond in a huge sports arena owned by Zbyszko's son, Lom. Before Widmark is thrown out of the arena for hustling customers to Sullivan's club, he learns that Zbyszko is disgusted by the fake wrestling matches his son offers to the public, that only his traditional Greco-Roman wrestling is a pure sport. Widmark later goes to Zbyszko and cons him into believing that he will promote the long neglected Greco-Roman wrestling and bring it back to the popularity it once enjoyed. The legendary wrestler agrees to lend his name to the enterprise, which incenses the powerful Lom, who threatens Widmark with extermination if he goes ahead with the scheme and misuses his father. On the other hand, if he truly promotes Greco-Roman wrestling, Lom tells Widmark, he can go ahead. Next Widmark goes to Withers, Sullivan's two-timing wife and Widmark's sideline paramour. He asks her for the money to establish his wrestling matches since Sullivan refuses to make a loan. Withers tells him yes, but only on condition that he bribe authorities into giving her a nightclub license so she can leave her dominating husband. Widmark provides Withers with a forged license and then gets enough money to have Sullivan match it. Withers leaves Sullivan, which infuriates the greasy fat man, who now believes Widmark has been having an affair with his wife. He goes to Lom and they work out a deal to ruin Widmark. Then Sullivan tells Widmark that he will not back his matches unless he uses big, murderous, phony wrestler Mazurki, the very man Zbyszko hates the most as the epitome of modern, fake wrestling. Trapped, Widmark engineers Mazurki into coming to his gym, where he challenges Richmond. Zbyszko agrees to the match but while Widmark, tasting triumph, prepares the contract for the match, Mazurki insults Zbyszko and the two go at each other in earnest in the ring. The older Zbyszko wins but the effort is too much for him and he has a stroke. Lom, livid, arrives to see his father die and Widmark tries to lie his way out of the disaster. He realizes he is a marked man and flees. Lom alerts the entire London underworld. Widmark goes to Withers—who ignores him—and then to Sullivan, who sneers as he explains how he entrapped him for dallying with his wife, adding: "You're a dead man, Harry Fabian, a dead man." Widmark keeps running through the dark streets of London, panting, sweating, afraid of every shadow as a thousand killers hunt him. He has nowhere to turn and nowhere to go and he knows it. He finally remembers an old barge lady, Delaney, who has dealt with him in black marketeering. He sits with her in a small cabin on her barge anchored on the Thames and pours out his fears, shaking, stating in a quavering voice: "How close I came...The things I did." Widmark is not remorseful about his conniving ways and merely uses the barge lady as an emotional sop, much the same way he has used everyone in his life, including Tierney, his one true love, who tracks him down to the barge in an effort to save him. But Lom's henchmen find him and, at the last minute, he shouts out statements in an attempt to clear Tierney of his own lethal machinations, then runs for his life—right into Mazurki, who kills Widmark and dumps his body into the murky waters of the Thames. NIGHT AND THE CITY is an uncompromising, exciting, but thoroughly anxious film that is seen through Widmark's desperate viewpoint. Director Dassin relentlessly displays London without charm and grace, showing only the seamy side where Widmark and his unsavory kind, except the lovely Tierney, dwell and live out their unscrupulous lives without thought of love or compassion. Everything is cold and calculating, one character using another in a greed for human control. The world Widmark desires to enter is that controlled by the Loms and Sullivans—who belong to a very exclusive club. They are as crooked and immoral as Widmark, but they have the money and the connections, and Widmark only aspires to be a loftier version of his own venal self. There is a consistent feeling of lonely helplessness throughout the film but it is shown in such a frenetic pace that it's utterly captivating while being repulsive. Widmark's performance is nothing short of remarkable. Greene's camerawork captures the stark reality of London's

tawdry side and Waxman's score is pulsating and emotionally powerful. The wrestling scene between Zbyszko, a former heavyweight wrestling champion, and Mazurki is one of the most heart-pounding matches ever filmed. Dassin does not spare the brutality, and the violence and implied violence will certainly upset youngsters.

p, Samuel G. Engel; d, Jules Dassin; w, Joe Eisinger (based on the novel by Gerald Kersh); ph, Max Greene [Mutz Greenbaum]; m, Franz Waxman; ed, Nick De Maggio, Sidney Stone; art d, C.P. Norman; cos, Oleg Cassini for Gene Tierney, Margaret Furse for Googie Withers.

Crime Drama   (PR:O   MPAA:NR)

NIGHT ANGEL, THE**   (1931) 75m PAR bw

Fredric March (*Rudek Berkem*), Nancy Carroll (*Yula Martini*), Alan Hale (*Biezal*), Alison Skipworth (*Countess de Martini*), Katherine Emmett (*Mrs. Berkem*), Phoebe Foster (*Theresa Masar*), Otis Sheridan (*Schmidt*), Hubert Druce (*Vincent*), Lewis Walker (*Kafka*), Clarence Derwent (*Rosenbach*), Charles Howard (*Clown*), Doris Rankin (*Matron*), Francine Dowd (*Mitzi*), Cora Witherspoon, Francis Pierlot, Estelle Winwood.

What started as a high-minded project for Goulding, who wrote and directed one of Nancy Carroll's most successful pictures, THE DEVIL'S HOLIDAY, in 1930, became poorly constructed, haphazard, and insincere for all involved. March plays a district attorney in Prague, forced to close down the cafe of Skipworth, a place of ill-fame, sending the keeper to jail. March relegates the daughter, Carroll, to a nurse's home instead of the reformatory, until the mother is released from jail. When the mother and daughter are re-united, March visits the establishment. He is attacked by the doorman, Hale, who is madly in love with Carroll and therefore jealous of March. March kills the man in self-defense, and then is tried for the murder. He is saved when Carroll gives a tear-filled speech, declaring her love for March. The loose script and poorly paced direction receive no help from the performers, with the possible exception of Hale who manages to be believable. March plows through his lines with no interest in the words, and Carroll, in a role originally designed for Marlene Dietrich, seems ill at ease in her ambiguous position.

d&w, Edmund Goulding (based on a story by Goulding); ph, William Steiner; ed, Emma Hill.

Drama   (PR:A   MPAA:NR)

NIGHT AT EARL CARROLL'S, A**   (1940) 62m PAR bw

Ken Murray (*Barney Nelson*), Rose Hobart (*Ramona Lisa*), Blanche Stewart (*Brenda Gusher*), Elvia Allman (*Cobina Gusher*), J. Carroll Naish (*Steve Kalkus*), Russell Hicks (*Mayor Jones*), Jack Norton (*Alonzo Smith*), John Laird (*Vic Murkil*), Ruth Rogers (*Miss Borgia*), Betty McLaughlin (*Miss de Milo*), Beryl Wallace (*Miss DuBary*), John Harmon (*Mac*), Ray Walker (*Jerry*), Billy Gilbert (*Machinist's Mate*), William B. Davidson (*Mayor Green*), Forbes Murray (*Mayor Brown*), Ralph Emerson (*Mayor Gray*), Allan Cavan (*Mayor White*), George McKay (*Mayor Stokes*), George Meeker (*Stage Manager*), Mary Lou Cook (*LaConga Singer*), Vera Lewis (*Maidy*), Florine McKinney (*Orchestra Leader*), Truman Bradley (*Radio Announcer*), Sterner Sisters (*Dancers*), The Three Normans (*Jugglers*), Lillian Cornell, Lela Moore.

A synthetic story was developed to show off talent at the famous Hollywood club, and even more to show the threadbare showgirls. It seems as if most of the picture is devoted to their endless parades across stage. The story centers around a gangster kidnaping Carroll and several of his main attractions on the night the mayor of Hollywood (none ever existed) is planning a party for visiting mayors. The gangster and the mayor are feuding, and this is the gangster's way of getting even. But the show must go on, so the remaining performers enlist some extra help and put on a whale of a show. Songs include: "Li'l Boy Love" (Frank Loesser, Frederick Hollander), "I Wanna Make with the Happy Times" (Loesser, Gertrude Niesen), "Cali-Con-Ga" (Earl Carroll, Dorcas Cochran, Nilo Menendez), "One Look at You" (Carroll, Ned Washington, Victor Young).

p, Earl Carroll; d, Kurt Neumann; w, Lynn Starling (based on a story by Starling); ph, Leo Tovar; ed, Alma Macrorie; md, Irvin Talbot; art d, Hans Dreier, Robert Odell.

Musical   (PR:A   MPAA:NR)

NIGHT AT THE OPERA, A****   (1935) 90m MGM bw

Groucho Marx (*Otis B. Driftwood*), Chico Marx (*Fiorello*), Harpo Marx (*Tomasso*), Kitty Carlisle (*Rosa Castaldi*), Allan Jones (*Riccardo Baroni*), Walter Woolf King (*Rodolfo Lassparri*), Siegfried "Sig" Rumann (*Herman Gottlieb*), Margaret Dumont (*Mrs. Claypool*), Edward Keane (*Captain*), Robert Emmett O'Connor (*Detective Henderson*), Gino Corrado (*Steward*), Purnell Pratt (*Mayor*), Frank Yaconelli (*Engineer*), Billy Gilbert (*Engineer's Assistant/Peasant*), Sam Marx (*Extra on Ship and at Dock*), Claude Peyton (*Police Captain*), Rita and Rubin (*Dancers*), Luther Hoobyar (*Ruiz*), Rodolfo Hoyos (*Count di Luna*), Olga Dane (*Azucena*), James J. Wolf (*Ferrando*), Inez Palange (*Maid*), Jonathan Hale (*Stage Manager*), Otto Fries (*Elevator Man*), William Gould (*Captain of Police*), Leo White, Jay Eaton, Rolfe Sedan (*Aviators*), Wilbur Mack, George Irving (*Committee*), George Guhl (*Policeman*), Harry Tyler (*Sign Painter*), Phillips Smalley, Selmer Jackson (*Committee*), Alan Bridge (*Immigration Inspector*), Harry Allen (*Doorman*), Lorraine Bridges (*Louisa*), Jack Lipson (*Engineer's Assistant*).

Songwriters-screenwriters Bert Kalmar and Harry Ruby, and gargantuan gagman Al Boasberg (over 300 pounds) did not receive any screen credit for this, the sixth and, perhaps, the funniest of the 13 Marx Brothers films. It was the Marx Brothers' first for MGM after they were dropped by Paramount and the first one without Zeppo. Thalberg had faith in the boys and thought that their other films for Paramount lacked cohesive stories and enough time to work out the routines, so he prevailed upon them to take a 50-minute precis of the best scenes on the road.

They toured four cities with Kaufman and Ryskind in the audience for 24 days and polished the gags until they were ready to film. The result was a huge success and the picture made more money than anyone could have expected (except Thalberg): the sum of $3 million profit. There were several famous scenes that are still talked about and one that never got on screen. The boys wanted to come through the MGM laurel wreath and roar like Leo, but someone in the executive office thought that amounted to desecration of the logo and the idea was tossed aside. Director Wood liked to shoot and re-shoot as many as 20 takes on each sequence and the Marxes weren't thrilled with that process, something that inhibited their free-wheeling. Groucho paid the most attention to what was happening and was always inventing new bits to crack up the studio technicians and the other actors. Chico spent his off-moments playing cards, and Harpo liked to work hard until near lunchtime, then begin asking for food until the crew had to break to feed him or suffer the consequences. Groucho is a tacky promoter who is trying to con rich ($8 million) Dumont into investing her money in an opera company run by Rumann. The stars of the company are King and Carlisle (who married co-screenwriter Kaufman's often-partner, Moss Hart) who are of two very different temperaments; she's darling and he has an ego as big as Texas. Dumont would like to crack New York's social set and Groucho swears he'll introduce her to all the "right people" if she comes across with the cash. All of the above takes place in Milan, home of La Scala (which they are definitely not associated with), and the group now boards an ocean liner where one of the funniest scenes in comedy history is played. Cabins have only been booked for a few of the people, but when Harpo (King's dresser) and Chico (agent for Jones, who is Carlisle's boy friend and a singer himself) join in, accompanied by Jones, also a stowaway, sparks fly. Groucho has a small cabin and the four men are trying to hide out there. Along come the maids, workmen, et al, and the tiny room is soon filled with 15 people, all of whom come pouring out on the padded Dumont at the end of the scene. (When they originally attempted the stateroom scene on the stage, it didn't get any yucks and the thought was to jettison it. Then Boasberg went to work and it came to life. He had promised to finish the scene and the Marxes went to his office to look for the revisions one night. What they found were hundreds of strips of paper tacked to Boasberg's office ceiling. They took down each strip, put them together in a session that required hours of jig-saw work and it all blended together.) Groucho, Chico, and Harpo get off the boat in New York and avoid capture when they cut beards from a trio of foreign dignitaries and glue them to their faces, thus receiving heroes' welcomes at New York City Hall. Eventually, Harpo is called upon to make a speech, and, stalling for time, takes a drink of water which causes his beard to fall off. Groucho shouts, "This means war!" as they race away. O'Connor, a New York detective, chases them to their hotel where they do a bed-switching bit between two rooms that leaves him confused and slow-burning a la Edgar Kennedy. King is after Carlisle but she spurns him, causing her to be fired as well as Groucho. He has a plan to exact revenge. It's opening night at the opera and they are to do "Il Trovatore." Chico and Harpo have fiddled with the orchestra's lead sheets and the group plays "Take Me Out to the Ballgame," which startles the opera-goers. They are further stunned when Groucho races through the audience selling peanuts. The sets fall, Harpo swings across the stage, and King gets kidnaped. Jones steps in with Carlisle, the opera goes forward, and they are, it should go without saying, sensations. By the time the picture ends, we have heard several songs, including selections from Giuseppe Verdi's *Il Trovatore*, Ruggiero Leoncavallo's *I Pagliacci* Jack Norworth's "Take Me Out to the Ballgame" (which always annoyed baseball fan Ruby who resented the fact that Norworth, a man who knew little about the game, wrote the best song about it), and "Alone" (Nacio Herb Brown, Arthur Freed, sung by Allan Jones, Kitty Carlisle), "Cosi-Cosa" (Ned Washington, Bronislau Kaper, Walter Jurmann) and "All I Do is Dream Of You" (Brown). Many of the jokes from the film are still quoted. When Groucho and Chico argue over a contract, Groucho tears off the offending clauses as the dispute heats up, and Groucho, at one point, says, "That is what we call a sanity clause." To which Chico replies, "You can't-a fool-a *me*! There *ain't* no Sanity Claus!" In the jam-packed stateroom scene, a manicurist arrives and asks Groucho if he wants his nails cut long or short. Groucho answers, "Better make them short. It's getting crowded in here." Another young girl arrives and asks if her aunt is in the cabin. Groucho retorts, "If she isn't, you can probably find someone just as good." The cleaning woman tries to get in the room to do her work and Groucho tells her, "Better start on the ceiling. It's the only place that isn't occupied." The description of the insanity can't possibly recreate it. See this movie and be prepared to wipe your eyes from laughter. Long-time MGM producer (LASSIE COME HOME, etc.) Sam Marx is seen as an extra.

p, Irving Thalberg; d, Sam Wood; w, George S. Kaufman, Morrie Ryskind, Al Boasberg, Bert Kalmar, Harry Ruby (based on a story by James Kevin McGuinness); ph, Merritt B. Gerstad; m, Herbert Stothart; ed, William Levanway; art d, Cedric Gibbons, Ben Carre; set d, Edwin B. Willis; cos, Dolly Tree; ch, Chester Hale.

Comedy **Cas.** **(PR:A MPAA:NR)**

NIGHT AT THE RITZ, A** (1935) 62m WB bw

William Gargan *(Duke Regan)*, Patricia Ellis *(Marcia)*, Allen Jenkins *(Gyp)*, Dorothy Tree *(Kiki Lorraine)*, Erik Rhodes *(Leopold)*, Berton Churchill *(Mr. Vincent)*, Gordon Westcott *(Scurvin)*, Bodil Rosing *(Mama Jaynos)*, Arthur Hoyt *(Mr. Hassler)*, Paul Porcasi *(Henri)*, William B. Davidson *(Connolly)*, Mary Treen *(Isabelle)*, Mary Russell *(Miss Barry)*.

Gargan plays a go-getter publicity man just fired from his hotel job, who tries to run a campaign selling his brother-in-law, Rhodes, as a master chef. Rhodes brags of being a great chef, but unknown to Gargan, he has never cooked a thing in his life and suffers from acute indigestion. Gargan discovers this the night a large convention has been scheduled to dine at the hotel where Rhodes has been enlisted. All is saved, however, when Rhodes' mother comes to the rescue. Simple story manages to deliver some well placed laughs. Rhodes carried most of the comedy, while Gargan acted frantic. Script needs some tightening.

d, William H. McGann; w, Albert J. Cohen, Robert T. Shannon, Manuel Seff; ph, James Van Trees; ed, Jack Killifer.

Comedy **(PR:A MPAA:NR)**

NIGHT BEAT*½ (1932) 61m Action-Mayfair bw

Jack Mulhall *(Johnny)*, Patsy Ruth Miller *(Eleanor)*, Walter McGrail *(Martin)*, Harry Cording *(Chill Scarpelli)*, Ernie Adams *(Weissenkorn)*, Richard Cramer *(Featherstone)*, Harry Semels *(Italian)*.

Routine story has Mulhall as a gangster who goes through a change of heart after returning from WW I. His old war buddy has become a district attorney and asks for Mulhall's help in battling a local gang. Mulhall accepts and in the process falls in love with the D.A.'s fiancee, Miller, further influencing him to go straight. Story suffers from over-predictability, with the miscasting of Mulhall as the macho type making matters worse.

p, Ralph M. Like; d, George B. Seitz; w, W. Scott Darling; ph, Jules Cronjager; ed, Byron Robinson.

Crime/Drama **(PR:A MPAA:NR)**

NIGHT BEAT* (1948, Brit.) 95m BL bw

Anne Crawford *(Julie Kendall)*, Maxwell Reed *(Felix Fenton)*, Ronald Howard *(Andy Kendall)*, Christine Norden *(Jackie)*, Hector Ross *(Don Brady)*, Fred Groves *(Police Constable Kendall)*, Sidney James *(Nixon)*, Nicholas Stuart *(Rocky)*, Frederick Leister *(Magistrate)*, Michael Medwin *(Spider)*, Philip Stainton *(Sergeant Slack)*, Michael Hordern.

Predictable crime drama has Reed and Howard as two army buddies who take to opposite sides of the law when the war is over. One becomes a cop, the other a black marketeer. As plots like this go, one winds up pursuing the other, thus allowing the screenwriters to pile on the emotional cliches.

p&d, Harold Huth; w, Guy Morgan, T. J. Morrison, Robert Westerby, Roland Pertwee (based on the story by Morgan); ph, Vaclav Vich; m, Benjamin Frankel; ed, Grace Garland; md, Dr. Hubert Clifford; cos, Beatrice Dawson.

Crime **(PR:A MPAA:NR)**

NIGHT BEFORE CHRISTMAS, A** (1963, USSR) 60m Gorky/Artkino c (VECHERA NA KHUTORE BLIZ DIKANKI)

Aleksandr Khvylya *(Chub)*, L. Myznikova *(Oksana)*, Y. Tavrov *(Vakula)*, L. Khityayeva *(Solokha)*, S. Martinson *(Osip, the Sacristan)*, Anatoliy Kubatskiy *(Panas)*, Vera Altayskaya *(Wife of Panas)*, D. Kapka *(Shanuvalenko)*, N. Yakovchenko *(Patsyuk)*, M. Sidorchuk *(Odarka)*, A. Radunskiy *(The Head)*, Georgiy Millyar *(The Devil)*, A. Ablova, V. Bubnova, M. Vasilyev, Y. Grigoryev, A. Demyanenko, L. Korolyova, I. Murzayeva, N. Skvortsova, A. Smirnov, Mark Troyanovskiy, Z. Chekulayeva, Y. Chekulayev.

Soviet farce on superstitious peasant life is a light-hearted combination of the devil's mischief, witchcraft, and blind love. The devil, Millyar, doesn't want Tavrov to marry the blacksmith's daughter, Myznikova, because he can't stand Tavrov's religious paintings. So he does whatever he can to keep the two apart, including stealing the moon so the blacksmith will be discouraged from going to a party and leaving his daughter alone. When Tavrov asks for the girl's hand in marriage, she accepts, but only on the condition that he bring a pair of the czarina's slippers. Tavrov does so by enlisting the help of the devil, which he achieves by grabbing him by the tail and forcing him to be Tavrov's assistant.

d&w, Aleksandr Rou (based on the story "Noch Pered Rozhdestvom" by Nikolay Gogol); ph, Dmitriy Surenskiy; m, A. Filippenko; ed, K. Blinova; art d, Aleksandr Dikhtyar; set d, A. Ivashchenko; spec eff, L. Akimov, V. Nikitchenko, Y. Lupandin.

Farce **(PR:A MPAA:NR)**

NIGHT BEFORE THE DIVORCE, THE** (1942) 62m FOX bw

Lynn Bari *(Lynn Thorndyke)*, Mary Beth Hughes *(Lola May)*, Joseph Allen, Jr. *(George Nordyke)*, Nils Asther *(Victor Roselle)*, Truman Bradley *(Bruce Campbell)*, Kay Linaker *(Hedda Smythe)*, Mary Treen *(Olga)*, Thurston Hall *(Bert Harriman)*, Spencer Charters *(Judge)*, Leon Belasco *(Leo)*, Tom Fadden *(Capt. Walt)*, Alec Craig *(Jitters)*.

Amusing tale of marital strife has Allen leaving his wife for a blonde bombshell. His reason is that his wife, Bari, is better at doing everything than he is. Bari dates a pianist, Asther, whose murder makes her a prime suspect and sends Allen back to her arms. Script begins to fall apart around halfway through, where the pace slackens and the sequences don't intertwine very well. A strong performance by Bari makes something of the poor material.

p, Ralph Dietrich; d, Robert Siodmak; w, Jerry Sackheim (based on a play by Gina Kaus, Ladislas Fodor); ph, Peverell Marley; ed. John Brady; md, Emil Newman.

Drama/Comedy **(PR:A MPAA:NR)**

NIGHT BIRDS* (1931, Brit.) 76m BIP bw

Muriel Angelus *(Dolly)*, Jack Raine *(Sgt. Harry Cross)*, Jameson Thomas *(Deacon Lake)*, Eve Gray *(Mary Cross)*, Franklyn Bellamy *(Charlo Bianci)*, Garry Marsh *(Archibald Bunny)*, Frank Perfitt *(Inspector Warrington)*, D. Hay Petrie *(Scotty)*, Harry Terry *(Toothpick Jeff)*, Margaret Yarde *(Mrs. Hallick)*, Ellen Pollock *(Flossie)*, Cyril Butcher *(Dancer Johnny)*, Barbara Kilner.

Haphazard production has Raine as a Scotland Yard detective on the trail of a notorious crook known as "Flash Jack." His search leads him into a run-in with another cop looking for the thief, an affair with the crook's mistress, and a fight on a roof. The worst sequence of all, though, is when Raine is able to pose as a dancer in a show without even single rehearsal. Raine's standoffish screen personality contributes to the deplorable quality of the production.

p&d, Richard Eichberg; w, Miles Malleson, Victor Kendall (based on a story by Kendall); ph, Henry Gartner.

Crime   **(PR:A   MPAA:NR)**

NIGHT BOAT TO DUBLIN**   (1946, Brit.) 91m ABF/Pathe bw

Robert Newton (*Capt. David Grant*), Raymond Lovell (*Paul Faber*), Guy Middleton (*Capt. Tony Hunter*), Muriel Pavlow (*Marion Decker*), Herbert Lom (*Keitel*), John Ruddock (*Bowman*), Martin Miller (*Prof. Hansen*), Marius Goring (*Frederick Jannings*), Brenda Bruce (*Lily Leggett*), Gerald Case (*Inspector Emerson*), Julian Dallas (*Lt. Allen*), Leslie Dwyer (*George Leggett*), Olga Lindo (*Mrs. Coleman*), Joan Maude (*Sidney Vane*), Valentine Dyall (*Sir George Bell*), Derek Elphinstone (*Naval Surgeon*), Carroll Gibbons, Edmundo Ros and his Rhumba Band, Bruce Gordon, George Hirste, Hubert Leslie, Gordon McLeod, Hay Petrie, Wilfrid Hyde-White, Stuart Lindsell, Lawrence O'Madden.

Plodding story of attempts to rescue a Swedish scientist from the Nazis, with a twist on the atom bomb theme to add some intrigue. Overall, the picture suffers from serious miscasting and off-paced direction. Some interesting moments in the portrayal of bit parts at a Dublin hotel, adding the charm of real Irish types.

p, Hamilton G. Inglis; d, Lawrence Huntington; w, Huntington, Robert Hall; ph, Otto Heller.

War/Spy   **(PR:A   MPAA:NR)**

NIGHT CALL NURSES**   (1974) 85m New World c

Patricia T. Byrne (*Barbara*), Alana Collins (*Janis*), Mittie Lawrence (*Sandra*), Clint Kimbrough (*Dr. Bramlett*), Felton Perry (*Jude*), Stack Pierce (*Sampson*), Richard Young (*Kyle Toby*), Dennis Dugan, Christopher Law, Dick Miller.

The ordeals of three nurses, Byrne, Collins, and Lawrence, all lovelies on the night shift at a psychiatric clinic, allow for another New World foray into sex, violence, and other profitable enterprises. Aside from the minimal horror angle, here a mixed-up male orderly with visions of becoming a head nurse, there's some dabbling into politics and the dangers of excessive drug taking. This picture never takes itself seriously for a single frame, with the performers obviously chosen more for their looks than any acting talent they may possess beneath their tight white uniforms. Roger Corman's exhortation to director Kaplan in this, his first directorial effort, was reported to be: "Frontal nudity from the waist up, total nudity from behind, and no pubic hair. Now go to work." Third of the Corman Nurse movies. Followed by THE YOUNG NURSES, 1973.

p, Julie Corman; d, Jonathan Kaplan; w, George Armitage; ph, (Metrocolor).

Drama/Horror   **(PR:O   MPAA:R)**

NIGHT CALLER, THE   (SEE: BLOOD BEAST FROM OUTER SPACE, 1965, Brit.)

NIGHT CALLER FROM OUTER SPACE   (SEE: BLOOD BEAST FROM OUTER SPACE, 1965, Brit.)

NIGHT CARGO*   (1936) 66m Marcy bw

Jacqueline Wells, Lloyd Hughes, Walter Miller, Carlotta Monti, Lloyd Whitlock, George Regas, Jimmy Aubrey, John Ince.

Mystery and intrigue swirl about the seedy ports of exotic Singapore in this low-low budget programmer starring former child star Wells who, by 1936, had grown into leading lady roles. To allow some breathing room between the murders, blackmail, and other melodramatic misdeeds, a bit of romance is thrown in to complete this potboiler. Wells, who began her career in the silents, would soon find the public a bit apathetic, so she changed her name to Julie Bishop in 1941 and started making films for Warner Bros.

d, Charles Hutchinson; w, Sherman L. Lowe; ph, Walter London; ed, Fred Bain.

Crime   **(PR:A   MPAA:NR)**

NIGHT CHILD*   (1975, Brit./Ital.) 91m Film Ventures c (AKA: THE CURSED MEDALLION)

Richard Johnson, Joanna Cassidy, Edmund Purdom, Evelyne Stewart, Nicole Elmi, Lila Kedrova.

Elmi, the young veteran of such films as ANDY WARHOL'S FRANKENSTEIN and BARON BLOOD, stars as a possessed child in this unimaginative ripoff of THE EXORCIST. Daddy Johnson is dating a lot of women his daughter doesn't particularly care for, which, of course, leads to lots of nasty Satanic business.

p, William C. Reich; d, Max Dallamano; w, Massimo Dallamano, Franco Marrottax, Jan Hartman.

Horror   **(PR:O   MPAA:R)**

NIGHT CLUB   (SEE: GIGOLETTE, 1935)

NIGHT CLUB GIRL**   (1944) 61m UNIV bw

Vivian Austin (*Eleanor*), Edward Norris (*Clark Phillips*), Maxie Rosenbloom (*Percival*), Judy Clark (*Janie*), Billy Dunn (*Charlie*), Leon Belasco (*Gaston*), Andrew Tombes (*Simmons*), Fred Sanborn (*Fred*), Clem Bevans (*Mayor*), Virginia Brissac (*Ma Kendall*), Emmett Vogan (*Captain*), George Davis (*Carlos*), Minna Gombell (*Rita*), Tom Dugan (*Eddie*), Ted Dunn (*Gus*), William B. Davidson (*Brenner*), The Mulcays, Paula Drake, Delta Rhythm Boys.

Silly yarn about the attempts of columnist Norris to get two poor kids, Austin and Dunn, a chance to perform at a Hollywood night club. But when their chance comes, they stuff themselves with hot dogs and are unable to perform well. Picture is only an excuse to show off some night club talent. Songs inlude: "Wo-Ho" (Jimmy Nolan, Jim Kennedy, sung by Paula Drake); "One O'Clock Jump" (Count

Basie, sung by the Delta Rhythm Boys); "The Peanut Song" (Nate Wexler, Red Maddock, Al Trace); " Vingo Jingo" (Don Raye, Gene De Paul, sung by the Delta Rhythm Boys); "I Need Love" (Milton Pascal, Edgar Fairchild); "What a Wonderful Day" (Harry Tobias, Al Sherman); and "Pagan Love Song" (Arthur Freed, Nacio Herb Brown).

p, Frank Gross; d, Eddie Cline; w, Henry Blankfort, Dick I. Hyland (based on the story "Night Life" by Adele Commandini); ph, Charles Van Enger; ed, Charles Maynard; art d, John B. Goodman, Martin Obzina; cos, Vera West; ch, Louis DaPron.

Musical   **(PR:A   MPAA:NR)**

NIGHT CLUB GIRL, 1947   (SEE: GLAMOUR GIRL, 1947)

NIGHT CLUB HOSTESS   (SEE: UNMARRIED, 1939)

NIGHT CLUB LADY**   (1932) 66m COL bw

Adolphe Menjou (*Thatcher Colt*), Mayo Methot (*Lola Carewe*), Skeets Gallagher (*Tony*), Ruthelma Stevens (*Kelly*), Blanche Frederici (*Mrs. Carewe*), Gerald Fielding (*Everett*), Nat Pendleton (*Mike*), Albert Conti (*Vincent Rowland*), Greta Granstedt (*Eunice*), Ed Brady (*Bill*), Lee Phelps (*Joe*), George Humbert (*Andre*), Niles Welch (*Dr. Baldwin*), William von Brincken (*Dr. Lengle*), Teru Shimada (*Mura*).

Menjou plays a police commissioner out to solve the murder of a night club owner who was killed even though she was under heavy police security. Menjou pins it on the woman posing as the owner's mother, who used a scorpion to commit the crime. Menjou pulls off his role fairly well, without any romantic flings for a change, and he even gets to speak a little French. Pace is somewhat slack, with a lot of attention given to extraneous details that add nothing to the story.

d, Irving Cummings; w, Robert Riskin (based on the novel by Anthony Abbott); ph, Teddy Tetzlaff.

Mystery/Crime   **(PR:A   MPAA:NR)**

NIGHT CLUB MURDER   (SEE: ROMANCE IN RHYTHM, 1934, Brit.)

NIGHT CLUB QUEEN**   (1934, Brit.) 80m Universal-Twickenham/ UNIV bw

Mary Clare (*Mary Brown*), Lewis Casson (*Edward Brown*), Jane Carr (*Bobbie Lamont*), George Carney (*Hale*), Lewis Shaw (*Peter Brown*), Merle Tottenham (*Alice Lamont*), Drusilla Wills (*Aggie*), Syd Crossley (*Jimmy*), Felix Aylmer (*Prosecution*), The Eight Black Streaks, The Sherman Fisher Girls.

Poignant story has Casson as a lawyer who was paralyzed in a railway accident. When he is forced to give up his career, his wife, Clare, opens a night club to support the family. When Clare's partner, Carney, is killed, she is accused of the murder, and the crippled Casson is forced to reenter the courtroom to defend his wife. Strong cast and well-paced direction help to keep this overly sentimental story from drifting all the way into pathos.

p, Julius Hagen; d, Bernard Vorhaus; w, H. Fowler Mear (based on a play by Anthony Kimmins).

Drama   **(PR:A   MPAA:NR)**

NIGHT CLUB SCANDAL**½   (1937) 72m PAR bw

John Barrymore (*Dr. Ernest Tindal*), Lynne Overman (*Russell Kirk*), Louise Campbell (*Vera Marsh*), Charles Bickford (*Capt. McKinley*), Harvey Stephens (*Frank Marsh*), J. Carroll Naish (*Jack Reed*), Evelyn Brent (*Julia Reed*), Elizabeth Patterson (*Mrs. Elvira Ward*), Cecil Cunningham (*Mrs. Alvin, Cook*), Barlowe Borland (*Dr. Sully*), John Sheehan (*Duffy*), George Guhl (*Broun*), Frank O'Connor (*Alcott*), Leonard Willey (*Dr. Goodman*), John Hamilton (*Governor*), George Offerman, Jr., Lee Shumway, Dorothy Howe, Herbert Ashley, Jack Raymond, Mack Gray, Robert Brister, Dick Cramer, Fred Warren, Spec O'Donnell, Dudley Clements, Franklin Parker, Reginald Simpson.

Routine formula crime drama has Barrymore as a man who's murdered his wife and blamed it on her lover. Bickford is the not-too-bright cop trying to solve the case, but the witty newspaper reporter finally brings the culprit to justice. Script is much too obvious to hold any suspense, with Overman as the newspaper reporter providing the only moments of worthwhile acting in the film. Remake of GUILTY AS HELL, 1932.

d, Ralph Murphy; w, Lillie Howard (based on the play by Daniel N. Rubin); ph, Leo Tover; ed, Archie Marshek; art d, Hans Dreier, Earl Hedrick.

Crime   **(PR:A   MPAA:NR)**

NIGHT COMES TOO SOON**   (1948, Brit.) 52m Federated-British Animated/BUT bw (AKA: THE GHOST OF RASHMON HALL)

Valentine Dyall (*Dr. Clinton*), Anne Howard, Alec Faversham, Beatrice Marsden, Howard Douglas, Anthony Baird, David Keir, Frank Dunlop, Monte de Lyle, Nina Erber, John Desmond.

When ghosts inhabit an Englishwoman's home, Dyall, a ghost hunter of sorts, takes on the poltergeists. The findings reveal a trio of spirits that includes a sailor, the seaman's late wife, and her lover, whom the sailor had shot. The thrills are poorly developed, resulting in a horrid horror picture.

p, Harold Baim; d, Denis Kavanagh; w, Pat Dixon (based on the play, "The Haunted and the Haunters" by Lord Lytton); ph, Ray Densham.

Horror/Thriller   **(PR:C   MPAA:NR)**

NIGHT COURT***   (1932) 90m MGM bw (GB: JUSTICE FOR SALE)

Phillips Holmes (*Mike Thomas*), Walter Huston (*Judge Moffett*), Anita Page (*Mary Thomas*), Lewis Stone (*Judge Osgood*), Mary Carlisle (*Elizabeth Osgood*), John Miljan (*Crawford*), Jean Hersholt (*Janitor*), Tully Marshall (*Grogan*), Noel Francis (*Lil Baker*), Warner Richmond (*Ed*).

Gripping story about a taxi driver, Holmes, forced to seek vengeance on a crooked judge, Huston, for putting his wife, Page, in jail on a trumped-up charge after she accidentally comes into some information that could harm Huston's career. Direction emphasizes individual personalities of the characters, which may harm the general movement of the plot but helps create a fascinating atmosphere. Holmes and Huston are captivating playing against each other.

d, W.S. Van Dyke; w, Bayard Veiller, Lenore Coffee (based on the play by Mark Hellinger, Charles Beahan); ph, Norbert Brodine; ed, Ben Lewis.

Crime   (PR:A MPAA:NR)

NIGHT CRAWLERS, THE   (SEE:
NAVY VS. THE NIGHT MONSTERS, THE, 1966)

NIGHT CREATURE*   (1979) 83m Dimension c (AKA:
OUT OF THE DARKNESS; FEAR)

Donald Pleasence (Axel MacGregor), Nancy Kwan (Leslie), Ross Hagen (Ross), Lesly Fine (Peggy), Jennifer Rhodes (Georgia).

Pointless attempt at a jungle thriller has Pleasence as a macho hunter frightened for the first time in his life by a man-eating black leopard that is stalking the area. In his quest for the cat he is joined by his two daughters and one of their boy friends, who all abandon the island to the beast. Pleasence is badly miscast in the main role, further hindering this hopeless enterprise.

p, Ross Hagen; d, Lee Madden; w, Hubert Smith (based on a story by Madden); ph, Pemylot Cheydon (CFI Color); m, Jim Helms; ed, Martin Draffke.

Adventure   Cas.   (PR:A MPAA:PG)

NIGHT CREATURES½**   (1962, Brit.) 81m Hammer-Major/UNIV c
(GB: CAPTAIN CLEGG)

Peter Cushing (Dr. Blyss/Capt. Nathaniel Clegg), Yvonne Romain (Imogene), Patrick Allen (Capt. Collier), Oliver Reed (Harry Crabtree), Michael Ripper (Jeremiah Mipps), Martin Benson (Rash), David Lodge (Bosun), Derek Francis (Squire), Daphne Anderson (Mrs. Rash), Milton Reid (Mulatto), Jack McGowran (Frightened Man), Peter Halliday (Jack Pott), Terry Scully (Dick Tate), Sydney Bromley (Tom Ketch), Rupert Osborn (Gerry), Gordon Rollings (Wurzel), Bob Head (Peg-Leg), Colin Douglas (Pirate Bosun).

Another costume thriller from England's Hammer studios has Cushing as a vicar in a small town where a smuggling trade has been exporting liquor. Cushing's religious garb masks his true identity as a famous pirate believed to have been hanged years earlier and now operating the smuggling ring. A group of sailors, headed by Allen, comes across ghost-like images and other mysterious illuminations in the swamps during their nighttime investigations. One of Allen's men, mulatto Reid, recognizes Cushing as the man who had tortured him and cut out his tongue. Allen is forced to arrest Cushing, bringing an end to the smuggling trade despite its benefits for the poor village. Picture's aura of mystery and the supernatural help to keep the suspense going. Cushing gives his usual effective performance as the mysterious vicar.

p, John Temple-Smith; d, Peter Graham Scott; w, Barbara S. Harper, Anthony Hinds (based on the novel Dr. Syn by Russell Thorndike); ph, Arthur Grant (Eastmancolor); m, Don Banks; ed, Eric Boyd-Perkins; prod d, Bernard Robinson; md, Philip Martell; art d, Don Mingaye; spec eff, Les Bowie.

Adventure/Drama   (PR:A MPAA:NR)

NIGHT CROSSING*½   (1982) 106m BV c

John Hurt (Peter Strelzyks), Jane Alexander (Doris Strelzyks), Doug McKeon (Frank Strelzyks), Keith McKeon (Fitscher Strelzyks), Beau Bridges (Gunter Wetzel), Glynnis O'Connor (Petra Wetzel), Geoffrey Liesik (Little Peter Wetzel), Michael Liesik (Andreas Wetzel), Ian Bannen (JosefKeller) Anne Stallybrass (Magda Keller), Mathew Taylor (Lucas Keller), Gunter Meisner (Maj. Koerner), Klaus Lowitsch (Schmolk), Sky Dumont (Ziegler), Jan Niklas (Lt. Fehler), Kay Walsh (Petra's Mother), Carola Hohn (Petra's Mother), Irene Prador (Mrs. Roseler), Jan Paulus Biczycki (Pharmacist), Osman Ragheb (Store Supervisor), Ursula Ludwig (1st Store Clerk), Jenny Thelen (2nd Store Clerk), Katharina Seyferth (Shopper), Gavin James (Pilot).

Film depiction of the true story of two families who escape from East to West Germany via hot-air balloon makes for dull screen material. Mainly plodding account is the fault of the high moralistic tone the picture takes, instead of the human, suspenseful one.

p, Tom Leetch; d, Delbert Mann; w, John McGreevey; ph, Tony Imi (Technicolor); m, Jerry Goldsmith; ed, Gordon D. Brenner; prod d, Rolf Zehetbauer; art d, Herbert Strabel.

Adventure   Cas.   (PR:C MPAA:PG)

NIGHT DIGGER, THE   (1971, Brit.) 110m Yongestreet-Tacitus/
MGM c (AKA: THE ROAD BUILDER)

Patricia Neal (Maura Prince), Pamela Brown (Mrs. Prince), Nicholas Clay (Billy Jarvis), Jean Anderson (Mrs. McMurtrey), Graham Crowden (Mr. Bolton), Sebastian Breaks (Dr. Robinson), Brigit Forsyth (District Nurse), Diana Patrick (Mary Wingate), Yootha Joyce (Mrs. Palafox), Peter Sallis (Rev. Palafox), Jenny McCracken (Farmwife), Bruce Myles (Bank Clerk), Zoe Alexander (Stroke Patient), Christopher Reynalds (Young Billy), Elaine Ives Cameron (Gypsy), Sibylla Kay (Whore).

Film has all the makings of a gothic horror classic—a psychopathic rapist and a blind woman watched over by her middle-aged spinster daughter in their Victorian mansion. But what develops is a love affair between Neal, as the daughter, and Clay, as the psychotic young handyman for the woman's estate, who is being protected by Neal while the police search for him. This gives Neal, who has never had much of her own life because of her invalid mother, her moment to defy

convention in the name of true love. Players give excellent portrayals, but the picture is lacking in both setting and direction.

p, Alan D. Courtney, Norman S. Powell; d, Alistair Reid; w, Roald Dahl (based on the novel Nest in a Falling Tree by Joy Crowley); ph, Alex Thomson (Metrocolor); m, Bernard Herrmann; ed, John Bloom; art d, Anthony Pratt; cos, Gabriella Falk; makeup, Ernie Gasser.

Horror   (PR:O MPAA:R)

NIGHT EDITOR½**   (1946) 65m COL bw (GB: THE TRESPASSER)

William Gargan (Tony Cochrane), Janis Carter (Jill Merrill), Jeff Donnell (Martha Cochrane), Coulter Irwin (Johnny), Charles D. Brown (Crane Stewart), Paul E. Burns (Ole Strom), Harry Shannon (Capt. Lawrence), Frank Wilcox (Douglas Loring), Robert Stevens (Doc Cochrane), Roy Gordon (Benjamin Merrill), Michael Chapin (Doc as a Boy), Robert Emmett Keane (Max), Anthony Caruso (Tusco), Edward Keane (Chief of Police Burnes), Jack Davis (District Attorney Halloran), Lou Lubin (Necktie), Charles Marsh (Swanson), John Tyrell (Street Sweeper Driver), Jimmy Lloyd (Clerk), Murray Leonard (Proprietor), Douglas Wood (Bank Manager), Ronnie Ralph (Small Boy), William Kahn (Newsboys), Joseph Palma (Newsboys), Emmett Vogan (Coroner), Johnny Calkins (Boy), Donald Kerr (Reporter), Betty Hill (Elaine), Frank Dae (Butler), Herman Marks, Frank McLure, Cy Malis (Men), Harry Tyler (Bartender), Charles Wagenheim (Phillips), Jack Frack (Reporter), Wally Rose (Photographer), Ed Chandler (Dickstein), Vernon Dent (Fat Man).

Noir-ish thriller has Gargan as a New York detective whose affair with "femme fatale" Carter leads to his eventually leaving the police department. While the two lovers are on a rendezvous, they witness a brutal murder. Gargan, a married man, chooses to remain silent to avoid scandal. But Carter uses the opportunity to blackmail the murderer, taking pleasure in the power her scheme gives her. When an innocent man is held for the murder, Gargan pursues the real killer. Approaching Carter to force her to come forward with the truth, he is greeted with an ice pick in his stomach. This is a classic example of film noir with its analogies between sex and violence, women who use sex to get what they want, and basic negativity toward people in general. Gargan is dull and ineffectual in his role as detective-narrator, but this may have been the intention.

p, Ted Richmond; d, Henry Levin; w, Hal Smith (based on the story "Inside Story" by Scott Littleton from the radio program "Night Editor" by Hal Burdick); ph, Burnett Guffey, Philip Tannura; m, Mischa Bakaleinikoff; ed, Richard Fantl; art d, Robert Peterson; set d, James Crowe.

Crime   (PR:A MPAA:NR)

NIGHT ENCOUNTER½**   (1963, Fr./Ital.) 80m SNE Gaumont-
Film Costellazione/Shawn bw (LA NUIT DES ESPIONS; LA NOTTE DELLE
SPIE; AKA: THE DOUBLE AGENTS

Robert Hossein (Peter), Marina Vlady (Helene), Robert Le Beal, Roger Crouzet, Clement Harari, Georges Vitaly, Michel Etcheverry.

Contrived WW II espionage drama starring, directed and co-written by Hossein in which a female German secret agent is to deliver some important documents to a German officer in an isolated cabin on the Normandy coast. Once she turns over the documents, the officer is to give her secret information regarding future Nazi espionage in Britain. The British, however, learn of the plot and plan to intercept the woman and put a British agent in her place. Then they will send another British agent to kill the German officer and escort the female British agent back to headquarters. Unfortunately, when the two parties meet, neither is certain as to whether or not the other is actually British or German. While the two attempt to ascertain each other's identity, they fall in love, further complicating the mystery.

d, Robert Hossein; w, Hossein, Louis Martin, Alain Poire (based on a story by Hossein); ph, Jacques Robin; m, Andre Gosselain; ed, Gilbert Natot; set d, Rino Mondellini.

Spy Drama   (PR:A MPAA:NR)

NIGHT EVELYN CAME OUT OF THE GRAVE, THE½**   (1973,
Ital.) 99m Phase One c (LA NOTTE CHE EVELYN USCA DALLA TOMBA)

Anthony Steffen (Lord Alan Cunningham), Marina Malfatti (Gladys), Rod Murdock (George), Erica Blanc (Susan), Giacomo Rossi-Stuart, Umberto Raho, Roberto Maldera, Joan C. Davies.

Typical Italian horror outing starring Steffen as a morbid playboy who enjoys torturing women in his specially built dungeon. Victim number one is Blanc, whom he meets in a nightclub after she performs her striptease act, which involves a velvet-lined coffin. Unfortunately, Steffen begins to believe that his dead wife has risen from her tomb to spoil his nocturnal pleasures. Effactually dubbed into English, though.

d, Emilio P. Miraglia; w, Fabio Pittoru, Massimo Felisatti, Miraglia; ph, Gastone DiGiovanni (Technicolor); m, Bruno Nicolai; ed, Romeo Ciatti; art d, Lorenzo Baraldi.

Horror   (PR:O MPAA:R)

NIGHT EXPRESS, THE   (SEE: WESTERN LIMITED, THE, 1932)

NIGHT FIGHTERS, THE**   (1960) 89m DRM/UA bw (GB:
A TERRIBLE BEAUTY)

Robert Mitchum (Dermot O'Neill), Anne Heywood (Neeve Donnelly), Dan O'Herlihy (Don McGinnis), Cyril Cusack (Jimmy Hannafin), Richard Harris (Sean Reilly), Marianne Benet (Bella O'Neill), Niall MacGinnis (Ned O'Neill), Harry Brogan (Patrick O'Neill), Eileen Crowe (Kathleen O'Neill), Geoffrey Golden (Sgt. Crawley), Hilton Edwards (Father McCrory), Wilfrid Downing (Quinn), Christopher Rhodes (Malone), Eddie Golden (Corrigan), Joe Lynch (Tim), Jim Neylan, T. R. McKenna (McIntyre Boys).

A WW II film shot in Ireland and featuring Mitchum, who reluctantly joins the IRA to help expel the British from Northern Ireland. When the IRA decides to collaborate with the Nazis against the British, Mitchum thinks they have lost sight of their values and he betrays the cause. He blows the whistle on his comrades, escaping to Liverpool by boat. Good action scenes and fine use of Irish locations help to smooth over some of the screenplay's rough edges.

p, Raymond Stross; d, Tay Garnett; w, Robert Wright Campbell (based on the novel *A Terrible Beauty* by Arthur Roth); ph, Stephen Dade; m, Cedric Thorpe Davis; ed, Peter Tanner; md, Dock Mathieson; art d, John Stoll.

War (PR:A MPAA:NR)

NIGHT FLIGHT*** (1933) 84m MGM bw

John Barrymore (*Riviere*), Helen Hayes (*Mme. Fabian*), Clark Gable (*Jules*), Lionel Barrymore (*Robineau*), Robert Montgomery (*Auguste Pellerin*), Myrna Loy (*Brazilian Pilot's Wife*), William Gargan (*Brazilian Pilot*), C. Henry Gordon (*Daudet*), Harry Beresford (*Roblet*), Ralf Harolde (*Pilot Number Five*), Leslie Fenton, Frank Conroy (*Radio Operators*).

MGM selected the popular Saint-Exupery story for this film in hopes of creating another GRAND HOTEL or DINNER AT EIGHT, loading the cast with superstars, but it missed. Still, NIGHT FLIGHT is full of gritty excitement and offers some splendid though splintered performances by Hayes, Gable, Loy, Montgomery, and the inimitable Barrymore brothers in their fifth and last film together. John Barrymore is the driving, rigid head of a South American airline who insists that the mail contracts be upheld at any costs, including the lives of his pilots. He demands that they fly through bad weather and, especially, navigate their rickety crates at night over the dangerous Andes Mountains. Barrymore's ruthless disregard for the lives of his pilots earns him the hatred of all but he bears up nobly in the pursuit of pioneering air mail. Gable, in his first film with Loy, is married to Hayes and he proves one of the most courageous of the pilots, although he reports via radio on one dangerous mission that he has only thirty minutes of fuel left and then there is silence. It falls to John Barrymore to break the news of Gable's death to Hayes. The same fate befalls Gargan, Loy's pilot husband, but John Barrymore's only response is to order up more pilots to risk their lives so letters will be delivered a few days earlier. Commiserating with the pilots is Lionel Barrymore, chief foreman, who is called on the carpet by John for fraternizing with the fliers. John Barrymore carries the film and Brown's direction is taut and often exciting, particularly the aerial sequences. The theme of this film would be used again with better effect in ONLY ANGELS HAVE WINGS and there are overtones of THE DAWN PATROL here, especially in the John Barrymore role where he is bound by duty to send men to certain death. This was a "man's film," with Hayes and Loy used as cameo props for the love interest. Gable spent most of his time in a mock airplane cockpit and he grew to distrust producer Selznick for typecasting him as a dispensible hero, a wary attitude that existed even when Gable went to work on Selznick's masterpiece, GONE WITH THE WIND, five years later. The Barrymore brothers are outstanding and the inevitable happened again, with Lionel stealing his one big scene from brother John, even though director Brown bet $10 with John that Lionel couldn't do it. In the scene, Lionel merely stands before John and takes a berating lecture, having no words. When the scene was shot, Lionel stood mute, his face twitching, eyes rolling, but the script had silenced even his notorious whine. He turned to go, but when he reached the door, he found a way to steal the scene; with his back to the camera, he reached his hand behind him and scratched his bottom. Beamed John to Brown: "Now there, sir, is a brother to be proud of! Pay me the ten dollars!" The film had a deep interest for many of those involved in making it. Director Brown was a flier himself as was Arnold "Buddy" Gillespie, who handled the special effects on the film (Gillespie was married to the famous aviatrix Ruth Elder). This was the first time an MGM film carried a producer's credit, that of Selznick, causing a rush of studio executives to have their names tacked on films they were producing. Only the imperial Irving Thalberg refused to take credit for productions he was overseeing.

p, David O. Selznick; d, Clarence Brown; w, Oliver H.P. Garrett (based on the story by Antoine de Saint-Exupery); ph, Oliver T. Marsh, Elmer Dyer, Charles Marshall; ed, Hal C. Kern; art d, Cedric Gibbons; spec eff, Arnold Gillespie.

Adventure (PR:A MPAA:NR)

NIGHT FLIGHT FROM MOSCOW (SEE: SERPENT, THE, 1973, Fr.)

NIGHT FLOWERS* (1979) 92m Willow/Leonard Franklin c

Jose Perez, Sabra Jones, Gabriel Walsh.

Tasteless, short-sighted drama about two disturbed Vietnam vets, one Irish-American, the other Hispanic, who get themselves into all sorts of sleazy trouble in Hoboken. The Hispanic has a sexual problem that compels him to rape and murder a girl, and the Irishman kills a thief who threatens to reveal his phony alibi. Another misguided attempt to metaphorically illustrate the readjustment problems of Vietnam vets.

p, Sally Faile; d&ed, Luis San Andres; w, Gabriel Walsh; ph, Larry Pizer; m, Harry Manfredini.

Drama (PR:O MPAA:NR)

NIGHT FOR CRIME, A*½ (1942) 75m PRC bw

Glenda Farrell (*Susan*), Lyle Talbot (*Joe*), Lina Basquette (*Mona*), Donald Kirke (*Hart, Studio Head*), Ralph Sanford (*Hoffman*), Forrest Taylor (*Williams*), Lynn Starr (*Carol*), Ricki Vallin (*Arthur*), Edna Harris (*Telephone Operator*), Marjorie Manners (*Ellen Smith*), Joseph DeVillard, Neils Bagge, Ruby Dandridge, Florence O'Brien, Bob Frazer, Jimmy Starr, Erskine Johnson, Edwin Schallert, Harry Crocker.

Shoddy murder mystery set on the Hollywood back lots, involving the disappearance of film star Basquette during the shooting of a movie. When Basquette turns up dead, bumbling cop Sanford investigates and soon everyone is under suspicion.

p, Lester Cutler; d, Alexis Thurn-Taxis; w, Arthur St. Claire, Sherman Lowe (based on a story by Jimmy Starr); ph, Marcel Le Picard; ed, Fred Bain.

Mystery (PR:A MPAA:NR)

NIGHT FREIGHT*½ (1955) 79m AA bw

Forrest Tucker (*Mike Peters*), Barbara Britton (*Wanda*), Keith Larsen (*Don Peters*), Thomas Gomez (*Haight*), Michael Ross (*Louis*), Myrna Dell (*Sally*), Lewis Martin (*Crane*), G. Pat Collins (*Kelly*), Sam Flint (*Gordon*), Ralph Sanford (*Engineer*), George Sanders (*Disc Jockey*), Joe Kirk (*Bartender*), Jim Alexander (*First Newsman*), Charles Fredericks (*Workman*), Guy Rennie (*Fireman*), Michael Dale (*Detective*).

Tucker stars as a short-line railroad operator who runs afoul of truck line owner Gomez, who believes the railroad is putting him out of business. When Gomez plans to blow up a munitions train and ruin Tucker, the railway man and his brother Larsen (who have been feuding over lovely gal Britton) team up and defeat the bad guy. Routine in all respects.

p, Ace Herman; d, Jean Yarbrough; w, Steve Fisher; ph, William Sickner; m, Edward J. Kay; ed, Chandler House; md, Kay.

Drama (PR:A MPAA:NR)

NIGHT FULL OF RAIN, A (SEE: END OF THE WORLD IN OUR USUAL BED IN A NIGHT FULL OF RAIN, 1978)

NIGHT GAMES** (1966, Swed.) 90m Sandrews bw (NATTLEK)

Ingrid Thulin (*Irene*), Keve Hjelm (*Jan (Grown Up)*), Jorgen Lindstrom (*Jan (Boy)*), Lena Brundin (*Mariana*), Naima Wifstrand (*Aunt Astrid*), Rune Lindstrom (*Homosexual*), Monica Zetterlund, Lauritz Falk, Christian Blatt.

Fairly revolting, but nonetheless interesting, film from feminist director Mai Zetterling in which Hjelm, on the eve of his marriage, returns to the castle of his youth to discover why he is impotent. Through flashbacks we see the aristocratic debauchery indulged in by his mother, including orgies and incest. With the help of his fiancee, Hjelm eventually blows up the castle and embarks on a new, normal sexuality, but not until nearly every sexual taboo known to man is paraded across the screen. Though very disturbing in parts, Zetterling, incredibly, handles the material with skill. Her attempts at deflating the aristocracy by showing them wallowing in sexual perversion are naive, however, to say the least.

d, Mai Zetterling; w, Zetterling, David Hughes (based on the novel by Zetterling); ph, Rune Ericson; m, Jan Johansson, George Riedel; ed, Paul Davies.

Drama (PR:O MPAA:NR)

NIGHT GAMES** (1980) 100m AE c

Cindy Pickett (*Valerie*), Joanna Cassidy (*Julie*), Barry Primus (*Jason*), Paul Jenkins (*Sion*), Gene Davis (*Timothy*), Juliet Fabriga (*Alicia*), Clem Parsons (*Jun*), Carla Reynolds (*Valerie at 13*), Rene Knecht (*Blake*), Pamela Mellish (*Sandra*), Walter Fagerstrom (*Rapist*), Clarke Reynolds (*Medavoy*), Hermin Aslanian (*Jewelry Shop Salesgirl*), Mario Munder (*Dress Shop Salesman*), George Weber, Bob Mallett (*Policemen*).

Roger Vadim failed to make a comeback with this soft-core epic muddled up with pretentious psychoanalysis. Vadim "discovery" Pickett (she had done lots of American TV before this, her debut in films) plays a disturbed Beverly Hills housewife whose memories of a childhood rape have made her frightened of sex. This threatens to ruin her marriage, and Pickett's only means of escape is elaborate sexual fantasies in which she makes love to several different men clothed in increasingly silly costumes, in unlikely locations. The fantasies, neither interesting nor erotic after being cut so that the film could get an R rating, form the core of the film and are its only excuse for existence.

p, Andre Morgan, Roger Lewis; d, Roger Vadim; w, Anton Diether, Clarke Reynolds (based on a story by Diether, Barth Jules Sussman); ph, Dennis Lewiston (Technicolor); m, John Barry; ed, Peter Hunt; prod d, Robert Laing; art d, Frank Israel; spec eff, Gene Grigg.

Drama **Cas.** (PR:O MPAA:R)

NIGHT GOD SCREAMED, THE* (1975) 85m Cinemation c (AKA: SCREAM)

Jeanne Crain, Alex Nicol, Daniel Spelling, Michael Sugich, Barbara Hancock, Dawn Cleary, Gary Morgan.

Crain, who had been nominated for an Oscar for her performance as a black passing for white in the 1949 film PINKY, stars as a damsel in distress here. She's being pursued by a hooded murderer because she testified against some blood-thirsty Jesus freaks. The film is as intelligent as the synopsis implies.

p, Gil Lasky, Ed Carlin; d, Lee Madden; w, Lasky.

Horror (PR:O MPAA:R)

NIGHT HAIR CHILD* (1971, Brit.) 89m Leander/Towers c (AKA: CHILD OF THE NIGHT)

Mark Lester, Britt Ekland, Lilli Palmer, Hardy Kruger, Harry Andrews, Collette Jack, Conchita Montez.

A pretty inept psychodrama starring Lester (of OLIVER! fame) as a young boy with a sexual fascination for his stepmother. The filmmakers tend to sensationalize the subject matter rather than deal with it on a mature, insightful level, which ultimately renders the film distasteful and pointless.

p, Graham Harris; d, James Kelly; w, Trevor Preston; ph, Harry Waxman (Movielab); m, Stelvio Cipriani.

Drama (PR:O MPAA:NR)

NIGHT HAS A THOUSAND EYES*** (1948) 80m PAR bw

Edward G. Robinson (*John Triton*), Gail Russell (*Jean Courtland*), John Lund (*Elliott Carson*), Virginia Bruce (*Jenny*), William Demarest (*Lt. Shawn*), Richard Webb (*Peter Vinson*), Jerome Cowan (*Whitney Courtland*), Onslow Stevenson (*Dr. Walters*), John Alexander (*Mr. Gilman*), Roman Bohnen (*Melville Weston, Special Prosecutor*), Luis Van Rooten (*Mr. Myers*), Henry Guttman (*Butler*), Mary Adams (*Miss Hendricks*), Philip Van Zandt (*Chauffeur/Cigar Attendant*), Douglas Spencer (*Dr. Ramsdell*), Jean King (*Edna, Maid*), Dorothy Abbott (*2nd Maid*), Bob Stephenson (*Gowan*), William Haade (*Bertelli*), Stuart Holmes (*3rd Scientist*), Jean Wong, Anna Tom (*Young Chinese Women*), Weaver Levy (*Young Chinese Man*), Artarne Wong (*Chinese Waiter*), Jane Crowley (*Newstand Woman*), Joey Ray (*Radio Announcer/Policeman*), Eleanore Vogel (*Scrubwoman*), Minerva Urecal (*Bit Woman, Italian*), Renee Randall (*1st Secretary*), Marilyn Gray (*2nd Secretary*), Lester Dorr (*Mr. Byers*), Harland Tucker (*Husband of Frantic Mother*), Violet Goulet (*Deb's Mother*), Edward Earle (*Bit Man*), Julia Faye, Rae Patterson (*Companions*), Margaret Field (*Agnes*), Major Sam Harris (*Deb's Father*), John Sheehan (*Elderly Doorman*), Betty Hannon (*Secretary*), James Davies (*Jailer*), Helen Chapman (*Secretary*), Jerry James, Len Hendry, Billy Burt (*Policemen*), Antonio Filauri, Weaver Levy (*Men*), Frank Hagney (*Truckman*), Lyle Latell, Jim Drumm, Jimmie Dundee, Pat Flaherty (*Policemen*), Harry Allen (*MacDougall*), Gladys Blake (*Mrs. Byers*), Frances Morris (*Mother*), Regina Wallace (*Mother-in-Law*), Marie Thomas (*Girl*), George Nokes (*Newsboy*), Audrey Saunders, Raymond Saunders, Russell Saunders, Walter Cook (*Tumbling Act*), Albert Pollet (*Frenchman Toto*).

It's hokey but scary and so well done that this film approaches classic *film noir*, even though the premise is harebrained and so far out on a limb as to break it and cause the sap to run wildly. Lund saves his fiancee Russell from committing suicide and then the couple contacts spiritualist Robinson who meets them in a restaurant where he is told that Russell's attempt was caused by his prediction that he envisioned her lying beneath the stars. She believed, coupled to Robinson's other too-accurate predictions, that this meant her death and tried to end her life rather than wait for the inevitable. Robinson then explains how he has been cursed with a gift to see not only the future but to predict especially tragic events, chiefly death. "I had become a reverse zombie," he tells them, "the world was dead and I was living." In flashback we see Robinson as a stage spiritualist who is assisted by Bruce. One night he actually has a vision and suddenly tells a woman in the audience to rush home, that her small boy is about to die in a fire. The child is saved but the incident frightens Robinson, even though he casually but accurately picks racetrack winners for his partner Cowan, which makes the partner rich. He then envisions Bruce dying in childbirth and this so unnerves Robinson that he quits the act and retreats to an abandoned mine where he lives for five years as a hermit. He then learns that Bruce had married Cowan, now a famous industrialist, and had died in childbirth. Another vision shakes him; he sees Cowan dying in a plane crash during a coast-to-coast speed contest. Robinson moves to Los Angeles to be near Cowan and his child, Russell, and tries to communicate with them, warning Russell that her father is about to meet his death. He begs Russell to stop Cowan's flight. Lund thinks Robinson is cracked but Russell believes him and vainly tries to halt the flight. Her father dies and then Robinson falls into deep depression when he envisions Russell's death by accident. In a flash forward to the present Lund now expresses his anger. He has had enough. First Robinson obliquely predicts Russell's suicide, now he is saying she will die in an accident. Lund goes to the police and has Robinson arrested. A case against the seer is strengthened when police learn that Cowan's plane has been tampered with. Robinson, meanwhile, is growing desperate, begging police to release him so he can save Russell. He convinces his captors that he is genuine when he correctly predicts a prisoner's suicide. He is freed and rushes to Russell's home, arriving just in time to prevent one of Cowan's crooked partners—the man who had sabotaged the plane—from shooting Russell. As he dashes forward to save Russell, the police on hand mistake his motives and fatally shoot him. In Robinson's pocket police find a note he had written where he predicted his own death. NIGHT HAS A THOUSAND EYES is packed with suspense and is expertly directed by Farrow with Robinson giving a superb performance. (In his biography, Robinson labeled the film "unadulterated hokum that I did for the money.") Young's score for NIGHT HAS A THOUSAND EYES is eerie and exceptional, setting the chilling tone for the movie, and Seitz's shadowy camerawork lends just the right atmosphere to all the creepy possibilities presented by Robinson's futuristic gaze. The ability to see the future, particularly a future full of death and destruction, has been the theme for many films, including those starring Robinson. He appeared as a man afflicted by lethal vision in FLESH AND FANTASY and NIGHTMARE, in addition to NIGHT HAS A THOUSAND EYES. Claude Rains suffered the same gift in one of the classics of this genre, THE CLAIRVOYANT, only his specialty was major disasters. George Macready was burdened with the soothsayer curse in I LOVE A MYSTERY, as were Mervyn Johns in the classic British thriller DEAD OF NIGHT, Michael Hordern in THE NIGHT MY NUMBER CAME UP, and Dick Powell in IT HAPPENED TOMORROW.

p, Endre Bohem; d, John Farrow; w, Barre Lyndon, Jonathan Latimer (based on the novel by Cornell Woolrich); ph, John F. Seitz; m, Victor Young; ed, Eda Warren; art d, Hans Dreier, Franz Bachelin; set d, Sam Comer, Ray Moyer; cos, Edith Head; makeup, Wally Westmore.

Mystery **(PR:C MPAA:NR)**

NIGHT HAS EYES, THE (SEE: TERROR HOUSE, 1942, Brit.)

NIGHT HAWK, THE*½ (1938) 63m REP bw

Robert Livingston (*Slim*), June Travis (*Della*), Robert Armstrong (*McCormick*), Ben Welden (*Otto Miller*), Lucien Littlefield (*Parrish*), Joseph Downing (*Lefty*), Roland L. Got (*Willie*), Cy Kendall (*Capt. Teague*), Paul Fix (*Spider*), Billy Burrud (*Bobby McCormick*), Charles Wilson (*Lonigan*), Dwight Frye (*Colley*), Paul McVey (*Larsen*), Robert E. Homans (*Mulruney*).

Absolutely unbelievable film starring Livingston as a superhuman newspaper reporter who declares war on the mob after hoods have killed his best friend, who was a customs agent. While trying to solve that murder, he gets involved with a soft-hearted mob hit man, Armstrong, who is out to get revenge on other gangsters who stole an iron lung which was meant for Armstrong's dying kid brother. Livingston hides inside the lung, and, when the time is right, he leaps out and steals the truck carrying the device. Wait, there's more! Livingston also manages to bust up two gangs, uncover a whiskey-smuggling ring, nearly get steamed to death, turn his girl's home into a target for hundreds of mob bullets, and incur his editor's wrath when his marriage announcement is scooped by a rival paper. All this flashes by in a little over an hour at breathtaking speed.

d, Sidney Salkow; w, Earl Felton; ph, Jack Marta; ed, Ernest Nims; md, Cy Feuer; art d, John Victor Mackay; cos, Irene Saltern; m/l, "Never a Dream Goes By," Walter Kent, Manny Kurtz, Al Sherman.

Crime **(PR:A MPAA:NR)**

NIGHT HEAVEN FELL, THE** (1958, Fr.) 91m Kingsley

International c (LES BIJOUTIERS DU CLAIR DE LUNE; GB: HEAVEN FELL THAT NIGHT)

Brigitte Bardot (*Ursula Desfontaines*), Alida Valli (*Florentine*), Stephen Boyd (*Lamberto*), Pepe Nieto (*Count Ribera*), Maruschi Fresno (*Conchita*), Adriano Dominguez (*Fernando*), Jose Marco Davo (*Chief Policeman*), Antonio Vico (*Count's Driver*), Mario f Moreno (*Alfonso*), Tosi (*The Captain*), Jose Tasso Tena (*Stableman*), Nicolas Perchicaut (*Priest*), Dr. Rafael Torrobo (*Veterinarian*).

Another silly Vadim-Bardot collaboration which sees Bardot as a convent girl on holiday in Spain who meets and runs off with Boyd, a good-for-nothing crook who has murdered her uncle and seduced her aunt. With Bardot's help he escapes and together they spend illicit days in the mountains having all manner of sex while running from the cops. Eventually, the law catches up and Bardot dies in a hail of bullets. The production was plagued with problems. Everything from the weather (some of the worst in Spanish history) to thespian temperament (Boyd and Bardot loathed each other) seemed to have combined to sabotage the film. After calling the film "the worst thing that ever happened to me," Boyd recanted and stated that Bardot was a refreshing actress because she didn't take herself very seriously. Neither did the critics. They lambasted the film when it was released. (In French; English subtitles.)

p, Raoul J. Levy; d, Roger Vadim; w, Vadim, Jacques Remy (based on the novel *The Moonlight Jewelers* by Albert Vidalie); ph, Armand Thirard (CinemaScope, Eastmancolor); m, George Auric; ed, Victoria Mercanton; md, Jacques Metehen; art d, Jean Andre.

Crime **(PR:O MPAA:NR)**

NIGHT HOLDS TERROR, THE*** (1955) 86m COL bw

Jack Kelly (*Gene Courtier*), Hildy Parks (*Doris Courtier*), Vince Edwards (*Victor Gosset*), John Cassavetes (*Robert Batsford*), David Cross (*Luther Logan*), Edward Marr (*Capt. Cole*), Jack Kruschen (*Detective Pope*), Joyce McCluskey (*Phyllis Harrison*), Jonathan Hale (*Bob Henderson*), Barney Phillips (*Stranske*), Charles Herbert (*Steven*), Nancy Dee Zane (*Deborah*), Joel Marston (*Reporter*).

A tense *film noir* based on a true story and starring Kelly as a middle-class family man returning to his desert home after a business trip into L.A. On the road he picks up a hitchhiker, Edwards, who jams a gun in his ribs and forces him to pick up his bloodthirsty accomplices, Cassavetes and Cross. The crooks move in with Kelly and his family and terrorize them until Kelly can sell his car to raise enough money to get rid of them. The hoods take the money but then kidnap Kelly when they learn that his father is rich. The FBI becomes involved and together with the phone company traces the crooks to their lair. In the end the kidnapers are killed and Kelly is reunited with his family. A well-constructed, powerful film.

p,d&w, Andrew Stone; ph, Fred Jackman, Jr.; m, Lucien Cailliet; ed, Virginia Stone; md, Cailliet; m/l, "Every Now and Then," Stone.

Crime **(PR:C MPAA:NR)**

NIGHT HUNT (SEE: IF HE HOLLERS, LET HIM GO! 1968)

NIGHT IN BANGKOK**½ (1966, Jap.) 105m Toho-Taiwan-Cathay/ Toho c (BANKOKKU NO YORU)

Chang Mei Yao (*Meilan*), Yuzo Kayama (*Shuichi*), Yuriko Hoshi (*Masayo*), Praprapon Pureem, Takashi Shimura.

Japanese melodrama starring Kayama as a young doctor. His foster sister, Hoshi, has loved him for years, but his romance with Yao, the daughter of a Chinese trader, causes her to lose interest in him. When Kayama attains a post in a major Bangkok hospital, things look promising for him and Hoshi, but the couple soon learn that her father has sold her to a Thai prince. The couple must part, but they declare their undying love for each other.

p, Sanezumi Fujimoto; d, Yasuki Chiba; w, Ryozo Kasahara; ph, Taiichi Kankura (Tohoscope, Eastmancolor); m, Naozumi Yamamoto.

Romance **(PR:A MPAA:NR)**

NIGHT IN CAIRO, A (SEE: BARBARIAN, THE, 1933)

NIGHT IN CASABLANCA, A*** (1946) 85m UA bw

Groucho Marx (*Ronald Kornblow*), Harpo Marx (*Rusty*), Chico Marx (*Corbaccio*), Lisette Verea (*Beatrice Reiner*), Charles Drake (*Pierre*), Lois Collier (*Annette*), Dan Seymour (*Capt. Brizzard*), Lewis Russell (*Galloux*), Harro Mellor (*Emil*), Frederick Gierman (*Kurt*), Sig Rumann (*Count Pfefferman*).

Not one of the Marx Brothers' better films, but as critic James Agee stated upon its release, ". . .the worst they might ever make would be better worth seeing than most other things I can think of." The plot revolves around Groucho, who finds himself as the new manager of the Casablanca Hotel. Little does he know, however, that the previous three managers have all been killed. Harpo is first seen leaning against a building minding his own business when a policeman (who's been told to "round up all the usual suspects" by police chief Seymour after the most recent hotel manager murder) spots him and asks, "What do you think you're doing? Holding the building up?" Harpo nods "Yes", the angry cop pulls him away, and the building collapses. Soon after we learn that Harpo is employed as sadistic Nazi Rumann's valet. Rumann, who has assumed a different identity, enjoys subjecting Harpo to all manner of abuse, abuse that Harpo cleverly circumvents (at one point he dons a catcher's uniform to protect himself) much to the dismay of Rumann. Chico, the president of the Yellow Camel Company, arrives in time to pester Groucho, who now finds himself the focus of a new set of assassination attempts. Eventually it is revealed that Rumann and his beautiful accomplice, Verea, have been killing off the managers of the hotel so that he can gain control of the establishment in order to locate a cache of valuable art that was stolen during WW II and hidden on the premises. After several attempts, Rumann gets frustrated by Harpo and Chico's constant interference (they save Groucho's life many times) and he decides to leave for Tunis. The brothers, who have by now figured out the plot, try to drive the Nazi crazy by sneakily moving his clothes around the room while he tries to pack his bags. Hiding in Rumann's wardrobe, the brothers manage to board the Nazi's escape plane. They waste no time overpowering the crew and they take over the plane with Harpo at the controls. It proves to be a glorious experience for Harpo, who delights in turning every knob and pushing every button in the cockpit, until he crashes the plane into a nightclub and Rumann is revealed as a Nazi and apprehended. A NIGHT IN CASABLANCA might never have been made if it hadn't been for Chico, who needed the money and convinced Groucho to do the film. Groucho, who was frustrated with his floundering radio career, agreed to do the film to help resolve his brother's financial troubles. Legal difficulties soon popped up when the legal department at Warner Bros. threatened to sue if the producers insisted on using the name "Casablanca" (Warner Bros. had produced Bogart's CASABLANCA). This led to some of Groucho's funniest and most biting letter writing, in which he harangued Warner Bros. unmercifully with a tirade of words pointing out just how ridiculous the threatened lawsuit was. After receiving two of Groucho's nasty letters, the Warner Bros. legal department gave up. The best bits in A NIGHT IN CASABLANCA belong to Harpo. A virtually unknown gag writer by the name of Frank Tashlin, later to become one of the brightest comedy directors of the 1950s (THE GIRL CAN'T HELP IT, WILL SUCCESS SPOIL ROCK HUNTER?), was hired to write Harpo's comedy bits. The Tashlin-Harpo collaboration proved to be the best material in the film, but a still-naive Tashlin never received the valuable screen credit he deserved for the work. Nevertheless, the Marx Brothers look old and tired in the film, and though it contains some very funny moments it falls far short of being among one of their classics.

p, David L. Loew; d, Archie Mayo; w, Joseph Fields, Roland Kibbee; ph, James Van Trees; m, Werner Janssen; ed, Gregg C. Pallas; m/l, "Who's Sorry Now?" Bert Kalmar, Harry Ruby, Ted Snyder.

Comedy **Cas.** **(PR:A MPAA:NR)**

NIGHT IN HAVANA (SEE: BIG BOODLE, THE, 1972)

NIGHT IN HEAVEN, A* (1983) 83m Koch/Kirkwood FOX c

Christopher Atkins *(Rick)*, Lesley Ann Warren *(Faye)*, Robert Logan *(Whitney)*, Deborah Rush *(Patsy)*, Deney Terrio *(Tony)*, Sandra Beall *(Slick)*, Alix Elias *(Shirley)*, Carrie Snodgress *(Mrs. Johnson)*, Amy Levine *(Eve)*, Fred Buch *(Jack Hobbs)*, Karen Margret Cole *(Louise)*, Don Cox *(Revere)*, Veronica Gamba *(Tammy)*, Joey Gian *(Pete)*, Bill Hindman *(Russel)*, Linda Lee *(Ivy)*, Rosemary McVeigh *(Alison)*, Gail Merrill *(Grace)*, Cindy Perlman *(Linda)*, Brian Smith *(Osgood)*, Scott Stone *(Lee)*, Andy Garcia *(T. J.)*, Craig Nedrow *(Man Mountain Dean)*, Anthony Avildsen *(Scooter)*, Harold Bergman *(Sladkus)*, Butch Warren *(Orshan)*, Robert Goodman *(Disick)*, John Archie *(Raymer)*, Will Knickerbocker *(Larry)*, Spatz Donovan *(Heaven M. C.)*, Dan Fitzgerald *(Guard)*, Sherry Moreland, Robbie Wolf, Tiffany Myles, Sally Ricca, Pam Tindal, Judy Arman, Mary Teahan.

Rotten sexploitation film masquerading as a serious drama. Warren plays a college teacher who is dragged to a male strip-tease club, "Heaven," by her femme friends for a night of titillation. There she is shocked to discover that Atkins, one of her students (whom she's flunking), is a male stripper. When an obnoxious emcee grabs Warren's hand and drives it into Atkins' crotch, it is only a matter of minutes before Hollywood explores another taboo romance. Dull, trite, and uninteresting, much of the film was obviously left on the cutting room floor, because very few major studio releases are released with such a short running time.

p, Gene Kirkwood, Howard W. Koch, Jr.; d, John G. Avildsen; w, Joan Tewkesbury; ph, David Quaid (DeLuxe Color); m, Jan Hammer; ed, Avildsen; prod d, William Cassidy; set d, Nicholas Romanac; cos, Anna Hill Johnstone; ch, Deney Terrio.

Drama **Cas.** **(PR:O MPAA:R)**

NIGHT IN HONG KONG, A½** (1961, Jap.) 119m Toho-Cathay/ Toho c (HONKON NO YORU)

Akira Takarada *(Hiroshi Tanaka)*, Yu Ming *(Wu Li Hung)*, Yoko Tsukasa *(Keiko Kimura)*, Mitsuko Kusabue, Ken Uehara, Daisuke Kato, Yu Fujiki, Won Inn, Ma Ree, Kang Pak King, Tetsu Nakamura, Hiroshi Koizumi, Michiyo Kogure, Mie Hama.

Another Japanese romantic melodrama directed by Yasuki Chiba. This one stars Takarada as a journalist on assignment in Hong Kong who meets and falls in love with Chinese girl Ming. When Takarada leaves to go back to Japan, he vows to return to Hong Kong and rekindle their romance. Back home, Takarada is met by childhood sweetheart Tsukasa who has loved him for years. Obsessed with Ming, Takarada returns to Hong Kong and is dismayed to discover that Ming is engaged to her boss' son. Declaring his love for her, Takarada proposes marriage, but Ming refuses because of her distaste for mixed marriages; her mother was Japanese and deserted her family during WW II. Enter Tsukasa who has jealously followed Takarada and is shocked when confronted with the relationship between her boy friend and Ming. Rejected, Tsukasa goes to Paris. In an effort to win Ming's love, Takarada locates her mother and tries unsuccessfully to reunite them. Eventually Ming agrees to marriage and a joyous Takarada flies off to Laos to finish his journalistic duties. On the eve of the wedding, Ming's hopes are shattered when it is announced that Takarada has been killed on the Laotian front.

d, Yasuki Chiba; w, Toshiro Ide; ph, Rokuro Nishigaki (Tohoscope, Eastmancolor); m, Hachiro Matsui.

Romance **(PR:A MPAA:NR)**

NIGHT IN JUNE, A½** (1940, Swed.) 86m Svenskfilmindustri bw (JUNINATTEN)

Ingrid Bergman *(Kerstin Nordback/Sara Nordana)*, Olof Widgren *(Stefan Von Bremen)*, Gunnar Sjoberg *(Nils Asklund)*, Carl Strom *(Dr. Berggren)*, Marianne Lofgren, Lill-Tollie Zellman, Marianne Aminoff, Gabriel Alw, Olof Winnerstrand, Sigurd Wallen, Hasse Ekman, Maritta Marke, Gudrun Brost, John Botvid, Karin Swanstrom, Mimi Pollak, Charlie Paterson, Ernst Brunman, Alf Kjellin, Karin Nordgren, Mona Geijer-Falkner, David Eriksson, Douglas Hage, Carl Deurell, Sven-Goran Alw, Richard Lund, Nils Jacobsson, Sol-Britt Agerup, Kerstin Ekwall, Britta Larsson, Viran Rydkvist, Erik Forslund.

A lengthy drama featuring Bergman as a small-town girl who falls into an affair with rootless sailor Sjoberg. Soon it is obvious to her that they are incompatible and she tries to break off the relationship. Sjoberg, however, draws a gun and threatens to commit suicide. The gun accidentally goes off and hits Bergman near the heart and only after hours of delicate surgery is her life saved. Sjoberg is tried for attempted murder, but Bergman supports his attempted-suicide story and the court gives him a light sentence. The whole sordid affair has sent the town into an uproar, forcing Bergman to leave. She changes her name and moves to Stockholm, where she meets a nice young man and settles down to a life of unpublicized marital bliss. Fine acting and beautiful photography compensate to some extent for the excessive running time of this early Bergman effort.

d, Per Lindberg; w, Ragnar Hylten-Cavallius (based on a story by Tora Nordstrom-Bonnier); ph, Ake Dahlquist; m, Jules Sylvain; ed, Oscar Rosander.

Drama **(PR:A MPAA:NR)**

NIGHT IN MONTMARTE, A*½ (1931, Brit.) 70m Gainsborough/ GAU bw

Horace Hodges *(Lucien Borell)*, Franklin Dyall *(Max Levine)*, Hugh Williams, *(Philip Borell, Artist)*, Heather Angel *(Annette Lefevre)*, Austin Trevor *(Paul de Lisle)*, Kay Hammond *(Margot)*, Edmund Willard *(Alexandre)*, Arthur Hambling *(Inspector Brichot)*, Reginald Purdell *(Tino)*, Binnie Barnes *(Therese)*, John Deverell, Charles Costello.

Dyall plays a rotten-to-the-core restaurant owner who indulges in heavy doses of blackmail to supplement his income. When he turns up stabbed to death, suspicion falls on Williams and it is up to his doddering old detective father Hodges to clear his name. This was the feature-film premiere of angelic actress Angel, who made a sufficiently good impression in such early talkies as to be imported from England to Hollywood by 20th Century-Fox in 1933. Her U.S. roles tended to be pallid, and by the late 1930s she was appearing in B pictures. This film presaged things to come for her; her third husband, Walter B. Sinclair (who directed such films as THE CAPTAIN IS A LADY and MR. AND MRS. NORTH for MGM) was stabbed to death by a prowler in 1970. This was also the first major feature appearance of caustic beauty Barnes, who made the trip west a year later than Angel.

p, Michael Balcon; d, Leslie Hiscott; w, Angus Macphail (based on the play by Miles Malleson, Walter Peacock).

Crime **(PR:A MPAA:NR)**

NIGHT IN NEW ORLEANS, A** (1942) 75m PAR bw

Preston Foster *(Steve Abbott)*, Patricia Morison *(Ethel Abbott)*, Albert Dekker *(Lt. Richards)*, Charles Butterworth *(Edward Wallace)*, Dooley Wilson *(Shadrach Jones, Butler)*, Paul Hurst *(Sgt. Riordan)*, Jean Phillips *(Janet Price)*, Cecil Kellaway *(Dan Odell)*, William Wright *(George Wallace)*, Noble Johnson *(Carney)*, Joseph Pope *(Carlson)*, Yola D'Avril *(Mme. Lamballe)*, George Chandler *(Taxi Driver)*, Henry Brandon *(Croupier)*, Arthur Loft *(Sgt. Bliss)*, Charles Williams.

Foster stars as a police lieutenant assigned to bust up the gang of a big-time gambler. When he finds the gambler's body, fellow police lieutenant Dekker suspects Foster of the murder. Foster then spends the rest of the film one step ahead of his colleagues (who are tyring to nab him) while trying to clear his name.

p, Sol C. Siegel; d, William Clemens; w, Jonathan Latimer (based on the story "Sing a Song of Homicide" by James R. Langham); ph, Merritt Gerstad, Leo Tover, John Mescall; ed, Ellsworth Hoagland; art d, Hans Dreier, Haldane Douglas.

Crime **(PR:A MPAA:NR)**

NIGHT IN PARADISE, A** (1946) 84m UNIV c

Merle Oberon *(Delarai)*, Turhan Bey *(Aesop, "Jason")*, Thomas Gomez *(King Croesus)*, Gale Sondergaard *(Attossa)*, Ray Collins *(Leonides)*, George Dolenz *(Frigid Ambassador)*, John Litel *(Archon)*, Ernest Truex, Jerome Cowan, Marvin Miller *(Scribes)*, Douglas Dumbrille, Moroni Olsen, Francis McDonald *(High Priests)*, Paul Cavanagh *(Cleomenes)*, Richard Bailey *(Lieutenant)*, Wee Willie Davis *(Salabaar)*, Roseanne Murray *(Marigold)*, Hans Herbert *(Priest)*, Julie London, Barbara Bates, Duan Kennedy, Ruth Valmy, Karen X. Gaylord, Kathleen O'Malley, Karen Randle, Kerry Vaughn, Audrey Young *(Palace Maidens)*, Eula Morgan, Art Miles, Al Chosis, Myrtle Ferguson, Frank Hagney *(Townspeople)*,

James Hutton *(Delarai Messenger)*, Juli Lynne *(Song Specialty)*, Jean Trent *(Iris)*, Jane Adams *(Lotus)*, John Merton *(Sailor)*, Don Stowell *(Sentinel)*, Pedro De Cordoba *(Magus)*, Harry Cording *(Captain)*, Ann Everett, Dorothy Tuomi, Marguerite Campbell, June Frazer *(Flower Girls)*, Colin Campbell *(Goatman)*, Nikki Kerkes, Mercedes Mockaitis *(Special Water Girls)*, Harlan Miller *(Slave)*, Denny Burke *(Contortionist)*, Neal Young *(Nobleman)*, Joe Bernard *(Old Man)*, John Berkes, Al Ferguson, Pietro Sosso *(Beggars)*, *Dick Alexander, Earle Ozman (Temple Guards)*, Rex Evans *(Chef)*, Jack Overman *(Man)*, Wade Crosby *(Rough Man)*, Charles Bates, Clyde Flynn, Joel Goodkind, Jimmy Fresco, Mickey Fresco, Juan Estrada, Robert Espinosa, Louis Montoya *(Boys)*, Kit Guard *(Man in Crowd)*.

Basically a fable, this film features Oberon as a princess in a mythical land a few centuries before Christ, a place that one never can identify other than that the name of the country is Lydia. Oberon is engaged to Gomez, a fat, oily Croesus who is, of course, the richest man in the world. Along comes Bey, as Aesop, and he pretends to be very old and feeble, as he learned that no one will take advice from a young person so he is masquerading as being ancient. Bey woos and wins Oberon away from Gomez while managing to save his small country (a place called Samos, which sounds more like one of Jupiter's moons) and his life. Sondergaard wants to marry Gomez and resents his attraction to Oberon. And was there anyone who could portray resentment and scheming better than Sondergaard? It's a very posh production with lots of beautiful costumes and sets but the dialog is so anachronistic and so reminiscent of the mid-1940s that we can't believe a word of it. A good cast is hampered by the dumb words they have to speak. Among the cast are Ray Collins, whom Orson Welles said was the "best radio actor in the world," and Marvin Miller, who was the busiest voice in the U.S. during the halcyon days of radio drama. He would appear on as many as 40 shows some weeks, playing many different parts on the same programs. Look for a very young Julie London as one of the palace maidens.

p, Walter Wanger; d, Arthur Lubin; w, Ernest Pascal, Emmett Lavery (based on the novel *Peacock's Feather* by George S. Hellman); ph, Hal Mohr, W. Howard Greene (Technicolor); m, Frank Skinner; ed, Milton Carruth; md, Skinner; art d, John B. Goodman, Alexander Golitzen; set d, Russell A. Gausman, E. R. Robinson; cos, Vera West; spec eff, John P. Fulton; m/l, "Night in Paradise," Skinner, Jack Brooks.

Drama/Fantasy **(PR:A MPAA:NR)**

NIGHT INTO MORNING**½ (1951) 86m MGM bw

Ray Milland *(Phillip Ainley)*, John Hodiak *(Tom Lawry)*, Nancy Davis *(Katherine Mead)*, Lewis Stone *(Dr. Horace Snyder)*, Jean Hagen *(Girl Next Door)*, Rosemary De Camp *(Anne Ainley)*, Dawn Addams *(Dotty Phelps)*, Jonathan Cott *(Chuck Holderson)*, Celia Lovsky *(Mrs. Niemoller)*, Gordon Gebert *(Russ Kirby)*, Katherine Warren *(Mrs. Anderson)*, Harry Antrim *(Mr. Anderson)*, Mary Lawrence *(Edith the Waitress)*, Herb Vigran *(Bartender)*, Wheaton Chambers *(Conductor)*, John Eldredge, Matt Moore *(Instructors)*, Whit Bissell *(Stone Yard Proprietor)*, Percy Helton, John "Skins" Miller *(Drunks)*, Otto Waldis *(Dr. Franz Neimoller)*, John Maxwell *(Dr. Huntington)*, John Jeffrey *(Timmy Ainley)*.

Adult drama starring Milland as a university professor who loses his wife and child in a gas explosion which occurred at his home while he was teaching classes. Suppressing his emotions, Milland finds solace in the bottle, much to the dismay of his friends, Hodiak and Davis. One evening, when Davis senses that Milland might end it all, she saves him from jumping out a window. The mindlessness and futility of his act having snapped him back to reality, Milland allows himself to live again.

p, Edwin H. Knopf; d, Fletcher Markle; w, Karl Tunberg, Leonard Spigelgass; ph, George J. Folsey; m, Carmen Dragon; ed, George White, Robert Watts; art d, Cedric Gibbons, James Basevi.

Drama **(PR:A MPAA:NR)**

NIGHT INVADER, THE**½ (1943, Brit) 81m WB-FN bw

Anne Crawford *(Karen Lindley)*, David Farrar *(Dick Marlow)*, Carl Jaffe *(Count von Biebrich)*, Sybilla Binder *(Baroness von Klaveren)*, Jenny Lovelace *(Liesje von Klaveren)*, Marius Goring *(Oberleutenant)*, *Martin Walker (Jimmy Archer)*, John Salew *(Witsen)*, George Carney *(Conductor)*, Kynaston Reeves *(Sir Michael)*, Philip Godfrey, Ernest Verne, Ronald Shiner, Harry Charman, Walter Gotell.

Farrar parachutes into Holland in order to retrieve an important war document. He poses as a reporter from the U.S. and holes up with Binder, a baroness who supports the British war effort. The two fall in love and end up escaping, evading capture by the Nazis. Though the story is wholly unbelievable, this film moves well. The pacing quickly covers any holes in logic, making for an okay wartime thriller.

p, Max Milder; d, Herbert Mason; w, Brock Williams, Edward Dryhurst, Roland Pertwee (based on the novel *Rendevous with Death* by John Bentley); ph, Otto Heller.

Thriller/War **(PR:C MPAA:NR)**

NIGHT IS ENDING, THE (SEE: PARIS AFTER DARK, 1943)

NIGHT IS MY FUTURE**½ (1962, Swed.) 87m Terrafilm/Embassy bw (MUSIK I MORKER)

Mai Zetterling *(Ingrid Olofsdotter)*, Birger Malmsten *(Bengt)*, Bengt Eklund *(Ebbe)*, Olof Winnerstrand *(The Vicar)*, Naima Wifstrand *(Mrs. Schroder)*, Bibi Skoglund *(Agneta)*, Hilda Borgstrom *(Lovis the Housekeeper)*, Douglas Hage *(Druge the Restaurant Owner)*, Gunnar Bjornstrand *(Klasson)*, Ake Claesson, John Elfstrom, Sven Lindberg, Bengt Logardt, Marianne Gyllenhammar, Barbro Flodquist, Ulla Andreasson, Rune Andreasson.

Very early Bergman film (he had directed 16 films before all the critical acclaim) starring Malmsten as a man blinded while in the military who struggles with his affliction. Wanting to be treated as an equal, not a cripple, he spurns help from anyone. He hires Zetterling (who would go on to direct films herself) to be his maid and companion. He teaches her about literature and music and soon a deep relation develops. Malmsten applies to the music academy, and when he is rejected he takes a job playing piano in a restaurant. This job ends abruptly when he discovers that the owner and another employee are crooks. Trying to regain some self-respect, Malmsten enrolls in a school for the blind. The classes work, but he is shattered when he learns that Zetterling has a boy friend. Dejected and lonely, Malmsten wanders near the railroad tracks and is almost killed. Zetterling and her boy friend find him on a bridge, and, after a quarrel, the boy friend knocks him down and leaves. Having gained confidence from being treated as an equal, Malmsten asks Zetterling to marry him and she accepts.

p, Lorens Marmstedt; d, Ingmar Bergman; w, Dagmar Edqvist (based on his novel); ph, Goran Strindberg; m, Erland von Koch; ed, Lennart Wallen; art d, P.A. Lundgren.

Drama **(PR:A MPAA:NR)**

NIGHT IS OURS*½ (1930, Fr.) 90m Lutetia-Froehlich bw (LA NUIT)

Marie Bell, Roussell, Jean Murat, Jim Gerald, Mary Costes, May Vincent, Kitty Kelly.

Early foreign talkie which was shot in French and German versions at the same time, and cost a staggering (at that time) $200,000. The plot revolves around a routine romance between Bell and Murat which is complicated by the appearance of a woman claiming to be his wife. Eventually the wife admits she has gotten a divorce after stalling for two years. Producer Froehlich directed the German version. A third negative was also made, sound-synchronized for the international market.

p, Carl Froehlich; d, Henry Roussell; w, (based on a play by Henry Kistemaeker).

Drama **(PR:A MPAA:NR)**

NIGHT IS THE PHANTOM (SEE: WHAT!, 1965, Fr./Brit./Ital.)

NIGHT IS YOUNG, THE** (1935) 78m MGM bw

Ramon Novarro *(Paul Gustave)*, Evelyn Laye *(Lisl Gluck)*, Charles Butterworth *(Willy)*, Una Merkel *(Fanni)*, Henry Stephenson *(Emperor)*, Edward Everett Horton *(Szereny)*, Rosalind Russell *(Countess Rafay)*, Donald Cook *(Toni)*, Charles Judels *(Riccardi)*, Herman Bing *(Nepomuk)*, Christian Rub *(Cafe Proprietor)*, Alberti Conti *(Moehler)*, Elspeth Dudgeon *(Duchess)*, Gustav von Seyffertitz *(Ambassador)*, Carlos J. de Valdez *(Adjutant)*, Snub Pollard *(Drummer)*.

Tedious Romberg-Hammerstein operetta starring Novarro as an archduke who dumps a princess for the love of ballet dancer Laye, but eventually succumbs to the wishes of the emperor and marries the princess. The film yielded two hit songs, "The Night Is Young" and "When I Grow Too Old to Dream," but it was Novarro's last screen appearance for 14 years, and Laye returned to England for good after its release. Other songs: "My Old Mare," "The Noble Duchess," "Lift Your Glass," "There's a Riot in Havana."

p, Harry Rapf; d, Dudley Murphy; w, Edgar Allan Woolf, Franz Schulz (based on a story by Vicki Baum); ph, James Wong Howe; ed, Conrad A. Nervig; cos, Dolly Tree; m/l, Sigmund Romberg, Oscar Hammerstein II.

Musical **(PR:A MPAA:NR)**

NIGHT JOURNEY** (1938, Brit.) 76m BN/BUT bw

Geoffrey Toone *(Johnny Carson)*, Patricia Hilliard *(Mary Prentice)*, Alf Goddard *(Tiny)*, Edward Lexy *(Milstone Mike)*, Ronald Ritchie *(Lemmy)*, Zillah Bateman *(Nan)*, Charles Farrell *(Dave)*, Richard Norris *(Harry)*, Phyllis Morris *(Mrs. Prentice)*, Johnnie Schofield, Charles Groves, Yolande Terrell, Douglas Stewart, George Street.

Toone is a truck driver who must transport a load of dynamite. His girl friend, Hilliard, becomes involved with a gang that deals in hot furs. Through an unimaginative and slow-moving series of events, the film leads to a terrific climax with Toone rescuing his beloved as the bad guys and their stolen loot are blown to smithereens.

p, John Corfield; d, Oswald Mitchell; w, Jim Phelan, Maisie Sharman (based on the novel *Tenapenny People* by Jim Phelan); ph, Geoffrey Faithfull.

Crime **(PR:A MPAA:NR)**

NIGHT KEY**½ (1937) 68m UNIV bw

Boris Karloff *(Dave Mallory)*, Jean Rogers *(Joan Mallory)*, Warren Hull *(Travers)*, Hobart Cavanaugh *(Petty Louie)*, Samuel S. Hinds *(Steve Ranger)*, Alan Baxter *(John Baron, the Kid)*, David Oliver *(Mike)*, Edwin Maxwell *(Kruger)*, Ward Bond *(Finger Man)*, Frank Hagney, Frank Reicher, Ethan Laidlaw, George Cleveland, Charles Wilson, Antonio Filauri, Ralph Dunn.

Karloff stars as a good guy for once in this fun, low-budget thriller. He plays a nearly blind old scientist who is robbed of his burglar alarm invention by his evil partner, Hinds, who owns the security company. Though ill, Karloff decides to invent a superior burglar alarm to provide for his daughter Rogers after his death. Karloff sells the new alarm to Hinds' company for royalties, but Hinds refuses to sell the device. Seeking to force Hinds to live up to their agreement, Karloff invents an apparatus that nullifies the old burglar alarms. At night he uses his device to gain entry into stores protected by Hinds' old alarms. Knowing he'll be ruined if this continues, Hinds hires trouble-shooter Hull to stop Karloff. Karloff, however, has been kidnaped by a group of thieves who want to use his gizmo to rob stores and offices. Karloff refuses, but after the crooks kidnap his daughter, he relents. Soon the gang has a crime spree through the city. Discovered by Hull, Karloff escapes and persuades Hinds to follow his guidelines for capturing the crooks. Eventually Karloff's daughter is rescued and the criminals apprehended. A grateful Hinds promises to pay Karloff in full for his inventions.

p, Robert Presnell; d, Lloyd Corrigan; w, Tristram Tupper, John C. Moffitt (based on a story by William Pierce); ph, George Robinson; ed, Otis Garrett; md, Lou Forbes; art d, Jack Otterson; spec eff, John P. Fulton; makeup, Jack Pierce.

Crime (PR:A MPAA:NR)

NIGHT LIFE IN RENO*

(1931) 72m Supreme/Artclass bw

Virginia Valli, Jameson Thomas, Dixie Lee, Dorothy Christy, Carmelita Geraghty, Arthur Housman, Pat O'Malley, Clarence Wilson.

Poorly done melodramatic tale of a husband leaving his wife and the consequences his actions bring. She takes off for Reno and takes up with a new man of her own. Unfortunately the new beau happens to be married and is shot by his jealous wife. The woman returns to home sweet home, making up with her philandering husband for a sappy happy ending. Bad filmmaking at its most atrocious. This was the last screen appearance for Valli. Best known for her work as a leading player in silents, she left acting at the age of 36 after marrying actor Charles Farrell.

d, Ray Cannon; w, Arthur Hoerl; ph, M. A. Anderson, M. Santacross; ed, Don Hayes, Martha Dresback.

Drama (PR:A MPAA:NR)

NIGHT LIFE OF THE GODS**½

(1935) 74m UNIV bw

Alan Mowbray (Hunter Hawky), Florine McKinney (Meg), Peggy Shannon (Daphne Lambert), Richard Carle (Grandpa Lambert), Theresa Maxwell Conover (Alice Lambert), Phillips Smalley (Alfred Lambert), Wesley Barry (Alfred Lambert, Jr.), Gilbert Emery (Betts), Ferdinand Gottschalk (Old Man Turner), Douglas Fowley (Cyril Sparks), William "Stage" Boyd (Mulligan), Henry Armetta (Roigi), Arlene Carroll (Stella), Raymond Benard (Apollo), George Hassell (Bacchus), Irene Ware (Diana), Geneva Mitchell (Hebe), Paul Kaye (Mercury), Robert Warwick (Neptune), Pat De Cicco (Perseus), Marda Deering (Venus), Ann Doran (Girl).

Silly comedy starring Mowbray as a man who discovers he can make statues come to life, or turn people to stone, with the help of a magic ring. For starters he turns his obnoxious relatives into museum pieces, then takes off on the town to celebrate. He meets McKinney, who, her father declares, is 900 years old, and they revive some statues and show them around town. Eventually Mowbray realizes that his stoic friends don't belong in society and neither does he, so he turns everybody, including himself, into stone.

p, Carl Laemmle, Jr.; d, Lowell Sherman; w, Barry Trivers (based on a novel by Thorne Smith); ph, John J. Mescall; ed, Ted Kent.

Comedy (PR:A MPAA:NR)

NIGHT LIKE THIS, A***

(1932, Brit.) 72m British and Dominions/WF bw

Ralph Lynn (Clifford Tope), Tom Walls (Michael Mahoney), Winifred Shotter (Cora Mellish), Mary Brough (Mrs. Decent), Robertson Hare (Miles Tuckett), Claude Hulbert (Archie Slott), Boris Ranevsky (Kosky), C.V. France (The Mailer), Joan Brierley (Molly Dean), Norma Varden (Mrs. Tuckett), Kay Hammond (Cocktail Shaker).

Playboy Lynn falls for Shotter, a nightclub dancer. She's being blackmailed by her club's owner because of a necklace she's borrowed, but thanks to her beau (along with the help of Irish cop Walls) all works out happily. Pretty good British comedy with some really hysterical moments. This was one of the "Aldwych Farces," a group of comedies which were brought to the screen after being produced for the stage by A NIGHT LIKE THIS director Tom Walls, and the cast here is loaded with "Aldwych" regulars. Playing a cop shouldn't have seemed too unfamiliar for Walls, as he had worked as a policeman (among other occupations) before involving himself with theater and film.

p, Herbert Wilcox; d, Tom Walls; w, W. P. Lipscomb, Walls, Ben Travers (based on the play by Travers); ph, F. A. Young.

Comedy (PR:A MPAA:NR)

NIGHT MAIL**½

(1935, Brit.) 53m BL/MGM bw

Henry Oscar (Mancini), Hope Davy (Wendy March), C. M. Hallard (Sir Jacob March), Richard Bird (Billy), Jane Carr (Lady Angela Savage), Garry Marsh (Capt. Ronnie Evans), Edmond Breon (Lord Ticehurst), Doris Hare, Tonie Edgar Bruce, Frank Atkinson, Viola Lyel, Wilfrid Hyde-White.

Intrigue and danger abound aboard the overnight mail train as Oscar, a crazed musician, tries to do in judge Hallard. Hallard wouldn't grant Oscar a divorce, which was enough to incite the man to murder. Hallard is saved in the nick of time by the lover of his would-be killer's wife. This thriller is helped along by its quick pacing and unusual assortment of quirky characters. The sort of underhanded conniver portrayed here by Oscar was his specialty.

p&d, Herbert Smith; w, Charles Bennett, Billie Bristow.

Thriller (PR:C MPAA:NR)

NIGHT MAYOR, THE**½

(1932) 68m COL bw

Lee Tracy (The Mayor, Bobby Kingston), Evalyn Knapp (Doree Dawn), Eugene Pallette (Hymie Shane), Warren Hymer (Riley), Donald Dillaway (Fred Field), Vince Barnett (Louis Mossbaum, Tailor), Astrid Allwyn (Patsy), Barbara Weeks (Nutsy), Gloria Shea (Gwen), Emmett Corrigan (Lt. Gov. Robertson), Tom O'Brien (Delaney), Wade Boteler (Clancy), Harold Minjir (Ashley Sparks), Wallis Clark (Crandall).Opportunistic newsman seeking to capitalize on a scandal in New York mayor Jimmy Walker's office before his name was out of the newspapers. Tracy plays "The Mayor" who has a penchant for the night life, sports, the theater, and an actress, Knapp. When scandal rocks his administration, Tracy has his girl friend marry Dillaway, a writer friend, so that the press will leave him alone.

d, Ben Stoloff; w, Gertrude Purcell (based on a story by Sam Marx); ph, Ted Tetzlaff, ed, Maurice Wright.

Drama (PR:A MPAA:NR)

NIGHT MONSTER**

(1942) 73m UNIV bw (AKA: HOUSE OF MYSTERY)

Bela Lugosi (Rolf the Butler), Lionel Atwill (Dr. King), Leif Erickson (Laurie the Chauffeur), Irene Hervey (Dr. Lynne Harper), Ralph Morgan (Kurt Ingston), Don Porter (Dick Baldwin), Nils Asther (Agor Singh), Fay Helm (Margaret Ingston), Frank Reicher (Dr. Timmons), Doris Lloyd (Miss Judd the Housekeeper), Francis Pierlot (Dr. Phipps), Robert E. Homans (Cap Beggs), Janet Shaw (Millie Carson), Eddy Waller (Jeb Harmon), Cyril Delevanti (Torque, Gateman at the Estate).

Somewhat creepy thriller starring Morgan as a legless homicidal maniac who wanders about a mansion (he wears false limbs) killing off the doctors responsible for amputating his legs. Lugosi got top billing, but he has a pathetically small role as the butler. Elyse Knox originally had the role of the maid, but was replaced by Janet Shaw due to illness. The picture was shot in 11 days. Beebe directed some fairly atmospheric sequences, but the climactic fire scene was actually stock footage from the end of THE GHOST OF FRANKENSTEIN.

p&d, Ford Beebe; w, Clarence Upson Young; ph, Charles Van Enger; ed, Milton Carruth; md, Hans J. Salter; art d, Jack Otterson, Richard Riedel; makeup, Jack Pierce.

Mystery (PR:A MPAA:NR)

NIGHT MOVES**½

(1975) 100m Hiller-Layton/WB c

Gene Hackman (Harry Moseby), Susan Clark (Ellen Moseby), Edward Binns (Ziegler), Harris Yulin (Marty Heller), Kenneth Mars (Nick), Janet Ward (Arlene Iverson), James Woods (Quentin), Anthony Costello (Mary Ellman), John Crawford (Tom Iverson), Melanie Griffith (Delly Grastner), Jennifer Warren (Paula), Ben Archibek (Charles), Maxwell Gail, Jr. (Tony), Victor Paul, Louis Elias, Carey Loftin, John Moio (Cops), Susan Barrister, Larry Mitchell (Airline Ticket Clerks), Tim Haldeman (Delivery Boy), Jacque Wallace (Man), Dennis Dugan (Young Man), C. J. Hincks (Girl), Phil Altman, Bob Templeton (Crewmen), Terry Leonard, Fred Waugh, Ron Rondell, Chuck Parkison, Jr. Glen Wilder, Betty Raymond, Dean Englehardt, Chuck Hicks, Ted Grossman, Richard Hackman, Rick Lockwood, Walter Scott, Ernie Orsatti (Stunt and Stunt Doubles), Avril Gentles, Sandra Diane Seacat, Rene Enriquez, Simon Deckard, Michael Ebert (Voices).

Hackman had already done the film-noir disenchanted private eye in THE CONVERSATION and this was a weak follow-up to that superior film. Hackman is an ex-footballer now operating a small-time investigation agency who is compulsive about getting to the bottom of things and not easily deterred. He had spent many years looking for his missing father, and when he finally located him, that was enough and he refused to say one word to the man. He's married to Clark, who is having an affair with Yulin, and his domestic life is a shambles. Ward, a blowsy actress who has seen better days (but not many), hires Hackman to find her missing daughter, Griffith. It's not that she loves the runaway, but only that the child has a trust fund of some consequence and Ward wants to get her hands on it. She thinks that her ex-husband, Crawford, may have enticed Griffith to Florida. Hackman begins his investigation of the flight of Griffith and hears that she's in residence with a stunt man at a movie location. When he gets there, Griffith is no longer where she was supposed to be, so he hies back to Crawford's fishing cabin in the Florida Keys where he finds her. Crawford is a smuggler and living with Warren. Griffith is located but she won't leave with Hackman, so he stays a while and is soon attracted to Warren, and the two of them have a fling. When Griffith finds that her former lover, the stunt man, has crashed his plane beneath the surface of the sea, she is thunderstruck and agrees to accompany Hackman back to Ward. Hackman brings the child home and goes back to Clark. The following day Griffith is beheaded by a seaplane while performing a movie stunt, and Hackman looks into that by viewing the film footage and reckons that the girl was deliberately murdered and that it wasn't an accident. Hackman goes to Florida and uncovers the truth; Warren and Crawford are smugglers of pre-Columbia artifacts and have been guilty of many murders to keep their cottage industry going. There's a battle, a chase, and finally the plane crash that kills Crawford and Warren. In the final scene, Hackman is bleeding from bullet wounds and seated in a motorboat that's aimlessly putt-putting in the sea. Mars and Dugan are totally wasted in their small roles as both are excellent character men. Griffith is the daughter of Tippi Hedren and somewhat better than her mother as an actress. Penn used Hackman well in BONNIE AND CLYDE, but it was downhill from there to this film and 1985's TARGET. Penn's associate producer on this movie, as well as many of Penn's others, was Gene Lasko, an excellent Broadway veteran who chose films over the stage.

p, Robert M. Sherman; d, Arthur Penn; w, Alan Sharp; ph, Bruce Surtees (Technicolor); m, Michael Small; ed, Dede Allen; prod d, George Jenkins; set d, Ned Parsons; cos, Rita Riggs; spec eff, Marcel Vercoutere, Joe Day; makeup, Bob Stein.

Mystery **Cas.** (PR:C MPAA:R)

NIGHT MUST FALL****

(1937) 117m MGM bw

Robert Montgomery (Danny), Rosalind Russell (Olivia), Dame May Whitty (Mrs. Bransom), Alan Marshall (Justin), Merle Tottenham (Dora), Kathleen Harrison (Mrs. Terence), Matthew Boulton (Belsize), Eily Malyon (Nurse), E.E. Clive (Guide), Beryl Mercer (Saleslady), Winifred Harris (Mrs. Laurie).

A shocking, nerve-tingling thriller, NIGHT MUST FALL was a smash stage play by Williams that was improved on by this superb and frightening film. Most of its success is due to an amazing performance by Montgomery. Whitty is a fussy, domineering grande dame living in a cottage in Essex, England with her niece Russell and several cowed servants. Just after Russell and Whitty hear that a "very flashy type" of woman guest in a nearby inn has vanished, Montgomery appears.

He explains that he has been working as a page boy at the inn but is now looking for new work. He carries with him a heavy hatbox and places this carefully on a shelf in a closet after being hired as a handyman by Whitty, whom he has easily charmed. He waits hand and foot upon the wheelchair-bound Whitty, flattering her at every opportunity and exchanging barbs with Russell, who distrusts him. When asked about the woman missing from the inn, Montgomery admits that he knew her and replies to Whitty: "What's she like? She's...on the tall side. Thin ankles with one of them bracelets on one of 'em. Fair hair...thin eyebrows, with white marks where they was pulled out, to be in fashion, you know. Her mouth—a bit thin as well, with red stuff painted round it, to make it look more; you can rub it off, I suppose. Her neck—rather thick...She's—very lively." With these chilling words, Montgomery reveals his sly psychopathic personality, which Russell wisely discerns. When Montgomery finds the family safe, he puts in motion a plan to kill Whitty. By then Russell has learned of Montgomery's murderous backround but she, like the 72-year-old Whitty, is mesmerized by the killer and does nothing. Russell must suddenly leave her aunt and when she returns she finds Whitty's corpse, rightly assuming she has been murdered by Montgomery. She almost becomes a victim but manages to escape. Montgomery is then arrested by police but insists upon taking his hat box with him. Inside it, of course, is the severed head of the woman from the inn he has killed and dissected, lugging her remains about with him as one would a trophy. NIGHT MUST FALL is directed with great care by Thorpe who draws forth every bit of suspense and subtle horror intended by author Williams. (The playwright actually played the role of the killer on stage but Montgomery made of the role a much more subtle and thus deadlier characterization.) Producer Stromberg saw the original play in London and insisted that he make it into a film, but MGM boss Louis B. Mayer thought it an awful idea. "You want to make a picture in which a man carries a woman's head around in a hatbox?" Mayer queried his most successful producer. Stromberg—then earning $8,000-a-week, plus profits on his films—said yes, and Mayer reluctantly agreed to let him go ahead. But Mayer was even more upset when Stromberg cast Montgomery in the role of the killer, this top MGM star having been known only for frothy but big box office comedies. Of course, Montgomery went after the part right from the start, insisting he play the spine-tingling killer to prove that he was really an actor of the first rank, and he did. The actor added all sorts of mannerisms to his weird character and opted for a slight Irish accent to give him that boyish charm that bedazzled Whitty and Russell. The studio converted one of its back lots for the English countryside setting and Mayer kept tight hold of the budget, trying to starve the film out of existence. Mayer felt the film completely projected the wrong image of his studio and cringed in his chair at Grauman's Chinese Theater on the night of May 4, 1937 during its premiere. He had taken extraordinary measures to disassociate MGM and himself from NIGHT MUST FALL. Mayer had handbills distributed to all theatergoers that night and during the following weeks in which MGM more or less disclaimed the film and he personally supervised the making of a trailer that preceded the film in which the studio admitted making the film but asked audiences to think of it as nothing more than experimental, hardly a main-line MGM product. Then the rave reviews poured in and Mayer cancelled the handbills and cut the prelude to the film. Montgomery was praised as a startlingly gifted actor and later won an Oscar nomination (he would lose to Spencer Tracy in CAPTAINS COURAGEOUS, also produced by MGM). Montgomery and Russell had been teamed before in FORSAKING ALL OTHERS and TROUBLE FOR TWO, and they would later appear together in LIVE, LOVE AND LEARN and FAST AND LOOSE, the latter a detective film in the THIN MAN mold. Whitty's marvelous performance in NIGHT MUST FALL earned her a Supporting Actress Oscar nomination but she lost to Alice Brady in IN OLD CHICAGO. Rumors later had it that Mayer got back at the film he so disliked by instructing his people not to vote for Oscars of any kind for NIGHT MUST FALL. The film was remade by the studio in 1964, starring Albert Finney, Susan Hampshire, and Mona Washbourne, but the remake lacked the tautness and dramatic impact of the powerful original.

p, Hunt Stromberg; d, Richard Thorpe; w, John Van Druten (based on a play by Emlyn Williams); ph, Ray June; m, Edward Ward; ed, Robert J. Kern; art d, Cedric Gibbons.

Thriller   **(PR:O MPAA:NR)**

NIGHT MUST FALL***   (1964, Brit.) 101m MGM bw

Albert Finney (Danny), Mona Washbourne (Mrs. Bramson), Susan Hampshire (Olivia Bramson), Sheila Hancock (Dora), Michael Medwin (Derek), Joe Gladwin (Dodge), Martin Wyldeck (Inspector Willet), John Gill (Foster).

A fair remake of the classic 1937 MGM film, this time starring Finney as the crazed ax murderer who weasels his way into the home of Washbourne and her daughter Hampshire on the pretense of redecorating. While living with the women, Finney plays bizarre games with Washbourne and has an affair with Hampshire. In the privacy of his room, Finney performs elaborate rituals with the severed heads of his female victims, which he keeps in a hatbox. When the police close in, Finney goes berserk and kills Washbourne, but ends up huddled in the corner of the bathroom like a little boy when Hampshire scolds him. Soon the police arrive and take him away. Atmospheric, but Finney's performance is not as subtle or chilling as Robert Montgomery's in the earlier version. Director Reisz used imaginative transitions, jump-cutting, and often overlapped the visuals of one scene into the audio of the following one. Nonetheless, the result was a disappointment.

p, Albert Finney, Karel Reisz; d, Reisz; w, Clive Exton (based on the play by Emlyn Williams); ph, Freddie Francis; m, Ron Grainer; ed, Fergus McDonell, Philip Barnikel; md, Grainer; prod d, Timothy O'Brien; art d, Lionel Couch; cos, Dolly Tree.

Drama   **(PR:O MPAA:NR)**

NIGHT MY NUMBER CAME UP, THE***½   (1955, Brit.) 94m Michael Balcon-EAL/CD bw

Michael Redgrave (Air Marshal John Hardie), Sheila Sim (Mary Campbell), Alexander Knox (Owen Robertson), Denholm Elliott (Flight Lt. McKenzie), Ursula Jeans (Mrs. Robertson), Ralph Truman (Lord Wainwright), Michael Hordern (Comdr. Lindsay), Nigel Stock (Walker the Pilot), Bill Kerr, Alfie Bass (The Soldiers), George Rose (Walter Bennett), Victor Maddern (Engineer), David Orr (Co-Pilot), David Yates (Navigator), Doreen Aris (Miss Robertson), Charles Perry (Kent), Geoffrey Tyrrell (Bennett's Secretary), Hugh Moxey (Wing Commander), Richard Davies (Wireless Operator), Stratford Johns (Sergeant), Nicholas Stuart, John Fabian, Percy Herbert, Robert Bruce, Philip Vickers.

An odd drama in the DEAD OF NIGHT tradition, this is exciting and well shot by Norman (making his feature debut), with good performances by all. Redgrave is an air marshal in the Far East and he's had a nightmare about crashing in a Dakota plane in an isolated spot off the Japanese coast. He is due to fly to Tokyo with his aide, Elliott, in a Liberator plane, so the uneasiness of his dream (which has eight people on the airship) is put aside. Then, due to a series of circumstances beyond his control, Redgrave and Elliott are diverted from the Liberator and placed aboard a Dakota with the same people he's dreamed about, including Knox and Sim. Little by little, all the worst parts of the dream come to pass. The plane is trapped in a storm, gets tossed around the sky, the oxygen becomes thin, etc. The only part of the dream that does not come true is the ultimate crash. Instead, the plane makes a forced landing and the group is saved. A frightening movie for anyone who has ever boarded a flight and wondered if this was the one which would go down in flames. Don't see it before taking an air trip or you may never even drive to the airport again.

p, Tom Morahan; d, Leslie Norman; w, R.C. Sheriff (based on a magazine article by Air Marshal Sir Victor Goddard); ph, Lionel Banes; m, Malcolm Arnold; ed, Peter Tanner; art d, Jim Morahan.

Drama   **(PR:A-C MPAA:NR)**

NIGHT NURSE*   (1931) 72m WB bw

Barbara Stanwyck (Lora Hart), Ben Lyon (Mortie), Joan Blondell (Maloney), Charles Winninger (Dr. Arthur Bell), Charlotte Merriam (Mrs. Ritchey), Edward Nugent (Eagan, an Interne), Blanche Frederici (Mrs. Maxwell), Allan [Rocky] Lane (2nd Interne), Walter McGrail (Mack, a Drunk), Ralf Harolde (Dr. Milton Ranger), Clark Gable (Nick), Vera Lewis (Miss Dillon), Marcia Mae Jones (Nanny), Betty Jane Graham (Desney), Betty May (Nurse), Jed Prouty (Archie, Father-To-Be), Willie Fung (Patient), James Bradbury, Jr. (Wounded Prisoner).

A somewhat risque pre-production code story about a nurse (Stanwyck) who uncovers a plot to murder two children, fatherless heirs to a large fortune, Jones and Graham. The children's mother, Merriam, is an evil drunk who plans on starving them to death and then marrying her opportunistic chauffeur, Gable, with the trust fund. Stanwyck confides in her roommate, Blondell, who suggests that she go to the police with the information. Gable, however, threatens to kill her if she starts talking. In order to make his threat more substantive, he delivers a savage fist to her jaw (he would do the same thing some twenty years later in TO PLEASE A LADY). Instead of turning to the law, Stanwyck asks an amiable bootlegger (Lyon) for help. With gun in hand, Lyon confronts Gable, saving the children's lives and winning Stanwyck in the process. The finale has Lyon agreeing to give up his life of crime in exchange for Stanwyck's love. A neglected Wellman picture, NIGHT NURSE followed in the shadow of his PUBLIC ENEMY and was to have been the third Wellman-Blondell-James Cagney picture. Cagney, however, had found such success with PUBLIC ENEMY that he was cast in SMART MONEY instead. On Wellman's urging Gable was loaned to Warners, where he was fitted in a morbid black chauffeur's suit and given a completely villainous role. Luckily for Gable, Warners refused to sign him to a contract which probably would have relegated him to sinister roles. Instead he moved on to MGM. While most critics of the day admitted that NIGHT NURSE found an audience because of Stanwyck's and Blondell's numerous dressing and undressing scenes, Stanwyck disagreed. According to Jane Ellen Wayne's biography, Stanwyck has said, "Joan Blondell and I were in awe. He was just the kinda guy who made you look at him all the time...It was Gable who brought the crowds to see NIGHT NURSE because the public couldn't get enough of him." Director Wellman, a busy man, helmed four other features this same year, all of them action-packed, filled with sound and fury.

d, William A. Wellman; w, Oliver H.P. Garrett, Charles Kenyon (based on the novel by Dora Macy [Grace Perkins Oursler]); ph, Barney "Chick" McGill; ed, Edward McDermott; art d, Max Parker; cos, Earl Luick.

Drama/Crime   **(PR:A-C MPAA:NR)**

NIGHT OF A THOUSAND CATS   (1974, Mex.) 95m Ellman c
                                                      (LA NOCHE DE LOS MIL GATOS)

Anjanette Comer, Zulma Faiad, Hugo Stiglitz, Christa Linder.

Though unashamedly sick, this is a pretty funny horror comedy for those who can stomach it. Cardona, who directed the unbelievably dreadful SURVIVE! (which had been based on the true story of the survivors of an airplane crash who were forced to turn to cannibalism), once more looks at this taboo subject in a decidedly more macabre fashion. A millionaire, faced with a horde of hungry kitties, decides to use human resources to feed his felines. The heads of decapitated women are also kept by the lunatic for reasons of his own mad understanding.

p, Avant; d, Rene Cardona, Jr.; w, Mario Marzac (based on his story); ph, Alex Phillips.

Horror/Comedy   **(PR:O MPAA:R)**

NIGHT OF ADVENTURE, A**   (1944) 65m RKO bw

Tom Conway (Mark Latham), Audrey Long (Erica), Edward Brophy (Steve), Louis Borell (Tony Clark), Addison Richards (Branson), Jean Brooks (Julie

Arden), Nancy Gates (Connie), Russell Hopton (Benny Sarto), Claire Carleton (Ruby La Rue), Emory Parnell (Judge), Edmund Glover (Andrews).

A remake of 1934's HAT, COAT AND GLOVE (which starred Ricardo Cortez) sees Conway (taking a break from the FALCON series) as a dedicated lawyer who is shocked to find that his neglected wife has taken up with an artist accused of murdering his model. The noble Conway rises to the man's defense and clears him —and his own wife—of the charges while managing to keep the whole affair from becoming a scandal in the newspapers.

p, Herman Schlom; d, Gordon Douglas; w, Crane Wilbur (based on the play "Hat, Coat and Glove" by Wilhelm Speyer); ph, Frank Redman; m, Leigh Harline; ed, Les Millbrook; md, C. Bakaleinikoff; art d, Albert S. D'Agostino, Ralph Berger; cos, Renie.

Drama (PR:A MPAA:NR)

NIGHT OF ANUBIS (SEE: NIGHT OF THE LIVING DEAD, 1968)

NIGHT OF BLOODY HORROR zero (1969) 89m Taste of Blood-Cinema IV/Howco c

Gerald McRaney (Wesley Stuart), Gaye Yellen (Angelle Miliot), Herbert Nelson (Dr. Bennett Moss), Evelyn Hendricks (Agatha Stuart), Lisa Dameron (Susan Collins), Charlotte White (Kay Jensen), Nicholous R. Krieger (Lt. James Cole), Michael Anthony (Mario Spenelli), Bert Roberts (Mark Lewis), Gordon Ogden (Tucker Fredricks), Murray Solow (Bartender), Nigel Strangeways, Burt Love, Louis Grapes (Hoods), George Spelvin (Priest), Anthony Herrero (Man in Club), Mark Fleming, Philip Fleming (Altar Boys), Farley Dennis (Wesley as a Boy), Emile Weaver III (Jonathan), John Barber, Sheri Sherwood, The Bored.

Inept, overly gory independent horror film shot in 16mm "Violent Vision." Story involves McRaney, who is a former mental patient accused of the cleaver killings of all his girl friends and cutting his psychiatrist's hand off before hacking him up. Eventually it is revealed that McRaney's mom Hendricks has been doing all the bloodletting. The producers offered to give $1,000 cash to the family of anyone who died of fright while watching the movie. The patrons should have been paid the money just for surviving it.

p&d, Joy N. Houck, Jr.; w, Robert A. Weaver, Houck; ph, Weaver (Violent Vision); m, General Music Corp.; ed, Weaver; makeup, Philip St. Jon.

Horror (PR:O MPAA:R)

NIGHT OF DARK SHADOWS* (1971) 97m MGM c (AKA: CURSE OF DARK SHADOWS)

David Selby (Quentin/Charles Collins), Lara Parker (Angelique), Kate Jackson (Tracy Collins), Grayson Hall (Carlotta Drake), John Karlen (Alex Jenkins), Nancy Barrett (Claire Jenkins), James Storm (Gerard Styles), Diana Millay (Laura Collins), Christopher Pennock (Gabriel Collins), Thayer David (Rev. Strack), Monica Rich (Sarah Castle), Clarisse Blackburn (Mrs. Castle).

Even the rabid fans of the television soap opera "Dark Shadows" will have to admit there's not much to like here. The second "Dark Shadows" motion picture (the first was HOUSE OF DARK SHADOWS) collapses from the absence of Jonathan Frid and Joan Bennett. The story sees Selby, the last of the Collins clan, inherit the family mansion and move in with his new bride. In his sleep he is plagued by nightmares in which he is propelled 150 years into the past and witnesses the sordid activities of his ghoulish ancestors. Eventually the spirits of the house possess him and he turns into a crazed monster and tries to kill his own wife. This really dull, low-budget production was shot entirely at millionaire Jay Gould's mansion in Tarrytown, New York.

p, Dan Curtis; d, Curtis, Alex Stevens; w, Sam Hall (based on a story by Hall, Curtis from the TV series "Dark Shadows"); ph, Richard Shore (Metrocolor); m, Robert Cobert; ed, Charles Goldsmith; md, Cobert; art d, Trevor Williams; makeup, Reginald Tackley.

Horror (PR:C MPAA:GP)

NIGHT OF EVIL* (1962) 88m Galbreath/Astor-Sutton bw

Earl Wilson (Narrator), Lisa Gaye, (Dixie Ann Dikes), William Campbell, Lynn Bernay, Remo Pisani, George Dietsel, Joseph Garri, Don De Leo, Burtt Harris, Gary Gage, Sammy Mannis, Patricia Dahling, David Dunstone, Barbara Bricker, Marjorie Suter, Eric Anthony Pregent, Ira Gaskill, Jack Morey, Barbara Meyers, Lary Beauchamp, Walt Rearick, Virginia Carter, Les Podwell, Margaret Silverman, James Foland, George Fruechtenicht, James Voors, Paul Dawson, Manny Silverman, Lois Broad, John Renforth, Morey Copeland, Karlton Kadell, Bob Durham, Merrill C. Johnson, Sara Gage, John Himes, Jack Nichols.

Probably the only film shot entirely in Fort Wayne, Indiana (thank goodness!) and the producers thought it looked enough like Colorado (?!) to set the movie there. NIGHT OF EVIL chronicles the decline and fall of high-school girl Gaye, who is wrongly sent to a girls' home. After getting out of the home, Gaye meets a promoter who enters her in the Miss Colorado contest. She wins the competition, but soon after falls in love with and marries an ex-convict. Her chance at becoming Miss America is ruined when her hubby tries to kidnap a cop and is caught, bringing the secret marriage into the public eye. Ruined, she becomes a stripper and eventually buys a gun for an attempted suicide. This too fails and she holds up a drugstore, is caught and sent to prison. Good for unintentional-laughter addicts.

p, Richard Galbreath, Lou Perry; d, Galbreath; w, Louis Perino (based on a story by Perry); m, Arnold Holop.

Drama (PR:C MPAA:NR)

NIGHT OF JANUARY 16TH* (1941) 80m PAR bw (AKA: THE NIGHT OF JANUARY 16TH; NIGHT OF JAN. 16TH)

Robert Preston (Steve Van Ruyle), Ellen Drew (Kit Lane), Nils Asther (Bjorn Faulkner), Donald Douglas (Attorney Polk), Margaret Hayes (Nancy Wakefield),

Clarence Kolb (Tilton), Rod Cameron (District Attorney's Assistant), Alice White (Flashy Blonde), Roy Gordon (Wakefield), Cecil Kellaway (Drunk), Harry Hayden (Williamson), Edwin Stanley (Hemingway), Paul Stanton (District Attorney), Willard Robertson (Inspector Donegan), James Flavin (Patrolman Kelly), George Renavent (Man with Brief Case).

Dull, insipid mystery wherein any half-awake moviegoer will be hit over the head with the solution in the first five minutes. Drew stars as the innocent secretary of rich businessman Asther, who is believed to have been murdered. After a circumstantial case is trumped up against her, worried investor Preston enters and proves the girl innocent. Based on a stage play by philosopher-novelist Rand that recruited audience members to sit in the jury box in the final act. Not even that gimmick could save this film.

p, Sol C. Siegel, Joseph Sistrom; d, William Clemens; w, Delmer Daves, Robert Pirosh, Eve Greene (based on the play by Ayn Rand); ph, John Mescall; ed, Ellsworth Hoagland; art d, Hans Dreier, Haldane Douglas.

Mystery (PR:A MPAA:NR)

NIGHT OF JUNE 13*½** (1932) 70m PAR bw

Clive Brook (John Curry), Lila Lee (Trudie Morrow), Charlie Ruggles (Philo Strawn), Gene Raymond (Herbert Morrow), Frances Dee (Ginger Blake), Mary Boland (Mazie Strawn), Adrianne Allen (Elna Curry), Charley Grapewin (Grandpop Strawn), Helen Jerome Eddy (Martha Blake), Billy Butts (Junior Strawn), Edward LeSaint (Mr. Morrow), Helen Ware (Mrs. Morrow), Richard Carle (Otto), Arthur Hohl, Wallis Clark.

Fine drama detailing the lives of a small group of families in a New York suburb who suddenly find themselves involved in a murder trial. Allen, an extremely disturbed and neurotic woman, commits suicide and leaves a note blaming her husband's (Brook) dalliance with young neighbor Lee. Brook discovers the note and destroys it to protect Lee. This action leads the police to suspect murder and soon Brook is before the court. Any of a number of witnesses in the neighborhood could clear him of the charge, but a code of silence develops because all have their own, personal reasons for lying about their activities on the night of the murder. Eventually an old man, Grapewin, comes forward and testifies, simultaneously exposing the petty weaknesses of his neighbors.

d, Stephen Roberts; w, Agnes Brand Leahy, Brian Marlow, William Slavens McNutt (based on the story "Suburb" by Vera Caspary); ph, Harry Fischbeck.

Drama (PR:A MPAA:NR)

NIGHT OF LUST*½ (1965, Fr.) 58m Les Films Univers-Aurora/Olympic International bw (LE CONCERTO DE LA PEUR; NOTTE EROTIQUE; AKA: NIGHT OF LOVE)

Hans Verner (Eric Voltay), Jean-Pierre Kalfon (Sacha Markriff), Marcel Champel (Fred Voltay), Yvonne Monlaur (Nora), Michel Lemoine, Regine Rumen, Willy Braque, Andre Rouyer, Jean Claude, Christiane Arnaud.

French crime potboiler starring Verner and Kalfon as rival gang leaders who clash over control of the narcotics trade. The U.S. distributors added footage of a lesbian nightclub act to liven things up a bit.

p&d, Jose Benazeraf; w, Guy Fanelli, Benazeraf, R. L. Frost; ph, Edmond Richard; m, Chet Baker; ed, George Marschalk.

Crime (PR:C MPAA:NR)

NIGHT OF MAGIC, A* (1944, Brit.) 56m Berkeley/Premier bw

Robert Griffith (Reggie), Billy "Uke" Scott (His Pal), Marian Olive (Princess Raviola), Vera Bradley, Dot Delavine, Gordon Ray, The Broadway Boys, The Gordon Ray Girls.

Griffith has a dream about receiving an Egyptian mummy from his uncle. The 3000-year-old bundle awakes, proving to be Olive, a party-mad Egyptian princess. After doing up old London town, Olive takes her new guy back to her time so he can see that the ancient Egyptians also knew how to throw a party. Though this is an imaginative idea that brims with all sorts of comic possibilities, the treatment here is simplistic and below par. Rather than contrast historical periods and personalities, the filmmakers have simply tossed together a musical revue with little wit or professionalism to speak of. Still, this was the sort of escapist film that provided nights of magic for Britons anxious to forget for a while the war and buzz bombs.

p, Burt Hyams; d, Herbert Wynne; w, Eversley Bracken; ph, W. Richards.

Comedy Revue (PR:A MPAA:NR)

NIGHT OF MYSTERY* (1937) 66m PAR bw

Grant Richards (Philo Vance), Roscoe Karns (Sgt. Heath), Helen Burgess (Ada Greene), Ruth Coleman (Sibella Greene), Elizabeth Patterson (Mrs. Tobias Greene), Harvey Stephens (Dr. Von Blon), June Martel (Barton), Terry Ray [Ellen Drew] (Secretary), Purnell Pratt (John F. X. Markham), Colin Tapley (Chester Greene), James H. Bush (Rex Greene), Ivan F. Simpson (Sproot), Greta Meyer (Mrs. Mannheim), Leonard Carey (Lister), Nora Cecil (Hemming), George Anderson (Detective Snitkin), Barlowe Borland (Medical Examiner), Myra Marsh (Police Nurse).

Poor remake of a previous Philo Vance mystery, THE GREENE MURDER CASE (which featured William Powell). This one stars unknown Grant Richards as Vance, investigating the murder of a New York millionaire. When the suspects begin to die off, the dashing amateur detective begins digging and finds out that Burgess is the killer. (see PHILO VANCE Series, Index).

d, E.A. Dupont; w, Frank Partos, Gladys Unger (based on the novel Greene Murder Case by S. S. Van Dine); ph, Harry Fischbeck; ed, James Smith; md, Boris Morros.

Mystery (PR:A MPAA:NR)

NIGHT OF NIGHTS, THE½ (1939) 85m PAR bw

Pat O'Brien (Dan O'Farrell), Olympe Bradna (Marie-Alyce O'Farrell/Alyce Martelle), Roland Young (Barry Keith-Trimble), Reginald Gardiner (J. Neville Prime), George E. Stone (Sammy Kayne), Murray Alper (Muggins, Chauffeur), Frank Sully (Taxi Driver), Russ Powell (Pop the Doorman), Charles Miller (Wilton), Pat O'Malley, D'Arcy Corrigan (Actors), Frank Shannon (Frank the Bartender), Ronnie Rondell (Attendant), Oscar O'Shea (Mr. Conway), Aileen Pringle (Perfume/Dress Saleslady), Laura Treadwell (Mrs. Abigail Keith-Trimble), Doodles Weaver (Flower Delivery Man), Wyndham Standing (Naval Commander), Frank Melton (Newcomb the Author), Theodore Von Eltz (John, Man with Silk Hat), Mary Gordon (Pencil Woman), Richard Denning (Call Boy), Larry Steers (Well-Wisher), Ethan Laidlaw (Roustabout in Play), A.L. Sherwood.

Fair backstage drama starring O'Brien as a playwright-actor-producer who abandoned a brilliant career and went into seclusion after his wife left him. Years later, his daughter, Bradna, finds him and encourages him to revive his talents. Aided by his close friends Young and Gardiner, O'Brien slowly and carefully sets about bringing one of his old hit plays back to the boards. His revival is met with critical acclaim and popular success.

p, George M. Arthur; d, Lewis Milestone; w, Donald Ogden Stewart; ph, Leo Tovar; ed, Doane Harrison.

Drama (PR:A MPAA:NR)

NIGHT OF PASSION (SEE: DURING ONE NIGHT, 1962, Brit.)

NIGHT OF SAN LORENZO, THE (SEE: NIGHT OF THE SHOOTING STARS, 1981, Ital.)

NIGHT OF TERROR* (1933) 61m COL bw (AKA: HE LIVED TO KILL)

Bela Lugosi (Degar), Sally Blane (Betty Jane Young), Wallace Ford, George Meeker, Tully Marshall, Edwin Maxwell, Bryant Washburn, Gertrude Michael, Mary Frey, Matt McHugh, Pat Harmon, Oscar Smith.

Inane "Old Dark House"-type murder mystery featuring the usual case of suspects being bumped off by an unknown killer. This one has a reporter, a homicidal maniac (not the killer—too obvious), a couple of mysterious Hindu servants, a swami played by Lugosi (who was appearing in THE DEVIL'S IN LOVE during the day and this one at night), and a pretty heroine. Story involves a formula that can put people in suspended animation, and the killer rises from the grave at the end and warns the audience not to reveal his identity. Probably the only time a character on screen actively threatened the viewer.

d, Benjamin Stoloff; w, Beatrice Van, William Jacobs, Lester Neilson (based on a story by Willard Mack); ph, Joseph Valentine; ed, Arthur Hilton.

Mystery (PR:A MPAA:NR)

NIGHT OF TERRORS (SEE: MURDER CLINIC, THE, 1967, Ital./Fr.)

NIGHT OF THE ASKARI** (1978, Ger./South African) 97m Lord and Eichberg/Topar c (AKA: WHISPERING DEATH)

Christopher Lee (Bill), James Faulkner (Terrick), Trevor Howard (Johannes), Horst Frank (Whispering Death), Sybil Danning (Sally), Sascha Helen (Peter), Sam Williams (Katchemu), Erik Schumann (Capt. Turnbull).

This tale of racial strife in an unnamed southern African country (could it be anywhere but South Africa?) merely reinforces the prejudices that are behind the region's violent upheaval. Faulkner, a white man, seeks vengeance for the rape and murder of his fiancee by a group of black terrorists led by Frank, an albino. Although the tension of the situation is effectively portrayed, little attempt is made to create characters that are well-rounded.

d, Juergen Goslar; w, Goslar, Scot Finch (based on the novel by Daniel Carney); ph, Wolfgang Treu; m, Erich Ferstl; ed, Richard Meyer.

Drama (PR:C MPAA:R)

NIGHT OF THE BEAST (SEE: HOUSE OF THE BLACK DEATH, 1965)

NIGHT OF THE BIG HEAT (SEE: ISLAND OF THE BURNING DOOMED, 1967, Brit.)

NIGHT OF THE BLOOD BEAST½ (1958) 65m AIP bw

Michael Emmet (Maj. John Corcoran), Angela Greene (Dr. Julie Benson), John Baer (Steve Dunlap), Ed Nelson (Dave Randall), Tyler McVey (Dr. Alex Wyman), Georgianna Carter (Donna Bixby), Rose Sturlin (The Creature).

Bizarre sci-fi film produced by Roger Corman's brother Gene which tells the tale of astronaut Emmet, who returns from space dead. An ugly looking alien revives his corpse and uses it as a breeding ground for more aliens. The alien does not seek to destroy the Earth, only to use part of it so that his people may survive his dying world. Of course, the earthlings don't see it that way and they burn him to death.

p, Gene Corman; d, Bernard L. Kowalski; w, Martin Varno (based on a story by Varno, Corman); ph, John Nicholaus; m, Alexander Laszlo; ed, Jodie Copelan, Dick Currier; art d, Dan Haller.

Science Fiction (PR:A MPAA:NR)

NIGHT OF THE BLOODY APES zero (1968, Mex.) 82m Jerand/Unistar c (LA HORRIPLANTE BESTIA HUMANA, HORROR Y SEXO; AKA: GOMAR-THE HUMAN GORILLA)

Jose Elias Moreno, Carlos Lopez Moctezuma, Armando Silvestre, Norma Lazareno, Agustin Martinez Solares, Gina Moret, Noelia Noel, Gerard Zepeda.

Gross and unbelievably inept Mexican horror film about a scientist who puts the heart of a gorilla into the chest of his dead son. Holding true to the unwritten horror film laws of anatomy and biology, the boy awakens and turns into a pug-ugly,

marauding killer who rapes and rips apart every living being in sight. Lazareno, the heroine, also happens to be a feline costumed wrestler and her boy friend is a Mexican law enforcement officer. The film, dubbed in English, becomes especially hard to watch with the addition of some actual open-heart surgery footage.

p, G. Calderon Stell, Alfredo Salazar; d, Rene Cardona; w, Cardona, Rene Cardona, Jr.; ph, Raul Martinez Solares; m, Antonio Conde; ed, Jorge [George] Bustos; spec eff, Javier Torres Torija.

Horror **Cas.** (PR:O MPAA:NR)

NIGHT OF THE CLAW (SEE: ISLAND CLAWS, 1980)

NIGHT OF THE COBRA WOMAN* (1974, U.S./Phil.) 85m New World c

Joy Bang (Joanna), Marlene Clark (Lena), Roger Garrett (Duff), Slash Marks (Sgt. Merkle), Vic Diaz (Lope).

Less-than-horrifying horror film shot in the Philippines by New York experimental filmmaker Andrew Meyer. The story involves Clark, a jungle priestess who needs the venom of cobras to remain young, and the services of young men to prevent her turning into a cobra permanently. Bang, a female biology student, is somewhat dismayed when her boy friend Garrett is seduced by Clark and becomes one of her minions. Pretty lame; the most exciting things about this one are the chosen screen names of some of the players. The film was said to have been lensed in "Slitherama" by its publicists.

p, Kerry Magness, Harvey Marks; d, Andrew Meyer; w, Meyer, Magness.

Horror **Cas.** (PR:O MPAA:R)

NIGHT OF THE DARK FULL MOON (SEE: SILENT NIGHT, BLOODY NIGHT, 1972)

NIGHT OF THE DEMON (SEE: CURSE OF THE DEMON, 1958, Brit.)

NIGHT OF THE DEMON (SEE: TOUCH OF SATAN, THE, 1971)

NIGHT OF THE EAGLE (SEE: BURN, WITCH, BURN!, 1962, Brit.)

NIGHT OF THE FLESH EATERS (SEE: NIGHT OF THE LIVING DEAD, 1968)

NIGHT OF THE FOLLOWING DAY, THE* (1969, Brit.) 93m Gina/UA c

Marlon Brando (Bud the Chauffeur), Richard Boone (Leer), Rita Moreno (Vi), Pamela Franklin (Girl), Jess Hahn (Wally), Gerard Buhr (Cop/Fisherman), Jacques Marin (Bartender), Hughes Wanner (Father), Alfredo Lettieri (Pilot).

Brando would be well-advised never to make another film for Universal Studios, as they have all been among his most minor efforts. For the San Fernando Valley lot, he made THE UGLY AMERICAN, THE COUNTESS FROM HONG KONG, THE APPALOOSA, BEDTIME STORY, and now this pot of tripe. It's a fraud from start to finish, another one of co-executive producer Elliott Kastner's "deals" that can never quite be called a motion picture. Rich Franklin arrives in Paris where she is kidnaped by Brando and Boone. (Brando's name in the picture is "Bud," which was, oddly enough, his nickname for those who had known him since childhood.) They take her to a country road where her limousine is switched for a car being driven by her stewardess, Moreno (in a silly blonde wig). They take her to an isolated house on a French beach and contact Franklin's father, Wanner, by phone, in an ingenious fashion Boone has invented which precludes the call being traced by the phone company. Moreno is a heroin addict and her brother, Hahn, is also part of the plot. When Brando sees Moreno's addiction and learns that Boone would like to have his way with Franklin, he is all for calling off the kidnaping. Buhr, a fisherman who turns out to be a cop, stops by the house and Moreno says she's taken this tranquil place as a resting spot for her husband. Franklin tries to get away but is caught. Brando tries to help Franklin and Moreno jealously resents that. Boone goes to Paris to talk to Wanner about the ransom. Wanner flies to the small local airport and gets phone instructions from Moreno to meet her and Hahn at the local bistro. At the cafe, Marin (the bartender-owner) smells something is up, goes for his gun, and wounds Hahn. Then Buhr arrives, and after more gunplay Buhr is shot. The money is taken and they go back to the cottage, where Boone, who has evidently just finished raping Franklin, is putting on his gloves and thanking her for her body. Brando, Moreno, and Hahn are machine-gunned by Boone, but Brando manages to escape the hail of bullets. Brando follows Boone on the sand and eventually slays him, then returns to find Franklin stripped and bleeding in the cottage. He cuts her loose and then (are you ready for this?) she wakes up in the airplane that is arriving at Orly. Y'see, it's all been a dream (what a creative twist that is!) that may, or may not, have been caused by a radio play she's been listening to on a tiny transistor. Good photography and interesting locations and a characterization from Brando that is not categorizable. He looked wonderful in the movie, lithe, blond, and strong. It was just before he probably said "The hell with it" and began eating his way into the Orson Welles battleship class. The author of the novel that this film is based upon also wrote the book that was the basis for Kubrick's little classic, THE KILLING. Would that Kubrick had done this one as well.

p&d, Hubert Cornfield; w, Cornfield, Robert Phippeny (based on the novel The Snatchers by Lionel White); ph, Willi Kurout, Jean Klissak (Technicolor); m, Stanley Myers; ed, Gordon Pilkington, Anne Vogler; art d, Jean Boulet; cos, Pierre Marcade; m/l, "One Early Morning," Myers, John Hendricks (sung by Annie Ross); makeup, Jackie Reynal.

Crime/Drama (PR:O MPAA:R)

NIGHT OF THE FULL MOON, THE* (1954, Brit.) 67m Hedgerley/UA bw

Dermot Walsh (Robby), Kathleen Byron (Jane), Philip Saville (Dale Merritt),

Anthony Ireland (Watercan Man), Tim Turner (George), Everley Gregg (Mrs. Jeans), Elizabeth Wallace (Helen), George Merritt (Charlie).

After crashing into an English countryside village, American FBI man Saville finds himself being chased by enemy agents for some secret information he had obtained. All avenues of escape fail, but the accidental maneuverings of a local policeman end up saving Saville. Utterly ridiculous, and poorly done to boot.

p&d, Donald Taylor; w, Taylor, Carl Koch; ph, Gerald Gibbs.

Spy/Thriller   **(PR:C MPAA:NR)**

NIGHT OF THE GARTER*½   (1933, Brit.) 86m British and Dominions/ UA bw

Sydney Howard (Bodger), Winifred Shotter (Gwen Darling), Elsie Randolph (Jenny Warwick), Connie Ediss (Fish), Austin Melford (Bunny Phipps), Harold French (Teddy Darling), Jack Melford (Kenneth Warwick), Marjorie Brooks (Barbara Phipps), Arthur Chesney (Vicar).

Dim-witted British comedy about a newlywed husband trying to retrieve his bride's garter.

p, Herbert Wilcox; d, Jack Raymond; w, Austin Melford, Marjorie Gaffney (based on the play "Getting Gertie's Garter" by Avery Hopwood, Wilson Collison); ph, F.A. Young.

Comedy   **(PR:A MPAA:NR)**

NIGHT OF THE GENERALS, THE*   (1967, Brit./ Fr.) 148m Horizon-Filmsonor/COL c (LA NUIT DE GENERAUX)

Peter O'Toole (Gen. Tanz), Omar Sharif (Maj. Grau), Tom Courtenay (Cpl. Hartmann), Donald Pleasence (Gen. Kahlenberge), Joanna Pettet (Ulrike von Seidlitz-Gabler), Philippe Noiret (Inspector Morand), Charles Gray (Gen. von Seidlitz-Gabler), Coral Browne (Eleanore von Seidlitz-Gabler), John Gregson (Col. Sandauer), Nigel Stock (Otto), Christopher Plummer (Field Marshal Rommel), Juliette Greco (Juliette), Yves Brainville (Liesowski), Sacha Pitoeff (Doctor), Charles Millot (Wionczek), Raymond Gerome (Colonel in War Room), Veronique Vendell (Monique), Pierre Mondy (Kopatski), Eleonore Hirt (Melanie), Nicole Courcel (Raymonde), Jenny Orleans (Otto's Wife), Gerard Buhr (Von Stauffenberg), Michael Goodliffe (Hauser), Gordon Jackson (Capt. Engel), Patrick Allen (Col. Mannheim), Harry Andrews (Gov. Stupnagel), Mac Ronay (Tanz's Driver).

In Warsaw in 1942, a prostitute who doubles as an agent for the Germans is sadistically murdered by one of her clients. Sharif, from the German intelligence service that employed the unfortunate girl, sets out to track down the killer and soon narrows the field of suspects down to three generals, O'Toole, Pleasence, and Gray. Eventually, Sharif's nearly obsessive mission to prove one of the three guilty annoys his superiors and he is transferred to Paris. Two years later, all the suspected generals are present in Paris when another prostitute is murdered in the same fashion as the first. By now it is plain that O'Toole is the wanted psychopath, especially after he visits a museum and upon looking at a Vincent Van Gogh self-portrait nearly faints with the shock of recognition of his own madness in the tortured brushstrokes. Sharif works with Noiret, a Paris detective and underground member who tells the German about a plot to kill Hitler, but Sharif is uninterested, pursuing his general. O'Toole plants evidence to indicate that his orderly, Courtenay, is the killer, but Sharif doesn't believe it. He confronts O'Toole, but just as he's about to arrest him word comes over the radio of the failure of the assassination plot and the attempts of certain officers to seize power. The radio goes on to warn against the traitors and O'Toole uses this excuse to murder Sharif and brand him an executed traitor. From there the story moves up 20 years. Another prostitute has been murdered almost immediately after O'Toole's release from prison for war crimes. Noiret, now with Interpol, tracks down Courtenay, living under an assumed name, and, after getting his statement that O'Toole indeed was the murderer in 1944, confronts O'Toole with him. The former general is at a banquet given in his honor by his old unit and when he realizes that the game is up he excuses himself to go into the next room and blow his brains out. The film is not entirely successful in its attempt to parallel illegal private killings with the legally sanctioned mass murder of war, chiefly because of an overlong and frequently confusing multiple flashback structure and constant cutting between one plot line and another. Also, O'Toole gives a wooden performance at best, but despite these drawbacks the film has a few terrific moments, particularly the destruction of a vast chunk of Warsaw on O'Toole's orders as an act of reprisal, and a scene when Sharif confronts O'Toole only to have the heretofore irrelevant subplot of the Hitler assassination scheme suddenly fall into place in the main story, giving O'Toole an excuse to murder his accuser. Apart from O'Toole, most of the performers are very good, with Pleasence, Noiret, and Sharif standouts.

p, Sam Spiegel; d, Anatole Litvak; w, Joseph Kessel, Paul Dehn (based on the books Die Nacht der Generale by Hans Helmut Kirst and The Wary Transgressor by James Hadley Chase); ph, Henri Decae (Panavision, Technicolor); m, Maurice Jarre; ed, Alan Osbiston; md, Jarre; prod d, Alexander Trauner; art d, Auguste Capelier; set d, Maurice Barnathan; cos, Rosine Delamare, J. Claude Philippe; makeup, Jean Zay.

Crime   **Cas.**   **(PR:O MPAA:NR)**

NIGHT OF THE GHOULS zero   (1959) 60m Atomic/ Crown International TV bw (AKA: REVENGE OF THE DEAD)

Criswell (Himself), Tor Johnson (Lobo), Maila "Vampira" Nurmi (Black Ghost), Keene Duncan (Dr. Acula), Valda Hansen (Fake Ghost), Lon Chaney, Jr..

Another low-budget masterwork of unintentional hilarity from Ed Wood, Jr., the man who gave us the greatest bad film of all time, PLAN 9 FROM OUTER SPACE. Unfortunately NIGHT OF THE GHOULS doesn't quite live up to its "classic" predecessor. Noted "psychic" Criswell returns to the screen once again as the narrator and star of the film (he, Johnson, Murmi, and Bela Lugosi were Wood's

constant troupe of players who appeared in nearly every one of his little masterpieces), who comes out of a coffin to relate another horrifying tale. The story concerns phony spiritualist Duncan, his lovely assistant Hansen, and big brute Johnson as they perform bogus seances to scare the money out of dim-witted customers looking to contact deceased loved ones. These ignorant crooks have been fooling with the supernatural, however, and one night they find that they have really brought the dead to life. The disturbed corpses exact revenge by burying the shady spiritualist and his crew alive. This was one of Wood's last efforts (thankfully) and it was never released theatrically, though local TV stations had no compunctions about airing it as a late-night feature, much to the delight of Wood, who used to call his friends and tell them to stay up and watch it.

p,d&w, Edward Wood, Jr.

Horror   **Cas.**   **(PR:O MPAA:NR)**

NIGHT OF THE GRIZZLY, THE*½   (1966) 102m PAR c

Clint Walker (Jim Cole), Martha Hyer (Angela Cole), Keenan Wynn (Jed Curry), Nancy Kulp (Wilhelmina Peterson), Kevin Brodie (Charlie Cole), Ellen Corby (Hazel Squires), Jack Elam (Hank), Ron Ely (Tad Curry), Med Flory (Duke Squires), Leo Gordon (Cass Dowdy), Don Haggerty (Sam Potts), Sammy Jackson (Cal Curry), Victoria Paige Meyerink (Gypsy Cole), Candy Moore (Meg), Regis Toomey (Cotton Benson).

Walker plays a retired lawman who travels to Hope, Wyoming in 1880 with his wife and family to begin a new life in the wilderness at the ranch he inherited from his grandfather. Trouble pops up in the form of a marauding grizzly bear that invades the ranch and terrorizes the family, killing Walker's prize bull and several of local citizen Wynn's sheep. To add to his troubles, Walker is stalked by Gordon, a man whom he had sent to prison years ago, who is now out and seeking revenge. Eventually Gordon is killed by the bear and the bear is killed by Walker. Photography director Griggs became ill after filming most of the lovely location shots at Holcomb Valley, California, near Lake Arrowhead; filming was completed by Lipstein. Songs include "Angela" (Jay Livingston, Ray Evans) and "Pine Tree Tall" (Clint Walker, Charlie Aldrich).

p, Burt Dunne; d, Joseph Pevney; w, Warren Douglas; ph, Harold Lipstein, Loyal Griggs (Techniscope, Technicolor); m, Leith Stevens; ed, Philip W. Anderson, art d, Hal Pereira, William Campbell; set d, Robert R. Benton, Anthony Mondell.

Western   **Cas.**   **(PR:A MPAA:NR)**

NIGHT OF THE HUNTER, THE***   (1955) 93m UA bw

Robert Mitchum (Preacher Harry Powell), Shelley Winters (Willa Harper), Lillian Gish (Rachel), Evelyn Varden (Icey Spoon), Peter Graves (Ben Harper), Billy Chapin (John), Sally Jane Bruce (Pearl), James Gleason (Birdie), Don Beddoe (Walt Spoon), Gloria Castillo (Ruby), Mary Ellen Clemons (Clary), Cheryl Callaway (Mary), Corey Allen (Young Man in Town), Paul Bryar (Hangman Bart).

In the only film ever directed by actor Laughton, Mitchum gives the performance of his life as a psychopathic killer in search of stolen loot. During the Depression-gripped early 1930s, Graves robs a West Virginia bank, killing two people, and rushes home with $10,000, hiding it in his little daughter's doll and having his little boy, Chapin, and girl, Bruce, swear they will never reveal the hiding place. Hot on his trail, police arrive and drag Graves off. Mitchum is then shown sitting in a burlesque house and, while the other male patrons ogle a well-endowed stripper in action on stage, he stares with eyes full of hate at the undulating, hip-swaying dancer. His hand slips into his coat pocket and he impulsively opens his switchblade knife, leaving the viewer with no doubt as to what he would like to do to the sexy performer. A hand descends upon his shoulder, the long arm of the law. Mitchum is taken into custody for stealing a car and sent to prison. Graves awaits execution in prison with stoical silence but his cellmate, the strange and calculating Mitchum, hangs on Graves' every word, trying to overhear what the bank robber is muttering even in his sleep, trying to coax the apparently unconscious Graves into revealing where he has hidden his loot. But Graves is only shamming sleep and, as Mitchum leans over the top bunk in the cell to learn more, he receives a hard smash to his face. After Graves is hanged, Mitchum, a self-appointed back country preacher who uses the scriptures for his own ends, is released from prison and heads for Graves' home. Mitchum proceeds to the community where Graves' family lives and ingratiates himself to the busybody neighbors, Varden and Beddoe, who run the local sweetshop. Mitchum impresses the sanctimonious couple with his powers as an evangelist, explaining why he has the words "love" and "hate" written on the fingers of his right and left hands: to demonstrate the struggle between good and evil. Mitchum then goes into a wrestling match where his right and left hands struggle for supremacy, one where "love" wins. Graves' widow Winters is quickly wooed and mesmerized by the psychopathic Mitchum, and, with Varden and Beddoe goading her, she quickly marries the psalm-quoting preacher. On their wedding night Winters lies down on a bed while Mitchum stands grimacing in the shadows. She calls to him and he turns to her, asking if she has "procreation" in mind. When she admits she wants no more children than the two she already has, Mitchum lectures her on sinful lust. She prays with him, then lies back and Mitchum raises his knife. Praying like a zealot, eyes wide open at the knife above her, Winters meets her death. Next Mitchum goes to work on the children, Chapin and Bruce, pretending to be their protector while spreading the story that Winters has run off with a salesman and gaining also the sloppy sympathies of Varden and Beddoe. The boy, Chapin, distrusts Mitchum from the start but little Bruce succumbs to his pretended affection for her. When she refuses to tell him where her father, Graves, had hidden the $10,000 in stolen money, Mitchum explodes. Frightened, the children hide from him, running to the cellar. Mitchum frantically searches the house for them and then sweetly calls to them in the cellar. They do not answer. Slowly, Mitchum descends, calling out, making promises, stumbling about, and then shouting threats. The children dash past him and he lunges forward, but Chapin drops a shelf laden with heavy jars on his head and knocks Mitchum flat. The children escape from the house and run to a barge where

Gleason, a kind old man who has shown the children affection, is rolling about in a drunken stupor. While fishing in the river, he has seen Winters strapped into her open car, tied to a seat beneath the waters, her long hair flowing with the underwater current, terror-shocked after seeing her throat slashed "like another mouth." Chapin cannot revive Gleason and he grabs his little sister and makes a race for the river, finding a small boat. He puts his sister into it—she is still carrying the doll with the money hidden inside it—and shoves off, getting in just as Mitchum bursts through the underbrush, sees them, and wades out after the fast-receding boat. They are beyond his grasp and Mitchum lets loose a blood-curdling, animal-like scream of frustration. The children float down the river, exhausted. They fall asleep while the creatures of the night look upon them, floating aimlessly under the stars. Chapin awakens and manages to bring the boat ashore. He and his sister take refuge in a barn and fall asleep. Then Chapin hears in the distance Mitchum's voice singing a familiar refrain: "Leaning, leaning! Safe and secure from all alarms. Leaning, leaning. Leaning on the everlasting arms!" Chapin looks from the barn window to see, on a ridge, Mitchum approaching on horseback. Director Laughton was inventive in this scene, as he was in so many others, confined to a small set but masking it in night shadows so that it appeared to be a rural exterior, with only Mitchum's silhouette and that of the horse he was riding shown on a ridge in the distance; in reality, the rider is a midget and the horse is a pony, Laughton using a scaled-down version of everything. "Doesn't he ever sleep?" Chapin says aloud, and then wakes Bruce and races back to the boat and the safety of the river. They continue to float downriver, sleeping, the boat drifting ashore. They are awakened by the stern voice of Gish the next morning, who orders Chapin and Bruce to get out of the boat and follow her to her home. Gish is a warm-hearted spinster who is addicted to taking in stray children. Although Bruce takes an immediate liking to her, Chapin is as distrustful of Gish as he was of Mitchum. However, at Christmas, he receives a gift from Gish—as do all the other children—and he seeks to return the affection by wrapping an apple in a doily and giving this to Gish, who tells him that it's the finest gift of all. Then the oldest girl of the clan, Castillo, while shopping in town, reveals to a stranger, Mitchum, that the children he is searching for are at Gish's rural home. He appears the next day to tell Gish that he is a preacher. He goes into his "love" and "hate" routine but this doesn't impress the savvy old lady. Next he demands that Gish turn over the two children to him. Gish turns to Chapin, who looks her in the eye and says: "He ain't my Pa." "No," she says, "nor a preacher, either!" Gish swiftly grabs a shotgun and aims it at Mitchum, ordering him from her property. He lets loose a stream of curses, calling Gish "the spawn of the devil,"and retreats. That night, Gish lines up all her children in her kitchen and marches back and forth in front of them with her shotgun like a resolute sentinel. She hears noises outside through the screened-in porch and then Mitchum's voice booms out of the darkness: "I want them kids!" Gish spits defiance at him and he begins to sing "Leaning, leaning..." with Gish filling in the words Mitchum—in his perverted view of God and religion—invariably leaves out: "Leaning on the Almighty." Moments later there is a crash and then Gish's gun goes off and Mitchum shrieks like a madman. Gish goes to the phone and calls the police, telling an officer over the phone: "I've got something trapped in my barn." At dawn police arrive and drag the wounded Mitchum forth. The trauma of seeing his surrogate father, no matter how evil the man is, being treated the same way as his natural father is too much for Chapin who runs forth, grabbing the doll from from his sister's hand, smashing the doll over Mitchum's head, shouting for him to take the money which spills forth. The boy is thus relieved of the terrible secret his father had sworn him to keep. Mitchum is hauled away and Gish is left to heal Chapin's wounds. Later, while shopping in town with her children, Gish leads them clear of a violent, shouting mob, led by Varden and Beddoe—who are now heading a lynch mob toward the jail where Mitchum is being kept—Varden, ever the hypocrite, shouting for the blood of the man she once admired. Another shot shows Mitchum being led out the side door of the jail to a car which will take him to prison and certain execution. THE NIGHT OF THE HUNTER was not a box-office hit but it certainly is a *film noir* classic with horror captured in almost every frame. Laughton's direction is superb and great performances were given by Mitchum, Gish, and even the normally overacting Winters and fine support came from Varden, Beddoe, and Gleason. Chapin and Bruce are exceptional as the harassed children and the overall film, though disturbing, is utterly faithful to the frightening Grubb novel. Laughton employed many a classical directorial device in this film, drawing heavily from the German directors Lang and von Sternberg, utilizing shadows and darkness for mood, apprehension, and terror, surrounding Mitchum with the kind of blackness that fills his sinister heart. Moreover, Laughton showed his obvious admiration for the great silent film director, D.W. Griffith, employing such techniques as irising up and down, particularly in scenes involving the feisty, wonderful Gish, Griffith's finest protege. Writer Agee was faithful to the book and produced an arresting screenplay (he died shortly after the film was completed). One report has it that Agee, who had been paid $30,000 for the script, was not the final author. Elsa Lanchester, Laughton's wife, claimed in her autobiography that Agee "turned in a script as large as a telephone book," and that Laughton had to entirely rewrite it. If true, the effort, including the lyrical, often beautiful composition Laughton created for the film, with cameraman Cortez's considerable help, was for naught since THE NIGHT OF THE HUNTER failed at the box office and did not budge the stick-in-the-mud critics at the time. He was never again given the chance to direct. Laughton called the film "a nightmarish sort of Mother Goose tale," but he felt that Mitchum was the only one who could really project the homicidal religious crackpot. The director-actor called Mitchum and explained the part by telling him that "you play a diabolical crud." Replied Mitchum: "Present!" Then Laughton added: "I'm not supposed to know about such things. I'm a professional non-crud." "I will take care of that department," Mitchum assured Laughton, and not only did the actor create one of the most horrific characters ever to appear on film but he assumed many of Laughton's responsibilites—or, at least that is what Mitchum later claimed, especially when it came to Chapin and Bruce. "Charles loathed those children. He made *me* direct them." The sadistic, vicious-minded character the actor so chillingly essayed later haunted Mitchum and, as some reports had it, he was disinclined to discuss the part years afterward. Cinematographer Cortez was the brother of Ricardo Cortez, one-time Latin lover of the silent screen; Stanley Cortez was the cameraman who filmed THE MAGNIFICENT AMBERSONS for Orson Welles and much of the gloom, murk, and incredible contrast of that film is evidenced in THE NIGHT OF THE HUNTER.

p, Paul Gregory; d, Charles Laughton; w, James Agee (based on the novel by Davis Grubb); ph, Stanley Cortez; m, Walter Schumann; ed, Robert Golden; md, Schumann; art d, Hilyard Brown; set d, Al Spencer; cos, Jerry Bos; spec eff, Jack Rabin, Louis De Witt; makeup, Don Cash.

Horror/Crime **(PR:O MPAA:NR)**

NIGHT OF THE IGUANA, THE½** (1964) 125m Seven Arts/MGM bw

Richard Burton *(Rev. T. Lawrence Shannon)*, Ava Gardner *(Maxine Faulk)*, Deborah Kerr *(Hannah Jelkes)*, Sue Lyon *(Charlotte Goodall)*, James Ward *(Hank Prosner)*, Grayson Hall *(Judith Fellowes)*, Cyril Delevanti *(Nonno)*, Mary Boylan *(Miss Peebles)*, Gladys Hill *(Miss Dexter)*, Billie Matticks *(Miss Throxton)*, Emilio Fernandes *(Barkeeper)*, Eloise Hardt, Thelda Victor, Betty Proctor, Dorothy Vance, Liz Rubey, Bernice Starr, Barbara Joyce *(Teachers)*, Roberto Leyva *(Pedro)*, C.G. Kim *(Chang)*; Fidelmar Duran *(Pepe)*.

Based on the Williams play that won the New York Drama Critics Award for 1961-62, THE NIGHT OF THE IGUANA is alternately fascinating and boring. It served to put the sleepy little village of Puerto Vallarta on the Mexican vacation map, and visitors to the town are still shown the rotting sets for the movie as part of their "official" tour. The cinematographer and Hall were nominated for Oscars but bypassed by their rivals in ZORBA THE GREEK. Burton is a defrocked Episcopalian who now earns his living as a tour guide. He's taking a group of schoolteachers around and Lyon, the junior member of the group, finds him attractive, so he squires her to his ratty hotel room where they are discovered by Hall. She threatens to have him sacked for his dalliance with Lyon unless he ceases and desists. The group is supposed to be quartered in a plush inn, but Burton takes them to a rundown place owned by Gardner, who has just been widowed. The teachers balk, but Burton strands them by tinkering with their bus and they must now remain at the seedy hotel. Burton falls ill with fever and tells Gardner that Hall means to have him fired, so Gardner won't let Hall use the phone to call Burton's employers. Kerr, a poor artist, and her grandfather, Delevanti, a poorer poet, have been working their way across Mexico by selling her sketches, and they arrive at the hotel to rest. Ward is the tour's bus driver and he is soon Lyon's boy friend. He fixes the bus, gathers the teachers, and they leave, with Ward as the tour leader. Kerr, Burton, Delavanti, and Gardner remain at the hotel and Kerr and Burton become closer, as Burton's mind seems to be on the verge of crumbling. Gardner loves Burton, although she sees that his existence would be better served by Kerr, so she offers her hotel to the two of them. Delavanti has been working on the same poem for 20 years, and when he finishes it, he dies. Kerr leaves after burying Delavanti, and Burton and Gardner stay on at the shuttered hostelry as the picture ends. We're never certain if Hall is in love with Burton or Lyon and that remains cloudy. Gardner is depicted as an old nymphomaniac who maintains two male whores to serve her, Duran and Leyva. The off-screen conduct of cast and crew was almost as weird as the film itself. Burton's wife, Elizabeth Taylor, was on hand throughout the filming, sticking like glue to Burton's side, reportedly to make sure her husband's eyes didn't roll too far over in Gardner's direction. Gardner, however, spent most of her time driving a sports car wildly through the surf along the beach. Lyon was chaperoned by her mother and director Huston made it seem all the more harrowing by giving each of the leading players a gun to protect themselves from unknown dangers. Lyon, who began her career as the title character in LOLITA, was making her second film appearance. Her movie life was, at best, erratic (TONY ROME, SEVEN WOMEN, etc.) and she has since retired to become a teacher in Los Angeles. The iguana mentioned in the title refers to a long lizard that can be seen roaming the streets and hotels of Puerto Vallarta and looks far more ferocious than it is. Matter of fact, many of the local people keep iguanas as pets. Puerto Vallarta, which sits on a huge bay that is much larger than Acapulco's, remains a pleasant place to holiday.

p, Ray Stark; d, John Huston; w, Anthony Veiller, Huston (based on the play by Tennessee Williams); ph, Gabriel Figueroa (CinemaScope); m, Benjamin Frankel; ed, Ralph Kemplen; md, Frankel; art d, Stephen Grimes; cos, Dorothy Jeakins; makeup, Jack Obringer, Eric Allwright.

Drama **Cas.** **(PR:O MPAA:NR)**

NIGHT OF THE JUGGLER* (1980) 100m COL c

James Brolin *(Sean Boyd)*, Cliff Gorman *(Gus Soltic)*, Richard Castellano *(Lt. Tonelli)*, Linda G. Miller *(Barbara)*, Barton Heyman *(Preacher)*, Sully Boyar *(Larry)*, Julie Carmen *(Marie)*, Abby Bluestone *(Kathy Boyd)*, Dan Hedaya *(Barnes)*, Mandy Patinkin *(Cabbie)*, Marco St. John *(H.R. Clayton III)*, Frank Adu *(Wino)*, Nancy Andrews *(Mrs. Logan)*, Rick Anthony *(M.C.)*, Tony Azito *(Cashier)*, Tally Brown *(Peep Show Operator)*, Blair Burrows, Joseph Carberry, Rosanna Carter, Rony Clanton, Mila Conway, Tito Goya, Delphi Harrington, Murray Horwitz, Frank Irizzary, Dorothy Lyman, Ruth Maynard, Ellen Parker, Samm-Art Williams, Arthur French, Richard Gant, James Moriarty.

Obnoxious, violent, and racist revenge movie starring Brolin as a tough ex-cop who tears apart most of New York City in pursuit of psychopath Gorman who has kidnaped Brolin's daughter. After innumerable car wrecks, beatings, stabbings, foul utterances, and far-fetched plot twists, the film comes to a fitful end with a shootout in the New York sewer system, which is where the editor should have dropped the final cut of this trash.

p, Jay Weston; d, Robert Butler; w, Bill Norton, Sr., Rick Natkin (based on the novel by William P. McGivern); ph, Victor J. Kemper (Technicolor); m, Artie

Kane; ed, Argyle Nelson; prod d, Stuart Wurtzel; set d, John Godfrey; cos, Peggy Farrell; stunts, Chris Howell.

Crime **Cas.** **(PR:O MPAA:R)**

NIGHT OF THE LAUGHING DEAD (SEE: HOUSE IN NIGHTMARE PARK, 1973, Brit.)

NIGHT OF THE LEPUS* (1972) 88m MGM c

Stuart Whitman *(Roy Bennett)*, Janet Leigh *(Gerry Bennett)*, Rory Calhoun *(Cole Hillman)*, DeForest Kelley *(Dr. Elgin Clark)*, Paul Fix *(Sheriff Cody)*, Melanie Fullerton *(Amanda Bennett)*, Chris Morrell *(Jackie Hillman)*, Chuck Hayward *(Jud)*, Henry Wills *(Frank)*, Francesca Jarvis *(Mildred)*, William Elliott *(Dr. Leopold)*, Robert Hardy *(Prof. Dirkson)*, Richard Jacome *(Deputy Jason)*, Inez Perez *(Housekeeper)*, G. Leroy Gaintner *(Walker)*, Evans Thornton *(Maj. White)*, I. Stanford Jolley *(Dispatcher)*, Robert Gooden *(Leslie)*, Walter Kelley *(Truck Driver)*, Frank Kennedy *(Doctor)*, Don Starr *(Cutler)*, Peter O'Crotty *(Arlen)*, Phillip Avenetti *(Officer Lopez)*, Russell Morell *(Priest)*, Donna Gelgur *(Wife in Car)*, Stephen De France *(Husband in Car)*, Sherry Hummer, Rick Hummer *(Children in Car)*, Jerry Dunphy *(TV Newscaster)*.

Believe it or not giant carnivorous bunny rabbits terrorize Arizona in this silly monster movie. Rancher Calhoun gets fed up with all the hungry bunnies eating his cattle's grass (they're still small at this point) so he enlists the aid of husband and wife scientists Whitman and Leigh who develop a hormone injection to halt the rabbits' breeding capabilities. Unfortunately the experiment goes awry and before you can say "Bugs Bunny," Arizona is lousy with 25-foot, man-eating bunnies that stomp like thunder and roar like lions. Eventually Whitman leads the rabbits to an electrified section of railway track which turns them into giant rabbit fricassee. Unintentionally hilarious, the special effects are handled by using normal rabbits, shot in slow motion and allowed to destroy miniature ranches, and people dressed like rabbits hopping around pretending to be monster bunnies. The mind marvels at the bravery of the person who walked into the producer's office to pitch this idea.

p, A.C. Lyles; d, William F. Claxton; w, Don Holliday, Gene R. Kearney (based on the novel *The Year of the Angry Rabbit* by Russell Braddon); ph, Ted Voigtlander (Metrocolor); m, Jimmie Haskell; ed, John McSweeney; prod d, Stan Jolley; set d, William Calvert; spec eff, Howard A. Anderson Company; makeup, Wes Dawn; animal trainers, Lou Schumacher, Henry Cowl.

Science Fiction/Horror **(PR:C MPAA:PG)**

NIGHT OF THE LIVING DEAD*** (1968) 90m Image Ten/ Continental bw (AKA: NIGHT OF THE FLESH EATERS)

Judith O'Dea *(Barbara)*, *Russell Streiner (Johnny)*, Duane Jones *(Ben)*, Karl Hardman *(Harry Cooper)*, Keith Wayne *(Tom)*, Judith Ridley *(Judy)*, Marilyn Eastman *(Helen Cooper)*, Kyra Schon *(Karen)*, Bill Heinzman, Charles Craig, Frank Doak, George Kosana.

Pittsburgh-based industrial filmmaker George Romero gathered together a loyal cast and crew of local Pittsburgh talent, scrounged up enough money to shoot on weekends, and committed to film one of the most terrifying pictures ever to hit the screen. NIGHT OF THE LIVING DEAD begins simply enough, with O'Dea and her smart-aleck brother Streiner visiting their father's grave in a lonely backwoods cemetery. The pair is accosted by a bizarre-looking man who seems to move with almost comical difficulty. The man tries to grab O'Dea, but Streiner intervenes and the crazy old man tries to bite him. In the ensuing struggle, Streiner is knocked unconscious on a tombstone. Terrified, O'Dea runs for help with the crazy man stumbling after her. After stupidly wrecking the car, O'Dea dashes to a nearby farmhouse to call for help, but she soon learns that no one is home and the phone is disconnected. Looking out the window, she sees that the crazy man is trying to find a way into the house. O'Dea runs upstairs only to find the partly devoured body of a woman. Dumbstruck, she becomes hysterical and starts to run outside. When she opens the door she is blinded by the bright headlights of a truck owned by a black man, Jones, who also has arrived at the house seeking refuge. As Jones pushes O'Dea back inside, we see that the crazy man has been joined by a few equally strange-looking men. Jones goes outside and kills a few of them with a tire iron (including one who found his way into the house). He then sets about a fortifying the house by nailing boards over the doors and windows without much help from O'Dea, whose mind has snapped. While working, Jones explains that most of the nearby towns have become infested with these deadly maniacs and many people have been killed by them. After securing the main floor, Jones is shocked to learn that a group of people have been huddled in the basement all along, led by cowardly family-man Hardman, who had taken refuge with his wife, Eastman, and a young teenage couple, Wayne and Schon, after Hardman's daughter was bitten by one of the creatures. Angered that the group stayed in the basement despite the fact that they heard O'Dea screaming for help, Jones takes an immediate dislike to Hardman and refuses his suggestion that they all barricade themselves in the basement until help arrives. To keep Hardman in his place, Jones retains sole ownership of the only rifle on the premises. A quick check out the window confirms that dozens of the zombie-people have gathered outside the door, and a new plan of action is needed. The news on the television announces that the crazed people are not escaped mental patients, but actually dead people who have come back to life seeking the flesh of the living. The newsmen are just as confused as anyone else, and announce the locations of some emergency shelters. The group decides to make a run for it in Jones' truck, and Wayne volunteers to make his way to the vehicle and gas it up (there are gas pumps behind the barn) while Jones and Hardman distract the zombies with Molotov cocktails. Wayne makes a run for it and is joined by his girl friend at the last minute. As he tries to fill the truck's tank, he is attacked from all sides by the zombies and accidentally sets the truck on fire. Bravely, he jumps in the burning truck and tries to get away but he and his girl friend are caught in the explosion. When the flames die down the ravenous ghouls descend on the vehicle and feast on the couple's remains. The setback drives the trapped survivors to the brink of madness and Hardman pathetically tries to trap Jones outside with the zombies. Jones makes it back into the house and shoots Hardman. Dying, Hardman stumbles down the stairs and stares at his daughter who, having died from her wound, comes back to life and devours her father. Eastman interrupts her daughter's feast and is murdered by the young zombie. Meanwhile, hundreds of zombies have attacked the house and are breaking through the barricades upstairs. O'Dea snaps out of her catatonic state long enough to help resist the monsters, but is dragged out of the house by her dead brother, Streiner, now a zombie. Alone in the house, Jones barricades himself in the basement and waits to die while listening to the zombies shuffling around on the floor above. The next morning Jones is awakened by the sound of gunfire and dogs. Cautiously he makes his way upstairs and finds the house empty. Peering out the window, Jones sees a sheriff's posse making its way across the field shooting every zombie in sight. Before he can call for help, an overeager posse member spots the man in the house and shoots him through the head, mistaking him for a ghoul. During the final credits sequence, seen in optically enhanced stills, we watch as Jones' body is thrown on a huge pile of zombie corpses and burned. Produced for less than $150,000 and shot in grainy black and white, Romero managed to send shock waves throughout the movie-going community with the film. Stodgy bastions of film criticism such as *Variety* spat out scathingly negative reviews of unbridled moral indignation, while other critics hailed the film as a masterpiece of modern horror. After being booked in a haphazard manner, rejected by Columbia because it wasn't in color and by American International Pictures because it had no romance and a downbeat ending, the film turned up at kiddie matinees, scaring the daylights out of the unprepared youngsters. NIGHT OF THE LIVING DEAD found a healthy niche on the midnight TV show circuit where it belonged and went on to become one of the most successful independent films ever made. Financial success notwithstanding, Romero's true brilliance is the film itself. Romero used all the budget handicaps to his advantage. The cheap, grainy film stock enhances the film's nightmarish quality, while his visual style relies on skillfully framed compositions edited together for maximum impact. The concept itself is horror at its most basic: a group of strangers trapped together in a small house being attacked by the living dead, once friends, relatives and neighbors, who want only to devour them. Much has been made of the gore level in NIGHT OF THE LIVING DEAD, but most of the horror is actually suggested or off-screen with a few, sparse visualizations brought in to punctuate the horror. What has not been noticed by most critics is that Romero is one of the few directors in America consistently giving lead roles to minorities. Jones, who is black, was cast as the voice of reason, the calm, smart, honorable, and brave man determined to survive the night against the zombies. This was in 1968 when Sidney Poitier was the only black man accepted by Hollywood for leading roles and no producer would have shown him shooting a white man, justifiably or not. In his subsequent DAWN OF THE DEAD and DAY OF THE DEAD, Romero cast blacks and women in strong, lead roles where they are in charge. He conceived the films as a trilogy from the beginning and all are equally brilliant. A landmark American film, NIGHT OF THE LIVING DEAD, while definitely not for most tastes, is an important, masterfully executed exercise in horror. A soundtrack to the movie was released 14 years after it was made.

p, Russell Streiner, Karl Hardman; d, George Romero; w, John A. Russo (based on a story by Romero); ph&ed, Romero; prod d, Vincent Survinski; spec eff, Regis Survinski, Tony Pantanello; makeup, Hardman, Marilyn Eastman.

Horror **Cas.** **(PR:O MPAA:NR)**

NIGHT OF THE PARTY, THE* (1934, Brit.) 60m GAU bw

Leslie Banks *(Sir John Holland)*, Ian Hunter *(Guy Kennington)*, Jane Baxter *(Peggy Studholme)*, Ernest Thesiger *(Chiddiatt)*, Viola Keats *(Joan Holland)*, Malcolm Keen *(Lord Studholme)*, Jane Millican *(Anna Chiddiatt)*, Muriel Aked *(Princess)*, John Turnbull *(Ramage)*, Laurence Anderson, W. Graham Browne.

An unbelievable murder mystery stars Banks as a police inspector investigating the murder of a newspaper magnate during a parlor game at a dinner party. The victim's secretary is arrested for the murder, but Banks isn't convinced. In fact, he even suspects his own daughter who confided that she was being blackmailed into a tryst with the deceased. All turns out well for the innocent woman, however, when a crazed novelist confesses to the killing at the trial (his books had gotten bad reviews in the dead man's newspaper) and then blows his brains out in front of the packed courtroom.

p, Jerome Jackson; d, Michael Powell; w, Ralph Smart (based on a play by Roland Pertwee, John Hastings Turner); ph, Geoffrey Faithfull.

Mystery **(PR:A MPAA:NR)**

NIGHT OF THE PROWLER** (1962, Brit.) 60m BUT bw

Patrick Holt *(Robert Langton)*, Colette Wilde *(Marie Langton)*, Bill Nagy *(Paul Conrad)*, Mitzi Rogers *(Jacky Reed)*, John Horsley *(Inspector Cameron)*, Benny Lee *(Benny)*, Marianne Stone *(Mrs. Cross)*, Mark Singleton *(Anders)*, Anthony Wager *(Sgt. Baker)*.

In order to control a major auto company, an executive must frame a man for murder. His victim is a seemingly natural patsy, a reformed embezzler. Run-of-the-mill British thriller, typical for the period.

p, John I. Phillips; d, Francis Searle; w, Paul Erickson.

Crime Drama **(PR:C MPAA:NR)**

NIGHT OF THE PROWLER, THE zero (1979, Aus.) 90m Chariot/ International Harmony c

Ruth Cracknell, John Frawley, Kerry Walker, John Derum, Maggie Kirkpatrick, Terry Camilleri.

Walker, an overweight, unhappy young woman, takes to wearing leather and to involving herself in criminal activities in a search for the meaning of life. Her unhappy family life and mismatched romance force her to find herself amidst the denizens of the night. Walker isn't the only one with trouble in finding understanding, as most audiences will be confused, bored, and maybe even asleep by the time the film wraps up. Directed by the same man who gave us THE ROCKY HORROR PICTURE SHOW, this tries for instant camp and settles for instant trash. Sharman fills this picture with incomprehensible flashbacks and flash forwards, resulting in an unattractive telling of an unattractive subject. This is the sort of film that provides a good argument for the concept of new and unlimited sources for guitar picks.

p, Anthony Buckley; d, Jim Sharman; w, Patrick White (based on his short story); ph, David Sanderson; m, Cameron Alan.

Comedy/Drama   **(PR:O MPAA:NR)**

NIGHT OF THE QUARTER MOON*   (1959) 95m MGM bw (AKA: FLESH AND FAME)

Julie London (Ginny Nelson), John Drew Barrymore (Roderic "Chuck" Nelson), Nat King Cole (Cy Robbin), Anna Kashfi (Maria Robbin), Dean Jones (Lexington Nelson), Agnes Moorehead (Cornelia Nelson), Cathy Crosby (The Singer), Ray Anthony (Hotel Manager), Jackie Coogan (Sgt. Bragan), Charles Chaplin, Jr. (The Neighbor), Billy Daniels (The Headwaiter), James Edwards (Asa Tully), Arthur Shields (Capt. O'Sullivan), Edward Andrews (Clinton Page), Robert Warwick (The Judge), Marguerite Belefonte (The Hostess), Bobi Byrnes (The Girl in the Woods), Charlotte Hawkins (Singer).

This tasteless drama stars Barrymore as a wealthy Korean War vet who falls in love with and marries London while on a fishing trip in Mexico with his brother, Jones. He brings his bride back to San Francisco and the society pages scream with the news that one of London's grandparents was black. Somehow, Nat King Cole and Agnes Moorehead were talked into appearing in this exploitative mess. Cole sings "To Whom it May Concern" while Bing Crosby's niece, Cathy, makes her screen bow singing "Blue Moon."

p, Albert Zugsmith; d, Hugo Haas; w, Frank Davis, Franklin Coen; ph, Ellis Carter (CinemaScope); m, Albert Glasser; ed, Ben Lewis; md, Glasser; art d, William A. Horning, Malcolm Brown.

Drama   **(PR:C MPAA:NR)**

NIGHT OF THE SEAGULL, THE*½   (1970, Jap.) 90m Toho c (SUNA NO KAORI)

Mic Hama (Woman), Jin Nakayama (Young Man), Megumi Matsumoto, Jitsuko Yoshimura, Natsuko Kahara.

The film tells the tale of a woman who has a brief, intense affair with a younger man while awaiting her trial for the murder of her husband's mistress. She is acquitted on grounds of self-defense and returns to her husband.

d, Katsumi Iwauchi; w, Mitsura Majima, Iwauchi (based on the novel Mermaid by Matsutaro Kawaguchi); ph, Choichi Nakai (Eastmancolor); m, Chemei Watanabe.

Drama   **(PR:C MPAA:NR)**

NIGHT OF THE SHOOTING STARS, THE**   (1982, Ital.) 106m RAI Radiotelevisione-Ager Cinematografica-Premier/UA c (GB: THE NIGHT OF SAN LORENZO)

Omero Antonutti (Galvano), Margarita Lozano (Concetta), Claudio Bigagli (Corrado), Massimo Bonetti (Nicole), Norma Martelli (Ivana), Enrica Maria Modugno (Mara), Sabina Vannucchi (Rosanna), Dario Cantarelli (Priest), Sergio Dagliana (Olinto), Giuseppe Furia (Requiem), Paolo Hendel (Dilvo), Laura Mannucchi, Rinaldo Mirannalti, Donata Piacentini, Franco Piacentini, Antonio Prester, David Riondino, Gianfranco Salemi, Massimo Sarchielli, Mario Spallino, Mirio Guidelli, Titta Guidelli, Antonella Guidelli, Giovanni Guidelli, Micol Guidelli, Miriam Guidelli, Samanta Boi, Beatrice Bardelli, Sauro Baschieri, Andrea Di Bari, Luca Canardi.

On the night of Saint Lawrence (a magical evening where Europeans believe that wishes may become fulfilled), a shooting star darts across the sky sending a grown woman into a recollection of her childhood. As the star passes her window, the woman relates the events that took place in her small town during the last days of WW II. With the advancing Allies pushing the last remnants of the German army out of Italy, the Nazis enact sick, desperate revenge on the townsfolk by staging vicious attacks on the old men, women, and children who remained in the villages. The members of the small town of San Miniato are divided in their opinions as to whether to remain in their village and risk dealing with the Nazis, or to attempt traveling across the back roads while dodging attacks from the sadistic Blackshirts in an effort to meet the advancing Allies. One group made up of various segments of the town's population sets out on the journey, with all the old forms of segregation breaking down as the people pull together in an effort to survive. An elderly peasant man with a natural ability to lead is chosen to guide the group to safety. Despite a few voices of dissent, the old man brings a clever ingenuity to his assignment and keeps the group's spirits up by showing a humane concern for every person and encouraging them to watch out for one another. During the journey, the old man develops a romantic friendship for an aristocratic woman who had always admired him, but could never let him know because of their class separation. Eventually he guides the group out of danger and observes the townspeople immediately adopting the societal roles that had divided them before the crisis. The Tavianis had previously gained international attention with PADRE PADRONE in 1977, which won the Golden Palm at Cannes. They approached THE NIGHT OF THE SHOOTING STARS in much the same manner by using an imaginative combination of events and showing how they are remembered through the eyes of a narrator as she reminisces about the magical moments of her childhood. (In Italian; English subtitles.)

p, Giuliani G. De Negri; d, Paola Taviani, Vittorio Taviani; w, Tavianis, De Negri, Tonino Guerra; ph, Franco di Giacomo (Agfacolor); m, Nicola Piovani; ed, Roberto Perpignani; art d, Gianni Sbarra.

Drama/War   **Cas.**   **(PR:O MPAA:R)**

NIGHT OF THE SILICATES   (SEE: ISLAND OF TERROR, 1967)

NIGHT OF THE STRANGLER*   (1975) 88m Howco c

Mickey Dolenz (Vance), Chuck Patterson (Priest), James Ralston (Dan), Michael Anthony, Susan McCullough, Katie Tilley, Ann Barrett.

When a black man becomes romantically involved with a white woman, their affair instigates a chain of events which leads to a series of brutal murders. Fans of the old "Monkees" TV series might want to take a peek to watch former sensation Dolenz sink to a new depth; otherwise it's a forgettable murder mystery.

p, Albert J. Salzer; d, Joy N. Houck, Jr.

Murder Mystery   **Cas.**   **(PR:O MPAA:R)**

NIGHT OF THE TIGER, THE   (SEE: RIDE BEYOND VENGEANCE, 1966)

NIGHT OF THE WITCHES zero   (1970) 78m Matchpoint/Medford c (AKA: NIGHT OF WITCHES)

Keith Erik Burt [Keith Larsen] (Preacher), Kathryn Loder (Cassandra, the High Priestess), Marta, Juana (Black Witches), Ron Taft (Frank Evans), Randy Stafford (Athena), Leon Charles (Mr. Greenstreet), John Jones (Timothy Gruper), Susie Edgell (Rosita), Ernest Lawrence Rossi, Beverly LaRue, Louise Blain.

This Charles Manson-inspired film, starring, produced and directed by Burt, tells of a bogus preacher who rapes and murders on the side. He stumbles across a coven of witches in California and tries to blackmail them (they kill people whom they believe are evil). Fortunately, the High Priestess (Loder) poisons him before he gets the chance.

p, Keith Erik Burt [Keith Larsen], Vincent Forte; d&w, Burt; ph, Herbert Theis (DeLuxe Color); ed, Anthony de Laune; art d, Ted Jonson; m/l, "Me and God and You," "Man of Many Pleasures," Sean Bonniwell (sung by The Baby).

Crime   **(PR:O MPAA:GP)**

NIGHT OF THE ZOMBIES zero   (1981) 88m NMD c (AKA: GAMMA 693; NIGHT OF THE WEHRMACHT ZOMBIES)

Jamie Gillis (Nick Monroe), Ryan Hilliard (Dr. Proud), Samantha Grey (Susan), Ron Armstrong (Capt. Fleck), Richard de Faut (Sgt. Freedman), Juni Kulis (GRO Officer Schuller), Alphonse de Noble (C.I.A. Agent), Joel M. Reed (Neo-Nazi), Shoshana Ascher (Prostitute), Lorin E. Price (Priest), Ron Dorfman (C.I.A. Chief), Ranate Schlessinger (Madame), Kuno Sponholtz (Doorman), Dick Carballo (Man in Bar), John Barilla, Michael Casconi, Gordon C. Dixon, Bob Laconi, Charlene Matus, Lee Moore, Glen A. Pence, Donald K. Wallace, Bill Williams, Carl Woerner, Kai Wulff.

A bizarre, bloody horror film, it was made by the man who brought you BLOODSUCKING FREAKS, Joel M. Reed. Porno star Gillis plays a CIA agent hot on the trail of a bunch of cannibalistic WW II zombie soldiers who continue to fight the war despite the fact that it's over and they're dead. This one would be great on a double bill with the Dana Andrews classic THE FROZEN DEAD.

p, Lorin E. Price; d&w, Joel M. Reed; ph, Ron Dorfman (TVC Color); m, Onomatopoeia Inc, Matt Kaplowitz, Maggie Nolin; ed, Samuel Pollard, Victor Kanefsky; cos, Eaves; spec eff, Peter Kunz; makeup, David E. Smith.

Horror   **Cas.**   **(PR:O MPAA:R)**

NIGHT OF THE ZOMBIES zero   (1983, Span./Ital.) 100m Dara Films/MPM-Beatrice Film c (APOCALIPSIS CANIBAL; INFERNO DEI MORTI-VIVENTI; VIRUS, INFERNO DEI MORTI-VIVENTI; AKA: HELL OF THE LIVING DEAD; ZOMBIE CREEPING FLESH)

Margit Evelyn Newton (Lea), Frank Garfield, Selan Karay, Robert O'Neil, Luis Fonoll, Gaby Renom, Ester Mesina, Victor Israel.

Once again the foreign horror film industry jumped on the George Romero (NIGHT OF THE LIVING DEAD; DAWN OF THE DEAD; DAY OF THE DEAD) zombie bandwagon and came up with another stinker. Borrowing ideas from Romero's "Living Dead" films and THE CRAZIES, this offering details the results of a disastrous chemical leak in Papua, New Guinea, that has turned the natives into flesh-eating zombies. Soon an Italian TV news crew led by tough female reporter Newton, accompanied by a squad of trigger-happy soldiers, arrives and the non-stop gore soon splatters over the screen. Cheap makeup effects, unintentionally funny dialog, and lots of blood are the order of the day for this film. While director Mattei (hiding under the pseudonym "Vincent Dawn" in the American release prints) may have gotten the inspiration for this trash from Romero's movies, he certainly displays no understanding of the humor, social insight, or skillful visual style that made Romero's films work.

d, Bruno Mattei [Vincent Dawn or Darum]; w, Claudio Fragasso, J. M. Cunilles; ph, John Cabrera (Telecolor); m, Goblin; ed, Claudio Borroni; prod d, Antonio Velart; makeup, Giuseppe Ferranti.

Horror   **(PR:O MPAA:NR)**

NIGHT PARADE**   (1929, Brit.) 72m RKO bw (GB: SPORTING LIFE)

Hugh Trevor (Bobby Murray), Lloyd Ingraham (Tom Murray), Dorothy Gulliver (Doris), Aileen Pringle (Paula Vernoff), Robert Ellis (John Zelli), Lee Shumway (Sid Durham), Ann Pennington (Dancer), Charles Sullivan (Huffy), Walter Kane (Jake), Barney Furey (Bennie), James Dugan (Artie), Nate Slott (Phil), Marie Astaire (Ethel), Heinie Conklin, Ann Greenway.

Routine boxing movie wherein Trevor, a middleweight champion, is seduced by femme fatale Pringle—who works for hoodlum Ellis—into throwing the big fight. Luckily their evil plot is revealed by good-girl Gulliver and her understanding father Ingraham and Trevor has enough time to pull himself off the mat and beat the stuffings out of his worthless opponent. The film has a few innovative touches, such as the climactic fight scene, which is staged in a blinding rainstorm. Unusual for a talkie of the time, this picture has no music, save for a popular song sung behind some dialog during a party sequence.

p, William LeBaron; d, Malcolm St. Clair; w, James Gruen, George O'Hara (based on the play "Ringside" by George Abbott, Edward Paramore, Gene Buck, Hyatt Daab); ph, William Marshall; ed, Jack Kitchen; art d, Max Ree.

Drama   (PR:A MPAA:NR)

NIGHT PASSAGE**½   (1957) 90m UNIV c

James Stewart (Grant McLaine), Audie Murphy (The Utica Kid), Dan Duryea (Whitey Harbin), Dianne Foster (Charlotte Drew), Elaine Stewart (Verna Kimball), Brandon de Wilde (Joey Adams), Jay C. Flippen (Ben Kimball), Herbert Anderson (Will Renner), Robert J. Wilke (Concho), Hugh Beaumont (Jeff Kurth), Jack Elam (Shotgun), Tommy Cook (Howdy Sladen), Paul Fix (Mr. Feeney), Olive Carey (Miss Vittles), James Flavin (Tim Riley), Donald Curtis (Jubilee), Ellen Corby (Mrs. Feeney), John Day (Latigo), Kenny Williams (O'Brien), Frank Chase (Trinidad), Harold Goodwin (Pick Gannon), Harold Tommy Hart (Shannon), Jack C. Williams (Dusty), Boyd Stockman (Torgenson), Henry Wills (Pache), Chuck Roberson (Roan), Willard Willingham (Click), Polly Burson (Rosa), Patsy Novak (Linda), Ted Mapes (Leary).

An Anthony Mann western without Anthony Mann. Mann was originally slated to direct this all-star oater, but he walked after voicing strong opinions regarding the quality of the script. Stewart, who was advised to follow Mann to the exit (they had collaborated earlier and come up with one of their best films, WINCHESTER 73), opted to stay and stick it out (reportedly to show off his musical talent—his character plays the accordion). The resulting film is a fair-to-average western that no one would remember for too long. The typical story line sees Stewart as the good brother and Murphy as the evil one, who cross paths when Stewart is hired to safeguard the railroad delivery of a $10,000 payroll. Murphy and his gang hold up the train and make off with the loot, leaving Stewart to hunt down his brother and retrieve the money. Despite his best efforts to convince his sibling to abandon his crooked ways, Stewart is unable to entice Murphy to leave before the inevitable showdown with the gang. When it looks as if Stewart is doomed, Murphy has a predictable change of heart and unites with his brother against his former comrades. Murphy is killed, as is the scene-stealing Duryea, leader of the gang, and Stewart makes sure the payroll is delivered. Routine direction by Neilson fails to create any sparks from the hackneyed material.

p, Aaron Rosenberg; d, James Neilson; w, Borden Chase (based on a story by Norman A. Fox); ph, William Daniels, Clifford Stine (Technirama, Technicolor); m, Dimitri Tiomkin; ed, Sherman Todd; art d, Alexander Golitzen, Robert Clatworthy; cos, Bill Thomas; m/l, Tiomkin, Ned Washington.

Western   (PR:A MPAA:NR)

NIGHT PEOPLE***½   (1954) 93m FOX c

Gregory Peck (Col. Van Dyke), Broderick Crawford (Leatherby), Anita Bjork (Hoffy), Rita Gam (Miss Cates), Walter Abel (Foster), Buddy Ebsen (Sgt. McColloch), Casey Adams (Frederick S. Hobart), Jill Esmond (Frau Schindler), Peter Van Eyck (Petrechine), Marianne Koch (Kathy), Ted Avery (Johnny), Hugh McDermott (Burns), Paul Carpenter (Col. Whitby), John Horsely (Stanways), Lionel Murton (Lakeland), Harold Benedict, Tom Boyd, T. Schaank, Sgt. Cleary, E. Haffner (Men), Ruth Garcia (Nurse), Peter Beauvais (Driver), A. Faerber (Mr. Schindler), Otto Reichow (Russian Major).

A topflight Cold War drama, this film depicts a clever and harrowing cat-and-mouse game between U.S. military people and Russian spies in postwar Berlin. Peck is an intelligence officer who learns that a U.S. Army corpsman has been kidnaped by the Communists and taken into the Russian zone. Worse, the young man's father is a magnate and political power broker, Crawford, who arrives from the U.S. and loudly demands that immediate action be taken to get his son released. Peck by then has learned that the Russians are insisting on the return of two elderly Germans—a retired general, Faerber, and his wife, Esmond, who supports her husband by playing piano in a seedy nightclub. Peck takes Crawford to the club so he can see for himself the harmless human beings Crawford insists be traded for his son. That problem is quickly solved when the two attempt to commit suicide. (The Russians inexplicably want Faerber so he can be turned over to some SS men wanting revenge against the general because of his involvement in the 1944 plot to kill Adolf Hitler!) Peck, with aides Gam and Ebsen at his side, manages to get the couple into a hospital where their critical condition is kept secret. Meanwhile, Bjork, an East German woman who has been spying for the U.S. and who is mildly involved with Peck, lobbies for the trade. Peck knows, of course, that the couple will be killed once they are turned over, but they die from their self-inflicted wounds and now he has nothing to trade for the American soldier. Then, thanks to Ebsen and Gam uncovering Bjork's background, Peck learns that his German lady is really a Russian counterspy. He arranges a trade for the American soldier and has a truck driver deliver the boy—who is drugged—giving the Russians who they think is Faerber's wife (but he really sends a drugged Bjork back to them, outwitting them in the end). The Johnson script is taut and the dialog is splendid, as is Johnson's economical direction. Peck does an outstanding job as the problem-plagued CIC officer who almost loses the deadly game. This was Johnson's first full-authority direction of a film but he was told by Fox chief Zanuck that Peck's contract permitted him to veto any director. Peck and Johnson had worked on THE GUNFIGHTER together four years earlier and the actor's confidence in Johnson was so high that he did not hesitate to approve of his friend as director.

p,d,&w, Nunnally Johnson (based on a story by Jed Harris, Thomas Reed); ph, Charles G. Clarke (CinemaScope, Technicolor); m, Cyril J. Mockridge; ed, Dorothy Spencer; md, Lionel Newman; art d, Hanns Kuhnert, Theo Zwierski.

Drama   (PR:A MPAA:NR)

NIGHT PLANE FROM CHUNGKING**½   (1942) 69m PAR bw

Robert Preston (Capt. Nick Stanton), Ellen Drew (Ann Richards), Stephen Geray (Rev. Dr. van der Lieden), Sen Young (Capt. Po), Soo Yong (Madame Wu), Otto Kruger (Albert Pasavy), Ernest Dorian (Maj. Brissac), Tamara Geva (Countess Olga Karagin), Allen Jung (Lt. Tang).

Typical Sino-Japanese War thriller starring Preston as an American pilot serving with the Chinese army who is assigned to fly a group of civilians to the Indian border. Unfortunately, the plane is shot down by the Japanese and a Nazi spy—who was on board disguised as a priest—leads them into a Japanese prison camp. Eventually, with help from Dorion, a French officer, the tiny group makes good its escape. A remake of the 1932 thriller SHANGHAI EXPRESS. Look for a terrific stint by veteran actor Kruger as a brash businessman (rather than his customary suave self) who appears to be dealing with the enemy.

p, Walter MacEwen, Michel Kraike; d, Ralph Murphy; w, Earl Fenton, Theodore Reaves, Lester Cole, Sidney Biddell (based on a story by Harry Harvey); ph, Theodor Sparkuhl; ed, Ellsworth Hoagland; art d, Hans Dreier, William Flannary.

War   (PR:A MPAA:NR)

NIGHT PORTER, THE**½   (1974, Ital./U.S.) 117m Edwards-Esae De Simone/AE c (IL PORTIERE DI NOTTE)

Dirk Bogarde (Max), Charlotte Rampling (Lucia), Philippe Leroy (Klaus), Gabriele Ferzetti (Hans), Giuseppe Addobbati (Stumm), Isa Miranda (Countess Stein), Nino Bignamini (Adolph), Marino Mase (Atherton), Amedeo Amodio (Bert), Piero Vida (Day Porter), Geoffrey Copleston (Kurt), Manfred Freiberger (Dobson), Ugo Cardea (Mario), Hilda Gunther (Greta), Nora Ricci (The Neighbor), Piero Mazzinghi (Concierge), Kai S. Seefield (Jacob), Claudio Steiner (Dobson).

Italian writer-director Cavani had visited one of the Nazi concentration camps after the war and interviewed a woman who had been involved in a sado-masochistic relationship with one of the guards. She used that story as the basis for this often powerful (and sometimes heavy-handed) film, and evidently wrote it specifically for Bogarde after having seen his work in DARLING and THE SERVANT. The year is 1958 and Bogarde works as the night porter in a Viennese hotel where his duties go far beyond the usual work of a man in his position. The ex-Nazi guests and the woman who owns the place, Miranda, allow themselves to be "dealt with" by ex-storm trooper Bogarde in a masochistic fashion that can only be dubbed "perverted." Bogarde and the others at the hotel are all Germans who think that they have managed to eliminate any witnesses to their war crimes. Bogarde is about to come up on trial, but he thinks he's safe, until Rampling and her husband check into the hotel. He recognizes her as a one-time camp victim in a place where he had masqueraded as a physician and taken photographs of her and many of the other inmates, and, in general, used her body for his own pleasures. The picture flashes forward and back as the two of them recall what happened during the war, and the scenes are most explicit, with rape, sodomy, torture, etc. And yet, Rampling seemed to be enjoying what happened. The daughter of an Austrian Socialist, she must have had a serious mental instability to have responded in the way she did. Bogarde and Rampling reawaken their "love" (that term may be debatable but that's the emotion that Cavani seeks to make us believe) and he hides her from the other Nazis when he realizes that they want to murder her for fear of being exposed. After laying low in his apartment, the two of them understand that there is no way out, as the others are waiting to get them, so they don the clothes they wore at the camp (he wears the Nazi uniform that he's kept all these years) and they are killed at the picture's conclusion. A strange and unforgettable picture that delves deeply into the psyches of torturers and the tortured. Presented by Joseph E. Levine in a non-exploitative campaign, it never caught fire with the public.

p, Robert Gordon Edwards; d, Liliana Cavani; w, Cavani, Italo Moscati (based on a story by Cavani, Barbara Alberti, Amedeo Pagani); ph, Alfio Contini (Technicolor); m, Daniele Paris; ed, Franco Arcalli; art d, Nedo Azzini, Jean Marie Simon; cos, Piero Tosi.

Drama   **Cas.**   (PR:O MPAA:R)

NIGHT RAIDERS*½   (1952) 52m MON bw

Whip Wilson (Whip), Tom Farrell (Jim Dugan), Fuzzy Knight (Texas), Lois Hall (Laura Davis), Steve Clark (Davis), Terry Frost (Lorch), Marshall Reed (Sheriff Hodkins), Lane Bradford (Talbot), Iron Eyes Cody (Cherokee), Carol Henry (Blair), Ed Cassidy (Banker), Forrest Taylor (Chairman), Stanley Price (Telegraph Man), Roy Butler (Merchant), Boyd Stockman.

Wilson must figure out who is ransacking the property of local ranchers during nightly raids, and not stealing anything. Eventually, the Whip discovers that the answer lies with Sheriff Reed who is searching for $15,000 in loot he has hidden from a train robbery for which saloonkeeper Frost took the rap.

p, Vincent M. Fennelly; d, Howard Bretherton; w, Maurice Tombragel; ph, Ernest Miller; md, Raoul Kraushaar; ed, Sam Fields.

Western   (PR:A MPAA:NR)

NIGHT RIDE**   (1930) 60m UNIV bw

Joseph Schildkraut (Joe Rooker, Reporter), Barbara Kent (Ruth Kearns), Edward G. Robinson (Tony Garotta), Harry Stubbs (Bob O'Leary), DeWitt Jennings (Capt. O'Donnell), Ralph Welles (Blondie), Hal Price (Mac), George Ovey (Ed).

Schildkraut plays a newlywed reporter who is pulled away from his wedding reception to cover a sensational bank robbery. Gathering evidence, Schildkraut deduces that the robber is none other than Robinson, a gang leader. The reporter makes a case against Robinson and files a story outlining his facts. Robinson kidnaps the nosy newshound and another reporter and intends to take them for a ride. To torture Schildkraut, Robinson claims he has bombed the reporter's home and killed his new bride. Before Robinson can kill the newsmen, he falls into a police trap and is captured leaving a relieved Schildkraut to learn that his wife is alive. Only Robinson's second talkie, and the first to cast the veteran stage actor in his oft-repeated role as a big-time mobster.

d, John S. Robertson; w, Edward T. Lowe, Jr. (based on a story by Henry La Cossit); ph, Alvin Wyckoff; ed, A. Ross, Milton Carruth.

Crime (PR:A MPAA:NR)

NIGHT RIDE** (1937, Brit.) 70m British and Dominions/PAR bw

Julien Vedey (Tony Spinelli), Wally Patch (Alf Higgins), Jimmy Hanley (Dick Benson), Joan Ponsford (Jean Morley), Frank Petley (Mr. Wilson), Elizabeth Kent (Ruth Wilson), Kenneth Buckley (Claude), Clelia Matania (Lucia Spinelli), Moore Marriott (Miner), Blake Dorn.

When drivers Hanley and his partner leave a crooked trucking magnate to form their own company, their former employer sends his daughter, Kent, to use her charms on Hanley. Along with some goons for hire, Kent nearly succeeds in her mission but the two young truckers prove themselves after rescuing people from a flooded mine. A shallow, wholly unbelievable drama with a contrived feel from start to finish.

p, Anthony Havelock-Allan; d, John Paddy Carstairs; w, Ralph Gilbert Bettinson (based on a story by Julien Vedey); ph, Francis Carver.

Drama (PR:C MPAA:NR)

NIGHT RIDER, THE*½ (1932) 72m Supreme/Artclass bw

Harry Carey, Eleanor Fair, George Hayes, Julian Rivero, Jack Weatherby, Walter Shumway, Bob Kortman, Nadja, Tom London, Cliff Lyons.

Bottom-of-the-barrel production sees Carey disguising himself as an infamous hooded outlaw in order to catch him. Carey had to sue low-budget producer Weiss' Supreme Features company to get his $5,000 salary out of this fiasco; the prospect of the lawsuit may have been what dimmed his personal luster in this altogether lackluster film. Hayes—later "Gabby"—does a sidekick stint in this one unusual for the time; he usually played villains. Not until THE LUCKY TEXAN (1934) did he again essay a comic-sidekick role.

p, Louis Weiss; d, William Nigh; w, Harry P. Christ [Harry Fraser]; ph, James Diamond.

Western **Cas.** (PR:A MPAA:NR)

NIGHT RIDERS, THE** (1939) 58m REP bw

John Wayne (Stony Brooke), Ray Corrigan (Tucson Smith), Max Terhune (Lullaby Joslin), Doreen McKay (Soledad), Ruth Rogers (Susan Randall), George Douglas (Pierce Talbot/Don Luis De Serrano), Tom Tyler (Jackson), Kermit Maynard (Sheriff Pratt), Sammy McKim (Tim), Walter Wills (Hazelton), Ethan Laidlaw (Andrews), Edward Peil, Sr. (Harper), Tom London (Wilson), Jack Ingram (Wilkins), William Nestell (Allen), Cactus Mack, Lee Shumway, Hal Price, Hank Worden, Roger Williams, Olin Francis, Francis Walker, Hugh Prosser, Jack Kirk, Yakima Canutt, Glenn Strange, David Sharpe, Bud Osborne, Georgia Summers.

Low-budget quickie shot in five days featuring Wayne, Corrigan and Terhune as the Three Mesquiteers who are forced to don masks and capes to expose an evil Spanish nobleman who has snatched their ranch from them. Wayne was at the lowest point in his career, having abandoned Republic to freelance in an attempt to dissociate himself from westerns. After a year of starving, he returned to a pay cut of over $6,000 dollars a picture. By the time THE NIGHT RIDERS was released, John Ford's STAGECOACH had hit the theaters and Wayne's star would rise and never fall again. (See THREE MESQUITEERS series, Index.)

p, William Berke; d, George Sherman; w, Betty Burbridge, Stanley Roberts (based on characters created by William Colt MacDonald); ph, Jack Marta; m, William Lava; ed, Lester Orlebeck.

Western **Cas.** (PR:A MPAA:NR)

NIGHT RIDERS OF MONTANA*½ (1951) 60m REP bw

Allen "Rocky" Lane (Himself), Chubby Johnson (Sheriff Davis), Roy Barcroft (Brink Stiles), Claudia Barrett (Julie Bauer), Arthur Space (Roger Brandon), Myron Healey (Steve Bauer), Mort Thompson (Jim Foster), Marshall Bradford (Sam Foster), Lester Dorr (Drummer), Ted Adams (Connors), George Chesebro (Jamison), Don Harvey (Janney), Zon Murray (Joe), Black Jack (Lane's Stallion).

Lane rides out in search of rustlers who have ruined every ranch in the territory except that of hot-headed loner Barrett. The ranchers decide that he is the most likely suspect. Luckily cooler heads prevail, and Lane learns that blacksmith Space and the always-rotten Barcroft are the real culprits.

p, Gordon Kay; d, Fred C. Bannon; w, M. Coates Webster; ph, Jack MacBurnie; m, Stanley Wilson; ed, Irving M. Schoenberg; art d, Frank Hotaling.

Western **Cas.** (PR:A MPAA:NR)

NIGHT RUNNER, THE*** (1957) 79m UNIV bw

Ray Danton (Roy Turner), Colleen Miller (Susan Mayes), Willis Bouchey (Loren Mayes), Merry Anders (Amy Hansen), Harry Jackson (Hank Hansen), Eddy C. Waller (Vernon), Robert Anderson (Ed Wallace), Jean Inness (Miss Dodd), Jane Howard (Typist), John Stephenson (Dr. Crawford), Richard Cutting (Man Interviewer), Alexander Campbell (Dr. Royce), Steve Pendleton (Capt. Reynolds), John Pickard (Dr. Fisher), Paul Weber (Dr. Rayburn), Jack Lomas (Real Estate Man), Natalie Masters (Miss Lowell), William Erwin (McDermott), George Barrows (Bus Driver), Ethyl May Halls (Elderly Woman), Sam Flint (Elderly Man), Marshall Bradford (Mailman), Diana Darrin (Waitress), Lola Kendrick (Secretary), Dale Van Sickel (Bus Driver), Alex Sharp (Deputy), Jay Berniker (Boy).

Powerful, disturbing film noir starring Danton as a schizophrenic mental patient who is forced to out-patient status due to hospital overcrowding. Before gaining his freedom, the doctors advise him to avoid stressful situations. Danton boards a bus to a beachside motel and finds that he is attracted to the area, and the motel

owner's daughter Miller. The two begin a romance, but their happiness is shattered when Miller's father discovers that Danton is a mental patient. Threatening to have him recommitted unless he leaves his daughter alone, the motel owner pushes Danton too far. The stress snaps Danton's mind momentarily and he kills the motel owner. Panic sets in and Danton flees down the beach with Miller. He decides to kill her and then himself, but when he pushes her into the water, the shock brings him back to his senses and he saves her. In the end, Danton gives himself up to the police. An interesting precursor to Hitchcock's PSYCHO which bears many coincidental similarities (the schizophrenia, a run-down motel, Danton's fascination with birds) and some sharply different interpretations of similar material (THE NIGHT RUNNER is much more sympathetic to its mentally ill character).

p, Albert J. Cohen; d, Abner Biberman; w, Gene Levitt (based on a story by Owen Cameron); ph, George Robinson; m, Joseph Gershenson; ed, Al Joseph; art d, Alexander Golitzen, Robert Boyle; set d, Russell A. Gausman, Ray Jeffers; cos, Rosemary Odell.

Thriller (PR:A MPAA:NR)

NIGHT SCHOOL* (1981) 88m Lorimar/PAR c (AKA: TERROR EYES)

Leonard Mann (Lt. Judd Austin), Rachel Ward (Eleanor Adjai), Drew Snyder (Prof. Millett), Joseph R. Sicari (Taj), Nicholas Cairis (Gus).

Thankfully forgettable Boston-made horror starring Mann as a police investigator, trying to solve the brutal decapitation murders of women who attend a local night school. Of course the heads turn up in a wide variety of places, and Mann narrows the suspects down to an amorous college professor, Snyder, and/or his pregnant, live-in sweetie and assistant, Ward. The plot thickens when Mann learns that the killings are part of a bizarre, demonic ritual practiced by primitive tribes. Reportedly actress Ward's first film. She would go on to appear with Burt Reynolds in SHARKEY'S MACHINE and with Jeff Bridges in AGAINST ALL ODDS.

p, Larry Babb, Ruth Avergon; d, Kenneth Hughes; w, Avergon; ph, Mark Irwin (Movielab Color); m, Brad Fiedel; ed, Robert Reitano; stunts, Ted Duncan.

Horror (PR:O MPAA:R)

NIGHT SHIFT*** (1982) 105m Ladd/WB c

Henry Winkler (Chuck Lumley), Michael Keaton (Bill Blazejowski), Shelley Long (Belinda Keaton), Gina Hecht (Charlotte Koogle), Pat Corley (Edward Koogle), Bobby DiCicco (Leonard), Nita Talbot (Vivian), Basil Hoffman (Drollhauser), Tim Rossovich (Luke), Clint Howard (Jefferey), Joe Spinell (Manetti), Cheryl Carter (Tanya), Becky Gonzalez (Lupe), Corki Corman (Sylvia), Ildiko Jaid (Joyce), Ava Lazar (Sharon), Robbin Young, Ola Ray, Cassandra Gava, Mimi Lieber, Ashley Cox, Elizabeth Carder, Dawn Dunlap, Jeanne Mori, K. C. Winkler, Catherine Gilmour, Monique Gabriel, Jim Staahl, Barbara Ann Grimes, Richard Belzer, Badja Djola, Marc Flanagan, Beau Billingslea, Kevin R. Sullivan, Grand Bush, Julius Leflore, Floyd Levine, Reid Cruickshanks, Charles Fleisher, Tom Mahoney, Vincent Schiavelli, Jack Perkins, Jim Ritz, John Boyle, Brett Clark, Paul Kaufman, Joy Michael Vogelbacher, Hugo Napier, Tom Candela, Edward G. Betlow, Horace Long, Angelo Vignari, Kevin Costner, Rick Starr, Russell Forte, Jim Greenleaf, Jason Fitz-Gerald, Jeremy Lawrence, Shannen Doherty, The Solid Gold Dancers.

Surprisingly tasteful and funny comedy starring Winkler as a dippy morgue attendant whose boring, mundane life changes when he is assigned to work the night shift with crazed schemer Keaton. Winkler, who secretly longs for some excitement in his life, becomes embroiled in Keaton's wild get-rich-quick plans. When the duo meet nice-girl hooker Long, who has just lost her pimp, the boys turn the morgue into a nighttime brothel using Long's other prostitute pals. Ron Howard's direction is carefully balanced, and he treats his characters with humanity and respect. Winkler turns in the best performance of his career, and Keaton is wonderful.

p, Brian Grazer; d, Ron Howard; w, Lowell Ganz, Babaloo Mandel; ph, James Crabe (Technicolor); m, Burt Bacharach; ed, Robert J. Kern, Jr., Daniel P. Hanley, Mike Hill; prod d, Jack Collis; art d, Pete Smith; m/l, Carole Bayer Sager, Bacharach; spec eff, Allen Hall.

Comedy **Cas.** (PR:C MPAA:R)

NIGHT SONG*½ (1947) 101m RKO bw

Dana Andrews (Dan), Merle Oberon (Cathy), Ethel Barrymore (Miss Willey), Hoagy Carmichael (Chick), Artur Rubinstein (Himself), Eugene Ormandy (Himself), Jacqueline White (Connie), Donald Curtis (George), Walter Reed (Jimmy), Jane Jones (Mamie), Whit Bissell (Ward Oates), Lennie Bremen (Headwaiter-Chez Mamie), Jack Gargan, Alex Melesh (Waiters), Vic Romito, Charles Cirillo (Sailors), Eva Mudge, Angela Clarke (Women), Hercules Mendez (Headwaiter), Harry Harvey (Postman), Suzi Crandall (Girl on Street), George Cooper (Bellboy), Luis Alberni (Flower Vendor), Howard Keiser (Newsboy), Herbert Evans (Butler), George Chandler (Bartender), Antonio Filauri (Chef), Hector Sarno (Proprietor), Ervin Richardson (Artist).

Incredibly soppy tear-jerker starring Andrews as a brilliant pianist who abandons writing his masterful concerto after being struck blind in an accident. Socialite Oberon takes sympathy on the composer, and feigns blindness and destitution to gain his confidence. Meanwhile, in her real identity, she offers a large cash prize for the best musical composition, while encouraging him—as the poor, blind girl—to finish his concerto and enter it in the contest. Andrews finally relents and finishes the piece, wins the prize, and then uses the money to restore his sight. He soon falls in love with the wealthy Oberon, whom he considers his benefactress, until he realizes his heart truly belongs to the poor, blind girl, whom he is delighted to find is the very same woman. Entirely too contrived a plot line to be taken seriously, NIGHT SONG is maudlin as the day is long and can only be suffered through by rabid fans of melodrama. Musically, however, the film rates higher. Backed by the New York Philharmonic Symphony Orchestra, conducted by Eugene Ormandy, Artur Rubinstein's performance of the Piano Concerto in C Minor is top notch.

p, Harriet Parsons; d, John Cromwell; w, DeWitt Bodeen, Frank Fenton, Dick

Irving Hyland (based on a story by Hyland); ph, Lucien Ballard; m, Leith Stevens; ed, Harry Marker; md, C. Bakaleinikoff; art d, Albert S. D'Agostino, Jack Okey; set d, Darrell Silvera, Joseph Kish; spec eff, Russell A. Cully; m/l, Jack Brooks, Stevens, "Who Killed 'Er?" Hoagy Carmichael, Fred Spielman, Janice Torre (sung by Carmichael).

Drama/Musical (PR:A MPAA:NR)

NIGHT SPOT*½ (1938) 60m RKO bw

Parkyakarkus [Harry Einstein] (Gashouse), Allan Lane (Pete Cooper), Gordon Jones (Riley), Joan Woodbury (Marge Dexter), Lee Patrick (Flo), Bradley Page (Marty Davis), Jack Carson (Shallen), Frank M. Thomas (Headwaiter), Joseph Crehan (Wayland), Crawford Weaver (Smokey), Cecil Kellaway (Loreyweather), Rollo Lloyd (Vail).

Uneasy mixture of comedy and crime as lead buffoon Parkyakarkus (who had gained a considerable amount of popularity from regular appearances on Eddie Cantor's radio show) tries to drum up some laughs while undercover cop Lane gathers evidence from the orchestra pit (he poses as a trumpet player) to prove that gangster/club owner Page is in fact running a gem-smuggling operation. This was Allan "Rocky" Lane's [Harry Albertshart] first role as a leading man; he went on to become a major figure in B westerns. This was the premiere screen appearance for the singing, dancing Woodbury, who went on to play in more than 70 features in a 15-year period, then retired from the cinema to produce and direct stage plays and operas.

p, Robert Sisk; d, Christy Cabanne; w, Lionel Houser (based on a story by Anne Jordan; ph, Nicholas Musuraca; ed, Harry Marker; m/l, "There's Only One Way to Say 'I Love You,'" Sam H. Stept, Herman Ruby.

Comedy/Crime (PR:A MPAA:NR)

NIGHT STAGE TO GALVESTON** (1952) 61m COL bw

Gene Autry (Himself), Pat Buttram (Himself), Virginia Huston (Ann Bellamy), Thurston Hall (Col. Bellamy), Judy Nugent (Cathy Evans), Robert Livingston (Adj. Gen. Slaydon), Harry Cording (Ted Driscoll), Robert Bice (Capt. Yancey), Frank Sully 3(Kelly), Clayton Moore (Clyde Chambers), Frank Rawls (Capt. Kramer), Steve Clark (Old Ranger), Harry Lauter (Evans), Robert Peyton (T. J. Wilson), Lois Austin (Mrs. Wilson), Kathleen O'Malley, Riley Hill, Dick Alexander, Boyd Stockman, Bob Woodward, Sandy Sanders, Ben Welden, Gary Goodwin, "Champion, Jr."

This time out, Autry becomes incensed by the misuses of power practiced by the Texas law enforcement officers (beatings, bribings, killings, and robbings) and he dons his old Texas Ranger uniform (the Rangers having been retired years ago) and puts an end to the corruption. Between bouts of self-righteous indignation he manages to sing a few sagebrush tunes including "Down In Slumberland," "Eyes Of Texas," and "A Heart as Big as Texas." Sidekick Pat Buttram warbles "Yellow Rose of Texas." The black-and-white prints were toned by the Sepiatone process. (See GENE AUTRY series, Index.)

p, Armand Schaefer; d, George Archainbaud; w,Norman S. Hall; ph, William Bradford; m, Mischa Bakaleinikoff; ed, James Sweeney; art d, Charles Clague.

Western Cas. (PR:A MPAA:NR)

NIGHT THE CREATURES CAME (SEE: ISLAND OF TERROR, 1967)

NIGHT THE LIGHTS WENT OUT IN GEORGIA, THE** (1981) 110m New Realm/AE c

Kristy McNichol (Amanda Child), Dennis Quaid (Travis Child), Mark Hamill (Conrad), Sunny Johnson (Melody), Don Stroud (Seth), Arlen Dean Snyder (Andy), Barry Corbin (Wimbish), Lulu McNichol (Boogie Woogie), Royce Clark (Luther), Marilyn Hickey (Woman on Bus), Jerry Rushing (L.C.), Jerry Campbell (Odie), Maxwell Morrow, Bill Bribble, Lonnie Smith (Boys), Elaine Falone (Verna), Terry Browning (Wanda), Barrie Geisinger (B.G.), Ellen Saland (Nellie), J. Don Ferguson (Hawkins), S. Victoria Marlowe (Woman with Hawkins), William Phillips (Texan), Fred Covington (Man in Jail), Ralph Pace (Judge), Nikola Colton (Court Officer), Cindy Partlow (Mavis), Peter Bridgemen (Cook), Wanda Strange (Woman), Bobby Leroux (Elmer), Harry Wilcox (Norman), Rita Teeter (Fat Woman), Robert Harrison, Jr. (Dishwasher), Lisa Riblet (Luther's Daughter), Lit Connah, Elsie Sligh (Elderly Women), Roger Teeter (Clerk), Charles Franzen (Bus Driver), Terry Beaver (Sheriff), Luther McLaughlin 3(Clerk), Anne Haney (Waitress), Joan Riordan 1(Barmaid), Ron Maxwell (Policeman), Debbie Strudas, Anita Haynes, Danny Nelson, R. P. Noren, Michael Massey, Linda Stephens, Wayne Sharpnack, Keith Allison, Jim Stabile, Robert "Bubba" Dean, Scott MacLellan, Kirk Johnson, Ruth Cameron, John Edson, White Trash Band.

Ho-hum country music saga starring Quaid as an aspiring singer, and McNichol as his pesky, ambitious younger sister who drags him kicking and screaming (for what seems interminably longer than 110 minutes) to fame and fortune in Nashville. Just for the record, the film has nothing whatsoever to do with the song on which it was supposed to be based.

p, Elliot Geisinger, Howard Kuperman, Ronald Saland, Howard Smith; d, Ronald F. Maxwell; w, Bob Bonney (based on a song by Bobby Russell); ph, Bill Butler, Fred Batka (CFI Color); m, David Shire; ed, Anne Goursaud; prod d, Gene Rudolf; cos, Joseph G. Aulisi.

Drama Cas. (PR:C MPAA:PG)

NIGHT THE SILICATES CAME (SEE: ISLAND OF TERROR, 1967)

NIGHT THE SUN CAME OUT, THE (SEE: WATERMELON MAN, 1970)

NIGHT THE WORLD EXPLODED, THE*½ (1957) 64m Clover/COL bw

Kathryn Grant (Laura Hutchinson), William Leslie (Dr. David Conway), Tris Coffin (Dr. Ellis Morton), Raymond Greenleaf (Gov. Cheney), Charles Evans (Gen. Bartes), Frank Scannell (Sheriff Quinn), Marshall Reed (General's Aide), Fred Coby (Ranger Brown), Paul Savage (Ranger Kirk), Terry Frost (Foreman).

The title just about sums up the plot of this dull science-fiction outing which sees scientists Leslie, Coffin, and their assistant Grant fretting over the discovery of E-112, a new element from the center of the Earth which explodes rocks when exposed to air. The solution, you ask? Simple. Flood all the low-lying areas of the world so that it is impossible for air to reach the rocks and the Earth won't explode. What would we do without these heroic, quick-thinking eggheads? Grant married Bing Crosby the year of this dull film's release, which guaranteed her a good living despite the impact of such offerings as this.

p, Sam Katzman; d, Fred F. Sears; w, Luci Ward, Jack Natteford; ph, Benjamin H. Kline; ed, Paul Borofsky; md, Ross DiMaggio; art d, Paul Palmentola.

Science Fiction (PR:A MPAA:NR)

NIGHT THEY KILLED RASPUTIN, THE** (1962, Fr./Ital.) 87m Vanguard-Faro-Explorer/Brigadier bw (LES NUITS DE RASPOUTINE; L'ULTIMO ZAR; AKA: GIANT MONSTER; THE NIGHTS OF RASPUTIN)

Edmund Purdom (Rasputin), Gianna Maria Canale (Czarina Alexandra), John Drew Barrymore (Prince Yousoupoff), Jany Clair (Irina Yousoupoff), Ugo Sasso (Czar), Giulia Rubini, Livio Lorenzon, Nerio Bernardi, Miranda Campa, Marco Guglielmi, Ivo Garrani, Maria Grazia Buccella, Michele Malaspina, Rita Rubirosa, Feodor Chaliapin, Enrico Glori, Yvette Lebon, Elida Day.

Fairly inaccurate biography of the rise and fall of the mad monk Rasputin (played with a certain amount of flair by Purdom), with specific concentration given to the several attempts on his life. Barrymore plays the heroic prince who lures the monk to his eventual, though almost comically difficult, doom. Barrymore's father had played the same role in 1932. Though released in color in Europe, American theater prints are in black and white. For a closer look at the real story, and terrific performances, see the French RASPUTIN of 1939 with Harry Baur playing the mad monk, and RASPUTIN AND THE EMPRESS, 1932 with Lionel Barrymore wildly essaying the role.

p, Vincent Fotre; d, Pierre Chenal; w, Ugo Liberatore, Chenal, Andre Tabet (based on a story by Chenal, Tabet); ph, Adalberto Albertini; m, Angelo Francesco Lavagnino; ed, Antonietta Zita; art d, Arrigo Equini.

Historical (PR:C MPAA:NR)

NIGHT THEY RAIDED MINSKY'S, THE*** (1968) 100m Tandem/UA c (GB: THE NIGHT THEY INVENTED STRIPTEASE)

Jason Robards [Jr.] (Raymond Paine), Britt Ekland (Rachel Schpitendavel), Norman Wisdom (Chick Williams), Forrest Tucker (Trim Houlihan), Harry Andrews (Jacob Schpitendavel), Joseph Wiseman (Louis Minsky), Denholm Elliott (Vance Fowler), Elliott Gould (Billy Minsky), Jack Burns (Candy Butcher), Bert Lahr (Professor Spats), Gloria LeRoy (Mae Harris), Eddie Lawrence (Scratch), Dexter Maitland (Duffy), Lillian Hayman (Singer in Speakeasy), Richard Libertini (Pockets), Judith Lowry (Mother Annie), Will B. Able (Clyde), Mike Elias, Frank Shaw (Immigration Officers), Chanin Hale (Valerie), Ernestine Barrett, Kelsey Collins, Marilyn D'Honau, Kathryn Doby, Joann Lehmann, Dorothea MacFarland, Billie Mahoney, Carolyn Morris, June Eve Story, Helen Wood (Minsky's Girls), Herbie Faye (Waiter), Joe E. Marks (Costume Shop Proprietor), Fats Thomas, Reno Pesauri (Stagehands), Rudy Vallee (Narrator).

The rise of burlesque theater is chronicled in this lively, bawdy, and charmingly tasteless comedy produced and co-written by Norman Lear and directed by William Friedkin. The main thrust of the plot involves Amish-raised girl Ekland who rejects her upbringing and travels to the New York City of the 1920s seeking to convert lost souls as a religious-scene dancer. Soon she finds herself embroiled in the wild world of Robards, Jr. who is the main attraction of the National Winter Garden theater leased from him by Minsky (Gould). Robards, Jr. circulates the rumor that new-girl-in-town Ekland will soon be performing a famed risque dance number at a special midnight show, when in reality she intends to do a very innocent Bible dance (he wants to embarrass a conservative vice-fighting society when they send the cops in to raid the joint). That night, Ekland's father appears to reclaim his daughter, a gangster wants to make her his moll, and a fight ensues between Robards, Jr. and his partner Wisdom over her affections. When Ekland gets on stage before a packed house to do her dance, her father tries to stop her and accidentally rips her dress. The enthusiastic response of the crowd eggs Ekland on and she proceeds to strip off her clothes in a dance of wild abandon. Down to the bare essentials, she reaches out to the disapproving Robards and the top of her dress falls off, which is greeted by a surprised roar of approval from the crowd, and the door being kicked open by the cops. The patrons scramble for the exits, and a new American art form, the striptease, is born. A fun film filled with loads of laughs, atmosphere, and nostalgia. The period flavor of the picture is superb. Producer Lear was able to talk the New York City authorities into delaying demolition of a whole block of condemned buildings on the East Side until the location shots had been completed. Songs include: "The Night They Raided Minsky's," sung by Vallee; "Take Ten Terrific Girls But Only 9 Costumes," sung by Vallee and Maitland; "How I Love Her," and "Perfect Gentleman," sung by Robards, Jr. and Wisdom; "You Rat, You," sung by Hayman, "Penny Arcade," and "Wait For Me."

p, Norman Lear; d, William Friedkin; W, Arnold Schulman, Sidney Michaels, Lear (based on the novel by Rowland Barber); ph, Andrew Laszlo (DeLuxe Color); m, Charles Strouse; ed, Ralph Rosenblum; prod d, William and Jean Eckart; md, Philip J. Lang; art d, John Robert Lloyd; set d, John Godfrey; cos, Anna Hill Johnstone; ch, Danny Daniels; m/l, Strouse, Lee Adams.

Comedy Cas. (PR:C-O MPAA:M)

NIGHT THEY ROBBED BIG BERTHA'S, THE zero (1975) 87m Scotia American c

Hetty Galen *(Big Bertha)*, Robert Nichols *(Professor)*, Doug Hale *(Corncob)*, Gary Allen *(Wilbur)*, Josie Johnson *(Sara Sue)*, Bill Moses *(Rufus)*, Walter Guthrie *(Sheriff)*, Frank Nastasi *(Chief White Eagle)*, Laura Sayer *(Priscilla)*, Terrell Bennett *(Preacherman)*, Kathleen Devine *(Savannah)*, Mary Mendum *(Veronica)*, Mike Tucci *(Lou)*, Harrison Ressler *(Manny)*, Chuck Ransdell *(Robbie)*, Bob Wier *(George)*, Christa Kale *(Urchin)*, Glenda Pierce *(Flora Mae)*, George Ellis *(Henry)*, Don Higdon *(Barnibus)*, Jay Mann *(Newscaster)*, Emily Bell *(Faith)*, Joan Jaffe *(Mrs. Oxhammer)*, Joyce Lee *(Mrs. Hornsby)*, Paige Connor *(Orphan)*, Maurice Hunt *(Dean)*, Larry Robinson *(Narrator)*.

Galen is the proprietor of the local massage parlor. On the night in question, the evening's usual goings-on are interrupted by the shenanigans of an inept burglar. About as insightful, witty, and intelligent as the title implies.

p&d, Peter Kares; w, (based on a story by Albert T. Viola, Robert Vervoordt from an idea by Robert N. Langworthy).

Comedy Cas. (PR:O MPAA:R)

NIGHT TIDE½** (1963) 84m Virgo AIP bw

Dennis Hopper *(Johnny Drake)*, Linda Lawson *(Mora)*, Gavin Muir *(Capt. Murdock)*, Luana Anders *(Ellen Sands)*, Marjorie Eaton *(Mme. Romanovitch)*, Cameron *(Woman in Black)*, H. E. West *(Lt. Henderson)*, Tom Dillon *(Merry-Go-Round Owner)*, Ben Roseman, Bruno Ve Sota.

Well-done, CAT PEOPLE-inspired drama starring Hopper as a sailor on leave who becomes attracted to, and then obsessed with, orphan girl Lawson, who plays a mermaid at a seaside resort sideshow. Muir, the sideshow owner, warns Hopper to stay away from the girl, for two men have turned up dead after having been seen in her company. Hopper then learns that Lawson believes herself to be descended from Sea People who must kill during the full moon. Despite these disturbing facts, Hopper accepts an invitation from Lawson to go skindiving. Remaining true to her beliefs, Lawson tries to kill Hopper while underwater, but he escapes and she disappears. Several days later Hopper returns to the sideshow and is shocked to see Lawson's lifeless body on display. Hopper calls the police and Muir is arrested. Muir confesses that he had convinced Lawson she was truly a sea devil from a very young age, and that rather than kill again she drowned herself.

p, Aram Kantarian; d&w, Curtis Harrington; ph, Vilis Lapenieks; m, David Raksin; ed, Jodie Copelan; prod d, Paul Mathison; ch, Benjamin Zemach.

Drama (PR:C MPAA:NR)

NIGHT TIME IN NEVADA½** (1948) 67m REP c

Roy Rogers *(Roy Rogers)*, Adele Mara *(Joan Andrews)*, Andy Devine *(Cookie Bullfincher)*, Grant Withers *(Ran Farrell)*, Marie Harmon *(Toni Bordon)*, Joseph Crehan *(Casey)*, George Carleton *(Jason Howley)*, Holly Bane *(Mort Oakley)*, Steve Darrell *(1st Tramp)*, Jim Nolan *(Jim Andrews)*, Hank Patterson *(2nd Tramp)*, Bob Nolan and the Sons of the Pioneers, Trigger.

Fast-paced, action-packed Rogers outing which opens with a thrilling train robbery perpetrated by villain Withers who needs the cattle (which he will convert to cash) to cover a theft from Mara's trust fund. Unfortunately for him, the cattle belong to Rogers, and Roy rides out to capture the varmint. Eventually Rogers confronts Withers, and a vicious fist-fight ensues in the back of a runaway truck. Roy catches his breath while singing the tunes: "Big Rock Candy Mountain," "Night Time in Nevada," "Sweet Loredo Lou," and "Over Nevada" (the last two songs are backed by The Sons of the Pioneers who made their final appearance with Rogers in this film).

p, Edward J. White; d, William Witney; w, Sloan Nibley; ph, Jack Marta (Trucolor); m, Dale Butts; ed, Tony Martinelli; md, Morton Scott; art d, Frank Hotaling; set d, John McCarthy, Jr.; spec eff, Howard Lydecker, Theodore Lydecker; m/l, Richard W. Pascoe, Will E. Dulmage, H. O'Reilly Clint, Tim Spencer, Edward Morrissey, Bob Nolan.

Western Cas. (PR:A MPAA:NR)

NIGHT TO REMEMBER, A½** (1942) 91m COL bw

Loretta Young *(Nancy Troy)*, Brian Aherne *(Jeff Troy)*, Jeff Donnell *(Anne Carstairs)*, William Wright *(Scott Carstairs)*, Sidney Toler *(Inspector Hankins)*, Gale Sondergaard *(Mrs. DeVoe)*, Donald MacBride *(Bolling)*, Lee Patrick *(Polly Franklin)*, Don Costello *(Eddie Turner)*, Blanche Yurka *(Mrs. Walter)*, Richard Gaines *(Lingle)*, James Burke *(Pat Murphy)*, Billy Benedict *(Messenger Boy)*, Cyril Ring *(Man)*, Eddie Dunn *(Mathews)*, George Chandler *(Taxi Driver)*, John H. Dilson *(Coroner)*, Cy Kendall *(Louis Kaufman)*, Ralph Curly *(Detective)*, Ralph Peters *(Taxi Driver)*, Gary Owen *(Mailman)*, William "Billy" Newill.

Aherne is a novelist who specializes in murder mysteries. His wife, Young, persuades him to leave their apartment, moving instead to a basement flat located in Greenwich Village. There she hopes he will find the ambience to at last complete a romantic story he has been trying to write. But Young's intentions go awry when this new address proves to be the worst place imaginable for a writer trying to keep his mind off murder. Some strange things start happening, though neither can quite put a finger on what is really going on. An almost entirely naked corpse turns up in the back yard. The cops take up the case without much success, which is all Aherne needs to get his juices flowing. He sets out to solve the murder himself, eventually piecing together the clues until the crime is solved. A thriller of the most ordinary order, this film is troubled with too many ingredients put into too small a package. The script is overwritten, dragging on the proceedings much longer than need be, with some extraneous characters that would best have been left out. The result is an overlong programmer that clearly could have used some cutting. What makes the film work on any level is good lead performances by Aherne and Young. These two thespians give weight to their characters, making what could have been routine just a little better than average. Young's career was marked with ups and downs and this was a rather forgettable addition to her body of work.

p, Samuel Bischoff; d, Richard Wallace; w, Richard Flournoy, Jack Henley (based on the story by Kelley Roos); ph, Joseph Walker; m, Werner R. Heymann; ed, Charles Nelson; md, Morris Stoloff; art d, Lionel Banks.

Crime (PR:A MPAA:NR)

NIGHT TO REMEMBER, A**** (1958, Brit.) 123m RANK bw

Kenneth More *(Herbert Lightoller)*, Ronald Allen *(Clarke)*, Robert Ayres *(Peuchen)*, Honor Blackman *(Mrs. Lucas)*, Anthony Bushell *(Capt. Rostron)*, John Cairney *(Murphy)*, Jill Dixon *(Mrs. Clarke)*, Jane Downs *(Mrs. Lightoller)*, James Dyrenforth *(Col. Gracie)*, Michael Goodliffe *(Thomas Andrews)*, David McCallum *(Bride)*, George Rose *(Joughin)*, Ralph Michael *(Yates)*, Kenneth Griffith *(Phillips)*, Frank Lawton *(Chairman)*, Michael Bryant *(Moody)*, Harriette Johns *(Lady Richard)*, Richard Leech *(Murdoch)*, Alec McCowen *(Cottan)*, Tucker McGuire *(Mrs. Brown)*, John Merivale *(Lucas)*, Laurence Naismith *(Capt. Smith)*, Russell Napier *(Capt. Lord)*, Redmond Phillips *(Hoyle)*, Joseph Tomelty *(Dr. O'Laughlin)*, Patrick Waddington *(Sir Richard)*, Jack Watling *(Boxhall)*, Geoffrey Bayldon *(Evans)*, Cyril Chamberlain *(Q.M. Rowe)*, Richard Clarke *(Gallagher)*, Bee Duffell *(Mrs. Farrell)*, Harold Goldblatt *(Guggenheim)*, Gerald Harper *(3rd Officer*, Carpathia*)*, Richard Hayward *(Victualling Manager)*, Thomas Heathcote *(3rd Steward)*, Danuta Karell *(Polish Mother)*, Andrew Keir *(Engineer Officer Hesketh)*, Christina Lubicz *(Polish Girl)*, Barry MacGregor *(Gibson)*, Eddie Malin *(Steward No. 5)*, Patrick McAlinney *(Farrell)*, Helen Misener *(Mrs. Straus)*, Mary Monahan *(Kate)*, Howard Pays *(Lowe)*, Philip Ray *(Clergyman*, Carpathia*)*, Harold Siddons *(Stone)*, Julian Somers *(Bull)*, Tim Turner *(Groves)*, Meier Tzelniker *(Straus)*, Alan Frank, Tom Naylor, John Richardson, Sean Connery.

The sinking of the great luxury liner *Titanic* is the subject of this spectacular, well-acted, and brilliantly directed film. The night all the world remembers is April 14, 1912 when the great ship struck an iceberg and sank, taking to the bottom with her 1,513 passengers and crew members (out of a total complement of 2,224 on board), sinking on the fifth day of her maiden voyage from Queenstown to New York. Although Kenneth More is ostensibly the star of this film, the production is the result of a great team effort with more than 200 speaking parts. The story, based on Lord's popular book, recounts the sailing of the *Titanic*, billed as the "unsinkable ship," and its inevitable voyage toward the Grand Banks of Newfoundland and doom. Brief scenes of the passengers are shown—those in first class, those in steerage—as well as the crew members, from officers to stewards and seamen, the central figure being More. As second officer Lightoller, More's perspective is the focal point of the events surrounding the mammoth tragedy. He witnesses the passengers settling into their quarters and the routine operations of the ship's progress as it ploughs across the tranquil Atlantic. We see the rich in their luxurious suites, and the second-class passengers envying them, and the steerage travelers just happy to be making the voyage to America despite their cramped quarters below decks. Early on, the communications cabin is swamped with messages from the wealthy passengers asking for stock prices, and arranging for their receptions in Manhattan. Ominously, the wireless operator is so swamped with these messages that he falls behind in sending to the bridge the all-important weather reports, particularly those sightings of icebergs drifting south from the polar regions to the sea lanes. "Slices of life" show McCallum as the ship's radio operator, Naismith as the ship's captain, Goodliffe as the ship's designer, McGuire as the robust "Unsinkable" Molly Brown, and Bushell as the heroic captain of the ancient *Carpathia* who drove his ship near destruction to cover the 58 miles between it and the *Titanic* after receiving the SOS signal. (The *Carpathia* almost burst its boilers in steaming to the rescue in four-and-a-half hours to pluck 711 passengers from their lifeboats. Most of the film depicts in detail exactly *how* the disaster occurred, with the 46,000-ton liner striking the berg and having a 300-foot gash made through three of her four watertight boiler rooms by an underwater spur of the berg which ripped the vessel open like a tin can. Fast cuts show how the passengers are calmly roused and taken to the lifeboats—of which there were too few—so that only the women and children and crew members needed to man the boats are lowered while paupers and millionaires remain on board. Those remaining heroically sing along with the ship's band the tunes of the day, particularly an old hymm, "Nearer My God to Thee." Using the facts of the event, Baker constructed a brillant and startling film and Ambler's script is uncluttered with fictional side episodes; here the facts are as dramatic as any imagined tale. The film received a small budget, only $1,680,000, but it suggests a much more expensive price tag. All the acting is superb and underplayed. Costumes, settings, and special effects are outstanding. A NIGHT TO REMEMBER is superior to the Fox production TITANIC of 1953 (albeit that film, despite its melodramatic core and the fact that it was shot in the studio tank, was technically impressive). A weaker effort was made by the British in 1929 in a film called ATLANTIC. A NIGHT TO REMEMBER was a critical success but received only lukewarm box-office support.

p, William McQuitty; d, Roy Baker; w, Eric Ambler (based on the book by Walter Lord); ph, Geoffrey Unsworth; m, William Alwyn; ed, Sidney Hayers; md, Muir Matheson; art d, Alex Vetchinsky; cos, Yvonne Caffin.

Historical Disaster Cas. (PR:A MPAA:NR)

NIGHT TRAIN***** (1940, Brit.) 90m GAU/FOX bw (GB: GESTAPO; NIGHT TRAIN TO MUNICH)

Margaret Lockwood *(Anna Bomasch)*, Rex Harrison *(Gus Bennett)*, Paul [Henreid] von Hernreid *(Karl Marsen)*, Basil Radford *(Charters)*, Naunton Wayne *(Caldicott)*, James Harcourt *(Axel Bomasch)*, Felix Aylmer *(Dr. Federicks)*, Wyndham Goldie *(Dryton)*, Roland Culver *(Roberts)*, Eliot Makeham *(Schwab)*, Raymond Huntley *(Kampenfeldt)*, Austin Trevor *(Capt. Prada)*, Kenneth Kent *(Controller)*, C.V. France *(Adm. Hassinger)*, Frederick [Fritz] Valk *(Gestapo Officer)*, Morland Graham *(Attendant)*, Billy Russell, Irene Handl, Pardoe Woodman, Albert Lieven, Edward Baxter, J.H. Roberts, David Horne, G.H. Mulcaster, Ian

Fleming, Wilfrid Walter, Jane Cobb, Charles Oliver, Torin Thatcher, Pat Williams, Winifred Oughton, Hans [John] Wengraf.

One of the finest spy dramas ever made, this film reflects the immense talents of the brilliant British director, Reed, and of scripters Launder and Gilliat. The film opens with a tranquil scene of the Alps, the camera closing upon a mansion, a wall, then a window—behind which uniformed men stand about a ranting figure, obviously Hitler haranguing his generals. His fist smashes down upon a map of Czechoslovakia. Newsreel footage then shows German troops entering that conquered country; Lockwood is shown being arrested. She is Harcourt's daughter and the Nazis are seeking him; he is an armor-plate expert with secrets the Nazis want, but he has fled to England. As an inmate of a Nazi concentration camp, Lockwood meets another prisoner, Henreid. Together the two plan and execute an escape, fleeing to England where Lockwood is instructed to contact music hall performer Harrison in order to see her father. Harrison is really a British secret agent who vies with Henreid for Lockwood's affections. She is attracted more to Harrison and his whimsical ways than to the more unbending Henreid. In a short time Lockwood and Harcourt are duped into accompanying Henreid, and they are abducted by U-boat and taken to Germany where the Nazis plan to extract information on armor-plating from Harcourt. Harrison follows and penetrates the Reich Naval Ministry in Berlin, posing as a German major. His credentials are minutely inspected but he convinces officials in the hierarchy that he is the genuine article, a junker, and learns the whereabouts of Lockwood and Harcourt, using the Imperial backgrounds of officials (who have photos on their desks of Hindenburg and the Kaiser, not of Hitler, the upstart) and their natural dislike for the Nazis to win them over. Harrison discovers that Lockwood and Harcourt are on the night train to Munich, actually the last peacetime train traveling from Germany to Switzerland. On board the train Harrison contacts Lockwood and Harcourt and, with the help of Wayne and Radford (the aloof funny characters in Alfred Hitchcock's THE LADY VANISHES), he is able to free the two from the Nazis. Henreid and a special squad of SS men trail the trio as it makes for the border and the final chase ends on cable cars with Harrison and Henreid dueling with pistols. (The switching of cable cars and Harrison's diving leap onto a passing car were later used expansively in the WW II film WHERE EAGLE'S DARE.) In the end, Harrison escorts Harcourt and Lockwood, the object of his heart, to Switzerland and safety. NIGHT TRAIN is not only action-jammed, with one harrowing scene piled upon another, but it is not broadly played; Reed employed subtlety instead of bravado. This film was made early in 1940 when WW II had just begun and it does not evidence the kind of bitter viewpoint the British would later adopt toward the subhuman Nazis. In this film the Germans remain an enemy of old but with some vestiges of chivalry and honor; at least Henreid's character evinces some of these qualities. Harrison is perfect as the daring, suave British spy and Lockwood gives a fine performance as does Henreid. Although it is obvious from the start that he is the enemy, he deceptively presents an image of basic decency, although there in really none in him. Reed provides a gripping, razor-edge melodrama that mounts to a stunning climax. This film is one of the 10 top spy productions ever made.

p, Edward Black; d, Carol Reed; w, Sydney Gilliat, Frank Launder (based on a story by Gordon Wellesley); ph, Otto Kanturek; ed, R.E. Dearing; md, Louis Levy; art d, Vetchinsky.

Spy Drama **Cas.** **(PR:A MPAA:NR)**

NIGHT TRAIN FOR INVERNESS½** (1960, Brit.) 69m Danzigers/PAR bw

Norman Wooland *(Roy Lewis)*, Jane Hylton *(Marion)*, Denis Waterman *(Ted Lewis)*, Silvia Francis *(Ann Lewis)*, Irene Arnold *(Mrs. Wall)*, Valentine Dyall *(Ken)*, Howard Lang *(Sergeant)*, Colin Tapley *(Jackson)*, Nancy Nevinson, Kaplan Kaye, Arnold Bell, Alastair Hunter, Rosamund Lesley, John Moulder-Brown, Josephine Stuart, Anton Rodgers, Larry Noble, Brian Nissen, Eric Dodson, Paddy Webster, Jack Melford, Adrian Blount.

Wooland is released from prison after serving a sentence for embezzlement. He kidnaps his son (Waterman), not knowing the boy is diabetic. Without his twice daily insulin injections Waterman will die, so a manhunt is launched by the police to find the pair and tragedy is averted. Good drama but nothing spectacular by one of Danziger's ablest directors of tidy little thrillers.

p, Edward J. Danziger, Harry Lee Danziger; d, Ernest Morris; w, Mark Grantham; ph, Jimmy Wilson.

Drama **(PR:C MPAA:NR)**

NIGHT TRAIN TO MEMPHIS*½ (1946) 66m REP bw

Roy Acuff *(Roy)*, Allan ["Rocky"] Lane *(Dan Acuff)*, Adele Mara *(Constance)*, Irving Bacon *(Rainbow)*, Joseph Crehan *(Stevenson)*, Emma Dunn *(Ma Acuff)*, Roy Barcroft *(Chad Morgan)*, Kenne Duncan *(Asa Morgan)*, LeRoy Mason *(Wilson)*, Nicodemus Stewart *(Porter)*, Nina Mae McKinney *(Maid)*, Francis McDonald *(Doctor)*, Smoky Mountain Boys.

Tedious hillbilly drama starring Acuff as a happy-go-lucky Tennessee mountain lad who tries to convince his fellow mountain folk, and his brother Lane, that the nasty railroad that runs through the area isn't all bad. After all, Lane is in love with the railroad owner's daughter Mara (he doesn't know who she is, of course). Racist treatment of Stewart and McKinney for comedy's sake leaves a bad taste.

p, Dorrell and Stuart McGowan; d, Lesley Selander; w, D. and S. McGowan; ph, William Bradford; m, Dale Butts; ed, Tony Martinelli; md, Morton Scott; art d, Fred A. Ritter; set d, John McCarthy, Jr.; spec eff, Howard and Theodore Lydecker; m/l, Beasley Smith, Marvin Hughes, Owen Bradley, Mel Force, Fred Rose, Roy Acuff, Odell McLeod.

Drama **(PR:A MPAA:NR)**

NIGHT TRAIN TO MUNDO FINE* (1966) 89m Cardoza-Francis/Hollywood Star Pictures bw

Coleman Francis *(Griffin)*, Anthony Cardoza *(Landis)*, Harold Saunders *(Cook)*, John Carradine *(Train Engineer)*, John Morrison *(Joe)*, George Prince *(Cherokee Jack)*, Lanell Cado *(Ruby Chastain)*, Tom Hanson *(Bayieu Chastain)$, Julian Baker (Sheriff)*, Charles Harter *(Old Man)*, Elaine Gibford *(Old Man's Daughter)*, Bruce Love *(Newspaper Reporter)*, Nick Raymond, Clarence Walker *(Policemen)*, Richard Lance *(Priest/Jaime Russell)*.

Director Francis plays an escaped convict who hooks up with aimless adventure-seeker (and coproducer) Cardoza. They join a band of mercenary soldiers who intend to invade Cuba. Though Francis and Cardoza merely want to make some quick cash and have no vested interest in the struggle, they find themselves dragged onto the island anyway, where they are captured by Castro's army. Eventually they escape and make their way back to the U.S., where Francis is re-arrested. Shot on 16-mm stock with a reported budget of only $30,000, and looking its cost, the film was theatrically released on 35 mm. *Mundo Fine* means the end of the world. The end of the line seems more like it for this cheap thriller made by the team responsible for THE BEAST OF YUCCA FLATS (1961).

p, Anthony Cardoza, Coleman Francis; d&w, Francis; ph, Herb Roberts; m, John Bath; ed, J. H. Russell; m/l, Ray Gregory.

Adventure **(PR:A MPAA:NR)**

NIGHT TRAIN TO MUNICH (SEE: NIGHT TRAIN, 1940, Brit.)

NIGHT TRAIN TO PARIS** (1964, Brit.) 65m Lippert/FOX bw

Leslie Nielsen *(Alan Holiday)*, Alizia Gur *(Catherine Carrel)*, Dorinda Stevens *(Olive Davies)*, Eric Pohlmann *(Krogh)*, Edina Ronay *(Julie)*, Andre Maranne *(Louis Vernay)*, Cyril Raymond *(Inspector Fleming)*, Stanley Morgan *(Plainclothesman)*, Hugh Latimer *(Jules Lemoine)*, John Quayle *(Jackson)*, Simon Oates *(Saunders)*, John Busby *(Bearman)*, Jenny White *(Vernay's Model)*, George Little *(Train Porter)*, Jacques Cey *(Coffier)*, Jack Melford *(P.C. Inspector)*, Trevor Reid *(Policeman on Train)*, Neal Arden *(Inspector Escalier)*, Alexandra Beauclerc *(Anna)*, Sylvia Lewis Jones *(Christine)*, Juliet Hunt *(June)*, Patricia Maynard *(Gail)*.

Average espionage thriller starring Nielsen as a former OSS agent who agrees to help Gur get some important tapes to Paris as a favor to old friend Latimer. When Latimer is killed, Nielsen realizes that the tapes contain important defense information and he spends the rest of the film trying to stay one step ahead of the rival agents. Eventually he learns that Gur is actually working for the other side, but he is able to defeat her and turn her and the tapes over to the authorities. Nice scenery doesn't help much. Songs include: "Night Train to Paris," "Chit Chat," "Look After My Baby," "Hey There Girl" (Brian Potter, Graham Dee; sung by Troy Dante and the Infernos).

p, Robert L. Lippert, Jack Parsons; d, Robert Douglas; w, Henry Cross [Harry Spalding]; ph, Arthur Lavis; m, Kenny Graham; ed, Robert Winter; md, Phillip Martell; art d, George Provis; makeup, Harold Fletcher.

Spy **(PR:A MPAA:NR)**

NIGHT UNTO NIGHT** (1949) 84m WB bw

Ronald Reagan *(John)*, Viveca Lindfors *(Ann)*, Broderick Crawford *(Shawn)*, Rosemary De Camp *(Thalia)*, Osa Massen *(Lisa)*, Craig Stevens *(Tony)*, John McGovern *(Willie Shawn)*, Lillian Yarbo *(Josephine)*, Art Baker *(Dr. Poole)*, Erskine Sanford *(Dr. Altheim)*, Lois Austin *(Mrs. Rose)*, Almira Sessions *(Maid)*, Irving Bacon *(Real Estate Agent)*, Ross Ford *(Bellboy)*, Dick Elliott *(Auto Court Manager)*, Ann Burr *(Willa Shawn)*, Jack Mower, Larry Rio, Ramon Ros, Leo White, Paul Panzer, Jack Wise, Billy Bletcher *(Men in Hotel)*, Philo McCullough *(Bus Driver)*, Creighton Hale *(Workman)*, Bing Conley, Joe Devlin *(Truckmen)*, William Haade *(Man in Art Museum)*, Dennis Donnelly *(David the Child)*, Dick Johnstone *(Man with Dog)*.

Reagan plays a biochemist who travels to a secluded area on the Gulf Coast of Florida when he learns that he has been stricken with epilepsy. He rents a beach house from the recently widowed Lindfors to convalesce and continue his work in private. As the days go by the doctor and the lonely widow grow close, but Reagan keeps his medical problem a secret. The dark and beautiful Lindfors has a few secrets as well. Each time she enters the house she and her husband lived in (the one Reagan is renting) she hears her departed spouse's voice. Soon she confides in Reagan and he tries to convince her that the house is not haunted, and it seems to him that her problems are of the mental variety. More trouble arises when Reagan is hit by a violent epileptic fit and his doctor, Baker, informs him that his condition is irreversible and terminal. Deeply depressed, Reagan attempts suicide by walking into a hurricane. Lindfors learns of Reagan's problems and, now in love with him, saves his life and vows to stay by his side. A plodding psychological drama, NIGHT UNTO NIGHT meanders through its underdeveloped script with only a few moments of effectively atmospheric direction to liven things up. The supporting cast is given nothing of interest to do, especially Crawford, who plays a friend of the suffering stars. Reagan's second film after his return from service in WW II, it was also director Siegel's second picture (THE VERDICT, 1946, was the first), and the film was designed as a vehicle for Warner's newest starlet, Swedish actress Lindfors. Unfortunately, the resulting film was so disappointing that Warner Bros. shelved it for two years and it wasn't released until after Lindfors had left the studio. The collaboration did benefit Siegel and Lindfors for a time, however, because they were married in 1949 (divorced in 1953). Siegel would direct Reagan again in THE KILLERS (1964), the actor's last film before seeking the governorship of California.

p, Owen Crump; d, Don Siegel; w, Kathryn Scola (based on the novel by Philip Wylie); ph, Peverell Marley; m, Franz Waxman; ed, Thomas Reilly; md, Leo F.

Forbstein; art d, Hugh Reticker; set d, G. W. Berntsen; cos, Leah Rhodes; spec eff, Harry Barndollar; makeup, Ward Hamilton.

Drama/Romance **(PR:A MPAA:NR)**

NIGHT VISITOR, THE*½ (1970, Swed./U.S.) 102m Hemisphere/UMC c

Max von Sydow *(Salem)*, Trevor Howard *(Inspector)*, Liv Ullmann *(Esther Jenks)*, Per Oscarsson *(Dr. Anton Jenks)*, Rupert Davies *(Clemens the Attorney)*, Andrew Keir *(Dr. Kemp)*, Arthur Hewlett *(Pop)*, Gretchen Franklin *(Mrs. Hansen)*, Jim Kennedy *(Carl)*, Hanne Bork *(Emmie)*, Bjorn Watt Boolsen *(Tokens)*, Lottie Freddie *(Britt)*.

A disappointing thriller made all the more unpalatable by the talent of those involved. Ullmann and Von Sydow became available when MGM turned thumbs down on Fred Zinnemann's picture, A MAN's FATE, so they jumped feet first into this one and one wonders if they bothered to read the silly script. Von Sydow is being housed in a Swedish prison for the insane because he has been convicted of killing his farmhand with an axe. The truth is that he's innocent and the murder was actually done by Ullmann and her physician husband, Oscarsson, when the dead man came upon them as they were burning down Von Sydow's farm buildings. The prison is supposedly impervious to a breakout, but Von Sydow, dressed only in boots and underwear, gets out of the place by using his other clothes as a ladder with which he lowers himself to the icy ground. He races across the frozen wastes to kill his sister, Bork, and Freddie, his one-time girl friend, both of whom refused to testify in his behalf at his trial. Next, he arranges some phony evidence to point the finger at Oscarsson for the murders, then he gets back inside the prison with no one being any the wiser. Oscarsson saw Von Sydow but nobody believes him. Howard is the local police inspector and he thinks that Von Sydow may have done the deed, but the head of the prison says escape is not possible. Von Sydow gets out again, kills Davies (a crooked lawyer), then goes to his own home to finally don an overcoat before he freezes to death. While there, he hacks Ullmann to bits with a hatchet and smears her blood on Oscarsson, who shivers with fear and just hopes that Von Sydow doesn't turn the hatchet on him. Von Sydow gets back inside the prison and Howard arrives at the bloodbath. Oscarsson is raving about what happened and Howard believes him enough to go to the prison where he finds Von Sydow sleeping like a baby in his cell. Howard is ready to call it quits when he hears the peep of a bird. Oscarsson's pet parakeet had secreted himself in the overcoat Von Sydow stole from the house. The picture ends as Von Sydow shrugs; his plot is over. How such eminent people could have become involved with this is a larger mystery than how Von Sydow managed to pull off the escape. Director Benedek, after all, had done THE WILD ONE and DEATH OF A SALESMAN for Stanley Kramer. Then again, he was also responsible for THE KISSING BANDIT, and that should explain a few things. The mixture of accents, Swedish and British, doesn't help, either, and the only reason to see this film is to sit back in bewilderment at something gone so awry.

p, Mel Ferrer; d, Laslo Benedek; w, Guy Elmes (based on the story "Salem Came to Supper" by Samuel Roecca); ph, Henning Kristiansen (Eastmancolor); m, Henry Mancini; ed, Bill Blunden; prod d, P. A. Lundgren; art d, Viggo Bentzon.

Thriller **Cas.** **(PR:C MPAA:GP)**

NIGHT WAITRESS*½ (1936) 59m RKO bw

Margot Grahame *(Helen Roberts)*, Gordon Jones *(Martin Rhodes)*, Vinton Haworth *(Skinner)*, Marc Lawrence *(Dorn)*, Billy Gilbert *(Torre, Cafe Owner)*, Donald Barry *(Mario Rigo)*, Otto Yamaoka *(Fong)*, Paul Stanton *(District Attorney)*, Arthur Loft *(Borgum)*, Walter Miller *(Inspector)*, Anthony Quinn, Charles Murphy *(Hoods)*, Frank Faylen, Dick Miller *(Cops)*, Barbara Pepper *(Blonde)*, Ernie S. Adams *(Crook)*.

Dull waterfront gangster tale starring Grahame as an innocent gal framed on a bond theft who leaves prison and accepts a job as a waitress in a wharf restaurant owned by Gilbert. She soon finds herself in hot water again when a small-time hood is murdered in the cafe while she is on duty. She doesn't want to reveal what she knows about the killing because she is in love with Jones, whom the victim was going to meet. Jones tells Grahame that he was arranging to haul a load of gold bullion for the dead man in his charter boat. Soon Grahame and Jones find themselves trapped between inquisitive police and an angry bunch of hoodlums, both wanting to get their mitts on the gold. Routine and uneventful. Look quickly for an unbilled Anthony Quinn as a mob hit man out to do in Donald Barry.

p, Joseph Henry Steele; d, Lew Landers; w, Marcus Goodrich (based on a story by Golda Draper); ph, Russell Metty; ed, Desmond Marquette; art d, Van Nest Polglase; cos, Edward Stevenson.

Crime **(PR:A MPAA:NR)**

NIGHT WALK (SEE: DEATHDREAM, 1972, Can.)

NIGHT WALKER, THE*½ (1964) 86m UNIV bw

Barbara Stanwyck *(Irene Trent)*, Robert Taylor *(Barry Morland)*, Lloyd Bochner *(The Man in the Dream)*, Hayden Rorke *(Howard Trent)*, Judith Meredith *(Joyce)*, Rochelle Hudson *(Hilda)*, Marjorie Bennett *(Manager)*, Jess Barker *(Malone)*, Pauelle Clark *(Pat)*, Tetsu Komai *(Gardener)*, Ted Durant *(Narrator)*, Kathleen Mulqueen *(Customer)*.

Co-stars Taylor and Stanwyck had been married for 11 years once and the studio thought that they might be able to work with each other with no problems. They were right. There was mutual respect from the pair (who had made two films while wooing but none during their marriage) and they did as well as they could with this confused script by Bloch and cheap-jack effects by Castle. He was 53 and she was 57 when they did the movie and they were both ill-advised to jump into this genre, but the prospect of hefty fees, a piece of the action, and a script by the man who wrote PSYCHO was too much to decline. What they didn't realize was that Bloch wrote the novel upon which Hitchcock based the film and the script was done by Joseph Stefano. Bloch, like Ray Bradbury, is excellent at writing prose, but dialog and the ability to tell a movie story seems to elude them both. Stanwyck is married to blind electronics wizard Rorke and she talks in her sleep. That makes Rorke believe she is having a romantic liaison with someone else. Rorke thinks that someone else is his lawyer, Taylor, but he is innocent of that charge. Stanwyck tells Taylor that she often has dreams of a lover but doesn't know who he is. Stanwyck and Rorke have an argument and she leaves her home. Later, Rorke, while experimenting in his workshop, blows himself to bits. Stanwyck's odd dreams keep going and she is transported to a chapel peopled by waxen images where she is part of a weird wedding ceremony. She is frightened by these nightly mental trips and tells Taylor, who informs her that Rorke had hired a private eye to keep tabs on her. This is Bochner and he is the man who keeps appearing in her dream. Stanwyck's beautician, Meredith, is killed by someone who looks like Rorke, but that's impossible, as Rorke is dead. Or is he? Now Taylor says that Rorke is alive and tried to kill him. Stanwyck and Taylor go into the wrecked laboratory, and Taylor reveals that he was wearing a Rorke mask (Castle used this gimmick in STRAIT-JACKET) and that he is responsible for Rorke's death because he made himself the beneficiary of the man's will, which the blind man signed, not knowing what he was signing. Taylor attempts to kill Stanwyck and is wounded by Bochner, who shows up in the nick of time. Bochner, who was also part of the plot, says that he was married to Meredith and he moves in on Stanwyck. Taylor and Bochner battle each other and fall through the weakened floor of the lab, and Stanwyck can finally sigh with relief. It's a hopeless hodge-podge and the special effects aren't worth the effort. A few chilling moments and a good score are all to recommend this, other than seeing Taylor and Stanwyck togther for the first time in 27 years.

p&d, William Castle; w, Robert Bloch (based on the story "Witches' Friday" by Elizabeth Kata); ph, Harold Stine; m, Vic Mizzy; ed, Edwin H. Bryant; md, Joseph Gershenson; art d, Alexander Golitzen, Frank Arrigo; set d, John McCarthy, Julia Heron; cos, Helen Colvig; spec eff, Charles Spurgeon; makeup, Bud Westmore, Dick Blair, Carl Silvera.

Horror **(PR:C MPAA:NR)**

NIGHT WAS OUR FRIEND*½ (1951, Brit.) 61m Association of Cinema Technicians/Monarch bw

Elizabeth Sellars *(Sally Raynor)*, Michael Gough *(Martin Raynor)*, Ronald Howard *(Dr. John Harper)*, Marie Ney *(Emily Raynor)*, Edward Lexy *(Arthur Glenville)*, Nora Gordon *(Kate)*, John Salew *(Mr. Lloyd)*, Cyril Smith *(Reporter)*, Michael Pertwee *(Young Man)*, Roger Maxwell, Edie Martin, Linda Gray, Felix Felton, Cecil Beran.

After being given up for dead after two years in the jungles of Brazil, Gough reappears. His ordeal has changed the man, leaving his mind unhinged. His wife, Sellars, though now in love with Howard, takes care of her husband. When Gough attacks a man, Sellars tries to get him hospitalized. Finally Gough commits suicide, Sellars is thought to have murdered him but eventually her name is cleared. Potentially interesting psychological material is wasted under the bleak drama, produced with little care or feeling for the material.

p, Gordon Parry; d, Michael Anderson; w, Michael Pertwee (based on the play by Pertwee); ph, Moray Grant.

Drama **(PR:C-O MPAA:NR)**

NIGHT WATCH, THE****** (1964, Fr./Ital.) 118m Playart-FS-Titanus/Consort-Orion bw (LE TROU; IL BUCO)

Michel Constantin *(Geo Cassid)*, Jean Keraudy *(Roland Darban)*, Philippe Leroy *(Manu Borelli)*, Raymond Meunier *(Monseigneur)*, Marc Michel *(Claude Gaspard)*, Andre Bervil *(Warden)*, Eddy Rasimi *(Guard Bouboule)*, Jean-Paul Coquelin *(Guard Grinval)*, Catherine Spaak *(Nicole)*.

Outstanding drama was the last film to be directed by Becker who died shortly after its completion. While awaiting trial for the attempted murder of his wife, Michel is moved into a cell with Keraudy, Constantin, Leroy, and Meunier, who decide to include him in their elaborate escape plan. The film goes into great detail on the mechanics of the escape. Dummies are made, a tunnel is dug, the men build a periscope out of a mirror and a toothbrush to watch for guards, a medicine bottle filled with sand is used as an hourglass so the conspirators can time their shifts, and eventually the tunnel connecting to the city's sewer system is complete. On the day they are to make their escape, Michel is called into the warden's office. There he is informed that his wife has dropped the charges against him. He relates the news to his cellmates, who eye him suspiciously. But he intends to go through with the escape anyway because he still faces a five-year term. As the men are about to make their way down the tunnel, alarms ring and guards appear and stop them; the men then realize that Michel had betrayed them to lighten his sentence. Using a cast of non-professionals, Becker paints a powerful portrait of men in desperate circumstances forced to trust one another out of necessity, against their better instincts. The film is shot in a documentary-like style and contains no music, using only the natural sounds of the prison to convey suspense and tension. American director Don Siegel was surely influenced by THE NIGHT WATCH when he made ESCAPE FROM ALCATRAZ starring Clint Eastwood.

p, Georges Charlot; d, Jacques Becker; w, Becker, Jose Giovanni, Jean Aurel (based on the novel *Le Trou* by Giovanni); ph, Ghislain Cloquet; ed, Marguerite Renoir, Genevieve Vaury; set d, Rino Mondellini; spec eff, Philippe Arthuys.

Prison Drama **(PR:A MPAA:NR)**

NIGHT WATCH** (1973, Brit.) 105m Brut/AE c

Elizabeth Taylor *(Ellen Wheeler)*, Laurence Harvey *(John Wheeler)*, Billie Whitelaw *(Sarah Cooke)*, Robert Lang *(Appleby)*, Tony Britton *(Tony)*, Bill Dean *(Inspector Walker)*, Michael Danvers-Walker *(Sgt. Norris)*, Rosario Serrano *(Dolores)*, Pauline Jameson *(Secretary)*, Linda Hayden *(Girl in Car)*, Kevin Colson *(Carl)*, Laon Maybanke *(Florist)*.

Disappointing murder mystery that fails to thrill—despite a decent performance from Taylor—takes its plot from the 1945 film LADY ON A TRAIN, starring Deanna Durbin, and also reminds one of GASLIGHT and SORRY, WRONG NUMBER (also written by Lucille Fletcher, whose play this was based on). Taylor plays a recently remarried woman (her first husband was killed in an automobile accident while in the company of his mistress) who thinks she sees a murder committed in the deserted house across the courtyard. Harvey, her husband, tells her she imagined it, her girl friend humors her, and soon Taylor begins to think she's going mad. Filled with red herrings and a predictable "twist" ending, NIGHT WATCH is a sorry failure of a suspense film.

p, Martin Poll, George W. George, Barnard Straus; d, Brian G. Hutton; w, Tony Williamson, Evan Jones (based on a play by Lucille Fletcher); ph, Billy Williams (Panavision, Technicolor); m, John Cameron; ed, John Jympson; art d, Peter Murton; set d, Peter James; cos, Valentino; m/l, "The Night Has Many Eyes," George Barrie, Sammy Cahn.

Mystery (PR:C MPAA:PG)

NIGHT WE DROPPED A CLANGER, THE (SEE: MAKE MINE A DOUBLE, 1961, Brit.)

NIGHT WE GOT THE BIRD, THE*½ (1961, Brit.) 82m Rix-Conyers/BL bw

Brian Rix (Bertie Skidmore), Dora Bryan (Julie Skidmore), Leo Franklyn (Victor), Irene Handl (Ma), Liz Fraser (Fay), John Slater (Wolfie Green), Reginald Beckwith (Chippendale Charlie), Robertson Hare (Dr. Vincent), Kynaston Reeves (Mr. Warre-Monger, J.P.), John LeMesurier 3(Clerk of the Court), Ronald Shiner (Cecil Gibson), Basil Lord (Bus Conductor), Vera Pearce (Aunt), Terry Scott (P. C. Lovejoy).

Sophomoric British comedy starring Rix and Bryan as a newlywed couple harassed on their honeymoon by her deceased first husband who has been reincarnated as a South American parrot. The script finds lots of excuses for people to lose their pants and make vulgar, inane sexual jokes that wouldn't amuse a 10-year-old.

p, Brian Rix, Darcy Conyers; d, Conyers; w, Ray Cooney, Tony Hilton, Conyers (based on the play "The Love Birds" by Basil Thomas); ph, S. D. Onions; m, Tommy Watts; ed, Thelma Connell.

Comedy (PR:C MPAA:NR)

NIGHT WIND* (1948) 68m FOX bw

Charles Russell (Ralph Benson), Virginia Christine (Jean Benson), Gary Gray (Johnny Benson), John Ridgely (Walters), James Burke (Sheriff Hamilton), Konstantin Shayne (Dr. Ulding), William Stelling (Barlow), Guy Kingsford (Wilson), Charles Lang (John Steele), Deanna Woodruff (Margie Benson), Flame (Big Dan).

Silly canine drama featuring a brave hound named Flame who is trained for service in WW II. Unfortunately, Flame's master is killed by the Nazis and the pooch retires to a hunting lodge in the States. Those painful puppy memories come back to haunt the veteran doggie years later when three strangers arrive at the lodge. Realizing that one of the men is wearing the trenchcoat worn by his master's killer, the dog attacks the three and reveals them to be German agents spying on an atomic project near the lodge.

p, Sol M. Wurtzel; d, James Tinling; w, Arnold Belgard, Robert G. North (based on a story by North); ph, Benjamin Kline; m, Ralph Stanley; ed, William F. Claxton; art d, George Van Marter; set d, Fay Babcock.

Drama (PR:A MPAA:NR)

NIGHT WITHOUT PITY** (1962, Brit.) 56m Parroch/Golden Era bw

Sarah Lawson (Diana Martin), Neil McCallum (O'Brien), Alan Edwards (Randall), Dorinda Stevens (Girl Friend), Michael Browning (Philip), Patrick Newell (Doctor), Beatrice Varley (Mother), John Moulder Brown (Geoffrey Martin), Brian Weske (Arthur), Vanda Godsell (Tart).

In order to rob a man's factory, two thieves split up. One holds the factory owner's wife and child hostage as the other ransacks the place. A very minor British crime film.

p, Jack Parsons; d, Theodore Zichy; w, Aubrey Cash.

Crime (PR:C MPAA:NR)

NIGHT WITHOUT SLEEP** (1952) 77m FOX bw

Linda Darnell (Julie Bannon), Gary Merrill (Richard Morton, Composer), Hildegarde Neff (Lisa Muller), Joyce MacKenzie (Laura Harkness), June Vincent (Emily Morton), Donald Randolph (Dr. Clarke), Hugh Beaumont (John Harkness), Louise Lorimer (Mrs. Carter), William Forrest (Mr. Carter), Steven Geray (George), Mauri Lynn (Singer), Bill Walker (Henry), Mae Marsh (Maid), Ben Carter (Benny), Sam Pierce (Sam), Sylvia Simms (Phone Operator), Beverly Tyler (Singer), Charles Tannen (Steve Brooks), Harry Seymour (Ned).

Hard-to-believe suspense film featuring Merrill as a psychotic composer who has been warned by his shrink that he has violent tendencies. Awaking one morning out of a drunken stupor, Merrill can't shake the feeling he has murdered a woman during the night. Panicked, he calls his ex-mistress Neff to see if she's all right. She says she's fine, so the distraught composer phones his old friend, movie actress Darnell, who is also doing quite well. (While dialing we are treated to lengthy flashback scenes involving his relationships with these women.) Relieved to find that he hasn't killed either of them, he goes to his bedroom to tell his wife and finds her dead.

p, Robert Bassler; d, Roy Baker; w, Frank Partos, Elick Moll (based on a story by Moll); ph, Lucien Ballard; m, Cyril Mockridge; ed, Nick DeMaggio; md, Lionel Newman; art d, Lyle Wheeler, Addison Hehr; set d, Thomas Little, Paul S. Fox;

cos, Renie; m/l, "Too Late for Spring," Alfred Newman, Haven Gillespie, "Look at Me," Alfred Newman, Ken Darby.

Mystery (PR:C MPAA:NR)

NIGHT WITHOUT STARS*½ (1953, Brit.) 75m Europa/RKO bw

David Farrar (Giles Gordon), Nadia Gray (Alix Delaisse), Maurice Teynac (Louis Malinay), Gilles Queant (Deffand), Gerard Landry (Pierre Chaval), June Clyde (Claire), Robert Ayres (Walter), Clive Morton (Doctor Coulson), Eugene Deckers (Armand), Ina De La Haye ("Mere Roget"), Martin Benson (White Cap).

Farrar stars as a partially blind Britisher in self-imposed exile on the Riviera who meets and falls in love with Gray, the widow of a famed French resistance fighter. When it appears that Gray is somehow involved in smuggling and murder, Farrar ferrets out the truth by having his blindness cured through a delicate operation and then faking his former affliction to gather evidence. Predictable and dull.

p, Hugh Stewart; d, Anthony Pelissier; w, Winston Graham (based on a novel by Graham); ph, Guy Green; m, William Alwyn; ed, John Seabourne; art d, Vetchinsky; cos, Balmain, Julie Harris; m/l, "If You Go," Michel Emer, Geoffrey Parsons.

Crime (PR:A MPAA:NR)

NIGHT WON'T TALK, THE½** (1952, Brit.) 60m Corsair/ABF-Pathe bw

Hy Hazell (Theo Castle), John Bailey (Clayton Hawkins), Mary Germaine (Hazel Carr), Ballard Berkeley (Inspector West), Elwyn Brook-Jones (Martin Soames), Grey Blake (Kenneth Wills), Duncan Lamont (Sgt. Robbins), Sarah Lawson (Susan), Helene Burns, Leslie Weston, Raymond Young, Stuart Pearson.

After an artist's model is found murdered, suspects grow like flowers in spring. The late woman's fiance, Bailey, and his new sweetheart, Germaine, are considered suspects, but when Germaine is nearly murdered herself the cops set a trap. The real killer proves to be Hazell, a sculptress, who had been in love with Bailey herself and wanted no one to get between them. Though a touch predictable, this is fairly intelligent for a minor crime thriller.

p, Harold Richmond; d, Daniel Birt; w, Brock Williams (based on a story by Roger Burford); ph, Brendan J. Stafford.

Crime/Mystery (PR:C MPAA:NR)

NIGHT WORK½** (1930) 94m Pathe bw

Eddie Quillan (Willie), Sally Starr (Mary, Nurse), Frances Upton (Aggie), John T. Murray (Calloway), George Duryea [Tom Keene/Richard Powers] (Harvey Vanderman), Ben Bard (Pinkie), Robert McWade (Phil Reisman), Douglas Scott (Oscar), Addie McPhail (Trixie), Kit Guard (Squint), Georgia Caine (Mrs. Ten Eyck), George Billings (Buster), Charles Clary (Mr. Vanderman), Tom Dugan (Johnny Harris), Arthur Hoyt (George Twining), Billie Bennett (Miss Brown), Tempe Pigott (Flora), Ruth Lyons (Miss Allenby), Nora Lane (Arlene Ogalthorpe), Marjorie "Babe" Kane (Cabaret Singer), Jack Mack (Biff Miller), Arthur Lovejoy (Effeminate Man), Marion Ballou (Mrs. Morgan), Martha Mattox (Mrs. McEvoy), James Donlan (Mr. McEvoy), Harry Bowen (Cabdriver), Ruth Hiatt (Violet Harris), Vincent Barnett (Headwaiter).

Quillan plays a good-hearted department store employee who willingly takes the blame when customers find something wrong with the merchandise. One day his selfless deeds are rewarded when a patron slips him a @10 bill as a tip. Excited by this good fortune, Quillan immediately goes to his bank to deposit the bill. On the way, he inadvertently gives the bill to Starr, a nurse seeking contributions for an orphanage. Soon Quillan learns that he has committed himself to supporting a child, and having taken a liking to Starr and little Scott, he gets another job to beef up his income. His bliss is short-lived however, and Quillan is shocked to learn that a wealthy man, Clary, believes Scott to be his grandson. Claiming that the baby is his son's child, Clary adopts the boy, leaving Quillan to plot ridiculous kidnaping schemes to regain custody. Eventually Quillan proves that Scott is not related to Clary and the child is returned to him. Wanting to give Scott a complete life, Quillan proposes to Starr and she accepts.

p, E. B. Derr; d, Russell Mack; w, Walter De Leon; ph, John Mescall; ed, Joseph Kane; md, Josiah Zuro; art d, Edward Jewell; m/l, "Deep In Your Heart," "I'm Tired of My Tired Man" (Mort Harris, Ted Snyder).

Comedy/Drama (PR:A MPAA:NR)

NIGHT WORK** (1939) 62m PAR bw

Mary Boland (Sybil Fitch), Charlie Ruggles (Homer C. Fitch), Billy Lee (Joe Fitch), Donald O'Connor (Butch Smiley), Clem Bevans (Smokestack Smiley), William Frawley (Bruiser Brown), Joyce Mathews (Patricia Fitch), John Hartley (Windy Wilson), William Haade (Mr. Turk), Edward Gargan (Officer Flannigan).

Ruggles and Boland once again star as husband and wife in this domestic comedy which sees them as apartment managers in a building owned by Ruggles' friend. The couple is left to care for O'Connor, who was orphaned when his father died, and the brunt of the film involves the boy's grandfather being conned into letting his grandson be adopted by the looney couple and their family. Most of the humor is primitive slapstick, but it works.

p, William H. Wright; d, George Archainbaud; w, Monte Brice, Lloyd Corrigan, Lewis R. Foster; ph, Harry Hallenberger; ed, Stuart Gillmore.

Comedy (PR:A MPAA:NR)

NIGHT WORLD½** (1932) 60m UNIV bw

Lew Ayres (Michael Rand), Mae Clarke (Ruth Taylor), Boris Karloff ("Happy" MacDonald), Dorothy Revier (Mrs. "Mac"), Russell Hopton (Klauss, Show Producer), Bert Roach (Tommy), Dorothy Peterson (Edith Blair), Paisley Noon (Clarence), Hedda Hopper (Mrs. Rand), Clarence Muse (Tim Dolan, Doorman), George Raft (Ed Powell), Robert Emmett O'Connor (Policeman), Florence Lake

(Miss Smith), Huntley Gordon *(Jim)*, Gene Morgan *(Joe)*, Greta Granstedt *(Blonde)*, Louise Beavers *(Maid)*, Sammy Blum *(Salesman)*, Harry Woods *(Gang Leader)*, Eddie Phillips *(Vaudevillian)*, Tom Tamarez *(Gigolo)*, Geneva Mitchell *(Florabelle)*, Arletta Duncan *(Cigarette Girl)*, Pat Somerset *(Guest)*, Joe Wallace, Charles Giblyn, Dorothy Granger, Frank Beale, John K. Wells *(Bits)*, Hal Grayson's Recording Orchestra *(Themselves)*, Frankie Farr *(Trick Waiter)*, Amo Ingraham, Alice Adair *(Chorines)*.

Jam-packed programmer with enough plot, stars, and behind-the-camera talent to fill at least two movies, shoe-horned into a B picture format. Gangster Karloff's New York nightclub is the central location for the paths of a wide variety of character types to cross. Hoofer Clarke spots wealthy-but-miserable young souse Ayres drinking himself to death night after night and decides to woo him away from the bottle, which will also solve her problem regarding slimy gangster Raft, who has fixed his sights on her. Ayres' drinking is caused by the fact that he has just learned his mother, Hopper (who was recently acquitted of murdering his father), killed her husband—not out of jealousy—but because she just hated the sight of him. Meanwhile, Karloff becomes enraged when he discovers his wife, Revier, is having an affair with show producer Hopton, so she removes the bullets from his gun, which leaves him helpless when rival racketeers gun him down. Clarke and Ayres witness the murder, but are saved from the gangsters' guns when the cops arrive. A strange and historically fascinating amalgamation of performers who were all rising to stardom after appearing in other films. Karloff and Clarke had just been in FRANKENSTEIN, Raft was fresh from SCARFACE (Karloff was in that one also), and Ayres was coming off an incredible debut in ALL QUIET ON THE WESTERN FRONT. A real curiosity.

p, Carl Laemmle, Jr.; d, Hobart Henley; w, Richard Schayer (based on a story by P. J. Wolfson, Allen Rivkin); ph, Merritt Gerstad; m, Alfred Newman; ed, Maurice Pivar; md, Hal Grayson; ch, Busby Berkeley.

Crime/Drama **(PR:A MPAA:NR)**

NIGHTBEAST*½ (1982) 80m Cinema Enterprises/Amazing Films c

Tom Griffith *(Sheriff Cinder)*, Jamie Zemarel *(Jamie)*, Karin Kardian *(Lisa)*, George Stover *(Steven)*, Don Leifert *(Drago)*, Anne Frith *(Ruth)*, Eleanor Herman *(Mary Jane)*, Richard Dyszel *(Mayor)*, Greg Dohler *(Greg)*, Kim Dohler *(Kim)*, Monica Neff *(Suzie)*, Glenn Barnes *(Glenn)*, Rose Wolfe *(Glenn's Girl)*, Richard Ruxton *(Governor)*, Dennis McGeehan *(Beast)*, Gary Svehla, Dick Svehla, Christopher Gummer, Anne Frith.

In a film clearly inspired by the science fiction monster films of the 1950s, director Dohler has a giant people-munching monster attack the good people of Earth after the creature's ship crash-lands. Nothing appears to stop the bloodthirsty behemoth until an electrical coil is used to fire 30,000 volts through the monster. The strengths of this film lie in its effects. There are some startling uses of gore makeup and other standards of the "man vs. monster" genre. However, the actors aren't given much to do other than stand around and talk. This film doesn't know where to go when there are no special effects to titillate the audience and the final result is disappointing.

p,d&w, Don Dohler; ph, Richard Geiwitz; ed, Dohler; m, Rob Walsh, Jeffrey Abrams, Arlon Ober, Leonard Rogowski; spec eff, John Dods, Ernest D. Farino, Kinetic Image; makeup, Larry Schlechter, James Chai, David Donoho, Amodio Giordano.

Science Fiction/Horror **Cas.** **(PR:C-O MPAA:R)**

NIGHT COMERS, THE* (1971, Brit.) 95m Scimitar/AE c

Marlon Brando *(Peter Quint)*, Stephanie Beacham *(Miss Margaret Jessel)*, Thora Hird *(Mrs. Grose)*, Harry Andrews *(Master of the House)*, Verna Harvey *(Flora)*, Christopher Ellis *(Miles)*, Anna Palk *(New Governess)*.

Marlon Brando is one of the most gifted actors of this century and he can do just about anything, but he can't manage to turn this sow's ear into much more than a slightly improved sow's ear. It's loosely based on Henry James' *Turn Of The Screw*, which also served as the basis for the excellent film, THE INNOCENTS, but that's where the resemblance stops. This is a preamble to that film (the way BUTCH AND SUNDANCE: THE EARLY DAYS was a forerunner to BUTCH CASSIDY AND THE SUNDANCE KID, although made later) and fails to satisfy on most levels. The two children in THE INNOCENTS were younger and so it is silly to see Harvey and Ellis as being at least three years older in this. It's England in the early 1900s and Ellis and Harvey are living at an old, dark house, being tended by Beacham, their governess, and Hird, the housekeeper. Their parents have been killed in an accident and their uncle, Andrews, has entrusted their care to the aforementioned two women, as he is busy living in London. Brando is an Irish gardener and stableman and keeps to himself. The two children like Brando and he is very gentle with them, explaining how they will eventually be with their parents in death and that their folks have gone to a better place. Harvey and Ellis have no one else to talk to that they like, so Brando becomes their surrogate father. They soon have their illusions shattered when they find that Brando enjoys tying up Beacham and whacking her around a bit before they make love. They can't quite fathom that and begin to imitate Beacham and Brando until Hird catches them as Ellis is tying up his sister. She is enraged and tosses Brando out of the mansion when she learns how the kids came to know of such matters. Beacham is ready to quit, as she is guilty about what's transpired and the kids are disturbed that their tranquil home will be split, so they do what they think is right to make certain that Brando and Beacham will be together forever: they tell Beacham that Brando is waiting for her on a small island in the middle of the deep lake on the property. When Beacham rows out on the lake late at night, the boat sinks, having been rigged that way by the kids, and she goes to a watery grave. On the following morning, Brando arrives and he is stunned by the discovery of Beacham's bloated body. He walks toward the mansion and Ellis sends a steel-tipped arrow through the man's head. No one finds the bodies, and when Palk, the new governess, arrives to take over Beacham's duties, she is assured by Hird that Ellis and Harvey are the very picture of perfect little angels. It's filled with sex, graphic language, and empty of taste, wit, and good sense. Winner, who made some of the worst pictures ever, continues his pattern here. Brando's career might have vanished entirely were it not for the fact that THE GODFATHER opened a few weeks later. Co-exec-producers Elliott and Jay Kanter and Alan Ladd, Jr. were reunited when Ladd took over the reins at MGM in the 1980s, after having an abortive run with his own company for a while.

p&d, Michael Winner; w, Michael Hastings (based on characters from *The Turn of the Screw* by Henry James); ph, Robert Paynter (Technicolor); m, Jerry Fielding; ed, Frederick Wilson; md, Fielding; art d, Herbert Westbrook; makeup, Richard Mills.

Drama **(PR:C-O MPAA:R)**

NIGHTFALL*½** (1956) 78m Copa/COL bw

Aldo Ray *(James Vanning)*, Brian Keith *(John)*, Anne Bancroft *(Marie Gardner)*, Jocelyn Brando *(Laura Fraser)*, James Gregory *(Ben Fraser, Insurance Investigator)*, Frank Albertson *(Dr. Edward Gurston)*, Rudy Bond *(Red)*, George Cisar *(Bus Driver)*, Eddie McLean *(Taxi Driver)*, Lillian Culver, Maya Van Horn *(Women)*, Orlando Beltran, Maria Belmar *(Spanish Couple)*, Walter Smith *(Shoeshine Boy)*, Monty Ash *(Clerk)*, Art Bucaro *(Cashier)*, Arline Anderson *(Hostess)*, Gene Roth *(Bartender)*, Robert Cherry *(Man)*, Jane Lynn, Betty Koch, Lillian Kassan, Joan Fotre, Pat Jones, Annabelle George *(Models)*, Winifred Waring *(Fashion Narrator)*.

Terrific *film noir*, expertly directed by Tourneur, stars Ray as an innocent man on the lam from a murder and robbery he didn't commit. The film opens as fugitive Ray meets Bancroft in a restaurant. When they leave, he is kidnaped by Keith and Bond who take Ray to a deserted oil derrick and torture him for the whereabouts of their stolen money. Ray manages to escape his tormentors, then tracks down Bancroft at her apartment, suspecting she set him up. When she claims ignorance, Ray takes her and flees, fearing Keith and Bond may find them. In a flashback Ray relates the events that got him in trouble. It seems he and a doctor friend were on their way to a hunting trip in the mountains of Wyoming when they discovered a car wreck and stopped to help. The passengers turned out to be Keith and Bond, two bank robbers who kidnaped the hunters and killed the doctor and then grabbed his medical bag, mistaking it for their loot. Ray, wounded from the shooting, took the bag of money and buried it in a snowbank for fear of being implicated in the crime. After hearing the story, Bancroft agrees to help Ray retrieve the money and, along with Gregory, an insurance investigator who believes he's innocent, they return to the scene of the crime. Discovering the cash is gone, Ray and his troupe see Bond kill Keith in a fight over the loot. Bond then mounts a snowplow and tries to run over Bancroft and Gregory, but Ray pulls him out of the cab and Bond is crushed under the plow. Similar in structure to Tourneur's OUT OF THE PAST, NIGHTFALL reverses the normal symbols of pain and suffering associated with *film noir* by showing that the only places Ray can hide are dark streets and musty restaurants, as opposed to the bright snowbanks and open spaces where he was shot and nearly killed by the thugs who would turn his life upside-down.

p, Ted Richmond; d, Jacques Tourneur; w, Stirling Silliphant (based on a novel by David Goodis); ph, Burnett Guffey; m, George Duning; ed, William A. Lyon; md, Morris Stoloff; art d, Ross Bellah; set d, William Kiernan, Louis Diage; cos, Jean Louis; m/l, "Nightfall," Sam M. Lewis, Peter DeRose, Charles Harold (sung by Al Hibbler); makeup, Clay Campbell.

Crime **(PR:A MPAA:NR)**

NIGHTFLIGHT FROM MOSCOW (SEE: SERPENT, THE, 1973, Fr./Ger.)

NIGHTHAWKS** (1978, Brit.) 113m Four Corner bw

Ken Robertson *(Jim)*, Tony Westrope *(Mike)*, Rachel Nicholas James *(Judy)*, Maureen Dolan *(Pat)*, Stuart Craig Turton *(Neal)*, Clive Peters *(Peter)*, Robert Merrick *(John)*, Frankl Dilbert *(American)*, Peter Radmall *(Artist)*.

This drama deals with the subject of homosexual schoolteachers. The film's protagonist must hide his sexual predilections from the community during the day, and ventures out in the evening to fulfill the empty half of his life. Filmed in stark black-and- white, the cast of largely nonprofessional actors gives this a realistic, gritty feeling.

p, Ron Peck, Paul Hallam; d, Peck; w, Peck, Hallam; ph, Joanna Davis; m, David Graham Ellis; ed, Richard Taylor, Mary Pat Leece; m/l, Ellis, Stuart Craig Turton.

Drama **(PR:O MPAA:NR)**

NIGHTHAWKS*½** (1981) 99m UNIV c

Sylvester Stallone *(Deke DaSilva)*, Billy Dee Williams *(Matthew Fox)*, Lindsay Wagner *(Irene)*, Persis Khambatta *(Shakka)*, Nigel Davenport *(Peter Hartman)*, Rutger Hauer *(Wulfgar)*, Hilarie Thompson *(Pam)*, Joe Spinell *(Lt. Munafo)*, Walter Mathews *(Commissioner)*, E. Brian Dean *(Sergeant)*, Caesar Cordova *(Puerto Rican Proprietor)*, Charles Duval *(Dr. Ghiselin)*, Tony Munafo *(Big Mike)*, Howard Stein *(Disco Manager)*, Tawn Christian *(Disco Hostess)*, Jamie Gillis *(Designer)*, Luke Reilly *(Conductor)*, Yvette Hawkins *(Mrs. Ntembwe)*, Einar Perry Scott *(Sostrom)*, Erle Bjornstad *(Mrs. Sostrom)*, Jacques Roux *(French Ambassador)*, Clebert Ford *(Nigerian Ambassador)*, Eivind Harum *(Swedish Ambassador)*, Obaka Adedunyo *(Mr. Ntembwe)*, Corine Lorain *(Suzanne Marigny)*, Jean-Pierre Stewart *(Rene Marigny)*, Thomas Rosales, John Shamsul Alam, Jose Santana *(Rippers)*, Patrick Fox *(Reporter)*, John Cianfrone, Tim Marquart, Tony Maffatone *(Muggers)*, Tom Degidon *(Immigration Officer)*, Rita Tellone *(Brunette)*, Al Gerrullo, Jr., Karl Wickman *(Helicopter Pilots)*, Brian Osborne *(Orchard)*, Robert Pugh *(Kenna)*, Catherine Mary Stewart *(Salesgirl)*, Frederick Treves *(Chief Police Inspector)*, Susan Vanner *(Girl at Party)*, Cliff Cudney, Joe Dabenigno, Steve Daskawisz, John Devaney, Paul Farentino, Edward Fox, Randy Francklan, Al Levitsky, Richard Noyce, Dar Robinson, Judee Wales, Luke Walter *(A.T.A.C. Men)*.

Stallone is a tough New York City cop who undergoes special anti-terrorist training while struggling to maintain his rocky marriage to Wagner. In Europe, Hauer, a rabid terrorist, plants a bomb in a London department store which results in the deaths of many school children; this causes him to fall out of favor with terrorist leaders. To regain his image as the top terrorist, Hauer journeys to New York and there—with the fanatical Khambatta at his side—he holds some officals hostage, kills several people, and escapes. Stallone, in a clever ruse, entraps Hauer in a bloody shootout and kills him. The action is swift and the direction and writing above average, thanks to Stallone's acceptance of acting duties alone. He is believable as the cantankerous detective and Williams is fine as the sidekick. Wagner is a pretty prop, no more, but Hauer is riveting as the evil terrorist whose only allegiance is to death and whose only human compunction is to kill. He is as frightening here as he was as the near-unstoppable replicant in BLADE RUNNER. Unfortunately, the film is rife with gratuitous violence, foul language, and sex scenes. Shot on location in New York.

p, Martin Poll; d, Bruce Malmuth; w, David Shaber (based on a story by Shaber, Paul Sylbert); ph, James A. Contner (Technicolor); m, Keith Emerson; ed, Christopher Holmes; prod d, Peter Larkin; cos, Bob DeMora, John Falabella.

Crime Drama **Cas.** **(PR:O MPAA:R)**

NIGHTMARE*** (1942) 80m UNIV bw

Diana Barrymore *(Leslie Stafford)*, Brian Donlevy *(Dan Shane)*, Henry Daniell *(Capt. Stafford)*, Eustace Wyatt *(Angus)*, Arthur Shields *(Sergeant)*, Gavin Muir *(Lord Abbington)*, Stanley Logan *(Inspector Robbins)*, Ian Wolfe *(Abbington's Butler)*, Hans Conried *(Hans)*, John Abbott *(Carl)*, David Clyde *(Jock)*, Elspeth Dudgeon *(Angus' Wife)*, Harold de Becker *(London Cabby)*, Ivan Simpson *(Money Changer)*, Keith Hitchcock *(London Bobby)*, Arthur Gould-Porter *(Freddie)*, Anita Bolster *(Mrs. McDonald)*, Lydia Bilbrook *(Mrs. Bates)*, Pax Walker *(Gladys)*, Bobbie Hale *(Old Gaffer)*.

A fast-paced, although at times a bit silly, espionage-suspense film starring Donlevy as a down-and-out and starving American gambler who breaks into the home of London lady Barrymore looking for food. There he finds a corpse, Barrymore's husband, in the study with a knife in its back. Barrymore catches Donlevy and gives him the option of waiting for the police to arrive or giving her a hand in disposing of the body for a price. Donlevy opts for the latter, but the cops get wise, forcing the pair to flee to Barrymore's family estate in Scotland. There Donlevy meets with Barrymore's adopted cousin Muir, who runs a distillery. While hiding out, Donlevy and Barrymore find things a bit strange at the estate and soon discover that Muir is a spy for the Nazis whose compatriots are being flown from Germany and parachuted over the secluded distillery. Deciding it is more noble to risk jail on a murder charge than blithely watch as the fate of the free world grows dimmer, Donlevy and Barrymore set a plan into action that will smash the spy ring. Eventually the Nazis are routed, Donlevy and Barrymore fall in love, and everybody buys more war bonds. Donlevy, Barrymore, and director Whelan establish an engrossing thriller in the first part of the film, but then dismantle it to get to the Nazis. When the viewer realizes that the murder was only a plot device to get the characters out of London and off to Scotland, there is a feeling of betrayal and manipulation. While NIGHTMARE is really nothing more than a competently crafted thriller anyway, the point is moot, but perhaps it may have been something special if it had proceeded along the opening story line.

p, Dwight Taylor; d, Tim Whelan; w, Taylor (based on the story "Escape" by Philip MacDonald); ph, George Barnes; ed, Frank Gross; art d, John Goodman.

Spy Drama/Suspense **(PR:C MPAA:NR)**

NIGHTMARE*** (1956) 89m Pine-Thomas-Shane/UA bw

Edward G. Robinson *(Rene Bressard)*, Kevin McCarthy *(Stan Grayson)*, Connie Russell *(Gina)*, Virginia Christine *(Sue)*, Rhys Williams *(Torrence)*, Gage Clarke *(Belnap)*, Barry Atwater *(Warner)*, Marian Carr *(Madge)*, Billy May *(Louie Simes)*.

Creepy, atmospheric remake of FEAR IN THE NIGHT (1947), which was also directed by Shane. McCarthy is superb as a New Orleans jazz musician who dreams he has stabbed a man to death in a mirrored room housed in a large mansion. When he wakes up with cuts and bruises on his body, he believes the dream was reality. Worried, he tells his brother-in-law Robinson, a police detective, who humors him and advises him to forget about it. Haunted by a strange sounding jazz tune that he heard in his dream, he searches the Bourbon Street clubs, hoping to hear the tune again. On a picnic with his wife and Robinson, McCarthy discovers the house in his dream, complete with a mirrored room and a phonograph and a record with the very song he couldn't forget. Later, when Robinson learns a murder has recently been committed there, he gives McCarthy 24 hours to leave town before he turns him in. Eventually Robinson, who begins to believe that McCarthy was hypnotized by the owner of the house to cover the murder of his wife, traps the killer and frees his brother-in-law from his dream. A truly creative, expressionistic film which uses distorted visuals, a stylized jazz score, and great performances from a fine cast to powerful effect.

p, Howard Pine, William C. Thomas; d&w, Maxwell Shane (based on the short story by William Irish [Cornell Woolrich]); ph, Joe Biroc; m, Herschel Burke Gilbert; ed, George Gittens; art d, Frank Sylos; set d, Edward Boyle; m/l, "What's Your Sad Story?" Dick Sherman, "The Last I Ever Saw of My Heart" Gilbert, Doris Houck.

Crime **(PR:C MPAA:NR)**

NIGHTMARE** (1963, Brit.) 83m Hammer/UNIV bw

David Knight *(Henry Baxter)*, Moira Redmond *(Grace)*, Brenda Bruce *(Mary)*, Jennie Linden *(Janet)*, George A. Cooper *(John)*, Irene Richmond *(Mrs. Gibbs)*, John Welsh *(Doctor)*, Timothy Bateson *(Barman)*, Clytie Jessop *(Woman in White)*, Hedger Wallace *(Sir Dudley)*, Julie Samuel *(Maid)*, Elizabeth Dear *(Janet as a Child)*, Isla Cameron *(Mother)*.

Routine suspense film about Linden who, as a child, saw her mother stab her father to death. The mother was then committed to an insane asylum, and Linden was left in the care of a guardian, Knight, and nurse-companion Redmond. The girl has recurring nightmares which terrorize her to the verge of a nervous breakdown. It is finally revealed that Knight and Redmond have conspired to drive her insane.

p, Jimmy Sangster; d, Freddie Francis; w, Sangster; ph, John Wilcox (Hammerscope); m, Don Banks; ed, James Needs; prod d, Bernard Robinson; art d, Don Mingaye, Ken Ryan; spec eff, Les Bowie; makeup, Roy Ashton.

Suspense **(PR:O MPAA:NR)**

NIGHTMARE zero (1981) 97m 21st Century c

Baird Stafford *(George Tatum)*, Sharon Smith *(Susan Temper)*, C.J. Cooke *(C.J. Temper)*, Mik Cribben *(Bob Rosen)*, Kathleen Ferguson *(Barbara)*, Danny Ronan *(Kathy, the Babysitter)*, John L. Watkins *(Man with Cigar)*.

Revolting gore film which was released unrated by the MPAA because it would have received an "X" for extreme violence. Stafford stars as a mental patient who, as a kid, witnessed his father and his mistress participating in violent sexual acts and was so shaken that he later hacked them to pieces with an axe. Stafford is put on antipsychotic drugs to calm his homicidal tendencies but they wear off and he then dismembers his ex-wife Smith, and her new family. Totally reprehensible, the ads for this film boasted gore effects by expert Tom Savini. When Savini claimed he had nothing to do with the film and threatened to sue, the advertising was quickly altered. A sleazebag production from start to finish.

p, John L. Watkins; d&w, Romano Scavolini; ph, Gianni Fiore (Technicolor); m, Jack Eric Williams; ed, Robert T. Megginson; spec eff, Les Larraine, William Milling; makeup, Edward French.

Horror **(PR:O MPAA:NR)**

NIGHTMARE (SEE: CITY OF THE WALKING DEAD, 1983, Span./Ital.)

NIGHTMARE ALLEY**** (1947) 111m FOX bw

Tyrone Power *(Stanton Carlisle)*, Joan Blondell *(Zeena)*, Coleen Gray *(Molly)*, Helen Walker *(Dr. Lilith Ritter)*, Taylor Holmes *(Ezra Grindle)*, Mike Mazurki *(Bruno)*, Ian Keith *(Pete)*, Julia Dean *(Mrs. Peabody)*, James Flavin *(Clem Hoatley)*, Roy Roberts *(McGraw)*, James Burke *(Town Marshal)*, Maurice Navarro *(Fire Eater)*, Leo Gray *(Detective)*, Robert Karnes *(Hotel Bellboy)*, Harry Hays Morgan *(Headwaiter)*, Albin Robeling *(Captain)*, George Beranger *(Geek)*, Marjorie Wood *(Mrs. Prescott)*, Harry Cheshire *(Mr. Prescott)*, Edward Clark *(Farmer)*, Eddy Waller *(Old Farmer)*, Mike Lally *(Charlie)*, George Davis *(Waiter)*, Hollis Jewell *(Delivery Boy)*, Laura Treadwell *(Woman)*, Nina Gilbert *(Worried Mother)*, Bill Free *(Man in Spode Room)*, Henry Hall *(Man)*, Jerry Miley *(Friend in Spode Room)*, Gilbert Wilson *(Husband in Spode Room)*, June Bolyn *(Maid in Grindle Room)*, Gene Stutenroth [Eugene Roth] *(Masseur)*, Charles Flickinger *(Bellboy)*, Florence Auer *(Housekeeper)*, Al Herman *(Cab Driver)*, George Chandler, Oliver Blake, Emmett Lynn, George Lloyd, Jack Raymond *(Hoboes)*, John Wald *(Radio Announcer)*, Clancy Cooper *(Stage Manager)*, George Matthews *(Knife Thrower)*.

Power is simply terrific as the sideshow hustler who makes it to the big time through underhanded methods, which also bring about his horrific ruination. Power gets a menial job with a cheap carnival and becomes fascinated with a mind-reading act conducted by Keith and Blondell. He soon becomes this show's barker, enticing customers to see the mind readers in action. Another attraction for the rural rubes is an illegal geek show, the geek being billed as half-man, half-beast, who works in a pit and bites the heads off live chickens. (Geek shows were prevalent circa 1900-1935 in chiefly Midwestern country carnivals and fairs and featured human derelicts who not only chewed the heads off chickens but also of live snakes.) Here the geek is a fallen carney performer who is now a dipsomaniac conducting his ghastly routines so he can be paid off with a quart of booze each evening. Power finds the man thoroughly repugnant: "How do you get a guy to be a geek? I can't understand how anybody can get so low." Power is quickly made a part of the mind reading act, collecting questions from the audience members written on pieces of paper. He switches these questions with blank pieces of paper which are given to the blindfolded Blondell—billed as "Miracle Woman of the Ages"—who burns them in a vase. The real questions are slipped to Keith who is hiding beneath the stage and he writes the questions on a blackboard which is reflected through mirrors into Blondell's crystal ball. Blondell simply reads off the questions and gives ambiguous answers that sound as if they have meaning. A pretty sideshow artist, Gray, who is in love with Power, tells him that the mind-reading act is good but it's no match to the spectacular act Blondell and Keith used to perform as big-time vaudevilleans, one where Keith stayed in the audience and merely held up the written question which Blondell would answer, a never-miss system which was controlled by a secret word code. Power goes to Keith and begins to feed liquor to him, pumping him for information about the old act. Keith toys with the gullible youth, telling him: "You should have seen me work." He pretends to stare into a crystal ball, saying: "Throughout the ages man has sought to look behind the veil that hides him from tomorrow...Wait! The shifting shape begins to clear. I see fields of grass and rolling hills and a boy—a boy is running barefoot through the hills. A dog is with him." Power is awestruck, saying: "His name was Gip. Go on." Keith laughs loudly and says: "See how easy it is to hook 'em? Stock reading. Fits everybody. Every boy has a dog." Keith explains that the great act he and his wife had went to pieces after he took to drink. Power keeps after Keith to get the secret word code but he mistakenly gives Keith some wood alcohol and the drunk dies the next day. Power goes to work on Blondell who admits she is promiscuous, quipping: "I have a heart like an artichoke—a leaf for everyone." He learns the secret word code during an affair with Blondell, and together they revive the old act, with Power in the audience holding up items given to him by patrons and Blondell accurately describing them even though she is blindfolded. Power cheats on Blondell by seducing Gray, which brings down the wrath of the carnival people, who insist that the scoundrel marry the poor girl. Power and Gray wed and then move to Chicago where Power installs himself as a great spiritualist in a swanky nightclub, with Gray assisting him. He mesmerizes audiences and becomes the city's sensation. He meets psychologist Walker, who is enamored of him, and they strike a deal. In exchange for confidential information about her clients, the richest people in town, she will share in fifty percent of the profits. Through Walker's high-society contacts, Power becomes rich by giving rigged seances, putting magnates and tycoons in touch with their dead loved ones. Holmes is so moved by seeing a vision of his deceased sweetheart that he promises to give the sharpster $150,000 to build a spiritual temple. Now Power aims to establish a religious cult that will make him millions. But Gray balks at posing as a dead woman, lecturing Power: "You make it sound so sacred and holy when all the time it's just a gag with you....You're just laughing your head off at those chumps. You think God's going to stand for that?" When Gray poses as the spirit of Holmes' dead girl friend, Holmes falls to his knees pathetically praying to God. Gray breaks down and shouts: "No, no—I can't stand it!" She admits she's Power's wife and Holmes explodes in anger: "You crook! You dirty sacrilegious thief!" Power hits Holmes, knocking him down, then runs to Walker but she tells him to leave her alone. If he ever dares come near her again, she will tell police how Keith came to die, a secret she has learned form the scorned Blondell. Power is finished, ruined. He takes to the road, loses all his money, and begins to drink heavily—living in cheap rooming houses, then, penniless, hobo jungles—until he is nothing more than an alcoholic derelict. He appears filthy and gaunt at a tawdry carnival, begging for work. The manager tells him he has no jobs but as Power begins to walk away, the manager tells him he's looking for a geek. Power tells him he'll take the job, stating: "Mister, I was made for it!" After performing the hideous act the first day Power is seen screaming as he runs hysterically through the carnival grounds. Gray, who is a performer in the same carnival, steps from a trailer and stops Power, comforting him and taking him in, suggesting that she will rehabilitate her errant husband. This last scene was added to the powerful film at the insistence of the Hays Office (Hollywood's then censoring board) which demanded that the film be softened and Power shown to be redeemed from his disgusting fate. The final scene of the movie shows the carnival manager talking to a roustabout. "How can a guy get so low?" asks the roustabout. "He reached too high," replies the stage manager. Furthman's script, although it could not include all of the terrifying details of Gresham's shocking novel, is potent and revealing as it examines the sleazy world of the spiritual con artist. Goulding was merciless in his inspection of a character rotten through and through, one where he carefully constructs Power's insidious rise and abruptly takes him down the mountain to the swamp. Power, who asked to play the part and had Fox buy the rights of the novel for him, gives the performance of his career, proving that he was not merely a matinee idol but a player who could dig deep inside himself and produce a characterization that was both memorable and telling. Goulding was then Power's favorite director; they had worked together in the 1946 production of THE RAZOR'S EDGE, presenting a stunning version of the Somerset Maugham tale. Goulding was noted for bringing forth excellent performances from actors thought to be one-dimensional or routine, as proven by such films as GRAND HOTEL (1932), DARK VICTORY (1939), THE GREAT LIE (1941), and CLAUDIA (1943). Walker is a standout as the cold-blooded psychologist amd Blondell excels as the frowzy but calculating spritualist (she is the essence of cheapness, an image she had cultivated for years). Gray is also fine as the stupid but loving wife who can forgive any crime. Mockridge's score is eerie and perfectly suited to the shadowy images captured in Garmes' photography. The public responded well to the film, if only to see Power in his offbeat role, but the world wondered why he wanted to play the corrupt Stan Carlisle. He later commented: "Stan Carlisle fascinated me. He was such an unmitigated heel. I've played other disreputable fellows...but never one like Carlisle. Here was a chance to create a character different from any I had ever played before. But aside from Carlisle himself, the story had the tough realism and the dramatic impact that many modern novels lack." When the rave reviews came in about Power's performance, Goulding told the world that Power was "the greatest actor of his generation."

p, George Jessel; d, Edmund Goulding; w, Jules Furthman (based on the novel by William Lindsay Gresham); ph, Lee Garmes; m, Cyril Mockridge; ed, Barbara McLean; md, Lionel Newman; art d, Lyle Wheeler, J. Russell Spencer; set d, Thomas Little, Stuart Reiss; cos, Bonnie Cashin; spec eff, Fred Sersen.

Crime Drama/Horror (PR:C-O MPAA:NR)

NIGHTMARE CASTLE½** (1966, Ital.) 90m Produzione Cinematografica Emmeci/AA bw AMANTI D'OLTRETOMBA; GB: NIGHT OF THE DOOMED; AKA: THE FACELESS MONSTERS; LOVERS FROM BEYOND THE TOMB)

Barbara Steele *(Muriel/Jenny)*, Paul Miller *(Dr. Stephen Arrowsmith)*, Helga Line *(Solange)*, Lawrence Clift *(Dr. Derek Joyce)*, Rik Battaglia *(David)*, John McDouglas [Giuseppe Addobbati] *(Jonathan)*.

Steele plays the unfortunate wife of crazed scientist Miller who decides to use her and her lover Battaglia in his experiments involving human blood and electricity. After electrocuting them, he drains their blood and injects it into his faithful and aging servant, Line, who is suddenly rejuvenated and beautiful. He then places the hearts of Steele and Battaglia in an urn. Shocked when he learns that Steele's fortune was left to her mentally unbalanced sister (also played by Steele), Miller marries her and tries to drive the woman insane so he can collect the inheritance. Her doctor (Clift), however, refuses to declare her insane and begins to sense danger in the house. Miller, meanwhile, is preparing another blood solution to continue Line's rejuvenation. Clift discovers the hearts in the urn and unleashes the ghosts of Steele and her lover who take their revenge by burning Miller alive and sucking the blood from Line which reduces her to nothing but a skeleton. One of cult-actress Steele's best, with fine direction provided by Grunewald.

p, Carlo Caiano; d, Allen Grunewald [Mario Caiano]; w, Caiano, Fabio de Agostini; ph, Enzo Barboni; m, Ennio Morricone; ed, Renato Cinquini; art d, Massimo Tavazzi; cos, Mario Giorsi.

Horror/Science Fiction Cas. (PR:C MPAA:NR)

NIGHTMARE CITY (SEE: CITY OF THE WALKING DEAD, 1983, Span./Ital.)

NIGHTMARE HONEYMOON* (1973) 115m MGM c

Dack Rambo, Rebecca Dianna Smith, John Beck, Pat Hingle, Jeanette Nolan, Roy Jenson.

Rambo and Smith's idyllic honeymoon is shattered when they witness a murder and the killers give chase. Sadistic high point comes when the murderers rape Smith. Director Nicholas Roeg (WALKABOUT, PERFORMANCE, THE MAN WHO FELL TO EARTH) walked off the set after five days of shooting and was replaced by CAT BALLOU director Elliott Silverstein. Cast includes Beck of the 1960s underground rock group, The Leaves.

p, Hugh Benson; d, Elliott Silverstein; w, S. Lee Pogostin (based on a novel by Lawrence Block); m, Elmer Bernstein.

Crime (PR:O MPAA:NR)

NIGHTMARE IN BLOOD*½ (1978) 90m Xeromega/PFE c

Kerwin Matthews *(Prince Zaroff)*, Jerry Walter *(Malakai)*, Dan Caldwell *(Prof. Seabrook)*, Barrie Youngfellow *(Cindy O'Flaherty)*, John J. Cochran *(Scotty)*, Ray K. Goman *(B.B.)*, Hy Pyke *(Harris)*, Irving Israel *(Ben-Halik)*, Drew Eshelman *(Arlington)*, Morgan Upton *(George Wilson)*, Justin Bishop *(Dr. Unworth)*, Stan Ritchie *(Marsdon)*, Charles Murphy *(Flannery)*, Yvonne Young *(Barbara)*, Mike Hitchcock *(Lt. Driscoll)*, Erika Stanley *(Girl in Graveyard)*.

Pretty bad low-budget picture about a horror film actor who turns out to be a real vampire. Director Stanley was a popular television horror movie host in San Francisco.

p, John Stanley, Kenn Davis; d, Stanley; w, Stanley, Davis; ph, Charles Rudnick (Techniscope, Technicolor); ed, Alfred Katzman.

Comedy/Horror (PR:O MPAA:R)

NIGHTMARE IN THE SUN*½ (1964) 80m Afilmco/Zodiac c

John Derek *(Hitchhiker)*, Aldo Ray *(Sheriff)*, Arthur O'Connell *(Sam Wilson)*, Ursula Andress *(Marsha Wilson)*, Sammy Davis, Jr. *(Truckdriver)*, Allan Joslyn *(Scoutmaster)*, Keenan Wynn *(Junk Dealer)*, Chick Chandler *(Bartender)*, Richard Jaeckel, Robert Duvall *(Motorcyclists)*, Lurene Tuttle, George Tobias *(Married Couple)*, Douglas Fowley, John Marley, William Challee, Michael Petit, James Waters, John Sebastian.

Poorly done crime tale starring Derek as a drifter unfortunate enough to allow himself to be seduced by Andress, the bored wife of wealthy-but-old rancher O'Connell. When O'Connell spots Derek leaving his wife's boudoir, he kills her. Corrupt sheriff Ray seizes the opportunity and blackmails O'Connell in exchange for his silence and then arrests Derek, who knows nothing of the killing. The ending sees O'Connell kill Ray and then confess to both murders.

p, Marc Lawrence, John Derek; d, Lawrence; w, Ted Thomas, Fanya Lawrence (based on a story by M. Lawrence, George Fass); ph, Stanley Cortez (DeLuxe Color); m, Paul Glass; ed, Douglas Stewart, William Shenberg; md, Glass; art d, Paul Sylos; set d,

Ray Boltz.

Crime (PR:O MPAA:NR)

NIGHTMARE IN WAX zero (1969) 95m A&E Film-Paragon-Productions Enterprises/Crown c (AKA: CRIMES IN THE WAX MUSEUM)

Cameron Mitchell *(Vincent)*, Anne Helm *(Marie)*, Scott Brady *(Detective Haskell)*, Berry Kroeger *(Max Black)*, Victoria Carroll *(Carissa)*, Phillip Baird *(Tony Deane)*, Hollis Morrison *(Nick)*, John Cardos *(Sgt. Carver)*, James Forrest *(Alfred)*, The T-Bones, The Gazzari Dancers, Reni Martin.

Sub-standard horror film rip-off of HOUSE OF WAX (itself a rip-off of MYSTERY OF THE WAX MUSEUM) starring Mitchell as a badly scarred, psychotic owner of a wax museum who abducts the stars of a movie studio as revenge for his disfigurement (he was injured by studio-head Kroeger during an argument over pretty actress Helm). Mitchell, of course, doesn't kill his victims and dump the bodies in the river—he injects them with a suspended animation formula, and then uses them in his exhibits. Eventually this scheme is figured out (all the cops have to do is try to make the obviously unstatuesque actors blink or twitch—which they can clearly be seen doing, despite editing) and Mitchell is lowered into a vat of boiling wax after the drug wears off and the performers gang up on him. Amateurish in all respects. Filmed at Movieland Wax Museum in Los Angeles.

p, Herbert Sussan, Martin B. Cohen; d, Bud Townsend; w, Rex Carlton; ph, Glen Smith (Pathe); ed, Leonard Kwit; set d, James Freiberg; makeup, Martin Varnaud.

Horror Cas. (PR:O MPAA:M)

NIGHTMARES** (1983) 99m UNIV c

Terror in Topanga: Cristina Raines *(Wife)*, Joe Lambie *(Husband)*, Anthony James *(Clerk)*, Clare Nono *(Newswoman)*, Raleigh Bond *(Neighbor)*, Robert Phelps *(Newsman)*, Dixie Lynn Royce *(Little Girl)*, Lee James Jude *(Glazier)*; Bishop of Battle: Emilio Estevez *(J.J.)*, Mariclare Costello *(Mrs. Cooney)*, Louis Giambalvo *(Cooney)*, Moon Zappa *(Pamela)*, Billy Jacoby *(Zock)*, Joshua Grenrock *(Willie)*, Gary Cervantes *(Mazenza)*, C. Stewart Burns *(Root)*, Andre Diaz *(Pedro)*, Rachel Goslins *(Phyllis)*, Joel Holman *(Z-Man)*, Christopher Bubetz *(Jeffrey)*, Rudy Negretl *(Emiliano)*, James Tolkan *(Bishop's Voice)*; The Benediction: Lance Henriksen *(MacLeod)*, Tony Plana *(Del Amo)*, Timothy Scott *(Sheriff)*, Robin Gammell *(Bishop)*, Rose Marie Campos *(Mother)*; Night of the Rat: Richard Masur *(Steven)*, Veronica Cartwright *(Claire)*, Bridgette Andersen *(Brooke)*, Albert Hague *(Mel)*, Howard F. Flynn *(Announcer)*.

This quartet of scary tales is, like any compilation film, a mixed bag. Two stories work and two don't. The best are "Bishop of Battle" featuring Estevez (one of the better actors of what had been dubbed"The Brat Pack" generation) as a teenager who becomes so good at a video game that he's consumed by the machine, becoming part of the game itself. "Night of the Rat," featuring Masur and Cartwright, is a strange bit of black humor about a suburban couple who must fight off a pony-sized rat that has invaded their home fresh from its stint in the 17th Century. The other stories, "Terror in Topanga" and "The Benediction," are simplistic mad slasher and "Duel"-inspired fantasies respectively, showing little imagination or wit. Surprisingly, this was never given much of a release in either the U.S. or England.

p, Christopher Crowe; d, Joseph Sargent; w, Crowe, Jeffrey Bloom; ph, Mario DiLeo, Gerald Perry Finnerman (Panavision, Technicolor); m, Craig Safan; ed, Rod Stephens, Michael Brown; prod d, Dean Edward Mitzner; art d, Jack Taylor; spec eff, Bo Gehring; makeup, James Scribner.

Science Fiction/Horror Cas. **(PR:O MPAA:PG)**

NIGHTS IN A HAREM (SEE: SON OF SINBAD, 1955)

NIGHTS OF CABIRIA*** (1957, Ital.) 110m Les Films Marceau/ Lopert bw (LE NOTTI DI CABIRIA; AKA: CABIRIA)

Giulietta Masina *(Cabiria)*, Francois Perier *(Oscar D'Onofrio, the Accountant)*, Amedeo Nazzari *(Alberto Lazzari, the Movie Star)*, Aldo Silvani *(Hypnotist)*, Franca Marzi *(Wanda, Cabiria's Friend)*, Dorian Gray *(Jessy, Lazzari's Girl Friend)*, Mario Passante *(Cripple in the "Miracle" Sequence)*, Pina Gualandri *(Matilda, the Prostitute)*, Polidor *(The Monk)*, Ennio Girolami, Christian Tassou, Jean Molier, Ricardo Fellini, Maria Luisa Rolando, Amedeo Girard, Loretta Capitoli, Mimmo Poli, Giovanna Gattinoni.

As with LA STRADA, Fellini directed his wife (Masina) as an innocent woman thrust into the middle of a cold and cruel world. NIGHTS OF CABIRIA lacks the lyrical simplicity that made LA STRADA such a magical film, but was an impressive enough display of Fellini's fascinating visual style to warrant the Academy Award for Best Foreign Film. Set in a district on the outskirts of Rome, Masina plays a near perfect embodiment of the old cliche "prostitute with a heart of gold." She's the type who understands misfortune to be part and parcel of life, but never loses faith in the value of life itself (an aspect of Fellini's own existential philosophy). When misfortune does come her way she shrugs it off her shoulder and continues walking the streets for a buck, as when a handsome movie star picks her up during a brawl with his girl friend. He takes her to his fabulous home, but quickly discards her after he is through with Masina's services. The shy and withdrawn Perier does fall in love with Masina, or at least she believes this to be the case. He is a simple sort of fellow with whom she could create a nice home and family. Selling her home and withdrawing her money from the bank, Masina makes plans to marry Perier, only to have him take advantage of her kindness by stealing all her money and leaving her out in the cold. Such an act would lead to the destruction of even the strongest person, but once Masina realizes her situation, she looks into the camera smirking a "that's life" smile, and sets off to take up her former profession—a scene reminiscent of Charlie Chaplin's Little Tramp. Perhaps the most difficult aspect of NIGHTS OF CABIRIA is accepting Masina as a prostitute; this sweet and naive looking woman, who stole audiences hearts with her childlike innocence in LA STRADA, just doesn't seem to conjure up thoughts of a woman selling herself on the streets. But it expresses the dismal view that fate makes no exceptions. As in the majority of Fellini's films (a result of his neorealist background), the emphasis here is on visual elements instead of a straight narrative form. It is the small details that create Masina's character and the environment in which she exists. This also was the basis for the Broadway musical (and subsequent film) "Sweet Charity." (In Italian; English subtitles.)

p, Dino De Laurentiis; d, Federico Fellini; w, Fellini, Ennio Flaiano, Tullio Pinelli, Pier Paolo Pasolini; ph, Aldo Tonti, Otella Martelli; m, Nino Rota; ed, Leo Catozzo; art d&cos, Piero Gherardi; makeup, Eligio Trani.

Drama **(PR:C MPAA:NR)**

NIGHTS OF LUCRETIA BORGIA, THE*½ (1960, Ital.) 108m Fides-Musa/COL c (LE NOTTI DI LUCREZIA BORGIA)

Belinda Lee *(Lucretia Borgia)*, Jacques Sernas *(Federico)*, Michelle Mercier *(Diana d'Alva)*, Arnoldo Foa *(Astorre)*, Franco Fabrizi *(Cesare Borgia)*, Marco Tulli, Lily Scaringi, Germano Longo, Nando Tamberlani, Raf Baldassarre, Gianni Loti, Stelio Candelli.

Absurd historical drama starring Lee in the title role as an impulsive woman hopelessly in love with Sernas, a young swordsman in her brother's employ. She is dismayed to learn that he is in love with family arch enemy Mercier, who is loved from afar by the nutty Count Borgia (Fabrizi).

p, Carlo Caiano; d, Sergio Grieco; w, Mario Caiano, Aldo Segri; ph, Massimo Dallamano (Totalscope, Eastmancolor); m, Alexander Derevitsky.

Historical Drama **(PR:A MPAA:NR)**

NIGHTS OF PRAGUE, THE*** (1968, Czech.) 92m Felix Broz Unit bw (PRAZSKE NOCI; AKA: PRAGUE NIGHTS)

Jan Klusak *(Rabbi Chaim)*, Jana Brezkova *(Mute Girl)*, Teresa Tuszynska, Josef Somr, Josef Abrham, Lucie Novot, Jan Libicek, Milos Kopecky, Milena Dvorska, Vaclav Kotva.

A trio of Prague-situated stories released as one film. The first two stories—"The Bread Shoes" and "The Poisoned Poisoner," directed by Schorm and Makovek respectively—are tales set in the Middle Ages. But the story that is the most interesting in this collection is a new version of the Yiddish legend, "The Golem." In this re-telling, Klusak plays a Polish rabbi who is asked to create a living clay man by Rudolph II. The famous Rabbi Loew learns of this and has Brezkova, a mute girl, seduce Klusak. She wipes the magic formula that gives the golem its powers off the creature's forehead, and the golem crumbles to pieces, destroying Klusak as well. It is then learned that Brezkova was also a man-made being, created by Rabbi Loew. As directed by Brdecka, who was well known for his animations, the story

has a glowing sense of atmosphere with an art decoration reminiscent of the silent German film, DER GOLEM: WIE ER IN DIE WELT KAM (1920).

d, Jiri Brdecka, Evald Schorm, Milos Makovek; w, Brdecka; ph, Jan Kallis, Frantisek Uldrych.

Drama **(PR:C MPAA:NR)**

NIGHTS OF SHAME½** (1961, Fr.) 81m Vascos Films/ Union Film bw (MARCHANDES D'ILLUSIONS)

Nicole Courcel *(Maria)*, Raymond Pellegrin *(Rene)*, Giselle Pascal *(Marie-Therese)*, Philippe Lemaire *(Pierre)*, Louise Carletti *(Marcelle)*, Michel Ardan *(Ferdinand)*, Gina Manes *(Mathilde)*, Abel Jacquin, Paul Demange, Lisette Lebon, Evelyne Corman, Rene Blancard, Jerome Goulven, Rene Havard, Simone Logeart, Jacques Muller, Simone Berthier, Julia Maffre, Rita Stoya.

Love and shame are set against the background of the Parisian underworld as Pascal plays a social worker trying to rehabilitate prostitutes. Pellegrin and his artist friend Lemaire both become enchanted with two of the "ladies of the night," unaware of their former profession. Carletti, Lemaire's girl, comes under suspicion when her older friend Manes is murdered by Carletti's ex-employer, gangster Ardan, who is then killed in an auto accident. Pascal tries to clear the girl's name by telling police that Lemaire and Carletti were together at the time of the murder. Eventually Lemaire and Pellegrin discover the former professions of their respective loves and, though the latter is accepting of this, Lemaire is appalled and leaves Carletti. The film opened in France seven years earlier than the U.S. release.

p&d, Raoul Andre; w, Raymond Caillava, Rene Blancard; ph, Roger Fellous; m, Daniel Lesur; ed, Gabriel Rongier; art d, Louis Le Barbenchon; cos, Almine; makeup, Louis Dor.

Drama **(PR:O MPAA:NR)**

NIGHTS WHEN THE DEVIL CAME (SEE: DEVIL STRIKES AT NIGHT, THE, 1959, Ger.)

NIGHTWING* (1979) 103m COL c

Nick Mancuso *(Youngman Duran)*, David Warner *(Phillip Payne)*, Kathryn Harrold *(Anne Dillon)*, Stephen Macht *(Walker Chee)*, Strother Martin *(Selwyn)*, George Clutesi *(Abner Tasupi)*, Ben Piazza *(Roger Piggott)*, Donald Hotton *(John Franklin)*, Charles Hallahan *(Henry)*, Judith Novgrod *(Judy)*, Alice Hirson *(Claire Franklin)*, Pat Corley *(Vet)*, Charlie Bird *(Beejay)*, Danny Zapien *(Joe)*, Peter Prouse *(Doctor)*, Jose Toledo *(Harold)*, Richard Romancito *(Ben)*, Flavio Martinez III *(Isla Lalama)*, Lena Carr, Virginia P. Maney, Wade Stevens, Robert Dunbar, John R. Leonard, Sr., James Arnett, Glynn Rubin, Gary Epper, Craig Baxley.

What do you get when you cross THE BIRDS with JAWS, adding just a touch of WILLARD? The influence of the three is obvious in this boring little horror film where a group of rabid bats goes on the rampage. Warner plays a surly, ever-wisecracking scientist who's tracking the flying rodents in an effort to get revenge on them for eating his father. Mancuso's a copy who doesn't believe in the tribal mumbo jumbo that has this as all part of some sort of spiritual revenge. Clutesi, fresh from his role as an Indian seer in the equally insipid PROPHECY, once more finds himself playing such a part. Any attempts to make this nonsense scary are ultimately defeated by cheesy special effects and gaping logic holes. The location shooting from the American Southwest is nicely photographed, though poorly used. Incredible that Smith, who co-scripted this based on his novel, was also the author of the fine novel *Gorky Park*.

p, Martin Ransohoff; d, Arthur Hiller; w, Steve Shagan, Bud Shrake, Martin Cruz Smith (based on the novel by Smith); ph, Charles Rosher (Metrocolor); m, Henry Mancini; ed, John C. Howard; prod d, James Vance; set d, Richard Kent; spec eff, Carlo Rambaldi

Horror Cas. **(PR:O MPAA:PG)**

NIHON NO ICHIBAN NAGAI HI (SEE: EMPEROR AND A GENERAL, THE, 1968)

NIJINSKY** (1980, Brit.) 129m Hera/PAR c

Alan Bates *(Sergei Diaghilev)*, George De La Pena *(Vaslav Nijinsky)*, Leslie Browne *(Romola De Pulsky)*, Alan Badel *(Baron De Gunzburg)*, Carla Fracci *(Tamara Karsavina)*, Colin Blakely *(Vassili)*, Ronald Pickup *(Igor Stravinsky)*, Ronald Lacey *(Leon Bakst)*, Vernon Dobtcheff *(Sergei Grigoriev)*, Jeremy Irons *(Mikhail Fokine)*, Frederick Jaeger *(Gabriel Astruc)*, Anton Dolin *(Maestro Cecchetti)*, Janet Suzman *(Emilia Marcus)*, Stephan Chase *(Adolph Bolm)*, Henrietta Baynes *(Magda)*, Sian Philips *(Lady Ripon)*, Charles Kay *(Argentinian Ambassador)*, Tomas Milian, Jr. *(Young Man on Beach)*, Monica Mason *(Maria Piltz)*, Valerie Aitken *(Lydia Nelidova)*, Genesia Rosato *(Ludmilla Schollar)*, June Brown *(Maria Stepanova)*, Blaise Mills *(Lisl)*, Kim Miller *(Marie Rambert)*, Dean McMillan *(Page)*, Mart Crowley *(Baron Adolphe De Meyer)*, Olga Lowe *(Signora Cerchetti)*, Geoffrey Hughes *(Gavrilov)*, Patricia Ruanne *(The Doll)*, Ben Van Cauwenbergh *(Max Froman)*.

Long-time dealmaker Harry Saltzman put this one together and it comes close to falling apart. Co-producer Kaye, a former ballerina who tired of it all one day and tossed her shoes out the window of husband Herbert Ross' sports car, returns to the ballet world to oversee this movie. The scenes of the dancing are wonderful and Ross, a choreographer in his early years, knows how to shoot them (as witnessed by the fact that he directed THE TURNING POINT), but the picture bogs down once the dancing stops. It only shows two years of Nijinsky's life, with the final 33 years of his incarceration in a mental hospital being dealt with by a printed epilog. De La Pena has the title role and acquits himself well in all his dances. (Why not? He's a member of the American Ballet Theatre and knows of what he pirouettes.) It's a triangular love story between De La Pena, his lover-teacher Bates, and the wife he acquires on a rare heterosexual sortie, Browne. Badel, another homosexual, is De La Pena's benefactor until he comes up against Bates, who monopolizes the youth's time. Side stories include Pickup (as Stravinsky) being annoyed that his masterwork, "Le Sacre du Printemps," was balleted and booed by audiences. It gets distasteful (although, perhaps, true) when De La Pena's mind starts to crack under the pushing by Bates, and the young dancer begins to masturbate on stage while performing "The Afternoon Of A Faun." Playwright Mart Crowley (THE BOYS IN THE BAND) does a small role, as do Irons and Suzman. Other ballets include "Scheherezade," "Jeux," "Spectre of the Rose," and "Petrouchka." We can only be happy that Ross did this and not Ken Russell. A good-looking movie, but if you don't like ballet, there's little reason to see it.

p, Nora Kaye, Stanley O'Toole; d, Herbert Ross; w, Hugh Wheeler (based on the book *Nijinsky* by Romola Nijinsky and *The Diary of Vaslav Nijinsky*); ph, Douglas Slocombe (Metrocolor); m, John Lanchbery; ed, William Reynolds; prod d, John Blezard; art d, Tony Roman, George Richardson; cos, Alan Barrett.

Biography **(PR:C-O MPAA:R)**

NIKKI, WILD DOG OF THE NORTH*½** (1961, U.S./Can.) 74m Disney-Cangary, Ltd.-WEST/BV c

Jean Coutu *(Andre Dupas)*, Emile Genest *(Jacques Lebeau)*, Uriel Luft *(Makoki)*, Robert Rivard *(Durante)*, Nikki *("The Malemute Wonder Dog")*, Neewa the Bear *(Himself)*, Taao *(Old Champion Fighting Dog)*, Jacques Fauteux *(Narrator)*, The Nomads *(Performers of French-Canadian Folk Songs)*.

Coutu is a trapper in the Canadian woods whose dog Nikki runs into the forest and returns with a new-found friend, Neewa, a bear cub. Coutu ties the two animals together, loads them into his canoe and heads downstream, but they are separated from him when the canoe overturns in the rapids. The two animals, still leashed together, must learn to fend for themselves in this unusual manner. The rope finally breaks but they continue together on their adventures. When winter approaches, however, Neewa goes into hibernation and Nikki is forced to fend for himself. He raids trapper Genest's campsite for food but is caught by the cruel man, who later trains him to become a pit fighter. A local authority comes to stop the illegal proceedings but gets beaten up by Genest who then tries to sic Nikki on the man. But the dog recognizes the authority as his old master Coutu and instead turns on Genest who ultimately falls on his own knife. Nikki returns to Coutu and together they head off for new adventures. Unlike many films of this type NIKKI...is a well made and exciting animal-action piece. Nikki and Neewa are quite a team and surprisingly natural actors. Some of the sequences will make the viewer wonder how the producers ever got these animal thespians to behave with such realism. There's excellent use of hand-held camera during the fight scene (which itself is unusually brutal for a Disney picture) and point-of-view shots from Nikki's perspective. The combination of fiction and Disney's "True-Life Adventures" works well in this overall fine film. Perfect for the kids (though the fight scene may be a little too much for the youngest in the family), and the adults will be charmed as well. Two versions of NIKKI...were shot: one in English for U.S. audiences, the other in French for French-Canadians.

p, Walt Disney, Winston Hibler; d, Jack Couffer, Donald Haldane; w, Hibler, Ralph Wright, Dwight Hauser (based on the novel *Nomads of the North* by James Oliver Curwood); ph, Lloyd Beebe, Couffer, Ray Jewell, William V. Bacon III, Donald Wilder (Technicolor); m, Oliver Wallace; ed, Grant K. Smith; set d, Jack McCullagh; cos, Jan Kemp; makeup, Ken Brooke, Barry Nye.

Animal Adventure **(PR:AAA MPAA:NR)**

NIKUTAI NO GAKKO (SEE: SCHOOL OF LOVE, 1966, Jap.)

NINE DAYS A QUEEN (SEE: LADY JANE GREY, 1936, Brit.)

NINE DAYS OF ONE YEAR*** (1964, USSR) 107m Mosfilm/Artkino bw (DEVYAT DNEY ODNOGO GODA)

Aleksey Batlov *(Dmitriy Gusev)*, Innokentiy Smoktunovskiy *(Ilya Kulikov)*, Tatyana Lavrova *(Lyolya)*, Nikolay Plotnikov *(Prof. Sintsov)*, Yevgeniy Teterin *(Surgeon)*, Nikolay Sergeyev *(Gusev's Father)*, Zinoviy Gerdt *(Narrator)*, S. Blinnikov, Yevgeniy Yevstigneyev, Mikhail Kozakov, I. Grabbe, V. Nikulin, P. Shpringfeld, A. Pelevin, Ada Voytsik, V. Belyayeva, Lyudmila Ovchinnikova, Yu. Kireyev, B. Yashin, I. Dobrolyubov, A. Smirnov, A. Pavlova, R. Esadze, Georgiy Yepifantsev, L. Durov, N. Batyroyova, Z. Chekulayeva, I. Yasulovich.

Batlov is a Soviet nuclear physicist working in Siberia with his professor, Plotnikov. There is an accident and both men are exposed to dangerously high amounts of radiation, causing Plotnikov's death. Batlov is warned that further radiation will kill him as well, but his work is far too important to him and he refuses to take a safer job. His devotion to his work affects his relationship with Lavrova, who nearly leaves him for a mutual friend (Smoktunovskiy), but finally marries Batlov. Smoktunovskiy, in the meantime, comes to work with his friend. When Batlov makes another important breakthrough and is once more exposed to radiation, he swears Smoktunovskiy to secrecy until the experiment can be completed. Lavrova begins to think she has failed her husband in some way for he spends more time away from her than before. Meanwhile he makes a secret trip to his family in Moscow and arranges for a life-saving bone marrow transplant at a clinic. Smoktunovskiy visits his friend the day before the operation with the news that they have made an important scientific discovery. The end sees Lavrova, who now knows of her husband's condition, waiting with Smoktunovskiy at the hospital in anticipation of the operation's outcome. They receive a note from him promising a grand celebration.

d, Mikhail Romm; w, Romm, Daniil Khrabrovitskiy; ph, German Lavrov; m, D. Ter-Tatevosyan; ed, Ye. Ladyzhenskaya; art d, G. Kolganov; cos, V. Kiselyova; makeup, V. Fetisov.

Drama **(PR:O MPAA:NR)**

NINE FORTY-FIVE½** (1934, Brit.) 59m WB-FN bw

Binnie Barnes *(Ruth Jordan)*, Donald Calthrop *(Dr. Venables)*, Violet Farebrother *(Mrs. Randall)*, Malcolm Tod *(James Everett)*, James Finlayson *(P. C. Doyle)*, George Merritt *(Inspector Dickson)*, Ellis Irving *(Turner)*, Cecil Parker *(Robert Clayton)*, Janice Adair *(Molly Clayton)*, Margaret Yarde *(Margaret Clancy)*, Rene Ray *(Mary Doane)*.

A man, hated by many, is found dead, and three people confess to murdering him. Enter inspector Merritt and doctor Calthrop who find each person has confessed to protect others, while the actual cause of death was a suicide. Typical of British murder mysteries of the time but competently handled by King, known in England as "King of the Quickies."

p, Irving Asher; d, George King; w, Brock Williams (based on a play by Owen Davis, Sewell Collins).

Murder Mystery **(PR:A MPAA:NR)**

NINE GIRLS½** (1944) 78m COL bw

Ann Harding *(Grace Thornton)*, Evelyn Keyes *(Mary O'Ryan)*, Jinx Falkenburg *(Jane Peters)*, Anita Louise *(Paula Canfield)*, Leslie Brooks *(Roberta Holloway)*, Lynn Merrick *(Eve Sharon)*, Jeff Donnell *("Butch" Hendricks)*, Nina Foch *(Alice Blake)*, Shirley Mills *("Tennessee" Collingwood)*, Marcia Mae Jones *(Shirley Berke)*, Willard Robertson *(Capt. Brooks)*, William Demarest *(Walter Cummings)*, Lester Matthews *(Horace Canfield)*, Grady Sutton *(Photographer)*.

Harding plays a sorority chaperone at a small California college. Her charges are nine of the wittiest wisecrackers Hollywood could put into one film. Everyone has a smart line for any situation that crops up—including murder. Louise plays the nastiest of the bunch, with her cruel insults and attempts at boy friend-stealing. She also threatens to blackmail Foch, a nervous and intelligent girl, claiming she will expose a huge loan to Foch's proud-but-poor parents, to get the unhappy student to write her a paper. Keyes catches Louise and condemns her actions, but the wily gal counteracts by threatening to expose Keyes' brother and his legal troubles, thus hampering Keyes' chance to receive an important teaching position. When the sorority girls go off to a lodge for the weekend, it's discovered that their nemesis has been murdered. Suspicious fingers go pointing in all directions, but it's quickly revealed that Harding is the culprit. She tries to get Keyes to write a self-incriminating letter and then attempts to shoot the poor girl when the cops burst in and arrest her. Harding's motive was passion, for she had wanted to marry Louise's father (Matthews) and the girl was the only thing in her way. NINE GIRLS is a really entertaining piece with a nice mix between the comedy and suspense. The wisecracking never grows tiresome and smartly gives way to the suspense when it's necessary. Louise is delightfully nasty, and Harding plays her part with the exact amount of prim social class that's expected. The supporting cast works well together, with Merrick as a stand-out in a hilarious imitation of Katharine Hepburn. The direction is well handled as the comedy builds up, and then we are directly plunged into a moment of terror. Though this clearly was a B feature, the photography is a cut above most other films of this level. There is a lush quality to it that is rarely found in B movies. Overall this is an entertaining "night at the movies."

p, Burt Kelly; d, Leigh Jason; w, Karen deWolf, Connie Lee (based on the play by Wilfrid H. Pettitt); ph, James Van Trees; m, John Leopold; ed, Otto Meyer; md, Morris Stoloff; art d, Lionel Banks, Ross Bellah.

Comedy/Suspense **(PR:C MPAA:NR)**

NINE HOURS TO RAMA*** (1963, U.S./Brit.) 125m Red Lion/FOX c(AKA: NINE HOURS TO LIVE)

Horst Buchholz *(Naturam Godse)*, Jose Ferrer *(Supt. Gopal Das)*, Valerie Gearon *(Rani Mehta)*, Don Borisenko *(Naryan Apte)*, Robert Morley *(P.K. Mussadi)*, Diane Baker *(Sheila)*, Harry Andrews *(Gen. Singh)*, Jairaj *(G.D. Birla)*, David Abraham *(Detective Munda)*, Achla Sachdev *(Mother)*, Marne Maitland *(Karnick)*, Harold Goldblatt *(Selvrag Prahlad)*, Wolfe Morris *(Detective Bose)*, Francis Matthews *(Rampure)*, Nagendra Nath *(Magin Mehta)*, Jack Hedley *(Kilpatrick)*, Bobby Naidoo *(Retiring Room Manager)*, Allan Cuthbertson *(Capt. Goff)*, Peter Illing *(Frank Ramamurti)*, Jagdev *(Detective)*, Frank Olegario *(Barburao)*, Joseph Cuby *(Chacko)*, Shay Gorman *(Duty Officer)*, Nigel Phoenix *(S.N.S. Boy)*, Harold Kasket *(Datta)*, Christopher Carlos *(Shankar)*, S.N. Selk *(Father)*, Julian Sherrier *(P.K.'s Secretary)*, M.Y. Shaikh, Manohargin *(Policemen)*, Jagdish Raj, Keshov Singh, Sheri Mohan *(Detectives)*, Kurt Christian *(Young Natu)*, Shashi Pameholi *(Young Apte)*, Thali Kouri *(The Madame)*, Ishaq Bux *(Gardener)*, Kunlan Malik *(Bus Conductor)*, Lal Bahadur *(Beggar)*, R.S. Bansal *(Astrologer)*, Rani Verma *(Sita)*, Baseo Panday *(Laundryman)*, J.S. Casshyap *(Mahatma Gandhi)*.

Based on the nine hours spent by assassin Naturam Godse (Buchholz) before he murdered India's greatest spiritual leader, Mahatma Gandhi (Casshyap), this film is a startling study of India and the turmoil between its two vying religious sects, Hindu and Moslem. Buchholz is a Hindu, a member of Gandhi's own party, who believes that the religious leader, in preaching non-violence, has allowed the Moslems to seize control of the country. He fanatically believes he must kill Gandhi to save India and sets out to shoot him. Buchholz has been carrying on an affair with beautiful Gearon, a married woman, but they argue about Gandhi—she being a firm supporter of the leader—and split up. Feeling rejected—Buchholz has also been turned down in his application to the British Army because of his Brahmin ancestry—the fanatic spends a little time with attractive prostitute Baker, but returns full of remorse to Gearon, who again sends him on his way. At this moment, Buchholz decides to kill Gandhi. En route to Gandhi's retreat, Buchholz thinks back on his life, which is shown in flashback—the killing of his father and child bride during a riot, his vow to his mother to see justice done by violence, and his enrollment in a fanatical group dedicated to Gandhi's extermination. While Buchholz is traveling toward his goal, Ferrer, the local police chief, learns of the assassination plot and warns Casshyap (who is almost a doppelganger for Gandhi) but the great leader will do nothing to alter his routine and rituals. Buchholz simply shoots the inspired pundit and allows himself to be dragged away by police, knowing he will pay with his life for the crime. Although Buchholz, Baker, and Gearon all seem to be miscast, the film is well-directed and-written, although it could have been shortened by twenty minutes. Arnold's score is moving and dynamic and Ibbetson's camerawork is outstanding. The 64-year-old Casshyap, a former teacher, is amazing in his resemblance, speech, and manner to the great Mahatma.

p&d, Mark Robson; w, Nelson Gidding (based on the book by Stanley Wolpert); ph, Arthur Ibbetson, Ted Moore (CinemaScope, DeLuxe Color); m, Malcolm Arnold; ed, Ernest Walter; md, Arnold; art d, Elliot Scott, Ram Yedekar; set d, John Jarvis; makeup, Harold Fletcher, Wally Schneiderman.

Historical Drama **(PR:C MPAA:NR)**

NINE LIVES ARE NOT ENOUGH**½ (1941) 63m WB bw (AKA: NINE LOVES ARE NOT ENOUGH)

Ronald Reagan (Matt Sawyer), Joan Perry (Jane Abbott), James Gleason (Sgt. Daniels), Peter Whitney (Roy Slocum), Faye Emerson (Rose Chadwick), Howard da Silva (Murray, the City Editor), Edward Brophy (Officer Slattery), Charles Drake ("Snapper" Lucas), Vera Lewis (Mrs. Slocum), Ben Welden (Moxie Karper), Howard Hickman (Col. Andrews), Tom Stevenson (Charles), John Ridgely (Mechanic), Paul Phillips (Hot-Foot), Cliff Clark (Lt. Buckley), Walter Soderling (Dr. Lynen), Joseph Crehan (Yates), John Maxwell (Gillis), John Hamilton (Chief Turner), Thurston Hall (J. B. Huntley), Billy Dawson (Copy Boy), Creighton Hale (Mahan), Olaf Hytten (Butler), Eddy Chandler (Cop), Jimmy O'Gatty (Muley), Hank Mann (Newspaper Man).

This hard-driven crime reporter film features Reagan in a made-to-order role. He's the reporter with a nose for news, always brash and ready for action, who writes an expose on gangster Welden. When Welden sues for libel and wins, Reagan is demoted to police-reporting by da Silva, who plays the perfect caricature of a hard-bitten city editor. Gleason and Brophy are a pair of bumbling officers who help Reagan prove himself as they discover the body of a millionaire whom, it is believed, committed suicide. Reagan writes a story that this is really a murder, though the coroner still believes otherwise. That's enough for da Silva, who fires Reagan. But, with the help of Perry, the murdered man's daughter, Reagan proves Welden to be the murderer. In the end Perry falls for Reagan and buys the newspaper, making her new guy the city editor and relegating da Silva to the lonely-hearts column. This is classic B film making with every stereotype and cliche firmly in place. Reagan is his usual gung-ho self, carried along by direction that nearly breaks the land-speed record for story movement.

p, William Jacobs; d, A. Edward Sutherland; w, Fred Niblo, Jr. (based on the novel by Jerome Odlum); ph, Ted McCord; ed, Doug Gould.

Crime **(PR:A MPAA:NR)**

NINE MEN***½ (1943, Brit.) 68m EAL/UA bw

Jack Lambert (Sgt. Jack Watson), Gordon Jackson (Young 'Un), Frederick Piper (Banger Hill), Grant Sutherland (Jock Scott), Bill Blewett (Bill Parker), Eric Micklewood ("Booky" Lee), John Varley ("Dusty" Johnstone), Jack Horsman (Joe Harvey), Richard Wilkinson (John Crawford), Giulio Finzi (Italian Mechanic), Trevor Evans.

An intelligent, gripping war film has a group of army recruits being told the story of nine British soldiers attacked by enemy planes while on patrol in North Africa. The commander is killed, leaving the sergeant and seven men to fight off the enemy until help can arrive. A powerfully told feature; the ensemble is excellent, hooking the audience from the early moments and holding on until the bitter end. This was inspired by a similar Russian film, THE THIRTEEN (1937), which also inspired a Hollywood version, SAHARA (1943). Director Watt is credited with making some of England's finest documentaries, and so it is little wonder that NINE MEN takes on a great deal of para-documentary feel, highlighted by the human verity of the characters. Shot for around $160,000, the North African desert was perfectly simulated at Margam Sands in North Wales, where the movie was made, and timely made, too, since its object was to convince the restless recruits that training made the fighting easier, and the skills with which the seven soldiers fought their way to freedom were the skills they themselves were learning in training camp.

p, Charles Crichton; d&w, Harry Watt (based on a story by Gerald Kersh); ph, Roy Kellino; m, John Greenwood; ed, Charles Crichton; art d, Duncan Sutherland.

War Drama **(PR:A MPAA:NR)**

NINE MILES TO NOON**½ (1963) 67m Daron/Falcon-Taurus bw

Renato Baldini (Dio Dimou), Dolores Sutton (Julia Dimou), Peter Lazer (Jamie Dimou), Morgan Sterne (Jeff Faulkner), Shelly Leder (Pazzo), Anna Marie Ralli (Nella).

Sterne plays an American arriving in Athens in search of his ex-wife Sutton, whom he had abandoned nine years earlier, following their son's birth. Sutton is now married to Baldini, a wealthy Greek architect who stands to inherit a fortune from Sutton's family. It's Sterne's goal to get that money at any cost. He meets his young son (Lazer) and discovers the boy doesn't get along with Baldini. Sterne promises to help the boy find his real father, not letting on his true identity. He then convinces Lazer to put some poison in the thermos Baldini takes to work every day. After the boy does so, he realizes it was wrong and he and his deaf-mute friend Leder run to the construction site where Baldini works. Sterne intercepts the boys and tells Lazer that he is his real father. The boys get away and Sterne chases them to the construction site and up 15 flights of scaffolding to the place where Baldini always eats his noontime meal. A fight ensues and Sterne shoots Baldini, wounding the man. Leder bravely tries to get the gun away from Sterne but falls to his death. Sterne gives himself up and Lazer begins to reconcile with Baldini at Leder's funeral. This routine drama was filmed on location in Athens.

p, Herbert J. Leder, Norman Kantor; d&w, Leder; m&md, Manos Hadjidakis.

Drama **(PR:C MPAA:NR)**

9/30/55***½ (1977) 101m UNIV c

Richard Thomas (Jimmy J.), Susan Tyrrell (Melba Lou), Deborah Benson (Charlotte), Lisa Blount (Billie Jean), Thomas Hulce (Hanley), Dennis Quaid (Frank), Mary Kai Clark (Pat), Dennis Christopher (Eugene), Collin Wilcox (Jimmy J's Mother), Ben Fuhrman (Coach), Ouida White (Aunt Ethel), Bryan Scott (Dickie), Glen Irby (Band Director), Mike Farris (Edgar), Tom Bonner (Radio Announcer), Bush Satterfield (Charlotte's Father), Katherine Satterfield (Charlotte's Mother), Betty Harford (Nurse), James Dombek (Mr.Brown), Belynda Dix (Girl in Car), Melody Hamilton (Girl with Corsage), Ray Hemphill (Young Man in Truck), Tex Biggs (Old Man in Truck), John Pearce (TV Man), Peter Boggs (Mr. Phillips), Mark Thomas, Paula Sanford, Freeman Mobley, Charles McCrary, George Johnson, Neal Moore, Mark Andrews, Ron Campbell, Brian Brandt.

Fine and sensitive drama features Thomas (John-Boy of television's "The Waltons") as a teenager who is crushed on September 30, 1955, when his hero, James Dean, is killed in a car crash. Blount is his wild friend who goes into hysterics over the teen idol's death. The pair join with other Dean-worshiping friends for an occult-mystical ceremony honoring their hero. The liquor-infested ceremony results in the accidental disfiguring of Blount's face. Themes of hero-worship and death are well handled in this unusual film. Thomas breaks from his nice-guy (John-Boy of "The Waltons") TV image, giving a powerfully effective performance. Unlike so many films of this sort, teenagers are treated as human beings. What's more, the adults are also well-handled, being given fine characterizations to work with. The excellent music score is by Rosenman, who wrote the music for James Dean's first two films as well. This film unfortunately never saw wide release and ironically was put out at the time of the death of another 1950s teen idol, Elvis Presley.

p, Jerry Weintraub; d&w, James Bridges; ph, Gordon Willis (Technicolor); m, Leonard Rosenman; ed, Jeff Gourson; art d, Robert Luthardt; set d, Sharon Thomas; cos, Kent Warner, Patricia Zinn, Mina Mittleman; stunts, R. A. Rondell.

Drama **(PR:C MPAA:PG)**

NINE TILL SIX** (1932, Brit.) 75m Associated Talking Pictures/RKO bw

Louise Hampton (Madam), Elizabeth Allan (Gracie Abbott), Florence Desmond (Daisy), Isla Bevan (Ailene Pennarth), Richard Bird (Jimmie Pennarth), Frances Doble (Clare), Jeanne de Casalis (Yvonne), Kay Hammond (Beatrice), Sunday Wilshin (Judy), Alison Leggatt (Freda), Moore Marriott (Doorman), George de Warfaz, Hilda Simms.

Episodic romance follows the lives of several employees of a well-known London dress shop. Hampton is the head dressmaker who borrows one of her own creations to go to a big dance with a high-ranking gentleman. However, the woman is accused of stealing the outfit, though predictably enough her name is cleared by film's end. Working on the script was Alma Reville, the wife of Alfred Hitchcock.

p&d, Basil Dean; w, Beverley Nicholls, Alma Reville, John Paddy Carstairs (based on the play by Aimee and Philip Stuart); ph, Bob Martin, Robert de Grasse.

Romance **(PR:A MPAA:NR)**

NINE TO FIVE*** (1980) 110m IPC/FOX c

Jane Fonda (Judy Bernly), Lily Tomlin (Violet Newstead), Dolly Parton (Doralee Rhodes), Dabney Coleman (Franklin Hart, Jr.), Sterling Hayden (Tinsworthy), Elizabeth Wilson (Roz), Henry Jones (Hinkle), Lawrence Pressman (Dick), Marian Mercer (Missy Hart), Ren Woods (Barbara), Norma Donaldson (Betty), Roxanna Bonilla-Giannini (Maria), Peggy Pope (Margaret), Richard Stahl (Meade), Ray Vitte (Eddie), Edward Marshall (Bob Enright), Alan Haufrect (Chuck Strell), Earl Boen (Perkins), Jeffrey Douglas Thomas (Dwayne Rhodes), Tom Tarpey (Norman Lane), Terrence McNally (Policeman), Barbara Chase (Buffy), David Price (Josh Newstead), Michael Delnao, Gavin Mooney, Peter Hobbs, Esther Sutherland, Helene Heigh, Vicki Belmonte, Jerrold Ziman, Jessica Badovinac, Eric Mansker, Shirley Anthony, Michael Hehr, Gary Bisig, Raymond O'Keefe.

Five years after this picture was released, a young couple sued the producers and Dolly Parton and claimed that they had written and submitted a song that was similar to the Oscar-nominated tune Parton wrote which helped this movie do well at the box office. They lost the case, although many musicologists found the music to be more than unusually alike. Fonda is a newly divorced woman who has taken an office job and is soon palling with two other secretaries, Tomlin and Parton (in a sensational movie debut that was soured by her appearance in RHINESTONE). Their boss is male chauvinist Coleman who is trying very hard to land Parton in bed. Tomlin is the woman who trained Coleman in his work but can't get a promotion due to her sex. Coleman is the bane of their existence and the threesome smoke some dope one night and dream about how they will get even with him. (Tomlin's fantasy, an animated sequence with her as a misguided Snow White who poisons Coleman, is particularly good.) They each have a different dream and Coleman finally spots the cabal against him. (Tomlin thinks she really has poisoned Coleman and they all go to a hospital where she steals a dead body, then they have to return same when they realize it never happened.) Coleman is kidnaped by the women; they chain him to his own bedroom ceiling and force him to watch banal soap operas. In his absence, the office becomes a better place to work and efficiency improves while Coleman's dotty wife, Mercer, is out of town. In the end, the women prevail in as unlikely a conclusion as could be imagined. Lots of laughs, not much sense, and the resemblance between this office and any real one is solely in Higgins' mind. Produced by Fonda's company, NINE TO FIVE is an amusing way to spend 110 minutes but as memorable as a mayor's speech. Charles Fox's music helps keep matters bouncing along and all credits are professional. There are several men in the picture and they are treated with disdain, much the same way Spielberg did it to the entire masculine gender in THE COLOR PURPLE. It was a pleasure to see some work by Higgins in which he didn't imitate Alfred Hitchcock.

When and if he ever gets around to doing something truly original, he might become a good director-writer. In this picture, the story was by his co-screenwriter, Resnick. Later made into a TV series.

p, Bruce Gilbert; d, Colin Higgins; w, Higgins, Patricia Resnick (based on a story by Resnick); ph, Reynaldo Villalobos (DeLuxe Color); m, Charles Fox; ed, Pembroke J. Herring; prod d, Dean Mitzner; art d, Jack Gammon Taylor, Jr.; set d, Ann McCulley; cos, Ann Roth; spec eff, Chuck Gaspar, Matt Sweeney; animation, Mishkin, Hellmuch, Virgien & Friends; m/l, "Nine to Five," Dolly Parton (sung by Parton).

Comedy **Cas.** **(PR:C-O MPAA:PG)**

1984½** (1956, Brit.) 94m Holiday/COL bw

Michael Redgrave *(Gen. O'Connor)*, Edmond O'Brien *(Winston Smith)*, Jan Sterling *(Julia)*, David Kossoff *(Charrington the Junk Shop Owner)*, Mervyn Johns *(Jones)*, Donald Pleasence *(Parsons)*, Carol Wolveridge *(Selina Parsons)*, Ernest Clark *(Outer Party Announcer)*, Patrick Allen *(Inner Party Official)*, Ronan O'Casey *(Rutherford)*, Michael Ripper, Ewen Solon *(Outer Party Orators)*, Kenneth Griffiths *(Prisoner)*.

Great liberties were taken with the story written by Orwell and published in 1949, a year before Orwell passed away. Those liberties were to the detriment of one of the most powerful and depressing books ever written. The year is, of course, 1984 and London is the capital of one of three world communities, Oceania. It's after the first atomic war and everyone in London (and everywhere else) is constantly watched by TV cameras (which are also screens) and by "Big Brother" and his faceless aides. The surroundings are drab and no individuality will be tolerated. The walls are festooned with posters which read "War Is Peace," "Freedom Is Slavery," and "Big Brother Is Watching You." And he is. O'Brien works for the state and finds that he cannot handle the stultifying atmosphere of being ruled by the Minsitry of Love because he is falling for Sterling. They begin to have a clandestine affair which will be life-threatening if ever uncovered by The Anti-Sex League or The Thought Police. Sterling and O'Brien make plans to overthrow Big Brother and they are joined in their cabal by Redgrave, but he is, in reality, a member of the Government and he eventually informs on them. Since there are two-way microphones in every residence, the deepest fears of every citizen have been audiotaped and are known to the authorities. When someone is brought in, they are taken to Room 101 where they have to confront their innermost fears. In the case of O'Brien, it's rats, and when he must face the little furry things, he breaks. The end of the movie is varied, depending on which country you see it in. The British version has Sterling and O'Brien killed. The American version has O'Brien betraying Sterling and so successfully brainwashed that he shouts for the love of Big Brother rather than "down with Big Brother"—the words he screams as his last epithet in England. The last words of the book are also different. After O'Brien's character is bumped off, the comment is made that "he loved Big Brother." Another version of the film was made in the 1980s which was equally depressing and ultimately unsuccessful with the critics and the public. Perhaps this is one of those novels that defies cinematization and must be savored in one's brain, rather than with the ears and eyes. The same could be said for Huxley's *Brave New World*.

p, N. Peter Rathvon; d, Michael Anderson; w, William P. Templeton, Ralph Gilbert Bettinson (based on the novel by George Orwell); ph, C. Pennington-Richards; m, Malcolm Arnold; ed, Bill Lewthwaite; md, Louis Levy; art d, Terence Verity; cos, Barbara Gray; spec eff, B. Langley, G. Blackwell, N. Warwick.

Drama **(PR:A-C MPAA:NR)**

1941½** (1979) 118m UNIV-COL-A-Team/UNIV c

Dan Aykroyd *(Sgt. Tree)*, Ned Beatty *(Ward Douglas)*, John Belushi *(Wild Bill Kelso)*, Lorraine Gary *(Joan Douglas)*, Murray Hamilton *(Claude)*, Christopher Lee *(Von Kleinschmidt)*, Tim Matheson *(Birkhead)*, Toshiro Mifune *(Comdr. Mitamura)*, Warren Oates *(Maddox)*, Robert Stack *(Gen. Stilwell)*, Treat Williams *(Sitarski)*, Nancy Allen *(Donna)*, Lucille Bensen *(Gas Mama)*, Jordan Brian *(Macey)*, John Candy *(Foley)*, Elisha Cook *(Patron)*, Patti LuPone *(Lydia Hedberg)*, Penny Marshall *(Miss Fitroy)*, Slim Pickens *(Hollis Wood)*, Lionel Stander *(Scioli)*, Dub Taylor *(Malcomb)*, Ignatius Wolfington *(Meyer Mishkin)*, Joseph P. Flaherty *(USO M.C.)*, *Eddie Deezen (Herbie)*, Bobby DiCicco *(Wally)*, Dianne Kay *(Betty)*, Perry Lang *(Dennis)*, J. Patrick McNamara *(DuBois)*, Frank McRae *(Ogden Johnson Jones)*, Steven Mond *(Gus)*, Wendie Jo Sperber *(Maxine)*, Christian Zika *(Stevie)*, Mark Carlton *(Stilwell Aide)*, Gary Cervantes *(Zoot Suiter)*, Paul Cloud *(Stilwell Aide)*, Luis Contreras *(Zoot Suiter)*, Carol Culver, Marjorie Gaines, Trish Garland *(Anderson Sisters)*, Dian Gallup, Denise Gallup *(Twins)*, Lucinda Dooling *(Lucinda)*, Gray Frederickson *(Lt. Bressler)*, Brian Frishman *(USO Goon)*, Sam Fuller *(Interceptor Commander)*, Barbara Gannen *(Interceptor Assistant)*, Brad Gorman *(USO Nerd)*, Jerry Hardin *(Map Man)*, Diane Hill *(Interceptor Assistant)*, Bob Houston *(Maddox's Soldier)*, Audrey Landers *(USO Girl)*, John Landis *(Mizerany)*, John R. McKee *(Reporter)*, Ronnie MacMillan *(Winowski)*, Dan McNally *(Reporter)*, Richard Miller *(Officer Miller)*, Akio Mitamura *(Ashimoto)*, Antoinette Molinari *(Mrs. Scioli)*, Walter Olkewicz *(Hinshaw)*, Mickey Rourke *(Reese)*, Whitney Ridbeck *(Daffy)*, Donovan Scott *(Kid Sailor)*, Kerry Sherman *(USO Girl)*, Hiroshi Shimizu *(Ito)*, Geno Silva *(Martinez)*, David Lander *(Joe)*, Michael McKean *(Willy)*, Susan Backlinie *(Polar Bear Woman)*, E. Hampton Beagle *(Phone Man)*, Deborah Benso *(USO Girl)*, Don Calfa *(Telephone Operator)*, Dave Cameron *(Reporter)*, Vito Carenzo *(Vito, Shore Patrol)*, Rita Taggart *(Reporter)*, Maureen Teefy *(USO Girl)*, Andy Tennant *(Babyface)*, Jack Thibeau, Galen Thomas $2(Stilwell Aides), Frank Verroca, John Volstadt *(USO Nerds)*, Carol Ann Williams, Jenny Williams *(USO Girls)*, Elmer *(Himself)*.

It's raucous slapstick and mindless mirth in the lowbrow tradition of The Three Stooges and much of it doesn't work, but what does is spectacular. The Japanese sneak attack on Pearl Harbor on December 7, 1941 sends Southern California into a near-panic state, especially among the military. Stack (playing General Stilwell) is appointed commander of the West Coast and is ordered to repel any Japanese invasion. Tanks are placed in downtown Los Angeles, anti-aircraft guns on the rooftops of buildings, and along the beaches, 40mm cannon are positioned. One such cannon is placed outside the seaside home of Beatty, a patriotic private citizen. Belushi, as a Japanese-hating fighter pilot, begins flying his warplane toward Los Angeles, stopping off at a remote airfield commanded by jittery commander Oates. After shooting up the place, Belushi has his plane refueled, and he again flies off. Meanwhile Matheson, a young officer, becomes enamored of Allen, Stack's pulchritudinous assistant, but learns that she will not respond amorously unless she's in a flying airplane. To that end Matheson commandeers a transport plane and amateurishly flies it around Los Angeles, drawing American anti-aircraft fire as the plane is mistaken for a Japanese bomber. Mifune surfaces his submarine and duels with Beatty who is operating the 40mm cannon, the Japanese next attacking a beachside carnival and destroying a ferris wheel. Belushi crash-lands on a Los Angeles street which is being destroyed by a tank crew—Candy, Aykroyd, etc. Stack, who is dragged from a theater where he has been weeping over the perils of DUMBO, thinks the world has gone mad (and it has). Belushi jumps onto a motorcycle and races to the carnival, diving into the ocean and landing on the submarine. Aykroyd drives his tank to the end of a pier which is destroyed and Belushi becomes a prisoner of the Japanese, taking an involuntary trip to Tokyo. Although this $31 million dollar bomb (three times the cost of E.T.) was a spectacular hit in Japan (where it was perceived to be sympathetic to the Japanese and showed their military men to be less idiotic than Americans but not much), 1941 did $23 million in box-office receipts. Director Spielberg remembered later that "when I first read the script I gagged on it. Moments were so funny that I vomited from laughter...The whole film is a noisy drunken brawl...For me, it was like making huge toys." It was considered tasteless, unfunny, and crude by most critics but there are some belly laughs and the production credits are good.

p, Buzz Feitshans; d, Steven Spielberg; w, Robert Zemeckis, Bob Gale (based on a story by Zemeckis, Gale, John Milius); ph, William A. Fraker (Panavision, Metrocolor); m, John Williams; ed, Michael Kahn; prod d, Dean Edward Mitzner; art d, William F. O'Brien; set d, John Austin; cos, Deborah Nadoolman; ch, Paul DeRolf, Judy Van Wormer; spec eff, A.D. Flowers: stunts, Terry Leonard; m/l, "Down By the O-Hi-O," Abe Olman, Jack Yellen, "Daddy," Bob Troup (sung by The Andrews Sisters).

Comedy **Cas.** **(PR:C-O MPAA:PG)**

1900*** (1976, Ital.) 245m PEA-Artistes Associes/PAR-UA-FOX c (NOVECENTO)

Burt Lancaster *(Alfredo Berlinghieri, Grandfather)*, Romolo Valli *(Giovanni)*, Anna-Maria Gherardi *(Eleonora)*, Laura Betti *(Regina)*, Robert De Niro *(Alfredo Berlinghieri, Grandson)*, Paolo Pavesi *(Alfredo as a Child)*, Dominique Sanda *(Ada)*, Sterling Hayden *(Leo Dalco)*, Gerard Depardieu *(Olmo Dalco)*, Roberto Maccanti *(Olmo as a Child)*, Stefania Sandrelli *(Anita Foschi, Olmo's Wife)*, Donald Sutherland *(Attila)*, Werner Bruhns *(Octavio)*, Alida Valli *(Signora Pioppi)*, Francesca Bertini *(Sister Desolata)*.

It took three major studios to put this epic together, Paramount, United Artists, and Twentieth Century-Fox. The picture was shown at Cannes where it occupied the entire day, and Bertolucci spent three years writing, directing, and editing it. This is the largest Italian movie to date, and for sheer scope, applause must be given. However, the undertaking is even too large to be called a movie and would have been better released as two or three films or shown as a mini-series. The American version is somewhat shorter at 245 minutes, but rear ends will still squirm at that length, no matter how fascinating the film. All of the action takes place in and around Parma, a medium-sized city in north central Italy. Bertolucci has used the area as a microcosm for all of Italy in the 20th Century. It begins in April, 1945, on the day of Italy's "liberation" from the Fascist forces (although there are those who will argue that Italy wanted the Fascists and it was that party that united the country), then flashes back to the day that Verdi died, in late January of 1901, for the birth of two young boys whose stories we follow for the rest of the picture. De Niro is the grandson of Lancaster, a well-to-do landowner. In a difficult role, he manages to convince the audience that he is a wimp. Depardieu is the bastard grandson of Hayden, a peasant farmer who tills the soil owned by Lancaster. As the boys grow up, De Niro becomes more and more of a weakling and fears Sutherland, the foreman, and Depardieu, who takes up communism and seeks to organize a peasant union. There's a strike in 1908 that puts all of the farmhands at bay with the bourgeoisie. The two young men fight in WW I and come home to take their places in the social strata. Fascism begins, De Niro inherits the property and marries Sanda, and Depardieu's wife, Sandrelli, dies in childbirth. He leaves the area when his Communist activities become too blatant, and he returns at the end of the war to oversee a trial of De Niro, who is eventually allowed to stay alive. There is far too much political theorizing and pulpit-pounding in the script, something that works against the grandeur and flattens any complexity that might have been engendered had Bertolucci just presented the facts with no bias. Two separate points are made: the first is the dual-telling of the stories of the families and the second is the political overtones of Fascism versus Communism. One or the other could have been excised and the picture would have been shorter and much better. One cannot dismiss the enormity of the enterprise lightly. Bertolucci's attention to detail and the splendid cast make 1900 better than anything Visconti did. There is very little camera trickery, a plus, but too much time in sidebar stories that meander in and out with no beginning or ending to them. A flawed masterpiece.

p, Alberto Grimaldi; d, Bernardo Bertolucci; w, Franco Arcalli, Bernardo and Giuseppe Bertolucci; ph, Vittorio Storaro (Technicolor); m, Ennio Morricone; ed, Arcalli; art d, Enzo Frigerio; cos, Gitt Magrini.

Drama **(PR:C-O MPAA:R)**

1914** (1932, Ger.) 80m Atlas/CAP bw (AKA: 1914: THE LAST DAYS BEFORE THE WAR)

Albert Basserman *(Count Hollweg)*, Herrman Wlach *(Count von Jagow)*, Wolfgang von Schwindt *(Count von Moltke)*, Robert Hartberg *(Count Hoyos)*, Reinhold Schuenzel *(Czar Nicholas II)*, Lucie Hoeflich *(The Czarina)*, Ferdinand Hart *(Archduke Nicholas)*, Oskar Homolka *(Sazanow)*, A. E. Licho *(Suchomlinow)*, Hans Peppier *(Count Pourtales)*, Theodore Loos *(Pateologue)*, Fritz Alberti *(Buchanan)*, Eugene Kloepfer *(Emperor Franz Josef)*, Alfred Abel *(Count Berchtold)*, Victor Jensen *(Count Tisza)*, Ferdinand von Alten *(Viviana)*, Bruno Ziemer *(Count von Schoen)*, Heinrich George *(Jean Jaures)*, Alexander Granach *(His Confidant)*, Paul Mederow *(Sir Edward Grey)*, Fritz Odemar *(Prince Lichnowsky)*, Dr. Eugene Fischer.

A well-acted history of Germany's involvement in WW I that benefits from some fine characterizations. However, the film is poorly photographed and the sound is an unacceptable recording considering the technology that was available. The American release also suffered from an unnecessary prolog and epilog in English with historian Fischer. Though the film blames the war on Russia and Czar Nicholas II, the film surprisingly was banned for a time in Germany. (In German.)

d, Richard Oswald; w, Heinz Goldberg, Fritz Wendhausen; ph, Mutz Greenbaum [Max Greene]; set d, Franz Schroedter.

Historical Drama **(PR:C MPAA:NR)**

1921 (SEE: RISING OF THE SUN, THE, 1957)

1990: THE BRONX WARRIORS** (1983, Ital.) 84m Deaf Films/United Film Distribution c (1990: I GUERRIERI DEL BRONX; AKA: BRONX WARRIORS)

Vic Morrow *(Hammer)*, Christopher Connolly *(Hot Dog)*, Fred Williamson *(The Ogre)*, Mark Gregory *(Trash)*, Stefani Girolami *(Anne)*, John Sinclair *(Ice)*, Enio Girolami, George Eastman, Betty Dessy, Rocco Lerro, Massimo Vanni, Angelo Ragusa.

It's 1990 and street gangs have taken over the Bronx. Morrow is hired to find an heiress who has taken up with a biker. Morrow locates the girl and puts a stop to the biker's plan to use her as a pawn in a war between two rival gangs. An uninspired attempt to cash in on the success of films such as THE WARRIORS and ESCAPE FROM NEW YORK.

p, Fabrizio De Angelis; d, Enzo G. Castellari, Dardana Sachetti, Elisa Livia Brighanti (based on a story by Sachetti); ph, Sergio Salvati (Panavision, Eastmancolor); m, Walter Rizzati; ed, Gianfranco Amicucci; cos, Massimo Lentini; spec eff, Antonio Corridori, Walter Battistelli, Pasquino Benassati, Pasquale Sarao; makeup, Maurizio Trani.

Crime **(PR:C MPAA:R)**

90 DEGREES IN THE SHADE½** (1966, Czech./Brit.) 90m CFD/Landau-Unger bw (TRICET JEONA VE STINU)

Anne Heywood *(Alena)*, James Booth *(Vorell)*, Rudolf Hrusinsky *(Kurka)*, Ann Todd *(Mrs. Kurka)*, Donald Wolfit *(Bazant)*, Jirina Jiraskova *(Vera)*, Jorga Kotrbova *(Hanka)*, Vladimir Mensik *(Emil)*, Jiri Sovak *(Director)*, Valtr Taub *(Doctor)*, Vera Tichankova *(Vavrova)*, Vera Uzelacova *(Prochazkova)*, Jan Skopecek *(Head Waiter)*, Stella Zazvorkova *(Salesgirl)*, Tafana Vavrincova *(Secretary)*, Jan Cmiral *(Judge)*, Vlasta Jelinkova, Eva Svobodova *(Women)*, Jiri Sasek *(Man with Briefcase)*, Jan Libicek *(Man in the Booth)*, Mirko Musil *(Saloon Keeper)*, Karel Pavlik *(Salesman)*, Ladislav Potmesil *(Jirka Kurka)*, Olbdrich Velen *(Criminal Investigator)*.

Heywood plays a young grocery clerk who is having an affair with Booth, her store's married manager. She realizes the man is no good because he steals liquor from the store. But her sexual passions are overwhelming and she cannot bring herself to end the affair. When store inventory is conducted, 80 bottles of brandy are found to contain tea. Hrusinsky and Wolfit, two company auditors, question the employees. Heywood, fearing exposure of the affair, runs from the store and Hrusinsky decides that she is to blame. Hrusinksy is a cold-hearted, calculating man whose blind loyalties have affected his marriage. Heywood confronts Booth and asks for his advice. He tells her to take the blame. The worst thing that could happen to her would be probation while he would probably receive a jail sentence. Heywood comes to believe her life is ruined and she kills herself. This unexpected turn of events moves Hrusinsky and he realizes that his own life needs a reexamination. Booth, ever the cad, remains aloof. He goes back to his job and hires a new girl to replace Heywood. The drama here is a little overblown but the love scenes are as hot as they come. This was made in Czechoslovakia with a predominantly British cast.

p, Raymond Stross; d, Jiri Weiss; w, David Mercer (based on a story by Weiss, Jiri Mucha); ph, Bedrich Batka; m, Ludek Hulan; ed, Jan Chaloupek, Russell Lloyd; art d, Bohuslav Kulic, Vera Liznerova.

Drama **(PR:O MPAA:NR)**

99 AND 44/100% DEAD** (1974) 97m FOX c (GB: CALL HARRY CROWN)

Richard Harris *(Harry Crown)*, Edmond O'Brien *(Uncle Frank)*, Bradford Dillman *(Big Eddie)*, Ann Turkel *(Buffy)*, Constance Ford *(Dolly)*, David Hall *(Tony)*, Katherine Baumann *(Baby)*, Janice Heiden *(Clara)*, Chuck Connors *(Marvin "Claw" Zuckerman)*, Max Kleven *(North)*, Karl Lukas *(Guard)*, Anthony Brubaker *(Burt)*, Jerry Summers *(Shoes)*, Roy Jenson *(Jake)*, Bennie Dobbins *(Driver)*, Chuck Roberson *(Gunman)*.

A perplexing muddle of styles clash and sputter when screenwriter Dillon's satiric, quirky parody of gangster movies meets flashy director Frankenheimer's slick and inventive visuals, neither of which complement the other. Coupled with Harris' typically irritating performance, this project must have seemed doomed from the start. O'Brien, a gruff and aging gang lord, hires hit-man Harris to kill Dillman, a rival gangster who is muscling in on his rackets. The milieu Harris enters is a strangely futuristic realm where almost anything can happen. High-speed car chases, a society of cement-shoed corpses in the river, and a sewer full of albino alligators are just some of the bizarre sights to be seen. Perhaps the strangest creation is that of Connors' character, dubbed the "Claw." This crazed killer has a metal stump for a hand that can be fitted with dozens of detachable appliances from household (a corkscrew) to lethal. All in all, the film is wildly inventive but uneven to the point of distraction with moments of funny satire being punctuated with outbursts of sadism and violence. Surprisingly, Dillon and Frankenheimer teamed up again, this time much more successfully, for FRENCH CONNECTION II (1975).

p, Joe Wizan; d, John Frankenheimer; w, Robert Dillon; ph, Ralph Woolsey (Panavision, DeLuxe Color); m, Henry Mancini; ed, Harold F. Kress; art d, Herman Blumenthal; cos, Ron Talsky; m/l, "Easy Baby," Mancini, Alan and Marilyn Bergman.

Crime/Satire **Cas.** **(PR:C-O MPAA:PG)**

99 RIVER STREET** (1953) 83m UA bw

John Payne *(Ernie Driscoll)*, Evelyn Keyes *(Linda James)*, Brad Dexter *(Victor Rawlins)*, Frank Faylen *(Stan Hogan)*, Peggie Castle *(Pauline Driscoll)*, Jay Adler *(Christopher)*, Jack Lambert *(Mickey)*, Eddy Waller *(Pop Dudkee)*, Glen Langan *(Lloyd Morgan)*, John Day *(Bud)*, Ian Wolfe *(Walde Daggett)*, Peter Leeds *(Nat Finley)*, William Tannen *(Director)*, Gene Reynolds *(Chuck)*.

Payne is a down-on-his-luck fighter reduced to driving a cab. He is married to Castle who is having an affair with Dexter, a jewel thief. Keyes is a would-be actress accused of murdering a stage producer. Payne offers to help her but finds he must clear his name as well when Castle's lifeless body turns up in the back of his cab. Dexter is the guilty party and Payne redeems himself once more in a climactic fight scene. The action is well staged in this otherwise routine work. Camera operator Planer occasionally comes up with some unusual shots, though an overabundance of close-ups slows the film's pacing. Unfortunately Keyes plays her part with excessive gusto. In this example of *film noir*, the contrasts between reality and the stage and between violence as an individual's fate and as pure show are illustrated. Karlson made two other movies reflecting the *film noir* style.

p, Edward Small; d, Phil Karlson; w, Robert Smith (based on a story by George Zuckerman); ph, Franz Planer; m, Emil Newman, Arthur Lange; ed, Buddy Small; art d, Frank Sylos.

Crime **(PR:C MPAA:NR)**

99 WOUNDS* (1931) 56m TIF bw

Tom Tyler *(Hank Johnson)*, Franklyn Farnum *(Reese)*, Jean Dumas *(Rose Purdue)*, Trilby Clark *(Carmencita Esteban)*, Iron Eyes Cody *(Running Bear)*, Fred Kohler *(Monty Vale)*, Wally Wales *(Chief Slow Water)*, Chief Thunder Cloud *(Medicine Man)*, Frank Ellis *(Moreland)*.

Border skirmishes, with a band of marauding "Indians" attacking settlers, bring marshal Tyler to Sonora. With the assistance of Mexican saloon girl Clark, Tyler discovers that the renegades, who find refuge by crossing the border, are really whites in war paint led by Kohler. Recruiting a band of real Indians, who feel they have been unfairly tagged with treachery, he disposes of the rascals and finds romance with Kohler's innocent daughter Dumas.

d, Spencer Gordon Bennett; w, Frank W. Othile (based on a story by George Fencroft); ph, Melvin Antwerp; ed, Fred S. White.

Western **(PR:A MPAA:NR)**

92 IN THE SHADE* (1975, U.S./Brit.) 88m ITC/UA c

Peter Fonda *(Tom Skelton)*, Warren Oates *(Nichol Dance)*, Margot Kidder *(Miranda)*, Burgess Meredith *(Goldsboro)*, Harry Dean Stanton *(Faron Carter)*, Sylvia Miles *(Bella Knowles)*, Elizabeth Ashley *(Jeannie Carter)*, William Hickey *(Mr. Skelton)*, Louise Latham *(Mrs. Skelton)*, Joe Spinell *(Ollie Slatt, Tourist)*, William Roerick *(Rudleigh)*, Evelyn Russell *(Mrs. Rudleigh)*, John Quade *(Roy)*, John Heffernan *(Myron, Carter's Assistant)*, Warren Kemmerling *(James Powell the Boat Builder)*, Robert Kruse *(Waiter)*, Scott Palmer *(Michael)*.

Another turkey from executive producer Elliott Kastner, the American-born dealmaker who spends much of his time in England. Kastner seems to be running the cinematic equivalent of a poultry farm and has made more bombs than a terrorist. Director-writer McGuane had two of his novels done by other directors and didn't like the way they turned out (they were THE SPORTING CLUB, directed by Larry Peerce, and RANCHO DELUXE, directed by Arthur Penn), so he decided to do this one himself. Perhaps novelist McGuane is better read than seen, because this one turned out no better than those. It's an aimless character piece that starts out going nowhere and ends up having been there. Fonda is a drifter who comes home to Key West after years of travel. He plans to be a fishing guide for the wealthy easterners who come south looking for marlins and a tan they can brag about over dinner at Lutece. His whacked-out parents, Latham and Hickey, pay little attention to his return, as she's too busy tending her flowers, and he won't get off the veranda, preferring to sit under the mosquito netting and bitch about the way the world has deteriorated. Meredith is Fonda's randy old grandfather, a rich eccentric, who spends most of his time in bed with his private secretary, Miles. Fonda wants some peace in his life, but local guide Oates and his buddy Stanton don't think there's room for another man in the fishing business, so they do everything they can to get him out, including filching Fonda's clients and telling him to beware of Oates' allegedly violent ways. Fonda won't buckle under to their threats and retaliates by placing an explosive device in the boat owned by Oates, and it's destroyed in the blast and fire. Fonda talks Meredith into lending him enough cash to get a plush craft, while Oates has to make do with an old scow he buys with his last few dollars. By this time, Fonda has established a relationship with

Kidder, a local teacher, and she defends him in a battle with Ashley, the dingbat, pregnant wife of Stanton. The fight between the two women has a calming effect on the men and they back off from each other for the time being. Kidder wishes Fonda would stay away from Oates, as she thinks Oates is capable of killing her lover. Hickey tries to convince Fonda that it's not worth all the effort, but Fonda is determined to make a success out of his venture. Spinell arrives and charters Fonda's boat. They sail out where Oates, wielding a gun, comes up alongside and threatens Fonda's life. Fonda goes for Oates and the two men fight as the boats move closer to shore in the tide. Spinell jumps out of Fonda's boat and makes his way into the shore while the men struggle for control of the firearm. The fight ends and the two men stare at each other. Neither is the victor, but they both begin laughing, as they realize that it's a big ocean out there and there's room for both of them to make a living. And that's it. If this picture is any indication of what life is like in Key West, spare us. Tennessee Williams used to favor the area and also wrote of the weird characters who inhabit the U.S.' southernmost territory (if you don't count Puerto Rico and the various Virgin Islands) and it's enough to make one want to keep away from there. McGuane and Ashley fell in love for a while, but that was as brief as his directorial career. The picture originally ended with Oates firing at Fonda and, presumably, killing him, but audiences at previews must have objected, and they changed the conclusion to offer some hope for the characters. It's interesting in that, for all the supposed emotion, the picture is so understated that we never feel blood boiling, and the result is a very detached movie that never ignites. The language is very graphic, unnecessarily so most of the time, so if you're watching it on cable with a tyke, put earmuffs on the child.

p, George Pappas; d&w, Thomas McGuane (based on his novel); ph, Michael C. Butler (Eastmancolor); m, Michael J. Lewis; ed, Ed Rothkowitz; md, Lewis; spec eff, Joe Day; makeup, Irv Buchman.

Drama **(PR:C MPAA:R)**

NINGEN NO JOKEN (SEE: HUMAN CONDITION, THE, 1959)

NINGEN NO JOKEN II (SEE: ROAD TO ETERNITY, 1961)

NINGEN NO JOKEN III (SEE: SOLDIER'S PRAYER, 1970)

NINJUTSU, SORYU HIKEN (SEE: SECRET SCROLLS (PART II), 1968, Jap.)

NINOTCHKA***** (1939) 110m MGM bw

Greta Garbo *(Lena Yakushova "Ninotchka")*, Melvyn Douglas *(Count Leon Dolga)*, Ina Claire *(Grand Duchess Swana)*, Sig Rumann *(Michael Ironoff)*, Felix Bressart *(Buljanoff)*, Alexander Granach *(Kopalski)*, Bela Lugosi *(Commissar Razinin)*, *Gregory Gaye (Count Alexis Rakonin)*, Richard Carle *(Vaston)*, Edwin Maxwell *(Mercier)*, Rolfe Sedan *(Hotel Manager)*, George Tobias *(Russian Visa Official)*, Dorothy Adams *(Jacqueline, Swana's Maid)*, Lawrence Grant *(Gen. Savitsky)*, Charles Judels *(Pere Mathieu, Cafe Owner)*, Frank Reicher, Edwin Stanley *(Lawyers)*, Peggy Moran *(French Maid)*, Marek Windheim *(Manager)*, Mary Forbes *(Lady Lavenham)*, Alexander Schonberg *(Bearded Man)*, George Davis *(Porter)*, Armand Kaliz *(Louis, the Headwaiter)*, Wolfgang Zilzer *(Taxi Driver)*, Tamara Shayne *(Anna)*, William Irving *(Bartender)*, Bess Flowers *(Gossip)*, Elizabeth Williams *(Indignant Woman)*, Paul Weigel *(Vladimir)*, Harry Semels *(Neighbor-Spy)*, Jody Gilbert *(Streetcar Conductress)*, Florence Shirley *(Marianne)*, Elinor Vandivere, Sandra Morgan, Emily Cabanne, Symona Boniface, Monya Andre *(Gossips)*, Kay Stewart, Jenifer Gray *(Cigarette Girls)*, Lucille Pinson *(German Woman at Railroad Station)*.

Garbo appears in her first comedy here and could have had no better director than the inimitable Lubitsch who presented a mirthful, delightful farce which poked fun at (and recognized, for the first time in a major American film) the Soviets and Stalin-dominated Russia. Garbo is magnificent and so is the film. NINOTCHKA opens with a Soviet committee-Bressart, Rumann, and Granach-arriving in Paris with orders to sell imperial jewels so that food-starved Russia can purchase tractors to harvest crops. Incensed by the mission is Claire, once the Grand Duchess Swana before the Russian revolution eradicated the monarchy and displaced the nobility. It is her jewels that the committee members are selling, jewels confiscated during the Bolshevik takeover. Claire has Douglas, lover and count, investigate the committee's activities in an effort to regain the jewels. He obtains a court injunction preventing the sale of the jewels and then corrupts the committee members with lavish living which so turns their heads that they could care less about returning to Russia with tractors. (Lubitsch accomplished the seduction of the committee to capitalism by merely stationing his cameras before the doors to the hotel suite of the committee, showing an army of waiters entering with trays of food and drink, each wave of new delights met with a roar of approval from the unseen committee members, culminating with the entry of three fetching cigarette girls which causes the committee to explode in a crescendo of acceptance.) At home, Commissar Lugosi is troubled over the lack of communication with Rumann, Bressart, and Granach. He dispatches his most able assistant, Garbo, to bring the errant Soviets into line. Garbo appears in Paris in drab clothes, with a rigid attitude and an unsmiling countenance. Everything about her is severe; she is all business and no nonsense, as the suave Douglas soon finds out. She is a Communist to the marrow but Douglas perseveres, making valiant amorous advances which cause Garbo to tell him that love is no more than "a chemical reaction." During the tour of Paris Douglas conducts, Garbo sees the great edifices and monuments of the City of Light only as illogical structures; she is more concerned with the functional, asking how much steel is in the Eiffel Tower. Once in his apartment, Douglas makes his move, kissing Garbo. She begins to melt a little, telling him that "that was restful." Then she tells Douglas that she has kissed another man before, a Polish lancer who was later killed in battle. Douglas takes her to lunch the next day and labors hard to get Garbo to laugh, a feat equal to taking Leningrad by storm. There obviously isn't a funny bone in her long, lean, beautiful body but Douglas courageously goes after even the smallest chuckle. He says: "When I first heard this joke I laughed myself sick! Here goes. A man comes into a restaurant. He sits down at the table and he says: 'Waiter, bring me a cup of coffee without cream.' Five minutes later the waiter comes back and says: 'I'm sorry, sir, we have no cream. Can it be without milk?' " Garbo glumly stares at Douglas and he snaps: "Oh, you have no sense of humor! None whatsoever. Not a grain of humor in you. There's not a laugh in you!" He's so upset that in gesturing wildly Douglas tips his chair and topples over backward. Garbo bursts forth laughing that deep-throated laugh, a laugh that startled and delighted audiences all over the world. The iceberg is quickly thawing. In the meltdown, the drab, dreary exterior is discarded and Garbo begins to buy and wear Parisian gowns, silk stockings, perfume. Douglas takes her dancing and wins her heart. She is no longer the ruthless Soviet official hunting down confiscated jewels, but a radiant, blossoming woman in love for the first time in her life. Politics now becomes a cavalier subject in Garbo's mind. She gets tipsy in a nightclub with Douglas, calls the customers "comrades," and encourages the female attendants in the washroom to go on strike. That night Douglas takes her to her hotel suite where she goes to sleep in her evening gown and Claire enters, removing her jewels from the safe. Claire confronts Garbo the next morning in a classic confrontation. The refined but bitchy Claire makes a comment about Garbo wearing an evening gown and Garbo responds by saying: "You see, it would have been very embarrassing for people of my sort to wear low-cut gowns in the old Russia. The lashes of the Cossacks across our backs were not very becoming, and you know how vain women are." Replies Claire without batting an eyelash: "Yes, you're quite right about the Cossacks. We made a great mistake when we let them use their whips. They had such reliable guns." Claire is really less concerned about the jewels than she is about her lover, Douglas, knowing he has fallen for Garbo. She wants him and to get him back she proposes that she sign over the jewels to Garbo but only on the proviso that Garbo leave immediately for Russia and get out of Douglas' life. Garbo realizes that she has been whipsawed and has no other choice but to accept Claire's offer. Garbo flies out of France on the next plane for Russia but Claire's plan goes awry. Douglas is hopelessly in love with Garbo and is no longer interested in the scheming duchess. Douglas attempts to get into Russia but he is denied a visa. Then he learns that the Soviet committee of three has been sent to Constantinople to sell furs, a choice assignment gleaned over Garbo's triumph with the jewels. Douglas expects a repeat of the Paris scenario and is correct. Rumann, Bressart, and Granach are again easily corrupted with lavish foreign living and Lugosi again dispatches Garbo to bring the easygoing comrades into line. When she arrives in Constantinople, Garbo finds her three errant comrades in a Russian restaurant which they have opened. Their financial backer? Douglas. He welcomes Garbo into his arms and the two plan to marry. No one plans to return to Russia—ever. This wonderful spoof of Communist Russia was Garbo's 26th film and is one of her finest. She is effervescent and still down to earth, a silent screen goddess adored for a mystique which becomes in NINOTCHKA exquisitely human. When Garbo made ANNA CHRISTIE in 1930, her first talking film, MGM bannered its promotion with the words "Garbo Talks!" Now that she had appeared in her first comedy, the studio blared: "Garbo Laughs!" Then the publicity department added that audiences going to see NINOTCHKA could also see Garbo "flirt, dance, drink, howl, romance and kiss!" The great actress was never so much at ease (except, perhaps, in her European silent film THE JOYLESS STREET, directed by G.W. Pabst) as she was in NINOTCHKA and she manages a subtle metamorphosis from austere, humorless Communist to ebullient female in love, one that is both enchanting and rewarding. How Garbo came to make NINOTCHKA is related through a story that may or may not be apochryphal. Reportedly, Lubitsch called Garbo and said: "Greta, vy don't you tell those idiots in your studio to let us do a picture together? Gott, how I vould love to direct a picture vith you." Garbo replied: "You tell them, Ernst. I'm far too tired to talk to studio executives." Lubitsch did some talking and then Garbo signed with MGM to do a single film, receiving $125,000, half of what she had demanded and gotten from the studio for ANNA KARENINA. She then announced to the press: "My next film will be a comedy...Will I be allowed to keep my lover in it? Certainly I am hoping so. Don't you think it is high time they let me end a picture happily with a kiss? I do. I seem to have lost so many attractive men in the final scene." Her scenes with Claire were electric since Claire was the widow of John Gilbert who had been Garbo's longtime lover on and offscreen. The film began production on May 19, 1939 in Culver City and took only fifty-eight days to complete, such was Lubitsch's demanding schedule and economical (and imperialistic) direction. Garbo stunned everyone with her performance, which earned her her fourth and final nomination for an Oscar as Best Actress. She was overwhelmed by GONE WITH THE WIND and Vivien Leigh walked off with the Oscar that year. Actually, it was Garbo who insisted that she do NINOTCHKA and pressured MGM to cooperate. At first studio chief Louis B. Mayer rejected the script altogether. He felt Garbo would be entering an unknown medium with comedy and he also found the subject of Communism repulsive in any form, even a satire where Communists, Russians, and the Soviet government were spoofed, not supported in any way. Garbo actually risked her career to make NINOTCHKA and proved her instincts correct, although Mayer continued to make fun of the film, later stating: "NINOTCHKA got everything but money. A Hardy picture cost $25,000 less than Lubitsch was paid alone. But any good Hardy picture made $500,000 more than NINOTCHKA made." For a long period of time the film went unnamed; even during production it was simply titled "The Garbo Film." Dozens of titles were suggested including WE WANT TO BE ALONE (which was discarded when it was remembered how Garbo's line "I vant to be alone" in ANNA CHRISTIE had been broadly mimicked and satirized), GIVE US THIS DAY, A KISS FROM MOSCOW (this one was rejected immediately as irritating to an American public that wanted no part of Moscow, kisses or otherwise), THIS TIME FOR KEEPS, THE LOVE AXIS, INTRIGUE IN PARIS, TIME OUT FOR LOVE, SALUTE FOR LOVE, A FOREIGN AFFAIR (later used in another production), A KISS FOR THE COMMISSAR, A KISS IN THE DARK, and finally NINOTCHKA which was decided upon by Nicholas Schenck, president of Loew's Inc. which controlled MGM. The studio got around the title by stating in one release: "What makes Garbo blush and laugh in NINOTCHKA? Don't pronounce it....See it." Garbo would make one more film, the poorly produced and received TWO-FACED WOMAN, before going into permanent retirement. NINOTCHKA would see several spin-offs and remakes, including COMRADE X (1940), with Clark Gable and Hedy Lamarr, and the unfunny, brittle THE IRON PETTICOAT (1956) with Katharine Hepburn and Bob Hope. Cole Porter's Broadway musical "Silk Stockings" was NINOTCHKA put to music and starred Don Ameche and Hidegarde Neff on the stage. The Rouben Mamoulian film SILK STOCKINGS appeared in 1957 starring Fred Astaire, Cyd Charisse (as a sexy commissar), and Janis Paige.

p&d, Ernst Lubitsch; w, Charles Brackett, Billy Wilder, Walter Reisch (based on a story by Melchior Lengyel); ph, William Daniels; m, Werner R. Heymann; ed, Gene Ruggiero; art d, Cedric Gibbons, Randall Duell; set d, Edwin B. Willis; cos, Adrian; makeup, Jack Dawn.

Comedy   Cas.   (PR:A MPAA:NR)

NINTH CIRCLE, THE***   (1961, Yugo.) 90m Jadran/Interprogress bw
(DEVETI KRUG)

Dusica Zegarac (Ruth), Boris Dvornik (Ivo), Ervina Dragman (Mrs. Vojnovic), Branko Tatic (Vojnovic), Dragan Milivojevic (Zvonko), Beba Loncar (Magda), Mihajilo Kostic, Vera Misita, Bozidar Drnic, Djurdjica Delic.

To help out Zegarac, a 17-year-old Jew, Tatic arranges a marriage for her and his son, Dvornik. Since the boy has been raised a Catholic, this marriage of convenience will protect Zegarac from the Nazis. Dvornik rebels at first and is ostracized by his friends and former girl friend. Gradually he comes to know and trust his new wife and soon falls deeply in love with her. However his Catholicism is not enough to save her and on an outing, Nazis arrest her. He follows her to a Nazi concentration camp where she is forced to work as a prostitute. The camp itself is run by a former friend of Dvornik. He manages to break in and tries to help her escape but she is too weak. Unable to help her climb the barbed wire fence, Dvornik takes Zegarac's hand and the two die together as the electric current is turned on.

d, France Stiglic; w, Stiglic, Vladimir Koch (based on a story by Zora Dirnbach); ph, Ivan Marincek; m, Branimir Sakac; ed, Lidija Branis; art d, Zeliko Zagota; cos, Vanda Pavelic.

Drama   (PR:O MPAA:NR)

NINTH CONFIGURATION, THE***   (1980) 105m WB c (AKA: TWINKLE, TWINKLE, KILLER KANE)

Stacy Keach (Col. Kane), Scott Wilson (Capt. Cutshaw), Jason Miller (Lt. Reno), Ed Flanders (Col. Fell), Neville Brand (Groper), George DiCenzo (Capt. Fairbanks), Moses Gunn (Maj. Nammack), Robert Loggia (Lt. Bennish), Joe Spinell (Spinell), Alejandro Rey (Lt. Gomez), Tom Atkins (Sgt. Krebs), Steve Sandor (1st Cyclist), Richard Lynch (2nd Cyclist).

Blatty, best known as the author of "The Exorcist," makes his debut as producer, director, and screenwriter with this adaptation of his novel. Keach plays an army psychiatrist brought to a sanitarium for military mental basket cases. Of course he is much crazier than any patient in the asylum. The dialog is really weird and often incomprehensible. Blatty has a good sense of the absurd however and handles the direction well. Things are never quite what they seem to be. The supporting cast is just as strange as Keach and utterly believable. Wilson is particularly effective as a former astronaut gone mad. Unfortunately the studio did not understand what the film was about and released several different versions with varying lengths. THE NINTH CONFIGURATION can be viewed at 105 minutes, 99 minutes, 104 minutes, or 118 minutes. The latter was the cut Blatty approved and probably the best version.

p,d&w, William Peter Blatty (based on the novel by Blatty); ph, Gerry Fisher; m, Barry DeVorzon; ed, T. Battle Davis, Peter Lee-Thompson, Roberto Silvi; prod d, Bill Malley, J. Dennis Washington; set d, Sydney Ann Kee.

Drama   (PR:O MPAA:R)

NINTH GUEST, THE½**   (1934) 67m COL bw

Donald Cook (Jim Daley), Genevieve Tobin (Jean Trent), Hardie Albright (Henry Abbott), Edward Ellis (Tim Cronin), Edwin Maxwell (Jason Osgood), Vincent Barnett (William Jones, Assistant Butler), Helen Flint (Sylvia Inglesby), Samuel S. Hinds (Dr. Murray Reid), Nella Walker (Margaret Chisholm), Sidney Bracey (Butler).

This is a nifty though predictable little mystery. Eight people are invited to a mysterious dinner party. No one knows who the host is. After everyone has been seated, the radio goes on and announces that the ninth guest has been killed and everyone else will be dead before the evening is through. With the house sealed shut everyone panics. Sure enough, guests start getting knocked off hourly until Tobin, Cook, and madman Albright are the only ones left. The suspense holds well under the well-paced direction, although by the time Cook, Tobin, and Albright are faced off the rest is highly predictable. The story also suffers from a lack of humor. Barnett has a few turns as a comic butler but it is a weak attempt and not well played.

d, Roy William Neill; w, Garnett Weston (based on the play by Owen Davis and the novel The Invisible Host by Gwen Bristow, Bruce Manning); ph, Benjamin Kline; ed, Gene Milford.

Mystery   (PR:A MPAA:NR)

NINTH HEART, THE***   (1980, Czech.) 90m Czeskoslovensky Film-export c

Ondrej Pavelka (Martin), Julie Juristova (Princess), Anna Malova (Toncka), Frantisek Filipovsky (Clown), Josef Kemr (Principal), Juraj Kukura (Astrologist), Premyal Koci (Grand Duke), Ruzena Rudnicka (Grand Duchess), Josef Somr (Captain).

Juristova is a beautiful princess held captive by evil astrologer Kukura. Pavelka plays a student who undergoes a year-long quest to rescue her, helped by Filipovsky, Pavelka's sidekick clown friend. This is a wonderful fantasy made with great wit and charm. The set design is impressive with Kukura lurking about in an elaborate Dracula-inspired castle.

d&w, Juraj Herz (based on a story by Josef Hanzlik); ph, Jiri Machane; m, Petr Hapka; set d, Vladimir Labsky.

Fantasy   (PR:A MPAA:NR)

NIPPER, THE   (SEE: BRAT, THE, 1930, Brit.)

NIPPON KONCHUKI   (SEE: INSECT WOMAN, THE, 1964)

**NIPPON NO ICHIBAN NAGAI HI   (SEE:
                            EMPEROR AND A GENERAL, THE, 1968)**

NITWITS, THE½**   (1935) 81m RKO bw

Bert Wheeler (Johnnie), Robert Woolsey (Newton), Fred Keating (Darrell), Betty Grable (Mary Roberts), Evelyn Brent (Mrs. Lake), Hale Hamilton (Lake), Arthur Aylesworth (Lurch), Erik Rhodes (Clark), Charles Wilson (Capt. Jennings), Willie Best (Sleepy), Lew Kelley (J. Gabriel Hazel), Dorothy Granger (Phyllis).

Wheeler and Woolsey are a pair of cigar salesmen working out of the same building as Grable. When the song publisher she works for is shot, the comedy team takes the blame. After much confusion the real killer is found and all ends happily. This is an adequate vehicle for Wheeler and Woolsey. The climactic slapstick finish is reminiscent of Keystone two-reelers from the 1920s. Grable is somewhat stiff in this early film appearance. The direction is fine for the fare, though too much time is spent on the ins and outs of the music publishing business.

p, Lee Marcus; d, George Stevens; w, Fred Guiol, Al Boasberg (based on a story by Stuart Palmer); ph, Edward Cronjager; ed, John Lockert; m/l, "Music in My Heart," "The Black Widow Will Get You if You Don't Watch Out," Dorothy Fields, Jimmy McHugh, "You Opened My Eyes," L. Wolfe Gilbert, Felix Bernard.

Comedy   (PR:A MPAA:NR)

NIX ON DAMES**   (1929) 67m FOX bw

Mae Clarke (Jackie Lee), Robert Ames (Bert Wills), William Harrigan (Johnny Brown), Maude Fulton (Stella Foster), George MacFarlane (Ed Foster), Camille Rovelle (Miss Woods), Grace Wallace (Bonnie Tucker), Hugh McCormack (Jim Tucker), Marshall Ruth (Billy), Benny Hall (Cliff), Billy Colvin (Hoffman), Frederick Graham (Baring), Louise Beavers (Magnolia).

This is a so-so backstage drama as were many of the early song-and-dance films that were created mainly to use the new device of sound. Ames and Harrigan play a vaudeville acrobatic team who have partnership problems when both fall for dancer Clarke. The direction shows some imagination, including a sequence involving a postcard coming to life. But the film ultimately suffers from its lack of purpose and turns into little more than just another showcase for song and dance.

d, Donald Gallaher; w, Maude Fulton, Frank Gay; ph, Charles G. Clarke; ed, Dorothy Spencer; set d, Duncan Cramer; cos, Sophie Wachner; m/l, "Fading Away" (sung by Mae Clarke), "One Sweetheart," "I'm Wingin' Home," "Two Pals, " "Say The Word," "The Song of My Heart," "Oh, Lord, Pour Down Your Waters and Baptize Me," L. Wolfe Gilbert, Abel Baer.

Musical   (PR:A MPAA:NR)

NO BLADE OF GRASS**   (1970, Brit.) 96m Symbol/MGM c

Nigel Davenport (John Custance), Jean Wallace (Ann Custance), John Hamill (Roger Burnham), Lynne Frederick (Mary Custance), Patrick Holt (David Custance), Anthony May (Andrew Pirrie), Wendy Richard (Clara), Nigel Rathbone (Davey), George Coulouris (Mr. Sturdevant), Ruth Kettlewell (Fat Woman), M. J. Matthews (George), Michael Percival (Police Constable), Tex Fuller (Mr. Beaseley), Simon Merrick (TV Interviewer), Anthony Sharp (Sir Charles Brenner), Max Hartnell (Lieutenant), John Lewis (Corporal), Norman Atkyns (Dr. Cassop), Christopher Lofthouse (Spooks), John Avison (Yorkshire Sergeant), Jimmy Winston, Richard Penny, R. C. Driscoll (Huns), Geoffrey Hooper (Tweed Jacket), Christopher Wilson (Farmer), William Duffy (Murdered Farmer), Mervyn Patrick (Joe Ashton), Denise Mockler (Emily Ashton), Ross Allan (Alf Parsons), Karen Terry (Parsons' Daughter), Joan Ward (Mrs. Parsons), Brian Crabtree (Joe Harris), Susan Sydney (Liz Harris), Michael Landy (Jess Arkwright), Louise Kay (Susan Arkwright), Bruce Myers (Bill Riggs), Margaret Chapman (Prudence Riggs), Christopher Neame (Locke), Bridget Brice (Jill Locke), Reg Staniford (Mr. Blennit), Maureen Rutter (Mrs. Blennit), Derek Keller (Scott), Suzanne Pinkstone (Mrs. Scott), Surgit Sood (Surgit), Dick Offord (Joe), Joanna Annin (Joe's Wife), John Buckley (Captain), Malcolm Toes (Sergeant Major).

It's the end of civilization as an environmental plague sweeps Britain. Davenport is persuaded by his friend Hamill to take the family and flee London. They are invited to hole up on Hamill's well-stocked family farm. Davenport and family leave, later joining outlaw May and his wife, Richard. From there on it's an orgy of violence as Davenport's party is faced by a group of crazed bikers and internal group struggles. The party eventually reaches the farm only to find that Hamill's brother, Holt, will not allow them to join him. Davenport leads an attack on the farm, killing Holt. His family takes over, determined to start life anew. This is potentially powerful material but is unfortunately dealt with on too melodramatic a level. The script is too conventional with a confusing use of flash forwarding. This dramatically harms the suspense levels, especially during climactic action sequences. Characters are often stereotypes, especially bad guys like the bikers. However there is a certain bleakness to the mise-en-scene that makes this film worth a look. Crops lie destroyed, and fields are littered with bodies of the dead. This pre-dates the apocalyptic visions of George Romero's DAWN OF THE DEAD or the Stephen King novel The Stand. This spotty, yet visually effective direction is by Wilde, who starred in numerous swashbucklers during the 1940s and 1950s after being an American Olympic Fencing team member.

p&d, Cornel Wilde; w, Sean Forestal, Jefferson Pascal (based on the novel *Death of Grass* by John Christopher); ph, H. A. R. Thomson (Panavision, Metrocolor); m, Burnell Whibley; ed, Frank Clarke, Eric Boyd-Perkins; md, Whibley; art d, Elliot Scott; cos, Tony Armstrong Boutique; spec eff, Terry Witherington; m/l, "No Blade of Grass," Louis Nelius, Charles Carroll (sung by Roger Whittaker), "Lead Us On," Carroll; makeup, George Blackler.

Science Fiction/Drama   **(PR:O   MPAA:R)**

NO BRAKES   (SEE: OH, YEAH, 1929)

NO DEADLY MACHINE   (SEE: YOUNG DOCTORS, THE, 1961)

NO DEFENSE*   (1929) 60m WB bw

Monte Blue (*Monte Collins*), May McAvoy (*Ruth Harper*), Lee Moran (*Snitz*), Kathryn Carver (*Lois Harper*), William H. Tooker (*Harper, Sr.*), William Desmond (*John Harper*), Bud Marshall (*Construction Laborer*).

Blue is the foreman of a bridge construction team. He falls for the young daughter of a Boston engineer, but their love is endangered when a bridge collapse appears to be Blue's fault. But no, it was her wicked brother all along and the couple ends up together. With only 50 percent of this spoken dialog and the rest silent, NO DEFENSE is a minor and completely boring exercise in early sound technology. Blue is too pure-hearted to be taken the least bit seriously and the special effects are terrible even by 1929 standards.

d, Lloyd Bacon; w, Robert Lord (based on a story by J. Raleigh Davis); ph, Frank Kesson; ed, Tom Pratt; md, Louis Sullivan; m/l, "West of the Great Divide"; titles, Joe Jackson.

Drama/Romance   **(PR:A   MPAA:NR)**

NO DEPOSIT, NO RETURN**   (1976) 112m Disney/BV c (AKA: DOUBLE TROUBLE)

David Niven (*J. W. Osborne*), Darren McGavin (*Duke*), Don Knotts (*Bert*), Herschel Bernardi (*Sgt. Turner*), Barbara Feldon (*Carolyn*), Kim Richards (*Tracy*), Brad Savage (*Jay*), John Williams (*Jameson*), Charlie Martin Smith (*Longnecker*), Vic Tayback (*Big Joe*), Bob Hastings (*Peter*).

Richards and Savage are a pair of poor little rich kids who dread spending Easter vacation with their grandfather, Niven. McGavin and the ever-bumbling Knotts are a pair of crooks the kids con into staging a kidnaping. Richards and Savage want to use the would-be kidnapers/benefactors so that they can join their mother in Hong Kong. The comedy is dumb and slow-moving with an insipid and predictable script. The film's saving grace is its marvelous comic cast which somehow manages to pull off this otherwise routine Disney film. Knotts has a particularly good scene chasing Savage's pet skunk along the girders of a building under construction. Niven is his usual charming self.

p, Ron Miller; d, Norman Tokar; w, Arthur Alsberg, Don Nelson (based on a story by Joe L. McEveety); ph, Frank Phillips (Technicolor); m, Buddy Baker; ed, Cotton Warburton; art d, John B. Mansbridge, Jack Senter; cos, Chuck Keehne.

Comedy   **(PR:AAA   MPAA:G)**

NO DOWN PAYMENT**½   (1957) 105m FOX bw

Joanne Woodward (*Leola Boone*), Sheree North (*Isabelle Flagg*), Tony Randall (*Jerry Flagg*), Jeffrey Hunter (*David Martin*), Cameron Mitchell (*Troy Boone*), Patricia Owens (*Jean Martin*), Barbara Rush (*Betty Kreitzer*), Pat Hingle (*Herman Kreitzer*), Robert H. Harris (*Markham*), Aki Aleong (*Iko*), Jim Hayward (*Mr. Burton*), Mimi Gibson (*Sandra Kreitzer*), Charles Herbert (*Michael Flagg*), Donald Towers (*Harmon Kreitzer*), Mary Carroll (*Mrs. Burnett*), Nolan Leary (*Reverend*).

A multi-character story that was bought by Fox to showcase eight of their contract players, NO DOWN PAYMENT is a social documentary about the phenomenon that was gripping the U.S. at the time: the exodus to the suburbs and the inability to pay for the homes beyond each monthly mortgage check. It takes place in a housing development known as "Sunrise Hills," a typical suburban tract where all the homes look alike but the people are vastly different. Hunter is an electrical engineer married to Owens. She's raped by drunken Mitchell, who is then killed by Hunter. Randall is a fast-talking used-car salesman with big plans that are constantly dashed by fate. He takes to drink and that causes his wife, North, to think about divorce. Mitchell is a decorated war veteran who cannot find himself in the post-war era and now works as a gas-station manager. He wants to be the subdivision's police chief. His wife is Woodward and her only desire in life to have babies. Hingle, the only solid citizen among them, runs a hardware store and wants to find a way for his assistant, Aleong, to live in the area. The fact that Aleong is a Japanese-American sticks in the craw of Hingle's wife, Rush, who wants to keep anyone but a lilywhite out of the neighborhood. The stories are told side by side, in much the same way as a soap opera on television, with occasional forays into each other's territories. In the end, everyone goes to church except widow Woodward, who leaves in a taxi. Aleong was a nightclub performer who had some success with a few Calypso records while pursuing an acting career. Focusing more on any one of the stories might have made more sense because, as it is, the film is too diffuse and jumps around so much that it's not easy to get close to any of the people. This was Ritt's second film after EDGE OF THE CITY and followed another career as a TV director of "live" programs as well as many acting roles, something he continued from time to time.

p, Jerry Wald; d, Martin Ritt; w, Philip Yordan (based on the novel by John McPartland); ph, Joseph La Shelle (CinemaScope); m, Leigh Harline; ed, Louis Loeffler; md, Lionel Newman; art d, Lyle Wheeler, Herman A. Blumenthal; cos, Mary Wills; spec eff, L. B. Abbott.

Drama   **(PR:C   MPAA:NR)**

NO DRUMS, NO BUGLES**½   (1971) 85m Cinerama Releasing Corp. c

Martin Sheen (*Ashby Gatrell*), Davey Davidson (*Callie Gatrell*), Rod McCary (*Lieutenant*), Denine Terry (*Sarah*), Carmen Costi, Ray Marsh, Frank Stubock, Bob Wagner, Edward Underwood (*Foxhunters*).

Sheen gives a fine performance as a lone man who runs off from the Civil War. He cannot bring himself to kill anyone and hides out in a cave for the war's duration. The camera records Sheen's life with great vigor, using the West Virginia locations nicely. The shots are well composed carrying the story well. This never bogs down with slow pacing or sticky sentimentality. Sheen pulls off his difficult task with sensitivity. He is completely believable and makes the film work.

p,d&w, Clyde Ware; ph, Richard McCarthy, Parker Bartlett (Techniscope, Technicolor); m, Lyle Ritz; ed, David Bretherton, Richard Halsey; cos, Melba; m/l, (theme song sung by Shelby Flint); makeup, Melba.

Drama   **Cas.**   **(PR:A   MPAA:G)**

NO ESCAPE**½   (1934, Brit.) 70m WB-FN bw

Binnie Barnes (*Myra Fengler*), Ralph Ince (*Lucky*), Ian Hunter (*Jim Brandon*), Molly Lamont (*Helen Arnold*), Charles Carson (*Mr. Arnold*), Philip Strange (*Kirk Fengler*), Madeleine Seymour (*Mrs. Arnold*), George Merritt (*Inspector Matheson*).

When Hunter repels the advances of Barnes, the wife of his partner in a rubber plantation, the woman tries to kill him. Her plans go awry, however, as her husband ends up the poisoned man. Hunter is suspected of murder so he flees from the Malaysian plantation for his home in England. There he is found to be a carrier of bubonic plague, which infects Barnes and kills her. Before passing away however, she confesses all, leaving Hunter a free man. An unusual thriller, farfetched but handled with style.

p, Irving Asher; d, Ralph Ince; w, W. Scott Darling.

Crime/Drama   **(PR:C   MPAA:NR)**

NO ESCAPE**½   (1936, Brit.) 85m Pathe Welwyn bw (AKA: NO ESCAPE/NO EXIT)

Valerie Hobson (*Laura Anstey*), Leslie Perrins (*Anthony Wild*), Robert Cochran (*Beeston*), Billy Milton (*Billy West*), Henry Oscar (*Cyril Anstey*), Ronald Simpson (*Scoop Martin*), Margaret Yarde (*Bunty*), Hal Gordon (*County Constable*), J. Neil More (*Commissioner of Police*), Hilda Campbell Russell (*Barmaid*), Kenneth Law (*Jenner*).

A novelist bets that he can keep a friend hidden for a month. They pack the "victim" in a car trunk and spirit him away to the country. When the boy fails to show up, his parents call the cops. Meanwhile a small-town journalist mistakes liquor bottle drippings for blood and chases after the pair himself. One night, the novelist goes rabbit shooting and fires at a moving figure. His target is none other than the boy he is hiding. But it turns out the boy was shot by a man whose wife was having an affair with the novelist. The man is arrested leaving the novelist and wife free to marry. The story is a little slow to start but once things are underway, this turns into an effective, though minor thriller. The acting and production credits are adequate.

d, Norman Lee; w, George Goodchild, Frank Witty (based on the play "No Exit" by Goodchild, Witty); ph, Bryan Langley.

Crime/Mystery   **(PR:C   MPAA:NR)**

NO ESCAPE, 1943   (SEE: I ESCAPED FROM THE GESTAPO, 1943)

NO ESCAPE**   (1953) 76m UA bw (AKA: CITY ON A HUNT)

Lew Ayres (*John Tracy*), Marjorie Steele (*Pat Peterson*), Sonny Tufts (*Detective Simon Shayne*), Lewis Martin (*Lt. Bruce Gunning*), Charles Cane (*Wilbur K. Grossett*), Gertrude Michael (*Olga Lewis*), Renny McEvoy (*Turnip*), Jess Kirkpatrick (*Mac, the Waiter*), James Griffith (*Peter Hayden*), Robert Watson (*Mr. Duffy*), Robert Bailey (*Detective Bob*), Leon Burbank (*Office Boy*), Robert Carson (*Dr. Seymour*), Barbara Morrison (*Mrs. Beresford*), Carleton Young (*Don Holden*), Hans Schumm (*Mr. Platoff*), Jim Vosper (*Mr. Crockett*), Joseph Kim (*Chinese Barman*), Maudie Prickett (*Bookstore Clerk*), Tim Graham (*Drunk*).

Ayres plays a down-and-out songwriter reduced to playing piano in a San Francisco bar. When an artist, Griffith, turns up dead, the clues point toward Steele but her police detective boy friend, Tufts, fixes things so Ayres will take the fall. She cannot let this happen though and tries to help Ayres escape. The city is crawling with cops and the pair end up in Griffith's apartment. There they are cornered by the real killer, Tufts. Just as he is about to kill them too, the police enter and arrest him. The plot seems suspenseful but the lackluster direction has no feel for thriller pacing. Things move too slowly with overwritten dialog mouthed in only average performances by the ensemble. However, the music captures the film's potential mood nicely. It's a pity the film does not live up to the score.

p, Matt Freed, Hugh MacKenzie; d&w, Charles Bennett; ph, Benjamin Kline; m, Bert Shefter; ed, Roy V. Livingston; m/l, "No Escape," Shefter, Bennett.

Crime   **(PR:O   MPAA:NR)**

NO EXIT**   (1930, Brit.) 69m WB bw

John Stuart (*Bill Alden*), Muriel Angelus (*Ann Ansell*), James Fenton (*Mr. Ansell*), Janet Alexander (*Mrs. Ansell*), John Rowal (*Harry Matthews*).

Stuart is a struggling writer who meets Angelus, the daughter of a publisher. She believes him to be a novelist who is making a lot of money for her father, and a romance ensues with all the complications one might expect. In the end the publisher's wife is proven to be the pseudonymous author making the money and one wouldn't have to think too hard to guess how the young people end up. This is, to say the least, no relation to Jean-Paul Sartre's play of the same title.

p,d&w, Charles Saunders; ph, Bryan Langley.

Romance/Comedy (PR:A MPAA:NR)

NO EXIT* (1962, U.S./Arg.) 85m Aries Cinematografica/Zenith bw
(HUIS CLOS; AKA: SINNERS GO TO HELL; STATELESS)

Viveca Lindfors (*Inez*), Rita Gam (*Estelle*), Morgan Sterne (*Garcin*), Ben Piazza (*Camarero*), Susana Mayo (*Florence*), Orlando Sacha (*Gomez*), Manuel Roson (*Capitan*), Mirtha Miller (*Carmencita*), Miguel A. Irarte (*Robert Miguel*), Elsa Dorian (*Shirley*), Mario Horna (*Albert*), Carlos Brown (*Roger Delaney III*).

This is a filmed adaptation of the famous existentialist drama by Sartre. Three total strangers—a noted journalist (Sterne), a narcissistic social climbing wife (Gam), and a lesbian (Lindfors)—are ushered into a brightly lit hotel room. It becomes apparent that this is eternity and they are to spend it together in this uncomfortable fashion. The group splits up and each tries to kill the others but eventually develops little more than contempt for one another. Their real stories are soon discovered: Garcin was shot for cowardice; Gam was a sex-crazed woman who married for money then killed her baby before destroying her husband; and Lindfors killed herself after seducing a married woman and driving her to suicide as well. There is a terrific fight and Gam tries to stab Lindfors with a paper knife. Finally the three realize that this is how they are to spend eternity and they break out in a hysterical fit of laughter before falling silent.

p, Fernando Ayala, Hector Olivera; d, Tad Danielewski; w, George Tabori (based on the play by Jean-Paul Sartre); ph, Ricardo Younis; m, Vladimir Ussachevsky; ed, Atilio Rinaldi, Carl Lerner, Jacques Bart; art d, Mario Vanarelli; cos, Horace Lannes; makeup, Aida Fernandez.

Drama (PR:O MPAA:NR)

NO FUNNY BUSINESS* (1934, Brit.) 60m F.P.I./UA-Principal bw

Gertrude Lawrence (*Yvonne*), Laurence Olivier (*Clive*), Jill Esmond (*Anne*), Gibb McLaughlin (*Florey*), Edmond Breon (*Edward*), Muriel Aked (*Mrs. Fothergill*).

Lame comedy that did nothing for any of the people involved. Lawrence and Breon are married and want to get a divorce, so they each goes to the same detective agency to get the goods on the other. Olivier and Esmond, who work for the company, are sent to the French Riviera to do that job. Olivier and Esmond have never met and mistake each other for the wrong person. They fall in love and Lawrence and Breon eventually decide to stay in their marriage. There's a mix-up in the hotel suites, a few stabs at sophisticated Noel Coward-type bantering, and a happy ending for the picture. Along the way, a couple of tunes written by Gay and sung by Lawrence, most notably "No Funny Business," but the other songs are best suited for deaf ears. Lousy photography, bad sound recording, and clunky dialog. Despite all of that, the picture was re-released in 1951. Believe it or not, NO FUNNY BUSINESS took *two* directors to make, although it's hard to see where one's bad work ends and the other's worse work begins. It might have made more sense as an episode on TV's "Love, American Style" because it doesn't even hold audience interest for the brief 60-minute length. Olivier and Esmond were married from 1930 through 1940, but he left her for Vivian Leigh, to whom he was married tempestuously for 20 years. The title is quite apt, as there was virtually "no funny business" in the script.

p, John Stafford; d, Stafford, Victor Hanbury; w, Hanbury, Frank Vosper (based on a story by Dorothy Hope); ph, W. Blakeley, D. Langley; m, Noel Gay; ed, Elmer McGovern.

Comedy (PR:A MPAA:NR)

NO GREATER GLORY** (1934) 117m COL bw

George Breakston (*Nemecsek*), Jimmy Butler (*Boka*), Jackie Searl (*Gereb*), Frankie Darro (*Feri Ats*), Donald Haines (*Csonakos*), Rolf Ernest (*Ferdie Pasztor*), Julius Molnar (*Henry Pasztor*), Wesley Giraud (*Kolnay*), Beaudine Anderson (*Csele*), Bruce Line (*Richter*), Samuel S. Hinds (*Gereb's Father*), Christian Rub (*Watchman*), Ralph Morgan (*Father*), Lois Wilson (*Mother*), Egon Brecher (*Racz*), Frank Reicher (*Doctor*), Tom Ricketts (*Janitor*).

This excellent film accomplishes a feat rarely found in the cinema: an accurate and moving portrayal of childhood's joys and agonies. Breakston plays a frail youngster who idolizes gang leader Butler. Butler is in charge of a group run like a miniature army, complete with uniforms, caps, and a flag. Breakston's ill health makes him an outcast to the more robust group but he is allowed to join up as a "private," the only member of this rank in an army full of officers. Butler despises the new member for his weaknesses because his army is built on strength and ability. Yet Breakston cannot see this, such is his admiration and his need to belong. When their flag is stolen by a rival gang of older boys called "The Red Shirts" Breakston takes it upon himself to retrieve the sacred banner. In a driving rain he invades the enemy camp and confronts their leader Darro. Darro grabs the younger boy and shoves his head under water over and over. But he cannot break the boy's spirit and gradually they come to respect his pluck. Breakston catches pneumonia resulting from the dunkings and is forced to remain in bed. Word reaches him that Butler and company are taking on the Red Shirts so Breakston sneaks from his bed and joins the battle. The excitement is too much for him though and he dies fighting for his cause. Butler, realizing the true meaning of strength and courage, tearfully watches as Breakston's mother, Wilson, carries away the limp body of her son. NO GREATER GLORY is a fine and honest film with excellent performances by its youthful cast. Breakston is all heart and innocent emotion, the epitome of admiring, loyal youth. His blind devotion and need to be accepted by peers is competely honest. Butler, whose career was tragically cut short by his death during WW II combat, is equally fine. His portrayal of the handsome, serious-minded idol is believable and moving. This film also serves as an allegory on the futility of war and the cold-hearted way it takes the best of men. It is a doubly ironic message when one considers the tragedy of Butler's own death in France 11 years later. This is based on an autobiographical novel by the noted Hungarian playwright Molnar with

a sensitive adaptation and direction that brought out the honesty and spirit of the book.

d, Frank Borzage; w, Jo Swerling (based on the novel *The Paul Street Boys* by Ferenc Molnar); ph, Joseph August; ed, Viola Lawrence.

Drama (PR:A MPAA:NR)

NO GREATER LOVE, 1931 (SEE: ALOHA, 1931)

NO GREATER LOVE* (1932) 70m COL bw

Dickie Moore (*Tommy Burns*), Alexander Carr (*Sidney Cohen*), Richard Bennett (*Surgeon*), Beryl Mercer (*Mrs. Burns*), Hobart Bosworth (*Doctor*), Betty Jane Graham (*Mildred*), Alec B. Francis (*Priest*), Mischa Auer (*Rabbi*), Helen Jerome Eddy (*Superintendent*), Martha Mattox (*Investigator*), Tom McGuire (*Policeman*).

This film is about as contrived as can be. Carr plays a Jewish delicatessen owner who adopts an orphaned Irish girl. But she is not just orphaned, she has a disability as well. The courts naturally want to take the kid away from Carr but he proves that he is a worthy parent despite the cultural differences. Carr plays a stereotypical Jew, mumbling Yiddish phrases and singing Yiddish lullabies. The cast really does an admirable job considering all the cliches and stock situations they are up against. Considering that Hollywood moguls were overwhelmingly Jewish it's a real surprise that such stereotypes were prevalent throughout the films of the 1930s and 1940s.

p, Benjamin Stoloff; d, Lewis Seiler; w, Isadore Bernstein, Lou Breslow; ph, William Thompson.

Drama (PR:A MPAA:NR)

NO GREATER LOVE* (1944, USSR) 68m Central Artfilm Studios/
Artkino bw

Vera Mertskaya (*Pasha*), Anna Smirnova (*Fenya*), Peter Aleinikov (*Senya*), Alexander Violmov (*Nikolai*), Irina Fedorova (*Oriova*), I. Peltzer (*Stepan Orlov*), Nikolai Boguliubov (*Lukyanov*), W. Gremin, B. Domchovsky, G. Kozshoun, V. Medvedyev, E. Memtchenko, G. Semenov, A. Chepurnon.

This Russian war film deals with a subject most Americans found unthinkable: women in combat positions. Mertskaya plays a woman whose husband and son have died by Nazi hands. Consequently, she is out for revenge. She catches up with the Nazi tank commander who crushed her loved ones and kills him in a similar fashion. The rest of the film follows her and her comrades as they wreak havoc on Nazi troops. Some of the violence is quite graphic though well executed and not the least bit gratuitous. Americans saw a censored version of this film. Apparently one scene where Mertskaya has revenge on a German general proved to be too much for American censors who replaced the offending sequence with a simple title that said "He Talked." The film was dubbed into English though this was not detrimental to the overall effect. Some of the photography is not what it should be but the ensemble performances and powerful sequences make up for the technical problems.

p&d, Frederick Ermler; w, M. Bleiman, I. Bondin, William C. White, Alexander Bakshy, I. Elman, I.K. Lopert, W.A. Pozner; ph, V. Rappaport, A. Zavialov; m, G. Popov; ed, Geraldine Lutten.

War (PR:O MPAA:NR)

NO GREATER LOVE, 1970 (SEE: HUMAN CONDITION, THE, 1970, Jap.)

NO GREATER LOVE THAN THIS½** (1969, Jap.) 106m Nikkatsu/
Toho c (KOTO NO TAIYO)

Fumie Kashiyama (*Hatsuko Araki*), Homare Suguro (*Dr. Takaoka*), Izumi Ashikawa, Jukichi Uno, Gin Maeda, Terumi Niki, Jun Hamamura.

Okino-shima is a small island off southwestern Japan. The people there are not used to civilization and are wary when a nurse, Kashiyama, comes to help them. Eventually the people accept her. When a mysterious parasite is causing islanders to fall ill Kashiyama brings in a doctor, Suguro. He discovers the source of the disease and falls in love with the nurse. They become engaged and prepare to leave the island but Kashiyama calls everything off at the last minute when she realizes her place is with the people of Okino-shima.

d, Kenji Yoshida; w, Shigeki Chiba (based on a story by Keiichi Ito); ph, Kenji Hagiwara (Nikkatsu Scope, Fuji Color); m, Riichiro Manabe; art d, Motozo Kawahara.

Drama (PR:C MPAA:NR)

NO GREATER SIN* (1941) 85m University Films bw (GB:
SOCIAL ENEMY NO. 1)

Leon Ames (*Dr. Cavanagh*), Luana Walters (*Sandra, Reporter*), John Gallaudet (*Townsend*), George Taggart (*Bill Thorne*), Adele Pearce (*Betty*), Guy Usher (*Pa James*), Bodil Ann Rosing (*Ma James*), William Gould (*Benton*), Tristram Coffin (*Dr. Raleigh*), Henry Roquemore (*Mayor*), Frank Jaquet (*Dr. Hobson*), Ralf Harolde (*Scaturo*), Lee Shumway (*Jarvis*), Paul Phillips.

The horror of syphilis is explored in this turgid story. Ames is a health commissioner out to clean up his town and the legion of prostitutes spreading the dread disease. Walters is the reporter who helps him investigate the problem. A subplot involves Taggart as a naive young man who contracts the disease and gives it to his pregnant wife, Pearce. When a quack doctor takes his money but fails to cure him, Taggart comes back and accidentally kills the man in a fight. His lawyer manages to get Taggart to confess his reasons for killing the doctor and Taggart's name is cleared. Meanwhile Ames and Walters have predictably fallen in love. The town council, worried about local image, finally consents to giving Ames the money he needs to clean up the town. The story reads well for a 1940s film but the production is laughably bad. The direction is amateur quality as is the often fuzzy photography. NO GREATER SIN has not aged well and plays as high camp in the post-sexual revolution era. Its melodramatic handling and naively serious feeling may have served as a warning to its original audiences but it is unintentionally funny by modern standards.

p, Edward Golden; d, William Nigh; w, Michael Jacoby (based on a story by Mary C. Ransone); ph, Harry Neumann; ed, Robert Golden; md, Edward Kay.

Drama   (PR:A MPAA:NR)

NO GREATER SIN   (SEE: EIGHTEEN AND ANXIOUS, 1957)

NO HANDS ON THE CLOCK**½   (1941) 76m PAR bw

Chester Morris (Humphrey Campbell), Jean Parker (Louise), Rose Hobart (Mrs. West), Dick Purcell (Red Harris), Astrid Allwyn (Gypsy Toland), Rod Cameron (Tom Reed), George Watts (Oscar Flack), James Kirkwood (Warren Benedict), Billie Seward (Rose Madden), Robert Middlemass (Chief Bates), Grant Withers (Harry Belding), Lorin Baker (Copley), George Lewis (Paulson), Ralph Sanford (Officer Gimble), Frank Faylen, Keye Luke.

Private eye Morris and his new bride Parker head off to Reno for a honeymoon. Upon arrival they find themselves embroiled in a kidnaping-murder case involving the disappearance of a wealthy rancher's son. The husband and wife investigate and solve the crime with the typical "all the suspects in one room" scene. This is a nifty little thriller, with freshly paced direction. Morris and Parker are a fine team, combining for good chemistry. Unfortunately the film is marred by a number of loose ends, the most significant being what ever happened to the kidnaped victim!

p, William H. Pine, William C. Thomas; d, Frank McDonald; w, Maxwell Shane (based on the novel by Geoffrey Homes); ph, Fred Jackman, Jr.; ed, William Ziegler.

Mystery/Crime   (PR:A MPAA:NR)

NO HAUNT FOR A GENTLEMAN**   (1952, Brit.) 58m Anglo-Scottish/Apex bw

Anthony Pendrell (John Northwick), Sally Newton (Miriam Northwick), Jack Mac-Naughton (Fitz-Cholmondley), Patience Rentoul (Mother), Dorothy Summers (Mrs. Mallett), Peter Swanwick (Brother Ravioli), Rufus Cruiekshank (Angus McDingle), Barbara Shaw (Lady Medeline de Boudoir), Joan Hickson (Mme. Omskaya), Hattie Jacques (Mrs. Fitz-Cholmondley), Joan Sterndale-Bennett (Mother Skipton), David King-Wood.

After heading off on their honeymoon, newlyweds Pendrell and Newton find themselves haunted by the constant shadow of mother-in-law Rentoul. However, while traveling in Scotland the couple meet a ghost (MacNaughton) who is more than accommodating in helping the pair rid themselves of the woman. A pointless comedy, using old jokes with little effect.

p, Charles Reynolds; d, Leonard Reeve; w, Julian Caunter, Gerard Bryant, Reeve (based on a story by Frederick Allwood); ph, Ted Lloyd.

Comedy/Fantasy   (PR:A MPAA:NR)

NO HIGHWAY   (SEE: NO HIGHWAY IN THE SKY, 1951, Brit.)

NO HIGHWAY IN THE SKY***½   (1951, Brit.) 98m FOX bw (GB: NO HIGHWAY)

James Stewart (Theodore Honey), Marlene Dietrich (Monica Teasdale), Glynis Johns (Marjorie Corder), Jack Hawkins (Dennis Scott), Ronald Squire (Sir John, the Director), Janette Scott (Elspeth Honey), Niall MacGinnis (Capt. Samuelson), Elizabeth Allan (Shirley Scott), Kenneth More (Dobson), David Hutcheson (Penworthy), Hugh Wakefield (Sir David Moon), Ben Williams (Guard), Maurice Denham (Maj. Pearl), Wilfrid Hyde-White (Fisher), Hector MacGregor (1st Engineer), Basil Appleby (2nd Engineer), Michael Kingsley (Navigator), Peter Murray (Radio Operator), Dora Bryan (Rosie), Jill Clifford (Peggy), Felix Aylmer (Sir Philip), Karel Stepanek (Mannheim), Wilfrid Walter (Tracy), John Salew (Symes), Marcel Poncin (Scientist), Cyril Smith (Airport Officer), Tom Gill (RAF Pilot), Hugh Gross (Director's Secretary), Arthur Lucas, Dodd Mehan, Maxwell Foster, Gerald Kent, John Lennox, Douglas Bradley Smith (Staff of Directors at Farnborough), Stuart Nichol, Philip Vickers (Control Officers), Philip Ray (Burroughs), Roy Russell (Butler), Diana Bennett (Stewardess), Michael McCarthy (Bus Conductor), Robert Lickens, Catherine Leach (Autograph Hunters).

Stewart is both humorous and compelling as an eccentric scientist working for the Royal Aircraft Establishment which has just produced a new airplane, the Reindeer. Stewart has studied this craft closely and goes to his superior, Hawkins, to tell him that the plane has a serious defect, that its tail assembly will break away from sheer fatigue at approximately 1,440 flying hours. Hawkins thinks Stewart is unduly alarmed and is unconvinced since the scientist has yet to conduct elaborate tests to prove his theory. Yet he sends widower Stewart to Labrador to investigate the inexplicable crash of a new Reindeer. En route he learns that the Reindeer in which he is flying has logged 1,420 hours and he insists that the plane turn back, but the pilot refuses. Stewart explains the problem to Dietrich, a famous musical star, and to stewardess Johns. Both are convinced of Stewart's sincerity but the plane lands without mishap and is examined. Nothing amiss is found and the Reindeer prepares to take off once more. Stewart wrecks the undercarriage of the plane to prevent loss of life and he is returned to England to face charges from his company. Dietrich shows up, as does Johns, and both women support Stewart and his little girl, Scott. Johns practically moves in with Stewart and Scott as it appears that Stewart is off his rocker but Hawkins backs him up and allows him to conduct exhaustive and expensive tests on the Reindeer aircraft. For weeks Stewart sleeplessly labors with the problems and just when Hawkins is about to call off the costly experimenting, the tail section falls off and Stewart is vindicated. His dogged beliefs eventually save many lives.Stewart is very convincing as the bumbling scientist and Johns is pert and appealing but Dietrich steals every scene in which she appears. She dresses in snug suits, veils, and furs designed by Christian Dior. Dietrich simply played Dietrich in this film and she was captivating.

p, Louis D. Lighton; d, Henry Koster; w, R.C. Sherriff, Oscar Millard, Alec Coppel (based on the novel No Highway by Nevil Shute); ph, Georges Perinal; ed, Manuel Del Campo; art d, C.P. Norman; cos, Christian Dior (Marlene Dietrich's wardrobe).

Aviation Drama   (PR:A MPAA:NR)

NO HOLDS BARRED**½   (1952) 65m MON bw

Leo Gorcey (Terrence Aloysius "Slip" Mahoney), Huntz Hall (Horace Debussy "Sach"/Hammerhead/Steel Fingers/Iron Elbow/Terrible Toes"), David Condon (Chuck), Bennie Bartlett (Butch), Bernard Gorcey (Louie Dumbrowski), Leonard Penn (Pete Taylor), Marjorie Reynolds (Rhonda Nelson), Hombre Montana (Terrible Tova), Henry Kulky (Mike the Mauler), Murray Alper (Barney), Barbara Grey (Gertie Smith), Lisa Wilson (Betty), Nick Stewart (Stickup Man), Ted Christy (Himself), Pat Fraley (Challenger), "Brother" Frank Jares (Crusher Martin), Leo "Ukie" Sherin (Sam), John Indrisano, Mike Ruby (Referees), Count John Maximillian Smith (Himself), Tim Ryan (Mr. Hunter), Sandra Gould (Mildred), Bob Cudlip (1st Mug), Mort Mills (2nd Mug), Ray Walker (Max), Bill Page (Pete), George Eldredge (Dr. Howard), Meyer Grace (Arena Messenger), Jimmy Cross (Announcer).

This is a better-than-average outing for Gorcey and company. Through some sort of odd biological quirk Hall is able to withstand pain in his head. Gorcey enters his pal in the wrestling arena, changing Hall's fighting name as the condition mysteriously changes from one part of the body to another. Real-life wrestlers are featured in the film's matches. The power finally ends up in Hall's hind quarters, which leads to an amusing exchange between he and Gorcey. The direction is well-paced for comedy and the broad humor of the script well fits the picture. (See BOWERY BOYS series, Index.)

p, Jerry Thomas; d, William Beaudine; w, Tim Ryan, Jack Crutcher, Bert Lawrence; ph, Ernest Miller; ed, William Austin; md, Edward J. Kay; art d, David Milton; set d, Robert Priestley; cos, Frank Beetson; spec eff, Ray Mercer.

Comedy   (PR:A MPAA:NR)

NO KIDDING   (SEE: BEWARE OF CHILDREN, 1961, Brit.)

NO KNIFE   (SEE: FRISCO KID, THE, 1979)

NO LADY*   (1931, Brit.) 70m GAU bw

Lupino Lane (Mr. Pog), Renee Clama (Sonia), Sari Maritza (Greta Gherkinski), Wallace Lupino (Ptomanian Ptough), Lola Hunt (Mrs. Pog), Denis O'Neil (Singer), Cyril McLaglen, Herman Darewski and His Blackpool Tower Band, Charles Stone, Roy Carey, Eddie Jay, Sam Lee.

Lane is a henpecked husband who goes for a holiday at a seaside resort. There he gets involved with a glider competition and some Ruritanian spies out to destroy the British entry via radio control. This plays like an overlong Mack Sennett comedy. The gags are fast and furious. Unfortunately the 70 minute running time is far too long for nonstop slapstick and the comedy grows weary before long. Lane, who also directed and co-wrote the film, overplays his role. His behind-the-camera abilities also leave much to be desired. There's no sense of comic timing and the recording is awful considering the technology available by 1931.

p, L'Estrange Fawcett; d, Lupino Lane; w, George Dewhurst (based on a story by Lane, Fawcett, Bert Lee, R.P. Weston); ph, Percy Strong.

Comedy   (PR:A MPAA:NR)

NO LEAVE, NO LOVE*½   (1946) 119m MGM bw

Van Johnson (Sgt. Michael Hanlon), Keenan Wynn (Slinky), Pat Kirkwood (Susan Malby Duncan), Edward Arnold (Hobart Canford Stiles), Marie Wilson (Rosalind), Leon Ames (Col. Elliott), Marina Koshetz (Countess Strogoff), Selena Royle (Mrs. Hanlon), Wilson Wood (Mr. Crawley), Vince Barnett (Ben), Frank "Sugarchile" Robinson (Boy Piano Player), Walter Sande (Sledgehammer), Arthur Walsh (Nick), Joey Preston (Boy Drummer Specialty), The Garcias (Dance Team), Xavier Cugat and His Orchestra, Guy Lombardo and His Orchestra.

Van Johnson is due to receive the Medal of Honor for his efforts during WW II. He and his buddy Wynn decide to live it up in London before heading home. He can't wait to reunite with his fiancee, but unbeknownst to Johnson, his intended had taken up with another while he was off fighting. Kirkwood is the radio singer who somehow manages to soothe Johnson's slightly ruffled feathers. The plot is standard programmer stuff and so poorly handled that it's an embarrassment. Kirkwood was brought to the U.S. for this film and was given the star treatment upon arrival. As it turned out this was her first and last Hollywood film. The script is a series of witless gags and routines, giving the two male leads no real chance to show their talents. Lombardo and Cugat each lead their respective bands for a few numbers, the only bright spots in this standard sub-par outing. Songs and musical numbers include: "All the Time" (Ralph Freed, Sammy Fain, sung by Pat Kirkwood), "Isn't It Wonderful" (Kay Thompson, sung by Kirkwood), "Love on a Greyhound Bus" (Thompson, Ralph Blane, Georgie Stoll), "It'll Be Great to be Back Home" (Charles Martin), "Old Sad Eyes" (Irving Kahal, Fain), "When It's Love" (Edgar De Lange, Nicholas Kharito), "Oye Negra" (performed by Xavier Cugat and His Orchestra).

p, Joe Pasternak; d, Charles Martin; w, Martin, Leslie Kardos; ph, Harold Rosson, Robert Surtees; ed, Conrad A. Nervig; md, Georgie Stoll; art d, Cedric Gibbons; cos, Irene; ch, Stanley Donen.

Musical/Comedy   (PR:A MPAA:NR)

NO LIMIT**   (1931) 78m PAR bw

Clara Bow (Helen "Bunny" O'Day), Stuart Erwin (Ole Olsen), Norman Foster (Douglas Thayer), Harry Green (Maxie Mindil), Dixie Lee (Dotty "Dodo" Potter), Mischa Auer (Romeo), Kenne Duncan (Curley Andrews), G. Pat Collins (Charlie), Maurice Black (Happy), Frank Hagney (Battling Hannon), Paul Nicholson (Chief of Detectives Armstrong), William B. Davidson (Wilkie the Building Superintendent), Lee Phelps (Ticket Taker), Robert Grieg (Doorman), Allan Cavan (Board Member), Bill O'Brien (George the Butler), Perry Ivins (Butterfly Man), Syd Saylor (Reporter).

Bow plays an innocent movie theater usherette who falls in love with a patron. She finally meets him and knocks him off his feet. After they marry she discovers her man is really a jewel thief and he is soon imprisoned. She moves in with Lee, one of her girl friends. Lee lives in a futuristic (by 1931 Hollywood standards) apartment that actually is a front for gamblers. Poor Bow is once more caught up in bad situations, but all is righted in the end when her man is sprung from jail. He reclaims his bride and they begin life anew. This is fairly sappy stuff played as light comedy. It doesn't work for several different reasons. The story is too helter-skelter in development and there are too many heavy moments that are played for laughs. The direction is plodding and does little with the hapless material.

d, Frank Tuttle; w, Viola Brothers Shore, Salisbury Field (based on a story by George Marion, Jr.); ph, Victor Milner; ed, Tay Malarkey.

Comedy (PR:A MPAA:NR)

NO LIMIT* ½** (1935, Brit.) 80m Associated Talking Pictures/ABF bw

George Formby (George Shuttleworth), Florence Desmond (Florrie Dibney), Howard Douglas (Turner), Beatrix Fielden-Kaye (Mrs. Horrocks), Peter Gawthorne (Mr. Higgins), Alf Goddard (Norton), Florence Gregson (Mrs. Shuttleworth), Jack Hobbs (Bert Tyldesley), Eve Lister (Rita), Edward Rigby (Grandfather), Evelyn Roberts (B.B.C. Commentator), Ernest Sefton (Mr. Hardacre), Arthur Young (Doctor).

Formby is wonderfully funny as a local yokel determined to become a champion dirt-bike racer. He builds his own machine and enters into competitions. The plot is relatively simple but works well, thanks in part to the comic talents of the lead. Formby was a popular British comedian (as was his father), who could handle seemingly mundane situations with originality. The climactic race on the Isle of Man is nicely photographed, with plenty of action and laughs mixed together. Banks was one of the best of England's comedy directors. His work here shows why. Pacing and rhythms are nicely drawn out with a good sense of comic timing. The balance between comedy and action is well maintained. Some of the musical and action sequences run a little longer than necessary, no doubt to add to the film's appeal to different audiences. Otherwise this is a wonderful little comedy.

p, Basil Dean; d, Monty Banks; w, Tom Geraghty, Fred Thompson (based on a story by Walter Greenwood); ph, Robert G. Martin; m/l, Harry Parr Davies, Clifford and Cliffe.

Comedy (PR:A MPAA:NR)

NO LIVING WITNESS** (1932) 65m Ralph M. Like/Mayfair bw

Gilbert Roland (Jerry Bennett), Noah Beery, Sr. (Clyde Corbin), Barbara Kent (Carol Everett), Carmel Myers (Emilia), Otis Harlan ("Pop" Everett), Dorothy Revier (Miss Thompson), J. Carrol Naish (Nick), Ferike Boros (Nick's Mother), John Ince (Police Captain), Monte Carter (Looey), Broderick O'Farrell (District Attorney), Arthur Millett (Harry Newton), James Cooley (Fatty Raskin), Gordon DeMain (Eddie Schrabe).

This is a cookbook film employing elements from various programmers and popular films. The result is a mixed bag containing some good performances and occasional spurts of creativity. Beery plays an unethical attorney. He's trying to cheat an out-of-town businessman with a phony race track scam. Roland is the good attorney who exposes Beery and saves the day. The ending, involving the comic efforts of the district attorney, an engagement ring, and his girl waiting at the train station, is right out of THE FRONT PAGE. The standout here is Naish in a relatively minor role. The dialog is a little bland considering the subject, but the direction moves briskly.

p, Cliff Broughton; d, E. Mason Hopper; w, Norman Houston; ph, Jules Cronjager; ed, Byron Robinson.

Drama (PR:A MPAA:NR)

NO LONGER ALONE** (1978) 99m World Wide c

Belinda Carroll (Joan Winmill), Roland Culver (A. E. Matthews), James Fox (Alan Richards), Wilfrid Hyde-White (Lord Home), Simon Williams (William Douglas Home), Helen Cherry (Miss Godfrey), Samantha Gates (Joan, Age 12), Karen Dines (Joan, Age 6), Gordon Devol (Robert Kennedy), Reginald Marsh (Producer), John Alkin (Bruce), Mary Kerridge (Lady Home), Robert Rietty (Joan's Father), Helen Cotterill (Elaine), John Clive (Basil), Vivienne Burgess (Grandmother).

Carroll plays the noted British actress Joan Winmill, who suffered from suicidal tendencies until she finally had a religious conversion. The story is told mainly in flashback. We see the actress' unhappy childhood and the death of her mother and a cousin. Her grandmother also suffers from similar psychological troubles and falls victim to a nervous breakdown. Winmill's affair with Robert Kennedy (played by Devol) is unfortunately overplayed. The scenes don't work, as Kennedy was too recent a historical figure to be successfully interpreted by an actor. The affair was also a minor part of Winmill's life and is unfortunately capitalized on by the producers. The film is nicely photographed and the director handles the material with sensitivity. Carroll's religious experiences are not overstated, which is an asset. The two children (Gates and Dines) who play Winmill in childhood are surprisingly accomplished performers.

p, Frank R. Jacobson; d, Nicholas Webster; w, Lawrence Holben (based on the autobiography by Joan Winmill Brown); ph, Michael Reed; m, Tedd Smith; ed, J. Michael Hooser; prod d, John Lageu; cos, Klara Kerpin.

Drama (PR:C MPAA:PG)

NO LOVE FOR JOHNNIE* ½** (1961, Brit.) 111m RANK-Five Star/EM bw

Peter Finch (Johnnie Byrne), Stanley Holloway (Fred Andrews), Mary Peach (Pauline West, Model), Donald Pleasence (Roger Renfrew), Billie Whitelaw (Mary), Dennis Price (Flagg), Hugh Burden (Tim Maxwell), Rosalie Crutchley (Alice Byrne), Michael Goodliffe (Dr. West), Mervyn Jones (Charlie Young), Geoffrey Keen (Prime Minister), Paul Rogers (Sydney Johnson), Peter Barkworth (Henderson), Fenella Fielding (Sheilah), Gladys Henson (Constituent).

In 1959 a controversial novel about the British House of Commons was published by Wilfred Fienburgh, a Socialist member of Parliament. Its insights into the inner workings of the British government understandably upset a few highbrows, though the public relished the fictionalized information. Fienburgh was killed in an auto accident shortly after publication of his book, two years before he could see the filmed version. Finch is Fienburgh's protagonist. He plays a member of Parliament re-elected to the House of Commons. But his political and social life is far from satisfying. He fails to receive an expected cabinet post and shortly after that, his Communist wife (Crutchley) leaves him. His life a shambles, Finch takes up with a militant left-wing faction. His upstairs neighbor (Whitelaw) takes Finch to a party where he meets Peach, a fashion model. They are soon lovers. He is so mad for her that he misses an important session in which he was to ask questions that would discredit the ruling party. Peach decides that marrying a man twice as old as she would be a mistake and she leaves London. Finch's fellow party members haul him onto the carpet for missing the important session because of the love of a woman. His life is once more a shambles, but he is surprised by the return of Crutchley. She wants to make a go of the marriage once more, and he nearly agrees. But a high official offers him a cabinet seat with the stipulation that Finch remain apart from his Communist wife. Finch is excellent as the man on a political and emotional roller coaster. The real key to this film, however, is the supporting cast. Keen as the prime minister, Holloway as an old veteran politico, Barkworth as a new member of the House of Commons, and Pleasence as a leftist all combine for some wonderful performances. Like real-life politics, this is a film studded with quirky and eclectic personalities that give a realistic feeling to the political proceedings. Though the film is more dramatic and less controversial than its source, NO LOVE FOR JOHNNIE is well-produced. The director moves things along with a great sense of drive. It may not exactly know where it's going (so much like the real political world), but it certainly brings us there. The personal elements staged against the panorama of important events are nicely handled. One is never sacrificed for the other, resulting in a fine mix of the human and the immense.

p, Betty E. Box; d, Ralph Thomas; w, Nicholas Phipps, Mordecai Richler (based on the novel No Love for Johnnie by Wilfred Fienburgh); ph, Ernest Steward (CinemaScope); m, Malcolm Arnold; ed, Alfred Roome; md, Arnold; art d, Maurice Carter; set d, Arthur Taksen; cos, Yvonne Caffin; makeup, William Partleton.

Drama (PR:O MPAA:NR)

NO LOVE FOR JUDY** (1955, Brit.) 51m Archway bw

Ellet Mauret (June), Zoe Newton (Judy).

A model and her friend vacation along the French Riviera. There the model raises the hackles of her companion by stealing her boy friends. Lovely scenery, lovely women, but not much else going on here.

d&w, Jacques de Lane Lea.

Comedy (PR:C MPAA:NR)

NO MAN IS AN ISLAND** (1962) 114m Gold Coast/UNIV (GB: ISLAND ESCAPE)

Jeffrey Hunter (George R. Tweed), Marshall Thompson ("Sonn" Sonnenberg), Barbara Perez ("Joe" Cruz), Ronald Remy (Chico Torres), Paul Edwards, Jr. (Al Turney), Rolf Bayer (Chief Schultz), Vincente Liwanag (Vincente), Fred Harris II (Roy Lund), Bert [Lamberto V.] Avellana (Mr. Shimoda), Chichay [Amparo Custodio] (Mrs. Nakamura), Antonio de la Mogueis (Florecito), Vic Silayan (Maj. Hondo), Bert LaForteza (Comdr. Oto Harada), Eddie Infante (Sus Quintagua), Nardo Ramos (Tumon), Rosa Mia (Primera Quintagua), Mike Anzures (Santos), Joseph de Cordova (Father Pangolin), Mario Barri (Limtiago), Stevie Joseph (Tommy Tanaka), Ding Tello (Japanese Sergeant Major), Burt Olivar (Antonio Cruz), Veronica Palileo (Josefa Cruz), Bruno Punzalan, Nena Ledesma, Segundo Veloria.

Hunter is a U.S. Navy radio operator on Guam when the Japanese invade the island. He avoids capture and with five other Americans hides in the jungles of the island interior. One by one the others are killed and Hunter is left by himself for 34 months. Aided by friendly natives, he at first hides in a leper colony run by priest de Cordova, using the hospital transmitter to broadcast to the island residents until the Japanese catch on and burn the building to the ground. He then hides in a cave, a friendly family bringing him food. When he spots American warships off the coast, he signals them with a hand mirror and that night swims out to a launch which takes him back to the ship. Using the information Hunter has gathered, the American forces easily recapture the island. At the conclusion, Hunter returns to the island and visits all the people who helped him. Loosely based on the experiences of George R. Tweed, the film takes major liberties with the facts, inevitable in this type of heroic biography. Hunter, fresh from playing the Messiah in Nicholas Ray's KING OF KINGS (1961), is too movie star-like to be really convincing as a sailor on the run in the jungle for nearly three years, but those qualms aside, the film works fairly well as wartime adventure. Numerous Japanese stragglers were still being found in the jungles of Guam even after this film was made, nearly 20 years after the war.

p, John Monks, Jr., Richard Goldstone, Rolf Bayer; d&w, Monks, Goldstone (based on the wartime experiences of George R. Tweed, USN); ph, Carl Kayser

(Eastmancolor); m, Restie Umali; ed, Basil Wrangell; art d, Benjamin Resella; spec eff, Robert R. Joseph; m/l, "Maulik Trabajo," Umali (sung by Barbara Perez).

War **(PR:C MPAA:NR)**

NO MAN OF HER OWN½** (1933) 85m PAR bw

Clark Gable *(Jerry "Babe" Stewart)*, Carole Lombard *(Connie Randall)*, Dorothy Mackaill *(Kay Everly)*, Grant Mitchell *(Charlie Vane)*, George Barbier *(Mr. Randall)*, Elizabeth Patterson *(Mrs. Randall)*, J. Farrell MacDonald *(Detective Dickie Collins)*, Tommy Conlon *(Willie Randall)*, Walter Walker *(Mr. Morton)*, Paul Ellis *(Vargas)*, Lillian Harmer *(Mattie)*, Frank McGlynn, Sr. *(Minister)*, Charley Grapewin *(Newsstand Clerk)*, Clinton Rosemond *(Porter)*, Oscar Smith *(Porter)*, Wallis Clark *(Thomas Laidlaw, Broker)*, Lionel Belmore *(Antique Dealer)*.

MGM loaned Clark Gable to Paramount for this picture and may have wished they hadn't, as it turned out better than had been expected and made a bundle for the Melrose Avenue lot that the Culver Cityites didn't reckon on. A deft blend of comedy, action, and romance, NO MAN OF HER OWN brought Gable and Lombard together for the first time, a union that would result in their happy marriage several years later. Mackaill is a bombshell whose job it is to lure high rollers into crooked card games with her beau, Gable. MacDonald is a New York City detective who has been trying to get the goods on Gable and can't manage to glean enough evidence, but he's rapidly amassing enough dope on the gambler to run him in. Gable knows he'd better run out of town before the heat gets too intense, so he decides to hide in a small town just outside New York until it's safe to return. Once there, Gable meets librarian Lombard, and she falls in love with him. On a bet with associate Ellis, Gable marries Lombard, but she is serious about the marriage and loves him dearly. She thinks he is a broker and has no idea that he earns his living by double-dealing at poker games with fat cats. They go to New York and Gable is up to his old tricks again but keeps the information from his adoring wife. Mackaill has been vacationing in the West Indies and returns to learn that Gable and Lombard are married. She's hurt and angry and plans to go to the local authorities to expose him. By this time, Gable has truly fallen in love with his own wife and understands that they can never stay together as long as he continues his illegal business, so he turns himself in to the cops and does a three-month sentence. Lombard thinks that he is off on a business trip to South America until Mackaill spills the beans to her. Once he is released, Gable is able to maintain his love and marriage with Lombard. It's a trifle, but there are many funny moments and the screen explodes whenever Gable and Lombard are in the same scenes. When Gable returns from his 90-day visit to the GrayBar hotel, Lombard is hip to where he's been, but doesn't let him know that and forces him to tell her the truth. It doesn't matter to her that he was a criminal because she realizes that he put himself away on her behalf and greater love hath no man for his woman.

p, Albert Lewis; d, Wesley Ruggles; w, Maurine Watkins, Milton Gropper (based on the story by Edmund Goulding, Benjamin Glazer); ph, Leo Tover; cos, Travis Banton.

Comedy/Drama **(PR:A MPAA:NR)**

NO MAN OF HER OWN½** (1950) 98m PAR bw

Barbara Stanwyck *(Helen Ferguson)*, John Lund *(Bill Harkness)*, Jane Cowl *(Mrs. Harkness)*, Phyllis Thaxter *(Patrice Harkness)*, Lyle Bettger *(Stephen Morley)*, Henry O'Neill *(Mr. Harkness)*, Richard Denning *(Hugh Harkness)*, Carole Mathews *(Blonde)*, Harry Antrim *(Ty Winthrop)*, Catherine Craig *(Rosalie Baker)*, Esther Dale *(Josie)*, Milburn Stone *(Plainclothesman)*, Griff Barnett *(Dr. Parker)*, Gaylord Pendleton, Stan Johnson *(Policemen)*, Georgia Backus *(Nurse)*, Dooley Wilson *(Dining Car Waiter)*, Ivan Browning *(Porter)*, William Haade *(Cop)*, Jean Andren *(Louise Russell)*, Selmer Jackson *(Minister)*, Laura Elliott, Charles Dayton *(Friends of the Family)*, Dick Keene *(Clerk)*, Johnny Michaels *(Delivery Boy)*, Virginia Brissac *(Justice of the Peace's Wife)*, Thomas Browne Henry *(Doctor at Hospital)*, Willard Waterman *(Jack Olsen)*, Dave Willock *(Jimmy Baker)*, Kathleen Freeman *(Clara Larrimore)*, Esther Howard *(Blowsy Boarding House Woman)*, Frank Marlowe *(Steve)*, Sumner Getchell *(John Larrimore)*, Gordon Nelson *(Justice of the Peace)*, Jean Ruth, Mary Lawrence, Jack Reynolds, Helen Mowery, Emmett Smith, Ashley Cowan, Jimmie Dundee, Phillip Tully, Ray Walker, Edna Holland.

Mystery writer Cornell Woolrich, using a pseudonym, wrote the novel upon which this soap opera is based and it was filled with all sorts of manipulations, most of which the audience could sense, but it didn't much matter. Stanwyck becomes pregnant by boy friend Bettger, who responds to that news by tossing her out on her ear, as though it were her fault and not his. He gives her a train ticket but nothing else. On the train, she meets Denning and Thaxter, an attractive young couple on their way home to meet Denning's parents, who have not yet met Thaxter. Stanwyck and Thaxter become friendly and have much in common, as Thaxter is also pregnant. The two women go into the ladies room aboard the hurtling train and Stanwyck admires Thaxter's wedding ring, so the other woman gives it to her to try on. At that moment, the train crashes. Thaxter and Denning are killed and Stanwyck gives birth to her child in the hospital, but is taken to be Thaxter because of the ring she wears. She goes to the home of Denning's wealthy parents, Cowl and O'Neill, and is welcomed as their surviving daughter-in-law, although there are several gaps in her memory (well, of course there are, as she hasn't lived any of the incidents referred to by O'Neill and Cowl, but they think it just may be temporary amnesia). Her life seems happy until Bettger finds her and threatens to expose the sham unless she comes up with some cash. Meanwhile, Lund, the older brother of the late Denning, has fallen in love with Stanwyck. The question now becomes, how to get rid of Bettger and keep her life intact? Lund and Stanwyck take care of that and wonder if they'll ever be discovered, but, not to worry, it all works out in the end. Barbara Stanwyck said, at the 1986 "Golden Globe" Awards, that she never felt pretty. She laughed and remarked that Kirk Douglas, who was standing at her side, was prettier than she was. She is wrong, of course, as her enduring and interesting looks have stood her in good stead for more than half a century of acting. This was stage actor Bettger's film debut. He has since become one of the busiest character actors around. Remade as I MARRIED A SHADOW.

p, Richard Maibaum; d, Mitchell Leisen; w, Sally Benson, Catherine Turney (based on the novel *I Married a Dead Man* by William Irish [Cornell Woolrich]); ph, Daniel L. Fapp; m, Hugo Friedhofer; ed, Alma Macrorie; art d, Hans Dreier, Henry Bumstead; set d, Sam Comer, Ray Myer; cos, Edith Head; spec eff, Farciot Edouart, Gordon Jennings; makeup, Wally Westmore, Bob Ewing.

Drama **(PR:A MPAA:NR)**

NO MAN WALKS ALONE (SEE: BLACK LIKE ME, 1964)

NO MAN'S LAND** (1964) 72m Cinema-Video International bw

Russ Harvey *(Cpl. Jerry Little)*, Kim Lee *(Anna Wong)*, Lee Morgan *(Old Sarge)*, Val Martinez, Tom Lytle, Henry Garcia, Eddie Retacy, Tom Drossis, Lyman Harrison, Don Russell, Percy Barbat.

Harvey (who also wrote, produced, and directed) stars as an American in the Korean War. He thinks he hears noises in an area dubbed "No Man's Land" and throws a grenade. This triggers a major battle between the U.S. forces and the North Koreans. Later he meets Lee, a young Korean girl who is walking her dog. They take a liking to one another and a friendship forms. Harvey and his troops go out on patrol once more and an old sergeant is killed by a sniper. Lytle takes volunteers back for medical treatment while Harvey finds the sniper. He kills the man and returns to Lee, whom he marries. Harvey shot this feature in San Antonio, Texas, of all places. He produced a number of these war-action flicks, including DUNGEONS OF HARROU, which was released the same month as NO MAN'S LAND.

p,d&w, Russ Harvey; ph, James Houston; m, Jaime Mendoza-Nava; ed, Charles Kimball; md, Mendoza-Nava; art d, Don Russell; makeup, Nan Ruckman; Military Advisor and Coordinator, T.E. Lytle.

War **(PR:O MPAA:NR)**

NO MAN'S RANGE** (1935) 55m Supreme/William Steiner bw (AKA: NO MAN'S LAND)

Bob Steele, Roberta Gale, Buck Connors, Steve Clark, Charles K. French, Jack Rockwell, Roger Williams, Earl Dwire, Ed Cassidy, Jim Corey.

Ever popular good guy Steele, with the curly mop of black hair, must go undercover as a renegade, using dynamite to trap the enemy. Standard action western with more than the usual amount of explosive action from little guy Steele, who always gave kids hope that in a world of big, bad people a welterweight could take care of the heavies. This was the first of 14 films Steele would make with his father, Bradbury, directing and writing the stories for independent producer Hackel.

p, A.W. Hackel; d, Robert N. Bradbury; w, Forbes Parkhill (based on a story by Bradbury).

Western **(PR:A MPAA:NR)**

NO MAN'S WOMAN** (1955) 70m REP bw

Marie Windsor, John Archer, Patric Knowles, Nancy Gates, Jil Jarmyn, Richard Crane, Fern Hall, Louis Jean Heydt, John Gallaudet, Douglas Wood, Percy Helton, Morris Ankrum.

A woman who shows no mercy in her dealings turns up dead. Five people are suspect in her murder and the investigation begins. A later release from staggering Republic Studios, produced by its founder, Yates, and one of the last films to be produced by the studio before its demise as a production company in 1958.

p, Herbert J. Yates; d, Franklin Adreon; w, John K. Butler (based on a story by Don Martin); ph, Bud Thackery; m, R. Dale Butts; ed, Howard Smith; md, Butts; art d, Walter Keller; cos, Adele Palmer.

Crime **(PR:C MPAA:NR)**

NO MARRIAGE TIES** (1933) 65m RKO bw

Richard Dix *(Bruce Foster)*, Elizabeth Allan *(Peggy Wilson)*, Alan Dinehart *(Perkins)*, David Landau *(Zimmer, Editor)*, Hilda Vaughn *(Olmstead)*, Hobart Cavanaugh *(Smith)*, Doris Kenyon *(Adrienne Deane)*, Charles Wilson.

Dix is an alcoholic newspaperman who is fired after being too soused to cover the Dempsey-Tunney fight. He ends up in a bar where he meets an advertising executive looking for some fresh ideas. He takes a liking to Dix and they form a partnership. Dix proves to be a ruthless businessman engaging in unethical practices. But when his fiancee (Kenyon) commits suicide, Dix's life crumbles. He drinks even more than previously and soon finds himself in danger of exposure for his ruthless tactics. An old girl friend (Allan on loan to RKO from MGM) lifts up her old flame from his degradation and helps him start life anew. There are elements of strong drama within the plot structure. Unfortunately the film is marred by overwriting—no less than five men worked on the story and screenplay. Dix gives a lively performance, but isn't quite believable as either newspaperman or ad executive. Eventually the film winds down into standard melodrama that is neither terrible nor exciting.

p, William Goetz; d, J. Walter Ruben; w, Arthur Caesar, Sam Mintz, H.W. Hanemann (based on the play "Ad-Man" by Arch A. Gaffney, Charles Curran); ph, Henry Cronjager; ed, George Hively.

Drama **(PR:A MPAA:NR)**

NO MERCY MAN, THE* (1975) 91m Cannon c (AKA: TRAINED TO KILL)

Steven Sandor, Rockne Tarkington, Richard X. Slattery, Heidi Vaughn, Michael Layne.

Cheap, exploitative story about a soldier returning from service in Viet Nam. As with so many films of this nature, all the vet needs is one thing to set off his explosive inner torments. Here it comes under the form of a stock gang of sadistic teens who try to take over the town. Ugly, mean-spirited, and forgettable.

p, Paul Rubey Johnson; d, Daniel Vance; w, Vance, Mike Nolin.

Drama/Action **(PR:O MPAA:R)**

NO MINOR VICES*** (1948) 96m Enterprise/MGM bw

Dana Andrews *(Dr. Perry Aswell)*, Lilli Palmer *(April Aswell)*, Louis Jourdan *(Ottavio Quaglini)*, Jane Wyatt *(Miss Darlington)*, Norman Lloyd *(Dr. Sturdivant)*, Bernard Gorcey *(Mr. Zitzfleisch)*, Roy Roberts *(Mr. Felton)*, Fay Baker *(Mrs. Felton)*, Sharon McManus *(Gloria Felton)*, Ann Doran *(Mrs. Faraday)*, Beau Bridges *(Bertram)*, Frank Kreig *(Cab Driver)*, Kay Williams *(Receptionist)*, Bobby Hyatt *(Genius)*, Jerry Mullins *(Boy)*, Inna Gest *(Mrs. Fleishgelt)*, Frank Conlan *(Window Cleaner)*, Joy Rogers, Eileen Coghlin *(Nurses)*.

Andrews plays a thriving young pediatrician who makes a mistake by hiring an artist to sketch some "real life" portraits of a doctor's office. The painter is madman Jourdan, who promptly turns the office into a shambles and makes a play for Andrews' wife (Palmer). Gorcey plays a cigar maker who watches the whole proceeding from his shop across the way. There are some nice moments of sophisticated humor within the film, but the overall production is hampered by its intellectual pretensions. Voice-overs of the lead characters' thoughts, a la "Strange Interlude," are nice at first but quickly become overdone. The presence of Gorcey, on leave from running his candy store for the BOWERY BOYS series, is also a nice touch that ends up being used too often. Jourdan is wonderful, appropriately nuts, as all eccentric artists should be. The support is fine, with Andrews and Palmer, normally dramatic actors, handling the light comedy well. In the end, NO MINOR VICES is passable and humorous, though not the sophisticated comedy it pretends to be. This was the first film from Enterprise Studios released world-wide through MGM. A previous outing (also directed by Milestone), ARCH OF TRIUMPH, died a miserable box-office death, causing United Artists to drop U.S. and Canadian distribution of Enterprise films. MGM had handled their overseas distribution. The co-founder of Enterprise was David Loew, who was son of MGM's Marcus Loew and the brother of Arthur Loew.

p&d, Lewis Milestone; w, Arnold Manoff; ph, George Barnes; m, Franz Waxman; ed, Robert Parrish; art d, Nicholas Remisoff; set d, Edward G. Boyle; cos, Marian Herwood; makeup, Gus Norim.

Comedy **(PR:A MPAA:NR)**

NO MONKEY BUSINESS*½ (1935, Brit.) 78m Radius Prod./GFD bw

Gene Gerrard *(Jim Carroll)*, June Clyde *(Clare Barrington)*, Renee Houston *(Jessie)*, Richard Hearne *(Charlie)*, Peter Haddon *(Arthur)*, Claude Dampier *(Roberts)*, Hugh Wakefield *(Prof. Barrington)*, Fred Duprez *(Theater Manager)*, Clifford Heatherley *(Baliff)*, O.B. Clarence, Robert Nainby *(Professors)*, Charles Paton *(Lodging House Keeper)*, Alexander Field *(Greengrocer)*, Hal Gordon *(Circus Proprietor)*, Reuben Castang and His Apes.

Gerrard is a circus star who is in love with Clyde, an anthropologist's daughter. He doesn't make headway with her until he gets pal Hearne, an acrobat, to dress up as an ape and make it look like Gerrard trained him. There's some imagination in the story, but it's never developed into anything substantial. Consequently, this ends up being about as stupid as it sounds. The production credits are acceptable for the material.

p, Julius Haemann; d, Marcel Varnel; w, Roger Burford, Val Guest (based on a story by Joe May, Karl Notl); ph, Claude Friese-Greene.

Comedy **(PR:A MPAA:NR)**

NO MORE EXCUSES** (1968) 62m Phantasma/Rogosin-Impact bw

Robert Downey *(Pvt. Stewart Thompson)*, Allen Abel *(Himself)*, Lawrence Wolf *(President James A. Garfield)*, Prentice Wilhite *(Charles Guiteau)*, Linda Diesem *(Mrs. Garfield)*, Amy Eccles *(Chinese Girl)*, Don Calfa *(Priest)*, Paula Morris *(His Woman/Prostitute)*, Singles People *(Themselves)*.

This is a strange underground work out of New York that has some fine surreal moments. Unfortunately it gets too carried away with itself to work and ends up being a confusing mess. Writer-director Downey plays a Civil War soldier who gets shot in the behind. He heads from the battlefield to modern day New York and runs into a variety of situations. Downey presents President Garfield and his assassin; SINA, or the Society for Indecency to Naked Animals, an organization dedicated to clothing the beasts of the world; some actual cinema-verite footage of singles bars; and a newsman who turns into a chimpanzee. It's a myriad of images and ideas that is often hysterical but just doesn't quite work. It's thrown together too haphazardly to be as effective as apparently intended. Some of the Civil War footage comes from a Downey short film called BALLS BLUFF. The soundtrack also contains music from GOLDFINGER and A MAN AND A WOMAN. A 55 minute version and 52 minute version were also released.

d&w, Robert Downey; ed, Robert Soukis.

Experimental Comedy **(PR:O MPAA:NR)**

NO MORE LADIES** (1935) 81m MGM bw

Joan Crawford *(Marcia Townsend)*, Robert Montgomery *(Sherry Warren)*, Edna May Oliver *(Fanny Townsend)*, Franchot Tone *(James Salston)*, Charlie Ruggles *(Edgar Holmes)*, Gail Patrick *(Theresa Germaine)*, Vivienne Osborne *(Lady Diana Moulton)*, Joan Burfield [Fontaine] *(Caroline Rumsey)*, Arthur Treacher *(Lord Moulton)*, David Horsley *(James McIntyre Duffy)*, Jean Chatburn *(Sally French)*, Charles Coleman *(Stafford the Butler)*, William Wagner *(Butler)*, Frank Mayo, Gertrude Astor, Jean Acker *(Nightclub Extras)*, Donald Ogden Stewart *(Drunk)*, Brooks Benedict *(Joe Williams, Bar Owner)*, Dave O'Brien *(Party Guest)*, Lew Harvey, David Thursby *(Bartenders)*, Isabel La Mai *(Jacquette)*, Frank Dawson *(Dickens)*, E.J. Babiel *(Desk Clerk)*, Ed Hart *(Taxi Driver)*, Tommy Tomlinson *(Dick)*, Charles O'Malley *(Bellboy)*, Sherry Hall *(Captain)*, Clem Beauchamp *(Drunk)*, Veda Buckland *(Maid)*, Mabel Colcord *(Cook)*, Reginald Denny *(Oliver Allen)*, Walter Walker.

NO MORE LADIES is a slick "formula" film with gorgeous costumes, lots of pseudo-witty lines, and an excellent cast, none of whom can make up for the manufactured nature of the screenplay. Nonetheless, it's still good fun and has enough humor going for it to make this a pleasant diversion. Crawford is a slim patron of cafe society who is tired of the sophisticated life and yearns for a deeper relationship with a man, unlike the ones she's been experiencing. She is moralistic, in that her attitude is one of commitment and she will stick with her guy once she finds him. Tone is pursuing her and would like nothing better than taking her home to his parents for an introduction. Despite his pleas, she meets and falls for Montgomery, a rakehell who hops in and out of womens' beds with great ease and no regrets. Crawford thinks she can reform Montgomery and manages to get him to marry her, but the various women in Montgomery's life refuse to leave. They include Patrick, Osborne, and Burfield. Tone waits patiently in the wings and lets Crawford know that the moment Montgomery decides to dump her he will gladly take her. Crawford wants to remain true to her pledge to love, honor, and cherish and declines Tone's advances. Meanwhile, Montgomery is still acting like a bachelor and Crawford is irate. She plans revenge and invites several people to a party at their home. These guests are all the men and women whom Montgomery has hurt by his philandering over the past decade. A cadre of angry women and angrier husbands are there to addle Montgomery; then, Crawford leaves with Tone to carry on what appears to be an affair, which is totally against the characterization they strove to establish up until now. That should give a clue to the audience about what later happens; Crawford can't go all the way" with Tone and she returns to Montgomery who now understands that he truly loves Crawford and he will mend his behavior to conform with her desires. Glamorous and well-produced, NO MORE LADIES made a few dollars for the studio. Good comedy relief from Oliver as a drunken grandmother and Treacher as a comic Englishman. Two directors received credit on the picture, Griffith and Cukor, although we can't see why.

p, Irving Thalberg; d, Edward H. Griffith, George Cukor; w, Donald Ogden Stewart, Horace Jackson (based on the play by A.E. Thomas); ph, Oliver T. Marsh; m, Edward Ward; ed, Frank E. Hull; art d, Cedric Gibbons; cos, Adrian.

Drama/Comedy **(PR:C MPAA:NR)**

NO MORE ORCHIDS*** (1933) 71m COL bw

Carole Lombard *(Anne Holt)*, Lyle Talbot *(Tony Gage)*, Walter Connolly *(Bill Holt)*, Louise Closser Hale *(Grandma Holt)*, Allen Vincent *(Dick)*, Ruthelma Stevens *(Rita)*, C. Aubrey Smith *(Cedric)*, Arthur Housman *(Serge)*, William V. Mong *(Burkehart)*, Jameson Thomas *(Prince Carlos)*, Charles Hill Mailes *(Merriwell)*, Ed Le Saint *(Captain of the Ship)*, William Worthington *(Cannon)*, Broderick O'Farrell *(Benton the Butler)*, Belle Johnstone *(Housekeeper)*, Harold Minjir *(Modiste)*, Sidney Bracey *(Holmes)*.

Lombard is the poor-little-rich-girl who falls in love with the penniless Talbot. Her father (Connolly) wants to see his daughter happy, but Lombard's uncle (Smith) is determined that she will marry into royalty. Connolly's bank faces financial disaster and he appeals to his brother for a loan. Smith agrees on the condition that Lombard marry a prince (Thomas). She reluctantly consents to the wedding, but Connolly and his mother (Hale) arrange for Lombard to reunite with Talbot out in the country. Connolly prepares to fly back to meet his brother. Knowing that his insurance policy will cover his financial troubles, Connolly crashes his airplane so his daughter can marry the man she loves. This early Lombard feature shows that the great comedic actress was equally capable of doing drama. She portrays her character well, with good support by the ensemble. Connolly is particularly effective as the ruined businessman. The suicide ending was a real shocker for its day and a disappointing surprise for audiences conditioned for happy endings. But the device works well in this entertaining, though very minor film. Script and direction are sharp, keeping the pace moving well.

d, Walter Lang; w, Gertrude Purcell, Keene Thompson (based on the novel by Grace Perkins); ph, Joe August.

Drama **(PR:A MPAA:NR)**

NO MORE WOMEN* (1934) 76m PAR bw

Edmund Lowe *(Three-Time)*, Victor McLaglen *(Forty-Fathom)*, Sally Blane *(Helen Young)*, Minna Gombell *(Annie Fay)*, Alphonz Ethier *(Capt. Brent)*, Harold Huber *(Iceberg)*, Christian Rub *(Big Pants)*, Tom Dugan *(Greasy)*, William Franey *(Oscar)*, J.P. McGowan *(The Hawk)*, Frank Moran *(Brownie)*.

Lowe and McLaglen are two deep-sea divers on different boats. Blane inherits McLaglen's boat and moves in. To guarantee that this business venture will be successful, she hires another diver, namely McLaglen's rival Lowe. The two constantly argue and finally duke it out while riding an amusement park roller coaster. McLaglen gets bumped from the car and falls in the ocean. He hides and is assumed to be dead. Lowe is arrested for murder. When a ship carrying a valuable load of gold sinks, McLaglen and another diver agree to split the booty. But the new man is greedy and engages McLaglen in an underwater battle. Lowe, mysteriously released from jail, comes to the rescue, though both men end up in the hospital. Still arguing, the two are stunned when Blane comes in and announces that she is marrying the ship's captain. This is a tired, overlong programmer with not much to offer. Both story and performances are flat and uninspired. There are some good action sequences, such as the roller coaster fight, but these stick out only because the rest of the film is so poor. The underwater photography looks as fake as can be. Production credits are way below average, with an absolutely wretched job of editing being the production low point.

d, Al Rogell; w, Delmar Daves, Lou Breslow (based on a story by Daves, Grant Leenhouts from the story "Underseas" by John Mikale Strong); ph, Harry Fischbeck, Theodore Sparkuhl; ed, Joseph Kane.

Drama **(PR:A MPAA:NR)**

NO, MY DARLING DAUGHTER½** (1964, Brit.) 85m RANK-Five Star/Zenith International bw

Michael Redgrave *(Sir Matthew Carr)*, Michael Craig *(Thomas Barclay)*, Roger Livesey *(Gen. Henry Barclay)*, Rad Fulton *(Cornelius Allingham)*, Juliet Mills *(Tansy Carr)*, Renee Houston *(Miss Yardley)*, Joan Sims *(2nd Typist)*, Peter Barkworth *(Charles)*, David Lodge *(Flanigan)*, Carole Shelley *(1st Typist)*, Victor Brooks *(Policeman)*, Court Benson *(Allingham)*, Ian Fleming *(Vicar)*, Terry Scott *(Constable)*.

Redgrave is an English nobleman who sends his daughter Mills to a Parisian finishing school. There she meets Fulton, an American student, and they promptly fall in love. As it turns out, Fulton's father is a business associate of Redgrave's. When Fulton forgets to deliver a letter to Redgrave, the older man flies out to New York to take care of business problems. He sends Mills off to Scotland for a fishing trip with his friend Livesey. Fulton follows her, prompting headlines suggesting an elopement. When Redgrave finds out who Fulton is, he agrees to a marriage, but it is too late, for Mills has met Livesey's son Craig and fallen head over heels. The two fathers are delighted when the new lovebirds elope. This simplistic "girl's" comedy served as Mills' screen debut. She handles the comedy well and ends up making the film believable. Otherwise, it's a stereotyped affair with stock situations and characters that moves a little too quickly for its own good.

p, Betty E. Box; d, Ralph Thomas; w, Frank Harvey (based on the play "Handful of Tansy" by Harold Brooke, Kay Bannerman); ph, Enest Steward; m, Norrie Paramor; ed, Alfred Roome; art d, Maurice Carter; set d, Arthur Taksen; cos, Yvonne Caffin; m/l, "No, My Darling Daughter," Herbert Kretzmer, David Lee; makeup, William Partleton.

Comedy **(PR:A MPAA:NR)**

NO NAME ON THE BULLET*½** (1959) 77m UNIV c

Audie Murphy *(John Gant)*, Joan Evans *(Ann)*, Charles Drake *(Dr. Luke Canfield)*, R.G. Armstrong *(Asa Canfield)*, Virginia Grey *(Mrs. Fraden)*, Warren Stevens *(Lou Fraden)*, Whit Bissell *(Thad Pierce)*, Karl Swenson *(Earl Sticker)*, Willis Bouchey *(Sheriff)*, Edgar Stehli *(Judge Benson)*, Jerry Paris *(Miller)*, Charles Watts *(Sid)*, Simon Scott *(Henry Reeger)*, John Alderson *(Ben Chaffee)*, Russ Bender, Jim Hyland.

Murphy, who usually played a good guy, is effective here as a man come to seek revenge in the Western town of Lordsburg. Everyone in town believes Murphy is out to kill someone. The question is who? The film moves slowly, building with a nice feeling of eerieness and paranoia that was a minor staple of 1950s filmmaking. Stelhi, the town judge who is confined to a wheelchair, is Murphy's intended victim. The sneering, mustached villain faces off against his victim who slowly tries to get out of his chair. . .The direction effectively builds up to the moment, creating great suspense and tension. This is undoubtedly one of Arnold's best moments.

p, Jack Arnold, Howard Christie; d, Arnold; w, Gene L. Coon (based on a story by Howard Amacker); ph, Harold Lipstein (CinemaScope, Eastmancolor); m, Herman Stein; ed, Frank Gross; md, Joseph Gershenson; art d, Alexander Golitzen, Robert E. Smith; cos, Bill Thomas.

Western **(PR:A MPAA:NR)**

NO, NO NANETTE*** (1930) 98m FN bw/c

Bernice Claire *(Nanette)*, Alexander Gray *(Tom Trainor)*, Lucien Littlefield *(Jim Smith)*, Louise Fazenda *(Sue Smith)*, Lilyan Tashman *(Lucille)*, Bert Roach *(Bill Early)*, ZaSu Pitts *(Pauline, Servant)*, Mildred Harris *(Betty)*, Henry Stockbridge *(Brady)*, Jocelyn Lee *(Flora)*.

This charming musical develops on the simplest plot line. Littlefield is a Bible salesman who innocently helps three different women in trouble. But he finds himself in troubles of his own when the three simultaneously arrive at his Atlantic City cottage. The farce is humorous in a naive way. The cast certainly is not the greatest for the material: Littlefield takes time to warm up and Gray is too young to be believed as the love interest, but somehow they manage to pull it off. There are two color production numbers in this otherwise black-and-white film. The first sequence is 8 minutes long and the second, 33 minutes. The latter takes up the final third of the film, squeezing in production numbers and the plot. NO, NO NANETTE was based on a 1925 Broadway musical. This version accurately translates the musical to film. The movie contains some delightful songs: "Dance of the Wooden Shoes" (Ned Washington, Herb Magidson, Michael Cleary), "As Long as I'm With You" (Grant Clarke, Harry Akst), "King of the Air," "No, No Nanette," "Dancing to Heaven" (Al Bryan, Ed Ward), "Tea for Two," and "I Want to be Happy" (Vincent Youmans, Irving Caesar).

d, Clarence Badger; w, Howard Emmett Rogers, Beatrice Van (based on the Broadway musical by Otto Harbach, Emil Nyitray, Vincent Youmans, Frank Mandel); ph, Sol Polito (Technicolor); ed, Mandel; ch, Larry Ceballos.

Musical **(PR:A MPAA:NR)**

NO, NO NANETTE*½ (1940) 96m RKO bw

Anna Neagle *(Nanette)*, Richard Carlson *(Tom)*, Victor Mature *(William)*, Roland Young *(Mr. Smith)*, Helen Broderick *(Mrs. Smith)*, ZaSu Pitts *(Pauline)*, Eve Arden *(Winnie)*, Tamara *(Sonya)*, Billy Gilbert *(Styles)*, Stuart Robertson *(Stillwater Jr./Stillwater Sr.)*, Dorothea Kent *(Betty)*, Aubrey Mather *(Remington)*, Mary Gordon *(Gertrude)*, Russell Hicks *(Hutch)*, Benny Rubin *(Max)*, Margaret Armstrong *(Dowager)*, George Nelson *(Messenger Boy)*, Lester Dorr *(Travel Agent)*, John Dilson, Cyril Ring, Joey Ray *(Desk Clerks)*, Sally Payne *(Maid)*, Torben Meyer *(Furtlemertle)*, Victor Wong *(Houseboy)*, Bud Geary *(Taxi Driver)*, Chris Franke *(Hansom Driver)*, Keye Luke, Ronnie Rondell *(Men)*, Muriel Barr, Georgianna Young, Marion Graham *(Show Girls)*, Minerva Urecal *(Woman in Airport)*, Julius Tannen *(Ship Passenger)*, Rosella Towne *(Stewardess)*, Frank Puglia, Maurice Cass, Paul Irving *(Art Critics)*, Mary Currier, Jean Fenwick, Joan Blair, Dora Clement *(Women at Smith Home)*.

This is the second version of the 1925 Broadway musical and is clearly inferior to its predecessor. NO, NO NANETTE, like many musicals of the 1920s, was a simple show whose charms lay within its musical numbers. The songs were probably the best thing in the 1930 movie version. In this remake, the songs are cut back and the story re-written. Young plays a wealthy man who is Neagle's uncle. He is being put into a precarious financial position by some women. Neagle decides to help her uncle using the talents of an artist (Carlson) and a theatrical producer (Mature, who was loaned to RKO by 20th Century-Fox for this film). Neagle soon finds she has troubles of her own when her fellow conspirators fall in love with her. Somehow Neagle manages to solve both her uncle's problems and her own and she winds up with Carlson. The plot is fairly standard for the day but was done a dozen times better by any romantic B picture. Direction plods through the story with no sense of comic timing. The lightness of the story is abused by the screenplay as well, given the standard characters and situations. Neagle is tolerable but not much more as she goes through the motions. Released at Christmas 1940, NO, NO NANETTE was box-office poison. However, the original musical was re-staged on Broadway in the late 1960s and achieved moderate success.

p&d, Herbert Wilcox; w, Ken Englund (based on the musical by Frank Mandel, Otto Harbach, Emil Nyitray, Vincent Youmans); ph, Russell Metty; ed, Elmo Williams; md, Anthony Collins; cos, Edward Stevenson; m/l, "I Want to be Happy," "Tea for Two," Youmans, Irving Caesar, "No, No Nanette," Al Bryan, Ed Ward.

Musical **(PR:A MPAA:NR)**

NO ONE MAN* (1932) 73m PAR bw

Carole Lombard *(Penelope Newbold)*, Ricardo Cortez *(Bill Hanaway)*, Paul Lukas *(Dr. Karl Bemis)*, Juliette Compton *(Sue Folsom)*, George Barbier *(Alfred Newbold)*, Virginia Hammond *(Mrs. Newbold)*, Arthur Pierson *(Stanley McIlvaine)*, Francis Moffett *(Delia)*, Irving Bacon *(License Clerk)*, Jane Darwell *(Patient)*.

Not much of a movie and one wonders why it was made, other than to display the comeliness of Lombard and the handsomeness of Cortez. Lombard is a Palm Beach, Florida, divorcee with a lot of money and a huge problem: she can't decide who to marry between kindly Lukas, an Austrian psychiatrist, and Cortez, a dashing, but shallow young man. Lombard is a confused woman and Lukas wants to help her in her quest for self-realization. Despite her head telling her that Lukas would be right for her, she follows her heart and marries Cortez, who immediately takes up with Compton, who almost commits suicide due to her relationship with ne'er-do-well Cortez. Cortez conveniently drops dead of a heart attack and Lombard winds up with Lukas, whom she had jilted earlier. Irving Bacon is seen in a small role, as is Barbier, but no one can help the essential emptiness of the piece, which, at 73 minutes, still felt long. Lukas, born in Hungary as Pal Lukacs, had been a matinee idol in Europe before coming to the U.S. at the behest of Adolph Zukor in 1927. He won the Oscar when he repeated his Broadway triumph in Lillian Hellman's WATCH ON THE RHINE, one of the few roles in which he played a sympathetic character. His first film in the U.S. was 1928's TWO LOVERS and he continued working until 1968's SOL MADRID, then died of heart failure in Tangier. Bacon specialized in hayseed roles like the clerk he played in this. He was in more than 200 films and is one of those character actors whom everyone recognizes but no one can name.

d, Lloyd Corrigan; w, Sidney Buchman, Agnes Brand Leahy, Percy Heath (based on the novel *No One Man* by Rupert Hughes); ph, Charles Lang; cos, Travis Banton.

Drama **(PR:A MPAA:NR)**

NO ORCHIDS FOR MISS BLANDISH zero (1948, Brit.) 102m Alliance-Tudor/REN bw

Jack La Rue *(Slim Grisson)*, Hugh McDermott *(Fenner)*, Linden Travers *(Miss Blandish)*, Walter Crisham *(Eddie)*, Leslie Bradley *(Bailey)*, Zoe Gail *(Margo)*, Charles Goldner *(Louis)*, MacDonald Parke *(Doc)*, Percy Marmont *(Mr. Blandish)*, Lilly Molner *(Ma Grisson)*, Frances Marsden *(Anna Borg)*, Danny Green *(Flyn)*, Jack Lester *(Brennan)*, Bart Norman *(Flagerty)*, Bill O'Connor *(Johnny)*, Irene Prador *(Olga)*, John McLaren *(Foster Harvey)*, Jack Durant, Halma and Konarski, Toy and Wing *(Cabaret Artists)*, Michael Balfour *(Barney)*, Gibb McLaughlin *(Butler)*, Sidney James *(Ted/Barman)*, Richard Nelson *(Riley)*, Annette Simmonds *(Cutie)*.

La Rue plays a sadistic gangster. He kills Travers' playboy fiance, then kidnaps the millionairess for himself. After numerous gangland killings, the police kill La Rue. Travis, orchid in hand, plunges to her death from a window. This is supposed to be an insightful gangster thriller but ends up being a sick exercise in sadism. Senseless violence exists merely for its own sake. The script and dialog are completely inane. The comic-book characterizations are equally bad and the "New York" sets have to be seen to be disbelieved. This is about as wretched as they come.

p, A.R. Shipman, Oswald Mitchell; d&w, St. John Legh Clowes (based on the novel by James Hadley Chase); ph, Gerald Gibbs; m, George Melachrino; ed, Manuel del Campo; art d, Harry Moore; makeup, Lester Garde.

Crime **(PR:O MPAA:NR)**

NO OTHER WOMAN*½ (1933) 58m RKO bw

Irene Dunne *(Anna Stanley)*, Charles Bickford *(Big Jim Stanley)*, J. Carroll Naish *(Bonelli)*, Eric Linden *(Joe Zarcobia)*, Gwili Andre *(Margot Von Dearing)*, Buster Miles *(Bobbie Stanley)*, Lelia Bennett *(Susie)*, Christian Rub *(Eli)*, Hilda Vaughn *(Governess)*, Brooks Benedict *(Chauffeur)*, Joseph E. Bernard *(Frank, Butler)*, Frederick Burton *(Anderson)*, Theodore Von Eltz *(Sutherland)*, Edwin Stanley *(Judge)*.

After wife Dunne figures out how to make her carefree steelworker husband Bickford a millionaire, their course is a tragic one. Bickford is overcome by his newfound wealth and ends up consoling himself in the arms of Andre. This leads to a scandalous divorce trial and doomed Bickford ends up imprisoned. Based in part on the play and film JUST A WOMAN, this is turgid stuff with no real emotion or honesty.

p, David O. Selznick; d, J. Walter Ruben; w, Wanda Tuchock (based on the play "Just A Woman" by Owen Francis); ph, Edward Cronjager; m, Max Steiner; ed, William Hamilton.

Drama (PR:A MPAA:NR)

NO PARKING** (1938, Brit.) 72m Wilcox/BL bw

Gordon Harker (*Albert*), Leslie Perrins (*Capt. Sneyd*), Irene Ware (*Olga*), Cyril Smith (*Stanley*), Charles Carson (*Hardcastle*), George Hayes (*James Selby*), Fred Groves (*Walsh*), Frank Stanmore (*Gus*), Blake Dorn, Alfred Atkins, George Merritt, Geraldo and His Orchestra.

A routine caper comedy that holds some interest because the story that it is based on was written by young director Carol Reed, who would eventually go on to direct one of the greatest British films ever made, THE THIRD MAN (1949). Already demonstrating a penchant for complicated plots, Reed's story concerns a hapless parking lot attendant (Harker) who unwittingly becomes involved with a ring of jewel thieves who mistake him for an American triggerman they've been waiting for. Of course on the day of the big robbery the real American gangster turns up and the climax turns into a free-for-all, with the cops arriving and Harker revealing himself as an undercover agent for the CID. While the ending does tend to get a bit ludicrous, it's all in good fun and fairly enjoyable.

p, Herbert Wilcox; d, Jack Raymond; w, Gerald Elliott (based on a story by Carol Reed); ph, Francis Carver.

Crime/Comedy (PR:A MPAA:NR)

NO PLACE FOR A LADY** (1943) 66m COL bw

William Gargan (*Jess Arno*), Margaret Lindsay (*June Terry*), Phyllis Brooks (*Dolly Adair*), Dick Purcell (*Rand Brooke*), Jerome Cowan (*Eddie Moore*), Edward Norris (*Mario*), James Burke (*Moriarity*), Frank Thomas (*Webley*), Thomas Jackson (*Capt. Baker*), Tom Dugan (*Rawlins*), Doris Lloyd (*Mrs. Harris*), Ralph Sanford (*Hal*), William Hunter (*Thomas*), Chester Clute (*Yvonne*).

Gargan is a private eye. He uncovers the murder of a wealthy widow and returns some stolen car tires as well. There are chances for humor that are unfortunately wasted in this routine programmer. The direction and dialog are lifeless. Gargan and Lindsay (as his fiancee) give fairly good performances despite the constraints.

p, Ralph Cohn; d, James Hogan; w, Eric Taylor; ph, James S. Brown; m, Lee Zahler; ed, Dwight Caldwell; art d, Richard Irvine.

Mystery (PR:A MPAA:NR)

NO PLACE FOR JENNIFER** (1950, Brit.) 89m ABF-Pathe bw

Leo Genn (*William*), Rosamund John (*Rachel Kershaw*), Beatrice Campbell (*Paula*), Guy Middleton (*Brian Stewart*), Janette Scott (*Jennifer*), Anthony Nicholls (*Baxter*), Jean Cadell (*Aunt Jacqueline*), Megs Jenkins (*Mrs. Marshall*), Edith Sharpe (*Doctor*), Ann Codrington (*Miss Hancock*), Brian Smith (*Martin Marshall*), Andre Morell (*Counsel*), Macdonald Hobley (*Salesman*), Harold Scott (*Man*), Philip Ray (*Mr. Marshall*), Chris Castor (*Schoolmistress*), Viola Lyel, William Simon, William Fox, Ruth Lodge, Jean Shepherd, Arnold Bell, Shirley Lorimer, Lockwood West, Harold Scott, Billy Thatcher, Anthony Wager, Jack McNaughton.

Genn and Campbell are a couple in the middle of a messy divorce case. At the center of their struggle is their 12-year-old daughter, Scott. Genn marries John and Campbell marries Middleton. They argue back and forth over custody rights and child psychiatry. This all proves to be too much for the sensitive girl and she runs away. She finally finds happiness with another family and the sympathetic Jenkins. Rather than playing this as a psychological portrayal of an unhappy child, the sentimental and sugary aspects of the drama are emphasized. Motivations and resolutions are simplistic and predictable. The players are believable but really not much more. Scott manages to get past the cliches of her role but without much effectiveness. To no one's surprise this was a box office smash.

p, Hamilton G. Inglis; d, Henry Cass; w, J. Lee-Thompson (based on the novel *No Difference to Me* by Phyllis Hambledon); ph, William McLeod; m, Allan Gray; ed, Monica Kimick; md, Louis Levy; art d, Charles Gilbert; set d, Terrence Verity.

Drama (PR:A MPAA:NR)

NO PLACE LIKE HOMICIDE (SEE: WHAT A CARVE UP!, 1962, Brit.)

NO PLACE TO GO*** (1939) 57m FN/WB bw

Dennis Morgan (*Joe Plummer*), Gloria Dickson (*Gertrude Plummer*), Fred Stone (*Andrew Plummer*), Sonny Bupp (*Tommy*), Aldrich Bowker (*Heffernan*), Charles Halton (*Mr. Bradford*), Georgia Caine (*Mrs. Bradford*), Frank Faylen (*Pete Shafter*), Dennie Moore (*Harriet Shafter*), Alan Bridge (*Frank Crowley*), Joe Devlin (*Spud*), Bernice Pilot (*Birdie*), Greta Meyer (*Hulda*), Christian Rub (*Otto Schlemmer*), Wright Kramer (*Banning*), James Conlon (*Rivers*), Thomas Pogue (*Lockwood*).

When Morgan comes into a good deal of money he takes his pop, Stone, out of the veteran's home and into his own household. Naturally havoc ensues in this film adaptation of a minor play by the great writers Kaufman and Ferber. Stone is marvelously funny with good support from Morgan and from Dickson as Morgan's social climbing wife. Bupp is an absolute delight as the young bootblack befriended by the old soldier. The play had previously been filmed as THE EXPERT in 1932.

p, Bryan Foy; d, Terry Morse; w, Lee Katz, Lawrence Kimble, Fred Niblo Jr.

(based on the play "Old Man Minick" by George S. Kaufman, Edna Ferber); ph, Arthur Edeson; ed, Benjamin Liss; cos, Howard Shoup.

Comedy (PR:A MPAA:NR)

NO PLACE TO HIDE** (1956) 71m AA c

David Brian (*Dr. Dobson*), Marsha Hunt (*Anne Dobson*), Hugh Corcoran (*Greg Dobson*), Ike Jarlego Jr. (*Ramon*), Celia Flor (*Miss Diaz*), Eddie Infante (*Col. Moreno*), Manuel Silos (*Manuel*), Lou Salvador (*Priest*), Pianing Vidal (*Dr. Lorenzo*), Alfonso Carvajal (*Dr. Mateo*), Vicenta Advincula (*Consuel*), Pompom the Dog.

American doctor Brian goes to the Philippines to continue experimenting with a cure for a deadly disease. He isolates the germ in small round capsules which his son, Corcoran, mistakes for marbles. The lad takes the pellets and goes off to play. From there it's a mad chase to find the boy before the capsules melt and the disease is spread. This film has its moments but the production is marred by the obnoxious performance by Corcoran. He is an impossible little brat who can barely enunciate his dialog. The film's saving grace is the on-location photography in the Philippines. The climactic chase through the streets of Manila almost makes up for the picture's lesser qualities.

p&d, Joseph Shaftel; w, Norman Corwin (based on a story by Shaftel); ph, Gilbert Warrenton (DeLuxe Color); m, Herschel Burke Gilbert; ed, Arthur H. Nadel; md, Gilbert; art d, Teodi Carmona.

Drama (PR:A MPAA:NR)

NO PLACE TO HIDE* (1975) 84m Galaxy/American c

Antony Page (*Tommy*), Sylvester E. Stallone (*Jerry*), Vickey Lancaster (*Estelle*), Dennis Tate (*Ray*), Barbara Lee Govan (*Marlena*).

This is a minor entry in the "conspiracy cinema" trend that enjoyed a brief vogue in the Hollywood films of the mid-1970s after the Watergate crisis had jarred America's conscience. The short-lived subgenre paints a grim portrait of the American government and depicts bureaucratic institutions as fundamentally corrupt and dangerous. While many of the films that sprang from this artistic mood are solid, interesting thrillers (THREE DAYS OF THE CONDOR, ALL THE PRESIDENT'S MEN, TWILIGHT'S LAST GLEAMING), many seem to be nothing more than leftwing, knee-jerk reactions to Nixon and J. Edgar Hoover. Among these simpleminded films is NO PLACE TO HIDE (the title alone betrays the sense of paranoia extolled by the filmmakers), a thin drama about a group of antiwar hippies being destroyed by the evil FBI which has planted an undercover agent in their midst. The FBI man seduces the otherwise peaceful radicals into performing terrorist activities so that they all can be put away for life. In the cast is a young Stallone (billed here as Sylvester E. Stallone) just a few short years before his ego and biceps would inflate to monstrous proportions and bring to the American screen in the 1980s a trend of right-wing, xenophobic films (RAMBO, ROCKY IV).

p&d, Robert Allen Schnitzer; w, Schnitzer, Larry Beinhart; ph, Marty Knoph (Technicolor); m, Michael Smith Combination; ed, Schnitzer.

Crime (PR:C-O MPAA:R)

NO PLACE TO LAND* (1958) 78m REP bw (GB: MAN MAD)

John Ireland (*Jonas Bailey*), Mari Blanchard (*Iris Lee*), Gail Russell (*Lynn Dillon*), Jackie Coogan (*Swede*), Robert Middleton (*Buck Lavonne*), Douglas Henderson (*Roy Dillon*), Bill Ward (*Chick*), Robert E. Griffin (*Mr. Bart*), John Carpenter (*Lepley*), Bill Coontz (*Bill*), Whitey Hughes (*Franklin*), Bill Blatty (*Policeman*), James Macklin (*Dr. Carter*), Patric Dennis Leigh (*Drunk*), Burt Topper (*Miles*).

Tedious romantic melodrama starring Ireland as a noncommital crop-duster whose girl friend, having grown tired of his attitude, rejects him to marry another man. She does this on the chance that Ireland may finally get jealous and attempt to woo her away from her marriage of convenience, but he doesn't and simply zooms off in his crop-dusting plane.

p&d, Albert C. Gannaway; w, Vance Skarstedt; ph, John Nickolaus, Jr. (Naturama); ed, Asa Clark; md, Alec Compinsky; art d, Dan Haller.

Drama (PR:A-C MPAA:NR)

NO QUESTIONS ASKED½** (1951) 81m MGM bw

Barry Sullivan (*Steve Kelver*), Arlene Dahl (*Ellen Sayburn*), George Murphy (*Inspector Matt Duggan*), Jean Hagen (*Joan Brenson*), Richard Anderson (*Detective Walter O'Bannion*), Moroni Olsen (*Henry Manston*), Dan Dayton (*Harry Dycker*), Dick Simmons (*Gordon N. Jessman*), Howard Petrie (*Franko*), William Reynolds (*Floyd*), Mauritz Hugo (*Marty Calbert*), Mari Blanchard (*Natalie*), Robert Sheppard (*Detective Eddie*), Michael Dugan (*Detective Howard*), Howland Chamberlin (*Beebe*), Richard Bartlett (*Betz*), Robert Osterloh (*Owney*), William Phipps (*Roger*).

Sullivan is an insurance attorney who gets dumped by girl friend Dahl for Simmons. He is distraught but soon is lavishing his affections on Hagen. But Dahl re-enters his life - and the old passions heat up. Sullivan falls for her once more, only to discover he is being duped to take a fall by Dahl and Simmons. This is an effective thriller though the suspense is never drawn as tautly as it should be. The script is by Sheldon who went on to produce TV situation comedies including "GI Dream of Jeannie."

p, Nicholas Nayfack; d, Harold F. Kress; w, Sidney Sheldon (based on a story by Berne Giler); ph, Harold Lipstein; m, Leith Stevens; ed, Joseph Dervin; art d, Cedric Gibbons, Paul Groesse.

Crime (PR:A MPAA:NR)

NO RANSOM** (1935) 78m Liberty bw (GB: BONDS OF HONOUR)

Leila Hyams (*Barbara Winfield*), Phillips Holmes (*Tom Wilson*), Jack La Rue (*Larry Romero*), Robert McWade (*John Winfield*), Hedda Hopper (*Mrs. John*

Winfield), Vince Barnett *(Bullet)*, Eddie Nugent *(Eddie Winfield)*, Carl Miller *(Ashton Woolcott)*, Irving Bacon *(Heinie)*, Christian A. Rub, Gerry Owen, Fritz Ridgeway, Mary Foy, Arthur Hoyt.

McWade plays a wealthy steel company executive. He has family troubles with a wife who will not let him drink or smoke, a daughter gone wild, and a ne'er-do-well son. Desperate for some family attention McWade hires gangster La Rue to kill him. But La Rue cannot bring himself to murder McWade and stages a phony kidnaping. This way he hopes to scare the family and make them realize how much they love and need the old man. Of course he does not count on falling in love with Hyams, McWade's daughter. McWade is funny, carrying an otherwise simplistic programmer. It has its entertaining moments, but is ultimately standard stuff.

d, Fred Newmeyer; w, Albert DeMond (based on the story "The Big Mitten" by Damon Runyon); ph, Harry Neumann; ed, Mildred Johnston.

Comedy **(PR:A MPAA:NR)**

NO RESTING PLACE** (1952, Brit.) 80m ABF/Classic bw

Michael Gough *(Alec Kyle)*, Eithne Dunne *(Meg Kyle)*, Noel Purcell *(Guard Mannigan)*, Brian O'Higgins *(Tom Kyle)*, Jack McGowran *(Billy Kyle)*, Diana Campbell *(Bess Kyle)*, Maureen O'Sullivan *(Nan Kyle)*, Christy Lawrence *(Paddy)*, Esther O'Connor *(Tam's Daughter)*, Billy O'Gorman *(The Gamekeeper)*, Robert Hennessey *(Superintendent Davison)*, Austin Meldon *(Station Sergeant)*, Frederick Johnson *(Baliff)*.

Gough is a wandering Irish tinker, married to Dunne. He accidentally kills O'Gorman, a game-keeper, and runs from the Civil Guard. There is potential for some interesting drama here but it is defeated by the unsympathetic characters and somewhat sappy plot development. However, the location work is excellent, with a nice use of the Irish landscapes. Director Rotha was a former documentary filmmaker and this was his first feature effort. His use of natural settings and detailed development works to some advantage but unfortunately not enough to save the picture.

p, Colin Lesslie; d, Paul Rotha; w, Rotha, Lesslie, Michael Orrom, Gerard Healy (based on the novel by Ian Niall); ph, Wolfgang Suschitzky; m, William Alwyn; ed, Betty Orgar, Orrom.

Drama **(PR:A MPAA:NR)**

NO RETURN ADDRESS½** (1961) 76m Westwind/Century bw

Harry Lovejoy *(Raymond Carver)*, Alicia Hammond *(Selma Carver)*, Shauna Dietlien *(Mary Carver)*, Jo Armstrong *(Grandmother)*, Paul Spencer *(Moegle)*, Paul Timcho *(Ritter)*, Jack Hammond *(Lover)*, John Vitale *(Gomez)*, Cliff Medaugh *(Psychiatrist)*, Chuck Hasting *(Truck Driver)*.

Lovejoy plays a man telling his life story to a psychiatrist. In flashback we see him turn to theft, egged on by his neurotic wife, Hammond. But his boss, Spencer, catches him dipping into the till and he is promptly arrested. After coming home from prison Lovejoy is distraught when he discovers his wife has taken a lover. He tries to find work to support his 9-year-old daughter and senile mother. His daughter bruises her knee and that gives Lovejoy an idea. He has her pose as a cripple to cash in on an insurance policy. The scam works, but all too well, for his daughter believes she really is crippled. Lovejoy's life is destroyed.

p&d, Alexander Grattan; w, Grattan, Robert Springer, Clark Bell; ph, Andrew Janczak.

Drama **(PR:A MPAA:NR)**

NO ROAD BACK*½ (1957, Brit.) 83m Gibraltar/RKO bw

Skip Homeier *(John Railton)*, Paul Carpenter *(Clem Hayes)*, Patricia Dainton *(Beth)*, Norman Wooland *(Inspector Harris)*, Margaret Rawlings *(Mrs. Railton)*, Eleanor Summerfield *(Marguerite)*, Alfie Bass *(Rudge Haven)*, Sean Connery *(Spike)*, Robert Bruce *(Sgt. Brooks)*, Philip Ray *(Garage Man)*, Thomas Gallagher *(Night Watchman)*, Romulus of Welham *(Rummy the Dog)*.

Homeier plays a young medical student whose blind and deaf mother, Rawlings, put him through school. She owns a nightclub but cannot make enough money to support her boy. She turns to fencing jewels and finds that she is good at it despite her handicaps. When Homeier returns from school in America, he discovers how his mother supported him when he is nearly framed for a botched robbery and murder. This is a tedious suspense film hampered by its constant use of sign language to move the story forward. There really was no point to making Rawlings blind and deaf other than to evoke audience sympathy. The drama is unconvincing though Homeier manages to give a good performance in his British screen debut. Also making his film debut was Connery in a minor role.

p, Steven Pallos, Charles Leeds; d, Montgomery Tully; w, Leeds, Tully (based on the play "Madame Tictac" by Falkland D. Cary, Philip Weathers); ph, Lionel Banes; m, John Veale; ed, James Connock.

Crime **PR:A MPAA:NR)**

NO ROOM AT THE INN*** (1950, Brit.) 88m BN/Stratford bw

Freda Jackson *(Mrs. Voray)*, Joy Shelton *(Judith Drave)*, Hermione Baddeley *(Mrs. Waters)*, Joan Dowling *(Norma Bates)*, Ann Stephens *(Mary O'Rane)*, Harcourt Williams *(Reverend Allworth)*, Niall MacGinnis *(O'Rane)*, Sydney Tafler *(Spiv Stranger)*, Frank Pettingell *(Burrells)*, Betty Blackler *(Lily)*, Jill Gibbs *(Irene)*, Robin Netscher *(Ronnie)*, Wylie Watson *(Councilor Green)*, James Hayter *(Councilor Trouncer)*, Eliot Makeham *(News Editor)*, Billy Howard, Jack Melford, Bartlett Mullins, Frederick Morant, Dora Bryan, Harry Locke, Joyce Martyn, Pamela Deacon, Veronica Haley, Beatrice Varley, Bee Adams, Marie Ault, Vera Bogetti, Basil Cunard, O. B. Clarence, Eleanor Hallam, Jack May, Robert McLachlan, Cyril Smith, Ernie Priest, Vi Kaley, Stanley Escane.

Jackson is a drunken cockney landlady who takes in some evacuees and orphans. However, she denies them basic comforts, feeding them only scraps as if they were worse than dogs. She forces them to live in filth while she soaks up bottle after bottle of gin. At last her brutal reign ends when she dies in a drunken rage. This is definitely a strange comedy and certainly not for everyone. It is based on a stage play that was enormously popular in London's West End. Jackson re-creates her nasty stage triumph, giving a vile and utterly fascinating performance. Her supporting players are excellent with Baddeley giving an outstanding performance in this early bit part. The direction wisely lets the characters tell the story, retaining some of the theatrical setting as well. This film may be a problem for American audiences as the cockney accents are often difficult to understand. The screenplay was co-written by the great writer Dylan Thomas.

p, Ivan Foxwell; d, Dan Birt; w, Foxwell, Dylan Thomas (based on the play by Joan Temple); ph, James Wilson, Moray Grant; m, Hans May; ed, Charles Hasse; md, May.

Comedy **(PR:A MPAA:NR)**

NO ROOM FOR THE GROOM* (1952) 82m UNI bw

Tony Curtis *(Alvah Morrell)*, Piper Laurie *(Lee Kingshead)*, Don DeFore *(Herman Strouple)*, Spring Byington *(Mamma Kingshead)*, Jack Kelly *(Will Stubbins)*, Lillian Bronson *(Aunt Elsa)*, Paul McVey *(Dr. Trotter)*, Stephen Chase *(Mr. Taylor)*, Lee Aaker *(Donovan Murray)*, Frank Sully *(Cousin Luke)*, James Parnell *(Cousin Mike)*, Lee Turnbull *(Cousin Pete)*, Dolores Mann *(Cousin Susie)*, Fess Parker *(Cousin Ben)*, Helen Noyes *(Cousin Emmy)*, Janet Clark *(Cousin Dorothy)*, Fred J. Miller *(Cousin Henry)*, Lynne Hunter *(Cousin Betty)*, Harold Lockwood, Catherine Howard, Lucille LaMarr, William O'Driscoll *(Relatives)*, David Janssen *(Soldier)*, Richard Mayer *(Man on Street)*, Jack Daly *(Customer at Bar)*, Alice Rickey *(Cousin Kate)*, Elsie Baker.

Curtis plays a soldier bound for Korea in this lifeless comedy. Before leaving he and girl friend Laurie elope to Las Vegas. Upon returning from the war Curtis finds himself fighting a different kind of battle. It seems Laurie lives with her mother and father along with more relatives than the family in CHEAPER BY THE DOZEN. He's got one other problem as well. Laurie has neglected to tell her mother (Byington) about the marriage and now mama wants her daughter to marry a rich man. Her intended is a cement tycoon (DeFore) who wants to run a new railroad through the populated household. The humor is forced and gradually grows weary in the unimaginative screenplay. Sirk's direction merely records action with no sense of timing or feel for the material. "I think I had to do it as a tryout for Tony Curtis," Sirk said later. "I can remember nothing about this picture at all." In this early Curtis film, he does a little better than a "tryout" but like the rest of the cast, he is so hampered by the material that none of his talent comes through.

p, Ted Richmond; d, Douglas Sirk; w, Joseph Hoffman (based on the novel *My True Love* by Darwin L. Teilhet); ph, Clifford Stine; m, Frank Skinner; ed, Russell Schoengarth; art d, Bernard Herzbrun, Richard H. Riedel; set d, Russell A. Gausman, Ruby R. Levitt; cos, Bill Thomas.

Comedy **(PR:A MPAA:NR)**

NO ROOM TO DIE** (1969, Ital.) 93m Junior bw
(UNA LUNGA FILA DI CROCI)

Anthony Steffen [Antonio De Teffe], William Berger, Nicholetta Machiavelli, Mario Brega, Riccardo Garrone, Mariangella Giordano.

Berger is a Bible-thumping bounty hunter in this Italian spaghetti western. He joins Steffen to round up a gang led by Garrone. Seems the bad guys are smuggling illegal immigrants across the border and selling them for slave labor. Berger gives a good performance that helps the film. The direction is not as tight as it could be and some poorly concocted sequences distract from the overall effect. This is an extremely violent film as well with a good deal of the action shot in no-holds barred close-ups.

p, Gabriele Crisanti; d&w, Sergio Carrone; ph, Franco Villa.

Western **(PR:O MPAA:NR)**

NO ROSES FOR OSS 117** (1968, Fr.) 105m PAC-DA-MA/Valoria c
(PAS DE ROSES POUR OSS 117; AKA: O.S.S. 117—DOUBLE AGENT)

John Gavin *(OSS 117)*, Margaret Lee *(Aicha)*, Curt Jurgens *(Major)*, Luciana Paluzzi *(Doctor)*, Robert Hossein *(Saadi)*, Piero Lulli, Rosalba Neri, Guido Alberti, George Eastman.

Gavin plays an American secret agent sent to the Middle East to foil an assassination attempt. He breaks up the ring of killers, saves a U.N. mediator and somehow manages to fit some smooching with Lee into his schedule. Jurgens is an appropriately hammy head of the assassins' ring. Otherwise, this is a fairly dull spy film from a series that tried to make Gavin another James Bond. It lacked the dry wit and silly gadgets of the Bond films, instead going for the routine situations. The script is colorless and the fight scenes lack believability. Gavin later made a career for himself as the American ambassador to Mexico, being sent there by another former-actor-turned-politician, President Ronald Reagan.

d, Andre Hunebelle; w, Michel Levine, Jean-Pierre Desganat, Renzo Cerrato, Pierre Foucauld (based on the novel by Josette Bruce); ph, Tonino Delli Colli; m, Piero Piccioni.

Action/Spy Drama **(PR:C MPAA:NR)**

NO SAD SONGS FOR ME** (1950) 89m COL bw

Margaret Sullavan *(Mary Scott)*, Wendell Corey *(Brad Scott)*, Viveca Lindfors *(Chris Radna)*, Natalie Wood *(Polly Scott)*, John McIntire *(Dr. Ralph Frene)*, Ann Doran *(Louise Spears)*, Richard Quine *(Brownie)*, Jeanette Nolan *(Mona Frene)*, Dorothy Tree *(Frieda Miles)*, Raymond Greenleaf *(Mr. Caswell)*, Urylee Leonardos *(Flora)*, Harlan Warde *(Lee Corbett)*, Margo Woode *(Doris Weldon)*, Harry Cheshire *(Mel Fenelly)*, Douglas Evans *(Jack Miles)*, Sumner Getchell *(George Spears)*, Lucile Browne *(Mrs. Hendrickson)*.

This tragedy is saved from being just another piece of maudlin claptrap by Sullavan's superior acting, Mate's knowledgeable direction, and a fine score by Duning that nabbed an Oscar nomination. Corey and Sullavan are happily married with one daughter, Wood, when family doctor McIntire tells Sullavan that she only has six more months to live. She's pregnant with another child and consciously decides to keep this information from Corey and continues to live out the rest of her brief existence in as close to normal a fashion as she can. Meanwhile, Corey starts an affair with Lindfors, and Sullavan, upon learning this forgives him because she knows that he doesn't know her condition. Further, she actually encourages Lindfors to stick around after they bury her. Corey and Sullavan go off on a final holiday and she dies while Lindfors is baby-sitting Wood. Anyone who has ever been around a cancer victim can tell you that they don't look nearly as glamorous as Sullavan does when she dies. In other films that deal with a lingering disease, the actor or actress usually gets a few pats of white makeup and some rings under the eyes to demonstrate the illness. Not so here. Sullavan chose this picture as her comeback after a five-year exile from the movie business. It was a hit with all those viewers who like nothing better than a good cry. Director Richard Quine, who was still doing some acting at the time this was made, does a small role.

p, Buddy Adler; d, Rudolph Mate; w, Howard Koch (based on a story by Ruth Southard); ph, Joseph Walker; m, George Duning; ed, William Lyon; md, Morris Stoloff; art d, Cary O'Dell.

Drama   **(PR:A-C   MPAA:NR)**

NO SAFETY AHEAD*   (1959, Brit.) 68m Danzigers/PAR bw

James Kenney (Clem, Bank Clerk), Susan Beaumont (Jean), Denis Shaw (Inspector), Gordon Needham (Richardson), Tony Doonan (Don), John Charlesworth (Jeff), Brian Weske (Bill), Robert Raglan (Langton), Mark Singleton, William Hodge, Terence Cooper, Vanda Godsell, Robert Dorning, Ursula Camm, Walter Horsburgh, Hal Osmond, Neil Wilson, Garard Green, John Brooking, Frank Coda, Tom Naylor, Tony Harrison, Edward Judd, Walter Gotell.

Lethargic crime programmer starring Kenney as a poor bank clerk who turns to robbery to raise enough money so he can marry his fiancee, Beaumont. Conveniently for Kenney, his brother happens to be an established crook, so he simply joins his sibling's gang. The crooks decide to rob a bank, but the heist goes awry and Kenney suddenly finds himself involved in murder. A life on the run doesn't suit Kenney so he gives himself up to the police after the rest of the gang has been killed or captured. Well-worn material is given nothing more than rudimentary treatment.

p, Edward J. Danziger, Harry Lee Danziger; d, Max Varnel; w, Robert Hirst; ph, Jimmy Wilson.

Crime   **(PR:C   MPAA:NR)**

NO SEX PLEASE—WE'RE BRITISH½   (1979, Brit.) 90m COL c

Ronnie Corbett, Beryl Reid, Arthur Lowe, Ian Ogilvy, Susan Penhaligon, Michael Bates, Cheryl Hall, David Swift, Deryck Guyler, Valerie Leon, Margaret Nolan, Gerald Sim, Michael Robbins.

A pleasing performance from Corbett (seen in the U.S. on PBS-TV as one of "The Two Ronnies") saves this otherwise average British farce from the usual doldrums. When the postman accidentally delivers a parcel of pornographic postcards to a stuffy bank, the uptight, repressed employees undergo a drastic change of sexual outlook, which sends the bank up for grabs. An amusing, harmlessly ribald comedy.

p, John R. Sloan; d, Cliff Owen; w, Anthony Marriott, Johnnie Mortimer, Brian Cooke (based on the play by Marriott, Alistair Foot); ph, Ken Hodges (Technicolor); m, Eric Rogers; ed, Ralph Kemplen.

Comedy   **(PR:C   MPAA:NR)**

NO SLEEP TILL DAWN   (SEE: BOMBERS B-52, 1957)

NO SMOKING½   (1955, Brit.) 72m Tempean/Eros bw

Reg Dixon (Reg Bates), Belinda Lee (Miss Tonkins), Lionel Jeffries (George Pogson), Myrtle Rowe (Milly), Ruth Trouncer (Joyce), Peter Martyn (Hal).

Intrepid local chemist Dixon stumbles upon the formula for a pill that will cause smokers to lose their desire to light up. Seeing an obvious market for his discovery, Dixon announces his find but discovers that the worldwide tobacco industry has the power to squash distribution. After the prime minister himself pleads with Dixon to abandon his scheme, the chemist reluctantly agrees, but begins work on a new drug that will make people stop drinking. A potentially funny idea is driven into the ground by a poor script and indifferent direction.

p, Robert S. Baker, Monty Berman; d, Henry Case; w, Kenneth R. Hayles (based on a teleplay by Rex Rienits, George Moresby-White); ph, Berman.

Comedy   **(PR:A   MPAA:NR)**

NO SURVIVORS, PLEASE*   (1963, Ger.) 93m Shorcht bw
(DER CHEF WUENSCHT KEINE ZEUGEN; AKA:
                                    THE CHIEF WANTS NO SURVIVORS)

Maria Perschy, Uwe Friedrichsen, Robert Cunningham, Karen Blanguernon, Gustavo Rojo, Ted Turner, Stefan Schnabel, Burr Jerger, Wolfgang Zilzer, Dirk Hansen, Rolf von Naukhaff.

This oddball feature tries so hard to be serious you cannot help but smile. The simplistic plot, a direct rip-off of the classic INVASION OF THE BODY SNATCHERS, has alien beings from Orion taking over the bodies of politicians and generals they have murdered. This way they can take over the world in no time at all. Those little buggers work fast as the scenery keeps changing every few minutes. This film is often wretched but does have occasional glimmering moments.

p, Hans Albin; d, Albin, Peter Berneis; w, Berneis, Istvan [Steve] Szekely; ph, Heinz Schnackertz.

Science Fiction   **(PR:C   MPAA:NR)**

NO TIME FOR BREAKFAST**   (1978, Fr.) 100m Action Filmedis-
Societe-Francais de Production/Daniel Bourla c
                                    (DOCTEUR FRANCOISE GAILLAND)

Annie Girardot (Francoise Gailland), Jean-Pierre Cassel (Daniel Letessier), Francois Perier (Gerard Gailland), Isabelle Huppert (Elisabeth Gailland), William Coryn (Julien Gailland), Suzanne Flon (Genevieve Lienard), Anouk Ferjac (Fabienne Cristelle), Michel Subor (Regis Chabret), Josephine Chaplin (Helen Varese), Andre Falcon (Jean Rivemale), Jacqueline Doyen, Margolion, Jacques Richard.

Girardot plays a busy French doctor. She is admired by her co-workers and patients but has problems at home, a dull husband (Perier). Huppert plays her pregnant teen-age daughter and Coryn her neglected son. Somehow Girardot manages to fit in time for a lover, played by Cassel. Her world seemingly comes crashing down around her when she discovers she has cancer. But she remains brave and optimistic, facing her operation with uncanny pluck. This plotless film ambles nicely from situation to situation all spun around the marvelous performance of Girardot. For her role in NO TIME FOR BREAKFAST, she received the 1976 Cesar as "Best Actress," the French equivalent to an Oscar.

p, Yves Gasser; d, Jean-Louis Bertucelli; w, Andre G. Brunelin, Bertucelli (based on the novel Un Cri by Noelle Loriot); ph, Claude Renoir (Eastmancolor); m, Catherine Lara; ed, Francois Ceppi.

Drama   **(PR:O   MPAA:NR)**

NO TIME FOR COMEDY**½   (1940) 93m FN-WB bw (AKA:
                                    GUY WITH A GRIN)

James Stewart (Gaylord Esterbrook), Rosalind Russell (Linda Esterbrook), Charles Ruggles (Philo Swift), Genevieve Tobin (Amanda Swift), Louise Beavers (Clementine, Actress-Maid), Allyn Joslyn (Morgan Carrel, Theatrical Director), Clarence Kolb (Richard Benson), Robert Greig (Robert), J.M. Kerrigan (Jim), Lawrence Grossmith (Frank), Robert Emmett O'Connor (Desk Sergeant), Herbert Heywood (Doorman), Frank Faylen (Cab Driver), James Burke (Sergeant), Edgar Dearing (Sweeney), Herbert Anderson (Actor), Arthur Housman (Drunk Wanting Directions), Peter Watkin (Swift's Butler), Nella Walker (Theatergoers), Olaf Hytten (Swift's Butler), John Ridgely (Cashier), Selmer Jackson (First-Nighter).

An excellent adaptation by the Epstein brothers makes this Behrman Broadway play come to life on screen. It starred Katherine Cornell on New York stage, although Russell more than fills Kit's shoes. Stewart is a Minnesota journalist who writes a New York play despite the fact that he's never been near the city. The play is taken for production and will star Russell. They send for Stewart to come in and make revisions and he takes the long way around, via the Grand Canyon, just because he's never been there. He's a stammering, likable guy and a breath of fresh air for Russell, who has been accustomed to the smart-alec types, like her director, Joslyn. Stewart and Russell meet, fall in love, and he takes up residence in New York where he becomes the 1930s version of Neil Simon (or, actually, Moss Hart) and pens four smash comedies in as many years. Soon, the hayseed is fancying himself as a Manhattan sophisticate and much of his charm has been replaced by a snobbish kind of cynicism. Tobin enters the scene. She's a married matron (to Ruggles) who thinks that Stewart is wasting his talent and time on such folderol as comedy and that he should strive for something deeper, like the Great American Tragedy. Stewart doffs his fool's cap and dons his Chekhovian coat to write what the New York critics think may be the worst drama to ever play that city. Stewart, at the same time, thinks he may have fallen for Tobin, and Russell, desperate to hold their marriage together, fakes an affair with Ruggles. When Stewart realizes that the shoemaker should stay with his last, he dumps Tobin and any ideas of becoming Eugene O'Neill and decides that Russell and comedy are both what he needs. The same twist was used by Preston Sturges in SULLIVAN'S TRAVELS. In that film, a great comedy director wants to make a film tragedy and comes to the conclusion that what the world needs now is laughs. That was the truth then and remains the truth to this day.

p, Jack L. Warner, Hal B. Wallis; d, William Keighley; w, Julius J. and Phillip G. Epstein (based on the play by S.N. Behrman); ph, Ernest Haller; m, Leo F. Forbstein; ed, Owen Marks.

Comedy   **(PR:A   MPAA:NR)**

NO TIME FOR ECSTASY½   (1963, Fr.) 100m Les Films Universal/
                              European Producers International bw (LA FETE ESPAGNOLE)

Peter Van Eyck (Michel Georgenko), Daliah Lavi (Nathalie Conrad), Roland Lesaffre (Marcel Nancini), Helmo Kindermann (Walter), Anne-Marie Coffinet (Gina), Henri Le Monnier, Billy Kearns, Emilio Carrere.

Van Eyck portrays a Ukranian idealist who joins the International Brigade during the 1936 Spanish Civil War. Shortly after his enlistment, Van Eyck meets Lavi, a young American journalist, and it's love at first sight. After arriving at the front, Van Eyck deserts when his comrade Lesaffre is tortured and mutilated by his captors. He runs off with Lavi just before his unit is to execute a group of their own prisoners. The two try to escape but are caught at the French border by anarchists. Van Eyck is taken away and the film ends with Lavi screaming as she hears her lover being shot.

p, Jose Benazeraf; d, Jean-Jacques Vierne; w, Henri-Francois Rey, Vierne (based on the novel La Fete Espagnole by Rey); ph, Raymond Lemoigne; m, Ricardo Biasco; ed, Claudine Bouche, Eric Pluet; art d, Rene Moulaert.

Drama   **(PR:O   MPAA:NR)**

NO TIME FOR FLOWERS*½   (1952) 83m Morjay/RKO bw

Viveca Lindfors (*Anna Svoboda*), Paul Christian (*Karl Marek*), Ludwig Stossel (*Papa Svoboda*), Adrienne Gessner (*Mama Svoboda*), Peter Preses (*Emil Dadak*), Manfred Inger (*Kudelka*), Peter Czeyke (*Stefan Svoboda*), Frederick Berger (*Anton Novotny*), Oscar Wegrostek (*Johann Burian*), Helmut Janatsch (*Milo*), Karl Bachmann (*Lawyer*), Hilde Jaeger (*Mrs. Pilski*), Pepi Glockner-Kramer (*Flower Woman*), Reinhold Seigert (*Police Guard*), Willi Schumann (*Police Sergeant*), Ilka Windisch (*Woman Drunk*), Toni Mitterwurzer (*Sedlacek*), Theodore Prokof (*Czech Peasant*), Robert Eckertt (*Taxi Driver*), Peter Brand (*1st Soldier*), Karl Schwetter (*2nd Soldier*).

NINOTCHKA was a wonderful romantic comedy about a Soviet agent who discovers love doesn't quite click with Party standards. NO TIME FOR FLOWERS is essentially the same thing without any of the wit, style, or Garbo. This was made during a phase of the Cold War in an obvious appeal to show how "superior" the West's capitalistic ways were to those behind the Iron Curtain. Lindfors has the Garbo role, playing a Czechoslovakian party member who is secretary to government official Christian. He's just returned from the U.S. and is assigned to see if Lindfors can control herself among the temptations of the West. At first she is shocked by her employer's "traitorous" behavior when he offers her cosmetics and an evening gown. But gradually he wears her down (with the help of such torture devices as bubble bath, champagne, and *nylons!*) and she decides that the West is for her. The whole scheme has backfired for Christian has fallen in love with Lindfors and they decide to defect. They run off and safely embrace in front of Austria's U.S. Zone. The sudden switch from comedy to drama is unnatural and simply does not work. The view of life behind the Iron Curtain is heavily slanted which is no surprise considering the political climate of the day. The U.S. State Department and Armed Forces cooperated in making this film (shot in occupied Austria) which no doubt influenced the anti-Communist message. Situations are standard and the characters are the worst sort of stereotypes imaginable. A good number of German actors make up the supporting cast assumedly because of their heavy accents. The direction is plodding with no feel for the material at all. The acting itself is no help making the entire project laughable rather than a comedy to laugh with. Siegel was to do a much better film with 1950s political overtones in the classic INVASION OF THE BODY SNATCHERS.

p, Mort Briskin; d, Don Siegel; w, Laslo Vadnay, Hans Wilhelm; ph, Toni Braun; m, Herschel Burke Gilbert; ed, Henrietta Brunsch, Arthur H. Nadel; art d, Edward Stolba.

Comedy   **(PR:A   MPAA:NR)**

NO TIME FOR LOVE***   (1943) 83m PAR bw

Claudette Colbert (*Katherine Grant*), Fred MacMurray (*Jim Ryan*), Ilka Chase (*Hoppy Grant*), Richard Haydn (*Roger, Composer*), Paul McGrath (*Henry Fulton, Magazine Publisher*), June Havoc (*Darlene, Chorus Girl*), Marjorie Gateson (*Sophie*), Bill Goodwin (*Christley*), Robert Herrick (*Kent, Sandhog*), Morton Lowry (*Dunbar*), Rhys Williams (*Clancy, Sandhog*), Murray Alper (*Moran, Sandhog*), John Kelly (*Morrisey*), Jerome De Nuccio (*Leon Brice*), Grant Withers (*Pete Hanagan*), Rod Cameron (*Taylor*), Willard Robertson (*President of Construction Company*), Arthur Loft (*Vice President*), Fred Kohler, Jr., Tom Neal, Max Laur, Oscar G. Hendrian, Tex Harris, Ted Jacques, Art Potter, Sammy Stein, Jack Roper (*Sandhogs*), Alan Hale, Jr. (*Union Checker*), Woody Strode (*Black Sandhog*), Faith Brook (*Pert Brunette*), Mitchell Ingraham (*City Commissioner*), Ben Taggart (*City General Manager*), Pat West (*Waiter at Murphy's Place*), Frank Moran (*Erector Tender*), Mickey Simpson (*Doctor*), Lillian Randolph (*Hilda*), Keith Richards (*Reporter*), Walter Soderling (*Gate Man*), Lorin Raker (*Sweetzer the Stage Manager*), Frederic Henry (*Man at Party*), Paul Phillips (*Office Worker*), Pat McVey (*City Chief Engineer*), Jack Shay (*2nd Engineer*), Kenneth Christy, Jack Gardner (*Photographers*), Charles Irwin (*O'Conner*), Jack Roberts (*Captain of Waiters*), Dave Wengren (*Jack Tender*), Robert E. Homans (*Pop Murphy*), Ronnie Rondell, George Dolenz.

A sweet comedy-romance picture that sees usually fastidious Colbert get involved in some of the muckiest scenes ever shot. She's a top-notch fashion photographer who is well-known in New York and who haunts the swank parties with her acerbic sister, Chase, and a coterie of admirers which includes her fiance, McGrath, and Haydn. She battles with her editor on an assignment and gets the job of shooting photos down in the depths of the city where a host of tunnel diggers are hard at work. She meets MacMurray, a sandhog who would rather she would go topside, as women are regarded as albatrosses down there. MacMurray is about to be hit by a falling piece of steel when Colbert pushes him out of the way. Another of the workmen thinks he's arranged it that way and MacMurray responds by knocking the guy out as Colbert snaps the photograph of the one-punch bout. Colbert and MacMurray snipe at each other in the time-honored tradition of two people who will eventually get together and she exits, but forgets(?) to take her tripod with her. MacMurray picks up the camera equipment and uses the return of it as a ruse to get to know Colbert a bit more. Colbert is at her apartment and telling her pals about MacMurray and how strong he is and the fact that she has dubbed him "Superman." When he arrives, the guys poke fun at the "Superman" designation, so MacMurray promptly smashes their heads together to show that he won't take any ridicule. The photos of MacMurray's fight in the tunnel are published and he loses his job for a half-year. Colbert feels terrible about that turn of events, contacts MacMurray, and asks if he would like to be her assistant. With no employment in sight, he takes the job and, in that capacity, meets one of Colbert's models, dancer Havoc, and makes eyes at her. Colbert has come to like MacMurray and resents the way Havoc is making eyes at him. Their love grows, but MacMurray is angered when he learns that she had given the job to him as suffrage, and that she really thinks he is an ill-educated man, despite the fact that she has grown attracted to him. MacMurray finds out that work has been suspended on the tunnel where all his pals were toiling because mud has been seeping through. Now we, and Colbert, learn that MacMurray is not just another laborer. He is, in fact, an engineer and he

invents a special device that he thinks will put everything in order. Colbert goes below to photograph the attempt to save the site and the machine doesn't work, so she and he are covered with mud. But her photos show that the machine will work when it has been developed a bit more. MacMurray and Colbert get together at finale (did you think they wouldn't?) and it ends happily. Some funny scenes where Colbert lets her coiffed hair down, including a fight with Havoc and another battle in an Irish bar to which Colbert and her snooty pals come slumming and meet MacMurray and his tough buddies. A fun romp with good lines from the screenwriters and engaging secondary playing by Haydn, Gateson, and Withers. Rod Cameron does a small role and is barely noticed. Tom Neal is also briefly seen as one of the sandhogs.

p, Fred Kohlmar, Mitchell Leisen; d, Leisen; w, Claude Binyon, Warren Duff (based on a story by Robert Lees, Fred Rinaldo); ph, Charles Lang, Jr.; m, Victor Young; ed, Alma Macrorie; art d, Hans Dreier, Robert Usher; set d, Sam Comer; cos, Edith Head, Irene; spec eff, Gordon Jennings, Farciot Edouart.

Comedy/Romance   **(PR:A   MPAA:NR)**

NO TIME FOR SERGEANTS***½   (1958) 111m WB bw

Andy Griffith (*Will Stockdale*), Myron McCormick (*Sgt. King*), Nick Adams (*Ben Whitledge*), Murray Hamilton (*Irvin Blanchard*), Howard Smith (*Gen. Bush*), Will Hutchins (*Lt. Bridges*), Sydney Smith (*Gen. Pollard*), James Milhollan (*Psychiatrist*), Don Knotts (*Manual Dexterity Corporal*), Jean Willes (*W.A.F. Captain*), Bartlett Robinson (*Captain*), Henry McCann (*Lt. Cover*), Dub Taylor (*Draft Board Man*), William Fawcett (*Pa Stockdale*), Raymond Bailey (*Colonel*), Jameel Farah [Jamie Farr] (*Lt. Gardella*), Bob Stratton (*Lt. Kendall*), Jack Mower (*Sheriff*), Malcolm Atterbury (*Man with Applications*), Peggy Hallack (*Rosabelle*), Sammy Jackson, Rad Fulton (*Inductees*), Dan Barton (*Tiger*), Francis De Sales (*Supervising Sergeant*), Robert Sherman (*Oculist*), Dick Wessel (*Infantryman*), Tom Browne Henry (*Senator*), Tom McKee (*Charles the Aide*), George Neise (*Baker*), Benny Baker (*Abel*), Fred Coby (*Sentry*), John Close (*M.P.*), Verne Smith (*Announcer's Voice*), Mary Scott (*Cigarette Girl*).

Mac Hyman's hilarious novel, which then became a television special, which then became a Broadway smash (script by Ira Levin), now comes to the screen with all of the fun intact. Andy Griffith played the role on TV and the stage and gets his chance to show how humorous he is in this, his second film, after a sensational debut in A FACE IN THE CROWD. He's a Georgia backwoods boy who is inducted into the peacetime Air Force when his country sends him "Greetings." His sergeant is McCormick (also repeating his Broadway role), a man who thinks that being in the service is a fine way to spend one's life, as long as nobody creates a ruckus. But that's exactly what Griffith does, as his warm naivete and questioning ways throw a monkey wrench into the sedate peacetime service. It's an episodic farce with one bright scene after another and some terrific acting by everyone. Griffith is sent to psychiatrist Milhollan and totally confounds the doctor. After he and Adams fall out of a plane and are posted as "missing, presumed dead," they turn up at their own funeral in a scene reminiscent of Mark Twain's *Tom Sawyer*. Griffith's characterization as he faces the constantly fuming McCormick may well be the inspiration for TV's "Gomer Pyle" and the way Jim Nabors worked with his sergeant, Frank Sutton. The story works so well that we're surprised no one has done it yet as a musical. Roddy McDowall was also in the Broadway play, but he declined the chance to appear in the movie, and his role was taken by Adams, who had a meteoric career in TV as "The Rebel" and was nominated for a Best Supporting Actor in TWILIGHT OF HONOR before dying at 37 of an accidental overdose of the drugs he was taking to correct a medical problem. Service comedies have long been popular as the basis for movies and this one must rank up there with STALAG 17 and MR. ROBERTS as being one of the best. Note Don Knotts and veteran Benny Baker in small roles as well as a man who went on to star in TV's M*A*S*H after he changed his name from Jameel Farah to Jamie Farr.

p&d, Mervyn LeRoy; w, John Lee Mahin (based on the play by Ira Levin from the novel by Mac Hyman); ph, Harold Rosson; m, Ray Heindorf; ed, William Ziegler; md, Heindorf; art d, Malcolm Brown; set d, Robert R. Benton; spec eff, Louis Lichtenfield.

Comedy   **Cas.**   **(PR:A   MPAA:NR)**

NO TIME FOR TEARS, 1951   (SEE: PURPLE HEART DIARY, 1951)

NO TIME FOR TEARS***½   (1957, Brit.) 86m ABF/ABF-Pathe

Anna Neagle (*Eleanor Hammond, the Matron*), George Baker (*Nigel Barnes*), Sylvia Sims (*Margaret*), Anthony Quayle (*Dr. Seagrave*), Flora Robson (*Sister Birch*), Alan White (*Dr. Hugh Storey*), Daphne Anderson (*Marian*), Sophie Stewart (*Sister Willis*), Patricia Marmont (*Sister Davies*), Rosalie Crutchley (*Theater Sister*), Joan Sims (*Sister O'Malley*), Angela Baddeley (*Mrs. Harris*), Christopher Witty (*George*), Lucille Mapp (*Maya*), Marjorie Rhodes (*Cleaner*), Jonathan Ley (*Timmy*), Josephine Stuart (*Timmy's Mother*), The Boulting Twins (*The Twins*), Victor Brooks (*Mr. Harris*), Adrienne Poster (*Cathy*), Mary Steele (*The Twins' Mother*), Judith Scott (*Bridie*), Viola Keets (*Bridie's Mother*), Brian Smith (*Don*), Richard O'Sullivan (*William*), Jessie Evans (*William's Mother*), Cyril Chamberlain (*Hall Porter*), George Rose (*Theater Porter*), Jessica Cairns (*Lawrie*), Marjorie Rhodes (*Cleaner*), Gillian Owen (*Night Nurse*), Loretta Parry (*Jackie*), Christopher Frost (*Peter*), Carla Challoner (*Jenny*), Joan Hickson (*Sister Duckworth*).

Standard hospital soap opera intertwining the lives (and deaths) of various patients and staff members. Though the situations are clearly out of the movie medical bag, the ensemble manages to rise above cliches and stereotypes. Neagle carries the film as the head nurse with good support from Syms as the new nurse on her staff. Since this is a children's hospital the opportunity to cast precocious youngsters must have been tempting. However the kids in this film are natural, with only a hint of saccharine in a few of the performances. The Boulting twins are the identical sons of British film director Ray Boulting. The various story lines include Neagle's concern for some neglected children; the child who may die without an operation;

and, of course, a few intra-hospital romances. The final sequence, a Christmas show for the patients, features good pantomime by Syms.

p, W. A. Whittaker; d, Cyril Frankel; w, Anne Burnaby; ph, Gilbert Taylor (CinemaScope, Eastmancolor); m, Francis Chagrin; ed, Gordon Pilkington.

**Drama					(PR:A MPAA:NR)**

NO TIME TO BE YOUNG**					(1957) 82m COL bw (GB: TEENAGE DELINQUENTS)

Robert Vaughn (Buddy Root), Roger Smith (Bob Miller), Tom Pittman (Stuart Bradley), Dorothy Green (Mrs. Doris Dexter), Merry Anders (Gloria Stuben), Kathy Nolan (Tina Parner), Sarah Selby (Helen Root), Fred Sherman (Mr. Stuben), Ralph Clanton (Mr. Parner), Don C. Harvey (Drive-In Manager), Bonnie Bolding (Sandra).

Vaughn plays a college dropout avoiding the draft. He decides to hold up a supermarket so he can finance a boat and sail away from his troubles. Smith and Pittman are his cohorts who have got troubles of their own: Smith needs money to pay off the medical bills of cheap hustler Anders, injured while on a date with him. Pittman is a failed writer who's just lost his wife (Nolan) because of his constant lying. The three attempt the heist but Vaughn gets carried away and kills the store's manager. His pals are picked up by the cops, but Vaughn steals a truck and tries to flee to Mexico. There's a spectacular chase that ends in a fiery death for Vaughn when his truck's brakes give out. This "New Faces" presentation from Columbia is a fairly routine and turgid melodrama which uses the "young people in trouble" theme without much insight. It's all action and reaction without any feel for character motivation. Many of the principal actors became television stars in the 1960s: Vaughn in "The Man From U.N.C.L.E.," Smith in "77 Sunset Strip," and Nolan in "The Real McCoys."

p, Wallace MacDonald; d, David Lowell Rich; w, John McPartland, Raphael Hayes (based on a story by McPartland); ph, Henry Freulich; m, Mischa Bakaleinikoff; ed, Jerome Thoms; art d, Carl Anderson.

**Drama					(PR:O MPAA:NR)**

NO TIME TO DIE					(SEE: TANK FORCE, 1958, Brit.)

NO TIME TO KILL**½					(1963, Brit./Swed./Ger.) 70m Frejafilm AB/ A.D.P. bw (MED MORD I BAGAGET)

John Ireland (Johnny Greco), Ellen Schwiers (Nina Christians), Brigitta Andersson (Helle), Frank Sundstrom (Hopkins), Hans Straat (Inspector Bergman), Ralph Brown (Jens), Erik Strandmark (Concierge), Charles Fawcett (Marine), Marcia Ford (Receptionist), John Starck (Bartender).

After serving eight years on a false arson conviction, Ireland is freed from prison. He goes to Sweden in search of the businessman he believes framed him. There he confronts the man's wife (Schwiers) and has an affair with her. He continues the search for her husband but his trail ends at the cemetery where the man is buried. The evidence begins to point to Schwiers and she tries to kill Ireland. He kills her defending himself and realizes that she was the one who set him up on the arson charge. This minor drama was made in Sweden in 1958 and released in England in 1961. It finally opened in Stockholm five years after production, in 1963.

p, Tom Younger, Sven Nicou; d&w, Younger; ph, Bengt Lindstrom; m, Harry Arnold; ed, Lennart Wallen.

**Drama					(PR:C MPAA:NR)**

NO TIME TO MARRY**½					(1938) 63m COL bw

Richard Arlen (Perry Brown), Mary Astor (Kay McGowan), Lionel Stander (Al Vogel), Virginia Dale (Eleanor Winthrop), Marjorie Gateson (Mrs. Pettensall), Thurston Hall (Pettensall), Arthur Loft (Wyatt Blake), Jay Adler (Hess), Matt McHugh (Abernathy), Paul Hurst (Sergeant), George Humbert (Buenocasa).

Arlen and Astor are a pair of reporters who are trying to get married. Various assignments for both of them cause them to keep postponing the big day until they finally decide on a date. Astor, however, discovers a missing person her fiance has been looking for. She is faced with a dilemma: Should she let Arlen know or go with her reporter's instincts and hand in the scoop herself? There are some amusing moments in this routine programmer but the cast fails to pull off the comic possibilities. The quick pacing helps save some of the comedy, but unfortunately, it is not enough.

d, Harry Lachman; w, Paul Jarrico (based on a story by Paul Gallico); ph, Allen G. Siegler; ed, Otto Meyer; md, Morris Stoloff; cos, Robert Kalloch.

**Comedy					(PR:A MPAA:NR)**

NO TOYS FOR CHRISTMAS					(SEE: ONCE BEFORE I DIE, 1966)

NO TRACE***					(1950, Brit.) 76m Tempean/Eros bw

Hugh Sinclair (Robert Southley), Dinah Sheridan (Linda), John Laurie (Inspector MacDougall), Barry Morse (Harrison), Michael Brennan (Fenton), Dora Bryan (Maisie), Madeleine Thomas (Mrs. Green), Michael Ward (Salesman), Michael Evans.

Sinclair plays a crime novelist who gives a weekly radio broadcast. Most of his stories are based on his real-life experiences, though this is a secret kept from his admiring public. Brennan, an American gangster who was once a partner in crime with the novelist, comes to England and tries to blackmail Sinclair. Sinclair kills him and then joins his friend Laurie, a Scotland Yard detective, as they try to solve the murder. Sinclair is seemingly off scot-free, but is unwittingly exposed by his secretary Sheridan. Though a tightly controlled, well-paced thriller, there are few surprises. The characterizations are well played however, and the direction shows a good feel for excitement.

p, Robert Baker, Monty Berman; d, John Gilling; w, Baker; ph, Eric Befche; ed, Gerald Landeau.

**Crime					(PR:A MPAA:NR)**

NO TREE IN THE STREET**					(1964, Brit.) 96m Allegro/Seven Arts bw (GB: NO TREES IN THE STREET)

Sylvia Syms (Hetty), Herbert Lom (Wilkie), Ronald Howard (Frank), Stanley Holloway (Kipper), Joan Miller (Jess), Melvyn Hayes (Tommy), Liam Redmond (Bill), Carole Lesley (Lova), Lana Morris (Marje), Lilly Kann (Mrs. Jacobson), Marianne Stone (Mrs. Jokel), Edwin Richfield (Jackie), Lloyd Lamble (Superintendent), Campbell Singer (Inspector), David Hemmings (Kenny), Richard Shaw (Reg), Rita Webb (Mrs. Brown), Fred Griffiths (Street Orator), Victor Brooks (Bookie's Clerk).

Lom plays a petty thief who controls a London slum area in 1938. Miller is a mother who wants her children to do better than she and escape from the slums. She talks her son Hayes into working for Lom in the hope that the neighborhood hero will be their ticket out. Miller tries to get her daughter Syms romantically interested in Lom as well, but the girl will have nothing to do with him. When she tries to leave home on her own, Miller gets the girl drunk. She takes her inebriated daughter to Lom who seduces the luckless Syms. Afterward, he humiliates her in front of an old lover. Meanwhile Hayes has gotten himself into trouble by committing murder, and he returns home to his mother and sister. Syms kills her brother so that he won't be hanged, and then confronts the man who brought the family such horror. Left alone, Miller has little left to do but scream in the streets. NO TREE. . . suffers from an artificial feeling within the plot and dialog. Characterizations are reduced to mere stereotypes in standard situations. Occasionally the proceedings are so unbelievable, the tone shifts from drama to an unintended self-parody. However, there are some notable exceptions within the drama. Syms is surprisingly moving, giving a sensitive performance despite the film's constraints. Holloway's characterization of a bookie's tout is comical and charming, not unlike the character he created a few years later in the Broadway musical "My Fair Lady." The camera work attempts a realistic documentary look which manages to succeed in capturing the details of slum life, making the setting seem surprisingly naturalistic. The finer points of the film, however, are overshadowed by its faults.

p, Frank Godwin; d, J. Lee Thompson; w, Ted Willis (based on the play by Willis); ph, Gilbert Taylor; m, Laurie Johnson; ed, Richard Best; art d, Robert Jones.

**Drama					(PR:A MPAA:NR)**

NO WAY BACK**					(1949, Brit.) 72m Concanen/Eros bw

Terence de Marney (The Croucher, Boxer), Eleanor Summerfield (Beryl), Jack Raine (Joe Sleet), John Salew (Sammy Linkman), Shirley Quentin (Sally), Denys Val Norton (Harry), Gerald C. Lawson (Mike), Tommy McGovern (Himself).

Depressing crime melodrama starring de Marney as a dull-witted boxer who is forced to retire from the ring after receiving serious eye damage in a vicious bout. Things only get worse for the ex-pugilist when he loses his life savings and then his wife. Completely down-and-out, the demoralized de Marney is brought out of his depressive abyss by Summerfield, a girl he knew in his childhood. Unfortunately this friendship leads to tragedy when the pair get involved with a sleazy gangster, Raine, who causes all of them to be gunned down by the police. While the unrelenting despair of the film gets to be a bit much by the climax, the central performances are surprisingly good and lend some credibility to an otherwise unpleasant melodrama.

p, Derrick de Marney; d, Stefan Osiecki; w, Osiecki, de Marney (based on the story "Beryl and the Croucher" by Thomas Burke); ph, Robert Navarro.

**Crime					(PR:C MPAA:NR)**

NO WAY BACK zero					(1976) 91m Po' Boy/Atlas c

Fred Williamson (Jess Crowder), Charles Woolf (Pickens), Tracy Reed (Candy), Virginia Gregg (Mrs. Pickens), Stack Pierce (Bernie), Argy Allen (Pickens' Brother), Paula Sills (Crowder's Secretary), Don Cornelius.

Williamson stars as an unethical black detective. The minimal plot concerns his efforts to capture Pierce, a gangster who's after money embezzled by Woolf. Williamson, who also wrote, directed, and produced this film, has made a mean-spirited anti-woman, anti-white diatribe. He flexes his macho muscle as he gets his white adversaries, while engaging in brutal rapes that supposedly leave women begging for more. This was one of the many supermacho black exploitation films (known as "blaxploitation") made during the 1970s aimed at the angry black urban male.

p,d&w, Fred Williamson; ph, Robert Hopkins (CFI Color); ed, James E. Nownes.

**Action					Cas.					(PR:O MPAA:R)**

NO WAY OUT***					(1950) 106m FOX bw

Richard Widmark (Ray Biddle), Linda Darnell (Edie), Stephen McNally (Dr. Wharton), Sidney Poitier (Dr. Luther Brooks), Mildred Joanne Smith (Cora), Harry Bellaver (George Biddle), Stanley Ridges (Dr. Moreland), Dots Johnson (Lefty), Amanda Randolph (Gladys), Bill Walker (Mathew Tompkins), Ruby Dee (Connie), Ken Christy (Kowalski), Ossie Davis (John), Frank Richards (Mac), George Tyne (Whitey), Robert Adler (Assistant Deputy), Bert Freed (Rocky), Jim Toney (Deputy Sheriff), Maude Simmons (Luther's Mother), Ray Teal (Day Deputy), Will Wright (Dr. Cheney), Jack Kruschen (Man), Eileen Boyer, Johnnie Jallings, Marie Lampe, Gertrude Tighe (Telephone Operators), Frank Jaquet (Reilly), John Whitney (Assistant), Howard Mitchell (Bailiff), Charles J. Flynn (Deputy), Kitty O'Neil (Landlady), Emmett Smith (Joe), Ralph Hodges (Terry), Thomas Ingersoll (Priest), Wade Dumas (Jonah), Fred Graham (Ambulance Driver), William Pullen (Ambulance Doctor), Jasper Weldon (Henry), Ruben Wendorf (Polish Husband), Laiola Wendorf (Polish Wife), Dick Paxton (Johnny Biddle), Stan Johnson, Frank Overton (Interns), Ralph Hodges (Terry), Thomas Ingersoll (Priest), Harry Lauter, Harry Carter, Don Kohler, Ray Hyke (Orderlies), Ann Tyrrell, Ann Morrison, Eda

Reis Merin *(Nurses)*, Kathryn Sheldon *(Mother)*, Ralph Dunn, Ruth Warren, Robert Davis, Ernest Anderson, Victor Kilian, Sr., Mack Williams, Eleanor Audley, Doris Kemper, Phil Tully, J. Louis Johnson, Ian Wolfe.

A powerful social drama that sent Poitier's stock soaring. Prior to this film, he'd only made a documentary and NO WAY OUT proved to be the picture that made him an actor to be reckoned with. Poitier is a doctor in a county hospital that dominates a slum area. The place is run by McNally, who believes in giving young physicians a chance to show their mettle no matter what color they are. Widmark and Bellaver are brought in, the result of having been in a gun battle. They are in the prison ward of the hospital and Poitier attempts to save Bellaver's life, but the man dies, as the result of more than the gunshot wound. Widmark, in another of his "crazy" roles, hates blacks and wants to kill Poitier. He engineers a riot, after refusing to allow an autopsy on Bellaver that would prove Poitier correct. In response to the onslaught, a group of blacks rallies to help and there is a bloody confrontation that winds up with Widmark being badly injured. Poitier, true to his Hippocratic Oath, tends to Widmark until the cops get there, late as usual. Poitier, who'd been helped by Bellaver's widow, Darnell, walks out of the hospital when the mother of one of the hoodlums spits in his face. A heavy drama that points the finger at prejudice and asks no quarter, NO WAY OUT takes a while getting started, but once it does, hearts pound and we are tightly caught in the drama that follows. Zanuck was running the studio and took time off from the executive office to personally produce this picture. He believed in what it had to say and his mark of excellence is stamped on every frame. Mankiewicz had just won two Oscars for his work as director and screenwriter on A LETTER TO THREE WIVES the year before. He also took an Oscar for writing the screenplay for ALL ABOUT EVE the same year as this was released, as well as a nomination for having co-written NO WAY OUT. It was his year.

p, Darryl F. Zanuck; d, Joseph L. Mankiewicz; w, Mankiewicz, Lesser Samuels; ph, Milton Krasner; m, Alfred Newman; ed, Barbara McLean; md, Newman; art d, Lyle Wheeler, George W. Davis; cos, William Travilla.

Drama **(PR:A MPAA:NR)**

NO WAY OUT*½ (1975, Ital./Fr.) 100m Lira-Adel-Mondial-Tefi/ Cinema Shares International c (AKA: TONY ARZENTA; BIG GUNS)

Alain Delon *(Tony Arzenta)*, Richard Conte *(Nick Gusto)*, Carla Gravina *(Sandra)*, Marc Porel *(Dennino)*, Roger Hanin *(Frenchman)*, Anton Diffring *(Boss)*, Nicoletta Machiavelli *(Prostitute)*, Guido Alberti, Silvano Tranquilli, Lino Troisi, Corrado Gaipa, Giancarlo Sbragia, Umberto Orsini.

Tedious, violent, and ultimately pointless gangster drama from Italy redeemed somewhat by the performances of Delon and Conte (it was to be one of Conte's last). Delon plays a respected and loyal Mafia hit man who decides he's had enough of killing and announces his retirement. The news does not sit well with the bosses of the four top mob families because they feel that Delon knows too much about their operations to be trusted outside the fold. The mob chieftains agree to kill Delon to ensure his silence. When Delon's wife and child are blown up in the family car (a bomb that was meant for him), the former killer gets the message and vows vengeance. The rest of the film sees Delon trapping and killing off the mob leaders one by one, but not without some difficulty. Having been wounded during the second hit, Delon seeks shelter from fellow criminal Porel. Porel harbors Delon and nurses him back to health so that he can complete his vendetta. After the third murder, the remaining mafioso, Conte, asks for a truce and a tired and disgusted Delon agrees. To show solidarity, Conte invites Delon to the wedding of his daughter, and it is there that Delon is murdered by his friend Porel. Routine and unimaginative, it is a sad end for the career of Conte, who had played dozens of gangsters in the 1950s and had a brief revival after Francis Coppola cast him as the rival mob boss, Don Barzini, in THE GODFATHER. Visually, the film is adept; it resembles a TV commercial, filled with fine Italian furniture. The characters continually hold the brand names of products toward the camera, which may account for much of its financing.

p, Luciano Martino; d, Duccio Tessaro; w, Franco Verucci, Ugo Liberatore, Gandus; ph, Silvano Ippoliti (Techniscope, Eastmancolor); m, Gianni Ferrio; ed, M. Masso.

Crime **(PR:O MPAA:NR)**

NO WAY TO TREAT A LADY*½** (1968) 108m PAR c

Rod Steiger *(Christopher Gill)*, Lee Remick *(Kate Palmer)*, George Segal *(Morris Brummel)*, Eileen Heckart *(Mrs. Brummel)*, Murray Hamilton *(Inspector Haines)*, Michael Dunn *(Mr. Kupperman)*, Martine Bartlett *(Alma Mulloy)*, Barbara Baxley *(Belle Poppie)*, Irene Dailey *(Mrs. Fitts)*, Doris Roberts *(Sylvia Poppie)*, Ruth White *(Mrs. Himmel)*, Val Bisoglio *(Detective Monaghan)*, David Doyle *(Lt. Dawson)*, Kim August *(Sadie)*, Joey Faye *(Superintendent)*, Patricia Ripley *(Woman ¡1)*, Jay Sidney *(Medical Examiner)*, Don Blair *(Reporter)*, Tom Ahearne *(Father O'Brien)*, Richard Nicholls *(Man in Sardi's)*, R. Bernard *(Indignant Man)*, John Gerstad *(Dr. Shaffer)*, Bill Fort *(Staff Editor)*, Zvee Scooler *(Old Man)*, Eddie Philips *(News Vendor)*, John Dutra *(Man With Dog)*, Burr Smidt *(Detective Sergeant)*, Linda Canby *(Teenage Girl)*, Jim Dukas *(Police Artist)*, Don Koll *(Detective)*, Vincent Sardi, J. Molinski *(Themselves)*, Bob O'Connell, Tony Major, Glen Kezer *(Officers)*, Al Nesor, Sam Coppola, Louis Basile *(Customers)*.

A black comedy in every sense of the word, this picture is quick, witty, and grisly. Steiger top-lines as a mother-obsessed theater owner in New York City who hates his dead parent (an actress) so much that he is exacting vengeance on every other woman. Based on the novel by William Goldman (BUTCH CASSIDY AND THE SUNDANCE KID numbers among his screenplay credits), it tells the story of wealthy Steiger, a man who grew up in and around the Broadway stage, who uses his masterful knowledge of disguise and his ability to secure costumes to essay seven roles. He plays a hairdresser, a woman, a waiter, and a plumber among others, as he murders several innocent victims by strangulation, thus becoming what has since been deemed a "serial killer" because his modus operandi includes leaving a lipstick kiss on the forehead of each dead woman. Segal is a Jewish detective with a cliche Jewish mother, Heckart, and he is assigned to the case. His comments to the media include one to the effect that this killer is most intelligent, which delights Steiger enough to prompt him to call Segal at headquarters. This is the first of a number of calls Steiger makes, each in a different voice and accent, as the battle of wits commences. Segal encounters witness Remick, who met the killer briefly when he was disguised as a man of the cloth, and the two fall quickly in love. Steiger begins to tail Segal and sees his relationship deepening with the woman. In one of his phone calls, Steiger subtly drops a clue that Segal pounces on; then Segal, in an attempt to flush out the madman, plants the story of another murder with the same modus operandi, which goads Steiger into calling Segal and denying the new crime. Segal keeps him on the line long enough for the phone company to get a trace on the call. Steiger decides to punish Segal by murdering Remick, so he shows up as a waiter who is carrying a gala dinner as a gift from Segal. Segal realizes the inner workings of the killer's mind and races to Remick's apartment before Steiger can do the deed. Steiger runs to his theater and is chased by Segal, who guns him down there. Once again, Segal does the same sort of role he did in BYE, BYE BRAVERMAN before and THE BLACK BIRD, BLUME IN LOVE, and WHERE'S POPPA? afterwards: the quintessential Jewish schlepp. This is a well-crafted film shot in New York City and it doesn't slow down at all, even in some of the lovey scenes between Remick and Segal, which are a bit too quick and glib. Remick looks marvelous and does what she can in a subordinate role, even though she's billed above Segal. A combination of Freud, fraud, and frou-frou, NO WAY TO TREAT A LADY got good notices and did a fair turn at the wickets.

p, Sol C. Siegel; d, Jack Smight; w, John Gay (based on a novel by William Goldman); ph, Jack Priestley (Technicolor); m, Stanley Myers; ed, Archie Marshek; art d, Hal Pereira, George Jenkins; set d, Jenkins; cos, Theoni V. Aldredge; m/l, "A Quiet Place," Myers, Andrew Belling (sung by the American Breed); "The Miller of Dee"; makeup, Robert O'Bradovich; hairstyles, Ernest Adler.

Comedy/Mystery **Cas.** **(PR:C-O MPAA:NR)**

NOAH'S ARK*** (1928) 135m WB bw

Dolores Costello *(Mary/Miriam)*, George O'Brien *(Travis/Japheth)*, Noah Beery, Sr. *(Nickoloff/King Nephilim)*, Louise Fazenda *(Hilda/Tavern Maid)*, Guinn "Big Boy" Williams *(Al/Ham)*, Paul McAllister *(Minister/Noah)*, Nigel De Brulier *(Soldier/High Priest)*, Anders Randolf *(German/Leader of Soldiers)*, Armand Kaliz *(Frenchman/King's Guard)*, Myrna Loy *(Dancer/Slave Girl)*, William V. Mong *(Innkeeper/Guard)*, Malcolm Waite *(Balkan/Shem)*, Noble Johnson, Otto Hoffman, Joe Bonomo.

A true "spectacular" in every sense of the word, NOAH'S ARK cost more than $1.5 million to produce and had several interesting sidelights about it. Based on a story by Darryl F. Zanuck, it's two films in one, as we see the story of the Hebrew Patriarch told side by side with modern times and all the parallels implicit. Note the credits list and you'll see that two cameramen were used. The reason for this is that Mohr knew that Grot's sets, when destroyed in the huge water sequence, would be dangerous to the extras. Grot refused to change his designs and Mohr quit. The result was that scenes were not faked and several of the extras drowned! Costello developed pneumonia from having been in the water too long, O'Brien lost a couple of toenails, and Williams lost two ribs. There was no such person as a "stunt man" in those days and actors were expected to perform their own derring-do, no matter how dangerous. The first 35 minutes of the film are totally silent (this was just shortly after Warner Brothers issued THE JAZZ SINGER) and the first voices we hear are those of Costello and O'Brien in a love scene. The story cuts back and forth from the familiar Biblical tale of Noah to shots of WW I and a wreck of the Orient Express as it goes from Paris to Constantinople. All of the actors do double roles, as the picture intercuts modern and Biblical sequences and it's sometimes confusing to watch both stories at the same time. But there is no question that director Curtiz has crafted a movie one won't soon forget—especially when we know that many lives were lost making it. It's very violent with murders, floods, and war. Not for the squeamish and surely not for the light of heart.

d, Michael Curtiz; w, Anthony Coldeway, B. Leon Anthony, Harold McCord (based on a story by Darryl F. Zanuck); ph, Hal Mohr, Barney McGill; m, Louis Silvers; ed, McCord; art d, Anton Grot; spec eff, Fred Jackman; m/l, "Heart O' Mine," Silvers, Billy Rose.

Biblical/Epic **(PR:A-C MPAA:NR)**

NOB HILL½** (1945) 95m FOX c

George Raft *(Johnny Angelo)*, Joan Bennett *(Harriet Carruthers)*, Vivian Blaine *(Sally Templeton)*, Peggy Ann Garner *(Katie Flanagan)*, Alan "Falstaff Openshaw" Reed *(Dapper Jack Harrigan)*, B.S. Pully *(Joe the Bartender)*, Emil Coleman *(Pianist)*, Edgar Barrier *(Lash Carruthers)*, George Anderson *(Rafferty)*, Don Costello *(Fighting Bartender)*, Joseph J. Greene *(Headwaiter)*, J. Farrell MacDonald *(Cabby)*, The Three Swifts *(Specialty)*, William Haade *(Big Time)*, Mike Mazurki *(Rafferty's Fighter)*, *Beal Wong, George T. Lee (Chinese Servants)*, Rory Calhoun *(Jose)*, Robert Greig *(Butler)*, Charles Cane *(Chips Conlon)*, Arthur Loft *(Turner)*, Nestor Paiva *(Luigi)*, Jane Jones *(Ruby)*, Otto Reichow *(Swedish Sailor), Chick Chandler (Guide)*, Harry Shannon, Tom Dillon, Ralph Peters, Brooks Hunt, Harry Strang *(Policemen)*, Frank Orth, Lester Dorr, Harry Harvey, Sr., Julius Tannen, Will Stanton, Syd Saylor, Marshall Ruth, Alphonse Martell, Peter Michael, Antonio Filauri, Jean De Briac *(Men)*, Almira Sessions, Polly Bailey, Leila McIntyre, Gwen Donovan *(Women)*, Edna Mae Jones *(Dance Hall Girl)*, Chief Thundercloud *(Indian Chief)*, Virginia Walker, Carol Andrews, Susan Scott, Harrison Greene *(Slummers)*, Ralph Sanford, Arthur Thalasso, Edward Keane, Eddie Hart, George Lloyd, Sam Flint *(Politicians)*, Byron Foulger *(Usher)*, Benson Fong *(Chinese Boy)*, Olive Blakeney *(Housekeeper)*, Joe Bernard *(Printer)*, Lillian Salvaneschi, Mario Salvaneschi *(Specialty Dance Team)*, George Reed *(Black Man)*, Bill "Red" Murphy *(Sailor)*, Sven-Hugo Borg, George Blagoi *(Swedish Sailors)*, Joe Smith,

Charles Dale, George E. Stone, Veda Ann Borg, George McKay, Helen O'Hara, Dorothy Ford, Paul Everton, Anita Bolster, Russell Hicks.

This film is a familiar period musical. Set in turn-of-the-century San Francisco during the heyday of the Barbary Coast, Raft is the well-respected proprietor of the Gold Coast Saloon who enjoys a hearty business, a steady stream of likable clients, and a promising relationship with the club's star singer, Blaine. His life takes a turn when he meets a teenaged girl, Garner, who's come to San Francisco from Ireland in search of her uncle. The helpless lass' innocent face fills with tears when Raft informs her that her uncle has died. Not knowing what else to do, Raft extends his generosity to Garner and invites her to stay with him. It is through Garner that Raft meets Bennett, an aggressive and flashy lady from snobbish, upper-class Nob Hill. Raft represses the attraction he feels for Bennett by trying to convince himself of the differences between them. "The Hill and the Coast are like champagne and beer," he states, "They don't mix." Bennett eventually invites Raft to dinner and daringly plants a kiss on the surprised saloonkeeper. A marriage proposal follows, as does the severing of the relationship between Raft and Blaine. As expected, Raft grows disillusioned with the insincere ways of Bennett, and the dishonest political scheming of her brother, who is making an election bid to be the city's district attorney. Bennett dumps Raft and Raft hits the bottle when he discovers that Blaine wants nothing to do with him. It takes Garner and her matchmaking ways to reunite the two. Assuming that three is a crowd, Garner plans to leave the lovers, but the finale has Raft and Blaine taking the young lass with them. A reworking of two Alice Faye vehicles, HELLO, FRISCO, HELLO (l943) and KING OF BURLESQUE (1935), NOB HILL offers a standard serving of entertaining, though cliched, scenes which are thankfully injected with a lively dose of music. Originally intended as a vehicle for Fred MacMurray and Lynn Bari, NOB HILL went over just as well with Raft and Bennett, especially with the addition of Garner to the cast list. Given a special Academy Award in 1945 as the "outstanding child performer of the year" (not for this film, but for her stunning performance in A TREE GROWS IN BROOKLYN), Garner is a fresh shot in the arm for the somewhat stale script. The film includes a number of tunes penned by Jimmy McHugh and Harold Adamson, including three highlights delivered by Blaine- "I Walked In," "I Don't Care Who Knows It" and "Touring San Francisco." Other songs include "Paris of the U.S.A." (McHugh, Adamson), "What Do You Want to Make Those Eyes at Me For?" (Howard Johnson, Joseph McCarthy, James V. Monaco), "San Francisco" (Gus Kahn, Bronislau Kaper, Walter Jurmann), "On San Francisco Bay" (Vincent Bryan, Gertrude Hoffman), "King Chanticleer (Texas Tommy)" (Nat D. Ayer), "Chinatown, My Chinatown" (William Jerome, Jean Schwartz), "Too-ra-loo-ra-loo-ra" (James Royce Shannon).

p, Andre Daven; d, Henry Hathaway; w, Wanda Tuchock, Norman Reilly Raine (based on a story by Eleanore Griffin); ph, Edward Cronjager (Technicolor); m, David Buttolph; ed, Harmon Jones; md, Emil Newman, Charles Henderson; art d, Lyle Wheeler, Russell Spencer; set d, Thomas Little, Walter M. Scott, Joseph C. Wright; spec eff, Fred Sersen; ch, Nick Castle.

Musical **(PR:A MPAA:NR)**

NOBI (SEE: FIRES ON THE PLAIN, 1959, Jap.)

NOBODY LIVES FOREVER*** (1946) 100m WB bw

John Garfield *(Nick Blake)*, Geraldine Fitzgerald *(Gladys Halvorsen)*, Walter Brennan *(Pop Gruber)*, Faye Emerson *(Toni)*, George Coulouris *(Doc Ganson)*, George Tobias *(Al Doyle)*, Robert Shayne *(Chet King)*, Richard Gaines *(Charles Manning)*, Dick Erdman *(Bellboy)*, James Flavin *(Shake Thomas)*, Ralph Peters *(Windy Mather)*, Allen Ray *(Art)*, Roger Neury *(Headwaiter)*, Jack Chefe *(Waiter)*, Harry Seymour *(Master of Ceremonies)*, Rudy Friml, Jr. *(Orchestra Leader)*, Fred Kelsey *(Railroad Conductor)*, Wallace Scott *(Drunk)*, Albert Von Antwerp *(Tough Waiter)*, Charles Sullivan *(Bartender-Waiter)*, Alex Havier *(Telesfero)*, Paul Power *(Hotel Clerk)*, George Meader *(Evans)*, Virgina Patton *(Switchboard Operator)*, Robert Arthur *(Bellhop)*, Marion Martin *(Blonde)*, Cyril Ring *(Blonde's Escort)*, William Edmunds *(Priest)*, William Forrest *(Mr. Johnson)*, Grady Sutton *(Counterman)*, Adrian Droeshout *(Man at Slot Machine)*, Joel Friedkin *(Storekeeper)*, Ralph Dunn *(Ben)*, Lee Phelps *(Police Officer)*.

Returning to New York after having served some harrowing duty in WW II, Garfield, an ex-gambler and confidence man, discovers that his girl friend, Emerson, has taken his money and run off with another man. In addition, Garfield's gambling interests have been taken over by a rival faction. Left without income or love, Garfield decides to force his rivals to pay him for his interest in the gambling operation and then cut all his ties with New York. Accompanied by one of his cronies, Tobias, Garfield heads for the space and light of California. There he runs into Brennan, an old man who served as Garfield's crime mentor. Brennan has been hired by a group led by Coulouris to persuade Garfield to finance the fleecing of a young widow who has inherited a fortune. Garfield is interested, but when he sees the beautiful young widow, Fitzgerald, he decides to pull the job personally and divide the cash with Coulouris. As he romances Fitzgerald, Garfield actually begins to fall in love with her and decides to end the game by offering to pay Coulouris out of his own pocket. Meanwhile, Garfield's former flame Emerson has arrived. Upon hearing of Garfield's offer, she convinces Coulouris that Garfield is trying to cheat him. Seeking revenge, Coulouris kidnaps Fitzgerald and holds her for ransom. Brennan learns that Fitzgerald is being held captive at a deserted pier and Garfield shows up to rescue her. In the ensuing gun battle, Brennan and Coulouris shoot each other dead, leaving Garfield to begin a new life with Fitzgerald. Scripted by W.R. Burnett from his own short story, "I Wasn't Born Yesterday," NOBODY LIVES FOREVER is an interesting, if minor, early *film noir*. Garfield is strong in a role that Warner Brothers had originally announced for Humphrey Bogart. Although Garfield was itching to get out of his Warner Bros. contract and entered into the project with little enthusiasm, he did look forward to working with Fitzgerald, an actress whose work he admired. Director Negulesco made the most of the contrast between New York City and the Pacific coast of California where Garfield finally makes his bid for a new life. Since the plot elements of the story were hackneyed, Negulesco and Garfield went for subtlety and mood to create an effective character study of a man who feels he no longer belongs to the society he left behind when he went to war.

p, Robert Buckner; d, Jean Negulesco; w, W.R. Burnett (based on his story "I Wasn't Born Yesterday"); ph, Arthur Edeson; m, Adolph Deutsch, Jerome Moross; ed, Rudi Fehr; md, Leo F. Forbstein; art d, Hugh Reticker; set d, Casey Roberts; cos, Milo Anderson; spec eff, William McGann, William Van Enger.

Drama **(PR:A MPAA:NR)**

NOBODY LOVES A DRUNKEN INDIAN (SEE: FLAP, 1970)

NOBODY LOVES A FLAPPING EAGLE (SEE: FLAP, 1970)

NOBODY RUNS FOREVER (SEE: HIGH COMMISSIONER, THE, 1968, Brit.)

NOBODY WAVED GOODBYE** (1965, Can.) 80m National Film Board of Canada/Cinema V bw

Peter Kastner *(Peter)*, Julie Biggs *(Julie)*, Claude Rae *(Father)*, Toby Tarnow *(Sister)*, Charmion King *(Mother)*, Ron Taylor *(Boy Friend)*, Robert Hill *(Patrolman)*, Jack Beer *(Sergeant)*, John Sullivan *(Probation Officer)*, Lynne Gorman *(Julie's Mother)*, Ivor Barry *(Interviewer)*, Sharon Bonin *(Waitress)*, Norman Ettlinger *(Landlord)*, John Vernon *(Lot Supervisor)*.

Kastner plays a rebellious high schooler. He refuses to listen to his mother and gets in trouble with the law after he drives away in a demonstrator model from his father's car dealership. The only person he can talk to is his girl friend, Biggs. Though more mature, she admires his reckless ways and tries to emulate him. Kastner finally leaves his parents and moves into a rooming house. They insist he return home and go to college. Their provisions also forbid him to ever see Biggs again. After she runs away as well, the two of them steal a car. When she realizes that nothing good will ever come of this, she asks to go back. She reveals that she is pregnant, gets out of the car, and Kastner rides off alone. NOBODY WAVED GOODBYE is a mixed bag. The story and script are routine, often dipping to a soap-opera level. The direction is simplistic and predictable, with pretentious camera work. The acting, however, is competent. The two leads are good despite their inexperience, and Rae and King as Kastner's parents are excellent counterpoints to the teenagers, giving the film some intelligence.

p, Roman Kroiter, Don Owen; d&w, Owen; ph, John Spotton; m, Eldon Rathburn; ed, Spotton, Donald Ginsberg.

Drama **(PR:C MPAA:NR)**

NOBODY'S BABY½** (1937) 67m MGM bw

Patsy Kelly *(Kitty)*, Lyda Roberti *(Lena)*, Lynne Overman *(Detective Littleworth)*, Robert Armstrong *(Scoops Hanford)*, Don Alvarado *(Cortez)*, Tom Dugan *(Bus Conductor)*, Orrin Burke *(Maurice)*, Dora Clement *(Miss McKenzie)*, Rosina Lawrence *(Yvonne)*, Laura Treadwell *(Mrs. Hamilton)*, Ottola Nesmith *(Head Nurse)*, Florence Roberts *(Mrs. Mason)*, Si Wills *(Master of Ceremonies)*, Herbert Rawlinson *(Radio Executive)*, Jimmie Grier's Orchestra, The Rhythm Rascals, The Avalon Boys.

Kelly and Roberti are a pair of nursing students. When ballroom dancer Lawrence is about to have a baby, she abandons her husband (Alvarado) so that no one will know she is really married to her dance partner. Of course all turns out happily in the end, but not before there's plenty of music, slapsticky laughs, and some fine dance numbers. NOBODY'S BABY was produced by Hal Roach, who was known for his comedy two-reelers. At different points in Kelly's career, Roach tried to make her into one-half of a female Laurel and Hardy comedy team by pairing her with ZaSu Pitts or Thelma Todd in a number of two-reelers. Here she is paired with Roberti. Songs include: "Quien Sabe," "I Dreamed About This," "All Dressed Up in Rhythm," "Nobody's Baby" (Marvin Hatley, Walter Bullock).

p, Hal Roach; d, Gus Meins; w, Harold Law, Hal Yates, Pat C. Flick; ph, Norbert Brodine; ed, Ray Snyder; spec eff, Roy Seawright; ch, Roy Randolph.

Comedy **(PR:A MPAA:NR)**

NOBODY'S CHILDREN** (1940) 65m COL bw

Edith Fellows *(Pat)*, Billy Lee *(Tommy)*, Georgia Caine *(Mrs. Marshall)*, Lois Wilson *(Miss Jamieson)*, Walter White, Jr. *(Himself)*, Ben Taggart *(Mr. Miller)*, Mary Currier *(Mrs. Miller)*, Mary Gordon *(Mary)*, Lillian West *(Miss Spellman)*, William Gould *(Dr. Tovar)*, Russell Hicks *(Sen. Hargreave)*, Janet Chapman *(Peggy)*, Mary Ruth *(Carol)*, Cynthia Crane *(Selma)*, Ivan Miller *(Mr. Stone)*, Dorothy Adams *(Mrs. Stone)*, John Marston *(Mr. Ferber)*, Mira McKinney *(Mrs. Ferber)*, William Forrest *(Mr. Gregg)*, Edward Earle *(Mr. Rogers)*, Edythe Elliott *(Mrs. King)*, Lloyd Whitlock *(Mr. Gibney)*, Georgia Backus *(Mrs. Wynn)*, Jean Hunt *(Flo)*, James Crane *(Jimmie)*, James Mackey *(Mickey)*, Fred Chapman *(Hal)*, Charles Flickinger *(Walt)*, Sally Martin *(June)*, Evelyn Young *(Nurse)*, Joel Friedkin *(Grocery Man)*, Nell Craig *(Receptionist)*, Lee Millar *(Dr. Gireaux)*, Stanley Brown *(Intern)*, Ed Thomas *(Martin)*, Joel Davis *(Vincent)*, Ruddy Hartz *(Junior Gregg)*.

A programmer designed to wear out the best of handkerchiefs. White, playing himself (as this was based on his radio show), broadcasts from an orphanage. He has the children say a few words to the radio audience in an obvious ploy to be adopted. The central focus is on 9-year-old Lee and his crippled 13-year-old sister, Fellows. Though he could easily be adopted by himself, Lee refuses to be separated from his sister. Overly sentimental.

d, Charles Barton; w, Doris Malloy (based on the radio program by Walter White, Jr.); ph, Benjamin Kline; ed, Richard Fantl; art d, Lionel Banks.

Drama **(PR:AAA MPAA:NR)**

NOBODY'S DARLING**   (1943) 71m REP bw

Mary Lee, Louis Calhern, Gladys George, Jackie Moran, Lee Patrick, Bennie Bartlett, Marcia Mae Jones, Roberta Smith, Lloyd Corrigan, Jonathan Hale, Sylvia Field, Billy Dawson, Beverly Boyd.

Director Mann's third film is another lackluster programmer to which he lent his budding talents (he really wouldn't hit stride until the 1950s when he directed an outstanding series of low-budget westerns, among them WINCHESTER 73 (1950), BEND OF THE RIVER (1952), THE MAN FROM LARAMIE (1955), and MAN OF THE WEST (1958)) after working as an assistant director for a few years. Lee stars as the yet-to-bloom daughter of a famous movie star. Frustrated by her parents' separation and the fact that no one notices her, Lee sets out to make a name for herself in Hollywood and succeeds. It would be nice to recommend the film to Mann devotees as an example of his early work, which would shed some new light on his later masterworks. However, NOBODY'S DARLING is indistinguishable from other Republic musicals. The studio was trying virtually every genre in an effort to grab mass audiences and distance itself from Poverty Row. Republic's musical comedy cycle began with FOLLOW YOUR HEART (1936) and continued with occasional releases through a 10-year period. Songs include: "It Had to Be You" (Gus Kahn, Isham Jones), "Blow, Gabriel, Blow" (Cole Porter), "I'm Always Chasing Rainbows" (Joseph McCarthy, Harry Carroll), "On the Sunny Side of the Street" (Dorothy Fields, Jimmy McHugh); "Row, Row, Row Your Boat."

p, Harry Grey; d, Anthony Mann; w, Olive Cooper (based on a story by F. Hugh Herbert); ph, Jack Marta; ed, Ernest Nims; md, Walter Scharf; art d, Russell Kimball; ch, Nick Castle.

Musical   **(PR:A   MPAA:NR)**

NOBODY'S FOOL***   (1936) 62m UNIV bw

Edward Everett Horton (*Will Wright*), Glenda Farrell (*Ruby Miller*), Cesar Romero (*Dizzy Rantz*), Frank Conroy (*Jake Cavendish*), Clay Clement (*Fixer Belmore*), Warren Hymer (*Sour Puss*), Henry Hunter (*Doc*), Florence Roberts (*Mary Jones*), Ed Gargan (*Tom*), Diana Gibson (*Blondie*), Pierre Watkin (*George Baxter*), Ivan Miller (*District Attorney*), Robert Middlemass.

Horton plays a mild-mannered small-town waiter in Iola, Kansas. He accidentally bursts in on a meeting of realtors, and before he knows what's going on, he's off to Manhattan. There he negotiates some realty dealings with gangsters, nearly triggering a gang war. He also falls in love with gun moll Farell. This film was tailor-made for Horton's comedic talents, and he plays his role with a comic innocence, bumbling his way through the easy going screenplay. The romance is a little weak but manages to be believable. Director Collins times the comedy scenes well, building the sequences nicely.

p, Irving Starr; d, Arthur Greville Collins; w, Ralph Block, Ben Markson, Jerry Sackheim (based on a story by Frank M. Dazey, Agnes C. Johnston); ph, Norbert Brodine; ed, Morris Wright.

Comedy   **(PR:A   MPAA:NR)**

NOBODY'S PERFECT**   (1968) 103m UNIV c

Doug McClure (*Doc Willoughby*), Nancy Kwan (*Tomiko Momoyama, Nurse*), James Whitmore (*Capt. Mike Riley*), David Hartman (*Boats McCafferty*), Gary Vinson (*Walt Purdy*), James Shigeta (*Toshi O'Hara, Diver*), Steve Carlson (*Johnny Crane*), George Furth (*Hamner*), Keye Luke (*Gondai-San*), Jill Donohue (*Marci Adler*), Bea Bradley (*Lt. Large*), Jim Creech (*Mr. Bayless*), Jerry Fujikawa (*Watanabe*), Edward Faulkner (*John Abelard*), Marian Collier (*Terry Abelard*), Ella Edwards, Maida Severn.

Another wacky Navy comedy in the same vein as the television series "McHale's Navy." Its episodic format contains many of the same gags seen in countless other movies. The film begins aboard the U.S.S. *Bustard*, a submarine rescue vehicle, during WW II. McClure and his fellow sailors steal a smiling Buddha from the local population and hide it in a cave. Years later, when the ship returns to Japan, McClure attempts to return the object. The funniest scene involves cockroaches being dumped into the captain's cabin so that McClure can go ashore on the pretext of getting exterminating supplies. However, the story line and comic situations, for the most part, are all too familiar.

p, Howard Christie; d, Alan Rafkin; w, John D.F. Black (based on the novel *The Crows of Edwina Hill* by Allan R. Bosworth); ph, Robert Wyckoff (Techniscope, Technicolor); m, Irving Gertz; ed, Gene Palmer; art d, Alexander Golitzen, Alexander A. Mayer; set d, John McCarthy, Robert C. Bradfield; cos, Rosemary Odell; makeup, Bud Westmore; technical advisers, Bernard M. Hillman, Marcus G. Klein, U.S. Defense Department, U.S. Navy.

Comedy   **(PR:A   MPAA:NR)**

NOBODY'S PERFEKT zero   (1981) 96m COL c

Gabe Kaplan (*Dibley*), Alex Karras (*Swaboda*), Robert Klein (*Walter*), Susan Clark (*Carol*), Paul Stewart (*Dr. Segal*), Alex Rocco (*Boss*), Arthur Rosenberg (*Mayor*), James Cromwell (*Dr. Carson*), Bobby Ramsen (*New Yorker*), John DiSanti (*Knuckles*), Ric Applewhite (*Louie*), Will Knickerbocker (*Mechanic*), Peter Bonerz (*Randall Kendall*), Harold Bergman (*Captain*), Roz Simmons (*Mrs. Freeman*), Alden McKay (*Freeman*), Omkar Spencer (*Young Wife*), Keshav Haeseler (*Young Husband*), Al Kiggins (*Col. Brogan*), Ray Forchion (*Army Officer*), Luke Halpin (*Deckhand*), Julio Mechoso, Jose Fong, Jorge Gil (*Gang Members*), John Archie, Lee Krug (*Mayor's Aides*), Jeff Gillen, Dan Rambo, Lillian Zuckerman, Clarence Thomas, Henry LeClair, Sean Brennan, Laurie Stark.

Three social misfits, Kaplan, Karras, and Klein (in a role that wastes his talents), drive their car into a cavernous pothole. They concoct various schemes to be reimbursed for the damages, eventually getting in the way of some mob members. This film is moronic, without a single funny idea, and is badly directed by television actor Bonerz (formerly of "The Bob Newhart Show"). Most recently, Bonerz has made a better reputation for himself as a television sitcom director.

p, Mort Engelberg; d, Peter Bonerz; w, Tony Kenrick (based on the novel *Two for the Price of One* by Kenrick); ph, James Pergola (Metrocolor); m, David McHugh; ed, Neil Travis; art d, Don K. Ivey; set d, Richard Helfritz.

Comedy   **Cas.**   **(PR:C   MPAA:PG)**

NOBORIRYU TEKKAHADA   (SEE: FRIENDLY KILLER, THE, 1970)

NOCTURNA zero   (1979) 85m Compass International c (AKA: NOCTURNA, GRANDDAUGHTER OF DRACULA)

Nai Bonet (*Nocturna*), John Carradine (*Count Dracula*), Yvonne De Carlo (*Jugulia*), Tony Hamilton (*Jimmy*), Brother Theodore (*Theodore*), Sy Richardson (*RH Factor*), Ivery Bell, Michael Harrison, Norris Harris, William H. Jones, Jr. (*The Moment of Truth*), Adam Keefe (*BSA President*), Monica Tidwell (*Brenda*), Tony Sanchez (*Victim*), Thomas Ryan (*Policeman*), Ron Toler (*Taxi Driver*), Pierre Epstein (*John*), Albert M. Ottenheimer (*Dr. Bernstein*), John Blyth Barrymore, Toby Handman, Angelo Vignari, Shelly Wyant (*BSA Members*), Frank Irizarry (*Disc Jockey*), Irwin Keyes, Marcus Anthony (*Transylvania Characters*), Al Sapienza, Jerry Sroka, A.C. Weary (*Musicians*).

Bonet, a former belly dancer who traded in her naval diamond for some cheap plastic fangs, plays the granddaughter of the famous vampire (Carradine, at an all-time low). Tired of the old man's outdated ways, she becomes involved with a musician and runs away to Manhattan. The film was not actually intended to be scary, but was made as a disco horror-comedy. Any way it's viewed, NOCTURNA is a mindless and pathetic attempt at filmmaking. The film was financially backed by former actor William Callahan, who was shot gangland style for embezzling funds in 1981.

p, Vernon Becker; d&w, Harry Tampa; ph, Mac Ahlberg (Metrocolor); ed, Ian Maitland; art d, Jack Krueger, Steve Davita; m/l, Reid Whitelaw, Norman Bergen.

Horror/Comedy   **(PR:O   MPAA:R)**

NOCTURNE**½**   (1946) 88m RKO bw

George Raft (*Lt. Joe Warne*), Lynn Bari (*Frances Ransom*), Virginia Huston (*Carol Page*), Joseph Pevney (*Fingers*), Myrna Dell (*Susan*), Edward Ashley (*Paul Vincent*), Walter Sande (*Halberson*), Mabel Paige (*Mrs. Warne*), Bernard Hoffman (*Torp*), Queenie Smith (*Queenie*), Mack Gray (*Gratz*), Pat Flaherty (*Cop with Susan*), Lorin Raker (*Police Chemist*), William Challee (*Police Photographer*), Greta Granstedt (*Clara*), Lillian Bond (*Mrs. Billings*), Carol Forman (*Receptionist*), Robert Malcolm (*Earn*), Jim Pierce, William [Willie] Bloom, Ed Dearing, Roger Creed (*Cops*), Phil Baribault (*Darkroom Assistant*), John Banner (*Shawn*), Rudy Robles (*Eujemio*), Janet Shaw (*Grace*), Ted O'Shea (*Dancer*), Tex Swan, Mel Wixon, Bob Terry (*Men*), Harry Harvey (*Police Doctor*), Lee Frederick (*Attendant*), Robert Anderson (*Pat*), Will Wright (*Mr. Billings*), Broderick O'Farrell (*Billings' Butler*), Virginia Edwards (*Mrs. O'Rourke*), Virginia Keiley (*Lotus Evans*), James Carlisle (*Elderly Man*), Paul Stader (*Practical Life Guard*), Antonio Filauri (*Nick Pappas*), Jack Norton (*Drunk*), Betty Farrington, Connie Evans, Doris Stone, Monya Andre, Eleanor Counts, Norma Brown (*Women*), John Rice (*Doorman*), Al Hill (*Cop at Brown Derby*), Edward Clark (*Apartment House Clerk*), Dorothy Adams (*Woman Tenant*), Lillian Bronson (*Cashier at Gotham*), Gladys Blake (*Ticket Seller*), Betty Hill, Carol Donell (*Girls*), Al Rhein (*Keyboard Club Waiter*), Benny Burt (*Keyboard Club Bartender*), Matt McHugh (*Coffee Attendant*), Lucille Casey (*Bessie*), Donald Kerr (*Gaffer*), Dick Rush (*Studio Cop*), Bert Moorehouse (*Director*), George Goodman (*Keyboard Club Manager*), Sam Flint, Lloyd Dawson (*Men*).

A popular composer is found shot to death and police lieutenant Raft is assigned to investigate. He believes the deceased has been slain by one of the ten cast-off women in his life but his superiors surprisingly conclude that the dead man ended his own life. Raft refutes the suicide theory and pushes on with his investigation until he so annoys his superiors that he is suspended from the force. Now obsessed with finding the killer, Raft goes after Bari, his main suspect, and he discovers that he is attracted to her. In the end, Bari inadvertently leads Raft to her sister, Huston, who is also the mysterious singer in the composer's life known only as "Dolores." Huston, Raft learns, is involved with her accompanist, Pevney, who turns out to be the real killer. Pianist Pevney provides Raft with the final clue to his identity as the murderer by playing the titled "Nocturne," which had been composed by the victim. Though the script is slight and drags in spots, Marin's direction and Wild's traveling shots and effective shadows and contrasts present a dark and brooding picture that is definitely *film noir*. Not a classic by any means but an offbeat production that is more than a curiosity thanks to Raft's mask-like performance. This was producer Harrison's first production for RKO; she had been a writer for Alfred Hitchcock on several films and she put to good use his brilliant ideas. Marin happily incorporated Harrison's ideas into NOCTURNE, which turned out to be a moneymaker, earning $568,000 the first time around.

p, Joan Harrison; d, Edwin L. Marin; w, Jonathan Latimer (based on an unpublished story by Frank Fenton, Rowland Brown); ph, Harry J. Wild; m, Leigh Harline; ed, Elmo Williams; md, Constantin Bakaleinikoff; prod d, Robert Boyle; art d, Albert S. D'Agostino, Boyle; set d, Darrell Silvera, James Altwies; cos, Renie; spec eff, Russell A. Cully; m/l, title song, Harline, Mort Greene, "Why Pretend," "A Little Bit is Better Than None," Eleanor Rudolph.

Crime Drama   **(PR:C   MPAA:NR)**

NOBODY IN TOYLAND**   (1958, Brit.) 87m Luckwell c

Colin Spaull (*Noddy*), Gloria Johnson (*Silky*), Leslie Sarony (*Mr. Pinkwhistle*), Peter Elliott (*Police Constable Plod*).

Disaster strikes in Toyland when a number of strange happenings threaten to destroy the magical kingdom. Spaull finds himself framed for acts of subversion and arrested by the Toyland police. Unknown to everyone is the fact that the crimes have been committed by the evil Red Goblins. Eventually the plot is discovered, the Red Goblins dealt with, and Spaull cleared.

p, Kay Luckwell; d, Maclean Rogers; w, Bill Luckwell, Michael Luckwell (based on the book by Enid Blyton).

Fantasy (PR:A MPAA:NR)

NOISY NEIGHBORS★★★ (1929) 74m Pathe bw

Eddie Quillan (Eddie), Alberta Vaughn (Mary), Quillan Family (Family), Theodore Roberts (Col. Carstairs), Ray Hallor (David), Russell Simpson (Ebenezer), Robert Perry, Mike Donlin, Billy Gilbert (Three Sons).

Quillan plays the head of a small-time vaudeville family that suddenly inherits a southern plantation. They head for the hills, only to find themselves caught up in the midst of a long-running hillbilly feud. Roberts is excellent as the head of one of the feuding clans. Though billed as a talkie, the film contained dialog only in its last five minutes. The comedy is well handled throughout, and while the sound seems to be an afterthought by the producers, its brief addition is put to good use. Unfortunately, Roberts died shortly before the film's release.

d, Charles Reisner; w, W. Scott Darling, John Krafft (based on a story by F. Hugh Herbert); ph, Dave Abela; ed, Anne Bauchens.

Comedy (PR:A MPAA:NR)

NOMADIC LIVES★★ (1977) 60m c

Marcia Jean Kurtz (Gretchen), James Carrington (Wesley).

A short independent feature from New York about a pair of young lovers—go-go dancer Kurtz and quick-sketch artist Carrington—whose relationship teeters between romance and boredom. Set in a less-than-affluent New Jersey trailer park, NOMADIC LIVES offers two fresh performances but suffers from the lack of development that accompanies its short 60-minute running time.

d&w, Mark Obenhaus.

Drama (PR:C MPAA:NR)

NON TIRATE IL DIAVOLO PER LA CODA (SEE: DEVIL BY THE TAIL, THE, 1969, Fr./Ital.)

NONE BUT THE BRAVE★★ (1963) 87m Ken-San/Parallel bw

James E. McLarty (Patrol Member).

During World War II, a pair of U.S. patrols are assigned to destroy two German radar stations. The first patrol completes its mission and waits for the second. However, the other patrol never arrives and the first unit must complete the entire mission. One lieutenant refuses to order his men to attack the station, believing it to be a suicide mission. When he is killed, a sergeant leads the patrol to success. A minor and forgettable film, shot on location near Austin, Texas.

p, Earl Podolnik, Wroe Owens; d, Ken Richardson; w, James E. McLarty (based on a story by Ken Richardson, Sandra Richardson); ph, Ronald Perryman; ed, Perryman.

War (PR:C MPAA:NR)

NONE BUT THE BRAVE, 1960 (SEE: FOR THE LOVE OF MIKE, 1960)

NONE BUT THE BRAVE★★ (1965, U.S./Jap.) 105m Tokyo Eiga-Artanis/WB c

Frank Sinatra (Chief Pharmacist's Mate Maloney), Clint Walker (Capt. Dennis Bourke), Tommy Sands (2nd Lt. Blair), Brad Dexter (Sgt. Bleeker), Tony Bill (Air Crewman Keller), Tatsuya Mihashi (Lt. Kuroki), Takeshi Kato (Sgt. Tamura), Sammy Jackson (Cpl. Craddock), Richard Bakalyan (Cpl. Ruffino), Rafer Johnson (Pvt. Johnson), Jimmy Griffin (Pvt. Dexter), Christopher Dark (Pvt. Searcy), Don Dorrell (Pvt. Hoxie), Phillip Crosby (Pvt. Magee), John Howard Young (Pvt. Waller), Roger Ewing (Pvt. Swensholm), Homare Suguro (Lance Cpl. Hirano), Kenji Sahara (Cpl. Fujimoto), Masahiko Tanimura (Lead Pvt. Ando), Hisao Dazai (Pvt. Tokumaru), Susumu Kurobe (Pvt. Goro), Takashi Inagaki (Pvt. Ishii), Kenichi Hata (Pvt. Sato), Toru Ibuki (Pvt. Arikawa), Ryucho Shumputei (Pvt. Okuda), Laraine Stephens (Lorie), Richard Sinatra (Pvt. Roth).

This is Sinatra's debut as a director and nothing other than a spectacular bloodbath is the result. The mediocre story has a dedicated Japanese force stranded on a remote island. The war has long passed them by but the commander, Mihashi, nevertheless rigidly maintains order, drilling his men constantly and driving them to complete the building of a boat that will take them to their distant headquarters. An American bomber crash-lands on the island after being damaged by a Japanese fighter. The Americans and Japanese do battle but come to a quick truce. Frank Sinatra, a pharmacist's mate, operates on a seriously injured Japanese soldier, amputating his leg but saving his life. The truce is to continue, agree American commander Walker and Mihashi, but the Japanese insist that whichever country sends aid, the fighting is to commence once again. The Americans repair their radio and signal for help. An American destroyer hoves into view and the Japanese attack, being killed to a man. Only five Americans survive the spectacular killing spree. The direction is poor to awful and the cast members walk about the island like zombies looking for Charles Laughton to turn them into beasts (ISLAND OF LOST SOULS). The script is cliche-ridden and Sinatra's heroics are embarrassing. Only excellent photography by Lipstein saves this posturing mess.

p&d, Frank Sinatra; w, John Twist, Katsuya Susaki (based on a story by Kikumaru Okuda); ph, Harold Lipstein (Panavision, Technicolor); m, Johnny Williams; ed, Sam O'Steen; md, Morris Stoloff; art d, LeRoy Deane, Haruyoski Oshita; set d, George James Hopkins; spec eff, Eiji Tsuburaya.

War (PR:O MPAA:NR)

NONE BUT THE LONELY HEART★★★★ (1944) 113m RKO bw

Cary Grant (Ernie Mott), Ethel Barrymore (Ma Mott), Barry Fitzgerald (Twite), June Duprez (Ada), Jane Wyatt (Aggie Hunter), George Coulouris (Jim Mordiney), Dan Duryea (Lew Tate), Konstantin Shayne (Ike Weber), Eva Lernard Boyne (Ma Chalmers), Morton Lowry (Taz), Helene Thimig (Sister Nurse), William Challee (Knocker), Joseph Vitale (Cash), Roman Bohnen (Dad Pettyjohn), Renie Riano (Flo), Marcel Dill (Percy), David Clyde (Policeman with Stripes), Roy Thomas (Rookie Policeman), Amelia Romano (Lame Girl), Queenie Vassar (Ma Snowden), Art Smith (Marjoriebanks), Rosalind Ivan (Mrs. Tate), Herbert Heywood (Dad Fitchitt), Helena Grant (Old Woman in Shop), Virginia Farmer (Ma Segwiss), Claire Verdera (Barmaid), Elsie Prescott (Old Lady), Katherine Allen (Millie Wilson), Diedra Vale (Miss Tate), Walter Soderling (Pa Floom), Polly Bailey (Ma Floom), Bill Wolfe (Blind Man), George Atkinson (Man with Gramophone), Barry Regan, Rosemary Blong, Jack Jackson, Rosemary La Planche (Dancers), Ted Billings (Cockney Bum), Milton Wallace (Ike Lesser), Eric Wilton, David Thursby (Prison Guards), Sammy Blum, Alec Harford (Drunks), Skelton Knaggs (Slush), Forrester Harvey (Bloke), Al Rhein, Al Murphy (Henchmen), Yorke Sherwood (Call Block Cop), Matthew Boulton, Herbert Evans (Police Sergeants), Joe North (Old Man), Ida Shoemaker (Old Lady), Chef Milani (Rossi), Keith Hitchcock (Roly Poly Man), Lita Gordon, Nancy Russell, Marina Bohnen (Girls), Robin Sanders Clark, Sayre Dearing, Ernie Shield (Men), William Ambler (Bus Driver), Marie De Becker (Mme. La Vaka), Bill O'Leary (Cab Driver), Leyland Hodgson, John Meredith (Cops), Diane Dyer (Baby), Charles Irwin (Cop at Crash), Tiny Jones (Woman), Colin Kenny (Cop Outside).

This was a daring and inventive film for its day and Grant, as the dedicated outsider, is superb, as is his cockney mother, Barrymore. The time is just prior to WW II and the setting is Whitechapel in the East End of London, the hardscrabble slums where Jack the Ripper freely roamed in murk and gloom a half-century earlier. Through these mean streets wanders Grant, a young man without a purpose, a shiftless but lighthearted fellow whose mother, Barrymore, runs a dingy second-hand furniture store. Grant and his mother exchange barbs whenever they meet which is infrequently since he is seldom home to occupy his room above the store. He vagabonds his way through the area, cadging cigarettes and food from friendly shopkeepers who have known him since boyhood. Particularly solicitous of Grant and protective of his mother is the local pawnbroker, Shayne, who dispenses wisdom and wit, as does family friend and drifter Fitzgerald. Though cellist Wyatt is in love with Grant he forsakes her for the sultry, alluring Duprez, the divorced wife of British underworld leader Coulouris. The gangster persuades Grant that he should join Coulouris' band of thieves and get rich quick, knowing full well that Grant's only ambition is to obtain wealth to spend it on the high-living Duprez. Grant takes part in some robberies and feels guilty about it, withdrawing from Coulouris' evil web while Duprez demands more and more luxuries. Then Grant learns from Shayne that his mother Barrymore has been concealing cancer, and is on the brink of death. Grant becomes a dutiful son to ease his mother's pain, not letting her know he knows about the cancer, repairing furniture and clocks, working all hours and cheering Barrymore whenever he can. Never close, mother and son now draw close but Barrymore knows that Grant is impoverished and cannot even contemplate marriage or a future without a nest egg so Barrymore, to leave Grant a legacy, begins to receive stolen property and is arrested. Grant visits her in the prison hospital where she is dying. At first it's stiff upper lip, then Grant breaks down after Barrymore tells him she's disgraced him. "Didn't disgrace me, Ma," Grant tells her, "this is your son, Ernie Mott. Ma! This is the boy who loves you, needs you, wants you!" She smiles, finally happy. Grant leaves, promising to visit again tomorrow, but Barrymore dies. Later, Grant talks to philosopher-drifter Fitzgerald and tells him he's going off to "fight with the men who'll fight for a human way of life." Fitzgerald tells him, leaving, that he'll see him "sooner." "How sooner?" says Grant. "Who knows," winks Fitzgerald, "it's all written in the book." Grant goes his separate way, into the future, supposedly to become—as the opening narration suggests—the unknown soldier of WW II. Odets' powerful script does well by the Llewellyn novel, as does his direction, but the film is unyielding, uncompromising in its portrayal of slum life and the fragile dreams lost in the gutter. it does not shrink from the depressing, the sordid, and only in Grant's indomitable spirit is there hope. NONE BUT THE LONELY HEART was not a box office winner, losing some money, but it has remained a classic portrayal of London slum life, enhanced by a dedicated cast. RKO, to get Barrymore in to the film during its hurried production schedule, paid the expenses of closing the long-running play "The Corn Is Green," in which the actress was starring.

p, David Hempstead; d&w, Clifford Odets (based on the novel by Richard Llewellyn); ph, George Barnes; m, Hanns Eisler; ed, Roland Gross; md, C. Bakaleinikoff; prod d, Mordecai Gorelik; art d, Albert S. D'Agostino, Jack Okey; set d, Darrell Silvera, Harley Miller; cos, Renie; spec eff, Vernon L. Walker.

Drama Cas. (PR:A MPAA:NR)

NONE SHALL ESCAPE★★★½ (1944) 85m COL bw

Marsha Hunt (Marja Pacierkowski), Alexander Knox (Wilhelm Grimm), Henry Travers (Father Warecki), Erik Rolf (Karl Grimm), Richard Crane (Willie Grimm as a Man), Dorothy Morris (Janina), Richard Hale (Rabbi Levin), Ruth Nelson (Alice Grimm), Kurt Kreuger (Lt. Gersdorf), Shirley Mills (Anna Oremska), Elvin Field (Jan Stys as a Boy), Trevor Bardette (Jan Stys as a Man), Frank Jaquet (Dr. Matek), Ray Teal (Oremski), Art Smith (Stys), George Lessey (Presiding Judge).

Knox plays a German soldier crippled during WW I. He returns to his home along the German-Polish border and resumes teaching school. Slowly he grows embittered with his life and becomes involved with hateful ideologies that eventually cause his fiancee (Hunt) to leave him. After sexually attacking one of his female students, Knox is banished from his village. He joins the Nazi party and soon rises to power. He returns home once more, this time as a Nazi commandant and creates a wave of terror in the village. This is an intelligent film that portrays the tribulations of German life after the war, and suggests that those conditions lead to WW II. Knox's performance is keen and searing, showing how a good man can become an instrument of evil. The supporting cast is equally fine with Hale a standout as a persecuted rabbi. NONE SHALL ESCAPE won an Oscar for its excellent screenplay.

p, Samuel Bischoff; d, Andre De Toth; w, Lester Cole (based on a story by Alfred Neumann, Joseph Than); ph, Lee Garmes; m, Ernest Toch; ed, Charles Nelson; art d, Lionel Banks.

Drama **(PR:A MPAA:NR)**

NON-STOP NEW YORK½** (1937, Brit.) 72m GAU/GB bw

Anna Lee *(Jennie Carr)*, John Loder *(Inspector Jim Grant)*, Frank Cellier *(Sam Pryor)*, Desmond Tester *(Arnold James)*, William Dewhurst *(Mortimer)*, James Pirrie *(Billy Cowper)*, Francis L. Sullivan *(Hugo Brandt)*, Drusilla Wills *(Ma Carr)*, Jerry Verno *(Steward)*, Athene Seyler *(Aunt Veronica)*, Ellen Pollock *(Miss Harvey)*, Arthur Goullett *(Henry Abel)*, Peter Bull *(Spurgeon)*, Tony Quinn *(Harrigan)*, Danny Green, Bryan Herbert, Tom Scott, Aubrey Pollack, Sam Wilkinson, Atholl Fleming, Alf Goddard, H.G. Stoker, Jack Lester, Hal Walters, Albert Chevalier, Phyllis Morris, Andrea Malandrinos, Roy Smith, Billy Watts, Frederick Piper, Edward Ryan, Percy Parsons, Alexander Sarner.

Lee (at the time, director Stevenson's wife) plays a London chorus girl who accidentally gets involved with gangsters. A hobo is accused of murder but Lee can provide him with an alibi. Consequently, the mob frames her for robbery, and she is sent to prison. Upon her release she discovers the police are looking for a missing witness in the murder case. She comes forward but her story is disbelieved. Still chased by the gang, she stows away on a transatlantic flight to New York. The gangsters knock out the pilots and parachute from the plane. A crash is averted because of the heroics of Loder, a detective who's been following Lee. Her name is cleared and the murder case is solved. Naturally, Lee and Loder fall in love. Routine and silly fare, though competently told and nicely acted. At the time, transatlantic passenger planes were still three years away, thus the film could be considered a futuristic melodrama.

p, Michael Balcon; d, Robert Stevenson; w, Kurt Siodmak, Roland Pertwee, J. O. C. Orton, Derek Twist, E. V. H. Emmett (based on the novel *Sky Steward* by Ken Attiwill); ph, Mutz Greenbaum; ed, A. Barnes.

Drama **(PR:A MPAA:NR)**

NOOSE (SEE: SILK NOOSE, THE, 1948, Brit.)

NOOSE FOR A GUNMAN½** (1960) 69m Premium/UA bw

Jim Davis *(Case Britton)*, Lyn Thomas *(Della Haines)*, Ted de Corsia *(Cantrell)*, Walter Sande *(Tom Evans)*, Barton MacLane *(Carl Avery)*, Harry Carey, Jr. *(Jim Ferguson)*, Lane Chandler *(Ed Folsey)*, John Hart *(Barker)*, Leo Gordon *(Link Roy)*, Bill Tannen *(Willetts)*, Jan Arvan *(Hallop)*, Bob Tetrick *(Anders)*, William Remick *(Man on Stagecoach)*, Kermit Maynard *(Carter)*, William Challee *(Gorse)*, Cecil Weston *(Mrs. Franklyn)*.

By 1960 the formula western was almost extinct, replaced by TV westerns and films that featured antiheros instead of traditional leading men. NOOSE FOR A GUNMAN was among the last of the B style westerns with clear-cut good guys and bad guys. Davis plays an honest gunslinger banished from a town after being falsely accused of murder. MacLane is an evil cattle baron, the murderer of Davis' brother, who has accused the hero of killing MacLane's sons. But Davis returns to foil MacLane, and his sidekick De Corsia, in a robbery attempt. At times the plot seems overly complicated, but Davis' professional performance is worth noting. De Corsia is wonderful, almost evil personified in his villainous role. Cahn's direction is simplistic and effective. NOOSE FOR A GUNMAN has a nice feeling for a type of film that no longer existed. Ironically, this was the last film for actor Kermit Maynard, who was the star of several B-westerns during their heydey, and was also the brother of Ken Maynard (one of the most popular of the cowboy heroes during the 1930s.

p, Robert E. Kent; d, Edward L. Cahn; w, James B. Gordon (based on a story by Steve Fisher); ph, Al Cline; ed, Grant Whytock; art d, Bill Glasgow.

Western **(PR:A MPAA:NR)**

NOOSE FOR A LADY** (1953, Brit.) 73m Insignia/Anglo-Amalgamated bw

Dennis Price *(Simon Gale)*, Rona Anderson *(Jill Hallam)*, Ronald Howard *(Dr. Evershed)*, Pamela Allan *(Margaret Allan)*, Alison Leggatt *(Mrs. Langdon-Humphries)*, Melissa Stribling *(Vanessa Lane)*, Charles Lloyd Pack *(Robert Upcott)*, Colin Tapley *(Maj. Fergusson)*, George Merritt *(Inspector Frost)*, Robert Brown, Doris Yorke, Esma Cannon, Joe Linnane, Ian Wallace, Gabriel Blount, Marguerite Young, Millicent Wolf, Alexis Milne.

Overly chatty whodunit starring Allan as a woman sentenced to prison for the murder of her husband, though no one really blames her because the deceased was universally despised. Price, her cousin, cuts short his vacation to investigate the murder because he believes Allan to be innocent. Aided by Allan's stepdaughter Anderson, the pair discover that the murder victim was a reprehensible blackmailer whose life style could have motivated any number of people to kill him. Unfortunately, further digging reveals that Price's helper Anderson murdered the blackguard.

p, Victor Hanbury; d, Wolf Rilla; w, Rex Rienits (based on the novel *Whispering Woman* by Gerald Verner); ph, Jimmy Harvey.

Crime **(PR:A MPAA:NR)**

NOOSE HANGS HIGH, THE*** (1948) 77m EL bw

Bud Abbott *(Ted Higgins)*, Lou Costello *(Homer Hinchcliffe)*, Cathy Downs *(Carol Scott)*, Joseph Calleia *(Mike Craig)*, Leon Errol *(Julius Caesar McBride)*, Mike Mazurki *(Chuck)*, Jack Overman *(Joe)*, Fritz Feld *(Psychiatrist)*, Vera Martin *(Elevator Girl)*, Joe Kirk, Matt Willis *(Gangsters)*, Ben Welden *(Stewart)*, Jimmy Dodd, Ben Hall *(Messengers)*, Ellen Corby *(Maid)*, Isabel Randolph *(Miss Van Buren)*, Frank O'Connor *(Postman)*, Bess Flowers *(Patient)*, Pat Flaherty *(Tough Driver)*, Elvia Allman *(Bit Woman)*, Lois Austin *(Woman on Street)*, Herb Vigran *(Man with Coat)*, James Flavin *(Traffic Cop)*, Minerva Urecal *(Husky Woman)*, Russell Hicks *(Manager)*, Arno Frey *(Headwaiter)*, Lyle Latell *(Workman)*, Irmgard Dawson *(Girl)*, Joan Myles *(Secretary)*, Harry Brown *(Upson)*, Benny Rubin *(Chinaman)*, Murray Leonard *(Crazy Dentist)*, Sandra Spence *(Dentist's Assistant)*, Alvin Hammer *(Tipster)*, Jerry Marlowe *(Cashier)*, Paul Maxey *(Jewel Proprietor)*, Fred Kelsey *(Cop)*, James Logan *(Valet)*, Oscar Otis *(Race Track Announcer)*, Fred M. Browne, Ralph Montgomery *(Waiters)*, Tim Wallace, Chalky Williams *(Cab Drivers)*.

Abbott and Costello play a pair of window washers. They are mistaken for gamblers and get mixed up with a group of gangsters led by Calleia. The plot is minimal as this is really a vehicle designed for the talents of the comedy team. Though the bits are as old as the movies, a nice twist of fresh humor is worked in. There's a well-timed bit with a pair of pants that is an excellent display of physical comedy. There's also some word play in the same vein as the "Who's on first" bit as the boys fool around with the phrase "You can't be here." A good supporting cast as well as fine comedy direction give this film some genuinely funny moments. (See ABBOTT AND COSTELLO series, Index.)

p&d, Charles Barton; w, John Grant, Howard Harris (based on a story by Daniel Taradash, Julian Blaustein, Bernard Fins); ph, Charles Van Enger; m, Walter Schumann; ed, Harry Reynolds; md, Irving Friedman; art d, Edward L. Ilou; set d, Armor Marlowe; makeup, Ern Westmore.

Comedy **(PR:AAA MPAA:NR)**

NOR THE MOON BY NIGHT (SEE: ELEPHANT GUN, 1958, Brit.)

NORA INU (SEE: STRAY DOG, 1963, Jap.)

NORA PRENTISS*** (1947) 111m WB bw

Ann Sheridan *(Nora Prentiss)*, Kent Smith *(Dr. Richard Talbot)*, Bruce Bennett *(Dr. Joel Merriam)*, Robert Alda *(Phil McDade)*, Rosemary DeCamp *(Lucy Talbot)*, John Ridgely *(Walter Bailey)*, Robert Arthur *(Gregory Talbot)*, Wanda Hendrix *(Bonita Talbot)*, Helen Brown *(Miss Judson)*, Rory Mallinson *(Fleming)*, Harry Shannon *(Police Lieutenant)*, James Flavin *(District Attorney)*, Douglas Kennedy *(Doctor)*, Don McGuire *(Truck Driver)*, Clifton Young *(Policeman)*, John Newland, John Compton, Ramon Ros *(Reporters)*, Jack Mower *(Sheriff)*, Philo McCullough *(Warden)*, Fred Kelsey *(Turnkey)*, Louis Quince *(Judge)*, Lottie Williams *(Agnes)*, Gertrude Carr *(Mrs. Dobie)*, Richard Walsh *(Bystander)*, Tiny Jones *(Flower Woman)*, Georgia Caine *(Mrs. Sterritt)*, Dean Cameron *(Rod the Piano Player)*, Roy Gordon *(Oberlin)*, David Fresco *(Newsboy)*, Jack Ellis, Lee Phelps *(Doormen)*, Creighton Hale *(Captain of Waiters)*, Ed Hart, Clancey Cooper, Alan Bridge *(Policemen)*, Ross Ford *(Chauffeur, Billie)*, Adele St. Maur *(Nurse)*, Ralph Dunn, Ed Chandler *(Detectives)*, Charles Marsh *(Bailiff)*, Matt McHugh, Wallace Scott *(Drunks)*, George Campeau *(Man)*, Charles Jordan *(Clerk at Court)*, John Elliott *(Chaplain)*, Herb Caen, Bill McWilliams, Mike Musura, Jerry Baulch, Fred Johnson, Jack Dailey, Bill Best, Seymore Snaer, James Nickle *(Newspapermen at Ferry Building)*.

Smith plays a successful San Francisco doctor who is unhappily married to DeCamp. He begins an affair with Sheridan, a nightclub singer, but can't work up the nerve to ask his wife for a divorce. Sheridan takes advantage of an opportunity to move to New York to open up at a new nightclub. Smith is depressed in her absence but sees a way out of his plight when his partner unexpectedly dies. He fakes his own death, then leaves for New York and his beloved. He later discovers that his California "death" is being investigated as a possible murder. Smith becomes paranoid and frightened, refusing to leave Sheridan's apartment. He turns to alcohol as his only refuge and watches Sheridan's career take off. He begins to think she is having an affair with her boss (Alda) and gets into a fight with the man. In his alcoholic stupor, Smith believes he's killed Alda. He flees in his car, only to wind up in a terrible accident that disfigures his face. After undergoing emergency plastic surgery, Smith becomes a new person and is relieved, until he is arrested for his own murder back in California. None of his former friends or family realize that it is he who is on trial. He is convicted of his own murder and sentenced to death. He convinces Sheridan to keep quiet about his real identity so as to avoid any further emotional difficulty for his family. The former lovers bid farewell in Death Row. Though intended to be a "woman's picture," the unusual story and expressionistic camera work make NORA PRENTISS an attractive *film noir*. The ironic, almost existential ending works well on this level. The cinematography (by famed cameraman Howe) also pushes the film beyond its intentions, capturing Smith's paranoia and despair quite nicely. He uses the seedy hotels and darkly lit nightclubs to their best advantage, giving the film an overall moodiness that heightens the drama.

p, William Jacobs; d, Vincent Sherman; w, N. Richard Nash, Philip McDonald (based on "The Man Who Died Twice" by Paul Webster, Jack Sobell); ph, James Wong Howe; m, Franz Waxman; ed, Owen Marks; md, Leo F. Forbstein; art d, Anton Grot; set d, Walter Tilford; cos, Travilla; spec eff, Harry Barndollar, Edwin DuPar; m/l, "Would You Like A Souvenir," "Who Cares What People Say," (Moe K. Jerome, Jack Scholl, Eddie Cherkose); makeup, Perc Westmore.

Drama **(PR:A MPAA:NR)**

NORAH O'NEALE*½ (1934, Brit.) 70m DuWorld bw (GB: IRISH HEARTS)

Lester Matthews *(Dr. Dermot Fitzgerald)*, Nancy Burne *(Norah O'Neale)*, Molly Lamont *(Nurse Otway)*, Patric Knowles *(Pip Fitzgerald)*, Kyrle Bellew *(Matron)*, Torren [Torin] Thatcher *(Dr. Hackey)*, Patrick Barr *(Dr. Connellan)*, Sarah Allgood *(Mrs. Gogarty)*, Arthur Sinclair *(Farmer)*, Joyce Chancellor *(Sheila Marr)*, Cathleen Drago *(Dublin Mother)*, Maire O'Neill *(Mrs. Moriarty)*, Mehan Hartley *(Fanninby)*, Tom Collins *(Dr. Joyce)*, Pegeen Mair *(Ward Nurse)*, May Warren *(Allannah Kenny)*, Theresa McCormac *(Mrs. Kenny)*, Mary O'Reilly *(Nurse Chambers)*,

Georgina Leech *(Girl)*, Iya Abdy *(Casualty Nurse)*, Mary Warren, Leo Rownson, Sean Dempsey, The Cummerford Dancers.

An Irish hospital is the setting for this melodrama, which is much like a soap opera in terms of its plot. Matthews plays an eligible young doctor, being ardently chased by two women. He is attracted to Burne, but her tastes run high and his finances can't afford her. Lamont deceives Matthews into becoming engaged after they share a kiss. Confused, he leaves for the country to help fight a typhoid epidemic. While the epidemic is thwarted, he succumbs to the disease himself. Everyone in his profession thinks he is incurable, but Burne nurses him back and only their true love for each other saves him. The film features several members of the famed acting ensemble, the Irish Abbey Players, and is often referred to as the first all-Irish talkie.

p, Harry Clifton; d&w, Brian Desmond Hurst (based on the story "Night Nurse" by J. Johnson Abraham); ph, Eugene Schefftan, Walter Blakeley; m, Herbert Hughes.

Drama **(PR:A MPAA:NR)**

NORMA RAE**** (1979) 110m FOX c

Sally Field *(Norma Rae)*, Beau Bridges *(Sonny)*, Ron Leibman *(Reuben)*, Pat Hingle *(Vernon)*, Barbara Baxley *(Leona)*, Gail Strickland *(Bonnie Mae)*, Morgan Paull *(Wayne Billings)*, Robert Broyles *(Sam Bolen)*, John Calvin *(Ellis Harper)*, Booth Colman *(Dr. Watson)*, Lee DeBroux *(Lujan)*, James Luisi *(George Benson)*, Gilbert Green *(Al London)*, Bob Minor *(Lucius White)*, Mary Munday *(Mrs. Johnson)*, Gregory Walcott *(Lamar Miller)*, Noble Willingham *(Leroy Mason)*, Lonnie Chapman *(Gardner)*, Bert Freed *(Sam Dakin)*, Bob E. Hannah *(Jed Buffum)*, Edith Ivey *(Louise Pickens)*, Scott Lawton *(Craig)*, Frank McRae *(James Brown)*, Gerald Okuneff *(Pinkerton Man)*, Gina Kaye Pounders *(Millie)*, Henry Slate *(Policeman)*, Melissa Ann Wait *(Alice)*, Joe A. Dorsey *(Woodrow)*, Sherry Velvet Foster *(Velma)*, Grace Zabriskie *(Linette)*, Stuart Culpepper *(Ray)*, Weona T. Brown *(Vendor)*, Carolyn Danforth *(Mavis)*, James W. Harris *(Worker)*, Charlie Briggs *(Warren)*, Billie Joyce Buck *(Agnes)*, Fred Covington *(Alston)*, J. Don Ferguson *(Peter)*, Sandra Dorsey *(Matron)*, Harold E. Finch *(Agent)*, Clayton Landey *(Teddy)*, William Pannell *(Billy)*, George Robertson *(Farmer)*, Thomas D. Samford III *(J.P.)*, J. Roy Tatum *(Woodrow Bowzer)*, Vernon Weddle *(Rev. Hubbard)*, Jack Stryker *(J.J. Davis)*.

Sally Field won her first Oscar for this role, a complex portrayal of an ill-educated southern woman who matures into a complete person when she is faced with union woes and must grow up or fall by the wayside. Field is one of many overworked and underpaid workers at a cotton mill that doesn't seem to realize the days of slavery are over. Her father, Hingle, dies when he is not accorded the correct medical diagnosis and attention, while her mother, Baxley, is rapidly losing her hearing due to the incessant din of the factory's equipment. The place is functioning without a union and when New York labor organizer Leibman arrives to forge a union, the workers fear for their jobs under the yoke of management. Field is a divorced woman who has two children (one of whom is illegitimate) and marries Bridges near the midway point of the picture. Bridges is jealous of the relationship between Leibman and Field when she decides to join him in his quest for solidarity among the workers. This unlikely duo seeks to unite the workers, despite the vague threats by the people who run the business and the annoyance of Bridges, who wishes that Leibman would just pack up and leave his motel. When they first meet, Leibman's grating personality rankles Field, and her lack of ambition does the same to him, but as the movie progresses, so does the mutual respect mount. Field begins undermining management from the inside and eventually convinces her fellow workers that they can achieve better conditions if they are willing to put themselves at the risk of losing their jobs. In the end, she manages to rally the workers into a strike, production at the mill ceases, and management must capitulate in order to keep production rolling. It's not a complicated story and could have even been dull were it not for the intelligent screenplay that had more than its share of compassion. Field's work was perfection. Shire's music took the Oscar and he won another for co-writing the song "It Goes Like It Goes" with Norman Gimbel. The screenplay was nominated, as was the picture, but BREAKING AWAY took the writing award and KRAMER VS. KRAMER won the accolade as Best Picture. The deck was stacked against management in the movie (in much the same way that Steven Spielberg stacked it against every man in THE COLOR PURPLE, another southern film) and their side is never presented. That didn't stop audiences from racing to see the movie and it made more money than just about any union movie, with the possible exception of the best union movie ever made, ON THE WATERFRONT. All the roles were cast well and it was a pleasure to see Baxley actually do something, after having spent many years on TV as "Barney Miller's" wife and seldom appearing in the show once they realized that the fun was at the station house, not in Miller's domestic life. As is the case in most of Ritt's films about the South, the technical credits were all excellent because he likes using the same people as often as he can and they function almost by instinct. Alonzo, Levin, and Herndon have a history of working with each other and with Ritt, and the results were proven at the box office, where the picture grossed well over $10 million on the first go-round.

p, Tamara Asseyev, Alex Rose; d, Martin Ritt; w, Irving Ravetch, Harriet Frank, Jr.; ph, John A. Alonzo (Panavision, DeLuxe Color); m, David Shire; ed, Sidney Levin; prod d, Walter Scott Herndon; art d, Tracy Bousman; set d, Gregory Garrison; m/l, "It Goes Like It Goes," Shire, Norman Gimbel (sung by Jennifer Warnes).

Drama **Cas.** **(PR:A-C MPAA:PG)**

NORMAN CONQUEST* (1953, Brit.) 75m BA Productions/Lippert bw (GB: PARK PLAZA 605)

Tom Conway *(Norman Conquest)*, Eva Bartok *(Nadina Rodin)*, Joy Shelton *(Pixie Everard)*, Sidney James *(Superintendent Williams)*, Richard Wattis *(Theodore Feather)*, Carl Jaffe *(Boris Roff)*, Frederick Schiller *(Ivan Burgin)*, Robert Adair *(Baron von Henschel)*, Anton Diffring *(Gregor)*, Ian Fleming, Edwin Richfield, Michael Balfour, Martin Boddey, Terence Alexander, Victor Platt, Leon Davey, Richard Marner, Tony Hilton, Alan Rolfe, Derek Prentice, Frank Seiman, Brian Moorhead, Billie Hill, Anthony Woodruff.

A faint, low-budget thriller starring Conway as a private detective who suddenly finds himself drugged and set up on a murder charge. The villain who perpetrated the frame-up turns out to be femme-fatale Bartok, an exotic evildoer who heads a diamond smuggling operation. Enter ex-Nazi Adair, the actual trigger man, who decides to grab more power for himself by framing Bartok. Bartok switches sides and becomes Conway's ally, but ends up giving her life to save his in the traditional bad-girl-turned-good manner. Less than overcome by grief, Conway is able to go on and destroy the diamond smuggling operation.

p, Bertram Ostrer, Albert Fennell; d, Bernard Knowles; w, Knowles, Fennell, Ostrer, Clifford Witting (based on the novel *Daredevil Conquest* by Berkeley Gray); ph, Eric Cross; m, Philip Green.

Crime **(PR:A MPAA:NR)**

NORMAN. . .IS THAT YOU?** (1976) 91m MGM/UA c

Redd Foxx *(Ben Chambers)*, Pearl Bailey *(Beatrice Chambers)*, Dennis Dugan *(Garson Hobart)*, Michael Warren *(Norman Chambers)*, Tamara Dobson *(Audrey)*, Vernee Watson *(Melody)*, Jayne Meadows *(Mrs. Hobart)*, George Furth, Barbara Sharma *(Bookstore Clerks)*, Sergio Aragones, Sosimo Hernandez *(Desk Clerks)*, Wayland Flowers *(Larry)*, Allan Drake *(Cab Driver)*.

An unsuccessful film version of the unsuccessful Broadway play. The film is a balky, occasionally funny comedy with a host of black stars. Bailey and Foxx appear as a married couple, but Bailey leaves him to go to Mexico with his brother. Depressed, Foxx heads to California to see his son Warren in Hollywood. To add to Foxx's misery, he finds out that his son is a homosexual, and has taken a white lover. This gives Foxx a chance to reel off one-liner after one-liner, which makes the film resemble a television sitcom—a fact that is not surprising since producer-director Schlatter directed the innovative television series "Laugh-In." Also, Foxx, a nightclub comedian known for his off-color humor, was starring in the sitcom "Sanford and Son" at the time the film was made. Visually, the film may seem below standard as it was shot on videotape and transferred to film. Its most outstanding feature is the Motown soundtrack.

p&d, George Schlatter; w, Ron Clark, Sam Bobrick, Schlatter (based on the play by Clark, Bobrick); ph, Gayne Rescher (Metrocolor); m, William Goldstein; ed, George Folsey, Jr.; art d, Stephen M. Berger; set d, Fred R. Price; cos, Michael Travis; m/l, "Norman. . .Is That You?" (Goldstein, Ron Miller), "One Out of Every Six" (Goldstein, Miller, sung by Thelma Houston), "An Old-Fashioned Man" (sung by Smokey Robinson).

Comedy/Drama **(PR:C MPAA:PG)**

NORMAN LOVES ROSE** (1982, Aus.) 98m Norman/Atlantic c

Carol Kane, Tony Owen, Warren Mitchell, Myra De Groot, David Downer, Barry Otto, Sandy Gore, Virginia Hey, Louise Pajo, Valerie Newstead, Betty Benfield, Julie Herbert, Olivia Brown, Herbert Newstead, Sid Feldheim, Johnny Lockwood, Arthur Sherman, Gypsey Dorney, Aaron Nitties, Theo Stevens, Gary Kliger, Josef Drewniak, Geoffrey Smith, Michael Rothner, Paul Schonberger, David Lilienthal, Joel Pearlman, Darren Cohen, Anthony Wolf, Leonardo Gesto, Wayne Shapiro, David Spicer, Sue Stenmark, Michael Adams, Shane Tapper.

Turtle-paced comedy from Australia about a 13-year-old boy who is completely infatuated with his voluptuous, and much older, sister-in-law, Kane. She takes him under her wing, teaches him about sex, and then discovers she is pregnant by him.

p, Henri Safran, Basil Appleby; d&w, Safran; ph, Vince Monton; m, Mike Perjanik; prod d, Darrell Lass; md, Perjanik; ed, Don Saunders.

Comedy **Cas.** **(PR:O MPAA:R)**

NORSEMAN, THE** (1978) 90m AIP c

Lee Majors *(Thorvald)*, Cornel Wilde *(Ragnar)*, Mel Ferrer *(King Eurich)*, Jack Elam *(Death Dreamer)*, Chris Connelly *(Rolf)*, Kathleen Freeman *(Indian Woman)*, Denny Miller *(Rauric)*, Seamon Glass *(Gunnar)*, Jimmy Clem *(Olaf)*, Susie Coelho *(Winnetta)*, Jerry Daniels *(Kiwonga)*, Deacon Jones *(Thrall)*, Bill Lawler *(Bjorn)*, Jesse Pearson *(Narrator)*, Fred Biletnikoff, David Kent, Frank Anderson, Curtis Jordan, Glen Hollis, John Welsh, Kevin Myers, Anthony Vitale, Cecil Kent, Steve Denny, Mike Kaminsky, Eric Crandall, Sandy Sanders, Ron Britt, Bob Hewlett, Gary Roy, Bill Twofeathers, Cyrus Strongshield, Mike Gallagher, Mike Rivera, Mike Vincent, Greg Rivera, Mark Wiles, Rick Merino, Wayne Harht, Joe Lopez.

A stodgy 11th-century drama, featuring Majors in the starring role. He portrays a Viking prince, who sets out across the Atlantic from his Greenland home in search of his father, the King. Accompanying him is his Viking horde, decked out in their best: furs, armor, and horned hats. They travel to North America, where Majors' father, Ferrer, and his party have been captured by Indians. With the help of a friendly Indian maiden, Coelho, they do find the king and his party, but their eyes have been gouged out. The Vikings engage in a few battles with the Indians (shot in a lot of gratuitous slow motion), and bring the prisoners back home.

p,d&w, Charles B. Pierce; ph, Robert Bethard (Panavision, Movielab Color); m, Jaime Mendoza-Nava; ed, Stephen Dunn, Shirak Kojayan, Aladar Klein, Sarah Legor, Robert Bell; set d, John Ball, Henry Peterson; cos, Bonney Langfitt.

Adventure **Cas.** **(PR:C MPAA:PG)**

NORTH AVENUE IRREGULARS, THE½** (1979) 99m Disney/BV c

Edward Herrmann *(Michael Hill)*, Barbara Harris *(Vickie)*, Susan Clark *(Anne)*, Karen Valentine *(Jane)*, Michael Constantine *(Marv)*, Cloris Leachman *(Claire)*, Patsy Kelly *(Rose)*, Douglas V. Fowley *(Delaney)*, Virginia Capers *(Cleo)*, Steve Franken *(Tom)*, Dena Dietrich *(Mrs. Carlisle)*, Dick Fuchs *(Howard)*, Herb Voland

(Dr. Fulton), Alan Hale, Jr. *(Harry the Hat)*, Melora Hardin *(Carmel)*, Bobby Rolofson *(Dean)*, Frank Campanella *(Max)*, Ivor Francis *(Rev. Wainwright)*, Louise Moritz *(Mrs. Gossin)*, Marjorie Bennett *(Mother Thurber)*, Ruth Buzzi *(Dr. Rheems)*, Ceil Cabot, Cliff Osmond, Carl Ballantine, Damon Bradley Raskin, Linda Lee Lyons, John Kerry, Dave Morick, Darrow Igus, Dennis Robertson, Ed McCready, Dave Ketchum, John Wheeler, David Rode, Mickey Morton, Pitt Herbert, Chuck Henry, Rickie Layne, Jack Perkins, Tom Pedi, Bill McLean, Roger Creed, Walt LaRue, Jack Griffin, Len Ross, Douglas Hume, Gary Morgan, Jack Cameron White, Michael Lloyd, Kim Bullard.

One of Disney's better efforts from the late 1970s, a poor time for Disney films. The story concerns Herrmann, a slightly clutzy and overly optimistic young priest who decides to delegate church authority to the women of his parish. He gives the church funds to Kelly, who invests the whole lot on a horse race. Of course she loses it, and Herrmann tries to get the money back from the bookie. Herrmann uncovers a huge ring of organized crime in the town, and bands the women together into a crime-fighting unit. The cast takes this routine story and helps turn it into an entertaining film, even for adults.

p, Ron Miller, Tom Leetch; d, Bruce Bilson; w, Don Tait (based on the book by Rev. Albert Fay Hill); ph, Leonard J. South (Technicolor); m, Robert F. Brunner; ed, Gordon D. Brenner; art d, John B. Mansbridge, Jack T. Collis; set d, Norman Rockett; cos, Chuck Keehne, Emily Sundby; spec eff, Eustace Lycett, Art Cruickshank, Danny Lee; m/l, Al Kasha, Joel Hirschhorn; stunts, Eddy Donno.

Comedy Cas. (PR:A MPAA:G)

NORTH BY NORTHWEST***** (1959) 136m MGM c

Cary Grant *(Roger Thornhill)*, Eva Marie Saint *(Eve Kendall)*, James Mason *(Phillip Vandamm)*, Jessie Royce Landis *(Clara Thornhill)*, Leo G. Carroll *(Professor)*, Philip Ober *(Lester Townsend)*, Josephine Hutchinson *(Handsome Woman)*, Martin Landau *(Leonard)*, Adam Williams *(Valerian)*, Edward Platt *(Victor Larrabee)*, Robert Ellenstein *(Licht)*, Les Tremayne *(Auctioneer)*, Philip Coolidge *(Dr. Cross)*, Patrick McVey, Ken Lynch *(Chicago Policemen)*, Edward Binns *(Capt. Junket)*, John Beradino *(Sgt. Emile Klinger)*, Nora Marlowe *(Anna the Housekeeper)*, Doreen Land *(Maggie)*, Alexander Lockwood *(Judge Anson B. Flynn)*, Stanley Adams *(Lt. Harding)*, Lawrence Dobkin *(Cartoonist)*, Harvey Stephens *(Stock Broker)*, Walter Coy *(Reporter)*, Madge Kennedy *(Housewife)*, Tommy Farrell *(Elevator Starter)*, Jimmy Cross, Baynes Barron *(Taxi Drivers)*, Harry Seymour *(Captain of Waiters)*, Frank Wilcox *(Weltner)*, Robert Shayne *(Larry Wade)*, Carleton Young *(Fanning Nelson)*, Ralph Reed *(Bellboy)*, Paul Genge *(Lt. Hagerman)*, Robert B. Williams *(Patrolman Waggonner at Glen Cove)*, Maudie Prickett *(Elsie the Maid)*, James McCallion *(Valet)*, Sally Fraser, Maura McGiveney, Susan Whitney *(Girl Attendants)*, Doris Singh *(Indian Girl)*, Ned Glass *(Ticket Agent)*, Howard Negley *(Conductor)*, Jesslyn Fax *(Woman)*, Jack Daly *(Steward)*, Tol Avery, Tom Greenway *(Detectives)*, Ernest Anderson *(Porter)*, Malcolm Atterbury *(Man on Road)*, Andy Albin *(Farmer)*, Carl Milletaire *(Clerk)*, John Damler, Len Hendry *(Police Lieutenants)*, Sara Berner *(Telephone Operator)*, Bobby Johnson *(Waiter)*, Taggart Casey *(Man with Razor)*, Bill Catching *(Attendant)*, Dale Van Sickel *(Ranger)*, Frank Marlowe *(Dakota Cab Driver)*, Harry Strang *(Assistant Conductor)*, Alfred Hitchcock *(Man Who Misses Bus)*, Olan Soule Cutts *(Assistant Auctioneer)*, Lucile Curtis, Sid Kane, Hugh Pryor, Charles Postal, Anne Anderson.

One of Hitchcock's best, NORTH BY NORTHWEST has everything—thrills, suspense, intrigue, mystery, humor, and no little comedy, black as a coal pit, of course, in keeping with the darkly whimsical perspective of that pantheon director. Grant, Saint, Mason, and Carroll are simply marvelous in their intricate roles, and, aside from Grant, it's hard to tell whether they're good or bad until the film has dragged the viewer feet-first into the complex plot. Peril of the common man or not-so-common man is always at the apex of any Hitchcock tale and this film is no exception. Grant is a successful advertising executive in New York City, Roger A. Thornhill, who amusingly has his personal matchbooks embossed with his initials "R.A.T." His wealthy mother, wonderfully played by Landis, indulges herself at every turn and thinks Grant's bachelor life is shallow, unimportant, and a waste, although she's no amateur at waste when it comes to shopping. Grant, two-times divorced, is having lunch with his mother at the Plaza when he answers the wrong page, one for a George Kaplan, and is suddenly mistaken for someone else, an identity he cannot shake and one that takes him into lethal hazard. He and his mother wind up investigating the mysterious Kaplan, going to Kaplan's room where they find several suits and other effects but no Kaplan. Grant answers the phone and is in even more trouble. As he leaves the floor by elevator with Landis, Grant boldly tells her that the two men standing behind him in the crowded elevator are trying to kidnap him. She smiles, then breaks into uncontrollable laughter, causing the two men, Williams and Ellenstein, to burst into laughter as do all the other passengers. Only Grant does not laugh and when they reach the lobby floor, he races out of the elevator with the two men on his tail. They overtake him and spirit him to the country home of Ober, where he is grilled by Landau, chief lieutenant to clever, erudite Russian spymaster Mason. He denies he is George Kaplan and Mason sneers that he is lying, that he has answered a page for Kaplan and even answered Kaplan's hotel room phone. Mason's minions force-feed Grant great quantities of liquor and then place him in a Mercedes convertible, sending him down a dangerous mountain road. He regains consciousness just as he is about to go off a cliff and, drunk as he is, manages to wildly steer the car to a halt, but not before wrecking it and sideswiping several cars and structures. Grant is arrested for drunken driving and thrown into jail. His mother arrives to bail him out and Landis continues denigrating her son in a wisecracking way, which makes the hungover Grant all the more miserable. The police and Landis accompany Grant to the Ober estate but none of the spies is present and Grant's mentality is questioned. He learns that the owner of the house, Ober, is a UN diplomat, and goes to the assembly, asking to see Ober. By then he has obtained a photo of Mason and shows this to Ober. The diplomat suddenly stares at the photo bug-eyed, gasping with wide open mouth. The he begins to fall forward and Grant clutches him, seeing he has a long knife driven into his back. Impulsively, Grant grabs the knife handle and yanks the blade free, letting Ober fall dead to the floor. He stands there, stupidly staring at the knife, in shock, as a news photographer rushes forward to take a photo of Grant holding the murder weapon. Grant flees, now realizing that he has been set up as a murderer, as well as a homicidal drunk. He goes to Grand Central Station, slipping on board a train bound for Chicago, barging in on Saint who allows him to hide in her stateroom as detectives comb the train for him. She adroitly lies to a detective when he enters her compartment to ask if she's seen Grant. Later, Grant and Saint form a friendly alliance which develops into romance. Upon their arrival in Chicago, the couple slip past detectives with Grant impersonating a porter. He changes his clothes in the men's room and later goes to the Ambassador East Hotel where Saint is staying. He asks Saint if he can clean up in her room and also sends his suit to be pressed. Inside the bathroom, he turns on the shower, whistles "I'm Singin' in the Rain," but keeps the door ajar so that he can hear Saint talking to Mason, the spymaster who had him abducted in the first place. Now that he knows Saint is involved somehow in the plot, he persuades her to help him find the secret agent named Kaplan. Saint tells him to go to a rendezvous in northern Indiana and he arrives there by bus. When the bus pulls away, Grant finds himself at a deserted crossroads without a soul in sight. He stands there waiting for Kaplan to show up but instead a car arrives and a man, Atterbury, gets out, but he stands on the opposite side of the road without making a move toward Grant. The man stares at Grant who tries to start a conversation, thinking he is Kaplan. But the man tells him he's only waiting for the bus. The man squints skyward and says to Grant, "That's funny." Peeved, Grant replies: "What is?" He follows the man's skyward gaze to see a double-winged airplane skooting at low-level, leaving a trail of smoke. "That plane's dustin' crops where there ain't no crops," the man says. The bus arrives and the man gets on and Grant is left standing alone once more. Then the plane turns and starts right for him as he watches disbelieving. The plane is almost at ground level and roaring forward when Grant instinctively begins to run as the plane swoops downward, its wheels almost touching the ground, machinegun fire spitting at him, chewing up the ground around him. Grant drops flat as the plane roars past him. He guts up and runs into a cornfield as the plane circles and, making another pass over him, begins to spray the entire area with lethal fumes. Grant plunges through the corn, hiding beneath the tall stalks. He then crosses an open field and the plane is fast behind him, catching up, spraying the field with bullets that miraculously miss Grant. As he flops downward, the plane, only a few feet above the ground, cannot pull upward and slams into a gas truck, causing a terrific explosion. Grant manages to escape along with the truck drivers but the pilot is roasted to death. Several drivers have stopped their cars to gape in shock at the inferno and Grant, having had enough of this game, jumps into a vacated pickup truck and races off with the owner running behind him, screaming for him to stop. Grant abandons the pickup truck in Chicago and trails Saint to an antique auction where he finds her with Mason. When he charges her with setting him up, Saint annoyingly turns to Mason who motions to his goons to close in on Grant, telling the victimized advertising executive that his hours are numbered. Seeing no way to escape, Grant decides to make a scene and begins bidding ridiculous amounts for the priceless objects, which turns the austere auction into a shambles. Grant is so obnoxious and preposterous toward the auctioneer and fellow bidders that police are called, which is exactly what he has hoped for. He is taken outside and put into a squad. While driving to headquarters, he identifies himself and the sergeant receives special instructions on the radiophone to take Grant to the airport. Here he meets American spymaster Carroll who tells him that Saint had no other choice but to set him up and pretend she was betraying him since she is an American agent trying to get the goods on Mason, a Russian agent who is smuggling important information out of the country in an upcoming trip. It's Saint's job to find out what that information is. Carroll futher explains that Saint's life is now in danger and he asks that Grant help save her by pretending to be the American agent Kaplan, a man who never existed at all, one created by Carroll's group to hoodwink Mason and his people. Grant lambastes Carroll for putting Saint in jeopardy but agrees to help anyway. They fly to Mt. Rushmore Memorial in South Dakota where Mason has a mountaintop retreat. In the crowded restaurant of the main resort the next day, Grant approaches Saint who is with Mason and other henchmen. Saint suddenly pulls out a gun and shoots Grant several times and he topples to the floor. He is instantly pronounced dead and taken out while Saint is hustled from the scene by Mason. Now Mason is convinced that she is loyal to him and that she must leave the country with him, which is what Saint wants so she can obtain the information Mason is taking with him. Of course the shooting is a ruse; Grant is perfectly all right but is held in a hospital incommunicado by Carroll to keep him out of trouble. He nevertheless escapes, believing that Carroll intends to sacrifice Saint for the top-secret information. Grant makes his way to Mason's retreat and manages to climb into a bedroom. He slips into a corridor which has a balcony overlooking a large living room to see Saint, Mason, and chief henchman Landau talking about the plane that is coming to pick them up. When Mason and Landau aren't looking, Grant tosses one of his monogrammed matchbooks down, so that it lands at Saint's feet. Inside he has written a message that he is upstairs. Saint picks it up, reads the note, and excuses herself to powder her nose. Qucikly, she huddles with Grant, telling him that he's about to foul everything up, that he is to leave her alone so she can complete her mission. While she is really powdering her nose Grant peeks over the balcony to see Landau and Mason arguing, Landau finally insulting Mason so that the spymaster, enraged, grabs a gun, the same one used by Saint to shoot Grant, and fires several shots into Landau who falls backward, then gets up with a sinister smile on his face. Mason looks at the gun with a stunned expression and then Landau tells him that it is loaded with blanks which he had earlier discovered and took such dramatic license as a way of proving to Mason that his girl friend Saint is a double agent. Now Mason realizes that he must rid himself of her and suggests that she be shoved out of the airplane when it reaches a great height. Saint appears and the trio leaves to take the plane which has just landed at a nearby field. Grant, knowing she is about to be killed, races downstairs to follow them, only to be stopped by the beefy housekeeper who holds a gun on him and tells him he is staying right where he is until Mason and company are safely away. But just as Saint is about to get on the plane with Mason, Grant arrives driving a car and shouts for her to grab the antique idol Mason had purchased at the Chicago auction and join him. Saint takes the figurine out of Mason's hands and dashes to the car and she and Grant speed away with Mason and henchmen in pursuit. Grant explains to Saint as they speed away that it took him some time to realize that the overweight housekeeper was holding him at bay with "that same silly little gun of yours," the one with the blanks, and he had quickly dispatched the housekeeper. They drive to a dead end, then get out and race through the woods, coming to a sheer cliff. "This is no good," Grant tells Saint. "We're on the monument." They stand, nowhere to go, on the bald cliff which bears the distinguished giant faces of Washington, Lincoln, Theodore Roosevelt, and Jefferson carved out of the side of the mountain. Mason's people are fast approaching and Grant and Saint take the only course left open to them. They slide down the face of the monument, almost falling as they work their way along the narrow ledges. Grant is grabbed by Williams as he turns a crevice and they struggle, with Grant sending Williams over the edge to his screaming death. When Grant turns around he finds that Landau is holding Saint and they are fighting over the precious figurine. Landau tears it out of Saint's hands and pushes her over the ledge but she manages to grab a lower ledge and hang on while Grant inches his way to her, reaching down with one hand to grasp hers, then reaching to an upper ledge. He cannot pull himself up and then sees Landau standing above him. He begs for help and Landau responds by stepping on Grant's fingers, smashing them. Grant winces in pain but will not let go of the ledge. He and Saint are about to slip away to their doom when a shot rings out. Landau's maniacal smile changes into an expression of pain and shock. He begins to fall sideways, the figurine dropping from his grasp to smash on the ledge and reveal a small strip of microfilm, the reason for the whole incredible adventure, and then Landau silently collapses, falling into oblivion. High above the monument Carroll and police have Mason in custody. The disgusted spymaster sees Landau being shot and tells Carroll, "Not very sporting of you." Grant, meanwhile, reaches downward to Saint who tells him she cannot make it and he tells her she can. There is a quick cut to show Grant pulling Saint not up to the safety of the ledge but into an upper berth of a Pullman car stateroom. They are married. Says the pajama-clad Saint:"This is silly." Grant responds by embracing and kissing her. The train is then shown speeding away, carrying its now secure passengers to a happy life. Of all of Hitchcock's tricky thrillers, NORTH BY NORTHWEST is one of the trickiest, with a new and mostly unexpected twist at every turn. Here the great suspense director went to the zenith of his imagination in creating a nonstop action film where the hero can meet an ugly fate from frame to frame. Though Lehman wrote the script, Hitchcock rewrote it verbally with the screenwriter through many months of wild mental imaginings. The director once stated (in Jay Robert Nash's *The Innovators*): "NORTH BY NORTHWEST" didn't end on Mt. Rushmore in one version. We got up into Siberia nearly with it, Ernie Lehman and I. I remember I had a sequence where the girl is kidnaped. They get her across the straits and they're going along a road in Siberia in an open car and a helicopter from the Alaskan side is chasing the car with a rope hanging from it and they were saying to the girl 'Grab the rope!' And she's rescued from the car but the heavies try to grab her back...it was the most daring rescue you've ever seen." This scene was never included in the film, nor were many other scenes the director wanted desperately to make. "I remember one scene I wanted. I said: 'Can't we work it in somehow? We ought to have a scene showing a vast plain of ice and two little black figures walking towards each other...enemies or something.' I don't know what would have happened when they got together...they are going along and there is a hole in the ice, and, suddenly, a hand comes out of the hole. You've got to go wild and then tone it down. Where would the hand come from? I don't know. That's what you have to work out afterwards....That's the hard work. Get the idea, which is a startling thing, then you've got to say how you came by that. You shock 'em first and explain later. That's the power of technique." The title of the film stems from a line appearing in "Hamlet," Act II, Scene 2, when Hamlet states to Rosenkrantz and Guildenstern: "I am but mad north-north-west; when the wind is southerly I know a hawk from a handsaw." Hitchcock's tongue-in-cheek idea here was that neither he nor the tragic Hamlet were mad, although some of the scenes of NORTH BY NORTHWEST suggest madness in the filmic finite, such as the terrifying seven minutes in which Grant is strafed and pursued by an unseen, maniacal crop-dusting pilot. And the great director even makes lighthearted fun of his common man victim, Grant, or rather, has Grant himself emphasize his own peril by mocking it. As he is dragged from the auction, he passes one of Mason's sinister minions and remarks: "I'm sorry, old boy, keep trying." Earlier he tells Saint in a wry and ironic comment that "My wives divorced me. They said I led too dull a life." Hitchcock considered, according to one report, the film to be "one big joke," and was later quoted as saying that "when Cary Grant was on Mt. Rushmore I would have liked to put him into Lincoln's nostril and let him have a sneezing fit." The impressive Mt. Rushmore scene was actually done on a gigantic MGM set accomplished by Hitchcock with the Schufftan process. Hitchcock supervised every technical aspect of the film which gives it that extremely smooth, glossy look, although he later claimed that he intended no specially designed Freudian images except one (as quoted in *Cahiers du Cinema*, No. 102): "There are no symbols in NORTH BY NORTHWEST. Oh yes! One. The last shot. The train entering the tunnel after the love scene between Grant and Eva Marie Saint. It's a phallic symbol but don't tell anyone." Hitchcock had been put under contract by MGM to direct THE WRECK OF THE MARY DEARE (1959). He worked a month on trying to produce a script with Lehman and then got bored and gave up. (The film was later directed by Michael Anderson.) The director kept talking about making a film in which the hero is chased across the faces on Mt. Rushmore and he later stated: "Now it so happened that a New York journalist had given me an idea about an ordinary businessman being mistaken for a decoy spy. I took that and, with Ernie Lehman, worked up the whole thing. It took about a year to write." Although almost all of NORTH BY

NORTHWEST seems fresh and original and the script sparkles with witty and humorous dialog, there is much that is reminiscent of THE 39 STEPS and SABOTEUR, two earlier superlative Hitchcock vehicles where the victim is accused of murdering someone and gets mistaken as a spy. SABOTEUR fits the mold more aptly; Robert Cummings in that film—a factory worker accused of sabotaging an airplane factory—must traverse America, as Grant does in NORTH BY NORTHWEST, only he ends up on top of another great American monument, The Statue of Liberty, fighting for his life. But it's the bad guy, Norman Lloyd, in that film, who dangles in mid-air. Hitchcock received a $4 million budget for this film and a personal salary of $250,000 with 10% of the gross over $8 million (the film went on to earn $6.5 million in its initial release, but added another $14 million in rereleases). Grant, who is wonderful as the suave but utterly trapped victim, received $450,000 for his performance plus whopping weekly overtime payments. He had appeared in three other Hitchcock films (SUSPICION, NOTORIOUS, and TO CATCH A THIEF) and this would be his last film with the great director of suspense. So familiar with each other were actor and director that Hitchcock hardly directed Grant at all and often took the actor's suggestions about angles and setups. Saint was a Hitchcock creation, another cool, aloof blonde (one of the best of this type, far superior to Tippie Hedren and Kim Novak) whom he transformed from "the mousey" type seen in ON THE WATERFRONT to a sleek, sexy, and sophisticated woman, selecting every bit of Saint's wardrobe for her. The supporting cast is superb, with Mason as the introspective but ruthless spymaster and Landau, Williams, and Ellenstein doing journeyman work as a trio of despicable villains. Landis is a standout as Grant's capricious mother and Carroll is convincing as the world-weary American chief of intelligence (this was Carroll's sixth film with Hitchcock, certainly a record; the previous five included REBECCA, SUSPICION, SPELLBOUND, THE PARADINE CASE, and STRANGERS ON A TRAIN). Herrmann's score is full of the same kind of insouciance and brightness that permeates the rest of the production credits of this stellar classic.

p&d, Alfred Hitchcock; w, Ernest Lehman; ph, Robert Burks (VistaVision, Technicolor); m, Bernard Herrmann; ed, George Tomosini; prod d, Robert Boyle; art d, William A. Horning, Merrill Pye; set d, Boyle, Henry Grace, Frank McKelvey; spec eff, A. Arnold Gillespie, Lee le Blanc; makeup, William Tuttle.

Spy Drama **Cas.** **(PR:A MPAA:NR)**

NORTH DALLAS FORTY***½ (1979) 119m PAR c

Nick Nolte (*Phillip Elliott*), Mac Davis (*Maxwell*), Charles Durning (*Coach Johnson*), Dayle Haddon (*Charlotte*), Bo Svenson (*Jo Bob Priddy*), Steve Forrest (*Conrad Hunter*), G.D. Spradlin (*B.A. Strothers*), Dabney Coleman (*Emmett*), Savannah Smith (*Joanne*), Marshall Colt (*Art Hartman*), Guich Koock (*Eddie Rand*), Deborah Benson (*Mrs. Hartman*), James F. Boeke (*Stallings*), John Bottoms (*VIP*), Walter Brooke (*Doctor*), Carlos Brown (*Balford*), Danny J. Bunz (*Tony Douglas*), Jane Daly (*Ruth*), Rad Daly (*Conrad, Jr.*), Cliff Frazier (*Monroe*), Stanley Grover (*March*), John Matuszak (*O.W. Shaddock*).

Fans of professional football are bound to be disillusioned by this excellent and often brutal satire of the game. It's simply one of the most honest pictures ever made about any sport where the players work for money. Nolte is a veteran pass-catcher for a club that resembles "America's Team"—The Dallas Cowboys. He is thought to have an attitude problem because he questions getting doped for pain before a game, and because he doesn't care to be part of "the family." His best friend is quarterback Davis (making an impressive film debut after a decade of picking and singing country ditties) and his girl friends are Haddon and Smith. The owner of the team, Forrest, and his coaches, Spradlin and Durning, demand obedience and conformity from their players, but Nolte feels he cannot knuckle under to their abusive leadership and resents the fact that there is no individuality allowed. The action off the field is far more interesting that what happens on the gridiron and the macho relationship between players is deeply limned to great advantage. The National Football League refused to help the production of this film in any way, so don't expect to see re-creations of games. The language is crude but feels right and the inside information about how it is in the locker room before and after the games smacks of authenticity. Producer Yablans co-wrote the screenplay, although we wonder how much he actually did when we also note that he co-wrote the screenplay for MOMMIE DEAREST. The picture made a great deal of money in the U.S. and deserved every penny. NORTH DALLAS FORTY makes its points without spiking the ball. Bo Svenson does a good job as a randy lineman. In real life, he is an excellent athlete and specializes in the European version of handball which is only seen in the U.S. during the TV broadcasts of the Olympics. Don't expect the baloney bravura of THE LONGEST YARD or the platitudes of NUMBER ONE. This is as close to the truth of how it is to play football as you may ever see.

p, Frank Yablans; d, Ted Kotcheff; w, Yablans, Kotcheff, Peter Gent (based on the novel by Gent); ph, Paul Lohmann (Panavision, Metrocolor); m, John Scott; ed, Jay Kamen; prod d, Alfred Sweeney; set d, Art Parker; cos, Dorothy Jeakins.

Sports/Drama **Cas.** **(PR:C-O MPAA:R)**

NORTH FROM LONE STAR** (1941) 58m COL bw

Bill Elliott (*Wild Bill Hickok*), Richard Fiske (*Clint Wilson*), Dorothy Fay (*Madge Wilson*), Dub Taylor (*Cannonball*), Arthur Loft (*Flash Kirby*), Jack Roper (*Rawhide Fenton*), Chuck Morrison (*Spike*), Claire Rochelle (*Lucy Belle*), Al Rhein (*Slats*), Edmund Cobb (*Dusty Daggett*), Art Mix, Steve Clark, Tex Cooper, Hank Bell, Dick Botiller.

Elliott takes on the job of sheriff so he can rid a frontier town of villain Fiske and his thugs, Loft and Roper. Fay and Rochelle compete for Elliott's affections. Comic relief is handled by Taylor, who appeared in 10 B westerns with Elliott. This film is one in a series for Columbia in which Elliott starred as Wild Bill Hickok. (See WILD BILL HICKOK series, Index.)

p, Leon Barsha; d, Lambert Hillyer; w, Charles Francis Royal; ph, Benjamin Kline; ed, Mel Thorsen.

Western **(PR:A MPAA:NR)**

NORTH OF NOME*½ (1937) 64m COL bw

Jack Holt *(John Raglan)*, Evelyn Venable *(Camilla)*, Guinn "Big Boy" Williams *(Haage)*, John Miljan *(Dawson)*, Roger Imhof *(Judge Bridle)*, Paul Hurst *(Carlson)*, Dorothy Appleby *(Ruby)*, Robert Gleckler *(Bruno)*, Ben Hendricks *(Grail)*, Frank McGlynn, Sr. *(Marshall)*, Mike Morita, George Cleveland, Blackhawk.

An average Holt vehicle, which casts him as a seal hunter in Alaska. He hunts on a small rock-bound island off the coast that has been claimed by a large company. Holt unexpectedly becomes host to the owner of the company, Imhof, when he and his entourage get shipwrecked near the island. Many personality conflicts occur during the city folks' stay. When a scuffle breaks out between Holt and Miljan, Venable, who has become sweet on Holt, is shot in the shoulder. Holt decides to signal a passing boat, so that Venable and the rest of the party can be rescued. Holt discovers, to his horror, that the captain of the boat, is Williams, a hijacker. At first, Holt gives his furs to Williams peacefully, but when the hijacker hits Imhof, Holt gets angered and takes control of the boat.

p, Larry Darmour; d, William Nigh; w, Albert DeMond (based on a story by Houston Branch); ph, James S. Brown, Jr.; ed, Dwight Caldwell.

Western **(PR:A MPAA:NR)**

NORTH OF SHANGHAI*½ (1939) 59m COL bw

James Craig *(Jed Howard)*, Betty Furness *(Helen Warner)*, Keye Luke *(Jimmy Riley)*, Morgan Conway *(Bod Laird)*, Joseph Danning *(Chandler)*, Russell Hicks *(Rowley)*, Dorothy Gulliver *(Sue)*, Honorable Wu *(Ming)*.

A dull tale of a female reporter, Furness, and a newsreel cameraman, Craig, who are covering the Sino-Japanese war. Furness is on a forced vacation after exposing an important scandal stateside, and she meets Craig on a boat headed for the war zone. They meet Luke, a Chinese cameraman, who helps them uncover a gang of spies working in the Shanghai office of Furness' newspaper. War buffs will find plenty of action shots from newsreels of the time, including hand-to-hand fighting and air raids.

d, D. Ross Lederman; w, Maurice Rapf, Harold Buchman; ph, Franz Planer; ed, Al Clark.

War/Drama **(PR:A MPAA:NR)**

NORTH OF THE GREAT DIVIDE*½ (1950) 67m REP c

Roy Rogers *(Roy Rogers)*, Penny Edwards *(Ann Keith)*, Gordon Jones *(Splinters)*, Roy Barcroft *(Banning)*, Jack Lambert *(Stagg)*, Douglas Evans *(Sgt. Douglas)*, Keith Richards *(Dacona)*, Noble Johnson *(Nogura)*, Foy Willing and Riders of Purple Sage, Iron Eyes Cody, Trigger the Horse.

A below par Rogers vehicle with Roy playing an Indian agent in Canada trying to prevent hostilities between Oseka Indians and a salmon cannery. The cannery, owned by Barcroft, is overfishing the salmon before they can travel upstream to where the Indians are camped. As a result, the Indians are starving. Rogers sorts things out and has time to sing three Jack Elliott songs, "By the Laughing Spring," "Just Keep a' Movin'," and the title song. Republic was engaging in a little greediness (called "conservation program") at the time it was making this film about greed. To save money, former Rogers' love interest Dale Evans was replaced by Edwards, funnyman sidekick Gabby Hayes was replaced by Jones, and the Riders of the Purple Sage took over the musical accompanying job from the Sons of the Pioneers.

p, Edward J. White; d, William Witney; w, Eric Taylor; ph, Jack Marta (Trucolor); m, Jack Elliott; ed, Tony Martinelli.

Western **Cas.** **(PR:A MPAA:NR)**

NORTH OF THE RIO GRANDE** (1937) 70m PAR bw

William Boyd *(Hopalong Cassidy)*, George Hayes *(Windy)*, Russell Hayden *(Lucky Jenkins)*, Stephen Morris *(Henry Stoneham/Lone Wolf)*, Bernadene Hayes *(Faro Annie)*, John Rutherford *(Crowder)*, Lorraine Randall *(Mary Cassidy)*, Walter Long *(Bull)*, Lee [J.] Cobb *(Goodwin)*, John Beach *(Clark)*, Al Ferguson *(Plunkett)*, Lafe McKee *(Joe)*.

Above average B western has Boyd, in the 11th entry in the Hopalong Cassidy series, on the trail of the people responsible for the murder of his brother. To catch them he makes himself appear as a man wanted by the law. Versatile character actor Lee J. Cobb made his first screen appearance in this horse opera. (See HOPALONG CASSIDY series, Index.)

p, Harry Sherman; d, Nate Watt; w, Jack O'Donnell (based on the story "Cottonwood Gulch" by Clarence E. Mulford); ph, Russell Harlan; ed, Robert Warwick; art d, Lewis Rachmil.

Western **(PR:A MPAA:NR)**

NORTH OF THE YUKON** (1939) 62m COL bw

Charles Starrett *(Jim Cameron)*, Linda Winters [Dorothy Comingore] *(Jean Duncan)*, Bob Nolan *(Bob Cameron)*, Paul Sutton *(Pierre Ledoux)*, Robert Fiske *(Mart Duncan)*, Vernon Steele *(Inspector Wylie)*, Edmund Cobb *(Cpl. Hawley)*, Tom London *(Carter)*, Lane Chandler *(Atkins)*, Richard Botiller *(Barton)*, Kenne Duncan *(Meeker)*, Harry Cording *(MacGregor)*, Hal Taliaferro, Ed Brady, Sons of the Pioneers.

Starrett is a Canadian Mountie on the trail of some fur thieves, and to crack the gang, his superiors pretend to have drummed him out of the Mounties and forced him to run the gauntlet of fellow Mountie's whips. When the gang invites him to their secret hideout to persuade him to join them, Starrett rescues the girl and tips off his fellow Mounties on the location of the hideout. Songs are provided by Sons of the Pioneers. The title of NORTH OF THE YUKON during shooting was NORTHWEST MOUNTED and all the advertising material was prepared that way. It is believed that Cecil B. DeMille had a hand in getting the title changed, perhaps to cover up the fact that the story is no more than a reworking of the Buck Jones drummed-from-the-service story used in BORDER LAW, THE FIGHTING RANGER, BORDER BRIGANDS, and LAW OF THE TEXAN.

d, Sam Nelson; w, Bennett R. Cohen; ph, George Meehan; m, Bob Nolan; ed, William Lyon; md, M.W. Stoloff; m/l, Bob Nolan.

Western **Cas.** **(PR:A MPAA:NR)**

NORTH SEA HIJACK (SEE: FFOLKES, 1979, Brit.)

NORTH SEA PATROL* (1939, Brit.) 64m Alliance bw (GB: LUCK OF THE NAVY)

Geoffrey Toone *(Cmdr. Clive Stanton)*, Judy Kelly *(Cynthia Maybridge)*, Clifford Evans *(Lt. Peel)*, John Wood *(Sub. Lt. Wing Eden)*, Albert Burdon *(Noakes)*, Alf Goddard *(Tomkins)*, Henry Oscar *(Cmdr. Perrin)*, Edmund Breon *(Adm. Maybridge)*, Doris Hare *(Mrs. Maybridge)*, Daphne Raglan *(Dora Maybridge)*, Kenneth Kent *(Col. Suvaroff)*, Marguerite Allen *(Anna Suvaroff)*, Olga Lindo *(Mrs. Rance)*, Leslie Perrins *(Briggs)*, Frank Fox *(Francois)*, Diana Beaumont *(Millie)*, Joan Fred Emney *(Cook)*, Laurence Kitchin *(Crump)*, Nigel Stock, Michael Ripper, Doris Hare, Carla Lehmann.

A strikingly poor British film made just before the outbreak of WW II but released soon after it began. Enemy spies plot to land an army on British shores and pose as house servants to an admiral to steal his secret orders. A derring-do naval commander and the admiral's daughter save the navy and the empire with a series of incredible and unbelievable acts. Stock company performances are a discredit to old-time director Lee, who, amazingly, once ran an acting school.

p, Walter C. Mycroft; d, Norman Lee; w, Clifford Grey (based on the play "Luck of the Navy" by Mrs. Clifford Mills); ph, Walter Harvey; ed, Walter Stokvis.

Spy **(PR:A MPAA:NR)**

NORTH STAR, THE½** (1943) 105m Goldwyn/RKO bw (AKA: ARMORED ATTACK!)

Anne Baxter *(Marina)*, Farley Granger *(Damian)*, Jane Withers *(Claudia)*, Eric Roberts *(Grisha)*, Dana Andrews *(Kolya)*, Walter Brennan *(Karp)*, Dean Jagger *(Rodion)*, Ann Harding *(Sophia)*, Carl Benton Reid *(Boris)*, Ann Carter *(Olga)*, Walter Huston *(Dr. Kurin)*, Erich von Stroheim *(Dr. Otto von Harden)*, Esther Dale *(Anna)*, Ruth Nelson *(Nadya)*, Paul Guilfoyle *(Iakin)*, Martin Kosleck *(Dr. Max Richter)*, Tonio Selwart *(German Captain)*, Peter Pohlenz *(German Lieutenant)*, Gene O'Donnell *(Russian Gunner)*, Robert Lowery *(Russian Pilot)*, Frank Wilcox *(Petrov)*, Charles Bates *(Petya)*, George Lynn *(German Pilot)*, Minna Phillips *(Old Lady in Wagon)*, Edmund Cobb *(Farmer)*, Bill Walker, Clarence Straight *(Young Men in Wagon)*, Jerry Mickelson *(Farmer's Son)*, Grace Cunard *(Farmer's Wife)*, Martin Faust, Jack Perrin, Bill Nestell, Al Ferguson, Henry Hall, John Judd *(Farmers)*, Bill Borzage *(Accordian Player in Wagon)*, Emma Dunn, Sarah Padden *(Old Ladies)*, Teddy Infuhr *(Little Stinker)*, Grace Leonard *(Woman on Bridge)*, Loudie Claar *(Woman on Hospital Cot)*, Lynne Winthrop *(Guerrilla Girl)*, Joyce Tucker *(Little Girl in Hospital)*, John Bagni *(Guard at Desk)*, John Beverly *(Orderly)*, Ferdinand Schumann-Heink *(Doctor's Assistant)*, Patricia Parks *(Sonya)*, Frederick Brunn, Ray Teal *(German Motorcycle Officers)*, Crane Whitney *(German Soldier)*, Lane Chandler, Harry Strang *(Guerrillas)*, Serge Protzenko, Ilia Khmara *(Accordion Players)*, Constant Franke *(Boris' Aide)*, Florence Auer *(Woman Farmer)*, Tommy Hall, Ronn Harvin, George Kole, Jack Vlaskin, William Sabbot, Clair Freeman, Eric Braunsteiner, Tamara Laub, Marie Vlaskin, Inna Gest *(Specialty Dancers)*, Art Baker *(Radio Voice)*.

During WW II, President Franklin Delano Roosevelt called upon the American film industry to pay tribute to America's Russian allies who were valiantly fighting their Nazi invaders. Roosevelt's son, James, was the president of Samuel Goldwyn Studios at the time and Goldwyn decided he would be the first filmmaker to heed the President's call. He enlisted playwright Lillian Hellman to write the script and intended to have it directed by William Wyler and photographed by Gregg Toland. Wyler, though, went into the service after completing MRS. MINIVER and director Milestone was hired, bringing cinematographer James Wong Howe with him to make the picture. The story concerned one Ukrainian collective farm village, The North Star, and its reaction when the Germans invade. Baxter, her boy friend Granger, her pilot brother Andrews, and friends Withers and Roberts are on their way to the big city of Kiev, catching a ride on Brennan's wagon, when Stuka dive bombers plunge down on the wagon train, strafing it. Baxter and her contingent manage to escape and head back to their village as fast as they can. Meanwhile, at the village, the men are preparing to take to the hills to fight a guerrilla war against the invaders, while doctor Huston organizes the destruction of the village, burning anything that might be of use to the enemy. Before the flames can claim everything, though, the Germans arrive and quickly put out the fires. Trying to discover where the men have gone, the Nazis torture Harding. Her arms and legs are broken and she is left to crawl home. The children of the village are rounded up and forcibly drained of some of their blood to provide transfusions for wounded Germans by doctor Von Stroheim. One child dies after too much blood is taken and Huston, horrified at the atrocities, goes into the hills where the guerrillas are hiding and persuades them to attack. He returns to the village and confronts Von Stroheim, who tells him that he hates the Nazis but is just following orders. Huston tells him this makes him worse than his superiors and, as the partisans begin their attack, Huston pulls out a pistol and shoots the doctor. Although casualties are heavy among the villagers, the occupiers are destroyed and the surviving Soviets join the exodus toward the west, preparing for the long struggle to free Mother Russia. Originally Teresa Wright had been scheduled to star, but she became ill and was replaced by Baxter. Her romantic interest, Granger—18 years old at the time—here has his first starring role. Goldwyn discovered the young actor through an advertisement in a newspaper. The film, while certainly competent and reasonably entertaining, does come off too obviously as propaganda. Screenwriter Hellman was quite upset when she saw what had happened to her script and in later years called the film "...a big-time, sentimental, badly directed, badly acted mess." Most of the reviews were positive (after all, you can hardly pan a film the president of the United States has asked to be made), although the Hearst papers, after printing about a million copies of a good review of the film, stopped the presses on orders from above and replaced the review with one calling the film Bolshevik propaganda and suggesting the film had been backed by Stalin. At the height of the McCarthy witch-hunts of the 1950s, the filmmakers were called before the House Un-American Activities Committee to explain their reasons for making the film. In 1957 the film was re-edited, with 22 minutes cut out, including most of the character development and every mention of the word "comrade". A spokesman from NTA, the company that released this politically corrected version under the title ARMORED ATTACK! said "The only thing we couldn't take out was Dana Andrews running around in a damn Soviet uniform."

p, William Cameron Menzies; d, Lewis Milestone; w, Lillian Hellman (based on a story by Hellman); ph, James Wong Howe; m, Aaron Copland; ed, Daniel Mandell; art d, Perry Ferguson, McClure Capps; set d, Howard Bristol; spec eff, R.O. Binger, Clarence Slifer; ch, David Lichine; m/l, "Song of the Guerrillas," "No Village Like Mine," "Younger Generation," Copland, Ira Gershwin.

War　　　　　　　　**Cas.**　　　　　　　　**(PR:A-C MPAA:NR)**

NORTH STAR, THE**　　　(1982, Fr.) 120m Sara-Antenne 2/Parafrance c
(L'ETOILE DU NORD)

Philippe Noiret (Edouard Binet), Simone Signoret (Mrs. Baron), Fanny Cottencon (Sylvie Baron), Julie Jezequel (Antoinette Baron), Jean Rougerie (Mons. Baron), Jean-Pierre Klein (Moise), Jean-Yves Chatelais (Valesco).

A poor adaptation of the prolific Belgian writer Georges Simenon's novel *The Tenant*, written in 1934. Noiret, a penniless Turkish Jew, is traveling with a Belgian girl, Cottencon, whom he met in the Near East. Noiret robs and murders a diamond merchant on a train to Paris and Cottencon takes him to Charleroi, where her mother runs a boarding house. Signoret is drawn to the man by his stories of his country and its customs, and Noiret, lulled into a sense of safety by her attentions, grows careless and allows himself to be captured by the police. Signoret makes a long journey to La Rochelle to see him shipped off to a penal colony and after a regretfully skimpy emotional scene Noiret vanishes. (In French.)

p, Alain Sarde; d, Pierre Granier-Deferre, w, Granier-Deferre, Jean Aurenche, Michel Grisolia (based on the novel *The Tenant* by Georges Simenon); ph, Pierre-William Glenn (Fujicolor); m, Philippe Sarde; ed, Jean Ravel; art d, Dominique Andre; cos, Catherine Leterrier.

Drama　　　　　　　　　　　　　　**(PR:C MPAA:NR)**

NORTH TO ALASKA***½　　　(1960) 122m FOX c

John Wayne (Sam McCord), Stewart Granger (George Pratt), Ernie Kovacs (Frankie Canon), Fabian (Billy Pratt), Capucine (Michelle "Angel"), Mickey Shaughnessy (Peter Boggs), Karl Swenson (Lars Nordquist), Joe Sawyer (Land Commissioner), Kathleen Freeman (Lena Nordquist), John Qualen (Logger), Stanley Adams (Breezy), Stephen Courtleigh (Duggan), Douglas Dick (Lieutenant), Jerry O'Sullivan (Sergeant), Ollie O'Toole (Mack), Tudor Owen (Boat Captain), Lilyan Chauvin (Jenny Lamont), Marcel Hillaire (Jenny's Husband, Butler), Richard Deacon (Angus, Desk Clerk), James Griffith (Salvationist), Max Hellinger (Bish the Waiter), Richard Collier (Skinny Sourdough), Esther Dale (Woman at Picnic), Fortune Gordien, Roy Jensen (Loggers), Charles Seel, Rayford Barnes (Gold Buyers), Fred Graham (Ole), Alan Carney (Bartender with Hat), Peter Bourne (Olaf), Tom Dillon (Barber), Arlene Harris (Queen Lil), Frank Faylen (Arnie), Kermit Maynard (Townsman), Joey Faye (Sourdough), Oscar Beregi (Captain), Pamela Raymond (Pony Dancer), Maurice Delamore (Bartender), Patty Wharton (Specialty Dancer), Johnny Lee (Coachman), Tudor Owen (Purser), Paul Maxey, Hobo (Clancy the Dog).

After years of hinting at a fun-loving, broad sense of humor in his movies, Wayne pulls out all the stops and plays NORTH TO ALASKA strictly for laughs. It is a big, bruising, sprawling, western comedy which proved so successful for Wayne that he played many of his last roles in this endearing style of gentle self-parody. The film is set in north Alaska circa 1890 and sees Wayne, Granger, and Granger's kid brother, Fabian, partners in a gold mine. Having struck it rich, Wayne travels to Seattle to buy more machinery and retrieve Granger's French-born fiancee who was supposed to wait while they dug out a fortune. Granger has sent Wayne on the mission because he intends to stay at the mine site and put the finishing touches on the honeymoon cabin he has built for the occasion. Unfortunately, when Wayne locates the girl in Seattle it turns out she is married to another man. Dreading having to return to Alaska with the bad news, Wayne visits a Seattle brothel to console himself with drink and women. There he meets another young French girl, Capucine, and figures that one French girl is as good as another and decides to bring her back with him as a replacement. Capucine likes Wayne and thinks that he is bringing her to Alaska to make her his bride, not Granger's. Meanwhile, oily con man Kovacs (whom Wayne had run into before he left) has slyly befriended Granger and Fabian with an eye toward their gold mine. Such is the trust between Kovacs and Granger that Granger buys a "diamond" ring from the trickster as a wedding present to his bride (of course it is fake). On the ship back to Alaska Capucine is dismayed to learn that Wayne intends to marry her off to his partner and not himself. Beside himself, because the girl is upset, Wayne tries to offer her money for wasting her time, but she throws the cash overboard. Back home, Wayne gets a room for Capucine in a hotel now owned by the wily Kovacs, while he returns to the mine. As it turns out, Kovacs and Capucine used to be lovers, and now the delighted con man wants to revive the relationship so that she can help him steal Wayne and Granger's mine. Eventually Capucine makes her way to the mine, but while Wayne and Granger are away defending their spread against some

claim jumpers, she finds herself left alone with Fabian, who develops a quick crush on the woman. After defending herself from the adolescent advances of Fabian, Capucine is shocked when Granger, after learning the truth about his original fiancee, rejects her and condemns Wayne. Seeking to mend the bridges between the two friends, Capucine explains the whole situation to Granger and tells him that it is Wayne she truly loves. Snapping out of his doldrums, Granger devises a plan to make Wayne jealous enough to admit his attraction to Capucine. He pretends to have changed his mind about his "bride" and together they enter the honeymoon cabin, making sure Wayne is within earshot. They then make plenty of noise popping champagne corks and clinking glasses, the sounds of which begin to drive Wayne crazy. After several minutes Capucine gets discouraged (she can't see Wayne outside doing one of the longest "slow burns" in history), so Granger makes her laugh. Her giggles finally push Wayne over the edge and the big man lets out a blood-curdling yell while heading for the door of the honeymoon cabin. Before Wayne can break it down, Granger wisely opens the door, sending the Duke crashing across the room. Failing to understand what has just happened and feeling humiliated, Wayne packs his bags. Before he can leave, however, the soldiers arrive and impound the mine because a cross-claim on the land has been filed due to the insidious efforts of Kovacs. Wayne, Granger, Fabian, and Capucine are reunited in the battle to retain ownership of their land. The climax of the film sees the heroes catch up with Kovacs and start a huge, rollicking, and extremely funny fight in the streets of Nome with dozens of participants slugging it out in the mud. After finally having been snapped (beaten?) to his senses, Wayne tells Capucine he loves her and they kiss, much to the delight of the townsfolk. NORTH TO ALASKA is pure, unabashed Hollywood hokum done to perfection. The entire cast plays it with relish and seems to actually be having fun while doing it. Wayne is a joy to watch and the comic scene where he works up an insane jealousy over Capucine and Granger in the honeymoon cabin has become one of the beloved actor's quintessential screen moments. Kovacs, whose brilliant career was cut tragically short by his death in an auto accident in 1962, gives a wonderfully malevolent performance as the con man. A wholly enjoyable film.

p&d, Henry Hathaway; w, John Lee Mahin, Martin Rackin, Claude Binyon, (uncredited) Wendell Mayes (based on the play "Birthday Gift" by Laszlo Fodor and an idea by John Kafka); ph, Leon Shamroy (CinemaScope, DeLuxe Color); m, Lionel Newman; ed, Dorothy Spencer; md, Newman; art d, Duncan Cramer, Jack Martin Smith; set d, Walter M. Scott, Stuart A. Reiss; cos, Bill Thomas; spec eff, L.B. Abbott, Emil Kosa, Jr.; ch, Josephine Earl; m/l, "If You Knew" Russell Faith, Robert P. Marcucci, Peter DeAngelis (sung by Fabian); makeup, Ben Nye.

Western　　　　　　　　　　　　**(PR:A MPAA:NR)**

NORTH TO THE KLONDIKE**　　　(1942) 58m UNIV bw

Broderick Crawford (John Thorn), Evelyn Ankers (Mary Sloan), Andy Devine (Klondike), Lon Chaney, Jr. (Nate Carson), Lloyd Corrigan (Dr. Curtis), Willie Fung (Waterlily), Keye Luke (Wellington Wong), Stanley Andrews (Jim Allen), Dorothy Granger (Mayme Cassidy), Monte Blue (Burke), Roy Harris (Ben Sloan), Jeff Corey (Man), Paul Dubov, Fred Cordova.

Chaney, Jr., is hellbent on driving a bunch of farmers off their land so he can mine the fertile area for gold in this cold tale set in Alaska. Aside from a thrilling canoe ride through the rapids and a bangup fist fight at the end between good guy Crawford and bad guy Chaney, this one stacks up as only an average actioner.

p, Paul Malvern; d, Erle C. Kenton; w, Clarence Upson Young, Lou Sarecky, George Bricker (based on a story by William Castle from the short story "Gold Hunters of the North" by Jack London); ph, Charles Van Enger; ed, Ted Kent.

Western　　　　　　　　　　　　**(PR:A MPAA:NR)**

NORTH WEST FRONTIER　　　(SEE: FLAME OVER INDIA, 1960, Brit.)

NORTHERN FRONTIER**　　　(1935) 56m Ambassador bw

Kermit Maynard (MacKenzie), Eleanor Hunt (Beth Braden), Russell Hopton (Duke Milford), J. Farrell MacDonald (Inspector Stevens), LeRoy Mason (Bull Stone), Ben Hendricks, Jr. (Sam Keene), Gertrude Astor (Mae), Walter Brennan, Dick Curtis, Kernan Cripps, Jack Chisholm, Lloyd Ingraham, Lafe McKee, Tyrone Power, Artie Ortego, Charles King, Rocky the Horse.

Kermit rides a second time with the Northwest Mounties in this outdoor adventure as he is given the unenviable task of having to join a group of gangsters incognito to get enough evidence to put them behind bars. He goes up against machine guns and outwits them with hard riding, the old stunts of his cowboy pictures, and a cowboy air that is less Mountie than western sheriff. An early outing for Brennan and Power, before they climbed into the big time.

p, Maurice Conn; d, Sam Newfield; w, Barry Barringer (based on the story "Four Minutes Late" by James Oliver Curwood); ph, Edgar Lyons; ed, Jack English.

Western　　　　　　　　　　　　**(PR:A MPAA:NR)**

NORTHERN LIGHTS**½　　　(1978) 90m Cine Manifest bw

Robert Behling (Ray Sorenson), Susan Lynch (Inga Olsness), Joe Spano (John Sorenson), Marianne Astrom-De Fina (Kari), Ray Ness (Henrik Sorenson), Helen Ness (Jenny Sorenson), Thorbjorn Rue (Thor), Nick Eldridge (Sven), Jon Ness (Howard), Gary Hanisch (Charlie Forsythe), Melvin Rodvold (Ole Olsness), Adelaide Thornveit (Adelaide Olsness), Mabel Rue (Grandma), Krist Toresen (Krist), Bill Ackeridge, Gordon Smaaladen, Harold Aleshire, Don DeFina, Henry Martinson.

Black-and-white film whose stark images leave an indelible impression on the mind. Set in the harsh land of North Dakota in 1915, it follows the fight to live of a Scandinavian couple. Not only do they have to battle weather, but foreclosing banks and indifferent politicians as they fight for their land and for the Nonpartisan League, formed to protect farmers' rights. Artistically done, but too slow-paced for most viewers. The film is subtitled when the characters speak Scandinavian.

p,d&w, John Hanson, Rob Nilsson; ph, Judy Irola; m, David Ozzie Ahlers; ed, Hanson, Nilsson; prod d, Marianne Astrom-De Fina; art d, Richard Brown.

Drama **(PR:A MPAA:NR)**

NORTHERN PATROL* (1953) 62m AA bw

Kirby Grant *(Cpl. Rod Webb)*, Marion Carr *(Quebec Kid)*, Bill Phipps *(Frank Stevens)*, Claudia Drake *(Oweena)*, Dale Van Sickel *(Jason)*, Gloria Talbot *(Meg Stevens)*, Richard Walsh *(Ralph Gregg)*, Emmett Lynn *(Old Timer)*, Frank Lackteen *(Dancing Horse)*, Frank Sully *(Bartender)*, Chinook the Dog.

Run-of-the-mill film starring a Canadian Mountie and his trusty dog. Chinook, the dog, sniffs out a dead body of a trapper and it has all the signs of a suicide. But the Mountie's instincts tell him it is murder. They track down the plot by Carr, a leather-clad gunslinger, who happens to be a woman. She is after some buried treasure that is located in the Valley of Death, an Indian burial ground, and wants her henchmen to steal it. A hackneyed bowl of sweet gruel for dog lovers only.

p, Lindsley Parsons; d, Rex Bailey; w, Warren Douglas (based on a story by James Oliver Curwood); ph, William Sickner; ed, Leonard W. Herman; art d, David Milton.

Western **(PR:A MPAA:NR)**

NORTHERN PURSUIT*** (1943) 94m WB bw

Errol Flynn *(Steve Wagner)*, Julie Bishop *(Laura McBain)*, Helmut Dantine *(Von Keller)*, John Ridgely *(Jim Austin)*, Gene Lockhart *(Ernst)*, Tom Tully *(Inspector Barnett)*, Bernard Nedell *(Dagor)*, Warren Douglas *(Sergeant)*, Monte Blue *(Jean)*, Alec Craig *(Angus McBain)*, Tom Fadden *(Hobby)*, Carl Harbaugh *(Radio Operator)*, Glen Cavender *(Workman)*, Fred Kelsey *(Conductor)*, Herbert Heywood *(Farmer)*, Ben Erway *(Immigration Officer)*, Robert Ashley, Robert Dayne, John Lannon, Jr., Cliff Storey, Eddie Searles *(German Ski Troopers)*, Arno Frey *(Submarine Captain)*, J. Pat Moriarity *(Recruiting Sergeant)*, John Alvin *(Orderly)*, Martin Noble *(German Cook)*, John Forsythe, Robert Kent *(Soldiers)*, Sam Waagenaar *(German Assistant Cook)*, Richard Allord *(Preisser)*, Clay Martin, Bob Gary *(Nazi Soldiers)*, Hugh Prosser *(Corporal)*, Milton Kibbee, George Kirby *(Hotel Clerks)*, Russell Hicks *(Chief Inspector)*, Charles Marsh *(Man in Camel Hair Coat)*, Arthur Gould-Porter *(Little Man on Train)*, Wallis Clark *(Judge)*, James Farley *(Turnkey)*, Ken Christy *(Warden)*, Paul Irving *(Lawyer)*, George Sherwood *(Ticket Seller)*, Bill Kennedy *(Mountie)*, Richard Allen *(Heinzmann)*, George Lynn *(Johnson the Mountie)*, Rose Higgins *(Alice, Wife of the Mayor)*, Guy Kingsford *(Campbell the Mountie)*, James Millican *(Army Driver)*, Joe Herrera, Jay Silverheels, George Urchel *(Indians)*, Joseph Hawroth, Jimmy Dugan *(Mounties)*, John Royce *(German Aviator)*, Robert Hutton *(Guard)*, Lester Matthews *(Colonel)*.

Good action film sees the heroic Flynn as a Canadian Mountie whose parents were born in Germany. Flynn and Ridgely, two Mounties on routine patrol, come across Dantine who is unconscious at a campsite. They take him to a remote cabin and nurse him back to health, learning that he is German. Flynn tells Ridgely to report back to headquarters and he will be along with Dantine when the injured man is well enough to travel. During their time alone, Flynn reveals his sympathies for Germany and Dantine admits that he is a Nazi officer whose plane crashed. Flynn later defects from the Mounties and agrees to lead Dantine, Lockhart, and other Nazis across rough terrain to a rendezvous point to meet a German bomber which will bomb strategic targets. Dantine doesn't completely trust Flynn and compels him to take along his fiancee, Bishop, as sort of an unofficial hostage. Flynn, of course, is only feigning loyalty to the Nazis and, when they reach the rendezvous point, foils the German efforts to commit sabotage and vindicates his Mountie status with authorities, winning back Bishop's heart. This was Flynn's first film after his notorious rape trial and there is one telling scene where he informs Bishop that she's the only woman in the world for him and then faces the camera in an aside, arches his eybrow, and declares: "What am I saying?" Flynn collapsed during the making of this fast-paced film and the publicity department at Warners stated that he had a momentary respiratory ailment but in truth it was a bout with tuberculosis. NORTHERN PURSUIT, for all its comic book heroics, is nevertheless entertaining and expertly directed by action helmsman Walsh. The great swashbuckler Flynn had lost none of his dash and Bishop is as alluring as Dantine is repulsive as the heavy.

p, Jack Chertok; d, Raoul Walsh; w, Frank Gruber, Alvah Bessie (based on the story *Five Thousand Trojan Horses* by Leslie T. White); ph, Sid Hickox; m, Adolph Deutsch; ed, Jack Killifer; md, Leo F. Forbstein; art d, Leo K. Kuter; set d, Casey Roberts; cos, Leah Rhodes; spec eff, E. Roy Davidson, Don Siegel, James Leicester; makeup, Pete Westmore.

Adventure/War Drama **Cas.** **(PR:A MPAA:NR)**

NORTHFIELD CEMETERY MASSACRE, THE (SEE: NORTHVILLE CEMETERY MASSACRE, THE, 1976)

NORTHVILLE CEMETERY MASSACRE, THE zero
(1976) 81m Cannon c (AKA: THE NORTHFIELD CEMETERY MASSACRE, THE)

David Hyry, Carson Jackson, Jan Sisk, J. Craig Collicut.

Wretchedly produced biker movie shot in the outskirts of Detroit with a cast of local people. When an outlaw biker gang rides into town looking for some fun, a few of the ladies decide to submit to the gang members' sexual demands. One of the bikers, a sensitive type, retreats to a barn with one of the girls. Unfortunately, a town deputy arrives, rapes the girl, and pins it on the bikers. This leads to an all-out war between the town and the unjustly accused bikers, which results in the usual exploitation film carnage. Unimaginatively directed and too bloody for words.

p,d&ph, William Dear, Thomas L. Dyke (Technicolor)

Crime **Cas.** **(PR:O MPAA:R)**

NORTHWEST MOUNTED POLICE*** (1940) 125m DeMille/PAR c

Gary Cooper *(Dusty Rivers)*, Madeleine Carroll *(April Logan)*, Paulette Goddard *(Louvette Corbeau)*, Preston Foster *(Sgt. Jim Brett)*, Robert Preston *(Constable Ronnie Logan)*, George Bancroft *(Jacques Corbeau)*, Lynne Overman *(Tod McDuff)*, Akim Tamiroff *(Dan Duroc)*, Walter Hampden *(Chief Big Bear)*, Lon Chaney, Jr. *(Shorty)*, Montagu Love *(Inspector Cabot)*, Francis McDonald *(Louis Riel)*, George E. Stone *(Johnny Pelang)*, Willard Robertson *(Supt. Harrington)*, Regis Toomey *(Constable Jerry More)*, Richard Denning *(Constable Thornton)*, Douglas Kennedy *(Constable Carter)*, Robert Ryan (Constable Dumont), Clara Blandick *(Mrs. Burns)*, Ralph Byrd *(Constable Ackroyd)*, Lane Chandler *(Constable Fyffe)*, Julia Faye *(Wapiskau)*, Jack Pennick *(Sgt. Field)*, Rod Cameron *(Cpl. Underhill)*, James Seay *(Constable Fenton)*, Jack Chapin *(Bugler)*, Eric Alden *(Constable Kent)*, Evan Thomas *(Capt. Gower)*, Davison Clark *(Surgeon Roberts)*, Chief Thundercloud *(Wandering Spirit)*, Harry Burns *(The Crow)*, Lou Merrill *(Lesure)*, Ynez Seabury *(Mrs. Shorty)*, Phillip Terry *(Constable Judson)*, Soledad Jiminez *(Grandmother)*, Kermit Maynard *(Constable Porter)*, Anthony Caruso *(Half Breed at Riel's Headquarters)*, Nestor Paiva *(Half Breed)*, Jim Pierce, John Laird *(Corporals)*, Ray Mala, Monte Blue, Chief Yowlachie, Chief Thunderbird, Paul Sutton *(Indians)*, Norma Nelson *(Niska)*, Eva Puig *(Ekawo)*, Jack Luden *(Constable Douglas)*, John Hart *(Constable Norman)*, Emory Parnell *(Constable Higgins)*, James Flavin *(Mountie)*, Bud Geary *(Constable Herrick)*, Wallace Reid, Jr. *(Constable Rankin)*, George Regas *(Freddie)*, James Dundee *(Constable Grove)*, Weldon Heyburn *(Constable Cameron)*, William Haade, Donald Curtis, Jane Keckley, Noble Johnson, Ethan Laidlaw, Archie Twitchell.

It's history again according the the gospel of DeMille but it's exciting and lavish and a great spectacle in the bargain. Set in 1885, at the time of the Riel Rebellion in Canada, Indians and half-breeds unite under the leadership of McDonald, goaded by renegade Bancroft. Foster is a courageous and by-the-book sergeant in the Mounties who is in love with Anglican nurse Carroll. Preston, Carroll's younger brother, is also a Mountie but he is hopelessly in love with Bancroft's half-breed sister, Goddard, a vixen who, though she loves Preston, is utterly loyal to her murderous father Bancroft. Into this turbulent world rides Cooper, a Texas Ranger in search of Bancroft who is wanted on a murder charge in the Lone Star state. Inspector Love tells Cooper that Bancroft is also wanted by the Mounties for murder but that he wishes to cooperate with U.S. authorities. He will think it over. While Love is deciding, Cooper moves into the Mountie barracks and befriends the hearty policemen with the red coats. He also meets and is smitten by the lovely blonde Carroll, and this causes Preston some angst and no little jealousy when he sees his intended respond to the the earthy Cooper. At one point, Cooper is describing his expansive native state and Carroll states: "Texas must be heaven." Says Cooper: "It will be when you get there." (DeMille's epics were known for corny dialog but the unsophisticated audiences of the 1930s nevertheless enjoyed it; though vaudeville had one foot in the grave and burlesque was still lingering, the broader the remark, the more the uneducated spectator felt knowledgeable and rewarded by his ability to discern the most basic sexual, social and political inferences.) When Bancroft and McDonald plan to ambush the 50 Mounties Love can muster against the thousands of half- breeds and Indians, Bancroft displays a newly-acquired Gatling gun (precursor to the machine gun). McDonald surveys the devastating fun and says ominously: "Blood will run like water." Replies the sadistic and callous Bancroft: "Blood? You won't notice it much. The Mounted Police wear red coats." The love scenes between Preston and the wildcat Goddard (who always overacted in any DeMille film as a matter of policy) are downright embarrassing, even for the audiences of that day. Says Goddard in her thick accent to Preston: "I think I eat your heart out, maybe!" And then she says: "My heart sings like a bird!" Preston is out-and-out mushy with lines like: "You're the sweetest poison that ever got into a man's blood! I love you! I want you!" When she turns on him, Preston lashes out at Goddard with a stream of invective that only DeMille could create: "You sneaking she-wolf! You dirty squaw! I'll kill you when I get loose." Before the Mounties are ambushed, Preston and another Mountie, Toomey, are sent to an outpost to keep watch and report back if they see the half-breeds approaching. But Preston deserts his post to see sexy Goddard and she ties him up so he will be safe from her father's bloodthirsty half-breeds. Toomey is punctured with arrows and the Mountie fort is savagely attacked, with Cooper saving Carroll and taking her from the carnage in a canoe (much the same way he would later save Goddard in UNCONQUERED). Moreover, Cooper later performs some breakneck riding to lasso the Gatling gun and drag it over a cliff so that it sinks into a lake and saves the rest of the Mountie force—a feat he attributes to Preston so that the youthful Mountie, by then dead, will be thought of as a hero, not a deserter—a Beau Geste he renders for the sake of the woman he loves, Carroll. Foster, meanwhile, with survivors of the near-massacre, rides boldly into the camp of Indian chief Big Bear (Hampden) to confront the bully Bancroft. The renegade shouts to the Indians to kill the Mounties but Preston steps forward, flips the powerful Bancroft on his back and, in the same startling motion, handcuffs him so that he immediately loses face in front of his Indian allies. Foster then offers Hampden a medal from Queen Victoria and asks the chief if he is worthy of such an honor. Hampden kneels in obedience to British authority and says: "The Cree are brothers to the brave!" (Hampden's makeup, like all of that applied to those playing Indians, including real Indians, was a dark mahogany but his eyes were bright blue and the studio had to spend more than $500 in fitting the character actor with an early-day set of contact lenses to change the color of his eyes to brown.) Bancroft, as a gesture of good will, is turned over to Cooper to be taken back to Texas for trial. The slow-speaking Texan, however, only gets his man, not the girl. Carroll decides that Foster is the man for her and, though she is fond of Cooper, she loves the stoical Mountie. This was DeMille's first Technicolor film and he made the most of it, presenting lavish and stunning color, although he was told by Paramount at the last minute that he could not shoot the film on location in Canada as he originally planned. (Throughout 1939, DeMille's associate producer, Bill Pine, scouted locations in Canada, selecting sites in Regina, Banff, Calgary, Ottawa, and Lake Louise, along with getting Canadian approval for the shooting.) DeMille did his own research on the

Riel Rebellion and then turned it over to a bevy of writers who provided a rather disjointed and episodic script but DeMille was satisfied and felt he could "fill in the blanks" as he went along. The original working title for the film was THE ROYAL CANADIAN MOUNTED and this was changed to SCARLET RIDERS, but someone at Paramount stated that this might be interpreted as horseback riding prostitutes so the final title, NORTHWEST MOUNTED POLICE came into being. Cooper was a natural in the film, playing his usual low-key character, which DeMille had liked since they had made THE PLAINSMAN in 1936. This was also the first Technicolor film for Cooper, although he had appeared in a color sequence in an entertainment documentary, PARAMOUNT ON PARADE (1930). DeMille sang Cooper's praises during the film, telling interviewers: "The thing about Gary Cooper that has impressed me most is his amazing alertness. From the time we made our first picture I have realized that he never misses a thing that goes on before the camera. People who see Cooper lounging off-camera don't know what's going on behind those half-closed eyes. But I know he's developing the business and characterization that bring naturalness and humaneness to his parts in my pictures." Foster, who brought a resolute and tough image to his role as leading Mountie, had appeared in a Cooper film, HIS WOMAN nine years earlier, but as an extra. (Conversely, David Newell, who had appeared with Cooper in the color sequence in PARAMOUNT ON PARADE, and who was being groomed for stardom in 1930 by that studio, had slipped into obscurity, appearing in NORTHWEST MOUNTED POLICE as an extra.) When it came to actors, DeMille was at best, ambivalent. He originally selected Joel McCrea to play the Texas Ranger but when McCrea had commitments elsewhere, DeMille easily accepted Cooper as his substitute. The director was less enthusiastic when Paramount told him it would save $62,000 by not shooting some scenes in Canada and called off the on-location shooting. The total company man, however, DeMille publicly supported the decision to shoot only on the studio lot with some additional scenes shot around Eugene, Oregon. Most of the Saskatchewan setting was achieved by converting the backlot into the Canadian wilds; more than 300 pine trees were planted and a forest ranger was reportedly hired to patrol the man-made pine forest so that no careless worker burned it down. His real job was to drive off the seagulls that were forever perching on the branches when the cameras were turned on. DeMille defended the backlot setting, even though it gives a confining, almost claustrophobic look to the film. Said the director: "The trouble with filming the real thing is that on the screen it looks sham. Overmuch confidence in Nature won't do." The backlot setting also allowed DeMille to plant no less than two dozen loudspeakers through which he could cue his hordes of extras during the battle scenes. Before the film was completely cast, DeMille expressed his worries over getting just the right actress to play the fiery half-breed female second lead. And from the beginning, Goddard went after the part. Marlene Dietrich was suggested for the role but she was nearing forty and DeMille thought her too sophisticated for the role. (Dietrich would surprise DeMille and the rest of the world, however, by later playing—at 47—a dark-skinnned, earthy, and fire-eating gypsy in a memorable role in GOLDEN EARRINGS, costarring with Ray Milland.) Rita Hayworth, then twenty-one, was also considered by DeMille but the budding star had no influence in the studio system at the time and neither did Simone Simon, who had also been suggested for the half-breed role. Goddard finally sent DeMille a note which read "Are you going to give me that part?" DeMille did not respond, except to tell friends that he resented pushy actresses. Hearing nothing, Goddard sent another note, this time correcting the script itself which she had read and researched. Said Goddard to DeMille: "C.B.—Loupette, the character in the script, means little he-wolf. Shouldn't you change it to Louvette, little she-wolf?" DeMille was surprised to learn that the actress was correct. He had the script changed but he still refused to cast Goddard. The actress was as stubborn as DeMille. She went to makeup genius Wally Westmore, who headed Paramount's makeup department. Westmore gave the actress a new black dye and stringy hairdo, coating her body with a dark tint and the costume department adorned her in greasy buckskins. She then showed up in DeMille's offices. The director, busy with elaborate sketches on his set-up shots, was told by his secretary that "Louvette is here to see you." Absent-mindedly, DeMille, without looking up from the sketches, said: "Send Louvette in." In swaggered the made-up Goddard. In DeMille's own words: "A dark girl, with eyes that could smolder or melt, came in, made up as a half-breed and costumed as such a girl would dress on the wild Canadian frontier in the 1880s." Goddard carried a bullwhip which she snaked along with her slinky movements. Once at his side, she raised her pretty leg and put her foot on his desk. (She knew DeMille had a foot fetish where he admired small feet in women and her feet were petite.) Said the actress in her best French-Indian accent: "You teenk you wan beeg director, hah? Me, Louvette, show you!" Such antics never sat well with the very formal DeMille but the actress so impressed him with her desire to have the part that he relented. "That was enough," he later admitted, "Paulette Goddard had the part." Sometimes DeMille had to subdue his actors for the sake of sanity. Though Overman was very low-key as a skinflinty but kind-hearted Scotsman, his rival and friend, Tamiroff, could not help but overplay any scene he was in, no matter how many times DeMille ordered the Russian-born actor to subdue his raging emotions. But the worst offender in the scene-chewing category was a real native American. Among the hundreds of Indian extras DeMille used in NORTHWEST MOUNTED POLICE was a Navajo warrior named Tom Hightree whose war whoop was so loud and blood-curdling that DeMille yelled "cut" and approached the Indian actor, telling him: "Mr. Hightree, please! If you could just moderate a little. It's too harrowing. After all, this is only a massacre." NORTHWEST MOUNTED POLICE went on to be one of the top six box-office grossers of 1940 and reaped a fortune for Paramount, as well as getting five Academy Award nominations. These included Bauchens for Best Editing (which won), Milner for Best Cinematography, Young for Best Musical Score, Dreier and Anderson for Best Art Direction, and Loren Ryder for Best Sound.

p&d, Cecil B. DeMille; w, Alan LeMay, Jesse Lasky, Jr., C. Gardner Sullivan (based on the book *Royal Canadian Mounted Police* by R.C. Fetherston-Haugh); ph, Victor Milner, W. Howard Green (Technicolor); m, Victor Young; ed, Anne Bauchens; art d, Hans Dreier, Roland Anderson; set d, Dan Sayre Groesbeck, Joe De Yong; cos, Natalie Visart, De Yong; spec eff, Gordon Jennings, Farciot Edouart; makeup, Wally Westmore; tech adv., Maj. G.F. Griffin, RCMP, Sgt. George A. Pringle, NWMP.

Adventure/Historical Epic **(PR:A MPAA:NR)**

NORTHWEST OUTPOST**½

(1947) 91m REP bw (GB: END OF THE RAINBOW)

Nelson Eddy *(Capt. James Laurence)*, Ilona Massey *(Natalia Alanova)*, Joseph Schildkraut *(Count Igor Savin)*, Hugo Haas *(Prince Nickolai Balinin)*, Elsa Lanchester *(Princess "Tanya" Tatiana)*, Lenore Ulric *(Baroness Kruposny)*, Peter Whitney *(Volkoff, Overseer)*, Tamara Shayne *(Olga, Natalia's Maid)*, Erno Verebes *(Kyril, Balinin's Aide)*, George Sorel *(Baron Kruposny)*, Rick Vallin *(Dovkin)*, Henry Brandon *(Chinese Junk Captain)*, Michael Visaroff *(Capt. Tikhonoff)*, Muni Seroff *(Sentry)*, Max Willenz *(Peasant)*, Nina Hansen *(Princess Tatiana's Maid)*, Eugene Sigaloff *(Priest)*, Michael Mark *(Small Convict)*, Dick Alexander *(Large Convict)*, George Paris *(Ship's Officer)*, Ray Teal *(Wounded Trapper)*, Zola Karabanova, Inna Gest *(Women)*, John Bleifer *(Groom)*, Molio Sheron *(Naval Officer)*, Gene Gary *(2nd Sentry)*, Gregory Golubeff Peter Seal *(Men)*, Nicco Romoff, Henry Kulky *(Peasants)*, John Peters *(Officer)*, Jay Silverheels *(Indian Scout)*, Constantine Romanoff *(Convict)*, Peter Gurs *(Trumpeter)*, Marvin Press *(Young Man)*, Abe Dinovitch *(Rough Man)*, Nicholas Kobliansky *(Deacon)*, Countess Rosanska, Dian Smirnova, Antonina Barnett, Lola De Tolly, Myra Sokolskaya *(Noble Ladies)*, George Blagoi, Sam Savitsky, Igor Dolgoruki, Nestor Eristoff *(Noble Gentlemen)*, The American GI Chorus.

Eddy's last film has him back saving fruity-voiced Massey, who played the woman in trouble in two of his previous films. Set at a trading fort when Russia controlled parts of California. Eddy, a true-blue American soldier hero, meets Massey, who is in California trying to save her imprisoned husband, Schildkraut. The two fall in love but face the usual obstacles. It seems that Massey had to marry to save her father from shame. She helps Schildkraut escape and he confronts Eddy. In between songs, Eddy is forced to kill him before he takes off again and the couple can sing together happily ever after. Eddy retired from films to make it on the nightclub circuit after this charming attempt to find "a story" to follow KNICKERBOCKER HOLIDAY three years before. Director Dwan, always deft and competent, seems to have regarded NORTHWEST OUTPOST as beneath the sharper edges of his skill, but he still found fun in the turgid story by poking fun at Eddy and his singing. Consequently, Eddy often is seen with his mouth open as he gallops to the rescue of Massey with a song on the soundtrack. As for the musical pieces, composer Friml was prolific but undirected in his work. For NORTHWEST OUTPOST the studio actually had to send a recording crew to his home to catch the outpouring of keyboard improvisations the 69-year-old musician was creating. Out of the endless tapes, songs were constructed for the film, and, of these, the only one that was memorable was the unfortunately named "Weary." Songs pieced together this way (except the Russian Easter Hymn by Friml and Edward Heyman) included: "Raindrops on a Drum" (performed by the American GI Chorus, later by Eddy, Massey), "Tell Me With Your Eyes" (sung by Massey, reprised by Hugo Haas), "One More Mile to Go" (sung by Eddy with the Chorus), Russian Easter Hymn (Eddy and Chorus), "Love is the Time" (Massey), "Nearer and Dearer" (Chorus, Eddy, Massey), "Weary" (performed by the American GI Chorus).

p, Herbert J. Yates; d, Allan Dwan; w, Elizabeth Meehan, Laird Doyle, Richard Sale (based on a story by Angela Stuart); ph, Reggie Lanning; m, Rudolf Friml; ed, Harry Keller; md, Robert Armbruster; art d, Hilyard Brown, Fred Ritter; set d, John McCarthy, Jr., James Redd; spec eff, Howard Lydecker, Theodore Lydecker; cos, Adele Palmer; makeup, Bob Mark.

Western Musical **(PR:A MPAA:NR)**

NORTHWEST PASSAGE*****

(1940) 125m MGM c

Spencer Tracy *(Maj. Robert Rogers)*, Robert Young *(Langdon Towne)*, Walter Brennan *(Hunk Marriner)*, Ruth Hussey *(Elizabeth Browne)*, Nat Pendleton *(Capt. Huff)*, Louis Hector *(Rev. Browne)*, Robert Barrat *(Humphrey Towne)*, Lumsden Hare *(Gen. Amherst)*, Donald MacBride *(Sgt. McNott)*, Isabel Jewell *(Jennie Coit)*, Douglas Walton *(Lt. Avery)*, Addison Richards *(Lt. Crofton)*, Hugh Sothern *(Jesse Beacham)*, Regis Toomey *(Webster)*, Montagu Love *(Wiseman Clagett)*, Lester Mathews *(Sam Livermore)*, Truman Bradley *(Capt. Ogden)*, Andrew Pena *(Konkapot)*, Tom London, Eddie Parker *(Rangers)*, Don Castle *(Richard Towne)*, Rand Brooks *(Eben Towne)*, Kent Rogers *(Odiorne Towne)*, Verna Felton *(Mrs. Towne)*, Richard Cramer *(Sheriff Packer)*, Ray Teal *(Bradley McNeil)*, Edward Gargan *(Capt. Butterfield)*, John Merton *(Lt. Dunbar)*, Gibson Gowland *(MacPherson)*, Frank Hagney *(Capt. Grant)*, Gwendolen Logan *(Mrs. Browne)*, Addie McPhail *(Jane Browne)*, Helen MacKellar *(Sarah Hadden)*, Arthur Aylesworth *(Flint, Innkeeper)*, Ted Oliver *(Farrington)*, Lawrence Porter *(Billy, Indian Boy)*, Tony Guerrero *(Capt. Jacobs)*, Ferdinand Munier *(Stoodley)*, George Eldredge *(McMullen)*, Robert St. Angelo *(Solomon)*, Denis Green *(Capt. Williams)*, Peter George Lynn *(Turner)*, Frederic Worlock *(Sir William Johnson)*, Hank Worden *(Ranger)*.

One of the great adventure-action films of all times, this Vidor classic owes much of its success to the rugged Tracy who plays the indefatigable Robert Rogers, one of America's greatest pioneers. Tracy is earthy, eloquent, and utterly awesome as the frontier leader who knows no fear in a wilderness rife with terror and bloodshed. The film opens with talented artist Young arriving home in Portsmouth, New Hampshire, to sheepishly explain to his family that he has been expelled from Harvard because of his snide political comments inserted into his cartoons. The criticism in this year of 1759 is aimed at the British, which alienates his in-laws-to-be, a Tory family of which Hussey is the prize daughter and Young's fiancee. Young and his roughneck sidekick Brennan get drunk in a pub one night and tell off Tory Love and Hussey's stuffed-shirt father Hector. His arrest is ordered but he and Brennan escape into the wilderness and on their travels they stop at a wayside inn where they meet Tracy who is trying to sober up his best Indian scout. He accomplishes this in a weird fashion, by getting the Indian even drunker on hot buttered rum, along with getting Young and Brennan soused, too. The pair wake up outside of the military post of Crown Point, headquarters of Tracy's rangers (Rogers' Rangers, the celebrated Indian fighters). Tracy entices Young to join him, explaining that his rangers are about to embark upon a great adventure and he needs a mapmaker. Brennan tags along and soon the pair are boating along with hundreds of other leather-clad veterans of many an Indian war. Their goal is St. Francis, the headquarters of the French-backed Abernaki tribe, a vicious Indian nation that has conducted bloody raids into colonial territory under British authority. The rangers tell tales of how the inhuman Abernakis have slaughtered their friends and families, how they have torn captives limb from limb, pried the ribs right out of the living, severed the heads of rangers, and used these gory trophies to play ball with. To stop the raids into the Ohio Valley, upstate New York, and New England, Tracy is ordered to annihilate the Abernakis and then escape by a tricky, uncharted route. The rangers work their way through the wilderness but disaffected Indian guides cause trouble and some of the powder carried by the rangers accidentally explodes, wounding several dozen men. Tracy sends a quarter of his force back to Crown Point with the Indians and proceeds, his men portaging their huge boats over impossible hills and through woods until they find waterways feeding off Lake Champlain which is controlled by the French. Then, when they can no longer row to their destination, the rangers hide their boats and slog through swamps to cover their tracks. Some fall ill or are injured and are left behind to face the merciless enemy, a fate they have accepted early on. Toomey is one of these, having broken a leg in the swamp. He positions himself on a tree limb just above the water level of the swamp, takes a long chaw of tobacco, and is grateful for the extra ammunition and food Tracy leaves with him in his death watch. Young is stunned by all of this but he soon learns the lessons of survival in the wilderness. At one point, a wild river blocks the path of the rangers but they form a human chain, with Tracy at the base, holding on to a tree at one end and stretching it to the other side so that the other men can move along it to the opposite bank. (This is only one of the spectacular scenes in a film that surpasses itself from frame to frame in physical feats and scenes of incredible endurance.) When the rangers arrive at St. Francis, they plan well, following Tracy's scheme to attack the Indian village and the French fort at its center from four sides at dawn. At sun-up the rangers race through the village, setting the huts and tepees on fire and overpowering the few French soldiers in the fort. The savages spill out of their shacks screaming but are driven back on four sides. The rangers close in until the savage horde is reduced to a massed huddle of terrified Indians. They are slaughtered as they attempt to escape. Tracy then gathers up all the food available, only a few baskets of corn, and discovers that the main French force is away but will soon return. He orders the white captives taken back with him, including Jewell, who has been with the Abernakis so long that she is half-savage herself, cursing Tracy and his men. After the battle, Young is found wounded, a bullet in his stomach. Tracy knows he must either motivate Young to stay on his feet and keep moving or leave him behind. He challenges Young who bandages his wound with Brennan's help, and then stumbles after the retreating rangers, Jewell helping him on Tracy's orders. He improves as he moves, his bleeding stops and he slowly regains his strength. The rangers, with the French hot on their trail, flee through the wilderness, with Tracy splitting his group. They head for Lake Memphremagog but find no food or British troops waiting for them as expected. Now they push on, starving, emaciated, exhausted, toward old Fort Wentworth, going solely on Tracy's promise that the British will be waiting for them with great stores of food. When they do stumble into the abandoned fort, they find nothing. Tracy tries to get them going again but his force is spent. All seems lost when they hear the fifes and drums of the approaching British relief force. Tracy and his skeletal force stand bravely to attention as the British march in bearing succulent armloads of food. Not until they officially receive the British salute do the marvelously disciplined rangers break ranks and race for the food. The rangers return to Portsmouth where they recuperate from their ordeal. Then Tracy orders them to prepare for another adventure, one that will make their recent exploit seem like nothing more than "a duck hunt." He explains how they are going to Fort Detroit and then push westward to find a northwest passage to the Pacific and a route to the Orient that will open up trade routes for the colonies to the world. Young, however, has decided to stay behind and pursue his art. He and Hussey watch the rangers march forth and Tracy approaches them, bidding them farewell. He shakes Young's hand and tells him: "I'll see you at sundown." Then off he goes, following his men, as Young and Hussey look after him. Hussey asks Young if there truly is a northwest passage and the artist replies: "I don't know…It's every man's dream to find a short route to his heart's desire. If there is one, he'll find it." Tracy, alone at the top of a hill, turns and waves at Young who tells Hussey: "That man will never die!" NORTHWEST PASSAGE is rousing adventure all the way, a man's film, if you will, one of stirring courage and thundering action which bears amazing authenticity of the era, thanks to the perfectionist techniques of director Vidor. The film was based on book one of Roberts' graphic and well-researched tale of Rogers' exploits, confining itself to the Indian wars instead of Rogers' struggle to raise funds and find a water route to the Pacific. The real Rogers was every bit the pioneer and hearty woodsman as Roberts and, subsequently Tracy, portrayed him. The great patriot Rogers (1717-1795) called his famous company of rangers to arms in 1755 and won fame and honors in the French and Indian wars. Rogers' dream to find a northwest passage was put on paper, estimates and plans that were later put to good use by Lewis and Clark in their trailblazing expedition of 1803-06. The commanding authority of Tracy is never challenged by any cast member although Brennan does tell him he's always right and that's not good. "If you ever meet me as just a man," Tracy replies, "you may need a little charity." Director Vidor, with a $2 million budget, went at NORTHWEST PASSAGE as one obsessed, certainly equalling the vigor and relentless energy of Robert Rogers himself. Without a completed script, Vidor took his almost all-male cast and technicians into the wilds of Idaho, around Lake Payette, which resembled the New England terrain of 200 years earlier (New England by then being criss-crossed with roads and pock-marked with telephone poles and thereby unacceptable for this wilderness film). Here, for 70 days, Vidor drove his cast and crew nonstop. Originally, MGM had slated the colossal adventure tale for Tracy, Robert Taylor, Wallace Beery, and Franchot Tone but only Tracy remained as the star, with Young and Brennan brought in for support. Young and Tracy were later to state that the ordeal was excruciating but exhilarating. Tracy had once stated that "the physical labor actors have to do wouldn't tax an embryo." After a few days of working under Vidor in Idaho, he had a completely different perspective, later commenting how he really earned his money in NORTHWEST PASSAGE. In the river-crossing sequence, which was shot in two days (with some scenes added in this sequence in the studio tank), no doubles were employed and Tracy wore out two pair of leather pants as he anchored himself to a tree next to the river to begin the human chain. (When not in any scenes, Tracy steered clear of the boisterous and hard-drinking cast members, remaining in his small cabin and reading every book Agatha Christie had written up to that time.) Although he appreciated the workout, or said he did, the physical demands under the rigid Vidor got on Tracy's nerves. "I don't care how good an actor you are," Tracy later stated, "you can't speak lines while standing up to your neck in ice water, unless you're in good physical shape. That's what happened to all of us on NORTHWEST PASSAGE. It isn't exactly fun to work in bitter cold, and sloshing through mud all day." The more than 300 Indians hired as warriors and extras in the film actually had less to do than the white actors and were under less strain. The local Indians hired for the film refused to act for the $5-a-day fee Vidor was offering, insisting upon $10. Tracy told Vidor to tell them they were only playing half-breeds and therefore not entitled to full pay. He did and the Indians surprisingly accepted the $5-a-day fee. Tracy got along with Vidor but reportedly later refused to work with him again because of the director's slave-driving techniques. Vidor was always uncompromising in his praise for this sterling actor (from *King Vidor on Filmmaking*): "Tracy along with Robert Donat just about head my list of the best actors I've worked with. Everything that Spence did came over with tremendous conviction…He played strong courageous parts with absolute conviction and physically—and emotionally—he was hardly a strong, courageous man. While working in Idaho on a tough location for NORTHWEST PASSAGE, he repeatedly threatened to leave the location and return to Los Angeles before the job was finished. I had to use several unusual methods to placate his fears and calm him into finishing the location work." The film was shot with parts of the script being flown to Vidor daily in Idaho, a vexing situation since MGM did not know whether or not the film would proceed to tell Robert's tale of Rogers' attempt to actually set out to find the northwest passage. As Vidor later stated: "NORTHWEST PASSAGE was a peculiar thing—it's a book in two parts. I made all the first part, which was the prolog; we were still supposed to do the second part of the book, and the producer, Hunt Stromberg, never could make up his mind about the second part…I started shooting, believing they would send me the pages up there [to Idaho] and they never arrived. I went to New York for some reason and they had another director [Jack Conroy] shoot the ending. So we came home. And then they released the prolog." The title bore the words NORTHWEST PASSAGE, Book One, Rogers' Rangers. A splintered tale though it might be, the film is nevertheless a powerful and moving picture, Vidor's first in Technicolor and he made good use of the verdant location sites; Wagner and Skall's cinematography is absolutely breathtaking, capturing the rich blues of the lakes and the deep greens of the forests, although Vidor had some trouble with the drab greens of the ranger costumes, until ordering special dyes to tone down the kelly green hues. The film was a great box- office and critical success and is considered to be one of Vidor's true masterworks. The story was remade in a TV series in 1959-59 for NBC, starring Keith Larsen as Rogers, Buddy Ebsen as Mariner, and Don Burnett as Towne.

p, Hunt Stromberg; d, King Vidor, Jack Conway (uncredited); w, Laurence Stallings, Talbot Jennings (based on the novel by Kenneth Roberts); ph, Sidney Wagner, William V. Skall (Technicolor consultants, Natalie Kalmus, Henri Jaffa); m, Herbert Stothart; ed, Conrad A. Nervig; art d, Cedric Gibbons, Malcolm Brown; set d, Edwin B. Willis; makeup, Jack Dawn.

Adventure **(PR:A-C MPAA:NR)**

NORTHWEST RANGERS** (1942) 64m MGM bw

James Craig *(Frank "Blackie" Marshall)*, William Lundigan *(James Kevin Gardiner)*, Patricia Dane *(Jean Avery)*, John Carradine *(Martin Caswell)*, Jack Holt *(Duncan Frazier)*, Keenan Wynn *("Slip" O'Mara)*, Grant Withers *(Fowler)*, Darryl Hickman *(Blackie as a Boy)*, Drew Roddy *(Jim as a Boy)*.

Indians leave two boys orphans who grow up under the auspices of a Canadian Mountie. The two have vastly different interests. One, Lundigan, wants to be a Mountie while the other, Craig, has a penchant for heavy gambling. After being cheated he vows revenge on the sleazy owner of the town's gambling establishment. He returns a few years later, with his pal, now a Mountie in charge of keeping the peace. Craig wins the whole gambling house playing roulette but ends up committing two murders. While Lundigan still loves his "brother," he is forced to carry out his duty and kills Craig in a gun battle. Craig was MGM's hope to take the place of Clark Gable, who had joined the Army Air Corps that year soon after the tragic death of his wife, Carole Lombard, in an air crash. Craig had the same muscularity and the manner and voice of Gable. He turned in a robust performance in NORTHWEST RANGERS, but he never rose above being a star of the second magnitude.

p, Samuel Marx; d, Joseph Newman; w, Gordon Kahn, David Lang (based on a story by Arthur Caesar); ph, Jackson Rose; ed, Frank E. Hull; art d, Cedric Gibbons; m/l, Earl Brent, Ralph Freed.

Western **(PR:A MPAA:NR)**

NORTHWEST STAMPEDE** (1948) 79m EL c

Joan Leslie *(Chris Johnson)*, James Craig *(Dan Bennett)*, Jack Oakie *(Mike Kirby)*, Chill Wills *(Mileaway)*, Victor Kilian *(Mel Saunders)*, Stanley Andrews *(Bowles)*,

Ray Bennett (*Barkis*), Lane Chandler (*Scrivner*), Harry Shannon, Kermit Maynard, Flame the Dog.

This light, romantic western centers most of its attention on a wild horse and a police dog. The story concerns a star rodeo performer, Craig, who inherits a ranch in Calgary, Canada, left to him by his father. Craig tries to settle down and make the ranch a profitable venture, but he longs for the days of the rodeo. Leslie plays his foreman, once a rodeo show girl herself, who believes Craig is neglecting his duties and that he ought to settle down and forget all about the rodeo. In between the friction of these two is a subplot concerning Craig's desire to capture a white wild stallion that roams the nearby countryside. It's Flame, the dog, however, who's the real star of this picture, and he proves it by stealing the show.

p&d, Albert S. Rogell; w, Art Arthur, Lillie Hayward (based on the *Saturday Evening Post* story, "Wild Horse Roundup" by Jean Muir); ph, John W. Boyle (Cinecolor); m, Paul Sawtell; ed, Philip Cahn; md, Irving Friedman; art d, Edward L. Ilou; set d, Armor Marlowe; cos, Frances Ehren; spec eff, R.O. Binger; makeup, Ern Westmore, Del Armstrong.

Western (PR:A MPAA:NR)

NORTHWEST TERRITORY*½ (1952) 61m MON bw

Kirby Grant (*Rod Webb*), Chinook (*Dog*), Gloria Saunders (*Ann DuMere*), Pat Mitchell (*Billy Kellogg*), John Crawford (*LeBeau*), Duke York (*Dawson*), Warren Douglas (*Morgan*), Tristram Coffin (*Kinkaid*), Don Harvey (*Barton*), Sam Flint (*Kellog, Prospector*).

Grant and Chinook the dog join forces again in another film that glorifies the Canadian Mounties. An old prospector, Flint, shows up with a map detailing the whereabouts of rich oil deposits. He's supposed to meet Grant at Ft. McKenzie where Grant will turn his grandson, Mitchell, over to him. But the prospector is killed before Grant arrives. Grant then sets after the killers, dragging along his amazing dog and Mitchell. He disguises himself as a rookie prospector in the hope that the killers will expose themselves. With a long drawn-out scene of Grant and Chinook chasing the murderers through the woods, they finally catch the killers, bring them to justice, and give back the oil claims to the rightful heir, Mitchell.

p, Lindsley Parsons; d, Frank McDonald; w, William Raynor (based on a story by James Oliver Curwood); ph, William Sickner; art d, Dave Milton.

Western (PR:A MPAA:NR)

NORTHWEST TRAIL* (1945) 66m Action/Lippert c

Bob Steele, John Litel, Joan Woodbury, Madge Bellamy, George Meeker, Ian Keith, Raymond Hatton, Poodles Hanneford, John Hamilton, Charles Middleton, Grace Hanneford, Bill Hammond, Bud Osborne, Al Ferguson, Bob Duncan, Josh [John] Carpenter.

A poor picture for even a low-budget western has Steele as a Canadian Mountie (looking as though his britches are too tight), escorting a young woman carrying a bundle of cash to her father. Their trek through the wilds of Canada (that looks anything but), brings on a few problems, allowing Steele his mandatory heroics. The cheap color process only makes this thing look more shoddy and ridiculous, and Steele appears to be only going through the motions.

p, William B. David, Max M. King; d, Derwin Abrahams; w, Harvey Gates, L. J. Swabacher; ph, Marcel Le Picard (Cinecolor); m, Frank Sanucci; ed, Thomas Neff.

Western Cas. (PR:A MPAA:NR)

NORWOOD** (1970) 96m PAR c

Glen Campbell (*Norwood Pratt*), Kim Darby (*Rita Lee Chipman*), Joe Namath (*Joe William Reese*), Carol Lynley (*Yvonne Phillips*), Pat Hingle (*Grady Fring*), Tisha Sterling (*Marie*), Dom De Luise (*Bill Bird*), Leigh French (*Vernell Bird*), Meredith MacRae (*Kay*), Sammy Jackson (*Wayne T.E.B. Walker*), Billy Curtis (*Edmund B. Ratner*), Merie Earle (*Grandma Whichcoat*), Jack Haley, Sr. (*Mr. Reese*), Jimmy Boyd (*Jeeter*), David W. Huddleston (*Uncle Lonnie*), Edith Atwater (*Irate Bus Passenger*), Gil Lamb (*Mr. Remley*), Cass Daley (*Mrs. Remley*), Joe Oakie (*Tilmon Fring*), Virginia Capers (*Ernestine*), Jay Ripley (*Pete*), Joann the Wonder Hen.

A lightweight film starring Campbell as a Marine Vietnam veteran. He leaves Texas to seek out Army buddy as well as some success as a performer, in New York, unwittingly transporting two stolen cars along the way. He abandons the cars after being chased by the police, and hitchhikes his way to New York. Upon his arrival, he discovers Namath has already left for Arkansas, leaving Campbell to have a short fling with Sterling, a hippie living in Namath's apartment. Finding the Greenwich Village audiences tough to please, he hops on a bus and meets Darby. Darby is on her way to marry Jackson, a Marine. Jackson refuses to marry her, and Campbell is stuck traveling with Darby, a chicken that does tricks, and a midget. After he finally tracks down Namath, Darby announces she is pregnant. Campbell offers to do the right thing and marry her, but Darby declines. Jackson suddenly appears, beats up Campbell, and takes Darby with him. Campbell finally gets his audition and, while singing, he sees Darby watching him, and the two realize they are in love. The film represents Namath's acting debut, and reunites Campbell and Darby after their success in TRUE GRIT.

p, Hal B. Wallis; d, Jack Haley, Jr.; w, Marguerite Roberts (based on the novel by Charles Portis); ph, Robert B. Hauser (Technicolor); m, Al De Lory; ed, Warren Low, John W. Wheeler; art d, Walter Tyler; set d, Arthur Parker; cos, Luster Bayless, Agnes Henry; spec eff, Bob Dawson; m/l, "Ol' Norwood's Comin' Home, " "Marie" (Mitchell Torok, Ramona Redd, sung by Glen Campbell), "The Repo Man," "I'll Paint You a Song," "Norwood [Me and my Guitar]," "Down Home," "Everything a Man Could Ever Need" (Mac Davis, sung by Campbell), "Country Girl," "The Bass Ensemble of Ralph, Texas," "Hot Wheels," "The Fring Thing," "Chicken Out [Joanne's theme]," "A Different Kind of Rock" (Al DeLory), "Village Raga" (Bill Plummer), "Smoke on the Water" (Earl Nunn, Zeke Clements), "Rock

of Ages" (Thomas Hastings, A.M. Toplady); makeup, Sue Bower, Jack Wilson, Ben Nye, Jr.

Comedy/Drama (PR:A MPAA:G)

NOSE ON MY FACE, THE (SEE: MODEL MURDER CASE, THE, 1970)

NOSFERATU, THE VAMPIRE*** (1979, Fr./Ger.) 107m FOX c
(NOSFERATU, PHANTOM DER NACHT; AKA: NOSFERATU, THE VAMPYRE)

Klaus Kinski (*Count Dracula*), Isabelle Adjani (*Lucy Harker*), Bruno Ganz (*Jonathan Harker*), Roland Topor (*Renfield*), Walter Ladengast (*Dr. Van Helsing*), Dan Van Husen (*Warden*), Jan Groth (*Harbormaster*), Carsten Bodinus (*Schrader*), Martje Grohmann (*Mina*), Ryk De Gooyer (*Town Official*), Clemens Scheitz (*Town Employee*), Lo Van Hartingsveld (*Councilman*), Tim Beekman (*Coffinbearer*), Jacques Dufilho (*Captain*), Beverly Walker (*Nun*).

After capturing the attention of the American critics and public with films as ambitious, unique, and powerful as AGUIRRE, WRATH OF GOD (1972), EVERY MAN FOR HIMSELF AND GOD AGAINST ALL (1974), and HEART OF GLASS (1976) eccentric German director Werner Herzog remade what he considers to be the most visionary and important of all German films, F. W. Murnau's silent masterpiece NOSFERATU (1922). He was only partly successful. Held together by the sheer power of Kinski's performance as the vampire, NOSFERATU evokes several scenes (practically shot-for-shot) from the Murnau classic while changing some of the thematics slightly. In Murnau's, the vampire is pure evil invading a small German community (Herzog feels that the 1922 film predicted the rise of Nazism in Germany). Herzog's vampire is much more sympathetic. An outcast from society (as are all of Herzog's protagonists), Kinski longs for contact, acceptance, and even love from the humans who fear and revile him. Sadly, his curse and death's head appearance forever prevent this. The vampire's undead state and need for blood seem to be portrayed as a horrible, irreversible *disease*, rather than an inherently evil harbinger from hell. While this isn't exactly a fresh innovation in the development of the horror film (Tod Browning's DRACULA, 1931, as played by Lugosi had moments of pathos, as does George Romero's MARTIN, 1978, where the vampire may not be a monster at all, but just a sick, mentally ill teenager), Herzog and Kinski do succeed because they convey a sense of pity for a being so visually repulsive (Kinski's makeup is an exact duplicate of Max Schreck's hideous visage in the 1922 silent) that he is hard to look at. Unfortunately the other aspects of the film aren't handled so well. While NOSFERATU is as visually stunning, haunting, and beautiful as Herzog's other films, the pace, acting (with the exception of Kinski), and denouement are at times slow, stilted, and unintentionally funny. Murnau's 1922 film manages to build at a deliberate, steady pace and does not hesitate to linger on a moment in order to achieve a supreme degree of terror without bogging down the whole film (it runs only 63 minutes). Herzog however, holds on moments for what seems like days, stretching vague points and seemingly unimportant nuances of character to the point where even art house audiences used to the unconventional begin to giggle. The end of the film (after Kinski has been destroyed when Adjani sacrifices her life by seducing him to stay until morning), which sees Ganz smiling to reveal a set of fangs and then riding off down the beach, cape flapping in the wind, comes off as an almost comic moment, totally negating the mood of the climax and the beauty and foreboding of the final image. As with most of Herzog's films, the story behind the production is almost more interesting than the film itself. Unable to shoot in Bremen where Murnau did in 1922, Herzog had to settle for the Dutch town of Delft. Still bitter from the occupation by the Nazis during WW II, the citizens of Delft were less than enthusiastic about welcoming this small army of German filmmakers into their town. When Herzog announced his plan to release 11,000 rats into the streets of Delft for the scene where Nosferatu arrives (the director wanted grey rats but ended up with white ones, so he had his crew paint them grey), the burgermeister categorically refused and told the apparently insane German that his town had just spent months clearing the canals of their own home-grown rats, leaving little enthusiasm for re-infesting the area with laboratory rats from Hungary. Nonplussed, Herzog moved his rats to a more accommodating city, Schiedam, where he was allowed to shoot, albeit on a smaller scale. Another problem that arose had little to do with Herzog himself, but with 20th Century Fox, which, in its infinite wisdom (and because it had paid for part of the movie), insisted that the director shoot an English-language version despite the fact that he and the rest of the cast spoke little English. When the resulting version was premiered in America it was met with gales of laughter as the German actors stumbled across lines of dialog they barely understood. Finally realizing that the whole idea had been a mistake, Fox pulled the prints and reissued a subtitled German-language version for general release. Despite the many problems with Herzog's version of NOSFERATU, the effective moments outweigh the unsuccessful ones, making it an interesting but flawed film that contains one magnificent performance worth relishing—Kinski as the vampire. (In German; English subtitles.)

p,d&w, Werner Herzog (based on the novel *Dracula* by Bram Stoker and the film script NOSFERATU by Henrik Galeen); ph, Jorg Schmidt-Reitwein (Eastmancolor); m, Popol Vuh, Florian Fricke, Richard Wagner, Charles Gounod; ed, Beate Mainka-Jellinghaus; prod d, Henning Von Gierke, Ulrich Bergfelder; art d, Von Gierke; cos, Gloria Storch; spec eff, Cornelius Siegel; makeup, Reiko Kruk, Dominique Colladant.

Horror Cas. (PR:C-O MPAA:PG)

NOT A HOPE IN HELL* (1960, Brit.) 77m Parkside/Archway bw

Richard Murcoch (*Bertie*), Sandra Dorne (*Diana Melton*), Jon Pertwee (*Dan*), Judith Furse (*Miss Appleton*), Tim Turner (*Cy Hallam*), Humphrey Lestocq (*Cricklegate*), Claude Hulbert (*Police Constable Salter*), Stuart Saunders (*Bulstrode*), Zoreen Ismael (*Jean*).

Inane farce about an unlikely threesome, a female British customs official, an American excise agent, and a TV star, combining their efforts to catch a gang of smugglers. Some laugh-filled comic performances, but as for the whole idea, refer back to the title.

p, Roger Proudlock; d, Maclean Rogers; w, Raymond Drewe.

Comedy (PR:A MPAA:NR)

NOT AGAINST THE FLESH (SEE: VAMPYR 1932, Fr./Ger.)

NOT AS A STRANGER½ (1955) 135m UA bw

Olivia de Havilland (*Kristina Hedvigson*), Robert Mitchum (*Lucas Marsh*), Frank Sinatra (*Alfred Boone*), Gloria Grahame (*Harriet Lang*), Broderick Crawford (*Dr. Aarons, Medical Professor*), Charles Bickford (*Dr. Runkleman*), Myron McCormick (*Dr. Snider*), Lon Chaney, Jr. (*Job Marsh*), Jesse White (*Ben Cosgrove*), [Henry] Harry Morgan (*Oley*), Lee Marvin (*Brundage*), Virginia Christine (*Bruni*), Whit Bissell (*Dr. Dietrich*), Jack Raine (*Dr. Lettering*), Mae Clarke (*Miss O'Dell*).

After producing several blockbusters (CHAMPION, THE WILD ONE, HIGH NOON, and DEATH OF A SALESMAN), Kramer decided to try his hand at directing and chose Morton Thompson's gargantuan (almost 1000 pages) novel to adapt. He partially succeeded, but was, in the end, defeated by Mitchum's lethargic performance. It's one thing for an actor to conceal emotions and expect the audience to fathom those enigmatic looks, but Mitchum was on his way to being comatose in many of the scenes. The Anhalts did a good job paring down the huge novel and trying to make it work without becoming too long. Mitchum was in his late 30s and Sinatra was near 40 when they attempted to play young interns. Their wrinkles worked against the believability of the picture. Mitchum is in medical school and can't pay the tuition, so he is in danger of being tossed out, thus ending his lifelong dream of being a doctor. He tries to borrow the cash from his best pal, Sinatra, and from one of his instructors, Crawford, but they can't help. Then he learns that nurse de Havilland has a tidy little nest egg, so he woos, then weds her and keeps going to school on her money. He soon thinks that he can walk on water and becomes insufferable in every way. They move to a small town where Mitchum goes to work for Bickford, a crusty but lovable general practitioner, and has an affair with Grahame, a rich patient. Bickford has a heart condition but, like so many physicians, refuses to see anyone about it. Mitchum has a battle with the head of the small-town hospital, McCormick, over a charity patient who turns out to be a typhoid carrier. In the crisis, de Havilland returns to nursing, and when the typhoid is defeated, Mitchum requests that she continue, but she declines when she learns that she's pregnant after an examination by Sinatra, who also tells Mitchum. At the same time, Bickford has a heart attack. Add to that de Havilland's desire to separate from Mitchum and one can see why he is so distressed when he tries to save Bickford with surgery and fails. Mitchum's error causes the old man's demise and he is destroyed by his surgical mistake, which causes him to, at last, realize that he is just a man, not a god. He returns to de Havilland, tells her he needs her compassion and her tenderness and her loyalty, and she is more than delighted to take him back. The book was very "hot," with lots of sexy scenes. This is, at best, cool and dispassionate and Mitchum's facial expressions seem to fall into two categories: sullen and sour. Good technical work from everyone involved and a popular song, "Not as a Stranger" (Buddy Kaye, Jimmy Van Heusen), helped make this a hit.

p&d, Stanley Kramer; w, Edna and Edward Anhalt (based on the novel by Morton Thompson); ph, Franz Planer; m, George Antheil; ed, Frederick Knudtson; prod d, Rudolph Sternad; md, Antheil; art d, Howard Richmond; set d, Victor Gangelin; cos, Joe King, Don Loper; makeup, Bill Wood; technical advisers, Morton Maxwell, M.D., Josh Fields, M.D., Marjorie Lefevre, R.N.

Drama (PR:A-C MPAA:NR)

NOT DAMAGED½ 1930) 72m FOX bw

Lois Moran (*Gwen Stewart*), Walter Byron (*Kirk Randolph*), Robert Ames (*Charlie Jones*), Inez Courtney (*Maude Graham*), George Corcoran (*Elmer*), Rhoda Cross (*Jennie*), Ernest Wood (*Peebles*).

Sweet romantic story about Moran searching for that perfect marriage partner. She longs for a big church wedding with all the extras. While dreaming, she works in a music store with her offbeat roommate, Courtney, who does fortune telling on the side. Moran has a nightmare about walking down a street naked, and Courtney tells her she will meet a handsome stranger. Moran, who has a steady boy friend, scoffs at Courtney as Byron enters the store. Moran is lured by his charm and goes to his apartment where she gets drunk at his party. Byron takes the inebriated girl to his bedroom and it appears he will take advantage of her. But, the next morning, it turns out he has slept in a different room, and he then proposes marriage to her.

d, Chandler Sprague; w, Frank Gay, Harold Attridge (based on "Solid Gold Article" by Richard Connell); ph, Chet Lyons; ed, Alexander Troffey; ch, Danny Dare.

Comedy (PR:C MPAA:NR)

NOT EXACTLY GENTLEMEN (SEE: THREE ROGUES, 1931)

NOT FOR HONOR AND GLORY (SEE:LOST COMMAND, 1966)

NOT MINE TO LOVE½ (1969, Israel) 90m S.Y.V./
Edward Meadow bw (SHLOSHA YAMIN VE YELED; AKA:
THREE DAYS AND A CHILD)

Oded Kotler (*Eli*), Shuy Osherov (*Shuy*), Judith Soleh (*Noa*), Misha Asherov (*Shuy's Father*), Illy Gorlitzky (*Zvi*), Germaine Unikovsky (*Yael*), Stella Avni (*Neighbor*), Baruch David (*Neighbor's Husband*), Shoshana Duer (*Yael's Mother*), Nissan Yatir (*Yael's Father*).

A heart-tugging Israeli film that centers around lost love. A former girl friend

(Soleh) calls Kotler and asks him to look after her 3-year-old son for a few days. Kotler starts thinking that the boy might be his and agrees, hoping it will bring back Soleh's love for him. The child immediately takes to Kotler, but Kotler is confused, alternating between feeling love and hate for the child. He loves the child, but despises it at the same time because, if it is his, he can never claim it for his own. As the time passes, and he hears nothing from Soleh, his hatred builds to such a degree that he puts a poisonous snake in the child's room while the boy is sleeping. After his current girl friend is almost bitten by the reptile instead, he snaps to his senses and realizes Soleh is lost to him forever.

p, Amatsia Hiuni; d, Uri Zohar; w, Zohar, Hiuni, David Gurfinkel, Dan Ben-Amotz (based on a story by A. B. Yehoshua); ph, Gurfinkel; m, Dov Seltzer; ed, Jacques Erlich.

Drama (PR:A MPAA:NR)

NOT NOW DARLING½ (1975, Brit.) 93m LMG-Sedgemoor/
Dimension c

Leslie Phillips, Ray Cooney, Moira Lister, Julie Ege, Joan Sims, Cicely Courtneidge, Derren Nesbitt, Barbara Windsor, Jackie Pollo, Trudi Van Doren.

Silly cheapie with illusions of grandeur centers around romantic trifles in the fur business, specifically the antics of one seller who uses his position to pick up girls. A few witty moments but not enough to sustain a feature.

p, Peter J. Thompson, Martin C. Shute; d, David Croft, Ray Cooney; w, John Chapman.

Comedy (PR:O MPAA:R)

NOT OF THIS EARTH½ (1957) 67m AA bw

Paul Birch (*Paul Johnson*), Beverly Garland (*Nadine Storey, Nurse*), Morgan Jones (*Harry Sherbourne*), William Roerick (*Dr. Frederick W. Rochelle*), Jonathan Haze (*Jeremy Perrin, Handyman*), Dick Miller (*Joe Piper*), Anne Carroll (*Davanna Woman*), Pat Flynn (*Officer Simmons*), Roy Engel (*Sgt. Walton*), Tamar Cooper (*Joanne Oxford*), Harold Fong (*Oriental Specimen*), Gail Ganley (*Girl*), Ralph Reed (*Boy*).

Roger Corman, master of low-budget horror and science-fiction films, comes up with a winner this time. Well-paced, it tells the story of an alien being (Birch), who comes to Earth to scout the planet for another blood source. He takes blood from humans for the people of his own planet, Davana. To kill his victims, he looks at them with his pupil-less eyes, so that he spends a majority of the movie in wrap-around sunglasses and a gray-flannel suit. A frail, but still frightening figure, he dies when the high-pitched whine of a motor bike causes him to crash his car. Earth is still not safe, however, as Davana sends another alien down to keep the blood flowing.

p&d, Roger Corman; w, Charles Griffith, Mark Hanna; ph, John Mescall; m, Ronald Stein; ed, Charles Gross; spec eff, Paul Blaisdell.

Science Fiction/Horror (PR:A MPAA:NR)

NOT ON YOUR LIFE (SEE: ISLAND OF LOVE, 1963)

NOT ON YOUR LIFE** (1965, Ital./Span.) 90m Naga-Zebra/Pathe bw
(EL VERDUGO; LA BALLATA DEL BOIA)

Nino Manfredi (*Jose Luis*), Emma Penella (*Carmen*), Jose Luis Lopez Vazquez (*Antonio*), Angel Alvarez (*Alvarez*), Jose Isbert (*Amedeo*), Maria Luisa Ponte (*Stefania*), Guido Alberti (*Governor of Prison*), Maruja Isbert (*Ignacia*), Feliz Fernandez (*1st Sacristan*), Alfredo Landa (*2nd Sacristan*), Jose Luis Coll (*Organist*), Julia Caba Alba (*1st Woman at Works*), Xan Des Bolas (*Watchman*), Jose Sazatornil (*Administrator*), Lola Gaos (*2nd Woman at Works*), Chus Lampreabe (*3rd Woman at Works*).

Death and the people who make a living from it are the subjects of this black comedy. A couple want to marry—he is an undertaker's assistant and she is the daughter of an executioner. Her father, Isbert, is ready to quit his executioner duties, but if he does, he will lose his new apartment awarded by the government. Young groom Manfredi is talked into taking the role but vows to quit before his first call to duty. A short time later, an execution is scheduled, but luckily it is to happen right before a carnival and fiesta, when many sentenced people are reprieved. Penella, the bride, wishes to enjoy the festivities and the couple travels to the place of execution, all the time hoping for the reprieve. It never happens, and Manfredi has to carry out his assigned duties. He says that the execution will be his last, but the look on his face reminds Isbert of his own reaction many years ago and he knows in his heart the boy will continue.

d, Luis Garcia Berlanga; w, Berlanga, Rafael Azcona, Ennio Flaiano (based on a story by Berlanga); ph, Tonino Delli Colli; m, Miguel Asins Arbo; ed, Alfonso Santacana; art d, Jose Antonio de la Guerra.

Comedy (PR:C-O MPAA:NR)

NOT QUITE DECENT** (1929) 58m FOX bw

June Collyer (*Linda Cunningham*), Louise Dresser (*Mame Jarrow*), Allan Lane (*Jerry Connor*), Oscar Apfel (*Canfield*), Paul Nicholson (*Al Bergon*), Ben Hewlett (*1st Crook*), Jan Kenney (*2nd Crook*), Marjorie Beebe (*Margie*).

A part-talkie, with only the last 15 minutes containing any spoken dialog. Dresser plays a matronly nightclub performer who takes Collyer under her guidance. Collyer gets involved with a shady character and Dresser comes to her rescue. As the two become closer, it becomes known that Collyer is Dresser's daughter, who was taken from her when her husband passed away. Most of the sound portion of the film is made up of songs. The film was made during Prohibition, and contains scenes involving speakeasies and characters connected with bootleggers.

d, Irving Cummings; w, Marion Orth, Edwin Burke (based on a story by Wallace

Smith); ph, Charles Clarke; m, S. L. Rothafel; ed, Paul Weatherwax; titles, Malcolm Stuart Boylan.

Drama/Musical (PR:A MPAA:NR)

NOT RECONCILED, OR "ONLY VIOLENCE HELPS WHERE IT RULES"**

(1969, Ger.) 51m New Yorker bw

(NICHT VERSOHNT ODER "ES HILFT NUR GEWALT, WO GEWALT HERRSCHT"; AKA: UNRECONCILED; NOT RECONCILED)

Heinrich Hargesheimer (*Heinrich Fahmel at Age 80*), Carlheinz Hargesheimer (*Heinrich Fahmel at Age 30-35*), Martha Standner (*Johanna Fahmel at Age 70*), Daniele Straub (*Johanna Fahmel as a Young Woman*), Henning Harmssen (*Robert Fahmel at Age 40*), Ulrich Hopmann (*Robert Fahmel at Age 18*), Joachim Weiler (*Joseph Fahmel*), Eva-Maria Bold (*Ruth Fahmel*), Hiltraud Wegener (*Marianne*), Ulrich von Thuna (*Schrella at Age 35*), Ernst Kutzinski (*Schrella at Age 15*), Heiner Braun (*Nettlinger at Age 35-40*), Georg Zander (*Hugo/Ferdinand Progulske*), Lutz Grubnau (*1st Abbot*), Martin Trieb (*2d Abbot*), Karl Bodenschatz (*Hotel Porter*), Walter Bruhl (*Trischler*), Wendelin Sachtler (*Mull*), Erika Bruhl (*Edith*), Anita Bell (*Old Woman Playing Cards*), Margrit Borstel (*Blonde Knitting Stockings*), Eduard von Wickenburg (*M*), Huguette Sellen (*Robert's Secretary*), Helga Bruhl (*Frau Trischler*), Joachem Gruner, Gunter Gobel, Peter Berger, Klaus Weyer, Eberhard Ellrich, Norbert Pritz, Bernd Wagner, Michael Kruger, Joseph Vollmert, Dieter Hornberg, Egbert Meiers, Ralf Kurth, Jurgen Beier, Michael Holy, Engelbert Greis, Wolfgang Kuck, Herbert Gammersbach, Rolf Buhl, Peter Kneip, Gerd Lenze, Erdmann Dortschy, Piero Poli, Diana Schlessinger, Karin Kraus, Claudia Wurm, Frouwke von Herwynen, Ise Maassen, Dagmar von Netzer, Hartmut Kirchner, Jurgen Kraeft, Achim Wurm, Max Dietrich Willutzki, Hannelore Langhoff, Johanna Odry, Gunther Becker, Willy Bruno Wange, Stefan Odry, Paul Esser, Hans Zander, Walter Brenner, Rudolf Thome, Claudio Domberger, Hans Schonberger, Karsten Peters, Kai A. Niemeyer, Franz Menzel, Kim Sachtler, Walter Talman-Gros, Joe Hembus, Max Zihlmann, Maurie Fischbein, Christel Meuser, Kathrin Bold, Annie Lautner, Johannes Buzalaki, Gottfried Bold, Victor von Halem, Beate Speith.

A detailing of the hard life of three generations of one family that lived during the most trying times of Germany. The family meets in Cologne in 1956, and begins to remember the past. Hargesheimer and Standner, who head the family, talk about the death of their children in WW I, her confinement to a mental institution for slandering the Kaiser, and the death of their Nazi son during WW II. At a party for Hargesheimer's 80th birthday, Stander makes a vow to assassinate a prominent minister in government. Her attempt fails, but her husband comforts the family with the knowledge that she will probably be freed because of her past mental problems. Another complex film by the husband-wife team of Jean-Marie Straub and Daniele Huillet, whose avant-garde sensibilities and typically dense filmmaking style may make the film difficult viewing for some audiences.

p, Jean-Marie Straub, Danielle Huillet; d, Straub; w, Straub, Huillet (based on *Billard um Halbzehn* by Heinrich Boll); ph, Wendelin Sachtler; m, "Mus: Sonata for Two Pianos and Percussion," Bela Bartok, "Suite No. 2 in B Minor, BMV 1067," Johann Sebastian Bach; ed, Straub, Huillet; md, Francois Louis.

Drama (PR:C MPAA:NR)

NOT SO DUMB*

(1930) 75m MGM bw

Marion Davies (*Dulcy*), Elliott Nugent (*Gordon*), Raymond Hackett (*Bill*), Franklin Pangborn (*Leach*), Julia Faye (*Mrs. Forbes*), William Holden (*Mr. Forbes*), Donald Ogden Stewart (*Van Dyck*), Sally Starr (*Angela*), George Davis (*Perkins*), Ruby Lafayette (*Grandma*).

Based on the Broadway play "Dulcy," NOT SO DUMB borders on farce. Davies, in her third film for Vidor, is driving everyone crazy with her penchant for saying or doing the wrong thing all the time. She is trying to carry off a party for her fiance, who wants to impress some important people willing to invest in his company. Dulcy's antics are routine, causing havoc all the way through to the end when everything turns out fine. An early film for Stewart, a noted humorist and novelist who had turned to acting only two years before.

d, King Vidor; w, Wanda Tuchock, Edwin Justus Mayer (based on the play "Dulcy" by Marc Connelly, George Kaufman); ph, Oliver Marsh; ed, Blanche Sewell; art d, Cedric Gibbons; cos, Adrian; titles, Lucille Newmark.

Comedy (PR:A MPAA:NR)

NOT SO DUSTY**½

(1936, Brit.) 69m GS Enterprises/RKO bw

Wally Patch (*Dusty Gray*), Gus McNaughton (*Nobby Clark*), Muriel George (*Mrs. Clark*), Phil Ray (*Dan Stevens*), Johnny Singer (*Johnny Clark*), Isobel Scaife (*Mary*), Ethel Griffies (*Miss Miller*), H. F. Maltby (*Mr. Armstrong*), Raymond Lovell (*Mr. Holding*), Nancy Pawley, Heather White, Leonard Bullen, Aubrey Mallalieu.

A fairly amusing little comedy starring Patch and McNaughton as two cockney garbagemen who stumble across a rare and valuable book that was inadvertently thrown away. A group of thieves learns of the garbagemen's discovery and soon the chase is on for possession of the irreplaceable publication. To complicate things a bit, a bogus book is introduced into the adventure, resulting in various cases of mistaken identity. Most of the film is a bit silly, but in any case it's a lot of fun.

p, A. George Smith; d, Maclean Rogers; w, Kathleen Butler, H. F. Maltby (based on a story by Wally Patch, Frank Atkinson); ph, Geoffrey Faithfull.

Comedy (PR:A MPAA:NR)

NOT SO DUSTY*½

(1956, Brit.) 81m Jaywell/Eros bw

Joy Nichols (*Lobelia*), Bill Owen (*Dusty*), Leslie Dwyer (*Nobby Clark*), Harold Berens (*Driver*), Robby Hughes (*Mr. Layton*), Ellen Pollock (*Agatha*), Wally Patch (*Porter*), Dandy Nichols (*Mrs. Clark*), William Simons (*Derek Clark*), Totti Trueman Taylor (*Miss Duncan*), Bill Shine (*Alistair*).

Pointless remake of the 1936 Patch and McNaughton comedy about a pair of cockney garbagemen who suddenly find themselves in possession of a priceless book. This time out lesser talents Owen and Dwyer play the garbagemen and the plot sees the evil sister of the man who discarded the book (Pollock) trying every nasty trick she can think of to regain possession. Eventually Owen and Dwyer manage to sell the book to a collector who appreciates its true worth. For some reason director Maclean Rogers, who had also directed the first version, remade his own movie—and badly at that.

p, Bill Luckwell, D. E. A. Winn; d&w, Maclean Rogers (based on a story by Kathleen Butler, H. F. Maltby); ph, Jimmy Wilson.

Comedy (PR:A MPAA:NR)

NOT SO QUIET ON THE WESTERN FRONT**½

(1930, Brit.) 50m BIP/Wardour bw

Leslie Fuller (*Bill Smith*), Mona Goya (*Fifi*), Wilfred Temple (*Bob*), Stella Browne (*Yvonne*), Gladys Cruickshank (*Mimi*), Gerald Lyle (*Pvt. Very*), Dmitri Vetter (*Pvt. John Willie*), Syd Courtenay (*Lieutenant*), Frank Melroyd (*Sergeant*), Marjorie Loring (*Diane*), Olivette (*Dancer*).

Silly comedy has a cook, Fuller, reminiscing about his days during WW I as he chats with customers of the cafe where he's employed. This is really just a clothesline plot designed to hang numerous song and dance numbers on, along with a few comic turns. Certainly nothing heavy duty in the musical comedy genre, but enjoyable on an unsophisticated level. This cheap film served as a kickoff by British International Pictures in the buildup of Fuller into a big box-office star in England. These efforts were usually directed by Banks, himself a comic veteran—in silent movies—before he became a director.

d, Monty Banks; w, Victor Kendall (based on a story by Syd Courtenay, Lola Harvey); ph, James Rogers.

Musical/Comedy (PR:A MPAA:NR)

NOT WANTED**½

(1949) 91m Emerald/Film Classics bw (AKA: STREETS OF SIN)

Sally Forrest (*Sally Kelton*), Keefe Brasselle (*Drew Baxter*), Leo Penn (*Steve Ryan*), Dorothy Adams (*Mrs. Kelton*), Wheaton Chambers (*Mr. Kelton*), Rita Lupino (*Joan*), Audrey Farr (*Nancy*), Carole Donne (*Jane*), Ruth Clifford (*Mrs. Stone*), Ruthelma Stevens (*Miss James*), Virginia Mullin (*Infant's Mother*), Marie Harmon (*Irene*), Roger Anderson (*Bill*), Greg Barton (*Patrolman*), Charles Seel (*Dr. Williams*), Larry Dobkin (*Assistant District Attorney*), Patrick Whyte (*Rev. Culbertson*), Dr. Maurice Bernstein (*Doctor in Delivery Room*).

A film with a message for unwed mothers co-written and co-produced by movie star Ida Lupino. A naive girl, Forrest, becomes infatuated with musician Penn and gives in to temptation. Penn doesn't want to be tied down, which is unfortunate for Forrest when she discovers she is pregnant. While going through the agony of being an unwed mother, she meets crippled veteran Brasselle who wants to marry her. She shuns him and enters a home for unwed mothers to sort out her problems. After she works things out, she reunites with Brasselle to begin life anew.

p, Ida Lupino, Anson Bond; d, Elmer Clifton; w, Paul Jarrico, Lupino (based on a story by Jarrico, Malvin Wald); ph, Henry Freulich; m, Leith Stevens; ed, William Ziegler; art d, Charles D. Hall; m/l, Harry Revel, Raymond Scott, George Greeley.

Drama (PR:A MPAA:NR)

NOT WANTED ON VOYAGE, 1938, Brit.

(SEE: TREACHERY ON THE HIGH SEAS, 1936, Brit.)

NOT WANTED ON VOYAGE**

(1957, Brit.) 82m Byron-Ronald Shiner/Renown bw

Ronald Shiner (*Steward Albert Higgins*), Brian Rix (*Steward Cecil Hollebone*), Griffith Jones (*Guy Harding*), Catherine Boyle (*Julie Haines*), Fabia Drake (*Mrs. Brough*), Michael Brennan (*Chief Steward*), Michael Shepley (*Col. Blewton-Fawcett*), Dorinda Stevens (*Pat*), Martin Boddey (*Captain*), Janet Barrow (*Lady Maud Catesby*), Therese Burton (*Mrs. Rose*), John Chapman (*Mr. Rose*), Peter Prowse (*Strang*), Eric Pohlmann (*Pedro*), Larry Noble (*Steward Bleeding*), Michael Ripper (*Steward Macy*), Hugh Moxey (*1st Officer*).

Too much corn stops this comedy from popping. Shiner and Rix perform one gag after another while aboard an ocean liner filled with seemingly slow-witted passengers. When not hustling tips from the passengers or clowning with each other, the two become involved with finding an expensive necklace that was stolen from a wealthy woman. Between laughs, the two manage to catch the thieves. Remake of the 1933 film TROUBLE, on which Price and Atwill based their play.

p, George Minter, Henry Halsted, Jack Marks; d, Maclean Rogers; w, Michael Pertwee, Evadne Price, Roland Pertwee, Marks (based on a screenplay by Dudley Sturrock from the play "Wanted on Voyage" by Price, Ken Attiwill; ph, Arthur Grant; m, Tony Lowry; ed, Helen Wiggins.

Comedy (PR:A MPAA:NR)

NOT WITH MY WIFE, YOU DON'T!**½

(1966) 118m Fernwood-Reynard/WB c

Tony Curtis (*Tom Ferris*), Virna Lisi (*Julie Ferris*), George C. Scott (*Tank Martin*), Carroll O'Connor (*Gen. Parker*), Richard Eastham (*Gen. Walters*), Eddie Ryder (*Sgt. Gilroy*), George Tyne (*Sgt. Dogerty*), Ann Doran (*Doris Parker*), Donna Danton (*Nurse Sally Ann*), Natalie Core (*Lillian Walters*), Buck Young (*Air Police Colonel*), Maurice Dallimore (*BBC Commentator*), Robert Cleaves ("*Time*" *Reporter*), Karla Most (*Italian Maid*), Betty Bresler (*Miss Ephron*), Alfred Shelley (*Bartender*).

Curtis, Scott, and Lisi star in this lightweight romantic comedy. Lisi had been the romantic interest for both Curtis and Scott, buddies in the Air Force during the Korean conflict. Curtis had won her hand through sabotage by telling her Scott had been killed in action. Now an aide to a general, Curtis is kept so busy that he neglects his wife. When Scott returns to the picture, much to the surprise of both Curtis and Lisi, he uses some trickery of his own, and has Curtis shipped to the Arctic. When Curtis finds out his wife might divorce him and is in Rome with Scott, he steals a jet and flies there to win her back. By that time, Lisi is ready to make up and Scott tells him that he doesn't want to change his single ways.

p&d, Norman Panama; w, Panama, Larry Gelbart, Peter Barnes (based on a story by Panama, Melvin Frank); ph, Charles Lang, Paul Beeson (Technicolor); m, Johnny Williams; ed, Aaron Stell; md, Williams prod d, Edward Carrere; md, Williams; set d, George James Hopkins; cos, Edith Head; ch, Shelah Hackett; m/l, "A Big Beautiful Ball," "My Inamorata," (Williams, Johnny Mercer); makeup, Gordon Bau; aviation liaison, Hamish Mahaddie.

Romance **(PR:A MPAA:NR)**

NOTEBOOKS OF MAJOR THOMPSON (SEE: FRENCH THEY ARE A FUNNY RACE, THE, 1956, Fr.)

NOTHING BARRED½** (1961, Brit.) 83m Rix-Conyers/BL bw

Brian Rix *(Wilfred Sapling)*, Leo Franklin *(Barger)*, Naunton Wayne *(Lord Whitebait)*, Charles Heslop *(Spankworth)*, Ann Firbank *(Lady Katherine)*, John Slater *(Warder Lockitt)*, Vera Pearce *(Lady Millicent)*, Arnold Bell *(Governor)*, Alexander Gauge *(Policeman)*, Jack Watling *(Peter Brewster)*, Irene Handl *(Elsie)*, Bernard Cribbins, Wally Patch *(Newspapermen)*, Wilfrid Lawson *(Albert)*, Terry Scott *(Policeman)*, Henry Kendall *(Parson)*, Duke of Bedford *(Convict)*.

A British lord finds himself broke and in trouble. When he mistakes an innocent plumber for a burglar, the two combine forces to help the lord steal one of the paintings he owns. Another amusing farce by the Rix-Conyers team.

p, Brian Rix, D'Arcy Conyers; d, Conyers; w, John Chapman.

Comedy **(PR:A MPAA:NR)**

NOTHING BUT A MAN*** (1964) 95m Du Art/Cinema V bw

Ivan Dixon *(Duff Anderson)*, Abby Lincoln *(Josie Dawson)*, Gloria Foster *(Lee)*, Julius Harris *(Will Anderson)*, Martin Priest *(Driver)*, Leonard Parker *(Frankie)*, Yaphet Kotto *(Jocko)*, Stanley Greene *(Rev. Dawson)*, Helen Lounck *(Effie Simms)*, Helene Arrindell *(Doris)*, Walter Wilson *(Car Owner)*, Milton Williams *(Pop)*, Melvin Stewart *(Raddick)*, Alfred Puryear *(Barney)*, Charles McRae *(Joe)*, Ed Rowan *(Willie)*, Tom Ligon, William Jordan *(Teenagers)*, Gertrude Jeanette *(Mrs. Dawson)*, Richard Webber *(Bud Ellis)*, Eugene Wood *(Schoolteacher)*, Jim Wright *(Bartender)*, Jary Banks *(Bessie)*, Dorothy Hall, Gil Rogers, Arland Schubert, Bill Riola, Pater Carew, Jay Brooks, Richard Ward, Moses Gunn, Sylvia Ray, Esther Rolle, Esther Davis.

A well-intentioned, independently made film describing the life of a black man in the 1960s South. Basically, all the title character (Dixon) wants to do is live simply. While working for the railroad in Alabama, he falls in love with Lincoln, the daughter of the minister (Greene). Greene does not like Dixon so the couple go to Birmingham to see Dixon's father, a dying alcoholic. Dixon also visits his illegitimate son, who has been abandoned by his mother and left in the care of a woman not related to him. Lincoln wants to marry, but Dixon does not want to assume the responsibility. The couple finally wed, and Dixon gets a job at the town sawmill. When he won't kowtow to his racist white employers, he is fired and labeled a troublemaker. He then finds work at a gas station but is still harassed by the townspeople. After beating and berating his wife out of frustration, he returns to Birmingham to watch his father die. The reality of the situation leads him to take a step toward manhood, and he gets his son and goes back to Lincoln to try to live in peace and dignity. The film garnered a great deal of praise at the time of its release for its accuracy in detailing the life of a black laborer in the South, and for not sentimentalizing the subject matter.

p, Robert Young, Michael Roemer, Robert Rubin; d, Roemer; w, Roemer, Young; ph, Young; ed, Luke Bennett; prod d, William Rhodes; cos, Nancy Ruffing; m/l, Eddie Holland, Lamont Dozier, Brian Holland (sung by Mary Wells, The Gospel Stars, Martha and the Vandellas, The Miracles, Little Stevie Wonder, The Marvelettes, Wilbur Kirk).

Drama **(PR:A MPAA:NR)**

NOTHING BUT THE BEST** (1964, Brit.) 99m Domino/Royal c

Alan Bates *(Jimmy Brewster)*, Denholm Elliott *(Charlie Prince)*, Harry Andrews *(Mr. Horton)*, Millicent Martin *(Ann Horton)*, Pauline Delany *(Mrs. March)*, Godfrey Quigley *(Coates)*, Alison Leggatt *(Mrs. Brewster)*, Lucinda Curtis *(Nadine)*, Nigel Stock *(Ferris)*, James Villiers *(Hugh)*, Drewe Henley *(Denis)*, Avice Landon *(Mrs. Horton)*, Ernest Clark *(Roberts)*, William Rushton *(Gerry)*, Peter Madden *(Ex-Politician)*, Robert Bruce *(Basil)*, Howard Lang *(Jutson)*, Paul Curran *(Mr. Brewster)*, Joe Levine *(Taxi Driver)*, Donald Pickering *(Adrian Slater)*, Joanna Morris *(Jimmy's Secretary)*, June Watts *(Waitress)*, Angus MacKay *(Clergyman)*, Diane Appleby *(Secretary)*, Bernard Levin *(Himself)*.

Stanley Ellin wrote some of the best and most chilling short stories ever, including the famous "Specialty of the House" that was made into an eerie Alfred Hitchcock half-hour. He is not given his due with this spotty adaptation by Raphael, who is usually much better than this. Bates is a lower-class real estate clerk who aspires to have some of that Room at the Top that he's been hearing so much about. He will stop at nothing to achieve social status and hires Elliott, a degenerate character, to teach him manners and the proper way to behave in the upper-crust society that Bates means to crack. Elliott instructs Bates (the way Higgins did with Eliza) in all the niceties and Bates moves in on his boss' daughter, Martin. Her father, Andrews, watches carefully as Bates calculatedly makes his approach. Martin sees right through Bates, but he is handsome and lots more fun than the twits who surround her. After Elliott wins a bundle at the races, he is of a mind to blow the whistle on Bates, who puts an end to those thoughts by putting an end to Elliott. He strangles Elliott with his necktie and, with the help of landlady Delany (who has the hots for Bates), stows the dead body in a huge trunk and hides it in her basement. With Elliott out of the way, Bates continues his wooing of Martin and they are soon married. While they are on their honeymoon, Delany takes a trip to South Africa, after having sold her property. Bates and Martin return and he thinks that his life is now a bowl of cherries, as he has been made Andrews' partner. The smile soon disintegrates when he sees that Delany's house is being razed by workmen, and the picture ends as Bates watches and winces and worries if Elliott's body will be uncovered. It's an immoral picture that attempts to be a comedy in the grisly tradition of KIND HEARTS AND CORONETS, but Bates has neither the comedic skill nor the sex appeal to pull it off. Martin is beautiful and does what she can with the slim material given her. Good cinematography from Roeg who went on to be a confusing director.

p, David Deutsch; d, Clive Donner; w, Frederic Raphael (based on the short story "The Best of Everything" by Stanley Ellin); ph, Nicolas Roeg (Eastmancolor); m, Ron Grainer; ed, Fergus McDonell; md, Grainer; art d, Reece Pemberton; set d, Helen Thomas; m/l, "The Best of Everything," Grainer, Raphael (sung by Millicent Martin).

Comedy **(PR:C MPAA:NR)**

NOTHING BUT THE NIGHT** (1975, Brit.) 90m Charlemagne/Cinema Systems c (AKA: THE RESURRECTION SYNDICATE)

Christopher Lee *(Col. Bingham)*, Peter Cushing *(Sir Mark Ashley)*, Georgia Brown *(Joan Foster)*, Diana Dors *(Anna Harb)*, Kathleen Byron *(Dr. Rose)*, Duncan Lamont *(Dr. Knight)*, Keith Barron *(Dr. Haynes)*, Fulton MacKay *(Cameron)*, Gwyneth Strong *(Mary Valley)*, John Robinson *(Lord Fawnlee)*, Michael Gambon *(Inspector Grant)*, Morris Perry *(Dr. Yeats)*, Shelagh Fraser *(Mrs. Allison)*, Geoffrey Frederick *(Computer Operator)*, Louise Nelson *(Nurse)*, Robin Wentworth *(Head Porter)*, Michael Wynne *(Donald)*, Andrew McCulloch *(Malcolm)*, Michael Segal *(1st Reporter)*, John Kelland *(2nd Reporter)*, Ken Watson *(Jamie)*, Paul Humpoletz *(Angus)*, Stanley Lebor *(Policeman)*, Stuart Saunders *(Police Sergeant)*, Michael Brennan *(Deck Hand)*, Janet Bruce *(Naureen Stokes)*, Beatrice Ward *(Helen Van Trayler)*, Geoffrey Denton *(Paul Anderson)*.

Children who have been injected with a serum containing the life essence of dead people retain the memories of those dead and become killers, wreaking havoc on London. Lee is the Scotland Yard detective assigned to solve the mystery. It was the first and last film made by Lee's own production company.

p, Anthony Nelson-Keys; d, Peter Sasdy; w, Brian Hayles (based on a novel by John Blackburn); ph, Ken Talbot; m, Malcolm Williamson; ed, Keith Palmer; md, Philip Martell; art d, Colin Grimes; spec eff, Les Bowie; makeup, Eddie Knight.

Horror/Mystery **(PR:A MPAA:PG)**

NOTHING BUT THE TRUTH½** (1929) 78m PAR bw

Richard Dix *(Robert Bennett)*, Berton Churchill *(E. M. Burke)*, Louis J. Bartels *(Frank Connelly)*, Ned Sparks *(Clarence Van Dyke)*, Helen Kane *(Mabel Riley)*, Wynne Gibson *(Sabel Riley)*, Dorothy Hall *(Gwen Burke)*, Madeline Gray *(Mrs. E. M. Burke)*, Nancy Ryan *(Ethel Clark)*.

An early comedy originally made in 1920 as a silent by MGM, and then remade in 1941 with Bob Hope as the star. This time Dix is the man who takes a bet for $10,000 that he cannot go for 24 hours without telling a lie. The money has been put up by his fiancee Hall, because if he wins and doubles the money, her father Churchill will double the amount again. Churchill also happens to be in on one-third of the bet himself, further complicating matters. Features Dix in his first talking film.

d, Victor Schertzinger; w, John McGowan, William Collier, Sr. (based on a story by McGowan and the play by James Montgomery); ph, Edward Cronjager; ed, Morton Blumenstock, Robert Bassler; m/l, "Do Something," Bud Green, Sammy Stept.

Comedy **(PR:A MPAA:NR)**

NOTHING BUT THE TRUTH*** (1941) 90m PAR bw

Bob Hope *(Steve Bennett)*, Paulette Goddard *(Gwen Saunders)*, Edward Arnold *(T. T. Ralston)*, Leif Erickson *(Tommy Van Deusen)*, Willie Best *(Samuel)*, Glenn Anders *(Dick Donnelly)*, Grant Mitchell *(Mr. Bishop)*, Catharine Doucet *(Mrs. Van Deusen)*, Rose Hobart *(Mrs. Donnelly)*, Clarence Kolb *(Mr. James P. Van Deusen)*, Leon Belasco *(Dr. Lothar Zarok)*, Mary Forbes *(Mrs. Ralston)*, Helene Millard *(Miss Turner)*, William Wright *(Mr. Pritchard)*, Oscar Smith *(Shoeshine Boy)*, Wilson Benge *(Fredericks)*, Jack Chapin, Rod Cameron *(Sailors)*, Dick Chandler *(Office Boy)*, Catherine Craig *(Receptionist)*, Edward McWade *(Elderly Clerk)*, Keith Richards *(Boy)*, James Blaine *(Doorman)*, Jack Egan *(Elevator Starter)*, Jim Farley *(Watchman)*, Victor Potel *(Pedestrian)*, Lee Shumway *(Cop)*, Eleanor Counts *(Maid)*, Buck Woods *(Porter)*, Billy Dawson *(Newsboy)*, Helen Vinson *(Linda Graham)*.

Hope is a habitual liar who has to tell the truth for 24 hours to win a bet in this cute comedy that keeps the jokes rolling for Hope. Goddard is his fiancee, who has handed him $10,000 for charity, hoping that he will double that amount in three days by winning the bet. Arnold, Erickson, and Anders are the ones who bet against him and provide the impetus for Hope's usual double-talk. This is the third and best version of this story, originally filmed in 1920 and then in 1929.

p, Arthur Hornblow, Jr.; d, Elliott Nugent; w, Don Hartman, Ken Englund (based on the play by James Montgomery, from the novel by Frederick S. Isham); ph, Charles Lang; ed, Alma Macrorie; art d, Hans Dreier, Robert Usher.

Comedy **(PR:A MPAA:NR)**

NOTHING BUT TROUBLE½** (1944) 69m MGM bw

Stan Laurel *(Himself)*, Oliver Hardy *(Himself)*, Henry O'Neill *(Basil Hawkley)*, Mary Boland *(Mrs. Elvira Hawkley)*, David Leland f2(King Christopher), John Warburton *(Ronetz)*, Matthew Boulton *(Prince Prentiloff of Marshovia)*, Connie

Gilchrist *(Mrs. Flannagan)*, Philip Merivale *(Prince Saul)*, Paul Porcasi *(Italian Restaurateur)*, Jean de Briac *(French Restaurateur)*, Joe Yule, Sr., Eddie Dunn, Forbes Murray, Ray Teal *(Officers)*, Howard Mitchell, Steve Darrell *(Zoo Attendants)*, William Frambe *(Ocean Liner Passenger)*, Garry Owen *(Periwinkle)*, Robert Emmett O'Connor *(Mulligan)*, Robert E. Homans *(Jailer)*, William J. Holmes, Mayo Newhall, Toby Noolan *(Royal Couriers)*, Chester Clute *(Doolittle)*.

Stan and Ollie are from a family that provided domestics to the landed gentry. They need work and can't find any in the U. S., so they go off to Europe. There they encounter the same problem there, so they return to the States and become the chef and butler to Boland and O'Neill, a chi chi couple who are tossing a swank bash in honor of Leland, the boy king of the mythical country of Orlandia. He is now in exile and looked over by his villainous uncle, Merivale. Laurel and Hardy leave the mansion to buy food for the party and run into Leland who is playing football with a bunch of street kids. He has fled an attempt on his life by one of Merivale's henchmen, and when Stan and Ollie learn of this, they hide the lad in the mansion until the heat is off. They never did get the meat they went out to buy, so they go to the local zoo and purloin a slab of horseflesh from the lion, who is not too thrilled about seeing his dinner disappear. At the dinner, the meat is too tough for anyone to cut, much less chew. When Merivale hears that Leland is missing, he departs the party to search for his nephew. Stan and Ollie get the sack for their faux pas and exit the mansion with Leland. With no place to stay, they wind up at a mission where Leland is recognized by a wino who promptly phones the authorities. Our heroes are tossed in the clink and Merivale has Leland in his clutches once again. The boy king says that Stan and Ollie are not kidnapers and they are released and given jobs as butler and chef for Leland. Merivale is intending to have a poisonous dish set before the king, but Stan and Ollie, upon noticing that Leland has a smaller portion of the salad than Merivale, switch the two plates. Merivale spots the switch and exits, saying that he doesn't feel well from all the stress of the last few days. Hardy mistakenly places the poison pill in a caviar hors d'oeuvre. Leland finally gets wise to Merivale's machinations and accuses him of plotting. Merivale pulls a gun on Leland, Laurel, and Hardy. The boy leaps out a window onto a platform attached to the house where a painter was doing some touch-up work. He quickly calls the cops. The workmen take the platform away from the side of the house as Merivale is motioning to Stan and Ollie that it's now their turn to jump out the window. While Merivale wields the gun with one hand, he pops the caviar goody into his mouth with the other and hits the deck in less time than you can say Beluga. Leland and the coppers race in, just as Laurel and Hardy are about to go out the window. Not one of the team's best efforts and it was their final MGM film. Sam Taylor, mostly noted as a screenwriter, received assistance from Bert Glazer on this. (See LAUREL AND HARDY series, Index.)

p, B. F. Ziedman; d, Sam Taylor; w, Russell Rouse, Ray Golden, Bradford Ropes, Margaret Gruen; ph, Charles Salerno, Jr.; m, Nathaniel Shilkret; ed, Conrad A. Nervig; art d, Cedric Gibbons, Harry McAfee; set d, Edwin B. Willis, Jack Bonar; cos, Irene.

Comedy   **(PR:AA MPAA:NR)**

NOTHING LIKE PUBLICITY**½   (1936,
                                    Brit.) 64m Greenspan & Seligman Enterprises/RKO bw

Billy [William] Hartnell *(Pat Spencer)*, Marjorie Taylor *(Denise Delorme)*, Moira Lynd *(Miss Bradley)*, Ruby Miller *(Sadie Sunshine)*, Max Adrian *(Bob Wharncliffe)*, Isobel Scaife *(Maid)*, Gordon McLeod *(Sir Arthur Wharncliffe)*, Dorothy Hammond *(Lady Wharncliffe)*, Aubrey Mallalieu *(Mr. Dines)*, Michael Ripper.

A tale of mixed up identities has hyperactive press agent Hartnell attempting to help a struggling young actress by getting her to pose as an heiress from the States. Complications arise when both a female crook pulling a similar impersonation, as well as the real heiress herself, show up. Fairly routine with a few good laughs by veteran comedy director Rogers.

p, A. George Smith; d, Maclean Rogers; w, Kathleen Butler, H. F. Maltby (based on a story by Arthur Cooper); ph, Geoffrey Faithfull.

Comedy   **(PR:A MPAA:NR)**

NOTHING PERSONAL*   (1980, Can.) 97m AIP-Filmways c

Donald Sutherland *(Prof. Roger Keller)*, Suzanne Somers *(Abigail Adams)*, Lawrence Dane *(Robert Ralston)*, Roscoe Lee Browne *(Mr. Paxton)*, Dabney Coleman *(Tom Dickerson)*, Saul Rubinek *(Peter Braden)*, Catherine O'Hara *(Janet Samson)*, Maury Chakin *(Kanook)*, Kate Lynch *(Audrey Seltzer)*, Hugh Webster *(Ralph Henry Emerson)*, Sean McCann *(Jake Barnes)*, Ben Gordon, Eugene Levy, Rummy Bishop, Richard Monette, Gabe Cohen, Bonnie Brooks, Robert Benson, Ken Lamaire, Sam Moses, Pat Collins, Jack Duffy, Tony Rasato, Robert Christie.

A good example of how a deal gets made and a picture doesn't, NOTHING PERSONAL was one of those Canadian tax shelter movies that are manufactured to take advantage of the concessions north of the border. The film's executive producers were Alan Hamel, Jay Bernstein, and Norman Hirschfield. Hamel is the female star's husband, Bernstein was her manager, and Hirschfield may have been the man who put it all together. These kinds of movies get done when there are several Canadians attached to the project, as the whole thing works on a point system, with a certain amount of points being allowed for the director, the writer, and the stars. Scanning the cast list, note that Canadians Sutherland, Rubinek, Levy, and O'Hara have featured roles. Kaufman can be brilliant, as in LOVE AT FIRST BITE, but he can also be a dreary writer, as in most of his other works. Sutherland is a liberal professor who objects to the clubbing of baby seals and Somers is a Harvard-educated attorney who is going to aid him in stopping the slaughter. In their mission, they come up against the man who runs the huge conglomerate that is responsible, Dane, and his flunky, Coleman. Sutherland and Somers then enlist Browne, a hotel owner, in their wish to find an Indian who can put a stop to it. The whole thing is tedious, witless, and has more holes than a Texas oil field. The direction is non-existent and the editing must have been done with a scythe. Somers and Sutherland wind up paired at the finish, but they have

so little dimension in their characters that one couldn't care less. This was Somers's first major film role after a successful television career. She and husband Hamel should have used a bit more taste in choosing it, as she almost disappeared from sight after this disaster. In a small role, look for the brilliant Eugene Levy, who did so well on TV's "SCTV" (with O'Hara) and scored in SPLASH.

p, David M. Perlmutter; d, George Bloomfield; w, Robert Kaufman; ph, Laszlo George, Arthur Ibbetson (Movielab Color); ed, George Appleby; art d, Mary Kerr; set d, Mark Freeborn, Anthony Greco; cos, Lynda Kemp.

Comedy   **Cas.**   **(PR:A-C MPAA:PG)**

NOTHING SACRED*****   (1937) 75m Selznick/UA c

Carole Lombard *(Hazel Flagg)*, Frederic March *(Wally Cook)*, Charles Winninger *(Dr. Enoch Downer)*, Walter Connolly *(Oliver Stone)*, Sig Rumann *(Dr. Emile Egglehoffer)*, Frank Fay *(Master Of Ceremonies)*, Maxie Rosenbloom *(Max Levinsky)*, Margaret Hamilton *(Drug Store Lady)*, Troy Brown *(Ernest Walker)*, Olin Howland *(Baggage Man)*, Hedda Hopper *(Dowager)*, John Qualen *(Swede Fireman)*, Art Lasky *(Mug)*, Monty Woolley *(Dr. Vunch)*, Hattie McDaniel *(Mrs. Walker)*, Alex Schoenberg *(Dr. Kerchinwisser)*, Alex Novinsky *(Dr. Marachuffsky)*, Katherine Shelton *(Downer's Nurse)*, Ernest Whitman, Everett Brown *(Policemen)*, Ben Morgan, Hans Steinke *(Wrestlers)*, George Chandler *(Photographer)*, Nora Cecil *(Schoolteacher)*, Claire Du Brey *(Miss Rafferty, Nurse)*, A.W. Sweatt *(Office Boy)*, Vera Lewis *(Miss Sedgewick)*, Ann Doran *(Telephone Girl)*, Jinx Falkenburg *(Katinka)*, Bill Dunn, Lee Phelps *(Electricians)*, Cyril Ring *(Pilot)*, Mickey McMasters *(Referee)*, Bobby Tracy *(Announcer)*, Betty Douglas *("Helen of Troy")*, Eleanor Troy *("Catherine of Russia")*, Monica Bannister *("Pocahontas")*, Margaret Lyman *("Salome")*, Shirley Chambers *("Lady Godiva")*, Billy Barty *(Little Boy)*, Wimpy the Dog, Raymond Scott and His Quintet.

A marvelous black comedy full of wit and journalistic wisdom in the grand and capricious style of Hecht (who co-authored, with Charles MacArthur, THE FRONT PAGE), this film is all the more stunning thanks to the outrageous and hilarious performance of super comedienne Lombard. This was one of the first of the screwball comedies and it is a classic of the genre which is just as funny today as when it was first filmed. March is an ambitious newsman who gets into big trouble when he tries to pass off a New York Negro as the "Sultan of Marzipan," a potentate who is about to donate $500,000 to establish an art institute. The Negro is actually penniless and doesn't know Marzipan from Manhattan. When Connolly, the editor of March's sensation-seeking tabloid, finds out about the impersonation he becomes livid and demotes March to writing obituaries. Meanwhile, Lombard, a working girl in Warsaw, Vermont, who longs to visit New York City, is routinely examined by her less than competent doctor, Winninger; the bumbling doctor sadly tells Lombard that she has radium poisoning and will only live a short while. News of this tragedy reaches March and he sets out to write a great sob story but by the time he reaches Lombard, Winninger has changed his diagnosis and has informed Lombard that she will live a long time since she isn't poisoned after all. March won't hear of it; he has a great story and he refuses to allow the truth to ruin his fabulous tale. He persuades Lombard to go through with the charade, promising that she will not only see New York but will enter the great city in style. She agrees and by the time March begins grinding out the tragedy in daily installments in his paper, New York is weeping loudly. Lombard arrives and is given the key to the city and installed in one of Manhattan's most lavish hotels, her suite and every convenience, including expensive clothes, jewels, nonstop service, all provided for by Connolly, Rumann, and other magnates wishing to look good to the world. March takes Lombard out dining and she gets drunk, passing out. The shocked sob sisters are quickly informed that Lombard has had a relapse due to her deadly illness and this causes another rash of city-wide bawling. Everywhere Lombard goes, women weep and men gulp down sorrow. In public places such as a wrestling match in Madison Square Garden, her appearance causes authorities to demand "minutes of respect," where crowds stand in sorrowful silence for the soon-to-be-deceased Lombard. But the beautiful blonde continues to thrive and her condition appears much too robust for editor Connolly's liking. Suspicious of his star reporter March, Connolly orders a team of expert physicians to examine Lombard. Just before the medical people arrive in her suite, March arranges to rough up the now disgusted Lombard, so she'll be properly run-down. He not only bruises and pummels her, but lands a terrific right cross to her face. (This lady-beating scene became one of the most famous and hilarious sequences in Hollywood history.) Still, Lombard cannot conceal her good health forever and a group of her financial backers, suddenly wise to her ruse, ask her, please, to find a way to die and save them all further spiritual mortification. March and Lombard prepare an elaborate but fake suicide for the lady and then they sail away in disguise, wearing sunglasses, en route to a new life together. Hecht had a great deal of fun writing NOTHING SACRED for the screen, plucking his backround from his own newspaper experiences. The fake sultan, for instance, was based upon a prank Hecht himself had concocted, one in which his eccentric poet friend Maxwell Bodenheim, then unknown, pretended to be a foreign potentate visiting Chicago, where Hecht was then working as a spectacular journalist. Like the fake poisoning shown in NOTHING SACRED, Hecht himself had "created" many a news story during his days in Chicago as a journalist, sprucing up slow news days with reports of nonexistent earthquakes, fires, and untraceable tragedies. Of course, the role of the errant reporter is based on his incredible and kindred exploits. Lombard is wonderful and funny to the bone in NOTHING SACRED, enacting a role that was made for her madcap talent, and March, one of the fine serious actors, showed his considerable flair for comedy in this delightful farce. Director Wellman squirmed with delight inside Hecht's spoofing script and his amused attitude affected every aspect of the film production. He was overheard by Lombard and March to say that "a little fun is the best tonic between scenes," and the leading lady and man jumped on that line. Lombard was vexed when she tried to talk to Wellman about her scenes; he would only shake his head and walk away. She fixed Wellman by having several technicians grab him one day, slip him into a straightjacket and tie him to his director's chair so she could have his undivided attention. She even infected March with her penchant for zany antics and the two of them spent their off-camera hours driving madly about the Selznick lot in a rented fire engine. Wellman began to talk like Lombard before the film was finished and his direction took on her wisecracking attitude. At one point he stated (as quoted in William R. Meyer's *Warner Brothers Directors*: "Miss Lombard, I know it must be tough for a woman to look into Freddie March's frozen puss and pretend to be in love with him. But close your eyes or something and let's do it just once more." The pace of this great film is so brisk that the viewers will have to remind themselves about just what scene caused the laughter to start, and it's a film with a laugh a minute throughout. Frank Capra borrowed some of this story line for MEET JOHN DOE and the film would be remade as a Broadway musical entitled HAZEL FLAGG. Dean Martin and Jerry Lewis appeared in a disastrously poor remake, LIVING IT UP.

p, David O. Selznick; d, William Wellman; w, Ben Hecht, additional dialog Ring Lardner, Jr., Budd Schulberg (based on the story *Letter to the Editor* by James H. Street); ph, W. Howard Greene (Technicolor); m, Oscar Levant; ed, James E. Newcom; md, Louis Forbes; art d, Lyle Wheeler; set d, Edward G. Boyle; cos, Travis Banton, Walter Plunkett; spec eff, Jack Cosgrove.

Comedy   **Cas.**   **(PR:A MPAA:NR)**

NOTHING TO LOSE   (SEE: TIME GENTLEMEN PLEASE, 1953, Brit.)

NOTHING VENTURE**½   (1948, Brit.) 73m BL bw

Peter Artemus, Philip Artemus, Jackie Artemus (*Tom, Dick, and Harry*), Terry Randal (*Diana Chaice*), Patric Curwen (*The Author*), Michael Aldridge (*Michael Garrod*), Paul Blake (*The Boss*), Wilfred Caithness (*The Professor*), Howard Douglas (*Badger*), Ben Williams (*Spike*), Peter Gawthorne (*Scotland Yard Official*), Arthur Denton (*Hotel Porter*), Alfred A. Harris (*Hotel Guest*), Jack Simpson and His Sextet (*Band*), Maureen Morton (*Singer*).

Helping Randal after her horse has been frightened by a gunshot, the plucky Artemus brothers learn some crooks are after her father. A scientist has invented a special ray gun the crooks want. When Randal and her father are held in a secret underground hideout, the Artemus' employ the help of a government agent to save them and bring the criminals to justice. This tale of intrigue and adventure was made with younger audiences in mind, but the outlandish plot developments may prove to be a little too much to take for the more sophisticated children of today.

p&d, John Baxter; w, Geoffrey Orme (based on his story); ph, Jo Jago; m, Kennedy Russell; ed, Vi Burdon; md, Russell; art d, Denis Wreford.

Children's Adventure   **(PR:AAA MPAA:NR)**

NOTORIOUS*****   (1946) 101m RKO bw

Cary Grant (*Devlin*), Ingrid Bergman (*Alicia Huberman*), Claude Rains (*Alexander Sebastian*), Louis Calhern (*Paul Prescott*), Mme. Konstantin (*Mme. Sebastian*), Reinhold Schunzel (*Dr. Anderson*), Moroni Olsen (*Walter Beardsley*), Ivan Triesault (*Eric Mathis*), Alex Minotis (*Joseph*), Wally Brown (*Mr. Hopkins*), Gavin Gordon (*Ernest Weylin*), Sir Charles Mendl (*Commodore*), Ricardo Costa (*Dr. Barbosa*), Eberhard Krumschmidt (*Hupka*), Fay Baker (*Ethel*), Antonio Moreno (*Senor Ortiza*), Frederick Ledebur (*Knerr*), Luis Serrano (*Dr. Silva*), William Gordon (*Adams*), Charles D. Brown (*Judge*), Ramon Nomar (*Dr. Silva*), Peter Von Zerneck (*Rossner*), Fred Nurney (*Huberman*), Herbert Wyndham (*Mr. Cook*), Aileen Carlyle (*Woman at Party*), Harry Hayden (*Defense Counsel*), Dink Trout (*Clerk at Court*), Howard Negley, Frank Marlowe, George Lynn (*Photographers*), Warren Jackson (*District Attorney*), Howard Mitchell (*Bailiff*), Sandra Morgan, Lillian West, Beulah Christian, Leota Lorraine, Almeda Fowler (*Women*), Garry Owen, Lester Dorr (*Motor Cops*), Patricia Smart (*Mrs. Jackson*), Tina Menard (*Maid*), Richard Clark, Frank McDonald (*Men*), Frank Wilcox (*FBI Man*), John Vosper, Eddie Bruce, Don Kerr, Ben Erway, Emmett Vogan, Paul Bryan, Alan Ward, James Logan (*Reporters*), Bea Benaderet, Virginia Gregg, Bernice Barrett (*File Clerks*), Ted Kelly (*Waiter*), Alfredo De Sa (*Ribero*).

This brilliant Hitchcock masterpiece combines romance and suspense in a smooth blend of mystery and action and presents startling performances from Grant and Bergman. She is the daughter of a man convicted of spying for the Nazis, a playgirl of dubious reputation who is known well in the international set. After her father's conviction, Grant, an American agent, is assigned to watch Bergman and he quickly meets and falls in love with her, engineering her to Rio de Janeiro. Although Grant knows through phone taps and correspondence that Bergman is utterly opposed to her father's Nazi philosophy and is a patriot loyal to America, he continues to conduct surveillance of her activities. Then spy chief Calhern orders Grant to set up Bergman with Rains, head of the German chemical cartel, I.G. Farben, operating in Brazil. Bergman agrees to not only meet Rains but to marry him if necessary to learn what the Germans are up to in Rio. All of this is unsavory to Grant who is now in love with Bergman but he stands by and watches his lady become involved with the suave Nazi cabal. At a party in Rains' magnificent mansion, Grant and Bergman investigate Rains' mysterious wine cellar and find some strange ore contained in the wine bottles instead of vintage wine. This is the top secret material they are looking for, but before samples can be analyzed Rains comes to believe that his wife is a spy and, with the help of his domineering mother, Konstantin, he begins to systematically and slowly poison Bergman. Just before succumbing, Bergman calls Grant, who drives to the mansion and rescues her, exposing Rains as incompetent to his German masters and leaving the shifty little Nazi to his lethal fate. Grant and Bergman go on to have a happy life together. NOTORIOUS is one of Hitchcock's most sophisticated thrillers, one where he employs a subtle touch in every frame, his actors underplaying their roles as they go about their deadly business. Early on Hitchcock and Hecht developed a "MacGuffin" (the Hitchcockian term for the reason or the item around which the plot of the film revolved) which producer David O. Selznick could not accept, Selznick then having Hitchcock and all properties developed by him under exclusive contract. The director and writer had gone to great lengths to develop an

enviable "MacGuffin," one that dealt with uranium, a rare ore which Hecht had read about and believed had something to do with the development of the atomic bomb, a bomb only rumored to exist in science fiction terms. Hecht took Hitchcock to see scientist Dr. Robert Andrew Millikan at Cal Tech where Millikan talked with them for several hours about the *possibility* of splitting the hydrogen atom, but when Hecht brought up uranium, Millikan rejected the idea of this substance being involved. Feeling that they would not be tampering with anything the government was then working on (the A-bomb was nearing completion at the time, toward the end of WW II), Hecht and Hitchcock went ahead, using the uranium angle, not realizing that uranium was a vital part of the makeup of the A-bomb. Also unknown to them was the fact that the minute they left Cal Tech, according to Hitchcock years later, a team of FBI agents was assigned to watch him and Hecht for months while the film was in production to see that they did not accidentally reveal any U.S. top secrets. When Hitchcock went back to Selznick to sell him on NOTORIOUS, the mogul still thought the idea about the uranium harebrained and that the public wouldn't buy such a preposterous "MacGuffin." Hitchcock was determined to make the film and Selznick was equally determined not to make it under the Selznick International banner so he appeased his top director and made enormous profits to boot by selling the NOTORIOUS package, Hitchcock, Hecht, Grant, Bergman, the script, to RKO for $800,000 plus 50 percent of the profits in 1944. On top of that, RKO spent $2 million producing the film. Still, everyone was happy when the film met with tremendous critical and public approval, eventually grossing $9 million. There is much in this film that proves Hitchcock a technical genius as well as a conceptual filmic mastermind. NOTORIOUS contains one of the great crane shots on record, one where Hitchcock positioned his camera at the top of a magnificent stairway, overlooking a huge crowd of party guests in Rains' sprawling mansion. The camera, in one sweeping take, moves down the stairs, over and through the crowd, into the main ballroom, and over to Bergman, to zero in on a tight closeup of the key to Rains' mysterious wine cellar clutched in Bergman's hand. (This incredible shot has some Hitchcockian precedents, one being a great tracking shot in YOUNG AND INNOCENT where the camera works its way across a crowded dance floor and closes in on the blinking eyes of a murderer in blackface playing among the band, the other being a stairway shot showing Robert Cummings and Priscilla Lane descending a stairway to a mammoth ballroom in a New York mansion in SABOTEUR.) Just as elaborate but technically correct is the plotting of this film, each scene carefully worked out in detail *in advance* by Hitchcock. The film also contains one of the longest and most passionate kissing scenes on record between Grant and Bergman (a little more than three minutes). He has arrived in her Rio apartment overlooking the magnificent bay and she is about to serve him a chicken dinner. But they take their time getting to it, Grant nibbling at Bergman's ears as if they were hors d'oeuvres, kissing and nibbling and caressing each other's lips, necks, and ears while they make mindless talk about the meal they are going to have after the meal of love they are then devouring. All of this was designed by Hitchcock to avert the then Hollywood censors from their restrictions on prolonged kissing scenes. The methodology even baffled the crafty Hecht when he showed up on the set to see this now famous kissing scene while the lover absent-mindedly discussed the forthcoming chicken dinner. "I don't get all this talk about chicken!" Hecht told Hitchcock, who only smiled in response. The director later recalled a strange memory that had lingered for years in his mind and had prompted, he said, the scene, one where the public had "the great privilege of embracing Cary Grant and Ingrid Bergman together. It was kind of a temporary menage a trois. . .I felt that they should reamin in an embrace and that we should join them. So when they got to the phone, the camera followed them, never leaving the closeup all the way, right over to the door, all in one continuous shot. . .The idea came to me many, many years ago when I was on a train going from Boulogne to Paris. There's a big, old, red brick factory, and at one end of the factory was this huge, high brick wall. There were two little figures at the bottom of the wall, a boy and a girl. The boy was urinating against the wall but the girl had hold of his arm and she never let go. She'd look down at what he was doing, and then look around at the scenery, and down again to see how far he'd got on. And that was what gave me the idea. She couldn't let go. Romance must not be interrupted, even by urinating." The stars later told Hitchcock that "they felt very awkward in that scene in NOTORIOUS. But I told them not to worry, it would look great on film, and that's all that mattered. It's one of my most famous scenes." Bergman's personal life at the time of production was very much in turmoil and she had only been in America for a few years and was still unsure of the English language. In one scene she could not get the right line, no matter how many takes Hitchcock ordered. The director took her aside and said quietly to her: "Ingrid, do you know what this scene is all about?" She replied: "Oh, yes, Hitch." He nodded. "Then let's try it again." But for another hour of takes Bergman was still fumbling about. Then, in the middle of her speech, her face brightened and she caught on and delivered her lines correctly. The director yelled "cut!" Hitchcock turned to Bergman and said: "Good morning, Ingrid." "Good morning, Hitch," the sterling actress replied, ready to give a real performance. Grant, having done SUSPICION earlier with Hitchcock, was never a problem. He moved effortlessly through his role exuding sophistication and confidence but lacking his usual charm since his part called for a clinical agent whose emotions reluctantly take over a no-nonsense mentality. But one scene did find Grant asking Hitchcock a ridiculous question. He carped to the director that he had to open a door with his right hand while he was holding his hat with the same hand. Said Hitchcock in that slow prosaic manner: "Have you considered the possibility of transferring the hat to the other hand?" Nothing could really perturb Hitchcock. Even when a life-threatening fire broke out on the set, the director was unflappable. He was in a conference with his brilliant cinematographer Tetzlaff, discussing the wonderful shadings and contrasting lighting effects the cameraman established for NOTORIOUS, when cries pierced the sound stage that a blaze was eating up the scenery. Hitchcock finished his sentence to Tetzlaff, then turned to some stagehands and cooly remarked: "Will someone please put that fire out?" He went back to his conversation without blinking another eye in the direction of the fire which was soon extinguished. Giving great sound support to this lush, glamorous film is Webb's superb score which emphasizes and enhances the nuances of the clever spy plot. Though Hecht receives full credit for developing NOTORIOUS, the story is loosely based upon a 1921 magazine story by John Taintor Foote entitled "Song of the Dragon" which was made into a silent film, CONVOY, in 1927, starring Dorothy Mackaill.

p&d, Alfred Hitchcock; w, Ben Hecht; ph, Ted Tetzlaff; m, Roy Webb; ed, Theron Warth; md, Constantin Bakaleinikoff; art d, Albert S. D'Agostino, Carroll Clark; set d, Darrell Silvera, Claude Carpenter; cos, Edith Head; spec eff, Vernon L. Walker, Paul Eagler.

Suspense/Spy Drama   Cas.   (PR:A MPAA:NR)

NOTORIOUS AFFAIR, A*½   (1930) 70m FN-WB bw

Billie Dove (*Patricia Hanley Gherardi*), Basil Rathbone (*Paul Gherardi*), Kay Francis (*Countess Balakireff*), Montagu Love (*Sir Thomas Hanley*), Kenneth Thomson (*Dr. Allen Pomroy*), Philip Strange, Gino Corrado, Elinor Vanderveer.

A melodrama that almost seems unfinished. Dove is a wealthy woman who gives up her social status to marry musician Rathbone. After giving up her stand in the community, she finds out he is having an affair with a countess. Instead of throwing him out, she returns briefly to a former suitor. When Rathbone becomes seriously ill, Dove nurses him back to health. Afterward, he changes his weak-willed ways to stay faithful forever.

p, Robert North; d, Lloyd Bacon; w, J. Grubb Alexander (based on the play "Fame" by Audrey Carter, Waverly Carter); ph, Ernest Haller; ed, Frank Ware; set d, Anton Grot; cos, Edward Stevenson.

Drama   (PR:A MPAA:NR)

NOTORIOUS BUT NICE*   (1934) 65m Batcheller/Chesterfield bw

Marian Marsh, Betty Compson, Donald Dillaway, Rochelle Hudson, John St. Polis, Henry Kolker, J. Carrol Naish, Dewey Robinson, Robert Ellis, Wilfred Lucas, Jane Keckley, Robert Frazer, Louise Beavers.

Dillaway and Marsh fall in love in this unstable melodrama. Dillaway's guardian, however, wants him to wed his daughter instead. Marsh, fearing her sweetheart will no longer be financially supported if they wed, puts a stop to their romance. Giving up all hope for marriage to Dillaway, Marsh marries a sleazy gambler, who is eventually shot. Marsh is arrested for the crime. A witness, who is about to be executed, comes forward and names the real killer, setting Marsh free. With their troubles behind them, Marsh and Dillaway can now be married.

d, Richard Thorpe; w, Carol Webster (based on a story by Adeline Leitbach); ph, M.A. Anderson.

Drama   (PR:A MPAA:NR)

NOTORIOUS CLEOPATRA, THE*½   (1970) 88m Global/Boxoffice International c

Sonora (*Cleopatra*), Johnny Rocco (*Marc Antony*), Jay Edwards (*Caesar*), Dixie Donovan (*Charmian*), Mason Bakman (*Enobarbus*), Christopher Stone (*Demetrius*), Michael Cheal (*Cicero*), Ron Smith (*Lepius*), Woody Lee (*Cassius*), Tom Huron (*Brutus*), Tai Hamilton (*High Priest*), James Brand (*Centurion*), Bobby Love (*Devil Dancer*), Joe Pepi (*Auctioneer*), Jess White (*Dungeon Guard*), Frank James (*Messenger*), Tommy Davis (*Nubian Guard*).

A new view of ancient Rome as seen through the romance of Cleopatra (Sonora) and Marc Antony (Rocco), and then Cleopatra and Julius Caesar (Edwards). The film glosses over historical fact and focuses instead on the characters' sex lives. It insinuates that actual historical events, such as the death of Caesar, Antony's suicide, and the death of Cleopatra, are the direct result of the jealousies and passions of both men for the Queen of the Nile. The plot is clouded by many sexual encounters between Sonora, as Cleopatra, and various centurions, and even her lady in waiting. An exploitation film disguised as historical drama.

p&d, A. P. Stootsberry; w, Jim Macher; ph, Dwayne Rayven (Eastmancolor); m, Vic Lance; ed, Rayven; art d, Earl Marshall; cos, Logan Costumes; makeup, Ray Sebastian.

Drama   (PR:O MPAA:NR)

NOTORIOUS GENTLEMAN, A**   (1935) 75m UNIV bw

Charles Bickford (*Kirk Arlen*), Sidney Blackmer (*Clayton Bradford*), Helen Vinson (*Nina Thorne*), Onslow Stevens (*John Barrett*), Dudley Digges (*Marleybone*), John Darrow (*Terry Bradford*), John Larkin (*Joshua*), Evelyn Selbie (*Carlena*), Alice Ardell (*Maid*).

An unraveled ending hurts this film about a perfect crime. Bickford is the scorned man, whose marriage proposal is turned down by Vinson. To gain revenge, he plots to kill her lover, Blackmer, and implicate Vinson. He succeeds on all counts but then takes the blame for the murder to protect the girl in a seemingly gallant gesture. He even has Blackmer's nephew (John Darrow) convinced that Darrow did it while in a drunken rage. The youth believes he did do it and writes a confession admitting his guilt. But wily Stevens is not convinced and in a weak courtroom scene wraps up the mystery.

p, Jerry Sackheim; d, Edward Laemmle; w, Leopold Atlas, Robert Trasker, Karen DeWolf, Rufus King (based on a story by Colin Clements, Forence Ryerson); ph, David Abel; ed, Albert Akst.

Crime Drama   (PR:A MPAA:NR)

NOTORIOUS GENTLEMAN***½   (1945, Brit.) 108m Individual/UNIV-RANK bw (GB: THE RAKE'S PROGRESS)

Rex Harrison (*Vivian Kenway*), Lilli Palmer (*Rikki Krausner*), Godfrey Tearle (*Col. Kenway*), Griffith Jones (*Sandy Duncan*), Margaret Johnston (*Jennifer Calthrop*), Guy Middleton (*Fogroy*), Jean Kent (*Jill Duncan*), Marie Lohr (*Lady Parks*), Garry Marsh (*Sir Hubert Parks*), David Horne (*Sir John Brockley*), Alan Wheatley

(*Edwards*), Brefni O'Rorke (*Bromhead*), Charles Victor (*Old Sweat*), Joan Maude (*Alice*), Patricia Laffan (*Miss Fernandez*), Howard Marion Crawford (*Guardsman*), Emrys Jones (*Bateson*), John Salew, Olga Lindo, David Wallbridge, John Dodsworth, Jack Vyvyan, Frederick Burtwell, George Cross, Kynaston Reeves, Jan van Loewen, Howard Douglas, Joy Frankau, Maureen McDermot, Jack Melford, David Ward, Sheila Huntington, Frank Phillips, Sidney Gilliat (*Voices Only*).

Harrison is excellent as a British cad who ultimately has an inglorious death in battle. After being tossed out of Oxford, he becomes involved with Kent, the wife of his best friend, Jones. When this ends he marries Palmer, a rich Austrian, to get at her money. Palmer tries to kill herself when she learns her husband is having an affair with Johnston, his father's secretary. In the end, it is Harrison who ends up unheroically killed in WW II. The film is presented well, with genuine style. It does not treat its unattractive subject with sympathy, yet remains sensitive and touching. However, Harrison's roguish affairs proved to be a bit much for Hollywood censors, who gave some problems to the film's distribution on its initial run.

p, Frank Launder, Sidney Gilliat; d, Gilliat; w, Launder, Gilliat (based on a story by Val Valentine); ph, Wilkie Cooper; m, William Alwyn; ed, Thelma Myers; art d, Norman Arnold.

Drama   (PR:C MPAA:NR)

NOTORIOUS LANDLADY, THE***   (1962) 123m COL bw

Kim Novak (*Carlye Hardwicke*), Jack Lemmon (*William Gridley*), Fred Astaire (*Franklyn Ambruster*), Lionel Jeffries (*Inspector Oliphant*), Estelle Winwood (*Mrs. Dunhill*), Maxwell Reed (*Miles Hardwicke*), Philippa Bevans (*Mrs. Brown*), Henry Daniell (*Stranger*), Ronald Long (*Coroner*), Doris Lloyd (*Lady Fallott*), Richard Peel (*Dillings*), Florence Wyatt (*Ambruster's Secretary*), Frederic Worlock (*Elderly Colonel*), Dick Crockett (*Carstairs*), Scott Davey (*Henry*), Jack Livesey (*Counsel*), Tom Dillon (*Coroner's Officer*), Benno Schneider, Clive Halliday, Antony Eustrel (*Men*), Carter De Haven, Sr., David Hillary Hughes, Nelson Welch (*Old Men*), Cecil Weston, Mavis Neal, Cicely Walper, Queenie Leonard (*Women*), Betty Fairfax (*Woman in Bathrobe*), Clive Morgan (*Man in Smoking Jacket*), Julie Scott (*Flousy*), Eric Micklewood (*Man with a Hangover*), Mark Burke (*Little Girl*), Ottola Nesmith (*Flower Lady*), Milton Parsons (*Mysterious Man*), Bru Mysak (*Ambruster's Driver*), Iris Bristol (*Girl*), Ross Brown (*Boy*), Gwen Watts (*Wife*), James Logan (*Bobby*), Bryan Herbert (*Husband*), Michael St. Clair (*Fire Chief*), Mary Scott (*Waitress*), Tudor Owen (*Farmer*), Tom Symonds (*Alf*), Laurence Conroy (*Clerk*), Barry Bernard (*Attendant*), Mary O'Brady (*Mrs. Oliphant*), Towyna Thomas (*Dowager*), Harold Innocent (*Young Escort*), Marjorie Bennett (*Autograph Seeker*), Alex Finlayson, Jackson Halliday, Ogden Dangerfield, Joe Palma (*Reporters*), Jacqueline Squire (*Woman Reporter*), Brian Gaffikin (*TV Reporter*), George Pelling (*Ticket Agent*), John Uhler Lemmon II (*Old Man in Wheelchair*).

Shot entirely in California (which was made to look like London), this was Lemmon's fifth picture with Quine, his third with Novak, and his first with Astaire. A clever mystery-comedy, it has many witty lines, some hysterical slapstick, and a generally good plot to whisk us along. Lemmon is a State Department employee who has been transferred from Saudi Arabia to London, where he rents a flat from Novak, who is under surveillance by Scotland Yard as a suspect in the case of her missing husband. Lemmon's boss, Astaire, and inspector Jeffries of the Yard ask him to snoop around and he reluctantly agrees. Novak's husband, Reed, shows up and she kills him after a battle over some jewels he'd stolen and can't find in the house. The cops tow Novak to jail and she goes on trial. It's self-defense, of course (you didn't really think Novak was a cold-blooded killer, did you?) and that's made clear in the testimony of Bevans, who lives with rich, old Winwood in the next house. But Bevans is lying. Winwood saw it all and told Bevans, who has testified because she wants to find the pawn ticket Reed referred to before Novak did him in. Bevan wants to use the information to blackmail Novak so she can get the gems. Then she plans to kill Winwood, who has been placed in an old age home in Penzance, by the sea. A wild chase to get to Winwood begins because Bevans got the ticket, obtained the candelabra in which Reed had placed the jewels, and then killed the pawnbroker. In Penzance, Bevans pushes Winwood's wheelchair toward the edge of a cliff, but Lemmon arrives in time to save the old lady. Novak tackles Bevans as Astaire and Jeffries arrive by helicopter, after losing their way and being forced to land and ask a farmer for directions. Kim Novak designed her own gowns for this cute film.

p, Fred Kohlmar; d, Richard Quine; w, Blake Edwards, Larry Gelbart (based on the story "The Notorious Tenant" by Margery Sharp); ph, Arthur E. Arling; m, George Duning; ed, Charles Nelson; art d, Cary Odell; set d, Louis Diage; cos, Kim Novak, Elizabeth Courtney; spec eff, David Koehler; m/l, "A Foggy Day in London Town," George Gershwin, Ira Gershwin, "Come Friends, Who Plough the Sea," "I Am the Very Model of a Modern Major-General" William S. Gilbert, Arthur Sullivan; makeup, Ben Lane.

Comedy/Mystery   (PR:A-C MPAA:NR)

NOTORIOUS LONE WOLF, THE**   (1946) 64m COL bw

Gerald Mohr (*Michael Lanyard*), Janis Carter (*Carla Winter*), Eric Blore (*Jamison*), John Abbott (*Lal Bara*), William B. Davidson (*Inspector Crane*), Don Beddoe (*Stanley*), Adelle Roberts (*Rita Hale*), Robert Scott (*Dick Hale*), Peter Whitney (*Harvey Beaumont*), Olaf Hytten (*Prince of Rapur*), Ian Wolfe (*Adam Wheelright*), Edith Evanson (*Olga*), Maurice Cass (*Assistant Hotel Manager*), Eddie Acuff (*Jones*), Virginia Hunter (*Lili*).

After a short hiatus, the "Lone Wolf" film series returned, with the character more debonair than ever. In this film, Mohr plays the jewel thief turned detective. Because of his notorious past, Mohr is the main suspect in the theft of a museum jewel. Much like the "Thin Man" series starring William Powell, Mohr coolly and smoothly works on catching the real crooks and maintaining his innocence, all the while eluding the authorities until he is proven right. (See LONE WOLF series, Index.)

p, Ted Richmond; d, D. Ross Lederman; w, Martin Berkeley, Edward Dein (based on a story by William J. Bowers); ph, Burnett Guffey; ed, Richard Fantl; md, Mischa Bakaleinikoff; art d, Perry Smith; set d, Frank Kramer.

Crime/Mystery/Comedy (PR:A MPAA:NR)

NOTORIOUS MR. MONKS, THE** (1958) 70m Ventura/REP bw

Vera Ralston (Angela Monks), Don Kelly (Dan Flynn), Paul Fix (Benjamin Monks), Leo Gordon (Chip Klamp), Luana Anders (Gilda Hadley), Tom Brown (Neilson), Lyle Talbot (Leonardo), Emory Parnell (Cobus Anders), Fuzzy Knight (Tom), Hank Worden (Pete), Grandon Rhodes (Mr. Hadley).

On the road hitchhiking, a young man is picked up by a drunken driver. Taken to the man's home, the young man meets his benefactor's wife, which leads to a murder. Though the material tries its best to be lurid, this production plays as merely bad camp under a rather tame treatment from a studio that itself was slowly settling into the dust, the star of THE NOTORIOUS MR. MONKS with it.

p, Rudy Ralston; d, Joe Kane; w, Richard C. Sarafian (based on a story by Peter Paul Fix); ph, Jack Marta; ed, Fred Knudtson; md, Gerald Roberts; art d, Ralph Oberg; set d, John McCarthy, Jr.; cos, Alexis Davidoff; makeup, Bob Mark.

Drama (PR:C MPAA:NR)

NOTORIOUS SOPHIE LANG, THE*½ (1934) 64m PAR bw (AKA: SOPHIE LANG)

Gertrude Michael (Sophie Lang/Elisa Morgan), Paul Cavanagh (Max Bernard/Sir Nigel Crane), Arthur Byron (Inspector Parr), Alison Skipworth (Aunt Nellie), Leon Errol (Peltz), Norman Ainsley (Robin), Arthur Hoyt, Edward McWade (Jewelers), Ferdinand Gottschalk (Augustus Telfen), Lucio Villegas (French Marshal), Ben Taggart (Capt. Thompson), Mme. Jacoby (Countess De Cesca), Del Henderson (House Detective), Stanhope Wheatcroft (Floor Walker), Adrian Rosley (Oscar), Joe Sawyer (Building Guard), Jack Pennick (Bystander), Clara Lou [Ann] Sheridan (Extra), William Jeffries, Jack Mulhall, Perry Ivins, Alphonse Martell (Clerks).

The first in an unexceptional series in which Michael plays a crook much sought after by the police; though she never really seems to commit any crime, she is wanted nevertheless. To catch her, police chief Byron enlists the aid of Cavanagh, another notorious criminal, from the other side of the Atlantic. A macabre chase sequence ensues in which the actors take a breather only when resting in a jail cell, but they soon escape and start running again. The comic talents of Errol help to soothe some of the running pains. (See SOPHIE LANG series, Index.)

p, Bayard Veiller; d, Ralph Murphy; w, Veiller (based on the story by Frederick Irving Anderson); ph, Al Gilks; art d, Hans Dreier, Robert Odell; cos, Travis Banton.

Comedy (PR:A MPAA:NR)

NOTRE DAME DE PARIS (SEE: HUNCHBACK OF NOTRE DAME, THE, 1957, Fr.)

NOTTI BIANCHE, LA (SEE: WHITE NIGHTS, 1957, Ital.)

NOUS IRONS A PARIS** (1949, Fr.) 98m Unidex bw

Philippe Lemaire (Jacques Lambert, Crooner), Francoise Arnoul (Micheline Grosbois), Christian Duvalleix (Paul, Composer), Henri Genes (Julien, Office Boy), Max Elloy (Honorin), Pasquali (Mons. Grosbois), Georges Lannes (Radio Manager), Maryse Martin (Maman Terrine), Ray Venture and Orchestra (Themselves), The Peter Sisters, Henri Salvador, George Raft, Martine Carol, Mons. Champagne (Guest Stars).

An entertaining French musical about three young people, Duvalleix, Lemaire, and Genes, who leave their jobs at a French radio station to operate their own clandestine station, called Radio X. They broadcast breezy entertainment and satirize contemporary advertising, especially The Lotus Girdle Company, which is managed by Pasquali, whose daughter Arnoul loves Lemaire. The three are soon joined by a strange assortment of characters, and the station becomes popular. However, they are forced to keep on the move with police who are looking for them. On their travels they encounter Raft, the Peter Sisters, Carol, and Champagne. When they reach Paris they are arrested, but the radio authorities agree to their release and offer them a special program on legal radio. This was one of the films in the sad later career of Raft, who, after his popularity sank in the mid-1940s, made some films in Europe in an effort to revive it. The fact that he was unsuccessful is no surprise after his cameo in NOUS IRONS A PARIS when the trench-coated "tough-guy" is stopped by the youngsters on the highway and kidded but does not seem to realize it. (In French.)

d, Jean Boyer; w, Franz Tanzler, Serge Veber, Boyer; ph, Charles Juin; m, Paul Misraki; ed, Franchette Mazin; art d, Raymond Negre; m/l, Andre Horner.

Comedy (PR:A MPAA:NR)

NOVEL AFFAIR, A**½ (1957, Brit.) 97m BL/Continental bw-c (GB: THE PASSIONATE STRANGER)

Ralph Richardson (Roger Wynter/Sir Clement Hathaway), Margaret Leighton (Judith Wynter/Leonie Hathaway), Patricia Dainton (Emily/Betty), Carlo Justini (Carlo/Mario), Ada Reeve (Old Woman), Andree Melly (Marla), Frederick Piper (Mr. Poldy), Michael Shepley (Miles Easter), Thorley Walters (Jimmy), George Woodbridge (1st Landlord), Allan Cuthbertson (Doctor), John Arnatt (Maurice), Barbara Archer (Barmaid), Marjorie Rhodes (Mrs. Poldy), Megs Jenkins (Millie), Michael Trubshawe (2nd Landlord), Alexander Gauge (MC at Dance), Barbara Graley (Secretary), C. Witty (Peter), Fred Tooze (Amos), Pat Ryan (Guard).

Justini is hired by Richardson and wife Leighton to be their new chauffeur. Leighton is a writer, and she uses the Italian chauffeur as the model for the romantic lead in her new novel. Justini reads the manuscript and gets the idea that his employer is in love with him. This turns out to be false and causes many humorous situations.

Segments of Leighton's novel come to life with Richardson, Justini, Dainton and Leighton playing these roles as well. The story-within-a-story sequences are in color, and the main story is in black and white.

p, Peter Rogers, Gerald Thomas; d, Muriel Box; w, M. Box, Sydney Box; ph, Otto Heller (Eastmancolor); m, Humphrey Searle; ed, Jean Barker; cos, Norman Hartnell.

Comedy (PR:A MPAA:NR)

NOW ABOUT ALL THESE WOMEN (SEE: ALL THESE WOMEN, 1964, Swed.)

NOW AND FOREVER** (1934) 81m PAR bw

Gary Cooper (Jerry Day), Carole Lombard (Toni Carstairs), Shirley Temple (Penelope Day), Sir Guy Standing (Felix Evans), Charlotte Granville (Mrs. J.H.P. Crane), Gilbert Emery (James Higginson), Henry Kolker (Mr. Clark), Tetsu Komai (Mr. Ling), Jameson Thomas (Chris Carstairs), Harry Stubbs (Mr. O'Neill), Egon Brecher (Doctor), Andre Cheron (Inspector), Agostino Borgato (Fisherman), Richard Loo (Hotel Clerk), Look Chan (Assistant Manager), Akim Tamiroff (French Jeweler), Buster Phelps (Boy with Skates), Rolfe Sedan (Hotel Manager), Ynez Seabury (Girl), Sam Harris (Man at Pool), Ronnie Cosbey (Little Boy), Grace Hayle (Lady in Store), George Webb, Buster the Dog.

Some good acting from a stellar cast can't save this Damon Runyon-like story from imploding. Cooper is an international con man and swindler whose wife died many years ago and whose child, Temple, now lives with his brother-in-law, Emery, who would like to have permanent custody. Cooper is amenable to that, but requires the tidy sum of $75,000 as compensation. Cooper and Lombard are lovers and conning companions, and when she hears what he plans, after they pull off a swindle in China, she is angered at the idea of selling a child and departs for Paris. Meanwhile, Cooper meets his daughter for the first time since she's been in diapers and finds her an engaging tot (Temple had the ability to melt the steeliest heart) who is eager to spread her little wings but cannot because Emery holds a tight rein over her curly locks. Cooper switches his plans and takes his tyke with him, using the money he gets by bilking wealthy, aged Standing on a phony stock deal for gold shares in a mine that doesn't exist. Cooper and Lombard are reunited and it seems that all will be well, as Cooper decides to tread the straight and narrow and go into real estate. Standing reappears and admits that he knew Cooper was a fraud and that he let Cooper bilk him because Standing himself is a jewel thief and now wants Cooper to aid him in his chicanery. Cooper decides against it. Granville, a rich widow, loves Temple and wants to adopt her. Cooper doesn't have a cent left in his wallet, so he steals Granville's expensive necklace and tries to fence it through Standing. Before he can get to the urbane Standing, Temple finds it in her teddy bear and worries that her daddy is a crook, but Lombard, wanting to shield the child, fraudulently admits the theft. Standing has the necklace now and Cooper wants to return it to Granville but Standing won't hear of that. A gun battle follows, Cooper is wounded, and Standing is killed. Bleeding, Cooper allows Temple to take Granville as her adopted mother, then waves farewell to the child and the older woman at the train station. Lombard takes Cooper to a hospital to have his wounds worked on, he goes into unconsciousness, and when he awakens, Lombard assures him that Temple will understand, at some later date, why he did what he did. It's not a comedy or a drama, just a picture. Cooper, the soul of Mr. Good Guy, is hard to take as a rat. Lombard has little to do to stretch her abilities and Temple steals the show. The script was co-written by Irving Thalberg's sister, toiling in a lot other than MGM.

p, Louis D. Lighton; d, Henry Hathaway; w, Vincent Lawrence, Sylvia Thalliery (based on the story "Honor Bright" by Jack Kirkland, Melville Baker); ph, Harry Fischbeck; ed, Ellsworth Hoagland; art d, Hans Dreier, Robert Usher; cos, Travis Banton; m/l, Harry Revel, Mack Gordon, "The World Owes Me a Living," Larry Morey, Leigh Harline.

Drama (PR:A MPAA:NR)

NOW AND FOREVER** (1956, Brit.) 91m ABF-Pathe c

Janette Scott (Janette Grant), Vernon Gray (Mike Pritchard), Kay Walsh (Miss Muir), Jack Warner (Mr. Pritchard), Pamela Brown (Mrs. Grant), Charles Victor (Farmer), Marjorie Rhodes (Farmer's Wife), Ronald Squire (Waiter), Wilfrid Lawson (Gossage), Sonia Dresdel (Miss Fox), David Kossoff (Pawnbroker), Moultrie Kelsall (Doctor), Guy Middleton (Hector), Michael Pertwee (Reporter), Henry Hewitt (Jeweler), Bryan Forbes (Frisby), Jean Patterson (Rachel), Harold Goodwin.

Scott's first adult role after a big career as a child star in Britain finds the rich girl head over heels in love with Gray, an auto mechanic who does not measure up to the social standards of her mother. Scott tries suicide but it miscarries. The pair then elope to Gretna Green, but are stopped by the police at the Scottish border because Scott is under age. A fresh performance by Scott helps to fan mild interest along the way, otherwise it cloys from a surfeit of sweets.

p&d, Mario Zampi, w, R.F. Delderfield, Michael Pertwee (based on a play "The Orchard Walls" by Delderfield); ph, Erwin Hillier (Technicolor); m, Stanley Black; ed, Richard Best.

Romance/Drama (PR:A MPAA:NR)

NOW AND FOREVER** (1983, Aus.) 93m Inter Planetary c

Cheryl Ladd (Jessie Clark), Robert Coleby (Ian Clark), Carmen Duncan (Astrid Bonner), Christine Amor (Margaret Burton), Aileen Britton.

Ladd is a fashionable young woman with some heavy-duty marital problems. First her husband cheats on her, then he's jailed on a phony rape charge. Heavy on the melodrama, this undoubtedly will please any soap opera fan. The film is based on a novel by Danielle Steel, an author who has hacked quite a nice living churning out things like this.

p, Treisha Ghent, Carnegie Fieldhouse; d, Adrian Carr; w, Richard Cassidy (based on the novel by Danielle Steel); ph, Don McAlpine; m, Graham Russell.

Drama   **Cas.**   **(PR:O MPAA:R)**

NOW BARABBAS   (SEE: NOW BARABBAS WAS A ROBBER, 1949, Brit.)

NOW BARABBAS WAS A ROBBER**½   (1949, Brit.) 87m WB bw
(AKA: NOW BARABBAS)

Richard Greene *(Tufnell)*, Cedric Hardwicke *(Governor)*, Kathleen Harrison *(Mrs. Brown)*, Ronald Howard *(Roberts, Bank Cashier)*, Stephen Murray *(Chaplain)*, William Hartnell *(Warder Jackson)*, Beatrice Campbell *(Kitty)*, Richard Burton *(Paddy)*, Betty Ann Davies *(Rosie)*, Leslie Dwyer *(Brown)*, Alec Clunes *(Gale)*, Harry Fowler *(Smith)*, Kenneth More *(Spencer)*, Dora Bryan *(Winnie)*, Constance Smith *(Jean)*, Lily Kahn *(Woman)*, David Hannaford *(Erb Brown)*, Julian d'Albie, Peter Doughty, Percy Walsh, Glyn Lawson, Gerald Case, Victor Fairley, Dandy Nichols.

The motivations of a group of English criminals come alive in this decently made British drama. It tells the stories of various prisoners, from the meek bank cashier caught embezzling to pay for his fiancee's expensive tastes in rings to the Irishman in jail for sabotage. Other characters include death row inmate Greene and a black smuggler and even a bigamist. Compelling with excellent camera work. This was Burton's third film since he entered pictures the year before from the British stage.

p, Anatole de Grunwald; d&w, Gordon Parry (based on the play by William Douglas Home); ph, Otto Heller; m, George Melachrino, Leighton Lucas; ed, Gerald Turney-Smith.

Prison Drama   **(PR:A MPAA:NR)**

NOW I LAY ME DOWN   (SEE: RACHEL, RACHEL, 1958)

NOW I'LL TELL**½   (1934) 72m FOX bw (GB: WHILE NEW YORK SLEEPS)

Spencer Tracy *(Murray Golden)*, Helen Twelvetrees *(Virginia Golden)*, Alice Faye *(Peggy Warren)*, Robert Gleckler *(Al Mositer)*, Hobart Cavanaugh *(Freddie)*, Henry O'Neill *(Doran)*, G. P. Huntley, Jr. *(Hart)*, Shirley Temple *(Mary Doran)*, Theodore Newton *(Joe Ready)*, Ray Cooke *(Traylor)*, Donald Haines *(Messenger Boy)*, Selmer Jackson *(Decker)*, Lane Chandler *(Friend)*, Irving Bacon *(Attendant)*, Leon Ames *(Mac)*, James Murray, Jack Norton *(Bits)*, June Lang *(Girl at Beach)*, Mary Forbes *(Mrs. Drake)*, Gertrude Astor *(Freddie's Wife)*, Mae Madison *(Waitress)*, Claude King *(Captain of Ship)*, Jim Donlon *(Honey Smith)*, Vince Barnett *(Peppo)*, Barbara Weeks *(Wynne)*, Clarence Wilson *(Davis)*, Ronnie Cosbey *(Tommy Jr.)*, Frank Marlowe *(Curtis)*.

A few films were made about the life of notorious bookie Arnold Rothstein. It served as the basis for STREET OF CHANCE, with William Powell as the urbane gangland leader; then David Janssen did it several years later in THE BIG BANKROLL. In between, bits and pieces of Rothstein's character emerged in various pictures, but this is the one that purports to tell the truth, as it was based on a story written by Rothstein's widow. The names were changed and the casting of Tracy seemed awry to anyone who knew what Rothstein looked and sounded like. Tracy is a gambler in a race with time. He means to make his bundle in a hurry and won't allow anyone to stand in his way. This ambition soon propels him to the top of his ill-advised profession and his pockets are bulging with money, but his domestic life is a shambles, as he seldom sees his wife, Twelvetrees. She is a social climber who yearns for invitations from the Four Hundred, although her husband's "work" seems to make that impossible. Tracy says he'll quit as soon as he reaches his goal of amassing $200,000, but once he has that amount, he ups the figure to $500,000, and when that's in the coffers, Tracy reneges on his word. As so often happens to a man with lots of new money, Tracy meets a bombshell, Faye, who toils in a nightspot, and takes her as his mistress. Faye would like Tracy to dump Twelvetrees and marry her, but he enjoys things the way they are. His wife represents stability and security and his mistress gives him the outside stimulation he desperately desires. Gleckler is another gambler who suspects that Tracy fixed a prize fight which cost Gleckler a pile of money. The second gambler is eager to nail the first so he abducts Twelvetrees. Racing back to the Big Apple to try and rescue his wife, Tracy is involved in a car accident in which he is badly hurt and Faye is killed. (This is the only film in which Faye bit the dust.) Twelvetrees can't put up with another minute of Tracy's behavior, so she leaves and goes to Europe where she will get a divorce from him. Gleckler continues to hound Tracy at every turn and Tracy is distraught and confused with both of the women in his life gone. He has nowhere to go, so he buys a large insurance policy with the money he gets by pawning Twelvetrees' expensive jewels. There is a confrontation with Gleckler and Tracy is shot. He is dying when Twelvetrees comes to his side and assures him that he'll get better and that they can resume their lives together. It's to no avail and Tracy's toes turn up at the conclusion. The full title of the movie was NOW I'LL TELL BY MRS. ARNOLD ROTHSTEIN, but theater managers thought that was a bit lengthy, especially since they had double features in those days and there would be no room for anything else on the marquee. Shirley Temple, then only six, performed one of a quartet of roles she did in 1934 and has a small four-liner as Henry O'Neill's daughter. The idea that Tracy deliberately staged his own assassination may just be a bit of fancy on the part of Mrs. Rothstein because he was hardly the type for a *beau geste*. Twelvetrees was not right in the role of the long-suffering wife, but Faye couldn't have been better as The Other Woman. She also got the chance to sing "Foolin' Around with the Other Woman's Man" in an all-black satin outfit, replete with black feathers and a black fan. The contrast against her blonde locks and pale skin was stunning. The other song was "Harlem Versus The Jungle." Both tunes were written by Lew Brown and Harry Akst. Rothstein was a fascinating human being who arranged many things, including the "Black Sox" scandal (or so it was alleged) in baseball, but the thought that he also arranged his own death is a bit much.

p, Winfield Sheehan; d&w, Edwin Burke (based on the book by Mrs. Arnold Rothstein); ph, Ernest Palmer; m, Hugo Friedhofer, Arthur Lange, David Buttolph; md, Lange; art d, Jack Otterson; cos, Rita Kaufman.

Crime/Biography   **(PR:A-C MPAA:NR)**

NOW IT CAN BE TOLD   (SEE: SECRET DOOR, THE, 1964)

NOW THAT APRIL'S HERE*½   (1958, Can.) 84m International Film Distributors bw

"Silk Stockings": Don Borisenko *(David Munro)*, Judy Welch *(Anne Greenleaf)*, Michael Mann *(Boy Friend)*, Beth Amos *(Mrs. Greenleaf)*, Sheila Billing, Pam D'Orsay *(Salesgirls)*; "Rocking Chair": John Drainie *(Tom Boultbee)*, Katherine Blake *(Hilda Adams)*, Alan Hood *(Henry)*, Art Jenoff *(Salesman)*; "The Rejected One": Nancy Lou Gill *(Mamie)*, Tony Grey *(Karl Henderson)*, Paisley Maxwell *(Helen Henderson)*, Fred Diehl *(John Henderson)*, Josephine Barrington *(Mrs. Henderson)*; "A Sick Call": Walter Massey *(John Williams)*, Anne Collings *(Elsa Williams)*, Kathy McNeil *(Jane Stanhope)*, Georges Toupin *(Father MacDowell)*, Rolf Carston *(The Doctor)*.

The first of its kind—a completely Canadian film, from production to actors. Filmed around Toronto, it deals with four stories by Morley Callaghan set in the 1920s. "Silk Stockings" is about the undying love of a clumsy man for his landlady's daughter at the boarding house he resides in. But she happens to be in love with someone else while he pines away. "Rocking Chair" has a widower who turns down the advances of a willful boarder because the memory of his late wife still controls his life. "The Rejected One" has a busty but illiterate blonde, who has a wealthy man fall in love with her. Despite the objections of his family, he swoons for the girl from the other side of the tracks. The final story, "A Sick Call," has a woman, a lapsed Catholic, on her death bed, who wants to revert back to Catholicism though her Protestant husband is against it. Poor acting sank this Canadian attempt to elbow into the fast track of filmmaking.

p, Norman Klenman, William Davidson; d, Davidson; w, Norman Klenman (based on four short stories by Morley Callaghan, introduced and narrated by Raymond Massey); ph, William Gimmi; m, John Hubert Bath.

Drama   **(PR:A MPAA:NR)**

NOW, VOYAGER***½   (1942) 117m WB bw

Bette Davis *(Charlotte Vale)*, Paul Henreid *(Jerry D. Durrance)*, Claude Rains *(Dr. Jaquith)*, Gladys Cooper *(Mrs. Henry Windle Vale)*, Bonita Granville *(June Vale)*, John Loder *(Elliott Livingston)*, Ilka Chase *(Lisa Vale)*, Lee Patrick *("Deb" McIntyre)*, James Rennie *(Frank McIntyre)*, Charles Drake *(Leslie Trotter)*, Katherine Alexander *(Miss Trask)*, Janis Wilson *(Tina Durrance)*, Mary Wickes *(Dora Pickford)*, Michael Ames [Tod Andrews] *(Dr. Dan Regan)*, Franklin Pangborn *(Mr. Thompson)*, David Clyde *(William)*, Claire du Brey *(Hilda)*, Don Douglas *(George Weston)*, Charlotte Wynters *(Grace Weston)*, Frank Puglia *(Manoel)*, Lester Matthews *(Captain)*, Mary Field, Bill Edwards, Isabel Withers, Frank Dae *(Passengers)*, Hilda Plowright *(Justine)*, Tempe Pigott *(Mrs. Smith)*, Ian Wolfe *(Lloyd)*, Reed Hadley *(Henry Montague)*, Elspeth Dudgeon *(Aunt Hester)*, Constance Purdy *(Rosa)*, George Lessey *(Uncle Herbert)*, Corbett Morris *(Hilary)*, Yola d'Avril *(Celestine)*, Georges Renavent *(Mons. Henri)*, Dorothy Vaughan *(Woman)*, Sheila Hayward *(Katie)*, Hamilton Hunneker *(Bill Kennedy)*.

In Walt Whitman's *Leaves Of Grass*, he wrote "The untold want, by life nor land ne'er granted, now voyager, sail thou forth to seek and find." Olive Higgins Prouty, who also penned *Stella Dallas*, took that phrase and wrote the novel upon which this film, the most popular of Davis' 1940s pictures, was based. Davis made 19 movies in that decade and some of them were better (THE LITTLE FOXES, THE LETTER), but none was more popular with the women who bought the hankies they sniffled into. Here is a huge sob story that Davis took more than an acting interest in. She claims to have worked extensively on Robinson's screenplay, deleting some of his dialog and using the words from the novel in its place. Davis, unlike Claudette Colbert and some others of her generation, was willing to take chances, which included removing all her makeup, adding weight, padding out her slim figure, and, in general, excising any vestige of attractiveness in order to make the point of her characterization. She is the dowdy and frustrated daughter of a masochistic mother, Cooper. They live in a Boston mansion and Davis is close to a nervous breakdown because she can't get any affection from Cooper, who forces her to dress in "sensible shoes" and wear spectacles that make her look like an owl. Chase is Davis' sister-in-law and she is worried about the mental state of Davis, so she enlists famed psychiatrist Rains to come in and help. He sees that she is near a collapse and recommends that she leave this house where no love grows and take refuge at his sanitarium. Once there, Davis begins a regimen that causes her to achieve mental and physical health as she drops 25 pounds and begins having more confidence about herself with each passing day. In three months, the ugly duckling has been transformed into an attractive woman who knows herself as well as anyone can. Rains now suggests she get aboard a liner and sail to South America. It's on this cruise that she meets married Henreid who has a wife who holds on to him by affecting bad health as an excuse. They arrive in Rio and enjoy a wonderful day and night together, and when they wake up in the morning, they learn that their ship has already left the port. They stay in Rio for a few days and Davis experiences passionate love for the first time in her life, but understands from the start that Henreid will never leave his wife. She decides to not see him again and goes home to Boston where Cooper, ice cold and thin-lipped, is waiting. Chase loves what she sees in the "new" Davis and makes an introduction to rich widower Loder, who falls for Davis instantly and soon asks for her hand in marriage. Davis teeters over that until she accidentally meets Henreid again and realizes how much she loves him. Davis tells Loder that it can never be and Cooper, upon hearing that, begins a slam-bang argument with Davis, which results in Cooper dying of a coronary. Davis feels guilty and depressed and again winds up at Rains' sanitarium, where she encounters Wilson, the young daughter of Henreid who reminds her so much of the way she used to be. Davis prevails on Rains to allow her to take Wilson under her wing and the young girl is happy, as she has found a surrogate mother. Later, Henreid comes to Davis' house to see his daughter and finds that the young girl has been magically changed and is, for once, content. Henreid is grateful for what Davis has done and agrees to allow Wilson to stay with her. As long as he's still married, there is no way the two of them can get together, but Davis has an answer to that, which she states in the film's last memorable line: "Don't ask for the moon when we have the stars." Davis, in the end, is also happy, as she has the child that she never bore and the feeling is that this is "their" child that she can now raise. Lots of tears and the famous scene where Henreid lights two cigarettes simultaneously and hands one to Davis. Max Steiner won an Oscar for his great score for this film, and Davis and Cooper were nominated but lost to Greer Garson and Teresa Wright for their roles in MRS. MINIVER.

p, Hal B. Wallis; d, Irving Rapper; w, Casey Robinson (based on the novel by Olive Higgins Prouty); ph, Sol Polito; m, Max Steiner; ed, Warren Low; md, Leo F. Forbstein; art d, Robert Haas; cos, Orry-Kelly; m/l, "It Can't Be Wrong," Steiner, Kim Gannon.

Drama Cas. (PR:A-C MPAA:NR)

NOW YOU SEE HIM, NOW YOU DON'T*** (1972) 88m Disney/BV c

Kurt Russell *(Dexter Riley)*, Cesar Romero *(A. J. Arno)*, Joe Flynn *(Dean Higgins)*, Jim Backus *(Timothy Forsythe)*, William Windom *(Prof. Lufkin)*, Michael McGreevey *(Richard Schuyler)*, Joyce Menges *(Debbie Dawson)*, Richard Bakalyan *(Cookie)*, Alan Hewitt *(Dean Collingsgood)*, Kelly Thordsen *(Sgt. Cassidy)*, Neil Russell *Alfred)*, George O'Hanlon *(Ted)*, John Myhers *(Golfer)*, Pat Delany *(Secretary)*, Robert Rothwell *(Driver)*, Frank Aletter *(TV Announcer)*, Dave Willock *(Mr. Burns)*, Edward Andrews *(Mr. Sampson)*, Jack Bender *(Slither Roth)*, Frank Welker *(Myles)*, Mike Evans *(Henry Fathington)*, Ed Begley Jr. *(Druffle)*, Paul Smith *(Road Block Officer)*, Billy Casper, Dave Hill *(Themselves)*.

Same cast, same production people in this sequel to the Disney film, THE COMPUTER WORE TENNIS SHOES (1969), again starring Kurt Russell. A humorous piece, Russell is a college student who finds a serum that can make him invisible. His school, Medfield College, is in money trouble, and he uses the serum to stop a planned takeover. Wanting the school is gangster Romero. Flynn, trying to get some money out of the rich Backus, plays golf and is aided in his game by Russell. Romero gets his hands on some of the serum and uses it to rob a bank, but in one of the best scenes gets caught in a wild car chase involving invisible cars. Quick-moving, pleasing to all, with some fine special effects.

p, Ron Miller; d, Robert Butler; w, Joseph McEveety (based on a story by Robert L. King); ph, Frank Phillips (Technicolor); m, Robert F. Brunner; ed, Cotton Warburton; art d, John B. Mansbridge, Walter Tyler; set d, Emile Kurl, Frank R. McKelvy; cos, Chuck Keehne, Emily Sunby; spec eff, Eustace Lycett, Danny Lee.

Juvenile (PR:AAA MPAA:G)

NOWHERE TO GO½** (1959, Brit.) 87m EAL/MGM bw

George Nader *(Paul Gregory)*, Bernard Lee *(Vic Sloane)*, Bessie Love *(Harriet Jefferson)*, Maggie Smith *(Bridget Howard)*, Geoffrey Keen *(Inspector Scott)*, Andree Melly *(Rosa)*, Howard Marion Crawford *(Cameron)*, Arthur Howard *(Dodds I)*, John Welsh *(Dodds II)*, Margaret McGrath *(Rosemary)*, Harry Corbett *(Sullivan)*, Harry Locke *(Bendel)*, Lilly Kahn *(Anna Berg)*, Lionel Jeffries *(Pet Shop Man)*, John Turner *(Policeman)*, Lane Meddick *(Welsh Garageman)*, Charles Price *(Man on Tractor)*, Noel Howlett *(Mr. Howard)*, Oliver Johnston *(Strongroom Official)*, Beckett Bould *(Gamekeeper)*.

Solid story line and fine British cast make this crime story passable. Nader, in his first role outside Hollywood, is a crook on the run. He has broken out of prison, after being sentenced for cheating a wealthy widow out of $154,000. After showing how he swindled the woman, the film returns to the present, where Nader is scheming to get back the money. However, since there is no honor among thieves, his friend, Lee, double-crosses him, his other sleazy buddies give him away, and the safety box key where he has the money stashed is stolen from him. To top it off, he gets back at Lee, and while beating him up, Lee dies. With a murder charge hanging over him, he is aided by Smith. But his paranoia gets to him and he thinks she will hand him over to the cops, so he takes off once again. He is finally gunned down by a Welsh farmer and killed.

p, Michael Balcon; d, Seth Holt, W. Holt, Kenneth Tynan (based on a novel by Donald MacKenzie); ph, Paul Beeson (Metroscope); m, Dizzy Reece; ed, Harry Aldous; art d, Alan Withy.

Crime (PR:A MPAA:NR)

NOZ W WODZIE (SEE: KNIFE IN THE WATER, 1963)

NUDE BOMB, THE*½ (1980) 94m UNIV c (AKA: THE RETURN OF MAXWELL SMART)

Don Adams *(Maxwell Smart)*, Sylvia Kristel *(Agent 34)*, Rhonda Fleming *(Edith Von Secondberg)*, Dana Elcar *(Chief)*, Pamela Hensley *(Agent 36)*, Andrea Howard *(Agent 22)*, Norman Lloyd *(Carruthers)*, Bill Dana *(Jonathon Levinson Seigle)*, Gary Imhoff *(Jerry Krovney)*, Sarah Rush *(Pam Krovney)*, Vittorio Gassman *(Nino Salvatore Sebastiani)*, Walter Brooke *(American Ambassador)*, Thomas Hill *(President)*, Ceil Cabot *(Landlady)*, Joey Forman *(Agent 13)*, Patrick Gorman *(French Delegate)*, Earl Maynard *(Jamaican Delegate)*, Alex Rodine *(Russian Delegate)*, Richard Sanders *(German Delegate)*, Vito Scotti *(Italian Delegate)*, Byron Webster *(English Delegate)*, Horst Ehrhardt *(Polish Delegate)*, James Noble *(Secretary of Defense)*, James Gavin, Gary Young, Anthony Herrera.

A feeble try at bringing back the characters from the popular TV series, "Get Smart." This was a dumb move. The film is almost a copy of the TV show without the sharp humor that made it so popular. Adams is back with new partner Howard trying to stop bad guy Gassman, who, of course, wants to rule the world. He has developed a bomb that can destroy all clothing fabric leaving everyone completely naked at one time and ripe for the takeover by his army. All the gadgets and tricks in the world couldn't help this one. Better left covered.

p, Jennings Lang; d, Clive Donner; w, Arne Sultan, Bill Dana, Leonard B. Stern (based on characters created by Mel Brooks, Buck Henry); ph, Harry L. Wolf (Technicolor); m, Lalo Schifrin; ed, Walter Hannemann, Phil Ticker; prod d, William Tuntke; set d, Marc E. Meyer, Jr.; cos, Burton Miller.

Comedy (PR:A MPAA:PG)

NUDE HEAT WAVE (SEE: TOUCHABLES, THE, 1961)

NUDE IN A WHITE CAR½** (1960, Fr.) 87m Champs Elysees/Trans-Lux bw (AKA: BLONDE IN A WHITE CAR)

Marina Vlady *(Eva)*, Robert Hossein *(Pierre)*, Odile Versois *(Helene)*, Helena Manson *(Amelia)*, Henri Cremieux *(The Doctor)*.

After being seduced by a beautiful naked woman sitting in a white car near the Riviera, Hossein's life becomes embroiled in a drama beyond his wildest imaginings. He follows the woman to her home, where she lives with her equally beautiful disabled sister. Hossein finds himself in the middle of a game, trying to figure out which sister seduced him. He moves in and both fall in love with him. Eventually he takes to Vlady, the paralyzed woman, and Versois, her able-bodied sister, walks out in anger. One day Hossein surprises Vlady in her room, finding her on her feet. She has been faking disability all along to gain sympathy from those around her and to keep Versois in her power. Vlady falls down a flight of stairs, screaming for her beloved as he walks out of the house in disgust. A strange and unusual psychological mystery, which makes good use of the house setting to achieve an air of claustrophobia. Vlady and Versois add to that feeling, keeping Hossein (and thus the audience) always on edge about what is taking place. Though nothing special, this film does have its moments.

d&w, Robert Hossein (based on the novel *Toi Le Ve* by Frederic Dard).

Mystery (PR:C MPAA:NR)

NUDE IN HIS POCKET** (1962, Fr.) 82m Madeleine-SNE GAU-Contact Organisation Cosmic bw (AMOUR DE POCHE; AKA: GIRL IN HIS POCKET)

Jean Marais *(Prof. Jerome)*, Genevieve Page *(Edith)*, Agnes Laurent *(Monette)*, Regine Lovi, Amedee, Pasquali, Joelle Janin, Jean-Claude Brialy, Flip the Dog.

A little on the different side for this French comedy. A professor, Marais, is fascinated with suspended animation and conducts countless experiments. Page, his fiancee, thinks he is wasting his time and wants him to go into a more stable profession—the soft drink business. During his final day in his lab, Marais knocks over his experimental solution and his dog laps it up. To Marais' amazement, the dog becomes a three-inch statue. To get it back to normal, he immerses the dog in salt water. He chucks the soft drink business and goes after some more experiments with a renewed vigor. While doing so, he starts falling in love with his assistant, Laurent. During a close encounter, Page shows up outside the lab door, demanding she be let in. To hide, Laurent drinks the formula and becomes a three-inch nude statue which Marais stashes in his pocket. Thus they are able to share many intimate moments together. Finally, Marais realizes where his love lies and dumps the domineering Page.

p, Gilbert de Goldschmidt; d, Pierre Kast; w, France Roche (based on the story "The Diminishing Draft" by Waldemar Kaempfert); ph, Ghislain Cloquet; m, Cogo Goragher, Georges Delerue, Marc Lanjean; ed, Robert Isnardon; art d, Sidney Bettex, Daniel Villerois; makeup, Alexandre Marcus, Blanche Picot.

Comedy (PR:A MPAA:NR)

NUDE ODYSSEY** (1962, Fr./Ital.) 97m PCM Cineriz-Francinex/Royal Films International c (L'ODYSSEE NUE; ODISSEA NUDA; AKA: LOVE—TAHITI STYLE; DIARY OF A VOYAGE IN THE SOUTH PACIFIC)

Enrico Maria Salerno *(Enrico)*, Venantino Venantini *(Filmmaker)*, Patricia Dolores Donlon *(Margaret)*, Elizabeth Logue *(Matae)*, Nathalie Gasse *(Tepare)*, Pauline Rey *(Hinano)*, Vaea Bennett *(Turere)*, Jack Russel, Karl Schonbourg, Charles Mau, Giulia Meserve, Arona.

Life has not been good to Salerno, a film director, so he takes off to Polynesia to do some filming. While there, he meets Donlon, an American, looking for her husband. He goes from one odyssey to another, following a Tahitian woman and joining her hedonistic lifestyle, then going on to live in a deserted mansion with two women. At the mansion, he finds out about his mother's death and retreats to a small island. He befriends a young boy and priest on the island and comes to the conclusion he cannot avoid life, he must take part. With a new outlook, he heads back to his real home—Rome.

p, Golfiero Colonna, Luciano Ercoli, Alberto Pugliese; d, Franco Rossi; w, Ennio DeConcini, Rossi, Colonna, Ottavio Alessi (based on a story by Rossi, De Concini, Colonna); ph, Alessandro D'Eva (Totalscope, Eastmancolor); m, Angelo Francesco Lavagnino; ed, Otello Colangeli; md, Lavagnino; set d, Giuseppe Ranieri; m/l, "Roi Mata," "The Legend of Hinano," Yves Roche, "Bon Voyage," Danny Small.

Drama (PR:A MPAA:NR)

NUDE...SI MUORE (SEE: YOUNG, THE EVIL AND THE SAVAGE, THE, 1968, Ital.)

NUDES ON CREDIT (SEE: LOVE NOW. . .PAY LATER, 1966)

NUISANCE, THE½** (1933) 83m MGM bw (AKA: THE CHASER; ACCIDENTS WANTED; AMBULANCE CHASER; NEVER GIVE A SUCKER A BREAK)

Lee Tracy *(Joe Phineas Stevens)*, Madge Evans *(Dorothy Mason)*, Frank Morgan

(Dr. Prescott), Charles Butterworth *(Floppy Phil)*, John Miljan *(Calhoun)*, Virginia Cherrill *(Miss Rutherford)*, David Landau *(Kelley)*, Greta Meyer *(Mrs. Mannheimer)*, Herman Bing *(Willy)*, Samuel S. Hinds *(Beaumont)*, Syd Saylor *(Fred)*.

Tracy stars as a smooth-talking ambulance chaser in this cheery comedy. No matter how small the injury, Tracy always comes away with big settlements. One company, victimized more than a few times by Tracy and his clients, moves to get him disbarred. They send Evans to get the goods on him, but their plot is foiled when the two have eyes for each other. Morgan is Tracy's doctor pal, who can make any injury look bad at any time. He's great in front of a jury, describing internal injuries that have been caused by accidents.

p, Lawrence Weingarten; d, Jack Conway; w, Sam Spewack, Bella Cohen [Spewack] (based on a story by Chandler Sprague, Howard Emmett Rogers); ph, Gregg Toland; ed, Frank Sullivan.

Comedy **(PR:A MPAA:NR)**

NUIT DE VARENNES, LA (SEE: LA NUIT DE VARENNES, 1983, Fr.)

NUITS ROUGES (SEE: SHADOWMAN 1974, Fr./Ital.)

NO. 96*½ (1974, Aus.) 113m Cash-Harmon-0-10 Network/Regent Trading-Cemp Films c

Johnny Lockwood *(Aldo Godolus)*, Philippa Baker *(Roma Godolfus)*, Pat McDonald *(Dorrie Evans)*, Ron Shand *(Herb Evans)*, Joe Hasham *(Don Finlayson)*, Sheila Kennelly *(Norma Whittaker)*, Gordon McDougall *(Les Whittaker)*, Tom Oliver *(Jack Sellars)*, Elaine Lee *(Vera Collins)*, Elisabeth Kirkby *(Lucy Sutcliffe)*, James Elliott *(Alf Sutcliffe)*, Jeff Kevin *(Arnold Feather)*, Bunney Brooke *(Flo Patterson)*, Bettina Welch *(Maggie Cameron)*.

Australian film based on the successful and long-running soap opera of the same name on Australian television. Same people who star in the TV series star in this film about a group of apartments, No. 96. Too many intersecting stories confuse the plot as it introduces too many characters at once. All the diverging stories finally end up on the same path and are summed up in one happy ending.

p, Bill Harmon; d, Peter Bernados; w, David Sale, Johnny Whyte; ph, John McLean (Eastmancolor); md, Tommy Tycho; art d, John Northcote.

Drama **(PR:C MPAA:NR)**

NUMBER ONE*½ (1969) 105m UA c (GB: THE PRO)

Charlton Heston *(Ron "Cat" Catlan)*, Jessica Walter *(Julie Catlan)*, Bruce Dern *(Richie Fowler)*, John Randolph *(Coach Jim Southerd)*, Diana Muldaur *(Ann Marley)*, G.D. Spradlin *(Dr. Tristler)*, Richard Elkins *(Kelly Williams)*, Mike Henry *(Walt Chaffee)*, Ernie Barnes *(Deke Coleman)*, Steve Franken *(Robin)*, Bart Burns *(Ed Davis)*, Forrest Wood *(Attendant)*, George Sperdakos *(Dr. Overstreet)*, Roy Jenson *(Roy Nelson)*, Bob Bennett *(Penny Forber)*, Billy Holiday *(Trainer)*, Bobby Troup *(Harvey Hess)*, Al Hirt *(Himself)*, The New Orleans Saints *(Themselves)*.

Ridiculous story sinks smooth film that has Heston join the jock set. Heston is a professional football player near the end of the line as far as his playing days are concerned for the New Orleans Saints, a team that is the end of the line for anybody. With his career coming to a close, his marriage also starts falling apart. A knee injury in the final pre-season game tells him the handwriting is on the wall: Elkins will be the new starting quarterback; painkillers just will not cut it for Heston anymore. While Heston is wallowing in his own selfish concerns, his wife has become a famous fashion designer, almost overshadowing Heston's achievements. He mopes around most of the film, has an affair, turns down a job offer, and starts drinking heavily after seeing what happened to another old pro who was forced to quit. But trooper that he is, he shoots himself up with painkillers and wears a knee brace so he can still compete. He gets called on to play and is booed by the crowd. He turns the jeers into cheers by leading the team to a quick touchdown and has the team on the march again. In a depressing ending, he sets up to pass and is completely wiped out by several defensive linemen. The film ends stoically with him crumpled on the field in one last symbolic shot.

p, Walter Seltzer; d, Tom Gries; w, David Moessinger; ph, Michel Hugo, Kirk Wooster (DeLuxe Color); m, Dominic Frontiere; ed, Richard Brockway; art d, Art Lowel; cos, Rita Riggs.

Sports/Drama **(PR:C MPAA:M)**

NUMBER SEVENTEEN*½ (1928, Brit./Ger.) 72m Fellner & Somio/Wolfe & Freedman bw

Guy Newall *(Ben)*, Lien Dyers *(Elsie Ackroyd)*, Carl de Vogt *(Gilbert Fordyce)*, Fritz Greiner *(Shelldrake)*, Ernst Neicher *(Harold Brant)*, Hertha von Walter *(Nora Brant)*, Craighall Sherry *(Sam Ackroyd)*, Frederick Solm *(Henry Jobber)*.

Sailor Newall helps the police bag a gang of jewel smugglers by getting a reformed female thief to point him in the right direction. This German-British coproduction was first made as a silent in Germany, and an English soundtrack was added a year later. The jumbled soundtrack makes sustaining interest almost impossible. Alfred Hitchcock would make his own version of this same Farjeon play in another four years.

p, Joseph Somlo; d&w, Geza M. Bolvary (based on the play by J. Jefferson Farjeon).

Crime **(PR:A MPAA:NR)**

NUMBER SEVENTEEN*** (1932, Brit.) 63m BIP/Wardour bw

Leon M. Lion *(Ben, Tramp)*, Anne Grey *(Nora Brant)*, John Stuart *(Gilbert Fordyce, Detective)*, Donald Calthrop *(Brant)*, Barry Jones *(Henry Doyle)*, Ann Casson *(Rose Ackroyd)*, Garry Marsh *(Sheldrake)*, Henry Caine *(Mr. Ackroyd)*, Herbert Langley *(Guard)*.

A technically compelling Hitchcock film which, while early in his career and rather crude, displays his genius at creating visual suspense. Trying to avoid the usual confines of theater (the film was based on a play), Hitchcock chose to begin his picture with a dizzying camera move that carries the audience up the staircase of a creepy gothic gangster hideout. It is this staircase, with its rickety bannister, that serves as the setting for the first half of NUMBER SEVENTEEN. A corpse is soon discovered by Lion, who finds himself in the middle of a jewelry scheme. In parody of horror and suspense pictures, the stairway fills with characters—including detective Stuart, the lovely Grey, and a trio of robbers—all of whom let a valuable necklace slip through their fingers. With Grey and Stuart handcuffed to the banister, suspense builds as the audience wonders who will be the first to fall victim to the unsteady railing. It finally gives way, suspending the handcuffed couple in the air. At the halfway point, the film switches to a speeding train carrying the same cast of characters still in search of the necklace. Gunshots are fired and the conductor is killed, setting the stage for a collision between the runaway train and a ferryboat and leaving the heroic Stuart in the arms of his love. Though a studio assignment for Hitchcock, NUMBER SEVENTEEN is filled with foreshadowings of his future films—a keen sense of humor, visually supplied suspense, and a love of miniature model special effects. As fun as the film can be, it is hampered by a cloudy plot which, unfortunately, distracts rather than informs. One incident which occurred on the set seems particularly tuned to Hitchcock's personality. He had planned to have the gangster's hideout double as a neighborhood refuge for stray cats. The plan was for dozens of cats to dart down the staircase when a gunblast was heard. The axiom about never working with animals came into play when, at the sound of the gunshot, the cats ran in the wrong direction. Instead of a comical visual joke, Hitchcock ended up with a horde of cat owners trying to chase down and identify their pets.

p, John Maxwell; d, Alfred Hitchcock; w, Hitchcock, Alma Reville, Rodney Ackland (based on the play and novel by Jefferson Farjeon); ph, Jack Cox, Bryan Langley; ed, A.C. Hammond; art d, C.W. Arnold.

Crime/Comedy **Cas.** **(PR:A MPAA:NR)**

NUMBER SIX** (1962, Brit.) 59m Merton Park/Anglo-Amalgamated bw

Ivan Desny *(Charles Valentine)*, Nadja Regin *(Nadia Leiven)*, Michael Goodliffe *(Supt. Hallett)*, Brian Bedford *(Jimmy Gale)*, Joyce Blair *(Carol Clyde)*, Leonard Sachs *(Welland)*, Michael Shaw *(Luigi Pirani)*, Harold Goodwin *(Smith)*.

A band of criminals plan to rob an heiress of her money. However, a secret agent gets wind of the plot and manages to stop the crooks before the damage is done. A minor, low-budget British crime film, based on the Edgar Wallace mystery and one of Jack Greenwood's taut, short films shot under the umbrella title "Edgar Wallace Mystery Theater," targeted eventually for English and American television.

p, Jack Greenwood; d, Robert Tronson; w, Philip Mackie (based on a novel by Edgar Wallace).

Crime **(PR:A MPAA:NR)**

NO. 13 DEMON STREET (SEE: DEVIL'S MESSENGER, THE, 1962)

NUMBER TWO** (1975, Fr.) 88m Sonimage-Bela/SNC c (NUMERO DEUX)

Sandrine Battistella *(Wife)*, Pierre Dudry *(Husband)*, Alexandre Rignault *(Grandpa)*, Rachel Stefanopoli *(Grandma)*.

Announced by Godard as a remake of BREATHLESS (a ploy to get financing), this video project has almost nothing to do with his 1959 masterpiece. It is a film with equal importance placed on politics as on sex, for Godard sees no reason why a film cannot be about both. The main characters could be seen as Battistella and Dudry, a dissatisfied couple who are both unhappy with their roles and suffer from physical ailments. Battistella is stricken with chronic constipation, while her husband is unable to perform sexually. In the meantime the parents teach their children about sex by showing them, and the grandparents, naked, speak directly to the camera. As Richard Roud writes, "although NUMERO DEUX is a frustrating film about frustration, a constipated film about constipation, it is not entirely without a sense of hope." Shot on videotape (and later transferred to film), the majority of the picture uses only a portion of the screen, usually the upper-left and the lower-right portions. The finish, however, relieves the tension this creates by opening up the entire screen. To further his interests in video, Godard built a studio in Grenoble where his tape experiments for French television continued until 1980 with the release of EVERY MAN FOR HIMSELF, marking his much awaited return to commercial filmmaking and international distribution.

d&w, Jean-Luc Godard.

Drama **(PR:O MPAA:NR)**

NUMBERED MEN** (1930) 65m FN-WB bw

Conrad Nagel *(Bertie Gray)*, Bernice Claire *(Mary Dane)*, Raymond Hackett *(Bud Leonard)*, Ralph Ince *(King Callahan)*, Tully Marshall *(Lemuel Barnes)*, Maurice Black *(Lou Rinaldo)*, William Holden *(Warden Lansing)*, George Cooper *(Happy Howard)*, Blanche Frederici *(Mrs. Miller)*, Ivan Linow *(Pollack)*, Frederick Howard *(Jimmy Martin)*.

An early prison picture much like all the rest that would follow it in the coming years. The story illustrates how one convict finds out that another prisoner has been seeing his woman. From this comes two murders and a prison riot which do not add that much to the film.

d, Mervyn LeRoy; w, Al Cohn, Henry McCarthy (based on the play "Jailbreak" by Dwight Taylor); ph, Sol Polito; ed, Terrill Morse; art d, Jack Okey.

Prison/Drama **(PR:A MPAA:NR)**

NUMERO DEUX (SEE: NUMBER TWO, 1975, Fr.)

NUN, THE*½** (1971, Fr.) 130m Rome-Paris-Societe Nouvelle de Cinematographie/Altura c (SUZANNE SIMONIN, LA RELIGIEUSE DE DIDEROT; LA RELIGIEUSE)

Anna Karina *(Suzanne Simonin)*, Liselotte Pulver *(Mme. de Chelles)*, Micheline Presle *(Mme. de Moni)*, Christine Lenier *(Mme. Simonin)*, Francine Berge *(Sister St. Christine)*, Francisco Rabal *(Dom Morel)*, Wolfgang Reichmann *(Father Lemoine)*, Catherine Diamant *(Sister St. Cecile)*, Yori Bertin *(Sister St. Therese)*.

A riveting religious drama set in 18th Century France which casts French New Wave favorite Karina as a young nun forced into the convent for financial reasons. Her stay, however, is anything but blessed, becoming instead a nightmare of sadistic persecution. A wicked mother superior (played to the extreme by Pulver) locks her in her cell with only a little food and water, restricting her from even simple hygiene. An attempt to contact a lawyer and annul her vows is met with refusal and an attempted seduction by Pulver. Karina finally finds her ray of hope in Rabal, who empathizes with her plight since he, too, was forced into the clergy. She escapes with Rabal's help, but when he also attempts to have his way with her she flees, winding up in a bordello. Tortured to the furthest limits, Karina throws herself from the window landing onto the pavement—her arms and legs sprawled out like a cross. Based on a novel by Denis Diderot (published in 1796, though a written in 1760), THE NUN is based not on a true story but on a practical joke. To get a friend to come from the country to Paris, Diderot wrote him letters in the name of Suzanne Simonin—a nun who made an unsuccessful attempt to rescind her vows. When Diderot heard that his friend (the Marquis de Croismare) was planning to visit Simonin, he promptly wrote that the nun had killed herself. Rivette (whose first film, PARIS BELONGS TO US, was a forerunner in the New Wave) first adapted the story for the stage and only after a number of performances did he bring it to the screen. Without actually being about the theater, as are all Rivette's other pictures, THE NUN oddly is his most theatrical. "It is," in Rivette's words, "extremely written, because it came out of the experience of working on the stage, and finally because the subject deals with Catholicism, which is the absolute peak of theater." As accessible as the film is (Rivette and Karina both found themselves at the height of their commercial careers), THE NUN still managed to be banned in France. Presumably the censors objected to the subject matter, though they did approve the script before production began. When it came time for the picture's release in 1966, there was a change of heart and for two years Rivette fought to have the ban lifted. In the meantime, however, the picture was chosen as an official selection at the Cannes Film Festival. The ban was lifted in 1968, not after editing but after a title change from LA RELIGIEUSE (THE NUN) to SUZANNE SIMONIN, LA RELIGIEUSE DE DIDEROT—a change in name, not content. (In French; English subtitles.)

p, Georges de Beauregard; d, Jacques Rivette; w, Rivette, Jean Gruault (based on the novel *Memoirs of a Nun* by Denis Diderot); ph, Alain Levent (Eastmancolor); m, Jean-Claude Eloy; ed, Denise de Casabianca, Francoise Geissler; art d, Jean-Jacques Fabre; cos, Gitt Magrini; English subtitles, Harold Salemson.

Historical/Religious Drama (PR:C MPAA:GP)

NUN AND THE SERGEANT, THE** (1962) 73m Eastern/UA bw

Robert Webber *(Sgt. McGrath)*, Anna Sten *(Nun)*, Leo Gordon *(Dockman)*, Hari Rhodes *(Hall)*, Robert Easton *(Nupert)*, Dale Ishimoto *(Pak)*, Linda Wong *(Bok Soon)*, Linda Ho *(Soon Cha)*, Tod Windsor *(Nevins)*, Valentin De Vargas *(Rivas)*, Kenny Miller *(Quill)*, Norman Du Pont *(Mossback)*, Roger Torrey *(Turnbridge)*, Gregori F. Kris *(Johnson)*, Caroline Kido *(Myung Hee)*, King Moody *(Pollard)*, Yashi *(Kil Cha)*, Anna Shin *(Ok-Cha)*.

Even the war action cannot save this film. Set during the Korean War, Webber is the tough GI given an important assignment that might cost him his life. Instead of wasting top soldiers, he recruits the worst of the lot (aka DIRTY DOZEN) and tries to get the losers into some semblance of a group. They hate his guts and plan to kill him and take off at the first chance. Once behind enemy lines, they encounter American nun Sten, who has an injured leg, and a group of schoolgirls left at the scene they are supposed to blow up. Webber takes the group along and slowly wins the respect of his men and, of course, the girls. All the men decide to stick with Webber, with the exception of Gordon who tries to rape one of the girls. As Sten's injury worsens, it becomes apparent she will die if she receives no treatment. He lets the girls take her to a village and goes on to lead his men on their mission and to glory.

p, Eugen Frenke; d, Franklin Adreon; w, Don Cerveris; ph, Paul Ivano; m, Jerry Fielding; ed, John Hoffman, Carl Mahakian; art d, Bob Kinoshita; cos, Marjorie Corso; spec eff, Norman Breedlove; makeup, Carlie Taylor.

War (PR:A MPAA:NR)

NUN AT THE CROSSROADS, A** (1970, Ital./Span.) 99m Izaro-Cinematografica/UNIV c (VIOLENZA PER UNA MONACA; ENCRUCIJADA PARA UNA MONJA; AKA: CROSSROADS FOR A NUN)

Rosanna Schiaffino *(Sister Maria)*, John Richardson *(Dr. Pierre Lemmon)*, Mara Cruz *(Lisa)*, Angel Picazo *(Father Raymond)*, Paloma Valdes *(Sister Blanche)*, Lili Murati *(Mother Claire)*, Lex Monson *(Nangu)*, Margot Cottens *(Madeleine)*, Andres Mejuto *(Michel)*, Willie P. Elie *(Isaku)*, Claudia Gravy *(Yvonne)*, Lorenzo Terzon *(Jean)*, Maria Fernanda Ladron de Guevara *(Mother Superior)*, Antonio Pica *(Officer)*, Alicia Altabella *(Sister Genevieve)*, Porfiria Sanchis *(Sister Marcella)*, Matilde Munoz Sampedro *(Sister Herminia)*, Petra Lacey *(Sister Lucille)*.

A heavy story about a nun who is caught in the turbulent Congo after it becomes an independent nation. It is a story of great soul-searching. Belgian nuns have a convent in the Congo and a leader of black Simba rebels, Elie, tells them to leave. He says all whites and colonists will probably be killed, but the nuns cannot leave without their bishop's permission. Schiaffino helps a woman and is attacked and raped by a group of marauders. The attackers arrive at the convent and ruthlessly kill the mother superior, Landron de Guevara, and Elie. White mercenaries come to the rescue and all return to Brussels. There, Schiaffino discovers she is pregnant and is scorned by her family. To add to her misery, the Vatican issues an ultimatum: renounce her vows or give up the child. Richardson, who has always loved her, offers to marry her and accept the child but she turns him away because she already is married to Christ.

p, Jose Maria Reyzabal; d, Julio Buchs; w, Frederico de Urrutia, Manuel Sebares, Victor Auz, Jose Luis Hernandez Marcos, Buchs (based on a story by Jose Frade); ph, Gabor Pogany (Totalvision, Eastmancolor); m, Giovanni Fusco; ed, Gaby Penalba; md, Carlo Savina; art d, Ottavio Scotti, Jaime P. Cubero; cos, Leon Revuelta, Marisa Crimi; spec eff, Manuel Baquero; makeup, Manuel Martin, Otello Fava.

Religious Drama (PR:A MPAA:GP)

NUN OF MONZA, THE (SEE: LADY OF MONZA, THE, 1970)

NUN'S STORY, THE***** (1959) 149m WB c

Audrey Hepburn *(Sister Luke, Gabrielle Van Der Mal)*, Peter Finch *(Dr. Fortunati)*, Edith Evans *(Mother Emmanuel, Superior General)*, Peggy Ashcroft *(Mother Mathilde)*, Dean Jagger *(Dr. Van der Mal)*, Mildred Dunnock *(Sister Margharita)*, Beatrice Straight *(Mother Christophe)*, Patricia Collinge *(Sister William)*, Eva Kotthaus *(Sister Marie)*, Ruth White *(Mother Marcella)*, Niall McGinnis *(Father Vermeuhlen)*, Patricia Bosworth *(Simone)*, Barbara O'Neil *(Mother Katherine)*, Lionel Jeffries *(Dr. Goovaerts)*, Margaret Phillips *(Sister Pauline)*, Rosalie Crutchley *(Sister Eleanor)*, Colleen Dewhurst *(Archangel)*, Stephen Murray *(Chaplain)*, Orlando Martins *(Kalulu)*, Errol John *(Illunga)*, Jeannette Sterke *(Louise Van Der Mal)*, Richard O'Sullivan *(Pierre Van Der Mal)*, Diana Lambert *(Lisa)*, Marina Wolkonsky *(Marie Van Der Mal)*, Penelope Horner *(Jeannette Milonet)*, Ave Ninchi *(Sister Bernard)*, Charles Lamb *(Pascin)*, Ludovice Bonhomme *(Bishop)*, Dara Gavin *(Sister Ellen)*, Elfrida Simbari *(Sister Timothy)*, Dorothy Alison *(Sister Aurelie)*, Molly Urquhart *(Sister Augustine)*, Frank Singuineau, Juan Aymerich, Giovanna Galletti.

It's hard to believe that this rare and moving film did not win one single Oscar of the six for which it was nominated. The film, the direction, the screenplay, the photography, the music, and Miss Hepburn were all in the running, but 1959 saw the emergence of another religious-based film, BEN-HUR, which took most of those awards with the others going to Simone Signoret and the screenplay for ROOM AT THE TOP. The story begins with the autobiographical best-seller by a one-time nun who chose to let the world know what it was like inside the walls of a convent. Several years later, a satirical film, NASTY HABITS, was made about the subject and Dame Edith Evans played the Abbess in that, as she did in this one. Less knowledgeable handling of this story might have resulted in an overly sentimental or even melodramatic telling, but director Zinnemann and screenwriter Anderson resisted all temptation and have presented the eye and the soul with one of the best pictures ever made about the subject of man's struggle to understand God. Zinnemann chose his shots carefully and with an accent on simplicity, rather than resorting to any cinematic tricks, and we must be grateful, for at no time does the style overcome the story. Hepburn is radiant and gives one of her best performances ever, and every role, no matter how miniscule, has been cast and played with excellence. Hepburn is the daughter of Belgian surgeon Jagger and she has the desire to become a nursing nun in the Congo, which was still overseen by Belgium at the time, several years prior to WW II. She enters a convent and the first 30 minutes or so become an uneditorialized documentary segment about how it is for the young novitiate and the development from postulant to nun. The Order, which is never identified, is run by Evans, who admits that the life of a nun is, in many ways, a life against nature, but if one is willing to adhere to the principles, there are rewards to be found on Earth as well as in Heaven. After watching the rigors of the cloistered existence, Hepburn is finally a nun and goes off to a school where she learns tropical medicine. Her desire to go to the Congo is sidetracked, as she is first assigned to a mental hospital in Belgium where she is almost killed by a maniacal patient whom she thought she could handle. The authorities had asked her to stay away from the person, but she was guilty of the sin of pride and believed that she was capable of taking care of the patient. Eventually, she travels to the Congo where she is disappointed by her appointment. She'd hoped to do her nursing with natives, but is, instead, sent to a hospital for Europeans where she meets crusty Finch, a dedicated surgeon who has no room in his life for women or religion and devotes himself to his medical work. Hepburn understands that she must shed herself of her old ways and plunges her life into work. The result is that she is stricken with a mild case of tuberculosis, although she is cured after her brief bout with it. Hepburn wants to be one with God and thinks that by staying in Africa, she will expunge her brain of the memories she has and achieve that exalted state. Finch reckons she wants to remain in the Congo because she fears going back to the rigidity of the convent and that's the reason why she came down with TB. Her next assignment is to squire a Belgian official back to the motherland and she arrives there just as the war is beginning. Travel restrictions force her to stay in Europe and she's sent to a hospital near Holland. She sees what kind of people the invading Nazis are, but she is told to turn the other cheek to the enemies of Belgium and maintain her Christian attitude when dealing with them. When Jagger is killed by Nazis as he's helping refugees escape, she makes the conscious decision to involve herself in the struggle and joins the underground. It doesn't take much time before she realizes that she is incapable of keeping her dispassionate attitude and that she must leave the convent in order to fight against the oppressors. With her superior's permission, she goes through the steps necessary to unbind her from her vows and the picture fades out as Hepburn is walking away from the convent, totally alone. This was, perhaps, the only movie from this studio (Warners) where there was no music over the final titles. No one could decide if Waxman should write an upbeat or a downbeat theme because the choice would imply an editorial decision on the part of the filmmakers, something that Zinnemann zealously and successfully avoided all the way through. Jack Warner fought against that viewpoint but Zinnemann prevailed and the end credits are accompanied by silence. Assistant director Piero Mussetta used 70 members of Rome's Royal Opera Ballet to stage a sequence in which nuns are involved in various rituals. That sequence should be viewed by every film student as an exercise in how to handle a large group. Hepburn is Belgian-born of a Dutch mother and a British father. She spent the war in Holland where she and her mother were caught at the start of the battles and she could identify with the plight of the character she played. THE NUN'S STORY has it all—warmth, drama, humor, and a sense of taste that is hard to find these days. There was a story going around Hollywood in late 1985 that Zinnemann went to a meeting with a young studio chief who had come out of television and was still not 35. Zinnemann entered the youth's office, sat down, and the executive said. . ."Well, Mr. Zinnemann, I've heard of you, of course, but your credits slip my mind. What have you done?" Zinnemann smiled, nodded, leaned forward and replied, "You first." It may only be apocryphal but we thought it was worth repeating.

p, Henry Blanke; d, Fred Zinnemann; w, Robert Anderson (based on the book by Kathryn C. Hulme); ph, Franz F. Planer (Technicolor); m, Franz Waxman; ed, Walter Thompson; art d, Alexander Trauner; set d, Maurice Barnathan; cos, Marjorie Best; makeup, Alberto De Rossi.

Biography (PR:A MPAA:NR)

NUNZIO**½ (1978) 85m UNIV c

David Proval (Nunzio), James Andronica (Jamesie), Morgana King (Mrs. Sabatino), Joe Spinell (Angelo), Tovah Feldshuh (Michelle), Maria Smith-Caffey (Carol Sabatino), Vincent Russo (JoJo), Jamie Alba (Bobby), Theresa Saldana (Mary-Ann), Glenn Scarpelli (Georgia), Tony Panetta (Georgie's Friend), Steve Gucciardo (Carmine), Charlet Oberley (Customer), Sal Maneri, Anthony Esemplare, Robert Hayden (JoJo's Friends), Sonia Zomina (Mrs. Shuman), Crystal Hayden (Crystal Sabatino), Vincent Igneri (Vincent Sabatino), Tom Quinn (Pete), Joseph Sullivan (Priest), Joseph Tripi, Anthony Gilberti, Jennifer Gilberti, Guy Spennato, Nicole DeMaio, Jerry Tambasco, John Di Giso, Jr., Brian Brennan, Bill Hickey, Walter Gorney, Monica Lewis, Dorene Belleus, Lenore Volpe, Angela Pietropinto, Amanda Hope Lipnick, P. W. Williams, Zoe Clarke-Williams, Filomena Spagnuolo, Joe Adamo, Tony DiBenedetto, Leo Ciani, Jack Meeks, Bob Scarantino, Larry Silvestri, James Anthony, Jenny Shawn, Pasquale Igneri, Randall Andronica, Sal LaPera.

Proval plays a good-hearted mentally retarded man with the mind of a 10-year-old. To help his mother, he works delivering groceries while his older brother, Andronica (also the film's writer), protects him from the neighborhood bullies. Proval often fantasizes about being Superman and marrying Feldshuh, who works in a nearby bakery. Much of the story concerns his brother who has to balance his macho image with a real love for his younger brother. Proval's Superman fantasy comes to life when he rescues a child from a burning building. Simple, but touching story.

p, Jennings Lang; d, Paul Williams; w, James Andronica; ph, Edward R. Brown (Panavision, Technicolor); m, Lalo Schifrin; ed, Johanna Demetrakas; prod d, Mel Bourne; art d, Richard Fuhrman; set d, George DeTitta; cos, Ann Roth.

Drama (PR:O MPAA:R)

NUR TOTE ZEUGEN SCHWEIGEN (SEE: HYPNOSIS, 1966)

NUREMBERG* (1961) 72m CR Enterprises/Unitel bw

Lee Bonnell, Roy Bennett, Marta Mithovitch.

While two soldiers question a German woman, U.S. Supreme Court Justice Robert Jackson gives an opening statement against war criminals at Nuremberg. While the woman denies she is a Nazi, her description of life under fascism reveals her true feelings. Interspersed is Nazi Germany film footage, Hitler speeches, and shots of concentration camps. As the woman finishes her speech, she is found innocent and set free.

p, Alan Kane.

War/Drama (PR:A MPAA:NR)

NURSE EDITH CAVELL*** (1939) 95m Imperadio/RKO bw

Anna Neagle (Nurse Edith Cavell), Edna May Oliver (Countess de Mavon), George Sanders (Capt. Heinrichs), May Robson (Mme. Rappard), ZaSu Pitts (Mme. Moulin), H. B. Warner (Mr. Gibson), Sophie Stewart (Sister Watkins), Mary Howard (Nurse O'Brien), Robert Coote (Bungey), Martin Kosleck (Pierre), Gui Ignon (Cobbler), Lionel Royce (Gen. Von Ehrhardt), Jimmy Butler (Jean Rappard), Rex Downing (Francois Rappard), Henry Brandon (Lt. Schultz), Fritz Leiber (Sadi Kirschen), Gilbert Emery (Brank Whitlock), Lucien Prival (Lt. Schmidt), Richard Deane (Lt. Wilson, Airman), Bert Roach (George Moulin), Halliwell Hobbes (British Chaplain), Ernst Deutsch (Dr. Schroeder, Public Prosecutor), Egon Brecher (Dr. Gunther), Will Kaufman (Baron von Weser), Gustave von Seyferttitz (President of Trial Court), Frank Reicher (Baron von Bissing), Joseph de Stefani (Manager), Henry Victor (Jaubec).

When the silent version first came out in 1928, NURSE EDITH CAVELL made a great stir because of its realistic and sometimes brutal depiction of war. Producer and director Herbert Wilcox brought it back with sound in 1939 and it opened just a few days after WW II was declared on the European side. Neagle is the good nurse Cavell, who is devoted to moving political prisoners and refugee soldiers from German-occupied Belgium in WW I. Neagle uses women and an underground railroad network to move the men. She finally is caught by the Germans and they graphically execute her for espionage. Rather dramatic for the time, but the country's attitude toward Germans and war must be remembered. Gripping throughout. Although the film was not financially successful, it helped to give RKO a reputation for serious, high-minded movies.

p&d, Herbert Wilcox; w, Michael Hogan (based on the novel Dawn by Capt. Reginald Berkeley); ph, F. A. Young, Joseph H. August; ed, Elmo Williams; md, Anthony Collins; art d, L. P. Williams; spec eff, Vernon L. Walker.

War/Drama Cas. (PR:A MPAA:NR)

NURSE FROM BROOKLYN** (1938) 67m UNIV bw

Sally Eilers (Elizabeth Thomas), Paul Kelly (Jim Barnes), Larry Blake (Larry Craine), Maurice Murphy (Danny Thomas), Morgan Conway (Inspector Donohue), David Oliver (Detective Branch), Lucille Gleason (Ma Hutchins).

A crime drama with a twist of romance. Eilers' brother is killed in a shoot-out. She is told by a low-life friend of his that the policeman they fought killed her brother in cold blood. Eilers believes the crook but starts falling for the wounded policeman, who finds out she is the dead boy's sister. The officer hunts the real killer and clears the dead boy's name and wins his sister.

p, Edmund Grainger; d, S. Sylvan Simon; w, Roy Chanslor (based on the story "If You Break My Heart" by Steve Fisher); ph, Milton Krasner; ed, Paul Landres; md, Charles Previn; art d, Jack Otterson.

Crime/Romance (PR:A MPAA:NR)

NURSE ON WHEELS**½ (1964, Brit.) 86m G. H. W. Anglo Amalgamated/Janus bw

Juliet Mills (Joanna Jones), Ronald Lewis (Henry Edwards), Joan Sims (Deborah Walcott), Athene Seyler (Miss Farthingale), Norman Rossington (George Judd), Barbara Everest (Nurse Merrick), Ronald Howard (Dr. Harold Golfrey), Joan Hickson (Mrs. Wood), George Woodbridge (Mr. Beacon), Renee Houston (Mrs. Beacon), Jim Dale (Tim Taylor), David Horne (Dr. Golfrey), Deryck Guyler (Examiner), Noel Purcell (Abel Worthy), Esma Cannon (Mrs. Jones), Brian Rawlinson (Policeman), Amanda Reiss (Ann Taylor), Virginia Vernon (Miss Maitland), Raymond Huntley (Vicar).

A British comedy that contains few laughs. Mills is the new nurse in a country town in England. She is pretty and follows a floozy predecessor. She becomes the subject of nasty gossip but eventually makes friends with the local doctor, his son, and a local shop owner. Mills, a bad driver, causes an accident with a rich farmer who falls for her. Lewis wants to evict a young couple whose vehicle is on his property. They fight over it because Mills thinks eviction would be terrible since the woman is near the end of her pregnancy. Mills delivers the child in the fields and is supported by the townspeople and Lewis in the end.

p, Peter Rogers; d, Gerald Thomas; w, Norman Hudis (based on the novel Nurse is a Neighbour by Joanna Jones); ph, Alan Hume; m, Eric Rogers; ed, Archie Ludski; md, Rogers; art d, Lionel Couch.

Comedy (PR:O MPAA:NR)

NURSE SHERRI** (1978) 88m Independent c (AKA: BEYOND THE LIVING)

Jill Jacobson, Geoffrey Land, Marilyn Joi, Mary Kay Pass, Prentiss Moulden, Clayton Foster.

Jacobson is a young nurse whose body is taken over by a religious fanatic. He had died while in surgery, so everyone who was part of the operation must die. Jacobson gets the assignment and goes after her co-workers with meat cleavers and a pitchfork. One of the most gruesome scenes occurs in a foundry.

p, Mark Sherwood; d, Al Adamson; w, Michael Bockman, Gregg Tittinger.

Horror (PR:O MPAA:R)

NURSEMAID WHO DISAPPEARED, THE**½ (1939, Brit.) 86m WB-FN/WB bw

Arthur Margetson (Antony Gethryn, Detective), Peter Coke (Tom Sheldon, Playwright), Lesley Brook (Avis Bellingham), Edward Chapman (Jenks), Coral Browne (Mabel Barnes), Joyce Kennedy (Lucia Gethryn), Dorice Fordred (Janet Murch), Martita Hunt (Lady Ballister), Marion Gerth (Ada Brent), Ian Maclean (Inspector Pike), Ian Fleming (Sir Egbert Lucas), Eliot Makeham, Scott Harold, Phil Ray, Mavis Villiers.

Playwright Coke overhears some men involved in a kidnaping ring. With detective Margetson's help, it's learned that the ring operates out of a phony employment agency that sends people to spy on would-be victims. After two attempts are made on Coke's life, a suicide, and a murder, the gang is finally captured. This programmer mystery pretty well holds its own in suspense. Thrills are well built into the script, which suffers only from a little more dialog than it needs.

p, Jerome Jackson; d, Arthur B. Woods; w, Paul Gangelin, Connery Chappell (based on the novel by Philip Macdonald); ph, Basil Emmott.

Mystery/Crime (PR:A MPAA:NR)

NURSE'S SECRET, THE**½ (1941) 65m FN/WB bw

Lee Patrick (Ruth Adams), Regis Toomey (Inspector Tom Patten), Julie Bishop (Florence Lents), Ann Edmonds (Paula Brent), George Campeau (Charles Elliott), Clara Blandick (Miss Juliet Mitchell), Charles D. Waldron (Dr. Stewart), Charles Trowbridge (Arthur Glenn), Leonard Mudie (Hugo), Virginia Brissac (Mary), Frank Reicher (Mr. Henderson), Georgia Caine (Miss Griffin), Keith Douglas (Dr. Keene), Faye Emerson (Telephone Girl), Lucia Carroll (Nurse).

A fairly suspenseful whodunit starring Patrick as a young nurse sent to care for an ancient, wealthy woman who lives in a large, creepy mansion. Soon afterwards, a death that appears to be a suicide occurs in the house, and police inspector Toomey is sent to investigate. Together the nurse and cop unravel the mystery (which has to do with an insurance scam) and fall in love. Surprisingly brisk direction by Smith, coupled with snappy dialog make this a pleasing little thriller.

p, William Jacobs; d, Noel M. Smith; w, Anthony Coldeway (based on the story "Miss Pinkerton" by Mary Roberts Rinehart); ph, James Van Trees; ed, doug Gould; art d, Stanley Fleischer.

Mystery (PR:A MPAA:NR)

NUT FARM, THE**   (1935) 65m MON bw

Wallace Ford (*Willie Barton*), Joan Gale (*Agatha*), Oscar Apfel (*Mr. Bent*), Bradley Page (*Holland*), Betty Alden (*Mrs. Bent*), Florence Roberts (*Mrs. Barton*), Spencer Charters (*Sliscomb, Landlord*), Lorin Raker (*Biddleford*), Arnold Gray (*Van Norton*).

Page plays an unscrupulous con-man who zeros in on Apfel and his wife, Alden, and persuades them to give up the nut farm to make a career in motion pictures. He enrolls them into a bogus Hollywood acting school and soon takes them for every penny. An OK comedy.

p, Trem Carr, William T. Lackey; d, Melville Brown; w, George Waggner (based on the play by John C. Brownell); ph, Harry Neumann; ed, Carl Pierson.

Comedy   **(PR:A   MPAA:NR)**

NUTCRACKER zero   (1982, Brit.) 101m Jershaw/RANK c

Joan Collins (*Mme. Carrere*), Carol White (*Margaux Lasselle*), Paul Nicolas (*Mike McCann*), Finola Hughes (*Nadia*), William Franklyn (*Sir Arthur Cartwright*), Murray Melvin, Leslie Ash, Fran Fullenwider, Gess Whitfield, Dan Meaden, Debbie Goodman, Raymond Christodoulou, Cherry Gillespie, Jane Wellman, John Vye, Patrick Wood, Patti Hammond, Liz Green, Anita Mahadervan, Victoria Shellard, Stephen Beagley, Tony Edge, Helen Mason, Pauline Crawford, Julia De Peyer, Rosemarie Ford, Seeta Indrani, Ed Bishop, Christopher Farris, Ewen Solon, Olivier Pierre, Trevor Baxter, Morgan Sheppard, Martin Burrows, Vernon Dobtcheff, Geraldine Gardner, Jo Warne, Richard Marner, Paul Mari, Peter Pacey.

Another trashy Joan Collins hubba-hubba film following hot on the heels of THE BITCH, THE STUD, featuring the over-hyped "Dynasty" TV star as the administrator of a London ballet school who seduces the lead male dancer and sells out her pupils to local politicos as high-priced hookers. Of course the young and innocent Russian ballerina Hughes did not defect for this so she gives up and goes home (which is what the audience should have done after the opening credits). Pure junk, not even unintentionally funny.

p, Panos Nicolaou; d, Anwar Kawadri; w, Raymond Christodoulou; ph, Peter Jessop (Eastmancolor); m, Simon Park; ed, Max Benedict; prod d, Geoff Sharpe; cos, Sharpe.

Drama   **(PR:O   MPAA:NR)**

NUTCRACKER FANTASY**½   (1979) 82m Sanrio c

Michele Lee (*Narrator*), Melissa Gilbert (*Clara*), Lurene Tuttle (*Aunt Gerda*), Christopher Lee (*Uncle Drosselmeyer/Street Singer/Puppeteer/Watchmaker*), Jo Anne Worley (*Queen Morphia*), Ken Sansom (*Chamberlain/Poet/Wiseman*), Dick Van Patten (*King Goodwin*), Roddy McDowall (*Franz Fritz*), Mitchel Gardner (*Indian Wiseman/Viking Wiseman*), Jack Angel (*Chinese Wiseman/Executioner*), Gene Moss (*Otto Von Atra/French Wiseman/Clovis*), Eva Gabor (*Queen of Time*), Joan Gerber, Maxine Fisher (*Mice Voices*), Robin Haffner (*Princess Mary*).

A well-animated children's adventure produced in Japan, and dubbed into English for American release. A young girl's dream takes her to an enchanted land where a King's daughter has been transformed into a sleeping mouse when an army of evil mice steal her heart. Luckily a young hero arrives and retrieves the princess' heart so that she can become a normal person once again. Of course they fall in love and everybody's happy at the end. Outstanding voice talent from Gilbert, Lee, and McDowall combined with cute songs make this a good one for the kiddies.

p, Walt deFaria, Mark L. Rosen, Arthur Tomioka; d, Takeo Nakamura; w, Thomas Joachim, Eugene Fornier (based on *The Nutcracker and the Mouse King* by E. T. A. Hoffman, adaptation by Shintaro Tsuji); ph, Fumio Otani, Aguri Sugita, Ryoji Takamori (DeLuxe Color); m, Peter Illych Tchaikovsky (adapted and arranged by Akihito Wakatsuki, Kentaro Haneda); ed, Jack Woods, Noboo Ogawa, Nakamura; set d, Mayasa Kaburagi, Hiroshi Yamashita; ch, Tetsutaro Shimizu; m/l, Randy Bishop, Marty Gwinn.

Fantasy   **(PR:AAA   MPAA:G)**

NUTTY, NAUGHTY CHATEAU**   (1964, Fr./Ital.)
102m Les Films Corona-Spectacles Lubroso-Euro International/Lopert c
(CHATEAU EN SUEDE; IL CASTELLO IN SVEZIA)

Monica Vitti (*Eleanore Falsen*), Curt Jurgens (*Hugo Falsen*), Jean-Claude Brialy (*Sebastian*), Suzanne Flon (*Agathe*), Jean-Louis Trintignant (*Eric*), Francoise Hardy (*Ophelie*), Sylvie (*Grandmother*), Daniel Emilfork (*Gunther*), Michel Le Royer (*Gosta*).

Jurgens is the insanely jealous and crazed owner of a lonely castle located in the hinterlands of Sweden that houses his equally loony family. His young and attractive wife, Vitti, is constantly on guard due to her husband's paranoia, and loyally aids her demented brother, Brialy. Flon, Jurgens' older sister, insists that everyone dress in 18th-Century fashions so as not to destroy her illusions of the past. One day Jurgens' cousin Trintignant arrives for a visit and falls in love with Vitti. Soon after, he is haunted by the ghost of Jurgens' first wife, but it turns out that the woman is very much alive but now crazy due to her near drowning in the lake. Because he could not divorce her, Jurgens declared she was dead and then locked her up in a bedroom. Vitti also informs Trintignant that Jurgens had murdered a man he had suspected of being one of her lovers. Trintignant decides to watch himself, and his instincts prove correct because Jurgens and his sister soon attempt to kill him. Trintignant escapes and runs home to inform the authorities of the strange goings-on at the house, but he is shocked to learn that a major magazine has just arrived to do a cover story on the family of lunatics. Another dull Vadim comedy.

d, Roger Vadim; w, Vadim, Claude Choublier (based on the play by Francoise Sagan); ph, Armand Thirard (Franscope, Technicolor); m, Raymond Le Senechal; ed, Victoria Mercanton; art d, Jean Andre.

Farce   **(PR:C   MPAA:NR)**

NUTTY PROFESSOR, THE***½   (1963) 107m PAR c

Jerry Lewis (*Prof. Julius Ferris Kelp/Buddy Love*), Stella Stevens (*Stella Purdy*), Del Moore (*Dr. Hamius R. Warfield*), Kathleen Freeman (*Millie Lemmon*), Ned Flory, Skip Ward, Norman Alden (*Football Players*), Howard Morris (*Father Kelp*), Elvia Allman (*Mother Kelp*), Milton Frome (*Dr. Leevee*), Buddy Lester (*Bartender*), Marvin Kaplan (*English Boy*), David Landfield, Celeste Yarnall, Francine York, Julie Parrish, Henry Gibson (*College Students*), Dave Willock (*Bartender*), Doodles Weaver (*Rube*), Mushy Callahan (*Cab Driver*), Gavin Gordon (*Salesman Clothier*), Joe Forte (*Faculty Member*), Terry Higgins (*Cigarette Girl*), Murray Alper (*Judo Instructor*), Gary Lewis (*Boy*), Les Brown and His Band of Renown.

This is Jerry Lewis' best film, but it's no masterpiece of comic genius. Lewis plays Julius F. Kelp, a bumbling professor of chemistry at a small college, who falls hopelessly in love with one of his students, Stevens. Stevens dates boys from the football team and goes to a steamy nightclub called the Purple Pit. Seeking to improve his looks, Lewis tries bodybuilding. He fails miserably (his arms get stretched out by the barbells) and decides to change himself by whipping up a chemical potion. That night he drinks his creation and is transformed into an overbearing, obnoxious, though dashing singer who calls himself Buddy Love. Though totally conceited, Buddy Love (Lewis) succeeds in winning over the entire student body by appearing at the Purple Pit and wooing the audience, including Stevens, with his piano playing and singing. Lewis now finds himself the rage at the college, but his formula has the unfortunate habit of wearing off at the wrong times. forcing him to make ridiculous explanations as to why Buddy Love suddenly disappeared, leaving Julius F. Kelp to make excuses for his behavior. The truth is revealed on the night of the big dance when Buddy Love performs at the function and changes into Julius before a shocked audience. In a maudlin ending, Lewis explains to the students why he deceived them and ends by telling them that they must like themselves as they are or never expect anyone else to like them. Stevens, of course, really loved Julius all along and they plan to be married. Much has been made of buddy Love's resemblance to Lewis' former partner, Dean Martin, and the connection is there, but who Love really resembles is the Lewis of the talk shows, telethons, and interviews. Pompous, self-important, and overly bitter about the manner in which his "art" has been received, Lewis worked hard at alienating himself from everybody but the French (they think he's a genius) for 20 years. THE NUTTY PROFESSOR is a funny film, but only fitfully so. The gags are scattered and at times infantile and insulting to anyone over the age of three. Lewis fans harp at how brilliant his performance is in THE NUTTY PROFESSOR, but aside from the Buddy Love character everything else is standard Lewis. For the superlative Lewis performance, one must see Martin Scorsese's overlooked comic masterpiece THE KING OF COMEDY. There Lewis allows us to see his dark side, and it seems that by the 1980s he had enough guts to come to grips with the complexities of his public persona and present them on screen in a film he didn't direct. His performance is brilliant, it overshadows DeNiro and should have been nominated for an Academy Award. Perhaps Lewis was finally ready to admit that Buddy Love was the dark side of Jerry Lewis and chose to show it honestly, openly, and brilliantly 20 years later.

p, Jerry Lewis, Ernest D. Glucksman; d, Lewis; w, Lewis, Bill Richmond (based on a story by Lewis); ph, W. Wallace Kelley (Technicolor); m, Walter Scharf; ed, John Woodcock; art d, Hal Pereira, Walter Tyler; set d, Sam Comer, Robert R. Benton; cos, Edith Head; spec eff, Paul K. Lerpal; m/l, "We've Got A World That Swings," Louis Y. Brown, Lil Mattis; makeup, Wally Westmore.

Comedy   **Cas.**   **(PR:A   MPAA:NR)**

NVUIIRANDO NO WAKADAISHO   (SEE:
                                     YOUNG GUY ON MT. COOK, 1969), Jap.)

NYUJIRANDO NO WAKADAISHO   (SEE:
                                     YOUNG GUY ON MT. COOK, 1969)

O

O. HENRY'S FULL HOUSE*½** (1952) 117m FOX bw (GB: FULL HOUSE)

"The Gift of the Magi": Jeanne Crain *(Della)*, Farley Granger *(Jim)*, Sig Rumann *(Menkie)*, Harry Hayden *(Mr. Crump)*, Fred Kelsey *(Santa Claus)*, Richard Hylton *(Bill)*, Richard Allen *(Pete)*, Fritz Feld *(Maurice)*, Frank Jaquet *(Butcher)*. "The Last Leaf": Anne Baxter *(Joanna)*, Jean Peters *(Susan)*, Gregory Ratoff *(Behrman)*, Richard Garrick *(Doctor)*, Steven Geray *(Radolf)*, Warren Stevens *(Druggist)*, Martha Wentworth *(Mrs. O'Brien)*, Ruth Warren *(Neighbor)*, Bert Hicks *(Sheldon Sidney)*, Beverly Thompson *(Girl)*, Hal J. Smith *(Dandy)*. "The Cop and the Anthem": Charles Laughton *(Soapy)*, Marilyn Monroe *(Streetwalker)*, David Wayne *(Horace)*, Philip Tonge *(Man with Umbrella)*, Thomas Browne Henry *(Manager)*, Richard Karlan *(Headwaiter)*, Erno Verebes *(Waiter)*, William Vedder *(Judge)*, Billy Wayne *(Bystander)*, Nico Lek *(Owner)*, Marjorie Holliday *(Cashier)*, James Flavin *(Cop)*. "The Clarion Call": Dale Robertson *(Barney Woods)*, Richard Widmark *(Johnny Kernan)*, Joyce MacKenzie *(Hazel)*, Richard Rober *(Chief of Detectives)*, Will Wright *(Manager)*, House Peters, Sr. *(Bascom)*, Tyler McVey *(O. Henry)*, Phil Tully *(Guard)*, Frank Cusack *(Waiter)*, Stuart Randall *(Detective)*, Abe Dinovitch *(Bartender)*. "The Ransom of Red Chief": Fred Allen *(Sam)*, Oscar Levant *(Bill)*, Lee Aaker *(J.B.)*, Kathleen Freeman *(J.B.'s Mother)*, Alfred Mizner *(J.B.'s Father)*, Irving Bacon *(Mr. Dorset)*, Gloria Gordon *(Ellie Mae)*, Robert Easton, Robert Cherry, Norman Leavitt *(Yokels)*, John Steinbeck *(Narrator)*.

A hearty and entertaining compendium of O. Henry's best stories sees some energetic performances and, in the case of a few of the stories, marvelous direction. The first tale, "The Cop and the Anthem" (19 minutes) shows Laughton as a haughty, persnickety tramp who dislikes cold weather and, just as winter blows upon the scene, plans to have himself arrested so he can enjoy the warm comfort of a jail cell, his usual seasonal routine. But fate and the long arm of the law turn against him. No matter what Laughton does, he cannot offend the law, including a mashing attempt with Monroe; the lady, and not Laughton, is arrested for street-walking. It's so hopeless that Laughton turns to the church, gets religion, and seeks honest employment for the first time in his miserable life. And it's at this decisive juncture that the tramp is arrested and taken to jail against his wishes. "The Clarion Call" is a terse 22-minute slice of life where decent cop Robertson must arrest old friend Widmark, who snorts his famous maniacal laugh in a battle of wits that ends with the triumph of justice. In "The Last Leaf" (23 minutes) Anne Baxter is dying in a small room, watching the leaves wither in the late fall wind, coming to believe in her delirious state that when the last leaf on the wall outside her window dies and blows away, she too will die. Winter comes and the leaves vanish, one by one, until a single leaf remains, stubbornly clinging to the wall. It will not die and the image of its valiant presence gives Baxter hope. She recovers only to find upon close inspection that the leaf is not real, that it is the creation of impoverished painter Ratoff, who has destroyed himself in the savage winter to scale a ladder and paint the leaf at night when Baxter is sleeping. Allen, Levant, and Aaker provide a laugh a minute in the 26-minute filming of the hilarious "The Ransom of Red Chief," the story of a boy so bad that his parents could care less when inept kidnapers Allen and Levant grab Aaker. The roughhouse kid makes life so miserable for his abductors that Allen and Levant *offer the parents money* to take back the insufferable brat. In "The Gift of the Magi" (21 minutes) young newlyweds Granger and Crain are so impoverished that they sacrifice the most cherished possessions to buy each other gifts at Christmas, sacrifices that humorously backfire. The direction and writing in all these sequences are above average and the entire film is a great treat, enhanced by Steinbeck's narration which is an homage to a fine writer, the mysterious O. Henry.

p, Andre Hakim; d, Henry Hathaway, Henry Koster, Henry King, Howard Hawks, Jean Negulesco; w, Lamar Trotti, Richard Breen, Ben Roberts, Ivan Goff, Walter Bullock, Nunnally Johnson (based on the stories by O. Henry); ph, Lloyd Ahern, Lucien Ballard, Joe MacDonald, Milton Krasner; m, Alfred Newman; ed, Nick DiMaggio, Barbara McLean, William B. Murphy; art d, Lyle Wheeler, Chester Gore, Joseph C. Wright, Richard Irvine, Addison Hehr; set d, Claude Carpenter, Thomas Little, Bruce MacDonald, Fred J. Rode.

Comedy/Drama **(PR:AAA MPAA:NR)**

O.M.H.S. (SEE: YOU'RE IN THE ARMY NOW, 1937, Brit.)

O LUCKY MAN!**** (1973, Brit.) 186m Memorial-Sam/WB c

Malcolm McDowell *(Mick Travis)*, Ralph Richardson *(Monty/Sir James Burgess)*, Rachel Roberts *(Gloria Rowe/Mme. Paillard/Mrs. Richards)*, Arthur Lowe *(Mr. Duff/Charlie Johnson/Dr. Munda)*, Helen Mirren *(Patricia Burgess)*, Dandy Nichols *(Tea Lady/Neighbor)*, Mona Washbourne *(Sister Hallett/Usher/Neighbor)*, Michael Medwin *(Army Captain/Power Station Technician/Duke of Belminster)*, Mary MacLeod *(Mrs. Ball/Vicar's Wife/Salvation Army Woman)*, Vivian Pickles *(Welfare Lady)*, Graham Crowden *(Dr. Millar/Prof. Stewart/Meths Drinker)*, Peter Jeffrey *(Factory Chairman/Prison Governor)*, Philip Stone *(Interrogator/Jenkins/Salvation Army Major)*, Wallas Eaton *(Col. Steiger/John Stone/Warder/Meths Drinker/Film Executive)*, Anthony Nicholls *(General/Judge/Foreman)*, Michael Bangerter *(Interrogator/William/Released Prisoner/Assistant)*, Jeremy Bulloch *(Car Crash Victim/Pig-Boy/Placard Bearer)*, Warren Clarke *(Master of Ceremonies/Male Nurse/Warner)*, Geoffrey Palmer *(Doctor/Basil Keyes)*, Geoffrey Chater *(Vicar/Bishop)*, Christine Noonan *(Coffee Trainee/Girl at Stag Party)*, Margot Bennett *(Coffee Bean Picker)*, Bill Owen *(Superintendent Barlow/Inspector Carding)*, Edward Judd *(Oswald)*, Brian Glover *(Foreman/Power Station Guard)*, David Daker, Edward Peel *(Policemen)*, James Bolam *(Attenborough/Doctor)*, Patricia Healey *(Hotel Receptionist)*, Paul Dawkins *(Man at Stag Party/Meths Drinker)*, Ian Leake *(Roadie)*, Pearl Nunez *(Mrs. Naidu)*, Colin Green *(Colin)*, Clive Thacker *(Clive)*, Dave Markee *(Dave)*, Alan Price *(Alan)*, Lindsay Anderson *(Director)*, Bart Alison, Ben Aris, John Barrett, Sue Bond, Constance Chapman, Peter Childs, Frank Cousins, Brian Coucher, Allen Cullen, Anna Dawson, Kymoke Debayo, Michael Elphick, Eleanor Fazan, Geoff Hinsliff, Jo Jeggo, Patricia Lawrence, Stephanie Lawrence, Brian Lawson, Terence Maidment, Tuesday Miller, Ken Oxtoby, Stuart Perry, Brian Pettifer, Bill Pilkington, Cyril Renison, Irene Richmond, Roy Scammell, Peter Scofield, Frank Singuineau, Patsy Smart, David Stern, Adele Strong, Hugh Thomas, Betty Turner, Glen Williams, Cathering Willmer.

O LUCKY MAN! is an awesome cinematic achievement that just misses being included in the classic stratum because there is too much to see. They cut 20 minutes from the original and even at the ultimate U.S. length of 166 minutes, many felt it was short and wished the entire picture were shown. The idea for the movie came from McDowell, whom director Anderson had starred in the movie IF. . .and their relationship continued through the making of this film. It is quite unlike anything you may have ever seen and defies categorizing. McDowell is a young salesman for a coffee company. He is an adherent to the Protestant "work ethic" which states that ambition and the willingness to toil long and hard hours are all the requirements for success. He is a smiling, innocent young man and his guileless ways soon attract the coffee company's public relations executive, Roberts, who promptly seduces him, then gives him the plum position of a supervisor. While driving to his new area, he witnesses an accident in which two drivers are killed. When he attempts to give his account to the two policemen (Daker, Peel) on the scene, he is ordered to leave at once and notes that the cops are more interested in looting the sports car and van which were involved in the fatal crash. McDowell puts up for the night at a small hotel operated by MacLeod. Then he meets Lowe, a lecherous customer of the coffee company, who takes him to a wild and very drunken party where the entertainment consists of X-rated films and real women performing unspeakable acts. When he returns to his room, MacLeod awaits him in his bed. They make love and McDowell gets a call from Roberts informing him that he has already been promoted to run the company's operations in Scotland. He's about to depart the following morning when Richardson, an aged resident of the hotel, gives him the gift of a gold suit with the warning "Try not to die like a dog." Ignoring that, McDowell discovers that the suit fits him well and takes off for Scotland. He gets to the address and is immediately arrested by uniformed guards, then taken to a research facility where they torture him until he signs a confession for having performed several crimes of which he is innocent and unaware. Just then, a warning siren sends his guards running from the edifice. He gets away through the aid of Nichols, a tea lady, and watches as the factory blows up in an atomic blast which levels the surrounding area as well. He finds what's left of his car, grabs the gold suit, and roams through the afflicted area until coming upon a peaceful valley and walking into a church where he falls asleep. He is awakened by the vicar's wife, MacLeod (or didn't we tell you that almost all of the leads play several parts?), and her children take him to a road where he hitches a ride with male nurse Clarke. On the ride, Clarke talks McDowell into becoming a guinea pig for medical research and promises that he will be paid handsomely. Once at the medical lab, McDowell learns that the doctor, Crowden, wants nothing less than to sterilize him. McDowell also notes the result of one of Crowden's earlier experiments: a huge pig with the head of a young man having been transplanted onto it. McDowell escapes and is picked up by a rock band and their in-house bird, Mirren. They travel to London in the group's small van and he spends the night with Mirren. Next day, he learns that she is the daughter of one of the richest and vilest men in England, Richardson again, whom he finally meets and goes to work for as his assistant. When one of Richardson's crooked deals falls apart, McDowell takes the rap and gets five years in the jug, while Mirren decides to marry Medwin, a young peer. His years in jail are not wasted, as he finds God and decides to devote himself to religion upon his release. He begins lecturing for the Salvation Army and has his pockets picked by a couple of thieves. In attempting to save the life of would-be suicide Roberts (in one of her three roles), he fouls that up and she dies and he nearly does as well. There's a band of drunks and druggies that McDowell seeks to aid with food and advice and he is shocked to find Mirren and Medwin, now poverty-stricken, among them. His life is in a shambles and he has nothing in which to believe and not a farthing in his pockets. McDowell sees a poster advertising the quest for an unknown to play the lead in a new film. Hundreds show up at the audition hall and McDowell is instantly picked by director Anderson (as himself) to be the star. When McDowell finds it difficult to smile (on Anderson's request), the director whacks him across the face with the script. McDowell smiles finally. The picture is made, becomes a hit, and McDowell is a new movie force. At a fete for the cast and crew of the film, McDowell wears his gold suit, dances with the others, and is now a Lucky Man. Thirteen of the actors play multiple roles, which would ordinarily confuse, except that they are so good at what they do there is no mistaking the parts they are playing. As black as the synopsis seems to be, that's how hilarious the picture is. Add that to the excellent songs written and performed by Alan Price, and you can see that this is no ordinary movie. Matter of fact, it may be quite the most unusual picture done in the 1970s out of England. The cuts came in the Salvation Army sequence and the Roberts' suicide and a few trims in some other places. Anderson pulls out all the stops in technique and there's hardly a film trick missed. Since this is essentially a fantasy, the gimmickry never gets in the way. Songs include, "O Lucky Man!" "Changes," "Sell, Sell," "Poor People," "Look Over Your Shoulder," "Justice," "My Home Town" (Alan Price).

p, Michael Medwin, Lindsay Anderson; d, Anderson; w, David Sherwin (based on an idea by Malcolm McDowell); ph, Miroslav Ondricek (Technicolor); m, Alan Price; ed, David Gladwell, Tom Priestley; prod d, Jocelyn Herbert; art d, Alan Withy; set d, Harry Cordwell; cos, Elsa Fennell; spec eff, John Stears; makeup, Paul Rabiger, Basil Newall.

Fantasy/Comedy Cas. (PR:O MPAA:R)

O, MY DARLING CLEMENTINE* (1943) 70m REP bw (AKA: OH MY DARLING CLEMENTINE)

Roy Acuff *(Sheriff)*, Harry "Pappy" Chesire *(Mayor)*, Isabel Randolph *(Mrs. Uppington)*, Frank Albertson *(Dan Franklin)*, Lorna Gray *(Clementine)*, Irene Ryan *(Irene/Princess Sheba)*, Eddie Parks *(Luke Scully)*, Lois Bridge *(Ellie Scully)*, Patricia Knox *(Bubbles)*, Tom Kennedy *(Bill Collector)*, Edwin Stanley *(Hartfield)*, Emmett Vogan *(Brown)*, Tennessee Ramblers, Radio Rogues.

A group of road musicians end up in a high-class Dixie town in this weak film that depended on Acuff's country following to save it from box-office failure. Their manager, Albertson, tries to put on a show and that's basically the plot. A few weak laughs surrounded by some Acuff songs. Lorna Gray and Albertson set off some mild fireworks as love interests.

p, Armand Schaefer; d, Frank McDonald; w, Dorrell and Stuart McGowan; ph, Bud Thackery; ed, Arthur Roberts; md, Morton Scott; art d, Russell Kimball; ch, Dave Gould.

Musical (PR:A MPAA:NR)

O SLAVNOSTI A HOSTECH (SEE: REPORT ON THE PARTY AND THE GUESTS, A, 1968, Czech.)

O.S.S.*½** (1946) 107m PAR bw

Alan Ladd *(John Martin)*, Geraldine Fitzgerald *(Ellen Rogers)*, Patric Knowles *(Comdr. Brady)*, John Hoyt *(Col. Meister)*, Gloria Saunders *(Mary Kenny, "Sparks")*, Richard Benedict *(Bernay)*, Harold Vermilyea *(Amadeus Braun)*, Don Beddoe *(Gates)*, Onslow Stevens *(Field)*, Gavin Muir *(Col. Crawson)*, Egon Brecher *(Marcel Aubert)*, Joseph Crehan *(Gen. Donovan)*, Bobby Driscoll *(Gerard)*, Julia Dean *(Mme. Prideaux)*, Crane Whitley *(Arnheim)*, Leslie Denison *(Lt. Col. Miles)*, Roberta Jonay *(Gracie Archer)*, Jean Ruth *(Brady's Secretary)*, Frederick Voltz, Lawson Houghton, George J. Fannon, Harlan Warde, Fred Zendar, Paul Lees, William Meader, Albert Ruiz, Charles Victor, Robert Cordell *(Trainees)*, Catherine Craig *(Williams' Secretary)*, Albert Van Antwerp *(Guard)*, Frank Ferguson *(Research Man)*, Murray F. Yeats *(Tall Man)*, Edward Harvey *(Mr. Williams)*, Pat McVey, Tom Schamp *(Plainclothesmen)*, Walter S. Pietila *(Mansion Attendant)*, Robert Wegner *(Gateman)*, James Westerfield *(Stout Man)*, Tom Stevenson *(Instructor)*, Vern Anders *(Sentry)*, Janna de Loos *(Woman Refugee)*, Andre Charlot *(French Importer)*, Archie Twitchell *(Officer)*, Will Thunis *(Young Man)*, George Sorel *(Husky Refugee)*, Jena Del Val *(Conductor)*, Frank Dae *(Scientist)*, George Barton *(Handyman)*, Jean Ransome *(Elevator Operator)*, Dorothy Barrett *(Brady's Secretary in London)*, Ed Kerr *(Courier)*, Herbert Wyndham *(Copilot)*, Anthony Marsh, Paul Barrett *(British Pilots)*, James Craven *(Jumpmaster)*, John Bogden *(Assistant Jumpmaster)*, Carl Ekberg, Leo Schlesinger, Eric Steiner, Eddie Bauer, Walter Rode, Zane Megowan, Jack Sterling, Bob Templeton, Paul Stupin, Len Hendry *(German Soldiers)*, Holder Bendixen *(German Sergeant)*, Frederick J. Waugh *(British Noncom)*, Robert Cordell *(Major at Airport Shack)*, Jack Lambert *(German Lieutenant)*, Monica Folts *(Little Girl with Kitten)*, George Bruggeman *(M.P., Noncom)*, Rene Dussaq *(French Artillery Officer)*, John Maxwell *(LaFevre)*, Albert Petit, Paul Diamond *(Resistance Men)*, Carmen Beretta *(Resistance Woman)*, Tony Merle *(Reynal)*, Helen Chapman *(Resistance Girl)*, Kathleen Terry *(Operator Next to Kenny)*, Philip Ahlm *(German Officer)*, Edmund Porada *(German Sergeant, Operator)*, John Dehner *(German Radar Captain)*, Jon Gilbreath *(German Radar Lieutenant)*, Henry Vroom *(German Corporal)*, Peter Michael *(German Noncom)*, Fred Kohler, Jr. *(Fireman)*, Jimmie Dundee *(Sentry)*, Joseph Granby *(Engineer)*, Edward Clark *(French Waiter)*, Renee Randall *(Cashier)*, Louise Colombet *(Old Frenchwoman)*, Maj. Fred Darrell *(Old Frenchman)*, Dorothy Adams *(Claudette)*, John Harmon *(Pierre)*, Fred Nurney *(Major Courier)*, Frank Pulliam, Jr. *(B-25 Pilot)*, George Taylor *(Gestapo Plainclothesman)*, Hans Moebus *(Gestapo Man)*, Dick Elmore *(German Army Private)*, Gene Garrick *(Operator)*, Henry Guttman *(German Major)*, Jerry James *(Pilot)*, Byron Poindexter *(Copilot)*, James Andrews *(Radio Operator)*, Carl Saxe, Roger Creed *(S.S. Men)*, Carl Andre *(Col. Hesiter's Aide)*, Jerome Alden *(British Noncom)*, George Fannon *(Marine Captain)*, Billy Burt *(Lieutenant J.G.)*, Billy Lechner, Carl Russell, Fred Datig, Jr., Frank Chalfant, George Billings, Charles Ferguson *(U.S. Soldiers)*.

Though fanciful liberties are taken with American espionage during WW II, O.S.S. (standing for Office of Strategic Services, the precursor to the CIA), offers a Ladd vehicle packed with suspense and excitement. The film opens by following a group of volunteers through spy school, including Ladd, a former public relations executive, sculptress Fitzgerald, railroad equipment salesman Beddoe, and hockey player Benedict. Fitzgerald has the benefit of having spent many years in France while working with her art. When completing their training, the new members are parachuted into France with the assignment of destroying the Corbett Mallon tunnel, along the main artery of the French railway system. Ladd early on shows his lack of faith in Fitzgerald's ability but she proves to be an adroit and effective spy, ingratiating herself to German staff officer Hoyt and learning secrets from him. Feeding his vanity in having some knowledge of art, Fitzgerald even gets Hoyt to pose for her and does a bust of him. She discovers that Hoyt will be taking a train through the tunnel she and the other American agents are to blow up. Hiding plastic explosives in the bust, Fitzgerald accompanies Hoyt and her work of art on the train which is stalled in the tunnel by French partisans. Ladd arrives and takes Fitzgerald off the train just before it and the tunnel are blown to bits. But Fitzgerald is not grateful to Ladd, telling him that he has violated the first rule of espionage by disobeying orders. "Never come back for me again," Fitzgerald tells Ladd. "Do you understand? *Never* come back!" When Ladd and Fitzgerald join a stream of refugees they are stopped by Gestapo agents but their venal leader, Vermilyea, sells Ladd information which is transmitted later by Benedict over a secreted short-wave radio to England. Hoyt surprisingly appears on the scene, scarred for life, an eyepatch where a perfectly good orb had once blinked, blown out by the tunnel explosion. He lives only to find and punish Fitzgerald. But all he snares is Vermilyea as Ladd and Fitzgerald escape once more. They run into Beddoe who briefly aids them but he gives himself away through a forgetful gesture. While eating, he neglects to fork his food with his left hand, in the custom of European dining, and is arrested. Later Ladd and Fitzgerald find a haven in a French farmhouse where Driscoll, a precocious boy, lives with his grandmother, Dean. The Americans next play host to a bunch of drunken German soldiers, among whom is Webb, another American agent, who passes vital information about the impending Normandy invasion to them. Ladd goes to a distant field and signals a British aircraft, relaying the secret information. Driscoll arrives to beg him to come back to the farmhouse because Gestapo officials have arrested Fitzgerald and Dean, but this time Ladd heeds Fitzgerald's caution of never going back for her. He continues sending out the message until the plane acknowledges receipt. Then he races back only to find the farmhouse empty and the woman he loves gone. Knowing Fitzgerald will be executed, Ladd sinks helplessly into a chair and sobs loudly. Ladd and Knowles, one of the O.S.S. commanders who trained Ladd's group, are later seen standing along a French roadway beneath a gnarled tree, watching American troops, fresh from the landings at Normandy, advancing up the road. Their victory, it is obvious, is due much to the efforts of the American agents who have sacrificed their lives. Ladd typically understates his role and is well-suited to the tough and dedicated spy he essays while Fitzgerald is lovely, warm, and vulnerable as a woman ready to die for a cause, which she does. Beddoe the bungler is unbelievable and too old for his role but Hoyt and Vermilyea are perfect as the sleazy, slimy Germans who will murder or sell out their own kind to satisfy personal lust and greed. Pichel's direction is taut and economical but the script is sometimes a bit too melodramatic. For three weeks in 1946 the O.S.S. allowed Hollywood studios, if executives were of a mind, to inspect their WW II files. Paramount jumped at the chance and culled many of the agency's best stories for the production of O.S.S. The studio used 30 ex-O.S.S. agents who had seen heroic service behind enemy lines during the war, employing them as technical advisors and bit players in the film. Ladd, who had refused to come to the studio after months of receiving lame scripts, was given his choice role in O.S.S. and reported for work without complaint. While still in production for O.S.S., Paramount offered Ladd the lead in THE GREAT GATSBY; Geraldine Fitzgerald heard about the offer and went to Ladd, telling him: "Oh, do. Do Gatsby. You're perfect for it. You're exactly what Scott Fitzgerald had in mind." Ladd replied: "I won't be able to do it, because I can't act, you know." Yet he did play Jay Gatsby and Fitzgerald was right. He was perfect in the role. Although O.S.S. was not as effective as the semi-documentary THE HOUSE ON 92ND STREET, or 13 RUE MADELEINE it presented high voltage entertainment and thrills.

p, Richard Maibaum; d, Irving Pichel; w, Maibaum; ph, Lionel Linden; m, Daniele Amfitheatrof, Heinz Roemheld; ed, William Shea; art d, Hans Dreier, Haldane Douglas; set d, Sam Comer, Stanley J. Sawley; spec eff, Gordon Jennings, Farciot Edouart; tech adv, Comdr. John H. Shaheen, USNR, Lt. Raphael G. Beugnon, AUS.

Spy Drama (PR:C MPAA:NR)

OSS 117—MISSION FOR A KILLER½** (1966, Fr./Ital.) 84m P.A.C.-P.C.M.-DA. MA./EM c (FURIA A BAHIA POUR OSS 117; OSS 117 FURIA A BAHIA)

Frederick Stafford *(OSS 117)*, Mylene Demongeot *(Anna Maria Sulza)*, Raymond Pellegrin *(Leandro)*, Perrette Pradier *(Consuela 1)*, Annie Andersson *(Consuela 2)*, Francois Maistre *(Carlos)*, Jacques Riberolles *(Miguel)*, Yves Furet *(Clark)*, Guy Delorme *(Karl)*, Jean-Pierre Janic *(Ludwig)*, Claude Carliez *(Thomas Ellis)*.

One of a series of French James Bondish pictures, this film stars Stafford (TOPAZ) as the secret agent. After the occurrence of mysterious government assassinations in which the assassins are also killed, Stafford is sent to Rio de Janeiro to investigate. He discovers that a drug is administered to the killers, placing them in a trance. Stafford learns that the drug comes from an Indian village and gets an offer from Pellegrin to visit the tribe. Instead Stafford is taken prisoner by an international organization bent on world domination. The grand finale has Brazilian paratroopers coming to the aid of Stafford and quelling the group's plot.

p, Paul Cadeac; d, Andre Hunebelle; w, Hunebelle, Jean Halain, Pierre Foucard (based on the novel *Le Dernier Quart d' Heure* by Jean Bruce); ph, Marcel Grignon (Franscope, Eastmancolor); m, Michel Magne; ed, Jean Feyte; art d, Paul-Louis Boutie; cos, Jo Ranzato.

Action/Adventure (PR:C MPAA:NR)

OBEY THE LAW*½ (1933) 64m COL bw

Leo Carrillo *(Tony Pasqual)*, Dickie Moore *(Dickie Chester)*, Lois Wilson *(Grace Chester)*, Henry Clive *(Big Joe Riordan)*, Eddie Garr *(Bob Richards)*, Gino Corrado *(Giovanni)*, Ward Bond *(Kid Paris)*.

Carrillo is an immigrant barber who becomes a citizen and fights for his personal freedom and rights. His heart is so pure and his faith in the system so strong that even when he is the victim of a holdup, he turns the other cheek, staking the destitute robber to a meal and finding him a job. Clive, a ward boss, tries to tell the immigrant and everyone else how to vote, but Carrillo's example helps turn the election away from Clive. Carillo's portrayal of the virtuous barber is the best thing about this otherwise lackluster film, a remake of a 1926 Columbia silent of the same name.

d, Benjamin Stoloff; w, Arthur Caesar (based on a story by Harry Sauber); ph, Joseph Valentine.

Drama **(PR:A MPAA:NR)**

OBJECTIVE, BURMA!**** (1945) 142m WB bw

Errol Flynn *(Maj. Nelson)*, James Brown *(Sgt. Treacy)*, William Prince *(Lt. Jacobs)*, George Tobias *(Gabby Gordon)*, Henry Hull *(Mark Williams)*, Warner Anderson *(Col. Carter)*, John Alvin *(Hogan)*, Mark Stevens *(Lt. Barker)*, Richard Erdman *(Nebraska Hooper)*, Anthony Caruso *(Miggleori)*, Hugh Beaumont *(Capt. Hennessey)*, John Whitney *(Negulesco)*, Joel Allen *(Brophy)*, George Tyne [Buddy Yarus] *(Soapy)*, Rodric Redwing *(Sgt. Chattu)*, William Hudson *(Hollis)*, Asit Koomar *(Ghurka)*, Lester Matthews *(Maj. Fitzpatrick)*, John Sheridan *(Copilot)*, Carlyle Blackwood, Jr. *(Pilot)*, Kit Carson, Neil Carter, Helmert Ellingwood, Shephard Houghton, Peter Kooy, Harlan Miller *(Paratroopers)*, Erville Anderson *(Gen. Stilwell)*.

This is one of the finest WW II films made during the war and Flynn, discarding his usual impudent and pranksterish posture, is terrific as the straightforward and very human leader of 50 American parachutists who drop behind enemy lines to destroy a Japanese radar station. The film opens with newsreel scenes of British, American, Indian, and other Allied troops fighting and losing ground to the steadily advancing Japanese hordes. American general Stilwell, played by Erville Anderson, a startling doppleganger, orders a paratroop raid behind Japanese lines and Flynn gets the assignment. He and his hand-picked men—Prince, Brown, Tobias, Erdman, Caruso, Tyne, and others, including aging journalist Hull—board two transports and head for the drop zone. Hull records for his newspaper back home the attitudes and emotional state of the paratroopers, seeing that some are nervous, others nonchalant, others eager for battle. Flynn jokes with one particularly nervous soldier, Caruso, to ease his tension but Caruso later freezes in the door and Tobias nudges him into space before jumping himself. The landing goes well and the soldiers proceed to the Japanese camp, going through torturous jungles and swamps to the objective. Flynn and his men catch the Japanese utterly by surprise and wipe out the entire garrison to the last man. But a Japanese spotter has seen the men land and has alerted other Japanese garrisons which now march in several directions against the Americans. Amelcan planes rendezvous with Flynn and his troops, preparing to pick them up on a deserted field, but just as the planes begin to descend word is brought that Japanese forces are closing in. Flynn calls off the planes and tells pilot Stevens to meet him and his troops at another rendezvous spot in a few days where supplies are to be dropped. The supplies are dropped and Flynn is ordered to walk out of Burma, 150 miles to Allied lines, since no other landing spots are available. He then spilts his forces, believing his men will be safer by moving in two groups. His good friend Prince heads one group and Flynn another; they plan to link up later. At the next drop zone, American planes unload supplies but when Flynn's men go to pick them up, Japanese snipers cut them down in a clearing and the rest retreat into the jungle. Later, when Flynn's men enter a native village they find the other half of the force slaughtered, left in mutilated pieces by the Japanese. Flynn discovers Prince still alive, barely, and is in agony when his friend begs him to kill him. Price dies painfully and Hull, witnessing his awful death—a journalist having a normally dispassionate nature—becomes enraged, spitting out his hatred for the Japanese:"They're immoral, degenerate idiots! Wipe them out, I say! Wipe them off the face of the earth!" (Bessie, who wrote the story, objected to these lines inserted by scriptwriter MacDougall, writing Jack Warner and asking him to delete the phrase as being "unfair" to *all* Japanese, but Warner stood firm and refused to change the slashing indictment. He considered it appropriate at a time when fever-pitch propaganda was the order of the day. The very real widespread atrocities committed by Japanese on Bataan, at Singapore, and earlier in China where thousands of Chinese troops were bayoneted in assembly-line executions which the Japanese arrogantly photographed themselves, were very much in the public mind which Warner and his executives knew well.) The Japanese return in great strength and Flynn orders his men to retreat even farther and the men bitterly leave their dead comrades behind without being able to bury them. They fight a vicious rear guard battle until escaping. The Japanese pursue them relentlessly and Flynn is further hampered by not having his radio to contact the planes looking for them. He finally manages to signal a lone plane piloted by Stevens, using a mirror to reflect sunlight. A rendezvous is arranged but Flynn has a hard time getting his men to move any farther. He starts off alone, his exhausted troopers looking after him. "Come on," Tobias wearily says, getting up, going after Flynn, "I'd follow him down the barrel of a cannon!" The small group struggles up to the top of a huge hill, believing there will be supplies or even reinforcements waiting for them. When they fall panting at the summit they see nothing. Now Flynn's orders to dig in and make foxholes are completely ignored. Flynn himself begins to dig frantically and the embarrassed men finally join him. When all seems hopeless, Stevens appears in his transport plane above and Flynn signals him again with the mirror. Food, ammunition, and grenades are dropped and now, well supplied, Flynn's men resolutely build their tight circle of foxholes and trenches at the top of the hill. A Japanese spotter has seen the parachutes of the supplies dropped and reports the American position. Hundreds of Japanese soldiers converge on the area. That night Flynn's men wait tensely in the darkness for the inevitable attack, waiting in silence as the Japanese first send infiltrators up the hill to crawl snakelike into the American trenches. Most of these invaders are killed but a few Americans pay with their lives, one for believing an English-speaking Japanese soldier is a friend, calling to him, "Are you all right?" The American trooper tells him where he is and is knifed to death. The same Japanese soldier approaches Whitney's foxhole, loudly whispering: "Where are you, Joe?" Whitney smiles, pulls the pin from a grenade, and whispers back: "Over here—here I am, sweetheart!" He rolls the grenade in the direction of the approaching enemy and then curls down in his foxhole. When the grenade goes off and kills the infiltrator, Whitney sits up and says softly, "By the way, my name ain't Joe!" Then the Japanese make a full-scale attack up the hill but Flynn's men open up with a withering fire, hurling dozens of grenades, slaughtering the enemy, and sending their remnants back in screaming retreat. At dawn, Whitney finds Hudson's body, telling Flynn as he hands over the dead soldier's dogtag: "So much for Mrs. Hollis' nine months of pain and 20 years of hope." Also found dead is newspaperman Hull. All seems hopeless when the deep droning of planes is heard. The haggard, ragged survivors look anxiously to the sky and then instinctively take refuge in their foxholes, waiting to be bombed to death. But they soon realize that the approaching planes are American and they jubilantly jump out of their holes and happily watch as scores of planes appear and thousands of American paratroopers fill the skies. "It's raining parachutes!" Erdman yells. The others cheer the sight in wild delight. The parachutists land as do dozens of gliders, disgorging men, howitzer cannon, jeeps, and tractors. Flynn and his ragtail men, 12 survivors in all, make their way down to the American lines and Warner Anderson, their commander, greets Flynn, congratulating him on a job well done. "Here's what it cost, not much to send home," Flynn tells him, filling Anderson's hand with dogtags, "a handful of Americans." Anderson orders Flynn and his men out of the combat zone. They are taken to a glider and enter it, Flynn pausing at the door to look back at the savage jungle land that has claimed the lives of his men. He steps inside and the glider is then shown being picked up by a passing transport, whisked into the air, and soaring skyward, outward, diminishing in the dawning sky. Flynn gives one of his most convincing and powerful performances in OBJECTIVE, BURMA! Walsh's direction is nothing less than excellent, the great action director maintaining a harrowing pace and providing one thrilling scene after another, keeping his cameras fluid with fast tracking shots, dolly and boom shots, framing his scenes so that the broad sweep of battle is contained and recorded in them with astounding effectiveness. Bessie, who would later become one of the "Hollywood Ten" writers indicted by HUAC, provided a marvelously witty, clever, and realistic story. Exceptional, too, is the dynamic, masterful score by Waxman, one that fits the mood and menace of the clammy, thick jungle, interspersed with the sounds of wild animals and exotic birds. Howe's splendid photography captures the jungle atmosphere with frightening accuracy and battle scenes are recorded with devastating authenticity. The film was shot almost entirely on the "Lucky" Baldwin Santa Anita ranch outside of Pasadena where the Burmese jungle was realistically recreated. Flynn, normally a heavy drinker during any production, had only an occasional drink with cast members which surprised director Walsh until the director learned that Flynn was busy writing another autobiography and had no time for carousing. The film received rave reviews and heavy box-office support in the U.S., but when OBJECTIVE, BURMA! was released in England, the British press exploded, claiming that the film minimized the efforts of the British in Burma (a theater of operations Britain had always considered exclusively their own, despite the fact that thousands of American soldiers were dying in Burma while heroically performing their duties). The British press niggardly and unjustly attacked the film and it was actually banned after some brutal British illustrations showed Flynn standing with a submachine gun on the grave of a British officer. As far as certain xenophobic British critcs were concerned, no one but the British had fought for Burma. It wasn't until 1952 that the film was shown again in England and it was the better received, but Warner Bros. had taken the precaution of inserting a conciliatory prolog to the film which showed British troops and others—depicted in newsreel cuts, which also showed Gen. Joseph "Vinegar Joe" Stilwell—involved in the Burma campaign. This still did not alter the fact that OBJECTIVE, BURMA! is one of the most moving and stirring WW II productions.

p, Jerry Wald; d, Raoul Walsh; w, Ranald MacDougall, Lester Cole (based on a story by Alvah Bessie); ph, James Wong Howe; m, Franz Waxman; ed, George Amy; md, Leo F. Forbstein; art d, Ted Smith; set d, Jack McConaghy; spec eff, Edwin DuPar; makeup, Perc Westmore; tech adv, Maj. Charles S. Galbraith, U.S. Army Parachute Troops.

War Drama **(PR:C MPAA:NR)**

OBJECTIVE 500 MILLION** (1966, Fr.) 92m Rome-Paris/Imperia bw (OBJECTIF 500 MILLION)

Marisa Mell *(Yo)*, Bruno Cremer *(Reichau)*, Jean-Claude Rolland *(Pierre)*, Etienne Berry *(Douard)*.

This film concerns a former French army captain who is released from prison and gets involved with cover girl Mell. She wants him to help her hijack a plane that takes $1 million from Paris to Bordeaux every month. The ex-captain learns that the man who set him up to go to prison is also involved. The plan calls for the ex-captain to stow away on the plane, steal the money, and parachute out of the plane, leaving an explosive to destroy the plane and the evidence. However, he doesn't plant the bomb, but jumps instead with a sack full of fake money. When he reaches the ground, he kills the man who turned him in and is in turn shot by the police. A reactionary political stance underlies and confuses the film, presenting the violent, near-fascist captain as an heroic figure.

p, Georges De Beauregard; d&w, Pierre Schoendoerffer; ph, Alain Levent; ed, Armand Psenny.

Crime **(PR:C MPAA:NR)**

OBLIGING YOUNG LADY*½ (1941) 80m RKO bw

Joan Carroll *(Bridget Potter)*, Edmond O'Brien *(Red Reddy)*, Ruth Warrick *(Linda Norton)*, Robert Smith *(Charles Baker)*, Eve Arden *(Space O'Shea)*, Charles Lane *(Detective Smith)*, Franklin Pangborn *(Prof. Gibney)*, George Cleveland *(Tom Birth, Hotel Manager)*, Marjorie Gateson *(Mira Potter)*, John Miljan *(George Potter)*, Luis Alberni *(Riccardi)*, Fortunio Bonanova *(Hotel Chef)*, Andrew Tombes *(Conductor)*, Almira Sessions *(Maid)*, Pierre Watkin *(John Markham)*, Florence Gill *(Hallyrod)*, Sidney Blackmer *(Attorney)*, Virginia Engels *(Bonnie)*, George Watts *(Judge Knox)*, Hal K. Dawson *(Pullman Bore)*, Dudley Dickerson *(Dining Car Waiter)*, Fred "Snowflake" Toones *(Porter)*, Dora Clement *(Aunt Lucy)*, John Dilson *(Uncle Joe)*, Charles Peck *(Johnny)*, Cecil Weston *(Aunt)*, Ruth Cherrington *(Dowager)*, Isabelle La Mal *(Wife)*, Jame Carlisle *(Husband)*, Jimmy Conlin *(McIntyre)*, George Chandler *(Skip)*, Max Wagner *(Jerry)*, George Lloyd *(Court

Bailiff), Vera Marshe *(Helen)*, Harry Harvey *(Court Clerk)*, Jed Prouty *(Judge Rufus)*, Frank M. Thomas *(Keenan)*, John Farrell *(Bottle)*, Ralph Sanford *(Pudgy, Bailiff)*, Murray Alper *(Station Wagon Driver)*, Gloria Whitney, Jean Acker, Walter Anthony Merrill, John Sylvester *(Cousins)*, Emory Parnell, Ted Oliver, Eddie Parker, Mickey Simpson *(Motor Cops)*, Benny Rubin, Ernie Stanton, Nora Cecil, Count Cutelli, Dot Farley, Ronnie Rondell, Marian Darlington, Tex C.C. Gilmore, Mary Lawrence, Eddie Borden *(Bird Lovers)*.

Boring is the word for this soap-sudsy melodrama about a 9-year-old child, Carroll, who is taken away by a secretary, Warrick, in an effort to reunite the child's separated parents. The film turns into one big chase, using outdated slapstick gags. However, O'Brien and Arden work well as the competitive reporters, and the wisecracking comedienne provides one of the picture's best moments when she adopts the guise of a post-bellum belle.

p, Howard Benedict; d, Richard Wallace; w, Frank Ryan, Bert Granet (based on a story by Arthur T. Horman, Jerry Cady); ph, Nicholas Musuraca; m, Roy Webb; ed, Henry Berman; md, Constantin Bakaleinikoff.

Comedy **(PR:A MPAA:NR)**

OBLONG BOX, THE* (1969, Brit.) 91m AIP c (AKA: EDGAR ALLEN POE'S "THE OBLONG BOX")

Vincent Price *(Julian Markham)*, Christopher Lee *(Dr. Neuhartt)*, Alistair Williamson *(Sir Edward Markham)*, Hilary Dwyer *(Elizabeth Markham)*, Peter Arne *(Samuel Trench)*, Harry Baird *(N. Galo)*, Carl Rigg *(Mark Norton)*, Maxwell Shaw *(Tom Hackett)*, Michael Balfour *(Ruddock)*, Godfrey James *(Weller)*, Rupert Davies *(Joshua Kemp)*, Sally Geeson *(Sally Baxter)*, Ivor Dean *(Hawthorne)*, Uta Levka, James Mellor, Danny Daniels, John Barrie, Hira Talfrey, John Wentworth, Betty Woolfe, Martin Terry, Anne Clune, Jackie Noble, Ann Barrass, Janet Rossini, Zeph Gladstone, Tara Fernando, Tony Thawton, Anthony Bailey, Richard Cornish, Colin Jeavons, Andreas Maladrinos, Hedger Wallace, Martin Wyldeck, Oh! Ogunde Dancers.

A fuzzy plot line hinders this Edgar Allen Poe story translated to film. Price plays, of course, the baddie who keeps his horrible looking brother locked in the upstairs of the house. Price wants nothing more to do with his brother, so he arranges through shady lawyer Arne to remove him from the house. Arne procures a secret box that keeps Price's brother (Williamson) alive while appearing dead. To show everyone his brother has died, Price gets Arne to commit a murder and substitutes that body for his brother's. But Lee's grave-robbing cronies give him Williamson's still-breathing body and Williamson starts working toward his revenge. He then goes on a murderous rampage that shows the viewer plenty of blood before he is shot and killed by Price. But the story isn't over yet. Price admits that his brother was tortured for his crimes and leaves the audience with a chilling sight as his face takes on the form of his mutilated late brother.

p&d, Gordon Hessler; w, Lawrence Huntingdon, Christopher Wicking (based on the story by Edgar Allen Poe); ph, John Coquillon (Berkey Pathe Color); m, Harry Robinson; ed, Max Benedict; art d, George Provis.

Horror **(PR:O MPAA:M)**

OBSESSED** (1951, Brit.) 78m Elvey-Gartside/UA bw (GB: THE LATE EDWINA BLACK)

David Farrar *(Gregory Black)*, Geraldine Fitzgerald *(Elizabeth)*, Roland Culver *(Inspector)*, Jean Cadell *(Ellen, Housekeeper)*, Mary Merrall *(Lady Southdale)*, Harcourt Williams *(Dr. Prendergast)*, Charles Heslop *(Vicar)*, Ronald Adam *(Schoolmaster)*, Sydney Monckton *(Horace)*, Irene Arnaud, Ernest Metcalfe.

When Edwina Black is found poisoned, her husband, Farrar, is considered a murder suspect, along with his mistress Fitzgerald. Detective Culver enters the case and proves that the housekeeper (Cadell), who had discovered her employer's corpse, had actually given the late woman arsenic so she could successfully kill herself. Though the performances are competent, this mystery isn't developed with any sense of style. The killer's real identity will be obvious to anyone watching. This telegraphed ending is coupled with cliches and stereotyped situations that don't add anything to the film.

p, Ernest Gartside; d, Maurice Elvey; w, Charles Frank, David Evans (based on the play "The Late Edwina Black" by William Dinner, William Morum); ph, Stephen Date; m, Allan Gray; ed, Douglas Myers; art d, George Provis; cos, Elizabeth Haffenden.

Crime/Mystery **(PR:C MPAA:NR)**

OBSESSION (SEE: HIDDEN ROOM, THE, 1949, Brit.)

OBSESSION*½ (1954, Fr./Ital.) 105m Gibo-Franco-London/Pathe c

Michele Morgan *(Helene)*, Raf Vallone *(Aldo)*, Jean Gaven *(Alex)*, Marthe Marcadier *(Arlette)*, Olivier Hussenot *(Louis)*, Robert Dalban *(Inspector)*, Jacques Castelot *(Lawyer)*.

A poor suspense film that is little more than a French soap opera featuring Morgan and Vallone as trapeze artists. Vallone is in love with Morgan, but doesn't tell her because he has murdered a man. When he learns that she plans to marry another man, Vallone confesses his love and admits to the murder. Morgan agrees to marry him and everything is fine until Vallone injures his arm. His substitute is Gaven, a friend of the man Vallone killed, who believes his friend's death was a suicide. Later, when Gaven is killed, a friend of Vallone and Morgan's is convicted of the crime. Morgan, believing that Vallone has killed Gaven, turns him in to the police, but it turns out that the convicted man was the real killer. However, Morgan has already told the police about Vallone's dark past and the scales of justice tip painfully into balance.

d, Jean Delannoy; w, Antoine Blondin, Roland Laudenbach, Delannoy (based on a novel by William Irish); ph, Pierre Montazel (Eastmancolor); ed, James Cuenet.

Crime/Drama **(PR:C MPAA:NR)**

OBSESSION** (1968, Swed.) 104m Nordisk Tonefilm/O.R.P. c (KUNGSLEDEN; AKA: THE ROYAL TRACK)

Matthias Henrikson *("You")*, Maude Adelson *(Leni Wodak)*, Lars Lind *(The Other Man)*, Guy De la Berg *(German Tourist)*, Johannes Blind *(Andreas)*.

Henrikson is on a desolate mountain trail in Lapland and thinks back to 10 years earlier, when he spent three days in the area with Adelson, a young Jewish refugee from a concentration camp. In his reverie he reconstructs their strained relationship, which ended in his rape of her. Back in the present, he discovers signs indicating that she may be near at hand, only to find her dead body in a stream. Filled with guilt and a sense of revenge, he finds and kills the man he suspects of Adelson's murder. The film ends with Henrikson walking off toward a future as clouded as the mountain air—an enigmatic ending to an enigmatic film.

p, Georg Eriksson, Lars Werner; d, Gunnar Hoglund; w, Hoglund, Bosse Gustafson (based on the book *Kungsleden* by Gustafson); ph, Bertil Wiktorsson (Eastmancolor); m, Karl-Erik Welin; ed, Jan Persson.

Drama **(PR:C MPAA:NR)**

OBSESSION** (1976) 98m COL c

Cliff Robertson *(Michael Courtland)*, Genevieve Bujold *(Elizabeth Courtland/Sandra Portinari)*, John Lithgow *(Robert LaSalle)*, Sylvia Kuumba Williams *(Maid)*, Wanda Blackman *(Amy Courtland)*, Patrick McNamara *(3rd Kidnaper)*, Stanley J. Reyes *(Inspector Brie)*, Nick Kreiger *(Farber)*, Stocker Fontelieu *(Dr. Ellman)*, Don Hood *(Ferguson)*, Andrea Esterhazy *(D'Annunzio)*.

Another one of De Palma's "homages" to Hitchcock, but this one comes off better than most of the erratic director's work because he hadn't yet fallen into his excessive ways. Robertson, Bujold, and De Palma were all partners in this project and made a good deal of money when it was finally released, after a year of attempting to find a company to send it out. The resistance was due to the incestuous element in the script which was modified by making it into a dream sequence. The executive producer, Robert S. Bremson, was a wealthy Kansas City photographic supplies magnate who put up the seed money and got that credit. He later joined with producer Brandon Chase and was involved in THE SWORD AND THE SORCEROR. Shot in Florence, New Orleans, and Los Angeles, the picture came in under $2 million and returned many times that. It was Lithgow's first feature assignment. The original title was "Deja Vu," but they decided to rename it and ran into difficulty with United Artists, who owned the title of MAGNIFICENT OBSESSION. After considerable negotiations, the new title was given. It is alleged that Hitchcock was not thrilled at the way De Palma and screenwriter Schrader adapted his VERTIGO plot, which was altered enough to make any legal action a losing cause. In 1959, Robertson's wife (Bujold) and daughter are kidnaped. The police, wanting to put an end to that cottage industry, tell him they will back him and to not pay the ransom. So he sends cut pieces of blank paper in the ransom package and the result is the disappearance of his family. Robertson and Lithgow are business partners and good friends, and when Robertson meets Bujold on a trip to Europe 16 years later, he becomes obsessed by her, a fact that Lithgow objects to. Robertson thinks that Bujold is his late wife and never takes into account the years that have passed. The story dares us to wonder if she is his wife or his daughter? When another kidnaping takes place, we learn that nothing is what it seems and there's a surprise twist at the conclusion better left for you to discover. Herrmann's overblown score won an Academy nomination, though everything else about the picture was overlooked. Robertson is also a director-writer and one had the feeling that he wanted to be behind the cameras as well as in front of them as the picture unspooled. There is more suspense than violence here, a rare occurrence in a De Palma picture for which we must be grateful.

p, George Litto, Harry N. Blum; d, Brian De Palma; w, Paul Schrader (based on a story by De Palma, Schrader); ph, Vilmos Zsigmond (Technicolor); m, Bernard Hermann; ed, Paul Hirsch; art d, Jack Senter; set d, Jerry Wunderlich.

Suspense/Romance **Cas.** **(PR:C MPAA:PG)**

OBVIOUS SITUATION, AN (SEE: HOURS OF LONELINESS, 1950, Brit.)

OCCHI SENZA VOLTO (SEE: HORROR CHAMBER OF DR. FAUSTUS, THE, 1962, Fr./Ger.)

OCEAN BREAKERS** (1949, Swed.) 64m AB Skandinavien/Hyperio bw (BRANNIGAR; AKA: THE SURF)

Ingrid Bergman *(Karin Ingman)*, Sten Lindgren *(Daniel Nordeman)*, Bror Ohlsson *(Pelle)*, Carl Strom *(Karin's Father)*, Weyler Hildebrand *(Elder Pastor)*, Stig *(Karin's Child)*, Tore Svennberg *(Mr. Nordeman)*, Knut Frankman, Carin Swenson, Georg Skarstedt, Henning Ohlsson, Vera Lindby, Viktor Ost, Emmy Albiin, Viktor Andersson, Helga Brofeldt, Carl Browallius, Ole Grenberg, Holger Lowenadler, E. Rosen.

Bergman is a fisherman's daughter who becomes the desire of minister Lindgren. The minister, who is not a true believer, seduces the young woman. Upset at what he has done, Lindgren rushes out into a storm and is struck by lightning, causing him to become an amnesiac. He is taken away to a hospital and Bergman discovers that she is pregnant. She has the child and refuses to give the name of the father. When Lindgren returns, he admits in a sermon that the child is his and trades in his collar for a farmer's pitchfork. Released in Sweden in 1935, it was 12 years before OCEAN BREAKERS was distributed in the U.S. under the title THE SURF. The film is most notable for the presence of Bergman, fresh from the boards of Stockholm's Royal Dramatic Theater School, making one of her first screen appearances. Her captivating but unpolished performance is a harbinger of greater things to come. (In Swedish; English subtitles.)

d&w, Ivar Johansson (based on an idea by Henning Ohlssen); ph, Julius Jaenzon.

Drama **(PR:A MPAA:NR)**

OCEAN'S ELEVEN½** (1960) 127m Dorchester/WB c

Frank Sinatra *(Danny Ocean)*, Dean Martin *(Sam Harmon)*, Sammy Davis, Jr. *(Josh Howard)*, Peter Lawford *(Jimmy Foster)*, Angie Dickinson *(Beatrice Ocean)*, Richard Conte *(Anthony Bergdorf)*, Cesar Romero *(Duke Santos)*, Patrice Wymore *(Adele Ekstrom)*, Joey Bishop *("Mushy" O'Conners)*, Akim Tamiroff *(Spyros Acebos)*, Henry Silva *(Roger Corneal)*, Ilka Chase *(Mrs. Restes)*, Buddy Lester *(Vincent Massler)*, Richard Benedict *("Curly" Steffens)*, Jean Willes *(Mrs. Bergdorf)*, Norman Fell *(Peter Rheimer)*, Clem Harvey *(Louis Jackson)*, Hank Henry *(Mr. Kelly)*, Charles Meredith *(Mr. Cohen)*, Red Skelton *(Client)*, Shirley MacLaine *(Tipsy Girl)*, George Raft *(Jack Strager)*, Don "Red" Barry *(McCoy)*, Murray Alper *(Deputy)*, Joan Staley *(Helen)*, George E. Stone *(Proprietor)*, Richard Sinatra *(Attendant)*, Harry Drucker *(Barber)*, Anne Neyland *(Delores)*, John Eiman, Gary Stafford *(Boys)*, H.T. Tsiang *(Houseboy)*, Wesley Gale *(Sky Cap)*, David Carlile *(Attendant)*, Myrna Ross *(Passenger)*, Norma Yost *(Airline Hostess)*, Marjorie Bennett *(Customer)*, Louis Quinn *(De Wolfe)*, Laura Connell *(Sugarface)*, John Indrisano *(Texan)*, Dick Hudkins *(Drunk)*, Al Silvani *(Boss)*, Shiva *(Snake Dancer)*, Mike Jordan *(Bartender)*, James Waters *(Disposal Attendant)*, Steve Pendleton *(Maj. Taylor)*, Ronnie Dapo *(Timmy)*, R. John Slosser, Howard Roth *(Squad Leaders)*, Perri Bova *(Maid)*, James Canino *(Elevator Operator)*, Carmen Phillips *(Hungry Girl)*, Jay Gerard *(Cab Driver)*, Edward Cable, Andy Martin, Edward Warren *(Security Cops)*, Leonard George *(Police Operator)*, David Landfield *(Flamingo M.C.)*, Garr Nelson *(Sands M.C.)*, Robert Bock *(Desert Inn M.C.)*, Eddie Gomez *(Riviera M.C.)*, Tony DeMilo *(Sahara M.C.)*, Tom Middleton *(TV Newscaster)*, Sparky Kaye *(Riviera Manager)*, Hoot Gibson *(Road Block Deputy)*, June Michele *(Lady Driver)*, Barbara Sterling, Louise Black, Helen Jay *(Girls)*, Forrest Lederer *(Sands Manager)*, Rummy Bishop *(Castleman)*, Gregory Gay *(Freeman)*, Ted Otis, Robert "Buddy" Shaw, Jack Santoro, Rex Devereaux, Joe Gallerani, Art Stewart, Bob Whitney, Dave White, John Craven *(Cashiers)*, David Leonard *(Rabbi)*, Nicky Blair *(Usher)*, Robert Gilbreath *(Pilot)*, William Justine *(Parelli)*, Harry Wilson *(Extra)*.

A free-wheeling, uninhibited all-star romp that set the pace for the "caper" films of the 1960s and 1970s, this was a good example of that genre and far better than most of those which followed. Sinatra, Davis, and Martin were all busy performing in Las Vegas every night and filming this by day and the good time they all were having fairly jumped off the screen. Tamiroff comes up with the idea of knocking off five Vegas casinos at the same time on New Year's Eve. The hotels are the Sahara, the Flamingo, The Riviera, The Sands, and the Desert Inn. The plot calls for the crooks, all veterans of the 82nd Airborne Division, led by Sinatra, to use their military knowledge and commando-like timing to plunge the casinos into darkness by shutting off their electrical supplies. To do this, they have to explode a power tower outside the town. Then the back-up systems at the hotels will be dealt with so the electronically controlled doors to the cages and the safes will swing open. Next, all the money will be taken and dumped in garbage cans outside each casino where they will be picked up by a disposal truck driven by Davis. The planning takes about a week and we have the opportunity to learn a bit about each man. Conte is the group's electrician and, like the others, basically an honest man. He needs his share of the loot to provide for his small son. Lawford is the son of much-married Chase, who is about to make Cesar Romero, a local gangster, her fifth husband. And each of the others has a brief background flash so they are not just stick figures. Sinatra is apart from his wife, Dickinson, and would like to see her but he knows she would just be in the way, so he sends her a telegram saying they can't get together. This, of course, brings her immediately to Las Vegas, where she is just in the way. Wymore, a former girl friend of Sinatra's arrives. Dickinson wants Sinatra to go back to New York with her, and when he doesn't, and can't tell her why, she exits, having been only a stage wait for the action to come. It's the big night. The robbery runs well, like a Rolex's innards, and then matters begin to fall apart—as they always seem to do in this sort of movie. Conte has a heart attack and dies. Romero has found out about the caper and who did it and now demands half the action. Romero makes it impossible for the gang to get the money out of town, so they come up with the idea of smuggling the loot out in Conte's coffin, figuring that no one would ever look there. What they don't reckon on, however, is Conte's widow, Willes. She decides to have Conte cremated and Sinatra and his cohorts look on in stunned silence as all the money (and their pal) goes up in smoke. The ending is not unlike the finale to THE KILLING, in which Sterling Hayden watches helplessly as the suitcase containing his racetrack money is tipped over when a dog races in front of a baggage cart at an airport and the money flies off in the propwash of a plane. The other similar ending is, you guessed it, the gold being sent to the wind in THE TREASURE OF THE SIERRA MADRE. Lawford had found the story, then he and Sinatra formed a production company, with Martin also buying in. George Raft and Red Skelton do small cameos, as does Shirley MacLaine, in an unbilled bit as a drunken floozy. MacLaine was busy making THE APARTMENT and took off a day to fly to Las Vegas and appear in a scene that reputedly took less than 10 minutes to shoot. She meets Martin and loses the key to her car. She bends over to pick it up and can't straighten her body. Martin helps her stand, she kisses him and thinks that he might like to take her home, then is disappointed when Martin is preoccupied with other matters. There were many interesting bits among the cast, including Hoot Gibson, Red Barry, and everyone's favorite jokester, Louis Quinn (who was "Roscoe"—the bookie—on TV's "77 Sunset Strip"). Quinn works all the time and one of the reasons is that he knows just about every gag ever created and keeps the set happy by telling them. Benedict eventually gave up acting to become a busy TV director. Two songs by Sammy Cahn and Jimmy Van Heusen, "Ain't That a Kick in the Head?" (sung by Dean Martin), "Ee-O-leven," (sung by Sammy Davis, Jr.). Three or four more tunes and this would have been a heckuva musical comedy.

p&d, Lewis Milestone; w, Harry Brown, Charles Lederer (based on a story by George Clayton Johnson, Jack Golden Russell); ph, William H. Daniels (Panavision, Technicolor); m, Nelson Riddle; ed, Philip W. Anderson; md, Riddle; art d, Nicolai Remisoff; set d, Howard Bristol; cos, Howard Shoup; makeup, Gordon Bau.

Comedy/Crime Cas. (PR:A MPAA:NR)

OCHAZUKE NO AJI (SEE: TEA AND RICE, 1964, Jap.)

OCTAGON, THE** (1980) 103m American Cinema c

Chuck Norris *(Scott James)*, Karen Carlson *(Justine)*, Lee Van Cleef *(McCarn)*, Art Hindle *(A.J.)*, Carol Bagdasarian *(Aura)*, Kim Lankford *(Nancy, Dancer)*, Tadashi Yamashita *(Seikura)*, Kurt Grayson *(Doggo)*, Yuki Shimoda *(Katsumoto)*, Larry D. Mann *(Tibor)*, John Fujioka *(Isawa)*, Jack Carter *(Sharkey)*.

THE OCTAGON is Chuck Norris' third martial arts action film and is no different from his first two kung fu pictures, GOOD GUYS WEAR BLACK and FORCE OF ONE. Norris, a retired martial arts champion, is asked by wealthy Carlson to protect her from a group of Ninjas. He agrees only when he learns that his longtime nemesis Yamashita is leading the martial arts killers. Bagdasarian, a former terrorist trained by the Ninjas, leads Norris to their secret base and aids him in destroying the camp and Yamashita. Lee Van Cleef (master of the menacing grin) makes the most of his role as the leader of a vengeful group of anti-terrorists.

p, Joel Freeman; d, Eric Karson; w, Leigh Chapman (based on a story by Paul Aaron, Chapman); ph, Michel Hugo (CFI Color); m, Dick Halligan; ed, Dann Cahn; prod d, James Schoppe; set d, Jim Hassinger; stunts, Aaron Norris; karate fight ch, Chuck Norris, Aaron Norris.

Martial Arts Cas. (PR:O MPAA:R)

OCTAMAN zero (1971) 90m Filmers Guild c (AKA: OCTOMAN)

Kerwin Matthews, Pier Angeli, Jeff Morrow, Jerry Guardino, Norman Fields, Robert Warner, David Essex.

Laughable horror film directed by Essex, who borrowed heavily from his own screenplay for THE CREATURE FROM THE BLACK LAGOON, which he had written nearly 20 years before. Brave-but-stupid explorers Matthews, Angeli, and company venture into the wilds of Mexico and discover a rather silly looking monster-octopus that lumbers about the terra firma on two legs like a man. Not only is the Octaman malformed, but he possesses only six tentacles as opposed to the usual eight (a budgetary consideration that make-up man Rick Baker was forced to contend with—a similar situation arose for Ray Harryhausen during the filming of IT CAME FROM BENEATH THE SEA (1955) which involved a huge octopus that attacks San Francisco), which makes the creature less than terrifying. The usual monster-wreaks-havoc-on-the-expedition scenes are filmed with little skill or imagination. Angeli, former James Dean flame, came out of semi-retirement to star in this one, but died tragically from a barbiturate overdose while the film was still in production. The young makeup man, Baker, would soon go on to bigger and better things including the special makeup effects for IT'S ALIVE, THE INCREDIBLE MELTING MAN, the remake of KING KONG (he played Kong as well), and perhaps his greatest achievement, the werewolf transformation scenes in AN AMERICAN WEREWOLF IN LONDON.

p, Michael Kraike; d, Harry Essex; w, Lawrence Morse; ph, Robert Caramico; m, Post Prod; spec eff & makeup, Rick Baker, Doug Bestwick, George Barr.

Horror Cas. (PR:O MPAA:NR)

OCTOBER MAN, THE½** (1948, Brit.) 91m TC/EL bw

John Mills *(Jim Ackland)*, Joan Greenwood *(Jenny Carden)*, Edward Chapman *(Mr. Peachey)*, Kay Walsh *(Molly)*, Joyce Carey *(Mrs. Vinton)*, Catherine Lacey *(Miss Selby)*, Frederick Piper *(Godby)*, Felix Aylmer *(Dr. Martin)*, Adrianne Allen *(Joyce Carden)*, Patrick Holt *(Harry)*, George Benson *(Mr. Pope)*, Ann Wilton *(Miss Parsons)*, Jack Melford *(Wilcox)*, Esme Beringer *(Miss Heap)*, John Boxer *(Troth)*, Edward Underdown *(Passport Official)*, Juliet Mills *(Little Girl)*, John Salew *(Ticket Inspector)*, Philip Ray *(Stebbins)*, George Woodbridge *(Grey)*, John Miller *(Mr. Newman)*, Kathleen Boutall *(Mrs. Newman)*, James Hayter *(Garage Man)*.

A psychological whodunit that has the main character struggle more within himself than with the struggle of finding a murderer. An industrial chemical accident leaves Mills with a severe brain injury and inclinations toward suicide after a friend's child is killed in the accident. With his release from the hospital, Mills goes to live in a suburban hotel which contains people from all walks of life. One of them is Molly, a struggling fashion model played by Walsh. She is being pursued by the lecherous Chapman, who figures that if he pays her rent it entitles him to go to her bed. She and Mills have only crossed paths once in the hotel, but she borrows money from him to pay her rent and the next day is found dead. Mills, because of his history, becomes a prime suspect and even can't figure out himself if he did it. It becomes a matter of him keeping hold of himself while seeking the real killer. The film is deep in the Hitchcock vein, but that's because it was directed by Baker a one-time Hitchcock assistant.

p, Eric Ambler; d, Roy Baker; w, Ambler (based on his novel); ph, Erwin Hillier; m, Kenneth Pakeman; ed, Alan Jaggs; md, Muir Mathieson; art d, Alexander Vetchinsky.

Mystery/Drama (PR:A MPAA:NR)

OCTOBER MOTH** (1960, Brit.) 54m Independent Artists/RANK bw

Lee Patterson *(Finlay)*, Lana Morris *(Molly)*, Peter Dyneley *(Tom)*, Robert Cawdron *(Police Constable)*, Sheila Raynor *(The Woman)*.After accidentally causing Raynor to be involved in an auto accident, Patterson, a mentally retarded man, brings her home to the farm he lives on with his sister (Morris). Patterson is convinced Raynor is his late mother but Morris tries to get

Dyneley, a telephone lineman, to help her brother get over this obsession. Patterson soon comes to believe Dyneley is his late father, a brutal man, and becomes bent on killing him. The sordid events come to a grisly close as Morris accidentally shoots her brother. Had this been done with some sensitivity, it could have been an interesting drama. However, the treatment here is depressing, catering to the basest elements of melodramatic structure and ends up a standard, lower-class production.

p, Arthur Alcott, Julian Wintle, Leslie Parkyn; d&w, John Kruse; ph, Michael Reed.

Drama   **(PR:O MPAA:NR)**

OCTOMAN   (SEE: OCTAMAN, 1971)

OCTOPUSSY**   (1983, Brit.) 130m Eon/MGM-UA c

Roger Moore (*James Bond*), Maud Adams (*Octopussy*), Louis Jourdan (*Kamal*), Kristina Wayborn (*Magda*), Kabir Bedi (*Gobinda*), Steven Berkoff (*Gen. Orlov*), David Meyer, Tony Meyer (*Twins*), Vijay Amritraj (*Vijay*), Desmond Llewelyn ("*Q*"), Robert Brown ("*M*"), Walter Gotell (*Gogol*), Geoffrey Keen (*Minister of Defense*), Suzanne Jerome (*Gwendoline*), Cherry Gillespie (*Midge*), Albert Moses (*Sadruddin*), Douglas Wilmer (*Fanning*), Andy Bradford (*009*), Lois Maxwell (*Miss Moneypenny*), Michaela Clavell (*Penelope Smallbone*), Philip Voss (*Auctioneer*), Bruce Boa (*U.S. General*), Richard Parmentier (*U.S Aide*), Paul Hardwick (*Soviet Chairman*), Dermot Crowley (*Kamp*), Peter Porteous (*Lenkin*), Eva Reuber-Staier (*Rublevitch*), Jeremy Bullock (*Smithers*), Tina Hudson (*Bianca*), William Derrick (*Thug with Yo-Yo*), Stuart Sanders (*Maj. Clive*), Patrick Barr (*British Ambassador*), Gabor Vernon (*Borchoi*), Hugo Bower (*Karl*), Ken Norris (*Col. Toro*), Tony Arjuna (*Mufti*), Gertan Klauber (*Bubi*), Brenda Cowling (*Schatzl*), David Grahame (*Petrol Pump Attendant*), Brian Coburn (*South American VIP*), Michael Halphie (*South American Officer*), Susanne Dando (*Gymnast Supervisor*), Roberto Germains (*Circus Ringmaster*), Richard Graydon (*Francisco the Fearless*), Mary Stavin, Carolyn Seaward, Carole Ashby, Cheryl Anne, Jani-Z, Julie Martin, Joni Flynn, Julie Barth, Kathy Davies, Helene Hunt, Gillian De Terville, Safira Afzal, Louise King, Tina Robinson, Alison Worth, Janine Andrews, Lynda Knight (*Octopussy Girls*), Teresa Craddock, Kirsten Harrison, Christine Cullers, Lisa Jackman, Jane Aldridge, Christine Gibson, Tracy Llewellyn, Ruth Flynn (*Gymnasts*), Ravinder Singh Revett, Gurdial Sira, Michael Moor, Sven Surtees, Peter Edmund, Ray Charles, Talib Johnny (*Thugs*), Carol Richter, Josef Richter, Vera Fossett, Shirley Fossett, Barrie Winship, The Hassani Troupe, The Flying Cherokees (*Circus Performers*).

From all indications (OCTOPUSSY and A VIEW TO A KILL being the major ones) the James Bond series was in its death throes. The only real excitement generated by OCTOPUSSY was whether or not it would beat Sean Connery's rival Bond production NEVER SAY NEVER AGAIN (they should have said it) to the theaters in the summer of 1983. It did. Moore once again sleepwalks through the role of 007, and this time he's out to stop evil Russian general Berkoff and his allies Adams, Jourdan, and Wayborn from launching a first-strike nuclear attack on the Western world. Berkoff is convinced that the West won't retaliate due to a powerful peace movement that has swept Europe. Bond, of course, won't allow that and sets out to spoil the mad Russian's plans by stopping the sale of bogus Faberge eggs, which are making the evildoers enough cash to proceed with their Earth-shattering plan. Adams is too beautiful to stay a villainess too long, and she joins up with Moore to defeat her former comrades. OCTOPUSSY featured the usual array of fine stunt work and special effects, but all this business was beginning to get very tiresome. (See JAMES BOND series, Index.)

p, Albert R. Broccoli; d, John Glen; w, George MacDonald Fraser, Richard Maibaum, Michael G. Wilson (based on the stories "Octopussy" and "The Property of a Lady" by Ian Fleming); ph, Alan Hume (Panavision, Technicolor); m, John Barry; ed, John Grover, Peter Davies, Henry Richardson; prod d, Peter Lamont; art d, John Fenner; set d, Jack Stephens; cos, Emma Porteous; spec eff, John Richardson; m/l, "All Time High," Barry, Tim Rice (sung by Rita Coolidge); stunts, Remy Julienne, Martin Grace, Paul Weston, Bill Burton, Dorothy Ford, Clive Curtis, Del Baker, Pat Banta, Jim Dowdall, Wayne Michaels, Nick Hobbs, Jazzer Jeyes, Christopher Webb, Malcolm Weaver; makeup, George Frost, Peter Robb-King, Eric Allwright.

Espionage   **Cas.**   **(PR:C MPAA:PG)**

ODD ANGRY SHOT, THE**   (1979, Aus.) 90m Samson/Roadshow c

Graham Kennedy (*Harry*), John Hargreaves (*Bung*), John Jarratt (*Bill*), Bryan Brown (*Rogers*), Graeme Blundell (*Dawson*), Richard Moir (*Medic*), Ian Gilmour (*Scott*), John Allen (*Lt. Golonka*), Brandon Burke (*Isaacs*), Graham Rouse (*Cook*), Tony Barry (*Black Ronnie*), Max Cullen (*Warrant Officer*), John Fitzgerald (*Intelligence Corporal*), Johnny Garfield (*Padre*), Ray Meagher (*Range Corporal*), Frankie J. Holden (*Spotted Soldier*), Roger Newcombe (*Clifford*), Brian Evis (*Mayberry*), Rose Ricketts (*Nurse*), Chuck McKinney (*1st Marine*), Freddie Paris (*2nd Marine*), Joy Westmore (*Bill's Mum*), Brian Wenzel (*Bill's Dad*), Sharon Higgins (*Bill's Girl*), Sarah Lee (*Bar Girl*), Brian Anderson (*Barman*).

An Australian film about that country's involvement in the Vietnam War. The story centers on a group of Australian volunteers who go into the Special Air Service, an elite fighting unit. They approach the fighting like competitive athletes looking forward to a sporting contest until things become violent and bloody. Director Jeffrey goes to great pains to convey a detailed sense of the sights and sounds of the war, both on the front lines (indistinct though they were) and behind them. He is aided in that pursuit by the evocative lensing of Don McAlpine, who worked as a cameraman in Vietnam during the war, and by the Department of Defense, which provided the necessary military hardware. But Jeffrey's real emphasis is on the way his soldiers react to the chaos that surrounds them, and he manages to wrench comedy from their attempts to survive in one piece. Kennedy, in particular, is persuasive as a career soldier who becomes disillusioned with the army life that he had used to escape the pressures of civilian existence.

p, Tom Jeffrey, Sue Milliken; d, Jeffrey; ph, Don McAlpine (Eastmancolor); m,

Michael Carlos; ed, Brian Kavanagh; prod d, Bernard Hides; spec eff, Brett Nolen; stunts, Grant Page.

War/Comedy   **Cas.**   **(PR:C MPAA:NR)**

ODD COUPLE, THE****   (1968) 105m PAR c

Jack Lemmon (*Felix Ungar*), Walter Matthau (*Oscar Madison*), John Fiedler (*Vinnie*), Herbert Edelman (*Murray*), David Sheiner (*Roy*), Larry Haines (*Speed*), Monica Evans (*Cecily*), Carole Shelley (*Gwendolyn*), Iris Adrian (*Waitress*), Heywood Hale Broun (*Sportswriter*), John C. Becher (*Hotel Clerk*), Roberto Clemente, Matty Alou, Maury Wills, Vernon Law, Ken Boyer, Bud Harrelson, Jerry Buchek, Ed Kranepool (*Themselves, Baseball Players*).

Neil Simon has the unique ability of depicting life, enhancing it a bit, and winding up with gold. His older brother, Danny (a successful writer in his own right who toiled on many TV shows), was divorced and living with Roy Gerber, a veteran agent, and, occasionally, with Les Colodny, a writer, then a TV studio executive, and later an advertising man. Danny Simon is a self-confessed fussbudget who insists on neatness, and Gerber and Colodny couldn't care less. They lived in California in a house above Hollywood that Danny attempted to keep neat but failed to do, as the debris kept piling up. Danny thought about writing a play about the experiences and told his brother some of the incidents. When Neil made him an offer he couldn't refuse (a piece of the action), Danny okayed it and the rest is stage, film, and TV history. Neil realized that doing "The Odd Trio" might be a bit unwieldy, so he made it into a couple instead. To outline the story might even make it sound like a tragedy. After all, it's the tale of two lonely men who have recently split from their wives: one is suicidal and the other is grumpy. They battle with each other over the difference in their ways and it could almost serve as a plot for a dramatic situation. But Simon's honest screenplay adaptation of his stage play is even better and adds to the more than 250 laughs (by actual count) in the play's script. Matthau and Art Carney did it on the stage (with Carney being replaced from time to time by Paul Dooley, "Wimpy" in POPEYE and father of the lead in BREAKING AWAY), but Paramount paged Lemmon for the coveted role of Felix. Billy Wilder had wanted to do the direction, although his price was allegedly higher than Saks, who directed the stage version, so that went out the window. The other actors were all from the stage play, with the addition of Adrian, Broun, Becher, and the ballplayers who played themselves. It was shortly after this picture that superstar Roberto Clemente was killed in a plane crash attempting to help some of his stricken fellow Puerto Ricans. Simon received an Oscar nomination for his script, although the film was otherwise overlooked by the Motion Picture Academy. Lemmon's wife has left him and he wants nothing more than to end his life. He's a TV newswriter and is so depressed that he is forever building dungeons in the air. After failing at his first suicide attempt, he goes to his regular Friday night poker game, which is being held at the huge apartment of his friend, Matthau, a divorced sportswriter for whom cleanliness is next to impossible. The others in the game, Fiedler, Sheiner, Haines, and Edelman (who also appeared as the phone repairman in the play and movie BAREFOOT IN THE PARK), all fear for Lemmon's life, so Matthau allows the distressed man to move in with him. What the heck, it's a big apartment and they won't get on each other's nerves, will they? Well you *know* they will: Lemmon's obsessive-compulsive behavior is soon gnawing at Matthau's vitals. The apartment is turned into a model of attractiveness, but Matthau is thinking that perhaps Lemmon's wife had a good idea when she left him. The riotous domestic quarrels sound like a typical husband-and-wife battle (and therein lies the fun when Lemmon nags Matthau about the overflowing cigarette butts, footprints in the kitchen, a souffle that falls, and like that). Before Matthau throttles Lemmon, he suggests that they get together and double-date two English women who live in the building, Evans and Shelley. Lemmon doesn't feel he is ready to talk to anyone who has a higher voice than his, but finally agrees when Matthau allows him to cook dinner. Lemmon's dinner is a shambles: his meat loaf burns, everything goes wrong, and he disintegrates into a river of sobs when the sisters ask about his wife and he tearfully recalls his lost marriage. Matthau is seething at the destruction of the sexy "mood" he was trying to create, but Evans and Shelley do their best to comfort Lemmon and are soon in tears themselves. When Lemmon won't take the sisters back to their apartment (Matthau was hoping for some action up there), Matthau finally cracks and begins breaking things and putting his now immaculate apartment back in the original sloppy condition it was in when Lemmon first arrived. Lemmon leaves, and when the poker cronies come by and no one has heard from Lemmon, they fear the worst and go around the city looking for him, to no avail. Later, at the Matthau apartment, Lemmon enters to gather his remaining possessions and tells them all that he is moving upstairs with the two sisters while he contemplates his next decision. Lemmon exits and the men sit down for their regular poker game and Matthau carps at them for spilling some of their ashes on the table as the picture ends. The barrage of one-liners that snaps off the screen is like sped-up waves on the sea. No sooner have your cheeks settled down from laughing than another fusillade begins and the best thing about the jokes is that they are all to the point and never out of character. So funny are these gags and so character-oriented that many of them would mean nothing without the framework that surrounds them. Simon usually writes about his own life. COME BLOW YOUR HORN showed him and Danny when he was breaking out of the house. BAREFOOT IN THE PARK depicted his first year of marriage to his late wife. CHAPTER TWO was the story of how he felt after his wife died and he met Marsha Mason, who starred in that film as herself. In this case, it was brother Danny's life that provided Simon with his biggest and best hit. When Simon departs from these familiar family themes, he runs aground, as in THE STAR-SPANGLED GIRL and THE SLUGGER'S WIFE. The TV series that came from this movie is a rare example of a film being transferred to the little screen without losing the flavor. Typical of the socko jokes is the one where one of the sisters asks Lemmon what he does for a living and he replies that he writes the news for television. She replies, "Isn't that interesting. Where on earth do you get all your ideas?" Other than the few scenes they added to take the action out of the stifling atmosphere of the apartment, this is essentially a filmed version of the play.

p, Howard W. Koch; d, Gene Saks; w, Neil Simon (based on his play); ph, Robert B. Hauser (Panavision, Technicolor); m, Neal Hefti; ed, Frank Bracht; art d, Hal Pereira, Walter Tyler; set d, Robert R. Benton, Ray Moyer; cos, Jack Bear; spec eff, Paul K. Lerpae; makeup, Wally Westmore, Harry Ray, Jack Petty.

Comedy   Cas.   (PR:A MPAA:G)

ODD JOB, THE   (1978, Brit.) 86m Tavlorda/COL c

Graham Chapman (*Arthur Harris*), David Jason (*The Odd Job Man*), Diana Quick (*Fiona Harris*), Simon Williams (*Tony Sloane*), Edward Hardwicke (*Inspector Black*), Bill Paterson (*Sgt. Mull*), Michael Elphick (*Raymonde*), Stewart Harwood (*Bernaard*), Carolyn Seymour (*Angie*), Joe Melia (*Headwaiter*), George Innes (*Caretaker*).

A British comedy starring Monty Python's Graham Chapman as an insurance executive who thinks he wants to die. He hires handy man Jason to murder him. Chapman has a change of heart, but because he has instructed Jason not to listen to anything he says, the odd job man plans to carry out the murder anyway. The rest of the film has Chapman trying to find a way out of his predicament. There is one chase after another, with Chapman meeting a wide range of strange characters: a racist caretaker, a gay underworld boss, and a swarm of constables. Finally, Chapman and his wife (Quick), thinking they're safe, fall off the terrace of their apartment, which had been booby trapped by Jason earlier.

p, Mark Forstater, Graham Chapman; d, Peter Medak; w, Bernard McKenna, Chapman; ph, Ken Hodges; m, Howard Blake; ed, Barrie Vince; prod d, Tony Curtis; cos, Shuna Harwood.

Comedy   Cas.   (PR:O MPAA:NR)

ODD MAN OUT***   (1947, Brit.) 116m TC/GFD/UNIV bw (AKA: GANG WAR)**

James Mason (*Johnny McQueen*), Robert Newton (*Lukey*), Kathleen Ryan (*Kathleen*), Robert Beatty (*Dennis*), William Hartnell (*Barman*), F.J. McCormick (*Shell*), Fay Compton (*Rosie*), Beryl Measor (*Maudie*), Cyril Cusack (*Pat*), Dan O'Herlihy (*Nolan*), Roy Irving (*Murphy*), Maureen Delany (*Theresa*), Kitty Kirwan (*Granny*), Min Milligan (*Housekeeper*), Joseph Tomelty (*Cabby*), W.G. Fay (*Father Tom*), Arthur Hambling (*Alfie*), Denis O'Dea (*Head Constable*), Elwyn Brook-Jones (*Tober*), Anne Clery, Maura Milligan, Eddie Byrne, Maureen Cusack, Pat McGrath, Dora Bryan, Guy Rolfe, Geoffrey Keen.

Reed established himself as a master director with this haunting, lyrical masterpiece film about a doomed fugitive, Mason, who gives one of the greatest portrayals of his illustrious career. He is an IRA leader who breaks out of jail and then plans a payroll holdup of a mill in Belfast, Northern Ireland, to fund his underground operations. Though Mason abhors violence, he uses his gun during the holdup and accidentally kills a man and is himself critically wounded. The driver of the escape car panics and leaves Mason to stumble away from the robbery. From that point on, Mason descends into a nightmare as he becomes more and more delirious from his wound. He is harbored by a bunch of strange people who either want to help him or sell him to the British authorities looking for him. Meanwhile, Ryan, Mason's sweetheart, is frantically searching for Mason, as are his IRA pals. The fugitive is hidden in deserted buildings, even in a bathtub in a junkyard for a while. On another occasion, two spinsters take him in, serve him tea, and then discover he is wounded, superficially bandaging him until he departs. He finally falls into the clutches of eccentric painter Newton who takes him to this ratty loft and there has Mason pose for a portrait of death. Mason finally struggles to free himself of the mad Newton and makes his way toward the docks in a final desperate effort to escape. Ryan catches up with him and both head for the harbor, getting to the gates that lead to freedom. It begins to snow lightly and just then the police show up. Ryan pulls a gun with the spotlights on her as Mason sags on her shoulder. She is determined to die with her man and she fires on the officers closing in on them. Police return the fire and the last scene shows two pathetically crumpled bodies at the harbor's edge, slowly being covered with a blanket of snow. Mason's performance as the dying fugitive is nothing less than great; in fact, this is truly the greatest role of his career. Ryan, who debuted here, is wonderful as the dedicated sweetheart, and marvelous performances are rendered by Cusack and O'Herlihy as Mason's chief lieutenants. McCormick is fascinating as a rag-picking bum who hides Mason, and Newton positively gorges himself on the scenery in a wild portrait of an artist whose sanity is questionable. The overall mood of the film, powerfully transmitted through Krasker's gritty cinematography, is early on established by Reed as a modern odyssey to doom and death in an uncaring world where charity and compassion are absent in human hearts. Each frame is another lethal step for Mason as Reed calculates, with a great air of poetry, his last moments on earth. The plot and character development are touchingly constructed and enhanced by a magnificent score by Alwyn. Though he is initially postured as a culprit, Mason's agonizing plight slowly transfigures him into a sort of Christ figure. At some points John Ford's THE INFORMER can be recalled, but only as a visual similarity. Ford's THE FUGITIVE is also reminiscent of ODD MAN OUT, at least insofar as both films present a grim hopelessness and an intolerable fate for a man who is basically decent but is trapped and condemned for his own altruistic beliefs. ODD MAN OUT is a great work of art, almost a painting on celluloid evoking the best canvases of Goya and Velasquez. This was not a popular box office production upon release but it quickly won worldwide plaudits and established Reed as a pantheon director with few peers.

p&d, Carol Reed; w, F.L. Green, R.C. Sheriff (based on the novel by Green); ph, Robert Krasker; m, William Alwyn; ed, Fergus McDonnell; md, Muir Mathieson; prod d, Roger Furse; art d, Ralph Brinton; spec eff, Stanley Grant, Bill Warrington.

Drama   (PR:C-O MPAA:NR)

ODD OBSESSION   (1961, Jap.) 96m Daiei/Harrison c (KAGI)

Machiko Kyo (*Ikuko Kenmochi*), Ganjiro Nakamura (*Mr. Kenji Kenmochi*), Junko Kano (*Toshiko Kenmochi*), Tatsuya Nakadai (*Kimura*), Tanie Kitabayashi (*Hana*),

Ichiro Sugai (*Masseur*), Jun Hamamura (*Dr. Soma*), Mantaro Ushio (*Dr. Kodama*), Kyu Sazanka (*Curio Dealer*).

A strange film about an elderly art critic (Nakamura) who has problems with his virility. Unbeknownst to his young wife (Kyo), he takes injections to help his sex life, but they don't seem to have any effect. Nakamura persuades Nakadai, a young intern, to have an affair with his wife, which arouses both the critic and his jealousy. The couple's daughter, Kano, who has fallen in love with Nakadai, becomes jealous of her mother. Nakamura has a stroke while in bed with his wife, and Kyo has to take care of him during the day and see Nakadai at night. Nakamura has a second stroke (brought on by the sight of his wife disrobing in preparation for a visit by Nakadai) and dies. Nakadai moves in with both the mother and daughter, and the three are poisoned by the family's servant, Kitabayashi, who is infuriated by their selfishness. The police read Kyo's diary and assume that the three have committed suicide over Nakamura's death. (In Japanese; English subtitles.)

p, Hiroaki Fujii; d, Kon Ichikawa; w, Natto Wada, Keiji Hasebe, Ichikawa (based on the novel *Kagi* by Junichiro Tanizaki); ph, Kazuo Miyagawa (DaieiScope, Daiei-Agfa Color); m, Yasushi Akutagawa; ed, Fujii, Ichikawa; art d, Tomoo Shimogawara; English titles, Frederick Laing.

Drama   (PR:O MPAA:NR)

ODDO zero   (1967) 61m Montgomery-C.I.T./I.R.M.I. bw

Martin Donley (*Alan Jaffeo/"Dick"*), Nicki Holt, Brigitta Reim.

A strange, brutal, and meaningless film made in 1967, long before it was popular to make movies about deranged Vietnam veterans. Donley, a war hero, returns to his San Francisco home and finds his father passed out on the floor. As if this is not enough of a shock, he discovers his stepmother making love to another woman and kills them both. Later, he meets a prostitute, kills her, and breaks into a woman's apartment, murdering her as well. Finally, the veteran returns home and puts a gun to himself.

d, Joe Davis; ph, V. Rodney; cos, Anna Saro.

Drama   (PR:O MPAA:NR)

ODDS AGAINST TOMORROW*   (1959) 95m Harbel/UA bw

Harry Belafonte (*Johnny Ingram*), Robert Ryan (*Earl Slater*), Shelley Winters (*Lorry*), Ed Begley (*Dave Burke*), Gloria Grahame (*Helen*), Will Kuluva (*Bacco*), Richard Bright (*Coco*), Lou Gallo (*Moriarity*), Fred J. Scollay (*Cannoy*), Carmen de Lavallade (*Kitty*), Mae Barnes (*Annie*), Kim Hamilton (*Ruth*), Lois Thorne (*Eadie*), Wayne Rogers (*Soldier*), Zohra Lampert (*Girl in Bar*), William Zuckert (*Bartender*), Burtt Harris (*George*), Clint Young (*Policeman*), Ed Preble (*Hotel Clerk*), Mel Stewart (*Elevator Operator*), Ronnie Stewart (*Fan with Dog*), Marc May (*Ambulance Attendant*), Paul Hoffman (*Garry*), Cicely Tyson (*Fra*), Lou Martini (*Captain of Waiters*), Robert Jones (*Guard*), Floyd Ennis (*Solly*), William Adams (*Bank Guard*), Fred Herrick (*Bank Manager*), Mary Boylan (*Bank Secretary*), John Garden (*Bus Station Clerk*), Allen Nourse (*Police Chief*).

A crackling crime caper that includes an overlay of racial tension, ODDS AGAINST TOMORROW was the first film out of Belafonte's own producing entity and proved that he wasn't just another pretty face and froggy voice. Robert Ryan, who was a liberal in real life, again plays a psychotic racist, nearly the same character he did in CROSSFIRE as a vicious anti-Semite. He essayed that role so well that people believed he was really that way and rumors abounded. Belafonte is a gambling junkie, a man whose love for the horses has caused his marriage to fall apart. He's a childish nightclub singer and is now in danger from the harassment of Kuluva, a gay gangster in the employ of the people who hold Belafonte's IOUs. Ryan is an ex-con looking for a big score and Begley is a former cop who has been cashiered from the force for illegal dealings. This unlikely trio unites to rob an upstate New York bank of $150,000. Belafonte desperately needs his share of the swag to call off Kuluva, who is now threatening to kill Belafonte's wife and daughter. Ryan is married to Winters, though dallying with Grahame, who gets vicarious thrills before they make love when she pleads with Ryan to tell her how it feels to murder someone. Ryan's anti-black feelings are overcome by Begley and the robbery takes place. But everything goes awry. A gas station jockey spots Ryan. Belafonte witnesses an accident and must give his version of the incident; then he switches places with the food delivery man who brings the bank's night workers their refreshments. The regular guy shows up and so do the cops. Begley is shot, and when he can't get the getaway car's keys to his compatriots, he takes his own life, rather than suffer the ignominy of arrest. Ryan and Belafonte escape and flee to an oil storage area not unlike the one in the final scenes of WHITE HEAT. By this time, the black-white tension has reached an apex; both men shoot at each other and the oil tanks blow up, incinerating Ryan and Belafonte. After the resulting fire has cooled, the two charred corpses are found and cannot be told apart, an indication that in death there is no color differential. In small roles, note Cicely Tyson, Wayne Rogers, and Zohra Lampert. This *film noir* picture had the added twist of race relations and didn't get the kind of box-office attention it deserved, perhaps due to that element. Terrific jazz score by John Lewis, pianist for the Modern Jazz Quartet.

p&d, Robert Wise; w, John O. Killens, Nelson Gidding (based on the novel by William P. McGivern); ph, Joseph Brun; m, John Lewis; ed, Dede Allen; art d, Leo Kerz; set d, Fred Ballmeyer; cos, Anna Hill Johnstone; makeup, Robert Jiras.

Crime   (PR:C MPAA:NR)

ODE TO BILLY JOE*   (1976) 105m WB c

Robby Benson (*Billy Joe McAllister*), Glynnis O'Connor (*Bobbie Lee Hartley*), Joan Hotchkis (*Mrs. Hartley*), Sandy McPeak (*Mr. Hartley*), James Best (*Dewey Barksdale*), Terence Goodman (*James Hartley*), Becky Brown (*Becky Thompson*), Simpson Hemphill (*Brother Taylor*), Ed Shelnut (*School Bus Driver*), Eddie Tair (*Tom Hargitay*), William Hallberg (*Dan McAllister*), Frannye Capelle (*Belinda Wiggs*), Rebecca Jernigan (*Mrs. Thompson*), Ann Martin (*Mrs. Hunnicutt*), Will

Long *(Trooper Bash)*, John Roper *(Trooper Ned)*, Pat Purcell, Jim Westerfield, Jack Capelle *(Youths in Car)*, Al Scott *(Master of Ceremonies)*.

A moving melodrama based on Bobbie Gentry's 1967 hit song about a 17-year-old boy who commits suicide by jumping off the Tallahatchie Bridge. The film is set in 1953 and stars Benson and O'Connor as two teenagers who meet and fall in love one summer. The film details the intricacies of southern small town life as the couple attend to their various obligations and then dash off to meet each other at the Tallahatchie Bridge. Tragedy strikes on the night of the local dance, when Benson gets drunk and is pushed into a homosexual act that destroys him emotionally. Devastated by the encounter, Benson goes to the bridge that he and O'Connor had made so many plans on, and commits suicide, leaving O'Connor to carry on alone. Though the film's climax has some very sensationalistic aspects, the material is handled with sensitivity and dignity and its characters are all human and complex. ODE TO BILLY JOE did surprisingly well at the box office, grossing over $10 million.

p, Max Baer, Roger Camras; d, Baer; w, Herman Raucher (based on the song by Bobbie Gentry); ph, Michel Hugo (Technicolor); m, Michel Legrand; ed, Frank E. Morriss; art d, Philip Jefferies; set d, Harry Gordon; m/l, "There'll Be Time," Alan and Marilyn Bergman.

Drama **Cas.** **(PR:O MPAA:PG)**

ODESSA FILE, THE*½** (1974, Brit./Ger.) 128m Domino-Oceanic/COL c

Jon Voight *(Peter Miller)*, Maximilian Schell *(Eduard Roschmann)*, Maria Schell *(Frau Miller)*, Mary Tamm *(Sigi)*, Derek Jacobi *(Klaus Wenzer)*, Peter Jeffrey *(David Porath)*, Klaus Lowitsch *(Gustav MacKensen)*, Kurt Meisel *(Alfred Oster)*, Hans Messemer *(Gen. Glucks)*, Garfield Morgan *(Israeli General)*, Shmuel Rodensky *(Simon Wiesenthal)*, Ernst Schroder *(Werner Deilman)*, Gunter Strack *(Police Official Kunik)*, Noel Willman *(Franz Bayer)*, Martin Brandt *(Marx)*, Hans Caninenberg *(Dr. Ferdinand Schultz)*, Heinz Ehrenfreund *(Shapira)*, Alexander Golling *(Colonel)*, Towje Kleiner *(Solomon Tauber)*, Gunter Meisner *(Gen. Greifer)*, Gunnar Miller *(Karl Braun)*, Elizabeth Neumann-Viertel *(Frau Wenzer)*, Christine Wodetzky *(Gisela)*, Werner Bruhns *(Magazine Publisher Hoffmann)*, Til Kiwe *(Medal Shop Proprietor)*, Georg Marischka *(Lawyer)*, Hans Wyprachtiger *(Landlord)*, Cyril Shaps *(Tauber's Voice)*, Miriam Mahler *(Esther Tauber)*, Joachim Dietmar Mues *(Wehrmacht Captain)*.

The same producer, Woolf, and screenwriter, Ross, came back to make this film after having done the more successful Forsyth adaptation of THE DAY OF THE JACKAL. This was not quite as exciting or cinematic, but it still remains a fine, fast, and edge of the seat international thriller. It's a bit too long and very convoluted and the story "beats" may be one too many, although if one concentrates on the subtleties, it's a rewarding experience. Voight is the son of a German soldier in Deutschland and currently a reporter attempting to track down the whereabouts of some of the sadistic SS men who mysteriously vanished after the war. The time is December, 1963. John F. Kennedy has been assassinated and the temper of the times is angry. Voight reads the diary of a suicide, a person who had been one of the death camp survivors. It is this chilling document that causes him to search for Maximilian Schell, a Nazi who has gone into hiding. (Schell has played these roles so often—THE MAN IN THE GLASS BOOTH, etc.—that it's enough already!) Voight's investigating is sidetracked by various officials of Odessa—a real group that actually exists—and the more they seek to keep him away, the more he continues. Israeli agents are also on the case and they come across Voight and enlist him in their cause with an innovative scheme. Although he is far too young to have been in WW II, they age him with makeup, provide him with another identity, and then train him hard until he assumes that persona and is unleashed into the dark world of Odessa. Israeli Willman is his trainer, and by the time his indoctrination is over, Voight's answers are automatic. Meanwhile, members of the Odessa are on to him and are shadowing his girl friend, Tamm. One of their group, Lowitsch, is sent out to erase this threat to their secrecy. There's a terrifying scene in the shop of Jacobi, a printer, that is a marvel of suspenseful restraint. Voight finally gets to Schell, and in what must be the most frightening scene in the film, the Nazi casually explains why he did what he did and why he feels he was right. He delivers his rationale with total sincerity and no guilt about what he's done and we must believe that people like this still exist, a shuddering possibility. There is a plot twist at the end that defies synopsizing because to reveal it would be to do the film disservice. Stick around for it, though, and be prepared for a sharp intake of breath. Maria Schell, as Voight's mother, does a small cameo and proves again that the amount of time a performer gets on screen makes no difference: The impact is what counts. Although Maria Schell is only a dozen years older than Voight, that differential is hardly noticeable. The two production companies, Domino Productions and Oceanic Filmproductions, may be tax shelter firms formed for the purpose of making this picture. It was not a huge grosser, but did respectably enough and served as another portrait in Voight's gallery of superior performances. When he's good, as in MIDNIGHT COWBOY, COMING HOME, and RUNAWAY TRAIN, he's sensational. When he's not so good, as in FEARLESS FRANK, THE ALL-AMERICAN BOY, and THE CHAMP, he's still better than most.

p, John Woolf; d, Ronald Neame; w, George Markstein, Kenneth Ross (based on the novel by Frederick Forsyth); ph, Oswald Morris (Panavision, Eastmancolor); m, Andrew Lloyd Webber; ed, Ralph Kemplen; prod d, Rolf Zehetbauer; cos, Monika Bauert; m/l, Webber, Tim Rice, Andre Heller (sung by Perry Como).

Adventure **Cas.** **(PR:C MPAA:PG)**

ODETTE*** (1951, Brit.) 123m Wilcox-Neagle-Imperiado/Lopert-Dowling-UA bw

Anna Neagle *(Odette)*, Trevor Howard *(Capt. Peter Churchill)*, Marius Goring *(Henri)*, Peter Ustinov *(Arnaud)*, Bernard Lee *(Jack)*, Col. Maurice Buckmaster *(Himself)*, Marie Burke *(Mme. Gliere)*, Gilles Queant *(Jacques)*, Guyri Wagner *(Interrogator)*, Wolf Frees *(Major)*, Frederick Windhousen *(Colonel)*, Alfred Shieske *(Commandant)*, Marianne Waller *(SS Wardress)*, Catherine Paul *(Mother Superior)*, John Hunter *(American Officer)*, Campbell Gray *(Paul)*, Derek Penley *(Jules)*.

Neagle is a Frenchwoman married to a British soldier and living in London during the opening days of WW II. After her husband is killed in action during the fall of France, she listens to a radio appeal for photos of the French coast for the British navy to use. She sends in her holiday snapshots, but she gets the address wrong and they end up at the War Office, where she is recruited as an intelligence agent. She tells her children that she is going to Scotland for a war job but instead undergoes intense training under control officer Howard. Later she is sent to France along with radio operator Ustinov and stationed in Marseilles, from which she sends back vital intelligence while playing a cat-and-mouse game with suave Gestapo man Goring. At last she is captured in a trap and undergoes brutal torture, including hot pokers buring her flesh and having her toenails ripped out with pliers. She endures it all without talking and is eventually sent to the Ravensbruck concentration camp and scheduled to be executed. Luckily, though, on the day the sentence is to be carried out, American troops near the camp and the Nazi commander decides that she will be a valuable item to have with him when he surrenders. Returned to Britain, Neagle and Howard later marry. Based on the true story of Odette Sansom Churchill, the filmmakers hired the real Odette as technical advisor and shot the film in many of the same locations in which the events actually occurred, including the rooms at Gestapo headquarters where she was tortured. The part of the head of British intelligence in London was played by the real gentleman, Col. Maurice Buckmaster. Producer-director Wilcox bought the rights to Odette's story and first tried to enlist Michele Morgan to play her part, but Morgan refused, as did Ingrid Bergman. It was only when Odette told Wilcox that she had assumed his wife—and longtime collaborator—Neagle would play the part, that Neagle was cast. Neagle's performance was one of her best in a long career filled with portrayals of British heroines from Nell Gwyn through Queen Victoria and nurse Edith Cavell. the other performances are also good, particularly Ustinov's. Only Goring's slightly swishy Gestapo man lends a false note to the proceedings. Howard's real-life counterpart was Winston Churchill's nephew. Producer-director Wilcox, with some 30 collaborative feature-film efforts in concert with with his wife, stated that ODETTE was the film by which he would most like to be remembered.

p&d, Herbert Wilcox; w, Warren Chetham-Strode (based on the book by Jerrard Tickell); ph, Max Greene [Mutz Greenbaum]; m, Anthony Collins; ed, W. Lewthwaite; art d, William C. Andrews; cos, Maude Churchill; makeup, Harold Fletcher; tech adv, Odette Sansom Churchill.

Spy Drama **(PR:A-C MPAA:NR)**

ODISSEA NUDA (SEE: NUDE ODYSSEY, 1962)

ODONGO** (1956, Brit.) 85m Warwick/COL c

Rhonda Fleming *(Pamela Muir)*, Macdonald Carey *(Steve Stratton)*, Juma *(Odongo)*, Eleanor Summerfield *(Celia Watford)*, Francis De Wolff *(George Watford)*, Earl Cameron *(Hassan)*, Dan Jackson *(Walla)*, Michael Carridia *(Lester Watford)*, Errol John *(Mr. Bawa)*, Leonard Sachs *(Game Warden)*, Paul Hardmuth *(Mohammed)*, Bartholomew Sketch *(Leni)*, Lionel Ngakane *(Leni's Brother)*.

A sappy tale about a small East African boy (Juma) who is the sidekick of Carey, a trapper who captures wild animals for zoos and circuses. Trouble starts when a vengeful native, fired by Carey, lets the animals out of their corral on the day a big buyer is to look them over. Juma is accused and the hurt boy runs away and is taken hostage by the guilty man. Fleming, a veterinarian who doesn't approve of Carey's profession, and the trapper put aside their differences to help the boy they both love.

p, Islin Auster; d&w, John Gilling (based on a story by Auster); ph, Ted Moore (CinemaScope, Technicolor); m, George Melachrino; ed, Alan Osbiston, Jack Slade; md, Melachrino; art d, Elliott Scott.

Juvenile Drama **(PR:A MPAA:NR)**

ODYSSEY OF THE PACIFIC** (1983, Can./Fr.) 78m Cine-Pacific-Babylone bw

Mickey Rooney *(Emperor of Peru)*, Jonathan Starr *(Toby)*, Anick *(Liz)*, Ky Huot Uk *(Han)*, Jean-Louis Roux *(Uncle Alex)*, Monique Mercure *(Aunt Elsa)*, Vera Dalton *(Flora)*.

A children's fantasy film about a young boy (Starr) and his sister (Anick) who live with their aunt (Mercure). The two kids get a new brother when Mercure adopts a Cambodian orphan (Uk). The children meet an elderly crippled eccentric (Rooney) who tells them he is the emperor of Peru. The former locomotive engineer fills their heads with wild stories and takes them to see his train engine, "The Pacific." Uk thinks that he can get home using the engine and his adopted brother and sister agree to help him. The old railroad man shows the trio how to run the train, but stays behind when the kids head off on their journey.

p, Claude Leger; d, Fernando Arrabal; w, Arrabal, Roger Lemelin; m, Edith Butler; prod d, Rene Petit.

Juvenile Fantasy **Cas.** **(PR:AA MPAA:NR)**

OEDIPUS REX** (1957, Can.) 87m Motion Pictures c (AKA: KING OEDIPUS)

Douglas Rain *(Messenger)*, Douglas Campbell *(Oedipus)*, Eric House *(Priest)*, Robert Goodier *(Creon)*, Donald Davis *(Tiresias)*, Eleanor Stuart *(Jocasta)*, Tony van Bridge *(Man from Corinth)*, Eric House *(Old Shepherd)*, William Hutt *(Chorus Leader)*, Gertrude Tyas *(Nurse)*, Nomi Cameron, Barbara Franklin *(Ismene and Antigone)*.

Stagy presentation of Yeats' version of the classic Greek tragedy starring Campbell as the doomed king who unknowingly murders his father and subsequently marries his mother. The cast—made up of the Stratford [Ontario] Festival Players—is superb, but this production belongs on the stage and not the screen. Famed actor, playwright, and stage producer Guthrie picked up the directing credit for this picture. Rain went on to be the voice of the Hal 9000 computer in Stanley Kubrick's 2001: A SPACE ODYSSEY.

p, Leonard Kipnis; d, Tyrone Guthrie; w, William Butler Yeats' translation of the tragedy "Oedipus the King" by Sophocles; ph, Roger Barlow (Eastmancolor); m, Cedric Thorpe Davie; art d, Arthur Price; set d, Tanya Moiseiwitsch.

Drama (PR:A MPAA:NR)

OEDIPUS THE KING***½ (1968, Brit.) 97m Crossroads-World Film-UNIV/UNIV c

Christopher Plummer (*Oedipus*), Lilli Palmer (*Jocasta*), Richard Johnson (*Creon*), Orson Welles (*Tiresias*), Cyril Cusack (*Messenger*), Roger Livesey (*Shepherd*), Donald Sutherland (*Chorus Leader*), Alexis Mantheakis (*Palace Official*), Dimos Starenios (*Priest*), Friedrich Ledebur (*King Laius*), Oenone Luke (*Antigone*), Cressida Luke (*Ismene*), Minos Argyrakis, Manos Destounis, George Dialegmenos, Takis Emmanouel, Alexandros Maniatakis, George Oekonomou, Pan Panagiotopoulos, Nikos Paschalides, Paul Roche, Achilleas Skordilis, Grigoris Stefanides, Kostas Themos, George Zaifides (*The Chorus*), Mary Xenoudaki, Jenny Damianopoulou, Diana J. Reed (*Jocasta's Handmaidens*).

The same thing that happened to the two films about Oscar Wilde happened here. There were a pair of motion picture companies making the same story at the same time. The other Oedipus story was the Italian version, EDIPO RE, directed by Pier Paolo Pasolini. In NEVER ON SUNDAY, Melina Mercouri's character satirically speaks of Oedipus as a "nice boy who loves his mother" and goes no further. The tragedy of this story goes deep into the veins and doesn't stop bloodletting until the bodies are pale. The old city of Thebes has been cursed by the Gods Up There because the king has been murdered. The only way this curse can be lifted is if the current ruler, Plummer, can locate and kill that criminal. As Plummer begins his investigation, he uncovers some of his own history and learns that he not only mistakenly killed his father, but he also made love to his own mother, Palmer, and sired children. She commits suicide by hanging and Plummer rips out his own eyes and becomes a blind mendicant as part of his guilt at the close. Not much of a plot for a musical, you must admit, but the Greeks knew how to get to the bottom of things when it came to stirring horror. Filmed in Greece in a unique style (they used an old amphitheater to serve as the background for much of the action), this film is suspenseful and emotional and shows a great deal of restraint where over emoting seemed to be just around the corner. Plummer is superb and Welles, holding himself in check as the Prophet of Doom, runs a close second in the acting department. Each smaller role is well-done and Sutherland is noteworthy as a one-person Greek Chorus, something that was part of every Hellenic play at the time. Sophocles would have nodded approval, although some of the story-telling is a bit surface and doesn't get down into the depths, a place where the play's author spent a great deal of his time. The translation is understandable and opts for some current colloquialisms to make it palatable for the modern ear. They wisely avoid much of the gore and stick to the talk, and yet it doesn't seem too verbal, probably due to the 97-minute length.

p, Michael Luke; d, Philip Saville; w, Luke, Saville (based on the Paul Roche translation of the play "Oedipus Rex" by Sophocles); ph, Walter Lassally (Technicolor); m, Jani Christou; ed, Paul Davies; art d, Yannis Migadis; cos, Denny Vachlioti.

Drama (PR:C MPAA:NR)

OF BEDS AND BROADS (SEE: TALES OF PARIS, 1962, Fr./Ital.)

OF FLESH AND BLOOD** (1964, Fr./Ital.) 83m Copernic-Saphrene-Dear/Times c (LES GRANDS CHEMINS; IL BARO)

Robert Hossein (*Samuel*), Renato Salvatori (*Francis*), Anouk Aimee (*Anna*), Bervil (*Garage Owner*), Jean Lefebvre (*Card Player*), Andree Turcy (*Old Woman*), Serge Marquand (*Mechanic*), Fernand Sardou (*Gendarme*), Robert Dalban (*Man in Fairground*).

An overwrought melodrama billed as "A Film by Roger Vadim", but actually written and directed by Christian Marquand. Salvatori is given the task of delivering a Jeep. While on the road he meets Hossein and the two strike up a friendship. Their friendship ends abruptly, however, when Hossein steals part of the Jeep's engine and disappears. While playing cards with some farmers, Hossein is caught cheating and the angry men break his hands. Hossein goes to Salvatori and his lover Aimee for help and they let him stay. After a spell, Hossein wanders off, still bitter over the mutilation. He meets an old woman and after she angers him, his mind snaps and he kills her. A posse is soon formed, among whose members are Salvatori and the farmers who broke Hossein's hands. They track him down, but Hossein kills the farmers who had crippled him. Salvatori kills Hossein so that he will not be taken by the authorities.

p, Raymond Danon; d, Christian Marquand; w, Paul Gegauff, Marquand, Pierre La Salle; ph, Andreas Winding (FranScope, Eastmancolor); m, Michel Magne; ed, Nadine Trintignant; art d, Jean Andre.

Drama (PR:C MPAA:NR)

OF HUMAN BONDAGE**** (1934) 83m RKO bw

Leslie Howard (*Philip Carey*), Bette Davis (*Mildred Rogers*), Frances Dee (*Sally Athelny*), Reginald Owen (*Thorpe Athelny*), Reginald Denny (*Harry Griffiths*), Kay Johnson (*Norah*), Alan Hale (*Emil Miller*), Reginald Sheffield (*Dunsford*), Desmond Roberts (*Dr. Jacobs*), Tempe Pigott (*Landlady*).

Maugham's classic tragic story of a clubfooted, sensitive painter-turned-physician, and the emotional hell a scheming, spiteful waitress makes of his life is brought to the screen with electric performances by Howard and Davis. As the star-crossed Philip Carey, Howard studies painting in Paris but realizes that his work will never

be anything more than second-rate. The club-footed Howard returns to England and there begins to study medicine. He meets in a restaurant a blonde vamp waitress, Davis, who manipulates his affection for her in cruel and crafty ways. She breaks a date with Howard to go out with loutish salesman Hale and later emotionally wounds Howard by bluntly telling him that she could never love a cripple. Davis goes on to state that Hale has promised to marry her and she intends to take him up on his offer. Rejected, Howard goes off to tend his injuries of the heart. He later meets sophisticated and decent Johnson, author of romantic novels, who aggressively courts him but Howard can only think of the vixen Davis. Before this relationship can bloom, Davis comes abruptly back into Howard's life, appearing at his apartment to explain that she has been deserted by Hale and is now pregnant. Howard cannot help himself in promising to marry Davis and abandon Johnson. But Davis is no more faithful to Howard than she is to herself; she encourages Denny, one of Howard's fellow medical students, eventually running off with him. Howard returns sadly to his studies but he is not rid of Davis who comes back once more with her child, begging for a place to stay. Howard givers her shelter but refuses her lame offer of sex, and when he leaves she destroys his belongings, even burning some bonds he needs to finance his studies. (This scene is almost identitical to that of Ida Lupino destroying Ronald Colman's masterpiece painting in THE LIGHT THAT FAILED, 1939.) Without tuition fees, Howard must leave school; he becomes a salesman but depression sets in and his health fails. Dee and her father Owen nurse back his strength and he later inherits money which allows him to complete his education and have his clubfoot fixed. He then hears that Davis is dying in a charity ward and he goes to see her but she dies before he arrives. Howard is finally free of the emotional chains that have created his human bondage to the vicious slattern Davis, free to wed Dee who loves him. This version of the Maugham novel is certainly the finest (the 1946 and 1964 versions being nothing more than dismal and uninspired remakes), thanks to Cromwell's sensitive and intelligent direction and the wonderful roles essayed by the leads. Howard, that cerebral, cultured British actor (he became so popular in American films that in England he was later called "that American actor"), is riveting in his role of the victimized medical student, one who evokes tremendous empathy. Davis, as the tawdry tart Mildred, gives her first bravura performance on the screen, one that established her as a major actress of deep and startling talents. After RKO acquired the Maugham novel for production, studio executives were shocked to learn that all of RKO's leading ladies wanted no part of the sluttish Mildred, the role being rejected by Katharine Hepburn, Ann Harding, and, of course, Irene Dunne. Davis, however, was languishing in unimportant roles at Warner Bros. and she began to lobby Jack Warner to loan her to RKO for the part, a six-month campaign that wore the normally steel-willed mogul down. Warner finally relented and loaned out Davis but he confided to friends that he was doing his tough lady star no favor, that the part would not only drain her but she would create such a repugnant image playing such a disgusting character that she would return gratefully to the Warner Bros. fold to repair a badly damaged career, taking whatever ingenue roles Warner deigned to toss in her direction. Director Cromwell was not concerned, however; he knew well the depth of Davis' acting talent. The actress threw herself into the role with the fury of a whirlwind, adopting a Cockney accent which she refused to discard when off camera, even employing the accent at home when answering the phone, which confused and amused her friends. Howard, when Davis first appeared on the set, did not approve of the 26-year-old Davis taking over the role of a British girl. He and others were quick to point out how Joan Crawford mangled her foreign accent when attempting to play a British lady in TODAY WE LIVE (1933). Moreover, the dignified, aesthetic Howard sat off camera reading a book and indifferently feeding Davis her lines during rehearsals, almost treating his interaction with the actress as an annoying chore. Then Cromwell told Howard that the actress was running away with the film and Howard jumped to attention, taking Davis seriously and putting forth his all. In addition to her supercharged deliveries of venomous lines, Davis supervised her own makeup so that she was shown to gradually disintegrate as a human being on screen, right up to the last scene where she is dying of syphilis, appearing emaciated, ghost-white with eyes blackened with illness, a horrible shocking transition. It is obvious that Davis relished her role, her despicable posture, and acid-dripping lines. The scene where she reveals her true nature and verbally destroys the pathetic Howard is one of the most startling ever put to film. Davis stands like a tart on a street corner, spewing forth the emotions of the gutter she truly represents: "You cad, you dirty swine. I never cared for you—not once! I was always making a fool of you. You bored me stiff. I hated you. It made me sick when I had to let you kiss me. I only did it because you begged me. You hounded me, you drove me crazy! And after you kissed me, I always used to wipe my mouth! Wipe my mouth! But I made up for it—for every kiss I had to laugh. We laughed at you, Miller and me and Griffiths and me. We laughted at you because you were such a mug, a mug, a monster! You're a cripple, a cripple!" At the premiere of this powerful film, RKO executives were horrified to find members of the audience laughing at the most poignant and dramatic scenes but they later reasoned that this had been triggered by a wholly misconceived musical score that was telegraphing wrong emotions and the studio ordered Steiner to rewrite the score; the new score was much more telling and to the point of the story, providing motifs identified with the leading players, including what Steiner termed a "musical limp" for the crippled Howard. By the time OF HUMAN BONDAGE went into general release, Davis received universally praising reviews. She was heralded as a great actress and a star of the first order, completely disproving Jack Warner's theory. Moreover, she believed that she would win the 1934 Academy Award for Best Actress and she was profoundly depressed when Claudette Colbert won for IT HAPPENED ONE NIGHT. Yet this film was her watershed picture and she would go on to glean Oscars for JEZEBEL and DANGEROUS. Davis was later quoted (in *Mother Goddam* by Whitney Stine) as saying: "I was heartbroken not to win my first Academy Award for OF HUMAN BONDAGE, not that I honestly ever have approved of my performance as Mildred, as I have upon only a *very* few occasions approved of other performances. But due to the reviews and acclaim given me by friends in my profession I just took it for granted I would win. One must never take anything for granted—especially Academy Awards."

p, Pandro S. Berman; d, John Cromwell; w, Lester Cohen (based on the novel by W. Somerset Maugham); ph, Henry W. Gerrard; m, Max Steiner; ed, William Morgan; art d, Van Nest Polglase, Carroll Clark; cos, Walter Plunkett.

Drama **Cas.** **(PR:C-O MPAA:NR)**

OF HUMAN BONDAGE½** (1946) 105m WB bw

Eleanor Parker *(Mildred Rogers)*, Paul Henreid *(Philip Carey)*, Alexis Smith *(Nora Nesbitt)*, Edmund Gwenn *(Athelny)*, Janis Paige *(Sally Athelny)*, Patric Knowles *(Griffiths)*, Henry Stephenson *(Dr. Tyrell)*, Marten Lamont *(Dunsford)*, Isobel Elsom *(Mrs. Athelny)*, Una O'Connor *(Mrs. Foreman)*, Eva Moore *(Mrs. Gray)*, Richard Nugent *(Emil Miller)*, Doris Lloyd *(Landlady)*.

In the second film version of W. Somerset Maugham's novel, Henreid stars as the doctor-artist crippled by both his physical problem and intense self-pity. Henreid's miserable life is interrupted by Smith, a novelist, but it is another woman, waitress Parker, with whom he becomes obsessed. His interest in the brash, crude woman grows into an attraction beyond his understanding, an overwhelming obsession that soon dominates all he does. Parker in turn mistreats Henreid, growing more sadistically abusive as their relationship develops. Eventually they reach a self-destructive conclusion and Henreid meets a new love interest, Paige, the daughter of bohemian Gwenn. Receiving a mixed critical reaction at the time of release, the second telling of this London-based story has both its strong and weak points. Henreid and Parker do admirable jobs, giving life to their parts though they certainly don't match Leslie Howard or Bette Davis in the first filmed version 12 years before. The production was fraught with troubles. In his autobiography, *Ladies Man*, Henreid described the shooting as a series of problems resulting from director Goulding's shooting methods. Taking Turney's original screenplay, Goulding decided to rewrite over the course of shooting, changing what Henreid felt was already a fine work. The two also disagreed over motivations for Henreid's character. Henreid described Goulding's methods as "childish" and, while he tried to hide his animosity from the director, bad feelings emerged between the two that lasted throughout production. Goulding also was a firm believer in the long take, never shooting closeups or other inserts to cover himself. As a result if a take didn't work the entire shot would have to be redone, causing delays and adding to the film's budget. Producer Blanke grew more frantic about these escalations and sought Henreid's help in putting an end to them. "I finally agreed to fluff my lines whenever I thought the take was too long," the actor recalled. "This would force Goulding to stop the shot and go back to a point before my fluff and reshoot. The camera angle was usually somewhat changed and it would force a cut at that point unless he was willing to reshoot the entire take. He had sense enough not to try that." The initial screening of the final product showed a film that could prove to be a box-office disaster, for Henreid's attempts to add variety in the shots were only partially successful. Henreid then got the bright idea of perhaps using an optical bench, one of the new devices available to filmmakers, which was capable of pulling closeups and medium shots out of a master shot. With the encouragement of friend Lew Wasserman, Henreid went over a shooting script penning down the moments he felt some shot variations would improve the film. "The next morning," wrote the actor, "I gave my notes to Lew and to my amazement [he] memorized all the changes in half an hour. 'This way,' he assured me, 'Blanke is going to think the changes came from me, not you—and I believe he'll put them in, at least I hope to hell he will!'" Indeed, Blanke not only bought the changes wholeheartedly but informed Henreid that these changes had been a brainstorm of his! The results were not bad, giving dramatic life to what could have been a disaster. Though by no means a great picture, the second version of OF HUMAN BONDAGE is certainly an entertaining one.

p, Henry Blanke; d, Edmund Goulding; w, Catherine Turney (based on the novel by W. Somerset Maugham); ph, Peverell Marley; m, Erich Wolfgang Korngold; ed, Clarence Kolster; md, Leo F. Forbstein; art d, Hugh Reticker, Harry Kelso.

Drama **(PR:O MPAA:NR)**

OF HUMAN BONDAGE** (1964, Brit.) 98m Seven Arts/MGM bw

Kim Novak *(Mildred Rogers)*, Laurence Harvey *(Philip Carey)*, Robert Morley *(Dr. Jacobs)*, Siobhan McKenna *(Norah Nesbitt)*, Roger Livesey *(Thorpe Athelny)*, Jack Hedley *(Griffiths)*, Nanette Newman *(Sally Athelny)*, Ronald Lacey *(Mathews)*, David Morris *(Young Philip Carey)*, Anthony Booth *(Martin)*, Anna Manahan *(Waitress)*, Jacqueline Taylor *(Cook/Woman Patient)*, Derry O'Donovan *(2nd Waitress)*, Helen Robinson *(Mangeress-Cashier)*, Michael Doolan *(Man with Club Foot)*, John Sutton *(Kingsford)*, Leo McCabe *(Elderly Man in Railway Carriage)*, Olive White *(Griffith's Girl Friend)*, Blanaid Irvine *(Distinguished Girl)*, Eamonn Morrisey *(Bespectacled Student)*, Ann Manceer *(Girl Patient)*, Robin Lepler *(Jeweler)*, Evelyn McNeice *(Mrs. Harding)*, Norman Smythe *(Attendant in Dissecting Theater)*, Caroline Swift *(Nurse)*, Cecil Nash *(Father of Boy with Club Foot)*, Peter Nash *(Young Boy)*, May Cluskey *(Sister)*, Terry Clinton *(Barmaid)*, Danny O'Shea *(Headwaiter)*, Martin Crosbie, Alex Dignam *(Porters)*, Brendan Mathews *(Technician)*, Bryan Forbes, Peter Moray *(Students)*.

This third version of Somerset Maugham's autobiographical story is clearly the least successful, marred by production troubles and miscasting of the lead roles. This time Harvey is the clubfoot who turns to medicine after failing as an artist. He leaves Paris for Edwardian England where he begins his studies, then meets Novak. This coarse, Cockney waitress becomes the great passion of Harvey's life. Though impressed by his social standing, Novak rejects his love and marries another man. Soon after, Harvey takes up with writer McKenna (in a solid performance) and under her guidance returns wholeheartedly to his studies. But this is short-lived as Novak returns to his life pregnant and alone. She moves in with Harvey and after the child is born Novak takes up with Harvey's close friend, Hedley. Harvey finds out, then confronts Novak. The two argue and Novak reveals her only interest in Harvey was for financial support, for his clubfoot only made her loathe the man. Once again Novak leaves and Harvey throws himself back into his work. He receives internship at a hospital where he meets bohemian Livesey and daughter Newman. His life appears to be headed in a solid direction but once more he is brought down by Novak when he hears the woman has become a low-class hooker. He finds the object of his obsession working in a cheap bawdy house, her once fiery personality now weakened by the life she leads. Harvey takes Novak and her child away from the brothel, resettling them in his apartment. Once again Novak rejects Harvey's attempts at kindness by destroying things in his apartment, then walking out. Novak returns to the street life only to see her child die and then she contracts syphilis herself. Ironically, she ends up in the hospital Harvey works at, where she dies in her spurned benefactor's arms. Harvey honors Novak's final wish by giving her a grand funeral. Broken by the events he has been subjected to in London, Harvey decides to return to Paris and once again take up a career in art. As he prepares to leave he is surprised to see Newman standing above him, apparently in love with him despite his tragic obsession with Novak. As the doomed pair, Novak and Harvey are passable but little more than that. Harvey looks too old for the role and fails to give his character much life, while Novak, though making a valiant attempt, never creates enough passion to make her role believable. Futher denying any dramatic potential is Forbes' unspired adaptation of Maugham's novel. Rather than probe the psychological makeup of the drama's players the script consistently chooses basic motivations with all the emotional convictions of a high school drama society production. Direction was begun by Hathaway but he wisely bowed out shortly after production was begun. Forbes was then tried out to helm his own work (he also appears in a minor nonspeaking role) but eventually Hughes was brought in to finish the film. The result was simple, straightforward storytelling which probably suited the material best. Considering the script quality and abilities of the cast, any stylized elaborations could have turned a mediocre picture into a turkey.

p, James Woolf; d, Ken Hughes, Henry Hathaway, Bryan Forbes; w, Forbes (based on the novel by W. Somerset Maugham); ph, Oswald Morris; m, Ron Goodwin; ed, Russell Lloyd; prod d, John Box; cos, Beatrice Dawson; makeup, George Frost.

Drama **(PR:O MPAA:NR)**

OF HUMAN HEARTS*½** (1938) 100m MGM bw

Walter Huston *(Ethan Wilkins)*, James Stewart *(Jason Wilkins)*, Beulah Bondi *(Mary Wilkins)*, Guy Kibbee *(Mr. George Ames)*, Charles Coburn *(Dr. Charles Shingle)*, John Carradine *(President Lincoln)*, Ann Rutherford *(Annie Hawks)*, Charley Grapewin *(Mr. Meeker)*, Gene Lockhart *(Quid)*, Leona Roberts *(Sister Clarke)*, Arthur Aylesworth *(Mr. Inchpin)*, Clem Bevans *(Elder Massey)*, Gene Reynolds *(Jason at Age 12)*, Leatrice Joy Gilbert *(Annie Hawks at Age 10)*, Sterling Holloway *(Chauncey at Age 18)*, Charles Peck *(Chauncey at Age 12)*, Robert McWade *(Dr. Crum)*, John Miljan *(Capt. Griggs)*, Rosina Galli *(Mrs. Ardsley)*, Anne O'Neal *(Mrs. Hawks)*, Esther Dale *(Mrs. Cantwell)*, Brenda Fowler *(Mrs. Ames)*, William Stack *(Salesman)*, Ward Bond, Frank McGlynn, Jr. *(Louts)*, Stanley Fields *(Horse Owner)*, Roger Moore *(Attendant)*, Guy Bates Post *(Horse Buyer)*, Jack Mulhall *(Soldier)*, Phillip Terry, Joe Forte *(Internes)*, Morgan Wallace *(Dr. Crandall)*.

Rural life in the Ohio Valley before the Civil War is the setting for Brown's superlative and poignant OF HUMAN HEARTS. Huston is a stern religious leader who forces his family to endure near poverty to set an example for his parishioners, and all this really does is make a drudge of his wife Bondi and compel his son—Reynolds as a boy, Stewart as a man—to resent and later dislike him. By the time Stewart reaches early manhood he yearns to break free of his father's stranglehold and go East to study medicine, but he is so impoverished that it is impossible. Bondi, however, defying her husband, sells off some of her dowry and finances her son's dream. Stewart becomes so engrossed with his own ambitions that he all but ignores his family and returns only when his father lies dying. He goes off to the Civil War as a doctor and Bondi, widowed, pines alone at home. Again, Stewart ignores the mother who has scrimped and saved and is now literally starving since Stewart has not even sent her enough money with which to live. Bondi, not having heard from Stewart, thinks he has been killed on the battlefield and writes President Lincoln, Carradine, to ask if he will see if her boy is alive or dead. Carradine discovers that Stewart is very much alive and sends for him. Gently but firmly Carradine reprimands Stewart for ignoring his mother in her time of need and sends him home on furlough. Stewart returns to the loving arms of Bondi, repentant and vowing she will never suffer again. Brown's direction is topnotch and he draws forth excellent performances from Huston, Bondi, and Stewart. Reynolds, playing Stewart as a boy, is also superb as are the wonderful supporting players, Kibbee, Grapewin, Rutherford, and Carradine as Lincoln. The story is on the melodramatic side and is often syrupy but Brown overcomes these inherent story line faults with a lively eye and spritely visuals.

p, John W. Considine, Jr.; d, Clarence Brown; w, Bradbury Foote (based on the story "Benefits Forgot" by Honore Morrow); ph, Clyde Devinna; m, Herbert Stothart; ed, Frank E. Hull; art d, Cedric Gibbons, Harry Oliver, Edwin B. Willis.

Drama **(PR:A MPAA:NR)**

OF LOVE AND DESIRE* (1963) 97m FOX c

Merle Oberon *(Katherine Beckman)*, Steve Cochran *(Steve Corey)*, Curt Jurgens *(Paul Beckman)*, John Agar *(Gus Cole)*, Steve Brodie *(Bill Maxton)*, Eduardo Noriega *(Mr. Dominguez)*, Rebecca Iturbide *(Mrs. Renard)*, Elsa Cardenas *(Mrs. Dominguez)*, Tony Carbajal *(Dr. Renard)*, Aurora Munoz *(Maria)*, Felix Gonzalez *(Engineer)*, Felipe Flores *(Julio)*.

OF LOVE AND DESIRE, Oberon's bizzare return to the screen after an absence of seven years, was shot in her actual 16th Century villa in Mexico, and tells the sordid tale of a socialite nymphomaniac. Oberon lives with her half-brother, Jurgens, who is sexually obsessed with her. Enter American engineer Cochran, whom Jurgens has hired for some mining operations. Soon Oberon seduces

Cochran, but sex turns to love, much to the dismay of Jurgens, who becomes insanely jealous. Jurgens tries to destroy the relationship by having Oberon's former lover, Agar, drop in. Agar tries to seduce Oberon, but she refuses. Desperate, he gets her drunk and rapes her. On awakening the next morning, Oberon attempts to slash her wrists, but is rescued by Cochran. Cochran assures her that he holds no malice and insists on marriage. Oberon begins packing and a distraught Jurgens confronts her with his obsessive desires, causing an upset Oberon to flee. Eventually Cochran finds her and they leave Mexico together. Overblown, badly written, and unintentionally funny.

p, Victor Stoloff; d, Richard Rush; w, Laslo Gorog, Rush (based on a story by Stoloff, Jacqueine Delessert); ph, Alex Phillips (Cinemascope, DeLuxe Color); m, Ronald Stein; ed, Harry Gerstad; art d, Roberto Silva; m/l, "Katherine's Theme," Stein (sung by Sammy Davis, Jr.).

Drama   **(PR:O MPAA:NR)**

OF MICE AND MEN***   (1939) 107m Hal Roach/UA bw

Burgess Meredith (George), Betty Field (Mae), Lon Chaney, Jr. (Lennie), Charles Bickford (Slim), Roman Bohnen (Candy), Bob Steele (Curley), Noah Beery, Jr. (Whit), Oscar O'Shea (Jackson), Granville Bates (Carlson), Leigh Whipper (Crooks), Leona Roberts (Aunt Clara), Helen Lynd (Susie), Barbara Pepper (2nd Girl), Henriette Kay (3rd Girl), Eddie Dunn (Bus Driver), Howard Mitchell (Sheriff), Whitney de Rhan, Baldy Cooke, Charles Watt, Jack Lawrence, Carl Pitti, John Beach (Ranch Hands).

Steinbeck's moving and power-packed story of two ranch hands trying to find a safe haven in a hostile world comes to the screen with penetrating compassion under the deft hand of director Milestone. Right from the opening credits, where Meredith and Chaney are shown fleeing a posse, the pace of the film is set and is maintained by Milestone who discarded overlaps and controlled his cameras with the precision of a bombardier. Having escaped the clutches of the law, Meredith and Chaney wander about the rural West, looking for work in the Depression era. They find odd jobs and hostility everywhere they go until they reach the San Joaquin Valley in California and a mean-minded barley ranch owner hires them as hands. They live in the bunkhouse with the other workers who soon realize that Chaney is dim-witted to the point of being non compos mentis and Meredith has, for inexplicable reasons, appointed himself Chaney's guardian. The two fantasize about owning their own small ranch and Chaney brightens at the thought of Meredith's promise that he can tend the rabbits and stroke their soft furry bodies. Meanwhile, the son of the owner, cruel and vicious Steele, begins bullying the much larger Chaney about, even though Bickford, the decent foreman, tries to shield the halfwit from Steele's sadistic attacks. The seething hatred deep in Steele has been implanted by his sexy wife, Field, who has dallied with some of his ranch hands in the past and, he suspects, even with foreman Bickford. Bohnen, another ranch worker who is missing a hand and is followed about by an ancient, smelly dog, overhears Meredith and Chaney talking about how they will soon "live off the fatta the lan' " and begs them to take him along with them when they get their little ranch. Bickford asks about Chaney's mental state and is told that the big fellow has a clouded brain "on accounta he'd been kicked in the head by a horse," The brawny Chaney does not know his own strength. He finds little animals and tries to keep them as pets but his affectionate strokes often turn to crushing and killing blows as his mind drifts. At the beginning Meredith finds him carrying about a dead mouse he has crushed to death and he later crushes a little puppy without knowing what he has done. But usually the giant is gentle and he cannot comprehend violence. Realizing that his wife has been looking for a healthy farm hand to satisfy her, and that Field has been flirting with Chaney, Steele barges into the bunkhouse and confronts the big man. He yells at the dumfounded Chaney and then begins to punch him viciously. Chaney does nothing but take one slashing punch after another from the vindictive Steele. Chaney looks to Meredith for guidance and Meredith shouts to his friend: "Fight him, Lennie, fight him!" Steele is like a windmill, throwing an avalanche of punches against the seemingly defenseless man, but finally Chaney scowls and grabs Steele's gloved hand in mid-swing, crushing it so that the sound of the cracking bones is heard by Meredith, Bickford, and the others. Steele screams in agony and then drops to the floor after Meredith tells Chaney to let him go. Later, when Field approaches the baffled Chaney in the barn, trying to seduce him, the giant begins stroking her hair, much the way he has stroked the puppy's fur, but he winds up killing her. Realizing what he has done and how "George will be mad at me," Chaney flees to the woods. Meredith runs ahead of a posse looking for Chaney and finds him first. He begins to tell him the tired story of how they will soon have their little ranch. As Chaney joyously nods his head, looking across a river, Meredith withdraws a gun and shoots his friend in the back of the head. This he has done to spare Chaney the anguish of a trial and resulting publicity where he will be held up to the world as a freak before he is executed. Though a grim and offbeat tale, OF MICE AND MEN is a noble morality tale that can be appreciated for its simplicity. The acting is faultless and Copland's score is magnificent. Steinbeck's THE GRAPES OF WRATH was brought to the screen under John Ford's masterful direction in the same year as this picture but neither suffered from the other's presence. Chaney is outstanding, as are Meredith, Bickford, and even B-film cowboy star Steele.

p&d, Lewis Milestone; w, Eugene Solow (based on the novel by John Steinbeck); ph, Nobert Brodine; m, Aaron Copland; ed, Bert Jordan; art d, Nicolai Remisoff; spec eff, Roy Seawright.

Drama   **(PR:O MPAA:NR)**

OF STARS AND MEN**   (1961) 53m Storyboard c

Voices of: Dr. Harlow Shapley, Mark Hubley, Hamp Hubley.

Evolution and man's place in the universe are explored in this charming animated fable, created by John and Faith Hubley. Using Dr. Harlow Shapley's book, Of Stars and Men, as a basis (a volume written "to tell the people in simple language what man is and where he is in the universe of atoms, protoplasms, stars, and

galaxies") the Hubleys begin their tale showing the evolution of the earth and its animal life. Man is introduced in the form of an arrogant boy who slowly comes to realize he's not alone in the universe. Though the ideas expressed in the story aren't anything new, the presentation is pure visual delight. The stylized pictures are brimming with humor and a touch of pathos. The soundtrack is well-crafted to the images, using the voice of the Hubley's children, Mark and Hamp, along with Dr. Shapley, as commentators of the various actions. OF STARS AND MEN is another standout in John Hubley's productive career. He had worked with Disney on such films as SNOW WHITE and DUMBO before leaving to help form UPA Productions. There he created such memorable cartoon characters as Gerald McBoing Boing and the irrepressible Mr. Maggo. In the late 1950s he left this studio to form his own Storyboard Productions, creating such animated pieces as ADVENTURES OF AN ASTERISK and WINDY DAY.

p, John, Faith Hubley; d, John Hubley; w, John, Faith Hubley, Harlow Shapley (based on the book Of Stars and Men by Shapley); ph, John Buehre (Eastmancolor); ed, Faith Hubley; md, Walter Trampler; animation d, William Littlejohn, Gary Mooney.

Animated Fantasy   **(PR:AAA MPAA:NR)**

OF UNKNOWN ORIGIN½   (1983, Can.) 88m David-Nesis-CFDC/WB c

Peter Weller (Bart), Jennifer Dale (Lorrie), Lawrence Dane (Eliot), Kenneth Welsh (James), Louis Del Grande (Clete), Shannon Tweed (Meg), Keith Knight (Salesman), Maury Chaykin (Dan), Leif Anderson (Peter), Jimmy Tapp (Meg's Father), Gayle Garfinkle (Janis), Earl Pennington (Thompson), Bronwen Mantel (Florence), Monik Nantel (Secretary), Jacklin Webb (News Vendor).

Strange, offbeat, and really not too bad thriller has Weller facing off against a horde of rats. After his wife and son go off on vacation, Weller is left in their New York townhouse, which he has personally renovated. His nemesis is a seemingly indestructable rat, a female—supposedly the more vicious half of the species. The battle grows into a full-fledged obsession, played with some real fervor by Weller. Though not for the weak of stomach, this is a well-done example of the rat-monster movie genre, told with a truly black sense of humor.

p, Claude Heroux; d, George Pan Cosmatos; w, Brian Taggert (based on the novel The Visitor by Chauncey G. Parker III); ph, Rene Verzier; m, Ken Wannberg; ed, Robert Silvi; prod d, Anne Pritchard; art d, Rosemarie McSherry; cos, Paul-Andre Guerin; spec eff, Jacques Godbout, Louis Craig; makeup, Stephan Dupuis.

Horror   **Cas.**   **(PR:O MPAA:R)**

OF WAYWARD LOVE   (1964, Ital./Ger.) 91m Spa Cinematografica-Eichberg/Pathe bw (L'AMORE DIFFICILE; EROTICA)

"The Women": Enrico Maria Salerno (Antonio), Catherine Spaak (Valeria), Claudia Mori (Bruna); "The Serpent": Lilli Palmer (Hilde Brenner), Bernhard Wicki (Prof. Brenner), Gastone Moschin (Police Marshal); "The Soldier": Nino Manfredi (Tomagra the Soldier), Fulvia Franco (The Widow).

Another Italian comedy anthology film about romance, sex, and marriage. "The Women" stars Salerno as a bored philanderer who, upset that his regular entourage of mistresses is too busy to see him, focuses his attentions on Mori, a casual fling from the past. She tells him that she is married, but joins him in bed anyway. Later, Salerno is seduced by Spaak, a young girl who informs him she was a virgin the next morning, leaving the experienced stud a bit confused by the day's events. "The Serpent" details frustrated wife Palmer's efforts to get her husband, Wicki, to pay some attention to her while on holiday in Sicily. After "crying wolf" over a deadly snake, which only annoys Wicki, Palmer finds herself stranded on the road when their car breaks down. She is aided by two truckdrivers, who take her to town, and still seeking to get her husband's attention, she cries rape. The men are arrested, but Wicki arrives and tells the police of his wife's recent problem and vows to pay more attention to her. "The Soldier" was directed by its star, Manfredi, who plays a lonely soldier trying to seduce gorgeous widow Franco while riding on a train. She ignores him, but when the other passengers leave, she makes love to him without saying a word. When the train arrives at the station, Franco leaves and Manfredi tries to follow, but he is stopped by her relatives who put her in a car and take her away.

p, Achille Piazzi; m, Piero Umiliani; ed, Eraldo Da Roma; "The Women": d, Sergio Sollima; w, Alessandro Continenza, Ettore Scola (based on a story by Ercole Patti); ph, Carlo Carlini; "The Serpent": d, Alberto Bonucci; w, Fabio Carpi, Guglielmo Santangelo, Renato Mainardi (based on a story by Mario Soldati); ph, Erico Meneczer; "The Soldier": d, Nino Manfredi; w, Fabio Carpi, Giuseppe Orlandini, Scola, Manfredi (based on a story by Italo Calvino); ph, Carlini.

Comedy   **(PR:O MPAA:NR)**

OFF LIMITS½   (1953) 89m PAR bw (GB: MILITARY POLICEMAN)

Bob Hope (Wally Hogan), Mickey Rooney (Herbert Tuttle), Marilyn Maxwell (Connie Curtis), Eddie Mayehoff (Karl Danzig), Stanley Clements (Bullet Bradley), Jack Dempsey (Himself), Marvin Miller (Vic Breck), John Ridgely (Lt. Cmdr. Parnell), Tom Harmon (Himself), Norman Leavitt (Chowhound), Art Aragon (Himself), Kim Spalding (Seaman Harker), Jerry Hausner (Fishy), Mike Mahoney (M.P. Huggins), Joan Taylor (Helen), Carolyn Jones (Deborah), Mary Murphy (Wac).

A fairly amusing comedy starring Hope as the manager of lightweight boxer Clements who has fought his way into the championship. Trouble arises, however, when Hope is forced to join the Army by his mobster partners, who want him to keep an eye on the pugilist, who has just been drafted. Clements turns out to be 4F, but Hope is not and gets inducted without Clements. In the Army, Hope is pestered by boxing hopeful Rooney, who wants the manager to make him a good boxer. Hope isn't interested until he learns that Rooney's aunt is the lovely Miss Maxwell, who runs the local nightclub. Desperate to strike up a relationship with Maxwell, Hope takes Rooney on in order to have an in with the aunt. Eventually, after lots of army gags involving MP's, Hope enters Rooney in a fight against Clements in an effort to get back at his ex-partners.

p, Harry Tugend; d, George Marshall; w, Hal Kanter, Jack Sher (based on a story by Kanter); ph, J. Peverell Marley; m, Van Cleave; ed, Arthur Schmidt; art d, Hal Pereira, Walter Tyler; m/l, "All About Love," Jay Livingston, Ray Evans (sung by Marilyn Maxwell, Bob Hope), "Military Policeman," Livingston, Evans (sung by Hope, Mickey Rooney).

Comedy   **(PR:A MPAA:NR)**

OFF THE BEATEN TRACK   (SEE: BEHIND THE EIGHT BALL, 1942)

OFF THE DOLE**½   (1935, Brit.) 89m Mancunian bw

George Formby (John Willie), Beryl Formby (Grace, Charm, and Ability), Constance Shotter (Irene), Dan Young (The Inimitable Dude), James Plant (Crisp and Debonair), Stan Pell (The Most Inoffensive Parson), Stan Little (Little Jack), Tully Comber (Measured For His Part), Clifford McLaglen (A Villian and Proud Of It), Wally Patch (Revels In His Part), The Twilight Blondes, The Boy Choristers, The London Babes, Arthur L. Ward and His Band.

Unable to hang onto a job for various reasons, Formby becomes a detective after inheriting his late uncle's investigation business. Though wholly unsuited for the job, Formby throws himself into the work and catches McLaglen, a big-time crook who's evaded the cops for years. Cute comedy that marked a turning point in Formby's career. This was the second Manchester-based effort for Formby, a Lancashire lad who afterwards forsook the north of England for the bright lights of London's soundstages. Portions of OFF THE DOLE later appeared in several British compilation films.

p, John E. Blakely; d, Arthur Mertz; w, Mertz, George Formby.

Comedy   **(PR:A MPAA:NR)**

OFF THE RECORD**   (1939) 62m WB bw

Pat O'Brien (Thomas "Breezy" Elliott), Joan Blondell (Jane Morgan), Bobby Jordan (Mickey Fallon), Alan Baxter (Joe Fallon), William B. Davidson (Scotty), Morgan Conway (Lou Baronette), Clay Clement (Jaeggers), Selmer Jackson (Detective Mendall), Addison Richards (Brand), Pierre Watkin (Barton), Joe King (Brown), Douglas Wood (J.W.), Armand Kaliz (Chatteau), Sarah Padden (Mrs. Fallon), Howard Hickman (Doctor), Mary Gordon (Mrs. Finnegan), Lottie Williams (Woman), David Durand (Blackie), Norman Phillips, Jr. (Nick), Tommy Bupp (Boy), Wade Boteler (Deputy), Sibyl Harris (Woman), Stanley Fields (Big Bruiser), Emmett Vogan (Priest), Al Hill, Jr. (Kid), Frank Coghlan, Jr. (Copy Boy), William Gould (Swede Captain), Emory Parnell (Policeman), Guy Usher (Inspector), Barbara Pepper (Flossie the Telephone Operator), Charles Seel (Veterinary), Pat Flaherty (Bartender), Dick Rush, Galan Galt (Railroad Cops), Isabel Withers, Betty Mack, Maris Wrixon, Ila Rhodes, Fern Barry, Caroline Clare, Alice Connors (Telephone Operators).

Blondell and O'Brien star as newspaper reporters (romantically involved) who inadvertently send young boy Jordan to reform school after they write an expose on the illegal slot-machine racket the boy was a spotter for. Guilt-ridden, Blondell convinces O'Brien that they should marry in order to adopt Jordan and get him out of reform school. Maudlin material, but Blondell and O'Brien's capable presences carry the weak script.

d, James Flood; w, Niven Busch, Lawrence Kimble, Earl Baldwin (based on the story "Fourth Estate" by Saul Elkins, Sally Sandlin); ph, Charles Rosher; m, Adolph Deutsch; ed, Thomas Richards; md, Leo F. Forbstein.

Drama   **(PR:A MPAA:NR)**

OFF THE WALL*½   (1977) 83m Gregory bw

Harvey Waldman (John Little), Gary Schnell (Dan), John French (Rob), Katy Roberts (Jane), Judy Feil (Betsy), Pat Crowley (Lennie Howe).

Low-budget independent film that suffers from a film-schoolish concept. Story involves a television documentary crew filming a day in the life of Waldman. Getting more than they bargained for, the crew members film Waldman robbing a bank and then he steals their camera and shoots his own film about his exploits as a fugitive. Eventually he leaves the camera in a bus terminal. Interesting but naively scripted and executed.

p, James Gregory; d, Rich King; w, King, Marly Swick, Harvey Waldman; ph, Chris Beaver, Jon Else, Judy Irving; ed, Gregory.

Drama   **(PR:C MPAA:NR)**

OFF THE WALL**½   (1983) 85m Hot Dog/Jensen Farley c

Paul Sorvino (Warden), Rosanna Arquette (Governor's Daughter), Patrick Cassidy (Randy), Billy Hufsey (Rico), Ralph Wilcox (Johnny), Dick Chudnow (Miskewicz), Monte Markham (Governor), Brianne Leary (Jennifer), Mickey Gilley, Gary Goodrow, Biff Manard, Stu Gilliam, Jenny Neumann, Lewis Arquette, Jeana Tomasino, Roselyn Royce.

After being framed on phony charges, two hitchhikers are jailed. They escape, which leads to a wild chase in this southern- produced comedy. One of several smaller features Arquette made before achieving some popularity in the film world with DESPERATELY SEEKING SUSAN. Look also for an appearance by Mickey Gilley, well-known country singer and the proprietor of the bar made famous in URBAN COWBOY.

p, Frank Mancuso; d, Rick Friedberg; w, Ron Kurz, Dick Chudnow, Friedberg; ph, Donald R. Morgan (Movielab Color); m, Dennis McCarthy; ed, George Hively; prod d, Richard Sawyer.

Comedy   **Cas.**   **(PR:O MPAA:R)**

OFF TO THE RACES**   (1937) 59m FOX bw

Slim Summerville (Uncle George), Jed Prouty (John Jones), Shirley Deane (Bonnie Jones), Spring Byington (Mrs. John Jones), Russell Gleason (Herbert Thompson), Kenneth Howell (Jack Jones), George Ernest (Roger Jones), June Carlson (Lucy Jones), Florence Roberts (Granny Jones), Billy Mahan (Bobby Jones), Ann Gillis (Winnie Mae), Fred "Snowflake" Toones (Ebbie), Chick Chandler (Spike), Ruth Gillette (Rosabelle).

This time out the Jones family, once again led by Prouty, help out uncle Summerville who has just purchased a trotting horse and intends to ride it in a race at the fairgrounds. When Summerville's ex-wife arrives in search of alimony, Summerville flees, leaving Prouty to ride the steed to victory. (See JONES FAMILY series, Index.)

p, Max Golden; d, Frank R. Strayer; w, Robert Ellis, Helen Logan (based on characters created by Katherine Kavanaugh); ph, Barney McGill; ed, Alex Troffey; md, Samuel Kaylin; m/l, "Meet the Family," L. Wolfe Gilbert, Felix Bernard.

Drama/Comedy   **(PR:A MPAA:NR)**

OFFBEAT**½   (1961, Brit.) 72m BL bw (AKA: THE DEVIL INSIDE)

William Sylvester (Steve Layton/Steve Ross), Mai Zetterling (Ruth Lombard), John Meillon (Johnny Remick), Anthony Dawson (James Dawson), Neil McCarthy (Leo Farrell), Harry Baird (Gill Hall), John Phillips (Supt. Gault), Victor Brooks (Inspector Adams), Diana King (Maggie Dawson), Gerard Heinz (Jake), Ronald Adam (J.B. Wykeham), Neil Wilson (Pat Ryan), Joseph Furst (Paul Varna), Nan Munro (Sarah Bennett), Anthony Baird (Constable).

Good programmer starring Sylvester as a Scotland Yard agent assigned to infiltrate and expose the members of a gang of gem thieves. Unfortunately, Sylvester falls in love with Zetterling, the young widow of one of the gang members, and he develops a camaraderie with the group. When she discovers his true identity and threatens to expose him, Sylvester denounces the police and decides to continue his life of crime. This is not to be, however, when he unwittingly allows the gang to be played right into the hands of the police.

p, E.M. Smedley Aston; d, Cliff Owens; w, Peter Barnes; ph, Geoffrey Faithfull; m, Ken Jones; ed, Anthony Gibbs; art d, George Provis.

Crime   **(PR:A MPAA:NR)**

OFFENDERS, THE zero   (1980) 100m B Movies c

Adele Bertei (Laura), Bill Rice (Dr. Moore), John Lurie (The Lizard), Johnny O'Kane, Robin Winters, Pat Place, Laura Kennedy, Judy Nylon, Marcia Resnick, Evan Lurie, Walter Lure, Anna Sui, Barvara Klar, Cynthia Womersley, Diego Cortez, Lydia Lunch, Kristian Hoffman, Bradley Field, Edit De Ak, Robert Smith, Terry Robinson, Clio Young, Harry Spitz, Gerard Hovagimyan, Kirsten Bates, Scott B., Kristof Kolhofer.

The New Wave music and fashion movement produced many revolutionary ideas, but unfortunately one of the most popular was that talent wasn't a necessity for working artists. Such is the case with this film, created as a "punk melodrama" and originally shown in serial format at Max's Kansas City, one of the tres chic New York punk clubs. Shot on Super 8 film (and with all the aesthetic qualities of the average low-budget home movie), the story is typical for the punk movement, a quirky tale of young turks involved with the kidnaped Bertei and her father, Rice. Though there's an occasional offbeat moment or two, these bright spots are lost in the muddle of out-of-focus sequences and confused by the amateur acting being fobbed off as alienation. The color and clothing styles are typical for New Wavers, but one could find the same visual treats at the local art school. This is a typical example of no-talents wrapping themselves in the all-protective flag of "art" to shield themselves from any intelligent criticism of their so-called work. Just the same, THE OFFENDERS is notable for the early screen appearances by musicians-cum-actors Adele Bertei and John Lurie, who would present more convincing portrayals in BORN IN FLAMES and STRANGER THAN PARADISE respectively.

d,w&ph, Scott B, Beth B; m, Bob Mason, Adele Bertei, Lydia Lunch, John Lurie, Scott B, Beth B, Terry Burns, Ed Steinberg, Alley.

Drama   **(PR:O MPAA:NR)**

OFFENSE, THE***   (1973, Brit.) 112m UA c (AKA: SOMETHING LIKE THE TRUTH)

Sean Connery (Detective Sgt. Johnson), Trevor Howard (Lt. Cartwright), Vivien Merchant (Maureen Johnson), Ian Bannen (Baxter), Derek Newark (Jessard), John Hallam (Panton), Peter Bowles (Cameron), Ronald Radd (Lawson), Anthony Sagar (Hill), Howard Goorney (Lambeth), Richard Moore (Garrett), Maxine Gordon (Janie).

Connery is superb in this psychological drama in which he plays a police officer who overzealously beats accused child molester Bannen to death during an interrogation. Eventually it is revealed that Connery lost control due to a traumatic molestation incident in his own childhood. A powerful and complex performance by Connery is somewhat weakened by Lumet's typically stiff and stagey direction, which tends to sap the life out of the film.

p, Denis O'Dell; d, Sidney Lumet; w, John Hopkins; ph, Gerry Fisher (Deluxe Color); ed, John Victor Smith; art d, John Clark; cos, Vangie Harrison.

Drama   **(PR:O MPAA:R)**

OFFERING, THE**½   (1966, Can.) 80m Secter c

Kee Faun (Mei-lin), Ratch Wallace (Gordon), Ellen Yamasaki (Jung-ling), Marvin Goldhar (Jack), Gene Mark (Tien).

When the Peking Opera visits Toronto, a Canadian stagehand falls in love with one of the principal singers. He pursues the romance despite the singer's initial shyness. However, what little chance their love has to succeed is ultimately doomed, for the troupe eventually returns to Red China. Though the drama is a simplistic story, the cast bring a certain fresh quality to their roles, helped along by the quick-paced direction that is so often found in minor independent features like this. Some sharp photography makes good use of the Toronto locations. Producer-director Secter was 23 years old when he made this film.

p&d, David Secter; w, Secter, Martin Lager, Iain Ewing, Jan Steen, Gillian Lennox; ph, Stanley Lipinski; m, Paul Hoffert; ed, Tony Lower; cos, Warren Hartman.

Drama   (PR:C   MPAA:NR)

OFFICE GIRL, THE* (1932, Brit.) 80m Gainsborough/RKO bw (AKA: SUNSHINE SUSIE)

Renate Muller (*Susie Surster*), Jack Hulbert (*Herr Hasel*), Owen Nares (*Herr Arvray*), Morris Harvey (*Klapper*), Sybil Grove (*Secretary*), Gladys Hamer (*Maid*), Daphne Scorer (*Elsa*), Barbara Gott.

Banal remake of the German film PRIVATE SECRETARY (this was the third time) starring Muller as the proverbial country girl who goes to the big city seeking fame and fortune by working in a bank. She catches the eye of bank president Hulbert, who poses as a lowly clerk to meet her, and they are soon blissfully happy. Muller, who is German and sounds it, is miscast against Hulbert who is very British in a film supposedly set in Vienna. Presented as a musical, the songs and production numbers are weak and the script hopeless. A total misfire. Songs: "Today I Feel So Happy," "Just Because I Lost My Heart to You," "I'll Get There in the End," "I Have My Aunt Eliza" (Paul Abraham, Desmond Carter).

p, Michael Balcon; d, Victor Saville; w, Angus Macphaill, Robert Stevenson, Saville, Noel Wood-Smith (based on the play "The Private Secretary" by Franz Schultz, Szomahazy); ph, Mutz Greenbaum; m, Paul Abraham; ed, Ian Dalrymple.

Musical   (PR:A   MPAA:NR)

OFFICE GIRLS zero (1974) 86m International c

Karin Field, Emely Reuer, R. Glemnitz.

The affairs and sexual intrigues which transpire within the confines of a seemingly innocent business office are chronicled in this waste of time. It's about all one could expect from a film carrying a title such as this one.

p, Wolf C. Hartwig; d, Ernst Hofbauer.

Drama   (PR:O   MPAA:R)

OFFICE PICNIC, THE*** (1974, Aus.) 85m Tom Cowan bw

John Wood (*Clyde*), Kate Fitzpatrick (*Mara*), Phillip Deamer (*Peter*), Patricia Kennedy (*Mrs. Rourke*), Gay Steele (*Elly*), Ben Gabriel (*The Boss*), Max Cullen (*Paddy*).

Charming and well-made low-budget Australian film about the employees of the Public Service Department whose unbelievable boredom is broken by the much anticipated company picnic. At the picnic all the office tensions are released and it is a day of true confessions and the releasing of repressed passions. A witty, touching, and insightful look at the office worker.

p,d&w, Tom Cowan; ph, Michael Edols; m, Don Mow; ed, Kit Guyatt.

Drama/Comedy   (PR:C   MPAA:NR)

OFFICE SCANDAL, THE*½ (1929) 70m Pathe Exchange bw

Phyllis Haver (*Jerry Cullen*), Raymond Hatton (*Pearson*), Margaret Livingston (*Lillian Tracy*), Leslie Fenton (*Andy Corbin*), Jimmie Adams (*Delaney*), Jimmy Aldine (*Freddie*), Dan Wolheim.

Early talkie (practically a silent) starring Haver as a newspaper reporter who persuades a judge to release the suspected killer of a wealthy racetrack dandy, because he used to be a newshound who has become a drunk. Hatton, the suspect, gets a job on Haver's paper. The city editor, however, is not convinced and does some digging himself. At the morgue he learns of Hatton's close relationship with the dead man's widow, vampish Livingston, and he builds a strong case against Hatton, which Haver overturns in a neat coup for a scoop in the end. THE OFFICE SCANDAL was to be the next to last movie ever made by the 1920's popular sex queen, tall, blonde Haver, before she married a New York millionaire and retired from the screen.

d, Paul Stein; w, Paul Gangelin, Jack Jungmeyer; ph, Jake Badaracco; ed, Doane Harrison.

Drama   (PR:A   MPAA:NR)

OFFICE WIFE, THE** (1930) 59m WB bw

Dorothy Mackaill (*Anne Murdock*), Lewis Stone (*Lawrence Fellows*), Hobart Bosworth (*Mr. McGowan*), Blanche Frederici (*Kate Halsey*), Joan Blondell (*Catherine Murdock*), Natalie Moorhead (*Linda Fellows*), Brooks Benedict (*Mr. Jameson*), Dale Fuller (*Miss Andrews*), Walter Merrill (*Ted O'Hara*).

Melodramatic tale of office hanky-panky starring breezy Mackaill as the secretary of the much older Stone, who dumps her boy friend to freely seduce the married man, upon learning that bored wife Moorhead has taken up with younger men, allows himself to become involved with Mackaill. As luck would have it, Moorhead soon files for divorce, and everybody is happy, including the Hays Office. Blondell's second film for Warner Bros. (her first, SINNER'S HOLIDAY, was released after THE OFFICE WIFE).

d, Lloyd Bacon; w, Charles Kenyon (based on the novel by Faith Baldwin); ph, William Rees; ed, George Marsh.

Drama   (PR:A   MPAA:NR)

OFFICER AND A GENTLEMAN, AN***½ (1982) 126m Lorimar/ PAR c

Richard Gere (*Zack Mayo*), Debra Winger (*Paula Pokrifki*), David Keith (*Sid Worley*), Robert Loggia (*Byron Mayo*), Lisa Blount (*Lynette Pomeroy*), Lisa Eilbacher (*Casey Seeger*), Louis Gossett, Jr. (*Sgt. Emil Foley*), Tony Plana (*Emiliano Della Serra*), Harold Sylvester (*Perryman*), David Caruso (*Topper Daniels*), Victor French (*Joe Pokrifki*), Grace Zabriskie (*Esther Pokrifki*), Tommy Petersen (*Young Zack*), Mara Scott Wood (*Bunny*), David Greenfield (*Schneider*), Dennis Rucker (*Donny*), Jane Wilbur (*Nellie Rufferwell*), Buck Welcher (*Thraxton*), Vern Taylor (*Tom Worley*), Elizabeth Rogers (*Betty Worley*), David R. Marshall, Gary C. Stillwell (*Drill Instructors*), Tee Dennard (*Dilbert Dunker Instructor*), Norbert M. Murray (*Altitude Instructor*), Daniel Tyler (*New Recruit*), William Graves (*Capt. Graves*), Brian D. Ford (*Aerodynamics Instructor*), Keith J. Harr (*Air Officer Candidate*), Pia Boyer, Danna Kiesel (*Paula's Sisters*), Marvin Goatcher (*Marvin Goatcher*), John Laughlin (*Troy*), Jeffrey P. Rondeau (*His Friend*), Michael Lee Bolger (*Man in Crowd*), Mark L. Graves (*Bartender*), Meleesa Wyatt, Jo Anna Keane (*Prostitutes*), Michael C. Pavey.

Lou Gossett (who only took the "junior" after his dad died) waited for a lifetime to get this role and he made the most of it, completely acting rings around everyone else in the picture and getting his first Oscar, as Best Supporting Actor. Following a bit part in an Abraham Lincoln High School (in Coney Island) play, he was about the 450th teenager to audition for a Broadway drama called "Take a Giant Step" and he got the starring role at the age of 17. After getting excellent reviews, he decided that to live in Manhattan would not be right for someone that young, so he commuted the hour by train and occasionally stayed in a friend's apartment in the city on matinee days. His next role was as an office boy in "The Desk Set" and, oddly enough, he was bypassed for the film versions of both pictures. He was an excellent athlete and received a basketball scholarship at N.Y.U., which he attended while working in and around New York in various shows and paying his dues. With AN OFFICER AND A GENTLEMAN, at long last, he became a full-fledged star. Gere is a slum boy who leaves his home and his drunken father, Loggia, to enter the 13-week cadet course prior to navy flight training. It's grueling, difficult, and strips the plebes of their pride, as they must face up to a tough sergeant, Gossett, who takes no backtalk and is determined to make these sniveling kids into officers and gentlemen, or wash them out quickly. Writer Stewart knew of what he spoke, as he'd been a Navy officer and drew upon his own experiences to create this screenplay. Gere and Gossett are at odds immediately and most of the center of the film has to do with their battles. On a brief leave, Gere meets Winger, who works at a local mill and wants someone to take her away from this "Norma Rae" life. Meanwhile, Gere's pal, Keith, meets millworker Blount (in a fine debut) and the couples become a foursome. Some false moments of drama where there should not have been any, as well as a few scenes where the acting gets out of hand, but Gossett is the force throughout and holds the picture together with his presence. At the end, Gere and Winger get together when Gere arrives, like a knight in naval armor, to carry her from the mill. Keith and Blount argue, part, and he commits suicide when she spurns him. Gere challenges Gossett to a fight and Gossett welcomes the confrontation and takes Gere apart, proving again that old age and wisdom will beat youth and enthusiasm every time. Gere graduates, after experiencing some doubts, and watches as Gossett dresses down the new recruits with the same disdain he showed Gere's class upon their arrival. One of Gere's best jobs, in a career that has been spotty at best and included AMERICAN GIGOLO, YANKS, and KING DAVID. Winger was nominated for an Oscar as Best Actress and was on the verge of becoming a major figure in films, which she did with her work in the overrated TERMS OF ENDEARMENT. The song, "Up Where We Belong" (Nitzsche, Buffy St. Marie, Will Jennings) won an Oscar.

p, Martin Elfand; d, Taylor Hackford; w, Douglas Day Stewart; ph, Donald Thorin (Metrocolor); m, Jack Nitzsche; ed, Peter Zinner; prod d, Philip M. Jeffries; art d, John Cartwright.

Drama   Cas.   (PR:O   MPAA:R)

OFFICER AND THE LADY, THE*½ (1941) 59m COL bw

Rochelle Hudson (*Helen Regan*), Bruce Bennett (*Bob Conlon*), Roger Pryor (*Johnny Davis*), Richard Fiske (*Ace Quinn*), Sidney Blackmer (*Blake Standish*), Tom Kennedy (*Bumps O'Neil*), Oscar O'Shea (*Dan Regan*), Joe McGuinn (*Frank*), Charles Wilson (*Capt. Hart*), William Hall (*Dawson*).

First feature film directed by Hollywood gag man Sam White was a routine police story starring hard-boiled Hudson as the girl friend of policeman Bennett, who hedges from a romantic commitment to his man because her father, O'Shea, also a cop, was crippled in the line of duty. Bennett, however, is luckier than the father and is able to smash a crime gang and rescue Hudson and her dad from the clutches of an escaped convict without receiving a scratch.

p, Leon Barsha; d, Sam White; w, Lambert Hillyer, Joseph Hoffman (based on a story by Hillyer); ph, George Meehan; ed, Richard Fantl; md, M.W. Stoloff; art d, Lionel Banks.

Crime   (PR:A   MPAA:NR)

OFFICER O'BRIEN*½ (1930) 72m Pathe bw

William Boyd (*Bill O'Brien*), Ernest Torrence (*John P. O'Brien*), Dorothy Sebastian (*Ruth Dale*), Russell Gleason (*Johnny Dale*), Clyde Cook (*Limo Lewis*), Ralf Harolde (*Mike Patello*), Arthur Housman (*Tony Zurick*), Paul Hurst (*Capt. Antrim*), Tom Maloney (*Detective*), Toyo Fujita (*Kono*).

Boyd stars as an honest cop who has trouble living with the fact that his father, Torrence, is a gangster. The old man redeems himself, however, when he kills the evil head of the gang. Boyd vows to quit the force to avoid any more embarrassment, but when duty calls, he answers. The skillful directorial touch of former screen and gag writer Garnett keeps the film engrossing throughout.

d, Tay Garnett; w, Tom Buckingham; ph, Arthur Miller; ed, Jack Ogilvie; art d, Edward Jewell; set d, Theodore Dickson; cos, Gwen Wakeling.

Crime   (PR:A   MPAA:NR)

OFFICER 13*   (1933) 62m AA/FD bw

Monte Blue, Lila Lee, Seena Owen, Charles Delaney, Robert Ellis, Frances Rich, Joseph Girard, Jackie Searle, Mickey McGuire, Lloyd Ingraham, Florence Roberts, George Humbert, Dot Meyberg, Charles O'Malley, Alan Cavan, Edward Cooper.

Rich and bored thrill-seeker Lee finds more than she bargained for when she hangs around gangsters for kicks. Mediocre story is saved from obscurity by the careful work of the veteran Lee and tough guy lover Blue.

d, George Melford; w, Frances Hyland (based on a story by Paul Edwards); ph, Harry Neumann, Tom Galligan; ed, Leete Brown; art d, Gene Hornbostel.

Crime   (PR:A   MPAA:NR)

OFFICER'S MESS, THE**½   (1931, Brit.) 98m PAR bw

Richard Cooper (Tony Turnbull), Harold French (Budge Harbottle), Elsa Lanchester (Cora Melville), Mary Newland (Kitty), Max Avieson (Bolton), Margery Binner (Phoebe), George Bellamy (Inspector Bedouin), Annie Esmond (Mrs. Makepiece), Fewlass Llewellyn (Adm. Harbottle), Helen Haye (Mrs. Harbottle), Faith Bennett (Ann Telford), Gordon Begg.

To make the man she loves jealous, actress Lanchester poses as a Navy officer's wife. However, an unexpected twist complicates Lanchester's plot when her jewels turn up missing. An unassuming comedy from England, typical for the period.

p, Harry Rowson; d, Manning Haynes; w, Douglas Hoare, Eliot Stannard (based on a play by Hoare, Sidney Blow).

Comedy   (PR:A   MPAA:NR)

O'FLYNN, THE   (SEE: FIGHTING O'FLYNN, THE, 1949)

OGGI, DOMANI E DOPODOMANI, 1968   (SEE:
KISS THE OTHER SHEIK, 1968, Ital./Fr.)

OGGI, DOMANI E DOPODOMANI, 1968   (SEE:
MAN WITH THE BALLOONS, THE, 1968, Fr./Ital.)

OGNUNO PER SE   (SEE: RUTHLESS FOUR, THE, 1969, Ital./Ger.)

OH, ALFIE   (SEE: ALFIE DARLING, 1975, Brit.)

OH BOY!**   (1938, Brit.) 73m ABF bw

Albert Burdon (Percy Flower), Mary Lawson (June Messenger), Bernard Nedell (Angelo Tonelli), Jay Laurier (Horatio Flower), Robert Cochran (Albert Bolsover), Edmon Ryan (Butch), Maire O'Neill (Mrs. Baggs), Syd Walker (Sergeant), Charles Carson (Governor), Jerry Verno (Shopwalker), John Wood (Man), Billy Milton (Conductor), Edmund Dalby, Boris Ranevsky.

After taking a special formula in hopes of turning into a caveman, scientist Burdon instead reverts to a childlike state of consciousness. This man-child overhears the plans of three American crooks to steal the Crown Jewels, and upon returning to his normal state, is able to stop the crooks in time. Fairly witless low-budget British comedy with an inane gimmick.

p, Walter C. Mycroft; d, Albert de Courville; w, Dudley Leslie (based on a story by Douglas Furber).

Comedy   (PR:A   MPAA:NR)

OH BROTHERHOOD   (SEE: FRATERNITY ROW, 1977)

OH! CALCUTTA! zero   (1972) 108m Elkins/Cinemation c

Raina Barrett, Mark Dempsey, Samantha Harper, Patricia Hawkins, Bill Macy, Mitchell McGuire, Gary Rethmeier, Margo Sappington, Nancy Tribush, George Welbes.

OH! CALCUTTA! is probably better remembered as the first nude musical comedy revue to play off Broadway, rather than the hapless film presentation this turkey is. Originally shown in theaters via a special closed-circuit television broadcast, the resulting videotape was cleaned up of technical problems and rereleased in theaters two years later. They needn't have bothered. Though controversial for live theater, nudity in the cinema was no longer shocking or daring, thus making this somewhat of a dinosaur. Unimaginatively photographed, with a tame treatment of the show's most controversial elements, the result plays more like a third-grader's jokes about sex rather than a sophisticated adult revue. Considering the writing talents involved (Sam Shepard, Jules Feiffer, and John Lennon among others) one might have hoped for better results than this. Sketches include a newlywed couple who hope for a better sex life with the husband ending up with a mannequin. Another has some self-induced fantasies of a male trio destroyed by a television projection of "The Lone Ranger." It's not just that this film fails on its own level: OH! CALCUTTA! desperately pretends to be something it woefully is not, which makes it all the more repellent.

p, Patrick Pleven; d, Gillaume Martin Aucion; w, Jules Feiffer, Dan Greenburg, John Lennon, Jacques Levy, Leonard Melfi, David Newman/Robert Benton, Sam Shepard, Clovis Trouille, Kenneth Tynan, Sherman Yellen (based on the theatrical revue devised by Tynan); ph, Jerry Sarcone, Frank Biondo, Arnold Giordano (Technicolor); ed, Frank Herold; art d, Eugene Gurlitz; ch, Margo Sappington; m/ l, Robert Dennis, Peter Schickele, Stanley Walden.

Musical Revue   Cas.   (PR:O   MPAA:PG)

OH DAD, POOR DAD, MAMA'S HUNG YOU IN THE CLOSET AND I'M FEELIN' SO SAD*½   (1967) 86m Seven Arts/PAR c

Rosalind Russell (Mme. Rosepettle), Robert Morse (Jonathan), Barbara Harris (Rosalie), Hugh Griffith (Commodore Roseabove), Jonathan Winters (Dad/Narrator), Lionel Jeffries (Airport Commander), Cyril Delavanti (Hawkins), Hiram Sherman (Breckenduff), George Kirby (Moses), Janis Hansen (The Other Woman).

The title of this movie was far longer than the lines of people waiting to rush in to

see it. This was one of the all-time busts at the box office, but it did have its moments. Based on Arthur Kopit's play, they held up release of the film for quite a while until a new director (Mackendrick) came in to shoot a prolog and some other scenes in a vain attempt to make some sense out of the shambles. It didn't help. A terrific cast was hampered by the screenplay (and the original idea) and even a later narration by two of the best gagmen around, McCormick and Baker, couldn't raise the level of humor. Russell is the domineering mother of Morse. The two go to the Caribbean (Jamaica) with her collection of Venus flytraps and a coffin in which resides the stuffed body of her dead husband, Winters (who narrates this film from On High). Morse is a whipped son and Russell wants to get him to stand on his own feet. To that end, she fixes him up with Harris, a sexy woman who will babysit the 25-year-old. Meanwhile, Russell is after wealthy Griffith, an old rakehell. Morse secretly looks at some of Russell's old home movies which she is showing to Griffith and is so shocked that he responds by wrecking everything she owns in the next room. Harris comes into the room and tries to seduce Morse and won't stop, even when Winters' stuffed body comes out of the coffin and falls on top of them. Morse proceeds to strangle Harris (in a substitution for Russell, or so it seems) to death and then exits. Russell marries Griffith and comes back to the house to see what's transpired. There's a chase and Griffith dies of a heart attack in an attempt to save Morse, who is in a mad motorboat which he cannot control. Morse comes back to Russell, who is now in mourning for her second husband, and she leaves the island with her assemblage and two coffins. Meanwhile, Winters' ghostly persona comments on the activities and goes back to Heaven or wherever. Everybody mugs unmercifully and there's hardly a joke that doesn't wheeze. Neil Hefti's score was taken, almost en toto, and used for another film, A NEW LEAF, as Paramount was trying to salvage something, anything, out of this disaster. What they were attempting was lost. A black comedy it ain't, because the very word "comedy" should indicate some laughter. As it was, this picture was slightly funnier than MEDEA, but not much. The only reason to see it is to witness such fine performers running around like mice in a maze trying to figure out how to exit. Winters worked on the film only a few days and tried mightily to impart some laughter with his narration, but the film was unfixable, as they never had the right slant on it from the start.

p, Ray Stark, Stanley Rubin; d, Richard Quine, Alexander Mackendrick; w, Ian Bernard, Pat McCormick, Herbert Baker (based on the play by Arthur L. Kopit); ph, Geoffrey Unsworth (Technicolor); m, Neal Hefti; ed, Warren Low, David Wages; art d, Phil Jeffries; set d, William Kiernan; cos, Galanos, Howard Shoup; spec eff, Charles Spurgeon, Farciot Edouart; makeup, Robert Schiffer.

Comedy   Cas.   (PR:C   MPAA:NR)

OH DADDY!*½   (1935, Brit.) 75m Gainsborough/GAV bw

Leslie Henson (Lord Pye), Frances Day (Benita de Lys), Robertson Hare (Rupert Boddy), Barry Mackay (Jimmy Ellison), Marie Lohr (Lady Pye), Alfred Drayton (Uncle Samson), Tony de Lungo (Count Duval), Daphne Courtney (Phillis Pye).

British "naughty" farce starring Henson as a hypocritical moralist and member of the local Purity League, who, when he misses his train to attend a meeting of the conservative society, winds up in a cabaret where he is led astray by a showgirl who turns out to be the stepdaughter he had never met. After a wild night on the town, Henson changes his views on life among the misbehaving. A fast and furious little farce.

p, Michael Balcon; d, Graham Cutts, Austin Melford; w, Melford.

Comedy   (PR:A   MPAA:NR)

OH DOCTOR**   (1937) 67m UNIV bw

Edward Everett Horton (Edward J. Billop), Donrue Leighton (Helen Frohman), William Hall (Rodney Cummings), Eve Arden (Shirley Truman), Thurston Hall ("Doc" Erasmus Thurston), Catherine Doucet (Martha Striker), William Demarest (Marty Short), Edward Brophy (Meg Smith), Minerva Urecal (Death Watch Mary Mackleforth), Wilson Benge (Butler), James Donlan (Mr. Stoddard), Kitty McHugh (Nurse), Cornelius Keefe (Ship's Officer), Ben Taggart (Policeman), Edward Le Saint (Dr. Evans), Lloyd Ingraham (Dr. Bower), Henry Roquemore (Auto Salesman), Frank B. Hammond (Patient), Carol Halloway (Woman), Heinie Conklin, Charley Sullivan (Men).

Nervous wreck Horton saves this macabre comedy in which he stars as a hypochondriac conned by crooks who offer him $50,000 that he can spend immediately if he signs over his soon-to-be-inherited fortune of $500,000 to them (Horton is afraid he'll die before he sees the money). Horton's nurse, Leighton, however, instills a new will to live in her boss through her affections, and they devise a plot to regain the money. Horton threatens to commit suicide unless the crooks give him back his agreement with them (his suicide would nullify the contract).

p, Edmund Grainger; d, Raymond B. McCarey; w, Harry Clork, Brown Holmes (based on the play by Harry Leon Wilson); ph, Milton Krasner; ed, Bernard W. Burton; md, Lou Forbes; art d, Jack Otterson; spec eff, John P. Fulton.

Comedy   (PR:A   MPAA:NR)

OH, FOR A MAN!**½   (1930) 78m FOX bw

Jeanette MacDonald (Carlotta Manson), Reginald Denny (Barney McGann), Marjorie White (Totsy Franklin), Warren Hymer (Pug Morin the "Walloping Wop"), Alison Skipworth (Laura), Albert Conti (Peck), Bela Lugosi (Frescatti), Andre Cheron (Costello), William B. Davidson (Kerry Stokes), Bodil Rosing (Masseuse), Donald Hall, Evelyn Hall, Althea Henly.

A bright, fast, and funny farce that shows off MacDonald's comedic abilities, with hardly any singing. MacDonald and Denny make a fine pairing and win over the audience despite a very skinny story. She's a diva with a huge operatic following and her life has become filled with ennui. She's doing "Isolde" on stage and is angered by the indifference of the crew. She also hates the attentions of the stage door Johnnies and has her maid, Skipworth, keep everyone away from her. Davidson adores her and would like to marry MacDonald, but she puts him off by saying that her career is her total focus in life. She goes home to bed after the show and is visited by second-story man Denny, who is there to rob her residence. He's about to chloroform her when she pushes him away, saying that he might ruin "the world's most beautiful voice." Now Denny recognizes his victim and it turns out that he is her biggest fan. They are soon pals and he asks if she will give him her opinion of his voice. He sings an old standard and his voice is not bad, although a little rough in the high register. She thinks she can reform this thief and make a singer out of him, so she arranges to have her conductor and her manager listen to him the next day. Denny worries that she may be trapping him, but she allays those fears by giving him a pearl ring as a token of her sincerity. Next day, Denny sings for Conti and Lugosi in German, but they are not impressed. She thinks they are just prejudiced and demands they sign Denny for the opera. (Denny was faking his lousy notes and really could sing. At one point, he'd been considered for the male lead in THE MERRY WIDOW.) She prevails on them to give Denny a job in the chorus (at $100 per week, a prince's ransom in those days) and let him move up in the ranks. When Conti, who runs the opera, sees he has no choice, Denny gets the job and begins his singing lessons. MacDonald's own teacher, Cheron, takes on the task as Denny leaves his regular vocation because he doesn't want to expose his golden throat to night work. Denny is as disgusted with his lessons as Cheron is in giving them and the thief, is about to leave when MacDonald proposes to him. Much as Denny has fallen for MacDonald, he can't picture himself carrying her luggage and doing all the things stage husbands do, so she agrees to stop working and devote herself to him. They go off to Italy where she owns a villa. Soon enough, they are on each others' nerves as she practices scales in one room, while he pounds a punching bag in another. She's invited to a local charity bazaar where she agrees to sing, while Denny grumbles. It's there she runs into White, an old friend, who has married one of Denny's pals, Hymer, a boxer. MacDonald sings; then White does a tune. Denny walks out on MacDonald and she goes back to New York where she is going to sing again. Late one night, she is once more visited by Denny, back at work as a thief it seems. He'd been to the opera that night, liked the first act, but didn't care much for the last and just wanted to tell her. They kiss and the picture fades out with the two of them reunited. Based on a story in *The Saturday Evening Post* by Mary F. Watkins, it was shot before the Production Code made it necessary for criminals to have retribution. Once that code was established, the movie could not be reissued and the studio lost a bit of money because MacDonald became quite popular and it might have turned a handsome penny. Lugosi had already established himself as a stage star in "Dracula," but his film version was not out yet and so audiences didn't laugh when he limned the Italian singing teacher. Music includes: "The Liebestod" from *Tristan and Isolde* (Richard Wagner, sung by MacDonald), "Believe Me If All Those Endearing Young Charms" (traditional, Thomas Moore, sung by Denny), German art song (composer unknown, sung by Denny), "On a Summer Night" (William Kernell, sung by MacDonald), "I'm Just Nuts About You" (Kernell, sung by Marjorie White).

p, William Fox, Hamilton McFadden; d, McFadden; w, Lynn Starling, Philip Klein (based on the story "Stolen Thunder" by Mary F. Watkins); ph, Charles Clarke; ed, Al De Gaetano; md, Arthur Kay; art d, Stephen Goosson; cos, Sophie Wachner.

Comedy **(PR:A MPAA:NR)**

OH! FOR A MAN!, 1957 (SEE: WILL SUCCESS SPOIL ROCK HUNTER, 1957)

OH, GOD!½** (1977) 104m WB c

George Burns *(God)*, John Denver *(Jerry Landers)*, Teri Garr *(Bobbie Landers)*, Ralph Bellamy *(Sam Raven)*, Dinah Shore *(Herself)*, Barry Sullivan *(Bishop Reardon)*, Donald Pleasence *(Dr. Harmon)*, William Daniels *(George Summers)*, Barnard Hughes *(Judge Baker)*, Paul Sorvino *(Rev. Willie Williams)*, Jeff Corey *(Rabbi Silverstein)*, George Furth *(Briggs)*, David Ogden Stiers *(Mr. McCarthy)*, Titos Vandis *(Bishop Makros)*, Moosie Drier *(Adam Landers)*, Rachel Longacker *(Becky Landers)*, Carl Reiner *(Interview Guest)*, Zane Buzby *(Girl)*.

Back in the 1930s and 1940s this kind of movie was almost a sub-genre with pictures like HERE COMES MR. JORDAN, ANGEL ON MY SHOULDER, THE HORN BLOWS AT MIDNIGHT. Then the fad slackened off, so it was a refreshing waft of air when Gelbart wrote the adaptation of Corman's novel. He received an Oscar nomination for his script, the only nod from the Academy for this film, but that didn't stop it from making more than $30 million on the first release and inspiring a sort-of sequel that didn't come close to the excellence of the first one. Denver, in his film debut, is married to Garr and working as an assistant manager in a supermarket. For some reason, he is chosen by Burns (God) to be the man who spreads The Good Word on Earth. Nobody believes him, of course, and Denver is soon a pariah in his job, his town, and even in his own home. But he has faith and manages to win in the end, as he's at a trial and Burns shows up to defend him. Lots of sharp one-liners and a hysterical turn from Sorvino as a Billy Graham/Oral Roberts (or you can name your own evangelist) TV tub-thumper who is in the religion business for big bucks. Reiner does one of his best directing jobs and never resorts to some of the silliness he's demonstrated in other films. Denver is very affable and could have had a good career given the right material. Burns, who was coming off his Oscar in THE SUNSHINE BOYS, delivers the goods and can turn an average joke into a scream with his impeccable timing. Good work from all the other actors, but the talented Pleasence is wasted in a tiny role. Furth alternates between acting and writing and it was he who did the book for the Broadway shows "Company" and "Twigs." Dinah Shore and Reiner do cameos on a TV talk show.

p, Jerry Weintraub; d, Carl Reiner; w, Larry Gelbart (based on the novel by Avery Corman); ph, Victor Kemper (Technicolor); m, Jack Elliott; ed, Bud Molin; art d, Jack Senter; set d, Stuart Reiss; cos, Michael J. Harte, Nancy McArdle; makeup, Leo Lotito.

Comedy **Cas.** **(PR:A-C MPAA:PG)**

OH GOD! BOOK II** (1980) 94m WB c

George Burns *(God)*, Suzanne Pleshette *(Paula)*, David Birney *(Don)*, Louanne *(Tracy)*, John Louie *(Shingo)*, Conrad Janis *(Mr. Benson)*, Anthony Holland *(Dr. Jerome Newell)*, Hugh Downs *(Newscaster)*, Dr. Joyce Brothers *(Herself)*, Hans Conried *(Dr. Barnes)*, Wilfrid Hyde-White *(Judge Miller)*, Marian Mercer, Bebe Drake Massey, Mari Gorman, Vernon Weddle, Alma Beltran.

This is a weak followup to OH, GOD, although not really a sequel because it does not have John Denver or anyone else from the original except for Burns. It took five writers to do the script and it appears that too many cooks were present. Louanne (no second name, like Liberace or Charo) is a cute tyke who runs into Burns (God, for the second time, and alleged to be older than Him) at a Chinese restaurant. (Don't all deities love Moo Goo Guy Pan?) Burns is annoyed at the way things are going and thinks that a child should lead everyone back to the Lord's arms. If the children can be enlisted in God's name, perhaps the adults will follow. Louanne's father is advertising man Birney and it must be in the genes, as she invents a "Think God" campaign and spreads the word with posters and wall-scrawlings. She enlists Louie and some of her other chums to help and the result is that she's tossed out of school. As in most pictures like this, only the lead, Louanne, can see Burns and other people think she's daft and talking to herself. She's brought before a corps of psychiatrists and is saved when Burns appears and gets her off the hook before they toss her into a rubber room. Birney and Pleshette are apart and become reconciled through the doings of their daughter. The picture is very talky, the gags fall flat upon the ear, and the whole thing is a mild piece at best. Co-screenwriters Fox and Jacobs are veteran Bob Hope gagmen, with credits as long as Kareem Jabbar's legs. Goldman was a Jack Benny writer and director Cates was responsible for a number of fine and sensitive films, including I NEVER SANG FOR MY FATHER, so it is surprising that this one doesn't work. Some gratuitous language takes this away from being a totally family film.

p&d, Gilbert Cates; w, Josh Greenfeld, Hal Goldman, Fred S. Fox, Seaman Jacobs, Melissa Miller (based on a story by Greenfeld); ph, Ralph Woolsey (Technicolor); m, Charles Fox; ed, Peter E. Berger; prod d, Preston Ames; set d, Chris Westlund.

Comedy **Cas.** **(PR:A-C MPAA:PG)**

OH, HEAVENLY DOG!** (1980) 103m Mulberry Square/FOX c

Chevy Chase / Benji *(Benjamin Browning)*, Jane Seymour *(Jackie Howard)*, Omar Sharif *(Malcolm Bart)*, Robert Morley *(Bernie)*, Alan Sues *(Freddie)*, Donnelly Rhodes *(Montanero)*, *(Higgins)*, John Stride *(Alistair Becket)*, Barbara Leigh-Hunt *(Margaret)*, Frank Williams *(Mr. Easton)*, Albin Pahernik *(Pelican Man)*, Susan Kellerman *(German Clerk)*, Lorenzo Music *(Carlton)*, Marguerite Corriveau *(Patricia Elliott)*, Harry Hill *(Jeffrey Edgeware)*, Margaret Courtenay *(Lady Chalmers)*, Richard Vernon *(Quimby Charles)*, Joe Camp, David Samain, Neil Affleck, Gerald Iles, Jennifer Foote, Dan Witt, Jerome Tiberghien, Norman Tavis, George E. Zeeman, Wendy Dawson, Jeannette Casenave, Gayle Garfinkle, Doris Malcolm, Mary Rathbone, Steve Michaels, Henry Hardy.

Misfired attempt at combining a children's doggy film and a fairly "adult" comedy by starring Chase and Benji in the same movie. A reversal of the 1951 Dick Powell comedy YOU NEVER CAN TELL (wherein a murdered dog returns to Earth as a human to find his killer), Chase plays a detective who is murdered in London while investigating a seamy political scandal. Chase is reincarnated as cutesy pooch Benji and he continues the investigation as the dog. Most of the laughs are derived from Benji-Chase's romantic pursuit of sexy magazine reporter Seymour as he is able to jump into her bath and lie in her lap because he's her faithful mutt. Silly and slow-moving.

p&d, Joe Camp; w, Rod Browning, Camp; ph, Don Reddy (Panaflex, DeLuxe Color); m, Evel Box; ed, Leon Seith; prod d, Garrett Lewis; art d, George Richardson; m/l, Elton John, Gary Osborne, Paul McCartney; dog trainers, Frank, Juanita Inn.

Comedy **Cas.** **(PR:A MPAA:PG)**

OH JOHNNY, HOW YOU CAN LOVE!*½ (1940) 64m UNIV bw

Tom Brown *(Johnny Sandham)*, Peggy Moran *(Kelly Archer)*, Allen Jenkins *(Ed "The Weasel")*, Donald Meek *(Mr. Thistlebottom)*, Juanita Quigley *(Junior)*, Isabel Jewell *(Gertie)*, Horace MacMahon *(Lefty)*, Betty Jane Rhodes *(Betty)*, Joseph Downing *("Doc")*, Thomas Jackson *(Chief of Police)*, John Hamilton *(Jonathan Archer)*, Jack Arnold *(Young Man in Roadster)*, Matt McHugh *(Charlie)*, Billy Burt *(Dance Speciality)*, Renie Riano *(Lady in Window)*, Laird Cregar *(Mechanic)*, Kernan Cripps *(Cop)*, Hugh McArthur *(Gas Station Attendant)*, Harris Berger *(Newsboy)*.

Silly programmer stars Brown as a traveling salesman who aids spoiled heiress Moran after she wrecks her car on her way to an elopement rendezvous. On the road the pair fall into misadventures involving an escaping bank robber and a nutty tourist camp. Inevitably, the salesman and the rich girl realize they were meant for each other and clinch for the fade. Songs include "Oh Johnny, How You Can Love" (Abe Olman, Ed Rose, sung by Betty Jane Rhodes), "Maybe I Like What You Like," "Swing Chariot Swing," "Make Up Your Mind" (Paul Gerard Smith, Frank Skinner).

p, Ken Goldsmith; d, Charles Lamont; w, Arthur T. Horman (based on a story "Road to Romance" by Edwin Rutt); ph, Milton Krasner; md, Charles previn.

Musical/Romance **(PR:A MPAA:NR)**

OH, MEN! OH, WOMEN!*** (1957) 90m FOX c

Dan Dailey *(Arthur Turner)*, Ginger Rogers *(Mildred Turner)*, David Niven *(Dr. Alan Coles)*, Barbara Rush *(Myra Hagerman)*, Tony Randall *(Cobbler)*, Natalie Schafer *(Mrs. Day)*, Rachel Stephens *(Miss Tacher)*, John Wengraf *(Dr. Kraus)*, Cheryll Clarke *(Melba)*, Charles Davis *(Steward)*, Clancy Cooper *(Mounted Policeman)*, Joel Fluellen *(Cab Driver)*, Renny McEvoy *(Bartender)*, Franklin Pangborn

(Steamship Clerk), Franklyn Farnum (Passenger), Hal Taggert, Alfred Tonkel, Monty O'Grady, Les Raymaster, Harry Denny (Clergymen).

Based on Ed Chodorov's successful play, this hit-and-miss psychiatric spoof had more hits than misses and tickled many funnybones. It was Randall's film debut, after having played on Broadway in "Inherit the Wind" and having done a good run on TV as pal to "Mr. Peepers." Niven is a sedate psychiatrist who keeps his medical practice and his domestic life apart, then is shocked to see that they are coming together. Rogers is the bored wife of film star Dailey. She lives a "Nora" existence (from Ibsen's "A Doll's House") and she is complaining that often-drunk husband Dailey is paying too much attention to Rush. What stuns Niven is that Rush is his intended and they are about to take an ocean voyage and be married by the captain aboard the liner. Enter Randall, another patient. Randall is having a fling with a nutty girl and then he reveals that girl is also Rush. Niven is beside himself and considering going back for more analysis. Niven manages to hold his heart and temper somewhat in check, gets Rogers and Dailey back together after a struggle, and plans to go on his cruise. On the ocean liner, Niven waits for Rush and when she doesn't arrive he tells the steward to put his luggage ashore. Just as he's about to get off the boat, Rush arrives to say goodbye to him. Seeing Niven changes Rush's feelings about him and now she wants to stay. It's all a lot of frou-frou and everyone winds up with whom they are supposed to wind up with in the end. Niven is suave, Rogers (she seems to like playing women who consult psychiatrists, as she did in LADY IN THE DARK among others) is energetic, but the best comedy comes from Randall and Rush, both of whom fairly explode off the screen with their eccentric characters. Chodorov had been one of the writers blacklisted by the House Unamerican Activities Committee and was not allowed to have his name on screen. As a symbol of solidarity, Johnson asked that his writing credit be erased as well. With such an admirable cast, one wishes this film could have been better. As it is, OH, MEN! OH, WOMEN! is a mild copy of a Moliere farce. Even so, it's more fun that most of the alleged comedies being made in the 1980s.

p,d&w, Nunnally Johnson (based on the play by Edward Chodorov); ph, Charles G. Clark (CinemaScope, DeLuxe Color); m, Cyril J. Mockridge; ed, Marjorie Fowler; art d, Lyle R. Wheeler, Maurice Ransford; set d, Walter M. Scott, Stuart A. Reiss; cos, Charles LeMaire; spec eff, Ray Kellogg; makeup, Ben Nye; hairstyles, Helen Turpin.

Comedy   **(PR:A-C MPAA:NR)**

OH, MR. PORTER!**   (1937, Brit.) 85m Gainsborough/GFD bw

Will Hay (William Porter), Moore Marriott (Jeremiah Harbottle), Graham Moffatt (Albert Brown), Sebastian Smith (Charles Trimbletow), Agnes Lauchian (Mrs. Trimbletow), Percy Walsh (Superintendent), Dennis Wyndham (Grogan), Dave O'Toole (Postman), Frederick Piper.

Amusing comedy starring Hay as the problem son of a family that arranges to get rid of him by finding him a job as stationmaster of an obscure railway post in Ireland where no trains stop. On his arrival, Hay finds only a doddering old clerk and an overweight boy porter as his employees. Hay sets about revitalizing the premises. After sprucing up the station, he books a train to transport the local soccer team. When the train vanishes, Hay hunts it down and discovers it is being used by gun smugglers. Quickly, Hay couples the car to an old engine and sends the train speeding to the police station, where the crooks are caught and Hay is hailed as a hero.

p, Edward Black; d, Marcel Varnel; w, J.O.C. Orton, Val Guest, Marriott Edgar (based on a story by Frank Launder); ph, Arthur Crabtree.

Comedy   **(PR:A MPAA:NR)**

OH MY DARLING CLEMENTINE   (SEE: O, MY DARLING CLEMENTINE, 1943)

OH NO DOCTOR!**   (1934, Brit.) 62m George King/MGM bw

Jack Hobbs (Montagu Kent), Dorothy Boyd (Josephine Morrow), James Finlayson (Axminster), Cecil Humphreys (Dr. Morrow), Peggy Novak (Tessa Burnett), Jane Carr (Protheroe), Abraham Sofaer (Skelton), David Wilton (Villain).

Mad scientist Humphreys uses the money of Boyd, his legal ward, to finance one of his inventions. When playwright Hobbs wants to marry Boyd, Humphreys sets up an unsuccessful evening wherein he plans to scare the young suitor to death. Dumb haunted house comedy with no real thrills or scares; reissued in a shorter version in 1943.

p,d&w, George King.

Comedy   **(PR:A MPAA:NR)**

OH ROSALINDA**½   (1956, Brit.) 101m AFB-Pathe c

Michael Redgrave (Col. Eisenstein), Ludmilla Tcherina (Rosalinda), Anton Walbrook (Dr. Falke), Mel Ferrer (Capt. Westerman), Dennis Price (Maj. Frank), Anthony Quayle (Gen. Orlofsky), Anneliese Rothenberger (Adele, Maid), Oska Sima (Frosh), Richard Marner (Judge), Olga Lowe, Nicholas Bruce, Ray Buckingham, Jill Ireland, Sari Barabas, Alexander Young, Denis Dowling, Walter Berry (Voices).

Modernized film version of the Strauss opera "Die Fledermaus" set in post-WW II Vienna. Redgrave is the French officer whose wife, Tcherina, is caught in a compromising situation with former flame Ferrer, an officer in the U.S. Army, by an escort guard who thinks Ferrer is her husband whom the guard has been assigned to jail. Seeking to maintain Tcherina's reputation, Ferrer allows himself to be jailed in Redgrave's place. Tcherina goes to a costume ball and flirts with her own husband and later gets back at him by showing him the watch he gave her during the flirtation. Generally entertaining, but lacks sparkle. Redgrave, Rothenberger, and Quayle sing their own roles.

p,d&w, Michael Powell, Emeric Pressburger (based on the opera "Die Fledermaus"

by Johann Strauss); ph, Christopher Challis (CinemaScope, Technicolor); m, Strauss; ed, Reginald Mills; m/l, Dennis Arundell.

Musical   **(PR:A MPAA:NR)**

OH! SAILOR, BEHAVE!**½   (1930) 70m WB bw

Irene Delroy (Nanette Dodge), Charles King (Charlie Carroll), Lowell Sherman (Prince Kosloff), Vivian Oakland (Kunegundi), Noah Beery, Sr. (Roumanian General), Ole Olsen (Simon), Chick Johnson (Peter), Lotti Loder (Louisa), Charles Judels (De Medici), Elsie Bartlett (Mitzi), Lawrence Grant (Von Klaus), Gino Corrado (Stephan).

The way-out comedy team of Olsen and Johnson made its film debut in this amusing comedy based on a failed Broadway play of Elmer Rice. Reworked for the team's talents, the story has the duo playing a pair of American sailors stationed in Naples. Their mission is to find a man with a wooden leg who has robbed a Navy storehouse. The humor is pretty basic but enjoyable nonetheless. The studio recreated the Bay of Naples on its back lots for this film, with amazingly good results. Release of this film was held up because of a prevailing attitude against musicals which was growing on the Warner's lot. Songs: "Love Comes in the Moonlight," "Leave a Little Smile," "Tell Us Which One You Love," "Highway to Heaven" (Al Dubin, Joe Burke), "The Laughing Song" (Olsen, Johnson).

d, Archie Mayo; w, Joseph Jackson, Sid Silvers (based on the play "See Naples and Die" by Elmer Rice); ph, Dev Jennings; ed, Robert Crandall.

Musical Comedy   **(PR:AAA MPAA:NR)**

**OH, SUSANNA*½   (1937) 59m REP bw

Gene Autry (Himself), Smiley Burnette (Frog), Frances Grant (Mary Ann), Earl Hodgins (Professor), Donald Kirke (Flash Baldwin), Boothe Howard (Wolf Benson), Clara Kimball Young (Mrs. Lee), Frankie Marvin (Hank), Ed Piel, Sr. (Sheriff Cole), Carl Stockdale (Jeff Lee), Gerald Roscoe, Roger Gray, Fred Burns, Walter James, Fred "Snowflake" Toones, Earl Dwire, Bruce Mitchell, Jack Kirk, George Morell, Light Crust Doughboys Band, Champion the Horse.

This Autry oater finds Gene unceremoniously tossed from a speeding train after thieves rob him while on his way to Mineral Springs. Drifters Burnette and Hodgins find Autry, brush him off, then join him on the road to Mineral Springs and revenge. Eventually Autry finds the baddies and decks them soundly. Songs include the title tune and "I'll Go Ridin' Down That Texas Trail" (Autry, Burnette). Too much singing in this sagebrusher weighs down the eyelids.

p, Nat Levine; d, Joseph Kane; w, Oliver Drake; ph, William Nobles; md, Harry Grey; m/l, Sam H. Stept, Drake, Gene Autry, Smiley Burnette.

WesternCas.   **(PR:A MPAA:NR)**

OH! SUSANNA**   (1951) 90m REP c (AKA: OH, SUSANNA)

Rod Cameron (Capt. Calhoun), Adrian Booth (Lia Wilson), Forrest Tucker (Lt. Col. Unger), Chill Wills (Sgt. Barhydt), William Ching (Cpl. Donlin), Jim Davis (Ira Jordan), Wally Cassell (Trooper Muro), James Lydon (Trumpeter Benton), Douglas Kennedy (Trooper Emers), William Haade (Trooper Riorty), John Compton (Lt. Cutter), James Flavin (Capt. Worth), Charles Stevens (Charlie Grass), Alan Bridge (Jake Ledbetter), Marion Randolph (Mrs. Worth), Marshall Reed (Trooper Murray), John Pickard (Rennie), Ruth Brennan (Young Wife), Louise Kane (Mary Bannon).

Typical B-western has cavalryman Cameron watching over Black Hills gold miners to assure that Indian treaties are kept. Head man Tucker cares little for Native Americans which makes it difficult for Cameron to carry out his duties. Eventually a war breaks out, with the Indians respectfully sparing only Cameron's life. Characterizations are short in this stereotypical action piece, but the battle scenes are well handled. Songs: "Oh! Susanna," "Is Someone Lonely," "The Regular Army, Oh," (Ed Harrigan, Jack Elliott).

p&d, Joseph Kane; w, Charles Marquis Warren; ph, Jack Marta (Trucolor); m, R. Dale Butts; ed, Arthur Roberts; art d, Frank Arrigo.

Western   **(PR:A MPAA:NR)**

OH! THOSE MOST SECRET AGENTS   (SEE: 00-2 MOST SECRET AGENTS, 1965, Ital.)

OH WHAT A DUCHESS!   (SEE: MY OLD DUCHESS, 1933, Brit.)

OH! WHAT A LOVELY WAR*½   (1969, Brit.) 144m Accord/PAR c

Ralph Richardson (Sir Edward Grey), Meriel Forbes (Lady Grey), Wensley Pithey (Archduke Franz Ferdinand), Ruth Kettlewell (Duchess Sophie), Ian Holm (President Poincare), John Gielgud (Count Berchtold), Kenneth More (Kaiser Wilhelm II), John Clements (Gen. von Moltke), Paul Daneman (Czar Nicholas II), Pamela Abbott (Czarina), Stella Courtney (Poincare's Lady), Kathleen Helme (Berchtold's Lady), Ruth Gower (Von Moltke's Lady), Elizabeth Craven (Kaiserin), Joe Melia (The Photographer), Anthony Morton (Italian Military Attache), Steve Plytas (Turkish Military Attache), Jack Hawkins (Emperor Franz Josef), John Hussey (Soldier on Balcony), Kim Smith (Dickie Smith), Mary Wimbush (Mary Smith), Paul Shelley (Jack Smith), Wendy Allnutt (Flo Smith), John Rae (Grandpa Smith), Kathleen Wileman (Emma Smith at Age 4), Corin Redgrave (Bertie Smith), Malcolm McFee (Freddie Smith), Colin Farrell (Harry Smith), Maurice Roeves (George Smith), Angela Thorne (Betty Smith), John Mills (Field Marshal Sir Douglas Haig), Julia Wright (His Secretary), Jean-Pierre Cassel (French Colonel), David Scheuer (French Soldier), Michael Wolf (German Officer), Jeremy Child (Wealthy Young Man), Ambrose Coghill (His Father), Penny Allen (Solo Chorus Girl), Sheila Cox, Sue Robinson, Hermione Farthingale, Joyce Franklin, Carole Gray, Dinny Jones, Delia Linden (Chorus Girls), Maggie Smith (Music Hall Star), David Lodge (Recruiting Sergeant), Michael Redgrave (Gen. Sir Henry Wilson), Laurence Olivier (Field Marshal Sir John French), Peter Gilmore (Pvt. Burgess), Derek Newark (Shooting Gallery Proprietor), Richard Howard (Young Soldier at Mons), John

Trigger *(Officer at Station)*, Ron Pember *(Corporal at Station)*, Juliet Mills, Nanette Newman *(Nurses at Station)*, Susannah York *(Eleanor)*, Dirk Bogarde *(Stephen)*, Norman Jones *(lst Scottish Soldier)*, Andrew Robertson *(2nd Scottish Soldier)*, Ben Howard *(Pvt. Garbett)*, Angus Lennie *(3rd Scottish Soldier)*, Brian Tipping *(4th Scottish Soldier)*, Christian Doermer *(Fritz)*, Tony Vogel *(German Soldier)*, Paul Hansard *(German Officer)*, John Woodnutt *(British Officer)*, Tony Thawnton *(Officer on Telephone)*, Frank Coda, Kim Grant, Richard Loring, Tom Mashall *(Soldiers in "Goodbyee")*, Annie Bee, Valerie Smith, Isabelle Metcalfe, Jenny Morgan *(Girl Friends in "Goodbyee")*, Cecil Parker *(Sir John)*, Zeph Gladstone *(His Chauffeuse)*, Stanley McGeagh, Stanley Lebor *(Soldiers in Gassed Trench)*, Robert Flemying *(Staff Officer in Gassed Trench)*, Thorley Walters, Norman Shelley *(Staff Officers in Ballroom)*, Isabel Dean *(Sir John French's Lady)*, Guy Middleton *(Gen. Sir William Robertson)*, Natasha Parry *(His Lady)*, Cecilia Darby *(Sir Henry Wilson's Lady)*, Phyllis Calvert *(Lady Haig)*, Raymond S. Edwards *(3rd Staff Officer in Ballroom)*, Freddie Ascott *("Whizzbang" Soldier)*, Edward Fox, Geoffrey Davies *(Aides)*, Pippa Steel, Elisabeth Murray *(Scoreboard Girls)*, Christian Thorogood, Paddy Joyce, John Dunhill, John Owens, P.G. Stephens *(Irish Soldiers)*, Vanessa Redgrave *(Sylvia Pankhurst)*, Clifford Mollison, Dorothy Reynolds, Harry Locke, George Ghent, Bette Vivian *(Hecklers)*, Michael Bates *(Drunken Lance Corporal)*, Charles Farrell *(Policeman)*, Pia Colombo *(Estaminet Singer)*, Vincent Ball *(Australian Soldier)*, Anthony Ainley *(3rd Aide)*, Gerald Sim *(Chaplain)*, Maurice Arthur *(Soldier Singer in Church Parade)*, Richard Davies *(Sergeant in Burial Party)*, Arthur White *(Sergeant in Dugout)*, Christopher Cabot *(Soldier in Shell Hole)*, Lind Joyce, Mary Yeomans *(Other Scoreboard Girls)*, Fanny Carby, Christine Noonan, Marianne Stone *(Mill Girls)*, Charlotte Attenborough *(Emma Smith at Age 8)*, Joanne Browne *(Singer)*, Frank Forsyth *(Woodrow Wilson)*, John Gabriel *(Nikolai Lenin)*.

An amazing, sprawling, and not entirely successful attempt to make a musical satire of WW I. The film opens as a number of members of European royalty gather for a group portrait. The camera explodes and Archduke Franz Ferdinand (Pithey) is killed. The kings and emperors trade insults and accusations, choose up sides, and declare war. At the amusement pier at Brighton, England, a flashing sign announces the new attraction, World War I. The Smith Family buys tickets and one by one the five sons go off to the war, one following the siren song of music-hall singer Maggie Smith. Another stops at the shooting gallery on the pier and his winning prize is an army uniform and a trip to the front. A giant scoreboard tallies the dead. Aristocrat Bogarde and wife York do their bit for the war effort by refusing to drink German wine and ordering their nanny to knit mittens for the soldiers. General Haig (Mills) orders the Somme offensive and later tells the British public the good news that although no ground was taken, only 60,000 died. One by one the Smith sons are killed, the last one on the last day of the war, just as the scoreboard reaches nine million. The final shot has the surviving Smiths, the women, picnicking in a cemetery beside the five graves of their sons and brothers. The camera tilts up to show thousands and thousands of identical white crosses extending over the hills as far as the eye can see. The film had its origins in a BBC radio program circa 1960 called "The Long, Long Trail," a retrospective of songs from the "War to End All Wars" that inevitably made them sound so jingoistic and ridiculous that the antiwar bias of the show was implicit. In 1963 it was transformed into a stage show in London's East End. A major hit, the rights were purchased by producer Brian Duffy and writer Len Deighton (a bestselling novelist). They hired actor Attenborough to direct, although he had never helmed a film before. Deighton later had his name removed from the credits when he and Attenborough argued about the course the film was taking, Deighton feeling the director was being too soft with the material. Of course this was officially denied and the reason for Deighton's absence from the credits was given as "contractual disputes." Everyone wanted to be in the film, and it is the only film ever to boast no less than five Knights of the Realm (Sir Laurence Olivier, Sir Ralph Richardson, Sir John Gielgud, Sir Michael Redgrave, and Sir John Clements). The film received rave reviews and was a major success in Britain, but it did disappointing business in the U.S. Songs: "Oh! What a Lovely War," "Oh I Do Like to Be Beside the Seaside," "Belgium Put the Kibosh on the Kaiser" (sung by Cassel), "Are We Downhearted?" "Your King and Country Need You" (sung by Allen), "I'll Make a Man of You" (sung by Maggie Smith), "Send for the Boys of the Girls' Brigade" (sung by Richard Howard), "We're 'Ere Because We're 'Ere," "Pack Up Your Troubles," "Heilige Nacht," "Christmas Day in the Cookhouse" (sung by Ben Howard), "Goodbyee" (sung by Joe Melia, Corin Redgrave), "Gassed," "Roses of Picardy," "Row, Row, Row," "Comrades" (sung by Melia), "La Paloma," "She Was One of the Early Birds," "Hush Here Comes a Whizzbang," "There's a Long, Long Trail," "Rule Britannia," "I Don't Want to be a Soldier," "Mademoiselle from Armentieres," "The Moon Shines Bright on Charlie Chaplin," "Adieu la Vie" (sung by Pia Colombo), "They Were Only Playing Leapfrog," "Forward Joe Soap's Army," "When This Lousy War Is Over" (sung by Maurice Arthur), "Whiter Than the Whitewash on the Wall," "I Want to Go Home," "The Bells of Hell," "Never Mind," "Far, Far from Wipers" (sung by Richard Howard), "If You Want the Old Battalion," "Keep the Home Fires Burning," "Over There," "They'll Never Believe Me."

p, Brian Duffy, Richard Attenborough, Len Deighton [uncredited]; d, Attenborough; w, Deighton [uncredited] (based on Joan Littlewood's stage production of Charles Chilton's play "The Long, Long Trail"); ph, Gerry Turpin (Panavision, Technicolor); m, Alfred Ralston; ed, Kevin Connor; prod d, Don Ashton; md, Ralston; art d, Harry White; set d, Peter James; cos, Anthony Mendleson; spec eff, Ron Ballanger; ch, Eleanor Fazan; makeup, Stuart Freeborn; military adv, Maj. Gen. Douglas Campbell.

War/Musical (PR:A-C MPAA:G)

OH, WHAT A NIGHT*½ (1935) 58m British Sound Film Productions bw

Molly Lamont *(Pat)*, James Carew *(Mortimer B. Gregory)*, Valerie Hobson *(Susan)*, Martin Walker, Roland Culver *(Marmaduke)*, Kathleen Kelly *(Miss Wyley)*, Ernest Stidwell *(Dawson)*, Nina Boucicault *(Althea Gregory)*, Stanella Perry.

British comedy wherein the nasty relatives of a missing millionaire convince an amnesia victim that he is the millionaire's long lost son and heir to the fortune. Well-bred and graceful Hobson, who would later go to Hollywood and quit it a year later in disgust at her skimpy roles, was only 18 years old when OH, WHAT A NIGHT was filmed.

p, Edward G. Whiting; d, Frank Richardson (based on the play "The Irresistible Marmaduke" by Ernest Denny).

Comedy (PR:A MPAA:NR)

OH, WHAT A NIGHT*½ (1944) 72m MON bw

Edmund Lowe *(Rand)*, Marjorie Rambeau *(Lil Vanderhoven)*, Jean Parker *(Valerie)*, Pierre Watkin *(Tom Gordon)*, Alan Dinehart *(Detective Norris)*, Claire DuBrey *(Petrie)*, Ivan Lebedeff *(Boris)*, Karin Lang *(Sonya)*, Charles Miller *(Sutton)*, Olaf Hytten *(Wyndy)*, George Lewis *(Rocco)*, Crane Whitley *(Sullivan)*, Charles Jordan *(Murphy)*, Dick Rush *(Healy)*.

Parker plays the niece of dowager Rambeau, whose diamonds are wanted by international jewel thieves. Her uncle is the mastermind behind the gang, but he is turned in by his young partner who has fallen in love with Parker. Good-looking Parker retired from the screen the year OH, WHAT A NIGHT came out, and did not return to films until 1950.

p, Scott R. Durlap; d, William Beaudine; w, Paul Gerard Smith (based on a story by Marion Orth); ph, Mack Stengler; ed, Dan Milner; md, Edward Kay.

Crime (PR:A MPAA:NR)

OH, YEAH!** (1929) 74m Pathe bw (GB: NO BRAKES)

Robert Armstrong *(Dude)*, James Gleason *(Dusty)*, Patricia Caron *(Pinkie)*, ZaSu Pitts *(The Elk)*, Bud Fine *(Pop Eye)*, Frank Hagney *(Hot Foot)*, Harry Tyler *(Splinters)*, Paul Hurst *(Superintendent)*.

Gleason and Armstrong play two rough drifters who land jobs as railroad brakemen after they prove their strength to the foreman. Thoughts of abandoning their nomadic lifestyle are considered seriously by the pair when they fall in love. Armstrong falls for Caron, who happens to be the paymaster and commissary chief of the railroad, and Gleason goes for Pitts, a dumb but likable waitress. Their happiness is threatened when Armstrong loses his nest egg in a crap game and then gets framed for a theft. The pals accidentally discover the identity of the real crooks and bring them to justice. Multitalented Gleason (actor, screenwriter, playwright), who was to become the big-city character type with a heart of gold beneath a gruff exterior, saved OH YEAH from perishing at the turnstiles by writing much of the witty dialog.

d, Tay Garnett; w, Garnett, James Gleason (based on the story "No Brakes" by A.W. Somerville); ph, Arthur Miller; m, George Green, George Waggner; song, "Love Found Me When I Found You" (sung by Robert Armstrong).

Drama (PR:A MPAA:NR)

OH, YOU BEAUTIFUL DOLL½** (1949) 93m FOX c

June Haver *(Doris Breitenbach)*, Mark Stevens *(Larry Kelly)*, S.Z. "Cuddles" Sakall *(Fred Fisher)*, Charlotte Greenwood *(Anna Breitenbach)*, Gale Robbins *(Marie Carle)*, Jay C. Flippen *(Lippy Brannigan)*, Andrew Tombes *(Ted Held)*, Eduard Franz *(Gottfried Steiner)*, Dick Rich *(Burly Man)*, Al Klein, Don Kerr, Warren Jackson, Sam Ash *(Quartette)*, Eula Morgan *(Mme. Zaubel)*, Nestor Paiva *(Lucca)*, Curt Bois *(Zaltz)*, Torchy Rand *(Sophie)*, Ray Walker *(Box Office Attendant)*, Frank Kreig *(Headwaiter)*, Victor Sen Yung *(Houseboy)*, Myrtle Anderson *(Cook)*, John Mylong *(Toastmaster)*, Robert Gist *(Musician)*, Marion Martin *(Big Blonde)*, James Griffith, Billy Wayne *(Reporters)*, John Davidson *(Steiner's Secretary)*, Edward Clark *(Cooper)*, Robert B. Williams *(Police Lieutenant)*, Phil Tully *(Police Sergeant)*, Maurice Samuels *(Italian)*, Harry Seymour *(Nightclub M.C.)*, Sam Finn *(Man)*, Maj. Sam Harris *(Composer)*.

Beloved character actor Sakall was given the biggest role of his career in OH, YOU BEAUTIFUL DOLL when he was cast as popular turn-of-the-century songwriter Fred Fisher (real name Breitenbach) in this musical biography. Playing fast-and-loose with the facts, the story chronicles Fisher's efforts at becoming a serious composer, though his work goes unrecognized. When he hooks up with song publisher Stevens, who advises him to arrange his melodies in a more up-tempo manner and sell them as popular tunes, Breitenbach changes his name to Fisher (so as not to ruin his chances with the highbrow community) and soon becomes the rage with tunes like the title song, "Peg 'O My Heart," "Chicago," and "There's a Broken Heart for Every Light on Broadway." This career change meets with great approval from Sakall's daughter, Haver, who is a singer and dancer. Wealthy, but unhappy with his station in the musical world, Sakall remains in seclusion until a respected conductor, Franz, decides to perform one of his pieces at Aeolian Hall. Excited by the acceptance of his tunes in the serious musical world, Sakall comes out of hiding and regains his pride as a composer. Other songs include: "I Want You to Want Me to Want You" (Bob Schafer, Alfred Bryan), "Come Josephine In My Flying Machine," "Who Paid the Rent for Mrs. Rip Van Winkle?" (Bryan), "Daddy You've Been More Than a Mother to Me," "When I Get You Alone Tonight" (Joseph McCarthy, Joe Goodwin), "Dardanella" (Felix Bernard, Johnny S. Black, Fred Fisher), "Ireland Must Be Heaven For My Mother Came From There" (McCarthy, Johnson).

p, George Jessel; d, John M. Stahl; w, Albert, Arthur Lewis; ph, Harry Jackson, Fred Sersen (Technicolor); ed, Louis Loeffler; md, Alfred Newman; art d, Lyle Wheeler, Maurice Ransford; ch, Seymour Felix.

Musical/Biography (PR:A MPAA:NR)

O'HARA'S WIFE**   (1983) 87m Davis-Panzer c

Edward Asner (*Bob O'Hara*), Mariette Hartley (*Harry O'Hara*), Jodie Foster (*Barbara O'Hara*), Perry Lang (*Rob O'Hara*), Tom Bosley (*Fred O'Hara*), Ray Walston (*Walter Tatum*), Allen Williams (*Billy Tatum*), Mary Jo Catlett (*Gloria*), Nelson Welch (*Nelson Attleby*), Richard Schaal (*Jerry Brad*), Nehemiah Persoff (*Dr. Fischer*), Kelly Bishop (*Beth Douglas*), Eric Kilpatrick (*Police Officer*).

Topper-like tale starring Asner as the faithful husband who loses his wife after she collapses and must be put on a life-support system. Rather than see her spend the rest of her life hooked to machines, Asner pulls the plug and Hartley dies. Much to his surprise, he is greeted at home by Hartley's ghost, which only he can see and hear. The ghost aids her husband in overcoming his grief, and then she pushes him to fulfill his life-long ambition of quitting his law practice and traveling. Conflicts at home are provided by estranged son Lang, constantly barraged by younger sister Foster who supports her dad wholeheartedly. Typical family comedy outing that has been done better elsewhere.

p, Peter S. Davis, William N. Panzer; d, William S. Bartman; w, James Nasella, Bartman (based on a story by Bartman, Joseph Scott Kierland); ph, Harry Stradling (DeLuxe Color); m, Artie Butler; ed, George Berndt, James A. Borgardt; art d, Robert Zentis; set d, Chuck Rutherford, Pamela Bennett; cos, Madeline Ann Graneto; m/l, Molly-Ann Leikin.

Comedy/Drama   Cas.   (PR:C MPAA:PG)

OHAYO***   (1962, Jap.) 93m Shochiku/
                              Shochiku Films of America bw (AKA: GOOD MORNING)

Koji Shidara (*Minoru the Elder Brother*), Masahiko Shimazu (*Isamu the Younger Brother*), Chishu Ryu (*Their Father*), Kuniko Miyake (*Their Mother*), Yoshiko Kuga (*Their Aunt*), Keiji Sada (*Their Teacher*), Haruo Tanaka (*Tatsuko*), Haruko Sugimura (*Kikue, His Wife*), Teruko Nagaoka, Toyoko Takahashi (*Neighbors*), Eijiro Tono.

One of Japanese master director Yasujiro Ozu's last films, a remake of one of his earlier films, I WAS BORN, BUT. . .(1932). Released in Japan in 1959, OHAYO tells the story of a small community in a middle-class housing development outside of Tokyo. Only one family owns a television set, and the local boys love to gather there and watch wrestling matches. Two brothers, Shidara and Shimazu, try desperately to convince their parents that they should also have a television set, but are told to shut up. In protest, the youngsters go on a silence strike which irritates their parents because the neighbors are offended at their (the parents') cruelty. If that isn't enough, the brothers run away, but are soon brought home by their teachers. The homecoming is a happy one, however, because a television set awaits the boys upon their arrival. A simple, witty, well-told family tale that suffers from Ozu's willingness to let his reputation carry the film, rather than attempting any new, less predictable, techniques. Even so, OHAYO is a beautiful and profoundly honest picture, and, in that sense, quintessentially Japanese.

p, Shizuo Yamanouchi; d, Yasujiro Ozu; w, Kogo Noda, Ozu; ph, Yushun Atsuta; m, Toshiro Mayuzumi; art d, Tatsuo Hamada.

Comedy/Drama   (PR:A MPAA:NR)

OIL FOR THE LAMPS OF CHINA***   (1935) 95m COS/WB-FM bw

Pat O'Brien (*Stephen Chase*), Josephine Hutchinson (*Hester Chase*), Jean Muir (*Alice Wellman*), John Eldredge (*Don Wellman*), Lyle Talbot (*Jim*), Arthur Byron (*Ross, No. 1 Boss*), Henry O'Neill (*Hartford*), Donald Crisp (*MacCargar*), Ronnie Cosby (*Bunsy*), Willie Fung (*Kim*), George Meeker (*Kendall*), Edward McWade (*Dan*), Christian Rub (*Dr. Jorgen*), Florence Fair (*Miss Cunningham, the Secretary*), William B. Davidson (*Swaley*), Joseph Crehan (*Clements*), Keye Luke (*Young Chinese*), Willard Robertson (*Speaker*), Tetsu Komai (*Ho*), Samuel S. Hinds (*George*), Miki Morita (*Japanese Tailor*), Teru Shimada (*Japanese Proprietor*), Cyril Ring (*Graves*), George Irving (*Man*), Bess Flowers, Lotus Liu (*Secretaries*).

A grim look at the brutality of American corporations abroad, greatly weakened by a hokey ending that nearly saps the film of its power. O'Brien stars as an ambitious oil company representative in China whose blind faith in the company almost ruins his life. Overly devoted to saving the corporation money, O'Brien's first baby dies in childbirth because he refused more expensive delivery. His best friend and coworker, Eldredge, loses a minor sales contract, so the fanatical O'Brien fires him. These events nearly cause his wife, Hutchinson, to walk out on him, but then O'Brien risks his life to save $15,000 the Chinese Communists have their eye on and he is shot. After a long hospital stay, O'Brien finds himself rewarded by the company with a demotion. Here's where Hollywood steps in and ruins a perfectly realistic ending. Soon after his demotion, the managing director of the oil company in New York hears of the injustice and places a phone call setting things straight and giving the film a happy ending. Remade in 1941 as LAW OF THE TROPICS.

p, Robert Lord; d, Mervyn LeRoy; w, Laird Doyle (based on the novel by Alice Tisdale Hobart); ph, Tony Gaudio; ed, William Clemens; md, Leo F. Forbstein; art d, Robert M. Haas; cos, Orry-Kelly.

Drama   (PR:A MPAA:NR)

OIL GIRLS, THE   (SEE: LEGEND OF FRENCHIE KING, THE, 1971,
                                                Fr./Ital./Span./Brit.)

OIL TOWN   (SEE: LUCY GALLANT, 1955)

O.K. CONNERY   (SEE: OPERATION KID BROTHER, 1967, Ital.)

OKAY AMERICA*½   (1932) 80m UNIV bw (GB: PENALTY OF FAME)

Lew Ayres (*Larry Wayne*), Maureen O'Sullivan (*Miss Barton*), Louis Calhern (*Mileaway Rosso*), Walter Catlett (*City Editor*), Alan Dinehart (*Jones*), Edward

Arnold (*Alsotto*), Rollo Lloyd (*Joe Morton*), Margaret Lindsay (*Ruth Drake*), Gilbert Emery (*Secretary Drake*), Nance O'Neill (*Mrs. Drake*), Frederick Burton (*President*), Frank Sheridan (*Commissioner*), Marjorie Gateson (*Mrs. Wright*), Henry Armetta (*Sam*), George Dow Clark (*Obituary Editor*), Emerson Treacy (*Jerry Robbins*), Ruth Lyons (*Phyllis*), Berton Churchill (*Baron*), Frank Darien (*O'Toole*), Onslow Stevens, James Flavin, Al Hall, William Daly, Neely Edwards, Caryl Lincoln, Akim Tamiroff, Willard Robertson, Virginia Howell, The Three Cheers, The Bluettes, Everett Hoagland's Band.

A hopelessly miscast Ayres struggles through this grim crime drama which features him as a Walter Winchell-type radio reporter. Ayres becomes embroiled in the kidnaping of an important Washington politician's daughter by mobster Arnold, who is obviously patterned after Al Capone. Arnold has kidnaped the girl so that he can strike a bargain with the President of the U.S. Ayres arranges for the girl's release after a ransom of $100,000 is paid. No happy ending for Ayres, however, when Arnold and his goons murder him while he is on the air during his broadcast. This film, with its obvious intent on exposing newspaper columnists who grew rich by ruining reputations, was one of the cycle launched in Hollywood when Darryl Zanuck, then production head at Warner Bros., decreed that henceforth his studio would produce films based on spot news. Topicality immediately became the byword and, as the pattern emerged and jelled, topical pictures like OKAY AMERICA succeeded in voicing a general indictment of Depression America, which reflected the discontent then prevalent in the nation. Remade as RISKY BUSINESS (1939).

d, Tay Garnett; w, William Anthony McGuire, Scott Pembroke (based on a story by McGuire); ph, Arthur Miller.

Crime   (PR:A MPAA:NR)

OKAY BILL**   (1971) 91m Cake/Four Star Excelsior c (AKA:
                                                        SWEET DREAMS)

Bob Brady (*Bill Thornberry*), Nancy Salmon (*Nancy Thornberry*), Gordon Felio (*Zachary Armstrong Lynn*), Roz Kelly (*Roz*).

Overly arty, self-conscious drama directed by John Avildsen (JOE, ROCKY) and starring Brady as a young, successful stockbroker who zips off to Greenwich Village on his motorcycle when no one's looking to venture into the hippy counterculture world. His wife, Salmon, is the dream of every middle-class male. She is liberated enough to go around bra-less, enjoy sex, and be the perfect mother for their child. Salmon, however, is unaware of her husband's excursions, and happily attends the local ecology awareness meetings without Brady. Brady soon becomes involved with Felio, an Andy Warhol-type character whose protege, Kelly, fascinates the square young businessman. After witnessing a wild party on Fire Island, Brady realizes that this crowd is not for him (shallow, lifeless) and that he does not even want to have sex with Kelly because he is lonely for his wife. Salmon arrives unexpectedly on the island to reclaim her husband and together they walk off into the sunset hand in hand.

p, David Disick; d,w&ph, John Avildsen (Berkey Pathe Color); m, Charles G. Morrow; ed, Avildsen.

Drama   (PR:O MPAA:R)

OKAY FOR SOUND**   (1937, Brit.) 86m Gainsborough/GFD bw

Fred Duprez (*Hyman Goldberger*), Enid Stamp-Taylor (*Jill Smith*), Graham Moffat (*Albert*), Meinhart Maur (*Guggenheimer*), H.F. Maltby (*John Rigby*), Jan Gotch, Louis Pergantes (*All-in-Wrestlers*), Jimmy Nervo Teddy Knox, Bud Flanagan [Dennis O'Keefe], Chesney Allen, Charlie Naughton, Jimmy Gold (*Studio Disorganizers*), Lucienne and Ashour, Patricia Bowman, Radio Three, The Robenis, Peter Dawson, Sherman Fisher Girls.

Silly but fun comedy starring Nervo, Knox, Flanagan, Allen, Naughton, and Gold as six goofy, unemployed brothers whose relative, a page boy at a movie studio, gets them jobs as extras. Through a series of misunderstandings, the boys are mistaken for studio executives and put in charge of running the place. Typical situation performed with energy and vigor.

p, Edward Black; d, Marcel Varnel; w, Marriott Edgar, Val Guest, Bud Flanagan, Chesney Allen, Jimmy Nervo, Teddy Knox, Charlie Naughton, Jimmy Gold; ph, Jack Cox.

Comedy   (PR:A MPAA:NR)

OKEFENOKEE*   (1960) 78m Filmservice bw

Peter Coe (*Indian Guide*), Henry Brandon (*Smuggler*), Peggy Maley (*His Girl*), Serena Sande (*Indian Girl*), Walter Klavun (*Henchman*).

Brandon and girl friend Maley are smuggling illegal aliens and drugs into southern Florida using the help of Seminole Indians and airboats. After Indian guide Coe's girl friend forcibly blinds herself (she stares into the sun and loses her eyesight after one of Brandon's goons has his way with her!) the Seminoles rise up to attack the bad men. Great garbage for the Southern drive-in market.

p, Aaron Danches; d, Roul Haig; w, Jess Abbott.

Action/Drama   (PR:O MPAA:NR)

OKINAWA**   (1952) 67m COL bw

Pat O'Brien (*Lt. Cmdr. Hale*), Cameron Mitchell (*Grip*), Richard Denning (*Lt. Phillips*), Rhys Williams (*Roberg*), James Dobson (*Emerson*), Richard Benedict (*Delgado*), Rudy Robles (*Felix*), Don Gibson (*Lt. Sanders*), George Cooper (*Yeoman*), Alan Dreeban (*Chief Pharmacist's Mate*), Norman Budd (*Smith*), Alvy Moore (*Quartermaster*).

Routine WW II film with the usual set of cliches. Action involves the gun crew of a destroyer stationed off Okinawa. Lots of stock battle footage pads the weak script as the stereotypical crew dukes it out with the Japanese. O'Brien is the tough-as-nails commander, Mitchell is the loudmouth-with-a-heart-of-gold powderman, Williams the kindly-but-tough old man, Denning the well-liked, but equally tough lieutenant, Dobson the homesick kid, and Benedict the fun-loving ladies' man.

p, Wallace MacDonald; d, Leigh Jason; w, Jameson Brewer, Leonard Stern, Arthur Ross (based on a story by Ross); ph, Henry Freulich; ed, Jerome Thoms; md, Mischa Bakaleinikoff; art d, George Brooks.

War (PR:A MPAA:NR)

OKLAHOMA****** (1955) 145m Magna Theatres c

Gordon MacRae *(Curly)*, Gloria Grahame *(Ado Annie)*, Gene Nelson *(Will Parker)*, Charlotte Greenwood *(Aunt Eller)*, Shirley Jones *(Laurey)*, Eddie Albert *(Ali Hakim)*, James Whitmore *(Carnes)*, Rod Steiger *(Jud Fry)*, Barbara Lawrence *(Gertie)*, J.C. Flippen *(Skidmore)*, Roy Barcroft *(Marshal)*, James Mitchell *(Dream Curly)*, Bambi Linn *(Dream Laurey)*, Jennie Workman, Kelly Brown, Marc Platt, Lizanne Truex, Virginia Bosler, Evelyn Taylor, Jane Fischer *(Dancers)*, Ben Johnson *(Cowboy at Train Depot)*.

Even though she was co-starred, Shirley Jones only received fifth billing on this, her first movie. Jones became an instant star after the movie and remained that through the 1980s. She was only 19 when the picture began the year-long shoot. Since there was no suitable location to be found in Oklahoma, the company went to an area outside Nogales, Arizona, and began a year before filming by planting a field of corn which took a full 12 months until it was as high as an elephant's eye. It was Rodgers and Hammerstein's first Broadway play that was set for the screen, the first of many hits they would have together until their last, "Pipe Dream," after which Hammerstein passed away. They opened their play on Broadway at the end of March, 1943, for a run that would last more than 2200 performances. The stage version starred Betty Garde, Alfred Drake, Celeste Holm, Howard Da Silva, Joseph Buloff, Lee Dixon, Joan Roberts, Joan McCracken, and Bambi Lynn—who was the only one to be in the film, 12 years later. The Todd A-O system was a bit shaky at the start, but later prints were corrected and the story and songs burst forth with the same energy and elan as had been seen on the stage. It's a paean of nostalgia for the early days of the first "Sooner" settlers in Oklahoma and the story isn't much at all. Boys, MacRae and Nelson, meet Girls, Jones and Grahame; Boys almost lose Girls; Boys Get Girls. In the meantime, Steiger, the villain, tries to come between Jones and MacRae and eventually loses his life. Until "Oklahoma" came to the stage, the traditional Broadway opening had a line of high-stepping chorus girls with razzle-dazzle outfits. In this, the set is quiet and we hear MacRae's voice extolling the pleasures of "Oh, What a Beautiful Morning," and we know right away that something is different. Comedy is provided by Albert, as the fast-talking traveling salesman, and Whitmore, as an angry shotgun-carrying farmer. Choreographer DeMille did an unprecedented thing on the stage which she repeated here. In the Dream Ballet, she replaced Jones and MacRae with dancers Linn and Mitchell and no one seemed to mind, so a new theatrical convention was born that has since been duplicated whenever the leads can't dance. (See ON THE TOWN.) They'd thought Nogales would be a good place to shoot, as it promised endless sunshine. That was not the case and the company had to stay there for eight months and wait out many squalls. They waited so long that Sheila MacRae, Gordon's wife, had enough time to arrive, get pregnant, and deliver her son before the picture was done. The rain caused several flash floods and it was while one of these occurred that the limousine carrying one whole week's worth of film was washed away and the film was lost, necessitating a week's re-shoot. Despite the length of time it took, Zinnemann never did too many takes. With his background as a film editor, he knew exactly what he wanted and didn't have the actors do endless scenes, preferring to edit it in his sharp mind while he shot, in much the same way Hitchcock, another former film cutter, did. When the time came to cast the role of "Laurey," it was almost as huge a task as finding "Scarlett O'Hara," as everyone and her sister tried out and screen-tested for the plum role. Jones had been in the chorus of "South Pacific" and Rodgers and Hammerstein were already eyeing her for the part, but as she had so little experience, they put that thought away. She then went on the road with another R&H show, "Me And Juliet," and was in Chicago when the call came for her to go to Hollywood. She was, of course, absolutely right for the part from the beginning, but it took a screen test with MacRae, who was also testing, for everyone to realize that. When interviewed by your editors, Jones said: "It was such a different experience for me. First of all, I had to go on a diet. I'd never been on a diet, coming from the small town, Smithton, Pennsylvania, where five starches a day was the usual norm. And the entire process of moviemaking was terribly confusing, so it took a while to get used to it." The score is, by this time, deeply imbedded in the minds of anyone who has ears, but the people they chose to play some of the roles were off-center and that very avoidance of on-the-nose casting is what makes this so constantly surprising. Despite the huge success it rightfully had, and continues to have whenever it's shown in revival houses or on TV, only the score received an Oscar, with but two other nominations: to Surtees for his cinematography and to Bennett, Blackton, and Deutsch for their musical direction. The Rodgers and Hammerstein songs include: "Oh, What a Beautiful Morning" (sung by Gordon MacRae), "Surrey with the Fringe on Top" (sung by MacRae, Shirley Jones, Gene Nelson), "I Cain't Say No" (sung by Gloria Grahame), "Many a New Day" (sung by Jones), "People Will Say We're in Love" (sung by MacRae, Jones), "Poor Jud Is Dead" (sung by Rod Steiger, MacRae), "All 'Er Nuthin" (sung by Nelson, Grahame), "Everything's Up to Date in Kansas City" (sung by Nelson, Charlotte Greenwood, chorus), "The Farmer and the Cowman" (sung by Jones), "Out of My Dreams" (sung by MacRae, Jones, danced by Bambi Linn, James Mitchell), and "Oklahoma" (sung by MacRae, Jones, Nelson, Greenwood, James Whitmore, J.C. Flippen, chorus). In a tiny role, look for Ben Johnson as the cowboy at the train depot. Of particular interest is Hammerstein's lyric for "People Will Say We're in Love." He'd always felt that a declaratory love song in act one was much too early, so he wrote songs for the first act that would state the facts but with certain drawbacks, such as this one and "If I Loved You," among the many he penned. If there had been an Oscar for choreography, DeMille would have won it.

p, Arthur Hornblow, Jr.; d, Fred Zinnemann; w, Sonya Levien, William Ludwig (based on the musical by Richard Rodgers, Oscar Hammerstein II, from the play "Green Grow the Lilacs" by Lynn Riggs); ph, Robert Surtees (Todd-AO, Eastmancolor); m, Rodgers; ed, Gene Gruggiero; prod d, Oliver Smith; md, Jay Blackton, Robert Russell Bennett, Adolph Deutsch; art d, Joseph Wright; cos, Orry-Kelly, Motley; ch, Agnes DeMille.

Musical Cas. (PR:AAA MPAA:G)

OKLAHOMA ANNIE** (1952) 90m REP c

Judy Canova *(Judy, Queen of Cowgirls)*, John Russell *(Dan Fraser)*, Grant Withers *(Bull McCready)*, Roy Barcroft *(Curt Walker)*, Emmett "Pappy" Lynn *(Paydirt)*, Frank Ferguson *(Eldridge Haskell)*, Minerva Urecal *(Mrs. Fling)*, Houseley Stevenson *(Blinky)*, Almira Sessions *(Mrs. Fudge)*, Allen Jenkins *(Bartender)*, Maxine Gates *(Tillie)*, Emory Parnell *(Judge Byrnes)*, Denver Pyle *(Skip)*, House Peters, Jr. *(Tullett)*, Andrew Tombes *(Mayor)*, Fuzzy Knight *(Larry)*, Si Jenks *(Old Man)*, Marion Martin *(Le Belle La Tour)*, Herb Vigran *(Croupier)*, Hal Price *(Sheriff)*, Fred Hoose *(Bookkeeper)*, Lee Phelps *(Taylor)*, Bobby Taylor *(Bobby)*, William Fawcett *(Painter)*.

Canova stars as a country-girl shopkeeper who is in love with the town's new sheriff, Russell. He was installed after it was discovered that the old sheriff was a crook. Canova wants to be an officer herself, and is deputized after she captures a bank robber. Together the male-female, sheriff-deputy team cleans up the county of all its corrupt and dishonest citizens—including local politicians—led by Ferguson, who runs a gambling den. When Russell is captured by the crooks, Canova rallies all the area's angry women and they raid the gambling house and throw the bums in jail. Because of her heroics, Canova becomes sheriff and Russell becomes county supervisor. Canova was known for her backwoods charm and enthusiastic singing style.

p, Sidney Picker; d, R.G. Springsteen; w, Jack Townley (based on a story by Townley, Charles E. Roberts); ph, Jack Marta (Trucolor); m, Nathan Scott; ed, Richard L. Van Enger; md, Scott; art d, Frank Arrigo; spec eff, Howard Lydecker, Theodore Lydecker; m/l, "Blow the Whistle," S. Sherwin, Harry McClintock, "Have You Ever Been Lonely," George Brown, Peter De Rose, "Never, Never, Never," Jack Elliott, Sonny Burke (all sung by Judy Canova).

Musical/Western (PR:A MPAA:NR)

OKLAHOMA BADLANDS** (1948) 59m REP bw

Allan "Rocky" Lane *(Himself)*, Eddy Walker *(Nugget Clark)*, Mildred Coles *(Leslie Rawlins)*, Roy Barcroft *(Sanders)*, Gene Stutenroth *(Oliver Budge)*, Earle Hodgins *(Jonathan Walpole)*, Dale Van Sickel *(Sharkey)*, Jay Kirby *(Ken Rawlins)*, Claire Whitney *(Agatha Scragg)*, Terry Frost *(Sheriff Heyman)*, Hank Patterson *(Fred)*, House Peters, Jr. *(Wilkins)*, Jack Kirk *(Marsden)*, Bob Woodward, Black Jack the Horse.

Veteran stuntman Yakima Canutt directed this Lane western which displays the cowboy and his horse outwitting a gang of unscrupulous landgrabbers, led by a corrupt newspaper publisher, who seek to drive newly arrived female rancher Coles off her land. Canutt began his directorial career in the mid-1940s.

p, Gordon Kay; d, Yakima Canutt; w, Bob Williams; ph, John MacBurnie; ed, Arthur Roberts; md, Mort Glickman; art d, Frank Arrigo; set d, John McCarthy, Jr., James Redd; spec eff, Howard Lydecker, Theodore Lydecker; makeup, Bob Mark.

Western Cas. (PR:A MPAA:NR)

OKLAHOMA BLUES** (1948) 56m MON bw

Jimmy Wakely, Dub "Cannonball" Taylor, Charles King, Virginia Belmont, George J. Lewis, Zon Murray, I. Stanford Jolley, Steve Clark, Frank LaRue, Milburn Morante, Don Weston, Arthur "Fiddlin" Smith, Bob Woodward, J.C. Lytton, Richard Reinhardt.

In the Oklahoma territory, two towns must duke it out to win the title of county seat. Typical western for singing hero Wakely.

p, Louis Gray; d, Lambert Hillyer; w, Bennett Cohen; ph, Harry Neumann; ed, Fred Maguire; md, Edward J. Kay.

Western (PR:A MPAA:NR)

OKLAHOMA CRUDE½** (1973) 108m COL c

George C. Scott *(Noble "Mase" Mason)*, Faye Dunaway *(Lena Doyle)*, John Mills *(Cleon Doyle)*, Jack Palance *(Hellman)*, William Lucking *(Marion)*, Harvey Jason *(Wilcox)*, Ted Gehring *(Wobbly)*, Cliff Osmond *(Massive Man)*, Rafael Campos *(Jimmy)*, Woodrow Parfrey *(Lawyer)*, John Hudkins *(Bloom)*, Harvey Parry *(Bliss)*, Bob Herron *(Dulling)*, Jerry Brown *(Rucker)*, Jim Burk *(Moody)*, Henry Wills *(Walker)*, Hal Smith *(C.R. Miller)*, Cody Bearpaw *(Indian)*, James Jeter *(Stapp)*, Larry D. Mann *(Deke Watson)*, John Dierkes *(Farmer)*, Karl Lukas, Wayne Storm *(Hoboes)*, Billy Varga *(Cook)*.

The title of this film can easily be applied to its cast members, as well as the black oil it signifies, for all of the players essay characters that are about as empathic as rattlesnakes. Scott is a sleazy, drunken roustabout whose breath, if it could be smelled by the viewer, would certainly collapse a healthy lung. He has no scruples, ambitions, or decency. Survival in the Oklahoma oil field area is all he knows and he doesn't know much of that anyway. Dunaway is a mean-spirited lady who owns a small piece of land which features a towering hill upon which she has constructed a derrick to wildcat for oil. Working with her is an Indian, Campos, and she disdains any other human contact, especially entreaties from a huge oil firm, Pan-Oklahoma, which seeks to obtain her rig. Mills, the estranged father of Dunaway, arrives to offer his daughter help but she contemptuously rejects him, sending him on his way. Mills goes to a hobo camp where he meets the hunkering Scott and asks him to help his daughter, promising him a share in the profits when the well comes gushing in. More out of caprice than commitment, Scott shows up and his help is grudgingly accepted by Dunaway but she makes it clear to him that she's not interested in him nor in any other man. In fact, she goes so far as to tell him that she wishes she had been born with the organs of both sexes so she could have sex with herself and thereby avoid any contact with males, whom she hates with an abiding passion, all males, young and old. While Scott, Dunaway, and Campos sleep, the area is invaded by sadistic Palance and his thugs, all doing henchman service for Pan-Oklahoma. They beat up Dunaway and Scott and so severely punish Campos that he dies of his wounds. Scott and Dunaway are driven off the land and go to town where they join forces with Mills. They go to a lawyer, Parfrey, who tells them it's useless to take Pan-Oklahoma to court for its barbaric land grabbing since the firm owns the judges. The attorney simply advises them to retake the property by force. Obtaining supplies, guns, and some hand grenades, the three drive Palance's goons from the land and take over the well once more. As they keep it methodically pumping, the trio must stand guard from attack day and night. Palance and goons surround the hilltop derrick and pot shoot at the occupants around the clock. As the ordeal continues, Dunaway's attitude softens and she becomes more friendly with Scott and, especially, her father, Mills. When a cable breaks, Mills affixes a metal sheet to his back and climbs the derrick to repair it, sniper bullets twanging off the metal shield. He gets to the top, makes the repairs, and is about to descend when he is fatally shot and falls to his death. Sorely pressed, Scott and Dunaway continue to operate the well and finally Palance decides to rush the derrick stronghold once more. Just as his men charge up the hill, the well comes in, blasting crude oil skyward. Dunaway has brought in her well under a deadline and, instead of being shot, she is instantly approached by representatives of oil firms offering her huge amounts of money for distributing the black gold. Triumphant, she is about to take the highest bid when the well suddenly fizzles out and runs dry. The oil people leave and Dunaway has come up a big loser. Scott tells her that he's planning to go to Mexico and starts to walk off the miserable property. Just then Dunaway calls him by his first name, a call that signifies her attraction to and need for him. Scott stops dead still, eyebrow arched in anticipation of sexual delights to come, a sneaky smile on Dunaway's thin lips, all captured in a final freeze frame. OKLAHOMA CRUDE is both drama and comedy and sometimes has a hard time making up its mind which to really be. Scott slides through his graceless role but sometimes is brilliant, while Dunaway does a hillbilly rendition of THE TAMING OF THE SHREW. Mills is outstanding as the errant father who had deserted his family and tries to redeem himself at the end. Palance, on the other hand, is a caricature of the old-fashioned villain; all he needs is the long black mustache to twirl as he contemplates the fate of his next victim. Yet the movie is highly entertaining since Kramer distains his usual "message" and plays for the straight story. The film is nevertheless vulgar for its own sake, packed with sadism and gutter talk. Mancini's tedious score misses and the special effects are lifeless. The violence is often extraordinary and bloody. This tale was much better made and told in BOOM TOWN, 1940, with Spencer Tracy, Clark Gable, Claudette Colbert, and Hedy Lamarr. OKLAHOMA CRUDE was not filmed in Oklahoma because a suitable setting for its time frame, 1913, could not be found in that state when the film was made in 1973. Instead an oil field near Stockton, California, was used.

p&d, Stanley Kramer; w, Marc Norman; ph, Robert Surtees (Panavision, Technicolor); m, Henry Mancini; ed, Folmar Blangsted; prod d, Alfred Sweeney; set d, Maury Hoffman; cos, Bill Thomas, Seth Banks; spec eff, Alex Weldon; m/l, "Send a Little Love My Way," Mancini, Hal David; stunts, John Hudkins.

Drama/Comedy **(PR:O MPAA:PG)**

OKLAHOMA CYCLONE**
(1930) 64m TIF bw

Bob Steele *(Oklahoma Cyclone)*, Al St. John *(Slim)*, Nita Ray *(Carmelita)*, Charles L. King *(McKim)*, Hector Sarno *(The Don)*, Slim Whitaker *(Rawhide)*, Shorty Hendrix *(Shorty)*, Emilio Fernandez *(Panchez Gomez)*, Fred Burns, Cliff Lyons, John Ince.

The adventures of a group of bronco busters, engaged in some two-fisted action, are chronicled in this early western outing for cowboy star Steele. This was the second of eight talkies in a series Steele made for the short-lived Tiffany, and the first in which the diminutive cowboy actor crooned a few songs—three, in fact, in rapid succession, followed by one from love interest Ray. Fortunately for Steele's career he soon ceased vocalizing.

p, Trem Carr; d, John P. McCarthy; w, Ford Beebe (based on a story by McCarthy).

Western **Cas.** **(PR:A MPAA:NR)**

OKLAHOMA FRONTIER**
(1939) 58m UNIV bw

Johnny Mack Brown *(Jeff McLeod)*, Bob Baker *(Tom Rankin)*, Fuzzy Knight *(Windy Day)*, Anne Gwynne *(Janet Rankin)*, James Blaine *(George Frazier)*, Robert Kortman *(J.W. Sanders)*, Charles King *(Soapy)*, Harry Tenbrook *(Grimes)*, Horace Murphy *(Mushy)*, Lloyd Ingraham *(Judge)*, Anthony Warde *(Wayne)*, Robert Cummings Sr. *(Rankin)*, Lane Chandler *(Sergeant)*, Hank Bell *(Corporal)*, Dick Bush *(Settler)*, Frank Mayo *(Marshal)*, Joe De LaCruz, Al Bridge, Hank Worden, Blackie Whiteford, Roy Harris [Riley Hill], George Magrill, George Chesebro, Tom Smith, the Texas Rangers.

Brown stars in his second horse opera for Universal as a former marshal who puts an end to evil land grabber Kortman's scheme to snatch all the best territory after Oklahoma is opened for homesteading. Climax features Brown marrying heroine Gwynne whose brother, Baker, was killed early in the film. A well-directed scene involving the race of settlers' wagons across the territory when the governor legalizes their claims is the highlight.

p, Albert Ray; d&w, Ford Beebe; ph, Jerome Ash; ed, Louis Sackin; md, Charles Previn.

Western **(PR:A MPAA:NR)**

OKLAHOMA JIM*½
(1931) 61m MON bw

Bill Cody, Marion Burns, Andy Shuford, William Desmond, Si Jenks, Franklyn Farnum, John Elliott, Ed Brady, G.D. Woods [Gordon DeMain], Iron Eyes Cody, J.W. Cody, Ann Ross, Art Ortego, White Eagle.

Short Cody vehicle overly packed with plot has the cowboy on the run from Indians. They hold him responsible for the suicide of a girl who claimed a white man seduced her on her wedding day. They chase him to Massachusetts where he helps heroine Burns collect her deceased father's estate, before Indian sidekick Shuford can persuade the marauding redskins that Cody is not the guy they want.

p, Trem Carr; d, Harry Fraser; w, G.A. Durham (based on a story by Fraser); ph, A.J. Stout.

Western **(PR:A MPAA:NR)**

OKLAHOMA JUSTICE**
(1951) 56m MON bw

Johnny Mack Brown, James Ellison, Phyllis Coates, Barbara Allen, Kenne Duncan, Lane Bradford, Marshall Reed, Zon Murray, Stanley Price, I. Stanford Jolley, Bruce Edwards, Richard Avonde, Carl Mathews, Edward Cassidy, Lyle Talbot, George DeNormand.

When outlaws reign in Oklahoma, something must be done, so Brown saves the day with the usual gunfights and fisticuffs found in his horse operas. Strictly for western action fans and aficionadoes of expert horsemanship.

p, Vincent M. Fennelly; d, Lewis Collins; w, Joseph O'Donnell.

Western **(PR:A MPAA:NR)**

OKLAHOMA KID, THE***
(1939) 85m WB bw

James Cagney *(Jim Kincaid)*, Humphrey Bogart *(Whip McCord)*, Rosemary Lane *(Jane Hardwick)*, Donald Crisp *(Judge Hardwick)*, Harvey Stephens *(Ned Kincaid)*, Hugh Sothern *(John Kincaid)*, Charles Middleton *(Alec Martin)*, Ward Bond *(Wes Handley)*, Edward Pawley *(Doolin)*, Lew Harvey *(Curley)*, Trevor Bardette *(Indian Jack Pasco)*, John Miljan *(Ringo)*, Arthur Aylesworth *(Judge Morgan)*, Irving Bacon *(Hotel Clerk)*, Wade Boteler *(Sheriff Abe Collins)*, Joe Devlin *(Keely)*, Dan Wolheim *(Deputy)*, Ray Mayer *(Professor)*, Bob Kortman *(Juryman)*, Tex Cooper *(Old Man in Bar)*, John Harron *(Secretary)*, Stuart Holmes *(President Cleveland)*, Jack Mower *(Mail Clerk)*, Frank Mayo *(Land Agent)*, Don Barclay *(Drunk)*, Horace Murphy, Robert Homans, George Lloyd *(Bartenders)*, Soledad Jiminez *(Indian Woman)*, Ed Brady *(Jury Foreman)*, Jeffrey Sayre *(Times Reporter)*, Spencer Charters, Joe Rickson, William Worthington, Elliott Sullivan, Tom Chatterton *(Homesteaders)*, Al Bridge *(Settler)*, Rosina Galli *(Manuelita)*, George Rigas *(Pedro)*, Clem Bevans *(Postman)*, Elliott Sullivan *(Henchman)*, Whizzer the Horse.

Both Cagney and Bogart are out of their elements in this fanciful western but they make the best of it and provide some great campy scenes. Cagney is the title character, a sort of Robin Hood type who is the black sheep of a do-good family. The film opens at the time of the Oklahoma land rush in 1893, when the government opened up the fertile lands of the Cherokee Strip to homesteaders. Thousands of frontier families rush for the land at the sound of the gun and these include Sothern and his son Stephens, who have already picked out a site for a new town. But by the time they arrive at the spot, they are greeted by Bogart and his outlaw band, who have ignored the proper starting time and arrived earlier, thus earning the sobriquet of "Sooners." (This would be a nickname thereafter for anyone born and raised in the state of Oklahoma.) Rather than give up the site, Sothern and Stephens agree to let Bogart have the saloon and gambling hall concessions of the new town if he will turn over the claim. He does, but it's the worst mistake Sothern and Stephens could make. Under Bogart's ruthless guidance, the new town, Tulsa, becomes a hellhole, with lawlessness and vice rampant. Sothern, now the town's leading citizen, decides to clean up Tulsa. He runs for mayor as a reform candidate with his son Stephens running for the post of sheriff. But Bogart knows that once Sothern is in office his own days are numbered. He frames Sothern on a phony murder charge. While Sothern awaits trial, Cagney hears of the frame-up and heads for Tulsa, meeting Lane en route. He confesses that he is the errant son of Sothern and also the notorious outlaw, "The Oklahoma Kid". After hearing the details of his father's frame-up from Lane, who is also his brother's sweetheart, Cagney rides fast for Tulsa. Meanwhile, Bogart has replaced an honest judge, Crisp, with another vest-pocket judge and Sothern is quickly tried and condemned. To make sure the phony conviction and death sentence stick, Bogart orders his men to lynch Sothern, which they do. By the time Cagney arrives there is little he can do but join with his brother, now a U.S. marshal, and seek revenge. He and Stephens blast their way into Bogart's saloon and Cagney shoots and kills Bogart in a wild battle but his brother Stephens is also mortally wounded. Stephens dies in Cagney's arms, asking him to go straight and to take care of Lane, both of which he promises to do. THE OKLAHOMA KID is hokey, corny, and wholly unbelievable but it's so contrived—and Cagney's performance is so outlandish, as is Bogart's heavy—that the film is oddly appealing. It's a treat just to watch and listen to Cagney play a guitar and sing "Rockabye Baby" and "I Don't Want to Play in Your Yard," when trying to soothe a crying Mexican baby. He is thoroughly disarming as he pranks his way through the movie. Bogart tries to stay up with Cagney's antics but he's no match for the twitching, jumping, hopping Bowery Boy suddenly stomping around in riding boots. Cagney and Bogart were never friends, although they became the top Warner Bros. stars. Cagney attributed this to Bogart's feisty antisocial attitude and it was during this production that Cagney had his only "outing" with Bogart, a late night dinner—no drinks—at Chasen's Restaurant. The evening was captioned by Mayo Methot, Bogart's then-mercurial firebrand of a wife, who stormed into the restaurant and accused Bogart of sitting around with "drunken friends." Said Cagney of Bogart at this time: "He hated just about everybody, but that was his aim—to hate them first. When it came to fighting, he was about as tough as Shirley Temple." Bogart, who slightly resented having to play second fiddle to Cagney in a host of Warner Bros. gangster films during the 1930s, took one look at the star of THE OKLAHOMA KID when he first stepped onto the set and said: "In that ten-gallon hat, you look like a mushroom!" During the production, Cagney was driving home one night and stopped for a traffic light. He looked over to see Bogart at the wheel of a sports car. Bogart was staring straight ahead, picking his nose. Cagney went home and wrote the following ditty: "In this silly town of ours/One sees odd primps and poses/But movie stars in fancy cars/Shouldn't pick their noses." He sent it to Bogart but never got a response.

p, Samuel Bischoff; d, Lloyd Bacon; w, Warren Duff, Robert Buckner, Edward E. Paramore (based on a story by Paramore, Wally Klein); ph, James Wong Howe; m, Max Steiner; ed, Owen Marks; art d, Esdras Hartley; cos, Orry-Kelly; makeup, Perc Westmore.

Western   **(PR:A MPAA:NR)**

OKLAHOMA RAIDERS**   (1944) 57m UNIV bw (GB: MIDNIGHT RAIDERS)

Tex Ritter (Steve), Fuzzy Knight (Banjo), Jennifer Holt (Donna), Dennis Moore (Todd), Jack Ingram (Arnold Drew), George Eldridge (James Prescott), John Elliott (Judge Masters), Slim Whitaker (Sheriff Banning), I. Stanford Jolley (Higgins), Dick Alexander (Duggan), Herbert Rawlinson (Colonel), Ethan Laidlaw (Williams), Stephen Keyes, Lane Chandler, Frank Ellis, William Desmond, Bob Baker, Johnny Bond and his Red River Valley Boys.

Loose remake of COME ON DANGER (1932) features Ritter and Knight sent to buy horses for the U.S. Cavalry, only to discover crooks Ingram and Eldridge up to their usual misdeeds, and a female masked vigilante, Holt (sister of Tim). The film includes massive amounts of stock footage from KING OF THE STALLIONS (1942). This was Ritter's last film for Universal.

p, Oliver Drake; d, Lewis D. Collins; w, Betty Burbridge; ph, William Sickner; ed, Norman Cerf; md, Paul Sawtell.

Western   **(PR:A MPAA:NR)**

OKLAHOMA RENEGADES**   (1940) 57m REP bw

Robert Livingston (Stony Brook), Raymond Hatton (Rusty Joslin), Duncan Renaldo (Rico), Lee "Lasses" White, Florine McKinney, Al Herman, William Ruhl, Eddie Dean, James Seay, Harold Daniels, Jack Lescoulie, Frosty Royce, Yakima Canutt.

The Spanish-American war is over and the three Mesquiteers (Livingston, Hatton, and Renaldo), are homeward bound to further adventures. This was one of eight movies the Mesquiteers made in 1940, with Bob Steele (who was to take over the Livingston role the next year), and Rufe Davis assuming the Hatton and Renaldo roles before the year was over. (See THREE MESQUITEERS series, Index.)

p, Harry Grey; d, Nate Watt; w, Earl Snell, Doris Schroeder (based on the story by Charles Condon from characters created by William Colt MacDonald); ph, Reggie Lanning; ed, Tony Martinelli.

Western   **(PR:A MPAA:NR)**

OKLAHOMA TERRITORY**½   (1960) 67m Premium/UA bw

Bill Williams (Temple Houston), Gloria Talbott (Ruth Red Hawk), Ted de Corsia (Buffalo Horn), Grant Richards (Bigelow), Walter Sande (Rosslyn), X Brands (Running Cloud), Walter Baldwin (Ward Harlen), Grandon Rhodes (Blackwell), John Cliff (Larkin).

District Attorney Williams prosecutes Indian chief De Corsia on a murder charge, gets a conviction, and then arranges his escape when he discovers De Corsia is innocent. Evil railway agent Richards is really responsible for the death because he had been trying to start an Indian war to clear land for his railroad. Climax features Williams, with guns drawn, forcing a federal judge to reopen the case. Fairly bizarre.

p, Robert E. Kent; d, Edward L. Cahn; w, Orville H. Hampton; ph, Walter Strenge; m, Albert Glasser; ed, Grant Whytock.

Western   **(PR:A MPAA:NR)**

OKLAHOMA TERROR*½   (1939) 60m MON bw

Jack Randall (Jack), Al St. John (Fuzzy), Virginia Carroll (Helen), Davison Clark (Cartwright), Glenn Strange (Haddon), Warren McCollum (Don), Nolan Willis (Yucca), Brandon Beach (Reynolds), Tristram Coffin (Mason), Ralph Peters (Reb), Slim Whitaker, Rusty the Horse.

Post Civil War western showcases Union soldier Randall returning home from battle to find his father has been murdered by hoods who are terrorizing the area. Joined by pal St. John, Randall organizes the local ranchers, who are fed up with the gang, and wipes out the crooks. In the end, it is revealed that the town's richest and most respected citizen was the mastermind behind the gang.

p, Lindsley Parsons; d, Spencer Bennett; w, Joseph West (based on a story by Parsons); ph, Bert Longenecker; ed, Robert Golden.

Western   **Cas.**   **(PR:A MPAA:NR)**

OKLAHOMA WOMAN, THE*   (1956) 71m SUN/ American Releasing bw

Richard Denning (Steve Ward), Peggie Castle (Marie "Oklahoma" Saunders), Tudor Owen (Ed Grant), Martin Kingsley (Sheriff Bill Peters), Cathy Downs (Susan Grant), Touch [Mike] Connors (Sheriff), Jonathan Haze, Richard "Dick" Miller, Thomas Dillon, Edmund Cobb, Bruno Ve Sota, Aaron Saxton, Joe Brown.

Part of Roger Corman's quartet of westerns, this one stars Denning as a gunfighter who returns home after serving a federal prison sentence, only to discover that the town has split into two factions. Much to his dismay, his girl friend, Castle, has become the villainous leader of the "bad" side and she will stop at nothing to ensure that lawlessness prevails. Repulsed by Castle's obnoxious personality (and her gunslinger Connors), Denning joins the "good" folks, led by politician Owen and his daughter Downs with whom he becomes enamored. Things come to a head when the sheriff and Owen are killed. Ex-con Denning is framed and about to be hung for his crimes, when Downs forces Castle to sign a confession implicating Connors. There was as much off-screen antagonism as on-screen between the female leads because Corman had signed Castle to get first female billing which outraged Downs. Eventually a compromise was struck that Castle's name would indeed be listed first, but that the typeface would be the same size as for Downs. In addition, Downs was promised to be featured in another production and she would receive top billing.

p&d, Roger Corman; w, Lou Rusoff; ph, Fred West (Superscope); m, Ronald Stein; ed, Ronald Sinclair.

Western   **(PR:C MPAA:NR)**

OKLAHOMAN, THE**½   (1957) 80m AA c

Joel McCrea (Dr. John Brighton), Barbara Hale (Anne Barnes), Brad Dexter (Cass Dobie), Gloria Talbott (Maria Smith), Verna Felton (Mrs. Waynebrook), Douglas Dick (Mel Dobie), Michael Pate (Charlie Smith), Anthony Caruso (Jim Hawk), Esther Dale (Mrs. Fitzgerald), Adam Williams (Bob Randell), Ray Teal (Jason, Stableman), Peter Votrian (Little Charlie), John Pickard (Marshal Bill), Diane Brewster (Eliza), Sheb Wooley (Cowboy/Henchman), Harry Lauter (Grant), I. Stanford Jolley (Storekeeper), Mimi Gibson (Louise Brighton), Robert Hinkle (Ken the Driver), Doris Kemper, Dorothy Neumann, Gertrude Astor (Women), Wheaton Chambers (Lounger), Earle Hodgins (Sam the Bartender), Watson Downs, Tod Farrell (Farmers), Rankin Mansfield (Doctor), Don Marlowe (Rider), Laurie Mitchell, Jenny Lea (Girls), Scotty Beckett (Messenger at Ranch), Lennie Geer (Bushwacker), Al Kramer (Wild Line), Kermit Maynard (Townsman), Bill Foster (Dobie Henchman).

Fine low-budget western starring McCrea as a doctor on his way to California when his wife dies during childbirth in Oklahoma. Not having the heart to travel any farther, McCrea decides to stay and build a practice in the town where his wife is buried. His practice thrives in the small community, but McCrea runs afoul of evil cattle barons Dexter and Dick after he helps an Indian whose land they were about to grab. Eventually McCrea faces Dexter in a gunfight and is wounded while Dexter is killed.

p, Walter Mirisch; d, Francis D. Lyon; w, Daniel B. Ullman; ph, Carl Guthrie (CinemaScope, DeLuxe Color); m, Hans Salter; ed, George White; md, Salter; art d, Dave Milton.

Western   **(PR:A MPAA:NR)**

OLD ACQUAINTANCE**½   (1943) 110m WB-FN bw

Bette Davis (Kitty Marlowe), Miriam Hopkins (Millie Drake), Gig Young (Rudd Kendall), John Loder (Preston Drake), Dolores Moran (Deirdre), Philip Reed (Lucian Grant), Roscoe Karns (Charlie Archer), Anne Revere (Belle Carter), Leona Maricle (Julia Brondbank), Esther Dale (Harriet), George Lessey (Dean), Joseph Crehan (Editor), James Conlin (Photographer), Marjorie Hoshelle (Margaret Kemp), Tommye Adams, Kathleen O'Malley, Timmy Sabor, Frances Ward, Virginia Patton, Lucille LaMarr, Harriett Olsen, Dorothy Schoemer (College Girls), Francine Rufo (Deirdre as a Child), Ann Codee (Mademoiselle), Creighton Hale (Stage Manager), Pierre Watkin (Mr. Winter), Frank Darien (Stage Doorman), Philip Van Zandt (Clerk), Charles Jordan (Bootlegger), Herbert Rawlinson (Chairman), Gordon Clark (Usher), Ann Doran (Saleslady), Frank Mayo, Jack Mower, Maj. Sam Harris (Army Officers), Charles Sullivan (Taxi Driver).

Davis and Hopkins had been teamed by producer Blanke in another "old" picture when they did THE OLD MAID in 1939. Despite the friction between the two women, they got together again for this less-successful duet. Van Druten's play had been on Broadway about three years before and he collaborated with Lenore Coffee on the screenplay, taking some liberties with the original text. Davis is a best-selling author who comes back to her small town to acknowledge the plaudits of the folks. She stays at the home of Hopkins, a childhood girl friend, who is now pregnant and happily married to Loder. Hopkins is envious of her pal's success and writes a steamy novel of her own which Davis manages to get to the right eyes at her publishing company and Hopkins is soon a best-selling writer. Hopkins becomes the Jaqueline Susann of her era and turns out one hot potboiler after another, while Davis spends her time writing what she considers to be more important creations. Years pass and Hopkins, Loder, and their daughter, Rufo, come to see Davis' new stage offering in New York. Loder is smitten by Davis, tells her he loves her, and even though she discourages him, he leaves Hopkins, who has changed a great deal for the worse due to her new status as an author. Ten years later, Loder is now an officer during WW II, and meets Davis again. He's about to get married and so is she, to Young, a Navy officer 10 years younger. Hopkins tries to find Loder and tries to put their marriage back together but to no avail. When Loder admits he once loved Davis, Hopkins goes through the roof and screams at Davis for stealing her husband. Davis responds to the false charges by throttling Hopkins, then exiting. Davis now learns that Loder and Hopkins' daughter (played by Moran as a grown-up) is in love with Young and he with her; Davis bows out and wishes the two kids well, knowing that her marriage to Young wasn't right for her anyhow. Davis visits Hopkins to tell her of Young and Moran and they are pals again. Hopkins says she is going to write a roman a clef about her relationship with Davis, if that's all right with Davis. The two women cement their old rifts and decide to remain bosom buddies as they face the rest of their lives with no one to talk to but each other. This could have been a wonderful comedy given that plot, but they opted for pathos and the result was just another okay picture. Remade as RICH AND FAMOUS.

p, Henry Blanke; d, Vincent Sherman; w, John Van Druten, Lenore Coffee (based on the play by Van Druten); ph, Sol Polito; m, Franz Waxman; ed, Terry Morse; md, Leo F. Forbstein; art d, John Hughes; set d, Fred MacLean; cos, Orry-Kelly.

Drama   **PR:A-C MPAA:NR)**

OLD BARN DANCE, THE**   (1938) 60m REP bw

Gene Autry (Gene), Smiley Burnette (Frog), Helen Valkis (Sally), Sammy McKim (Johnny), Walter Shrum and His Colorado Hillbillies (Hillbilly Band), Stafford Sisters (Trio), Maple City Four (Orchestra), Dick Weston [Roy Rogers] (Singer), Ivan Miller (Thornton), Earl Dwire (Clem), Hooper Atchley (Maxwell), Raphael [Ray] Bennett (Buck), Carleton Young (Peabody), Frankie Marvin (Cowboy), Earle Hodgins (Terwilliger), Gloria Rich (Singer), Champion the Horse.

Average Autry outing puts the singing cowboy and his pals in the horse selling business. Their main clientele are ranchers, but a tractor company that persuades the cattlemen that horses are a thing of the past puts the group out of business. Forced to work as singers on the radio, Autry and company find themselves being sponsored by the same tractor company that drove them out of business. When Autry learns that the company's tractors have been nothing but trouble for the ranchers (they constantly break down), the singing cowboy surmises that the tractor company is crooked and kicks the outfit out of town. Republic Studios noticed a young singing cowboy in the background named Dick Weston and signed him as Roy Rogers to replace Autry who left the studio after this picture because of a contractual dispute.

p, Sol C. Siegel; d, Joseph Kane; w, Bernard McConville, Charles Francis Royal; ph, Ernest Miller; ed, Lester Orlebeck; md, Alberto Columbo; m/l, Jack Lawrence, Peter Tinturin, Smiley Burnette, Frankie Marvin, Colorado Hillbillies.

Western   **Cas.**   **(PR:A MPAA:NR)**

OLD BILL AND SON**   (1940, Brit.) 96m Legeran/GFD bw

Morland Graham (Old Bill Busby), John Mills (Young Bill Busby), Mary Clare (Maggie Busby), Renee Houston (Stella Malloy), Rene Ray (Sally), Gus McNaughton (Alf), Ronald Shiner (Bert), Janine Darcey (Francoise), Roland Culver (Colonel), Donald Stuart (Canuck), Manning Whiley (Chimp), Nicholas Phipps (Commentator), Allan Jeayes (Willoughby), Percy Walsh (Gustave).

Cockney comedy starring Graham as the embodiment of the popular WW I doughboy cartoon character. Graham, in his old age, follows his son to France in WW II by joining the Pioneer Corps because the other branches of the armed services try to persuade him that his participation in this war is unnecessary.

p, Josef Somlo, Harold Boxall, Alexander Korda; d, Ian Dalrymple; w, Bruce Bairnsfather, Arthur Wimperis, Dalrymple (based on cartoons by Bairnsfather); ph, Georges Perinal; ed, Charles Crichton; prod d, Vincent Korda; md, Muir Mathieson.

Comedy   **(PR:A MPAA:NR)**

OLD BONES OF THE RIVER***   (1938, Brit.) 90m Gainsborough/GFD bw

Will Hay (Prof. Benjamin Tibbetts), Moore Marriott (Jerry Harbottle), Graham Moffatt (Albert), Robert Adams (Bosambo), Jack Livesey (Capt. Hamilton), Jack London (M'Bapi), Wyndham Goldie (Commissioner Sanders), The Western Brothers (Narrators).

After being sent into deepest Africa to open up schools for local tribesmen, teacher Hay finds himself becoming the acting commissioner when Goldie comes down with malaria. His tax-collecting methods, coupled with Moffatt and Marriott's help, cause unrest among the natives and Hay barely makes it out of the territory alive. Some great moments of hilarity in this British comedy of errors. A sequel to the 1935 film SANDERS OF THE RIVER from the Korda Brothers, starring Paul Robeson.

p, Edward Black; d, Marcel Varnel; w, Marriott Edgar, Val Guest, J.O.C Orton (based on the novels Bones and Lieutenant Bones by Edgar Wallace); ph, Arthur Crabtree.

Comedy   **(PR:A MPAA:NR)**

OLD BOYFRIENDS**   (1979) 103m AE c

Talia Shire (Diane Cruise), Richard Jordan (Jeff Turrin), Keith Carradine (Wayne Van Til), John Belushi (Eric Katz), John Houseman (Dr. Hoffman), Buck Henry (Art Kopple), Nina Jordan (Dylan Turrin), Gerritt Graham (Sam the Fisherman), P.J. Soles (Sandy), Bethel Leslie (Mrs. Van Til), Joan Hotchkis (Pamela Shaw), William Bassett (David Brinks).

Somewhat pointless but nonetheless interesting drama starring Shire as a clinical psychologist who, after a failed suicide attempt, decides to relive her past by finding her old boy friends. The trip takes her across the country where she meets Jordan, her college heartthrob, now a documentary filmmaker. From there she finds Belushi, her high school sweetheart, now the leader of a rock 'n' roll band whom she humiliates in revenge for a previous humiliation he had heaped upon her. Eventually she makes her way back to her home town to find her first childhood crush. To her surprise, he has died and she is consoled by his brother, Carradine. All the performances are fine, but the film as written by Paul and Leonard Schrader is as lifeless as it is pointless. Director Tewkesbury, with her first feature after having worked extensively with Robert Altman (she wrote NASHVILLE), does not seem to have a handle on the point of all this, though she provides some insightful and interesting moments along the way.

p, Edward R. Pressman, Michele Rappaport; d, Joan Tewkesbury; w, Paul Schrader, Leonard Schrader; ph, William A. Fraker; m, David Shire; ed, Bill Reynolds; art d, Peter Jamison; cos, Tony Faso, Suzanne Grace.

Drama   **Cas.**   **(PR:O MPAA:R)**

OLD CHISHOLM TRAIL**   (1943) 61m UNIV bw

Johnny Mack Brown (Dusty Gardner), Tex Ritter (Montana Smith), Fuzzy Knight (Polario), Jennifer Holt (Mary Lee), Mady Correll (Belle Turner), Earle Hodgins (Chief Hopping Crow), Roy Barcroft (Ed), Edmund Cobb (Joe Rankin), Budd Buster (Hank), Mike Carey (George Sherwood), Roy Butler (Larry), Michael Vallon (Sheriff), Jimmy Wakely, Scotty Harrel, Johnny Bond (Jimmy Wakely Trio).

Brown and Ritter star as two cowpokes on a drive down the Chisholm Trail. They defeat the evil duo of Correll and Barcroft by opening a locked water hole the bad guys control.

p, Oliver Drake; d&w, Elmer Clifton (based on a story by Harry Fraser); ph, William Sickner; ed, Ray Snyder; md, H.J. Salter; art d, Jack Otterson; m/l, Oliver Drake, Jimmy Wakely, Milton Rosen.

Western   **(PR:A MPAA:NR)**

OLD CORRAL, THE, 1936   (SEE: SONG OF THE GRINGO, 1936)

OLD CORRAL, THE*   (1937) 52m REP bw (GB: TEXAS SERENADE)

Gene Autry (Gene), Smiley Burnette (Frog), Hope Manning (Eleanor), Sons of Pioneers (O'Keefe Bros.), Cornelius Keefe (Simms), Lon Chaney, Jr. (Garland), John Bradford (Scarlotti), Milburn Morante (Snodgrass), Abe Lefton (Abe), Merrill McCormick (Joe), Charles Sullivan (Frank), Buddy Roosevelt (Tony), Lynton Brent (Dunn), Frankie Marvin (First Prisoner), Oscar and Elmer [Ed Platt and Lou Fulton] (Themselves), Jack Ingram, Dick Weston [Roy Rogers], Champion the Horse.

Badly conceived Autry western that has everything but the kitchen sink thrown into it. Autry stars as the singing sheriff of a small sagebrush town who meets a young singer, Manning, who left her club in Chicago after witnessing a murder. With the police and gangsters hot on her trail, Manning hides in the western town. Recognized by Autry and local bad guy Keefe, the girl soon finds herself in danger. The mobsters arrive armed with machine guns and Autry kicks the city-slicker varmints out of town. In the end Autry kisses Manning for the fade. Sub-plots see the less-than-worrisome Sons of the Pioneers as bandits and a very young and as of yet undiscovered Dick Weston (soon to be Roy Rogers) duke it out with Autry.

p, Armand Schaefer; d, Joseph Kane; w, Joseph Poland, Sherman Love (based on a story by Bernard McConville); ph, Edgar Lyons; ed, Lester Orlebeck; m/l, "So Long Old Paint," "In the Heart of the West," Sons of Pioneers, Flemming Allen, Oliver Drake.

Western   **Cas.**   **(PR:A MPAA:NR)**

OLD CURIOSITY SHOP, THE**½   (1935, Brit.) 90m Alliance/FD bw

Ben Webster (Grandfather Trent), Elaine Benson (Nell Trent), Hay Petrie (Quilp), Beatrix Thompson (Mrs. Quilp), Gibb McLaughlin (Sampson Brass), Lily Long (Sally Brass), Reginald Purdell (Dick Swiveller), Polly Ward (The Marchioness), James Harcourt (Single Gentleman), J. Fischer-White (Schoolmaster), Dick Tubb (Tommy Codlin), Roddy Hughes (Short), Amy Veness (Mrs. Jarley), Peter Penrose (Kit Nubbles), Vic Filmer (Tom Scott), Wally Patch (George), Fred Groves (Showman).

Lushly produced adaptation of a Dickens tale starring Webster as an old gambler and Benson as his granddaughter. Their lives are ruined when their landlord, a miserly old dwarf played with relish by Petrie, evicts them, forcing them into a life of poverty. Petrie was a renowned character actor who specialized in the odd duck roles. The film was remade in 1957 as MR. QUILP.

p, Walter C. Mycroft; d, Thomas Bentley; w, Margaret Kennedy, Ralph Neale (based on the novel Old Curiosity Shop and Reprinted Pieces by Charles Dickens); ph, Claude Friese-Greene; m, Eric Coates; ed, L. Norman; art d, Cedric Dawe; cos, Michael Weight.

Drama   **(PR:A MPAA:NR)**

OLD CURIOSITY SHOP, THE, 1975   (SEE: MR. QUILP, 1975, Brit.)

OLD DARK HOUSE, THE***½   (1932) 70m UNIV bw

Boris Karloff (Morgan), Melvyn Douglas (Roger Penderel), Charles Laughton (Sr. William Porterhouse), Gloria Stuart (Margaret Waverton), Lillian Bond (Gladys DuCane), Ernest Thesiger (Horace Femm), Eva Moore (Rebecca Femm), Raymond Massey (Philip Waverton), Brember Wills (Saul Femm), John [Elspeth] Dudgeon (Sir Roderick Femm).

A wonderfully funny and frightening haunted house film with an all-star cast helmed by a brilliant director, James Whale. Loosely based on J.B. Priestley's novel Benighted, the story sees a group of stranded travelers forced to seek refuge at the strange house of Femm. Massey, his wife Stuart and their friend Douglas are the first to arrive at the Femms' door. Inside lurks the bizarre Femm family presided over by the bedridden patriarch Dudgeon (age 102), his aged, atheist son Thesiger (in his best role, BRIDE OF FRANKENSTEIN notwithstanding), Moore, Thesiger's sister and a religious fanatic, and their older brother Wills who is a crazed pyromaniac kept locked up by their hulking, mute, scarred, and slightly psychotic butler Karloff (in his first starring role). When two more stranded travelers, Laughton and Bond, arrive, the evening's festivities begin. While sitting out the storm, the guests slowly realize the nature of the Femm house and the loonies who inhabit it. While Thesiger and Moore exchange quips, Karloff gets drunk and makes menacing advances on Stuart, but is knocked unconscious by Massey. When he comes to, a furious Karloff unleashes Wills who tries to set the house on fire. Douglas kills Wills during a struggle and the travelers vacate the crazy household upon the morning light. While the story is quite simple, the film is filled with quirky, lively performances and a masterful blend of comedy and horror. The former stage actor and director Whale gives special emphasis to characters' entrances and exits, heightening the terror and comedy.

p, Carl Laemmle, Jr.; d, James Whale; w, Benn W. Levy, R.C. Sherriff (based on the novel *Benighted* by J.B. Priestley); ph, Arthur Edeson; ed, Clarence Kolster; art d, Charles D. Hall; spec eff, John P. Fulton; makeup, Jack P. Pierce.

Horror/Comedy **(PR:A MPAA:NR)**

OLD DARK HOUSE, THE**½ (1963, Brit.) 86m COL c

Tom Poston *(Tom Penderel)*, Robert Morley *(Roderick Femm)*, Janette Scott *(Cecily)*, Joyce Grenfell *(Agatha Femm)*, Peter Bull *(Jasper Femm/Casper Femm)*, Mervyn Johns *(Potiphar)*, Fenella Fielding *(Morgana)*, Danny Green *(Morgan Femm)*.

Inferior remake of the 1932 James Whale classic starring Poston as an American car salesman in London who is plunged into a nightmare when he delivers a car to an old Welsh mansion. When he learns that the man who ordered the car has died, Poston attempts to leave but he crashes the car in a storm and must spend the night at the mansion. There he meets two sisters, Scott and Fielding (one nice, one evil); Bull, in a dual role as brothers Jasper and Casper; Johns, who is building an ark in anticipation of another great flood; Grenfell, Casper and Jasper's mother; and the head of the eccentric household, Morley. During the night, a different family member is killed every hour by an unseen murderer. Eventually Poston realizes that the killer is a woman and he immediately suspects Fielding. But Scott confesses to the crimes explaining that she wanted the family fortune all to herself. She flees the house, but not before Poston learns that she has planted time bombs throughout the mansion. Racing against time, Poston manages to clear the house of all the bombs, throwing the last one out the window only seconds before it explodes. The bomb lands at Scott's feet, and justice is done.

p, William Castle, Anthony Hinds; d, Castle; w, Robert Dillon (based on the novel *Benighted* by J.B. Priestley); ph, Arthur Grant (Eastmancolor); m, Benjamin Frankel; ed, James Needs; md, Frankel; art d, Bernard Robinson; spec eff, Les Bowie.

Horror/Comedy **(PR:A MPAA:NR)**

OLD DRACULA*½ (1975, Brit.) 89m World Film Services/AIP c (GB: VAMPIRA; OLD DRAC)

David Niven *(Count Dracula)*, Teresa Graves *(Countess Vampira)*, Peter Bayliss *(Maltravers)*, Jennie Linden *(Angela)*, Nicky Henson *(Marc)*, Linda Hayden *(Helga)*, Bernard Bresslaw *(Pottinger)*, Cathy Shirriff *(Nancy)*, Andrea Allan *(Eve)*, Veronica Carlson *(Ritva)*, Minah Bird *(Rose)*, Christopher Sandford *(Milton)*, Freddie Jones *(Gilmore)*, Frank Thornton *(King)*, Aimi MacDonald, Patrick Newell *(Couple in Hotel)*, Hoima McDonald, Nicola Austine, Penny Irving *(Playboy Bunnies)*.

Botched attempt at a horror/comedy starring Niven as the title character who, in modern times, has had to resort to guided tours of his castle to lure new victims in range of his fangs. He rents his castle to *Playboy* magazine for a photo shoot with some of their bunnies. Seeking to revive his long-dead mate, he gives her corpse a blood transfusion from a beautiful black victim. The experiment works and his love is revived, but her skin has turned black and she comes out of the coffin as Teresa Graves. By the end of this ridiculous film, Niven, too, turns black.

p, Jack H. Wiener; d, Clive Donner; w, Jeremy Lloyd; ph, Tony Richmond (Movielab Color); m, David Whitaker; ed, Bill Butler; art d, Philip Harrison; cos, Vangie Harrison; m/l, "Vampira," Anthony Newley (sung by The Majestics), "When You Look for a Dream," John and Rosalind (sung by John and Rosalind).

Comedy/Horror **(PR:C MPAA:PG)**

OLD ENGLISH**½ (1930) 85m WB bw

George Arliss *(Sylvanus Heythorp)*, Leon Janney *(Jock)*, Doris Lloyd *(Mrs. Larne)*, Betty Lawford *(Phyllis Larne)*, Ivan Simpson *(Joe Phillin)*, Harrington Reynolds *(Farney)*, Reginald Sheffield *(Bob Phillin)*, Murray Kinnell *(Charles Ventnor)*, Ethel Griffies *(Adela Heythorp)*, Henrietta Goodwin *(Letty)*.

Hopelessly stagebound adaptation of a once-popular play saved by the timeless performance of Arliss as the title character. Arliss stars as the elderly managing director of a shipbuilding firm whose harsh treatment of his daughter leads to his ultimate doom. Preferring to shower the teen-age children of his illegitimate son with affection, Arliss makes a fraudulent financial deal that he feels will ensure their future. Caught with his hand in the till, Arliss decides the only honorable way to avoid scandal is to commit suicide. He arranges to be served a bountiful gourmet meal, the consumption of which means certain death. He eats the meal, and after finishing a last after-dinner liqueur, dies quietly in his armchair. Visually dull (the different acts of the play are easily discernible by the set changes within the film illustrating the nearly insufferable lack of movement), but an interesting chance to see Arliss at work. The death scene is almost duplicated in DIAMOND JIM.

d, Alfred E. Green; w, Walter Anthony, Maude Howell (based on the play by John Galsworthy); ph, James Van Trees; ed, Owen Marks; md, Erno Rapee, Louis Silvers; cos, Earl Luick.

Drama **(PR:A MPAA:NR)**

OLD FAITHFUL**½ (1935, Brit.) 67m GS Enterprises/RKO bw

Horace Hodges *(Bill Brunning)*, Glennis Lorimer *(Lucy Brunning)*, Bruce Lister *(Alf Haines)*, Wally Patch *(Joe Riley)*, Isobel Scaife *(Lily)*, Muriel George *(Martha Brown)*, Edward Ashley Cooper *(Edwards)*.

Hodges is an old-time hansom driver who refuses to modernize by giving up his horse for a motorized taxicab. When his daughter Lorimer falls for one of the hated taxi drivers, her would-be suitor must pose as a plumber in order to please Hodges. Though dated, this retains some moments of charm, thanks to Hodges' wonderful characterization.

p, A. George Smith; d, Maclean Rogers; w, Kathleen Butler, H.F. Maltby (based on a story by Irving Dennes, Harry Dawes).

Romance/Comedy **(PR:A MPAA:NR)**

OLD-FASHIONED GIRL, AN** (1948) 82m Vinson/EL bw

Gloria Jean *(Polly Milton)*, Jimmy Lydon *(Tom Shaw)*, John Hubbard *(Mr. Sydney)*, Frances Rafferty *(Frances Shaw)*, Mary Eleanor Donahue *(Maud Shaw)*, Irene Ryan *(Mrs. Shaw)*, Douglas Wood *(Mr. Shaw)*, Barbara Brier *(Trix Parker)*, Claire Whitney *(Miss Mills)*, Rosemary La Planche *(Emma Davenport)*, Quenna Norla *(Miss Perkins)*, Shirley Mills *(Belle)*, Saundra Berkova *(Irma)*, Milton Kibbee *(Farmer Brown)*.

Routine LITTLE WOMEN inspired tale starring Jean as the independent music teacher who would rather scrape by on her own meager earnings than give in to her rich and domineering relatives. Jean was a popular actress in the 1940s, but never achieved real fame in her adult years.

p&d, Arthur Dreifuss; w, Dreifuss, McElbert Moore (based on the novel by Louisa May Alcott); ph, Philip Tannura; ed, Arthur A. Brooks; m/l, "Where," "Kitchen Serenade," Charles Previn, Moore, Bobby Worth, Al Sendry (sung by Gloria Jean).

Drama **(PR:A MPAA:NR)**

OLD-FASHIONED WAY, THE***½ (1934) 66m PAR bw

W.C. Fields *(The Great [Mark Anthony] McGonigle/Squire Cribbes in Play)*, Joe Morrison *(Wally Livingston/William Dowton in Play)*, Judith Allen *(Betty McGonigle/Agnes Dowton in Play)*, Jan Duggan *(Cleopatra Pepperday)*, Nora Cecil *(Mrs. Wendelschaffer)*, Baby LeRoy [Overacker] *(Albert Wendelschaffer)*, Jack Mulhall *(Dick Bronson)*, Joe Mills *(Charles Lowell)*, Samuel Ethridge *(Bartley Neuville)*, Emma Ray *(Mother Mack)*, Ruth Marion *(Agatha Sprague)*, Clarence Wilson *(Sheriff Prettywillie)*, Richard Carle *(Barnesville Sheriff)*, Otis Harlan *(Mr. Wendelschaffer)*, Tammany Young *(Marmaduke Gump)*, Dorothy Ray *(Bertha)*, Oscar Smith *(Porter)*, Maxine Elliott Hicks *(Waitress)*, Lew Kelly *(Sheriff Walter Jones)*, Davidson Clark *(Passenger Who Loses Ticket)*, Edward Le Saint *(Conductor)*, Larry Grenier *(Drover Stevens in Play)*, William Blatchford *(Landlord of the Saloon in Play)*, Jeffery Williams *(Mr. Arden Rencelaw in Play)*, Donald Brown *(The Minister in Play)*, Tom Miller *(The Villager in Play)*, Adrienne Ames *(Girl in Audience)*, Billy Bletcher *(Tomato Throwing Man)*, Robert McKenzie *(Checkers Player)*, Georgie Billings *(Kid in Railroad Car)*, Oscar Apfel *(Mr. Livingston, Wally's Father)*, Marvin Lobach *(Man Sleeping Beneath Fields)*, Sam McDaniels *(Porter)*, Duke York *(Stagehand)*, Sam Flint *(Man with Mallet)*.

Another romp for the great W.C., but this time he is an impoverished but still pompous manager of a group of hammy actors. The film opens with a sheriff waiting on a train platform with the acting troupe which is about to depart for another engagement of that weary stage vehicle "The Drunkard." The sheriff holds a summons for Fields which charges him with bad debts. Fields, as The Great (Mark Anthony) McGonigle, approaches from behind the sheriff, spots the summons, and lights it with a match. He then steps in front of the sheriff who gives him a sinister grin and says: "I have something for you!" He whips out the now-blazing summons from behind his back and Fields nods a thank you, lights his cigar from the fiery document, and steps on board the train with his actors, leaving the sheriff nonplussed, mouth agape, on the platform. This sets the stage and mood for the entire film, set in the gaslight era, with Fields always one step ahead of sheriffs trying to get him to pay his bills which have piled up over the decades all over America. He also has to contend with his daughter, Allen, and her romance with singer Morrison, while fending off his eternal nemesis, Baby LeRoy. Included in the film is a revamped segment of Field's old vehicle POPPY and a terrific juggling act which the master himself performs. Fields was probably *the* foremost juggler of the 20th Century and proves it in this film, balancing 12 cigar boxes, four balls, and a stick on one foot which he kicks to the other foot while all the while retrieving his so-called "mistakes" at the last moment and dropping nothing. The whole film is worth the sight of this incredible display of dexterity. Fields had a brief affair with the alluring Allen during the production but he spent most of his time posting complaints on studio walls about Baby LeRoy. One such read: "I am mad at Baby LeRoyoff. Baby LeRoyoff has libeled me! He says I stole his bottle! Baby LeRoyoff is all wet! Baby LeRoyoff is a menace; he steals scenes!" The precocious child star actually tweaked Fields' nose in one scene, an impulsive act not called for in the script. Instead of exploding, as the cast and crew expected, the great comedian only gave the child a wry smile. Later he was asked by the Hollywood press if he was sensitive about his large nose. "To the contrary, " he replied. "I take inordinate pride in my nose. Indeed, I have treatment done on it every day." With that he lifted a glass containing his then-favorite drink, rum and pineapple juice, to his lips, gave the newsmen a wink, and said: "My daily treatment!"

p, Willian LeBaron; d, William Beaudine; w, Garnett Weston, Jack Cunningham (based on an original story by Charles Bogle [W.C. Fields]); ph, Benjamin Reynolds; m, Harry Revel; art d, John Goodman; m/l, "Rolling in Love," "A Little Bit of Heaven Known as Mother," "The Sea Shell Song," Revel, Mack Gordon.

Comedy **(PR:A MPAA:NR)**

OLD FRONTIER, THE*½ (1950) 60m REP bw

Monte Hale *(Barney Regan)*, Paul Hurst *(Skipper Horton)*, Claudia Barrett *(Betty Ames)*, William Henry *(Dr. Creighton)*, Tristam Coffin *(John Wagner)*, William Haade *(Pills Fowler)*, Victor Kilian *(Judge Ames)*, Lane Bradford *(Spud)*, Denver Pyle *(George)*, Almira Sessions *(Mrs. Smedley)*, Tom London *(Banker)*.

Hale stars as the new sheriff of a town terrorized by a gang of bank robbers led by criminal mastermind Coffin, who is the community's most respected attorney. Hale, of course, finds out the truth and cleans up the town. Bizarre addition to the cast is Hurst, Hale's sidekick, a salty-talking sailor who somehow wound up out West.

p, Melville Tucker; d, Philip Ford; w, Bob Williams; ph, Ellis W. Carter; ed, Harold Minter.

Western **(PR:A MPAA:NR)**

OLD GREATHEART (SEE: WAY BACK HOME, 1932)

OLD GROUCHY (SEE: GROUCH, THE, 1961, Gr.)

OLD HOMESTEAD, THE** (1935) 72m Liberty bw

Mary Carlisle (Nancy), Lawrence Gray (Bob), Dorothy Lee (Elsie Wilson), Willard Robertson (Uncle Jed), Eddie Nugent (Rudy Nash), Lillian Miles (Peggy), Fuzzy Knight (Lem), Eddie Kane (Mr. Wertheimer), Harry Conley (Press Agent), Verne Spence, Bob Nolan, Leonard Slye [Roy Rogers], Hugh Farr, Sons of the Pioneers.

Country singers wind up in the big city to win fame and fortune on the radio. Carlisle stars as a girl in love with farm-boy Gray until his new-found success pulls them apart. After brief flirtations with others, the romance returns and the country couple are reunited. Fuzzy Knight and Sons of the Pioneers provide the backup and comedy. Western great Roy Rogers has a small part under his real name of Leonard Slye in the same year he broke into films. Songs include: "Moonlight in Heaven" (Jack Scholl, Louis Alter, sung by Gray); "Somehow I Know" (Harry Tobias, Neil Moret, Charles Rosoff), "The Plowboy" (J. Keirn Brennan, Ted Snyder, sung by Gray), and "When the Old Age Pension Check Comes to Our Door" (Manny Stone).

p, M.H. Hoffman; d, William Nigh; w, W. Scott Darling; ph, Harry Neumann; m, Howard Jackson; ed, Mildred Johnston.

Musical **(PR:A MPAA:NR)**

OLD HOMESTEAD, THE*½ (1942) 68m REP bw

Leon Weaver (Abner, Chief of Police), Frank Weaver (Cicero), June Weaver [Elviry] (Mayor), Dick Purcell (Scarf Lennin), Jed Prouty (Councilman Bell), Anne Jeffreys (Goldie), Maris Wrixon (Mary Jo Weaver), Robert Conway (Fred Morgan), Linda Brent (Bunny).

Another Weaver family vehicle starring June Weaver as the mayor and Leon Weaver as the chief of police in the small town of Farmington. The town is hit by a crime wave that soon has the citizenry talking of a recall vote. Getting overly clever, June Weaver pretends to be crooked and hires mobster Purcell to eliminate the opposition. The plan backfires however, when crooked councilman Prouty aligns with the mob and crusading journalist Conway begins a front-page tirade. Leon Weaver comes to the rescue and arrests Prouty, Purcell, and their henchmen. (See WEAVER FAMILY series, Index.)

p, Armand Schaefer; d, Frank MacDonald; w, Dorrell McGowan, Stuart McGowan; ph, Ernest Miller; ed, Arthur Roberts; md, Cy Feuer; art d, Russell Kimball; m/l, "In the Town Where I Was Born," (sung by Leon Weaver, Frank Weaver, and June Weaver).

Drama **(PR:A MPAA:NR)**

OLD HUTCH**½ (1936) 80m MGM bw

Wallace Beery (Hutch), Eric Linden (Dave), Cecilia Parker (Irene), Elizabeth Patterson (Mrs. Hutchins), Robert McWade (Jolly), Caroline Anne Perkins (Sally), Julia Ellen Perkins (Florrie), Delmar Watson (Allie), Harry Watson (Freddie), James Burke (Teller), Virginia Grey (Girl), Donald Meek (Gunnison), Scotty Beckett (Roy), Frank Reicher (District Attorney), Norman Willis (Surveyor), Wilbur Mack (Judge), Frank Jenks (Crook), Zeffie Tilbury (Elderly Woman), George Chandler (Cigar Store Clerk).

Beery plays the good-for-nothing father of a large family who accidentally finds $100,000 in buried loot. He must become a hard-working, respectable citizen to justify the dough because the whole town knows he has not worked a day in his life. Life takes a nasty turn when bank robbers snatch his fortune, but his boastful posturing while trying to explain the money's loss turns out to be in his favor when it leads to the crooks' capture.

p, Harry Rapf; d, J. Walter Ruben; w, George Kelly (based on the story "Old Hutch Lives Up to It" by Garret Smith); ph, Clyde De Vinna; ed, Frank Sullivan; md, Dr. William Axt; art d, Cedric Gibbons, Stan Rogers; set d, Edwin B. Willis.

Comedy **(PR:A MPAA:NR)**

OLD IRON** (1938, Brit.) 80m TW/BL bw

Tom Walls (Sir Henry Woodstock), Eva Moore (Lady Woodstock), Cecil Parker (Barnett), Richard Ainley (Harry Woodstock), David Tree (Michael), Veronica Rose (Lorna Barnett), Enid Stamp-Taylor (Eileen Penshaw), Leslie Perrins (Richard Penshaw), Arthur Wontner (Judge), Henry Hewitt (Wilfred), O. B. Clarence (Gordon), Hubert Harben, Nancy Pawley, Frank Daly.

Walls is a tyrannical shipping magnate who cuts off his daughter without a farthing after he disapproves of her marriage. When son Ainley marries Rose, Walls throws her father off of his board of directors. In a rage Ainley tears off in his car, accidentally killing a man. After his son is charged with manslaughter, Walls realizes that something must change and the family is reconciled. Though the drama has some moments of interest, the piece as a whole doesn't quite work.

p&d, Tom Walls; w, Ben Travers; ph, Mutz Greenbaum [Max Greene].

Drama **(PR:A MPAA:NR)**

OLD LOS ANGELES*½ (1948) 87m REP bw

William Elliott (Bill Stockton), John Carroll (Johnny Morrell), Catherine McLeod (Marie Marlowe), Joseph Schildkraut (Luis Savarin), Andy Devine (Sam Bowie), Estelita Rodriguez (Estelita Del Rey), Virginia Brissac (Senora Del Rey), Grant Withers (Marshal Luckner), Tito Renaldo (Tonio Del Rey), Roy Barcroft (Clyborne), Henry Brandon (Larry Stockton), Julian Rivero (Diego), Earle Hodgins (Horatius P. Gassoway), Augie Gomez (Miguel).

Routine musical western starring Elliott and Devine as the hero and sidekick out to stop the villainous Carroll and Schildkraut. Only surprise is Rodriguez, who, posing as a cafe singer, turns out to be a federal agent after the same crooks. Dull musical

numbers bog down the already hackneyed script. Among them were "Ever Faithful," sung by McLeod and Rodriguez.

p&d, Joseph Kane; w, Gerald Adams, Clements Ripley (based on a story by Ripley); ph, William Bradford; m, Ernest Gold; ed, Richard L. Van Enger; md, Morton Scott; art d, James Sullivan; set d, John McCarthy, Jr., Charles Thompson; cos, Adele Palmer; spec eff, Howard Lydecker, Theodore Lydecker; m/l, Aaron Gonzales, Nathan Scott, Quirino F. Mendoza y Cortes, Jack Elliott; makeup, Bob Mark.

Western **(PR:A MPAA:NR)**

OLD LOUISIANA*½ (1938) 63m Cresent bw (GB: TREASON; AKA: LOUISIANA GAL)

Tom Keene (John Colfax), Rita Cansino [Hayworth] (Angela Gonzales), Robert Fiske (Gilmore), Ray "Raphael" Bennett (Flint), Allan Cavan (President Thomas Jefferson), Will Morgan (Steve), Budd Buster (Kentucky), Carlos De Valdez (Gov. Gonzales), Wally Albright (Davey), Ramsey Hill (James Madison), Iron Eyes Cody.

Dull Keene frontier saga featuring the star as the American representative in the then-Spanish territory of Louisiana. Outraged by the Spaniards' attempts at halting their river-based trade, Keene travels to Washington to talk with the President. The Spanish, however, plan to keep him from Washington. Look for a very young Rita Hayworth [Cansino] as the daughter of the Spanish governor. It was her fifth film appearance, and when a clever distributor came across a print of OLD LOUISIANA at the height of Hayworth's popularity in the mid-1940s, he retitled it LOUISIANA GAL and gave her star billing.

p, E.B. Derr; d, Irvin Willat; w, Mary Ireland (based on a story by John T. Neville); ph, Arthur Martinelli; ed, Donald Barratt; art d, Edward C. Jewell; md, Abe Meyer; cos, Lou Brown; makeup, Steve Corso.

Adventure **(PR:A MPAA:NR)**

OLD MAC** (1961, Brit.) 53m Border/Carlyle bw

Charles Lamb (Father), Vi Stevens (Mother), Children of the Corona Academy.

Children find a dog and save it from its hobo owner. With this problem out of the way, they must now figure out a way to keep the canine from their parents. Simple drama that the kids will probably enjoy. An early directorial effort for Winner, who later made DEATH WISH.

p, O. Negus Fancey; d, Michael Winner; w, Richard Bayley.

Drama **(PR:A MPAA:NR)**

OLD MAID, THE***½ (1939) 95m FN-WB bw

Bette Davis (Charlotte Lovell), Miriam Hopkins (Delia Lovell Ralston), George Brent (Clem Spender), Jane Bryan (Tina), Donald Crisp (Dr. Lanskell), Louise Fazenda (Dora), James Stephenson (Jim Ralston), Jerome Cowan (Joe Ralston), William Lundigan (Lanning Halsey), Cecilia Loftus (Grandmother Henrietta Lovell), Rand Brooks (Jim Ralston, Jr.), Janet Shaw (Dee), DeWolf [William] Hopper (John Ward), Marlene Burnett (Tina as a Child), Rod Cameron (Man), Doris Lloyd (Aristocratic Maid), Frederick Burton (Mr. Halsey).

Bette Davis had already distinguished herself in DARK VICTORY and JEZEBEL, but her performance in this was a revelation, as she plumbed new emotional depths. She always liked to stretch and here she allows herself to be aged to 60 and manages to convey that, despite the fact that she had just turned 30 when she made this. Davis and Hopkins had many battles on the set and Hopkins did her best to upstage and scene-steal as much as she could, but that's like trying to upstage Dumbo or Jumbo or even Moby Dick. You might get away with it for a while but in the end you'll be swallowed up. Goulding and Robinson had collaborated on DARK VICTORY and the task of adapting this Pulitzer Prize play fell to them. There were no awards given to the film and that was not an oversight. It was just that 1939 was the year of so many huge and successful pictures that there was no way anyone could squeeze this on their Academy ballot when facing the likes of GONE WITH THE WIND; GOODBYE, MR. CHIPS; STAGECOACH; WUTHERING HEIGHTS; MR. SMITH GOES TO WASHINGTON, and about 10 other great films. It's the Civil War. Hopkins has been engaged to Brent but he's been away from home for two years and she decides to marry Stephenson, a rich man, instead. Brent is a handsome, dashing type who thinks Davis, Hopkins' cousin, is sweet, but his heart beats fast for Hopkins and he is stunned when she weds the wealthy Philadelphian. Davis tries her best to allay Brent's pain and they sleep together, which causes him to see a little more in her than he did before. When he comes back from his service in the war, perhaps something will come of this. But that's not to be, as Brent is killed fighting for his side at Vicksburg. However, Davis now carries Brent's child, and through the intercession of the family doctor, Crisp, Davis goes off to Arizona to cure the bogus "lung problem" that she's manufactured to cover her pregnance. After the war, Davis comes back to the City of Brotherly Love to run an orphanage for the children whose parents have died in the conflict. In doing that, she is able to hide her daughter, Burnett, in the orphanage population. Meanwhile, Cowan, Hopkins' brother-in-law, finds Davis attractive and is considering marrying her. Then Hopkins learns that Burnett is Davis' child by the late Brent and she lies to Cowan and says that Davis is too "sick" to marry. The two cousins split after Hopkins' lie and remain that way until Cowan dies in an accident. Now Hopkins invites Davis and her daughter to live at her house. Little Burnett grows up to be Bryan, who thinks that Davis is her old maid aunt and that Hopkins has rescued her from the orphanage. This odd lineage causes a problem when Bryan falls in love with rich Lundigan. The fact that she's an "orphan" mitigates against acceptance by Lundigan's family. Hopkins wants to officially adopt Bryan to give her a good family name and Davis agrees, promising herself that she will reveal the truth to Bryan on the girl's wedding night. It rolls around and Davis can't bring herself to "spoil" Bryan's happiness. Bryan and Lundigan prepare to depart on their honeymoon and Bryan bids everyone goodbye, then saves the last kiss for her old maid aunt, Davis, who knows that she will never be able to tell her daughter the truth and must spend the rest of her life with Hopkins, who cannot forgive her for having the child by Brent. Bring lots of hankies for this one and be prepared to watch a star turn by Davis, who has seldom been better.

p, Hal B. Wallis, Henry Blanke; d, Edmund Goulding; w, Casey Robinson (based on the play by Zoe Akins from the novel by Edith Wharton); ph, Tony Gaudio; m, Max Steiner; ed, George Amy; md, Leo F. Forbstein; art d, Robert Haas; cos, Orry-Kelly.

Drama **(PR:C MPAA:NR)**

OLD MAN, THE** (1932, Brit.) 75m BL-Gainsborough/GAU bw

Maisie Gay *(Mrs. Harris)*, Anne Grey *(Lady Arranways)*, Lester Matthews *(Keith Keller)*, Cecil Humphreys *(Lord Arranways)*, D. A. Clarke-Smith *(John Lorney)*, Diana Beaumont *(Millie Jeans)*, Gerald Rawlinson *(Dick Mayford)*, Frank Stanmore *(Charles)*, Finlay Currie *(Rennett)*.

Lackluster Edgar Wallace mystery wherein the guests at a country hotel are being terrorized by a mysterious "old man" who has killed a crook trying to blackmail Grey. Eventually Gay, a servant in the hotel, helps reveal the killer's identity and solve the mystery.

p, S.W. Smith; d, Manning Haynes; w, Edgar Wallace (based on a play by Wallace).

Mystery **(PR:A MPAA:NR)**

OLD MAN AND THE BOY, THE (SEE: THE TWO OF US, 1967, Fr.)

OLD MAN AND THE SEA, THE**** (1958) 86m WB c

Spencer Tracy *(The Old Man)*, Felipe Pazos *(The Boy)*, Harry Bellaver *(Martin)*, Donald Diamond, Don Blackman, Joey Ray, Richard Alameda, Tony Rosa, Carlos Rivera, Robert Alderette, Mauritz Hugo.

This was an impossible film to make but Warner Bros. and Sturges tackled the job and, with Tracy giving a virtuoso, bravura performance, the picture became a minor classic. Tracy plays a semiliterate old Cuban fisherman, a man who has been a toiler on the seas all his life. His only possessions are a shack and a small boat and he has not had any luck at catching anything significant for years. Tracy's pedantic efforts to remain a fisherman only cause snickers of derision from his Spanish community where he is thought of as an old, simple-minded fool. Only a small boy, Pazos, believes in Tracy and admires him, bringing him his coffee in the morning to get him started for the ritual of the sea. Tracy is up before dawn and moves out with the other men, carrying the mast to his boat on his shoulder, portrayed as a heavy burden not unlike the cross Christ carried, then shoving off into an azure ocean. Once at sea, he makes ready for the day's catch, hoping that he will have luck, putting out his lines and introspectively thinking back on his life, from the few women he has known to such prosaic but exultant experiences as winning an arm-wrestling contest that took hours to finish. During his wistful daydreams, Tracy passes comments in his narration about the high principles of fishing and, while dreaming and thinking, he doesn't realize that he has gone too far beyond his usual limit into the Gulf Stream. A little bird alights on his small craft and he talks to it, telling it to take a short rest but then reminding it that it must soon fly off and take its chances with nature, as is the case with all living things. Then, with his lines out, Tracy hooks a huge fish, a mammoth marlin which has to be the greatest marlin in any ocean, larger than his boat, one that puts up a titanic struggle with the old man who uses up all his line to catch it, using his back as a brace for the line and his hands which are turned to bloody pulp as the line whirs through them. The battle between the fish and the old man is Homeric, legendary, unthinkable. Yet, after many hours of painful struggle, Tracy wins the battle, killing the fish and tying it next to his boat, then setting sail for home. But he is out very far and the voyage home is now fraught with peril. Many sharks are beckoned to the boat, following the trail of the marlin's blood, and they attack the dead fish as Tracy again puts up a fight to save his miraculous catch, slashing at the sharks with his knife and spearing them and slamming them with his oars as they make constant runs at the marlin, tearing it apart piece by piece until only its skeletal remains drift pathetically next to the boat in which the old man sits exhausted, defeated. "You went out to far, old man," Tracy tells himself, as a way of finding reason for his great triumph turned to tragedy. He had overextended himself and made himself vulnerable to the very elements of nature he had always believed he understood and could control. He had lived all his life for this victory and now he sits as a hunkering human hulk, the vanquished, apologizing to the magnificent marlin for bringing it to disgraceful mutilation. "Fish, I respect you and I love you," he says in his prosaic way and weeps for its miserable fate which is his own. He drifts homeward and by the time he sees the lights of Havana, there is hardly anything left to the marlin, only its head and part of its tail and a long, hideous skeleton, so grim and grisly that the old man cannot bear to look at it. He leaves his boat next to a seaside cafe (where tourists gape at the skeleton the next day) and struggles home to his shack, his mast so heavy on his back that Tracy sinks to the ground, exhausted with physical and mental fatigue. The boy finds him a wreck the next morning, dying. THE OLD MAN AND THE SEA is an allegorical tale providing Tracy with his greatest one-man show and he delivers powerful impact, humor, and an overwhelming image of stoic heroism that only Tracy possessed. Sturges' direction, given the confining nature of the settings, is masterful and the cinematography headed by Howe and pieced together by many others is largely eye-popping. (The contribution of much of the footage by many sources, however, has a tendency to present alternating and inconsistent color patterns from scene to scene.) Schmidt's clever editing of Howe's basic photography and that of others is a superb job of integrating and crosscutting shots without interrupting the visual plot. The responsibility for bringing Hemingway's classic novella to the screen wholly rests with Broadway producer Hayward who visited his old friend Hemingway at his home outside Havana in 1952 and, after Hemingway's wife Mary, was the first person to read *The Old Man and the Sea*. Hayward was so impressed with the tale that he personally hand-carried the manuscript to Hemingway's publisher, Scribner's, in New York. *Life* magazine serialized the novella in September, 1952, and the entire issue was sold out the very day it was issued, all on the strength of the great book. By the time the Book-of-the-Month grabbed the novella, Warner Bros., through Hayward, was already arranging to buy the film rights, paying Hemingway $175,000. Hemingway was asked for his choice of screenwriters and suggested that his friend Viertel adapt the tale for the screen. Hayward and Hemingway actually formed a partnership concerning the film and both men selected Tracy to star as the old man. Howe began initial photography in 1955, shooting background shots of the Cuban coast. Many fishing parties, including one with Hemingway which sailed as far as Peru's Capo Blanco, made desperate excursions into deep water to try and hook a huge marlin and get footage for the film but all were unsuccessful in landing a fish anywhere near as big as that described in the novella (indeed, if there ever could be a marlin that big). Fred Zinnemann was hired by Hayward to direct the film but after four months only a little footage had been actually shot, with Tracy lounging around a huge villa in Cuba with scores of servants to wait on him. He was restless and complained of nothing to do. Moreover, it was rumored that Hayward and Zinnemann had run into great difficulties concerning the Viertel script which was utterly faithful to the novella. Zinneman reportedly wanted to change the story and producer Hayward wouldn't hear of it. Suddenly, Zinnemann was fired by Hayward, the director stating that it was over a "technical" problem. When asked about it, Tracy said: "It's a matter between Hayward and Zinnemann. I don't know what it's about. Maybe it's the schedule, and maybe Fred just couldn't stand my face." Sturges replaced Zinnemann, much to the urging of Tracy; he and Sturges had produced the marvelous BAD DAY AT BLACK ROCK in 1955. Meanwhile, enormous costs on the lingering production kept mounting as more and more fishing footage was obtained. Backround footage was obtained from the Disney studio and also from private sportsmen like Houston's Alfred Glassnell. Tons of equipment were called for, with more than $400,000 in additional cameras and other technical devices shipped from Warner Bros. The overall production would exceed $6 million and Sturges would wind up shooting most of the film in five weeks in the Warner Bros. tank. Since Hemingway and scores of other big-time fishermen came up empty-handed, Sturges opted for a huge mechanically operated rubber fish to pass for the giant marlin. (This later prompted Hemingway to state that "no picture with a f]]]]]] rubber fish ever made a dime!") The tank used at Warners contained more than 750,000 gallons of water which had to pass for the sea. Tracy cropped his hair and dyed it snowy white for the role but by the time the film was completed, his hair had turned stark white anyway. Hemingway became disillusioned with the film and began to criticize Tracy, blaming him for the delays when it was really a matter of technical problems. "This picture is becoming my life's work," complained Tracy in 1957. "By now there isn't a chance to make back all the money we will spend, so we're just concentrating on making it worthwhile." Later he was widely quoted as saying he would sell his interest in the film for 15 cents. "This is for the birds," he added. When the film was released, Tracy received kudos from almost all the critics but Hemingway grouched that the film looked like the work of "a rich, fat actor," a remark that forever tore apart the relationship between the actor and writer. Tracy deservedly won an Oscar nomination for his incredible performance but lost to David Niven for SEPARATE TABLES. He later admitted that he himself had voted for Niven, explaining that his reasons were simple: "It's my integrity. There are six, maybe seven of us out here who still have it. It doesn't count much." Hemingway's problems with THE OLD MAN AND THE SEA continued after its release. He was sued by a 70-year-old Cuban fisherman, Miguel Ramirez, for reportedly stealing his tale and reaping a fortune on a film that rightly belonged to him. The suit was eventually dismissed as ludicrous.

p, Leland Hayward; d, John Sturges; w, Peter Viertel (based on the novella by Ernest Hemingway); ph, James Wong Howe, Floyd Crosby, Tom Tutwiler, Lamar Boren; m, Dimitri Tiomkin; ed, Arthur P. Schmidt; md, Tiomkin; art d, Art Loel, Edward Carrere; set d, Ralph Hurst; spec eff, Arthur S. Rhoades.

Drama **(PR:A MPAA:NR)**

OLD MAN RHYTHM** (1935) 74m RKO bw

Charles "Buddy" Rogers *(Johnny Roberts)*, George Barbier *(John Roberts, Sr.)*, Barbara Kent *(Edith Warren)*, Grace Bradley *(Marion Beecher)*, Betty Grable *(Sylvia)*, Eric Blore *(Phillips)*, Erik Rhodes *(Frank Rochet)*, John Arledge *(Pinky Parker)*, Johnny Mercer *(Colonel)*, Donald Meek *(Paul Parker)*, Dave Chasen *(Andy)*, Joy Hodges *(Lois)*, Douglas Fowley *(Oyster)*, Evelyn Poe *(Honey)*, Margaret Nearing *(Margaret)*, Ronald Graham *(Ronald)*, Sonny Lamont *(Blimp)*, William Carey *(Bill)*, Lucille Ball, Marian Darling, Jane Hamilton, Maxine Jennings, Kay Sutton *(College Girls)*, Jack Thomas, Erich Von Stroheim, Jr., Carlyle Blackwell, Jr., Bryant Washburn, Jr., Claude Gillingwater Jr. *(College Boys)*, Maj. Sam Harris *(Board Member)*.

The song "There's Nothing Like a College Education" sums up this musical campus farce which has father Barbier enroll in the college his son, Rogers, is attending. He plans to keep an eye on the boy's romantic activities. Rogers falls into golddigger Bradley's trap, but in the end she leaves him upon hearing that his family fortune has been drained in a bad business deal. Lots of mediocre musical numbers pad this otherwise dull comedy. Songs by Johnny Mercer and Lewis Gensler include: "Old Man Rhythm," "I Never Saw a Better Night," "There's Nothing Like a College Education," "Boys Will Be Boys," "When You Are in My Arms," and "Come the Revolution Baby."

p, Zion Myers; d, Edward Ludwig; w, Sid Herzig, Ernest Pagano, H. W. Hanemann (based on a story by Lewis Gensler, Herzig, Don Hartman); ph, Nick Musuraca; m, Lewis Gensler; ed, George Crone; md, Roy Webb; art d, Van Nest Polglase; ch, Hermes Pan.

Musical **(PR:A MPAA:NR)**

OLD MOTHER RILEY*½ (1937, Brit.) 75m BUT-Hope-Bell/BUT bw
(AKA: THE RETURN OF OLD MOTHER RILEY;
THE ORIGINAL OLD MOTHER RILEY)

Arthur Lucan (*Mrs. Riley*), Kitty McShane (*Kitty Riley*), Barbara Everest (*Mrs. Briggs*), Patrick Ludlow (*Edwin Briggs*), J. Hubert Leslie (*Capt. Lawson*), Edith Sharpe (*Matilda Lawson*), Syd Crossley (*Butler*), Edgar Driver (*Bill Jones*), Dorothy Vernon (*Aggie Sparks*), Zoe Wynn (*Kay Stewart*), G. H. Mulcaster (*Prosecution*), Charles Carson (*Defense*), Elma Slee, Balliol and Tiller, F. B. J. Sharp, Charles Sewell, Charles Paton.

The genesis of a long-running British series (1937-1952), OLD MOTHER RILEY tells the outrageous tale of a match magnate who dies and leaves his fortune to his family. The only condition is that they must shelter the first person they see selling matches. They are unfortunately blessed with the presence of a loud Irish washerwoman, Old Mother Riley, who is heartily portrayed, in drag, by Arthur Lucan. Her presence in the household is far from welcome, as is that of her daughter, McShane, Lucan's real-life wife. Far from being impressive pieces of cinema, the OLD MOTHER RILEY series provided for some innocuous and occasionally hysterical entertainment. (See OLD MOTHER RILEY series, Index.)

p, Norman Hope-Bell; d, Oswald Mitchell; w, Con West (based on a story by John Argyle); ph, Jack Parker.

Comedy   (PR:A   MPAA:NR)

OLD MOTHER RILEY**   (1952, Brit.) 69m REN/Bell bw (GB: OLD MOTHER RILEY'S NEW VENTURE)

Arthur Lucan (*Mrs. Riley*), Kitty McShane (*Kitty Riley*), Chili Bouchier (*Cora*), Willer Neal (*David*), Maureen Riscoe (*Mabel*), Wilfred Babbage (*Major*), Sebastian Cabot (*Potentate*), C. Denier Warren (*Hillick*), John Le Mesurier (*Karl*), Arthur Gomez (*Chef*), Paul Sheridan (*Saunders*), Fred Groves (*Grigsby*).

Lucan's Mother Riley character is put in charge of a hotel when the proprietor decides to take time off after being victimized by a series of robberies. Trouble strikes soon thereafter when a jewel theft is blamed on Lucan, sending her to prison. By the final reel she manages to regain her freedom, but not until a chaotic pie-throwing scene is complete. A couple of songs are also squeezed in, with McShane and Neal delivering "I'll Take You Home Again, Kathleen" and "Galway Bay." Oddly, OLD MOTHER RILEY (released in Britain in 1949) wasn't seen in the U.S. until the long-running OLD MOTHER RILEY series had ended. Since the British title, OLD MOTHER RILEY'S NEW VENTURE, made little sense to American audiences (they had yet to see an old "venture"), the distributors saw fit to tag the picture OLD MOTHER RILEY, ignoring the fact that the title was previously used in the series starter back in 1937. (See OLD MOTHER RILEY series, Index.)

p, Harry Reynolds; d, John Harlow; w, Con West, Jack Marks; ph, James Wilson; m, George Melachrino.

Comedy   (PR:A   MPAA:NR)

OLD MOTHER RILEY AT HOME*½   (1945, Brit.) 76m BN/Anglo-American bw

Arthur Lucan (*Mrs. Riley*), Kitty McShane (*Kitty Riley*), Freddie Forbes (*Mr. Bumpron*), Richard George (*Dan*), Willer Neal (*Bill*), Wally Patch (*Bouncer*), Kenneth Warrington (*Boss*), Angela Barrie (*Duchess*), Janet Morrison (*Mary*), Elsie Waggstaffe (*Mrs. Ginochie*).

Lucan, again donning his female attire, must chase down his runaway daughter, McShane, who has skipped off with her new boy friend, Neal. Lucan, with help from McShane's true love, George, finds her in a gambling den and after some camp hysterics manages to get her back home. One of the weaker series entries. (See OLD MOTHER RILEY series, Index.)

p, Louis H. Jackson; d, Oswald Mitchell; w, Mitchell, George A. Cooper (based on a story by Joan Butler, Ralph Temple); ph, James Wilson.

Comedy   (PR:A   MPAA:NR)

OLD MOTHER RILEY CATCHES A QUISLING   (SEE: OLD MOTHER RILEY IN PARIS, 1938, Brit.)

OLD MOTHER RILEY, DETECTIVE*½   (1943, Brit.) 80m BN/Anglo-American bw

Arthur Lucan (*Mrs. Riley*), Kitty McShane (*Kitty Riley*), Ivan Brandt (*Inspector Victor Cole*), Owen Reynolds (*Kenworthy*), George Street (*Inspector Moresby*), Johnnie Schofield (*Constable Jimmy Green*), Hal Gordon (*Bill*), Valentine Dunn (*Elsie*), Marjorie Rhodes (*Cook*), H. F. Maltby (*H. G. Popplethwaite*), Peggy Cummins (*Lily*), Alfredo Campoli, Edgar Driver, Michael Lynd, Nellie Bowman, Jimmy Rhodes, Eddie Stern, Pat Kavanagh, Gerry Wilson, Pat Keogh, Charles Paton, Jack Vyvyan, Eve Chipman, Frank Webster, Charles Doe, Vi Kaley, Ernest Metcalfe, Mike Johnson, Louise Nolan, Mary Norton, Hilde Palmer, Bryan Herbert, Nino Rossini, Noel Dainton, Ben Williams, Harry Terry, Bombardier Billy Wells, Leo de Pokorny, Arthur Dent, Stanley Paskin, Geoffrey Roberts.

A lifeless effort which has Lucan working as a cleaning woman until the police decide to use her in a black market crackdown. The gangster premise is merely an excuse for Lucan to try out some humorous bits (in drag, of course), but the picture is too padded to hold much interest. (See OLD MOTHER RILEY series, Index.)

p, John Baxter; d, Lance Comfort; w, Austin Melford, Geoffrey Orme, Barbara K. Emary, Arthur Lucan; ph, James Wilson.

Comedy   (PR:A   MPAA:NR)

OLD MOTHER RILEY, HEADMISTRESS*   (1950, Brit.) 75m REN bw

Arthur Lucan (*Mrs. Riley*), Kitty McShane (*Kitty Riley*), Enid Hewitt (*Miss Carruthers*), Jenny Mathot (*Mlle. Leblanc*), Ethel Royale (*Lady Meersham*), Harry Herbert (*Simon*), Cyril Smith (*Maltby*), Paul Sheridan (*Nixon*), Willer Neal (*Travers*), C. Denier Warren (*Clifton Hill*), Luton Girls Choir, George Melanchrino and His Orchestra, Alfred Waller, Bill Stevens, Eve Dewhurst, Graham Tunbridge, Myrette

Morven, Dorothy Darke, Beth Ross, Madge Brindley, Vi Kaley, Jacqueline Stanley, Catherine Carleton [*Boyle*], Patricia Owens.

A poor addition to the OLD MOTHER RILEY stable, this entry has Lucan taking his music hall Irish washerwoman to the screen as a laundry owner who winds up heading a girls' school. When plans for a railroad threaten to bring down the school, Lucan fights a winning battle, and, in the process, manages to get his daughter, McShane, reinstated as the choir leader. If only one OLD MOTHER RILEY film is to be seen in a lifetime, don't make it this one. (See OLD MOTHER RILEY series, Index.)

p, Harry Reynolds; d, John Harlow; w, Con West, Jack Marks; ph, Ken Talbot.

Comedy   (PR:A   MPAA:NR)

OLD MOTHER RILEY IN BUSINESS**   (1940, Brit.) 80m BN/Anglo-American bw

Arthur Lucan (*Mrs. Riley*), Kitty McShane (*Kitty Riley*), Cyril Chamberlain (*John Halliwell*), Charles Victor, Wally Patch, Ernest Butcher, Ernest Sefton, O. B. Clarence, Edgar Driver, Edie Martin, Roddy Hughes, Morris Harvey, Ruth Maitland.

Lucan comes to the aid of some local shopkeepers when Golden Stores, a heartless chain, makes its presence felt. The heroic Irish lass gives the Golden Stores boss a shove into the river and soon finds herself on the lam, donning a nurse's outfit to escape from the hospital in which she has hidden. Needless to say, the strongwilled and vociferous Lucan saves the day. (See OLD MOTHER RILEY series, Index.)

p, John Corfield; d, John Baxter; w, Geoffrey Orme; ph, James Wilson.

Comedy   (PR:A   MPAA:NR)

OLD MOTHER RILEY IN PARIS½**   (1938, Brit.) 76m BUT bw (AKA: OLD MOTHER RILEY CATCHES A QUISLING)

Arthur Lucan (*Mrs. Riley*), Kitty McShane (*Kitty Riley*), Jerry Verno (*Joe*), Magda Kun (*Mme. Zero*), C. Denier Warren (*Commissioner*), Stanley Vilven (*Hotelier*), George Wolkowsky (*Apache*), Douglas Stewart, Frank Terry, Rex Alderman, Richard Riviere, Edward Wild, Charles Castella, Harold B. Hallam.

One of the most farfetched and yet most entertaining of the OLD MOTHER RILEY series, this entry places Lucan against a Parisian backdrop in the middle of an espionage-counterespionage adventure. After heading to Paris to find her daughter, Irish washerwoman Lucan is mistakenly identified as a spy, only to snare a real one himself. Daring deeds and Lucan's sharp characterization make for an irresistable romp. (See OLD MOTHER RILEY series, Index.)

p&d, Oswald Mitchell; w, Con West.

Comedy   (PR:A   MPAA:NR)

OLD MOTHER RILEY IN SOCIETY*½   (1940, Brit.) 81m BN/Anglo-American bw

Arthur Lucan (*Mrs. Riley*), Kitty McShane (*Kitty Riley*), John Stuart (*Tony Morgan*), Dennis Wyndham (*Tug Mulligan*), Minnie Rayner, Athole Stewart, Charles Victor, Ruth Maitland, Margaret Halstan, Peggy Novack, Diana Beaumont, Aubrey Dexter, Cyril Chamberlain.

On a par with the typical series entry, OLD MOTHER RILEY IN SOCIETY casts Lucan in his familiar dressed-in-drag role as the wardrobe lady for his chorus girl daughter, McShane. When she falls in love with the wealthy Stuart, Old Mother Riley puts on her maid's outfit and enters their household as a servant. Inevitable disasters follow and the maid's real identity is revealed. Again the series served its purpose and kept the theater patrons laughing. (See OLD MOTHER RILEY series, Index.)

p, John Corfield; d, John Baxter; w, Austin Melford, Barbara K. Emary, Mary Cathcart Borer (based on a story by Kitty McShane, Bridget Boland); ph, James Wilson.

Comedy   (PR:A   MPAA:NR)

OLD MOTHER RILEY JOINS UP*½   (1939, Brit.) 75m BN/Anglo-American bw

Arthur Lucan (*Mrs. Riley*), Kitty McShane (*Kitty Riley*), Bruce Seton (*Lt. Travers*), Martita Hunt (*Commandant*), H. F. Maltby (*Gen. Hogsley*), Garry Marsh (*Rayful*), Jeanne Stuart, Bryan Powley, Dorothy Dewhurst, Glen Alyn.

Lucan is cast as a nurse this time and ends up involuntarily joining the Auxiliary Territorial Service. After a series of madcap adventures, she manages to keep some important documents out of a German spy's hands. A tolerable romp which kept the patriotic English fires burning during the early part of WW II. (See OLD MOTHER RILEY series, Index.)

p, John Corfield; d, Maclean Rogers; w, Jack Marks, Con West; ph, James Wilson.

Comedy   (PR:A   MPAA:NR)

OLD MOTHER RILEY MEETS THE VAMPIRE   (SEE: MY SON, THE VAMPIRE, 1963, Brit.)

OLD MOTHER RILEY MP**   (1939, Brit.) 77m BUT bw

Arthur Lucan (*Mrs. Riley*), Kitty McShane (*Kitty Riley*), Torin Thatcher (*Jack Nelson*), Henry Longhurst (*Wicker*), Patrick Ludlow (*Archie*), Dennis Wyndham (*Emperor of Rocavia*), Cynthia Stock (*Supervisor*), Rex Alderman, Kenneth Henry.

Graced with an insane plot, this fast-paced comedy has washerwoman Lucan losing her job at the laundry. Sparked with an enthusiasm for justice, she runs for Parliament against the powerful landlord who gave her the boot. She not only wins, but manages to recover a massive debt owed to Britain by a foreign government. Nonsensical but full of laughs. (See OLD MOTHER RILEY series, Index.)

p, F. W. Baker; d, Oswald Mitchell; w, Mitchell, Con West; ph, James Wilson.

Comedy **(PR:A MPAA:NR)**

OLD MOTHER RILEY OVERSEAS** (1943, Brit.) 80m BN/Anglo-American bw

Arthur Lucan (*Mrs. Riley*), Kitty McShane (*Kitty Riley*), Morris Harvey (*Barnacle Bill*), Fred Kitchen, Jr. (*Pedro Quentos*), Magda Kun, Antony Holles, Ferdy Mayne, Freddie William Breach, Bob Lloyd, Jack Vyvyan, Paul Erikson, Eda Bell, Ruth Meredith, Stanelli, Rosarito and Paula.

Following the successful formula of OLD MOTHER RILEY IN PARIS, this less impressive entry has Lucan traveling to Portugal in search of daughter McShane, who has taken work with a wine company. Mother Riley is mistakenly believed to be a famed pianist (in Paris she was thought to be a spy) and manages to save her daughter from a kidnaping scheme, as well as rescue some stolen port wine. (See OLD MOTHER RILEY series, Index.)

p&d, Oswald Mitchell; w, H. Fowler Mear, Arthur Lucan (based on a story by L.S. Deacon, Albert Mee); ph, James Wilson.

Comedy **(PR:A MPAA:NR)**

OLD MOTHER RILEY'S CIRCUS** (1941, Brit.) 80m BN/Anglo-Amalgamated bw

Arthur Lucan (*Mrs. Riley*), Kitty McShane (*Kitty Riley*), John Longden (*Bill*), Roy Emerton (*Santley*), Edgar Driver (*Bobo*), Beckett Bould (*Davis*), O. B. Clarence (*Lawyer*), Syd Crossley (*Bailiff*), Hector Abbas (*Wizista*), W. T. Holland, John Turnbull, Iris Vandeleur, Norah Gordon, Jennie Gregson, Lawrence Hanray, Ernest Sefton, Ben Williams, The Hindustans, The Balstons, Harry Koady, Jean Black, The Carsons, Reading and Grant, Medlock and Marlow, Speedy, Isabel and Emma, Eve and Joan Banyard.

A harmless piece of entertainment which puts Old Mother Riley in the center of a circus as head ringmaster. Although the big top is plagued by the disappearance of its owner, the show manages to go on. The money pours in, financial ruin is avoided, and Lucan discovers that her long-lost daughter (McShane) is actually the star of the show. The usual padding that plagues the "Old Mother Riley" series is avoided thanks to a jolly atmosphere and some decent acts. (See OLD MOTHER RILEY series, Index.)

p, Wallace Orton; d, Thomas Bentley; w, Con West, Geoffrey Orme, Barbara K. Emary, Arthur Lucan; ph, James Wilson.

Comedy **(PR:A MPAA:NR)**

OLD MOTHER RILEY'S GHOSTS** (1941, Brit.) 82m BN/Anglo-American bw

Arthur Lucan (*Mrs. Riley*), Kitty McShane (*Kitty Riley*), John Stuart (*John Cartwright*), A. Bromley Davenport (*Warrender*), Dennis Wyndham (*Jem*), John Laurie (*McAdam*), Peter Gawthorne (*Mr. Cartwright*), Henry B. Longhurst, Ben Williams, Charles Paton, Henry Woolston, Eric Stuart.

Sure to garner up a couple of hardy laughs, this series addition has Lucan living in a supposedly haunted castle while battling the efforts of a notorious group of spies. It seems that they are after an inventor's plans and are using phantoms and ghouls as a way of scaring Ma Riley out of her wits. However, she gives them a dose of their own medicine and makes the castle safe again. Some fun "scares" (a knight whose head flies off) help pass the time. Lucan would again give the horror genre a try in 1952's MY SON THE VAMPIRE. (See OLD MOTHER RILEY series, Index.)

p&d, John Baxter; w, Con West, Geoffrey Orme, Arthur Lucan; ph, James Wilson; m, Kennedy Russell; art d, Holmes Paul.

Comedy/Horror **(PR:A MPAA:NR)**

OLD MOTHER RILEY'S JUNGLE TREASURE** (1951, Brit.) 75m Oakland/REN bw

Arthur Lucan (*Mrs. Riley*), Kitty McShane (*Kitty Riley*), Garry Marsh (*Kim*), Roddy Hughes (*Mr. Orders*), Sebastian Cabot (*Morgan, the Pirate*), Cyril Chamberlain (*Capt. Daincourt*), Anita D'Ray (*Estelle*), Willer Neal (*Harry Benson*), Peter Butterworth (*Steve*), Robert Adams (*Chief Stinker*), Roddy Hughes (*Mr. Orders*), Peter Stanwick (*Mr. Benson*), Harry Lane (*Slim*), Michael Ripper (*Jake*), Bill Shine (*Officer Prang*), Maria Mercedes (*Air Hostess*), Gerald Rex (*Ted*).

A relentlessly absurd farce which has Lucan as Mother Riley working in an antique shop with daughter McShane. Upon recovering a secret treasure map, they head for the South Seas and begin their hunt. Not only do they find a fortune, but Lucan is turned into a native queen. A film in the stylized vein of British comedy (as are all the pictures in the OLD MOTHER RILEY series which continues through the films of Monty Python. (See OLD MOTHER RILEY series, Index.)

p, George Minter; d, Maclean Rogers; w, Val Valentine; ph, James Wilson.

Comedy **(PR:A MPAA:NR)**

OLD MOTHER RILEY'S NEW VENTURE (See: OLD MOTHER RILEY, 1952, Brit.)

OLD OKLAHOMA PLAINS*½ (1952) 60m REP bw

Rex Allen (*Himself*), Slim Pickens (*Himself*), Elaine Edwards (*Terry Ramsey*), Roy Barcroft (*Arthur Jensen*), John Crawford (*Chuck Ramsey*), Joel Marston (*Lt. Spike Connors*), Russell Hicks (*Col. Bigelow*), Fred Graham (*Nat Cameron*), Stephen Chase (*Maj. Gen. Parker*), The Republic Rhythm Riders, Koko the Horse.

Strange series western has Allen helping the Army clear cattle from an area of range so that they can conduct tank maneuvers circa 1926. The ranchers, however, do not like the idea because they fear the Army will no longer buy their horses

if tanks replace the cavalry. Barcroft, the rancher with the most to lose if the tank tests are successful, plots to sabotage the maneuvers and it's up to Allen to stop him. Bizarre highlight is a race between a tank and a cavalry troop which is lifted nearly verbatim from Republic's 1938 epic ARMY GIRL. One of the last gasps of the series western.

p, Edward J. White; d, William Witney; w, Milton Raison (based on a story by Albert DeMond); ph, John MacBurnie; m, Stanley Wilson; ed, Tony Martinelli; art d, Fred Hotaling; set d, John McCarthy, Jr., James Redd; m/l, "Dese Bones" (sung by Rex Allen and The Republic Rhythm Riders).

Western **(PR:A MPAA:NR)**

OLD OVERLAND TRAIL* (1953) 60m REP bw

Rex Allen (*Himself*), Slim Pickens (*Himself*), Roy Barcroft (*John Anchor*), Virginia Hall (*Mary Peterson*), Gil Herman (*Jim Allen*), Wade Crosby (*Draftsman*), Leonard Nimoy (*Black Hawk*), Zon Murray (*Mack*), Harry Harvey (*Proprietor*), The Republic Rhythm Riders, Koko the Horse.

Late entry in the Allen series of westerns has the hero as an agent for the Bureau of Indian Affairs assigned to stop villainous railroad contractor Barcroft from inciting the Indians to war. Barcroft gives booze and guns to the Indians in the hopes that they will drive the immigrants from the land and into his cheap labor camps. Allen gives chase, but is shocked to find his estranged brother is one of Barcroft's henchmen. Look hard and fast for "Star Trek's" Leonard Nimoy in an early role as one of the Indians. The musical highlight is "Just a Wanderin' Buckaroo" done with an echo-chamber effect.

p, Edward J. White; d, William Witney; w, Milton Raison; ph, John MacBurnie; ed, Harold Minter; md, R. Dale Butts; art d, Frank Arrigo; m/l, "Cowboy's Dream of Heaven," Jack Elliott (sung by Rex Allen, Virginia Hall, The Republic Rhythm Riders), "Just a Wanderin' Buckaroo," "Work for the Night Is Coming," (sung by Allen, Hall, The Republic Rhythm Riders).

Western **(PR:A MPAA:NR)**

OLD ROSES*½ (1935, Brit.) 60m FOX bw

Horace Hodges (*Johnnie Lee, "Old Roses"*), Nancy Burne (*Jenny Erroll*), Bruce Lister (*Chris Morgan*), Charles Mortimer (*John Morgan*), Felix Aylmer (*Lord Sandebury*), Wilfrid Walter (*Sweeton*), Esme Church (*Mrs. Erroll*), George Hayes (*Simes*), Eric Portman (*Lou*), Trefor Jones (*Singing Gypsy*), Philip Ray, Con Brierley, Eileen Senton.

A harmless but ineffective tale about a small-town gardener with a love for roses who befriends a pair of young lovers. His devotion to them leads him so far as to confess to a murder which the young man is accused of commiting. By the finale "Old Roses" (played with a dose of charm by Hodges) admits his fakery and goes on with his life.

p&d, Bernard Mainwaring; w, Anthony Richardson; ph, Alex Bryce.

Drama **(PR:A MPAA:NR)**

OLD SCHOOL TIE, THE (SEE: WE WENT TO COLLEGE, 1936)

OLD SHATTERHAND** (1968, Ger./Yugo./Fr./Ital.) 122m CCC/Constantin c (AKA: APACHES LAST BATTLE; SHATTERHAND)

Lex Barker (*Old Shatterhand*), Pierre Brice (*Winnetou*), Daliah Lavi (*Paloma*), Guy Madison (*Bradley*), Ralf Wolter (*Sam Hawkens*), Gustavo Rojo (*Bush*), Rik Battaglia (*Dixon*), Kitti Mattern (*Rosemary*), Alain Tissier (*Tunjunga*), Bill Ramsey.

The first in a long series of German westerns based on the novels of Karl May. Barker stars as the cowboy who, along with his good and noble Indian friend Brice, chief of the Apaches, must end a nasty war between the Comanches and Apaches. Unscrupulous white men seeking to steal the land in the ensuing confusion started the war. Standard B western plot helped somewhat by outstanding photography. Some American prints are cut to a 98-minute running time.

p, Arthur Brauner; d, Hugo Fragonase; w, Ladislas Fodor, Robert A. Stemmle (based on the novels by Karl May); ph, Siegfried Hold (Superpanorama, Eastmancolor); m, Riz Ortolani; ed, Alfred Srp.

Western **(PR:A MPAA:NR)**

OLD SOLDIERS NEVER DIE*½ (1931, Brit.) 58m BIP/Wardour bw

Leslie Fuller (*Bill Smith*), Max Nesbitt (*Sam Silverstein*), Alf Goddard (*Sergeant*), Molly Lamont (*Ada*), Mamie Holland (*Jane*), Wellington Briggs (*Colonel*), Wilfred Shine (*Padre*), Nigel Barrie (*Doctor*), Harry Nesbitt (*Harry Silverstein*), Hal Gordon (*Recruit/Sentry*).

Cheap British comedy starring Fuller and Nesbitt as two buddies (one cockney, the other Jewish) who accidentally walk into a recruiting office thinking it a movie theater. Before they know it they're in the army harassing their cruel sergeant Goddard.

p&d, Monty Banks; w, Val Valentine (based on a story by Syd Courtenay, Lola Harvey).

Comedy **(PR:A MPAA:NR)**

OLD SPANISH CUSTOM, AN*½ (1936, Brit.) 61m British and Continental/MGM bw (GB: THE INVADER)

Buster Keaton (*Leander Proudfoot*), Lupita Tova (*Lupita Malez*), Esme Percy (*Jose*), Lyn Harding (*Gonzalo Gonzalez*), Webster Booth (*Serenader*), Andrea Malandrinos (*Carlos*), Hilda Moreno (*Carmita*), Clifford Heatherley (*David Cheeseman*).

Keaton stars in another of his unfortunately dismal sound efforts, this time as a well-to-do yachtsman. While docked in Spain he falls for the attractive Tova, who freely returns his affections. He soon finds that he is merely a pawn in her game of playing two of her lovers against each other with the aim of getting one of them killed. Not surprisingly, audiences and distributors alike felt that the film was unwatchable—a fault that can be attributed chiefly to Keaton. On the very first day of shooting, director Brunel received a note which warned of Keaton's love of liquor: "Don't let him drink!" But drink he did, causing ill feelings on the set and driving the film over its meager budget. As bad as the film was, the producers insisted that its 61 minutes weren't enough, and brought in a new editor to lengthen it. However, since no extra scenes were filmed, the only option was to add frames to the already existing shots. It was finally released in the U.S. in its pared-down version, doing nothing to prolong Keaton's sagging career. It was to be Keaton's last starring performance until a 1946 appearance in the negligible EL MODERNO BARBA AZUL, a Mexican "Bluebeard" tale which mercifully never saw a U.S. release.

p, Sam Spiegel, Harold Richman; d, Adrian Brunel; w, Edwin Greenwood; ph, Eugene Schuftan; m, John Greenwood, George Rubens; ed, Dan Birt.

Comedy (PR:A MPAA:NR)

OLD SPANISH CUSTOMERS   (1932, Brit.) 69m BIP/MGM bw

Leslie Fuller (Bill), Binnie Barnes (Carmen), Drusilla Wills (Martha), Wallace Lupino (Pedro), Hal Gordon (Manuelito), Ernest Sefton (Tormillo), Betty Fields, Syd Courtenay, Hal Walters, Lola Harvey, Allan Woodburn.

Fuller stars as a Britisher vacationing in Spain who winds up in the bullfighting arena when he is erroneously believed to be a matador. A formula plot which delivers predictable results. Former music-hall comedian Fuller recreated the put-upon character "Bill" in a number of 1930s "quota quickie" comedies.

p, John Maxwell; d, Lupino Lane; w, Syd Courtenay, Lola Harvey.

Comedy (PR:A MPAA:NR)

OLD SUREHAND, 1. TIEL   (SEE: FLAMING FRONTIER, 1968, Ger./Yugo.)

OLD SWIMMIN' HOLE, THE*   (1941) 81m MON bw (GB: WHEN YOUTH CONSPIRES)

Jackie Moran (Chris), Marcia Mae Jones (Betty), Leatrice Joy (Julie), Charles Brown (Elliott), Theodore Von Eltz (Baker), George Cleveland (Harper), Dix Davis (Jimmy), Dorothy Vaughan, Sonny Boy Williams, Si Jenks.

Maudlin, dull melodrama starring Moran and Jones as two kids trying to get their single parents interested in each other. Sub-plot has Moran wanting to become a doctor, but forced by his mother's poverty to stay out of school.

p, Scott R. Dunlap; d, Robert McGowan; w, Dorothy Reid (based on a story by Gerald Breitigam); ph, Harry Neumann; ed, Russell Schoengarth.

Drama (PR:A MPAA:NR)

OLD TEXAS TRAIL, THE**   (1944) 60m UNIV bw (GB: STAGECOACH LINE)

Rod Cameron (Jim), Virginia Christine (Queenie Leone), Eddie Dew (Dave), Fuzzy Knight (Pinky), Ray Whitley (Amarillo), Joseph J. Greene (Jeff Talbot), Marjorie Clements (Mary), George Eldredge (Sparks Diamond), Edmund Cobb (Joe Gardner), Jack Clifford (Sheriff), Merle Travis (Jake), Dick Purcell, Harry Strang, Ray Jones, William Desmond, George Turner, Art Fowler, Henry Wills, The Bar-6 Cowboys.

Rod, Fuzzy, and their pals help a stagecoach line fend off a malicious pack of outlaws who want to retain the rights to the coach line themselves. A rip-snortin' 60 minutes of western cliches that raise dust in the Lone Star state.

p, Oliver Drake; d, Lewis D. Collins; w, William Lively; ph, William Sickner; ed, Saul Goodkind; md, Paul Sawtell; art d, John B. Goodman, Harold H. MacArthur.

Western   **Cas.** (PR:A MPAA:NR)

OLD WEST, THE**½   (1952) 61m COL bw

Gene Autry (Himself), Pat Buttram (Panhandle Gibbs), Gail Davis (Arlie Williams), Lyle Talbot (Doc Lockwood), Louis Jean Heydt (Jeff Blecker), House Peters, Sr. (Parson Brooks), House Peters, Jr. (Saunders), Dick Jones (Pinto), Kathy Johnson (Judie), Don Harvey (Hod Evers), Dee Pollock (Eddie Jamison), Raymond L. Morgan (Duffield), James Craven (Daniels), Tom London (Chadwick), Frank Marvin (Watkins), Syd Saylor, Bob Woodward, Buddy Roosevelt, Tex Terry, Pat O'Malley, Bobby Clark, Robert Hilton, John Merton, Frank Ellis, Champion the Horse, Champ Jr. the Horse.

Autry battles the evil Talbot and his goons who are trying to steal Autry's contract to supply horses for the stagecoach line in this saga. Preacher Peters teams with Autry to clean up the town of Saddlerock and throw out the bums. The first Autry film for director Archinbaud, who would guide Autry until the end of the series.

p, Armand Schaefer; d, George Archainbaud; w, Gerald Geraghty; ph, William Bradford; ed, James Sweeney; md, Mischa Bakaleinikoff; art d, Charles Clague; m/l, "Somebody Bigger than You and I," "Music by the Angels" (sung by Gene Autry, chorus).

Western (PR:A MPAA:NR)

OLD WYOMING TRAIL, THE**   (1937) 56m COL bw

Charles Starrett (Bob Patterson), Donald Grayson (Sandy), Barbara Weeks (Elsie Halliday), Dick Curtis (Ed Slade), Edward Le Saint (Jeff Halliday), Guy Usher (Lafe Kenney), Bob Nolan, Roy Rogers, Tim Spencer, Hugh Farr, Karl Farr (Sons of the Pioneers), George Chesebro, Edward Piel, Edward Hearn, Art Mix, Slim Whitaker, Alma Chester, Ernie Adams, Dick Botiller, Frank Ellis, Joe Yrigoyen, Charles Brinley, Fred Burns, Si Jenks, Curley Dresden, Ray Whitley, Blackie Whiteford, Tom London, Art Dillard, Ray Jones, Jerome Ward, Ed Javregi, Tex Cooper.

Starrett must stop a gang of land-grabbers before they can snatch all the territory that will be intersected by new railroad. Good fist-fight between Starrett and Curtis.

p, Harry Decker; d, Folmer Blangsted; w, Ed Earl Repp (based on a story by J. Benton Cheney); ph, Allen G. Siegler; ed, William Lyon.

Western   **Cas.** (PR:A MPAA:NR)

OLD YELLER**½   (1957) 83m Disney/BV c

Dorothy McGuire (Katie Coates), Fess Parker (Jim Coates), Tommy Kirk (Travis Coates), Kevin Corcoran (Arliss Coates), Jeff York (Bud Searcy), Beverly Washburn (Lisbeth Searcy), Chuck Connors (Burn Sanderson), Spike the Dog (Old Yeller).

Disney Studios' first attempt at a boy-and-his-dog film, and their best. Set in Texas in 1869, OLD YELLER tells the story of a farm family whose father, Parker, is forced to leave on a cattle drive for three months to earn enough money so that they can settle down. While he is gone, Parker leaves his 15-year-old son, Kirk, in charge. When his younger brother, Corcoran, finds a stray yellow dog and decides to adopt him, Kirk is frustrated at this breach of his authority. But his mother, McGuire, approves of the dog's presence and reminds Kirk of how lonely his little brother is. Soon Old Yeller has won the hearts of the whole family and proves useful on the farm. One day, a lone cowboy arrives and tells the family that the dog is his. When he sees how attached the family is to the dog, especially Corcoran, the cowboy agrees to swap for the dog. Corcoran gives him a horned toad in trade, and Old Yeller is on the farm to stay. Kirk takes the dog to trap some wild pigs. But Kirk gets trapped in the midst of the wild, vicious animals. Old Yeller courageously fights the pigs off Kirk, and both boy and dog are wounded. Both of them heal, but Old Yeller is kept in confinement until Kirk can determine if he has contracted rabies. Eventually, Kirk decides the danger has passed, but he is shocked one day when the dog turns very vicious for no apparent reason. Realizing that Old Yeller has indeed contracted rabies, Kirk shoots the dog. The depressed Kirk rejects all advice or help, including a puppy fathered by Old Yeller. When Parker finally returns to the farm, McGuire tells him what has happened and he has a long talk with his son regarding responsibility, love, and loss. Kirk tells his father that he has been trying to deal with the dog's death, but it is not easy. After visiting Old Yeller's grave, Kirk is greeted by the puppy, and for the first time he sees Old Yeller embodied in his pup. Kirk adopts the dog and takes it back to the farm. A heartwarming (in the best sense of the word), powerful children's film, well-scripted, -paced and -performed. Sequel: SAVAGE SAM.

p, Walt Disney; d, Robert Stevenson; w, Fred Gipson, William Tunberg (based on the novel by Gipson); ph, Charles P. Boyle (Technicolor); m, Oliver Wallace; ed, Stanley Johnson; md, Clifford Vaughan; art d, Carroll Clark; set d, Emile Kuri, Fred MacLean; cos, Chuck Keehne, Gertrude Casey; m/l, "Old Yeller," Wallace, Gil George (sung by Jerome Courtland); makeup, Pat McNalley.

Drama   **Cas.** (PR:A MPAA:G)

OLDEST CONFESSION, THE   (SEE: HAPPY THIEVES, THE, 1961)

OLDEST PROFESSION, THE*   (1968, Fr./Ital./Ger.) 97m Gibe-Francoriz-Franco London-Rialto-Rizzoli/Goldstone-VIP c (LE PLUS VIEUX METIER DU MONDE; L'AMORE ATTRAVERSO I SECOLI; DAS ALTESTE GEWERBE DER WELT)

"Prehistoric Era": Michele Mercier (Brit), Enrico Maria Salerno (Braque), Gabriele Tinti (Seaman); "Roman Nights": Elsa Martinelli (Empress), Gastone Moschin (Caesar; "Mademoiselle Mimi": Jeanne Moreau (Mimi), Jean-Claude Brialy (Philibert), Jean Richard (Constable); "The Gay Nineties": Raquel Welch (Nini), Martin Held (Banker), Siegfried Schurenberg (Edouard), Tilly Lauenstein; "Paris Today": Nadia Gray (Nadia), France Anglade (Catherine), Jacques Duby (Doctor), Francis Blanche (Visitor), Marcel Dalio (Older Man); "Anticipation": Anna Karina (Miss Conversation), Marilu Tolo (Miss Physical), Jacques Charrier (Space Traveler), Jean-Pierre Leaud (Bellboy), Daniel Bart, Jean-Patrick Lebel.

The history of prostitution is carelessly traced from prehistoric times (Indovina's episode) up through the future of sex (Godard's episode). None of the segments is good, especially in comparison to other works by the directors. Godard's segment is the most talked about only because he directed it—it is barely better than the rest, looking like a color version of his earlier ALPHAVILLE. This episode (and the film) ends quite simply with a kiss, which is perhaps an intentional return to THE KISS (1896), one of the earliest films made. A fine troupe of actors is wasted: Moreau, Brialy, Welch, Dalio, Karina, and Leaud.

p, Joseph Bergholz; d, Franco Indovina ("Prehistoric Era"), Mauro Bolognini ("Roman Nights"), Philippe De Broca ("Mademoiselle Mimi"), Michael Pfleghar ("The Gay Nineties"), Claude Autant-Lara ("Paris Today"), Jean-Luc Godard ("Anticipation"); w, Ennio Flajano ("Prehistoric Era," "Roman Nights"), Daniel Boulanger ("Mademoiselle Mimi"), Georges Tabet, Andre Tabet ("The Gay Nineties"), Jean Aurenche ("Paris Today"), Jean-Luc Godard ("Anticipation"); ph, Pierre Lhomme (all episodes except "The Gay Nineties"), Heinz Holscher ("The Gay Nineties") (All Eastmancolor); m, Michel Legrand; ed, Susanne Paschen ("The Gay Nineties"), Agnes Guillemot ("Anticipation"); art d, Max Douy, Bernard Evein, Maurice Petri (all episodes except "The Gay Nineties"), Herta Hareiter ("The Gay Nineties").

Comedy/Drama (PR:O MPAA:NR)

O'LEARY NIGHT   (SEE: TONIGHT'S THE NIGHT, 1954, Brit.)

OLGA'S GIRLS zero   (1964) 70m American Film Distributing bw

Audrey Campbell (Olga), Rickey Bell (Collette), Ava Denning (Susie), Darlene Bennett (Connie), Jean Laloni (Bunny), Ann Pepper (Kitty), Cynthia Grey (Lela), Giselle Swan (Dolores), Dolly Simmons (Judy), Jane Hill (Lorraine), Rita Barrie (1st Party Girl), June Vega (2nd Party Girl), Gil Adams (White Slaver), Perry Peters, Audrey Campbell (Narrators).

Sadistic "adults only" feature starring Campbell as a disgusting drug dealer and white slaver who rules her domain by brutally torturing all who oppose her. Bell, one of Campbell's assistants, leaves to start her own prostitution business. Enraged, Campbell kidnaps Bell's most popular girl, Hill, to force a confrontation. After a vicious fight, Campbell wins and business goes back to normal. Sequel to WHITE SLAVES OF CHINATOWN.

p, George Weiss; d, Joseph P. Mawra; ph, Werner Rose; m, Clyde Otis; set d, Sande Johnsen.

Crime (PR:O MPAA:NR)

OLIVE TREES OF JUSTICE, THE½** (1967, Fr.) 81m Societe Algerienne/Pathe bw (LES OLIVIERS DE LA JUSTICE)

Pierre Prothon *(Jean/Narrator)*, Jean Pelegri *(His Father)*, Marie Decaitre *(His Mother)*, Huguette Poggi *(Cousin Louise)*, Said Achaibou, Mohamed Bennour, Boralfa, Mathilde Gau, Kaoudoune, Amar Metchiek, Fatima Moktari, Ali Moulahcene, Djama Precigout, Gesomina Ros, Alexandre Sagols, Mohamed Saour, Bounedine Sekkal, Mustapha Smaili, Josiane Solal, Lucienne Terrades, Janine Vila.

Overly sentimental, but with its heart in the right place, THE OLIVE TREES OF JUSTICE tells the story of Prothon, a Parisian who returns to Algiers (he was raised there) during the war of independence to be with his dying father. His memories of a happy childhood are sparked by the rubble-strewn streets of Algeria and he wonders why French and Algerian children cannot play together as he and his friends did as children. After his father dies, dozens of friends, French and Arab, come to pay their respects. Touched by this reunion, Prothon is encouraged by an Arab friend to stay in Algeria. He declines, however, and explains that he must return to the life he has built in Paris. Things change for Prothon when his normally racist aunt runs to the aid of an Arab boy who was struck by a car. Encouraged by this display of human emotion, Prothon decides to stay in Algeria. Released in France in 1962.

p, Georges Derocles; d, James Blue; w, Jean Pelegri, Sylvain Dhomme, Blue (based on the novel *Les Oliviers de la Justice* by Pelegri); ph, Julius Rascheff; m, Maurice Jarre; ed, Suzanne Gaveau, Marie-Claude Barlset.

Drama (PR:A MPAA:NR)

OLIVER!*** (1968, Brit.) 153m Warwick-Romulus/COL c

Ron Moody *(Fagin)*, Shani Wallis *(Nancy)*, Oliver Reed *(Bill Sikes)*, Harry Secombe *(Mr. Bumble)*, Mark Lester *(Oliver Twist)*, Jack Wild *(The Artful Dodger)*, Hugh Griffith *(The Magistrate)*, Joseph O'Conor *(Mr. Brownlow)*, Peggy Mount *(Widow Corney)*, Leonard Rossiter *(Mr. Sowerberry)*, Hylda Baker *(Mrs. Sowerberry)*, Kenneth Cranham *(Noah Claypole)*, Megs Jenkins *(Mrs. Bedwin)*, Sheila White *(Bet)*, Wensley Pithey *(Dr. Grimwig)*, James Hayter *(Mr. Jessop)*, Elizabeth Knight *(Charlotte)*, Fred Emney *(Chairman of Workhouse Governors)*, Edwin Finn, Foy Evans *(Workhouse Paupers)*, Norman Mitchell *(Arresting Policeman)*, Robert Bartlett, Graham Buttrose, Jeffrey Chandler, Kirk Clugeston, Dempsey Cook, Christopher Duff, Nigel Grice, Ronnie Johnson, Nigel Kingsley, Robert Langley, Brian Lloyd, Peter Lock, Ian Ramsey, Peter Renn, Bill Smith, Kim Smith, Freddie Stead, Raymond Ward, John Watters *(Fagin's Boys)*, Clive Moss *(Charlie Bates)*, Veronica Page *(Oliver's Mother)*, Henry Kay *(Doctor)*, Jane Peach *(Rose the Maid)*, Keith Roberts *(Policeman in Magistrate's Court)*, Peter Hoar *(Court Clerk)*, John Baskcombe, Norman Pitt, Arnold Locke, Frank Crawshaw *(Workhouse Governors)*.

It was eight years after Lionel Bart's musicalization of Dickens' book hit the state that this film was done. It was also the eighth version (that we can count) of the classic and perhaps the finest. First done in 1909 by Pathe, then by Vitaphone in 1910, followed by a Nat Goodwin starrer (as Fagin) in 1912, then the Tully Marshall version in 1916 (which had Marie Doro, a female, playing Oliver), then the one that the British censored with Lon Chaney as Fagin and Jackie Coogan as Oliver in 1922. The first talkie starred Irving Pichel and Dickie Moore and then there was the Lean picture in 1948. Bart, who was born Lionel Begleitner, had been writing since the mid-1950s and had already had one London stage hit, "Fings Ain't What They Used To Be," before this blockbuster at about the time he turned 30 years of age. His subsequent works, "Blitz" and "Maggie May," did not achieve one gram of the success of this musical, and if he were to never write another thing, OLIVER! would be enough. Carol Reed was wise when he hired Harris to write the screenplay, as the original needed very little to make it work for the screen and Harris tastefully left well enough alone. Many times, a screenwriter will attempt to plant his or her stamp on someone else's work and that often ruins the original theme. Harris, who did not have all that many credits (REACH FOR THE SKY, FERRY TO HONG KONG, THE ADMIRABLE CRICHTON, LIGHT UP THE SKY among them) did a smashing job and the result was his being nominated for Best Screenplay. Other nominations went to Morris' cinematography and Moody's Fagin, as well as Wild's Artful Dodger, for Best Supporting Actor. OLIVER! rightfully won as Best Picture, for Best Direction, Best Art Direction, and, of course, Best Musical Score. Yet another Oscar went for Best Sound and Onna White received a "special" Oscar for her choreography (since that field is not covered by the Academy's voting). OLIVER! was a very expensive picture and every farthing shows up on the screen in every frame. The way the boy got to be at the workhouse is deleted and the picture begins as Lester is having a meal at the orphanage where he lives. The boys are all hungry after the tiny bowl of gruel they are given and Lester loses at the drawing of straws, so he must ask the proprietor, Secombe, for a second helping. "More!" bellows Secombe. "You want MORE!??" Stunned by Lester's request for two reasons (first, no one had ever done that before and second, the gruel was so awful, who would want any more?), Secombe takes the blond youth by the ear and leads him through London's snow as he seeks someone, anyone who will take this audacious child off his hands. Secombe finally finds a taker, the undertaker Rossiter, who lives in the shop with his wife, Baker, and his assistant, Cranham. They work Lester until his bones ache and the child attempts to be a good undertaker's apprentice, but when Cranham questions Lester's heritage and passes some scurrilous remarks about his dead mother, Lester rebels and runs into the teeming streets. He encounters Wild, a small, top-hatted youth who lives by his wits. Wild takes Lester back to his abode, a drafty attic where he lives with several other street boys under the eye of Moody, a crook who takes care of the lads and trains them to be pickpockets. Lester is welcomed into the den of thieves and taught lessons on how to pick a pocket or two. Satisfied that Lester is now ready to help increase his coffers, Moody sends the boy out on his first job with Wild close by to watch the boy's progress. Wild and another boy try to nick the wallet of O'Conor, a well-to-do man. The two others get away, but Lester is too slow and he is arrested. A trial takes place after the boy has cooled his heels in jail for a bit. In court, Lester insists that he's innocent and touches O'Conor's heart. The rich man takes Lester home with him and the boy is now living in absolute luxury. One of Moody's heinous associates is Oliver Reed who fears that Lester might blow the whistle on their nefarious criminality. The only way to keep the boy silent is to nab him back. Reed convinces his live-in mate, Wallis, that he won't hurt the boy and just wants to make sure Lester promises to keep mum. The truth is that Reed means to cosh the boy's skull as soon as he grabs him. When they kidnap Lester, Wallis wakes up to Reed's plan and immediately gets in touch with O'Conor. Then she grabs Lester and will deliver the boy to O'Conor in neutral territory at midnight on London Bridge (the same one that was sold to McCulloch in Lake Havasu City, Arizona). Reed smells a rat and tails them, grabs Lester, and kills Wallis. When Wallis's body is found with Reed's ugly dog near it, there's no question about who did her in. A mob forms and they, plus the police, follow the dog. Meanwhile, Reed is taking the high road and dragging Lester along the rooftops with him. At one point, Reed has to let go of Lester to grab a rope, but a police marksman shoots him dead. O'Conor, by this time, has learned that Lester is his nephew, the son of his long-missing niece. He takes the boy back to a life of riches, and Moody and Wild, now just the two of them, decide that they'll stay together and continue their lives as crooks. Moody, who had amassed a fortune and lost it all in a deep stream, has nothing but Wild and his wits, and that will be enough. Moody was sensational in the role he created in London (but did not play on Broadway) and stole the picture from everyone. He was nowhere near as semitic as Alec Guiness so there was no problem with his portrayal. Although it cost 10 million 1960 dollars, it doubled that amount on the first go-round and continues to make money on TV. If this wasn't the best musical to come out of England, then it must be among the top five, although we can't think of any we like better. The wonderful songs by Lionel Bart include: "Food, Glorious Food" (sung by Mark Lester, chorus), "Oliver!" (sung by Harry Secombe, Peggy Mount, chorus), "Boy For Sale" (sung by Secombe), "Where Is Love?" (sung by Lester), "Consider Yourself" (sung by Jack Wild, Lester, ensemble), "Pick a Pocket or Two" (sung by Ron Moody, chorus), "I'd Do Anything" (sung by Wild, Shani Wallis, Sheila White, Lester, Moody, chorus), "Be Back Soon" (sung by Moody, chorus), "As Long as He Needs Me" (sung by Wallis), "Who Will Buy?" (sung by Lester, ensemble), "It's A Fine Life" (sung by Wallis, White, chorus), "Reviewing the Situation" (sung by Moody), "Oom-Pah-Pah" (sung by Wallis, chorus).

p, John Woolf; d, Carol Reed; w, Vernon Harris (based on the musical play by Lionel Bart, from the novel *Oliver Twist* by Charles Dickens); ph, Oswald Morris (Panavision, Technicolor); m, Bart; ed, Ralph Kemplen; prod d, John Box; md, John Green; art d, Terence Marsh; set d, Vernon Dixon, Ken Mugglestone; cos, Phyllis Dalton; spec eff, Allan Bryce; ch, Onna White; makeup, George Frost.

Musical Comedy (PR:AAA MPAA:G)

OLIVER TWIST ** (1933) 74m Herbert Brenon/MON bw

Dickie Moore *(Oliver Twist)*, Irving Pichel *(Fagin)*, William "Stage" Boyd *(Bill Sikes)*, Doris Lloyd *(Nancy Sikes)*, Barbara Kent *(Rose Maylie)*, Alec B. Francis *(Brownlow)*, George K. Arthur *(Toby Crackit)*, Clyde Cook *(Chitling)*, Sonny Ray *(The Artful Dodger)*, George Nash *(Charlie Bates)*, Lionel Belmore *(Bumble)*, Tempe Pigott *(Mrs. Corney)*, Nelson McDowell *(Sowerberry)*, Virginia Sale *(Mrs. Sowerberry)*, Bobby Nelson *(Noah Claypole)*, Harry Holman *(Grimwig)*.

Low-budget production of the Charles Dickens classic which pales in comparison to the 1948 and 1968 British versions. Five-year-old cherub Moore makes a less-than-successful Oliver Twist, due to his youth and his obvious lack of the range required for the part. Pichel is fine as Fagin, but Boyd's (not Hopalong Cassidy, but a different actor) Bill Sykes is less than that of nightmares. A competent, if uninspired effort, it spawned a short Dickens craze among the Hollywood studios.

p, I. E. Chadwick; d, William Cowen; w, Elizabeth Meehan (based on the novel by Charles Dickens); ph, J. Roy Hunt; ed, Carl Pearson.

Drama Cas. (PR:A MPAA:NR)

OLIVER TWIST**** (1951, Brit.) 105m Cineguild/RANK-UA bw

Robert Newton *(Bill Sikes)*, Alec Guinness *(Fagin)*, Kay Walsh *(Nancy)*, Francis L. Sullivan *(Mr. Bumble)*, Henry Stephenson *(Mr. Brownlow)*, Mary Clare *(Mrs. Corney)*, John Howard Davies *(Oliver Twist)*, Josephine Stuart *(Oliver's Mother)*, Henry Edwards *(Police Official)*, Ralph Truman *(Monks)*, Anthony Newley *(The Artful Dodger)*, Hattie Jacques, Betty Paul *(Sibgers)*, Kenneth Downey *(Workhouse Master)*, Gibb McLaughlin *(Mr. Sowerberry)*, Kathleen Harrison *(Mrs. Sowerberry)*, Amy Veness *(Mrs. Bedwin)*, W. G. Fay *(Bookseller)*, Maurice Denham *(Chief of Police)*, Frederick Lloyd *(Mr. Grimwig)*, Ivor Barnard *(Chairban of the Board)*, Deidre Doyle *(Mrs. Thingummy)*, Edie Martin *(Annie)*, Fay Middleton *(Martha)*, Diana Dors *(Charlotte)*, Michael Dear *(Noah Claypole)*, Graveley Edwards *(Mr. Fang)*, Peter Bull *(Landlord of "Three Cripples")*, John Potter *(Charlie Bates)*, Maurice Jones *(Workhouse Doctor)*.

When Lon Chaney made his silent version of OLIVER TWIST in 1922, the British censors objected because they felt that the film might encourage hooliganism in England and did not depict the Dickens classic in the way they wished. It took 26 years and a relaxation of the standards to get this one made and the U.S. censors rankled against Guinness' portrayal of Fagin as being "anti-Semitic" because of the size of the actor's false nose. Thus, three years passed from the completion of the film until a slightly expurgated version made it to America's shores. The first uncut version was only seen at a Lean festival in 1970, in New York, when the Museum of Modern Art saw fit to screen it. Lean had just finished his magnificent GREAT EXPECTATIONS and thought he should follow up with one of the master's best. In the pivotal title role, he chose a young boy who had never appeared on screen before. He worked closely with Davies, didn't give him much to say in the script, and the result was a cinematic achievement insofar as he allowed the lad's expressive face to do all his talking for him. Davies eventually quit acting and became a TV producer, responsible for such classics as "Fawlty Towers" and "Monty Python's Flying Circus." If we were to compare GREAT EXPECTATIONS with OLIVER TWIST, the latter would be slightly wanting, but it still remains a classic of the genre. The picture begins as a storm rages and a young woman makes her way to a workhouse in the throes of labor. She pushes herself to the huge doors, rings the bell, and is taken in, where she delivers a son and then dies. Davies is raised in the workhouse and makes the tactical error of asking for some more when he finishes his meager meal of gruel. This so enrages the man in charge, Sullivan (who was also the attorney for Mills in GREAT EXPECTATIONS), that Davies is let out as an apprentice to undertaker McLaughlin, and his wife, Harrison. Davies is treated so poorly that he escapes and soon falls in with a pre-teen gang of pickpockets led by Newley. The boys escort Davies to their home, a tacky attic where they live and bring their booty to the man who takes care of them, Guinness, who thinks of all these boys as his sons. When Davies is caught pickpocketing the wallet of wealthy Stephenson, he almost goes to jail but Stephenson decides to take the child instead, and his life is turned around. It turns out that Davies' mother was the niece of Stephenson and the old fellow is thrilled to have his nephew with him. Newton, a murderer, kidnaps Davies back, against the wishes of his barmaid girl friend, Walsh. When she helps the youth escape, Newton kills her for her efforts. At the end, a crowd gathers to catch Newton, who has Davies in tow, and there is a chase across the rooftops. Newton is killed and Davies is taken back to Stephenson. Many of the Dickensian characters have had to be either excised or compressed to fit the time frame of the film, but only the most diehard fans of Dickens will protest. The sets are as much a part of the story as the words the actors speak and Bryan's accomplishment should not go unnoticed. All the acting is first-quality and there is not a false moment in the cast. In a small role, note Diana Dors, who grew up to be the sexpot star of A KID FOR TWO FARTHINGS as well as many other films of the 1950s. As good as this picture was, it was even better when done as a musical. Newley is excellent in his role as the Artful Dodger, before he got into the overacting habits for which he became famous.

p, Ronald Neame, Anthony Havelock-Allan; d, David Lean; w, Lean, Stanley Haynes (based on the novel by Charles Dickens); ph, Guy Green; m, Sir Arnold Bax; ed, Jack Harris; md, Muir Mathieson; set d, John Bryan; cos, Margaret Furse; spec eff, Joan Suttie, Stanley Grant.

Period Drama   Cas.   (PR:AA MPAA:NR)

OLIVER'S STORY*   (1978) 92m PAR c

Ryan O'Neal (Oliver Barrett IV), Candice Bergen (Marcie Bonwit), Nicola Pagett (Joanna Stone), Edward Binns (Phil Cavilleri), Benson Fong (John Hsiang), Charles Haid (Stephen Simpson), Kenneth McMillan (James Francis), Ray Milland (Mr. Barrett), Josef Sommer (Dr. Dienhart), Sully Boyar (Mr. Gentilano), Swoosie Kurtz (Gwen Simpson), Meg Mundy (Mrs. Barrett), Beatrice Winde (Waltereen), Sol Schwade (Arlie), Father Frank Toste (Fr. Giamatti), Cynthia McPherson (Anita), Gloria Irizarry (Cleaning Woman), Louis Turenne (Waiter), Victor Gil de la Madrid (Newscaster), Deborah Rush, Ann Risley, Jose L. Torres, Miguel Loperana, Sarah Beach, Wilfredo Hernandez, Dora Collazo-Levy, Herb Braha, Peter Looney.

More unbearable maudlin sentiment from Erich Segal. This sequel to the inexplicably successful 1970 tearjerker LOVE STORY begins as Ali McGraw's casket is being lowered into the grave. A distraught O'Neal attempts to go on with his life, working as a busy lawyer in a prestigious firm, while still spewing his mawkish 1960s liberal sentiments, with an overdose of self-pity that continually frustrates his close friends. Then one fine day, he meets the beautiful heir to the Bonwit Teller fortune, Bergen, and it's rich-loves-rich, a distinct contrast to the original film. From there it's the usual Segal nonsense, highlighted by Milland's reprise of his role as O'Neal's father. Eventually O'Neal loses Bergen when she walks out after having heard enough of his banal whimpering.

p, David V. Picker; d, John Korty; w, Erich Segal, Korty (based on the novel by Segal); ph, Arthur Ornitz (Panavision, Movielab Color); m, Lee Holdridge; ed, Stuart H. Pappe; art d, Robert Gundlach; set d, Phil Smith; cos, Peggy Farrell; m/l, "Oliver's Theme," Francis Lai.

Romance   Cas.   (PR:C MPAA:PG)

OLLY, OLLY, OXEN FREE*½   (1978) 83m Rico Lion/Sanrio c (AKA: THE GREAT BALLOON ADVENTURE)

Katharine Hepburn (Miss Pudd), Kevin McKenzie (Alby), Dennis Dimster (Chris), Peter Kilman (Mailman), Obie (Joshua).

The mammoth Japanese toy company Sanrio put up the money for this and thought they had something with Hepburn in the lead. After all, would such a great lady do a turkey? They didn't reckon with Hepburn's occasional lapses of taste (THE MADWOMAN OF CHAILLOT, GRACE QUIGLEY, etc.) and this picture had more holes in the story than a colander and was not as interesting. The childhood title had nothing to do with the content and that was their first mistake. Their second mistake was making the picture in the first place. McKenzie and Dimster are two kids who come across an old balloon once piloted by McKenzie's grandfather, who used to sail the device around county fairs and the like many years before. They'd like to put the balloon aloft again and turn to junkyard owner Hepburn for the wherewithal. The balloon goes up (in a lovely scene), flies around the wine country of California, and comes down in the Hollywood Bowl while an

orchestra is playing Peter Ilyich Tchaikovsky's "1812 Overture." There's a hint that a sequel would follow, but that was just a gleam in the producer's eye and never came to pass. Other than the splendid aerial photography and the pleasure of watching Hepburn, there's little to recommend this to anyone over the age of thumb-sucking.

p&d, Richard A. Colla; w, Eugene Poinc (based on a story by Maria L. de Ossio, Poinc, Colla); ph, Gayne Rescher (Metrocolor); m, Bob Alcivar; ed, Lee Burch; prod d, Peter Wooley; cos, Edith Head.

Children's Adventure   (PR:A MPAA:G)

OLSEN'S BIG MOMENT*½   (1934) 70m FOX bw (AKA: OLSEN'S NIGHT OUT)

El Brendel (Knute Olsen), Walter Catlett (Robert Brewster III), Barbara Weeks (Jane Van Allen), Susan Fleming (Virginia West), John Arledge (Harry Smith), Maidel Turner, Edward Pawley, Joseph Sauer [Sawyer].

Brendel plays a Swedish janitor who is constantly frustrated in his attempts to enjoy his night off. Complications involving a girl about to marry a rich souse for his money, a gangster attempting to prevent his kid sister from getting embroiled in high society, and other inanities combine to form the basis of this none-too-funny chuckler. An unusual film in that it employs the talents of two of the finest character actors of the time, Brendel and Catlett, in leading roles. Brendel, whose perpetually perplexed expression and whose phrase "Yumpin' Yiminy" made him the stock Swedish comic, and the google-eyed, fidgety Catlett were not a regular team.

d, Malcolm St. Clair; w, Henry Johnson, James Tynan (based on a story by Geroge Marshall); ph, L.W. O'Connell.

Comedy   (PR:A MPAA:NR)

OLSEN'S NIGHT OUT   (SEE: OLSEN'S BIG MOMENT, 1934)

OLTRAGGIO AL PUDORE   (SEE: ALL THE OTHER GIRLS DO, 1966, Fr./Ital.)

OLYMPIC HONEYMOON   (SEE: HONEYMOON MERRY-GO-ROUND, 1939, Brit.)

OMAHA TRAIL, THE**   (1942) 61m MGM bw

James Craig (Pat Candel), Pamela Blake (Julie Santley), Dean Jagger ("Pipestone" Ross), Edward Ellis (Mr. Vane), Chill Wills (Henry), Donald Meek (Jonah McCleod), Howard da Silva (Ben Santley), Henry Morgan (Nat), Morris Ankrum (Job), Kermit Maynard.

Craig stars as a brave stranger who helps desperate railroadman Ellis get his locomotive to Omaha so that he can get first dibs on the lucrative westward line. Unfortunately, the duo must contend with the villainous Jagger, who is determined to stop the railroad's expansion for fear his wagon-train business will be ruined. If that isn't enough to contend with, there are always those pesky Indians who are constantly on the warpath. Good cast, plenty of action. One of his first two leading-man roles for the handsome Craig during 1942.

p, Jack Chertok; d, Edward Buzzell; w, Jesse Lasky, Jr., Hugh Butler (based on a story by Lasky); ph, Sidney Wagner; ed, Conrad A. Nervig; art d, Cedric Gibbons; m/l, "Bang, Bang, Bang," Buzzell, Earl Brent.

Western   (PR:A MPAA:NR)

O'MALLEY OF THE MOUNTED*½   (1936) 59m FOX bw

George O'Brien (O'Malley), Irene Ware (Edith Hyland), Stanley Fields (Red Jagger), James Bush (Bud Hyland), Victor Potel (Gabby), Reginald Barlow (Commissioner), Dick Cramer (Butch), Tom London (Lefty), Charles King (Brody), Olin Francis (Andy), Crauford Kent (McGregor), Blackjack Ward.

O'Brien stars as the title lawman who is assigned the task of patrolling the Canadian/U.S. border and halting the activities of a gang of outlaws terrorizing the small American border towns. To do this, O'Brien goes undercover and joins the gang to gather enough evidence to arrest the lot of them during a bank hold-up. The story is the work of famed silent-screen matinee cowboy actor William S. Hart.

p, Sol Lesser; d, David Howard; w, Dan Jarrett, Frank Howard Clark (based on a story by William S. Hart); ph, Frank B. Good; ed, Arthur Hilton.

Adventure   (PR:A MPAA:NR)

OMAR KHAYYAM**   (1957) 101m PAR c

Cornel Wilde (Omar), Michael Rennie (Hasani), Debra Paget (Sharain), Raymond Massey (The Shah), John Derek (Malik, the Young Prince), Yma Sumac (Karina), Margaret Hayes (Zarada), Joan Taylor (Yaffa), Sebastian Cabot (Nizam), Perry Lopez (Prince Ahmud), Morris Ankrum (Imam Mowaffak), Abraham Sofaer (Tutush), Edward Platt (Jayhan), James Griffith (Buzorg), Peter Adams (Master Herald), Henry Brandon (1st Commander), Kem Dibbs (Tutush Bodyguard), Paul Picerni (2nd Commander), Valeria Allen (Harem Wife), Charles La Torre (Army Physician), Dale Van Sickel (Officer), John Abbott (Yusuf), Len Hendry (Courier), Joyce Meadows (Harem Girl), Abdel Salam Moussa (Shah's Soldier).

Silly costume drama set in medieval Persia starring Wilde as the hero, a brilliant example of Eastern manhood, who becomes embroiled in a dangerous romance with Paget (the real Omar preferred boys), the fiancee of Shah Massey who is busy fighting the Persian/Byzantine war. In addition, his court is rife with evil assassins secretly led by Wilde's boyhood friend Rennie and the Shah's first and former wife Hayes, who are out to overthrow Massey. Director Dieterle, who was responsible for such prestigious filmed biographies as ZOLA and PASTEUR, gave up the ghost with this one after spending 27 years directing fine films in the U.S. He returned to Europe, where he directed films in Italy and Germany before retiring. OMAR KHAYYAM was not exactly a well-fitting crown to his illustrious American career. The lavish production and fine cast are hampered somewhat by a contrived and overly complicated screenplay that delves into every conceivable cliche in less than two hours. Songs rendered by Sumac, "The Andean Nightingale," a singer with a remarkable vocal range, include "The Loves of Omar Khayyam" (Jay Livingston, Ray Evans), "Take My Heart" (Victor Young, Mack David), and "Lament" (Moses Vivanco).

p, Frank Freeman, Jr.; d, William Dieterle; w, Barre Lyndon; ph, Ernest Laszlo (VistaVision, Technicolor); m, Victor Young; ed, Everett Douglas; art d, Hal Pereira, Joseph MacMillan Johnson; cos, Ralph Jester; spec eff, Farciot Edouart, John P. Fulton.

Adventure **(PR:A MPAA:NR)**

OMBRE BIANCHE (SEE: SAVAGE INNOCENTS, THE, 1961)

OMEGA MAN, THE** (1971) 98m WB c

Charlton Heston *(Robert Neville)*, Anthony Zerbe *(Matthias)*, Rosalind Cash *(Lisa)*, Paul Koslo *(Dutch)*, Lincoln Kilpatrick *(Zachary)*, Eric Laneuville *(Richie)*, Jill Giraldi *(Little Girl)*, Anna Aries *(Woman in Cemetery Crypt)*, DeVeren Bookwalter, John Dierkes, Monika Henreid, Linda Redfearn, Forrest Wood *(Family Members)*, Brian Tochi *(Tommy)*.

Another misfired adaptation of Richard Matheson's fine science-fiction novel *I Am Legend* (the first, THE LAST MAN ON EARTH, starring Vincent Price, fared a bit better) starring Heston as one of the few survivors of a post-apocalypse Los Angeles who hasn't been turned into one of an army of pale-skinned mutants called "vampires" who only go out at night. The vampires are led by Zerbe, who has become obsessed with destroying what is left of the scientific culture that made nuclear war possible. The film boils down to a violent battle of wits between a machine-gun-toting Heston and Zerbe's minions, who eventually win and literally crucify Heston for trying to save mankind. Badly dated and clumsily allegorical, THE OMEGA MAN has some fairly interesting moments, the most memorable being the view of a devastated, empty downtown Los Angeles. Heston was instrumental in bringing Matheson's novel to the screen for this unsatisfactory second try. He had been introduced to the book by Orson Welles, no slouch himself at doomsday tales.

p, Walter Seltzer; d, Boris Sagal; w, John William Corrington, Joyce H. Corrington (based on the novel *I Am Legend* by Richard Matheson); ph, Russell Metty (Technicolor); m, Ron Grainer; ed, William Ziegler; art d, Arthur Loel, Walter M. Simonds; set d, William L. Kuehl; cos, Margo Baxley, Bucky Rous; makeup, Gordon Bau.

Science Fiction **(PR:C MPAA:GP)**

OMEN, THE** (1976) 111m FOX c (AKA: BIRTHMARK)

Gregory Peck *(Robert Thorn)*, Lee Remick *(Katherine Thorn)*, David Warner *(Jennings)*, Billie Whitelaw *(Mrs. Baylock)*, Leo McKern *(Bugenhagen)*, Harvey Stevens *(Damien)*, Patrick Troughton *(Father Brennan)*, Martin Benson *(Father Spiletto)*, Anthony Nichols *(Dr. Becker)*, Holly Palance *(Young Nanny)*, John Stride *(Psychiatrist)*, Robert MacLeod *(Mr. Horton)*, Sheila Raynor *(Mrs. Horton)*, Tommy Duggan *(Priest)*, Robert Rietty *(Monk)*, Roy Boyd *(Reporter)*, Nancy Manningham *(Nurse)*, Nicholas Campbell *(Marine)*.

Silly, bloody, but at times a very effective horror film that takes THE EXORCIST one step further by concentrating, not on a devil-possession, but on the Antichrist himself. Peck stars as the highly respected American ambassador to England who, when his wife Remick gives birth to a stillborn child, is encouraged by a priest to switch his dead child with the living baby of a mother who died during childbirth. Five years later, strange things begin happening in the Peck household and they can all be traced to the boy, Stevens. At his birthday party, his nanny hangs herself in full view of all his little friends (a *very* disturbing scene). She is replaced by Whitelaw, his new nanny, who just happens to be an agent of the Devil (unknown to the kid's parents of course). When nosy priest Troughton arrives warning Peck and Remick that they have adopted the Antichrist and that he should seek help from an old exorcist (McKern), he is killed shortly thereafter by a falling lightning rod. Soon after, Warner, a photographer friend of the family, notices odd things in his photos which weren't seen with the naked eye, and he convinces Peck, who by this time is getting a bit concerned, to go with him to Italy in search of McKern. McKern confirms their suspicions and informs Peck that the only way he can get rid of the little devil is to kill him on a sacrificial altar using a special set of daggers. Back in England, Remick is killed by not one, but two rather nasty falls (one over a balcony, the second out of the ambulance window). In Italy, Warner is decapitated by a sliding sheet of glass (the film's most clever and memorable gore effect) for his part in the devilish revelations. Peck finally decides he's had enough and returns to England determined to do the deed. First, he kills nanny Whitelaw (who more or less forces him to) and then drags the boy off to a nearby church where he prepares to stab the kid in the proper sequence. Before he can strike his first blow for Christianity, the cops arrive, misinterpret what Peck is up to, and shoot him dead. Luckily for him, the now-orphaned anti-christ is adopted by Peck's close friend, the President of the United States. Regardless of its rather questionable premise, execution (unintentionally funny dialog abounds), or taste, THE OMEN went on to make an obscene amount of money and spawned two sequels, DAMIEN—OMEN II and THE FINAL CONFLICT, neither of which was very good (the films were originally conceived in four parts, tracing Damien's rise to power from his childhood through adulthood and eventually to Armageddon, but patron interest slacked off considerably after the second film, forcing the wise producers to cut it short at three). Director Richard Donner's (SUPERMAN, THE GOONIES) first feature film. The incubus aspects of the film caused the United States Catholic Conference to call the film one of the most distasteful ever to be released by a major studio; the moguls no doubt were contrite all the way to the bank. When asked whether the devil made him do it, author Seltzer recounted his artistic credo: "I did it strictly for the money. I was flat broke. . ."

p, Harvey Bernhard; d, Richard Donner; w, David Seltzer; ph, Gilbert Taylor (Panavision, DeLuxe Color); m, Jerry Goldsmith; ed, Stuart Baird; art d, Carmen Dillon; set d, Tessa Davies; spec eff, John Richardson; m/l, "Ave Satani," Goldsmith; makeup, Stuart Freeborn.

Horror **Cas.** **(PR:O MPAA:R)**

OMICRON** (1963, Ital.) 102m Lux-Ultra-Vides/PAR bw

Renato Salvatori *(Omicron/Angelo)*, Rosemary Dexter *(Lucia)*, Gaetano Quartaro *(Midollo)*, Mara Carisi *(Mrs. Midollo)*, Ida Serasini *(Widow Piattino)*, Calisto Calisti *(Torchio)*, Danti di Pinto *(Police Inspector)*.

A fairly interesting Italian science-fiction comedy starring Salvatori as a dead worker whose body is brought back to life when an alien creature (an Omicron) inhabits it. The alien soon masters Salvatori's old job and works the machines with amazing speed. Later, he even gets involved in a strike and, of course, falls in love. Eventually the alien's host body convinces him he would be happier back home on Venus.

p, Franco Cristaldi; d&w, Ugo Gregoretti; ph, Carlo di Palma.

Science Fiction/Comedy **(PR:A MPAA:NR)**

OMOO OMOO, THE SHARK GOD* (1949) 58m Esla/Screen Guild bw (AKA: OMOO-OMOO) (GB: THE SHARK GOD)

Ron Randell *(Jeff)*, Devera Burton *(Julie)*, Trevor Bardette *(Captain)*, Pedro de Cordoba *(Tari)*, Richard Benedict *(Richards)*, Rudy Robles *(Tembo)*, Michael Whalen *(Chips)*, George Meeker *(Doc)*, Lisa Kinkaid *(Tala)*, Jack Raymond *(Tex)*.

A South Seas curse afflicts sea captain Bardette when he plucks the black pearl eyes from a native Shark God. The curse proves fatal for the captain, but before it can kill his daughter, Burton, order is restored. Loaded with stock footage of supposedly dangerous animals, this bottom-rung adventure tale fails to put a spell on anyone. Far removed from its nominal source—Melville's famed semi-autobiographical novel *Omoo*, a sequel to his *Typee*—which shared with the film little more than the exotic locale.

p, Leonard S. Picker; d, Leon Leonard; w, Leonard, George Green (based on the novel *Omoo* by Herman Melville); ph, Benjamin Kline; m, Al Glasser; ed, Stanley Frazen; art d, Fred Ritter.

Adventure **(PR:A MPAA:NR)**

ON A CLEAR DAY YOU CAN SEE FOREVER**½ (1970) 129m Howard W. Koch-Alan Jay Lerner/PAR c

Barbra Streisand *(Daisy Gamble)*, Yves Montand *(Dr. Marc Chabot)*, Bob Newhart *(Dr. Mason Hume)*, Larry Blyden *(Warren Pratt)*, Simon Oakland *(Dr. Conrad Fuller)*, Jack Nicholson *(Tad Pringle)*, John Richardson *(Robert Tentrees)*, Pamela Brown *(Mrs. Fitzherbert)*, Irene Handl *(Winnie Wainwhistle)*, Roy Kinnear *(Prince Regent)*, Peter Crowcroft *(Divorce Attorney)*, Byron Webster *(Prosecuting Attorney)*, Mabel Albertson *(Mrs. Hatch)*, Laurie Main *(Lord Percy)*, Kermit Murdock *(Hoyt III)*, Elaine Giftos *(Muriel)*, John Le Mesurier *(Pelham)*, Angela Pringle *(Diana Smallwood)*, Leon Ames *(Clews)*, Paul Camen *(Millard)*, George Neise *(Wytelipt)*, Tony Colti *(Preston)*.

The play on which this is based was not a huge hit and neither was the movie, despite the presence of Streisand and some good tunes by Lerner and his new partner, Lane. The longer version of the film had four more scenes including a song by Jack Nicholson and a production number. They might have been wiser to have cut some of the other songs and a lot more of the dialog and to have left Nicholson's work in. Streisand is a chain-smoker who won't go on an airplane because she worries about the "no smoking" sign on takeoffs and landings. She's engaged to prig Blyden, a man studying at a business school who is so stiff that he is basing his future on which prospective employer offers the best pension plan. Blyden hates her smoking habit and they are about to have dinner with a recruiter from a large company, so she goes to doctor Montand's hypnotism class to see if he can help her stop the habit. When Montand puts her under, he's shocked to learn that she can do many ESP tricks including making flowers grow quickly. Going deeper, she regresses to a past life where she was a 19th Century peeress. (Seeing the Brooklyn-born Streisand attempt to play the British lady is an unintentional howl.) Streisand continues meeting Montand and being sent back to the previous century and we discover that her character is a cockney woman who had masqueraded as a lady to get where she was (shades of MY FAIR LADY?). The more she sees Montand, the more Blyden gets annoyed. More sessions take place and Streisand is seen in the orphanage where her mother works. She finds the birth records and makes notes of the important men who've sired the waifs and uses that information to blackmail her way into polite society. Newhart runs the medical school where Montand toils and threatens to fire Montand when the media catches hold of the experiments he's involved with. (The real-life equivalent of this was the story of Bridey Murphy, which was made into a film called THE SEARCH FOR BRIDEY MURPHY which may, or may not, have been a hoax.) Nicholson is Streisand's former stepbrother, a guitar-strumming beatnick not unlike many other roles he's played, and it looks as though they may get together at one point. Cut back and forth between the two eras (slipshod work here and shaky direction by Minnelli) until Streisand walks into Montand's office and plays back a tape recording of his and learns that he finds her current persona a drudge but he adores the woman she was in the 1800s. She leaves and comes back when he *thinks* he wants to see her again. At the last session, she reveals that she has lived at least a dozen times and that she will live again and marry Montand in the year 2038. In the end, she exits. It was never a great script and the editing left much of the story fuzzy. Good-looking sets and costumes, but they do not a picture make. And no matter how much makeup Streisand wears, there's no doubt that hers is the face that launched a thousand tugboats. Filmed in New York and in Brighton, England, it was an odd premise for a musical and never fulfilled any of the creator's wishes. Barbara Harris played the role on Broadway and was more convincing in the dual role. Songs include: "On A Clear Day, You Can See Forever," "Come Back to Me," "What Did I Have That I Don't Have?" "He Isn't You," "Hurry, It's Lovely Up

Here," "Go To Sleep," "Love with All the Trimmings," "Melinda" (Burton Lane, Alan Jay Lerner).

p, Howard W. Koch; d, Vincente Minnelli; w, Alan Jay Lerner (based on the musical play by Lerner, Burton Lane); ph, Harry Stradling, Sr. (Panavision, Technicolor); m, Lane; ed, David Bretherton; prod d, John De Cuir; md, Nelson Riddle; cos, Cecil Beaton, Arnold Scassi; ch, Howard Jeffrey; makeup, Harry Ray.

Musical Cas. (PR:AA MPAA:G)

ON AGAIN—OFF AGAIN** (1937) 60m RKO bw

Bert Wheeler *(William Hobbs)*, Robert Woolsey *(Claude Horion)*, Marjorie Lord *(Florence Cole)*, Patricia Wilder *(Gertie Green)*, Esther Muir *(Nettie Horton)*, Paul Harvey *(Mr. Applegate)*, Russell Hicks *(George Dilwig)*, George Meeker *(Tony)*, Maxine Jennings *(Miss Meeker)*, Kitty McHugh *(Miss Parker)*, Hal K. Dawson *(Sanford)*, Alec Harford *(Slip Grogan)*, Pat Flaherty *(Mr. Green)*, Jane Walsh *(Nurse)*, Alan Bruce *(Attendant)*.

A fair Woolsey-and-Wheeler comedy which sees the two comedians as partners in a pill factory. The always-quarreling businessmen decide to settle their differences by agreeing to hold a wrestling match, wherein the winner gets to run the company for a year, making the loser serve as his valet. From there the laughs are derived from typical master-servant bits that are funny, but nothing special. The same story was filmed in 1918 as A PAIR OF SIXES, then again as a musical, QUEEN HIGH, in 1930. Songs, in Wheeler's nasal tenor, are "Thanks to You" and "One Happy Family" (Dave Dreyer, Herman Ruby).

p, Lee Marcus; d, Edward Cline; w, Nat Perrin, Benny Rubin (based on the play "A Pair of Sixes" by Edward H. Peple); ph, Jack Mackenzie; ed, John Lockert; md, Roy Webb; art d, Van Nest Polglase.

Comedy (PR:A MPAA:NR)

ON AN ISLAND WITH YOU*** (1948) 107m MGM c

Esther Williams *(Rosalind Reynolds)*, Peter Lawford *(Lt. Lawrence Y. Kingslee)*, Ricardo Montalban *(Ricardo Montez)*, Jimmy Durante *(Buckley)*, Cyd Charisse *(Yvonne Torro)*, Leon Ames *(Cmdr. Harrison)*, Kathryn Beaumont *(Penelope Peabody)*, Dick Simmons *(George Blaine)*, Marie Windsor *(Jane)*, Arthur Walsh *(2nd Assistant Director)*, Nina Ross *(Mrs. Peabody)*, Betty Reilly *(Vocalist)*, Kay Norton *(Martha the Hairdresser)*, Nolan Leary *(Cameraman)*, Chester Clute *(Tommy the Waiter)*, Carl Leviness *(Desk Clerk)*, Cosmo Sardo *(Barber)*, Dick Winslow *(Bald Radio Operator)*, Jimmy Dale *(Navigator)*, Sam Tubuo *(Native Chief)*, Lester Dorr *(Photographer)*, Franklin Parker *(Lieutenant/Technical Advisor)*, Emelia Leovalli *(Grandmother)*, Uluao Letuli *(Sword Dancer)*, Xavier Cugat and His Orchestra.

Lavish Esther Williams musical which sees the swimming star (Fannie Brice stated, "Wet, she's a star; dry, she ain't") play a movie star on location in Hawaii. When Navy technical advisor Lawford falls in love with the star, trouble begins. She rebuffs him at a dance. Not one to take no for an answer, Lawford kidnaps Williams in his Navy plane and takes her to a nearby island to make her dance with him to the music from his portable radio. Durante punctuates the silliness with a hysterical performance as the movie's harried assistant director. Montalban and Charisse team up for some fancy dance numbers, but it is Williams' show all the way and she delivers with her usual fantastic swimming numbers performed to the strains of Xavier Cugat and His Orchestra. The film was one of 1948's top grossers at the box office. Songs include: "On an Island with You"; "If I Were You"; "Taking Miss Mary to the Ball"; "Dog Song"; "Buenas Noches, Buenos Aires" (Nacio Herb Brown, Edward Heyman); "Wedding Samba" (Abraham Ellstein, Allan Small, Joseph Liebowitz); "I Can Do Without Broadway, But Can Broadway Do Without Me" (Jimmy Durante).

p, Joe Pasternak; d, Richard Thorpe; w, Dorothy Kingsley, Dorothy Cooper, Charles Martin, Hans Wilhelm (based on an original story by Martin, Wilhelm); ph, Charles Rosher (Technicolor); ed, Douglas Biggs, Ferris Webster; md, Georgie Stoll, art d, Cedric Gibbons, Edward Carfagno; set d, Edwin B. Willis, Richard Pefferle; cos, Irene; ch, Jack Donahue.

Musical (PR:A MPAA:NR)

ON ANY STREET (SEE: LA NOTTE BRAVA, 1962, Fr./Ital.)

ON APPROVAL*½ (1930, Brit.) 100m British and Dominions/W&F Film Service-GAU bw

Tom Walls *(Duke of Bristol)*, Yvonne Arnaud *(Maria Wislak)*, Winifred Shotter *(Helen Hayle)*, Edmond Breon *(Richard Wemys)*, Mary Brough *(Emerald)*, Robertson Hare *(Hedworth)*.

Adaptation of a long-running London stage comedy starring Walls as a near-broke Duke who persuades rich pickle-heiress Arnaud to submit to a month-long trial marriage.

p, Herbert Wilcox; d, Tom Walls; w, W. P. Lipscomb (based on the play by Frederick Lonsdale); ph, F. A. Young.

Comedy (PR:A MPAA:NR)

ON APPROVAL½** (1944, Brit.) 80m GAU/EFI bw

Clive Brook *(George, Duke of Bristol)*, Beatrice Lillie *(Maria Wislack)*, Googie Withers *(Helen Hale)*, Roland Culver *(Richard Halton)*, O. B. Clarence *(Dr. Graham)*, Lawrence Hanray *(Parkes)*, Elliot Mason *(Mrs. McCosh)*, Hay Petrie *(Landlord)*, Marjorie Rhodes *(Cook)*, Molly Munks *(Jeanne)*, E. V. H. Emmett *(Narrator)*.

Livelier remake of the 1930 British comedy, this time starring Brook as the destitute Duke who cleverly cons rich American girl Lillie to agree to a month-long trial marriage to be spent in a Scottish castle. A better cast than the original helps immensely, and Lillie, who had clicked mightily on Broadway but was practically ignored by Hollywood, finally had an outing worthy of her talents, thanks to England. It is Lillie who makes ON APPROVAL richly amusing and sometimes uproarious, in spite of mediocre directing by Clive Brook.

p, Sydney Box, Clive Brook; d, Brook; w, Brook, Terence Young (based on the play by Frederick Lonsdale); ph, Claude Friese-Greene; m, William Alwyn; ed, Fergus McDonnel; md, Muir Matheson; art d, Tom Morahan.

Comedy Cas. (PR:A MPAA:NR)

ON BORROWED TIME*** (1939) 99m MGM bw

Lionel Barrymore *(Julian Northrup, "Gramps")*, Sir Cedric Hardwicke *(Mr. Brink)$ Beulah Bondi (Nellie)*, Una Merkel *(Marcia Giles)*, Bobs Watson *(Pud)*, Nat Pendleton *(Mr. Grimes)*, Henry Travers *(Dr. Evans)*, Grant Mitchell *(Mr. Pilbeam)*, Eily Malyon *(Demetria Riffle)*, James Burke *(Sheriff Burlingame)*, Charles Waldron *(Rev. Murdock)*, Ian Wolfe *(Charles Wentworth)*, Phillip Terry (Bill Lowry), Truman Bradley *(James Northrup)*.

Barrymore is a crotchety old man (as usual) trying to raise his grandson, Watson, after the death of the latter's parents and the death of the former's wife. With Death such a frequent visitor, Barrymore has little trouble recognizing him in the form of Hardwicke when the reaper comes for the grandfather. Barrymore proves too cagey for him, though, and chases him up an apple tree, from which he is unable to come down until the old man releases him. The two engage in long, philosophical discussions about life and death while Hardwicke tries to make Barrymore understand the importance of his mission. Barrymore begins to realize that since his incarceration of Death, no one in town has been dying, a mixed blessing. Barrymore knows he can't hold Hardwicke up the tree forever, and he tries to prepare for his passing, especially to ensure that Watson won't have to be raised by maiden aunt Malyon. Hardwicke manages to use his wiles to coax Watson into climbing the tree, where Death still has powers (as demonstrated when he strikes a squirrel dead with a point of his finger to show Barrymore what he can do), and then makes the boy fall. His neck is broken and, unable to die, he will have to live as a quadriplegic the rest of his life. Barrymore now realizes the folly of his actions and lets Hardwicke down from the tree to claim him and the boy, who are last seen walking through a celestial sheep pasture. Charming allegory doesn't pack the punch of the original Broadway production, mostly due to the considerable bad language used by the old man and emulated by his grandson, which had to be cut for the sake of movie audiences. Still, the film's message about the folly of fearing and trying to stave off death comes through. The performances are mostly first rate, particularly Hardwicke's, who claimed this was his favorite film role, and who more or less abandoned the stage to take up residence in Hollywood and concentrate on his film career afterwards.

p, Sidney Franklin; d, Harold S. Bucquet; w, Alice D. G. Miller, Frank O'Neill, Claudine West (based on a play by Paul Osborne, from a novel by Lawrence Edward Watkin); ph, Joseph Ruttenberg; ed, George Boemler.

Drama (PR:A MPAA:NR)

ON DANGEROUS GROUND*** (1951) 82m RKO bw

Ida Lupino *(Mary Malden)*, Robert Ryan *(Jim Wilson)*, Ward Bond *(Walter Brent)*, Charles Kemper *(Bill Daly)*, Anthony Ross *(Pete Santos)*, Ed Begley *(Capt. Brawley)*, Ian Wolfe *(Carrey)*, Sumner Williams *(Danny Malden)*, Gus Schilling *(Lucky)*, Frank Ferguson *(Willows)*, Cleo Moore *(Myrna)*, Olive Carey *(Mrs. Brent)*, Richard Irving *(Bernie)*, Pat Prest *(Julie)*, Bill Hammond *(Fred)*, Gene Persson, Tommy Gosser, Ronnie Garner, Dee Garner, Harry Joel Weiss *(Boys)*, Ruth Lee *(Helen)*, Kate Lawson, Esther Zeitlin *(Women)*, William Challee *(Thug)*, Eddie Borden, Steve Roberts, Budd Fine, Mike Lally, Don Dillaway, Al Murphy, Art Dupuis, Frank Arnold, Homer Dickinson *(Men)*, Ken Terrell *(Crook)*, W.J. O'Brien *(Hotel Clerk)*, Nita Talbot *(Woman in Bar)*, Joe Devlin *(Bartender)*, Jim Drum *(Stretcher Bearer)*, A.I. Bezzerides *(Gatos)*, Tracy Roberts *(Peggy Santos)*, Vera Stokes *(Mother)*, Nestor Paiva *(Bagganierri)*, Leslie Bennett *(Sgt. Wendell)*, Jimmy Conlin *(Doc Hyman)*, John Taylor *(Hazel)*.

A realistic and often grippng crime yarn, ON DANGEROUS GROUND tells the story of tough cop Ryan. He has been brutalized by the "human garbage" he must clean up in New York City and is on the verge of a nervous breakdown. Ryan is so filled with hate that he lets his fists speak for him when interrogating any suspect and, rather than suspend a normally good policeman, captain Begley sends Ryan into the country to help investigate a rural killing. Ryan is confronted with a vengeance-seeking father, Bond, who lives every moment of his life just to be able to catch the killer of his daughter and empty his shotgun into him, a man seething with so much hatred that he becomes for Ryan a mirror image. He also meets Lupino, the blind sister of the wanted killer, and through her compassionate view of the world, he becomes more human and understanding, realizing that the youth wanted for the crime is mentally disturbed. Lupino begs Ryan to take her brother alive and prevent him from falling into Bond's hands. This the cop attempts to do, tracking the youth, Williams, across vast tracts of snow. Cornered, Williams panics and, instead of taking Ryan's help, falls from a cliff to his death. Ryan consoles Lupino and then plans to head back to New York. He realizes he loves Lupino but he knows no other work than law enforcement. Before returning to the city, however, Ryan comes to accept the fact that there is nothing in New York for him but misery. He returns to Lupino with the resolve of beginning a new life. ON DANGEROUS GROUND is tautly directed by that master of stark dramas, Ray. Ryan and Lupino give sterling performances but the story line is broken up into two distinct segments which lessens the film's impact and cohesiveness. It failed to hit at the box office and RKO lost $425,000 on this above-average *film noir* entry.

p, John Houseman; d, Nicholas Ray; w, A.I. Bezzerides, Ray (based on the novel *Mad with Much Heart* by Gerald Butler); ph, George E. Diskant; m, Bernard Herrmann; ed, Roland Gross; md, Constantin Bakaleinikoff; art d, Albert S. D'Agostino, Ralph Berger; set d, Darrell Silvera, Harley Miller; spec eff, Harold Stine; makeup, Mel Burns.

Crime Drama (PR:C MPAA:NR)

ON DRESS PARADE   (SEE: DEAD END KIDS ON DRESS PARADE, 1939)

ON FRIDAY AT ELEVEN   (SEE: WORLD IN MY POCKET, THE, 1962, Fr./Ital./Ger.)

ON GOLDEN POND**   (1981) 109m ITC-IPC-UNIV-AFD c

Katherine Hepburn (*Ethel Thayer*), Henry Fonda (*Norman Thayer, Jr.*), Jane Fonda (*Chelsea Thayer Wayne*), Doug McKeon (*Billy Ray*), Dabney Coleman (*Bill Ray*), William Lanteau (*Charlie Martin*), Chris Rydell (*Sumner Todd*).

The odds were against ON GOLDEN POND from the start. It was a "little" play that only ran 126 performances off-Broadway, and despite the fact that it had a good life in the hinterlands, no one thought a movie version would mean much, given the market for sex and violence which seemed to be the norm in the early 1980s. Henry Fonda had always preferred the stage to the screen but didn't get a chance to see the play, as he was busy on a vehicle of his own in Washington when this show was in New York. Scripts were sent to him and Hepburn and both found it delightful and agreed to make the picture. Without those two powerhouses, one wonders if this would have ever been done. That's not meant to denigrate the quality of Thompson's script (which won an Oscar), but the moguls of Hollywood are not given to sentiment. Jane Fonda raised the money for the film and took the unaccustomed small role as Henry Fonda's daughter. It was the first and last time they would appear together on screen as adults and the script reflected much of their own familial woes, which had been publicized for years. Jane Fonda had always been a tough daughter to raise for the quiet Henry Fonda. She'd appeared with him in a 1954 play in Nebraska, then became a model, and eventually married French director Roger Vadim, who thought he had another Bardot sexpot on his hands. Later, her political beliefs clashed with those of her father's and there was no love lost between them for a spell. Henry Fonda was 75 when this picture was made and must have known he didn't have much time. There could not have been a better final curtain for him than this. He died nine months later after receiving his first Oscar for this film. Hepburn also won an Oscar, her fourth, and nominations went to director Rydell, Jane Fonda, composer Grusin, and editor Wolfe, who also passed away and to whom the movie is dedicated. To everyone's surprise, ON GOLDEN POND was a huge box office hit despite the very simple (though timeless) plot. It all takes place at the New England summer cottage of retired professor Henry Fonda, a man approaching 80, and his wife, Hepburn, who is near that age. Fonda is a cantankerous, crusty man who realizes that his time is nigh and makes many remarks about the subject (all the more touching when one knows that he died not much later). This will mark almost a half-century of visiting the cottage and Fonda fears it may be his last holiday. Hepburn is wise to Fonda's "act" (for it is an "act," in that she's seen the other side of him as well, the side that caused her to stay with him all these years) and ignores most of it. It isn't easy being a friend to Fonda because of his ways, but once you get past the crust, there's a lot to be found. She's hoping that Fonda and their daughter can come to terms after so many years of bickering. Jane Fonda is about to arrive with her fiance, Coleman, and his son, McKeon, from a previous marriage. The couple are about to take a European trip and will drop McKeon off for the summer while they holiday. McKeon is a tough kid given to four-letter words and a smart-ass attitude. After a birthday party for the old man, Coleman and Jane Fonda wonder if they can leave McKeon. Hepburn is all for it, but the old man and the boy, who have been carping at each other from the start, are not keen on the idea. Nevertheless, McKeon is accepted as their charge for the summer and Coleman and Jane Fonda depart. Coleman is as much the martinet as Henry Fonda, but McKeon begins to like the old fellow and the two begin a bond that takes them fishing. McKeon likes the outdoor life and blossoms under Fonda's tutelage. Fonda has been attempting to catch a huge trout in the lake for years. He's come to call the fish "Walter" and goes after it like Ahab went for Moby Dick. While making their way through a craggy area, the boat has the side ripped out of it and both Fonda and McKeon are tossed into the water. When they don't return for dinner, Hepburn goes looking for them and finally locates the duo as they are holding on to a rock. After they've come back to the house, Hepburn attempts to keep them there, but the two conspire to continue their adventures together. McKeon, in essence, has become the son that Fonda never had. Little hints are tossed in about that and we begin to understand his disappointment in his daughter. Jane Fonda comes back to the cottage alone. She and Coleman had been married in Belgium and he's on his way back to California where she'll join him with McKeon. When Jane Fonda sees Henry Fonda and McKeon on the lake having a marvelous time, she is more than a little resentful because she never got that sort of treatment from her father. Hepburn upbraids her for being childish and pleads with her daughter to at least make an attempt to understand her father. Later, Jane Fonda does that and sees that Henry Fonda is not the ogre she'd been thinking he was. Maybe it's age or maybe it's the relationship that he and McKeon have established, but Henry Fonda seems a new man in his daughter's eyes. The summer draws to a close and Jane Fonda and McKeon are about to leave. For the first time in as long as the two of them can remember, Jane and Henry Fonda put their arms around each other. After they've left, Henry Fonda has a mild heart palpitation when he tries to lift something too heavy and both he and Hepburn think maybe this is the end. She gives him a heart pill and he comes back from death's door and the two of them make a few jokes about the grim reaper and wonder if they'll be back to see the loons again next summer. A beautifully photographed (by Billy Williams) movie with some very funny lines and just as many poignant moments. The four-letter words were gratuitous and there were a few places where confrontations should have happened, rather than been avoided. Jane Fonda and Coleman were to team again when he became her chauvinist boss in NINE TO FIVE, but the father and daughter team would never work together again. Lanteau does a neat job as Jane Fonda's childhood pal, a full-time resident of the Golden Pond area and the local mailman. It's about families, old age, lack of communication, and reconciliation. In short, it's honest. Shot in New Hampshire at Squam Lake near Laconia, the settings are

almost as breathtaking as the two venerable veterans who did their only picture together, after a lifetime of barely knowing one another but always admiring the other's work.

p, Bruce Gilbert; d, Mark Rydell; w, Ernest Thompson (based on his play); ph, Billy Williams; m, Dave Grusin; ed, Robert L. Wolfe; prod d, Stephen Grimes; set d, Emad Helmy; cos, Dorothy Jeakins.

Comedy/Drama   **Cas.**   **(PR:A-C MPAA:PG)**

ON GUARD   (SEE: OUTPOST OF THE MOUNTIES, 1939)

ON HER BED OF ROSES zero   (1966) 104m Famous Players bw

Ronald Warren (*Stephen Long*), Sandra Lynn (*Melissa Borden*), Barbara Hines (*Joanna Borden*), Lee Gladden (*Dr. Richard von Krafft-Ebing*), Ric Marlow (*Arthur Borden*), Regina Gleason (*Rachel Long*), Lovey Song (*Sally Marsh*), Richard Clair (*Detective*), Ned York (*Jimmy Blake*), Pat Barringer (*Belly Dancer*), Pamebla Woolman (*Tahitian Dancer*), Elaine Poulos (*Middle Eastern Dancer*), Karen Arney (*Flower Shop Girl*), Sarah Nade (*Francine*), Richard Tretter (*Drake*).

Rotten filmmaker Zugsmith strikes again. This time it's an epic psychological melodrama starring Lynn as a distraught fiancee who goes to famed psychiatrist Gladden after her betrothed, Warren, murders his mother, mows down innocent bystanders, and eventually commits suicide. After lengthy, investigative flashbacks, Dr. Gladden determines that it was all caused by Long's repressed upbringing, combined with the total domination of his psyche by his mother. This led to Long's sexual impotence (revealed in a moving scence where fiancee Lynn unsuccessfully tries to seduce Long in a rose garden) which required the terrible catharsis of violence to purge his tortured soul. Ridiculous excuse for some exploitive moviemaking masquerading as an insightful psychological study.

p, Robert Caramico; d&w, Albert Zugsmith (based on the book *Psychopathia Sexualis: Eine Klinischforensische Studie* by Richard von Krafft-Ebing.; ph, Caramico; m, Joe Greene; ed, Herman Freedman; prod d, Ruth Zugsmith.

Drama   **(PR:C MPAA:NR)**

ON HER MAJESTY'S SECRET SERVICE*½   (1969, Brit.) 140m UA c

George Lazenby (*James Bond*), Diana Rigg (*Tracy Draco*), Telly Savalas (*Ernst Stavro Blofeld*), Ilse Steppat (*Irma Bunt*), Gabriele Ferzetti (*Marc Ange Draco*), Yuri Borienko (*Gruenther*), Bernard Horsfall (*Campbell*), George Baker (*Sir Hilary Bray*), Bernard Lee ("M"), Lois Maxwell (*Miss Moneypenny*), Desmond Llewelyn ("Q"), Angela Scoular (*Ruby*), Catherina von Schell (*Nancy*), John Gay (*Hammond*), Dani Sheridan (*American Girl*), Julie Ege (*Scandinavian Girl*), Joanna Lumley (*English Girl*), Mona Chong (*Chinese Girl*), Anoushka Hempel (*Australian Girl*), Ingrit Black (*German Girl*), Jenny Hanley (*Italian Girl*), Zara (*Indian Girl*), Sylvana Henriques (*Jamaican Girl*), Helena Ronee (*Israeli Girl*), Geoffrey Cheshire (*Toussaint*), Irvin Allen (*Che Che*), Terry Mountain (*Raphael*), James Bree (*Master Gumpold*), Virginia North (*Olympe*), Brian Worth (*Manuel*), Norman McGlen (*Janitor*), Dudley Jones (*Hall Porter*), John Crewdson (*Draco Copter Pilot*), Josef Vasa (*Piz Gloria Attendant*), Leslie Crawford (*Felsen*), George A. Cooper (*Braun*), Reg Harding (*Blofeld's Driver*), Richard Graydon (*Draco's Driver*), Bill Morgan (*Klett*), Bessie Love (*American Casino Guest*), Steve Plytas (*Greek Tycoon*), Robert Rietty (*Chef de Jeu*), Elliott Sullivan (*American*), Martin Leyder (*Chef de Jeu Huissier*).

This could have been the best of the James Bond series if it had starred Sean Connery instead of Australian model George Lazenby, whom the producers grabbed after a frantic talent search. Based on the best of Ian Fleming's Bond novels, the film version of ON HER MAJESTY'S SECRET SERVICE sported an extremely well-written script, which finally revealed a bit more of Bond's character. The film opens as Lazenby, searching in Portugal for the elusive villain Blofeld (this time played by Savalas), spots the beautiful Rigg drowning. He saves her life and is shocked to learn that he has just foiled her suicide attempt. Soon after, he is recalled to London by Lee and told to stop his obsessive manhunt for Savalas. Frustrated, Lazenby quits the service and cleans out his desk. On his own, he returns to Portugal in search of Savalas, but he rescues Rigg once again when he bails her out of a heavy gambling debt. They soon become lovers, but the next morning Lazenby finds himself being taken to the headquarters of international gangster Ferzetti, who informs him that Rigg is his daughter. To maintain her honor, Ferzetti offers Lazenby one million dollars to marry her. He refuses, but persuades the gangster to help him trace Savalas. The trail leads to Switzerland where Lazenby learns that Savalas is attempting to buy the title of count to bestow upon himself. Upon investigation of Savalas' incredible mountain hideaway (actually a newly built restaurant that the producers borrowed in exchange for paying to decorate the interior after the film crew left), Lazenby learns that the villain is up to his usual tricks, and plans to rule the world by introducing sterility spores into the world's agricultural supplies. Revealed as a spy by one of the 12 women Savalas has employed for the distribution of the spores, Lazenby is forced to flee on skis (some of the Bond series' best stunt work is performed here). Meeting him in a small skiing village, Rigg rescues Lazenby by picking him up in her car. Realizing he's in love with her, Lazenby proposes marriage and Rigg accepts. With Savalas hot on their heels, the couple must don skis and continue their escape down the mountain. After failing in an attempt to kill them in an avalanche, Savalas manages to kidnap Rigg and take her back to his headquarters. Using her as a bargaining tool, Savalas demands that he be awarded the title of count, and be given complete and total amnesty for his crimes against the world. His offer is rebuffed immediately, and the Secret Service, aided by Ferzetti, bombs Savalas' headquarters by helicopter. Rigg is rescued, and Lazenby fights it out with Savalas on a speeding bobsled, which sends the villain to his apparent doom. After things settle down, Lazenby and Rigg are married. While on their honeymoon, Savalas suddenly appears and machine-guns Rigg to death, leaving Lazenby crying over her body. Less emphasis on gadgets, and more on Bond's character, adds greatly to the series, but Lazenby's lackadaisical performance (he had never acted before) hurts the entire film. What he lacked in thespian talents, he made up for in his incredible physical skills, which impressed his stunt trainers. Director Hunt reportedly gave up on Lazenby's acting and concentrated more on Rigg and Savalas, which began to make the Australian model nervous, and then angry. This lack of attention drove Lazenby to become an overly temperamental star, and it threw a cloud over the whole production. All-in-all, despite the obvious weaknesses, ON HER MAJESTY'S SECRET SERVICE has proven to be one of the most interesting and entertaining of the Bond series. (See JAMES BOND series, Index.)

p, Albert R. Broccoli, Harry Saltzman; d, Peter Hunt; w, Richard Maibaum, Simon Raven (based on the novel by Ian Fleming); ph, Michael Reed, Egil Woxholt, Roy Ford, John Jordan, Willy Bogner, Jr., Alex Barbey, Ken Higgins, (Panavision, Technicolor); m, John Barry; ed, John Glen; prod d, Syd Cain; art d, Bob Laing; set d, Peter Lamont; cos, Marjorie Cornelius; spec eff, John Stears; m/l, Barry, Hal David, Monty Norman; stunts, George Leech.

Spy/Adventure   Cas.   (PR:C   MPAA:M)

ON HIS OWN   (1939, USSR) 96m Soyuzdetfilm/Amkino bw (AKA: AMONG PEOPLE)

V.O. Massalitinova (Akulina Ivanovna), M. Troyanovsky (Grandfather Kashirin), Alexei [Alyosha] Lyarsky (Alexei Peshkov [Gorky]), I. Kudriavtsev (Sergeyev), N. Berezovskaya (Sergeyeva), E. Lilina (Matrena Ivanovna), F. Seleznev (Viktorushka), I. Zarubina (Natalia), D. Zerkalova ("Queen Margot"), A. Timontayev (Smurl), M. Povolotski (Seriozhka), N. Plotnikov (Zhikharev), I. Chuvelev (Sitanov), Chugunov (Ivan Larlonovich), V. Terentiev (Kapendiukhin), V. Novikov (Yakev Kashirin), M. Gorlov (Steward), B. Maruta (Mitropolski).

Dull adaptation of Gorky's autobiography in this sequel to the CHILDHOOD OF MAXIM GORKY starring Lyarsky as the now-grown Gorky who finds himself trapped working for a rich family as a serf. He escapes his servitude and finds a job as a dishwasher on a small riverboat. Eventually we watch as Gorky grows to manhood and begins his battle for freer education. Stiff, boring, and overlong, padded with some Soviet songs. The third film in this trilogy, UNIVERSITY OF LIFE, was released in the U.S. in 1941. Interestingly, Gorky was quite an advocate of the new medium of motion pictures; during his exile in Capri, he watched a French silent comedy with his friend, V. I. Lenin. Later, he made post-revolution plans for a panoply of historical films, plans which were never realized by the new Soviet film industry. The great writer might have been describing this very picture when he wrote—upon first seeing Lumiere's cinematograph in 1896—"This mute, grey life finally begins to disturb and depress you."

d, Mark Donskoi; w, I. Gruzdev (based on the autobiography V. Lyudakh (In the World) by Maxim Gorky [Alexei Peshkov]); m, L. Schvarts.

Biography   (PR:A   MPAA:NR)

ON MOONLIGHT BAY*   (1951) 95m WB c

Doris Day (Marjorie Winfield), Gordon MacRae (William Sherman), Jack Smith (Hubert Wakeley), Leon Ames (George Winfield), Rosemary DeCamp (Mrs. Winfield), Mary Wickes (Stella), Ellen Corby (Miss Stevens), Billy Gray (Wesley Winfield), Jeffrey Stevens (Jim Sherman), Esther Dale (Aunt Martha), Suzanne Whitney (Cora), Eddie Marr (Barker), Sig Arno (Dancing Instructor), Jimmy Dobson (Soldier), Rolland Morris (Sleeping Soldier), Silent Movie Cast: Lois Austin (Mother), Creighton Hale (Father), Ann Kimball (Daughter), Ray Spiker (Bartender), Hank Mann, Jack Mower, Ralph Montgomery (Salesmen), Henry East.

If it weren't for the presence of some musical standards and the standout job by young Billy Gray as the incorrigible kid brother, this would have sunk without a trace. They wanted to get the nostalgic glow of MEET ME IN ST. LOUIS when they adapted some of Tarkington's "Penrod" stories as well as a bit from his Alice Adams, but it didn't quite fill the time up. Set in a tiny Indiana town around 1917, Day is a lively miss in her late teens (hah!) who meets and falls for MacRae, a college student in the area. Day is a tomboy more given to baseball than ballroom dancing and her father, Ames, doesn't like MacRae. Ames is a bank employee and MacRae is not thrilled about people who handle other people's money and take a cut. When Gray gets into trouble at school, he blames it all on his father, who, he tells everyone, has taken to drink. The whole town is in an uproar and MacRae believes the story about Ames, so he races to the house to save Day from her father's "drunken" wrath. MacRae eventually joins the Army and Ames is placated enough to allow his daughter to marry the lad. Some good comedy performances by Corby as the schoolmistress who is taken in by Gray's fibs, Wickes as the sharp-tongued family maid, and Ames and DeCamp as Day's parents. But the best comedy goes to Gray (as a "Penrod" character) and he makes the most of it. He is not to be confused with comedian Billy Gray, an older comic who appeared in SOME LIKE IT HOT and THE SPECTER OF THE ROSE. Only one original song in the film, "Love Ya" (Charles Tobias, Peter DeRose, sung by Doris Day, Jack Smith), with the others all being culled from various sources. They include: "On Moonlight Bay" (Percy Wenrich, Edward Madden, sung by Gordon MacRae), "Till We Meet Again" (Richard Whiting, Ray Egan, sung by Day, MacRae), "Pack Up Your Troubles In Your Old Kit Bag" (George Asaf, Felix Powell, sung by MacRae), "I'm Forever Blowing Bubbles" (Jean Kenbrovin, John W. Kellette, sung by Smith), "Christmas Story" (Pauline Walsh), "Tell Me Why Nights Are Lonely" (W.J. Callahan, Max Kortlander, sung by Day, MacRae), "Cuddle Up a Little Closer" (Otto Harbach, Karl Hochna, sung by MacRae), "Every Little Movement Has a Meaning All Its Own" (Harbach, Hochna, sung by Smith). Sequel: BY THE LIGHT OF THE SILVERY MOON.

p, William Jacobs; d, Roy Del Ruth; w, Jack Rose, Melville Shavelson (based on the novel Alice Adams and the "Penrod" stories by Booth Tarkington); ph, Ernest Haller (Technicolor); m, Max Steiner; ed, Thomas Reilly; md, Ray Heindorf; art d,

Douglas Bacon; set d, William Wallace; cos, Milo Anderson, Marjorie Best; ch, LeRoy Prinz; makeup, Gordon Bau.

Musical/Comedy   (PR:AAA   MPAA:NR)

17927

ON MY WAY TO THE CRUSADES, I MET A GIRL WHO. . .
          (SEE: CHASTITY BELT, THE, 1969, U.S./Ital.)

ON OUR LITTLE PLACE   (SEE: ON OUR SELECTION, 1930, Aus.)

ON OUR MERRY WAY**   (1948) 107m UA bw (AKA: A MIRACLE CAN HAPPEN)

Burgess Meredith (Oliver Pease), Paulette Goddard (Martha Pease), Fred MacMurray (Al), Hugh Herbert (Elisha Hobbs), James Stewart (Slim), Dorothy Lamour (Gloria Manners), Victor Moore (Ashton Carrington), Eilene Janssen (Peggy Thorndyke), Henry Fonda (Lank), William Demarest (Floyd), Dorothy Ford (Lola), Charles D. Brown (Mr. Sadd), Betty Caldwell (Cynthia), David Whorf (Sniffles Dugan), Frank Moran (Bookie), Tom Fadden (Deputy Sheriff), Walter Baldwin (Livery Stable Man), Paul E. Burns (Boss—Want Ad Dept), Lucien Prival (Jackson), Almira Sessions (Mrs. Cotton), Nana Bryant (Housekeeper), Greta Grandstedt (Secretary), Joe Devlin, Peggy Norman (Parents), Paul Causey Hurst (Sheriff), George Davis, George Lloyd, Max Wagner (Movers), Chester Clute (Bank Teller), Leo Kaye (Bartender), Eduardo Ciannelli (Maxim Cordova), Daniel Haight (Squirt), Charles Tony Hughes, Jack Cheatham (Cops), Carl Switzer (Zoot), John Qualen (Mr. Atwood), Harry James (Guest Star).

They changed the name of this film just a few days after it was released to less than breathtaking business or reviews. The change didn't help this segmented piece unified by the question "How has a child changed your life?" asked by Meredith, a classified ad salesman for a newspaper who has but one lifelong ambition: to be the paper's "Inquiring Reporter." Meredith and Goddard are married (as they were in real life while making this film) and he's fibbed to her that he's the man who asks the questions for the paper. Now he has to actually do that or lose the love of his new wife. Lamour and Moore are Hollywood bit players and she is advised by a child star to don a sarong. She does and becomes a household word in a satirical episode. Fonda and Stewart are a pair of itinerant jazz musicians and their "child" is a voluptuous jazz-baby, Ford, who altered their lives by winning a "fixed" music contest in the slapstick segment. Demarest and MacMurray are two con men who come up against a brat, Whorf, and have their lives changed in the "O. Henry irony" chapter. The picture doesn't merit much attention but there are several interesting sidelights to note. Stewart and Fonda had their choice of writers and author John O'Hara gave them the best segment of the bunch (also the most musical, with Harry James doing a cameo). Their work was directed by John Huston and George Stevens, not a bad duo. Huston had begun the directing, then Fonda had to do something else and when he returned, Huston was not able to take up the chores, so Stevens stepped in. Neither one took screen credit. Fonda and Stewart were old pals and had never worked with each other before. They waited 22 years before doing it again in THE CHEYENNE SOCIAL CLUB. Whorf, the rotten kid in the Demarest-MacMurray segment, was actor-director Richard Whorf's son and later became an assistant director on "Batman" and then a TV producer. MacMurray and Demarest must have liked working with each other and again teamed on TV's "My Three Sons" for what seemed to be a lifetime. Hollywood enjoyed making these episodic pictures for a while. Sometimes they worked (as in O. HENRY'S FULL HOUSE, TALES OF MANHATTAN) and sometimes they didn't, as in this.

p, Benedict Bogeaus; d, King Vidor, Leslie Fenton; w, Laurence Stallings, Lou Breslow (based on stories by John O'Hara, Arch Oboler); ph, John Seitz, Ernest Laszlo, Gordon Avil, Joseph Biroc, Edward Cronjager; m, Heinz Roemheld; ed, James Smith; md, David Chudnow, Skitch Henderson; art d, Ernst Fegte, Duncan Cramer; set d, Eugene Redd, Robert Priestly; cos, Greta; m/l, Skitch Henderson, Donald Kahn, Frank Loesser.

Comedy/Drama   (PR:A   MPAA:NR)

ON PROBATION**   (1935) 71m PEER bw

Monte Blue (Al Murray), Lucile Browne (Jane Murray), William Bakewell (Bill Coleman), Barbara Bedford (Mable Gordon), Matthew Betz (Dan), Edward J. LeSaint (Judge), Betty Jane Graham (Jane at Age 12), Arthur Loft (Benson), Henry Rocquemore (Lambert), Lloyd Ingraham (Horne), King Kennedy (Clarence), James "Hambone" Robinson (Negro Lad), Henry Hall (District Attorney), Margaret Fealy (Fagan Woman), John Webb Dillon, Roy Rice (Detectives), Marie Werner (Housekeeper), Gino Corrado (Waiter), Charles Hutchison (Man at Station).

A surprisingly skillful melodrama from Poverty Row starring Blue as a shady politician who seeks to boost his public image by becoming the guardian of a poor young girl he has met on the street. The girl, Graham, is employed as a pickpocket by fortune teller Fealy. Outraged that Blue wants to steal away her meal ticket, Fealy lays a curse on the politician's head and predicts that he will be killed by a lion. Blue laughs off the curse and proceeds with his plan. As the years go by, Blue's money, influence, and power grow, and the girl (now played by Browne), returns home from finishing school an attractive young woman. Blue is instantly smitten with his charge and proposes marriage. Browne gently rejects her guardian's offer by stating that she would prefer to continue her studies. Blue, however, suspects otherwise and sends one of his goons off to shadow Bakewell, a young man to whom Browne is obviously attracted. Though Browne is in love with Bakewell, she rejects his proposal as well because she is ashamed of her past. Seeking to wrest Browne from Bakewell, Blue tells the youth of her streetwise ways, but the information does nothing to deter Bakewell. Frustrated, Blue has his hoodlums work Bakewell over and hold him captive. Luckily, Bakewell manages to escape, leaving Browne at Blue's mercy. The crooked politician gets into a violent fight with Browne, and she hits him over the head with a decorative bronze lion. Terrified that she has fulfilled the old fortune teller's prophecy, Browne flees and confesses the crime to Bakewell. Bakewell decides to dispose of the body and runs upstairs, interrupting one of Blue's hoods who is stuffing the boss' body in a trunk. The youth takes the trunk and, together with Browne, he boards the next train out of town. Unknown to the pair, detectives are following them. Plagued with guilt, Browne tries to confess to the police, but just as she is about to leave, the train collides head-on with another locomotive. Bakewell and Browne escape the carnage and assume that Blue's body will be incinerated in the wreckage. Much to their surprise, Blue's henchman emerges and tells them that the boss is very much alive and just hiding from the police in the trunk (it seems the law had gotten wind of Blue's questionable political dealings and he was looking for an excuse to disappear). Bakewell risks his life to save Blue from the fire and succeeds, only to hand the bewildered crook over to the detectives. While the plot tends to get a bit ludicrous at times, ON PROBATION is a fine example of Poverty Row films at their best. When buoyed by decent production values, these films can be entertaining, even vital, examples of Hollywood on a shoestring.

p, Sam Efrus; d, Charles Hutchison; w, Sherman L. Lowe (based on a story by Crane Wilbur); ph, Henry Kurse; ed, Fred Bain; set d, Jennett.

Drama/Crime   **(PR:A MPAA:NR)**

ON OUR SELECTION½   (1930, Aus.) 85m Cinesound/
                                  Greater Union bw (AKA: ON OUR LITTLE PLACE)

Bert Bailey, Alfred Bevan, Fred MacDonald.

An early talkie from Australia which was the feature film directing debut of former editor Ken Hall. Notable because it was one of the first Australian films to have a firm grasp on all the technical elements, ON OUR SELECTION is a humorous drama chronicling the life of a rancher and his family.

d, Ken Hall (based on the play by Steele Rudd); ph, Walter Sully.

Comedy/Drama   **(PR:A MPAA:NR)**

ON SECRET SERVICE, 1933   (SEE: SECRET AGENT 1933, Brit.)

ON SECRET SERVICE, 1936   (SEE: TRAILIN' WEST, 1936)

ON SPECIAL DUTY   (SEE: BULLETS FOR RUSTLERS, 1940)

ON STAGE EVERYBODY**   (1945) 76m UNIV bw

Peggy Ryan (Molly Sullivan), Johnny Coy (Danny Rogers), Jack Oakie (Michael Sullivan), Julie London (Vivian Carlton), Otto Kruger (James Carlton), Esther Dale (Ma Cassidy), Wallace Ford (Emmet Rogers), Milburn Stone (Fitzgerald), Stephen Wayne (Tom), Jimmy Clark (Dick), Charles Teske, Eddie Cutler (Dancers), Ruth Lee (Barbara), Warren Jackson (Guard), Tom Daley (Frank), Donald Kerr (Cab Driver), Syd Saylor (Clem), Cy King, Rex Lease (Onlookers), Grady Sutton (Cathcart), Carey Harrison (Man Boarder), Margaret Bert (Woman Boarder), Sherry Hall (Ernest Hilliard (Sponsors), John Hamilton (Mr. Smoothasilk), Chester Clute (Tupper), Pat Gleason (Performer), Ralph Peters (Carter), Felice Richmond (Woman with Broom), Charles Hall (Painter), Billy Newell (Mason), Marion Martin (Bubbles), Arthur Loft (Fulton), Dorothy Granger (Marlow), Eddie Acuff (George), Audley Anderson (Porter), Emmett Vogan (Mr. Peppycornflakes), Sidney Miller (Radio/Racetrack Announcer), Earl Keen (Dog Impersonation), King Sisters (Themselves), Jean Richey (Skater), Billy Usher, Georgiana Bannister, Ilene Woods, Bob Hopkins, June Brady, Cyril Smith, Ronnie Gibson, Jean Hamilton, Beatrice Fung Oye, Ed "Strawberry" Russell (Winners of Radio Show Contest).

Comedy musical which sees father Oakie and daughter Ryan partnered in a vaudeville act. Oakie, a staunch opponent of radio (it will ruin vaudeville) one day finds himself hosting a radio talent show where he introduces a group of youngsters who have won a radio show contest. The real-life winners of the real-life contest appeared as themselves. Donald O'Connor had originally been scheduled to fill the juvenile spot held by Coy, but O'Connor enlisted—this was WW II, after all—and went off to training camp. The camera lingered long on the sweater of Julie London in her first featured role in films. Songs include: "For Him No Love," "It'll All Come Out in the Wash," "I'm So at Home with You" (Inez James, Sidney Miller), "Stuff Like That There" (Ray Evans, Jay Livingston), "What Do I Have to Do to Be a Star?" (Bobby Kroll), and "Dance With a Dolly With a Hole In Her Stocking" (Terry Shand, Jimmy Eaton, Mickey Leader), "Put Put Put Your Arms Around Me" (Mann Curtis, Al Hoffman, Jerry Livingston), "Take Me In Your Arms" (Mitchell Parrish, Fred Markush, Fritz Rotter).

p, Lou Goldberg; d, Jean Yarbrough; w, Warren Wilson, Oscar Brodney; ph, Charles Van Enger; m, Milton Rosen; ed, Philip Cahn; md, Rosen; art d, John B. Goodman, Martin Obzina; set d, Russell A. Gausman, Charles Wyrick.

Musical   **(PR:A MPAA:NR)**

ON SUCH A NIGHT**   (1937) 71m PAR bw

Grant Richards (Nicky Last), Karen Morley (Gail Stanley), Roscoe Karns (Joe Flynn), Eduardo Ciannelli ("Ice" Richmond), Milli Monti (Mlle. Mimi), Alan Mowbray (Prof. Richard Candle), Esther Dale (Miss Belinda Fentridge), Robert McWade (Col. Fentridge), John Alexander (District Attorney), John Wray (Guard Rumann), Frank Reicher (Horace Darwin), Jim Marcus (Judge), Ruth Robinson (Matron Nurse), Paul Fix (Maxie Barnes), Philo McCullough (Defense Attorney), Etta McDaniel (Samantha), Eddie Anderson (Henry Clay Washington), Bernice Pilot (Emmie Lou), Lew Payton (George Washington Fentridge).

Mississippi River tale starring Richards as a low-level hoodlum who is framed for murder by his boss and sentenced to be hanged. The execution never happens, however, because the mighty Mississippi overflows its banks and sends everyone scurrying for shelter, which enables Richards to escape from his guard. Suddenly Morley appears announcing she is Richard's wife and they flee the flood to a genteel southern plantation where they are treated hospitably until the real killer,

Ciannelli, tracks the pair down. When the river threatens to sweep them all away, Richards sees his opportunity, captures the gangster, and brings him to justice.

p, Emanuel Cohen; d, E.A. Dupont; w, Doris Malloy, William Lipman (based on a story by Morley F. Cassidy, S.S. Field, John D. Klorer); ph, Charles Schoenbaum; m, Ernst Toch; ed, Ray Curtiss; md, George Stoll; spec eff, Fred Jackman.

Crime Drama   **(PR:A MPAA:NR)**

ON THE AIR**   (1934, Brit.) 78m BL bw

Davy Burnaby (Davy), Reginald Purdell (Reggie), Betty Astell (Betty), Anona Winn (Chambermaid), Max Wall (Boots), Hugh E. Wright (Vicar), Clapham and Dwyer, Scott and Whaley, Derek Oldham, Mario de Pietro, Jane Carr, Eve Becke, Edwin Styles, Teddy Brown, Harry Champion, Wilson, Keppel and Betty, Roy Fox and His Band, Jimmy Jade, Buddy Bradley's Rhythm Girls.

A collection of popular British radio personalities are put through their paces on the thin plot pretext of having them appear in a charity show staged by village vicar Wright. Some of the acts are still fun to watch in this slightly above-average musical.

p&d, Herbert Smith; w, Michael Barringer (based on a story by Samuel Woolf Smith); ph, Alex Bryce.

Musical   **(PR:A MPAA:NR)**

ON THE AIR LIVE WITH CAPTAIN MIDNIGHT½
          (1979) 93m Sebastian International c (AKA: CAPTAIN MIDNIGHT)

Tracy Sebastian, John Ireland, Dena Detrich, Ted Gehring, Mia Kovacs.

Exploitation filmdom's favorite couple, Ferd and Beverly Sebastian, set their sights a bit higher than with their previous efforts (GATOR BAIT and THE HITCHHIKERS, for example) in this story of an alienated youth who finds happiness as a disk jockey on a pirate radio station operating out of the back of a van. Sebastian offspring Tracy looks uncomfortable in the lead.

p,d&w, Beverly and Ferd Sebastian.

Drama   **Cas.**   **(PR:C MPAA:PG)**

ON THE AVENUE***   (1937) 90m FOX bw

Dick Powell (Gary Blake), Madeleine Carroll (Mimi Caraway), Alice Faye (Mona Merrick), The Ritz Brothers (Themselves), George Barbier (Commodore Caraway), Alan Mowbray (Frederick Sims), Cora Witherspoon (Aunt Fritz Peters), Walter Catlett (Jake Dribble), Douglas Fowley (Eddie Eads), Joan Davis (Miss Katz), Stepin Fetchit (Herman), Sig Rumann (Herr Hanfstangel), Billy Gilbert (Joe Papaloupas), E.E. Clive (Binns the Cabby), Douglas Wood (Mr. Trivet), John Sheehan (Stage Manager), Paul Irving (Harry Morris), Harry Stubbs (Kelly), Ricardo Mandia (Luigi), Lynn Bari (Chorus Girl), Geneva Sawyer (Chorine), Hank Mann (Footman in Sketch), Edward Cooper (Potts), Paul Gerrits (Joe Cherry), Frank Darien.

The presence of The Ritz Brothers made this one of the funnier musicals of the 1930s. It was so highly touted that it played the Radio City Musical Hall as their February film in 1937. Berlin's tuneful score helped the flimsy material and the result was a rollicking satire of the hoity-toity set. Powell, borrowed from Warners, concocts and appears in a new Broadway musical which stars Faye as "The Richest Girl In The World"—a direct whack at Carroll, who is that in the flesh. Carroll, in a carbon of the life of Doris Duke, attends the show and becomes outraged when she sees the resemblance between herself and the character depicted. She goes backstage to Powell in an attempt to get him to scissor the offending material but he won't hear of it and turns a deaf ear. Nevertheless, he is somewhat intrigued by Carroll; they make a date and are soon in love, which results in Powell promising to soft-pedal the sketch that Carroll got angry over. Faye, who has been Powell's best girl, is angered by the intrusion of this cafe society debutante, sees things another way, and when Carroll's father, Barbier, plus boy friend Mowbray, aunt Witherspoon, and Carroll come to the show, Faye zings even harder. Barbier is so annoyed that he brings proceedings against Powell for the scandalous libel. Carroll won't talk to Powell after Faye's behavior and she retaliates by purchasing the entire show from producer Catlett and has the show changed in such a way that Powell looks like a fool. She even hires an entire audience to walk out on him while he's on stage and his response is to quit the show and be in breach of contract. Carroll is set to marry Mowbray, an adventurer-explorer, but Witherspoon knows that Carroll is still in love with Powell, so she races into the wedding area, grabs her niece away, and gets Powell and Carroll married at New York's City Hall. Lest you worry about Alice Faye's romantic life, it is indicated that she has something of an interest in Carroll's father, the immensely wealthy Barbier, at the conclusion. Harry Ritz's in-drag imitation of Faye in the Brothers' version of "O Chi Chornia" is hysterical. Other tunes by Irving Berlin include: "He Ain't Got Rhythm," "You're Laughing at Me," "This Year's Kisses," "Slumming on Park Avenue," "The Girl on the Police Gazette," and the hugh hit, "I've Got My Love to Keep Me Warm." Three other songs were tossed out before the final print. They were "On the Steps of Grant's Tomb," "Swing Sister," and, inexplicably, the title song, "On the Avenue." Remade as LET'S MAKE LOVE in 1960.

p, Darryl F. Zanuck; d, Roy Del Ruth; w, Gene Markey, William Conselman; ph, Lucien Andriot; m, Irving Berlin; ed, Allen McNeil; md, Arthur Lange; art d, William Darling, Mark-Lee Kirk; set d, Thomas Little; cos, Gwen Wakeling; ch, Seymour Felix; m/l, Berlin.

Musical/Comedy   **(PR:AA MPAA:NR)**

ON THE BEACH**½   (1959) 133m Kramer/UA bw

Gregory Peck (Dwight Towers), Ava Gardner (Moira Davidson), Fred Astaire (Julian Osborn), Anthony Perkins (Peter Holmes), Donna Anderson (Mary Holmes), John Tate (Adm. Bridie), Lola Brooks (Lt. Hosgood), John Meillon (Swain), Lou Vernon (Davidson), Guy Doleman (Farrel), Ken Wayne (Benson), Richard Meikle (Davis), Harp McGuire (Sundstrom), Jim Barrett (Chrysler), Basil

Buller Murphy *(Sir Douglas Froude)*, Keith Eden *(Dr. Fletcher)*, John Royle *(Senior Officer)*, Frank Gatcliff *(Radio Officer)*, Paddy Moran *(Portman)*, John Casson *(Salvation Army Captain)*, Kevin Brennan *(Dr. King)*, C. Harding Brown *(Dykers)*, Grant Taylor *(Morgan)*, Peter Williams *(Prof. Jorgenson)*, Harvey Adams *(Sykes)*, Stuart Finch *(Jones)*, Joe McCormick *(Ackerman)*, Audine Leith *(Betty)*, Jerry Ian Seals *(Fogarty)*, Carey Paul Peck *(Boy)*, Katherine Hill *(Jennifer Holmes)*, Peter O'Shaughnessy *(Jorgenson Associate)*, Rita Pauncefort, Elwyn Peers, Jerry Duggan, Harvey Adams, Mayne-Lynton, Collins Hilton, Cyril Gardner, Brian James, Ronald Fortt, Paddy Fitzallen, Richard Webb, John Morgan, Paul Maloney, Colin Crane, Peter Ashton, Jack Boyer, Joe Jenkins, Mario Vecci, Hugh Wills, Lucian Endicott, Ken Baumgartner.

A grim end-of-the-world drama, this Kramer semi-message film has all the people in the world dead except those in Australia (where the film was shot) or those on board Peck's submarine which probes the southern Pacific for the approaching radiation death cloud. Peck is the captain of the U.S. *Sawfish*, a submarine patrolling Australian waters when, in the year 1964, a nuclear war of unexplained origins has wiped out the Northern Hemisphere of the Earth and a radioactive cloud is rolling toward Australia, expected to arrive five or six months hence when it will destroy all life. A strange, unexplained radio signal seems to be coming from the area of San Diego, California, and Peck is sent to investigate the source. Accompanying him and his crew is Australian scientist Astaire, who has taken to booze to drown his sorrow at the end of the world. Also assigned to the mission is Perkins, a supposed British officer whose accent vanishes in the first few minutes of his appearance. Peck and the others arrive along the California coast to find San Francisco and San Diego dead cities shrouded in radioactive clouds (but there is not a body in sight). A crew member in a special suit goes ashore at San Diego and finds that the signal is being made by a bottle caught in a cord of a flapping window shade, the bottle tapping against a telegrapher's key. Peck sadly takes his submarine back to Australia where doom is predicted. Now the film turns to a study in human disintegration. Astaire buys a sports car to run in a race where participants plan on crashing and immolating themselves. He wins, fulfilling a lifetime ambition. Astaire then drives to his home, puts the car in the closed garage and turns on the ignition, committing suicide. Perkins and Anderson kill their child, then themselves. Everybody starts taking suicide pills and Gardner, a party girl, tries to console Peck who has lost his wife and children in America. Peck and his crew members decide to die in the U.S. and depart from Australia. Gardner is invited along but she is late in arriving at the pier and the *Sawfish* steams out of Melbourne Harbor without her, despite the fact that she has driven 100 mph to get there. (Oddly, long before this event, it is reported that no one has gasoline, yet Gardner has it for her car.) The whole thing is so depressing, despite some credible acting by Peck and Astaire, that the terror and impact of the doomsday story is lessened. Gardner overacts terribly in her small supporting role and Perkins is a twitching embarrassment. Though Kramer's good intentions of spreading his warnings of nuclear irresponsibility are good, the film fails for the most part to make its point, mostly because Shute's basic story is full of scientific holes, implausibilities, and gross exaggerations. The most effective element of this film was the song, "Waltzing Matilda," which became a big hit after being used as the picture's theme song. Another film, THE WORLD, THE FLESH AND THE DEVIL, developed the same end-of-the-world theme and didn't do much better. FAIL SAFE and even Terry Southern's black comedy, DR. STRANGELOVE, captured the basic fears and horror of the doomsday idea better.

p&d, Stanley Kramer; w, John Paxton, James Lee Barrett (based on the novel by Nevil Shute); ph, Giuseppe Rotunno, Daniel Fapp; m, Ernest Gold; ed, Frederic Knudtson; prod d, Rudolph Sternad; art d, Fernando Carrere; cos, Joe King, Fontana Sisters; spec eff, Lee Zavitz; m/l, "Waltzing Matilda," Marie Cowan, A.B. Patterson; makeup, John O'Gorman, Frank Prehoda.

Drama **Cas.** **(PR:O MPAA:NR)**

ON THE BEAT** (1962, Brit.) 105m RANK bw

Norman Wisdom *(Norman Pitkin/Guilio Napolitani)*, Jennifer Jayne *(Rosanna)*, Raymond Huntley *(Sir Ronald Ackroyd)*, David Lodge *(Inspector Hobson)*, Esma Cannon *(Mrs. Stammers)*, Eric Barker *(Doctor)*, Eleanor Summerfield *(Sgt. Wilkins)*, Ronnie Stevens *(Oberon)*, Terence Alexander *(Chief Supt. Belcher)*, Maurice Kaufmann *(Vince)*, Dilys Laye *(American Lady)*, George Pastell *(Manzini)*, Jack Watson *(Police Sergeant)*, Campbell Singer *(Bollington)*, Lionel Murton *(Man in Train)*, Robert Rietty *(Italian Lawyer)*, Marjie Lawrence *(Crying Lady)*, Peggy Ann Clifford *(Guilio's Mother)*, John Blythe *(Chauffeur)*, Mario Fabrizi *(Newspaper Seller)*, Monty Landis *(Mr. Bassett)*, Alfred Burke *(Trigger O'Flynn)*, Cyril Chamberlain *(Cafe Proprietor)*, Jean Aubrey *(Lady Hinchingford)*.

Dimwitted British comedy starring Wisdom as a recently fired parking lot attendant whose dream of becoming a policeman comes true when Scotland Yard hires him to catch an Indian jewel thief who just happens to be his exact double. The criminal is posing as an effeminate hairdresser, and Wisdom assumes his identity to get the goods on him. Pretty silly stuff.

p, Hugh Stewart; d, Robert Asher; w, Jack Davies, Norman Wisdom, Eddie Leslie; ph, Geoffrey Faithfull; m, Philip Green; ed, Bill Lewthwaite.

Comedy **(PR:A MPAA:NR)**

ON THE BRINK (SEE: THESE ARE THE DAMNED, 1965, Brit.)

ON THE BUSES* (1972, Brit.) 88m Hammer/EMI c

Reg Varney, Doris Hare, Anna Karen, Michael Robbins, Stephen Lewis.

Yet another feature film version of a popular British television comedy series that is wholly without style, humor, or interest. Despite the picture's obvious handicaps, it was the most successful film at the British box offices in 1971 and ensured that a rash of imitations would follow. The story, such as it is, concerns the trials and tribulations of life in a bus depot involving women drivers. The humor is sexist, of course, and infantile, with no wit or sophistication, which of course ensured its mass appeal.

p, Ronald Woolfe, Ronald Chesney; d, Harry Booth; ph, Mark McDonald (Technicolor); m, Max Harris.

Comedy **(PR:C MPAA:PG)**

ON THE CARPET (SEE: LITTLE GIANT, 1946)

ON THE COMET½** (1970, Czech.) 88m Studio Barrandov Czech State c (NA KOMETE; AKA: HECTOR SERVADAC'S ARK)

Emil Horvath, Jr. *(Servadec)*, Magda Vasarykova *(Angelika)*, Frantisek Filipovsky *(Captain)*, Josef Vetrovec, Cestmir Randa.

The fourth Jules Verne adaptation directed by Czech director Zeman. Based on Verne's novel *Hector Servadac*, the film details how a piece of Earth suddenly becomes a comet and floats through space with all the residents of that chunk of land as its passengers. Beautifully executed visuals help this fairly fantastic story.

d, Karel Zeman; w, Zeman, Jan Prochazka (based on the novel *Hector Servadac* by Jules Verne); ph, Rudolf Stahl (Eastmancolor); m, Lubos Fiser; art d, Jiri Hlupy.

Science Fiction **(PR:A MPAA:NR)**

ON THE DOUBLE*** (1961) 92m DENA-CAPRI/PAR c

Danny Kaye *(Pfc. Ernest Williams/Gen. Sir Lawrence Mackenzie-Smith)*, Dana Wynter *(Lady Margaret Mackenzie-Smith)*, Wilfrid Hyde-White *(Col. Somerset)*, Margaret Rutherford *(Lady Vivian)*, Diana Dors *(Sgt. Bridget Stanhope)*, Allan Cuthbertson *(Capt. Patterson)*, Jesse White *(Cpl. Joseph Praeger)*, Gregory Walcott *(Col. Rock Houston)*, Terrence de Marney *(Sgt. Colin Twickenham)*, Rex Evans *(Gen. Carleton Browne-Wiffingham)*, Edgar Barrier *(Blankmeister)*, Rudolph Anders *(Oberkommandant)*, Ben Astar *(Gen. Zlinkov)*, Bobby Watson *(Hitler)*, Pamela Light.

Very funny Kaye comedy which sees the star as a lowly GI stationed in England during WW II shortly before the invasion of Normandy. One day he is caught impersonating England's most important battle commander (for whom he is an exact double) for laughs, and the military intelligence community decides to use him to confuse the Nazis as to the whereabouts of the important general. Kaye agrees to the assignment and he manages to fool the general's loyal chauffeur Dors into believing he is actually the general. He is not so lucky with Wynter, the estranged wife of the general, but she agrees to keep quiet for the good of the country. When the real general is killed in a plane crash, Kaye is told to continue the deception so that the Nazis will think he still lives. Eventually it is revealed that Dors is actually a Nazi spy, and she kidnaps Kaye and takes him to Germany to be interrogated. Kaye give the Nazis false information and manages to escape, but not before having to don a series of ridiculous disguises (including a hilarious impersonation of Marlene Dietrich). Finally Kaye makes it back to England where he exposes one of the deceased general's closest friends—another general, Evans—as the chief Nazi spy in Britain and the Allied invasion of Normandy proceeds without a hitch. Songs by Kaye's long-time wife, Sylvia Fine, include "Darlin' Meggie," "The Mackenzie Hielanders," and "On the Double."

p, Jack Rose; d, Melville Shavelson; w, Rose, Shavelson; ph, Harry Stradling, Geoffrey Unsworth (Panavision, Technicolor); m, Leith Stevens; ed, Frank Bracht; md, Stevens; art d, Hal Pereira, Arthur Lonergan; set d, Sam Comer, Frank R. McKelvy; cos, Edith Head; spec eff, John P. Fulton, Farciot Edouart; ch, Bill Foster; makeup, Wally Westmore.

Comedy **(PR:A MPAA:NR)**

ON THE FIDDLE (SEE: OPERATION SNAFU, 1965, Brit.)

ON THE GREAT WHITE TRAIL* (1938) 58m GN bw (AKA: RENFREW OF THE ROYAL MOUNTED ON THE GREAT WHITE TRAIL; RENFREW ON THE GREAT WHITE TRAIL)

James Newill *(Renfrew)*, Terry Walker *(Kay Larkin)*, Robert Fraser *(Andrew Larkin)*, Richard Alexander *(Doc Howe)*, Richard Tucker *(Inspector Newcomb)*, Robert Terry *(Sgt. Kelly)*, Eddie Gribbon *(Patsy)*, Walter McGrail *(Garou)*, Philo McCullough *(Williams)*, Charles King *(LaGrange)*, Juan Duval *(Pierre)*, Vic Potel *(Parker)*, Carl Mathews, Silver King the Wonder Dog, Bruce Warren.

Second outing for Newill (the first was GREAT WHITE TRAIL) which sees Fraser, a frustrated fur trader who gets so fed up with his trading posts being robbed that he sets out to the North country in pursuit of the thieves. Luckily for him, his loyal-but-concerned daughter Walker follows with Mountie Newill in tow. Based on a popular radio program of the 1930s, the RENFREW series with Newill comprised eight films, shifting studios in mid-series from Grand National to Monogram. Songs crooned by tuneful Mountie Newill include "Je t'Aime," "Beautiful," and "Mounted Men," which has nothing to do with taxidermy. (See RENFREW OF THE MOUNTIES series, Index.)

p&d, Al Herman; w, Charles Logue, Joseph F. Poland (based on an original story by Laurie York Erskine); ph, Ira Morgan; ed, Duke Goldstone; m/l, Lew Porter, Bob Taylor, Betty Laidlaw, Robert Lively.

Adventure **(PR:A MPAA:NR)**

ON THE ISLE OF SAMOA** (1950) 65m COL bw

Jon Hall *(Kenneth Crandall)*, Susan Cabot *(Moana)*, Raymond Greenleaf *(Peter Appleton)*, Henry Marco *(Karaki)*, Al Kikume *(Chief Tihoti)*, Rosa Turich *(Waini)*, Leon Lontoc *(Laki)*, Neyle Morrow *(Mutu)*, Jacqueline de Wit *(Papita)*, Ben Welden *(Nick Leach)*.

Hall stars in this adventure tale as a crook who steals his gambling partner's loot and a transport plane as well. Experiencing trouble, Hall is forced to crash land on an uncharted South Seas island. There he is greeted by the gentle, loving natives and he soon falls in love with local girl Cabot. Greenleaf, a missionary who was shipwrecked years before, has civilized the populace, and Hall soon becomes indoctrinated by the kindly old man's teachings. Nevertheless, once his plane is repaired, Hall decides to leave the island. Before he can go, however, a volcanic eruption threatens the island and wrecks his newly repaired plane. He realizes that his true happiness lies with Cabot and the island people. Hailing a conveniently passing ship (unlike taxicabs, one seems always to be available on such islands), Hall departs to pay his debt to society, vowing to return to this island paradise.

p, Wallace MacDonald; d, William Berke; w, Brenda Weisberg, Harold Greene (based on a story by Joseph Santley); ph, William Bradford; m, Mischa Bakaleinikoff; ed, Aaron Stell.

Adventure   **(PR:A MPAA:NR)**

ON THE LEVEL*½   (1930) 76m FOX bw

Victor McLaglen (Biff Williams), Fifi D'Orsay (Mimi), William Harrigan (Danny Madden), Lilyan Tashman (Lynn Crawford), Arthur Stone (Don Bradley), Leila McIntyre (Mom Whalen), Ben Hewlett (Buck), Harry Tenbrook (Dawson), R. O. Pennell (Professor), Mary McAlister (Mary Whalen).

Iron-man ironworker McLaglen, who only smokes when he has a red-hot rivet with which to light his cigarette, leaves New Orleans with fellow he-man Harrigan to pursue a beam-walking job on a New York City skyscraper. Cajun queen D'Orsay, resentful at his departure, expresses her ire with a pistol, placing some bullets in the vicinity of his retreating figure. She then trails after him to the big city, where she finds work as an entertainer in a nightclub. Her missing macho man becomes the head of the ironworker's union and the target of some slick crooks who want to divert the union's treasury into their own pockets. The chief negotiator for the crooks is the tantalizing Tashman, who bats her eyelashes at the big boob. In the nick of time, D'Orsay pulls her pistol on the mob, and McLaglen re-takes the treasury money. The prune-faced proletarian then promises to be true.

d, Irving Cummings; w, William K. Wells, Andrew Bennison, Dudley Nichols (based on a story by Wells); ph, L.W. O'Connall, Dave Ragin; ed, Al DeGaetano; set d, William Moll; cos, Sophie Wachner.

Comedy   **(PR:A MPAA:NR)**

ON THE LOOSE**   (1951) 74m Filmakers/RKO bw

Joan Evans (Jill Bradley), Melvyn Douglas (Frank Bradley), Lynn Bari (Alice Bradley), Robert Arthur (Larry Lindsay), Hugh O'Brian (Dr. Phillips), Constance Hilton (Susan Tanner), Michael Kuhn (Bob Vance), Susan Morrow (Catherine), Lillian Hamilton (Miss Druten), Elizabeth Flournoy (Mrs. Tanner), John Morgan (Mr. Tanner), Lawrence Dobkin (Ruegg), Tristram Coffin (Judge), Edwin Reimers (Prosecuting Attorney), Mark Tangner (Roy Marsh), Don Brodie (Bartender Grove), Jesse Kirkpatrick (Teacher at Fight), Don Megowan (Headwaiter), Jack Larson, Diane Ware (Charleston Bits), Leonard Penn (Dance Judge), Allen Harris (Dr. Wayne), Jerry Hausner (Gus), Lela Bliss (Nurse), Marc Rohm, Robert Marlowe (Court Clerks).

Overly melodramatic "problem" picture illustrating the roots of juvenile delinquency—the parents. Douglas and Bari play the inattentive, thoughtless parents of teenager Evans who is moved to get attention by becoming the town's bad girl. Her boy friend doesn't understand the change in her, and her female friends no longer relate. Driven to desperation by loneliness, she attempts suicide—an act that finally brings her parents out of their self-possessed stupor. The script, written by husband-and-wife team Eunson and Albert (Evans' parents in real life) is weak and pat, lending no valuable insight into a very common problem.

p, Collier Young; d, Charles Lederer; w, Dale Eunson, Katherine Albert (based on a story by Young, Malvin Wald); ph, Archie Stout; m, Leigh Harline; ed, Desmond Marquette; md, C. Bakaleinikoff; art d, Albert D'Agostino, Walter E. Keller.

Drama   **(PR:A MPAA:NR)**

ON THE MAKE   (SEE: DEVIL WITH WOMEN, A, 1930)

ON THE NICKEL*½   (1980) 96m Rose's Park c

Donald Moffat (Sam), Ralph Waite (C. G.), Hal Williams (Paul), Penelope Allen (Rose), Jack Kehoe (Bad Mood), Danny Ades (God Bless), Paul Weaver (Hill), Ina Gould (Estelle), Jack O'Leary, (Big William), Cano Graham, (Sliver), James Gammon (Peanut John), Arthur Space (Soapy Post), Bert Conway (Bert), Jamie Sanchez (Joe), Tom Mahoney (Bobby D), Edmund Villa (Henry), Lane Smith (Preacher), Ellen Geer (Louise), Gayle Vance (Beatrice), Mike Robelo, Nathan Adler, Pattick Tovatt, George Loros, Melvin F. Allen, Hirsch Adell, Herb Evans, John Ryan, Peter Alsop, Charles Comfort, Kerry Shear Waite, Lou Gilbert, Cecil Jordan, Allen Buck, Sosimo, Charles Parks, John Perryman, Frank Savino, Steve Tucker, LeRoy Wheeler, Arnold Johnson, Carmen Filpi, Pat Corley.

Independent production which attempts to make "Skid Row" the setting for an overly sentimental and indulgent dissertation on an individual's responsibility for his own fate. Moffat plays a reformed drunk who has worked himself out of the gutter, only to have to face this hopeless life style once again when his good pal, Ralph Waite, is in trouble. Moffat gives a strong performance, but is unable to lift the material out of the gutter. Filmed over a long period of time by Ralph Waite, who himself had a drinking problem at one time, and who did a series of TV commercials to underscore the help available to alcoholics.

p,d&w, Ralph Waite; ph, Ric Waite (TVC Labs Color); m, Fredric Myrow; ed, Wendy Greene Bricmont; cos, Patrick Norris; m/l, Tom Waits.

Drama   **Cas.**   **(PR:O MPAA:R)**

ON THE NIGHT OF THE FIRE   (SEE: FUGITIVE, THE, 1940, Brit.)

ON THE OLD SPANISH TRAIL**   (1947) 75m REP c

Roy Rogers (Himself), Tito Guizar (Ricco), Jane Frazee (Candy Martin), Andy Devine (Cookie Bullfincher), Estelita Rodriguez (Lola), Charles McGraw (Harry Blaisdell), Fred Graham (Marco the Great), Steve Darrell (Al), Marshall Reed

(Gus), Wheaton Chambers (Silas MacIntyre), Bob Nolan and The Sons of the Pioneers.

Routine western fare has Rogers teaming up with Guizar, a Mexican Robin Hood type, to put a stop to the crooked ways of McGraw. Lots of songs and lots of action in a script that slackens in believability, but manages to wade its way through. Rogers gave up his fancy outfit for this one, instead wearing casual denims, the customary garb of the real West. The songs are mostly traditional western ballads, but Guizar sings an excerpt from "Una Furtiva Lagrima" from Gaetano Donizetti's opera "l'Elisire d'Amore."

p, Edward J. White; d, William Witney; w, Sloan Nibley (based on a story by Gerald Geraghty); ph, Jack Marta (Trucolor); ed, Tony Martinelli; md, Morton Scott; art d, Frank Hotaling; set d, John McCarthy, Jr., Helen Hansard; spec eff, Howard Lydecker, Theodore Lydecker; m/l, Bob Nolan.

Western   **Cas.**   **(PR:A MPAA:NR)**

ON THE RIGHT TRACK*½   (1981) 97m TLD-Zephyr/FOX c

Gary Coleman (Lester), Maureen Stapleton (Mary/Big Lady), Normal Fell (Mayor), Michael Lembeck (Frank), Lisa Eilbacher (Jill), Bill Russell (Robert), Herb Edelman (Sam), David Selburg (Felix), C. Thomas Cuncliffe (Shoeshine Concessioner), Belinda Bremner (Lady with Suitcase), Nathan Davis (Mario), Mike Bacarella (Sean), Jack Wasserman (Vito), Fern Persons (Flower Lady), Arthur Smith (Gerald), Mike Genovese (Louis), Harry Gorsuch (Harry), George Brengel (Bookstore Man), Corin Rogers (Mark), Page Hannah (Sally), I.W. Klein (IRS Man), Muriel Bach (Beauty Salon Boss), Ronda Pierson, Linda Golla, Brenda Lively (Salon Girls), John Mohrlein (Thief), Sally Benoit (Interview), Thom Brandolino (Crewman), Jerry McKay (Pantyhose Peddler), Mario Tanzi (Racetrack Window Man), Rick LeFevour (Mugger), Edna Moreno (Old Lady), Bert Weineberg (Monkey Man), James Hogan, Jr. (Minister), Debbie Hall (Bride), Jamie Gertz (Big Girl), Steve Marmer (Customer with Cold), Gil Cantanzaro, Sr. (Cab Driver), Gil Cantanzaro, Jr. (Truck Driver), Chelcie Ross, Felix Shuman (Customers), James Andelin, Al Nuti (Transit Cops), Mark Hutter, T.W. Miller (Policemen).

Producer Jacobs, director Philips, and actor Coleman in their first feature production, having done all their previous work in television, which explains a lot about this picture. Coleman plays a 10-year-old shoeshine boy who lives out of a locker at a train station, never leaving the station for fear of the outside. Everyone is extremely fond of the young boy, with the various people who work at the station taking care of his needs, the most prominent being bag lady Stapleton who gives him motherly advice. Fondness for Coleman grows when it is discovered that he can predict winners at the racetrack. Other than a few cute lines and situations, there's little else of value in this absurd and extremely naive picture.

p, Ronald Jacobs; d, Lee Philips; w, Tina Pine, Avery Buddy, Richard Moses; ph, Jack Richards (CFI Color); m, Arthur B. Rubenstein; ed, Bill Butler; art d, William Fosser.

Comedy   **Cas.**   **(PR:C MPAA:PG)**

ON THE RIVERA**   (1951) 90m FOX c

Danny Kaye (Henri Duran/Jack Martin), Gene Tierney (Lilli), Corinne Calvet (Colette), Marcel Dalio (Philippe Lebrix), Jean Murat (Periton), Henri Letondal (Louis Forel), Clinton Sundberg (Antoine), Sig Rumann (Gapeaux), Joyce MacKenzie (Mimi), Monique Chantal (Minette), Marina Koshetz (Mme. Cornet), Ann Codee (Mme. Periton), Mari Blanchard (Eugenie), Ethel Martin, George Martin, Vernal Miller (Dance Team), Ellen Ray, Gwyneth [Gwen] Verdon (Specialty Dancers), Rosario Imperio (Spanish Dancer), Antonio Filauri, Charles Andre, Franchesca De Scaffa, Joi Lansing, Eugene Borden, Albert Pollet, Andre Toffel, Albert Morin, George Davis, Tony Laurent, Peter Camlin, Jack Chefe.

A remake of FOLIES BERGERE (1935), which had already been redone as THAT NIGHT IN RIO (1941), this film proved to be an excellent vehicle for the multi-talented Kaye. He's cast as an American nightclub entertainer working on the Riviera who bears a striking resemblance to a famed French aviator, also played by Kaye. When the entertainer is asked to double as the flier at an important party, the expected comedy of mistaken identities ensues. Confusion reaches its zenith the following morning when Tierney, as the aviator's wife, awakens not knowing which of the men she spent the night with. The film provides plenty of opportunities for Kaye to sing, dance, joke, and act, and he acquits himself well on all accounts. Kaye's real-life wife Sylvia Fine wrote four of the songs he performed in ON THE RIVIERA, again lending credence to the actor's quote, "I am a wife-made man." The prolific Lang handles the directing with aplomb, and it's a very satisfying entertainment experience. Gwen Verdon (here billed as Gwyneth), who would achieve stardom as a dancer on Broadway and some success in the movies, made her film debut, appearing in a dance routine. Kaye performs "Popo the Puppet," "On the Riviera," "Rhythm of a New Romance," and "Happy Ending" (Sylvia Fine) and "Ballin' the Jack" (Jim Burris, Chris Smith).

p, Sol C. Siegel; d, Walter Lang; w, Valentine Davies, Phoebe Ephron, Henry Ephron (based on a play by Rudolph Lothar, Hans Adler); ph, Leon Shamroy (Technicolor); ed, J. Watson Webb, Jr.; md, Alfred Newman; art d, Lyle Wheeler, Leland Fuller; ch, Jack Cole.

Musical/Comedy   **(PR:A MPAA:NR)**

ON THE ROAD AGAIN   (SEE: HONEYSUCKLE ROSE, 1980)

ON THE RUN**   (1958, Brit.) 70m Danziger/UA bw

Neil McCallum (Wesley), Susan Beaumont (Kitty Casey), William Hartnell (Tom Casey), Gordon Tanner (Bart Taylor), Philip Saville (Driscol), Gilbert Winfield (Joe).

U.S.-style prizefighting programmer has McCallum a boxer who takes a job at a garage while hiding from gangsters who expected him to throw a fight. He falls in love with Beaumont, the owner's daughter, and she urges him to beat up the gangsters when they come for him. Adequate entertainment with some good fight scenes.

p, Edward J. and Harry Lee Danziger; d, Ernest Morris; w, Brian Clemens, Eldon Howard; ph, Jimmy Wilson.

Crime (PR:A MPAA:NR)

ON THE RUN   (1967, Brit.) 59m Merton Park/Schoenfeld bw

Emrys Jones (*Frank Stewart*), Sarah Lawson (*Helen Carr*), Patrick Barr (*Sgt. Brent*), Delphi Lawrence (*Yvonne*), Kevin Stoney (*Wally Lucas*), William Abney (*Jock Mackay*), Katy Wild (*Jean Stewart*), Philip Locke (*Dave Hughes*), Richard Warner (*Prison Governor*), Brian Haines (*Vance*), Garfield Morgan (*Meredith*), Brian Wilde (*Chief Warden*), Ken Wayne (*Bryce*), Bee Duffell (*Mrs. Thomas*).

Jones is doing time in prison for his part in a major theft. Stoney, the brains behind the robbery, wants information from Jones on the location of the loot, and springs him from prison. Jones won't cooperate until Stoney kidnaps his girl friend, Lawson. The police arrest both before either can get to the treasure. Routine crime drama released in the U.S. four years after its British run.

p, Jack Greenwood; d, Robert Tronson; w, Richard Harris (based on a story by Edgar Wallace); ph, James Wilson; ed, Derek Holding; md, Bernard Ebbinghouse; art d, Peter Mullins.

Crime (PR:A MPAA:NR)

ON THE RUN   (1969, Brit.) 56m Children's Film Fund c

Dennis Conoley (*Ben Mallory*), Robert Kennedy (*Thomas Okapi*), Tracey Collins (*Lil*), Gordon Jackson (*Mr. Mallory*), Bari Johnson (*Uncle Joseph*), John Hollis (*Baldy*), Olwen Brooks (*Miss Fisher*), Dan Jackson (*Chief Okapi*), Harry Locke (*Removal Man*).

Pleasant enough children's film has children from the London slums helping an African prince (Kennedy) evade kidnapers. Children should like it.

p, Derick Williams; d&w, Pat Jackson (based on a novel by Nina Bawden).

Children (PR:A MPAA:NR)

ON THE RUN   (1983, Aus.) 101m Pigelu/Cineworld c

Paul Winfield (*Harry*), Rod Taylor (*Payette*), Beau Cox (*Paul*), Shirley Cameron, Ray Meagher, Danny Adcock.

A predictable but quirky Australian action picture which stars Winfield as an American convict in Sydney who befriends a French-speaking youngster, Cox. Danger erupts when Cox witnesses a murder and is targeted for death by Taylor, Winfield's hit-man boss. Accompanied by a dwarf, the pair take to a mountaintop where a hair-raising skirmish ensues. Winfield's performance is solid, but the picture never becomes any more involving than its shallow title. Taylor, a native Australian who made it big in the U.S., is unconvincing in his role. Black actor Winfield, who got an Oscar nomination for SOUNDER (1972), is excellent in a part that might otherwise have smacked of gimmickry.

p&d, Mende Brown; w, Michael Fisher; ph, Paul Onorato (Colorfilm Color); m, Laurie Lewis; ed, Richard Hindley; stunts, Grant Paige.

Crime (PR:C MPAA:NR)

ON THE SPOT*½   (1940) 62m MON bw

Frankie Darro (*Frankie*), Mantan Moreland (*Jefferson*), John St. Polis (*Doc Hunter*), Robert Warwick (*Cyrus Haddon*), Mary Kornman (*Ruth Hunter*), Maxine Leslie (*Gerry*), Lillian Elliot (*Mrs. Kelly*), Leroy Mason (*Smiling Bill*).

Street-tough kid Darro tries to go straight by getting a job as a soda jerk. Trouble follows him, however, when a gangster phones his cronies from Darro's work place, saying he's leaving an important message with the kid. The gangster is killed before he can share his message, but his pals still think Darro has the needed information. It turns out that Warwick, posing as a banker, is really a criminal mastermind, and all the plot lines are resolved when this is revealed. Not much action in this one, and the performances are only average.

p, Grant Withers; d, Howard Bretherton; w, Joseph West, Dorothy Reid (based on a story by West); ph, Harry Neumann; ed, Russell Schoengarth.

Crime/Drama (PR:A MPAA:NR)

ON THE STROKE OF NINE   (SEE: MURDER ON CAMPUS, 1934)

ON THE SUNNYSIDE   (1936, Swed.) 95m Svenskfilmindustri bw (PA SOLSIDAN)

Lars Hanson (*Harold Ribe*), Ingrid Bergman (*Eva Bergh*), Edvin Adolphson (*Joakim Brink, Writer*), Marianne Lofgren (*Kajsa Ribe*), Karin Swanstrom, Einar Axelson, Carl Browallius, Bullen Berglund, Eddie Figge, Olga Andersson, Viktor Andersson, Eric Gustafsson.

Bergman plays the bank clerk daughter of a Bohemian artist father who takes a liking to the lifestyle of artists. She finally falls for and marries the conservative Hanson, moving to his country estate. Worried that Bergman may miss the exciting life she led in the city, Hanson invites some of her friends to come stay at their home, only to find jealousy when an old flame of Bergman arrives with the group. His fears prove unfounded, however, as Bergman is quite content with her life with him. A somewhat slow-moving story, elevated considerably by Bergman's performance. She had already conquered the Swedish film industry, and now was gaining the attention of Hollywood.

d, Gustaf Molander; w, Oscar Hemberg, Gosta Stevens (based on the play by Helge Krog); ph, Ake Dahlquist; md, Eric Bengtsson.

Drama (PR:A MPAA:NR)

ON THE SUNNY SIDE   (1942) 69m FOX bw

Roddy McDowall (*Hugh Aylesworth*), Jane Darwell (*Annie*), Stanley Clements (*Tom Sanders*), Katherine Alexander (*Mrs. Andrews*), Don Douglas (*Mr. Andrews*), Freddie Mercer (*Don Andrews*), Ann Todd (*Betty*), Jill Esmond (*Mrs. Aylesworth*), Freddie Walburn (*Dick*), Leon Tyler (*Flip*), Billy Benedict (*Messenger*), Stuart Robertson (*Broadcast Announcer*), Whiskers (*Angus*).

English boy McDowall is sent by his parents to the U.S. while WW II rages in Europe. An American family living outside Cleveland takes the boy in and conflicts arise almost immediately between McDowall and Mercer, son of McDowall's American "parents." The two boys compete with one another and learn from one another over the course of the film. The movie is filled with the antics of the two young rivals and other neighborhood kids, making it good fare for the children.

p, Lou Ostrow; d, Harold Schuster; w, Lillie Hayward, George Templeton (based on the story "Fraternity" by Mary C. McCall, Jr.); ph, Lucien Andriot; ed, Fred Allen; md, Emil Newman.

Drama (PR:AA MPAA:NR)

ON THE THRESHOLD OF SPACE***   (1956) 98m FOX c

Guy Madison (*Capt. Jim Hollenbeck*), Virginia Leith (*Pat Lange*), John Hodiak (*Maj. Ward Thomas*), Dean Jagger (*Dr. Hugh Thornton*), Warren Stevens (*Capt. Mike Bentley*), Martin Milner (*Lt. Morton Glenn*), King Calder (*Lee Welch*), Walter Coy (*Lt. Col. Masters*), Ken Clark (*Sgt. Ike Forbes*), Donald Murphy (*Sgt. Zack Deming*), Barry Coe (*Communications Officer*), Richard Grant (*Medic*), Donald Freed (*Paramedic Officer*), Ben Wright (*Taxi Driver*), Carlyle Mitchell (*George Atkins*), Robert Cornthwaite (*Dawson*), Jo Gilbert (*Secretary*), Juanita Close (*Nurse*), Helen Bennett (*Mrs. Lange*), Charles Lind, David Armstrong, Joe Locke.

Something of an early version of THE RIGHT STUFF (1983), ON THE THRESHOLD OF SPACE paid tribute to the men who were laying the groundwork for man's exploration of space. (The title may have been more prophetic than the makers realized, since men would be in space within five years after the film's release.) The filmmakers tried for an accurate depiction of the ongoing research and testing, relying heavily on U.S. Air Force input and shooting on location at air bases in Florida (Eglin) and New Mexico (Holloman). Madison stars as an Air Force physician who undergoes extensive tests in an effort to determine how the human body will respond to the expected stress and strain of space travel. The rigors include being ejected in a space capsule from a jet at the altitude of 45,000 feet, traveling at 1,000 miles per hour in a rocket sled, and a 100,000 foot balloon ascent. All is suspensefully captured by the camera, and Madison is effective as the dedicated man of science. Leith plays his concerned but supportive wife. Hodiak is the research head who can't resist getting involved in some of the testing himself. This would be his last film, as he died of a heart attack at the age of 41 before the picture's release. Excused from military service during WW II because of hypertension, Hodiak made his film debut with a supporting role in I DOOD IT (1943). Following the war, he primarily filled supporting roles in films up until the time of his death.

p, William Bloom; d, Robert D. Webb; w, Simon Wincelberg, Francis Cockrell; ph, Joe MacDonald (CinemaScope, DeLuxe Color); m, Lyn Murray; ed, Hugh S. Fowler; md, Lionel Newman; art d, Lyle R. Wheeler, Lewis H. Creber; spec eff, Ray Kellogg.

Drama (PR:A MPAA:NR)

ON THE TOWN*****   (1949) 98m MGM c

Gene Kelly (*Gabey*), Frank Sinatra (*Chip*), Betty Garrett (*Brunhilde Esterhazy*), Ann Miller (*Claire Huddesen*), Jules Munshin (*Ozzie*), Vera-Ellen (*Ivy Smith*), Florence Bates (*Mme. Dilyouska*), Alice Pearce (*Lucy Shmeeler*), George Meader (*Professor*), Bern Hoffman (*Worker*), Lester Dorr (*Subway Passenger*), Bea Benaderet (*Working Girl*), Walter Baldwin (*Sign Poster*), Don Brodie (*Photo Layout Man*), Sid Melton (*Spud*), Robert B. Williams (*Officer*), Tom Dugan (*Officer Tracy*), Murray Alper (*Cab Company Owner*), Hans Conried (*Francois*), Claire Carleton (*Redhead*), Dick Wessel (*Sailor Simpkins*), William "Bill" Phillips (*Sailor*), Frank Hagney (*Cop*), Carol Haney (*Dancer in Green*), Eugene Borden (*Waiter*), Judy Holiday (*Voice of a Sailor's Date*).

New York never looked so beautiful or more exciting than in ON THE TOWN, a breakthrough musical that took this kind of movie out of the claustrophobic sound stages and out onto the streets. In the following years, many other films would imitate that innovation, but it is here that it was first done. The plot is as fragile as a soap bubble and twice as thin, but it doesn't matter one bit because it is so energetic, so vital, so filled with power that the screen has trouble holding it at times and the actors almost leap off and dance up the aisles. No, it's not as good as SINGIN' IN THE RAIN and it's not as monumental or prestigious as AN AMERICAN IN PARIS, but in its own way, ON THE TOWN is just as important to anyone who loves movies because it was the first real fusion of story, songs, and dances with nary a moment taken out to stage a pretentious production number just for its own sake. Kelly, Sinatra, and Munshin are three jolly tars on a 24-hour pass in New York City. They come off their ship filled with high hopes for a memorable day. Sinatra suggests that the first order of business is to find some willing wenches; then see the sights. They board a New York subway train and note that this month's "Miss Turnstiles" picture is being mounted in the car. (For years the New York Subway System had a regular "Miss Subways" each month, some of whom went on to become actresses, such as Diana Lynn.) The picture is of comely Vera-Ellen and Kelly likes the photo so much that he takes it out of the frame and wants to keep it for those long nights at sea. They arrive at the next station and Vera-Ellen is there, being photographed by newsmen, so Kelly asks if he can take a picture with her. They do, and when Kelly turns to talk to his pals, Vera-Ellen vanishes into the rush-hour crowd (it's early in the morning and millions are hurrying to work). The sailors go topside and get into a cab driven by Garrett. They think they might be able to catch up with Vera-Ellen, who is still on the train. They miss connections with Vera-Ellen's train at Columbus Circle and sadly return to the taxi, which is due to go back to the garage, as Garrett has finished her all-night stint. By this time, Garrett has found Sinatra more than passably attractive and she agrees to help the sailors in their quest for Kelly's amour. The first place they go to is the Museum of Anthropological History, where they meet Miller. She's doing a paper on prehistoric man and is admiring a statue. When Munshin strolls in and is a duplicate of said sculpture, Miller is thrown for a loop. They unerringly wreck a dinosaur replica and leave the museum before they are arrested, now a group of five. Garrett thinks they might be able to find Vera-Ellen if they separate and go to different places. Sinatra will go with Garrett, Munshin with Miller, and they'll all meet that night atop the observation tower of the then-World's Tallest Building, the Empire State, on the corner of Fifth Avenue at 34th Street, the same place where King Kong met his fate from those machine-gunning planes. Garrett really just wants to get close to Sinatra, but her best-laid plans don't work out, as her roommate, Pearce, is unexpectedly at the apartment, suffering from a very bad cold. Kelly visits Symphonic Hall and learns that Vera-Ellen is taking a dance class from Bates, in a Maria Ouspenskaya ballet teacher role. Kelly is smitten. They make a date to meet that night with all the others at the Empire State Building. Kelly, a small-town boy, thinks that "Miss Turnstiles" is a huge New York celebrity and Miller and Garrett are not about to tell him how fleeting that fame is. The six of them get together and go out on the town. At a nightclub run by Conried, Miller slips the man a few bucks to make a lot of noise about Vera-Ellen's being "Miss Turnstiles." She has to leave the evening's fun before midnight and Kelly is without a female to drape over his arm, so Garrett gets him Pearce, whom he'll meet later. Kelly takes Vera-Ellen home and feels bad that she doesn't want to stay with him, but he doesn't know that she now has to go to her job. She dances in a cooch place in Coney Island in order to pay for her dancing lessons. The party continues and they all run into Bates at a bar where she explains that Vera-Ellen had to leave or lose her job. They all clamber into a Brooklyn-bound cab and are followed by the police, who have been tailing them because they've been told to be on the lookout for the sailors who destroyed the dinosaur earlier. After a bit of searching at Sodom by the Sea, they find Vera-Ellen and she tells Kelly that she is not a big star at all, just an aspiring dancer from a town he's probably never even heard of, Meadowville, Indiana. She almost reels when Kelly retorts that Meadowville is his hometown as well! The pursuing cops, Williams and Dugan, finally get to the boys, who must think fast in order to escape, so they all dress in female clothing and become part of the women who are dancing in the Coney Island show. When they think that they can make a safe getaway, they race outside and go right into a paddy wagon run by the Navy's shore patrol. The girls persuade the cops to back off and allow the guys to return to their ship, which they do at six a.m. exactly, 24 hours to the minute from the time they left. Garrett, Miller, and Vera-Ellen sadly wave farewell as the men board. 98 minutes have gone by and it feels like five. There were only four songs from the original show and only one actress, Pearce. Louis B. Mayer bought the show for $250,000 before it was produced but didn't like the play when he saw it, deeming it "smutty" and "communistic" because there was one scene that had a white sailor dancing with a black woman. Freed prevailed on Mayer to give him a green light for a $2 million budget, including $110,000 to Comden and Green for rewrites and new lyrics to the music by associate producer Roger Edens. Freed didn't like much of Bernstein's play music, but Bernstein had other fish to fry and relinquished the rights so that Edens could write new tunes. Mayer didn't want the film to go on location and Kelly wanted to shoot the entire picture in New York. They compromised and Kelly was allowed one frantic week of filming in Manhattan, during which time he managed to show us the Bronx, the Battery, Coney Island, Brooklyn, The Empire State Building, Times Square, The Statue of Liberty, Fifth Avenue, Radio City, The Bronx Zoo, Central Park, Carnegie Hall, the Subway, Wall Street, Grant's Tomb, and the Brooklyn Navy Yard, where the ship docked. Perhaps it was this short work schedule that contributed to the frantic pace of the film, jamming, cramming, packing until there wasn't a wasted second. It was as though the actors weren't allowed to breathe in, only out, and when they did that, they had better be singing or speaking. It was a shame to lose some of Bernstein's music, which included the lovely "Lonely Town," but Freed, a well-known songwriter on his own, had strong ideas and didn't like Bernstein's moody tunes. There may have been another factor, though, and that is that all film studios have their own music publishing arms and don't like to use music that's been published by someone else unless they are absolutely forced to. The movie had a shooting schedule of 47 days with five weeks' rehearsal. It won only a solo Oscar for Edens and Hayton, a gross oversight by the members of the Academy. Kelly and Donen co-directed the first of their triumphs with ON THE TOWN and it is to be assumed that Kelly handled the dance pieces while Donen did the dialog. There was one serious ballet sequence and Kelly knew that his compadres couldn't handle the footwork, so he took a leaf from Agnes DeMille's ballet in OKLAHOMA and substituted other dancers for the leads. Sinatra, Munshin, Garrett, and Miller were replaced by Alex Romero (now a choreographer in his own right), Gene Scott, Carol Haney (who was to star on Broadway in "Pajama Game" before an early death), and Marie Grosscup. There were many hysterical gags in the picture and the one that ran all the way through was a commentary on New York nightlife, as every club the sailors visited had the exact same floor show going on. There may have been better songs and even better performances in other musicals, but for effervescence and raw pow! nothing has yet come close to ON THE TOWN. Shooting in New York has never been easy, with all the rubberneckers who seem to have nothing better to do than watch, so cinematographer Rosson used many hidden cameras and Manhattanites must have been shocked to see themselves on screen when the picture opened at Radio City Music Hall in December, 1949, to a waiting crowd of more than 10,000 eager people. Later, there would be many musicals that owed their genesis to ON THE TOWN. They include WEST SIDE STORY, FUNNY GIRL, HIT THE DECK, and SKIRTS AHOY, among many others. The score included: "New York, New York," "I Feel Like I'm Not Out of Bed Yet," "Come Up to My Place (Leonard Bernstein, Betty Comden, Adolph Green), "Miss Turnstiles Ballet" (Bernstein), "Main Street," "You're Awful," "On the Town," "You Can Count on Me," "Pearl of the Persian Sea," "Pre-Historic Man," and "That's All There Is, Folks" (Roger Edens, Comden, Green). The excellent orchestrations were by Conrad Salinger and the vocal arrangements were by Saul Chaplin, who later became a producer.

p, Arthur Freed; d, Gene Kelly, Stanley Donen; w, Adolph Green, Betty Comden (based on the musical play by Comden, Green, Leonard Bernstein from the ballet "Fancy Free" by Jerome Robbins); ph, Harold Rossen (Technicolor); m, Bernstein, Roger Edens, Saul Chaplin, Conrad Salinger; ed, Ralph E. Winters; md, Lennie Hayton, Roger Edens; art d, Cedric Gibbons, Jack Martin Smith; set d, Edwin B. Willis, Jack D. Moore; cos, Helen Rose; spec eff, Warren Newcombe; ch, Kelly, Donen; m/l, Bernstein/Comden, Green, Edens; makeup, Jack Dawn; hairstyles, Sydney Guilaroff.

Musical/Comedy Cas. (PR:A MPAA:NR)

ON THE WATERFRONT***** (1954) 108m COL bw

Marlon Brando *(Terry Malloy)*, Karl Malden *(Father Barry)*, Lee J. Cobb *(Johnny Friendly)*, Rod Steiger *(Charley Malloy)*, Pat Henning *("Kayo" Dugan)*, Eva Marie Saint *(Edie Doyle)*, Leif Erickson *(Glover)*, James Westerfield *(Big Mac)*, Tony Galento *(Truck)*, Tami Mauriello *(Tillio)*, John Hamilton *("Pop" Doyle)*, John Heldabrand *(Mott)*, Rudy Bond *(Moose)*, Don Blackman *(Luke)*, Arthur Keegan *(Jimmy)*, Abe Simon *(Barney)*, Barry Macollum *(J.P.)*, Mike O'Dowd *(Specs)*, Marty Balsam *(Gillette)*, Fred Gwynne *(Slim)*, Thomas Handley *(Tommy)*, Anne Hegira *(Mrs. Collins)*, Pat Hingle *(Bartender)*, Nehemiah Persoff *(Cab Driver)*.

A tour de force both for director Kazan and actor Brando, ON THE WATERFRONT is a gritty, no-holds-barred drama of the corruption-glutted New York docks. It is also the story of the excruciating struggle to make a living among the dockworkers and the awesome power of the unions that control the workers. Cobb is the gangster union-boss and Steiger his crooked lawyer. Steiger's brother, Brando, is an ex-pug who hangs around the docks and runs errands for Cobb who doles handouts to those who do his bidding. Most of the time Brando keeps pigeons on a rooftop and dreams about his days as a hopeful fighter, a once-was ambition, even for this young man. Cobb tells Brando to contact a truculent union worker who is holed up in his apartment, asking him to meet him on the roof of his tenement building. The worker goes to the roof and two of Cobb's goons push him off to his death. Brando, in shock, watches this happen and says to some of Cobb's other thugs: "I thought they were only gonna lean on him a little." Replies the human fireplug Galento ("Two-ton" Tony Galento, a 1930s boxer who was known for butting his head into the chests of his opponents), "The canary could sing but he couldn't fly!" Brando later meets pretty Saint, the dead man's sister, and begins to feel responsible for the death. She introduces him to a gritty priest, Malden, who tells Brando that the dead man was killed because he was going to expose racket boss Cobb and his brutal henchmen and he exhorts Brando to provide the crime commission with information that will smash the dock racketeers. Another dockworker, Henning, does cooperate with the crime commission, loudly bragging that he will bring Cobb down. While working in the hold of a ship, a huge packing crate is "accidentally" dropped on Henning and he is killed. Malden shows up and gives the man the last rites, then addresses the longshoremen in the hold. Malden tells the men that God is down in that hold with them and he asks them to put an end to the system which can snuff out a life on a boss' orders. thugs Galento and Mauriello—perhaps the most repulsive goons ever to besmirch the screen—begin to shout down Malden. Mauriello throws a can and strikes the priest and Brando steps forth and warns the goons to stop it. Malden continues to address the workers, head bleeding, his clothes soiled by the rotten food hurled at him. Mauriello steps up again and starts to hurl another object when Brando jumps in front of him and hits him with powerhouse blows that send the hulk backward and unconscious. Malden continues, saying: "Boys, this is my church. And if you don't think Christ is down here on the waterfront, you got another guess coming!" Later Brando falls in love with Saint and Malden's persuasive ways begin to edge him into cooperating with Erickson and others with the crime commission. Seeing that Brando is straying, Cobb orders Steiger to get his brother in line or face the fatal consequences. Steiger takes Brando for a cab ride (the taxi driven by Persoff, a Cobb henchman) and the two have a brotherly heart-to-heart talk. Steiger tells Brando that he is getting a new job, plenty of money, and all kinds of favors, but he must keep silent and not talk to the crime commission. Brando is now thoroughly disillusioned with his older, educated brother. Steiger pulls a gun on Brando, insisting that he do as he is told, but Brando shoves the gun away in disgust. Steiger realizes what he's done and then gets nostalgic, saying Brando could have been another Billy Conn in the ring and that "the skunk we got you for a manager brought you along too fast." "It wasn't him, Charley," Brando responds. "It was you. Remember that night in the Garden and you came down to my dressing room and you said 'Kid, this ain't your night. We're going for the price on Wilson.' You remember that? This ain't your night! My night! I could have taken Wilson apart! So what happens? He gets a title shot outdoors in a ballpark and I get a one-way ticket to palookaville! You was my brother, Charley, you should've looked out for me just a little bit so I wouldn't have to take them dives for the short-end money." Steiger shrugs: "We had some bets down for you—you saw some money." Brando winces: "You don't understand! I could have had class. I could've been a contender! I could've been *somebody*, instead of a bum, which is what I am! It was you, Charley." Steiger tells Brando that he will tell Cobb that he couldn't find him and then hands him the gun, letting him out of the cab. Persoff, overhearing everything, drives Steiger into a garage where Cobb's goons are waiting. Brando runs to Saint and forces himself on her, and while they begin to make love, Cobb's goons call up from the street: "Your brother's down here—he wants to see you!" Brando leaves and goes down an alley and Saint joins him and then a truck barrels down the alley after them; they barely escape being run over. Then Brando sees Steiger, hanging from a hook in the alley, bullet holes in him, dead. Gently, he removes the body from the hook, lowering it. "I'm gonna take it out of their skulls!" Brando vows. He tells Saint to take care of his brother's body. He goes to Cobb's saloon headquarters looking for the boss, holds several goons at bay with the gun Steiger has given him but they escape when Malden shows up and talks Brando into going to the crime commission to smash Cobb's murderous stranglehold on the dockworkers. "Don't fight him down here in the jungle 'cause that's just what he wants!" He tells Brando to get rid of the gun and orders a beer. Brando joins him and then throws the gun into a picture of Cobb on the wall, smashing it. The next day Brando goes before the crime commission and testifies against Cobb and his thugs. Shrieking curses and vowing revenge, Cobb tells Brando he's a dead man. Though disenfranchised, Cobb still exercises control of his union, his straw boss, Westerfield, handing out jobs to everyone the next day on the docks, all except Brando. Enraged, Brando runs down a gangplank to a barge where Cobb and his goons are hiding and he tears the racketeer apart, despite the fact that he receives a brutal beating from the thugs. He is a bloody mess but the scores of workers shout that they will not go to work without Brando. He struggles to his feet, half conscious, and staggers up the gangplank, working his way through the crowd, toward the warehouse, to be the first worker to enter and take his job. The men follow him, indicating a clearcut defeat for the mob and a victory for the workers. ON THE WATERFRONT is nerve-jarring, nonstop high drama and Brando is spectacular as the ex-fighter who finds his conscience and risks his principles with his life. The dialog is realistic, simple but almost poetic in its simplicity, and the grimy, seedy tenements and clammy, greasy docks are captured in all their sinister forms. Kazan sets every scene with menace and suspense and within the framework of his vision is a steel gray world without pity, but one with the kind of tough hope it takes to survive in such a subhuman atmosphere. Cobb is a great villain, one who exercises his power with a payoff, a sneering smile, and a booming voice, and his goons are really ugly, frightening characters, many of them former real-life boxers with faces scarred and mutilated by years in the ring. Saint is an island of sanity and decency as is Malden who gives one the finest performances of his career. His speech in the ship's hold is a magnificent indictment of evil and reaffirmation of Christianity. The film is a draining experience from beginning to end, relentless is its portrayal of inhumanity, shown all the more grim in its startling documentary approach by cinematographer Kaufman. It is also extremely violent, bloody, and more frightening than a Boris Karloff horror film. Not for young children, certainly. Controversy surrounded ON THE WATERFRONT at the time of its release. It was accused of being anti-American and union leaders denounced it, but it has stood the test of time and emerges as a great portrait of a nonconforming individual who is not an informer but rather a man who experiences a moral transformation for the good of his fellow man. Schulberg's literate, uncompromising screenplay made sure that no one could mistake Brando's intentions. Schulberg was the logical choice of director Kazan to write the script, after having crusaded against the criminal elements and horrible abuses in the so-called sport of boxing, as shown in THE HARDER THEY FALL. His script was based on a fascinating and heroic series of newspaper articles written by Malcolm Johnson who was assigned by his editors of the old New York *Sun* to investigate waterfront crime in New York. What he unearthed and later revealed in a 24-part series, following the murder of a New York dock hiring boss in April, 1948, shocked America. Johnson's hard-hitting series described in detail the killings, bribery, kickbacks, thievery, shakedowns, and extortion that were everyday occurrences along New York's waterfront. He won the Pulitzer Prize for his great work. When Kazan took over the project, he had fallen into disfavor in Hollywood, chiefly because he had cooperated with the House Un-American Activities Committee (HUAC) and armed some Hollywood Communists during the McCarthy era (as had Schulberg), but this film reaffirmed Kazan's wonderful and supercharged talent. Courageously, Columbia decided to make a film on a subject that Hollywood had always considered taboo—unions and labor. Studio mogul Harry Cohn was not orignally in favor of doing the film but since his New York office had made the production deal with producer Spiegel, he did not interfere. He did view the film at his private screening room in his home, however, with Kazan at his side. He only commented on one scene, where Brando tells priest Malden to "go to hell." Snorted Cohn to Kazan: "Boy, are you going to have trouble with the Breen Office [the then official Hollywood censor] over that 'go to hell' scene. They'll never pass it." Cohn was shocked when the Breen Office did not object to the scene, so much so that he barraged the censor with angry questions about why other films Columbia had produced had been clipped and cut and censored for what he thought were lesser offenses. Kazan insisted on shooting the film on location and almost every scene was photographed in Hoboken, New Jersey, much to the dislike of Cohn, who thought it better to shoot it on his back lot in California. (Oddly, writer Schulberg had earlier refused to ever write another film for Cohn but he would contract with independent producer Spiegel and Spiegel's arrangement with Columbia guaranteed no interference from Cohn.) Kazan was noted for taking his films on location to give them a thoroughly authentic look. In 1947 he made the crime film drama BOOMERANG in Stamford, Connecticut, and in 1950 he took cast and crew to New Orleans to make the superb and tense drama PANIC IN THE STREETS. Kazan proved to be so packed with personal energy during the production that he worked cast and crew around the clock. He only took a breast of chicken sandwich on toast (no butter, no mayonnaise) for lunch. When he was asked where he got his energy, Kazan replied: "I never get tired making a film. But at a cocktail party, listening to all that genteel bull——, I'd collapse from fatigue within a half hour." Kazan's first choice for the role of the fighter was Brando but Brando reportedly could not make up his mind to take the role. Next Kazan offered the part to Frank Sinatra, who had just made a memorable comeback in FROM HERE TO ETERNITY and was one of the hottest actors on the scene. Before the deal was signed, however, Brando decided he wanted to appear in ON THE WATERFRONT and was signed for the part. Sinatra later loudly complained, according to one report, that he had been misled by Kazan. No matter. Brando's career choice was another acting coup among many. (This would be the last film Brando would do with Kazan, although the dynamic director would offer him roles and get rejections for BABY DOLL, A FACE IN THE CROWD, and THE ARRANGEMENT.) Although Harry Cohn had prophesied doom for ON THE WATERFRONT, a film that cost only $902,000 to make, the picture was a whopping success, grossing $9,500,000 in its initial release. Moreover, it went on to win eight Academy Awards in 1954, including Best Picture, Brando for Best Actor, Saint for Best Actress, Kazan for Best Director, and Schulberg for Best Screenplay.

p, Sam Spiegel; d, Elia Kazan; w, Budd Schulberg (based on a story suggested by a series of articles by Malcolm Johnson); ph, Boris Kaufman; m, Leonard Bernstein; ed, Gene Milford; art d, ed, Gene Milford; art d, Richard Day; makeup, Fred Ryle.

Crime Drama **Cas.** **(PR:O MPAA:NR)**

ON THE YARD*** (1978) 103m Midwest Film c

John Heard *(Juleson)*, Thomas Waites *(Chilly)*, Mike Kellin *(Red)*, Richard Bright *(Nunn)*, Joe Grifasi *(Morris)*, Lane Smith *(Capt. Blake)*, Richard Hayes *(Stick)*, Hector Troy *(Gasolino)*, Richard Jamieson *(Lt. Carpenter)*, Thomas Toner *(Warden)*, Ron Faber *(Manning)*, David Clennon *(Psychiatrist)*, Don Blakely *(Tate)*, J. C. Quinn *(Luther)*, Dominic Chianese *(Mendoza)*, Eddie Jones *(Lt. Olson)*, Ben Slack *(Clemmons)*, James Remar *(Larson)*, Dave McCalley *(Redmond)*, Ludwick Villani *(Candy)*, John Taylor *(Schulte)*, Ivan Yount *(Inmate)*, Ralph Hobbs *(Zeke)*, David Berman *(Caterpillar)*, Joseph Mazurkiewicz, Lowell Manfall, Peg French *(Parole Board)*, Ralph Basalla *(Processor)*, Walter Sanders *(Cool Breeze)*, Roland Jackson *(Cadillac)*, Leon J. Cassady, Frank Conrad, Leroy Newsome *(Bakery Workers)*, Robert Johnson *(Mechanic)*, Fred Jones, James Johnson, George Gamble, John Demmitt *(Therapy Session)*, John Kephart, Alan Gramley, Jan Chwiej *(Prison Squad)*, John Berhosky *(Bus Guard)*, William Carver *(Night Guard)*, Morris Pratt *(Office Guard)*.

An effective attempt to realistically portray prison life, ON THE YARD focuses on four inmates, with Waites portraying the acknowledged leader of the prisoners. Heard is a convicted wife murderer, Kellin is a habitual criminal who has spent more time in jail than out, and Grifasi is Waites' errand boy. The film offers revealing portraits of the leads and succeeds in providing a compelling examination of the relationships and how they are shaped by the prison environment. Veteran actor Kellin is memorable as the con who can't con the parole board into granting him an early release. The rest of the cast is made up of unknowns, although Remar would go on to more than adequately fill villainous roles in 48 HOURS (1982) and THE COTTON CLUB (1984). Braly had done a good job of adapting his critically acclaimed novel for the screen, and the husband-wife team of the Silvers has competently evoked the prison atmosphere. The couple traded hats on this project —previously Raphael served as producer to Joan's director on HESTER STREET (1975) and BETWEEN THE LINES (1977).

p, Joan Micklin Silver; d, Raphael D. Silver; w, Malcolm Braly (based on his novel); ph, Alan Metzer; m, Charles Gross; ed, Evan Lottman; art d, Leon Harris; cos, Robert Harris.

Drama **Cas.** **(PR:O MPAA:R)**

ON THEIR OWN** (1940) 63m FOX bw

Spring Byington *(Mrs. John Jones)*, Ken Howell *(Jack Jones)*, George Ernest *(Roger Jones)*, June Carlson *(Lucy Jones)*, Florence Roberts *(Granny Jones)*, Billy Mahan *(Bobby Jones)*, Marguerite Chapman *(Margaret)*, John Qualen *(Peters)*, Charles Judels *(Giuseppe Galentoni)*, Chick Chandler *(Doc Duggan)*, Forrester Harvey *(Mr. Pim)*, Isobel Randolph *(Hortense Dingwell)*, Walter Soderling *(Mr. Flint)*, Inez Palange *(Mrs. Galentoni)*, William B. Davidson *(Judge Bull)*, Charles Lane *(Johnson)*.

When Papa Jones suffers a heart attack the Jones family moves to California where dad is to enter a sanitarium for a rest cure. They buy a bungalow court and rent out to families with children, much to the consternation of a neighbor who does not like all the noise. Well-produced piece of escapist entertainment. At the time of production, Jed Prouty was in a battle with Fox over his contract, so he was conveniently written out of the script. Roberts, who had played Granny Jones since the series began in 1936, died shortly after the picture's release at the age of 79. Her first screen appearance took place during the silent era, but her film career really didn't get going until 1930, when she was 69. During the 1930s she had supporting roles in more than 30 films. (See JONES FAMILY series, Index.)

p, Sol. M. Wurtzel; d, Otto Brower; w, Harold Buchman, Val Burton (based on a story by Burton, Jack Jungmeyer, Jr. and Edith Skouras, and characters created by Katherine Kavanaugh); ph, Arthur Miller; ed, Nick de Maggio; md, Samuel Kaylin.

Comedy **(PR:A MPAA:NR)**

ON THIN ICE*½ (1933, Brit.) 62m Hall Mark/EPC British bw

Ursula Jeans *(Lady Violet)*, Kenneth Law *(Harry Newman)*, Viola Gault *(Mabel)*, Stewart Thompson *(Corry)*, Cameron Carr *(Mr. Newman)*, Dorothy Bartlam.

A confusing and paper-thin crime mystery which has Law caught in the middle of a blackmail plot against his wealthy father. His planned wedding to Jeans is threatened when he gets himself entangled in a web with actress Gault who, according to Bartlam, is actually an impostor.

d&w, Bernard Vorhaus; ph, Eric Cross.

Crime **(PR:A MPAA:NR)**

ON TOP OF OLD SMOKY*½ (1953) 59m COL bw

Gene Autry *(Himself)*, Smiley Burnette *(Himself)*, Gail Davis *(Jen Larrabee)*, Grandon Rhodes *("Doc" Judson)*, Sheila Ryan *(Lila Maryland)*, Kenne Duncan *(McQuaid)*, Robert Bice *(Kirby)*, Zon Murray *(Bud)*, Fred S. Martin *(Freddie Cass)*, Jarry Scoggins *(Jerry Cass)*, Bert Dodson *(Bert Cass)*, The Cass County Boys, Champion, Jr. the Horse.

One of six films Autry made in 1953, his last year as a movie actor. In this one he and the Cass County Boys are mistaken for Texas Rangers after they help out Davis, the operator of a toll road. Davis is being harassed by poachers who want her land because of its valuable mineral content. Weak story offers some good songs including the ever popular "On Top of Old Smoky," sung by Autry.

p, Armand Schaefer; d, George Archainbaud; w, Gerald Geraghty (based on his story); ph, William Bradford (Sepiatone); ed, James Sweeney; md, Mischa Bakaleinikoff; art d, George Brooks.

Western   **Cas.**   **(PR:A MPAA:NR)**

ON TOP OF THE WORLD   (SEE: EVERYTHING OKAY, 1936, Brit.)

ON TRIAL**   (1928) 91m WB bw

Pauline Frederick (Joan Trask), Bert Lytell (Robert Strickland), Lois Wilson (May Strickland), Holmes Herbert (Gerald Trask), Richard Tucker (Prosecuting Attorney), Jason Robards, Sr. (Defense Attorney), Johnny Arthur (Stanley Glover), Vondell Darr (Doris Strickland), Franklin Pangborn (Turnbull), Fred Kelsey (Clerk), Edmund Breese (Judge), Edward Martindel (Dr. Morgan).

Screen treatment of the popular play (done more successfully on the screen in 1939) has Lytell on trial for the murder of his friend, Herbert, who, it turns out, was a cad. Attorney Robards, a young and inexperienced counsel, manages to convince the jury that the murder was justifiable because it allowed Lytell to preserve his wife's honor. Adaptation is rather weak, but a good cast makes the most of it. This film is of primary interest for its early and unsuccessful use of sound techniques. Muffled dialog, hissing "s" sounds, and distracting scratching noises combined to make listening to the Vitaphone sound track a chore.

d, Archie Mayo; w, Robert Lord, Max Pollock (based on the play by Elmer Rice); ph, Byron Haskins; ed, Tommy Pratt; cos, Earl Luick.

Drama   **(PR:A MPAA:NR)**

ON TRIAL½   (1939) 60m WB bw

John Litel (Robert Strickland), Margaret Lindsay (Mae Strickland), Edward Norris (Arbuckle), Janet Chapman (Doris Strickland), James Stephenson (Gerald Trask), Nedda Harrigan (Joan Trask), Larry Williams (Glover), William B. Davidson (Gray), Earl Dwire (Judge), Gordon Hart (Dr. Morgan), Charles Trowbridge (Henry Dean), Sidney Bracey (Joe Burke), Kenneth Harlan (Mr. Trumbell), Vera Lewis (Mrs. Leeds), Nat Carr (Clerk), Stuart Holmes (Mr. Summers), Cliff Saum (Bailiff), Jack Mower (Court Stenographer), John Dilson (Jury Foreman), Lola Cheaney (Mrs. Rosenblatt), Edgar Edwards (1st Reporter), John Harron (2nd Reporter).

The second filming of Elmer Rice's popular 1919 play stars Norris as a lawyer assigned to defend an uncooperative Litel against a murder charge. Litel killed Stephenson and Norris proves it was necessary to preserve the honor of Litel's wife, Lindsay. She had disappeared after the crime, but Norris also succeeds in finding her, reuniting the happy couple. Drama offers some intrigue and is competently handled by Morse, who was beginning his directorial career in 1939. He would go on to do a number of B pictures, with his most notable contribution being the director of the American version of GODZILLA (1956).

p, Bryan Foy; d, Terry Morse; w, Don Ryan (based on the play by Elmer Rice); ph, L. W. O'Connell; ed, James Gibbons.

Drama   **(PR:A MPAA:NR)**

ON VELVET*   (1938, Brit.) Associated Industries/COL bw

Wally Patch (Harry Higgs), Joe Hayman (Sam Cohen), Vi Kaley (Mrs. Higgs), Mildred Franklin (Mrs. Cohen), Jennifer Skinner (Mary), Leslie Bradley (Monty), Ambrose Day (Waterbury), Nina Mae McKinney, Julie Suedo, Garland Wilson, Sidney Monckton, Olive Delmer, Bob Field, George Sims, Cleo Fauvel, Andree Sacre, Queenie Lucy, Eric Barker, Gordon Little, Mark Stone, Collinson & Dean, Helga & Jo, Bellings' Dogs, Rex Burrows and His Orchestra, The Columbia Choir.

A nearly unwatchable musical comedy about a pair of gamblers who lose their savings at the races and then try to make a fortune with a television station. Somehow they manage to make ends meet and even get back in their wives' good graces.

p&d, Widgey R. Newman; w, John Quin.

Musical   **(PR:A MPAA:NR)**

ON WINGS OF SONG   (SEE: LOVE ME FOREVER, 1935)

ON WITH THE SHOW**½   (1929) 120m WB c

Betty Compson (Nita), Louise Fazenda (Sarah), Sally O'Neil (Kitty), Joe E. Brown (Ike), Purnell B. Pratt (Sam Bloom), William Bakewell (Jimmy), Fairbanks Twins (Twins), Wheeler Oakman (Durant), Sam Hardy (Jerry), Thomas Jefferson (Dad), Lee Moran (Pete), Harry Gribbon (Joe), Arthur Lake (Harold), Josephine Houston (Harold's Fiancee), Henry Fink (Father), Otto Hoffman (Bert), Ethel Waters (Herself), Harmony Quartet (Harmony 4 Quartet), Four Covans, Angelus Babe.

The first film in all natural color is a musical that revolves around the backstage actions of a troupe trying to put a show together, the same type of story that would make a big hit with 42ND STREET four years later. The show is about to make its out-of-town opening when the backer walks out because the coat check girl has turned him down. The producer then is unable to pay the cast or meet expenses, with more pressure added when the prima donna refuses to continue with the show until she is paid. The little money the company has is stolen by the doorman. In between all this farrago are rehearsals for the musical and dance numbers. Prime among these are two tunes sung by Ethel Waters, "Am I Blue" and "Birmingham Bertha." Crude photography and sound recording techniques acted as drawbacks to the filming of these numbers. Large camera booths were placed much too far from the stage, making for long static shots with no closeups of the performers. Compson is miscast in the lead, as she has no singing or dancing ability, forcing the use of an obvious substitute (Josephine Houston dubbed her vocals). Direction is well paced, but more effort could have been put forth in the editing room. It was

elastic-faced Brown's debut for Warner Bros., and he was roundly panned for a poor performance. Other songs include: "In the Land of Let's Pretend," "Let Me Have My Dream," "Welcome Home," "Don't It Mean a Thing to You," "Lift the Julips to My Lips," "On with the Show" (Harry Akst, Grant Clark).

d, Alan Crosland; w, Robert Lord (based on the play "Shoestring" by Humphrey Pearson); ph, Tony Gaudio; ed, Jack Killifer; ch, Larry Ceballos.

Musical   **(PR:A MPAA:NR)**

ON YOUR BACK*½   (1930) 70m FOX bw

Irene Rich (Julianne), Raymond Hackett (Harvey, Her Son), H.B. Warner (Raymond Pryer), Wheeler Oakman ("Lucky" Jim Seymour), Marion Shilling (Jeanne Burke), Ilka Chase (Dixie Mason), Charlotte Henry (Belle), Rose Dione (Mrs. Dupinnet), Arthur Hoyt (Victor).

Rich plays a struggling New York dressmaker whose ambition and desire to give her son the good life push her to success. She opens a boutique on Fifth Avenue at the time her son enters college. Rich is shocked when her son falls for a chorus girl, who later attaches herself to sugar daddy Warner and builds a big tab at Rich's boutique. The boy comes back from college still in love with the girl. Rich tries to get the girl to break it off by forcing the girl to pay her bill under the threat of exposure. The drastic change in sympathy of the Rich character, from a devoted mother to a conniving woman, hurts the flow of the story, and is not compensated for either in performances or other aspects of the script.

d, Guthrie McClintic; w, Howard J. Green (based on the story by Rita Weiman); ph, Joseph August; ed, Frank Hull; art d, Jack Schulze; cos, Sophie Wachner.

Drama   **(PR:A MPAA:NR)**

ON YOUR TOES*½   (1939) 93m WB-FN bw

Zorina (Vera), Eddie Albert (Phil Dolan, Jr.), Alan Hale (Sergei Alexandrovitch), Frank McHugh (Paddy Reilly), James Gleason (Phil Dolan, Sr.), Leonid Kinskey (Ivan Boultonoff), Gloria Dickson (Peggy Porterfield), Queenie Smith (Mrs. Dolan), Erik Rhodes (Konstantin Morrisine), Berton Churchill (Donald Henderson), Donald O'Connor (Phil as a Boy), Sarita Wooten (Vera as a Girl), Paul Hurst (Bartender), Alex Melesh (Pavlov).

Some fine talent was gathered for this picture but a dreadful script put a dull edge to the exquisite musical numbers. Albert plays a composer who has ditched vaudeville to try the legitimate theater. He becomes involved with a visiting Russian ballet company which includes his childhood sweetheart, Zorina, but trouble erupts when members of the company mistake him for a traitor. Adaptation of this Broadway hit did not take to the screen as well as would have been expected, mainly because the characters lacked the depth to carry a film. Notable in this sadly failed attempt at musical comedy is the fact that it was Norwegian Zorina's second film and her first starring role, and that her husband was at the time, Balanchine, choreographed the never-to-be-forgotten ballet sequence "Slaughter on Tenth Avenue." Also, the film marked the 12th appearance for 14-year-old O'Connor in his three years as a breezy hoofer before the cameras. Musical numbers include: "There's a Small Hotel," "Quiet Night," "On Your Toes," "Princess Zenobia Ballet" (Richard Rodgers, Lorenz Hart).

p, Robert Lord; d, Ray Enright; w, Jerry Wald, Richard Macaulay, Sig Herzig, Lawrence Riley (based on the play by Richard Rodgers, Lorenz Hart, George Abbott); ph, James Wong Howe, Sol Polito; ed, Clarence Kolster; cos, Orry-Kelly; ch, George Ballanchine.

Musical/Comedy   **(PR:A MPAA:NR)**

ONCE*   (1974) 100m Communication Design c

Christopher Mitchum (Creation), Marta Kristen (Humanity), Jim Malinda (Destruction).

An overlong, arty allegory which is played without dialog. Mitchum (son of Robert) stars as Creation and decides to give himself a companion, Kristen, the embodiment of Humanity. An attempt at idyllic surroundings is squelched by Malinda, who destroys Mitchum's creations and steals Kristen away. The finale avoids apocalypse as Creation and Humanity unite. Shot entirely on a West Coast beach with the actors wearing only loincloths.

p, Marianne Heilig, Morton Heilig; d,w&ph, Morton Heilig; m, Aminadav Aloni.

Allegory   **(PR:C MPAA:R)**

ONCE A CROOK**½   (1941, Brit.) 78m FOX bw

Gordon Harker (Charlie Hopkins), Sydney Howard (Hallelujah Harry), Kathleen Harrison (Auntie), Carla Lehmann (Estelle), Bernard Lee (The Duke), Cyril Cusack (Bill Hopkins), Diana King (Bessie), Joss Ambler (Inspector Marsh), Charles Lamb (Joseph), Raymond Huntley (Prison Governor), Felix Aylmer (King's Counsel), John Salew (Solicitor), Wally Patch (Warder), Frank Pettingell (The Captain).

Intriguing crime drama has Harker as a reformed safecracker whose former partner, Lee, sent to prison for shooting a cop, wants to get even with him. Lee's plan of attack is to set up Harker's son on a phony rap, using his daughter as bait. The son, Cusack, becomes attracted to the life of crime, having the same talents at opening a safe as his father had. But the daughter winds up falling for Cusack and points the finger at her own father to shield him. Script is shaky in spots, but sound direction by the efficient maker of family films, Mason, moves the story along. Comical Harker, always good as cop or crook, and Howard of the eccentric acting style, stately and always strange of gesture, stand out in this droll little story.

p, Edward Black; d, Herbert Mason; w, Roger Burford (based on the play by Evadne Price, Ken Atwill); ph, Arthur Crabtree.

Crime/Drama   **(PR:A MPAA:NR)**

ONCE A DOCTOR**   (1937) 59m FN-WB bw

Jean Muir (*Paula Nordland*), Donald Woods (*Steven Brace*), Gordon Oliver (*Jerry Brace*), Joseph King (*Dr. Brace, Sr.*), Henry Kolker (*Dr. Nordland*), Gordon Hart (*Dr. Lewis*), Joseph Crehan (*Capt. Andrews*), Louise Stanley (*Ruby Horton*), David Carlyle [Robert Paige] (*Dr. Burton*), Cy Kendall (*Dr. Deardon*), Ed Stanley (*Dr. Adams*), Houseley Stevenson, Sr. (*Magistrate*), Harlan Tucker (*Prosecuting Attorney*), Guy Usher (*Warden*), Thomas Pogue (*Dr. Artimus Dade*), Ed Keane (*Capt. Littleton*).

Woods and Oliver are foster brothers trying to become doctors, following in the footsteps of their father, King, a prominent surgeon. The brothers also love the same woman, tall, blonde Muir. The real son, Oliver, is a rakehell, whose lack of self confidence drives him to drink and to blame Woods for the death of a patient, causing Woods' expulsion from the medical profession. But Oliver admits his mistake and Woods is taken back in the world of medicine and wins the hand of Muir. Plot is a predictable tale of the struggles of a devoted doctor with no new insights to offer. Woods gives a good performance in a role that is too cliche-ridden to allow him to show his abilities. Another in a long series of disappointing B pictures for beautiful, warm-hearted Muir, in which her talents continued to be wasted in Hollywood. The year of ONCE A DOCTOR's release, she left Tinseltown and temporarily returned to the New York stage from where she had begun her career.

p, Bryan Foy; d, William Clemens; w, Robertson White, Ben G. Kohn (based on a story by Frank Daughterty, Paul Perez), ph, L. William O'Connell; ed, Clarence Kolster; cos, Milo Anderson.

Drama   (PR:A   MPAA:NR)

ONCE A GENTLEMAN**   (1930) 85m Sono Art-World Wide bw

Edward Everett Horton (*Oliver*), Lois Wilson (*Mrs. Mallin*), Francis X. Bushman (*Bannister*), King Baggot (*Van Warner*), Emerson Treacy (*Junior*), George Fawcett (*Col. Breen*), Frederick Sullivan (*Wadsworth*), Gertrude Short (*Dolly*), Estelle Bradley (*Gwen*), William J. Holmes (*Oglethorpe*), Cyril Chadwick (*Jarvis*), Evelyn Pierce (*Natalie*), Drew Demarest (*Timson*), William O'Brien (*Reeves*), Charles Coleman (*Wuggins*).

Horton plays a butler faithful to the same master for more than 15 yers. He takes a well-deserved vacation and is mistaken as a colonel from India, a situation he allows to ride until it lands him in hot water. Everything works out in the end, with Horton meeting a widowed housekeeper he brings back to his place of employment. Thin plot is given life and charm through a rare performance on the part of Horton and the facile direction of the energetic and reliable Cruze.

p&d, James Cruze; w, Walter Woods, Maude Fulton (based on a story by George F. Worts); ph, Jackson Rose.

Comedy   (PR:A   MPAA:NR)

ONCE A JOLLY SWAGMAN   (SEE: MANIACS ON WHEELS, 1951, Brit.)

ONCE A LADY**   (1931) 80m PAR bw

Ruth Chatterton (*Anna Keremazoff*), Ivor Novello (*Bennett Cloud*), Jill Esmond (*Faith Penwick, the Girl*), Suzanne Ransom (*Faith Penwick, the Child*), Geoffrey Kerr (*Jimmy Fenwick*), Doris Lloyd (*Lady Ellen*), Herbert Bunston (*Roger Fenwick*), Gwendolen Logan (*Mrs. Fenwick*), Stella Moore (*Alice Fenwick*), Edith Kingdon (*Caroline Gryce*), Bramwell Fletcher (*Allen Corinth*), Ethel Griffies (*Miss Bleeker*), Theodore von Eltz (*Harry Cosden*), Claude King (*Sir William Gresham*), Lillian Rich (*Jane Vernon*).

Chatterton plays a woman from Russia married to an aristocratic Englishman, by whom she has a daughter. When the man runs for Parliament, the stuffy family asks Chatterton to leave because her Russian background may prove too eccentric. Years later in Paris, Chatterton meets the daughter she left behind, without the daughter realizing Chatterton is her mother. The girl finds herself in a predicament not too dissimilar from that of her mother, in that she is in love with a man her father objects to. Chatterton offers the girl some good advice. Chatterton's performance is marred by her having to strut a phony Russian accent that does not sound in the least convincing. British matinee idol Novello, who wrote "Keep the Home Fires Burning," made his only Hollywood talkie appearance in the film, which was also marred by Britons speaking the mother tongue in accents U.S. audiences could not understand.

d, Guthrie McClintic; w, Zoe Akins, Samuel Hoffenstein (based on the play "The Second Life" by Rudolf Bernauer, Rudolf Oesterreicher); ph, Charles Lang.

Drama   (PR:A   MPAA:NR)

ONCE A RAINY DAY**½   (1968, Jap.) 85m Toho c (AKOGARE)

Michiyo Aratama, Yoko Naito, Ryo Tamura, Daisuke Kato, Nobuko Otowa, Fukuko Sayo, Shoichi Ozawa.

This Japanese picture, steeped in tradition, has a young man and woman meeting after being playmates years earlier. They discuss the childhood they had together, which was interrupted when the boy was deserted by his mother, and the girl by her father. The young couple's meeting develops into a romance, but they are separated from each other again when their relationship is met with disapproval by their guardians.

d, Hideo Onchi; w, Taichi Yamada (based on the story by Keisuke Kinoshita); ph, Aizawa Yuzuru (Tohoscope, Eastmancolor); m, Toru Takemitsu.

Drama   (PR:A   MPAA:NR)

ONCE A SINNER*½   (1931) 71m FOX bw

Dorothy Mackaill (*Diana Barry*), Joel McCrea (*Tommy Mason*), John Halliday (*Richard Kent*), C. Henry Gordon (*Serge Ratoff*), Ilka Chase (*Kitty King*), Clara Blandick (*Mrs. Mason*), Myra Hampton (*Mary Nolan*), George Brent (*James Brent*), Sally Blane (*Hope Patterson*), Ninette Faro (*Marie*), Theodore Lodi (*Pierre*).

A plodding story about Mackaill falling in love with clean-cut McCrea, then nearly losing him when her sordid past is discovered. They are a married couple living a sort of innocent bliss in the country when McCrea decides he must move to the big city if he is to get anywhere in his work as an inventor. There, he overhears a conversation about his wife having been a "kept" woman at one time and falls into a jealous rage. Of course, all is forgiven in the end. The slow pace here tries to make it seem as though there were some depth behind these characters, but there is none.

d, Guthrie McClintic; w, George Middleton; ph, Arthur L. Todd; ed, Ralph Dietrich.

Drama   (PR:A   MPAA:NR)

ONCE A SINNER*½   (1952, Brit.) 78m John Argyle/Hoffberg bw

Pat Kirkwood (*Irene James*), Jack Watling (*John Ross*), Joy Shelton (*Vera Lamb*), Sydney Tafler (*Jimmy Smart*), Thora Hird (*Mrs. James*), Humphrey Lestocq (*Lewis Canfield*), Harry Fowler (*Bill James*), Gordon McLeod, Edith Sharpe, Danny Green, R. Stuart Lindsell, Olive Sloane, George Street, Charles Paton, Stuart Latham, Rose Howlett.

Dull story about a bank clerk, Watling, who falls for Kirkwood, a girl from the wrong side of the tracks and the mistress to a counterfeiter. He marries Kirkwood, only to have her desert him when his job becomes jeopardized. Cast is adequate, but the story lacks credibility.

p, John Argyle; d, Lewis Gilbert; w, David Evans (based on the novel *Irene* by Ronald Marsh); ph, Frank North, Len Harris; m, Ronald Binge.

Drama   (PR:A   MPAA:NR)

ONCE A THIEF**   (1935, Brit.) 67m British & Dominions/PAR British bw

John Stuart (*Roger Drummond*), Nancy Burne (*Marion Ashley*), Lewis Shaw (*Frank Ashley*), Derek Gorst (*George Marston*), Frederick Culley (*Sir John Chirwin*), Lola Duncan (*Mrs. Eagle*), Joan Kemp-Welch (*Alice*), Ronald Shiner (*Man*).

A chemist, Stuart, is sent to prison when a handbag he finds and "borrows" some money from is also missing a valuable piece of jewelry. He, naturally, is implicated. His problems continue when a work associate steals a special formula of his for making paint. Upon his release from prison, Stuart hunts down the culprit and proves his innocence.

p, Anthony Havelock-Allan; d, George Pearson; w, Basil Mason (based on a story by Robert Dargavel).

Crime   (PR:A   MPAA:NR)

ONCE A THIEF*   (1950) 87m UA bw

Cesar Romero (*Mitch*), June Havoc (*Margie*), Marie McDonald (*Flo*), Lon Chaney, Jr. (*Gus*), Iris Adrian (*Pearl*), Jack Daly (*Eddie*), Marta Mitrovich (*Nickie*), Ann Tyrrell (*Dr. Borden*), Phil Arnold (*Ollie*), Kathleen Freeman (*Phoebe*), Joseph Jefferson (*Crime Lab Officer*), Michael Mark (*Milton*), Dana Wilson (*Jane*), Bill Baldwin (*Bondsman*), Peter Dunne (*Liquor Store Clerk*), Fred Kelsey (*Police Sergeant*).

Haphazard film has Havoc as a young girl who surrenders to the police after murdering Romero. She then relates the events that led up to the murder of the heel. Slack direction and plodding script turned the competent cast into lifeless characters. Director Wilder is the older brother of big moneymaker producer-director-screenwriter Billy Wilder.

p, W. Lee Wilder; d, Wilder; w, Richard S. Conway, Wilder (based on the story by Max Colpet, Hans Wilhelm); ph, William H. Clothier; ed, Asa Boyd Clark.

Crime   (PR:A   MPAA:NR)

ONCE A THIEF, 1961   (SEE: HAPPY THIEVES, THE, 1962)

ONCE A THIEF**½   (1965) 106m CIPRA-Ralph Nelson-Fred Engel/ MGM bw

Alain Delon (*Eddie Pedak*), Ann-Margret (*Kristine Pedak*), Van Heflin (*Mike Vido*), Jack Palance (*Walter Pedak*), John Davis Chandler (*James Sargatanas*), Jeff Corey (*Lt. Kebner*), Tony Musante (*Cleve Shoenstein*), Steve Mitchell (*Frank Kane*), Zekial Marko (*Luke*), Tammy Locke (*Kathy Pedak*), Russell Lee (*Drummer*), Yuki Shimoda (*John Ling*).

Author-screenwriter Marko also takes a small role in this run-of-the-mill gangland epic that is only saved by some sterling acting by the four stars. Produced by director Nelson, ex-agent Engel, and Frenchman Jacques Bar, doing his first American film, it has some nice touches, including Palance, Chandler, and Musante as three brutal killers one would not want to meet in, or even near, an alley. Delon and Ann-Margret are married with a child, Locke. Delon is an ex-con and determined to make a new life for his family and himself in San Francisco. Heflin is a police inspector who thinks Delon shot him years ago in an unsolved crime and he is eager to clap the Frenchman (who claims he is from Trieste, Italy, in order to justify his accent) in jail. Delon is framed by Chandler for a murder (we can't figure out why after seeing the film twice) and Heflin arrests Delon, then can't make the charges stick due to a lack of hard evidence. However, Delon's legit job is lost because of Heflin's doggedness, and his wife has to get a job in a tawdry North Beach nightclub. Palance is Delon's brother and he is planning a big platinum caper that will net him and his cohorts, Chandler and Musante, a cool million. Palance invites Delon to join in and he does. The robbery turns out well and they come away with the loot, but Chandler kills Palance in a double-cross and then is surprised when Delon gets away with the loot. In order to recover the money, Chandler kidnaps daughter Locke. Meanwhile, Heflin has gotten to the bottom of things and now knows Delon didn't do the killings at the top of the film. Delon calls on Heflin to help him get Locke, then admits to Heflin what he'd been denying all along—that he was the man who shot the cop so many years before. Despite that, Heflin agrees to help save Locke and does. The child is okay but Delon is killed in the gun battle while trying to shield Heflin. It's an okay crime story with the feeling that we've seen it before.

p, Jacques Bar; d, Ralph Nelson; w, Zekial Marko (based on the novel *Scratch a Thief* by Marko); ph, Robert Burks (Panavision); m, Lalo Schifrin; ed, Fredric Steinkamp; md, Schifrin; art d, George W. Davis, Paul Groesse; set d, Henry Grace, Jack Mills; makeup, William Tuttle.

Crime **(PR:C MPAA:NR)**

ONCE BEFORE I DIE*½ (1967, U.S./Phil.) F.8/Goldstone c

Ursula Andress *(Alex)*, John Derek *(Maj. Bailey)*, Rod Lauren *(Captain)*, Richard Jaeckel *(Lt. Custer)*, Ron Ely, Vance Skarstedt, Allen Pinson, Gregg Martin, Renato Robles, Fred Galang, Nello Nayo, Mario Taquibulos, Rob Francisco, Eva Vivar, Lola Boy, Armando Lucero.

WW II drama set in the Philippines has Derek as captain of a small outfit on an island which is under Japanese attack. The men, along with Derek's fiancee, Andress, attempt to escape by trekking through the jungle. But the group walks into disaster, with everyone being killed except for Andress, who continues to the beach. Picture gets its title from a sequence in which Andress has sex with a virgin soldier before the young man is killed.

p&d, John Derek; w, Vance Skarstedt (based on the story "Quit for the Next" by Anthony March); ph, Arthur Arling (Eastmancolor); m, Emanuel Vardi; ed, John Davisson; md, Vardi; m/l, title song, Norman Gimbel, Ralph London.

War **(PR:C MPAA:NR)**

ONCE IN A BLUE MOON* (1936) 65m PAR bw

Jimmy Savo *(Gabbo the Great)*, Nikita Balieff *(Gen. Onyegio)*, Cecelia Loftus *(Duchess)*, Whitney Bourne *(Nina)*, Edwina Armstrong *(Princess Ilena)*, Sandor Szabo *(Ivan)*, J. Charles Gilbert *(Captain)*, Hans Steinke *(Count Bulba)*, George Andre *(Kolia)*, Jackie Borene *("The General")*, Michael Dalmatoff *(Nikita)*.

This attempt to produce a satire on pre-Soviet Russian life style just didn't stack up. The film was marred by poor photography, unintelligible recording, and other facets of production that were below par. Savo had been billed as the new Chaplin, but this picture fails to prove he had any comic talents at all. It may not have been his fault, for if he were given something to work with he might have proved to be a worthwhile comedian.

p,d&w, Ben Hecht, Charles MacArthur; ph, Lee Garmes; m, George Antheil.

Comedy **(PR:A MPAA:NR)**

ONCE IN A LIFETIME½** (1932) 90m UNIV bw

Jack Oakie *(George Lewis)*, Sidney Fox *(Susan Walker)*, Aline MacMahon *(May Daniels)*, Russell Hopton *(Jerry Hyland)*, ZaSu Pitts *(Miss Leighton)*, Louise Fazenda *(Helen Hobart)*, Gregory Ratoff *(Herman Glogauer)*, Onslow Stevens *(Lawrence Vail)*, Robert McWade *(Mr. Walker)*, Jobyna Howland *(Mrs. Walker)*, Claudia Morgan *(Miss Chasen)*, Gregory Gaye *(Rudolph Kammerling)*, Eddie Kane *(Meterstein)*, Johnnie Morris *(Weisskopf)*, Mona Maris *(Phyllis Fontaine)*, Carol Tevis *(Florabel Leigh)*, Sam "Deacon" McDaniel *(Porter)*, Frank LaRue *(Sign Painter)*, Alan Ladd *(Projectionist)*, Margaret Lindsay *(Secretary)*, Leyland Hodgson *(Reporter)*.

Satire on Hollywood during the early talkie days has three New York vaudevillians who travel there with the get-rich-quick scheme of opening a school of elocution. One of the group, Oakie, almost immediately insults a big shot producer, Ratoff, and because of this is considered to be some sort of genius and given a job as a movie supervisor. He then goes on to make a masterpiece out of a script that had been tossed away. Picture suffers from an over-exaggeration of characters and comic details, resulting in some unsuitable slapstick. But Oakie has the energy to carry off his role well, with some topnotch back- up performances. Look for a bit part by Alan Ladd, who made his debut in this film after enrolling in a class Universal had organized to develop new talent. The original authors of the play had actually never been in Hollywood but managed to infer the material needed for the play through reading *Variety*. The impression they received of the magic land of filmmaking through these writings was that it is one of the most absurd and insane places on the map.

p, Carl Laemmle, Jr.; d, Russell Mack; w, Seton I. Miller (based on the play by Moss Hart, George S. Kaufman); ph, George Robinson.

Comedy **(PR:A MPAA:NR)**

ONCE IN A MILLION (SEE: WEEKEND MILLIONAIRE, 1937, Brit.)

ONCE IN A NEW MOON** (1935, Brit.) 63m FOX British bw

Eliot Makeham *(Harold Drake)*, Rene Ray *(Stella Drake)*, Morton Selten *(Lord Bravington)*, Wally Patch *(Syd Parrott)*, Derrick de Marney *(Hon. Bryan-Grant)*, Sir John Clements *(Edward Teale)*, Mary Hinton *(Lady Bravington)*, Gerald Barry *(Col. Fitzgeorge)*, Richard Goolden *(Rev. Benjamin Buffett)*, H. Saxon-Snell *(K. Pilkington-Bigge)*, John Turnbull *(Capt. Crump)*, Cecil Landau, Ralph Howard, Vernon Kelso, Thorley Walters, Walter Roy, Charles Paton, Franklyn Kelsey, William Fazan.

An interesting but ultimately unsatisfying picture which has a British village catapulted into space when a star collides with the moon. Makeham, scientific member of the community, is elected to head the newly formed independent state, though battles begin when the local conservatives become upset with his socialist stand. Once daring both in its content and its political tone, time has extinguished its flame. This was the first film for distinguished stage actor and director Clements, who was knighted in 1968.

d&w, Anthony Kimmins (based on a novel *Lucky Star* by Owen Rutter).

Fantasy **(PR:A MPAA:NR)**

ONCE IN PARIS ***½ (1978) 100m Leigh-McLaughlin c

Wayne Rogers *(Michael Moore)*, Gayle Hunnicutt *(Susan Townsend)*, Jack Lenoir *(Jean-Paul Barbet)*, Phillippe March *(Marcel Thery)*, Clement Harari *(Abe Wiley)*, Tanya Lopert *(Eve Carling)*, Marthe Mercadier *(Jean-Paul's Wife)*, Yves Massard *(1st Man at Party)*, Sady Rebbot *(2nd Man at Party)*, Max Fournel *(1st Waiter)*, Gerard Croce *(Mons. Farny)*, Victoria Ville *(Mme. Farny)*, Frank Peyrinaud *(Young Man at Party)*, Matt Carney *(Lars Brady)*, Doris Roberts *(His Ex-Wife)*, Jean-Jacques Charriere *(His Friend)*, Sylviane Charlet *(Woman in Restaurant)*, Pierre Dupray *(Her Friend)*, Patrick Aubree *(Desk Clerk)*, Stephane Delcher *(Bell Boy)*, Jean-Jacques Rousselet *(2nd Waiter)*, Jacques Bovanich *(1st Chauffeur)*, Henri Attal *(2nd Chauffeur)*, Beatrice Chatelier *(Girl in Car)*, Marta Andras, Chouky Sergent, Manny Fuchs *(Party Guests)*, Andre Fetet *(Freddie)*, Caroline Carliez, Edgar Croce, Nicole Teboul, Michael Teboul *(Jean-Paul's Children)*.

Highly influenced by director-writer Gilroy's own experiences when sent to Paris to work on the script for THE ONLY GAME IN TOWN. There Gilroy met Lenoir, who worked as his chauffeur. Lenoir plays a chauffeur in this production, in which Rogers is a scripter sent to Paris to try and salvage the remains of a screenplay that is in the middle of production. Rogers is told that Lenoir is not to be trusted, but discovers the contrary as the two men strike up a quick friendship, with Lenoir taking Rogers throughout Paris and giving him insights on street life. At the same time Rogers has an affair with Hunnicutt, a British aristocrat staying in the hotel room next to his. The picture is a warm, sympathetic look at the friendship between three people, joined together for a short period of time. There are few of the usual dramatic situations, but instead we are given a revelatory character study. The Parisian backdrops are hardly the usual picturesque settings we've seen in so many movies. Instead, Lenoir takes Rogers to his private haunts, the Paris that only a Parisian knows. Lenoir's casting as himself was a great break for the Moroccan-born chauffeur-actor. Until this film, he'd never done anything more than a bit role and had appeared in Woody Allen's LOVE AND DEATH a few years before. His near-flawless English came as the result of having met many American soldiers who occupied his country during the war. Lenoir came to the U.S. to plug the movie, but this film made very little noise so his dreams of becoming another Maurice Chevalier soon disappeared and he returned to Paris. This little gem was far better than the movie Gilroy worked on when he met Lenoir and stands as a good example of a superb "little picture."

p, Frank D. Gilroy, Gerard Croce, Manny Fuchs; d&w, Gilroy; ph, Claude Saunier (TVC Labs Color); m, Mitch Leigh; ed, Robert Q. Lovett.

Drama **Cas.** **(PR:C MPAA:PG)**

ONCE IS NOT ENOUGH* (1975) 121m PAR c (AKA: JACQUELINE SUSANN'S ONCE IS NOT ENOUGH)

Kirk Douglas *(Mike Wayne)*, Alexis Smith *(Deidre Milford Granger)*, David Janssen *(Tom Colt)*, George Hamilton *(David Milford)*, Melina Mercouri *(Karla)*, Gary Conway *(Hugh)*, Brenda Vaccaro *(Linda)*, Deborah Raffin *(January Wayne)*, Lillian Randolph *(Mabel, Maid)*, Renata Vanni *(Maria, Maid)*, Mark Roberts *(Rheingold)*, John Roper *(Franco)*, Leonard Sachs *(Dr. Peterson)*, Jim Boles *(Scotty)*, Ann Marie Moelders *(Girl in El Morocco)*, Trudi Marshall *(Myrna)*, Eddie Garrett *(Maitre D' Polo Lounge)*, Sid Frohlich *(Waiter)*, Kelly Lange *(Weather Lady)*, Maureen McCluskey, Harley Farber, Michael Millius, Tony Ferrara *(Four Beautiful People)*.

Dull adaptation of Susann's soaper focusing on a group of jet-setters. Douglas plays a has-been movie producer, whose only remaining desire is to please his daughter Raffin. This leads him to a marriage with the wealthy Smith, who has been involved in a lesbian love affair with Mercouri for several years. The marriage allows Raffin to live the expensive lifestyle she is used to, while being romanced by playboy Hamilton and down-and-out author Janssen. Characters are little more than stereotypes, with the film failing to give needed depth to some intense relationships.

p, Howard W. Koch; d, Guy Green; w, Julius J. Epstein (based on the novel by Jacqueline Susann); ph, John A. Alonzo (Panavision, Movielab Color); m, Henry Mancini; ed, Rita Roland; prod d, John DeCuir; set d, Ruby Levitt; cos, Moss Mabry; m/l, Larry Kusik.

Drama **(PR:O MPAA:R)**

ONCE MORE, MY DARLING½** (1949) 92m Neptune/UNIV bw

Lillian Randolph *(Mamie, the Maid)*, Robert Montgomery *(Collier Laing)*, Jane Cowl *(Mrs. Laing)*, Steven Geray *(Kalzac)*, John Ridgely *(Burke, FBI Man)*, Roland Winters *(Col. Head)*, Maurice Cass *(Dr. Grasser)*, Ann Blyth *(Marita Connell)*, Taylor Holmes *(Jed Connell)*, Charles McGraw *(Herman Schmelz, Chauffeur)*, Don Beddoe *(Judge Fraser)*, Louise Lorimer *(Mrs. Fraser)*, Wilton Graff *(Mr. Frobisher)*, Sally Corner *(Mrs. Frobisher)*, D.J. Thompson *(Mary Frobisher)*, George Carleton *(Mr. Grant)*, Edna M. Holland *(Mrs. Grant)*, Ray Teal *(Truck Driver)*, Bert Hicks *(Peter Vellon)*, Ann Pearce *(Receptionist)*, Barbara Payton *(Girl Photographer)*, John Harmon *(Georgie)*, George Chandler *(Motel Proprietor)*, Jack Overman *(Grip)*, Bert Conway *(Assistant Director)*, Maurice Marsac *(Henri)*, Del Henderson *(Hotel Clerk)*, William Vedder *(Alfred)*, Michael Cisney *(Alfred)*, Phyllis Kennedy *(Waitress)*, Isabel Withers *(Woman)*, Jim Toney *(Fruit Dealer)*, Donald Gordon *(Kid)*, John Pickard *(Inspector)*, James Linn *(Gaffer)*, Jack Gargan *(Mixer)*, Betty Roche *(Script Clerk)*, Robert Coudy *(Parking Attendant)*.

Montgomery starred in and directed this farce in which he plays an actor-lawyer called up for a special assignment. His job is to romance Blyth in order to figure out where she received the Nazi jewelry she wears. Montgomery is reluctant to take up the assignment, which becomes even more intense when he realizes what Blyth is really like—an uninhibited and romantic girl. Within 24 hours the pair elopes to Las Vegas, followed closely behind by a number of concerned parties. Direction is shaky in some parts, but the script is filled with fast and witty dialog. Blyth proves to be able to handle a comic role well, giving her character plenty of life.

p, Joan Harrison; d, Robert Montgomery; w, Robert Carson, Oscar Saul (based on the story "Come Be My Love" by Carson); ph, Frank Planer; m, Elizabeth Firestone; ed, Ralph Dawson; md, Frank Skinner; art d, Bernard Herzbrun, Bert Clatworthy; set d, Russell A. Gausman, Ruby R. Levitt; cos, Orry Kelly; spec eff, David S. Horsley; makeup, Bud Westmore, John Holden.

Comedy **(PR:A MPAA:NR)**

ONCE MORE, WITH FEELING*** (1960) 92m COL c

Yul Brynner *(Victor Fabian)*, Kay Kendall *(Dolly Fabian)*, Gregory Ratoff *(Maxwell Archer)*, Geoffrey Toone *(Dr. Hilliard)*, Maxwell Shaw *(Jascha Gendel/Grisha Gendel)*, Mervyn Johns *(Mr. Wilbur, Jr.)*, Martin Benson *(Bardini)*, Harry Lockhart *(Chester)*, Shirley Ann Field *(Angela Hopper)*, Grace Newcombe *(Mrs. Wilbur)*, C.S. Stuart *(Manning)*, Colin Drake *(Doctor)*, Andrew Paulds *(Interviewer)*, C.E. Joy *(Sir Austin Flapp)*, Barbara Hall *(Secretary)*.

"Once more, with feeling" is a musical expression usually shouted by conductors after the orchestra has failed to bring bravura to their rehearsal. This was Kay Kendall's last luminous moment on the screen, as she died less than 90 days after the picture finished shooting, although you'd never know whe was suffering from leukemia by the way she darted around the sets, delivering the crackling dialog with elan. Kendall and Brynner are long-time mates and he is an insufferable and temperamental conductor of the London Symphony given to breaking batons and puncturing personalities with his saber-sharp tongue. He is also very talented and that allows him to get away with such petulance. Kendall spends most of her time balming bruised egos and repairing torn pride. She adores him and will tolerate all of his often-childish behavior. The only thing she will *not* allow is his trifling with another woman. And when Brynner takes the opportunity to dally with Field, a hot-blooded and determined young pianist, Kendall storms out of their relationship and remains out, despite his constant attempts to win her back. Immediately, his life begins to come apart at the seams. Brynner and his agent, Ratoff, tell the bosses at the symphony that Kendall is returning to the fold so they'll renew Brynner's contract. The truth is that Kendall has taken up with Toone, a physicist, and is planning to marry him. She returns to Brynner's side to arrange for a divorce from him, and while she's there, manages to persuade his bosses to renew. Brynner now tells her that, if she recalls (and how she couldn't recall *this*, we'll never know), they never actually got married. If she wants to get the divorce papers legally, she'll have to first marry him in order to do that. The marriage takes place and the expected happens as the two of them fall in love again and Kendall finds Brynner's presence so exhilarating that she realizes Toone is a lump of meat by comparison. The play was set in New York and Kurnitz switched it to Europe to accommodate the accents of the leads. Great fun, scintillating words, and plenty of good music from Sousa, Wagner, Liszt, Beethoven, and many others. Preston Sturges touched upon the same egomaniacal conductor in UNFAITHFULLY YOURS with Kendall's husband, Rex Harrison, in that role. Mervyn Johns, as the symphony's chief benefactor, gets one of the funniest lines when he rushes in looking for Brynner, spies a musician, and says, "Take me to your leader!"

p&d, Stanley Donen; w, Harry Kurnitz (based on his play); ph, Georges Perinal (Technicolor); m, Ludwig van Beethoven, Franz Liszt, Richard Wagner, John Philip Sousa; ed, Jack Harris; prod d, Alex Trauner; md, Muir Mathieson; cos, Givenchy.

Comedy **(PR:A-C MPAA:NR)**

ONCE THERE WAS A GIRL*** (1945, USSR) 71m Soyuzdet/Artkino bw

Nina Ivanova *(Nastenka)*, Natasha Zashipina *(Katia)*, Ada Voyst Voystik *(Nastenka's Mother)*, Vera Altaiskaya *(Katia's Mother)*, Leda Shtykan *(Tonja)*, Alexander Larinov *(Makar Ivanovich)*, Nikolai Korn *(Nastenka's Father)*.

Starkly realistic portrayal of the plight of two girls, 9-year-old Ivanova and 5-year-old Zashipina, during the seige of Russia by the Nazis in WW II. The girls have close encounters with death several times, yet manage to live through it all. The story's slow pace helps to enforce just what type of turmoil the girls had to face. (In Russian; English subtitles.)

d, Victor Eisimont; w, Vladimir Nedobrovo; ph, George Gariblan.

War **(PR:C MPAA:NR)**

ONCE TO EVERY BACHELOR** (1934) 72m Liberty bw

Marian Nixon, Neil Hamilton, William Austin, Raymond Hatton, Aileen Pringle, Bradley Page, Kathleen Howard, Ralf Harolde, George Irving, Don Alvarado.

Nixon plays a young girl caught up with a group of gangsters. To throw police off her trail, she takes up with society man Hamilton. He hopes it will help him shake off his affair with a married woman, a relationship that worries his wealthy aunt. Though at first only looking for an escape from their problems, the two eventually fall in love. Good cast is unable to take up the slack in this rather weak story.

p, M.H. Hoffman; d, William Nigh; w, George Waggner (based on a story by Eleanor Gates); ph, Harry Neumann; ed, Mildred Johnston.

Drama **(PR:A MPAA:NR)**

ONCE TO EVERY WOMAN** (1934) 70m COL bw

Ralph Bellamy *(Dr. Barclay)*, Fay Wray *(Head Nurse Fanshawe)*, Walter Connolly *(Dr. Selby)*, Mary Carlisle *(Doris Andros)*, Walter Byron *(Dr. Preston)*, J. Farrell MacDonald *(Flannigan)*, Billie Seward *(No. 5)*, Kathrin Clare Ward *(Mrs. Flannigan)*, Mary Foy *(Miss Baxter)*, Ben Alexander *(Joe)*, Rebecca Wassam *(Gail Drake)*, Leila Bennett *(Sally)*, Jane Darwell *(Mrs. Wood)*, Nora Cecil *(Baxter's Sister)*, Ed Le Saint *(Priest)*.

Bellamy plays a young doctor and protege to Connolly, an aging medic who refuses to realize his time is almost up. That is, until he attempts to perform a delicate brain operation in which Bellamy must push his superior out of the way in order to complete it successfully himself. Story suffers from some unbelievable moments and shaky direction, but a good cast helps the picture through.

d, Lambert Hillyer; w, Jo Swerling (based on the story by A.J. Cronin); ph, John Stumar; ed, Richard Cahoon.

Drama **(PR:A MPAA:NR)**

ONCE UPON A COFFEE HOUSE*½ (1965) 91m Fred Berney c

Vince Martin *(Rival)*, Karen Thorsell *(Coffee House Barmaid)*, Curtis Taylor *(Playboy)*, Jerry Newby *(Coffee House Owner)*, Pedro Roman, Eve Tellegen, Oscar Brand, John Rivers, Deanna Lund, Sherry Lou Shepherd, The Goldebriars, The Freewheelers, Jim, Jake and Joan.

Taylor is a rich playboy who meets and falls in love with Thorsell, the folksinging barmaid of a Miami coffeehouse. Her boss tries to persuade Taylor to buy his business so the couple can be near one another, while rival Martin makes a pain of himself, jealously believing Thorsell has posed in the nude for Taylor.

p, Fred Berney; d, Shepherd Traube; w, Carl Yale; ph, (Eastmancolor); ch, Johnny Conrad; m/l, Yale.

Drama **(PR:A MPAA:NR)**

ONCE UPON A DREAM** (1949, Brit.) 87m Rank/GFD bw

Googie Withers *(Mrs. Carol Gilbert)*, Griffith Jones *(Jackson)*, Guy Middleton *(Maj. Gilbert)*, Betty Lynne *(Mlle. Louise)*, David Horne *(Registrar)*, Geoffrey Morris *(Registrar's Clerk)*, Raymond Lovell *(Mr. Trout)*, Noel Howlett *(Solicitor)*, Agnes Lauchlan *(Aunt Agnes)*, Mirren Wood *(Conductress)*, Hubert Gregg *(Capt. Williams)*, Maurice Denham *(Vicar)*, Mona Washbourne *(Vicar's Wife)*, Gibb McLaughlin *(Pontefact)*, Dora Bryan *(Barmaid)*, Anthony Steel, Nora Nicholson, Hal Osmond, Arthur Denton, Eric Messiter, Cecil Bevan, Wilfred Caithness.

Lighthearted story has attractive comedy star Withers dreaming she's been involved in an affair with one of her husband's wartime aides, now his domestic servant, only to wake up the next morning to think that her dream was a reality. Predictable zaniness follows, kept on track by capable commercial-oriented director Thomas.

p, Antony Darnborough; d, Ralph Thomas; w, Patrick Kirwan, Victor Katona; ph, Jack Cox, Len Harris; m, Manning Sherwin; ed, Jean Barker; art d, George Provis; cos, Julie Harris.

Comedy **(PR:A MPAA:NR)**

ONCE UPON A HONEYMOON*½ (1942) 117m RKO bw

Ginger Rogers *(Katie O'Hara)*, Cary Grant *(Pat O'Toole)*, Walter Slezak *(Baron Von Luber)*, Albert Dekker *(LeBlanc)*, Albert Basserman *(Gen. Borelski)*, Ferike Boros *(Elsa)*, Harry Shannon *(Cumberland)*, John Banner *(Kleinoch)*, Natash Lytess *(Anna the Hotel Maid)*, Peter Seal *(Polish Orderly)*, Major Nichols, Dina Smirnova, Alex Davidoff, Leda Nicova *(Travelers in Warsaw)*, Ace Bragunier *(Plane Pilot)*, Emil Ostlin *(German Captain)*, Del Henderson *(American Attache)*, Carl Ekberg *(Hitler)*, Fred Niblo *(Ship Captain)*, Oscar Lorraine *(Ship Steward)*, Claudine De Luc *(Hotel Proprietor)*, Brandon Beach *(Civilian)*, Russell Gaige, Gohr Van Vleck Walter Stahl, *(Baron's Guests)*, Joe Diskay *(Warsaw Desk Clerk)*, Eugene Marum *(Anna's Son)*, Gordon Clark, Jack Martin, Manart Kippen, George Sorel, Walter Bonn, Bill Martin, Arno Frey, Hans Von Twardowski *(German Officers)*, Lionel Royce *(Marshal Mocha)*, Jacques Vanaire *(French Radio Announcer)*, Frank Alten *(Spontaneity)*, Boyd Davis *(Chamberlain)*, Emory Parnell *(Quisling)*, Albert Petit, Eddie Licho *(French Waiters)*, Bob O'Connor *(Polish Operator)*, Rudolph Myzet, Joseph Kamaryt *(Czech Officials)*, George Irving *(American Consul)*, Hans Schumm, Hans Furberg, Bob Stevenson, Henry Victor, Fred Aldrich, Johnny Dime, Henry Guttman *(Storm Troopers)*, Alex Melesh *(Hotel Clerk in Warsaw/Bar Waiter)*, Felix Basch *(Herr Kelman)*, Fred Giermann, Ernst Hausman *(Germans)*, Otto Reichow *(German Private)*, John Peters *(Kleinoch's Driver)*, Hans Conried *(French Fitter)*, William Vaughn *(German Colonel)*, Walter Byron *(Guard)*, Hans Wollenberger *(Waiter)*, Bert Roach *(Bartender)*.

This was a flawed attempt at the TO BE OR NOT TO BE genre, mixing comedy with Nazis. The two are as compatible as escargot and sauerkraut. It's 1938 and Grant is an American radio broadcaster (like Ed Murrow) in Europe, where he's reporting on the approaching war. Rogers is a Brooklyn girl who'd spent some time peeling off her clothes for bald men but she's now posing as a society woman and has married Slezak, a big man in the Nazi scheme of things. She doesn't know that and thinks he's just a rich Austrian nobleman. His job is to help the Hitler gang get into the other countries. Grant knows Slezak is a member of the hierarchy, and as he and Rogers get closer, she leaves with him during a bombing in Poland and they race across Scandinavia and wind up in France where they join forces with Dekker, an American spy, to help fight the Germans. Grant and Rogers leave for the U.S. and Slezak drowns as he's on his way to spy in the States. The few comedy scenes are funny but there is a lot of talk and no action in most of the other sequences. It's far too realistic to be comedic (in the Nazi scenes) and not consistently funny to be mirthful. They spent some money making the picture and the use of newsreel clips was excellent. Taken section by section, the parts add up to somewhat more than the whole.

p&d, Leo McCarey; w, Sheridan Gibney (based on a story by Gibney, McCarey); ph, George Barnes; m, Robert Emmett Dolan; ed, Theron Warth; art d, Albert S. D'Agostino, Al Herman; set d, Darrell Silvera, Claude E. Carpenter; spec eff, Vernon L. Walker; makeup, Mel Burns.

Drama/Comedy **Cas.** **(PR:A MPAA:NR)**

ONCE UPON A HORSE** (1958) 85M UNIV bw (AKA: HOT HORSE)

Dan Rowan *(Dan Casey)*, Dick Martin *(Doc Logan)*, Martha Hyer *(Miss Amity Babb)*, Leif Erickson *(Granville Dix)*, Nita Talbot *(Miss Dovey Barnes)*, James Gleason *(Postmaster)*, John McGiver *(Mr. Tharp)*, Paul Anderson *(Blacksmith)*, David Burns *(Bruno de Gruen)*, Dick Ryan *(Henry Dick Coryell)*, Max Baer *(Ben)*,

Buddy Baer *(Beulah's Brother)*, Steve Pendleton *(Milligan)*, Sydney Chatton *(Engineer)*, Sam Hearn *(Justice of the Peace)*, Ingrid Goude *(Beulah)*, Ricky Kelman *(Small Boy)*, Joe Oakie *(Fireman)*, Tom Keene, Bob Livingston, Kermit Maynard, Bob Steele *(Themselves)*.

Cult comedians Rowan and Martin made their film debut in this farcical look at the western film. The two are cowpokes who can't decide whether to turn criminal or go straight. Neither way really matters, because they are unsuccessful no matter what their path. Weak story was just a structure for a number of gags, many genuinely funny. Rowan and Martin were later to achieve fame as the cohosts for their popular television series "Rowan and Martin's Laugh-In."

p,d&w, Hal Kanter (based on a story by Henry Gregor Felsen); ph, Arthur E. Arling (CinemaScope); m, Frank Skinner; ed, Milton Carruth; md, Joseph Gershenson; art d, Alexander Golitzen, Robert Clatworthy; cos, Bill Thomas; spec eff, Clifford Stine; m/l, Jay Livingston, Ray Evans.

Comedy **(PR:A MPAA:NR)**

ONCE UPON A SCOUNDREL½** (1973) 90m Carlyle c

Zero Mostel *(Carlos del Refugio)*, Katy Jurado *(Aunt Delfina)*, Titos Vandis *(Dr. Fernandez)*, Priscilla Garcia *(Alicia)*, A. Martinez *(Luis)*.

Unpretentious, charming story stars Mostel as a wealthy Mexican land baron, madly in love with young Garcia. To get her fiance out of the way, Mostel accuses him of stealing a duck, thus sending the youth to prison. The traditional law states that the young man cannot be released until Mostel forgives him, which Mostel doesn't plan on doing. Fearing that she will never see her loved one again, Garcia and her aunt, Jurado, conceive a plan which will make Mostel believe himself to be dead—that he is just a wandering souls who can never rest in peace. Mostel ultimately repents and frees the fiance, then goes on to do good deeds everywhere. Exceptional photography blends in the beautiful Mexican scenery very well with the story.

p, James S. Elliot; d, George Schaefer; w, Rip Van Ronkel; ph, Gabriel Figueroa; m, Alex North; ed, Albert Valenzuela; cos, Noel Taylor.

Comedy **Cas.** **(PR:A MPAA:G)**

ONCE UPON A SUMMER (SEE: GIRL WITH GREEN EYES, 1964, Brit.)

ONCE UPON A THURSDAY (SEE: AFFAIRS OF MARTHA, 1942)

ONCE UPON A TIME*½ (1944) 89m Alexander Hall/COL bw

Cary Grant *(Jerry Flynn)*, Janet Blair *(Jeannie Thompson)*, James Gleason *(The Moke)*, Ted Donaldson *(Pinky Thompson)*, Howard Freeman *(McKenzie)*, William Demarest *(Brandt)*, Art Baker *(Gabriel Heatter)*, Paul Stanton *(Dunhill)*, Mickey McGuire *(Fatso)*, Ed Gargan, Harry Strang, Billy Bevan *(Cops)*, Cliff Clark, Emory Parnell *(Radio Cops)*, Torben Meyer *(Hotel Manager)*, William Austin *(Assistant Hotel Manager)*, Isabel Withers, Almeda Fowler, Nell Keller *(Women)*, Lane Chandler *(Doorman)*, Esther Howard, Eddie Bruce *(Clerks)*, Nolan Leary *(Elevator Man)*, John Abbott, Ian Wolfe, Jack Lee, Charles Arnt *(Reporters)*, Don Barclay, Fred Howard *(Photographers)*, Alex Melesh, George Davis *(Waiters)*, William Gould *(Editor)*, George Eldredge, Dick Gordon, Lewis Wilson, Freeman Wood, Cy Ring *(Men)*, Pedro de Cordoba, Vaughan Glaser, Erwin Kaiser *(Scientists)*, Lucille Brown *(Miss Flemmin)*, Anne Loos, Mary Currier *(Secretaries)*, Charles Bates, Hugh McGuire, Tom Brown, Gary Gray, Cecil Weston *(Bits)*, Garry Owen *(Mug)*, Harrison Greene, George Anderson, John Dilson, James Flavin, Emmett Vogan, Vernon Dent *(Business Men)*, Nelroy Ashley *(Business Woman)*, Christian Rub *(Janitor)*, Robert Williams *(Stage Manager)*, Vi Athens, Marilyn Johnson, Sybil Merritt, June Millarde, Thelma Joel *(Chorus Girls)*, Ronnie Rondell, Robert Tafur *(Gauchos)*, Lionel Braham *(Weight Lifter)*, Joseph Greene *(Rajah Pirate)*, Murray Alper *(Soldier)*, Iris Adrian *(Girl)*, Tom Kennedy, John Kelly *(Truckmen)*, Spec O'Donnell, John Tyrrell *(Ushers)*, Pierre Watkin *(Radio Stage Manager)*, Alan Stone *(Radio Technician)*, Phyllis Kennedy, Sandra Coles, Eula Guy, Grace Lenard, Pauline Drake *(Telephone Operators)*, Syd Saylor *(Shipyard Worker)*, Tom Dugan *(Police Announcer)*, Buddy Yarus *(Jitterbug)*, Jeff Donnell *(Brooklyn Girl)*, Fern Emmett *(Teacher Type)*, Ida Moore *(Gossipy Woman)*, Mary Field, Barbara Pepper *(Taxi Girls)*, William Yip, Jing Lim *(Chinese Men)*, Ruth Warren *(Fatso's Mother)*, Ray Teal, Eddie Acuff *(Shipyard Workers)*, Charles Coleman, Leonard Carey *(English Bobbies)*, Norval Mitchell *(Masseur)*, Charles Waldron *(Preacher)*, Walter Pietila, George Bruggeman *(Trapeze Artists)*, Eddie Hall *(Bike Rider)*, Frank Hagney *(Assistant Cyclist)*, Clyde Fillmore *(FBI Executive)*, Kirk Alyn *(Attendant)*, Walter Fenner *(Walt Disney Double)*, Bill Chaney, Lawrence Lathrop *(Call Boys)*, Henry Armetta *(Barber)*, Jack Norton *(Customer)* Lloyd Bridges *(Captain)*, George Neise, Robert Lowell *(Lieutenants)*, Gary Bruce *(Technical Sergeant)*.

Based on a radio play by Norman Corwin (from an idea by Lucille Fletcher Herrmann), this film should have stayed a radio play. Attempting to expand it to a film was a mistake, despite the frantic attempts by Grant and the rest of the cast to elevate it to a passable farce. Grant is a quick-witted producer in grave financial trouble. His theater is about to be shuttered and he doesn't know what to do. Standing on a New York street, he throws a nickel over his shoulder and it's picked up by Donaldson (making his debut). The young lad carries a shoe box and opens it to show Grant a caterpillar that dances when Donaldson plays "Yes Sir, That's My Baby." Grant thinks he can use this fuzzy terpsichorean to his advantage, maybe even get his theater back from the bankers. (Baker) Gabriel Heatter (he was a famous news man on radio who began each broadcast with "Ah yes, there's good news tonight!") hears about the phenomenon and details the story on his broadcast as part of the human interest segment. The radio show is listened to by everyone and Grant, Donaldson, and the caterpillar become overnight sensations. Donaldson's guardian-sister, Blair, doesn't like the publicity and lets Grant know that in no uncertain terms. The moment these two battle we know that they'll be clinching at the fadeout. Grant makes a deal with Walt Disney, (Fenner) for $100,000 but backs out at the last minute, understanding at last how low he has sunk. The caterpillar has flown the box and no one can find him; Donaldson is heartbroken. Grant attempts to get into Donaldson's good graces, but the boy will have none of it. At the end, Grant sits at a piano and begins tinkling "Yes Sir, That's My Baby" and a colorful butterfly makes its way out of a cocoon. Donaldson is called for, plays his harmonica, and the butterfly responds to the music. At the close, everything wraps with Grant and Blair and Donaldson preparing to be a happy, if caterpillar-less, family. The fairy-tale title gives away the nature of the material.

p, Louis Edelman; d, Alexander Hall w, Lewis Meltzer, Oscar Saul, Irving Fineman (based on the radio play, "My Client Curly" by Norman Corwin, Lucille Fletcher Herrmann); ph, Franz F. Planer; m, Frederick Hollander; ed, Gene Havlick; md, M.W. Stoloff; art d, Lionel Banks, Edward Jewell; set d, Robert Priestley; m/1, "Yes Sir, That's My Baby," Walter Donaldson, Gus Kahn.

Comedy **(PR:A MPAA:NR)**

ONCE UPON A TIME (SEE: MORE THAN A MIRACLE 1967, Fr./Ital.)

ONCE UPON A TIME IN THE WEST***** (1969, U.S./Ital.) 165m Rafran-San Marco/PAR c

Henry Fonda *(Frank)*, Claudia Cardinale *(Jill McBain)*, Jason Robards, Jr. *(Cheyenne)*, Charles Bronson *(The Man "Harmonica")*, Frank Wolff *(Brett McBain)*, Gabriele Ferzetti *(Morton)*, Keenan Wynn *(Sheriff)*, Paolo Stoppa *(Sam)*, Marco Zuanelli *(Wobbles)*, Lionel Stander *(Barman)*, Jack Elam *(Knuckles)*, Woody Strode *(Stony)*, John Frederick *(Member of Frank's Gang)*, Enzo Santianello *(Timmy)*, Dino Mele *(Harmonica as a Boy)*, Benoit Stefanelli, Salvo Basile, Aldo Berti, Luigi Ciavarro, Livio Andronico, Marco Zuanelli, Marilu Carteny, Spartaco Conversi.

Simply stated, this is Sergio Leone's masterpiece. In ONCE UPON A TIME IN THE WEST, Leone pulls together all the themes, characterizations, visuals, humor, and musical experiments of the three "Dollars" films and comes up with a true epic western. It is a stunning, operatic film of breadth, detail, and stature that deserves to be considered among the greatest westerns ever made. Though the film's original release in America was a severely edited version (Paramount wanted to cram an extra show in every night to sell more popcorn) the film was re-released in 1984 uncut. The videotape is uncut as well, and it is this version that will be described here. ONCE UPON A TIME IN THE WEST's credit sequence is perhaps one of the most famous in cinema history. It unfolds slowly, deliberately as Leone lingers on the strange behavior of Fonda's three hired killers (two of whom are Elam and Strode in unforgettable cameos) who await the arrival of a train containing Bronson, a stranger who has asked for an audience with Fonda. The slow rhythmic squeak of a rusty windmill provides an eerie accompaniment to the scene as the three gunmen occupy themselves while waiting for the train to arrive. The set pieces: water dripping on Strode's bald head, Elam trying to shoo a pesty fly, and the third member of the gang cracking his knuckles, bring a vital, detailed life to the scene accompanied by an almost unbearable sense of anticipation. Today's Spielberg-ized audiences, one supposes, couldn't sit still for this supposed lack of "action". Suddenly the sound of a shrill train whistle cuts through the tension like a knife and heralds the arrival of Bronson. When the train pulls out, it leaves Bronson on the opposite side of the tracks, playing a tuneless, mournful song on his harmonica. When Bronson realizes that these men have no intention of bringing him to a meeting with Fonda, he guns them down without batting an eye. From this opening, the film shifts to the lonely McBain farm where Wolff prepares himself and his three children for the arrival of his new wife, Cardinale, a whore whom he met in New Orleans. Before Wolff's eldest son has a chance to go to the station, a shot rings out and the farmer's daughter falls dead. In a matter of seconds the entire family is wiped out by unseen assassins with the exception of Wolff's nine-year-old son who comes running out of the house to investigate. Accompanied by the chilling electric guitar chords of composer Ennio Morricone, the killers emerge from the brush, dust swirling around them. The men are dressed in tan-colored, ankle-length "dusters," and as they approach the scene of their carnage, we see that their leader is none other than Henry Fonda. He stares at the small boy coolly. One of his henchman asks, "What do we do with this one, Frank?" Fonda spits, glances at his men, and calmly states, "Now that you called me by name. . .," gives the boy a reassuring smile and shoots him. From this point on the film expands into a land war between Cardinale (aided by Bronson and charming outlaw Robards) and Fonda who is employed by crippled railroad magnate Ferzetti to "clear the tracks." Cardinale inherits the land from her murdered husband and learns that he intended to build a lucrative train station on the property because it contains water necessary for the railroad. Ferzetti, of course, wants the land for free. Where Robards helps Cardinale because he admires (or loves?) her, Bronson's motives are much darker. He wants Fonda for mysterious reasons of his own. Fonda, however, has ambitious plans and Bronson's pursuit of him is a mild annoyance. An aging gunfighter, he becomes fascinated with Ferzetti's money and power and decides to become a "businessman" by slowly pushing the crippled railroad man out of the picture. Unfortunately for Fonda, he fails to understand that in the new America money is more powerful than the gun. When Ferzetti realizes that Fonda is trying to take over, he buys off some of Fonda's own men to assassinate him. Bronson, of course, sees that Fonda's own men are about to ambush him, so he helps the gunfighter survive. This finally pushes Fonda over the brink and he decides to abandon his grandiose ambitions to pursue Bronson. Meanwhile, Robards has gathered his men and slaughtered Fonda's henchmen—a massacre that kills Ferzetti as well. The film's major concerns and characters finally all assemble at the McBain farm, with Cardinale's train station and the railroad tracks nearby. Robards, wounded from the battle, visits Cardinale for the last time and they both watch the confrontation between Fonda and Bronson from the house. Fonda admits to Bronson, "Morton (Ferzetti) once told me I could never be like him. Now I understand why. It wouldn't have bothered him knowing you were around somewhere alive." Bronson responds, "So you found out you weren't a businessman after all."

Fonda states that he's, "Just a man." Bronson muses that they are an ancient race that's dying out. Fonda finally asks Bronson who he is and what it is he wants. Bronson says he'll only know ". . .at the point of dyin'." In the long-standing Leone tradition, the men square off against each other in a circular area and just as they are about to draw, we cut to a flash-back (presumably shared by both men) which shows a much younger Fonda grinning malevolently at a man with a noose around his neck who is standing on the shoulders of his younger brother. The young man is obviously tired and struggles mightily to support his sibling. Fonda shoves a harmonica in the boy's mouth and says, "Keep your lovin' brother happy." Fonda's henchmen laugh. The older brother looks at his torturers with disgust, utters a final epithet and purposely kicks his brother out from under him, sending the boy face down in the dust, while hanging himself. It is obvious that the young boy is Bronson. Leone cuts to Bronson shooting Fonda once in the heart before the evil man can even draw his gun. As Fonda lies dying, Bronson takes the harmonica he has carried since that day so many years ago, and shoves it in Fonda's mouth. Fonda finally understands and breathes his last breath into the harmonica. Having completed his long-standing vendetta, Bronson enters Cardinale's house to get his gear. Though it is obvious she would like him to stay, she lets him go. Robards leaves as well and joins Bronson. Not far from the house, Robards' wounds prove too much and he falls off his horse. Dying, he tells Bronson to go away and let him die alone. Bronson does as requested and after Robards has died, he rides off into the desert with his friend's body head down over a saddle, leaving Cardinale to serve water to the thirsty workers bringing the railroad to the West. The paths Leone was struggling to develop in his previous three westerns finally merge and take shape in one of the most original and stunning westerns ever made. Called a "Dance of Death" by some critics, the film is an operatic eulogy for the western hero. Leone's men are titans of mythic stature, ". . .an ancient race," as Bronson states, and ONCE UPON A TIME IN THE WEST deals with their demise. By the end of the film, all the major male characters are dead (except for Bronson, but one gets the impression he is riding off to die somewhere) leaving a woman, Cardinale, to build this brave new world. Guns are no longer needed, only money, the railroad, and water. From the beginning, Leone wanted to make a western that was different from the "Dollars" films. United Artists offered Leone such major stars as Kirk Douglas, Gregory Peck, and Charlton Heston, but the director was already feeling some unpleasant pressure from the studio, and he really wanted to work with Henry Fonda, so he took his picture to Paramount. Leone had been courting Fonda since A FISTFUL OF DOLLARS, because he wanted to exploit the underlying hardness he found in the actor's performances, especially in the westerns of John Ford. Unfortunately all the scripts Leone submitted to Fonda were badly translated from Italian to English and were a nightmare to read. Fonda's reaction was the same to the script for ONCE UPON A TIME IN THE WEST, but on a hunch he called his friend Eli Wallach, who had worked with Leone on THE GOOD, THE BAD AND THE UGLY. Wallach told Fonda to ignore the script and do the film because Leone was a "genius." Soon Fonda arranged for a private screening of Leone's previous work and sat through all three "Dollars" films in one afternoon. Excited by the uniqueness and humor he found in the films, Fonda agreed to play the villain for Leone. In the weeks before Fonda was due on the set, the actor acquired a set of contact lenses that would turn his blue eyes to brown, and he grew a thick, dark moustache so that he would appear more villainous. When Fonda arrived on the set, Leone took one horrified look at Fonda and insisted that the brown eyes and moustache be taken off immediately. He wanted the Fonda face that the movie-going public throughout the world loved so well. Besides the casting of Fonda as a cold-blooded killer, one of the other major distinctions of ONCE UPON A TIME IN THE WEST is its brilliant musical score. Composed by Ennio Morricone (who had also written the memorable music for the director's other westerns), the score contains distinct themes for each of the four main characters (tuneless harmonica for Bronson, biting electric guitar for Fonda, humorous banjo for Robards, and a lush, romantic score for Cardinale). Perhaps the most unusual aspect of the score is the fact that Morricone composed it on the basis of the script, and it was done before one frame of film was exposed. Leone loved the music and played it on the set for all the actors so that they could adapt their body rhythms to the music that would be played over their performance. By using this rather unorthodox method of scoring a film (or perhaps one should say filming a score) Leone and Morricone created the most complete integration of music, movement, and visual imagery to be found in Hollywood films. Despite the undeniably brilliant result of his visuals, themes, casting, and music, Leone's epic western was dumped by an American studio system that didn't understand it. Cut to pieces in order to shorten its length, the editing rendered the original U.S. release almost unintelligible, which confused critics and ensured that it would bomb at the box office. In Europe, however, where the film was released intact, it did fantastic business and even broke all box office records in Paris where it played steadily for *four* years. (The film even started a fashion craze—everyone in Paris wanted the western "dusters" worn by Fonda's and Robards' men.) Finally, in 1984, Paramount re-released the film uncut and it is only now getting the respect from American critics it truly deserves.

p, Fulvio Morsella; d, Sergio Leone; w, Leone, Sergio Donati (based on a story by Dario Argento, Bernardo Bertolucci, Leone); ph, Tonino Delli Colli (Techniscope, Technicolor); m, Ennio Morricone; ed, Nino Baragli; md, Morricone; art d, Carlo Simi; set d, Carlo Leva; cos, Simi; makeup, Alberto De Rossi.

Western   **Cas.**   **(PR:O   MPAA:M)**

ONCE YOU KISS A STRANGER*   (1969) 106m WB-Seven Arts c

Paul Burke *(Jerry)*, Carol Lynley *(Diana)*, Martha Hyer *(Lee)*, Peter Lind Hayes *(Peter)*, Philip Carey *(Mike)*, Stephen McNally *(Lt. Gavin)*, Whit Bissell *(Dr. Haggis)*, Elaine Debry *(Sharon)*, Kathryn Givney *(Aunt Margaret)*, Jim Raymond *(Johnny Parker)*, George Fenneman *(Announcer)*, Orville Sherman *(Raymond)*, Maura McGiveney *(Harriet Parker)*, Ann Doran *(Lee's Mother)*.

Remake of Alfred Hitchcock's STRANGERS ON A TRAIN, but with the madman

Bruno being replaced by the pretty psychotic, Lynley. Lynley seduces golf pro Burke at a country club, then suggests to him that she will murder his arch rival if he kills the psychiatrist who wants to commit her to an asylum. Thinking her to be joking, Burke agrees only to find out later that Lynley had recorded the conversation and now threatens to blackmail him if he does not go through with the bargain. Lynley kills the golfing rival, Carey, by running him over with a golf cart, then continues pestering Burke until he confers with her psychiatrist. Neither Lynley nor Burke are believable in their roles, with little support from the rest of the cast. What suspense the story has comes through chase sequences or other such moments; the plot carries little. Director Sparr died three months before the official release of ONCE YOU KISS A STRANGER, from injuries he received while hunting locations for another film.

p, Harold A. Goldstein; d, Robert Sparr; w, Frank Tarloff, Norman Katkov (based on the novel *Stranger On A Train* by Patricia Highsmith); ph, Jacques Marquette (Movielab Color); m, Jimmie Fagas; ed, Marjorie Fowler; md, Fagas; art d, Art Loel; set d, Jerry Miggins; m/l, title song, Fagas, Ken Darby (sung by Dick Addrisi); makeup, Perc Westmore.

Mystery/Drama   **(PR:O   MPAA:M)**

ONDATA DI CALORE   (SEE: DEAD OF SUMMER, 1970, Ital./Fr.)

ONE AGAINST SEVEN   (SEE: COUNTER-ATTACK, 1945)

ONE AND ONLY, THE***   (1978) 98m First Artists/PAR c

Henry Winkler *(Andy Schmidt)*, Kim Darby *(Mary Crawford)*, Gene Saks *(Sidney Seltzer)*, William Daniels *(Mr. Crawford)*, Harold Gould *(Hector Moses)*, Polly Holliday *(Mrs. Crawford)*, Herve Villechaize *(Milton Miller)*, Bill Baldwin *(Announcer in Des Moines)*, Anthony Battaglia *(Little Andy)*, Ed Begley, Jr. *(Arnold the King)*, Peter Vrocco *(Autograph Hound)*, Brandon Cruz *(Sherman)*, Lucy Lee Flippin *(Agatha Franklen)*, Charles Frank *(Paul Harris)*, Chavo Guerrero *(Indian Joe)*, H.B. Haggerty *(Capt. Nemo)*, Dennis James, *(Himself)*, Richard Karron *(The Elephant)*, Jean LeBouvier *(Wrestling Fanatic)*, Ralph Manza *(Bellman)*, Ken Olfson *(Mr. Arnold)*, Jack Scalici *(Waiter)*, Will Seltzer *(Eddie)*, Amzie Strickland *(House Mother)*, Mary Woronov *(Arlene)*.

A 1950s milieu picture has Winkler as an obnoxious young cad who wants to make it big in show business. His first pursuit is the courtship of Darby, who he wins over despite his disrespectful treatment of her parents. The two marry and are off to New York where Winkler's attempts at show biz only land him jobs in carnivals as a wrestler. Promoter Saks helps push Winkler to the top in the professional wrestling field, where the big-headed youth gets his chance to show off. Director Reiner has managed to give a human treatment to this topic bringing to life a loathsome character such as Winkler plays.

p, Steve Gordon, David V. Picker; d, Carl Reiner; w, Gordon; ph, Victor J. Kemper, (Panavision, Movielab Color); m, Patrick Williams; ed, Bud Molin; prod d, Edward Carfagno; set d, Ruby Levitt; m/l, title song, Alan, Marilyn Bergman (sung by Kacey Cisy).

Drama   **Cas.**   **(PR:C   MPAA:PG)**

ONE AND ONLY GENUINE ORIGINAL FAMILY BAND, THE*½
          (1968) 110m Disney/BV c

Walter Brennan *(Grandpa Bower)*, Buddy Ebsen *(Calvin Bower)*, John Davidson *(Joe Carder)*, Lesley Ann Warren *(Alice Bower)*, Janet Blair *(Katie Bower)*, Kurt Russell *(Sidney Bower)*, Steve Harmon *(Ernie Stubbins)*, Richard Deacon *(Charlie Wrenn)*, Wally Cox *(Mr. Wampler)*, Debbie Smith *(Lulu Bower)*, Bobby Rhia *(Mayo Bower)*, Smitty Wordes *(Nettie Bower)*, Heidi Rook *(Rose Bower)*, John Walmsley *(Quinn Bower)*, Pamelyn Ferdin *(Laura Bower)*, John Craig *(Frank)*, William Woodson *(Henry White)*, Goldy Jeanne Hawn *(Giggly Girl)*, Jonathan Kidd *(Telegrapher)*.

True story of the attempts of an aging diehard Democrat, Brennan, and the head of a family of staunch Republicans who Brennan tries to bring to the 1888 Democratic convention. Tiresome feature which never lived up to the expectations of such a fine cast. But the material is even too much for a tried veteran such as Brennan, who could do little with the poor script. Meteoric is the story of "Giggly Girl" Goldy Hawn. A bit player in her first motion picture, she was already a TV star in "Laugh-In" by the time the film was released. Songs included: "The One and Only Genuine Original Family Band," "Dakota," "Drummin' Drummin' Drummin'," "The Happiest Girl Alive," "Oh Benjamin Harrison," "West of Wide Missouri" (Richard M., Robert B. Sherman).

p, Bill Anderson; d, Michael O'Herlihy; w, Lowell S. Hawley (based on the autobiography *Nebraska 1888* by Laura Bower Van Nuys); ph, Frank Phillips (Technicolor); m, Richard M. Sherman, Robert B. Sherman; ed, Cotton Warburton;) art d, Carroll Clark, Herman Blumenthal; set d, Emile Kuri, Hal Gausman; cos, Bill Thomas, Chuck Keehne, Emily Sundby; makeup, Gordon Hubbard.

Drama   **Cas.**   **(PR:AA   MPAA:G)**

ONE APRIL 2000*½   (1952, Aust.) 105m Wien Film bw (AKA: APRIL 1ST 2000)

Josef Meinrad, Hilde Krahl, Judith Holzmeister, Otto Tressler, Paul Hoerbiger, Hans Moser, Curt Jurgens.

A product of the Austrian government as a plea to the Allied forces to grant them independence. Gist of the story is that everything in the country has been going fine, so they are eventually granted independence on April 1st, in the year 2000. Heavy-handed direction and weighty government interest sapped any life from the story that was there to begin with. Jurgens had a brief appearance prior to gaining international fame. Wagner, the cinematographer for THE CABINET OF DR. CALAGARI, was the photographer on this project. (In German.)

p, Karl Ehrlich; d, Wolfgang Liebeneiner; w, Ernst Maboe, Rudolf Brunngraber; ph, Fritz Arno Wagner.

Drama (PR:A MPAA:NR)

ONE BIG AFFAIR** (1952) 80m UA bw

Evelyn Keyes (Jean Harper), Dennis O'Keefe (Jimmy Donovan), Mary Anderson (Hilda Jones), Connie Gilchrist (Miss Marple), Thurston Hall (Mr. G), Gus Schilling (Mr. Rush), Jose Torvay (Charcoal Wagon Driver), Charles Musqued (Police Chief), Andrew Velajquez (Orphan Boy).

Plodding story has Keyes as a school marm on vacation in Mexico. Tired of sightseeing, she takes a rest, only to miss the bus. Her companions think she has been kidnaped, but in reality she has met lawyer O'Keefe, forging the makings of a new romance. Predictable story has a few instances of comic relief, but the Mexican scenery is the picture's highpoint.

P, Benedict Bogeaus; d, Peter Godfrey; w, Leo Townsend, Francis Swann (based on the story by George Bricker); ph, Jose Orty Ramos; m, L. Hernandez Breton; ed, George Crome; art d, Edward Fitzgerald.

Drama (PR:A MPAA:NR)

ONE BODY TOO MANY**½ (1944) 74m PAR bw

Jack Haley (Albert Tuttle), Jean Parker (Carol Dunlap), Bela Lugosi (Larchmont, Butler), Bernard Nedell (Atty. Gellman), Blanche Yurka (Matthews), Douglas Fowley (Henry Rutherford), Dorothy Granger (Mona), Lyle Talbot (Jim Davis), Lucien Littlefield (Kenneth), Fay Helm (Estelle), Maxine Fife (Margaret), William Edmunds (The Professor).

Mystery thriller stars Haley as an insurance salesman sent in to guard the body of a recently deceased millionaire until the reading of his will. During his stay the corpse disappears, and two other murders occur. Well-paced thriller keeps up suspense, with Lugosi adding extra chills as the servant. Scriptwriter Miller, who was serving with the Marines in the South Pacific at the time, wrote the story in between his military chores. Anybody who was there knows how hard it was to come by any paper, but Miller managed, mailing envelopes filled with little scraps of paper dealing with the story to producer Thomas in Hollywood. Then cowriter Shane would polish the pieces into a finished script.

p, William Pine, William Thomas; d, Frank McDonald; w, Winston Miller, Maxwell Shane; ph, Fred Jackson, Jr.; ed, Howard Smith; art d, F. Paul Sylos.

Mystery Cas (PR:A MPAA:NR)

ONE BORN EVERY MINUTE (SEE: FLIM-FLAM MAN, THE, 1967)

ONE BRIEF SUMMER* (1971, Brit.) 86m Twickenham Film Associates/Cinevision c

Felicity Gibson (Susan Long), Clifford Evans (Mark Stevens), Jennifer Hilary (Jennifer), Jan Holden (Elizabeth), Peter Egan (Bill Denton), Fanny Carby (Mrs. Shaw), Richard Vernon (Hayward), Helen Lindsay (Mrs. Hayward), Basil Moss (John Robertson), David Leland (Peter), Brian Wilde (Lambert), Lockwood West (Ebert), Neville Martin (Rooley), Keith Smith (Gavin), Susan Harvey (Victoria), Carolyn Seymour (Mark's Secretary), Robert Wilde (Boy in Train), Virginia Balfour (Virginia), Moira Foot, Pauline Challoner (Girls at "Way In").

Evans plays a divorced tycoon who falls for the young girl friend of his daughter. He abandons his mistress and marries the girl despite his daughter's jealousy. But Gibson, as the girl, falls in love with a young neighbor and runs off with him. This was the directorial debut for Mackenzie, and his lack of experience shows, as he adds very little color to the story or the characters. Story pretty much just drags along, lacking a catalyst to get it moving.

p, Guido Coen; d, John Mackenzie; w, Wendy Marshall (based on a story by Coen, Harry Tierney and the play "Valkyrie's Armour" by Tierney); ph, David McDonald (Eastmancolor); m, Roger Webb; ed, John Colville; md, Webb; art d, Roger Andrews; m/l, "All Thre Is—Is Now!" by Webb, Norman Jewell (sung by Watson T. Brown and The Detroit Affiliation).

Drama (PR:A MPAA:R)

ONE CROWDED NIGHT*½ (1940) 68m RKO bw

Billie Seward (Gladys), William Haade (Joe), Anne Revere (Mae), Paul Guilfoyle (Jim), Emma Dunn (Ma), George Watts (Pa), Dick Hogan (Vince), Gale Storm (Annie), Don Costello (Lefty), Gaylord [Steve] Pendleton (Mat), Charles Lang (Matson), Adele Pearce (Ruth), J.M. Kerrigan (Doc Joseph), Casey Johnson (Bobby), Harry Shannon (McDermot), Ferris Taylor (Lansing).

GRAND HOTEL in a California auto court, this film features just about every stereotypical character RKO could dig up. The film covers a single night in the court, jumping from one story to another until all the loose ends are tied up nicely by the film's finish. Among the players are an escaped convict and the mobsters pursuing him; a sailor AWOL from the Navy to be with his soon-to-deliver wife, and the authorities pursuing him; a woman with a shady past and the straight-arrow type who loves her; and a drunken doctor who's selling an elixir to cure any ailment. The cast performs creditably, but the story is so predictable that it doesn't really matter much. Reis made his directorial debut with this film. He would go on to do a number of entries in the FALCON series before achieving what was probably his greatest success with THE BACHELOR AND THE BOBBY-SOXER (1947).

p, Cliff Reid; d, Irving Reis; w, Richard Collins, Arnaud d'Usseau (based on a story by Ben Holmes); ph, J. Roy Hunt; ed, Theron Warth; art d, Van Nest Polglase.

Drama (PR:A MPAA:NR)

ONE DANGEROUS NIGHT** (1943) 77m COL bw

Warren William (Michael Lanyard), Marguerite Chapman (Eve Andrews), Eric Blore (Jamison), Mona Barrie (Jane Merrick), Tala Birell (Sonia), Margaret Hayes

(Patricia), Ann Savage (Vivian), Thurston Hall (Inspector Crane), Warren Ashe (Sidney), Fred Kelsey (Dickens), Frank Sully (Hertzog), Eddie Marr (Mac), Gerald Mohr (Harry Cooper), Louis Jean Heydt (Arthur), Roger Clark (John Sheldon), Gregory Gaye (Dr. Eric), Ed Laughton (Drunk), Dick Rush (Doorman), Symona Boniface (Woman), John Tyrell (Attendant), Joe McGuinn (Motor Cop), Chuck Hamilton, Bill Lally, Pat Lane (Cops), George Calliga (Headwaiter), George Ghermanoff (Waiter), Ann Hunter (Coatroom Girl), Hal Price (Doorman), Ralph Peters (House Detective), Wedgewood Nowell (Attendant).

Competent second feature has William the suave jewel thief-turned-detective known as the Lone Wolf. Here he has to clear himself after being accused of the murder of a criminal who was shot in the presence of the three women he was blackmailing. Evading both the police and the dead man's henchmen, William identifies the killer. William's seventh appearance as the Lone Wolf is an entertaining diversion and his next to last before ill health forced him to abandon the series. Gerald Mohr, who has a minor role in this film, then took over the lead for two more films. (See LONE WOLF series, Index.)

p, David Chatkin; d, Michael Gordon; w, Donald Davis (based on a story by Arnold Phillips, Max Nosseck and characters created by Louis Joseph Vance); ph, L.W. O'Connell; ed, Viola Lawrence; md, Morris W. Stoloff; art d, Lionel Banks; Robert Peterson.

Crime (PR:A MPAA:NR)

ONE DARK NIGHT** (1939) 81m Sack Amusement bw

Mantan Moreland, Betty Treadville, Josephine Pearson, John Thomas, Arthur Ray, Jessie Grayson, Bobby Simmons, Lawrence Criner, Monte Hawley, Alfred Grant, Ruby Logan, Guernsey Morrow, Herbert Skinner and The Four Tones.

An attempt to duplicate the success of the HARDY FAMILY series with an all-black cast, ONE DARK NIGHT was the first entry in a proposed series dealing with the Brown family. Moreland stars as the father of the clan who is thrown out of the house when his fellow family members tire of his lazy ways. He travels to the desert where he discovers radium and becomes a rich man. He buys a night club owned by Criner and then thwarts the villainous man's attempts to woo daughter Pearson. The film included some extremely poor production work, which did little to enhance the plodding story. The music was the highlight with numbers including "West of Harlem" (performed by Skinner and The Four Tones); "Shake and Break It" (performed by Logan, Thomas, Pearson); "Sharpest Man In Town" and "Alone Again" (performed by Logan), all by Lew Porter and Johnny Lange.

p, Harry M. Popkin; d, Leo C. Popkin; w, Billie Meyers.

Musical/Comedy (PR:A MPAA:NR)

ONE DARK NIGHT**½ (1983) 89m ComWorld c

Meg Tilly (Julie), Melissa Newman (Olivia), Robin Evans (Carol), Leslie Speights (Kitty), Donald Hotton (Dockstader), Elizabeth Daily (Leslie), David Mason Daniels (Steve), Adam West (Allan), Leo Gorcey, Jr. (Barlow), Rhio H. Blair (Coroner), Larry Carroll (TV Reporter), Katee McLure (Reporter), Kevin Peter Hall (Eddie), Ted Lehman (Drunk), Nancy Mott (Lucy), Martin Nosseck (Caretaker), Albert Cirimele (Reporter), Shandor (Russian Minister), Julie Chase, Peaches Johnson.

A teenage shocker with a bit more substance than normal, has Tilly as a sweet girl desperate to be accepted by her peers, a rather tough and nasty bunch. One of the girls, Evans, was jilted by Tilly's present boy friend, so she is anxious to make it as tough on Tilly as possible. Tilly's final chore to gain her acceptance in a club is to spend the night in a mausoleum, where Evans plans to scare the girl out of her wits. The mayhem begins in the mausoleum when a dead man with telekinetic powers uses his skills to drain the energies from the pranksters. The direction manages to develop the tension and the cast is adequate.

p, Michael Schroeder; d, Tom McLoughlin; w, McLoughlin, Michael Hawes; ph, Hal Trussel (Movielab Color); m, Bob Summers; ed, Charles Tetoni, Michael Spence; art d, Craig Stearns, Randy Moore; cos, Linda Bass; spec eff, Tom Burman, Ellis Burman, Bob Williams.

Horror Cas. (PR:C MPAA:PG)

ONE DAY IN THE LIFE OF IVAN DENISOVICH** (1971, U.S./ Brit./Norway) 108m Group W-Leontes-Norsk/Cinerama c

Tom Courtenay (Ivan Denisovich), Espen Skjonberg (Tiurin), James Maxwell (Captain), Alfred Burke (Alyosha), Eric Thompson (Tsezar), John Cording (Pavlo), Mathew Guinness (Kilgas), Alf Malland (Fetiukov), Frimann Falck Clausen (Senka), Jo Skjonberg (Gopchick), Odd Jan Sandsdalen (Eino), Torstein Rustdal (Vaino), Wolfe Morris, Paul Connell, Lars Nordrum, Sverre Hansen, Kjell Stormoen, Hans Stormoen, Roy Bjornstad.

Alexander Solzhenitsyn's popular novel of life in a Soviet prison camp was brought to the screen the year after the author won the Nobel Prize for literature. Set in the early 1950s, it depicts 24 hours in the life of a prisoner (Courtenay) who is in the eighth year of a 10-year term in one of Josef Stalin's Siberian labor camps. Over the course of the day, Courtenay conspires to get extra food and to avoid punishment, while also engaging in competitive wall-building with a fellow prisoner. The film accurately captures the bleakness of the camp and serves as a worthy tribute to the indomitable spirit of its subjects, yet fails to bring the audience closer to the characters. Instead, the players are isolated, treated more as symbols than humans. This is particularly the case with Courtenay, whose Leontes Production company was one of the film's three coproducers. Nykvist's contribution is the film's greatest strength as he brilliantly photographed the location scenes at Roros, Norway, near the Arctic Circle. This was the second filming of Solzhenitsyn's novel, the first being in 1963 for NBC's "Chrysler Theatre," starring Jason Robards, Jr.

p&d, Casper Wrede; w, Ronald Harwood (based on the novel by Alexander

Solzhenitsyn); ph, Sven Nykvist (Eastmancolor); m, Arne Nordheim; ed, Thelma Connell; art d, Per Schwab; cos, Ada Skolmen; makeup, Nurven Bradangen.

Drama (PR:A MPAA:G)

ONE DESIRE**½ (1955) 94m UNIV c

Anne Baxter (Tacey Cromwell), Rock Hudson (Clint Saunders), Julie Adams (Judith Watrous), Carl Benton Reid (Sen. Watrous), Natalie Wood (Seely), Betty Garde (Mrs. O'Dell), William Hopper (MacBain), Barry Curtis (Nugget), Adrienne Marden (Marjorie Huggins), Fay Morley (Flo), Vici Raaf (Kate), Lynne Millan (Bea), Smoki Whitfield (Sam), Robert Hoy, John Daheim (Firemen), Betty Jane Howarth (May), William Forrest (Mr. Wellington), Howard Wright (Judge Congin), Alan De Witt (John), Joe Mell (Franklin), Paul McGuire (Vernon), Guy Wilkerson (Marshal Coe), Paul Levitt (Brogan), Edward Earle (Mr. Hathaway), Edmund Cobb (Driver), Barbara Knudson (Alice), Charles Gray (Vernon's Son), Joe Golbert (Dealer), Dennis Moore, Donald Kerr (Miners), Terry Frost (Jack), Forbes Murray (Man at Party), Paul Keast (Wyatt), Joel Allen (Mr. Ribbling).

Set in the West at the turn of the century, the story focuses on Hudson, owner of a gambling den, and Baxter, his girl friend who's addicted to making bets. The pair decides to go straight and they head for a new town and a new lifestyle, taking Hudson's kid brother, Curtis, along. When they encounter the orphaned Wood, they decide to take her in as well. Hudson gets a new job and all is going well until the venomous Adams arrives. She has eyes for Hudson and she uses her banker father's money to gain legal custody of the children. Baxter leaves town and Hudson marries Adams so as not to lose the youngsters. When Adams is killed in a fire, Baxter returns and the foursome are happily reunited. It was a real tear-jerker, but mounted with a sincerity that kept it from degenerating into a soap opera. The glossy photography and handsome settings give the film a visual appeal.

p, Ross Hunter; d, Jerry Hopper; w, Lawrence Roman, Robert Blees (based on the novel Tacey Cromwell by Conrad Richter); ph, Maury Gertsman (Technicolor); m, Frank Skinner; ed, Milton Carruth; md, Joseph Gershenson; art d, Alexander Golitzen, Carroll Clark; cos, Bill Thomas.

Drama (PR:AA MPAA:NR)

ONE DOWN TWO TO GO*½ (1982) 84m Almi c

Fred Williamson (Cal), Jim Brown (J), Jim Kelly (Chuck), Richard Roundtree (Ralph), Paula Sills (Teri), Laura Loftus (Sally), Tom Signorelli (Mario), Joe Spinell (Joe Spangler), Louis Neglia (Armando), Peter Dane (Rossi), Victoria Hale (Maria Rossi), Richard Noyce (Hank), John Guitz (Bob), Warrington Winters (Sheriff Lucas), Arthur Haggerty (Mojo), Irwin Litvack (Banker), Addison Greene (Pete), Dennis Singletary (Boy), John Dorish (Deputy), Robert Pastner (Slim), Patty O'Brien (Nurse), Aaron Banks (Armando's Trainer).

Black exploitation films had enjoyed some popularity in the late 1960s and early 1970s before wearing out. For ONE DOWN TWO TO GO, producer-director Williamson has assembled some of the stars of those films (himself, Brown, and Roundtree) and added kung fu movie veteran Kelly in an apparent attempt to revive the genre. The plot has Williamson, Brown, and Kelly battling an assortment of white villains after their friend Roundtree has been cheated out of the profits from a martial arts tournament he promoted. Roundtree gives a respectable performance, while the other stars seem to be going through the motions. Williamson exhibits no particular flair for directing and the whole project is pretty dismal.

p&d Fred Williamson; w, Jeff Williamson; ph, James Lemmo; m, Joe Trunzo, Herb Hetzer; ed, Daniel Loewenthal.

Crime/Adventure **Cas.** (PR:O MPAA:R)

ONE EMBARRASSING NIGHT**½ (1930, Brit.) 90m British and Dominions/MGM bw (GB: ROOKERY NOOK)

Ralph Lynn (Gerald Popkiss), Tom Walls (Clive Popkiss), Winifred Shotter (Rhoda Marley), Mary Brough (Mrs. Leverett), J. Robertson Hare (Harold Twine), Ethel Coleridge (Mrs. Twine), Griffith Humphreys (Mr. Putz), Doreen Bendix (Poppy Dickey), Margot Grahame (Clara Popkiss).

Ben Travers was the author of a number of successful plays known as the "Aldwych farces" and Lynn, Walls, and Hare became known as the "Aldwych farceurs" by starring in several screen adaptations of the plays. This was the first to be made as a sound film, with Walls starring and making his directorial debut. It's an amusing comedy in which Shotter plays a girl who has left home to escape her stepfather. She becomes friendly with a married man and an assortment of complications arises as he tries to hide her from pursuing family members, as well as his own wife and mother-in-law. The pace is brisk, the dialog well-written, and the proper number of pratfalls, mistaken identities, and chases are all in place.

p, Herbert Wilcox; d, Tom Walls, Byron Haskin; w, Ben Travers, W.P. Lipscomb (based on a play by Travers); ph, Dave Kessan; ed, J. Maclean Rogers.

Comedy (PR:A MPAA:NR)

1=2?*½ (1975, Fr.) 90m Societe Generale De Production c

Bernard Fresson (Boss), Claude Rich (Borel), Andrea Ferreol (Wife), Rita Renoir (Secretary), Michel Aumont (Watchman), Guy Trejean (Minister).

French satire has a large computer company developing an extensive advertising campaign to promote a program which offers people a double life, giving them the chance to be what they always wanted to be. Party sequences make for some interesting caricatures, but as a whole the story is lacking any development or clear-cut motivation.

d&w, Dolores Grassjan; ph, Alain Derobe (Eastmancolor); ed, Francoise Bonnot.

Comedy (PR:C MPAA:NR)

ONE EXCITING ADVENTURE**½ (1935) 70m UNIV bw

Binnie Barnes (Rena Sorel), Neil Hamilton (Walter Stone), Paul Cavanagh (Lavassor), Grant Mitchell (Fussli), Eugene Pallette (Kleinsilber), Ferdinand Gottschalk (The Jeweler), Henry Kolker, Doris Lloyd (Customers), Dick Winslow (Boy), Edward Keane (Hotel Manager), G.P. Huntley, Jr., William Worthington (Men), Dorothy Christy (Woman with Earrings), Edward McWade (Grouchy Man), Bess Flowers (Woman), Ann Doran, Joan Woodbury (Girls), Jason Robards, Sr., Edna Searle.

Barnes is a kleptomaniac who can't resist jewels, which she hides in her chandelier. Mitchell and Pallette are a couple of detectives who attempt to track the thief down via the scent of her perfume. Cavanagh is an international jewel thief and Barnes saves herself when she inadvertently helps Pallette capture the criminal. The plot is rather cloudy, but a good script and crisp direction make the movie an entertaining romp. Barnes sings "The Road to You."

d, Ernst L. Frank; w, Samuel Ornitz, William Hurlbut (based on a story by Franz Schulz and Billy Wilder); ph, Norbert Brodine; ed, Murray Seldeen.

Comedy (PR:A MPAA:NR)

ONE EXCITING NIGHT** (1945) 64m Pine-Thomas/PAR bw

William Gargan (Pete Wills), Ann Savage (Sue Gallagher), Leo Gorcey (Clutch), Don Beddoe (Max Hurley), Paul Hurst (Murphy), Charles Halton (Miggs), George Zucco (Jelke), Robert Barron (Cop), George E. Stone (Joe Wells).

Gargan and Savage are rival reporters who discover the corpse of a gangster in a wax museum. The gangster's death hasn't been reported, so the two vie for the scoop, but there's a complication—the corpse keeps disappearing. Zucco is the gangster's killer who is also seeking the corpse. He wants it gone for good to avoid a murder charge and to cover his theft of some valuable jewels. The plot devices are handled well and Halton, as the manager of the wax museum, and Gorcey, his assistant, offer the comic relief. Thomas, co-owner of the film's production company, tried his hand at directing the film and did a competent job.

p, Maxwell Shane, d, William C. Thomas; w, David Lang (based on his story); ph, Fred Jackman, Jr.; m, Alexander Laszlo; ed, Henry Adams; art d, Paul Sylos; set d, Ray Berk.

Crime/Comedy (PR:A MPAA:NR)

ONE EXCITING NIGHT, 1946 (SEE: YOU CAN'T DO WITHOUT LOVE, 1946)

ONE EXCITING WEEK** (1946) 69m REP bw

Al Pearce (Dan Flannery), Pinky Lee (Itchy), Jerome Cowan (Al Carter), Shemp Howard (Marvin), Arlene Harris (Lottie Pickett), Mary Treen (Mabel Taylor), Lorraine Krueger (Helen Pickett), Maury Dexter (Jimmy Curtis), Will Wright (Otis Piper), Arthur Loft (Charlie Pickett), Chester Clute (Mayor Teeple), The Teen-Agers.

One-time radio personality Pearce plays an amnesiac in a plot with a twist—Pearce winds up impersonating himself. He plays a Merchant Marine hero on his way home to join in a celebration, when a blow sustained in a fight with a group of crooks causes him to lose his memory. The crooks then tell Pearce that he is their gang leader and convince him to assume the identity of the hero in order to receive the $10,000 the town plans to give him. Script is filled with some interesting developments and Lee and Howard supply laughs as the crooks. The direction lacks pacing, but it's still an entertaining outing.

p, Donald H. Brown; d, William Beaudine; w, Jack Townley, John K. Butler (based on a story by Dennis Murray); ph, John Alton; ed, William P. Thompson; md, Morton Scott; art d, Frank Hotaling; set d, John McCarthy, Jr., George Milo; spec eff, Howard Lydecker, Theodore Lydecker; m/l, Don Raye and, Hughie Prince, John Pettis, Billy Meyers, Elmer Schoebel, Jack Lawrence (performed by the Teenagers).

Comedy (PR:A MPAA:NR)

ONE-EYED JACKS ***½ (1961) 141m Pennebaker/PAR c

Marlon Brando (Rio), Karl Malden (Dad Longworth), Katy Jurado (Maria), Pina Pellicer (Louisa), Slim Pickens (Lon), Ben Johnson (Bob Amory), Sam Gilman (Harvey), Larry Duran (Modesto), Timothy Carey (Howard Tetley), Miriam Colon (Redhead), Elisha Cook, Jr. (Bank Teller), Rudolph [Rodolfo] Acosta (Rurales Officer), Ray Teal (Bartender), John Dierkes (Barber-Photographer), Margarita Cordova (Nika, Flamenco Dancer), Hank Worden (Doc), Nina Martinez (Margarita, Castilian Girl), Philip Ahn (Uncle), Clem Harvey (Tim), William Forrest (Banker), Shichizo Takeda (Owner of Cantina), Henry Wills (Posseman), Mickey Finn (Blacksmith), Fenton Jones (Squaredance Caller), Joe Dominguez (Corral Keeper), Margarita Martin (Mexican Vendor), John Michael Quijada (Rurales Sergeant), Francy Scott (Cantina Girl), Felipe Turich (Card Sharp), Nesdon Booth (Townsman), Nacho Galindo (Mexican Townsman), Jorge Moreno (Bouncer in Shack), Snub Pollard (Townsman), Joan Petrone, Tom Webb.

This offbeat western is almost as strange as the Brando opus, THE MISSOURI BREAKS, which he made a decade and a half later, but it packs a wallop and no few surprises. Brando and Malden are bandits who rob a Mexican bank in 1880. Both men ride the same horse after fast-approaching possemen shoot one of their mounts; Malden is also without shoes since the lawmen had rousted the pair while Malden was pitching woo at a curvy Latin lady and had to leave sans boots. The bandits stop on top of a hill, realizing that they cannot outdistance the posse while riding one horse, and it is decided that Malden will ride off and return for Brando with another mount. He goes, leaving Brando on the hilltop, duelling with the lawmen below. Coming to a small ranch, Malden tries to buy a horse and then realizes that by the time he rides back for Brando, he will undoubtedly become a prisoner, too, or at least that is his rationale. He rides away to safety with all the gold he and Brando have stolen. Brando is slowly surrounded on the hilltop and taken prisoner after running out of ammunition. He spends five years being brutalized in the stinking Sonora prison and then joins forces with Duran in a daring escape. Later Brando and Duran meet Johnson and Gilman, two mean-streaked desperadoes, and the four travel—wary of each other—to Monterey, California to rob a bank. The town, however, is controlled by none other than Malden, who has gone straight and is now the town sheriff, having married Jurado and adopting her grown Mexican daughter, Pellicer. Brando and his associates arrive in Monterey just as the town is to have a fiesta and the outlaw tells a surprised Malden that he escaped the posse five years earlier and has been moving aimlessly around the West. But he seethes with revenge and spitefully seduces the virginal Pellicer as a way of getting back at Malden. Meanwhile, he and the others plot to rob the bank but Brando gets sidetracked when sitting in a bar with Duran and watching drunken bully Carey abuse a whore. He beats Carey up and then kills him when Carey tries to shoot him and for this act of self-defense, the wily Malden takes Brando to a hitching post, publicly whips him, and then smashes his shooting hand, just to make sure Brando has no plans to draw on him in the future. While his hand mends, Brando can only think of killing Malden. Johnson and Gilman can only think of robbing the bank and grow insultingly impatient with Brando as they wait for his hand to heal. They finally set out to rob the bank, killing Duran and later, when looting, they accidentally kill a little girl. The innocent Brando is grabbed by Malden and held for the crime. Brando is thrown in the Monterey jail; he asks Malden if he'll get a fair trial. "Sure," Malden says smilingly, "you'll get a fair trial—and then I'm gonna hang you!" Brando stares at Malden and tells him: "You're a real one-eyed Jack in this town, Dad, but I seen the other side of your face." Brando is insulted and abused by fat-gutted Pickens, a sadistic deputy, but he turns the trick on the deputy, shoots him, and escapes. He and Malden then shoot it out in the town square and Malden is killed. Brando, before riding away, embraces Pellicer and promises to come back for her. ONE-EYED JACKS is Brando's only directorial achievement, the star having taken over the film from the famous Stanley Kubrick after he and Kubrick disagreed on character development. The story draws heavily upon the legend of Billy the Kid (the father-son relationship between Malden and Brando is almost identical to that between lawman Pat Garrett and the outlaw William Bonney; the escape from jail and the abusive guard are obviously drawn from the Kid's own experiences). It is also fraught with too many pensive moments where Brando, unlike any real outlaw on the dodge in the Old West, broods and ponders instead of naturally going for his gun or mounting his horse. (There simply wasn't time in the Old West for introspection in lawman or outlaw.) But the ever-careful and painfully exacting Brando took all the time in the world when assuming the mantle of director. Producer Rosenberg didn't like the idea but by the time the star and Kubrick had clashed, too much money had already been spent on preproduction and Paramount's front office was screaming for completion. The film was supposed to be shot on a 60-day shooting schedule but Brando used six months to get the film in the can. Said Rosenberg later: "He [Brando] pondered each camera set-up while 120 members of the company sprawled on the ground like battle-weary troops...every line every actor read, as well as every button on every piece of wardrobe got Brando's concentrated attention until he was completely satisfied." Brando exposed more than one million feet of film which Rosenberg considered "a new world's record." The company—Brando produced under his own production company, Pennebaker Productions—printed about 250,000 feet of film (the normal total exposed footage is about 150, 000 feet for any major film, of which 40,000 feet are printed for rushes). Marshek and others edited the huge film down to 141 minutes and it was still overlong, with scenes that played up Brando's martyr-like character (the whipping scene is almost a duplication of the Crucifixion but is oddly sadistic and, like a lot of the film, crammed with gratuitous violence). The film was completed on June 2, 1959 but Brando went back for one day's shooting, on October 14, 1960, to reshoot the final scene, before the film was released that year. Lang's photography of the spectacular Monterey Peninsula, the windswept, ocean-lapped coast and rocky coastline, is outstanding, and Brando's performance, weird or not, is dynamic and intriguing. Malden is a classic study in guile but Jurado is only a prop and Pellicer, reportedly a Rosenberg discovery, in unconvincing and unattractive as the naive girl. (This was Pellicer's only U.S. film; after a shortlived career in Mexican pictures, she committed suicide at the age of 24.) The film was not a financial success, costing Paramount more than $6 million (with an original budget of only $1.8 million); it returned, in its initial release, only $4.3 million. This tale of basic revenge shows man as vile and contemptuous of his fellow man, a view repeatedly seen through the eyes of the often smug but never boring Brando.

p, Frank P. Rosenberg; d, Marlon Brando; w, Guy Trosper, Calder Willingham (based on the novel *The Authentic Death of Hendry Jones* by Charles Neider); ph, Charles Lang, Jr. (VistaVision, Technicolor); m, Hugo Friedhofer; ed, Archie Marshek; art d, Hal Pereira, J. McMillan Johnson; set d, Sam Comer, Robert R. Benton; cos, Yvonne Wood; spec eff, John P. Fulton, Farciot Edouart; ch, Josephine Earl; makeup, Wally Westmore (Marlon Brando's makeup, Phil Rhodes); tech adv, Rodd Redwing, Rosita Moreno.

Western Cas. (PR:O MPAA:NR)

ONE-EYED SOLDIERS** (1967, U.S./Brit./Yugo.) 83m Avala Film-BACO British/United Screen Arts c

Dale Robertson *(Richard Owen)*, Luciana Paluzzi *(Gava Berens)*, Guy Deghy *(Harold Schmidt)*, Andrew Faulds *(Col. Ferrer)*, Mila Avramovic *(Antonio Caporelli)*, Dragan Nikolic *(The Mute)*, Bozidar Drnie *(Dr. Charles Berens)*.

An international criminal, a sadistic dwarf, and $15 million in a Swiss bank vault are the main ingredients in this international thriller. Paluzzi plays the daughter of a United Nations official whose dying words to her are "one-eyed jacks." Hardly a moving farewell, but Paluzzi appreciates the goodbye message because it provides a valuable clue to the whereabouts of a key that opens the vault containing the fortune. She goes off in pursuit of the money, followed by criminal Deghy. The trail takes her to Yugoslavia where she enlists the aid of Robertson, an American newsman, in eluding Deghy. Avramovic, the dwarf (who used to be an SS agent), proves to be a formidable foe in the quest for the key, so Paluzzi, Robertson, and Deghy join forces against the little fellow. Avramovic is eventually killed by Nikolic, Deghy's assistant who was a victim of Avramovic's torture during WW II. The trio then retrieve the key from a one-eyed statue, only to be arrested by Faulds, the local police chief. Deghy then does some fast talking and he and Faulds depart with the key, leaving Robertson and Paluzzi locked in a hotel room. Entertaining in a way only truly bad movies can be.

p, Clive Sharp; d&w, Jean Christophe (based on a story by Richard Fraink); ph, Branko Ivatovic (Techniscope, Technicolor); m, Avala Studios.

Crime (PR:C MPAA:NR)

ONE FAMILY*½ (1930, Brit.) 70m British Instructional-Empire Marketing Board/PP bw

Douglas Beaumont *(The Boy)*, Sam Livesey *(The Policeman)*, Michael Hogan *(The Father)*, Joan Maude *(The Mother)*, Phyllis Neilson-Terry *(Australia)*, Lady Keble *(Canada)*, Lady Ravensdale *(New Zealand)*, Lady Carlisle *(South Africa)*, Lady Lavery *(Irish Free State)*, Miss Dadabhoy *(India)*.

An unimaginative pseudo-travelog of the British Empire masquerading as a children's fantasy film. Beaumont plays a young boy who dreams that policeman Livesey takes him on a guided tour through Buckingham Palace and then it's on to the rest of the empire, represented by Australia, New Zealand, South Africa, Northern Ireland, and India. While the film is nothing more than a wistful trip down imperialism lane, it holds some historical interest since the scenes in Buckingham Palace were the first ever allowed to be shot inside the royal residence.

d, Walter Creighton.

Fantasy/Historical (PR:A MPAA:NR)

ONE FATAL HOUR (SEE: FIVE STAR FINAL, 1931)

ONE FATAL HOUR (SEE: TWO AGAINST THE WORLD, 1936)

ONE FLEW OVER THE CUCKOO'S NEST**** (1975) 129m Fantasy/UA c

Jack Nicholson *(Randle Patrick McMurphy)*, Louise Fletcher *(Nurse Mildred Ratched)*, William Redfield *(Harding)*, Michael Berryman *(Ellis)*, Brad Dourif *(Billy Bibbit)*, Peter Brocco *(Col. Matterson)*, Dean R. Brooks *(Dr. John Spivey)*, Alonzo Brown *(Miller)*, Sherman "Scatman" Crothers *(Turkle)*, Mwako Cumbuka *(Warren)*, Danny De Vito *(Martini)*, William Duell *(Jim Sefelt)*, Josip Elic *(Bancini)*, Lan Fendors *(Nurse Itsu)*, Nathan George *(Washington)*, Ken Kenny *(Beans Garfield)*, Mel Lambert *(Harbor Master)*, Sydney Lassick *(Charlie Cheswick)*, Kay Lee *(Night Supervisor)*, Christopher Lloyd *(Taber)*, Dwight Marfield *(Ellsworth)*, Ted Markland *(Hap Arlich)*, Louisa Moritz *(Rose)*, Phil Roth *(Woolsey)*, Will Sampson *(Chief Bromden)*, Mimi Sarkisian *(Nurse Pilbow)*, Vincent Schiavelli *(Frederickson)*, Marya Small *(Candy)*, Delos V. Smith, Jr. *(Scanlon)*, Tim Welch *(Ruckley)*, Tim McCall *(News Commentator)*.

A deeply disturbing film, this romp through a lunatic ward with the energetic and wise-cracking Nicholson is nevertheless compelling to the point of obsession. Nicholson is doing time on a prison farm and, to get out of work detail and escape the rigors of prison life, he pretends to be crazy. Shipped to a mental asylum, he becomes the prisoner of a much more hateful system, presided over by a quietly sadistic head nurse, Fletcher. To his amazement, Nicholson finds that his fellow inmates are"no crazier than any other s.o.b. on the the street," and he finds that all have distinctive personalities with strange and pathetic quirks, although a few have retreated into entirely monistic states. To bring life to the dead atmosphere, Nicholson introduces card games (with pornographically illustrated cards), organizes basketball games, and even conducts a field trip for his fellow inmates, but at every turn Fletcher is there to administer vicious punishment, attempting to break Nicholson's spirit and will. At one point Nicholson smuggles two girl friends, Small and Moritz, into the ward and passes out a cache of booze, giving a wild midnight party for the inmates and initiating the emotionally disturbed Dourif into sex. Fletcher finds Dourif in bed with one of the girls the next morning and vindictively tells the impressionable youth that she will inform his mother. Dourif commits suicide and Nicholson goes berserk, trying to strangle Fletcher. He is later lobotomized and returned to the ward a human vegetable. Incensed at this, a huge Indian, Sampson, who has also faked his insanity to escape a brutal world, smothers Nicholson to death in a mercy killing, then goes to the washroom, tears out a massive sink, and uses this as a battering ram to break through the walls to freedom. Beyond jarring and electrifying drama, ONE FLEW OVER THE CUCKOO'S NEST is a naked study in rebellion and mistreatment, wonderfully enacted by a mostly nonprofessional cast. Nicholson is in his usual but powerful mold (FIVE EASY PIECES, THE LAST DETAIL) as a cagy anti-hero ready to poke and jab the system at every opportunity, even knowing he cannot win against it, or change it, and is even prepared to die before submitting to it. Fletcher appears in her one and only effective role. (The woman as an actress is close to pathetic, speaking in a monotone, her face immobile, her body as rigid as the starch in her immaculate uniform; in many scenes she resmbles photos of those tall blonde female SS guards who had brutalized concentration camp prisoners during WW II.) Nicholson, who won the Oscar for Best Actor, gives a performance that is nothing less than great; in fact, this was his greatest role to date, albeit the psychological posture is so traumatic (not to mention distasteful) that no young child should be subjected to this performance or the film itself. Misread as humorous in spots, the entire utterly depressing and drab film is a juggernaut indictment of an uncaring, destructive medical system that makes prisoners of the mentally disturbed, rather than working toward their health and happiness. Actor Kirk Douglas acquired the rights to Wasserman's play (originally written by Kesey as a novel) and had a great success acting in it on Broadway in the 1960s, but by the time this film was made in 1975, he realized that he was too old to play the lead and turned the property over to his son Michael. The fledgling producer-actor brought in Forman as director and this minor masterpiece was produced. In addition to Nicholson's Oscar, the movie swept the top 1975 Academy Awards, winning Oscars as Best Picture, and for Best Director (Forman), Best Actress (Fletcher), and Best Screenplay (Hauben, Goldman). This picture marked the screen debuts of gigantic Creek Indian painter Sampson, of Dourif and Lloyd, and of Dr. Brooks (who was superintendent of the Oregon State Hospital in Salem, where the picture was filmed). The news commentator was played by McCall, a former governor of Oregon.

p, Saul Zaentz, Michael Douglas; d, Milos Forman; w, Lawrence Hauben, Bo Goldman (based on the novel by Ken Kesey and the play by Dale Wasserman); ph, Haskell Wexler, William Fraker, Bill Butler (DeLuxe Color); m, Jack Nitzsche; ed, Richard Chew, Lynzee Klingman, Sheldon Kahn; prod d, Paul Sylbert; art d, Edwin O'Donovan; cos, Agnes Rodgers; makeup, Fred Phillips.

Drama   **Cas.**   **(PR:O MPAA:R)**

ONE FOOT IN HEAVEN***½   (1941) 106m WB bw

Fredric March (*William Spence*), Martha Scott (*Hope Morris Spence*), Beulah Bondi (*Mrs. Lydia Sandow*), Gene Lockhart (*Preston Thurston*), Grant Mitchell (*Clayton Potter*), Moroni Olsen (*Dr. John Romer*), Harry Davenport (*Elias Samson*), Elisabeth Fraser (*Eileen Spence at 17*), Frankie Thomas (*Hartzell Spence at 18*), Laura Hope Crews (*Mrs. Thurston*), Jerome Cowan (*Dr. Horrigan*), Ernest Cossart (*John E. Morris*), Nana Bryant (*Mrs. Morris*), Mary Field (*Louella Digby*), Hobart Bosworth (*Richard Hardy Case*), Roscoe Ates (*George Reynolds*), Clara Blandick (*Mrs. Watkins*), Charles Halton (*Haskins*), Paula Trueman (*Miss Peabody*), Virginia Brissac (*Mrs. Jellison*), Casey Johnson (*Fraser Spence at 10*), Carlotta Jelm (*Eileen Spence at 11*), Peter Caldwell (*Hartzell Spence at 10*), Milt Kibbee (*Alf McAfee*), Harlan Briggs (*Druggist MacFarlan*), Olin Howland (*Zeke Harris*), Frank Mayo (*Drummer*), Fred Kelsey (*Conductor*), Vera Lewis (*Mrs. Simpson*), Dorothy Vaughan (*Mrs. Erlich*), Tempe Pigott (*Mrs. Dibble*), Sarah Edwards (*Mrs. Spicer*), Herbert Heywood (*Storekeeper*), Dick Elliott (*Casper Cullenbaugh*), Charlotte Treadway (*Ella Hodges*), Ann Edmonds (*Bride*), Byron Barr [Gig Young] (*Groom*), Ruth Robinson, Cathy Lipps.

In one of his finest performances, March plays a Methodist minister who devotes his life to building up floundering parishes into strong pillars of faith. Episodic in construction, ONE FOOT IN HEAVEN, begins in 1904 in Canada where March is busy attending medical school. After listening to an evangelist, he decides to pack his bags and travel with his devoted wife, Scott, to a small Iowa community which is desperately in need of spiritual guidance. In an effort to fit in with the locals, March and Scott live at the poverty level, casting aside the luxuries, elegant clothing, and fine food to which they have been accustomed. After their work in one parish is complete they travel ahead to the next, adding children to their family in the process. Over the next 20 years, March and Scott fight a number of uphill battles waged by unaccepting parishioners in every town. Thomas, the family's eldest son, becomes the center of controversy in one such town when a rumor is spread that he has impregnated a local girl. March manages to prove the gossipmongers wrong and even shames them into contributing financially to the construction of a new church. In another town, Thomas exposes his father to movies by dragging him along to a moralistic William S. Hart western film. March is so enthralled that he sings the praises of movies at his next sermon. One memorable sequence has March replacing a haggard, monotonous choir of aging parishioners with a group of fresh, angelic-voiced children. When it appears as if March and his family are finally going to settle down comfortably, word reaches them of another troubled parish. Faithful to his calling, March again travels to where he is needed. The entire town comes out to bid him farewell and, in a teary but joyful finish, March leaves as a tune plays on the church's new carillon. A huge audience pleaser, ONE FOOT IN HEAVEN, was based on the actual exploits of the Rev. William Spence, whose story was told in a book written by his son (portrayed in the film by Thomas). Adding to the film's authenticity is Rev. Dr. Norman Vincent Peale (the representative of the nation's Protestant denominations) as technical advisor. What makes the film so enjoyable, however, isn't its religious message, but March's portrayal of Spence as a real man—one with morals and common sense, who can also show aggression when necessary. Although Anatole Litvak was originally slated to direct, the job was handed over to Rapper, a new but competent name at Warner Bros. Rapper recalls the enthusiasm he felt for the project in his description of a scene of a blazing fire, "I was so fascinated by it that I kept forgetting to give cues. We had houses burning down and a whole block of traffic snarled up, with children running everywhere, firemen and crowds, and terrific excitement. We had rehearsed several times without setting the building on fire. Then we started the fire and it was even more exciting. Suddenly I realized people were calling on me, and they were asking me about cues. I had forgotten all about directing." ONE FOOT IN HEAVEN received an Academy Award nomination for Best Picture.

p, Jack L. Warner, Hal B. Wallis; d, Irving Rapper; w, Casey Robinson (based on the biography by Hartzell Spence of his father); ph, Charles Rosher; m, Max Steiner; ed, Warren Low; tech adv, Norman Vincent Peale.

Drama   **(PR:AA MPAA:NR)**

ONE FOOT IN HELL**   (1960) 89m FOX c

Alan Ladd (*Mitch Barrett*), Don Murray (*Dan Keats*), Dan O'Herlihy (*Harry Ivers*), Dolores Michaels (*Julie Reynolds*), Barry Coe (*Stu Christian*), Larry Gates (*Doc Seltzer*), Karl Swenson (*Sheriff Olson*), John Alexander (*Sam Giller*), Rachel Stephens (*Ellie Barrett*), Henry Norell (*George Caldwell*), Harry Carter (*Mark Dobbs*), Ann Morriss (*Nellie*).

Adaptation of a story which had originally been made in 1957 for TV's "Playhouse 90" under the title "The Last Man." Ladd stars as an offbeat hero who schemes to destroy a town that refused him help when his wife was dying. Laden with guilt over the woman's death, the townspeople offer Ladd the job of deputy sheriff. Ladd kills the sheriff, but says the man died in an ambush and is promoted to the dead man's post. This enables him to band together an unlikely group of misfits

(Murray, Coe, O'Herlihy, and Michaels to go through with his plan to rob the town's bank and kill those people who earlier refused him help. After pulling off the robbery, Ladd decides to do away with his cohorts as well. But Murray decides to go straight and kills Ladd. Plot manages to be both trite and implausible and isn't helped by Clark's plodding direction. Ladd handles the role of the deranged figure well, wearing a faint smirk which indicates something lurking beneath his calm exterior.

p, Sidney Boehm; d, James B. Clark; w, Aaron Spelling, Boehm (based on the story by Spelling); ph, William C. Mellor (CinemaScope, Deluxe Color); m, Dominic Frontiere; ed, Eda Warren; art d, Duncan Cramer, Leland Fuller.

Western   **(PR:A MPAA:NR)**

ONE FOR ALL   (SEE: PRESIDENT'S MYSTERY, THE, 1936)

ONE FOR THE BOOKS   (SEE: VOICE OF THE TURTLE, THE, 1947)

ONE FRIGHTENED NIGHT**   (1935) 64m Mascot bw

Charley Grapewin (*Jasper Whyte*), Mary Carlisle (*Doris Waverly*), Arthur Hohl (*Arthur Proctor*), Evalyn Knapp (*1st Doris*), Wallace Ford (*Joe Luvalle*), Hedda Hopper (*Laura Proctor*), Lucien Littlefield (*Dr. Denham*), Regis Toomey (*Tom Dean*), Rafaela Ottiano (*Elvira*), Fred Kelsey (*Jenks*), Clarence H. Wilson (*Felix, Lawyer*), Adrian Morris (*Deputy Sheriff*).

Mascot was mainly engaged in producing serials, but the company sometimes created features, and ONE FRIGHTENED NIGHT is one of their better efforts. Based on a story by Stuart Palmer, author of the Hildegarde Withers mystery novels, the film stars Grapewin as a wealthy old man who gathers his relatives together to hear a reading of his will. The relatives all stand to substantially profit from the will, provided Grapewin's long lost granddaughter isn't found. The remainder of the film includes the appearance of a couple of women claiming to be the granddaughter, a murder, and some frantic plotting until Littlefield is revealed as the villain and Carlisle as the rightful heir. Grapewin is very good as the old eccentric, as is Ford as an ex-vaudevillian. The pace is quick and the music heightens the suspense. The score featured original compositions by Charles Dunworth, Jean de la Roche, Josiah Zuro, Francis Gromon, Milan Roder, Rex Bassett, Rudolph Friml, Oscar Potoker, and Constantin Bakaleinikoff.

p, Nat Levine; d, Christy Cabanne; w, Wellyn Totman (based on the story by Stuart Palmer); ph, Ernie Miller, William Nobles; ed, Joseph H. Lewis; md, Arthur Kay; spec eff, Jack Coyle, Howard Lydecker.

Mystery/Comedy   **Cas.**   **(PR:A MPAA:NR)**

ONE FROM THE HEART**   (1982) 107m Zoetrope/COL c

Frederic Forrest (*Hank*), Teri Garr (*Frannie*), Raul Julia (*Ray*), Nastassia Kinski (*Leila*), Lainie Kazan (*Maggie*), Harry Dean Stanton (*Moe*), Allan Goorwitz [Garfield] (*Restaurant Owner*), Jeff Hamlin (*Airline Ticket Agent*), Italia Coppola, Carmine Coppola (*Couple in Elevator*), Larry Albright, Mitchell Amundsen, Mary Andrews, James Austin, Elizabeth Bailey, Steve Calou, Jim Jack Campbell, Daniel Candib, Stephen Cohn, Ronald Colby, Tom Dahlgren, Foster Denker, Tony Dingman, Jim Dunn, Don Elmblad, Laura Fine, Michael Fink, Merrilisa Formento, Suzanne Fox, William George, Lyn Gerry, Ronald Gress, Michael Hacker, Tess Haley, Karl Herrman, Clark Higgins, Pete Jasper, Nancy Jencks, Roy Thomas Johns, Jill Kearney, Tom Koster, Kenneth Larson, Jack Lindauer, Loolee de Leon, Dan Lutz, Bonnie Macker, Michael Magill, Cathy Masom, Barbara McBane.

If this trifling love story had cost $1 million, it might have been welcomed, but critics were waiting with sharpened quills (dipped in curare) because it came in at the staggering sum of $27 million (with about half of that out of Coppola's own pocket, causing his dream of Zoetrope studios to be shattered as the banks took the lot back from him) and returned less than $2 million on the first release. The razzle-dazzle gimmickry and the photographic techniques dwarf the trivial story, as though C.B. DeMille had shot MY DINNER WITH ANDRE. Coppola built a replica of Las Vegas on his lot for about $6 million (he should have used the one George Stevens had to build for THE ONLY GAME IN TOWN, when Liz Taylor insisted on shooting that very American story in Paris because her husband, Richard Burton, was making a film there and she didn't want to be separated from him). The original script by Bernstein was non-musical and set in Chicago. Coppola had only done one musical, FINIAN'S RAINBOW, and that died, so he wanted to prove he could handle a film with singing and dancing and no machine guns blazing. It's a fantasy of romance among the blue-collar set. Garr and Forrest are a couple who love each other but feel they have to see what other lovers may be like. So he takes Kinski and she opts for Julia and they get back together at the end. Before that happens, the eye has been treated to such a display of technology and visual novelties that it is all one can remember. Coppola, who is one of the better screenwriters around and specializes in revealing his characters layer by layer like the unpeeling of an onion, forgets his training and leaves the heart behind. It is a sterile film—we never get involved with the people because we are so struck by the hardware. There's nothing wrong with any of the actors and they do their best with what they have to say, although they are one-dimensional from start to finish. Nevertheless, it's worthwhile seeing, if only to watch Garr, Stanton, and Goorwitz. Forrest seems to be walking around most of the time like a confused man looking for his lost dog. If nothing else, Coppola is willing to attempt different things and will put his money where his lens cap is.

p, Gray Frederickson, Armyan Bernstein, Fred Roos; exec p, Bernard Gersten; d, Francis Coppola; w, Bernstein, Coppola (based on a story by Bernstein); ph, Vittorio Storaro, Ronald V. Garcia (Metrocolor); m, Tom Waits; ed, Anne Goursand, Rudi Fehr, Randy Roberts; prod d, Dean Tavoularis; art d, Angelo Graham; cos, Ruth Morley; spec eff, Robert Swarthe; ch, Kenny Ortega; m/l, Waits (sung by Crystal Gayle, Waits).

Romance   **Cas.**   **(PR:O MPAA:R)**

ONE GIRL'S CONFESSION*½   (1953) 74m COL bw

Cleo Moore (Mary Adams), Hugo Haas (Dragomie Damitrof), Glenn Langan (Johnny), Ellen Stansbury (Judy), Anthony Jochim (Father Benedict), Burt Mustin (Gardener), Leonid Snegoff (Old Gregory), Jim Nusser (Warden), Russ Conway (Police Officer), Mara Lea (Girl), Gayne Whitman (District Attorney), Leo Mastovoy (Gambler), Martha Wentworth (Old Lady).

Haas produced, directed, wrote, and starred in this tale of a waitress, Moore, who gets revenge on her boss—the man who previously robbed her father—by stealing $25,000 from him. She confesses to her crime, but hides the money to have it waiting when she is released from jail. Once free, Moore takes a job as a waitress at Haas' cafe. When Haas is almost forced to close the cafe because of his gambling debts, Moore offers to lend him the needed money from her stash. But Haas starts wildly spending money making Moore believe that he has found her money. She hits him over the head with a bottle, then turns herself in to the police believing she killed the man. Haas isn't dead and Moore is released to go off with her lover, Langan. Mundane plot is performed and directed in an equally mundane manner.

p,d&w, Hugo Haas; ph, Paul Ivano; m, Vaclav Divina; ed, Merrill G. White; art d, Rudi Feld.

Drama   **(PR:C MPAA:NR)**

ONE GOOD TURN*½   (1936, Brit.) 72m ABF bw

Leslie Fuller (Bill Parsons), Georgie Harris (Georgie), Hal Gordon (Bert), Molly Fisher (Dolly Pearson), Basil Langton (Jack Pearson), Clarissa Selwyn (Ma Pearson), Arthur Finn (Townsend), Faith Bennett (Violet), Arthur Clayton, Arnold the Horse.

Fuller and Harris are the operators of a coffee stall who long to become music hall comedians. Fisher, the daughter of their landlady, is duped by a fraudulent movie producer who persuades her mother to put up her life savings to back the show in which her daughter is supposed to star. Fuller and Harris check into the producer's shady past and become involved with a gang of Chinese gangsters. Not especially funny in 1936 and the intervening years have added nothing.

p, Joe Rock; d, Alfred Goulding; w, Syd Courtenay, Georgie Harris, Jack Byrd (based on a story by Con West, Herbert Sargent); ph, Cyril Bristow.

Comedy   **(PR:A MPAA:NR)**

ONE GOOD TURN**   (1955, Brit.) 90m TC/GFD bw

Norman Wisdom (Norman), Joan Rice (Iris), Shirley Abicair (Mary), Thora Hird (Cook), William Russell (Alec), Richard Caldicot (Bigley), Marjorie Fender (Tuppeny), Keith Gilman (Jimmy), Joan Ingram (Matron), Harold Kasket (Ivor Petrovitch), Fred Kitchen, Jr. (Cinema Manager), David Hurst (Prof. Dofee), Michael Balfour (Hypnotist's Stooge), Ricky McCullough (Gunner Mac), Harold Goodwin.

Beginning in 1954 and continuing for the rest of the 1950s, popular British comedian Wisdom turned out a picture a year, starring as a bumbling do-gooder. This was his second effort and it's an enjoyable yarn in which Wisdom works as a handyman at a failing orphanage. To save the orphanage from financial ruin, Wisdom gets involved in a walkathon and a boxing match, and also conducts a symphony orchestra. Most of the bits work and the likable Wisdom carries the film nicely. While his movies were very successful in England, they never gained much support in the U.S.

p, Maurice Cowan; d, John Paddy Carstairs; w, Cowan, Carstairs, Ted Willis (based on the story by Dorothy Whipple, Sid Colin, Talbot Rothwell); ph, Jack Cox; m, John Addison; ed, Geoffrey Foot; m/l, Norman Newell, Norman Wisdom.

Comedy   **(PR:A MPAA:NR)**

ONE HEAVENLY NIGHT**   (1931) 82m Goldwyn/UA bw

Evelyn Laye (Lilli), John Boles (Count Mirko Tibor), Leon Errol (Otto), Lilyan Tashman (Fritzi Vyez), Hugh Cameron (Janos), Marian Lord (Liska), Lionel Belmore (Zagen), George Bickel (Papa Lorenc), Vincent Barnett (Egon), Henry Victor (Almady), Henry Kolker (Police Chief), Luis Alberni (Violinist).

On a trip to Europe, Samuel Goldwyn saw Evelyn Laye on the British stage and was captivated by her. Upon returning to America, he set out to create a vehicle that he was certain would catapult the actress/singer to stardom. He hired Pulitzer Prize-winning authors Louis Bromfield and Sidney Howard to come up with a story and their collaboration resulted in ONE HEAVENLY NIGHT. Set in Budapest, the film stars Laye as a flower girl who is persuaded to pose as Tashman, a sultry cabaret singer. As the entertainer, she is pursued by Boles, a dashing count. Laye falls for the count, but Tashman complicates matters when she reveals the duplicity and attempts to woo Boles herself. Boles knows true love though, and he finds Laye, who has fled after being exposed, and claims her for his wife. Laye made a memorable debut in the film, and the rest of the cast is good, as is the score, but the entire project was undone by the trite story. The movie proved to be a box office failure for Goldwyn's production company and he was so unnerved by it that he never made another operetta, nor did he ever again cast Laye, Boles, Tashman or Errol in any of his films. As for Laye, she made four more films in Hollywood, ending with PRINCESS CHARMING (1935), then returned to the British stage where she remained a popular star into the 1950s. Musical numbers in ONE HEAVENLY NIGHT include "I Belong to Everybody" (Tashman); "Along the Road of Dreams" (Laye); "My Heart is Beating," "Heavenly Night (When Evening is Near)" (Boles, Laye); "Goodnight Serenade" (Boles, Laye, men's chorus), all with music by Nacio Herb Brown and Bruno Granichstadten and lyrics by Edward Eliscu and Clifford Grey.

p, Samuel Goldwyn; d, George Fitzmaurice; w, Sidney Howard (based on a story

by Louis Bromfield); ph, George Barnes, Gregg Toland; ed, Stuart Heisler; md, Frank Tours; art d, Richard Day.

Musical/Drama   **(PR:A MPAA:NR)**

ONE HORSE TOWN   (SEE: SMALL TOWN GIRL, 1936)

ONE HOUR LATE*½   (1935) 75m PAR bw

Joe Morrison (Eddie Blake), Helen Twelvetrees (Betty Dunn), Conrad Nagel (Stephen Barclay), Arline Judge (Hazel), Ray Walker (Cliff Miller), Edward Craven (Maxie), Toby Wing (Maizie), Gail Patrick (Mrs. Ellen Barclay), Charles Sellon (Sampson), George E. Stone (Benny), Jed Prouty (Mr. Finch), Jack Mulhall (Whittaker), Edward Clark (Mr. Meller), Raymond [Ray] Milland (Tony St. John), Bradley Page (Jim), Sidney Miller (Orrville), Gladys Hulette (Gertrude), Billy Bletcher (Smith), Betty Farrington (Miss Jones), Arthur Hoyt (Barlow), Matty Fain (The Crook), Hallene Hill (Sick Woman), Diana Lewis (Her Daughter), Frank Mayo (Kearney), Eddie Phillips (Elevator Starter), Phil Tead (Wally), James P. Burtis (Art), Maxine Elliot Hicks (Elsie Kelsey), Jack Norton (Manager), Sam Ash (Phil Romaine), William Norton Bailey (Clayton), William H. Strauss (Man Who is Robbed), Carol Holloway (Nurse), George Lloyd (Collier), Frank Rice (Engineer), Robert Kent (Soda Clerk), Harry Depp (Fiddle Player), Billy Dooley (Attendant in Radio Station), Rhea Mitchell (Stage Mother), Shirley Jeanne Rickert (Child), Charles Morris (Man Outside Radio Room), William Jeffrey (M.C.), Genevieve Phillips (Information Girl), Buck Mack (Property Man), Jack Raymond (Musician), Robert Littlefield (Orchestra Leader), Ann Sheridan (Girl), Frank Losee, Jr., Alfred Delcambre (Friends), Monte Vandegrift, Lee Shumway (Detectives), Francis Sayles, Duke York (Mixers).

Morrison plays a would-be singer working as a shipping clerk while trying to make it as a singer. He is involved in a juvenile type of romance with Twelvetrees, a stenographer for the same company. Morrison becomes jealous when his sweetheart continually flirts with her lonely boss while at the same putting off their engagement. But Morrison gets his chance to prove himself when he is stalled in an elevator with the boss' wife and the president of a radio station. This also gives us a rest from Morrison's tedious acting and a chance to hear his fine singing voice.

p, Albert Lewis; d, Ralph Murphy; w, Kathryn Scola, Paul Gerard Smith (based on the story by Libbie Block); ph, Ben Reynolds; m/l, "Last Roundup," "A Little Angel Told Me So," "Me Without You," Sam Coslow, Leo Robin, Lewis Gensler.

Drama/Comedy   **(PR:A MPAA:NR)**

ONE HOUR TO DOOM'S DAY   (SEE: CITY BENEATH THE SEA, 1953)

ONE HOUR TO LIVE*½   (1939) 59m UNIV bw

Charles Bickford (Lt. Sid Brady), Doris Nolan (Muriel Vance), John Litel (Rudy Spain), Samuel S. Hinds (Commissioner), Paul Guilfoyle (Stanley Jones), Robert Emmett Keane (Maxie Stanton), Jack Carr (Riki/Tiger), John Gallaudet (Jimmy Marco), Emory Parnell ("Fats"), Olin Howland (Clerk), Theresa Harris (High Yaller Girl), Jack Roper (Referee), Ernie Alexander (Intern), Eddy Chandler (Petrie), Mary Foy (Jail Matron), James Green (Browning), Clarence Gordon (Fighter), Charles Sullivan (Fight Second), Buck Woods, Napoleon Simpson, Al Grant, Bud Harris (Black Men), Frank Marlowe, Charles Sherlock (Cab Drivers), Ed Piel, Sr. (Fingerprint Expert), Ralph Dunn, Jimmie Lucas (Heavies), Jack Gardner (Cab Driver).

Uninspired gangster drama has Bickford as a detective chasing after the crook who has stolen and married his girl, Nolan. After several brushes with death, Bickford finally pins down the hood, as well as the surprising revelation that Hinds, the Police Commissioner, is the actual brains behind the whole operation. It only took 23 days to write and shoot this film, and it shows.

p, George Yohalem; d, Harold Schuster; w, Roy Chanslor; ph, George Robinson; ed, Edward Curtis.

Crime   **(PR:A MPAA:NR)**

ONE HOUR WITH YOU***   (1932) 80m PAR bw

Maurice Chevalier (Dr. Andre Bertier), Jeanette MacDonald (Colette Bertier), Genevieve Tobin (Mitzi Olivier), Charles Ruggles (Adolph), Roland Young (Professor Olivier), George Barbier (Police Commissioner), Josephine Dunn (Mlle. Martel), Richard Carle (Detective), Charles Judels (Policeman), Barbara Leonard (Mitzi's Maid), Florine McKinney (Girl), Donald Novis (Singer), Charles Coleman (Marcel the Butler), Eric Wilton (Butler), George Davis (Cabby), Bill Elliott (Dance Extra) Sheila Mannors (Colette's Downstairs Maid), Leonie Pray (Collette's Upstairs Maid), Bess Flowers (Party Extra).

This is one of those very rare remakes that's better than the original, although the same director had a hand in both. Lubitsch made THE MARRIAGE CIRCLE as a silent in 1924, which starred Adolphe Menjou, Florence Vidor, Monte Blue, Creighton Hale and Marie Prevost. With the advent of sound, he thought a musical version might work and he was right. Chevalier was signed and wanted Kay Francis and Carole Lombard as his costars (both of whom he had his Gallic eye on) but Lubitsch knew that there might be a problem with that so he convinced Chevalier to accept MacDonald and Tobin. It began with Cukor at the directorial helm and Lubitsch running all of Paramount's production. After shooting quite a bit, Lubitsch began coming on the set to make suggestions and Cukor became fed up and quit. Consequently, Lubitsch finished the movie and sought solo credit as director. Cukor asked for a Director's Guild arbitration and won a co-director credit, although in some prints, Lubitsch gets a singular credit with Cukor being listed as Dialogue Director. At the same time this was being shot, a French version was lensed with everyone in the cast remaining except for Tobin, Young, Ruggles and Barbier, who were replaced by Lily Damita, Ernest Ferny, Pierre Etchepare and Andre Cheron, in that order. Chevalier and MacDonald are strolling in the Bois de Boulogne in Paris and begin necking furiously. An offended policeman, Judels, tells them to stop but they explain that they are married. He won't believe them and suggests that if what they say is true, they go home and practice their lovemaking in the privacy of their own boudoir. They do just that and Chevalier does his first 'camera take' to look at the audience and explain that they really are married and weren't kidding the gendarme. (He uses that technique several times during the movie to narrate and bridge any gaps.) Chevalier is a doctor with an eye that tends to rove. Tobin is MacDonald's best girlfriend although she's willing to toss that aside in favor of an affair with Chevalier, so she pays him a professional call and her intentions become evident. Tobin is married to Young, a professor who suspects his wife of dallying so he hires Carle, a private detective, to follow her and bring him evidence. When Carle arrives with proof that Tobin has visited Chevalier, Young tells Chevalier that he is about to divorce Tobin and will name the doctor as the reason for that splituation. Chevalier tells MacDonald what's happened and she is stunned, then decides what's fair for the gander is fair for the goose, so she has a fling with Ruggles, who has been patiently waiting in the wings for her. Chevalier is miffed but MacDonald says that it's now time for them to cease this merry-making and get down to marriage. She promises to never stray again if he won't and he happily agrees. A minor plot at best but the dialog crackles and the singing is wonderful. Not one of Lubitsch's best, perhaps because there was not a single guiding hand from the first day's shooting. Nevertheless, a good example of the romantic comedy-musicals of the 1930s. Songs include: "One Hour with You" (Richard A. Whiting, Leo Robin, sung by MacDonald, Chevalier, Tobin, Ruggles, Novis), "Three Times a Day" (Whiting, Robin), "Now I Ask You What Would You Do?" (Whiting, Robin, sung by Chevalier) "What a Little Thing Like a Wedding Ring Can Do" (Oscar Straus, Robin) "Oh That Mitzi" (Straus, Robin, sung by Chevalier), "It Was Only a Dream Kiss," "Mitzi-Colette Talk Song" (Straus, Robin), "Police Station Talk Song" (John Leipold, sung by Barbier, Chorus), "We Will Always Be Sweethearts" (Straus, Robin, sung by MacDonald, Chevalier).

p, Ernst Lubitsch; d, Lubitsch, George Cukor; w, Samson Raphaelson (based on the play "Only a Dream" by Lothar Schmidt [Goldschmidt]); ph, Victor Milner; m, Oscar Straus, Richard Whiting; ed, William Shea; md, Nathaniel W. Finston; art d, Hans Dreier; set d, A.E. Freudeman; cos, Travis Banton.

Musical Comedy   **(PR:A-C MPAA:NR)**

ONE HUNDRED AND ONE DALMATIANS***½

(1961) 79m Disney/BV c

Voices: Rod Taylor (Pongo), Lisa Davis (Anita), Cate Bauer (Perdita), Ben Wright (Roger Radcliff), Frederick Worlock (Horace), J. Pat O'Malley (Jasper/Miscellaneous Dogs), Betty Lou Gerson (Cruella De Vil/Miss Birdwell), Martha Wentworth (Nani/Goose/Cow), Tom Conway (Collie), George Pelling (Great Dane), Micky Maga (Patch the Puppy), Barbara Beaird (Holly the Puppy), Queenie Leonard, Marjorie Bennett (Cows), Tudor Owen, Mimi Gibson, Sandra Abbott, Paul Wexler, Mary Wickes, Barbara Luddy, Lisa Daniels, David Frankham, Ramsay Hill, Sylvia Marriott, Thurl Ravenscroft, Bill Lee, Max Smith, Bob Stevens, Helene Stanley, Donald Barclay, Dal McKennon, Jeanne Bruns.

Three hundred artists worked on this project for three years to come up with one of the best feature cartoons ever to come out of the Disney studios. The story is a nice blend of a romantic theme and an interesting detective twist, combined with exquisite caricatures of both humans and dogs. The plot revolves around a dog, Pongo, and his master, Roger, who fall for Anita and her dog Perdita. Roger and Anita marry, which also allows Pongo and Perdita to be together and to produce an offspring of 15 Dalmatian puppies. A wicked woman named Cruella De Vil is overly persistent in her desires to have all 15 puppies. But Roger refuses her, prompting the wealthy woman to hire a pair of Cockney crooks to stage a heist of the pups. Roger and Anita resort to all types of measures to locate the lost pups, but to no avail. This makes Pongo resort to the "twilight bark", a system of barking signals which locates the puppies in a deserted mansion on the outskirts of London. Pongo, assisted by a dog named the Colonel, a horse, and a cat, then rescues the puppies from the mansion. In doing so he also uncovers a total of 99 Dalmatians, whom the wicked woman has gathered to make herself a rare coat. When all the dogs are safely back at Roger's house, he decides to keep the whole bunch. Throughout the story are subtle visual elements that give it an atmosphere that transcends a cartoon sense of reality. Among these evocative touches are several highly dramatic sequences, such as when Roger massages the heart of one of the puppies that has just been delivered. Additional depth is given to the caricatures through the voices used to compliment the personalities. Note the physical resemblance between many of the dogs and their masters. The Disney crew also had a fine time poking fun at TV, parodying the medium with a game show called "What's My Crime" and with another program sponsored by a Kanine Krunchies. The animators benefitted from the then-new process known as xerography. Copy machine systems may not seem particularly revolutionary from today's vantage point, but in 1961 they must have seemed truly marvelous to the Disney animators faced with the prospect of an untold number of scenes filled with 101 Dalmatians. Interestingly, they combined this new technology with a "rough-line" drawing technique that took some of the gloss off the traditional polish of the Disney animation style. Songs include: "Remember When" (Franklyn Marks), "Cruella de Vil," "Dalmatian Plantation" (Mel Leven, sung by Jeanne Bruns, Bill Lee), "Kanine Krunchies Kommercial" (Leven, sung by Lucille Bliss).

p, Walt Disney; d, Wolfgang Reitherman, Hamilton S. Luske, Clyde Geronimi; w, Bill Peet (based on a book by Dodie Smith); m, George Bruns; ed, Donald Halliday, Roy M. Brewer, Jr; prod d&art d, Ken Anderson; animation, Milt Kahl, Marc Davis, Oliver Johnston, Jr., Franklin Thomas, John Lounsbery, Eric Larson, Hal King, Cliff Nordberg, Eric Cleworth, Art Stevens, Hal Ambro, Bill Keil, Dick Lucas, Les Clark, Blaine Gibson, John Sibley, Julius Svendsen, Ted Berman, Don Lusk, Amby Paliwoda; backgrounds, Albert Dempster, Ralph Hulett, Anthony Rizzo, Bill Layne.

Animation   **(PR:AAA MPAA:G)**

$100 A NIGHT**½

(1968, Ger.) 85m Rex/ William Mishkin bw MADCHEN FUR DIE MAMBOBAR)

Kai Fischer (Olga), Gerlinde Locker (Eva), Tommy Rupp (Tommy Kersten), Jimmy Makulis (Jimmy), Rolf Kutschera (Martini), Rolf Olsen (Rutka) Wolf Albach-Retty (Kruger), Horst Beck, Edith Elmay, Guido Wieland, Alfred Bohm, Raoul Retzer, Inge Rassaert, Renate Rohm, Aina Capell, Gaby King, Josef Hendrichs, Hansi Prinz, Mona Baptiste, Dalida, Macky Kasper, Habiba, Latin Bob Stars, Fatty George and His Orchestra.

This look at the underworld life of Germany has Locker as a singer trying to make a success of herself. She gets a job as booking agent at an agency next to a nightclub run by Kutschera, a man also involved in drug dealing, espionage, and illegal massage parlors. The trumpeter of the jazz band playing at the club talks Locker into singing at the club; enraging jealous dancer Fischer, who attempts to kill Locker, but falls to her own death instead. The trumpet player, Rupp, turns out to be an undercover cop, out to pin down the activities of Kutschera.

d, Wolfgang Gluck; w, Hellmut Andics, August Rieger; ph, Walter Tuch; m, Willi Hoffman, Gilbert Becaud, Klaus Ogermann, Perez Prado, Sten Clift; ed, Ursula Norkus; art d, Felix Smetana; ch, Willy Dirtl.

Crime/Drama   **(PR:C MPAA:NR)**

100 MEN AND A GIRL**½

(1937) 85m UNIV bw

Deanna Durbin (Patricia Cardwell), Leopold Stokowski (Himself), Adolphe Menjou (John Cardwell), Alice Brady (Mrs. Frost), Eugene Pallette (John R. Frost), Mischa Auer (Michael Borodoff), Billy Gilbert (Garage Owner), Alma Kruger (Mrs. Tyler), Jack [J. Scott] Smart, (Marshall, the Doorman), Jed Prouty (Tommy Bitters), Jameson Thomas (Russell), Howard Hickman (Johnson), Frank Jenks (Taxi Driver), Christian Rub (Gustave Brandstetter), Gerald Oliver Smith (Stevens, the Butler), Jack Mulhall (Rudolph, a Bearded Musician/Boarder), James Bush (Music Lover), John Hamilton (Manager), Eric Wilton (Butler), Mary Forbes (Theater Patron), Rolfe Sedan, Charles Coleman, Hooper Atchley (Guests), Leonid Kinskey (Pianist), Edwin Maxwell (Ira Westing, Music Editor), Rosemary La Planche (Girl), Bess Flowers (Party Guest).

There are many child stars who have been horrors to work with but that was not the case with Deanna Durbin, who was a delight for everyone and surely one of the most agreeable tykes to ever don the greasepaint. She began her career with Judy Garland in an MGM short, EVERY SUNDAY, but the studio dropped her and kept Garland. It wasn't that her voice wasn't resonant, it was merely that the studio felt there was only room for one of that type and opted for Judy. Durbin was signed by Universal, cast in THREE SMART GIRLS, and did so well that they top-lined her in this one, which turned out to be a box office winner that took the studio from the brink of bankruptcy. Menjou is a trombonist without a place to blow. The same problem is happening to many of his musician friends. Durbin, realizing the difficulty, forms an orchestra and convinces the eminent Leopold Stokowski to conduct the aggregation in a concert. The orchestra is a hit and all ends well. An excellent mix of classical and pop music, the numbers included: "Hungarian Rhapsody No. 2" (Franz Liszt), the drinking song from "La Traviata" (Verdi), excerpts from "Lohengrin" (Wagner), "Symphony No. 5" (Tschaikovsky), "Alleluja" (Mozart), "It's Raining Sunbeams" (Sam Coslow, Frederick Hollander), "A Heart That's Free" (Alfred G. Robyn, Thomas T. Railey). An Oscar went to Previn for his musical supervision plus nominations for the score, recording, editing, the story, and best of all it was even named as one of the finalists for Best Picture along with THE AWFUL TRUTH, DEAD END, IN OLD CHICAGO, CAPTAINS COURAGEOUS, LOST HORIZON, STAGE DOOR, and A STAR IS BORN. Pretty stiff competition for the ultimate winner, THE LIFE OF EMILE ZOLA.

p, Joe Pasternak, Charles R. Rogers; d, Henry Koster; w, Bruce Manning, Charles Kenyon, James Mulhauser, Hans Kraly (based on a story by Kraly); ph, Joseph Valentine; ed, Bernard W. Burton; md, Charles Previn.

Musical   **(PR:AAA MPAA:NR)**

ONE HUNDRED PERCENT PURE

(SEE: GIRL FROM MISSOURI, THE, 1934)

100 RIFLES**

(1969) 110m FOX c

Jim Brown (Lyedecker), Raquel Welch (Sarita), Burt Reynolds (Yaqui Joe), Fernando Lamas (Verdugo), Dan O'Herlihy (Grimes), Hans Gudegast [Eric Braeden] (Von Klemme), Michael Forest (Humara), Aldo Sambrell (Sgt. Paletes), Soledad Miranda (Girl in Hotel), Alberto Dalbes (Padre Francisco), Carlos Bravo (Lopez), Jose Manuel Martin (Sarita's Father).

A violent western, much in the vein of THE WILD BUNCH (in fact, having several similarities which appear to be something more than mere coincidence), and shot in Spain. Brown plays a sheriff on the trail of Reynolds, a Yaqui Indian who has robbed a bank in order to supply his people with money to buy rifles. Though he is committed to bringing his man back, once Brown is exposed to the type of mistreatment the Indians have had at the hands of Lamas (a sadistic military leader whose methods include the hanging of corpses from telephone poles), he also joins in the fight. Welch plays the leader of the Indian rebels, whose father has recently been killed at the hands of Lamas. Though spoken for by Reynolds, she and Brown have a go at it in a love scene filled with more violence than tenderness. When Brown and Reynolds are captured by Lamas, and all seems lost, the Yaquis stage an attack with their newly acquired rifles, freeing the sheriff and the fugitive. Brown returns to Arizona, but without Reynolds, who has been left behind to bring order to the newly freed Indians. Beneath all the fierce fighting sequences, is just another routine western plot.

p, Marvin Schwartz; d, Tom Gries; w, Clair Huffaker, Gries (based on the novel The Californio by Robert MacLeod); ph, Cecilio Paniagua (DeLuxe Color); m,

Jerry Goldsmith; ed, Robert Simpson; art d, Carl Anderson; spec eff, L.B. Abbott, Art Cruickshank; makeup, Ramon de Diego.

Western Cas. (PR:O MPAA:R)

125 ROOMS OF COMFORT* (1974, Can.) 80m Nulvano/Art Films c

Tim Henry, Jackie Burroughs, Bob Warner, Bob Silverman, Les Barker.

Inexpensive Canadian independent production centers on an ex-rock star whose inability to cope with life off the stage sends him to a mental hospital. After a brief recuperation he is released only to sell the hotel he has inherited to a pushy American. The hotel is the setting for a number of peculiar occurrences, none of which combine in a very cinematic manner. The talents of Burroughs are wasted in this one.

p, Don Haig; d, Patrick Loubert; w, Loubert, Bill Freut; ph, H. Fike.

Drama Cas. (PR:O MPAA:NR)

ONE HYSTERICAL NIGHT** (1930) 75m UNIV bw

Reginald Denny *(William Judd/"Napoleon")*, Nora Lane *(Nurse/"Josephine")*, E.J. Ratcliffe *(Wellington)*, Fritz Feld *(Paganini)*, Slim Summerville *(Robin Hood)*, Joyzelle *(Salome)*, Jules Cowles *(William Tell)*, Walter Brennan *(Paul Revere)*, Henry Otto *(Dr. Hayden)*, Margaret Campbell *(Mrs. Bixby)*, Peter Cawthorne *(Mr. Bixby)*, D.R.O. Hatswell *(Claude Bixby)*, Rolfe Sedan *(Arthur Bixby)*, Lloyd Whitlock *(Attorney Thurston)*.

About to inherit a fortune, Denny is persuaded by his aunt and uncle to dress as Napoleon for a costume ball; then they drive him to an asylum and have him committed as suffering delusions of grandeur. He escapes and, with nurse Lane and a host of other inmates, returns to his home and sees his place restored and his avaricious relatives ousted. Denny, who had been occasionally dabbling in screenwriting, took on both the writing and editing of this mediocre comedy. He never tried either again. This film was released in both silent and sound versions.

d, William James Craft; w, Reginald Denny; ph, Arthur Todd; ed, Denny.

Comedy (PR:A MPAA:NR)

ONE IN A MILLION* (1935) 66m IN/CHES bw

Dorothy Wilson *(Dorothy Brooks)*, Charles Starrett *(Donald Cabot)*, Guinn "Big Boy" Williams *(Spike McGafferty)*, Gwen Lee *(Kitty Kennedy)*, Holmes Herbert *(Cabot, Sr.)*, Francis Sayles *(Dickman)*, Fred Santley *(Frankie)*, Barbara Rogers *(Patsy)*, Robert Frazer.

The haphazardness of this production takes its toll on what could have been an interesting story. Poor direction, dull photography, and unacceptable editing mar any worth this project might have had. Wilson plays a shopgirl who goes into hiding after she thinks she has killed her boss. While at the resort where she has taken refuge, she falls for a rich and handsome young man, who turns out to be the son of her former boss.

p, Maury M. Cohen; d, Frank Strayer; w, Karl Brown, Robert Ellis; ph, M.A. Anderson; ed, Roland Reed.

Drama (PR:A MPAA:NR)

ONE IN A MILLION** (1936) 95m FOX bw

Sonja Henie *(Greta Muller)*, Adolphe Menjou *(Tad Spencer)*, Jean Hersholt *(Heinrich Muller)*, Ritz Brothers *(Themselves)*, Arline Judge *(Billie Spencer)*, Dixie Dunbar *(Goldie)*, Don Ameche *(Bob Harris)*, Ned Sparks *(Danny Simpson)*, Montagu Love *(Ratoffsky)*, Leah Ray *(Leah)*, Shirley Deane, June Gale, Lillian Porter, Diana Cook, Bonnie Bannon, June Wilkins, Clarice Sherry, Pauline Craig *(Members of Girls' Band)*, Albert Conti *(Manager of St. Moritz Hotel)*, Julius Tannen *(Chapelle)*, Margo Webster *(French Skater)*, Frederic Gierman *(German Announcer)*, Bess Flowers *(Woman in Box)*, Egon Brecher *(Chairman)*, Paul McVey *(Announcer, Madison Square Garden)*, Borrah Minevitch and his Harmonica Rascals *(Adolph and His Gang)*.

This was the movie that served to introduce Norwegian skating whiz Henie to America and it was a smash debut. She'd taken the Olympic medal in Germany the year before and was hot news. The big surprise was that she could also speak as well as she skated without tripping over her tongue. Henie and Jesse Owens were the stars of that 1936 Olympiad but he wasn't as blonde and squeaky-clean as she was and no one rushed to sign the magnificent Owens to a film contract. She never did become an actress but her nice smile and her ability to skate gave her more films than anyone else in that sport. She was also a wise businesswoman and amassed a fortune with investments reaped from being the producer and star of her own touring ice shows until her retirement from skating at the age of 57 in 1960. The ice is thicker than the plot for this movie. Menjou is a two-bit Ziegfeld touring Europe with his troupe that includes the Ritz Brothers, Dunbar, Minnevitch and more. They're short of money and food and on a train to do a show in Switzerland when Menjou spies Henie practicing her craft on a frozen lake. She's about to go to the Olympics and see if she can bring home the same medal her father, Hersholt, won many years before. She wins, signs on with Menjou has an attraction to newsman Ameche, who is trying to protect her from Menjou's profit-making schemes, and winds up at Madison Square Garden where she delights America. Good comedy from the Ritz Brothers, Minnevitch and Ned Sparks but the unquestioned star is Henie, who skated as beautifully as Fred and Ginger danced. Tunes include: "One in a Million," "We're Back in Circulation Again," "Who's Afraid of Love?" "Lovely Lady in White," "The Moonlight Waltz" (Sidney D. Mitchell, Lew Pollack).

p, Darryl F. Zanuck; d, Sidney Lanfield; w, Leonard Praskins, Mark Kelly; ph, Edward Cronjager; ed, Robert Simpson; md, Louis Silvers; skating ensembles, Jack Haskell.

Musical/Comedy (PR:AA MPAA:NR)

ONE IS A LONELY NUMBER*** (1972) 97m MGM c (AKA: TWO IS A HAPPY NUMBER)

Trish Van Devere *(Amy Brower)*, Monte Markham *(Howard Carpenter)*, Janet Leigh *(Gert Meredith)*, Melvyn Douglas *(Joseph Provo)*, Jane Elliot *(Madge Frazier)*, Jonathan Lippe *(Sherman Cooke)*, Mark Bramhall *(Morgue Attendant)*, Paul Jenkins *(James Brower)*, A. Scott Beach *(Frawley King)*, Henry Leff *(Arnold Holzgang)*, Dudley Knight *("King Lear")*, Maurice Argent *(Pool Manager)*, Thomas McNallan *(Hardware Clerk)*, Morgan Upton *("Earl of Gloucester")*, Joseph Spano *("Earl of Kent")*, Kim Allen *(Ronnie Porter)*, Peter Fitzsimmons *(Employment Office Clerk)*, Christopher Brooks *(Marvin Friedlander)*.

An underrated picture that came and went before it got a chance to find an audience, this was two years ahead of its time in theme and execution. These days, there is a surfeit of "women's films" which examine all the problems of modern-day divorcehood but this one does it better than most of those. Van Devere and Jenkins have been what she thought was happily married for a number of years. Then, without a word of warning, Jenkins, a college professor, leaves and starts divorce proceedings. Though she's still young at 27, Van Devere has never had to be independent and fears that responsibility. Elliot is Van Devere's best friend and she takes the shocked woman to meet Leigh, who is the president of a divorced women's club. After a meeting with Leigh that disintegrates into booziness, Van Devere gets a job as a lifeguard (despite her excellent education) but she can't fulfill some of the requirements as she suffers from mild acrophobia and fears the high diving board. Douglas is Van Devere's local grocer and he is as lonely as she because his beloved wife of nearly 40 years has recently passed away. Van Devere and Douglas find much in common and establish a bond between them, disregarding the difference in their ages. Elliot takes Van Devere to an art gallery opening party and Markham steps into Van Devere's life. He's a handsome and charming man and he dances enough attention on her to take her to dinner and back to his posh apartment. She knows what's going to happen and tries to change the subject but Markham makes the expected move and she reacts in panic and exits hastily. Douglas escorts her to see Shakespeare in the Park, a performance of *King Lear*, but once the two begin talking about how lonely they feel, tears begin to flow and the evening is ruined. She goes home and Markham awaits her. Now a bit more confident about herself, she goes to bed with Markham, then realizes that she's been had in more ways than one when he admits he's already married. Van Devere next learns that Jenkins is happy living in Nevada with a teenage female young enough to be his daughter and her response is to tell her attorney, Beach, to go for her ex-husband's throat and wallet in the settlement. She seeks out Douglas but the store is shuttered and no one has seen him for a few days. She's worried that something may have happened to the kindly grocer and searches the city morgues where she sees scores of dead old men, none of whom is Douglas. The following morning, as she is going to court with Elliot and Leigh to help her through the day, she spots Douglas and is glad to learn that he was away on a small vacation and there was no cause to worry. Once in court, the defendants, led by Jenkins's lawyer, Leff, are surprised to hear her state that she wants nothing from the man who left her, not one cent. All she needs right now is her freedom. That done, Van Devere heads straight for her job at the swimming pool, climbs to the top of the diving platform and does a perfect swan into the pool. Along the way, she has come up against some chauvinists like Lippe, her employment agent; her own attorney, Beach, and a couple of others who think that a divorced woman is fair game for any man. The picture gets a bit glib at times and the denouement is not motivated enough but there are so many good things about this film that it's worthwhile. Director Stuart has had a spotty career making some of the best and the worst films, from the sublime, WILLIE WONKA AND THE CHOCOLATE FACTORY, to the ridiculous, I LOVE MY WIFE. In order to fill the empty seats, they changed the title for a while to TWO IS A HAPPY NUMBER but it didn't help. In one scene, an attorney hands Van Devere an ice cream cone filled with raspberry ripple and both Seltzer and Stuart thought that the title of the film should have been "A Fine Day for Raspberry Ripple." If nothing else, that would have been remembered but MGM had bombed with THE STRAWBERRY STATEMENT just two years before and wasn't into flavors despite having a 1941 hit with THE CHOCOLATE SOLDIER.

p, Stan Margulies; d, Mel Stuart; w, David Seltzer (based on the short story "The Good Humor Man" by Rebecca Morris); ph, Michel Hugo (Metrocolor); m, Michel Legrand; ed, David Saxon; md, Legrand; art d, Walter M. Simonds; set d, George Gaines.

Drama (PR:C MPAA:PG)

ONE IS GUILTY** (1934) 64m COL bw

Ralph Bellamy *(Inspector Trent)*, Shirley Grey *(Sally)*, Warren Hymer *(Walters)*, Rita La Roy *(Lola Deveroux)*, J. Carrol Naish *(Jack Allan)*, Wheeler Oakman *(Toledo Eddie)*, Ruth Abbott *(Miss Kane)*, Willard Robertson *(Wells Deveroux)*.

Bellamy is a detective on the trail of a murder, but he is crossed up when another murder is committed after he is certain he has already nailed down the culprit. Evenly paced schemer, which manages a few twists to keep the suspense flowing. One of many such 1930s detective films in which Bellamy played the lead.

d, Lambert Hillyer; w, Harold Shumate; ph, John Stumar.

Crime (PR:A MPAA:NR)

ONE JUMP AHEAD** (1955, Brit.) 66m Kenilworth/GFD bw

Paul Carpenter *(Paul Banner)*, Diane Hart *(Maxine)*, Jill Adams *(Judy)*, Freddie Mills *(Bert Tarrant)*, Peter Sinclair *(Old Tarrant)*, Arnold Bell *(Supt. Faro)*, David Hannaford *(Brian)*, Roddy Hughes *(Mac)*, Edward French, Jane Ashley, Rose Howlett, Freddie Watts, Mary Jones, Charles Lamb, Arthur Gross.

Occasionally witty dialog enhances this B-bracket programmer. Carpenter is a reporter on the trail of the killer of a blackmailing young lady and a schoolboy believed to have witnessed the crime. He discovers that Adams, an ex-lover, is the murderer and he leaves her a pistol with one bullet in it to take the proper way out. Carpenter and Hart repeat roles originated by Peter Reynolds and Honor Blackman in THE DELAVINE AFFAIR.

p, Guido Coen; d, Charles Saunders; w, Doreen Montgomery (based on a novel by Robert Chapman); ph, Brendan J. Stafford.

Crime (PR:A MPAA:NR)

ONE JUST MAN* (1955, Brit.) 55m AB-Pathe bw

Alexander Knox (Judge Craig), Peter Reynolds (Playboy), Ron Randell, Joan Haythorne, Maureen Swanson, Cyril Raymond, Eunice Gayson, John Warwick.

A short feature which is actually two featurettes strung together. The first has judge Knox taking it upon himself to deal with law-breakers, though his plans take a wrong turn. The second tale has Reynolds attempting to dupe an insurance company with a false claim, but instead is duped himself. Both episodes are nothing more than second-rate suspensers.

p, Edward J. Danziger, Harry Lee Danziger; d, David Macdonald; w, James Eastwood, Kate Barley; ph, Jimmy Wilson.

Crime (PR:A MPAA:NR)

ONE LAST FLING* (1949) 74m WB bw

Alexis Smith (Olivia Pearce), Zachary Scott (Larry Pearce), Douglas Kennedy (Victor Lardner), Ann Doran (Vera Thompson), Ransom Sherman (Judge Boulton), Veda Ann Borg (Gay Winston), Jim Backus (Howard Prichard), Helen Westcott (Annie Mae Hunter), Barbara Bates (June Payton), Jody Gilbert (Amy Deering).

Dull, clinche-ridden attempt at comedy has Smith returning to work at her husband's music store, only to erupt in a jealous rage when her husband wants to hire his attractive ex-girl friend. Good camera work and set design are wasted in this effort.

p, Saul Elkins; d, Peter Godfrey; w, Richard Flournoy, William Sackheim (based on a story by Herbert Clyde Lewis); ph, Carl Guthrie; m, David Buttolph; ed, Frederick Richards; md, Leo F. Forbstein; art d, John Hughes; set d, Howard Winterbottom; cos, Milo Anderson; makeup, Perc Westmore.

Comedy Cas. (PR:A MPAA:NR)

ONE LIFE (SEE: END OF DESIRE, 1962, Fr./Ital.)

ONE LITTLE INDIAN**½ (1973) 91m Disney/BV c

James Garner (Clint Keyes), Vera Miles (Doris), Pat Hingle (Capt. Stewart), Morgan Woodward (Sgt. Raines), John Doucette (Sgt. Waller), Clay O'Brien (Mark), Robert Pine (Lt. Cummins), Bruce Glover (Schrader), Ken Swofford (Pvt. Dixon), Jay Silverheels (Jimmy Wolfe), Andrew Prine (Chaplain), Jodie Foster (Martha), Walter Brooke, Rudy Diaz, John Flinn, Tom Simcox, Lois Red Elk, Hal Baylor, Terry Wilson, Paul Sorenson, Boyd "Red" Morgan, Jim Davis.

Garner plays a deserter from the U.S. Cavalry sentenced to hanging after disregarding orders. His crime was saving the lives of Indian women and children during a raid. During his trek through the desert on the camel Rosy, he comes across a young white boy, O'Brien, who was raised as an Indian and is trying to get back to his lost tribe. Garner takes the boy under his wing as he escapes pursuit from Woodward, putting up for a bit at the ranch of Miles. Sincere portrayals give this rather bland story some life, with the camel Rosy holding up the comic end.

p, Winston Hibler; d, Bernard McEveety; w, Harry Spalding; ph, Charles F. Wheeler (Technicolor); m, Jerry Goldsmith; ed, Robert Stafford; art d, John B. Mansbridge, LeRoy G. Deane; cos, Chuck Keehne, Emily Sunbay.

Western (PR:AA MPAA:G)

ONE MAD KISS* (1930) 67m FOX bw

Don Jose Mojica (Jose Salvedra), Mona Maris (Rosario), Antonio Moreno (Don Estrada), Tom Patricola (Paco).

Formula drama taking the Robin Hood story and placing it in a Spanish setting. Mojica is the bandit who robs from the rich to help the oppressed subjects of a crooked official. He states his love for Maris in a letter, but the tyrannical governor confiscates the missive and uses it to track down Mojica. The entire production is crude, with little offered to make it worthwhile. Songs include: "Oh, Where Are You," "One Mad Kiss" (Jose Mojica, Troy Saunders), "Behind the Mask," "Monkey on a String," "Oh: Have I a Way with the Girls" (James Hanley, Joseph McCarthy), "Only One," "The Gay Heart" (Dave Stamper, Clare Kummer), "Once in a While" (Stamper, Kummer, Cecil Arnold), "In My Arms," "I Am Free" (William Kernell), "Lament" (Dudley Nichols, Mojica).

d, Marcel Silver; w, Dudley Nichols (based on a play by Adolph Paul); ph, Charles Van Enger; ed, Louis Loeffler.

Musical (PR:A MPAA:NR)

ONE MAN**½ (1979, Can.) 87m National Film Board of Canada c

Len Cariou (Jason Brady), Jayne Eastwood (Alicia Brady), Carol Lazare (Marian Galbraith), Barry Morse (Colin Angus Campbell), August Schellenberg (Ernie Carrick), Jean Lapointe (Ben Legault), Sean Sullivan (Rodney Porter), Terry Haig (Dr. Gendron), Marc Legault (Leo), Danny Freedman, Gilles Renaud (Hoods), Bob Girolami (TV Announcer), Jacques Godin (Jaworski), Donovan Hare (Donovan), Kevin Hare (Kevin), Jesse Brown, Peter MacNeil, Michel Maillot, Jerome Tiberghien, Larry Kent, Jean-Pierre Bergeron, John Boylan, Dave Patrick, Richard Comar, Gary Plaxton, Joan Heeny, Miguel Fernandez, Elizabeth Chouvalidze, Terrence Ross, Julie Anna, Paul Loughlin, Yvon Leroux, Paul Haynes, Bronwen Mantel, Barry Lane, Janice Bryan, Helen Mullins, Laurent Poirier, Jean-Pierre Hallee, Pietro Bertolissi, Elizabeth Suzuki, Joan Blackman, Vlasta Vrana.

Predictable story has Cariou as a TV/Newsman involved in a story about a large factory that is polluting a poor section of the city and seriously endangering the lives of the children who live in the slum. Cariou and his family are harassed by henchmen from the offending company, while his own bosses are loath to take any action for fear of stirring up problems with big business. A rare sense of conviction to the problems posed makes this story more gripping than the usual social conscience film.

p, Michael Scott; d, Robin Spry; w, Spry, Peter Pearson, Peter Madden; ph, Douglas Kiefer (Eastmancolor); m, Ben Low; ed, John Kramer; art d, Denis Boucher.

Drama (PR:C MPAA:PG)

ONE MAN JURY* (1978) 98m Cal-Am Artists c

Jack Palance (Wade), Christopher Mitchum (Blake), Pamela Shoop (Wendy), Cara Williams (Nancy), Joe Spinell (Mike), Jeff McCracken (Billy Joe), Alexandra Hay (Tessie), Angel Tompkins (Kitty), Andy Romano (Chickie), Tom Pedi (Angie), Chuck Bergansky (Kayo), Anthony Sirico (Charlie), Richard Foronjy (Al), Patrick Wright (Kinky), Frank Pesce (Freddie), Dick Yarmy (Customer), Donald "Red" Barry (Murphy), James Bacon (Reporter), Kirk Scott (Cole), Royal Dano (Bartender), John Blythe Barrymore (Policeman), Elizabeth Kerr (Maid), Alfred T. Williams (Detective), John E. Neukum, Jr., (Cop), Lindsay Workman (Judge), George Deaton, Alex Hakobian (Pool Players), Myrna Dell (Landlady), Geraldine Smith (Barmaid), Mike Mazurki (Handler), Hany Ghorra (Floorman), Betty Hager, Sampa Tacorda (Chip Girls).

Ultra-violent DIRTY HARRY knockoff has Palance a tough cop disgusted by a system that turns dangerous punks loose because of technicalities. He turns in his badge, takes gun in hand, and goes out blasting a vicious gang particularly in need of extermination.

p, Theodor Bodnar, Steve Bono; d&w, Charles Martin; ph, (CFI Color); m, Morton Stevens.

Crime Cas. (PR:O MPAA:R)

ONE MAN JUSTICE*** (1937) 59m COL bw

Charles Starrett (Larry Clarke), Barbara Weeks (Mary Crockett), Hal Taliaferro [Wally Wales] (Neal King), Jack Clifford (Sheriff), Alan Bridge (Red Grindy), Walter Downing (Doc Willat), Mary Gordon (Bridget), Jack Lipson (Slim), Edmund Cobb (Tex Wiley), Dick Curtis (Hank Skinner), Matson Williams (Lefty Gates), Harry Fleischman (Joe Craig), Art Mix, Hank Bell, Steve Clark, Frank Ellis, Ethan Laidlaw, Eddie Laughton, Ted Mapes, Lew Meehan, Merrill McCormick.

Action-packed western has Starrett arriving in Mesa as the exact double of a man long believed to be dead. In truth, Starrett is this same man, having had a bout with amnesia five years earlier, but slowly beginning to recover his memory after his stay in the town. Starrett helps to clean up the general lawlessness of the town by calling in some of his buddies from Texas. At the same time he regains the wife and ranch which were his before he lost his memory. Nonstop action is given a perceptive guiding hand by director Barsha.

p, Peter B. Kyne; d, Leon Barsha; w, Paul Perez (based on a story by William Colt MacDonald); ph, John Stumar.

Western (PR:A MPAA:NR)

ONE-MAN LAW** (1932) 61m COL bw

Buck Jones, Shirley Grey, Robert Ellis, Murdock McQuarrie, Harry Todd, Henry Sedley, Ernie Adams, Dick Alexander, Wesley Giraud, Edward J. LeSaint, "Silver".

Ellis plays a city slicker from Chicago who buys up land to have it developed by one set of tenants, while at the same time the deeds are being sold to someone else back in the city. When the new owners come to stake their claims, trouble erupts. But sheriff Jones settles everything for both parties, preventing Ellis from pulling off his dastardly plan. Well-paced action and good development make this familiar story an above par western.

d&w, Lambert Hillyer; ph, Mack Stengler.

Western (PR:A MPAA:NR)

ONE-MAN MUTINY (SEE: COURT-MARTIAL OF BILLY MITCHELL, THE, 1955)

ONE MAN'S JOURNEY**½ (1933) 72m RKO bw

Lionel Barrymore (Dr. Eli Watt), May Robson (Sarah Twiddle), Dorothy Jordan (Letty McGinnis), Joel McCrea (Jimmy Watt), Frances Dee (Joan Stockton), David Landau (McGinnis), James Bush (Bill Radford), Buster Phelps (Jimmy Watt, Age 6), Oscar Apfel (John Radford), June Filmer (May Radford), Samuel S. Hinds (Doctor Babcock), Hale Hamilton (Dr. Tillinghas).

Barrymore plays a small-town doctor whose search for success and prominence within his field is continually thwarted because of his devotion to the people he serves. He is a self-sacrificing sort who will accept vegetables or a chicken as payment for his services. Barrymore finally gets recognition for his career when a large medical society honors him. At the same time, the son he reared alone becomes a successful doctor and marries his childhood sweetheart. An uplifting story about one man's devotion to humanity, which at times plods through the details a bit, but overall gives a good character study. Barrymore's portrayal never allows the doctor to wallow in self-pity or to look with contempt upon the people who have kept him from success. Remade in 1938 as A MAN TO REMEMBER.

p, Pandro S. Berman; d, John Robertson; w, Lester Cohen, Sam Ornitz (based on the short story "Failure" by Katherine Haviland Taylor); ph, Jack Mackenzie; ed, Arthur Roberts.

Drama (PR:A MPAA:NR)

ONE MAN'S LAW**   (1940) 57m REP bw

Don "Red" Barry (Jack), Janet Waldo (Joyce), George Cleveland (Judge Wingate), Dub Taylor (Nevady), Edmund Cobb (Mathews), Dick Elliott (Pendergrast), James H. McNamara (Martin), Robert Frazer (Fletcher), Rex Lease (Hudkins), Edward Piel, Sr. (Winters), Fred "Snowflake" Toones, Bud Osborne, Horace B. Carpenter, Jack Kirk, Cactus Mack, Jim Corey, Curley Dresden, Roy Brent, William Kellogg, Barry Hays, Guy Usher, Matty Roubert, Jack Ingram, Charles King, Stanley Price.

Familiar cowboy story has Barry persuaded to become sheriff after his pal, Taylor, brags about his reputation as a "tough hombre." In reality Barry is just a friendly cowpoke. Nevertheless, he does a successful job in uniting the citizens of the town to ward off a gang sent by a nearby town that is in competition to draw the railroad through their locale. Taylor in a secondary role offers the brightest performance in this picture, with Barry unconvincing in his role.

p&d, George Sherman; w, Bennett Cohen, Jack Natteford; ph, Reggie Lanning; m, Cy Feuer; ed, Lester Orlebeck.

Western   **(PR:A MPAA:NR)**

ONE MAN'S WAY**   (1964) 105m UA bw

Don Murray (Norman Vincent Peale), Diana Hyland (Ruth Peale), William Windom (Rev. Clifford Peale), Virginia Christine (Anna Peale), Carol Ohmart (Evelyn), Veronica Cartwright (Mary), Liam Sullivan (Dr. Gordon), June Dayton (Mrs. Gordon), Ian Wolfe (Bishop Hardwick), Charles Lampkin (Lafe), Arthur Peterson, Jr. (Instructor), Hope Summers (Mrs. Thompson), Virginia Sale (Miss Collingswood), Rory O'Brien (Leonard Peale as a Child), David Bailey (Robert Peale as a Child), Mickey Sholdar (Norman Peale as a Child), Paul Marin (Feldman), Hank Stanton (Jack Wilson), Bryan O'Byrne (Organist), Eddie Ryder (Gas Station Attendant), Ed Peck (Harry the Reporter), John Harmon (Elder Marcus), Joseph Hamilton (Elder Thompson), Tom Palmer (Prof. Aiken), Sandra Gale Bettin (Alma), Wendy Ferdin (Margaret Peale), Butch Patrick (John Peale), Sharyl Locke (Elizabeth Peale), Gerald Gordon (Robert Peale, Grown), Tom Skerritt (Leonard Peale, Grown), Vernon Rich (Mr. Melton), Bing Russell (Tom Rayburn), Ann Morgan Guilbert (Receptionist), Edward Prentiss (Mr. Boardman), Arthur Marshall (Rod Allenberry), Geraldine Wall (Mae Michaels), Jon Lormer (John Hellman), Jean Carson (Woman Who Shoots Husband).

Murray plays Norman Vincent Peale in this film based on Arthur Gordon's book about the inspirational leader. The son of a cruel Ohio clergyman, Murray works as a crime reporter before turning to the cloth himself as a means of combating the misfortune he has been reporting on. Because of his rather unorthodox beliefs—that God is a loving God, rather than a vengeful one—he is regarded as a rebel. He becomes a popular figure, attracting a large following, as well as appearing on the radio and in his own syndicated newspaper column. He eventually publishes a book, The Power of Positive Thinking, and considers resigning from the church, but his faith is renewed after a critically ill child is brought back to health. Murray is appropriately devout, charismatic, and loquacious as the appealing-appalling minister. Windom turns in a fine performance, as does Hyland, who was "introduced" to the moviegoing public in this picture.

p, Frank Ross; d, Denis Sanders; w, Eleanore Griffin, John W. Bloch (based on the book Norman Vincent Peale: Minister to Millions by Arthur Gordon); ph, Ernest Laszlo; m, Richard Markowitz; ed, Philip W. Anderson; md, Willard Jones; art d, Edward Jewell; set d, Morris Hoffman; cos, Jack Angel, Grace Kuhn; makeup, Ben Lane, Joe De Bella.

Drama   **(PR:A MPAA:NR)**

ONE MILE FROM HEAVEN**   (1937) 68m FOX bw

Claire Trevor (Lucy "Tex" Warren), Sally Blane (Barbara Harrison), Douglas Fowley (Jim Tabor), Fredi Washington (Flora Jackson), Joan Carol (Sunny), Ralf Harolde (Moxie McGrath), John Eldredge (Jerry Harrison), Paul McVey (Johnny), Ray Walker (Mortimer Atlas), Russell Hopton (Peter Brindell), Chick Chandler (Charlie Milford), Eddie "Rochester" Anderson (Henry Bangs), Howard Hickman (Judge Clarke), Bill Robinson (Officer Joe).

Trevor plays a newspaper reporter assigned to fill in for a colleague at police headquarters. When sent on a bum tip to the "colored" section of the city, she comes across a young black woman claiming to be the mother of the white child she is raising. Further investigation by Trevor reveals the real mother to be a wealthy society woman. A court battle ensues between the real mother and the black woman who has raised the child, with the outcome that the wealthy woman gets the child, and the black woman comes along as a nurse. A potentially volatile subject is here treated in a nonchalant manner, but at least the film does not fall into a trap of being overly stereotypic. Robinson, as a Harlem police officer, performs a nice tap number.

p, Sol M. Wurtzel; d, Allan Dwan; w, Lou Breslow, John Patrick, Robin Harris, Alfred Golden (based on stories by Judge Ben B. Lindsey); ph, Sidney Wagner; ed, Fred Allen; md, Samuel Kaylin; art d, Bernard Herzbrun.

Drama/Comedy   **(PR:A MPAA:NR)**

ONE MILLION B.C.***   (1940) 80m UA bw (AKA: THE CAVE DWELLERS; CAVE MAN; GB: MAN AND HIS MATE)

Victure Mature (Tumak), Carole Landis (Loana), Lon Chaney, Jr. (Akhoba), Conrad Nagel (Archaeologist/Narrator), John Hubbard (Ohtao), Robert Kent (Mountain Guide), Mamo Clark (Nupondi), Mary Gale Fisher (Wandi), Nigel De Brulier (Peytow), Inez Palange (Tohana), Edgar Edwards (Skakana), Jacqueline Dalya (Ataf), Adda Gleason, Rosemary Theby, Audrey Manners, Patricia Pope, Ed Coxen, Creighton Hale, Ben Hall, Jimmy Boudwin, Chuck Stubbs, Boots Le

Baron, Dick Simons, Jean Porter, Katherine Frye, Ora May Carlson (Shell People), Ricca Allen, Harry Wilson, John Northpole, Harold Howard, Henry Sylvester, Norman Budd, Lorraine Rivero, Aida Hernandez, Betty Greco, Frank Tinajero, James Coppedge (Klang People).

Veteran comedy producer Hal Roach decided to try a change of pace, creating this thrilling epic about the early days of mankind. Unfortunately, the film is somewhat silly and inaccurate with regard to dinosaurs and man roaming the plains at the same time. Back in the Stone Age, mankind seems divided into two tribes: the warlike mountain dwellers known as the Rock People, and the more peaceful beach folk who are called the Shell People. Chaney, the grizzled oppressive patriarch of the Rock People, has a falling out with his son, Mature, and banishes him from the tribe. Wandering the wasteland alone, Mature is forced to fend off several "dinosaurs" (real-life lizards made up to look mean and then matted into the frame to appear enormous) before finding the lair of the Shell People. The kindly beachcombers take the big lug in and soon one of the women, Landis, is in love with Mature. Landis teaches Mature a crude form of table manners and he becomes a bit more civilized. Not surprisingly, the inter-tribal relationship causes a bit of tension between the two peoples. Luckily, through a series of disasters (including a volcanic explosion), and battles with prehistoric beasts, the Rock People and the Shell People put aside their differences and join together in the fight for survival. The production history of ONE MILLION B.C. was almost as titanic a struggle as the fight for existence in prehistoric days. Looking to lend some credibility to his project, producer Roach, Sr. sought out legendary producer-director D.W. Griffith, who had made a one-reeler about prehistoric people called MAN'S GENESIS in 1912 (he remade it in 1913 as BRUTE FORCE). Griffith had virtually disappeared from the motion picture business and hadn't directed a film in nine years. Interested by Roach's offer to let him "supervise" the project, Griffith arrived at the studio to report for work. Roach sent out three conflicting press releases announcing Griffith's participation in the project. The first said that he was directing, the second that he was producing, and in the third he was back at directing. After having cast Landis and Mature (he also shot their screen tests), Griffith found that his opinions and advice were being virtually ignored. He seemed to spend the rest of his time on the project with the special-effects crew and was heard to praise their work. When the production was completed, Griffith picked up his last paycheck and demanded his name be taken off the credits. Roach complied, and to this day no one is really certain whether Griffith actually directed any of ONE MILLION B.C. The film was also something of a frustration for one of its stars, Lon Chaney, Jr. Fresh from his triumph as Lennie in OF MICE AND MEN, Chaney was cast as the patriarch of the Rock People even before his previous film was released. Chaney's enthusiasm for the project was such that he created his own special makeup for the role, echoing the skills of his famed father. From all accounts the makeup was quite impressive, but Chaney was unable to use it because the cosmetician's union wouldn't allow an actor to apply his own makeup. Hollywood had definitely changed since Chaney's father was in movies. The special effects in ONE MILLION B.C. are a disappointment. To save money, Roach Sr. opted for dressing up lizards instead of building realistic models of prehistoric animals and animating them the way Willis O'Brien had done in THE LOST WORLD (1925) and KING KONG (1933). Considering the cheapness of the approach, the effects work fairly well. Well enough, in fact, to have been reused dozens of times in other films. ONE MILLION B.C. was remade in 1967 by Hammer Studios as ONE MILLION YEARS B.C., using the top-notch stop-motion animation talents of Ray Harryhausen. Though the effects are superior, star Raquel Welch caused more excitement in her animal-skin bikini.

p, Hal Roach, Sr.; d, Hal Roach, Sr., Hal Roach, Jr. (D.W. Griffith, uncredited); w, Mikell Novak, George Baker, Joseph Frickert, Grover Jones (based on the story by Novak, Baker, and Frickert); ph, Norbert Brodine; m, Werner R. Heymann; ed, Ray Snyder; art d, Charles D. Hall; spec eff, Roy Seawright; stunts, Yakima Canutt.

Adventure   Cas.   **(PR:A-C MPAA:NR)**

ONE MILLION DOLLARS**   (1965, Ital.) 110m Ceiad-COL c (LA CONGIUNTURA)

Vittorio Gassman (Don Giuliano), Joan Collins (Jane), Jacques Bergerac (Sandro), Hilde Barry (Dana), Adolfo Eibenstein (Grandfather).

Gassman is an Italian nobleman, and Collins is part of a gang which smuggles money across the Italian border to be deposited in a Swiss bank. Their excursion together takes them from Rome through the picturesque Alps, to a scenic Swiss lake resort. Pleasant chase film, which doesn't take itself too seriously, but at times is faltering in its pace. Collins shows little talent in her role, but manages to look nice.

p, Mario Cecchi Gori; d, Ettore Scola; w, Scola, Ruggero Maccari; ph, Sandro D'Eva (Techniscope, Technicolor); m, Luis Enriquez Bacalov, Marcello Malvestiti.

Comedy   **(PR:A MPAA:NR)**

$1,000,000 DUCK**½   (1971) 91m Disney/BV c

Dean Jones (Prof. Albert Dooley), Sandy Duncan (Katie Dooley), Joe Flynn (Finley Hooper), Tony Roberts (Fred Hines), James Gregory (Rutledge), Lee Harcourt Montgomery (Jimmy Dooley), Jack Kruschen (Dr. Gottlieb), Virginia Vincent (Eunice Hooper), Jack Bender (Arvin Wadlow), Billy Bowles (Orlo Wadlow), Sammy Jackson (Frisby), Arthur Hunnicutt (Mr. Purdham), Frank Wilcox (Bank Manager), Bryan O'Byrne (Bank Teller), Ted Jordan (Mr. Forbes), Neil Russell (Mr. Smith), Pete Renoudet (Mr. Beckert), Frank Cady (Assayer), George O'Hanlon (Parking Attendant), Jonathon Daly (Purchasing Agent), Hal Smith (Courthouse Guard), Edward Andrews (Morgan), Stu Gilliam, Fran Ryan, Vaughn Taylor, Bernard Fox, Ed Reimers, Hank Jones.

Dean Jones plays a research scientist who takes home a duck that has been exposed to radiation. When the duck is frightened by the dog next door it lays what appear, and in fact turn out to be, gold eggs. This all-American family finds itself exceedingly rich, as well as involved in a search by the U.S. Treasury to find what it believes to be a vast underworld plot. This light-hearted fun is made to work through the performances of a well-chosen cast, though the overall pacing drags and the editing is rough. It may be that Charley the duck's lineage can be traced back to the top-billed, uranium-laying bird in the 1950s British comedy MR. DRAKE'S DUCK. But while that fowl caused a stir in military circles, Charlie had more to do with greed and greenbacks. In fact, Walt Disney Studios underestimated the value of the web-footed moneymaker; and when the receipts were counted, the feathered-creature feature had brought in a surprising $4.7 million. $1,000,000 DUCK also brought to the screen for the first time perky Broadway star Sandy Duncan.

p, Bill Anderson; d, Vincent McEveety; w, Roswell Rogers (based on a story by Ted Key); ph, William Snyder (Technicolor); m, Buddy Baker; ed, Lloyd L. Richardson; art d, John B. Mansbridge, Al Roelofs; set d, Emile Kuri, Hal Gausman; cos, Chuck Keehne, Emily Sundby; spec eff, Eustace Lycett; makeup, Robert J. Schiffer.

Comedy **(PR:AA MPAA:G)**

$1,000,000 RACKET* (1937) 66m Victory bw

Herman Brix [Bruce Bennett] *(Lawrence Duane)*, Joan Barclay *(Molly Henessey)*, Bryant Washburn *(Herbert Marvin)*, Vane Calvert *(Mrs. Henessey)*, Sam Adams *(Tim Henessey)*, Jimmy Aubrey *(Melton)*, David O'Brien *(Johnny Henessey)*, Monte Carter *(Lefty)*, Frank Wayne *(Eddie)*, Bob Terry *(Luke)*, Lyn Arden *(Nan)*.

Haphazard production in which (Bruce Bennett, still acting under his given name) and Barclay fall in love, to find themselves later the object of some greedy gangsters. Cliche-ridden script has little plot development, with performances and direction being exceedingly poor.

p, Sam Katzman; d, Bob Hill; w, Basil Dickey; ph, William Hyer; ed, Holbrook Todd.

Comedy/Drama **(PR:A MPAA: NR)**

1,000,000 EYES OF SU-MURU (SEE: MILLION EYES OF SUMURU, THE, 1967, Brit.)

ONE MILLION YEARS B.C.** (1967, Brit./U.S.) 91m Hammer/FOX c

Raquel Welch *(Loana)*, John Richardson *(Tumak)*, Percy Herbert *(Sakana)*, Robert Brown *(Akhoba)*, Martine Beswick *(Nupondi)*, Jean Wladon *(Ahot)*, Lisa Thomas *(Sura)*, Malya Nappi *(Tohana)*, Richard James *(Young Rock Man)*, William Lyon Brown *(Payto)*, Frank Hayden *(1st Rock Man)*, Terence Maidment *(1st Shell Man)*, Mickey De Rauch *(1st Shell Girl)*, Yvonne Horner *(Ullah)*.

Basically a remake of the 1940 film ONE MILLION B.C., this is a story which takes a rather naive perspective toward prehistoric humans, portraying them as grunting animals who walk fully upright. Richardson is a man banished from his aggressive and warring tribe, the Rock People, for fighting with his father. After wandering the savage desert and nearly dying, he stumbles to the shore and is nursed back to health by the Shell People, a kind and gentle tribe. Richardson's naturally aggressive ways make him distrustful, so he picks a fight with the leader of the Shell People, and is banished again, but not before Welch falls in love with him. She leaves with him, following him to the place where the Rock people dwell. After discovering the whereabouts of these new people, Welch goes back to her own tribe to inform them of the developments. Unfortunately, this information leads to a small war between the two groups, but a massive earthquake interrupts the battle, killing most of the participants. Realizing their war is folly, the survivors make peace. Not surprisingly there is little fine acting to be found among the rocks and dinosaurs, which is just as well for Welch because she is only around to show off her body in tight-fitting animal skins. Though Welch's dubious contribution to the film may have meant lots of press and decent boxoffice returns in 1967, the enduring star of the show is, as always, the outstanding special effects by Ray Harryhausen. During the course of the film we are treated to such prehistoric creatures as a giant sea turtle, a brontosaurus, an allosaur, a triceratops, a ceratosaur, and even a real-live iguana lizard made into a giant as an homage to the monsters in the original ONE MILLION B.C. While far from being one of Harryhausen's best films (the quality of which had little to do with his abilities), the effects are superb and worth a look for fans of his work.

p, Michael Carreras; d, Don Chaffey; w, Carreras (based on a story by Mickell Novak, George Baker, Joseph Frickert); ph, Wilkie Cooper (DeLuxe Color); m, Mario Nascimbene; ed, Tom Simpson; art d, Robert Jones; cos, Carl Toms; spec eff, Ray Harryhausen; makeup, Wally Schneiderman.

Adventure **(PR:A MPAA:NR)**

ONE MINUTE TO ZERO** (1952) 105m RKO bw

Robert Mitchum *(Col. Steve Janowski)*, Ann Blyth *(Linda Day)*, William Talman *(Col. John Parker)*, Charles McGraw *(Sgt. Baker)*, Margaret Sheridan *(Mary Parker)*, Richard Egan *(Capt. Ralston)*, Eduard Franz *(Dr. Gustav Engstrand)*, Robert Osterloh *(Maj. Davis)*, Robert Gist *(Maj. Carter)*, Roy Roberts *(Gen. Thomas)*, Wally Cassell *(Pvt. Means)*, Eddie Firestone *(Lt. Stevens)*, Peter Thompson *(Lt. Cronin)*, Steve Flagg *(Lt. Martin)*, Ted Ryan *(Pvt. Noblè)*, Larry Stewart *(Pvt. Weiss)*, Lalo Rios *(Pvt. Chico Mendoza)*, Hal Baylor *(Pvt. Jones)*, Tom Carr *(Pvt. Clark)*, Tom Irish *(Sgt. Cook)*, Alvin Greenman *(Pvt. Lane)*, Maurice Marsac *(M. F. Villon)*, Dorothy Granger, Karen Hale *(Nurses)*, Kay Christopher *(Mrs. Stuart)*, Wallace Russell *(Pilot Norton)*, Stuart Whitman *(Officer)*, Owen Song *(Interpreter)*, Monya Andre *(French UN Woman)*, John Mallory *(Soldier)*, Buddy Swan, William Forrest, Tyler McVey, Robert Bray, Ray Montgomery, Al Murphy.

Costly war epic set during the Korean War, starring Mitchum as a toughened soldier trying to figure out methods to outmaneuver the North Koreans, while at the same time romancing Blyth. The picture is little more than a cliche-filled army story, with actual footage used to try to create a greater sense of realism. Some fairly humorous incidents help to soften the tedious story, such as the scene in which Greenman, a private, tries to teach a group of Korean kids how to blow bubblegum. Mitchum and Blyth offer performances far beyond the material they are given, with the couple singing an English translation of the popular Japanese song "Tell Me Golden Moon."

p, Edmund Grainger; d, Tay Garnett; w, Milton Krims, William Wister Haines; ph, William E. Snyder; m, Victor Young; ed, Robert Belcher, Frank McWhorter; md, C. Bakaleinikoff; art d, Albert S. D'Agostino, Jack Okey; m/l, "When I Fall in Love," (Young), "Tell Me Golden Moon (China Night)," (Norman Bennett, Nobuyuki Takeoda).

War **(PR:A MPAA:NR)**

ONE MORE RIVER*** (1934) 85m UNIV bw (GB: OVER THE RIVER)

Diana Wynyard *(Clare Corven)*, Frank Lawton *(Tony Croom)*, Mrs. Patrick Campbell *(Lady Mont)*, Jane Wyatt *(Dinny Cherrell)*, Colin Clive *(Sir Gerald Corven)*, Reginald Denny *(David Dornford)*, C. Aubrey Smith *(Gen. Charwell)*, Henry Stephenson *(Sir Lawrence Mont)*, Lionel Atwill *(Brough)*, Alan Mowbray *(Forsyte)*, Kathleen Howard *(Lady Charwell)*, Gilbert Emery *(Judge)*, E.E. Clive *(Chayne)*, Robert Greig *(Blore)*, Gunnis Davis *(Bonjy)*, Tempe Piggott *(Mrs. Purdy)*.

Excellent screen adaptation of the best-selling final novel by John Galsworthy, published after his death. The story centers around a young woman, Wynyard, who is seriously mistreated by her sadistic husband, Clive. After being severely beaten by him, she leaves home and meets Lawton, who falls madly in love with her. The husband spies on the couple, which leads to the divorce court and a long, but compelling trial in an English court of law, which has a stricter code in regard to divorce. A well-chosen cast is handled smoothly through the direction by Whale, filling the story with suspense—quite an achievement, considering the majority of the action occurs in the courtroom.

d, James Whale; w, R.C. Sherriff (based on the novel by John Galsworthy); ph, John Mescall.

Drama **(PR:A MPAA:NR)**

ONE MORE SPRING*** (1935) 86m FOX bw

Janet Gaynor *(Elizabeth Cheney)*, Warner Baxter *(Jaret Otkar)*, Walter Woolf King *(Morris Rosenberg)*, Jane Darwell *(Mrs. Sweeney)*, Roger Imhof *(Mr. Sweeney)*, Grant Mitchell *(Mr. Sheridan)*, Lee Kohlmar *(The Flutist)*, Stepin Fetchit *(Zoo Attendant)*, Nick [Dick] Foran *(Park Policeman)*, Rosemary Ames *(Sheridan's Secretary)*, John M. Qualen *(Auctioneer)*, Astrid Allwyn *(Girl at Auction)*, Jack Norton *(Drunk)*, Harry Harvey *(Taxi Driver)*, Michael Visaroff *(Russian)*, Jill Bennett *(Tart)*, William Wagner *(Bookkeeper)*, Bobby Dunn *(Bum)*, Walter Downing *(Spectator)*, Tina Marshall *(Crying Woman)*.

Amusing tale of a group of down-and-outers who team together during strange circumstances and help each other live through a lowered material existence. Baxter is an antique dealer, with nothing left but a bed which belonged to Napoleon. He runs into King, a musician, who after years of study, is unable to find a job. The two roll the bed to the park and are all set to make camp, when the local park attendant allows them to use his tool shed as a shelter. The two men run into Gaynor, a chorus girl who has just lost her job, and invite her to stay at their shed. When an overwrought banker, Mitchell, attempts suicide, the threesome talk him out of it, giving him back the attitude he needs to make it in a competitive world. When spring comes along, King finally finds a job, and Baxter opens a new business through the aid of the banker. This gives Baxter the chance to propose marriage to Gaynor. Gaynor and Baxter team up for some very amusing moments, playing off each other very well. The direction makes for an intimate look at a situation which never takes itself too seriously.

p, Winfield Sheehan; d, Henry King; w, Edwin Burke (based on the novel by Robert Nathan); ph, John Seitz; m, Arthur Lange; art d, Jack Otterson.

Comedy **(PR:A MPAA:NR)**

ONE MORE TIME*½ (1970, Brit.) 95m Chrislaw-Trace-Mark/UA c

Sammy Davis, Jr. *(Charlie Salt)*, Peter Lawford *(Chris Pepper/Lord Sydney Pepper)*, Maggie Wright *(Miss Tomkins)*, Leslie Sands *(Inspector Crook)*, John Wood *(Figg)*, Sydney Arnold *(Tombs)*, Edward Evans *(Gordon)*, Percy Herbert *(Mander)*, Bill Maynard *(Jenson)*, Dudley Sutton *(Wilson)*, Glyn Owen *(Dennis)*, Lucille Soong *(Kim Lee)*, Esther Anderson *(Billie)*, Anthony Nicholls *(Candler)*, Allan Cuthbertson *(Belton)*, Cyril Luckham *(Magistrate)*, Moultrie Kelsall *(Priest)*, Julian D'Albie *(Gen. Turpington-Mellish)*, Gladys Spencer *(Lady Turpington-Mellish)*, Joanna Wake *(Claire Turpington-Mellish)*, Juliette Bora, Florence George, Amber Dean Smith, Lorraine Hall, Carmel Stratton, Thelma Neal *(Salt & Pepper Nightclub Girls)*, Davie Trevena, Norman Mitchell, Richard Goolden, Geoffrey Morris, Norman Pitt, George McGrath, Mischa De La Motte, Walter Hopsburgh, John Nettles, Peter Reeves, Christopher Lee, Peter Cushing.

A sequel to the successful SALT AND PEPPER has the same two detectives, Davis and Lawford, retired from the force and running a nightclub. When the club is closed down, Lawford goes to London to try and persuade his wealthy and stuffy twin brother to lend him a hand. He refuses, but after a brief sampling of the local night spots, Lawford gives it another try, only to find his brother has been murdered. Lawford switches clothes with the corpse and poses as the wealthy one, giving the impression that Lawford is the one murdered. Lawford then invites Davis over, and the two discover the truth behind the supposed upright brother. He was actually a smuggler, whose enemies still think he is alive. Script offers some new laughs, but the material drags out what was interesting about the original. The only film directed by Jerry Lewis in which he does not appear.

p, Milton Ebbins; d, Jerry Lewis; w, Michael Pertwee; ph, Ernest W. Steward (DeLuxe Color); m, Les Reed; ed, Bill Butler; prod d, Jack Stevens, spec eff, Terry Witherington; m/l, "One More Time," (Reed, Jackie Rae, sung by Davis),

"When the Feeling Hits You," (Bobby Doyle, sung by Davis) "Where Do I Go from Here?" (Reed, Geoff Stephens, sung by Davis); makeup, George Frost.

Comedy **(PR:A MPAA:PG)**

ONE MORE TOMORROW** (1946) 88m WB bw

Ann Sheridan *(Christie Sage)*, Dennis Morgan *(Tom Collier)*, Jack Carson *(Pat Regan)*, Alexis Smith *(Cecilia Henry)*, Jane Wyman *(Fran Connors)*, Reginald Gardiner *(Jim Fisk)*, John Loder *(Owen Arthur)*, Marjorie Gateson *(Edna)*, Thurston Hall *(Rufus Collier)*, John Abbott *(Joseph Baronova)*, Marjorie Hoshelle *(Illa Baronova)*, Sig Arno *(Poppa Diaduska)*, William Benedict *(Office Boy)*, John Alvin *(Announcer)*, Henri DeSoto *(Headwaiter)*, Hal K. Dawson *(Guest)*, Otto Hoffman *(Stationmaster)*, Mary Field *(Maude Miller)*, Frances Morris *(Young Woman)*, Fred Essler *(Picard)*, Danny Jackson *(Orson Curry)*, Frank Coghlan, Jr. *(Telegraph Boy)*, Lynne Baggett, Gertrude Carr, Robert Hutton, Juanita Stark, Lottie Williams, Joan Winfield *(Party Guests)*.

Dull adaptation of the play "The Animal Kingdom," which had been filmed earlier in 1932 by RKO. This version stars Sheridan as a leftist photographer who falls in love with a rich playboy, Morgan. When Sheridan refuses to put up with Morgan's wealth and carefree lifestyle, he turns to Smith. The two marry, but Morgan's heart still belongs to Sheridan, making for a dismal time for Smith. Morgan and Sheridan cross paths again, this time sticking it out together, with Smith headed to Reno for a divorce. Though the cast is good, the script falls short because the film chooses not to deal with the radical vs. conservative theme of the play.

p, Henry Blanke; d, Peter Godfrey; w, Charles Hoffman, Catherine Turney, Julius J. Epstein, Philip G. Epstein (based on the play "The Animal Kingdom" by Philip Barry); ph, Bert Glennon; m, Max Steiner; ed, David Weisbart, md, Leo F. Forbstein; art d, Anton Grot; set d, George James Hopkins.

Drama **(PR:A MPAA:NR)**

ONE MORE TRAIN TO ROB*** (1971) 108m UNIV c

George Peppard *(Harker Fleet)*, Diana Muldaur *(Katy)*, John Vernon *(Timothy X. Nolan)*, France Nuyen *(Ah Toy)*, Steve Sandor *(Jim Gant)*, Soon-Taik Oh *(Yung)*, Richard Loo *(Mr. Chang)*, C.K. Yang *(Wong)*, John Doucette *(Sheriff Monte)*, Robert Donner *(Sheriff Adams)*, George Chandler *(Conductor)*, Marie Windsor *(Louella)*, Joan Shawlee *(Big Nellie)*, Harry Carey, Jr. *(Red)*, Timothy Scott *(Slim)*, Hal Needham *(Bert Gant)*, Jim Burk *(Skinner)*, Ben Cooper *(1st Deputy)*, Guy Lee *(Sen)*, Ray Dimas *(Herbert)*, Pamela McMyler *(Cora May Jones)*, Merlin Olsen *(Eli Jones)*, Phil Olsen *(Luke Jones)*, Jon Drury *(Wilson)*, John Mitchum *(Guard)*.

Lighthearted western starring Peppard as a train robber sent to prison after being framed by Vernon, a member of his gang. Vernon wants Peppard out of the way so he can marry Peppard's girl. Peppard gets his vengeance on Vernon by assisting a group of Chinese, who have a cache of gold Vernon attempts to appropriate through the kidnaping of an aged patriarch. The two men have a showdown at the end, with Peppard winning and getting his girl back. The direction is fast paced, managing to blend the vengeance theme with that of the Chinese gold nicely, and Peppard gives a solid performance as the antihero. Hal Needham, stunt coordinator extraordinaire and now a director of action films, appears in a small role and also organized the stunts for this film.

p, Robert Arthur; d, Andrew V. McLaglen; w, Don Tait, Dick Nelson (based on a story by William Roberts); ph, Alric Edens (Technicolor); m, David Shire; ed, Robert Simpson; art d, Alexander Golitzen, Henry Bumstead; set d, Charles Thompson; cos, Grady Hunt; spec eff, Albert Whitlock; m/l, "Havin' Myself a Fine Time," Shire, Richard Maltby, Jr., sung by Tim Morgan; stunts, Hal Needham.

Western **(PR:A MPAA:GP)**

ONE MYSTERIOUS NIGHT** (1944) 61m COL bw (GB: BEHIND CLOSED DOORS)

Chester Morris *(Boston Blackie)*, Richard Lane *(Inspector Farraday)*, Janis Carter *(Dorothy Anderson)*, William Wright *(Paul Martens)*, Robert Williams *(Matt Healy)*, George E. Stone *(The Runt)*, Dorothy [Malone] Maloney *(Eileen Daley)*, Robert E. Scott *(George Daley)*, Lyle Latell *(Matthews)*, George McKay *(Sgt. McNulty)*, Early Cantrell *(Margaret Dean)*, Joseph Crehan *(Jumbo Madigan)*, John Tyrell *(Austin)*, Ann Loos *(Newstand Clerk)*, Henry Jordan *(2nd Man)*, Ben Taggart *(Traffic Officer)*.

Morris plays former jewel thief Boston Blackie, who is called by the police to help find a stolen diamond from an exhibit to raise money for war victims. He is assisted by sidekick Stone, and throughout the search they are followed by a female reporter out to get Morris' picture. Solid cast makes up for the rather slow-moving story. (See BOSTON BLACKIE series, Index.)

p, Ted Richmond; d, Oscar [Budd] Boetticher, Jr.; w, Paul Yawitz (based on the character created by Jack Boyle); ph, L.W. O'Connell; ed, Al Clark; md, Mischa Bakaleinikoff; art d, Lionel Banks, George Brooks.

Crime **(PR:A MPAA:NR)**

ONE NEW YORK NIGHT½** (1935) 71m MGM bw (AKA: THE TRUNK MYSTERY)

Franchot Tone *(Foxhall)*, Una Merkel *(Phoebe)*, Conrad Nagel *(Kent)*, Harvey Stephens *(Collis)*, Steffi Duna *(Louise)*, Charles Starrett *(George)*, Louise Henry *(Ermine)*, Tommy Dugan *(Selby)*, Harold Huber *(Blake)*, Henry Kolker *(Carlisle)*.

Tone plays a man from Wyoming who has come to the big city in the hopes of finding a wife, but winds up in the midst of a murder mystery. The man in the room next to his is found dead by Tone, who hopes a lost bracelet discovered in the room will lead him to the real murderer. He is helped in his search by the hotel phone operator, Merkel, whom he eventually takes back to Wyoming as his wife. Though lacking in suspense, the neat pacing and comic interludes make for passable entertainment. Actor Charles Starrett, who has a small role here, became a cowboy star the next year after this film's release in a series of B-westerns for Columbia.

p, Bernard H. Hyman; d, Jack Conway; w, Frank Davis (based on the play "Order, Please" by Edward Childs Carpenter, Walter Hackett); ph, Oliver T. Marsh; ed, Tom Held.

Mystery/Comedy **(PR:A MPAA:NR)**

ONE NIGHT. . .A TRAIN** (1968, Fr./Bel.) 85m Parc-Fox Europa-Films du Siecle/FOX c (UN SOIR. . .UN TRAIN)

Yves Montand *(Mathias)*, Anouk Aimee *(Anne)*, Francois Beukelaers *(Val)*, Hector Camerlynck *(Hernhutter)*, Adriana Bogdan *(Moira)*, Senne Rouffaer *(Elkerlyk)*, Dom De Gruyter *(Werner)*, Jacqueline Royaards *(Grandmother)*, Jan Pere *(Death)*.

An ambitious project by director Delvaux, which ultimately fails because of his attempt to include complex symbolism and narrative devices without developing any single theme sufficiently. Montand plays a linguistics professor in Belgium, where his Flemish-speaking students are staging a rebellion against the French-speaking political and cultural forces. At the same time his girl friend, Aimee, is beginning to demand a commitment from Montand. The two fight, but she joins Montand when he leaves by train for another city. Aimee mysteriously disappears on the train, and after Montand and his companions get off the train, it crashes and Aimee is killed. Intermixed with the narrative are dream sequences, flash backs, and flash forwards, similiar to the work of Alain Resnais. Other obvious influences are Antonioni and Ingmar Bergman, particularly in the film's atmosphere and technique. Montand never appears at ease in his role as an intellectual battling with love, and Aimee's charactor is too limited.

p, Mag Bodard; d&w, Andre Delvaux (based on the book by Johan Daisne); ph, Ghislain Cloquet (Eastmancolor); ed, Suzanne Baron.

Drama **(PR:C MPAA:NR)**

ONE NIGHT AT SUSIE'S½** (1930) 85m FN-WB bw

Billie Dove *(Mary)*, Douglas Fairbanks, Jr. *(Dick Rollins)*, Helen Ware *(Susie)*, Tully Marshall *(Buckeye Bill)*, James Crane *(Houlihan)*, John Loder *(Hayes)*, Claude Fleming *(Drake)*.

Ware plays the owner of a boarding house, who is always willing to help or counsel gangsters and racketeers in trouble. Her foster son, Fairbanks, takes the blame for a murder committed by his girl friend, Dove. While Fairbanks is in jail, Dove tries to have his play produced, resorting to any means at her disposal. Meanwhile, double crosser Crane is romantically interested in Dove, making it difficult for the couple when Fairbanks is finally released. Ware's gangster friends are on to Crane's plan and discreetly get him out of the way. Ware's performance is the show's highpoint, making the top name stars seem secondary. The story lapses into sentimentality, but otherwise contains some interesting twists, with some well-placed comic routines. Marshall, a former burglar resigned to being Ware's butler, is particularly charming.

d, John Francis Dillon; w, Forrest Halsey, Katherine Scola (based on a story by Frederick Hazlitt Brennan); ph, Ernest Haller.

Drama **(PR:A MPAA:NR)**

ONE NIGHT IN LISBON½** (1941) 97m PAR bw

Fred MacMurray *(Dwight Houston)*, Madeleine Carroll *(Leonora Perrycoate)*, Patricia Morison *(Gerry Houston)*, Billie Burke *(Catherine Enfilden)*, John Loder *(Comdr. Peter Walmsley)*, Dame May Whitty *(Florence)*, Edmund Gwenn *(Lord Fitzleigh)*, Reginald Denny *(Erich Strasser)*, Billy Gilbert *(Popopopoulos)*, Marcel Dalio *(Concierge)*, Bruce Wyndham *(Strasser's Aide)*, Jerry Mandy *(Popopopoulos' Waiter)*, Billy Bevan *(Lord Fitzleigh's Aide)*, Mikhail Rasumny *(Manager of Restaurant)*, Douglas Walton *(Frank)*, Walter Byron *(Dinner Guest)*, Barbara Denny *(Party Guest)*, Catherine Craig, Keith Richards *(Guests)*, Herbert Evans *(John the Butler)*, David Clyde *(Cab Driver)*, James Finlayson, Harry Allen *(Air Raid Wardens)*, Keith Hitchcock *(Policeman)*, Evan Thomas *(Diplomat)*, Lumsden Hare *(Doorman)*, Francisco Maran *(Waiter)*, Antoinette Valdez *(Fado Singer)*, Loulette Sablon *(French Maid)*, Gavin Muir *(Aide)*, Pete Peterson *(Sailor)*.

A spirited romantic comedy set in London during WW II starring MacMurray as an airman from Texas who ferries warplanes from the U.S. to England. While hiding out in a London air-raid shelter, MacMurray meets Carroll, a proper, well-mannered English girl who has learned to expect the most formal of behavior from men. MacMurray, with his Texas twang, is completely foreign to her, but he does manages to win her over by singing an off-key rendition of "Home on the Range." When the skies clear, MacMurray and Carroll set out to have themselves a carefree time, but obstacles get in their way. Loder, MacMurray's rival for Carroll's affections —a very proper Royal Navy commander—consistently makes a crowd of their twosome. MacMurray's former wife, Morison, also pops up, similarly cramping the lovebirds' style. They take a trip to neutral Lisbon, where they get ensnarled in a spy ring. Of course, it's up to them to crack it, which they do before MacMurray proposes to Carroll and invites her to return to America with him. Pretty average in it execution, ONE NIGHT IN LISBON benefits from an excellent supporting cast, including Burke and Gwenn, who are sympathetic to the couple's desires, as well as Whitty, Denny, Gilbert, and Dalio. This film was the fourth, and final, pairing for MacMurray and Carroll, who had previously appeared in CAFE SOCIETY (1939), HONEYMOON IN BALI, and VIRGINIA (both 1940).

p&d, Edward H. Griffith; w, Virginia Van Upp (based on the play "There's Always Juliet" by John Van Druten); ph, Bert Glennon; ed, Eda Warren; md, Sigmund Krumgold; art d, Hans Dreier, Ernst Fegte.

Romance/Spy Drama **(PR:A MPAA:NR)**

ONE NIGHT IN PARIS**

(1940, Brit.) 62m Alliance bw (GB: PREMIERE)

John Lodge (Inspector Bonnard), Judy Kelly (Carmen Daviot), Hugh Williams (Rene Nissen), Joan Marion (Lydia Lavalle), Edmond Breon (Morel), Wallace Geoffrey (Renoir), Geoffrey Sumner (Capt. Curry), Steve Geray (Frolich), Edward Chapman (Lohrmann), Joss Ambler (Spectator).

Lodge plays the inspector on the case of the murder of a financial backer of a musical, shot during the Paris premiere of the show. It is quickly established that the shot came from the stage, making everyone in the cast a suspect in the murder. Lodge gives a formidable performance as the inspector, but the story is unable to maintain any consistent level of suspense throughout.

p, Walter C. Mycroft; d, Walter Summers; w, F. McGrew Willis, Max Wallner, F. D. Andam; ph, Otto Kanturek; ed, Lionel Tomlinson; m/l, Dones V. Buday, Hans Schachtner, Peter Fenn, Clifford Gray.

Crime/Musical (PR:A MPAA:NR)

ONE NIGHT IN THE TROPICS**½

(1940) 82m UNIV bw

Allan Jones (Jim Moore), Robert Cummings (Steve Harper), Nancy Kelly (Cynthia), Mary Boland (Aunt Kitty), Bud Abbott (Abbott), Lou Costello (Costello), Peggy Moran (Mickey Fitzgerald), William Frawley (Roscoe), Leo Carrillo (Senor Escobar), Don Alvarado (Rudolfo), Theodore Rand, Mina Farragut (The Theodores), Nina Orla (Nina), Richard Carle (Mr. Moore), Edgar Dearing (Man), Barnett Parker (Thompson), Francis McDonald (Escobar's Aide), Jerry Mandy (Vendor), Eddie Dunn (Edwards), Vivian Fay (Dancer), Eddie Acuff (Steward), Frank Penny (Waiter), William Alston (Orchestra Leader), Charles B. Murphy (Drunk), Charlie Hall (Steward), Kathleen Howard, Tyler Brooke, Sally Payne, Cyril Ring, Barry Norton.

Abbott and Costello made their film debut in this picture, proving to be the only worthwhile aspect of an otherwise tedious story. The pair used some of their routines already popular through their radio show for effective comedy relief. The story stars Jones as an insurance salesman selling a policy to soon-to-be-married Cummings, but Jones elopes with the bride, Kelly, before any wedding can take place. Songs include: "Back in My Shell," "Remind Me," "You and Your Kiss" (Jerome Kern, Dorothy Fields);" "Your Dream is the Same as My Dream" (Kern, Oscar Hammerstein II, Otto Harbach).

p, Leonard Spigelgass; d, A. Edward Sutherland; w, Gertrude Purcell, Charles Grayson, Kathryn Scola, Francis Martin (based on the novel Love Insurance by Earl Derr Biggers); ph, Joseph Valentine; ed, Milton Carruth; md, Charles Previn; art d, Jack Otterson; cos, Vera West; ch, Larry Ceballos.

Musical Comedy (PR:A MPAA:NR)

ONE NIGHT OF LOVE**

(1934) 84m COL bw

Grace Moore (Mary Barrett), Tullio Carminati (Giulio Monteverdi, Impresario), Lyle Talbot (Bill Houston), Mona Barrie (Lally), Jessie Ralph (Angelina, Housekeeper), Luis Alberni (Giovanni, Monteverdi's Assistant), Andres De Segurola (Galuppi), Rosemary Glosz (Frappazini), Nydia Westman (Muriel), Jane Darwell (Mary's Mother), William Burress (Mary's Father), Frederick Burton (Impresario), Henry Armetta (Cafe Proprietor), Sam Hayes (Radio Announcer), Reginald Barlow (Stage Manager), Frederick Vogeding (1st Doctor), Arno Johnson (2nd Doctor), Olaf Hytten (Viennese Valet), Leo White (Florist), Herman Bing (Vegetable Man), Edward Keane (Stage Director), Reginald Le Borg (Opera Director), Paul Ellis (Pinkerton), Joseph Mack (Captain of Italian Yacht), Marion Lessing (German Girl), Hans Joby (Taxi Driver), Victoria Stuart (Cora Florida), John Ardizoni (Radio Judge), Kurt Furberg (Stage Manager), Spec O'Donnell (Call Boy), Michael Mark (Flower Store Man), Richard La Marr (Steward), Wadsworth Harris (Judge), Arthur Stuart Hull (Sugar Daddy), Wilfred Lucas, Edmund Burns, Rafael Storm (Men).

Moore is a struggling opera singer who goes to Europe after losing a radio talent contest. Singing teacher Carminati is impressed after hearing her sing in a cafe. He takes her on as a student and develops her voice, while she falls in love with him. She becomes jealous when he takes on another female singer as a pupil, which almost ruins her opening night. She is triumphant, however, proving her star talent at the New York Metropolitan Opera House. Songs include: "One Night of Love" (Victor Schertzinger, Gus Kahn), "Ciri-Biri-Bin" (A. Pestaloza, Rudolf Thaler), and extracts from "Lucia de Lammermoor" (Gaetano Donizetti), "Madame Butterfly" (Giacomo Puccini), "Carmen" (Georges Bizet, all sung by Moore).

p, Harry Cohn d, Victor Schertzinger; w, S.K. Lauren, James Gow, Edmund North (based on a story by Dorothy Speare, Charles Beahan); ph, Joseph Walker; m, Louis Silvers; ed, Gene Milford; md, Dr. Pietro Cimini; art d, Stephen Goosson; cos, Robert Kalloch; spec eff, John Hoffman.

Musical (PR:A MPAA:NR)

ONE NIGHT STAND**

(1976, Fr.) ONS/La Boetie c

Richard Jordan (Paul), Ting Pei (Anya), Tien Ni (Sonya), Mei Fang (Sandy), Tsang Kong (Arthur), Ken Wayne (Harry), Marie Daems (Countess).

Filmed in English and shot in Hong Kong, ONE NIGHT STAND casts Jordan as a young American searching for himself and companionship. He ventures to Asia when his former wife (who has fled with their child) attempts suicide. In his travels he encounters a few lovely Asian girls, leaving them behind just as quickly as he meets them. Skillfully handled by both director Rissient and star Jordan, with an added plus coming from the exotic locale.

d, Pierre Rissient; w, Rissient, Kenneth White; ph, Alain Derobe (Eastmancolor); ed, Bob Wade.

Drama Cas. (PR:O MPAA:NR)

ONE NIGHT WITH YOU*½

(1948, Brit), 92m Two Cities/UNIV bw

Nino Martini (Giulio Moris), Patricia Roc (Mary Santell), Bonar Colleano (Piero Santellini), Hugh Wakefield (Santell), Guy Middleton (Matty), Stanley Holloway (Tramp), Charles Goldner (Fogliati), Irene Worth (Lina Linari), Willy Feuter (Pirelli), Miles Malleson (Jailer), Richard Hearne (Stationmaster), Christopher Lee (Pirelli's Assistant), Stuart Latham (Script Writer), Judith Furse (2nd Script Writer), Brian Worth (3rd Script Writer).

Martini is a famous tenor who meets Roc at an English train station. Both miss their trains when Martini saves Roc's dog from a fight, and the tenor finds that his luggage is missing. A tramp has stolen it who is then mistaken for the singer and ushered off to a studio in Rome. Meanwhile, Martini and Roc have to sing for their supper as they wait for their next train. Complications arise when they are arrested for passing a forged money note. The two get out of jail just in time to get to Rome and fix the situation created by the tramp. A remake of the Italian film FUGA A DUE VOCI (1941).

p, Josef Somlo; d, Shaun Terence Young; w, Caryl Brahms, S. J. Simon (based on a story by Carlo Bragaglia); ph, Andre Thomas, Norman Warwick; m, Lambert Williamson; ed, Douglas Meyers; md, Muir Mathieson; art d, Tom Verity; set d, F. Pearson; cos, Joy Ricardo; spec eff, Henry Harris, George Blackwell; m/l, Bixio; makeup, Tony Sforzini.

Musical (PR:A MPAA:NR)

ONE OF OUR AIRCRAFT IS MISSING***½

(1942, Brit.) 90m BN-Archers/UA bw

Godfrey Tearle (Sir George Corbett), Eric Portman (Tom Earnshaw), Hugh Williams (Frank Shelley), Bernard Miles (Geoff Hickman), Hugh Burden (John Glyn Haggard), Emrys Jones (Bob Ashley), Googie Withers (Jo de Vries), Pamela Brown (Else Meertens), Joyce Redman (Jet van Dieren), Hay Petrie (Burgomeister), Arnold Marle (Pieter Sluys), Robert Helpmann (De Jong), Peter Ustinov (Priest), Alec Clunes (Organist), Roland Culver (Naval Officer), Stewart Rome (Commander), David Evans, John Salew (Sentries), William D'Arcy (Officer), David Ward, Robert Duncan (Airmen), Selma Van Dias (Burgomeister's Wife), Hector Abbas (Driver), James Carson (Louis), Bill Akkerman (Willem), Peter Schenke (Hendrik), Valerie Moon (Jannie), Robert Beatty (Hopkins), Joan Akkerman (Maartje), Michael Powell (Dispatching Officer).

Squadrons of heavy Wellington bombers take off from Britain at dusk and cross the English Channel for a raid on Stuttgart. They encounter flak on the return flight and six crewmen on one plane are forced to bail out over Nazi-occupied Holland. They are found by Dutch children who help them evade a German patrol; then, disguised, they are passed from person to person until they reach the coast and are spirited back to Britain in a small boat. Almost immediately after being reunited with their squadron they are back in the air, flying more dangerous missions into Germany. The second Powell-Pressburger collaboration (the script garnered an Academy Award nomination), this film does not reach the heights of the first (THE INVADERS, 1941), which its plot more than slightly resembles. The best sequences are the opening ones, detailing the raid with almost documentary precision as the men concentrate on their duties, adjusting instruments as their planes shake from the antiaircraft fire all around them. The performances—although necessarily of the stiff-upper-lip variety—are all good, especially Tearle's as the aircraft commander, Withers' as an important link in the chain of rescuers, and Scottish character actor Petrie's as an apoplectic burgomeister. The film's worth as a propaganda piece was considerable, and it is the weight of too many long-winded speeches about people uniting to fight the Germans that makes the film somewhat dated now.

p,d&w, Michael Powell, Emeric Pressburger; ph, Roland Neame; ed, David Lean; art d, David Rawnsley.

War Drama Cas. (PR:A MPAA:NR)

ONE OF OUR DINOSAURS IS MISSING**

(1975, Brit.) 93m Disney/BV c

Peter Ustinov (Hnup Wan), Helen Hayes (Hettie), Clive Revill (Quon), Derek Nimmo (Lord Southmere), Joan Sims (Emily), Bernard Bresslaw (Fan Choy), Natasha Pyne (Susan), Roy Kinnear (Supt. Grubbs), Joss Ackland (B. J. Spence), Deryck Guyler (Harris), Andrew Dove (Lord Castleberry), Max Harris (Truscott).

A tedious Disney adventure about a dinosaur skeleton which contains top secret microfilm. Chinese agents steal the fossil from the British Natural History Museum and nanny Hayes and her friends help the British Intelligence chief retrieve the dinosaur and the microfilm. Hayes and her fellow nannies return the stolen fossil after a number of inane slapstick scenes. Even the youngest in the family will walk away from this one.

p, Bill Walsh; d, Robert Stevenson; w, Walsh (based on the novel The Great Dinosaur Robbery by David Forrest); ph, Paul Beeson (Technicolor); m, Ron Goodwin; ed, Hugh Scaife; art d, Michael Stringer; cos, Anthony Mendleson.

Adventure (PR:AA MPAA:G)

ONE OF OUR SPIES IS MISSING**

(1966) 91m MGM c

Robert Vaughn (Napoleon Solo), David McCallum (Illya Kuryakin), Leo G. Carroll (Mr. Alexander Waverly), Maurice Evans (Sir Norman Swickert), Vera Miles (Madame de Sala), Ann Elder (Joanna Sweet), Bernard Fox (Jordin), Dolores Faith (Lorelei Lancer), Anna Capri (Do Do), Harry Davis (Alexander Gritsky), Yvonne Craig (Wanda), Monica Keating (Olga), Cal Bolder (Fleeton), Robert Easton (Texan), James Doohan (Phillip Bainbridge), Ollie O'Toole (Corvy), Antony Eustrel (Steward), Richard Peel (Cat Man), Barry Bernard (Pet Shop Owner).

Episodes of the popular television series "The Man From U.N.C.L.E." edited together to make a theatrical feature. Several cats from the Soho area of London disappear, and members of U.N.C.L.E. begin to suspect their rival organization, THRUSH, of being behind it. Top agents Vaughn and McCallum trace the clues to

Miles, who runs a fashion salon in Paris. She has access to a rejuvenation formula, first used on the cats, which is scheduled to be tested on her former lover, retired statesman Evans, resulting in dire consequences for England. THRUSH wants the formula for its own evil purposes, but Vaughn and McCallum are successful in rescuing Evans and thwarting their archenemies as well. Features all the leading actors from the series, in addition to other TV actors from other series, such as Doohan from "Star Trek."

p, Boris Ingster; d, E. Darrell Hallenbeck; w, Howard Rodman (based on a story by Henry Slesar); ph, Fred Koenekamp (Metrocolor); m, Gerald Fried; ed, Henry Berman, William B. Gulick; art d, George W. Davis, James Sullivan; set d, Henry Grace, Charles S. Thompson, Jack Mills; m/l, "One of Our Spies Is Missing," Jerry Goldsmith.

Spy Adventure   (PR:A MPAA:NR)

ONE OF THE MANY   (SEE: HE COULDN'T TAKE IT, 1933)

ONE ON ONE**   (1977) 98m WB c

Robby Benson (Henry Steele), Annette O'Toole (Janet Hays), G. D. Spradlin (Coach Moreland Smith), Gail Strickland (B. J. Rudolph), Melanie Griffith (Hitchhiker), James G. Richardson (Malcolm), Hector Morales (Gonzales), Cory Faucher (Tom), Doug Sullivan (Young Henry), Lamont Johnson (Barry Brunz).

A predictable sports film starring Benson, who lands a basketball scholarship to a large university only to discover that he's not as good as he thought. Benson, who doesn't look anything like a basketball player, is berated by the other players and harassed by his coach, Spradlin. O'Toole is the coed he falls in love with. In the end Benson comes off the bench to save the climactic game. The script was co-written by Benson and his father, Jerry Segal.

p, Martin Hornstein; d, Lamont Johnson; w, Robby Benson, Jerry Segal; ph, Donald M. Morgan (Panavision, Technicolor); m, Charles Fox; ed, Robbe Roberts; art d, Sherman Loudermilk; set d & cos, Donfeld; m/l, Fox, Paul Williams (sung by Seals and Crofts).

Drama   Cas.   (PR:A MPAA:PG)

ONE-PIECE BATHING SUIT, THE   (SEE: MILLION DOLLAR MERMAID, 1952)

ONE PLUS ONE zero   (1961, Can.) 114m Fluorite, Ltd./ Selected bw [AKA: 11 (EXPLORING THE KINSEY REPORT)

Leo G. Carroll (Professor Logan), Hilda Brawner (Clare Hollister), William Traylor (Hollister), Kate Reid (Julia Bradley), Ernest Graves (John Bradley), Richard Janaver (Carlton), June Duprez (Margaret Gaylord), Austin Willis (Sam Tooray), Jane Rose (Mrs. Kingsley), Truman Smith (Mr. Kingsley), Winifred Dennis (Gertrude), Virginia MacLeod (Miss Pom), Rita Gardner (Peggy Cannon), Jack Betts (Bill Cannon), Alice Hill (The Nurse), Arch McDonnell, Herman Ettlinger, Margot Christie, Norman Welsh, Daryl Masters, Eleanor Beecroft, Madeleine Christie, Garrick Hagon, Toby Tarnow, Michael Stewart, Sharon Acker, Robert Christie, Alfred Scopp, Peggi Loder, Douglas Rain, Leslie Yeo, Barbara Hamilton, Sydney Brown, Susan Fletcher, Frances Tobias, Ruth Springford, Judith Orban, Bena Schuster, William Ferguson, Cal Whitehead, Sammy Sales.

Why anyone would try to adapt the Kinsey sex survey into a film is beyond reason, and this film is beyond bad. The film has an episodic structure broken down into five segments, none of which is entertaining or well done. It begins with a lecture by Carroll and then moves to re-enactments of certain experiences of the audience members. For example: Traylor was worried that the premarital sex he had with his wife would ruin their honeymoon; Reid is worried about telling her husband of her brief affair. Other experiences and questions about divorce, extramarital affairs, and babies are discussed by the lecture audience and re-enacted for the viewer as well.

p,d&w, Arch Oboler (based on the play "Mrs. Kingsley's Report" by Oboler); ph, George Jacobson; m, John Bath; ed, Chester W. Schaeffer; makeup, Irene Kent; animation, Pistafilm.

Drama   (PR:C-O MPAA:NR)

ONE PLUS ONE**   (1969, Brit.) 99m Cupid/New Line c (AKA: SYMPATHY FOR THE DEVIL)

The Rolling Stones (Themselves), Anne Wiazemsky (Eve Democracy), Iain Quarrier (Bookman), Frankie Dymon, Jr. (Black Power Militant), Sean Lynch (Narrator), Danny Daniels, Illario Pedro, Roy Stewart, Linbert Spencer, Tommy Ansah, Michael McKay, Rudi Patterson, Mark Matthew, Karl Lewis, Bernard Boston, Nike Arrighi, Francoise Pascal, Joanna David, Monica Walters, Glenna Forster-Jones, Elizabeth Long, Jeanette Wild, Harry Douglas, Colin Cunningham, Graham Peet, Matthew Know, Barbara Coleridge.

Godard's didactic film essay based on the themes of construction and destruction was not only his first non-French picture, but featured The Rolling Stones. They are photographed in a documentary manner while in the studio recording "Sympathy for the Devil," one of their classic songs. The rest of the film deals with revolution, Black Power, political slogans, and filmmaking. Anne Wiazemsky, Godard's wife at the time, plays Eve Democracy, a girl who answers only "yes" and "no" to the questions asked her. One can extract only the barest thread of narrative from ONE PLUS ONE, but that is of little or no importance to Godard, nor does it shed any light on an explanation. Fortunately or unfortunately (depending on one's sentiments), the film gained more recognition for being a Rolling Stones film than for being a Godard film. The producers recognized this fact and without authorization changed the film's end. Throughout the film, Mick Jagger and the band repeat and repeat rehearsals of their song, but Godard's version of the film never plays the final cut of the song as it was recorded. The producers decided to use the finished song at the picture's end, and fill up screen time with monochromatic stills of the band. Depending on what day a viewer went to the theater, he would either see Godard's

ONE PLUS ONE or the producer's SYMPATHY FOR THE DEVIL. Needless to say, the producer's film has long since vanished from the annals of film history.

p, Michael Pearson, Iain Quarrier; d&w, Jean-Luc Godard: ph, Tony Richmond (Eastmancolor); m, The Rolling Stones; ed, Ken Rowles; m/l, "Sympathy for the Devil," Keith Richard, Mick Jagger (sung by the Rolling Stones).

Film Essay   (PR:O MPAA:NR)

ONE POTATO, TWO POTATO**   (1964) 92m Bawalco/Cinema V bw

Barbara Barrie (Julie Cullen Richards), Bernie Hamilton (Frank Richards), Richard Mulligan (Joe Cullen), Harry Bellaver (Judge Powell), Marti Mericka (Ellen Mary), Robert Earl Jones (William Richards), Vinette Carroll (Martha Richards), Sam Weston (Johnny Hruska), Faith Burwell (Ann Hruska), Jack Stamberger (Minister), Michael Shane (Jordan Hollis).

Barrie, the mother of a young child, is deserted by her husband Mulligan. He leaves for South America and she gets a divorce and a job at a local plant. She meets Hamilton, a black co-worker. They fall in love and marry, and move to Hamilton's parents' farm. Mulligan returns and, when he finds out that his ex-wife has married a black man, files for custody of his child. Hamilton is told to take his family out of state because the chances of keeping custody are slim. The couple decides to stay and fight. The judge, influenced by social prejudices, awards the child to Mulligan. An engaging, independent production shot on a small budget in Ohio.

p, Sam Weston; d, Larry Peerce; w, Raphael Hayes, Orville H. Hampton (based on a story by Hampton); ph, Andrew Laszlo; m, Gerald Fried; ed, Robert Fritch; md, Fried.

Drama   (PR:C MPAA:NR)

ONE PRECIOUS YEAR**   (1933, Brit.) 76m British & Dominions/ PAR British bw

Anne Grey (Dierdre Carlton), Basil Rathbone (Derek Nagel), Owen Nares (Stephen Carton), Flora Robson (Julia Skene), Ben Webster (Sir Richard Pakenham), Evelyn Roberts (Mr. Telford), H. G. Stoker (Sir John Rome), Robert Horton (Dr. Hibbert), Violet Hopson (Woman at Party), Jennie Robins, Olga Slade, Ronald Simpson, Western Brothers, Casa Nuova Girls.

Finding that she has a terminal disease and only a year to live, classy Grey embarks on an affair with Rathbone, a charming cad of the type frequently found in British films. Her husband, Nares, learns of the affair only after Rathbone dumps her, and he forgives her. Tears are dried when the doctor enters with news that he has discoverd a cure for Grey's malady. Strictly routine melodrama with a better than usual cast.

p, Herbert Wilcox; d&w, Henry Edwards (based on the play "Driven" by E. Temple Thurston).

Drama   (PR:A MPAA:NR)

ONE RAINY AFTERNOON**   (1936) 75m Pickford-Lasky/UA bw

Francis Lederer (Philippe Martin), Ida Lupino (Monique Pelerin), Hugh Herbert (Toto), Roland Young (Maillot), Erik Rhodes (Count Alfredo Donstelli), Joseph Cawthorn (M. Pelerin), Countess Liev de Maigret (Yvonne), Donald Meek (Judge), Georgia Caine (Cecile), Richard Carle (Minister of Justice), Mischa Auer (Leading Man), Angie Norton (Hortense), Eily Malyon (President of Purity League), Ferdinand Munier (Prosecutor), Murray Kinnell (Theater Manager), Phyllis Barry (M. Pelerin's Secretary), Lois January (Malliot's Secretary), Seger Ellis, Margaret Warner (Singers on Screen), Iris Adrian (Cashier), Jack Mulhall (Ice Rink Announcer), Billy Gilbert (Court Clerk), Florence Lawrence, Florence Turner, Eric Mayne, Donald Reed, Alfred Valentino, Francis Powers, Edward Bibby.

Producer Lasky, who had brought Maurice Chevalier to Hollywood to star in THE SMILING LIEUTENANT, brought European actor Francis Lederer from Paris to star in this slight story. Lederer sits down in the wrong seat at a movie theater, and thinking that his date is next to him he kisses her only to find out it's Lupino. She has him arrested and there's a big scandal. Lederer becomes famous and Lupino falls in love with him. A light farce, which has a bare bones story that was adapted from a German film.

p, Jesse Lasky; d, Rowland V. Lee; w, Stephen Morehouse Avery, Maurice Hanline (based on the film MONSIEUR SANS GENE from a story by Emeric Pressburger, Rene Pujal); ph, Peverell Marley; m,Ralph Irwin; ed, Margaret Clancy; md, Alfred Newman, Merritt Gerstad; art d, Richard Day; cos, Omar Kiam; m/l, Irwin, Jack Stern, Harry Tobias, Preston Sturges.

Comedy   Cas.   (PR:A MPAA:NR)

ONE ROMANTIC NIGHT*½   (1930) 73m UA bw

Lillian Gish (Alexandra), Rod La Rocque (Prince Albert), Conrad Nagel (Dr. Nicholas Haller), Marie Dressler (Princess Beatrice), O.P. Heggie (Father Benedict), Albert Conti (Count Lutzen), Edgar Norton (Col. Wunderlich), Billie Bennett (Synphorosa), Philippe De Lacy (George), Byron Sage (Arsene), Barbara Leonard (Mitzi).

ONE ROMANTIC NIGHT was Lillian Gish's first talkie and was adapted from Molnar's play "The Swan." The film was almost totally reshot by uncredited director George Fitzmaurice after Stein was released from the picture, and after second director Harry d'Abbadie d'Arrast was also released. The acting, except for Gish's and Dressler's, is wooden, and the film didn't help Gish's transition into sound pictures.

d, Paul L. Stein, George Fitzmaurice; w, Melville Baker (based on the play "The Swan" by Ferenc Molnar); ph, Karl Struss; ed, James Smith; set d, William Cameron Menzies, Park French.

Romantic Comedy   (PR:A MPAA:NR)

ONE SINGS, THE OTHER DOESN'T**   (1977, Fr.) 105m Cine-Tamaris-SFP-Institute National de l'Audiovisuel and Contretemps-Paraidise-Population/Cinema 5 c (L'UNE CHANTE L'AUTRE PAS)

Valerie Mairesse (Pauline [Apple]), Therese Liotard (Suzanne), Ali Raffi (Darius), Robert Dadies (Jerome), Jean-Pierre Pellegrin (Pierre), Francois Wertheimer (Francois II).

A self-conscious film about a 15-year relationship between two Frenchwomen—the older, more conservative Liotard and the outgoing Mairesse. The singer of the title is Mairesse, who falls in love with Raffi, an Iranian student. She agrees to return to Iran with him, but soon finds herself treated with traditional Mideastern scorn toward women. Meanwhile, Liotard's long-time romance with Dadies ends with his suicide. She takes refuge with her children in her parents' provincial cottage. Mairesse, an activist in women's rights, finally meets up with Liotard at a legalized abortion rally and the two help each other cope with their problematic lives. Not a bad movie by any means, just one with ideas that tend to seem heavy-handed. A more insightful and better developed film is Diane Kury's ENTRE NOUS (1983). (In French; English subtitles.)

d&w, Agnes Varda; ph, Charlie Van Damme, Nurith Aviv, Elisabeth Prouvost (Eastmancolor); ed, Joelle Van Effenterre, Francoise Thevenot, Elisabeth Pistorio; m/l, Francois Wertheimer, Orchid, Vagna.

Drama   **Cas.**   **(PR:C-O MPAA:NR)**

ONE SPY TOO MANY**   (1966) 101m Arena/MGM c

Robert Vaughn (Napoleon Solo), David McCallum (Illya Kuryakin), Rip Torn (Alexander), Dorothy Provine (Tracey Alexander), Leo G. Carroll (Mr. Alexander Waverly), Yvonne Craig (Maude Waverly), David Opatoshu (Kavon), David Sheiner (Paviz), Donna Michelle (Princess Nicole), Leon Lontoc (Gen. Bon-Phouma), Robert Karnes (Col. Hawks), Clarke Gordon (Claxon), James Hong (Prince Phanong), Cal Bolder (Ingo Lindstrum), Carole Williams (Receptionist), Teru Shimada (President Sing-Mok), Arthur Wong (Gen. Man-Phang), Robert Gibbons (Farrell).

Another "The Man From U.N.C.L.E." feature assembled by editing two of the episodes of the TV series together. Torn is a crazed scientist who plans to take control of the world by using his "will gas." Vaughn and McCallum track Torn to his Greek underground palace, but the secret agents are caught and left to die as Torn rushes to America to carry out his plan. Though perhaps enjoyable on the small screen, as a theatrical feature it just doesn't hold up. Torn's performance is enjoyable, dwarfing those of the other actors.

p, David Victor; d, Joseph Sargent; w, Dean Hargrove; ph, Fred Koenekamp (Metrocolor); m, Gerald Fried, Jerry Goldsmith; ed, Henry Berman; art d, George W. Davis, Merrill Pye.

Spy Drama   **(PR:A MPAA:NR)**

ONE STEP TO HELL*½   (1969, U.S./Ital./Span.) 94m Copercines-Metheus-Harris Associates/World c (CACCIA AI VIOLENTI; REY DE AFRICA; AKA: KING OF AFRICA)

Ty Hardin (King Edwards), Pier Angeli (Ann Peterson), Rossano Brazzi (Dr. Hamilton), George Sanders (Capt. Phillips), Helga Line (Deborah Vinton), Dale Cummings (Bartender), George [Jorge] Rigaud, Julio Pena, Charles Fawcett, Alan Collins [Luciano Pigozzi], Pamela Tudor, Michael [Miguel del] Castillo, John Anthony [Antonio] Mayans, Fred Coplan, Martha Valardi, Fernando Villena, Salvadore Lago, Simon Sibela, Aldo Bufi-Landi, Valentino Macchi.

A dull Italian adventure film starring Hardin as a South African police officer tracking down three escaped murderers. The convicts have killed the owner of a gold mine and kidnaped his wife, Line, who unwittingly leads them to the mine. The police officer pursues the convicts to the mine, rescues Line, and kills the convicts by setting off an explosion in the mine.

p&d, Sandy Howard; w, Jack DeWitt, Howard, Robert L. Joseph, Eduardo M. Brochero; ph, Julio Ortas, Sven Persson (Eastmancolor); m, Gianni Marchetti; ed, Juan Serra; md, Marchetti; art d, Jaime Perez Cubero, Jose Luis Galicia; m/l, title song, Bob Harris.

Adventure   **Cas.**   **(PR:C MPAA:G)**

ONE STOLEN NIGHT*½   (1929) 58m WB bw

Betty Bronson (Jeanne), William Collier, Jr. (Bob), Mitchell Lewis (Mons. Blossom), Nina Quartero (Chyra), Rose Dione (Mme. Blossom), Harry Todd (Balzar), Otto Lederer (Abou-ibn-Adam), Angelo Rossitto (Dwarf), Jack Santoro (Brandon), Harry Schultz (Sheik), Charles Hill Mailes (Daoud).

This remake of Vitagraph's 1923 production THE ARAB stars Collier as a soldier in the British cavalry stationed in the Sudan. After he takes the blame for a theft his brother committed, he deserts to join a vaudeville troupe, and falls in love with Bronson. Problems arise when a sheik, Schultz, buys her. He throws her out, however, when he discovers she's a white woman. Only about 50 per cent of the film has spoken dialog. One song, "My Cairo Love."

d, Scott R. Dunlap; w, Edward T. Lowe, Jr. (based on the story "The Arab" by D.D. Calhoun); ph, Frank Kesson.

Adventure   **(PR:A MPAA:NR)**

ONE SUMMER LOVE*   (1976) 95m AIP c (AKA: DRAGONFLY)

Beau Bridges (Jesse Arlington), Susan Sarandon (Chloe), Mildred Dunnock (Mrs. Barrow), Michael B. Miller (Gabriel Arlington), Linda Miller (Willa Arlington), Martin Burke (Lonnie Arlington), James Otis (Clifford), James Noble (Dr. Leo Cooper), Ann Wedgeworth (Pearlie Craigle), Fredrick Coffin (Walter Craigle), Harriet Rogers (Mrs. Patterson).

One of American International's occasional attempts to present serious material. Bridges tries to adjust to the real world after being a patient in a mental hospital.

Thinking that he killed his mother, he tries to find a surrogate in Sarandon, Wedgeworth, and Miller. His mother isn't actually dead, but their reunion does turn to violence. A heavy-handed script sinks this film into melodrama.

p&d, Gilbert Cates; w, N. Richard Nash; ph, Gerald Hirschfeld (Movielab Color); m, Stephen Lawrence; ed, Barry Malkin; art d, Peter Dohanos; set d, Dick Merrell; cos, Ruth Morley.

Drama   **(PR:C MPAA:PG)**

ONE SUNDAY AFTERNOON***   (1933) 75m PAR bw

Gary Cooper (Biff Grimes), Fay Wray (Virginia Brush), Neil Hamilton (Hugo Barnstead), Frances Fuller (Amy Lind), Roscoe Karns (Snappy Downer), Jane Darwell (Mrs. Lind), Clara Blandick (Mrs. Brush), Sam Hardy (Dr. Startzman), Harry Schultz (Schneider), James Burtis (Dink Hoops), A.S. Byron (Foreman), Jack Clifford (Watchman), Johnny St. Clair.

Cooper is a dentist who feels that he married the wrong girl, Fuller. The woman wanted, Wray, was stolen from him by Hamilton. He seeks some form of revenge on Hamilton, but can't find a satisfactory way to go about it. Slowly, Cooper realizes how right Fuller is for him and how Hamilton got what he deserved when he married the nagging Wray. This was the first of three adaptations of James Hagan's play by Warner Bros. including another version in 1941 under the title THE STRAWBERRY BLONDE starring James Cagney, Olivia de Havilland, and Rita Hayworth, and directed by Raoul Walsh. Warner remade it another time in 1948, again with Walsh directing, under the original title and starring Dennis Morgan, Dorothy Malone, and Janis Paige.

p, Louis D. Lighton; d, Stephen Roberts; w, William Slavens McNutt, Grover Jones (based on the play by James Hagan); ph, Victor Milner; ed, Ellsworth Hoagland; art d, Hans Dreier, W.B. Ihnen; cos, Travis Banton.

Drama   **(PR:A MPAA:NR)**

ONE SUNDAY AFTERNOON**   (1948) 90m WB c

Dennis Morgan (Biff Grimes), Janis Paige (Virginia Brush), Don DeFore (Hugo Barnstead), Dorothy Malone (Amy Lind), Ben Blue (Nick), Oscar O'Shea (Toby), Alan Hale, Jr. (Marty), George Neise (Chauncey), Jimmy Nolan, Douglas Kennedy, Wilson Wood, Doria Caron, June Whittey, Layne Arlene, Emmett Vogan, Gail Bonney, Ray Montgomery, Ray Teal, Maude Prickett, Dorothy Ford.

The third and weakest version of the James Hagan play, starring Morgan as the dentist who loses his dream girl to DeFore and marries Malone on the rebound. In the end Morgan realizes that he has married the right girl. Walsh, who directed THE STRAWBERRY BLONDE (the second version of Hagan's play), directed this as well, but with less enthusiasm and energy. Songs include: "Girls Were Made to Take Care of Boys," "Some Day," "Johnny and Lucille," "Sweet Corner Girl," "The Right to Vote," "One Sunday Afternoon" (Ralph Blane), "Amy, You're a Little Bit Old Fashioned" (Marion Sunshine, Henry I. Marshall), "Daisy Bell" (Harry Dacre), "In My Merry Oldsmobile" (Vincent Bryan, Gus Edwards), "Auld Lang Syne" (Robert Burns), "Deck the Hall With Boughs of Holly."

p, Jerry Wald; d, Raoul Walsh; w, Robert L. Richards (based on the play by James Hagan); ph, Sid Hickox, Wilfred M. Cline (Technicolor); ed, Christian Nyby; art d, Anton Grot, Fred M. McLean; cos, Leah Rhodes; m/l, Ralph Blane.

Musical   **(PR:A MPAA:NR)**

ONE THAT GOT AWAY, THE**½   (1958, Brit.) 111m Rank bw

Hardy Kruger (Franz von Werra), Colin Gordon (Army Interrogator), Michael Goodliffe (RAF Interrogator), Terence Alexander (RAF Intelligence Officer), Jack Gwillim (Commandant Grizedale), Andrew Faulds (Lt. Grizedale), Julian Somers (Booking Clerk), Alec McCowen (Duty Officer Hucknall), John Van Eyssen, Harry Lockhart, Robert Crewdson, George Mikell, George Roubicek, Frederick Jaeger, Richard Marner, Paul Hansard (German Prisoners), Stratford Johns, Glyn Houston.

The true story of a German Luftwaffe pilot who is captured by the British during the early days of WW II. Kruger is the brash pilot who brags to his captors that he'll escape. He makes two unsuccessful tries in England and then he's transported to Canada. On a train to Montreal, he escapes and makes his way to the U.S. border, neutral at the time.

p, Julian Wintle; d, Roy Baker; w, Howard Clewes (based on a novel by Kendal Burt, James Leasor); ph, Eric Cross; m, Hubert Clifford; ed, Sidney Hayers; art d, Edward Carrick.

War Drama   **(PR:A MPAA:NR)**

ONE THIRD OF A NATION**   (1939) 78m PAR bw

Sylvia Sidney (Mary Rogers), Leif Erickson (Peter Cortlant), Myron McCormick (Sam Moon), Hiram Sherman (Donald Hinchley), Sidney Lumet (Joey Rogers), Muriel Hutchison (Ethel Cortlant), Percy Waram (Arthur Mather), Otto Hulett (Assistant District Attorney), Horace Sinclair (John, Butler), Iris Adrian (Myrtle), Charles Dingle (Mr. Rogers), Edmonia Nolley (Mrs. Rogers), Hugh Cameron (Mr. Cassidy), Julia Fassett (Mrs. Cassidy), Baruch Lumet (Mr. Rosson), Byron Russell (Inspector Castle), Robert George (Building Inspector), Wayne Nunn (Inspector Waller), Max Hirsch (Mr. Cohen), Miriam Goldina (Mrs. Cohen), Bea Hendricks (Min).

Adapted from a controversial play originally produced by the Federal Theatre Project (part of the WPA), this Depression-era film contrasts the lifestyles of tenement dwellers with the upper class in New York City. The phrase "one third of a nation" was derived from Franklin D. Roosevelt's statement that one-third of America's population was not adequately housed. The plot concerns Erickson, a member of a very wealthy family, who learns that he has inherited a block of slum tenements. In one of these dwellings, a raging fire had crippled the young Lumet. Erickson meets the boy some time after the fire, and eventually falls in love with his older sister, Sidney. Producer-director Murphy shot in the New York slum district to give the film the realism needed to convey its message. This was Sidney's last film under her Paramount contract, and she returned to stage work, appearing in only an occasional movie over the next 40 years. The young Sidney Lumet, here in his only film appearance, grew up to become a prominent feature-film director (THE PAWNBROKER, DOG DAY AFTERNOON).

p&d, Dudley Murphy; w, Oliver H. P. Garrett, Murphy (based on the play by Arthur Arent); ph, William Miller, Edward Hyland; m, Nathaniel Shilkret; ed, Duncan Mansfield.

Drama **(PR:A MPAA:NR)**

1,000 CONVICTS AND A WOMAN zero (1971, Brit.) 92m AIP c
(AKA: FUN AND GAMES)

Alexandra Hay (Angela Thorne), Sandor Eles (Paul Floret), Harry Baird (Carl), Neil Hallett (Warden Thorne), Robert Brown (Ralph), Frederick Abbott (Forbus), David Bauer (Gribney), Peter J. Elliott (Matthews), Tracy Reed (Linda), Stella Tanner (Mrs. Jackson), Peter Weston, Stanley Davies, Dinny Powell, Ronnie Brody, Joe Dunne, Terry Richards.

A tame sexploitation film with Hay as the daughter of a British prison governor who slips in between the sheets with practically every man in the compound, including guards and prisoners. Two prisoners set a trap to reveal to the girl's father her true nature.

p, Philip N. Krasne; d, Ray Austin; w, Oscar Brodney; ph, Gerald Moss (DeLuxe Color); m, Peter J. Elliott; ed, Philip Barnikel; md, Frank Barber; art d, James Weatherup; m/l, "Fun and Games," Elliott Austin (sung by Mike Felix).

Drama **(PR:O MPAA:R)**

$1,000 A MINUTE½** (1935) 70m REP bw

Roger Pryor (Wally Jones), Leila Hyams (Dorothy), Edgar Kennedy (McCarthy), Edward Brophy (Benny), Purnell Pratt (Editor), Morgan Wallace (Big Jim), Sterling Holloway (Pete), Herman Bing (Vanderbrocken), Franklin Pangborn (Reville), William Austin (Salesman), Arthur Hoyt (Jewel Clerk), George ["Gabby"] Hayes ("New Deal" Watson), Russell Hicks (Sonny), Claude King (Robinson), Spencer Charters (Robinson), Lee Phelps (Ryan), Ian Wolfe (Davidson), James Burtis (Flanagan), Harry C. Bradley (Dr. Cromley), Rolfe Sedan (Louie), Fern Emmett (Irene).

Two wealthy men bet that a person can't spend $720,000 in 12 hours (720 minutes). News reporter Pryor is the person picked to spend the money and when the police discover that he has $720,000 and he covered a recent bank robbery they make the reporter their No. 1 suspect. The film then becomes one giant race as Pryor tries to spend the money and keep one step in front of the cops. Kennedy plays a police officer and Holloway is a cab driver.

p, Nat Levine; d, Aubrey Scotto; w, Joseph Fields, Jack Natteford, Clair Church (based on a story by Everett Freeman); ph, Jack Marta, Ernest Miller; ed, Ray Curtiss; cos, I. Magnin.

Comedy **(PR:A MPAA:NR)**

$1,000 A TOUCHDOWN* (1939) 71m PAR bw

Joe E. Brown (Marlowe Mansfield Booth), Martha Raye (Martha Madison), Eric Blore (Henry), Susan Hayward (Betty McGlen), John Hartley (Bill Anders), Syd Saylor (Bangs), Joyce Mathews (Lorelei), Tom Dugan (Popcorn Vendor), Matt McHugh (Brick Benson), Hugh Sothern (King Richard), Josef Swickard (Hamilton McGlen, Sr.), Adrian Morris (Two Ton Terry), Dewey Robinson (Cab Driver), William Haade (Guard), Jack Perrin (McGlen's 1st Son), Phil Dunham (McGlen's 2nd Son), Constantine Romanoff (Duke), Charles Middleton (Stage Manager), Dot Farley (Hysterical Woman), Emmett Vogan (Coach), Fritzie Brunette, Gertrude Astor (McGlen's Sons' Wives), John Hart (Buck), Wanda McKay (Babe), Cheryl Walker (Blondie), Wayne "Tiny" Whitt (Big Boy), Bob Layne (Irish), George McKay (Mr. Fishbeck), Edward Gargan (Ironmansky), Grace Goodall (Nurse), Frank M. Thomas (Dr. Black), Bob Milasch (Tramp), Jimmy Conlin (Sheriff), Johnny Morris (Newsboy), George Barton (Truck Driver), D'Arcy Corrigan (Cecil), Dorothy Dayton (Gen), Jack Shea (Dimples), Jolly Rowlings (Harry), Harry Templeton (Hank), Jack Chapin (Red), James F. Hogan (Spud), Don Evan Brown (Jack), Arthur Bernard (Dick), Linda Brent (Bertie), Maxine Conrad (Sally), Mary Ray (Toots), Paula De Cardo (Dora), Judy King (Honey), Patsy Mace (Ginger), Jane Webb (Billie).

Unsuccessful actor Brown and actress Raye transform a school Raye has inherited into a dramatic college, but they can't get any students. With the help of butler Blore and romance teacher Hayward they form a football team, hoping for publicity, and now they can't find any school that will play them. Finally they set up a game with a pro football team and Raye bets all her money on her boys. Brown enters the game in the final minutes and wins it for her, concluding a harmless comedy that was strictly routine stuff for grimacing Brown and boisterous Raye and that was soundly and unanimously panned by critics when it came out.

p, William C. Thomas; d, James Hogan; w, Delmer Daves; ph, William Mellor; ed, Chandler House; art d, Hans Dreier, William Flannery; m/l, "Love with a Capital U," Ralph Rainger, Leo Robin.

Comedy **(PR:A MPAA:NR)**

1,000 FEMALE SHAPES (SEE: 1,000 SHAPES OF A FEMALE, 1963)

1,000 PLANE RAID, THE½** (1969) 94m Oakmont/UA c

Christopher George (Col. Greg Brandon), Laraine Stephens (WAC Lt. Gabrielle Ames), J.D. Cannon (Gen. Cotten Palmer), Gary Marshall (RAF Wing Comdr. Trafton Howard), Michael Evans (British Group Comdr. Leslie Hardwicke), Ben Murphy (Lt. Archer), James Gammon (Maj. Varga), Gavin MacLeod (Sgt. Kruger), Scott Thomas (Richman), Tim McIntire (Quimby), Bo Hopkins (Douglas), Henry Jaglom (Worchek), Noam Pitlik (Jacobi), Barry Atwater (Gen. Conway),

John Carter (Middleton), Charles Dierkop (Railla), Mac McLaughlin, Wayne Sutherlin (Waist Gunners), Philip Proctor (Turret Gunner), Larry Perkins (Navigator), Carl Reindel (Bombardier).

George is a U. S. Air Force colonel who convinces the Allies during WW II that a daylight bombing raid of Germany will bring a quick end to the war. The plan is approved though it is extremely dangerous. Discord develops because he demands that normal bombing operations continue until the daylight raid. George dislikes brash Marshall and cautious Murphy, but this changes when he flies with the pair during the raid and witnesses their bravery. The filmmakers try to pass Santa Maria, California, as wartorn England, which gives a clue to the quality of this war film.

p, Lewis J. Rachmil; d, Boris Sagal; w, Donald S. Sanford (based on a story by Robert Vincent Wright); ph, William W. Spencer (Deluxe Color); m, Jimmie Haskell; ed, Henry Batista, Jodie Copelan; md, Haskell; art d, Harold Michelson; spec eff, Justus Gibbs, Henry Millar, Jr.

War **(PR:A MPAA:G)**

1,000 SHAPES OF A FEMALE*½ (1963) 79m Artlife/
Cinema Syndicate-Chancellor c (AKA: 1,000 FEMALE SHAPES)

Dan Craig, Marty Devine, Byron Mabe, Sande Johnsen, Al Ruban, Faith Gilbert, Kimberly Harris, Doris Dane, Linda Bennet, Christine Kingsley, Jimmy Gavin, Monica Davis, Bob Bensen, Alicia Douglas, Vernon Marsh, Patricia Darling, Joey Naudic, Terri Powers, Rosebud O'Toole, Irene Charles, Nell Murray, Gigi Darlene, Jane Day, Priscilla Hadley, Andrea Sinclair.

An art gallery owner shows his friend his new collection of nudies by New York artists, and then the film flashes back to how the artists created their work. Each artists uses a strange technique that to today's audience will seem cliched (one artist paints using his hair, another uses his feet, and one covers the model in paint and rolls her around on the canvas). The early 1960s New York art scene with little to recommend it today.

p&d, Barry Mahon; w, Sande N. Johnsen; ph, Mahon (Eastmancolor); m, Arlene Corwin; ed, Maurice McEndree; art d, Johnson.

Comedy **(PR:A MPAA:NR)**

1001 ARABIAN NIGHTS** (1959) 76m UPA/COL c

Voices: Jim Backus (Uncle Abdul Azziz Magoo), Kathryn Grant (Princess Yasminda), Dwayne Hickman (Aladdin), Hans Conried (The Wicked Wazir), Herschel Bernardi (The Jinni), Alan Reed (The Sultan), Daws Butler (Omar the Rug Maker), Clark Sisters (Three Maids from Damascus).

Mr. Magoo is a lamp seller in Old Baghdad, named Abdul Azziz Magoo, who finds a genie in one of his lamps in this first animated feature with the well-known cartoon character. The discovery gets the near-sighted bumbler into a number of situations as he helps his nephew to marry the beautiful princes. Actor Jim Backus supplies Magoo's voice. An enjoyable entry for the kids.

p, Stephen Bosustow; d, Jack Kinney; w, Czeni Ormonde (based on a story by Dick Shaw, Dick Kinney, Leo Salkin, Pete Burness, Lew Keller, Ed Nofziger, Ted Allan, Margaret Schneider, Paul Schneider); ph, Jack Eckes (Technicolor); m, George Duning; ed, Joe Siracusa, Skip Craig, Earl Bennett; md, Morris Stoloff; prod d, Robert Dranko; m/l, Duning, Ned Washington; animation director, Abe Levitow; sequence directors, Rudy Larriva, Gil Turner, Osmond Evans, Tom McDonald, Alan Zaslove,; animators, Harvey Toombs, Phil Duncan, Clarke Mallery, Bob Carlson, Hank Smith, Ken Hultgren, Jim Davis, Casey Onaitis, Sanford Strother, Ed Friedman, Jack Campbell, Herman Cohen, Rudy Zamora, Stan Wilkins; background, Barbara Beggs, Boris Gorelick, Rosemary O'Connor.

Animation **Cas.** **(PR:AA MPAA:NR)**

ONE THRILLING NIGHT** (1942) 69m MON bw

John Beal (Horace Jackson), Wanda McKay (Millie Jason), Tom Neal (Frankie Saxton), Barbara Pepper (Dottie), Warren Hymer (Pat Callahan), J. Farrell MacDonald (Sgt. Haggerty), Ernie Adams (Pete), Lynton Brent (Joe), Jerome Sheldon (Duke Keesler), Jimmy O'Gatty (Tubby), Pierce Lyden, Gene O'Donnell, Tom Herbert, Charles Williams.

Beal marries McKay before he goes off to his WW II Army unit, and they spend their honeymoon in a New York City hotel room. The room is invaded by gangsters hunting a buried cache of money, and Beal is kidnaped by the criminals, escapes, and is kidnaped again. Gangsters and police are in and out of the honeymoon suite, and the couple never gets to enjoy their first night together.

p, A.W. Hackel; d, William Beaudine; w, Joseph Hoffman; ph, Marcel LePicard; ed, Martin G. Cohn; md, Frank Sanucci.

Comedy **(PR:A MPAA:NR)**

ONE TOO MANY* (1950) 110m Hallmark bw (GB;
KILLER WITH A LABEL)

Ruth Warrick (Helen Mason), Richard Travis (Bob Mason), Ginger Prince (Ginger Mason), Rhys Williams (Sully), William Tracy (Billy Leighton), Onslow Stevens (Dr. Foster), Mary Young (Mrs. Sullivan), Thurston Hall (Simes), Larry J. Blake (Walt Williams), Victor Kilian (Frank Emery), "Buzzy" Bookman (Johnny Emery), Cecil Elliott (Bar Woman), Luther Crockett (The Minister), Gilbert Fallman (The Priest), Lester Sharpe (The Rabbi), Lelah Tyler (Mrs. Adams), Helen Spring (Mrs. Johnson), Harry Stanton (Mr. Harrison), Lyle Talbot (Mr. Boyer), George Eldredge (City Editor), Roy E. Butler (Beer Man), Harry Hines (Shiskey Man), Jack Reitzen (Sherry Man), Robert Malcolm (Sgt. Peterson), William Baldwin (Newhope Doctor), Dan Rense (Policeman), William Kahn (Barroom Drunk), Sara Perry (Liquor Store Woman), Eddie Parker (Motorcycle Officer), Tony Layng (Ambulance Driver), Bobo Scharffe (Carrier Boy), Jane Hampton, Claire James (Nurses), Harmonaires, Louis Da Pron, Ern Westmore, Carlos Molina Orchestra (Themselves).

An exploitation film about alcoholism which wasn't shown in theaters but in Hallmark's road show markets. Warrick is a former concert pianist and mother who is an alcoholic. The story centers around the problems she brings her husband, Travis, and their daughter. Preachy, longwinded, and boring sums this film up. Hallmark was known for its exploitative potboilers. This is the last film Warrick, the star of the TV soap opera "All My Children," made before she absented herself from the screen until the late 1960s.

p, Kroger Babb; d, Erie C. Kenton; w, Malcolm Stuart Boylan (based on a story by Babb); ph, Carl Berger; m, Bert Shefter; ed, Edward Mann; md, Shefter; m/l, Irving Bibo, Johnny Stephens, Nelly Goletti, Bunny Lewis, Bill Copeland, the Harmonaires.

Drama **(PR:A MPAA:NR)**

ONE TOUCH OF VENUS½** (1948) 81m UNIV bw

Robert Walker *(Eddie Hatch)*, Ava Gardner *(Venus, Goddess of Love/Venus Jones)*, Dick Haymes *(Joe)*, Eve Arden *(Molly Grant)*, Olga San Juan *(Gloria)*, Tom Conway *(Whitfield Savory)*, James Flavin *(Corrigan)*, Sara Allgood *(Mrs. Gogarty, the Landlady)*, Hugh Herbert *(Mercury)*, Arthur O'Connell, Kenneth Patterson, Anne Nagel, Mary Benoit, Russ Conway, Joan Miller, Jerry Marlowe, Ralph Brooks *(Reporters)*, George J. Lewis, Eddie Parker *(Detectives)*, Pat Shade *(Newsboy)*, Helen Francell, Harriett Bennett *(Women)*, Josephine Whittell *(Dowager)*, John Valentine *(Stammers)*, Phil Garris *(Counter Man)*, Ralph Peters *(Taxi Driver)*, George Meeker *(Mr. Crust)*, Dick Gordon *(Guest)*, Martha Montgomery *(Pretty Girl)*, Yvette Renard, Pat Parrish *(Girls)*.

Anyone who was privileged to see the original play, which starred Mary Martin and had a wonderful score with sixteen songs, will be miffed at this cinematic yawn. Walker is a department store window dresser in the employ of Conway. There's a statue of the goddess Venus and Walker talks to it as he does his work. When he kisses the sculpture, it comes to life and is Ava Gardner, looking scrumptious in the nightie and slip that the goddess wears. Gardner's loving ways bring peace to the store and couples fall in love and she is soon a statue again. That is it, folks. No wit in the adaptation, dull direction and only a few of the glorious tunes by Ogden Nash and Kurt Weill are retained. They include "Speak Low," and "The Trouble with Women." "That's Him," "Don't Look Now But My Heart Is Showing," and "My Week" with new lyrics by Ann Ronnell, which was added to expand the story. The dancing numbers were routine and the only consistent humor was delivered by Arden as Conway's secretary. Gardner was looped musically by Eileen Wilson. Briefly seen were Olga San Juan and Sara Allgood. Dick Haymes sings a bit but even his mellow sound couldn't raise this picture to any level beyond tepid.

p, Lester Cowan; d, William A. Seiter; w, Harry Kurnitz, Frank Tashlin (based on the musical play "The Tented Venus" by Kurt Weill, S.J. Perelman, Ogden Nash, suggested by the novel *The Tinted Venus* by F. Anstey); ph, Franz Planer; m, Kurt Weill; ed, Otto Ludwig; md, Leo Arnaud; art d, Bernard Herzbrun, Emrich H. Nicholson; set d, Russell A. Gausman, Al Fields; cos, Orry-Kelly; spec eff, David Horsley; ch, Billy Daniels; m/l, Weill, Nash, Ann Ronnell.

Musical Comedy **Cas.** **(PR:A MPAA:NR)**

ONE-TRICK PONY*** (1980) 98m WB c

Paul Simon *(Jonah)*, Blair Brown *(Marion)*, Rip Torn *(Walter Fox)*, Joan Hackett *(Lonnie Fox)*, Allen Goorwitz [Garfield] *(Cal Van Damp)*, Mare Winningham *(Modeena Dandridge)*, Michael Pearlman *(Matty Levin)*, Lou Reed *(Steve Kunelian)*, Steve Gadd *(Danny Duggin)*, Eric Gale *(Lee-Andrew Parker)*, Tony Levin *(John DiBatista)*, Richard Tee *(Clarence Franklin)*, Harry Shearer *(Bernie Wepner)*, Daniel Stern *(Hare Krishna)*, Lisa Carlson, Sameen Tarighati *(Groupies)*, Joe Smith *(Narrator at Convention)*, Noel L. Silverman *(Lawyer)*, Jordan Cael *(Lee Perry)*, Susan Forristal *(Cal's Girl Friend)*, Ann Karell *(Moto Inn Clerk)*, Freda Scott *(Chambermaid)*, The B 52's, The Lovin' Spoonful, Sam and Dave, Tiny Tim, Acappella Singers.

Pop singer Paul Simon (Simon and Garfunkel) wrote the screenplay and the score and starred in this film of a singer in a downward slide in his popularity and his personal life. Simon was on top of the charts 10 years ago and now opens for punk bands in New York clubs. He is divorced from his wife Brown, but she is still in love with Simon and wants him to grow up. Simon's record company is still expecting a hit record and record producer Reed (a rock singer in real life) throws in a bag of studio tricks to get that hit record for the floundering singer. The film works because the story never goes into melodrama, thanks to Simon and to director Young (formerly a documentary filmmaker) who underplays most scenes and avoids the cliched and obvious.

p, Michael Tannern, Michael Hausman; d, Robert M. Young; w, Paul Simon; ph, Dick Bush (Technicolor); m, Simon; ed, Edward Beyer, Barry Malkin, David Ray; prod d, David Mitchell; art d, Woods MacIntosh; set d, Justin Scoppa; cos, Hilary Rosenfeld.

Drama **Cas.** **(PR:O MPAA:R)**

ONE, TWO, THREE*½** (1961) 115m Mirisch-Pyramid/UA bw

James Cagney *(C.R. MacNamara)*, Horst Buchholz *(Otto Ludwig Piffl)*, Pamela Tiffin *(Scarlett Hazeltine)*, Arlene Francis *(Phyllis MacNamara)*, Lilo Pulver *(Ingeborg)*, Howard St. John *(Hazeltine)*, Hanns Lothar *(Schlemmer)*, Lois Bolton *(Mrs. Hazeltine)*, Leon Askin *(Peripetchikoff)*, Peter Capell *(Mishkin)*, Ralf Wolter *(Borodenko)*, Karl Lieffen *(Fritz)*, Henning Schluter *(Dr. Bauer)*, Red Buttons *(Military Police Sergeant)*, John Allen *(Tommy MacNamara)*, Christine Allen *(Cindy MacNamara)*, Hubert Van Meyerinck *(Count von Droste-Schattenburg)*, Tile Kiwe *(Newspaperman)*, Karl Ludwig Lindt *(Zeidlitz)*, Rose Renee Roth *(Bertha)*, Ivan Arnold *(Military Police Corporal)*, Jacques Chevalier *(Pierre)*, Paul Bos *(Krause)*, Helmut Schmid *(East German Police Corporal)*, Otto Friebel *(East German Interrogator)*, Werner Buttler *(East German Police Sergeant)*, Klaus Becker, Siegfried Dornbusch *(Policemen)*, Max Buchsbaum *(Tailor)*, Jaspar von Oertzen *(Haberdasher)*, Inga De Toro *(Stewardess)*, Werner Hassenland *(Shoeman)*, Abi von Hasse *(Jeweler)*.

James Cagney left the movie business for more than twenty years after finishing his role in ONE, TWO, THREE and it's no wonder; he needed at least that much time to rest up after the fastest-moving comedy made in the 1960s and surely one of the funniest. This film begins at mach one and gets somewhere near the speed of light by the time it finishes. Matter of fact, it's often too furiously quick for its own good as the dialog comes at the ears with Uzi-like speed. Cagney is the fast-talking, hard-driving, self-made man who heads up Coca-Cola's bottling interests in Germany. His attitude is similar to the man who once ran General Motors and said "What's good for General Motors is good for America." And since there is nothing in Europe more American than Coca-Cola, Cagney is determined to bring it to everyone with two lips and a gullet. Cagney would like to become chief of all the European operations and is working toward that end when Tiffin, the teenage daughter of St. John—one of the heavyweights at Coca-Cola's Georgia headquarters—arrives and Cagney has to baby-sit her for two weeks as she makes her way through a tour of the Continent. Cagney does his best to squire the dippy Tiffin, in the hope that his behavior will get him his desired promotion, but things go awry when she falls hard for Buchholz, a dedicated East Berlin Communist hippy. Cagney learns that St. John is coming to Germany at the same time he discovers Tiffin has married Buchholz. He plants a copy of that most capitalistic of papers, *The Wall Street Journal* on Buchholz, figuring the youth will be clapped in irons and an annulment can be secured. Then he learns that Tiffin is expecting Buchholz's baby so he has to get the kid out of jail and train him to be a capitalist in order to make him a suitable son-in-law for St. John (who was doing the same role he played in Broadway's "L'il Abner" as "General Bullmoose," which he repeated in the filmed version). Cagney successfully springs Buchholz, spends a few bucks to purchase a royal title for him, and gives him a crash course in American business. Buchholz impresses St. John so much that the pleased father-in-law hands the plum job of running Europe to his new relation, the father of his unborn grandchild. Cagney winds up going back to Atlanta with wife Francis. He did his job too well and lost the promotion he'd hoped for. Cagney plays this part with such verve and energy that he seems to be a much younger man than he was (62) and even appears to be a new actor eager to impress the studio with his abilities. But that was always the way Cagney played things—to the hilt. Many of the jokes were taken right from the period's headlines and were already dated by the time the film was released. It was based on a one-act play by the master farceur Molnar and expanded beautifully by Wilder and Diamond. Filmed on location in West Berlin and at the studios in Munich (where Wilder had been before the war), it won no awards except the laughter of those who saw it. Fapp got an Oscar nomination for his cinematography. Previn's score was perfect and the use of several old ditties was excellent, including "Yes, We Have No Bananas" (Frank Silver, Irving Cohn). It would be better to watch this alone as the sound of chuckling in a theater will drown out many of the clever lines.

p&d, Billy Wilder; second unit d, Andre Smagghe; w, Wilder, I.A.L. Diamond (based on the play "Egy, Ketto, Harom" by Ferenc Molnar); ph, Daniel Fapp (Panavision); m, Andre Previn; ed, Daniel Mandell; md, Previn; art d, Alexander Trauner; spec eff, Milt Rice; makeup, Josef Coesfeld.

Comedy **(PR:A MPAA:NR)**

1 2 3 MONSTER EXPRESS** (1977, Thai.) 125m Narong Poomin c (1 2 3 DUAN MAHAPHAI)

Krung Srivilai *(Ekasid)*, Sorapong Chatri *(Padet)*, Patravadi Sritrairatana *(Patra)*, Piyamatr Monjakul *(Tipawan)*, Naiyana Chivanand *(Sichan)*, Nawarat Yukthanan *(Lapipan)*, Niroot Sirichanya *(Anocha)*, Lak Apichat *(Cherd)*, Setta Sirichaya *(Chesta)*, Anyarat Suthat Na Ayudhaya *(Tik)*, Banchong Nilpet *(Tan)*, Sulaliwan Suwanatat *(Menh)*, Bu Vibulnan *(Siaoh)*, Ratanaporn Noi *(Sarapi)*, Pinyo Panui *(Yoh)*, Ratanaporn Indrakamhaeng *(Ratana)*, Muang Apollo *(Muang)*, Tawin Jaengsawang *(Tawin)*, Somboon Sukinan *(Buem)*, Kitti Daskorn *(Peurd)*, Somchai Samipak *(Chai)*.

A luxury film by Thailand standards, 1 2 3 MONSTER EXPRESS (a luxury bus) went through almost as many mishaps in the making as the coach does in the film. Budgeted at about $150,000, almost twice the ordinary amount spent on the making of a Thai movie, the unfortunate death of its original director, Prinya Lilason, early in the filming, and the job passing through many hands before it was finished gives it a curiously disjointed look. The story deals with a bus trip from Bangkok to the provinces, and several murders that take place among the passengers along the way. Finally they learn that a time bomb has been placed on the bus, and the panic continues. The most that can be said for this ill-fated endeavor is that it seems to be an attempt to upgrade the local product, and not imitate film imports as is the wont of Thailand filmmakers.

p, Narong Poomin; d, Prinya Lilason, Vinai Poomin, Narong Poomin; w, Rom Bunnag, Narong Poomin (based on a story by Narong Poomin); ph, Pisan Prasingh; m, Seksan Sonimsat; ed, Manat Topayat; prod d & art d, Ulai Sirisombat; m/l, "A New Lease On Life," Sonimsat (sung by Setha Sirichaya, Anyarat Suthat Na Ayudhaya).

Drama **(PR:C MPAA:NR)**

ONE WAY OUT (SEE: CONVICTED, 1950)

ONE WAY OUT*½ (1955, Brit.) 61m Major/Rank bw

Jill Adams *(Shirley Harcourt)*, Eddie Byrne *(Supt. Harcourt)*, Lyndon Brook *(Leslie Parrish)*, John Chandos *(Danvers)*, Olive Milbourne *(Mrs. Harcourt)*, Arthur Howard *(Marriott)*, Ryck Rydon *(Harry)*, Anne Valery *(Carol Martin)*, Doris Gilmore, Nicholas Tanner.

Hardworking cop Byrne quits the force after his efforts to convict a crime kingpin are ruined when his daughter takes part in a robbery. The former officer then continues in his pursuit of the crook, but gets himself killed in the process. The plot is never believable for a moment, a near tragedy considering the effort applied by the actors in attempting to make this nonsense communicable to an audience.

p, John Temple-Smith, Francis Edge; d, Francis Searle; w, Jonathan Roche (based on the story by Temple-Smith and Jean Scott-Rogers); ph, Walter Harvey.

Crime   (PR:A MPAA:NR)

ONE WAY PASSAGE***   (1932) 69m WB bw

William Powell (Dan Hardesty), Kay Francis (Joan Ames), Frank McHugh (Skippy), Aline MacMahon (Betty the Countess), Warren Hymer (Steve Burke), Frederick Burton (Doctor), Douglas Gerrard (Sir Harold), Herbert Mundin (Steward), Wilson Mizner (Singing Drunk), Mike Donlin (Hong Kong Bartender), Roscoe Karns (Bartender on Ship), Dewey Robinson (Honolulu Contact), Bill Halligan (Agua Caliente Bartender), Stanley Fields (Captain), Willie Fung (Curio Dealer), Heinie Conklin (Singer), Allan Lane, Ruth Hall (Friends), Harry Seymour (Ship's Officer).

A better-than-average melodrama. Powell is a convict being transported from Hong Kong to San Quentin to be executed for murder, and stylish Francis is a young woman dying of heart disease. They meet on board a ship heading to San Francisco and fall in love. McHugh and MacMahon supply comic relief as the matchmakers who keep San Francisco cop Hymer temporarily out of the way of the lovers. Robert Lord won an Oscar for Best Original Story. A haunting quality pervades the tale of the doomed lovers that is unusual in the assembly-line programming Warner Bros. churned out in the early 1930s. Part of this was due to the leisurely way its two stars went about their business in a film only 69 minutes long. Another factor in its success was certainly its director, Garnett, known for his love of sea stories. The picture often has been called his best in a career that spanned the late 1920s to the 1960s, for many different studios, mostly heavy melodramas, but always efficiently and capably directed. Garnett actually wrote the story treatment, working from an idea of Lord's. He intended to take credit for this work but producer Wallis told Garnett: "Let me remind you of Sam Taylor." Taylor had directed Mary Pickford and Douglas Fairbanks, Sr. in THE TAMING OF THE SHREW (1928) and took an additional credit which later became celebrated, if not notorious: "By William Shakespeare, with Additional Dialog by Sam Taylor." Garnett decided to forego the story credit and, ironically, Lord, who only contributed the idea but who had the exclusive credit for the story, won an Oscar, not Garnett. Songs include: "Where was I?" (W. Frank Harling, Al Dubin), "If I Had My Way."

p, Hal Wallis; d, Tay Garnett; w, Wilson Mizner, Joseph Jackson (based on a story by Robert Lord); ph, Robert Kurrle; ed, Ralph Dawson; cos, Orry-Kelly.

Drama   (PR:A MPAA:NR)

ONE WAY PENDULUM***   (1965, Brit.) 90m Woodfall Film/Lopert bw

Eric Sykes (Mr. Groomkirby), George Cole (Defense Counsel/Friend), Julia Foster (Sylvia), Jonathan Miller (Kirby), Peggy Mount (Mrs. Gantry), Alison Leggatt (Mrs. Groomkirby), Mona Washbourne (Aunt Mildred), Douglas Wilmer (Judge/Maintenance Man), Kenneth Farrington (Stan), Glyn Houston (Detective Inspector Barnes), Graham Crowden (Prosecuting Counsel/Caretaker), Walter Horsbrugh (Clerk of the Court/Drycleaner's Assistant), Frederick Piper (Usher/Office Clerk), Vincent Harding (Policeman/Bus Conductor), Tommy Bruce (Voice of Gormless).

A wacky British comedy about a family of eccentrics. Sykes, the father, is building a replica of Old Bailey courts in the living room. His wife, Leggatt, hires a maid to eat the family's leftovers, and their daughter, Foster, spends her time watching apes in the zoo. Son Miller is trying to get his collection of weight scales to play a musical piece. Sykes holds a mock trial with his son as the murder defendant and his wife playing the main witness. His son is found innocent and that night he gets his scales to play George Frederick Handel's "Hallelujah Chorus" from "The Messiah," making it impossible for his father to sleep. Antic happenings by these spirited characters skirt chaos, but director Yates keeps a rein on it all throughout.

p, Michael Deely; d, Peter Yates; w, N.F. Simpson (based on a play by Simpson); ph, Denys Coop; m, Richard Rodney Bennett; ed, Peter Taylor; md, Marcus Dods; prod d, Reece Pemberton; makeup, Tom Smith.

Comedy   (PR:A MPAA:NR)

ONE WAY STREET*½   (1950) 79m UNIV bw

James Mason (Doc Matson), Marta Toren (Laura), Dan Duryea (Wheeler), William Conrad (Ollie), King Donovan (Grieder), Jack Elam (Arnie), Tito Renaldo (Hank Torres), Basil Ruysdael (Father Moreno), Rodolfo Acosta (Francisco Morales), Margarito Lama (Antonio Morales), George Lewis (Capt. Rodriguez), Emma Roldan (Catalina), Robert Espinoza (Santiago), Jose Dominguez (Bias), Julia Montoya (Juanita), Marguerite Martin (Frasca), Rock Hudson (Truck Driver), Paul Fierro (Bandit), Freddie Letuli (A Weaver).

Mason is a doctor who gets involved with criminals in this pointless melodrama. After a robbery from which the crooks bring back a bundle of money, Mason informs them that he's poisoned their boss, Duryea, and if they don't give him the money and Duryea's girl friend, Toren, he won't give them the antidote. Mason and Toren escape to Mexico and end up in a small village. Mason starts a hospital in the village and hears that Duryea is after him (the "poison" was only aspirin). Mason returns the money and at the exchange point a gang member kills Duryea and Mason kills him. Mason himself is killed when he falls in front of a car as he returns to a waiting Toren. Soundly panned by critics and avoided by the public after its release, ONE WAY STREET quickly sank into oblivion, leading Mason to later remark, "I never encountered anyone who saw this film, other than studio personnel. It must have been a leftover project from some previous regime, for you'd think Universal would no longer have afforded the floor space for this sort of pretentious melodrama."

p, Leonard Goldstein; d, Hugo Fregonese; w, Lawrence Kimble (based on the

story "Death on a Side Street" by Kimble); ph, Maury Gertsman; m, Frank Skinner; ed, Milton Carruth; art d, Bernard Herzbaum, Al Ybarra; cos, Orry-Kelly.

Crime Drama   (PR:A MPAA:NR)

ONE-WAY TICKET*½   (1935) 72m COL bw

Lloyd Nolan (Jerry), Peggy Conklin (Ronnie), Walter Connolly (Capt. Bourne), Edith Fellows (Ellen), Gloria Shea (Willa), Nana Bryant (Mrs. Bourne), Thurston Hall (Mr. Ritchie), George McKay (Martin), Robert Middlemass (Bender), Willie Fung (Wing), Jack Clifford (Charlie), James Flavin (Ed).

Nolan robs the bank whose president had swindled him out of his savings and is sent to jail. After a group of prisoners are brutally machine-gunned attempting an escape, Nolan pulls off his own escape, marries the warden's daughter, Conklin, and they live as fugitives. In the end justice wins out and Nolan is returned to his cell. Mainly a preachy story about the harshness of prisons rather than the futility of swindling.

p, B.P. Schulberg; d, Herbert Biberman; w, Vincent Lawrence, Joseph Anthony, Oliver H.P. Garrett, Grover Jones (based on a novel by Ethel Turner); ph, Henry Freulich; ed, John Rawlins.

Crime Drama   (PR:A MPAA:NR)

ONE WAY TICKET TO HELL*   (1955) 90m Exhibitors Productions/
                                                                 Eden bw

Barbara Marks (Cassandra Light), Bamlet L. Price, Jr. (Cholo Martinez), Robert A. Sherry (Lt. David Jason), Robert Norman (Johnny Adams), Elaine Lindenbaum (Margo Rossi), William Kendall (Russel Packard), Anthony Gorsline (Jimmy Sanchez), Joe Popovich (Stutzman), Joel Climenhaga (Sven Bergman), Lucile Price (Mrs. Leigh), Bamlet L. Price, Sr. (Mr. Leigh), Victor Schwartz (Sgt. Schwartz), Kurt Martell (Narrator).

Another lifeless melodrama about the dangers of drug abuse, produced so humorlessly that it has absolutely nothing worthwhile to offer. Marks is the one-time sweet and innocent girl who gets hooked on pot, then pills, which leads to heroine addiction. It's all downhill from there as her life falls apart in her mad efforts to remain high. She gets into a horrible car crash due to her drug abuse, and it lands her in the hospital. Almost immediately upon her release she's back on the street, this time selling as well as using drugs. As a pusher she is in danger of being arrested, and when things get too hot, she tries to make a run for it, but is caught and forced to go straight. The cheapness of this feature is best revealed in the absence of dialog. Instead a narrator is used to convey much of the action. As such, plot and characters remain undeveloped, and the film relies on trite sociological concepts rather than insightful characterizations.

p,d&w, Bamlet L. Price, Jr.

Drama   (PR:A MPAA:NR)

ONE WAY TO LOVE*½   (1946) 83m COL bw

Willard Parker (Mitchell Raymond), Marguerite Chapman (Marcia Winthrop), Chester Morris (Barry Cole), Janis Carter (Josie Hart), Hugh Herbert (Eustace P. Trumble), Dusty Anderson (Capt. Henderson), Jerome Cowan (A.J. Gunther), Irving Bacon (Train Conductor), Roscoe Karns (Hobie Simmons), Frank Sully (Hopkins), Frank Jenks (Jensen), Lewis Russell (Roger Winthrop).

A nice comedy that grows dull as it grows complex. Morris and Parker are radio script writing partners in Chicago until Parker takes a job with his fiancee's father and Morris is forced to write commercial jingles. Their agent gets them a $1,000-a-week assignment in Hollywood, but both must work at the job. Morris and Parker board a train to Tinseltown with their respective girl friends. On the train they meet the president of the company sponsoring the show, and also a millionaire who offers them twice the money, if they will work for him. They accept, and here is where the fun comes in. Two lunatic chasers board the train and grab the millionaire as an escapee, and the pair promptly re-sign with the president of the company. When they get to Los Angeles, it turns out that the company president is the lunatic, and the millionaire is not, so the four get back on the train to chase the millionaire back to Chicago.

p, Burt Kelly; d, Ray Enright; w, Joseph Hoffman, Jack Henley (based on a story by Lester Lee, Larry Marks); ph, Charles Lawton, Jr.; ed, Richard Fantl; art d, Stephen Goosson, George Brooks; set d, Albert Rickerd; cos, Jean Louis.

Comedy   (PR:A MPAA:NR)

ONE WAY TRAIL, THE**½   (1931) 60m COL bw

Tim McCoy (Tim Allen), Doris Hill (Helen Beck), Carroll Nye (Terry Allen), Polly Ann Young (Mollie), Al Ferguson (Coldeye Carnell), Bud Osborne, Slim Whitaker, Jack Ward, Herman Hack.

McCoy, the fastest draw of all screen cowboys, goes after menacing Ferguson, who shot McCoy's brother when he found him cheating at cards, in this nicely constructed story of filial loyalty. Gunplay and rollicking scraps provide nonstop action in a superior McCoy entry.

p, Irving Briskin; d, Ray Taylor; w, George Plympton (based on a story by Claude Rister); ph, John Hickson; ed, Otto Meyer.

Western   (PR:A MPAA:NR)

ONE WAY WAHINI*   (1965) 80m Continental/United Screen Arts c
                                                                 (AKA: ONE WAY WAHINE)

Joy Harmon (Kit Williams), Anthony Eisley (Chick Lindell), Adele Claire (Brandy Saveties), David Whorf (Lou Talbot), Edgar Bergen (Sweeney), Lee Krieger (Charley Rossi), Ken Mayer (Hugo Sokol), Harold Fong (Quong), Alvy Moore (Maxwell), Aime Luce (Tahitian Dancer), Ralph Nanalei (Paulo).

Harmon and Claire head for Hawaii to enjoy the sun and surf, and get mixed up in a scheme to rip off a couple of crooks. Whorf meets the girls and tells them about two swindlers who stole a large sum of money from a bank in Chicago, and he gets the girls to distract the two while he and pal Eisley grab the money. The girls meet the two crooks and Harmon is almost raped by one of them in a wild struggling match, but manages to drop the money down to Eisley in a plastic bag, which breaks, and Eisley is forced to hide the money in a trash can. The four discover that the two men are gangsters and when they go to get the money they find that a beach bum has found it and has given it to the police. A nice offbeat story with good comedy touches and plenty of dancing, but not the routine hula kind.

p&d, William O. Brown; w, Rod Larson; ph, John Morrill (Techniscope, Technicolor); m, Jo Hansen; ed, George White; songs, "One Way Wahine" (sung by Jody Miller), "When the One Way Wahine Does the Bird," "When I Look at You" (sung by Ray Peterson); makeup, Lillian Lawson.

Comedy **(PR:C-O MPAA:NR)**

ONE WILD NIGHT* (1938) 63m FOX bw

June Lang (Jennifer Jewel), Dick Baldwin (Jimmy Nolan), Lyle Talbot (Singer Martin), J. Edward Bromberg (Norman), Sidney Toler (Lawton), Andrew Tombes (Chief Nolan), William Demarest (Editor Collins), Romaine Callender (Heppie), Jan Duggan (Mrs. Halliday), Spencer Charters (Lem Halliday), Harlan Briggs (Mayor).

Four wealthy men set up their own kidnapings to escape from their wives and get a little vacation. One of them, Bromberg, a bank manager, steals the ransom money and law student Baldwin and tasteful reporter Lang go on the trail of the doublecrosser. Not much in this for the players or the audience, though some good names grace the cast. In the case of Toler, he had been doing such good work as a character actor since he entered films early in the sound era, that he was entrusted with the title role in the "Charlie Chan" series soon after the release of ONE WILD NIGHT, following the death of all-time favorite Chan Warner Oland.

p, John Stone; d, Eugene Forde; w, Charles Belden, Jerry Cady (based on an idea by Edwin Dial Torgenson); ph, Harry Davis; m, Samuel Kaylin; ed, Nick De Maggio; md, Kaylin; art d, Bernard Herzbrun, Haldane Douglas.

Comedy **(PR:A MPAA:NR)**

ONE WILD OAT** (1951, Brit.) 78m Coronet/Eros bw

Robertson Hare (Humphrey Proudfoot), Stanley Holloway (Alfred Gilbey), Sam Costa (Mr. Pepys), Andrew Crawford (Fred Gilbey), Vera Pearce (Mrs. Gilbey), June Sylvaine (Cherrie Proudfoot), Robert Moreton (Throstle), Constance Lorne (Mrs. Proudfoot), Gwen Cherrill (Audrey Cuttle No. 1), Irene Handl (Audrey Cuttle No. 2), Ingeborg Wells (Gloria Samson), Charles Groves (Charles), Joan Rice (Annie, Maid), Audrey Hepburn, Fred Berger, William [James] Fox.

Successful stage play is transferred to the screen with little to differentiate it from the play. Hare and Holloway are two enemies whose children decide to unite the families by marrying, an event neither man relishes. To see that the marriage never takes place, Hare does a bit of snooping about the enemy, forcing Holloway to devise an underhanded scheme to blemish Hare's past. Good performances help to make this slightly amusing film worth a glance. Watch for Audrey Hepburn, appearing here in her first feature.

p, John Croydon; d, Charles Saunders; w, Vernon Sylvaine, Lawrence Huntington (based on the play by Sylvaine); ph, Robert Navarro; m, Stanley Black; ed, Marjorie Saunders.

Comedy **(PR:A MPAA:NR)**

ONE WISH TOO MANY½** (1956, Brit.) 55m Realist Film Unit/ Sterling Educational Films-Children's Film Foundation bw

Anthony Richmond (Peter), Rosalind Gourgey (Nancy), John Pike (Ian), Terry Cooke (Bert), Arthur Howard (Headmaster), Gladys Young (Miss Mint), Sam Costa (Mr. Pomfrett), Bay White (Mrs. Brown), Frank Hayden (Mr. Brown), Paddy Joyce (Barrow Boy).

Richmond is a schoolboy who finds a magic marble that grants wishes. He uses it to escape into his own fantasy world, get revenge on bullies, and pull pranks on his teachers. This gets out of hand when he makes a toy steam roller into a real one which runs wild in London. Richmond's father comes to his rescue and the boy is happy to learn that he's lost the marble. Grand prize winner for Best Children's Film at the Venice Children's Film Festival in 1956, which, in retrospect, makes one wonder, since it has a condescending air and much of the photography is murky. But, maybe that's London.

p, Basil Wright; d, John Durst; w, John Eldridge, Mary Cathcart Borer (based on a story by Norah Pulling); ph, Adrian Jeakins; m, Douglas Gamley; ed, James Clark; art d, Bernard Sarron; spec eff, Bowie and Margutti.

Comedy **(PR:A MPAA:NR)**

ONE WITH THE FUZZ, THE (SEE: SOME KIND OF NUT, 1969)

ONE WOMAN'S STORY** (1949, Brit.) 91m GFD/UNIV bw (GB: THE PASSIONATE FRIENDS)

Ann Todd (Mary Justin), Claude Rains (Howard Justin), Trevor Howard (Steven Stratton), Isabel Dean (Pat), Betty Ann Davies (Miss Layton), Arthur Howard (Servant), Guido Lorraine (Hotel Manager), Marcel Poncin (Hall Porter), Natasha Sokolova (Chambermaid), Helen Burls (Flowerwoman), Jean Serrett (Emigration Official), Frances Waring (Charwoman), Wanda Rogerson (Bridge Guest), Wilfrid Hyde-White (Solicitor), Helen Piers, Ina Pelly, John Hudson, Max Earl.

Todd is a young woman who marries banker Rains for wealth and position, but finds that material things don't bring fulfillment. In Switzerland she meets Howard, with whom she had a love affair nine years before and her life is suddenly complicated by the passion she still feels toward her former lover. The film's script was adapted from the novel by H. G. Wells.

p, Ronald Neame; d, David Lean; w, Eric Ambler, Lean, Stanley Haynes (based

on H. G. Wells' novel The Passionate Friends); ph, Guy Green, Oswald Morris; m, Richard Addinsell; ed, Geoffrey Foot; md, Muir Mathieson; art d, Hopewell Ashe; set d, John Bryan; cos, cos, Margaret Furse.

Drama **(PR:A MPAA:NR)**

ONE YEAR LATER** (1933) 65m AA bw

Mary Brian (Molly Collins), Russell Hopton (Tony Richards), Donald Dillaway (Jim Collins), George Irving (J. Atwell Hunt), Will Ahern (Himself), Gladys Ahern (Joyce Carewe), DeWitt Jennings (Deputy Russell), Jackie Searl (Clarence), Pauline Garon (Vera Marks), Pat O'Malley (Reporter), Marjorie Beebe, All Hill, Myrtle Steadman, Edward Keene, Harry Holman, William Humphrey, Lloyd Whitlock, Nina Guilbert, John Ince, James Mack, Walter Brennan, Herbert Evans, Jane Keckley, Kit Guard, Al Klein, Tom London, Virginia True Boardman.

Dillaway is on a train heading to the prison where he is to be hanged. His wife, "nice girl" Brian, is with him and she tells reporter Hopton how her husband had gotten into a fight to protect her and killed a man. Hopton, who is dying of tuberculosis decides to help the couple. He knocks out the guard, helps Dillaway escape, and jumps off the train. Hopton's body is found and the police assume it's the body of Dillaway, allowing the couple to start a new life. A novel story handled diligently by director Hopper and a long cast of competent performers.

p, H.H. Hoffman; d, E. Mason Hopper; w, F. Hugh Herbert, Paul Perez, Will Ahern; ph, Faxon Dean, Tom Galligan; ed, Mildred Johnston.

Drama **(PR:A MPAA:NR)**

ONEICHAN MAKARI TORU (SEE: THREE DOLLS FROM HONG KONG, 1966, Jap.)

ONI NO SUMU YAKATA (SEE: DEVIL'S TEMPLE, THE, 1969, Jap.)

ONI SHLI NA VOSTOK (SEE: ITALIANO BRAVA GENTE, 1965, Ital./ USSR)

ONIBABA*½ (1965, Jap.) 104m Kindai Eiga Kyokai-Tokyo Eiga/ Toho International bw (AKA: THE DEMON; THE DEVIL WOMAN; THE HOLE)

Nobuko Otowa (The Mother), Jitsuko Yoshimura (The Daughter-in-Law), Kei Sato (Hachi, Farmer), Jukichi Uno (The Warrior), Taiji Tonomura (Ushi, the Merchant).

In medieval Japan a mother and her daughter-in-law survive by killing samurais and warriors and selling their weapons and armor. Sato comes to them and reveals that the woman's son has been killed in battle. He then begins an affair with the daughter-in-law, and the mother schemes to find a way to break them apart. She comes across a wounded warrior in a swamp, who wears a horrible mask and tells the old woman the mask hides his face, which is beautiful. She kills him and takes off the mask to find a terribly disfigured face and then puts the mask on to scare her daughter-in-law. The mask shrinks on the woman's face, and when the daughter-in-law breaks it off, the old woman's face has decomposed.

p, Toshio Konya; d&w, Kaneto Shindo; ph, Kiyomi Kuroda (Tohoscope); m, Hikaru Hayashi [Mitsu Hayashi]; ed, Toshio Enoki; art d, Shindo.

Horror **(PR:C MPAA:NR)**

ONIMASA** (1983, Jap.) 146m Toei c

Tatsuya Nakadai (Onimasa), Masako Natsume (Matsue), Shima Iwashita (Uta), Tetsuro Tamba (The Big Boss), Kaori Tagasugi (Hanako), Akika Kana (Hanako's Mother), Emi Shindo (2nd Mistress), Akika Nakamura (3rd Mistress), Mari Natsuki (Opponent's Mistress).

Nakadai has been a gangster boss in the Japanese town of Shikoku since 1921. Somewhat crazed, he is married and has two mistresses, but no children. He adopts Natsume, a girl in her early teens, and they become very close even when Nakadai fathers a daughter of his own. This is a very brutal film, which falls into heavy melodramatics. The production quality is flawless, but credibility is stretched by scenes such as Nakadai's attempted rape of his adopted daughter who then tries to kill herself when they later become closer. This film was Japan's official submission for the 1982 foreign language Academy Award.

p, Shigeiu Okada; d, Hideo Gosha; w, Koje Takata, Gosha (based on a novel by Tomiko Miyao); ph, Fujio Morita (Fujicolor); m, Mitsukai Karno; ed, Isamu Ichida; prod d, Yoshindon Nishioka.

Drama **(PR:O MPAA:NR)**

ONION FIELD, THE** (1979) 122m AE c

John Savage (Karl Hettinger), James Woods (Greg Powell), Franklyn Seales (Jimmy Smith), Ted Danson (Ian Campbell), Ronny Cox (Pierce Brooks), David Huffman (District Attorney Phil Halpin), Christopher Lloyd (Jailhouse Lawyer), Diane Hull (Helen Hettinger), Priscilla Pointer (Chrissie Campbell), Beege Barkett (Greg's Woman), Richard Herd (Beat Cop), Le Tari (Emmanuel McFadden), Richard Venture (Glenn Bates), Lee Weaver (Billy), Phillip R. Allen (District Attorney Marshall Schulman), Pat Corley (Jimmy's 1st Lawyer), K. Callan (Mrs. Powell), Sandy McPeak (Mr. Powell), Lillian Randolph (Nana), Ned Wilson (LAPD Captain), Jack Rader (IAD Captain), Raleigh Bond (2nd Judge), Brad English (Red-Haired Cop), Stanley Grover (Greg's 2nd Lawyer), Michael Pataki (District Attorney Dino Fulgoni), Steve Conte (1st Prison Guard No.

After have some of his earlier works altered, Wambaugh decided to write the screenplay for this version of his true story about two Los Angeles cops and the killers of one of them. Danson and Savage are a pair of plainclothes officers working the Hollywood beat. They go after two lowlifes in a car, Woods and Seales, and are shocked when a gun is put in their faces. The cops are disarmed, kidnapped, and taken to a field a distance from Los Angeles where Danson is assassinated. Savage gets away and his description soon nabs the killers. The rest of the picture concerns the justice system and how it favors the felon over the victim. Both killers are amenable to cooperation (in return for a deal from the D.A.'s office) and both claim it was the other who pulled the trigger on Danson, a happy-go-lucky man of Scottish heritage who loved to play the bagpipes. The judicial system of the state of California is raked over the coals as Woods, just this side of being psychotic, makes mincemeat of the law and the trials drag on for years. Meanwhile, Savage is so wracked with guilt for his partner's death that he begins to break down mentally. An authentic look at police work (and that is where it shines), the picture gets confused in the court scenes and doesn't sustain the power of the opening sequences. Good acting and careful direction by Becker make it worth seeing, but the violence and the language may be too graphic for some tastes. It is strictly from the point of view of the police, something that may annoy the bleeding hearts who thump for prisoners' rights and forget about the people who died at the hands of murderers. Although Wambaugh himself was a cop with the Los Angeles Police Department, he had technical assistance on this from Richard Falk. Advice on courtroom procedures came from Phillip Halpin and Dino Fulgoni, who were portrayed by Huffman and Pataki. The crime took place in 1963 and Smith (Seales) was released in the 1980s, over strenuous objections.

p, Walter Coblenz; d, Harold Becker; w, Joseph Wambaugh (based on his book); ph, Charles Rosher; m, Eumir Deodato; ed, John W. Wheeler; prod d, Brian Eatwell; set d, Joe Hubbard, Dick Goddard.

True Police Story **Cas.** **(PR:C-O MPAA:R)**

ONIONHEAD** (1958) 110m WB bw

Andy Griffith *(Al Woods)*, Felicia Farr *(Stella)*, Walter Matthau *("Red" Wildoe)*, Erin O'Brien *(Jo Hill)*, Joe Mantell *("Doc" O'Neal)*, Ray Danton *(Ensign Dennis Higgins)*, James Gregory *("The Skipper")*, Joey Bishop *(Gutsell)*, Roscoe Karns *("Windy" Woods)*, Claude Akins *(Poznicki)*, Ainslie Pryor *(Chief Miller)*, Sean Garrison *(Yeoman Kaffhamp)*, Dan Barton *(Ensign Fineberg)*, Mark Roberts *(Lt. Bennett)*, Peter Brown *(Clark)*, Tige Andrews *(Charlie Berger)*, Karl Lukas *(Agnelli)*.

Griffith is a college student who isn't doing well with his classes or his girl O'Brien so he joins the Coast Guard during WW II. He becomes a cook on the USS Periwinkle where Matthau is the chief cook. Griffith soon gets involved with Farr who, while planning to marry Matthau, can't keep her hands off other men. She does marry him, and Griffith returns to "nice girl" O'Brien. An uneven comedy which doesn't measure up to Griffith's starring film NO TIME FOR SERGEANTS, but it does have its moments, and Matthau is a standout in most of them.

p, Jules Schermer; d, Norman Taurog; w, Nelson Gidding (based on a novel by Weldon Hill); ph, Harold Rosson; m, David Buttolph; ed, William Ziegler; md, Ray Heindorf; art d, Leo K. Kuter; cos, Howard Shoup.

Drama **(PR:A MPAA:NR)**

ONKEL TOMS HUTTE (SEE: UNCLE TOM'S CABIN, 1969, Fr./Ital./Ger.)

ONLY A WOMAN*½ (1966, Ger.) 86m Rialto/Comet c
(ICH BIN AUCH NUR EINE FRAU)

Maria Schell *(Dr. Lilli Konig)*, Paul Hubschmid [Christian] *(Martin Bohlen)*, Hans Nielson *(Dr. Katz)*, Anita Hofer *(Pauline)*, Ingrid van Bergen *(Annabella)*, Hannelore Auer *(Gerda)*, Tilly Lauenstein *(Mrs. Starke)*, Agnes Windeck *(Housekeeper)*.

Hubschmid is a fashion photographer who poses as a patient of psychiatrist Schell after she tells his girl friend (her patient) that he is a terrible lover. He wants to get back at Schell but they end up falling in love.

p, Horst Wendlandt; d, Alfred Weidenmann; w, Johanna Sibelius, Eberhard Keindorff; ph, Heinz Holscher; m, Peter Thomas; ed, Walter Wischniewsky; art d, Helmut Nentwig; cos, Hannelore Wessel.

Comedy **(PR:A MPAA:NR)**

ONLY ANGELS HAVE WINGS**** (1939) 121m COL bw

Cary Grant *(Geoff Carter)*, Jean Arthur *(Bonnie Lee)*, Richard Barthelmess *(Bat McPherson)*, Rita Hayworth *(Judith McPherson)*, Thomas Mitchell *(Kid Dabb)*, Sig Rumann *(Dutchman)*, Victor Killian *(Sparks)*, John Carroll *(Gent Shelton)*, Allyn Joslyn *(Les Peters)*, Donald [Don "Red"] Barry *(Tex Gordon)*, Noah Beery, Jr. *(Joe Souther)*, Melissa Sierra *(Lily)*, Lucio Villegas *(Dr. Logario)*, Forbes Murray *(Hartwood)*, Cecilia Callejo *(Felice)*, Pat Flaherty *(Mike)*, Pedro Regas *(Pancho)*, Pat West *(Baldy)*, Manuel Maciste *(Balladeer)*, Sammee [Sam] Tong *(Native Cook)*, Candy Candido *(Musician)*, Charles Moore *(Servant)*, Inez Palange *(Lily's Aunt)*, Rafael Corio *(Purser)*, Lew Davis, Jim [James] Millican, Al Rhein, Curley Dresden, Ed Randolph, Ky Robinson, Bud Wolfe, Eddie Foster *(Mechanics)*, Stanley Brown *(Hartwood, Jr.)*, Victor Travers Francisco Maran *(Planter Overseers)*, Wilson Benge *(Assistant Purser)*, Vernon Dent *(Ship Captain)*, Elana Duran *(Spanish Blonde Girl)*, Budd Fine *(First Mate)*, Jack Lowe, Tex Higginson *(Banana Foremen)*, Enrique Acosta, Raoul Lechuga, Dick Botiller, Harry Bailey, Amora Navarro, Tessie Murray *(Tourists)*.

An amazing adventure film where the adventure is confined to a shabby saloon and a few side rooms, ONLY ANGELS HAVE WINGS is a Grant-Arthur vehicle that sharply bears the Hawks mark. Grant is the head of a broken-down air mail and freight service where he has to send courageous civilian pilots over the treacherous Andes mountains in Peru. Arthur becomes involved with a young pilot, Beery, but quickly switches her attention to Grant after meeting the hard-boiled pilot chief. She is surrounded by other pilots—Joslyn, Carroll, and Barry—who are attracted to her, but she can't make headway with the all-business Grant, who seems to have nerves of steel and a heart of iron. Into this group comes Barthelmess, a pilot who tarnished his reputation in an accident years earlier in which another pilot was killed. The other fliers blame Barthelmess for the death of flier Mitchell's brother and the guilt-ridden pilot, washed up as a professional, is at the end of his rope until Grant gives him a job. Hayworth, Barthelmess' sexy, cuckolding wife, tries to seduce Grant and almost succeeds until Grant realizes he has genuine affection for the smart-talking Arthur. Barthelmess, though a pariah among his peers, proves that he's made of courageous stuff by volunteering to take on the most hazardous missions. Meanwhile, Mitchell—an elderly pilot who acts as surrogate father to Grant—is losing his sight but won't admit it. Grant keeps him on the ground to protect him. Then Grant learns that he has no pilot to assign to an important and dangerous mission and plans to make the flight himself. Mitchell goes in his place and is killed. The hard-boiled exterior Grant has maintained throughout the film finally disintegrates with the death of his dearest friend and Arthur sees him as human after all. It is strongly suggested that Grant and Arthur will end up together, but will pursue a life that is no less hectic. ONLY ANGELS HAVE WINGS is a powerful character study and director Hawks pinpoints his almost all-male cast with deadly accuracy, carefully developing the personalities of the fine cast. Though much of the dialog is predictable and even banal in spots, the story is strong and the acting outstanding. Hawks' direction is sharp and his cameras move with fluid grace through the confining sets. There are many similar films that established the theme of this film, including CEILING ZERO, THE DAWN PATROL, and NIGHT FLIGHT, but its true predecessor is the surprisingly good low-budget FLIGHT FROM GLORY, with Chester Morris and Van Heflin. Made two years earlier, FLIGHT FROM GLORY bears an uncanny plot resmblance to Hawks' film: the valiant, manly pilot-supervisor, the brash flier thought to be cowardly, the isolated company of males disrupted by a beautiful woman. The side story of Mitchell's failing sight and resulting death because of this near-blindness is repeated in THE FLYING TIGERS. The strained love story between Grant and Arthur is one that is nearly identical to that of RED DUST, yet is has wonderfully poignant moments, including an ending right out of THE FRONT PAGE. Even at the finish, when he knows he is in love with Arthur and he's about to take off in a plane, Grant plays it tough. He flips a coin, telling her that she goes if the coin turns up tails, but stays and waits for him if it's heads. It's heads and she smiles but it's a half-hearted smile; she feels that he really doesn't care. When Grant flies off, she turns the coin and sees that it's a trick coin with two heads and that Grant, after all, wasn't taking any chances on losing her. Hayworth gives a notable performance as a vamp in the film and supporting players Joslyn and Carroll are live wires full of sardonic wit and jaded views. Barthelmess, having the most complex character in the film, plays his role stoically and little is gained from his dispassionate personality. This was an important film for him, a comeback film, since he had seen lean years since his days of being a silent screen star (a superstar, really, under the direction of D.W. Griffith in WAY DOWN EAST), but the meaty part he was given was left on the kitchen table, half eaten. Barthelmess never again appeared in a major film as a lead. The special effects, particularly the fine aerial sequences, earned Roy Davidson and Edwin C. Hahn an Oscar nomination in a category recognized for the first time by the academy.

p&d, Howard Hawks; w, Jules Furthman [uncredited, William Rankin, Eleanor Griffin] (based on a story by Hawks); ph, Joseph Walker, Elmer Dwyer; m, Dimitri Tiomkin, Manuel Maciste, Morris W. Stoloff; ed, Viola Lawrence; md, Stoloff; art d, Lionel Banks; cos, Robert Kallock; spec eff, Roy Davidson, Edwin C. Hahn; stunts&tech adv, Paul Mantz.

Aviation Drama **(PR:A MPAA:NR)**

ONLY EIGHT HOURS (SEE: SOCIETY DOCTOR, 1935)

ONLY GAME IN TOWN, THE*½ (1970) 113m FOX c

Elizabeth Taylor *(Fran Walker)*, Warren Beatty *(Joe Grady)*, Charles Braswell *(Thomas J. Lockwood)*, Hank Henry *(Tony)*, Olga Valery *(Woman with Purple Wig)*.

This was one of the most expensive flops in Fox's history when the cost of the film is analyzed against the return. Although set in Las Vegas, Taylor insisted that it be filmed in Paris because her husband, Burton, was there making a British film with Rex Harrison called STAIRCASE, another bust. So the studio spent a fortune building Vegas sets at the Studios de Boulogne which cost about three times as much as if they'd done the whole thing in Nevada. Add that to the nearly two million paid the stars and it's easy to see how the ante mounted. Gilroy had written a play that lasted less than two weeks on Broadway with Tammy Grimes and Barry Nelson but Fox gave him a half-million or so for the rights before it died, so they went ahead. Sinatra was orignially tapped to play the male lead but when Taylor became ill and the production was temporarily detained, he had to fulfill another commitment and bowed out. George Stevens, who had previously directed Taylor in GIANT and A PLACE IN THE SUN was coming back after taking five years off, probably due to the disastrous results of his last film, THE GREATEST STORY EVER TOLD. Beatty took the part after having turned down BUTCH CASSIDY AND THE SUNDANCE KID as well as BOB AND CAROL AND TED AND ALICE so one wonders if he actually read those scripts. The shooting took more than 80 days in France and that still wasn't enough, so the company went to Las Vegas for ten more, including location photography under the reins of second unit director Bob Swink. With all of that, the plot can be summed up in just a few words. Taylor is a tired Vegas showgirl who has been having an affair with married swinger Braswell, a wealthy San Francisco businessman who pays her rent and buys her fabulous wardrobe (Fonssagrives and Tiel) and pays for her bouffant hairdo by Alexandre of Paris. Beatty is a gambling junkie who plays piano for knockabout comic Henry to pay off the money he owes around town. He's trying to get even, then raise enough money to go to New York and further his ivory-tinkling career. Taylor has been seeing Braswell for five years and he keeps promising to rid himself of his wife but she is losing hope of that ever happening. Beatty moves in with Taylor on a "no commitment beyond sex" basis but the inevitable happens and they fall in love. When Braswell shows up, having shed his mate, Taylor tosses him aside for the man she has come to love, Beatty. Pretty slim stuff and very talky; some of the dialogue sparkles but it's basically a programmer dressed up in ermine. Much of the play takes place in Taylor's apartment with only a few moves outside. In the only sequence that stands out in memory, Taylor and Beatty have an argument, he races off to the casinos where he has a terrific run, then it shifts and he loses it all. He sits down at one of the garish fountains outside the hotel (it looked like Caesar's Palace), takes out his last remaining money, a one hundred dollar bill, makes it into a tiny green-and-white boat, puts it in the water and watches as it sails away, which is exactly what Fox did when they agreed to make this film. The picture opened in January of 1970 in Las Vegas and audiences stood in line waiting to get out. A monumental waste of money, second only to the government's Pentagon expenditures, it cost more than $11 million and returned less than $2 million. Far more interesting than this film is Gilroy's ONCE IN PARIS, which was an autobiographical account of what happened to him while he was in The City of Light working on THE ONLY GAME IN TOWN. His chauffeur was one of the most incredible characters he'd ever met so he decided to write and direct a film about those weeks and instead of hiring Jean Gabin or Louis Jourdan to play the driver, he cast the man to play himself.

p, Fred Kohlmar; d, George Stevens; w, Frank D. Gilroy (based on the play by Gilroy); ph, Henri Decae (DeLuxe Color); m, Maurice Jarre; ed, John W. Holmes, William Sands, Pat Shade; md, Jarre; art d, Herman Blumenthal, Auguste Capelier; set d, Walter M. Scott, Jerry Wunderlich; cos, Mia Fonssagrives, Vicki Tiel; spec eff, L. B. Abbott, Art Cruickshank; makeup, Frank Larue, John Jiras.

Drama   **(PR:C MPAA:M)**

ONLY GIRL, THE   (SEE: HEART SONG, 1933, Brit.)

ONLY GOD KNOWS*   (1974, Can.) 95m Canart and Queensbury c

Gordon Pinsent (Father John Hagan), John Beck (Rev. Philip Norman), Paul Hecht (Rabbi Isaac Sherman), Tisa Farrow (Terry Sullivan), Toby Tarnow (Frances Sherman), Louis Tanno (Don Dominic), Lawrence Dane (Vincenzo), Albert Bernardo (Paulo), Nick Nichols (Angelo), George Touliatis (Giorgio), Paul Bertoya (Enrico).

A ridiculous clergy-meets-gangsters comedy which groups a minister, a priest, and a rabbi together in running a drug rehabilitation center. When funding runs dry, they enter a deal with failing local mafioso Tanno in exchange for absolving him of his sins. When Tanno dies, the trio is forced to steal the promised money from his safe. Instead of paying for their sins in jail, the holy criminals are given their freedom and allowed to keep the money.

p, Lawrence Z. Dane; d, Peter Pearson; w, Haskell Gray (based on an idea by Dane); ph, Don Wilder; m, Ben McPeek; art d, Roy Force-Smith.

Comedy   **(PR:A MPAA:NR)**

ONLY ONCE IN A LIFETIME*   (1979) 97m Sierra Madre-
                                         Montezuma Esparza/Movietime c

Miguel Robelo (Dominguez), Estrellita Lopez (Counsuelo), Sheree North (Sally), Claudio Brook (Jimenez).

Dull, predictable story of a Mexican-American artist who has given up on life since his wife has died and whose only friend is an old dog. He won't paint in the style that will get him some buyers and avoids a Chicano teacher who's taken a liking to him. He finally comes to his senses and manages to change his lifestyle and begin a relationship with the schoolteacher.

p, Montezuma Esparza, Alejandro Grattan; d&w, Grattan; ph, Turner Browne; m, Robert O. Ragland; ed, Esperanza Vasquez.

Drama   **(PR:C MPAA:PG)**

ONLY ONE NIGHT**   (1942, Swed.) 89m AB Svenskfilmindustri/
                                         Scandia bw (EN ENDA NATT)

Ingrid Bergman (Eva), Edvin Adolphson (Valdemar Moreaux), Alno Taube (Helga Martensson), Olof Sandborg (Magnus von Brede), Erik "Bullen" Berglund, Marianne Lofgren, Magnus Kesster, Sophus Dahl, Ragna Breda, John Eklof, Tor Borong, Viktor "Kulorten" Andersson, Ka Nerell, Folke Helleberg, Nila Nordstahl.

Adolphson is a circus attendant who discovers he's the illegitimate son of Sandborg, a rich aristocrat. He leaves his girl friend, Taube, and begins his new upper society life. Sandborg matches him up with Bergman, but neither likes the idea at first. Slowly, Adolphson begins to fall in love with her, and one night he makes a drunken pass at her. When Bergman rejects him, Adolphson returns to his old life and Taube. This was one of the last films Bergman made in Sweden before coming to Hollywood. ONLY ONE NIGHT was almost considered risque in its time, dealing with illegitimacy and pre-marital sex, two subjects Hollywood rarely dealt with in those days. (In Swedish; English subtitles.)

d, Gustaf Molander; w, Gosta Stevens (based on the story "En Eneste Natt" by Harald Tandrup).

Comedy Drama   **(PR:C MPAA:NR)**

ONLY SAPS WORK**   (1930) 77m PAR-Publix bw

Leon Errol (James Wilson), Richard Arlen (Lawrence Payne), Mary Brian (Barbara Tanner), Stuart Erwin (Oscar), Anderson Lawler (Horace Baldwin), Charles Grapewin (Simeon Tanner), George Irving (Dr. White), Nora Cecil (Mrs. Partridge), Charles Giblyn (Dr. Jasper), Fred Kelsey (Murphy), G. Pat Collins (Rafferty), George Chandler (Elevator Boy), Jack Richardson (Chef), Clarence Burton (Sgt. Burns), Clifford Dempsey (Detective Smith).

Light-hearted farce sees Errol as a kleptomaniac who begins by pilfering small items like cigars from passersby and works his way up to bank robbing. There's a hilarious scene where Errol vists a health farm, posing as a detective, and gives bellhop Erwin lessons on becoming a private eye. Arlen plays his law-abiding friend who, unknowingly, aides Errol in his robberies. The great title reflects the effort of a few in this cast.

d, Cyril Gardner, Edwin H. Knopf; w, Sam Mintz, Percy Heath, Joseph L.

Mankiewicz (based on the play "Easy Come, Easy Go" by Owen Davis); ph, Rex Wimpy; ed, Edward Dmytryk; md, Leo Reisman.

Comedy   **(PR:A MPAA:NR)**

ONLY THE BEST   (SEE: I CAN GET IT FOR YOU WHOLESALE, 1951)

ONLY THE BRAVE*½   (1930) 66m PAR bw

Gary Cooper (Capt. James Braydon), Mary Brian (Barbara Calhoun), Phillips Holmes (Capt. Robert Darrington), James Neill (Vance Calhoun), Morgan Farley (Tom Wendell), Guy Oliver (Gen. U. S. Grant), John H. Elliott (Gen. Robert E. Lee), E. H. Calvert (The Colonel), Virginia Bruce (Elizabeth), Elda Voelkel (Lucy Cameron), William Le Maire (The Sentry), Freeman S. Wood (Elizabeth's Lover), Lalo Encinas (Gen. Grant's Secretary), Clinton Rosemond (Butler), William Bakewell (Young Lieutenant).

One of Cooper's worst films has him playing a Union cavalry captain who volunteers to be a spy when he's jilted by his girl friend. He goes behind enemy lines and ends up at the mansion of Brian. They fall in love and each time Cooper tries to get himself arrested and get the fake battle plans into Confederate hands, Brian always intervenes. Cooper finally manages to pull it off and ends up in front of a firing squad because of it. A Union detachment arrives in the nick of time, and after the war is over Cooper and Brian are married. The script is stilted and the direction uninspired.

d, Frank Tuttle; w, Edward E. Paramore, Jr., Agnes Brand Leahy, Richard H. Digges, Jr. (based on a story by Keene Thompson); ph, Harry Fischbeck; ed, Doris Drought.

War   **(PR:A MPAA:NR)**

ONLY THE FRENCH CAN   (SEE: FRENCH CAN-CAN, 1956, Fr.)

ONLY THE VALIANT*½**   (1951) 105m Cagney/WB bw

Gregory Peck (Capt. Richard Lance), Barbara Payton (Cathy Eversham), Ward Bond (Cpl. Timothy Gilchrist), Gig Young (Lt. William Holloway), Lon Chaney, Jr. (Trooper Kebussyan), Neville Brand (Sgt. Ben Murdock), Jeff Corey (Joe Harmony), Warner Anderson (Trooper Rutledge), Steve Brodie (Trooper Onstot), Dan Riss (Lt. Jerry Winters), Terry Kilburn (Trooper Saxton), Herbert Heyes (Col. Drumm), Art Baker (Capt. Jennings), Hugh Sanders (Capt. Eversham), Michael Ansara (Tucsos), Nana Bryant (Mrs. Drumm).

A disappointing western with a routine plot which is somewhat redeemed by its star and a solid supporting cast. Peck plays a hard-nosed Army captain who is assigned to lead a detachment of men to guard a narrow pass that will be used by the Apaches to attack an undermanned fort. Their job is to hold off the warring Apaches until a reinforcement unit of 400 arrives. The by-the-book captain selects the toughest, most unruly men in the cavalry for the mission (Bond, Chaney, Young, Brand, and Brodie among them), all of whom hate his guts. Then, through rigorous training and discipline, Peck manages to whip the men into shape and transforms them into a dedicated group of soldiers. Love interest is provided by Payton, the only woman in the film, and though she has struck up a romance with Young, she gives Peck some encouraging signs. The rivalry between the two men causes trouble, especially after Peck sends Young out on a suicide mission in his place. Peck's decision is viewed as romantically self-serving by his men and Payton, a move which further erodes his authority. Eventually the Indians attack and in the heat of battle Peck redeems himself in the eyes of his men. Though only three soldiers survive, the mission is a success. The script of ONLY THE VALIANT never rises above the intelligence of a B western and the production design is obviously artificial, but the cast makes all the difference. Bond's performance as the alcoholic corporal is the real standout among the unit of misfits and he is well complemented by the swarthy likes of Chaney, Brand, and Corey, who plays a scout. Peck's participation in the film was arranged against his will by David O. Selznick. Selznick's company was sinking fast after the twin financial disasters of THE PARADINE CASE (1948) and PORTRAIT OF JENNIE (1949) and he needed to raise some quick cash. Having secured several big name actors under contract, the producer began selling their talents to rival studios for big fees. Soon Peck's came up, and though the actor disliked the script, his services were sold to Warner Bros. for $150,000. Peck himself was paid an additional $60,000, but he was unhappy with the film and somewhat offended that he had to play opposite a no-name actress like Payton after having worked with the likes of Ingrid Bergman, Greer Garson, and Jennifer Jones. Despite his reservations, Peck turned in a decent performance and pulled the film out of the doldrums.

p, William Cagney; d, Gordon Douglas; w, Edmund H. North, Harry Brown (based on a novel by Charles Marquis Warren); ph, Lionel Lindon; m, Franz Waxman; ed, Walt Hannemann, Robert S. Seiter; prod d, Wiard Ihnen; set d, Armor E. Marlowe.

Western   **(PR:A MPAA:NR)**

ONLY THING YOU KNOW, THE**   (1971, Can.) 86m c

Ann Knox, John Denos, Alan Royal, Iain Ewing, Linda Huffman, Hugh and Eileen McIntyre.

A young woman leaves home and moves in with her teacher boy friend and finds that life on one's own isn't some romantic dream. This was the first feature film from documentary filmmaker Mackey. Most of the dialog is improvised and the acting is not up to par even for low-budget independents.

p,d&w, Clarke Mackey; ph, Paul Lang; m, Paul Craven, Iain Ewing.

Drama   **(PR:C MPAA:NR)**

ONLY TWO CAN PLAY*½**   (1962, Brit.) 106m Vale-BL/Kingsley-
                                                              COL bw

Peter Sellers (John Lewis), Mai Zetterling (Elizabeth Gruffydd-Williams), Virginia Maskell (Jean Lewis), Richard Attenborough (Gareth Probert), Kenneth Griffith

(Iaeun Jenkins), Maudie Edwards *(Mrs. Davies)*, Frederick Piper *(Davies)*, Graham Stark *(Hyman)*, John Arnatt *(Bill)*, Sheila Manahan *(Mrs. Jenkins)*, John Le Mesurier *(Salter)*, Raymond Huntley *(Vernon)*, David Davies *(Beynon)*, Meredith Edwards *(Clergyman)*, Eynon Evans *(Town Hall Clerk)*, Marjorie Lawrence *(Girl in Bus)*.

Sort of a Welsh version of THE SEVEN YEAR ITCH, this takes some very funny turns and the laughs come quicly as we watch Sellers in another of his deft characterizations. Sellers is one of the staff at a Welsh library in Swansea. He is bored with his wife, Maskell, annoyed at his children, angry at his lot in life which has caused him to be living in cramped quarters overseen by his dragon of a landlady, Edwards, and just fed up in general. He escapes mentally by dreaming of affairs with gorgeous women and, one day, a gorgeous woman actually walks into his dull existence and knocks it for a loop. This is Zetterling, the rich, sensuous wife of dull Huntley, one of the town's leading lights. She finds Sellers intriguing and they plan to have a fling. She has some influence with the town biggies and will get him a higher position that includes a raise in wages. The middle of the movie concerns their abortive attempts to consummate this passion but it just never seems to work out—therein lies the comedy. Sellers reviews the local stage productions and Zetterling talks him into taking a car ride with her instead of going to the show. She has a brand new automobile with all sorts of newfangled stuff on it and he presses all the wrong buttons in the first part of this slapstick scene. Then they are interrupted when a cow peeks into the car. They'd parked in a lonely field and thought they were totally alone. Next thing, Huntley shows up and the result is sexual frustration for both. Sellers writes a review of the play he never saw, not knowing that the play didn't come off because the theater burned to the ground. His newspaper is enraged but that's balmed by Zetterling's getting him the job of head librarian. Meanwhile, Maskell has been having a casual flirtation with two-bit poet Attenborough (in a role not unlike Tom Conti's in REUBEN, REUBEN). Sellers understands that if he takes that job he might be unable to do the litte extra things he likes to do, so he says ta-ta to the position and Zetterling and returns to Maskell. He will now run a mobile library that will keep him close to his wife and children. Anyone who has ever been in a dull marriage will recognize the reality of this funny movie. It never goes too far.

p, Leslie Gilliat; d, Sidney Gilliat; w, Bryan Forbes (based on the novel *That Uncertain Feeling* by Kingsley Amis); ph, John Wilcox; m, Richard Rodney Bennett; ed, Thelma Connell; md, Muir Mathieson; art d, Albert Witherick; set d, Robert Cartwright; makeup, Phil Leakey.

Comedy   **(PR:C   MPAA:NR)**

ONLY WAY, THE***   (1970, Panama/Den./U.S.) 98m Hemisphere/
                                                      Laterna/UMC c

Ove Sprogoe *(Petersen)*, Jane Seymour, Martin Potter.

When the occupying Germans decide to export Danish Jews to the concentration camps in WW II, Sprogoe must confront his feelings on his nationalism as well as the fate of his Jewish neighbors. Rather than see his friends Seymour and Potter taken away by the Nazis, Sprogoe helps them escape to Sweden along with the 7,000 other Danish Jews that were spirited away to safety. The action unfolds along predictable lines. However, the ensemble effort, particularly with Sprogoe's quiet, anchoring performance, creates something more than one might expect with the material.

d, Bent Christensen; w, Christensen, Leif Panduro, John Gould; ph, Henning Kristiansen (Eastmancolor); m, Carl Davis.

Drama   **Cas.**   **(PR:A   MPAA:G)**

ONLY WAY HOME, THE**   (1972) 86m Washita Ventures/REG c

Bo Hopkins *(Orval)*, Beth Brickell *(Marcia)*, Steve Sandor *(Billy Joe)*, G.D. Spradlin *(Philip)*, Walt Jones *(Orval's Boss)*, Jack Isaacs *(Bobby)*, Jean Abney *(Orval's Mother)*, Maurice Eaves *(Henderson)*, Stanley Zenor *(Church Custodian)*, Tom Kroutil *(Deliveryman)*, Jane Hall *(Waitress)*, Lynn Hickey *(Car Salesman)*, Beverly Osborne *(Cowboy)*, Edgar Springer *(Motorist)*, Matthew Smith *(Little Boy)*, Ida B. *(Boy's Mother)*, Jo Peters *(Drunk Lady)*, Linda Capetta *(Model)*, Louise Chester *(Waitress)*, Clyde Martin *(Gunshop Clerk)*, Nancy Harris *(Proprietress)*, Francine Shed *(Billy Joe's Wife)*, George Clow *(Uncle John)*, Joseph Taft *(Barfly)*, Ross Cummings *(Driver)*, Mary Gordon Taft *(Driver's Wife)*, Ann Ault *(Marcia's Mother)*, George Keyes *(Workman)*.

Hopkins and Sandor get bored with their lifeless jobs and take their motorcycles to the open road where they meet a well-to-do couple who have a flat tire. The two men help them fix it, but then the husband talks down to Sandor who becomes enraged. He starts a fight with the wealthy man who leaves him lying dead on the road. Hopkins and Sandor take the wife, Brickell, and the three hide-out in a farmhouse. Sandor wants to kill her, but Hopkins won't let him. The film has an ending that will catch everyone offguard. This was the first film directed by actor G.D. Spradlin and was shot entirely in Oklahoma.

p&d, G.D. Spradlin; w, Jeeds O'Tilbury; ph, Henning Schellerup (Eastmancolor); m, Dan Foliart, Uke Hart, Tom Shapiro; ed, Donald W. Ernst.

Drama   **(PR:C   MPAA:PG)**

ONLY WHEN I LARF**½   (1968, Brit.) 103m Beecord/PAR c

Richard Attenborough *(Silas)*, David Hemmings *(Bob)*, Alexandra Stewart *(Liz)*, Nicholas Pennell *(Spencer)*, Melissa Stribling *(Diana)*, Terence Alexander *(Gee Gee Gray)*, Edric Connor *(Awana)*, Clifton Jones *(Gen. Sakut)*, Calvin Lockhart *(Ali Lin)*, Brian Grellis *(Spider)*, David Healy *(Jones)*, Alan Gifford *(Poster)*.

Attenborough, Hemmings, and Stewart are con artists who work out a scheme to sell crates of weapons, which are really filled with scrap metal, to a militant African. Things backfire when they accidentally ship the revolutionary back to Africa in one of the crates. Hemmings takes over as the brains and plans to rip-off Pennell, a wealthy young man, and then double-cross Attenborough, who is trying to get

Pennell's money first. Everyone converges in Lebanon and, through a slapstick set of events, Stewart drives off with the money leaving Attenborough, Hemmings, and Stribling stranded in the desert.

p, Len Deighton, Brian Duffy; d, Basil Dearden; w, John Salmon (based on the novel by Deighton); ph, Tony Richmond (Eastmancolor); m, Ron Grainer (performed by Whistling Jack Smith); ed, Fergus McDonell; art d, John Blezard; cos, Beatrice Dawson; makeup, Freddie Williamson.

Crime Comedy   **(PR:A   MPAA:G)**

ONLY WHEN I LAUGH**½   (1981) 120m COL c (GB:
                                                    IT HURTS ONLY WHEN I LAUGH)

Marsha Mason *(Georgia)*, Kristy McNichol *(Polly)*, James Coco *(Jimmy)*, Joan Hackett *(Toby)*, David Dukes *(David)*, John Bennett Perry *(Lou, the Actor)*, Guy Boyd *(Man)*, Ed Moore *(Dr. Komack)*, Byron Webster *(Tom)*, Peter Coffield *(Mr. Tarloff)*, Mark Schubb *(Adam Kasabian)*, Ellen LaGamba *(Receptionist)*, Venida Evans *(Nurse Garcia)*, Nancy Nagler *(Heidi)*, Dan Monahan *(Jason)*, Michael Ross *(Paul)*, Tom Ormeny *(Kyle)*, Ken Weisbrath *(Waiter)*, Henry Olek *(George, the Director)*, Jane Atkins *(Doreen)*, Kevin Bacon *(Don)*, Ron Levine *(Gary)*, Rebecca Stanley *(Denise Summers)*, Nick LaPadula *(Bartender)*, Phillip Lindsay *(Super)*, Birdie Hale *(Super's Wife)*, Wayne Framson *(Father)*, Jon Vargas *(Manuel)*.

Not satisfied with just making people laugh, Neil Simon occasionally ventures into territories where he attempts to blend laughter and tears and often succeeds, but audiences are always surprised when he aims for the heart. His play "The Gingerbread Lady" was not one of his huge successes and neither was this film version of it, although that does not detract from the basic quality of the film and appreciation for what Simon tried to do. Mason (who received an Oscar nomination for her role) is a divorced acress who has just come back from a 90-day stay in a drying-out hospital where she has ostensibly kicked her dependence on alcohol. She is trying to reestablish her relationship with McNichol, her teenage daughter, after having neglected the child in favor of booze for several years. Her former lover is Dukes, a playwright who has written a new vehicle for her return to the Broadway stage, based on their hurricane relationship. Mason's best pals are Coco, a gay actor who never made it, and Hackett, a tart-tongued egotist who gets all the good laugh lines with her bitchy comments on the situation. As Mason's pressures mount and her pals have their own problems, she predictably goes back to drinking, has a bad time and finally winds up patching up her differences with McNichol in an honest rapprochement that never gets saccharine. There was similarity between this and OPENING NIGHT in that they both concerned actresses, the Broadway stage and the neurotic pressures of being in show business. Some have said this story was drawn from the true-life tale of Judy Garland and Liza Minnelli, and there is credence there although Simon adds his own dimension and this ends on an upbeat note, whereas Garland's life did not. Coco and Hackett also nabbed Oscar nominations for their supporting work. A rare foray into the "R" ratings for Simon, who usually writes lily-white dialogue that overlooks swear words.

p, Roger M. Rothstein, Neil Simon; d, Glenn Jordan; w, Simon (based on his play "The Gingerbread Lady"); ph, David M. Walsh (Metrocolor); m, David Shire; ed, John Wright; prod d, Albert Brenner; art d, David Haber; cos, Ann Roth.

Comedy/Drama   **Cas.**   **(PR:C   MPAA:R)**

ONLY YESTERDAY**½   (1933) 108m UNIV bw

Margaret Sullavan *(Mary Lane)*, John Boles *(James Stanton Emerson)*, Billie Burke *(Julia Warren)*, Reginald Denny *(Bob)*, Jimmy Butler *(Jim, Jr.)*, Edna May Oliver *(Leona)*, Benita Hume *(Phyllis Emerson)*, George Meeker *(Dave Reynolds)*, June Clyde *(Deborah)*, Marie Prevost *(Amy)*, Oscar Apfel *(Mr. Lane)*, Jane Darwell *(Mrs. Lane)*, Tom Conlon *(Bob Lane)*, Berton Churchill *(Goodheart)*, Onslow Stevens *(Barnard)*, Franklin Pangborn *(Tom)*, Walter Catlett *(Barnes)*, Noel Francis *(Letitia)*, Barry Norton *(Jerry)*, Arthur Hoyt *(Burton)*, Natalie Moorhead *(Lucy)*, Joyce Compton *(Margot)*, Betty Blythe *(Mrs. Vincent)*, Grady Sutton *(Charlie Smith)*, Ruth Clifford *(Eleanor)* Dorothy Grainger *(Sally)*, Geneva Mitchell *(Patty)*, Bramwell Fletcher *(Scott Hughes)*, Dorothy Christy *(Rena)*, Julia Faye, Crauford Kent, Vivian Oakland, Bert Roach, Robert Ellis, Cissy Fitzgerald, Leo White, Huntley Gordon, Herbert Corthell, Richard Tucker.

Although the title is drawn from Allen's retrospective commentary of the period between 1918 and 1933, this has nothing to do with that scholarly work. It was a brilliant debut for Sullavan and she transcended the material. It was also the debut of Jimmy Butler, an excellent child actor who would only do a couple of other films before passing away at an early age. Basically a BACK STREET-type film (it even had Boles in the male lead, the same man who had starred with Irene Dunne in that movie the year before), ONLY YESTERDAY was a very successful draw for Depression audiences and established Sullavan as a star in her first movie. It's 1929 and the stock market is crashing. Boles is a broker who has lost everything and is about to take his own life, a fate that many of his compatriots shared in those dark days. He raises a revolver for that purpose, then notices a letter he'd missed reading. He lays the gun down and opens the missive to find that it's from Sullavan, recounting their experiences together. Flashback to 1917 where Boles, a handsome young officer, is training in Virginia for The War To End All Wars and meets Sullavan at a festive ball. They are instantly attracted to each other, have one night of love, and he is sent to fight in France soon afterward. Boles is seen to be a decent chap, not a rakehell, a man who would understand what happened to Sullavan if he had only known. She becomes pregnant, travels north to New York to stay with her aunt, Burke (in a wonderful turn as one of moviedom's first liberated women) and has the boy baby. The war comes to a halt on the eleventh day of the eleventh month of 1918 and the lads come home to have their traditional parade down Fifth Avenue. Sullavan goes to the parade and looks for Boles among the happy warriors and, miracle of miracles, she finds him. But her hopes are shattered when he doesn't recognize her. (This is a huge credibility gap in the story as anyone as sympathetically portrayed as Boles would have recalled someone as sweet and attractive as Sullavan, unless he was suffering from "shell-shock" which was a regularly used gimmick of convenience in many films.) Sullavan backs off without telling him of his parenthood. When she reads that he has married Hume, she erases any thoughts of reunification and concentrates on her own life as a mother and businessperson. She makes a few bucks in her work and sends son Butler to military school. Ten years go by in a trice and Boles and Sullavan meet again at a New Year's Eve function. Her love life has been presumably empty for a decade and when they get together that night, it's right back to bed for the duo, although Boles still doesn't know that she's the same Virginia reeler he met in 1917. As far as Boles is concerned, it was a lovely way to spend an evening, nothing more. She leaves in the morning without having revealed what the audience knows. Flash forward and we discover that she has a weak ticker and is on the brink of departing and just wanted Boles to know he had an offspring. He discards his thoughts of suicide and quickly goes to her home, to discover that she's already given up the ghost. The last scene is particularly touching as Boles meets Butler for the first time and tells him that he now has a father. Except for the large lapse of memory that Boles has, this is a pretty good movie. It was remade in 1948 with Joan Fontaine in the lead. The title was changed for that to LETTER FROM AN UNKNOWN WOMAN.

d, John M. Stahl; w, William Hurlbut, Arthur Richman, George O'Neill (based on the book by Frederick Lewis Allen); ph, Merritt Gerstad; ed, Milton Carruth.

Drama   **(PR:C MPAA:NR)**

ONNA GA KAIDAN O AGARUTOKI   (SEE: WHEN A WOMAN ASCENDS THE STAIRS, 1963, Jap.)

ONNA GOROSHI ABURA JIGOKU   (SEE: PRODIGAL SON, THE, 1964, Jap.)

ONNA NO MIZUUMI   (SEE: LAKE, THE, 1970, Jap.)

ONNA NO NAKANI IRU TANIN   (SEE: THIN LINE, THE, 1967, Jap.)

ONNA NO REKISHI   (SEE: WOMAN'S LIFE, A, 1964, Jap.)

ONNA NO UZU TO FUCHI TO NAGARE   (SEE: WHIRLPOOL OF WOMAN, 1966, Jap.)

ONNA NO ZA   (SEE: WISER AGE, THE, 1962, Jap.)

ONNA UKIYOBURO   (SEE: HOUSE OF STRANGE LOVES, THE, 1969, Jap.)

ONSEN GERIRA DAI SHOGEKI   (SEE: HOTSPRINGS HOLIDAY, 1970, Jap.)

OOH, YOU ARE AWFUL   (SEE: GET CHARLIE TULLY, 1972, Brit.)

OPEN ALL NIGHT**   (1934, Brit.) 62m REA/RKO bw

Frank Vosper (Anton), Margaret Vines (Elsie Warren), Gillian Lind (Maysie), Lewis Shaw (Bill Warren), Leslie Perrins (Ranger), Colin Keith-Johnson (Henry), Geraldine Fitzgerald (Jill), Michael Shepley (Hilary).

Vosper is an exiled Russian duke who now works as the manager at an all-night restaurant. His boss informs him that he's being let go because they want new blood, and Vosper painfully finishes his last night. That same night, a young man becomes involved with a murder in the restaurant and Vosper takes the blame so the man can take his dying wife to Vienna. Vosper goes home, writes a confession note for the murder, and kills himself.

p, Julius Hagen; d, George Pearson; w, Gerard Fairlie (based on a play by John Chancellor).

Drama   **(PR:O MPAA:NR)**

OPEN CITY****   (1946, Ital.) 105m Excelsa/Mayer-Burstyn bw (ROMA, CITTA APERTA; AKA: ROME, OPEN CITY)

Anna Magnani (Pina), Aldo Fabrizi (Don Pietro Pellegrini), Marcello Pagliero (Giorgio Manfredi), Maria Michi (Marina), Harry Feist (Maj. Bergmann), Francesco Grandjacquet (Francesco), Giovanna Galletti (Ingrid), Vito Annichiarico (Marcello, Pina's Son), Carla Revere (Lauretta), Nando Bruno (Agostino), Carlo Sindici (Police Superintendent), Joop Van Hulzen (Hartmann), Akos Tolnay (Austrian Deserter), Eduardo Passarelli (Policeman), Amalia Pelegrini (Landlady).

With this film, director Rosselini introduced what later came to be termed Italian Neorealism, which was more like a documentary approach to drama. OPEN CITY is so realistic that it is more effective than many a real documentary, made up of many stories all based on the German occupation of Rome during WW II, and the considerable resistance battle against that occupation by Italian partisans between September 1943 and June 1944 when the city was liberated by American-British troops. It is brutally honest and deals with a broad section of Italian society, not the least Magnani, one of Italy's greatest actresses. Here she is a working-class woman who is pregnant but still fearlessly trying to aid her lover, who is part of the resistance. She tries to persuade the Germans to release her man but to no avail and, when he is taken away by truck, she runs after the vehicle and is shot down in the gutter. Fabrizi, as a patriotic priest who aids the underground fighters and is put before a firing squad for his efforts, is outstanding. Feist, as the German officer who is superficially sympathetic to the plight of the Italians, is excellent, even though he was not a name actor (as was the case with most of the cast) Rosselini actually wrote the script with some friends after the Gestapo invaded Rome and his secreted cameras recorded the awful occupation right under the noses of the Germans. The inventive director later stated (in The Italian Cinema by Pierre Leprohon): "I shot this film on a tiny budget, scraped together as I went along. There was only enough to pay for the raw film, and no hope of getting it developed since I didn't have enough to pay the laboratories. So there was no viewing of rushes until shooting was completed. Some time later, having acquired a little money, I edited the film and showed it to a few people in the cinema, critics and friends. It was a great

disappointemt to most of them." But when the film was released to the public, and especially when prints arrived in England and the U.S., it became a huge critical and solid financial success. Rossellini's poverty and the fact that he was compelled to use real streets and cheap film that projected that faded grayish look—and the abrupt, almost amateur cutting, due to lack of proper editing facilities—created unintentionally the so-called Neorealist look. Magnani and Fabrizi were not stars at the time, but unemployed music-hall actors who did the work cheaply to survive the Nazi occupation. Magnani became an overnight sensation and remained a star thereafter. OPEN CITY is now a minor classic of stark and often brutal reality during a time when half the world was enslaved by lunatics and the other half busied itself with ways to get them back into the asylum.

p&d, Roberto Rossellini; w, Sergio Amidei, Federico Fellini, Rossellini (based on a story by Amidei, Alberto Consiglio); ph, Ubaldo Arata; m, Renzo Rossellini; English titles, Pietro Di Donato, Herman G. Weinberg.

War Drama   **Cas.**   **(PR:O MPAA:NR)**

OPEN ROAD, THE*½   (1940, Fr.) 85m Robert Mintz bw (LE CHEMINEAU)

Victor Francen (The Vagabond), Tania Fedor (Toinette), Georges Colin (Francois), Lurville (Master Pierre), Morton (Martin), Rivers Cadet (Thomas), Eymont (Toinet), Jeanne Marken (Catherine), Lucy Leger (Aline).

Francen is a hobo who has an affair with a female farm worker and then returns 20 years later to find he has a son. The son, who thinks that the man married to his mother is his father, find his parents object to his girl friend. Francen smoothes things out for his son and his relationship before he takes off on the road again. (In French; English subtitles.)

p&d, Fernand Rivers; w, (based on a play by Jean Richepin); ph, Mundviller; ed, Datlowe; subtitles, Ralph Roeder.

Drama   **(PR:A MPAA:NR)**

OPEN SEASON*   (1974, U.S./Span.) 103m Impala-Arpa/COL c

Peter Fonda (Ken), Cornelia Sharpe (Nancy), John Phillip Law (Greg), Richard Lynch (Art), Albert Mendoza (Martin), William Holden (Wolkowski), Helga Line (Sue), Didi Sherman (Helen), Conchita Cuetos (Joyce), Norma Castel (Annie), May Heatherly (Alicia Rennick), Gudrun McCleary (Mrs. Rennick), Simon Andreu (Barman), William Layton (District Attorney), Beatrix Savon (Sandy), Loretta Tovar (Moonmaid), Mabel Escano (Waitress), Scott Miller (Prucell), Jaime Doria (Carter), Lorreaine Clewes (Hostess), Judith Stephen (Manageress), Amory Fitzpatrick (Connie Frazer), Jerry Boudreaux (Tommy Frazer), Mike Sambeck (Petey).

Fonda, Law, and Lynch are three hunters who find more enjoyment in pursuing humans than animals. Sharpe and Mendoza are the two lucky victims in this dud, and Holden makes an appearance in the ending of the film. Shot in Spain and Michigan.

p, Jose S. Vicuna; d, Peter Collinson; w, David Osborn, Liz Charles-Williams; ph, Fernando Arribas (Eastmancolor); m, Ruggero Cini; ed, Alan Pattillo; art d, Gil Parrondo; spec eff, Antonio Balandin; stunts, Juan Majan; makeup, Cristobal Criado.

Action   **(PR:O MPAA:R)**

OPEN SECRET**   (1948) 70m Marathon/EL bw

John Ireland (Paul Lester), Jane Randolph (Nancy Lester), Roman Bohnen (Locke), Sheldon Leonard (Mike Frontelli), George Tyne (Harry Strauss), Morgan Farley (Mitchell), Ellen Lowe (Mrs. Locke), Anne O'Neal (Mrs. Tistram), Arthur O'Connell (Carter), John Alvin (Ralph), Bert Conway (Mace), Rory Mallinson (Hill), Helena Dare (Mrs. Hill), Leo Kaye (Bartender), King Donovan (Fawnes), Tom Noonan (Bob), Charles Waldron, Jr..

An action melodrama about anti-Semitism sees Ireland as a police lieutenant who tries to expose a gang of racist thugs. Ireland is helped by a victimized photography store owner,Tyne, who gets pictures of the gang in acts of vandalism and violence against Jews. Most of the film circles around the gang's attempts to get their hands on the pictures.

p, Frank Satenstien; d, John Reinhardt; w, Henry Blankfort, Max Wilk, John Bright (based on a story by Wilk, Ted Murkland); ph, George Robinson; m, Herschel Gilbert; ed, Jason Bernie; md, Gilbert; art d, George Van Marter; set d, Earl Wooden.

Drama   **(PR:A MPAA:NR)**

OPEN THE DOOR AND SEE ALL THE PEOPLE**½
(1964) 82m Jerome Hill/Noel-Barney Pitkin-FilmMakers' Cooperative bw

Maybelle Nash (Alma Blake/Thelma Fahnstock), Alec Wilder (Dan, Alma's Husband), Jeremiah Sullivan (Jerry), Charles Rydell (Andrew), Chris Schroll (Chris), Johanna Hill (Jo), Paul Chu (Luke), Melvina Boykin (Melvina), Ellen Martin (Mimosa), Lester Judson (Raoul), Louise Rush (Veronica), Harry Rigby (Steadman), Tony Ballen (Paul), Day Tuttle (Wei No. 1), Douglas Ho (Wei No. 2), Chao Li Chi (Wei No. 3), John Holland (Antoine), Susana De Mello (Amaryllis), Gwen Davies (Gypsy Mother), Gene Fallon (Mayor), Astride Lance (Solitary Girl), Sheilah Chang (Cashier), Taylor Mead (Tramp), Billy Leavitt (Archiband Davies, Jr.).

Nash plays two elderly identical twins who are complete opposites. One is a wealthy, cranky hypochondriac, and the other is a fun-loving supermarket cashier. Both have families, and the film looks and pokes fun at the differing social values of the sisters. A small film with an offbeat sense of humor.

p,d&w, Jerome Hill; ph, Gayne Rescher; m, Alec Wilder; ed, Henry A. Sundquist; md, Samuel Baron.

Comedy   **(PR:A MPAA:NR)**

OPENED BY MISTAKE*½ (1940) 67m PAR bw

Charlie Ruggles *(Buzz Nelson)*, Janice Logan *(Margaret Nichols)*, Robert Paige *(Jimmie Daniels)*, William Frawley *(Matt Kingsley)*, Florence Shirley *(Elizabeth Stiles)*, Lawrence Grossmith *(Jarvis Woodruff)*, Rafael Corio *(Mr. DeBorest)*, Esther Dale *(Mrs. DeBorest)*, James Burke *(Sgt. Wilkins)*, Jack Norton *(Al)*.

News reporter Paige and sports editor Ruggles get their hands on a trunk containing a body. Insurance company investigator Logan arrives, and she and Paige become fugitives from the law as they track down the murderer who turns out to be a crazed chemist.

p, Stuart Walker; d, George Archainbaud; w, Stuart Palmer, Garnet Weston, Louis S. Kaye (based on a story by Hal Hudson, Kenneth Earl); ph, Theodore Sparkuhl; ed, Arthur Schmidt; art d, Hans Dreier, Earl Hedrick.

Comedy/Mystery **(PR:A MPAA:NR)**

OPENING NIGHT** (1977) 144m Faces c

Gene Rowlands *(Myrtle Gordon)*, John Cassavetes *(Maurice Aarons)*, Ben Gazzara *(Manny Victor)*, Joan Blondell *(Sarah Goode)*, Paul Stewart *(David Samuels)*, Zohra Lampert *(Dorothy Victor)*, Laura Johnson *(Nancy Stein)*, John Tuell *(Gus Simmons)*, Ray Powers *(Jimmy)*, John Finnegan *(Prop Man)*, Louise Fitch *(Kelly)*, Fred Draper *(Leo)*, Katherine Cassavetes *(Vivian)*, Lady Rowlands *(Melva Drake)*, Sharon Van Ivan *(Doorman)*, Jimmy Christie *(Shirley)*, James Karen *(News Stand Operator)*, Jimmy Moyce *(Bell Boy)*, Sherry Bain *(Bartender)*, Sylvia Davis Shaw *(Bar Maid)*, Peter Lampert *(Maitre d')*, Briana Carver *(Lena)*, Angelo Grisanti *(Charlie Spikes)*, Carol Warren *(Carla)*, Meade Roberts *(Eddie Stein)*, Eleanor Zee *(Sylvia Stein)*.

Another of Cassavetes' puzzling, personal, neurotic and often brilliant productions that would have benefited from editing with a scythe. Rowlands is a nervous actress on the brink of a breakdown as she prepares to star in a show called "The Second Woman" which was written by Blondell. The entire movie takes place in the few days prior to the Broadway opening and shows the backstage turmoil of a show about to happen. Rowlands begins to fall apart when a fan of hers dies in an accident and she is forced to look hard at her life and determine what's important about it. Cassavetes usually does movies about average Joes and Janes and this time focuses on show business to prove that those shining stars one sees on the stage are subject to the same frailties as anyone else. He is an "actor's director" in that he always seems to get superb performances. The only problem is that he never knows when to stop and every scene could be cut down without losing importance. If he could have been controlled and allowed some other person's creativity in the script or editing, he might have turned out a masterpiece in his lifetime but he insisted on being Orson Welles and having the final say, something Welles may have regretted in the end.

p, Al Ruban; d&w, John Cassavetes; ph, Ruban (Metrocolor); m, Bo Harwood; ed, Tom Cornwell; md, Booker T. Jones; art d, Brian Ryman; cos, Alexandra Corwin-Hankin.

Drama **(PR:C MPAA:NR)**

OPERACION GOLDMAN (SEE: LIGHTNING BOLT, 1967, Ital./Span.)

OPERACION LOTO AZUL (SEE: MISSION BLOODY MARY, 1967, Fr./Ital./Span.)

OPERATION AMSTERDAM** (1960, Brit.) 105m RANK/FOX bw

Peter Finch *(Jan Smit)*, Eva Bartok *(Anna)*, Tony Britton *(Maj. Dillon)*, Alexander Knox *(Walter Keyser)*, Malcolm Keen *(Johann Smit)*, Christopher Rhodes *(Alex)*, Tim Turner *(Lieutenant)*, John Horsley *(Cmdr. Bowerman)*, Keith Pyott *(Dealer)*, Melvyn Hayes *(Willem Lubka)*, Oscar Quitak *(Dealer)*, John Bailey *(Officer)*, John Richardson.

The true story about the removal of $10 million worth of industrial diamonds out of Amsterdam before the Nazis arrived. Finch, diamond expert Knox, British officer Britton, and Dutch contact Bartok are the foursome who attempt to get the diamonds out. They have 14 hours to catch a boat to England while avoiding local Nazi fifth columnists and beating the Germans. A routine war drama with enough action and suspense to keep interest.

p, Maurice Cowan; d, Michael McCarthy; w, McCarthy, John Eldridge (based on the *Adventure in Diamonds* by David E. Walker); ph, Reginald Wyer; m, Philip Green; ed, Arthur Stevens; art d, Alex Vetchinsky; cos, Eleanor Abbey.

War **Cas.** **(PR:A MPAA:NR)**

OPERATION BIKINI** (1963) 84m Alta Vista/AIP bw-c

Tab Hunter *(Lt. Morgan Hayes)*, Frankie Avalon *(Seaman Joseph Malzone)*, Scott Brady *(Capt. Emmett Carey)*, Jim Backus *(Bosun's Mate Ed Fennelly)*, Gary Crosby *(Seaman Floyd Givens)*, Michael Dante *(Lt. William Fourtney)*, Jody McCrea *(Seaman William Sherman)*, Eva Six *(Reiko)*, Aki Aleong *(Seaman Ronald Davayo)*, David Landfield *(Lt. Cale)*, Richard Bakalyan *(Seaman Hiller)*, Joe Finnegan *(Seaman Morris)*, Vernon Scott *(Seaman Fowler)*, Raymond Guth *(Seaman Rich)*, Tony Scott *(C.P.O Perez)*, Steve Mitchell *(Seaman Nolan)*, Mickey McDermott *(Seaman Fairly)*, Wayne Winton *(Seaman Patterson)*, Duane Ament *(Seaman Kingsley)*, Jody Daniels *(Seaman Jones)*, Marc Cavell *(Paul)*, Raynum K. Tsukamoto *(Kawai)*, Lan Nam Tuttle *(Mika)*, Alicia Li *(3rd Native Girl)*, Nancy Dusina *(Dream Girl Back Home)*, Judy Lewis *(Dream Siren)*.

No, it's not another beach movie, but a WW II melodrama about a navy demolition team. Hunter, Avalon, and Brady must destroy a sunken submarine before the Japanese get the top-secret equipment aboard the vessel. The crew lands on Bikini Island and is aided by the guerrillas to find the location of the sub. Hunter falls in love with female guerrilla Six who is later killed by the Japanese. They complete their mission and Avalon, of course, sneaks in a song.

p, James H. Nicholson, Lou Rusoff; d, Anthony Carras; w, John Tomerlin; ph, Gilbert Warrenton; m, Les Baxter; ed, Carras, Homer Powell; art d, Daniel Haller; spec eff, Charles Moody; m/l, "The Girl Back Home," Bob Marcucci, Russ Faith (sung by Frankie Avalon); makeup, Ted Coodley; tech adv, retired Navy Capt. Charles L. Freeman.

War **(PR:A MPAA:NR)**

OPERATION BLUE BOOK (SEE: BAMBOO SAUCER, THE, 1968)

OPERATION BOTTLENECK* (1961) 76m Zenith/UA bw

Ron Foster *(Lt. Voss)*, Miiko Taka *(Ari)*, Norman Alden *(Cpl. Merc)*, John Clarke *(Sgt. Marty)*, Ben Wright *(Manders)*, Dale Ishimoto *(Matsu)*, Jane Chang *(Atai)*, Lee Moichu *(Lolo)*, Tiko Ling *(Tai)*, June Kawai *(Danue)*, Jin Jin Mai *(Saiobu)*, Ben Bennett *(Benjy)*, Marc Eden *(Tom)*, George Yoshiniga *(Koju)*, Ken Wales *(1st Commander)*, John Durren *(2nd Commander)*.

Unexciting depiction of the attempts of a handful of WW II soldiers to rescue a buddy from the clutches of the Japanese. This man, along with his would-be rescuers, was part of a mission which parachuted into Burma, but when he injured himself during the fall he became easy prey for the enemy. Not enough action to sustain its 76 minutes.

p, Robert E. Kent; d, Edward L. Cahn; w, Orville H. Hampton.

War **(PR:A MPAA:NR)**

OPERATION BULLSHINE** (1963, Brit.) 84m Associated British Picture/Seven Arts-Manhattan Films International c

Donald Sinden *(Lt. Gordon Brown)*, Barbara Murray *(Pvt. Betty Brown)*, Carole Lesley *(Pvt. Marge White)*, Ronald Shiner *(Gunner Slocum)*, Naunton Wayne *(Maj. Pym)*, Dora Bryan *(Pvt. Cox)*, John Cairney *(Gunner Willie Ross)*, Fabia Drake *(Jr. Cmdr. Maddox)*, Joan Rice *(Pvt. Finch)*, Daniel Massey *(Bombardier Palmer)*, Peter Jones *(Gunner Perkins)*, Barbara Hicks *(Sgt. Merrified)*, John Welsh *(Brigadier)*, Judy Grinham *(P.T. Instructress)*, Cyril Chamberlain *(Orderly Sergeant)*, Ambrosine Phillpotts *(Reporter)*, Naomi Chance *(Subaltern Godfrey)*, Marianne Stone *(Sgt. Cook)*, Harry Landis *(Gunner Wilkinson)*, Brian Weske *(Gunner Pooley)*, George Mikell *(German Airman)*, Blockbuster Bridget *(A Bulldog)*, Dorinda Stevens, Amanda Barrie, Marigold Russell, Julie Hopkins, Beverly Prowse, Margaret Simons, Pamela Searle, Eve Eden, Julie Alexander, Pat Gibson.

At an anti-aircraft station on the British coast, lieutenant Sinden is joined by his wife, Murray, and other A.T.S. (Auxiliary Territorial Service) women. No one on the base knows that Sinden and Murray are man and wife, and the major, Wayne, suspects the lieutenant is having an affair with Lesley. She's been chasing after him, and he tries hard to keep her away without revealing his wife. Wayne sends Sinden home on leave to visit his wife, and he's followed closely behind by Lesley, as well as his wife, who is beginning to suspect some hanky-panky. The major goes to London and finds the couple and Lesley together, and angrily sends them back to base. The girls manage to save the day, though, by shooting down an enemy plane and capturing the pilot.

p, Frank Godwin; d, Gilbert Gunn; w, Anne Burnaby, Rupert Lang, Gunn (based on the story "Mixed Company" by Burnaby); ph, Gilbert Taylor (Technicolor); m, Laurie Johnson; ed, E. B. Jarvis; art d, Robert Jones; m/l, Johnson, Godwin (sung by The Polka Dots); makeup, Eric Aylott.

Comedy **(PR:A MPAA:NR)**

OPERATION CAMEL** (1961, Den.) 74 m Merry Filmproduktion-Dansk-Svensk Film/AIP bw (SOLDATERKAMMERATER PA VAGT)

Nora Hayden *(The Dancer)*, Paul Hagen, Ebbe Langberg, Preben Kaas, Carl Ottosen, Louis Miehe-Renard, Klaus Pagh, Svend Johansen, Ole Dixon, Tor Stokke, Lisbet Kurt, Mogens Brandt, Vera Stricker, Annie Birgit Garde, Raggah Jussef, Maria Velasco, Major Poulsen, Addison Mayers.

After completing their training, a group of Danish soldiers is assigned as part of the U.N. peace-keeping force in Gaza. There the zany fellows get involved in a series of comic episodes. Their major contribution is to free Hayden from a group of evil-doers who are holding her captive in a night club and forcing her to perform for their customers. When it was released in Denmark in 1960, the film was in color, one of several comedies made as part of a "Soldaterkammerater" series. The series, needless to say, was not a hit in the U.S. Strangely, OPERATION CAMEL had its premiere in the U.S. in Omaha, Nebraska.

p, Henrik Sanberg; d, Sven Methling, Jr.; w, Bob Ramsing, Preben Kaas; ph, Aage Wiltrup, Ole Lytken, Ib Lonvang, Per Staehr; m, Ib Glinderman, Simon Rosenbaum, Gustav Winckler, George Swensson.

Comedy **(PR:A MPAA:NR)**

OPERATION CIA*½ (1965) 90m Hei-Ra-Matt/AA bw (AKA: LAST MESSAGE FROM SAIGON)

Burt Reynolds *(Mark Andrews)*, Kieu Chinh *(Kim-chinh)*, Danielle Aubry *(Denise, French Agent)*, John Hoyt *(Wells)*, Cyril Collick *(Withers)*, Vic Diaz *(Prof. Yen)*, Bill Catching *(Frank Decker)*, Marsh Thomson *(Stacey)*, John Laughinghouse, Frank Estes *(American Officers)*, Chaiporn *(Terrorist)*, Santi *(Porter)*, Juanita *(Ming-tah)*, Michael Schwiner *(Embassy Marine)*, Robert Gulbranson *(Man in Bed)*, Janet Russell *(Girl in Bed)*.

Reynolds is sent to Saigon during the Vietnam War to investigate a fellow agent's murder and stumbles onto a plot to kill the U.S. ambassador. He's helped by Chinh and escapes from kidnaper Diaz to prevent the ambassador's murder by double agent Aubry. Some footage was shot in Saigon but, even with authentic locations, the story was just too stock to keep interest.

p, Peer J. Oppenheimer; d, Christian Nyby; w, Bill S. Ballinger, Oppenheimer (based on a story by Oppenheimer); ph, Richard Moore; m, Paul Dunlap; ed, Joseph Gluck, George Watters; cos, Thelma Nyby.

Action/Adventure **(PR:A MPAA:NR)**

OPERATION CONSPIRACY* (1957, Brit.) 69m Balblair/REP bw (GB: CLOAK WITHOUT DAGGER)

Philip Friend (*Maj. Felix Gratton*), Mary Mackenzie (*Kyra Gabaine*), Leslie Dwyer (*Fred Borcombe*), Allan Cuthbertson (*Col. Packham*), John G. Heller (*Peppi Gilroudian, Dress Designer*), Chin Yu (*Yan Chu*), Bill Nagy (*Mario Oromonda*), Patrick Jordan (*Capt. Wallis*), Patricia Haines, Stuart Mitchell, Ivor Dean, Marianne Stone, Maria Mercedes, Frank Thornton, Gerry Levey, Boris Ranevsky.

Silly spy drama starts out in WW II with Mackenzie and Friend lovers, the latter an intelligence officer on the trail of a spy. After Friend fails to capture the spy as a result of Mackenzie's interference, the plot jumps forward several years. Mackenzie is now a reporter covering a fashion show at a place where Friend is working as an undercover agent in the guise of a waiter. The pair take up where they left off, only this time Mackenzie is instrumental in helping her lover catch the spy. Absurd premise and undeveloped material leave performers totally handicapped.

p, A. R. Rawlinson; d, Joseph Sterling; w, Rawlinson; ph, Gerald Gibbs; m, Wilfred Burns; ed, Carmen Beliaeff; md, Burns; art d, John Stoll.

Spy Drama (PR:A MPAA:NR)

OPERATION CROSS EAGLES** (1969, U.S./Yugo.) 90m Noble Productions-Triglav Film/Continental c (UNAKRSNA VATRA)

Richard Conte (*Lt. Bradford*), Rory Calhoun (*Sgt. Sean MacAfee*), Aili King (*Anna*), Phil Brown (*Sgt. Tunley*), Rada Djuriein, Relja Basic, Abdul Rahman, Rick West.

During WW II, Calhoun and two men from his command unit successfully complete a mission behind enemy lines and join up with some Yugoslavian partisans. Conte, an American lieutenant, is the leader of the partisans. He enlists Calhoun's aid in capturing a German commandant whom he hopes to exchange for an American general who is being held by the Germans. Problems arise because there's a traitor within the unit. The German is captured but Conte's plotting succeeds in freeing the American without giving up the commandant. The traitor is identified and killed and Conte reveals that the purpose of the mission had always been to capture the German. Conte is credited with the direction of this uninspired tale, the only time in his career he ever filled that post.

p, Ika Panajotovic; d, Richard Conte; w, Vincent Fotre; ph, Nenad Jovicic; art d, Bob Radley.

War (PR:A MPAA:NR)

OPERATION CROSSBOW** (1965, U.S./Ital.) 118m MGM c (OPERAZIONE CROSSBOW; AKA: THE GREAT SPY MISSION; CODE NAME: OPERATION CROSSBOW)

Sophia Loren (*Nora*), George Peppard (*Lt. John Curtis*), Trevor Howard (*Prof. Lindemann*), John Mills (*Boyd of M.I.6*) Richard Johnson (*Duncan Sandys*), Tom Courtenay (*Robert Henshaw*), Jeremy Kemp (*Phil Bradley*), Anthony Quayle (*Bamford*), Lilli Palmer (*Frieda*), Paul Henreid (*Gen. Ziemann*), Helmut Dantine (*Gen. Linz*), Barbara Rueting (*Hanna Reitsch*), Richard Todd (*Wing Cmdr. Kendall*), Sylvia Syms (*Constance Babington Smith*), John Fraser (*Flight Lt. Kenny*), Maurice Denham (*R.A.F. Officer*), Patrick Wymark (*Prime Minister Winston Churchill*), Karel Stepanek (*Prof. Hoffer*), Moray Watson (*Col. Kenneth Post*), Richard Wattis (*Sir Charles Sims*), Allan Cuthbertson (*German Technical Examiner*), Robert Brown (*Air Commodore*), Wolf Frees, William Mervyn, Milo Sperber, George Mikell, Ferdy Mayne.

Producer Ponti assembled a star-studded cast and spared no expense in telling a story based on the British efforts during WW II to find and destroy Nazi rocket bases. Film begins with Johnson being assigned to investigate reports that the Nazis are on the verge of unleashing lethal rockets on England. Johnson finds evidence to support the report and when V-1 rockets hit London, Peppard, Courtenay and Kemp are chosen for a suicide mission to find the rocket base. They parachute into Germany and pose as scientists who are assigned to the project. Courtenay meets a quick demise when his cover is blown, but he reveals nothing about his cohorts. Peppard has a narrow escape when Loren, the wife of the man he is pretending to be, encounters him at a hotel. Peppard persuades her not to reveal the charade to the authorities, and Palmer, an Allied agent, makes sure of it by killing Loren. Peppard and Kemp succeed in locating the base. They guide Allied bombers to the installation which is destroyed, the heroes perishing in the bombing. This epic contained some excellent action footage and a briskly paced story which was nicely handled by the cast. Loren's star billing is somewhat misleading since her screen time is minimal, and she functions only as a sex prop; most of the other major names in the cast fill what amount to cameos, but they acquit themselves admirably. It was a quality production that never found much of an audience. In fact, after its premiere in the U.S. garnered a lukewarm reception, MGM tried changing the title to THE GREAT SPY MISSION, believing that the word "operation" in the original title might lead people to think it was a medical film, a genre which wasn't doing well at the box office in the mid-1960s.

p, Carlo Ponti; d, Michael Anderson; w, Richard Imrie, Derry Quinn, Ray Rigby (based on a story by Duilio Coletti, Vittoriano Petrilli); ph, Erwin Hillier (Panavision, Metrocolor); m, Ron Goodwin; ed, Ernest Walter; md, Goodwin; art d, Elliott Scott; spec eff, Tom Howard.

War Drama (PR:A MPAA:NR)

OPERATION CUPID* (1960, Brit.) 65m Twickenham/Rank bw

Charles Farrell (*Charlie Stevens*), Wallas Eaton (*Cecil*), Avice Landone (*Mrs. Mountjoy*), Wally Patch (*Bookmaker*), Harold Goodwin (*Mervyn*), David Saire (*Claude*), Beth Rogan (*Barmaid*), Bruce Seton (*Representative*), Pauline Shepherd, Charles Clay, Martin Sterndale, Eddie Malin, Colin Rix, Neil Hallett, Audrey Nicholson, George Patterson, Roy Jefferies.

What could have been a pleasant romantic comedy turns into hogwash because of incompetent scripting and direction. Three ne'er-do-wells get involved in a match-

making service, a job they approach half-heartedly until they realize its prospects. This comes in the form of Landone, who, posing as a millionaire, does a good job of pulling the wool over the eyes of one of the three who is trying to deceive her as well. Everything turns out for the best, though, when the two discover the truth about the other's identity, having declared their love for each other by this time. Laughs are few and far between.

p, Guido Coen; d, Charles Saunders; w, Brock Williams (based on the story by Jack Taylor); ph, Jimmy W. Harvey.

Comedy (PR:A MPAA:NR)

OPERATION DAMES*½ (1959) 74m Camera Eye/AIP bw (GB: GIRLS IN ACTION)

Eve Meyer (*Lorry Evering*), Chuck Henderson (*Sgt. Valido*), Don Devlin (*Tony*), Ed Craig (*Hal*), Cindy Girard (*Roberta*), Barbara Skyler (*Marsha*), Chuck Van Haren (*Billy*), Andrew Munro (*Dinny*), Byron Morrow (*Benny Sullivan*), Alice Allyn (*Marge*), Ed Lakso (*George*), Joe Maierhouser (*Col. Bradley*).

USO troupe headed by Meyer is lost behind enemy lines during the Korean War. Henderson leads a squadron of soldiers to find and lead the entertainers back to safety. A low-budget production with a typical war story line. Camera Eye Productions was primarily known for its documentaries and had won an Oscar in 1957 for the best documentary, THE TRUE STORY OF THE CIVIL WAR. Former "Playboy" centerfold Meyer was at the time married to director Russ Meyer who would later that year burst upon the movie scene with his IMMORAL MR. TEAS.

p, Stanley Kallis; d, Louis Clyde Stouman; w, Ed Lasko (adapted from a story by Kallis); ph, Edward R. Martin; ed, Stouman; m, Richard Margowitz; m/l, "Girls, Girls, Girls," "Regular Man" by Lasko.

War/Comedy (PR:C MPAA:NR)

OPERATION DAYBREAK** (1976, U.S./Brit./Czech.) 118m Vista-Schuster-American Allied-Ceskoslovensky-Barrandov/WB c (AKA: PRICE OF FREEDOM)

Timothy Bottoms (*Jan Kubis*), Martin Shaw (*Karel Curda*), Joss Ackland (*Janak*), Nicola Pagett (*Anna*), Anthony Andrews (*Joseph Gabcik*), Anton Diffring (*Reinhard Heydrich*), Diana Coupland (*Aunt Marie*), Ronald Radd (*Her Husband*), Kim Fortune (*Ata*), Pavla Matejovska (*Jindriska*), Carl Duering (*Karl Frank*), Cyril Shaps (*Father Petrek*), Ray Smith (*Hajek*), Timothy West (*Vaclav*), Ann Lonnberg (*Sonja*), Vernon Dobtcheff (*Piotr*), Reinhardt Kolldehoff (*Fleisher*), George Sewell (*Panwitz*), William Lucas (*Doctor*), Frank Gatliff (*Surgeon*), Dr. Josef Stoll (*Sefrna*), Ludvik Wolf (*Klein*), Nigel Stock (*General*), Philip Madoc (*Sgt. Major*), Josef Abraham, Jaroslav Drbohlav, Aubrey Woods, Cyril Cross, Radoslav Dubansky, Josef Laufer, Vitezslav Jandek, Neil McCarthy, Gertan Klauber, John Abineri, Keith James.

An attempt to recreate the assassination of the brutal Nazi Reinhard Heydrich by the Czech underground during WW II. Heydrich was the leader of the Nazi occupation forces in Czechoslovakia and this callous treatment of the Czechs earned him the nickname of "The Hangman." Bottoms, Shaw, and Ackland play British-trained Czechs who leave their London base and parachute into their homeland to kill Heydrich. They miss their first opportunity, but are successful the second time around when they toss a grenade into his car. In retaliation for the assassination, the Nazis annihilate the entire town of Lidice. Shaw, in an effort to protect his wife and child, turns his cohorts in and they are trapped, with other freedom fighters, in a cathedral where they valiantly hold off a Nazi battalion. Eventually, Bottoms and Shaw are the only survivors, and they kill themselves to avoid capture. The story sticks pretty closely to actual events, but it still is lacking in drama. Bottoms is miscast as the hero, never quite conveying the strength and determination the role required. This was the second time this story had been the basis for a film. Fritz Lang filmed a less accurate but no more successful version in 1943, called HANGMEN ALSO DIE.

p, Carter De Haven; d, Lewis Gilbert; w, Ronald Harwood (based on the novel *Seven Men at Daybreak* by Alan Burgess); ph, Henri Decae (Technicolor); m, David Hentschel; ed, Thelma Connell; art d, William McCrow, Bob Kulic; spec eff, Roy Whybrow.

War (PR:A MPAA:PG)

OPERATION DELILAH*½ (1966, U.S./Span.) 86m S.W.P. Productions-Esamer Films/Comet c (OPERACION DALILA)

Rory Calhoun (*Rory*), Gia Scala (*Delilah*), Marvin Kaplan, Enrique Guitart, Manolo Moran, Angel Alvarez, Jose Manuel Martin, Jose Isbert, Jackie Mason, Angel Del Pozo, Jose Luis Lopez Vazquez, Jorge [George] Rigaud.

A superficial political satire about the overthrow of a Caribbean island by a man whose beard means he's a Marxist. The U.S. and other Western powers want the new leader out and they send Calhoun, the owner of a razor company, to head the covert operation. He hooks up with Scala, who bumps and grinds her way into the new leader's heart. She drugs him and prepares to shave him when she discovers that the beard is false and that the new leader is really the old leader. Filmed in Madrid and Barcelona.

p, Sidney W. Pink, Henry Eller; d, Luis de los Arcos; w, Arcos, Pink; ph, Mario Pacheco (Eastmancolor); m, Adolfo Waitzmann; ed, Margarita Lauvergeon [Ochoa], Kurt Herrnfeld; art d, Antonio Simont.

Comedy (PR:A MPAA:NR)

OPERATION DIAMOND** (1948, Brit.) 53m Cine-Industrial/REN bw

Frank Hawkins (*Maj. Dane*), Michael Medwin (*Sullivan*), Beth Ross (*Hilda*), Campbell Singer (*Bert*), Gerik Schelderupp (*Jan van der Meer*), Archie Duncan, Donald Ferguson, Toni McMillan, Alastair Hunter, Martin Wyldeck, Hamish Menzies, Arthur Mullard, Fred Beck, Sydney Benson, Cyril Conway.

Intriguing war drama about the efforts of a Dutch and an English soldier to save a precious diamond belonging to the Dutch government from the grasp of the Nazis. A preface to the action shows how the diamond, the world's largest, was discovered and brought to Holland, giving the film an air of authenticity, as well as highlighting the importance of the soldier's mission.

p, Patrick Matthews; d, Ronnie Pilgrim; w, Anthony Richardson; ph, Pilgrim.

War   **(PR:A   MPAA:NR)**

OPERATION DIPLOMAT**   (1953, Brit.) 70m Nettlefold/BUT bw

Guy Rolfe (Dr. Mark Fenton), Lisa Daniely (Lisa Durand, Nurse), Patricia Dainton (Sister Rogers), Sydney Tafler (Wade), Brian Worth (Geoffrey Terry), Anton Diffring (Shroder), Ballard Berkeley (Inspector Austin), James Raglan (Sir Oliver Peters), Edward Dain, Michael Golden, Avice Landone, Eric Berry, Ann Bennett, Jean Hardwicke, Alexis Chesnakov.

Fast-paced drama centering on the efforts of physician Rolfe to save the life of the mystery figure he was forced to operate on under shady circumstances. Rolfe's secretary is murdered for revealing the patient's identity to Rolfe. In the knick of time, the police and Rolfe save the mystery figure, a diplomat, from being smuggled out of the country. This film is hard to swallow, but the nonstop action helps cover up the gaping holes of the plot.

p, Ernest G. Roy; d, John Guillermin; w, A. R. Rawlinson, Guillermin (based on a television serial by Francis Durbridge); ph, Gerald Gibbs.

Crime   **(PR:A   MPAA:NR)**

OPERATION DISASTER**   (1951, Brit.) 102m GFD/UNIV bw (GB: MORNING DEPARTURE)

John Mills (Lt. Comdr. Armstrong), Helen Cherry (Helen), Richard Attenborough (Stoker Snipe), Lana Morris (Rose Snipe), Nigel Patrick (Lt. Harry Manson), Andrew Crawford (Warrant Officer McFee), Michael Brennan (CPO Barlow), James Hayter (A. B. Higgins), Wylie Watson (A. B. Nobby Clark), Jack Stuart (L/Sea Kelly), Roddy McMillan (L/Sea Andrews), Frank Coburn (L/Sea Brough), Peter Hammond (Sub/Lt. Oakley), Victor Maddern (L/Tlg. Hillbrook), George Cole (E.R.A. Marks), Bernard Lee (Cmdr. Gates), Kenneth More, Alastair Hunter, George Thorpe, Zena Marshall, Arthur Sandifer.

An actual event, the sinking of the British submarine "Truculent," provides the basis for an uneven drama starring Mills as the commander of a submarine that strikes a mine, killing all but 12 men and leaving them trapped beneath the ocean. Most of the action concentrates on the mechanics of the rescue attempt, while the men below try to decide who among them will survive (the rescue equipment can only save eight men). Fast-paced and interesting at first, the film slows down considerably and spends too much time depicting the stiff-upper-lip heroics.

p, Jay Lewis; d, Roy Baker; w, W.E.C. Fairchild (based on the play "Morning Departure" by Kenneth Woollard); ph, Desmond Dickinson; ed, Alan Osbiston; art d, Alex Vetchinsky.

Drama   **(PR:A   MPAA:NR)**

OPERATION EICHMANN**   (1961) 92m Bischoff-Diamond/AA bw

Werner Klemperer (Adolf Eichmann), Ruta Lee (Anna Kemp), Donald Buka (David), Barbara Turner (Sara), John Banner (Rudolf Hoess), Hanna Landy (Fran Hoess), Lester Fletcher (Kurt Kessner), Steve Gravers (Jacob), Jim Baird (David, as a Boy), Debbie Cannon (Sara, as a Girl), Jackie Russo (Jacob, as a Boy), Paul Thierry (Lopez), Rodolfo Hoyos (Sanchez), Norbert Schiller (Uri Goldmann), Luis Van Rooten (Heinrich Himmler), Oscar Beregi (Kuwait Chief of Police), Theodore Marcuse (Felsner), Otto Reichow (Rostich), Walter Linden (Eichmann's Driver), Hans Hermann (Hans), Hans Gudegast [Eric Braeden] (Klaus), Robert Christopher (Ben, Pilot), Carl Lucerne (Cafe Singer), Austin Green, Robert H. Harris.

A quickie project, rushed into production for release on the eve of Adolf Eichmann's trial in Israel for war crimes. Klemperer plays the Nazi madman and the first part of the film depicts Eichmann's personal role in the holocaust which resulted in the slaughter of six million Jews. The second half is set after WW II and focuses on the hunt for Eichmann by Israeli agents Buka and Gravers. The trail takes them from the Middle East to Spain and finally to South America where they nab Klemperer, who is still spouting Nazi philosophy. The film ends with Klemperer being flown to Israel for his trial. Klemperer is properly repellant as Eichmann, and the film gains some interest with the search for the murderer, but overall it's a pretty slipshod affair. The haste is evident throughout, particularly in the sometimes disjointed narrative. The film was released in March and within a matter of a few months, Eichmann would be convicted for his atrocities and hanged on May 21, 1961.

p, Samuel Bischoff, David Diamond; d, R. G. Springsteen; w, Lewis Copley; ph, Joseph Biroc; m, June Starr; ed, Roy Livingston; md, Alex Alexander; art d, Rudi Feld; spec eff, Charles Duncan; m/l, "The Right One Must Come Along," by Gustav Heimo, Franz Steininger, "The Prayer" (sung by Cantor Sholom Katz); makeup, Anthony Lloyd.

Drama   **(PR:A   MPAA:NR)**

OPERATION ENEMY FORT*½   (1964, Jap.) 95m Toho c (YAMANEKO SAKUSEN)

Makoto Sato, Yuriko Hoshi, Yosuke Natsuki, Toru Ibuki, Kumi Mizuno, Jun Tazaki.

Set during the Sino-Japanese conflict (1937-45), the story concerns a Japanese battalion and its attempts to combat guerrilla attacks in the northern mountains of China. The Japanese protect a warehouse owner, believing him to be a sympathizer, and help him transport a shipment of goods which he says might be stolen by the guerrillas. A lieutenant learns the warehouse owner is really the guerrilla leader and the goods are actually an arms shipment, but he is taken prisoner by the Chinese before he can reveal his discovery. The Chinese attempt to force him to

lead the battalion into a trap, but he escapes and destroys the guerrillas' arms supply.

p, Senkichi Taniguchi; w, Shinichi Sekizawa; ph, Fukuso Koizumi (Tohoscope, Eastmancolor); m, Masaru Sato.

Drama   **(PR:A   MPAA:NR)**

OPERATION GANYMED**½   (1977, Ger.) 126m Pentagramma-Zweites Deutsches Fernsehen c

Horst Frank, Dieter Laser, Uwe Friedrichsen, Juergen Prochnow, Claus Theo Gaestner, Vicky Roskilly, Wolf Mittler.

The winner of the first prize at the Trieste Science Fiction Film Festival in 1978, OPERATION GANYMED is the work of Germany's leading science fiction director, Erler, whose films are primarily done for German TV. The film tells the story of a space mission sponsored by the U.N. which has been given up for lost after more than four years in space. One of the craft returns to Earth, however, landing in a Mexican desert. The crew have evidence of life on other planets, but they are unable to cope with the hardships of the desert. The five space travelers are driven insane by thirst, start murdering one another, and engage in cannibalism until only one man is left. Completely mad, he stumbles into a Mexican village. Prochnow, one of the crew members, would achieve stardom in the U.S. with the release of DAS BOOT in 1981, going on to appear in American made-for-TV movies.

p,d&w, Rainer Erler; ph, Wolfgang Grasshoff.

Science Fiction   **(PR:C   MPAA:NR)**

OPERATION HAYLIFT**   (1950) 73m Lippert bw

Bill Williams (Bill Masters), Ann Rutherford (Clara Masters), Tom Brown (Tom Masters), Jane Nigh (Pat), Joe Sawyer (George Swallow), Richard Travis (Max), Raymond Hatton (Sandy), Jimmy Conlin (Ed North), Tommy Ivo (Roy Masters), Dink Dean (Lt. Richter), Joanna Armstrong (Hannah), M'Liss McClure (Mary), Frank Jaros (Luigi), Capt. H.G. Fisher, USAF (2nd Pilot), Sgt. Victor Rogers, USAF (Crew Chief), Sgt. Wm. Dooms, USAF (Radio Operator), Roger Norton, USAF (Navy Officer), The United States Air Force.

Story depicts a true incident in which the U.S. Air Force saved cattle and sheep herds threatened with starvation when crippling blizzards struck Nevada in January of 1949. Intertwined with the rescue story is the tale of two brothers, Williams and Brown, portraying ranchers who stand to be ruined by the disaster. It's a reasonably effective offering, though most of the interest derives from the fact that it's a true story. The film benefited from the full cooperation of the Air Force, which loaned numerous planes and equipment for use in the film. Several Air Force servicemen fill roles in the film, which was shot entirely on location in Ely, Nevada. Sawyer, who had appeared in many films throughout the 1930s and 1940s, usually as a villain, tried his hand at producing and writing with this film.

p, Joe Sawyer; d, William Berke; w, Sawyer, Dean Reisner; ph, Benjamin Kline.

Drama   **(PR:A   MPAA:NR)**

OPERATION KID BROTHER*½   (1967, Ital.) 104m Produzione D.S./UA c (O.K. CONNERY)

Neil Connery (Himself), Daniela Bianchi (Maya), Adolfo Celi (Thair Beta), Agata Flori (Mildred), Bernard Lee (Commander Cunningham), Anthony Dawson [Antonio Margheriti] (Alpha), Lois Maxwell (Max), Yachuco Yama (Yachuco), Guido Lollobrigida (Kurt), Franco Giacobini (Juan), Nando Angelini (Ward Jones), Mario Soria (Gamma), Anne-Marie Noe (Lotte), Leo Scavini, Francesco Tensi, Enzo Consoli, Mirella Pamphili, Antonio Gradoli, Franco Ceccarelli.

What better way to spoof James Bond films than to pull together actors from the 007 series (Lee, Celi, Maxwell, Bianchi) and to use Sean Connery's brother, Neil as the lead? Sounds good, but like most spy spoofs it's a five-minute sketch dragged out to feature length. Connery is a plastic surgeon who is recruited to stop Celi from achieving world domination. Lots of gadgets and pretty women in an uninvolving story. Neil Connery never claimed to be an actor, and this, his only film appearance, proved he wasn't.

p, Dario Abatello; d, Alberto de Martino; w, Paolo Levi, Frank Walker, Stanley Wright, Stefano Canzio, Vincenzo Mannino, Carlo Tritto; ph, Alejandre Ulloa, Gianni Bergamini (Technicope, Technicolor); m, Bruno Nicolai, Ennio Morricone; ed, Otello Colangeli; art d, Franco Fontana; set d, Massimo Tavazzi; cos, Gaia Romanini; spec eff, Gagliano; m/l, "The Man For Me" by Nicolai, Morricone, Audrey Nohra.

Action/Comedy   **(PR:A   MPAA:NR)**

OPERATION LOTUS BLEU   (SEE: MISSION BLOODY MARY, 1967, Fr./Ital./Span.)

OPERATION LOVEBIRDS*   (1968, Den.) 102m Nordisk/Emerson c (SLA FORST, FREDE!)

Essy Persson (Sonja), Morten Grunwald (Freddy), Ove Sprogoe (Smith), Poul Bundgaard (Kolick), Martin Hansen (Dr. Pax), John Wittig, Frankie Steele, Jorgen Blaksted, Edward Fleming, Valso Holm, Lisbeth Frandsen, Soren Rode, Philippe Decaux, Freddy Koch, Karl Stegger, Andre Sallyman, Knud Rex, Arthur Jensen, Ebba With, Else Marie, Anna Marie Lie, Jan Priiskorn Schmidt, Michael Sprehn, Olaf Lindfors, Bjorn Spiro, Hans Ejner Jensen, Gunnar Stromvad, Anne Werner Thomsen.

Unsuspecting salesman Grunwald accidentally finds his suitcase full of trick novelty items switched with that of Sprogoe, a secret agent on the trail of a crazed doctor who wants to start a nuclear missile attack. Because he has become privy to the plan, Grunwald is inducted into the secret service and used to help thwart the mad doctor's plans, which he does, at one point using his bag of tricks to confuse the enemy. Absurd premise fails to generate anything other than embarrassment.

p, Bo Christensen; d, Erik Balling; w, Bengt Janus, Benning Bahs, Balling; ph,

Jorgen Skov, Arne Abrahamsen (Eastmancolor); m, Bent Fabricius-Bjerre; art d, Bahs.

Comedy **(PR:A MPAA:NR)**

OPERATION M (SEE: HELL'S BLOODY DEVILS, 1970)

OPERATION MAD BALL*** (1957) 105m COL bw

Jack Lemmon *(Pvt. Hogan)*, Kathryn Grant *(Lt. Betty Bixby)*, Ernie Kovacs *(Capt. Paul Locke)*, Arthur O'Connell *(Col. Rousch)*, Mickey Rooney *(M/Sgt. Yancy Skibo)*, Dick York *(Cpl. Bohun)*, James Darren *(Pvt. Widowskas)*, Roger Smith *(Cpl. Berryman)*, William Leslie *(Pvt. Grimes)*, Sheridan Comerate *(Sgt. Wilson)*, L.Q. Jones *(Ozark)*, Jeanne Manet *(Mme. LaFour)*, Bebe Allen *(Lt. Johnson)*, Mary LaRoche *(Lt. Schmidt)*, Dick Crockett *(Sgt. McCloskey)*, Paul Picerni *(Pvt. Bullard)*, David McMahon *(M/Sgt. Pringle)*, Otto Reichow *(German Prisoner of War)*.

Lemmon received his first starring role in this military service comedy which also served as the screen debut of the brilliant television comedian Ernie Kovacs. Based on a play, OPERATION MAD BALL details the efforts of a group of bored WW II GIs stationed at an Army medical unit in France who try to improve moral by throwing a "Mad Ball" for the nurses. Unfortunately, all the nurses are officers and the enlisted men are forbidden to fraternize with them. The mastermind behind this plan is Lemmon, a fast-talking private who sneaks around behind the back of his by-the-book captain, Kovacs. Lemmon arranges for the party to be held at a hotel run by Manet, a shifty French local out to make a fast buck off the GIs. Rooney shines as the clever master sergeant who can dig up anything Lemmon needs at a moment's notice and Grant (Mrs. Bing Crosby) is likable as Lemmon's disapproving girl friend. The film is filled with some funny rapid-fire dialog adapted by playwright Carter and producer Harris with help from a young Blake Edwards. OPERATION MAD BALL was the obsession of actor Richard Quine who saw the property as his ticket into directing. Quine brought the screenplay to Columbia studio chief Harry Cohn and refused to sell it unless he could direct. Cohn balked at first but gave in with the proviso that Cohn and Jed Harris, who produced the show on Broadway and whom Cohn hated, would never meet. One day Cohn called both Quine and Harris to his office, a command that sent a chill down the spine of Harris. Quine assured Harris that he could handle the notoriously volatile Cohn. As Norman Zierold relates in his book *Moguls*, Cohn demanded a chunk of dialog be taken out of a scene on page one of the script. Quine flatly refused, claiming it to be a necessary speech. "I don't give a damn. Take it out." Cohn said. "You can't just take a speech out without giving a solid reason," Quine responded. "The hell I can't. It's my studio." "Then keep your f]]]]]] studio," Quine said, and stormed out of Cohn's office with Harris following sheepishly. "I thought you handled that very well," Harris said. Cohn eventually capitulated. Later in the shooting, Quine decided to shoot the climactic party scene at night and served the cast real alcohol so that everyone would be relaxed and in a party mood. When Cohn learned of the costly overtime shoot he stormed onto the set and demanded an explanation. Quine explained his logic and invited the mogul to stay, have a drink, and watch the shooting. This seemed to appease Cohn and he sat out of camera range sipping a drink and had a good time. Lemmon fondly remembers the shooting of OPERATION MAD BALL and cites it as one of his personal favorites. He greatly enjoyed working with both Rooney and Kovacs (he would make two more films with Kovacs, BELL, BOOK AND CANDLE and IT HAPPENED TO JANE), but Rooney had him laughing so much that 30 takes were required for one scene. Director Quine states in Don Widener's biography of the actor entitled *Lemmon*, "Mickey never did the scene twice the same way and every time he'd add a new touch, Jack would just fall over backwards. It was the only time I ever saw Lemmon unable to handle an acting chore. He had only one line in the scene and I don't think he ever got it out." As for Kovacs, he grabbed eagerly at the chance to work his special magic on the big screen. He tackled the role of Capt. Paul Locke with verve and a malevolent zest and garnered good reviews. Unfortunately, Hollywood didn't really know what to do with Kovacs and typecast him in the role for much of his brief movie career. Of the nine movies Kovacs appeared in, he played a captain four times (OPERATION MAD BALL, OUR MAN IN HAVANA, WAKE ME WHEN IT'S OVER, and SAIL A CROOKED SHIP). Frustrated by this short-sighted casting which handcuffed his creativity, Kovacs took out an ad in *Variety* which simply read, "No more * !! captains."

p, Jed Harris; d, Richard Quine; w, Harris, Blake Edwards, Arthur Carter (based on the play by Carter); ph, Charles Lawton, Jr.; m, George Duning; ed, Charles Nelson; md, Morris W. Stoloff; art d, Robert Boyle; set d, William Kiernan, Bill Calvert; m/l, Fred Karger, Quine.

Comedy **(PR:A MPAA:NR)**

OPERATION MANHUNT½** (1954) 77m UA bw

Harry Townes *(Igor Gouzenko)*, Irja Jensen *(Katya Gouzenko)*, Jacques Aubuchon *(Volov)*, Robert Goudier *(Victor Collier)*, Albert Miller *(Chertok)*, Caren Shaffer *(Jean Gouzenko)*, Kenneth Wolfe *(Stephen Gouzenko)*, Will Kuluva *(Rostovich)*, Ovila Lagare *(Inspector Boucher)*, Igor Gouzenko *(Epilogue)*.

Townes is a Russian code clerk who defects to the west and is stalked by a Russian agent. The Soviets want to kill the defector, who has made his home in Canada. The film cuts from Townes enjoying life with his wife and children to the Soviet efforts to locate the traitor. An agent finally finds Townes, but he defects too. Based on the true story of Igor Gouzenko who delivers the film's epilogue. He worked as a code clerk in the Russian Embassy in Ottawa, and exposed a Soviet spy ring. That incident, which took place nine years before the release of this film, was the basis for THE IRON CURTAIN (1948), starring Dana Andrews.

p, Fred Feldkamp; d, Jack Alexander; w, Paul Monash; ph, Akos Farkus, Benoit Jobin; ed, David Gazalet; md, Jack Shaindlin.

Drama **(PR:A MPAA:NR)**

OPERATION MASQUERADE (SEE: MASQUERADE, 1965, Brit.)

OPERATION MERMAID (SEE: BAY OF SAINT MICHEL, 1963)

OPERATION MURDER* (1957, Brit.) 66m Danzingers/UA bw

Tom Conway (Dr. Wayne), Sandra Dorne *(Pat Wayne)*, Patrick Holt *(Dr. Bowen)*, Rosamund John *(Head Nurse)*, Robert Ayres *(Larry Winton)*, Virginia Keiley *(Julie)*, John Stone *(Inspector Price)*, Alastair Hunter *(Williams)*, Frank Hawkins, Gilbert Winfield, Timothy Fitzgerald, Tony Quinn.

When their private hospital is in danger of closing because of money problems, doctors Conway and Holt devise a scheme to kill Conway's rich cousin for an inheritance. The plan blows up when Conway's alibi crumples like a plot line of this ridiculous story from the usually brisk thriller director Morris.

p, Edward J. Danzinger, Harry Lee Danzinger; d, Ernest Morris; w, Brian Clemens; ph, Jimmy Wilson.

Crime **(PR:A MPAA:NR)**

OPERATION PACIFIC*** (1951) 111m WB bw

John Wayne *("Duke" Gifford)*, Patricia Neal *(Mary Stuart)*, Ward Bond *("Pop" Perry)*, Scott Forbes *(Larry)*, Philip Carey *(Bob Perry)*, Paul Picerni *(Jonesy)*, William [Bill] Campbell *(The Talker)*, Kathryn Givney *(Comdr. Steele)*, Vincent Forte *(Soundman)*, Martin Milner *(Caldwell)*, Cliff Clark *(Comsubpac)*, Jack Pennick *(The Chief)*, Virginia Brissac *(Sister Anne)*, Lewis Martin *(Squad Commander)*, Louis Mosconi *Radarman)*, Carleton Young *(Capt. McAllister)*, Gordon Gebert *(Tommy Kirby)*, Steve Flagg *(Lt. Jorgenson)*, Brett King *(Lt. Ernie Stark)*, Dick Wessell *(Mess Sergeant)*, Gail Davis *(Virginia Blithe)*, Milburn Stone *(Ground Control Officer)*, Sam Edwards *(Junior)*, Gayle Kellogg *(Herbie)*, Keith Larsen, Mack Williams.

A solid WW II action film, OPERATION PACIFIC offers more than the usual Wayne heroics. It presents subtle doubts about the invincibility of Wayne, while allowing the foxy Neal to assert her strong personality upon him. Wayne and Neal had been married and are now divorced after she lost a child he had fathered. He stumbles out of the jungle with a baby he has just saved and later turns the child over to a base hospital where Neal is stationed as a nurse. She arranges to accidentally meet Wayne again to see if she still has that old feeling for him. She does, but refuses to yield to her emotions, even though he admits that their breakup was his fault: "We had something—I guess I kicked it around." Meanwhile, young Navy flier Carey is hotly pursuing Neal, begging her to marry him. With Wayne back in her life, even by a toehold, Neal hesitates. Wayne goes off to sea on his submarine with skipper Bond who happens to be the father of Carey. During a battle, Bond is wounded and orders his ship submerged, even though he will be left to drown topside. Wayne obeys and is later guilt-haunted, as well as hated by Carey. Neal is his only source of comfort and he later soothes his guilt by saving Carey, whose plane has been shot down and who has been forced to survive in the sea. Wayne is still a little too tough for Neal who tells him off near the end, bitterly reminding him how he deserted her when their son died. "You went off into some corner alone, never realizing that by comforting you I could have helped my own grief. You don't need anybody but yourself!" But Neal's superior, Brissac, gives her a comeuppance, telling her: "You married him for what he is and then tried to make something else out of him, but you couldn't!" Neal and Wayne wind up together while the problems of defective torpedoes are solved. There's plenty of action here, especially when Wayne sails submerged into the middle of a Japanese fleet and then fires off all his torpedoes in all directions to see if they will work. Clips from an earlier Warner Bros. submarine film, DESTINATION TOKYO, were used in OPERATION PACIFIC; in one brief scene, the star of the former film, Cary Grant, can be briefly glimpsed. The film was shot partly on location in Honolulu and was mirrored by another production that year, SUBMARINE COMMAND, where William Holden is also afflicted by debilitating doubt and guilt.

p, Louis F. Edelman; d&w, George Waggner; ph, Bert Glennon; m, Max Steiner; ed, Alan Crosland, Jr.; art d, Leo K. Kuter.

War Drama **(PR:A MPAA:NR)**

OPERATION PETTICOAT*½** (1959) 124m Granarte/UNIV c

Cary Grant *(Adm. Matt Sherman)*, Tony Curtis *(Lt. Nick Holden)*, Joan O'Brien *(Lt. Dolores Crandall)*, Dina Merrill *(Lt. Barbara Duran)*, Arthur O'Connell *(Sam Tostin)*, Gene Evans *(Molumphrey)*, Richard Sargent *(Stovall)*, Virginia Gregg *(Maj. Edna Hayward)*, Robert F. Simon *(Capt. J. B. Henderson)*, Robert Gist *(Watson)*, Gavin MacLeod *(Ernest Hunkle)*, George Dunn *(Prophet)*, Dick Crockett *(Harmon)*, Madlyn Rhue *(Lt. Claire Reid)*, Marion Ross *(Lt. Ruth Colfax)*, Clarence E. Lung *(Ramon)*, Frankie Darro *(Dooley)*, Tony Pastor, Jr. *(Fox)*, Nicky Blair *(Kraus)*, John W. Morley *(Williams)*, Robert Hoy *(Reiner)*, Glenn Jacobson *(Control Talker)*, Nino Tempo, William Bryant *(Crewmen)*, Leon Lontoc *(Filipino Farmer)*, James F. Lanphier *(Lt. Cmdr. Daly)*, Alan Dexter *(Navy Chief)*, Preston Hanson *(Lt. Col. Simpson)*, Hal Baylor *(M.P. Sergeant)*, Bob Stratton *(Marine Lieutenant)*, Vi Ingraham *(Pregnant Filipino Woman)*, Alan Scott *(Chief of Demolition Crew)*, Francis L. Ward *(Third Class Petty Officer)*, William R. Callihan *(Lt. Morrison)*, Gordon Casell *(Col. Higginson)*, Tusi Faiivae *(Witch Doctor)*, Robert Keys, Dale Cummings *(M.P.'s)*, Joseph Kim *(Filipino)*, Malcolm Cassell, Larry Gilliland, Fred Harlfinger II *(Sailors)*, Harry Harvey Jr., Haile Chase, Howard Venezia *(Soldiers)*, Vince Deadrick, William Kinney *(Ad Libs)*, Robert C. Youmans *(Lieutenant)*, Robert Gibson *(Seaman)*, Bert Beyers *(Bowman)*, Tony Corrado *(Fireman Lye)*.

Tony Curtis had always wanted to be Cary Grant and even did a good impression of him in the picture before this, SOME LIKE IT HOT, where he pretended to be a wealthy British oil man in an attempt to romance Monroe. Now he gets his chance to work opposite the master and just about steals the show. Grant had a piece of the action of this hugely successful film and an early edition of the *Guiness Book of World Records* indicates that Grant was the highest paid actor in the business due to the money he took in from his share. That claim has since been relinquished a few times to other performers. It's after WW II and Grant is going over his log book of the submarine he captains. He is about to turn over the command of the ship to Curtis who will squire the sub to a fate of being destroyed before it is replaced by a nuclear sub. He recalls some of the events of the sub's life and the picture unwinds in flashback. It's December, 1941, and Grant's tired sub can only function after dog-robber Curtis secures supplies and gear to make it work. Curtis picks up five stranded nurses plus a couple of Filipino families and a goat to ferry them out of harm's way. The minute these nurses come aboard, chaos erupts. O'Brien, Merrill, Gregg, Rhue and Ross take over matters and hilarious incidents commence which wind up in the sub being painted pink. Most of the jokes are sexist by today's standards but that doesn't make them any less humorous. When the busty nurses attempt to pass the hot young sailors in the very narrow corridors of the sub, well, you can imagine what happens. By the time the picture ends, Merrill and Curtis are married and so are Grant and O'Brien. There's no thrust to the story other than one gag after another, most of which are bright and original. Screenwriters Shapiro and Richlin had previously teamed for PILLOW TALK and their excellent hand at dialogue is also heard to great advantage in this film. Some of the actors have gone on to other professions including Tony Pastor, Jr. (son of the Italian performer but no relation to the Irish boniface who ran nightclubs in New York at the start of the century), who became the creative director of Marvel Productions where he oversees all of that company's cartoon operation. Nicky Blair opened several restaurants and became a popular host along the Sunset Strip. Standout comedy performances from every actor on the screen, and special plaudits for Curtis who was at the top of his comedic form in a career that has been a rollercoaster. The script was nominated for an Oscar but the Academy seldom gives Oscars for funniness, with the notable exception of ANNIE HALL. Blake Edwards' direction kept matters running like a new Mercedes-Benz. It was filmed in Key West, Florida, and aboard the submarine, "Balboa." A TV series was attempted later and never came close to the joie de vivre of the movie.

p, Robert Arthur; d, Blake Edwards; w, Stanley Shapiro, Maurice Richlin (based on a story by Paul King, Joseph Stone); ph, Russell Harlan, Clifford Stine (Eastmancolor); m, David Rose; ed, Ted J. Kent, Frank Gross; art d, Alexander Golitzen; Robert E. Smith; set d, Russell A. Gausman, Oliver Emert; cos, Bill Thomas; makeup, Bud Westmore.

Comedy Cas. (PR:A MPAA:NR)

OPERATION ST. PETER'S* (1968, Ital.) 88m PAR c (OPERAZIONE SAN PIETRO)

Lando Buzzanca *(Napoleon)*, Edward G. Robinson *(Joe)*, Heinz Ruhmann *(Cardinal Braun)*, Jean-Claude Brialy *(Cajella)*, Pinuccio Ardia *(The Baron)*, Dante Maggio *(The Captain)*, Ugo Fancareggi *(Agonia)*, Marie-Christine Barclay *(Marisa)*, Uta Levka *(Samantha)*, Antonella Delle Port *(Cesira)*.

An inane caper farce with Buzzanca stealing Michelangelo's Pieta. The statue is worth $30 billion, but he has no one to sell it to. American gangster Robinson buys it for $40 and a spaghetti dinner. The Vatican doesn't want word to leak out that the statue has been stolen so they send out their own priest to track down the thieves. Priests involved in a high-speed film chase are a rare sight, but they prove to be quite adept at it—understandable, since Ruhmann admits that he won the Indianapolis 500 as a youth. A very weak comedy. Robinson made several films in Europe during the mid-1960s, none of them particularly memorable, but this was surely one of the worst.

p, Turi Vasile; d, Lucio Fulci; w, Ennio De Concini, Adriano Baracco, Roberto Gianviti, Fulci; ph, Erico Menczer; art d, Giorgio Giovannini.

Action/Comedy (PR:A MPAA:G)

OPERATION SAN GENNARO (SEE: TREASURE OF SAN GENNARO, 1968, Fr./Ital./Ger.)

OPERATION SECRET½** (1952) 108m WB bw

Cornel Wilde *(Peter Forrester)*, Steve Cochran *(Marcel Brevoort)*, Phyllis Thaxter *(Maria)*, Karl Malden *(Maj. Lautrec)*, Paul Picerni *(Armand)*, Lester Matthews *(Robbins)*, Jay Novello *(Herr Bauer)*, Dan O'Herlihy *(Duncan)*, Ed Foster *(Claude)*, Claude Dunkin *(Rene)*, Wilton Graff *(French Official)*, Baynes Barron *(Henri)*, Philip Rush *(Zabreski)*, Robert Shaw *(Jacques)*, Henry Rowland *(German M.P.)*, Dan Riss *(Sergeant)*, Gayle Kellogg *(Corporal)*, John Beattie *(Radio Operator)*, George Dee, Rudy Rama, Monte Pittman, Tony Eisley, Joe Espitallier, Harry Arnie *(Maquis)*, Paula Sowl *(Hostess)*, Peter Michael *(Legionnaire)*, Gary Kettler *(Nazi NCO)*, John Logan *(Nazi Soldier)*, Tom Browne Henry *(Monk)*, Ted Lawrence *(Didot)*, Don Harvey *(Guard)*, Roy Jenson *(Michel)*, Craig Morland *(British M.P.)*, Elizabeth Flournoy *(Woman Marine)*, Harlan Warde *(Maj. Dawson)*, William Leicester *(Capt. Hughes)*, Kenneth Patterson *(General)*, John Nelson *(Crewman)*, William Slack *(Pvt. Korst)*, Frank Jaquet *(Bartender)*, Larry Winter, Greg Barton *(Sentries)*, Frances Zucco *(Elsa)*, Len Hendry *(Gestapo Officer)*, John Marshall *(Driver)*, Charles Flynn *(German Civil Officer)*, John Pickard *(Soldier)*, Bob Stevenson *(Fireman)*, George Magrill *(Brakeman)*, Jack Lomas *(Engineer)*, Carlo Tricoli *(Old Peasant)*, Wayne Taylor *(Etienne)*.

Wilde stars as an American officer and former French Foreign Legion member who has turned his energies to assisting the French underground in WW II. Years after the war's end, however, he is accused of murdering Picerni, an officer of the French underground group. This reckless act is contradictory to Wilde's actual heroic nature during the war, seen in flashback. Sent on a dangerous mission behind German lines, Wilde was to report on Allied the bomb damage done to the ball-bearing factories at Schweinfurt. Not only does he accomplish that, but he also captures some valuable Nazi films (actual German Signal Corp footage) of the first Messerschmidt jet plane and V-1 pilotless bomb. On his return flight, however, Wilde is downed and reported dead. Years later the French secret police investigate the murder of Maquis Picerni and call on a number of witnesses to testify. The facts are revealed by each witness—Cochran, a fellow Maquis who was secretly working as a Communist agent; Malden, an ex-Maquis and friend of Wilde's; Novello, a one-time Gestapo agent; Matthews, a representative of the British Foreign Office; and Thaxter, a former underground worker and love interest of Wilde's. Cochran delivers the most indicting testimony of Wilde's guilt but before a verdict is reached Wilde makes a surprise entrance into the courtroom. He clears himself of any wrongdoing and points the finger at the guilty Cochran. Although based on the actual exploits of Lt. Col. Peter Ortiz, OPERATION SECRET fails to arouse any strong emotions. Instead of being drawn into this fascinating and heroic tale, the audience is distanced by the many flashbacks. Fortunately, the wartime footage and the adventures of the underground are adroitly directed with strong action scenes. The acting is average, except for a stirring performance from Malden, who plays a humorous, granite-hard soldier with a strong affection for alcohol.

p, Henry Blake; d, Lewis Seiler; w, Harold Medford, James R. Webb, Alvin Josephy, John Twist (suggested by "The Life of Peter Ortiz" by Lt. Col. Peter Ortiz, USMCR); ph, Ted McCord; m, Roy Webb; ed, Clarence Kolster; md, Ray Heindorf; set d, William T. Kuehl.

War/Courtroom Drama (PR:A MPAA:NR)

OPERATION SNAFU** (1965, Brit.) 97m AIP bw (GB: ON THE FIDDLE; AKA: WAR HEAD; OPERATION WAR HEAD)

Alfred Lynch *(Horace Pope)*, Sean Connery *(Pedlar Pascoe)*, Cecil Parker *(Group Capt. Bascombe)*, Stanley Holloway *(Mr. Cooksley)*, Alan King *(T/Sgt. Buzzer)*, Eric Barker *(Doctor)*, Wilfrid Hyde-White *(Trowbridge)*, Kathleen Harrison *(Mrs. Cooksley)*, Eleanor Summerfield *(Flora McNaughton)*, Terence Longdon *(Air Gunner)*, Victor Maddern *(1st Airman)*, Harry Locke *(Huxtable)*, Lance Percival *(MacTaggart)*, John Le Mesurier *(Hixon)*, Viola Keats *(Sister)*, Peter Sinclair *(Mr. Pope)*, Jack Lambert *(Police Constable)*, Cyril Smith *(Ticket Collector)*, Graham Stark *(Sgt. Ellis)*, Miriam Karlin *(WAAF Sergeant)*, Bill Owen *(Corporal Gittens)*, Ian Whittaker *(Lancing)*, Monty Landis *(Conductor)*, Barbara Windsor *(Mavis)*, Toni Palmer *(Ivy)*, Kenneth J. Warren *(Dusty)*, Ann Beach *(Iris)*, Gary Cockrell *(U.S. Snowdrop)*, Edna Morris *(Lil)*, Thomas Heathcote *(Sergeant)*, Brian Weske *(Corporal)*, Simon Lack *(Flight Lt. Baldwin)*, Jean Aubrey *(WAAF Corporal)*, Harold Goodwin *(Cpl. Reeves)*, Beatrix Lehmann *(Lady Edith)*, Jack Smethurst, Patsy Rowlands, Priscilla Morgan, Richard Hart, Stuart Saunders, Norman Coburn, Michael Sarne.

Typical British WW II comedy notable only for the early appearance of Connery (as a gypsy no less!). Lynch stars as a conniving Britisher who talks his buddy Connery into joining the military with him so that they can make big bucks fleecing the soldiers. They soon set up shop in every conceivable racket from rations to leave passes. Eventually Lynch even outsmarts himself and both he and Connery wind up as unlikely war heroes. Released in Britain in 1961, when Connery was just beginning his JAMES BOND series, the picture might never have made it to the U.S. but for the success of those films.

p, S. Benjamin Fisz; d, Cyril Frankel; w, Harold Buchman (based on the novel *Stop at a Winner* by R.F. Delderfield); ph, Edward Scaife; m, Malcolm Arnold; ed, Peter Hunt; md, Arnold; art d, John Blezard.

Comedy (PR:A MPAA:NR)

OPERATION SNATCH½** (1962, Brit.) 83m Keep/CD bw

Terry-Thomas *(Lt. "Piggy" Wigg)*, George Sanders *(Maj. Hobson)*, Lionel Jeffries *(Evans)*, Jackie Lane *(Bianca Tabori)*, Lee Montague *(Miklos Tabori)*, Michael Trubshawe *(Col. Marston)*, James Villiers *(Lt. Keen)*, Dinsdale Landen *(Capt. Whittington)*, Jeremy Lloyd *(Capt. James)*, John Gabriel *(Maj. Frink)*, Warren Mitchell *(Contact Man)*, Mario Fabrizi *(Tall Man)*, Bernard Hunter *(Capt. Baker)*, Mark Singleton *(Prime Minister's Secretary)*, John Meillon *(Medical Officer)*, Gerard Heinz *(Col. Waldock)*, Howard Lang *(P.T. Sergeant)*, Graham Stark *(1st Soldier)*, John Scott *(Lt. Gen. Hepworth)*, Ian Whittaker *(Dyson)*.

Thomas is stationed in Gibraltar during WW II and is assigned to watch over the famous Barbary apes. According to legend, as long as the apes are on the rock, Gibraltar will stay under English rule. The only male ape dies and everyone fears the apes will die and the Germans will use it as propaganda. Thomas and Jeffries go to Zurich and steal an ape from a German circus. This saves the ape colony, Thomas is promoted, and he and Jeffries are transferred to watch over the ravens in the Tower of London.

p, Jules Buck; d, Robert Day; w, Alan Hackney, John Warren, Len Heath (adapted from a story by Paul Mills); ph, Geoffrey Faithfull; m, Ken Jones; ed, Bert Rule; md, Jones; art d, Ivan King.

Comedy (PR:A MPAA:NR)

OPERATION THIRD FORM** (1966, Brit.) 58m World Wide/Children's Film Foundation bw

John Moulder Brown *(Dick)*, Kevin Bennett *(Tom)*, Sidney Bromley *(Paddy)*, Derren Nesbitt *(Skinner)*, Michael Crockett *(Alan)*, Ronnie Caryl *(Brian)*, Roberta Tovey *(Jill)*, George Roderick *(Boss)*.

Enjoyable tale strictly for children in which a group of boys combine their efforts to clear a friend accused of the theft of the school bell. They manage to discover the real crooks, and prove the friend's innocence.

p, Hindle Edgar; d, David Eady; w, Michael Barnes (based on the story by Edgar and Eady).

Children (PR:AA MPAA:NR)

OPERATION THUNDERBOLT½** (1978, ISRAEL) 120m Golan-Globus-G.S. Films/Cinema Shares International c (AKA: ENTEBBE; OPERATION THUNDERBOLT)

Yehoram Gaon *(Jonathan)*, Assaf Dayan *(Shuki)*, Ori Levy *(Air Force Commander)*, Arik Lavi *(Dan Shomron)*, Klaus Kinski *(Boese)*, Sybil Danning *(Halima)*,

Oded Teomi (*Dan Zamir*), Hi Kelos (*American Reporter*), Henry Czerniak (*Pilot*), Gila Almagor (*Nurit Aviv*), Rachel Marcus (*Devora Bloom*), Reuben Bar Yotam (*Ben David*), Shoshik Shani (*Alma Raviv*), Shaike Ophir (*Gadi Arnon*), Shlomo Vishinsky (*Moshe Bloom*), Shmuel Rodenski (*Family Representative*), Ben Yosef (*Prof. Tal*), Yitzhak Neeman (*Jabbar*).

The Israel verison of the Entebbe raid in which a crack Israeli army squad rescued Israeli hostages held by German terrorists in Uganda. The film gives a better insight to the Israeli government's decision and training of the soldiers than the two American TV movie versions. Gaon plays the officer who was killed in the raid and Kinski is the terrorist leader. Golan and Globus would go on to form Cannon Films, and this film is better than most of the ones they cranked out.

p, Menahem Golan, Yoram Globus; d, Golan; w, Clark Reynolds; ph, Adam Greenberg; m, Dov Seltzer; ed, Dov Henig; art d, Kuli Sander; cos, Rochelle Zaltzman.

Action Drama   **Cas.**   **(PR:C   MPAA:PG)**

OPERATION UNDER COVER   (SEE: REPORT TO THE COMMISSIONER, 1975)

OPERATION WAR HEAD   (SEE: OPERATION SNAFU, 1965, Brit.)

OPERATION X*½   (1951, Brit.) 79m BL-LFP/COL bw (GB: MY DAUGHTER JOY)

Edward G. Robinson (*George Constantin*), Nora Swinburne (*Ava Constantin*), Peggy Cummins (*Georgette Constantin*), Richard Greene (*Larry Boyd*), Finley Currie (*Sir Thomas MacTavish*), Gregory Ratoff (*Marcos*), Ronald Adam (*Col. Fogarty*), Walter Rilla (*Andreas*), James Robertson Justice (*Prof. Karol*), David Hutcheson (*Ennix*), Don Nehan (*Polato*), Peter Illing (*Sultan*), Ronald Ward (*Dr. Schindler*), Robert Villa (*Prince Alzar*), Harry Lane (*Barboza*).

A disappointing picture despite the presence of good acting by Robinson, OPERATION X is a picture that never gets on its feet. Robinson is a tough, megalomaniacal businessman who can never forget his early years as a shoeshine boy in Constantinople. He would like to be the richest man in the world and will stop at nothing in that attempt. Next to his love of money, he loves his daughter, Cummins, far beyond his affection for his colorless wife, Swinburne. He has a master plan to amass a fortune which he calls "Operation X." In order to put that in place, he must secure a rare material that can only be found in an unnamed Arab country ruled by the Sultan, Illing. His Machiavellian mind concocts a plan to marry Cummins to Illing's son, Villa. With that taken care of, he can tap the country's resources. But Cummins is affianced to Greene, a bright young newsman who has been doing some undercover investigation about Robinson's plan. When Robinson learns of Greene's snooping, he tosses the man out. Swinburne knows how much Cummins loves Greene so she steps in to make a plea to allow the young woman to have happiness with Greene, rather than putting her into a marriage of financial convenience. Robinson refuses and Swinburne then tosses the bombshell at him that Cummins is not his real daughter! Well, that puts a crimp in Robinson's collar (which he gets very hot under) and Robinson goes nuts. The picture is told in a flashback so we already know his elevator doesn't reach the top floor and it's only a matter of unspooling the story to get to the end. Bland and boring, despite Robinson's attempts to raise the level of the movie from the bargain basement.

p&d, Gregory Ratoff; w, Robert Thoeren, William Rose (based on the novel *David Golder* by Irene Nemirowsky); ph, Georges Perinal, Andre Back; m, R. Gallois-Montbrun; ed, Raymond Poulton; md, Dr. Hubert Clifford; set d, Andre Andrejew.

Drama   **(PR:A-C   MPAA:NR)**

OPERATION X   (1963, Jap.) 102m Toho bw (DOBUNEZUMI SAKUSEN)

Yuzo Kayama, Yosuke Natsuki, Makoto Sato, Kumi Mizuno, Ichiro Nakatani, Tadao Nakamaru, Kunie Tanaka, Mickey Curtis, Nami Tamura.

A young Japanese officer takes over a garrison in northern China during the final days of WW II. Against advice, he leads an attack against the Chinese, his men are killed, and he is taken prisoner. A reward is put up for the officer. The leader of a Chinese guerrilla group, with four soldiers, heads out to free the Japanese officer. The guerrilla leader would rather have the Japanese rule than the communists. The guerrilla group races against a Chinese intelligence agent who wants the reward. The guerrillas save the officer and he joins the group and the fight.

p, Tomoyuki Tanaka, Ken-ichiro Tsunoda; d&w, Kihachi Okamoto; ph, Yuzuru Aizawa (Tohoscope); m, Massaru Sato.

War   **(PR:C   MPAA:NR)**

OPERATOR 13   (1934) 86m MGM bw (GB: SPY 13)

Marion Davies (*Gail Loveless/"Ann Claibourne"*), Gary Cooper (*Capt. Jack Gailliard*), Jean Parker (*Eleanor*), Katharine Alexander (*Pauline Cushman*), Ted Healy (*Dr. Hitchcock*), Russell Hardie (*Littledale*), Henry Wadsworth (*John Pelham*), Douglas Dumbrille (*Gen. "Jeb" Stuart*), Willard Robertson (*Capt. Channing*), Fuzzy Knight (*Sweeney*), Sidney Toler (*Maj. Allen*), Robert McWade (*Col. Sharpe*), Marjorie Gateson (*Mrs. Shackleford*), Wade Boteler (*Gaston*), Walter Long (*Operator 55*), Hattie McDaniel (*Cook*), Francis McDonald (*Denton*), William H. Griffith (*Mac*), James Marcus (*Staff Colonel*), Sam McDaniel (*Old Bob*), Buddy Roosevelt (*Civilian*), Frank McGlynn Jr., Wheeler Oakman (*Scouts*), Don Douglas (*Confederate Officer*), Si Jenks (*White Trash*), Reginald Barlow (*Col. Storm*), Ernie Alexander, Richard Powell (*Confederate Sentries*), Belle Daube (*Mrs. Dandridge*), Wilfred Lucas (*Judge*), Bob Stevenson (*Guard*), Martin Turner (*Wickman*), Frank Burt (*Confederate Lieutenant*), Wallie Howe (*Clergyman*), William Henry (*Young Lieutenant*), Richard Tucker (*Execution Officer*), Arthur Grant (*Chaplain*), Sherry Tansey (*Officer*), Lia Lance (*Witch Woman*), Charles Lloyd (*Union Private*), De Witt C. Jennings (*Artillery Man*), Sam Ash (*Lieutenant*), Ernie

Adams (*Orderly*), Clarence Hummel Wilson (*Claybourne*), Franklin Parker (*John Hay*), Claudia Coleman (*Nurse*), Sterling Holloway (*Wounded Soldier*), Sherry Hall (*Army Officer*), Douglas Fowley (*Union Officer*), Fred Warren (*Gen. U. S. Grant*), John Elliott (*Gen. Robert E. Lee*), Frank Leighton (*Union Major*), James C. Morton (*Secret Service Man*), Hattie Hill, John Kirkley (*Slaves*), John Larkin, Poppy Wilde (*Party Guests*), The Four Mills Brothers.

Davies is an actress during the Civil War who becomes a Northern spy. She goes behind Confederate lines with experienced spy Alexander and they end up at the mansion Gen. "Jeb" Stuart uses for his headquarters. Alexander is a guest at the mansion and Davies is hired as a washerwoman. Davies meets Cooper, who is a scout. Alexander is discovered as a spy and sentenced to death. Davies helps her escape back to Union lines and learns that Cooper is organizing Southern sympathizers in the North. She pretends to be a Southern belle at a mansion in Richmond, meets Cooper again and they fall in love. Eventually, Davies is discovered and makes her escape with another Union spy. Cooper tracks them down as a Union column approaches. The other spy wants to kill Cooper, but Davies handcuffs herself to her lover and they hide in a well. The Union soldiers shoot the other spy, who is dressed as a Confederate soldier but they leave when they cannot find Davies. Cooper and Davies come out of the well, Cooper breaks the handcuffs, kisses her goodbye, and goes back to his outfit. This was Cooper's third loan-out from Paramount for this strictly Davies film. Folsey was nominated for an Academy Award for his photography.

p, Lucien Hubbard; d, Richard Boleslavsky; w, Harry Thew, Zelda Sears, Eve Greene (based on novel by Robert W. Chambers); ph, George Folsey; m, Dr. William Axt; ed, Frank Sullivan; art d, Cedric Gibbons, Arnold Gillespie; cos, Adrian; m/l, "Sleepy Head" sung by The Four Mills Brothers), "Jungle Fever," "Once in a Lifetime," Walter Donaldson, Gus Kahn.

Drama   **(PR:A MPAA:NR)**

OPERAZIA GOLDMAN   (SEE: LIGHTNING BOLT, 1965, Ital)

OPERAZIONE CROSSBOW   (SEE: OPERATION CROSSBOW, 1965, U.S./Ital.)

OPERAZIONE PARADISO   (SEE: KISS THE GIRLS AND MAKE THEM DIE, 1967, U.S./Ital.)

OPERAZIONE PAURA   (SEE: KILL BABY KILL, 1966, Ital.)

OPERETTA½**   (1949, Ger.) 106m Wien-Film/Interfilm-Discina bw

Willy Forst (*Franz Jauner*), Maria Holst (*Marie Geistinger*), Dora Komar (*Emmi Krall*), Paul Hoerbiger (*Alexander Girardi*), Leo Slezak (*Franz von Suppe*), Edmund Schellhammer (*Johann Strauss*), Curd [Curt] Jurgens (*Karl Millocker*), Siegfried Breuner (*Count Hohenburg*), Alfred Neugebauer (*Count Esterhazy*).

A German musical with Forst as an operatic producer who becomes famous in Vienna. His rival is Holst, a famed opera singer, who was top of the hill in Vienna until Forst showed up. She leaves and returns later to fall in love with her rival. There are musical numbers from "Barber of Seville," "Beggar Student," "Bocaccio," "Fatinitza," "Gypsy Baron," and Strauss' "Die Fledermaus." (In German, English subtitles.)

d, Willy Forst; w, Forst, Exel Aggebrecht (based on a story by Forst); ph, Hans Schneeberger; md, Willy Schmidt-Gentner.

Musical   **(PR:A MPAA:NR)**

OPHELIA zero   (1964, Fr.) 100m Boreal/New Line bw

Alida Valli (*Claudia Lesurf*), Claude Cerval (*Adrien Lesurf*), Andre Jocelyn (*Yvan Lesurf*), Juliette Mayniel (*Lucie*), Robert Burnier (*Andre Lagrange*), Jean-Louis Maury (*Sparkos*), Sacha Briquet (*Gravedigger*), Liliane David (*Ginette*), Pierre Vernier (*Paul*), Serge Bento (*Francois*), Roger Carol (*Worker*), Laszlo Szabo (*Foolish Guard*), Henri Attal, Dominique Zardi, Jean-Marie Arnoux (*Guards*).

Released in Paris in 1962, OPHELIA is one of Chabrol's worst films and certainly one of the least flattering examples of the New Wave. Jocelyn, upset with his mother;s marriage to his uncle, patterns his revenge after Shakespeare's "Hamlet," an idea which occurs to him after seeing Olivier's version of the film. You would have thought Jocelyn would have learned a little something about acting by watching Olivier, but no. . . he turns in an atrocious performance, as does everyone else in the cast. OPHELIA is made to look even worse when measured against Chabrol's successes, although those are few and far between. (In French, English subtitles.)

d, Claude Chabrol; w, Chabrol, Martial Matthieu, Paul Gegauff; ph, Jean Rabier; m. Pierre Jansen; ed, Jacques Gaillard; md, Andre Girard.

Drama   **(PR:C MPAA:NR)**

OPIATE '67   (1967, Fr./Ital.) 87m Fair-Incei-Mountfluor Dicifrance/ McAbbe-Janus bw (LES MONSTRES; I MOSTRI; AKA: 15 FROM ROME)

Vittorio Gassman, Ugo Tognazzi, Marisa Merlini, Michele Mercier, Lando Buzzanca, Luisa Ruspoli, Marino Mase, Rick Tognazzi, Franco Castellani, Nino Nini, Angela Portaluri, Rika Dialina, Daniele Vargas, Riccardo Paladini, Carlo Ragno, Ugo Attanasio, Mario Laurentino, Maria Mannelli, Luciana Vincenzi, Salvatore Borgese, Francesco Caracciolo, Yacinto Yaria, Carlo Kechler, Mario Brega, Luia Modugno.

An episodic film about 15 so-called "monsters of modern Rome," with Gassman and Tognazzi playing most of these monsters. There is a film crew that uses an old woman and repeatedly throws her into a pool, a man who watches soap operas while his wife fools around with other men, a father who has a large family he cannot afford to support who gets his wife pregnant again so he will get a larger welfare check. There is a priest who goes on TV to talk about vanity, two unsuccessful womanizers, a young boy who kills his father, and more. They all act pathetic in large and small ways. Not an uplifting film, and it's hard to get involved in a film where everyone is a disgusting jerk.

p, Mario Cecci Gori; d, Dino Risi; w, Age and Scarpelli [Agenore Incrocci, Furio Scarpelli], Elio Petri, Ettore Scola, Ruggero Maccari, Risi; ph, Alfio Contini; m, Armando Trovajoli; ed, Maurizio Lucidi; art d, Ugo Pericoli.

Drama (PR:C MPAA:NR)

OPPOSITE SEX, THE** (1956) 115m MGM c

June Allyson (Kay Hilliard), Joan Collins (Crystal Allen), Dolores Gray (Sylvia Fowler), Ann Sheridan (Amanda Penrose), Ann Miller (Gloria Dell), Leslie Nielsen (Steve Hilliard), Jeff Richards (Buck Winston), Agnes Moorehead (Countess Lavaliere), Charlotte Greenwood (Lucy), Joan Blondell (Edith Potter), Sam Levene (Mike Pearl), Bill Goodwin (Howard Fowler), Alice Pearce (Olga), Barbara Jo Allen [Vera Vague] (Dolly), Sandy Descher (Debbie Hilliard), Carolyn Jones (Pat), Jerry Antes (Leading Male Dancer), Alan Marshal (Ted), Jonathan Hale (Phelps Potter), Harry James (Himself), Art Mooney (Himself), Dick Shawn (Singer), Jim Backus (Psychiatrist), Celia Lovsky (Lutsi), Harry McKenna (Hughie), Ann Moriss (Receptionist), Dean Jones (Assistant Stage Manager), Kay English (Aristocratic Woman), Gordon Richards (Butler), Barrie Chase, Ellen Ray (Specialty Dancers), Gail Bonney, Maxine Sermon, Jean Andren (Gossips), Bob Hopkins (Drunk in 21 Club), Janet Lake (Girl on Train), Jo Gilbert (Woman Attendant), Donald Dillaway (Box Office Man), Joe Karnes (Pianist), Juanita Moore (Maid), Vivian Marshal (Girl), Marc Wilder (Dancer), Marjorie Helen (Leg Model), Trio Ariston (Specialty Act).

This all-star cast could not please the critics in this musical which satirized women and how they hold on to their men. THE OPPOSITE SEX is a movie adaption of Clare Booth Luce's 1936 Broadway Hit, THE WOMEN and the film of the same title released in 1939, which starred Norma Shearer, Joan Crawford, Rosalind Russell, Mary Boland, Paulette Goddard, Joan Fontaine, and Marjorie Main. Producer Pasternak added music and men to the highly-successful play. Allyson plays a woman who almost loses her man to the sexy Collins. She learns if she wants to win her man back, she must adapt to the predatory ways of Collins. The rest of the cast provides comic relief as people in assorted states of marriage who help Allyson form her own ideas. Songs by Nicholas Brodszky, Sammy Cahn, George Stoll, and Ralph Freed include: "The Opposite Sex," "Dere's Yellow Gold on de Trees (De Banana)" (sung by Joan Collins), "A Perfect Love" (sung by June Allyson), "Rock and Roll Tumbleweed" (sung by Jeff Richards with Art Mooney), "Now! Baby, Now" (sung by Collins), "Jungle Red," "Young Man with a Horn" (sung by Allyson with Harry James).

p, Joseph Pasternak; d, David Miller; w, Fay and Michael Kanin (based on the play "The Women" by Clare Boothe [Luce]); ph, Robert Bronner (CinemaScope, Metrocolor); m, Nicholas Brodszky; ed, John McSweeney Jr.; md, Albert Sendrey, Skip Martin; art d, Cedric Gibbons, Daniel B. Cathcart; set d, Edwin B. Willis; cos, Helen Rose; spec eff, A. Arnold Gillespie, Warren Newcombe; ch, Robert Sidney; makeup, William Tuttle.

Musical/Comedy (PR:A MPAA:NR)

OPTIMIST, THE (SEE: BIG SHOT, THE, 1931)

OPTIMISTIC TRAGEDY, THE*½ (1964, USSR) 120m Mosfilm/ Artkino bw (OPTIMISTICHESKAYA TRAGEDIYA)

Margarita Volodina (The Commissar), Boris Andreyev ("The Boss"/"Vozhak"), Vyacheslav Tikhonov (Aleksey), Vsevolod Sanayev ("Husky"/"Siplyy"), Orko Byerninen (Vaynonen), Vsevolod Safonov (Bering), I. Zhevago (Boatswain), D. Netrebin ("Pock-marked"/"Ryaboy"), Grigoriy Mikhaylov (Old Sailor), P. Sobolevskiy (Ship's Doctor), Erast Garin (Vozhachok), Oleg Strizhenov (1st Officer), Gleb Strizhenov (2nd Officer), A. Glazyrin, V. Belokhvostik (Leaders), I. Vankov (Tattooed Sailor), V. Nedobrovo-Buzhinskaya (Woman in Black), V. Shulgin (Tall Sailor), I. Bychkov, I. Bondar, V. Grave, V. Demidovskiy, V. Zabavin, Ye. Zosimov, Yu. Kireyev, L. Knyazev, N. Kondratyev, P. Konoykhin, A. Milyukhin, V. Novikov, D. Orlovskiy, V. Prikhodko, A. Sakhnovskiy, S. Svashenko, V. Skuridin, A. Stroyev, N. Khryashchikov.

After the October Revolution in 1917, an officer and a woman are sent on a naval craft to convert the crew to communism. After some political propaganda and rhetoric, the crew becomes full-fledged Communists and the woman is killed by the White Army and becomes a martyr.

d, Samson Samsonov; w, Sofia Vishnevetskaya, Samsonov, N. Glagoleva (based on the play "Optimisticheskaya Tragediya" by Vsevolod Vitaliyevich Visnevskiy); ph, Vladimir Monakhov; m, Vasiliy Dekhteryov; ed, A. Kamagorova; md, V. Dudarova; art d, I. Novoderezhkin, Sergev Voronkov; cos, V. Perepyolov; spec eff, I. Felitsyn, A. Klimenko; m/l, M. Matusovskiy; makeup, S. Kalinin.

Drama (PR:A MPAA:NR)

OPTIMISTS, THE* (1973, Brit.) 110m Cheetah/PAR c (GB: THE OPTIMISTS OF NINE ELMS)

Peter Sellers (Sam), Donna Mullane (Liz), John Chaffey (Mark), David Daker (Bob Ellis), Marjorie Yates (Chrissie Ellis), Katyana Kass (Ellis Baby), Patricia Brake (Dog's Home Secretary), Michael Graham Cox (Park Keeper), Bruce Purchase (Park Policeman), Bernie Searl, Tommy Wright (Dustmen), Pat Ashton (Mrs. Bonini), Pat Becket, Daphne Lawson, Candyce Jane Brandl, Hilary Pritchard (Laundry Ladies).

Sellers is an old vaudevillian living in the London slums and making a meager living by performing with his dog on street corners. He befriends the young Mullane and Chaffey. Sellers instills in them the child-like dreams the two youngsters have lost living in poverty, and they give him companionship. An enjoyable, sentimental family film that makes no qualms about tugging at your heart strings. An under-rated film with an excellent performance by Sellers.

p, Adrian Gaye, Victor Lyndon; d, Anthony Simmons; w, Simmons, Tudor Gates (based on the novel The Optimists of Nine Elms by Simmons); ph, Larry Pizer (Eastmancolor); m, Lionel Bart; ed, John Jympson; md, George Martin; art d, Robert Cartwright.

Drama (PR:A MPAA:PG)

OPTIMISTS OF NINE ELMS, THE (SEE: OPTIMISTS, THE, 1973, Brit.)

OR POUR LES CESARS (SEE: GOLD FOR THE CAESARS, 1964, Fr./Ital.)

ORACLE, THE (SEE: HORSE'S MOUTH, THE 1953, Brit.)

ORAZIO E COURIAZI (SEE: DUEL OF CHAMPIONS, 1964, Ital./ Span.)

ORBITA MORTAL (SEE: MISSION STARDUST, 1968, Ital./Span.)

ORCA* (1977) 92m Dino De Laurentiis/PAR c (AKA: ORCA— KILLER WHALE)

Richard Harris (Capt. Nolan), Charlotte Rampling (Rachel Bedford, Oceanologist), Will Sampson (Umilak), Bo Derek (Annie), Keenan Wynn (Novak, First Mate), Robert Carradine (Ken), Scott Walker (Swain), Peter Hooten (Paul), Wayne Heffley (Priest), Vincent Gentile (Gas Station Attendant), Don "Red" Barry (Dock Worker).

Dino De Laurentiis' attempt to cash in on JAWS fails totally. Harris is a whaler who makes the mistake of killing the pregnant mate of a killer whale. The whale takes his revenge on everyone and everything associated with Harris. Harris, himself, becomes possessed with killing the whale and they have a laughable standoff on an ice flow. Bo Derek has her leg bitten off and Wynn is killed by the whale. Only Rampling is left as the ending credits come on in this non-exciting action/adventure film. Morricone, who does all of Sergio Leone's scores, is wasted in this waterlogged yawn where the whale outacts the arrogant Harris.

p, Luciano Vincenzoni, d, Michael Anderson; w, Vincenzoni, Sergio Donati; ph, Ted Moore, Vittorio Dragonetti (Panavision, Technicolor); m, Ennio Morricone; ed, Ralph E. Winters, John Bloom, Marion Rothman; prod d, Mario Garbuglia; md, Morricone; art d, Boris Juraga, Ferdinando Giovannoni; set d, Armando Scarano, John Godfrey; cos, Jost Jakob, Philippe Pickford; spec eff, Alex C. Weldon; m/l, "My Love, We Are One," Morricone, Carol Conners; makeup, Neville Smallwood; stunts, Romano Puppo, Emilio Messina.

Adventure **Cas.** (PR:C MPAA:PG)

ORCHESTRA WIVES** (1942) 98m FOX bw

George Montgomery (Bill Abbott), Ann Rutherford (Connie), Glenn Miller (Gene Morrison), Cesar Romero (Sinjin), Lynn Bari (Jaynie), Carole Landis (Natalie), Virginia Gilmore (Elsie), Mary Beth Hughes (Caroline), Nicholas Brothers (Specialty), Tamara Geva (Mrs. Beck), Frank Orth (Rex Willet), Grant Mitchell (Dr. Ward), Henry [Harry] Morgan (Cully Anderson), Jackie Gleason (Beck), Edith Evanson (Hilda), Alec Craig (Henry Fink), Tex Beneke, Marion Hutton, The Modernaires (Themselves).

There were many behind-the-scenes type pictures made in the 1940s but ORCHESTRA WIVES may be the finest example of the genre, due in great part to the presence of Glenn Miller (in his final appearance before that ill-fated flight over the English Channel. More about that later.) Rutherford is the new wife of musician Montgomery. He's touring with Miller's band, the couple meet at a one-nighter in Rutherford's small town, and fall in love, and she goes with the aggregation as it continues touring. The other wives in the band are old hands at the scene and none of them feels the Rutherford-Montgomery marriage can last, mainly due to the presence of band singer Bari, who is a sensuous type who likes other women's men. Bari (whose tunes were looped by vocalist Pat Friday) has her eye on Montgomery and won't stop until she gets him. The wives in the band cause some hassling between the players and the group is on the verge of breaking up upon return from a West Coast engagement to the Midwest. It all ends happily as dapper Romero, the band's pianist, gets the couple and the band together. The picture swings with the Miller music from start to finish, all tunes having been written by those aces of movie tunes, Harry Warren and Mack Gordon. The songs include: "Serenade in Blue," "People Like You and Me," "At Last," "I've Got a Gal in Kalamazoo," and "That's Sabotage." When interviewed by your editors, delicious Rutherford (the long-time wife of producer William Dozier) said that she'd been under contract at MGM for years (she was Andy Hardy's heartthrob) and was due to start a picture for that studio called SEVEN SWEETHEARTS (based on Pride and Prejudice) but she had been on a War Bond tour in Chicago and came home with a case of German measles so she couldn't go to work. MGM topper Mayer thought she was faking it because she'd told Mayer earlier that she didn't like the tiny role she'd been given so he loaned her to Zanuck for this picture. She further said that Jackie Gleason (he played the bass man in the band) was a delight on the set and kept everyone laughing between takes. It was Gleason's third effort. According to Rutherford, Glenn Miller was the "sweetest, loveliest, and dearest gentleman" she'd met in years. He was never impressed with himself and his huge success, and was one of the boys all the way. Landis does a small role but she had already peaked as far as the studio was concerned. She committed suicide in 1948 when her lover, Rex Harrison, married Lilli Palmer. Miller died in a crash that had been mysterious until late in 1985 when some British pilots came forward to explain it. Miller was on a plane over the English Channel and flying under a squadron of bombers that had been told to jettison all of their explosives because they couldn't deliver them to their targets due to weather problems. Miller perished in the mistake. A great loss to anyone who loves to hear melodies and loved his unique brand of music.

p, William LeBaron; d, Archie Mayo; w, Karl Tunberg, Darrel Ware (based on a story by James Prindle); ph, Lucien Ballard; ed, Robert Bischoff; md, Alfred Newman; art d, Richard Day, Joseph C. Wright.

Musical (PR:A MPAA:NR)

ORCHIDS TO YOU**

(1935) 74m FOX bw

John Boles (*Thomas Bentley*), Jean Muir (*Camellia Rand*), Charles Butterworth (*Teddy Stuyvesant*), Ruthelma Stevens (*Evelyn Bentley*), Harvey Stephens (*George Draper*), Arthur Lake (*Joe*), Spring Byington (*Alice Draper*), John Qualen (*Smith*), Patricia Farr (*Polly*), Arthur Treacher (*Morton*), Sidney Toler (*Nick Corsini*).

Muir owns a flower shop in a hotel and Boles is an attorney who is trying to kick her out. When she discovers that another man is sending Boles' wife flowers, she refuses to testify so as not to break his heart. Muir is tossed into jail for 10 days for contempt of court. When she gets out she finds herself in Boles' arms. Some good moments, but the story does not hold up as a whole.

p, Robert T. Kane; d, William A. Seiter; w, Howard Estabrook, William Hurlbut, Bartlett Cormack, Glenn Tryon (based on a story by Gordon Rigby, Robert Dillon); ph, Merritt B. Gerstad; md, Arthur Lange.

Drama (PR:A MPAA:NR)

ORDERED TO LOVE**

(1963, Ger.) 82m Alfa-Film-FTR/ Transocean bw (LEBENSBORN)

Maria Perschy (*Doris Korff*), Joachim Hansen (*Klaus Steinbach*), Harry Meyen (*Dr. Hagen*), Emmerich Schrenk (*Meyer Westroff*), Joachim Mock (*Kempe*), Marisa Mell (*Erica Meuring*), Gert Gunter Hoffmann (*Mertens*), Waldemar Tepel (*Hellmich*), Lothar Mann (*Koss*), Michael Welchberger (*Guhne*), Helmut Lange (*Nietermann*), Eva Bubat (*Irmgard*), Rosemarie Kirstein, Renate Kuster, Hannalore Juterbock, Birgitt Bergen, Elke Eichwede, Dinah Berger.

Perschy is one of many women ordered to participate in a Nazi program to breed the master race during WW II. The men are chosen from soldiers and the SS. The head of the camp, Meyen, falls in love with Perschy. She falls in love with Hansen, who has taken the identity of a dead SS man to avoid his own execution. The two attempt to escape to Switzerland, but Hansen is killed and Perschy is spared only because she is pregnant. The baby is killed after it is born, and Perschy escapes the camp during a bombing raid.

p, Wolf Brauner; d, Werner Klingler; w, Will Berthold, Jack Dunn Trop (based on stories by Berthold); ph, Igor Oberberg; m, Gerhard Becker; art d, Paul Markwitz, Max Vorberg.

Drama (PR:O MPAA:NR)

ORDERS, THE***

(1977, Can.) 107m Les Productions Prisma/ Films 13 bw/c (LES ORDRES)

Jean Lapointe (*Taxi Driver*), Helene Loiselle (*Wife*), Claude Gauthier (*Lavoie*), Louis Forestier (*Social Worker*), Guy Provost (*Doctor*).

This film is based on the events that took place after the Liberation Front of Quebec took hostages in 1970. Documentary filmmaker Brault uses his skills to bring a realistic feel to the story. The government called for martial law and 450 people were arrested for no reason and without warrants. Most of the film deals with the cruel and inhuman way these people were treated in prison. The police would break into houses and drag people to jail and then subject them to mental torture. A strong film that shows how dangerous and out-of-control a police state can become.

d, Michael Brault; w, Brault, Guy Defresne; ph, Brault; m, Philippe Gagon.

Drama (PR:C-O MPAA:NR)

ORDERS ARE ORDERS*½

(1959, Brit.) 78m Group 3/BL bw

Brian Reece (*Capt. Harper*), Margot Grahame (*Wanda Sinclair*), Raymond Huntley (*Col. Bellamy*), Sidney James (*Ed Waggermeyer*), Tony Hancock (*Lt. Wilfred Cartroad*), Peter Sellers (*Pvt. Goffin*), Clive Morton (*Gen. Grahame-Foxe*), June Thorburn (*Veronica Bellamy*), Maureen Swanson (*Joanne Delamere*), Peter Martyn (*Lt. Broke*), Bill Fraser (*Pvt. Slee*), Edward Lexy (*Capt. Ledger*), Barry Mackay (*RSM Benson*), Donald Pleasence (*Lance-Cpl. Martin*), Eric Sykes (*Pvt. Waterhouse*), Reginald Hearne, Barry Steele, Maureen Pryor, Mark Baker, Stephen Vercoe, Donald Hewlett, Michael Trubshawe, David Green, Harold Ayer, Leonard Williams, Peter Haig.

A Hollywood film unit invades two British army barracks when the commanding officer is away. The officer suddenly turns up, putting a slight delay in the filming until the makers are able to charm him, using a pretty starlet, voluptuous blonde Grahame, into allowing them to continue. However, when an army big shot decides to make a snap inspection, the film unit is unable to explain its reasons for being in the camp. Except for a couple of decent comic performances, the good cast, including both Peter Sellers and Donald Pleasence in early roles, are wasted by the film's haphazard construction.

p, Donald Taylor; d, David Paltenghi; w, Taylor, Geoffrey Orme, Eric Sykes (based on the play by Ian Hay, Anthony Armstrong); ph, Arthur Grant.

Comedy (PR:A MPAA:NR)

ORDERS IS ORDERS***

(1934, Brit.) 62m GAU bw

Charlotte Greenwood (*Wanda, Ed's Assistant*), James Gleason (*Ed Waggermeyer, Hollywood Director*), Cyril Maude (*Col. Bellamy*), Finlay Currie (*Dave*), Percy Parsons (*Zingbaum*), Cedric Hardwicke (*Brigadier*), Donald Calthrop (*Pavey*), Ian Hunter (*Capt. Harper*), Jane Carr (*Patricia Bellamy*), Ray Milland (*Dashwood*), Edwin Lawrence (*Quartermaster*), Eliot Makeham (*Pvt. Slee*), Hay Plumb (*Pvt. Goffin*), Wally Patch (*Regimental Sergeant Major*), Jane Cornell (*Starlet*), Glennis Lorimer, Sydney Keith.

A funny satire on Hollywood filmmaking that was adapted from a series of plays

about the military. A Yank director, Gleason, is using a British army barracks and soldiers for a Foreign Legion film. A lot of the comedy comes from the filmmaking efforts and Gleason's inept efforts to get the film shot and "in the can." Hardwicke plays a brigadier who tells Gleason his portrayal of the military is not correct. Gleason continually answers: "You know, and I know, but they don't know in Kansas City." Gleason not only wants the barracks and soldiers at his disposal but the whole British army as well. Greenwood is his assistant and dresses exactly as Gleason does. No one realizes the American director does not have permission to use the British soldiers. Maude plays the British colonel, and Carr is his daughter. The satire keeps falling into farce, but it is still funny. The film was remade in 1954 with a more grammatically correct title, ORDERS ARE ORDERS.

p, Michael Balcon; d, Walter Forde; w, Leslie Arliss, Sidney Gilliat; James Gleason (based on a play by Ian Hay, Anthony Armstrong); ph, Glen MacWilliams.

Comedy (PR:A MPAA:NR)

ORDERS TO KILL**

(1958, Brit.) 93m Lynx/United Motion Picture bw

Eddie Albert (*Maj. MacMahon*), Paul Massie (*Gene Summers*), Lillian Gish (*Mrs. Summers*), James Robertson Justice (*Naval Commander*), Irene Worth (*Leonie*), Leslie French (*Marcel Lafitte*), John Crawford (*Maj. Kimball*), Lionel Jeffries (*Interrogator*), Sandra Dorne (*Blonde*), Nicholas Phipps (*Lecturer Lieutenant*), Anne Blake (*Mme. Lafitte*), Miki Iveria (*Louise*), Lillie Bea Gifford (*Mauricette*), Launce Maraschal (*Gen. Nolan*), Robert Henderson (*Col. Snyder*), William Greene (*Mitchell*), Selma Vaz Dias (*Patronne*), Ralph Nossek (*Psychiatrist*), Ann Walford (*F.A.N.Y.*), Boris Ranevsky (*Old German Officer*), Jacques Brunius (*Comdr. Morand*), Henzie Raeburn, Peter La Trobe, Philip Bond, Michael Kelly, Denyse MacPherson, Frederick Wendhausen, Bernard Rebel, Geoffrey Hibbert, Sam Kydd, Andrea Malandrinos.

Massie is a grounded American pilot during WW II who goes into the espionage branch. He is trained to kill a Paris lawyer who is suspected of giving the Nazis names and locations of radio operators. Massie trains vigorously under the supervision of Justice and then has second thoughts about his mission. After he meets his target, French, his mission does not seem so clear-cut and he begins to wonder if the lawyer is really guilty. Even with his doubts, Massie follows through on his assignment and then learns the man he killed was innocent. An engaging psychological study of the effect killing, even in the name of justice, can have on a person.

p, Anthony Havelock-Allan; d, Anthony Asquith; w, Paul Dehn, George St. George (based on a story by Donald C. Downes); ph, Desmond Dickinson; m, Benjamin Frankel; ed, Gordon Hales; art d, John Howell.

War Drama (PR:A MPAA:NR)

ORDET**½

(1957, Den.) 126m Palladium/Kingsley International bw (AKA: THE WORD)

Henrik Malberg (*Morten Borgen*), Emil Hass Christensen (*Mikkel Borgen*), Preben Lerdorff-Rye (*Johannes Borgen*), Cay Kristiansen (*Anders Borgen*), Birgitte Federspiel (*Inger, Mikkel's Wife*), Ejner Federspiel (*Peter Skraedder*), Ove Rud (*Pastor*), Ann Elisabeth Rud (*Maren Borgen, Mikkel's Daughter*), Susanne Rud (*Lilleinger Borgen, Mikkel's Daughter*), Gerda Nielsen (*Anne Skraedder*), Sylvia Eckhausen (*Kirstine Skraedder*), Henry Skjaer (*Doctor*), Hanne Agesen (*Karen, a Servant*), Edith Thrane (*Mette Maren*).

An inspirational drama about the Christian faith which comes from Dreyer (THE PASSION OF JOAN OF ARC, 1928), perhaps the most profoundly religious of cinema directors. Taking place in a staunch God-fearing village, ORDET tells the story of Malberg and his three sons—Christensen, who is filled with religious doubts; Kristiansen, who is involved in a romance that is tarnished by differences of faith; and the central character, Lerdorff-Rye, who believes himself to be Jesus Christ. Lerdorff-Rye's extreme devotion is passed off as madness until he is visited by the Holy Spirit. This miraculous happening is followed by his resurrecting Christensen's dead wife at her funeral. By the film's end, Christensen (his wife once again at his side) has returned to the faith, while Kristiansen is given permission to marry the girl he desires. Solely because of its subject matter, ORDET is an overwhelmingly intellectual experience. Dreyer, however, successfully simplifies not only the religious and philosophical aspects of the picture, but also its visual style (the film contains only 114 shots in 126 minutes), resulting in a meditative, faith-stirring mood. A film which shows Dreyer's superb control of *mise-en-scene*, and one not to be missed by fans of THE PASSION OF JOAN OF ARC. Dreyer had hoped that Poul Schierbeck would write the music for ORDET, but Schierbeck died before he could take on the assignment officially. Among his papers Dreyer found several themes he thought Schierbeck may have composed with ORDET in mind, and so he used them in the film. The playwright, Munk, was a clergyman as well as a dramatist who wrote this play in two days after witnessing the death of one of his young parishioners in childbirth. Known all over Scandinavia for the strength of his belief in Christianity, he was also a target of the Nazis during their occupation of his country. And, fatal irony, the theme of his great ORDET—the struggle between faith and its opposite, life-hostile fanaticism—was present at his death. On the night of January 4, 1944, he received the nightmarish knock on the door by a heinous Nazi. The next day his lifeless body was found in a ditch. (In Danish; English subtitles.)

p,d&w, Carl Theodor Dreyer (based on the play by Kaj Munk); ph, Henning Bendtsen; m, Poul Schierbeck; ed, Edith Schussel; art d, Erik Aaes.

Religious Drama (PR:A-C MPAA:NR)

ORDINARY PEOPLE***½

(1980) 124m Wildwood/PAR c

Donald Sutherland (*Calvin*), Mary Tyler Moore (*Beth*), Judd Hirsch (*Berger*), Timothy Hutton (*Conrad*), M. Emmet Walsh (*Swim Coach*), Elizabeth McGovern (*Jeannine*), Dinah Manoff (*Karen*), Fredric Lehne (*Lazenby*), James B. Sikking (*Ray*), Basil Hoffman (*Sloan*), Quinn Redeker (*Ward*), Mariclare Costello

(Audrey), Meg Mundy (Grandmother), Elizabeth Hubbard (Ruth), Adam Baldwin (Stillman), Richard Whiting (Grandfather), Scott Doebler (Bucky).

This picture just about swept everything the year it was released, winning the Oscar for Best Movie, Best Direction, Best Screenplay, and Best Supporting Actor. Hirsch and Moore were also nominated. It was a nice movie but not a great one and with a different cast it would have been a typical TV picture. The box office returns were astounding when one considers that this was an understated family drama which no one thought would capture the public's fancy to the tune of more than $60 million in film rentals. Hutton is a disturbed young man who has just attempted suicide because he feels guilty about not having saved his brother in a sailing accident. The boy drowned and Hutton wears that mantle of remorse. His parents are Sutherland and Moore. He is a conservative man and she is an ice princess, and Hutton thinks they have always loved the dead brother more and he cannot elicit any compassion from either one, so when the domestic situation becomes explosive, they send him to see psychiatrist Hirsch. Hutton and McGovern, a classmate at their suburban Chicago school, have a mild romance in between the psychiatric sequences, while Moore's dispassionate manner keeps her son, and, later, her husband, at arm's length. By the time the picture ends, Hutton has been relieved of his anxiety and Moore and Sutherland are about to part, as he has become increasingly hostile to her aloof attitude. Moore's character is so unsympathetic and so accurate that we hate her all the way through and don't even feel sorry when her husband leaves. She lost her own son about the same time as this picture was being made and probably plumbed her emotional depths for the role. There is so little cinema in the film that it could have been a two-set play just as easily. Lots of gratuitous rough language gives it our O rating.

p, Ronald L. Schwary; d, Robert Redford; w, Alvin Sargent (based on the novel by Judith Guest); ph, John Bailey (Technicolor); ed, Jeff Kanew; art d, Phillip Bennett, Michael Riva; set d, Jerry Wunderlich, William Fosser; cos, Bernie Pollack.

Drama   Cas.   (PR:O MPAA:R)

OREGON PASSAGE   (1958) 80m AA c

John Ericson (Lt. Niles Ord), Lola Albright (Sylvia Dane), Toni Gerry (Little Deer), Edward Platt (Roland Dane), Judith Ames (Marion), H. M. Wynant (Black Eagle), Jon Shepodd (Lt. Baird Dobson), Walter Barnes (Sgt. Jed Erschick), Paul Fierro (Nato), Harvey Stephens (Capt. Boyson).

A routine western with Ericson wanting to capture an Indian chief and finding that he must battle more with his commander, Platt. Platt thinks that Ericson has had an affair with his wife, Albright, years ago and this affects Platt's decision making. After two cavalry patrols are wiped out, Albright is captured by Indians. Platt goes after her and both of them are killed. Ericson organizes his men, repels an attack on the fort, and kills the Indian chief in hand-to-hand combat.

p, Lindsley Parsons; d, Paul Landres; w, Jack DeWitt (adapted from the novel by Gordon D. Shirreffs); ph, Ellis Carter (CinemaScope, DeLuxe Color); m, Paul Dunlap; ed, Maury Wright.

Western   (PR:A MPAA:NR)

OREGON TRAIL, THE½   (1936) 59m REP bw

John Wayne (Capt. John Delmont), Ann Rutherford (Anne Ridgley), Joseph Girard (Col. Delmont), Yakima Canutt (Tom Richards), Frank Rice (Red), E. H. Calvert (Jim Ridgley), Ben Hendricks Jr. (Maj. Harris), Harry Harvey (Tim), Fern Emmett (Minnie the Old Maid), Jack Rutherford (Benton), Marian Farrell (Sis), Roland Ray (Markey), Gino Corrado (Forrenza), Edward J. LeSaint (Gen. Ferguson), Octavio Giraud (Don Miguel).

A remake of the BIG TRAIL (the film that gave Wayne his first starring role) which was just another of the Republic Wayne westerns. Wayne seeks revenge against the men who killed his father. Rutherford is the Duke's love interest in this nondescript western.

p, Paul Malvern; d, Scott Pembroke; w, Jack Natteford, Robert Emmett, Lindsley Parsons (based on a story by Emmett, Parsons); ph, Gus Peterson; ed, Carl Pierson.

Western   (PR:A MPAA:NR)

OREGON TRAIL*½   (1945) 55m REP bw

Sunset Carson (Sunset), Peggy Stewart (Jill Layton), Frank Jaquet (George Layton), Si Jenks (Andy), Mary Carr (Granny Layton), Lee Shumway (Capt. Street), Bud Geary (Fletch), Kenne Duncan (Johnny Slade), Steven Winston (Pendleton), Tex Terry (Moyer), Tom London (Marshal), Earle Hodgins (Judge), Monte Hale, Rex Lease (Cowboys), John Merton, Cactus Mack, Bud Osborne.

Carson leads a wagon train out west and crushes Duncan's plans to build a personal empire. This was Carson's third top-billed western for Republic and Mary Carr, silent film star and mother of the director, had a small part. She lived to the ripe old age of 99 years.

p, Bennett Cohen; d, Thomas Carr; w, Betty Burbridge (based on a story by Frank Gruber); ph, Bud Thackery; ed, Richard L. Van Enger; md, Richard Cherwin; art d, Gano Chittenden.

Western   Cas.   (PR:A MPAA:NR)

OREGON TRAIL, THE**   (1959) 86m FOX c

Fred MacMurray (Neal Harris), William Bishop (Capt. George Wayne), Nina Shipman (Prudence Cooper), Gloria Talbott (Shona Hastings), Henry Hull (Seton), John Carradine (Zachariah Garrison), John Dierkes (Gabe Hastings), Elizabeth Patterson (Maria Cooper), James Bell (Jeremiah Cooper), Ralph Sanford (Mr. Decker), Tex Terry (Brizzard), Arvo Ojala (Ellis), Roxene Wells (Flossie Shoemaker), Gene N. Fowler (Richard Cooper), John Slosser (Johnny), Sherry Spalding (Lucy), Ollie O'Toole (James G. Bennett), Ed Wright (Jesse), Oscar Beregi (Ralph Clayman), Addison Richards (President James K. Polk), Lumsden Hare (British Ambassador).

MacMurray is a New York reporter sent to cover the opening of the Oregon territory in 1846. The reporter is investigating whether President James Polk is sending troops under the disguise of pioneers to hold the land. MacMurray is captured by Indians and escapes with the help of Indian maiden Talbott. He quits his newspaper job, helps the soldiers fight the Indians, and settles down with Talbott in the new territory. A routine western directed by Gene Fowler, Jr., who also directed I WAS A TEENAGE WEREWOLF and I MARRIED A MONSTER FROM OUTER SPACE. This was the fifth movie called either OREGON TRAIL or THE OREGON TRAIL. Universal made a silent version in 1923 starring Art Acord who reportedly committed suicide while in a drunken stupor. Next, in 1936 Paul Malvern produced a John Wayne film for Republic called OREGON TRAIL. In 1939, Universal again picked up THE OREGON TRAIL and turned it into a 15-chapter photoplay. Ford Beebe directed John Mack Brown in this version. Republic recycled the name THE OREGON TRAIL in 1945. This version featured Sunset Carson. And Twentieth Century-Fox appropriated the name for this film.

p, Richard Einfeld; d, Gene Fowler Jr.; w, Louis Vittes, Fowler (based on a story by Vittes); ph, Kay Norton (CinemaScope, DeLuxe Color); m, Paul Dunlap; ed, Betty Steinberg; m/l, "Ballad of the Oregon Trail," Dunlap, Charles Devlan, "Never Alone," Will Miller; makeup, Del Acerdo.

Western   (PR:A MPAA:NR)

OREGON TRAIL SCOUTS**   (1947) 58m REP bw

Allan Lane (Red Ryder), Bobby Blake (Little Beaver), Martha Wentworth (The Duchess), Roy Barcroft (Hunter), Emmett Lynn (Bear Trap), Edmund Cobb (Jack), Earle Hodgins (Judge), Edward Cassidy (Bliss), Frank Lackteen (Running Fox), Billy Cummings (Barking Squirrel), Jack Kirk (Stage Coach Driver), Jack O'Shea, Chief Yowlachie.

Lane was the third actor to play the hero in the Red Ryder series, replacing "Wild Bill" Elliott who took over for Don "Red" Barry. This installment tells how Lane got his sidekick, Blake. Lane sets up a treaty with the Indians so that he can trap fur on their land. Bad guy Barcroft kidnaps the Indian chief's grandson, Blake, so that he can secure the fur trapping rights for himself. Lane saves the day with fists and guns blazing, and the young Blake joins up with the hero. (See RED RYDER series, Index.)

p, Sidney Picker; d, R. G. Springsteen; w, Earle Snell (based on a story by Snell, from the comic strip by Fred Harman); ph, Alfred Keller; ed, Harold R. Minter; md, Mort Glickman; art d, Paul Youngblood, set d, John McCarthy, Jr., George Milo; spec eff, Howard Lydecker, Theodore Lydecker.

Western   Cas.   (PR:A MPAA:NR)

ORFEU NEGRO   (SEE: BLACK ORPHEUS, 1959, Fr./Ital./Braz.)

ORGANIZATION, THE**   (1971) 105m UA c

Sidney Poitier (Lt. Virgil Tibbs), Barbara McNair (Valerie Tibbs), Gerald S. O'Loughlin (Lt. Jack Pecora), Sheree North (Gloria Morgan), Fred Beir (Bob Alford), Allen Garfield [Goorwitz] (Benjy), Bernie Hamilton (Lt. Jessop), Raul Julia (Juan Mendoza), Ron O'Neal (Joe Peralez), James A. Watson, Jr. (Stacy Baker), Charles H. Gray (Night Watchman Morgan), Jarion Monroe (Larry French), Dan Travanty (Sgt. Chassman), Billy "Green" Bush (Dave Thomas), Maxwell Gail, Jr. (Rudy), Ross Hagen (Chet), Paul Jenkins (Tony), John Lasell (Zach Mills), Lani Miyazaki (Annie Sekido), Garry Walberg (Capt. Stacy), Demond Wilson (Charlie Blossom), George Spell (Andy Tibbs), Wanda Spell (Ginny Tibbs), Graham Jarvis (William Martin), Colin Adams (Dan), Johnny Haymer (John Bishop).

Poitier poorly recreates the character from the movies IN THE HEAT OF THE NIGHT and THEY CALL ME MR. TIBBS, in which he starred as homicide detective, Virgil Tibbs. He becomes involved with a group of young people who are trying to clean up a local drug ring. The group breaks into a furniture warehouse which is fronting the drug operation and the store manager is killed. The group gets in contact with Poitier and tells him they were the ones that broke into the warehouse, but they didn't kill anyone. Poitier risks his job and follows the group without reporting it to his superiors. Soon after, Poitier is suspended from the police force, but this enables him to make the moves to crack the drug ring.

p, Walter Mirisch; d, Don Medford, w, James R. Webb (based on a character created by John Ball); ph, Joseph Biroc (DeLuxe Color); m, Gil Melle; ed, Ferris Webster; prod d, James F. McGuire; art d, George B. Chan; set d, Marvin March; cos, Angela Alexander, Wes Jefferies, John K. Lemons; spec eff, Sass Bedig, Norman O. Skeete; makeup, Del Armstrong.

Crime Drama   Cas.   (PR:C MPAA:GP)

ORGANIZER, THE***   (1964, Fr./Ital./Yugo.) 126m Lux-Vides-Mediterranee-Avala/CD bw (LES CAMARADES; I COMPAGNI; AKA: THE STRIKERS)

Marcello Mastroianni (Prof. Sinigaglia), Renato Salvaroti (Raoul), Annie Girardot (Niobe), Gabriella Giorgelli (Adele), Bernard Blier (Martinetti), Folco Lulli (Pautasso), Francois Perier (Maestro Di Meo), Vittorio Sanipoli (Baudet), Giuseppe Cadeo (Cenerone), Elvira Tonelli (Cesarina), Giamopiero Albertini (Porro), Pippi Starnazza (Bergamasco), Pippo Mosca (Cerioni), Franco Ciolli (Omero), Raffaella Carra (Bianca), Antonio Casa Monica (Arro), Enzo Casini (Antonio), Kenneth Kove (Luigi), Mario Pisu (Manager), Gino Manganello (Uncle Spartaco), Edda Ferronao (Maria), Anna Di Silvio (Gesummina), Antonio Di Silvio (Pietrino), Sara Simoni (Cenerone's Wife), Piero Traiannoni (Bookkeeper), Anna Glori (Signora Cravetto), Bruno Scipioni, Anselmo Silvio, Giuseppe Marchetti, Fred Borgognoni, Giulio Bosetti.

A coproduction of several companies, this powerful labor film won a number of awards, including four at the Argentina Film Festival in 1964. Workers are toiling ungodly hours at a Turin textile plant in the late 1800s. A worker is hurt due to weariness and three of his fellows, Tonelli, Lulli, and Blier, approach the company's bosses for some relief, but Sanipoli, the foreman, spurns them. The workers respond by planning to leave work an hour before quitting time in retaliation. Lulli gives the order, but Sanipoli won't let the workers go and Lulli is rewarded for his independence attempt by being suspended fron his job for a fortnight with no wages. The workers turn to Mastroianni, a professor who has come to stay in Turin with his pal, Perier, a schoolteacher. Mastroianni has made some political noises and he is semi-hiding but surfaces long enough to help the workers plan a strike. The bosses agree to cease Lulli's suspension and erase any fine but that's all they'll do, so a strike occurs. Management calls in the goons, but the angered workers meet the scabs at the train station and violence follows, during which Lulli is killed. Newspapers get the story and it becomes a cause celebre; then the commissioner of Turin's police tells the scabs that they must depart the city before any more deaths occur. Management, realizing that Mastroianni is behind it all, uses coercion to get the police to arrest the professor. He escapes the long arm of the law by staying with Girardot, a local lady of the evening. Sanipoli manages to talk Blier into going back to the mill, saying that it would actually be a good thing and would convince the others. At that, Mastroianni emerges from Girardot's apartment and makes an impassioned speech that galvanizes the other mill employees. As one, they descend on the factory where they are met by waiting army men who fire guns and a young teenager is killed. Mastroianni is taken in by the police and the workers go back to their labors. In the end, nothing much has happened to the workers' plight, but they have made their presence felt and unionism is the next step. Excellent film with good performances, although 20 minutes could have been cut out easily. Directed by the man who did what may be the best Italian comedy ever, BIG DEAL ON MADONNA STREET. (In Italian; English subtitles.)

p, Franco Cristaldi; d, Mario Monicelli; w, Age, Scarpelli, Monicelli; ph, Giuseppe Rotunno; m, Carlo Rustichelli; ed, Ruggero Mastroianni; md, Pierluigi Urbini; art d, Mario Garbuglia; cos, Piero Tosi; English subtitles, Herman G. Weinberg.

Drama   **(PR:A MPAA:NR)**

ORGY OF BLOOD   (SEE: BRIDES OF BLOOD, 1968)

ORGY OF THE DEAD zero   (1965) 82m Astra/F.O.G.-Crest c

Criswell (The Emperor), Pat Barringer (Shirley/Gold), Fawn Silver (Black Ghoul), William Bates (Bob), Louis Ojena (The Mummy), John Andrews (The Wolfman), Rod Lindeman (Giant), John Bealy (Detective), Arlene Spooner (Nurse), Colleen O'Brien (The Street Walker), Barbra Norton (The Skeleton), Mickey Jines (Hawaiian), Nadejda Dobrev (The Slave), Dene Starnes (The Zombie), Texas Starr (The Cat), Bunny Glaser (Indian), Rene De Beau (Seven Veils), Stephanie Jones (The Skull).

After his famous shockers GLEN OR GLENDA and PLAN 9 FROM OUTER SPACE, Wood went on to write this film that used professional strippers as the stars. Plot involves a writer and her fiance who decide to visit a cemetery one night to gather material for her next book. They run into the Master of the Dead, Criswell, and his partner the princess of Darkness, Silver, performing a ceremony to judge recently deceased sinners. The two are tied up and forced to watch the ceremony that includes a Main Street prowler who robbed then murdered her clients, a bride who killed her husband and now must spend eternity with his skeleton, and a cat lover who is turned into a cat, to name just a few of the many colorful characters. In the end, Silver decides to take the fiance as her personal slave, but he is saved from this fate by the morning sun which returns the dead to dust. Features famous strippers Texas Starr and Bunny Glaser.

p&d, A. C. Stephen; w, Edward Davis Wood, Jr. (based on the novel by Wood); ph, Robert Caramico; art d, Robert Lathrop; cos, Robert Darieux; ch, Mark Desmond.

Horror   **(PR:O MPAA:NR)**

ORGY OF THE GOLDEN NUDES   (SEE: HONEYMOON OF HORROR, 1964)

ORIENT EXPRESS*½   (1934) 71m FOX bw

Heather Angel (Coral Musker, Dancer), Norman Foster (Carlton Myatt, Date Merchant), Ralph Morgan (Dr. Czinner, Anarchist), Herbert Mundin (Mr. Peters), Una O'Connor (Mrs. Peters), Irene Ware (Janet Pardoe), Dorothy Burgess (Mabel Warren), William Irving (Conductor), Roy D'Arcy (Crook), Lisa Gord, Perry Ivins, Fredrik Vogeding, Marc Lobell.

The story in this picture revolves around two main characters, Angel as a dancer on her way to an engagement, and Morgan as a revolutionary returning in disguise to raise money for his cause. The production is clean and the scenery well done, with Hollywood as a stand-in for what is supposed to be Europe, but the characters never develop fully, leaving the viewer with just a surface insight into their personalities.

p, Sol M. Wurtzel; d, Paul Martin; w, William Conselman, Carl Hovey, Oscar Levant, Martin (based on a novel by Graham Greene); ph, George Schneiderman.

Drama   **(PR:A MPAA:NR)**

ORIENTAL DREAM   (SEE: KISMET, 1944)

ORIGINAL OLD MOTHER RILEY, THE   (SEE: OLD MOTHER RILEY, 1937, Brit.)

O'RILEY'S LUCK   (SEE: ROSE BOWL, 1936)

ORLAK, THE HELL OF FRANKENSTEIN*   (1960, Mex.) 103m Filmadora Independiente/COL bw (ORLAK, EL INFIERNO DE FRANKENSTEIN)

Joaquin Cordero (Jaime/Orlak), Andres Soler (Dr. Frankenstein), Rosa de Castilla

(Estela), Irma Dorantes (Elvira), Armando Calvo, Pedro de Aguillon, David Reynoso, Carlos Ancira, Carlos Nieto.

A Mexican version of the Frankenstein story has Dr. Frankenstein (Soler) being sprung from jail by ex-convict Cordero. The con wants to use Soler's creature, also played by Cordero, to reap revenge on all the people responsible for his incarceration. The creature's face is melted when the doctor revives him with 100,000 electrical volts, so he is forced to wear a metal can on his head. Plot ends with the monster walking off with Cordero's love, Dorantes. Director Baledon was a Mexican matinee idol in the 1940s, famous for filming remakes of American films, including Ford's MY DARLING CLEMENTINE, retitled MI ADORADA CLEMENTINA, in 1953.

p&d, Rafael Baledon; w, Alfredo Ruanova, Carlos Enrique Taboada; ph, Fernando Alvarez Garces Colin.

Horror   **(PR:C-O MPAA:NR)**

O'ROURKE OF THE ROYAL MOUNTED   (SEE: SASKATCHEWAN, 1954)

ORPHAN OF THE PECOS**   (1938) 57m Victory bw

Tom Tyler (Rayburn), Jeanne Martel (Ann), Marjorie Beebe (Mrs. Barnes), Howard Bryant (Pete), Forrest Taylor (Brand), Charles "Slim" Whitaker (Sheriff), Ted Lorch (Mathews), Roger Williams (Slim), Lafe McKee (Gelbert), John Elliott.

Tyler searches for the man who murdered Martel's father and robbed his safe. He's successful thanks to the aid of ventriloquist Lorch, who throws his voice which makes the killer confess. Martel, as the standard romantic interest, was Tyler's real-life wife. A minimum of talk and a maximum of action.

p&d, Sam Katzman; w, Basil Dickey; ph, Bill Hyer; ed, Holbrook Todd.

Western   **(PR:A MPAA:NR)**

ORPHAN OF THE RING   (SEE: KID FROM KOKOMO, THE, 1939)

ORPHAN OF THE WILDERNESS½**   (1937, Aus.) 85m Cinesound/British Empire bw

Gwen Munro (Margot), Brian Abbott (Tom Henton), Ethel Saker (Mrs. Henton), Harry Abdy (Shorty McGee), Joe Valli (Andrew McMeeker), Ron Whelan (Mell), Sylvia Kellaway (Nell), June Munro (June), Edna Montgomery (Jill).

Kangaroos steal the scene in this picture about a kangaroo left abandoned in the wilderness to fend for itself. Finally it is taken in by a kindly farmer who teaches it how to box. But when a group of shearers tease the animal during the farmer's absence, the kangaroo almost tears one of the men to pieces. The farmer decides that the animal might be better off with the circus his girl friend belongs to and sells it to a trainer there. But the poor animal is neglected and so, nearly driven mad with thirst and hunger, it breaks out of its cage to freedom. Upon learning of the trainer's brutality, the farmer rescues the animal from the circus men who have been instructed to find it. Audiences anywhere in the world will be charmed by this unusual and warmly played and directed story.

d, Ken Hall; w, Edmund Seward (based on a story by Dorothy Cotterell); ph, George Heath; animal trainer, Ken Hall.

Drama   **(PR:A MPAA:NR)**

ORPHANS OF THE NORTH*   (1940) 56m MON bw

Bob Webster (Brown), Mary Joyce (Mary), Ann Henning (Joy), Eleanor Phillips (Joy's Mother), John Pool (Trapper).

Webster ventures into the northern wilderness to locate his prospector friend who has been missing for some time. But when he becomes entrapped in a caved-in mine where his pal is also trapped, Joyce, the prospector's daughter, decides to locate both men herself. Most of the screen-time is filled with her search, shots of baby bear cubs (the titled orphans), and the Alaskan scenery. Dull story line and poor acting.

p,d,w&ph, Norman Dawn; ed, Charles Hunt.

Adventure   **(PR:AA MPAA:NR)**

ORPHANS OF THE STREET*½**   (1939) 64m REP bw

Tommy Ryan (Tommy), Robert Livingston (Bob), June Storey (Lorna), Ralph Morgan (Sands), Harry Davenport (Doc Ramsey), James Burke (Manning), Sidney Blackmer (Parker), Victor Kilian (Farmer), Hobart Cavanaugh (Grant), Herbert Rawlinson (Adams), Reed Gleckler (Hughes), Ian Wolfe (Bunting), Reed Hadley (Miller), Don Douglas (Col. Daniels), Paul Everton (Judge), Ace (Skippy).

An entertaining but implausible tale of young Ryan who, after learning that his dead father's inheritance can no longer cover the costs of military school, is sent to a state home. He runs away, taking with him a trusty police dog. He soon gets mixed up in a dog show and a murder. The dog is tried for murder, and having nothing to say to his defense, except "woof," is sentenced to death. Ryan clears everything up by finding the real murderer, and wins himself a scholarship to the military academy. Farfetched but fun.

p, Herman Schlom; d, John H. Auer; w, Eric Taylor, Jack Townley, Olive Cooper (based on the story by Earl Felton); ph, Ernest Miller; ed, Murray Seldeen, Ernest Nims.

Drama/Crime   **(PR:AAA MPAA:NR)**

ORPHEE   (SEE: ORPHEUS, 1950, Fr.)

ORPHEUS***   (1950, Fr.) 112m Productions Andre Paulve/Palais-Royal bw (OPRHEE)

Jean Marais (Orpheus), Maria Casares (The Princess), Marie Dea (Eurydice), Francois Perier (Heurtebise), Juliette Greco (Aglaonice), Edouard Dermit (Cegeste), Henri Cremieux (Friend in Cafe), Pierre Bertin (Police Commissioner), Roger Blin

(Writer), Jacques Varennes, Andre Carnege, Rene Worms *(Judges)*, Renee Cosima *(Bacchante)*, Jean-Pierre Melville *(Hotel Manager)*, Jean Cocteau *(Narrator)*.

Equalled only by his BEAUTY AND THE BEAST, Cocteau's ORPHEUS is a brilliant example of the poet-playwright's creative cinematic genius. Marais plays Orpheus, a famous young poet who is married to Dea. A fellow poet, Dermit, is hit by a passing motorcyclist in front of the cafe they frequent. Casares, Dermit's patroness, orders Marais into her Rolls Royce to accompany them to the hospital, since he witnessed the accident. He goes with her, but is surprised when they pull up to a chalet instead of a hospital. Here, Casares brings Dermit "back to life." (By ingeniously running the film backwards for that one shot, Cocteau was able to make it appear that Dermit was magically rising up from the ground.) Casares and Dermit then exit the room by walking through a mirror which leads to the Underworld. Marais returns home in Casares' Rolls Royce, which is chauffeured by Perier. His waking hours are spent at the car's radio deciphering coded messages and turning them into poetry. While he sleeps, Casares watches over him at the foot of his bed. While Marais is preoccupied with his secret messages, Perier becomes involved with Dea, who longs for her husband's affections. She seeks advice from Greco, but on the way is struck down by the morbid motorcyclists. Casares quickly sends her to the Underworld to prepare her for her life after death, much to the chagrin of Perier who believes that Casares simply wanted to get rid of her competition. Together Marais and Perier pass through the mirror using a special glove that Casares left behind. Perier has hopes of finding Dea; Marais, however, is obsessed with thoughts of Casares. Marais overhears an interrogation of Casares by a board of judges where she proclaims her love for Marais. The judges agree to free her if she returns Dea to her world, but on the condition that Marais never lay eyes on Dea again. Tense and comical moments take place upon Dea's return home as Marais does all he can to avoid looking at his wife. Eventually, however, he glimpses her in a mirror and she is sent back to the Underworld. It is then that a furious mob appears outside of Marais' home. Led by Greco, they believe that Marais killed Dermit in order to steal his poems. Avenging the death of Dermit, the mob kills Marais. He is united with Casares in the Underworld. Acting beyond her limits, she symbolically strangles Marais so that he may return to his own world where he is destined to be a poet, and the husband of Dea. Awarded the top prize at the 1950 Venice Film Festival, ORPHEUS was instantly heralded as a masterpiece. It was blessed with perfect casting (though Cocteau had considered both Greta Garbo and Marlene Dietrich for Casares' role), photographic innovation, and an exceptional score by Georges Auric. It is as much a film about the creative process as it is about death, but even those who miss these meanings will still be hypnotized by its style and beauty. As with all Cocteau's films, the written word cannot accurately describe the visual sensations he creates, sensations which are not diminished with the passage of time.

p,Emil Darbon; d&w, Jean Cocteau (based on the play by Cocteau); ph, Nicholas Hayer; m, Georges Auric, plus themes from Christophe Willibald Gluck's opera "Orfeo ed Euridice"; ed, Jacqueline Sadoul; art d, Jean d'Eaubonne.

Fantasy **Cas.** **(PR:A MPAA:NR)**

OSAKA MONOGATARI (SEE: DAREDEVIL IN THE CASTLE, 1969, Jap.)

OSCAR, THE* (1966) 119m Greene-Rouse/EM c

Stephen Boyd *(Frank Fane)*, Elke Sommer *(Kay Bergdahl)*, Milton Berle *(Kappy Kapstetter)*, Eleanor Parker *(Sophie Cantaro)*, Joseph Cotten *(Kenneth H. Regan)*, Jill St. John *(Laurel Scott)*, Tony Bennett *(Hymie Kelly)*, Edie Adams *(Trina Yale)*, Ernest Borgnine *(Barney Yale)*, Ed Begley *(Grobard)*, Walter Brennan *(Orrin C. Quentin)*, Broderick Crawford *(Sheriff)*, James Dunn *(Network Executive)*, Peter Lawford *(Steve Marks)*, Jack Soo *(Sam)*, Jean Hale *(Cheryl Barker)*, Eddie Ryder *(Marriage Broker)*, Chris Alcaide *(Ledbetter)*, John Dennis *(Sid)*, Peter Leeds *(Bert)*, John Holland *(Stevens)*, Jean Bartel *(Secretary)*, John Crowther *(Wally)*, Ross Ford *(Lochner)*, Walter Reed *(Pereira)*, Edith Head, Hedda Hopper, Bob Hope, Merle Oberon, Frank Sinatra, Nancy Sinatra *(Themselves)*.

A campy film made interesting by the fact that Hollywood could stumble with a story about itelf. THe plot is so melodramatic and so far stretched from reality that the film becomes a hilarious hodgepodge. Boyd, as movie star Frank Fane, is up for the Best Actor Oscar at the Academy Awards ceremony. As he sits waiting for the winner to be announced, the audience is subjected to his life story told by his ex-best friend, Bennett. Not surprisingly, he comes from a slimy past, and he steps on everyone to get to the top in Hollywood. Boyd begins his career as an announcer at a striptease club. He is discovered by drama coach Parker, who shows him more than just the finer points of acting, and he lands his first film role. Parker gets talent agent Berle to represent Boyd and the actor is on his way. He is joined by his best friend Bennett, who is appointed as his public relations man. Boyd continues to step on and use whomever he can. When his career begins to hit bottom, he is able to get the lead in a television series, but drops it when he hears he's been nominated for an Oscar. He has a private investigator expose his sordid past to get sympathy from Academy voters. That backfires, however, when his friends and family discover his ruthlessness and dishonesty, and leave him. He goes to the ceremony alone, and when the Best Actor award is read by Merle Oberon, Boyd stands up as he hears the first name of the winner, Frank, announced; but, the award goes to Frank Sinatra, not Frank Fane. Boyd falls dejected back into his chair. No awards go for *best* acting here, but plenty for *bad* acting. Singer Bennett heads the list, followed closely by Berle and Sommer. Brainless Hollywood trash that could be enjoyed for its camp qualities. The comeuppance ending of this film is really the reason for its existence and it was based upon a real incident occurring at the Academy Awards ceremonies for 1932-33. Will Rogers was making the award for Best Director and announced in his folksy way: "and the best director of the year is. . . Well, well, well, what do you know! I've watched this young man for a long time. . . Saw him come up from the bottom, and I *mean* the bottom. It couldn't happen to a nicer guy. Come up and get it, Frank!" With that director Frank Capra, who had been nominated as Best Director for LADY FOR A DAY (which received four Oscar nominations), rose from his table and began working his way nervously through the crowded Biltmore Hotel ballroom. The spotlight picked him up just as he stepped on the dance floor but then swung sharply away to shed its bright light upon another director, Frank Lloyd, who had actually won the Oscar for CAVALCADE. Capra was in shock and later said: "That walk back—through applauding VIPs yelling 'Sit down! Down in front! Sit down!' as I obstructed their view—was the longest, saddest, most shattering walk in my life. I wished I could have crawled under the rug like a miserable worm. When I slumped into my chair I felt like one. All my friends at the table were crying." The tears disappeared the following year when the great Capra won an Oscar for Best Director for IT HAPPENED ONE NIGHT. He would go on to take statuettes for MR. DEEDS GOES TO TOWN, 1936, and for YOU CAN'T TAKE IT WITH YOU, 1938. Unlike the sleazy Boyd of this film, Frank Capra was never a loser.

p, Clarence Greene; d, Russell Rouse; w, Harlan Ellison, Rouse, Greene (based on the novel by Richard Sale); ph, Joseph Ruttenberg (Pathe Color), m, Percy Faith; ed, Chester W. Schaeffer; art d, Hal Pereira, Arthur Lonergan; set d, Robert R. Benton, James Payne; cos, Edith Head; spec eff, Paul K. Lerpae; ch, Steven Peck, m/l, "Thanks for the Memory," Ralph Rainger, Leo Robin, "All the Way," James Van Heusen, Sammy Cahn; makeup, Wally Westmore.

Drama **Cas.** **(PR:A MPAA:NR)**

OSCAR WILDE*½** (1960, Brit.) 96m Vantage/Four City bw

Robert Morley *(Oscar Wilde)*, Phyllis Calvert *(Constance Wilde)*, John Neville *(Lord Alfred Douglas)*, Ralph Richardson *(Sir Edward Carson)*, Dennis Price *(Robert Ross)*, Alexander Knox *(Sir Edward Clarke)*, Edward Chapman *(Marquis of Queensberry)*, Martin Benson *(George Alexander)*, Robert Harris *(Justice Henn Collins)*, Henry Oscar *(Justice Wills)*, William Devlin *(Solicitor-General)*, Stephen Dartnell *(Cobble)*, Ronald Leigh-Hunt *(Lionel Johnson)*, Martin Boddey *(Inspector Richards)*, Leonard Sachs *(Richard Legallienne)*, Tony Doonan *(Wood)*, Tom Chatto *(Clerk of Arraigns)*.

For some strange reason two separate companies were making the exact same story at the same time, the life and trials of Oscar Wilde. In one Peter Finch starred as the famed Irish writer (THE TRIALS OF OSCAR WILDE), and in this it was Robert Morley. The Finch film was in color and the Morley picture, which was rushed out for release just a few days before, was in black-and-white and was also the superior film. Morley is married to Calvert, but she stays mostly in the background as he meets and falls in love with Neville (who makes his movie debut), a young lord-about-town who hates his father, Chapman, with as much passion as he returns Morley's love. Chapman is The Marquis of Queensberry, the same man who gave us the rules for boxing, and he and Neville are forever battling. Neville is a college student and Morley is already a legendary wit, successful playwright, and sometime performer. Chapman sends Morley a note and accuses him of posing as "a sodomite." Morley, under Neville's goading, brings a suit against Chapman for libel and the case goes to trial, with Morley breaking down on the witness stand. Morley is then tried for gross indecency and there is a clash of wits between him and Richardson, as the queen's counsel, that should be studied by actors as one of the best examples of courtroom histrionics. Morley is convicted and sentenced to two years hard labor. He comes out of jail a broken man and dies in Paris. Morley was 52 when he made the picture and Wilde died at age 46, but that's a quibble. His performance was brilliant, as was Richardson's. Although the Finch picture covered the exact same ground, it didn't have the fire of this one, specifically in the courtroom scenes, which snap and crackle like a blazing fireplace.

p, William Kirby; d, Gregory Ratoff; w, Jo Eisinger (based on the play by Leslie and Sewell Stokes); ph, Georges Perinal; m, Kenneth V. Jones; ed, Tony Gibbs.

Biography **(PR:C MPAA:NR)**

OSETROVNA (SEE: SIGN OF THE VIRGIN, 1969, Czech.)

O'SHAUGHNESSY'S BOY½** (1935) 88m MGM bw

Wallace Beery *(Windy)*, Jackie Cooper *(Stubby)*, George "Spanky" McFarland *(Stubby as a Child)*, Henry Stephenson *(Maj. Winslow)*, Sara Haden *(Martha)*, Leona Maricle *(Cora)*, Willard Robertson *(Hartings)*, Clarence Muse *(Jeff)*, Ben Hendricks *(Franz)*, Wade Boteler *(Callahan)*, Jack Daley *(Mack)*, Oscar Apfel *(Lawyer)*, Wally Albright, Jr. *(Child)*, Hooper Atchley *(Secretary)*, Alf James *(Farmer)*, Al Williams, Ernie Alexander *(Acrobats)*, Mable Waldman *(Fat Lady)*, Charles Ludwig *(Midget)*, Frank LaMont *(Human Skeleton)*, Jack Baxley, Nick Copeland *(Barkers)*, Lee Shumway *(Detective)*.

Beery and Cooper are teamed again in a film that follows their earlier success, THE CHAMP (1931), in almost every respect. Only settings and other incidental elements have been changed. This one takes place inside the circus, where Beery is the animal trainer and his wife is an acrobat. Everything goes fine for the threesome (Spanky is the third family member, playing a younger version of Cooper) until Beery's sister-in-law pays a visit and tears into him with her claws outstretched. When Beery comes back drunk from a party thrown in his honor by the owner of the circus, Haden (the sister-in-law) convinces her sister that Beery is a ne'er-do-well. The woman believes her, taking her son and moving in with Haden. Beery discovers his wife and child gone just prior to opening a new act involving a tiger and an elephant, placing him in an unstable condition and unfit for the ring. Beery loses his arm to the tiger, and eventually his confidence. Meanwhile, his wife dies and Cooper is left in the care of Haden, who continually fills the boy's head with visions of his father as worthless and responsible for his mother's early death. When Cooper is old enough to attend military school, he starts to spend the summer with his father. At first their relationship is strained, with Cooper distrustful of Beery, seeing him through the eyes of his aunt. As the boy gets to know what his father is like, he also understands the things Haden has been telling him are lies. The presence of Cooper helps to build Beery's confidence enough to get him back inside the cage with a tiger, leading to the animal trainer's comeback. The film is designed to wrench out as much sympathy as possible, relying on the earlier teamings of Cooper and Beery to evoke immediate emotional responses. Neither Beery nor Cooper do much acting in roles that are basically walk-throughs for them by this time, though Hayden is brilliant as the catty and cunning aunt. As in THE CHAMP and later, TREASURE ISLAND, Cooper did not enjoy the company of Beery, later stating that he "really disliked him. . . there was no warmth to the man." Beery, in all his films with Cooper, tried to steal every scene from the boy, mugging and gesturing so fiercely as to draw down the wrath of directors. As much as W. C. Fields flaunted his dislike of Baby Leroy, Beery showed his contempt for having to act across from Cooper whenever possible. Cooper was fatherless at the time and sought any tidbits of affection he could from Beery; he got none. Beery's notorious skinflintery was never more in evidence than during this production. On one occasion Cooper and his mother were in the studio commissary and watched Beery walk from his table without leaving a tip. Cooper's mother offered to loan Beery some change so he could leave something for the waitress. He sneered, then patronizingly explained to the puzzled woman that he did not believe in tipping, that tips were left for only very special service and since he was Wallace Beery and got very special service all the time, the service was therefore not really special and so no tip was actually earned!

p, Philip Goldstone; d, Richard Boleslawski; w, Leonard Praskins, Wanda Tuchock, Otis Garrett (based on the story by Harvey Gates, Malcolm Stuart Boylan); ph, James Wong Howe; m, William Axt; ed, Frank Sullivan; art d, Cedric Gibbons, Stan Rogers; set d, Edwin B. Willis.

Drama **(PR:A MPAA:NR)**

OSSESSIONE*** (1959, Ital.) 112m ICI Roma bw

Clara Calamai *(Giovanna)*, Massimo Girotti *(Gino)*, Juan de Landa *(The Husband)*, Elia Marcuzzo *(Lo Spagnuolo)*, Dhia Cristani *(Anita)*, Vittorio Duse *(The Lorry Driver)*, Michele Riccardini, Michele Sakara.

The first directorial effort in the brilliant, though sporadic, career of Visconti was originally made in 1942 but not shown outside Italy for several years because of copyright problems. Based on the novel *The Postman Always Rings Twice* by American James M. Cain (previously filmed in France in 1939, later in the U.S. in 1946, starring John Garfield and Lana Turner, and most recently in 1981, with Jack Nicholson and Jessica Lange), Visconti created a sizzling love story set against a background of murder and adultery along the backroads of the Italian countryside. The nomadic Gino (Girotti), a man living under the illusion that attachments only act as a hindrance, happens upon the roadside inn run by Calamai and her older, grotesque-looking husband de Landa. One look at this couple tells their entire story; she is young, beautiful, and full of passionate energy, but married to a man unequal to her in all capacities except one, money. Calamai has only married this man to keep her from a life of poverty and/or prostitution. Girotti agrees to take care of some chores for de Landa in exchange for food and a place to sleep. Calamai soon takes a romantic interest in the visitor that she was never able to find in her relationship with her husband. At first Girotti is not very receptive to Calamai's advances; his moral conscience does not allow him to take advantage of the kindness and friendship that de Landa has shown. But the demanding wife eventually entices the drifter into a heated affair that exists in dark corners and out of the way places to avoid the seemingly ever present de Landa. When Girotti starts to despise himself for having to sneak around to carry on this liaison, he suggests to Calamai they leave together. But, at the last moment, after her clothes have been packed for the journey, she refuses. Whatever excitement and freedom the trip with the drifter may hold, she opts for the security and stability she can maintain at the inn. Girotti leaves by himself, finding a temporary traveling companion in Marcuzzo, a fellow drifter and a homosexual who pays for Girotti's train ticket. The two establish a friendship based on the unspoken laws of eternal travellers who never allow themselves to become tied down by a home or wife. This quick relationship is shattered when Marcuzzo discovers that Girotti's suitcase is full of women's clothes, an indication of Girotti's disloyalty to Marcuzzo and his code, the same ideals Girotti held before his affair with Calamai. Later Calamai and de Landa bump into Girotti while on a trip to a neighboring village. Totally ignorant of the affair between his wife and this man, de Landa persuades Girotti to accompany them back to the inn. Fearful that she may lose her lover again, Calamai devises a scheme, with Girotti's assistance, to kill her husband while making it appear as an accident. Not only will she receive life insurance for the death, but she can continue carrying on with her lover without the constant fear of being caught in the act. Her happiness is short-lived however; driven by moralistic guilt and the suspicion that Calamai was only using him as part of a far-fetched scheme, Girotti finds it almost impossible to remain at the inn. He leaves again, but only for an afternoon to carry on a quick fling with a dancer, returning when Calamai convinces him that she is pregnant. Meanwhile, the police are suspicious of the openness with which the lovers live and start their own investigation. Realizing the danger, Calamai and Girotti attempt to flee but are stopped by a car crash that kills Calamai, and leaves Girotti to take the blame for her death. An ironic ending in light of the fake car crash Calamai devised in order to make her husband appear as if he had died accidentally. Prior to embarking upon his own carrer as a director, Visconti worked as an assistant director and prop master for Jean Renoir. This apprenticeship had quite an effect in developing Visconti's own style. Instead of filming inside a studio, as other Italian filmmakers did prior to OSSESSIONE, he went into the countryside to show the Italian people in their environment, not in an idealized setting. OSSESSIONE was vital as a forerunner of the neorealist movement, which had its beginnings in Roberto Rossellini's OPEN CITY a couple of years later. Because the Fascist government of 1942 had complete control over film production in Italy, Visconti had to have his script okayed before shooting. The government saw nothing wrong with the script that Visconti presented, but was quite shocked with the final product that displayed an Italy in contrast to the stylized depiction common to Italian films. Fearful of possible political overtones, OSSESSIONE was temporarily shelved by the Fascist government, only to be put back into circulation after Mussolini saw the film and indicated how much he enjoyed it. When the Fascists were fleeing to the north to escape the advancing Allied forces, they took the negative of OSSESSIONE and recut it to look like an entirely different film. Luckily Visconti kept a print of the original, which was copied and put into release at the end of the war. As a portrayal of the conflict between moral conscience and uncontrolable passion, between the need to maintain a secure existence and the desire to remain free of any confining forces, OSSESSIONE is a powerful statement, even though Visconti was later accused of copyright violation of the Cain story. (In Italian; English subtitles.)

p, Libero Solaroli; d, Luchino Visconti; w, Mario Alicata, Antonio Pietrangeli, Gianni Puccini, Giuseppe De Santis, Visconti (based on the novel *The Postman Always Rings Twice* by James M. Cain); ph, Aldo Tonti, Domenico Scala; m, Giuseppe Rosati; ed, Mario Serandrei; art d, Gino Rosati.

Drama **(PR:C MPAA:NR)**

OSTATNI ETAP (SEE: LAST STOP, THE, 1949, Pol.)

OSTERMAN WEEKEND, THE** (1983) 102m FOX c

Rutger Hauer *(John Tanner)*, John Hurt *(Lawrence Fassett)*, Craig T. Nelson *(Bernard Osterman)*, Dennis Hopper *(Richard Tremayne)*, Chris Sarandon *(Joseph Cardone)*, Burt Lancaster *(Maxwell Danforth)*, Meg Foster *(Ali Tanner)*, Helen Shaver *(Virginia Tremayne)*, Cassie Yates *(Betty Cardone)*, Sandy McPeak *(Stennings)*, Christopher Starr *(Steve Tanner)*, Cheryl Carter *(Marcia)*, John Bryson, Anne Haney *(Honeymoon Couple)*, Kristen Peckinpah *(Secretary)*, Jan Triska *(Mikalovich)*, Hansford Rowe *(Gen. Keever)*, Merete Van Kamp *(Zuna)*, Bruce Block *(Manager)*, Buddy Joe Hooker *(Kidnaper)*, Tim Thomerson *(Motorcycle Cop)*, Deborah Chiariamonte *(Nurse)*, Walter Kelley *(1st Agent)*, Brick Tilley *(2nd Agent)*, Eddy Donno *(3rdAgent)*, Den Surles *(Assailant)*, Don Shafer *(Helicopter Agent)*, Irene Gorman Wright *(ExecutiveAssistant)*, Gregory Joe Parr *(Helicopter Pilot)*, Buckley F. Norris *(Technician)*, Robert Kensinger, Janeen Davis *(Stage Managers)*, Marshall Ho'o *(Martial Arts Instructor)*.

There are some novelists whose work remains unadaptable by screenwriters. So it is with Robert Ludlum, who has written a slew of best sellers, after having been an actor and a stage manager at a Paramus, New Jersey theater. So much of Ludlum's fun happens in the back-stories and in the mind of the characters that it looks convoluted and unconvincing on screen and they have yet to make it work. Peckinpah, after a bomb with CONVOY, took five years off (whether it was forced or not has never been determined) before returning to the screen with this picture, the first of Ludlum's novels to achieve great popularity. The chief of the CIA, Lancaster, gets Hurt, a ruthless operative, to convince Hauer, the news director of a TV network, to participate in a plot to ferret out some spies who are pals of Hauer's. Still with us? Hauer is shocked to hear that his friends, Nelson, Hopper, Sarandon, and their wives, Shaver and Yates, are Soviet agents. Nelson is a TV writer who says that he is "a nihilist anarchist living on residuals" and he is Osterman, the man who throws the annual weekend of the title. Hauer's house has been rigged with state-of-the-art snooping equipment by Hurt (his wife was killed by the CIA and he knows it, so he is going to get even with Lancaster with this ploy). In the end, the weekenders are not spies at all, just people getting together to discuss ways and means of avoiding their high income taxes. The CIA operatives are the villains (aren't they always?) and the picture soon disintegrates into a high-tech video game, then a totally unmotivated shoot out. Peckinpah supposedly didn't like the story or the script and his disdain seems evident in every frame, although he couldn's resist putting his stylish direction into the twisted story in a vain attempt to make some sort of sense of the whole thing. He failed. The actors pretend that they know what's going on in the script, but it's a fair bet they had no idea at all. The only Ludlum book that reads like a movie is the one that he can't seem to get made, THE ROAD TO GANDOLFO, a very funny story about the kidnaping of the pope.

p, Peter S. Davis, William N. Panzer; d, Sam Peckinpah; w, Alan Sharp, Ian Masters (based on the book by Robert Ludlum); ph, John Coquillon (DeLuxe Color); m, Lalo Schifrin; ed, Edward Abroms, David Rawlins; art d, Robb Wilson King; set d, Keith Hein.

Spy Drama **Cas.** **(PR:C-O MPAA:R)**

OSTRE SLEDOVANE VLAKY (SEE: CLOSELY WATCHED TRAINS, 1967, Czech.)

OTCHI TCHORNIA (SEE: DARK EYES, 1938, Fr.)

OTCHIY DOM (SEE: HOME FOR TANYA, A, 1961, USSR)

OTEL U POGIBSHCHEGO ALPINISTA (SEE: DEAD MOUTAINEER HOTEL, THE, 1979, USSR)

OTETS SOLDATA (SEE: FATHER OF A SOLDIER, 1966, USSR)

OTHELLO** (1955, U.S./Fr./Ital.) 90m Mercury/UA bw

Orson Welles *(Othello)*, Michael MacLiammoir *(Iago)*, Suzanne Cloutier *(Desdemona)*, Robert Coote *(Roderigo)*, Hilton Edwards *(Brabantio)*, Michael Lawrence *(Cassio)*, Fay Compton *(Emilia)*, Nicholas Bruce *(Lodovico)*, Jean Davis *(Montano)*, Doris Dowling *(Bianca)*, Joseph Cotten *(Senator)*, Joan Fontaine *(Page)*.

Orson Welles' version of the classic Shakespearean play in which Welles cast himself as the tragic title character. Welles took great liberties with the play, employing dnynamic editing and flashy camera work, as well as revealing the film's ending in the opening moments. Though Welles spent only three weeks shooting his MACBETH, he devoted three years of continually interrupted production to this picture. In an effort to raise the necessary cash to complete OTHELLO, Wells appeared in three films—Henry King's PRINCE OF FOXES, Henry Hathaway's THE BLACK ROSE, and Carol Reed's THE THIRD MAN, all three of which were superior to the picture he was trying to finance.

p,d&w, Orson Welles (based on the play by William Shakespeare); ph, Anchise Brizzi, Aldo Graziati [G.R. Aldo], Georges Fanto, Obadan Troiani, Alberto Fusi; m, Francesco Lavagnino, Alberto Barberis; ed, Jean Sacha, John Shepridge, Renzo Lucidi, William Morton; md, Willy Ferrero; art d, Alexandre Trauner; cos, Maria de Matteis.

Drama **(PR:C MPAA:NR)**

OTHELLO½** (1960, U.S.S.R.) 108m Mosfilm/UNIV c

Sergei Bondarchuk *(Othello)*, Andrei Popov *(Iago)*, Irina Skobtseva *(Desdemona)*, Vladimir Soshalsky *(Cassio)*, E. Vesnik *(Roderigo)*, A. Maximova *(Emilia)*, E. Teterin *(Brabantio)*, M. Troyanovsky *(Doge of Venice)*, A. Kelberer *(Montano)*, N. Brilling *(Lodovico)*, L. Ashrafova *(Bianca)*, A. Blach, V. Borzho, V. Lebedev, I. Melamed, S. Troitsky, Y. Fried.

Released in Russia in 1955, this version of the Shakespearean play is inexcusably damaged by Universal's insistence in dubbing the picture instead of subtitling. The poorly done job detracts from the beautiful Soviet landscape, which releases the story from the usually confined quarters of the stage. Bondarchuk's performance and Khachaturian's score are the prime assets to Yutkevich's script, which was first conceived in 1938.

d&w, Sergei Yutkevitch (based on the play by William Shakespeare); ph, E. Andrikanis; m, Aram Khachaturian; ed, G. Mariamov; art d, A. Vaisfeld, V. Dorrer, M. Karykin; cos, O. Kruchinina.

Drama **(PR:A MPAA:NR)**

OTHELLO*½** (1965, Brit.) 166m British Home Entertainments/WB c

Laurence Olivier *(Othello)*, Frank Finlay *(Iago)*, Maggie Smith *(Desdemona)*, Robert Lang *(Roderigo)*, Anthony Nicholls *(Brabantio)*, Roy Holder *(Clown)*, Derek Jacobi *(Cassio)*, Joyce Redman *(Emilia)*, Sheila Reid *(Bianca)*, Harry Lomax *(Duke of Venice)*, Michael Turner *(Gratiano)*, Kenneth Mackintosh *(Lodovico)*, Terence Knapp *(Duke's Officer)*, Keith Marsh *(Senator)*, Tom Kempinski *(Sailor)*, David Hargreaves, Malcolm Terris *(Senate Officers)*, Nicholas Edmett *(Messenger)*, Edward Hardwicke *(Montano)*, William Hobbs, Trevor Martin, Christopher Timothy *(Cypriot Officers)*, Petronella Barker, Janie Booth, Andrew Bradford, Peter Cellier, Mike Gambon, Reginald Green, Peter John, Lewis Jones, John McEnery, Bruce Purchase, Dan Meaden, Malcolm Reynolds, Robert Russell, Clive Rust *(Senators, Soldiers, Cypriots)*.

Orson Welles had attempted Shakespeare's OTHELLO 14 years before, but that version paled next to this. It began at the Chichester Festival in 1964 and then was taken to London for the National Theatre. The man who directed that version, John Dexter, staged the action, but the film director gets the credit here, although this is such a stage-bound affair that one can't perceive where Dexter ends and Burge commences. Jocelyn Herbert's stage sets were transformed for the screen by Kellner, although all of them seem to have been physically transported, rather than redesigned. The main reason for seeing this is, of course, Olivier, in another of his towering performances. Olivier, in blackface, is the Moor who wears a crucifix and crosses himself but who, every now and then, reverts to his Islamic background. Never before has Othello seemed so human, so able to be touched, so vulnerable. Olivier's voice is a heavenly instrument upon which Shakespeare's verbal tunes are given celestial playing. He is more than ably counterpointed by Smith's Desdemona, a sweet, gullible, and totally innocent creature who has the misfortune of being betrayed. Finlay, as Iago, is too old to make us believe he is the 28 years of age the script calls for him to be and he has been directed to play the villain in a more quiet fashion than was customary. Olivier chose to make us care more for Othello than, perhaps even Shakespeare himself intended. That decision was correct and we empathize with the wracking jealousy he puts forth. Jacobi, who was not to be recognized internationally until he did TV's "I, Claudius," is a wonder of restraint in the role of Cassio, a part that has been played many times before with rolling eyes and stentorian speech. As a movie, this was a great play and was nominated by the Academy for the work of Olivier, Finlay, Redman, and Smith.

p, Anthony Havelock-Allan, John Brabourne; d, Stuart Burge; w, Margaret Unsworth (based on the play by William Shakespeare); ph, Geoffrey Unsworth (Panavision, Technicolor); m, Richard Hampton; ed, Richard Marden; art d, William Kellner; cos, Jocelyn Herbert; makeup, George Partleton.

Drama **Cas.** **(PR:A MPAA:NR)**

OTHER, THE*** (1972) 108m FOX c

Uta Hagen *(Ada, Grandmother)*, Chris Udvarnoky *(Niles Perry)*, Martin Udvarnoky *(Holland Perry)*, Diana Muldaur *(Alexandra Perry)*, Norma Connolly *(Aunt Vee)*, Victor French *(Angelini)*, Loretta Laversee *(Winnie)*, Lou Frizzell *(Uncle George)*, Portia Nelson *(Mrs. Rowe)*, Jenny Sullivan *(Torrie)*, John Ritter *(Rider)*, Jack Collins *(Mr. P.C. Pretty)*, Ed Bakey *(Chan-yu)*, Clarence Crow *(Russell)*.

A chilling tale of two twin brothers set in the sweltering heat of a 1930's Connecticut farm town. A number of strange happenings begin to worry the town elders, as well as Muldaur, the widowed mother of the two boys. The only adult with even the slightest grip on sanity is Hagen, the philosophical grandmother who offers explanations of the inexplicable. She makes every attempt to treat the good twin, Chris Udvarnoky, with the maximum of healthy attention. The boy is negatively influenced, however, by his twin, Martin Udvarnoky, an evil (and possibly dead) youngster who is responsible for the grotesque killings that occur, including a baby found floating in a wine cask, a playful child jumping onto a pitchfork hidden in a haystack, and a morbid attempt at removing a buried ring from a corpse's hand. A truly frightening film based on the first novel by Thomas Tryon, who also scripted and acted as executive producer.

p&d, Robert Mulligan; w, Thomas Tryon (based on the novel by Tryon); ph, Robert L. Surtees (DeLuxe Color); m, Jerry Goldsmith; ed, Folmar Blangsted, O. Nicholas Brown; prod d, Albert Brenner; set d, Ruby Levitt; cos, Tommy Welsh, Joanne Haas; makeup, Joe Di Bella.

Horror **(PR:O MPAA:PG)**

OTHER LOVE, THE*½ (1947) 95m Enterprise/UA bw (AKA: MAN-KILLER)

Barbara Stanwyck *(Karen Duncan)*, David Niven *(Dr. Anthony Stanton)*, Maria Palmer *(Nurse Huberta)*, Joan Lorring *(Celestine)*, Richard Conte *(Paul Clermont)*, Richard Hale *(Prof. Linnaker)*, Edward Ashley *(Richard Shelton)*, Natalie Schafer *(Dora Shelton)*, Lenore Aubert *(Yvonne)*, Jimmy Horne *(Pete)*, Mary Forbes *(Mme. Gruen)*, Ann Codee *(The Florist)*, Kathleen Williams *(Florist's Assistant)*, Gilbert Roland *(Croupier)*, Mary Fields *(Nurse)*, Michael Romanoff.

Enterprise, headed by David Lewis, didn't make too many movies before giving up the ghost, and this picture serves as a good example of why. Lewis had been Thalberg's assistant and worked on many MGM films, including CAMILLE and he returns to that theme with THE OTHER LOVE. The working title for this soap was "No Other Love" and it was released in the 1950s as MAN-KILLER, a title which had nothing to do with the content. Erich Maria Remarque wrote the short story on which it was based and they expanded it to feature length with some padded sequences. Stanwyck is a successful concert pianist with tuberculosis. She goes to a swank sanitarium in the Swiss Alps where she is immediately entranced by her doctor, the dashing Niven, a man whose bedside manner is legendary. Stanwyck is not long for this world and Niven knows that, so he attempts to keep her calm and rested, thus limiting her devil-may-care attitude. He forces her to rest and she indicates her disagreement with that prescription. She becomes friendly with another patient, Lorring, and it is her death that causes Stanwyck to reconsider her own mortality and rebel against Niven's wishes. She takes off with race driver Conte (who almost steals the movie with his carefree characterization of an early day Mario Andretti) and has a mad fling in Europe while her body can still stand the rigors of high living. Eventually, she returns to the hospice and she and Niven are marrried, as he lies and tells her that she will soon be well enough to return to her usual life. One night, while he's playing Chopin (badly) on the piano, she just closes her eyes and dies—and none too soon, as Niven's piano playing is atrocious. Lots of glitz, good production values, but the more than a passing nod to CAMILLE makes this a bit too familiar to be taken seriously. Stanwyck's appearance, as she becomes increasingly sicker, never changes and she looks, in death, the same way she looked in life, a great deal like Barbara Stanwyck. Gilbert Roland plays a gambling-house croupier in a parody of a gambling house croupier. One added note about the credits: both Keller and Milner are variously listed as cinematographer, both Glickman and Polk have been listed as musical director, and Moreland as well as the Lydeckers have been given credit, from various sources, for the special effects. We could't tell you which were correct, so we've given them all.

p, David Lewis; d, Andre de Toth; w, Ladislas Fodor, Harry Brown (based on the short story "Beyond" by Erich Maria Remarque); ph, Victor Milner, Alfred Keller; m, Miklos Rozsa; ed, Walter Thompson; md, Rudolph Polk, Mort Glickman; art d, Nathan Juran; set d, Edward G. Boyle; cos, Edith Head, Edward P. Lambert; spec eff, Robert Moreland, Howard and Theodore Lydecker; makeup, Bob Ewing.

Drama **(PR:A MPAA:NR)**

OTHER MEN'S WOMEN*½ (1931) 70m WB-Vitaphone bw (AKA: THE STEEL HIGHWAY)

Grant Withers *(Bill)*, Mary Astor *(Lily)*, Regis Toomey *(Jack)*, James Cagney *(Ed)*, Fred Kohler, Sr. *(Haley)*, J. Farrell MacDonald *(Pegleg)*, Joan Blondell *(Marie)*, Walter Long *(Bixby)*, Bob Perry, Lee Moran, Kewpie Morgan, Pat Hartigan *(Railroad Workers)*, Lillian Worth *(Waitress)*.

The working title for this film was "The Steel Highway," which was a much better designation for what the story was about, but someone at the studio must have felt that the misleading title of OTHER MEN'S WOMEN would bring in the customers. It's another one of Warner Brothers' proletariat pictures about the average Joe and the problems of being a blue-collar man. Toomey is a railroad engineer happily married to Astor. Toomey's pal, fireman Withers, needs a place to stay and the couple allow him to take up residence with them—a mistake. Astor and Withers are soon making eyes at each other behind Toomey's back. It doesn't take too much time for Toomey to see their mutual attraction and Withers decides it might be better to find accommodations elsewhere. The two men go on a train ride together and begin to quarrel. That erupts into a physical conflict and Toomey falls out of the engine and is injured badly. He loses his vision due to the skirmish and Withers appears ready to move in on Astor, but he is shocked to see that she dearly loves Toomey and will stay by him forever. A huge rainstorm is followed by torrential floods in the area and a railroad bridge is in danger of being swept away by the roiling tides. Withers reckons that the only way to keep the bridge from going down is to add weight to it, so he decides to take a train and stall it on the bridge until the raging waters recede. Toomey leaps aboard the train and blindly tosses Withers off; then he pilots the engine to the bridge and his ultimate demise as the train crashes through the water-soaked span. James Hall and Marian Nixon were to have played the Toomey and Astor roles but were replaced just prior to shooting. Cagney, who was appearing in his third film (the others were SINNER'S HOLIDAY and DOORWAY TO HELL) didn't have much to do and was still a film away from the movie that made him a star, THE PUBLIC ENEMY. Blondell, who had also played in SINNER'S HOLIDAY, was in her seventh movie in less that 18 months, but neither she nor Cagney played an important role in this programmer. Good action sequences by Wellman and the picture only bogs down when the triangular love interest is featured.

d, William A. Wellman; w, William K. Wells, Maude Fulton (based on a story by

Fulton); ph, Barney "Chick" McGill; ed, Edward McDermott; md, Leo F. Forbstein; cos, Earl Luick; makeup, Perc Westmore.

Drama   (PR:A-C MPAA:NR)

OTHER ONE, THE½**   (1967,Fr.) 81m Ancinex/CD c
                                         (L'UN ET L'AUTRE)

Malka Ribovska (Anne), Philippe Noiret (Andre), Marc Cassot (Julien), Francoise
Prevost (Simone), Christian Alers (Remoulin), Claude Dauphin (Serebriakov).

Ribovska is an actress with a repertory company who is experiencing a creative
block. She places the blame on her live-in boy friend, a photographer whom she
believes has sold out to the advertising world. She decides to pose as her sister,
whom her boy friend has never met, but eventually discloses her true feelings.
Director Rene Allio's follow-up to his fine THE SHAMELESS OLD LADY, which
also starred his wife, Ribovska, is not quite the expected success. His homages to
Chekhov and Ophuls, however, are endearing.

p, Nicole Stephane; d&w, Rene Allio; ph, Jean Badal; m, Serge Gainsbourg; ed,
Chantal Delattre.

Drama   (PR:C MPAA:NR)

OTHER PEOPLE'S BUSINESS   (SEE: WAY BACK HOME 1932)

OTHER PEOPLE'S SINS**   (1931, Brit.) 63m Associated Picture/
                                         PDC bw

Horace Hodges (Carfax), Stewart Rome (Anthony Vernon, Barrister), Anne Grey
(Anne Vernon), Arthur Margetson (Bernard Barrington, Impresario), Mrs. Hayden
Coffin (Mrs. Vernon), A. Harding Steerman (Prosecution), Clifton Boyne (Juror),
Arthur Hambling (Fireman), Sam Wilkinson (Actor), Arthur Bawtree, Russell Car,
Laura Smithson, J. Hubert Leslie, C. Disney Roebuck, Claude Maxted, John
Hope.

When Grey kills a man who attempts to force himself upon her, her father
(Hodges) takes the blame and goes on trial for murder. Grey's husband, who
knows nothing of his wife's involvement, defends him fruitlessly until Grey breaks
down and admits her guilt. Intriguing film, considering it takes place almost entirely
inside the courtroom.

p&d, Sinclair Hill; w, Leslie Howard Gordon; ph, Desmond Dickinson.

Crime/Drama   (PR:A MPAA:NR)

OTHER SIDE OF BONNIE AND CLYDE, THE*   (1968) 75m Dal-
                                                Art bw

Joe Enterentree [Bonnie Shefield] (Bonnie Parker), Lucky Mosley [Sonny Wayne]
(Clyde Barrow), Floyd Hamilton, Mrs. Frank Hamer, Frank Hamer, Jr. (Themselves), Burl Ives (Narrator).

A bizarre attempt to cash in on Arthur Penn's BONNIE AND CLYDE, by telling the
"other side" of the legendary killers. Filled mostly with newsreel footage of the
actual couple, it contains a few re-enactments by Enterentree and Mosley. It is
worthwhile mainly for the interview material with ex-gangster Floyd Hamilton and
Texas sheriff, Frank Hamer. . .and his family! If anything, it's more truthful than
Penn's glamorized version.

p&d, Larry Buchanan.

Biography   (PR:O MPAA:NR)

OTHER SIDE OF MIDNIGHT, THE*   (1977) 165m FOX c

Marie-France Pisier (Noelle Page), John Beck (Larry Douglas), Susan Sarandon
(Catherine Douglas), Raf Vallone (Constantin Demeris), Clu Gulager (Bill Fraser),
Christian Marquand (Armand Gautier), Michael Lerner (Barbet), Sorrell Booke
(Lanchon), Louis Zorich (Demonides), Antony Ponzini (Paul Metaxas), Charles
Cioffi (Chotas), Dimitra Arliss (Madame Rose), Jan Arvan (Warden), Josette Banzet
(Madame Rose), John Chappell (Doc Peterson), Eunice Christopher (Female
Guard), Roger Etienne (Jacques Page), Howard Hesseman (O'Brien), Carrie Kelly
(Susie), Curt Lowens (Henri Correger), Peter Mamakos (Cocyannis), Louis
Mercier (Paris Cab Driver), Jacques Marin (Philippe Sorel), Lina Raymond (Sultry
Girl), Charles Siebert (Steve), George Skaff (Doctor), George Sperdakos (Spyros),
Roger Til (Hotel Detective), Titos Vandis (President of Council), Than Wyenn
(Greek Priest), John Blackwell (Beverly Hills Bellhop), Lilyan Chauvin (Mrs.
Page), George Keymas (Dr. K). Lidia Kristen (Housekeeper), Denise De Mirjian
(Nun), Matilda Calnan (Old Dressmaker).

Using WW II as a backdrop, Beck plays an American pilot who falls in love with a
young French girl, Pisier. When the time comes for him to return to the States, he
promises her that he will return in three weeks to marry her. She waits for the
appropriate date, but Beck never shows. Heartbroken, she aborts the baby she has
been carrying and decides that men are to be used for personal gain. She evetually
becomes a great French actress and marries a Greek tycoon, Vallone. But over the
years she has also been keeping tabs on Beck, his disastrous career as a commercial
pilot, and his shaky marriage to Sarandon. Eventually, she arranges for Beck to
come to Greece to be her personal pilot. He fails to recognize her, so she makes his
life miserable. When he finally realizes that she is the young Parisian girl he loved,
they are reunited again as lovers. Sarandon becomes a problem for the pair,
however, because she won't grant Beck a divorce. They plot her murder, and
when she overhears, she rushes out to the boat docked behind their apartment and
is swept out to sea. Going on circumstantial evidence, Beck and Pisier are charged
with her murder. Vallone convinces them to plead guilty in the hopes that they'll
get a lighter sentence, but the judge views them as two cold unrepentant murderers
and gives them the death penalty. Picture concludes with Beck and Pisier being put
to death, and Vallone, who has had the last laugh as the jilted husband, visiting
Sarandon at a convent where she had been cared for since the nuns found her
adrift at sea.

p, Frank Yablans; d, Charles Jarrott; w, Herman Raucher, Daniel Taradash (based

on the novel by Sidney Sheldon); ph, Fred J. Koenekamp (Panavision, DeLuxe
Color); m, Michel Legrand; ed, Donn Cambern, Harold F. Kress; prod d, John De
Cuir; set d, Raphael Bretton, Tony Mondell; cos, Irene Sharaff; makeup, Lee
Harman.

Drama   **Cas.**   (PR:O MPAA:R)

OTHER SIDE OF PARADISE, THE   (SEE: FOXTROT, 1977, Mex./
                                                    Swiss.)

OTHER SIDE OF THE MOUNTAIN, THE*½**
        (1975) 101m Filmways-Peerce/UNIV c (GB: A WINDOW TO THE SKY)

Marilyn Hassett (Jill Kinmont), Beau Bridges (Dick Buek), Belinda J. Montgomery
(Audra-Jo), Nan Martin (June Kinmont), William Bryant (Bill Kinmont), Dabney
Coleman (Dave McCoy), Bill Vint (Buddy Werner), Hampton Fancher (Lee
Zadroga), William Roerick (Dr. Pittman), Dori Brenner (Cookie), Walter Brooke
(Dean), Jocelyn Jones (Linda Meyers), Greg Mabrey (Bob Kinmont), Tony Becker
(Jerry Kinmont), Griffin Dunne (Herbie Johnson), Warren Miller (Dr. Enders),
Robin Pepper (Skeeter Werner), Brad Savage (Boy In Wheelchair), John Perell
(Ambulance Driver), Terry Hall (Ambulance Attendant), Bruce Dennis Cosbey
(Head of Ski Patrol), Sharri Zak (Nurse), Dick Winslow (Man in Car), Candy
McCoy (Andrea Mead Lawrence), John David Garfield, Kenneth Dorsey, William
Johnson, Frank Foeldi, Frank Willis, William Woolard, Jack Ross Sharp, Richard
Malone, Michael Murdock, Samuel Dwyer (CRC Patients).

The heroic tale of real-life skier Jill Kinmont (played by Hassett), whose 1956
Olympic hopes were shattered when she took a paralyzing fall in Utah's Snow Cup
race. Movie takes you through Kinmont's depression over her fate, her break-up
with her fiance who can't accept her paralysis, her romance with Bridges and how
he helps her fight back to go on to become a grammar school teacher in California.
Ending has Bridges, a daredevil pilot, getting killed in a plane crash, and Hassett's
acceptance of his death. Sequel: THE OTHER SIDE OF THE MOUNTAIN, PART
TWO.

p, Edward S. Feldman; d, Larry Peerce; w, David Seltzer (based on the book A
Long Way Up by E. G. Valens); ph, David M. Walsh (Technicolor); m, Charles
Fox; ed, Eve Newman; set d, Philip Abramson; cos, Grady Hunt; m/l, "Richard's
Window," Norman Gimbel, Fox (sung by Olivia Newton-John).

Drama/Biography   **Cas.**   (PR:A MPAA:PG)

OTHER SIDE OF THE MOUNTAIN—PART 2, THE*½**
                                    (1978) 105m Filmways/UNIV c

Marilyn Hassett (Jill Kinmont), Timothy Bottoms (John Boothe), Nan Martin (June
Kinmont), Belinda J. Montgomery (Audra-Jo), Gretchen Corbett (Linda), William
Bryant (Bill Kinmont), James A. Bottoms (Mr. Boothe), June Dayton (Mrs.
Boothe), Curtis Credel (Roy Boothe), Carole Tru Foster (Beverly Boothe), Charles
Frank (Mel), George Petrie (Doctor in Los Angeles), Ross Durfee (Presenter at
Luncheon), Jackie Russell (Woman at Bar), Gerri Nelson (Waitress), Tom Jordan
(Bob Kinmont), Harry Moses (Jerry Kinmont), Myron Healey (Doctor in Bishop),
Rev. Bee Landis (Minister), Steve Conte (Wrangler), Craig Chudy (Gary), David
Yanez (Indian Boy), Marlina Vega (Indian Girl).

Hassett returns in an update to the life of quadruplegic ex-skier Jill Kinmont. After
being named "Woman of the Year" for her courageous will to live, she takes a
vacation and falls in love with truck driver Bottoms. She gets over her fear of falling
in love, as Bottoms makes her "feel like a woman for the first time." Although most
of the dramatics of the ex-skier's life were already accounted for in the original, this
movie is strong enough by itself. Told via flashbacks, viewers can appreciate this
film, even if they haven't seen the first.

p, Edward S. Feldman; d, Larry Peerce; w, Douglas Day Stewart; ph, Ric Waite
(Panavision, Technicolor); m, Lee Holdridge; ed, Eve Newman, Walter Han-
nemann; art d, William Campbell; set d, John Dwyer; spec eff, Art Brewer; m/l,
Molly-Ann Leikin, Holdridge (song sung by Merrily Webber).

Drama/Biography   **Cas.**   (PR:A MPAA:PG)

OTHER SIDE OF THE UNDERNEATH, THE*   (1972,
                                            Brit.) 133m Bond c

Sheila Allen, Liz Danciger, Elaine Donovan, Susanka Fraey, Ann Lynn, Jenny
Moss, Penny Slinger.

A tiresome and confused independent production which focuses on the schizophrenia of a group of girls in a therapy session. Bordering on surrealism, it never quite
reveals the causes of their disease.

p, Jack Bond; d&w, Jane Arden (based on the play by Arden); ph, Aubrey Dewar,
Bond; m, Sally Minford; ed, David Mingay.

Drama   (PR:O MPAA:R)

OTHER TOMORROW, THE*½**   (1930) 64m WB-FN bw

Billie Dove (Edith Larrison), Kenneth Thomson (Nort Larrison), Grant Withers
(Jim Carter), Frank Sheridan (Dave Weaver), William Granger (Drum Edge), Otto
Hoffman (Ted Journet), Scott Seaton (Ed Conover).

A sizzling love story with Dove and Withers as one-time sweethearts who discover
that their feelings for each other have not changed despite years of separation.
However, Dove is now married to a self-absorbed man who is insanely jealous of
her. To keep from damaging Dove's honor, Withers acts like a coward. Eventually
Withers and Dove do become lovers, though only after Dove's husband is accidentally killed. Silent star Dove is as refined and beautiful as ever, adding strength to a
script that is overly contrived.

d, Lloyd Bacon; w, Fred Myton, James A. Starr (based on the story by Octavus
Roy Cohen); ph, Lee Garmes.

Drama   (PR:A MPAA:NR)

OTHER WOMAN, THE* (1931, Brit.) 64m Majestic/UA bw

Isobel Elsom (*Roxanne Paget*), David Hawthorne (*Anthony Paget*), Eva Moore (*Mrs. Wycherley*), Pat Paterson (*Prudence Wycherly*), Gladys Frazin (*Minerva Derwent*), Jane Vaughan (*Marian*), Mervin Pearce, Sam Wilkinson.

Elsom plays the hedonistic and self-centered wife of Hawthorne, whom she treats without respect. Her attitude takes a turnabout when she becomes fearful of losing him to another woman. Feature films aren't made much worse than this wretched romantic drama whose cast includes the future Mrs. Charles Boyer, Paterson.

p, Gordon Craig; d&w, G. B. Samuelson (based on the story "The Slave Bracelet" by Olga Hall Brown).

Drama (PR:A MPAA:NR)

OTHER WOMAN, THE*½ (1954) 81m FOX bw

Hugo Haas (*Darman*), Cleo Moore (*Sherry*), Lance Fuller (*Ronnie*), Lucille Barkley (*Mrs. Darman*), Jack Macy (*Lester*), John Qualen (*Papasha*), Jan Arvan (*Collins*), Karolee Kelly (*Marion*), Steve Mitchell (*1st Assistant Director*). Mark Lowell (*2nd Assistant Director*), Melinda Markey (*Actress*), Sue Casey, Sharon Dexter, Ivan Haas, Jan Englund, Art Marshall.

Another one of Hugo Haas' interesting failures casts Haas in a true-to-life role: an emigre producer-director. In the film, he marries the daughter of a studio head and soon gets on would-be actress Moore's bad side when he doesn't cast her for the part she wants. She slips him a spiked drink and arranges for a frame- up. She demands $50,000 from him or she'll produce "evidence" that he had an affair with her. He decides to kill Moore and place the blame on Qualen, an unsuspecting bum. Haas' happy ending is thrown by the wayside when he ends up in jail for the crime. Haas' seventh one-man show (producer, director, writer, actor) is as consistently bad/good (depending on your sentiments) as his previous works.

p,d&w, Hugo Haas; ph, Eddie Fitzgerald; m, Ernest Gold; ed, Robert S. Eisen; art d, Rudi Feld.

Drama/Crime (PR:C-O MPAA:NR)

OTKLONENIE (SEE: DETOUR, 1968, Bulgaria)

OTLEY**½ (1969, Brit.) 90m Open Road/COL c

Tom Courtenay (*Gerald Arthur Otley*), Romy Schneider (*Imogen*), Alan Badel (*Sir Alex Hadrian*), James Villiers (*Hendrickson*), Leonard Rossiter (*Johnston*), Freddy Jones (*Philip Proudfoot*), Fiona Lewis (*Lin*), James Bolam (*Albert*), James Cossins (*Jeffcock*), James Maxwell (*Rollo*), Edward Hardwicke (*Lambert*), Ronald Lacey (*Curtis*), Phyllida Law (*Jean*), Geoffrey Bayldon (*Hewett*), Frank Middlemass (*Bruce*), Damian Harris (*Miles*), Robert Brownjohn (*Paul*), Maureen Toal (*Landlady*), Barry Fantoni (*Larry*), Bernard Sharpe (*Tony*), Paul Angelis (*Constable*), David Kernan (*Ground Steward*), Sheila Steafel (*Ground Stewardess*), Katherine Parr (*Newsagent*), Kathleen Helm (*Dietician*), Norman Shelley, John Savident, Ken Parry (*Businessmen*), Jonathan Cecil (*Young Man at Party*), Georgina Simpson (*Young Girl at Party*), Ron Owen (*Hotel Walter*), Stella Tanner (*Traffic Warden*), Robin Askwith (*1st Kid*), Kevin Bennett (*2nd Kid*), Kenneth Cranham (*3rd Kid*), Robert Gillespie (*Policeman*), Donald McKillop (*Police Driver*), Jimmy Young, Pete Murray, The Herd.

The bumbling Courtenay visits a friend on the night the man is killed. It turns out the man was a member of a gang that smuggles state secrets, and the gang now believes Courtenay holds information it covets. He is kidnaped, beaten up, and questioned by gang members Villiers and Schneider. Set free, he is recaptured by another group. He then discovers he has unknowingly been carrying a tobacco holder that contains a tape-recorded message all the spies want. Schneider is revealed as a member of a Parliament-sanctioned counterspy organization, and there are other unexpected twists and turns in identifying some of the aforementioned characters. A spotty Bond-influenced spoof that showcases Courtenay and not much else.

p, Bruce Cohn Curtis; d, Dick Clement; w, Ian Le Frenais, Clement (based on the novel *Otley* by Martin Waddell); ph, Austin Dempster (Perfect Pathe); m, Stanley Myers; ed, Richard Best; art d, Carmen Dillon; m/l, "Homeless Bones," Myers, Don Partridge (sung by Partridge); makeup, Michael Morris.

Spy/Comedy (PR:C MPAA:M/PG)

OTOKO TAI OTOKO (SEE: MAN AGAINST MAN, 1961, Jap.)

OTROKI VO VSELENNOI (SEE: TEENAGERS IN SPACE, 1975, USSR)

OTTO E MEZZO (SEE: 8½, 1963, Ital.)

OUANGA*½ (1936, Brit.) 63m GT Films/J.H. Hoffberg bw

Fredi Washington, Philip Brandon, Sheldon Leonard, Marie Paxton, Winifred Harris, Sid Easton, Babe Joyce, George Spink.

Washington is a voodoo princess in Jamaica who decides to kill Paxton, the fiancee of plantation owner Leonard, whom she loves. Natives carry Paxton off to the place of sacrifice, but Leonard learns of the plan and rescues his intended. Washington flees into the jungle and dies. The production had a fascinating history, opening with Terwilliger (who gained prominence as a screenwriter for D. W. Griffith) and Berger (who had shot most of Frank Buck's BRING 'EM BACK ALIVE) arriving in Haiti to shoot, but being run off by voodoo curses and strange accidents. They returned to the capital, Port au Prince, and hired drummers, dancers, and extras to take to Jamaica where they planned to film. But before they could leave all the dancers disappeared and the rest of the cast was put in jail. Finally arriving in Jamaica, Terwilliger and Berger put together another cast and began shooting. The heat of the day was too much for the crew so they took to shooting at night under floodlights. Two natives died in a cloudburst, and a cyclone leveled the sets. Disease claimed the life of one American crew member. After two

months, the film was completed but it received virtually no bookings. In 1939, the script was rewritten and shot as POCOMANIA, also known as THE DEVIL'S DAUGHTER, with an all-black cast led by Nina Mae McKinney and Hamtree Harrington. A fascinating but hard-to-find film.

p,d&w, George Terwilliger; ph, Carl Berger.

Drama (PR:A MPAA:NR)

OUR BETTERS***½ (1933) 80m RKO bw

Constance Bennett (*Lady Pearl Grayston*), Gilbert Roland (*Pepi d'Costa*), Charles Starrett (*Fleming Harvey*), Anita Louise (*Bessie*), Grant Mitchell (*Thornton Clay*), Hugh Sinclair (*Lord Henry Bleane*), Alan Mowbray (*Lord George Grayston*), Minor Watson (*Arthur Fenwick*), Violet Kemble-Cooper (*The Duchess*), Tyrell Davis (*Ernest*), Harold Entwistle (*Poole*), Virginia Howell (*Mrs. Saunders*), Walter Walker (*Mr. Saunders*), Phoebe Foster (*The Princess*).

Bennett plays an American hardware heiress married to a stuffy English lord. She gets angry with him and proceeds to scandalize London society with her wild ways. Bennett does such outrageous things as wear black to social events that call for white and throws a wild tea party that ignores all decorum. The style is veddy, veddy British with the polite manner and sophistication. Cukor, in one of his earliest films, handles the comedy well with a smart pacing that never drags. Bennett is good fun, handling her comic turns with ease. The only low point is Davis as an effeminate dancing teacher. Because films made in the 1930s could not portray homosexuals directly, Davis' role is that of the classic stereotyped pansy with rouged lips and mincing behavior. After this film was made, producer Selznick eventually defected to MGM at the invitation of his father-in-law, Louis B. Mayer. He brought Cukor with him from RKO to direct his first film for the new studio.

p, David O. Selznick; d, George Cukor; w, Jane Murfin, Harry Wagstaff Gribble (based on a play by W. Somerset Maugham); ph, Charles Rosher; ed, Jack Kitchin; md, Max Steiner; art d, Van Nest Polglase; cos, Hattie Carnegie.

Comedy (PR:C MPAA:NR)

OUR BLUSHING BRIDES**½ (1930) 79m MGM bw

Joan Crawford (*Jerry Marsh*), Anita Page (*Connie*), Dorothy Sebastian (*Franky*), Robert Montgomery (*Tony Jardine*), Raymond Hackett (*David Jardine*), John Miljan (*Martin W. Sanderson*), Hedda Hopper (*Mrs. Weaver*), Albert Conti (*Mons. Pantoise*), Edward Brophy (*Joe Munsey*), Robert Emmett O'Connor (*The Detective*), Martha Sleeper (*Evelyn Woodforth*), Mary Doran, Norma Drew, Gwen Lee, Claire Dodd, Catherine Moylan, Wilda Mansfield (*Models-Mannequins*), Louise Beavers (*Amelia the Maid*).

Three small-town women—Crawford, Page, and Sebastian—share an apartment and work as department store mannequins in a large city. Page and Sebastian, tired of their drab existence, decide to find suitors but end up making unwise choices. Page eventually commits suicide, and Sebastian finds herself in trouble with the law. Only Crawford keeps her head above water by rejecting the advances of the store owner's son, Montgomery, even though she is head-over-heels in love with him. She ends up in his arms, but not without retaining her sensibility. It's Crawford's picture all the way, as she struts about in sophisticated fashion.

d, Harry Beaumont; w, Bess Meredyth, John Howard Lawson, Edwin Justus Mayer (based on a story by Meredyth); ph, Merritt B. Gerstad; ed, George Hively, Harold Palmer; art d, Cedric Gibbons; cos, Adrian; ch, Albertina Rasch.

Drama (PR:A MPAA:NR)

OUR DAILY BREAD*** (1934) 74m Viking/UA bw (GB: MIRACLE OF LIFE)

Karen Morley (*Mary Sims*), Tom Keene (*John Sims*), John Qualen (*Chris*), Barbara Pepper (*Sally*), Addison Richards (*Louie*), Harry Holman, Bill Engel, Frank Minor, Henry Hall, Ray Spiker, Lynton Brant, Alex Schumberg, Bud Ray, Harry Samuels.

This was part of an intended film trilogy by Vidor, one which he felt throughout his life was equal to his majestic silent classic THE CROWD. It is not, but it has a certain poignancy and quaintness, told in simple terms, that makes it umbilical to the hard times of the early 1930s. At the depth of the Depression, Morley and Keene, down and out like most Americans, inherit a dilapidated farm and seek to save it and themselves by inviting homeless but hard-working people to join them in a farm collective, or loosely organized commune. While everyone slaves away at tilling the soil and eking out a few meals a day, Keene grows restless and depressed. Then Pepper—a slovenly, slatternly city girl—arrives and quickly seduces Keene, persuading him to run away with her. He deserts Morley and his fellow workers and heads for the city in the middle of a drought with the wheat withering under a blazing sun. As he makes his way with Pepper, Keene suddenly discovers a hidden stream and his thoughts go back to the needy people of his farm. He cannot desert them after all and races back to tell one and all that water is at hand and, if they all work like demons, they might be able to divert the stream and irrigate the crops, saving their future. Men, women, and children pour forth with tools and form a chain of workers one run ahead of the diverted stream, furiously digging a ditch and shoring it up with boulders, chopping down trees, bushes, anything in the water's path, until it flows freely downhill into the valley where the farm and thirsty crops await. The jubilant farm workers (some so excited that they cartwheel across the screen) are saved and so, too, is Morley's marriage. The ever-faithful wife is reunited with her errant husband Keene and the world is once more bearable if not overly hopeful. The film was shot on a shoestring after Irving Thalberg, production chief at MGM, told Vidor that he wanted no part of a film dealing with farm communes (or any kind of picture offering a strong Socialist message). Vidor nevertheless went ahead and produced a film of sincerity and powerful emotions, even though his actors, except for Morley and a few others, were amateurs. One report stated that Vidor was compelled to use Pepper—a thoroughly inept actress—at the insistence of one of Vidor's financial backers. She nevertheless is surprisingly convincing as the city tramp and has become a minor cult-film figure. Most of the film reflects Vidor's great vitality, especially the spectacular irrigation scenes at the end, some of the most dramatic and dynamic scenes ever put on celluloid. Yet much of the film lacks the overall polish and professionalism that a first-rate budget would have given it. It is obvious that Vidor was inspired by the Soviet film, THE EARTH THIRSTS (1930) by Yuli Rayzman, but it is also true that the scenes showing crowds of Chinese farmers massing to ward off the locusts in THE GOOD EARTH (1936) were inspired by this Vidor production.

p&d, King Vidor; w, Vidor, Elizabeth Hill, Joseph L. Mankiewicz; ph, Robert Planck; m, Alfred Newman; ed, Lloyd Nossler.

Drama   **Cas.**   **(PR:A MPAA:NR)**

OUR DAILY BREAD**½   (1950, Ger.) 110m Deutsche Film Studio/ Central Cinema bw

Paul Bildt (*Herr Webers, the Father*), Harry Hindemith (*Ernst*), Paul Edwin Roth (*Harry*), Victoria von Ballasko (*The Mother*), Inge Landgut (*Inge*), Helmut Helsig (*Peter*), Ina Halley (*Kate*), Angelika Hurwicz (*Niki*).

This German remake of Vidor's classic film is an interesting work. Made in post-World War II Germany, this version deals with a young German family trying to struggle through the ravages of their postwar life. The film, heavily influenced by the leftist politics that were sweeping the land, brings the family to realize that Socialism is the best route to take. However, the message is not heavy-handed and is woven into the personal drama nicely. The story builds with a quiet dignity that brings the important message through with sympathy and feeling. Director/writer Dudow is best known for his second film, KUHLE WAMPE (1932), a radical, Communist-inspired look at Germany's social and economic conditions. The controversial film was banned in Germany and Dudow, a member of the German Communist Party, fled to Switzerland. He returned to East Germany after WW II, where he resumed his directorial career and went on to win the state award three times. (In German; English subtitles.)

d, Slatan Dudow; w, Dudow, Hans Joachim-Beyer, Ludwig Turek; ph, Robert Baberakd; m, Hanns Eisler; English subtitles, Charles Clement.

Drama   **(PR:O MPAA:NR)**

OUR FIGHTING NAVY   (SEE: TORPEDOED, 1939, Brit.)

OUR GIRL FRIDAY   (SEE: ADVENTURES OF SADIE, THE, 1955, Brit.)

OUR HEARTS WERE GROWING UP**½   (1946) 83m PAR bw

Gail Russell (*Cornelia Otis Skinner*), Diana Lynn (*Emily Kimbrough*), Brian Donlevy (*Tony Minnetti*), James Brown (*Avery Moore*), Bill Edwards (*Dr. Tom Newhall*), William Demarest (*Peanuts Schultz*), Billy De Wolfe (*Roland Du Frere*), Sharon Douglas (*Suzanne Carter*), Mary Hatcher (*"Dibs" Downing*), Sara Haden (*Miss Dill*), Mikhail Rasumny (*Bubchanko*), Isabel Randolph (*Mrs. Southworth*), Frank Faylen (*Federal Agent*), Virginia Farmer (*Miss Thatcher*), Ann Doran (*Monica Lonsdale*), Douglas Walton (*Terence Marlowe*), Charles Williams, Matt McHugh (*Taxi Drivers*), Nell Craig (*Teacher*), Garry Owen (*Bellboy*), Byron Barr (*Roger*), Eddie Carnegie (*Clerk in Newstand*), Roland Dupree, Charles Saggau (*Freshmen*), John Indrisano (*Maxie*), Cy Ring (*Hotel Desk Clerk*), Mona Freeman (*Girl*), Gladys Gale (*Mrs. Appley*), Al Hill (*Louie*), Guy Zanette (*Barney*), Sam Finn, Benny Burt, Theodore Rand, Sam Bazley (*Gangsters*), Arthur Loft (*Desk Sergeant*), James Millican (*Stage Manager*), Pierre Watkin (*Producer*), John "Skins" Miller (*Cab Driver*), Carol Deere, Maggie Mahoney, Ada Ruth Butcher, Gwen Martin, Dorothy Jean Reisner, Mary Kay Jones, Patricia Murphy (*Lowell Schoolgirls*).

Russell and Lynn are a pair of college students swinging through the 1920s a la raccoon coats, flappers, and bobbed hair. They get mixed up with kindhearted bootlegger Donlevy, who helps them get their boy friends back. A truly enjoyable sequel to OUR HEARTS WERE YOUNG AND GAY.

p, Daniel Dare; d, William D. Russell; w, Norman Panama, Melvin Frank (based on the story by Frank Waldman); ph, Stuart Thompson; m, Victor Young; ed, Doane Harrison; art d, Hans Dreier, Haldane Douglas, set d, Sam Comer.

Comedy   **(PR:A MPAA:NR)**

OUR HEARTS WERE YOUNG AND GAY**½   (1944) 81m PAR bw

Gail Russell (*Cornelia Otis Skinner*), Diana Lynn (*Emily Kimbrough*), Charles Ruggles (*Mr. Otis Skinner*), Dorothy Gish (*Mrs. Otis Skinner*), Beulah Bondi (*Miss Abigail Horn*), James Brown (*Avery Moore*), Bill Edwards (*Tom Newhall*), Jean Heather (*Frances "Smitty" Smithers*), Alma Kruger (*Mrs. Lamberton*), Helen Freeman (*Mrs. Smithers*), Joy Harrington, Valentine Perkins (*English Girls*), Georges Renavent (*Mons. Darnet*), Roland Varno (*Pierre Cambouille*), Holmes Herbert (*Captain*), Reginald Sheffield (*Purser*), Edmond Breon (*Cockney Guide*), Nina Koshetz (*Herself*), Noel Neill, MaxineFife, Carmelle Bergstrom (*Girls*), Will Stanton (*Cockney Room Steward*), Olaf Hytten (*Deck Steward*), Roland Dupree (*Boy at Dance*), Nell Craig (*Mother of Little Girl*), Maurice Marsac (*Headwaiter*), Ronnie Rondell (*Waiter*), Will Thunis, Alphonse Martell (*Guards*), Ottola Nesmith (*Fur Shop Owner*), Evan Thomas (*Bus Driver*), Eugene Borden (*Coachman*), Marie McDonald (*Blonde*), Queenie Leonard (*Maid*), Frank Elliott (*Doctor*), Betty Farrington (*Woman*).

Russell and Lynn become part of the 1920 tourist trade to London and Paris with some genuinely funny results. They adapt to foreign customs after a few at-sea romances, an episode in a swanky restaurant involving shedding rabbit capes, and an evening locked in Paris' Notre Dame Cathedral. An equally enjoyable sequel, OUR HEARTS WERE GROWING UP, made it to the screen two years later. Gish's appearance marked her return to Paramount after a 17-year absence. Russell and Lynn as the two authors who blithely careened around Europe in the 1920s and then wrote about it, were delightful ingenues at the time, although Russell suffered

the agonies of the damned from stage fright, which continued all during her brief career. Both dead now—raven-haired Russell tragically at the age of 36, and Lynn, the daughter-in-law of New York Post publisher Dorothy Schiff, of a stroke at the age of 45—neither lived up to her early promise.

p, Sheridan Gibney; d, Lewis Allen; w, Gibney (based on the book by Cornelia Otis Skinner, Emily Kimbrough); ph, Theodor Sparkuhl; m, Werner Heymann; ed, Paul Weatherwax; art d, Hans Dreier, Earl Hedrick; spec eff, Gordon Jennings; m/l, Kermit Goell, Ted Grouya.

Comedy   **(PR:A MPAA:NR)**

OUR HITLER, A FILM FROM GERMANY***   (1980, Ger.)
450m OMNI Zoetrope c (HITLER, EIN FILM AUS DEUTSCHLAND; AKA: OUR HITLER; HITLER, A FILM FROM GERMANY)

Heinz Schubert, Peter Kern, Hellmut Lange, Rainer von Artenfels, Martin Sperr, Peter Moland, Johannes Buzalski, Alfred Edel, Amelie Syberberg, Harry Baer, Peter Luhr, Andre Heller.

Simply put, this is both a magnificent and horrifying work about the dark side of human nature. German director Syberberg, who was born in 1935 and grew up under Nazi rule, presents an epic nightmare ruminating on the effect Adolf Hitler had and continues to have, not only on Germany, but all mankind. Originally this was presented on German television in four parts, but the American release (at 7½ hours) is generally shown in two halves. Subtitling the respective chapters "From the World Ash Tree to the Goethe Oak of Buchenwald," "A German Dream. . .Until the End of the World," "The End of a Winter's Tale and the Final Victory of Progress," and "We Children of Hell Recall the Age of the Grail," Syberberg's theme is as simple as the film is complex. Such evil as existed in the mind of Adolf Hitler, argues the director, could never have existed without the support—however unwitting—of the rest of humanity (the adverb "OUR" was added to the American release by its distributor, Francis Ford Coppola, driving the point home with clarity). The presentation itself is the stuff of nightmares. Hitler is alternatively characterized by actors, old radio broadcasts, and a ventriloquist dummy. The music of the Fuehrer's beloved Richard Wagner is worked in, creating a sort of decadent modern Wagnerian opera in the course of the film. One of the more haunting images presented is a toga-clad Hitler, rising from the composer's grave, an image inspired by some noted illustrations from Dante's *Inferno*. Syberberg's own theory of cinema saw film as *the* art of the 20th Century, and here he created what he hoped was a filmed equivalent of a great symphonic score. Like music, the film has recurring motifs and ideas, clashing and working in harmony throughout the piece. Syberberg's vision is not an optimistic one; it is forthright and brutal in it's hallucinatory honesty. He presents, much like Franz Kafka's *The Metamorphosis*, a vision of dark and unsettling dreams. And, that dream is us.

p, Bernd Eichinger; d&w, Hans-Jurgen Syberberg; ph, Dietrich Lohmann; m, Richard Wagner; ed, Jutta Brandstaedter; art d, Hans Gailling; cos, Barbara Gailling, Brigitte Kuhlenthal; puppets, Barbara Buchwald, Hans M. Stummer.

Drama   **(PR:O MPAA:NR)**

OUR LADY OF FATIMA   (SEE: MIRACLE OF OUR LADY OF FATIMA, THE, 1952)

OUR LEADING CITIZEN*½   (1939) 89m PAR bw

Bob Burns (*Lem Schofield*), Gene Lockhart (*J.T. Tapley*), Susan Hayward (*Judith Schoefield*), Joseph Allen, Jr. (*Clay Clinton*), Charles Bickford (*Shep Muir*), Elizabeth Patterson (*Aunt Tillie Clark*), Clarence Kolb (*Jim Hanna*), Paul Guilfoyle (*Jerry Peters*), Fay Helm (*Tonia*), Kathleen Lockhart (*Mrs. Barker*), Otto Hoffman (*Stony*), Kathryn Sheldon (*Miss Swan*), Hattie Noel (*Drusilla*), James Kelso (*Chief of Police Donovan*), Russell Hicks (*Chairman*), Gus Glassmire (*Doctor*), Thomas Louden (*Frederick the Butler*), Olaf Hytten (*Charles the Butler*), Harry C. Bradley (*Director*), Harry Smiley, Jack H. Richardson, Thomas A. Curran, Hayden Stevenson, Broderick O'Farrell, Frank O'Connor, Harry B. Stafford, Helen Dickson, Ethel May Halls (*Members*), Sid D'Albrook, Harry Tenbrook, Galan Galt, Oscar G. "Dutch" Hendrian, Paul Kruger, George Magrill (*Workmen*), Ruth Robinson (*Mrs. Hanna*), Nell Craig, Peggy Leon, Lillian West (*Bridge Players*), Heinie Conklin, C.L. Sherwood (*Porters*), Syd Saylor (*Sam the Porter*), Gertrude Messinger, Florence A. Dudley, Jane Webb (*Telephone Operators*), Wally Maher (*Convention Clerk*), Cyril Ring, Larry Steers, Arthur Arlington (*Delegates*), Monte Blue (*Frank*), Frances Morris (*Maid*), Phil Dunham (*Janitor*).

Ever since Will Rogers died in 1935, producers had been attempting to find someone who could replace his "down-home" humor on screen and they thought they had that someone with bazooka-playing Arkansas Philosopher Bob Burns. They were wrong. This very naive picture has Burns as an attorney who welcomes the son of his late partner, Allen, into lawyering, much to the delight of Burns' daughter, Hayward. Allen had been practicing in New York and has now returned to his roots. Lockhart is the local heavyweight factory owner and Allen is all for becoming his attorney despite the fact that Burns says Lockhart doesn't care much about his workers and has been slashing people and production costs in order to make more money. Lockhart's workers strike when he gives them a 10 percent wage cut and Burns drops Lockhart as a client, but Allen remains and Hayward is disappointed with that decision. Bickford leads a group of scab-goons to break the strike, the factory explodes from a bomb, and a man is killed. This causes the locals to have a meeting where Burns pleads for them to be calm, follow the Golden Rule, and try to smooth out the problems. Lockhart backs Burns, then puts Allen up as a candidate for U.S. senator from the unnamed state. Allen is thrilled, but Burns sees right through Lockhart's ploy, so he tells Lockhart to cease the nomination for Allen or he will be exposed by Burns as having wrongfully taken the property of Patterson, a mountain woman who didn't know what was happening. Lockhart agrees to pay Patterson back and Burns shows Allen the Lockhart-signed IOU; then Burns says he'd like to nominate Allen. At the finale, Burns triumphs when he has Bickford tossed out of town. Lockhart nominates someone else at the convention, Allen proposes Burns as a candidate, and the picture ends with Allen and Hayward in each other's arms again. Not funny and not fast, it was a B film all the way, despite the fact that Paramount attempted to elevate it by inviting a score of state governors to the premiere.

p, George Arthur; d, Alfred Santell; w, John C. Moffitt (based on a story by Irvin S. Cobb); ph, Victor Milner; ed, Hugh Bennett; art d, Hans Dreier, Roland Anderson.

Drama   (PR:A   MPAA:NR)

OUR LITTLE GIRL½   (1935) 64m FOX bw

Shirley Temple (Molly Middleton), Rosemary Ames (Elsa Middleton), Joel McCrea (Dr. Donald Middleton), Lyle Talbot (Rolfe Brent), Erin O'Brien-Moore (Sarah Boynton), Poodles Hanneford (Circus Performer), Margaret Armstrong (Amy), Rita Owin (Alice), Leonard Carey (Jackson), J. Farrell MacDonald (Mr. Tramp), Jack Baxley (Leyton), Warren Hymer.

When Temple's folks drift apart—her dad involved with his work, her mom involved with their neighbor—she runs away in an attempt to reconcile the pair. Second only to Curly Top's appearance in importance is a location known as "Heaven's Gate," the favorite family spot where the couple reunites. The young star makes this one worth watching, despite its slow-moving plot and weak script.

p, Edward Butcher; d, John Robertson; w, Stephen Avery, Allen Rivkin, Jack Yellen (based on the story "Heaven's Gate" by Florence Leighton Pfalzgraf); ph, John Seitz; md, Oscar Bradley; m/l, Paul Francis Webster, Lew Pollack.

Drama   (PR:AAA   MPAA:NR)

OUR MAN FLINT*   (1966) 107m FOX c

James Coburn (Derek Flint), Lee J. Cobb (Cramden), Gila Golan (Gila), Edward Mulhare (Malcolm Rodney), Benson Fong (Dr. Schneider), Shelby Grant (Leslie), Sigrid Valdis (Anna), Gianna Serra (Gina), Helen Funai (Sakito), Michael St. Clair (Gruber), Rhys Williams (Dr. Krupov), Russ Conway (American General), Ena Hartman (WAC), William Walker (American Diplomat), Peter Brocco (Dr. Wu), James Brolin (Technician).

James Coburn's first starring role casts him as secret agent Derek Flint, an expert 007-type who is picked by a computer to put a stop to GALAXY, a secret organization with plans of world domination via weather control. He sets out with his cigarette lighter, which has some 83 uses, and locates the three scientists who have masterminded the plot. He is captured, but escapes and switches clothes with one of GALAXY'S guards. Before time runs out (the world is given one hour to surrender) Coburn blows up enemy headquarters and saves the world. The script is loaded with holes and the direction is tired, but it's still one of the better Bond spoofs. Jerry Goldsmith's lively score helps. IN LIKE FLINT, the 1967 sequel, also starred Coburn.

p, Saul David; d, Daniel Mann; w, Hal Fimberg, Ben Starr (based on a story by Fimberg); ph, Daniel L. Fapp (CinemaScope, DeLuxe Color); m, Jerry Goldsmith; ed, William Reynolds; art d, Jack Martin Smith, Ed Graves; set d, Walter M. Scott, Raphael Bretton; cos, Ray Aghayan; spec eff, L.B. Abbott; makeup, Ben Nye.

Spy Drama/Satire   (PR:A   MPAA:NR)

OUR MAN IN HAVANA*   (1960, Brit.) 111m Kingsmead/COL bw

Alec Guiness (Jim Wormold), Burl Ives (Dr. Hasselbacher), Maureen O'Hara (Beatrice Severn), Ernie Kovacs (Capt. Segura), Noel Coward (Hawthorne), Ralph Richardson ("C"), Jo Morrow (Milly Wormold), Paul Rogers (Hubert Carter), Gregoire Aslan (Cifuentes), Jose Prieto (Lopez), Timothy Bateson (Rudy), Duncan Macrae (MacDougal), Maurice Denham (Navy Officer), Raymond Huntley (Army Officer), Hugh Manning (RAF Officer), Maxine Audley (Teresa), Yvonne Buckingham (Striptease Girl), Ferdy Mayne (Prof. Sanchez), Karel Stepanek (Dr. Braun), Gerik Schjelderup (Svenson), Elizabeth Welsh (Beautiful Woman), Rachel Roberts.

Subtle, sly espionage agents go bumbling through the sultry Cuban night with master comic Guinness in a droll comedy that is as hilarious as it is absurd. The real world of spies is ridiculous enough and here that great British director Reed takes those absurdities and crams them into the twisting, gyrating, and Machiavellian mind of vacuum cleaner salesman Guinness. the innocuous Guinness has a small store in Havana where he is suddenly approached by Coward, a master spy who enlists Guinness as one of his agents in a "weak" area of information. Realizing he will be making good money for every tidbit of information he passes along to headquarters in London, and knowing there is no real information to gather, Guinness, to provide the good things in life for his teenage daughter Morrow, begins to invent information. Kovacs, the reportedly brutal chief of police who has cast a covetous eye on Morrow, gets reports that Guinness has been acting in a furtive manner. He spies on Guinness, while Guinness spies on him, and the whole thing begins to crazily expand into a massive intrigue where no intrigue exists. Now out of control, the situation blows up with Ives being killed and Guinness dispatching a very real enemy to save himself. Moreover, he has delivered preposterous drawings of giant weird-looking war machines in the mountains around Havana but these are nothing more than huge fabrications based on what he knows—vacuum cleaners. Unable to bear the pressure any longer, Guinness admits to hoaxing the British intelligence service and he is ordered back to London with Morrow where he meets an unexpected fate. OUR MAN IN HAVANA is probably Guinness' most droll comedy and it mixes its subtle mirth with some fearful and sinister consequences. Guinness is superb as the greedy, imaginative shop owner, but Kovacs, as the posturing police chief, and Coward, as the British spy chief, really steal the film. The production is more of an inside joke among Coward, Guinness, Reed, and Greene than something for a general audience, but the black humor seeps through the soggiest and most obtuse scenes. The cast and crew shot this film in Havana shortly after Fidel Castro's takeover. There were no tourists in Havana then, only starving people, prisoners in caged carts en route to interrogation, and a few forlorn Americans. Guinness and his wife dined with writer Ernest Hemingway

and the actor later met critic Kenneth Tynan in a bar who said he had two tickets to an event that night and asked Guinness to join him. When the actor asked Tynan what he was going to see, the drama critic replied (as quoted from Blessings in Disguise by Alec Guinness): "They are shooting a couple of 16-year-olds, a boy and a girl. I thought you might like to see it." Guinness declined.

p&d, Carol Reed; w, Graham Greene (based on his novel); ph, Oswald Morris (CinemaScope); m, Hermanos Deniz; ed, Bert Bates; art d, John Box; cos, Phyllis Dalton.

Comedy   (PR:A   MPAA:NR)

OUR MAN IN MARRAKESH, 1966   (SEE: BANG! BANG!YOU'RE DEAD, 1966, Brit.)

OUR MAN IN MARRAKESH, 1967   (SEE: THAT MAN GEORGE, 1967, Fr./Ital./Span.)

OUR MISS BROOKS½   (1956) 84m Lute/WB bw

Eve Arden (Miss Constance Brooks), Gale Gordon (Osgood Conklin), Don Porter (Lawrence Nolan), Robert Rockwell (Phillip Boynton), Jane Morgan (Margaret Davis), Richard Crenna (Walter Denton), Nick Adams (Gary Nolan), Leonard Smith ("Stretch" Snodgrass), Gloria MacMillan (Harriet Conklin), Joe Kearns (Mr. Stone), William Newell (Dr. Henley), Philip Van Zandt (Mr. Webster), Marjorie Bennett (Mrs. Boynton), June Blair (Miss Lonelyhearts), Joe Forte (Butler), Leo Curley, David Alpert (Realty Men), Herb Vigran, Frank Mitchell (Reporters).

A long version of the celebrated television series also features Arden and Rockwell in starring roles. On the screen, she continues her pursuit of biology professor Rockwell, who is tied to his mother's apron strings. Arden is able to make him jealous, however, when she decides to tutor a student and the child's father shows interest in her. Redundant for those familiar with the weekly series, but pleasant viewing all the same.

p, David Weisbart; d, Al Lewis; w, Lewis, Joseph Quillan (based on an idea by Robert Mann, from the CBS television series); ph, Joseph LaShelle; m, Roy Webb; ed, Frederick Y. Smith; art d, Leo K. Kuter.

Comedy   (PR:AA   MPAA:NR)

OUR MISS FRED*   (1972, Brit.) 96m EMI/Willis Worldwide c

Danny La Rue, Alfred Marks, Lance Percival, Lally Bowers, Frances de la Tour, Walter Gotell.

Female impersonator La Rue and his troupe are captured in France during WW II and he manages to escape by dressing in women's clothes. A weak British comedy along the lines of the OLD MOTHER RILEY series.

p, Josephine Douglas; d, Bob Kellett; w, Hugh Leonard; ph, Dick Bush (Technicolor); m, Peter Greenwell.

Comedy   (PR:C   MPAA:PG)

OUR MODERN MAIDENS*½   (1929) 70m MGM bw

Joan Crawford (Billie Brown), Rod LaRocque (Abbott), Douglas Fairbanks, Jr. (Gil), Anita Page (Kentucky), Albert Gran (B. Bickering Brown), Josephine Dunn (Ginger), Edward Nugent (Reg).

In this sequel to OUR DANCING DAUGHTERS Crawford and Fairbanks both fall in love with other people before their wedding is to take place. Fairbanks becomes involved with Page, his fiancee's house guest. Guilt-ridden, he decides he must go through with his marriage to Crawford, but does not know that Page has become pregnant. The marriage takes place, and, just before the honeymoon, Page revels her secret. Crawford leaves to be with her true love, and Fairbanks obtains an annulment so that he and Page can be married. Films dealing with this somewhat racy subject matter were allowed in the days before the Motion Picture Production Code.

p, Hunt Stromberg; d, Jack Conway; w, Josephine Lovett (based on her story); ph, Oliver Marsh; m, Dr. William Axt; ed, Sam S. Zimbalist; art d, Cedric Gibbons; cos, Adrian; ch, George Cunningham; titles, Ruth Cummings, Marian Ainslee.

Drama/Romance   (PR:A   MPAA:NR)

OUR MOTHER'S HOUSE*½   (1967, Brit.) 104m Heron-Filmways/ MGM c

Dirk Bogarde (Charlie Hook), Margaret Brooks (Elsa Hook), Pamela Franklin (Diana Hook), Louis Sheldon Williams (Hubert Hook), John Gugolka (Dunstan Hook), Mark Lester (Jiminee Hook), Sarah Nicholls (Gerty Hook), Gustav Henry (Willy Hook), Parnham Wallace (Louis), Yootha Joyce (Mrs. Quayle), Claire Davidson (Miss Bailey), Annette Carell (Mother), Gerald Sim (Bank Clerk), Edina Ronay (Doreen), Diana Ashley (Girl Friend), Garfield Morgan (Mr. Moley), Faith Kent (Woman Client), John Arnatt (Man Client), Jack Silk (Motorcyclist), Anthony Nicholls (Mr. Halbert).

The seven Hook children live in a large Victorian home with their bedridden mother, taking care of the finances and upkeep themselves. Every evening they allow time to listen to their mother read to them from the Bible—"mothertime" as the children call it. When their mother dies, they secretly bury her in the backyard in an effort to avoid being sent to an orphanage. They set up a shrine in a backyard shed and continue their "mothertime" tradition. They go to school and do their chores and meet nightly to discuss money matters. A visiting schoolteacher is about to find out their secret when long-lost father Bogarde arrives. He is far less responsible than the children, however, and begins to frivolously spend their money and bring home women. He eventually reveals to them that they are all illegitimate, shattering the saintly illusions of their mother. Furious, one of the girls deals Bogarde a fatal blow with a fireplace poker, forcing the youngsters to dispense with their childish innocence and to leave the house.

p&d, Jack Clayton; w, Jeremy Brooks, Haya Harareet (based on the novel by

Julian Gloag); ph, Larry Pizer (Metrocolor); m, Georges Delerue; ed, Tom Priestly; art d, Reece Pemberton; set d, Ian Whittaker; makeup, Bill Lodge.

Drama **(PR:O MPAA:NR)**

OUR NEIGHBORS—THE CARTERS** (1939) 83m PAR bw

Fay Bainter *(Ellen Carter)*, Frank Craven *(Doc Carter)*, Edmund Lowe *(Bill Hastings)*, Genevieve Tobin *(Gloria Hastings)*, Mary Thomas *(Mattie Carter)*, Scotty Beckett *(Dickie Carter)*, Bennie Bartlett *(Junior Carter)*, Donald Brenon *(Paul Carter)*, Nana Bryant *(Louise Wilcox)* Thurston Hall *(Mr. Guilfoyle)*, Granville Bates *(Joseph Laurence)*, Edward McWade *(Pop Hagen)*, Norman Phillips *(Henry Laurence)*, Richard Clayton *(Peter Bush)*, Frank Reicher *(Dr. Proser)*, John Conte *(Reporter)*, Martha Mears *(Girl Reporter)*, Olaf Hytten *(Butler)*, Edward Marr *(Storekeeper)*, Guy Wilkerson *(Father)*, George Anderson *(Drug Co. Representative)*, Frances Morris *(Secretary to Mr. Guilfoyle)*, Richard Denning *(Pilot)*, Judith King *(Secretary)*, Grace Hayle, Betty Farrington *(Women)*, Frank O'Connor, Billy Engle *(Men)*, Janet Waldo, Patsy Mace *(Receptionists)*, Wanda Kay, Audrey Maynard *(Usherettes)*.

Craven is the head of the Carter clan and operator of a local drug store. When a cut-rate chain store opens, he and his family begin to panic. The day is saved upon the arrival from the big city of Lowe and his wife, Tobin. The story is stripped to its barest essentials, relying on strong characterizations to carry the picture.

p, Charles R. Rogers; d, Ralph Murphy; w, S.K. Lauren (based on the story by Renaud Hoffman); ph, George Barnes; ed, William Shea; md, Sigmund Krumgold; art d, Hans Dreier, Earl Hedrick.

Drama/Comedy **(PR:AAA MPAA:NR)**

OUR RELATIONS**** (1936) 65m Stan Laurel-Hal Roach/MGM bw

Stan Laurel *(Himself/Alfie Laurel)*, Oliver Hardy *(Himself/Bert Hardy)*, Sidney Toler *(Captain of the S.S. Periwinkle)*, Alan Hale, Sr. *(Joe Groagan the Waiter)*, Daphne Pollard *(Mrs. Daphne Hardy)*, Betty Healy *(Mrs. Betty Laurel)*, Iris Adrian *(Alice the Beer Garden Girl)*, Lona Andre *(Lily the Other Cafe Girl)*, James Finlayson *(Finn the Chief Engineer)*, Arthur Housman *(Inebriated Stroller)*, Jim Kilganon *(Other Drunk)*, Charlie Hall *(Pawnshop Extra)*, Harry Bernard, Harry Arras, Charles A. Bachman, Harry Neilman *(Officers)*, John Kelly *(1st Mate)*, Art Rowlands, Harry Wilson *(Seamen)*, Baldwin Cooke, Nick Copland, James C. Morton, Lee Phelps *(Bartenders)*, George Jimenez *(Cafe Manager)*, Bob Wilbur *(Cab Driver)*, Jim Pierce *(Doorman)*, Ruth Warren *(Mrs. Addlequist)*, Walter Taylor *(Finn's Friend, Snuffy)*, Constantine Romanoff *(Tuffy)*, Alex Pollard *(Waiter)*, Joe Bordeaux, Stanley "Tiny" Sandford, Billy Engle, Bob O'Connor *(Grubby Wharf Toughs)*, Bobby Dunn *(Messenger Boy)*, Ralf Harolde, Noel Madison *(Gangsters)*, Ham Kinsey *(Stunt Double for Laurel)*, Cy Slocum *(Stunt Double for Hardy)*, Del Henderson *(Judge Polk)*, Fred Holmes *(Bailiff)*, Bob Finlayson, Alex Finlayson, Foxy Hall, Jay Eaton, Jack Hill, Rita Dunn, Alice Cooke, Ed Brandenberg, Jack Egan, Bunny Bronson, Marvel Andre, Dick Gilbert, Jack Cooper, Jerry Breslin, Bill Madsen, Ernie Alexander, Tony Campenero, Polly Chase, Jay Belasco, Gertrude Astor, Buddy Messinger, Gertie Messinger Sharpe, David Sharpe, Rose Langdon, Johnny Arthur, Kay McCoy, Mrs. Jack W. Burns, Rheba Campbell, Margo Sage, Ed Parker, Leo Sulkey, Marvin Hatley, Sam Lufkin, Barney O'Toole, Ray Cooke, Art Miles, Crete Sipple, Dick French, Rosemary Theby.

Perhaps the best Laurel and Hardy feature, OUR RELATIONS marked Stan Laurel's first producer credit and he did a heck of a job in this most elaborate picture that owes a great deal to Shakespeare's "Comedy Of Errors." Based on a 1903 short story by the master of grisly, W. W. Jacobs (who also wrote "The Monkey's Paw"), OUR RELATIONS was later cut to a one-reeler known as SAILOR'S DOWNFALL, but it hardly captured the fun of the full-length version. Stan and Ollie are sailors who get shore leave and have a valuable diamond ring they are to deliver. In the past, they've spent all their money while on liberty and they are aware of their own shortcomings in the cash department, so they give their cash to Toler, their captain, and tell him to hold it in safekeeping and to not return it to them until after their ship has sailed. The town they are visiting is the same place where their twin brothers now live in domestic harmony with their wives, Pollard and Healy, two women who have raised the art of henpecking to new levels. Stan and Ollie meet two girls, Adrian and Lona Andre, in a local waterfront dive. Nearby, their twins are quaffing beer with their mates in another tavern. Need we say that the duos are soon mixed? The diamond ring turns up missing and the boys get involved with gangsters Harolde and Madison, and when they can't locate the jewel, they are placed in cement blocks and left on a pier where they will soon fall into the water. Naturally, it all comes together in the end with the right husbands rematched with the correct wives and the twins being reunited after a long separation. Several funny scenes include Laurel and Hardy's attempt to convince Toler to give them back their money, a set-piece in a hotel room where they have been placed without clothing, their difficulty (as the married men) to make beer-hall owner Hale understand that they had not been there earlier with Adrian and Andre, and an hysterical sequence with Finlayson where he has a light bulb in his mouth and his wig secured on his head by hot mustard. Amidst all the fun, there is real danger to the boys when they come up against the villains. This was the first and only time they worked with director Lachman, who was not known for his comedic skills (his most famous feature was DANTE'S INFERNO; he also did a couple of CHARLIE CHAN films) and he seemed to just turn on Mate's camera and let the boys have their way with the humor. This was a larger picture than Laurel and Hardy usually made and the nightclub set looks more like something Busby Berkeley might have used. A standout comedy role was played by Housman as a drunk, and Stanley Sandford, one of the wharf rats, was appearing in his final film of the 23 he made with Laurel and Hardy. It was one of Iris Adrian's first roles and she was developing the character she would play for the next several decades, the brash, loud blonde with a heart of gold. Despite the excellence of this film, other L&H movies are better remembered and no one seems to know why. (See: LAUREL AND HARDY series, Index)

p, Stan Laurel, L.A. French; d, Harry Lachman; w, Richard Connell, Felix Adler, Charles Rogers, Jack Jevne (based on the short story "The Money Box" by William Wymark Jacobs); ph, Rudolph Mate; m, LeRoy Shield; ed, Bert Jordan; md, Shield; art d, Arthur I. Royce, William L. Stevens; spec eff, Roy Seawright.

Comedy **Cas.** **(PR:AA MPAA:NR)**

OUR SILENT LOVE½** (1969, Jap.) 114m Tokyo Eiga/Toho bw (CHICHI TO KO)

Kinya Kitaoji, Keiju Kobayashi, Yoko Naito, Mayumi Ozora, Hideko Takamine, Izumi Hara, Daisuke Kato, Nobuko Otowa, Ryo Tamura.

The son of deaf-mute parents is offered a job by a factory owner who sees him as a prospect for his daughter, also a deaf-mute. He tries to break up his daughter's relationship with a deaf-mute boy because he fears their children will be born suffering the same affliction. The daughter and her lover agree to a suicide pact, but are saved with the encouragement of the young factory worker. A tender film from a one-time assistant to Keisuke Kinoshita (BALLAD OF NARAYAMA), who arranged the marriage of director Matsuyama and actress Takamine.

p, Sanezumi Fujimoto; d&w, Zenzo Matsuyama; ph, Kozo Okazaki (Tohoscope); m, Toru Funamura.

Drama **(PR:A MPAA:NR)**

OUR TIME*½ (1974) 90m WB c (AKA:DEATH OF HER INNOCENCE)

Pamela Sue Martin *(Abby)*, Betsy Slade *(Muffy)*, Parker Stevenson *(Michael)*, George O'Hanlon, Jr. *(Malcolm)*, Roderick Cook *(Headmaster)*, Edith Atwabter *(Mrs. Pendleton)*, Meg Wyllie *(Nurse)*, Marijane Maricle *(Miss Picard)*, Michael Gray *(Buzzy)*, Karen Balkin *(Laura)*, Debralee Scott *(Ann)*, Nora Heflin *(Emmy)*, Kathryn Holcomb *(Helen)*, Mary Jackson *(Miss Moran)*, Carol Arthur *(Gym Teacher)*, Hope Summers *(Biology Teahcer)*, Jerry Hardin *(Keats)*, Robert Walden *(Frank)*.

Set in the 1950s, OUR TIME tells the saccharine tale of a pair of young girls—Martin and Slade—and their first experiences with the opposite sex. Slade becomes pregnant and an abortion by a young medical student results in her death. Essentially a made-for-TV film (DEATH OF HER INNOCENCE was its TV title), the picture is totally void of any signs of life—the characters lack heart, the script lacks movement and the music is petrified. Directed by ex-news anchor Peter Hyams, who went on to tackle 2010, the sequel to 2001, A SPACE ODYSSEY. Martin and Stevenson both went on to teeny-bopper status with their roles in TV's NANCY DREW and THE HARDY BOYS, respectively.

p, Richard A. Roth; d, Peter Hyams; w, Jane C. Stanton; ph, Jules Brenner (Technicolor); m, Michel Legrand; ed, James Mitchell; art d, Peter Wooley; set d, Chuck Pierce.

Drama **(PR:A MPAA:PG)**

OUR TOWN**** (1940) 90m Principal Artists/UA bw

Frank Craven *(Mr. Morgan, the Narrator)*, William Holden *(George Gibbs)*, Martha Scott *(Emily Webb)*, Fay Bainter *(Mrs. Gibbs)*, Beulah Bondi *(Mrs. Webb)*, Thomas Mitchell *(Dr. Gibbs)*, Guy Kibbee *(Editor Webb)*, Stuart Erwin *(Howie Newsome)*, Phillip Wood *(Simon Stinson)*, Doro Merande *(Mrs. Soames)*, Ruth Tobey *(Rebecca Gibbs)*, Douglas Gardiner *(Wally Webb)*, Arthur Allen *(Prof. Willet)*, Spencer Charters *(The Constable)*, Tim Davis *(Joe Crowell)*, Dix Davis *(Si Crowell)*, Dan White *(Wedding Guest)*, Charles Trowbridge *(Reverend)*.

The classic Pulitzer Prize-winning Thornton Wilder play was brought to the screen with style and wonderful characterizations by an inspired cast. Small-town America is typified by the role of Craven, a down-home philosopher and narrator who profiles the lives of citizens living in Grover's Corners in New England. Scott is the idealistic but hard-working daughter of the local editor and Holden is the son of the local physician who falls in love with her, goes through a difficult courtship and finally wins Scott's hand in marriage, only to lose her during childbirth. Life in this peaceful, quaint small town is shown in three periods, 1901, 1904, and 1913, with attention basically focused upon two families, those of Holden and Scott, showing the adolescence and maturing of the boy and girl while an adult world looks on amused and delighted at the eventual bond between the two. The portrait is a microcosm of small-town America before WW II, and director Wood follows the Wilder script faithfully to show the laughter, the love, and pain in the lives of his heartwarming characters. Wood's techniques are marvelous to behold, a dazzling series of dissolves, moody and bright alternating lighting, wonderful detail, and montages that capture the flavor of the period and the simple life styles. In one fantastic five-minute montage, Scott takes a nightmare excursion through the village graveyard and sees all of her friends and relatives beyond her own death, even peering upward at her husband, Holden, and family members from her own grave, a fantasy she experiences while going through the agony of childbirth. Scott, in her first film role, is splendid, as is Holden. Mitchell as the physician and Kibbee as the editor are superb in their supporting roles, along with their wives, played by Bainter and Bondi. Erwin plays a colorful milkman and Charters a passionate cop. Wood's outstanding direction is enhanced by a stirring score by Copland and eye-filling sets by Menzies, whose genius for capturing any locale is much in evidence.

p, Sol Lesser; d, Sam Wood; w, Thornton Wilder, Frank Craven, Harry Chandlee (based on the play by Wilder); ph, Bert Glennon; m, Aaron Copland; ed, Sherman Todd; md, Irvin Talbot; prod d, William Cameron Menzies, Harry Horner.

Drama **Cas.(PR:A MPAA:NR)**

OUR VERY OWN** (1950) 92m Goldwyn/RKO bw

Ann Blyth *(Gail)*, Jane Wyatt *(Lois Macaulay)*, Donald Cook *(Fred Macaulay)*, Farley Granger *(Chuck)*, Joan Evans, *(Joan)*, Ann Dvorak *(Mrs. Lynch)*, Natalie Wood *(Penny)*, Gus Schilling *(Frank)*, Phyllis Kirk *(Zaza)*, Jessie Grayson *(Violet,*

Cook), Martin Milner *(Bert)*, Rita Hamilton *(Gwendolyn)*, Ray Teal *(Mr. Lynch)*, Harold Lloyd, Jr. *(Boy)*.

Shortly before her high school graduation 18-year-old Blyth learns that Wyatt and Cook are her foster parents, leaving her with curiosity about her real mother. She begins a search which ends at the doorstep of Dvorak, who is less than thrilled to see the girl. Blyth realizes how understanding and loving her foster parents are and includes this revelation in her graduation day speech. A less-than-average script which could have done better in the hands of the more masterful melodramatic director Douglas Sirk. A fine cast is wasted, including the pigtailed Natalie Wood. This marked the film debuts of Kirk and Lloyd.

p, Samuel Goldwyn; d, David Miller; w, F. Hugh Herbert; ph, Lee Garmes; m, Victor Young; ed, Sherman Todd; art d, Richard Day; cos, Mary Wills.

Drama **(PR:A MPAA:NR)**

OUR VINES HAVE TENDER GRAPES**** (1945) 105m MGM bw

Edward G. Robinson *(Martinius Jacobson)*, Margaret O'Brien *(Selma Jacobson)*, James Craig *(Nels Halverson)*, Agnes Moorehead *(Bruna Jacobson)*, Jackie "Butch" Jenkins *(Arnold Hanson)*, Morris Carnovsky *(Bjorn Bjornson)*, Frances Gifford *(Viola Johnson)*, Sara Haden *(Mrs. Bjornson)*, Louis Jean Heydt *(Mr. Faraasen)*, Francis Pierlot *(Minister)*, Greta Granstedt *(Mrs. Faraasen)*, Arthur Space *(Mr. Peter Hanson)*, Elizabeth Russell *(Kola Hanson)*, Dorothy Morris *(Ingborg Jenson)*, Charles Middleton *(Kurt Jensen)*, Arthur Hohl *(Dvar Svenson)*, Abigail Adams *(Girl)*, Johnny Berkes *(Driver)*, Rhoda Williams *(Marguerite Larsen)*, George Lloyd *(Farmer)*.

Few films touch the heart so deeply as this one and fewer still present such moving performances while doing it. Robinson is terrific as the Norwegian-born Wisconsin farmer who lives with daughter O'Brien, a widower who is strict with his precocious offspring but is also loving and tender. In O'Brien's world there are daily tragedies of great import such as the time she accidentally kills a squirrel and how her understanding father comforts her. Then Robinson hears that a huge circus is passing through town on a train, something his daughter will not have the opportunity to see; he drives with O'Brien in the middle of the night to the train station and offers one of the foremen of the circus a few dollars if he'll only bring one of the elepahnts off the train for a few minutes. He does and O'Brien is filled with wonder at the sight of the great, gentle beast. When attractive Gifford arrives in Benson Junction to teach school a great deal of excitement ensues, especially among the children and gossipy neighbors who observe how handsome town editor Craig is drawn to her. Craig proposes after a while but Gifford draws back, fearing that she will be bored to death in the small farming community with its dull day-to-day existence. Craig is called to serve in WW II and asks Gifford to wait for him but she cannot make such a commitment. Later, a near tragedy almost consumes the town when O'Brien and her cousin, Jenkins, disappear. The community is in an uproar as a frantic search for the children is conducted during torrential spring rains. They are found alive but soaking wet in a bathtub that has taken them on a perilous journey through the swollen waters of a nearby stream. Robinson doesn't know whether to spank or hug his adventurous child and opts for the latter. But he is severe with O'Brien when she refuses to let Jenkins borrow her skates. Robinson is the personification of a man who knows when to display emotion, such as explaining to his daughter, upset at Craig's induction into the service, that to preserve "peace on earth," one must be willing to fight for peace. All of the lessons taught by Robinson come to fruition when the town gathers to hear that a neighbor's farm has been struck by lightning and that the resultant fire has wiped him out. O'Brien is the first to stand up in church and offer her prize calf to the destitute farmer, which starts a run of charity through the parishioners. Robinson beams in pride at his daughter and then forgoes his own plans for a new barn to help the stricken neighbor. This wonderful outpouring of neighborly generosity and compassion is witnessed by schoolteacher Gifford who there and then decides that Benson Junction is not a dull place after all but one of the grandest spots on earth in which to live. She resolves to stay there and wait for Craig to return from the war. Supporting Robinson with marvelous performances are O'Brien, who furthered her juvenile career in films mightily with this entry, as did Jenkins, one of Louis B. Mayer's favorite child actors. Moorehead is excellent and sports a mild Norwegian accent in an underplayed part, and Morris, as the retarded neighbor who dies, displays a fine talent. Craig and Gifford made such convincing and gentle lovers that MGM teamed them again in SHE WENT TO THE RACES (1945) and LITTLE MR. JIM (1946). Released just after V-J Day, OUR VINES HAVE TENDER GRAPES was written with great care by the talented Trumbo whom Robinson had earlier befriended (and was later criticized for by citizens siding with HUAC during the Sen. Joseph McCarthy era when Trumbo was part of the "Hollywood Ten"). Robinson would recall in his autobiography, *All My Yesterdays*: "I'd known Trumbo for a long while; I knew he was hot-headed, wildly gifted, inordinately progressive, and, it seemed to me, intensely logical. My relationship with him professionally and socially became, not very many years later, a subject for official concern of the Congress."

p, Robert Sisk; d, Roy Rowland; w, Dalton Trumbo (based on the novel *For Our Vines Have Tender Grapes* by George Victor Martin); ph, Robert Surtees; m, Bronislaw Kaper; ed, Ralph E. Winters; art d, Cedric Gibbons, Edward Carfagno; spec eff, A. Arnold Gillespie, Danny Hall.

Drama **(PR:A MPAA:NR)**

OUR WIFE*** (1941) 95m COL bw

Melvyn Douglas *(Jerry Marvin)*, Ruth Hussey *(Susan Drake)*, Ellen Drew *(Babe Marvin)*, Charles Coburn *(Prof. Drake)*, John Hubbard *(Tom Drake)*, Harvey Stephens *(Dr. Cassell)*, Theresa Harris *(Hattie)*.

A cheery romantic romp which stars Douglas as a composer-musician who is thrown into a state of depression when his recent marriage to Drew fails. His career suffers and he takes a cruise to cheer himself up. On board ship he meets Hussey, her father, Coburn, and her brother, Hubbard. It doesn't take Douglas long to fall for Hussey and regain his creative spark. He invites Hussey and her family to join him in his Long Island home, an offer they gladly accept. The newly inspired Douglas pens a "Concerto for Trumpet" which premiers for an enthusiastic crowd and features Douglas on trumpet (actually played by Mannie Klein). The concerto is a success and Douglas once again soars to fame. With his new-found popularity, however, comes a renewed interest from Drew who makes a desperate attempt to recapture his love. Faking a fall down a flight of stairs, she pretends to be paralyzed from the waist down in order to gain his sympathy. Her ruse is soon discovered by Hussey, who manages to keep Douglas for herself. While far from being a profound and original comedy, OUR WIFE does serve as a pleasing piece of entertainment that includes some competent performances and a lush musical score by Shuken.

p&d, John M. Stahl; w, P.J. Wolfson (based on the play by Lillian Day, Lyon Mearson); ph, Franz E. Planer; m, Leo Shuken; ed, Gene Havlick; md, M.W. Stoloff; art d, Lionel Banks.

Comedy/Musical **(PR:A MPAA:NR)**

OUR WINNING SEASON*½ (1978) 92m AIP c

Scott Jacoby *(David Wakefield)*, Deborah Benson *(Alice Barker)*, Dennis Quaid *(Paul Morelli)*, Randy Herman *(Jerry McDuffy)*, Joe Penny *(Dean Berger)*, Jan Smithers *(Cathy Wakefield)*, P.J. Soles *(Cindy Hawkins)*, Robert Wahler *(Burton Fleishaur)*, Wendy Rastatter *(Susie Wilson)*, Damon Douglas *(Miller)*, Joanna Cassidy *(Sheila)*.

Jacoby is a high school track star who is not quite fast enough to beat his rival, Wahler, the leader of an opposing gang. The 1960s setting allows the writers to bring in a character who pals around with Jacoby and is killed in Vietnam. His death compels Jacoby into trying harder, eventually emerging as the No. 1 track runner. Another teen picture riddled with cliches from the brainless romances to the pot-smoking scenes to the ritualistic 18th birthday visit to the prostitute. Director Ruben pulls off a few nice moments, but he is still a far better mimic than a director.

p, Joe Roth; d, Joseph Ruben; w, Nick Niciphor; ph, Stephen Katz (Movielab Color); m, Charles Fox; ed, Bill Butler; art d, Angelo Graham; cos, Jimmy George; stunts, Mickey Gilbert.

Drama **(PR:C MPAA:PG)**

OURSELVES ALONE (SEE: RIVER OF UNREST, 1937, Brit.)

OUT½** (1982) 85m Eli Hollander/Cinegate c

Peter Coyote, O-Lan Shepard, Jim Haynie, Grandfather Semu Haute, Scott Beach, Danny Glover, Michael Grodenchik, Gail Dartez.

Interesting low-budget "road" movie has Coyote chucking his old life and taking to the highways in the quest for identity that is familiar in American culture from *Huckleberry Finn* to EASY RIDER. The twist here, though, is that none of it is played seriously. Coyote meets anarchists who foment revolution by extracting secret plans from bowls of alphabet soup, and he also encoutners a wise old Indian who seems to know all the mysteries of the universe but just wants to talk about his new boots. Worth checking out if you can find it.

p&d, Eli Hollander; w, Hollander, Ronald Sukenick (based on the novel by Sukenick); ph, Robert Ball; m, David Cope; ed, Hollander; prod d, Antony Chapman.

Drama **(PR:C-O MPAA:NR)**

OUT ALL NIGHT** (1933) 69m UNIV bw

Slim Summerville *(Ronald Colgate)*, ZaSu Pitts *(Bonny)*, Laura Hope Crews *(Mrs. Colgate)*, Shirley Grey *(Kate)*, Alexander Carr *(Rosemountain)*, Rollo Lloyd *(David Arnold)*, Gene Lewis *(Tracy)*, Billy Barty, Shirley Jane Temple [Shirley Temple], Philip Purdy *(Children)*, Florence Enright, Dorothy Bay, Mae Busch, Paul Hurst.

A satisfying minor comedy which has Summerville and Pitts getting locked in a store overnight. Because of this, they have to get married, but Summerville's mom is less than enthusiastic. She tries to get them to divorce and even goes along on their honeymoon. Cute stuff which is made even cuter by the presence of a 5-year old Shirley Temple in her third screen appearance.

d, Sam Taylor; w, William Anthony McGuire (based on the story by Tim Whelan); ph, Jerry Ash; ed, Bernard Burton.

Comedy **(PR:A MPAA:NR)**

OUT CALIFORNIA WAY** (1946) 67m REP c

Monte Hale *(Monte)*, Adrian Booth *(Gloria McCoy)*, Bobby [Robert] Blake *(Danny McCoy)*, John Dehner *(Rod Mason)*, Nolan Leary *(George Sheridan)*, Fred Graham *(Ace Carter)*, Tom London *(Johnny Archer)*, Jimmy Starr *(Himself)*, Edward Keane *(E.J. Pearson)*, Bob Wilke *(Assistant Director)*, Brooks Benedict *(Cameraman)*, St. Luke's Choristers, Foy Willing and the Riders of the Purple Sage, Roy Rogers, Dale Evans, Allan Lane, Donald Barry, Trigger the Horse.

An interesting western which features Hale and Dehner as competitive actors working for a mythical Hollywood studio. Little Bobby Blake (who became a dynamic actor as well as TV's "Baretta," Mickey in "The Little Rascals," and numerous other roles) provides the subplot as a tyke trying to get his horse, Pardner, a role in an upcoming movie. Roy Rogers and wife Dale Evans make a walk-on appearance which only adds to the movie set authenticity. Unfortunately, the picture is filmed in weak Trucolor, making it worthwhile to watch only on a black and white TV set. Republic chose to shoot OUT CALIFORNIA WAY in an effort to gain some attention for Hale, the singing cowboy they hoped would gain the same sort of popularity Gene Autry had managed to claim. Such was not the case with Hale's career, with the star quickly sliding into a nonentity by the time television had come into prominence. Songs by Paul Westmoreland, Foy Willing, Jack Meakin, Foster Carling, Tex Carlson, Jack Stratham, Gus Snow, Eddie Dean, and Hal Blair include: "Detour," "Rose of Santa Fe," "Hello Monte," "Out California Way," "Little Bronc of Mine," and "Boggie Woogie Cowboy."

p, Louis Gray; d, Lesley Selander; w, Betty Burbridge (based on the story by Barry Shipman); ph, Bud Thackery (Trucolor); ed, Charles Craft; md, Hilyard Brown; cos, Adele Palmer.

Western   Cas.   **(PR:A MPAA:NR)**

OUT OF IT**½   (1969) 95m UA bw

Barry Gordon (*Paul*), Jon Voight (*Russ*), Lada Edmund, Jr. (*Christine*), Gretchen Corbett (*Barbara*), Peter Grad (*Steve*), Martin Gray, Oliver Berry, Leonard Gelber, Richard Coyler.

Gordon, an introverted high school student asks Edmund, a beautiful blonde cheerleader, for a date. They go to a performance of "Romeo and Juliet," but Edmund fakes sickness and Gordon brings her back home, only to discover that she has a date with tough, but dumb, footballer Voight. Rejected, Gordon turns to his eager friend Corbett and the two of them go out. Voight, however, decides to muscle the frail Gordon and injures him during football practice. Tired of Voight's tough guy stance, Edmund goes back to Gordon. After the bully burns Gordon's varsity jacket, Gordon takes revenge and threatens Voight with a toy gun, humiliating him in front of his teammates. Edmund goes back to Voight, and Gordon is left to overcome the problems of being a teenager. Even though the script is completely out of date, the performances of Gordon (a taller version of Nick from A THOUSAND CLOWNS) and Voight (just before MIDNIGHT COWBOY) make this picture a treat. Independently produced in 1967, the film was bought by UA and held up for another year to ride the coattails of MIDNIGHT COWBOY's success. Photographed by ROCKY director John G. Avildsen.

p, Edward Pressman; d&w, Paul Williams; ph, John G. Avildsen; m, Michael Small, ed, Ed Orshan; md, Small; m/l, Small, Michael Benedikt (performed by the New York Rock And Roll Ensemble).

Comedy/Drama   **(PR:A MPAA:M)**

OUT OF SEASON***   (1975, Brit.) 90m Lorimar-Robert Enders/Athenaeum-EMI c (AKA: WINTER RATES)

Vanessa Redgrave (*Ann*), Cliff Robertson (*Joe*), Susan George (*Joanna*).

A small cast in a tight environment made this look like exactly what it was—a stage play adapted for the screen. It's England, a seaside village, and Robertson returns after having been away for a couple of decades. Redgrave owns a remote hotel and lives there with her daughter, George. Years before, Robertson and Redgrave had been lovers and the first question is whether or not George was the result of their affair, but that is never explained. The two women compete for the dark and somewhat enigmatic Robertson. Redgrave recalls the way it used to be between them and George employs a Lolita-like charm to seduce Robertson, so the thought of possible incest is introduced. It's very subtle in the insinuations and the script allows the audience to draw their own conclusions because the matter of which woman wins Robertson is never explained. George was 25 when the film was made and a bit too old to convince our eyes that she was still a pouty teenager. Although made in England, the two writers and executive producer Robert Enders are all Americans. Enders did several films with Glenda Jackson, some of which he wrote, and has had his greatest film success in England, after having produced TV shows in the U.S. in the 1960s. The unproduced play upon which the film was based was titled "Winter Rates" and had been optioned by producer Alexander Cohen, who wanted Harold Pinter to direct and Pinter's then wife Vivien Merchant to star. Pinter got another offer and the project lingered until John Roberts, formerly of the Royal Shakespeare Company, left that august body to open his own stage production firm. He optioned the play but died of a heart attack soon afterwards and writers Bercovici and Bercovitch (no relations) decided that the play was jinxed and put it on the shelf. Bercovitch then became the head of production at Lorimar, which was about to go into the film business. Lorimar, headed by Merv Adelson and Lee Rich, was heavily involved in television and wanted to expand but didn't care to risk a great deal of money, so Bercovitch suggested they do a European co-production. The bosses agreed and Bercovitch began searching for the right material. He read hundreds of scripts, books, articles, and couldn't find the right story. On a trip to Santa Barbara, he was telling his wife his problems as they walked along the beach and she suggested he film the play. Bercovitch hesitated, lest he be accused of being self-serving, but he pulled out the play, dusted it off, read it as objectively as he could, consulted with Bercovici, then decided to hand it to Adelson, and let him make the decision. Adelson thought it was well-written and gave the green light. The "Lady Or The Tiger" ending was quite deliberate on the parts of the authors, as the matter of which woman wound up with Robertson was deemed not to be important and secondary to the drama that led to the conclusion.

p, Eric Bercovici; d, Alan Bridges; w, Bercovici, Reuben Bercovitch; ph, Arthur Ibbetson (Technicolor); m, John Cameron; ed, Peter Weatherley; art d, Robert Jones.

Drama   Cas.   **(PR:C-O MPAA:R)**

OUT OF SIGHT*½   (1966) 87m UNIV c

Jonathan Daly (*Homer*), Karen Jensen (*Sandra*), Robert Pine (*Greg*), Carole Shelyne (*Marvin*), Wende Wagner (*Scuba*), Maggie Thrett (*Wipeout*), Deanna Lund (*Tuff Bod*), Rena Horten (*Girl from FLUSH*), John Lawrence (*Big Daddy*), Jimmy Murphy (*Mousie*), Norman Grabowski (*Huh!*), Forrest Lewis (*Mr. Carter*), Deon Douglas (*Mike*), Bob Eubanks (*M.C.*), Pamela Rodgers (*Madge*), Vicki Fee (*Janet*), Coby Denton (*Tom*), Billy Curtis (*FLUSH Assistant*), John Lodge (*John Stamp*), Gary Lewis and the Playboys, Freddie and the Dreamers, The Turtles, Dobie Gray, The Astronauts, The Knickerbockers, Jamie Farr.

Lame-brained Daly gets a chance to be a secret agent when he answers a call intended for his brother, a real agent. He investigates a plot to sabotage an upcoming beach event after teeny-booper Jensen overhears a plot concocted by Big Daddy Lawrence, who has been "driven mad by rock'n'roll." Lawrence's henchmen send a trio of voluptuous, bikini-clad gals to divert his attentions, but to

no avail. Not even the Girl from FLUSH, complete with an assistant in a sidecar, can keep Daly from doing his job. An abundance of music from top of the pops melodymakers is the highlight. Bob Eubanks, the host of TV's "The Dating Game," also makes an appearance in a familiar role, that of a master of ceremonies. Songs include: "Malibu Run" (Jim Karstein, Leon Russell, Gary Lewis, T. Leslie, sung by Gary Lewis and The Playboys), "Out on the Floor" (Fred Darian, Al De Lory, sung by Dobie Gray), "She'll Come Back" (Nita Garfield, Howard Kaylan, sung by The Turtles), "Baby Please Don't Go" (Joe Williams, sung by The Astronauts), "It's Not Unusual" (Gordon Mills, Les Reed, sung by The Knickerbockers), "Funny Over You" (Freddie Garrity, sung by Freddie and The Dreamers), "A Love Like You" (Quinn & Jones, sung by Freddie and The Dreamers), "What's Her Name," "Hip City" (Darian, De Lory).

p, Bart Patton; d, Lennie Weinrib; w, Larry Hovis (based on a story by Hovis, David Asher); ph, Jack Russell (Technicolor); m, Al de Lory, Fred Darian, Nick Venet; ed, Jack Woods; art d, Lloyd S. Papez; set d, Audrey Blasdel; cos, Helen Colvig; makeup, Bud Westmore.

Musical/Comedy   **(PR:A MPAA:NR)**

OUT OF SINGAPORE**½   (1932) 61m Goldsmith/William Steiner bw (AKA; GANGSTERS OF THE SEA)

Noah Beery (*1st Mate Woolf Barstow*), Dorothy Burgess (*Concha*), Miriam Seegar (*Mary Carroll*), Montagu Love (*Scar Murray*), George Walsh (*Steve Trent*), Jimmy Aubrey (*Bloater, Cook*), William Moran (*Capt. Carroll*), Olin Francis (*Bill*), Ethan Laidlaw (*2nd Mate Miller*), Leon Wong (*Wong, Merchant*), Horace B. Carpenter (*Capt. Smith*), Fred "Snowflake" Toones] (*Snowball*), Ernest Butterworth (*Sailor*).

A quick-moving Poverty Row potboiler with Beery as an unpalatable seaman who is hired to work on Moran's Singapore-bound cargo ship. Accompanied by Love, Beery plots to take control of the ship, poisoning Moran in the process. When the second mate hears of their plot, he promptly falls victim to the dark sea. The captain's daughter, Seegar, duped by Beery's mask of kindness, fails to recognize that Beery and Love are anything but friendly. While docked in Singapore, Beery arranges to have a supposedly valuable cargo loaded on board the ship. His plan is to then sink the ship and collect on the heavily insured cargo. Boarding the ship in Singapore is Walsh, a replacement for the drowned second mate, and Burgess, Beery's sensuous, dancing girl friend. Walsh soon learns of the ship's destiny and attempts to overpower Beery. Instead, he gets locked in an isolated cabin. The responsibility of saving the ship and crew is left up to Burgess, who convinces Seegar that Beery is nothing but a low-life murderer. Burgess manages to lock up Beery before he can carry out his plan, paving the way for Walsh and Seegar's escape. As they drift in their lifeboat, Beery and his ship meet an explosive finale. Another imitative film of THE SEA WOLF, but this time with some entertaining delights, first in the teaming of those two screen villains Beery and Love, and then in the revealing costumes worn by Beery's girl friend, Burgess—costumes that would not be allowed two years later when the Production Code went into effect.

p, Ken Goldsmith; d, Charles Hutchinson; w, John S. Natteford (based on a story by Fred Chapin); ph, Edward S. Kull; ed, S. Roy Luby.

Crime   **(PR:C MPAA:NR)**

OUT OF THE BLUE **   (1931, Brit.) 88m BIP/Pathe bw

Gene Gerrard (*Bill Coverdale*), Jessie Matthews (*Tommy Tucker*), Kay Hammond (*Angela Tucker*), Kenneth Kove (*Freddie*), Binnie Barnes (*Rosa*), David Miller (*Sir Jeremy Tucker*), Fred Groves (*Bannister Blair*), Averil Haley (*Judy Blair*), Hal Gordon (*Videlop*), Gordon Begg (*Mumford*), John Reynders and His Band.

Matthews is the daughter of Miller, an impoverished nobleman. While trying to make it as a singer, she falls in love with radio personality Gerrard, but he is engaged to Hammond, Matthews' sister, whom he doesn't love. Lightweight musical was Matthews' first; within a couple of years she would become one of the biggest stars in Britain, then almost as quickly forgotten, only to spend the next three decades unable to find work.

p, John Maxwell; d, Gene Gerrard, John Orton; w, Frank Miller, R. P. Weston, Bert Lee (based on the play "Little Tommy Tucker" by Caswell Garth, Desmond Carter); ph, Ernest Palmer, Arthur Crabtree.

Musical   **(PR:A MPAA:NR)**

OUT OF THE BLUE***   (1947) 90m EL bw

George Brent (*Arthur Earthleigh*), Virginia Mayo (*Deborah Tyler*), Turhan Bey (*David Gelleo*), Ann Dvorak (*Olive Jensen*), Carole Landis (*Mae Earthleigh*), Elizabeth Patterson (*Miss Spring*), Julia Dean (*Miss Ritchie*), Richard Lane (*Detective Noonan*), Charles Smith (*Elevator Boy*), Paul Harvey (*Holliston*), Alton E. Horton (*Detective Dombry*), Hadda Brooks (*Black Singer*), Robert Bilder (*Milkman*), Dorothy Douglas (*Hatcheck Girl*), Billy Newell (*Danny the Bartender*), Lee Phelps (*Motorcycle Cop*), Jerry Marlowe (*Cop*), Marcia Ralston (*Patricia*), Ralph Sanford (*Desk Sergeant*), Flame the Dog (*Rabelais*), Paul Palmer (*Doorman*), George Carleton (*Veterinarian*).

Brent gets himself into a fine mess when he invites the racy Dvorak to his apartment during his wife's absence. Dvorak puts away too much liquor and passes out, causing Brent to wrongly believe that she is sleeping the big sleep. He decides to stuff her on the terrace of a neighbor's apartment. She finally comes to, but the wily neighbor forces Brent to go through with the girl's burial. The screwball elements get screwier when wife Landis returns. It doesn't work all the time, but when it does it draws out a hearty laugh.

p, Isadore G. Goldsmith, Bryan Foy; d, Leigh Jason; w, Vera Caspary, Walter Bullock, Edward Eliscu (based on a story by Caspary); ph, Jackson Rose; m, Carmen Dragon; ed, Alfred De Gaetano, Norman Colbert; md, Irving Friedman; art d, Edward Jewell; set d, Armor Marlowe; spec eff, George J. Teague; m/l, Will Jason, Henry Nemo.

Comedy   Cas.   **(PR:A MPAA:NR)**

OUT OF THE BLUE½   (1982) 94m Robson Street/Discovery c

Linda Manz (CeBe), Sharon Farrell (Kathy), Dennis Hopper (Don), Raymond Burr (Brean), Don Gordon (Charlie), Eric Allen, Fiona Brody, David Crowley, Joan Hoffman, Carl Nelson, Francis Ann Pettit, Glen Pfiefer, David Ackridge, Jim Byrne, Glen Fyfe, Louis Gentle, Murdine Hirsh, John Anderson, Howard Taylor, Ron Charter, Ray Wallis, Trevor Wilkins, Nancy Gould, Michele Little, Valentina Fierro, Ray Isabelle, Sid Albina de Silva, Wayne McLeod, Eve Humber, Mike Spencer.

A fitful study of the Woodstock generation as failed adults from actor/director Hopper, who plays the father of Manz, a disaffected, confused, and fatalistic teenager with a passion for Elvis Presley and the Sex Pistols' pathetic, burned-out Sid Vicious. Hopper returns home after serving a five year prison term for being drunk and ramming his giant semi rig into a school bus full of children, killing several youngsters. Manz was riding with her father at the time of the accident and the gutted remains of the truck sit at the front of her parents' property and serve as a sort of hideout for the troubled girl. While Hopper has been in prison, his wife, Farrell, has developed quite a reputation as a floozy and drug addict. Hopper tries to reenter society, but the relatives of the children he killed get him fired from his new job and hound him back into a self-destructive pattern of behavior. Eventually Manz, who had hoped her life would get back to "normal" when her dad returned, decides to take it upon herself to end her family's pathetic existence, and she lures her parents into the burned-out shell of the truck and blows them and herself to kingdom come. it is a shocking and disturbing moment in a deeply brutal film. Hopper took a hard, bitter look at what his generation had become in adulthood and found that the free attitudes toward sex, booze, and drugs just led to irresponsible, mind-rattled, middle-aged losers pretending to be adults whose own children see things more clearly than they do. Considering Hopper came in at the last minute and replaced Yakir, the original director (who also cowrote the screenplay), the end result is nothing less than shocking. Hopper was able to extract some painfully real moments from himself and his cast, making OUT OF THE BLUE a cold, critical, unflinching gaze at the failed promise of a generation.

p, Leonard Yakir; d, Dennis Hopper; w, Yakir, Brenda Nielson, Gary Jules Jouvenat; ph, Marc Champion; m, Tom Lavin; ed, Doris Dyck; art d, David Hiscox.

Drama   Cas.   (PR:O MPAA:R)

OUT OF THE CLOUDS**   (1957, Brit.) 88m EAL/RANK c

Anthony Steel (Gus Randall), Robert Beatty (Nick Milbourne), David Knight (Bill Steiner), Margo Lorenz (Leah Roche), James Robertson Justice (Capt. Brent), Eunice Gayson (Penny Henson), Isabel Dean (Mrs. Malcolm), Gordon Harker (Taxi Driver), Bernard Lee (Customs Officer), Michael Howard (Purvis), Marie Lohr (Rich Woman), Esma Cannon (Her Companion), Abraham Sofaer (Indian), Melissa Stribling (Jean Osmond), Sidney James (Gambler), Nicholas Phipps (Hilton Davidson), Megs Jenkins (Landlady), Jill Melford (Eleanor), Arthur Howard (Booking Clerk), Cyril Luckham (Doctor), Jack Lambert (Designer), Katie Johnson (Passenger), Barbara Leake, Harold Kasket, William Franklyn.

The everyday life and drama of London Airport's employees is brought to the screen in this unlikely mishmash of characterizations. It has the feel of a soap opera crossed with a documentary as we watch Steel, the gambling pilot who gets involved in a smuggling ring; Beatty, the duty officer waiting for his chance to fly; Justice, the superstitious pilot; and Gayson, the hostess who is everyone's flame. OUT OF THE CLOUDS subscribes to the theory that there is drama in everyone's life, but this picture proves that such drama isn't always worth putting on the screen.

p, Michael Relph, Basil Dearden; d, Dearden, Relph; w, John Eldridge, Relph, Rex Reinits (based on the novel The Springboard by John Fores); ph, Paul Beeson, Jeff Seaholme (Eastmancolor); m, Richard Addinsell; ed, Jack Harris; md, Dock Mathieson; art d, Jim Morahan; cos, Anthony Mendleson.

Drama   (PR:A MPAA:NR)

OUT OF THE DARKNESS, 1958   (SEE: TEENAGE CAVEMAN, 1958)

OUT OF THE DARKNESS, 1979   (SEE: NIGHT CREATURE, 1979)

OUT OF THE DEPTHS½   (1946) 61m COL bw

Jim Bannon (Capt. Faversham), Ross Hunter (Clayton Shepherd), Ken Curtis (Buck Clayton), Loren Tindall (Pete Lubowsky), Robert Scott ("Pills" Wilkins), Frank Sully ("Speed" Brogan), George Khan (Lt. Ito Kaida), Coulter Irwin (Sparks), George Offerman, Jr. (Ten-to-One Ryan), Rodric Redwing (Mike Rawhide), Robert Williams (First Officer Ross), William Newell (Charlie Anderson), Warren Mills (Eddie Jones), John Tyrrell (Bailey).

The lives of four members of a submarine crew which survived an attack in Japanese waters are seen in flashback as the men set out on another mission. This time they must stop a Jap sub from launching a Kamikaze attack on the U.S. fleet. There are countless fine war films and this one isn't one of them. It's not that it is that bad, only that it is exceeded by so many others. Hunter went on in the 1950s to become best known as the producer of Douglas Sirk's melodramas, especially MAGNIFICENT OBSESSION and ALL THAT HEAVEN ALLOWS.

p, Wallace MacDonald; d, D. Ross Lederman; w, Martin Berkeley, Ted Thomas (based on a story by Aubrey Wisberg); ph, Philip Tannura; ed, Paul Borofsky; md, Mischa Bakaleinikoff; art d, Jerome Pycha, Jr.; set d, Richard Mansfield.

War Drama   (PR:A MPAA:NR)

OUT OF THE FOG*½   (1941) 93m WB bw

Ida Lupino (Stella Goodwin), John Garfield (Harold Goff), Eddie Albert (George Watkins), Thomas Mitchell (Jonah Goodwin), John Qualen (Olaf Johnson), George Tobias (Igor Propotkin), Aline MacMahon (Florence Goodwin), Jerome

Cowan (District Attorney), Odette Myrtil (Caroline Pomponette), Leo Gorcey (Eddie), Paul Harvey (Judge Moriarty), Charles Wilson, Jack Mower (Detectives), Konstantin Sankar (Bublitchki), Ben Welden (Boss), Murray Alper (Clerk), Barbara Pepper (Cigarette Girl), Frank Coghlan, Jr. (Newspaper Vendor), Charles Drake, Richard Kipling, Eddie Graham, Jack Wise, Alexander Leftwich (Reporters), Robert E. Homans (Officer Magruder).

Seldom does a handsome leading man render the kind of sinister and totally unsavory performance as Garfield powerpacks into OUT OF THE FOG. He is a sly but always menacing gangster who muscles in on poor fishermen, terrifying Mitchell and Qualen into turning over to him the money they have scrimped to save for years so they can buy a new boat. Many other citizens of Sheepshead Bay, Brooklyn, have been terrorized by racketeer Garfield into paying extortion money. Rather than completely surrender to the crafty crook, Mitchell and Qualen plot his death, even though the local cop later discovers their awkward plan and looks the other way when destiny lends a helping hand to the two fishermen. After inveigling Garfield into their boat, Mitchell and Qualen botch the job and Garfield is about to kill them but he stands up in the boat, loses his balance, and topples overboard to drown. Providentially, he drops his wallet in the boat and the fishermen discover that it contains their savings. Lupino, who plays Mitchell's daughter, is in love with hoodlum Garfield, though she knows he's rotten through and through. She turns in a fine performance, albeit she is on screen less than she was in THE SEA WOLF (1941) where she made an international impact. Mitchell and Qualen are excellent as the cowering juice victims but it's Garfield's vehicle all the way, one of his own favorites which he rightly felt was directed by Litvak with consummate skill. The fog-bound docks and the turn-of-the-century saloon, and other sets created by Weyl drip with eerie authenticity and Howe's photography captures the dark and pervasive mood of the story.

p, Hal B. Wallis; d, Anatole Litvak; w, Robert Rossen, Jarry Wald, Richard Macaulay (based on the play "The Gentle People" by Irwin Shaw); ph, James Wong Howe; ed, Warren Low; md, Leo F. Forbstein; art d, Carl Jules Weyl; spec eff, Rex Wimpy.

Crime Drama   (PR:C MPAA:NR)

OUT OF THE FOG*   (1962, Brit.) 68m Eternal Films/GN bw (AKA: FOG FOR A KILLER)

David Sumner (George Mallon), Susan Travers (June Lock), John Arnatt (Supt. Chadwick), James Hayter (Daniels), Jack Watson (Sgt. Tracey), Olga Lindo (Mrs. Mallon), Renee Houston (Ma), George Woodbridge (Chopper), Anthony Oliver (Chaplain).

After a mad killer, who only strikes when the moon is full, has claimed three blonde women as his victims, a young policeman sets a trap that captures him. Hardly noteworthy and mostly forgotten.

p, Maurice J. Wilson; d&w, Montgomery Tully.

Crime   (PR:A MPAA:NR)

OUT OF THE FRYING PAN   (SEE: YOUNG AND WILLING, 1943)

OUT OF THE NIGHT   (SEE: STRANGE ILLUSIONS, 1945)

OUT OF THE PAST**   (1933, Brit.) 51m FN-WB bw

Lester Matthews (Capt. Leslie Farebrother), Joan Marion (Frances Dane), Jack Raine (Eric Cotton), Henry Mollison (Gerald Brassard), Eric Stanley (Sir John Brassard), Margaret Damer (Lady Brassard), Aubrey Dexter (David Mannering), Wilfred Shine (Richard Travers).

After innocently being named co-respondent in a messy divorce case, Marion tries to commit suicide. She is saved, though, and after a few years she has an important position in a department store, and is engaged to the owner's son. Unexpectedly Matthews, the man into whose divorce she had been dragged, turns up. She breaks off her engagement to marry him. Dull melodrama, almost indistinguishable from a hundred others.

p, Irving Asher; d, Leslie Hiscott; ph, Basil Emmott.

Drama   (PR:A MPAA:NR)

OUT OF THE PAST***   (1947) 97m RKO bw (GB: BUILD MY GALLOWS HIGH)

Robert Mitchum (Jeff Bailey), Jane Greer (Kathie Moffett), Kirk Douglas (Whit Sterling), Rhonda Fleming (Meta Carson), Richard Webb (Jim), Steve Brodie (Fisher), Virginia Huston (Ann), Paul Valentine (Joe), Dickie Moore (The Kid), Ken Niles (Eels), Lee Elson (Policeman), Frank Wilcox (Sheriff Douglas), Mary Field (Marney), Jess Escobar, James Bush (Doormen), Hubert Brill (Car Manipulator), Brooks Benedict, Mike Lally, Homer Dickenson, Bill Wallace (Kibitzers), Primo Lopez (Bellhop), Mildred Boyd (Woman), Ted Collins (Man), Calib Peterson (Man with Eunice), Theresa Harris (Eunice), Wesley Bly (Headwaiter), Tony Roux (Jose Rodriguez), Jose Portugal, Sam Warren, Euminio Blanco, Vic Romito (Waiters), Michael Branden (Rafferty), Wallace Scott (Petey), John Kellogg (Baylord), Oliver Blake (Tillotson), William Van Vleck (Cigar Store Clerk), Phillip Morris (Porter), Charles Regan (Mystery Man), Harry Hayden (Canby Miller), Adda Gleason (Mrs. Miller), Manuel Paris (Croupier).

A film noir classic and masterwork by Tourneur, OUT OF THE PAST presents vintage Mitchum, a man always at low ebb who fatalistically falls for dazzling Greer, knowing it means his doom. The film opens to show hoodlum Valentine spotting a name on a gas station in Bridgeport, California, and he later discovers it is owned by Mitchum. He approaches Mitchum who doesn't seem too happy to see him. Valentine tells Mitchum that big shot gambler Douglas, for whom Mitchum once worked briefly, wants to see him in Lake Tahoe, Nevada. Mitchum realizes that it's not a request but an order, and he tells Valentine that he will go to see the big man. Mitchum goes to his girl friend's house (Huston), picks her up, and takes her for a drive, telling her the story of his sordid past, beginning at the point where he was a failing detective in New York City. In flashback we see Mitchum and his gumshoe partner Brodie summoned to the posh penthouse of gambler Douglas. The big shot wants Mitchum to find his girl friend, Greer, who, after shooting and wounding him, has vanished with $40,000 of his money. Douglas offers detective Mitchum $5,000 to bring Greer back, promising that he won't hurt her. Mitchum finds Greer's maid and discovers that her employer had taken a lot of luggage and gotten shots to ostensibly flee to Florida. But Mitchum states in narration that "you don't have to take shots to go to Florida," and rightly assumes that Greer has gone to Acapulco. He trails her there and manages to meet her in a bar she frequents. They are both attracted to each other and when Mitchum tells Greer that he's there to take her back to Douglas, she claims she has not stolen the money and he believes her) and go off together. He is smitten with her and easily gets stuck in the web of this "black widow" woman, a ravishing statuesque brunette with almond eyes. The couple go to San Francisco and live in obscurity, changing their names and living happily. Then one day Brodie, Mitchum's ex-partner in the private detective business, spots Mitchum at a racetrack and follows him to a mountain retreat where Mitchum and Greer are living. Brodie has been offered money by oily Douglas to locate Greer and ex-partner Mitchum but he tells Mitchum that he'll forget his whereabouts if Mitchum pays him off. Mitchum realizes that the blackmail will never stop and says no; he and Brodie get into a slam-bang fight and Greer shoots and kills Brodie, then races outside and drives away. Mitchum buries his ex-partner and later discovers Greer's bankbook which shows she has the $40,000 in her account, confirming that she did steal Douglas' money after all. Thoroughly disillusioned, Mitchum goes off to the mountain town of Bridgeport and opens a gas station, befriending mute Moore and falling in love with Huston. In a flash forward, Mitchum finishes his dark tale to Huston. They have now arrived in Lake Tahoe and Huston takes her car back to Bridgeport while Mitchum faces Douglas. The rattlesnake gambler is not coiled to kill him, however. To his surprise, Mitchum discovers that Douglas is not going to shoot him. The gambler tells him that he can square things by taking on another assignment; he must go to San Francisco and obtain Douglas' tax records which a lawyer, Niles, has been threatening to turn over to the IRS unless he's paid off. Then Mitchum finds Greer back with Douglas, although she says she's still in love with him and only went back to the gambler out of fear that Douglas would kill her. In San Francisco, Douglas contacts voluptuous Fleming, who works for lawyer Niles and is in liaison with Douglas. She, in turn, sets up a meeting between Niles and Mitchum but Mitchum smells betrayal. He warns the lawyer that he is in jeopardy but the smug Niles takes no heed. Niles is later murdered by Valentine and the killing is blamed on Mitchum. Now he knows he was called back by Douglas so that he could be set up. Moreover, Mitchum learns from Greer that the gambler forced her to sign an affidavit that Mitchum murdered his ex-partner, Brodie. Mitchum is now sought for two killings and he returns to hide out at Bridgeport, but before authorities can find him, Valentine, who is being paid by Greer, arrives to murder him. Moore, the mute boy who works for Mitchum at the station, however, leads the professional killer to a mountainous stream in the woods, pretending to take Valentine to Mitchum, and there kills the man. Mitchum has another showdown with Douglas, telling him that he will turn him over to the IRS with what he knows about his operations. Douglas offers him $50,000 to leave the country but tells him he wants the triple-crossing Greer turned over to the police for the killing of Brodie. Mitchum breaks up with Huston, telling her that his past has caught up with him and that they would never be happy together. He then returns to Douglas' estate to find the gambler dead, killed by Greer. He tells her that they should flee to Mexico and she agrees. While she is packing her bags, Mitchum calls police and a roadblock is set up. As the two drive toward the police trap Mitchum tells Greer what he knows about her and what she has done. The roadblock comes into view and Greer pulls a gun and viciously shoots Mitchum and, in turn, is shot to death by police. Moore later conveys to Huston that Mitchum died while going off with Greer, the woman he really loved, a lie designed to soften the blow of Mitchum's death. Huston, it is suggested, will now wed solid Bridgeport citizen Webb, who has patiently loved her while she flirted with the notion of marrying Mitchum. Though complex and terribly involved, the plot of OUT OF THE PAST is handled with meticulous care by Tourneur, who had proven to be a master of the macabre with such films as CAT PEOPLE (1942) and I WALKED WITH A ZOMBIE (1943). He cautiously sets his scenes and develops the tricky characters with great skill, mightily aided by a superb script from Homes (nee Mainwaring) who would go on to write the cult classic, INVASION OF THE BODY SNATCHERS (1957). For years, OUT OF THE PAST was considered an above average B film by critics who knew no better and had no appreciation of *film noir*, but it is today considered to be one of *the* top *film noir* productions, one that established Mitchum as an overnight star, projecting his droopy-lidded, cynical, laconic but quietly tough guy pose as an image he would retain throughout his long and spotty career. He would maintain his memorable image through such other *film noir* classics as PURSUED (1947), directed with elan by Raoul Walsh, and WHERE DANGER LIVES (1950). Other than THE STORY OF G.I. JOE (1945), Mitchum had not had a lead role until OUT OF THE PAST and he barely got this one. Humphrey Bogart had been the first choice for the lead but he turned it down, as did John Garfield and Dick Powell. Mitchum, an RKO contract player, was brought in to save money. It was felt that he was supported by such a strong cast that he could carry the film, although the studio hyped him as a brand new super tough guy with ads that stated: "It's like lightning kissing thunder when Mitchum makes love to a girl with a gun." RKO thought to compete with the Bogart-Lauren Bacall legend by showing Mitchum with that limp cigarette dangling from a lazy mouth and Greer holding a smoking gun in their ads. Greer is great as the double-dealing *femme fatale*, rendering a performance packed with guile and one that put her permanently in the *film noir* legend. Douglas is as slick a wheeler-dealer as ever slipped across the screen and Valentine is full of mystique as his loyal killer. Fleming, as another scheming vixen, does a good bit, as does good-good girl Huston, and Moore, as Mitchum's mute friend, is outstanding. The script was written by Homes-Mainwaring who later stated: "I wrote the first draft and then went on to something else. Producer Warren Duff put Jim [James M.] Cain on it, and Cain threw away my script and wrote a completely new one. They paid him twenty or thirty thousand and it had nothing to do with my novel or anything. He took it out of the country and set the whole in the city." Duff then rejected the Cain script and brought back Mainwaring, who reinstituted his orginal story line. True to his penchant for authenticity, Tourneur shot most of the film on location, giving it a wonderful episodic, transcontinental look, taking cast and crew to Los Angeles, San Francisco, Bridgeport, Lake Tahoe, New York, Mexico City, and Acapulco.

p, Warren Duff; d, Jacques Tourneur; w, Geoffrey Homes [Daneil Mainwaring] (James M. Cain, Frank Fenton, uncredited) (based on Homes' novel *Build My Gallows High*); ph, Nicholas Musuraca; m, Roy Webb; ed, Samuel E. Beetley; md, Constantin Bakaleinikoff; art d, Albert S. D'Agostino, Jack Okey; set d, Darrell Silvera; cos, Edward Stevenson; spec eff, Russell A. Cully; makeup, Gordon Bau.

Crime Drama **Cas.** **(PR:C MPAA:NR)**

OUT OF THE SHADOW

(SEE: MURDER ON THE CAMPUS, 1963, Brit.)

OUT OF THE STORM**

(1948) 61m REP bw

James Lydon *(Donald Lewis)*, Lois Collier *(Ginny Powell)*, Marc Lawrence *(Red Stubbins)*, Richard Travis *(R.J. Ramsey)*, Robert Emmett Keane *(Holbrook)*, Helen Wallace *(Martha Lewis)*, Harry Hayden *(Chief Ryan)*, Roy Barcroft *(Arty Sorenson)*, Charles Lane *(Mr. Evans)*, Iris Adrian *(Ginger)*, Byron Foulger *(Al Weinstock)*, Claire DuBrey *(Mrs. Smith)*, Smoki Whitfield *(Maintenance Man)*, Charlie Sullivan *(Plant Guard)*, Rex Lease *(Gus Clute)*, Edgar Dearing *(Ed Purcell)*.

Lydon, a clerk at a shipping plant, sees his big opportunity when a gang comes to steal the payroll. He hides $100,000 and takes it home with him. After struggling with his conscience, he returns the money and confesses to insurance investigator Travis. Over-acted performances throughout, with a badly written script.

p, Sidney Picker; d, R. G. Springsteen; w, John K. Butler (based on a story by Gordon Rigby); ph, John McBurnie; ed, Richard L. Van Enger; md, Morton Scott; art d, James Sullivan; set d, John McCarthy, Jr., George Milo; cos, Adele Palmer; spec eff, Howard Lydecker, Theodore Lydecker.

Crime **(PR:A MPAA:NR)**

OUT OF THE TIGER'S MOUTH**

(1962) 78m Pathe-America bw

Loretta Han-Yi Hwong *(Little Moon)*, David Fang *(Peaceful)*, Lillian Wai *(Grandma Yang)*, T'ang Juo Ch'ing *(Mme. Pang)*, Mario Barri *(Mario)*, Lolita Shek *(Su Mei)*, Feng Yi *(Boatman Feng)*, Victoria Chan *(Beggar Girl)*.

Two children are placed on a boat to Hong Kong, but before reaching the mainland are sold by an unscrupulous boatman to a brothel. The cliched "whore-with-a-heart-of-gold" helps them to get to Hong Kong, where they are to meet their uncle. On the way, however, they get robbed of the little money they have. They arrive, but only to receive the news that their uncle has died. An American production filmed on location in Hong Kong with a Hollywood-bred cast.

p, Wesley Ruggles, Jr.; d, Tim Whelan, Jr.; w, Ruggles, Jr., Whelan, Jr.; ph, Emmanuel I. Rojas; m, Howard Wells; ed, Jack Ruggiero.

Drama **(PR:A MPAA:NR)**

OUT OF THIS WORLD**½

(1945) 96m PAR bw

Eddie Bracken *(Herbie Fenton)*, Veronica Lake *(Dorothy Dodge)*, Diana Lynn *(Betty Miller)*, Cass Daley *(Fanny the Drummer)*, Parkyakarkus *(Gus Palukas)*, Donald MacBride *(J.C. Crawford)*, Florence Bates *(Harriet Pringle)*, Gary Crosby, Phillip Crosby, Dennis Crosby, Lindsay Crosby *(Children in the Audience)*, Olga San Juan, Nancy Porter, Audrey Young, Carol Deere *(Glamourette Quartet)*, Carmen Cavallaro, Ted Fiorito, Henry King, Ray Noble, Joe Reichman *(Themselves)*, Don Wilson *(Radio Announcer/Master of Ceremonies)*, Mabel Paige *(Mrs. Robbins)*, Charles Smith *(Charlie Briggs)*, Irving Bacon *(Irving Krunk)*, Toni LaRue *(Marimba Player)*, Mary Elliott *(Arlen, Trumpet Player)*, Carmelle Bergstrom *(Margy, Trombone Player)*, Betty Walker *(Guitar Player)*, Virginia Morris, June Harris *(Trumpet Players)*, Laura Gruver, Marguerite Campbell *(Violin Players)*, Inez Palange *(Mrs. Palukas)*, Esther Dale *(Abbie Pringle)*, Charles B. Williams *(Joe Welch)*, Gloria Saunders *(Vickie Kelly)*, Lorraine Krueger *(Maizie)*, Milton Kibbee *(Bald-Headed Man)*, Davison Clark *(Pullman Conductor)*, Nell Craig *(Woman)*, Virginia Sale *(Spinster)*, Charles R. Moore *(Porter)*, Norman Nesbitt *(Announcer)*, Jamiel Hasson *(Arabian Announcer)*, Michael Visaroff *(Russian Announcer)*, Jimmie Lono *(Eskimo Announcer)*, Sammee Tong *(Chinese Announcer)*, Lal Chand Mehra *(Hindu Announcer)*, Leon Belasco *(Himself)*, Selmer Jackson *(Doctor)*.

Bracken is a nobody who is accidentally pushed into singing a tune with Lynn's all-girl orchestra at a small-town benefit show. He opens his mouth and out comes the familiar swooning sounds of Bing Crosby. The audience goes wild and publicity soars. Lynn brings the pseudo-Crosby to New York with her and gets investors to put forward some cash. She mistakenly sells them shares totalling 125 percent of the profits. Her near-disastrous financial management is all cleared up by the finale. An agreeable little spoof on superstardom and the bobby-soxer crowd. The cast does a fine job of entertaining, though Lake is unfortunately wasted in a minor role as a booking agent. Bing never shows up on the screen, but his four sons do—as part of Bracken's audience. Songs include: "June Comes Around Every Year," "Out Of This World" (Johnny Mercer, Harold Arlen), "I'd Rather Be Me" (Eddie Cherkose, Felix Bernard, Sam Coslow), "All I Do Is Beat That Golden Drum" (Coslow, sung by Cass Daley), "It Takes A Little Bit More" (Coslow), "A Sailor With An Eight-Hour Pass" (Ben Raleigh, Bernie Wayne, sung by Daley) and a version of Chopin's "Minute Waltz," which the girls play as "The Ghost Of Mr. Chopin" (Coslow).

p, Sam Coslow; d, Hal Walker; w, Walter DeLeon, Arthur Phillips (based on stories by Elizabeth Meehan, Sam Coslow); ph, Stuart Thompson; ed, Stuart

Gilmore; md, Victor Young; art d, Hans Dreier, Haldane Douglas; set d, Kenneth Swartz; cos, Edith Head; ch, Sammy Lee.

Musical **(PR:A MPAA:NR)**

OUT OF TOWNERS, THE, 1964 (SEE: DEAR HEART, 1964)

OUT OF TOWNERS, THE**** (1970) 98m Jalem/PAR c

Jack Lemmon *(George Kellerman)*, Sandy Dennis *(Gwen Kellerman)*, Milt Kamen *(Counterman)*, Sandy Baron *(TV Man)*, Anne Meara *(Woman in Police Station)*, Robert Nichols *(Man in Airplane)*, Ann Prentiss *(Airline Stewardess)*, Ron Carey *(Boston Cab Driver)*, Phil Bruns *(Officer Meyers)*, Graham Jarvis *(Murray)*, Carlos Montalban *(Cuban Diplomat)*, Robert King *(Agent in Boston)*, Johnny Brown *(Waiter on Train)*, Dolph Sweet *(Police Sergeant)*, Jack Crowder *(Police Officer)*, Jon Korkes, Robert Walden *(Looters)*, Richard Libertini *(Boston Baggage Man)*, Paul Dooley *(Day Hotel Clerk)*, Anthony Holland *(Night Hotel Clerk)*, Billy Dee Williams *(Lost and Found Supervisor)*, Bob Bennett *(Man in Boston Phone Booth)*, Mary Norman *(Stewardess)*, Paul Jabara *(Ist Hippie)*, Hash Howard *(2nd Hippie)*, Maxwell Glanville *(Redcap)*, Meredith Vincent *(Washroom Lady)*, B. Paipert *(Sweeper)*, J. French *(Cleaning Woman)*, A.P. Westcott *(Porter)*, Ray Ballard *(Attendant)*.

Neil Simon is probably the most successful playwright in history, if we gauge success by money in the bank. As a person who has brought laughter to so many millions, he deserves it. In his original script for THE OUT-OF-TOWNERS, he mines gold from a field that had been virtually tapped out. Lemmon is an Ohio businessman who is on his way to New York with his wife, Dennis, to talk about the possibility of moving to that city in an executive position. They are flying in and have refused the food on the plane in favor of dining in one of Manhattan's fine restaurants. Their intention is to sup, check into a good hotel, have the appointment the following morning, and return to Dayton. But things never work out the way they were planned. The plane cannot land in New York because of fog, so it's shunted to Boston. Once in the Hub City, they learn that their luggage is missing and they have to take a crowded, foodless train back to New York. They arrive in a driving rainstorm and the city has been crippled by a number of strikes, including walkouts by the transit workers and the garbage collectors. They walk a distance to the Waldorf only to learn that the hotel has cancelled their reservation. They meet sweet Jarvis, a nice man who says he can find them a room, but he turns out to be a mugger who steals all of their money. With no cash, they decide to try the police, who tell them they can be put up at a local armory for the night. On their way there, the police car is hijacked by crooks, and they are tossed out in Central Park where they spend the night. They are robbed again and in the morning Lemmon is taken to be a rapist by two joggers who beat him up. Then Lemmon is chased by a police officer on a horse who thinks he is a child molester. Lemmon is trying to get to his interview and hitches a ride in the car of a Cuban official, Montalban, but that auto is sidetracked by angry protestors against Castro's rule. When he finally gets to his appointment, he looks seedy and totally unpresentable, but the company offers the job to him anyhow. Lemmon decides that New York is no place for him and Dennis, and he turns the job down, preferring to stay in quiet, tranquil Ohio. They happily board their plane back to Ohio and it is promptly hijacked to Cuba as the film ends. It's implausible, of course, for all of that to envelop a couple in 24 hours, but every single incident indicated has happened at one time or another and Simon has cleverly put them all together for one of his best screenplays. Director Hiller happily keeps Dennis' quirky mannerisms to a minimum and lets Lemmon do his thing (and a wonderful thing it is), with all secondary roles well-cast. The way New York is shown will keep newcomers away. Each incident is funny, but they come so thick and so fast that they cannot be believed. Fun City is no fun to these midwesterners. The picture grossed well at the box office and added some further feathers to Lemmon's comedy headdress. Many of Simon's plays have not translated to the screen (with the notable exceptions of THE ODD COUPLE and BAREFOOT IN THE PARK) because he writes differently for the stage. But when he tries his hand at the screen, he does quite well, as in this, THE GOODBYE GIRL, and THE HEARTBREAK KID. His unique ability to make people laugh without resorting to foul language and questionable situations make him a national treasure.

p, Paul Nathan; d, Arthur Hiller; w, Neil Simon; ph, Andrew Laszlo (Movielab Color); m, Quincy Jones; ed, Fred Chulack; art d, Charles Bailey, Walter Tyler; set d, Arthur Parker; cos, Forrest T. Butler, Grace Harris; makeup, Clay Lambert, Armand Delmar.

Comedy **Cas.** **(PR:A MPAA:G)**

OUT WEST WITH THE HARDYS*½** (1938) 84m MGM bw

Lewis Stone *(Judge Hardy)*, Mickey Rooney *(Andy Hardy)*, Cecilia Parker *(Marian Hardy)*, Ann Rutherford *(Polly Benedict)*, Fay Holden *(Mrs. Hardy)*, Sara Haden *(Aunt Milly)*, Don Castle *(Dennis Hunt)*, Virginia Weidler *(Jake Holt)*, Gordon Jones *(Ray Holt)*, Ralph Morgan *(Bill Northcote)*, Nana Bryant *(Dora Northcote)*, Thurston Hall *(H.R. Bruxton)*, Tom Neal *(Aldrich Brown)*, Anthony Allan *(Cliff Thomas)*.

America's model family goes West in this their fourth picture. Stone brings his clan to the ranch of a friend who is trying to keep from being run off his land. While Stone is upholding the law, daughter Parker is falling in love with the ranch foreman. Rooney, however, is again the favorite, as he overdresses in full cowboy regalia, and tries unsuccessfully to prove his ranch abilities to cute moppet Weidler. One of the best of the "Andy Hardy" series entries, an opinion which is reflected in the fact that it was one of the top-grossing films of the year. (See ANDY HARDY series, Index.)

p, J.J. Cohn; d, George B. Seitz; w, Kay Van Riper, Agnes Christine Johnston, William Ludwig (based on the characters created by Aurania Rouverol); ph, Lester White; ed, Ben Lewis.

Drama/Comedy **(PR:AAA MPAA:NR)**

OUT WEST WITH THE PEPPERS*½ (1940) 63m COL bw

Edith Fellows *(Polly Pepper)*, Dorothy Ann Seese *(Phronsie Pepper)*, Dorothy Peterson *(Mrs. Pepper)*, Charles Peck *(Ben Pepper)*, Tommy Bond *(Joey Pepper)*, Bobby Larson *(David Pepper)*, Victor Kilian *(Jim Anderson)*, Emory Parnell *(Ole)*, Helen Brown *(Alice Anderson)*, Pierre Watkin *(King)*, Ronald Sinclair *(Jasper King)*, Walter Soderling *(Caleb)*, Roger Gray *(Tom)*, Hal Price *(Bill)*, Rex Evans *(Martin)*, Millard Vincent, Wyndham Standing *(Specialists)*, Andre Cheron *(Frenchman)*, John Rogers *(Ship Steward)*, Ernie Adams *(Telegraph Operator)*, Kathryn Sheldon *(Abbie)*, Eddie Laughton *(Lumberjack)*, Harry Bernard *(Checker Player)*.

In their third picture, the Pepper family ventures West into mischief, and into territory already claimed by the far-superior Hardy family (See OUT WEST WITH THE HARDYS) in 1938. Based on the characters from Margaret Sidney's book, the film is soaked in sweetness and lacks the life of the Hardy clan. (See FIVE LITTLE PEPPERS series, Index.)

d, Charles Barton; w, Harry Rebuas (based on the book by Margaret Sidney); ph, Benjamin Kline; ed, James Sweeney; md, M. W. Stoloff; art d, Lionel Banks.

Drama/Comedy **(PR:AAA MPAA:NR)**

OUTBACK½** (1971, Aus.) 99m NLT-Group W/UA c

Donald Pleasence *(Doc Tydon)*, Gary Bond *(John Grant)*, Chips Rafferty *(Jock Crawford)*, Sylvia Kay *(Janette Hynes)*, Jack Thompson *(Dick)*, Peter Whittle *(Joe)*, Al Thomas *(Tim Hynes)*, John Meillon *(Charlie)*, John Armstrong *(Atkins)*, Slim De Grey *(Jarvis)*, Maggie Dence *(Receptionist)*, Norman Erskine *(Joe the Cook)*, Owen Moase, John Dalleen *(Controllers)*, Buster Fiddess *(Charlie Jones)*, Tex Foote *(Stubbs)*, Colin Hughes *(Stockman)*, Jacko Jackson *(Van Driver)*, Nancy Knudsen *(Robyn)*, Dawn Lake *(Joyce)*, Harry Lawrence *(Higgins)*, Bob McDarra *(Pig Eyes)*, Carlo Marchini *(Poker Player)*, Liam Reynolds *(Miner)*.

A powerful drama set in the "inferno of dust and sweat" known as the Outback of Australia. Unsuspecting schoolteacher Bond stops over in the Outback while on his way to a Sydney vacation. He is soon sucked into the vociferous goings on of a small group of villagers who live on booze, sex, and violence. Before he knows it he is stone drunk and carrying on with a crazed nympho (Kay) who thrives on sex. He then gets taken on a horrifying kangaroo hunt with the drunken adventurers. Pleasence is wonderfully grotesque as an alcoholic doctor who is unable to work in Sydney because of his dependency on drink. It doesn't present a very flattering view of Australia, especially in its lengthier 110 minute version. A similar real-life experience was the inspiration for Australian journalist Kenneth Cook's novel *Wake in Fright*, on which OUTBACK is based. It is said that British director Joseph Losey had hoped to use the novel as the source for a film to star Dick Bogarde in the Bond role, but instead the property was purchased by an Australian company. Although many of the key players and technical people are British, the film retains a distinctly Australian flavor; due in no small part to the presence of one of Australia's best known actors, Chips Rafferty, who died not long after the film's completion.

p, George Willoughby; d, Ted Kotcheff; w, Evan Jones (based on the novel *Wake in Fright* by Kenneth Cook); ph, Brian West (Technicolor); m, John Scott; ed, Anthony Buckley; art d, Dennis Gentle; makeup, Monica Dawkins.

Drama **(PR:O MPAA:R)**

OUTCAST, THE** (1934, Brit.) 74m BIP/Wardour bw

Leslie Fuller *(Bill Potter)*, Mary Glynne *(Eve Baxter)*, Hal Gordon *(Jim Truman)*, Jane Carr *(Nancy Acton)*, Gladdy Sewell *(May Truman)*, Jimmy Godden *(Harry)*, Wallace Geoffrey *(Ted Morton)*, Pat Aherne *(Burke)*, John Schofield.

England's Wembley Dog Track is the backdrop for this comedy about a pair of comedians who hit the skids when their manager takes off with their money. Attempting to recoup their losses, the duo (Fuller and Gordon) become race track bookies and run their own dog, The Outcast, in the big race. Although they have a second run-in with their shady manager, they still come out on top.

p, Walter C. Mycroft; d, Norman Lee; w, Syd Courtenay, Lola Harvey.

Comedy **(PR:A MPAA:NR)**

OUTCAST½** (1937) 77m PAR bw

Warren William *(Dr. Phillip Wendel Jones)*, Karen Morley *(Margaret Stevens)*, Lewis Stone *(Lawyer Anthony Abbott)*, Richard Carle *(Mooney)*, Jackie Moran *(Freddie)*, Christian Rub *(Olaf)*, Esther Dale *(Hattie Simmerson)*, John Wray *(Mr. John Simmerson)*, Virginia Sale, Ruth Robinson, Murray Kinnell, Jonathan Hale, Frank Melton, Lois Wilde, Tommy Jackson, Matthew Betz, Harry Woods, George Magrill, Dick Alexander.

William is a doctor recently acquitted of murder, but the court's decision doesn't satisfy the dead girl's sister-in-law (Morley), who is bent on avenging her brother's pain. She follows William to the small village where he is residing, and soon a lynch mob wants his neck. This picture doesn't measure up to Fritz Lang's superior treatment of the nation's lynching epidemic in FURY, but it still boasts an intelligent script and some fine performances, especially by Stone who would soon become a familiar face as Judge Hardy in the long-running ANDY HARDY series.

p, Emanuel Cohen; d, Robert Florey; w, Doris Malloy, Dore Schary (based on the novel *Happiness Preferred* by Frank R. Adams); ph, Rudolph Mate; ed, Ray F. Curtiss.

Drama **(PR:A MPAA:NR)**

OUTCAST, THE, 1951 (SEE: MAN IN THE SADDLE, 1951)

OUTCAST, THE½** (1954) 90m REP c

John Derek *(Jet Cosgrave)*, Joan Evans *(Judy Polsen)*, Jim Davis *(Maj. Cosgrave)*, Catherine McLeod *(Alice Austin)*, Ben Cooper *(The Kid)*, Taylor Holmes *(Andrew

Devlin), Nana Bryant (*Mrs. Banner*), Slim Pickens (*Boone Polsen*), Frank Fergu-son (*Chad Polsen*), James Millican (*Cal Prince*), Bob Steele (*Duke Rankin*), Nacho Galindo (*Curly*), Harry Carey, Jr. (*Bert*), Bill Walker (*Sam Allen*), Robert "Buzz" Henry (*Zeke Polsen*), Nicolas Coster (*Asa Polsen*).

Derek heads west and gets tough with Davis, a louse of an uncle who forged Derek's father's will and ended up with his ranch, instead of having it rightfully go to Derek. He's determined to get back what belongs to him, but his sights aren't so focused that he can't find time for women. Both Evans and McLeod hold his interest, with Evans being the gal he settles down with. Derek is almost too macho in his tough-guy role, constantly playing with his gun or battering his knuckles, but never really showing the vulnerability that makes a good actor great. This was one of the last efforts by director Witney for Republic, the studio he had long labored for, turning out serials and low-budget westerns.

p, William J. O'Sullivan; d, William Witney; w, John K. Butler, Richard Wormser (based on a story by Todhunter Ballard); ph, Reggie Lanning (Trucolor); m, R. Dale Butts; ed, Tony Martinelli.

Western Cas. (PR:A MPAA:NR)

OUTCAST LADY*½ (1934) 80m MGM bw (GB: A WOMAN OF THE WORLD)

Constance Bennett (*Iris March*), Herbert Marshall (*Napier Harpenden*), Mrs. Pat-rick Campbell (*Lady Eve*), Hugh Williams (*Gerald March*), Elizabeth Allan (*Ven-ice*), Henry Stephenson (*Sir Maurice Harpenden*), Robert Loraine (*Hilary*), Lums-den Hare (*Guy*), Leo [G.] Carroll (*Dr. Masters*), Ralph Forbes (*Boy Fenwick*), Alec B. Francis (*Truble*).

An endlessly confusing picture which has trouble when it comes to plot clarity. Bennett is the forlorn widow of Forbes, who all too suddenly commits suicide. She tries to find out why, with the answer hinging on a note she received as she entered the church on her wedding day. Her husband's death is just the first in a string of tragedies, including the death of her brother. All of this added together results in her eventual suicide. Bennett tries but is unsuccessful in her attempt to save this weak reworking of the Garbo vehicle A WOMAN OF AFFAIRS. That Clarence Brown-directed silent feature and the Michael Arlen novel, *The Green Hat*, on which it was based, both contained elements which the Hays Commission would certainly have found objectionable. Being that the Hays Code was put into "strict effect" a scant six months before the release of OUTCAST LADY, the film's creators had to treat their source carefully, which may partially account for the picture's plot confusion—though only partially.

d, Robert Z. Leonard; w, Zoe Akins (based on the novel *The Green Hat* by Michael Arlen); ph, Charles Rosher; ed, William LeVanway; cos, Adrian.

Drama (PR:A MPAA:NR)

OUTCAST OF BLACK MESA** (1950) 54m COL bw

Charles Starrett (*Steve Norman/The Durango Kid*), Smiley Burnette (*Himself*), Martha Hyer (*Ruth Dorn*), Richard Bailey (*Andrew Vaning*), Stanley Andrews (*Sheriff Grasset*), William Haade (*Dayton*), Lane Chandler (*Ted Thorp*), William Gould (*Walt Dorn*), Bob Wilke (*Curt*), Charles "Chuck" Roberson (*Kramer*), Ozie Waters.

Starrett is cast in his familiar role as The Durango Kid in this average serial oater. The hero is accused of the murder of his pal Gould and of an attempt to do away with Chandler. He digs up the real killer and uncovers a plot to take over the gold mine where Gould was killed. Includes a fair amount of scenes from past Starrett adventures. (See DURANGO KID series, Index.)

p, Colbert Clark; d, Ray Nazarro; w, Barry Shipman (based on a story by Elmer Clifton); ph, Fayte Browne; ed, Paul Borofsky; art d, Charles Clague.

Western (PR:A MPAA:NR)

OUTCAST OF THE ISLANDS***½ (1952, Brit.) 93m LFP/BL bw

Ralph Richardson (*Capt. Lingard*), Trevor Howard (*Peter Willens*), Robert Morley (*Mr. Almayer*), Kerima (*Aissa*), George Coulouris (*Babalatchi*), Wilfrid Hyde-White (*Vinck*), Frederick Valk (*Hudig*), Betty Ann Davies (*Mrs. Willens*), Peter Illing (*Alagappan*), James Kenney (*Ramsey*), A.V. Bramble (*Badavi*), Dharma Emman-uel (*Ali*), Annabel Morley (*Nina Almayer*), Marne Maitland (*Mate*).

One of Joseph Conrad's easier stories to translate to the screen, OUTCAST OF THE ISLANDS offers Howard in a memorable role as a trading post operator in the Far East who is suddenly dismissed from his post. He goes to his old friend Richardson, a salty sea captain, who takes Howard to another trading post he operates with his partner Morley who, in turn, is married to Richardson's adopted daughter, Hiller. Once in the islands, Howard finds working with the pompous, overbearing Morley stifling and he is soon in conflict with his nominal boss while Hiller finds the rebellious Howard attractive. He alienates her by falling in love with a beautiful native girl, Kerima. A local politician uses Kerima and Howard's attrac-tion to her to betray the trading post to competitors, so that Howard leads an Arab group through a secret channel but he is betrayed in the end and exposed. Howard and Kerima flee to another island where Richardson later finds him thoroughly disillusioned and no longer in love with his native siren. Kerima tries to persuade Howard to kill Richardson whom she feels is interfering with her love life, but Howard refuses. Richardson realizes that Howard has given up on life and is no longer interested in having anything to do with civilization and he leaves Howard and Kerima alone, so that the Englishman will be forever known as the "outcast of the islands." Howard is spellbinding as the rootless Englishman and he is superbly supported by those consummate actors Richardson and Morley, with some piquant scenes created by Hiller. Kerima is a sultry dark beauty who caused, in her love scenes with Howard, some anxious moments for the censors, so thinly clad was her curvacious body. The Breen Office (the then Hollywood censor) objected more to scenes showing naked native boys swimming than to the Kerima-Howard clinches.

The film was originally released in England at 102 minutes but cut to 93 minutes when released in the U.S.

p&d, Carol Reed; w, William Fairchild (based on the novel by Joseph Conrad); ph, Ted Scaife, John Wilcox; m, Brian Easdale; ed, Bert Bates; prod d, Vincent Korda; spec eff, Percy Day; ch, T. Ranjana, K. Gurunanse.

Drama (PR:A MPAA:NR)

OUTCASTS OF POKER FLAT, THE** (1937) 70m RKO bw

Preston Foster (*John Oakhurst*), Jean Muir (*Helen Colby*), Van Heflin (*Rev. Samuel Woods*), Virginia Weidler (*Luck*), Margaret Irving (*The Duchess*), Frank M. Thomas (*Redford*), Si Jenks (*Kentuck*), Dick Elliott (*Stumpy*), Al St. John (*Uncle Billy*), Bradley Page (*Sonoma*), Monte Blue (*Indian Jim*), Billy Gilbert (*Charley*), Dudley Clements (*Wilkes*), Richrd Lane (*High-Grade*), Barbara Pepper (*Tavern Lady*), George Irving (*Doctor*).

Foster is a reformed gambler and hard drinker who, with the encouragement of Muir and Heflin, adopts a young tot (Weidler) to help him take the straight road. Based on a pair of Bret Harte stories, the film never delivers the strong characteriza-tions that the written word achieved. A remake of John Ford's silent from 1919, the story was told again in 1952 with Anne Baxter and Dale Robertson as the principals.

p, Robert Sisk; d, Christy Cabanne; w, John Twist, Hary Segall (based on the Bret Harte stories, "The Outcasts Of Poker Flats" and "The Luck Of Roaring Camp"); ph, Robert DeGrasse; ed, Ted Cheseman; md, Roy Webb.

Western (PR:A MPAA:NR)

OUTCASTS OF POKER FLAT, THE**½ (1952) 80m FOX bw

Anne Baxter (*Cal*), Dale Robertson (*John Oakhurst*), Miriam Hopkins (*Duchess*), Cameron Mitchell (*Ryker*), Craig Hill (*Tom Dakin*), Barbara Bates (*Piney*), Billy Lynn (*Jake*), Dick Rich (*Drunk*), Tom Greenway, Harry Carter (*Townsmen*), Russ Conway, Bob Adler (*Vigilantes*), John Ridgely (*Bill Akeley*), Harry T. Shannon (*Bearded Miner*), Harry Harvey, Sr. (*George Larabee*), Lee Phelps, Kit Carson (*Men*), Jack Byron (*Miner*), Frosty Royce, Joe P. Smith, (*Possemen*), Albert Schmidt, Joe Haworth (*Gunmen*).

Mitchell is a murderous bandit holding a group of people hostage in a mountain cabin during a raging snowstorm. After killing a couple of his prisoners, gambler Robertson gets his chance to muscle Mitchell to the ground and kill him. A remake of a twice-filmed story (1937 by Christy Cabanne, 1919 by John Ford), which differs from its predecessors by preferring action to character study. It works, however, and makes for a fine picture.

p, Julian Blaustein; d, Joseph M. Newman; w, Edmund H. North (based on the stories "The Outcasts of Poker Flat" and "The Luck of Roaring Camp" by Bret Harte); ph, Joseph La Shelle; m, Hugo Friedhofer; ed, William Reynolds; md, Lionel Newman; cos, Dorothy Jeakins.

Western (PR:A MPAA:NR)

OUTCASTS OF THE CITY** (1958) 61m REP bw

Osa Massen (*Leda Mueller*), Robert Hutton (*Lt. Jerry Seabrook*), Maria Palmer (*Helen Schiller*), Nestor Paiva (*Pastor Skira*), John Hamilton (*Col. White*), George Neise (*Hans Welton*), Leon Tyler (*Biff*), Larry Blake (*Hecker*), Norbert Schiller (*Doctor*), Michael Dale (*Sgt. Hammond*), George Sanders (*GI Announcer*), John Close, John Clark, John Harding, James Wilson (*Army Officers*).

A love story set in post WW II Germany which has American officer Hutton falling in love with the German Massen. Their romance hits a snag, however, when Neise, a former lover of Massen, returns and seeks revenge on Hutton. A secret plot gets Neise killed, resulting in Hutton receiving the blame. Massen puts herself on the line and is able to prove Hutton's innocence, paving the way for their freedom and romance.

p&d, Boris L. Petroff; w, Stephen Longstreet; ph, Walter Strenge; m, Harry Sukman; ed, Frank Doyle; md, Sukman; art d, C. Daniel Hall; m/l, Victor Young, Stan Freberg.

Drama/Romance (PR:A MPAA:NR)

OUTCASTS OF THE TRAIL** (1949) 59m REP bw

Monte Hale (*Pat Garrett*), Paul Hurst (*Doc Meadowlark*), Jeff Donnell (*Lavinia White*), Roy Barcroft (*Jim Judd*), John Gallaudet (*Tom "Ivory" White*), Milton Parsons (*Elias Dunkenscold*), Tommy Ivo (*Chad White*), Minerva Urecal (*Mrs. Rysen*), Ted Mapes (*Fred Smith*), George W. Lloyd (*Horace Rysen*), Steve Darrell (*Sheriff Wilson*), Tom Steele, Lane Bradford.

The children of a convicted stagecoach robber (Gallaudet) are given the cold shoulder by their neighbors even though dad has gone straight and returned the money. In the meantime, however, the daughter (Donnell) gets herself mixed up in a robbery. With the help of Hale both names are cleared and the crooks captured.

p, Melville Tucker; d, Philip Ford; w, Olive Cooper; ph, Bud Thackery; m, Stanley Wilson; ed, Tony Martinelli; md, Morton Scott; art d, Frank Arrigo; set d, John McCarthy, Jr., James Redd.

Western (PR:A MPAA:NR)

OUTCRY***½ (1949, Ital.) 89m E.N.I.C./Crest bw
(IL SOLE SORGE ANCORA; AKA: THE SUN ALWAYS RISES; THE SUN RISES AGAIN)

Lea Padovani (*Laura*), Elli Parvo (*Donna Matilda*), Vittorio Duse (*Cesare*), Mas-simo Serrato (*Maj. Heinrich*), Egisto Olivieri (*Laura's Father*), Marco Sarri (*Cesare's Brother*), Lia Golmar (*Matilda's Cousin*), Carlo Lizzani (*Don Camillo, Priest*), M. Levi, G. Pontecorvo.

Released in Italy in 1946, OUTCRY quickly became one of the classics of the Italian cinema rising along side Roberto Rossellini's OPEN CITY (1946) and

PAISAN (1948). It dealt with the exploitation of a group of peasants in Lombardy, located outside of Milan. Duse is a deserter who hides there and soon becomes involved with Padovani, a partisan leader's daughter, and then with the wealthy Parvo. The film's climax comes when the Fascists murder a pair of hostages—a priest (played by co-writer Lizzani) and a Communist—while the crowd of peasants rebel. A masterful job of editing and Vergano's stark, neo-realist style brought this picture worthy praise, however it seems to have been forgotten today, overshadowed by Rossellini's great successes. Vergano was kept from making films for a period of time while serving a sentence for his involvement in a revolutionary movement. (In Italian; English subtitles.)

p, G.G. Agliani; d, Aldo Vergano; w, Guido Aristarco, Carlo Lizzani, Giuseppe DiSantis, Vergano (based on a story by Giuseppe Gorgerino); ph, Aldo Tonti; m, Giuseppe Rosati; art d, Fausto Gallil; subtitles, Herman G. Weinberg.

Drama **(PR:C-O MPAA:NR)**

OUTCRY, THE (SEE: IL GRIDO, 1962, U.S./Ital.)

OUTER GATE, THE** (1937) 62m MON bw

Ralph Morgan *(John Borden)*, Kay Linaker *(Lois Borden)*, Ben Alexander *(Bob Terry)*, Edward [Eddie] Acuff *(Todd)*, Charles Brokaw *(Carmody)*.

Alexander is a bookkeeper in love with his boss' daughter, though the boss doesn't approve. The boss wrongly accuses Alexander of theft and has him imprisoned. When the innocent bookkeeper gets out of jail, he becomes vindictive, even though the boss tries his best to right the wrong. A bit talky for a film which lasts just over an hour.

p, I.E. Chadwick; d, Ray Cannon; w, Laurie Brazee; ph, Marcel Le Picard; ed, Carl Pierson.

Drama **(PR:A MPAA:NR)**

OUTFIT, THE** (1973) 102m MGM c (AKA: THE GOOD GUYS ALWAYS WIN)

Robert Duvall *(Earl Macklin)*, Karen Black *(Bett Jarrow)*, Joe Don Baker *(Cody)*, Robert Ryan *(Mailer)*, Timothy Carey *(Jake Menner)*, Richard Jaeckel *(Chemey)*, Sheree North *(Buck's Wife)*, Marie Windsor *(Madge Coyle)*, Jane Greer *(Alma)*, Henry Jones *(Doctor)*, Joanna Cassidy *(Rita)*, Tom Reese *(1st Man)*, Elisha Cook, Jr. *(Carl)*, Bill McKinney *(Buck)*, Anita O'Day *(Herself)*, Archie Moore *(Packard)*, Tony Young *(Accountant)*, Roland LaStarza *(Hit Man)*, Edward Ness *(Ed Macklin)*, Roy Roberts *(Caswell)*, Toby Anderson *(Parking Attendant)*, Emile Meyer *(Amos)*, Roy Jensen *(Al)*, Philip Kenneally *(Bartender)*, Bern Hoffman *(Jim Sinclair)*, John Steadman *(Gas Station Attendant)*, Paul Genge *(Payoff Man)*, Francis De Sales *(Jim)*, James Bacon *(Bookie)*, Army Archerd *(Butler)*, Tony Trabert *(Himself)*, Carl Eller.

In an attempt to re-create the murder-and-mayhem gangster films of the 1930s and 1940s, the producers called upon several veterans of those early attempts to help this one succeed. So we get a chance to see the latter-day personas of Cook (who was Wilmer in THE MALTESE FALCON), Jaeckel (who never ages), Windsor (who will always be remembered for her role in Stanley Kubrick's THE KILLING), Carey (another Kubrick favorite), and several others. Duvall is a free-lance crook who has just been freed from a long prison stretch and comes home to learn that his brother was killed by gunmen in the employ of LCN (La Cosa Nostra, although they didn't call it that in the film). He thinks that he may be next in their cross-hairs and that fear is corroborated when his girl friend, Black, tells him that she has been coerced into setting him up by Carey, a gangster who works for The Outfit. Duvall, his late brother, and his pal (Baker) made the mistake of knocking over a bank that was run by the gangsters, and now they are to pay the price for their mistake with their lives. LaStarza is the hit man (which is an inside joke, as he was a heavy-hitter pugilist in real life) who is soon put out of the way by Duvall. Baker and Duvall unite again after Duvall buries his brother and the two men vengefully raid the mob's bookie rooms and gambling dens. The boss of the Mob, Ryan (in the penultimate film of his 81-movie career), tells Carey that Duvall and Baker must be stopped or Carey will get concrete shoes. Carey assembles a raiding party and ambushes Baker, Duvall, and Black on a lonely road. In the gunplay, Black is killed, as are Carey and his aides. Duvall and Baker now go after Ryan, get into his heavily guarded house and plant an explosive device. Next, Duvall stalks Ryan in the mansion and shoots him. Baker is wounded in the fray, but both men gleefully escape in the blast and fire while the cops and the fire department arrive. As a concession to the FCC, the TV version of the film does not have them escaping. Rather, they are seen trapped in a room with the fire raging around them. Since everyone in the picture is a thief or a murderer, the usual "justice and retribution" rules don't count. Sports fans will recognize tennis player Trabert, boxer Moore, and footballer Eller. Jazz buffs will enjoy Anita O'Day and knowledgeable show-business insiders will note columnists James Bacon and Army Archerd in tiny bits. THE OUTFIT is just another crime movie without much to recommend it other than a continuous stream of blood.

p, Carter De Haven; d&w, John Flynn (based on the novel by Richard Stark [Donald E. Westlake]); ph, Bruce Surtees (Metrocolor); m, Jerry Fielding; ed, Ralph E. Winters; art d, Tambi Larsen; set d, James I. Berkey; cos, Yvonne Wood; m/l, "Your Guess Is as Good as Mine." Steve Gillette, Jeremy Kronsberg; stunts, Ron Rondell.

Crime **(PR:C-O MPAA:PG)**

OUTLAND** (1981) 109m Ladd Company-WB c

Sean Connery *(O'Neil)*, Peter Boyle *(Sheppard)*, Frances Sternhagen *(Lazarus)*, James B. Sikking *(Montone)*, Kika Markham *(Carol)*, Clarke Peters *(Ballard)*, Steven Berkoff *(Sagan)*, John Ratzenberger *(Tarlow)*, Nicholas Barnes *(Paul O'Niel)*, Manning Redwood *(Lowell)*, Pat Starr *(Mrs. Spector)*, Hal Galili *(Nelson)*, Angus MacInnes *(Hughes)*, Stuart Milligan *(Walters)*, Eugene Lipinski *(Cane)*, Norman Chancer *(Slater)*, Ron Travis *(Fanning)*, Anni Domingo *(Morton)*, Bill Bailey *(Hill)*, Chris Williams *(Caldwell)*, Marc Boyle *(Spota)*, Richard Hammat *(Yario)*, James Berwick *(Rudd)*, Gary Olsen *(Worker)*, Isabelle Lucas *(Nurse)*, Sharon Duce *(Prostitute)*, P. H. Moriarty *(1st Man)*, Angelique Rockas *(Maintenance Woman)*, Judith Alderson, Rayner Bourton *(Prostitutes in Leisure Club)*, Doug Robinson *(2nd Man)*, Julia Depyer, Nina Francoise, Brendon Hughes, Philip Johnston, Norri Morgan *(Dancers in Leisure Club)*.

Connery is a marshal on Io, Jupiter's third moon, in a mining colony where a drug ring has caused a rash of violence. He has a code of morality he lives by which won't allow him to ignore the violence, even though his devotion to duty could mean his life. His angry wife packs up and leaves. Alone, he awaits the arrival of the company henchmen who plan to exterminate him. His waiting is intensified as the screen is filled with digital readouts of the amount of time remaining until the big showdown. If it sounds a little like an outer space version of HIGH NOON, that's because it is. Director and writer Hyams simply transposed the classic anti-western into an anti-science fiction adventure. Connery and Boyle, as the villain, are fine, but where are Gary Cooper, and Grace Kelly, and the great score by Dimitri Tiomkin? The film has an appealing look to it, though many of the visuals have a striking resemblance to those seen in ALIEN (1979). A third-rate project from the word "go."

p, Richard A. Roth; d&w, Peter Hyams; ph, Stephen Goldblatt (Panavision, Technicolor); m, Jerry Goldsmith; ed, Stuart Baird; prod d, Philip Harrison; art d, Malcolm Middleton; cos, John Mollo; spec eff, John Stears; ch, Anthony Van Laast.

Science-Fiction **Cas.** **(PR:O MPAA:R)**

OUTLAW, THE* (1943) 126m Hughes/RKO bw

Jack Beutel *(Billy the Kid)*, Jane Russell *(Rio)*, Thomas Mitchell *(Pat Garrett)*, Walter Huston *(Doc Holliday)*, Mimi Aguglia *(Guadalupe)*, Joe Sawyer *(Charley)*, Gene Rizzi *(Stranger)*, Frank Darien *(Shorty)*, Pat West *(Bartender)*, Carl Stockdale *(Minister)*, Nena Quartero *(Chita)*, Dickie Jones, Frank Ward, Bobby Callahan *(Boys)*, Ethan Laidlaw, Ed Brady, William Steele *(Deputies)*, Wally Reid, Jr. *(Bystander)*, Ed Peil, Sr. *(Swanson)*, Lee "Lasses" White *(Coach Driver)*, Ted Mapes *(Guard)*, William Newell *(Drunk Cowboy)*, Cecil Kellogg *(Officer)*, Lee Shumway *(Dealer)*, Emory Parnell *(Dolan)*, Martin Garralaga *(Waiter)*, Julian Rivero *(Pablo)*, Arthur Loft, Dick Elliott, John Sheehan *(Salesmen)*.

One of the shabbiest, contrived, and cornball westerns ever made, THE OUTLAW is nevertheless a marvelous curiosity whose undeserved fame was the result of the most clever ad campaign in decades. Howard Hughes literally created a salivating national appetite for a morsel so unappetizing as to make spoiled chopped liver the equal of Beluga caviar. This blatantly over-publicized film supposedly concerned itself with the legend of Billy the Kid but the real legends promoted by Hughes were Jane Russell's enormous breasts. The story line, such as it is, opens by showing Beutel, as Billy the Kid, meeting Huston, as Doc Holliday, and arguing over a horse. Beutel wins the debate and he and Huston become good friends. Lawman Mitchell, as Pat Garrett, tries to take Beutel prisoner but botches the job. Huston takes Beutel to his ranch where his mistress awaits—Russell in a blouse so low cut that it's hardly there to cover her jutting mammaries. Beutel is immediately taken with the sultry siren, little realizing that he's already gunned down Russell's brother. She takes a pot shot at him and he throws her into a haystack and forces himself on her. Later, Mitchell is more successful and wounds the outlaw, but Beutel manages to escape, returning to tempestuous Russell who bandages him up, puts him to bed, and then discovers that he is having alternating fevers and chills. To cure the chills, Russell crawls into bed with Beutel to warm him up. (These scenes were later cut, 11 minutes of them, to mollify the censor.) After nursing Beutel back to health in her peculiar way, Russell falls in love with the outlaw and they are married in a secret ceremony. When Huston discovers this union he is not upset, as one might expect, but further helps Beutel escape into the desert, just ahead of a posse led by Mitchell. They cannot last in the broiling heat, especially since Russell, in a fit of pique, has filled their canteens with sand instead of water. They turn back and Mitchell corners Huston and kills his old friend. Beutel returns to punish Russell for her spiteful betrayal (all she wanted to do by cutting off his water, she explains, was force him to come back sooner). He forgives her, however, and later tricks Mitchell by locking him to a porch with the lawman's own handcuffs, then leaves with sexy Russell for more adventures. Of course, this film and the facts about Billy the Kid (William H. Bonney) have nothing to do with each other. Hughes and scriptwriter Furthman made up their filmic tale out of thin air and their dialog was even thinner. Packed with cliches and bad acting by the monotone-voiced Beutel, and the flat delivery of Russell (the only thing about her that *was* flat), THE OUTLAW was unabashedly strung-together popcorn, stale and tasteless at that. Hughes, in typical dictatorial mood, hired Howard Hawks to direct and then argued with him for several weeks into production about every aspect of the film, then fired the great director, taking over the helm himself. He was impossible as usual, demanding hundreds of takes of the smallest scenes. Russell, who was 19 years old and was picked out of a batch of publicity photographs, had never acted in her life before this film and little realized that what Hughes was doing, working the crew from 3 p.m. until late at night and calling for as many as 100 takes of each scene, was not only highly unorthodox but unprofessional. Veteran actors Huston and Mitchell knew differently, however. Huston said nothing when Hughes had him repeat his lines 30 or 40 times but Mitchell constantly blew up, swore, stomped around the set, and glared at Hughes. The self-appointed director merely said: "Oh, Tommy, did you say something?" Remembered Russell in her autobiography: "I could have died when I finally saw the picture several years later. Jack [Beutel] wasn't good, but I was terrible." Though wonderman photographer Toland shot a fine film visually, providing moody lighting, Hughes' direction is static and unimaginative. He obviously spent most of his time ogling Russell's breasts. In one scene where she was tied between two posts and writhing and jiggling almost out of her low-cut blouse, Hughes suddenly yelled "Cut!" He had a great idea. Though he had manipulated his cameras to expose every angle of her breasts, something was missing. He decided that he would put his vast knowledge of aerodynamics to better use and design a special bra for Russell, one which would accentuate her mammaries at the yank of a string. He ordered a bra made and directed Russell to wear it. Once in her dressing room, however, she discarded the contraption and opted for her own specially designed bra. "So I put on my own bra," Russell later admitted after Hughes was dead, "covered the seams with tissue, pulled the straps over to the side, put on my blouse, and started out...I never wore his bra, and believe me, he could design planes, but a Mr. Playtex he wasn't." Hughes hired superb publicist Russell Birdwell to promote Russell and the film. Birdwell brought a bevy of cameramen to the set each day and they insisted that the scantily clad Russell pick up a pair of milk pails. "My boobs were bulging out of the top of my blouse every time I picked up those pails," Russell ruefully remembered. "But I didn't know it until I saw myself on the covers and in the centerfolds of practically every magazine on the newsstands...I honestly feel sorry if THE OUTLAW publicity campaign was responsible for the young girls who decided that the only way to make it in show business was to shove out their bosom or take their clothes off altogether." The campaign was national and expensive, Hughes spending tens of thousands of dollars to purposely agitate the censor and arouse public indignation. He released the film in San Francisco in 1943 after United Artists refused to distribute it. Hughes splashed the film at the Geary Theater and it was quickly closed down by civic groups which is just what he wanted. Birdwell, meanwhile, leased thousands of billboards from coast to coast for three years, plastering a suggestive photo of the half-naked Russell reclining on a bed of hay, gun in hand, breasts jutting and jutting. By 1946, when Hughes did release the film, premiering it in Los Angeles while rented blimps sailed overhead, he had created incredible interest in the nearly banned production, captioning it with the sleazy advertising query bannering all his ads: "What are the two reasons for Jane Russell's rise to stardom?" Russell, according to gossip columnist Sheilah Graham, received a 10-year contract from Hughes at $50,000 a year whether she acted or not. According to Russell, she barely had enough money to fill the gas tank of her car under the Hughes contract. Hughes never lost; he wound up selling Russell's contract to his own Hughes Tool Company for $100,000, some time after putting his signature to it.

p, Howard Hughes; d, Hughes, Howard Hawks; w, Jules Furthman; ph, Gregg Toland; ed, Walter Grissell; md, Victor Young; art d, Perry Ferguson; spec eff, Roy Davidson.

Western　　　　　　　Cas.　　　　　　　(PR:O　MPAA:NR)

OUTLAW AND THE LADY, THE　　　　　　(SEE: WACO, 1952)

OUTLAW BLUES**½　　　　　　　　(1977) 100m Sequoia/WB c

Peter Fonda (Bobby Ogden), Susan Saint James (Tina Waters), John Crawford (Chief Buzz Cavenaugh), James Callahan (Garland Dupree), Michael Lerner (Hatch), Steve Fromholz (Elroy), Richard Lockmiller (Associate Warden), Matt Clark (Billy Bob), Jan Rita Cobler (Cathy Moss), Jeffrey Friedman (TV Reporter), Gene Rader (Leon Warbeck), Curtis Harris (Big Guy), Jerry Greene (Disk Jockey), Dave Helfert (Anchorman), James N. Harrel (Cop Chauffeur).

In a story very similar to the Elvis Presley vehicle LOVING YOU (1957), Fonda is released from prison and travels to Texas in pursuit of Callahan, a country-western singer who stole a tune of Fonda's called "Outlaw Blues." When Callahan is accidentally shot, the police organize a manhunt to locate Fonda. Saint James, a singer in Callahan's band, befriends Fonda. The pair become lovers, and Saint James creates a publicity story which elevates Fonda to the top of the charts as a folk hero. It's all done in a rather tongue-in-cheek manner, which adds a certain charm to the picture though Fonda's singing is abysmal. Saint James is adorable in her first major film role. Songs include: "Outlaw Blues" (John Oates), "Jailbirds Can't Fly" (Harlan Sanders, R. C. O'Leary); "Whisper in a Velvet Night" (Lee Clayton); "I Dream Of Highways," "Beyond These Walls," "Water for My Horses" (Hoyt Axton), all sung by Fonda.

p, Steve Tisch; d, Richard T. Heffron; w, B. W. L. Norton; ph, Jules Brenner (Technicolor); m, Charles Bernstein; ed, Danford B. Green, Scott Conrad; art d, Jack Marty; cos, Rosanna Norton; spec eff, Milton Rice; makeup, Tom Lucas; stunts, Carey Loftin.

Drama　　　　　　　Cas.　　　　　　　(PR:A　MPAA:PG)

OUTLAW BRAND*½　　　　　　　　(1948) 57m MON bw

Jimmy Wakely, Dub "Cannonball" Taylor, Kay Morley, Bud Osborne, Leonard Penn, Nolan Leary, Christine Larson, Tom Chatterton, John James, Boyd Stockman, Frank McCarroll, Jack Rivers, Dick Reinhart, Ray Whitley, Louis Armstrong, Jay Kirby, Eddie Majors.

Singing western star Wakely takes on the role of a reliable cowhand whose job it is to tame a wild stallion. Trouble arises when he is also called upon to wrangle up a wily bandit, but everything is soon brought under control.

p, Louis Gray; d, Lambert Hillyer; w, J. Benton Cheney; ph, Harry Neumann; ed, Carl Pierson; md, Edward Kay.

Western　　　　　　　　　　　　(PR:A　MPAA:NR)

OUTLAW COUNTRY**½　　　　　　(1949) 72m Screen Guild bw

Lash LaRue (Lash LaRue/The Frontier Phantom), Al [Fuzzy] St. John (Fuzzy Q. Jones), Dan White (Jim McCord), House Peters, Jr. (Col. Saunders), Steve Dunhill (Turk), Lee Roberts (Buck), Ted Adams (Frank Evans), Nancy Saunders (Jane Evans), John Merton (Marshal Clark), Dee Cooper (Jeff Thomas), Jack O'Shea (Senor Cardova), Sandy Sanders, Bob Duncan (Fighting Deputies).

One of the best of the Lash LaRue pictures, OUTLAW COUNTRY relies on the gimmick of dual roles for LaRue. He plays both the law-minded, whip-crackin' marshal in pursuit of a gang of counterfeiters, and the outlaw who is part of the phony bill operation. The bad twin has a change of heart, however, and helps the good guys capture the gang.

p, Ron Ormond; d, Ray Taylor; w, Ormond, Ira Webb; ph, Ernest Miller; ed, Hugh Winn; md, Walter Greene; art d, Fred Preble.

Western　　　　　　　　　　　　(PR:A　MPAA:NR)

OUTLAW DEPUTY, THE**½　　　　　　(1935) 55m Puritan bw

Tim McCoy (Tim Mallory), Nora Lane (Joyce Rutledge), Bud Osborne (Cash), George Offerman, Jr. (Chuck Adams), Joseph Gerard (Rutledge), Si Jenks, Jack Montgomery, George Holtz, Hank Bell, Tex Cooper, Jim Corey.

McCoy is the unjust justice who takes the side of the outlaws, but he is really a law-and-order man at heart. He is denounced and jailed, but Lane comes to his aid and helps him clear his name. A respectable outing with fine performances and an appealing story.

p, Nat Ross; d, Otto Brower; w, Ford Beebe, Dell Andrews (based on the story "King of Cactusville" by Johnston McCulley); ph, James Diamond; ed, Robert Johns.

Western　　　　　　　　　　　　(PR:A　MPAA:NR)

OUTLAW EXPRESS*½　　　　　　　(1938) 56m UNIV bw

Bob Baker (Bob Bradley), Cecilia Callejo (Lorita), Don Barclay (Andy), LeRoy Mason (Summers), Forrest Taylor (Ferguson), Nina Campano (Lupe), Martin Garralaga (Don Ricardo), Carleton Young (Ramon), Carlyle Moore (Bill Cody), Jack Kirk (Phelps), Arthur Van Slyke (Postmaster), Ed Cassidy (Officer), Jack Ingram, Julian Rivero, Tex Palmer, Chief Many Treaties, Ray Jones, Bill Hazlett, Joe Dominguez, Wilbur McCauley, Apache the Horse.

Baker is a U.S. marshal who is assigned to put an end to a rash of raids on Spanish landowners. The dirty work is being done by U.S. outlaws just after the government annexed California into the Union. The actors are poorly cast and the story's insipid.

p, Trem Carr; d, George Waggner; w, Norton S. Parker (based on his story); ph, Harry Neumann; m, Frank Skinner; ed, Charles Craft.

Western　　　　　　　　　　　　(PR:A　MPAA:NR)

OUTLAW GOLD*½　　　　　　　　(1950) 51m MON bw

Johnny Mack Brown (Dave Willis), Jane Adams (Kathy), Myron Healey (Sonny Lang), Milburn Morante (Sandy Barker), Marshall Reed (Jackson), Hugh Prosser (Bigsby), Carol Henry (Joe), Bud Osborne (Sheriff), George DeNormand (Whitey), Frank Jacquet, Carl Mathews, Ray Jones, Steve Clark, Bob Woodward, Merrill McCormack.

Illogical story stars Brown as a U.S. marshal on the trail of gold robbers. Healey plays a gunman recently released from jail. He's out to get revenge on Brown who sent him to prison five years earlier. The chase leads to Reed's door, as the newspaper publisher who has murdered his partner and is leader of the gold heisting operation. Brown clears the way for the gold shipment's passage to Mexico, while fending off Healey and Reed.

p, Vincent M. Fennelly; d, Wallace W. Fox; w, Jack Lewis; ph, Gilbert Warrenton; ed, Fred Maguire; md, Edward Kay; art d, Dave Milton.

Western　　　　　　　　　　　　(PR:A　MPAA:NR)

OUTLAW JOSEY WALES, THE*****　　　(1976) 135m Malpaso/WB c

Clint Eastwood (Josey Wales), Chief Dan George (Lone Watie), Sondra Locke (Laura Lee), Bill McKinney (Terrill), John Vernon (Fletcher), Paula Trueman (Grandma Sarah), Sam Bottoms (Jamie), Geraldine Keams (Little Moonlight), Woodrow Parfrey (Carpetbagger), Joyce Jameson (Rose), Sheb Wooley (Cobb), Royal Dano (Ten Spot), Matt Clarke (Kelly), John Verros (Chato), Will Sampson (Ten Bears), William O'Connell (Carstairs), John Quade (Comanchero Leader).

This superb western is not only Eastwood's greatest achievement as an actor-director, but an important moment in the development of the western hero. The film opens as Missouri farmer and family man Eastwood plows his field aided by his young son. Later in the day his farm is attacked by a vicious band of Union guerrillas known as "Redlegs" because of their red boots. The bandits are led by McKinney, who hits Eastwood in the face with his saber. Eastwood falls to the ground with a deep gash on his face, and left for dead. When he awakens he finds that his house has been burned to the ground, with the charred corpses of his family in the rubble. He buries his family, kneels over the graves, breaks into sobs and cries, collapsing on the graves clutching the wooden marker. We see a pile of smoldering ashes. Eastwood's hands dig into the cinders and he retrieves a gun and holster. He practices. He is not a good shot. He becomes better, practicing with both hands. Sitting alone near the graves of his family, Eastwood's brooding is interrupted by a dozen men on horseback who ride up out of the woods. They are men led by "Bloody" Bill Anderson, a brutal Confederate guerrilla leader. Surveying the ruined farm, the rebel leader asks, "Redlegs?" Eastwood nods. "You'll find 'em up in Kansas. They're with the Union. And we're goin' up there and set things right." Eastwood looks up at the ragtag group of men, the gash on his face hardening into a scar. "I'll be comin' with ya," he replies. The credits sequence is a montage of Civil War footage (mostly culled from John Huston's THE RED BADGE OF COURAGE), intercut with shots of Eastwood riding and fighting with "Bloody" Bill Anderson's men. Eastwood ages during these years. A scruffy beard almost hides his scar. We see the death of "Bloody" Bill and the end of the war. As the credits end, we watch as Vernon, now in command of the guerrillas, announces that he plans to take the Union up on its offer of amnesty. All the rebels need do is take an oath to the Union and disarm. Reluctantly, all the men finally admit to themselves that the war is over, all, that is, except Eastwood. As the men go off to the Union camp to surrender, Eastwood once again sits alone. At the Union camp it is revealed that Vernon has been paid by the Union to talk his men into surrendering. McKinney, the man responsible for the murders of Eastwood's family, presides over the surprise execution of the rebels. Vernon, who knew nothing of the ambush, is prevented from retaliating. Out of the mist rides Eastwood. Singlehandedly he kills many Union soldiers and rescues a young rebel, Bottoms, who has been severely wounded. The Union sends McKinney and the reluctant Vernon south in pursuit of Eastwood and Bottoms. Bottoms, aware that he is dying from his wounds, encourages Eastwood to leave him behind, but, feeling close to the boy because he reminds him of his son, Eastwood refuses to abandon him. The next morning, the boy dies. This time Eastwood swallows his sorrow and sends the boy's body, head down over a saddle, back to the Union for a decent burial. He can no longer cry. The driving rain must do it for him. Continuing his journey, Eastwood next encounters an old Cherokee Indian, George, wearing a stovepipe hat and a long black coat, looking like a parody of Abraham Lincoln. George tells Eastwood about the time he and his tribe went to Washington, D.C., to talk to the President about getting their land back (hence the clothes). They were only allowed to talk to the secretary of the interior, who congratulated them for being so "civilized." George laments for the time when he wasn't so "civilized." The next morning, the Indian burns his Abe Lincoln suit. Although Eastwood acts as if he'd rather be alone, he allows George to accompany him on his journey. As they ride past a remote outpost, the men rescue a young Cherokee woman (Keams) from two trappers intent on raping her. Eastwood is dismayed when Keams decides to follow him on his trek as well. The next morning a stray dog appears and it, too, joins their little caravan. In an attempt to discourage the dog, Eastwood spits tobacco right between the beast's eyes. The dog stares at him and growls. Even the dog won't take Eastwood's tough loner facade seriously. That night at the camp, Eastwood works up enough nerve to make sexual contact with the Indian woman. This is the first time since his family was killed that we see Eastwood feeling some romantic passion. He walks up to Keams, whose back is to him, and touches her tenderly. She rolls over to reveal George underneath her. The old man got the girl before the hero. The next day the group witnesses an attack on a covered wagon owned by an old woman, Trueman, and her granddaughter, Locke. A group of Comancheros have pillaged the wagon and now attempt to rape Locke. Eastwood pulls his guns and takes aim, but his heroic action is circumvented by the Comanchero leader who stops the men from raping Locke because "the Chief likes 'em fresh." Soon after, George and Keams accidentally get themselves captured by the Comancheros and they are imprisoned alongside Trueman and Locke. Eastwood attacks the convoy and rescues his friends. Grateful for the help, Trueman invites Eastwood and his small troupe of travelers to live with her and Locke at the farmhouse her son built. The group accepts the invitation, but Eastwood worries that Vernon, McKinney, and now Sampson, the Comanchee warrior whose men he has just killed, will pick up their trail. En route, the voyagers discover a ghost town inhabited only by a bartender (Clarke), an aging prostitute (Jameson), an old Mexican (Verros), and a gambler (Dano). These lonely people pack their bags and join Eastwood and his "family" on the trip to the farmhouse. When they arrive, Eastwood is struck by how similar the farm is to his own. Trueman declares that they all can live together and make a go of it. Once again Eastwood sits alone and watches the small commune at work. Keams chops wood, Trueman beats a carpet, George, Dano, Clarke, and Verros clear the fields. Suddenly Locke, dressed in white, appears behind Eastwood. She smiles at him and runs off, disappearing with a haunting quickness. It is as if the ghost of Eastwood's murdered wife had come to visit him. Later in the day the group hold a prayer service led by Trueman, who intones, "Thanks a lot for Josey Wales, who you changed from a murderin' bushwhacker on the side of Satan to a better man tryin' to deliver us from the Philistines." The service is interrupted by the appearance of Sampson. Eastwood leaves the farm to meet with the Indian chief. At the encampment, Sampson tells Eastwood that he is tired of having to move because of the white man. Eastwood declares that he has nowhere else to go, "Dyin' ain't so hard for men like you and me. It's the livin' that's hard...I'm sayin' that men can live together without butcherin' one another." It is obvious that both men are tired of violence and killing. "It shall be life," declares Sampson. That night there is a celebration in Eastwood's honor at the farmhouse. Everyone sings and dances, even Eastwood. That night he relaxes his defenses enough to reach out to Locke, but tragically, his dreams are still filled with the screams of his murdered family. As dawn breaks, Eastwood, with great regret, saddles his horse and prepares to leave. His departure is interuppted by the arrival of McKinney and his Redlegs. McKinney gloats and smiles, "You're all alone now." "Not quite," replies George as a dozen rifles appear from the windows of the farmhouse. A full-scale battle ensues, and while the farmers defeat the Redlegs, Eastwood chases McKinney back to the ghost town for a final confrontation. The combat is hand-to-hand, and ends with Eastwood killing McKinney with his own sword. Wounded, Eastwood wanders into the bar only to be confronted by two Texas Rangers who are accompanied by Vernon, the man who had betrayed the rebels. Dano has been telling the men about the death of Josey Wales. Vernon recognizes Eastwood, but says nothing. Satisfied that their quarry is dead, the Rangers leave. Vernon stays behind and though fully expecting to be killed, tells Eastwood that the war is finally over. Eastwood replies, "I guess we all died a little in that damn war." Allowing Vernon to live, Eastwood mounts his horse and rides back to the farmhouse. Whereas Eastwood's homage to director Sergio Leone in HIGH PLAINS DRIFTER was bleak from start to finish with no hope of salvation and no alternatives to damnation, THE OUTLAW JOSEY WALES begins with life (Eastwood and his family) and ends with life (the communal family). In between is a long period of healing and rebuilding. Eastwood re-examines the screen persona he developed with director Leone in the Italian films and the image of the classic western hero. Eastwood's "man-with-no-name" character for the most part was an unattached, uncivilized avenger who possessed mystical gunfighting skills. The traditional western hero is also a loner. A man with a dark, pained past who, although he may have become briefly involved in the lives of others, can never settle down and reap the fruits of society. John Wayne in THE SEARCHERS and Alan Ladd in SHANE are the finest examples of the traditional western hero. While these men are certainly heroic, they are also sad and tragic. THE OUTLAW JOSEY WALES, however, is a cautiously optimistic epic, deeply rooted in the history of America. Eastwood, despite his efforts, is not a loner. The viewer has witnessed the great tragedy that brought him to this cold, hard, violent existence. We understand his pain and see that deep down he seeks to heal and start a new life. Eastwood changes his image and the western hero by allowing himself to take on more responsibilities, thus making himself more vulnerable. Though his skills in the art of killing are frequently demonstrated, his companions save his life more than once. He cannot survive without the people around him. Instead of surrendering and assimilating into the "rebuilt" post-war society full of carpetbaggers, Klansmen, and dishonor, Eastwood and his group head out on their own. The extended family of displaced persons provide for and protect one another. They create their own society, one steeped in honor, mutual respect, and love. The traditional western hero is shown to control his own destiny. In THE OUTLAW JOSEY WALES, Eastwood is never in control. His life was shattered by the Redlegs, the war was lost, he would have been murdered had he surrendered, his wish to be left alone after the war was not to be. He would have drifted to his own destruction had not fate crossed his path with people who understood that he really wanted to belong and not become the tragic loner that the genre expected him to be. THE OUTLAW JOSEY WALES was based on the first novel written by a middle-aged half-Cherokee Indian poet named Forrest Carter entitled *The Rebel Outlaw: Josey Wales* (the title was eventually changed to *Gone to Texas*). The book was published by a small company in Arkansas and only 75 hardcover editions went to press. The author sent a copy to Eastwood, unsolicited, but miraculously the star read it. Eastwood was impressed with the book and bought the screen rights. He then hired director Philip Kaufman, whose western THE GREAT NORTHFIELD, MINNESOTA RAID, Eastwood admired. Unfortunately, the star and director had strong differences of opinion and Eastwood took over the directing chores as well. The filming, which took place on locations in Utah, Nevada, and California, was completed in an incredibly swift eight and a half weeks. The cinematography by Bruce Surtees is magnificent, as is Jerry Fielding's musical score. Acting honors must go to Chief Dan George, who nearly steals the film from the star and serves as the emotional center of the film. His dry wit and dignified, loving presence serves to remind Eastwood's Josey Wales that life is always better than death and we must "Endeavor to persevere." Although THE OUTLAW JOSEY WALES was an uplifting affirmation of life that managed to expand the confines of the western genre, it was also one of the last westerns produced by Hollywood (Walter Hill's THE LONG RIDERS was the only notable one to follow). With the disaster of Michael Cimino's HEAVEN'S GATE and the disappointing box office of Lawrence Kasdan's childish SILVERADO, it seems as if the western is truly dead. Eastwood returned to the saddle with the financially successful, if somewhat artistically disappointing, PALE RIDER, but the film made money because of its star and not the genre. Judging from his popularity and obvious commitment to the genre, fans of the western must place all their hope in Eastwood to revitalize one of the American cinema's greatest creations.

p, Robert Daley; d, Clint Eastwood; w, Phil Kaufman, Sonia Chernus (based on the book *Gone to Texas* by Forrest Carter); ph, Bruce Surtees (Panavision, DeLuxe Color); m, Jerry Fielding; ed, Ferris Webster; prod d, Tambi Larsen; set d, Chuck Pierce; stunts, Walter Scott.

Western **Cas.** **(PR:O MPAA:R)**

OUTLAW JUSTICE** (1933) 57m Majestic bw

Jack Hoxie, Dorothy Gulliver, Chris-Pin Martin, Donald Keith, Kermit Maynard, Charles King, Jack Trent, Walter Shumway, Jack Rockwell, Tom London.

Hoxie poses as an outlaw in order to save Gulliver from doom, an act which gains him the respect of the local sheriff. This was Hoxie's first sound picture after making dozens of silent westerns. His voice wasn't well-suited to the talkies, however, and after five more low-budget westerns he left movies to appear in Wild West shows. One of Martin's earliest pictures and he plays a Mexican sidekick, a role which would become his specialty in films throughout the 1930s and 1940s.

p, Larry Darmour; d, Armand Schaefer; w, Oliver Drake (based on a story by W. Scott Darling); ph, William Nobles.

Western **(PR:A MPAA:NR)**

OUTLAW MOTORCYCLES* (1967) 80m Hollywood Star/Gillman Film c

A group of biker fanatics organize a variety of social events, including a state-wide race. A funeral procession and a wedding march are also on the agenda and serve as nothing more than a chance for everyone to show off their new chopper. Luckily for the cast and crew, they've all chosen to remain anonymous except for Titus Moody, who bears no relation to the Fred Allen radio show character.

p&d, Titus Moody [Titus Moede].

Action/Crime **(PR:O MPAA:NR)**

OUTLAW OF THE PLAINS* (1946) 56m PRC bw

Buster Crabbe, Al "Fuzzy" St. John, Patti McCarty, Charles King, Jr., Karl Hackett, Jack O'Shea, John L. "Bob" Cason, Bud Osborne, Budd Buster, Roy Brent, Charles "Slim" Whitaker.

St. John gets cheated by an outlaw who tells him that a worthless plot of land is rich in gold. When the gullible St. John tries to convince the locals to invest with him, Crabbe manages to expose the deception and save everyone from ruin. (See BILLY CARSON series, Index.)

p, Sigmund Neufeld; d, Sam Newfield; w, A. Frederic Evans (based on a story by Elmer Clifton); ph, Jack Greenhalgh; m, Lee Zahler; ed, Holbrook N. Todd.

Western **(PR:A MPAA:NR)**

OUTLAW STALLION, THE** (1954) 64m COL c

Phil Carey *(Doc Woodrow)*, Dorothy Patrick *(Mary Saunders)*, Billy Gray *(Danny Saunders)*, Roy Roberts *(Hagen)*, Gordon Jones *(Wagner)*, Trevor Bardette

(Rigo), Morris Ankrum (Sheriff Fred Flummer), Chris Alcaide (Truxton), Robert Anderson (Martin), Harry Harvey (Mace), Guy Teague (Trimble).

A widowed mother and her son live a quiet life on their ranch until the boy's white stallion kills a gang leader's black stallion. Roberts, the evil outlaw, is determined to avenge his stallion's death and kidnaps the kid, him mom, and the horse. As with the horse battle, however, the white hats put an end to the menacing ways of the black hats. Ankrum provides some interest as a sheriff plagued with nagging backache, but everything else is very predictable.

p, Wallace MacDonald; d, Fred F. Sears; w, David Lang; ph, Lester H. White (Technicolor); ed, Aaron Stell.

Western (PR:A MPAA:NR)

OUTLAW TERRITORY (SEE: HANNAH LEE, 1953)

OUTLAW: THE SAGA OF GISLI** (1982, Iceland) 106m Isfilm c
(UTLAGINN: GISLA SAGA SURSSONAR)

Arnar Jonsson, Ragheiour Steindorsdottir, Tinni Gunnlangsdottir, Bjarni Steingrimsson, Helgi Skulason.

A beautifully photographed tale of revenge among 10th-century Icelandic farmers. When two women carry on a conversation which is misinterpreted by a jealous husband, it leads to murder, and a seemingly endless cycle of retaliation begins. The peaceful Gisli is forced to live as an outcast in the mountains. He has a price on his head and, in the spirit of the Western, a number of people want to collect the reward. It takes some getting used to, however, when the characters are seen riding ponyback instead of on stallions. The plot gets thick, and confusing, but there is enough happening on the screen to maintain interest. Film indicates that the developing Icelandic film industry has a good command of current technology. (In Icelandic; English subtitles.)

p, Jan Hermannsson; d&w, Agust Gudmundsson; ph, Sigurdur Sverrir Palsson; m, Askell Masson; ed, William River; art d, Jan Porisson.

Drama (PR:C MPAA:NR)

OUTLAW TRAIL** (1944) 53m MON bw

Hoot Gibson (Hoot), Bob Steele (Bob), Chief Thundercloud (Thundercloud), Jennifer Holt (Alice Thornton), Cy Kendall ("Honest John" Travers), Rocky Camron (Sheriff Rocky Camron), George Eldridge (Carl Beldon), Charles King (Chuck Walters), Hal Price (H.A. Fraser), John Bridges (Ed Knowles), Bud Osborne (Blackie), Jim Thorpe (Spike), Frank Ellis, Al Ferguson, Warner Richmond, Tex Palmer.

Another entry in the TRAIL BLAZERS B Western series, with Chief Thundercloud filling the void left by Ken Maynard who quit the series after ARIZONA WHIRLWIND (1944). Kendall plays the not-so-honest civic leader who freely prints up money and has the rest of the town in his debt. The Blazers bring his reign to an expected end. Fine direction and an overflow of pistol poppin'. (See TRAIL BLAZERS series, Index.)

p&d, Robert Tansey; w, Frances Kavanaugh (based on a story by Alvin J. Neitz [Alan James]); ph, Edward Kull; ed, John C. Fuller; md, Frank Sanucci.

Western (PR:A MPAA:NR)

OUTLAW TREASURE* (1955) 65m American Releasing Corp./AIP bw

John Forbes [John Carpenter], Frank "REd" Carpenter, Adele Jergens, Glenn Langan, Hal Baylor, Michael Whalen, Frank Jenks, Harry Lauter.

Producer/writer/star Carpenter romps through post-Civil War California doing a lot of nothing. He's supposed to be working for the Army, trying to crack a case of missing gold shipments. The James Gang is brought in for good measure, but Carpenter seems to be more concerned with firing his cap gun than acting. Jergens is the tough blonde who comes to Carpenter's aid when her outlaw boy friend goes after Carpenter's dad (also played by Carpenter!). She spends almost no time on the screen, though she gets costar billing.

p, John Carpenter; d, Oliver Drake; w, Carpenter; ph, Clark Ramsey; m, Darrell Calker.

Western (PR:A MPAA:NR)

OUTLAW WOMEN** (1952) 76m Howco/Lippert c

Marie Windsor (Iron Mae McLeod), Richard Rober (Woody Callaway), Alan Nixon (Dr. Bob Ridgeway), Carla Balenda (Beth Larabee), Jacqueline Fontaine (Ellen Larabee), Jackie Coogan (Piute Bill), Maria Hart (Big Dora), Billy House (Barney), Richard Avonde (Frank Slater), Leonard Penn (Sam Bass), Lyle Talbot (Judge Dixon), Brad Johnson (Chuck).

A programmer with a gimmick—a Western town run by women. Windsor is the gambling queen who won't let male outlaws come into her town, Las Mujeres. Rober finally gets on her good side, and a witty ending has the girls still ruling the town. . .as wives.

p, Ron Ormond; d, Ormond, Sam Newfield; w, Orville Hampton; ph, Ellis W. Carter (Cinecolor); ed, Hugh Winn; m/l, "Frisco Kate" Ben Young, "Crazy Over You" June Carr (sung by Fontaine).

Western (PR:A MPAA:NR)

OUTLAWED GUNS** (1935) 62m UNIV bw

Buck Jones (Reece Rivers), Pat O'Brien (Babe Rivers), Frank McGlynn, Sr. (Slim Gordon), Roy D'Arcy (Jack Keeler), Ruth Channing (Ruth Ellsworth), Joseph Girard (Rocky Ellsworth), Joan Gale (Marj Ellsworth), Charles King, Monte Montague, Bob Walker, Carl Stockdale, Cliff Lyons, Babe DeTreest, Jack Montgomery, Lee Shumway, Jack Rockwell.

Jones is O'Brien's older brother who nearly gets pinned for O'Brien's illegal activities. O'Brien joins up with an outlaw gang and big brother has to save him. Buck

straightens everything out, but not before O'Brien is killed while leaving jail. Standard fare with some fine horse chases.

p, Buck Jones; d, Ray Taylor; w, Jack Neville (based on the story by Cliff Farrell); ph, William Sickner, Allen Thompson; ed, Bernard Loftus.

Western (PR:A MPAA:NR)

OUTLAW'S DAUGHTER, THE** (1954) 76m Regal/FOX c

Bill Williams (Jess), Jim Davis (Dan), Kelly Ryan [Sheila Connelly] (Kate), Elisha Cook, Jr. (Tulsa), George Cleveland (Lem), Guinn "Big Boy" Williams (Moose), Nelson Leigh (Dalton), Sara Haden (Mrs. Merril), George Barrows (Rock), Zon Murray (Duke, the Bartender), Zabuda (Mexican Dancer), Dick Powers (Bank Manager), Regina Gleason (Eastern Girl), Sam Flint (Doctor), Paul Stader, Danny Fisher (Stunt Men), Eugene Anderson, Jr. (Rider).

Ryan is the daughter of an outlaw whom she believes was killed by Marshal Davis. Even though she's romantically interested in Davis, she chooses the criminal life and goes with Williams' gang. The marshal tracks down the gang and kills everyone except Ryan. He then tells her that it was actually Williams who killed her father. He offers to let her go free, but she honorably agrees to do a jail term. Ryan, who at the time was married to Guy Madison, made her film debut here, beginning an abbreviated movie career.

p&d, Wesley Barry; w, Sam Roeca; ph, Gordon Avil (Eastmancolor); m, Raoul Kraushaar; ed, Ace Herman.

Western (PR:A MPAA:NR)

OUTLAWS IS COMING, THE½** (1965) 88m COL bw (AKA: THREE STOOGES MEET THE GUNSLINGER)

Larry Fine, Moe Howard, Joe De Rita (The Three Stooges), Adam West (Kenneth Cabot), Nancy Kovack (Annie Oakley), Mort Mills (Trigger Mortis), Don Lamond (Rance Roden), Rex Holman (Sunstroke Kid), Emil Sitka (Mr. Abernathy/Witch Doctor/Cavalry Colonel), Henry Gibson (Charlie Horse), Murray Alper (Chief Crazy Horse), Tiny Brauer (Bartender), Joe Bolton (Rob Dalton), Bill Camfield (Wyatt Earp), Hal Fryar (Johnny Ringo), Johnny Ginger (Billy the Kid), Wayne Mack (Jesse James), Ed T. McDonnell (Bat Masterson), Bruce Sedley (Cole Younger), Paul Shannon (Wild Bill Hickok), Sally Starr (Belle Starr), Marilyn Fox, Sidney Marion, Audrey Betz, Jerry Allan, Lloyd King.

This was the Three Stooges' last film, and it might even appeal to those who don't like the slapstick trio. The Stooges go West after a stint with the Preservation of Wildlife Society and get mixed up in a battle between gunslingers and an Indian tribe. The outlaws are trying to start an Indian uprising by killing off all the buffalo. With the help of Annie Oakley (Kovack) the Stooges battle a variety of Western mythic figures—Jesse James, Billy the Kid, the Dalton gang, Cole Younger—getting aid from good guys Wyatt Earp, Bat Masterson, and Wild Bill Hickok. A silly Western spoof which has a number of moments every bit as good as BLAZING SADDLES (1974). Producer/director Mauer is the son-in-law of Moe Howard. Though this was the end of the movie line for the Stooges, Moe would go on to make two more films before his death in 1975.

p&d, Norman Maurer; w, Elwood Ullman (based on a story by Maurer); ph, Irving Lippman; m, Paul Dunlap; ed, Aaron Nibley; art d, Robert Peterson; set d, James M. Crowe; spec eff, Richard Albain; makeup, Joe Dibella.

Western/Comedy (PR:A MPAA:NR)

OUTLAWS OF PINE RIDGE½** (1942) 55m REP bw

Don "Red" Barry (Chips Barrett), Lynn Merrick (Ann Hollister), Noah Beery, Sr. ("Honest" John Hollister), Donald Kirke (Jeff Cardeen), Emmett Lynn (Jackpot McGraw), Francis Ford (Bartender), Clayton Moore (Lane Mannion), Stanley Price (Steve Mannion), George Lewis (Ross), Forrest Taylor (Sheriff Gibbons), Wheaton Chambers, Roy Brent, Ken Terrell, Al Taylor, Tex Terry, Jack O'Shea, Cactus Mack, Tom Steele, Horace B. Carpenter, Duke Green, Duke Taylor, Jess Cavin.

A hard-hitting Western with Barry saving the little town of Pine Ridge from falling into the hands of the villains. He quells an attempt by the local outlaw gang to keep Beery from getting elected to the post of governor. Beery has promised to bring justice to the area, a promise no outlaw can contend with. A lot of well-staged action and some notable comic segments help this rise above the standard cowboy entries.

p, Eddy White; d, William Witney; w, Norman S. Hall; ph, Bud Thackery; m, Mort Glickman; ed, William Thompson; art d, Russell Kimball.

Western (PR:A MPAA:NR)

OUTLAWS OF SANTA FE** (1944) 56m REP bw

Don "Red" Barry (Bob Hackett/Bob Conray), Helen Talbot (Ruth Gordon), Wally Vernon (Buckshot), Twinkle Watts (Winky Gordon), Charles Morton (Jim Hackett), Herbert Heyes (Henry Jackson), Bud Geary (Steve), LeRoy Mason (Trigger McGurn), Kenne Duncan (Chuck), Nolan Leary (Mayor Ward), Walter Soderling (Judge Turner), Edmund Cobb (Marshal Billings), Frank McCarroll (Bill), Bob Kortman (Ed), Emmett Lynn (Saloon Drunk), Ernie Adams, Jack Kirk, Pierce Lyden, Forrest Taylor, Bob Burns, Jack O'Shea, Fred Graham.

Barry is an outlaw who turns his back on the criminal life in order to focus his intentions on finding the man who killed his father. He has a few run-ins with the marshal, but in the end gains the lawman's respect. The story is very similar to the O. Henry short story "Alias Jimmy Valentine."

p, Eddy White; d, Howard Bretherton; w, Norman S. Hall; ph, John McBurnie; m, Mort Glickman; ed, Charles Craft; art d, Fred Ritter.

Western (PR:A MPAA:NR)

OUTLAWS OF SONORA✶✶   (1938) 58m REP bw

Bob Livingston (*Stony Brooke*), Ray Corrigan (*Tucson Smith*), Max Terhune (*Lullaby Joslin*), Jack Mulhall (*Dr. Martin*), Otis Harlan (*Newt*), Jean Joyce (*Miss Burke*), Stelita Peluffo (*Rosita*), Tom London (*Sheriff Trask*), Gloria Rich (*Jane*), Edwin Mordant (*Pierce*), Ralph Peters (*Gabby*), George Chesebro (*Slim*), Frank LaRue (*Coroner*), Jack Ingram (*Nick*), Merrill McCormack (*Pete*), Curley Dresden, Jim Corey, George Cleveland, Earl Dwire, Jack Kirk.

Livingston is given the job of transporting a cache of money from a cattlemen's association to a nearby town. An outlaw also played by Livingston hears about the journey and, realizing that he looks like the good guy, goes to the cattlemen pretending to be Livingston. The finale has the good Livingston clearing up the mistaken identity and capturing his double. The average plot is made interesting by Livingston's dual assignment. Terhune provides a few comic moments with a ventriloquist act. (See THREE MESQUITEERS series, Index.)

p, William Berke; d, George Sherman; w, Betty Burbridge, Edmund Kelso (based on a story by Burbridge and on characters created by William Colt MacDonald); ph, William Nobles; ed, Tony Martinelli.

Western   **(PR:A MPAA:NR)**

OUTLAWS OF STAMPEDE PASS✶½   (1943) 58m MON bw

Johnny Mack Brown, Raymond Hatton, Ellen Hall, Harry Woods, Milburn Morante, Edmund Cobb, Sam Flint, Jon Dawson, Charles King, Mauritz Hugo, Art Mix, Cactus Mack, Artie Ortego, Eddie Burns, Bill Wolfe, Hal Price, Dan White, Kansas Moehring, Tex Cooper.

Stampede Pass is overrun by a gang of worthless outlaws who make life difficult for the town's inhabitants. Muscular Brown and sidekick Hatton ride into town and deal the gang members their just desserts. Another tight, well made low-budgeteer out of Gower Gulch.

p, Scott R. Dunlap; d, Wallace Fox; w, Jess Bowers [Adele Buffington] (based on a story by Johnston McCulley); ph, MarcelLe Picard; ed, Carl Pierson.

Western   **(PR:A MPAA:NR)**

OUTLAWS OF TEXAS✶✶¼   (1950) 56m MON bw

Whip Wilson (*Tom*), Andy Clyde (*Hungry*), Phyllis Coates (*Anne*), Terry Frost (*Jordan*), Stanley Price (*Moore*), Tom Farrell (*Jeff*), Zon Murray (*Wilkins*), George DeNormand (*Bilson*), Steve Carr (*Sheriff*).

Coates is the leader of a gang of bank robbers, and it's up to marshal Wilson to nab the criminals. He and his friend, Clyde, pose as outlaws and infiltrate the gang. Their true identities are discovered, but they still manage to bring about the downfall of Coates and her cronies. Western fans were disappointed in this offering, feeling it didn't provide enough action, but it stands as a reasonably appealing film. This would be Clyde's last appearance as Wilson's partner. The rest of his career would be primarily devoted to comedy shorts, with an occasional feature performance. Writer Ullman would go on to a successful TV career as producer-writer of "Laramie," and writer for other western series.

p, Vincent M. Fennelly; d, Thomas Carr; w, Dan Ullman; ph, Gilbert Warrenton; ed, Richard Heermance; md, Edward Kay; art d, Dave Milton.

Western   **(PR:A MPAA:NR)**

OUTLAWS OF THE CHEROKEE TRAIL✶½   (1941) 56m REP bw

Bob Steele (*Tucson Smith*), Tom Tyler (*Stony Brooke*), Rufe Davis (*Lullaby Joslin*), Lois Collier, Tom Chatterton, Rex Lease, Joel Friedkin, Roy Barcroft, Philip Trent, Peggy Lynn, Bud Osborne, Chief Yowlachie, John James, Lee Shumway, Karl Hackett, Chuck Morrison, Billy Burtis, Griff Barnett, Bud Geary, Al Taylor, Henry Wills, Sarah Padden, Iron Eyes Cody, Cactus Mack.

In yet another of his 23 MESQUITEERS series appearances, Steele finds himself in Indian territory pitted against an outlaw gang. When a local's daughter is kidnaped Steele and his pals get into gear and return her to safety. Another satisfying B western in the popular series. (See THREE MESQUITEERS series, Index.)

p, Louis Gray; d, Les Orlebeck; w, Albert DeMond (based on characters created by William Colt MacDonald); ph, Ernest Haller; m, Cy Feuer; ed, Ray Snyder.

Western   **(PR:A MPAA:NR)**

OUTLAWS OF THE DESERT✶½   (1941) 66m PAR bw

William Boyd (*Hopalong Cassidy*), Brad King (*Johnny Nelson*), Andy Clyde (*California*), Forrest Stanley (*Charles Grant*), Jean Phillips (*Susan Grant*), Nina Guilbert (*Mrs. Jane Grant*), Luli Deste (*Marie Karitza*), Albert Morin (*Nickie Karitza*), George Woolsley (*Major*), Duncan Renaldo (*Sheik Suleiman*), Jean Del Val (*Faran El Kalar*), Mickey Eissa (*Salim*), Jamiel Hasson (*Ali*), George Lewis (*Yussuf*).

Desperate for new material to continue the long-running Cassidy series, the writers sent Hopalong to Arabia to purchase horses. Accompanied by Clyde and King, Boyd finds that the Middle East has evil-doers just like the American West. The trio get involved with a sheik and his harem and also succeeds in thwarting a kidnaping plot while acquiring the needed horses. Renaldo, who had recently deserted THE THREE MESQUITEERS series, plays the sheik. King replaced Russell Hayden as one of Hoppy's pals in the series after the latter went to Columbia to fill a role in Charles Starrett's cowboy series. (See HOPALONG CASSIDY series, Index.)

p, Harry Sherman; d, Howard Bretherton; w, J. Benton Cheney, Bernard McConville (based on characters created by Clarence E. Mulford); ph, Russell Harlan; m, John Leipold; ed, Carrol Lewis; md, Irvin Talbot; art d, Ralph Berger.

Western   **(PR:A MPAA:NR)**

OUTLAWS OF THE ORIENT✶✶   (1937) 61m COL bw

Jack Holt (*Chet Eaton*), Mae Clarke (*Joan*), Harold Huber (*Ho-Fang*), Ray Walker (*Lucky*), James Bush (*Johnny*), Joseph Crehan (*Snyder*), Bernice Roberts (*Alice*), Harry Worth (*Sheldon*).

Holt is up against the malevolent ways of Huber, whose unethical manner of protectionism in the Gobi oil fields is soaking the money out of the pockets of a group of oil drillers. One of a pair of films directed, without much acclaim, for Columbia by Ernest "Shorty" Schoedsack, who four years previously had codirected KING KONG with Merian Cooper. Although he was called "Shorty" he stood six-foot-four.

d, Ernest B. Schoedsack; w, Charles Francis Royal, Paul Franklin (based on the story by Ralph Graves); ph, James S. Brown, Jr.; ed, Dwight Caldwell.

Western   **(PR:A MPAA:NR)**

OUTLAWS OF THE PANHANDLE✶✶   (1941) 59m COL bw

Charles Starrett (*Jim Endicott*), Frances Robinson (*Doris Burnett*), Stanley Brown (*Neil Vaughn*), Norman Willis ("Faro Jack" Vaughn), Ray Teal (*Walt Burnett*), Lee Prather (*Elihu Potter*), Bob Nolan (*Bob*), Steve Clark (*Lon Hewitt*), Bud Osborne (*Mart Monahan*), Eddie Laughton (*Chad*), Richard Fiske (*Britt*), Jack Low (*Dogger*), Pat Brady, Blackie Whiteford, Sons of the Pioneers.

Starrett comes to the aid of ranchers who are trying to get a railroad to come through their town so they can safely transport their cattle to market. Their main obstacle is Willis, who has built a drinking and gambling hall in an attempt to get the rail workers too drunk to drive stakes. Fast-moving Starrett fare.

p, Jack Fier; d, Sam Nelson; w, Paul Franklin; ph, George Meehan; ed, Arthur Seid; m/l, Bob Nolan, Tim Spencer.

Western   **(PR:A MPAA:NR)**

OUTLAWS OF THE PRAIRIE✶✶½   (1938) 56m COL bw

Charles Starrett (*Dart Collins*), Donald Grayson (*Slim Grayson*), Iris Meredith (*Judy Garfield*), Norman Willis (*William Lupton*), Dick Curtis (*Dragg*), Edward J. Le Saint (*Lafe Garfield*), Eddie Cobb (*Jed Stevens*), Art Mix (*Lawton*), Steve Clark (*Cobb*), Hank Bell (*Jim*), Earle Hodgins (*Neenah*), Lee Shumway (*Capt. MacMillan*), Dick Alexander, Frank Shannon, Fred Burns, Jack Rockwell, Jack Kirk, George Chesebro, Charles LeMoyne, Frank Ellis, Frank McCarroll, Curley Dresden, Vernon Dent, George Morrell, Buel Bryant, Ray Jones, Jim Corey, Blackie Whiteford, Bob Burns, Bob Nolan and The Sons of the Pioneers.

One of the more impressive Starrett oaters has the hero coming to the aid of a group of gold shippers who lose their profits to stagecoach robbers on a steady basis. Starrett overpowers the bad guys before the banks can foreclose on the shippers. Nolan and his Sons of the Pioneers add some punch with a few nice tunes and Grayson joins in on the warbling.

p, Harry L. Decker; d, Sam Nelson; w, Ed Earl Repp (based on the story by Harry F. Olmstead); ph, John Boyle; ed, William Lyon.

Western   **(PR:A MPAA:NR)**

OUTLAWS OF THE RIO GRANDE✶✶   (1941) 63m PRC bw

Tim McCoy (*Tim*), Virginia Carpenter (*Rita*), Charles King (*Trigger*), Ralph Peters (*Monty*), Karl Hackett (*Marlow*), Rex Lease (*Luke*), Phillips Turich (*Pancho*), Kenne Duncan (*Brett*), Thornton Edwards (*Alvarado*), Joe Dominguez (*Castro*), Frank Ellis, George Chesebro, Sherry Tansey.

McCoy finds himself used by a gang of outlaws who have kidnaped a Mexican engraver and forced him to help them in a counterfeit operation. He is given advice on how to put the gang behind bars by a mysterious Mexican. Plenty of gunslinging for those who hunger after action.

p, Sigmund Neufeld; d, Peter Stewart [Sam Newfield]); w, George H. Plympton; ph, Jack Greenhalgh; ed, Holbrook N. Todd.

Western   **(PR:A MPAA:NR)**

OUTLAWS OF THE ROCKIES✶½   (1945) 54m COL bw (GB: A ROVING ROGUE)

Charles Starrett (*Steve Williams*), Tex Harding (*Himself*), Dub Taylor (*Cannonball*), Carole Mathews (*Jane Stuart*), Philip Van Zandt (*Dan Chantry*), I. Stanford Jolley (*Ace Lanning*), George Chesebro (*Bill Jason*), Steve Clark (*Potter*), Jack Rockwell (*Sheriff Hall*), Carolina Cotton, Spade Cooley.

Sheriff Starrett is accused of being an outlaw when he helps friend Harding get out of jail. He's not an outlaw, of course, but the Durango Kid, fighting to preserve justice. Spade Cooley, billed as the "King of Western Swing," leaves much to be desired, although Cotton, as a cowboy yodeler, can climb up and down the decibels with the best of them. (See DURANGO KID series, Index.)

p, Colbert Clark; d, Ray Nazarro; w, J. Benton Cheney; ph, George Kelley; ed, Aaron Stell; art d, Charles Clague.

Western   **Cas.**   **(PR:A MPAA:NR)**

OUTLAWS OF THE WEST   (SEE: CALL THE MESQUITEERS, 1938)

OUTLAW'S PARADISE✶✶   (1939) 62m Victory bw

Tim McCoy ("Trigger" Mallory/Capt. William Carson), Benny Corbett (*Magpie*), Joan Barclay (*Jessie*), Ted Adams (*Slim*), Forrest Taylor (*Eddie*), Bob Terry (*Steve*), Don Gallagher (*Mort*), Dave O'Brien (*Meggs*), Jack Mulhall (*Warden*), Carl Mathews, Jack C. Smith, George Morrell.

McCoy fills the shoes of both a Justice Department investigator and the outlaw he is investigating. He successfully puts the lid on a gang that is trying to get rich by stealing negotiable bonds from the U.S. mail.

p, Sam Katzman; d, Sam Newfield; w, Basil Dickey; ph, Marcel Picard; ed, Holbrook Todd.

Western   **(PR:A MPAA:NR)**

OUTLAW'S SON** (1957) 89m Bel-Air/UA bw

Dane Clark (Nate Blaine), Ben Cooper (Jeff Blaine), Lori Nelson (Lila Costain), Ellen Drew (Ruth Sewall), Charles Watts (Marshal Elec Blessingham), Cecile Rogers (Amy Wentworth), Joseph Stafford (Jeff Blaine as a Child), Eddie Foy III (Tod Wentworth), John Pickard (Ed Wyatt), Robert Knapp (Deputy Marshal Ralph Striker), Les Mitchel (Bill Somerson), Guy Prescott (Phil Costain), George Pembroke (Paul Wentworth), Jeff Daley (Ridley), Wendy Stuart (Lila Costain as a Child), Ann Maria Nanasi (Amy Wentworth as a Child), James Parnell (Jorgenson), Scott Peters (Randall), Buddy Hart (Todd Wentworth as a Child), Ernie Dotson (Ben Jorgenson), Ken Christy (Mac Butler), Audley Anderson (Egstrom), Leslie Kimmell (Kessler).

Cooper is the deserted son of a short-tempered outlaw who gets on the town's bad side after killing a local banker. Years later, the son tries to fit into society by becoming a deputy marshal, but the temper he inherited from his dad begins to flare up. He teams with an outlaw gang, causing the father to return and keep his son from following in his footsteps. Ably directed by Selander.

p, Aubrey Schenck; d, Lesley Selander; w, Richard Alan Simmons (based on the novel *Gambling Man* by Clifton Adams); ph, William Margulies; m, Les Baxter; ed, John F. Schreyer.

Western (PR:A MPAA:NR)

OUTPOST IN MALAYA**½ (1952, Brit.) 88m Pinnacle/GFD bw (GB: THE PLANTER'S WIFE)

Claudette Colbert (Liz Frazer), Jack Hawkins (Jim Frazer), Anthony Steel (Inspector Hugh Dobson), Ram Gopal (Nair), Jeremy Spenser (Mat), Tom Macauley (Jack Bushell), Helen Goss (Eleanor Bushell), Sonja Hana (Ah Moy), Andy Ho (Wan Li), Peter Asher (Mike Frazer), Shaym Bahadur (Putra), Bryan Coleman (Capt. Dell), Don Sharp (Lt. Summers), Maria Baillie (Arminah), Bill Travers (Planter), John Stamp (Len Carter), John Martin (Harry Saunders), Myrette Mowen (Mildred Saunders), Alfie Bass, Patrick Westwood (Soldiers), Ny Cheuk Kwong (Ho Tang), Yah Ming (Ah Siong), Victor Maddern (Radio Operator).

Hawkins plays a British plantation owner in Malaya whose marriage is on the rocks. He tries to force his wife, Colbert, to return to England with their son to avoid the potential disaster they await at the hands of native rebels on the rampage. Colbert refuses to abandon the plantation and together the couple stays and fights off the uprising with help from Gopal, a loyal native aide. A fairly routine melodrama, the only unusual moment being a lengthy fight between a mongoose and a cobra that is wholly unrelated to the plot.

p, John Stafford; d, Ken Annakin; w, Peter Proud, Guy Elmes (based on the novel *The Planter's Wife* by S. C. George); ph, Geoffrey Unsworth; m, Allan Gray; ed, Alfred Roome; md, Ludo Philipp; art d, Ralph Brinton.

Drama (PR:A MPAA:NR)

OUTPOST IN MOROCCO** (1949) 92m UA bw

George Raft (Capt. Paul Gerard), Marie Windsor (Cara), Akim Tamiroff (Lt. Glysko), John Litel (Col. Pascal), Eduard Franz (Emir of Bel-Rashad), Erno Verebes (Bamboule), Crane Whitley (Caid Osman), Damian O'Flynn (Commandant Fronval).

Cynical bon vivant turned desert fighter Raft is sent on an assignment to extinguish a tribal rebellion among the Arabs. His mission gets detoured, however, when he falls in love with engaging Windsor, the daughter of the rebel leader. Raft's weary troops overpower the Arab forces, but Windsor is killed when she makes a ridiculous charge on a fort with Arab troops in a vain effort to make her father stop fighting. Hardly credible story.

p, Samuel Bischoff, Joseph N. Ermolieff; d, Robert Florey; w, Charles Grayson, Paul de Sainte-Colombe (based on the story by Ermolieff); ph, Lucien Andriot; m, Michel Michelet; ed, George Arthur; art d, Arthur Lonergan.

Adventure (PR:A MPAA:NR)

OUTPOST OF HELL** (1966, Jap.) 98m Toho Co. bw (DOKURITSU KIKANJUTAI IMADA SHAGEKICHU)

Tatsuya Mihashi, Makoto Sato, Yosuke Natsuki, Makoto Terada, Hiroshi Tachikawa.

Five Japanese soldiers are the last hold-outs on the Manchurian border during WW II. One by one they are killed by the advancing Soviet troops, until the outpost is captured. An average war adventure from Taniguchi, a director whose talent has diminished with time. Released in Japan in 1963.

d, Senkichi Taniguchi; w, Masato Ide; ph, Kazuo Yamada (Tohoscope).

War Drama (PR:A MPAA:NR)

OUTPOST OF THE MOUNTIES*½ (1939) 63m COL bw(GB: ON GUARD)

Charles Starrett (Sgt. Neal Crawford), Iris Meredith (Norma Daniels), Stanley Brown (Larry Daniels), Kenneth MacDonald (R. A. Kirby), Edmund Cobb (Burke), Bob

Nolan (Bob), Lane Chandler (Cooper), Dick Curtis (Beaumont), Albert Morin (Larue), Hal Taliaferro (Evans), Pat O'Hara (Inspector Wainwright), The Sons of the Pioneers.

A weak programmer which has Starrett cast as a Canadian mountie trying to calm a battle between miner Brown and trader Curtis. Curtis' high prices are putting a strain on everyone's pocketbook, but because of the ongoing feud, when Curtis is killed the blame is placed on Brown. Starrett points the guilty finger at Curtis' partners who thought they could get away with the murder and the theft of a safe full of gold dust. If they had known that Starrett always gets his man they would have never even tried.

d, C.C. Coleman, Jr.; w, Charles Francis Royal; ph, George Meehan; ed, Charles Nelson; m/l, Bob Nolan, Tim Spencer.

Western (PR:A MPAA:NR)

OUTRAGE**½ (1950) 75m RKO bw

Mala Powers (Ann Walton), Tod Andrews (Ferguson), Robert Clarke (Jim Owens), Raymond Bond (Mr. Walton), Lilian Hamilton (Mrs. Walton), Rita Lupino (Stella Carter), Hal March (Sgt. Hendrix), Kenneth Patterson (Mr. Harrison), Jerry Paris (Frank Marini), Angela Clarke (Mrs. Harrison), Roy Engel (Sheriff Hanlon), Lovyss Bradley (Mrs. Miller), Robin Camp (Shoeshine Boy), William Challee (Lee Wilkins), Tristram Coffin (Judge McKenzie), Jerry Hausner (Mr. Denker), Bernie Marcus (Dr. Hoffman), Joyce McCluskey (Office Worker), Albert Mellen (Scarface), John Morgan (Prosecuting Attorney), Victor Perrin (Andrew), John Pelletti (Fred Keith), Beatrice Warde (Marge).

Ida Lupino's first directorial outing was this thoughtful story of the effect of rape on Powers, a working girl engaged to a handsome young man. She is so shaken by the attack and the response it receives from the locals that she leaves home and settles in California under a new identity. She is befriended by Andrews, an understanding minister who helps her overcome her trauma and return to her fiance. A touchy subject for the time, which is admittedly overdone in spots, but on the whole is admirable. Lupino would go on to produce and direct other feature films and TV projects.

p, Collier Young; d, Ida Lupino; w, Lupino, Malvin Wald, Young; ph, Archie Stout; ed, Harvey Manger; md, C. Bakaleinikoff.

Drama (PR:C MPAA:NR)

OUTRAGE, THE*½ (1964) 95m MGM bw

Paul Newman (Juan Carrasco), Laurence Harvey (Husband), Claire Bloom (Wife), Edward G. Robinson (Con Man), William Shatner (Preacher), Howard Da Silva (Prospector), Albert Salmi (Sheriff), Thomas Chalmers (Judge), Paul Fix (Indian).

Based on the Kurosawa screenplay for his 1951 film and a play by the Kanins which starred Rod Steiger, Claire Bloom, and Noel Willman, this film is almost a parody of the former, despite Ritt's direction. Newman, in his desire to be authentic, plays his role like a second-rate Cisco Kid and that throws the film's delicate balance out of whack. It's the 1870s in the Southwest. Three men meet at a lonely railway station. They are Robinson, a confidence trickster; Shatner, a preacher; and Da Silva, a prospector. They talk about the trial of Newman, who was sentenced to die for killing Harvey and raping his wife, Bloom. There were three witnesses at the trial and all three had variant views of what happened, so different, in fact, that it seems like three stories, not one. Newman's contention was that he'd bound Harvey, raped Bloom, then had a duel with Harvey in which the Englishman was killed. Bloom says that she killed Harvey after he claimed she'd encouraged Newman's attentions. An aged Indian, Fix, says that he found Harvey with a knife sticking out of him and that the dying man claimed that he'd inflicted the wound on himself due to the humiliation of his wife being raped. That discussion (and the appropriate flashbacks) done, the three men hear the squawl of a baby. They investigate and find that the baby's clothes also contain gold, which Robinson promptly attempts to acquire. The three men argue and Da Silva admits that he also witnessed the rape and murder but failed to appear at the trail because he'd stolen the jeweled dagger from Harvey's bleeding chest. Da Silva says that Newman did rape Bloom and felt guilty about it, so he tried to convince her to leave with him. She enjoyed the attention of both men and the control she had, so she prodded Harvey into a fight with Newman, and, in the skirmish, Harvey was accidentally stabbed when he fell on the jeweled knife. Da Silva picks up the baby and offers to keep it, despite a quintet of his own kids at home. Shatner, who had been questioning his faith after hearing what he's just heard, is delighted by Da Silva's offer (made more out of guilt for not testifying than any altruistic purpose, we think) and smiles, as he believes again in man's humanity to man. Each of the tales is seen as it is told and Harvey's main job is to stay tied to a tree. There are some leavening slapstick moments, but the whole affair is sludge. Newman, despite his beard and accent (as thick as salsa on a tamale), is still Newman, and if you like him, you may like THE OUTRAGE. All others, please refer to the original for the right way to tell this kind of story. Newman's bogus South of the Border accent was so ludicrous that he should have been forced to fly to Mexico City, gone on Televisa (the main TV channel), and apologized to the entire country.

p, A. Ronald Lubin; d, Martin Ritt; w, Michael Kanin (based on stories by Ryunosuke Akutagawa, the Japanese film RASHOMON by Akira Kurosawa, and the play "Rashomon" by Fay and Michael Kanin); ph, James Wong Howe (Panavision); m, Alex North; ed, Frank Santillo; md, North; art d, George W. Davis, Tambi Larsen; set d, Henry Grace, Robert R. Benton; cos, Don Feld; spec eff, J. McMillan Johnson, Robert R. Hoag; makeup, Ron Berkeley, William Tuttle.

Western (PR:C MPAA:NR)

OUTRAGEOUS!***½ (1977, Can.) 100m Film Consortium of Canada-Canadian Film Development/Cinema 5 c

Craig Russell (Robin Turner), Hollis McLaren (Liza Connors), Richard Easley (Perry), Allan Moyle (Martin), David McIlwraith (Bob), Gerry Salzberg (Jason), Andree Pelletier (Anne), Helen Shaver (Jo), Martha Gibson (NurseCarr), Helen Hughes (Mrs. Connors), Jonah Royston (Dr. Beddoes), Richard Moffatt (Stewart), David Woito (Hustler), Rusty Ryan (Jimmy), Jackie Loren (Herself), Michael Daniels (Performer in Gold), Michel (Performer in Pink), Trevor Bryan (Miss Montego Bay), Mike Ironside (Drunk), Rene Fortier (Manatee D.J.), Maxine Miller (Peggy O'Brien).

A strange picture from first time director Benner, who brings to the screen a look at mental patients, homosexuals, and transvestites. Russell is a gay hairdresser who does female impersonations at a Toronto night club, his best being Tallulah Bankhead and Bette Davis. He meets up with recently released mental patient McLaren who is determined to have a child and lead a normal existence. The pair become closer and McLaren becomes pregnant by another man. Russell gets fired because of his night club act, but goes to New York where he becomes a hit. McLaren goes off to have her baby, but plummets into depression when it is still-born. Eventually the pair of crazies reunite with the hope of surviving in New York along with millions of other crazy people. Made on a miniscule budget of $165,000, OUTRAGEOUS! was considered as a project by a number of Hollywood studios, none of which wanted Benner to be at the helm. Luckily he held out and produced it himself. The laughs are continuous from beginning to end, the impersonations exceptional, and the performances far above the norm. Russell was even awarded the "Best Actor" prize at the Berlin Film Festival. While at times the film suffers from sub-standard production values, it is a revealing and intelligent film.

p, William Marshall, Hendrick J. Van Der Kolk; d&w, Richard Benner (based on the story "Making It" by Margaret Gibson); ph, James B. Kelly (Eastmancolor); m, Paul Hoffert; ed, George Appleby; art d, Karen Bromley; set d, Bruce Calnan; cos, Michael Daniels; m/l, Paul Hoffert, Brenda Hoffert.

Comedy/Drama   **(PR:O MPAA:R)**

OUTRIDERS, THE**   (1950) 93m MGM c

Joel McCrea (Will Owen), Arlene Dahl (Jen Gort), Barry Sullivan (Jesse Wallace), Claude Jarman, Jr. (Roy Gort), James Whitmore (Clint Priest), Ramon Navarro (Don Antonio Chaves), Jeff Corey (Keeley), Ted de Corsia (Bye), Martin Garralaga (Father Damasco).

McCrea, together with Sullivan and Whitmore, are Confederate soldiers on the lam from their Yankee captors. They join up with a rebel gang of raiders who are preparing to ambush a wagon train full of priceless bullion. They return to the side of the law, however, and prevent the theft. In the meantime, McCrea wins over attractive widow Dahl. Navarro, the great Latin lover of the silent days and star of the 1927 BEN-HUR, here made one of his rare talkie appearances. He successfully made the silent-to-sound transition, but worked in movies only when he had the urge to do so. He thrived in the real estate business until he was tragically murdered in 1968 by thieves who broke into his Hollywood Hills home. THE OUTRIDERS scenarist Ravetch would go on to write screenplays for HUD (1963) and HOMBRE (1967) both starring Paul Newman and directed by Martin Ritt.

p, Richard Goldstone; d, Roy Rowland; w, Irving Ravetch; ph, Charles Schoenbaum (Technicolor); m, Andre Previn; ed, Robert J. Kern.

Western   **(PR:A MPAA:NR)**

OUTSIDE IN*½   (1972) 90m Robbins International c (AKA: RED, WHITE, AND BUSTED)

Darrel Larson (Ollie Wilson), Heather Menzies (Chris), Dennis Olivieri (Bernard), John Bill (Rink Schroeder), Peggy Feury (Mrs. Wilson), Logan Ramsey (Uncle Albert).

Larson is a California draft-dodger who returns from his Canadian hide-away in order to attend his father's funeral. During his visit home he becomes involved in the problems of two former friends—a Viet Nam vet (Bill) and a fellow draft evader (Olivieri) whose life ends in suicide. This picture doesn't display any of the inventiveness of Baron's earlier films—BLAST OF SILENCE (1961) and PIE IN THE SKY (1964)—and its subject matter is given an uninspired treatment. The first release from Harold Robbins' short-lived production company.

p, George Edwards; d, Allen Baron; w, Robert Hutchinson (based on the story by Hutchinson, Baron); ph, Mario Tosi (DeLuxe Color); m/l, Randy Edelman (sung by Edelman).

Drama   **(PR:C MPAA:R)**

OUTSIDE MAN, THE**½   (1973, U.S./FR.) 104m UA c(UN HOMME EST MORT)

Jean-Louis Trintignant (Lucian), Ann-Margret (Nancy), Roy Scheider (Lenny), Angie Dickinson (Jackie), Georgia Engel (Jane), Felice Orlandi (Anderson), Carlo De Mejo (Karl), Umberto Orsini (Alex), Michel Constantin (Antoine), Carmine Argenziano (2nd Hawk), Rice Cattani (Butler), Ted de Corsia (Victor), Edward Greenberg (Hitchiker), Philippa Harris (Salesgirl), Jackie Haley (Eric), John Hillerman (Department Store Manager), Jon Korkes (1st Hawk), Connie Kreski (Rosie), Ben Piazza (Desk Clerk), Alex Rocco (Miller), Talia Shire (Make-up Girl), Lionel Vitrant (Paul).

Imported French hit man Trintignant comes to Los Angeles to knock off mob boss de Corsia. He accomplishes the task, but then goes on the run himself when American killer Scheider is hired to kill the Frenchman. Decidedly off-beat (a climactic shootout is set around de Corsia's corpse, embalmed in a sitting position), the film suffers from a lack of continuous structure, which unfortunately works against the film as a whole. Some excellent characterizations by the players do pick things up, making this work a must for genre fans.

p, Jacques Bar; d, Jacques Deray; w, Deray, Jean-Claude Carriere, Ian McLellan Hunter (based on a story by Deray, Carriere); ph, Terry K. Meade, Silvano Ippoliti; m, Michel Legrand; ed, Henri Lanoe, William K. Chulack; prod d, Harold Michelson; art d, Kenneth A. Reid; m/l, title song Charles Burr (sung by Joe Morton).

Crime Drama/Thriller   **(PR:C MPAA:PG)**

OUTSIDE OF PARADISE**½   (1938) 68m REP bw

Phil Regan (Danny), Penny Singleton (Mavourneen), Bert Gordon (The Mad Russian), Leonid Kinskey (Ivan), Ruth Coleman (Dorothy), Mary Forbes (Mrs. Stonewall), Lionel Pape (Mr. Stonewall), Ralph Remley (Timothy), Renie Riano (Ellen), Linda Hayes (Linda), Joe E. Marks (Bass), David Kerman (Felix), Billy Young (Johnny), Cliff Nazarro (Cliff), Harry Allen (Old Man).

Regan is an Irish singer/band leader in a Russian night club who learns that he has inherited half-interest in an Irish castle. He and the boys in the band, along with some Russian pals, head for Ireland and meet co-owner Singleton. She isn't

receptive to their plans to turn the castle into a nightclub, but eventually it all works out. Tunes include: "All for One," "Outside of Paradise," "Doing Shenanigans," "A Little Bit of Everything," "A Sweet Irish Sweetheart of Mine" (Peter Tinturin, Jack Lawrence).

p, Harry Sauber; d, John H. Auer; w, Sauber; ph, Jack Marta; ed, Ernest Nims.

Musical   **(PR:A MPAA:NR)**

OUTSIDE THE LAW*   (1930) 76m UNIV bw

Edward G. Robinson (Cobra Collins), Mary Nolan (Connie), Owen Moore ("Fingers" O'Dell), Edwin Sturges (Jake), John George (Humpy), Delmar Watson (The Kid), DeWitt Jennings (Police Chief), Rockliffe Fellowes (Police Captain O'Reilly), Frank Burke (District Attorney), Sidney Bracey (Assistant).

Robinson is a two-bit gangster who gets cut into a deal to knock over a bank, but becomes the target of a nasty trick played by gang leader Moore. He isn't told when the robbery is supposed to occur. Nolan, Moore's moll, tires to save him by telling him that the heist is taking place in a week, but Robinson learns that while they are gabbing the burglary is in progress. He rushes to the scene and is killed by the cops. Moore and Nolan end up doing time. A poor film on all fronts, including a vapid performance from Robinson. OUTSIDE THE LAW was one of a trio of gangster roles for Robinson (the others being NIGHT RIDE and THE WIDOW FROM CHICAGO) in 1930, a year before he got it right in LITTLE CAESAR. OUTSIDE THE LAW was previously filmed in 1921 by Tod Browning with Lon Chaney in the lead. The second version was undertaken after Browning gave up his plans to film THE SEA BAT. This abandoned project was to have been shot in Bermuda, incorporating actual voodoo ceremonies. He left his interest in the bizarre behind him for this uninspired picture, but would return to it two years later with FREAKS.

d, Tod Browning; w, Browning, Garrett Fort; ph, Roy Overbaugh; ed, Milton Carruth.

Crime   **(PR:A MPAA:NR)**

OUTSIDE THE LAW   (SEE: CITADEL OF CRIME, 1941)

OUTSIDE THE LAW*½   (1956) 81m UNIV bw

Ray Danton (Johnny Salvo), Leigh Snowden (Maria Craven), Grant Williams (Don Kastner), Onslow Stevens (Alec Conrad), Raymond Bailey (Philip Bormann), Judson Pratt (Maury Saxon), Jack Kruschen (Phil Schwartz), Floyd Simmons (Harris), Mel Welles (Milo), Alexander Campbell (Warden), Karen Verne (Mrs. Pulenski), Maurice Doner (Mr. Pulenski), Jesse B. Kirkpatrick (Bill MacReady), Arthur Ranson (Parker), Richard H. Cutting (Pomeroy), George Mather (Bus Station Clerk), Amapola del Vando (Mama Gomez), Vernon Rich.

Danton, after being paroled from prison into the Army, is called back to the U.S. to help crack an international counterfeiting operation which involves a former GI pal. He is needed to romance his pal's girl to see if she can supply any information. He gets nothing from her, but the importing firm where she is employed proves to be up to no good. The finale has him helping to do in the gang, win over the gal, and reunite with his father, a Treasury agent. Danny Arnold, the film's writer, would go on to a very successful career in TV, winning Emmies as producer/writer/creator of such comedies as "My World And Welcome To It" and "Barney Miller."

p, Albert J. Cohen; d, Jack Arnold; w, Danny Arnold (based on the story by Peter R. Brooke); ph, Irving Glassberg; ed, Irving Birnbaum; md, Milton Rosen; cos, Rosemary Odell.

Crime Drama   **(PR:A MPAA:NR)**

OUTSIDE THE 3-MILE LIMIT*½   (1940) 63m COL bw (GB: MUTINY ON THE SEAS)

Jack Holt (Treasury Agent Conway), Harry Carey (Capt. Bailey), Sig Rumann (Van Cleve), Eduardo Ciannelli (Dave Reeves, Gambling Ship Owner), Donald Briggs (Jimmy Rothaker, Reporter), Irene Ware (Dorothy Kenney), Dick Purcell (Agent Melvin Pierce), Ben Welden (Lefty Shores), Paul Fix (Bill Swanson), George Lewis (Ed Morrow).

Holt is hired by the government to investigate reports that a counterfeiting operation is peddling phony bills through a gambling boat. When a murder occurs on board, the ship's owner (Ciannelli) steers the boat out to sea, safely beyond the three-mile limit. A mutiny changes the captain's plans, making way for Holt to break up the ring. Clearly a cranked-out piece of studio product, this film seems to have been inspired by an attempt by Federal authorities to board gambling ships operating off the California coast in 1939.

p, Larry Darmour; d, Lewis D. Collins; w, Albert De Mond (based on the story by DeMond, Eric Taylor); ph, James S. Brown, Jr.; m, Lee Zahler; ed, Dwight Caldwell.

Drama/Crime   **(PR:A MPAA:NR)**

OUTSIDE THE WALL**½   (1950) 80m UNIV bw

Richard Basehart (Larry Nelson), Marilyn Maxwell (Charlotte), Signe Hasso (Celia), Dorothy Hart (Ann Taylor), Joseph Pevney (Gus Wormer), John Hoyt (Stoker), Henry [Harry] Morgan (Garth), Lloyd Gough (Chaney), Mickey Knox (Latzo).

Basehart is released from a Philadelphia prison at age 29, after serving a 15-year sentence. He finds life on the outside a bit difficult to adjust to, especially when it comes to women. He falls for Maxwell, a blonde money-grabber, who nearly has him involved with a $1 million Brinks robbery. He is befriended, however, by nurse Hart, who helps him go straight. Fine performances all the way down the list.

p, Aaron Rosenberg; d&w, Crane Wilbur (based on a story by Henry Edward Helseth); ph, Irving Glassberg; ed, Edward Curtiss; md, Milton Schwartzwald.

Drama   **(PR:A MPAA:NR)**

OUTSIDE THESE WALLS**½ (1939) 60m COL bw

Michael Whalen (Dan Sparling), Dolores Costello (Margaret Bronson, Virginia Weidler (Ellen), Don Beddoe (Dinky), Selmer Jackson John Wilson), Mary Forbes (Gertrude Bishop), Robert Emmett Keane (Sam Fulton), Pierre Watkin (Hewitt Bronson), Kathleen Lockhart (Miss Thornton), Dick Curtis (Flint).

Whalen is writer and editor of the prison news sheet in the joint where he is doing time. Even though he contributes to legit papers, he has trouble finding work when he gets out. He eventually buys a small printing press, with the help of a prison loan, and freely attacks the corrupt politicians whose power influences the news that the major papers print. Soon the prison warden is out of a job, but with Whalen's support he runs for governor and wins. A fine script and an equally compelling performance from Whalen add up to an entertaining picture.

d, Raymond B. McCarey; w, Harold Buchman (based on a story by Ferdinand Reyher); ph, Lucien Ballard; ed, James Sweeney.

Drama (PR:A MPAA:NR)

OUTSIDER, THE** (1933, Brit.) 67m Cinema House/MGM bw

Joan Barry (Lalage Sturdee), Harold Huth (Anton Ragatzy), Norman McKinnel (Jasper Sturdee), Frank Lawton (Basil Owen), Mary Clare (Mrs. Coates), Glenore Pointing (Carol), Annie Esmond (Pritchard), Sidney J. Gillett (Dr. Ladd), Randolph McLeod (Sir Nathan Israel), Fewlass Llewellyn (Sir Montague Tollemach), Clayton Greene, Freda Whittaker.

Huth is the inventor of a revolutionary new surgical tool which successfully treats crippled patients. He tries to convince the traditional men of medicine to give the new tool a whirl, but they'll have no part of it. He finally talks one of the men into testing the instrument on the man's daughter, Barry. The finale has the girl walking around as good as new and madly in love with Huth. MGM test released this British quota picture in the States and surprised themselves with its success. Co-penned by Alfred Hitchcock's wife, Alma Reville.

p, Eric Hakim; d, Harry Lachman; w, Lachman, Alma Reville (based on the play by Dorothy Brandon); ph, Gunther Krampf; ed, G. Pollatschik, Winifred Cooper.

Drama (PR:A MPAA:NR)

OUTSIDER, THE** (1940, Brit.) 90m ABF bw

George Sanders (Anton Ragatzy), Mary Maguire (Lalage Sturdee), Barbara Blair (Wendy), Peter Murray Hill (Basil Owen), Frederick Leister (Joseph Sturdee), Walter Hudd (Dr. Helmore), Kathleen Harrison (Mrs. Coates), P. Kynaston Reeves (Sir Montague Tollemach), Edmond Breon (Dr. Ladd), Ralph Truman (Sir Nathan Israel), Martin Walker, Ian Colin, Lesley Wareing, Edward Lexy, Eddie Pola), Elaine Hamill, Zillah Bateman, Fewlass Llewellyn, Picot Scholling, Jack Lambert, Stella, Arbenina, Roddy McDowall, Derek Farr.

Sanders is a young innovator of medical science who devises a treatment of muscles which can cure crippled patients. His advances are ignored by the traditional committee of doctors until he cures one of their daughters. In the end, Sanders gets the girl, who is now walking about with ease. Sander's only medical background comes from his study of the anatomy of cattle at the Chicago Stockyards, a method which may or may not have enhanced the crippled girl's chances. A remake of an earlier British picture with the same title and same cameraman.

p, Walter C. Mycroft; d, Paul L. Stein; w, Dudley Leslie (based on the play by Dorothy Brandon); ph, Gunthar Krampf; ed, Flora Newton.

Drama (PR:A MPAA:NR)

OUTSIDER, THE**½ (1949, Brit.) 98m Pilgrim/Variety bw (GB: THE GUINEA PIG)

Richard Attenborough (Jack Read), Sheila Sim (Lynne Hartley), Bernard Miles (Mr. Read), Cecil Trouncer (Mr. Hartley, Housemaster), Robert Flemyng (Nigel Lorraine), Edith Sharpe (Mrs. Hartley), Joan Hickson (Mrs. Read), Peter Reynolds (Grimmett), Timothy Bateson (Ronald Tracey), Clive Baxter (Gregory), Basil Cunard (Buckton), John Forrest (Fitch), Maureen Glynne (Bessie), Brenda Hogan (Lorna Beckett), Herbert Lomas (Sir James Corfield), Anthony Newley (Miles Minor), Anthony Nicholls (Mr. Stringer), Wally Patch (Uncle Percy), Hay Petrie, Oscar Quitak, Percy Walsh, Norman Watson, Robert Desmond, Kynaston Reeves, Jack McNaughton, Judy Manning, Lionel Stevens, Ambrose Day, Digby Wolfe, James Kenney, Peter Howes, Richard Hart, Michael Braisford, Michael McKeag, Edward Judd, Colin Stroud, Desmond Newling, George Bryden, Olive Sloane.

Attenborough (who would later win an Oscar for directing GANDHI) is in the title role here as a rural English student put into an expensive public school as an experiment. He experiences an internal conflict between his simple upbringing and the poshness of his new surroundings. Good supporting roles as well as Attenborough's thoroughly believable performance help make this a sincere, if minor, film.

p, John Boulting; d, Roy Boulting; w, Warren Chetham Strode, Roy Boulting, Bernard Miles (based on a stage play by Strode); ph, Gilbert Taylor; m, John Woolridge; ed, Richard Best; art d, John Howell, Stanley Yeomanson.

Drama (PR:A MPAA:NR)

OUTSIDER, THE** (1962) 108m UNIV bw

Tony Curtis (Ira Hamilton Hayes), James Franciscus (Jim Sorenson), Gregory Walcott (Sgt. Kiley), Bruce Bennett (Maj. Gen. Bridges), Vivian Nathan (Mrs. Nancy Hayes), Edmund Hashim (Jay Morago), Paul Comi (Sgt. Boyle), Stanley Adams (Noomie the Bartender), Wayne Heffley (Cpl. Johnson), Ralph Moody (Uncle), Jeff Silver (Mr. McGruder), James Beck (Tyler), Forrest Compton (Bradley), Peter Homer, Sr. (Mr. Alvarez), Mary Patton (Chairlady), Gertrude Michael (Clubwoman), Vincent Edwards (George), Miriam Colon (Anita), Ray Daley (Gagnon), Ronald Trujillo (Kenny Hayes), Walter Woolf King (Civilian), Al Hodge (Colonel), Kathleen Mulqueen (Mrs. Sorenson), John War Eagle (Mr. Goode),

Ted Bessell (Kid), Gregory Fio Rito (David), Lynda Day [George] (Kim), Jody Johnston (Jane), Tom Sherlock (Assistant), Riley Hill (Delivery Man), Charley Stevens (Joseph Hayes).

The famous news photograph of the men who raised the flag on Mount Suribachi after the bloody fight at Iwo Jima comes to life in this earnest but flawed attempt at telling the story of one of the survivors of the battle. It's almost like two films in one, as the first half is rapid, and the second half bogs down in the muddled relationship between the two men who are at the core of the story. Curtis was miscast in the film, something that wasn't the case when Lee Marvin did it in a totally different script (by Merle Miller) for a TV show a year before. It's the height of WW II and teenage Curtis, a Pima Indian living his entire life on an Arizona reservation, decides to join the Marines. In boot camp (the best scenes of the film), he finds one person who doesn't treat him like a second-class citizen, Franciscus. The two boys go off to war together and are part of the quintet of flag-raisers. When Franciscus is later killed by Japanese bullets, Curtis is destroyed. The war continues and Curtis is acclaimed a national hero and goes on a bond drive across the U. S. He can't handle all the accolades and feels guilty that he has survived, so he reaches for the whiskey to give him strength. His drinking is soon out of hand and the press has a field day. He goes back to his Marine unit and the war ends. He tries hard to be invisible back on the reservation, but the tribe needs a representative to go to Washington on an agricultural matter. Because of his fame, Curtis is chosen. He travels to the capital but booze gets the better of him and he spends some time in jail for drunk and disorderly conduct. Upon returning to the reservation, he is shunned by his fellow Indians and they do not elect him to the post on the tribal council, something he'd had his heart set upon. With no one in the world to counsel him, Curtis climbs a mountain with several bottles of liquor and is eventually found, dead of exposure. He was 32. A terrible tragedy that was totally true. One of the main problems with the script was the relationship between Curtis and Franciscus, which seemed almost, but just short of, beyond friendship. Had they looked deeper into that story, it might have not been as palatable to the general public, who want their heroes to kiss women and their horses only. Filmed at the Iwo Jima Memorial at Arlington, Camp Pendleton, Los Angeles' San Fernando Valley, San Diego, Camp Matthews, Chicago's Soldier Field, and the Arizona reservation of the Pima-Maricpa Indian tribe. Good intercutting of newsreel footage with the film makes the battle scenes come to life. . .and death. In small roles, note TV's Ted Bessell and Lynda Day George.

p, Sy Bartlett; d, Delbert Mann; w, Stewart Stern (based on the biography "The Hero of Iwo Jima" by William Bradford Huie); ph, Joseph LaShelle; m, Leonard Rosenman; ed, Marjorie Fowler; md, Rosenman; art d, Alexander Golitzen, Edward S. Haworth; set d, Oliver Emert; makeup, Bud Westmore; technical advisor, Lt. Col. Clement J. Stadler.

Biography PR:A-C MPAA:NR)

OUTSIDER, THE***½ (1980) 128m Cinematic Arts B.V./PAR c

Craig Wasson Michael Flaherty), Patricia Quinn (Siobhan), Sterling Hayden (Seamus Flaherty), Niall Toibin (Farmer), Elizabeth Begley (Mrs. Cochran), T.P. McKenna (John Russell), Frank Grimes (Tony Coyle), Bosco Hogan (Finbar Donovan), Niall O'Brien (Emmet Donovan), Joe Dowling (Pat), John Murphy (Flynn), Conal Kearney (Ted), J.G. Devlin (Tweeny), Avril Gentles (Mrs. Flaherty), John Seitz (Mr. Flaherty), Aiden Grennell (Hanlan), Desmond Cave (Kevin McCann), Des Nealon (Col. O'Darell), Joseph McPartland (McDermot), Joy Lynch (Thompson), Allan Cuthbertson (Stanley), Ray Macanally (Mac Whirter).

One of the finest films yet to deal with the tensions in Northern Ireland. Wasson is a young Irish-American who is inspired by his grandfather's tales of patriotism in fighting the British many years ago. Wasson's welcome to Belfast is less than warm, however, as he discovers that he is the target of an IRA plot. They plan to arrange his murder, making it appear that the British army killed him. By turning him into an American martyr, they hope to raise tremendous amounts of money from sympathetic Irish-Americans. The British soldiers receive an equally unflattering portrayal. In one scene, a British soldier guns down a 12-year-old boy, and later the soldiers are seen unmercifully torturing an IRA rebel. It is a harsh look at a harsh situation in which neither side can be portrayed favorably without stretching the truth. This production, which came in for under $3 million, begins and ends in Detroit, but most of it was shot in Dublin, where the streets of the Irish capital city stood in for the troubled lanes of Belfast.

p, Philippe Modave; d&w, Tony Luraschi (based on the novel The Heritage of Michael Flaherty by Colin Leinster); ph, Ricardo Aronovich; ed, Catherine Kelber; m Ken Thorne; art d, Franco Fumagalli; cos, Judy Dolan.

Drama (PR:O MPAA:R)

OUTSIDER IN AMSTERDAM** (1983, Neth.) 85m Verenigade Nederland c (GRIJPSTRA AND DE GIER)

Rutger Hauer (Brigadier Rinus de Gier), Rijk de Gooyer (Adjutant H.F. Grijpstro), Willeke Van Ammelrooy (Constanze), Donald Jones (Habberdoedas van Meteren), Frederik de Groot (Rechercheur Cardozo), Marina de Graaf (Helen).

Hauer and de Gooyer are a pair of plainclothes Dutch cops who, like the filmmakers, have seen too many episodes of American TV cop shows. They go on the beat cracking drug rings, putting straight sickly addicts, and trying to put a lid on the freakish sex trade which seems to overpower the entire city of Amsterdam. Of interest only for Hauer, who has begun to rise in popularity since his wonderful role in BLADERUNNER. (In Dutch; English subtitles.)

p, Rob Houwer; d, Wim Verstappen; w, Verstappen, Kees Holierhoek; ph, Marc Velperlaan; m, Rogier van Otterloo; ed, Jutta Brandstadter; art d, Roland de Groot.

Crime Drama (PR:O MPAA:NR)

OUTSIDERS, THE, 1964, Fr. (SEE: BAND OF OUTSIDERS, 1964, Fr.)

OUTSIDERS, THE*** (1983) 91m Zoetrope/WB c

Matt Dillon *(Dallas Winston)*, Ralph Macchio *(Johnny Cade)*, C. Thomas Howell *(Ponyboy Curtis)*, Patrick Swayze *(Darrel Curtis)*, Rob Lowe *(Sodapop Curtis)*, Emilio Estevez *(Two-Bit Matthews)*, Tom Cruise *(Steve Randle)*, Glenn Withrow *(Tim Shephard)*, Diane Lane *(Cherry Valance)*, Leif Garrett *(Bob Sheldon)*, Darren Dalton *(Randy Anderson)*, Michelle Meyrink *(Marcia)*, Gailard Sartain *(Jerry)*, Tom Waits *(Buck Merrill)*, William Smith *(Store Clerk)*, Tom Hillman, Hugh Walkinshaw, Teresa Wilkerson Hunt, Linda Nystedt, S.E. Hinton, Brent Beesley, John C. Meier, Ed Jackson, Dan Suhart.

Without a doubt Coppola remains one of modern-day Hollywood's most frustrating directors. His visual style is stunning and poetic, but he often prefers myth-making to filmmaking. With his GODFATHER films and the troubled APOCALYPSE NOW, the myths were inherent in the material. But in the early 1980s he began choosing projects that were essentially small films that he proceeded to blow up to preposterous proportions. Such is the case with THE OUTSIDERS, a film based on the fine teenage novel by S. E. Hinton (who wrote it while still in high school herself and who makes a cameo appearance here as a nurse.) It's the story about confrontations between a group of "greasers" and their more affluent high school peers, the "Socs." Dillon is an unofficial leader, a rebellious young punk who leads his buddies on a variety of typical teenage "adventures," such as sneaking into drive-ins and intimidating little kids. However, when fellow gang members Macchio and Howell are confronted by their rivals a boy is killed. With Dillon's help the two young culprits hide out in an abandoned church. Later Macchio dies from injuries he receives rescuing some children after a church catches fire. His death causes Dillon to snap, and he goes on a rampage, holding up a store before being gunned down by the cops. Both the film and the actors strike several sincere, realistic notes. Dillon gives a sensitive portrayal with good support from a cast that would go on to populate some of the best teenage films in the years to come. The fault lies in Coppola's interpretation which gives the story a reverence bordering on the religious. Using a 1950s setting, he tries to evoke images of REBEL WITHOUT A CAUSE, but he isn't really successful. THE OUTSIDERS is permeated with artistic pretension. It is pedantic in intent without any of the beautiful roughness found in Nicholas Ray's classic work. Coppola's grandiose visions do pay off in terms of the photography which is beautiful to the eye. Dillon's death scene is a carefully composed series of shots that overwhelm the viewer with their use of light and color. Coppola makes good use of natural elements as well, employing fire, wind, and water within the beautiful *mise-en-scene*. But beautiful images are not enough to make this everything Coppola had envisioned. At best, it's handsome to look at, but no more than a well-acted teen film.

p, Fred Roos, Gray Frederickson; d, Francis Ford Coppola; w, Kathleen Knutsen Rowell (based on the novel by S. E. Hinton); ph, Stephen H. Burum (Panavision, Technicolor); m, Carmine Coppola; ed, Anne Goursaud; prod d, Dean Tavoularis; set d, Gary Fettis; cos, Marge Bowers

Drama **Cas.** **(PR:C MPAA:PG)**

OUTWARD BOUND½** (1930) 82m WB bw

Leslie Howard *(Tom Prior)*, Douglas Fairbanks, Jr. *(Henry)*, Helen Chandler *(Ann)*, Beryl Mercer *(Mrs. Midget)*, Alec B. Francis *(Scrubby)*, Alison Skipworth *(Mrs. Cliveden-Banks)*, Lyonel Watts *(Rev. William Duke)*, Montagu Love *(Mr. Lingley)*, Dudley Digges *(Thompson the Examiner)*, Walter Kingsford *(The Policeman)*, Laddie the Dog.

Eerie and unusual for its time, OUTWARD BOUND deals with a cross-section of citizens on board a ship heading to an unspecified destination. Digges plays the Examiner, a man who controls the fates of all the passengers, the majority of whom prove to be dead souls. Howard is excellent as an alcoholic who meets his mother on this strange voyage. Fairbanks and Chandler are a young couple, the only living pair on the boat, who fail at a suicide when their dog breaks a window, saving them from suffocation. Based on a Broadway play of 1924, the unusual theme has unfortunately not aged well. The story lurches forward at much too slow a pace, hampered further by outdated dialog and acting styles. Still, film historians will probably want to look at this for its technical aspects, which were quite good for the time. Lighting and fog effects are used with excellent results in creating a supernatural atmosphere. To achieve the otherworldly setting, photographer Mohr had the set spray-painted a light gray, coupling it with gauze over the camera lens, and used fog machines. The first U.S. film for Leslie Howard, who had appeared in the stage play taking the role here played by Fairbanks. Mercer, Digges, and Watts reprise their stage roles. Remade in 1944 as BETWEEN TWO WORLDS and in 1961 as THE FLIGHT THAT DISAPPEARED.

p, J.L. Warner; d, Robert Milton; w, J. Grubb Alexander (based on the play by Sutton Vane); ph, Hal Mohr; ed, Ralph Dawson; cos, Earl Luick.

Drama **(PR:C MPAA:NR)**

OVER-EXPOSED*½ (1956) 80m COL bw

Cleo Moore *(Lila Crane)*, Richard Crenna *(Russell Bassett)*, Isobel Elsom *(Mrs. Payton Grange)*, Raymond Greenleaf *(Max West)*, Shirley Thomas *(Herself)*, James O'Rear, *(Roy Carver)*, Donald Randolph *(Coco Fields)*, Dayton Lummis *(Horace Sutherland)*, Jeanne Cooper *(Renee)*, Jack Albertson *(Les Bauer)*, William McLean *(Freddie)*, Edna M. Holland *(Mrs. Gulick)*, Edwin Parker *(Matt)*, John Cason *(Bud)*, Dick Crockett *(Jerry)*, Geraldine Hall *(Martha)*, Voltaire Perkins *(Judge Evans)*, Joan Miller *(Frank)*, Helyn Eby Rock *(Mrs. Grannigan)*, Frank Mitchell *(Steve)*, Norma Brooks *(Doris)*, Robert B. Williams *(Sergeant)*.

Moore plays a photographer who begins at the bottom and works her way to the top of her field. Greenleaf, an alcoholic photographer, teaches her the trade. Once she hits the big city, she takes up with Crenna, a newspaper reporter. She also meets Elsom, a rich widow who likes the young woman's work. OVER-EXPOSED starts off well when Moore is learning her craft. However, once she hits the big time, the script has nothing left to say. Moore, who is best known as Hugo Haas' leading lady in various spectacles, is passable but Crenna is an utter bore. The direction shows occasional flashes of intelligence but is mostly plodding and lifeless.

p, Lewis J. Rachmil; d, Lewis Seiler; w, James Gunn, Gil Orlovitz (based on a story by Richard Sale, Mary Loos); ph, Henry Freulich; m, Mischa Bakaleinikoff; ed, Edwin Bryant; art d, Carl Anderson; cos, Jean Louis.

Drama **(PR:C MPAA:NR)**

OVER MY DEAD BODY*** (1942) 67m FOX bw

Milton Berle *(Jason Cordry)*, Mary Beth Hughes *(Patricia Cordry)*, Reginald Denny *(Brenner)*, Frank Orth *(Detective)*, William B. Davidson *(Crole)*, Wonderful Smith *(Colored Boy)*, J. Patrick O'Malley *(Petie Stuyvesant)*, George M. Carleton *(Judge)*, John Hamilton *(District Attorney)*, Jill Warren *(Elsie)*, Milton Parsons *(Lawrin)*, Leon Belasco *(Pierre)*, Charles Trowbridge *(Mardley)*, Bud [Lon] McCallister *(Jimmie)*, Cyril Ring *(Court Clerk)*, Edwin August *(Bailiff)*, Emory Parnell *(Capt. Grady)*, Ed Gargan *(Sergeant)*, Don Dillaway, George Riley *(Reporters)*, George Andre Beranger *(Salesman)*, Frances Morris *(Woman Reporter)*, Joseph J. Weston *(Editor)*.

Unable to make it as a mystery writer, Berle must turn to his wife (Hughes) for financial support. His problem is that he writes mysteries so confusing that even he can't figure them out. Upon visiting his wife's office, he overhears a conversation among the business partners. It seems their boss committed suicide over their nefarious schemes. Berle is struck by inspiration. Here's a real mystery! He has himself arrested as the murderer, figuring he'll be able to concoct a nifty idea to work himself out of the rap. But this backfires and Berle ends up on trial for murder. At last in the courtroom he reveals the truth, but not before some close shaves. This is a clever, well-written little film. Though it requires the audience to suspend their disbelief for all of 67 minutes, it's well worth the effort. Berle, in one of his earliest appearances, is absolutely wonderful, making this comedy funny and nearly believable.

p, Walter Morosco; d, Malcolm St. Clair; w, Edward James (based on the novel by James O'Hanlon); ph, Lucien Andriot; m, Emil Newman, Cyril J. Mockridge; ed, J. Watson Webb.

Comedy/Mystery **(PR:A MPAA:NR)**

OVER SHE GOES*** (1937, Brit.) 74m ABF bw

John Wood *(Lord Drewsden)*, Claire Luce *(Pamela)*, Laddie Cliff *(Billy Bowler)*, Sally Gray *(Kitty)*, Stanley Lupino *(Tommy Teacher)*, Gina Malo *(Dolly Jordan)*, Judy Kelly *(Alice Mayhill)*, Max Baer *(Silas Morner)*, Syd Walker *(Inspector Giffnock)*, Richard Murdoch *(Sgt. Oliver)*, Bertha Belmore *(Lady Drewsden)*, Fred Hearne *(Lord Harry Drewsden)*, Archibald Batty *(Alfred)*.

Wood is an old vaudevillian who inherits the title of lord. He invites his old partners, Cliff and Lupino, to check out his new digs. But also arriving on the scene is Kelly, a girl Wood used to go with. She's bearing a two-year-old letter written by Wood in his leaner days, promising marriage. She wants to sue for breach of promise. His old pals help him out by disguising as ghosts to retrieve the letter. This is a witty little British comedy, well acted by the leads. The direction shows an excellent sense of timing with songs well integrated into the story.

p, Walter C. Mycroft; d, Graham Cutts; w, Elizabeth Meehan, Hugh Brooke (based on the play by Stanley Lupino); ph, Otto Kanturek; m/l, Billy Mayerl, Desmond Carter, Frank Byton, Michael Carr, Jimmie Kennedy.

Musical/Comedy **(PR:A MPAA:NR)**

OVER THE BORDER*½ (1950) 58m MON bw

Johnny Mack Brown *(Johnny Mack)*, Myron Healey *(Jeff Grant)*, Marshall Reed *(Bart Calhoun)*, Mike Ragan *(Duke Winslow)*, Robert House Peters *(Wade Shelton)* Wendy Waldron *(Tess Malloy)*, Pierre Watkin *(Rand Malloy)*, Hank Bell *(Sheriff)*, George De Normand *Tucker)*, Milburn Morante *(Mason)*, Frank Jaquet *(Doc Foster)*, Buck Bailey *(Ford)*, George Sewards *(Stage Driver)*, Carol Henry *(Stage Guard)*, Frank McCarroll *(Carl)*, Bud Osborne *(Stableman)*, Herman Hack, Ray Jones, Artie Ortego, Bob Woodward.

Watkin, a Wells Fargo agent and Brown's uncle, is murdered by bad guy Reed. Brown chases the outlaw and discovers the man is also the brains behind a silver smuggling operation. Healey is a seemingly respectable merchant who's in with Reed. This is a lesser entry in Brown's series for Monogram, with slow-paced direction that fails to hold much interest. As with most bad Westerns, the only saving grace is the two-fisted action.

p&d, Wallace Fox; w, J. Benton Cheney; ph, Harry Neumann; ed, John C. Fuller; md, Edward Kay.

Western **(PR:A MPAA:NR)**

OVER THE EDGE½** (1979) 95m Orion/WB c

Michael Kramer *(Carl)*, Pamela Ludwig *(Cory)*, Matt Dillon *(Richie)*, Vincent Spano *(Mark)*, Tom Fergus *(Claude)*, Harry Northup *(Doberman)*, Andy Romano *(Fred Willat)*, Ellen Geer *(Sandra Willat)*, Richard Jamison *(Cole)*, Julia Pomeroy *(Julia)*, Tiger Thompson *(Johnny)*.

This teenage rebellion picture sets itself apart from the others in its genre by using a suburban setting rather than the usual one of urban decay. A group of teenagers become bored with their lives in a planned suburban community. They see the same things over and over each day with no outlets for creativity or uniqueness. The kids turn to whiskey and violence to relieve the boredom, finally destroying the local high school at film's end. This is a mixed bag of a film with good points that outweigh the bad. Most notable is the cast. The teenagers here project a real sense of frustration and alienation with their freshness and honesty. Many of the cast, including Dillon (in his screen debut) and Spano went on to more notable projects. Kaplan's direction is gritty and perceptive. He knows how these kids feel and telegraphs it well. The film's score is kinetic, punched up by some hard-driving rock songs from the punk band The Ramones. There is a tendency to stereotype all the adults as bad authoritative figures, and there are some hammy performances, but all in all, OVER THE EDGE is definitely worth a look.

p, George Litto; d, Jonathan Kaplan; w, Charlie Hass, Tim Hunter; ph, Andrew Davis; m, Sol Kaplan; ed, Robert Bargere; prod d, Jim Newport; set d, A.C. Montenaro; spec eff, Richard Johnson.

Drama   Cas.   (PR:O MPAA:PG)

OVER THE GARDEN WALL**   (1934, Brit.) 68m BIP/Wardour bw

Bobby Howes (Bunny), Marian Marsh (Mary), Margaret Bannerman (Diana), Viola Lyel (Gladys), Bertha Belmore (Jennifer), Syd Crossley (Podds), Mary Sheridan (Tilda), Fred Watts (Thorold), Stewart Granger.

When Howes goes off to live with his aunt in the country at her modernized home, he falls for neighboring Marsh. She's the niece of the people next door, a mean-spirited pair who prefer life in their old-fashioned cottage. The romance is nearly squelched by all the elders, but of course love conquers all in this minor musical comedy.

p, Walter C. Mycroft; d, John Daumery; w, H.F. Maltby, Gordon Wellesley (based on the play "The Youngest of the Three" by Maltby); ph, Jack Cox.

Comedy/Musical   (PR:A MPAA:NR)

OVER THE GARDEN WALL*   (1950, Brit.) 95m Film Studios Manchester/Mancunian bw

Norman Evans (Fanny Lawton), Jimmy James (Joe Lawton), Dan Young (Dan), Alec Pleon (Alec), Sonya O'Shea (Mary Harrison), John Wynn (Tony Harrison), Frederick Bradshaw (Ken Smith).

Slow-moving comedy has James and Evans, a working class pair, dead set on giving their daughter O'Shea and her husband Wynn a grand welcome-home party. Problems arise when the son of James' boss (Bradshaw) shows up and shamelessly flirts with O'Shea. The comedy suffers from the real talents of the piece giving way to younger performers not seasoned enough to pull off the farce. The film was re-released in 1960 with some 40 minutes trimmed out.

p&d, John E. Blakeley; w, Anthony Toner; ph, Ernest Palmer.

Comedy   (PR:A MPAA:NR)

OVER THE GOAL**   (1937) 63m FN-WB bw

June Travis (Lucille Martin), William Hopper (Ken Thomas), Johnnie Davis (Tiny Waldron), Mabel Todd (Bee), Gordon Oliver (Benton), William Harrigan (Jim Shelly), Willard Parker (Duke Davis), Eric Stanley (Dr. Martin), Raymond Hatton (Abner), Herbert Rawlinson (Stanley Short), Douglas Wood (Dr. Marshall), Eddie Anderson (William), Hattie McDaniel (Hannah), Fred McKaye (Clay), Eddie Chandler (Peters), George Offerman, Jr. (Teddy), Jack Chapin (Pinky), Robert Hoover (Larkin), John Craven (King), Members of the USC Football Squad.

Hopper is a college football hero who promises girl friend Travis he'll hang up his cleats rather than risk injury. But team spirit and family finances deem otherwise and Hopper goes back to the gridiron to help his team win the big game. The film is all routine football cliches without much thought to originality or logic. Plenty of rah-rah enthusiasm is exhibited by the cast, and the USC football squad is featured. This was released in the fall of 1937 in order to capitilize on college football fever.

p, Bryan Foy; d, Noel Smith; w, William Jacobs, Anthony Coldeway (based on the story "Block That Kick" by Jacobs); ph, Warren Lynch; ed, Everett Dodd; m/l, "Scattin' with Mr. Bear," "As Easy as Rollin' Off a Log," M.K. Jerome, Jack Scholl.

Football drama   (PR:A MPAA:NR)

OVER THE HILL***½   (1931) 87m FOX bw

Mae Marsh (Ma Shelby), James Kirkwood (Pa Shelby), Joe Hachey (Isaac Shelby), Tom Conlon (Johnny Shelby), Julius Molnar (Thomas Shelby), Marilyn Harris (Susan Shelby), Nancy Irish (Isabel Potter), James Dunn (Johnny as an Adult), Sally Eilers (Isabel as an Adult), Edward Crandall (Thomas as an Adult), Claire Maynard (Phyllis, His Wife), Olin Howland (Isaac as an Adult), Eula Guy (Minnie, His Wife), Joan Peers (Susan as an Adult), William Pawley (Ben Adams), George Reed, Douglas Walton, David Hartford.

A fine, slightly dated melodrama features Marsh (D.W. Griffith's "Pet Sister" from BIRTH OF A NATION) as the widowed mother of a large brood. She has been consigned to the poorhouse by an ungrateful son. Another child returns from his wandering ways and sees what has happened. Angered, he goes to the home and brings his mother back to her rightful place. This drama boasts of some wonderful performances, particularly by Marsh. Her silent training does her well as she often emotes without having to say a word. The direction is restrained, allowing the drama to speak for itself. One shot has Marsh on her knees scrubbing a floor while the light and shadows from the windows frame her. The appearance is much like a fine etching, greatly adding to the drama. This is a remake of a 1920 silent film, and infinitely superior to the original.

d, Henry King; w, Tom Barry, Jules Furthman (based on the poem "Over the Hill to the Poorhouse" by Will Carleton); ph, John Seitz; ed, Frank Hull.

Drama   (PR:C MPAA:NR)

OVER THE MOON**   (1940, Brit.) 78m LFP-Denham/UA c

Merle Oberon (June Benson), Rex Harrison (Dr. Freddie Jarvis), Ursula Jeans (Lady Millie Parsmill), Robert Douglas (John Flight), Louis Borell (Count Pietro d'Altamura), Zena Dare (Julie Deethorpe), Peter Haddon (Lord Petcliffe), David Tree (Journalist), Mackenzie Ward (Lord Guy Carstairs), Carl Jaffe (Michel), Elizabeth Welch (Cabaret Singer), Herbert Lomas (Ladbrooke), Wilfred Shine (Frude), Gerald Nodin (Cartwright), Bruce Winston, Lewis Gilbert, Evelyn Ankers, Meriel Forbes, Billy Shine.

It took three years from the time this movie was completed until it was released in the U.S. and the wait was not quite worth it. A romantic comedy reminiscent of many others before (and since), it's the story of seemingly impoverished Oberon, who lives in a large, old, and drafty mansion with ancient servants. The place belongs to her uncle and she thinks that it is all he ever had. When he dies and leaves her almost $90 million, her life is tossed into chaos. She'd been happily engaged to poor local physician Harrison, but her sudden wealth causes him to step away, as he doesn't care to be a consort to her queen. Oberon goes on a trip to Europe, visits Monte Carlo, Switzerland, Italy, France, and is besieged by more than her share of gigolos and adventurers, all eager to lay their paws on her cash. In the course of the film, Oberon comes to the realization that love is all and money matters not in affairs of the heart, so she returns to patient Harrison and they marry and honeymoon on the continent with a third-class railway ticket Harrison has paid for with his own meager funds. Good production, some witty lines from the quartet of writers, and the general Korda patina of first class all the way. Two years after this film was made, Oberon married producer Korda. That marriage ended in 1945. OVER THE MOON was a pleasant, frothy farce that offended no one and is as easily forgotten as last year's second-place finisher in the National League East. We give Howard credit for direction, but it didn't appear on the screen.

p, Alexander Korda; d, Thornton Freeland, William K. Howard; w, Anthony Pelissier, Alec Coppel, Arthur Wimperis (based on a story by Robert E. Sherwood, Lajos Biro); ph, Harry Stradling, Robert Krasker (Technicolor); m, Mischa Spoliansky; ed, Pat Wooley; md, Muir Mathieson; prod d, Vincent Korda; cos, Rene Hubert; m/l, Spoliansky, Desmond Carter.

Comedy   PR:A MPAA:NR

OVER THE ODDS***   (1961, Brit.) 65m Jermyn/RANK bw

Marjorie Rhodes (Bridget Stone), Glynn Melvyn (George Summers), Cyril Smith (Sam), Esma Cannon (Alice), Thora Hird (Mrs. Carter), Wilfrid Lawson (Willie Summers), Frances Cuka (Hilda Summers), Gwen Lewis (Mrs. Small), Rex Deering (Butcher), Patsy Rowlands (Marilyn), Fred Griffiths (Fruit Vendor), Leslie Crowther (Fishmonger), Sheena Marshe (Blonde), Erica Houen (Bridesmaid).

A typical British farce with wacky developments and uproarious slapstick comedy. Melvyn is a bookmaker whose wife has walked out on him. He meets a new woman (Cannon) and decides to remarry. But complications arise when Rhodes, one of the meanest mothers-in-law in cinema, descends to cause problems for her ex-son-in-law. The editing is inconsistent, but otherwise the film is an effective comedy. The actors overplay without shame, clearly enjoying themselves.

p, Alec C. Snowden; d, Michael Forlong; w, Ernest Player (based on the play by Rex Howard Arundel); ph, Norman Wardwick; ed, Reggie Beck.

Comedy   (PR:A MPAA:NR)

OVER THE RIVER   (SEE: ONE MORE RIVER, 1934)

OVER THE WALL**   (1938) 72m WB bw

Dick Foran (Jerry Davis), June Travis (Kay Norton), John Litel (Father Connor), Dick Purcell (Ace Scanlon), Veda Ann Borg (Maxine), George E. Stone (Gyp), Ward Bond (Eddie Edwards), John Hamilton (Warden), Jonathan Hale (Governor), Tommy Bupp (Jimmy Davis), Robert E. Homans (John Davis), Mabel Hart (Mrs. Davis), Raymond Hatton (Convict), Alan Davis (Joe), Eddie Chandler (Keeper)

Foran exchanged his regular cowboy outfit for some prison stripes in this strange programmer. He plays a nice guy who's framed (naturally) for murder. Once inside Sing Sing, Foran meets the prison chaplain (Litel) who helps him prove his innocence. But Foran has another revelation inside the pokey. He's not just in Sing Sing, he learns how to Sing! Sing! And that he does with such ditties as "One More Tomorrow", "Have You Met My Lulu," and "Little White House on the Hill." Foran determines to become a crooner once he's sprung. While out on a singing venture for Litel's radio show, Foran makes a break and is recaptured. But things are righted in the end as he proves his innocence and is reunited with girl Travis. The film is well made with earnest performances (particularly that of Foran). The music is blended nicely into the plot. However, what worked for audiences in 1938 comes off as unbelievable, campy humor for the more cinematically sophisticated audiences of modern times. Author Lawes was a famed prison reform advocate who appeared on many radio programs of the time. He had actually been the long-time warden of Sing Sing prison. This was the second film made from his written works; the first was 20,000 YEARS IN SING SING (1933).

p, Bryan Foy; d, Frank McDonald; w, Crane Wilbur, George Bricker (based on the story "One More Tomorrow" by Lewis E. Lawes); ph, James Van Trees; ed, Frank Magee; m/l, M.K. Jerome, Jack Scholl

Musical/Prison Drama   (PR:A MPAA:NR)

OVER 21***   (1945) 104m COL bw

Irene Dunne (Paula Wharton), Alexander Knox (Max Wharton), Charles Coburn (Robert Gow), Jeff Donnell (Jan Lupton), Loren Tindall (Roy Lupton), Lee Patrick (Mrs. Foley), Phil Brown (Frank MacDougal), Cora Witherspoon (Mrs. Gates), Charles Evans (Col. Foley), Pierre Watkin (Joel I. Nixon), Anne Loos (Mrs. Dumbrowski), Nanette Parks (Mrs. Clark), Adelle Roberts (Mrs. Collins), Jean Stevens (Mrs. Greenberg), Billy Lechner (Little Boy), Robert Williams (Taxi Driver), Abigail Adams, Francine Ames, Pat Jackson, Marilyn Johnson, Carole Mathews, Jo Gilbert (Officer Candidates' Wives), Charles Marsh (Howell), Dan Stowell (Male Secretary), Robert Emmett Keane (Kennedy), Forbes Murray (Meredity), Cosmo Sardo (Barber), Alfred Allegro, Lillian Bronson (Secretaries), George Carleton (Hinkle), Doug Henderson, Michael Owen, George Peters, John James, Bob Meredith, William Hudson (Officer Candidates), James Flavin (Captain), Rube Schaefer (Athletic Instructor), George Bruggerman, Chuck Hamilton, LeRoy Taylor (Lieutenants), Gladys Blake (Girl), Wallace Pindell (Publicity Man).

Dunne and Knox are a pair of married writers living near an Army base. In order to find out more about the military life, Knox joins up. He finds there's more to the disciplined lifestyle than he thought as he tries to compete with kids half his age. Meanwhile, Dunne is stuck at home trying to cope with the domestic troubles that such a life brings. Coburn is the publisher who desperately wants Knox back at his old job. There are some wonderful parodies of Hollywood life as well when Dunne fights it out with film producer Watkin. This is based on a fine play by Ruth Gordon which she wrote after experiencing a similar situation during the war. Dunne is fun in the role (originated by Gordon on Broadway) and Coburn is the quintessential grumpy publisher. The direction is excellent with a good feel for comedy timing and some nifty satires on army life. Some of the humor is a little sophisticated and may be missed by the less astute members of the audience.

p, Sidney Buchman; d, Charles Vidor; w, Buchman (based on the play by Ruth Gordon); ph, Rudolph Mate; m, Marlin Skiles; ed, Otto Meyer; md, M.W. Stoloff; art d, Stephen Goossen, Rudolph Sternad; set d, Louis Diage; cos, Jean Louis.

Comedy   **(PR:C MPAA:NR)**

OVER-UNDER, SIDEWAYS-DOWN*   (1977) 86m CineManifest c

Robert Viharo (Roy), Sharon Goldman (Jan), Roy Andrews (Wilbur), Robert A. Behling (Frank), Michael Cavanaugh (Rich), Lonnie Ford (Luke), Fran Furey (A. J.), Esteban Oropreza (Tomas), Larry Patterson (Johnson).

Viharo plays a factory worker rapidly approaching middle-age. He sees his wife and children as roadblocks to his real dream of playing major league baseball. His wife (Goldman) tries to be supportive, but soon grows weary. Viharo will not allow her to take a job or attend school since her responsibility is raising the kids. The frustrations of the pair mount and they gradually grow apart. None of this material is new or particularly fresh. The handling here is muddled, with no depth or perception. The weak script was directed by no less than three men, resulting in a classic example of too many cooks spoiling the broth. Viharo and Goldman are not bad, just severely limited in what they can do.

p, Steve Wax; d, Wax, Eugene Corr, Peter Gessner; w, Corr, Gessner; ph, Stephen Lighthill; m, Ozzie Ahlers; ed, Corr, David Schickele.

Drama   **(PR:C MPAA:NR)**

OVERCOAT, THE**½   (1965, USSR) 78m Lenfilm/Cinemaster International bw (SHINEL)

Rolan Bykov (Akakiy Akakiyevich), Yuriy Tolubeyev (Petrovich), A. Yezhkina (Petrovich's Wife), Ye. Ponsova (Landlady), T. Teykh (Important Person), N. Urgant, Aleksandr Sokolov, V. Maksimov, R. Lebedev, P. Lobanov, G. Kolosov, M. Ladygin, G. Voropayev, N, Kuzmin.

Bykov plays an unimportant office clerk to whom work is everything. His fellow employees insult his devotion to the job and his otherwise mundane, boring life. He ignores these taunts and continues at his job, never taking his life beyond his financial means. Bykov takes his winter coat to be patched in anticipation of the cold Russian winter. However, the drunken tailor (Tolubeyev) tells him the coat is beyond repair and recommends getting a new one. Bykov receives a Christmas bonus and combining it with some money saved up through the years he decides that a new overcoat is indeed a possibility. He chooses the fabric and Tolubeyev sets out to design the best of overcoats. His fellow employees are impressed by the new garment and one of the wealthier office workers invites the man over for some champagne. Bykov leaves the poor neighborhood where he dwells for the unaccustomed wealthier area of town. At the party he is uncomfortable with the surrounding opulence, a feeling further created by the champagne. Long after his normal bedtime Bykov heads for home. Arriving in his neighborhood, the man is jumped by some thieves and his new overcoat is stolen. Fellow employees tell Bykov that the police would be useless but he should visit Teykh. Teykh meets with Bykov, but dismisses him from the interview to impress the lowly man with his importance. Bykov's spirit is broken and he tramps out into the snow. He catches a chill which subsequently leads to deliriums and his eventual death. He returns as a ghost, taking overcoats from the backs of St. Petersburg's finest citizens. When Teykh's coat is taken, the ghost's work is done and he disappears for good. This film is based on an 1842 story by famed Russian satirist, Gogol.

d, Aleksey Batalov; w, L. Solovyov (based on "Shinel" by Nikolai Vasilievich Gogol); ph, G. Marandzhyan; m, N. Sidelnikov; art d, B. Manevich, I. Kaplan.

Drama   **(PR:O MPAA:NR)**

OVERLAND BOUND**   (1929) 58m Presidio/Talking Pictures

Leo Maloney (Lucky Lorimer), Allene Ray (Mary Winters), Jack Perrin (Larry Withers/Jimmy Winters), Lydia Knott (Ma Winters), Wally Wales (Buck Hawkins), Charles K. French (Underwood), R.J. Smith (Reno Creager), William J. Dyer (Boss Wheeler), Joe Maloney, Bullet the Dog, Starlight the Horse.

This routine western is historically notable for several reasons. The overly melodramatic plot involves a crooked railroad agent trying to get a pair of widows to sign over their ranch. Perrin is the good guy who saves the day and wins the heart of the widow's daughter. OVERLAND BOUND was the second western with sound and the first of its genre produced by an independent studio. Though the sound is poorly recorded, this was a highly successful film that paved the way for numerous other independent companies dealing in programmer westerns. The direction makes up for the bad sound, with a vigorous energy that carries the story well. Maloney, who has a minor role, was an actor who turned to direction with this film. Sadly, it was his only directoral effort because he died of a heart attack a few days after OVERLAND BOUND's well-received New York premiere.

p&d, Leo Maloney; w, Ford I. Beebe (based on the story by Beebe, Joseph Kane); ph, William Nobles; ed, Fred Bain.

Western   **(PR:A MPAA:NR)**

OVERLAND EXPRESS, THE*½   (1938) 55m COL bw

Buck Jones (Buck Dawson), Marjorie Reynolds (Jean Greeley), Carlyle Moore (Tom Furness), Matson Williams (William Hawley), William Arnold Henry Furness), Lou Kelly (Fred Greeley), Bud Osborne (Overland Wilson), Ben Taggart (Adams), Ben Corbett, Gene Alsace [Rocky Camron], Blackie Whiteford, Bob Woodward, Silver the Horse.

Jones is a member of the Pony Express, riding the famous trail between St. Joseph, Missouri, and California. Along the way he meets up with the expected hostile Indians, as well as the rival operators of a stagecoach. Too much time is spent on detail and not enough on action which makes this a slow-going effort at best. There's a poor mismatch of stock Indian shots edited into the footage as well. The action is kept down to a minimum with the emphasis placed on the hard-riding men.

p, L.G. Leonard; d, Drew Eberson; w, Monroe Shaff (based on the story by Shaff); ph, Allen Q. Thompson; m, Edward Kilenyi; ed, Gene Milford; md, Kilenyi; art d, F. Paul Sylos.

Western   **(PR:A MPAA:NR)**

OVERLAND MAIL**½   (1939) 51m MON bw

Jack Randall (Jack), Vince Barnett (Porchy), Jean Joyce (Mary), Tristram Coffin (Polini), George Cleveland (Porter), Glenn Strange (Dawson), Dennis Moore (Duke), Merrill McCormick (Squint), Joe Garcia (Buck), Maxine Leslie (Blondie), James Sheridan [Sherry Tansey] (Joe), Hal Price (Lugo), Harry Semels (Pancho), Rusty the Horse.

Randall's a rider for the Pony Express. He meets Joyce, a disguised federal agent who enlists him in a battle against some counterfeiters. The female agent is a nice touch in this fairly routine outing. There are some inconsistencies within the plot's logic, but that's forgotten when the fists start flying. Rusty the Wonder Horse proves himself to be one of the better cowboy horses.

p, Robert Tansey; d, Robert Hill; w, Robert Emmett [Tansey]; ph, Bert Longnecker; ed, Robert Golden

Western   **(PR:A MPAA:NR)**

OVERLAND MAIL ROBBERY*½   (1943) 56m REP bw

Wild Bill Elliott (Wild Bill), George "Gabby" Hayes (Gabby), Anne Jeffreys (Judy Goodrich), Alice Fleming (Mrs. Patterson), Weldon Heyburn (John Patterson), Kirk Alyn (Tom Hartley), Roy Barcroft (David Patterson), Nancy Gay (Lola Patterson), Peter Michael (Jimmy Hartley), Bud Geary (Slade), Tom London (Sheriff), Jack Kirk, Kenne Duncan, Jack Rockwell, Frank McCarroll, Jack O'Shea, LeRoy Mason, Hank Bell, Cactus Mack, Ray Jones, Tom Steele, Frank Ellis, Maxine Doyle, Diane Henry.

An easterner heads west to take over the family stagecoach line. His brother is murdered and he must fight off a gang of siblings headed by their crooked and tough mother. Elliott, a friend of the murdered brother, arrives to save the day. A standard programmer without much originality. Even the fight sequences contain nothing fresh, and the direction is more sluggish than usual.

p, Louis Gray; d, John English; w, Bob Williams, Robert Yost; ph, John MacBurnie; m, Mort Glickman; ed, Charles Craft.

Western   **Cas.**   **(PR:A MPAA:NR)**

OVERLAND PACIFIC**½   (1954) 73m Reliance/UA c

Jack [Jock] Mahoney (Rose Granger), Peggie Castle (Ann Dennison), Adele Jergens (Jessie Lorraine), William Bishop (Del Stewart), Walter Sande (Mr. Dennison), Chubby Johnson (Sheriff Blaney), Pat Hogan (Dark Thunder), Chris Alcaide (Jason), Phil Chambers (Weeks), George Eldredge (Broden), Dick Rich (Saber), House Peters, Jr. (Perkins).

Undercover agent Mahoney is sent to the western village of Oaktown because it seems as though the Indians have been stirring up trouble and delaying the installation of the railroad. Actually, Bishop, a local saloon owner, wants the railroad to pass through some valuable property he owns so he can collect a small fortune. He's been supplying the Indians with rifles and other weapons in order to stop the railroad from going elsewhere. The plot develops nicely and contains some good action sequences, but the color process (by the Color Corporation of America) mars the film with a murky tone. Mahoney, who had been starring in TV's "Range Rider" series at the time, had previously worked with director Sears when they both served as actors in Charles Starrett's "Durango Kid" series.

p, Edward Small; d, Fred F. Sears; w, J. Robert Bren, Gladys Atwater, Martin Goldsmith (based on a story by Frederic Louis Fox); ph, Lester White (Color Corp. of America); ed, Bernard Small

Western   **(PR:A MPAA:NR)**

OVERLAND RIDERS**   (1946) 54m PRC bw

Buster Crabbe, Al "Fuzzy" St. John, Patty McCarty, Slim Whitaker, Bud Osborne, Jack O'Shea, Frank Ellis, Al Ferguson, John L. "Bob" Cason, George Chesebro, Lane Bradford, Wally West.

Billy the Kid is causing trouble out in the Old West. In rides Crabbe and sidekick St. John to save the day, but not before they go through the standard amounts of gunplay and two-fisted action. (See Billy Carson series, Index.)

p, Sigmund Neufeld; d, Sam Newfield; w, Ellen Coyle; ph, Jack Greenhalgh; md, Lee Zahler; ed, Holbrook N. Todd; set d, Gene Stone.

Western   **(PR:A MPAA:NR)**

OVERLAND STAGE COACH   (SEE: OVERLAND STAGECOACH, 1942)

OVERLAND STAGE RAIDERS*** (1938) 55m REP bw

John Wayne (Stony Brooke), Ray Corrigan (Tuscon Smith), Max Terhune (Lullaby Joslin), Louise Brooks (Beth Hoyt), Anthony Marsh (Ned Hoyt), Ralph Bowman [John Archer] (Bob Whitney), Gordon Hart (Mullins), Roy James (Harmon), Olin Francis (Jake), Fern Emmett (Ma Hawkins), Henry Otho (Sheriff), George Sherwood (Clanton), Archie Hall (Waddell), Frank LaRue (Milton), Yakima Canutt (Bus Driver), Slim Whitaker (Hawkins), Milt Kibbee, Jack Kirk, Bud Osborne, Dirk Thane, Edwin Gaffney, Bud McClure, John Beach, Curley Dresden, Tommy Coats, George Plues.

An entry in Republic's "Three Mesquiteers" series and the second to feature Wayne. This is more of a modern western, with the Mesquiteers protecting a Greyhound bus of all things! It's carrying some gold that eventually ends up in an airplane. Hijackers are after the cargo, but Wayne and company defeat them handily. The action, though routine, is well handled with a good sense of fun and excitement. Brooks plays Wayne's girl friend in what would be her last film—a sad comedown for the actress who had starred in the German masterpiece PANDORA'S BOX (1929). (See THREE MESQUITEERS series, Index.)

p, William Berke; d, George Sherman; w, Luci Ward (based on a story by Bernard McConville, Edmond Kelso, from characters created by William Colt McDonald); ph, William Nobles; ed, Tony Martinelli.

Western **Cas.** **(PR:A MPAA:NR)**

OVERLAND STAGECOACH** (1942) 61m PRC bw (AKA: OVERLAND STAGE COACH)

Bob Livingston, Al "Fuzzy" St. John, Smoky [Dennis] Moore, Julie Duncan, Glenn Strange, Charles King, Art Mix, Budd Buster, Ted Adams, Julian Rivero, John Elliott, Tex Cooper.

A stagecoach is robbed by a masked gunman. In rides Livingston, "the Lone Rider," along with sidekick St. John, to save the day and stop the nefarious outlaw. (See LONE RIDER series, Index.)

p, Sigmund Neufeld; d, Sam Newfield; w, Steve Braxton.

Western **(PR:A MPAA:NR)**

OVERLAND TELEGRAPH**½ (1951) 60m RKO bw

Tim Holt (Tim), Gail Davis (Terry), Hugh Beaumont (Brad), Mari Blanchard (Stella), George Nader (Paul Manning), Robert Wilke (Bellew), Cliff Clark (Muldoon), Russell Hicks (Colonel), Robert Bray (Steve), Fred Graham (Joe), Richard Martin (Chito Rafferty).

Someone is sabotaging the new transcontinental telegraph. It's up to Holt and sidekick Martin to discover who's behind the plot. A trail of vandalism and a murder leads to Nader, an Army outpost supplier who's afraid his business will dry up once the telegraph comes in. Nader is also romantically interested in Blanchard, a singer in a saloon run by Beaumont. Beaumont has designs on her as well and tries to frame Nader for murder. The busy plot keeps Holt and Martin active as they solve all the problems with the inevitable gunfight climax. The two separate plot lines could have been integrated better, but otherwise it's an average outing for Holt. TV fans might shudder to think that this is the mysterious job Beaumont always returned home from on "Leave it to Beaver."

p, Herman Schlom; d, Lesley Selander; w, Adele Buffington (based on a story by Carroll Young); ph, J. Roy Hunt; m, Paul Sawtell; ed, Samuel E. Beetley; art d, Albert D'Agostino.

Western **(PR:A MPAA:NR)**

OVERLANDERS, THE***½ (1946, Brit./Aus.) 91m EAL/UNIV bw

Chips Rafferty (Dan McAlpine), John Nugent Hayward (Bill Parsons), Daphne Campbell (Mary Parsons), Jean Blue (Mrs. Parsons), Helen Grieve (Helen Parsons), John Fernside (Corky), Peter Pagan (Sailor Sinbad), Frank Ransome (Charlie), Stan Tolhurst (Manager), Marshall Crosby (Minister), John Fegan (Police Sergeant), Clyde Combo (Jackie), Henry Murdoch (Aborigine Nipper).

This was the first film from Ealing Studios to be made in Australia. Producer Balcon sent one of his better directors (Watt) to Australia with orders to find a subject that could well represent the Land Down Under. After spending five months taking in the scenery, Watt met an official of the Federal Food Office. He related a story that took place during WW II. In anticipation of a Japanese invasion the Australian government decided to move over 500,000 head of cattle to a safe location. The drive covered over 2,000 miles and took 15 months. Watt concluded the meeting with the subject he had been searching for. The film begins in 1942. A meatpacking plant has been destroyed and Rafferty is ordered to kill 1,000 head of cattle. Rather than kill the much-needed prime beef, Rafferty decides to lead the cattle 2,000 miles across the continent. The long and hazardous journey is overwhelming. The cattle drivers' horses die after eating poisoned weeds and wild horses must be rounded up and broken in. A particularly harrowing sequence involves a mad stampede heading directly towards the men. This is all beautifully photographed against the setting of the Australian Outback. The scenery is well used, creating a fine mise-en-scene of men, cattle, and nature. Rafferty plays his part as the strong, silent man with a job to do. He was known as "the Australian Gary Cooper" and well demonstrates how that moniker was earned. The majority of the cast is comprised of non-actors, giving the film a realistic touch. The score is by noted British composer Ireland and is his first attempt at film music. This is an often beautiful film that features a careful balance of both large and small moments.

p, Michael Balcon, Ralph Smart; d&w, Harry Watt; ph, Osmond Borradaile; m, John Ireland; ed, Leslie Norman, E.M. Inman Hunter.

War Drama **(PR:C MPAA:NR)**

OVERLORD***½ (1975, Brit.) 85m EMI/Jowsend bw

Brian Stirner (Tom), Davyd Harries (Jack), Nicholas Ball (Arthur), Julie Neesam (Girl), Sam Sewell (Trained Soldier).

This WW II film tells the story of a young British soldier, taking him from his induction and training periods to his death at Normandy on D-Day. Stirner is excellent as the young man, giving a solemn and honest performance. The film's dialog and production values reflect a careful attention to detail. John Alcott's fine black-and-white photography is blended with old newsreel footage with good effect. Also included is rare footage of a rehearsal for D-Day held on a lonely British beach. There's a fine use of flash-backs, though the flash-forwarding is somewhat distracting. The overriding themes of the film are never broadly stated, but are subtly revealed. The horror and reality of war are quietly played out on both the human and panoramic levels with disturbing effect. This film was produced in association with the Imperial War Museum.

p, James Quinn; d, Stuart Cooper; w, Cooper, Christopher Hudson; ph, John Alcott; m, Paul Glass; ed, Jonathan Gili.

War **(PR:O MPAA:NR)**

OVERNIGHT**½ (1933, Brit.) 78m LFP/PAR bw (GB: THAT NIGHT IN LONDON)

Robert Donat (Dick Warren), Pearl Argyle (Eve Desborough), Miles Mander (Harry Tresham), Lawrence Hanray (Ribbles), Roy Emerton (Capt. Paulson), Graham Soutten (Bert), James Knight (Inspector Brody), Eugene Leahy (Bank Manager), James Bucton (Inspector Ryan), The Max Rivers Girls.

Donat is a small town bank clerk who grows bored with the country life. He embezzles some of the bank's cash and heads off to the bright lights of London. There, an underground character learns of the naive man's holdings and sends his dancer to try to entice the money out of Donat. However, she falls for Donat and helps him get back home where his old job is restored. Not much of a drama, but it manages to hold up on its own.

p, Alexander Korda; d, Rowland V. Lee; w, Dorothy Greenhill, Arthur Wimperis (based on the story by Greenhill); ph, Robert Martin; m, Peter Mendoza; ed, Stephen Harrison.

Crime Drama **(PR:C MPAA:NR)**

OVERTURE TO GLORY*** (1940) 85m G.&L. bw

Moishe Oysher (Joel-David Strashunsky), Florence Weiss (Chana, His Wife), Baby Winkler (Peretz, Their Son), Maurice Krohner (Reb Aaron), Lazar Freed (Rabbi), Benjamin Fishbein (Nute), Jack Mylong Munz (Moniuszko), Leonard Elliott (Tilchinski), Helen Beverly (Wanda), Luba Wesoly (Countess), Ossip Dymow (Count Parnofsky), Erika Zaranova (Prima Donna), Ivan Busatt (Director of the Opera).

Oysher is a Jewish cantor who longs for the world of opera. He leaves his wife and child to fulfill his passion, but eventually loses his voice and humbly returns to his village on Yom Kippur, the Jewish Day of Atonement. He learns that his son has passed away, and grief-stricken, he goes to the synagogue. There, Oysher regains his voice as he performs Kol Nidre in a passionate and melodious rendering. The film ends dramatically as Oysher collapses and dies upon the altar. It is not the best of films, hampered by slow direction and occasional lapses in the photography. However, it is an important film for several reasons. At the time of the film's release, the culture portrayed here was being effectively wiped out by Hitler and the Nazi regime. OVERTURE TO GLORY is thus an important record of Eastern European Jewry. Also, this story (based on a supposedly true Jewish folk tale) was specifically written for the talents of Oysher. He was one of the last of the great Yiddish performers and he gives a fine interpretation of the role. The Yiddish theater had been an important source for talent in turn-of-the-century New York, producing such names as Fanny Brice and George Jessel. OVERTURE TO GLORY gives the modern-day audience a brief glimpse at what one of those theater pieces may have looked like. (In Yiddish; English subtitles.)

p, Ludwig Landy, Ira Greene; d, Max Nosseck; w, Ossip Dymow, Jacob Gladstone; m, Alexander Olshanetsky; English subtitles, Julien Leigh.

Drama **(PR:C MPAA:NR)**

OWD BOB (SEE: TO THE VICTOR 1938, Brit.)

OWL AND THE PUSSYCAT, THE**½ (1970) 98m Raystar/COL c

Barbara Streisand (Doris), George Segal (Felix), Robert Klein (Barney), Allen Garfield [Goorwitz] (Dress Shop Proprietor), Roz Kelly (Eleanor), Jacques Sandulescu (Rapzinsky), Jack Manning (Mr. Weyderhaus), Grace Carney (Mrs. Weyderhaus), Barbara Anson (Ann Weyderhaus), Kim Chan (Theater Cashier), Stan Gottlieb (Coatcheck Man), Evelyn Lang [Marilyn Chambers] (Barney's Girl), Dominic T. Barto (Man in Bar), Buck Henry (Man Looking Through Doubleday's Bookstore), Joe Madden, Fay Sappington (Old Neighbors), Marshall Ward, Tom Atkins, Stan Bryant (Gang in Car).

For her first non-singing role, Streisand chose this bawdy adaptation of Manoff's hit 1964 play which starred white Alan Alda and black Diana Sands. The femme role has been altered to fit Streisand's ethnicity but many of the play's jokes remain intact. Former choreographer Ross was on his second film (the first was the unfortunate remake of GOODBYE, MR. CHIPS) and did well handling the two volatile stars. Segal is his usual nebbish, an author and clerk who makes his living in a bookstore. He suspects that neighbor Streisand is a prostitute and tells his landlord, Sandulescu, who responds by evicting Streisand. When she learns that her ouster was due to Segal's informing on her, she shows up at his apartment late one night and moves in with him, shrieking all the while that he is a gay fink. Segal is thunderstruck and allows her to stay. (Well, of course he does. If he didn't there would be no play or movie.) Streisand develops a case of incurable hiccups and Segal, in an attempt to scare the hics out of her, dons a skeleton suit. Her response is to scream so loudly that the neighbors complain and Segal is evicted. With no place to stay, they descend on Klein's apartment. He is there with his girl friend, Lang (which was a pseudonym for porno star Marilyn Chambers), and when Segal and Streisand erupt again, Klein and Lang leave the apartment, rather than stay awake all night to the noisy sounds of the battling couple. The argument continues until Streisand turns on her "charm" and beds Segal. The next day, they are at each other's throats once more. She takes a job as a dancer and quits when her male audience prefers to watch football on the bar's TV set. Segal attends a tacky movie and sees Streisand in a film called "Cycle Sluts." He can't help missing her and Streisand's pal, Kelly, tells him where she is. He squires Streisand to the home of his stuffy intended, Anson, and the two of them decide to take a bath together after puffing on some grass. When Anson and her parents, Manning and Carney, come home, Streisand immediately recognizes Manning as one of her kinkiest Johns. Streisand and Segal leave and walk in Central Park, alternately arguing, billing and cooing, and getting to know more about each other. They are in love at the finale, but if the movie went another 20 minutes, it would probably have ended with one of them killing the other. It made a fine profit at the box office and showed that Streisand didn't have to sing to make her presence felt. The reason for two cinematographers is that Stradling died while the film was in production and was replaced by Laszlo. Some very funny scenes but too much emphasis on smut to be called witty.

p, Ray Stark; d, Herbert Ross; w, Buck Henry (based on the play "The Owl and the Pussycat" by Bill Manhoff); ph, Harry Stradling, Andrew Laszlo (Panavision, Eastmancolor); m, Richard Halligan; ed, Margaret Booth, John F. Burnett; prod d, John Robert Lloyd; art d, Robert Wightman, Philip Rosenberg; set d, Leif Pedersen; cos, Ann Roth; m/l, Halligan, Blood Sweat and Tears (performed by Blood, Sweat and Tears); makeup, Joe Cranzano.

Comedy **Cas.** **(PR:C MPAA:R)**

OX-BOW INCIDENT, THE***** (1943) 75m FOX bw (GB: STRANGE INCIDENT)

Henry Fonda *(Gil Carter)*, Dana Andrews *(Donald Martin)*, Mary Beth Hughes *(Rose Mapen)*, Anthony Quinn *(Juan Martines, Mexican)*, William Eythe *(Gerald Tetley)*, Henry [Harry] Morgan *(Art Croft)*, Jane Darwell *(Ma Grier)*, Matt Briggs *(Judge Daniel Tyler)*, Harry Davenport *(Arthur Davies)*, Frank Conroy *(Maj. Tetley)*, Marc Lawrence *(Farnley)*, Victor Kilian *(Darby)*, Paul Hurst *(Monty Smith)*, Chris-Pin Martin *(Poncho)*, Ted [Michael] North *(Joyce)*, George Meeker *(Mr. Swanson)*, Almira Sessions *(Mrs. Swanson)*, Margaret Hamilton *(Mrs. Larch)*, Dick Rish *(Deputy Butch Mapes)*, Francis Ford *(Old Man)*, Stanley Andrews *(Bartlett)*, Billy Benedict *(Greene)*, Rondo Hatton *(Hart)*, Paul Burns *(Winder)*, Leigh Whipper *(Sparks)*, George Lloyd *(Moore)*, George Chandler *(Jimmy Cairnes)*, Hank Bell *(Red)*, Forrest Dillon *(Mark)*, George Plues *(Alec Small)*, Willard Robertson *(Sheriff)*, Tom London *(Deputy)*, Donald House, Dan Dix, Ben Watson, Walter Robbins, Frank McGrath, Ed Richard, Cap Anderson, Tex Cooper, Clint Sharp, Larry Dods, Tex Driscoll *(Posse)*.

One of the great westerns to date, THE OX-BOW INCIDENT, based on a real event occurring in 1885 in Nevada, is a powerful and ugly portrait of mob violence that equals majestic Greek tragedy. This is a Wellman masterpiece, shown through a glass darkly or not, one where he uncannily penetrates the psyche of his characters with brilliant exposure. Fonda and Morgan ride into Bridger's Wells, Nevada, a dying town, and head for the local saloon for a much-needed drink after finishing a throat-parching cattle drive. There Fonda gets into a row with local tough Lawrence, but before their battle ends, a cowboy comes riding hard into town to shout to one and all that popular rancher Larry Kinkaid has been shot by rustlers "right through the head, I tell you!" Lawrence, who is the dead man's best friend, explodes in wrath and whips up the townsfolk, demanding justice, insisting that everyone mount up and ride after the rustlers, wherever they might be. "Don't let's go off half-cocked and do something we'll be sorry for," cautions storekeeper Davenport. He points out that the sheriff is at the Kinkaid ranch and they should wait for his return before grabbing any strangers and making accusations or taking the law into their own hands. "If we hang these men ourselves...we'll be worse than murderers," he intones. Lawrence keeps lobbying for a posse to be formed, as does Conroy, a pompous ex-Confederate officer who suddenly appears in his old Civil War uniform. Briggs, a blowhard judge who never makes any kind of decision when not forced to it, sputters, "Of course, you can't flinch from what you believe to be your duty, but certainly you don't want to act hastily." Lawrence is almost beside himself at such ambiguous remarks and sneeringly shouts: "Whoever shot Larry Kinkaid ain't coming back for you to fuddle with your lawyer's tricks for six months, then be let off because Davies [Davenport], or some other whiny old woman claims he ain't bad at heart. Kinkaid didn't have six months to decide if he wanted to die." Conroy takes command and orders that a posse be formed. Brutish Rich, a deputy sheriff, deputizes 28 citizens, even though he doesn't have the authority to do so. These include Fonda and Morgan, reluctant volunteers who hate violence but who feel they had better join the posse rather than be hunted by it as prime suspects, being strangers in town. Conroy leads the dedicated posse forward, his reason for being there obvious; he is reveling in his uniform and the sudden acceptance of his long-lost authority. Moreover, he intends to show his sensitive son, Eythe, whom he has ordered to go along, what it is "to be a man!" With the others, the motives are varied. Darwell, a robust boarding house shrew with a will of iron and a face to match, considers this mission her solemn duty. With vicious bartender Hurst, becoming a posse member is a much-desired adventure, probably his last. Lawrence seeks revenge and Rich longs for sadistic punishment while a mild-mannered Negro, Whipper, joins the group to pray for the victims, whomever they may be. The posse rides aimlessly until nightfall when several members suggest they return. "What!" roars Darwell, "We'll be the laughingstock of the county if we turn back now!" A short time later they ride into the small camp of three exhausted, unemployed farmers, Andrews, Quinn, and Ford. Andrews is the boss and the other two his helpers. They are new to the area, Andrews explains, and intend to find a homestead site. But soon the posse discovers that the three men are prime suspects in the Kinkaid killing. Nearby 50 head of cattle with the Kinkaid brand are found. When Andrews cannot produce a bill of sale,he and the others are accused of murdering the rancher. Andrews protests, quickly explaining that he gave Kinkaid cash and that the rancher promised to mail him a receipt. Evidence mounts up fast against the three strangers. Kinkaid's gun is found on Quinn, who is identified as a wanted murderer. Quinn admits that he is wanted by the law but that he only found the gun and kept it. Andrews tells the grim posse members that he knows the circumstantial evidence mounting against him and his two friends is serious. Pleads Andrews: "Even in this godforsaken country, I've got a right to a trial." Conroy shows his dictatorial iron by replying: "You're getting a trial with 28 of the only kind of judges murderers and rustlers get in what you call this godforsaken country." Conroy then calls for a vote of the 28 posse members; only seven are in favor of sparing the lives of the three men. Andrews is told that they will be hanged. He begs for time, saying that he has a wife and two children and wants to write a farewell letter. Conroy tells him to go ahead, that the posse members are not uncivilized, and that he, Quinn, and Ford have until dawn to write their letters and make peace with God. Kindly Davenport receives Andrews' letter and reads it, much to Andrews' consternation. Davenport begs Andrews to let him read the letter aloud, since he believes it is so compassionate and sincere that it will probably save his life. Andrews adamantly refuses, saying that it is personal and that he will not bare his soul to a bunch of lynch mob members. Before the lynching, Quinn makes a break for it, and is shot in the leg. He grittily digs a bullet out of his own leg while spitting curses at the self-appointed executioners. Ford, a senile old man, doesn't seem to know what is happening, even when the trio is taken to the base of a gnarled tree and ropes put around their necks as they straddle horses, their hands tied behind their backs. Fonda speaks up for the condemned men but he is silenced by Darwell and others whose desire to see justice done is so frantic that they fanatically take pleasure, after Rich fires his gun, in whipping the horses ahead, to leave the three forlorn men to dangle to death. Only Eythe refuses to strike the horse. His father, Conroy, smashes his face with a pistol butt, knocking him unconscious. Conroy slaps his horse and then orders Lawrence to finish the job by firing bullets into all three men. The lynch mob departs, except for Whipper who stays behind to croon a hymn over the dead men. Before the posse reaches town, the sheriff, Robertson, meets them to tell them that rancher Kinkaid has not died of his wounds and that he has already arrested the rustlers who wounded Kinkaid. He learns of the lynching and snarls: "The Lord better have mercy on you. You won't get it from me!" Conroy goes to his home and, to make up for his unforgiveable error, shoots himself. The morose lynch mob gathers in the saloon where $500 in donations is taken up among them for Andrews' widow and children. Fonda then reads Andrews' letter to his wife. (These words do not appear in Clark's novel, but are made up from a speech given by Davies in the book.) The poignant last words of victim Andrews are movingly uttered by an emotional Fonda: "A man just naturally can't take the law into his own hands and hang people without hurting everybody in the world, because he's not just breaking one law but all laws. Law is a lot more than words you put in a book, or judges or lawyers or sheriffs you hire to carry it out. It's everything people have ever found out about justice and what's right and wrong. It's the very conscience of humanity. There can't be any such thing as civilization unless people have got a conscience, because if people touch God anywhere, where is it except through their conscience? And what is anybody's conscience except a little piece of the conscience of all men that ever lived?" Fonda and Morgan then ride off to take the letter to Andrews' widow. Fonda is prosaic and compassionate as the observer in this powerful anti-lynch-law film, the man through whose eyes the film is unraveled, although stunning performances are rendered by Davenport—the only person other than Fonda and Morgan voicing sanity and reason—Hurst, the hateful bartender who whips up the mob's lust for punishment, sanctimonious Darwell, and the tyrannical Conroy who kills himself more in shame over his son's pacificism than because he ordered three innocent men hanged. Quinn only has a small role as one of the victims but he is terrific as the angry and indignant lynch candidate who is about to be hanged not for past crimes but for something he did not do. Wellman's direction of this superb cast is nothing less than awesome, one where he draws forth subtle performances from some, properly bombastic renderings from others. The whole film is coated with shadow (for doubt and fear) and it has a gritty, worn-out feel to its atmosphere right down to the threadbare costumes on the actors, in keeping with the somber tale. Much of this is due to Miller's outstanding photography, supported by a downbeat score from Mockridge. Wellman wanted desperately to make this film and badgered Fox mogul Zanuck for permission to go ahead. He pointed to his past successes—PUBLIC ENEMY (1931), A STAR IS BORN (1937), NOTHING SACRED (1937)—where he had mixed drama with social message, yet Zanuck and other studio executives felt that the Clark novel was too overwhelming for moviegoers of the day. To persuade Zanuck, Wellman promised the mogul that he would direct two films, THUNDER BIRDS and BUFFALO BILL (which he did, sandwiching THE OX-BOW INCIDENT between the two films) if he were allowed to go ahead. Zanuck, during negotiations with the studio, was actually away from Fox in WW II service. William Goetz was running the studio in Zanuck's absence and his canvass of top executives drew a no on the film. Wellman sent a wire to Zanuck which read: "This is to remind you of our handshake; regards, Bill Wellman." (The wire referred to the prior agreement the director and studio boss had about the three-picture deal.) Zanuck wired Goetz within a few days: "Let Wellman go ahead." Doing this film was not that risky after all. Hollywood had earlier dealt with lynchings in films, notably Fritz Lang's FURY (1936) and THEY WON'T FORGET (1937), the latter dealing with the notorious Leo Frank-Mary Phagan rape-murder case of 1913 which resulted in Frank's lynching in 1915. Moreover, lynchings in America had dropped drastically by the time of THE OX-BOW INCIDENT, only three in 1943 against a record high of 231 in 1892. (About 2,000 persons had been lynched in the U.S. since records of such grim events were begun in 1882 by the Tuskegee (Alabama) Institute.) Originally, in 1940, Wellman had discussed making THE OX-

BOW INCIDENT with producer Harold Hurley who, for some inexplicable reason, wanted Mae West to star in the film, acting as sort of a wisecracking saloon hostess around whom the story would revolve. Hurley had acquired the book rights for $6,000 but Wellman refused to direct a film where the colorful West would be at the core of a very serious story and dropped out. When Hurley left Paramount, where he had been trying to package THE OX-BOW INCIDENT, he needed money and Wellman bought the rights to the Clark book for $6,500 and then went to Fox to begin his fight to make the film. He early on enlisted the aid of scriptwriter Trotti, a sterling scribe in matters of the past, one who had written brilliant scripts for such films as IN OLD CHICAGO (1938), YOUNG MR. LINCOLN (1939), and DRUMS ALONG THE MOHAWK (1939). Wellman easily convinced Fonda to play his sensitive cowboy role but the actor had to agree to play in a comedy planned for 1942, THE MAGNIFICENT DOPE. Andrews, the chief victim of the lynch mob, had appeared in only light comedies and battled to get his role, one which helped him greatly to star status. Although scenes at the beginning and the end of the film offer realistic-looking western exteriors, Wellman insisted that the bulk of the film be shot on a set with painted backdrops, mostly since the body of the movie occurred at night and so that he could better control the nuances of lighting he wanted. Some critics complained about the "claustrophobic" look and feel of the picture because of its set-bound image but it is exactly that atmosphere that helps to create the mood of pervasive doom and maniacal intent of the two dozen "average citizens" to commit a capital crime. When released, most critics praised the film, but a few grossly underrated this classic, one poorly envisioning reviewer likening it to a B western. It remained one of Wellman's favorite films all his days, despite the fact that it did poorly at the box office, and Fonda also looked back on THE OX-BOW INCIDENT as one of the few films he did at Fox in which he took great pride. (Interestingly enough, the film has similarities to the mood and posture of another blockbuster Fonda film, TWELVE ANGRY MEN.) An abbreviated version of the film, only 55 minutes, was made by Fox in 1955, directed by Gerd Oswald and starring Cameron Mitchell as Donald Martin, the chief victim. This was shown on TV in the U.S. only and released theatrically in England.

p, Lamar Trotti; d, William A. Wellman; w, Trotti (based on the novel by Walter Van Tilburg Clark); ph, Arthur Miller; m, Cyril J. Mockridge; ed, Allen McNeil; art d, Richard Day, James Basevi; set d, Thomas Little, Frank Hughes; cos, Earl Luick; makeup, Guy Pearce.

Western/Drama   **(PR:C-O MPAA:NR)**

OZ   (SEE: 20TH CENTURY OZ, 1977, Aus.)

P.C. JOSSER**½** (1931, Brit.) 90m Gainsborough/Woolf and Freedman bw

Ernie Lotinga (*Jimmy Josser*), Jack Frost (*Nobby*), Maisie Darrell (*Violet Newsome*), Robert Douglas (*Dick Summers*), Garry Marsh (*Carson*), Max Avieson (*Travers*), Elsie Percival.

Lotinga brings his bumbling Josser character, familiar to British audiences from a series of short movies, into feature-length life here. Lotinga is booted off the police force, but manages to regain his position after cracking a crooked racing scheme, that involved doping. One of the brighter British comedies of the early 1930s; the subsequent series did not live up to the promise of the first. (See JOSSER series, Index.)

p, Michael Balcon; d, Milton Rosmer; w, Con West, Herbert Sargent (based on the play "The Police Force" by Ernie Lotinga).

Comedy **(PR:A MPAA:NR)**

P.J.*** (1968) 109m UNIV c (GB: NEW FACE IN HELL)

George Peppard (*P.J. Detweiler*), Raymond Burr (*William Orbison*), Gayle Hunnicutt (*Maureen Preble*), Brock Peters (*Police Chief Waterpark*), Wilfrid Hyde-White (*Billings-Browne*), Jason Evers (*Jason Grenoble*), Coleen Gray (*Betty Orbison*), Susan Saint James (*Linette Orbison*), Severn Darden (*Shelton Quell*), H. Jane Van Duser (*Elinor Silene*), George Furth (*Sonny Silene*), Barbara Dana (*Lita*), Herbert Edelman (*Charlie*), John Qualen (*Poppa*), Bert Freed (*Police Lieutenant*), Ken Lynch (*Thorson*), Jim Boles (*Landlord's Agent*), Arte Johnson (*Jackie*), King Charles MacNiles (*Calypso Singer*), Don Haggerty (*Ape*), Kay Farrington (*Mrs. Thorson*), Lennie Bremen (*Greavy*).

Peppard is a down-and-out private eye who's hired as a bodyguard for Hunnicutt, the mistress of millionaire Burr. After a few attempts on her life, Burr moves Hunnicutt, Peppard, and Burr's entire family down to the Bahamas. When another attempt is made on Hunnicutt's life, Peppard kills the would-be assassin, who turns out to be Evers, Burr's business partner. Peppard is jailed for murder but later released. When he's freed Peppard discovers that he's been left behind while everyone else has flown to New York. Evidence proves that he was set up to murder Evers. He confronts Burr and Hunnicutt, who end up killing each other in a struggle. Peppard leaves their offices, free for new adventures. This is an excessively violent film with muddled plotting. The strange twist involving Evers' murder is never made clear enough for the audience, resulting in a confused and bloody picture without much thought behind it.

p, Edward J. Montagne; d, John Guillermin; w, Philip Reisman, Jr. (based on a story by Reisman and Montagne); ph, Loyal Griggs (Techniscope, Technicolor); m, Neal Hefti; ed, Sam E. Waxman; art d, Alexander Golitzen, Walter M. Simonds; set d, John McCarthy, Robert Priestly; cos, Jean Louis; m/l, "Welcome to St. Crispin," Percy Faith, Philip Reisman, Jr. (sung by King Charles MacNiles); makeup, Bud Westmore.

Crime **(PR:O MPAA:NR)**

PT RAIDERS (SEE: SHIP THAT DIED OF SHAME, THE, 1955, Brit.)

PACE THAT THRILLS, THE**** (1952) 63m RKO bw

Bill Williams (*Dusty*), Carla Balenda (*Eve Drake*), Robert Armstrong (*Barton*), Frank McHugh (*Rocket*), Steve Flagg (*Chris*), Cleo Moore (*Ruby*), John Mallory (*Blackie*), Diane Garrett (*Opal*), John Hamilton (*Sour Puss*), Claudia Drake (*Pearl*).

This routine programmer revolves around the mystery and intrigues of professional motorcycle racing. Williams is a pro racer and tester for a motorcycle factory. His best friend (Flagg) is a motorcycle designer who's working on a new transmission that will revolutionize the machine. In addition to their common love for motorcycles, they share an infatuation with Balenda, the woman who comes between them. There's not much more to this simplistic film than that, but there's plenty of stock motorcycle footage tossed in for excitement. The climactic race has Williams riding an experimental bike designed by Flagg. He wins the race, of course, as well as the affections of Balenda. There's really nothing fresh or original about this, and the motorcycle racing is not as exciting as the photographer thinks it is. Only dyed-in-the-wool bike fanatics will enjoy the racing sequences. Otherwise, it's pretty slow going. Mallory, who plays a minor role, is the younger brother of actor Robert Mitchum.

p, Lewis J. Rachmil; d, Leon Barsha; w, DeVallon Scott, Robert Lee Johnson (based on a story by Scott and Johnson); ph, Frank Redman; ed, Samuel E. Beetley; md, C. Bakaleinikoff; art d, Albert S. D'Agostino, Walter E. Keller.

Action **(PR:C MPAA:NR)**

PACIFIC ADVENTURE*** (1947, Aus.) 62m COL bw (GB: SMITHY)

Ron Randell (*Sir Charles Kingsford Smith*), Muriel Steinbeck (*Lady M. Kingsford Smith*), John Tate (*Charles Ulm*), Joy Nichols (*Kay Sutton*), Nan Taylor (*Nan Kingsford Smith*), Alec Kellaway (*Capt. G. Allan Hancock*), John Dease (*Sir Hubert Wilkins*), Joe Volti (*Stringer*), Marshall Crosby (*Arthur Powell*), John Dunne (*Harold Kingsford Smith*), Edward Smith (*Beau Sheil*), Alan Herbert (*Tommy Pethybridge*), Rt. Hon. W.M. Hughes, Capt. P.G. Taylor, John Strannage (*Themselves*), C.J. Montgomery Jackson (*Warner*), Gundy Hill (*Lyon*), John Fleetwing.

This Australian feature is a biography of Sir Charles Kingsford Smith, one of that country's early aviators. Randell stars as the pioneer aviator who goes through various adventures. He makes the first round-Australia flight and then, backed by the government, flies across the Pacific Ocean in his airplane, the "Southern Cross." He later tries to start his own airline, but meets with adversity. Finally Randell attempts to win a British-Australian mail contract and disappears on the flight home from London. Also portrayed is Smith's romance with Steinbeck, whom he eventually marries. None of this is terribly exciting or well thought out. The script gives Randell no room to act, and he's not helped any by the weak direction. The supporting cast is mediocre, with Steinbeck utterly useless in her underdeveloped role. The photography's not bad, but there's a preponderance of stock airplane footage that's mixed into the film. The story is told in a documentary style that just doesn't pay off.

d, Ken G. Hall; w, John Chandler, Alec Coppel (based on the story "Smithy" by Hall, Max Afford); ph, George Heath; ed, Terry Banks, md, Henry Krips; art d, Alan Kenyon.

Biography **(PR:A MPAA:NR)**

PACIFIC BLACKOUT*½** (1942) 76m PAR bw

Robert Preston (*Robert Draper*), Martha O'Driscoll (*Mary Jones*), Philip Merivale (*John Ronnel*), Eva Gabor (*Marie Duval*), Louis Jean Heydt (*Kermin*), Thurston Hall (*William*), Mary Treen (*Irene*), J. Edward Bromberg (*Pickpocket*), Spencer Charters (*Night Watchman*).

An unspectacular WW II tale about a fugitive spy, Preston, and the girl he falls in love with, O'Driscoll, set during a West Coast blackout. The blackout is intended to be a practice run for U.S. bombers, but saboteurs try to carry out an actual attack. This film's box office prospects weren't helped by its poor timing—it was released just five short weeks after Pearl Harbor.

p, Sol C. Siegel; d, Ralph Murray; w, Lester Cole, W. F. Lipscomb (based on a story by Frank Spencer, Curt Siodmak).

War **(PR:A MPAA:NR)**

PACIFIC DESTINY**** (1956, Brit.) 97m BL c

Denholm Elliott (*Arthur Grimble*), Susan Stephen (*Olivia Grimble*), Felix Felton, Peter Bathurst, Clifford Buckton (*Uncles*), Michael Hordern (*Resident Commissioner*), Gordon Jackson (*District Officer*), Inia Te Wiata (*Tauvela*), Henrietta Godinet (*Lama*), Ollie Crichton (*Taloa*), Hans Kruse (*Kitiona*), Moira MacDonald (*Voice-of-the-Tide*), Rosie Leavasa (*Sea-Wind*), Sani (*King's-Bundle-of-Mats*), Fiti (*Grandmother*), John Bryce (*Tulo*), Ezra Williams (*Tiki-Tiku*), Tulletefuga (*Matangi*), Aft Kalapu (*Teraloa*), Overlau Beruta (*Fa' afetai*), Cecilia Fabricious (*Movement-of-Clouds*), Polo (*Fa'alavelave*), Tusa (*Prisoner*), Noa (*Warder*).

Elliott stars in the story of the true-life adventures of a man who served as a British colonial officer in the South Seas. At the urgings of his uncles (Felton, Bathurst, and Buckton) Elliott takes his young wife (Stephen) and heads to Samoa for his first assignment. There he must deal with the resident commissioner (Hordern), a man who is not easily pleased. Elliott is constantly in trouble with his supervisor and is consigned to a smaller island. Elliott regards this as a sign of failure and decides to quit. However, Stephen refuses to let her husband give up so easily and encourages him to accept his new assignment as a challenge. Elliott comes around and finally proves himself in the new post. The Cinemascope photography of the Samoan locations is often stunning, the best part of an otherwise boring film. There's little in the way of action, and far too much dialog. Plot development is sluggish and predictable. Elliott does his best and delivers an earnest characterization, and Hordern's performance is right on the money in a good (though stereotyped) comic role. But these assets just aren't enough to overcome the fact that this is a routine and boring story with a pretty picture backdrop. PACIFIC DESTINY was the first independent feature by producer Lawrie. He had previously worked with the National Film Finance Corporation (of England) as managing director before making the switch to independent filmmaking.

p, James H. Lawrie; d, Wolf Rilla; w, Richard Mason (based on the autobiography *A Pattern of Islands* by Sir Arthur Grimble); ph, Martin Curtis (Cinemascope, Eastmancolor); m, James Bernard; ed, John Trumper.

Drama **(PR:A MPAA:NR)**

PACIFIC LINER**** (1939) 76m RKO bw

Victor McLaglen (*Crusher McKay*), Chester Morris (*Dr. Craig*), Wendy Barrie (*Ann Grayson*), Alan Hale (*Gallagher*), Barry Fitzgerald (*Britches*), Allan Lane (*Bilson*), Halliwell Hobbes (*Captain Mathews*), Cyrus W. Kendall (*Deadeyes*), Paul Guilfoyle (*Wishart*), John Wray (*Metcalfe*), Emory Parnell (*Olaf*), Adia Kuznetzoff (*Silvio*), John Bleifer (*Kovac*).

This programmer was a fairly gloomy story. An ocean liner bound for San Francisco from Shanghai is thrown into turmoil when one of its passengers proves to have cholera. People drop like flies (and oh so dramatically!) until McLaglen, the chief engineer, begins an investigation. Morris and Barrie are the ship's doctor and nurse, who find themselves working overtime. There are some unusual scenes for a cheap film like this, including bodies being burned in the ship's furnace. The cast is a tight ensemble, but they were much better than this film deserved. The direction tells the story with good straightforward action but can't overcome the morbid tone. However, this film was successful and proved to be a moneymaker for the studio.

p, Robert Sisk; d, Lew Landers; w, John Twist (based on a story by Anthony Coldeway, Henry Roberts Symonds); ph, Nicholas Musuraca; ed, Harry Marker; md, Russell Bennett; cos, Edward Stevenson.

Drama **(PR:C MPAA:NR)**

PACIFIC RENDEZVOUS** (1942) 75m MGM bw

Lee Bowman (Lt. Bill Gordon), Jean Rogers (Elaine Carter), Mona Maris (Olivia Kerlov), Carl Esmond (Andre Leemuth), Paul Cavanagh (Comdr. Brennan), Blanche Yurka (Mrs. Savarina), Russell Hicks (John Carter), Arthur Shields (Prof. Harvey Lessmore), William Post, Jr. (Lanny), William Tannen (Jasper Dean), Frederic Worlock (Dr. Jackwin), Curt Bois (Kestrin), Felix Basch (Dr. Segroff), Addison Richards (Gordon Trisby), Edward Fielding (Secretary of Navy), William Roberts (Operator), Hans Von Morhart (German Operator), Frances Carson (Mrs. Hendricks), Michael Visaroff (Col. Petroff), Edward Earle (Dr. Jackwin's Assistant), Grace Lem (Japanese Woman), Arno Frey (German), Syd Saylor (Navy Recruiting Officer), Tex Brodus (Officer), George Lollier (Marine), Hal Cooke (Orderly), Byron Foulger (Drum Man), Pat O'Malley (Ship's Captain), Phil Tead (Taxi Driver), George Carleton (Chaplain), Gayne Whitman (Barini), James Warren (FBI Agent), Bill Nind (Waiter), Milburn Stone (Clerk), Hans Conried (Bellboy), J. Anthony Hughes (Pat Riley), Louis Arco (Assistant German), Henry Rowland (Elevator Boy), Alphonse Martell (Stronskoff), Joyce Bryant (Girl), Eddie Lee, Tommy Lee (Japanese).

Bowman is a Navy code expert assigned to intelligence, but really wants to see action. He has a romance with Rogers, a flighty and silly woman. Bowman finally has his day when his talents help him crack an espionage ring. This is a minor film at best with weak plot development and trite dialog. It was a remake of the much better RENDEZVOUS, this time set one great war later. The production values are standard with okay performances by the leads.

p, B.F. Zeidman; d, George Sidney; w, Harry Kurnitz, P.J. Wolfson, George Oppenheimer; ph, Paul Vogel; m, David Snell; ed, Ben Lewis; art d, Cedric Gibbons; cos, Robert Kalloch.

War   (PR:A MPAA:NR)

PACK, THE**½ (1977) 99m WB c (AKA: THE LONG DARK NIGHT)

Joe Don Baker (Jerry), Hope Alexander-Willis (Millie), Richard B. Shull (Hardiman), R.G. Armstrong (Cobb), Ned Wertimer (Walker), Bibi Besch (Marge), Delos V. Smith, Jr. (McMinnimee), Richard O'Brien (Dodge), Sherry Miles (Lois), Paul Wilson (Tommy), Eric Knight (Guy), Steve Lytle (Paul), Rob Narke (Husband), Peggy Price (Wife), Steve Butts (Bobby).

A group of abandoned dogs band together on a small vacation island. They revert to their natural state and become a vicious pack of killer beasts. Baker is a marine biologist who leads the humans in their fight against the wild animals. This could easily have turned into a JAWS rip-off but instead is a nicely handled little horror piece. Lighting and editing are used to their best advantage, creating a creeping terror that mounts to the cataclysmic climax. The violence is never gratuitous, and it's kept within a range that's reasonable yet still frightening. This was made with the cooperation of the American Humane Society, which oversaw the treatment of the animals. The intelligent direction builds tension and the overall product is a cut above other films of this nature.

p, Fred Weintraub, Paul Heller; d&w, Robert Clouse (based on the novel by Dave Fisher); ph, Ralph Woolsey (Technicolor); m, Lee Holdridge; ed, Peter E. Berger; cos, Lynn Bernay.

Horror/Action   Cas.   (PR:O MPAA:R)

PACK TRAIN** (1953) 57m COL bw

Gene Autry (Himself), Smiley Burnette (Himself), Gail Davis (Jennifer Coleman), Kenne Duncan (Ross McLain), Sheila Ryan (Lola Riker), Tom London (Dan Coleman), Harry Lauter (Roy Wade), Melinda Plowman (Judy), B.G. Norman (Ted), Louise Lorimer, Frankie Marvin, Norman E. Westcoatt, Tex Terry, Wesley Hudman, Kermit Maynard, Frank Ellis, Frank O'Connor, Dick Alexander, Jill Zeller, Herman Hack, Champion the Horse.

Autry goes through his stock numbers in this average and unexciting piece. Duncan and Ryan are the heavies who are selling supplies to settlers at outrageous prices. Autry attempts to get supplies to the people and is trailed by the angry outlaws. There's a climactic gun battle, and naturally Autry comes out on top. He also finds time to sing "God's Little Candles" and "Wagon Train" in between the adventures. Burnette has a few good moments of comedy and his own song "Hominy Grits."

p, Armand Schaefer; d, George Archainbaud; w, Norman S. Hall; ph, William Bradford (Sepiatone); ed, James Sweeney; art d, George Brooks; m/l, Jimmy Kennedy, Gene Autry, Smiley Burnette.

Western   (PR:A MPAA:NR)

PACK UP YOUR TROUBLES**½ (1932) 68m MGM bw

Stan Laurel (Himself), Oliver Hardy (Himself), Tom Kennedy (Recruiting Sergeant), Grady Sutton (Eddie the Groom), Donald Dillaway (Eddie Smith), Jacquie Lyn (Eddie's Baby), Mary Carr (Woman), Billy Gilbert (Mr. Hathaway), C. Montague Shaw (Groom's Father), Muriel Evans (The Bride), James Finlayson (The General), Al Hallet, Bill O'Brien (Butlers), Mary Gordon (Mrs. MacTavish), Lew Kelly (Saunders the Bank Guard), Frank Brownlee (Irascible Drill Sergeant), George Marshall (Pierre the Army Post Cook), Charley Rogers (Rogers the Butler), Frank Rice (Parkins the Butler), James C. Morton, Gene Morgan, James Mason (Police Officers), Charles Dorety (Passerby), Charles Middleton, Nora Cecil (Officers in the Eastside Welfare Association), Jack Hill (New Recruit/Pedestrian), Ham Kinsey (Man who Delivers Telegram/Doughboy), Dorothy Layton (Bridesmaid), Charley Young (Crowd Extra), Marvin Hatley, Ben Hendricks, Jr., Pat Harmon, Bud Fine, Frank S. Hagney, Bob "Mazooka" O'Conor, Pete Gordon, Baldwin Cooke (Doughboys), Henry Hall (Drill Soldier), Ellinor Van Der Veer (Unperturbed Society Matron), Charlie Hall (Man), Robert Emmett Homans (Detective), George Miller, Chet Brandenberg (Street Extras), Richard Tucker (Bank President), Rychard [Richard] Cramer (Uncle Jack), Adele Watson (Uncle Jack's Wife Annie), Dick Gilbert (Jerry, Grubby Friend of Cramer).

Filmed the same year as the first Laurel and Hardy feature PARDON US (1931),

this follow-up was held from release until the following year while their money-making debut continued to rake in profits. For their second film the duo turned to an easy comic target—the Army. They play a couple of WW I recruits who experience nothing but trouble while trying to serve their country. They pal around with Dillaway, who makes them promise to look after his daughter, Lyn, if he should not return from the war. When Dillaway is killed, Laurel and Hardy heed his wish and take the darling 3-year-old away from her miscreant foster parents. They then begin a seemingly fruitless search for the girl's grandfather, whose name is Smith. To make their search even more difficult, they do not know the grandfather's first name. They peruse the phone book but have no luck. Laurel, on a hunch, travels to Poughkeepsie in search of the mysterious "Smith." When Hardy questions the trip, Laurel replies, "I went all the way to Poughkeepsie and this ain't them" as he holds out a box of Smith Brothers cough drops. Another lead has them attending a boxing match between Steamboat Smith and Kid McCarey (a play on the codirectorial credit given to Ray McCarey). When Hardy informs the brutish boxer that they have his granddaughter, he angrily responds "Blackmail, eh?" and belts Hardy in the jaw. Barely surviving on the meager profits of their lunch wagon, Laurel, Hardy, and Lyn decide to try their luck at requesting a bank loan. It turns out, coincidentally, that the banker, Tucker, is Lyn's grandfather. Extending his gratitude to the duo, Tucker invites Laurel and Hardy to his luxurious mansion for dinner. Before they can eat, however, the cook recognizes them as enemies from their days at the Army training camp and chases them out of the house. While not as funny as PARDON US, PACK UP YOUR TROUBLES does benefit from a somewhat more cohesive story line. Basically, PACK UP YOUR TROUBLES is a collection of humorous skits (the first half hour in the Army is only vaguely connected to the latter search). The funniest moment in the film's early half is when Laurel and Hardy are told by the Army cook (played wonderfully by director Marshall) to collect the garbage. When they ask what they should do with it, Marshall sarcastically responds, "Take it to the general." A confused Laurel asks his hefty pal, "What do you suppose the general wants with it?" To which Hardy replies, "There you go asking questions again. When will you learn to follow Army curriculum? If the General wants it he can have it." They then proceed to fill up the General's office with garbage. An even funnier moment occurs later when Laurel gives in to Lyn's wish for a bedtime story. Before long, Lyn has taken over the storytelling and has put Laurel into a sound sleep. Curiously, this scene was to have been played with Hardy in Laurel's role before Hardy suggested the change. Roach, the film's producer, had discovered the charismatic 3-year-old Lyn in England and subsequently made great use of her in his "Our Gang" comedy shorts. Although a codirector credit is given on PACK UP YOUR TROUBLES, Marshall reportedly was the sole man at the helm. McCarey, a veteran of Hal Roach shorts for the "Our Gang" series, "Charlie Chase" series, and Laurel and Hardy (as well as being the brother of Leo), is said to have been the chief gag writer.

p, Hal Roach; d, George Marshall, Raymond McCarey; w, H.M. Walker; ph, Art Lloyd; m, LeRoy Shield, Marvin Hatley; ed, Richard Currier.

Comedy   Cas.   (PR:AAA MPAA:NR)

PACK UP YOUR TROUBLES*** (1939) 75m FOX bw (GB: WE'RE IN THE ARMY NOW)

Jane Withers (Colette), The Ritz Brothers (Themselves), Lynn Bari (Yvonne), Joseph Schildkraut (Hugo Ludwig), Stanley Fields (Sgt. "Angel Face" Walker), Fritz Leiber (Pierre Ferrand), Lionel Royce (Gen. Von Boech), Georges Renavent (Colonel Giraud), Adrienne d'Ambricourt (Mme. Marchand), Leon Ames (Adjutant), William Von Brincken (Mueller), Ed Gargan (Sentry), Robert Emmett Keane (Kane), Henry Victor (Col. Schlager).

During WW I the zany Ritzes audition their new act for an agent. Unfortunately, the humor relies on German accents, and the boys bomb. They join the army and are sent to France to become mule skinners. They meet Withers, the American daughter of a French officer (Schildkraut). Mishaps occur when they are mistaken for German spies by some French soldiers. The Ritzes escape by balloon and end up in Germany. Somehow they make their way back to France, bringing with them a captured German general. This vehicle for the Ritz's talents was good fun and a lot of laughs, though just about every gag is forgotten as soon as the picture's over. Withers does a nice job with her part, beginning to make the transition from kid star to teen actress. After attending the premiere of this film, Harry Ritz walked out of the theater with his brothers and then turned to them and said: "Boys, we've gone from bad to Wurtzel!" The remark, of course, summed up Harry Ritz's estimate of the film's producer.

p, Sol M. Wurtzel; d, H. Bruce Humberstone; w, Lou Breslow, Owen Francis (based on a story by Breslow, Francis); ph, Lucien Andriot; ed, Nick De Maggio; md, Samuel Kaylin; art d, Richard Day, Albert Hogsett; cos, Helen A. Myron; m/l, "Who'll Buy My Flowers," Sidney Clare, Jule Styne (sung by Jane Withers).

Comedy   (PR:AA MPAA:NR)

PACK UP YOUR TROUBLES** (1940, Brit.) 75m BUT bw

Reginald Purdell (Tommy Perkins), Wylie Watson (Eric Sampson), Patricia Roc (Sally Brown), Wally Patch (Sgt. Barker), Muriel George (Mrs. Perkins), Ernest Butcher (Jack Perkins), Manning Whiley (Muller), G. H. Mulcaster (Col. Diehard), Meinhart Maur, Leonie Lamartine, Yvonne Andre.

Garage-owner Purdell and his ventriloquist buddy, Watson, join the army and go to France where they are promptly captured by the Germans. Using Watson's voice-throwing skills, they manage to overpower the camp commandant and a Gestapo man and return home. Lightweight comedy worth watching for Purdell and Watson's nice comic performances.

p, F.W. Baker; d, Oswald Mitchell; w, Reginald Purdell, Milton Hayward (based on a story by Con West); ph, Geoffrey Faithfull; m/l, "Beer Barrel Polka," Jaromir Vejvoda, Lew Brown, "Pack Up Your Troubles," "Goodbye Sally."

Comedy   (PR:A MPAA:NR)

PAD, THE. . .(AND HOW TO USE IT)* (1966, Brit.) 86m UNIV c

Brian Bedford (Bob Handman), Julie Sommars (Doreen Marshall), James Farentino (Ted), Edy Williams (Lavinia), Nick Navarro (Beatnik), Pearl Shear (Fat Woman on the Bus), Barbara London (Waitress), Barbara Reid (Girl on the Phone), Roger Bacon (Larry), Don Conreaux (Ralph).

There are a few funny moments in this farce, but mostly it's a cheap and insensitive film. It's based on a romantic one-act play by Peter Shaffer (author of "Equus" and "Amadeus") that explored the feelings of a shy and lonely man. In the hands of director Hutton, it turned into a free-wheeling comedy with a title designed to hook the audiences of THE KNACK. . .(AND HOW TO GET IT). Bedford plays a shy classical music lover who meets Sommars at a Mozart concert when he accidentally spills some pop on her. He apologizes and invites her to dinner at his place. But Bedford panics before the date and goes to his swinging pal Farentino for advice. Farentino coaches Bedford in the ways of the ultra-hip. When Sommars comes over she's fascinated with Farentino and all but ignores Bedford, who gets drunk and then argues with his pal. Farentino splits and Bedford puts on "Madama Butterfly" in order to make the mood more romantic. He makes an awkward pass at Sommars but she declines and leaves with Farentino's phone number. Bedford is doomed to remain eternally lonely. The setting for the story was changed from London to L.A., though Bedford (who originated the role on stage) kept his British accent. Location work was done at the famed Whiskey-A-Go-Go, where a number of famed rock groups got their start. As comedy, the film is passable, and the actors aren't bad. However, the farcical treatment just doesn't seem right, and Bedford's unhappy ending is out of place. What should have been a sensitive comedy is ultimately a travesty.

p, Ross Hunter; d, Brian G. Hutton; w, Thomas C. Ryan, Ben Starr (based on "The Private Ear" a one-act play by Peter Shaffer); ph, Ellsworth Fredricks (Techniscope, Technicolor); m, Russ Garcia; ed, Milton Carruth; art d, Alexander Golitzen, George Webb; set d, John McCarthy, George H. Henshaw; cos, Rosemary Odell; m/l, "The Pad (And How to Use It)," Robert Allen (sung by The Knickerbockers); makeup, Bud Westmore.

Comedy (PR:O MPAA:NR)

PADDY*** (1970, Irish) 97m Dun Laoghaire/AA c (AKA:GOODBYE TO THE HILL)

Milo O'Shea (Harry Redmond), Des Cave (Paddy Maguire), Dearbhla Molloy (Maureen), Maureen Toal (Mrs. Kearney), Peggy Cass (Irenee), Judy Cornwell (Breeda), Donal LeBlanc (Larry Maguire), Lillian Rapple (Mrs. Doyle), Desmond Perry (Cahill), Maire O'Donnell (Mrs. Maguire), Vincent Smith (Billy Maguire), Ita Darcy (Josie Maguire), Desmond Walter Ellis (Butcher's Apprentice), Dominic Roche (Duncan Stuart), Clive Geraghty (Tony Deugan), Alec Doran (Graveyard Priest), Mary Larkin (Liz O'Boyle), Pat Layde (Mr. Hayes), John Kavanagh (Willie Egan), John Molloy (Watchbox), Bill Foley (Priest), Brendan Dunne (Barney), Mary Jo Kennedy (Mary), Mark Mulholland (Jack Sloan), Danny Cummins (Taxi Driver).

Cave is a butcher boy who works to support his family. Their father has run out on them and he's ready to do the same, irked by their constant nagging and complaining. With the encouragement of his drinking pal O'Shea, Cave sets out on a series of amorous adventures. He has an affair with Toal (O'Shea's real-life wife), a lively widow who frequents the butcher shop. He becomes her paramour, then leaves her for a job with an insurance firm. There he gets involved with Molloy, a secretary. He also has an affair with Cornwell, a fiery woman who prefers a menage a trois. His younger brother dies, and Cave feels some remorse. His problems are compounded when Molloy announces that she is pregnant but intends to marry another because Cave is too irresponsible. He is consoled by O'Shea, who has taken up with Cass, an American tourist visiting Dublin. This film was made on a limited budget and though it suffers from financial limitations, PADDY is a gentle, charming comedy. The lighting is poorly done and the sound often amateurish, but Cave's amiable performance more than atones for these problems. The dialog is a delight, full of clever understatements. "I've got a feelin' Mrs. Kearney's not a virgin," claims the astonished lad as Toal seduces him. Cave and most of the supporting cast are veterans of Ireland's Abbey Theater. Their past work together has made them a tight ensemble whose members know how to play off one another with ease.

p, Tamara Asseyev; d, Daniel Haller; w, Lee Dunne (based on his novel Goodbye to the Hill); ph, Daniel Lacambre (Eastmancolor); m, John Rubenstein; ed, Christopher Holmes; set d, Tim Booth; m/l, "Paddy," John Rubenstein, David Colloff (sung by Emmy Lou Harris), "Maureen," Rubenstein, Stephen Michaels (sung by The Happenings), "Oop Oomp Ee Doo," Rubenstein, Colloff.

Comedy (PR:O MPAA:GP)

PADDY O'DAY*** (1935) 73m FOX bw

Jane Withers (Paddy O'Day), Rita Cansino [Hayworth] (Tamara Petrovitch), Pinky Tomlin (Roy Ford), Jane Darwell (Dora), Michael S. Visaroff (Popushka Petrovitch), Nina Visaroff (Momushka Petrovitch), Vera Lewis (Aunt Flora Ford), Louise Carter (Aunt Jane Ford), Russell Simpson (Benton, Butler), Francis Ford (Immigration Officer), Pat O'Malley (Wilson), Robert Dudley (Chauffeur), Selmer Jackson, Ruth Clifford, Larry Steers (First Class Passengers), Harvey Clark (Ship's Doctor), Jessie Pringle, Evelyn Selvie (Immigrant Women), Myra Marsh (Matron), Jane Keckley (Maid), Tommy Bupp, Sherwood Bailey, Harry Watson (Street Boys), Russ Clark (New York Traffic Policeman), Larry Fisher (Truck Driver), Hal K. Dawson (Motorist), Egon Brecher, Leonid Snegoff, Demetrius Alexis (Russian Musicians), Clarence H. Wilson (Brewster), Richard Powell (Taxi Driver), George Givot (Mischa).

This was a vehicle designed specifically to fit the talents of child star Withers. She plays a young Irish immigrant who's come to America in search of her mother. She escapes from immigration authorities with the help of a Russian dancer (Cansino)

and gets to the house where she believes her mother works as a cook. Unfortunately, her mother has died, leaving Withers an orphan in the storm. Tomlin is a boarder at the house who's charmed by the girl's talents and agrees to help her. Problems arise when the girl's two spinster aunts (Lewis and Carter) try to gain custody of her. But Tomlin marries Withers' friend Cansino and the couple adopts the little girl. Of course there's plenty of opportunity for Withers to strut her musical stuff as she sings and dances to the tunes "Keep the Twinkle in Your Eye" (Sidney Clare, Edward Eliscu, Harry Akst) and "Changing My Ambition" (Pinky Tomlin). For what it is, the film is enjoyable and not overly saccharine. Withers handles the turns from comedy to drama like a seasoned pro (which she was). Cansino later changed her name and achieved stardom as Rita Hayworth. She was cast in this film by Winfield Sheehan, the vice president of Fox. She had been his discovery and he was determined that she would become a star. He was going to use PADDY O'DAY to prove that Cansino could handle herself in a meaty role and thereby justify his decision to cast her in a Technicolor remake of RAMONA. But it was her bad luck to be involved with the Fox Studios just when it was merging with Twentieth Century. The new president, Darryl F. Zanuck, did not agree with Sheehan about Cansino's talents. He cast Loretta Young in RAMONA and stuck Cansino in a minor role in A MESSAGE TO GARCIA with Barbara Stanwyck. But after the preview Cansino's footage was cut altogether and she was dropped from the studio's payroll. A few years and one name change later, Zanuck came to regret his decision. Additional song: "I Like a Balalaika" (Clare, Eliscu, Akst).

p, Sol M. Wurtzel; d, Lewis Seiler; w, Lou Breslow, Edward Eliscu; ph, Arthur Miller; ed, Alfred DeGaetano; md, Sammy Kaylin; cos, Helen A. Myron; ch, Fanchon; makeup, Ernest Westmore.

Musical Comedy (PR:A MPAA:NR)

PADDY, THE NEXT BEST THING*** (1933) 75m FOX bw

Janet Gaynor (Paddy Adair), Warner Baxter (Lawrence Blake), Walter Connolly (Maj. Adair), Harvey Stephens (Jack Breen), Margaret Lindsay (Eileen Adair), Mary McCormick (Herself), Joseph M. Kerrigan (Collins), Fiske O'Hara (Mr. Davy), Merle Tottenham (Maid), Roger Imhof (Micky), Trevor Bland (Sellaby), Claire McDowell (Miss Breen).

This is a simplistic, amiable comedy about the problems of an Irish family. Connolly is an impoverished landowner with two daughters. He insists that the elder (Lindsay) marry local rich man Baxter. The money will help Connolly and he'll have one less daughter to worry about. But Lindsay loves Stephens and is caught in a quandary. Leave it to her tomboy sister (Gaynor) to save the day. Gaynor busts up the budding romance and wins Baxter for herself. Gaynor is an utter delight, making this marshmallow-soft story work. The locales are nicely used and there's some fine Irish music on the soundtrack.

d, Harry Lachman; w, Edwin Burke (based on the novel by Gertrude Page); ph, John Seitz.

Comedy (PR:A MPAA:NR)

PADRE PADRONE***½ (1977, Ital.) 114m Radio Italiano/Cinema V c (AKA: FATHER MASTER; MY FATHER, MY MASTER)

Omero Antonutti (Gavino's Father), Saverio Marconi (Gavino), Marcella Michelangeli (Gavino's Mother), Fabrizio Forte (Gavino as a Child), Marino Cenna (Servant/Shepherd), Stanko Molnar (Sebastiano), Nanni Moretti (Cesare).

This is a simple story about a boy's growth to manhood under the despotism of his patriarchal father. At age six, Forte is pulled out of school and taken by his father, Antonutti, into the mountains to become a sheepherder. Antonutti tries to control his son's life in every respect, with a comportment bordering on the sadistic. As the boy grows to manhood, he discovers things for himself and rebels against his father's authority. Marconi, playing the adolescent, enlists in the army to escape Antonutti's rule. His contact with people and sudden wealth of experiences change him for the better. The denouement finds Marconi meeting his father once more, finding him an embittered, pathetic individual. Originally filmed by the Taviani brothers for Italian television, the work is a fine example of letting a strong ensemble tell a story naturally without intrusion by the directors. Using both professional actors as well as local people from the Sardinian countryside, the story of the virtual imprisonment of young Sardinians by the sheep and pastures of their land unfolds simply and yet with great power. Winner of the grand prize at the Cannes Film Festival of 1977, the tale is based in truth. The real-life model for the film went through a similar experience before escaping at age 20, going on to become a linguistics professor, and writing a book about his experiences. (In Italian; English subtitles.)

p, Giuliani De Negri; d&w, Paolo and Vittorio Taviani (based on a book by Gavino Ledda); ph, Mario Masini (Eastmancolor); m, Egisto Macchi; ed, Roberto Perpignani; art d, Giovanni Sbarra; English subtitles, Paolo, Vittorio Taviani.

Drama Cas. (PR:C MPAA:NR)

PAGAN, THE**½ (1929) 83m MGM bw

Ramon Novarro (Henry Shoesmith, Jr.), Renee Adoree (Madge), Donald Crisp (Henry Slater), Dorothy Janis (Tito).

Novarro is a singing Polynesian storekeeper in this part-talkie romance which thrilled audiences who were itching to see the star's bare chest. He falls for Janis, an island girl who is taken away by the lecherous Crisp. When Crisp tries to force her into marriage, Novarro defends her and hauls her off to his mountain home.

Romance/Drama (PR:A-C MPAA:NR)

PAGAN HELLCAT (SEE: MAEVA, 1961)

PAGAN ISLAND** (1961) 67m Cinema Syndicate/Century bw

Edward Dew (Stanton), Nani Maka ("Princess" Nani Maka).

Dew finds himself shipwrecked on an island populated only by women, which might seem like paradise for any man. But after a feast in his honor, the women take him prisoner and set him out in the sun to die. It seems the women have despised all men ever since a group of pirates raped them and destroyed the underwater temple of their sea god. Maka, the young woman who is to be sacrificed to the sea god, saves Dew, and they fall in love. They escape on the day appointed for the sacrifice and find the temple of the sea god and three chests full of treasure. Maka is killed by a giant clam as they leave the ruins of the temple, and Dew is eventually picked up by a schooner. The underwater sequences in the film were shot at the Seaquarium in Miami, Fla.

p&d, Barry Mahon; w, Clelle Mahon; ph, Mark Dennis (Movielab Color); makeup, Richard Kereszi.

Adventure (PR:A MPAA:NR)

PAGAN LADY*
(1931) 70m COL bw

Evelyn Brent (Dut Hunter), Conrad Nagel (Ernest Todd), Charles Bickford (Dingo Mike), Roland Young (Dr. Heath), William Farnum (Mal Todd), Lucille Gleason (Nellie), Leslie Fenton (Jerry Willis), Gwen Lee (Gwen Willis), Wallace MacDonald (Francisco).

Nagel is a nice boy, the nephew of an evangelist. He meets up with Brent, a "pagan lady." Of course she steers the sweet young thing astray and his life is ruined. Aside from a terrific storm sequence, there's really not much to recommend in this turgid, insipid RAIN rip-off. Brent looks too angelic for her part and Nagel's acting is a joke. The script is full of hokey dialog and the director apparently gave up about halfway through the film. It's not helped any by the mediocre photography.

d, John Francis Dillon; w, Benjamin Glazer (based on the play by William DuBois); ph, Norbert Brodine, Gus Peterson; ed, Vi Lawrence.

Drama (PR:A MPAA:NR)

PAGAN LOVE SONG**
(1950) 76m MGM c

Esther Williams (Mimi Bennett), Howard Keel (Hazard Endicott), Minna Gombell (Kate Bennett), Charles Mauu (Tavae), Rita Moreno (Terru), Philip Costa (Manu), Dione Leilani (Tani), Charles Freund (Papera), Marcella Corday (Countess Mariani), Sam Maikai (Tua), Helen Rapoza (Angele), Birdie DeBolt (Mama Ruau), Bill Kaliloa (Mata), Carlo Cook (Mons. Bouchet).

Keel is an American schoolteacher who heads off for Tahiti to take over his late uncle's coconut plantation. There he meets Williams, another American whom he mistakes for an island native. He falls in love and goes out of his way to sweep her off her feet. He does this fairly successfully, to no one's surprise. The plot is as thin as they come and utter hokum. The only consolation is when Williams performs one of her patented water ballets, nicely choreographed with some good underwater photography. But that's about it for entertainment. Producer Freed normally had high production values which gave his work an artistic quality, but he let everything slide in this bomb. Freed helped pen the song lyrics and used a 1929 composition of his for the title tune. The lifeless direction was by Alton, who was better known for choreography. He went back to that trade shortly after finishing this film. Originally Freed had contracted the great Stanley Donen as director, but he was replaced when Williams refused to work with him.

p, Arthur Freed; d, Robert Alton; w, Robert Nathan, Jerry Davis (based on the book Tahiti Landfall by William S. Stone); ph, Charles Rosher (Technicolor); ed, Adrienne Fazan; md, Adolph Deutsch; art d, Cedric Gibbons, Randall Duell; set d, Edwin B. Willis, Jack D. Moore; cos, Helen Rose; spec eff, A. Arnold Gillespie, Warren Newcombe; m/l, "The House of Singing Bamboo," "Singing in the Sun," "Etiquette," "Why is Love So Crazy," "Tahiti," "The Sea of the Moon," Harry Warren, Freed, Nacio Herb Brown, "Coconut Milk," "Pagan Love Song," Freed, Roger Edens; makeup, William J. Tuttle.

Musical (PR:A MPAA:NR)

PAGE MISS GLORY**½
(1935) 90m COS/WB bw

Marion Davies (Loretta Dalrymple/"Dawn Glory"), Pat O'Brien (Dan "Click" Wiley), Dick Powell (Bingo Nelson), Mary Astor (Gladys Russell), Frank McHugh (Ed Olsen), Lyle Talbot (Slattery of the Express), Patsy Kelly (Betty), Allen Jenkins (Petey), Barton MacLane (Blackie), Hobart Cavanaugh (Joe Bonner), Joseph Cawthorn (Mr. Freischultz), Al Shean (Mr. Hamburgher), Berton Churchill (Mr. Yates, Assistant Hotel Manager), Helen Lowell (Loretta's Mother), Lionel Stander (Nick Papadopolis), Mary Treen (Beauty Operator), Gavin Gordon (Metz), Edward Cooper (Doorman), John Quillan, Ernie Alexander (Bellboys), Emmett Vogan (Hotel Clerk), Claudia Coleman (Elaine), Charles Irwin (Staff Announcer), Jack Norton, Jack Mulhall, Gordon "Bill" Elliott (Reporters), Huntley Gordon (Radio Official), Rudy Cameron, Edward Keane (Advertising Men), Irving Bacon (Waiter), Franklyn Farnum (Dance Extra), Edward Hearn (Detective), Phil Tead (Announcer), Charles R. Moore (Porter), Pat West (Cabby), Jonathan Hale (Man in Railroad Station), Selmer Jackson (Radio Broadcaster), Joseph Crehan (Detective Chief), Harry Beresford (Kimball), E.E. Clive.

This is a mildly amusing comedy that pokes fun at beauty contests. O'Brien enters a composite picture into competition. To his surprise, he's the winner. He needs someone to front for him and hires Davies, a hotel chambermaid. She becomes America's sweetheart, and O'Brien watches out for her. It's good fun that's well-played and effectively directed. Makeup and lighting help nicely with Davies' transition from chambermaid to beauty queen. This was the first Cosmopolitan picture released through Warner Bros. Previously Cosmopolitan's boss (and Davies' lover) William Randolph Hearst had been handling his distribution through MGM. But he made a deal which shifted the distributor as well as Miss Davies' celebrated and expensive personal bungalow. This served as her makeup and changing room and made quite a sensation.

d, Mervyn LeRoy; w, Delmer Daves, Robert Lord (based on the play by Joseph

Schrank and Philip Dunning); ph, George Folsey; ed, William Clemens; md, Leo F. Forbstein; art d, Robert M. Haas; cos, Orry-Kelly; m/l, Harry Warren, Al Dubin.

Comedy (PR:A MPAA:NR)

PAGLIACCI
(SEE: CLOWN MUST LAUGH, A, 1936, Brit.)

PAI-SHE CHUAN
(SEE: MADAME WHITESNAKE, 1963, Hong Kong)

PAID***
(1930) 83m MGM bw (GB: WITHIN THE LAW)

Joan Crawford (Mary Turner), Robert Armstrong (Joe Garson), Marie Prevost (Agnes Lynch), Kent Douglass [Douglas Montgomery] (Bob Gilder), John Miljan (Inspector Burke), Purnell B. Pratt (Edward Gilder), Hale Hamilton (District Attorney Demarest), Polly Moran (Polly), Robert Emmett O'Connor (Cassidy), Tyrell Davis (Eddie Griggs), William Bakewell (Carney), George Cooper (Red), Gwen Lee (Bertha), Isabel Withers (Helen Morris).

Studio chief Thalberg's wife was scheduled to play in this adaptation of the successful play, but when she became pregnant Crawford talked him into letting her have the role. Filmed as a silent in 1917 with Alice Joyce, then again with Norma Talmadge in 1923 (both with the original title of WITHIN THE LAW), this talkie version was an improvement over those, mainly because of Crawford's dynamic presence. Crawford is an innocent department store employee who is sent to prison for a crime she did not commit. Her sentence is three years and while in the stir, she meets fellow inmates Prevost and Moran while she plots vengeance on the District Attorney who prosecuted her, Hamilton, and the wealthy store owner, Pratt, who testified mistakenly against her. After her release, Prevost takes her to meet Armstrong, a successful crook. Armstrong and his strong-arm aides have some crimes in mind but Crawford, fresh out of jail, thinks there may be safer ways to make some money than engaging in illegal activities. Crawford and Prevost get ancient, lonely and rich men to write them love letters, then take legal action for "breach of promise" and collect large sums under the guise of "heart balm," which was a popular trick in those days. The plot pays off and Crawford is riding high but her dreams of revenge are not forgotten. She meets Pratt's son, Douglass, and gets him to fall for her. They get married without Pratt's knowledge. Meanwhile, the cops, led by Miljan, spread the word that the "Mona Lisa" is not in Paris. Rather, it is secretly reposing in Pratt's mansion. This is a ruse to bring out Armstrong and entrap him into robbing the house where the law will be waiting. At the same time, Crawford is actually falling in love with her own husband. Armstrong leads his men in the robbery by tying up electrical company workers and wearing their uniforms. The cops nab the crooks and get the truth out of them. Crawford, who was not part of the scheme, is happy that she wasn't and decides that enough is enough. She has her revenge as well as a husband she adores. Some good suspense during the robbery and a crackerjack job by Crawford as she goes from a soft woman to a tough cookie then back to sweet as sugar again.

d, Sam Wood; w, Lucien Hubbard, Charles MacArthur (based on the play "Within the Law" by Bayard Veiller); ph, Charles Rosher; ed, Hugh Wynn; art d, Cedric Gibbons; cos, Adrian.

Crime/Love Story (PR:A MPAA:NR)

PAID IN ERROR**
(1938, Brit.) 68m COL bw

George Carney (Will Baker), Lillian Christine (Joan Atherton), Tom Helmore (Jimmy Randle), Marjorie Taylor (Penny Victor), Googie Withers (Jean Mason), Molly Hamley-Clifford (Mrs. Jenkins), Jonathan Field (Jonathan Green), Aubrey Mallalieu (George), Michael Ripper.

Down and out, Carney manages to get by day to day on the good graces of his landlady. When bank clerk Taylor makes an error in Carney's favor, he gleefully runs out to spend the money. Taylor's boy friend, Helmore, the chief cashier, tries to help recover the money to save his sweetie's job, which he manages to do after winning a bet. Silly comedy, but there are some occasional moments that are genuinely amusing.

p, George Smith; d, Maclean Rogers; w, Basil Mason, H.F. Maltby (based on a story by John Chancellor); ph, Geoffrey Faithfull.

Comedy (PR:A MPAA:NR)

PAID IN FULL**½
(1950) 105m PAR bw

Robert Cummings (Bill Prentice), Lizabeth Scott (Jane Langley), Diana Lynn (Nancy Langley), Eve Arden (Tommy Thompson), Ray Collins (Dr. Fredericks), Frank McHugh (Ben), Stanley Ridges (Dr. Winston), Louis Jean Heydt (Dr. Carter), John Bromfield (Dr. Clark), Kristine Miller (Miss Williams), Laura Elliot (Tina), Ida Moore (Dorothy), James Nolan (Charlie Malloy), Geraldine Wall (Miss Ames), Rolland Morris (Bunny Howard), Laura Lee Michel (Joanne), Jane Novak (Mrs. Fredericks), Carole Mathews (Model), Margaret Field (Joanne's Mother), Carol Channing (Mrs. Peters), Dorothy Adams (Emily Burroughs), Arlene Jenkins, Christine Cooper (Secretaries), Byron Barr (Man at Bar), Laura Elliott (Bridesmaid), Marie Blake (Tired Woman), Jimmie Dundee (Truck Driver), Gladys Blake (Talkative Woman), Douglas Spencer (Crib Man), Dewey Robinson (Diaper Man), Charles Bradstreet (Marc Hickman), Harry Cheshire (Minister).

Scott and Lynn play a pair of sisters in this soap opera aimed at female audiences of 1949. Scott is the older and more caring of the two while Lynn is an obnoxious and selfish brat. Though Scott loves Cummings, she realizes her sister also loves the man and so sacrifices her own feelings. Lynn has a child that Scott accidentally kills. Later Cummings divorces Lynn and marries Scott. She, too, becomes pregnant but is warned that childbirth will kill her. Scott decides to have the baby anyway and present it to Lynn and Cummings in restitution. This is a delightfully turgid melodrama full of catty behavior from Lynn. She and Scott are fine as the sisters. Direction milks the material for every last teardrop, resulting in a good waste of time. It's based on a true story published in Reader's Digest, but don't expect to see believable drama.

p, Hal B. Wallis; d, William Dieterle; w, Robert Blees, Charles Schnee (based on a story by Dr. Frederic M. Loomis); ph, Leo Tover; m, Walter Lang, Victor Young; ed, Warren Low; art d, Hans Dreier, Earl Hedrick.

Drama **(PR:A MPAA:NR)**

PAID TO DANCE* (1937) 55m COL bw (AKA: HARD TO HANDLE)

Don Terry *(William Dennis)*, Jacqueline Wells [Julie Bishop] *(Joan Bradley)*, Rita Hayworth *(Betty Morgan)*, Arthur Loft *(Jack Miranda)*, Paul Stanton *(Charles Kennedy)*, Paul Fix *(Nifty)*, Louise Stanley *(Phyllis Parker)*, Ralph Byrd *(Nickels Brown)*, Beatrice Curtis *(Frances Mitchell)*, Bess Flowers *(Suzy)*, Beatrice Blinn *(Lois)*, Jane Hamilton *(Evelyn)*, Dick Curtis *(Mike Givens)*, Al Herman *(Joe Krause)*, Thurston Hall *(Governor)*, John Gallaudet *(Barney Wilson)*, Horace MacMahon *(LaRue)*, George Lloyd *(Sanders)*, Ruth Hilliard *(Ruth Gregory)*, Ann Doran *(Rose Trevor)*, Bud Jamison *(Lieutenant of Police)*, Bill Irving *(Salesman)*, Eddie Fetherston *(Skipper)*, Edward LeSaint *(Magistrate)*, Ernest Wood *(Francine)*, Lee Prather *(McDonald)*, Jay Eaton, Stanley Mack, Ethan Laidlaw, Arthur Stuart Hull *(Dance Hall Customers)*, Georgie Cooper *(Mrs. Daniels)*, Edward Hearn *(Butler)*, Bill Lally, Dan Wolheim, Dick Rush, Bruce Mitchell *(Cops)*, George Lollier *(Sailor)*, Jack Cheatham *(Radio Cop)*, Bud McTaggart *(Newsboy)*, Edward Peil, Sr. *(Conductor)*, Walter Lawrence *(News Vendor)*, Nell Craig *(Woman)*, Harry Strang *(Attendant)*.

Silly movie that uses the "ten cents a dance" racket as a background for criminal action. Terry is a dick who finds out gangsters are hustling in on the poor dance hall girls. One of the girls (Wells, who later changed her name to Julie Bishop) is as pure as freshly fallen snow, and a romance ensues. Terry breaks the ring and all is righted. The film was quickly ground out to capitalize on Warner's MARKED WOMAN, a much better film dealing with gangsters and their abuses of women in small-time bars. This drama is pocketed with illogical scenes and characters who refer to events that have yet to occur. At one point a gangster picks up a telephone and, without benefit of dialing or operator assistance, he is magically in touch with his boss. The film is full of continuity problems as well, a reflection of its cheap production. Hayworth, who had just finished a leading role in THE GAME THAT KILLS, somehow got relegated to this trash in a supporting role. She would regain her stature and become a major star.

p, Ralph Cohn; d, Charles C. Coleman, Jr.; w, Robert E. Kent (based on a story by Leslie T. White); ph, George Meehan; ed, Byron Robinson; md, Morris Stoloff; art d, Stephen Goosson; cos, Robert Kalloch.

Drama **(PR:C MPAA:NR)**

PAID TO KILL** (1954, Brit.) 72m Hammer/Executive bw (GB: FIVE DAYS)

Dane Clark *(James Nevill)*, Thea Gregory *(Andrea Nevill)*, Paul Carpenter *(Paul Kirby)*, Cecile Chevreau *(Joan)*, Anthony Forwood *(Glanville)*, Howard Marion Crawford *(McGowan)*, Avis Scott *(Eileen)*, Peter Gawthorne *(Bowman)*, Charles Hawtrey *(Bill)*, Hugo Schuster, Leslie Wright, Martin Lawrence, Arthur Young.

Faced with total financial ruin, businessman Clark blackmails his pal Carpenter into murdering him within the next five days so wife Gregory will have some money from the insurance policy. However, Clark's situation unexpectedly changes and he desperately searches for his friend in order to stop the killing. After coming close to being killed several times, Clark learns his partner Forwood is in cahoots with Gregory to murder him. They have kidnapped Carpenter and framed him, but the two would-be killers end up shooting themselves. Had this been done with any style, the film could have been another DOUBLE INDEMNITY. However the script only gives perfunctory scenes and motivations, which isn't helped any by the spotty talents of the cast.

p, Anthony Hinds; d, Montgomery Tully; w, Paul Tabori; ph, Jimmy Harvey; m, Ivor Slaney; ed, James Needs; art d, J. Elder Wills.

Crime **(PR:C MPAA:NR)**

PAINT YOUR WAGON** (1969) 166m PAR c

Lee Marvin *(Ben Rumson)*, Clint Eastwood *(Pardner)*, Jean Seberg *(Elizabeth)*, Harve Presnell *(Rotten Luck Willie)*, Ray Walston *(Mad Jack Duncan)*, Tom Ligon *(Horton Fenty)*, Alan Dexter *(Parson)*, William O'Connell *(Horace Tabor)*, Ben Baker *(Haywood Holbrook)*, Alan Baxter *(Mr. Fenty)*, Paula Trueman *(Mrs. Fenty)*, Robert Easton *(Atwell)*, Geoffrey Norman *(Foster)*, H.B. Haggerty *(Steve Bull)*, Terry Jenkins *(Joe Mooney)*, Karl Bruck *(Schermerhorn)*, John Mitchum *(Jacob Woodling)*, Sue Casey *(Sarah Woodling)*, Eddie Little Sky *(Indian)*, Harvey Parry *(Higgins)*, H.W. Gim *(Wong)*, William Mims *(Frock-Coated Man)*, Roy Jenson *(Hennessey)*, Pat Hawley *(Clendennon)*, The Nitty Gritty Dirt Band.

PAINT YOUR WAGON was not as awful as it was painted by the critics. Then again, how could it be? Never before had a "major" musical been so savaged by quills dipped in arsenic. It cost $20 million to make and didn't come close to recovering the outlay. Not that much of the money is seen on screen because there was more waste making this picture than the Pentagon is usually guilty of. The original play script was altered greatly by Chayefsky but even his touch couldn't baste this turkey. On Broadway, it had never been a real blockbuster hit, opening in November, 1951, and playing less than a year. The play starred James Barton, Olga San Juan, James Mitchell, Kay Medford and Tony Bavaar, and it went through several hands until Paramount made the mistake of filming it. Jack Warner thought Doris Day might be a good star, then backed off. For a while, Paramount considered it for Crosby and then Louis Mayer bought the rights after he'd left MGM, but he died in 1957 before he could put it before the cameras. Had he lived long enough to make the movie, it probably would have killed him. When THE SOUND OF MUSIC reaped a huge bonanza, Hollywood thought America wanted to see musicals. They were right, up to a point. America wanted to see *good* musicals and PAINT YOUR WAGON just wasn't that good. On paper, it looked as though it should have worked. A successful screenwriter-producer, Lerner, a big time Broadway and Hollywood director, Logan, plus three stars with some box office drawing power, Marvin, Eastwood, and Seberg. But movies are made on film, not paper, and therein lay the rub. Not only was the play's simplistic story tossed out, several of Loewe's tunes went the same way and Andre Previn was brought in, with Loewe's okay, to write some new melodies to Lerner's lyrics. Marvin and Eastwood are two California prospectors during the Gold Rush of 1849-50. They are sort of the western version of "The Odd Couple" with Eastwood as the calm, cool and restrained partner to drunken, noisy and rambunctious Marvin, in a role not unlike the one he did in CAT BALLOU. They search for gold and Marvin expresses the desire to have a wife of his own. A local Mormon is finding it tough to support both his wives so he sells one of them, Seberg, to Marvin for $800. There are very few women in the area and Marvin knows that she will become a target for the lonely miners. In order to make sure they'll leave Seberg be, Marvin hijacks a wagonload of hookers and takes them to the randy prospectors, just to get them off Seberg's case. The prostitutes are put up at Presnell's local hotel/bar and all seems well. Marvin has been away on this caper and while gone, Eastwood and Seberg discover there's a lot to like about the other, so when Marvin returns, he goes through the roof at what's transpired. Seberg thinks she can put an end to this and says it can work if she doesn't have to choose between them. Huh? She'd like them *both* as husbands! After all, if a Mormon man can have two wives, why can't a Mormon woman have two husbands? Since Marvin and Eastwood both love her and are unwilling to give her up, they decide to see if this unlikely menage can work. Things go well for a spell until there is a huge blizzard and the men save the lives of Baxter, Trueman and Ligon. Baxter is a solid citizen, decent, God-fearing and conservative. He and his wife are shocked at the relationship in the house where they are recuperating from being almost buried in snow. Further, when Ligon makes some comments about how much he admires Marvin and begins emulating him, the parents are livid. So, inside the house, there is one crisis, and outside, more trouble is bubbling because the gold in the area has been showing signs of disappearing. The trio decide to stay and think they can make a bundle with a plan. Through the years, thousands of miners have come through the town and they reckon that there must be a fortune in gold dust which has spilled through the cracks in the wooden floors of the town. So they, plus Walston and a few others, dig several tunnels and begin recovering some yellow stuff. This gets them to dig even more tunnels and soon enough, the underground area of the town is riddled with bunkers and tunnels. With Baxter and Trueman as her moral idols, Seberg is overcome with guilt about the way she's been living and tosses both her husbands out. At the same time, the tunnels all collapse and the whole town implodes, a scene that took seven months to build at a cost of more than $2 million. With no gold in the neighborhood and no buildings to speak of, it soon becomes a Ghost Town. Almost everyone leaves with just a few of the locals determined to stay and make things work. Marvin departs for greener pastures and leaves Eastwood and Seberg behind to work out their love and their lives together. Everyone does their own singing, a mistake except for Harve Presnell. Alan Jay Lerner and Frederick Loewe's songs include: "I Talk To The Trees" (Eastwood), "I Still See Elisa" (Eastwood), "I'm On My Way" (Eastwood, Marvin, Gim, Walston, Hawley, Norman, Bruck, O'Connell, Baker, Jenkins, Mitchum, Miners), "Hand Me Down That Can O' Beans" (Marvin, Miners, Nitty Gritty Dirt Band), "Whoop-Ti-Ay" (Miners), "They Call The Wind Maria" (Presnell, Miners), "There's a Coach Comin' In" (Miners), "Wandrin' Star" (Marvin, Miners). The songs by Lerner and Andre Previn were: "Best Things" (Marvin, Eastwood, Hawley, Norman, Walston), "The Gospel Of No Name City" (Dexter), "A Million Miles Away Behind The Door" (Seberg), "The First Thing You Know" (Marvin), "Gold Fever" (Eastwood, Miners, Dance Hall Girls). Eastwood followed the lead of Rex Harrison and talk-sang effectively. Marvin sounded like a combination of Eugene Pallette and Mickey Mouse. He sang so badly that his songs became camp classics. Shot in the Oregon wilderness near Baker, everything had to be flown in. The road was washed out and so badly eroded that the movie company paid to have it repaved, 46 miles at more than $10,000 per mile, all of which was added to the movie's cost. Gossip has it that Seberg must have liked the idea of two husbands. She was married to author Romain Gary at the time and allegedly conducted an affair with one of her costars (we won't tell which) and Gary flew to the location to straighten out that situation. Many hippies lived in the area and were hired as extras, eventually forming a union and demanding several concessions from the company which also added to the price. Through it all, there are some funny moments, and the scenery is marvelous although the actors kept getting in front of it.

p, Alan Jay Lerner; d, Joshua Logan; w, Lerner, Paddy Chayefsky (based on the musical play by Lerner, Frederick Loewe); ph, William A. Fraker (Panavision, Technicolor); 2nd unit ph, Loyal Griggs; aerial ph, Nelson Tyler; m, Loewe; ed, Robert C. Jones; prod d, John Truscott; md, Nelson Riddle; choral md, Roger Wagner; art d, Carl Braunger; set d, James I. Berkey; cos, Truscott; spec eff, Maurice Ayers, Larry Hampton; ch, Jack Baker; makeup, Frank McCoy.

Musical **Cas.** **(PR:C MPAA:M)**

PAINTED ANGEL, THE½** (1929) 68m FN/WB bw

Billie Dove *(Mamie Hudler/Rodeo West)*, Edmund Lowe *(Brood)*, J. Farrell MacDonald *(Pa Hudler)*, George MacFarlane *(Oldfield)*, Cissy Fitzgerald *(Ma Hudler)*, Norman Selby *(Jule)*, Nellie Bly Baker *(Sippie)*, Peter Higgins.

Dove plays a smalltime New Orleans singer. Through her initiative and pluck she becomes tops on the New York City night club circuit. She also has to contend with the affections of Lowe, whom she wants, and MacFarlane, whom she doesn't. The project is fairly bland but Dove (a former Ziegfeld girl) gives it a bit of class. The drama is really an excuse for some elaborate musical numbers. The visuals for these sequences are decidedly a cut above the rest of the film. Songs include: "Help Yourself To My Love," "Bride Without a Groom," "Only the Girl," "Everybody's Darling," "That Thing" (Herman Ruby, M.K. Jerome).

d, Millard Webb; w, Forrest Halsey (based on a story by Fannie Hurst); ph, John Seitz; ed, Harold Young.

Musical **(PR:A MPAA:NR)**

PAINTED BOATS   (SEE: GIRL ON THE CANAL, THE, 1947, Brit.)

PAINTED DESERT, THE½**   (1931) 79m Pathe bw

William Boyd (Bill Holbrook), Helen Twelvetrees (Mary Ellen Cameron), William Farnum (Cash Holbrook), J. Farrell MacDonald (Jeff Cameron), Clark Gable (Brett), Charles Sellon (Tonopah), Will Walling (Kirby), Edmund Breese (Judge Mathews), Al St. John (Buck), Guy Edward Hearn (Tex), Wade Boteler, William LeMaire, Dick Cramer, James Mason, Hugh Allen Adams, Jerry Drew, Brady Kline, Edward Hearn, Cy Clegg, James Donlon, George Burton.

Farnum and MacDonald stumble across infant Boyd in an abandoned covered wagon. Farnum adopts the baby, igniting a feud between the two men that continues for many years. Boyd returns from college with an engineering degree and tries to settle the bad blood between his father and his old friend. The young man starts a tungsten mine and falls for MacDonald's daughter, Twelvetrees, which sets off a battle with her other suitor, Gable. Gable blows up Boyd's mine, and there follows a showdown between the two men. Boyd comes out unscathed, marries Twelvetrees and brings Farnum and MacDonald together. This was one of the small group of westerns that Boyd did before his Hopalong Cassidy fame, and it was one of Gable's first appearances on the silver screen. The outstanding element of this film is Edward Snyder's breathtaking cinematography.

p, E. B. Derr; d, Howard Higgins; w, Higgins, Tom Buckingham; ph, Ed Snyder; ed, Clarence Kolster.

Western   **Cas.**   **(PR:A MPAA:NR)**

PAINTED DESERT, THE½*   (1938) 59m RKO bw

George O'Brien (Bob McVey), Laraine Johnson [Day] (Carol Banning), Ray Whitley (Steve), Stanley Fields (Placer Bill), Fred Kohler, Sr. (Fawcett), Max Wagner (Kincaid), Harry Cording (Burke), Lee Shumway (Bart), Lloyd Ingraham (Banning), Maude Allen (Yukon Kate), William V. Mong (Heist), Lew Kelly (Bartender), James Mason, Jack O'Shea, Ray Jones, Ken Card, The Phelps Brothers.

This is a remake of the far better Boyd western. O'Brien takes the lead, and the plot is reconstructed for his talents. This time the hero teams up with Johnson (also known with the surname "Day") to work on a tungsten mine. Kohler is a naughty mining agent who wants the metal for himself. He employs the aid of Mong, an equally corrupt banker. The film is weakly played and poorly scripted. The only really good moments are those pirated from the previous version, including the climactic mine explosion. The dialog is unnatural, and there are songs that get in the way of the action.

p, Bert Gilroy; d, David Howard; w, John Rathmell, Oliver Drake (based on a story by Jack Cunningham); ph, Harry Wild; ed, Frederic Knudston; m/l, "Moonlight on the Painted Desert," Oliver Drake, "My Days are Through on the Range," "Painted Desert," Ray Whitley.

Western   **Cas.**   **(PR:A MPAA:NR)**

PAINTED FACES**   (1929) 74m TIF/Stahl bw

Joe E. Brown (Hermann/Beppo), Helen Foster (Nancy, His Adopted Daughter), Richard Tucker (District Attorney), William B. Davidson (Ringmaster), Barton Hepburn (Buddy Barton, Ballyhoo Man), Dorothy Gulliver (Babe Barnes), Lester Cole (Roderick), Sojin (Cafe Proprietor), Jack Richardson (Stage Manager), Howard Truesdell, Baldy Belmont, Jerry Drew, Walter Jerry, Russ Dudley, Purnell Pratt, Clinton Lyle, Alma Bennett, Mabel Julienne Scott, Florence Midgley, May Wallace (Jurors).

Circus clown Brown is a member of a jury which is trying to convict the innocent Hepburn of murder. Brown refuses to be swayed by the other 11 jury members' guilty vote and keeps them "hung" for five days. Finally, it is revealed that Brown has committed the crime in order to save the murdered man's adopted daughter, Foster, from any more abuse. The court sympathizes with him and delivers an innocent verdict. An early film performance for Brown who began his career as a nine-year-old circus acrobat.

d, Albert Rogell; w, Frederic Hatton, Fanny Hatton (based on a story by Frances Hyland); ph, Benjamin Kline, Jackson Rose; ed, Richard Cahoon; m/l, "Somebody Just Like You," Abner Silver.

Drama   **(PR:A MPAA:NR)**

PAINTED HILLS, THE***   (1951) 65m MGM

Paul Kelly (Jonathan Harvey), Bruce Cowling (Lin Taylor), Gary Gray (Tommy Blake), Art Smith (Pilot Pete), Ann Doran (Martha Blake), Chief Yowlachie (Bald Eagle), Andrea Virginia Lester (Mita), "Brown Jug" Reynolds (Red Wing), Lassie ("Shep").

This was the famous collie's last film for MGM. The story stars Kelly, Lassie's master, as a goldminer in the 1870s. Kelly's partner in the mine is Cowling, who gets a bad case of gold fever. He wants it all for himself and tries to arrange his partner's death so that the blame goes to Lassie. Of course the canine heroine outsmarts the villain, who meets his doom falling over a cliff. The story is played with too much sentiment but otherwise THE PAINTED HILLS is a good adventure that's perfect for the kids. The action sequences are well put together giving a sense of excitement. The fine color photography makes good use of the beautiful mountain scenery. Kress was directing his first film, having previously worked as an editor for Metro. He did two films for the studio, both low-budget B films which were having a renaissance at MGM in the early 1950s. Producer Franklin was well known for his animal films.

p, Chester M. Franklin; d, Harold F. Kress; w, True Boardman (based on the novel Shep of the Painted Hills by Alexander Hull); ph, Alfred Gilks, Harold Lipstein (Technicolor); m, Daniele Amfitheatrof; ed, Newell B. Willis; art d, Cedric Gibbons, Leonid Vasian.

Adventure/Animal Drama   **(PR:AAA MPAA:NR)**

PAINTED SMILE, THE   (SEE: MURDER CAN BE DEADLY, 1963, Brit.)

PAINTED TRAIL, THE***   (1938) 50m MON bw

Tom Keene (Tom), Eleanor Stewart (Ann), LeRoy Mason (Boss), Walter Long (Driscoll), Ed Cassidy (Evans), Jimmy Eagles (Sammy), Ernie Adams (Bo), Glenn Strange (Sheriff), Frank Campeau, Bob Kortman, Dick Cramer, Tom London, Forrest Taylor, Harry Harvey, Bud Osborne.

Retired lawman Keene is called back into action in order to break a smuggling ring along the Mexican border. Mason and Long are the bad guys and Stewart is the waitress who gives Keene just what he ordered. The exciting climax takes place along the border as Keene blazes away on the U.S. side while Mason and Long fire back from Mexico. The routine story is a cut above other westerns thanks to the performance of the star. He's athletic and handsome, and takes his role to heart. This was his first film with western director Hill after a long absence from each other.

p, Robert Tansey; d, Robert Hill; w, Robert Emmett [Tansey]; ph, Bert Longenecker; ed, Howard Dillinger.

Western   **(PR:A MPAA:NR)**

PAINTED VEIL, THE***   (1934) 83m MGM bw

Greta Garbo (Katherine Koerber Fane), Herbert Marshall (Dr. Walter Fane), George Brent (Jack Townsend), Warner Oland (Gen. Yu), Jean Hersholt (Prof. Koerber), Beulah Bondi (Frau Koerber), Katherine Alexander (Mrs. Townsend), Cecilia Parker (Olga), Soo Yong (Amah), Billy Bevan (Bridegroom), Forrester Harvey (Waddington), Alice Cook (Curious Woman), Jane Kerr (Cruel Woman), Vernon Dent (Chief of Police), Gus Leonard (Major-Domo), Dorothea Wolbert (Stuttering Woman), Delmar Watson (Crying Boy), Lillian Lawrence (Spinster), Keye Luke (Shay Kee Seng, the Clerk), Olaf Hytten (Dr. Somerset), Herbert Farjean (Dr. Simmons), James Wang (Proprietor of Curio Shop), Ethel Griffies (Lady Coldchester), Margaret Mann (Mother Superior), Leonard Mudie (Secretary), Lawrence Grant (English Governor), Colin Kenny.

Garbo had just had a smash hit with QUEEN CHRISTINA when she went into this rather standard W. Somerset Maugham love story, although she brought into it her great mystique and her great talent, and made more of it than what was really there. She marries Marshall, a physician, journeying with him to China where his busy practice keeps him too busy to occupy Garbo's bed. She meets Brent, a political attache, who has plenty of leisure time and they spend it together. Marshall discovers the love affair and confronts the couple. He tells Garbo that he must go into the interior where a cholera epidemic has broken out and she can either accompany him or stay with Brent. Ever the politician, Brent backs away, explaining that he cannot risk the scandal. Marshall leaves for the provinces and Garbo goes with him. Once at work, Marshall tells Garbo that he is sorry for the way he has treated her. He must go even farther into the country, he tells her, and there's no reason why she should continue to risk her health, that she can return to civilization if she likes. Garbo does not leave, but stays on to nurse the myriad cholera victims; she is waiting for Marshall when he returns. The estranged couple fall in love again and renew their marriage vows. But before they can settle down, an irate Chinese stabs Marshall when he orders a section of the disease-infected city burned. Brent arrives in the city just as Garbo learns that Marshall is wounded but when he asks her to go away with him, she rejects him and goes to nurse Marshall back to health. Garbo is magnificent throughout this weak story, in one stunning scene after another. Terror, quiet and creeping, is present on her veiled face as she sits through a dinner with Marshall, wondering if he is aware of her affair or not. When she waits outside a hospital room to hear whether or not her husband will live, Garbo stoops in grief, her shoulders curved awkwardly inward, her form racked with sorrow. Here was an actress who acted with her face and body. MGM spent more than $1 million on this production and it did not do well at the box office, no fault of its stellar star. Reportedly, Garbo and her costar Brent had a short but torrid affair offscreen which abruptly ended when Brent insisted upon marriage. The plot line of THE PAINTED VEIL bears a remarkable likeness to that of a 1929 Garbo vehicle, WILD ORCHIDS.

p, Hunt Stromberg; d, Richard Boleslawski; w, John Meehan, Salka Viertel, Edith Fitzgerald (based on the novel by W. Somerset Maugham); ph, William Daniels; m, Herbert Stothart; ed, Hugh Wynn; art d, Cedric Gibbons; cos, Adrian; ch, Chester Hale.

Drama   **(PR:A MPAA:NR)**

PAINTED WOMAN*   (1932) 70m FOX bw

Spencer Tracy (Tom Brian), Peggy Shannon (Kiddo), William "Stage" Boyd (Captain Boynton), Irving Pichel (Robert Dunn), Raul Roulien (Jim), Murray Kinnell (Collins), Laska Winter (Tia), Chris-Pin Martin (Marquette), Paul Porcasi (Machado), Stanley Fields (Yank), Wade Boteler (Lefty), Jack Kennedy (Mack), Dewey Robinson (Bouncer).

This early Tracy effort is a standard film with a South Seas backdrop. Shannon plays a nightclub singer in Singapore. Boyd wants to marry her. She accidentally gets involved with a murder and has to hightail it out of town. She lies to Boyd about what happened and he allows her on his ship. When he finds out the truth, he leaves her on a small island. There she meets Tracy and falls in love. They marry despite her past about which she is honest with him. Boyd returns and is furious when he finds his old flame married. He's killed by Tracy's servant but Shannon is accused of the crime. Tracy walks out on her but at last the servant confesses and all is righted. As fine an actor as Tracy was, he couldn't help this lurid tale. The script is weak, and much unnecessary action is added as an attempt to fill it out. The direction is bland.

d, John Blystone; w, Guy Bolton and Leon Gordon (based on the play "After the

Rain" by Alfred C. Kennedy); ph, Ernest Palmer; m, Arthur Lange, Hugo Friedhofer; ed, Alex Troffey; md, George Lipshultz.

Drama **(PR:A MPAA:NR)**

PAINTING THE CLOUDS WITH SUNSHINE** (1951) 87m WB c

Dennis Morgan *(Vince Nichols)*, Virginia Mayo *(Carol)*, Gene Nelson *(Ted Lansing)*, Lucille Norman *(Abby)*, Tom Conway *(Bennington)*, Wallace Ford *(Sam Parks)*, Tom Dugan *(Barney)*, Jack Law *(Orchestra Leader)*, Abe Dinovitch *(Busboy)*, Harry Mendoza *(Rolondo)*, Dolores Castle *(Yvette)*, Tristram Coffin *(Manager)*, Eddie Acuff, Jack Daley *(Doormen)*, Brick Sullivan, Paul Gustine *(Housemen)*, Donald Kerr *(Dealer)*, Garnett Marks *(Manager)*, Joe Recht *(Bellboy)*, Crauford Kent, Frank Dae *(Board Members)*, William Vedder *(Cadwalder)*.

This is really just another GOLDDIGGERS film without the charm or innocence of the original films. Instead of Broadway showgirls, Mayo, Norman and Gibson are vending their talents in Las Vegas. Starting off in Los Angeles, the girls listen as Mayo gives them a pep talk on how to find a rich guy. Buoyed by her speech, they head off for that gambling town and end up in a hotel run by Sakall. He's just about broke, having made some poor gambling decisions. Morgan plays a disguised millionaire who goes for Norman. When his banking cousin from Boston (Conway) arrives on the scene, his plot to win Norman is nearly ruined, but all is righted in the end. It's routine, but competently acted and efficiently directed. The songs provide some fun, although numbers like "Tip-Toe Through the Tulips" and "With a Song in My Heart" hardly seem like Vegas material. The songs are: "Painting the Clouds With Sunshine," "Tip-Toe Through the Tulips," (Al Dubin, Joe Burke), "Vienna Dreams" (Irving Caesar, Rudolf Sieczy), "With a Song in My Heart," (Richard Rodgers, Lorenz Hart), "Birth of the Blues" (Buddy DeSylva, Lew Brown, Ray Henderson), "You're My Everything" (Harry Warren, Mort Dixon), "Jealousy" (Vera Bloom, Jacob Gabe), "Man is a Necessary Evil," "Mambo Man" (Jack Elliott, Sonny Burke).

p, William Jacobs; d, David Butler; w, Harry Clark, Roland Kibbee, Peter Milne (based on the play "Gold Diggers of Broadway" by Avery Hopwood); ph, Wilfred Cline (Technicolor); ed, Irene Morra; md, Ray Heindorf; art d, Edward Carrere; cos, Milo Anderson; ch, LeRoy Prinz.

Musical **(PR:A MPAA:NR)**

PAIR OF BRIEFS, A** (1963, Brit.) 90m Rank/Davis bw

Michael Craig *(Tony Stevens)*, Mary Peach *(Frances Pilbright)*, Brenda De Banzie *(Gladys Pudney)*, James Robertson Justice *(Justice Hadden)*, Roland Culver *(Sir John Pilbright)*, Liz Fraser *(Pearly Girl)*, Ron Moody *(Sid Pudney)*, Jameson Clark *(George Lockwood)*, Charles Heslop *(Peebles)*, Bill Kerr *(Victor)*, Nicholas Phipps *(Peter Sutcliffe)*, Joan Sims *((Beryl)*, John Standing *(Hubert Shannon)*, Amanda Barrie *(Golly)*, Judy Carne *(Maude)*, Barbara Ferris *(Gloria Lockwood)*, Myrtle Reed *(Barmaid)*, Terry Scott *(Court Attendant)*, Graham Stark *(Police Officer)*, Ronnie Stevens *(House Detective)*.

Two rookie lawyers, Craig and Peach, work for Peach's uncle's law firm and they find themselves at the opposite ends of the same case. Peach is defending De Banzie against her husband, Moody, (represented by Craig) who is suing for conjugal rights. Things in the courtroom don't go well for the green lawyers and the judge indicates he might disbar them. The case goes in favor of the wife until Craig discovers that De Banzie got the case rolling because she was afraid Moody would blackmail her if he found out that she married a millionaire. Once the dust is settled in the courtroom, Craig and Peach decide to get married.

p, Betty E. Box; d, Ralph Thomas; w, Nicholas Phipps (based on the play "How Say You?" by Harold Brooke, Kay Bannerman); ph, Ernest Steward; m, Norrie Paramor; ed, Alfred Roome; art d, Maurice Carter.

Comedy **(PR:A MPAA:NR)**

PAISA (SEE: PAISAN, 1948, Ital.)

PAISAN**** (1948, Ital.) 120m Organization Films International-Foreign Film/Mayer-Burstyn bw (PAISA)

Carmela Sazio *(Carmela)*, Robert Van Loon *(Joe from Jersey)*, Alfonsino Pasca *(Boy)*, Maria Michi *(Francesca)*, Renzo Avanzo *(Massimo)*, Harriet White *(Harriet)*, Dots M. Johnson *(Black MP)*, Bill Tubbs *(Capt. Bill Martin, Chaplain)*, Dale Edmonds *(Dale, O.S.S. Man)*, Carlo Piscane *((Peasant in Sicily Story)*, Mats Carlson *(Soldier in Sicily Story)*, Gar Moore *(Fred, American Soldier)*, Gigi Gori *(Partisan)*, Cigolani *(Cigolani, Partisan)*, Lorena Berg *(Maddalena)*, Benjamin Emmanuel, Raymond Campbell, Albert Heinz, Harold Wagner, Merline Berth, Leonard Parrish, Allen Dan, Merlin Hugo, Anthony La Penna.

PAISAN is one of those rare segmented films that never loses steam as it goes through six separate chronological sequences which begin with the Allied invasion of Sicily in 1943 and end as the Italians surrender in 1944. The word "paisa" is an alteration by the Anglo-Saxons of the Italian word "paese" which means homeland. And "paisan" means "countryman." The six episodes are vastly different in treatment and tone. In the first, Van Loon, a New Jerseyite, gets the job of guarding a young Sicilian woman, Sazio, in a deserted old castle. She won't say a word or even betray a single emotion and the entire sequence has to do with his attempt to win her over without being able to speak a word of the language. In Naples, Johnson, a black U.S. Military Policeman, is taking a nap when his shoes are stolen by Pasca, a young street urchin. He searches for the boy and finally finds him living in a cavern with a horde of poor, homeless Neapolitans. Upon seeing the way in which they must exist, Johnson decides against arresting anyone and goes off without his shoes. The Roman story has to do with the U.S. soldier Moore meeting a streetwalker, Michi. They had met several months before when she gave him a drink of water as his tank rolled into the Eternal City. Moore is drunk and talks about the girl he met back then, but Michi recognizes his ramblings as something that happened to her but he is far too drunk to participate in anything further than his memories of the girl, the same girl he is now with but cannot recognize. The Florentine tale has to do with U.S. nurse White and Italian partisan Gori as they make their way through German lines in a suspenseful episode that looks more like John Sturges than Rossellini. The fourth episode has three chaplains, a Catholic, a Protestant, and a Jew meeting a group of Franciscan monks at a monastery. The monks are unaccustomed to the Protestant and the Jew and eventually discover that they are all united under one God. The action sequence is the final one; a shoot-out between the Germans and the OSS and British soldiers working with the partisans. In the end, the heroes all die. PAISAN has humor, pathos, adventure, romance, tension, atmosphere and warmth. The fact that they came in separate stories did not work against the overall impression of the film. In later years, these same emotions would be attempted, to a lesser degree, in VIVA ITALIA! This was Rossellini's second post-war film. The first was OPEN CITY, which received more critical and financial success but may not have been as good as this one. He is the father of Isabella Rossellini, one of his two daughters by his "scandalous" (for the 1950s) relationship with Ingrid Bergman. The music was by his younger brother, Renzo, who did a good job despite being related to the director. (In Italian; English subtitles.)

p, Roberto Rossellini, Rod E. Geiger, Mario Conti; d, Rossellini; w, Sergio Amidei, Federico Fellini, Rossellini, Annalena Limentani (based on stories by Victor Haines, Marcello Pagliero, Amidei, Fellini, Rossellini, Klaus Mann, Vasco Pratolini); ph, Otello Martelli; m, Renzo Rossellini; ed, Eraldo Da Roma; English titles, Herman G. Weinberg.

War Drama **Cas.** **(PAR:C MPAA:NR)**

PAJAMA GAME, THE**** (1957) 101m WB c

Doris Day *(Kate "Babe" Williams)*, John Raitt *(Sid Sorokin)*, Carol Haney *(Gladys Hotchkiss)*, Eddie Foy, Jr. *(Vernon Hines)*, Reta Shaw *(Mabel)*, Barbara Nichols *(Poopsie)*, Thelma Pelish *(Mae)*, Jack Straw *(Prez)*, Ralph Dunn *(Hasler)*, Owen Martin *(Max)*, Jackie Kelk *(1st Helper)*, Ralph Chambers *(Charlie)*, Mary Stanton *(Brenda)*, Buzz Miller, Kenneth LeRoy *(Featured Dancers)*, Jack Waldron *(Salesman)*, Ralph Volkie *(2nd Helper)*, Franklyn Fox *(Pop Williams)*, William A. Forester *(Joe)*, Peter Gennaro *(Dancer)*, Elmore Henderson *(Waiter)*, Fred Villani *(Tony, the Headwaiter)*, Kathy Marlowe *(Holly)*, Otis Griffith *(Otis)*.

Out of a simple idea comes one terrific movie. Day is a worker in a pajama factory. She and her coworkers want a 7½-cent raise but management refuses. Day heads a grievance committee and takes the complaints to shop superintendent Raitt and spoils the whole movement by falling in love. Day is an utter delight in the role. She's funny and intelligent and sure can wear a pair of pajamas nicely. The choreography by Fosse (who would go on to direct Broadway shows and films) is as energetic as can be. The dancing isn't just left to the actors—camera moves are carefully planned to give the hoofing the best look possible. The inventive pans and tracking shots are wonderfully natural and have a lot of energy themselves. The camera sometimes serves as an additional dance partner, creating a unique and comic tango with Haney. This is a movie that knows how to move! The codirection by Abbott and Donen lifts the film from its Broadway roots and makes it a cinematic musical that everyone will enjoy. It has a vitality that makes it one of the best movie musicals of all time. The songs include: "I'm Not at All in Love," "Small Talk," "There Once was a Man," "Steam Heat," "Hernando's Hideaway," "Hey There," "Once-a Year-Day," "Seven and a Half Cents," "I'll Never Be Jealous Again," "Racing with the Clock," "The Pajama Game," "Her Is." (Richard Adler, Jerry Ross).

p&d, George Abbott and Stanley Donen; w, Abbott, Richard Bissell (based on their Broadway musical from Bissell's novel *Seven and a Half Cents*); ph, Harry Stradling (Warner Color); ed, William Ziegler; art d, Malcolm Bert; set d, William Kuehl; cos, William, Jean Eckart; ch, Bob Fosse; makeup, Gordon Bau.

Musical **(PR:A MPAA:NR)**

PAJAMA PARTY½** (1964) 82m AIP c

Tommy Kirk *(Go-Go)*, Annette Funicello *(Connie)*, Elsa Lanchester *(Aunt Wendy)*, Harvey Lembeck *(Eric Von Zipper)*, Jesse White *(J. Sinister Hulk)*, Jody McCrea *(Big Lunk)*, Ben Lessy *(Fleegle)*, Donna Loren *(Vikki)*, Susan Hart *(Jilda)*, Bobbi Shaw *(Helga)*, Cheryl Sweeten *(Francine)*, Luree Holmes *(Perfume Girl)*, Candy Johnson *(Candy)*, Buster Keaton *(Chief Rotten Eagle)*, Dorothy Lamour *(Head Saleslady)*, Andy Romano, Linda Rogers, Alan Fife, Alberta Nelson, Jerry Brutsche, Bob Harvey *(The Rat Pack)*, Renie Riano *(Maid)*, Joi Holmes *(Topless Bathing Suit Model)*, Kerry Kollmar *(Little Boy)*, Joan Neel, Patricia O'Reilly, Marion Kildany, Linda Opie, Mary Hughes, Patti Chandler, Laura Nicholson, Linda Benson, Carey Foster, Stacey Maxwell, Teri Hope, Margo Mehling, Diane Bond, Keva Page, Toni Basil, Kay Sutton, Connie Ducharme, Joyce Nizzari, Leslie Wenner *(The Pajama Girls)*, Ray Atkinson, Frank Alesia, Ned Wynn, Ronnie Rondell, Howard Curtis, John Fain, Mike Nader, Rick Newton, Guy Hemric, Ed Garner, Frank Mortiforte, Ronnie David, Gus Trikonis, Bob Pane, Roger Bacon, Ronnie Dayton *(The Pajama Boys)*, Nooney Rickett Four *(Themselves)*, Don Rickles, Frankie Avalon.

Former Disney kid Kirk plays a Martian sent by his cohorts to scout Earth for a possible invasion. He lands in Lanchester's garden and meets the muscular McCrea along with gal pal Funicello. She forgets all about her man when she meets this groovin' guy from way yonder. Lanchester's dress shop is in trouble when White and Lessy try to rob it for a fortune she's supposedly stashed away. Lembeck is a motorcycle gang leader who's jealous of McCrea's relationship to that busty gal. Kirk has a swell time trying to convince Funicello and her aunt he's really from outer space and his people want to invade Earth. Lanchester throws the title party for all the teens in town, bringing the usual beach scene found in this sort of movie to an indoor setting. White and Lessy are still after Lanchester's money, and with the help of Indian chief Keaton and the buxom Swede Shaw, they crash the party. Kirk saves the day by teleporting the bad guys to Mars and also taking care of the motorcycle gang. He and Funicello end up arm in arm and McCrea and the non-English speaking Shaw start a sort of romance. Songs include: "It's That Kind of

Day," "There Has to Be a Reason," "Where Did I Go Wrong?" "Pajama Party," "Beach Ball," "Among the Young," "Stuffed Animal" (Guy Hemric, Jerry Styner). This film was a follow-up to BEACH PARTY. The beach movies were enormously popular though extremely unvaried. This is no great work but it's fun in its own way. Avalon, the usual male lead for the beach films, makes a cameo appearance as does another beach veteran, Rickles. Shaw steals the show with her comic and sexy performance. The direction is competent and jaunty, working well withing the limitations of the genre. This was Lamour's last theatrical film—a rather undignified way to go. Even sadder is seeing the great silent clown Keaton reduced to playing "Chief Rotten Eagle." The "zany" name for his character seems patronizing and the role is unfit for a man who ranks as one of film's great comic genuises. Alcohol and a sordid personal life took its toll on the man, reducing the silent clown to doing films like this.

p, James H. Nicholson, Samuel Z. Arkoff; d, Don Weis; w, Louis M. Heyward; ph, Floyd Crosby (Panavision, Pathecolor); m, Les Baxter; ed, Fred Feitshans, Eve Newman; art d, Daniel Haller; set d, Harry Reif; cos, Marjorie Corso; spec eff, Butler-Glouner, Inc, Roger George, Joe Zomar; ch, David Winters; makeup, Bob Dawn.

Musical   **(PR:AA MPAA:NR)**

PAJAMA PARTY IN THE HAUNTED HOUSE   (SEE: GHOST IN THE INVISIBLE BIKINI, THE, 1966)

PAL FROM TEXAS, THE **   (1939) 56m Metropolitan bw

Bob Steele, Claire Rochelle, Jack Perrin, Josef Swickard, Betty Mack, Ted Adams, Carleton Young, Jack Ingram, Robert Walker.

When a gold mine becomes available, one man tries to take it over in a decidedly less than honest fashion. Leave it to perennial good guy Steele to right all wrongs.

p&d, Harry S. Webb; w, Carl Krusada (based on a story by Forrest Sheldon).

Western   **(PR:A MPAA:NR)**

PAL JOEY****   (1957) 111m Essex-George Sidney/COL c

Rita Hayworth (Vera Simpson), Frank Sinatra (Joey Evans), Kim Novak (Linda English), Barbara Nichols (Gladys), Bobby Sherwood (Ned Galvin), Hank Henry (Mike Miggins), Elizabeth Patterson (Mrs. Casey), Robin Morse (Bartender), Frank Wilcox (Col. Langley), Pierre Watkin (Mr. Forsythe), Barry Bernard (Anderson), Ellie Kent (Carol), Mara McAfee (Sabrina), Betty Utey (Patsy), Bek Nelson (Lola), Henry McCann (Shorty), John Hubbard (Stanley), James Seay (Livingston), Hermes Pan (Choreographer), Ernesto Molinari (Chef Tony), Jean Corbett (Specialty Dance Double), Robert Rietz (Boy Friend), Jules Davies (Red-Faced Man), Judy Dan (Hat Check Girl), Gail Bonney (Heavy-Set Woman), Cheryl Kubert (Girl Friend), Tol Avery (Detective), Robert Anderson (Policeman), Genie Stone (Girl), Raymond McWalters (Army Captain), Bob Glenn (Sailor), Sue Boomer (Secretary), Helen Eliot (Traveler's Aid), Hermie Rose (Bald Club Owner), Jack Railey (Hot Dog Vendor), Frank Wilimarth (Sidewalk Artist), Roberto Piperio (Waiter), Bobbie Lee, Connie Graham, Bobbie Jean Henson, Edith Powell, Jo Ann Smith, Ilsa Ostroffsky, Rita Barrett (Strippers), Howard Sigrist (Sidewalk Photographer), Paul Cesari, Everett Glass (Pet Store Owners), Maurice Argent, Michael Ferris (Tailors), Eddie Bartell, Albert Nalbandian, Joseph Miksak, Sydney Chatton, Frank Sully (Barkers), Andrew Wong (Chinese Club Owner), George Chan (Chinese Pianist), Allen Gin (Chinese Drummer), Barbara Yung, Pat Lynn, Jean Nakaba, Elizabeth Fenton, Lessie Lynne Wong, Nellie Gee Ching (Chinese Dancers), George DeNormand, Oliver Cross, Bess Flowers, Franklyn Farnum (Bits), Giselle D'Arc (Vera's Maid), Leon Alton (Printer Salesman), Jane Chung (Flower Lady), George Ford, Steve Benton (Electricians), Ramon Martinez, George Nardelli (Headwaiters).

PAL JOEY is a very rare story, in that the hero is an apparent rat and there is virtually no one in the tale with a saving grace. It's based on a series of "letters" written by author John O'Hara from a mythical dancer who signed all the missives, "Your Pal Joey." O'Hara, a national treasure when it comes to short stories, was approached by producer George Abbott, who talked him into adapting it as the book for a musical. Rodgers and Hart came aboard and the play was a success, although audiences were divided about the content. The tunes were sensational with double, and sometimes single entendres, and a sensational performance by the young lead, a Pittsburgh Irishman named Gene Kelly. It opened in December, 1940, and featured Vivienne Segal, Leila Ernst, June Havoc, and a red-headed chorus boy named Van Johnson. The stage run only lasted 198 performances. Columbia bought the rights, had several writers attempt to sanitize it for the screen, paged Cagney for the lead, then tried Cary Grant. (He always seems to be up there in studio chiefs' minds. Jack Warner, you may recall, wanted him to play Higgins in MY FAIR LADY). Gloria Swanson, Grace Moore, Ethel Merman, Irene Dunne, and several others were considered for the femme lead, but the war put an end to the project and it languished until the play was revived in the 1950s with Segal and Harold Lang. Columbia saw the throngs at the theater and their interest was again piqued. Brando was a thought for the male lead and Mae West was considered for the Segal role. Sinatra had just done GUYS AND DOLLS with Brando and knew that the part would be much better in his own mouth, so he raised a few bucks and took a piece of the action, thereby assuring himself the role. The play took place in Chicago and was about a dancer. The screenplay shifted the action to San Francisco and altered Joey to a singer, which was more in keeping with Sinatra's talents. Of the film's 14 songs, 10 came from the original and four others were taken from previous Rodgers and Hart scores for "Babes in Arms," "Too Many Girls," and "On Your Toes." When Columbia first bought the play for pictures, boss Cohn wanted Kelly but he was already contracted to MGM and Mayer wanted too much money, so the story was shelved for 17 years until Sinatra strolled in. Although he was the driving force behind the project and the title role, Sinatra backed off and let Hayworth get top billing because of her many years with the studio. She never could sing much and her vocals were looped by Jo Ann Greer.

Novak's voice was sung by Trudi Erwin. The Production Code called for several changes in the script and the result was more squeaky-clean than one would have hoped for, although it didn't seem to matter much to audiences who adored Sinatra and the others and made the picture a success. Director Sidney elicited some wonderful performances from everyone concerned, but the picture was almost overlooked by the Motion Picture Academy, gathering only four nominations: Best Art Direction and Set Decoration, Best Sound Recording, Best Film Editing, and Best Costume Design. It won none of them. Sinatra does a bang-up job as this Joe, not unlike another he played, Joe E. Lewis, in THE JOKER IS WILD. He's a saloon singer with a gleam in his eye, a tuxedo in his suitcase, and not a penny in his pocket as he arrives in San Francisco and gets a job at the nightclub owned by Hank Henry (the veteran Vegas burlesque comic whom Sinatra liked to have around, so he gave him roles in a number of films including OCEAN'S ELEVEN). It isn't long before Sinatra is having his way with most of the chorines who high-step at the club, with the only reluctant one being Novak, a sweet, ingenuous young woman who is working her first engagement. Sinatra and the band, led by real-life bandleader Sherwood, are paged to do a private soiree at the posh home of Hayworth, who lives up on Nob Hill. Hayworth is the widow of a wealthy man and Sinatra recognizes her as a one-time stripper who used to take it off with the best of 'em. She has eyes for Sinatra but he is rapidly falling in love with the one holdout at the club, Novak. Hayworth is willing to put her money where her heart is, so she decides to finance Sinatra in his own nightspot, the Chez Joey. Sinatra agrees to the deal but insists that Novak get a featured number in his new show. Hayworth didn't get where she is by chance and she slyly notes that there is more between Sinatra and Novak than an employer-employee relationship, so she holds back the money and says that he cannot open the club if Novak remains. Sinatra, in an unaccustomed selfless gesture, won't give in and the club never opens its doors. Novak goes to Hayworth and begs her to go ahead with the deal. Hayworth takes that under consideration and says she'll unbuckle her purse but only on the proviso that Novak makes a quick exit. Then Hayworth tells Sinatra that she'll even be willing to end his years of poverty by marrying him, a tempting prospect. Sinatra doesn't have to consider this very long and opts to stay with Novak. If he has any talent, it'll happen, and he will not spend his life as a gigolo married to a woman he doesn't love. Some of Rodgers and Hart's best songs ever are in this score. From the original play comes: "Zip" (Hayworth mouthing Greer's voice), "Bewitched, Bothered and Bewildered" (sung by Sinatra, Hayworth), "I Could Write a Book" (sung by Sinatra, Novak mouthing Erwin's voice), "That Terrific Rainbow" (sung by Novak), "Whad Do I Care for a Dame?" (sung by Sinatra), as well as "Happy Hunting Horn," "Plant You Now, Dig You Later," "Do It the Hard Way," and "Take Him." The other songs were "There's a Small Hotel" (sung by Sinatra, from "On Your Toes,"), "I Didn't Know What Time It Was" (sung by Sinatra, from "Too Many Girls"), "My Funny Valentine" (sung by Novak, from "Babes In Arms"), "In Our Little Den of Iniquity," "Great Big Town," and the huge hit from "Babes in Arms," Sinatra's driving rendition (arranged by Nelson Riddle) of "The Lady Is A Tramp." Gorgeous costumes, superior photography, excellent choreography, and snappy direction by George Sidney make this a don't-miss picture. Sure, it's a bit sentimental at the end and, yes, they have deleted some of the more explicit sexual situations, but it is still a bold subject for a musical and the result is 111 minutes of pleasure.

p, Fred Kohlmar; d, George Sidney; w, Dorothy Kingsley (based on the New Yorker stories by John O'Hara, the musical play by O'Hara, Richard Rodgers, Lorenz Hart); ph, Harold Lipstein (Technicolor); m, Nelson Riddle; ed, Viola Lawrence, Jerome Thoms; md, Morris Stoloff; art d, Walter Holscher; set d, William Kiernan, Louis Diage; cos, Jean Louis; ch, Hermes Pan; m/l, Rodgers, Hart; makeup, Ben Lane.

Musical Comedy   **(PR:C MPAA:NR)**

PALACE OF NUDES*½   (1961, Fr./Ital.) 96m Lutetia-UEC William Mishkin bw (CRIME AU CONCERT MAYOL; AKA: PALACE OF SHAME)

Claude Godard (Mado), Daniel Clerice (Max), Jean-Pierre Kerien (Inspector Million), Robert Berri (Fred), Jean Tissier (Grumeau), Magda, Paul Demange, Paul Ensia, Jean Daurand, Celia Cortez, Ariene Lancel, Monique Vivian, Gina Manes, Ballets d'Evelyne Gray.

A lame murder mystery takes place in a striptease joint. The star dancer is poisoned and then her understudy is shot to death while wearing one of the star's costumes. Kerien is the police inspector on the case and discovers that the understudy had been the target all along. Suspects pile up, but the prime suspect is Max, the star dancer's lover. Finally, the understudy's friend captures Max after the police discover that he's the killer. This film was shot at the Concert Mayol in Paris.

d, Pierre Mere; w, Jacques Chabannes, Lucien Rimmels; ph, Pierre Dolley; m, Marcel Landowski; makeup; Lala Janvier.

Crime Drama   **(PR:C MPAA:NR)**

PALE ARROW   (SEE: PAWNEE, 1957)

PALEFACE, THE***½   (1948) 91m PAR c

Bob Hope ("Painless" Peter Potter), Jane Russell (Calamity Jane), Robert Armstrong (Terris), Iris Adrian (Pepper), Robert [Bobby] Watson (Toby Preston), Jack Searl (Jasper Martin), Joseph Vitale (Indian Scout), Charles Trowbridge (Gov. Johnson), Clem Bevans (Hank Billings), Jeff York (Joe), Stanley Andrews (Commissioner Emerson), Wade Crosby (Web), Chief Yowlachie (Chief Yellow Feather), Iron Eyes Cody (Chief Iron Eyes), John Maxwell (Village Gossip), Tom Kennedy (Bartender), Henry Brandon (Wapato the Medicine Man), Francis J. McDonald (Lance), Frank Hagney (Greg), Skelton Knaggs (Pete), Olin Howlin (Undertaker), George Chandler, Nestor Paiva (Patients), Earle Hodgins (Clem), Arthur Space (Zach), Trevor Bardette, Alan Bridge (Horsemen), Edgar Dearing (Sheriff), Dorothy Grainger (Bath House Attendant), Charles Cooley (Mr. "X"), Eric Alden (Bob), Babe London (Woman on Wagon Train), Loyal Underwood

(Bearded Character), Billy Engle, Houseley Stevenson, Al M. Hill (Pioneers), Margaret Field, Laura Corbay (Guests), Duke York, Ethan Laidlaw (Henchmen), John "Skins" Miller (Bellhop), Wally Boyle (Hotel Clerk), Stanley Blystone, Bob Kortman (Onlookers), Lane Chandler (Tough-Looking Galoot), Oliver Blake (Westerner), Carl Andre, Ted Mapes, Kermit Maynard (Horsemen), Dick Elliott (Mayor), Betty Hannon, Charmienne Harker, Dee La Nore, Marie J. Tavares, Marilyn Gladstone, June Glory (B-Girls), Harry Harvey, Paul E. Burns (Justices of the Peace), Jody Gilbert (Woman in Bath House), Hall Bartlett (Handsome Cowboy), Syd Saylor (Cowboy), Sharon McManus (Child).

A very funny spoof on westerns that wavered between satire and farce, THE PALEFACE did so well at the box office that a sequel, THE SON OF PALEFACE, was made four years later, but it didn't come close to the fun of this one. Almost 20 years later, Don Knotts starred in a remake, THE SHAKIEST GUN IN THE WEST, and it was a pale imitation. Russell had been the star of Howard Hughes' THE OUTLAW and she makes good fun of herself here, while playing off the fast wisecracks of Hope. He's a dentist who got his degree by mail and is now hoping to earn a living in the rootin'-tootin' West. He encounters Russell (Calamity Jane), who has been on the run for some crimes she'd committed before the movie started. Russell is trying to nab the villain who has been selling guns to the Indians in the neighborhood. If she manages to do that, she hopes her prior felonies will be overlooked. To take the heat off her, Russell marries Hope, and then, of course, falls for him. Hope manages to capture the bad guys in an inadvertent fashion and is acclaimed a hero. The movie sat on the shelves for a while, and by the time it came out, one of the tunes, "Buttons and Bows" (Jay Livingston, Ray Evans) was already a hit, and later won the Oscar. Hope and Russell sang that one, while Iris Adrian did Livingston and Evans' "Meetcha Round the Corner" as well as Joseph J. Lilley's "Get a Man." Lots of jokes pepper the dialog and Russell shows she can trade quips with Hope without losing a smidgen of the fun. Whereas DUEL IN THE SUN and THE OUTLAW sought to bring steamy sex to the western genre, THE PALEFACE sought to make fun of that innovation and succeeded.

p, Robert L. Welch; d, Norman Z. McLeod; w, Edmund Hartman, Frank Tashlin, Jack Rose; ph, Ray Rennahan (Technicolor); m, Victor Young; ed, Ellsworth Hoagland; art d, Hans Dreier, Earl Hedrick; set d, Sam Comer, Bertram Granger; cos, Mary Kay Dodson; spec eff, Gordon Jennings; Farciot Edouart; ch, Billy Daniel.

Comedy   **Cas.**   **(PR:A   MPAA:NR)**

PALM BEACH***   (1979, Aus.) 88m Albie Thoms c

Nat Young (Nick Naylor), Ken Brown (Joe Ryan), Amanda Berry (Leilani Adams), Bryan Brown (Paul Kite), Julie McGregor (Kate O'Brien), John Flaus (Larry Kent), Bronwyn Stevens-Jones (Wendy Naylor), David Lourie (Zane Green), Peter Wright (Rupert Roberts), John Clayton (Eric Tailor), Lyn Collingwood (Mrs. Adams), Adrian Rawlins (David Litvinoff), P. J. Jones (Detective Sgt. Robinson), Mick Eyre (Magazine Editor), Jim Roberts (Art School Dean), Cathy Power (Art School Student), Mick Winter (Board Polisher), Tony Hardwick (Boardshop Owner), David Elfick (Projectionist).

This independent, avante-garde Australian feature has some unusual moments and interesting cinematic techniques. It carefully winds together the stories of four characters. Bryan Brown plays an unemployed man, desperate for money. He steals a gun and turns to robbery for his income. Ken Brown is another underworld figure, a petty thief who dabbles in drug deals. Also there is Berry, a loose teenage runaway who's being tailed by private detective Flaus. The film is shot in long takes with an overlapping soundtrack that gives mystique to the stories. There's a slight bizarre humor as well that permeates the different characters. One funny moment has a much-relieved Flaus sitting in the cops' offices after they have solved his case, removing his toupee to mop his brow. The actors give an interesting ensemble effort that never shows a hint of amateurism. That's quite an accomplishment from a group of mostly non-professional actors. Flaus was actually an Australian film lecturer. The film is not without its problems. The thick Australian accents may be difficult for an untrained ear to discern. PALM BEACH was shot in 16mm and blown up to 35mm, resulting in a far too grainy look that clearly was not intended.

p,d&w, Albie Thoms; ph, Oscar Scherl; m, Terry Hannigan; ed, Thoms.

Drama   **Cas.**   **(PR:O   MPAA:NR)**

PALM BEACH STORY, THE***   (1942) 90m PAR bw

Claudette Colbert (Gerry Jeffers), Joel McCrea (Tom Jeffers), Mary Astor (Princess Centimillia), Rudy Vallee (J.D. Hackensacker III), Sig Arno (Toto), Robert Warwick (Mr. Hinch), Arthur Stuart Hull (Mr. Osmond), Torben Meyer (Dr. Kluck), Jimmy Conlin (Mr. Asweld), Victor Potel (Mr. McKeewie), William Demarest, Jack Norton, Robert Greig, Roscoe Ates, Dewey Robinson, Chester Conklin, Sheldon Jett (Members of Ale and Quail Club), Robert Dudley (Wienie King), Franklin Pangborn (Manager), Arthur Hoyt (Pullman Conductor), Alan Bridge (Conductor), Fred "Snowflake" Toones (Black Bartender), Charles B. Moore (Black Porter), Frank Moran (Brakeman), Harry Rosenthal (Orchestra Leader), Esther Howard (Wife of Wienie King), Howard Mitchell (Man in Apartment), Harry Hayden (Prospect), Monte Blue (Doorman), Esther Michelson (Near-Sighted Woman), Edward J. McNamara (Officer in Penn Station), Harry Tyler (Gateman at Penn Station), Mantan Moreland (Waiter in Diner), Keith Richards (Shoe Salesman), Frank Faylen (Taxi Driver), Byron Foulger (Jewelry Salesman), Max Wagner (Rough-Looking Comic), Wilson Benge (Steward), John Holland (Best Man), J. Farrell MacDonald (O'Donnell), Julius Tannen (Proprietor of Store).

McCrea and Sturges had just come off the wonderful SULLIVAN'S TRAVELS which took many pot shots at Hollywood. They teamed again to snipe at the idle rich with this hysterically funny film that was almost a fairy tale in concept. The war was raging in 1942 and almost every movie coming out of Hollywood (except for the period pieces) had something to do with that conflict, so Sturges decided that what the country needed was some laughter and he more than succeeded with his script and direction. McCrea and Colbert have been married for five years, love

each other, and have everything—except money. He's an inventor with a few good ideas but without the wherewithal to finance them. Colbert loves him so much that she conceives a plan she feels will make sense: divorce McCrea, find a new and very rich husband, then use the man's money to help McCrea realize his ambitions. McCrea and Colbert have to give up their flat, and in walks Dudley, an impish old man with pockets stuffed with cash. (He is the 1940s equivalent of Ray Kroc, late owner of MacDonalds.) He gives Colbert a handful of bills and she immediately hops a train to the haunt of the very rich, Palm Beach, Florida. On the train she meets several millionaires on a spree. They are Demarest, Norton, Greig, Ates, Robinson, Conklin, and Jett. The group carries shotguns and laughingly shoots the windows out of the train. Meanwhile, Colbert has taken refuge in the club car and meets Vallee, an incredibly rich man who doesn't allow that wealth to get in the way of his kindliness. Vallee soon falls for Colbert and he invites her to be his guest and come aboard his yacht, where she meets his man-hungry sister, Astor, currently married to Arno (her fourth or fifth husband, no one is certain), a man who speaks in some unknown dialect that's uproarious. Astor is nicknamed "Princess" because she was once married to royalty. McCrea arrives with the express idea of dragging Colbert out of this den. Colbert talks him into posing as her brother (a plot twist seen in THE MONTE CARLO STORY 15 years later) so she can get money from Vallee. Astor wants McCrea as her next hubby and Vallee proposes to Colbert. All is well, though, when Colbert and McCrea (in a weak twist) reveal they have identical twins and a double wedding ends the proceedings. But until that sequence peters things out, this is a barrage of laughs. Vallee is terrific in the same sort of role played by Joe. E. Brown in SOME LIKE IT HOT.

p, Paul Jones; d&w, Preston Sturges; ph, Victor Milner; m, Victor Young; ed, Stuart Gilmore; art d, Hans Dreier, Ernst Fegte; cos, Irene; makeup, Wally Westmore.

Comedy   **(PR:A   MPAA:NR)**

PALM SPRINGS**   (1936) 71m PAR bw (GB: PALM SPRINGS AFFAIR)

Frances Langford (Joan Smyth), Sir Guy Standing (Capt. Smyth), Ernest Cossart (Starkey, Butler), Smith Ballew (Slim), David Niven (George Brittel), E. E. Clive (Bruce Morgan), Spring Byington (Aunt Letty), Sterling Holloway (Oscar), Grady Sutton (Bud), Sarah Edwards (Miss Pinchon), Ed Moose (Motorcycle Cop), Mary Jane Temple (Nurse), June Horn, Ann Doran, Ella McKenzie (School Girls), Fred "Snowflake" Toones (Porter), Frances Morris (Maid), David Worth (Leonard), Annabelle Brudie, Marianne Brudie (Twins), Lee Phelps (Bartender), Maidel Turner (Mrs. Baxter), Bert Gale (Caterer), Cyril Ring (Reception Clerk).

The great comic playwright George S. Kaufman was a stolid nonbeliever in the musical comedy. He felt that the songs were an annoyance that got in the way of jokes. PALM SPRINGS is a classic example of why his theory is correct. Standing plays a wealthy gambler who finds his funds quickly shrinking. He tries to get his daughter (Langford) to marry the ever-charming Niven, an English millionaire. She almost agrees but disappoints her father and his pocketbook when she falls for poor but honest cowboy Ballew. Potentially good moments in the story are sabotaged by the constant interruptions of musical numbers. This was Ballew's film debut, after a fine career on radio; Standing and Niven give the most effective performances. Songs include the hit tune "I'm in the Mood for Love" (Dorothy Fields, Jimmy McHugh), "The Hills of Old Wyoming" (Ralph Rainger, Leo Robin, sung by Smith Ballew, Frances Langford), "I Don't Want to Make History [I Just Want to Make Love]" (Rainger, Robin, sung by Langford), "Palm Springs," "Dreaming Out Loud" (Rainger, Robin), "Will I Ever Know" (Mack Gordon, Harry Revel, sung by Langford).

p, Walter Wanger; d, Aubrey Scotto; w, Joseph Fields, Humphrey Pearson (based on the story "Lady Smith" by Myles Connolly); ph, James Van Trees; md, Boris Morros; cos, Helen Taylor.

Musical Comedy   **(PR:A   MPAA:NR)**

PALM SPRINGS AFFAIR   (SEE: PALM SPRINGS, 1936)

PALM SPRINGS WEEKEND½**   (1963) 99m WB c

Troy Donahue (Jim Munroe), Connie Stevens (Gail Lewis), Ty Hardin (Stretch Fortune), Stefanie Powers (Bunny Dixon), Robert Conrad (Eric Dean), Andrew Duggan (Chief Dixon), Jack Weston (Coach Campbell), Carole Cook (Mrs. Yates), Jerry Van Dyke (Biff Roberts), Zeme North (Amanda North), Billy Mumy (Boom-Boom), Dorothy Green (Cora Dixon), Robert Gothie (Gabby), Greg Benedict (Hap), Gary Kincaid (Fred), Mark Dempsey (Mike), Jim Shane (Dave), Tina Cole (Ruth Stewart), Sandy Kevin, Roger Bacon, Margo Spinker, The Modern Folk Quartet.

Made during the era when beach films were popular with the teenage audience, PALM SPRINGS WEEKEND capitalized on the success of MGM's WHERE THE BOYS ARE (1960). Duggan plays the harried police chief of Palm Springs. Every spring the hotels are loaded with college kids looking for a good time with members of the opposite gender, including then teen idol Donahue, playing a medical student. Aboard his bus on the trip there is Stevens, a high-school girl pretending to be a wealthy college coed. The bus breaks down and Stevens hitches a ride with Conrad, a rich spoiled brat. Stevens also meets Hardin, a Hollywood stuntman, who becomes romantically interested in her. Donahue meets Powers, Duggan's daughter, and takes her to a party that turns into one rowdy affair. The cops burst in and arrest everyone, but Duggan lets them off with just a warning. Donahue is singled out by Duggan, and given the command to never see Powers again. Meanwhile, Stevens finds herself in trouble as Conrad tries to have his way with her. Hardin comes to her rescue and beats up the rich punk. Conrad is enraged and follows Hardin in his car, sideswiping the stuntman and causing him to crash in a fiery wreck. Donahue arrives on the scene and gets Hardin to a hospital. There he is visited by Stevens, who confesses her secret. A subplot concerns a college basketball coach, Weston, who manages to find romance with a Cook, a widow who runs the hotel where everyone is staying. Stevens' gawky roommate, North, also finds love in the klutzy form of Van Dyke. When it's finally time to leave, Donahue bids a tearful adieu to Powers, and she promises to wait for him. Even Duggan begins to change his mind about the college kids. Though the story is simplistic and the characters aren't anything more than the usual types, PALM SPRINGS WEEKEND is entertaining in its own way. The humor is innocuous enough and the players deliver their roles with an earnest freshness. The on-location shooting helps the story and the direction always manages to keep action on the screen. The screenplay is by Hamner, who went on to pen the fine television series "The Waltons."

p, Michael A. Hoey; d, Norman Taurog; w, Earl Hamner, Jr.; ph, Harold Lipstein (Technicolor); m, Frank Perkins; ed, Folmar Blangsted; art d, LeRoy Deane; set d, George James Hopkins; cos, B. Richards, M. Butler, Joyce Rogers, May Booth, Norma Brown; m/l, "Live Young," Larry Kusik, Paul Evans (sung by Troy Donahue); makeup, Gordon Bau, Norman Pringle, Fred Williams.

Teenage Comedy/Drama (PR:C MPAA:NR)

PALMY DAYS*** (1931) 80m UA bw

Eddie Cantor (Eddie Simpson), Charlotte Greenwood (Helen Martin), Spencer Charters (A.B. Clark), Barbara Weeks (Joan Clark), George Raft (Joe the Frog), Paul Page (Steve Clayton), Harry Woods (Plug Moynihan), Charles B. Middleton (Yolando), Loretta Andrews, Edna Callahan, Nadine Dore, Ruth Edding, Betty Grable, Amo Ingraham, Jean Lenivick, Betty Lorraise, Fay Pierre, Hylah Slocum, Betty Stockton, Nita Pike, Nancy Nash, Neva Lynn, Hazel Witter (The Goldwyn Girls), Walter Catlett.

A cute followup to Goldwyn's production of WHOOPEE, this farcical musical, like its predecessor, had the benefit of Berkeley's choreography, and the master was developing the style that was to make him famous. Lots of pretty girls, plenty of songs, and the incredible energy of Cantor triumphed over a fairly ordinary story that sees shy Cantor, a nervous type who sings when he gets too excited, working in a bogus spiritualist scam for his downstairs neighbor, Middleton. Charters owns a successful bakery and consults Middleton from time to time and is on the verge of being swindled by the phony medium. Through a mistake, Cantor is hired as the efficiency expert for the bakery and thinks he's in love with Charters' daughter, Weeks, but the company's physical culturist, Greenwood, isn't about to let that happen. Middleton gets Cantor to secure the bakery safe's combination, then Cantor won't give it to the villain. Middleton sends his henchmen, Raft and Woods, to "convince" Cantor to turn over the information. Cantor sees the hoods coming after him, hides in the company gym, dresses in drag, and tries to blend in with the Goldwyn Girls (as bakery workers). He darn near pulls it off until Greenwood, who can't see past the disguise, orders Cantor to take a shower with the other women. Cantor manages to escape Raft and Woods, goes to the office, takes out the weekly payroll cash, and slips it into a loaf of unbaked dough which is mistakenly baked into a bread. Middleton tells Charters that Cantor stole the money and suggests Cantor be turned over to the cops. Greenwood and Cantor race to the ovens to try and find the correct loaf containing all the money. There is a breakneck chase as Cantor and Greenwood attempt to locate the dough in the dough while the bad guys try to locate them. Cantor finally finds the missing money and gives it to Charters, who blows the whistle on Middleton and his malfeasants. When Cantor learns that the girl of his dreams, Weeks, is going to marry her longtime boy friend, Page, he shrugs it off and contents himself with Greenwood, whom everyone knew he would wind up with from the start. It's hokey and jokey but it never stops pleasing. Look hard at the Goldwyn Girls and note Betty Grable, in her seventh film appearance, a few of which were as one of Sam Goldwyn's nubile beauties. No smash hits in the score but the songs were pleasant enough and kept the action humming. Tunes include: "Bend Down, Sister" (Ballard MacDonald, Con Conrad, sung by Charlotte Greenwood, the Goldwyn Girls), "Goose Pimples" (MacDonald, Conrad, sung by Greenwood), "Dunk Dunk Dunk" (MacDonald, Conrad, sung by the Goldwyn Girls), "My Honey Said Yes, Yes" (Cliff Friend, sung by Canter, the Goldwyn Girls, reprised by Cantor, Greenwood, the Preacher [unbilled]), "There's Nothing Too Good for My Baby" (Cantor, Benny Davis, Harry Akst, sung by Cantor). Greenwood is delightful as the randy woman out to put stars in Cantor's banjo eyes. This acrobatic dancer and comedienne began in movies at the age of 18 and continued her high kicks until well into her sixties. Raft was appearing in his fourth film and added little to the picture, having not yet settled in on the screen persona which stood him in such good stead for many years. Cantor had a chance to do all his tricks, including his standard "blackface" number, a drag scene, and his usual frenetic chase.

p, Samuel Goldwyn; d, A. Edward Sutherland; w, Morrie Ryskind, Keene Thompson, David Freedman, Eddie Cantor (based on a story by Ryskind, Freedman, Cantor); ph, Gregg Toland; ed, Sherman Todd; md, Alfred Newman; art d, Richard Day; set d, Willy Pogany; cos, Chanel; ch, Busby Berkeley.

Musical/Comedy (PR:A MPAA:NR)

PALOMINO, THE**½ (1950) 73m COL c (GB: HILLS OF THE BRAVE)

Jerome Courtland (Steve Norris), Beverly Tyler (Maria Guevara), Joseph Calleia (Miguel Gonzales), Roy Roberts (Ben Lane), Gordon Jones (Bill), Robert Osterloh (Sam), Tom Trout (Williams), Harry Garcia (Johnny), Trevor Bardette (Brown), Juan Duval (Manuel).

Courtland plays the son of a meat packer who meets Tyler, the owner of a once highly successful breeding ranch for palominos. It's not exactly love at first sight as the two engage in constant fighting. However, when Tyler's prize colt is stolen by villain Roberts for his rustling operation, Courtland comes to the animal's rescue and wins Tyler's heart. The plot is standard, with ridiculously simplistic characters. But there's some beautiful mountain scenery and plenty of footage of the golden palominos. In spite of the plot's relatively unsophisticated development, THE PALOMINO does have some moments of genuine entertainment, particularly for children and horse lovers.

p, Robert Cohn; d, Ray Nazarro; w, Tom Kilpatrick; ph, Vincent Farrar (Technicolor); ed, Aaron Stell; md, M. Bakaleinikoff; art d, Perry Smith.

Western/Adventure (PR:AAA MPAA:NR)

PALOOKA*** (1934) 86m Reliance/UA bw (GB: THE GREAT SCHNOZZLE; AKA: JOE PALOOKA)

Jimmie Durante (Knobby Walsh), Lupe Velez (Nina Madero), Stuart Erwin (Joe Palooka), Marjorie Rambeau (Mayme Palooka), Robert Armstrong (Pete Palooka), Mary Carlisle (Anne), William Cagney (Al McSwatt), Thelma Todd (Trixie), Franklyn Ardell (Doc Wise), Tom Dugan (Whitey), Guinn "Big Boy" Williams (Slats), Stanley Fields (Blacky), Louise Beavers (Crystal), Fred "Snowflake" Toones (Smokey), Al Hill (Dynamite Wilson), Gordon De Main (Photographers' Official), Gus Arnheim and His Orchestra.

Durante plays the great fight manager from Ham Fisher's famed comic strip, who finds a young pugster Erwin knocking things around a gym and trains the kid for the "big fight." His opponent is Cagney, the younger (and less talented) brother of Jimmy. He plays a drunken champ who is easily defeated by Erwin. This is a fun comedy with all the right elements for a good time at the movies. Durante is wonderful in his first big role, and he even has an opportunity to sing his trademark "Ink-a-Dinka-Do!" (Ben Ryan, Durante). The dialog is clever with good direction on both the comedy and fight sequences. There is no connection with any of the other JOE PALOOKA films made in the late 1940s. Other songs include: "Like Me a Little Bit Less [Love Me a Little Bit More]" (Harold Adamson, Burton Lane), "Palooka, It's a Grand Old Name" (Ann Ronnell, Joe Burke), "Count Your Blessings" (Irving Caesar, Ferde Grofe, Edgar A. Guest). (See JOE PALOOKA series, Index.)

d, Benjamin Stoloff; w, Ben Ryan, Murray Roth, Gertrude Purcell, Jack Jevne, Arthur Kober (based on the comic strip by Ham Fisher); ph, Arthur Edeson; ed, Grant Whytock.

Comedy Cas. (PR:AA MPAA:NR)

PALS OF THE GOLDEN WEST** (1952) 78m REP bw

Roy Rogers (Himself), Dale Evans (Cathy Marsh), Estelita Rodriguez (Elena Madera), Pinky Lee (Pinky), Anthony Caruso (Jim Bradford), Roy Barcroft (Ward Sloan), Edwardo Jiminez (Pancho), Ken Terrell (Tony), Emmett Vogan (Col. Wells), Maurice Jara (Lopez), The Roy Rogers Riders, Trigger the Horse, Bullet the Dog.

The last film in Rogers' famous series. Barcroft and Caruso are trying to bring some diseased cattle into the U.S. Border Patrolman Rogers has to stop them from spreading the hoof-and-mouth disease. Though another patrolman is gunned down and there's a terrible sandstorm, Rogers manages to stop the villains and keep American cattle disease-free. Unfortunately Rogers' last outing is no different than any other average work in the series. Hoof-and-mouth disease was an oft recurring plot motif in his films. However, his real-life wife, Evans, makes an appearance, and there are a few good cowpoke tunes—"Slumber Trail," "Beyond the Great Divide," "You Never Know When Love May Come Along," as well as the title number (Jack Elliott, Aaron Gonzales, Jordan Smith). This was far from the end of Rogers' career for shortly after this picture was released, he and Evans began working on their first television series for NBC, which was essentially the same as his film work.

p, Edward J. White; d, William Witney; w, Albert DeMond, Eric Taylor (based on a story by Sloan Nibley); ph, Jack Marta; m, Stanley Wilson; ed, Harold Minter; art d, Frank Hotaling.

Western Cas. (PR:A MPAA:NR)

PALS OF THE PECOS**½ (1941) 56m REP bw

Robert Livingston (Stony Brooke), Bob Steele (Tucson Smith), Rufe Davis (Lullaby Joslin), Robert Winkler (Tim Burke), June Johnson (June), Pat O'Malley (Jim Burke), Dennis Moore (Larry Burke), Roy Barcroft (Keno Hawkins), John Holland (Buckley), Tom London (Sheriff), Robert Frazer (Stevens), George Chesebro, Chuck Morrison, Bud Osborne, Jack Kirk, Forrest Taylor, Frank Ellis, Eddie Dean.

Another in the THREE MESQUITEERS films finds the trio saving a stagecoach line from being shut down by the villain. The setting is 1858 in the Old West, one of the few Mesquiteers films that does not occur in the modern West. The dialog and action are clean and crisp despite the simplistic and routine plot. Johnson plays the love interest for Livingston. (See THREE MESQUITEERS series, Index.)

p, Louis Gray; d, Les Orlebeck; w, Oliver Drake, Herbert Delmas (based on a story by Drake from characters created by William Colt MacDonald); ph, Reggie Lanning; ed, Ray Snyder.

Western Cas. (PR:A MPAA:NR)

PALS OF THE RANGE** (1935) 57m Merrick/Superior bw

Rex Lease, Francis Wright [Morris], Yakima Canutt, George Chesebro, [Robert]Blackie Whiteford, Milburn Morante, Joey Ray, Tom Forman, Artie Ortego, Bill Patton, Art Mix, Bud Osborne, Ben Corbett, George Morrell.

After wrongly being jailed on cattle rustling charges, an honest and true-blue rancher breaks loose from the pokey in order to track down and nab the evil nasties behind the crime. Typical western actioner.

p, Louis Weiss, George M. Merrick; d, Elmer Clifton; w, Merrick, Clifton.

Western (PR:A MPAA:NR)

PALS OF THE SADDLE**½ (1938) 55m REP bw

John Wayne (Stony Brooke), Ray Corrigan (Tucson Smith), Max Terhune (Lullaby Joslin), Doreen McKay (Ann), Josef Forte (Judge Hastings), George Douglas (Paul Hartman), Frank Milan (Frank Paige), Ted Adams (Henry C. Gordon), Harry

Depp (Hotel Clerk), Dave Weber (Russian Musician), Don Orlando (Italian Musician), Charles Knight (English Musician), Jack Kirk (Sheriff), Monte Montague, Olin Francis, Curley Dresden, Art Dillard, Tex Palmer.

This addition to the THREE MESQUITEERS series marked the debut of Wayne, who replaced Bob Livingston in the role of Stony Brooke. Most of the Mesquiteers films involved present-day adventures in the West, as does this outing in which Wayne discovers some enemy agents trying to smuggle a deadly chemical, Monium, from which poisonous gas can be made, into Mexico. There they plan to sell it to foreign agents. But leave it to the Mesquiteers to save the day. The plot is overly complicated, but this enjoyable western is a good beginning for Wayne in the series. (See THREE MESQUITEERS series, Index.)

p, William Berke; d, George Sherman; w, Betty Burbridge, Stanley Roberts (based on characters created by William Colt MacDonald); ph, Reggie Lanning; ed, Tony Martinelli; md, Cy Feuer.

Western   Cas.   (PR:A MPAA:NR)

PALS OF THE SILVER SAGE   (1940) 52m MON bw

Tex Ritter (Tex Wright), Sugar Dawn (Sugar), Slim Andrews (Cactus), Clarissa Curtis (Ruth), Glenn Strange (Vic Insley), Carleton Young (Jeff), John McGuinn (Cowhide), Chester Gann (Ling), Warner Richmond (Sheriff), John Merton, Evelyn Daw, Gene Alsace, Harry Harvey, Fred Parker, White Flash the Horse.

Typical Ritter B-western finds him working for 6-year-old Dawn after her folks pass on. He discovers Dawn's foreman, also her cousin, is changing brands on her cattle. It's unexciting with unconvincing dialog, the usual amount of ritter tunes, and standard production values.

p, Edward Finney; d, Al Herman; w, George Martin; ph, Marcel Le Picard; ed, Robert Golden; m/l, Johnny Lange, Lew Porter.

Western   (PR:A MPAA:NR)

PAMPA SALVAJE   (SEE: SAVAGE PAMPAS, 1967, U.S./Span./Arg.)

PANAMA FLO*   (1932) 72m Pathe/RKO bw

Helen Twelvetrees (Flo Bennett), Robert Armstrong (Babe), Charles Bickford (McTeague), Marjorie Peterson (Pearl), Maude Eburne (Sadie), Paul Hurst (Al), Ernie Adams (Jake the Bartender), Reina Veles (Chaera), Hans Joby (Pilot).

Twelvetrees plays a showgirl mixed up with a gangster. To avoid going to jail, she is offered a job as a housekeeper to Bickford, a local businessman. After her boy friend (Armstrong) returns from supposedly being lost in an air accident, she finds out that he is merely using her to get to the rich man's money. She shoots Armstrong, and thinks she has killed him. Bickford sends her to New York and promises to join her there, where they will be married. As it turns out, she did not kill Armstrong because Bickford fired a second shot that proved to be the fatal bullet. This turgid programmer has many problems: the script is riddled with plot inconsistencies and the characters' motivations are confusing, with Armstrong, at first the romantic interest, becoming the heavy, and Bickford switching from bad guy to hero. It was all too pat and easy to be believed. Remade in 1939 as PANAMA LADY with Lucille Ball.

p, Harry Joe Brown; d, Ralph Murphy; w, Garrett Fort; ph, Arthur Miller; ed, Charles Craft.

Drama   (PR:A MPAA:NR)

PANAMA HATTIE**   (1942) 79m MGM bw

Ann Sothern (Hattie Maloney), Dan Dailey, Jr. (Dick Bulliet), Red Skelton (Red), Marsha Hunt (Leila Tree), Virginia O'Brien (Flo Foster), Rags Ragland (Rags), Alan Mowbray (Jay Perkins), Ben Blue (Howdy), Jackie Horner (Geraldine Bulliet), Carl Esmond (Lucas Kefler), Pierre Watkin (Adm. Tree), Stanley Andrews (Col. John Briggs), Lena Horne (Specialty), George Watts (Mac the Bartender), Lucien Prival (Hans), Joe Yule (Waiter), Duke York (Bruno), Fred Graham (Naval Policeman), Roger Moore (Spy), Max Wagner (Guard), Grant Withers (Shore Patrol), The Berry Brothers (Themselves), Carmen Amaya Dancers.

A terrific Broadway play was fiddled with until they changed it into a dull movie that was only highlighted by the few Porter tunes that were salvaged from the original stage show. MGM paid $130,000 for the rights to the play, then tossed much of it aside in favor of this ho-hum outing. In New York, it starred Ethel Merman, James Dunn, Arthur Treacher, Rags Ragland, Betty Hutton, and Joan Carroll and it ran over 500 performances following the 1940 opening. When the war began, they added the extra dimension of spies in the Canal Zone just to show they had been reading the newspapers and listening to Edward R. Murrow on the radio. This is a clunker with a story line so thin that it hardly can be synopsized. Sothern runs a nightclub in Panama, some sailors enter, a few spies are tossed in to relieve the vaudeville-like production numbers, and the picture is over. It ran less than 80 minutes and managed to pack in a host of songs, so you can get the idea that the story material was nearly nonexistent. Tunes by Cole Porter include: "It Was Just One Of Those Things" (sung by Lena Horne, in her second film), "Fresh as a Daisy" (sung by Virginia O'Brien), "I've Still Got My Health" (sung by Ann Sothern), "Let's Be Buddies" (sung by Sothern, Horner), "Make It Another Old Fashioned" (sung by Sothern). Other songs are: "Hattie from Panama," "Good Neighbors," "I'll Do Anything for You" (Roger Edens), "The Son of a Gun Who Picks on Uncle Sam" (Burton Lane, E. Y. "Yip" Harburg), "Did I Get Stinkin' at the Savoy?" (Walter Donaldson, Harburg, sung by O'Brien), "The Sping" (Phil Moore, J. Le Gon), "La Bumba Rhumba" (Alex Hyde), "Berry Me Not" (Moore), "Hail, Hail, the Gang's All Here" (Sir Arthur Sullivan's music from "The Pirates of Penzance" (lyrics by Theodore F. Morse). Off-stage music included "They Ain't Done Right by Our Nell" (Porter). Three songs were deleted from the final print. They were "Stop Off in Panama," "Salome" (Roger, Edens), and "Cookin with Gas" (Edens, Lenny Hayton). Despite the uncredited script work by Lillie Messinger, Mary C. McCall, Jr., Joseph Schrank, as well as uncredited direction by

Vincente Minnelli and Roy Del Ruth, plus sketches by Fred Finklehoffe and Minnelli, nothing could save this. Minnelli did take credit for staging the dances and there was something called "technical advice" by Sergio R. Orta. The excellent vocal and orchestration arrangements were by George Bassman and Conrad Salinger. With all the flaws, this trifle made more than $4 million on the first release, an indication of how much the U.S. wanted to forget that a war was going on. Good burlesque work from Skelton, Blue, and Ragland (the only repeater from Broadway) provided what little humor there was.

p, Arthur Freed; d, Norman Z. McLeod; w, Jack McGowan, Wilkie Mahoney (based on the play by Herbert Fields, B.G. De Sylva, Cole Porter); ph, George Folsey; ed, Blanche Sewell; md, George Stoll; art d, Cedric Gibbons; set d, Edwin B. Willis, Hugh Hunt; cos, Kalloch; ch, Danny Dare, Vincente Minnelli.

Musical/Comedy   (PR:A MPAA:NR)

PANAMA LADY*½   (1939) 64m RKO bw

Lucille Ball (Lucy), Allan Lane (McTeague), Steffi Duna (Cheema), Evelyn Brent (Lenore), Donald Briggs (Roy Harmon), Bernadene Hayes (Pearl), Abner Biberman (Elisha), William Pawley (Bartender), Earle Hodgins (Foreman), Joe Devlin (2nd Bartender).

Ball is a cabaret singer in Panama. She gets involved with Brent and Hayes in a scheme to rob drunken oilman Lane. When Ball gets caught she goes to work for the man in order to avoid jail. Duna is a jealous native girl whose temper flairs when Lane's affections swing towards the new housekeeper. The drama is dull, hampered by a witless script. Remake of RKO's PANAMA FLO (1932), which was worse.

p, Cliff Reid; d, Jack Hively; w, Michael Kanin (based on a story by Garrett Fort); ph, J. Roy Hunt; ed, Theron Warth; md, Roy Webb; art d, Van Nest Polglase; cos, Edward Stevenson; spec eff, Vernon L. Walker.

Drama   Cas.   (PR:A MPAA:NR)

PANAMA PATROL½**   (1939) 67m FA/GN bw

Leon Ames (Lt. Phillip Waring), Charlotte Wynters (Helen Lane), Weldon Heyburn (Lt. Murdock), Adrienne Ames (Lia Maing), Abner Biberman (Arlie Johnson), Hugh McArthur (Lt. Everett), Donald Barry (Lt. Loring), John E. Smart (Eli Maing), Lai Chand Mehra (Singh), William Von Brincken (Marlin), Richard Loo (Tommy Young), Frank Darien (Sam), Paul McVey (Baird), Gerald Mohr (Pilot), Harry Bradley (Clerk), Philson Ahn (Khantow), Philip Ahn (Suri), Lew Kelly (Knowles).

Ames and Wynters are a pair of army officers set to be married. While at the marriage license bureau, they are interrupted by a call from their office. Then they're off to the Panama Canal, where they have to stop a group of Chinese spies. The group's actions are foiled, and the happy couple can marry at last. Though a solid B film with good plot development and first-rate photography, too much detail is given to the workings of such things as code deciphering, which causes the film to drag in spots. There's also an absence of comic relief. Ames and Wynters make a good team, with Biberman fine in his role as a traitorous intelligence officer.

p&d, Charles Lamont; w, Arthur Hoerl (based on a story by Hoerl, Monroe Shaff); ph, Arthur Martinelli; ed, Bernard Loftus; md, David Chudnow; art d, Ralph Berger; set d, Glenn Thompson.

Spy Drama   (PR:A MPAA:NR)

PANAMA SAL*½   (1957) 70m Vineland/REP bw

Elena Verdugo (Sal Regan), Edward Kemmer (Dennis P. Dennis), Carlos Rivas (Manuel Ortego), Harry Jackson (Peter Van Fleet II), Joe Flynn ((Barrington C. Ashbrook), Christine White (Patricia Sheldon), Albert Carrier (Moray), Jose Gonzales Gonzales (Peon), Billie Bird (Woman Manager), Ukonu and his Afro-Calypsonians.

A "Pygmalion in Panama" as playboy Kemmer meets native girl Verdugo and tries to transform her into a Beverly Hills socialite. He meets her in a Panamanian waterfront saloon where she sings her heart out night after night. Kemmer promises her stardom in Hollywood so she goes back to the States with him. But the new setting proves to be too much and she runs away. Kemmer chases her for he realizes he loves her. Verdugo sings vigorously, but otherwise her performance is lackluster. The script develops slowly and contains insipid dialog. While the direction is little more than a camera pointed at the action, never adding anything to the proceedings. PANAMA SAL was filmed in black and white with a Naturama processing that falls off around the edges, causing further distraction to an already troubled film.

p, Edward J. White; d, William Witney; w, Arnold Belgard; ph, Jack Marta (Naturama); ed, Joseph Harrison; md, Gerald Roberts; art d, Ralph Oberg; ch, Roland Dupree; m/l, Joe Hooven, Marilyn Hooven.

Drama   (PR:A MPAA:NR)

PAN-AMERICANA½**   (1945) 84m RKO bw

Phillip Terry (Dan), Audrey Long (Jo Anne), Robert Benchley (Charlie), Eve Arden (Hoppy), Ernest Truex (Uncle Rudy), Marc Cramer (Jerry), Isabelita (Lupita), Bill Garvin (Sancho), Frank Marasco (Miguel), Armando Gonzales (Carlos), Joan Beckstead (Miss Peru), Valerie Hall (Miss El Salvador), Luz Vasquez (Miss Mexico), Betty Joy Curtis (Miss Bolivia), Goya Del Valle (Miss Panama), Carmen Lopez (Miss Paraguay), Aldonna Gauvin (Miss Uruguay), Velera Burton (Miss Dutch Guiana), Ruth Lorran (Miss Honduras), Alma Beltran (Miss Guatemala), Nina Bara (Miss Argentina), Shirley Karnes (Miss Dominican Republic), George Mendoza (Waiter), Bettejane [Jane] Greer (Miss Downing), Mary Halsey (Switchboard Operator), Nancy Marlowe (Pretty Office Girl), Elaine Riley (Girl), Hugh Hendrikson (Juan), Fernando Ramos (Jose), Leif Argo (Pedro), Albano Valerio (Mexican Ambassador), Tom Costello (Brazilian Ambassador), Evita Lopez (Mexican Flower Girl), Julian Rivero (Pablo), Jesus Castillion (Specialty), Douglas

Madore, Boots Le Baron (*Boys*), Francis Revel, David Cota (*Waiters*), Rita Corday, Patti Brill, Rosemary La Planche, Susan Walsh, Greta Christensen, Virginia Belmont (*Pan American Girls*), Rossario and Antonio, Miguelito Valdes, Chuy Castillion, Padillia Sisters, Chuy Reyes' Orchestra, Nestor Amaral's Samba Band, Chinita Marin, Harold and Lola, Louise Burnett.

Long plays the pretty feature writer for "Western World" magazine. She goes to South America in search of stories for the journal, as well as a long-awaited rendezvous with her fiance, Cramer, an American businessman living in Rio. But will her heart swoon for Terry, the handsome photographer who accompanies her? The plot is utter nonsense and little more than an excuse to showcase some great Latin American musical acts. The best of the lot includes flamenco dance team Rosario and Antonio. There's also some great songs, including "Ba-Ba-Lu" (Bob Russell, Marguerita Lecuna), which would later become a trademark song for Desi Arnaz. Narration was provided by Benchley, who was on loan from Paramount. Other songs include: "Stars in Your Eyes," "La Morine de Mi Copla" (Gabriel Ruiz, Mort Greene), "Rhumba Matumba" (Bobby Collazo, Greene), "Guadalajara" (Pepe Guizar, Greene), "Negra Leona" (A. Fernandez, Greene), "Baramba" (Lecuona, Greene).

p&d, John H. Auer; w, Lawrence Kimble (based on a story by Frederick Kohner, Auer); ph, Frank Redman; ed, Harry Marker; cos, Renie; ch, Charles O'Curran.

Musical   **(PR:A MPAA:NR)**

PANAMINT'S BAD MAN*½   (1938) 58m Principal/FOX bw

Smith Ballew (*Kimball*), Evelyn Daw (*Joan*), Noah Beery, Sr. (*Gorman*), Stanley Fields (*Black Jack*), Harry Woods (*Craven*), Pat O'Brien (*Carl Adams*), Armand "Curly" Wright (*Nicola*).

Ballew plays a U.S. deputy assigned to infiltrate a band of stagecoach robbers. The outlaws are led by the scowling Beery, who constantly twitches his moustache. All works out well in the end, with bad guy Fields seeing the light, and Daw listening to Ballew sing his affections. This was the fifth and last cowboy picture for Ballew. Producer Lesser had seen him play a cowboy in PALM SPRINGS (1936) and was convinced that this Gary Cooper look-alike would be a natural for a B-western series of his own. However Ballew's acting was barely adequate and, consequently, he never caught on as hoped.

p, Sol Lesser; d, Ray Taylor; w, Luci Ward, Charles Arthur Powell (based on a story by Edmund Kelso, Lindsley Parsons); ph, Allen Thompson; ed, Albert Jordan.

Western   **Cas.**   **(PR:A MPAA:NR)**

PANCHO VILLA*½   (1975, Span.) 90m Granada/Scotia International c

Telly Savalas (*Pancho Villa*), Clint Walker (*Villa's Lieutenant*), Anne Francis, Chuck Connors, Angel Del Pozo, Jose Maria Prada.

Savalas is the Mexican revolutionary in this uneventful and fictionalized account of the man. Savalas and his men cross the American border and take over an Army outpost after being duped in a deal for arms. Connors plays the officer in charge of the fort. The Mexican invaders are finally chased back across the border by General Pershing. Exciting conclusion involves a head-on collision with two trains.

p, Bernard Gordon; d, Eugene Martin; w, Julian Halevy; ph, Alejandro Ulloa.

Western   **Cas.**   **(PR:C MPAA:PG)**

PANCHO VILLA RETURNS**   (1950, Mex.) 95m Hispano Continental bw

Leo Carrillo (*Pancho Villa*), Esther Fernandez (*Teresa Mota*), Jeanette Comber (*Rosario*), Rodolfo Acosta (*Martin Corona*), Rafael Alcayde (*Serpio Reyna*), Jorge Trevino (*Col. Lopera*), Eduardo Gonzalez Pliego (*Father Romo*), Humberto Alamazan (*Tadeo Mota*).

This has more to do with Pancho Villa the myth rather than the man. He is presented as a good man, leading his revolutionaries against the men who killed Mexico's president. Carrillo (later to co-star in the television series "Cisco Kid") does well with his role as do the supporting cast members. Though there is plenty of expertly staged action, the direction is too soft. Also, Villa here is too nice, a kind-hearted disciplinarian who probably could never lead a revolution. Filmed by a Mexican production company in English dialog.

p,d,&w, Miguel Contreras Torres; ph, Alex Phillips; m, Elias Breeskin.

Western   **(PR:A MPAA:NR)**

PANDA AND THE MAGIC SERPENT**   (1961, Jap.) 76m Toei/Globe c (HAKUJA DEN)

Marvin Miller (*Narrator*).

A children's animated feature from Japan adapted from a Chinese fairy tale. A young boy falls in love with an immortal, who was transformed into human form from a white snake. They journey through China with a raccoon and a panda until a wizard tries to drown the two lovers in the Yangtze River. When he fails, he attempts to frame the boy on charges of theft. The raccoon and panda aid in the boy's escape, but he is killed in a fall while chasing the immortal girl's shadow. The girl gives up her immortality to the dragon god to bring the boy back to life so they can spend their lives together.

p, Hiroshi Okawa; d, Kazuhiko Okabe, Teiji Yabushita; w, Yabushita, Shin Uehara, Seiichi Yashiro; ph, Takamitsu Tsukahara (Eastmancolor); m, Chuji Kinoshita; ed, Shintaro Miyamoto; art d, Okabe, Kiyoshi Hashimoto; animator, Yasuo Otsuka, Yusaku Sakamoto; original drawings, Akira Daikubara, Yasuji Mori; background, Kazuo Kusano.

Animation   **Cas.**   **(PR:A MPAA:NR)**

PANDEMONIUM zero   (1982) 82m MGM/UA c (AKA: THURSDAY THE 12TH)

Tom Smothers (*Cooper*), Debralee Scott (*Sandy*), Candy Azzara (*Bambi*), Suzanne Kent, Phil Hartmann, Michael Kless, David L. Lander, Bradley Lieberman, Victoria Carroll, Teri Landrum, Alix Elias, Ebbe Roe Smith, Randy Bennett, Miles Chapin, Marc McClure, Pat Ast, David Becker, Paul Reubens, John Paragon, Don McLeod, David McCharen, Richard C. Adams, Nancy Ryan, Jim Boeke, Gary Allen, Eve Arden, Kaye Ballard, Tab Hunter, Sydney Lassick, Edie McClurg, Jim McKrell, Lenny Montana, Donald O'Connor, Richard Romanus, Izabella Telezynska, Carol Kane, Judge Reinhold, Randi & Candi Brough.

With the success of AIRPLANE! a series of film genre parodies followed. Most were mercifully ignored, including this mess. Taking the mad slasher/kill-a-teenager genre to task here, a mad killer haunts the campus of It Had To Be U., murdering the students in various silly ways (the "Cheerleader shish kebab, or five-on-a-javelin" surely must have been the fulfillment of a former scorned high-school student working on the film). Despite the relatively talented cast, this goes nowhere in a hurry. It tries to be "so bad it's good," but never develops its thin premise with any effect. The only slashing that should happen with this film is to cut it up into guitar picks. Paul Reubens, who later became known as Pee Wee Herman, makes a guest appearance.

p, Doug Chapin; d, Alfred Sole; w, Richard Whitley, Jaime Klein; ph, Michel Hugo (Panavision, Technicolor); m, Dana Kaproff; ed, Eric Jenkins; prod d, Jack DeShields; art d, James Claytor; cos, Roberta Weiner; spec eff, Bob Dawson; makeup, Bob Mills.

Comedy/Horror   **(PR:C MPAA:PG)**

PANDORA AND THE FLYING DUTCHMAN**   (1951, Brit.) 123m Dorkay-Romulus/MGM c

James Mason (*Hendrick van der Zee*), Ava Gardner (*Pandora Reynolds*), Nigel Patrick (*Stephen Cameron*), Sheila Sim (*Janet Fielding*), Harold Warrender (*Geoffrey Fielding*), Mario Cabre (*Juan Montalvo*), John Laurie (*Angus*), Pamela Kellino (*Jenny Ford*), Patricia Raine (*Peggy Ford*), Margarita d'Alvarez (*Senora Montalvo*), Marius Goring (*Reggie Demarest*), La Pillina (*Spanish Dancer*), Abraham Sofaer (*Judge*), Francisco Igual (*Vincente*), Guillermo Beltran (*Barman*), Lila Moinar [*Lily Molnar*] (*Geoffrey's Housekeeper*), Phoebe Hodgson (*Dressmaker*), John Carew (*Priest*), Edward Leslie (*Doctor*), Christina Forbes (*Nurse*), Gabriel Carmona, Antonio Martin (*Members of Montalvo's Quadrilla*), Helen Cleveley, Gerald Welsh.

Partly based on the folk tale of the same name, PANDORA AND THE FLYING DUTCHMAN is a painstakingly researched film that eventually gets too somber and sinks. The picture begins with two bodies being washed up on the Spanish coast and then proceeds to explain that Gardner, an expatriate American living in 1930s Spain is a devil-may-care woman who doesn't have the emotional ability to return any of the love that men lavish on her. She is stoic when a young man takes his own life over her, then she decides to marry Patrick, a race driver, more on an impulse than on a well thought-out decision. Before she can say "I do," she notes a large boat in the harbor. She swims out to see who is aboard and meets Mason, the captain, a Dutchman who is, to say the least, enigmatic about his background. Now we discover that Mason is a man condemned by Fate to sail the seas forever and can become human only once every seven years. If he can find one woman who is willing to give up her life for him, his eerie voyage can end and his soul can go to rest. Gardner is that woman but Mason loves her so much he doesn't want her to lose her life over him. One of Gardner's former fiances is Cabre, a matador, and he wants to get back into Gardner's affections, so he arranges a bullfight. Patrick wants to show how brave *he* is and tries to break the world's land speed record and crashes his auto. Later, not badly hurt, he comes back and Mason and Gardner have already gone. Cabre understands that Patrick is not his rival for Gardner's affections: Rather, his rival is Mason. Cabre tries to kill Mason, but, of course, since Mason is not alive, he can't be killed. Cabre dies in the bullfight and Mason and Gardner are united in death when they commit suicide together. Very lengthy for the material and ultimately unsatisfying, the movie looked wonderful under Cardiff's lensing of the Spanish land and seascape. Gardner sings two 1930s songs: "You're Driving Me Crazy" (Walter Donaldson) and "How Am I To Know?" (Jack King, Dorothy Parker). In a small role, Mason's wife, acting under her first husband's name, is featured. This is Pamela Killino (former wife of British director Roy Kellino), who chose to use that name instead of Ostrer, the name she was born with.

p, Albert Lewin, Joseph Kaufman; d&w, Lewin (based on the version of the Flying Dutchman legend in the opera by Richard Wagner); ph, Jack Cardiff (Technicolor); m, Alan Rawsthorne; ed, Ralph Kemplen; md, Dr. Hubert Clifford, Rawsthorne; art d, Tim Hopewell-Ash, John Bryan; set d, John Hawkesworth; cos, Beatrice Dawson, Julia Squire.

Drama   **(PR:A-C MPAA:NR)**

PANHANDLE***   (1948) 85m AA bw

Rod Cameron (*John Sands*), Cathy Downs (*Dusty Stewart*), Reed Hadley (*Matt Carson*), Anne Gwynne (*June O'Carroll*), Blake Edwards (*Floyd Schofield*), Dick Crockett (*Elliott*), Rory Mallinson (*Sheriff*), Charles Judels (*Barber*), Alex Gerry (*McBride*), Francis McDonald (*Crump*), J. Farrell MacDonald (*Doc Cooper*), Henry Hall (*Wells*), Stanley Andrews (*Tyler*), Jeff York (*Jack*), James Harrison (*Harland*), Charles LaTorre (*Juan*), Frank Dae (*Regan*), Bud Osborne.

Cameron gives a fine portrayal of a retired gunman who straps on his six-shooter once more to revenge his brother's death. Hadley is the murderer who wants to control the entire territory. Of course he's gunned down by the hero and loses his secretary to Cameron as well. A secretary in a Western? Who works for the bad guy no less? Gwynne's lively portrayal makes the character believable and funny but then again the production team on this B flick was a cut above most. The freshness and ingenuity are the work of none other than Blake Edwards, who served as co-producer and co-writer on this, his first film. He also gives a fine performance as Hadley's baby-faced gang member. Edwards' inventiveness was appreciated in this genre, usually ridden with cliches. He went on to great renown as a director with his PINK PANTHER films, as well as witty farces like VICTOR, VICTORIA. He did make one western as a director, the well received WILD ROVERS in 1971. Director Lesley Selander remade the movie in 1966 as THE TEXAN.

p, Blake Edwards, John C. Champion; d, Lesley Selander; w, Edwards, Champion; ph, Harry Neumann (Sepiatone); m, Red Dunn; ed, Richard Heermance; art d, Dave Milton.

Western   **(PR:A   MPAA:NR)**

PANIC   (SEE: PANIQUE, 1946, Fr.)

PANIC*½   (1966, Brit.) 69m Ingram/Schoenfeld bw

Janine Gray (*Janine Heining*), Glyn Houston (*Mike*), Dyson Lovell (*Johnnie Cobb*), Duncan Lamont (*Inspector Saunders*), Stanley Meadows (*Tom*), Brian Weske (*Ben*), Charles Houston (*Louis Cobb*), Philip Ray (*Jessop*), Marne Maitland (*Lantern*), John Horsley (*Inspector Malcolm*), Dermot Kelly (*Murphy*), Paul Carpenter (*Flight Commentator*), Sean Lynch (*Layabout in Cafe*), Colin Rix (*Detective Sgt. Rose*), Roland Curram (*Frinton*), Milton Reid (*Dan*), Julie Mendez (*Lucette*), Duncan Lewis (*Joe*), Jeremy Hawk (*Spike*), Leonard Sachs (*Len Collier*), Vic Wise (*Benny*), Garry Davis (*Bobby Shark*), Manning Wilson (*Policeman*).

A hollow crime melodrama about a Swiss woman, Gray, who works for a London diamond merchant and becomes inadvertently involved with her boy friend's scheme to exploit her boss. Her boy friend, Lovell, sends two of his friends to the merchant as German jewelers, but they are found out, the boss is killed, and Gray is knocked out. She wakes up with amnesia and begins wandering around London. Lovell is frantically searching for her thinking that she's gone to the police. A boxer, Houston, takes Gray in and decides to go back to the ring to earn the money to get Gray out of the country. Lovell finally tracks Gray down after the fight, begins to beat on the tired Houston, and Gray shoots her boy friend dead.

p, Guido Coen; d&w, John Gilling (based on a story by Coen, Gilling); ph, Geoffrey Faithfull; ed, Bill Lewthwaite; art d, Duncan Sutherland.

Crime Drama   **(PR:A   MPAA:NR)**

PANIC BUTTON**½   (1964) 90m Yankee/Gorton bw

Maurice Chevalier (*Philippe Fontaine*), Eleanor Parker (*Louise Harris*), Jayne Mansfield (*Angela*), Michael Connors (*Frank Pagano*), Akim Tamiroff (*Pandowski*), Carlo Croccolo (*Guido*), Vincent Barbi (*Mario*).

Chevalier is a washed up film star whose movies are never watched on television and whom no one wants to hire. Connors wants to produce a flop to use as a tax write-off. He hires Chevalier to play Romeo, and Mansfield, a small-time call girl, as his Juliet for a TV pilot he's sure will fail. Chevalier approaches his new role with care and distinction. He's got a lot of struggling to do, for the director (Tamiroff) is a sleazy dramatics coach who will just about assure Connors of his goal. Chevalier returns to the hotel he lives in, which is run by his ex-wife Parker, discovers the real reason behind the film, and becomes enraged. He steals a print and enters it in the Venice Film Festival. It's a big hit because everyone thinks it's a comedy. Chevalier is a star once more and producers clamor for Connors, each offering him a bad script for his talents. This is a minor but enjoyable little comedy. It certainly doesn't represent the best of Chevalier's work but he has a good time with it and ends up his usual charming self. He enjoyed working with Mansfield and was impressed with her flair for comedy. She is cute and funny in her role. Chevalier sings "I Can't Resist the Twist," and does the dance with Mansfield, and "It's Spring Every Day" (Georges Gavarentz). The film never got wide distribution, opening for a limited run in Los Angeles and hardly anywhere else. It was shot on location in Rome and Venice, using the scenery well. A similar idea was put to much better use a few years later with the uproarious Mel Brooks comedy, THE PRODUCERS.

p, Ron Gorton; d, George Sherman; w, Hal Biller (based on a story by Gorton, dramatized by Mort Friedman, Gorton); ph, Enzo Serafin (Totalscope); m, Georges Gavarentz.

Comedy   **(PR:A   MPAA:NR)**

PANIC IN NEEDLE PARK*½   (1971) 110m Dunne-Didion- Dunne/FOX c

Al Pacino (*Bobby*), Kitty Winn (*Helen*), Alan Vint (*Hotchner*), Richard Bright (*Hank*), Kiel Martin (*Chico*), Michael McClanathan (*Sonny*), Warren Finnerty (*Sammy*), Marcia Jean Kurtz (*Marcie*), Raul Julia (*Marco*), Angie Ortega (*Irene*), Larry Marshall (*Mickey*), Paul Mace (*Whitey*), Nancy MacKay (*Penny*), Gil Rogers (*Robins*), Joe Santos (*DiBono*), Paul Sorvino (*Samuels*), Arnold Williams (*Freddy*), Vic Ramano (*Santo*), Bryant Fraser (*Prep Schoolboy*), Dora Weissman (*Pawnshop Lady*), Sully Boyar (*Doctor*), Florence Tarlow (*Ward Nurse*), Ruth Alda (*Admitting Nurse*), Anthony Palmer (*Hotel Clerk*).

Pacino tried hard in his first starring role, but even his talents couldn't breath life into this dreary, exploitative, and ultimately distasteful look at heroin addicts in New York City. Winn, a pregnant young girl from the Midwest, goes to New York City and has an abortion. Recovering at the apartment of her former lover, Julia, Winn meets Pacino, a young dope dealer who has come by to drop off some marijuana. Soon Winn and Pacino take up together and she discovers that he is a heroin addict. Winn herself picks up the habit and the pursuit of heroin becomes an all-consuming obsession. Meanwhile, Pacino decides to help his brother Bright pull a warehouse robbery so that he can finance his habit and marry Winn. The robbery is poorly executed and Pacino is caught and sent to prison. The dope dealer is eventually released, but he soon learns that Winn has taken up with his brother and turned to prostitution to pay for her heroin habit. After a vicious confrontation, Pacino and Winn get back together but things are not the same. Pacino sets himself up as one of drug kingpin Ramano's heroin distributors and is assigned to handle the aptly named "Needle Park," where the highest concentration of junkies reside.

His dream of being a big-time dealer is shattered, however, when Winn is arrested for selling pills to youngsters. Vint, a narcotics officer who knows Pacino, offers to let Winn go if she will supply information regarding Ramano's drug operation, promising that Pacino will only get a light sentence. She agrees and soon after Pacino is dragged off by police. Realizing she informed, Pacino screams a string of vicious epithets at Winn. Vint is true to his word and six months later Pacino is released and finds Winn waiting for him. He ignores her and walks right by—but then turns around and joins her as they leave the prison. Supposedly a no-holds-barred look at the seamy heroin subculture, PANIC IN NEEDLE PARK is actually a boring romance between two dullards, intercut with lots of gratuitous close-ups of filthy needles being jabbed into scarred veins. Director Schatzberg's attempt to show the horrors of drug abuse by plunging the film into the sleazy underworld and letting his camera linger on the degradation is misguided because his characters are never fully developed. Of course the viewer is disgusted and repulsed by such scenes, but a higher level of understanding is never reached because we have not been shown what has brought the characters to such a place. PANIC IN NEEDLE PARK, therefore, is the cinematic equivalent of a yellow journalism expose—all sensation and no content.

p, Dominick Dunne; d, Jerry Schatzberg; w, Joan Didion, John Gregory Dunne (based on the book by James Mills); ph, Adam Holender (DeLuxe Color); ed, Evan Lottman; art d, Murray P. Stern; set d, Philip Smith; cos, Jo Ynocencio; makeup, Herman Buchman.

Drama   **Cas.**   **(PR:O   MPAA:R)**

PANIC IN THE CITY*½   (1968) 96m United Pictures/Commonwealth United c

Nehemiah Persoff (*August Best*), Anne Jeffreys (*Myra Pryor*), Howard Duff (*Dave Pomeroy*), Linda Cristal (*Dr. Paula Stevens*), Stephen McNally (*James Kincade*), Oscar Beregi (*Dr. Paul Cerbo*), Gregory Morton (*Steadman*), Dennis Hopper (*Goff*), George Barrows, John Hoyt, Steve Franken, Wesley Lau, Jim Adams, Hank Brandt, Eddie Firestone, John Pickard, Cal Currens, Jan Watson, Elaine Beckett, Stanley Clements, Walter Reed, Leon Lontoc, Deanna Lund, Edith Loder, Wendy Stuart, Robert Terry, Bee Tompkins, Mike Farrell, Eilene Janssen, Jim Kline, William Tannen, Dodie Warren, Rush Williams, Douglas Evans, Maurice Wells, James Seay, Al Shafran, Renee Redman, Tex Armstrong, Walter Scott, George Sawaya.

After an important nuclear scientist is murdered in the hospital while recovering from radiation burns, National Bureau of Investigation agent Duff is called in to investigate. With the help of the scientist's assistant (Cristal) Duff's trail leads him to an international Communist conspiracy. Persoff and Jeffreys are two scientists who want to start WW III by exploding a homemade nuclear bomb in Los Angeles. Duff corners Persoff at the local Communist headquarters where the bomb already has been triggered. Duff is exposed to a deadly dose of radiation. Having nothing left to lose, he flies the bomb over the middle of the ocean, sacrificing himself to save the city. The film probably would have worked in the mid-1950s when fears of the dangers of the supposed international Communist conspiracy were prevalent throughout conservative filmmaking. But by 1968 such a story was a joke, made funnier by the total seriousness the film projects. The direction shows little suspense, choosing to emphasize Persoff and his madness. The final sequences are too far-fetched for even the most rabid hater of Communism to swallow. The low-budget esthetics that permeate the film do not accomplish much. Motorcyclist Dennis Hopper has a brief role as a murderer and the film gives an early appearance to Mike Farrell who later scored with the television version of "M*A*S*H." The picture was presold to television before its release, as was common for Earle Lyons' United Picture Corp. and Harold Goldman's Commonwealth United Entertainment releases.

p, Earle Lyon; d, Eddie Davis; w, Davis, Charles E. Savage; ph, Alan Stensvold (Eastmancolor); m, Paul Dunlap; ed, Terry O. Morse; art d, Paul Sylos, Jr.

Drama   **(PR:O   MPAA:NR)**

PANIC IN THE PARLOUR**   (1957, Brit.) 81m Romulus/Distributors Corp. of America bw (GB: SAILOR BEWARE!)

Peggy Mount (*Emma Hornett*), Cyril Smith (*Henry Hornett*), Shirley Eaton (*Shirley Hornett*), Ronald Lewis (*Albert Tufnell*), Esma Cannon (*Edie Hornett*), Joy Webster (*Daphne*), Gordon Jackson (*Carnoustie Bligh*), Thora Hird (*Mrs. Lack*), Geoffrey Keen (*Rev. Mr. Purefoy*), Jack MacGowran (*Toddy*), Peter Collingwood (*Verger*), Eliot Makeham (*Uncle Brummell*), Henry McGee, Charles Houston, Anne Blake, Fred Griffiths, Douglas Blackwell, Edie Martin, Margaret Moore, Barbara Hicks.

Mount is the focus of this picture as a domineering mother who has to be in control of every last detail of her daughter's wedding, including where she will live. Mount's control of her family's life eventually costs her daughter her marriage as the sailor (Lewis) leaves the bride at the altar. The strained comedy didn't carry over well from stage to screen.

p, Jack Clayton; d, Gordon Parry; w, Philip King, Falkland L. Cary; ph, Douglas Slocombe; m, Peter Akister.

Comedy   **(PR: MPAA:NR)**

PANIC IN THE STREETS***   (1950) 93m FOX bw

Richard Widmark (*Clinton Reed*), Paul Douglas (*Police Capt. Tom Warren*), Barbara Bel Geddes (*Nancy Reed*), Walter [Jack] Palance (*Blackie*), Zero Mostel (*Raymond Fitch*), Dan Riss (*Neff*), Alexis Minotis (*John Mefaris*), Guy Thomajan (*Poldi*), Tommy Cook (*Vince Poldi*), Edward Kennedy (*Jordan*), H.T. Tsiang (*Cook*), Lewis Charles (*Kochak*), Raymond Muller (*Dubin*), Tommy Rettig (*Tommy Reed*), Lenka Peterson (*Jeanette*), Pat Walshe (*Pat*), Paul Hostetler (*Dr. Paul Gafney*), George Ehmig (*Kleber*), John Schilleci (*Lee*), Waldo Pitkin (*Ben*), Leo Zinser (*Sgt. Phelps*), Beverly C. Brown (*Dr. Mackey*), William Dean

(Cortelyou), H. Waller Fowler, Jr. *(Murray)*, Rex Moad *(Wynant)*, Irvine Vidacovich *(Johnston)*, Val Winter *(Commissioner Dan Quinn)*, Wilson Bourg, Jr. *(Charlie)*, Mary Liswood *(Angie Fitch)*, Aline Stevens *(Rita Mefaris)*, Stanley J. Reyes *(Redfield)*, Darwin Greenfield *(Violet)*, Emile Meyer *(Capt. Beauclyde)*, Herman Cottman *(Scott)*, Al Theriot *(Al)*, Juan Villasana *(Hotel Proprietor)*, Robert Dorsen *(Coast Guard Lieutenant)*, Henry Mamet *(Anson)*, Tiger Joe Marsh *(Bosun)*, Arthur Tong *(Lascar Boy)*.

This is a tense, offbeat, and mostly absorbing drama which has to do with modern New Orleans and an ancient medical scourge, the Bubonic Plague, once known as the Black Death, responsible for destroying half the population of Europe, 1348-1666. Police find a murdered man on a New Orleans dock and physician Widmark is called in to identify the strange disease infecting the body. He fearfully diagnoses the plague. Douglas is told by Widmark that news of the plague victim must be quashed until the killer and victim are identified and all those having to do with both persons are quarantined. Douglas is skeptical but goes along with Widmark's plan, giving him a deadline to settle the matter but pooh-poohing the possibility of the plague. Widmark conducts his own investigation, finding a rat-infested foreign vessel which has had a plague victim on board at one time. He traces the victim's movements to a dockside Armenian cafe where the terrified proprietor denies ever knowing the victim. But the owner's wife dies the next day of plague and the owner talks, giving information to Widmark that leads him to petty gangster Palance and his fat, sweaty toady Mostel, the men responsible for killing the man found on the dock. In the end, just as news of the plague is about to break in the press, Widmark manages to corner Palance. The hoodlum, attempting to escape, tries to climb on board a ship at dockside, shinnying up the rope hawser only to be stopped by a shield used to keep rats from boarding the ship (the symbolism of Palance, a killer and plague-carrier, similar to rats carrying the Black Death, is not lost in this graphic similarity). Palance, squirming and desperate, finally falls into the water and is captured, ending Widmark's quest. Widmark is outstanding as the dedicated and fearless physician and Bel Geddes as his patient wife is very good. Douglas plays his usual gruff, authoritarian role and Palance is exceptional as a conscienceless hoodlum oozing evil. Kazan directs with meticulous care and everywhere his special stamp of moodiness, shadow-life, and sinister atmospherics can be seen. Kazan later stated that PANIC IN THE STREETS "was done away from the studio in New Orleans with lots of nonactors. The most fun movie ever made. The only thing I didn't like was the title. It was half winging, a pseudo or semi-documentary."

p, Sol C. Siegel; d, Elia Kazan; w, Richard Murphy, Daniel Fuchs (based on the stories "Quarantine" and "Some Like 'em Cold" by Edna Anhalt, Edward Anhalt); ph, Joe MacDonald; m, Alfred Newman; ed, Harmon Jones; art d, Lyle Wheeler, Maurice Ransford; set d, Thomas Little, Fred J. Rode; cos, Travilla; spec eff, Fred Sersen; makeup, Ben Nye.

Drama **(PR:C MPAA:NR)**

PANIC IN YEAR ZERO!*** (1962) 92m Alta Vista/AIP bw (AKA: END OF THE WORLD)

Ray Milland *(Harry Baldwin)*, Jean Hagen *(Ann Baldwin)*, Frankie Avalon *(Rick Baldwin)*, Mary Mitchell *(Karen Baldwin)*, Joan Freeman *(Marilyn Hayes)*, Richard Garland *(Mr. Johnson)*, Richard Bakalyan *(Carl)*, Rex Holman *(Mickey)*, Neil Nephew *(Andy)*, Willis Bouchey *(Dr. Strong)*, O.Z. Whitehead *(Hogan)*, Byron Morrow *(Haenel)*, Shary Marshall *(Mrs. Johnson)*, Russ Bender *(Harkness)*, Hugh Sanders *(Becker)*, Andrea Lane, Scott Peters, Bud Slater, Kelton Crawford.

Milland and his wife Hagen, along with their two teenage children, Avalon and Mitchell, leave Los Angeles for a fishing trip. Two hours outside of the city they hear an enormous explosion. Nuclear war has begun and Milland decides to continue to the vacation spot since it's probably the safest place to be. They stop to get supplies and ammunition, then hole up in a cave that's safe from radiation. The family members notice Milland's demeanor slowly changing from serene to one of ugly vengeance. At first they don't understand but when Mitchell is raped by a group of roving punks the family demeanor changes too. Avalon and Milland kill the rapists and rescue Freeman, the woman the men have held hostage. A surviving member of the thugs tries to attack Freeman again but she grabs a rifle and kills him. Finally the family receives word that Los Angeles is safe and returns to help rebuild civilization. This is one of five films Milland directed and probably is the best of the lot. A good sense of tension overcomes some of the luridness in the plot. Nothing can overcome Avalon's acting, however. He's no better here than in any of his beach movies with Annette Funicello. Other performances are much better. Hagen is fine as the mother who slowly cracks around the edges. Looking back on the movie some 20 years after its release, PANIC IN YEAR ZERO! has a certain timelessness to it that is a sad reflection on a society unable to solve the question of nuclear holocaust.

p, Arnold Houghland, Lou Rusoff; d, Ray Milland; w, Jay Simms, John Morton (based on a story by Simms); ph, Gilbert Warrenton; m, Les Baxter; ed, William Austin, Anthony Carras; art d, Daniel Haller; set d, Haller; spec eff, Pat Dinga, Larry Butler; cos, Marjorie Corso; makeup, Ted Coodley.

Drama **(PR:O MPAA:NR)**

PANIC ON THE AIR (SEE: YOU MAY BE NEXT!, 1936)

PANIC ON THE TRANS-SIBERIAN TRAIN (SEE: HORROR EXPRESS, 1974, Span./Brit.)

PANIQUE** (1947, Fr.) 100m Film Sonor-Regina/Film Rights bw (AKA: PANIC)

Viviane Romance *(Alice)*, Michel Simon *(Mons. Hire)*, Paul Bernard *(Alfred)*, Charles Dorat *(Michelet)*, Lucas Gridoux *(Mons. Fortin)*, Max Dalban *(Capoulade)*, Emile Drain *(Breteuil)*, Guy Favieres *(Mons. Sauvage)*, Louis Florencie *(Inspector Marcelin)*, Marcel Peres *(Cermanutti)*, Louis Lions *(Marco)*, Michel Ardan *(Fernand)*, J.F. Martial *(Mons. Joubet)*, Lucien Paris *(Mons. Branchu)*, Olivier Darrieux *(Etienne)*, Balpo *(Le Client)*.

Simon plays a loner who becomes a target for murderer Bernard and his mistress Romance. The killer diverts the suspicions of angry neighbors to Simon, wrongly accused of being guilty. A mob grows more intense and Simon is killed, but leaves behind a photograph which implicates the real culprits. Julian Duvivier, in his first post-war French film, was far less optimistic than he had been during his Hollywood years, producing a film without any sympathetic characters. It received a special mention from the Venice Film Festival and is a fine example of *film noir*stylistics.

d, Julian Divivier; w, Duvivier, Charles Spaak (based on the novel *Les Fiancailles de M. Hire* by Georges Simenon); ph, Nicholas Hayer; m, Jacques Ibert; ed, Marthe Poncin.

Crime Drama **Cas.** **(PR:C MPAA:NR)**

PANTHER ISLAND (SEE: BOMBA ON PANTHER ISLAND, 1949)

PANTHER'S CLAW, THE½** (1942) 72m PRC bw

Sidney Blackmer *(Thatcher Colt)*, Byron Foulger *(Everett Digberry)*, Ricki Vallin *(Anthony Abbott)*, Herbert Rawlinson *(District Attorney)*, Gerta Rozan *(Nina Politza)*, Lynn Starr *(Miss Spencer)*, Barry Bernard *(Edgar Walters)*, John Ince *(Capt. Flynn)*, Martin Ashe *(Officer Murphy)*, Joaquin Edwards *(Endico Lombardi)*, Walter James *(Capt. Henry)*.

There's murder in an opera company and Blackmer's out to solve the case! Assisted by Vallin he investigates and meets such characters as Edwards, a drunken baritone; Rozan, a beautiful singer; and Foulger, the opera company's wigmaker. The latter is the focal point of this tightly controlled, better-than-average mystery. It's well-acted with some realistic dialog and sequences. The direction shows a good feel for mystery and suspense with its brisk pace.

p, Lester Cutler; d, William Beaudine; w, Martin Mooney (based on a story by Anthony Abbott); ph, Marcel Le Picard; ed, Fred Bain.

Mystery **(PR:A MPAA:NR)**

PANTHER'S MOON (SEE: SPY HUNT, 1950)

PAPA'S DELICATE CONDITION*** (1963) 98m Amro/PAR c

Jackie Gleason *(Jack "Papa" Griffith)*, Glynis Johns *(Ambolyn Griffith)*, Laurel Goodwin *(Augusta Griffith)*, Linda Bruhl *(Corinne Griffith)*, Charlie Ruggles *(Grandpa Anthony Ghio)*, Ned Glass *("Sparrow" Wildman)*, Murray Hamilton *(Mr. Harvey)*, Elisha Cook, Jr. *(Mr. Keith)*, Charles Lane *(Hiram Cosgrove)*, Benny Baker *(Douglas)*, Claude Johnson *(Norman)*, Ken Renard *(Walter)*, Don Beddoe *(Mr. Looby)*, Trevor Bardette *(Stanley Henderson II)*, Juanita Moore *(Ellie)*.

Silent screen star Corinne Griffith saw her career wane when sound marched in because her voice was, at best, thin. After her film demise, she turned to writing, published several books, including the one that served as inspiration for this film, parlayed her earnings into a multi-million-dollar real estate fortune (she owned much of South Beverly Drive in Beverly Hills), and lived out her life healthily and wealthily on South Beverwil Drive, about two blocks away from her vast holdings. For years, her small, exquisite home was a stop for the tour buses that prowl the area. She had the last laugh on the studio chiefs who said she was "beautiful, but dumb." This autobiographical movie takes place in her home town of Grangeville, Texas, before WW I. Gleason is Papa, a man given to taking a few more drinks than the average fellow and that is the "delicate condition" referred to in the title. His 6-year-old, Bruhl, adores him but his behavior is a constant thorn to his wife, Johns, and his older daughter, Goodwin. There's a "blue law" in Texas stating that a man can't buy a drink, so Gleason buys the local pharmacy to give him and his pals a place to imbibe. When Bruhl wants a pony and cart from a traveling circus, Gleason uses all of his savings to buy the entire shebang, including all the unpaid debts, and throws his family into financial chaos. Johns is disgusted and takes her daughters to Texarkana, moving back in with her father, Ruggles, who is mayor of that town. Gleason can't stand being away from his family. Ruggles is about to run for reelection and Gleason arrives with the flea-bitten circus troupe to help him garner the office. Gleason attempts to take Bruhl with him to Grangeville but Johns stops him and there is a struggle. In the fracas, Bruhl falls and is mildly hurt. Gleason is depressed about what he's done and vanishes. Months pass and Ruggles sees that Johns, Bruhl, and Goodwin truly miss the man, so he searches the South and finally locates Gleason in Louisiana, then convinces him to return to Texarkana. Gleason stands outside the Ruggles' house and can't bring himself to walk in until he hears Johns at the piano as she plays and sings the traditional "Bill Bailey, Won't You Please Come Home?" (Hughie Cannon). That convinces him, and the family is united for a happy ending. A lovely family film that you can take a tyke or your maiden aunt Shirley to see, PAPA'S DELICATE CONDITION is the movie in which the Sammy Cahn-Jimmy Van Heusen standard "Call Me Irresponsible" was first heard. It was a perfect tune for the story and won the Oscar as Best Song of 1963. Gleason didn't have that much of a chance to exercise his comedy in the constrained role, but there was some fine humor from Cook and Hamilton as the circus owners as well as from Baker, Glass, and Lane as Gleason's cronies. Bruhl, as Corinne Griffith, was delightful.

p, Jack Rose; d, George Marshall; w, Rose (based on the book by Corinne Griffith); ph, Loyal Griggs (Technicolor); m, Joseph J. Lilley; ed, Frank P. Keller; md, Lilley; art d, Hal Pereira, Arthur Lonergan; set d, Sam Comer, James Payne; cos, Edith Head; spec eff, Paul K. Lerpae.

Comedy **(PR:A MPAA:NR)**

PAPER BULLETS*** (1941) 69m PRC bw (AKA: GANGS, INC.)

Joan Woodbury *(Rita Adams)*, Jack LaRue *(Mickey Roma)*, Linda Ware *(Donna Andrews)*, John Archer *(Bob Elliott)*, Vince Barnett *(Schribbler)*, Allan [Alan] Ladd *(Jimmy Kelly)*, Gavin Gordon *(Kurt Parrish)*, Philip Trent *(Harold Dewitt)*, William Halligan *(Chief Flynn)*, George Pembroke *(Clarence Dewitt)*, Selmer Jackson *(District Attorney)*, Kenneth Harlan *(Jim Adams)*, Bryant Washburn *(Bruce King)*,

Alden Chase *(Joe Kent)*, Robert Strange *(Lou Wood)*, Alex Callam *(Fagan)*, Harry Depp *(John Mason)*.

This is a better-than-average thriller, the first release from the Kozinsky Brothers (also known as the King Brothers), after a failed deal with Cecil B. DeMille for a series of films to be shown on jukeboxes. The film is efficiently done, made in six days on a $30,000 budget. Woodbury is a woman forced to go to jail after taking the rap for a wealthy playboy's hit-and-run accident. She discovers the real driver's identity and vows vengeance on his father. It turns out the man is a political reformer whose career is ruined when Woodbury gets him involved in racketeering. She goes to prison once more but takes the man with her. The film moves fast, despite problems with the plot and additional hampering because of too many characters. PAPER BULLETS featured an actor named "Allan Ladd" in a minor role. It was re-released after the actor had achieved some fame, titled GANGS, INC. and billed as "starring Alan Ladd."

p, Maurice Kozinsky, Frank Kozinsky [the King Brothers]; d, Phil Rosen; w, Martin Mooney; ph, Arthur Martinelli; ed, Martin G. Cole; md, Johnny Lange, Lew Porter; art d, Frank Dexter, Sr.; m/l, Lange, Porter, Vic Knight, M. Kozinsky.

Crime **(PR:A MPAA:NR)**

PAPER CHASE, THE½** (1973) 112m FOX c

Timothy Bottoms *(Hart)*, Lindsay Wagner *(Susan Kingsfield)*, John Houseman *(Prof. Kingsfield)*, Graham Beckel *(Ford)*, Edward Herrmann *(Anderson)*, Bob Lydiard *(O'Connor)*, Craig Richard Nelson *(Bell)*, James Naughton *(Kevin)*, Regina Baff *(Asheley)*, David Clennon *(Toombs)*, Lenny Baker *(Moss)*.

John Houseman had already distinguished himself as a writer in films (JANE EYRE), as a producer (EXECUTIVE SUITE, THE BAD AND THE BEAUTIFUL, many more) and as the story editor of CITIZEN KANE before winning the Best Supporting Actor Oscar for this, only his second role. (He'd appeared in SEVEN DAYS IN MAY, nine years before.) They had a good idea when they began THE PAPER CHASE, but the execution was not up to the concept, although it was still running as a pay-cable TV series in the 1970s. Bottoms is a Minnesota-bred law student who comes to Harvard and has a tough time keeping up with the Cabots and the Lowells who sit next to him in the lecture hall of Houseman, a ruthless instructor who takes great pleasure in puncturing his students' egos. The scenes of how it is to go to Harvard are the best; then they drag in a totally dumb love story in which Bottoms just happens to be in love with Wagner who just happens to be Houseman's daughter. It becomes a triangle between the three, with Wagner as the female equivalent of a eunuch unable to do much. Other than the classroom scenes and the verbal battles between Houseman and Bottoms, it gets to be soggy stuff. Houseman is the aged Lou Gossett, and Bottoms is the confused Richard Gere, as this picture is the Boston version of AN OFFICER AND A GENTLEMAN (which actually came much later), a typical military school plot with only the venue changed. Bridges secured an Oscar nomination for his adaptation of the novel and manages to slip in some intellectual one-liners to ease the drama. A character study more than anything, THE PAPER CHASE ends on an unbelievable note as Bottoms, who has struggled long and hard on his labors, tosses away the letter containing his grades in a gesture that is a gratuitous attempt at showing his development as a human being. Anyone who has worked against all odds to get passing marks will spot the essential dishonesty of that move. Houseman's Oscar was deserved for his portrayal of a man determined to "wash out" the weaklings and keep only the most dedicated.

p, Robert C. Thompson, Rodrick Paul; d, James Bridges; w, Bridges (based on the novel by John Jay Osborn, Jr.); ph, Gordon Willis (Panavision, DeLuxe Color); m, John Williams; ed, Walter Thompson; art d, George Jenkins; set d, Gerry Holmes.

Comedy/Drama **Cas.** **(PR:A-C MPAA:PG)**

PAPER GALLOWS*** (1950, Brit.) 77m Advance/EL bw (GB: TORMENT)

Dermot Walsh *(Cliff Brandon)*, Rona Anderson *(Joan)*, John Bentley *(Jim Brandon)*, Michael Martin-Harvey *(Curley Wilson)*, Valentine Dunn *(Mrs. Crier)*, Dilys Laye *(Violet Crier)*.

Walsh and Bentley are brothers, a pair of crime novelists who share Anderson as a secretary. One of them kills a man (Martin-Harvey) in order to create a realistic plot for his next work. He takes Anderson with him and threatens to hang her. The other brother must find the corpse, Anderson, and his brother, all culminating in a wild car crash. The story here is nothing new, but direction is fresh and original. Taking this simplistic plot line, Guillermin manages to inject some good suspense into a modestly budgeted feature. Walsh, Bentley, and Anderson play their roles well and work off one another with skill. Although this is nothing special, PAPER GALLOWS is exciting and entertaining. Producer and writer John Guillermin went on to write and direct a number of TARZAN movies.

p, Robert Jordan Hill, John Guillermin; d&w, Guillermin; ph, Gerald Gibbs; m, John Wooldridge; ed, Hill.

Crime **(PR:A MPAA:NR)**

PAPER LION*** (1968) 105m UA c

Alan Alda *(George Plimpton)*, Lauren Hutton *(Kate)*, David Doyle *(Oscar)*, Ann Turkel *(Susan)*, Sugar Ray Robinson, Frank Gifford, Vince Lombardi, Joe Schmidt *(Themselves)*, Alex Karras, John Gordy, Mike Lucci, Pat Studstill, Roger Brown *(Themselves, Members of the Detroit Lions)*, Detroit Lions Coaching Staff and Team *(Themselves)*, Roy Schneider.

In 1966 George Plimpton wrote a series of articles for *Sports Illustrated* magazine based on his firsthand experiences in the world of professional sports. He pitched in baseball's All-Star Game, then fought a few rounds with one-time middleweight champ Sugar Ray Robinson. The story of PAPER LION begins when Plimpton, played by Alda in his film debut, tosses around a football with his editor Doyle. Doyle is hit by inspiration: What would it be like for Alda to experience the joys and woes of a rookie quarterback for a professional football team? The pair approaches several teams and finally is accepted by the Detroit Lions. Alda signs a waiver releasing the team from responsibility for injury. His status is kept secret but Alda's ignorance of football soon gives him away. He becomes the butt of jokes and subject to the wrath of a few team members who resent what he's doing. During an intersquad scrimmage one member tackles the hapless 175-pound writer and carries both him and the ball across the goal. Alda finally gains acceptance after defensive tackle Karras takes him under a protective wing. The other players come to realize Alda's sincerity and he soon is making progress. His secretary, Hutton, pays a visit and is surprised by her employer's new skills. Alda is finally awarded a jersey with the number "0" and allowed to play the final few minutes of a preseason game in which Detroit holds a comfortable lead. His performance is less than extraordinary as he manages to lose 32 yards in three plays, fumbles the ball, and knocks himself unconscious running into a goal post. But the players admire his spunk and Alda is awarded the game ball. PAPER LION is a pleasant comedy with simple humor that makes it work. Alda's performance is engaging, overcoming what is essentially a one-joke role. Karras as his benefactor is equally good in his film debut. He continued playing ball for a few more years, before going on to a surprisingly successful career in films and television. The portrayal of professional athletes is less than honest, with toned-down language and uniforms that are dirtied rather than bloodied. The team is pictured as a fraternity of fun-loving boys who wouldn't pull the wings off flies. Some of the players also could benefit from acting lessons as performances rank from good to unbelievably wooden. Hutton is wasted in her role which amounts to little more than a walk-on. The cameos by real-life sport figures such as Lombardi and Robinson are fun to watch. The direction gives the film a sweetness that makes PAPER LION enjoyable even for the non-football fan.

p, Stuart Millar; d, Alex March; w, Lawrence Roman (based on *Paper Lion* by George Plimpton); ph, Morris Hartzbrand, Peter Garbarini, Steve Sabol, Fred Hoffman, Al Taffet, Jack Schatz, Joseph Wheeler, Eugene Friedman, David Marx, Richard Pollister, Fred Porrett, Morris Kellman (Techniscope, Technicolor); m, Roger Kellaway; ed, Sidney Katz, John Carter, Louis San Andres; set d, Hank Aldrich.

Sports/Comedy **(PR:A MPAA:G)**

PAPER MOON*½** (1973) 102m Saticoy/PAR c

Ryan O'Neal *(Moses Pray)*, Tatum O'Neal *(Addie Loggins)*, Madeline Kahn *(Trixie Delight)*, John Hillerman *(Sheriff Hardin/Jess Hardin)*, P.J. Johnson *(Imogene)*, Jessie Lee Fulton *(Miss Ollie)*, Jim Harrell *(Minister)*, Lila Water *(Minister's Wife)*, Noble Willingham *(Mr. Robertson)*, Bob Young *(Gas Station Attendant)*, Jack Saunders *(Station Master)*, Jody Wilbur *(Cafe Waitress)*, Liz Ross *(Pearl the Widow Morgan)*, Yvonne Harrison *(Marie the Widow Bates)*, Ed Reed *(Lawman)*, Dorothy Price *(Ribbon Saleslady)*, Eleanor Bogart *(Elvira the Widow Stanley)*, Dorothy Foster *(Edna the Widow Huff)*, Lana Daniel *(Moses' Girl Friend)*, Herschel Morris *(Barber)*, Dejah Moore *(Salesgirl)*, Ralph Coder *(Store Manager)*, Harriet Ketchum *(Store Customer)*, Desmond Dhooge *(Cotton Candy Man)*, Kenneth Hughes *(Harem Tent Barker)*, George Lillie *(Photographer)*, Burton Gilliam *(Floyd the Desk Clerk)*, Floyd Mahaney *(Beau the Deputy)*, Gilbert Milton *(Leroy's Father)*, Randy Quaid *(Leroy)*, Tandy Arnold, Vernon Schwanke, Dennis Beden *(Leroy's Brothers)*, Hugh Gillin *(2nd Deputy)*, Art Ellison *(Silver Mine Gentleman)*, Rosemary Rumbley *(Aunt Billie)*.

Driving a model-T roadster in the Depression year of 1936, O'Neal stops to pay his respects at the funeral of one of his former girl friends. Neighbors quickly explain to him that the dead woman has left an "adorable" 9-year-old daughter an orphan and beg him to take the child to relatives in St. Joseph, Missouri. O'Neal takes Tatum O'Neal along with him out of reluctant civility and instantly regrets his generosity. The little girl smokes, swears, and exhibits a kind of premature sophistication that adults interpret as "cute" when such conduct is nothing more than obnoxious and/or repulsive in a child stripped of naivete and innocence. After taking sly vengeance on the brother of the man who caused the death of Tatum's mother in a car accident by defrauding him of $200, O'Neal buys a new car and then takes Tatum to a train station, buying her a ticket for St. Joseph. Rather than get on the train, Tatum creates a scene in the station restaurant and screams that O'Neal owes her $200, since he got it from the family that inadvertantly caused her mother's death and therefore her rightful inheritance (and that's the way of all of her logic), but he's probably her father to boot. O'Neal denies loudly such parentage but she continues to yell that "we got the same jaw!" Embarrassed but feeling an obligation to pay off the child, O'Neal takes her along on his roadway adventures through Kansas and Missouri, ambling towards St. Joseph. En route he plays soft con games on rubes, the gullible rural folk buying all sorts of items from him at inflated prices, such as widows purchasing monogrammed Bibles at steep prices, books allegedly ordered by their recently deceased spouses as gifts for their wives. At other times Tatum joins O'Neal in swindling busy department store cashiers in a money switch involving $20 bills. At a country carnival the amorous O'Neal picks up Kahn, a slatternly, buxom tart, and her teenage black maid who accompany Tatum and O'Neal, the black girl becoming Tatum's friend. Tatum learns that Kahn is not a real carnival dancer but a prostitute and resolves to get rid of her, arranging for a hotel clerk to visit Kahn and then, moments later, have O'Neal enter the bedroom to find the two in a compromising position. Kahn is quickly abandoned by O'Neal and he and Tatum return to the road. In a small town O'Neal swindles a bootlegger out of $625 but doesn't deliver the goods. He is later stopped by a vicious and venal sheriff, the bootlegger's brother, and is thrown in jail. Hillerman demands the return of the money which is hidden inside Tatum's hat, threatening the con man with a long prison term. O'Neal and Tatum manage to elude Hillerman and his deputies, escaping. Near St. Joseph, O'Neal asks Tatum to aid him in a "big score," and she willingly accepts. But Hillerman shows up with his goons and, before O'Neal can put through his swindle, he is beaten to a pulp. Later, driving a dilapidated truck, O'Neal manages to deliver Tatum to her relatives, who receive the child with open arms (and are they in for a surprise!). O'Neal starts to leave but his truck breaks down. Tatum runs up to him on the road and insists that he take her along. "I don't want you riding with me no more!" yells O'Neal, but Tatum yells back that "You still owe me $200!" She also still believes, it is obvious, that O'Neal is her real father. The truck begins to roll down a hill and O'Neal hops in, then Tatum gets in, too, and the two go racing down the hill to more adventures. For all of its manipulations of nostalgia—the severe black-and-white photography, the rural settings where time has stood still and it's still 1936 visually—PAPER MOON still offers brilliant, bittersweet images and a mild but highly entertaining story, despite Tatum's forced essay of a grownup child. Ryan O'Neal is excellent, although he takes his role not much beyond the shock of an adult constantly being victimized on an emotional level by a 9-year-old. Kahn is excellent as the hippy, bosomy slut. Her annoying high-pitched voice and forward-leaning posture, coupled to the most absurd dialog spawned by a woman, wholly captures the part she is playing. Hillerman, however, is too hammy to be the uneducated and brutal lawman he is supposed to be playing. Bogdanovich's direction is fast, furious, and full of fun, although larceny here passes for honest labor. As with THE LAST PICTURE SHOW (1971), the director opted for black-and-white cinematography (beautifully captured by Kovacs) in a world swimming in color celluloid, to achieve historical authenticity. "I have more affection, more affinity for the past," Bogdanovich later stated. "Since I am more interested in it, it comes easier for me." Originally, John Huston was to direct this film, after the book rights were acquired, and Paul Newman was to play the Ryan O'Neal role and his daughter, Nell Potts, was to play Tatum O'Neal's role. All this changed when Huston backed out and Bogdanovich entered the picture. Critics were mixed about the film, many endorsing it as a minor classic that almost perfectly recreated the 1930s, while others thought the film a preposterous and insincere replica of real 1930s films. It's really a little bit of both, having more charm and flavor, like a Whitman Sampler of ages ago, than the true grit of the windblown dust bowl when times were always and truly hard and survival had no room for caprice. The public was enamored of the film, or chiefly the O'Neals, and returned $16 million from the box office in the initial U.S. release. This was Tatum O'Neal's film debut and no one would ever forget it, especially Tatum O'Neal, who won a Best Supporting Actress Oscar for her performance (beating out costar Kahn). For Bogdanovich, Tatum O'Neal was big box office but her inexperience and pseudo-sophisticated attitude drove him to dark distraction. He later stated that the little grownup girl provided him with "one of the most miserable experiences of my life." Filmed on location nears Hays, Kansas, and St. Joseph, Missouri. The highly effective musical backdrop for the picture is a procession of nostalgia from the shellac-record collection of Rudi Fehr. Included are extracts from myriad 1930s classics such as "A Picture of Me Without You," "Mississippi Mud" (performed by Paul Whiteman and His Orchestra), "About A Quarter To Nine" (performed by Ozzie Nelson and His Orchestra), "Georgia On My Mind" (performed by Hoagy Carmichael and His Orchestra), "After You've Gone" (performed by Tommy Dorsey and His Orchestra), and "The Music Goes Round and Round" (performed by Nat Gonella and His Orchestra).

p&d, Peter Bogdanovich; w, Alvin Sargent (based on the novel *Addie Pray* by Joe David Brown); ph, Laszlo Kovacs; ed, Verna Fields; prod d, Polly Platt; set d, John Austin, James Spencer; cos, Pat Kelly, Sandra Stewart; spec eff, Jack Harmon; makeup, Rolf Miller.

Comedy/Drama Cas. (PR:C MPAA:PG)

PAPER ORCHID**½

(1949, Brit.) 86m Ganesh/COL bw

Hugh Williams *(Frank McSweeney)*, Hy Hazell *(Stella Mason)*, Sidney James *(Freddy Evans)*, Garry Marsh *(Johnson)*, Andrew Cruickshank *(Inspector Clement Pill)*, Ivor Barnard *(Eustace Crabb)*, Walter Hudd *(Briggs)*, Ella Retford *(Lady Croup)*, Hughie Green *(Harold Croup)*, Vida Hope *(Jonquil Jones)*, Frederick Leister *(Walter Wibberley)*, Kenneth Morgan, Vernon Greeves, Patricia Owens, Rolf Lefebvre, Roger Moore, The Ray Ellington Quartet.

Two competing newspapers try to top each other when a man is found murdered in gossip columnist Hazell's apartment. One rival reporter finally admits to killing the man in a drunken fit, and planting the body in Hazell's flat. He pays for his crime in suicide by throwing himself under a train. Though the story is well developed and the film has good production values, it is not convincing.

p, William Collier, John R. Sloan; d, Roy Baker; w, Val Guest (based on the novel by Arthur La Bern); ph, Basil Emmott.

Crime/Mystery (PR:C MPAA:NR)

PAPER TIGER*

(1975, Brit.) 101m MacLean c

David Niven *(Walter Bradbury)*, Toshiro Mifune *(Ambassador Kagoyama)*, Hardy Kruger *(Muller)*, Ando *(Koichi Kagoyama)*, Ivan Desny *(Foreign Minister)*, Irene Tsu *(Talah)*, Ronald Fraser *(Forster)*, Miiko Taka *(Mme. Kagoyama)*, Jeff Corey *(Mr. King)*, Patrica Donahue *(Mrs. King)*, Kurt Christian *(Harok)*, Jeanine Siniscal *(Foreign Minister's Girl)*.

Niven gives his charming best to this film but to no avail. He plays the English tutor of a Japanese ambassador's son, Ando, a kid so cute and dimpled he inspires diabetes. Niven regales Ando with tales of his daring during WW II, and when Ando and Niven are kidnaped, Ando looks to Niven for his escape. Yet Niven actually was a coward during the war and returns to timidity. Eventually he makes a successful effort to escape, though, and inspires peace and harmony among various nationalities, including the English, Japanese, and Germans, handily overcoming the traumas that haunted him for so long. The film also has some poorly choreographed karate sequences. The screenplay, a pale imitation of WEE WILLIE WINKIE with Shirley Temple, is tolerable but hampered by plodding direction. The Ray Coniff Singers provide the closing theme song, which could lull audiences to sleep.

p, Euan Lloyd; d, Ken Annakin; w, Jack Davies; ph, John Cabrera, Charly Steinberger, Tony Braun (Technicolor); m, Roy Budd; ed, Alan Pattillo; prod d, Herbert Smith; art d, Tony Reading, Peter Scharff; m/l, "My Little Friend," Sammy Cahn, Budd (sung by Ray Coniff Singers).

Drama Cas. (PR:A-C MPAA:PG)

PAPERBACK HERO**½

(1973, Can.) 93m Agincourt International/Rumson c

Keir Dullea *(Rick)*, Elizabeth Ashley *(Loretta)*, John Beck *(Pov)*, Dayle Haddon *(Joanna)*, Franz Russell *(Big Ed)*, George R. Robertson *(Burdock)*, Margot Lamarre *(Julie)*, Ted Follows *(Cagey)*, Linda Sorenson *(Mona)*, Les Ruby *(Jock)*, Jacquie Presly *(Marlene)*, Chet Robertson *(Father)*, Winnie Rowles *(Mother)*, Gerry Cooke *(Noogie)*, John Ottenberg *(Heavy)*, Linda Findlay *(Friend)*, Mike Shabaga *(Referee)*, Pat Scott *(Hippie)*, John Leffler *(Bus Driver)*, Jim Arnsten, Dave Steingard *(Policemen)*, Max Bentley *(Max)*.

This mixed-bag story features some fine moments of acting and cinematic technique. However, its good points are hampered by a lack of continuity in plot and characterizations. Dullea is a small-town punk whose status on the local hockey team makes him a hero to the ladies. When the local businessmen who finance the team decide to withdraw funding Dullea is knocked from his pedestal. His mental state declines and he takes to robbery, culminating in a shoot-out with the local police force. Dullea's performance is not one of the best in the movie as his accent fluctuates between small town and normal. Otherwise he's competent in the role. Ashley and Haddon as two of his female companions are fine. The smaller parts are handled effectively. The direction is good but faltering, and plot development lacks flow.

p, James Margellos, John F. Bassett; d, Peter Pearson; w, Les Rose, Barry Pearson; ph, Don Wilder (Eastmancolor); m, Ron Collier; ed, Kirk Jones; art d, Tom Hall; cos, Marion Mills; m/l, "If You Could Read My Mind," Gordon Lightfoot (sung by Lightfoot).

Drama (PR:O MPAA:R)

PAPILLON****

(1973) 150m Corona-General Production Co./AA c

Steve McQueen *(Henri Charriere, Papillon)*, Dustin Hoffman *(Louis Dega)*, Victor Jory *(Indian Chief)*, Don Gordon *(Julot)*, Anthony Zerbe *(Toussaint, Leper Colony Chief)*, Robert Deman *(Maturette)*, Woodrow Parfrey *(Clusoit)*, Bill Mumy *(Lariot)*, George Coulouris *(Dr. Chatal)*, Ratna Assan *(Zoraima)*, William Smithers *(Warden Barrot)*, Gregory Sierra *(Antonio)*, Barbara Morrison *(Mother Superior)*, Ellen Moss *(Nun)*, Don Hanmer *(Butterfly Trader)*, Dalton Trumbo *(Commandant)*, Val Avery *(Pascal)*, Victor [Vic] Tayback *(Sergeant)*, Dar Robinson *(McQueen's Cliff Stunt)*, Mills Watson *(Guard)*, Ron Soble *(Santini)*, E.J. Andre *(Old Con)*, Richard Angarola *(Commandant)*, Jack Denbo *(Classification Officer)*, Len Lesser *(Guard)*, John Quade *(Masked Breton)*, Fred Sadoff *(Deputy Warden)*, Allen Jaffe *(Turnkey)*, Liam Dunn *(Old Trustee)*, Anne Byrne Hoffman *(Mrs. Dega)*.

Superb prison yarn has McQueen in one of his best roles as the notorious French thief, Henri Charriere (better known as "Papillon"), who escaped from the inescapable Devil's Island. The grim and unrelentingly brutal film begins in the streets of Marseilles in the 1930s with French soldiers carrying rifles with fixed bayonets, escorting a large group of prisoners to the docks. Among them is McQueen, a convicted murderer (who claims he has been framed for killing a pimp), and Hoffman, a big time stock swindler who still has a lot of money hidden. On board the ship taking them to Cayenne in French Guiana the two meet and Hoffman is aloof. During the voyage, a couple of brutal murderers in the hold where all the prisoners sleep in hammocks, attempt to kill Hoffman (to slice him open, after learning that he has swallowed some jewels, his financial security against the upcoming rigors of prison life). McQueen attacks the two men, killing one, and saving Hoffman who later finds it difficult to thank his savior. Once in Cayenne all McQueen can do is think about escape. He attacks a guard who abuses Hoffman and then makes a break, only to be later recaptured. McQueen spends most of his time in solitary confinement where he is put for repeated escape attempts. Here he staves off starvation, madness, and disease while his body deteriorates. He and Smithers, the commandant of the solitary confinement compound, duel with wits (and age together, the hair of both men turning white over the years), especially when Smithers learns that someone (Hoffman) has been smuggling extra food to McQueen. Although starved and mentally punished by Smithers, McQueen will not reveal Hoffman's identity. He serves his full time and is received warmly by Hoffman at the main prison when released for not giving the swindler away. Hoffman is now living a cushy life, paying off guards and even the warden for favored treatment and he tries to persuade McQueen to serve out his time and wait for a parole. There is still only the stubborn thought of escape in McQueen's mind and he persuades another inmate to join him after he has bribed prison authorities (with Hoffman's money) to have a boat waiting for him. He and the other prisoner kill a trustee, slip outside to the compounds and, while Hoffman is serving cold drinks to guards and officers watching a concert, climb over the prison wall. A guard is about to alert others to the break, but Hoffman knocks him out and then goes over the wall, too, breaking an ankle. The three men make their way through the jungle to the waiting boat, only to find that it is rotten, a boat full of holes that is sold over and over to escaping prisoners. Quade intercepts them to show them the dead bodies of two bounty-hunters he has killed, men who were waiting for the prisoners. Quade explains that he was once a prisoner and now he lives in the jungle, surviving by his wits (his body is marked with strange tattoos) and giving help to escaping inmates when he can. He guides them to a leper colony where Zerbe gives them aid, a boat, and supplies but only after McQueen shows he is not afraid of the lepers nor of contacting their deadly disease by smoking on the same cigar as Zerbe. When Zerbe sees the trio off the next day he says to McQueen: "How did you know we have dry leprosy and that it cannot be communicated?" McQueen replies: "I didn't." The escaped convicts sail away and later, during the stormy voyage, Hoffman's broken ankle must be set. When the trio finally come ashore they run right into police walking on the beach with another prisoner, Sierra. Hoffman distracts the police while McQueen and Sierra take flight into the jungle.

Native tribesmen with poison dart blowguns are brought into the jungle by the police to track the two fleeing prisoners. Sierra runs into a booby trap of spiked stakes that pierce his body and kill him instantly while McQueen dashes on into the jungle. His back is suddenly struck with darts from native blowguns and he falls crazily over a cliff and into a river, floating away. He is later rescued by natives and taken to the colony of a nomadic Indian tribe. Here he is nursed by beautiful Assan until he is once more healthy. Jory, the chief, admires the colorful tattoo of the butterfly McQueen has on his chest (which has given him the sobriquet of "Papillon") and asks that the escaped prisoner tattoo the same image on his chest. Knowing this fierce tribe will turn on him if he does not perform the cosmetic surgery, McQueen shapes crude implements and begins a night-long operation that is successful and causes Jory great happiness, so much so that he rewards McQueen with a bag of priceless pearls. McQueen goes on living in this paradise but wakes up one morning to find that the entire tribe, including the lovely Assan, has departed, moved off to another location and leaving no forwarding address. He decides to make his way back to civilization, using his pearls to buy his freedom. At one stop, however, where McQueen stays at a nunnery, he offers a Mother Superior, Morrison, a pearl when she becomes suspicious. Morrison promptly turns McQueen over to police but does not turn over the pearl. Back to solitary confinement goes McQueen and he is later moved to the supposedly escape-proof Devil's Island off the French Guiana coast where vicious currents and no natural landfall will thwart any break. McQueen is now old, as is Hoffman, but they live in relative comfort, each having a small cottage and garden to tend. Yet the urge to be free still burns inside McQueen and he once again approaches Hoffman to join him in an escape. Hoffman at first resists and then tells McQueen that he will go with him. The two study the deadly, sheer cliffs slicing almost straight down to the ocean, and the currents and waves attacking the rocky shoreline. McQueen drops coconut shells into the water and sees them dashed onto the rocks until he discovers that "it's the seventh wave" that washes the coconut shells out to sea. Lashing together a huge raft of coconut shells, McQueen goes to the cliff accompanied by Hoffman. Just before the leap to freedom, Hoffman tells McQueen that he will not be going with him. McQueen nods, telling Hoffman that he has known that all along. The two old friends embrace and then McQueen hurls the makeshift raft into the water while counting the waves and leaps after it. He holds onto the raft as it clears the rocky crags and drifts out to sea, then climbs atop it to float to freedom as Hoffman, with a smile on his face, watches him diminish to a speck on the horizon. PAPILLON was produced with consummate technical skills and offers brilliant acting from McQueen and Hoffman and it drips of authenticity. Schaffner, who expertly captured the gritty story of PATTON does not flinch from showing every conceivable horror of the French penal system, from guillotined prisoners, filth, unspeakable punishment, and vile inmates to the nightmare terrors of the primitive jungles into which McQueen plunges in his insatiable quest for freedom. Excellent supporting roles are offered by Zerbe, the grotesque but compassionate leper chief, Jory, the stoic Indian chief, and Coulouris, a venal prison doctor. Even scriptwriter Trumbo, who had become a cult figure by the time of this film, gets into the act as the commandant of the penal colony at the film's beginning. Shot on location in Spain and in the wilds of Jamaica, PAPILLON was a costly film, with McQueen's salary at a reported $2 million and Hoffman at $1,250,000; Schaffner, according to one report, received $750,000 for his directorial efforts. The overall price tag for this excellent prison saga exceeded million with distributor Allied Artists contributing $7 million, money allegedly earned from that firm's blockbuster, CABARET. The movie gleaned $22 million through U.S. release. This film was originally given an R MPAA rating (and rightly so just for its extreme violence alone) but Allied Artists argued for and won a later PG rating.

p, Robert Dorfman, Franklin J. Schaffner; d, Schaffner; w, Dalton Trumbo, Lorenzo Semple, Jr. (based on the autobiographical novel by Henri Carriere); ph, Fred Koenekamp (Panavision, Technicolor); m, Jerry Goldsmith; ed, Robert Swink; prod d, Anthony Masters; art d, Jack Maxsted; set d, Hugh Scaife; cos, Anthony Powell; makeup, Charles Schram.

Prison Drama　　Cas.　　(PR:O MPAA:R/PG)

PAR LE FER ET PAR LE FEU　(SEE: INVASION 1700, 1965, Fr./Ital./Yugo.)

PARACHUTE BATTALION**　(1941) 75m RKO bw

Robert Preston (Donald Morse), Nancy Kelly (Kit Richards), Edmond O'Brien (Bill Burke), Harry Carey (Bill Richards), Buddy Ebsen (Jeff Hollis), Paul Kelly (Tex), Richard Cromwell (Spence), Robert Barrat (Col. Burke), Erville Alderson (Pa Hollis), Edward Fielding (Chief of Infantry), Selmer Jackson (Thomas Morse), Grant Withers (Captain), Walter Sande (Medical Officer), Kathryn Sheldon (Ma Hollis), Gayne Whitman (Staff Officer), Douglas Evans (Radio Announcer), Eddie Dunn (Recruiting Sergeant), Jack Briggs, Lee Bonnell, Robert Smith (Privates).

RKO was one of the last studios to realize war was imminent but finally caught up with the Hollywood propaganda films six months before the bombing of Pearl Harbor. This is a simplistic story about a group of Army trainees preparing for a parachute corps. Preston is an egotistical football hero who takes to jumping easily, O'Brien is the coward who learns to change his ways, and Ebsen provides comic relief. Kelly is the romantic interest who finds her affections wavering between O'Brien and Preston. The real star of this film is the parachute footage. This was made with the cooperation of the 51st Parachute Battalion at Fort Benning, Georgia, which performed all the jumps, which we see from the folding of the chute to the leap from the plane. As a feature this was not much of a movie, but as an educational piece there was a good deal to see. The war-conscious audiences of 1941 seemed to agree, giving the film a $128,000 profit. Co-writer Maj. Hugh Fite belonged to the U.S. Air Corps.

p, Howard Benedict; d, Leslie Goodwins; w, John Twist, Maj. Hugh Fite; ph, J.

Roy Hunt; m, Roy Webb; ed, Theron Warth; m/l, "Parachute Battalion," Webb, Herman Ruby.

War　　　　　　(PR:A MPAA:NR)

PARACHUTE JUMPER**½　(1933) 73m WB bw

Douglas Fairbanks, Jr. (Bill Keller), Leo Carrillo (Weber), Bette Davis (Alabama), Frank McHugh (Toodles), Claire Dodd (Mrs. Newberry), Sheila Terry (Secretary), Harold Huber (Steve), Thomas E. Jackson (Coffey), George Pat Collins (Crowley), Harold Healy (Wilson), Ferdinand Munier (Hocheimer), Pat O'Malley, Walter Miller.

Fairbanks and his pal McHugh are unemployed pilots fresh from the service. They're looking for work and meet fellow umemployment victim Davis wandering in Central Park. The trio decides to share an apartment to save money. Fairbanks takes a job as chauffeur for a racketeer's mistress (Dodd), not knowing her real business. She flirts with him and eventually her lover Carrillo catches the two of them in an embrace. But Carrillo's impressed with Fairbanks' calm attitude when threatened with death and decides to hire the young man as a bodyguard. Carrillo becomes charmed by Davis' southern accent and hires her as his secretary. The mobster discovers that his bodyguard is an expert pilot and dupes Fairbanks into flying narcotics runs. One day they're followed by government agents, and Fairbanks, believing the other plane to be piloted by hijackers, shoots it down. But he discovers what his cargo is (he thought it was liquor) and threatens to quit. Carrillo points a gun at him and tells him more flights are in his future. When they're chased again Fairbanks manages to disarm his employer and dump the cargo. He lands safely and hands over Carrillo to the authorities. His innocence is proved and all ends happily. This is a fairly exciting programmer with some good production values in the flying sequences. Newsreel and stock footage mixed in with the film makes a good effect. The acting is routine but passable. However, Davis hated this film (as she did so much of her early work) and later had some artistic revenge. In the catty classic WHAT EVER HAPPENED TO BABY JANE? (1962), her aging character watches a compilation of some old movies in which she starred. Among the footage is none other than PARACHUTE JUMPER.

p, Jack L. Warner; d, Alfred E. Green; w, John Francis Larkin (based on the story "Some Call it Love" by Rian James); ph, James Van Trees; ed, Ray Curtis; art d, Jack Okey.

Drama　　　　　(PR:A MPAA:NR)

PARACHUTE NURSE**　(1942) 65m COL bw

Marguerite Chapman (Glenda White), William Wright (Lt. Woods), Kay Harris (Dottie Morrison), Lauretta M. Schimmoler (Jane Morgan), Louise Albritton (Helen Ames), Frank Sully (Sgt. Peters), Diedra Vale (Ruby Stark), Evelyn Wahl (Gretchen Ernst), Shirley Patterson (Katherine Webb), Eileen O'Hearn (Mary Mack), Roma Aldrich (Nita Dominick), Marjorie Reardon (Wendie Holmes), Catherine Craig (Lt. Mullins), Douglas Wood (Maj. Devon), Forrest Tucker (Lt. Tucker), John Tyrell (Sgt. Tyrell), Ed Laughton (Sgt. Laughton), Mary Zavian, Sally Cairns, Ann Markall, Gwen Holubar, Ninette Crawford, Dona Dax, Helen Foster, Mary Milburn, Dorothy Trail, Diane Royal, Audrene Brier, Mary Windsor (Company "C" Girls), Barbara Brown (Mrs. Jordan), Elizabeth Dow (Doris), Alma Carroll (Mae), Kit Guard (Truck Driver), Theo Coleman (Nurse), June Melville (Meehan), Jan Wiley (Tenderfoot).

In the early 1940s programmers supporting the war effort were ground out by the dozens. PARACHUTE NURSE was one of these, only slightly different for its "woman's angle." It tells the story of a group of nurses trained to parachute into combat situations to help injured men on the battlefield who otherwise might die. The usual amount of in-fighting found in these films is here, none of it beyond a stereotyped level. One story line features a nurse of German heritage who is ostracized by her companions because her brother is fighting for the enemy. She is conveniently removed from the main story, however, when her parachute doesn't open. Another segment deals with Chapman who can't find the courage to jump. She soon changes her mind when boy friend Wright is injured and needs aid. The opening scenes of the film are forced and unrealistic but gradually the pace picks up, becoming a fairly entertaining (if far-fetched) story. Too much attention is paid to the nurses' jump training and not enough to character development, which made this film little more than a filler for B movie double features. Watch for Forrest Tucker in a bit part.

p, Wallace MacDonald; d, Charles Barton; w, Rian James (based on a story by Elizabeth Meehan); ph, Philip Tannura; ed, Mel Thorsen; md, M.W. Stoloff; art d, Lionel Banks.

Drama　　　　　(PR:A MPAA:NR)

PARADE D'AMOUR　(SEE: LOVE PARADE, THE, 1929)

PARADE OF THE WEST*½　(1930) 75m UNIV bw

Ken Maynard (Bud Rand), Gladys McConnell (Mary Owens), Otis Harlan (Prof. Clayton), Frank Rice (Swifty), Bobbie Dunn (Shorty), Jackie Hanlon (Billy Rand), Fred Burns (Copeland), Frank Yaconelli (Sicily Joe), Stanley Blystone (Dude), Blue Washington (Sambo), Tarzan, Rex (The Horses).

Maynard, who served as the film's producer, plays a daredevil rodeo rider. After a bad fall he loses his nerve for the hard-riding life and returns to the medicine show where he started. He befriends a young boy who falls ill. This causes Maynard to once more mount the dreaded horse, "Mankiller" which he does with great success. His fears are overcome, the boy recovers, and McConnell becomes the lady in his life. This is a poorly done western, padded with too much stock footage of rodeo trick-riding and roping. Maynard was capable of much better acting than this film indicates. A preponderance of old jokes haunts the film as well, dusted off from vaudeville and crammed into the early moments before giving way to the story's "drama."

p, Ken Maynard; d, Harry Joe Brown; w, Lesley Mason (based on a story by Bennett Cohen); ph, Ted McCord; ed, Fred Allen.

Western (PR:A MPAA:NR)

PARADES** (1972) 95m Confron/Cinerama c (AKA: BREAK LOOSE)

Russ Thacker ("Baby" Novick), Brad Sullivan (Sgt. Hook), David Doyle (Capt. Jinks), Lewis J. Stadlen (Potofski), Dorothy Chace (Mother), Anthony Holland (Filmmaker "T"), Joseph R. Sicari (Filmmaker "S"), Andrew Duncan (Chaplain), James Catusi (Brahmberg), Erik Estrada (Chicano), Michael Heit (Barrymore), Tim Riley (Crazyhorse), Michael McGowan (Dimedropper), Robert Capece (Wild One), Don Blakely (Blackass), John Pleshette (Murray), Madeline Lee (Bertha), Alice Whitfield (Mildred), Russell Horton (Wexley), Sab Shimono (Togo), Ruth McKinney (Nurse), Peggy Whitton (Jane).

The film tells the story of mistreatment of AWOL prisoners at the fictional Fort Nix. It's supposedly based on accounts taken from prisoners at Fort Dix, New Jersey and at other American army bases. The result is a mixture of overplayed drama and an uneven style of filmmaking that varies from the highly serious to moments of intense black comedy. The violence is extremely graphic with a strong anti-army sentiment. It was the first feature for the 28-year-old Siegel who was a noted documentary filmmaker. His training in that genre shows here with a realistic look and feel. Watch for an appearance by 1970s television heartthrob Estrada in a minor role.

p&d, Robert J. Siegel; w, George Tabori; ph, Sol Negrin (DeLuxe Color); m, Garry Sherman; ed, Richard Marks; md, Sherman; art d, Robert Wightman; m/l, "I Am Your Child," Marty Panzer, Barry Manilow (sung by Manilow).

Drama (PR:O MPAA:R)

PARADINE CASE, THE*** (1947) 125m SELZ-Vanguard/Selznick Releasing Organization-UA bw

Gregory Peck (Anthony Keane), Charles Laughton (Lord Horfield), Charles Coburn (Sir Simon Flaquer the Lawyer), Ann Todd (Gay Keane), Ethel Barrymore (Lady Sophie Horfield), Louis Jourdan (Andre Latour), [Alida] Valli (Maddalena, Anna Paradine), Leo G. Carroll (Sir Joseph Farrell), Joan Tetzel (Judy Flaquer), Isobel Elsom (Keeper at Inn), Alfred Hitchcock (Man Carrying Cello), John Goldsworthy, Lewter Matthews, Pat Aherne, Colin Hunter, John Williams.

Hitchcock tried mightily to overcome the rambling, overlong script, but in the end, he never could quite succeed. Producer Selznick wrote the words by the day and would send Hitchcock the scenes as he finished them, a practice Hitchcock hated. Alida Valli, in her U.S. film debut, has been accused of murdering her wealthy, blind husband. She engages top barrister Peck, who is married to Todd, to defend her. As the two of them spend much time together, Peck discovers himself falling for Valli and his love is what colors his sensibility. Just prior to the trial, Peck finds out that Valli and her stableman, Jourdan, had been having an affair. The case is being heard by judge Laughton, who doesn't much like Peck, probably due to the fact that Laughton had made some amorous advances to Todd and was rebuffed. Valli will not have Jourdan mentioned in the case and makes that clear to Peck. Nevertheless, Peck calls on Jourdan, grilling him on the stand in an attempt to show that it was he who killed Valli's husband. The man had been murdered by a fatal dose of poison and someone, probably the murderer, washed out the glass in which the poison resided. Jourdan, also making his U.S. debut, is disgraced and later takes his own life. When Peck questions Valli, she admits that she killed her husband and then blames Peck for her lover's suicide. Stunned, Peck exits the courtroom as the picture fades. This film cost more than 3 million 1947 dollars, a huge amount. They re-created the Old Bailey courtroom down to the last polished wood panel, at a cost of more than $70,000. Hitchcock thought that Olivier and Garbo might be the right protagonists, but Larry was busy preparing his HAMLET and Greta wanted to be alone, so he had to settle for Peck and Valli. Barrymore is Laughton's loony wife and played it well enough to get an Oscar nomination, the only notice that the Academy took of this movie. Hitchcock had four cameras going simultaneously for the courtroom sequences, then put the action together in the editing room, and these are the best scenes in the film. The use of four cameras and fast-cutting was exactly the opposite of what he did in his next film, ROPE, which he shot in single 10-minute "takes," using one camera only with not one cutaway in the proceedings. A TV version of THE PARADINE CASE was attempted in 1962, starring Richard Basehart, Viveca Lindfors, and Boris Karloff. It was savaged by the critics. As the Queen's prosecutor, Leo G. Carroll is outstanding. If you want to see courtroom theatrics of a much higher caliber, we refer you to WITNESS FOR THE PROSECUTION, which also starred Laughton, but in a far better role. Hitchcock's customary appearance is as a man carrying a cello, which may or may not have had any significance.

p, David O. Selznick; d, Alfred Hitchcock; w, Selznick, Alma Reville, James Bridie (based on the novel by Robert Hichens); ph, Lee Garmes; m, Franz Waxman; ed, Hal C. Kern, John Faure; prod d, J. McMillan Johnson; art d, Tom Morahan; set d, Joseph B. Platt, Emile Kuri; cos, Travis Banton; spec eff, Clarence Slifer.

Crime Drama (PR:A-C MPAA:NR)

PARADISE POUR TOUS** (1982, Fr.) 110m AJ Films/Films A2 c

Patrick Dewaere, Jacques Dutronc, Fanny Cottencon, Stephane Audran, Philippe Leotard, Jeanne Goupil.

Dewaere is a suicidal insurance salesman who finds a new lease on life when he meets Dutronc, a scientist experimenting with an anti-depressant. Dewaere becomes so accepting of his surroundings, however, that he soon drives everyone crazy. A plot to use Dutronc to pepper others with the anti-depressant soon results from the hands of the "conscienceless" guinea pigs. Ironically, the film's producer, director, and writer, Alain Jessua, killed himself before the picture's release, ending a long career committed to science-fiction satire.

p&d, Alain Jessua; w, Jessua, Andre Ruellan; ph, Jacques Robin; m, Rene Koening; art d, Constantine Mejinsky.

Science-Fiction/Satire (PR:C-O MPAA:NR)

PARADISE zero (1982) 100m EM c

Willie Aames (David), Phoebe Cates (Sarah), Richard Curnock (Geoffrey), Tuvia Tavi (The Jackal), Neil Vipond (Reverend), Aviva Marks (Rachel), Joseph Shiloach (Ahmed).

Two nubile teeny-boppers (Aames and Cates) find themselves abandoned at a desert oasis. The film features plenty of food, some adventures with a bloodthirsty Arab, and enough tanned, nude flesh to arouse the film's intended teenaged audience. The acting is laughable with a story that's as believable as honesty in government. PARADISE is little more than a rip-off of the 1980 teen sex film, THE BLUE LAGOON which featured the same basic plot on a desert island. The two films as a double feature would be perfect for an incurable insomniac.

p, Robert Lantos, Stephen J. Roth; d&w, Stuart Gillard; ph, Adam Greenberg (CFI Color); m, Paul Hoffert; ed, Howard Terrill; prod d, Claude Bonniere; cos, Julie Ganton, Mary-Jane McCarty.

Drama Cas. (PR:O MPAA:R)

PARADISE ALLEY** (1962) 81m Sutton/Pathe-America bw (AKA: STARS IN YOUR BACKYARD)

Hugo Haas (Himself), Carol Morris, Marie Windsor, Corinne Griffith, Billy Gilbert, Don Sullivan, Chester Conklin, Margaret Hamilton, William Forrest, Tom Fadden, Jesslyn Fax, Almira Sessions, Jan Englund, Tom Duggan, William Schallert, Clegg Hoyt, Tim Johnson, Bob Dennis, James Canino, Skipper McNally.

Haas, in another of his produced, directed, and written by grade-Z pictures, stars as an aging European film director who sets out to prove that the inhabitants of a sleazy boarding house are a likable lot. He pretends to make a film about them but has no film in the camera—the cast, however, is not clued in on his deception. A studio head soon hears of his plans and finances him to actually complete the project. In real life Haas had seen the last of his studio-backed cash flow. Of interest mainly for a fine veteran cast which stars in Haas' movie-within-the-movie (titled "The Chosen and the Condemned"). They include Griffith, Hamilton, Gilbert, Sessions, and Conklin.

p,d&w, Hugo Haas; m, Franz Steininger.

Drama/Comedy (PR:A MPAA:NR)

PARADISE ALLEY**** (1978) 107m Force Ten Productions/UNIV c

Sylvester Stallone (Cosmo Carboni), Lee Canalito (Victor), Armand Assante (Lenny), Frank McRae (Big Glory), Anne Archer (Annie), Kevin Conway (Stitch), Terry Funk (Franky the Thumper), Joyce Ingalls (Bunchie), Joe Spinell (Burp), Aimee Eccles (Susan Chow), Tom Waits (Mumbles), Chick Casey (Doorman), James J. Casino (Paradise Bartender), Fredi O. Gordon (Paradise Alley Hooker), Lydia Goya, Patricia Spann (Bar Room Hookers), Michael Jeffers (Paradise Alley Bum), Max Leavitt (Mr. Giambelli), Paul Mace (Rat), Polli Magaro (Fat Lady), Pamela Miller (Vonny), John Monks, Jr. (Mickey the Bartender), Leo Nanas (Store Owner), Frank Stallone, Jr. (Singer), Frank Pesce (Skinny the Hand), Stuart K. Robinson (Towel Boy), Ray Sharkey (Legs), Jeff Wald (Sticky).

Stallone did his usual universal thing (writing, directing, starring) in this above-average 1940s story about wrestling in the slums of New York's Hell's Kitchen, but he managed to create a near-great comedy/drama. He is one of three brothers hustling for a living and not making much doing it. Assante is an embittered WW II veteran, wounded in the leg so that he limps with a cane and hates the world for it, including his one-time girl friend, floozy dancehall hostess Archer. Stallone has eyes for his brother's girl friend but she's loyal to Assante. Meanwhile, Stallone uses up his spare time with Ingalls, a whore with the usual heart of gold, and looks for ways to enrich himself without working. He is a regular visitor to a dive called Paradise Alley where wrestling matches are regularly held. He takes a look at the resident champ, Big Glory, wonderfully played by McRae, a black who lives in the rat-infested cellar of the club, and decides that his behemoth brother, Canalito, can easily become the new champion. Canalito is a phlegmatic iceman, happily lugging huge blocks of ice up three-story staircases and patiently improving his mind with girl friend Eccles, a Chinese-American who believes his mind is more important than his brawn. After some hard arguments, Stallone gets Canalito to go into the ring against McRae and become the champ as "Kid Salami." Then local hoodlum Conway, a weird transvestite gangster, puts his vicious champion, Funk, known as Terry the Thumper, up against Canalito, but Stallone's brother manages to beat him in a Homeric battle. Assante acts as Canalito's coach, ruthlessly using his brother until he understands his own warped viewpoint and reverts to his true compassionate nature. The film is funny, tragic, sad, and happy with wonderful performances from all and Stallone's direction, his debut, is disjointed but electric and always stimulating. The film is evocative of the period which is reproduced in sets and costumes with meticulous care and what comes through is nostalgic drama of the first order. The overall mood, stylized with superb cinematography by Kovacs and Conti's score, is fascinating, although the violence is often excessive and the street level morality embodied by Stallone is sometimes offensive.

p, John F. Roach, Ronald A. Suppa; d&w, Sylvester Stallone; ph, Laszlo Kovacs (Panavision, Technicolor); m, Bill Conti; ed, Eve Newman; prod d, John W. Corso; art d, Deborah Beaudet; set d, Jerry Adams; cos, Sandra Berke, Lambert Marks; wrestling ch, Terry Funk; m/l, "Too Close To Paradise," Conti.

Drama/Comedy Cas. (PR:O MPAA:PG)

PARADISE CANYON**½ (1935) 59m MON bw

John Wayne (John Wyatt), Marion Burns (Linda Carter), Earle Hodgins (Dr. Carter), Yakima Canutt (Curly Joe Gale), Reed Howes (Trigger), Perry Murdock

(Ike), Gino Corrado *(Rurale Captain)*, Gordon Clifford *(Mike)*, Tex Palmer, Herman Hack, Earl Dwire.

This was to be the last official Monogram production to feature Wayne. Here the Duke plays a government agent who goes undercover. His job is to track down some counterfeiters who operate near the Mexican border. His first suspect is Hodgins, a medicine show operator, but the trail leads to Canutt. There's the usual amount of action and gun play with the highlight being a high dive off a cliff into a lake. Burns plays Hodgins' daughter who becomes Wayne's love interest. From Monogram Wayne went to Republic Studios using the character name "John Wyatt" once again in his first film there, WESTWARD HO (1935). This was no doubt done to capitalize on the popularity of the cowboy star. The direction and production here are average work and Wayne isn't bad. But you would never guess he was to become a great American legend by watching this film.

p, Paul Malvern; d, Carl Pierson; w, Lindsley Parsons, Robert Tansey [Robert Emmett] (based on a story by Parsons); ph, Archie Stout; ed, Gerald Roberts.

Western   Cas.   (PR:A MPAA:NR)

PARADISE EXPRESS½**   (1937) 60m REP bw

Grant Withers *(Larry Doyle)*, Dorothy Appleby *(Kay Carson)*, Arthur Hoyt *(Trotter)*, Maude Eburne *(Maggie Casey)*, Harry Davenport *(Jed Carson)*, Donald Kirke *(Armstrong)*, Arthur Loft *(Glover)*, Lew Kelly *(Tom Wilson)*, Anthony Pawley *(Stymie)*, Fern Emmett *(Proprietress)*, John Holland *(Gus)*, Bob McClung *(Harmonica Player)*, Bruce Mitchell *(Conductor)*, Guy Wilkerson *(Skinny Smith)*, George Cleveland *(Beasley)*, Ralph McCollough *(Dispatcher)*.

Old-timers are nearly forced to close down their railroad stations by some evil newcomers. However, their livelihood is saved when Withers, the handsome young hero, wins a railroad race to the town of Paradise. He gets the girl (Appleby) as well and all ends happily. This is a routine, harmless melodrama with a standard story and production values. There are some exciting sequences in the race and the outdoor settings are used well.

p, Nat Levine; d, Joseph Kane; w, Jack Netteford, Betty Burbridge (based on a story by Allan Elston, Paul Perez); ph, Jack Marta.

Action/Romance   (PR:A MPAA:NR)

PARADISE FOR THREE*   (1938) 75m MGM bw (GB: ROMANCE FOR THREE)

Frank Morgan *(Rudolph Tobler/Edward Schultze)*, Robert Young *(Fritz Hagedorn)*, Mary Astor *(Mrs. Mallebre)*, Edna Mae Oliver *(Aunt Julia Kunkel)*, Florence Rice *(Hilde Tobler)*, Reginald Owen *(Johann Kesselhut)*, Henry Hull *(Sepp, Hotel Kitchen Worker)*, Herman Bing *(Mr. Polter)*, Sig Rumann *(Karl Bold)*, Walter Kingsford *(William Reichenbach)*, George Ernest *(Office Boy)*, Greta Meyer *(Mrs. Traub)*, Mariska Aldrich *(Beauty Operator)*, Elsa Christian *(Woman)*, Lilyan Irene *(Maid)*, Maurice Cass, Edwin Maxwell, Gustav von Seyffertitz, Wedgwood Nowell *(Lawyers)*, Anna Q. Nilsson, Grace Goodall, Florence Wix, Hazel Laughton *(Women Bridge Players)*.

Morgan plays a soap manufacturer in desperate need of a vacation. He enters his company's jingle contest under an assumed name and to no one's surprise comes up the winner. He sneaks off to a mountain resort in the Alps ready for some rest and relaxation. But trouble arrives in the form of Astor who's convinced her man has run out on her. She bears a breach of promise suit against the multimillionaire and things get a mite busy for Morgan. Morgan and Astor are a funny duo with good comic chemistry. The supporting cast is equally fine with some veteran second bananas like Bing and Rumann providing laughs. Hull is particularly good in his minor role of kitchen worker. This was Astor's first film for MGM and the first for director Buzzell. His direction shows a good sense of the absurd as he gives sequences the right pacing and so keeps the film—and the laughs—moving right along.

p, Sam Zimbalist; d, Edward Buzzell; w, George Oppenheimer, Harry Ruskin (based on the novel *Three Men in the Snow* by Erich Kaestner); ph, Leonard Smith; m, Edward Ward; ed, Elmo Veron; art d, Cedric Gibbons, Stan Rogers; set d, Edwin B. Willis.

Comedy   (PR:A MPAA:NR)

PARADISE FOR TWO   (SEE: GAIETY GIRLS, THE, 1937, Brit.)

PARADISE, HAWAIIAN STYLE**   (1966) 91m PAR c

Elvis Presley *(Rick Richards)*, Suzanna Leigh *(Judy Hudson)*, James Shigeta *(Danny Kohana)*, Donna Butterworth *(Jan Kohana)*, Marianna Hill *(Lani)*, Irene Tsu *(Pua)*, Linda Wong *(Lehua)*, Julie Parrish *(Joanna)*, Jan Shepard *(Betty Kohana)*, John Doucette *(Donald Belden)*, Philip Ahn *(Moki)*, Grady Sutton *(Mr. Cubberson)*, Don Collier *(Andy Lowell)*, Doris Packer *(Mrs. Barrington)*, Mary Treen *(Mrs. Belden)*, Gigi Verone *(Peggy Holdren)*, Shanon Hale *(Blonde Applicant)*.

Presley plays an airline pilot who loses his job because of his wild ways, goes to Hawaii, and teams up with his old pal Shigeta to form a charter helicopter service. He hires the pretty Leigh as secretary *cum* love interest while continuing his playboy ways. While transporting some dogs, Presley is momentarily distracted and accidentally dips his helicopter. This forces the car of an FAA official to go into a ditch, and Presley's license is temporarily suspended. He is supposed to wait until a hearing before he can fly again, but violates the order when Shigeta breaks his leg and needs to get to a hospital. To compound his problems, Presley's playboy ways catch up with him when a bevy of angry beauties gang up on him at a party. But all is righted in the end when he wins both the hearing and the affections of his one true love, Leigh. Had anyone else done this film it might have been passable. But Presley had shown he was capable of better quality films early in his career, and is a disappointment in this poor attempt to recapture the feeling of BLUE HAWAII (1961). His off-screen high living was beginning to catch up with him, and he looks

overweight and puffy. It's sad to think that the man who once shocked a nation on the "Ed Sullivan Show" is reduced to singing such tripe as "A Dog's Life" and the most un-Presley-like song "Bill Bailey, Won't You Please Come Home?" The film isn't badly made; the direction and script have their entertaining moments. But Presley's great talent was woefully manipulated by a coterie of yes men. Col. Tom Parker served as "technical consultant" on this and other Presley features. In all, Presley sings "Paradise, Hawaiian Style," "Scratch My Back, (Then I'll Scratch Yours)," "Stop Where You Are," "This Is My Heaven" (Bill Giant, Bernie Baum, Florence Kaye); "House of Sand," "Queenie Wahine's Papaya" (Giant, Baum, Kaye, Donna Butterworth); "Datin'" (Fred Wise, Randy Starr, Butterworth); "Drums of the Islands" (Sid Tepper, Roy C. Bennett); "A Dog's Life" (Sid Wayne, Ben Weisman); "Sand Castles" (Herb Goldberg, David Hess, Butterworth); "Bill Bailey, Won't You Please Come Home?" (Hughie Cannon).

p, Hal Wallis; d, Michael Moore; w, Allan Weiss, Anthony Lawrence (based on an original story by Weiss); ph, W. Wallace Kelley (Technicolor); m, Joseph J. Lilley; ed, Warren Low; art d, Hal Pereira, Walter Tyler; set d, Sam Comer, Ray Moyer; cos, Edith Head; ch, Jack Regas.

Musical   Cas.   (PR:A MPAA:NR)

PARADISE ISLAND*   (1930) 68m TIF bw

Kenneth Harlan *(Thorne)*, Marceline Day *(Ellen)*, Tom Santschi *(Lutze)*, Paul Hurst *(Beauty)*, Betty Boyd *(Poppi)*, Victor Potel *(Swede)*, Gladden James *(Armstrong)*, Will Stanton *(Limey)*.

Bargain-basement South Seas musical romance starring Day as a sweet and innocent young thing who travels to the tropics to marry her beau, James. Upon her arrival she is shocked to learn that James has gambled away all his money and is deeply in debt to saloon owner Santschi. Seeing an opportunity to win Day, Santschi pretends to be sympathetic to James' plight. Before he gets too far, however, two wild sailors arrive, Harlan and Hurst, and win back James' money. Realizing that she is no longer in love with James, Day falls for Harlan instead. Songs include: "I've Got A Girl In Every Port," "Drinking Song," "Lazy Breezes," "Just Another Dream" (Val Burton, Will Jason).

d, Bert Glennon; w, Monte Katterjohn (based on a story by M.B. Deering); ph, Max Dupont; ed, Byron Robinson.

Musical/Romance   (PR:A MPAA:NR)

PARADISE ISLE*   (1937) 73m MON bw

Movita *(Ida)*, Warren Hull *(Kennedy)*, George Pilita *(Tono)*, William B. Davidson *(Hoener)*, John St. Polis *(Coxon)*, Pierre Watkin *(Steinmeyer)*, Kenneth Harlan *(Johnson)*, Russell Simpson *(Baxter)*.

This South Seas programmer is a cut above most in its unique approach to the story. Hull is the white man who falls in love with the native girl (Movita). The twist to the story has Hull as a blinded painter seeking a doctor who can help restore his sight. Though clearly a fantasy, PARADISE ISLE presents its story with grace and style. The two leads play sensitively without stooping to B-movie sentimentality. The film was shot in Samoa, assuring beautiful scenery.

p, Dorothy Reid; d, Arthur Greville Collins; w, Marion Orth (based on the story "The Belled Palm" by Allan Vaughan Elliston); ph, Gilbert Warrenton; m, Sam K. Tuiteleapaga, Lani McIntyre; ed, Russell Schoengarth; spec eff, Fred Jackman.

Drama   (PR:A MPAA:NR)

PARADISE LAGOON   (SEE: ADMIRABLE CRICHTON, THE, 1957, Brit.)

PARADISE ROAD   (SEE: BIG DADDY, 1969)

PARADISIO*   (1962, Brit.) 82m Tonylyn/Fanfare-Evelyn Place bw

Arthur Howard *(Prof. Sims)*, Eva Waegner *(Lisa Hinkle)*.

Leslie Howard's brother Arthur is a professor at Oxbridge who comes across a special pair of sunglasses that makes everyone he looks at appear naked. He soon becomes involved with a spy ring, but escapes to the sunny beaches on the Riviera with his wonder-glasses. Some sequences even appear in 3-D in this little oddity for which no director wanted to take credit.

p, Jacques Henrici; w, Lawrence Zeitlin, Henri Haile, Henrici; m, John Bath (played by Kurt Graunke Orchestra).

Comedy/Spy Satire   (PR:O MPAA:NR)

PARADISO DELL'UOMO   (SEE: MAN'S PARADISE, 1963, Ital.)

PARALLAX VIEW, THE*½   (1974) 102m PAR c

Warren Beatty *(Joseph Frady)*, Hume Cronyn *(Editor Edgar Rintels)*, William Daniels *(Austin Tucker)*, Paula Prentiss *(Lee Carter)*, Kelly Thorsden *(Sheriff L.D.)*, Earl Hindman *(Deputy Red)*, Chuck Waters *(Busboy/Assassin)*, Bill Joyce *(Sen. Carroll)*, Bettie Johnson *(Mrs. Carroll)*, Bill McKinney *(Art, an Assassin)*, Joanne Harris *(Chrissy)*, Ted Gehring *(Schecter)*, Lee Pulford *(Shirley)*, Doria Cook *(Gale)*, Jim Davis *(Sen. Hammond)*, Joan Lemmo *(Organist)*, Anthony Zerbe *(Schwartzkopf)*, Kenneth Mars *(Former FBI Agent Turner)*, Stacy Keach, Sr., Ford Rainey *(Commission Spokesmen)*, Walter McGinn *(Parallax Agent Jack Younger)*, William Jordan *(Tucker's Aide)*.

A popular senator is shot by a waiter at the Seattle Space Needle. Three years later TV reporter Prentiss, who was on the scene, goes to newspaper reporter Beatty frightened for her life. Assassination witnesses have been systematically killed, she says, and Prentiss knows that she's next. Beatty discounts her fears as irrational paranoia, but after her supposed suicide, doubt creeps into his mind. He begins investigating the story despite an argument from his editor (Cronyn) that this is creating news rather than reporting it. Beatty goes to the small fishing town where one of the witnesses was killed and nearly dies for his efforts. He gets hold of an application for a group called the Parallax Corporation that features some unusual questions. A psychologist explains that this test is designed to identify psychopathic traits, and has a murderer take the test for Beatty. He files the application and then meets with Daniels, a former aid to the late senator. Daniels shows Beatty some photographs suggesting that there was more than one killer at the assassination. The boat they are on explodes, but Beatty manages to escape. Back at his cheap motel Beatty is greeted by McGinn, an agent of Parallax. According to the application Beatty has a certain aggressiveness that would make him invaluable to certain corporations. At Parallax headquarters Beatty spots the man in Daniels' photographs. He follows the man to the local airport and watches as he loads a suitcase onto the plane. Beatty suspects a bomb and passes a note to the stewardess. After the plane has returned, it explodes. Meanwhile, Cronyn receives a tape recording from Beatty of the conversation with McGinn. Cronyn is interested and pays the new deliveryman who has brought his lunch from a local deli. But the deliveryman is a Parallax agent and the food poisoned with a chemical that makes it appear Cronyn has had a heart attack. Beatty later spots the delivery boy and follows him to a hall where another senator, a potential presidential candidate, is to make a speech. Beatty follows the man to the catwalks above the hall where the senator is practicing for the evening's events. The senator is suddenly shot and Beatty tries to escape. But it's a trap and he is killed. A few months later a commission declares that Beatty was a lone gunman who killed the senator for his own insane reasons. Case closed. THE PARALLAX VIEW takes its title from a photography term referring to the difference between viewfinder image and actual picture when looking through a camera. In the parallax view the subject appears normal but goes through very subtle changes. Such is the world in this powerful study of paranoia. Only Beatty and the audience know what reality is. Anyone else with a glimmer of the truth is killed. Pakula's direction maintains a neat balance between the real and the perceived. The film's opening sequence presents Beatty as a disheveled loner, not unlike Arthur Bremer or John Hinckley, lost in a crowd around a popular politician. Beatty immediately looks suspicious, but of course is not a dangerous psychopath. The film retains this pattern throughout. Things are not what they appear to be. Pakula's direction is at its best with disorienting shots and editing patterns. Characters are often filmed behind glass or curtains, allowing only a partial look at the whole scene. The music, a patriotic theme with ominous undertones, helps create the tense eerie mood. Perhaps the finest moment in the film comes when Beatty is asked to take a test at Parallax headquarters. He watches an Eisenstein-styled montage of pictures and words designed to draw anger. In five minutes the sequences carefully match the words "Father," "Mother," "Love," "God," "Country," and "Me" with a variety of pictures ranging from sentimental scenes of family life to distorted people trapped in mental homes. Political images from Hitler to the White House and the Pope are mixed in. This montage says a great deal about American life and how different images could produce enough anger to make someone kill. Beatty's performance is terrific. His characterization is controlled and supported by a certain naive honesty. The rest of the cast is equally fine, particularly Daniels as the frightened political aide and McGinn as the calmly sinister Parallax representative. The film is not without its problems, however. Pandering to its action/thriller elements, an early fight and car chase severely detract from the film's more ominous themes and were probably included to please action genre fans. The most compelling aspects are of course the political and historical overtones. Pakula wanted to create a film about ". . .a sort of American myth based on some things that have happened, some fantasies we may have had of what might have happened and a lot of fears many of us have had." The fictional assassination was a deliberate attempt to suggest a possible explanation for the John F. Kennedy assassination. Using historical parallels (the photographs which imply a second gunman at Dallas; the fact that many of the assassination witnesses died mysteriously in the years following 1963), Pakula created a possible, though fictional, explanation in a film steeped in Americana symbolism. The film was released in June of 1974, after the studio had let the controversial work sit for several months. Another case of political conspiracies and skullduggery was chronicled nicely by Pakula a few years later in ALL THE PRESIDENT'S MEN (1976).

p&d, Alan J. Pakula; w, David Giler, Lorenzo Semple, Jr. (based on the novel by Loren Singer); ph, Gordon Willis (Panavision, Technicolor); m, Michael Small; ed, John W. Wheeler; prod d, George Jenkins; art d, Jenkins; set d, Reg Allen; cos, Frank Thompson.

Thriller   **Cas.**   **(PR:O MPAA:R)**

PARALLELS*   (1980, Can.)92m Creswin/Group 3 c

David Fox (*Father Robert Dane*), Judith Mabey (*Judith Del Assandro*), Gerard Lepage (*Steven Del Assandro*), Kyra Harper (*Claire*), David Ferry (*Philip Calder*), Walter Kaasa (*Bishop Teller*), Howard Dallin (*Father Clifford*), Jennifer Raach (*Marianne*), Stephen Walsh (*Paul*).

A complex drama shot in Canada with what is apparently an all-Canadian cast and production crew, PARALLELS has its moments. Fox is a priest who runs a boys' university. Prior to becoming a man of the cloth, Fox had an affair with Mabey, whose son, Lepage, is now one of the students under Fox's care. The church is not thrilled with the liberal rector because of his open and outspoken views on abortion, birth control, and discipline, three items which the hierarchy feels are sacrosanct and above questioning. Lepage, a bit of a troublemaker, steals Harper away from her boy friend, Ferry, and this starts a ruckus on campus. Fox eventually has to take off his priestly garb and settle matters. The movie was made for about $300,000 and sometimes shows it. Good acting and some literacy in the screenplay by director Schoenberg and co-author Summers. Summers later became a novelist who specialized in plots concerning computers. In order to sell his books, he conceived of a most interesting ploy; he typed out the first chapter of his novel and sent it out, via modems, to as many computer "bulletin boards" as he could. The computer hackers would read the chapter and, hopefully, would rush out and buy the book so they could find out what happened. As for Schoenberg, this is a good

example of a "first picture" and as soon as he gets the right script, he'll be someone to watch.

p, Jack Wynters; d, Mark Schoenberg; w, Schoenberg, Jaron Summers; ph, Douglas Cole; m, Don Archbold; ed, Mark Slipp; art d, Drew Borland.

Drama   **(PR:A-C MPAA:NR)**

PARANOIA, 1968   (SEE: KISS THE OTHER SHEIK, 1968, Fr./Ital.)

PARANOIA, 1968   (SEE: MAN WITH THE BALLOONS, THE, 1968, Fr./Ital.)

PARANOIAC*½   (1963, Brit.) 80m Hammer/UNIV bw

Janette Scott (*Eleanor Ashby*), Oliver Reed (*Simon Ashby*), Liliane Brousse (*Francoise*), Alexander Davion (*Tony Ashby*), Sheila Burrell (*Aunt Harriet*), Maurice Denham (*John Kossett*), John Bonney (*Keith Kossett*), John Stuart (*Williams*), Colin Tapley (*Vicar*), Harold Lang (*RAF Type*), Laurie Leigh (*1st Woman*), Marianne Stone (*2nd Woman*), Sydney Bromley (*Tramp*), Jack Taylor (*Sailor*).

After the success of Hitchcock's classic PSYCHO there was a rush of imitation films, some good, some despicable. PARANOIAC, while nothing like its inspiration, ranks as one of the best of these efforts. Scott goes to a memorial service for her late parents. While there she glimpses a figure who bears a striking resemblance to a brother who committed suicide seven years previously. This is all the excuse her surviving brother Reed needs to prove she's mentally unbalanced and not worthy of an inheritance. Scott begins to doubt her sanity and tries to kill herself as well. Who should rescue her but Davion, the supposedly dead brother. He claims that there was no suicide, just a disappearance. He moves back to the family mansion and must fend off mysterious and violent attacks. He also finds himself falling in love with Scott and admits he is an impostor. Meanwhile, Reed's incessant organ playing rings throughout the castle, driving everyone just a shade madder. A la PSYCHO they confront him and discover he is the real killer, keeping the mummified remains of his brother in a chapel. He knocks out Davion and ties him up while Reed's equally crazy aunt Burrell sets the place ablaze to cover the crimes. Scott manages to rescue Davion from the flames, but Reed dies as he tries to save what's left of his kid brother. PARANOIAC has some great plot twists, well handled in a macabre stylization. Reed is wonderfully sick, combining a sly sort of wit with some gruesome behavior. It's a semi-comical characterization that never disappoints. This was the first directorial effort for Francis, who had worked for many years as a British cameraman. He builds the suspense well with some genuinely frightening sequences and good pace.

p, Anthony Hinds; d, Freddie Francis; w, Jimmy Sangster; ph, Arthur Grant (CinemaScope); m, Elisabeth Lutyens; ed, James Needs; prod d, Bernard Robinson; art d, Don Mingaye; spec eff, Les Bowie, Kit West; makeup, Roy Ashton.

Horror   **(PR:O MPAA:NR)**

PARASITE zero   (1982) 85m EM 3-D c

Robert Glaudini (*Dr. Paul Dean*), Demi Moore (*Patricia*), Luca Bercovici (*Ricus*), James Davidson (*Merchant*), Al Fann (*Collins*), Vivian Blaine (*Miss Daley*), Tom Villard (*Zeke*), Cherie Currie (*Dana*), James Cavan (*Buddy*), Joanelle Romero (*Bo*), Freddie Moore (*Arn*), Natalie May (*Shell*), Cheryl Smith (*Captive Girl*), Joel Miller (*Punk*).

"The First Futuristic Monster Movie in 3-D!" That's what the ads read and they were probably the most exciting part of this inane mess, quickly ground out to cash in on the 3-D renaissance of the early 1980s. Glaudini is a scientist who creates nasty little creatures that grow on victims' insides, then burst through right into audiences' laps. It all takes place on an old western movie set shortly after yet another in a never-ending string of cheap movie "nuclear holocausts." This blatantly rips off a number of popular movies, most notably ALIEN (1970) with bits of MAD MAX (1979) and Cronenberg's far superior THE PARASITE MURDERS (1974). There's little logic to the plot, but that's not what this movie is about. Currie's acting is about as accomplished as her singing with the rock group "The Runaways." Producer-director Band left the movie-making business after creating this mess for the more lucrative videocassette market. There he had great success marketing and distributing schlock horror films.

p&d, Charles Band; w, Alan Adler, Michael Shoob, Frank Levering; ph, Mac Ahlberg (Stereovision, 3-D, Metrocolor); m, Richard Band; ed, Brad Arensman; art d, Pamela B. Warner; spec eff, Stan Winston, James Kagel, Doug White, Lance Anderson; cos, Lesley Lynn Nicholson; stunts, Harry Wowchuk.

Horror   **Cas.**   **(PR:O MPAA:R)**

PARASITE MURDERS, THE   (SEE: THEY CAME FROM WITHIN, 1976, Can.)

PARATROOP COMMAND   (1959) 77m AIP bw

Richard Bakalyan (*Charlie*), Ken Lynch (*Lieutenant*), Jack Hogan (*Ace*), Jimmy Murphy (*Sergeant*), Jeffery Morris (*Pigpen*), Jim Beck (*Cowboy*), Carolyn Hughes (*Gina*), Patricia Huston (*Amy*), Paul Busch (*German Captain*), Sid Lassick (*Interpreter*), Brad Trumball (*Pilot*).

After Bakalyan accidentally kills a member of his own paratroop squadron, he must prove his courage in this war melodrama. To clear himself with the troops and with himself, Bakalyan sets off a series of land mines in the North African desert to open a way for a much-needed radio generator. In the process of performing these heroics, he is killed. This double bill filler is surprisingly engrossing, both in terms of plot and characterization. Screenwriter Stanley Shpetner resists the temptation to assign a wide range of ethnic stereotypes to the squadron members. They become real individuals to the viewer—unusual for a WW II action film, and even more so for a "B" programmer.

p, James H. Nicholson, Samuel Z. Arkoff; d, William Witney; w, Stanley Shpetner (based on his story); ph, Gilbert Warrenton; m, Ronald Stein; ed, Robert Eisen.

War Drama   (PR:A MPAA:NR)

PARATROOPER**½   (1954, Brit.) 88m Warwick/COL c (GB: THE RED BERET)

Alan Ladd (*Canada MacKendrick*), Leo Genn (*Maj. Snow*), Susan Stephen (*Penny Gardner*), Harry Andrews (*R.S.M.*), Donald Houston (*Taffy*), Anthony Bushell (*Gen. Whiting*), Patric Doonan (*Flash*), Stanley Baker (*Breton*), Lana Morris (*Pinky*), Tim Turner (*Rupert*), Michael Kelly (*Dawes*), Anton Kiffring (*The Pole*), Thomas Heathcote (*Alf*), Carl Duering (*Rossi*), John Boxer (*Sgt. Box*), Victor Maddern, Harry Locke, Michael Balfour, Guido Lorraine, Dermot Palmer, George Margo, Henry Longhurst, Guy De Monceau, Richard Shaw, Peter Burton, Richard Ford, Walter Gotell, Yvonne Stein.

Ladd stars as a guilt-ridden American Army officer who resigns his commission after ordering a friend and fellow officer to jump from a plane which was about to crash. Ladd, the plane's pilot, managed to safely land the plane, but his friend died when his chute failed to open. Determined to avoid life-or-death decisions, Ladd enlists in a British paratrooper training camp under the pretense that he is Canadian. He keeps his past secret and merely follows orders. Commanding officer Genn takes notice of Ladd's skill and digs into his past records to learn more. In the meantime, Ladd has fallen for Stephen, a friendly British girl who serves as a parachute packer. Ladd's unit is called on to fight in North Africa on a mission to recapture an airfield from the Nazis. Led by Genn, the troops soon find themselves stuck in the middle of a minefield with Nazis closing in around them. Genn is wounded, forcing Ladd into a position of command. Ladd arms himself with a bazooka and blows open a path in the minefield, clearing the way for his fellow soldiers to reach safety. Upon his return to the base, Ladd decides that he must face the responsibility before him and continue to lead his fellow soldiers in battle. The first of three pictures Ladd contracted to do in Britain (THE BLACK KNIGHT and HELL BELOW ZERO followed), PARATROOPER was met with controversy by some British critics who felt that a British actor should have been cast in the lead. Others, however, came to Ladd's defense and were thrilled that he was visiting their shores. Ladd even held a press conference to ease the growing tension. "Look," he explained, "I didn't come over to conquer anything or anybody. All I'm going to do is play the part of a guy who comes to England to learn to fight. Got that? I said learn to fight, not to teach." Regardless of what the critics wrote, British fans adored Ladd, voting him the most popular actor of that year. Even Winston Churchill gave a show of support by commending Ladd on his performance in the film.

p, Irving Allen, Albert R. Broccoli; d, Terence Young; w, Richard Miabaum, Frank S. Nugent, Sy Bartlett (based on the story "The Red Beret" by Hilary St. George Sanders); ph, John Wilcox (Technicolor); m, John Addison; ed, Gordon Pilkington.

War   (PR:A MPAA:NR)

PARBESZED   (SEE: DIALOGUE, 1967, Hung.)

PARDNERS**   (1956) 90m PAR c

Dean Martin (*Slim Mosely, Jr.*), Jerry Lewis (*Wade Kingsley, Jr.*), Lori Nelson (*Carol Kingsley*), Jeff Morrow (*Pete Rio*), Jackie Loughery (*Dolly Riley*), John Baragrey (*Dan Hollis*), Agnes Moorehead (*Mrs. Matilda Kingsley*), Lon Chaney, Jr. (*Whitey*), Milton Frome (*Hawkins, Butler*), Richard Aherne (*Chauffeur*), Lee Van Cleef (*Gus*), Stuart Randall (*Carol's Cowhand*), Scott Douglas (*Salvin*), Jack Elam (*Pete*), Bob Steele (*Shorty*), Mickey Finn (*Red*), Douglas Spencer (*Smith*), Philip Tonge (*Footman*), Emory Parnell (*Col. Hart*), Dorothy Ford (*Amanda*), Frances Mercer (*Sally*), William Forrest (*Hocker*), James Parnell (*Bank Teller*), Mary Newton (*Laura*), Len Hendry (*Western Cowboy*), Charles Stevens (*Indian*), Gavin Gordon, Robert Brubaker, Tony Michael, Johnstone White (*Businessmen*), Valerie Allen, Elaine Riley, Ann McCrae (*Dance Hall Girls*), Don House, Frank Cordell, Robert Garvey, Keith Wilson, Emily Belser, Stanley Blystone, Hank Mann, Bobby Barber (*Townspeople*).

Lewis plays a spoiled New York millionaire who becomes the town sheriff while Martin plays a ranch foreman in this musical western spoof of Bing Crosby's 1936 film, RHYTHM ON THE RANGE. Both Lewis and Martin continually play for laughs with Martin as straight man. As Lewis loses his fear of the West, he teams with Martin to rid the town of the bad guys. While getting rid of the heavies, Lewis is romanced by Loughery while Nelson does the same with Martin.

p, Paul Jones; d, Norman Taurog; w, Sidney Sheldon, Jerry Davis (based on the story "Rhythm on the Range" by Marvin J. Houser); ph, Daniel Fapp (VistaVision, Technicolor); ed, Archie Marshek; md, Frank De Vol; art d, Hal Pereira, Roland Anderson; cos, Edith Head; ch, Nick Castle; m/l, "Buckskin Beauty," James Van Heusen, Sammy Cahn (sung by Jerry Lewis), "Pardners," "The Wind! The Wind!" "Me 'N You 'N the Moon," Van Heusen, Cahn (sung by Dean Martin).

Comedy   (PR:A MPAA:NR)

PARDON MY BRUSH zero   (1964) 60m Active-Stardust/Gillman-S.I.E. c

Maureen Gaffney.

Idiotic sex comedy that features two house painters accidentally mixing up some vanishing cream with their paint supply. They are assigned to paint the walls of a building inhabited by young, beautiful women, and only someone with the intellect of a raisin cookie can't figure out where the film goes from there. One of the erstwhile painters falls into a swimming pool, where one young lady fires at him from an atomic submarine. The two are finally shot by the building's owner, who catches them in her bathroom.

p,d&w, John K. McCarthy.

Comedy   (PR:O MPAA:NR)

PARDON MY FRENCH*½   (1951, U.S./Fr.) 82m UA bw (GB: THE LADY FROM BOSTON)

Paul Henreid (*Paul Rencourt*), Merle Oberon (*Elizabeth Rockwell*), Maximilienne (*Mme. Bleubois*), Paul Bonifas (*Bleubois*), Jim Gerald (*Poisson*), Martial Rebe (*Mobet*), Dora Doll (*Yvette*), Lauria Daryl (*Mme. Mobet*), Lucien Callemand (*Inspector*), Victor Merenda (*Francois*), Gilberte Defoucault (*Marie-Claire*), Marina (*Jacqueline*), Gerard Rosset (*Michel*), Albert Cullaz (*Andre*), Andre Aversa (*Pierrot*), Nicole Monnin (*Marcelle*).

Merle Oberon plays a school teacher who inherits a chateau in Cannes in this predictable comedy. She arrives in France ready to take over the chateau and has some fun with the money left over. But the chateau is inhabited by a group of squatters led by Paul Henreid. It's not too hard to predict what happens as Oberon falls for Henreid and permits the squatters to stay.

p, Peter Cusick, Andre Sarrut; d, Bernard Vorhaus; w, Roland Kibbee; ph, Gerald Gibbs; m, Guy Bernard; ed, Derek Armstrong, Gordon Hales; art d, Emile Alex.

Comedy   (PR:A MPAA:NR)

PARDON MY GUN*   (1930) 67m Pathe bw

Sally Starr (*Mary*), George Duryea [Tom Keene/Richard Powers] (*Ted Duncan*), Mona Ray (*Peggy*), Lee Moran (*Jeff*), Robert Edeson (*Pa Martin*), Frank MacFarlane (*Hank*), Tom MacFarlane (*Tom*), Harry Woods (*Copper*), Stompie ("*Lightnin*"), Lew Meehan (*Denver*), Ethan Laidlaw (*Tex*), Harry Watson, Al Norman, Ida May Chadwick, Abe Lyman and His Band.

Cowpoke Duryea falls madly in love with his boss' daughter, Ray, but he must compete for the girl's affections with Woods, a rival rancher. Woods, in an effort to push Duryea out of the picture, tries to sabotage the annual relay race where the cowboy will be riding his boss' prize horse. A routine oater with music, PARDON MY GUN features a barn dance with drum solos, yodeling, and dancing. The song "Deep Down South" was written by George Green.

p, E.B. Derr; d, Robert De Lacy; w, Hugh Cummings (based on a story by Betty Scott); ph, Edward Snyder; ed, Fred Allen.

Western   (PR:A MPAA:NR)

PARDON MY GUN*½   (1942) 56m COL bw

Charles Starrett (*Steve Randall*), Alma Carroll (*Dodie Cameron*), Arthur Hunnicutt (*Arkansas*), Texas Jim Lewis (*Tex*), Noah Beery Sr. (*Judge*), Dick Curtis (*Clint*), Ted Mapes (*Ace*), Lloyd Bridges (*Whitey*), Dave Harper (*Corks*), Roger Gray (*Sheriff*), Jack Kirk, Art Mix, Joel Friedkin, Guy Usher, Denver Dixon, Texas Jim Lewis and His Lone Star Cowboys.

A rancher is killed for the money he is carrying out of town but the killers inadvertently throw the money satchel into the bushes which Carroll finds. She is under suspicion, but a survey engineer, Starrett, comes to her rescue. While they hunt the thieves, a romance develops between the two. It ends predictably with the two in the customary loving embrace.

p, Jack Fier; d, William Berke; w, Wyndham Gittens; ph, George Meehan; ed, Mel Thorsen; art d, Lionel Banks.

Western   (PR:A MPAA:NR)

PARDON MY PAST**½   (1945) 88m MUT/COL bw

Fred MacMurray (*Eddie York/Francis Pemberton*), Marguerite Chapman (*Joan*), Akim Tamiroff (*Jim Arnold*), William Demarest (*Chuck*), Rita Johnson (*Mary Pemberton*), Harry Davenport (*Grandpa Pemberton*), Douglas Dumbrille (*Uncle Wills*), Karolyn Grimes (*Stephani*), Dewey Robinson, Tom Moffatt (*Plainclothesmen*), Hugh Prosser (*Mr. Long*), Frank Moran (*Thug*), George Chandler (*Cab Driver*), Charles Arnt (*Clothes Salesman*), Herbert Evans (*Butler*).

PARDON MY PAST is a slick postwar comedy with lots of laughs, despite the old warhorse "mistaken identity" plot. MacMurray and Demarest have been just mustered out of the service and are traveling to Wisconsin where they plan to use their savings to begin a mink farm. Upon arriving, MacMurray is thought to be a gambling playboy who owes a lot of money around town for his losses, mainly to Tamiroff, whose aides, Prosser and Moran, are very tough-looking collectors indeed. MacMurray and Demarest go to the abode of the playboy and he is again mistaken for the man, who is supposed to be vacationing in Mexico. While at the estate, MacMurray meets and falls for Chapman, a poor relative of his alter ego. The playboy's grandfather, Davenport, doesn't much like his nephew and the uncle, Dumbrille, has plans to remove whatever money is in the family through an intricate plot. The playboy is about to be divorced from Johnson, through the efforts of Dumbrille. He has the backbone of a jellyfish and is easily manipulated. MacMurray gives enough of an acting job in both parts that we can distinguish which character he's playing without anyone having to identify him by name. (At no time in the picture do they engage in the "double image" technique.) In the end, MacMurray and Chapman get together and the playboy and his wife return to their old domestic bliss. Tamiroff is calmed and the picture ends peacefully with no mayhem to speak of. Good fun for all. Robert Aldrich did one of his first jobs as assistant director.

p&d, Leslie Fenton; w, Earl Felton, Karl Kamb (based on a story by Patterson McNutt, Harlan Ware); ph, Russell Metty; m, Dmitri Tiomkin; ed, Otho Lovering, Richard Heermance; md, Tiomkin; prod d, Bernard Herzbrun; set d, Edward C. Boyle.

Comedy   (PR:A MPAA:NR)

PARDON MY RHYTHM**　　　　　(1944) 61m UNIV bw

Gloria Jean (Jinx Page), Patric Knowles (Tony Page), Evelyn Ankers (Julia Munson), Marjorie Weaver (Dixie Moore), Walter Catlett (Michael O'Bannon), Mel Torme (Ricky O'Bannon), Patsy O'Connor (Doodles Weaver), Ethel Griffies (Mrs. Dean), Jack Slattery (Announcer), Linda Reed (Soda Fountain Waitress), Alphonse Martell (Headwaiter), Bob Crosby and His Orchestra, The Mel Torme Trio.

This lightweight musical focuses on the dreams of talented youth, much like the more recent and more emotional FAME. It follows the path of teen-ager Jean, whose romance with Torme goes through some tough times. Part of the trouble comes when bandleader Crosby sends Weaver after Torme to get him to sign a contract. Jean then sends her father after Weaver, but everything comes out in the end. Songs include: "I'll See You in My Dreams" (Gus Kann, Isham Jones, sung by Crosby), "Do You Believe in Dreams?" (Don George, Irving Bibo, Al Piantadosi), "Spell of the Moon," "Shame on Me," "Drummer Boy," and "You've Got to Hand it to the Band."

p, Bernard W. Burton; d, Felix E. Feist; w, Val Burton, Eugene Conrad (based on the story "Mis IQ" by Hurd Barrett); ph, Paul Ivano; ed, Edward Curtiss; md, H.J. Salter; art d, John B. Goodman, Ralph M. DeLacy.

Musical　　　　　　　　　　　　　**(PR:A　MPAA:NR)**

PARDON MY SARONG**½　　　　(1942) 83m UNIV bw

Bud Abbott (Algernon Shaw), Lou Costello (Wellington Phlug), Virginia Bruce (Joan Marshall), Robert Paige (Tommy Layton), Lionel Atwill (Dr. Varnoff), Leif Erickson (Whaba), William Demarest (Detective Kendall), Samuel S. Hinds (Chief Kolua), Orville Jones, Charles Fuqua, Bill Kenney, Deek Watson (Ink Spots), Raymond Winfield, Sammy Green, Teddie Fraser (Tip, Tap, Toe), Irving Bacon (Proprietor), Nan Wynn (Luana), Marie McDonald (Ferna), Elaine Morey (Amo), Susan Levine (Tagalong), Jack LaRue (Tabor), Hans Schumm (Moss), Joe Kirk, Frank Penny (Henchmen), Charles Lane (Superintendent), Chester Clute (Checker), Tom Fadden (Sven), George Chandler (Newsman), Eddie Acuff (Man), Sig Arno (Marco), Jane Patten, Florine McKinney, Marjorie Reardon, Audrey Long (Girls), Teddy Infuhr (Nemo), Katherine Dunham Dancers, The Sarango Girls, Sharkey the Seal.

A standard Abbott and Costello comedy follows the boys through their familiar routines in one misadventure after another. This time the boys, playing Chicago bus drivers, get involved with a fabulously wealthy playboy. They also meet a jewel thief and are chased through an island jungle. The pair pull out every chase trick imaginable to go for the laugh. Songs include: "Island of the Moon" (Don Raye, Gene De Paul, sung by Paige and Bruce), "Lovely Luana," "Vingo Jingo" (Raye, DePaul; sung by Wynn and chorus), "Do I Worry" (Bobby Worth, Stanley Cowan; sung by The Ink Spots), "Java Jive" (sung by The Ink Spots), "Shout, Brother Shout" (Clarence Williams, sung by The Ink Spots) and "If I Didn't Care" (Jack Lawrence). (See ABBOTT AND COSTELLO series, Index.)

p, Alex Gottlieb; d, Erle C. Kenton; w, True Boardman, Nat Perrine, John Grant; ph, Milton Krasner; ed, Arthur Hilton; md, Charles Previn; art d, Jack Otterson; ch, Katherine Dunham.

Comedy　　　　　　　　　　　　**(PR:AAA　MPAA:NR)**

PARDON MY STRIPES*½　　　　(1942) 64m REP bw

Bill Henry (Henry Platt), Shelia Ryan (Ruth Stevens), Edgar Kennedy (Warden Bingham), Harold Huber (Big George Kilraine), Paul Hurst (Feets), Cliff Nazarro (Nutsy), Tom Kennedy (Casino), Edwin Stanley (Andrews), Dorothy Granger (Peaches), George McKay (Old Timer), Maxine Leslie (Myrtle).

A weak comedy that pushes each situation far beyond its limit. Henry is a college football player who runs the wrong way for a touchdown, but still scores big when a gangster who won a bundle on the game gives him a job. He is assigned to take $117,000 from California to Chicago, but misses his plane when he meets a female reporter. He hires his own plane and then accidentally drops the money into the prison courtyard. The rest of this strained film has him trying to retrieve the money. Of course, he also gets the girl.

p, Albert J. Cohen; d, John H. Auer; w, Lawrence Kimble, Stuart Palmer (based on a story by Mauri Grashin, Robert T. Shannon); ph, John Alton; ed, Howard O'Neill; md, Cy Feuer; art d, John Victor MacKay.

Comedy　　　　　　　　　　　　**(PR:A　MPAA:NR)**

PARDON MY TRUNK　　　(SEE: HELLO, ELEPHANT, 1954, Ital.)

PARDON OUR NERVE**　　　　(1939) 67m FOX bw

Lynn Bari (Terry Wilson), June Gale (Judy Davis), Guinn "Big Boy" Williams (Samson Smith), Michael Whalen (Dick Malone), Edward Brophy (Nosey Nelson, Taxi Driver), John Miljan (Duke Page), Theodore von Eltz (Lucky Carson), Ward Bond (Kid Ramsey), Chester Clute (Mr. Flemingwell, Bill Collector), Helen Ericson (Arabella), Tom Kennedy (Bodyguard).

A couple of clever city girls, always one jump ahead of the bill collectors, get jobs with a dating service but are promptly fired. They overhear a phone call from a society matron who wants a boxer to perform at a party. They persuade a waiter to play the part and when he actually clobbers the champion, the women put him in the fight business. They pull every trick in the book to make their man a winner, but people finally become wise to their shenanigans.

p, Sol M. Wurtzel; d, H. Bruce Humberstone; w, Robert Ellis, Helen Logan (based on a story by Hilda Stone, Betty Reinhardt); ph, Charles Clarke; ed, Harry Reynolds; md, Samuel Kaylin.

Comedy　　　　　　　　　　　　**(PR:A　MPAA:NR)**

PARDON US**½　　　(1931) 55m MGM bw (GB: GAOL BIRDS; AKA: JAIL BIRDS)

Stan Laurel (Himself), Oliver Hardy (Himself), Walter Long ("The Tiger," a Wily Convict), James Finlayson (Schoolteacher), June Marlowe (Warden's Daughter), Charlie Hall (Dental Assistant/Deliveryman), Sam Lufkin, Silas D. Wilcox, George Miller (Prison Guards), Wilfred Lucas (The Warden), Frank Holliday (Officer in Classroom), Harry Bernard (Warren the Desk Sergeant), Stanley J. [Tiny]Sandford (Officer LeRoy Shields), Robert [Bobby] Burns (Prone Dental Patient), Frank Austin (Dental Patient in Waiting Room), Otto Fries (Dentist), Robert Kortman, Leo Willis (Pals of "the Tiger"), Jerry Mandy (Convict Who Can't Add), Bobby Dunn, Eddie Dunn, Baldwin Cooke, Charles Dorety, Dick Gilbert, Will Stanton, Jack Herrick, Jack Hill, Gene Morgan, Charles A. Bachman, John [Blackie] Whiteford, Charley Rogers (Insurgent Convicts), Gordon Douglas (Typist at Desk), James Parrott, Hal Roach (Prisoners Marching in Formation Near Hardy), Eddie Baker (Plantation Overseer), The Etude Ethiopian Chorus (Cotton Pickers), Bloodhound (Belle), Guido Trento, Boris Karloff.

In 1930, one of MGM's largest successes was THE BIG HOUSE, with Chester Morris and Wallace Beery. The sets were still standing and some of the additional footage was languishing on the editorial shelves, so Roach put this picture into the works. It was Laurel and Hardy's first feature film after delighting audiences with their two reelers and it looks rushed and padded, although there is more than enough humor along the way to satisfy all but the most finicky "Sons of the Desert" (which is the name of the Laurel and Hardy fan club, a group of several thousand who hold regular meetings and watch the old films and know every line of dialog by heart). The boys are outside a store that sells malts and hops, and plan to make their own beer and sell whatever they don't drink. Straightaway, they are taken to jail (the trial is never seen) and tossed into a mean, vicious prison population which includes Karloff. The warden, Lucas, does a satire of the welcoming speech in every jail movie, telling the men to obey the rules and they'll do all right, but if they stray, the prison will be "Hell On Earth!" Laurel has a loose tooth, and whenever he finishes a sentence, the tooth's vibrations make a Bronx Cheer noise. The jail's roughest con is Long, and when he meets Laurel and hears the "raspberry" sound, he is mightily impressed with the little guy's courage, as no one ever dared to do that to him before. Long has a break planned and he is caught, due to a mistake by Laurel and Hardy, but they get away, don blackface makeup and try to hide in a community of cotton-pickers (during this sequence they do a lovely song and dance number with Hardy's voice being featured). However, they are discovered when Lucas' car breaks down in the area. Their freedom is short and it's back in stir until Long starts a riot and the boys help to end it, again inadvertently (as were most of their brave deeds). They are rewarded for their "bravery" by being pardoned. Lucas wishes them well and hopes they can return to what they were doing before coming to jail. Laurel is reminded of his old occupation and instantly tries to sign Lucas up for a keg of beer. Anyone watching the film today will find fault with the jumpy editing and the ancient Prohibition premise because it's been more than a half-century since people were jailed for brewing or distilling.

p, Hal Roach; d, James Parrott; w, H.M. Walker; ph, Jack Stevens; ed, Richard Currier; m/l, LeRoy Shield, Edward Kilenyi, Arthur J. Lamb, H.W. Petrie, Will Marion Cook, Irving Berlin, Cole and Johnston, Abe Olman, M. Ewing, Frederic Van Norman, L.E. de Francesco, J.S. Zamecnik, Freita Shaw, Marvin Hatley.

Comedy　　　　**Cas.**　　　　**(PR:AAA　MPAA:NR)**

PARENT TRAP, THE***　　　　(1961) 124m Disney/BV c

Hayley Mills (Sharon McKendrick/Susan Evers), Maureen O'Hara (Maggie McKendrick), Brian Keith (Mitch Evans), Charlie Ruggles (Charles McKendrick), Una Merkel (Verbena), Leo G. Carroll (Rev. Mosby), Joanna Barnes (Vicky Robinson), Cathleen Nesbitt (Louise McKendrick), Ruth McDevitt (Miss Inch), Crahan Denton (Hecky), Linda Watkins (Edna Robinson)Nancy Kulp (Miss Grunecker), Frank DeVol (Mr. Eaglewood).

Mills plays twins in this innocent but fast-paced comedy. The twins are separated at birth—one goes off with the father and the other with the mother after the parents divorce. They are reunited at a summer camp where they discover their relationship despite their glaring personality differences. Their scheme to get their parents back together by switching places when camp is over. They discover that father is ready to marry a money-hungry woman and decide to put a stop to it. With all kinds of tricks and schemes the twins make the woman's life miserable and she leaves. The parents then decide to make a second trip to the altar.

p, George Golitzen; d&w, David Swift (based on the novel Das Doppelte Lottchen by Erich Kastner); ph, Lucien Ballard (Technicolor); m, Paul J. Smith; ed, Philip W. Anderson; art d, Carroll Clark, Robert Clatworthy; set d, Emile Kuri, Hal Gausman; cos, Bill Thomas; spec eff, Ub Iwerks; m/l, "The Parent Trap," "For Now for Always," "Let's Get Together" Richard M. Sherman, Robert B. Sherman (sung by Tommy Sands, Annette Funicello); makeup, Pat McNally.

Comedy　　　　**Cas.**　　　　**(PR:AA　MPAA:NR)**

PARENTS ON TRIAL*　　　　(1939) 58m COL bw

Jean Parker (Susan Wesley), Johnny Downs (Don Martin), Linda Terry (Linda Ames), Noah Beery, Jr. (Jerry Kearns), Henry Kolker (James Wesley), Virginia Brissac (Mrs. Martin), Nana Bryant (Margaret Ames), Richard Fiske (Lawrence Hastings), Mary Gordon (Martha).

In this dull film parents are blamed for what their children do. The potential is there, but there is not enough force in this picture to give it any depth. Dialog is predictable, which makes the story flat.

d, Sam Nelson; w, J. Robert Bren, Gladys Atwater, Lambert Hiller (adapted from a story by Bren and Atwater); ph, John Stumar; ed, James Sweeney.

Drama　　　　　　　　　　　　**(PR:A　MPAA:NR)**

PARIS** (1929) 97m FN bw-c

Irene Bordoni *(Vivienne Rolland)*, Jack Buchanan *(Guy Pennell)*, Louise Closser Hale *(Cora Sabbot)*, Jason Robards *(Andrew Sabbot)*, Margaret Fielding *(Brenda Kaley)*, ZaSu Pitts *(Harriet)*.

Hale is an over-protective mother who leaves Massachusetts for Paris with the purpose of preventing her son Robards from tying the knot with chorus girl Bordoni. The picture tries to use color sequences (39 minutes worth) to keep the audience awake, but for some reason left out the major selling point—the film was based on a play for which Cole Porter wrote the tunes, but they were omitted for the screen version. The new tunes by Al Bryan and Ed Ward include, "Crystal Girl, " "Miss Wonderful," "Paris," "I Wonder What Is Really on His Mind," "I'm a Little Negative," "Somebody Mighty Like You," "My Lover (Master of My Heart)." This film marks both Bordoni's and Buchanan's talkie debut. Bordoni reprised her stage role in this movie.

p&d, Clarence Badger; w, Hope Loring (based on the play by Cole Porter, Martin Brown, E. Ray Goetz); ph, Sol Polito (Technicolor) ed, Edward Schroeder; ch, Larry Ceballos.

Musical (PR:A MPAA:NR)

PARIS AFTER DARK½** (1943) 85m FOX bw (GB: THE NIGHT IS ENDING)

George Sanders *(Dr. Andre Marbel)*, Philip Dorn *(Jean Blanchard)*, Brenda Marshall *(Yvonne Blanchard)*, Madeleine LeBeau *(Collette)*, Marcel Dalip *(Michel)*, Robert Lewis *(Col. Pirosh)*, Henry Rowland *(Capt. Franck)*, Raymond Roe *(George Bennoit)*, Gene Gary *(Victor Durand)*, Jean Del Val *(Papa Benoit)*, Curt Bois *(Max)*, Ann Codee *(Mme. Benoit)*, Louis Borell *(Picard)*, John Wengraf *(Mannheim)*, Michael Visaroff *(Paul)*, Frank Lyon *(Nazi Agent in Homburg Hat)*, Simone D'Ambrogio *(Servant Girl)*, Curt Furberg *(Anesthetist)*, Robert Gilbert *(Gestapo Agent)*, George Davis *(Barfly)*, Eugene Borden *(Central Committee Member)*, Henry Le Baubigny *(Man)*, John Beverly, George Sorel, Arno Frey, Walter Bonn *(German Detectives)*, Wolfgang Zilzer *(German Radio Announcer)*, Otto Reicher *(German Gestapo Man)*, Jacques Lory *(Blind Man)*, Christiana Tourneur *(Max's Wife)*, Jack Pullen *(Del Val)*, Paul Weigel *(News Dealer)*, Chavo De Leon *(French Gunner)*, Guy Kingsford *(English Pilot)*, Dick French *(Mechanic)*, Frank Arnold, Maurice Marsac *(French Soldiers)*, Gaston Glass, Richard Ordynski *(Soldiers)*.

Moguy gives this film a good sense of direction because his background in the subject matter is impeccable; he escaped France during the German invasion. Sanders is the upper-class doctor who is able to continue his practice above suspicion even though he is a leader in the French resistance movement. His nurse supports his activities, but her Nazi-brainwashed husband provides the tension until he realizes the error of his ways.

p, Andre Daven; d, Leonide Moguy; w, Harold Buchman (based on a story by George Kessel); ph, Lucien Andriot; m, Hugo W. Friedhofer; ed, Nick De Maggio; md, Emil Newman; art d, James Basevi, John Ewing; spec eff, Fred Sersen.

War Drama (PR:A MPAA:NR)

PARIS AU MOIS D'AOUT (SEE: PARIS IN THE MONTH OF AUGUST, 1968, Fr.)

PARIS BELONGS TO US*** (1962, Fr.) 120m Ajym-Films du Carrosse/Merlyn bw (PARIS NOUS APPARTIENT; AKA: PARIS IS OURS)

Betty Schneider *(Anne Goupil)*, Giani Esposito *(Gerard Lenz)*, Francoise Prevost *(Terry Yok)*, Daniel Crohem *(Philip Kaufman)*, Francois Maistre *(Pierre Goupil)*, Jean-Claude Brialy *(Jean-Marc)*, Jean Marie Robain *(De Georges)*, Brigitte Juslin, Noelle Leiris, Monique Le Poirier, Malka Ribovska, Louise Roblin, Henri Poirier, Jean Martin, Anne Zamire, Paul Bisciglia, Claude Chabrol, Jean-Luc Godard, Jacques Demy, Jean-Pierre Delage, Andre Thorent.

Schneider, after overhearing a discussion on the suicide of a young Spaniard, is compelled to learn why the youth's life ended so tragically. She becomes involved with a theater director (Esposito) and takes a part in his production of Shakespeare's "Pericles." She becomes worried for Esposito's life when he tells her that the Spaniard was involved in a worldwide conspiracy and that he is targeted for murder by the same organization. She also meets Crohem, an American victim of McCarthyism, who is responsible for informing the Spaniard and Esposito of the organization. Eventually it is revealed that Crohem made the whole thing up, but not before Esposito's paranoia gets the better of him and he commits suicide. Along with Claude Chabrol's LE BEAU SERGE, this first feature by Jacques Rivette was the one that kindled the flame which became known as the French New Wave. Production began in the early summer of 1958 with money borrowed from the magazine he (and his New Wave counterparts) worked for, *Cahiers Du Cinema*. Technicians, actors, and lab fees were all on credit, with no money exchanged until the film's release in 1960. Without so much as a car, Rivette and his entourage of film enthusiasts worked whenever they could, spending Sundays trying to raise enough money to begin again on Mondays. With the help of Chabrol and Truffaut, whose first films were already receiving acclaim at the Cannes Film Festival, PARIS was finally released—a stepping stone in the development of French Cinema's rebirth.

p, Roland Nonin; d, Jacques Rivette; w, Rivette, Jean Gruault; ph, Charles Bitsch; m, Philippe Arthuys; ed, Denise de Casabianca.

Mystery/Drama (PR:A-C MPAA:NR)

PARIS BLUES½** (1961) 98m Pennebaker-Diane-Jason-Monica/UA bw

Paul Newman *(Ram Bowen)*, Joanne Woodward *(Lillian Corning)*, Sidney Poitier *(Eddie Cook)*, Louis Armstrong *(Wild Man Moore)*, Diahann Carroll *(Connie Lampson)*, Serge Reggiani *(Michel Duvigne)*, Barbara Laage *(Marie Seoul)*, Andre Luguet *(Rene Bernard)*, Marie Versini *(Nicole)*, Moustache *(Drummer)*, Aaron Bridgers *(Pianist)*, Guy Pederson *(Bass Player)*, Maria Velasco *(Pianist)*, Roger Blin *(Gypsy Guitarist)*, Helene Dieudonne *(The Pusher)*, Niko *(Ricardo)*.

The story is slim but the jazz is great, especially when legendary Louis Armstrong gets into the act. Newman and Poitier are friends and American expatriates living in Paris after WW II, playing jazz in a club run by Laage who is having a tepid affair with Newman. Living in Paris for Newman means dedicating himself to studying and composing classical music, while earning a comfortable living in a jazz joint. For Poitier, the expatriate life offers asylum from the racial hatreds in America. Then into their lives burst bubbling tourists Woodward and Carroll, who pair off with Newman and Poitier. Carroll convinces Poitier that it's better to go back to the U.S. and face his fears of bigotry than to hide out in a foreign country. They fall in love and plan to wed when returning to America. Newman, on the other hand, returns Woodward's deep affection with hesitant emotions; he doesn't want to give up his music career to become a second-rate musician at home. Yet he succumbs and leaves Paris after learning from his professor that his latest classical composition is considerably less than classical. But once he decides to marry Woodward and return to the States, Newman is nagged by the thought that he is deserting his great talent. He changes his mind at the last minute and tells Woodward at the train station that he cannot go with her, that he is staying in Paris to continue his career. PARIS BLUES is well-intentioned but Ritt's direction flags and the dialog is often bogged down with talky stretches where Poitier mouths generalities about racism and Newman waxes too eloquently about "pure" jazz. The appearance of Armstrong is the great highlight of this mostly turgid film. Newman is good in the thin role he was given but Poitier is merely a black prop designed to appease the growing concern over racial equality. This was Newman's second film with Ritt directing and was made just after he scored a great triumph in THE HUSTLER. This was also his fourth film with wife Woodward. Newman's trombone playing was dubbed by Murray MacEachern and Paul Gonsalves dubbed Poitier's saxophone exercises. The jazz numbers are outstanding and include: "Mood Indigo" (Duke Ellington, Irving Mills, Albany Bigard), "Take the 'A' Train" (Billy Strayhorn), "Sophisticated Lady" (Ellington, Mills, Mitchell Parish), "Paris Blues," "Paris Stairs, " "Unclothed Woman," "Autumnal Suite," "Wild Man Moore," "Nite" (Ellington), "Birdie Jingle," "Guitar D'Amour." There are some objectionable scenes dealing with dope addiction, excused on the naive basis that such addiction goes hand in hand with jazz and Paris nightclubs.

p, Sam Shaw; d, Martin Ritt; w, Jack Sher, Irene Kamp, Walter Berstein, Lulla Adler (based on a novel by Harold Flender); ph, Christian Matras; m, Duke Ellington; ed, Roger Dwyre; art d, Alexander Trauner.

Drama Cas. (PR:O MPAA:NR)

PARIS BOUND** (1929) 73m Pathe bw

Ann Harding *(Mary Hutton)*, Fredric March *(Jim Hutton)*, George Irving *(James Hutton, Sr.)*, Leslie Fenton *(Richard Parrish)*, Hallam Cooley *(Peter)*, Juliette Crosby *(Nora Cope)*, Charlotte Walker *(Helen White)*, Carmelita Geraghty *(Noel Farley)*, Ilka Chase *(Fanny Shipman)*.

This adaptation of the successful 1927 play has March and Harding as a liberated young husband and wife who decide that it is enough to remain "spiritually" faithful. Harding takes up with a musician, while March takes off for Europe. He returns and tells his wife that he had an affair with a French femme. Harding is hurt, never expecting him to take seriously their philosophy of infidelity. The finale has the two living happily together. An average picture which, like the play that preceeded it, caused a great deal of talk among the "respected" social circles for its modernistic approach to matrimony.

p, Arthur Hopkins; d, Edward H. Griffith; w, Horace Jackson, Frank Reicher (based on the play by Philip Barry); ph, Norbert Brodine, Norbert Scully; m, Josiah Zuro; ed, Helen Warne; cos, Gwen Wakeling.

Romance (PR:A MPAA:NR)

PARIS BRULE-T-IL? (SEE: IS PARIS BURNING?, 1966, Fr.)

PARIS CALLING** (1941) 93m Charles K. Feldman Group/UNIV bw

Elizabeth Bergner *(Marianne)*, Randolph Scott *(Nick)*, Basil Rathbone *(Benoit)*, Gale Sondergaard *(Colette)*, Lee J. Cobb *(Schwabe)*, Charles Arnt *(Lantz)*, Eduardo Ciannelli *(Mouche, Bartender)*, Elisabeth Risdon *(Mme. Jannetier)*, Georges Renavent *(Butler)*, William Edmunds *(Prof. Marceau)*, Patrick O'Malley *(McAvoy)*, Georges Metaxa *(Waiter)*, Paul Leysaac *(Chief of Underground)*, Gene Garrick *(Wolfgang Schmitt)*, Paul Bryar *(Paul)*, Otto Reichow *(Gruber)*, Adolph Milar *(Gestapo Agent)*, Marion Murray *(Cherie)*, Grace Lenard *(Marie)*, Yvette Bentley *(Simone)*, Marcia Ralston *(Renee)*, Pedro de Cordoba *(Speaker)*, Ian Wolfe *(Thin Workman)*, Rosalind Ivan *(Mama Picon)*, Mary Forbes *(Lady Guest)*, Howard Hickman *(French General)*, Ed Emerson *(Chauffeur)*, Harlan Briggs *(Papa Picon)*, Denis Green *(English Chauffeur)*, Charles Wagenheim *(French Waiter)*, Crauford Kent *(British Naval Officer)*, Fred Vogeding *(German Officer)*, Philip Van Zandt *(Thick Workman)*, Norma Drury *(French Lady)*, Jeff Corey *(Secretary)*, Jean Del Val *(Peasant)*, Roland Varno *(German Pilot)*, William Ruhl *(Nazi Radio Operator)*, Douglas Grant *(British Squadron Leader)*, Eric Lonsdale *(English RAF Lieutenant)*, John Meredith *(English Radio Operator)*, Jacques Vanaire *(Hotel Manager)*, Eugene Borden *(Aide)*, Hans Von Morhart *(German Corporal)*, Gene O'Donnell *(English Messenger)*, Dick Alexander *(German Guard)*, Alphonse Martel *(French Aide-Gendarme)*, Arno Frey *(Watchman)*, George Cathrey *(RAF Radio Operator)*, Ken Nolan *(German Sergeant)*, Eric Alden, Eddie Dew, William Yetter *(Gestapo Men)*, Joe Kamaryst, Marty Faust, Hans Furberg *(Men)*, John Bleifer, Pete Sosso *(Workmen)*.

A slow-moving film about a young Parisienne socialite who joins the French underground movement against the Germans during WW II. She eventually falls for an American fighter pilot (Scott) and is forced to shoot her former lover, who has betrayed the underground fighters.

p, Benjamin Glazer; d, Edwin L. Marin; w, Glazer, Charles S. Kaufman (based on a story by John S. Toldy); ph, Milton Krasner; m, Richard Hageman; ed, Edward Curtiss; md, H.J. Salter; art d, Jack Otterson.

War Drama (PR:A MPAA:NR)

PARIS DOES STRANGE THINGS*½ (1957, Fr./Ital.) 86m Franco-London Films-Films Gibe-Electra Compania/WB c (ELENA ET LES HOMMES)

Ingrid Bergman (*Princess Elena Sorokowska*), Jean Marais (*Gen. Francois Rollan*), Mel Ferrer (*Viscount Henri de Chevincourt*), Jean Claudio (*Lionel Villaret*), Jean Richard (*Hector, Rollan's Batman*), Magali Noel (*Lolotte, Elena's Maid*), Juliette Greco (*Miarka*), Pierre Bertin (*Martin-Michaud*), Jean Castanier (*Isnard*), Elina Labourdette (*Paulette*), Frederic Duvalles (*Gaudin*), Dora Doll (*Rosa la Rose*), Mirko Ellis (*Marbeau*), Jacques Hilling (*Lisbonne*), Jacques Jouanneau (*Eugene Godin*), Renaud Mary (*Fleury*), Gaston Modot (*The Leader of Gypsies*), Jacques Morel (*Duchene*), Michele Nadal (*Denise Godin*), Albert Remy (*Buchez*), Olga Valery (*Aunt Olga*), Leo Marjane (*The Street Singer*), Leon Larive (*Henri's Domestic*), Gregori Chmara (*Elena's Domestic*), Paul Demange (*A Spectator*), Jim Gerald (*Cafe Owner*), Robert Le Beal (*The Doctor*), Claire Gerard (*The Strolling Woman*), The Zavattas, Gerard Buhr, Jean Ozenne, Rene Berthier, Hubert de Lapparent, Pierre Duverger, Jaque Catelain, Simone Sylvestre, Corinne Jansen, Liliane Ernout, Louisette Rousseau, Palmyre Levasseur, Lyne Carrel.

Comparing the star of this picture with Venus, director Renoir said that for a long time he "had been dying to make something gay with Ingrid Bergman, I wanted to see her laughing and smiling on the screen." She did that and much more in this critically assaulted tale of a beautiful Polish princess in Paris in the 1880s. She finds herself romancing men in the hopes of bringing them great success after presenting each with a marguerite, her favorite flower. She funnels her affections to Marais, a general with plans of becoming a dictator after a coup d'etat. Because of her past experiences with catapulting men to fame and success, she believes she can do the same for Marais. It takes Ferrer, a young count and friend, to convince her to change her attitude towards immortalizing men. She realizes that Ferrer is her true love, and she lets an affair of the heart overshadow the affairs of state. As with so many truly great movies, the public harshly attacked the film, which had been re-cut and dubbed by Warner. "A mishmash," "a shock," and "a farrago" were just some of the stones thrown at Renoir, as was another suggestion that he throw the film in the Seine. On the film's plus side, however, Jean-Luc Godard calls it "the most intelligent film in the world." Though both descriptions are exaggerated, PARIS DOES STRANGE THINGS is a fantastic film. It's filled with patented "Renoirisms", from the utter sincerity of emotions to the exceptional impressionistic composition. Renoir's comparison of Bergman to Venus is by no means an over-statement. This goddess of an actress is placed in the film by the Olympian Renoir for the purpose of offering chosen men immortality through fame. An eloquent portrait, which is perhaps the greatest painted by Renoir in his later years.

p, Louis Wipf; d, Jean Renoir; w, Renoir (adapted by Renoir, Jean Serge); ph, Claude Renoir (Technicolor); m, Joseph Kosma; ed, Borys Lewin; set d, Jean Andre; cos, Rosine Delamare, Monique Plotin; m/l, "Mefiez-vous de Paris," Leo Marjane; "O Nuit," Juliette Greco (traditional songs arranged by Georges Van Parys).

Drama (PR:A MPAA:NR)

PARIS EROTIKA (SEE: PARIS OOH-LA-LA!, 1963, U.S./Fr.)

PARIS EXPRESS, THE*½ (1953, Brit.) 83m Raymond Stross/George Schaefer c (GB: THE MAN WHO WATCHED TRAINS GO BY)

Claude Rains (*Kees Popinga*), Michael Nightingale (*Clerk*), Felix Aylmer (*Merkemans*), Herbert Lom (*Julius de Koster, Jr.*), Gibb McLaughlin (*Julius de Koster, Sr.*), Marius Goring (*Lucas*), Lucie Mannheim (*Mrs. Popinga*), Joan St. Clair (*Frida Popinga*), Robin Alalouf (*Karl Popinga*), Marta Toren (*Michele*), Michael Alain (*Train Conductor*), Jean Deveaux (*Train Official*), Ferdy Mayne (*Louis*), Anouk Aimee (*Jeanne*), Roy Purcell (*Plainclothesman*), Eric Pohlmann (*Goin*), Macdonald Parke (*American Businessman*), Mary Mackenzie (*Mrs. Lucas*).

Rains plays a simple clerk who has long been faithful to his bosses. He has spent a lifetime watching trains go by to places like Paris and Brussels—places where a man of his means could never afford to go. Upon discovering that his bosses have been cheating the company to finance a French mistress, Rains takes a quick second look at his own principles. He then exits to Paris with the company's money and becomes involved with the French woman. One adventure follows another, including the murder of Rains' boss and the subsequent accusation of Rains as the murderer. The French woman stays involved because she is determined to get her own hands on the money.

p, Joseph Shaftel; d&w, Harold French (based on the novel *The Man Who Watched Trains Go By* by Georges Simenon); ph, Otto Heller (Technicolor); m, Ben Frankel.

Mystery **Cas.** (PR:A MPAA:NR)

PARIS FOLLIES OF 1956* (1955) 73m AA c (AKA: SHOWTIME; FRESH FROM PARIS)

Forrest Tucker (*Dan Bradley*), Margaret Whiting (*Margaret Walton*), Dick Wesson (*Chuck Russell*), Martha Hyer (*Ruth Harmon*), Barbara Whiting (*Barbara Walton*), Lloyd Corrigan (*Alfred Gaylord*), Wally Cassell (*Harry*), Fluff Charlton (*Taffy*), James Ferris (*Jim*), William Henry (*Wendell*), The Sportsmen (*Themselves*), Frank Parker (*Himself*).

Considering this musical was shot in just five days, it's not bad. Tucker stars as an enterprising producer who decides to open a new theater-restaurant in Hollywood with heavy backing from the wealthy Corrigan. Disaster strikes when Tucker learns that Corrigan is only a harmless looney pretending to be rich, forcing the producer to scramble for the cash. Shot on location at the "Moulin Rouge" in Hollywood. Songs include "Can This Be Love," "I Love A Circus," "Have You Ever Been To

Paris," "I'm All Aglow Again," "I'm in a Mood Tonight" (Pony Sherrell, Phil Moody), and the Sportsmen sing "The Hum Song" (Sid Kuller).

p, Bernard Tabakin; d, Leslie Goodwins; w, Milton Lazarus; ph, Ed DuPar (DeLuxe Color); ed, Gene Fowler, Jr.; md, Frank DeVol; ch, Donn Arden.

Musical (PR:A MPAA:NR)

PARIS HOLIDAY*½ (1958) 100m Tolda/UA c

Bob Hope (*Robert Leslie Hunter*), Fernandel (*Fernydel*), Anita Ekberg (*Zara*), Martha Hyer (*Ann McCall*), Andre Morell (*American Ambassador*), Preston Sturges (*Serge Vitry*), Jean Murat (*Judge*), Maurice Teynac (*Dr. Bernais*), Irene Tunc (*Shipboard Lovely*), Roger Treville (*Golfer Patient*), Ives Brainville (*Inspector Dupont*), Alan Gifford.

A light-hearted mystery has Hope going after a manuscript by a famous French playwright. He doesn't have the manuscript, but sexy Amazon Ekberg thinks he does as the two travel aboard an ocean liner. This sets the stage for some humorous chase scenes, including one with Hope being rescued via helicopter from a mental institution and escaping French gangsters.

p, Robert Hope; d, Gerd Oswald; w, Edmund Beloin, Dean Riesner (based on a story by Hope); ph, Roger Hubert (Technirama, Technicolor); m, Joseph L. Lilley; ed, Ellsworth Hoagland; md, Lilley; prod d, Georges Wakhevitch; cos, Pierre Balmain; m/l, "Every Day's a Holiday in Paris," Jimmy Van Heusen, Sammy Cahn.

Mystery **Cas.** (PR:A MPAA:NR)

PARIS HONEYMOON*½ (1939) 83m PAR bw

Bing Crosby ("*Lucky*" *Lawton*), Franciska Gaal (*Manya*), Akim Tamiroff (*Peter Karloca, Tavern Keeper*), Shirley Ross (*Barbara Wayne/Countess De Remi*), Edward Everett Horton (*Ernest Figg*), Ben Blue (*Sitska*), Rafaela Ottiano (*Fluschotska*), Luana Walters (*Angela*), Gregory Gaye (*Count De Remi*), Alex Melesh (*Pulka Tomasto*), Victor Kilian (*Old Villager*), Michael Visaroff (*Judge*), Keith Kenneth (*Butler*), Raymond Hatton (*Huskins*), Konstantin Shayne (*Hotel Porter*).

A wealthy Texan (Crosby) travels to Europe because he is infatuated with a member of the aristocracy (Ross). However, as he spends time in her home, he comes across a pretty girl who is not part of the social scene (Gaal). Crosby comes to prefer the angelic peasant girl to the cultured Ross, leading to a full blown love affair with Gaal. Songs include: "I Have Eyes," "Sweet Little Headache," "Funny Old Hills," "Joobalai," "The Maiden By The Brook," "Work While You May" (Ralph Rainger, Leo Robin), "I Ain't Got Nobody" (Roger Graham, Dave Peyton, Spencer Williams).

p, Harlan Thompson; d, Frank Tuttle; w, Frank Butler, Don Hartman (based on a story by Angela Sherwood); ph, Karl Struss; ed, Archie Marshek; art d, Hans Dreier, Ernst Fegte; set d, A. E. Freudeman.

Musical/Comedy (PR:A MPAA:NR)

PARIS IN SPRING* (1935) 80m PAR bw (GB: PARIS LOVE SONG)

Mary Ellis (*Simone*), Tullio Carminati (*Paul de lille*), Ida Lupino (*Mignon de Charelle*), Lynne Overman (*DuPont*), Jessie Ralph (*Grandma Leger*), James Blakeley (*Albert De Charelle*), Hugh Enfield [Craig Reynolds] (*Alphonse*), Joseph North (*Etienne*), Dorothea Wolbert (*Francine*), Harold Entwistle (*Charles, The Butler*), Arnold Korff (*Doctor*), Sam Ash (*Clerk*), Jack Raymond (*Elevator Man*), Akim Tamiroff (*Cafe Manager*), David Worth, Charles Martin, Jerry Miley, Fred Kohler, Jr. (*Collegians*), Elsa Peterson (*Hairdresser*), Arthur Housman (*Interviewer*), Michael Mark (*Bartender*), Nanette Lafayette, Alice Ardell (*Manicurists*), Rolfe Sedan, Jack Mulhall.

This worn-out idea has two people (not married to each other) deciding to make their respective spouses jealous by pretending to have an affair. They make this decision at the site of their first meeting, the top of the Eiffel Tower, where each has gone to contemplate a suicidal jump because of personal troubles with their respective loves. Songs include "Paris in Spring," "Bon Jour Mamselle," "Why Do They Call It Gay Paree?" "Jealousy" (Mack Gordon, Harry Revel).

p, Benjamin Glazer; d, Lewis Milestone; w, Samuel Hoffenstein, Franz Shulz, Keene Thompson (based on a play by Dwight Taylor); ph, Ted Tetzlaff; m, Harry Revel; ed, Eda Warren; art d, Hans Dreier, Ernst Fegte.

Musical (PR:A MPAA:NR)

PARIS IN THE MONTH OF AUGUST*½ (1968, Fr.) 94m Sirius/Trans-Lux bw (PARIS AU MOIS D'AOUT)

Charles Aznavour (*Henri Plantin*), Susan Hampshire (*Patricia Seagrave*), Michel de Re (*Gogaille*), Daniel Ivernal (*Civadusse*), Alan Scott (*Peter*), Etchika Choureau (*Simone Plantin*), Jacques Marin (*Bouvreuil*), Helena Manson (*Concierge*), Dominique Davray (*Model*), Leonce Corne, Andre Certes, Marcel Charvey, Bernard Musson, Ann Lewis, Dominique Zardi, Henri Attal, Joelle Cazal, Amarande, Max Amyl, Jean Sylvere, Patricia Aznavour.

Aznavour is a department store clerk on vacation with his wife and kids in Paris. Alone one day, he meets fashion model Hampshire and becomes her tour guide. They wander around Paris and Hampshire soon falls in love with Aznavour, who is pretending to be an artist. When the time comes for him to choose between a life in London with Hampshire or life with his family, he opts for the latter. A charmer which is made even more charming by Aznavour's personality.

p, Louis Emile Galey; d, Pierre Granier-Deferre; w, Rodolphe M. Arlaud, Henri Jeanson, Granier-Deferre (based on the novel by Rene Fallet); ph, Claude Renoir (Totalvision); m, Georges Garvarentz; ed, Jean Ravel; art d, Bernard Evein; m/l, "August Days in Paree," Garvarentz, Aznavour (sung by Aznavour).

Romance/Comedy (PR:A MPAA:NR)

PARIS INTERLUDE*½   (1934) 73m MGM bw

Madge Evans (*Julie Bell*), Otto Kruger (*Sam Colt*), Robert Young (*Pat Wells*), Una Merkel (*Cassie*), Ted Healy (*Jimmy*), Louise Henry (*Mary Louise*), Edward Brophy (*Ham*), George Meeker (*Rex Fleming*), Bert Roach (*Noble*), Richard Tucker (*Stevens*), James Donlin (*Jones*), Carlos J. de Valdez, Gene Perry (*Doctors*), Constant Franke, Maurice Brierre (*Interns*), Pauline High (*Nurse*), Rolfe Sedan (*Waiter*).

A little French girl is madly in love with a shiftless newspaperman from America. He spends most of his time swilling beer and talking romance with the rest of his fellow American journalists. A cub reporter is also in love with the girl, and when the American reporter is rumored to be killed in China, the younger reporter pushes her for marriage. The senior journalist reappears and, in a surge of decency, directs the girl toward his younger friend.

p, Lucien Hubbard; d, Edwin L. Marin; w, Wells Root (based on the play "All Good Americans" by S.J. Perelman, Laura Perelman); ph, Milton Krasner; ed, Conrad A. Nervig; art d, Cedric Gibbons, Merrill Pye; set d, Edwin B. Willis; cos, Adrian.

Drama   (PR:A MPAA:NR)

PARIS IS OURS   (SEE: PARIS BELONGS TO US, 1962, Fr.)

PARIS LOVE SONG   (SEE: PARIS IN SPRING, 1935)

PARIS MODEL**   (1953) 81m COL bw

Eva Gabor (*Gogo Montaine*), Tom Conway (*Maharajah of Kim-Kepore*), Laurette Luez (*Lisa*), Aram Katcher (*Louis-Jean Vacheron*), Bibs Borman (*Berta Courtallez*), Marilyn Maxwell (*Marion Parmelee*), Cecil Kellaway (*Patrick J. Sullivan*), Florence Bates (*Mrs. Nora Sullivan*), Robert Bice (*Jack Parmelee*), Byron Foulger (*Ernest Boggs*), Paulette Goddard (*Betty Barnes*), Leif Erickson (*Edgar Blevins*), Gloria Christian (*Cora Blevins*), Barbara Lawrence (*Marta Jensen*), Robert Hutton (*Charlie Johnson*), El Brendel (*Papa Jensen*), Prince Michael Romanoff (*Himself*).

A Paris designer gown is followed through four vignettes. The first has a stunning woman purchasing the gown, as she has a date with a very wealthy foreigner. Next, the gown is copied and bought by a secretary, who wants to use it to seduce her married boss. Unfortunately, when the two are at a party, his wife shows up in the same dress. The gown is then used by a married woman to tempt a retiring company president to name her husband as his replacement. The final vignette has the gown's wearer aiming for a marriage proposal from her longtime boy friend.

p, Albert Zugsmith; d, Alfred E. Green; w, Robert Smith; ph, William Bradford; m, Albert Glasser; ed, W. Donn Hayes; md, Glasser; art d, William Glasgow; set d, Alfred E. Spencer; cos, Ann Peck, Charles Keehne; spec eff, Jack Rabin, David Commons; makeup, Albert S. Greenway, Harry Thomas.

Drama   (PR:A MPAA:NR)

PARIS NOUS APPARTIENT   (SEE: PARIS BELONGS TO US, 1962, Fr.)

PARIS OOH-LA-LA!**   (1963, U.S./Fr.) 80m Les Films Univers-
American Film/American Film c (PARIS EROTIKA; 24 HEURES D'UN AMERI-
CAIN A PARIS)

Dick Randall (*Sam Smith*), Jessica Rubicon, Poupee La Rose, Dodo From Hamburg, The Heros, Roberto Talamo, Pamela Holhouse, Claudine Hogleenel, Stephanie Underdorn, Cosette Blanche, Ballet of the Folies Pigalle, Chantal Delor, Monique Sivers, Jane Jonason, Beatrice de L'Etang, Nancy Holloway.

A pleasant comedy about an American businessman on a one-day stopover in Paris. He tries all night to find a female companion, but his repeated attempts are foiled. Having given up, he returns to his hotel room, where a young woman from Peoria, Illinois, mistakes him for a Frenchman. He takes her to his room and they make love.

p,d&w, Jose Benazeraf; ph, Alain Derobe (CinemaScope, Eastmancolor); m, Louiguy.

Comedy   (PR:O MPAA:NR)

PARIS PICK-UP**   (1963, Fr./Ital.) 90m SNE Gaumont-Marianne-
Galatea/PAR bw (LE MONTE-CHARGE; LA MORTE SALE IN ASCENSORE)

Robert Hossein (*Robert Herbin*), Lea Massari (*Martha Dravet*), Maurice Biraud (*Adolphe Ferry*), Robert Dalban (*The Inspector*), Pascale Brouillard.

An ex-con is nearly accused of a murder he did not commit when he spends the evening with a dead man's wife. As he is about to be arrested, the woman (Massari) reveals to police that she drugged her husband in an attempt to make it appear to be suicide, then picked up a stranger (Hossein) who would, unfortunately, take the rap for her murder. An excellent score.

p, Alain Poire, Michel Bernheim; d, Marcel Bluwal; w, Frederick Dard, Bluwal (based on the novel by Dard); ph, Andre Bac; m, Georges Delerue; ed, Germaine Vaury; art d, Jean Manaroux.

Mystery/Crime   (PR:C MPAA:NR)

PARIS PLANE**   (1933, Brit.) 52m Sound City/MGM bw

John Loder, Allan Jeayes, Molly Lamont, Barry Livesey, Julie Suedo, Edwin Ellis, James Harcourt, Eileen Munro.

A claustrophobic thriller which sees a detective, Loder, chase a fugitive killer into an airport. The murderer, Jeayes, dons a disguise and boards a plane, but Loder is right behind him. Armed with the knowledge that his quarry is aboard a specific flight, Loder boards the plane and waits for the disguised killer to reveal himself. As the plane prepares to land, Jeayes accidentally betrays his identity and Loder captures him. A fairly interesting crime film that exploits its low budget successfully by containing the action in one enclosed area.

p, Ivar Campbell; d, John Paddy Carstairs; w, Charles Bennett.

Crime   (PR:A MPAA:NR)

PARIS PLAYBOYS**   (1954) 65m AA bw

Leo Gorcey (*Terence Aloysius "Slip" Mahoney*), Huntz Hall (*Horace Debussy "Sach" Jones/Prof. Maurice Gaston Le Beau*), Veola Vonn (*Mimi DuBois*), Steven Geray (*Gaspard*), John Wengraf (*Vidal*), Bernard Gorcey (*Louie Dumbrowski*), Marianne Lynn (*Celeste*), David Condon [David Gorcey] (*Chuck*), Bennie Bartlett (*Butch*), Alphonse Martell (*Pierre*), Gordon Clark (*Cambon*), Fritz Feld (*Marcel*).

Sach (Hall) is mistaken for a missing French scientist and is sent to Paris along with Slip (Leo Gorcey) and Louie (Bernard Gorcey) to impersonate him. The scientist had been working on a super rocket fuel, which Hall manages to perfect in his absence. Plenty of dull gags revolving around the boys trying to keep the formula out of the hands of spies. Definitely not one of the Bowery Boys better efforts. Very little is seen of Chuck and Butch (Condon and Bartlett) described as "excess baggage" in this film by screenwriter Bernds who explained that they were left in the Paris setting only as a symbol of the big gang Leo Gorcey had in all the other Eastside Kids pictures. According to Bernds, young Gorcey ribbed Condon (his real-life brother) about his small role and was not very kind on the set to his father, Bernard Gorcey. (See: BOWERY BOYS series, Index.)

p, Ben Schwalb; d, William Beaudine; w, Elwood Ullman, Edward Bernds; ph, Harry Neumann; m, Marlin Skiles; ed, John C. Fuller; md, Skiles; art d, David Milton; set d, Robert Priestley; cos, Smoke Kring.

Comedy   (PR:A MPAA:NR)

PARIS UNDERGROUND**   (1945) 97m UA bw (GB: MADAME
PIMPERNEL)

Constance Bennett (*Kitty de Mornay*), Gracie Fields (*Emmyline Quayle*), George Rigaud (*Andre de Mornay*), Kurt Kreuger (*Capt. Kurt von Weber*), Charles Andre (*Father Dominique*), Leslie Vincent (*Lt. William Gray*), Eily Malyon (*Mme. Bengler*), Gregory Gaye (*Tissier*), Richard Ryen (*Mons. Renard*), Adrienne d'Ambricourt (*Margot*), Vladimir Sokoloff (*Undertaker*), Roland Varno (*Lt. Comdr. Stowe*), Andrew McLaglen (*Sgt. McNair*), Andre Charlot, Harry Hayes Morgan, Dina Smyrnova, Otto Reichow, Fred Gierman, Erich Von Morhardt, Art Miles, Marcel de la Brosse, Anthony Ward, Georgette Rhodes, Peter Kooy, Loulette Sablon, Reska Law, Reni Revel, Mina Borget, Ray de Ravenne, Rene Mimieux.

A slow-starting suspense film that focuses on the lives of two women (Bennett and Fields) in France during the Nazi occupation. Their lives appear to be very sedate on the outside, but both are actually heavily involved with the French underground movement. Sloppy editing hurt the film—particularly the ending—when the women are captured and on the brink of being killed, then all of a sudden they're being rescued by American forces.

p, Constance Bennett; d, Gregory Ratoff; w, Boris Ingster, Gertrude Purcell (based on a novel by Etta Shiber); ph, Lee Garmes; m, Alexander Tansman; ed, James Newcom; prod d, Nicholai Remisoff; md, Tansman; art d, Victor Greene; set d, Sydney Moore; cos, Travis Banton.

War Drama   (PR:A MPAA:NR)

PARIS VU PAR   (SEE: SIX IN PARIS, 1968, Fr.)

PARIS WAS MADE FOR LOVERS   (SEE: TIME FOR LOVING, A,
1971, Brit.)

PARIS WHEN IT SIZZLES**   (1964) 110m Quine-Charleston/PAR c

William Holden (*Richard Benson*), Audrey Hepburn (*Gabrielle Simpson*), Gregoire Aslan (*Police Inspector*), Raymond Bussieres (*Gangster*), Christian Duvallex (*Maitre d'Hotel*), Noel Coward (*Alexander Meyerheimer*), Tony Curtis (*2nd Policeman*), Marlene Dietrich, Mel Ferrer (*Guest Stars*), Fred Astaire, Frank Sinatra (*Singing Voices*), Thomas Michel, Dominique Boschero, Evi Marandi.

A remake of the 1953 French picture HENRIETTE'S HOLIDAY (directed by Julien Duvivier) which here pairs Holden and Hepburn for the first time since 1954's SABRINA. Holden is a screenwriter under pressure from movie producer Coward to finish his latest script, "The Girl Who Stole the Eiffel Tower." Coward gives him 48 hours to finish, unaware that he has yet to begin. Hoping to hurry the process along, Holden hires a secretary, Hepburn. She moves in with him and during that short period they fall madly in love, while confusing their own lives with those of the script's characters. They imagine themselves in various scenes from the film—a western, a musical, a spy drama, a romance, a comedy—with their fantasies taking precedent over their work. When their time limit has expired they still have no script. Distraught, Holden tells Hepburn that he is not good enough for her. She leaves but before she can get too far Holden chases after her. Their relationship takes off with the promise of a Hollywood-style romance. Unfortunately, however, PARIS WHEN IT SIZZLES falls as flat as "The Girl Who Stole the Eiffel Tower." Although the locations and Hepburn both photograph brilliantly, the relationship between Hepburn and Holden never comes to life. This comes as no surprise, however, since Holden and Hepburn were on quite shaky ground in real life. It was during the filming of SABRINA that Holden found himself falling uncontrollably in love with Hepburn. Ten years after her refusal to marry him, they paired in PARIS WHEN IT SIZZLES. As quoted in Bob Thomas' biography *Golden Boy*, Holden once told Ryan O'Neal, "I remember the day I arrived at Orly Airport for PARIS WHEN IT SIZZLES. I could hear my footsteps echoing against the walls of the transit corridor, just like a condemned man walking the last mile. I realized that I had to face Audrey and I had to deal with my drinking. And I didn't think I could handle either situation." He couldn't, and director Quine and producer Axelrod were in for problems. On a visit to the set Shelia Graham, in her *Hollywood Revisited*, remembers: "Most of the heat was coming from the producer and director because of the delays caused by Mr. Holden's drinking. He and they had thought his alcoholism was under control, after he had undergone a devastating cure that consisted of the nurse giving him a glass of his favorite tipple every hour on the hour. Soon he would start retching just to hear the footsteps of the nurse." Quine took it upon himself to keep an eye on Holden. He even went so far as to rent a house next to Holden's and climb into a tree which offered a view of Holden's bedroom. When Holden, who was actually outside at his pond, saw Quine in the tree he asked, "What are you doing?" The quick-witted Quine responded, "Just getting a little air." "Oh? Well, you better get some sleep," Holden stated "we've got a lot work to do in the morning." Hepburn tried her best to make Holden comfortable (which only made Holden want her more) and ease tensions on the set. After the first days "rushes" were viewed, however, Hepburn was extremely dissatisfied with how she was photographed. She demanded that Renoir be fired (a gross insult to the highly respected family name in Paris). Franz Planer was the first choice, but when his schedule was found to be too busy, Lang was picked. After that delay, another more major setback followed. After a drinking binge with Jack Lemmon (who was in Paris to film IRMA LA DOUCE), Holden checked into a clinic to dry out. After a short rest, he emerged with a renewed desire to continue the picture but once again went off on a binge. This time Holden bought a Ferrari and decided to drive to Switzerland for Bastille Day. Ignoring the pleas of Quine and Axelrod, Holden drove off with only one more scene to complete. Not surprisingly, Holden's drinking didn't pair well with the Ferrari. He returned after a weekend to the set, suffering from minor injuries he sustained after driving into a brick wall. In what seemed like a desperate attempt to add some stronger box office potential to the film, Quine enlisted a number of big names to appear in a party scene. Among the names are Dietrich (who reportedly got to keep the limousine and the fur coat that she arrives in), Ferrer (Hepburn's husband), Curtis, and the singing voices of Sinatra and Astaire. All of this box office artillery, however, couldn't raise PARIS WHEN IT SIZZLES to anything more than an average piece of entertainment.

p, Richard Quine, George Axelrod; d, Quine; w, Axelrod (based on the story by Julien Duvivier, Henri Jeanson); ph, Charles Lang, Jr. (Technicolor); m, Nelson Riddle; ed, Archie Marshek; art d, Jean d'Eaubonne; set d, Gabriel Bechir; cos, Hubert de Givenchy, Christian Dior; spec eff, Paul K. Lerpae; makeup, Frank McCoy.

Romantic Comedy   **(PR:A   MPAA:NR)**

PARISIAN, THE**½   (1931, Fr.) 63m Pathe-Natan/CAP bw (MON GOSSE DE PERE)

Adolphe Menjou (Gerome), Roger Treville (Gerard), Redgie Williams (Stanley), Campion (Julien), Elissa Landi (Yvonne), Renee Savoye (Secretary), Valery (Mado), Pauline Carton (The Concierge).

A film—that had both French and U.S. versions—about a middle-aged Frenchman (Menjou) who is happy with his life. He doesn't work too hard, has a nice young wife, and lives a life of ease. An American-raised son (Treville), who had lived with Menjou's divorced wife, shows up and wants to make his father a rich man. The old man resists and eventually the kid adopts his father's life of leisure. The film was produced in France in 1930, shortly after Menjou parted ways with Paramount and moved to Paris. It went over much better with French audiences (in its native version) than it did in the English language version in which, for some unexplained reason, contrived French and British accents are mixed in throughout, making for a confusing story.

d, Jean de la Muir; w, Mary Murillo, Ray Horniman; ph, P.J. Faulener; ed, Stewart B. Moss.

Drama   **(PR:A   MPAA:NR)**

PARISIAN ROMANCE, A*½   (1932) 76m Allied bw

Lew Cody (Baron), Marian Shilling (Claudette), Gilbert Roland (Victor), Joyce Compton (Marcelle), Yola D'Avril (Pauline), Nicholas Soussanin (Emil), George Lewis (Pierre), Luis Alberni, James Eagles, Paul Porcasi, Helen Jerome Eddy, Nadine Dore, Bryant Washburn.

A trite film that relies on the somewhat repetitive action. Lew Cody dominates the film as he chases Parisian women and fights Gilbert Roland. A breezy love story with competent direction.

d, Chester M. Franklin; w, F. Hugh Herbert (based on the play by Octave Feuillet); ph, Harry Neumann, Tom Galligan; ed, Mildred Johnston.

Drama   **(PR:A   MPAA:NR)**

PARISIENNE   (SEE: LA PARISIENNE, 1958, Fr./Ital.)

PARK AVENUE LOGGER**   (1937) 65m RKO bw (GB: MILLIONAIRE PLAYBOY)

George O'Brien (Grant Curran), Beatrice Roberts (Peggy O'Shea), Willard Robertson (Ben Morton), Ward Bond (Paul Sanger), Bert Hanlon (Nick), Lloyd Ingraham (Mike Curran), George Rosener (Mat O'Shea), Dave Wengren, Robert E. O'Connor Gertrude Short, Al Baffert.

The head of a blue-blood family (Ingraham) thinks his son is less than a man and sends him off to a lumber camp to prove his manhood, not knowing that the kid is already a top wrestler. Up at the camp, the wrestling star (known as The Masked Marvel) exposes a couple of crooked foremen, beats up the lumberjacks, and wins the heart of a beautiful girl by helping save her father's logging operation.

p, George A. Hirliman; d, David Howard; w, Dan Jarrett, Ewing Scott (based on a story by Bruce Hutchison); ph, Frank B. Good; ed, Robert Crandall.

Drama   **(PR:A   MPAA:NR)**

PARK PLAZA 605   (SEE: NORMAN CONQUEST, 1953, Brit.)

PARK ROW**   (1952) 83m UA bw

Gene Evans (Phineas Mitchell), Mary Welch (Charity Hackett), Bela Kovacs (Ottmar Mergenthaler), Herbert Heyes (Josiah Davenport), Tina Rome (Jenny O'Rourke), George O'Hanlon (Steve Brodie), J.M. Kerrigan (Dan O'Rourke), Forrest Taylor (Charles A. Leach), Don Orlando (Mr. Angelo), Neyle Morrow (Thomas Guest), Dick Elliott (Jeff Hudson), Stuart Randall (Mr. Spiro), Dee Pollock (Rusty), Hal K. Dawson (Mr. Wiley), Charles Horvath (Man Battered by Mitchell Against Monument), Monk Eastman.

Scattered direction doesn't help this film about the evolution of the American press. Evans tries to start his own newspaper, but his former employer uses a variety of dirty tactics to try to put him under. In the end, she realizes her evil ways and comes to understand the importance of freedom of the press.

p,d&w, Samuel Fuller; ph, Jack Russell; m, Paul Dunlap; ed, Phillip Cahn; art d, Theobald Holsopple; set d, Ray Robinson; cos, Jack Miller; spec eff, Roscoe S. Cline.

Drama   **(PR:A   MPAA:NR)**

PARLIAMO DI DONNE   (SEE: LET'S TALK ABOUT WOMEN, 1964, Fr./Ital.)

PARMI LES VAUTOURS   (SEE: FRONTIER HELLCAT, 1966, Fr./Ital./W. Ger./Yugo.)

PARLOR, BEDROOM AND BATH**½   (1931) 69m MGM bw (GB: ROMEO IN PYJAMAS)

Buster Keaton (Reginald Irving), Charlotte Greenwood (Polly Hathaway), Reginald Denny (Jeffery Haywood), Cliff Edwards (Bell Hop), Dorothy Christy (Angelica Embrey), Joan Peers (Nita Leslie), Sally Eilers (Virginia Embrey), Natalie Moorhead (Leila Crofton), Edward Brophy (Detective), Walter Merrill (Frederick Leslie), Sidney Bracy (Butler), Eugene Pallette.

Keaton made the transition from silents to talkies with a bit of difficulty. He'd already done FREE AND EASY and DOUGHBOYS (both 1930) before this remake of the 1920 film of the same name which had starred Eugene Pallette and was based on a play that ran in 1918. While certainly nowhere near the quality of his masterful silents, PARLOR, BEDROOM AND BATH contains several funny moments. Keaton plays a man who earns his living nailing up advertisements on telegraph poles. While working one day, he is nearly killed by a car. The driver, Denny, is extremely upset because the girl he loves, Eilers, refuses to marry him until her older sister, Christy, is betrothed. Comedies being what they are, Christy meets Keaton and falls in love. Knowing that Christy will fly into a jealous rage if Keaton is caught flirting with another woman, the rest of the clan takes great pains to ensure this doesn't happen. Unfortunately Denny employs his lovely sister to train the dim-witted Keaton in the proper skills of proposing marriage. This of course leads to the teacher-student relationship blossoming into true love, with the resulting comedy gags following closely behind. The film was shot mostly on location at Keaton's palatial Beverly Hills home, and while supporting players Brophy and Edwards contribute some nice bits, it's Keaton's picture all the way. Director Sedgwick, who helmed most of the Great Stone Face's movies, ensured this and tried to protect the comedian when the studios took control of his career. Keaton also performed in the French and German versions of the film, speaking the foreign languages himself (the supporting players were all actors from the respective countries). Denny, an actor whose career spanned 50 years (he would go on to play the role of "Algy" in the BULLDOG DRUMMOND series), had a vocation in addition to acting: he designed the first radio-controlled airplane ever flown in the U.S., a feat that made him a force in the aviation industry.

d, Edward Sedgwick; w, Richard Schayer, Robert E. Hopkins (based on the play by Charles W. Bell, Mark Swan); ph, Leonard Smith; ed, William Levanway.

Comedy   **Cas.**   **(PR:A   MPAA:NR)**

PARNELL*   (1937) 115m MGM bw

Clark Gable (Charles Stewart Parnell), Myrna Loy (Katie O'Shea), Edna May Oliver (Aunt Bea), Edmund Gwenn (Campbell), Alan Marshal (Willie O'Shea), Donald Crisp (Davitt), Billie Burke (Clara), Donald Meek (Murphy), Montagu Love (William Ewart Gladstone), George Zucco (Sir Charles Russell), Neil Fitzgerald (Pigott), Phyllis Coghlan (Ellen), Brandon Tynan (Redmond), Byron Russell (Healy), Berton Churchill (The O'Gorman Mahon), Halliwell Hobbes, J. Farrell MacDonald, Randolph Churchill.

PARNELL was Clark Gable's biggest financial disaster. He was so struck by the thud that he vowed to never again play in a period piece. The failure of PARNELL caused the studio to have to convince him to accept the role of Rhett Butler in another period film that did somewhat better. Based on a play, the movie had the screenplay written by not one, but two eminent playwrights, Van Druten and Behrman, but it didn't help. The problem was the miscasting of Gable, whose attempts at an Irish accent were laughable. A 1936 popularity poll named Gable as "King of Hollywood" so he must have thought he could play the role of the "uncrowned King of Ireland" and he accepted. He was mistaken. "GG"The Troubles" in Ireland go much further back than yesterday's headlines from Belfast. Gable is in the U.S. attempting to secure donations for the wretched poor of Ireland. What they want is home rule and the cessation of the British government in their country. Gable goes back to Erin and the country rallies behind his desire for independence. Loy is separated from Marshal, a villainous man, and she is currently residing with her aunt, Oliver, a well-to-do woman who has plenty of space in her huge home. Oliver pays Marshal money so he keeps his distance, and he won't give her a divorce for fear of losing his stipend. Marshal wants to run for Parliament and needs to put up a front so he asks Loy if she will help and be a hostess to Gable, who is so powerful that if he gives his backing, Marshal will probably win the election. Loy goes to Gable's office to meet him and he says he recognizes her from having seen her at the opera a short time before. He knew at that time that they would meet. He agrees to come to her house for dinner but has to leave on an important emergency before cigars and brandy are served. Loy sees him to the door and he declares his love for her and an affair begins. (In real life, it went on for many years but in the picture they compress it to just a few months.) Gable continues his labors on behalf of his country and there seems to be a light at the end of the tunnel, then Marshal appears and uses blackmail. He wants Gable to appoint him to a high post once the country achieves independence. Gable won't hear of it and Marshal threatens to bring a messy divorce suit and name Gable as the reason for it. Love makes an announcement at a dinner that Gable's petition for home rule is going to be brought to Parliament, a great feather for Gable's cap. But there's a problem. While the reception takes place, newsboys are screaming the headlines that Marshal has, in fact, named Gable in the divorce. Gable's plans go to hell and the bill for home rule is not introduced and it looks as though Gable has betrayed his land for the love of a woman. Loy thinks she can solve matters by claiming that Marshal originally invited Gable to their home in order to do this nefarious deed but Gable won't hear of her sullying her good name and he allows the suit to continue with nolo contendere on his part. Gable vainly attempts to keep the political party together but his old pals turn their backs on him and the unit disintegrates. Gable has a heart attack at a political meeting, then is carried to Loy's home where his last words are: "You'll have to teach me all the things that are expected of me. It'll be strange to say 'my wife.' I'll have to practice. Only, you mustn't go away from me." Loy promises she won't and Gable replies, "I know you won't. One's destiny can't ever go away from one," and he dies. It's slow, pretentious, expensive, and boring. The studio spent $750,000 to make the movie and lost $600,000. They built an entire Irish Village in Chatsworth, in the San Fernando Valley, and used almost 2,000 extras. Good costumes, authentic sets, and a story that took liberties with the truth. Marshal's character was not the rat he was in the script and Gable was hardly a deacon of the church. The rotten way the British treated the Irish is never seen and that's a mistake because it's hard to engender any sympathy for the Irish cause unless the reasons are given for their behavior. The best parts in this film went to the secondary players. In a tiny role, an actual member of Parliament, Randolph Churchill, played a member of Parliament and said he earned more money acting it than living it.

p&d, John M. Stahl; w, John Van Druten, S.N. Behrman (based on a play by Elsie T. Schauffler); ph, Karl Freund; m, William Axt; ed, Fredrick Y. Smith; art d, Cedric Gibbons; cos, Adrian.

Biography   (PR:A-C MPAA:NR)

PAROLE*½   (1936) 67m UNIV bw

Henry Hunter (Russ Whalen), Ann Preston (Frances Crawford), Alan Dinehart (Richard K. Mallard), Noah Beery, Jr. (Bobby Freeman), Grant Mitchell (Marty Crawford), Alan Baxter (Percy "Okay" Smith), Alan Hale (John Borchard), Bernadene Hayes (Joyce Daniels, Mallard's Secretary), Berton Churchill (Rex Gavin), Charles Richman (Driscoll), John Miltern (The Governor), Selmer Jackson (Earl Bigbee), Clifford Jones [Philip Trent] (Reporter Gregory), Frank Mills (Dummy Watts), Anthony Quinn (Zingo Browning), Wallis Clark (The Warden), Edward Keane (District Attorney), Douglas Wood (Parole Board Chairman), Christian Rub (John), John Kennedy (Police Chief), Frank McGlynn, Sr. (Patton), Landers Stevens (State's Attorney), Zeffie Tilbury (Molly Smith), Stanley Andrews (Parole Board Member Williams), Tom Moore (Carmody), Arthur Loft (Special Prosecutor), William "Billy" Gilbert (Salvatore Arriolo), Guy Usher (Police Lieutenant), Walter Miller (Personnel Manager), Thomas Curran (Board Chairman), Ed Reinoch (Psychiatrist), Arnold Gray (Secretary), Harry C. Bradley (Dr. Arthur Carroll).

Plenty of action carries this story about paroled prisoners who try to make it on the outside. The outside pressures almost get to them, but eventually they stay on the straight and narrow and prove that the idea of parole is a good one.

p, Robert Presnell; d, Louis Friedlander [Lew Landers]; w, Kubec Glasmon, Joel Sayre, Horace McCoy (based on a story by Glasmon, Sayre, Robert Dillon, Kay Morris); ph, George Robinson; ed, Phil Cahn.

Crime Drama   (PR:A MPAA:NR)

PAROLE FIXER**   (1940) 68m PAR bw

William Henry (Scott Britton), Virginia Dale (Enid Casserly), Robert Paige (Steve Eddson), Gertrude Michael (Colette Menthe), Richard Denning (Bruce Eaton), Anthony Quinn (Francis "Big Boy" Bradmore), Marjorie Gateson (Mrs. Thornton Casserly), Lyle Talbot (Ross Waring), Harvey Stephens (Bartley Hanford), Paul McGrath (Tyler Craden), Richard Carle (Gustave Kalkus), Charlotte Wynters (Nellie), Louise Beavers (Aunt Lindy), Wilfred Roberts (Frank Preston), Jack Carson (George Mattison), John Galludet (Edward Bradshaw), Eddie Marr (Edward "Slim" Racky), Morgan Wallace (Ben), Sonny Bupp (Bobby Mattison), Billy Lee (Jimmy Mattison), Harry Shannon (Randall Porter), Russell Hicks (Judge), Edwin Maxwell (Edward Murkil), Mary Hart (Mrs. Tilden), Olaf Hytten (Carter), Ed Mortimer (Mr. Tilden), Byron Foulger (Florist), Doodles Weaver (Edward the Florist's Helper).

Based on a book by FBI director J. Edgar Hoover, the film looks at the seedy side of parole, showing how people with the right political connections can get anyone out of prison. A crooked lawyer controls the chairman of the parole board, but his stoolie is caught by the FBI. Most of the story is based on facts, with a few additions for dramatic flair.

d, Robert Florey; w, William R. Lipman, Horace McCoy (based on Persons in Hiding by J. Edgar Hoover); ph, Harry Fischbeck; m, Boris Morros; ed, Harvey Johnston; art d, Hans Dreier, John Goodman.

Crime Drama   (PR:A MPAA:NR)

PAROLE GIRL*½   (1933) 64m COL bw

Mae Clarke (Sylvia Day), Ralph Bellamy (Joe Smith), Marie Prevost (Jeanie), Hale Hamilton (Tony), Ferdinand Gottschalk (Taylor), Ernest Wood (Davidson), Sam Godfrey (Walsh), John Paul Jones (Harris), Lee Phelps (Burns).

Clarke gets thrown in jail when she unknowingly helps a con artist rip off store manager Bellamy. She gets paroled early after she puts out a blaze (which she had started herself) in the prison shop. She goes back to Bellamy to make amends and ends up falling in love with him. Problems arise when the store manager's wife gets out of prison. Clarke leaves the scene, but when Bellamy's wife, Prevost, informs him that she divorced him while she was in prison, Clarke comes running back.

d, Eddie Cline; w, Norman Krasna (based on his story "Dance of the Millions"); ph, Benjamin Kline.

Crime Drama   (PR:A MPAA:NR)

PAROLE, INC.*   (1949) 71m Orbit/EL bw

Michael O'Shea (Richard Hendricks), Turhan Bey (Barney Rodescu), Evelyn Ankers (Jojo Dumont), Virginia Lee (Glenda Palmer), Charles Bradstreet (Harry Palmer), Lyle Talbot (Police Commissioner), Michael Whalen (Kid Redmond), Charles Williams (Titus Jones), James Cardwell (Duke Vigili), Paul Bryar (Charley Newton), Noel Cravat (Blackie Olson), Charles Jordan (Monty Cooper).

A dull, cliched crime film with O'Shea as an FBI agent who goes undercover to get the goods on an underworld operation. Mobsters are getting criminals paroled before their sentences are up, and the G-man puts a swift end to their evildoings.

p, Constantin J. David; d, Alfred Zeisler; w, Sherman L. Lowe (based on a story by Lowe, Royal K. Cole); ph, Gilbert Warrenton; m, Alexander Laszlo; ed, John D. Faure; art d, Rudi Feld; set d, Jacque Mapes.

Crime   (PR:A MPAA:NR)

PAROLE RACKET*   (1937) 62m COL bw

Paul Kelly (Police Lt. Tony Roberts), Rosalind Keith (Betty Wilson, Reporter), Leona Maricle (Anna Gregg), Thurston Hall (Jameson, City Editor), Gene Morgan (Woresky), John Spacey (Tim Delevan), Francis McDonald (Nat Beldon), Raymond Brown (Capt. McArthur), Jack Daly (Sgt. O'Leary), C. Montague Shaw (Judge Grayson), Al Hill ("Dapper" Dunning).

Kelly is a police lieutenant who goes undercover to break up a mob-run parole operation. The gangsters have a few men on the parole board sitting in their pockets, and so Kelly must work his way into the gang's confidence to bust them all. Big yawns for the predecessor of PAROLE, INC. (1949).

d, C.C. Coleman Jr.; w, Harold Shumate; ph, George Meehan; ed, Dick Fantl.

Crime   (PR:A MPAA:NR)

PAROLED FROM THE BIG HOUSE*   (1938) 58m SYN bw (GB: MAIN STREET GIRL)

Jean Carmen (Pat Mallory), Richard Adams ("Slicker" Nixon), George Eldredge ("Red" Herron), Gwen Lee (Binnie Bell), Milburn Stone (District Attorney Downey), Walter Anthony (Joe "Killer" Britt), Ole Olesen ("Torchy"), Earl Douglas (Hoke "The Duke" Curtis), Eddie Kaye ("Gunner" Garson), Joe Devlin (Jed Cross), Eleanor De Van (Rita).

Another parole racket film that is as lame as PAROLE RACKET (1937) and PAROLE, INC. Stone plays the district attorney tracking down the man behind the racket, and Carmen seeks out the man who killed her father. A lot of yawns.

p, J.D. Kendis; d, Elmer Clifton; w, George Plympton; ph, Eddie Linden.

Crime   (PR:A MPAA:NR)

PAROLED—TO DIE*½   (1938) 55m REP bw

Bob Steele (Doug Redfern), Kathleen Eliot (Joan Blackman), Karl Hackett (Harvey Meline), Horace Murphy (Lucky Gosden), Steve Clark (Sheriff Blackman), Budd Buster (Spike Travers), Sherry Tansey (Heavy Matson), Frank Ball (Judge), Jack Smith (Prosecuting Attorney), Horace B. Carpenter.

Steele is a rancher innocently jailed for a bank robbery with Hackett, the town boss responsible for the frame-up. A government agent arrives to help Steele clear his name. With no surprise, Steele gets the goods on Hackett and his men.

p, A.W. Hackel; d, Sam Newfield; w, George H. Plympton (based on a story by Harry F. Olmsted); ph, Robert Cline; ed, Roy Claire.

Crime   **Cas.**   (PR:A MPAA:NR)

PAROXISMUS   (SEE: VENUS IN FURS, 1967)

PARRISH*½   (1961) 140m WB c

Troy Donahue (Parrish McLean), Claudette Colbert (Ellen McLean), Karl Malden (Judd Raike), Dean Jagger (Sala Post), Diane McBain (Alison Post), Connie Stevens (Lucy), Sharon Hugueny (Paige Raike), Dub Taylor (Teet Howie), Hampton Fancher (Edgar Raike), David Knapp (Wiley Raike), Saundra Edwards (Evaline Raike), Hope Summers (Mary Howie), Bibi Osterwald (Rosie), Madeleine Sherwood (Addie), Sylvia Miles (Eileen), Alfonso Marshall (Gladstone), John Barracudo (Willis), Terry Carter (Cartwright), Ford Rainey (John Donati), Sara Taft (Gramma), Edgar Stehli (Tully), Wade Dumas (Maples), John McGovern (Skipper), Hayden Rorke (Tom Weldon), Irene Windust (Maizie Weldon), Don Dillaway (Max Maine), Gertrude Flynn (Miss Daly), House Jameson (Oermeyer), Ken Allen (Lemmie), Karen Norris (Operator), Frank Campanella (Foreman), Carroll O'Connor (Fire Chief), Michael Sean (Bellhop), Fred Marlow (Butler—Post Home), Martin Eric (Mr. Gilliam), Vincent Gardenia (Gas Station Attendant), Bernie Richards (Bandleader).

A wooden Donahue walks stiffly as a young worker trying to fit in with the rich and ruthless life style of the Connecticut River Valley tobacco growers in this too-long tale. Part of his problem comes from falling in love with three different women along the way. When his mother marries a tobacco baron, Donahue goes to work for him but promptly quits because of his evil ways. After a stint in the navy, Donahue leases some land to start his own growing, but cannot hire workers because of their terror of reprisals by his stepfather. Finally, a young girl and her friends help out, and set the scene for the final fight between Donahue and his stepfather. Donahue beats down the baron's son when he tries to set fire to the fields, while the baron stands by and acknowledges his enemy's victory.

p,d&w, Delmer Daves (based on the novel by Mildred Savage); ph, Harry Stradling, Sr. (Technicolor); m, Max Steiner; ed, Owen Marks; art d, Leo K. Kuter; set d, William L. Kuehl; cos, Howard Shoup; m/l, John Barracudo, Alfonso Marshall, Terry Carter; makeup, Gordon Bau.

Drama (PR:A MPAA:NR)

PARSIFAL** (1983, Fr.) 255m GAU-TMS/Triumph c

Armin Jordan (Amfortas, Sung by Wolfgang Schone), Martin Sperr (Titurel, Sung by Hans Tschammer), Robert Lloyd (Gurnemanz), Michael Kutter (Parsifal 1), Karen Krick (Parsifal 2, Sung by Reiner Goldberg), Aage Haugland (Klingsor), Edith Clever (Kundry, Sung by Yvonne Minton), Rudolph Gabler, Urban von Klebelsberg, Bruno Romani-Versteeg (Knights of the Grail, Sung by Gilles Cachemaille, Paul Frey), Monika Gaertner, Thomas Fink, David Meyer, Judith Schmidt (Squires, Sung by Christer Bladin, Tamara Herz, Michael Roider, Hanna Schaer), Amelie Syberberg (Bearer of the Grail), David Luther (Young Parsifal, Sung by Gertrude Oertel), Anahita Farroschad, Miriam Feldmann, Johanna Fink, Alexandra Grunsberg, Vivian Kintisch, Martina Lanzinger, Antonia Preser, Catharina Preser, Claudia Schmann, Bettina Stiller, Anya Toelle, Annette Woll, Stephanie Corler, Eva Kessler, Catharina Klemm, Judith Klemm, Sabine Kuckelmann, Isabelle Malbrun, Caroline Riollot, Guillemette Riollot, Sofia Romani, Ina Schroter, Balthasar Thomass, Sophie von Uslar (Flowermaidens, Sung by Britt-Marie Aruhn, Jocelyne Chamonin, Tamara Herz, Gertrude Oertel, Eva Saurova, Hanna Schaer).

Syberberg's overlong version of Richard Wagner's overlong opera, produced by France's Gaumont, which has also brought other classic operas to the screen at the helm of well-respected directors—DON GIOVANNI by Joseph Losey, LA TRAVIATA by Franco Zeffirelli, and CARMEN by Francesco Rosi. This contemporized, abstract version, however, is in the same Wagnerian tradition as Syberberg's previous films (HITLER: A FILM FROM GERMANY)—long. A Wagnerian treatment of Wagner is more than all but the staunchest fans can handle. Presented by Francis Ford Coppola, who likewise has a fondness for keeping the audience in their seats for a while.

p, Henry Nap, Annie Nap-Oleon; d, Hans-Jurgen Syberberg; ph, Igor Luther; m, Richard Wagner; ed, Jutta Brandstaedter, Marianne Fehrenberg; md, Armin Jordan; set d, Werner Achmann; cos, Veronicka Dorn, Hella Wolter.

Opera (PR:A MPAA:PG)

PARSON AND THE OUTLAW, THE** (1957) 71m COL c

Anthony Dexter (Billy the Kid), Charles "Buddy" Rogers (Rev. Jericho Jones), Jean Parker (Mrs. Jones), Sonny Tufts (Jack Slade), Robert Lowery (Col. Morgan), Marie Windsor (Tonya), Madalyn Trahey (Elly McCloud), Bob Steele, Joe Sodja, Bob Duncan, Bob Gilbert, Jack Lowell, John Davis, Paul Spahn, Herman Pulver.

Dexter is Billy the Kid who hangs up his guns in an attempt to forget the past and start a new life. Things go well until the local preacher, Rogers, is shot down by a band of outlaws. Since the murdered man was a friend, Dexter has no choice but to reholster his gun and go after the killer. The film's style seems more in step with westerns made in the 1930s and 1940s by Republic and other B movie production companies. Director and co-writer Drake scripted for Tom Mix, George O'Brien, Johnny Mack Brown, and others.

p, Charles Rogers, Robert Gilbert; d, Oliver Drake; w, Drake, John Mantley; ph, Clark Ramsey (Technicolor); m, Joe Sodja; ed, Warren Adams.

Western (PR:A MPAA:NR)

PARSON OF PANAMINT, THE** (1941) 84m PAR bw

Charlie Ruggles (Chuckawalla Bill Redfield), Ellen Drew (Mary Mallory), Phillip Terry (Rev. Phillip Pharo), Joseph Schildkraut (Bob Deming), Porter Hall (Jonathan Randall), Henry Kolker (Judge Arnold Mason), Janet Beecher (Mrs. Tweedy), Clem Bevans (Crabapple Ellerton), Douglas Fowley (Chappie Ellerton), Paul Hurst (Jake Waldren), Frank Puglia (Joaquin), Minor Watson (Sheriff Nickerson), Harry Hayden (Timothy Hadley), Russell Hicks (Prosecuting Attorney), Hal Price, Rod Cameron.

Terry plays a minister who arrives in the mining town of Panamint to clean it up. He's as quick to use his fists as quote from the Bible. His successful attempts to reform the criminal element in the town is washed away by the flood that destroys Panamint. The story is told by the town's mayor, Ruggles, who also discovered the mine that the town was built around. This is a remake of two earlier editions: the 1916 Paramount version directed by William Desmond Taylor and starring Dustin Farnum, Winifred Kingston, and "Doc" Cannon, and the 1922 version under the title, WHILE SATAN SLEEPS, directed by Joseph Henabery, with Jack Holt, Wade Boteler, and Mabel Van Buren in the leads.

p, Harry Sherman; d, William McGann; w, Harold Shumate, Adrian Scott (based on the novel by Peter B. Kyne); ph, Russell Harlan; ed, Sherman Rose; md, Irvin Talbot; art d, Ralph Berger.

Western (PR:A MPAA:NR)

PART TIME WIFE**½ (1930) 72m FOX bw

Edmund Lowe (Jim Murdock), Leila Hyams (Mrs. Murdock/Betty Rogers), Tom Clifford (Tommy Milligan), Walter McGrail (Johnny Spence), Louis Payne (Butler),

Sam Lufkin (Caddie Master), Bodil Rosing (Maid), George "Red" Corcoran (Chauffeur).

When Lowe is too busy with his career to pay attention to wife Hyams, they separate, and she begins indulging in her favorite passion, golf, as well as making a living modeling. Lowe begins to play golf on his doctor's instructions, and, after the game has made him a different man, he finds himself paired with his wife. With their sport to share, they are soon reconciled. Okay comedy hampered by crude recording techniques.

d, Leo McCarey; w, Raymond L. Schrock, Howard Green, McCarey (based on the story "Shepper Newfounder" by Stewart Edward White); ph, George Schneiderman; ed, Jack Murray.

Comedy (PR:A MPAA:NR)

PART-TIME WIFE* (1961, Brit.) 70m Danziger/BL bw

Anton Rodgers (Tom), Nyree Dawn Porter (Jenny), Kenneth J. Warren (Drew), Henry McCarthy (Whitworth), Mark Singleton (Detective), Susan Richards (Miss Aukland), Raymond Rollett (Barnsdale), June Cunningham (Blonde).

An insurance salesman lends his wife to a friend who needs to impress a rich uncle, only the uncle turns out to be a fraud and a thief. Not very original vehicle from Max Varnel, son of the man who directed some of the funniest British movies of the 1930s and 1940s, Marcel Varnel.

p, Brian Taylor; d, Max Varnel; w, H.M. McCormack.

Comedy (PR:A MPAA:NR)

PART 2, SOUNDER (SEE: SOUNDER, PART 2, 1976)

PART 2, WALKING TALL (SEE: WALKING TALL, PART 2, 1975)

PARTINGS** (1962, Pol.) 101m Syrena/Telepix bw (POZEGNANIA; AKA: LYDIA ATE THE APPLE)

Maria Wachowiak (Lidka), Tadeusz Janczar (Mirek), Saturnin Zurawski (Felix), Irena Netto (Owner of the Villa "Quo Vadis"), Zdzislaw Mrozewski (Paul's Father), Stanislaw Milski (Professor), Hanna Skarzanka (Maryna), Helena Sokolowska (Paul's Aunt), Irena Starkowna (Countess).

A heavily politicized film about a pair of lovers separated by the war for five years. The soldier returns home to find that his girl has married a wealthy count, whom she cannot stand. They make love, she leaves her husband, and both escape the village in time to watch the Soviet tanks roll into town. Released in Poland in 1958.

d, Wojciech J. Has; w, Stanislaw Dygat, Has (based on the novel by Dygat); ph, Mieczyslaw Jahoda; m, Lucjan Kaszycki; ed, Zofia Dwornik.

Drama (PR:A MPAA:NR)

PARTLY CONFIDENTIAL (SEE: THANKS FOR LISTENING, 1937)

PARTNER, THE*½ (1966, Brit.) 58m Merton Park/Schoenfeld bw

Yoko Tani (Lin Siyan), Guy Doleman (Wayne Douglas), Ewan Roberts (Detective Inspector Simons), Mark Eden (Richard Webb), Anthony Booth (Buddy Forrester), Helen Lindsay (Helen Douglas), Noel Johnson (Charles Briers), Denis Holmes (Sgt. Rigby), John Forgeham (Adrian Marlowe), Virginia Wetherell (Karen), Yvette Wyatt (Pam), Norman Scace (Dr. Ambrose), John Forbes-Robertson (Alwood), Brian Haines (Surgeon), Earle Green (Peter), Neil Wilson (Security Officer), Guy Standeven (Counterhand), Norma Parnell (Day Nurse).

Standard mystery plot which has an accountant murdered while working on a deal with a film producer. The usual suspects are corralled and the blame is placed on a private detective who was hired to shadow the accountant. Released in England in 1963.

p, Jack Greenwood; d, Gerard Glaister; w, John Roddick (based on the novel The Million Dollar Story by Edgar Wallace); ph, James Wilson; m, Bernard Ebbinghouse; ed, Derek Holding; md, Ebbinghouse; art d, Scott MacGregor.

Mystery (PR:A MPAA:NR)

PARTNERS*½ (1932) 62m RKO-Pathe bw

Tom Keene, Nancy Drexel, Bobby Nelson, Otis Harlan, Victor Potel, Lee Shumway, Billy Franey, Carlton King, Ben Corbett, Fred Burns.

Keene is accused of the murder of old-timer Franey, and eludes putative justice to bring in the real killers. The hero has befriended the murdered man's grandson, Nelson, and with the help of his trusty horse, Flash, he captures the real criminal, Shumway. With his name cleared, Keene is able to start a family with Nelson and Drexel.

d, Fred Allen; w, Donald W. Lee; ph, Harry Jackson; ed, Walter Thompson.

Western (PR:A MPAA:NR)

PARTNERS** (1976, Can.) 96m Clearwater/Astral c

Denholm Elliott (John Grey), Hollis McLaren (Heather Grey), Michael Margotta (Paul Howard), Lee Broker (Philip Rudd), Judith Gault (Barbara), Robert Silverman (Hayes), Irene Mayeska (Aunt Margot).

McLaren is the daughter of the owner of a large Canadian paper firm who gets involved with criminal type Margotta. They have a torrid love affair while an American corporation tries to buy out her father, Elliott. When it becomes apparent that he won't sell out to them, the Americans hire thug Broker to kill him. McLaren takes over the company, and with the new self-assurance she has gained from her lover, runs the company with a sure hand. A mildly entertaining film that is hurt by some second-rate performances.

p, Chalmers Adams, Dan Owen; d, Owen; w, Norman Snider, Owen; ph, Marc Champion; m, Murray McLauchlan; ed, George Appleby.

Drama (PR:C MPAA:NR)

PARTNERS*   (1982) 93m PAR c

Ryan O'Neal (Benson), John Hurt (Kerwin), Kenneth McMillan (Chief Wilkens), Robyn Douglass (Jill), Jay Robinson (Halderstam), Denise Galik (Clara), Joseph R. Sicari (Walter), Michael McGuire (Monroe), Rick Jason (Douglas), James Remar (Edward K. Petersen), Jennifer Ashley (Secretary), Darrell Larson (Al), Tony March (2nd Aide), Seamon Glass (Gillis), Steve Reisch (Counter Boy), Carl Kraines (1st Aide), Bob Ozman (Detective), Carol Williard (Officer), Iris Alhanti (Jogger), Bob Bigelow (Man on Balcony), John Garber (Body Builder), Sherrie Lessard (Telephone Operator), Ed McCready (Doorman), Jackie Millines (Photo Assistant), Ray Sanders (Muscle Man), Luis Torres (Pablo), Gene Ross, Douglas Bruce, Bill Cross, Craig Shreeve, Gregory L. Hodal (Cops).

This is a moronic, dull comedy about straight and gay cops teamed together to track down a murderer. Mainstream Hollywood has seldom addressed homosexuality without stumbling over itself and this film is no exception with its cliches and superficial characterizations. O'Neal is the straight cop teamed up with gay police clerk Hurt to uncover the killer of a male model. The story follows the problems the men have as they pretend they're lovers living in a gay apartment building. The jokes are flat and predictable and the portrayal of gays sophomoric and embarrassing. It's understandable that O'Neal would get himself involved in a piece of junk like this since most of the films he has chosen to be in have been poor, but to see the superior actor Hurt in this is a shock.

p, Aaron Russo; d, James Burrows; w, Francis Veber; ph, Victor J. Kemper (Movielab Color); m, Georges Delerue; ed, Danford B. Greene; prod d, Richard Sylbert; set d, George Gaines; cos, Wayne Finkelman.

Comedy   Cas.   (PR:O MPAA:R)

PARTNERS IN CRIME*   (1937) 66m PAR bw

Lynne Overman (Hank Hyer), Roscoe Karns (Sim Perkins), Muriel Hutchison (Odette Le Vin), Anthony Quinn (Nicholas Mazaney), Inez Courtney (Lillian Tate), Lucien Littlefield (Mr. Twitchell), Charles Halton (Silas Wagon), Charles Wilson (Inspector Simpson), June Brewster (Mabel), Esther Howard (Mrs. Wagon), Nora Cecil (Housekeeper), Russell Hicks (Mayor Callahan), Don Brodie (Reporter), Archie Twitchell [Michael Branden] (Photographer), Arthur Hoyt (Callahan's Secretary), Oscar "Dutch" Hendrian (Cab Driver), Ruth Warren (Miss Brown).

Overman is a private eye who learns of a smear campaign against a mayoral candidate by dating a beautiful girl (Hutchison) who is in on the dirty dealings. The detective blows open the whole can of worms and gets his reporter friend elected instead. It turns out, however, that the new mayor isn't an American citizen, and so he's disqualified. An inept, mindless picture with a plot that is beyond comprehension.

p, Harold Hurley; d, Ralph Murphy; w, Garnett Weston (based on the novel Murder Goes to College by Kurt Steel); ph, Henry Sharp; m, Boris Morros; ed, Eda Warren; art d, Hans Dreier, Robert Odell.

Crime   (PR:A MPAA:NR)

PARTNERS IN FORTUNE   (SEE: ROCKIN' IN THE ROCKIES, 1945)

PARTNERS IN TIME*½   (1946) 74m RKO bw

Chester Lauck (Lum), Norris Goff (Abner), Pamela Blake (Elizabeth), John James (Tim), Teala Loring (Janet), Danny Duncan (Grandpappy Spears/Constable Spears), Grady Sutton (Cedric Weehunt/Caleb Weehunt), Dick Elliott (Squire Skimp), Phyllis Kennedy (Abagail), Ruth Lee (Miss Thurston), Charles Jordan (Gerald Sharpe), Ruth Caldwell (Josie).

This was the sixth and final Lum and Abner film (Lum 'n' Abner were radio stars) which tells the tale of how the two got started in the little town of Pine Ridge, Arkansas. In 1904 Goff arrives in town and meets up with Lauck and they romance the women, put out the town's first fire, and start up their Jot-Em-Down store. In between the flashbacks, the duo have to fight off Elliott and Jordan to keep their store and save the romance of two young lovers, James and Loring.

p, Ben Hersh; d, William Nigh; w, Charles E. Roberts; ph, Jack Mackenzie; ed, S. Roy Luby; md, Lud Gluskin; art d, Ralph Berger.

Comedy   (PR:A MPAA:NR)

PARTNERS OF THE PLAINS*½   (1938) 70m PAR bw

William Boyd (Hopalong Cassidy), Harvey Clark (Baldy), Russell Hayden (Lucky Jenkins), Gwen Gaze (Lorna Drake), Hilda Plowright (Aunt Martha), John Warburton (Ronald Harwood), Al Bridge (Scar Lewis), Al Hill (Doc Galer), Earle Hodgins (Sheriff), John Beach (Mr. Benson).

One of the stronger Hopalong Cassidy westerns has Boyd giving English lady Gaze a hand with her inherited ranch. Hopalong teaches her the finer points of ranching and takes care of bad guy Bridge. Producer Sherman made sure that the Hopalong Cassidy series stood head and shoulder above the other series westerns by putting the best talent in front of and behind the camera by refusing to cut corners. (See HOPALONG CASSIDY series, Index.)

p, Harry Sherman; d, Lesley Selander; w, Harrison Jacobs (based on a story by Clarence E. Mulford); ph, Russell Harlan; ed, Robert Warwick; art d, Lewis Rachmil; m/l, "Moonlight on the Sunset Trail," Ralph Freed, Burton Lane (sung by Gwen Gaze).

Western   Cas.   (PR:A MPAA:NR)

PARTNERS OF THE SUNSET*   (1948) 53m MON bw

Jimmy Wakely, Dub "Cannonball" Taylor, Christine Larson, Ray Whitley, Leonard Penn, Steve Darrell, Marshall Reed, Bob Woodward, Boyd Stockman, Don Weston, Jack Rivers, Jay Kirby, Arthur "Fiddlin'" Smith, J.C. Lytton, Carl Matthews, Carl Sepulveda, Agapito Martinez.

Wakely and Taylor foil Larson's plan to murder her husband. Substandard singing

cowboy actioner slightly enlivened by Taylor's comic antics and directorial touches by the veteran Hillyer, whose roots go back to the silent westerns of the William S. Hart days.

p, Louis Gray; d, Lambert Hillyer; w, J. Benton Cheney; ph, Harry Neumann; ed, Johnny Fuller; md, Edward J. Kay.

Western   (PR:A MPAA:NR)

PARTNERS OF THE TRAIL*½   (1931) 63m MON bw

Tom Tyler (John), Betty Mack (Ruby Gerard), Reginald Sheffield (John Durant), Lafe McKee (Sheriff McWade), Marguerite McWade (Mary Lopez), Horace B. Carpenter (Skeets Briggs), Pat Rooney (Burke).

Tyler is on the run out West for the murder of his wife's lover, and he lets his buddy Sheffield take the rap. Tyler goes on to rob banks and trains as Sheffield tries to clear his name. Tyler finally decides to give himself up to allow Sheffield to continue his romance with Mack.

d, Wallace Fox; w, G.A. Durlam (based on a story by Will Beale); ph, Archie Stout.

Western   (PR:A MPAA:NR)

PARTNERS OF THE TRAIL**   (1944) 57m MON bw

Johnny Mack Brown (Nevada), Raymond Hatton (Sandy), Christine McIntyre (Kate), Craig Woods (Joel), Robert Frazer (Edwards), Harry F. Price (Dobbey), Jack Ingram (Trigger), Lynton Brent (Lem), Marshall Reed (Baker), Ben Corbett (Duke), Steve Clark (Cobly), Lloyd Ingraham (Applegate), Ted Mapes.

Brown and Hatton are U.S. marshals trying to uncover a reason for the wanton murders of ranchers. The trail leads them to Ingraham and his band of outlaws, who provide plenty of gunplay and action to keep the film mildly entertaining.

p, Scott R. Dunlap; d, Lambert Hillyer; w, Frank H. Young; ph, Harry Neumann; ed, Carl Helm; md, Edward Kay.

Western   (PR:A MPAA:NR)

PARTS: THE CLONUS HORROR   (SEE: CLONUS HORROR, THE, 1979)

PARTY, THE**   (1968) 98m Mirisch-Geoffrey/UA c

Peter Sellers (Hrundi V. Bakshi), Claudine Longet (Michele Monet), Marge Champion (Rosalind Dunphy), Sharron Kimberly (Princess Helena), Denny Miller (Wyoming Bill Kelso), Gavin MacLeod (C.S. Divot), Buddy Lester (Davey Kane), Corinne Cole (Janice Kane), J. Edward McKinley (Fred Clutterbuck, Studio Head), Fay McKenzie (Alice Clutterbuck), Kathe Green (Molly Clutterbuck), Carol Wayne (June Warren), Tom Quine (Congressman Dunphy), Timothy Scott (Gore Pontoon), Elianne Nadeau (Wiggy), Al Checco (Bernard Stein), Steve Franken (Levinson), James Lanphier (Harry), Jerry Martin (Bradford), Danielle De Metz (Stella D'Angelo), Dick Crockett (Wells), Frances Davis (Maid), Allen Jung (Cook), Herb Ellis (Film Director), Natalie Borisova, Jean Carson, Paul Ferrara, Ken Wales.

Sellers is an actor from India who is brought to Hollywood to star in "Son of Gunga Din" and proceeds to destroy more property than an L.A. earthquake. When Sellers manages to blow up the film's most expensive set, the producer has him blackballed, but things get mixed up and the actor gets an invitation to the producer's party. The slapstick comes fast and furious as Sellers breaks up the party and demolishes the producer's mansion. With PINK PANTHER director Blake Edwards at the helm, it's not surprising that Sellers' character is an Indian version of Inspector Clouseau without any of the charm. The slapstick script quickly runs out of gas thanks to the one-joke story line and Blake's uninspired direction.

p&d, Blake Edwards; w, Edwards, Tom Waldman, Frank Waldman (based on a story by Edwards); ph, Lucien Ballard (Panavision, DeLuxe Color); m, Henry Mancini; ed, Ralph Winters; prod d, Fernando Carrere; cos, Jack Bear; spec eff, Norman Breedlove; m/l, "Nothing to Lose," Mancini, Don Black (sung by Claudine Longet); makeup, Allan Snyder, Lynn Reynolds.

Comedy   (PR:A MPAA:NR)

PARTY CRASHERS, THE*½   (1958) 78m PAR bw

Mark Damon (Twig Webster), Bobby Driscoll (Josh Bickford), Connie Stevens (Barbara Nickerson), Frances Farmer (Mrs. Bickford), Doris Dowling (Mrs. Webster), Gary Gray (Don Hartlow), Bob Padget (Mumps Thornberg), Skip Torgerson (Bill Leeds), Joe Sonessa (Larry Bronsen), Gene Perrson (Stan Osgood), Denver Pyle (Mr. Bickford), Walter Brooke (Mr. Webster), Cathy Lewis (Mrs. Nickerson), Onslow Stevens (Mr. Nickerson), Theodora Davitt (Sharon Lee).

Nothing new in this melodramatic trash about juvenile delinquents. Damon is the leader of a gang of spoiled suburban jerks who cruise in their sports cars looking for parties to crash. The reason behind these kids' bad habits is their parents' bad habits. (But the big question is who is behind the badly-written script?) This is made clear when Damon and friends crash a motel party and find Damon's mother, Dowling, the drunken center of attention. This shocking sight changes Damon's party habits and the adults realize what a poor example they have been setting. Frances Farmer, in her first film role since 1942, plays a concerned parent, and Oscar-winning child actor Bobby Driscoll, who would later become a drug addict, is a square teenager.

p, William Alland; d, Bernard Girard; w, Girard, Dan Lundberg (based on a story by Girard); ph, Eddie Fitzgerald; ed, Everett Douglas; art d, Tambi Larsen.

Drama   (PR:A MPAA:NR)

PARTY GIRL*½   (1930) 67m TIF bw

Douglas Fairbanks, Jr. (Jay Rountree), Jeanette Loff (Ellen Powell), Judith Barrie (Leeda Cather), Marie Prevost (Diana Hoster), John St. Polis (John Rountree), Lucien Prival (Paul Nucast), Sammy Blum (Sam Metten), Harry Northrup (Robert Lowry), Almeda Fowler (Maude Lindsay), Hal Price (Lew Albans), Charles Giblyn

(Lawrence Doyle), Sidney D'Albrook *(Investigator)*, Florence Dudley *(Miss Manning)*, Earl Burtnett's Biltmore Orchestra and Trio.

A Times Square escort service run by Fowler supplies girls for businessmen's parties. Prevost is the No. 1 party girl and Loff is a former escort who has become a secretary. Fairbanks, the son of a company president, is blackmailed into marrying one of the girls, who dies when she falls out of a window while trying to escape from the police. Thanks to censors and the morals of the time we're supposed to believe that these party girls just danced and drank with these anxious businessmen. A little too dated and corny to be entertaining. Prevost, a successful silent star, couldn't find her niche in sound films and began drinking heavily, which helped bring on her death in 1937.

p, Edward Halperin; d, Victor Halperin; w, Monte Katterjohn, George Draney, V. Halperin (based on the story by Katterjohn, V. Halperin); ph, Henry Cronjager, Robert Newhard; ed, Russell Schoengarth; cos, Helen Rose; m/l, Harry Stoddard, Marcy Klauber.

Drama **(PR:A MPAA:NR)**

PARTY GIRL*½** (1958) 99m Euterpe/MGM c

Robert Taylor *(Thomas Farrell)*, Cyd Charisse *(Vicki Gaye)*, Lee J. Cobb *(Rico Angelo)*, John Ireland *(Louis Canetto)*, Kent Smith *(Jeffery Stewart)*, Claire Kelly *(Genevieve)*, Corey Allen *(Cookie)*, Lewis Charles *(Danny Rimett)*, David Opatoshu *(Lou Forbes)*, Kem Dibbs *(Joey Vulner)*, Patrick McVey *(O'Malley)*, Barbara Lang *(Tall Blonde Party Girl)*, Myrna Hansen *(Joy Hampton)*, Betty Utey *(Showgirl)*, Jack Lambert *(Nick)*, Sam McDaniel *(Jesse)*, Floyd Simmons *(Assistant Prosecutor)*, Sydney Smith *(Judge Bookwell)*, Rusty Lane *(Judge John A. Dasen)*, Michael Dugan *(Jenks)*, Irving Greenberg, Richard Devine, Georges Saurel *(Rico's Hoods)*, Carl Thayler, Mike Pierce, John Franco, Ken Perry *(Cookie's Henchmen)*, Barrie Chase, Sanita Pelkey, Sandy Warner *(Showgirls)*, Burt Douglas *(P.A. Voice)*, Harry Tom McKenna *(Politician)*, Erich von Stroheim, Jr. *(Police Lieutenant)*, Herbert Armstrong *(Intern)*, Carmen Phillips *(Rico's Secretary)*, Pat Cawley *(Farrell's Secretary)*, Marshall Bradford *(District Attorney)*, Tom Hernandez *(Sketch Artist)*, David McMahon *(Guard)*, Andrew Buck *(Chauffeur)*, Aaron Saxon *(Frankie Gasto)*, Vaughn Taylor *(Dr. Caderman)*, Peter Bourne *(Cab Driver)*, Vito Scotti *(Hotel Clerk)*, Ralph Smiley *(Hotel Proprietor)*, Herbert Lytton *(Judge Alfino)*, Benny Rubin *(Mr. Field)*, Paul Keast *(Judge Davers)*, Jerry Schumacher *(Newsboy)*, John Damler *(Detective)*, Geraldine Wall *(Day Matron)*, Robert B. Williams *(Guard)*, Dolores Reed *(Woman)*, David Garcie *(Newsman)*, Harry Hines *(Newsboy)*, Jack Gargan *(Officer)*, Margaret Bert *(Wardrobe Woman)*, Hy Anzel *(Man)*, Maggie O'Bryne *(Woman)*.

A hard-hitting crime drama, PARTY GIRL is a portrait of the Roaring Twenties in Chicago and, in particular, the story of a criminal lawyer, Taylor, who represents crime czar Cobb whose role is based on the bestial Al Capone. Taylor is a brilliant attorney, crippled and walking with a cane, an affliction he uses to good ploy when addressing juries, pleading the cases of Cobb's lethal underlings. He gets hit man Ireland off on a murder charge. To celebrate, Cobb gives Ireland a big party, inviting dancers from one of his nightclubs, including leggy, sexy Charisse. Ireland makes a play for the curvacious showgirl but she rejects him, more interested in keeping company with the aloof Taylor. The lawyer slowly gets involved with Charisse and she begins working on him to quit Cobb and his mob and go straight. He tells her he's married to a woman who has rejected him because he is a cripple, even though he goes on supporting his wife. Disillusioned and hating the world, Taylor begins to soften as his affection deepens for Charisse. He then resolves to go to Sweden where experts claim they can repair his leg. Following the operation, he walks on two good legs and right into the arms of Charisse. The showgirl has been loyal to him, despite the fact that she's been visited by Taylor's wife, Kelly, and been told that she has no legal claim to the rich attorney, and now that her husband has been cured she intends to hold onto him. Taylor, however, plans to divorce his shrew of a wife and marry Charisse. He is also ready to break with Cobb but he takes on one more case. The defendant, one of Cobb's top guns, is killed along with other goons in a gang war and Taylor is wounded in the gun battle. Police arrest him as a material witness and prosecutor Smith tells him that he will go to prison and never see party girl Charisse again unless he testifies against Cobb. Taylor demands that Charisse be given police protection and Smith agrees. But when Taylor begins to reveal the mob secrets, Cobb's goons grab Charisse and the attorney finally goes to the crime boss and tries to reason with him. Cobb only sneers and tells Taylor that he's going to reduce Charisse's lovely face to pulp with acid but Taylor smashes him and the acid splashes onto Cobb, sending him reeling backward in screaming agony, toward a bank of windows. Police outside spray the gangster and he falls dead with myriad bullets in his corpulent body. Taylor and Charisse embrace, finally free of the mob. PARTY GIRL offers only a standard story but director Ray makes more of it through clever setups and inventive techniques, drawing forth excellent performances from Taylor (who is essaying a role loosely based on Dixie Davis, lawyer for mob boss Dutch Schultz of New York who later turned informant and who married a beautiful showgirl). Cobb turns out a "Wild-Man-of-Borneo" performance where he not only eats the scenery but spits it out and chews on it again and again. Charisse, who performs two sensuous nightclub dances, does a commendable job with her cliched role. Ireland is only a hulking thug hissing lascivious comments toward Charisse when on screen, calling her "Puss." Taylor was 47 years old at the time of this film, his last for MGM after serving the studio for 24 years.

p, Joe Pasternak; d, Nicholas Ray; w, George Wells (based on a story by Leo Katcher); ph, Robert Bronner (CinemaScope, Metrocolor); m, Jeff Alexander; ed, John McSweeney, Jr.; art d, William A. Horning, Randall Duell; set d, Henry Grace, Richard Pefferle; cos, Helen Rose; spec eff, Lee LeBlanc; ch, Robert Sidney; m/l, Nicholas Brodszky, Sammy Cahn (title theme sung by Tony Martin); makeup, William Tuttle.

Crime Drama **(PR:C MPAA:NR)**

PARTY GIRLS FOR THE CANDIDATE (SEE: CANDIDATE, THE, 1964)

PARTY HUSBAND* (1931) 73m WB-FN bw

Dorothy Mackaill *(Laura)*, James Rennie *(Jay Hogarth)*, Dorothy Peterson *(Kate)*, Donald Cook *(Horace Purcell)*, Mary Doran *(Bee Canfield)*, Joe Donahue *(Pat)*, Helen Ware *(Mrs. Duell)*, Paul Porcasi *(Henri Renard)*, Gilbert Emery *(Ben Holliday)*, Barbara Weeks *(Sally)*.

Rennie and Mackaill are a husband and wife who decide they'll try a modern approach to their marriage. The couple agree that they'll both live their own lives with no questions asked, but after a while things begin to fall apart. Rennie spends the night with his wife's friend, Peterson, and his wife spends the night on a boat with her boss, but she reneges at the last moment. Mackaill's mother, Doran, shows up to straighten out her daughter's and son-in-law's relationship.

d, Clarence Badger; w, Charles Kenyon (based on a novel by Geoffrey Barnes); ph, Sid Hickox; ed, Frank Ware.

Comedy/Drama **(PR:A MPAA:NR)**

PARTY PARTY zero (1983, Brit.) 98m Film and General-A&M Sound/FOX c

Daniel Peacock, Karl Howman, Perry Fenwick, Sean Chapman, Phoebe Nicholls, Gary Olsen, Clive Mantle, Caroline Quentin, Kim Thomson, Kate Williams, Kenneth Farrington, Philip Martin Brown, Annabel Mednick, Sallyanne Law, Sarah London, Paul Mari, Harvey Hillyer, Michele Winstanley, Peter Lovstrom, Robin Hayter, Debbie Bishop, Nick Berry, Ann Somers, Sharon Maiden, Geoffrey Drew, Graham Weston, Pat Ashton.

A confused British "comedy" about a young lad who throws a party while his parents are away. Of course they come home. . .and are oh so shocked. Recalling the dopiness of the CARRY ON series, PARTY PARTY is set somewhere in the mythical past of working-class England, occasionally jarred into the present by Elvis Costello music. Nothing here seems to fit. Financed by the Film Division of A&M Records, it was apparently conceived as a tool to sell a record which boasts hit tunes of 1982. A pathetic movie epitomizing everything that is wrong with the British film industry. Begun as a student film short, it should have stayed that way.

p, Davina Belling, Clive Parsons; d, Terry Winsor; w, Daniel Peacock, Winsor; ph, Sydney Macartney; ed, Eddy Joseph; art d, Deborah Gillingham.

Comedy **(PR:C MPAA:NR)**

PARTY WIRE** (1935) 66m COL bw

Jean Arthur *(Marge Oliver)*, Victor Jory *(Matthew Putnam)*, Helen Lowell *(Nettie Putnam)*, Charley Grapewin *(Will Oliver)*, Robert Allen *(Roy Daniels)*, Clara Blandick *(Mathilda Sherman)*, Geneva Mitchell *(Irene Sherman)*, Maude Eburne *(Clara West)*, Edward Le Saint *(Mason)*, Charles Middleton *(Johnson)*.

Jory has returned to his home town to run the dairy business he inherited. Being the town's most eligible bachelor, Jory is the center of attention. When he begins seeing Arthur, the town gossips cause them many problems after misconstruing information gathered by eavesdropping on a party line.

p, Robert North; d, Erle C. Kenton; w, Ethel Hill, John Howard Lawson (based on a story by Bruce Manning, Vera Caspary); ph, Al Seigler; ed, Viola Lawrence.

Comedy/Drama **(PR:A MPAA:NR)**

PARTY'S OVER, THE*½ (1934) 63m COL bw

Stuart Erwin *(Bruce)*, Ann Sothern *(Ruth)*, Arline Judge *(Phyllis)*, Chick Chandler *(Martin)*, Patsy Kelly *(Mabel)*, Catharine Doucet *(Sarah)*, Marjorie Lytell *(Betty)*, Henry Travers *(Theodore)*, William Bakewell *(Clay)*, Esther Muir *(Tillie)*, Rollo Lloyd *(Fred)*.

Erwin is a young accountant who finds himself supporting his whole family. His brother and sister marry people with no money and look to their brother for handouts. The same goes for Erwin's father. Problems arise when the family tries to interfere with Erwin's romance with Sothern. In the end, Erwin dumps his mooching family and gets his romance with Sothern on the right track.

d, Walter Lang; w, S.K. Lauren (based on a play by Daniel Kusell); ph, Benjamin Kline; ed, Viola Lawrence.

Comedy/Drama **(PR:A MPAA:NR)**

PARTY'S OVER, THE* (1966, Brit.) 94m Tricastle/AA bw

Oliver Reed *(Moise)*, Clifford David *(Carson)*, Ann Lynn *(Libby)*, Catherine Woodville *(Nina)*, Louise Sorel *(Melina)*, Mike Pratt *(Geronimo)*, Maurice Browning *(Tutzi)*, Jonathan Burn *(Phillip)*, Roddy Maude-Roxby *(Hector)*, Annette Robertson *(Fran)*, Mildred Mayne *(Countess)*, Alison Seebohm *(Ada)*, Barbara Lott *(Almoner)*, Eddie Albert *(Ben)*.

An overly melodramatic, moronic film about a man going to England to find his fiancee. David is sent by the girl's father, Albert, to find her and he discovers that she became involved with a group of beatniks and has disappeared. The story line drags as David goes through the tpyical paces to trace the whereabouts of his fiancee. The trail ends at the local morgue where David learns that she died in a drunken fall, after which one of the beatniks made love to her without noticing that she was dead. David sends her body back to her father and spares him the details of her demise.

p, Anthony Perry; d, Guy Hamilton; w, Marc Behm; ph, Larry Pizer; m, John Barry; ed, John Bloom; art d, Peggy Gick; m/l, title song, Barry (sung by Annie Ross).

Drama **(PR:O MPAA:NR)**

PAS DE MENTALITE (SEE: WORLD IN MY POCKET, THE, 1962, Fr./Ital./W. Ger.)

PAS QUESTION LE SEMEDI   (SEE: IMPOSSIBLE ON SATURDAY, 1966, Fr./Israel)

PASAZERKA   (SEE: PASSENGER, THE, 1970, Pol.)

PASQUALINO SETTEBELLEZZE   (SEE: SEVEN BEAUTIES, 1976, Ital.)

PASQUALINO: SEVEN BEAUTIES   (SEE: SEVEN BEAUTIES, 1976, Ital.)

PASS TO ROMANCE   (SEE: HI, BEAUTIFUL, 1944)

PASSAGE, THE zero   (1979, Brit.) 99m GEN/UA c

Anthony Quinn (*The Basque*), James Mason (*Prof. Bergson*), Malcolm McDowell (*Von Berkow*), Patricia Neal (*Ariel Bergson*), Kay Lenz (*Leah Bergson*), Christopher Lee (*Head Gypsy*), Michael Lonsdale (*Renoudot*), Marcel Bozzuffi (*Perea*), Paul Clemens (*Paul Bergson*), Rose Alba (*Madame*), Neville Jason (*Lt. Reincke*), Robert Rhys (*Son of the Gypsy*), James Broadbent (*German Soldier*), Peter Arne (*French Guide*), Frederick Jaeger (*German Major*), Terence York (*1st German Sentry*), Terence Maidment (*2nd German Sentry*).

Quinn is a Frenchman who takes American scientist Mason and his family through the mountains to Spain and freedom. SS officer McDowell heads the hunt for the scientist and leads Quinn and Mason in the uninspired acting category. The script is a jumbled bag of war movie cliches, and director Thompson seems to have been asleep through most of the production.

p, John Quested, Maurice Binder, Lester Goldsmith; d, J. Lee Thompson; w, Bruce Nicolaysen (based on his book *Perilous Passage*); ph, Mike Reed (Technovision); m, Michael J. Lewis; ed, Alan Strachan.

War Drama   **(PR:O MPAA:R)**

PASSAGE FROM HONG KONG**   (1941) 61m WB bw

Lucille Fairbanks, Keith Douglas, Paul Cavanagh, Richard Ainley, Marjorie Gateson, Gloria Holden, Lumsden Hare, Tom Stevenson, Boyd Irwin, Chester Gan.

Barely entertaining programmer has Douglas, a writer of crime stories, inventing a story that involves him in a murder, in an attempt to woo Fairbanks. The fact that the film was set in Hong Kong practically on the eve of the Japanese invasion in WW II did little to stir vitality in this loony tune.

p, William Jacobs; d, D. Ross Lederman; w, Fred Niblo, Jr. (based on the story "Agony Column" by Earl Derr Biggers); ph, Allen G. Seigler; ed, Frederick Richards.

Comedy/Crime   **(PR:A MPAA:NR)**

PASSAGE HOME*½   (1955, Brit.) 102m Group/GFD bw

Anthony Steel (*1st Mate Vosper*), Peter Finch (*Capt. Lucky Ryland*), Diane Cilento (*Ruth Elton*), Cyril Cusack (*Bohannon*), Geoffrey Keen (*Ike*), Hugh Griffith (*Pettigrew*), Duncan Lamont (*Llewellyn*), Gordon Jackson (*Burne*), Bryan Forbes (*Shorty*), Michael Craig (*Burton*), Robert Brown (*Shane*), Martin Benson (*Guiterres*), Patrick McGoohan (*McIsaacs*), Michael Bryant, Sam Kydd, Glyn Houston, Patrick Westwood, George Woodbridge, John Warren, Ian Whittaker, Scott Harold, Arthur Lovegrove, Leonard White, Peter Ventham, Gerald Anderson, Philip Ray.

Old standby melodrama has attractive blonde Cilento a passenger on a ship bound for England from South America. Tyrannical captain Finch tries to force himself on her but she is rescued by first mate Steel. Finch locks himself in his cabin and drinks until a storm allows him to regain his pride by saving the ship. A good cast and a fast pace cover up the holes in this effort, scripted by a writer who is also a sailor, Fairchild.

p, Julian Wintle; d, Roy Baker; w, William Fairchild (based on the novel by Richard Armstrong); ph, Geoffrey Unsworth.

Drama   **(PR:A MPAA:NR)**

PASSAGE OF LOVE   (SEE: TIME LOST AND TIME REMEMBERED, 1966, Brit.)

PASSAGE TO MARSEILLE*½   (1944) 110m WB bw

Humphrey Bogart (*Matrac*), Claude Rains (*Capt. Freycinet*), Michele Morgan (*Paula*), Philip Dorn (*Renault*), Sydney Greenstreet (*Maj. Duval*), Peter Lorre (*Marius*), George Tobias (*Petit*), Victor Francen (*Capt. Patain Malo*), Helmut Dantine (*Garou*), John Loder (*Manning*), Konstantin Shayne (*1st Mate*), Monte Blue (*2nd Mate*), Corinna Mura (*Singer*), Eduardo Ciannelli (*Chief Engineer*), Vladimir Sokoloff (*Grandpere*), Charles La Torre (*Lt. Lenoir*), Hans Conried (*Jourdain*), Mark Stevens (*Lt. Hastings*), Louis Mercier (*Engineer*), Billy Roy (*Mess Boy*), Donald Stuart (*Military Driver*), Walter Bonn (*Prison Official*), Carmen Beretta (*Petit's Wife*), Diane DuBois (*Petit's Daughter*), Jean Del Val (*Raoul*), Alex Papanao (*Lookout*), Peter Miles (*Jean*), Raymond St. Albin (*Medical Officer*), Peter Camlin (*French Sergeant*), Anatol Frikin (*Crazy Convict*), Frank Puglia (*Older Guard*), Harry Cording (*Chief Guard*), Adrienne D'Ambricourt (*Mayor's Wife*), Fred Essler (*Mayor*).

Curtiz offers a slam-bang action film with adventurer Bogart in the lead, one which has a tricky, flash-backing plot but is nevertheless exciting and absorbing all the way. The film opens as a squadron of Free French bombers takes off at night from an airfield in England en route to bomb Germany during the early days of WW II. One plane in the squadron always strays off course on the return flight back to England, the one carrying bombardier Bogart, so that he can drop a letter to his small son and wife, Morgan, who live in Nazi-occupied France. Loder, a journalist, picks up the story about Bogart when doing an article concerned with the Free French squadron. Rains, captain of the group, relates Bogart's story to Loder which

is then shown in flashback. A group of prisoners who have escaped the dreaded prison at Cayenne in French Guiana are picked up by a passing French freighter commanded by Francen, who is loyal to Free France but who hides such sympathies from fascist-minded Greenstreet, a French officer sypathetic to Vichy France and Marshall Petain, the collaborative government working with the Nazis occupying most of France. The rescued men claim they are survivors of a torpedoed ship but their true identities are learned in a second flashback (within the first flashback). They are Bogart, a French journalist who opposed the Nazi takeover of his country from within and such traitors as Pierre Laval, Lorre, a pickpocket, Dantine, a killer, Dorn, an army deserter, Tobias, an oafish farmer. In the second flashback, showing the prisoners at the miserable Cayenne prison, another flashback (a third within the second) describes how Bogart lived in Paris, married Morgan, and became a fugitive journalist while fighting fascists. Then, in a series of flash-forwards, Bogart and the escaped prisoners—they have fled their prison to fight for Free France upon hearing about the war—are shown on board the freighter which is headed for Marseille. News comes of France's surrender to Germany and Greenstreet insists that the ship's precious cargo of nickel ore be delivered to Marseille and into the hands of the fascists. Francen is opposed to this, intending to take the cargo to England. Greenstreet and his fascist henchmen then openly battle Francen, Rains, Bogart, and the other supporters of Free France for control of the ship. Bogart and his men win but the ship is attacked by a Nazi bomber which strafes the ship and kills several men, including Lorre, thief turned patriot. Bogart jumps to a machine gun and shoots the enemy plane out of the sky and then the German survivors are gunned down in the water rather than rescued. In another flash-forward, Bogart, Tobias, Dorn, and Dantine are shown as members of the Free French bomber squadron fighting the Germans during WW II. Loder completes his story when Bogart's plane returns, shot up and with Bogart dead. Rains reads the last letter Bogart has written to his small son, one in which he encourages the boy to believe in freedom, while Bogart is buried on a cliff overlooking the English Channel. Then Rains announces firmly: "That letter will be delivered!" The fadeout shot shows Free French bombers headed for Germany, one breaking away to deliver Bogart's letter to his waiting widow and son. Although Curtiz draws superb performances from his great cast, many of whom appeared in Warner Bros. recent smash hit, CASABLANCA (1942) (Bogart, Lorre, Greenstreet, Dantine, Rains, Mura, and Mercier), the story line is more than a bit confusing because of the unwieldly flashbacks used to tell the tale. Yet the great action director packs the film with marvelous adventure and exciting scenes, not to mention stirring with frenzy the steaming cauldron of patriotism with a giant ladle. Bogart, in the shipboard scenes, did not wear his customary part-toupee to make himself look aged and worn. Warners attempted to time the release of the film with what the studio thought would be the invasion of southern France, but when these landings did not take place the film was distributed without an international news event to boost the production (as had been the case with CASABLANCA, released just after American troops landed in Africa and Allied leaders met in that African city for top-level conferences). Howe's gritty photography helped set the mood and Steiner's music dynamically established the patriotic fervor of the cast. Warner Bros. bought this story by Nordhoff and Hall, a novella appearing in *The Atlantic Monthly*, for the then unheard-of price of $75,000. These writers commanded such financial attention due to their immense successes in the past with books that were turned into the blockbuster movies MUTINY ON THE BOUNTY (1935) and THE HURRICANE (1937).

p, Hal B. Wallis; d, Michael Curtiz; w, Casey Robinson, Jack Moffitt (based on the novel *Men Without a Country* by Charles Nordhoff, James Norman Hall); ph, James Wong Howe; m, Max Steiner; ed, Owen Marks; art d, Carl Jules Weyl; set d, George James Hopkins; cos, Leah Rhodes; spec eff, Jack Cosgrove, Edwin B. Du Par, Byron Haskin, E. Roy Davidson, Rex Wimpy; m/l, Steiner, Ned Washington; makeup, Perc Westmore.

War Drama   **Cas.**   **(PR:A MPAA:NR)**

PASSAGE WEST*½   (1951) 80m PAR c (GB: HIGH VENTURE)

John Payne (*Pete Black*), Dennis O'Keefe (*Jacob Karns*), Arleen Whelan (*Rose Billings*), Frank Faylen (*Curly*), Mary Anderson (*Myra Johnson*), Peter Hanson (*Michael Karns*), Richard Rober (*Mike*), Griff Barnett (*Papa Ludwig*), Dooley Wilson (*Rainbow*), Mary Field (*Miss Swingate*), Richard Travis (*Ben Johnson*), Mary Beth Hughes (*Nellie*), Arthur Hunnicutt (*Pop Brennan*), Lillian Bronson (*Mom Brenna*) Ilka Gruning (*Mama Ludwig*), Estelle Carr (*Minna Karns*), Susan Whitney (*Lea Johnson*), Paul Fierro (*Ramon*), Clint Stuart (*Burk*).

A low-key western with O'Keefe as a minister leading a wagon train to the territories. A group of escaped convicts join the train and force the settlers to run their wagons at a perilous pace. When the group arrives in California, the convicts decide to stay on with the settlers, influenced by their faith and example. But when it's learned that gold has been discovered, the convicts return to their old ways. Convict Payne then sacrifices his own and his fellow cons lives to destroy the gold mine and save the settlers.

p, William Pine, William Thomas; d, Lewis R. Foster; w, Foster (based on a story by Nedrick Young); ph, Loyal Griggs (Technicolor); m, Mahlon Merrick; ed, Howard Smith.

Western   **(PR:A MPAA:NR)**

PASSAGES FROM JAMES JOYCE'S FINNEGANS WAKE   (SEE: FINNEGAN'S WAKE, 1967)

PASSENGER, THE*½   (1970, Pol.) 60m Kamera Film Unit/Altura bw (PASAZERKA)

Aleksandra Slaska (*Liza*), Anna Ciepielewska (*Marta*), Jan Kreczmar (*Walter*), Marek Walczewski (*Tadeusz*), Maria Koscialkowska (*Inga*), Irena Malkiewicz ("*Ober*"), Leon Pietraszkiewicz (*Commandant*), Janusz Bylczynski (*Kapo*), A. Golebiowska (*Female Commandant*), John Rees (*English Narrator*), Vanda Jones

(Voice of Liza), Barbara Horawianka, Anna Jaraczowna, Andrzej Krasicki, S. Musial, L. Olszewska, W. Swaryczewska, Zbigniew Szymborski, Barbara Walkowna, Kazimierz Rudzki, Boguslaw Sochnacki, Elzbieta Czyzewska, Maria Ciesielska.

Slaska, a former overseer at Auschwitz and an SS member, is reunited with Ciepielewska, a prisoner in the concentration camp. The two had become friendly when Slaska arranged for the prisoner to meet with her lover, a fellow prisoner. Slaska also reveals the jealousy she felt for the woman's relationship, and how she used her power to control the prisoner. Before the film was completed, director Andrzej Munk was killed in an auto accident. The unfinished picture, later pieced together by his associates, could possibly have been a masterpiece had he lived. It received the International Critics Award at Cannes in 1964, a year after its Polish release. (Dubbed into English.)

d, Andrzej Munk; w, Zofia Posmysz-Piasecka, Munk (based on the book *Pasazerka* by Posmysz-Piasecka); ph, Krzysztof Winiewicz (Dyaliscope); m, Tadeusz Baird; ed, Zofia Dwornik, Witold Lesiewicz; md, Stanislaw Wislocki; art d, Jerzy Possack; set d, Tadeusz Wybult; cos, Wieslawa Chojkowska; makeup, Teresa Tomaszewska; English version, John Minchinton.

Drama **(PR:O MPAA:NR)**

PASSENGER, THE**** (1975, Ital.) 123m CIC-Concordia-C.I.P.I-Champion/MGM-UA c (AKA: PROFESSION: REPORTER)

Jack Nicholson *(David Locke)*, Maria Schneider *(Girl)*, Jennie Runacre *(Rachel Locke)*, Ian Hendry *(Martin Knight)*, Stephen Berkoff *(Stephen)*, Ambroise Bia *(Achebe)*, Jose Maria Cafarel *(Hotel Keeper)*, James Campbell *(Witch Doctor)*, Manfred Spies *(German Stranger)*, Jean Baptiste Tiemele *(Murderer)*, Angel Del Pozo *(Police Inspector)*, Chuck Mulvehill *(Robertson)*.

A visually stunning adventure which is rooted in philosophical meanderings but comes across as a portrait of a character stuck in a sand trap who is miraculously handed a way out. Nicholson is the imprisoned Locke, a reporter sent to Northern Africa on a mission to interview some guerrillas. After a battle with a Jeep that refuses to travel through sand, Nicholson winds up in a blisteringly hot run-down hotel. He is confused with another hotel guest, Mulvehill, to whom he bears a striking resemblance. When he discovers Mulvehill dead in his room, Nicholson is presented his chance on a silver platter. He switches passport photos, personal belongings, and places Mulvehill in his own room. Looking through "his" daily planner, he finds a number of women's names and various appointments. Curious, he decides to keep the rendezvous and discovers that Mulvehill was a gun runner who supplied foreign governments with plans and documents. At one point he meets with a terrorist group, hands over the necessary papers, accepts the money, and then apologizes (halfheartedly, and lucky not to be discovered) for failing to get the antiaircraft guns. In the meantime he has met Schneider, referred to only as "the girl." They are drawn together, she seeming to have no life of her own (we are told she is an architecture student) and he trying to understand his. Though Nicholson's wife and friend are searching for him, they never seem to be in the right place at the right time, or, if they are, they pass him without realizing it. Nicholson and Schneider take off together in his convertible, traveling to a small Spanish hotel after a brush with inquisitive police and a chase. Later, in the hotel, Schneider leaves Nicholson alone on the bed and through his window a car can be seen approaching. An African government official emerges along with some others as the camera begins a seven-minute-long tracking shot from the hotel room, through the window bars, and outside. A muffled crack is heard; it may be a car backfiring or gunshot. Eventually the police arrive with Nicholson's wife and Schneider. Nicholson is seen lying on the bed, lifeless. Both women are questioned as to his identity—his wife fails to recognize him, while Schneider confirms that she knows him. THE PASSENGER could probably be analyzed until the end of time, without getting anywhere. What is more interesting than the "whys" and "hows" of the film (the exact nature of his death, for example, doesn't seem important) is the "where" and "when." Nicholson and Schneider are very much a part of their environments whether that be the sandy wastelands of Northern Africa or the exquisite Gaudi architecture of Barcelona. Schneider's character has no history—it just is—a quality shared by Nicholson's acquired character. THE PASSENGER, for Antonioni, marks a return to his earlier successes and fully accomplishes the experiments he attempted in his other English-speaking films—the overrated BLOW-UP and the embarrassingly unperceptive ZABRISKIE POINT. Nicholson is perhaps the chief factor to this success, providing Antonioni, for the first time, with an expert actor to bring the intellect in the script down to a real, physical form, much the way that Brando (and again Schneider) worked on Bertolucci's sensibilities in LAST TANGO IN PARIS. THE PASSENGER also marked the first time Antonioni worked from someone else's story, though he did work on the script. From the original by the 25-year-old Mark Peploe came a collaboration with *Signs and Meaning in the Cinema* author Peter Wollen, originally titled PROFESSION: REPORTER and FATAL EXIT. What finally emerged is a hauntingly photographed journey for answers that don't exist and one of the most highly praised European films of all time.

p, Carlo Ponti; d, Michaelangelo Antonioni; w, Mark Peploe, Peter Wollen, Antonioni (based on a story by Peploe); ph, Luciano Tovoli (Metrocolor); ed, Franco Arcali, Antonioni; art d, Piero Poletto; set d, Osvaldo Desideri; cos, Louise Stjensward; makeup, Franco Freda.

Drama **(PR:C MPAA:PG)**

PASSENGER TO LONDON* (1937, Brit.) 57m FOX British bw

John Warwick *(Frank Drayton)*, Jenny Laird *(Barbara Lane)*, Paul Neville *(Vautel)*, Ivan Wilmot *(Veinberg)*, Aubrey Pollock *(Sir James Garfield)*, Victor Hagen *(Carlton)*, Nigel Barrie *(Sir Donald Frame)*, Sybil Brooke, Dorothy Dewhurst.

A train traveling from Eastern Europe to London is the setting for this unimaginative spy thriller. Warwick is the hero, saving the British empire by keeping secret documents from falling into the hands of the enemy. Nothing that hasn't been done better a hundred times over.

p&d, Lawrence Huntington; w, David Evans; ph, Stanley Grant.

Spy Drama **(PR:A MPAA:NR)**

PASSING OF THE THIRD FLOOR BACK, THE*** (1936, Brit.) 80m GAU bw

Conrad Veidt *(The Stranger)*, Rene Ray *(Stasia)*, Frank Cellier *(Wright)*, Anna Lee *(Vivian Tompkin)*, John Turnbull *(Maj. Tompkin)*, Cathleen Nesbitt *(Mrs. Tompkin)*, Ronald Ward *(Chris Penny)*, Beatrix Lehmann *(Miss Kite)*, Jack Livesey *(Larkcomb)*, Sara Allgood *(Mrs. de Hooley)*, Mary Clare *(Mrs. Sharpe)*, Barbara Everest *(Cook)*, Alexander Sarner *(The Gramophone Man)*.

Decent film adaptation of a popular Victorian morality play has Veidt a mysterious and gentle looking stranger who appears out of the night to take a room in a rundown boarding house run by avaricious landlord Cellier. He takes the only vacancy, the room in the back on the third floor, and soon becomes involved in the lives and travails of the other, mostly pathetic denizens of the shabby boarding house. In addition to Cellier preying on the poverty of the residents, there's aging dowager Allgood, Lehmann as a wayward woman now bitterly facing the loss of her looks, and others with their own petty problems, jealousies, and bickerings. Veidt manages to untangle some of their woes and show them a better way to treat each other during a boat outing, but the next day they return to their old ways, Veidt disappears as mysteriously as he came, and Cellier's greed (and eye for young ladies) gets him murdered. Veidt is better than the film in this static version of a mostly forgotten play by the author of the Victorian classic comic novel *Three Men in a Boat*. Several of the supporting players also turn in strong performances, but none of them can help this film's stagebound manner and basic lack of plot. Veidt gives one of the best performances of a career filled with memorable films, and his Christ-like manner is much played down compared to the way it was usually done on stage. Veidt was an intense actor who buried himself in roles and he called this film, where he absolutely radiates sprituality "my most difficult role."

p, Ivor Montagu; d, Berthold Viertel; w, Michael Hogan, Alma Reville (based on the short story and play by Jerome K. Jerome); ph, Curt Courant; m, Louis Levy; ed, Derek N. Twist.

Drama **(PR:A MPAA:NR)**

PASSING SHADOWS** (1934, Brit.) 67m BL/FOX British bw

Edmund Gwenn *(David Lawrence)*, Barry Mackay *(Jim Lawrence)*, Aileen Marson *(Mary Willett)*, D.A. Clarke-Smith *(Stranger)*, Viola Lyel *(Mrs. Willett)*, Wally Patch *(Sergeant)*, John Turnbull *(Inspector Goodall)*, Barbara Everest *(Mrs. Lawrence)*, Barry O'Neill, Philip Hewland.

Mackay is set upon by a thief and he shoots the culprit. Believing that he killed the man, he is torn by guilt. His parents persuade him not to turn himself in, and it is eventually revealed that the thief did not die but encouraged Mackay to think him dead to escape a murder charge. Takes too long to get anywhere interesting.

p, Herbert Smith; d, Leslie Hiscott; w, Michael Barringer; ph, Alex Bryce.

Crime **(PR:A MPAA:NR)**

PASSING SHOW, THE (SEE: HOTEL VARIETY, 1933)

PASSING STRANGER, THE** (1954, Brit.) 84m Harlequin/IF-BL bw

Lee Patterson *(Chick)*, Diane Cilento *(Jill)*, Duncan Lamont *(Fred)*, Olive Gregg *(Meg)*, Liam Redmond *(Barney)*, Harold Lang *(Spicer)*, Mark Dignam *(Inspector)*, Paul Whitsun-Jones *(Lloyd)*, Alfie Bass *(Harry)*, Cameron Hall *(Maxie)*, George Cooper *(Charlie)*, Lyndon Brook *(Mike)*, Charles Leno, Leonard Williams, John Garside, Warren Mitchell, George Luscombe, Harry H. Corbett, Patrick Westwood, Russell Waters, Joe Sterne, John Pitt, John Fabian, Joby Blanshard.

Patterson is a deserter from the U.S. Army who joins, then leaves a gang of gunrunners. He falls in love with Cilento but they do not have enough money to go to America, so he rejoins the gang for a robbery to get the money. Lamont, Cilento's former boy friend, informs the police and they catch Patterson at the airport. Decent second feature tries hard but fails because of script limitations.

p, Anthony Simmons, Leon Clore, Ian Gibson-Smith; d, John Arnold; w, Simmons, Arnold (based on a story by Simmons); ph, Walter Lassally.

Crime **(PR:A MPAA:NR)**

PASSING THROUGH½** (1977) 105m Larry Clark c

Nathaniel Taylor *(Warmack)*, Clarence Muse *(Papa Harris)*, Pamela Jones *(Maya)*.

Taylor stars as a jazz musician engaged in a battle with some crooked record company executives who prefer to let violence and money rule their business. With the encouragement of his mystical grandfather, Muse, he turns to his African heritage for answers to his dilemma. A battle ensues between Taylor and the mobster-run company, resulting in the death of Taylor's close friend. Inspired by the past achievements of his black race, Taylor succeeds in overpowering the killers and emerging victorious. Muse, a 78-year-old actor who first appeared on screen in 1929, turns in a commanding performance as the wise old grandfather. Clark directed the film as a degree requirement at UCLA, and writer Lange later appeared as "Isaac" on TV's "The Love Boat."

d, Larry Clark; w, Ted Lange, Clark; ph, Roderick Young, George Geddis; m, Pan African People's Arkestra; ed, Clark.

Drama/Crime **(PR:O MPAA:NR)**

PASSION** (1954) 84m RKO c

Cornel Wilde *(Juan Obregon)*, Yvonne De Carlo *(Rosa Melo/Tonya Melo)*, Raymond Burr *(Capt. Rodriguez)*, Lon Chaney, Jr. *(Castro)*, Rodolfo Acosta *(Salvador Sandro)*, John Qualen *(Gaspar Melo)*, Anthony Caruso *(Sgt. Munoz)*, Frank de Kova *(Martinez)*, Peter Coe *(Colfre)*, John Dierkes *(Escobar)*, Richard Hale

(Don Domingo), Rozene Kemper (Grandmother Melo), Belle Mitchell (Senora Carrisa), Alex Montoya (Manuel Felipe), Zon Murray (Barca), Rosa Turich (Maraquita), Stuart Whitman (Bernal Vaquero), James Kirkwood (Don Rosendo), Robert Warwick (Money Lender).

In old California Wilde's parents are killed by bandits. The killers, led by Acosta, want to drive out all the ranchers. When the law can't do anything because of a lack of evidence, Wilde seeks justice on his own. He wipes out the gang and forces a confession from Acosta which police chief Burr hears.

p, Benedict Bogeaus; d, Allan Dwan; w, Joseph Leytes, Beatrice A. Dresher, Howard Estabrook (based on a story by Dresher, Leytes, Miguel Padilla); ph, John Alton (Technicolor); m, David Raskin; ed, Carl [Carlos] Lodato; md, Louis Forbes; art d, Van Nest Polglase; set d, John Sturtevant; cos, Gwen Wakeling.

Western　　　　　　　　　　　　　　　　　　**(PR:A MPAA:NR)**

PASSION**　　　　　　　　　(1968, Jap.) 90m Daiei c (MANJI)

Ayako Wakao (Misuko Tokumitsu), Kyoko Kishida (Sonoko Kakiuchi), Yusuke Kawazu (Eijiro Watanuki), Eiji Funakoshi (Kotaro Kakiuchi).

Released in Japan in 1964, this picture tells the story of housewife Kishida who falls in love with a beautiful female model. Their lesbian relationship is confused by the presence of the other woman's male lover, as well as Kishida's husband. A faked suicide pact, followed by an authentic one, leaves Kishida the only one alive out of the four.

p, Yonejiro Saito; d, Yasuzo Masumura; w, Kaneto Shindo; ph, Setsuo Kobayashi (Daiei Scope, Eastmancolor); m, Tadashi Yamauchi.

Drama　　　　　　　　　　　　　　　　　　**(PR:O MPAA:NR)**

PASSION, 1969　　　　(SEE: PASSION OF ANNA, THE, 1969, Swed.)

PASSION***½　　　　(1983, Fr./Switz.) 88m Sara-Sonimage-Films A2-Film et Video Productions-SSR/Artificial Eye-UA Classics c

Jerzy Radzilwilowicz, Hanna Schygulla, Isabelle Huppert, Michel Piccoli, Lazlo Szabo, Sophie Loucachevski, Patrick Bonnel, Myriam Roussel, Magaly Campos, Jean-Francois Stevenin, Barbara Tissier, Serge Desarnauds, Agi Banfalvi, Ezio Ambrosetti, Manuelle Baltazar, Sarah Beauchesne, Bertrand Theubet, Sarah Cohen-Sali, Catherine van Cauwenberghe, Sophie Maire, Cornelia Mandry, Cathy Marchand, Marie-Annick Abgrall, Rene Mennotier, Frantizek Mandik, Attila Bokor.

Radziwilowicz (MAN OF MARBLE, 1979) plays a cigar-smoking director (much like Godard) from Poland who is filming in the style of the great painters—Rembrandt, Delacroix, Goya, and El Greco. The film he is making is a study of light and image, but he is far behind schedule because he can never get the lighting right. A noisy parody of an Italian filmmaker keeps asking what the "story" is. The director places his faith in the Americans, who always come through. Schygulla is a motel owner whose image on a video screen becomes an obsession with Radziwilowicz. Huppert plays a stuttering factory worker who is trying to stir up a revolt among her coworkers. A commercial failure, PASSION is the second film from the "new" Godard after his self-imposed exile into Marxist filmmaking and French television. It is, however, a superb film with more narrative than one usually expects from Godard and a surprising amount of humor. PASSION also boasts an excellent international cast. In addition to Radziwilowicz, it includes Rainer Werner Fassbinder regular Hanna Schygulla in perhaps her most visually striking screen appearance ever. Isabelle Huppert whom Godard perviously cast in his EVERY MAN FOR HIMSELF (1980), and Michel Piccoli who starred opposite Brigitte Bardot in Godard's CONTEMPT (1963). Equal credit must go to Raoul Coutard, whose camerawork and lighting is the center of the entire film. (In French; English subtitles.)

p, Alain Sarde; d&w, Jean-Luc Godard; ph, Raoul Coutard (Eastmancolor); ed, Godard; art d, Serge Marzolff, Jean Bauer.

Drama　　　　　　　　　　　　　　　　　　**(PR:O MPAA:R)**

PASSION FLOWER*½　　　　　　　(1930) 78m MGM bw

Kay Francis (Dulce Morado), Kay Johnson (Katherine Pringle Wallace), Charles Bickford (Dan Wallace), Winter Hall (Leroy Pringle), Lewis Stone (Antonio Morado), ZaSu Pitts (Mrs. Harney), Dickie Moore (Tommy), Raymond Milland (Bit).

Francis is Johnson's cousin and both are very rich with Johnson's fortune coming from her family, and Francis' from marriage. Johnson falls in love with the family chauffeur, Bickford, and Francis convinces her to marry him. A few years later Francis falls in love with Bickford and tries to break up his and Johnson's marriage.

d, William DeMille; w, Martin Flavin, Laurence G. Johnson, Edith Fitzgerald (based on the novel by Kathleen Norris); ph, Hal Rosson; ed, Conrad A. Nervig; art d, Cedric Gibbons; cos, Adrian.

Drama　　　　　　　　　　　　　　　　　　**(PR:A MPAA:NR)**

PASSION FOR LIFE**½　　　(1951, Fr.) 94m UGC-Cooperative Generale du Cinematographie Francias/AGDC-Brandon bw (L'ECOLE BUISSONNIERE; AKA: I HAVE A NEW MASTER)

Bernard Blier (Pascal Laurent), Juliette Faber (Lise Arnaud), Edouard Delmont (Arnaud), Pierre Coste (Albert), Jean-Louis Allibert (Innovator), Arius (Mayor), Aquistapace (Antique Dealer), Ardisson (Hairdresser) Maupi (Chemist), Danny Caron (Cecile), Lucien Callamand, Gaston Modot, Henri Poupon (The Examiners).

Appealing to popular sentiment, PASSION FOR LIFE tells the moving tale of Blier, an energetic teacher whose enthusiasm for teaching is met with negativism by his student's old-fashioned parents. Taking a new assignment in the French countryside, Blier works lovingly with his grateful students, instilling them with modern, intelligent ideas. The older generation, particularly Coste, regards education as an unnecessary waste of time. Blier's devotion pays off, however, and the parents learn to trust in his ways. Blier's son, Bertrand, received some acclaim when his 1978 film GET OUT YOUR HANDKERCHIEFS took Best Foreign Film honors at the Academy Awards.

d, Jean-Paul Le Chanois; w, Le Chanois, Elise Freinet; ph, Andre Dumaitre, Marc Fossard, Maurice Pecqueux; m, Joseph Kosma; ed, Emma Le Chanois; art d, Claude Bouxin.

Drama　　　　　　　　　　　　　　　　　　**(PR:A MPAA:NR)**

PASSION HOLIDAY*　　　　(1963) 75m Flamingo/Davis c (AKA: MIAMI RENDEZVOUS)

Christy Foushee (Cathy), Linda Hall (Anne), Yanka Mann (Dixie), Stella Palma (Betty), Bruce Brown (Frank), Harry Hocker (Harry), Fred Kost (Eddie), Bob Lee (George), Ed Ross (Emil), Larry Roberts (Sam), Dick Kennedy (Joe), Sam Segal, Jack Gundersen (Truck Drivers), Monroe Myers, Harold Richter (Crooks), Leon Label (Boss), Wynona, Habibi, Kismet (Exotic Dancers), Victor Charles, Peg Rayborn, Sharon Lee, Virginia Horn, Bobbi Shaw, Lanita Kent, Connie Crump, Ludovic Huot, Owen Negrin, Pearl Rubin, Gertrude Dean, Lou Horn, Ed Bell, Sid Katz, Marion Webber, Eva Bartfield, Charles Bartfield, John Wentz, Frances Glick, Bob Krantz, Jr.

Four women meet four men in Miami Beach and take off together on a rented yacht to a remote island. They get involved with crooks who are searching for jewels. Everything is just hunky-dory by the finale, with all eight returning to Florida.

p, Hal Marsh, Irwin Meyer, Herb Meyer; d, Wynn Miles; ph, Hal Carrington (Eastmancolor); ed, Larry Bennet; spec eff, Jack Johnson; makeup, Rudolph Liszt.

Comedy/Drama　　　　　　　　　　　　　**(PR:C MPAA:NR)**

PASSION IN THE SUN*　　　　(1964) 73m Trans American bw (AKA: PASSION OF THE SUN)

Dale Berry, Josette Valague, Sans Souci Girls.

Valague is taken hostage by foreign agents but escapes. She is dressed only in her underwear when she is captured by a circus freak. She is chased around a carnival by the freak, and gets on a ride. The freak finds her, starts up the ride, and is promptly hit and killed by one of its speeding cars.

p&d, Dale Berry; w, (based on a story by Enrique Madariaga).

Drama　　　　　　　　　　　　　　　　　　**(PR:O MPAA:NR)**

PASSION ISLAND**½　　　(1943, Mex.) 93m EMASA/Maya bw (LA ISLA DE LA PASION)

David Silva (Julio), Isabela Corona (Lolita), Pituka De Foronda (Maria), Chaflan (Alligator), Miguel Angel Ferritz (Capt. Allende), Pedro Armendariz (Toro), Antonio Bravo (Doctor), Chela Campos (Coquito).

Silva is a Mexican soldier and hero in this film about the annexation of Clipperton Island at the turn of the century. The soldiers dispatched to hold the island only expected to stay for a few months, but when war broke out they had to stay two years. The soldiers mutiny, killing their captain, but Silva makes a stand against them. The mutineers are killed and Silva restores military order. (In Spanish; English subtitles.)

d&w, Emilio Fernandez; English subtitles, Herman Weinberg.

Drama　　　　　　　　　　　　　　　　　　**(PR:A MPAA:NR)**

PASSION OF ANNA, THE***　　　　(1970, Swed.) 100m Filmindustri-Cinematograph/UA c (EN PASSION)

Liv Ullmann (Anna Fromm), Bibi Andersson (Eva Vergerus), Max von Sydow (Andreas Winkelman), Erland Josephson (Elis Vergerus), Erik Hell (Johan Andersson), Sigge Furst (Verner), Svea Holst (Verner's Wife), Annika Kronberg (Katarina), Hjordis Pettersson (Johan's Sister), Lars-Owe Carlberg, Brian Wikstrom (Policemen), Barbro Hiort af Ornas, Malin Ek, Britta Brunius, Brita Oberg, Marianne Karlbeck, Lennart Blomkvist.

Max von Sydow, an ex-convict who lives alone in an island farmhouse, is visited one day by the crippled Ullmann, who requests to use the phone. Ullmann soon leaves, but forgets to take her purse with her. Von Sydow looks through it, finds her name, address, and a letter from her husband which discusses their unhappy marriage. He returns the purse and is introduced to Josephson and Andersson, friends of Ullmann's. Eventually Ullmann moves into Von Sydow's farmhouse. Tensions between the two begin to rise, partially due to reports of a crazed murderer who is on the loose. In a fit of anger, Von Sydow goes after Ullmann with an ax. The maniac strikes at Von Sydow's farm, setting his barn on fire. Ullmann rescues Von Sydow from the scene of the blaze, and drives frantically down the road. Von Sydow accuses her of trying to kill him, perhaps as she killed her husband and son years earlier in an auto accident (the one which left Ullmann crippled). He gets out of the car and Ullmann drives off. Hailed by many to be a Bergman masterpiece, THE PASSION OF ANNA (only his second film in color) employs some interesting techniques, such as interviews with each of the four main actors, and also sheds some light on many of the usual baroque mannerisms and symbols which have come to be associated with the director. It still contains, however, that element of coldness which has turned many viewers against Bergman. Filmed on the island of Faro, a one-time home for Bergman.

p, Lars-Owe Carlberg; d&w, Ingmar Bergman; ph, Sven Nykvist (Eastmancolor); ed, Siv Kanalv; prod d, P.A. Lundgren; cos, Mago; spec eff, Ulf Nordholm; makeup, Cecilia Drott.

Drama　　　　　　　　　　　　　　　　　　**(PR:C MPAA:R)**

PASSION OF LOVE** (1982, Ital./Fr.) 117m Massfilm-Marceau Cocinor-Connoisseur/Putnam Square c (PASSIONE D'AMORE)

Bernard Giraudeau (Giorgio Bacchetti), Valeria D'Obici (Fosca), Laura Antonelli (Clara), Jean-Louis Trintignant (Doctor), Massimo Girotti (Colonel), Bernard Blier (Maj. Tarasso), Gerardo Amato (Lt. Baggi), Sandro Ghiani (Giorgio's Attendant), Alberto Incrocci (Capt. Rivolti), Rosaria Schemmari (Fosca's Maid), Francesco Piastra (Colonel's Attendant), Saverio Vallone (Blond Lieutenant), Franco Committeri (Clara's Husband).

A problematic Italian-French production that has no clear direction or theme. Giraudeau is a soldier who must leave Antonelli, the stunning but married woman he's been having an affair with, when he's transfered to an isolated fort. At the outpost, the only woman around is the beastly looking, terminally ill D'Obici, who quickly falls in love with the new soldier. Giraudeau finally gives in and falls in love with her. They make love, and D'Obici dies a happy woman while Giraudeau turns into a bear who has fits. The story can be interpreted in many ways, but it doesn't seem like director Scola gave it much thought. Exquisitely photographed in pastel colors with lavish turn-of-the-century costuming.

p, Franco Committeri; d, Ettore Scola; w, Scola, Ruggero Maccari (based on the novel Fosca by Iginio Ugo Tarchetti); ph, Claudio Ragona (Eastmancolor); m, Armando Trovajoli; ed, Raimondo Crociani; art d, Fiorenzo Senese; cos, Gabriella Pescucci.

Drama   Cas.   (PR:O MPAA:NR)

PASSION OF SLOW FIRE, THE**½ (1962, Fr.) 91m Cinephonic-Odeon/Trans-Lux bw (LA MORT DE BELLE; AKA: THE END OF BELLE)

Jean Desailly (Stephane Blanchon), Alexandra Stewart (Belle), Monique Melinand (Mme. Blanchon), Yvette Etievant (Judge's Secretary), Jacques Monod (Judge Bechman), Marc Cassot (Police Officer), Jacques Pierre (Belle's Admirer), Yves Robert (Bartender), Luisa Colpeyn (Belle's Mother), Van Doude (Doctor), Maurice Teynac (Stephane's Friend).

Stewart is an American student who boards at the home of professor Desailly and his frigid wife. When the girl is found murdered, the professor becomes the prime suspect. When the evidence appears strongly against the innocent Desailly, he changes his life and has an affair; but obsessed by Stewart's death, he kills the woman he becomes involved with. He becomes a murderer at the same time the police announce that they've received a confession from the man who really killed Stewart. An entertaining crime drama from a novel by the masterful Georges Simenon.

p, Francois Chavane; d, Edouard Molinaro; w, Jean Anouilh (based on the novel The Death of Belle by Georges Simenon); ph, Jean-Louis Picavet; m, Georges Delerue; ed, Robert Isnardon, Monique Isnardon; art d, Robert Clavel.

Mystery   (PR:C MPAA:NR)

PASSION OF THE SUN   (SEE: PASSION IN THE SUN, 1964)

PASSION PIT, THE, 1965   (SEE: SCREAM OF THE BUTTERFLY, 1965)

PASSION PIT, THE, 1969   (SEE: ICE HOUSE, THE, 1969)

PASSION STREET, U.S.A.* (1964) 90m Nu Wave/Gillman bw (AKA: PASSION STREET; PASSION STREETS; BOURBON STREET)

Tanya Conway (Lorrie Owens), Steve Ihnat (Dick Dudman), Gary Clarke (Joseph Redding).

Conway moves from her Memphis home to New Orleans' French Quarter where she becomes involved with a detective and a minister. She falls in love with the latter, and after the detective angrily tries to break the romance up, Conway sticks with the minister.

p, James C. Dunne, Oscar Daley; d, Daley; m, Bob Emenegger.

Drama   (PR:C MPAA:NR)

PASSIONATE DEMONS, THE** (1962, Norway) 86m Concord-Norsk/Manson-Albex bw (LINE)

Margaret Robsahm (Line), Toralv Maurstad (Jacob), Henki Kolstad (Gabriel Sand), Sissel Tuul (Hanne), Elisabeth Bang (Jacob's Sister), Ronnaug Alten (Jacob's Mother), Truuk Doyer (A Passionate Demon), Rolf Christensen (Jacob's Father), Atle Merton (Laffen), Per Lillo Stenberg (Jeno), Ragnhild Hjorthoy (Ellen), Per Christensen (Putte), Odd Borg (Kalle), Ulf Wengaard.

Maurstad, a Norwegian seaman, returns home after years at sea and refuses to see his sickly father, instead spending his time with Robsahm, a carefree girl. The romance cools when she becomes pregnant, and he nearly kills her on a yachting outing. He returns to the sea after realizing that he is no better than his father, whom he blames for his mother's insanity.

p, Sverre Gran; d, Nils Reinhardt Christensen; w, Pal Lokkeberg; ph, Ragnar Sorensen; m, Egil Monn-Iversen; ed, Olav Engebregtsen; art d, H.C. Hansen.

Drama   (PR:A MPAA:NR)

PASSIONATE FRIENDS, THE   (SEE: ONE WOMAN'S STORY, 1949, Brit.)

PASSIONATE PLUMBER**½ (1932) 73m MGM bw

Buster Keaton (Elmer Tuttle), Jimmy Durante (McCracken, Patricia's Chauffeur), Irene Purcell (Patricia Alden), Polly Moran (Albine), Gilbert Roland (Tony Lagorce), Mona Maris (Nina), Maude Eburne (Aunt Charlotte), Henry Armetta (Bouncer), Paul Porcasi (Paul Le Maire), Jean del Val (Chauffeur), August Tollaire (Gen. Bouschay).

Keaton never found material in his talkies that came close to his silent work, and even in 1932 his star had already dimmed greatly. The main problem with this film

is the overly rewritten script that was put through the ringer to make it fit Keaton's screen persona. The tone is inconsistent, and the script is unable to sustain interest for 73 minutes. Durante's performance is the highlight of the film. He manages to upstage Keaton in every scene they're in together.

d, Edgar Sedgwick; w, Laurence E. Johnson, Ralph Spence, Jacques Deval (based on the play "Her Cardboard Lover" by Frederick Lonsdale); ed, William S. Gray.

Comedy   (PR:A MPAA:NR)

PASSIONATE SENTRY, THE*** (1952, Brit.) 85m LFP/FA bw (GB: WHO GOES THERE?)

Nigel Patrick (Miles Cornwall), Peggy Cummins (Christine Deed), Valerie Hobson (Alex Cornwall), George Cole (Arthur Crisp), A.E. Matthews (Sir Arthur Cornwall), Anthony Bushell (Maj. Guy Ashley), Joss Ambler (Guide).

After Cummins is jilted by Cole, an English guardsman, the caddish ex-boy friend hides her away in St. James Palace. Returning home is Patrick, who is more than a little surprised to find a beautiful girl hidden in his apartment. Romantic complications of the very British sort set in, ending in a happy situation for all. There are some fine characterizations, backed with crisp dialog in this nicely handled British farce. There's a lot of fun, directed with a good sense for the material. Patrick originated his role in the stage version of this and repeated the performance with fine results.

p&d, Anthony Kimmins; w, John Dighton (based on a play by Dighton); ph, John Wilcox, Ted Scaife; m, Muir Mathieson; ed, Gerald Turney-Smith; prod d, Wilfred Shingleton; md, Mathieson

Comedy   (PR:C MPAA:NR)

PASSIONATE STRANGER, THE   (SEE: NOVEL AFFAIR, A, 1957, Brit.)

PASSIONATE STRANGERS, THE* (1968, Phil.) 78m MJP/RAF bw

Michael Parsons (Adam Courtney), Valora Noland (Margaret Courtney), Mario Montenegro (Roberto Valdez), Celia Rodriguez Lydia Trasmonte, Vic Diaz (Angel Mascardo), Butch Aquino (Julio Lazatin), Claude Wilson (J.V. Harrison), Jose Dagumboy (Yoyong), Bong Calumpang (Yoyong's Companion), Cesar Aguilar (Manuel Hidalgo).

An American mill owner accidentally murders a labor organizer, which causes anger and confusion among the local members of the labor union. Strong anti-American sentiments are expressed and the mill owner is eventually brought to trial. The case doesn't stand up in court, though, so one of the townsfolk stabs the mill owner to death. Cut from 101 minutes.

p, M.J. Parsons; d&w, Eddie Romero (based on a story by Cesar Amigo, Reuben Canoy); ph, Justo Paulino; m, Nestor Robles.

Drama   (PR:C MPAA:NR)

PASSIONATE SUMMER** (1959, Brit.) 104m RANK c

Virginia McKenna (Judy), Bill Travers (Douglas Lockwood), Yvonne Mitchell (Mrs. Pawley), Alexander Knox (Mr. Pawley), Carl Mohner (Louis), Ellen Barrie (Silvia), Guy Middleton (Duffield), Gordon Heath (Coroner), Pearl Prescod (Mrs. Morgan), Harry Quashie (Joe), Roscoe Holder (Cable Clerk), Danny Daniels (Boatman), Jan Holden (Air Hostess), John Harrison (Shopkeeper), Bruce Pitt (John), Waveney Lee (Norah), Martin Stephens (Alan).

Travers is a devoted schoolteacher at a progresssive school in Jamaica who is trying to help a problem student, Barrie. The teacher also has own problems stemming from his involvement with two women, the headmaster's wife (Mitchell) and an airline stewardess (McKenna). Mitchell is trying to sabotage Travers' romance with McKenna, and ultimately her jealousy destroys the trust that had been developing between Travers and his student. Barrie catches Travers and Mitchell kissing, and her jealous rage sends the young girl running out into a hurricane to her death. This brings Travers to his senses and he goes back to McKenna.

p, Kenneth Harper, George Willoughby; d, Rudolph Cartier; w, Joan Henry (based on the novel The Shadow and the Peak by Richard Mason); ph, Ernest Steward (Eastmancolor); m, Angelo Lavagnino; ed, Reginald Mills.

Drama   (PR:A MPAA:NR)

PASSIONATE SUNDAY   (SEE: DARK ODYSSEY, 1961)

PASSIONATE THIEF, THE*** (1963, Ital.) 95m Titanus-EM bw (RISATE DI GIOIA)

Anna Magnani (Tortorella), Toto (Umberto), Ben Gazzara (Lello), Fred Clark (The American), Edy Vessel (Mimi), Gina Rovere, Mac Ronay, Toni Ucci, Rik von Nutter, Marcella Rovena, Kurt Polter, Alberto De Amicis, Gianni Bonagura, Peppino De Martino, Mara Ombra, Dori Dorika, Carlo Pisacane.

Magnani meets a pair of pickpockets, Toto and Gazzara, who try to get rid of her before they prey on a wealthy American (Clark). Clark becomes interested in her, but his drunkeness results in his trying to jump in the Trevi Fountain where he is arrested. Later, Gazzara steals a necklace from a Madonna statue, but it is Magnani who is arrested. She serves a short jail term and finds Toto waiting for her. A fine comedy which owes much to Monicelli's fresh direction, a superb cast, and the source material by Alberto Moravia.

p, Silvio Clementelli; d, Mario Monicelli; w, Suso Cecchi D'Amico, Agenore Incrocci, Furio Scarpelli, Monicelli (based on the stories "Ladri in Chiesa" and "Risate di Gioia" by Alberto Moravia); ph, Leonida Barboni; m, Lelio Luttazzi; ed, Adriana Novelli; art d, Piero Gherardi, Giuseppe Ranieri.

Comedy/Crime   (PR:A MPAA:NR)

PASSIONE D'AMORE   (SEE: PASSION OF LOVE, 1982, Ital./Fr.)

PASSKEY TO DANGER**   (1946) 58m REP bw

Kane Richmond (*Tex Hanlon*), Stephanie Bachelor (*Gwen Hughes*), Adele Mara (*Renee Beauchamps*), Gregory Gay (*Mrs. Warren*), Gerald Mohr (*Malcolm Tauber*), John Eldredge (*Alex Cardovsky*), George J. Lewis (*Julian Leighton*), Fred Graham (*Bert*), Tom London (*Gerald Bates*), Donia Bussey (*Jenny*), Charles Williams (*Mr. Williams*), Charles Wilson (*Police Sergeant*).

A B film that is part mystery, part comedy stars Richmond as an advertising executive who turns detective when he discovers a team of embezzling brothers. A couple of mean-looking hoods are also on the brothers' trail, causing some humorous moments for Richmond. The brothers, whose last name is Spring, believe the ad man is trying to blackmail them when an ad campaign called "The Three Springs" fashions comes out.

p, William J. O'Sullivan; d, Lesley Selander; w, O'Leta Rhinehart, William Hagens; ph, William Bradford; m, Richard Cherwin; ed, Harry Keller; md, James Sullivan; spec eff, Howard Lydecker, Theodore Lydecker.

Mystery/Comedy   **(PR:A MPAA:NR)**

PASSOVER PLOT, THE*   (1976, Israel) 108m Atlas c

Harry Andrews (*Yohanan the Baptist*), Hugh Griffith (*Caiaphas*), Zalman King (*Yeshua*), Donald Pleasence (*Pontius Pilate*), Scott Wilson (*Judah*), Dan Ades (*Andros*), Michael Baseleon (*Mattai*), Lewis van Bergen (*Yoram*), William Burns (*Shimon*), Daniel Hedaya (*Yaacov*), Helena Kallianiotes (*Visionary Woman*), Kevin O'Connor (*Irijah*), Robert Walker (*Bar Talmi*), William Watson (*Roman Captain*).

This film on the life of Christ was adapted from the book by Hugh J. Schonfield that discusses Christ as a political revolutionary. King plays Christ, here called by His Hebrew name Yeshua, in this version of His life, where Christ sets up His own crucifixion as a plot against the Romans. The film is too talky with almost every scene dependent on explanatory dialog to pull the plot strings, which also accounts for the film's snail's pace. Surprisingly, it is typical of any Biblical film on Christ until the last few minutes when He doesn't rise from the dead.

p, Wolf Schmidt; d, Michael Campus; w, Millard Cohan, Patricia Knop (based on the book by Hugh J. Schonfield); ph, Adam Greenberg (Deluxe Color); m, Alex North; ed, Dov Hoenig; art d, Kuli Sander; cos, Mary Wills.

Drama   **(PR:C MPAA:PG)**

PASSPORT HUSBAND*½   (1938) 72m FOX bw

Stuart Erwin (*Henry Cabot*), Pauline Moore (*Mary Jane Clayton*), Douglas Fowley (*Tiger Martin*), Joan Woodbury (*Conchita Montez* (Robert Lowery (*Ted Markson*), Harold Huber (*Blackie Bennet*), Edward S. Brophy (*Spike*), Paul McVey (*H.C. Walton*), Lon Chaney, Jr. (*Bull*), Joseph Sawyer (*Duke Selton*).

A silly gangster comedy which fails because of the brainless script. Erwin is a bus boy working in a nightclub in South America, who gets involved with gun moll and singer Woodbury, and finds himself knee-deep in trouble with her gangster friends. The bus boy is forced to marry Woodbury so she won't be deported like many of her gangster cronies. Erwin finds himself in even more trouble when he inherits his uncle's pinball machine business and the gangsters want to move in on the operation. Woodbury falls in love with Erwin, but he is in love with cigarette girl Moore, and eventually drives the mobsters out of his hair.

p, Sol M. Wurtzel; d, James Tinling; w, Karen de Wolf, Robert Chapin (based on a story by Hilda Stone); ph, Edward Snyder; ed, Nick De Maggio; md, Samuel Kaylin.

Comedy   **(PR:A MPAA:NR)**

PASSPORT TO ADVENTURE   (SEE: PASSPORT TO DESTINY, 1944)

PASSPORT TO ALCATRAZ*½   (1940) 60m COL bw (AKA: PASSPORT TO HELL)

Jack Holt (*George Hollister*), Noah Beery, Jr. (*Ray Nolan*), Cecilia Callejo (*Karol Roy*), Maxie Rosenbloom (*Hank Kircher*), C. Henry Gordon (*Leon Fenten*), Guy Usher (*Thomas Lindsey*), Clay Clement (*Drexel Stuyvesant*), Ivan Lebedoff (*Bogen*), Ben Welden (*Bender*), Robert Fiske (*Reed*), Harry Cording (*Jeffers*).

Holt is a private detective tracking down foreign saboteurs in this routine B action fare. The saboteurs are blowing up U.S. munition factories and Holt poses as one of the criminals to give each one of them a one-way ticket to the titled prison. An early film for "Slapsie" Maxie Rosenbloom, former light-heavyweight boxing champion during the 1930s.

d, Lewis D. Collins; w, Albert DeMond; ph, James S. Brown Jr.; m, Lee Zahler; ed, Dwight Caldwell.

Action/Adventure   **(PR:A MPAA:NR)**

PASSPORT TO CHINA**   (1961, Brit.) 75m Hammer-Swallow/COL bw (GB: VISIT TO CANTON)

Richard Basehart (*Don Benton*), Lisa Gastoni (*Lola Sanchez*), Athene Seyler (*Mao Tai Tai*), Eric Pohlmann (*Ivano Kang*), Alan Gifford (*Charles Orme*), Bernard Cribbins (*Pereira*), Burt Kwouk (*Jimmy*), Hedgar Wallace (*Inspector Taylor*), Marne Maitland (*Han Po*), Milton Reid (*Bodyguard*), Yvonne Shima (*Liang Ti*), Robert Lee (*Chinese Officer*), Zoreen Ismail (*Swee Kim*), Paula Lee Shiu (*Girl Croupier*), Sorata Ra Fat (*Hostess*), Gerry Lee Yen (*Room Boy*), Ronald Ing (*Sentry*), Kevin Scott.

Basehart is a former WW II Pilot living in Hong Kong with no intention of doing the espionage work which the U.S. government is asking of him. He does, however, agree to help a Chinese woman find her son, a missing pilot. With the help of a Russian friend, Basehart locates the boy, but also gets mixed up with Gastoni, an American agent. She is trying to sell a secret formula, but dies as Basehart tries to

help her escape. After he returns to Hong Kong, Basehart again refuses to do undercover work for American intelligence.

p&d, Michael Carreras; w, Gordon Wellesley; ph, Arthur Grant; m, Edwin Astley; ed, James Needs, Alfred Cox; art d, Bernard Robinson, Thomas Goswell; makeup, Roy Ashton.

Adventure   **(PR:A MPAA:NR)**

PASSPORT TO DESTINY**   (1944) 65m RKO bw (AKA: PASSPORT TO ADVENTURE)

Elsa Lanchester (*Ella*), Gordon Oliver (*Franz*), Lenore Aubert (*Grete*), Lionel Royce (*Dietrich*), Fritz Feld (*Hausmeister*), Joseph Vitale (*Lt. Bosch*), Gavin Muir (*Lord Haw Haw*), Lloyd Corrigan (*Prof. Walthers*), Anita Bolster (*Agnes*), Lydia Bilbrook (*Millie*), Lumsden Hare (*Captain*), Hans Schumm (*Prison Warden*).

Lanchester is the widow of a British officer during WW II who decides to travel to Berlin to kill Hitler. She travels through France, and then makes her way into Germany as a deaf-mute, obtaining a job as a cleaning lady at the chancellery in Berlin. Lanchester never gets her chance at the dictator, but she does cause a lot of problems for the German staff. Oliver plays a German officer opposed to the Nazis who helps Lanchester escape along with his girl friend, Aubert. Implausible story made bearable by Lanchester's commanding performance.

p, Herman Schlom; d, Ray McCarey; w, Val Burton, Muriel Roy Bolton; ph, Jack Mackenzie; m, Roy Webb; ed, Robert Swink; art d, Albert S. D'Agostino, Jack Okey; cos, Edward Stevenson; spec eff, Vernon L. Walker.

Comedy/Drama   **(PR:A MPAA:NR)**

PASSPORT TO HELL*½   (1932) 75m FOX bw (GB: BURNT OFFERING)

Elissa Landi (*Myra Carson*), Paul Lukas (*Lt. Kurt Kurtoff*), Warner Oland (*Baron von Sydow, Police Commandant*), Alex Kirkland (*Lt. Erich von Sydow*), Donald Crisp (*Sgt. Snyder*), Earle Foxe (*Purser*), Vera Morrison (*Sheba*), Yola d'Avril (*Rosita*), Ivan Simpson (*Simms*), Eva Dennison (*Mrs. Butterworth*), Anders Van Hayden (*Immigration Officer*), Bert Sprotte (*Hotel Proprietor*), William Von Brincken (*Officer*).

A dull melodrama starring Landi, who is deported to Germany after being blamed for a man's suicide. WW I breaks and the woman marries the son of a German commandant to avoid being put into an alien prison camp. She has an affair with another officer, while her husband sells secrets to the English to pay for Landi to leave the country. He then commits suicide, but Landi rips up the confession note to save his honor. She leaves the country in hopes of seeing her lover once the war is over. Features Oland taking a break from his "Charlie Chan" series to play the commandant.

d, Frank Lloyd; w, Leon Gordon, Bradley King (based on a story by Harry Hervey); ph, John Seitz; ed, Harold Schuster; art d, William Darling; cos, Earl Luick.

Drama   **(PR:A MPAA:NR)**

PASSPORT TO HELL, 1940   (SEE: PASSPORT TO ALCATRAZ, 1940)

PASSPORT TO OBLIVION   (SEE: WHERE THE SPIES ARE, 1966, Brit.)

PASSPORT TO PIMLICO***   (1949, Brit.) 84m Ealing/EL bw

Stanley Holloway (*Arthur Pemberton*), Hermione Baddeley (*Eddie Randall*), Margaret Rutherford (*Prof. Hatton-Jones*), Paul Dupuis (*Duke of Burgundy*), Basil Radford (*Gregg*), Naunton Wayne (*Straker*), Jane Hylton (*Molly*), Raymond Huntley (*Mr. Wix*), Betty Warren (*Connie Pemberton*), Barbara Murray (*Shirley Pemberton*), John Slater (*Frank Huggins*), Frederick Piper (*Garland*), Sydney Tafler (*Fred Cowan*), Charles Hawtrey (*Bert Fitch*), James Hayter (*Commissionaire*), Philip Stainton (*P.C. Spiller*), Stuart Lindsell (*Coroner*), Michael Hordern (*Inspector Bashford*), Arthur Howard (*Bassett*), Bill Shine (*Captain*), Harry Locke (*Sergeant*), Sam Kydd (*Sapper*), Fred Griffiths (*Spiv*), Grace Arnold (*Woman in Underground*), E.V.M. Emmett (*Newsreel Commentator*), Roy Carr, Nancy Gabrielle, Gilbert Davis, Joey Carr, Lloyd Pearson, Arthur Denton, Tommy Godfrey, Masoni, Paul Demel, Michael Knight, Roy Gladdish, Bernard Farrel, Michael Craig.

A light British comedy about an unexploded bomb that suddenly goes off and unearths documents stating that that area of London belongs to Burgundy, France. Halloway becomes the head of the new government where new borders and customs barriers are drawn. A fresh comedy with some well-aimed satirical arrows from producer Balcon's Ealing Studios, famous for their sophisticated, irreverent comedies.

p, Michael Balcon; d, Henry Cornelius; w, T.E.B. Clarke; ph, Lionel Barnes, Cecil Cooney; m, Georges Auric; ed, Michael Truman; art d, Roy Oxley; cos, Anthony Mendleson.

Comedy   **Cas.**   **(PR:A MPAA:NR)**

PASSPORT TO SHAME   (SEE: ROOM 43, 1959, Brit.)

PASSPORT TO SUEZ**   (1943) 72m COL bw

Warren William (*Michael Lanyard*), Ann Savage (*Valerie King*), Eric Blore (*Jameson*), Robert Stanford (*Donald Jameson*), Sheldon Leonard (*Johnny Booth*), Lloyd Bridges (*Fritz*), Gavin Muir (*Karl*), Lou Merrill (*Rembrandt*), Frederick Worlock (*Sir Roger Wembley*), Jay Novello (*Cezanne*), Sig Arno (*Whistler*), John Tyrrel (*Wembly Man ¡1*), Frank O'Connor (*Wembley Man ¡2*), Eddie Kane (*Gay Man*), Stanley Price (*Native Cop*), Gene Stone (*Bartender*), Frank Arnold (*French Waiter*), Carl DeLord, Hercules Mendez, Janet Calionzes (*Greeks*), Jack Lee (*Drunk*), George Chermanoff, Adonis DeMilo, Tony Abdenour (*Turks*), Frances

Chan *(Chinese)*, Grace Lem *(Woman)*, Tanya Semova *(Russian)*, Jack Rice *(Hotel Clerk)*, Floyd Shackelford, Darby Jones *(Bellboys)*, Nick Thompson, Frank Lackteen *(Launderers)*, Mal Merrihugh *(Chauffeur)*.

This was William's eighth and last film as the super sleuth Lone Wolf, and this time the detective heads for Egypt. William goes undercover as a Nazi spy to break up a Nazi scheme to steal British plans for the Suez Canal. A good amount of gunplay and chase scenes, including one outstanding chase in airplanes, can't breathe fresh air into this film. (See LONE WOLF series, Index.)

p, Wallace MacDonald; d, Andre DeToth; w, John Stone (based on a story by Alden Nash); ph, L.W. O'Connell; ed, Mel Thorsen; md, Morris W. Stoloff.

Action/Adventure **(PR:A MPAA:NR)**

PASSPORT TO TREASON*½ (1956, Brit.) 70m Mid-Century/Astor bw

Rod Cameron *(Mike O'Kelly)*, Lois Maxwell *(Diane Boyd)*, Clifford Evans *(Orlando Sims)*, Peter Illing *(Giorgio Sacchi)*, Marianne Stone *(Miss Jones)*, Douglas Wilmer *(Dr. Randolph)*, Ballard Berkeley *(Inspector Threadgold)*, Andrew Faulds *(Barrett)*, John Colicos *(Pietro)*, Barbara Burke, Derek Sydney, Trevor Reid, Neil Wilson.

An overly complicated, muddled murder mystery with Cameron as a private investigator in London. When one of his associates is killed the detective takes on the case. The dead man was investigating a league for world peace. Cameron does some snooping with the help of Maxwell and discovers that the league is being run by fascists.

p, Robert S. Baker, Monty Berman; d, Baker; w, Norman Hudis, Kenneth R. Hayles (based on a novel by Manning O'Brine); ph, Berman; m, Stanley Black; ed, Henry Richardson; art d, John Stoll.

Mystery **(PR:A MPAA:NR)**

PASSWORD IS COURAGE, THE½** (1962, Brit.) 116m MGM bw

Dick Bogarde *(Charles Coward)*, Maria Perschy *(Irena)*, Alfred Lynch *(Cpl. Billy Pope)*, Nigel Stock *(Cole)*, Reginald Beckwith *(Unteroffizier)*, Richard Marner *(Schmidt)*, Ed Devereaux *(Aussie)*, Lewis Fiander *(Pringle)*, George Mikell *(Necke)*, Richard Carpenter *(Robinson)*, Margaret Whiting *(French Farmwoman)*, Olaf Pooley *(German Doctor)*, Ferdy Mayne *(German Officer)*, Colin Blakely *(1st German Goon)*, Michael Mellinger *(Feldwebal)*, Bernard Archard, George Pravda, Mark Eden, Douglas Livingstone, John Gardiner, Howard Pays, Tommy Elliott, Bernard Proctor, Philo Hauser.

Bogarde is a British officer captured during WW II by the Germans and never gives up trying to escape. As he's being marched to the P.O.W. camp, Bogarde lies down with wounded German soldiers and is taken to a hospital. He's given an Iron Cross before the Nazis realize his true identity. Back in prison camp he builds a tunnel, gets maps and such from the Polish underground, and escapes with Lynch, but both men are recaptured. Finally, the two men do escape by stealing a fire engine and driving it to freedom. The film is based on the true story of Sgt. Maj. Charles Coward.

p, Andrew Stone, Virginia Stone; d&w, Andrew Stone (based on the biography of Charles Coward by John Castle); ph, David Boultin (Metroscope); m, Derek New; ed, Noreen Ackland, Virginia Stone; art d, Wilfred Arnold, spec eff, Bill Warrington.

War Drama **(PR:A MPAA:NR)**

PAST OF MARY HOLMES, THE* (1933) 70m RKO bw

Helen MacKellar *(Mary Holmes)*, Eric Linden *(Geoffrey Holmes)*, Jean Arthur *(Joan Hoyt)*, Richard "Skeets" Gallagher *(Pratt)*, Ivan Simpson *(Jacob Riggs)*, Clay Clement *(Etheridge)*, Franklin Parker *(Brooks)*, Eddie Nugent *(Flannigan)*, Roscoe Ates *(Klondike)*, J. Carroll Naish *(Kent)*, John Sheehan *(Kinkaid)*, Rochelle Hudson, Jane Darwell.

A terribly acted film with MacKellar and Linden battling to upstage each other in every scene. MacKellar is a washed up opera star and she blames it on her son, Linden. In an attempt to put her name back in the headlines and get revenge on her son, she accuses Linden of killing a man. During the trial, though, mother has a change of heart and things end happily with the real killer put behind bars. The film was a remake of the silent picture, THE GOOSE WOMAN (1925).

p, Bartlett Cormack; d, Harlan Thompson, Slavko Vorkapich; w, Edward Marion Dix, Edward Doherty (based on the story "Goose Woman" by Rex Beach); ph, Charles Rosher; ed, Charles L. Kimball.

Drama **(PR:A MPAA:NR)**

PASTEUR* (1936, Fr.) 65m Lenauer International bw

Sacha Guitry *(Pasteur)*, Jean Perier *(Doctor)*, Jose Squinquel *(Pupil-Roux)*, Bonvallet *(President)*, Schutz *(Grandfather)*, Beuve *(Lister)*, Master Rodon *(Meister)*.

A boring and long-winded account of the life of French scientist Louis Pasteur. The film beat Warner Bros.' LIFE OF LOUIS PASTEUR into the theaters but is put to shame by the American film version. (In French.)

p, Maurice Lehman, Ferdinand Rivers; d&w, Sacha Guitry; ph, Jean Bachelet et Ribault.

Drama **(PR:A MPAA:NR)**

PASTOR HALL½** (1940, Brit.) 97m Charter/UA bw

Nova Pilbeam *(Christine Hall)*, Seymour Hicks *(Gen. von Grotjahn)*, Wilfred Lawson *(Pastor Frederick Hall)*, Marius Goring *(Fritz Gerte)*, Percy Walsh *(Veit)*, Brian Worth *(Werner von Grotjahn)*, Peter Cotes *(Erwin Kohn)*, Hay Petrie *(Nazi Pastor)*, Eliot Makeham *(Pipperman)*, Edmund Willard *(Freundlich)*, Manning Whiley *(Vogel)*, Lina Barrie *(Lina Veit)*, J. Fisher White *(Johann Herder)*, Barbara Gott *(Frau Kemp)*, Bernard Miles *(Heinrich Degan)*, Raymond Rollett.

A German pastor stands up against the tactics and teachings of the Nazis and finds himself in a concentration camp. He is beaten and tortured, but escapes to give one last sermon to his parish before being shot down. The story is inspired by the life of a German minister. When the film arrived in the U.S., the critics saw the film as pure propaganda since the U.S. was still uninvolved in the war in Europe, but PASTOR HALL is far less heavy-handed than most wartime films Hollywood cranked out after Pearl Harbor. In the American version, there is a prologue with Eleanor Roosevelt speaking against Hitler and his Nazi rule. Her son James Roosevelt presented the film in the U.S. through United Artists.

p, John Boulting; d, Roy Boulting; w, Leslie Arliss, Ann Reiner, Haworth Bromley (based on a play by Ernst Toller); ph, Mutz Greenbaum; m, Charles Brill, Mack Adams; ed, Jack Harris; md, Brill.

War Drama **(PR:A MPAA:NR)**

PAT AND MIKE**** (1952) 95m MGM bw

Spencer Tracy *(Mike Conovan)*, Katharine Hepburn *(Pat Pemberton)*, Aldo Ray *(Davie Hucko)*, William Ching *(Collier Weld)*, Sammy White *(Barney Grau)*, George Mathews *(Spec Cauley)*, Loring Smith *(Mr. Beminger)*, Phyllis Povah *(Mrs. Beminger)*, Charles Buchinski [Bronson] *(Hank Tasling)*, Frank Richards *(Sam Garsell)*, Jim Backus *(Charles Barry)*, Chuck Connors *(Police Captain)*, Owen McGiveney *(Harry MacWade)*, Joseph E. Bernard *(Gibby)*, Lou Lubin *(Waiter)*, Carl Switzer *(Bus Boy)*, William Self *(Pat's Caddy)*, Billy McLean, Frankie Darro, Paul Brinegar, "Tiny" Jimmie Kelly *(Caddies)*, Mae Clarke, Elizabeth Holmes, Helen Eby-Rock *(Women Golfers)*, Hank Weaver *(Commentator)*, Tom Harmon *(Sportscaster)*, Charlie Murray *(Line Judge)*, Don Budge, Helen Dettweiler, Betty Hicks, Beverly Hanson, Babe Didrikson Zaharias, Gussie Moran, Alice Marble, Frank Parker *(Themselves)*, Kay English, Jerry Schumacher, Sam Pierce, Bill Lewin, A. Cameron Grant *(Reporters)*, John Close, Fred Coby, Russ Clark *(Troopers)*, Tom Gibson, Kay Deslys *(Shooting Gallery Proprietors)*, Barbara Kimbrell, Elinor Cushingham, Jane Stanton *(Tennis Players, Louis Mason (Railway Conductor)*, King Mojave *(Linesman)*, Frank Sucack *(Chairman)*, Crauford Kent *(Tennis Umpire)*, Sam Hearn *(Lawyer)*.

MGM was wise to cast Babe Didrikson Zaharias as herself in this sports-oriented comedy because much of the story sounds like hers and there could have been a lawsuit if some shyster lawyer got hold of the case. The Kanin-Gordon script received an Oscar nomination, the only notice taken by the Academy, but that didn't stop hordes of fans from flocking to the theaters. It was the seventh Tracy-Hepburn film and their last one together for the Culver City lot. Hepburn, in a direct turnaround from the character she played in WOMAN OF THE YEAR, where she hated sports, is a perky, lively physical education teacher at a small California college. She also participates in various sports tournaments but never does well when her fiance, Ching, is there to watch. He's a professor at the school and adores her. Hepburn enters an amateur golf tournament and meets fast-talking Tracy, a sports promoter who thinks that he can make some money with this slim athlete. Since Tracy has a financial interest in who wins the tournament, he attempts to talk Hepburn into throwing the game with a bribe but she adamantly turns him down, although she does find him fascinating. At first, there is no love lost between the two as he convinces her to turn professional and begins to ballyhoo her prowess as a golfer and a tennis player. It all goes well and she makes some money until Ching arrives on the scene and she again plays poorly. Ching finds Tracy and Hepburn in what might be deemed a compromising position (although it is totally innocent) and he walks out on her. At first, she is thrown by Ching's exit, then she eventually realizes in the film, as she did in life, that Tracy is the only man for her. Along the way, Tracy takes a couple of crooked partners, including Bronson (while he was still known as Buchinski) and he is saved from being hurt by Hepburn. The movie was mostly shot at the Riviera Country Club in Pacific Palisades and it gave Hepburn an opportunity to show her abilities at golf, tennis, swimming, hiking, and basketball. Aldo Ray, on loan from Columbia, does a neat bit as a punchy boxer and Chuck Connors, on loan from his job as the Triple A Los Angeles Angels' first sacker, makes his film debut as a police captain. There are several real athletes in the picture (see cast list) and they also acquit themselves well. Bronson had appeared for director Cukor in THE MARRYING KIND and showed that he could handle comedy well in a Damon Runyon-type gangster role. The most famous line in the picture was the ad-lib pronunciation by Tracy that got the biggest laugh. He's watching Hepburn walk away from him as he leans over a drinking fountain and says to his crony, "Not much meat on 'er, but what there is is cherce." Cukor tried for another take and Tracy repeated the New York-style of saying "choice" and Cukor decided to let it remain. The result was a huge laugh from the audience and the scene was later used as part of the tribute to Tracy and Hepburn in the MGM compilation film, THAT'S ENTERTAINMENT, PART II. Many funny lines and easy, smooth direction by Cukor make this, perhaps, the best movie they made together.

p, Lawrence Weingarten; d, George Cukor; w, Ruth Gordon, Garson Kanin; ph, William Daniels; m, David Raksin; ed, George Boemler; art d, Cedric Gibbons, Urie McCleary; set d, Edwin B. Willis, Hugh Hunt; cos, Orry-Kelly; spec eff, Warren Newcombe; makeup, William Tuttle.

Comedy **(PR:A MPAA:NR)**

PAT GARRETT AND BILLY THE KID** (1973) 106m Gordon Carroll-Sam Peckinpah/MGM c

James Coburn *(Pat Garrett)*, Kris Kristofferson *(Billy the Kid)*, Bob Dylan *(Alias)*, Jason Robards, Jr. *(Gov. Lew Wallace)*, Richard Jaeckel *(Sheriff Kip McKinney)*, Katy Jurado *(Mrs. Baker)*, Slim Pickens *(Sheriff Baker)*, Chill Wills *(Lemuel)*, John Beck *(Poe)*, Rita Coolidge *(Maria)*, R.G. Armstrong *(Deputy Ollinger)*, Luke Askew *(Eno)*, Richard Bright *(Holly)*, Matt Clark *(Deputy J.W. Bell)*, Jack Dodson *(Llewellyn Howland)*, Jack Elam *(Alamosa Bill)*, Emilio Fernandez *(Paco)*, Paul Fix *(Pete Maxwell)*, L.Q. Jones *(Black Harris)*, Jorge Russek *(Silva)*, Charlie Martin Smith *(Bowdre)*, Harry Dean Stanton *(Luke)*, Claudia Bryar *(Mrs. Horrell)*, John Chandler *(Norris)*, Mike Mikler *(Denver)*, Aurora Clavel *(Ida Garrett)*, Rutanya

Alda (Ruthie Lee), Walter Kelley (Rupert), Rudolph Wurlitzer (Tom O'Folliard), Gene Evans (Mr. Horrell), Donnie Fritts (Beaver), Don Levy (Sackett), Sam Peckinpah (Will), Dub Taylor (Josh), Elisha Cook, Jr. (Cody).

After Peckinpah handed in his "final cut" of this, which he called "the best film I ever made," the hierarchy at MGM saw fit to re-edit it (with six editors credited) and turn it into a chopped salad. The 15 minutes which were removed consisted of a prolog and epilog which showed the murder of Coburn, many years after he had slain Kristofferson. Other scenes which bit the dust included a bit between Coburn and his wife, and the entire roles of Barry Sullivan, Elisha Cook, Jr., and Dub Taylor. Peckinpah was so incensed that he tried to have his name taken off the credits when he saw what had been done to the picture. Coburn is the aged outlaw and Kristofferson is Billy. Coburn feels that the time has come for him to settle down and grow old peacefully, so he goes to work as a lawman and is assigned by the wealthy railroad interests and cattlemen to hunt down his old buddy. Much as he dislikes the job, Coburn searches for Kristofferson and finds him in the New Mexico territory and tells him to clear out and save his skin. Kristofferson, with the confidence of being only 21, disregards the threat, so Coburn arrests him and claps him in jail for a former transgression. Kristofferson is sentenced to be the guest of honor at a necktie party and shoots his way out of jail with a gun he finds in the prison outhouse. (This firearm is never explained and it may have been excised in the deep cuts.) In doing so, he shoots and kills Clark and Armstrong, two deputies. He takes along Dylan, a former printer, and the two set out together. (Dylan's role must have been heavily edited because it consists mostly of dumb expressions and monosyllabic answers and the interminable use of his narrative songs over various scenes which drone on like a mosquito in the ear.) They end up back in New Mexico to put a gang together. Coburn hires Elam, an ex-criminal, to help him, while the governor, Robards, engages Beck as a man to help bring the youthful Kristofferson to justice. (Robards' character of Lew Wallace was an interesting historical sidelight. He'd been a Civil War hero and a general before he was 40. In later years, he was to become the author of the bestseller Ben Hur, A Tale of Christ, which was the basis for the BEN HUR films.) A hunt begins and Kristofferson reluctantly kills Elam, while Coburn guns down Kristofferson's best pal, Jones. One by one, Kristofferson's friends are being eliminated and he considers going to Mexico to escape. That idea disappears when he comes across the body of Fernandez, another cohort. The man has been tortured and murdered while attempting to flee to his home south of the border. This brings Kritofferson up short and he realizes that his fate may have already been sealed because there doesn't seem to be any way out. Kristofferson tries to hole up at Jones' ranch and Coburn gets the word on that and travels there with Beck and another lawman, Jaeckel. They get there late at night and Coburn peers through the window to see Kristofferson making love to Coolidge; Garrett gives them time to finish, and when Kristofferson walks outside, Coburn shoots him dead. Later, in a fit of guilt at having killed his old compadre, Coburn shoots at his own reflection in a mirror. The next day, he rides off as the folks of the town watch. The epilog showed that Coburn had been killed by the same men who ordered him to get Kristofferson, a fitting reward for his treachery. Billy the Kid (William Bonney) has been fodder for several films. Wallace Beery and Johnny Mack Brown played Garrett and Bonney in 1930; then Brian Donlevy and Robert Taylor did it in 1941. The story was told again in MY DARLING CLEMENTINE and THE LEFT-HANDED GUN, and even touched upon in BILLY THE KID VERSUS DRACULA. Enough already! This version of the tale is pretty to look at, and just when you think a scene is getting intriguing, it cuts away. Dylan's presence is as useful as a hearing aid for a snake. It was filmed in and around that favorite location for filmmakers, Durango, Mexico. Whereas a good story should have a beginning, a muddle and an end, this one only seems to have the muddle. Peckinpah and writer Wurlitzer do cameos. Coolidge and Kristofferson were married about this time but it didn't last very long.

p, Gordon Carroll; d, Sam Peckinpah; w, Rudolph Wurlitzer; ph, John Coquillon (Panavision, Metrocolor); m, Bob Dylan; ed, Roger Spottiswoode, Garth Craven, Robert L. Wolfe, Richard Halsey, David Berlatsky, Tony De Zarraga; art d, Ted Haworth; set d, Ray Moyer; spec eff, A.J. Lohman; m/l, "Knockin' on Heaven's Door," Dylan (sung by Dylan); makeup, Jack P. Wilson.

Western Biography   Cas.   (PR:C MPAA:R)

PATATE   (SEE: FRIEND OF THE FAMILY, 1965, Fr./Ital.)

PATCH   (SEE: DEATH OF A GUNFIGHTER, 1969)

PATCH OF BLUE, A*   (1965) 105m MGM bw**

Sidney Poitier (Gordon Ralfe), Shelley Winters (Rose-Ann D'Arcy), Elizabeth Hartman (Selina D'Arcy), Wallace Ford (Ole Pa), Ivan Dixon (Mark Ralfe), Elisabeth Fraser (Sadie), John Qualen (Mr. Faber), Kelly Flynn (Yanek Faber), Debi Storm (Selina, age 5), Renata Vanni (Mrs. Favaloro), Saverio LoMedico (Mr. Favaloro).

Hartman is an 18-year-old blind girl who lives with her prostitute mother, Winters, and her grandfather, Ford. Ford takes his granddaughter outside for the first time since she became blind, 13 years before, when her mother accidentally blinded her during an argument. In the park, Hartman meets Poitier and they become close friends in spite of pressure from Winters and Poitier's brother, Dixon. Poitier gets Hartman to go to a school for the blind but tells her that he won't marry her until she meets more people. A moving story that neatly avoids melodrama. Winters won an Oscar for best supporting actress for her performance.

p, Pandro S. Berman; d&w, Guy Green (based on the story "Be Ready With Bells and Drums" by Elizabeth Kata); ph, Robert Burks (Panavision); m, Jerry Goldsmith; ed, Rita Roland; art d, George W. Davis, Urie McCleary; set d, Henry Grace, Charles S. Thompson; makeup, William Tuttle.

Drama   (PR:A MPAA:NR)

PATERNITY   (1981) 94m PAR c

Burt Reynolds (Buddy Evans), Beverly D'Angelo (Maggie Harden), Norman Fell (Larry), Paul Dooley (Kurt), Elizabeth Ashley (Sophia Thatcher), Lauren Hutton (Jenny Lofton), Juanita Moore (Celia), Peter Billingsley (Tad), Jacqueline Brookes (Aunt Ethel), Linda Gillin (Cathy), Mike Kellin (Tour Guide), Victoria Young (Patti), Elsa Raven (Prenatal Nurse), Carol Locatell (Ms. Werner), Kay Armen (Claudia Feinstein), Murphy Dunne (Singing Telegram Man), Toni Kalem (Diane Cassabello), Kathy Bendett (Laurie), MacIntyre Dixon (Nature Walk Teacher), Alfie Wise (Cab Driver), Tony DiBenedetto (Butcher), Dick Wienad (Mario), Eugene Troobnick (Falalfel Vendor), Ken Magee (Man in Bar), Elaine Giftos (Woman in Bar), Sydney Daniels (Receptionist), Hector Troy (Carlos), Roger Etienne (Waiter), Jason Delgado, Aaron Jessup (Jugglers), Frank Bongiorno (News Vendor), Frank Hamilton (Old Man on Boat), James Harder (Doorman), Irena Ferris (Connie), Lee Ann Duffield (Girl with Mask), Clotilde (Emily), Brad Trumbull, John Gilgreen, Jeff Lawrence (Salesmen), Robin Blake (Nurse), Paula Holland (Pretty Girl), Laura Grayson (Receptionist), Susanna Dalton (Gloria), Buddy Micucci, Derek Thompson, Joseph Hamer, Bob Maroff, Kevin Rigney, Natalie Priest, Jane Cecil.

Reynolds is the manager of Madison Square Garden who is just hitting middle age and begins to realize, thanks to his friends (Fell and Dooley), that he has no one to continue his name; he will have nothing to say he existed. So Reynolds decides to have a child but not a wife. He searches for a woman willing to have a baby without making a commitment, and finds D'Angelo, a musician and waitress who needs money to go to school in Paris. She agrees, and the two fall in love just before the baby is to be born. A light comedy that suffers from a weak script. Reynolds holds his own, but the brainless material never gives him a real chance.

p, Lawrence Gordon and Hank Moonjean; d, David Steinberg; w, Charlie Peters; ph, Bobby Byrne (Movielab); m, David Shire; ed, Donn Cambern; prod d, Jack Collis; art d, Peter Smith; set d, John Anderson; cos, Albert Wolsky.

Comedy   Cas.   (PR:C MPAA:PG)

PATH OF GLORY, THE   (1934, Brit.) 68m Triumph/PDC bw

Maurice Evans (Anton Maroni), Valerie Hobson (Maria), Felix Aylmer (President of Thalia), Henry Daniell (King Maximillian), Athole Stewart (Gen. Ferranzi), Stafford Hilliard (Ferraldi), John Deverell (Paul), David Burns (Ginsberg), Frederick Burtwell (Pedro), Harvey Braban (Col. Conti), Frank Atkinson (Karl), Frank Lacey.

A humorous satire which has two mythical countries declaring war on each other, purely for economic reasons. The laughs start flowing when both sides become determined to lose. It contains some bright spots, but fails to live up to its promising premise.

p&d, Dallas Bower; w, L. DuGarde Peach (based on a radio play by Peach).

Comedy   (PR:A MPAA:NR)

PATHER PANCHALI*½   (1958, India) 112m West Bengal Government/Edward Harrison bw (AKA: THE SONG OF THE ROAD; THE SAGA OF THE ROAD; THE LAMENT OF THE PATH)**

Kanu Banerji (Harihar the Father), Karuna Banerji (Sarbojaya the Mother), Subir Banerji (Apu), Runki Banerji (Durga, as a child), Umas Das Gupta (Durga, as a young girl), Chunibala Devi (Indirtharkun the Old Aunt), Reva Devi (Mrs. Mookerji), Rama Gangopadhaya (Ranu Mookerji), Tulshi Chakraborty (Schoolmaster), Harimoran Nag (Doctor).

The first of Satyajit Ray's APU TRILOGY is also the director's first film. It tells the tale of a poverty-stricken family living in a Bengal village. The father, a struggling writer, leaves for the city, letting his wife take care of the children and an elderly relative. The old woman is driven to the countryside where she dies, and by the time the mother returns home, her daughter has also died. The remaining two films of the trilogy—APARAJITO and THE WORLD OF APU—follow the son, Apu, into manhood and then fatherhood. Based on a popular two-volume novel, the APU TRILOGY has proven Ray to be not only a great Indian director, but one of the world cinema's finest. Commissioned in 1945 to illustrate a children's version of PATHER PANCHALI, Ray became interested in bringing the novel to the screen, even though he had no previous film experience (nor did most of his crew). The production began sporadically on weekends, often being interrupted by cash shortages before the Bengal government helped finish the picture. Inspired by Jean Renoir (Ray visited the set of THE RIVER during its production in India) and the classics of western cinema, Ray's films are extremely unpretentious. PATHER PANCHALI's Cannes Festival premiere attracted little attention, thought to be slow moving (which it is) and boring (which it isn't). Only after receiving praise from critic Andre Bazin did it receive a special humanitarian prize from the jury. It was also chosen in 1962 as a runner-up in the prestigious Sight and Sound top 10 films of all time.

p,d&w, Satyajit Ray (based on the novel by Bibhutibhusan Bandopadhaya); ph, Subrata Mitra; m, Ravi Shankar; ed, Dulal Dutta; art d, Banshi Chandra Gupta.

Drama   Cas.   (PR:A MPAA:NR)

PATHFINDER, THE   (1952) 78m COL c

George Montgomery (Pathfinder), Helena Carter (Welcome Alison), Jay Silverheels (Chingachgook), Walter Kingsford (Col. Duncannon), Rodd Redwing (Chief Arrowhead), Stephen Bekassy (Col. Brasseau), Elena Verdugo (Lokawa), Bruce Lester (Capt. Bradford), Chief Yowlachie (Eagle Feather), Ed Coch, Jr. (Uncas), Russ Conklin (Togamak), Vi Ingraham (Ka-Letan), Adele St. Maur (Matron).

Montgomery is a scout sent by the British to infiltrate a French stronghold. With the help of Carter and Silverheels he learns that the French are planning to take control of the Great Lakes territory. The French unmask Montgomery and Carter, and British officer Lester and his troops save the couple from the firing squad. The script was adapted from James Fenimore Cooper's novel.

p, Sam Katzman; d, Sidney Salkow; w, Robert E. Kent (based on the novel by

James Fenimore Cooper); ph, Henry Freulich (Technicolor); ed, Jerome Thoms; md, Mischa Bakaleinikoff; art d, Paul Palmentola; set d, Sidney Clifford.

Action Adventure **(PR:A MPAA:NR)**

PATHS OF GLORY***** (1957) 86m Bryna Productions/UA bw

Kirk Douglas *(Col. Dax)*, Ralph Meeker *(Cpl. Paris)*, Adolphe Menjou *(Gen. Broulard)*, George Macready *(Gen. Mireau)*, Wayne Morris *(Lt. Roget)*, Richard Anderson *(Maj. Saint-Auban)*, Joseph Turkel *(Pvt. Arnoud)*, Timothy Carey *(Pvt. Ferol)*, Peter Capell *(Col. Judge)*, Susanne Christian *(The German Girl)*, Bert Freed *(Sgt. Boulanger)*, Emile Meyer *(Priest)*, Kem Dibbs *(Pvt. LeJeune)*, Jerry Hausner *(Pvt. Meyer)*, Frederic Bell *(Shell-Shocked Soldier)*, Harold Benedict *(Capt. Nichols)*, John Stein *(Capt. Rousseau)*.

Beyond all doubt this is one of the greatest anti-war films ever made, ranking with Lewis Milestone's ALL QUIET ON THE WESTERN FRONT (1930), a jarring, utterly harrowing masterpiece from Kubrick. Douglas, in one of his finest portrayals—and whose own production company brought this salient, magnificent film into existence—is the commander of the battle-decimated 701st Infantry Regiment of the French Army dug in along the Western Front in a brutal stalemated WW I. It is 1916 and the Allies have been struggling to overcome an equally determined German war machine for two years. Douglas, who has been a criminal lawyer during peacetime, hopes that his regiment will be relieved from front-line duty. The high command has other plans. Menjou, corps commander and suave representative of the high command, arrives at the placid, beautiful chateau which serves as headquarters for Macready, the divisional general in charge. General Menjou tells Macready that his division has been dormant and must now make an all-out attack against an impregnable German position nicknamed The Ant Hill and that this position must be captured within 48 hours. Macready at first tells Menjou that such a task is impossible but Menjou, totally ignoring reality, tells Macready that he's sure "your men can do it without too much difficulty." He then goes on to state that a victory such as taking The Ant Hill will certainly result in a fast promotion for Macready. The vainglorious Macready then assures Menjou that the task will be accomplished. Macready, pompous, his general's uniform immaculate, his air that of an owner of thoroughbreds inspecting his stables, visits the trenches where the 701st resides. Marching down the trenches, Macready sneeringly looks over the men he commands, stopping now and then to superficially inquire as to their well-being and moving on without waiting for a response. He finds one man, Bell, shell-shocked and orders him transferred out of the regiment as an undesirable mental imcompetent. A sergeant, Freed, tries to take the man's side but Macready slaps the soldier, trying to snap him out of his mental state, but it only reduces him to tears. (This face-slapping scene would be repeated with devastating impact in PATTON a decade later, and it is quite possible that the scene was drawn from the actual Patton incident during WW II.) Later, Macready informs Douglas that his men must take The Ant Hill. Douglas explodes, shouting that such a feat is not only impossible but that almost all of his men will be killed attempting such a suicidal attack. Macready is completely unruffled and adds, as a casual afterthought, that perhaps half of Douglas' men will be killed, not too high a price to pay for such a military prize, according to high command evaluation. The ensuing battle profiled here was drawn from the bloody fight for Fort Douamont during the battle of Verdun, a six-month struggle that turned into the greatest slaughterhouse blood bath of WW I, one which claimed the lives of 315,000 patriotic French soldiers vowing "*Ils ne passeront pas!*" ["They shall not pass!"] Douglas continues to argue with Macready who, in turn, slyly states that he will relieve him of his command unless he goes through with the attack. To stay close to his men and protect them as much as possible, Douglas agrees to lead the attack, knowing a replacement would waste the regiment with impersonal disdain. That night a patrol, led by cowardly, drunken lieutenant Morris (ironically one of America's most decorated flying aces during WW II), crawls through no-man's-land to survey the Ant Hill. The Germans send up flares and Morris becomes frightened, telling another soldier, Meeker, that they should return to their own lines and forget about an advance scout, Dibbs, whom he has sent ahead. Meeker tells him to wait for the scout but Morris panics and throws a grenade and runs back to the French lines. Meeker finds Dibbs killed, blown up by Morris' grenade. Morris, back in his dugout, is surprised to see Meeker return. Meeker accuses Morris of cowardice and of killing Dibbs, his own man, with a grenade. Morris tells him he cannot speak to an officer in such a manner and is risking a court-martial. Meeker calls him a "sneaky, booze-guzzling, yellow-bellied rat." Morris tells him that he could charge him with insubordination. Meeker tells him he can be charged with cowardice and wanton murder of one of his own men. Morris tries to appease him, then Douglas comes into the bunker and asks for a report. Morris congratulates Meeker on a good patrol and dismisses him. Rather than risk accusing an officer of wrong-doing, Meeker salutes and retires. Morris then tells Douglas that Dibbs was killed by machine gun fire when he coughed. The attack is set for the next morning with only minimal artillery support so as not to alert the enemy to a full-scale advance. The troops talk through the night; Turkel, a private, is mostly concerned about being killed by a bayonet. At dawn, Douglas walks solemnly through the trenches, inspecting his waiting men, who stand ready with fixed bayonets to go over the top. At the zero hour, Douglas climbs to the top of the trench, blows his whistle, and his men pour over, thousands of them, heading through no-man's-land. The attackers are slaughtered before reaching a halfway point. Macready sees through a rear telescope that a whole company has not left the trenches. He orders his artillery to open fire on his own trenches but the battery commander, Stein, refuses unless he has a written order. Douglas returns to the trenches and tries to get the men there to attack but they will not budge. Morris, drunk and in command, tells him that "it's impossible. . .the men are falling back all along the line. . .impossible." When Douglas attempts to lead the men out of the trenches he is knocked backward onto the duckboards by the bodies of soldiers falling on top of him. The attack is an utter failure. Macready, seeing this from a rear observation post, explodes, ordering the regiment out of the line, yelling: "If those little sweethearts won't face German bullets, they'll face French ones!" First Macready wants to court-martial the entire regiment, then, in a conference with Douglas and Menjou, demands that 100 men be shot as examples of extreme cowardice. Douglas argues that the regiment has shown bravery in the past. "They're scum, colonel," Macready sneers quietly. "The whole rotten regiment, a pack of sneaking, whining, tail-dragging curs." Douglas then mocks him with the ridiculous, saying, "Why not shoot the entire regiment?" Then Douglas offers himself and Menjou brushes off the notion. Menjou suggests reasonableness and Macready agrees that only three men will be selected, tried, and then shot. Douglas is appointed defense attorney for the three men to be picked at random by their officers. Turkel, a radical, Carey, a half-wit, and Meeker, selected by Morris to cover up his own sins, are picked to stand trial. Douglas appears before the court-martial and tries to defend the three men but at every turn the kangaroo court-martial dismisses his evidence, refuses the testimony of witnesses, and will not allow any real defense of the victimized men. Each man gives his version of what occurred during the attack and what he did or did not do. Carey explains that all in his platoon were killed, except himself and a private named Meyer. The arrogant chief of the court-martial, Capell, and Anderson—prosecuting attorney and yes-man to Macready—badger Carey into admitting that he only advanced about half way across no-man's-land before he turned back. Douglas then cross-examines Carey, pointing out that even though he and Meyer were the only ones left alive in his platoon, they should have gone ahead. "Why didn't you and Meyer attack the Ant Hill single-handed?" "Just me and Meyer, sir?" inquires the slow-witted Carey. "Yes." Carey gets the point finally and smirkingly replies, directing his comment to the court: "I knew we should have taken the Ant Hill but we came on back." Douglas tries to defend Turkel by trying to cite his medals—earned in previous engagements—but Capell cuts him off, saying that Turkel, who has been selected by lot to stand trial, is "not being tried for his former bravery but his current cowardice." Douglas then has Meeker testify that he was knocked unconscious as he tried to go over the top and has the scar on his head to prove it. None of this means anything to a court that considers the three men, in Anderson's pompous words, "a blot on the honor of the French nation." Douglas begins his summary by stating: "Gentlemen of the court, there are times when I'm ashamed to be a member of the human race, and this is one such occasion. It's impossible for me to summarize a case for the defense when I have never been allowed a reasonable opportunity to present a defense." Macready interrupts him with the challenge: "Are you protesting the authenticity of this court?" Douglas says he protests being prevented from introducing evidence which he considers "vital in the defense. The prosecution presented no witnesses, there has never been a written indictment against the defendants—and lastly, I protest the fact that no stenographic record of this trial has been kept!" He goes on to state that the court-martial "is a stain" and "a mockery of human justice." He begs for mercy from the court and gets none. All three men are condemned and a last meal is brought to them. Carey begins to eat heartily, then stops, thinking the food might be poisoned or drugged. Turkel and Meeker talk about escaping but Carey tells them there is no escape. Meeker looks down at a bug crawling on the table and says that it will be alive long after he's dead. Carey squashes the bug with his hand and says: "Now you got the edge on him." A priest, Meyer, enters the condemned cell, which is really a large stable, and comforts Carey, who breaks into tears; Meyer then hears Meeker's confession. Turkel mocks the priest and then hits him; Meeker slugs Turkel, who strikes his head on a concrete beam and receives a skull fracture. He is in an unconscious state but is still ordered to be executed. That night Douglas tells Morris that he will be in charge of the execution squad. When Morris begs to be relieved, Douglas growls: "Request denied—you've got the job. It's all yours." As Morris leaves, Stein, the captain of the battery of artillery for the division, arrives, saying he has something to tell Douglas that will have "a bearing on the court-martial." Later that evening, Douglas goes to a grand chateau and asks to see Menjou, who excuses himself from dancing at a ball and meets with Douglas in a huge, elegant library. Douglas begs Menjou to spare the three condemned men. Menjou has a drink with him and, projecting an avuncular image, tells him that "troops crave discipline and one way to maintain discipline is to shoot a man every now and then." As Menjou starts to go, Douglas tells him that he has sworn affidavits from two officers and an enlisted man stating that Macready ordered his own artillery to shell his own trenches. He suggests that such information, if it reaches the press, could be hurtful. Menjou keeps the affidavits but walks out, saying: "Will you pardon me, Colonel Dax, I've been rude to my guests too long." The next morning, Carey, Meeker, and Turkel—the latter carried unconscious on a stretcher—are marched before their regiment, tied to posts, and shot to death by a firing squad commanded by Morris. Just before ordering the squad to fire, Morris offers Meeker a blindfold; he can't bring himself to look at the man with whom he had gone to school years earlier and the man he has wronged. "I'm sorry," Morris whispers to Meeker. Following the execution, Macready and Menjou sit in the chateau eating a hearty breakfast. "The men died wonderfully," says Macready. Douglas enters and Macready tells Douglas: "Colonel Dax, your men died very well!" Menjou then confronts Macready with the charge by Douglas that he ordered his artillery to fire on his own men. Macready calls Douglas disloyal. Menjou smoothly says there must be an inquiry. Macready stands up in shock and says to Menjou: "So that's it—you're making me the goat of the whole affair!" He storms out. Then Menjou offers Douglas Macready's job with a promotion to general, stating that it is a "promotion you have so carefully planned for." Douglas angrily replies: "Sir, would you like me to suggest what you can do with that promotion?" Menjou yells that he must apologize at once or be placed under arrest. Douglas apologizes by saying: "I apologize for not being entirely honest with you. I apologize for not revealing my true feelings. I apologize, sir, for not telling you sooner that you're a degenerate, sadistic old man and you can go to hell before I apologize to you now or ever again!" The ever politically sly Menjou gives him a weak smile and sits down, saying, "Colonel Dax, you're a disappointment to me. You've spoiled the keenness of your mind by wallowing in sentimentality. You really did want to save those men and you were not angling for Mireau's command. You're an idealist and I pity you as I would the village idiot. We're fighting a war, Dax, a war we've got to win. Those men didn't fight and they were shot. You brought charges against General

Mireau and I insisted that he answer them. Wherein have I done wrong?" Douglas gives him a long look and says, "Because you don't know the answer to that question, I pity you." Douglas returns to his command to stand outside a pub where the proprietor has brought a young German girl, Christian (later Kubrick's wife), to entertain the French troops. The soldiers hoot and whistle and catcall loudly so that Christian cannot be heard singing her simple song; she is so terrified that she cries but keeps on singing until the shouting and whistles drop off so that only her plaintive, thin voice is heard singing a universally known song called "Soldier Boy." Soon, the French soldiers are humming along with her, their faces drawn, their eyes watery, some with tears sliding uncontrollably down their cheeks as the song evokes the memories of their youth, their homes, a world they will probably never again see. The girl sings in German, and the Frenchmen still hum along with her, a deep resonant humming that seems to reverberate from their very souls. Douglas stands outside, realizing that his men are not completely dehumanized, that passion and memory still cling to what is left of their entities. Freed tells him that the soldiers must move up to the front. Douglas tells Freed to give the men a few more minutes and then resolutely marches back to his headquarters. (This last scene in the pub is one of the greatest transformations of human behavior on celluloid, with Kubrick's sensitive cameras closing in on the most soulful faces to ever stare and weep in uniform, any uniform.) The martial music at the end of the film is a resonant, low-register delivery of the "Soldier Boy" song, where the opening of the film (the only two places where music is evident) presents a military version of "The Marseillaise." Kubrick's direction of this stirring and emotional film is flawless, every frame filled with great acting from Douglas, who was never better, to the smallest bit player. The old and self-indulgent generals who typified the unconcern most of the high command had for the lost lives of their men is embodied chillingly in patrician Macready and foxy Menjou, two absolutely vicious scoundrels who typify the responsibility for the eradication of a whole generation of young men. Morris is wonderful as the drunken coward, Anderson repulsive as the slick toady to Macready, and Meeker is terrific as the decent trooper who dies only because of his knowledge that his superior is a coward. Carey, as the incompetent victim, is also jarring, as is the disillusioned Turkel. The battle scenes showing the attack on The Ant Hill are devastating, brutally authentic, and the barrage through which Douglas leads his men—Kubrick's cameras tracking along in startling truck and boom shots—is a hurricane of death that comes closer to the real thing than anything ever dramatized. Of course, Kubrick's statement is one of overwhelming condemnation of war and its senseless waste but it is also a statement of human courage, human compassion, and the kind of white-heat will that insists upon survival despite the efforts of tyrants to wipe out their fellow man, to wipe out principle, honesty, and the greatness of human spirit. And, as PATHS OF GLORY certainly says with brilliance, that spirit will never die. Every general staff officer of every nation in the world should be compelled to watch this film at least once a year and hopefully they will remember that they command not armies but men, flesh and blood. The battle cry here is not for war and the death of others but for peace, for life, and that little time of freedom from conflict each generation nurtures in its youth before the bleating of bugles and the long, sorrowful muttering of drums begins to beckon. That sound is heard, Kubrick reminds us with painful memory, when we can no longer recall the shattered bodies of our sacred dead and when deceptive long green grass covers from realistic view the scarred geography of a cruel past. France did not wish to remember this past and banned PATHS OF GLORY from its theaters when it was released; in fact, it is still banned as a slander against French honor (it was briefly banned from American military bases). The script is literate, shrewd, and apt to the point Kubrick makes, the same as Cobb's provocative novel which appeared in 1934. (The novel—based on an actual occurrence—was not endorsed in France, either, and Cobb was not a welcome visitor to that country after penning his indictment of the French militarists.) Some of the shots used by Kubrick and marvelously photographed by Krause are almost identical to still photographs, particularly in the pub scene showing the French soldiers, appearing in an out-of-print pictorial called *The Great War*, written and edited by Laurence Stallings. This is a director's film, one where Kubrick profiles naked power with the kind of visual excitement seldom seen on the screen. Kubrick's presence is always felt but never interferes with the astounding traveling shots through the trenches where the common troops cringe in claustrophobic terror and the expansive ballrooms where the generals dally in contrast to the plight of their men. Then there is that terrible approaching shot as the three condemned men move inexorably toward the three black stakes against which they will end their lives, stakes that loom larger and larger as the men and the camera approach. There is grim irony everywhere, especially when Macready views the desperate, frenzied, and confused attack on The Ant Hill from his distant position as if enjoying it as a spectator sport, something akin to watching a horse race from a comfortable glass-encased box seat. In this brief scene alone Kubrick captures the hypocrisy and murderous power of the military caste system. Although the French had no love for PATHS OF GLORY, Winston Churchill viewed the film and stated his admiration for the authenticity of the battle scenes. These amazing sequences were shot outside the village of Pucheim, west of Munich (the entire film was shot in Germany). Douglas' company hired dozens of German workmen to change several acres into a vast moonscape of no-man's-land, gouging out the crater holes, bomb holes, huge ruts, and gullies, filling some with water, strewing the area with barbed wire and then planting hundreds of explosives throughout to be set off during the attack on The Ant Hill. Hundreds of German policemen were hired as extras to play the French troops while six cameras tracked the attack, recording the "deaths" of scores of actors who were given little maps showing their "dying zones" or the exact locations in the battle area where they were to dramatically be hit by machine gun bullets or shrapnel from bombs and fall dead. The composition for these scenes owed some debt to those battle scenes shown in two Warner Brothers WW I films, THE FIGHTING 69TH and SERGEANT YORK. It is also obvious that Kubrick was mightily influenced by Max Ophuls, who was known for his countless dolly shots, and the fluid styles of certain Russian directors. In order to allow room for Kubrick's rolling cameras, the trenches down which Douglas and Macready march were made six feet wide, about two feet wider than the real trenches of WW I. Douglas acquired the book rights to the Cobb novel and then hired the relatively unknown Kubrick to direct. Their union and achievement together with PATHS OF GLORY led to their later collaboration in producing the spectacle SPARTACUS. PATHS OF GLORY, though it appeared to be a very expensive film, cost only $900,000 to produce (where SPARTACUS would cost $10 million).

p, James B. Harris; d, Stanley Kubrick; w, Kubrick, Calder Willingham, Jim Thompson (based on the novel by Humphrey Cobb); ph, George Krause; m, Gerald Fried; ed, Eva Kroll; art d, Ludwig Reiber.

War Drama Cas. (PR:C MPAA:NR)

PATIENT IN ROOM 18, THE** (1938) 58m WB bw

Patric Knowles *(Lance O'Leary)*, Ann Sheridan *(Sara Keate)*, Eric Stanley *(Bentley, Valet)*, John Ridgely *(Jim Warren)*, Rosella Towne *(Maida Day)*, Jean Benedict *(Carol Lethany)*, Harland Tucker *(Dr. Arthur Lethany)*, Edward Raquelo *(Dr. Fred Hajek)*, Charles Trowbridge *(Dr. Balman)*, Vicki Lester *(Nurse)*, Cliff Clark *(Inspector Foley)*, Ralph Sanford *(Donahue)*, Frank Orth *(John Higgins)*, Greta Meyer *(Hilda)*, Walter Young *(Coroner)*, Ralph Dunn *(Hotel Clerk)*, George Offerman, Jr. *(Newsboy)*, Glen Cavender *(Doorman)*, Jack Richardson *(Cabby)*, Cliff Saum, Jack Mower *(Policemen)*, Spec O'Donnell *(Elevator Operator)*, William Hopper *(Grabshot)*, Owen King *(Day Clerk)*.

Knowles is a detective laid up in a hospital where one of the patients was murdered and $100,000 worth of radium was stolen. Knowles takes on the case as the nurse tries to keep him in his bed. Knowles pins the crimes on the crazed Trowbridge and wins over head nurse Sheridan.

p, Bryan Foy; d, Bobby Connolly, Crane Wilbur; w, Eugene Solow, Robertson White (based on a story by Mignon G. Eberhart); ph, James Van Trees; ed, Lou Hesse.

Mystery (PR:A MPAA:NR)

PATIENT VANISHES, THE*½ (1947, Brit.) 73m Pathe/FC bw (AKA: THIS MAN IS DANGEROUS)

James Mason *(Mick Cardby)*, Mary Clare *(Matron)*, Margaret Vyner *(Mollie Bennett)*, Gordon McLeod *(Inspector Cardby)*, Frederick Valk *(Dr. Moger)*, Barbara Everest *(Mrs. Cardby)*, Barbara James *(Lena Morne)*, G.H. Mulcaster *(Lord Morne)*, Eric Clavering *(Al Meason)*, Terry Conlin *(Detective-Sgt. Trotter)*, W.G. Fay *(Mr. Eslick)*, Brefni O'Rorke *(Dr. Crosbie)*, Viola Lyel *(Nurse)*, Anthony Shaw *(Sir Wallace Benson)*, Michael Rennie *(Inspector)*.

Mason is the detective son of Scotland Yard inspector McLeod, and both are assigned to the same case. An English lord's daughter has been kidnaped and father and son race to be the one to save the girl without paying the ransom. A dull mystery burdened with too much dialog. The film, based on a novel in the Mick Cardby detective series, was made in 1943, but went unreleased during the war. It was distributed in America four years later.

p, John Argyle; d, Lawrence Huntington; w, Argyle, Edward Dryhurst, David Hume (based on the novel *They Called Him Death* by Hume).

Mystery (PR:A MPAA:NR)

PATRICIA GETS HER MAN*½ (1937, Brit.) 68m WB-FN bw

Hans Sonker *(Count Stephan D'Orlet)*, Lesley Brook *(Patricia Fitzroy)*, Edwin Styles *(Brian Maxwell)*, Aubrey Mallalieu *(Col. Fitzroy)*, Cissy Fitzgerald *(Duchess Banning)*, Betty Lynne *(Marie)*, Yoshihide Yanai *(Suki)*, Leonard Barry, Scott Harold, Cecil Calvert, H.B. Passat.

A predictable comedy programmer which has Brook trying to snare film star Styles while on a stay in the South of France. She enlists Sonker, a philandering count, to court her and make Maxwell jealous. Brook's plot backfires when Sonker falls in love with her and devises a counterplot. Sonker and Styles abduct the girl, giving Styles a chance to offend her and send her running into the arms of Sonker.

p, Irving Asher; d, Reginald Purdell; w, Max Merritt, Maurice Kusell; ph, Basil Emmott.

Comedy/Romance (PR:A MPAA:NR)

PATRICK*** (1979, Aus.) 110m Australian International/Filmways c

Susan Penhaligon *(Kathy Jacquard)*, Robert Helpmann *(Dr. Roget)*, Robert Thompson *(Patrick)*, Rod Mullinar *(Ed Jacquard)*, Bruce Barry *(Dr. Wright)*, Julia Blake *(Matron Cassidy)*, Helen Hemingway *(Sister Williams)*, Maria Mercedes *(Nurse Panicale)*, Frank Wilson *(Detective Sgt. Grant)*, Peter Culpan *(Grant's Assistant (Marilyn Rodgers (Day Desk Nurse)*, Peggy Nichols *(Night Desk Nurse)*, Carole-Ann Aylett *(Patrick's Mother)*, Walter Pym *(Capt. Fraser)*, Paul Young *(The Lover)*.

A well-paced and intelligently written horror film from Australia similar to CARRIE in its subject matter involving psychokinesis. Thompson plays Patrick, a young man who has been in an irreversible coma for three years, ever since his mother and her lover were killed in an electrical accident. As it happens, Thompson killed them, and the comatose man has a powerful sixth sense. He falls in love with Penhaligon, the nurse that takes care of him. She begins to conclude that Patrick is causing strange occurrences in the hospital. Patrick begins killing the doctors and nurses that would like to accelerate his death. He also wants Penhaligon to commit suicide so she can join him in death. Director Franklin would go on to direct PSYCHO II. The U.S. version of PATRICK, like MAD MAX, has poorly dubbed American voices over the Australian ones.

p, Anthony I. Ginnane, Richard Franklin; d, Franklin; w, Everett De Roche; ph, Don McAlpine (Afgacolor); m, Brian May; ed, Edward Queen-Mason; art d, Leslie Binns; spec eff, Conrad Rothman.

Horror Cas. (PR:O MPAA:PG)

PATRICK THE GREAT** (1945) 88m UNIV bw

Donald O'Connor *(Pat Donahue, Jr.)*, Peggy Ryan *(Judy Watkin)*, Frances Dee *(Lynn Andrews)*, Donald Cook *(Pat Donahue, Sr.)*, Eve Arden *(Jean Mathews)*, Thomas Gomez *(Max Wilson)*, Gavin Muir *(Prentis Johns)*, Andrew Tombes *(Sam Bassett)*, Irving Bacon *(Mr. Merney)*, Emmett Vogan *(Alsop)*, Isabelle Mal *(Grand Dame)*, Robert Emmett Keane *(Henry Ames)*, Joel Allen *(Actor)*, Lee Phelps *(Prop Man)*, Ernie Adams *(Constable)*, Billy Benedict *(Joey)*, Douglas Wood), Sir Orville Armstrong), Sidney Miller *(Tony)*, Eddie Dunn *(Plumber)*, Buster Brodie *(Bellboy)*, Ray Walker *(Orchestra Leader)*, George Chandler *(Bellhop)*, George Lloyd *(Fisherman)*, Harry Harvey, Neely Edwards *(Waiters)*, Cal Rothenberg, Robert Coleman, John Truel, Joe "Corky" Geil, Walter Carter, Bobby Scheerer *(Jivin' Jacks)*, Grace Costello, Shirley Mills, Peggy Brant, Dolores Diane, Jean Davis, Patsy O'Connor *(Jivin' Jills)*.

O'Connor is the son of actor Cook, and family problems arise when O'Connor gets a part in a Broadway play that the father was bidding for. They squabble as they vacation at a mountain lodge, but find time for Ryan and Dee. Cook forgets about his lost role when Dee agrees to marry him. Songs include "Song of Love," "For the First Time," "Don't Move," "Ask Madam Zan," "The Cubacha," "When You Bump into Someone You Know" (Charles Tobias, David Kapp, Sidney Miller, Inez James, Charles Previn).

p, Howard Benedict; d, Frank Ryan; w, Dorothy Bennett, Bertram Millhauser (based on a story by Jane Hall, Frederick Block, Ralph Block); ph, Frank Redman; m, Hans J. Salter; ed, Ted J. Kent; art d, John B. Goodman, Abraham Grossman; art d, Vera West; ch, Louis DaPron.

Musical **(PR:A MPAA:NR)**

PATRIOT, THE*½** (1928) 113m PAR-FP bw

Emil Jannings *(Czar Paul I, Son of Catherine the Great and Mad Peter I)*, Lewis Stone *(Count Pahlen the "Patriot")*, Florence Vidor *(Countess Anna Ostermann)*, Neil Hamilton *(Crown Prince Alexander)*, Harry Cording *(Stefan)*, Vera Voronina *(Mlle. Lapoukhine, the Czar's Mistress)*.

A masterfully constructed picture which chronicles the last days in the life of yet another mad Russian czar, Paul I, played remarkably by Jannings as a stark-raving lunatic who does, on rare occasion, show strains of humanity. Set in 18th-Century Russia, Jannings retreats to the safety of his palace, fearing that an assassination plot will spoil his reign of lunacy. It is only Stone, a devoted count and the czar's longtime friend, that Jannings can trust. Although Stone feels a loyalty to the czar, he can no longer sit back and watch his people live in the misery of his rule. He enlists the aid of Cording, a palace guard whom Jannings viciously humiliates, to help carry out the assassination plot. Cording uses his mistress, Voronina, to lure the czar into the bedroom where the murder is to take place. Voronina, however, informs the czar of the scheme. Stone is called in and questioned about the accusations, but is able to reassure Jannings of his loyalty. A plot surely does exist, and later that night it is carried out. Cording and Stone enter Janning's bedroom and a shot is fired (by Cording) into the czar's body. Cording then turns the gun on the noble count and fires again. As he lies dying on the floor, Stone proclaims, "I have been a bad friend and lover—but I have been a Patriot." As fine as all the supporting roles are (Stone received a Best Actor nomination), it is Jannings who steals the picture. His leering animalistic czar is a tour-de-force whether he is throwing a harmless Pekinese puppy out a window or punching his endearing, playful mistress in the face with all his might. He is at his most disturbing when he berates Cording. During an inspection the czar notices that Cording is missing a button on his uniform. The enraged Jannings explodes, shoves his finger in Cording's face, plunges his thumb into his mouth, and then mercilessly whips him. THE PATRIOT was directed as a silent, but the advent of sound led to some post-synchronized dialog (Jannings beckons to his friend Stone: "Pahlen, Pahlen!")—none of which Lubitsch was involved with. Also noteworthy is Hans Dreier's magnificent marble set design, which received an Oscar nomination, along with Hans Kraly's adaptation.

d, Ernst Lubitsch; w, Hans Kraly, Julian Johnson (based on the novel *Der Patriot: Drama in 5 Akten* by Alfred Neumann, the stage adaptation by Ashley Dukes, and "Paul I" by Dimitri Merejkowski); ph, Bert Glennon; m, Domenico Savino, Gerard Garbonaro; ed, Lubitsch; set d, Hans Dreier; cos, Ali Hubert.

Historical Drama **(PR:C MPAA:NR)**

PATSY, THE*½ (1964) 100m PAR c

Jerry Lewis *(Stanley Belt)*, Ina Balin *(Ellen Betz)*, Everett Sloane *(Caryl Fergusson)*, Phil Harris *(Chic Wymore)*, Keenan Wynn *(Harry Silver)*, Peter Lorre *(Morgan Heywood)*, John Carradine *(Bruce Alden)*, Hans Conried *(Professor Mule-RRR)*, Richard Deacon *(Sy Devore)*, Scat Man Crothers *(Shoeshine Boy)*, Del Moore *(Police Officer)*, Neil Hamilton *(Barber)*, Buddy Lester *(M.C.)*, Nancy Kulp *(Theater-Goer)*, Lloyd Thaxton *(Disc Jockey)*, Norman Alden *(Bully at Gym)*, Jack Albertson *(Man)*, Henry Slate *(Paul)*, Gavin Gordon *(Executive on Golf Course)*, Ned Wynn *(Page)*, Phil Foster *(Sloan)*, Herbie Faye *(Tailor)*, Harry Spear *(Salesman)*, Lorraine Crawford *(Manicurist)*, June Smaney *(Pedicurist)*, Joan Swift *(Girl)*, Mabel Smaney *(Woman in Phone Booth)*, Harry V. Cheshire *(Police Sergeant)*, Robert May *(Fireworks Boy)*, John Macchia *(Student)*, Ed Rosa *(Band Leader)*, Joe Stabil *(Leader Musician)*, Sherwood Price *(Bellboy)*, Michael Ross *(Truck Driver)*, Dave Lipp *(Frozen Stare Man)*, Hollis Morrison *(Jute Box)*, Phil Arnold *(Bartender)*, Michael Mahoney *(Heckler)*, Dee Jay Mattis *(The Broad)*, Terry Naylor *(Customer)*, William Leyden *(TV Announcer)*, Sam Weston *(Man on Phone)*, Jerry Hausner *(Floorman)*, Darlene Lucht *(Check Room Girl)*, Quinn O'Hara *(Cigarette Girl)*, Fritz Feld *(Maitre D')*, Clyde Adler *(Bald-Headed Man)*, Kathleen Freeman *(Katie)*, John Gallaudet *(Barney)*, Jerry Dexter *(Radio Newscaster)*, Dave Willock *(Alex)*, Norman Leavitt *(Newsboy)*, John Marlowe, Bob Harvey *(Waiters)*, Bob Ivers, Richard Bakalyan *(Boys at Dance)*, Fay de Witt, Sheila Rogers, Eddie Ryder *(People at Party)*, William Wellman, Jr., Bob Denner, Billy Beck *(Band Members)*, Don Brodie, Murray Alper, Barbara Pepper, Peggy Mondo *(Bowlers)*, Adele Claire, Isabelle Dwan *(Elderly Ladies)*, Billy Bletcher, Byron Kane, Bob Carson *(Table Captains at Italian Cafe)*, Marianne Gaba, Layne Maddox, Nancy Patricia Fisher, Joanne C. Quakenbush *(Waitresses)*, William Enge, Rob Christian, Walter Smith, Bobby Johnson, Joey Johnson, Mantan Moreland *(Barbershop Porters)*, Rhonda Fleming, Hedda Hopper, George Raft, Mel Torme, Ed Wynn, Vernon Scott, Joe Finnigan, Richard Gehman, Ernest Schworck, Edward C. Widdis, The Step Brothers *(Themselves)*.

The management team of a famous singer who dies in a plane crash hastily looks for a new superstar to save their jobs. The team, consisting of Lorre, Wynn, Sloane, Harris, Carradine, and Balin, choose bellboy Lewis to groom for stardom. Things go badly as Lewis bombs his nightclub appearances and recording sessions. But somehow he gets invited to be on the Ed Sullivan show, and the management team abandons ship, fearing the worst. Lewis is a hit and does become a superstar. He hires the management team back and proposes to Balin. George Raft, Hedda Hopper, Ed Wynn and Ed Sullivan make cameo appearances. This is one of Lewis' lesser efforts, with his appearances on the Ed Sullivan Show drawing the only real laughs. The film was originally going to be called SON OF BELLBOY, as the sequel to Lewis' 1960 film, THE BELLBOY, but that was quickly dropped. Peter Lorre died four days after the filming of his scenes.

p, Ernest D. Glucksman; d, Jerry Lewis; w, Lewis, Bill Richmond; ph, W. Wallace Kelley (Technicolor); m, David Raksin; ed, John Woodcock; art d, Hal Pereira, Cary Odell; set d, Sam Comer, Ray Moyer; cos, Edith Head; m/l "I Lost My Heart in a Drive-In Movie," Raskin, Jack Brooks; makeup, Wally Westmore.

Comedy **Cas.** **(PR:A MPAA:NR)**

PATTERN FOR PLUNDER (SEE: BAY OF SAINT MICHEL, 1964, Brit.)

PATTERN OF EVIL (SEE: SATAN IN HIGH HEELS, 1962)

PATTERNS**** (1956) 83m UA bw (GB: PATTERNS OF POWER)

Van Heflin *(Fred Staples)*, Everett Sloane *(Walter Ramsey)*, Ed Begley *(William Briggs)*, Beatrice Straight *(Nancy Staples)*, Elizabeth Wilson *(Marge Fleming)*, Joanna Roos *(Miss Lanier)*, Elene Kiamos *(Sylvia Trammel)*, Shirley Standlee *(Miss Hill)*, Ronnie Welsh, Jr. *(Paul Briggs)*, Sally Gracie *(Ann)*, Michael Dreyfuss *(Billy)*, Adrienne Moore *(1st Secretary)*, Elaine Kaye *(2nd Secretary)*.

There wasn't one note of music in PATTERNS and the absence wasn't missed as Serling's words had a music of their own. It began as a television play for the "Kraft Theatre" and, like MARTY and other TV plays, it was turned into a film. The limited use of film technique (much of the movie takes place in the offices of a huge conglomerate and it is basically an interior story) does not work against this because the characters are so fascinating and the performances are universally superior. Heflin is brought in from Ohio (the same state Jack Lemmon lived in when visiting New York in THE OUT-OF-TOWNERS) to serve at the company's New York office. Boss of all bosses is Sloane, a ruthless company man who runs the firm like a benevolent dictator, with more emphasis on the dictatorial than the benevolence. Begley is an executive who has seen better days and is being eased out by Sloane, who intends Heflin to be Begley's replacement. There is no room in Sloane's mind for old loyalties and the company's interests must be above all feelings. Heflin truly likes Begley, who is always alibi-ing for Sloane's behavior and shrugging off the boss' insults. There are a few cutaways as Heflin discusses matters with his wife, Straight, but most of the action is strictly in the "executive suite," which was the name of a movie not unlike this one. Anyone who has ever worked in a large company will recognize the people and the situations depicted in the screenplay but some of the Machiavellian tactics may be lost on others. Brilliantly directed by another TV veteran, Cook, this picture did not garner any awards and didn't do much business, which was a darn shame. Sloane's work as the corporation chief is sensational, a portrait of a driven man who rules his roost like an emperor. Begley, who came out of radio where he appeared in more than 10,000 programs, was one of the most versatile actors in show business and proved so when he played the William Jennings Bryan role in Broadway's "Inherit The Wind" for more than 700 performances, then turned around and did Clarence Darrow after Paul Muni left the show.

p, Michael Myerberg; d, Fielder Cook; w, Rod Serling (based on his television play); ph, Boris Kaufman; ed, Dave Kummins, Carl Lerner; art d, Richard Sylbert; cos, Mary Merrill.

Drama **(PR:A MPAA:NR)**

PATTERNS OF POWER (SEE: PATTERNS, 1956)

PATTON***** (1970) 170m FOX c (GB: PATTON—LUST FOR GLORY; AKA: PATTON: A SALUTE TO A REBEL)

George C. Scott *(Gen. George S. Patton, Jr.)*, Karl Malden *(Gen. Omar N. Bradley)*, Michael Bates *(Field Marshal Sir Bernard Law Montgomery)*, Edward Binns *(Maj. Gen. Walter Bedell Smith)*, Lawrence Dobkin *(Col. Gaston Bell)*, John Doucette *(Maj. Gen. Lucian K. Truscott)*, James Edwards *(Sgt. William George Meeks)*, Frank Latimore *(Lt. Col. Henry Davenport)*, Richard Muench *(Col. Gen. Alfred Jodl)*, Morgan Paull *(Capt. Richard N. Jenson)*, Siegfried Rauch *(Capt. Oskar Steiger)*, Paul Stevens *(Lt. Col. Charles R. Codman)*, Michael Strong *(Brig. Gen. Hobart Carver)*, Karl Michael Vogler *(Field Marshal Erwin Rommel)*, Stephen Young *(Capt. Chester B. Hansen)*, Peter Barkworth *(Col. John Welkin)*, John Barrie *(Air Vice-Marshal Sir Arthur Coningham)*, David Bauer *(Lt. Gen. Harry Buford)*, Tim Considine *(Soldier Who Gets Slapped)*, Albert Dumortier *(Moroccan Minister)*, Gerald Flood *(Air Chief Marshal Sir Arthur Tedder)*, Jack Gwillim *(Gen. Sir Harold Alexander)*, David Healy *(Clergyman)*, Bill Hickman *(Gen. Patton's Driver)*, Carey Loftin *(Gen. Bradley's Driver)*, Lionel Murton *(3rd Army Chaplain)*, Sandy Kevin *(Correspondent)*, Douglas Wilmer *(Maj. Gen. Francis de Guingand)*, Patrick J. Zurica *(lst Lt. Alexander Stiller)*, Lowell Thomas *(Narrator of Fox*

Movietone Newsreels), Alan MacNaughtan *(British Briefing Officer)*, Clint Ritchie *(Tank Captain)*, Abraxas Aaran *(Willy the Dog)*.

This WW II spectacle is immense but Scott's virtuoso performance looms even larger than any battle or any personality of the war. He *is* Patton in body and mentality, providing one of the most acute and dynamic biographical portrayals ever seen. Early during the war, an American tank unit is wiped out at Kasserine Pass near Tunis by elements of Gen. Erwin Rommel's devastating Afrika Korps. Inspecting the wholesale carnage of his troops is Malden, playing Gen. Bradley. He quickly concludes that an uncompromising, hard-hitting U.S. general is needed to head his tank divisions and he names Scott to the post. The enigmatic Scott, as George Smith Patton, Jr., takes over the remnants of the American units in Africa and quickly turns a demoralized, sloppy, and undisciplined gang of men into a crack unit. He then fearlessly leads this division against Rommel, drawing the German "Desert Fox" into an enormous trap at El Guettar wherein he destroys the German tank units in a desert engagement. Scott is jubilant with triumph, yelling during the height of the battle as his men get the upper hand: "Rommel, you magnificant bastard, I read your book!" He quickly earns the sobriquet "Old Blood and Guts" (to which many a dogface under his command would later add, "our blood and his guts"). Scott quickly wins fame through his victories so that the German high command takes notice of him, studying his unorthodox manner, his sense of personal destiny, while other Allied commanders—chiefly British Field Marshal Montgomery (Bates)—become jealous and extremely competitive. Scott does not aid his own cause when meeting members of the press, expansively describing his theories of warfare and jocularly taunting his peers. Scott's next assignment is to invade Sicily but he fulminates against the high command when he learns that he and his American 7th Army are to support Montgomery and his British troops who will spearhead the attack across the island and have the honor of taking Messina. Scott, however, plays it his own way, without telling his superiors. He orders one of his commanders, Doucette, to skirt the German defenses and smash through them in all-out drive on Messina, beating Montgomery's forces into the city, further incurring the wrath of the British field marshal. When Bates arrives in Messina at the head of his troops, he is greeted in the main square by Scott and his massed tanks. Bates is completely deflated and instantly registers an emotion that is to be aimed at Scott for the duration of the war—hate. In a visit to a field hospital, Scott finds a battle-fatigued soldier, Considine. He asks Considine where he is wounded and the soldier breaks down and weeps. Scott, enraged and no believer in fatigue as an excuse for hospitalization, slaps Considine and then turns to doctors and shouts: "Get this coward out of here!" He is later upbraided by Malden and then ordered by General Dwight D. Eisenhower to apologize publicly through the ranks of his entire division. He does, with consummate grace and dignity. Removed from his command as a result of widespread publicity over the slapping incident, Scott is a frustrated general without a military mission. A visionary, he tells aides that he does not believe God will allow him to sit out the war and that he was meant to lead men into great battles. Yet he remains on inactive rolls and is finally used as a decoy to hoodwink German intelligence into believing that he will lead an invasion from Calais. The Normandy Invasion takes place without Scott but, after much conciliatory conversation with superior Malden, he is given the command of the 3rd Army, winning one mighty battle after another with his armored troops. When the 101st Airborne Division at Bastogne is encircled by masses of German troops, Scott leads his 3rd Army hundreds of miles across Europe in a Herculean effort to rescue the beleagured paratroopers. Just before the 101st is overwhelmed by German troops, Scott arrives with his 3rd Army and saves the day, smashing the encircling ring of Germans and ending Hitler's last great counteroffensive of the war in the Battle of the Bulge (officially known as Ardennes II, 1944-45). Then Scott turns his troops around and races for Czechoslovakia where he is about to crush the final Nazi resistance in that sector. At the last minute, his old competitor, Montgomery, is allowed to mop up the remnants of the German armies in that battle zone. Immediately following the end of the war in Europe, Scott becomes highly vocal in his criticism of America's ally, Russia, even suggesting that German armies be reactivated and used to crush communism. Again, Scott is removed from command and sent into involuntary retirement. He bids his faithful staff farewell and drives off, ostensibly to his death (since Patton was killed a short time later in a car accident). Scott is amazing to watch in his multi-dimensional role of the most controversial American general (except, perhaps, for General of the Armies Douglas MacArthur) in the 20th Century. He is insensitive to his men's plight on some occasions but gentle as a loving father to their needs at other times. The scene where he slaps Considine is balanced with a scene where Patton comes on a battlefield and receives a report from a dying American tank commander, kissing him on the forehead for his valor. Enigmatic and inexplicable, the total character of Patton is captured with subtle undertones and rich extravagance by Scott in his Academy Award-winning role (he refused to accept the Oscar). Wonderful support comes from Malden as Bradley, Bates as Montgomery, Binns as Bedell-Smith and Doucette as Truscott. Schaffner's direction is majestic and his handling of complex battles is masterful. The film is flawless and Scott, who disliked Malden's essaying of Bradley during the production (calling him "Old Smiley"), never gave a better performance before or since this film. Some of his lines remain memorable to this day, particularly his truthful admission about war: "God help me, I do love it so." His opening six-minute speech about the fighting spirit of Americans is a classic and worth the entire film. Schaffner shot the film in 70-millimeter Dimension 150 which allowed a broad look at the massive battles he staged, almost impersonal spectacles that have a macabre kind of beauty which somehow removes the viewer from the very real brutalities of modern warfare. Fox thought to duplicate the success of its black-and-white blockbuster, THE LONGEST DAY, by spending a fortune on this incredible film which was shot on location in England, Spain, Morocco, and Greece. PATTON gleaned more than $28 million in its initial release, becoming the first great box-office wonder of the 1970s. Oddly, the television showings of this film present strange editing. The one scene missing from TV airings is one where Scott kills a donkey and has it thrown over a bridge because it is blocking his army's advance; but the scenes depicting the brutal battle deaths of thousands of men are included.

p, Frank McCarthy, Frank Caffey; d, Franklin J. Schaffner; w, Francis Ford Coppola, Edmund H. North (based on material in the books *Patton: Ordeal and Triumph* by Ladislas Farago and *A Soldier's Story* by Gen. Omar N. Bradley); ph, Fred Koenekamp (Dimension 150, CinemaScope, DeLuxe Color); m, Jerry Goldsmith; ed, Hugh S. Fowler; art d, Urie McCleary, Gil Parrondo; set d, Antonio Mateos, Pierre-Louis Thevenet; spec eff, L.B. Abbott, Art Cruickshank; makeup, Del Acevedo; stunts, Joe Canutt.

War Drama/Biography **Cas.** **(PR:C MPAA:PG)**

PAUL AND MICHELLE*½

(1974, Fr./Brit.) 103m PAR c

Anicee Alvina *(Michelle Latour)*, Sean Bury *(Paul Harrison)*, Keir Dullea *(Garry)*, Ronald Lewis *(Sir Robert)*, Catherine Allegret *(Joanna)*, Georges Beller *(Daniel)*, Anne Lonnberg *(Susannah)*, Sara Stout *(Sylvie)*, Steve Gilbert *(Nic)*, Anthony Clarke *(Hush)*, Peggy Frankston *(Lilli)*, Peter Graves *(Sir Henry)*, Toby Robins *(Jane)*, Andre Maranne *(Bellancourt)*, Jenny Arasse *(Soeur Mercier)*, Michel Garland *(Doctor in Arles)*, Elizabeth Kaza *(Mother Superior)*, Albert Simono *(Dr. Duval)*, Sylvie Joly *(Receptionist)*, Robert Favart *(Professor)*, Carine Vogel *(Doctor's Receptionist)*, Lucy Arnold *(Girl at Patisserie)*, Jacqueline Fogt *(Mme. Bellancourt)*, Jack Berard *(Butler)*, Guy Harly *(Waiter)*.

The sequel to FRIENDS (1971) which continues the relationship between an English aristocratic teenager, Bury, and middle class French girl Alvina. An empty-headed story, with Bury graduating from prep school with Alvina and their baby, Stout, waiting for him. The sex scenes, arguments with parents, and other soap opera plot devices make for one dull film.

p&d, Lewis Gilbert; w, Angela Huth, Vernon Harris (based on a story by Gilbert); ph, Claude Renoir (Panavision, Technicolor); m, Michel Colombier; ed, Thelma Connell; art d, Pierre Guffroy; m/l, Steve Gilbert (sung by Gilbert), title Song, Colombier, Don Black (sung by Russell Stone).

Drama **(PR:O MPAA:R)**

PAUL TEMPLE RETURNS**

(1952, Brit.) 71m Nettlefold/BUT bw

John Bentley *(Paul Temple)*, Patricia Dainton *(Steve Temple)*, Valentine Dyall *(Supt. Bradley)*, Christopher Lee *(Sir Felix Reybourne)*, Ronald Leigh Hunt *(Inspector Ross)*, Ben Williams *(Roddy Carson)*, Grey Blake *(Storey)*, Arthur Hill *(Cranmer Guest)*, Robert Urquhart *(Slater)*, Dan Jackson *(Sakki)*, Peter Gawthorne *(Sir Graham Forbes)*, Andrea Malandrinos, George Patterson, Vi Kaley, Elizabeth Gilbert, Gerald Rex, Michael Mulcaster, Dennis Holmes, Sylvia Pugh.

Bentley stars in this standard murder mystery as an amateur novelist/sleuth who is on the trail of a celebrated murderer. The climax takes place in an uninviting mansion which is full of snakes. With the assistance of his wife, Dainton, the murder is solved and his career as a novelist receives a shot in the arm. This marked the last of the Temple films.

p, Ernest G. Roy; d, Maclean Rogers; w, Francis Durbridge (based on the radio serial "Paul Temple Intervenes" by Durbridge); ph, Geoffrey Faithfull.

Mystery **(PR:A MPAA:NR)**

PAUL TEMPLE'S TRIUMPH*½

(1951, Brit.) 80m Nettlefold/BUT bw

John Bentley *(Paul Temple)*, Dinah Sheridan *(Steve Temple)*, Jack Livesey *(Sir Graham Forbes)*, Beatrice Varley *(Mrs. Weston)*, Barbara Couper *(Mrs. Morgan)*, Jenny Mathot *(Jacqueline Giraud)*, Andrew Leigh *(Prof. Hardwicke)*, Hugh Dempster *(Oliver Ffollett)*, Bruce Seton *(Bill Bryant)*, Ivan Samson *(Maj. Murray)*, Dino Galvani, Leo de Pokorny, Michael Brennan, Joseph O'Conor, Shaym Bahadur, Gerald Rex, Ben Williams, Anne Hayes, Peter Butterworth, Hamilton Keene, Jean Packer, Frederick Morant, Denys Val Norton, Michael Hogarth.

An uninvolving series entry which has Bentley and his wife Sheridan on the hunt for a kidnaped scientist whose secret formula for atomic weaponry has fallen into enemy hands. He is located at the headquarters of "Z," a malevolent underground organization, and safely returned to the good guys.

p, Ernest G. Roy; d, Maclean Rogers; w, A.R. Rawlinson (based on the radio series "News of Paul Temple" by Francis Durbridge; ph; Brendan J. Stafford.

Crime/Mystery **(PR:A MPAA:NR)**

PAULA

(SEE: FRAMED, 1947)

PAULA**

(1952) 80m COL bw (GB: THE SILENT VOICE)

Loretta Young *(Paula Rogers)*, Kent Smith *(John Rogers)*, Alexander Knox *(Dr. Clifford Frazer)*, Tommy Rettig *(David Larson)*, Otto Hulett *(Lt. Dargen)*, Will Wright *(Raymond Bascom)*, Raymond Greenleaf *(Pres. Russell)*, Eula Guy *(Cora)*, William Vedder *(Dean Cornwall)*, Ann Doran *(Welfare Worker)*, Kathryn Card *(Gussie)*, Sidney Mason *(Dr. Morris Cull)*, Keith Larsen *(Intern)*, Ann Tyrrell *(Nurse)*, Clark Howat *(Attendant)*, Roy Engel *("Weagent")*, Brandon Beach *(Professor)*, Edna Holland *(Old Nurse)*, Jeanne Bates *(Attending Nurse)*, Maj. Sam Harris *(Professor)*, Edwin Parker *(Truck Driver)*, Gertrude Astor *(Mrs. Brown)*, Alice Mills *(Small Girl)*, Lawrence Williams *(Dr. Lazlo)*, Helen Dickson *(Mrs. Lazlo)*, Richard Gordon *(Mr. Brown)*.

Young tries to teach a young boy (Rettig) how to talk again, after a hit-and-run accident causes him to become mute. Unknown to both of them, Young was the driver of the car. But as Rettig begins to make progress, he realizes that Young caused his injuries and so decides to take revenge on her when the police investigation draws close. In a sappy and predictable ending, Young wins over the young boy and all charges against her are dropped.

p, Buddy Adler; d, Rudolph Mate; w, James Poe, William Sackheim (based on a story by Larry Marcus); ph, Charles Lawton, Jr.; m, George Duning; ed, Viola Lawrence; md, Morris Stoloff; art d, Ross Bellah; cos, Jean Louis.

Drama **(PR:A MPAA:NR)**

PAULINE A LA PLAGE (SEE: PAULINE AT THE BEACH, 1983, Fr.)

PAULINE AT THE BEACH*½** (1983, Fr.) 94m Les Films du Losange-Les Films Ariane/Orion c (PAULINE A LA PLAGE)

Amanda Langlet *(Pauline)*, Arielle Dombasle *(Marion)*, Pascal Greggory *(Pierre)*, Feodor Atkine *(Henry)*, Simon De La Brosse *(Sylvain)*, Rosette *(Louisette)*.

The third in Eric Rohmer's series of "Comedies and Proverbs" is the study of a lovely blonde French woman and her blossoming young cousin Pauline (Langlet). The pair get involved with three men during a beachside vacation, and Langlet emerges from the experiences the wiser of the two. Rohmer continues to forge along in his preoccupation with moral tales, comedies, and proverbs with an uncompromising charm. Very little (in terms of plot) happens in any of his pictures, but the audience is treated to superb performances, a deification of the female gender, and some of cinema's wittiest dialog. Photographed by Oscar-winning cameraman Nestor Almendros.

p, Margaret Menegoz; d&w, Eric Rohmer; ph, Nestor Almendros; m, Jean-Louis Valero; ed, Cecile Decugis.

Drama/Comedy **Cas.** **(PR:O MPAA:R)**

PAWNBROKER, THE**** (1965) 114m Landau-Unger-Pawnbroker/Landau Releasing Organization-AA-AIP bw

Rod Steiger *(Sol Nazerman)*, Geraldine Fitzgerald *(Marilyn Birchfield)*, Brock Peters *(Rodriguez)*, Jaime Sanchez *(Jesus Ortiz)*, Thelma Oliver *(Ortiz' Girl)*, Marketa Kimbrell *(Tessie)*, Baruch Lumet *(Mendel)*, Juano Hernandez *(Mr. Smith)*, Linda Geiser *(Ruth Nazerman)*, Nancy R. Pollock *(Bertha)*, Raymond St. Jacques *(Tangee)*, John McCurry *(Buck)*, Eusebia Cosme *(Mrs. Ortiz)*, Warren Finnerty *(Savarese)*, Jack Ader *(Morton)*, E.M. Margolese *(Papa)*, Marianne Kanter *(Joan)*, Ed Morehouse *(Robinson)*, Marc Alexander *(Rubin)*.

THE PAWNBROKER looked as though it had been drawn from a play rather than a novel because so much of the action took place in one spot. From the moment it was released, controversy surrounded it. Jewish groups felt it was anti-Semitic because they thought the character was shown to be an insensitive man who was only interested in money. Black organizations hated the portrayal of Peters as a rotten gangster. The Legion of Decency condemned the movie because of a scene where Oliver bares her breasts, which was just about the first time that had ever happened in a mainstream movie. Steiger is the pawnbroker, a man who was a professor and saw his wife, Geiser, raped by Nazi officers and his two children sent to their deaths. That he remained alive is a source of bewilderment and pain for him and he has lost faith in God, in man, in everything and everyone. He is emotionless, noninvolved, and totally apart from the world that surrounds his little pawnshop in New York's Spanish Harlem. His assistant, Sanchez, thinks that there may be a man with feelings under that icy exterior and tries to bring him out to no avail. Each time Sanchez, an ebullient and lovable Puerto Rican, tries to penetrate Steiger's facade, he gets nowhere. The same holds true for Fitzgerald, a local social worker. Meanwhile, Steiger is having an affair with Kimbrell, another survivor of the death camps, who lost her husband to the Nazi beasts and whose dying father, Lumet, disapproves of their relationship. Peters actually owns the shop and Steiger is working for him, and when Steiger learns that Peters is a pimp, he swears he had no idea of how Peters made his money. To keep this front going, Peters gets Steiger to admit that he did, in fact, know the source of the money. Oliver is Sanchez's girl friend and she comes in to pawn an item. When Steiger won't give her much money for the bauble, she bares her breasts to try to get him to raise the bid. That sets him back in a quick Resnais-type flashback and he sees his late wife in his mind's eye. (There are several flashbacks, almost subliminal in length, which pepper the film.) Sanchez continues his onslaught on Steiger, trying to get him to show any kind of response, and Steiger returns the attempt by being thoughtlessly cruel to Sanchez. The youth is hurt and arranges for some thugs to rob the pawnshop. They march in with weapons and Steiger won't give them the money and just about dares them to fire their guns. Sanchez has a change of heart and steps in front of the bullet meant for Steiger and dies in the pawnbroker's arms. It is only here, at the end, that Steiger shows some tenderness as Sanchez expires. Steiger puts his hand down hard on the metal spoke he uses for receipts and it goes through; then he walks the streets alone as the picture ends. Until Peters took the role, we had been treated to the whitest black men ever with Sidney Poitier always playing the hero in films like GUESS WHO'S COMING TO DINNER, THE SLENDER THREAD, and others. It was an unrealistic picture of blacks but studios always seemed to back off when it came to showing the race in anything but glowing terms. Just as there had been Jewish gangsters and Italian gangsters, so were there black gangsters and this movie must be commended for daring to break the barrier. Steiger was towering in the role and was denied the Oscar by Lee Marvin's work in CAT BALLOU, a lightweight comedy at best. New York City never looked as grim as it did under Lumet's direction and it became as much a character in the film as any of the humans. Ely Landau and Herbert Steinmann "presented" the film and Ulu Grosbard, who went on to be a director, was the production manager. Gritty, grotesque, and powerful, THE PAWNBROKER marked Steiger's first starring role in a major film. He had previously been seen as a supporting actor in many fine films and a few potboilers and got an Oscar nomination for his second movie, ON THE WATERFRONT. He is one of the few non-Jews who can convince audiences that he is. Then again, he was also able to convince people he was Irish in ON THE WATERFRONT, southern in IN THE HEAT OF THE NIGHT, and French in WATERLOO. A brilliant actor who has never received the accolades he's merited.

p, Roger Lewis, Philip Langner; d, Sidney Lumet; w, David Friedkin, Morton Fine (based on the novel by Edward Lewis Wallant); ph, Boris Kaufman; m, Quincy Jones; ed, Ralph Rosenblum; art d, Richard Sylbert; set d, Jack Flaherty; cos, Anna Hill Johnstone; makeup, Bill Herman.

Drama **Cas.** **(PR:C MPAA:NR)**

PAWNEE zero (1957) 80m REP c (GB: PALE ARROW)

George Montgomery *(Paul)*, Bill Williams *(Matt)*, Lola Albright *(Meg)*, Francis J. McDonald *(Tip)*, Robert E. Griffin *(Doc)*, Dabbs Greer *(Brewster)*, Kathleen Freeman *(Mrs. Carter)*, Charlotte Austin *(Dancing Fawn)*, Ralph Moody *(Wise Eagle)*, Anne Barton *(Mrs. Brewster)*, Raymond Hatton *(Obie Dilks)*, Charles Horvath *(Crazy Fox)*, Robert Nash *(Carter)*.

A moronic and cliched western with Montgomery as the adopted son of a Pawnee chief, who decides to learn more about his own people. He becomes a scout on a wagon train following the Oregon Trail, and when the wagon train is attacked by Montgomery's own tribe the adopted Indian decides that it's better to be a white man. The racial tone of the film alone deserves a low rating.

p, Jack J. Gross, Philip N. Krasne; d, George Waggner; w, Waggner, Louis Vittes, Endre Bohem; ph, Hal McAlpin (Trucolor); m, Paul Sawtell; ed, Kenneth G. Cranel; art d, Nicolai Remisoff.

Western **(PR:A MPAA:NR)**

PAY BOX ADVENTURE* (1936, Brit.) 68m British and Dominions/PAR bw

Syd Crossley *(Tom Furlong)*, Marjorie Corbett *(Mary Blake)*, Roxie Russell *(Enid Soames)*, Billy Watts *(Jimmy Trevor)*, Eric Fawcett *(Sidney Parke)*, Molly Hamley Clifford *(Mrs. Bartlett)*, George Turner *(Gus)*, Billy Saunders, Harold Thorne.

A lackluster crime yarn which details the attempts made by a group of employees trying to save the dying movie theater in which they work. When an evil lawyer learns that the young lady who works as a cashier stands to inherit a sizable sum, he engineers a plan to ruin the theater and obtain the fortune. A dreary production in all respects, PAY BOX ADVENTURE heralded the end of director Kellino's long and noteworthy career which had begun in the silent days.

p, Anthony Havelock-Allan; d, W.P. Kellino; w, Gerald Elliott.

Crime **(PR:A MPAA:NR)**

PAY OFF, THE* (1930) 65m RKO bw (GB: THE LOSING GAME)

Lowell Sherman *(Gene Fenmore)*, Marian Nixon *(Annabelle)*, Hugh Trevor *(Rocky)*, William Janney *(Tommy)*, Helene Millard *(Dot)*, Robert McWade *(Frank)*, Alan Roscoe *(District Attorney)*, Lita Chevret *(Margy)*, Bert Moorehouse *(Spat)*, George F. Marion *(Mouse)*, Walter McGrail *(Emory)*.

Sherman both directs and stars in this film about a master thief who only steals from other criminals and doesn't resort to violence against any of his victims. The Robin Hood-style crook falls in love with Nixon, who is engaged to Janney. In a gallant gesture, Sherman chooses to go to the electric chair to save Nixon and Janney from being prosecuted. The film represents Sherman's second effort as a director, but unfortunately he is better in front of the camera than behind it. The film is technically awkward and a crucial scene involving a jewelry heist is bungled by bad direction.

p, William LeBaron, Henry Hobart; d, Lowell Sherman; w, Jane Murfin (based on a play by Sam Shipman, John Hymer); ph, J. Roy Hunt; ed, Rose Smith; art d, Max Ree.

Crime **(PR:A MPAA:NR)**

PAY OR DIE*** (1960) 111m AA bw

Ernest Borgnine *(Lt. Joseph Petrosino)*, Zohra Lampert *(Adelina Saulino)*, Alan Austin *(Johnny Viscardi)*, Renata Vanni *(Mama Saulino)*, Bruno Della Santina *(Papa Saulino)*, Franco Corsaro *(Vito Zarillo)*, Robert F. Simon *(Commissioner)*, Robert Ellenstein *(Luigi Di Sarno)*, Howard Caine *(Enrico Caruso)*, John Duke *(Lupo Miano)*, John Marley *(Caputo)*, Mario Siletti *(Loria)*, Mimi Doyle *(Nun)*, Mary Carver *(Mrs. Rossi)*, Paul Birch *(Mayor)*, Vito Scotti *(Simonetti)*, Nick Pawl *(Palumbo)*, Vincent Barbi *(Fabraka)*, Sherry Alberoni *(Giulia De Sarno)*, Leslie Glenn *(Girl at Bombing)*, Sal Armetta *(Botti)*, Carlo Tricoli *(Don Cesare)*, Bart Bradley *(Nicolo)*, Marian Collier *(Girl from Opera)*, Joseph D. Sargent *(Sorgente)*, Sam Capuano *(Rossi)*, Judy Strangis *(Marisa Rossi)*, David Poleri *(Voice of Caruso)*.

Director Wilson had just come off a hit movie, CAPONE, for Allied Artists and went right back to the same Italian gangster territory for this, a true biography of the man who headed the New York "Italian Squad" for the police department. It covers three years in the life and death of a man who did his best to prove a link between the Sicilian parentage of the Mafia and the U.S. involvement. A similar story had been told in the MGM picture THE BLACK HAND in which Irish J. Carrol Naish played the real-life policeman. Both pictures did a fine job in recording the story although there were a few liberties taken in each film. The setting is that area just north of New York's Canal Street known as "Little Italy." It would be seen, in later years, as the backdrop for MEAN STREETS and several other films. Borgnine leads a squad of loyal officers in an attempt to get the neighborhood out of the grip of the secret society where, in the name of "protection," there is extortion, beatings, bombings, and murder. Borgnine is married to Lampert, making an impressive debut in movies, but he doesn't have too much time for a domestic life as he is dedicated to erasing the power of the Mafia and to restoring the good name of Italian immigrants, a reputation sullied due to the activities of the gangsters. Borgnine saves Caine (as Enrico Caruso) from a death plot and is saddened when several young Italian girls are killed in the bombing of a jewelry store. One of the girls is the daughter of the crook behind the plot, Ellenstein. Borgnine gets some city money to travel to Palermo to uncover some evidence and he is assassinated by unknown killers. Good character work from Barbi, Marley, and Scotti, the latter one of the busiest actors in Hollywood and who speaks five dialects of Italian as well as several other tongues. Austin, Borgnine's top aide in the film, eventually gave up full-time acting and opened a fabulously successful clothing store in Beverly Hills near the corner of Brighton Way and famed Rodeo Drive.

p&d, Richard Wilson; w, Richard Collins, Bertram Millhauser (based on the life of Lt. Joseph Petrosino); ph, Lucien Ballard; m, David Raksin; ed, Walter Hannemann; prod d, Fernando Carrere; md, Raksin; set d, Darrell Silvera; cos, Roger J. Weinberg; spec eff, Milt Olsen, Lou Lacava, Bob Mark.

Crime Drama (PR:C MPAA:NR)

PAY THE DEVIL (SEE: MAN IN THE SHADOW, 1957)

PAYDAY**** (1972) 102m Cinerama c

Rip Torn (*Maury Dann*), Anna Capri (*Mayleen*), Elayne Heilveil (*Rosamond*), Michael C. Gwynne (*Clarence*), Jeff Morris (*Tally*), Cliff Emmich (*Chauffeur*), Henry O. Arnold (*Ted*), Walter Bamberg (*Bridgeway*), Linda Spatz (*Sandy*), Eleanor Fell (*Galen Dann*), Clara Dunn (*Mama Dann*), Earle Trigg (*Disk Jockey*), Mike Edwards (*Restaurant Manager*), Winton McNair (*Highway Policeman*).

Torn is a fading country singer in this excellent and overlooked drama. The film chronicles the last 36 hours of Torn's life, as he travels from one honky-tonk to the next. The character is a cruel, egotistical performer who knows his career is on the skids. The grind of being on the road, the groupies, the payoffs and drugs are captured in unglamourized fashion by screenwriter Don Carpenter and director Daryl Duke. Every character in this film is three dimensional and none of them are either heroes or villains. Gwynne is Torn's ruthless manager, Capri the singer's mistress and Heilveil makes her debut as an innocent groupie. A powerful film that examines the dark side of performing and the struggle for success and fame. Torn's brilliant performance along with the film deserves more recognition.

p, Martin Fink, Don Carpenter; d, Daryl Duke; w, Carpenter; ph, Richard Glouner (CFI Color); ed, Richard Halsey; m/l, Shel Silverstein, Ian and Sylvia Tyson, Bob Smith, Tommy McKinney.

Drama **Cas.** (PR:O MPAA:R)

PAYMENT DEFERRED½** (1932) 75m MGM bw

Charles Laughton (*William Marble*), Neil Hamilton (*Gordon Holmes*), Maureen O'Sullivan (*Winnie Marble*), Dorothy Peterson (*Annie Marble*), Verree Teasdale (*Mme. Collins*), Ray Milland (*James Medland*), Billy Bevan (*Hammond*), William Stack (*A Doctor*), Halliwell Hobbes (*A Prospective Tenant*).

Laughton is excellent as a suburban murderer who buries his victim in his garden. The film's script was adapted from a play by Jeffrey Dell in which Laughton starred. O'Sullivan is gripping in a final scene. The film ends on an ironic note with Laughton being hung for a murder which was in reality a suicide.

d, Lothar Mendes; w, Ernest Vajda, Claudine West (based on a play by Jeffrey F. Dell); ph, Merritt Gerstad; ed, Frank Sullivan.

Drama (PR:A MPAA:NR)

PAYMENT IN BLOOD* (1968, Ital.) 89m Circus-Fona Roma/COL c
(WINCHESTER PER UN MASSACRO)

Edd Byrnes (*Stuart*), Guy Madison (*Col. Blake*), Louise Barrett [Luisa Baratto] (*Manuela*), Enio Girolami (*Chamaco*), Rick Boyd, Rosella Bergamonti, Mario Donen, Alfred Aysanoa, Marco Mariani, Attilio Severini, Adriana Facchetti, Guilio Maculani, Piero Vida, Mirella Pamphili.

A band of ex-Confederate soldiers led by Madison pillages towns on the Texas-Mexico border and bounty hunter Byrnes joins the gang. He tells Madison that he knows where a large amount of gold is hidden and when the bandits arrive in the town of Durango they realize Byrnes' true identity. Madison kills the town's sheriff and his posse and leaves Byrnes in a burning bar while his men dig up the treasure, which turns out to be Confederate money. Byrnes is saved by his partner, Barrett, and finishes off Madison and his gang. A clumsy western that's extremely violent, dubbed poorly into English.

d, E.G. Rowland [Enzo Girolani]; w, Tito Capri, Rowland; ph, Aldo Pennelli (Techniscope, Technicolor); m, Francesco De Masi, Fono Roma; ed, Antonietta Zita; art d, Saverio D'Eugenio; set d, Antonio Fratalocchi; cos, Giorgio Desideri; spec eff, F. Bacciucchi; m/l, "Seven Men," De Masi, Audrey Nohra, Alessandroni (sung by Raul); makeup, Massimo De Rossi.

Western (PR:O MPAA:R)

PAYMENT ON DEMAND* (1951) 90m RKO bw (AKA: THE STORY OF A DIVORCE)

Bette Davis (*Joyce Ramsey*), Barry Sullivan (*David Ramsey*), Jane Cowl (*Mrs. Hedges*), Kent Taylor (*Robert Townsend*), Betty Lynn (*Martha Ramsey*), John Sutton (*Tunliffe*), Frances Dee (*Eileen Benson*), Peggie Castle (*Diana Ramsey*), Otto Kruger (*Prescott*), Walter Sande (*Swanson*), Brett King (*Phil Polanski*), Richard Anderson (*Jim Boland*), Natalie Schafer (*Mrs. Blanton*), Katherine Emery (*Mrs. Gates*), Lisa Golm (*Molly*), Kathleen Ellis (*Receptionist*), Mack Williams (*Pinkins*), Ilka Gruning (*Mrs. Polanski*), David Leonard (*Mr. Polanski*), Barbara Davis, Sherry Merrill (*Diana, as a Child*), Ruth Lee (*Aunt Edna*), Jay Brooks (*Butler*), Lela Bliss (*Mrs. Filson*), Moroni Olsen (*David Ramsey's Attorney*).

PAYMENT ON DEMAND was made before Davis' much flashier performance in ALL ABOUT EVE and was held back until after that was released. After 18 years at Warner Bros., this was her first outside assignment and, while it doesn't come close to some of her more memorable roles, it's still a fine movie. The original title (see above) may have been more apt, as it is, truly, the story of a divorce, from start to finish, and yet it bypasses all the usual soapy stuff and offers an adult look at some of the reasons why people part company. Davis is married to Sullivan, who is a lawyer and a top executive in a large steelmaking firm. They've been a duo for 20 years and she thinks everything is swell. When he tells her he wants a divorce, she is stunned. Davis is a tough cookie in her own right and a woman who spends much of her time scaling the social ladder, something that has annoyed Sullivan

through the years. He moves to his club and Davis reveals the situation to their daughters, Lynn and Castle, then she flashes back in reverie and reviews the incidents leading up to this split and begins to understand what it is about her that caused the rift. It is now that she learns Sullivan has taken up with comely Dee, a schoolteacher. In anger, she threatens to countersue on the grounds of adultery and name Dee in the case. The only thing that will mollify her is if Sullivan settles a huge property sum on her and their daughters. Sullivan, seeking to avoid a scandal, tells his lawyer, Olsen, to give her whatever she wants, anything to get her out of his hair. While awaiting the final papers to be signed, Davis gets on a pleasure cruise ship and goes to Port-au-Prince, Haiti, where she visits Cowl, an aging and somewhat sad divorcee who has now settled into a life of rum and gigolos. Watching Cowl's behavior, Davis is aware of what life is going to be like for her as an over-the-hill unmarried woman. On the ship, Davis is having an affair with Sutton, a handsome businessman traveling alone who admits that he is married with a family. Davis gets a cablegram from Lynn stating that she is about to get married and she uses the wireless message to extricate herself from Sutton and race back home. The only advice she can give her daughter is to lay back and not be too aggressive with her husband in her desires or she might lose him, the way Davis lost Sullivan. The wedding ends, the honeymooners go off happily, and Sullivan, who was also there, offers to drive Davis home. While driving, Davis lets her hair down and tells Sullivan how terribly alone she's been without him and how she can't bear to be parted from the one man she's ever loved. Davis knows that Sullivan still adores her and felt forced to make his move because of her lack of respect for his wishes and the drifting apart they'd done when she was more interested in everyone and everything else but him. Sullivan admits he loves her and would like to reconcile. Davis wants nothing as much as that but she is also pragmatic and hopes that the suggestion was made sincerely and not out of sympathy for her plight. She tells Sullivan that she truly wants to be back in his arms but implores him to think about it for a spell and ask her again, sometime later, if he still feels the same way. The picture ends with the two of them having reawakened their feelings about each other and there is no doubt that they will try to make it work again and this time, they will succeed. An honest story with good acting and direction, PAYMENT ON DEMAND moves over familiar ground and needed only some solid humor to raise the level of the drama. People who have been married for so many years usually manage to get a few funny lines into their conversations but laughs are in no supply here and would have helped considerably.

p, Jack H. Skirball, Bruce Manning; d, Curtis Bernhardt; w, Manning, Bernhardt; ph, Leo Tover; m, Victor Young; ed, Harry Marker; md, C. Bakaleinikoff; art d, Albert S. D'Agostino, Carroll Clark; cos, Edith Head.

Drama (PR:A-C MPAA:NR)

PAYOFF, THE*½ (1935) 81m WB bw

James Dunn (*Joe McCoy*), Claire Dodd (*Maxine*), Patricia Ellis (*Connie*), Alan Dinehart (*Marty Bleuler*), Joseph Crehan (*Harvey Morris*), Frankie Darro (*Jimmie Moore*), Frank Sheridan (*George Gorman*), Eddie Shubert (*Beetles Davis*), Al Hill (*Mike*), Anita Kerry, Helen Lowell, Allen Wood, Andre Beranger, Paul Porcasi, George Humbert.

Dunn plays a sports columnist with money problems in this nondescript melodrama. Spurred on by his nagging wife Dodd, Dunn gets mixed up with a crooked wrestling promoter hoping to better his situation. Dodd leaves him for casino operator Dinehart, whom she eventually murders. Dodd commits suicide, leaving Dunn to be comforted by colleague Ellis.

p, Bryan Foy; d, Robert Florey; w, George Bricker, Joel Sayre (based on a story by Bricker); ph, Arthur Todd; ed, Harold McLernon; md, Leo F. Forbstein; art d, Carl Weyl; cos, Orry-Kelly.

Drama (PR:A MPAA:NR)

PAYOFF, THE*½ (1943) 74m PRC bw

Lee Tracy (*Brad McKay*), Tom Brown (*Guy Morris*), Tina Thayer (*Phyllis Walker*), Evelyn Brent (*Alma Dorene*), Jack La Rue (*John Angus*), Ian Keith (*Inspector*), John Maxwell (*Moroni*), John Sheehan (*Sgt. Brenen*), Harry Bradley (*Dr. Steele*), Forrest Taylor (*Hugh Walker*), Pat Costello (*Reporter*), Robert Middlemass.

Tracy, in one of his frequent roles as a newspaperman, plays an investigative newspaper reporter who tracks down the killer of the city's special prosecutor. The murdered man was gathering evidence against mob rackets, and with the help of cub reporter Brown, Tracy apprehends the killer.

p, Jack Schwarz; d, Arthur Dreifuss; w, Edward Dein (based on a story by Arthur Hohl); ph, Ira Morgan; ed, Charles Henkel, Jr; md, Charles Dent.

Mystery (PR:A MPAA:NR)

PAYROLL* (1962, Brit.) 94m Lynx/AA bw (AKA: I PROMISED TO PAY)

Michael Craig (*Johnny Mellors*), Francoise Prevost (*Katie Pearson*), Billie Whitelaw (*Jackie Parker*), William Lucas (*Dennis Pearson*), Kenneth Griffith (*Monty*), Tom Bell (*Blackie*), Barry Keegan (*Bert Landridge*), Edward Cast (*Detective Sgt. Mark Bradden*), Andrew Faulds (*Detective Inspector Carberry*), William Peacock (*Harry Parker*), Glyn Houston (*Frank Moore*), Joan Rice (*Madge Moore*), Vanda Godsell (*Doll*), Stanley Meadows (*Bowen*), Brian McDermott (*Brent*), Hugh Morton (*Mr. John*), Keith Faulkner (*Alf*), Bruce Beeby (*Worth*), Murray Evans (*Billy*), Kevin Bennett (*Archie*), Michael Barrington.

Whitelaw is the wife of a driver for an armored car who seeks revenge when her husband is killed during a heist. She learns that Lucas, an employee at the factory, was the inside man, and sends him letters and makes anonymous phone calls in an attempt to break him down. The criminals are led by Craig, who kills two of his men when the pressure from the police investigation and from Whitelaw become too much. He tries to flee the country, but Whitelaw shows up on the ship and he's killed when he jumps off the ship to rescue the overboard loot and is hit by a motorboat.

p, Norman Priggen; d, Sidney Hayers; w, George Baxt (based on a novel by Derek Bickerton); ph, Ernest Steward; m, Reg Owen; ed, Tristram Cones; md, Owen; art d, Jack Shampan; cos, Morris Angel; m/l, "It Happens Every Day" Tony Osborne (sung by Eddie Ellis); makeup, Trevor Crole-Rees.

Crime   (PR:A MPAA:NR)

PEACE FOR A GUNFIGHTER*

(1967) 82m Cable Springs/Crown International c

Burt Berger ("The Preacher"), JoAnne Meredith (Melody), Everett King (Smiley), Stirling Welker (Sloan), Danny Zapien (Igmagio), John Scovern (Rafe), Mark Farrington (The Minister), Bob Pollard (Old Man), Ray Odom (Gambler), Mark Sanchez (Boy), Allen Wood (Wells Fargo Agent).

Berger, tired of his image as the fastest gun alive, tries to settle down in the small town of Reata Pass, but finds that the locals won't let him lay down his shooting irons. He fights one last battle then starts a new life with dance hall girl Meredith.

p, Robert J. Allen, Harold W. Johnson; d, Raymond Boley; w, Michael W. Fuller; ph, Allen (Techniscope, Technicolor); m, Dolan Ellis; ed, James L. Royer; set d, Red Johnson; m/l, "Peace for a Gunfighter," "Sometime" Ellis.

Western   (PR:C MPAA:NR)

PEACE KILLERS, THE*

(1971) 88m Damocles/Transvue c

Clint Ritchie (Rebel), Jess Walton (Kristy), Paul Prokop (Alex), Michael Ontkean (Jeff), Lavelle Roby (Black Widow), Nino Candido (Snatch), Jon Hill (Whitey), Gary Morgan (Gadget), John Raymond Taylor (Cowboy), Robert Cornthwaite (Ben), Kres Mersky (Carol), Albert Popwell (Blackjack), Joey Rosendo (Joey), Candace Dupuy (Linda), Jack Starr (Detective), Milt Gold (Hippie).

A motocycle gang raises some dust in a commune in which the gang leader's girl is living. The gang wants her back and is willing to kill and lay tire tracks across the backs of the peace-loving inhabitants. Gory and self-conscious, the film features torture, gang rape, and bad acting.

p, Joel B. Michaels; d, Douglas Schwartz; w, Michael Berk (based on the story by Michaels, Diana Maddox); ph, Schwartz (DeLuxe Color); m, Kenneth Wannberg; ed, Schwartz; prod d, Carl Randall; set d, Stephen Oliker; spec eff, William Munns; m/l, "White Dove," "Rebel," Ruthann Friedman (sung by Friedman); makeup, John Elliott.

Action   (PR:O MPAA:R)

PEACE TO HIM WHO ENTERS***

(1963, USSR) 90m Mosfilm/ Artkino bw (MIR VKHODYASHCHEMU; AKA: PEACE TO HIM)

Viktor Avdyushko (Yamshchikov), Aleksandr Demyanenko (Ivlev), Stanislav Khitrov (Rukavitsyn), Lidiya Shaporenko (Barbara), V. Bokadoro (French Woman), N. Grinko (American), Nikolay Timofeyev (Battalion Commander), I. Izvitskaya (Traffic Controller), A. Fayt (Serb), Viktor Koltsov, G. Nikitin, V. Zhilkin, S. Krylov, M. Logvinov, E. Knausmyuller, V. Marenkov, V. Makarov, G. Samokhina, A. Seryozhkin.

Shaporenko, a pregnant German woman, is delivered to a field hospital near enemy lines by three men: a newly graduated officer, a friendly truck driver, and a shell-shocked mute. Their route is scarred with violence, death and hatred, but through it all they gain insight. Shaporenka finally gives birth to her child in safety. Released in Russia in 1961, the film won a Special Gold Medal at the Venice Film Festival.

d, Aleksandr Alov, Vladimir Naumov; w, Leonid Zorin, Alov, Naumov; ph, Anatoliy Kuznetsov; m, Nikolay Karetnikov; ed, N. Anikeyeva; art d, Ye. Chernyayaev; cos, T. Kasparova; makeup, Ye. Yevseyeva.

War/Drama   (PR:A MPAA:NR)

PEACEMAKER, THE**

(1956) 82m UA bw

James Mitchell (Terrall Butler), Rosemarie Bowe (Ann Davis), Jan Merlin (Viggo Tomlin), Jess Barker (Ed Halcomb), Hugh Sanders (Lathe Sawyer), Herbert Patterson (Gray Arnett), Dorothy Patrick (Edith Sawyer), Taylor Holmes (Mr. Wren), Robert Armstrong (Ben Seale), Philip Tonge (Elijah Maddox), David McMahon (Sam Davis), Wheaton Chambers (Doc Runyan), Jack Holland (Walt Kemper), Nancy Evans (Miss Smith), Harry Shannon (Cowpuncher).

Mitchell is a gunslinger turned preacher who has put down his weapons in favor of wisdom and the Lord's word in this small western with religious overtones. He gets mixed up in a feud between the farmers and ranchers, but ultimately brings law to the land. The first film directed by Ted Post, who would later direct Clint Eastwood in HANG EM' HIGH.

p, Hal R. Makelim; d, Ted Post; w, Hal Richards, Jay Ingram (based on the novel by Richard Poole); ph, Lester Shorr; m, George Greeley; ed, William Shea; art d, Frank Smith.

Western   (PR:A MPAA:NR)

PEACH O' RENO**

(1931) 63 RKO bw

Bert Wheeler (Wattles), Robert Woolsey (Swift), Dorothy Lee (Prudence), Joseph Cawthorn (Joe Bruno), Cora Witherspoon (Aggie Bruno), Sam Hardy (Judge Jackson), Zelma O'Neal (Pansy), Mitchell Harris (Crosby), Arthur Hoyt (Secretary).

The comedy team of Wheeler and Woolsey run a quickie divorce service in Reno, Nevada, by day and a gambling joint by night. They find trouble when a tough gambler wants to know who arranged for his wife's divorce. Wheeler is soon shaking in his stockings as he dresses in drag to avoid detection.

p, William LeBaron; d, William A. Seiter; w, Tim Whelan, Ralph Spence, Eddie Welch (based on a story by Whelan); ph, Jack Mackenzie; ed, Jack Kitchin; m/l, "From Niagara Falls to Reno," Richard A. Whiting, Harry Akst, Grant Clarke.

Comedy   (PR:A MPAA:NR)

PEACH THIEF, THE***

(1969, Bulgaria) 84m Sofiya/Brandon bw (KRADETSUT NA PRASKOVI)

Nevena Kokanova (Lisa), Rade Markovic (Ivo Obrenovich), Mikhail Mikhailov (The Colonel), Vasil Vachev (The Colonel's Orderly).

An engrossing Bulgarian picture about an inmate in a POW camp who steals peaches from a colonel's orchard. He meets the colonel's bored wife, and soon the two become lovers. The colonel eventually moves the prisoners out, but the lovers are compelled to remain together. The prisoner breaks free in the hope of getting his love to run away with him, but is killed by a guard who has been told to protect the peach garden from thieves. Released in Bulgaria in 1964.

d&w, Vulo Radev (based on a story by Emilian Stanev); ph, Todor Stoyanov; m, Simeon Pironkov; art d, Nedelcho Nanev.

Drama/Romance   (PR:C MPAA:M)

PEACOCK ALLEY*½

(1930) 63m TIF bw-c

Mae Murray (Claire Tree), George Barraud (Stoddard Clayton), Jason Robards, Sr. (Jim Bradbury), Richard Tucker (Martin Saunders), W.L. Thorne (Dugan), Phillips Smalley (Bonner), E.H. Calvert (Paul), Arthur Hoyt (Crosby), Billy Bevan (Walter).

In a fit of frustration, chorus girl Murray marries her childhood beau Robards in a desperate effort to make the man she really loves, millionare Barraud, jealous. While on their honeymoon in New York, the absent-minded Robards forgets to sign his new bride's name on the register and soon the house detective arrives. Claiming that he caught Murray in the room with another man the night before, he kicks the couple out into the street. Enraged at the thought that his bride has been with another, and concluding that the second party is none other than Barraud, Robards insists on a fight. Murray claims it is all just a misunderstanding, but the angry Robards leaves her anyway. Crushed, Murray becomes embroiled in her role in a new Broadway show, hoping to forget. Miraculously, millionaire Barraud arrives on opening night with a marriage proposal and Murray enthusiastically accepts. Unremarkable, somewhat maudlin romance which contains a few brief sequences in Technicolor.

d, Marcel De Sano; w, Frances Hyland, Wells Root, Carey Wilson (based on a story by Wilson); ph, Benjamin Kline, Harry Zech (Technicolor); ed, Clarence Kolster; art d, Hervey Libbert.

Romance   (PR:A MPAA:NR)

PEACOCK FEATHERS

(SEE: OPEN THE DOOR AND SEE ALL THE PEOPLE, 1964)

PEARL, THE***½

(1948, U.S./Mex.) 77m Aguila-Films Asociados Mexico-Americanos/RKO bw

Pedro Armendariz (Kino), Maria Elena Marques (Juana), Fernando Wagner (Buyer of Pearls), Charles Rooner (Village Doctor), Alfonso Bedoya (Godfather of Kino and Juana's Baby), Juan Garcia (Sapo), Enandine Diaz De Leon (Medicine Woman), Gilberto Gonzalez, Maria Cuadros.

John Steinbeck has always written well about the poor, the downtrodden, the people whom God may have forgotten when bestowing good fortune. He did it in The Grapes of Wrath when he detailed the plight of the "Okies" who came west to the promised land of Cailfornia. His stories about central California's poor folks, such as Cannery Row and Tortilla Flat were heart-tuggers. In THE PEARL, he turns his attentions on the west coast of Mexico and the fishermen who earn their livelihood by the grace of the sea. THE PEARL was not a hit at the box office but it remains one of the best pictures ever to come out of RKO, and surely stands up there with the top pictures ever made in Mexico. No question that it's an allegory and that may have been what turned off audiences who were more accustomed to a straightforward story with no hidden meanings. The thrusting of wealth upon a poor person has been seen in other films before, such as MAN WITH A MILLION, etc., and the new lotteries across the U.S. are bringing forth many more similar stories as blue-collar workers are becoming instantly rich, but THE PEARL does it as no other picture had done it before or since. Armendariz is a fisherman who finds a huge, perfect pearl. It's a treasure that he believes will change his life, bring him money and respect, and allow him to provide for his wife, Marques, and their son. Yes, his life does change, but it's for the worse. He is soon beset by avaricious hyenas who bilk him, physically hurt him, murder his child, and eventually turn him into a killer as well. As poor as he was, Armendariz was far happier when he was scuffling for his living and barely managing to eke by. At the end of the brief, beautifully photographed story, Armendariz realizes that this pearl has brought him nothing but pain and heartbreak, so he tosses it back into the Pacific Ocean from whence it came and hopes that the gesture will restore his former life to him. It was a "little" picture about the big things in people's lives. It was about wealth, power, joy, and sorrow, and it brought them all home in such a fashion that THE PEARL will never be forgotten by anyone who sees it. Director Fernandez, a man single-handedly responsible for the development of the Mexican cinema, was the first filmmaker in his country to garner international awards for his movies. His 1943 film MARIA CANDELARIA won the Grand Prize at Cannes and THE PEARL won the International Prize at San Sebastian. American audiences will recognize the Mexican filmmaker not for the films he has directed, but for the acting he's done in American movies. Fernandez became a close friend of Sam Peckinpah after the controversial director came to Mexico to shoot portions of MAJOR DUNDEE (1965). Fernandez generously guided the American production company through the complex ins and outs of filmmaking in Mexico. By this time the great Mexican director was devoting most of his energy to acting and Peckinpah cast him in his next film, THE WILD BUNCH (1969). In that film Fernandez created the unforgettable character of General Mapache, a complex and vicious renegade soldier fighting off Villa's uprising. The role is vital to the film and Fernandez turned in an incredible performance. Peckinpah used Fernandez's acting talents in two subsequent films, PAT GARRETT AND BILLY THE KID (1973)—though the studio savaged the film in the editing and most of the Fernandez footage wound up on the floor—and BRING ME THE HEAD OF ALFREDO GARCIA (1974). It is a shame that American audiences have only Fernandez's acting to savor, becuase the films he has directed are filled with beauty, drama, and simple truths of the human condition.

p, Oscar Dancingers; d, Emilio Fernandez; w, John Steinbeck, Fernandez, Jack Wagner (based on the story by Steinbeck); ph, Gabriel Figueroa; m, Antonio Diaz Conde; ed, Gloria Schoemann; art d, Javier Torres Tarija.

Drama   Cas.   (PR:A MPAA:NR)

PEARL OF DEATH, THE***   (1944) 69m UNIV bw

Basil Rathbone (Sherlock Holmes), Nigel Bruce (Dr. John H. Watson), Evelyn Ankers (Naomi Drake), Dennis Hoey (Inspector Lestrade), Miles Mander (Giles Conover), Ian Walfe (Amos Hodder, Antique Shop Proprietor), Charles Francis (Digby, Curator of Regent Museum), Holmes Herbert (James Goodram, Diamond Courier), Richard Nugent (Bates, Museum Guard), Mary Gordon (Mrs. Hudson, Sherlock Holmes' Housekeeper), Rondo Hatton (The Creeper), J. Welsh Austin (Sgt. Bleeker), Connie Leon (Ellen Carey), Charles Knight (Bearded Man), Al Ferguson, Colin Kenny (Guards), Audrey Manners (Teacher), Billy Bevan (Constable), Lillian Bronson (Maj. Harker's Housekeeper), Leslie Denison (Constable Murdock), John Merkyl (Dr. Boncourt), Harry Cording (George Gelder, Plaster Bust Manufacturer), Eric Wilton (Chauffeur), Harold de Becker (Boss), Arthur Mulliner (Sandeford), Wilson Benge, Arthur Stenning (Stewards), Leyland Hodgson (Customs Officer).

A fine entry in the SHERLOCK HOLMES series which has Rathbone again cast as the lead and Bruce as his bumbling assistant. They are out to stop Manders and his gruesome aide, Hatton, from stealing a precious pearl. Rathbone surmises that they hid it in one of six busts of Beethoven, and of course he's right. He has to kill Hatton, however, before he can find out for sure. Hatton plays the Oxford Creeper, a monstrous villain who consistently kills by breaking people's backs—always at the third vertebra. In real life, Hatton's looks were just as evil as on the screen. Afflicted with a disfiguring disease known as acromegaly, Hatton gained fame for his portrayal of toughs and became quite successful in Hollywood as a result of this film. Hatton died two years after this picture's release, famous as "the only film star to play monsters without makeup." (See SHERLOCK HOLMES series, Index.)

p&d, Roy William Neill; w, Bertram Millhauser (based on the story "The Six Napoleons" by Sir Arthur Conan Doyle); ph, Virgil Miller; ed, Ray Snyder; md, Paul Sawtell; art d, John B. Goodman, Martin Obzina.

Mystery   (PR:A MPAA:NR)

PEARL OF THE SOUTH PACIFIC*½   (1955) 86m RKO c

Virginia Mayo (Rita Delaine), Dennis Morgan (Dan Merrill), David Farrar (Bully Hayes), Murvyn Vye (Halemano), Lance Fuller (George), Basil Ruysdael (Michael), Lisa Montell (Momu), Carol Thurston (Mother).

Mayo, clad only in a sarong (her clothes were burned by a native), prances and jiggles around a small Pacific island with Morgan and Farrar, a pair of thieves intent on stealing a treasure of black pearls. The booty, however, is well protected by a giant octopus in an underwater burial grotto. The islanders get angry, kill Farrar, and destroy the adventurers' boat. Mayo and Morgan are content to live a quiet life among the natives. Another indistinguishable film from the prolific Allan Dwan.

p, Benedict Bogeaus; d, Allan Dwan; w, Talbot Jennings, Richard Landau, Jesse Lasky, Jr. (based on a story by Anna Hunger); ph, John Alton (Superscope, Technicolor); m, Louis Forbes; ed, James Leicester; art d, Van Nest Polglase.

Adventure   Cas.   (PR:A MPAA:NR)

PEARL OF TLAYUCAN, THE**   (1964, Mex.) 105m Matouk bw
                                                                (TLAYUCAN)

Andres Soler (Don Carlos), Julio Aldama (Euphemio, the Husband), Jorge Martinez de Hoyos (Priest), Norma Angelica (Wife), Anita Blanch (Spinster), Noe Murayama (Blind Man), Francisco Cordova, Jose Galvez, Antonio Bravo, Jose Chavez, Dolores Camarillo, Jose Carlos Ortiz.

In a Mexican peasant village, the local priest upbraids the parishioners for their lack of generosity. When a small boy becomes sick, his father steals a pearl from a statue in the church to pay for medicine, but is caught. He loses the pearl, which later turns up in a pig's manure. The man is freed after his neighbors rally to his support. When his wife returns the pearl to the statue, the locals are convinced a miracle has occurred. Released in Mexico in 1961.

d&w, Luis Alcoriza (based on a novel by Jesus Murcielago Velazquez); ph, Rosalio Solano; m, Sergio Guerrero; ed, Carlos Savage; art d, Jesus Bracho.

Comedy   (PR:A MPAA:NR)

PEARLS BRING TEARS**½   (1937, Brit.) 63m GS Enterprises/COL bw

John Stuart (Harry Willshire), Dorothy Boyd (Madge Hart), Eve Gray (Pamela Vane), Mark Stone (George Hart), Googie Withers (Doreen), Aubrey Mallalieu (Mr. Vane), Annie Esmond (Mrs. Vane), H.F. Maltby (Mr. Duffield), Hal Walters (Herbert), Syd Crossley (Bankes), Isobel Scaife (Mary), Michael Ripper, Elizabeth James.

A fast-paced and surprisingly witty comedy about a woman, Boyd, who breaks a valuable string of pearls that she has borrowed for a dance. The catch is that they are only on loan to her husband as security for a business deal. She takes them to

be repaired but they are stolen, forcing her to spend the latter half of the film in a frenzied search. As the title implies, no happiness is gained from the pearls and eventually they find their way back to their original owner.

p, A. George Smith; d, Manning Haynes; w, Roy Lockwood (based on a story by Clifford Grey); ph, Geoffrey Faithfull.

Comedy   (PR:A MPAA:NR)

PEARLS OF THE CROWN***½   (1938, Fr.) 100m Lenauer bw (LES
                                                      PERLES DE LA COURONNE)

Sacha Guitry (Francis I/Jean Martin/Barras/Napoleon III), Jacqueline Delubac (Francoise Martin/Mary, Queen of Scots/Josephine), Lyn Harding (King Henry VIII/An Equerry to His Majesty), Ermete Zacconi (Pope Clement VII), Enrico Glori (Chamberlain to Pope), Marguerite Moreno (Catherine de Medici/Empress Eugenie), Yvette Plenne (Queen Mary Tudor/Queen Elizabeth), Catalano (Spanelli), Arletty (Queen of Abyssinia), Percy Marmont (Cardinal Wolsey), Derrick de Marney (Darnley), Barbara Shaw (Anne Boleyn), Simone Renant (Madame Du Barry), Jean Louis Barrault (Gen. Bonaparte), Emile Drain (Napoleon I), Cecile Sorci (A Courtesan), Fred Duprez (An American), Germaine Aussey (Gabrielle D'Estress).

Sacha Guitry's interesting historical drama about the seven pearls of the English crown. Three were lost forever, but the remaining four found their way into a variety of hands (Napoleon, King Henry VIII, Queen Elizabeth were among their owners) over the generations. Guitry himself plays four roles (as well as writing and directing). Delubac plays three, Harding, Moreno and Plenne play two apiece. Guitry chose to push the audience's patience a bit by filming the story in three languages, having some characters speak French, while others speak either Italian or English, which makes subtitles a virtual necessity (unless one is trilingual, of course). One of Guitry's finest works, and perhaps his least theatrical. (In French, Italian, and English; English subtitles).

p, Serge Sandberg; d, Sacha Guitry, Christian Jaque; w, Guitry; ph, J. Kruger; md, Jean Francaix; English subtitles, Stuart Gilbert.

Historical Drama   (PR:A MPAA:NR)

PEAU DE BANANE   (SEE: BANANA PEEL, 1965, Fr.)

PEAU D'ESPION   (SEE: TO COMMIT A MURDER, 1970, Fr./Ital./W.
                                                                      Ger.)

PECCATORI IN BLUE-JEANS   (SEE: CHEATERS, THE, 1961, Fr./
                                                                      Ital.)

PECK'S BAD BOY**½   (1934) 70m FOX bw

Thomas Meighan (Dad Peck), Jackie Cooper (Bill Peck), Dorothy Peterson (Aunt Lily), Jackie Searl (Horace), O. P. Heggie (Duffy, Handy Man and Town Philosopher), Gertrude Howard (Martha the Maid), Charles Evans (Minister), Larry Wheat (M.C.), Harvey Clark (Spectator), Lloyd Ingraham.

Twelve-year-old Jackie Cooper finds out he's adopted when Peterson and her obnoxious son (Searl) move in with Meighan. Peterson tries to cause a split between father and son so that her boy can take his place in Meighan's affections, but nothing can come between the pair. Cooper is perfectly cast in this entertaining tale for kids.

p, Sol Lesser; d, Edward F. Cline; w, Bernard Schubert, Marguerite Roberts (based on the play by George W. Peck); ph, Frank B. Good; ed, Donn Hayes.

Drama   (PR:AAA MPAA:NR)

PECK'S BAD BOY WITH THE CIRCUS**   (1938) 78m RKO bw

Tommy Kelly (Bill Peck), Ann Gillis, (Fleurette), Edgar Kennedy (Bailey), Benita Hume (Myrna), Spanky MacFarland (Pee Wee), Billy Gilbert (Mr. Boggs), Grant Mitchell (Mr. Peck), Nana Bryant (Mrs. Peck), Wade Boteler, Murphy), Harry Stubbs (Hank), Fay Helm (Mrs. De Cava), Mickey Rentschler (Herman Boggs), Louise Beavers (Cassey), William Demarest (Daro).

A weak juvenile picture in comparison with the previous Peck pictures, (1921, with Jackie Coogan and 1934, with Jackie Cooper) starring young Tommy Kelly (THE ADVENTURES OF TOM SAWYER) as the homespun hero, Bill Peck. He heads for summer camp, but on the way meets up with a ten-year-old bareback rider from the circus. A kid romance starts up between the pair, but Kelly returns to camp on time to enter the big obstacle course race. Helped along by a fine cast which includes Gillis as the circus girl (also from TOM SAWYER, as is Nana Bryant), Edgar Kennedy as the lion tamer, Our Gang's Spanky MacFarland, William Demarest, Billy Gilbert and Grant Mitchell.

p, Sol Lesser; d, Edward F. Cline; w, Al Martin, David Boehm, Robert Neville (based on the character created by George W. Peck); ph, Jack Mackenzie; ed, Arthur Hilton.

Drama   Cas.   (PR:AAA MPAA:NR)

PECOS RIVER**   (1951) 55m COL bw (GB: WITHOUT RISK)

Charles Starrett (Steve Baldwin/the Durango Kid), Smiley Burnette (Himself), Jack [Jock] Mahoney (Himself), Delores Sidener (Betty Coulter), Steve Darrell (Whip Rockland), Edgar Dearing (Ol' Henry), Frank Jenks (Sheriff Dennig), Paul Campbell (Sniffy), Zon Murray (Mose), Maudie Prickett (Mrs. Peck), Edward [Eddie] Fetherston (Mr. Grey), Harmonica Bill.

Starrett is a government agent investigating some U.S. mail robberies. He dons his Durango Kid gear when the going gets tough, and takes time to teach young Jack Mahoney how to shoot a six-gun. (See DURANGO KID series, Index.)

p, Colbert Clark; d, Fred F. Sears; w, Barry Shipman; ph, Fayte Browne; ed, Paul Borofsky; md, Mischa Bakaleinikoff; art d, Charles Clague.

Western   (PR:A MPAA:NR)

PEDDLIN' IN SOCIETY** (1949, Ital.) 85m Lux bw (DA BANCARELLA A BANCAROTTA)

Anna Magnani (Gioconda), Vittorio De Sica (Count Gherani), Virgilio Riento (Don Nicola), Laura Gore (Anna the Maid), Zora Piazza (Lucia), Lauro Gazzolo (Col. Bonifazio), Vito Chiari (Tranqill, the Boy).

Magnani turns in a strong performance as a vegetable and fruit vendor who earns a fortune on the black market and leases a ritzy villa from a count. She lives life to the fullest before feeling the results of some bad investments, when she is forced to abandon the life of luxury and return to peddling. (In Italian; English subtitles.)

d, Gennaro Righelli; ph, Aldo Tonti; m, E. Montagnini; English subtitles, Clare Catalano.

Drama (PR:A MPAA:NR)

PEDESTRIAN, THE***½ (1974, Ger.) 97m Cinerama c (DER FUSSGANGER)

Gustav Rudolf Sellner (Heinz Alfred Giese), Ruth Hausmeister (Inge Maria Giese), Maximilian Schell (Andreas Giese), Manuel Sellner (Hubert Giese), Elsa Wagner (Elsa Giese), Dagmar Hirtz (Elke Giese), Michael Weinert (Michael Giese), Peter Hall (Rudolf Hartmann), Alexander May (Alexander Markowitz), Christian Kohlund (Erwin Gotz), Franz Seitz (Dr. Karl Peters), Herbert Mensching, Peter Moland (Reporters), Gertrud Bald (Henriette Markowitz), Walter Kohut (Dr. Rolf Meineke), Margarethe Schell von Noe (Frau Buchmann), Sigfrit (Auditor), Gila von Weitershausen (Karin), Fani Fotinou (Greek Woman), Gaddi Ben-Artzi (Greek Man), Walter Schmidinger (Policeman), Walter von Varndal (Dr. Kratzer), Silvia Hurlimann (Hilde), Norbert Schiller (Himself), Angela Salloker (Herself), Peggy Ashcroft (Lady Gray), Elisabeth Bergner (Frau Lilienthal), Lil Dagover (Frau Eschenlohr), Kate Haack (Frau von Rautenfeld), Johanna Hofer (Frau Bergedorf), Francoise Rosay (Frau Dechamps).

Maximilian Schell directs from his own script this story of a German industrialist whose past involvement with WW II destroys his life. A newspaper reveals that it was he who ordered the massacre of a Greek village, causing his family to become cold toward him and his eldest son to commit suicide. Schell uses some interesting camera devices such as slow motion, and a flashback style to illustrate his intentions. A well-conceived film that won Best Picture from the Golden Globe, and an Academy Award Best Foreign Film nomination.

p, Maximilian Schell, Zev Braun; d&w, Schell; ph, Wolfgang Treu, Klaus Koenig (Eastmancolor); m, Manos Hadjidakis; ed, Dagmar Hirtz; set d, Hertha Pischinger.

Drama Cas. (PR:C MPAA:PG)

PEEK-A-BOO* (1961, Fr.) 65m Optimax-C.C.F. Lux/Fanfare-U.S. c (AH! LES BELLES BACCHANTES)

Robert Dhery (Himself), Colette Brosset (Herself), Louis de Funes (Inspector Leboeuf), Raymond Bussieres (Plumber), Rosine Luguet (Plumber's Wife), Jacqueline Maillan (Theater Manager), Sophie Mallet, Simone Claris, Liliane Autran, Caccia, Jacques Legras, Robert Saget, Gerard Calvi, Francis Blanche, Michel Serrault, Guy Pierrault, Jacques Jouanneau, The Bluebell Girls, Ballets Colette Brosset, Ballets de la Loie Fuller.

When a small French theater opens a burlesque show, the local police inspector makes sure that no one is breaking any decency laws. He gets interested in the show and before long is up on the stage with the fleshy gals. Just an excuse to publicize the show, which is no better than the movie. First released in Paris in 1954.

p, Edgar Bacquet; d, Jean Loubignac; w, Robert Dhery, Francis Blanche; ph, Rene Colas (Agfacolor); m, Gerard Calvi; ed, Jacques Mavel; art d, Roger Briaucourt; cos, Catherine Raymonde; ch, Colette Brosset; m/l, Calvi, Blanche.

Comedy (PR:O MPAA:NR)

PEEPER* (1975) 87m FOX c (AKA: FAT CHANCE)

Michael Caine (Tucker), Natalie Wood (Ellen Prendergast), Kitty Winn (Mianne Prendergast), Thayer David (Frank Prendergast), Liam Dunn (Billy Pate), Dorothy Adams (Mrs. Prendergast), Timothy Agoglia Carey (Sid), Don Calfa (Rosie), Michael Constantine (Anglich), Snag Werris (Burlesque Comic), Liz Renay (Burlesque Dancer), Margo Winkler (Lady With Luggage), Guy Marks (Man in Alley), Gary Combs, Robert Ito, Buffy Dee.

Caine is a private eye a la Philip Marlowe in Los Angeles circa 1947 in this blase attempt to spoof the genre. He is hired by the wealthy Constantine to locate his daughter. Caine follows the clues to the home of the eccentric Prendergast family, who are housing Wood and Winn, one of whom is Constantine's flesh and blood. A barren script which has almost nothing going for it, except a nice impersonation of Bogie by Guy Marks over the opening credits. From there it goes downhill. . .and fast.

p, Irwin Winkler, Robert Chartoff; d, Peter Hyams; w, W.D. Richter (based on the novel Deadfall by Keith Laumer); ph, Earl Rath (Panavision, DeLuxe Color); m, Richard Clements; ed, James Mitchell; prod d, Albert Brenner; set d, Marvin March; stunts, Hal Needham.

Drama/Comedy (PR:A MPAA:PG)

PEEPING TOM**½ (1960, Brit.) 109m Anglo-Amalgamated/Astor c (AKA: FACE OF FEAR)

Karl Boehm (Mark Lewis), Moira Shearer (Vivian), Anna Massey (Helen Stephens), Maxine Audley (Mrs. Stephens), Esmond Knight (Arthur Baden), Bartlett Mullins (Mr. Peters), Shirley Ann Field (Diane Ashley), Michael Goodliffe (Don Jarvis), Brenda Bruce (Dora), Martin Miller (Dr. Rosan), Pamela Green (Milly), Jack Watson (Inspector Gregg), Nigel Davenport (Sgt. Miller), Brian Wallace (Tony), Susan Travers (Lorraine), Maurice Durant (Publicity Chief), Brian Worth (Assistant Director), Veronica Hurst (Miss Simpson), Miles Malleson (Elderly Gentleman), Alan Rolfe (Store Detective), Michael Powell (Mr. Lewis), John Dunbar.

A disturbing, sadistic, obsessive, voyeuristic, sometimes brilliant movie. . .that everyone with an interest in films should see. Boehm is a focus-puller at a film studio, who works part-time at a corner cigar store taking pornographic photos of women. He approaches a prostitute on the street one night and goes to her apartment. He carries with him a 16mm camera and films her as he stabs her with the sharpened leg of his tripod, then leaves. The next morning he films the police investigation of her murder. He meets Massey, a woman who lives downstairs from him with her blind mother, and the two become friendly. He lets her watch home movies of him as a young boy. She is horrified to see that the films are of his father scientifically torturing the boy. One scene has the child crying as a nearby couple make love, another has the father (played by director Powell) waking the boy up by throwing a lizard on his bed. He explains to Massey that the films were made as part of his psychologist father's studies in fear. It is not long before Boehm finds himself another model, Shearer. He promises her a screen test, but as the camera is rolling he places the pointy tripod at her throat, and as she watches her reflection in a mirror, she is killed. Again, Boehm films the police investigation. He becomes increasingly attracted to Massey and promises not to bring his camera along when they go out. He watches the films of his murders afterwards, but is interrupted by Massey's blind mother. She cannot see what Boehm is watching but is able to sense his instability. Boehm's conversation with a psychiatrist at the film studio arouses the suspicion of police. They follow him. He returns to his flat and finds Massey watching the films of his murders. He confesses his crimes and, as the police enter, he turns the camera on and films his suicide while watching his face in the mirror. Michael Powell, one of the cornerstones of the British film industry during the 1940s, was vilified by the British press following the release of this picture. The director of THE RED SHOES (1948) and co-director of THE THIEF OF BAGDAD (1940) had made a provocative psychological horror film, which critics in his homeland found completely repugnant. It was quickly re-cut (butchered is more accurate) by the studio and was shown briefly in U.S. second-run houses. It wasn't until 1979 that a restored version was released due to the efforts of Martin Scorsese, a devout fan of the picture. Shearer, who plays a ballerina in THE RED SHOES, also does a dance number in PEEPING TOM, one of many in-jokes in the film. Esmond Knight, interestingly, plays the role of a film director although in real life he was practically blind. Powell's career never recovered from the critical attacks and he made only a handful of features and shorts after PEEPING TOM.

p&d, Michael Powell; w, Leo Marks; ph, Otto Heller (Eastmancolor); m, Brian Easdale; ed, Noreen Ackland; md, Easdale; art d, Arthur Lawrence; set d, Ivor Beddoes; ch, Wally Stott.

Crime Drama Cas. (PR:O MPAA:NR)

PEER GYNT*½ (1965) 85m Willow/Brandon bw

Charlton Heston (Peer Gynt), Betty Hanisee (Aase), Mrs. Herbert Hyde (Old Woman), Lucielle Powell (Kari), Sue Straub (Old Woman), Charles Paetow (Aslak), Katherine Elfstrom (Solveig), Morris Wilson (Haegstad), George B. Moll (Drunk/Bedouin Chief), Betty Barton (Ingrid), Alan Eckhart (Mads Moen), Katharine Bradley, Anty Ball, Alice Badgerow (Three Cowherd Girls), Audrey Wedlock (Woman in Green), Roy Eggert, Jr. (Dovre-King/Mons. Ballon/Priest), Francis X. Bushman (Boyg, A Voice in the Darkness), Sarah Merrill (Woman in Green, as a Hag), Alan Heston (Ugly Urchin), David Bradley (Herr Trumpeterstraale/Bailiff), Warren McKenzie (MacPherson), Rose Andrews (Anitra), Robert Cooper (Man in Mourning), Rod Maynard (Lad), Jane Wilimovsky (Old Woman), Thomas A. Blair (Button Moulder/Thin Person).

Charlton Heston made his first screen appearance in 1941 at age 16 in this adaptation of Henrik Ibsen's play. Made silently as part of a Northwestern University project, the picture was shot in northern Illinois, Wisconsin, and along the northern shores of Lake Michigan. Heston's Gynt would be similar to other characters he would play in Hollywood, portraying the world adventurer who steals sacred robes and faithfully loves a maiden. The picture was re-edited with new footage and a voice-over by Francis X. Bushman for release in 1968.

p&d, David Bradley; w, (based on the verse drama by Henrik Ibsen); ph, Bradley, Richard Roth, Robert Cooper; m, Edvard Grieg; cos, Sally Hyde, Elizabeth Cole.

Fantasy/Adventure (PR:A MPAA:NR)

PEG O' MY HEART**½ (1933) 86m COS/MGM bw

Marion Davies (Peg O'Connell), Onslow Stevens (Gerald Markham), J. Farrell MacDonald (Patrick Shamus O'Connell), Juliette Compton (Ethel Chichester), Irene Browne (Mrs. Chichester), Tyrell Davis (Alaric Chichester), Alan Mowbray (Mr. Brent), Doris Lloyd (Mrs. Brent), Robert Grieg (Jarvis), Nora Cecil (Smythe), Geoffrey Gill (Terance), Mutt (Michael), Billy Bevan.

A screen adaptation of a popular play which had run on Broadway for two years beginning in 1912. Davies is the very Irish lass who is bequeathed the sum of 2 million pounds on the condition that she leave her homeland and live with the upper-crust Chichester family in England for three years. Though she is devoted to her father, MacDonald, and the terms forbid her to see him during the period, she reluctantly agrees after Dad convinces her that she can't afford to pass up the opportunity. A variety of comic episodes follows as the naive and uneducated Davies attempts to deal with the reserved Chichesters and their high-society acquaintances. Eventually, Davies gives up the game and happily returns to her father and her Irish village. The story was hardly new, but Davies gave a winning performance, offering some engaging songs, including "Sweetheart Darlin'."

d, Robert Z. Leonard; w, Francis Marion, Frank R. Adams (based on the play by J. Hartley Manners); ph, George Barnes; m, Herbert Stothart; ed, Margaret Booth.

Musical/Comedy (PR:A MPAA:NR)

PEG OF OLD DRURY*** (1936, Brit.) 74m British and Dominions/PAR bw

Anna Neagle *(Peg Woffington)*, Cedric Hardwicke *(David Garrick)*, Margaretta Scott *(Kitty Clive)*, Jack Hawkins *(Michael O'Taffe)*, Maire O'Neill *(Peg's Mother)*, Arthur Sinclair *(Peg's Father)*, Hay Peetrie *(Mr. Rich)*, Robert Atkins *(Dr. Johnson)*, George Barratt *(Doorkeeper)*, Stuart Robertson *(Singer)*, Pollie Emery *(Martha)*, Dorothy Robinson *(Miss Dalloway)*, Sara Allgood *(Irishwoman)*, Eliot Makeham *(Dr. Bowdler)*, Aubrey Fitzgerald *(Digby)*, Christopher Steele *(Oliver Goldsmith)*, Tom Heslewood *(William Pitt)*, Leslie French *(Pope)*.

The relationship between Peg Woffington and David Garrick, legendary stage performers in 18th Century England, is the subject of this well-made period piece. Neagle has the title role and the film opens with her leaving her home town of Dublin to follow her love, Hawkins, to England where he is trying to become an actor. Hawkins has found a new lady, however, so Neagle tries to make it in the theater herself, eventually gaining the attention of Hardwicke, portraying the popular actor Garrick. Under his guidance, Neagle becomes a highly regarded actress at the Drury Lane theater, and the two fall in love. Neagle has a weak heart, however, and at the finale she is seen collapsing during a performance of William Shakespeare's "As You Like It," and dying shortly afterwards. The film deviates somewhat from reality since Woffington actually lived for three years after her on-stage collapse, but the movie is still a very satisfying effort. Neagle and Hardwicke give impressive performances, and the stage excerpts from the works of Shakespeare and Ben Johnson are flawlessly mounted. Much of the film's power derives from the screenplay by Malleson, the actor's first screen-writing assignment.

p&d, Herbert Wilcox; w, Miles Malleson (based on the play "Masks and Faces" by Charles Reade, Tom Taylor); ph, F. A. Young; ed, Merrill White.

Historical Romance **(PR:A MPAA:NR)**

PEGGY½** (1950) 77m UNIV c

Diana Lynn *(Peggy Brookfield)*, Charles Coburn *(Prof. Brookfield)*, Charlotte Greenwood *(Mrs. Emelia Fielding)*, Barbara Lawrence *(Susan Brookfield)*, Charles Drake *(Tom Fielding)*, Rock Hudson *(Johnny Higgins)*, Connie Gilchrist *(Miss Zim, Nurse)*, Griff Barnett *(Dr. Wilcox)*, Charles Trowbridge *(Dean Stockwell)*, James Todd *(Mr. Gardiner)*, Jerome Cowan *(Mr. Collins)*, Ellen Corby *(Mrs. Privet, Librarian)*, Peter Brocco *(Mr. Winters)*, Donna Martell *(Contestant)*, Jack Gargan *(Chauffeur)*, Olan Soule *(Simmons)*, Marjorie Bennett *(Flossie)*, Sid Marion *(Photographer)*, Jack Kelley *(Lex)*, Wheaton Chambers *(Gateman)*, David MacMahon, Carl Sklover *(Taxi Drivers)*, John Wald *(Announcer)*, Smoki Whitfield, Dudley Dickerson *(Red Caps)*, Floyd Taylor *(Newsboy)*, Ann Pearce *(Pretty Girl)*, James Best *(Frank Addison)*, Jim Congdon *(Football Player on Train)*, Tim Graham *(Dr. Stanton)*, Jim Hayes, Bill Cassady *(Football Players in Dorm)*, Donald Kerr *(Taxi Driver)*, Paul Power, Art Howard *(Judges)*, Lucille Barkley *(Contestant)*, David Alison, Joe Recht, John McKee *(Photographers)*, Felippa Rock *(Mother)*, Michel Ross, Robert G. Anderson *(Van Men)*, Ralph Montgomery *(Milkman)*, Jim Leighton *(Harvey)*, David Stollery *(Small Boy)*, Harold De Garro *(Stilt Walker)*, Felice Richmond *(Woman)*, James Stark *(Attendant)*, Bill Kennedy, Michael Cisney, George Hoagland, Charles J. Conrad *(Reporters)*, Bill Walker, James Davis, Ivan H. Browning *(Porters)*, Mickey McCardle, Roger McKee, Bob DeLauer, Bob Porter, Sonny Howe, Larry Carr, Paul Devry *(Football Players)*.

Widower Charles Coburn retires from his post as professor at Ohio State University and moves with his daughters, Lynn and Lawrence, to Pasadena, California. Lynn is secretly married to Ohio football player Hudson, but she can't reveal the union because Coburn despises the young man. The sisters enter the contest which will determine who will preside as the 1950 Tournament of Roses queen. Since Lynn isn't single, she's ineligible to serve as queen, but she becomes a contestant to allay Coburn's suspicions. Complications multiply as Lynn is chosen queen and Hudson's team shows up to play in the Rose Bowl. When the truth comes out, Coburn accepts the marriage, Lynn relinquishes the crown, and her sister assumes the throne. Silly but entertaining fluff, with a lot of good footage from the 1950 Tournament of Roses parade and the game of that day which pitted OSU against California.

p, Ralph Dietrich; d, Frederick de Cordova; w, George W. George, George F. Slavin (based on a story by Leon Ware); ph, Russell Metty (Technicolor); ed, Ralph Dawson; md, Joseph Gershenson; art d, Bernard Herzbrun, Richard H. Fiedel; set d, Russell A. Gausman, Ruby R. Levitt; cos, Rosemary O'Dell; makeup, Bud Westmore.

Comedy **(PR:A MPAA:NR)**

PEKING BLONDE (SEE: BLONDE FROM PEKING, THE, 1968, Fr.)

PEKING EXPRESS½** (1951) 95m PAR bw

Joseph Cotten *(Michael Bachlin)*, Corinne Calvet *(Danielle Grenier)*, Edmund Gwenn *(Father Joseph Murray)*, Marvin Miller *(Kwon)*, Benson Fong *(Wong)*, Soo Yong *(Li Eiu)*, Robert W. Lee *(Ti Shen)*, Gregory Gay *(Stanislaus)*, Victor Sen Yung *(Chinese Captain)*, Peter Chong *(Restaurant Car Steward)*, Harold Fong *(Ticket Clerk)*, Eddie E. Lee *(Chinese Policeman)*, Beal Wong *(Chinese Pilot)*, Leon M. Lontok *(Chinese Boatman)*, Lane Nakano *(Driver of Jeep)*, George T. Lee *(Soldier)*, Wing Foo *(Soldier)*, Alfredo Santos *(Guard)*, Wei Fan HSueh *(Officer-Assistant to Kwon)*, James B. Leong *(Train Conductor)*, Jung Lim *(Train Porter)*, Rollin Moriyama *(Chinese Priest)*, Walter Ng *(Soldier)*, Si Lan Chen *(Old Woman)*, Gregory Merims *(Russian Plainclothesman)*, William Yip *(Chinese Nationalist)*, Vanya Dimitrova *(Woman)*, Weaver Levy *(Chinese Officer)*, Hom Wing Gim.

Put a bunch of very different people together in an enclosed location and you're off to the dramatic races. It can be brilliant, as in LOST HORIZON when everyone was on a plane, it can be exciting, as in THE HIGH AND THE MIGHTY, it can be dumb, as in THE CASSANDRA CROSSING or it can be somewhere in the middle, as in this picture. The scene is the Peking Express, a train that runs between Shanghai and Peking and is the Oriental version of the very Occidental Orient Express in Europe. Cotten is a doctor attached to the United Nations, on his way to perform a delicate operation on a man who runs the underground. Calvet, a one-time lover of Cotten, just happens to be on the train as well. Also on board are Gwenn, a charming old priest, and Fong, a newsman who leans so far to the left that he can barely make a right turn. Marvin Miller is a nefarious black marketeer who has arranged to have his brigade of bandits stop and rob the train. Miller's son is being held by the same man on whom Cotten is to operate and the reason for the kidnaping and hostage-taking is to get the boy free. Calvet offers herself to Miller if he lets Cotten and the others leave. In the end, the hostages get the upper hand and vanquish the villains. It's a remake of SHANGHAI EXPRESS, a picture that was far superior. Hollywood liked this type of film and also made NIGHT PLANE FROM CHUNGKING, another potboiler. Marvin Miller may have been the most versatile man in radio—announcing, acting, and even singing on more radio programs than any other person who ever stepped before a microphone.

p, Hal B. Wallis; d, William Dieterle; w, John Meredyth Lucas, Jules Furthman (based on a story by Harry Hervey); ph, Charles B. Lang, Jr.; m, Dimitri Tiomkin; ed, Warren Low, Stanley Johnson; art d, Hal Pereira, Franz Bachelin.

Drama **(PR:A MPAA:NR)**

PEKING MEDALLION, THE (SEE: CORRUPT ONES, THE, 1967, Ger.)

PENAL CODE, THE* (1933) 62m Monarch/Frueler bw

Regis Toomey, Helen Cohan, Pat O'Malley, Robert Ellis, Virginia True Boardman, Henry Hall, Leander de Cordova, John Ince, Murdock McQuarrie, Olin Francis, Jack Cheetham, Barney Furey, James Eagles, Julie Griffith, Dorothy Sinclair, Henry Henna, Jack Grant, Eliazabeth Poule, Jean Porter, Albert Richman.

This second-rate B picture opens with a commentary from New York Police Commissioner Mulrooney on the necessity of keeping one's kids off the streets and out of gangs. A lousy youngster takes the wrong road and finds himself writing letters to mom from behind bars. He eventually gets out, but has a tough time shaking his delinquent image. This one's claim to fame is the casting of George M. Cohan's daughter Helen. She had an appealing screen presence, but only made a few film appearances before retiring due to poor health.

d, George Melford; w, F.H. Herbert (based on a story by Edmund T. Lowe); ph, Edward Kull; ed, Fred Bain.

Crime Drama **(PR:A MPAA:NR)**

PENALTY, THE** (1941) 79m MGM bw

Edward Arnold *(Martin "Stuff" Nelson)*, Lionel Barrymore *("Grandpop" Logan)*, Marsha Hunt *(Katherine Logan)*, Robert Sterling *(Edward McCormick)*, Emma Dunn *("Ma" McCormick)*, Gene Reynolds *("Roosty"/Russell Nelson)*, Veda Ann Borg *(Julie)*, Richard Lane *(Craig)*, Gloria DeHaven *(Anne Logan)*, Grant Mitchell *(Judge)*, Phil Silvers *(Hobo)*, Warren Ashe *(Jay)*, William Haade *(Van)*, Ralph Byrd *(Brock)*, Edgar Barrier *(Burns)*, Al Hill *(Coney)*, Byron Foulger *(Bank Manager)*, Mimi Doyle *(Salesgirl)*, Tim Ryan *(Police Sergeant)*, Alonzo Price *(Capt. Harbridge)*.

Reynolds plays the son of vicious gangster Arnold. The father gets his son involved in a variety of illegal activities, and the young man is even present when Arnold brutally slays an FBI agent and a cab driver. The courts step in and feel Reynolds needs a change of scenery so he is sent off to a farm to live with Barrymore and his family. The country life appeals to him and he reforms under the guidance of the farmer's clan. When Arnold comes to reclaim him, Reynolds chases the gangster away at gunpoint. The violence was pretty graphic for the time, but the competent cast rises above the trite story to make this passably entertaining. Director Bucquet primarily worked on the DR. KILDARE films, but he had teamed with producer Chertok early in his career to work on the series of "Crime Does Not Pay" shorts, experience that was put to good use on THE PENALTY. Actor Gene Reynolds in later years became producer of the long-running phenomenally successful TV series M*A*S*H.

p, Jack Chertok; d, Harold S. Bucquet; w, Harry Ruskin, John Q. Higgins (based on the play by Martin Berkeley); ph, Harold Rosson; ed, Ralph Winters.

Crime **(PR:C MPAA:NR)**

PENALTY OF FAME (SEE: OKAY AMERICA, 1932)

PENDULUM½** (1969) 106m Pendulum/COL c

George Peppard *(Capt. Frank Matthews)*, Jean Seberg *(Adele Matthews)*, Richard Kiley *(Woodrow Wilson King)*, Charles McGraw *(Dep. Chief Hildebrand)*, Madeleine Sherwood *(Mrs. Eileen Sanderson)*, Robert F. Lyons *(Paul Martin Sanderson)*, Frank Marth *(Lt. Smithson)*, Marj Dusay *(Liz Tennant)*, Paul McGrath *(Sen. Augustus Cole)*, Stewart Moss *(Richard D'Angelo)*, Isabell Sanford *(Effie, Maid)*, Dana Elcar *(Det. "Red" Thornton)*, Harry Lewis *(Brooks Elliott)*, Mildred Trares *(Mary Schumacher)*, Robin Raymond *(Myra)*, Phyllis Hill *(Mrs. Wilma Elliott)*, S. John Launer *(Judge Kinsella)*, Jock MacKelvie *(U.S. Attorney Grady Butler)*, Logan Ramsey *(Det. Jelinek)*, Richard Guizon *(Dep. Marshal Barnes)*, Douglas Henderson *(Det. Hanauer)*, Gene Boland *(Garland)*, Jack Grimes *(Artie)*.

With its theme of "the law may be going too far to protect the criminal," PENDULUM was something of a precursor to the similarly themed Clint Eastwood and Charles Bronson movies which would prove to be so popular in the following decade. Peppard stars as the cynical Washington, DC police captain who is being honored for his capture of a psychotic rapist/murderer just as the courts are overturning the killer's conviction on a technicality and setting him free. Kiley is the lawyer whose dedication to civil liberties leads him to champion Lyons' cause, attaining his release because of Peppard's failure to read him his rights upon arrest. Peppard's personal life is also in a turmoil as he believes his wife, Seberg, is having an affair with Lewis. When Seberg and Lewis are murdered in bed together, Peppard is the likely suspect. He is arrested on murder charges and hires Kiley to defend him. Peppard escapes from jail and tracks down Lyons whom he believes is the real murderer of the lovers. His suspicion proves correct as Lyons confesses during a confrontation and is arrested, clearing Peppard. The film tries for an honest examination of the U.S. justice system, and is somewhat successful. Peppard is very good as the weary police captain, and Kiley gives a convincing performance as the committed lawyer. The whole project is undermined, however, by the very predictable story and plodding direction. This was one of the few features directed by Schaefer, who has mainly worked in television, where his projects such as "The Magnificnet Yankee" and "A War of Children" have won numerous Emmy Awards.

p, Stanley Niss; d, George Schaefer; w, Niss; ph, Lionel Lindon (Technicolor); m, Walter Scharf; ed, Hugh S. Fowler; prod d, Walter M. Simonds; set d, Morris Hoffman; m/l, "The Pendulum Swings Both Ways," Mack David, Scharf (sung by The Lettermen).

Drama   **Cas.**   **(PR:A-C MPAA:M)**

PENELOPE**   (1966) 97m Euterpe/MGM c

Natalie Wood (Penelope Elcott), Ian Bannen (James B. Elcott), Dick Shawn (Dr. Gregory Mannix), Peter Falk (Lt. Bixbee), Jonathan Winters (Prof. Klobb), Lila Kedrova (Sadaba), Lou Jacobi (Ducky), Norma Crane (Mildred), Arthur Malet (Maj. Higgins), Jerome Cowan (Bank Manager), Arlene Golonka (Honeysuckle Rose), Amzie Strickland (Miss Serena), Bill Gunn (Sgt. Rothschild), Carl Ballantine (Boom Boom), Iggie Wolfington (Store Owner).

Wood, disguised as a sweet little old lady, robs her husband's bank of $60,000 in an attempt to get his attention. She visits her psychoanalyst and confesses her crime, but he is of little help since he is loonier than most of his patients and in love with Wood. He tries to return the cash to the bank, but the situation only gets worse. Unfortunately, the picture is not all that funny, making the mistake of giving Winters a scene which is over in just a couple of minutes. Okay for fans of Wood, but that's it.

p, Arthur Loew, Jr.; d, Arthur Hiller; w, George Wells (based on the novel by E.V. Cunningham [Evan Hunter]); ph, Harry Stradling (Panavision, Metrocolor); m, Johnny Williams; ed, Rita Roland; art d, George W. Davis, Preston Ames; set d, Henry Grace, Keogh Gleason; cos, Edith Head, Ann Landers; makeup, William Tuttle; m/l, "The Sun is Gray," Williams, Gale Garnett, "Penelope," Williams, Leslie Bricusse.

Comedy   **(PR:A MPAA:NR)**

PENGUIN POOL MURDER, THE***   (1932) 70m RKO bw (GB: THE PENGUIN POOL MYSTERY)

Edna May Oliver (Hildegard Withers), James Gleason (Inspector Piper), Mae Clarke (Gwen Parker), Robert Armstrong (Barry Costello), Donald Crook (Philip Seymour), Clarence H. Wilson (Bertrand B. Hemingway), Edgar Kennedy (Donovan), Mary Mason (Secretary), Rochelle Hudson (Telephone Operator), Guy Usher (Gerald Parker), James Donlon (Fink), Joe Hermano (Chicago Lew), William Le Maire (Macdonald), Gustav von Seyffertitz.

Oliver undertakes the role of femme sleuth Hildegard Withers in this first picture in the short-lived series. While strolling through the Battery Park Aquarium in New York City she spots the body of a man floating in the penguin tank. With the help of the slow-witted Gleason, she solves the murder in a tricky courtroom escapade. Oliver and Gleason belted out their witty lines in two more pictures—MURDER ON THE BLACKBOARD and MURDER ON A HONEYMOON—but RKO foolishly broke up the team (ZaSu Pitts was later miscast as Withers), and changed the writing team. As the old saying goes—"why fix it when it ain't broke?"

d, George Archainbaud; w, Willis Goldbeck (based on the novel by Stuart Palmer and the story by Lowell Brentano); ph, Henry Gerrard; ed, Jack Kitchin.

Mystery   **(PR:A MPAA:NR)**

PENGUIN POOL MYSTERY, THE   (SEE: PENGUIN POOL MURDER, THE, 1932)

PENITENTE MURDER CASE, THE**   (1936) 70m Telepictures-The Stewart Productions-Kinotrade bw (AKA: LASH OF THE PENITENTES)

Jose Swickard (Dr. Robert Taylor), Marie de Forest (Raquel), William Marcos (Manuel), Jose Rubio (Chico).

In the remote mountains of New Mexico, a journalist arrives to do a feature story on the Penitentes, a secretive Catholic cult that practices flagellation and crucifixion of one chosen victim each year. He hires a houseboy (Rubio) who is a member of the cult, and the journalist bribes him to show him one of the secret ceremonies. Meanwhile, Rubio's ex-girlfriend, de Forest, has left the village and is posing nude for artist Marcos. Rubio denounces her before the cult elders and demands that she be punished. The journalist asks Rubio to be shown the Good Friday ritual, when the chosen Cristo of the village is scourged and lashed to a cross. Soon afterward Rubio is called before the council. They tell him that his actions in guiding the journalist have been discovered and that in atonement he must kill the meddler. While the reporter sits writing his story, Rubio shoots him in the back. That night de Forest is dragged from her bed by cultists, who strip her and tie her up. She is given 20 lashes for her lascivious behavior, while her little brother runs for help. She recovers from her injuries thanks to a friendly doctor, and Rubio is arrested and confesses to the killing. Based on a real incident in which a reporter was murdered by his houseboy while researching a piece on the Penitente cult. In the wake of that story, some actual footage of a Penitente scourging and crucifixion shot at great risk by Roland C. Price was dusted off and a framing story was concocted. Because of the nude scene involving de Forest, the producers had a great deal of difficulty distributing this film, and even after cuts were made the Hays Office refused to give the film its seal of purity. A version was shot at the same time with the same actors

speaking their parts in Spanish and was released under the title EL ASASENATO DE LOS PENITENTES. A difficult film to see, but overlooking the limitations of the amateur actors and $15,000 budget, a fascinating experience.

p, Roland C. Price, Harry J. Revier; d, Revier; w, Zelma Carroll (based on a story by Price); ph, Price; m, Lee Zahler.

Drama   **(PR:O MPAA:NR)**

PENITENTIARY**   (1938) 74m COL bw

Walter Connolly (Thomas Mathews), John Howard (William Jordan), Jean Parker (Elizabeth Mathews), Robert Barrat (Capt. Grady), Marc Lawrence (Jack Hawkins), Arthur Hohl (Finch), Dick Curtis (Tex), Paul Fix (Punch), Marjorie Main (Katie Mathews), John Gallaudet (State's Attorney), Edward Van Sloan (Dr. Reinewulf), Ann Doran (Blanche Williams), Dick Elliott (McNaulty), Charles Halton (Leonard Nettleford), Ward Bond (Prison Barber), James Flavin (Doran), Stanley Andrews (Capt. Dorn), Robert Allen (Doctor), Jack Dougherty, Ethan Laidlaw, Frank Mayo, Harry Hollingsworth, Frank Meredith (Cops), Lee Shumway (Guard), Lester Dorr (Reporter), Thurston Hall (Judge), Louise Stanley, Bess Flowers (Women), Perry Ivins (Lou), Billy Arnold (Fingerprint Man), Eric Wilton (Butler), Lee Prather (Sergeant).

Connolly is a district attorney who becomes a prison warden. He was responsible for sending convict Howard up the river. Complications arise when Connolly's daughter falls in love with the con. The plot may sound a bit familiar if you've seen CRIMINAL CODE (1931). It's almost an exact duplicate of the earlier picture, although Connolly's performance is miles below Walter Huston's, who played the role in the original.

p, Robert North; d, John Brahm; w, Seton I. Miller; Fred Niblo, Jr. (based on a play by Martin Flavin); ph, Lucien Ballard; ed, Viola Lawrence; md, Morris Stoloff.

Prison Drama   **(PR:A MPAA:NR)**

PENITENTIARY**½   (1979) 99m Jerry Gross c

Leon Isaac Kennedy (Too Sweet), Thommy Pollard (Eugene), Hazel Spears (Linda), Badja Djola (Wilson), Gloria Delaney (Inmate), Chuck Mitchell (Lt. Arnsworth), Wilbur "Hi-Fi" White (Sweet Pea).

A no-holds-barred look at prison life and the sexual appetites of the inmates. Kennedy is a tough, street-wise fighter who finds that to survive in the lock-up he must either play "girl" to his sexually hungry cellmates, or beat the tar out of them. He chooses the latter (thankfully for the film's sake) and soon becomes the prison's top boxer, a skill that wins him an early parole. A black exploitationer with more energy and intellect than most. Followed by the lifeless PENITENTIARY II.

p,d&w, Jamaa Fanaka; ph, Marty Ollstein; m, Frankie Gaye; ed, Betsy Blankett; art d, Adel Mazen.

Prison Drama   **Cas.**   **(PR:O MPAA:R)**

PENITENTIARY II zero   (1982) 103m Fanaka MGM-UA c

Leon Isaac Kennedy (Too Sweet Gordon), Ernie Hudson (Half Dead), Mr. T (Himself), Glynn Turman (Charles), Peggy Blow (Ellen), Cepheus Jaxon (Do Dirty), Marvin Jones (Simp), Donovan Womack (Jesse "The Bull"), Ebony Wright (Sugar), Eugenia Wright (Clarisse), Renn Woods (Nikki), Marci Thomas (Evelyn), Dennis Libscomb, Gerald Berns (Announcers), Joe Anthony Cox (Midget), Sephton Moody (Charles, Jr.), Malik Carter (Seldom), Stan Kamber (Sam).

Kennedy, after boxing his way to freedom in this pic's predecessor PENITENTIARY, decides that he'll turn a new life and enjoys girls and roller boogie. But Hudson and his pals have other ideas. They kill his girlfriend and in a ROCKY-esque finish Kennedy returns to prison to fight the prison champ. MGM saw the success the first picture had and corralled producer-writer-director Fanaka to duplicate his formula. All he did was give us a picture with as much imagination as the picture's title.

p,d&w, Jamaa Fanaka; ph, Steve Posey (DeLuxe Color); m, Jack W. Wheaton; ed, James E. Nownes.

Prison Drama   **Cas.**   **(PR:O MPAA:R)**

PENN OF PENNSYLVANIA   (SEE: COURAGEOUS MR. PENN, 1941, Brit.)

PENNIES FROM HEAVEN***   (1936) 80m COL bw

Bing Crosby (Larry), Madge Evans (Susan), Edith Fellows (Patsy), Donald Meek (Gramps), John Gallaudet (Hart), Louis Armstrong (Henry), Tom Dugan (Crowbar), Nana Bryant (Miss Howard), Charles Wilson (Warden), Harry Tyler (Concessionaire), William Stack (Carmichael), Tom Ricketts (Briggs), Nydia Westman, Louis Armstrong Band, Lionel Hampton.

An amusing musical notable mainly for its fine selection of songs, including the Academy Award-nominated title tune penned by Johnny Burke and Arthur Johnston. The film opens with Crosby serving a jail sentence for smuggling (for which he has been wrongly convicted). Before he is released he is given a note by a murderer who is about to meet his end in the gas chamber. The murderer's note contains the name and address of his victim's relatives. As a final request, he asks Crosby to locate the relatives and move them into his abandoned family estate. Crosby finds the relatives—a 10-year-old girl, Fellows, and her grandfather, Meek—living in squalor. At Crosby's urging Fellows and Meek pack their bags and head for their new home, only to find that it looks haunted. To make the place more inviting, Crosby comes up with the idea of turning it into a restaurant called the Haunted House Cafe. To draw the crowds he croons a number of Johnston and Burke tunes, including "One, Two, Button Your Shoe," "So Do I," "Let's Call a Heart a Heart," "Now I've Got Some Dreaming to Do," "What This Country Needs," and, with help from Louis Armstrong and His Orchestra, "Skeleton in the Closet."

p, Emmanuel Cohen; d, Norman Z. McLeod; w, Jo Swerling (based on the story

"The Peacock's Feather" by Katherine Leslie Moore); ph, Robert Pittack; m, Arthur Johnson; ed, John Rawlins; md, Georgie Stoll; art d, Stephen Goosson.

Drama (PR:A MPAA:NR)

PENNIES FROM HEAVEN½** (1981) 108m MGM c

Steve Martin *(Arthur)*, Bernadette Peters *(Eileen)*, Christopher Walken *(Tom)*, Jessica Harper *(Joan)*, Vernel Bagneris *(Accordion Man)*, John McMartin *(Mr. Warner)*, John Karlen *(Detective)*, Jay Garner *(Banker)*, Robert Fitch *(Al)*, Tommy Rall *(Ed)*, Eliska Krupka *(Blind Girl)*, Frank McCarthy *(Bartender)*, Raleigh Bond *(Mr. Barrett)*, Gloria LeRoy *(Prostitute)*, Nancy Parsons *(Old Whore)*, Toni Kaye, Shirley Kirkes *(Tarts)*, Jack Fletcher *(Elevator Operator)*, Hunter Watkins *(Boy)*, Arell Blanton, George Wilbur *(Motorcycle Police)*, M.C. Grainey *(Young Policeman)*, Mark Campbell *(Newsboy)*, Mark Martinez *(Schoolboy)*, Duke Stroud, Joe Medalis *(Countermen)*, Will Hare *(Father Everson)*, Richard Blum, William Frankfather, James Mendenhall, Jim Boeke, Robert Lee Jarvis, Luke Andreas, Joshua Cadman, Paul Valentine, Bill Richards, John Craig, Alton Ruff, Karla Bush, Robin Hoff, Linda Montana, Dorothy Cronin, Twink Caplan, Lillian D'Honau, Barbara Nordella, Dean Taliaferro, Wayne Storm, Gene Ross, Edward Heim, Dave Adams, Greg Finley, Paul Michael, Joe Ross, Conrad Palmisano, Richard E. Butler, Ronald G. Oliney.

Prolific British TV writer Dennis Potter did a series for the telly which starred Bob Hoskins and took the heart of Blighty. Someone at MGM thought that it could be condensed and made into a feature, so they tapped Steve Martin to play the Hoskins role and asked his then girl friend Peters to do the distaff part. The picture cost more than $20 million and barely recovered $4 million of that. It's a musical, although the singing is done to old records by famed performers. Martin is a Depression era sheet music salesman who falls for Peters, even though he's married to Harper. This is a huge movie with incredible sets, mammoth dance sequences, and a weird, underlying feeling of discontent. The movie was crunched by just about everyone when it came out and audiences preferred going to the dentist for a root canal over attending the theater to see this. It deserved better, if only for the attempt at something completely different. Telescoping several hours of a TV mini-series into 108 minutes was a mistake, as was the expenditure of so much money for a trifling story. There was so much time spent on style and songs that there was hardly a moment left for character development. By adding foul language and some sex, it lost whatever family audience it might have garnered and yet, there's no question that it is beautiful to look at and that Martin displays a hidden talent for dancing that should be used in another film. Martin had a meteoric career in the beginning but then made more depth bombs than a defense plant. Potter's script was nominated for an Oscar.

p, Herbert Ross, Nora Kaye; d, Ross; w, Dennis Potter (based on his television series); ph, Gordon Willis (Metrocolor); m, Marvin Hamlisch, Billy May; ed, Richard Marks; art d, Fred Tuch, Bernie Cutler; cos, Bob Mackie; ch, Danny Daniels.

Musical Cas. (PR:C-O MPAA:R)

PENNY PARADISE** (1938, Brit.) 72m ATP/ABF bw

Edmund Gwenn *(Joe Higgins)*, Jimmy O'Dea *(Pat)*, Betty Driver *(Betty Higgins)*, Maire O'Neill *(Widow Clegg)*, Jack Livesey *(Bert)*, Ethel Coleridge *(Aunt Agnes)*, Syd Crossley *(Uncle Lancelot)*, James Harcourt *(Amos Cook)*.

Gwenn is a devoted tugboat captain who throws an eventful party upon learning that he has won a soccer pool. His local pub fills with friends—some of whom want a share of the earnings. Even his daughter is targeted by a greedy chap who thinks he can sweet-talk his way into her purse. When Gwenn learns that his best friend, O'Dea, forgot to post the pool ticket, the problem of how to spend the money is quickly solved. As a consolation, Gwenn is put in charge of the best tugboat on the river—a prize worth much more to him than money.

p, Basil Dean, Jack Kitchin; d, Carol Reed; w, Thomas Thompson, Thomas Browne, W.L. Meade (based on a story by Dean); ph, Ronald Neame, Gordon Dines.

Comedy (PR:A MPAA:NR)

PENNY POINTS TO PARADISE*½ (1951, Brit.) 77m Advance-PYL/Adelphi bw

Harry Secombe *(Harry Flakers)*, Alfred Marks *(Edward Haynes)*, Peter Sellers *(The Major/Arnold P'Fringe)*, Paddy O'Neil *(Christine Russell)*, Spike Milligan *(Spike Donnelly)*, Bill Kerr *(Digger Graves)*, Freddie Frinton *(Drunk)*, Vicki Page *(Sheila Gilroy)*, Joe Linnane *(Policeman)*, Sam Kydd *(Porter/Taxi Driver)*, Felix Mendelssohn and His Hawaiian Serenaders.

Set in England's Brighton, PENNY POINTS TO PARADISE stars Secombe as the winner of a sizable soccer pool. Before he gets the chance to spend his cash, however, he is victimized by counterfeiters who replace the real money with bogus bills. A trifling comedy which would be completely forgotten had it not been Peter Sellers' debut. Sellers, along with fellow "Goon Show" stars Secombe and Milligan, received a whopping 100 pounds for their efforts.

p, Alan Cullimore; d, Tony Young; w, John Ormonde.

Comedy (PR:A MPAA:NR)

PENNY POOL, THE½** (1937, Brit.) 85m Mancunian bw

Duggie Wakefield *(Duggie)*, Billy Nelson *(Billy)*, Tommy Fields *(Tommy Bancroft)*, Luanne Shaw *(Renee Harland)*, Charles Sewell *(Henry Bancroft)*, Harry Terry *(Jerry Rogers)*, Chuck O'Neil *(Chuck)*, Jack Butler *(Jack)*, Mascotte, The Marie Louise Sisters, Macari and His Dutch Serenaders.

Shaw is a factory worker whose luck with winning pools is all bad. She is fired from her job for filling in her coupon on company time. Someone else finds the ticket, fills in his name, and wins the pool. Shaw's boy friend, Fields, the son of her former boss, manages to straighten out the mess, gets her compensation, and wins her over romantically.

p, John E. Blakeley; d, George Black; w, Arthur Mertz; ph, Germaine Burger.

Comedy (PR:A MPAA:NR)

PENNY PRINCESS*** (1953, Brit.) 91m Conquest/UNIV c

Yolande Donlan *(Lindy Smith)*, Dirk Bogarde *(Tony Craig)*, Edwin Styles *(Chancellor/Cobbler)*, Reginald Beckwith *(Finance Minister/Blacksmith)*, Kynaston Reeves *(Burgomeister/Policeman)*, A. E. Matthews *(Selby)*, Peter Butterworth *(Julien)*, Desmond Walter-Ellis *(Alberto)*, Laurence Naismith *(Louis)*, Paul Sheridan *(French Attache)*, Eric Pohlmann *(Paul)*, Anthony Oliver *(Selby's Valet)*, Mary Clare *(Maria)*, Robert Henderson *(Macy's Staff Manager)*, J. McDonald Parke, Alexander Gauge *(Lawyers)*, Fletcher Lightfoot, Derek Prentice, Raf de la Torre, Richard Wattis.

A lightweight British comedy, the first independent production from actress Donlan and all-around cineman Guest. The busty blonde Donlan, every bit as vapid as Judy Holliday in her role as a shopgirl who inherits a tiny European principality, decides to do her duty by her new people and get their struggling economy back on an even keel. Their sole product of any merit is a unique cheese, which happens to have a high alcoholic content, so one need not serve wine with it. Neighboring countries have closed their borders to the trade through excessive tariffs. Enter British cheese salesman Bogarde, who, though much set-upon, helps her find a solution. In the process, he falls in love with the vacuous damsel, who resigns her fiefdom to marry him. Bogarde solicited this role; he wanted to try his hand at light comedy. Producer-director-writer Guest tried to get Wiliam Holden, but failed. Bogarde said "I don't think he's [Guest] ever quite forgiven me".

p,d&w, Val Guest; ph, Geoffrey Unsworth (Technicolor); m, Philip Martell; ed, Alfred Roome; art d, Maurice Carter; cos, Beatrice Dawson.

Comedy (PR:A MPAA:NR)

PENNY SERENADE½** (1941) 125m COL bw

Irene Dunne *(Julie Gardiner Adams)*, Cary Grant *(Roger Adams)*, Beulah Bondi *(Miss Oliver)*, Edgar Buchanan *(Applejack)*, Ann Doran *(Dotty)*, Eva Lee Kuney *(Trina, Age 6)*, *Leonard Willey (Dr. Hartley)*, Wallis Clark *(Judge)*, Walter Soderling *(Billings)*, Baby Biffle *(Trina, Age 1)*, Edmund Elton *(Minister)*, Billy Bevan *(McDougal)*, Nee Wong, Jr. *(Sung Chong)*, Michael Adrian Morris *(Bill Collector)*, Grady Sutton, Stanley Brown *(Men)*, Beryl Vaughn *(Flower Girl)*, John Tyrrell *(Press Operator)*, Iris Han *(O-Hanna-San)*, Otto Han *(Sam, the Cook)*, Ben Taggart *Policeman)*, Frank Moran *(Cab Driver)*, Lynton Brent *(Reporter)*, Al Seymour *(Bootlegger)*, Dick Wessel *(Joe)*, Charles Flynn *(Bob)*, Arline Jackson, Mary Bovard, Georgia Hawkins *(Girls)*, Fred "Snowflake" Toones *(Train Porter)*, Ed Peil, Sr. *(Train Conductor)*, Eddie Laughton *(Cab Driver)*, Doris Herbert *(Minister's Wife)*, Bess Flowers *(Mother)*, John Ferguson *(Father)*, Lani Lee *(Chinese Waitress)*, Rollin Moriyama, Ben Kumagai *(Rickshaw Boys)*, Lillian West *(Nurse)*, Henry Dixon *(Old Printer)*, Dorothy Adams *(Mother)*, Albert Butterfield *(Boy)*.

After coming off the hysterical movie THE AWFUL TRUTH, audiences thought that Grant and Dunne would make another rollicking comedy and the very title, PENNY SERENADE, seemed to indicate a light-hearted romp. Not so. This is a weeper from the start, with only a few moments of comedy placed in so the audience can dry their eyes before the next sentimental barrage. Dunne is about to leave her husband, Grant, and she plays "Penny Serenade" on her Victrola, a tune which takes her, via flashback, to the early days of their marriage. Grant is a newspaper reporter and Dunne works in a music store. They meet, fall in love, marry and go off to Japan where he is on assignment. She becomes pregnant and loses the baby when there is a horrendous earthquake which causes a miscarriage. They return to the U.S. and Grant buys a small newspaper in a tranquil town. Dunne would like to have children but is no longer physically able to so they plan to adopt a baby. They are in no position financially and it looks as though it won't go through until Bondi, the head of the adoption agency, helps them. They get the child, Baby Biffle, and raise her until she becomes Kuney and dies suddenly. Their grief pours off the screen and they are about to part when they get the chance to adopt another baby which brings them back together. Dunne plays several records on her phonograph, including: "You Were Meant For Me" (Arthur Reed, Nacio Herb Brown), a tune that she recalls was playing when she first met Grant, their wedding song "Moonlight and Roses Bring Mem'ries of You" (Ben Black, Neil Moret [Charles N. Daniels]), and "Poor Butterfly," which covers their lives in Japan. Grant got an Oscar nomination, the only notice this picture had. It never quite made up its mind if it was a tragedy or a comedy although there was one hilarious scene where Grant has to bathe the baby that left audiences howling with laughter, a scene that showed up in many films. Buchanan, as a family pal, steals the picture with his on-the-nose portrait of a kindly, bumbling man who helps them through their crises.

p&d, George Stevens; w, Morrie Ryskind (based on the story by Martha Cheavens); ph, Joseph Walker; m, W. Franke Harling; ed, Otto Meyer; md, Morris Stoloff; art d, Lionel Banks.

Drama/Comedy Cas. (PR:A MPAA:NR)

PENNYWHISTLE BLUES, THE** (1952, South Africa) 63m Swan/Mayer-Kingsley bw (AKA: THE MAGIC GARDEN)

Tommy Ramokgopa *(Thief)*, Dolly Rathebe *(Lili)*, Harriet Qubeka *(Mrs. Sakabona)*, David Mnkwanazi *(Lucas Ranku)*, Victor Cwai *(John)*, Grinsell Nogauza *(Mr. Shabalala)*, Lucas Khosa *(Issac Wela)*, Linda Madikisa *(Mrs. Wela)*, Jonathan Mzamo *(Priest)*, Willard Cele *(Pennywhistle Player)*.

A film from South Africa featuring an all-black cast of nonprofessionals set in the small village of Alexandria located on the outskirts of Johannesburg. The film is a slice-of-life drama that revolves around the theft of a 40-pound donation made to the local church by an old man who wanted his life savings to go to a good cause. Responding to public outcry over the theft, the thief buries the loot in the garden of a poor widow for safekeeping until the heat dies down. The widow, however, finds the cash and exchanges it with a greedy grocer for a credit note. The thief re-steals the cash from the grocer, but soon loses it to a young man who uses the money to bail out his sweetheart's father who is heavily in debt. Once again the thief steals the money from the girl's father's creditor, but the cash ends up back at the church, from which he intends to steal it again

p&d, Donald Swanson; w, Ferinand Webb, Swanson, C. Pennington-Richards (based on a story bye James Brown); ph, Pennington-Richards; m, Ralph Trewhela, Matcome "Tommy" Ramokgopa; ed, Gerald Ehrlich

Drama **(PR:A MPAA:NR)**

PENROD AND HIS TWIN BROTHER (1938) 62m WB bw

Billy Mauch *(Penrod Schofield)*, Bobby Mauch *(Danny)*, Frank Craven *(Mr. Schofield)*, Spring Byington *(Mrs. Schofield)*, Charles Halton *(Mr. Bitts)*, Claudia Coleman *(Mrs. Bitts)*, Jackie Morrow *(Rodney Bitts)*, Philip Hurlic *(Verman)*, Bennie Bartlett *(Chuck)*, Bernice Pilot *(Delia)*, John Pirrone *(Sam)*, Billy Lechner *(Donald)*, Charley Foy *(Kraemer)*, Charles Jordan *(Shorty)*, Jay Adler *(Johnson)*, Max Wagner *(Blackie)*, Eddie Collins *(Captain)*, Fred Lawrence *(Clark)*, Cliff Soubier *(Sheriff)*, Robert E. Homans *(Chief Flynn)*, Eddie Chandler *(Officer McCarthy)*, Jack Mower *(Officer Clancy)*, Billy Wolfstone *(Piggy)*, Jarry Madden *(Slats)*, Ernie Wechbaugh *(Joe)*, Donald Hulbert, Jerry Tucker, Jack Cunningham *(Members of Penrod's Gang)*.

The Mauch twins start up a gang of pint-sized G-men and end up locating the hideout of a gang of real criminals. The cops come along and make the arrests. The kids' dog even gets a medal for its heroics. Fine fare for the kids. Made as a vehicle for the Mauch twins, with Bobby playing a tough big-city boy from Chicago and Billy the bucolic title whippersnapper, the story deviates markedly from author Tarkington's tales. (See PENROD series, Index)

p, Bryan Foy; d, William McGann; w, William Jacobs, Hugh Cummings (based on stories by Booth Tarkington); ph, Arthur Todd; ed, Doug Gould, Frank Dewar.

Comedy **(PR:AAA MPAA:NR)**

PENROD AND SAM** (1931) 70m FN bw

Leon Janney *(Penrod Schofield)*, Matt Moore *(Mr. Schofield)*, Dorothy Peterson *(Mrs. Schofield)*, Junior Coghlan *(Sam Williams)*, Johnny Arthur *(Mr. Bassett)*, ZaSu Pitts *(Mrs. Bassett)*, Charles Sellon *(Mr. Bitts)*, Wade Boteler *(Mr. Williams)*, Helen Beaudine *(Margaret)*, Nestor Aber *(Rodney)*, Billy Lord *(George)*, Margaret Marquis *(Marjorie)*, Betty Graham *(Baby Rensdale)*, James Robinson *(Herman)*, Robert Dandridge *(Verman)*, Cameo *(The Dog)*.

Janney and pal Coghlan are a pair of youngsters who have a knack for getting into mischievous situations. Reminiscent of the OUR GANG comedies, the PENROD series does its best to recapture turn-of-the-century youngsters, especially by placing them in a vacant-lot clubhouse which is off-limits to "sissies." A remake, again remade in 1937. Author Tarkington, who had served in the Indiana legislature, was well acquainted with the rural midwest of his boyhood, as his young hoosier heroes—extremely popular in the literature of the time—would attest. He later wrote the Pulitzer Prize-winning novel from which Orson Welles derived his fine second feature film THE MAGNIFICENT AMBERSONS (1942). (See PENROD Series, Index.)

d, William Beaudine; w, Waldemar Young (based on the story by Booth Tarkington); ph, Roy Overbaugh; ed, Leroy Stone

Comedy **(PR:AAA MPAA:NR)**

PENROD AND SAM** (1937) 68m FN/WB bw

Billy Mauch *(Penrod Schofield)*, Frank Craven *(Mr. Schofield)*, Spring Byington *(Mrs. Schofield)*, Craig Reynolds [Hugh Enfield] *(Roy "Dude" Hanson)*, Harry Watson *(Sam)*, Jackie Morrow *(Rodney Bitts)*, Philip Hurlic *(Verman)*, Charles Halton *(Mr. Bitts)*, Bernice Pilot *(Delia)*, Kenneth Harlan *(G-man)*, Allan Davis *(Lefty)*, Si Wills *(Suds)*, Billy Lechner *(Wienie)*, Billy Wolfstone *(Piggie Nelson)*, Jerry Madden *(Slats Fogarty)*, Robert E. Homans *(Sheriff)*, Mildred Gover *(Mrs. Diggs)*, George Billings, Jerry Tucker, Jack Cunningham, Don Hulbert, John Pirrone *(Members of Penrod's Gang)*.

This third treatment of author Tarkington's popular story deviates from it the most. Tarkington, who never patronized or sentimentalized his youthful rustic ruffians, should have been appalled to see them turned into Hoosier sleuths, rounding up a band of criminals. Black actor Hurlic, as a youth orphaned by gangland bullets, steals the show in this one. Many of the cast members went on to perform in a sequel, PENROD AND HIS TWIN BROTHER (1938), also featuring young Mauch's twin brother Bobby. It was equally bowdlerized, having a similar youthful-detective story. The twins and their peers did it once again that same year with the same basic plot in PENROD'S DOUBLE TROUBLE. (See PENROD Series, Index.)

p, Bryan Foy; d, William McGann; w, Lillie Hayward, Hugh Cummings (based on the story by Booth Tarkington); ph, L. William O'Connell; ed, Thomas Pratt.

Comedy **(PR:AAA MPAA:NR)**

PENROD'S DOUBLE TROUBLE** (1938) 63m FN/WB bw

Billy Mauch *Penrod Schofield)*, Bobby Mauch *(Danny)*, Dick Purcell *(Tex Boyden)*, Gene Lockhart *(Mr. Schofield)*, Kathleen Lockhart *(Mrs. Schofield)*, Hugh O'Connell *(Prof. Caligostro)*, Bernice Pilot *(Delia)*, Charles Halton *(Mr. Bitts)*, Jackie Morrow *(Rodney Bitts)*, Philip Hurlic *(Verman)*.

Warner Bros. beat its Penrod formula into the ground with this variation from Booth Tarkington's stories. Again the Mauch twins confuse the adults by looking so much alike, and by proving their worth as junior G-men. Let's not forget that little mutt of theirs, who this time leads the gang of kids to Penrod's kidnapers. (See PENROD series, Index.)

p, Bryan Foy; d, Lewis Seiler; w, Ernest Booth, Crane Wilbur (based on stories by Booth Tarkington); ph, Arthur Todd; ed, Frank Dewar.

Comedy **(PR:AAA MPAA:NR)**

PENTHOUSE*** (1933) 90m COS/MGM bw (GB: CROOKS IN CLOVER)

Warner Baxter *(Jackson Durant)*, Myrna Loy *(Gertie Waxted)*, Charles Butterworth *(Layton, Butler)*, Mae Clarke *(Mimi Montagne)*, Phillips Holmes *(Tom Siddall)*, C. Henry Gordon *(Jim Crelliman)*, Martha Sleeper *(Sue Leonard)*, Nat Pendleton *(Tony Grazotti)*, George E. Stone *(Murtoch)*, Robert Emmett O'Connor *(Stevens)*, Raymond Hatton, Arthur Belasco *(Bodyguards)*.

Pendleton shines as a powerful but sympathetic gangland chief, a pragmatist with a sense of humor whose self-constructed empire is threatened by rival gangster Gordon. Baxter is a successful corporation lawyer who, bored with the legalistic doings of the high and mighty, craves the company of criminal clients. He takes on the defense of Pendleton, who has been accused of murder. He wins the case, but as a result loses both his prestigious position with a firm of Harvard attorneys and his fiancee, Clarke. Pendleton—fearful that his new-found barrister buddy's life may be in jeopardy as a result of his successful courtroom battle—appoints two goons, Hatton and Belasco, to safeguard his legal savior. Clarke's new high-society romantic attachment is the victim of a murder frame-up at the instigation of bad gangster Gordon, and so Baxter defends his rival in romance. When Clarke is killed also, Baxter tries to solve the continuing series of crimes, this time with the help of Gordon's wisecracking moll, Loy. Wise to her betrayal, Gordon abducts his ex-mistress, holding her in his hideout. Baxter races to Loy's defense, arriving at the hideout to a tune of machinegun fire. He is greeted by his smiling hoodlum pal Pendleton, who has raided the place and pulled off the resuce. Pendleton then slumps to the floor, mortally wounded, having given his life on behalf of his new high-society friend. This interesting melding of bourgeoisie and *lumpenproletariat* presaged things to come in the THIN MAN series which began a year later, featuring the same director, W.S. "One-shot Woody" Van Dyke, the same team of scriptwriters, and the same leading lady. Loy was just breaking away from her ethnic "you touch me, I keel you" roles, which had her using her universal ethnic accent for every characterization ranging from East Indian to Egyptian. From now on, she would play high-society roles herself, albeit still with wisecracks.

p, Hunt Stromberg; d, W.S. Van Dyke; w, Frances Goodrich, Albert Hackett (based on the novel by Arthur Somers Roche); ph, Lucien Andriot, Harold Rossen; m, Dr. William Axt; ed, Robert J. Kern.

Crime Drama **(PR:A MPAA:NR)**

PENTHOUSE, THE zero (1967, Brit.) 100m Tahiti/PAR c

Suzy Kendall *(Barbara Willason)*, Terence Morgan *(Bruce Victor)*, Tony Beckley *(Tom)*, Norman Rodway *(Dick)*, Martine Beswick *(Harry)*.

An exercise in sadism and masochism that was well-done but totally made to satisfy an audience's basest instincts. It began as a play and looks it, as the bulk of the action is claustrophobically confined to the penthouse in an as-yet unfinished apartment building. Morgan is a realtor with access to the furnished model atop the edifice and he is using it for illicit trysts with Kendall. Morgan is a married man with children and he assured Kendall that he'll dump the family as soon as the right moment comes along (Hah!). They are at the flat early one day when the doorbell rings. Beckley stands there and says he has come to read the gas meter. Kendall allows him entrance and he walks in with his assistant, Rodway. Almost instantly, Beckley wields a knife and ties Morgan to a chair (a place where Morgan remains for most of the movie). Rodway and Beckley get Kendall to smoke some dope, then fill her full of whiskey and force her to do a strip. Next, each rapes her in the bedroom as Morgan watches in frustration. Rodway and Beckley leave and Kendall unties Morgan. They hesitate calling the police, as there is no way to explain why they were there together. The doorbell rings, they answer it and meet Beswick, who says she is the parole office assigned to Rodway and Beckley and that she has brought them back to say they are sorry for what they've done. Against Kendall's wishes, Morgan allows them inside the apartment. The men soon bind Kendall and Morgan and dance around them, then leave, just as mysteriously as they had come. Kendall and Morgan work themselves free and depart in opposite directions. Tasteless, made only to shock, and with some preposterous holes, THE PENTHOUSE had the benefit of better acting than the script demanded. Lisa Shane sings "World Full of Lonely Men" (John Hawksworth, Harold Shaper) over the end titles, and none too soon either. Not for children, nor anyone with sensitivity.

p, Harry Fine; d&w, Peter Collinson (based on the play "The Meter Man" by C. Scott Forbes); ph, Arthur Lavis (Eastmancolor); m, John Hawksworth; ed, John Trumper; art d, Peter Mullens; makeup, George Partleton.

Thriller **(PR:O MPAA:NR)**

PENTHOUSE PARTY** (1936) 60m Liberty bw (GB: WITHOUT CHILDREN)

Marquerite Churchill *(Sue)*, Bruce Cabot *(David)*, Evelyn Brent *(Shirley)*, Reginald Denny *(Phi1)*, Dorothy Lee *(Carol)*, William Janney *(Sonny)*, Dickie Moore *(Baby Sonny)*, Cora Sue Collins *(Baby Carol)*.

Churchill is the unloved mom whose husband takes up with other women, and whose kids don't return the love that she dished out. Her answer is to live it up and have a penthouse party where she downs all the cocktails she can handle. Ultimately, the now-grown kids, Lee and Janney, straighten mom out and reunite her with husband Cabot. This independent production was one of eight films in which B-movie queen Churchill appeared in 1936, the year she retired from movies to devote herself to housewifely duties with her real-life husband, cowboy star George O'Brien. She emerged from retirement 14 years later to appear in one more film, BUNCO SQUAD, following their divorce in 1948.

p, M.H. Hoffman, Jr.; d, William Nigh; w, Gertrude Orr (based on a story by Mrs. Wilson Woodrow); ph, Harry Neumann; ed, Mildred Johnston.

Drama   **(PR:A   MPAA:NR)**

PENTHOUSE RHYTHM*   (1945) 60m UNIV bw

Kirby Grant (Dick), Lois Collier (Linda), Edward Norris (Junior), Maxie Rosenbloom (Himself), Eric Blore (Ferdy Pelham), Minna Gombell (Taffy), Edward S. Brophy (Bailey), Judy Clark (Patty), Marion Martin (Irma), Donald McBride (Brewster), Henry Armetta (Joe), Jimmy Dodd (Jank), Bobby Worth (Johnny), Louis DaPron (Bill), George Lloyd (Nick), Paul Hurst (Sergeant), Harry Barris (Tim), Velasco and Lenee (Dance Specialty).

A musical combination comprising three brothers and a sister try to make it in the show-biz world, but find that the road to success is full of obstacles. . .and countless cliches. Nothing here sticks out except the running time which, at 60 minutes, is excessive. Includes the rhythm-less tunes "Society Numbers," "Let's Go American, " "When I Think of Heaven," "Up Comes Love," and "Peter Had a Wife and Couldn't Keep Her."

p, Frank Gross; d, Eddie Cline; w, Stanley Roberts, Howard Dimsdale (based on a story by Roberts, Min Selvin); ph, William Sickner; m, Jack Brooks, Norman Berens, Seymour Kramer, Inez James, Sidney Miller; ed, Russell Schoengarth; md, Edgar Fairchild; art d, John B. Goodman, Harold H. MacArthur.

Musical   **(PR:A   MPAA:NR)**

PEOPLE AGAINST O'HARA, THE***   (1951) 101m MGM bw

Spencer Tracy (James Curtayne), Pat O'Brien (Vincent Ricks), Diana Lynn (Ginny Curtayne), John Hodiak (Louis Barra), Eduardo Ciannelli (Knuckles Lanzetta), James Arness (Johnny O'Hara), Yvette Duguay (Mrs. Lanzetta), Jay C. Flippen (Sven Norson), William Campbell (Frank Korvac), Richard Anderson (Jeff Chapman), Henry O'Neill (Judge Keating), Arthur Shields (Mr. O'Hara), Louise Lorimer (Mrs. O'Hara), Ann Doran (Betty Clark), Emile Meyer (Capt. Tom Mulvaney), Regis Toomey (Fred Colton), Katherine Warren (Mrs. Sheffield), Paul Bryar (Detective Howie Pendleton), Peter Mamakos (James Korvac), Perdita Chandler (Gloria Adler), Frank Ferguson (Al), Don Dillaway (Monty), C. Anthony Hughes (George), Lee Phelps (Emmett Kimbaugh), Lawrence Tolan (Vincent Korvac), Jack Lee (Court Clerk), Tony Barr (Little Wolfie), Jan Kayne, Virginia Hewitt (Girls), Richard Landry (Sailor), "Billy" Vincent (William Sheffield), Frankie Hyers (Bartender), Michael Dugan (Charlie, Detective), Lennie Bremen (Harry), Jim Toney (Officer Abrams), Benny Burt (Sammy), John Maxwell (Thayer Connolly), Mae Clarke (Receptionist), Paul McGuire (Male Stenographer), Kay Scott (Secretary), Angi O. Poulis (Watchman), Julius Tannen (Toby Baum), Dan Foster (Assistant District Attorney), Harry Cody (Photographer), Ned Glass (Magistrate), John Butler (Court Clerk), Lou Lubin (Eddie), Michael Mark (Workman), Phyllis Graffeo (Mary), Maurice Samuels (Papa Lanzetta), Celia Lovsky (Mrs. Korvac), Charles Buchinsky [Bronson] (Angelo Korvac), Joyce Otis (Thelma), "Tiny" Jimmie Kelly (Leigh Keighly), Fred Essler (Augie), John Albright (Waiter), John Sheehan (Postal Clerk), Jack Kruschen (Detective), William Self (Technician), Jonathan Cott (Policeman), William Schallert (Intern), Sammy Finn, Brooks Benedict (Gamblers), Frank Sully, Ernesto Morelli (Fishmongers), Jeff Richards (Ambulance Driver), George Magrill (Court Attendant), Bud Wolfe (Fingerprint Technician), Bill Fletcher (Pete Korvac), Richard Bartlett (Tony Korvac).

A surprisingly grim crime film starring Tracy as an alcoholic district attorney forced into an early retirement because of his drinking problem. Having made a strong recovery after giving up the bottle, Tracy becomes determined to salvage his reputation by taking on the defense of Arness, the son of family friends who has been accused of murder. Tracy's daughter, Lynn, who has nursed him through his bad period, worries that the pressure to prove himself will drive him back to drink. Though Arness swears he is innocent of the shooting, he refuses to reveal his whereabouts on the night of the murder because he was with his former sweetheart, Duguay, who now is married to powerful mobster Ciannelli. Meanwhile, the state builds a strong case against Arness with information gleaned from Campbell, a friend of Arness' who has turned against him. With the help of detective O'Brien, Tracy learns the truth behind Arness' weak alibi and begins to suspect that Campbell is the real killer. The only witness to the shooting is a sailor who refuses to testify unless paid to do so. Desperate to revive his career, Tracy reluctantly pays the man. During the trial, Tracy's weakened physical condition works against him and district attorney Hodiak learns of the bribe. Tracy loses the case. Obsessed with clearing both Arness and himself, Tracy sets up a meeting with Campbell and his seedy family on the pretense of selling information. Tracy wears a recording device to the meeting which will broadcast what is said straight to a police van. The dialog is damning enough for the police to arrest the criminals, but when they move in, Tracy is killed in the crossfire. Directed with a dark eye for detail by Sturges, THE PEOPLE AGAINST O'HARA is an odd film for Tracy at this point in his career, and the fact that he is killed at the end makes for a very bleak film. Though his sacrifice can be seen as heroic, the mood of the film seems to indicate that Tracy never really had any choice about his fate and was doomed from the beginning. Surprisingly, THE PEOPLE AGAINST O'HARA was the first time Tracy and his old friend O'Brien appeared on screen together. O'Brien was having trouble getting decent roles after WW II and Hollywood seemed to be ignoring him. Anxious to help him, Tracy refused to do the film unless O'Brien got a part. Fans of Charles Bronson should look quickly to spot their hero in a bit part as one of the evil Korvac Brothers. This was the first time that Bronson had appeared in a Sturges film and he would soon become a familiar face in the director's works with bigger roles in NEVER SO FEW (1959), THE MAGNIFICENT SEVEN (1960), and THE GREAT ESCAPE (1963).

p, William H. Wright; d, John Sturges; w, John Monks, Jr. (based on the novel by Eleazar Lipsky); ph, John Alton; m, Carmen Dragon; ed, Gene Ruggiero; art d,

Cedric Gibbons, James Basevi; set d, Edwin B. Willis, Jacque Mapes; cos, Helen Rose; spec eff, A. Arnold Gillespie, Warren Newcombe; makeup, William Tuttle.

Crime   **(PR:C   MPAA:NR)**

PEOPLE ARE FUNNY*½   (1945) 93m Pine-Thomas/PAR bw

Jack Haley (Pinky Wilson), Helen Walker (Corey Sullivan), Rudy Vallee (Ormsby Jamison), Ozzie Nelson (Leroy Brinker), Philip Reed (John Guedel), Bob Graham (Luke), Barbara Roche (Aimee), Art Linkletter (Himself), Frances Langford (Herself), Clara Blandick (Grandma), Roy Atwell (Mr. Pippensiegal), Wheaton Chambers, Casey Johnson, Rosarita Varela, Lillian Molieri, The Vagabonds.

The title of this one comes from a radio show which did its best to persuade people to do ridiculous things in exchange for gifts. The screen version of this idea has a pair of rival producers trying to find an audience. Reed is the producer who pirates the "People Are Funny" idea from small-time announcer Haley in order to make station sponsor Vallee happy. Many of the performers were popular radio personalities of the time; this type of cinema-radio tie-in became a genre as picture producers attempted to capture the audiences of another medium. Songs include "I'm in the Mood for Love" (Dorothy Fields, Jimmy McHugh), "Angelina" (Doris Fisher, Allan Roberts), "The Old Square Dance is Back Again" (Don Reid, Henry Tobias), "Every Hour On the Hour" (Don George, Duke Ellington), and "Alouette" (traditional).

p&d, Sam White; w, Maxwell Shane, David Lang (based on the story by Lang, and on John Guedel's radio program "People Are Funny"); ph, Fred Jackman, Jr.; ed, Henry Adams; md, David Chudnow; art d, F. Paul Sylos; set d, Glenn Thompson; ch, Jack Crosby.

Musical   **Cas.**   **(PR:A   MPAA:NR)**

PEOPLE MEET AND SWEET MUSIC FILLS THE HEART**
(1969, Den./Swed.) 94m Nordisk-Sandrews/Trans-Lux bw (MENNESKER MODES OG SOD MUSIK OPSTAR I HJERTET; MANNISKOR MOTS OCH LJUV MUSIK UPPSTAR I HJARTAT)

Harriet Andersson (Sofia Petersen), Preben Neergaard (Sjalof Petersen), Erik Wedersoe (Hans Madsen), Eva Dahlbeck (Devah Sorensen), Lone Rode (Evangeline Hansen), Georg Rydeberg (Robert Clair de Lune), Lotte Horne (Mithra), Bent Christensen (Fanconetti), Mona Chong, Cassandra Mahon (Girls of the House), Elin Reimer (Mme. Calcura), Knud Rex (Ramon Salvador), Lotte Tarp (Kose), Eske Holm, Zito Kerras, Ove Rud, Benny Juhlin, Arne Weel, Claus Nissen, Armand Miehe, Jimmy Moore, Per Gundemann.

Andersson embarks on a sex-filled train trip to South America, which is spotted with murder and seduction, eventually landing her in a brothel. She soon makes for New York and becomes a dancing star, pursued by one of her train affairs. She ends up on another train, where she is forced by a masked assailant to remove her clothes, but this time she finds herself left alone in the morning. What does it all mean? Why does the title make it sound like a romantic musical from the 1940s? Who knows. . .but it does have its humorous moments.

p, Goran Lindgren, Henning Carlsen; d, Carlsen; w, Paul Borum, Carlsen (based on the novel Mennesker Modes og Sod Musik Opstar i Hjertet by Jens August Schade); ph, Henning Kristiansen; m, Krzysztof Komeda; ed, Carlsen; art d, P. A. Lundgren; cos, Ulla-Britt Soderlund, Lotte Ravnholt; ch, Eske Holm.

Drama/Comedy   **(PR:O   MPAA:NR)**

PEOPLE NEXT DOOR, THE*   (1970) 93m AE c

Eli Wallach (Arthur Mason), Julie Harris (Gerrie Mason), Deborah Winters (Maxie Mason), Stephen McHattie (Artie Mason), Hal Holbrook (David Hoffman), Cloris Leachman (Tina Hoffman), Don Scardino (Sandy Hoffman), Rue McClanahan (Della), Nehemiah Persoff (Dr. Salazar), Mike Kellin (Dr. Margolin), Sandy Alexander (Elliott), Anthony Call (Dr. Lauran), Matthew Cowles (Wally), Joseph Leon (Price Whitehead), Bruce Scott (Jack), Anita Dangler (Blonde Mother), Bobby Sandler, Jay Savino, Steve Kanyon, Ron Panvini (Party Musicians), The Bead Game (Artie's Group), Jan Sarno (Night Nurse), Paul Ganapoler (Club Owner), Marilyn Chris (Discotheque Waitress), Ben Yaffee (Discotheque Owner), John Batiste (Therapist).

A couple of suburban parents discover that their "little" daughter is strung out on LSD and wonder where they went wrong. The kid doesn't heed her parents' requests until Harris physically slaps some sense into her in a hospital. Goody-goody model boy Scardino, son of school-principal neighbor Holbrook, turns out to be the neighborhood dope dealer. Based on a CBS Television Playhouse drama, THE PEOPLE NEXT DOOR succeeds only in wasting a fine cast and clearly defining the word "cliche." Horribly dated, but aptly shot by Gordon Willis in his pre-Woody Allen days.

p, Herbert Brodkin; d, David Greene; w, J. P. Miller (based on his teleplay); ph, Gordon Willis (DeLuxe Color); m, Don Sebesky; ed, Brian Smedley-Aston, Arline Garson; prod d, Charles Bailey; set d, Richard Adee; cos, Ann Roth; songs, "Mama, Don't You Wait Up for Me" (sung by The Glass Bottle), "Sweet Medusa," "My Life in Review" (sung by The Bead Game).

Drama   **(PR:O   MPAA:R)**

PEOPLE THAT TIME FORGOT, THE*   (1977, Brit.) 90m Amicus/AIP c

Patrick Wayne (Maj. Ben McBride), Doug McClure (Bowen Tyler), Sarah Douglas (Lady Charlotte "Charly"), Dana Gillespie (Ajor), Thorley Walters (Dr. Edward Norfolk), Shane Rimmer (Hogan), Tony Britton (Capt. Lawton), John Hallam (Chang-Sha), David Prowse (Executioner), Milton Reid (Sabbala), Kiran Shah (Bolum), Richard Parmentier (Lt. Whitby), Jimmy Ray (Lt. Graham), Tony Hale (Telegraphist).

A pretty bad sequel to the slightly better THE LAND THAT TIME FORGOT which now has Patrick Wayne (John's son) flying to the tropical island of Caprona (somewhere in the icy Arctic) to rescue Doug McClure, who has been waiting to be saved since the end of the last picture. McClure has been fighting dinosaurs and dodging erupting volcanoes while growing his beard out during the wait. He's also managed to teach the English language to cave girl cutie Gillespie, whose diminutive furs no doubt help to keep him warm. The men manage to get their plane back in the air so they can hightail it out of there. The special effects are sub-Bert I. Gordon, but in color, turning THE PEOPLE THAT TIME FORGOT into the movie that people will forget. It made some bucks, but couldn't put AIP back on its feet. The second entry in the Burroughs-based trilogy, filmed in Britain and the Canary Islands.

p, John Dark; d, Kevin Connor; w, Patrick Tilley (based on the novel by Edgar Rice Burroughs); ph, Alan Hume (Movielab Color); m, John Scott; ed, John Ireland, Barry Peters; prod d, Maurice Carter; art d, Bert Davey, Fernando Gonzalez; set d, Simon Wakefield; cos, Brenda Dabbs, Daryl Bristow; spec eff, John Richardson, Ian Wingrove; makeup, Robin Grantham, George Prost.

Adventure/Fantasy   Cas.   (PR:AA MPAA:PG)

PEOPLE TOYS   (SEE: DEVIL TIMES FIVE, 1974)

PEOPLE VS. DR. KILDARE, THE**   (1941) 78m MGM bw (GB: MY LIFE IS YOURS)

Lew Ayres (Dr. James Kildare), Lionel Barrymore (Dr. Leonard Gillespie), Laraine Day (Mary Lamont), Bonita Granville (Frances Marlowe), Alma Kruger (Molly Byrd), Red Skelton (Vernon Briggs, Janitor), Diana Lewis (Fay Lennox), Paul Stanton (Mr. Reynolds), Walter Kingsford (Dr. Walter Carew), Nell Craig (Nurse Parker), Tom Conway (Mr. Channing), Marie Blake (Sally), Eddie Acuff (Clifford Genet, Janitor), George H. Reed (Conover), Chick Chandler (Dan Morton), Frank Orth (Mike Ryan), Gladys B. Lake (Maisie), Grant Withers (Policeman), Anna Q. Nilsson (Juror), Dwight Frye (Jury Foreman).

This addition to the DR. KILDARE series has Ayres spending most of his time in the courtroom defending himself against a malpractice suit. After operating on accident victim Granville's leg, Ayres is sued because the girl can no longer skate as she used to. She agrees to go under the knife again and this time Ayres has her zooming around the rink within hours. This one provides all the entertainment that previous episodes delivered. The British distributors removed the Kildare name from the title, feeling that their theater patrons were getting confused about which films of the popular series they had or had not seen. (See DR. KILDARE series, Index.)

d, Harold S. Bucquet; w, Willis Goldbeck, Harry Ruskin (based on the story by Lawrence P. Bachmann, Max Brand); ph, Clyde De Vinna; ed, Ralph Winters.

Medical Drama   (PR:A MPAA:NR)

PEOPLE WHO OWN THE DARK*   (1975, Span.) 87m Newcal/Sean Cunningham c (PLANETA CIEGO)

Paul Naschy, Maria Perschy, Tony Kendall.

An orgy in the basement of an old house is disturbed when nuclear war breaks out and everyone above ground is blinded. Clacking their canes and bumping into each other, the sightless survivors attack the house. Paul Naschy looks dangerous carrying a high-powered rifle to fight off the not very terrifying attackers and defends unknown starlets who are ringers for Sophia Loren, Britt Ekland, and other famous faces. Inspired by George Romero's NIGHT OF THE LIVING DEAD, this is a film that is not worth a look.

p, Salvadore Romero; d, Armando de Ossorio; w, Vencenzio Naranda.

Horror   Cas.   (PR:O MPAA:R)

PEOPLE WILL TALK½**   (1935) 67m PAR bw

Charles Ruggles (Henry Wilton), Mary Boland (Clarice Wilton), Leila Hyams (Peggy Trask), Dean Jagger (Bill Trask), Ruthelma Stevens (Doris McBride), Hans Steinke (Strangler Martin), Constantine Romanoff (Prettyboy Plotsky), Edward Brophy (Pete Ranse), John Rogers (Spider Murphy), Stanley Andrews (Willis McBride), Cecil Cunningham (Nellie Simpson), Jack Mulhall (Sam Baxter), Marina Schubert (Helen Baxter), Sam Flint, Aileen Carlyle.

A sprightly domestic comedy which again has Ruggles teamed with Boland as a husband-and-wife pair. Their daughter Hyams splits from her flirtatious husband after he is overly affectionate with the vampish Stevens at their one-year anniversary party. Ruggles and Boland stage a quarrel to teach Hyams a lesson, but they too end up splitting. It takes their newly sympathetic daughter to reunite them. Refreshing.

p, Douglas MacLean; d, Alfred Santell; w, Herbert Fields (based on the story by Sophie Kerr, F. Hugh Herbert); ph, Alfred Gilks; ed, Richard Currier.

Comedy   (PR:A MPAA:NR)

PEOPLE WILL TALK**   (1951) 110m FOX bw

Cary Grant (Dr. Noah Praetorius), Jeanne Crain (Annabel Higgins), Finlay Currie (Shunderson), Hume Cronyn (Prof. Elwell), Walter Slezak (Prof. Barker), Sidney Blackmer (Arthur Higgins), Basil Ruysdael (Dean Lyman Brockwell), Katherine Locke (Miss James), Will Wright (John Higgins), Margaret Hamilton (Miss Pickett), Esther Somers (Mrs. Pegwhistle), Carleton Young (Technician), Larry Dobkin (Business Manager), Jo Gilbert (Nurse), Ann Morrison (Dietician), Julia Dean (Old Lady), Gail Bonney (Secretary), William Klein (Student Manager), George Offerman (Haskins), Adele Longmire (Mabel), Billy House (Coonan), Al Murphy (Photographer), Irene Seidner (Cook), Parley Baer (Toy Salesman), Joyce MacKenzie (Gussie), Maude Wallace (Night Matron), Kay Lavelle (Bella), Jack Kelly, Paul Lees, William Mauch, Leon Taylor (Students), Stuart Holmes (Board Member), Ray Montgomery (Doctor).

Joseph L. Mankiewicz had just won two Oscars for ALL ABOUT EVE (writing, directing) and the year before that two more for the same tasks on A LETTER TO

THREE WIVES. Mankiewicz liked challenges and took on a big one when he chose to adapt Goetz's German play, "Dr. Praetorius," and make it into an odd amalgam of wit, satire, humanity, and high drama. The dialog almost glistens as the actors speak. Mankiewicz honed every line until it was hard to find one that wasn't a bon mot and that literacy worked, in part, against the picture because it's hard to believe so many people speak that brilliantly. Grant is an early crusader in the medical profession who thinks that the mind can cure just as well, if not better, than massive doses of prescribed medicine. He believes in treating the patient, rather than the single disease, a practice that delights his charges but horrifies his colleagues, who are far more traditional and hidebound in their diagnoses. Grant is teaching at a medical school and living what is thought to be a strange life. His servant and best friend is Currie, a murderer who has been sent to jail twice but that doesn't daunt his sense of humor. His other friend is Slezak, a rotund scientist who loves model trains and knockwurst, in no particular order. Grant's enemy at the school is Cronyn, a sourpuss anatomy instructor who feels more at home dissecting corpses than talking to humans. One day, Grant is teaching his students and Crain, a young aspiring doctor, faints during the lecture. Grant is soon aware that she's newly pregnant and when she tries to kill herself, he says that his first diagnosis was wrong, then marries her. Crain's father is Blackmer, a drunk and a loser, but a man with what Tennessee Williams called "the charm of the defeated." In between his classes, Grant conducts the school's orchestra in Wagner and Brahms. Cronyn hates Grant and the love others lavish on him so he contacts the dean, Ruysdael, and brings up a few interesting things about Grant's background, which causes Grant to have to face matters in front of the school's board of directors. Grant once gave some medical advice to people and told them he was a butcher. He explains that there are some patients who need to think a "miracle" has taken place and who just don't trust physicians, hence the masquerading as a man of meat. Grant explains his philosophy of medicine and eventually wins over the listeners. While all this is going on, Grant is spending his home front time convincing Crain that he really does love her and didn't marry her out of pity for her plight. The designation "sophisticated" applies well to PEOPLE WILL TALK and Grant gives one of his best-ever performances, a carefully controlled job of acting that never becomes farce. The movie is mature and frank and Mankiewicz uses the opportunity to take well-aimed pot shots at the hypocrisy rampant in the groves of Academe.

p, Darryl F. Zanuck; d&w, Joseph L. Mankiewicz (based on the play "Dr. Praetorius" by Curt Goetz); ph, Milton Krasner; m, Brahms, Wagner; ed, Barbara McLean; md, Alfred Newman; art d, Lyle Wheeler, George W. Davis; set d, Thomas Little, Walter M. Scott; cos, Charles LeMaire; spec eff, Fred Sersen; makeup, Ben Nye.

Comedy   (PR:A-C MPAA:NR)

PEOPLE'S ENEMY, THE**   (1935) 65m SEL/RKO bw

Preston Foster (Vince), Lila Lee (Catherine), Melvyn Douglas (Traps), Shirley Grey (Ann), Roscoe Ates (Slip), William Collier, Jr. (Tony), Sylbil Elaine (Mary), Herbert Rawlinson (Duke), Charles Coburn (Judge).

Foster is a thoroughly despicable underworld figure whose empire crumbles when he is jailed for income tax evasion—but not before he also turns his back on his imperiled wife and kid, eventually losing them to the kindly Douglas. This was one of the first Hollywood pictures to blatantly condemn the lives of the once-heroic gangland figures. RKO let its sentiments be known in the title, which implies that underworld activities are a threat to the common man. This appears to have been the studio's response to the toughening attitude of Joseph Breen's censorship office.

p, Burt Kelly; d, Crane Wilbur; w, Gordon Kahn, Edward Dean Sullivan (based on a story by Sullivan); ph, Joseph Ruttenberg; ed, William Thompson.

Crime   (PR:A MPAA:NR)

PEPE½**   (1960) 195m COL c

Cantinflas (Pepe), Dan Dailey (Ted Holt), Shirley Jones (Suzie Murphy), Carlos Montalban (Auctioneer), Vicki Trickett (Lupita), Matt Mattox (Dancer), Hank Henry (Manager), Suzanne Lloyd (Carmen), Stephen Bekassy (Jewelry Salesman), Ernie Kovacs (Immigration Inspector), William Demarest (Studio Gateman), Carol Douglas (Waitress), Francisco Reguerra (Priest), Joe Hyams (Charro), Carlos Rivas, Joey Bishop, Michael Callan, Maurice Chevalier, Charles Coburn, Richard Conte, Bing Crosby, Tony Curtis, Bobby Darin, Sammy Davis, Jr., Jimmy Durante, Zsa Zsa Gabor, voice of Judy Garland, Greer Garson, Hedda Hopper, Peter Lawford, Janet Leigh, Jack Lemmon, Dean Martin, Jay North, Kim Novak, Andre Previn, Donna Reed, Debbie Reynolds, Edward G. Robinson, Cesar Romero, Frank Sinatra, Billie Burke, Ann B. Davis, Jack Entratter, Col. E.E. Fogelson, Jane Robinson, Bunny Waters (Themselves), Shirley DeBurgh (Senorita Dancer), Steve Baylor, John Burnside (Parking Lot Attendants), James Bacon (Bartender), Jimmy Cavanaugh (Dealer), Jeanne Manet (French Woman), Robert B. Williams (Immigration Officer), Bonnie Green (Dancer), Lela Bliss (Dowager), Ray Walker (Assistant Director), David Landfield (Announcer's Voice), Margie Nelson (Patron), Dorothy Abbott, Kenner C. Kemp, Steve Carruthers, Jim Waters, Billy Snyder (Bits), Fred Roberto (Cashier).

Mexican actor Mario Moreno took the name of "Cantinflas" years ago and became the most popular performer in all the Spanish-speaking world, playing a character that was a mixture of Harry Langdon's gentleness, Charlie Chaplin's feistiness, and Buster Keaton's knockabout physicality. After the enormous success of Mike Todd's AROUND THE WORLD IN 80 DAYS, in which Cantinflas played an important role, Columbia decided to star him in another cameo-packed epic, using almost everyone who had ever made a movie on the Gower Street lot. The result was a nice family picture that ran three hours and 15 minutes, or just slightly longer than an average filibuster in the U.S. Senate. It was only marginally more entertaining. Cantinflas is a peon working on a ranch in Mexico. He has spent years grooming and tending a white stallion and is dismayed and distraught when the magnificent beast is sold to Dailey, a dissolute Hollywood film director. Dailey takes the animal back to California and Cantinflas follows them, then persuades Dailey to allow him to stay on and tend the horse. Next, Cantinflas meets and falls in love with Jones, an attractive waitress who hopes to be a star in films. When Dailey needs money to make a new movie, Cantinflas takes his meager savings to Las Vegas, wins a bundle, and gives it to his boss. The thrilled Bailey names Cantinflas producer of the picture and gives Jones the starring role. They begin to shoot but Dailey is soon low on money and has to sell the horse to Robinson, a big-time film mogul. Cantinflas is hurt by the sale but thinks he can have some happiness with Jones until he realizes that Dailey is the man she loves. Robinson wants to buy the movie from Dailey who refuses until Robinson promises to return the steed to Cantinflas. So everything works out for the best when Robinson gets the movie, Jones gets Dailey, and Cantinflas gets the horse, which is all he ever wanted since the first reel, several generations ago. Along the way, there are a number of guest appearances and several songs. Curtis and Leigh do a cute skit as Cantinflas delivers flowers to Leigh who is taking a bubble bath. She thinks he's someone else, gets him drunk and winds up dancing with him around an indoor pool, then dancing with Curtis, who eventually falls in the water. Sinatra, Romero, and Bishop play themselves in Las Vegas as they advise the naive Mexican how to gamble at the casino tables. Crosby is seen autographing a tortilla. Chevalier sings "September Song" and offers some advice on how to handle women. Durante is a frustrated dealer. Jack Lemmon dons his "Daphne" costume from SOME LIKE IT HOT for a drag bit and the list goes on until 35, count 'em, guests have had their moment in the lens. Two people who aren't normally seen on any screen are Colonel "Buddy" Fogelson, long-time husband of Greer Garson, and Jack Entratter, who ran the Sands Hotel in Las Vegas for many years after having co-owned the famed Copacabana in New York with Jules Podell. Songs include: "September Song" (Kurt Weill, Maxwell Anderson, sung by Maurice Chevalier), "Mimi" (Richard Rodgers, Lorenz Hart, sung by Chevalier), "Pennies From Heaven" (Johnny Burke, Arthur Johnston, sung by Bing Crosby), "Hooray For Hollywood" (Johnny Mercer, Richard Whiting, new lyrics by Sammy Cahn, sung by Sammy Davis, Jr.), "South of the Border" (Michael Carr, Jimmy Kennedy, sung by Michael Callan), "Let's Fall in Love" (Ted Koehler, Harold Arlen, sung by Callan), "Lovely Day" (Augustin Lara, Maria Teresa Lara, English lyrics by Dory Langdon, sung by Shirley Jones), "Pepe" (Langdon, Hans Wittstatt, sung by Jones). Previn and his wife Langdon, wrote such new tunes for the movie as "That's How It Went All Right" (sung by Bobby Darin, Callan, Matt Mattox, and Jones), and "Faraway Part of Town" (sung off-screen by Judy Garland as Jones and Dan Dailey danced). Previn instrumentals included "The Rumble" (danced by Callan, Jones, and Mattox) and "Suzy's Theme" (danced by Cantinflas and Debbie Reynolds). Previn also appeared on screen to play the piano in his "The Rumble" a highly sensual dance number that would have been more at home in WEST SIDE STORY. With all of the above, with all the stars and the tunes and the choreography, this was a bust at the box office and put an end to the U.S. career of Cantinflas. He went back to his roots and continues to be an enormous success to see whom audiences pay billions of pesos, pesetas, cruzieros, bolivares, escudios, soles, balboas, cordobas, lempiras, quetzales, colones, sucres—in other words, anything but dollars. Director Sydney, who knew his way around musicals as he proved with PAL JOEY and KISS ME KATE, was defeated by the sheer scope of this one.

p&d, George Sidney; w, Dorothy Kingsley, Claude Binyon (based on a story by Leonard Spigelgass, Sonya Levien, from the play "Broadway Magic" by Ladislas Bush-Fekete); ph, Joe MacDonald (CinemaScope, Technicolor); m, Johnny Green; ed, Viola Lawrence, Al Clark; art d, Ted Haworth; set d, William Kiernan; cos, Edith Head; ch, Eugene Loring, Alex Romero; makeup, Ben Lane.

Musical/Comedy   **(PR:AAA MPAA:NR)**

PEPE LE MOKO***   (1937, Fr.) 90m Hakim-Paris Film/MAYER AND BURSTYN-Commercial bw**

Jean Gabin (Pepe le Moko), Mireille Balin (Gaby Gould), Line Noro (Ines), Lucas Gridoux (Inspector Slimane), Gabriel Gabrio (Carlos), Fernand Charpin (Regis), Saturnin Fabre (Grandfather), Gilbert Gil (Pierrot), Roger Legris (Max), Gaston Modot (Jimmy), Marcel Dalio (L'Arbi), Frehel (Tania), Olga Lord (Aicha), Renee Carl (Mother Tarte), Rene Bergeron (Inspector Meunier), Charles Granval (Maxime Kleep), Philippe Richard (Inspector Janvier), Paul Escoffier (Commissioner Louvain), Robert Ozanne (Gendron), Georges Peclet (Barsac), Frank Maurice (An Inspector).

Although the French-made PEPE LE MOKO was shot before the English language remake, ALGIERS, it was released in the U.S. afterward. Both movies deserve to be listed in anyone's roster of superior romantic gangster movies. Filmed in Pathe's studio at Joinville, with exteriors shot in Algiers, Sete, and Marseille, PEPE LE MOKO is based on a real criminal who hid in the Casbah where he was protected by his pals. The actual man had come from Provence and his dark skin earned him the designation of "le moko." He was the Casanova of the Casbah and used to say that if he were ever killed by the police, hundreds of widows would come to hear his last rites. Gabin is the man who is helped by his pals to stay out of the eye of the police. He's a thief and a brigand and a charmer and has surrounded himself with loyal gang members, whom he keeps in line by the sheer force of his personality, never resorting to violence. Gabin's granfather Fabre not only dotes on his grandson, but acts as fence for the stolen goods the mob brings him. Informer Charpin tells the cops that they might just be able to nab Gabin at Fabre's house. But before the cops can get there Gabin's tentacles have already reached out and grasped the information (his men are everywhere!) and his mistress, Noro, tells him directly what's going to happen. There is a gunfight and Gabin is hit, but not badly. He gets away and sees gorgeous Balin, a Parisian tourist, being escorted by the local police inspector, Gridoux. She is fascinated by Gabin and the attraction is returned. It also doesn't hurt that she's wearing some valuable jewelry. Gridoux takes Balin back to her hotel, nods at Gabin and says, "It is written, Pepe." Gabin is tired of his life with Noro and being on the run and yearns for his old days in Paris. The cops use the services of Charpin to get one of Gabin's aides, Gil, out of the Casbah's haven on

the false pretext that his mother is sick. As soon as he leaves the Casbah, Gil is shot by the cops. Gabin and the others know who set him up, go after Charpin, and push him against a wall. Hysterically, he pleads for his life. He bumps into a jukebox, which starts the machine playing raucous music as Gil pumps bullets into Charpin just before he himself dies of the wounds inflicted at the hands of the cops. Meanwhile, Gabin and Balin are finding much to love about each other and it's expressed in a unique way. Each recalls a subway line in Paris and they begin to call out the stops (starting from either end of the Metro) until they meet and say, as one, "La Place Blanche." Noro angrily watches the attraction between Gabin and Balin grow and Gridoux means to use her against the thief. There is no way he can capture Gabin within the confines of the Casbah so he informs Balin's older, wealthy boy friend, Granval, about the affair his mistress is conducting. Upon hearing that, Granval absolutely forbids Balin to venture inside the Casbah again. She will not tolerate an ultimatum and leaves to see Gabin. Before entering the Casbah, Gridoux gets to her and falsely states that Gabin has been killed. Balin is shattered and makes her plans to leave the city at once. Inside the Casbah, Gabin waits vainly for Balin. When he learns that Balin is about to sail, he plans to get on the boat with her, never knowing that Gridoux is waiting for just that reaction. Noro tries to stop him from leaving and fails. She tells Gridoux what Gabin plans to do. Gabin departs the Casbah and races to the dock where the ship is building up steam prior to departure. He runs around the liner in a frenzied attempt to find Balin when Gridoux grabs him, just inches away from her, but neither knows that the other is that close. As Gabin is manacled and taken from the ship, he asks Gridoux for one final favor, to watch the boat depart. Gridoux, knowing that he has Gabin at last, can afford to be magnanimous and grants the request. The boat begins to move and Gabin sees Balin standing at the rail. He shouts her name but his voice is muffled by the wail of the ship's horn. Balin doesn't see the small figure behind the gates. Instead, she looks longingly over his head at the Casbah. He reaches into his pocket, pulls out a knife, and rips his guts out in a final gesture of frustration. When the war started, the French government banned the film as too depressing and demoralizing, especially since the news from the front was also bleak. The Germans took over and their puppet government retained the ban, but the moment the war ended, it was again shown and hailed as a classic. The novel upon which it was based was written by Henri La Barthe, using the nom de plume "Detective Ashelbe." La Barthe had actually worked in Algiers and knew the man of whom he wrote. Charles Boyer turned the part down, then starred in the U.S. version, ALGIERS, when Gabin didn't want to come to Hollywood for the film, explaining that he, like French wine, "didn't travel well." The Hakim Brothers shot the exteriors in Algiers and came back with a native, Yguerbouchen, to score the movie, giving it an authentic sound. MGM saw the success in France and bought the remake rights after Erich Von Stroheim informed them of the movie. Fearing the wrath of the Hays Office and the various cuts which would have to be made to satisfy the prudish censors, they sold the rights to Walter Wanger, who hired Boyer, Gurie, and his discovery, Hedy Lamarr. The 1948 CASBAH was a musical version starring Tony Martin and Yvonne De Carlo. In 1951, the French did their own remake, but it was a yawner. This may have been the movie after which the film noir genre was named. PEPE LE MOKO owes a great deal of its heritage to the early gangster films in the U.S., most notably SCARFACE, but Duvivier took the notion of mixing love and bullets and added a particular poetry of his own. The camera work is as though it were bathed in oil, the actors don't seem to be acting, and the lack of sentimentality deserves special praise. Making a criminal the lead is never easy. Coppola did it and so does Duvivier. They de-emphasize the felonious natures of their heroes by concentrating on their needs, their loneliness, their desperation, and their singularity of purpose in a corrupt society.

p, Robert Hakim, Raymond Hakim; d, Julien Duvivier; w, Duvivier, Henri Jeanson, Detective Roger d'Ashelbe [Henri La Barthe], Jacques Constant (based on the book by d'Ashelbe); ph, Jules Kruger, Marc Fossard; m, Vincent Scotto, Mohamed Yguerbouchen; ed, Marguerite Beauge; prod d, Jacque Krauss; set d, Strauss, Robert Vernay.

Crime/Romance   Cas.   (PR:C MPAA:NR)

PEPPER   (1936) 65m FOX bw**

Jane Withers (Pepper Jolly), Irvin S. Cobb (John Wilkes), Slim Summerville (Uncle Ben Jolly), Dean Jagger (Bob O'Ryan), Muriel Robert (Helen Wilkes), Ivan Lebedeff (Baron Von Stofel), Maurice Cass (Doctor), Romaine Callendar (Butler), Tommy Bupp (Jimmy), Carey Harrison, Reginald Simpson, George Humbert.

Withers is a scruffy youngster who pressures grouchy millionaire Cobb into stopping the eviction of a neighborhood family, but not without the aid of tomato-hurling moppets. She soon cons him into taking her to Coney Island, and later saves his daughter from marrying a phony count. Withers is likable as the devilish but well-meaning little star.

p, John Stone; d, James Tinling; w, Lamar Trotti (based on a story by Jefferson Parker, Murray Roth); ph, Daniel B. Clark; ed, Fred Allen; md, Samuel Kaylin

Drama/Comedy   (PR:AAA MPAA:NR)

PEPPERMINT SODA*½   (1979, Fr.) 97m Alma-Alexandre/GAU-New Yorker c (DIABOLO MENTHE)**

Eleonore Klarwein (Anne Weber), Odile Michel (Frederique Weber), Coralie Clement (Perrine Jacquet), Marie Veronique Maurin (Muriel Cazau), Valerie Stano (Martine Dubreuil), Anne Guillard (Sylvie Le Garrec), Corinne Dacla (Pascal Carimil), Veronique Vernon (Evelyne Delcroix), Francoise Berlin (Mlle. Sassy), Arlette Bonnard (Mme. Poliakoff), Jacqueline Boyen (Mlle. Petitbon), Dora Doll (Mme. Clou), Tsila Chelton (Mme. Colotte), Jacques Rispal (Superintendent), Anouk Ferjac (Mme. Weber), Puterflam (M. Weber), Yves Regnier (Philippe), Robert Rimbaud (M. Gazau).

A thoroughly charming picture (released in Paris in 1977), which brings to life the loves and fears of two teenaged sisters. Kurys marks her directing debut with a semi-autobiographical account starring Klarwein as the 13-year old sister (Kury's age in 1963—the setting of the film) and Michel as her 15-year old sibling. Living with their divorced mother, Ferjac, the girls discover and talk about the things that interest teenage girls—boys, sex, school, and politics (they *are* French). Klarwein, however, lacks the boy friend that her older sister has, and must resort to steaming open Michel's love letters. Her confused reaction to men is further illustrated by her dislike for her mother's boy friend. It is only from her father that she gets what she wants (a ski trip), but not until she shows her disapproval at his leaving home. A sensitive portrayal of teens which compares with Truffaut's Antoine Doinel series (THE 400 BLOWS through LOVE ON THE RUN) and George Roy Hill's A LITTLE ROMANCE. Kurys continued bringing her growing years (and her relationship with her sister) with her next two pictures COCKTAIL MOLOTOV (1980) and ENTRE NOUS (1983). For the curious, the film's title refers to an "adult" drink that Klarwein nearly gets a chance to taste, but to no avail. (In French; English subtitles.)

d&w, Diane Kurys; ph, Philippe Rousselot (Eastmancolor); m, Yves Simon; ed, Joelle Van Effenterre.

Drama/Comedy   **(PR:C MPAA:PG)**

PER IL BENE E PER IL MALE   (SEE: ANATOMY OF A MARRIAGE, 1964, Fr./Ital.)

PER QUALCHE DOLLARO IN PIU   (SEE: FOR A FEW DOLLARS MORE, 1964, Ital./Span./Ger.)

PER UN PUGNO DI DOLLARI   (SEE: FISTFUL OF DOLLARS, A, 1967, Ital./Span./Ger.)

PERCY*   (1971, Brit.) 100m Welbeck-Anglo-EMI/MGM c

Hywel Bennett (*Edwin Anthony*), Denholm Elliott (*Emmanuel Whitbread*), Elke Sommer (*Helga*), Britt Ekland (*Dorothy Chiltern-Barlow*), Cyd Hayman (*Moira Warrington*), Janet Key (*Hazel*), Tracey Crisp (*Miss Elder*), Antonia Ellis (*Rita La Rousse*), Tracy Reed (*Mrs. Penney*), Patrick Mower (*James Vaile*), Pauline Delany (*Sister Flanagan*), Adrienne Posta (*Maggie Hyde*), Julia Foster (*Marilyn*), Sheila Steafel (*Mrs. Gold*), Arthur English (*M.C.*), Angus Mackay (*TV Producer*), Rita Webb (*Mrs. Hedges*), Charles Hodgson (*TV Interviewer*), Sue Lloyd (*Bernice*), Denise Coffey (*Operator*), Margaretta Scott (*Rita's Mother*), Edward Malin (*Elderly Patient*), Graham Crowden (*Alfred Spaulton*), T. P. McKenna (*Meet the People Compere*), Anthony Haygarth, Ronnie Brody.

Bennett becomes the world's first recipient of a penis transplant, and grows curious about the previous owner. Bennett names his new addition "Percy," which is simply an example of the locker-room grade of humor this picture has to offer. The best thing about it is the score by Ray Davies, performed by The Kinks.

p, Betty E. Box; d, Ralph Thomas; w, Hugh Leonard, Terence Feel (based on the novel by Raymond Hitchcock); ph, Ernest Steward (Technicolor); m, Ray Davies; ed, Roy Watts; art d, Robert Jones; set d, Christopher Cook; cos, Emma Porteus; makeup, Edward Knight.

Comedy   **(PR:O MPAA:R)**

PERCY'S PROGRESS   (SEE: IT'S NOT THE SIZE THAT COUNTS, 1979, Brit.)

PERFECT ALIBI, THE**   (1931, Brit.) 78m Associated Talking Pictures/RKO bw (GB: BIRDS OF PREY)

Robert Lorraine (*Carter*), Warwick Ward (*Laverick*), Frank Lawton (*Jimmy Hilton*), C. Aubrey Smith (*Arthur Hilton*), Dorothy Boyd (*Mollie*), Ellis Jeffreys (*Mrs. Green*), Nigel Bruce (*Manager*), Jack Hawkins (*Alfred*), Tom Reynolds, David Hawthorne.

An interesting British murder mystery which quickly eliminates the "mystery" from the plot by revealing the killers from the start—a la Hitchcock. On a country estate, just before a grand dinner party, the host, Smith, is murdered by Lorraine and his villainous partner Ward (who previously appeared in the silent classic VARIETY). Their alibi is perfectly plotted out and even witnesses can verify their whereabouts. It appears to be a suicide, but young lovers Boyd and Lawton prove otherwise. As usual there is no such thing the "perfect alibi," and this time Lorraine and Ward find that out. Based on a play by A. A. Milne who is best known for his storybook creation *Winnie The Pooh*. Released in Britain at 98 minutes.

p&d, Basil Dean; w, A.A. Milne, Dean (based on Milne's play "The Fourth Wall"); ph, Jack McKenzie, I.C. Martin; ed, Jack Kitchen.

Crime/Mystery   **(PR:A MPAA:NR)**

PERFECT CLUE, THE**   (1935) 64m Majestic bw

David Manners (*David Mannering*), Skeets Gallagher (*Ronnie Van Zandt*), Dorothy Libaire (*Mona Stewart*), William P. Carleton (*Jerome Stewart*), Ralf Harolde (*Barkley*), Ernie Adams (*Carter*), Robert Gleckler (*Delaney*), Frank Darien (*Station Master*), Charles C. Wilson (*District Attorney*), Betty Blythe (*Ursula Chesebrough*), Jack Richardson (*Simms*), Pat O'Malley (*Police Officer*).

Libaire, the daughter of a millionaire, skips out on her boy friend while they are eloping and hires a car to take her to the nearest town. She is robbed by the chauffeur, who promptly dumps her by the roadside. He has a change of heart, however, and returns for her. The pair get mixed up in a murder and are jailed, but helped by her jilted boy friend and all her cash, the pair are able to clear their names.

p, Larry Darmour; d, Robert G. Vignola; w, Albert De Mond, Ralph Cedar, Don Brown (based on a story by Lolita Ann Westman); ph, Herbert Kirkpatrick; ed, Dwight Caldwell.

Crime/Comedy   **(PR:A MPAA:NR)**

PERFECT COUPLE, A*½   (1979) 110m Lion's Gate/FOX c

Paul Dooley (*Alex Theodopoulos*), Marta Heflin (*Sheila Shea*), Titos Vandis (*Panos Theodopoulos*), Belita Moreno (*Eleousa*), Henry Gibson (*Fred Bott*), Dimitra Arliss (*Athena*), Allan Nicholls (*Dana 115*), Ann Ryerson (*Skye 147, Veterinarian*), Poppy Lagos (*Melpomeni Bott*), Dennis Franz (*Costa*), Margery Bond (*Wilma*), Mona Golabek (*Mona*), Terry Wills (*Ben*), Susan Blakeman (*Penelope Bott*), Melanie Bishop (*Star*), Fred Bier, Jette Seear (*The Imperfect Couple*), Tom Pierson (*Conductor for Los Angeles Philharmonic Orchestra*), Mona Golabek (*Piano Soloist*); Keepin' 'Em Off The Streets: Ted Neeley (*Teddy*), Heather MacRae (*Mary*), Tomi-Lee Bradley (*Sydney-Ray*), Steven Sharp (*Bobbi*), Tony Berg (*Lead Guitar and Musical Director*), Craig Doerge (*Keyboards*), Jeff Eyrich (*Bass Guitar*), David Luell (*Saxophone*), Butch Sanford (*Guitar*), Art Wood (*Drums*), Ren Wood (*Guest Appearance*).

THE PERFECT COUPLE is another misfire from Altman's erratic cannon. His two previous pictures, A WEDDING and QUINTET, had done poorly at the box office and in most critic's minds and this movie continued that tradition. In an attempt to do a 1970s version of the Preston Sturges-Howard Hawks-George Cukor type comedies of the 1930s, Altman took an unlikely duo and sought to match them, not through the usual "cute-meet" followed by difficulties, then resolved with a "love conquers all" denouement, but with the use of a dating service known as Great Expectations, a company that really exists and has successfully matched more than 40,000 people. Dooley, an Altman favorite, is the son of Vandis, an old-world Greek who keeps a tight rein on the family. He is lonely, wants to meet someone to love, and finds her through the video dating company. She is Heflin, a manager for a rock group and, perhaps, the only actress in Hollywood who is skinnier than Shelley Duvall, another Altman pet. Dooley's sister, Moreno, is a cellist with the Los Angeles Philharmonic and Dooley squires Heflin to the Hollywood Bowl to hear Moreno on their first date together. The usual stuff happens. Dooley's sun roof jams open and the duo are drenched in a downpour and Heflin catches a cold. They kiss goodnight at her apartment and arrange another date but circumstances are such that each mistakenly thinks the other has stood them up. Intercuts between the dull life of Dooley and the exciting rehearsals of Heflin's band, complete with the usual rock 'n' roll cliche characters. The wooing continues and we have a chance to see the differences between the super-straight Dooley and the slightly bent Heflin. The picture ends as Dooley and Heflin are at the Bowl watching a concert by the Philharmonic and Heflin's band, "Keepin' 'Em Off the Streets." Ryerson does a neat turn as a sensuous veterinarian whom Dooley takes up with during a temporary lull in his relationship with Heflin. Arliss, a fine actress, is wasted and Gibson, another Altman favorite who stole NASHVILLE from 24 other actors, also doesn't get much of a chance as the smarmy brother-in-law. Songs include "Hurricane" (Tom Berg, Ted Neeley, Allan Nicholls) and "Fantasy" (Nicholls). If the leader of the rock group, Neeley, looks somewhat familiar, that's because you may recall him as Jesus Christ, Superstar, in the picture of the same name.

p&d, Robert Altman; w, Altman, Allan Nicholls; ph, Edmond L. Koons (Panavision, DeLuxe Color); m, Nicholls; ed, Tony Lombardo; m/l, Nicholls, "Keepin' 'Em Off the Streets."

Comedy/Romance   **(PR:A-C MPAA:PG)**

PERFECT CRIME, THE**   (1928) 83m FBO bw

Clive Brook (*Dr. Benson*), Irene Rich (*Stella*), Ethel Wales (*Mrs. Frisbie*), Carroll Nye (*Trevor*), Gladys McConnell (*Mrs. Trevor*), Edmund Breese (*Wilmot*), James Farley (*Jones*), Phil Gastrock (*Butler*), Tully Marshall (*Frisbie*), Jane LaVerne (*Trevor Baby*), Lynne Overman (*Newlywed*).

Originally made as a silent, sound was added just before release and it looks it as much of the picture unreels without much talk. However, the story is okay enough to be seen as a silent and still make sense. Overman and his wife are young marrieds in their apartment and he is sneaking a call to a woman he met the night before while they listen to the radio. The news says that Brook, a doctor assigned to the police department, has just solved a big crime. Cut to the cops' headquarters where Brook is handing in his resignation because his girl friend, Rich, wants him to get out of that business. The police wish he wouldn't as he is the U.S. equivalent of Sherlock Holmes (or "Crime Doctor," a later radio series which starred Ray Collins, House Jameson, Everett Sloane, and John McIntire at various times). The chief cop says that there is no such thing as "The Perfect Crime" but if there ever was one, Brook would know how to perform it. Brook goes home, looks out of the window, and sees Marshall, a mean-spirited man, belt his wife when she dares ask him for the rent, This gives Brook, who is teetering on the edge of madness, an idea. Brook owns the place and Marshall is his tenant. Later, Marshall comes over to pay the rent and Brook plies him with booze as the man has a toothache. Next he gives Marshall some pills, tells him to lock all the doors and windows in his room, take the pills and go to sleep and have Marshall's wife call him at 5 a.m. to check on his aching molar. When Marshall can't be awakened at 5 and the wife can't open the locked bedroom door, Brook is called in. She doesn't see that he has a razor hidden on his person. He breaks down the door, walks in, making sure the wife stays outside, then comes out and says that Marshall has slit his own throat and committed suicide. An investigation takes place and Nye is arrested and charged with the murder. The cops ask Brook to come in and solve the case but he refuses until Rich pleads with him to do so. Nye is framed and convicted and awaiting execution as his wife, McConnell, pleads to have Brook break the mystery. Brook eventually confesses his crime to the cops, Nye is freed and he and McConnell thank Brook for what he's done. Now there is a dissolve and Brook is seen at his desk reading. We are never sure if this entire story was true, or just a fanciful flight of imagination on Brook's part—a terrible cheat to the audience.

d, Bert Glennon; w, Ewart Adamson, Victor Currier, Randolph Bartlett, William Le

Baron (based on the story "The Big Bow Mystery" by Israel Zangwill); ph, James Wong Howe; ed, Archie F. Marshek.

Crime   **(PR:A-C MPAA:NR)**

PERFECT CRIME, THE, 1934   (SEE: ELLERY QUEEN AND THE PERFECT CRIME, 1934, Brit.)

PERFECT CRIME, THE½**   (1937, Brit.) 69m WB bw

Hugh Williams (*Charles Brown*), Glen Alyn (*Sylvia Burton*), Ralph Ince (*Jim Lanahan*), Iris Hoey (*Mrs. Pennypacker*), Philip Ray (*Newbold*), James Stephenson (*Parker*), Wilfrid Caithness (*Rawhouse*), John Carol (*Snodgrass*), Kate Cutler, Sam Springson, George Hughes, Ralph Roberts, Madge White.

The neat little British thriller features Williams as a mousy bank clerk who has finally had it with handling other people's money and now wants to get his hands on some of the cash. He robs the bank, writes a suicide note to establish the fact that he was remorseful for what he did, then goes aboard a ship. He also leaves a bit of money behind so there will be no question in the minds of the police. It will look as though he spent much of the cash, was overcome by guilt, and jumped overboard. Plans go awry when a ship's steward finds the note and the remaining money, steals the cash, and gets rid of the last letter. Then the steward is mysteriously killed. Williams has nowhere to turn until he meets Alyn, a beautiful young woman, and tells her what he's done. With her help and the aid of detective Ince (who also directed), they locate the murderer. In the end, Williams will have to do some time for the robbery but he knows Alyn will be waiting outside the prison to welcome him into her arms. Ince was an American actor who appeared in many films, including LITTLE CAESAR, THE BIG GAMBLE, and THE TENDERFOOT. In later life, he became a director and was responsible for a number of low-budget pictures out of Britain, including MURDER AT MONTE CARLO. He died in a traffic accident in England at the age of 50. His two brothers were John and Thomas Ince, after whom there is a street named in Culver City, California. Thomas Ince's death remains a mystery to this day. The official police report says he died of heart failure due to indigestion while aboard the yacht owned by William Randolph Hearst but rumors still abound that Hearst shot Ince for allegedly having an affair with Marion Davies. Nothing was ever proven in that department and yet tongues continue to wag.

p, Irving Asher; d, Ralph Ince; w, Basil Woon; ph, Basil Emmott.

Crime Drama/Mystery   **(PR:A MPAA:NR)**

PERFECT FLAW, THE½**   (1934, Brit.) 50m FOX bw

Naomi Waters (*Phyllis Kearnes*), D. A. Clarke-Smith (*Louis Maddox*), Ralph Truman (*Richard Drexel*), Wally Patch (*Bert*), Charles Carson (*Henry Kearns*), Romilly Lunge (*Jack Robbins*), William Hartnell (*Vickers*), Hal Walters (*Jennings*), Eric Hales.

Maddox is a clerk who enlists Truman in a get-rich-quick scheme that collapses. To protect himself he tries to murder a stockbroker, but that crime fails also. Routine programmer with nothing special to distinguish it.

p&d, Manning Haynes; w, Michael Barringer.

Crime   **(PR:A MPAA:NR)**

PERFECT FRIDAY***   (1970, Brit.) 94m Sunnymede/Chevron c

Ursula Andress (*Lady Britt Dorsett*), David Warner (*Lord Nicholas Dorsett*), Stanley Baker (*Mr. Graham*), Patience Collier (*Nanny*), T. P. McKenna (*Smith*), David Waller (*Williams*), Joan Benham (*Miss Welsh*), Julian Orchard (*Thompson*), Trisha Mortimer (*Janet*), Ann Tirard (*Miss Marsh*), Johnny Briggs, Fred Griffiths, Sidney Jennings (*Taxi Drivers*), Hugh Halliday (*Cyclist*), Max Faulkner (*Strongroom Guard*), Carleton Hobbs (*Elderly Peer*), Eric Longworth (*House of Lords Messenger*), Brian Peck (*Chauffeur*), Howard Lang (*Bank Commissioner*), Patrick Jordan (*Bank Guard*), Malcolm Johns (*Swiss Boy Friend*), Garfield Morgan, Derek Cox (*Airport Officials*), Barbara Ogilvie (*Woman Airport Official*), Georgina Simpson (*Stewardess*).

Andress, a wealthy bank patron, plans a bank heist with Warner and Baker. They devise a highly detailed, meticulously timed scheme. Andress' task is to seduce the chief security guard, while Warner, posing as a bank inspector, replaces real money with counterfeit bills. The plan is nearly foiled, but they get away with it. Unfortunately for Warner and Baker, Andress runs off without splitting up the money.

p, Jack Smith; d, Peter Hall; w, Anthony Grevill-Bell, C. Scott Forbes (based on a story by Forbes); ph, Alan Hume (Movielab Color); m, John Dankworth; ed, Rex Pyke; md, Dankworth; prod d, Terence Marsh; art d, Robert Laing; set d, Hugh Scaife; cos, Kiki Byrne, Rahuis; makeup, W. T. Partleton, John O'Gorman.

Crime/Comedy   **(PR:C MPAA:R)**

PERFECT FURLOUGH, THE**½   (1958) 93m UNIV c (GB: STRICTLY FOR PLEASURE)

Tony Curtis (*Cpl. Paul Hodges*), Janet Leigh (*Lt. Vicki Loren*), Keenan Wynn (*Harvey Franklin*), Linda Cristal (*Sandra Roca*), Elaine Stritch (*Liz Baker*), Marcel Dalio (*Henri*), Les Tremayne (*Col. Leland*), Jay Novello (*Rene*), King Donovan (*Maj. Collins*), Gordon Jones, Dick Crockett (*MPs*), Troy Donahue (*Sgt. Nickles*), Alvy Moore (*Pvt. Marvin Brewer*), Lilyan Chauvin (*French Nurse*), Eugene Borden (*French Doctor*), Marcel Rousseau (*Magistrate*), James Lanphier (*Assistant Hotel Manager*), Roger Etienne (*Bellboy*), Manuel Paris (*Doorman*), Phil Harvey (*Capt. Morgan*), Hugh Lawrence (*Capt. Johnson*), Vernon Rich (*Middle-Aged Man*), Carleton Young (*Maj. Morrow*), Sheila Keddy (*Mrs. Appleton*), Peter Camlin (*Winemaker*), Albert Carrier (*Hairdresser*), Genevieve Aumont (*Pregnant Woman*), Karen Scott (*French Waitress*), Gail Bonney (*Spinster*), Frankie Darro (*Man in Cast*), Jack Chefe (*Maitre d'*), Scotty Groves (*Medic*), Vic Romito (*Reporter*).

Army psychologist Leigh comes up with the idea of the "perfect furlough"—a scheme in which one of 105 army men stationed at her base would receive a three-week furlough to fit their desires. Meant to be a morale booster, the losers are expected to live vicariously off the winner's experiences. Womanizer Curtis takes the honors and chooses a famous actress to accompany him to Paris, a trip on which Leigh acts as a chaperone. Before long Curtis and Leigh are walking down the aisle, a walk they also took in real life.

p, Robert Arthur; d, Blake Edwards; w, Stanley Shapiro; ph, Philip Lathrop (CinemaScope, Eastmancolor); m, Frank Skinner; ed, Milton Carruth; md, Joseph Gershenson; art d, Alexander Golitzen; set d, Russell A. Gausman, Oliver Emert; cos, Bill Thomas; spec eff, Clifford Stine; m/l, Skinner, Diane Lampert, Richard Loring; makeup, Bud Westmore.

Comedy   **(PR:A MPAA:NR)**

PERFECT GENTLEMAN, THE**   (1935) 73m MGM bw (GB: THE IMPERFECT LADY)

Frank Morgan (*Maj. Chatteris*), Cicely Courtneidge (*April*), Heather Angel (*Evelyn*), Herbert Mundin (*Hitch*), Una O'Connor (*Harriet*), Richard Waring (*John*), Henry Stephenson (*Bishop*), Forrester Harvey (*Baxton*), Mary Forbes (*Lady Clyffe-Pembrook*), Doris Lloyd (*Kate*), Edward Cooper (*Alf*), Brenda Forbes (*Penelope*), Ivan Simpson, Clifford Severn.

Morgan meets Courtneidge on a train to London and she invites him to her opening night performance. Even though the audience boos her he stands by her and cheers. The sincerity of his defense, however, is taken as part of her act and he is soon called to the stage. The audience confirms the fact that the pair are a success, eventually leading to a marriage. The script has plot holes you can drive a truck through, but it is still enjoyable.

p, Harry Rapf; d, Tim Whelan; w, Edward Childs Carpenter (based on the story "The Prodigal Father" by Cosmo Hamilton); ph, Charles Clarke; ed, George Boemler; m/l, "There's Something in a Big Parade" Bronislau Kaper, Walter Jurmann, Ned Washington.

Comedy   **(PR:A MPAA:NR)**

PERFECT LADY, THE**   (1931, Brit.) 76m BIP/Wardour bw

Moira Lynd (*Anne Burnett*), Harry [Henry] Wilcoxon (*Larry Tindale*), Reginald Gardiner (*Lord Tony Carderay*), Betty Amann (*Jacqueline Dubarry*), Athene Seyler (*Lady Westhaven*), Frederick Lloyd (*Lord Westhaven*).

When Lynd's fiance (Gardiner) leaves her to pursue a mercenary French actress (Amann), she pretends to be a maid and gets a job with the seductress. Using her position to break up the romance, she also falls in love with Wilcoxon. Average British comedy of the period.

p&d, Milton Rosmer, Frederick Jackson; w, Jackson.

Comedy   **(PR:A MPAA:NR)**

PERFECT MARRIAGE, THE*½   (1946) 87m PAR bw

Loretta Young (*Maggie Williams*), David Niven (*Dale Williams*), Eddie Albert (*Gil Cummins*), Charlie Ruggles (*Dale Williams, Sr.*), Virginia Field (*Gloria*), Rita Johnson (*Mabel Manning*), ZaSu Pitts (*Rosa*), Nona Griffith (*Cookie Williams*), Jerome Cowan (*Addison Manning*), Nana Bryant (*Corinne Williams*), Luella Gear (*Dolly Haggerty*), Howard Freeman (*Peter Haggerty*), Catherine Craig (*Julie Camberwell*), John Vosper (*Jack Camberwell*), Ann Doran (*Secretary*), Carol Coombs (*Lola*), Lyle Latell (*Bulaski*), Boyd Davis (*Doctor*), Walter Baldwin (*Horse Ring Attendant*), Frank Ferguson (*Gentleman*), Georges Renavent (*Waiter Captain*).

After 10 years of marriage, Young and Niven realize that they cannot stand each other any more and begin to fight incessantly. As is always the case with this sort, the loving daughter is the one responsible for the kissy reunion. A fine cast overcomes the paper thin script.

p, Hal B. Wallis; d, Lewis Allen; w, Leonard Spigelgass (based on the play by Samson Raphaelson); ph, Russell Metty; m, Frederick Hollander; ed, Ellsworth Hoagland; art d, Lionel Banks; set d, Sam Comer, Grace Gregory; cos, Edith Head; m/l, "Stardust," Hoagy Carmichael.

Comedy   **(PR:A MPAA:NR)**

PERFECT SET-UP, THE   (SEE: ONCE YOU KISS A STRANGER, 1969)

PERFECT SNOB, THE**   (1941) 61m FOX bw

Charlie Ruggles (*Dr. Mason*), Charlotte Greenwood (*Martha Mason*), Lynn Bari (*Chris Mason*), Cornel Wilde (*Mike Lord*), Anthony Quinn (*Alex Moreno*), Alan Mowbray (*Freddie Browning*), Chester Clute (*Nibsie Nicholson*), LeRoy Mason (*Witch Doctor*), Jack Chefe (*Waiter*), Biddle Dorsay (*Boat Driver*), Matt McHugh (*Baggage Man*), Charles Tannen (*Chauffeur*), Frances Glaswin, Marilyn Kinsley (*Girls*), David Hopi, Salvadore Barroga (*Natives*).

Bari vacations in Hawaii with the intention of finding herself a husband. Her mother's advice is to marry for money, her father's belief is that love must come first. She lucks out and falls for Wilde, a handsome fellow who surprises her when he finally reveals that he owns a sugar plantation. It's Ruggles who steals the picture as Bari's wise veterinarian father.

p, Walter Morosco; d, Ray McCarey; w, Lee Loeb, Harold Buchman; ph, Charles Clarke; ed, J. Watson Webb; md, Emil Newman; art d, Richard Day, Albert Hogsett.

Comedy   **(PR:A MPAA:NR)**

PERFECT SPECIMEN, THE***   (1937) 97m FN-WB bw

Errol Flynn (*Gerald Beresford Wicks*), Joan Blondell (*Mona Carter*), Hugh Herbert (*Killigrew Shaw*), Edward Everett Horton (*Mr. Grattan*), Dick Foran (*Jinks Carter*), May Robson (*Mrs. Leona Wicks*), Beverly Roberts (*Alicia*), Allen Jenkins (*Pinky*), Dennie Moore (*Clarabelle*), Hugh O'Connell (*Hotel Clerk*), James Burke

(Snodgrass), Granville Bates (Hooker), Harry Davenport (Carl Carter), Tim Henning (Briggs), Lee Phelps (Head of State Patrol), John Heistand (Commentator), Eddy Chandler (State Police Captain), Wilfred Lucas (Deputy Sheriff), Spencer Charters (Station Master), Harry Hollingsworth, Frank Mayo (Detectives), Evelyn Mulhall (Sarah), Charlie Sullivan (Timekeeper), Pat West (Fight Announcer), Cliff Saum, Jack Kenney (Spectators), Al Herman (Copy Reader), James Burtis, Hal Craig (Cops), Tom Brewer (Sheriff), Larry McGrath (John Phillips).

An amusing comedy, Flynn's first such effort, that is the reverse of IT HAPPENED ONE NIGHT, which just happened to be based on a story by the same author who wrote that multi-award winner, Samuel Hopkins Adams. Flynn is an immensely rich and handsome young man being groomed to take over the family's vast business interests by his tyrannical relative Robson, who rules every moment of his life and has sheltered him like a Little Lord Fauntleroy. He lives on a huge estate and has been tutored in educational matters and physical culture and has never been outside the gates of the compound. This condition has left him bereft of any ability to communicate with his fellow man or woman. Blondell is a nosy news reporter determined to get the story of the reclusive millionaire so she crashes through the gates of the mansion at the same moment when Flynn, ever curious, is testing Newton's theory of gravity by falling out of a tree! She takes him out into the world and he is thought to have been kidnaped so a huge national dragnet is called and the resultant complications are what make for the merriment. At one point, Flynn dons boxing gloves and gives a very convincing account of himself in the ring, something he was to do when essaying the biography of Jim Corbett in GENTLEMAN JIM five years later. In an attempt to get some national publicity, the Warner Bros. press agents concocted the bogus tale that Flynn had represented his native country of Australia in the 1928 Olympic boxing competition in Holland. Flynn kept quiet about the ruse for quite some time and eventually labeled the report as untrue. Horton does a funny turn as Robson's private secretary and Dick Foran stands around looking handsome. Blondell is beguiling and adorable and Flynn shows some flair for comedy but it was not really his metier. The arch script needed four screenwriters and suffered, at times, from fallen archness.

p, Hal B. Wallis, Harry Joe Brown; d, Michael Curtiz; w, Norman Reilly Raine, Lawrence Riley, Brewster Morse, Fritz Falkenstein (based on the story by Samuel Hopkins Adams); ph, Charles Rosher; m, Heinz Roemheld; ed, Terry Morse; md, Leo F. Forbstein; art d, Robert Haas; cos, Howard Shoup; spec eff, Byron Haskin, Edwin DuPar, Rex Wimpy.

Comedy **(PR:A MPAA:NR)**

PERFECT STRANGERS (SEE: VACATION FROM MARRIAGE, 1945, Brit.)

PERFECT STRANGERS** (1950) 88m WB bw (GB: TOO DANGEROUS TO LOVE)

Ginger Rogers (Terry Scott), Dennis Morgan (David Campbell), Thelma Ritter (Lena Fassler), Margalo Gillmore (Isobel Bradford), Anthony Ross (Robert Fisher), Howard Freeman (Timkin), Alan Reed (Harry Patullo), Paul Ford (Judge Byron), Harry Bellaver (Bailiff), George Chandler (Lester Hubley), Frank Conlan (John Brokaw), Charles Meredith (Lyle Pettijohn), Frances Charles (Eileen Marcher), Marjorie Bennett (Mrs. Moore), Paul McVey (District Attorney), Edith Evanson (Mary Travers), Whit Bissell (Defense Attorney), Sumner Getchell (John Simon), Ford Rainey (Ernest Craig), Sarah Selby (Mrs. Wilson), Alan Wood (Clerk of Court), Ronnie Tyler (Newsboy), Isabel Withers (Woman), Max Mellenger (Official), Boyd Davis (Judge), Weldon Heyburn (Man), Ezelle Poule (Secretary), Mike Lally (Court Steno), Charles Lind (Thomas Luscomb), Russell De Vorkin (Newsboy), Donald Kerr (Busboy), Ned Glass (O'Hanlon), Paul Dubov (Vonderheit), Creighton Hale, John Albright, Frank Marlowe, Ed Coke (Reporters), Lou Marcelle (TV Announcer), Frank Pat Henry (Doctor), Joleen King (Nurse), Dick Kipling (Autopsy Surgeon), Sidney Dubin (Chemist), Art Miles (Sheriff), Joseph Kerr (Doctor), Richard Bartell (Weatherman), Frank Cady (Geologist), Hugh Murray (Minister), Pat Mitchell (Newsboy).

Ladislaus Bus-Fekete, the Hungarian author who was responsible for many Hollywood stories, wrote a play which Ben Hecht and Charles MacArthur adapted for the U.S. stage. That was turned into this film, with less than glowing results, by screenwriter Edith Sommer. Two stories take place side by side as Rogers and Morgan are jurors at a murder trial. Much of the action takes place in the jury room and the secondary characters are more interesting than the stars. Rogers is a divorcee, Morgan is a married man, and in the course of the trial the two fall in love, then go their separate ways when their jury duty is over, a sop to the Production Code, no doubt. All the laughs come from the others on the love-nest triangle panel. Ritter is a pregnant housewife with an I.Q. that's lower than her bra size, Reed is a barber, Ross is a Casanova, Meredith and Freeman are two pig-headed types, Bennett just knits like Madame De Farge, and Gillmore is the woman who wants the accused to go to the chair because her own wealthy husband left her and she has a 10-foot high grudge against husbands who are not faithful. Some cute lines and a good stage performance by Rogers but the picture is hardly more than a stage play with cameras rolling. It's sort of "Twelve Not-So-Angry Men (and Women)" and little more.

p, Jerry Wald; d, Bretaigne Windust; w, Edith Sommer, George Oppenheimer (based on the plays "Ladies and Gentlemen" by Ben Hecht, Charles MacArthur and "Twelve in the Box" by Ladislaus Bus-Fekete); ph, Peverell Marley; m, Leigh Harline; ed, David Weisbart; art d, Stanley Fleischer; set d, George James Hopkins; cos, Milo Anderson; makeup, Perc Westmore, Eddie Allen.

Comedy **(PR:A MPAA:NR)**

PERFECT UNDERSTANDING*½ (1933, Brit.) 80m Gloria Swanson-British/UA bw

Gloria Swanson (Judy Rogers), Laurence Olivier (Nicholas Randall), John Halliday (Ivan Ronnson), Sir Nigel Playfair (Lord Portleigh), Michael Farmer (George Drayton), Genevieve Tobin (Kitty Drayton), Nora Swinburne (Lady Stephanie Fitzmaurice), Charles Cullum (Sir John Fitzmaurice), Peter Gawthorne (Jackson, Butler), Rosalinde Fuller (Cook), Evelyn Bostock (Maid), O. B. Clarence (Dr. Graham), Mary Jerrold (Mrs. Graham).

Gloria Swanson had just married Michael Farmer, an Englishman, and had a daughter. When she lost her contract with Joe Schenck, she moved to England, and, having married a British subject, she learned that she could start her own movie company there. She starred in as well as produced this picture (and gave her hubby a part in the proceedings) but it was a total loss, both critically and financially and she even had to sell much of her stock in United Artists in order to complete the picture. Swanson is an American woman on holiday in England when she meets Olivier (sporting a mustache to look older than his 25 years as Swanson was 32 and looked every bit of it), an English aristocrat. They fall in love and decide to get married but insist on maintaining their own freedom and their own friends. They take a long honeymoon on the Riviera (many of these scenes are of such forced gaiety that they seemed ludicrous to Depression audiences and even more so today) and Swanson comes back to London to get their abode ready. Meanhwile, Olivier is mildly hurt in a speedboat race and taken to Cannes, where he is put up at the villa owned by Swinburne, a married woman who soon falls in love with him. They have a go at it one night and when Olivier goes home to London, he confesses his sexual transgression to Swanson. She gets even by going to see an admirer, Halliday, and though it looks like she's also strayed, the truth is that she chickens out before anything more serious than a mild flirtation occurs. Olivier is less than understanding of her behavior and when she tells him that she is expecting, he considers marching out on her but finally recovers from his fit of jealousy and they are united in a clinch. Wearing two hats was not easy for Swanson and her acting shows it. Add that to being a new mother and the constant bickering with her husband and it's easy to see why the picture suffered, despite being neatly shot in London and in the south of France. (Why do they call it "the south of France" but never the "north of France?" In Illinois, people talk of going "upstate" or "downstate" and in California, it's either "Northern California" or "Southern California." This has nothing to do at all with the movie but we like to occasionally digress and pique your curiosity about other matters.) Fans of Olivier will be disappointed in his role. He was just getting started in movies and had scenes stolen left and right by the mercurial Swanson, who knew her way around cameras.

p, Gloria Swanson; d, Cyril Gardner; w, Miles Malleson, Michael Powell (based on a story by Malleson); ph, Curt Courant; m, Henry Sullivan; ed, Thorold Dickinson.

Comedy/Drama **(PR:A-C MPAA:NR)**

PERFECT WEEKEND, A (SEE: ST. LOUIS KID, THE, 1934)

PERFECT WOMAN, THE½** (1950, Brit.) 89m RANK-TC/EL bw

Patricia Roc (Penelope), Stanley Holloway (Ramshead), Nigel Patrick (Roger Cavendish), Miles Malleson (Prof. Belmond), Irene Handl (Mrs. Butter, Housekeeper), Pamela Devis (Olga the Robot), Fred Berger (Farini), David Hurst (Wolfgang Winkel), Anita Sharp-Bolster (Lady Diana), Phillipa Gill (Lady Mary), Constance Smith (Receptionist), Patti Morgan, Noel Howlett.

A sharply directed comedy about a professor who invents a robot woman who perfectly obeys the standards of society. He then hires an escort for his invention, to show the "dummy" around town. The professor's daughter puts a damper on things when she takes the robot's place. She successfully pulls off the impersonation, but the appearance of the real robot reveals her deception. The professor learns a lesson when his creation goes on the blink.

p, George Black, Alfred Black; d, Bernard Knowles; w, Knowles, J. B. Boothroyd, George Black (based on the play by Wallace Geoffrey, Basil John Mitchell); ph, Jack Hildyard, Russell Thompson; m, Arthur Wilkinson; ed, Peter Graham Scott; art d, J. Elderwills.

Comedy **(PR:A MPAA:NR)**

PERFECTIONIST, THE** (1952, Fr.) 91m Discina bw (UN GRAND PATRON)

Pierre Fresnay (The Chief), Renee Devilliers (Florence), Marcel Andre (Tannard), Claire Duhamel (Catherine), Roland Alexandre (Jacques), Pierre Destailles (Gaston), Michel Vadet (Larmy), Christiane Barry (Jacqueline), Nadine Alari (Yvette), Maurice Ronet (Francois), Serge Lecointe (Albert), J. C. Pascal (Marcillac).

Fresnay is a renowned surgeon referred to by his colleagues as "The Chief." His success is met with disfavor by his wife who, naturally, feels that she is being ignored. He is more concerned with becoming a member of the prestigious Academy of Medicine than heeding his wife's requests for more time together. He finally gives in and agrees to go with her on a second honeymoon, but before they can leave, a seat in the Academy is vacated by a member's death. He ignores the trip and his wife resigns herself to being married to a success. An average film which surprisingly won great acclaim in France upon its release. It has since fallen from most moviegoers' memories, as has the body of work produced by director Ciampi. (In French; English subtitles.)

p, Andre Paulve; d, Yves Ciampi; w, Ciampi, Pierre Very; ph, Marcel Grignon; m, Joseph Kosma.

Drama **(PR:A MPAA:NR)**

PERFORMERS, THE½** (1970, Jap.) 94m Shochiku c (HANA TO NAMIDA TO HONOO)

Hibari Misora (Kasumi Fujihana), Shinichi Mori (Ryusuke), Shogo Shimada (Seijuro Fujihana), Yoichi Hayashi (Hiroshi), Yataro Kitagami (Kisaburo), Nana Ozaki (Hamako), Takamaru Sasaki, Osami Nabe, Shin-ichi Yanagizawa, Fujio Murakami, Ryusuke Kita, Kentaro Imai, Kyoko Mizuki, Natsuko Shiga, Michiko Yashima, Yoshisaburo Owa, Nobuko Suzuki, Fusako Maki.

Family melodrama about the turbulent relationship between the owner of a dance school, Shimada, and his rebellious daughter, Misora. Shimada hopes his daughter will take over the dance school, but she has no interest in the family business. She is too wrapped up in her affair with a jazz musician, much to the dismay of her father. Her affair soon ends, giving one of her father's prize pupils, Kitagami, the hope that he may marry her someday. This is shattered when she takes up with a singer, Mori, and they begin performing in nightclubs together. Shimada demands that Misora stop seeing Mori, but she refuses. Meanwhile, the angry Kitagami decides to open his own dance school and steals most of Shimada's staff to do it. Totally demoralized, Shimada falls ill and decides to forgive his daughter and apologize. Sensing that Mori needs to survive on his own for awhile, Misora dumps him and concentrates on her own career. When she needs money for an important recital, her old boy friend the jazz musician gives it to her. He tells her the money is from the advance Mori received when he signed with an agent. The film ends on an upbeat note with all the performers at work and successful.

d&w, Umeji Inoue; ph, Keiji Maruyama (Shochiku Grandscope, Eastmancolor); m, Seitaro Omuri; art d, Gohei Morita.

Drama **(PR:C MPAA:NR)**

PERIL FOR THE GUY** (1956, Brit.) 55m World Wide-Children's Film Foundation/BL bw

Christopher Warbey *(Freddie)*, Frazer Hines *(Kim)*, Ali Alleney *(Ali)*, Katherine Kath *(Anita Fox)*, Meredith Edwards *(Police Constable Durrant)*, Amanda Coxall *(Pat)*, Peter Copley *(Ritter)*, Paul Daneman.

When a scientist invents a machine to detect oil, he and four children are kidnaped by a gang of spies. One child escapes and fetches the police. Adequate for the kiddies.

p, Hindle Edgar; d&w, James Hill (based on a novel by John Kennett); ph, James Allen.

Children **(PR:A MPAA:NR)**

PERILOUS HOLIDAY½** (1946) 89m COL bw

Pat O'Brien *(Patrick Nevil)*, Ruth Warrick *(Agnes Stuart)*, Alan Hale *(Dr. Lilley)*, Edgar Buchanan *(George Richards)*, Audrey Long *(Audrey Latham)*, Willard Robertson *(Graeme)*, Eduardo Ciannelli *(Senor Aguirre)*, Minna Gombell *(Mrs. Latham)*, Martin Garralaga *(Manuel Perez)*, Jay Novello *(Luigi)*, Al Hill *(Benny Lockner)*, Pedro Regas *(Pedro)*, Nacho Galindo *(Proprietor)*, Manuel Paris *(Waiter)*, Ralph Navarro *(Maitre D')*, Joe Dominguez *(Police Car Driver)*, Don Avalier *(Police Lieutenant)*, Chris-Pin Martin *(Servant)*, David Cota *(Shoeshine Boy)*, Delmar Costello *(Pageboy)*, Jack Del Rio *(Bartender)*, Eddie LeBaron and his Continental Orchestra.

Treasury agent O'Brien teams up with newspaper columnist Warrick to battle vile counterfeiters Hale and Buchanan who are operating in Mexico. Hale killed Warrick's father and it was she who drove the illegal operation out of the U.S. and into Mexico after writing a series of exposes. Of course, the crime fighters fall in love and defeat the baddies. This was Warrick's first decent film since CITIZEN KANE. In later years, she made a name for herself in the highly successful TV soap operas "Peyton Place" and "All My Children."

p, Phil L. Ryan; d, Edward H. Griffith; w, Roy Chanslor (based on a story by Robert Carson); ph, Charles Lawton, Jr.; m, Paul Sawtell; ed, Viola Lawrence; md, M. W. Stoloff; art d, Stephen Goosson, Rudolph Sternad; set d, Frank Tuttle; spec eff, Ray Cory; m/l, Allan Roberts, Doris Fisher.

Crime **(PR:A MPAA:NR)**

PERILOUS JOURNEY, A (SEE: BAD BOY, 1939)

PERILOUS JOURNEY, A½** (1953) 90m REP bw

Vera Ralston *(Francie Landreaux)*, David Brian *(Monty Breed)*, Scott Brady *(Shard Benton)*, Charles Winninger *(Capt. Eph Allan)*, Hope Emerson *(Olivia Schuyler)*, Eileen Christy *(Susan)*, Leif Erickson *(Richards)*, Veda Ann Borg *(Sadie)*, Ian MacDonald *(Sprague)*, Virginia Grey *(Abby)*, Dorothy Ford *(Rose the Singer)*, Ben Cooper *(Sam Austin)*, Kathleen Freeman *(Leah)*, Barbara Hayden *(Cathy)*, Paul Fierro *(Pepe)*, Angela Greene *(Mavis)*, John Dierkes *(1st Mate)*, Fred Graham *(Whiskers the Stowaway)*, Trevor Bardette *(Whiskered Miner)*, Richard Reeves *(Stewart the Sailor)*, Bob Carney *(Barfly)*, Charles Evans *(Minister)*, Philip Van Zandt *(Tout)*, Byron Foulger *(Mr. Martin, the Desk Clerk)*, Denver Pyle *(Bartender)*, Harry Tyler *(Vagrant)*, Emil Sitka *(Drunk)*, Jack O'Shea *(Cook)*, Brandon Beach, Frank Hagney, Stanley Blystone *(Ad Libs)*, Dick Alexander *(Crying Miner)*, Charles Cane *(Miner)*, Gloria Clark *(Bride-to-Be)*, Alden Aldrich *(2nd Mate)*.

Set in 1850, A PERILOUS JOURNEY details the lengthy voyage of 49 East Coast women who hire a ship and head to California in search of men. Ralston leads the pack as a woman in search of her no-good husband who had left her years ago. Her search takes her into all the seedy joints from Panama to Sacramento where she finally sees the bum, only to watch him get shot down in a dispute. Veteran western director Springsteen manages to bring some zing to the routine proceedings.

p, William J. O'Sullivan; d, R. G. Springsteen; w, Richard Wormser (based on the novel *The Golden Tide* by Vingie Roe); ph, Jack Marta; m, Victor Young; ed, Richard L. Van Enger; art d, Frank Arrigo; m/l, "On the Rue de la Paix," "Bon Soir," "California," Young, Edward Heyman.

Western/Adventure **(PR:A MPAA:NR)**

PERILOUS WATERS** (1948) 64m MON bw

Don Castle *(Willie Hunter)*, Audrey Long *(Judy Gage, Publisher's Secretary)*, Peggy Knudsen *(Pat Ferris)*, Samuel S. Hinds *(Dana Ferris, Publisher)*, Gloria Holden *(Mrs. Ferris)*, John Miljan *(Carter Larkin)*, Walter Sande *(Franklin)*, Stanley Andrews *(Capt. Porter)*, Cy Kendall *(The Boss)*, Gene Garrick *(Fred)*, George Ramsey *(Bart)*, Mike Kilian *(Brooks)*, Julian Rivero *(Fisherman)*.

Castle plays a hired gun sent to kill Hinds, a crusading newspaper publisher out to stop gambling. The mob gets upset with Hinds' constant print barrages so they send out Castle to stop the presses. If that isn't bad enough, Miljan and Hinds' wife attempt to blackmail the poor, honest publisher. Castle finds Hinds when the publisher is on his private yacht sailing toward Mexico, but forsakes the mob and lets his intended victim live.

p, Jack Wrather; d, Jack Bernard; w, Richard Wormser; Francis Rosenwald (based on the story "Search" by Leon Ware); ph, Henry Sharp; ed, Stewart S. Frye; md, Dave Chudnow; art d, Lewis Creber.

Crime **(PR:A MPAA:NR)**

PERILS OF PAULINE, THE*½** (1947) 96m PAR c

Betty Hutton *(Pearl White)*, John Lund *(Michael Farrington)*, Billy De Wolfe *(Timmy)*, William Demarest *(Chuck McManus)*, Constance Collier *(Julia Gibbs)*, Frank Faylen *(Joe Gurt)*, William Farnum *(Hero—Western Saloon)*, Paul Panzer *(Gent—Interior Drawing Room)*, Snub Pollard *(Propman—Western Saloon)*, Creighton Hale *(Marcelled Leading Man)*, Chester Conklin, James Finlayson, Hank Mann *(Chef Comics)*, Bert Roach *(Bartender—Western Saloon)*, Francis McDonald *(Heavy—Western Saloon)*, Heinie Conklin *(Studio Cop)*, Franklyn Farnum *(Friar John)*, Eric Alden *(Officer)*, Ethel Clayton *(Lady Montague)*, Harry Hayden *(Stage Manager)*, Julia Faye *(Nurse)*, Chester Clute *(Willie Millick)*, Myrtle Anderson *(Maid)*, Frank Ferguson *(Theater Owner)*, Rex Lease, Stanley Blystone, Sidney D'Albrook *(Reporters)*, John "Skins" Miller *(Cameraman—Drawing Room Set)*, Bess Flowers, Paula Ray *(Reporters)*, Tom Dugan *(Balloonist)*, Eugene Borden *(French Doctor)*, Byron Poindexter *(Man)*, Raymond de Ravenne *(Call Boy)*, Jack Shea *(Workman)*.

A quick glance at the cast list will show you that the producers knew what they were doing and hired many of the old-time silent screen comics to play in this partially fabricated biography of Pearl White, the "Queen of the Serials." It's a patented combination of belly-laughs and nostalgia as Hutton essays the role of a young extra who went from $5 a day to stardom and retired happily with a huge fortune in less than a decade. Most of the film has to do with the haphazard way in which they shot the old films and it might have been more effective if the movie was made in black and white instead of Technicolor. The re-creation of many of the silent movie stunts and gags is excellent but the hokum story of the love affair between Hutton and Lund is only a stage wait for the laughs. Director Marshall went so far as to drag White's original villain, Paul Panzer, out of retirement to reprise his role in this tuneful comedy. Frank Loesser got an Oscar nomination for "I Wish I Didn't Love You So," but Hutton's record of Loesser's "Poppa Don't Preach to Me" was a larger hit at the time. He also wrote "Rumble, Rumble, Rumble" and the hilarious "The Sewing Machine" for the movie. The other tune was "Poor Pauline" (Raymond Walker, Charles McCarron). Fine character acting by Collier, as an old-time actress, and Demarest, in a satire of the megaphoned silent director. Pearl White had been a circus performer. After hurting her spine falling off a horse, she went to work as a secretary, was spotted by a producer and given a job in a three-reeler, THE LIFE OF BUFFALO BILL, when the leading actress was ill. That led her to her meeting with Louis Gasnier who cast her in his serial. She was unable to do many of her own stunts because of the back injury and was "doubled" by small men in several films. She eventually moved to France in 1924 and stayed there until her death in 1938 at the age of 49. Her two husbands were Victor Sutherland (seven years) and Wallace McCutcheon (two years), both actors.

p, Sol C. Siegel; d, George Marshall; w, P. J. Wolfson, Frank Butler (based on a story by Wolfson suggested by incidents in life of Pearl White and Charles W. Goddard's original serial, "The Perils of Pauline"); ph, Ray Rennahan (Technicolor); m, Robert Emmett Dolan; ed, Arthur Schmidt; art d, Hans Dreier, Roland Anderson; ch, Billy Daniels.

Comedy/Biography/Musical **Cas.** **(PR:A MPAA:NR)**

PERILS OF PAULINE, THE** (1967) 98m UNIV c

Pat Boone *(George)*, Terry-Thomas *(Sten Martin)*, Pamela Austin *(Pauline)*, Edward Everett Horton *(Casper Coleman)*, Hamilton Camp *(Thorpe)*, Doris Packer *(Mrs. Carruthers)*, Kurt Kasznar *(Consul General)*, Vito Scotti *(Frandisi)*, Leon Askin *(Commissar)*, Aram Katcher *(Vizier)*, Ric Natoli *(Prince Benji)*, Jeanne Gerson *(Pauline's Foster Mother)*, Joe Higgins *(Pauline's Foster Father)*, Keith Taylor *(Henry)*, Max Kleven *(Gorilla)*.

This picture had nothing to do with the superior biography that starred Betty Hutton. Instead, they've taken the same title and gone back to the original 20-episode serial Pearl White made in 1914. It was lensed as a TV pilot but when no network saw fit to put it on its schedule, the picture was released. Austin, who became famous doing automobile commercials, toplines with Boone and Thomas. The whiz-bang story has Boone and Austin as two young orphans who fall for each other while living at the home where they have been raised. Boone leaves first and promises to return for her when he becomes rich. Seven years pass and Boone is somehow the richest man in the world. He comes back for Austin but she's now living in Arabia , where she's the nanny for Natoli, the 12-year-old prince. Natoli has lecherous eyes for Austin and is already planning to begin his very own harem with Austin as the centerpiece. When she balks at that, he sells her into slavery to a band of pygmies in Africa. These little guys want to shrink her down to their size. A huge gorilla saves her from that fate (shades of KING KONG?) and she is then rescued by Terry-Thomas, an African hunter whose fame is legendary. Meanwhile, Boone has come down with a strange disease he picked up on the Dark Continent (odd they call it that when the pygmies seen are all white) and is in New York trying to get over it. Austin comes to the Big Apple, falls down a sewer, and is saved by 99 1/2-year-old Horton, the second richest man in the world, who would like her to marry his 1-year-old grandson. In order to effect that union, he tosses Austin into a deep-freeze to wait for the infant to grow. Boone has himself frozen as well, despondent over not being able to locate Austin. They both thaw ahead of schedule and Austin winds up in a spacewalk (don't ask how, just read!), having been coaxed there by Soviet agents. When she returns to Earth, she accepts a job in a movie directed by Scotti (very funny, as always) and costarring the gorilla who had saved her from the pygmies (Kleven in a costume). When the huge beast kidnaps Austin, Boone comes to her rescue. The two marry and go off to Venice where their gondola begins to sink as the film ends. They've crammed every possible stunt they could into this movie and there is absolutely no room for anything else. "Batman" was a huge TV hit at the time and they tried to do something equally campy but camp is a delicate matter and this is a sledgehammer.

p, Herbert B. Leonard; d, Leonard, Joshua Shelley; w, Albert Beich (suggested by the story by Charles W. Goddard); ph, Jack A. Marta (Eastmancolor); m, Vic Mizzy; ed, Sam E. Waxman; art d, Alexander Golitzen, John T. McCormack; set d, John McCarthy, Julia Heron; cos, Grady Hunt; m/l, "My Pretty Pauline," Mizzy (sung by Boone); makeup, Bud Westmore; stunts, Max Kleven.

Comedy/Adventure   **(PR:A   MPAA:NR)**

PERIOD OF ADJUSTMENT***   (1962) 112m MGM bw

Tony Franciosa (Ralph Baitz), Jane Fonda (Isabel Haverstick), Jim Hutton (George Haverstick), Lois Nettleton (Dorothea Baitz), John McGiver (Stewart P. McGill), Mabel Albertson (Mrs. Alice McGill), Jack Albertson (Desk Sergeant).

If anyone else but Williams had written this stage play, it might have been hailed by everyone but audiences and critics were so used to the author's delvings into deep, dark recesses that they were taken aback by a genial comedy, William's first. The title refers to that period of time that every young couple must face when first married. Hutton is a Korean War veteran who has just come out of a hospital where he was being treated for a nervous disorder brought about by his service. He meets and falls for his nurse, Fonda, a sweet and loving southern girl who wants nothing more than to make him happy. Their marriage is rocky from the start as Hutton quits his job and the two of them spend their wedding night in a tacky motel, after having driven there in what Hutton advertised as a station wagon but which was, in reality, an old hearse. Hutton gets drunk and passes out before he can consummate the marriage (which is a deliberate move on his part as he questions his own sexual ability). The following day they go to visit Franciosa in Tennessee. Franciosa had married his wife, Nettleton, for money but eventually grew to love her. That's being threatened by his relationship with Nettleton's parents, McGiver and Mabel Albertson, a domineering set of in-laws that would cause a lesser man to search for the rat poison. Franciosa quits McGiver's business and Nettleton, who is greatly influenced by her parents, leaves Franciosa when they convince her that he won't stay long with her now that he's out of the company. McGiver and Albertson arrive together to gather Nettleton's things from the Franciosa house and there is a brouhaha that ends when they're all hauled into the police station and face Jack Albertson, the desk sergeant. (The two Albertsons were brother and sister, not husband and wife.) At seeing all this happen, Fonda and Hutton realize they don't have it so bad and they do their best to help Nettleton and Franciosa get back together. Franciosa buys Nettleton a fur coat and the reconciliation is effected. The Hutton-Fonda marriage is still sexless and Hutton finally admits that he's frightened of being inadequate. She allays his fears and says that they have a whole lifetime to learn about each other and work things out. Fonda is the weakest link in the marital quartet and Franciosa emerges as the strongest. Given the right material, he can steal scenes from anyone.

p, Lawrence Weingarten; d, George Roy Hill; w, Isobel Lennart (based on the play by Tennessee Williams); ph, Paul C. Vogel (Panavision); m, Lyn Murray; ed, Fredric Steinkamp; art d, George W. Davis, Edward Carfagno; set d, Henry Grace, Dick Pefferle; makeup, William Tuttle.

Comedy/Drama   **(PR:A-C   MPAA:NR)**

PERMANENT VACATION**½   (1982) 75m Cinesthesia/Gray City c

Chris Parker (Aloysious Parker), Leila Gastil (Leila), Maria Duval (Latin Girl), Ruth Bolton (Mother), Richard Boes (War Veteran), John Lurie (Sax Player), Eric Mitchell (Car Fence), Lisa Rosen (Popcorn Girl), Frankie Faison (Man in Lobby), Suzanne Fletcher (Girl in Car), Felice Rosser (Woman by Mailbox), Chris Hameon (French Traveler), Charlie Spademan, Evelyn Smith (Patients), Sara Driver, Jane Fire (Nurses).

A road film, of sorts, about an alienated youth who wanders the deserted streets of New York City meeting a variety of people, and visiting his girl friend and his ailing mother. The film pays less attention to a traditional story than to the series of vignettes which the characters occupy. While it shows a definite talent and cinematic eye, it has a tendency to draw attention to its film school pretensions. Jarmusch, a former NYU student, produced this 16mm film on a miniscule budget. After befriending Nicholas Ray and Wim Wenders, Jarmusch pieced together a similar but far more successful picture, STRANGER THAN PARADISE, featuring John Lurie. Lurie, who is blessed with one of the most cinematic faces in recent years, contributes much to this picture's atmosphere with his moody sax solos.

p,d&w, Jim Jarmusch; ph, James A. Lebovitz, Thomas DiCillo, James A. Lebovitz (Duart Color); m, Jarmusch, John Lurie; ed, Jarmusch.

Drama   **(PR:C   MPAA:NR)**

PERMETTE SIGNORA CHE AMI VOSTRA FIGLIA   (SEE: CLARETTA AND BEN, 1983, Ital./Fr.)

PERMISSION TO KILL*½   (1975, U.S./Aust.) 93m Wien-Sascha/AE c

Dirk Bogarde (Alan Curtis), Ava Gardner (Katina Petersen), Bekim Fehmiu (Alexander Diakim), Timothy Dalton (Charles Lord), Nicole Calfan (Melissa Lascade), Frederic Forrest (Scott Alexander), Alf Joint (MacNeil), Peggy Sinclair (Lily), Anthony Dutton (Jennings), Klaus Wildbolz (Muller), John Levene (Adams), Dennis Blanch (Brewer), Vladimir Popovic (Kostas), Ratislav Plamenac (Pavlos), Peter

Garell (Carlo), Ermin Von Gross (Hotel Manager), Bob Sessions (Pete), Dr. Francois Baudet (French Doctor).

Dull drama starring Bogarde as a mysterious secret agent attempting to stop powerful Third World leader Fehmiu from returning to his home country. The film is slow, confusing, and ponderous, with a lackluster cast. Gardner is embarrassing as the former mistress of Fehmiu.

p, Paul Mills; d, Cyril Frankel; w, Robin Estridge (based on the novel by Estridge); ph, Freddie Young (Technicolor); m, Richard Rodney Bennett; ed, Ernest Walter; prod d, Elliot Scott; art d, Theo Harisch; cos, Peppi Wanke, Emmi Minnich, Franka; makeup, George Partleton.

Spy Drama   **(PR:C   MPAA:PG)**

PERRY RHODAN-SOS AUS DEM WELTALLO   (SEE: MISSION STARDUST, 1968 Ital./Span./Ger.)

PERSECUTION*½   (1974, Brit.) 88m Tyburn/Fanfare c (AKA: TERROR OF SHEBA; SHEBA)

Lana Turner (Carrie Masters), Trevor Howard (Paul Bellamy), Ralph Bates (David Masters), Olga Georges-Picot (Monique Kalfon), Suzan Farmer (Janie Masters), Mark Weavers (Young David), Patrick Allen (Robert Masters), Jennifer Guy (Waitress), Shelagh Fraser (Mrs. Banks), Ronald Howard (Dr. Ross), John Ryan (Gardener), Catherine Brandon (Mrs. Deacon).

The 28-year-old son of veteran movie maker Freddie Francis, Kevin, thought he really had something when he produced this Grand Guignol picture. Turner was following in the footsteps of Crawford and Davis in WHATEVER HAPPENED TO BABY JANE? and he hoped that her appeal would bring the people rushing in. Turner is the most possessive mother of all time, a wealthy American now living in England. She has been crippled by the husband who has since gone off somewhere and her son, Weavers, represents the father in her mind, so she spends most of her time terrorizing the boy. She accomplishes that by frightening the boy through the use of several cats, all named Sheba. Weavers can take it no longer so he gets revenge by drowning her latest feline in a saucer of milk. Turner gets even by supervising a funeral for the pussy and giving the tiny coffin to Weavers as his Christmas gift. Time goes by and Weavers grows up to become Bates, a young man married to Farmer. Turner didn't want to lose her son to another woman and attempted to make their marriage fall apart to no avail. Bates and Farmer have a child which is suffocated when Turner's current Sheba jumps into the crib. Both Bates and Farmer are understandably depressed and Turner, who wants to split the couple, hires Georges-Picot, a professional hooker, to act as a "nurse" for Farmer while the girl is still mentally reeling from the death of her baby. As Turner had hoped, Bates falls for Georges-Picot and they are soon sexually involved. In the midst of lovemaking, Farmer catches them and runs out of the room, then falls down a flight of stairs and dies. Bates, having lost a wife and child, goes over the edge, kills Georges-Picot, then rushes to the garden to unearth the bones of all the dead cats. While digging, he finds the bones of his father, whom he'd thought had deserted them years before. When he confronts Turner, she admits that she killed the man and that he wasn't Bates' father at all. Rather, the real father was Howard, the same man who crippled her. Bates' mind totally snaps and he winds up drowning Turner in her latest cat's milk. Howard stops by as the missing lover-father and his contribution is negligible. The best part of the movie is seeing the gorgeous home in which it was shot. The house was owned by producer Harry Saltzman (the man who produced many of the "James Bond" pictures) although he had nothing to do with this mish-mash. Shockingly, Turner received the Best Actress award at the Festival of Horror Films in Spain for her role in PERSECUTION. Another movie that asks the question: "Why in the world did they bother to make this?"

p, Kevin Francis; d, Don Chaffey; w, Robert B. Hutton, Rosemary Wootten, Frederick Warner; ph, Kenneth Talbot (Eastmancolor); m, Paul Ferris; ed, Michael Campbell; art d, Jack Shampan, Peter Williams; cos, Anthony Mendleson; makeup, Jimmy Evans, Roy Ashton.

Horror/Thriller   **Cas.**   **(PR:C   MPAA:PG)**

PERSECUTION AND ASSASSINATION OF JEAN-PAUL MARAT AS PERFORMED BY THE INMATES OF THE ASYLUM OF CHARENTON UNDER THE DIRECTION OF THE MARQUIS DE SADE, THE**   (1967, Brit.) 115m Marat Sade/UA c (GB: MARAT/SADE)

Clifford Rose (Mons. Coulmier), Brenda Kempner (Mme. Coulmier), Ruth Baker (Mlle. Coulmier), Michael Williams (Herald), Freddie Jones (Cucurucu), Hugh Sullivan (Kokol), Jonathan Burn (Polpoch), Jeanette Landis (Rossignol), Robert Lloyd (Jacques Roux), Glenda Jackson (Charlotte Corday), Ian Richardson (Jean-Paul Marat), Susan Williamson (Simonne Evrard), Patrick Magee (Marquis de Sade), John Steiner (Duperret), Mark Jones (Abbot), Morgan Sheppard (A Mad Animal), James Mellor (Schoolmaster), Ian Hogg (Military Representative), Mark Jones (Mother), Henry Woolf (Father), John Hussey (Newly Rich Lady), John Harwood (Voltaire), Leon Lissek (Lavoisier), Heather Canning, Jennifer Tudor (Nuns), Timothy Hardy, Stanford Trowell (Guards), Patrick Gowers, Richard Callinan, Michael Gould, Nicholas Moes, Rainer Schuelein, Paul Hiley (Musicians), Mary Allen, Michael Farnsworth, Maroussia Frank, Tamara Fuerst, Guy Gordon, Sheila Grant, Michael Percival, Lyn Pinkney, Carol Raymont (Patients).

Geoffrey Skelton and Adrian Mitchell translated Weiss' play, which opened in Berlin in April, 1964, prior to the London and New York premieres. If you think the English title is strange, try the German one: "Die Verfolgung Und Ermordung Jean Paul Marats, Dargestellt Durch Die Schauspielgruppe Des Hospizes Zu Charenton Anleintung Des Herrn De Sade." Phew! It's a play within a play, based on the fact that in the first years of the 1800s, Parisian sophisticates used to attend "theatrical" performances at mental hospitals. These shows were part of the inmates' therapies and a good, if weird, time was supposedly had by all. The members of the Royal Shakespeare Company, who did the play in the London production, are used again here for the tale. Magee is the man who gave sadism its name. He is residing at Charenton, the hospital where he will spend his last days. An audience arrives to see a show Magee has written the words and the music for. The audience is in a bathhouse at the asylum and settles down to watch the presentation, a mythical conversation with Marat, one of the forces behind the French Revolution. Marat is played by Ian Richardson and is seen in his tub as he screams for social changes through violence. Magee is opposed to Richardson and claims that death and destruction solve nothing, as the difficulties in living will continue no matter who is at the steering wheel of the government. Magee feels that pain is only effective when used to gratify one's deeper, sexual needs. The other actors are all inmates and become more involved in the show until the dividing line between the show and their lives is blurred. Jackson comes to the home of Richardson and finds it difficult to gain entrance. Once inside, she wields a knife from her bodice and stabs Richardson while he is seated in his tub. The "play" ends and Magee explains to the audience that it was presented in the spirit of stimulating the spectators to think about such matters, questions which cannot easily be answered. However, the patients who have been acting have, by this time, become so imbued with the words and cries for "freedom" that they rise up and begin attacking the guards, the audience, and each other. The acting was excellent but the script rambles and darts from free verse to street language to wild screaming and unjustified pauses, and in the end, one wonders what the authors meant. When the play ran in London, the actors had a good time counting the number of walkouts between the acts. The same happened in the film but the cost of making it was so low, just a bit over $500,000 with everything included, that the distributors rightly thought they could recover their investment in the art houses and in the 16mm after-market. They were correct. MARAT/SADE can only be done on a stage where the actors are on an Equity Waver (no pay) or else subsidized by some organization, as the cost of mounting such a hugely populated show is prohibitive these days, so if you must see the story, try to get hold of the movie.

p, Michael Birkett; d, Peter Brook; w, Peter Weiss, Geoffrey Skelton, Adrian Mitchell (based on the play by Weiss); ph, David Watkin (DeLuxe Color); m, Richard Peaslee; ed, Tom Priestley; prod d, Sally Jacobs; art d, Ted Marshall; cos, Gunilla Palmstierna-Weiss; ch, Malcolm Goddard; makeup, Bunty Phillips.

Historical Drama **(PR:C MPAA:NR)**

PERSECUTION OF HASTA VALENCIA (SEE: NARCO MEN, THE, 1971, Span./Ital.)

PERSONA**** (1967, Swed.) 81m Svensk Filmindustri/Lopert bw (AKA: MASKS)

Bibi Andersson *(Nurse Alma)*, Liv Ullmann *(Actress Elisabeth Vogler)*, Gunnar Bjornstrand *(Mr. Vogler)*, Margareta Krook *(Dr. Lakaren)*, Jorgen Lindstrom *(The Boy)*.

One of Bergman's masterworks, this film is a complex and difficult intellectual challenge to its audience that demands repeated viewings. Bergman's Brechtian techniques constantly reminding us that we are watching a film, pull us deep into the heart of this existential work. Opening with a bare bulb projected on the screen, we then see the countdown leader of the first reel, then short film clips from slapstick comedy and cartoons. Gradually the story gets under way. Ullmann is an actress who mysteriously has stopped speaking during a performance of "Electra." She is put into the care of Andersson, a nurse who takes the patient to a seaside cottage. Using light and shadow, Bergman accentuates the already strong resemblances between the two actresses and takes us into a psychodrama that is more the story of the nurse than of the patient. Andersson pours her soul out to the silent Ullmann in an effort to get her to speak again. Gradually we learn more about her, discovering she is just as troubled as her patient. In a memorable and revealing sequence Andersson and Ullmann are juxtaposed until gradually their faces melt together into one. The film finally comes to an abrupt full circle as we see the film slip out of the projector and once more we are left with the bare bulb. These are true *tour-de-force* roles for both women. Ullmann is only allowed to react with facial and body gestures, while Andersson (who early on describes herself "as a good listener") must speak for the two of them, slipping from sanity to madness in a deceptively subtle manner. This is vintage Bergman, dealing with his constant themes of reality, art, psychology, and life and death. Beautifully photographed by one of his best cameramen, Nykvist, and winner of the Swedish Film Industry's Best Picture Award for 1966-67. 85-minute and 90-minute versions are also in circulation.

p,d&w, Ingmar Bergman; ph, Sven Nykvist; m, Lars-Johan Werle; ed, Ulla Ryghe; prod d, Bibi Lindstrom; art d, Lindstrom; cos, Mago; spec eff, Evald Andersson; makeup, Borje Lundh, Tina Johansson.

Drama **Cas.** **(PR:O MPAA:NR)**

PERSONAL AFFAIR½** (1954, Brit.) 83m TC/UA bw

Gene Tierney *(Kay Barlow)*, Leo Genn *(Stephen Barlow)*, Glynis Johns *(Barbara Vining)*, Pamela Brown *(Evelyn)*, Walter Fitzgerald *(Henry Vining, Editor)*, Megs Jenkins *(Vi Vining)*, Thora Hird *(Mrs. Usher)*, Michael Hordern *(Headmaster)*, Martin Boddey *(Police Inspector)*, Norah Gaussen [Gorsen] *(Phoebe)*, Nanette Newman *(Sally)*.

Johns plays a 17-year-old high schooler who starts trouble when she falls hopelessly in love with her teacher, Genn. The small-town biddies begin their chatter when Johns disappears after Genn's wife, Tierney, confronts the teenager about her obsession. Soon after the girl's departure, her beret is found floating in the river, putting Genn under suspicion of murder. After three days of taking guff from townspeople, Johns returns and says she had been to London to visit some friends and think over her infatuation with Genn. Though everyone is relieved that she is alive and embarrassed that they suspected Genn, life will never be quite the same between the teacher and the community. Though the film suffers a bit from an overly preachy finale, the performances carry it through.

p, Anthony Darnborough; d&w, Anthony Pelissier (based on the play "A Day's Mischief" by Lesley Storm); ph, Reginald Wyer; m, William Alwyn; ed, Frederick Wilson.

Drama **(PR:C MPAA:NR)**

PERSONAL BEST** (1982) 124m Geffen/WB c

Mariel Hemingway *(Chris Cahill)*, Scott Glenn *(Terry Tingloff)*, Patrice Donnelly *(Tory Skinner)*, Kenny Moore *(Denny Stites)*, Jim Moody *(Roscoe Travis)*, Kari Gosswiller *(Penny Brill)*, Jodi Anderson *(Nadia "Pooch" Anderson)*, Maren Seidler *(Tanya)*, Martha Watson *(Sheila)*, Emily Dole *(Maureen)*, Pam Spencer *(Jan)*, Deby LaPlante *(Trish)*, Mitzi McMillin *(Laura)*, Jan Glotzer *(Karen)*, Jan Van Reenen *(Yelovitch)*, Allan Feuerbach *(Zenk)*, Jane Frederick *(Fern Wadkins)*, Cindy Gilbert *(Charlene Benveniste)*, Marlene Harmon *(Pam Burnside)*, Linda Waltman *(Debbie Floyd)*, Cindy Banks *(Kim Stone)*, Milan Tiff *(Willie Lee)*, Earl Bell *(Randy Van Zile)*, Larry Pennell *(Rick Cahill)*, Luana Anders *(Rita Cahill)*, George de la Pena *(Raoul)*, Robert Patten *(Colin Sales)*, Margaret Ellison *(Nellie Bowdeen)*, Charlie Jones, Frank Shorter *(TV Announcers)*, Jim Tracy *(Duane)*, Janet Hake *(Waitress)*, Sharon Brazell *(Hostess)*, Chuck Debus *(Coach)*, Gregory Clayton *(Trainer)*, David Edington *(Waiter)*, Robert Horn *(Water Polo Coach)*, Christopher Vargas *(Water Polo Player)*, Wendell Ray *(PA Announcer)*, Richard Martini *(Meet Manager)*, Len Dawson *(Announcer)*, Clim Jackson, John Smith *(Men's Team Members)*, Anna Biller, Susan Brownell, Desiree Gauthier, Sharon Hatfield, Linda Hightower, Joan Russell, Themis Zambrzycki *(Women's Team Members)*, Dr. Leroy R. Perry, Jr. *(Chiropractor)*.

PERSONAL BEST may have been director-writer Towne's personal worst picture. He tiffed with executive producer Geffen (a record mogul) while making the movie and must have won the battles because what came out on screen is a very personal and self-serving product. It has to do with the training of female athletes for the 1980 Olympics and is somewhat reminiscent of CHARIOTS OF FIRE in the attention to detail. It is a slow enough movie to begin with at 124 minutes, but it feels even slower as Towne trains his slow-motion camera on far too many scenes in an attempt to get us to realize how each muscle in the women's bodies function. Hemingway and Donnelly are both athletes and having a lesbian affair. Hemingway is a newcomer to the life of "Vice Versa," and when she finally breaks up with her older girl friend, she takes up with Moore, a one-time Olympian who offers her another shoulder to weep on. Glenn is the coach, a standard tough-talking character who decries his lot in life of having to train women rather than men. The action sequences are marred by the slo-mo and the dialog goes on for far more minutes than is needed, something that Towne was never guilty of in his other screenplays. Cliches abound and Towne's long-awaited directorial debut turns out to be just another sweat movie with some nudity and shock tossed in to get the "R" rating. Donnelly and Moore were making their film debuts and acquitted themselves well for non-actors. She had been a track star and he had worked as a writer for *Sports Illustrated*. Their contributions are excellent and both could have careers as actors. Good production design from Ron Hobbs, an Englishman who'd worked on many TV shows at Fox before getting his chance in films. Charlie Jones and Frank Shorter, the famed Olympic marathoner, play sports announcers. Many times a screenwriter needs someone else, another brain, to help the story and screenplay. In this case, the Emperor's Clothes worn by Towne were never pointed out to him and the picture is a disappointment. Towne was obviously trying for a different kind of sports story and the goal was admirable in the light of so many similar films which had come before. However, the use of the sex and the nudity made it so different, and the going-on-too-long made it so boring, that it turned off sports fans and movie fans alike and wound up crashing at the box office.

p,d&w, Robert Towne; ph, Michael Chapman, Allan Gornick, Jr. (Technicolor); m, Jack Nitzsche, Jill Fraser; ed, Ned Humphreys, Jere Huggins, Jacqueline Cambas, Walt Mulconery, Bud Smith; prod d, Ron Hobbs; set d, Rick Simpson; cos, Linda Henrikson, Ron Heilman; spec eff, Dale Newkirk; makeup, Christina Smith, Karl Silvera.

Sports Drama **Cas.** **(PR:C-O MPAA:R)**

PERSONAL COLUMN*** (1939, Fr.) 89m Pax bw (PIEGES)

Maurice Chevalier *(Robert Fleury)*, Erich von Stroheim *(Pears)*, Pierre Renoir *(Bremontiere)*, Marie Dea *(Adrienne)*, Andre Brunot *(Tenier)*, Temerson *(Batol)*, Jacques Varennes *(Maxime)*, Madeleine Geoffreoy *(Valerie)*, Rognoni, Andre Nicolle *(Police Inspectors)*, Julienne Paroli *(Housekeeper)*, Henri Bry *(Oglou)*, Mady Berry *(Cook)*, Henri Cremieux, Andre Roanne *(Patrons)*.

After a number of young women have disappeared, the Paris police hire the latest victim's roommate, Dea, to go undercover and investigate the newspaper ads asking for young, single girls (all the missing women had answered such ads in the personal column). Dea arranges interviews with numerous men seeking female employees. After having met with everyone from hotel managers to butlers, all of them proved innocent, Dea meets Chevalier, a nightclub entertainer seeking a new maid. Dea falls in love with the charming singer and the two make plans to marry. Just before the wedding, Chevalier is arrested and charged with the murders of the missing women. Though he claims he is innocent, the evidence looks increasingly grim and he is sentenced to die. Dea, however, is sure he has been framed and manages to ensnare the real murderer. As one of the last films produced in France before WW II, PERSONAL COLUMN had to be smuggled out of its home country and into America. Unfortunately, the American censors made up for what the Nazis missed, when they censored several scenes that detailed some of the more sensational aspects of the murder victims' sex lives. In 1947 PERSONAL COLUMN was remade as LURED.

p, Michel Safra; d, Robert Siodmak; w, Jacques Companeez, Ernest Neuville, Simon Gantillon; ph, R. Voinquel; m, Michel Michelet; ed, Yvonne Martin; art d&set d, Wakevich, Colasson; m/l, "Elle Pleurait Comme Une, Madeleine," Maurice Vander, R. Reville, "Mon Amour," Fredo Gardoni, Jean Chavoit, Willemetz (both sung by Maurice Chevalier).

Drama   (PR:C   MPAA:NR)

PERSONAL COLUMN   (SEE: LURED, 1946)

PERSONAL HONOR   (SEE: HELLO ANNAPOLIS, 1942)

PERSONAL MAID**½   (1931) 74m PAR bw

Nancy Carroll (Nora Ryan), Pat O'Brien (Peter Shea), Gene Raymond (Dick Gary), Hugh O'Connell (Kipp), Mary Boland (Mrs. Otis Gary), George Fawcett (Gary Gary), Ernest Lawford (Barrows), Terry Carroll (Anna Ryan), Jessie Busley (Ma Ryan), Donald Meek (Pa Ryan), Charlotte Wynters (Gwen Gary), Clara Langsaner (Mrs. Wurtz), Lewis Drayton, George Offerman, Francis Fraunie.

Tired of her turbulent home life on New York City's East Side, young Irish girl Carroll decides to fulfill her dreams by becoming a maid in swanky uptown homes. She soon finds herself as the personal maid to a family just as turbulent as her own, only richer. Luckily, her goodhearted presence manages to shape the family up and eventually she moves from maid to mate of the family's eldest son.

p, Lothar Mendes; d, Monta Bell; w, Adelaide Heilbron (based on the novel by Grace Perkins); ph, Karl Freund; ed, Arthur Ellis

Drama   (PR:A   MPAA:NR)

PERSONAL MAID'S SECRET**   (1935) 60m WB bw

Ruth Donnelly (Lizzie), Anita Louise (Her Daughter), Warren Hull (Tom Smith), Margaret Lindsay (Mrs. Smith), Frank Albertson (Her Brother), Arthur Treacher (Bentley's Brother), Ronnie Cosbey (Tom Smith, Jr.), Henry O'Neill, Gordon Elliott, Lillian Kemble Cooper, Maude Turner Gordon.

Donnelly plays a maid who has worked in the richest, most important homes who gives it all up to work for a young, up-and-coming insurance man and his family. Through her influence, the grateful family makes all the right decisions (emotional and financial) and they soon become one of the forces to be reckoned with on the social scene.

p, Bryan Foy; d, Arthur Greville Collins; w, F. Hugh Herbert, Lillie Hayward (based on a story by Lillian Day); ph, Byron Haskin; ed, Thomas Richards; md, Leo F. Forbstein; art d, Carl Weyl; cos, Orry-Kelly.

Drama   (PR:A   MPAA:NR)

PERSONAL PROPERTY**½   (1937) 88m MGM bw (GB: THE MAN IN
                                                        POSSESSION)

Robert Taylor (Raymond Dabney), Jean Harlow (Crystal Wetherby), Reginald Owen (Claude Dabney), Una O'Connor (Clara), E.E. Clive (Mr. Dabney), Henrietta Crosman (Mrs. Dabney), Cora Witherspoon (Mrs. Burns), Barnett Parker (Arthur Trevelyan), Forrester Harvey (Bailiff), Marla Shelton (Catherine Burns), Lionel Braham (Lord Carstairs), William Stack (Policeman), Jimmy Aubrey, Leyland Hodgson, Douglas Gordon (English Cabbies), Arthur Stuart Hull, Charles Requa (English Businessmen), Tom Ricketts (Elderly Man), Billy Bevan (Frank, the Waiter).

This was the penultimate picture for Harlow, who was already suffering from the illness that caused the uremic poisoning which took her life. It was also the only picture which she and Taylor made together. He was the darling of the MGM lot and worked with almost every leading lady in Culver City and had just come off a sensational appearance opposite Greta Garbo in CAMILLE. Making a comedy was just the ticket for Taylor, if only to get out of the tubercular mood of his last film, and this was a nice way to do that. Hard to believe but Van Dyke (known as "One-Take" because he moved so quickly) shot the entire movie in less than two weeks! Harlow is an American widow in England and in deep trouble paying her bills. Taylor is the scion of an important family, a devil-may-care playboy who does a short stretch in jail for having sold a car that he didn't own. His father, Clive, and his brother, Owen, don't think he can ever reform his ways. Harlow's house and personal property are being attached by creditors and Taylor gets the job of watching the place to make certain she doesn't try to move any of her possessions out in the dead of night. Harlow would like to marry Owen, even though she doesn't love him, in the hope that a wealthy marriage will erase her debts, thinking she can always shed him later. The truth is that Taylor's family is just as insolvent and Owen, thinking that Harlow is rich, wants to marry her to help their straits. Taylor knows what's happening and revels in his knowledge, going so far as playing the role of a butler at a party Harlow tosses for her prospective hubby. Owen sees Taylor and demands Harlow sack him, something she can't do as he is there on orders from the sheriff, although she doesn't tell Owen that. Owen hands Taylor a few pounds to leave. The wedding day dawns but the sheriff and the moving men enter to get all the expensive gear in the residence. Owen learns that Harlow is even more broke than he is so he makes a quick exit. Taylor and Harlow have been falling in love all through the movie and decide to cement that by hopping aboard the truck carrying the furniture and finding the nearest man of the cloth to now pronounce them man and wife. Not that much laughter but some good shots of Harlow in revealing clothes and one "beefcake" sequence with Taylor in a bathtub which was presumably put in to give the ladies' hearts something to flutter over. This is a remake of the 1931 film THE MAN IN POSSESSION.

p, John W. Considine, Jr.; d, W.S. Van Dyke II; w, Hugh Mills, Ernest Vajda (based on the play "The Man in Possession" by H.M. Harwood); ph, William Daniels; m, Franz Waxman; ed, Ben Lewis; art d, Cedric Gibbons, Henry McAfee; set d, Edwin B. Willis; cos, Dolly Tree.

Comedy   (PR:A   MPAA:NR)

PERSONAL SECRETARY**   (1938) 61m UNIV bw

William Gargan (Mark Farrell), Joy Hodges (Gale Rogers), Andy Devine ("Snoop" Lewis), Ruth Donnelly ("Grumpy"), Samuel S. Hinds (Alan Lemke), Frances Robinson (June Reese), Florence Roberts (Mrs. Farrell), Kay Linaker (Flo Sampson), Matty Fain ("Slim" Logan), Selmer Jackson (Blackmere), Jack Carr (Jack Murphy), Louise Stanley (Dixie Green).

Gargan and Hodges play rival columnists constantly at war. Gargan (who is patterned after Walter Winchell) is the big cheese and through his radio broadcasts and print columns, he consistently proclaims the guilt or innocence of the latest sensational murder trial suspects. Hodges is the underdog looking for a way to deflate Gargan, so she works as his personal secretary so she can collect enough information to embarrass him. Surprisingly, the couple fall in love and eventually get married while they work to prove socialite Linaker did not kill her philandering husband. Believe it or not, their dog provides the all-important clue.

p, Max H. Golden; d, Otis Garrett; w, Betty Laidlaw, Robert Lively, Charles Grayson (based on the story "The Comet" by Laidlaw, Lively); ph, Stanely Cortez; ed, Frank Gross; md, Charles Previn.

Drama   (PR:A   MPAA:NR)

PERSONALITY**   (1930) 66m COL bw

Sally Starr (Lil Morse), Johnny Arthur (Sandy Jenkins), Lee D. Kohlmar (Mr. Himmelschlosser), Vivian Oakland (Mrs. Keller), John T. Murray (Mr. Keller), Blanche Frederici (Ma), Frank Hammond (Pa), Buck Black (Junior), George Pearce (Mr. Abbott).

Arthur stars as an ambitious young man who marries his sweetheart, Starr, and proceeds to con his way into a high paying job for which he really is not qualified. Seeking to provide a ritzy life style for his new bride, Arthur buys all their furniture and appliances on credit. Tragedy strikes when the firm learns of Arthur's deception and gives him the boot. Soon the collection agency arrives and removes all the furnishings from the couple's home. Forced to sell vacuum cleaners to make ends meet, Arthur gloomily takes to the streets, while Starr goes home to her parents to wait for him to strike it rich. Contrived ending sees Arthur's old boss giving him back his old job with a raise, no less.

d, Victor Heerman; w, Gladys Lehman, Heerman; ph, Ted Tetzlaff; ed, David Berg; art d, Harrison Wiley.

Drama   (PR:A   MPAA:NR)

PERSONALITY KID, THE**   (1934) 67m WB bw

Pat O'Brien (Ritzy McCarthy), Glenda Farrell (Joan McCarthy), Claire Dodd (Patricia Merrill), Henry O'Neill (Jay Stephens), Robert Gleckler (Gavin), Thomas E. Jackson (Bill Rankin, Sports Writer), Arthur Vinton (McPhail), Clarence Muse (Shamrock), Clay Clement (Duncan King), George Cooper (Tiny), George Pat Collins (Ed), Pudgie White (Louie), Jack Perry (Sailor White), Harry Seymour (Referee), Mary Russell (Waitress), Mushy Callahan (Biff Sullivan), Paul Power (Freddie), Marvin Shechter (Kearney), Phil Regan (Murray, Sports Writer), Billy Arnold (Sam, Sullivan's Manager), Howard Russell (Doctor), Margaret Morris (Secretary), Landers Stevens (Executive), Jack Kennedy (Proprietor), Sailor Vincent (Spike), Bess Flowers (Nurse), Howard Hickman (Doctor), Al Hill (Al), Heinie Conklin (Drinker), Renee Whitney (Party Guest).

By 1934, the boxing film had already slipped into the unsavory world of ho-hum cliche and THE PERSONALITY KID did little to stem the tide. O'Brien stars as an egotistical pug who lets his prizefighting success go to his head. Thinking he is hot stuff, O'Brien dumps on his wife and goes out with fancy ladies. When he discovers that his wife had arranged for him to box only softies, O'Brien gets disgusted with her and leaves home. Eventually the couple get back together when his wife announces she is pregnant and he returns home. Sappy, contrived, and indifferently executed; even the boxing scenes in the film are poorly staged, with the performers obviously pulling their punches.

d, Alan Crosland; w, F. Hugh Herbert, David Boehm, Erwin Gelsey (based on the story "One Man Woman" by Gene Towne, C. Graham Baker); ph, William Rees; ed, Terry Morse; art d, John Hughes; cos, Orry-Kelly.

Drama   (PR:A   MPAA:NR)

PERSONALITY KID*½   (1946) 62m COL bw

Anita Louise (Laura Howard), Michael Duane (Harry Roberts), Ted Donaldson (Davey Roberts), Barbara Brown (Mrs. Roberts), Bobby Larson (Albert Partridge), Edythe Elliott (Mrs. Howard), Paul Maxey (Mr. Partridge), Martin Garralaga (Melendez), Oscar O'Shea (Officer O'Brien), Harlan Briggs (Mr. Howard), Regina Wallace (Mrs. Partridge).

Sugary kiddie fare starring Donaldson as a cute tyke who finds a donkey and decides to keep it as a pet. Most of the "heartwarming" humor comes from Donaldson's efforts to housebreak the burro, despite his family's objections. Meanwhile, older brother Duane is trying to make it in the commercial photography business, and succeeds when he takes a charming shot of the kid and his donkey to win a big contest. Pure tedium for anyone over the age of two.

p, Wallace MacDonald; d, George Sherman; w, Lewis Helmer Herman, William B. Sackheim (based on a story by Cromwell MacKechnie); ph, Henry Freulich; ed, Richard Fantl; md, Mischa Bakaleinikoff; art d, Cary Odell, set d, James Crowe.

Drama   (PR:AA   MPAA:NR)

PERSONALS, THE***   (1982) 90m New World c

Bill Schoppert (Bill), Karen Landry (Adrienne), Paul Eiding (Paul), Michael Laskin (David), Vicki Dakil (Shelly), Chris Forth (Jennifer), Patrick O'Brien (Jay).

A surprisingly well made, independently produced (in Minneapolis), romantic comedy starring Schoppert as a middle-aged, balding loser whose wife leaves him for another man. Pushed by his buddy into the singles scene, Schoppert has a series of funny and touching dates, most of which end in disaster. Eventually he falls in love with a fresh-faced young actress, Landry, but she is married and he becomes the third wheel. A good little film.

p, Patrick Wells; d&w, Peter Markle; ph, Markle, Greg Cummins (DuArt Color); m, Will Sumner; ed, Stephen E. Rivkin.

Romance/Comedy   **Cas.**   **(PR:C MPAA:PG)**

PERSONS IN HIDING, SEE BACK PAGE FOR PERSONS IN HIDING

PERSONS UNKNOWN   (SEE: BIG DEAL ON MADONNA STREET, 1958, Ital.)

PERSUADER, THE**   (1957) 72m World Wide/AA bw

William Talman (Matt Bonham/Mark Bonham), James Craig (Bick Justin), Kristine Miller (Kathryn Bonham), Darryl Hickman (Toby Bonham), Georgia Lee (Cora Nicklin), Alvy Moore (Willy Williams), Gregory Walcott (Jim Cleery), Rhoda Williams (Nell Landis), Paul Engle (Paul Bonham), Jason Johnson (Morse Fowler), Nolan Leary (Dan), John Milford (Clint), Frank Richards (Steve), Joyce Compton, Leilani Sorenson, Wendy Stuart.

A routine western starring Talman as a preacher who rides into town only to learn that his brother has been killed by rotten town-boss Craig because he would not knuckle under. Craig dominates the townsfolk, who choose to look the other way. Hickman, Talman's nephew, has turned hard and cold and is determined to get revenge. Talman, using the word of the Lord, preaches strength and dignity, eventually spurring the people to run Craig out of town. While THE PERSUADER is really nothing special, it spawned a whole series of religious westerns aimed at Bible Belt distribution.

p&d, Dick Ross; w, Curtis Kenyon, Ross; ph, Ralph A. Woolsey; m, Ralph Carmichael; ed, Eugene Pendleton; md, Carmichael; art d, Walter Keller; m/l, "The Pretender," Carmichael (sung by James Joyce).

Western   **(PR:A MPAA:NR)**

PERVYY DEN MIRA   (SEE: DAY THE WAR ENDED, THE, 1961, USSR)

PETE KELLY'S BLUES***   (1955) 95m Mark VII Ltd./WB c

Jack Webb (Pete Kelly, Narrator), Janet Leigh (Ivy Conrad), Edmond O'Brien (Fran McCarg), Peggy Lee (Rose Hopkins), Andy Devine (George Tenell), Lee Marvin (Al Gannaway), Ella Fitzgerald (Maggie Jackson), Martin Milner (Joey Firestone), Jayne Mansfield (Cigarette Girl), Than Wyenn (Rudy), Herb Ellis (Bedido), John Dennis (Guy Bettenhouser), Mort Marshall (Cootie Jacobs), Nesdon Booth (Squat Henchman), William Lazerus (Dako), Dick Cathcart (Cornetist), Matty Matlock (Clarinetist), Moe Schneider (Trombonist), Eddie Miller (Saxophonist), George Van Eps (Guitarist), Nick Fatool (Drummer), Ray Sherman (Pianist), Jud de Naut (Bass Player), Snub Pollard (Waiter in Rudy's), Joe Venuti, Harper Goff, Perry Bodkin (Featured Members of the Tuxedo Band), The Israelite Spiritual Church Choir of New Orleans.

Webb directs, produces, and stars in this interesting tale of jazz and gangsters in prohibition era Kansas City. Opening with the funeral of a black cornet player, the film moves on to show how Webb's combo is threatened when gangster O'Brien decides to diversify his operations by extorting agent fees out of the musicians. Webb and his boys try to stand up to him, but when drummer Milner is killed, Webb goes out for revenge, and after a shootout in a nightclub, O'Brien's gunman crashes through the ceiling onto the dance floor, taking the mirrored globe with him. Webb's direction is craftsman-like and exciting in a blunt way, but his performance is stiff and hardly different from his Joe Friday character from the DRAGNET movie and TV series. Leigh is only okay as his girl friend, and Marvin is quite good as his wise-cracking best friend. By far the best reason to check out this late movie perennial, though, is the impressive collection of top jazzmen like Matty Matlock, Moe Schneider, and George Van Eps. Also contributing are Ella Fitzgerald, who sings two songs and does a small supporting turn, and Peggy Lee, surprisingly effective as a singer on the skids and on the bottle who is eventually beaten into insanity by O'Brien, a performance that garnered her an Oscar nomination. The film has a certain edge of realism and unsentimentality not usually found in films about jazz before this time (the bars where the band plays are crowded and smoky, and the drinks are probably overpriced) and the music is good. Webb's cornet playing was dubbed by Dick Cathcart. Music includes "Pete Kelly's Blues" (Sammy Cahn, Ray Heindorf, sung by Ella Fitzgerald), "Sing a Rainbow," "He Needs Me" (Arthur Hamilton), "Somebody Loves Me," "Sugar" (Maceo Pinkard, Sidney Mitchell, Edna Alexander, sung by Peggy Lee), "I Never Knew" (Gus Kahn, Ted Fiorito), "Hard-Hearted Hannah" (Jack Yellen, Milton Ager, Bob Bigelow, Charles Bates, sung by Ella Fitzgerald), "Bye, Bye Blackbird" (Mort Dixon, Ray Henderson), "What Can I Say After I Say I'm Sorry" (Walter Donaldson, Abe Lyman), "Oh, Didn't He Ramble" (Bob Cole, J. Rosamond Johnson [Will Handy]).

p&d, Jack Webb; w, Richard L. Breen; ph, Hal Rosson (CinemaScope, WarnerColor); m, Ray Heindorf, Sammy Cahn, Arthur Hamilton; ed, Robert M. Leeds; prod d, Harper Goff; art d, Feild Gray; set d, John Sturtevant; cos, Howard Shoup; makeup, Gordon Bau.

Crime Drama   **(PR:C MPAA:NR)**

PETE 'N' TILLIE***½   (1972) 100m UNIV c

Walter Matthau (Pete Seltzer), Carol Burnett (Tillie Schlaine), Geraldine Page (Gertrude), Barry Nelson (Burt), Rene Auberjonois (Jimmy Twitchell), Lee H. Montgomery (Robbie Seltzer), Henry Jones (Mr. Tucker), Kent Smith (Father Keating), Philip Bourneuf (Dr. Willett), Whit Bissell (Minister), Timothy Blake (Lucy Lund), James McAllister (Baby Robbie Seltzer).

A very unusual love story with comedy and drama, this owed a bit to PENNY

SERENADE, which had the same sort of subject matter but not the same treatment. The unfortunate title sounded like a sitcom or an old comic strip or one of those pornographic cartoon books that kids looked at 40 years previously. It was only Burnett's second film, after waiting almost 10 years since her small role in WHO'S BEEN SLEEPING IN MY BED? She was very much under control and engaged in none of the mugging and hamminess that made her such a TV star. This was both good and bad. Had she overplayed, there would have been accusations of her not being able to sustain a characterization, so she chose to go for reality and her antics were missed. It's like hiring Julio Iglesias to act and not letting him sing. Burnett is on her way to becoming an old maid when her pals, Page and Nelson, toss a party at their San Francisco residence and use it to introduce her to Matthau, a man in the same domestic situation. He's a compulsive punster who works in motivational research, and although she's not all that impressed by his verbal byplay, she does allow him to take her home to her place, where they share a drink, but nothing else. He begins to woo her with a series of dinners at out-of-the-way (but not necessarily romantic) restaurants, and when they finally climb into bed together, it's wonderful. After a while, Matthau gets a raise and a better position and Burnett gives him an ultimatum: either get married or forget it. They wed and she has a son whom Matthau dotes upon and raises in a world filled with gags, puns, old movies, and the shared glee of pulling practical jokes on their neighbor, Jones, who always falls for them. Matthau begins a brief fling with Blake, a pretty office colleague, then Burnett goes to meet the woman and manages to convince her that the affair will lead nowhere. Their son, Montgomery, becomes a victim of leukemia and has less than 12 months to live. They don't tell him what's wrong but lavish much on the boy, including a camping holiday in the nearby mountains. Eventually, as they knew would happen, Montgomery dies and both are understandably devastated. Half a year goes by and Burnett and Matthau continue their mourning until they finally go out one evening to a party at Page and Nelson's, the same place where they met 10 years before. Matthau forces himself to be jolly, even going so far as to make a pass at one of the guests. Burnett and Matthau begin to drift apart and she considers a conversion to Catholicism in order to find some meaning in her life and their son's death. Matthau moves out and Burnett doesn't make any attempt to stop him, preferring to seclude herself. Page, trying to get Burnett out of her funk, asks her friend to join her while working on a charity drive. Page has to get an official police permit to do her benevolent work and that requires her to state her name, address, and age. Page has been keeping her true years a secret, and when asked the question, she can't handle it and faints on the spot. Burnett and Page get into an argument that winds up in an actual fight as the women batter each other with purses, water hoses, and whatever is handy. (It's about here that the picture opts for farce, and loses just about everyone.) All the while, Burnett has had a male friend, Auberjonois, a gay man who has always been there to give balm and solace, and he realizes she needs someone to be with, so he suggests that they might get married, with no sex, and become companions. Burnett is touched by his proposal and considers it briefly. Just as Burnett has recovered her mental and physical strength and is getting ready to return to her life, Matthau arrives and confesses that he has not had a moment's happiness since they drifted apart. They discuss the reasons for their estrangement and decide to have another go at it as he walks her to his car and a return to the life that once they led. The admixture of happiness and grief, laughter and sobs, reality and farce is what makes this film such an admirable attempt. It never quite settles in on what it is, but while it's playing, just about everyone in every audience can find something to like. Epstein and Page received Oscar nominations for their efforts and the picture made money, a tribute to moviegoers' taste, because the movie was not the kind of story that audiences were clamoring to see in the early 1970s.

p, Julius J. Epstein; d, Martin Ritt; w, Epstein (based on the novella Witch's Milk by Peter De Vries); ph, John A. Alonzo (Panavision, Technicolor); m, John Williams; ed, Frank Bracht; art d, George Webb; set d, Joe Stone, John Austin; cos, Edith Head.

Comedy/Drama   **(PR:A-C MPAA:PG)**

PETER IBBETSON***½   (1935) 88m PAR bw

Gary Cooper (Peter Ibbetson), Ann Harding (Mary, Duchess of Towers), John Halliday (Duke of Towers), Ida Lupino (Agnes), Douglas Dumbrille (Col. Forsythe), Virginia Weidler (Mimsey), Dickie Moore (Gogo), Doris Lloyd (Mrs. Dorian), Elsa Buchanan (Mme. Pasquier), Christian Rub (Maj. Duquesnoit), Donald Meek (Mr. Slade), Gilbert Emery (Wilkins), Marguerite Namara (Mme. Ginghi), Elsa Prescott (Katherine), Marcelle Corday (Maid), Adrienne D'Ambricourt (Nun), Theresa Maxwell Conover (Sister of Mercy), Colin Tapley, Clive Morgan, Ambrose Barker, Thomas Monk (Clerks), Blanche Craig (The Countess), Stanley Andrews (Judge).

There are some, including Luis Bunuel, who think that this picture is "one of the ten best films ever made." It's good, but not that good. The 1891 novel was first filmed as a silent, FOREVER, with Elsie Ferguson and Wallace Reid. Then it was made into a stage play which starred John and Lionel Barrymore and Constance Collier (who also adapted the play script for this movie). Noted musicologist Deems Taylor also turned it into an opera. It's surrealistic, mystical, and moody, and suffers only from the miscasting of Cooper in the title role. Well produced, it was a hit in Europe but did not fare that well in the U.S., although it is still shown in art houses from time to time. Cooper is an architect who visits Paris and goes to a huge garden area where he used to play as a child with another youngster. The garden is now heavily weeded and in a state of disarray. Halliday, a Duke, has hired Cooper's company to build new housing for his horses on the family property. Cooper gets the assignment from his bosses but has creative disagreements with Halliday's wife, Harding, and he is soon sacked from the job. That doesn't last very long, and she allows him to exercise his abilities as they develop a close friendship. Halliday mistakes their camaraderie for love and accuses Cooper of having an affair with Harding, then fires him. It is here that Cooper betrays an old habit, something so unique that Harding recognizes him as the boy with whom she played in the garden mentioned earlier. Knowing this, Harding and Cooper embrace, thereby sending Halliday into a jealous rage. Harding placates Halliday by explaining that they were childhood buddies and that apparently calms the angry peer. After finishing his work, Cooper is about to depart and once again embraces Harding, still in a friendly fashion. Just then, Halliday walks in with a pistol at the ready. Cooper thinks Halliday will shoot him so he tosses a chair at the man in self-defense. The weight of the chair kills Halliday. Cooper is tried, convicted, and sentenced to life imprisonment for having murdered Halliday. While incarcerated, Cooper begins dreaming of the days of yore (Cooper and Harding are played by Moore and Weidler as children) and shouts in his sleep. The prison guards are angered and, believing Cooper to be a troublemaker, beat him badly and injure his spine. He's semi-comatose when he sees Harding walk into his dank cell. She says that if they cannot be together in life, then they always will be in his dreams and that he must have faith in that. She will send him a token to prove her contention. It will be a ring he can always treasure. Cooper doesn't believe his dream but when the ring arrives the following day, he is convinced that she had come to him. Years go by and Cooper and Harding grow old in life but remain young in his dreams. She dies, telling him that they will be able to meet again in their beloved garden as soon as he wants to join her. Cooper dies and they are united. It is the dream sequences, which have a reality of their own, that set this apart from the usual parapsychological story and give it the interest that the Surrealists saw. Collier, who was such a delightful actress and appeared in many films, including ROPE, worked on the adaptation, then it was given to Lawrence and Young for the screenplay. Mayer and Meehan came in later to add additional scenes. Lupino, as Cooper's girl friend who loses him to Harding, doesn't have much to do but what she does, she does well. PETER IBBETSON is a story that transcends time and space and proves that love is stronger than everything.

p, Louis D. Lighton; d, Henry Hathaway; w, Vincent Lawrence, Waldemar Young, Constance Collier, John Meehan, Edwin Justus Mayer (based on the novel by George du Maurier and the play by John Nathaniel Raphael); ph, Charles Lang; m, Ernst Toch; ed, Stuart Heisler; md, Nat W. Finston; art d, Hans Dreier, Robert Usher; spec eff, Gordon Jennings.

Romance/Fantasy **(PR:A MPAA:NR)**

PETER PAN**** (1953) 76m Disney/RKO c

voices: Bobby Driscoll *(Peter Pan)*, Kathryn Beaumont *(Wendy)*, Hans Conried *(Capt. Hook/ Mr. Darling)*, Bill Thompson *(Mr. Smee)*, Heather Angel *(Mrs. Darling)*, Paul Collins *(Michael Darling)*, Tommy Luske *(John)*, Candy Candido *(Indian Chief)*, Tom Conway *(Narrator)*.

PETER PAN is a wonderful movie. The score is not as good as the one Mary Martin sang in the 1950s Broadway version, but it's like comparing grapes to watermelons. Disney knew as early as 1935 that this would make a fine animated film. In 1939, he contacted the heirs to the Barrie estate (The Great Ormond Street Hospital in London had been granted literary trusteeship of the play as part of Barrie's will) and they agreed to allow him to film Barrie's classic. Then the war began and Disney temporarily shelved plans for the movie. It cost more than $4 million to make, a huge amount. Lest you wonder why it came in so high, you should know that Disney filmed a live-action version of the movie first so his artists would have something to base their sketches upon. Once that was done, the drawing began. Dancer Roland Dupree was Peter and Hans Conried, who also did the voices of the father and Hook, dressed up in the costume of the captain. Too bad no one but the Disney employees has ever seen that version. Barrie's durable and delightful story has had many incarnations and has continued to be revived regularly with many different musical stars, including Sandy Duncan. Conried is the father of the house and annoyed that daughter Beaumont insists on telling stories to the other children about a mythical boy known as Peter Pan (Driscoll). He orders Beaumont and the dog out of the nursery; then he and his wife, Angel, leave for a night on the town. He doesn't believe that such a creature as Beaumont speaks of exists, but after the couple depart, Driscoll and Tinker Bell magically appear. It turns out that Beaumont had captured Driscoll's shadow and now the boy wants it back. The other kids (Collins, Luske) awaken and Driscoll agrees to take them all to a wonderful place called Never Neverland where they won't have to grow up. Tinker Bell gets annoyed at Driscoll's attentions to Beaumont and doesn't think it's such a good notion. Despite that, they all go off to Never Neverland, where they get involved in a series of incidents. Conried (Captain Hook) wants to nab Driscoll (this was the first time anywhere that Peter was actually played by a boy) and kidnap an Indian princess, but Driscoll foils that. Now Conried captures Tinker Bell and wants the creature to confess Driscoll's secret hideaway. She does and Conried puts an explosive there but Tinker Bell gets away in the blast. Meanwhile, Conried has caught Beaumont, Luske, and Collins and has them on his ship. There's a battle between Driscoll and Conried which ends when the captain falls over the side of the ship and is chased by the crocodile that had bitten off the captain's hand and has been waiting for the rest of him since then. "Pixie Dust" is applied to the ship by Tinker Bell and the kids are returned home. When their parents walk in, they excitedly tell the story of what they've done. Their father wonders and questions, then looks out at the sky and sees the shadow of the ship (as a cloud) across the moon and remembers that he saw the same thing many many years before. In all previous versions of PETER PAN, the audience is asked to clap their hands to revive Tinker Bell after the explosion. That was not done here, as it's basically a stage technique, although it was used in the Betty Bronson silent version of the movie. Lots of laughs, fabulous animation, and excellent voicing by the actors. Songs include "The Elegant Captain Hook," "The Second Star to the Right," "What Makes the Red Man Red?" "You Can Fly, You Can Fly," "Your Mother and Mine" (Sammy Cahn, Sammy Fain), "A Pirate's Life" (Oliver Wallace, Erdman Penner),"March of the Lost Boys (Tee Dum Tee Dee)" (Wallace, Ted Sears, Winston Hibler), "Never Smile at a Crocodile" (Frank Churchill, Jack Lawrence).

p, Walt Disney; d, Hamilton Luske, Clyde Geronimi, Wilfred Jackson; w, Ted Sears, Bill Peet, Joe Rinaldi, Erdman Penner, Winston Hibler, Milt Banta, Ralph Wright (based on the play by Sir James M. Barrie); ph, (Technicolor); m, Oliver Wallace, Edward H. Plumb; directing animators, Milt Kahl, Franklin Thomas, Wolfgang Reitherman, Ward Kimball, Eric Larson, Oliver Johnston, Jr., Marc Davis, John Lounsbery, Les Clark, Norman Ferguson; color and styling, Mary Blair, Claude Coats, John Hench, Donald Da Gradi; backgrounds, Ray Huffine, Art Riley, Albert Dempster, Eyvind Earle, Ralph Hylett, Thelma Witmer, Dick Anthony, Brice Mack; layout, Mac Stewart, Tom Codrick, A. Kendall O'Connor, Charles Philippi, Hugh Hennesy, Ken Anderson, Al Zinnen, Lance Nolley, Thor Putnam, Don Griffith; character animators, Hal King, Cliff Nordberg, Hal Ambro, Don Lusk, Ken O'Brien, Marvin Woodward, Art Stevens, Eric Cleworth, Fred Moore, Bob Carlson, Harvey Toombs, Judge Whitaker, Bill Justice, Hugh Fraser, Jerry Hathcock, Clair Weeks; effects animation, George Rowley, Blaine Gibson, Joshua Meador, Dan MacManus.

Animation/Children **(PR:AAA MPAA:G)**

PETER RABBIT AND TALES OF BEATRIX POTTER*** (1971, Brit.) 90m EMI/MGM c (GB: TALES OF BEATRIX POTTER)

Frederick Ashton *(Mrs. Tiggy-Winkle)*, Alexander Grant *(Pigling Bland/Peter Rabbit)*, Julie Wood *(Mrs. Tittlemouse)*, Keith Martin *(Johnny Town Mouse)*, Ann Howard *(Jemina Puddle-Duck)*, Robert Mead *(Fox)*, Gary Grant *(Alexander Town Mouse)*, Sally Ashby *(Mrs. Pettitoes/Tabitha Twitchit)*, Brenda Last *(Black Berkshire Pig)*, Wayne Sleep *(Tom Thumb/Squirrel Nutkin)*, Michael Coleman *(Jeremy Fisher)*, Lesley Collier *(Hunca Munca)*, Leslie Edwards *(Owl/Mr. Brown)*, Carole Ainsworth, Avril Bergen, Jill Cooke, Graham Fletcher, Bridget Goodricke, Suzanna Raymond, Rosemary Taylor, Anita Young *(Squirrels/Country Mice)*, Erin Geraghty *(Beatrix Potter)*, Joan Benham *(The Nurse)*, Wilfred Babbage *(Cox the Butler)*, The Royal Ballet Corps.

Based on the stories of Potter, the memorable creator of Peter Rabbit and his friends. Walt Disney Studios wanted to do her stories for a long time, but Bryan Forbes succeeded in bringing them to the screen. The stories were set to music and performed by the Royal Ballet. The film follows the life of the withdrawn Potter and how she blossoms when the toy animals in her room come to life and begin to take over. The film was a tremendous success in Britain, hitting it big with the younger set and with adults who grew up reading her books. Costumes stole the show, particularly the human-like masks created by Rostislav Douboujinsky. Ashton's choreography is also a standout.

p, Richard Goodwin; d, Reginald Mills; w, Goodwin, Christine Edzard (based on stories and characters created by Beatrix Potter); ph, Austin Dempster (Technicolor); ed, John Rushton; md, John Lanchberry; prod d, Edzard; art d, John Howell; cos, Edzard, ch, Frederick Ashton.

Ballet **(PR:AA MPAA:G)**

PETER THE CRAZY (SEE: PIERROT LE FOU, 1965, Fr./Ital.)

PETERSEN½** (1974, Aus.) 97m Hexagon/AE (AKA: "JOCK" PETERSEN)

Jack Thompson *(Tony "Jock" Petersen)*, Jacki Weaver *(Suzie Petersen)*, Joey Hohenfels *(Debbie)*, Amanda Hunt *(Carol)*, George Mallaby *(Executive)*, Arthur Dignam *(Charles Kent)*, David Phillips *(Heinz)*, Helen Morse *(Jane)*, Christine Amor *(Annie)*, Wendy Hughes *(Patricia Kent)*, Ann Pendlebury *(Peggy)*, Dina Mann *(Robin)*, Charles Tingwell *(Tony's Father)*, Belinda Giblin *(Moira)*, John Ewart *(Pete)*, Karen Petersen *(Teresa)*, John Orcsik *(Walter)*, Sandy McGregor *(Marg)*, Syd Conabere *(Annie's Father)*, Charmain Jacka *(Annie's Mother)*, Robert Hewitt, Lindsay Smith, Tim Robertson, Graham Mathrick *(Bikers)*, Moira Farrow *(Mrs. Blunden)*, Bill Bennett, Cliff Ellen *(Bushmen)*, David Ravenswood *(Dr. Fredericks)*, Tom Lake *(Library Attendant)*, Lynne Flanagan *(Car Yard Customer)*, Sheila Florence *(Tony's Mother)*, Warwick Randall *(Hotel Manager)*, Barry Barkla *(Police Sergeant)*, Alan Lee *(Police Constable)*, Sandy Gore *(Surburban Housewife)*.

A fairly well-written Australian film featuring Thompson as a dashing married man who gives up electrical work to go to college for a degree in the arts. One suspects his true motivation is to bed some young college girls, and he starts an affair with Hughes, an English tutor and wife of associate professor of English Dignam. This leads to all sorts of complications involving Thompson's grades (Dignam is his advisor), his wife, and his children. Sensitively written and played, PETERSEN is an interesting character study.

p&d, Tim Burstall; w, David Williamson; ph, Robin Copping; m, Peter Best; ed, David Bilcock; art d, Bill Hutchinson.

Drama **(PR:C MPAA:R)**

PETERVILLE DIAMOND, THE½** (1942, Brit.) 85m FN-WB bw

Anne Crawford *(Teri)*, Donald Stewart *(Charles)*, Renee Houston *(Lady Margaret)*, Oliver Wakefield *(The Robber)*, Charles Heslop *(Dilfallow)*, Bill [William] Hartnell *(Joseph)*, Felix Aylmer *(President)*, Charles Victor *(Dan)*, Joss Ambler *(Police Chief)*, Paul Sheridan *(Luis)*, Jeremy Hawk, Julian Somers, Rosamund Greenwood, Leo de Pokorny.

While on vacation with husband Stewart in Mexico, neglected wife Crawford grows bored when all her spouse can think of is business. To pacify her, Stewart buys Crawford the beautiful Peterville Diamond. Word of this reaches jewel thief Wakefield, who begins to woo the neglected woman in order to get his hands on the gem. An enjoyable light comedy, with some witty repartee.

p, Max Milner; d, Walter Forde; w, Gordon Wellesley, Brock Williams; ph, Basil Emmott.

Comedy **(PR:A MPAA:NR)**

PETE'S DRAGON** (1977) 134m Disney/BV c

Helen Reddy (Nora), Jim Dale (Dr. Terminus), Mickey Rooney (Lampie), Red Buttons (Hoagy), Shelley Winters (Lena Gogan), Sean Marshall (Pete), Jean Kean (Miss Taylor), Jim Backus (The Mayor), Charles Tyner (Merle), Gary Morgan (Grover), Jeff Conway (Willie), Cal Bartlett (Paul), Charlie Callas (Voice of Elliott), Walter Barnes (Captain), Robert Easton (Store Proprietor), Roger Price (Man with Visor), Robert Foulk (Old Sea Captain), Ben Wrigley (Egg Man), Joe Ross (Cement Man), Al Checco, Henry Slate, Jack Collins (Fishermen).

PETE'S DRAGON heralded the decline of Disney. Populated with a cast of Hollywood misfits and crammed with lackluster and forgettable musical numbers, PETE'S DRAGON is set in turn-of-the-century Maine and tells the oft-told tale of a lonely, orphaned little boy, Marshall, who runs away from his nasty foster family and encounters a charming dragon named Elliott (animated of course). While Elliot is a clever creation (he can disappear at will) and is sure to delight audiences, the story is boring and tedious whenever he is not on screen. Eventually Marshall is found by Reddy, the daughter of a lighthouse keeper, and finds happiness. The sets and production values are as fine as ever, but the film lacks imagination, nerve, or guts. While Disney was certainly capable of making some mature, insightful, and downright terrifying films for children that realistically dealt with childhood fears and concerns, by the time PETE'S DRAGON came along the company lacked the imagination and desire to make challenging children's films so instead wallowed in indifferently made, forgettable, maudlin tripe. Songs by Al Kasha and Joel Hirschhorn include "Candle on the Water," "I Saw a Dragon," "It's Not Easy," "Every Little Piece," "The Happiest Home in These Hills," "Brazzle Dazzle Day," "Boo Boo Bopbopbop (I Love You Too)," "There's Room for Everyone," "Passamashloddy," and "Bill of Sale." This was cut by 30 minutes for a 1984 release; a 121-minute version also exists.

p, Ron Miller, Jerome Courtland; d, Don Chaffey; w, Malcolm Marmorstein (based on a story by Seton I. Miller, S. S. Field); ph, Frank Phillips (Technicolor); m, Irwin Kostal; ed, Gordon D. Brenner; md, Kostal; art d, John B. Mansbridge, Jack Martin Smith; set d, Lucien M. Hafley; cos, Bill Thomas; spec eff, Eustace Lycett, Art Cruickshank, Danny Lee, ch, Onna White; animation, Ken Anderson, Don Bluth, Joe Hale, Dorse A. Lanpher.

Fantasy   Cas.   (PR:AAA MPAA:G)

PETEY WHEATSTRAW zero (1978) 93m Tronsue/Generation International c

Rudy Ray Moore, Jimmy Lynch, Leroy & Skillet, Eboni Wryte, Wildman Steve, G. Tito Shaw, Lady Reed, Doc Watson.

Another filmic outing for obnoxious comedian Moore (known as "Mr. Dolemite") which further demonstrates his talents for foul-mouthed, unfunny, and trashy characterizations. This one combines voodoo, karate, and violence when Moore leaves his humble "Uncle Tom's Cabin" beginnings to become a comedian. He shows up in a small town and becomes embroiled in a comedian gang war when a rival, mob-backed, comedy team seeks to eliminate him. The mobsters kill a young boy and then slaughter the kid's mourners at the funeral. Believe it or not, Satan arrives and agrees to return everyone to life if Moore will marry his (Satan's) hideous daughter in order to produce a grandchild. Moore agrees and is rewarded with a magic cane. Using the all-powerful cane, Moore gets his revenge on the comedy team and then tries to beat the devil by skipping town. Satan, however, sends his toadies out to get Moore and they chase him. Total garbage.

p, Theadore Toney; d&w, Cliff Roquemore; ph, Nickolas Von Sternberg (Pacific Film Lab Color); ed, Cecelia Hall, Jack Tucker.

Comedy   (PR:O MPAA:R)

PETRIFIED FOREST, SEE BACK PAGE FOR E) PETRIFIED FOREST

PETS zero (1974) 103m Dahlia c

Joan Blackman, Candy Rialson, Teri Guzman, Ed Bishop, K.T. Stevens, Berry Kroeger.

Vile misogynist trash involves the story of a whip-toting sadist who keeps women as "pets" for his own warped brand of pleasure. The real danger in the film is twofold: it reflects a genuine social sickness on the part of its producers, as well as the depraved types who would watch this for kicks.

p&d, Raphael Nussbaum; w, Richard Reich.

Exploitation   Cas.   (PR:O MPAA:R)

PETTICOAT FEVER** (1936) 80m MGM bw

Robert Montgomery (Dascom Dinsmore), Myrna Loy (Irene Campion), Reginald Owen (Sir James Felton), Otto Yamaoka (Kimo), George Hassell (Capt. Landry), Forrester Harvey (Scotty), Irving Bacon (Carl), Bo Ching (Big Seal), Iris Yamaoka (Little Seal), Winifred Shotter (Clara Wilson).

A silly little romance starring Montgomery as a lonely radio-operator at an Arctic weather post who goes bananas when a plane carrying Loy and her British fiance Owen is forced to land near his station. Loy is the first white woman he has seen in two years and he takes off after her, much to the dismay of Owen, who must compete for Loy's affections. Loy eventually gives in to Montgomery's advances, but trouble arrives in the form of his long-lost fiancee, Shotter, who has learned that her old beau has inherited a fortune and wants to marry him. After several hackneyed comedic situations, Loy and Montgomery give Owen and Shotter the brushoff and clinch for the fade.

p, Frank Davis; d, George Fitzmaurice; w, Harold Goldman (based on the play by Mark Reed); ph, Ernest Haller; ed, Frederick Y. Smith.

Romance/Comedy   (PR:A MPAA:NR)

PETTICOAT LARCENY*½ (1943) 61m RKO bw

Ruth Warrick (Pat Mitchell), Joan Carroll (Joan Mitchell), Walter Reed (Bill Morgan, Press Agent), Tom Kennedy (Pinky), Jimmy Conlin (Jitters), Vince Barnett (Stogie), Paul Guilfoyle (Joe Foster), Grant Withers (Detective Hogan), Earl Dewey (Mr. Crandall), Charles Coleman (Higgins), Cliff Clark (Lt. Hackett), Wally Brown (Sam Colfax, Columnist).

Carroll plays an 11-year-old radio actress who, dismayed about the quality of her scripts, joins the criminal underworld to research their speech habits (oh sure). The kid's aunt, Warrick, and the cops believe that the whole thing is a big publicity stunt masterminded by Warrick's beau Reed. His denials cause a rift between the pair, so he sets out to find the brat and drag her home. Unfortunately, Carroll gets kidnaped and Reed must rescue her. All turns out well when Carroll is safely returned to the airwaves (with a better grasp of gangland lingo one assumes) and Reed and Warrick make up.

p, Bert Gilroy; d, Ben Holmes; w, Jack Townley, Stuart Palmer; ph, Frank Redman; m, Roy Webb; ed, John C. Grubb; md, C. Bakaleinikoff; art d, Albert S. D'Agostino, Walter E. Keller.

Drama   (PR:A MPAA:NR)

PETTICOAT PIRATES** (1961, Brit.) 87m Associated British/WB-Pathe c

Charlie Drake (Charlie), Anne Heywood (Anne Stephens), Cecil Parker (C-in-C), John Turner (Capt. Michael Patterson), Maxine Audley (Superintendent), Thorley Walters (Lt. Jerome Robertson), Eleanor Summerfield (Mabel), Victor Maddern (C.O.C. Nixon), Lionel Murton (Admiral, U.S.N.), Barbara Hicks (P.T. Instructor), Kenneth Fortescue (Paul Turner), Dilys Laye (Sue), Michael Ripper (Tug), Anton Rodgers (Alec), Murray Melvin (Kenneth), Diane Aubrey (Gunnery Officer), Kim Tracy (Mess Attendant).

A very silly, and fairly sexist British comedy featuring Heywood as the commander of 150 WRENS (British equivalent of the WACS) who tries desperately to get the high command to allow women to serve on battleships. Her request is denied, so the impetuous Heywood and her crew invade a frigate containing a skeleton crew and pirate it. The women sail their way into an American/British practice maneuver (while using the deck for sunbathing on the way there) and prove themselves worthy of active service. Unfortunately a storm kicks up and the brave women just cannot seem to handle it without some men. If it was not for the reaffirmation of male dominance over women at the end (and the sunbathing), PETTICOAT PIRATES would have been a surprisingly progressive feminist testament to the strength and skill of women, but the filmmakers chickened out and gave the guys some reassurance that they are better than women.

p, Gordon L.T. Scott; d, David Macdonald; w, Lew Schwartz, Charlie Drake (based on a story by T.J. Morrison); ph, Gilbert Taylor (CinemaScope, Technicolor); m, Don Banks; ed, Ann Chegwidden.

Comedy   (PR:A MPAA:NR)

PETTICOAT POLITICS** (1941) 67m REP bw

Roscoe Karns (Joe Higgins), Ruth Donnelly (Lil Higgins), Spencer Charters (Grandpa), George Ernest (Sidney Higgins), Lois Ranson (Betty Higgins), Polly Moran (Widow Jones), Paul Hurst (Slats O'Dell), Pierre Watkin (Alfred Wilcox), Alan Ladd (Don Wilcox), Harry Woods (Guy Markwell), Claire Carleton (Tilly), Jeff Corey (Henry Trotter), Charles Moore (Newt), George Meader (Mayor Williams), Emmett Vogan (Bryant), Pom Pom (The Dog).

Another Higgins family comedy. This one opens as the patriarch, Karns, decides to retire from the candy factory rat race and spend the rest of his days quietly duck hunting. Unfortunately, his wife, Donnelly, has heard from the insurance man that retired people cannot just relax or they will die. Panicked, she pushes her old man into running for mayor and has the local women's reform movement, of which she and Moran are the charter members, endorse him. Wouldn't you know it that the man already entrenched in city hall is hooked up with the mob, and the usual set of complications arise. Look for a very young Alan Ladd once again playing Moran's beau. (See HIGGINS FAMILY series, Index.)

p, Robert North; d, Erle C. Kenton; w, Ewart Adamson, Taylor Cavan; ph, Jack Marta; ed, Edward Mann; md, Cy Feuer; art d, John Victor Mackay.

Comedy   (PR:A MPAA:NR)

PETTICOATS AND BLUEJEANS (SEE: PARENT TRAP, THE, 1961)

PETTY GIRL, THE*** (1950) 87m COL c (GB: GIRL OF THE YEAR)

Robert Cummings (George Petty), Joan Caulfield (Victoria Braymore), Elsa Lanchester (Dr. Crutcher), Melville Cooper (Beardsley), Audrey Long (Connie), Mary Wickes (Prof. Whitman), Frank Orth (Moody), John Ridgely (Patrolman), Raymond Largay (B.J. Manton), Ian Wolfe (President Webb), Frank Jenks (Kaye), Tim Ryan (Durkee), Mabel Paige (Mrs. Hibsch), Kathleen Howard (Prof. Langton), Sarah Edwards (Prof. Morrison), Everett Glass (Prof. Haughton), Douglas Wood (Prof. Stratton), Edward Clark (Prof. Ramsey), Philip Van Zandt (Senor Chameleon), Movita Castaneda (Carmelita), Lyn Thomas (Patti McKenzie), Dorothy Vaughn (Maid), Richard Avonde (M.C./Orchestra Leader), Ray Teal, Pat Flaherty (Policemen), Earle Hodgins (Boatman), Henry Hall (Faculty Member), Russell Hicks (Tycoon), Herbert Heywood (Doorman), Shirley Ballard (January-Petty Girl), Jetsy Parker (February), Barbara Freking (March), Shirley Whitney (April), Claire Dennis (May), Betsy Crofts (June), Joan Larkin (July), Lucille LaMarr (August), Eileen Howe (September), Carol Rush (October), Eloise Farmer (November), Dorothy Abbott (December), Tippi Hedren (Ice Box), Lois Hall (Coca Cola), Mona Knox (Mazola).

Calendar artist Cummings finds himself being pushed to be an "artist" by his sponsor, Long, who wants to see her find praised by the critics. Soon he meets prudish college professor Caulfield, who is in New York on a vacation, and is so enamored of her (he wants her to pose for him) that he follows her back to her college. His persistence gets her fired, so she takes the offensive and goes back to New York for a showdown with Long. To snare Cummings, Caulfield poses for him and they eventually marry. Watch for Tippi Hedren of Alfred Hitchcock fame in her film debut. Songs include "Petty Girl," "Fancy Free," "Calypso Song," "Ah Loves You" (Harold Arlen, Johnny Mercer).

p, Nat Perrin; d, Henry Levin; w, Perrin (based on a story by Mary McCarthy); ph, William Snyder; ed, Al Clark; md, Morris Stoloff; art d, Walter Holscher.

Musical (PR:A MPAA:NR)

PETULIA* (1968, U.S./Brit.) 105m Petersham/WB c

Julie Christie (*Petulia Danner*), George C. Scott (*Archie Bollen*), Richard Chamberlain (*David Danner*), Arthur Hill (*Barney*), Shirley Knight (*Polo*), Pippa Scott (*May*), Kathleen Widdoes (*Wilma*), Roger Bowen (*Warren*), Richard Dysart (*Motel Receptionist*), Ruth Kobart, Ellen Geer (*Nuns*), Lou Gilbert (*Mr. Howard*), Nate Esformes (*Mr. Mendoza*), Maria Val (*Mrs. Mendoza*), Vincent Arias (*Oliver*), Eric Weiss (*Michael*), Kevin Cooper (*Stevie*), Joseph Cotten (*Mr. Danner*), Austin Pendleton (*Intern*), Barbara Colby (*Patient*), Rene Auberjonois (*Salesman*), Josephine Nichols (*Neighbor*), De Ann Mears (*Nurse*), The Grateful Dead, Big Brother and the Holding Company, The Ace Trucking Company, The Committee, Members of the American Conservatory Theatre.

By the time PETULIA was released, audiences were tiring of the quick-cutting gimmickry used by Lester, a veteran of TV commercials, to tell his stories. Had he spent more time on content and less on sheer style, this might have had greater impact. To be sure, there are many wonderful pot shots satirically taken, but they are such throwaways that they get lost in the maelstrom. Scott is a middle-aged doctor who truly cares about his patients in his San Francisco practice. He has just left his wife, Knight, and their children but maintains a jealous attitude toward Knight's new intended, Bowen. Scott is not finding it easy to learn how to be single in the swinging scene. He goes to a party and meets Christie, a married woman who comes on very strong. They don't make love that night but she falls quickly for him and predicts that they will eventually marry. Scott is fascinated by Christie, as she is totally different from every woman he's ever met before. They make love, but that's the smallest part of their relationship, as Scott begins to feel younger and more energized by their affair. Scott doesn't know it but she had planned to meet him after having seen an operation he performed on Arias, a Mexican youth whom she subsidizes. Christie is married to Chamberlain, the weak-willed son of millionaire Cotten. They've been wed for six months, but he was impotent on the wedding night and she has since refused to share the marital bed with him, something that causes him to beat her regularly. Christie is at Scott's apartment one day and he's not there. Chamberlain arrives, beats her bloody, and leaves. When Scott does arrive home, he takes Christie to the hospital and supervises her treatment and recovery. Near the end of her stay, Scott comes to the hospital to check on her welfare and is shocked to learn that she's left with Chamberlain and moved back in with him at the family's huge home. Scott goes to the mansion and Christie opts to stay with Chamberlain, something Scott cannot understand one bit. Chamberlain swears he will never again hurt Christie and asks that she be patient with him and not expect miracles. He has a problem and hopes she will help him get over it. A year goes by and Christie is in the hospital again, this time on a more pleasant journey. She is about to have Chamberlain's child. Scott visits her and asks that she go away with him. She agrees, then, with all the unpredictability demonstrated earlier, changes her mind. Chamberlain arrives just after Scott has exited and she is put under sedation for the delivery. Her last word before the anesthesia takes effect is Scott's name. It's a strange movie that reflects the era of the 1960s in the inability of the characters to make commitments, other than Scott, who is a Dr. Kildare/Ben Casey combination. Lots of laughs in between the tears, including good barbs pointed at such things as topless waitresses, artificial flowers, Catholic hospitals, "hot pillow" motels, 24-hour supermarkets, and, most of all, the way people have become inured to the horrors of war and can engage in banal conversation as the TV news blares the latest body count in the background. Nick Roeg did the cinematography and his slick lensing is evident throughout. Director Lester was a man of the 1960s but as the decade drew to a close, his stylistic attempts at being new were becoming old hat. Producer Wagner had been an executive for many years at Universal Studios before striking out as an independent. Although shot in San Francisco and Tijuana (where Christie meets Arias after he's hit by a car), this is technically a British picture because of Lester's involvement, although he is an expatriate American. If that's confusing to you, it doesn't compare with some of the confusion in the movie.

p, Raymond Wagner; d, Richard Lester; w, Lawrence B. Marcus, Barbara Turner (based on the novel *Me and The Arch Kook Petulia* by John Haase); ph, Nicolas Roeg (Technicolor); m, John Barry; ed, Antony Gibbs; md, Barry; prod d, Tony Walton; art d, Dean Tavoularis; set d, Audrey Blasdel; cos, Walton, Arlette Nastat; makeup, Gus Norim.

Drama/Comedy (PR:C MPAA:R)

PEYTON PLACE*½ (1957) 162m FOX c

Lana Turner (*Constance MacKenzie*), Hope Lange (*Selena Cross*), Lee Philips (*Michael Rossi*), Lloyd Nolan (*Dr. Matthew Swain*), Diane Varsi (*Allison MacKenzie*), Arthur Kennedy (*Lucas Cross*), Russ Tamblyn (*Norman Page*), Terry Moore (*Betty Anderson*), Barry Coe (*Rodney Harrington*), David Nelson (*Ted Carter*), Betty Field (*Nellie Cross*), Mildred Dunnock (*Mrs. Thornton*), Leon Ames (*Harrington*), Lorne Greene (*Prosecutor*), Robert H. Harris (*Seth Bushwell*), Tami Connor (*Margie*), Staats Cotsworth (*Charles Partridge*), Peg Hillias (*Marion Partridge*), Erin O'Brien-Moore (*Mrs. Page*), Scotty Morrow (*Joey Cross*), Bill Lundmark (*Paul Cross*), Alan Reed, Jr. (*Matt*), Kip King (*Pee Wee*), Steffi Sidney (*Kathy*), Tom Greenway (*Judge*), Ray Montgomery (*Naval Officer*), Jim Brandt (*Messenger*), Edith Claire (*Miss Colton*), John Doucette (*Army Sergeant*), Alfred Tonkel (*Bailiff*),

Edwin Jerome (*Cory Hyde*), Bob Adler (*Jury Foreman*), Harry Carter (*Court Clerk*), Michael Lally (*Bailiff*).

Peyton Place was one of the best-selling novels of all time and no one thought it could be made into a decent movie. The subject matter was so steamy it was feared that it might be truncated and done as a pale soap opera. But the pundits were mistaken. Hayes' masterful adaptation of the book managed to keep all of the stories going on such a high level of taste that the Catholic Legion of Decency gave it their "A" rating, which meant it was "acceptable to all." Filmed in the small town of Camden, Maine, it's a terrific example of Hollywood's professionalism on all counts. The lives of seemingly "ordinary people" were examined in a suburban community and the result was a box-office smash as it became one of the biggest hits of the year. Set in the 1940s, it paved the way for a sequel, RETURN TO PEYTON PLACE, and a very successful TV series that was seen three nights per week in prime time. Mildred Dunnock, a loving teacher of the children at Peyton Place's high school, is overlooked by the powers-that-be for the job of principal, and Philips, a sharp Ph.D., is brought in for the job. He has many new ideas for educational advances and the town wants fresh blood. In no time at all, he meets Turner, a widow with a teenage daughter, Varsi. Since he is such a dashing type, Philips is surprised when Turner spurns his amorous advances and he retaliates by sniping at her for the way she treats Varsi, specifically when the teen's birthday party turns into an innocent-enough petting fest. Varsi and her pals are due to graduate this semester. Wealthy Coe marries Moore, a sensuous young woman, despite his father's annoyance. Meanwhile, Varsi is having a sincere friendship with Tamblyn, whose mother, O'Brien-Moore, is a domineering woman who resents his friendship with anyone. At the same time, Lange is the stepdaughter of the school's drunken caretaker, Kennedy. He rapes her and she later kills him accidentally. The war begins and things begin to change rapidly in the town. Varsi finds she must flee Turner's influence and goes to New York where she becomes the person who writes about life in the slow lane of Peyton Place. When Lange goes on trial for Kennedy's death, Varsi comes home to cover it and she is reunited with Turner and she learns her mother is finally going to marry Philips. The reason for her reluctance to marry and her doting attitude toward Varsi is that Varsi was born out of wedlock and Turner didn't want her daughter to go the same way. PEYTON PLACE is a jewel of a soap opera and manages to make all its points without ever becoming maudlin. The Academy gave it nine Oscar nominations, but it won none. The kudos went for Best Picture, Best Actress (Turner), Best Director, Best Script, Best Cinematography, and four nominations in supporting roles for Tamblyn, Kennedy, Lange, and Varsi. Only THE GODFATHER, PART II garnered that many Best Supporting nominations. The details of the story are what make it exciting. Lange gets pregnant by Kennedy and has an abortion by kindly Doctor Nolan; Field, Kennedy's wife, kills herself over the anguish; Coe joins the service and is one of the first soldiers to be killed; Tamblyn finally escapes his mother's forceful ways; the Lange trial ends when Nolan produces a document he's forced Kennedy to sign, admitting the parenthood of his stepdaughter's baby, and so on. In later years, another small town would be examined in THE LAST PICTURE SHOW and there are several similarities between the two, with the major difference being New England versus the Southwest in locale, but the same sort of behavior happening in both venues. If someone had judiciously pruned 20 minutes out of this, it would have been even better, but since so many millions had bought the book (someone figured it out to be one out of every 37 people in the U.S.), they feared a bad reaction from those who'd loved Metalious's work.

p, Jerry Wald; d, Mark Robson; w, John Michael Hayes (based on the novel by Grace Metalious); ph, William Mellor (CinemaScope, DeLuxe Color); m, Franz Waxman; ed, David Bretherton; md, Edward B. Powell; art d, Lyle R. Wheeler, Jack Martin Smith; set d, Walter M. Scott, Bertram Granger; cos, Adele Palmer, Charles Le Maire; spec eff, L.B. Abbott; makeup, Ben Nye.

Drama (PR:C MPAA:NR)

PHAEDRA½ (1962, U.S./Gr./Fr.) 115m Melinafilm-Jorilie/Lopert bw

Melina Mercouri (*Phaedra*), Anthony Perkins (*Alexis*), Raf Vallone (*Thanos*), Elizabeth Ercy (*Ercy*), Olympia Papadouka (*Anna*), George Saris (*Ariadne*), Andreas Philippides (*Andreas*), Giorgos Karoussos (*The Old Man*), Alexis Pezas (*Dimitri*), Kostas Baladimas (*Dimo*), Nikos Tzoyias (*Felere*), Depy Martini (*Heleni*), Stelios Vocovits (*Stravos*), Jules Dassin (*Christo*), Marc Bohan (*Himself*), Lillia Ralli (*Herself*).

After their smashing comedy success with NEVER ON SUNDAY, Dassin and Mercouri teamed again for this loose adaptation of *Hippolytus* by Euripides with the script changing the story to bring it up-to-date. Mercouri is married to Vallone, a powerful Greek shipping tycoon in the class of Onassis and Niarchos. She is his second wife and he dispatches her to London to convince his son by his first marriage, Perkins, to come home to Greece for the summer holiday. The moment they meet, Perkins and Mercouri are attracted to one another and are soon enmeshed in a steamy love affair which takes them to Paris. Vallone would like to teach his son the shipping business and Mercouri brings Perkins back to the small island of Hydra where they live. Perkins is tortured by guilt over having slept with his stepmother but happy to see his father, who has big plans for the boy. He wants Perkins to marry the daughter of another shipping magnate—forget about love, this is business and a marital merger will help seal their impending partnership. Mercouri is outraged by the arrangement and angrily admits that she has been having an affair with Perkins. Vallone's response is to beat up the sensitive Perkins and scream at Mercouri. Battered, Perkins prepares to leave and Mercouri begs to be allowed to go with him but he won't agree to that as his plan is to commit suicide, which he does by driving his car off a cliff. Mercouri, having nothing left to live for, takes a handful of sleeping pills and does herself in, thus leaving Vallone with the simultaneous loss of his son and spouse. Not a good subject for a musical comedy, right? PHAEDRA suffers from too much allegory and a heavy hand from Dassin, who also plays an old Greek. There is a Greek chorus of women who comment on matters in several tongues and are extraneous. The picture looks good, having been shot in Greece, England, and France, and they were wise to leave it in black and white as any sort of color might have ruined the atmosphere.

p&d, Jules Dassin; w, Dassin, Margarita Liberaki (based on a script by Liberaki and *Hippolytus* by Euripides); ph, Jacques Natteau; m, Mikis Theodorakis, Johann Sebastian Bach; ed, Roger Dwyre; art d, Max Douy; set d, Maurice Barnathan; cos, Denny Vachlioti; makeup, Jill Carpenter, Janine Casse.

Drama (PR:C MPAA:NR)

PHANTASM***½ (1979) 90m AE c

Michael Baldwin (*Mike*), Bill Thornbury (*Jody*), Reggie Bannister (*Reggie*), Kathy Lester (*Lady in Lavender*), Terrie Kalbus (*Granddaughter*), Ken Jones (*Caretaker*), Susan Harper (*Girl Friend*), Lynn Eastman (*Sally*), David Arntzen (*Toby*), Ralph Richmond (*Bartender*), Bill Cone (*Tommy*), Laura Mann (*Double Lavender*), Mary Ellen Shaw (*Fortune Teller*), Myrtle Scotton (*Maid*), Angus Scrimm (*Tall Man*).

A tour-de-force from 21-year-old producer/director/writer/photographer/editor Don Coscarelli (he was a veteran at this point, having directed his first feature, JIM —THE WORLD'S GREATEST, at age 18), PHANTASM is a wonderfully creative, bizarre, delightfully terrifying horror film that never fails to surprise. Told as if the whole experience were a nightmare, Baldwin stars as a 15-year-old orphan who lives with his older brother, Thornbury. After witnessing some strange happenings at the funeral of a murdered friend (shadowy gnome-like creatures lurking around the tombstones, etc.), Baldwin grabs his skeptical brother and returns to the creepy mausoleum to investigate. Once inside, they find it is actually the headquarters of the lanky and grotesque undertaker Scrimm, who is using the place as a connection with the nether world in order to take over the Earth. Scrimm has a number of insidious devices to ensure his success including a silver sphere that flies through the air, sprouts sharp spikes, plunges into the forehead of an unsuspecting victim, and then drills his brains out. From this point on the film is increasingly hard to describe, so just trust that this is one of the strangest, liveliest horror films in years and is well worth seeing. Not for the squeamish.

p, Don A. Coscarelli, Paul Pepperman; d,w,ph&ed, Coscarelli (Technicolor); m, Fred Myrow; Malcolm Seagrave; prod, S. Tyer; art d, David Gavin Brown; spec eff, Pepperman, Willard Green.

Horror Cas. (PR:O MPAA:R)

PHANTOM BROADCAST, THE*½ (1933) 71m MON/FD bw (GB: PHANTOM OF THE AIR)

Ralph Forbes (*Norman Wilder*), Vivienne Osborne (*Elsa Evans*), Paul Page (*Dr. Robert Brooks*), Gail Patrick (*Laura Hamilton*), [Guinn] "Big Boy" Williams (*Sandy Higgins*), Rockcliffe Fellowes (*Joe Maestro*), Carl Miller (*Lefty*), Arnold Gray (*Grant Murdock*), Pauline Garon, Mary MacLaren, Harlan Tucker, George Nash, Althea Henley, George ["Gabby"] Hayes.

A really strange murder mystery about a hunchbacked radio singer who hires a good-looking stand-in to double for him when he must make personal appearances. When a lovely young lady arrives at the station seeking the crooner's help in starting a singing career, the hunchback falls in love, but becomes upset when the woman thinks the stand-in is him. Thinking that his double is courting the girl, the hunchback decides to kill him, but discovers that someone has beaten him to it. The police think the hunchback is guilty, of course, and they shoot him after giving chase. In the end the girl turns out to be the real killer.

p, W.T. Lackey; d, Phil Rosen; w, Tristam Tupper; ph, Gilbert Warrington.

Crime (PR:A MPAA:NR)

PHANTOM COWBOY, THE** (1941) 56m REP bw

Don "Red" Barry (*Lawrence*), Virginia Carroll (*Elanita*), Milburn Stone (*Borden*), Neyle Marx (*Lobo*), Rex Lease (*Jeffers*), Nick Thompson (*Pancho*), Bud Osborne (*Dreer*), Ernest Wilson (*Memphis*), Burr Caruth (*Motley*), Frank Ellis, Art Dillard, Jack O'Shea, Chuck Baldra.

A fairly interesting Barry B-western, which finds our hero and his homesteader friends being driven off the land they inherited by Stone and his cohort Lease. Luckily a masked stranger known as "El Lobo" arrives to save their interests. Unfortunately the masked man is mortally wounded by the villains and passes his costume and persona to Barry in the hopes that "El Lobo" will ride again to aid the downtrodden.

p&d, George Sherman; w, Doris Schroeder; ph, Reggie Lanning; ed, Tony Martinelli; md, Cy Feuer.

Western (PR:A MPAA:NR)

PHANTOM EXPRESS, THE*½ (1932) 65m Majestic bw

William Collier, Jr. (*Bruce Harrington*), Sally Blane (*Carolyn Nolan*), J. Farrell McDonald (*Smokey Joe Nolan*), Alex Axelson (*Axel*), Hobart Bosworth (*President Harrington*), Lina Basquette, Huntley Gordon, Claire McDowell, Eddie Phillips, Jack Pennick, Robert Ellis, Carl Stockdale, David Rollins, Tom Wilson, Alan Forest, Alice Dahl, Tom O'Brien, Brady Kline, Jack Mower, Jack Trent, Bob Littlefield.

A mediocre suspense picture in which a group of villains fake a "phantom" train that runs down in the tracks forcing oncoming trains to think they're about to have a head-on collision and crash. The crooks hope that the constant brake slamming will sour the passengers on the railroad and they'll seek other modes of transportation. Eventually it is revealed that the "phantom" train is actually an airplane with a lowered headlight and a sound effects record played at full volume. The train sequences result from a combination of location shooting , incluinding a staged train wreck in the Mojave Desert, and some less effective miniatures.

p, Irving C. Franklin, Donald M. Stoner; d, Emory Johnson; w, Johnson, Laird Doyle; ph, Ross Fisher; ed, S. Roy Luby.

Mystery Cas. (PR:A MPAA:NR)

PHANTOM FIEND, THE*½ (1935, Brit.) 67m Twickenham/Olympic bw (GB: THE LODGER)

Ivor Novello (*Angeloff*), Elizabeth Allan (*Daisy Bunting*), A.W. Baskcomb (*Mr. Bunting*), Jack Hawkins (*Joe Martin*), Barbara Everest (*Mrs. Bunting*), Peter Gawthorne (*Lord Southcliffe*), P. Kynaston Reeves (*Bob Mitchell*), Shayle Gardner (*Detective Snell*), Drusilla Wills (*Mrs. Coles*), Antony Holles (*Sylvano*), George Merritt (*Commissioner*), Mollie Fisher (*Gladys*), Andrea Malandrinos (*Rabinovitch*), Iris Ashley.

In the light of Hitchcock's THE LODGER, none of the other film versions of this story even come close, but this one is commendable. Musician Novello appears to be a soft-spoken gentle sort to his girl friend and to the people in the boarding house where he lives. However, when a rash of Jack-the-Ripper-style murders occur, he is the man who is suspected. He is nearly done in by a lynch mob, but is saved when the real murderer is apprehended. This is the first remake of Alfred Hitchcock's classic (filmed silently in 1926). Other versions would follow in 1944, and in 1954 as THE MAN IN THE ATTIC, also starring Novello.

p, Julius Hagen; d, Maurice Elvey; w, Ivor Novello, Miles Mander, Paul Rotha, H. Fowler Mear (based on the novel *The Lodger* by Mrs. Marie Belloc-Lowndes); ph, Sidney Blythe, Basil Emmott.

Mystery (PR:A MPAA:NR)

PHANTOM FIEND, 1966 (SEE: RETURN OF DR. MABUSE, THE, 1966, Fr./Ital/W. Ger.)

PHANTOM FROM SPACE*½ (1953) 72m UA bw

Ted Cooper (*Lt. Hazen*), Rudolph Anders (*Dr. Wyatt*), Noreen Nash (*Barbara Randall*), James Seay (*Maj. Andrews*), Harry Landers (*Lt. Bowers*), Jack Daly (*Wakeman*), Dick Sands (*Phantom*), Lela Nelson, Michael Mark.

Billy Wilder's lesser-known brother W. Lee produced and directed this silly science-fiction film featuring Sands as an invisible alien from outer space who crashes on Earth near an American observatory. After the alien kills a few picnickers, the police take notice and, with the help of scientists Anders and Nelson, they discover that the alien must wear a helmet containing air from his own planet to survive. The intrepid scientists then trap the alien in the observatory, make him visible using an infra-red light machine, and take his helmet off, thereby killing him. So much for E.T.

p&d, W. Lee Wilder; w, Bill Raynor, Myles Wilder; ph, William Clothier; m, William Lava; ed, George Gale; spec eff, Alex Weldon, Howard Anderson.

Science Fiction (PR:A MPAA:NR)

PHANTOM FROM 10,000 LEAGUES, THE* (1956) 80m ARC bw

Kent Taylor (*Ted*), Cathy Downs (*Lois*), Michael Whalen (*King*), Helene Stanton (*Wanda*), Philip Pine (*George*), Rodney Bell (*Bill*), Pierce Lyden (*Andy*), Vivi Janis (*Ethel*), Michael Garth (*Sheriff*).

A badly made picture, but it was one of the first horror/science-fiction films released by Sam Arkoff and Jim Nicholson's new production company, American Releasing Company, which would soon turn into American International Pictures. Taylor stars as an oceanographer hired to investigate a giant sea monster that has been eating some unlucky swimmers and fishermen. Once underwater, Taylor discovers that the creature is a man-made mutant produced by evil scientist Whalen to guard some underwater uranium deposits. The creature gets its energy from an "atomic light" (whatever that is). Eventually the monster (obviously a badly operated hand puppet) decides that enough is enough, and it kills Whalen and itself in a massive explosion. "Freezing Horror!" screamed the ads, and they were right; the audience was numb from unintentional laughter. Released on a double bill with Corman's relatively superior THE DAY THE WORLD ENDED.

p, Jack Milner, Dan Milner; d, Dan Milner; w, Lou Rusoff (based on a story by Dorys Lukather); ph, Bryden Baker; m, Ronald Stein; ed, Jack Milner, Dan Milner.

Science Fiction (PR:A MPAA:NR)

PHANTOM GOLD** (1938) 56m COL bw

Jack Luden (*Breezy*), Beth Marion (*Mary*), Barry Downing (*Buddy*), Charles Whitaker (*Rattler*), Hal Taliaferro [Wally Wales] (*Dan*), Art Davis (*Happy*), Jimmy Robinson (*Pancakes*), Jack Ingram (*Pete*), Buzz Barton (*Pedro*), Marin Sais (*Mag*), Tuffy the Dog.

When looter Whitaker picks an old, dried-up gold mine and claims he's struck it rich, hero Luden arrives in town a bit suspicious. After surmising that the poor gold-fevered miners who arrive to dig have been taken for everything they own, Luden realizes that the whole thing is a scam for Whitaker and his cohorts to rob innocent miners. But then a strange thing happens. The miners actually do hit some gold and it turns out there is still a mother lode in the mine. Luden files a claim, and Whitaker tries to stop him but he loses.

p, Larry Darmour; d, Joseph Levering; w, Nate Gatzert; ph, James S. Brown, Jr.; m, Lee Zahler; ed, Dwight Caldwell.

Western (PR:A MPAA:NR)

PHANTOM HORSEMAN, THE (SEE: BORDER OUTLAW, 1950)

PHANTOM IN THE HOUSE, THE** (1929) 64m T/C/Continental Talking Pictures bw

Ricardo Cortez (*Paul Wallis*), Nancy Welford (*Dorothy Milburn*), Henry E. Walthall (*Boyd Milburn*), Grace Valentine (*Peggy Milburn*), Thomas A. Curran (*Judge Thompson*), Jack Curtis ("*Biffer*" *Bill*), John Elliott (*Police Captain*).

A complicated melodrama finds Valentine getting her inventor husband Walthall (the "Little Colonel" in THE BIRTH OF A NATION) in trouble for a murder she has committed. After Walthall's been sentenced to life, his wife changes her name and uses his inventions to make herself wealthy. Having achieved social recognition, she decides to marry off her daughter, Welford, to a respectable party, though the girl loves regular guy Cortez. Walthall returns from prison after 15 years and is introduced to his daughter as a "family friend." Valentine threatens to expose his past when Walthall sides with Welford's decision to marry for love. When judge Curran tells Cortez Walthall's story, a fight breaks out. Curran is killed by Curtis, Walthall's old prison mate, but Cortez is blamed for the murder. Walthall manages to right this wrong and Valentine repents. Husband and daughter reconcile with her as they all drift off to happily-ever-after-land. Like many early talkies, this film had both silent and sound versions to accommodate the technologies of the nation's different theaters.

d, Phil Rosen; w, Arthur Hoerl; ph, Herbert Kirkpatrick; m/l, "You'll Never Be Forgotten" Abner Silver, Maceo Pinkard.

Drama **(PR:A MPAA:NR)**

PHANTOM KILLER** (1942) 61m MON bw

Dick Purcell *(Edward Clark)*, Joan Woodbury *(Barbara Mason)*, John Hamilton *(John G. Harrison)*, Warren Hymer *(Sgt. Corrigan)*, Kenneth Harlan *(Lt. Brady)*, J. Farrell MacDonald *(Police Captain)*, Mantan Moreland *(Nicodemus)*, Gayne Whitman *(District Attorney)*, George Lewis *(Kramer)*, Elliott Sullivan *(Dave Rigby)*, Karl Hackett, Isabel Lamal, Robert Carson, Frank Ellis, Harry Depp.

A strange murder mystery starring Purcell as a crusading district attorney out to pin a murder on the community's local benefactor, Hamilton, a deaf-mute with a reputation beyond reproach. When Hamilton is acquitted of the murder charge, a disgusted Purcell quits his job and sets out to gather the damning evidence himself. Eventually he discovers that Hamilton has a normal twin brother with whom he worked as a team. While the handicapped Hamilton was out at a local public function, the healthy brother committed the murder. Monogram had done this material years earlier as THE SPHINX.

p, A.W. Hackel; d, William Beaudine; w, Karl Brown; ph, Marcel Le Picard; ed, Jack Ogilvie; md, Frank Sanucci.

Mystery **(PR:A MPAA:NR)**

PHANTOM LADY*½** (1944) 87m UNIV bw

Franchot Tone *(Jack Marlow)*, Ella Raines *(Carol "Kansas" Richman)*, Alan Curtis *(Scott Henderson)*, Aurora Miranda *(Estela Monteiro)*, Thomas Gomez *(Inspector Burgess)*, Fay Helm *(Ann Terry)*, Elisha Cook, Jr. *(Cliff March)*, Andrew Tombes *(Bartender)*, Regis Toomey, Joseph Crehan *(Detectives)*, Doris Lloyd *(Kettisha)*, Virginia Brissac *(Dr. Chase)*, Milburn Stone *(District Attorney)*, Jay Novello.

A corker of a mystery-crime film, PHANTOM LADY had that Germanic look of the 1930s, probably due to the direction of Teuton Robert Siodmak who used his camera and lighting so well that the words could have been erased from the sound track and the movie still would have made sense. Curtis has just walked out of his apartment after having had a huge argument with his wife. Feeling somewhat sorry for himself and needy for human companionship, he goes bar hopping and meets Helm, an interesting woman who is wearing a fascinating hat. Nothing much happens there and when he returns to his apartment, he finds that his wife has been strangled to death with his necktie. Since he and Helm had made an agreement to not reveal their names to each other, he can't use her as an alibi. They'd been to a musical show where the singer, Aurora, was wearing the same hat. (Note: Aurora was Carmen Miranda's sister and sang a Brazilian ditty by Jacques Press and Eddie Cherkose called "Chick-ee-Chick.") When Curtis can't find anyone who can corroborate that he was out during those hours on the fateful night, he is tried, convicted, and will die in less than three weeks (they did things much faster in the criminal courts back then). No one believes Curtis except his long-time secretary, Raines, and she sets out to solve the crime. She first convinces Gomez, a cop, that her boss has been framed, and the two of them unite in their quest. Raines visits the club where Curtis met Helm and gets the barkeep, Tombes, to agree to tell the truth. But before he can do that, he's killed in an auto crash. Now Raines pretends to be a hooker and goes after Cook, the show's drummer, who recalls the lady in question but admits that someone's given him cash to forget he ever saw her. Cook finds his own "rap sheet" from the cops in Raines's purse and goes after her. She gets away long enough to call Gomez and, at the same time, Cook is murdered by Tone, the real killer. Tone is a nutcake artist who killed Curtis' wife when she wouldn't go away with him after having had a long affair. Tone joins Raines at the jail as they visit Curtis and he agrees to "help" her find the killer. They trace the hat to Helm and she gives it to them as evidence but she is somewhat dotty and one wonders if her testimony will hold up. Raines goes to Tone's apartment, spots her purse (which she'd dropped when with Cook) and it dawns on her that Tone is the true murderer. Tone grips his scarf and prepares to throttle her when Gomez arrives. Tone leaps out the window to his death, Curtis leaves jail and is united with Raines. This was producer Harrison's first film after almost a decade of working with Hitchcock in several capacities. His later film, FRENZY, bears a slight resemblance to this.

p, Joan Harrison; d, Robert Siodmak; w, Bernard C. Schoenfeld (based on the novel by William Irish [Cornell Woolrich]); ph, Woody Bredell; ed, Arthur Hilton; md, Hans J. Salter; art d, John B. Goodman, Robert Clatworthy; set d, Russell Gausman, L.R. Smith; cos, Vera West, "phantom hat" created by Kenneth Hopkins.

Crime/Mystery **(PR:C MPAA:NR)**

PHANTOM LIGHT, THE*** (1935, Brit.) 75m Gainsborough/GAU bw

Binnie Hale *(Alice Bright)*, Gordon Harker *(Sam Higgins)*, Ian Hunter *(Jim Pearce)*, Donald Calthrop *(David Owen)*, Milton Rosmer *(Dr. Carey)*, Reginald Tate *(Tom Evans)*, Mickey Brantford *(Bob Peters)*, Herbert Lomas *(Claff Owen)*, Fewlass Llewellyn *(Griffith Owen)*, Alice O'Day *(Mrs. Owen)*, Edgar K. Bruce *(Sgt. Owen)*, Louie Emery *(Station Mistress)*, Barry O'Neill *(Capt. Pearce)*.

After a lighthouse keeper is murdered under mysterious circumstances, a series of strange shipwrecks and disappearances follow. A "phantom" light is consistently seen near the dead man's lighthouse along the Welsh shoreline, but lady detective Hale, along with a navy man and another lighthouse keeper, discover that a group of investors are behind the crimes. Balanced with good proportions of suspense, humor, and atmosphere, this minor feature rises above many budget restrictions as intelligent entertainment. One of the many programmers Powell directed in the 1930s.

p, Jerome Jackson; d, Michael Powell; w, J. Jefferson Farjeon, Austin Melford, Ralph Smart (based on the play "The Haunted Light" by Evadne Price, Joan Roy Byford); ph, Geoffrey Faithfull, Roy Kellino; m, Louis Levy; ed, Derek Twist; art d, Alex Vetchinsky.

Mystery/Crime **(PR:C MPAA:NR)**

PHANTOM OF CHINATOWN** (1940) 61m MON bw

Keye Luke *(Jimmy Wong)*, Lotus Long *(Win Len)*, Grant Withers *(Street)*, Paul McVey *(Grady)*, Charles Miller *(Dr. Benton)*, Virginia Carpenter *(Louise Benton)*, John Dilson *(Charles Fraser)*.

Finally an Oriental actor plays an Oriental detective. Someone at Monogram decided that they didn't need another white British man to replace Karloff as the Chinese detective in the Mr. Wong series so they let CHARLIE CHAN veteran, and actual Oriental, Luke take over. Besides the revolutionary racial casting, there's not much else to note about this routine murder mystery in which an archaeologist is murdered to obtain information found on an ancient Mongolian scroll about an oil-rich territory. Aided by the dead man's daughter Long (a Eurasian actress), Luke hunts the killer down. (See MR. WONG series, Index.)

p, Paul Malvern; d, Phil Rosen; w, Joseph West (based on a story by Hugh Wiley); ph, Fred Jackman, Jr.; ed, Jack Ogilvie.

Mystery **Cas.** **(PR:A MPAA:NR)**

PHANTOM OF CRESTWOOD, THE** (1932) 77m RKO bw

Karen Morley *(Jenny Wren)*, Ricardo Cortez *(Gary Curtis)*, H.B. Warner *(Priam Andes)*, Pauline Frederick *(Faith Andes)*, Robert McWade *(Walcott)*, Aileen Pringle *(Mrs. Walcott)*, Skeets Gallagher *(Mack)*, Mary Duncan *(Dorothy Mears)*, Gavin Gordon *(Will Jones)*, Anita Louise *(Esther Wren)*, Robert Elliott *(Tall Man)*, Ivan Simpson *(Henry T. Herrick)*, Hilda Vaughn *(Carter)*, George E. Stone *(The Cat)*, Sam Hardy *(Pete Harris)*, Matty Kemp *(Frank Andes)*, Tom Douglas *(The Boy)*, Eddie Sturgis *(Bright Eyes)*.

A contrived murder mystery that was subjected to one of the strangest marketing campaigns ever dreamed up. When RKO began production of THE PHANTOM OF CRESTWOOD, they immediately ran a radio dramatization of the same story with the same characters on NBC for six weeks. When it came to the last episode however, eager listeners were given the opportunity to send in their own ideas on how to end the story, with prizes offered to those who came up with the best endings. When the film was released, the loyal radio audience flocked to the theaters to see how the mystery *did* end. Morley plays a shady lady who summons five of her former male "friends" together and tells them they must give her large sums of money, or she will expose her relationship with each of them. She's soon found murdered and there are five likely suspects, of course. Enter detective Cortez who grills them all as we see their various relationships with the deceased through a series of flashbacks. Eventually the killer is pinpointed, much to the disappointment of the radio listeners who had probably come up with better solutions on their own.

p, David O. Selznick; d, J. Walter Ruben; w, Bartlett Cormack (based on a story by Cormack, Ruben); ph, Carroll Clark, Henry Gerrard; art d, Carroll Clark

Mystery **(PR:A MPAA:NR)**

PHANTOM OF 42ND STREET, THE** (1945) 58m PRC bw

Dave O'Brien *(Tony Woolrich, Drama Critic)*, Kay Aldridge *(Claudia Moore)*, Alan Mowbray *(Cecil Moore)*, Frank Jenks *(Romeo, Taxi Driver)*, Edythe Elliott *(Janet Buchanan)*, Jack Mulhall *(Lt. Walsh)*, Vera Marshe *(Ginger)*, Stanley Price *(Reggie Thomas)*, John Crawford *(John Carraby)*, Cyril Delevanti *(Robert)*, Paul Power *(Timothy Wells)*.

Murder among a family of Broadway actors makes up this whodunit starring O'Brien as a drama critic and Mulhall as a cop who team up to solve the backstage killing of a rich uncle. Aldridge plays the youngest member of the acting clan whose Broadway debut is spoiled when it is discovered her wealthy uncle was murdered backstage. Suspicion falls immediately on her father, Mowbray, a successful thespian in his own right who is known to be on the skids financially. Seeing that he's in line to inherit his brother's estate, he becomes the most likely suspect. Through perseverance and valuable plot twists, O'Brien and Mulhall sort things out and justice is served.

p, Martin Mooney, Albert Herman; d, Herman; w, Milton Raison (based on the story by Jack Harvey, Raison); ph, James Brown; m, Karl Hajos; ed, Hugh Winn; art d, Paul Palmentola; set d, Harry Reif.

Mystery **Cas.** **(PR:A MPAA:NR)**

PHANTOM OF LIBERTY, THE**** (1974, Fr.) 104m Greenwich/FOX c (LE FANTOME DE LA LIBERTE; AKA THE SPECTER OF FREEDOM)

Jean-Claude Brialy *(Mr. Foucauld)*, Monica Vitti *(Mrs. Foucauld)*, Milena Vukotic *(Nurse)*, Michel Lonsdale *(Hatter)*, Michel Piccoli *(2nd Prefect)*, Claude Pieplu *(Commissioner)*, Paul Frankeur *(Innkeeper)*, Julien Bertheau *(1st Prefect)*, Adriana Asti *(Prefect's Sister)*, Adolfo Celi *(Dr. Legendre)*, Pierre Maguelon *(Policeman Gerard)*, Francois Maistre *(Professor)*, Helen Perdriere *(Aunt)*, Jean Rochefort *(Mr. Legendre)*, Bernard Verley *(Captain)*, Paul Leperson.

An illogical collection of incidents which jump from place to place and time to time, in a manner which follows the logic of dreams. Any attempt to synopsize the plot would be feeble and miss the film's point—which seems to suggest that there isn't one. The film opens with a firing squad in Napoleonic times who shout "Down with Liberty." From there the film turns into a scene of a maid reading to a child the story we have just witnessed. Again the direction switches to a man selling supposedly pornographic postcards of French tourist attractions which are not pornographic at all. A nurse then makes the mistake of wandering into a poker game played by a group of monks. A man with a rifle kills passersby from the top of a Montparnasse building and is heroically received. A missing girl helps the police fill out a report on her disappearance. And in perhaps the most memorable sequence, a group of dinner guests sit on toilet seats and must raise their hands in order to go to the dining room. A crazy uproariously funny film for those who are not part of the upper class or devoutly religious. It was a joy to see that Bunuel could still ruffle as many feathers at age 75 as he did in 1928's UN CHIEN ANDALOU and 1930's L'AGE D'OR. (In French; English subtitles.)

p, Serge Silberman; d, Luis Bunuel; w, Bunuel, Jean-Claude Carriere; ph, Edmond Richard (Eastmancolor); ed, Helen Plemianikov.

Drama (PR:O MPAA:R)

PHANTOM OF PARIS, 1942 (SEE: MYSTERY OF MARIE ROGET, THE, 1942)

PHANTOM OF PARIS, THE**½ (1931) 72m MGM bw

John Gilbert (Cheri-Bibi), Leila Hyams (Cecile), Lewis Stone (Costaud), Jean Hersholt (Herman), C. Aubrey Smith (Bourrelier), Natalie Moorhead (Vera), Ian Keith (Marquis du Touchais), Alfred Hickman (Dr. Gorlin).

Convoluted murder mystery starring Gilbert as a magician wrongly accused of murdering the father of Hyams, his girl friend. After becoming a fugitive from the law, a confused Hyams marries her other suitor, Keith, who happens to be the actual killer. Keith dies (unbeknownst to Hyams), and after a bit of plastic surgery, Gilbert takes the dead man's place and gathers enough evidence to clear his name.

d, John S. Robertson; w, Bess Meredyth, Edwin Justus Mayer, John Meehan (based on the novel Cheri-Bibi by Gaston Leroux); ph, Oliver T. Marsh; ed, Jack Ogilvie.

Mystery (PR:A MPAA:NR)

PHANTOM OF SANTA FE** (1937) 75m Burroughs-Tarzan c

Norman Kerry, Nena Quartero, Frank Mayo, Monte Montague, Tom O'Brien, Carmelita Geraghty, Jack Mower, Frank Ellis, Merrill McCormack.

Strange goings on affect the life on the prairie, all the work of a mysterious phantom. A western packed with the typical gunfights, action, and an occasional chuckle or two. What makes this poverty-row western different than most is the use of color film stock, highly unusual for the time. Originally shot in 1931, the film features silent-screen star Kerry in one of his early talking roles. Kerry's trademark was a large, waxed mustache.

d, Jacques Jaccard; w, Charles Royal.

Western (PR:A MPAA:NR)

PHANTOM OF SOHO, THE** (1967, Ger.) 92m CCC-Filmkunst/
Producers Releasing Organization Film bw (DAS PHANTOM VON SOHO)

Dieter Borsche (Hugh Patton), Barbara Rutting (Clarinda Smith), Hans Sohnker (Sir Philip), Peter Vogel (Hallam), Helga Sommerfeld (Corinna Smith), Werner Peters (Dr. Dalmar), Hans Nielsen (Lord Malhouse), Stanislav Ledinak (Gilard), Otto Waldis (Liver-Spot), Hans W. Hamacher (Captain), Emil Feldmar (Daddy), Harald Sawade (Charlie), Elisabeth Flickenschildt (Joanna Filiati).

Once again the Germans try to make a British movie mystery, and are only fairly successful. Borsche stars as the Scotland Yard detective investigating the murders of a number of prominent London businessmen. When discussing the situation with his boss, Sohnker, he meets his superior's fiancee, Rutting, who is a mystery writer. She announces that the identity of the murderer will be revealed in the last chapter of her latest book. While digging for clues, Borsche learns that all the dead men had taken a pleasure cruise together. After running down all the various leads and still confused as to who the culprit is, Borsche is practically hit over the head with the answer when Rutting confesses to the crimes. She reveals that all the men had been involved in some sleazy sexual business and that they had all raped her on the pleasure cruise. After making her stunning revelation, she takes a cyanide pill and dies.

p, Arthur Brauner; d, Franz Josef Gottlieb; w, Ladislas Fodor (based on a story by Bryan Edgar Wallace); ph, Richard Angst (Ultrascope); m, Martin Bottcher; ed, Walter Wischniewsky; art d, Hans Jurgen Kiebach, Ernst Schomer.

Mystery (PR:C MPAA:NR)

PHANTOM OF TERROR, THE (SEE: BIRD WITH THE CRYSTAL PLUMAGE, THE, 1969, Ital./W. Ger.)

PHANTOM OF THE AIS (SEE: PHANTOM BROADCAST, 1933)

PHANTOM OF THE DESERT* (1930) 55m SYN bw

Jack Perrin (Jack Saunders), Eva Novak (Mary Van Horn), Josef Swickard (Col. Van Horn), Lila Eccles (Nora), Ben Corbett (Benny Mack), Edward Earle (Dan Denton), Robert Walker (Steve), Pete Morrison (Jim), Starlight ("Phantom" the Horse).

Another low-budget, independently produced bad B-western for cowboy star Perrin in which his horse, Starlight, gets better material than he does. See Perrin and Starlight try to stop evil rustlers! See Starlight eat a wanted poster with his picture on it! See the antics of the horse garner better reviews than the humans! See Perrin's movie career bite the dust!

p, Harry S. Webb, F.E. Douglas; d, Webb; w, Carl Krusada; ph, William Nobles; ed, Fred Bain.

Western (PR:A MPAA:NR)

PHANTOM OF THE JUNGLE** (1955) 75m Arrow/Lippert bw

Jon Hall, Ray Montgomery, Anne Gwynne, Kenneth McDonald, Carleton Young, James Griffith, Nick Stewart, Milton Wood.

When some American scientists venture into darkest Africa, they rile the local natives by stealing a sacred golden tablet. Enter a compatriot doctor, who saves the lives of the naughty party before it's too late. Standard jungle story.

p, Rudolph C. Flothow; d, Spencer Bennet; w, William Lively, Sherman L. Lowe.

Adventure (PR:A MPAA:NR)

PHANTOM OF THE OPERA, THE**** (1929) 93m UNIV bw/c

Lon Chaney (The Phantom), Mary Philbin (Christine Daae), Norman Kerry (Raoul de Chagny), Snitz Edwards (Florine Papillon), Gibson Gowland (Simon), Edward Martindel (Philippe de Chagny), Virginia Pearson (Carlotta), Arthur Edmund Carewe (Ledoux), Edith Yorke (Mama Valerius), Anton Vaverka (Prompter), Bernard Siegel (Joseph Buquet), Olive Ann Alcorn (La Sorelli), Cesare Gravina (Manager), George B. Williams (Mons. Ricard), Bruce Covington (Mons. Moncharmin), Edward Cecil (Faust), Alexander Bevani (Mephistopheles), Grace Marvin (Martha), Ward Crane (Count Ruboff), Chester Conklin (Orderly), William Tryoler (Director of Opera Orchestra).

The classic silent horror film was reissued with the advent of sound. A few scenes between Philbin and Kerry were reshot with dialog, and Martindel completely replaced John Sainpolis as Kerry's father in the new version. Additionally, dubbed vocals from the opera "Faust" were added to the scenes where that work is being performed. Chaney does not speak, nor would he until THE UNHOLY THREE, the following year. (SEE: MPG Volume X.)

p, Carl Laemmle; d, Rupert Julian, Edward Sedgwick (director of sound sequences, Ernst Laemmle); w, Raymond Schrock, Elliott J. Clawson, Tom Reed, Frank M. McCormack (based on the story "Le Fantome de l'Opera" by Gaston Leroux); ph, Virgil Miller, Milton Bridenbecker, Charles Van Enger; ed, Maurice Pivar; prod d, Charles Hall, Ben Carre.

Horror (PR:A MPAA:NR)

PHANTOM OF THE OPERA*** (1943) 92m UNIV c

Nelson Eddy (Anatole Garron), Susanna Foster (Christine DuBois), Claude Rains (Enrique Claudin), Edgar Barrier (Inspector Raoul de Chagny), Leo Carrillo (Signor Feretti), Jane Farrar (Biancarolli), J. Edward Bromberg (Amiot), Fritz Feld (Lecours), Frank Puglia (Villeneuve), Steven Geray (Vercheres), Barbara Everest (Aunt), Hume Cronyn (Gerard), Fritz Leiber (Frans Liszt), Nicki [Nicole] Andre (Lorenzi), Gladys Blake (Jennie), Elvira Curci (Biancarolli's Maid), Hans Herbert (Marcel), Kate Lawson (Marie), Miles Mander (Pleyel), Rosina Galli (Christine's Maid), Walter Stahl (Dr. Lefours), Paul Marion (Desjardines), Tudor Williams, Anthony Marlow (Martha Singers), Beatrice Roberts (Nurse), Marek Windheim (Renfrit), Muni Seroff (Reporter), Belle Mitchell (Feretti's Maid), Ernest Golm (Office Manager), Renee Carson (Georgette, Pleyel's Girl Friend), Lane Chandler, Stan Blystone (Officers), Cyril Delevanti (Bookeeper), John Walsh (Office Boy), Dick Bartell, Jim Mitchell (Reporters), Alphonse Martell (Policeman), Wheaton Chambers (Reporter), Edward Clark (Usher), William Desmond, Hank Mann (Stagehands).

Universal Studios elaborate and expensive remake of their classic 1925 silent horror film THE PHANTOM OF THE OPERA boasts fabulous sets, gorgeous costumes, and stunning Technicolor photography—but fails in the horror department due to too much music and low comedy. Draining much of the fear, suspense, and mystery out of the original Gaston Leroux material (elements which the 1925 film exploited memorably), this 1943 remake sees Rains—the future "Phantom"—as a somewhat frail, middle-aged violinist with the Paris Opera orchestra. In love from afar with Foster, a pretty and talented singer in the chorus, the love-sick Rains even secretly pays for lessons to help her improve her singing. Foster, however, is being courted by the opera's tenor, Eddy, and a French police inspector, Barrier, and doesn't even realize that Rains exists. After a performance, Rains is called into the office of Puglia, the director of the opera. There he is informed that his playing isn't good enough (due to a partially paralized hand) and he must be replaced. Stunned and upset, Rains visits singing instructor Carrillo and begs him to continue Foster's lessons even though he is unable to pay. Carrillo won't hear of it and declares that he will give Foster a few more lessons and then tell her that she no longer needs training. Knowing that Foster can be a first class diva if given the chance, a desperate Rains submits the concerto he has written—his life's work—to a music publisher. Through a misunderstanding Rains comes to believe that the company has stolen his composition and he insanely strangles the owner, Mander. During the struggle, Mander's girl friend Carson tries to help her lover by throwing acid in Rains' face. Wracked with pain, Rains runs off into the night and hides from the police in the sewers. Weeks later, strange happenings seem to plague the opera house. Costumes, masks, props, and food disappear and the stagehands begin a rumor that the opera is haunted. While practicing in her dressing room, Foster hears a voice through the wall telling her that she will become the greatest singer in Paris. At that night's performance, diva Farrar (niece of soprano Geraldine Farrar) suddenly falls ill (she was drugged by Rains) and Foster must take her place. She gives the performance of her life while Rains—now wearing a stage mask to hide his scarred visage—hides in his lair beneath the opera house and listens. When the opera is over, the public gives Foster their thundering approval. When Farrar awakes from her drugged state, she immediately accuses Eddy of committing the deed to further the career of his girl friend Foster. Inspector Barrier thinks the charge ridiculous, but Farrar gets even by restricting Foster to the chorus for the length of her contract. Learning of this, the mad Rains later appears in Farrar's dressing room and strangles her. Rains is spotted however, and a chase ensues within the stage rigging. Unfortunately, Eddy is wearing a costume similar to that of Rains and he is mistakenly caught by Barrier while the real Phantom escapes. The opera house closes its doors during the investigation and Rains sends angry notes demanding that Foster replace the dead Farrar as star of the opera. Unable to find Rains' hideout, Barrier decides to reopen the opera with another singer, Andre (in her U.S. screen debut), replacing Farrar. This is sure to anger Rains and once again bring him out into the open. Barrier's plan does bring Rains out of hiding, but the crazed phantom cuts the chain that holds the huge chandelier over the orchestra pit, sending it crashing into the audience below. During the ensuing pandemonium, Rains whisks Foster into his lair where he tells her of his mad scheme to make her diva of the opera. Eddy and Barrier manage to trace Rains to his subterranean hideout and notice that the ancient structure is about to collapse. Curious as to the identity of the phantom, Foster snatches the mask off Rains' face and is horrified at the hideous scars underneath. At the same moment, Eddy and Barrier burst in and a fight ensues. The underground passage begins to crumble as Eddy and Barrier grab Foster and take her to safety. Rains is caught in a hail of falling stones and rushing rock and disappears, leaving only his mask and violin behind. Back at street level, heros Eddy and Barrier are a bit dismayed that Foster has chosen her career over the both of them—so they walk off together to have dinner. Universal spent $1.5 million on THE PHANTOM OF THE OPERA and every dollar is on screen. While the opera house set was the original one that was built for the original 1925 silent film, many additional sets were constructed and dressed up with elaborate and expensive wares. Rains, who had just finished playing what would later become his best-remembered role—that of Capt. Louis Renault in CASABLANCA—managed to bring a sense of pathos and menace to the role of the phantom. The sparse and briefly seen makeup of the disfigured violinist is merely servicable and wisely no attempt was made to duplicate or surpass Lon Chaney's amazing visage in the silent version. Perhaps more shocking to audiences was that blond singer Eddy had his hair dyed black and sported a thin black mustache for his role (which made him look alarmingly like his rival for Foster's affections, actor Barrier—the men are practically indistinguishable). While this version of THE PHANTOM OF THE OPERA can be quite entertaining at times, it is frustrating that the horror elements were used merely as a plot device to propel the story along to the next elaborate opera scene. This structure pleased neither horror film fans nor opera buffs, who were a bit dismayed at the cut-and-paste nature of the musical numbers. Musical director Ward used parts of Friedrich von Flotow's *Martha* and created two "original" operas, *Le Prince de Caucasie* and *Amour et Glorie*, by borrowing sections of Tchaikovsky's *Symphony No 4* for the former and some Chopin themes for the latter. Eddy does some of his finest singing here, as does Foster. Foster, who was kept on the Universal lot as a threat to keep star Deanna Durbin in her place, was never in another production as large as THE PHANTOM OF THE OPERA and quickly sank into obscurity. Musical numbers include: "Lasst Mich Euch Fragen" (sung by Eddy) and "Mag der Himmel Euch Verbegen" (sung by Williams, with chorus, both from the opera *Martha*by Von Flowtow, special libretto by George Waggner), "Lullaby of the Bells" (Edward Ward, Waggner, sung by Eddy and Foster), "Grand Polonaise," "Nocturne in E Flat," "Waltz in G Minor" (Chopin, French lyrics by William von Wymetal, sung by Eddy, Farrar), "Le Prince de Causasie" (an opera based on the Fourth Symphony of Peter Ilich Tchaikovsky, libretto by Waggner, excerpts sung by Andre, Eddy, chorus, others). THE PHANTOM OF THE OPERA won three Academy Awards: for cinematography, art direction, and interior decorations. Another remake of THE PHANTOM OF THE OPERA was attempted by Britain's Hammer Studios starring Herbert Lom in 1962.

p, George Waggner; d, Arthur Lubin; w, Eric Taylor, Samuel Hoffenstein (based on the novel *Le Fantome de l'Opera* by Gaston Leroux, adapted by John Jacoby); ph, Hal Mohr, W. Howard Greene (Technicolor); m, operatic score, Edward Ward, George Waggner; ed, Russell Schoengarth; md, Ward; art d, John B. Goodman, Alexander Golitzen; set d, R.A. Gausman, Ira S. Webb; cos, Vera West; makeup, Jack Pierce.

Horror/Drama **(PR:A MPAA:NR)**

PHANTOM OF THE OPERA, THE*** (1962, Brit.) 84m Hammer/UNIV c

Herbert Lom *(The Phantom)*, Heather Sears *(Christine Charles)*, Thorley Walters *(Lattimer)*, Edward De Souza *(Harry Hunter)*, Michael Gough *(Lord Ambrose D'Arcy)*, Martin Miller *(Rossi)*, Miles Malleson *(Philosophical Cabby)*, Miriam Karlin *(Charwoman)*, John Harvey *(Vickers)*, Harold Goodwin *(Bill)*, Ian Wilson *(Dwarf)*, Marne Maitland *(Xavier)*, Michael Ripper *(Longfaced Cabby)*, Sonya Cordeau *(Yvonne)*, Patrick Troughton *(Rat Catcher)*, Liane Aukin *(Maria)*, Leila Forde *(Teresa)*, Geoffrey L'Oise *(Frenchman)*, Renee Houston *(Mrs. Tucker)*, Liam Redmond, Miriam Karlin.

Following successful reinterpretations of such horror film icons as Frankenstein, Dracula, the Mummy, and the Wolfman, Hammer Studios turned its attention to the classic tale of THE PHANTOM OF THE OPERA. Fully aware that its small-budget efforts would be closely compared with the two previous big-budget American versions (in 1925 starring Lon Chaney, Sr., and again in 1943 starring Claude Rains), Hammer bravely forged ahead and managed to produce a film that, while no classic, stands as a well-crafted thriller with some memorable moments. Shifting the action from Paris to London, the film opens during the first performance of "Saint Joan," a new opera written by the wealthy and influential Lord Gough. In the middle of a scene, the body of a hanged stagehand swings into view from the wings. The audience is thunderstruck, as is the prima donna, Aukin, who immediately quits. The producers soon replace the skittish singer with a new discovery, Sears. Unfortunately, Sears refuses to knuckle under to Gough's lecherous advances and the powerful benefactor rejects her for the role. Sears' tribulations continue when she is kidnaped by a strange dwarf, Wilson, and brought into the bowels of the opera house. There she meets Lom, a bizarre man whose face is hidden behind a crudely crafted, one-eyed mask. Lom admires Sears' vocal talents and has decided to train her to sing an opera he has written. The mysterious composer vows that she soon will be given the lead in a new show. Meanwhile, Sears' fiance, De Souza, has discovered that Gough had stolen his opera from an obscure composer who was believed to have drowned in the Thames. Curious about the dead man, De Souza traces his last hours and discovers a sewer tunnel which leads underneath the opera house. There he finds Sears with Lom and he unmasks the composer. Beneath the mask is a badly scarred visage. When confronted by De Souza, Lom admits that he is the composer whose work was stolen by Gough. Lom discovered that the copyright to his opera had been made in Gough's name. A struggle broke out between the men and during the fight, Lom's face was horribly burned by acid. Screaming in pain, Lom had run to the river and thrown himself in. There he found the sewer tunnel and decided to take up residence beneath the opera. Because he did not resurface, police assumed he had drowned. Sympathetic to Lom's plight, De Souza agrees to let Sears' vocal training continue. Eventually, Sears is given the lead in the opera and during the opening night performance De Souza notices Wilson, the dwarf, watching from the catwalk above the stage. Others see Wilson, and in his attempt to escape he knocks loose the huge chandelier that hangs directly above Sears. Seeing that she is about to be killed, Lom pulls off his mask, leaps onto the stage, and pushes Sears out of the way before the chandelier crushes him. Hammer's THE PHANTOM OF THE OPERA was originally to have starred the studio's favorite Dracula, Christopher Lee, but a last-minute switch was made in favor of Herbert Lom. While he could not hope to equal Chaney's classic tour-de-force,' or even Rains' memorable portrayal, Lom succeeded admirably in creating an alternately malevolent, sympathetic, and even tragic character. Hammer had hired professional maskmakers to create the phantom's mask, but they failed to come up with a suitable design. Director Fisher tried to shoot around Lom's masked scenes while awaiting the result of the maskmaker's work, but he finally grew impatient and had Hammer's makeup man, Roy Ashton, construct a crude mask out of cloth, tape, and gauze. The effect is perfect because the mask looks like something Lom would have made for himself while combing the dank sewers beneath the opera house. Despite the film's low budget, the production has the usual Hammer eye for detail and looks as if it had an expensive treatment. Gough turns in his usual fine performance as the evil opera benefactor, while Sears (whose singing was dubbed by opera singer Pat Clark) and De Souza are serviceable as the standard hero and heroine. Hammer's penchant for graphic bloodletting was suspended for this effort and the film manages to pack some memorable chills into its gothic melodrama.

p, Anthony Hinds; d, Terence Fisher; w, John Elder (based on a story by Gaston Leroux); ph, Arthur Grant (Technicolor); m, Edwin Astley; ed, Alfred Cox; prod d, Bernard Robinson; art d, Don Mingaye; makeup, Roy Ashton.

Horror **(PR:C-O MPAA:NR)**

PHANTOM OF THE PARADISE**½ (1974) 91m Harbor/FOX c

Paul Williams *(Swan)*, William Finley *(Winslow the Phantom)*, Jessica Harper *(Phoenix)*, George Memmoli *(Philbin)*, Gerrit Graham *(Beef)*, Jeffrey Comanor, Archie Hahn, Harold Oblong *(The Juicy Fruits, The Beach Bums, The Undeads)*, Gene Gross *(Warden)*, Henry Calvert *(Nightwatchman)*, Ken Carpenter, Sam Forney *(Stagehands)*, Leslie Brewer, Celia Derr, Linda Larimer, Roseanne Romine *(Surfgirls)*, Nydia Amagas, Sara Ballantine, Kristi Bird, Cathy Buttner, Linda Cox, Jane Deford, Bibi Hansen, Robin Jeep, Deen Summers, Judy Washington, Susan Weiser *(Dancers)*, Janet and Jean Savarino *(Singing Twins)*, Keith Allison *(Country and Western Singer)*, Bobby Birkenfeld *(Guy)*, Sandy Catton *(Black Singer)*, William Donovan, Scott Lane, Dennis Olivieri, Adam Wade *(Reporters)*, Nancy Moses, Diana Walden *(Backup Singers)*, Sherri Adeline *(Girl in Ticket Line)*, Carol O'Leary *(Betty)*, Mary Bongfeld, Coleen Crudden, Bridgett Dunn *(Mini-Boppers)*, William Shephard *(Rock Freak)*, Andrew Epper, Jim Lovelett *(Winslow's Doubles)*, Steven Richmond, James Gambino *(Swan's Doubles)*.

A rock 'n' roll parody better than THE ROCKY HORROR PICTURE SHOW, but not much better. One of director Brian De Palma's more original efforts, PHANTOM OF THE PARADISE combines elements of THE PHANTOM OF THE OPERA and "Faust" into a fairly entertaining, but only sporadically successful, horror/music/comedy. Finley stars as an unknown songwriter whose best composition is stolen by evil and unscrupulous record producer Williams (a questionable piece of casting, the man wrote sappy songs for groups like The Carpenters and he's supposed to represent the rock 'n' roll industry) who wants to use it as the basis for a new "sound" with which to open his glittery rock palace, the Paradise. Finley accuses Williams of the theft, but the record producer frames the songwriter on a phony drug charge and Finley is thrown in prison. After hearing that his song is now a hit, an angry Finley breaks out of jail and goes to Williams record company in order to destroy it. There he suffers a horrible accident and is scarred for life. Seeking revenge he dons a bizarre helmet and a black cape and begins to creep about the Paradise. Eventually Williams and the "Phantom" meet and strike an unholy pact in which Finley agrees to finish a rock 'n' roll symphony for Williams, only if Harper (whom Finley loves) is allowed to perform it. Unknowingly Finley is now satanically beholding to Williams because Williams sold his soul to the Devil many years before. Of course Williams tries to renege on the deal and marry Harper himself, but Finley puts an end to the evil, defeating Williams and then dying himself. While some of the attacks an the music industry, "glitter" rock, and success are right on target, the film suffers from a bad pace and overly complicated script that tries to comment on far too many aspects of pop culture to ever really nail down one of them. FOX had to pay Universal Studios a large sum of money because Universal sued over the similarities between PHANTOM OF THE PARADISE and PHANTOM OF THE OPERA, which the latter studio owned the rights to. Songs include: "Goodbye, Eddie, Goodbye," "Faust," "Upholstery," "Special to Me," "Old Souls," "Somebody Super Like You," "Life At Last," "The Hell of It," "The Phantom's Theme (Beauty and the Beast" (Williams, Tipton).

p, Edward R. Pressman; d&w, Brian De Palma; ph, Larry Pizer (Movielab Color); m, Paul Williams, George Aliceson Tipton; ed, Paul Hirsch; prod d, Jack Fisk; set d, Sissy Spacek; cos, Peter Jamison, Rosanna Norton; ch, William Shephard, Harold Oblong; spec eff, Greg Auer.

Comedy/Horror/Musical   **(PR:C MPAA:PG)**

PHANTOM OF THE PLAINS**   (1945) 56m REP bw

Bill Elliott (Red Ryder), Bobby Blake (Little Beaver), Alice Fleming, Ian Keith, William Haade, Virginia Christine, Bud Geary, Henry Hall, Fred Graham, Jack Kirk, Jack Rockwell, Tom London, Earle Hodgins, Rose Plummer.

In this entry in the Red Ryder B-western series, the duo of Elliott and Blake help a duchess who wants to marry a seemingly charming Englishman. Together they prove that her would-be husband is actually a wife murderer. (See RED RYDER SERIES, Index.)

p, R.G. Springsteen; d, Lesley Selander; w, Earle Snell, Charles Kenyon; ph, William Bradford; ed, Charles Craft; md, Richard Cherwin; art d, Hilyard Brown; set d, Charles Thompson.

Western   **(PR:A MPAA:NR)**

PHANTOM OF THE RANGE, THE**   (1938) 58m Victory bw

Tom Tyler, Beth Marion, Sammy Cohen, Soledad Jiminez, Forrest Taylor, Charles King, John Elliott, Dick Cramer.

Tyler stars as a wandering cowpoke who hooks up with pretty sagebrush girl Marion. She is traveling through the badlands to sell her dead grandpa's debt-ridden property. The only catch is that her crazy grandad's "ghost" is riding around scaring the wits out of everybody who comes near his "buried treasure." In reality the "ghost" is perpetrated by treasure hunters King, Taylor, Elliott, and Jimenez, who are trying to keep any curious folk away from their digs.

p, Sam Katzman; d, Bob Hill; w, Basil Dickey; ph, Bill Hyer; ed, Charles Henker.

Western   **Cas.**   **(PR:A MPAA:NR)**

PHANTOM OF THE RUE MORGUE*½   (1954) 83m WB c/3-D

Karl Malden (Dr. Marais), Claude Dauphin (Inspector Bonnard), Patricia Medina (Jeannette Rovere), Steve Forrest (Prof. Paul Dupin), Allyn McLerie (Yvonne), Veola Vonn (Arlette), Dolores Dorn (Camille), Anthony Caruso (Jacques), Merv Griffin (Georges Brevert), Paul Richards (Rene), Rolphe Sedan (LeBon), Erin O'Brien-Moore (Wardrobe Woman), Charles Gremora (Sultan), The Flying Zacchinis, Frank Lackteen, Henry Kulky.

Another Warner Bros. color, 3-D horror extravaganza, but unfortunately it is nowhere near as good as their previous effort, HOUSE OF WAX. Basically a remake of the 1932 MURDERS IN THE RUE MORGUE, this version starred an unbelievably hammy Karl Malden as a crazed scientist/zookeeper who hypnotizes a big ape (again played by Charles Gremora, in a monkey suit, who appeared in the 1932 version) and sends it out to kill all the good-looking women who won't have anything to do with him. Malden sets up professor Forrest as the murderer so that he can move in on Forrest's girl Medina. The ape falls in love with her also, which causes a considerable amount of tension between Malden and his hairy buddy. The climax sees most of the animals in the zoo running loose while Malden goes completely off his rocker. The only highlight of this film is trying to spot Merv Griffin in the background as a college student.

p, Henry Blanke; d, Roy Del Ruth; w, Harold Medford, James R. Webb (based on the story "Murders in the Rue Morgue" by Edgar Allan Poe); ph, J. Peverell Marley (3-D, Warner Color); m, David Buttolph; ed, James Moore; makeup, Gordon Bau.

Horror   **(PR:C MPAA:NR)**

PHANTOM PATROL*   (1936) 60m Ambassador bw

Kermit Maynard, Joan Barclay, Paul Fix, Julian Rivero, Eddie Phillips, Roger Williams, Lester Dorr, Dick Curtis, Harry Worth, George Cleveland, Rocky the Horse.

Ken's brother Kermit once again plays an intrepid Canadian Mountie wandering through the Northwest forests in search of trouble. Fix plays an evil crook who bursts into the secluded cabin of a famous mystery writer, ties him up, and then impersonates him. After more than enough of this nonsense, Maynard finally puts two and two together and gets his man.

p, Maurice Conn; d, Charles Hutchinson; w, Stephen Norris (based on the story "The Fatal Note" by James Oliver Curwood); ph, Arthur Reed.

Adventure   **Cas.**   **(PR:A MPAA:NR)**

PHANTOM PLAINSMEN, THE**   (1942) 57m REP bw

Bob Steele (Tuscon Smith), Tom Tyler (Stony Brooke), Rufe Davis (Lullaby Joslin), Robert O. Davis (Col. Eric Hartwig), Lois Collier (Judy Barrett), Charles Miller (Capt. Marvin), Alex Callam (Kurt Redman), Monte Montague (Muller), Henry Rowland (Lindrick), Richard Crane (Tad), Jack Kirk (Joe), Vince Barnett (Deputy Short), Lloyd Ingraham (Doctor), Al Taylor, Bud Geary (Outlaws), Herman Hack (Townsman), Edward Cassidy (Sheriff).

A wartime Three Mesquiteers B-western, which sees our heroes working on the horse ranch of their war-hating boss, Miller, who refuses to sell his steeds to any army. The boys soon find out that Nazis traveling incognito have been purchasing Miller's horses, so they set out to stop them from shipping the ponies to Germany. Unfortunately the boss' son is vacationing in Europe and gets nabbed by the Gestapo and held hostage until the old man allows the horses to be shipped to Der Fuhrer. The Three Mesquiteers won't let that happen so after lots of riding and shooting, they save the day. (See THREE MESQUITEERS series, Index.)

p, Louis Gray; d, John English; w, Robert Yost, Barry Shipman (based on a story by Yost from characters created by William Colt McDonald); ph, Bud Thackery; ed, William Thompson; md, Cy Feuer; art d, Russell Kimball.

Western   **(PR:A MPAA:NR)**

PHANTOM PLANET, THE**   (1961) 82m Four Crown/AIP bw

Dean Fredericks (Capt. Frank Chapman), Coleen Gray (Liara), Anthony Dexter (Herron), Dolores Faith (Zetha), Francis X. Bushman (Seson), Richard Weber (Lt. Makonnen), Al Jarvis (Judge Eden), Dick Haynes (Col. Lansfield), Earl McDaniel (Pilot Leonard), Michael Marshall (Lt. White), John Herrin (Capt. Beecher), Mel Curtis (Lt. Cutler), Jimmy Weldon (Navigator Webb), Akemi Tani (Communications Officer), Lori Lyons (Radar Officer), Richard Kiel (Solarite), Susan Cembrowska, Marissa Mathes, Gloria Moreland, Judy Erickson, Marya Carter, Allyson Ames, Marion Thompson, Warrene Ott.

A strange science fiction film starring Fredericks as an astronaut forced to crash land on an asteroid and make repairs. When he breathes the air on the asteroid, he shrinks to six inches tall and discovers a whole race of little people who have made the asteroid their spaceship. Resigning himself to the fact that he's going to stay small for awhile, the astronaut makes friends with the tiny people and helps them in their battle against the evil "solarites" (ugly, cannibalistic monsters) led by Richard Kiel. After defeating the monsters, Fredericks once again dons his space suit, breathes Earth oxygen, and returns back to normal size. He leaves the asteroid and heads back to Earth. Believe it or not, a 79-year-old Francis X. Bushman (noted for romantic leads in silent films as well as playing Messala to Ramon Navarro's title part in BEN HUR, 1926) plays the leader of the little people.

p, Fred Gebhardt; d, William Marshall; w, William Telaak, Fred de Gortner, Gebhardt; ph, Elwood J. Nicholson; m, Hayes Pagel; ed, Hugo Grimaldi, Donald Wolfe; art d, Bob Kinoshita; set d, Joe Kish; cos, Marla Craig; spec eff, Studio Film Service; makeup, David Newell.

Science Fiction   **(PR:A MPAA:NR)**

PHANTOM PRESIDENT, THE**½   (1932) 80m PAR bw

George M. Cohan (T.K. Blair/Doc Peter Varney), Claudette Colbert (Felicia Hammond), Jimmy Durante (Curly Cooney), George Barbier (Jim Ronkton), Sidney Toler (Prof. Aikenhead), Louise MacKintosh (Sen. Sarah Scranton), Jameson Thomas (Jerrido), Julius McVicker (Sen. Melrose), Paul Hurst (Sailor), Hooper Atchley (Announcer), Charles Middleton (Lincoln), Alan Mowbray (Washington).

Notable only as George M. Cohan's first (and almost last) talkie, THE PHANTOM PRESIDENT is a predictable political comedy which sees the "Yankee Doodle Dandy" playing a dual role: one as a lackluster presidential candidate with all the charm of a sofa; the other as his exact double, a smooth talking medicine man. Desperate to win, the candidate and his men hire the medicine man to impersonate their boss so the crowds will think he's got some spunk. Of course identities get confused, as does the candidates girl friend Colbert. The candidate gets so upset at these developments that he arranges for the medicine man to be bopped on the head and shipped out to sea, but the goons goof and he's the one taking the slow boat out. THE PHANTOM PRESIDENT was not a pleasant experience for those involved because an egotistical Cohan tried to grab control of the production, thinking he was the only one capable of writing, producing, and directing a George M. Cohan show. He even went so far as to refuse any publicity outings (i.e. interviews, magazine articles, radio) and the film died at the box office. Rodgers and Hart did the songs, which included the unmemorable: "Give Her a Kiss," "The Country Needs a Man," "Somebody Ought to Wave a Flag," and "The Convention."

d, Norman Taurog; w, Walter DeLeon, Harlan Thompson (based on a novel by George F. Worts); ph, David Abel; m/l, Richard Rodgers, Lorenz Hart.

Musical   **(PR:A MPAA:NR)**

PHANTOM RAIDERS***   (1940) 70m MGM bw

Walter Pidgeon (Nick Carter), Donald Meek (Bartholomew), Joseph Schildkraut (Al Taurez), Florence Rice (Cora Barnes), Nat Pendleton (Gunboat Jacklin), John Carroll (John Ramsell, Jr.), Steffi Duna (Dolores), Cecil Kellaway (Franklin Morris), Matthew Boulton (John Ramsell, Sr.), Alec Craig (Andy MacMillan), Thomas Ross (Dr. Grisson), Dwight Frye (Eddie Anders).

The second of the Nick Carter mysteries (Pidgeon would make two more after this) is a well-paced and finely directed low-budgeter with the super sleuth and his assistant, Meek, off to Panama to investigate the sinkings of a British company's ships when they leave the canal laden with supplies for the Allies. Eventually Pidgeon discovers that a big-time American gangster, Schildkraut, is behind the operation, and he perseveres to get the evidence to end the crook's activities. Jacques Tourneur's careful direction (he also directed the first Nick Carter picture) is visually fascinating as usual. (See NICK CARTER series, Index.)

p, Frederick Stephani; d, Jacques Tourneur; w, William R. Lipman (based on a story by Jonathan Latimer); ph, Clyde De Vinna; m, David Snell; ed, Conrad A. Nervig.

Mystery   **(PR:A MPAA:NR)**

PHANTOM RANCHER**   (1940) 61m Colony bw

Ken Maynard (Mitchell), Dorothy Short (Ann), Harry Harvey (Gopher), Ted Adams (Collins), Dave O'Brien (Luke), Tom London (Parker), John Elliott (Markham), Reed Howes (Lon), Steven Clark (Burton), Carl Matthews (Hank), Sherry Tansey (Joe), Sherry Tansey, Wally West, George Morrell, Herman Hack, Tarzan the Horse.

Maynard travels to a strange territory to collect the land his deceased uncle left him, only to find that his uncle was considered a miserly, mean-hearted mortgage grabber who terrorized the local farmers. Upset by this development, Maynard sets out to right things with the locals and discovers that his uncle wasn't mean at all, that actually it was an evil real-estate agent who used his relative as a front to commit his dirty deeds. Maynard dons a masked costume and rides off to every farmer in the area giving them enough money to pay off their mortgage, while taking abuse from the very same people when his mask is off. He eventually confronts the evil real-estate tycoon and all is well between Ken and the farmers.

p, Max Alexander, Arthur Alexander; d, Harry Fraser; w, Bill Lively; ph, William Hyers; m, Lew Porter; ed, Fred Bain.

Western **Cas.** **(PR:A MPAA:NR)**

PHANTOM RANGER*½ (1938) 54m MON bw

Tim McCoy (Tim Hayes), Suzanne Kaaren (Joan Doyle), Karl Hackett (Sharpe), John St. Polis (Pat Doyle), John Merton (Bud), Harry Strang (Jeff), Charles King (Dan), Dick Cramer (Barton), Tom London (Reynolds), Herbert Holcombe, Wally West, Horace B. Carpenter, Sherry Tansey, George Morrell, Herman Hack.

Federal agent McCoy uses the tried and true method of posing as a crook to catch the real crooks when he goes after a gang of counterfeiters who have kidnaped heroine Kaaren's father, a government engraver. The plucky cowgirl also goes undercover, posing as a dance-hall floozie in order to get some clues as to her father's whereabouts. Standard action marred somewhat by the weak dialog.

p, Maurice Conn; d, Sam Newfield; w, Joe O'Donnell (based on a story by Stanley Roberts, O'Donnell); ph, Jack Greenhalgh; ed, Richard Wray.

Western **Cas.** **(PR:A MPAA:NR)**

PHANTOM SHIP** (1937, Brit.) 80m Hammer/Guaranteed Pictures bw
(AKA: THE MYSTERY OF THE MARIE CELESTE; SECRETS OF THE MARY CELESTE)

Bela Lugosi (Anton Lorenzen), Shirley Gray (Sarah Briggs), Arthur Margetson (Capt. Briggs), Edmund Willard (Toby Bilson), George Mozart (Tommy Duggan), Ben Welden (Boas Hoffman), Dennis Hoey (Tom Goodschard), Gibson Gowland (Andy Gillings), Cliff McLaglen (Capt. Morehead), Herbert Cameron (Volkerk Grot), James Carew (James Winchester), Terence de Marney (Charlie Kaye), Ben Soutten (Jack Samson), Bruce Gordon (Olly Deveau), Johnny Schofield (Peter Tooley), Edgar Pierce (Arlan Harbens), (J.B. Williams), (Judge), Charles Mortimer (Attorney General), Wilfred Essex (U.S. Consul), Alec Fraser (Comdr. Mohon), Gunner Moir (Ponta Katz), Monti de Lyle (Portunato).

In the late 19th Century an American windjammer was found drifting off the English coast. The crew was gone and no trace of them was ever found. This film speculates what might have taken place on board the ill-fated ship. Lugosi is excellent as the sea captain who slowly descends into madness. He is hired to pilot a boat he had worked on six years previously, when the original crew had mistreated Lugosi until he was emotionally and physically ruined. Now he has the same first mate under his command and can finally exact his maddened revenge. Interesting as this sounds, the film is a disappointment. The weak supporting cast is unconvincing, with British accents abounding in a supposedly American crew. The illusion of a ship alone at sea is well-conveyed by the photography and direction, which carefully masks the studio sets. Yet the film is too tragic to be the gruesome psychological drama it aspires to be. The second film produced by Britain's Hammer Studios.

p, M. Fraser Passmore; d, Denison Clift; w, Charles Lackworthy; ph, Geoffrey Faithfull, Eric Cross.

Mystery **Cas.** **(PR:A MPAA:NR)**

PHANTOM SPEAKS, THE*½ (1945) 69m REP bw

Richard Arlen (Matt Fraser, Reporter), Stanley Ridges (Dr. Paul Renwick), Lynne Roberts (Joan Renwick), Tom Powers (Harvey Bogardus), Charlotte Wynters (Cornelia Willmont, Housekeeper), Jonathan Hale (Owen McAllister, District Attorney), Pierre Watkin (Charlie Davis, Editor), Marian Martin (Betty Hanzel), Garry Owen (Louis Fabian), Ralf Harolde (Frankie Teel), Doreen McCann (Mary Fabian).

Powers plays an executed killer who returns to earth and assumes the form of a mild-mannered scientist. From the scientist's body he continues to commit his heinous crimes. Intrepid reporter Arlen figures out what's up before the cops do.

p, Armand Schaefer; d, John English; w, John E. Butler; ph, William Bradford; ed, Arthur Roberts; md, Richard Cherwin; art d, Russell Kimball; set d, George Milo; cos, Adele Palmer.

Crime **(PR:A MPAA:NR)**

PHANTOM STAGE, THE** (1939) 57m Trem Carr/UNIV bw

Bob Baker (Bob), Marjorie Reynolds (Mary), George Cleveland (Grizzly), Forrest Taylor (Lawson), Reed Howes (Denver), Tex Palmer (Runt), Murdock MacQuarrie (Scott), Glenn Strange (Sheriff), Jack Kirk (Stage Driver), Dick Rush, Ernie Adams.

Baker plays a helpful cowpoke who assists lady stagecoach owner Reynolds in the mysterious disappearance of a gold cargo from her passengers' luggage with no apparent robbery having taken place. As it turns out, the villains have stuffed a midget into a trunk, and during the bumpy ride the little crook climbs out and pilfers the passengers' goods. A strange western.

p, Paul Malvern; d, George Waggner; w, Joseph West; ph, Harry Neumann; md, Frank Sanucci.

Western **(PR:A MPAA:NR)**

PHANTOM STAGECOACH, THE*½ (1957) 69m COL bw

William Bishop (Glen Hayden), Kathleen Crowley (Fran Maroon), Richard Webb (Tom Bradley), Hugh Sanders (Martin Maroon), John Doucette (Harry Farrow), Frank Ferguson (Joe Patterson), Ray Teal (Sheriff Ned Riorden), Percy Helton (Mr. Wiggins), Maudie Prickett (Mrs. Wiggins), Lane Bradford (Langton), John Lehmann (Williams), Eddy Waller (Sam), Robert Anderson (Varney).

A dull stagecoach war is the basis of this tired western. Innocent stage owner Ferguson finds his operation being attacked by a mysterious, armor-plated stagecoach owned by rival operator Sanders. Bishop rides in as a Wells Fargo investigator determined to get to the bottom of this nonsense.

p, Wallace MacDonald; d, Ray Nazarro; w, David Lang; ph, Henry Freulich; ed, Edwin Bryant; md, Mischa Bakaleinikoff; art d, Ross Bellah.

Western **(PR:A MPAA:NR)**

PHANTOM STALLION, THE** (1954) 54m REP bw

Rex Allen, Slim Pickens, Carla Balenda, Harry Shannon, Don Haggerty, Peter Price, Rosa Turich, Zon Murray, Koko the Horse.

Problems arise along the trail as a wagonmaster runs into a series of harrowing adventures. A good chance to see the great western sidekick Pickens in an early role.

p, Rudy Ralston, Herbert J. Yates; d, Harry Keller; w, Gerald Geraghty; ph, Bud Thackery; m, R. Dale Butts; ed, Harold Minter.

Western **(PR:A MPAA:NR)**

PHANTOM STOCKMAN, THE** (1953, Aus.) 67m Platypus/UNIV bw

Chips Rafferty (The Sundowner), Henry Murdoch (The Dancer), Jeanette Elphick (Kim Marsden), Guy Dolman (Mr. Stapleton), Max Osbiston (Frank McLeod), Albert Namatjira (Himself).

Rafferty plays an Australian Robin Hood who rides throughout the territory righting the wrongs done by bad men. During the course of the film he tracks down a killer, finds some cattle thieves, and generally makes himself a legend, especially with Elphick with whom he falls in love. Real-life aborigine painter Namatjira appears as himself.

d&w, Lee Robinson; ph, George Heath.

Adventure **(PR:A MPAA:NR)**

PHANTOM STRIKES, THE**½ (1939, Brit.) 58m Ealing-Northwood-Capad-ATP/MON bw (GB: THE GAUNT STRANGER)

Wilfrid Lawson (Maurice Meister), Sonnie Hale (Sam Hackett), Alexander Knox (Dr. Lomond), Louise Henry (Cora Ann Milton), Patrick Barr (Inspector Wembury), John Longden (Central Inspector Bliss), Patricia Roc (Mary Lenley), Peter Croft (Johnny Lenley), Charles Eaton (Col. Walford), George Merritt (Sgt. Carter), Arthur Hambling (Detective Sgt. Richards).

An average adaptation of an Edgar Wallace tale featuring Barr as a Scotland Yard investigator and Knox as a police doctor who team up to find the mysterious killer known only as "The Ringer" because he is a master of disguise. When lawyer Lawson receives a bouquet of flowers informing him that he'll be dead in 48 hours, the cops get to work trying to uncover the killer. As the hours tick away, the cops learn that Lawson's secretary had recently committed suicide and "The Ringer" holds the lawyer responsible. At the fated hour Lawson dies, but Barr reveals his partner Knox as the murderer. Third of four film versions of Wallace's novel.

p, Michael Balcon; d, Walter Forde; w, Sidney Gilliat (based on the novel The Ringer by Edgar Wallace); ph, Ronald Neame, Gordon Dines; ed, Charles Saunders; art d, O.F. Werndorff.

Mystery **(PR:A MPAA:NR)**

PHANTOM SUBMARINE, THE* (1941) 70m COL bw

Anita Louise (Madeleine Neilson), Bruce Bennett (Paul Sinclair), Oscar O'Shea (Capt. Valsar), John Tyrell (Dreux), Pedro De Cordoba (Henri Jerome), Victor Wong (Willie Ming), Charles McMurphy (2nd Mate), Harry Strang (Chief Engineer), Don Beddoe (Bartlett), Richard Fiske, Eddie Laughton (Cab Drivers), Budd Fine (Chalon), Henry Zynda (Sub Commander), Mildred Shay (Cigarette Girl), Jacques Vanaire (Headwaiter), William Ruhl (Lt. Morrissey), William Forrest (Jonas), Paul Scott (Assistant Editor), Max Barwyn (Butler), Charles Sullivan (Helmsman), Brick Sullivan, Al Rhein, George Barton, Myron Geiger, John Kascier, Ward Arnold, Bernard Breakston, Dutch Hendrian (Sailors).

Uneventful sea adventure starring Louise as a newspaper columnist hired by the Navy to assist in their investigation of reports involving an enemy submarine mysteriously crusing near the Panama Canal. Also in the area is a salvage ship manned by Bennett who is looking for gold in a sunken ship. Bennett finds the gold, Louise finds the sub (it was planting mines), and the two find romance in each other.

p, Ralph Cohn; d, Charles Barton; w, Joseph Krumgold (based on a story by Augustus Muir); ph, Barney McGill; ed, William Lyon; md, M. W. Stoloff; art d, Lionel Banks.

Adventure **(PR:A MPAA:NR)**

PHANTOM THIEF, THE**½ (1946) 65m COL bw

Chester Morris (Boston Blackie), Jeff Donnell (Anne Duncan), Richard Lane (Inspector Farraday), Dusty Anderson (Sandra), George E. Stone (Runt), Frank Sully (Sgt. Matthews), Marvin Miller (Dr. Nejino), Wilton Graff (Rex Duncan), Murray Alper (Eddie Alexander, Chauffeur), Forbes Murray (Dr. Purcell Nash), Joseph Crehan (Jumbo Madigan, Pawnbroker), Edward F. Dunn (Police Sergeant), George Magrill (Patrolman), Eddie Featherstone (Police Sergeant No. 2), Edmund Cobb (Policeman No. 1).

When some valuable gems are heisted, Morris, as reformed thief Boston Blackie, is hot on the trail. He follows the clues to a medium with shady methods and wraps up the case. Director Lederman began in films in 1913 as an extra in Mack Sennett comedies, and later worked as Fatty Arbuckle's prop man. He started directing films in the 1920s, and was responsible for several Rin Tin Tin features, serials, low-budget westerns, and action films. (See BOSTON BLACKIE series, Index.)

p, John Stone; d, D. Ross Lederman; w, Richard Wormer, Richard Weil (based on a story by G.A. Snow); ph, George B. Meehan, Jr.; ed, Al Clark; md, Mischa Bakaleinikoff; art d, Robert Peterson; set d, George Montgomery.

Crime/Mystery **(PR:A MPAA:NR)**

PHANTOM THUNDERBOLT, THE*½   (1933) 62m KBS/FOX-World Wide bw

Ken Maynard, Frances Lee, Frank Rice, William Gould, Bob Kortman, Harry Holman, Frank Beal, Wilfred Lucas, William Robyns, Nelson McDowell, Tarzan the Horse.

A fairly unusual Maynard B-western with our hero as a peace-loving cowpoke who hires a publicity man to spread the reputation that he's a gunslinger, figuring that gunslingers are usually left alone. Unfortunately, under his new guise as a gunman, he is hired by some scared townsfolk to chase away the villains who have invaded their homes. Stuck between a rock and a hard place, Maynard figures out a way to get rid of the bad guys and romance local girl Lee.

p, Burt Kelly, Sam Bischoff, William Saal; d, Alan James; w, Forrest Sheldon, Berry Burbridge; ph, Jackson Rose.

Western   Cas.   (PR:A MPAA:NR)

PHANTOM TOLLBOOTH, THE***½   (1970) 90m MGM c

Butch Patrick (Milo), Voices: Mel Blanc, Daws Butler, Candy Candido, Hans Conried, June Foray, Patti Gilbert, Shep Menken, Cliff Norton, Larry Thor, Les Tremayne.

A fine adaptation of Norton Justin's children's book which was Chuck Jones' and MGM's first animated feature. Patrick stars (in the live-action sequences) as Milo, a bored youngster who cannot maintain an interest in anything. One day the "phantom tollbooth" appears in his bedroom and Patrick drives his toy car into it. He is then transported (and animated) into a strange and wonderful world where society is broken up into two camps, letters and numbers. Unfortunately letters and numbers are at war with each other (each think that they are more important to society) and Patrick soon finds himself in the middle. Aided by a dog called Tock, Patrick restores the land to peace. A charming film that combines some fairly sophisticated ideas (demons from the "Mountains of Ignorance" cause much of the trouble and Patrick tries to restore "Rhyme and Reason" to the land) with cute and likable characters that are sure to grab a child's attention. Songs include: "Milo's Song," "Time Is a Gift," "Word Market," "Numbers Are the Only Things That Count," "Rhyme and Reason Reign" (Lee Pockriss, Norman Gimbel), "Don't Say There's Nothing to Do in the Doldrums," "Noise, Noise, Beautiful Noise" (Pockriss, Paul Vance).

p, Chuck Jones, Abe Levitow, Les Goldman; d, Jones, Levitow, David Monahan; w, Jones, Sam Rosen (based on the book by Norton Juster); ph, Lester Shorr (Metrocolor); animation ph, Jack Stephens; m, Dean Elliott; ed, Jim Faris; prod d, Maurice Noble; art d, George W. Davis, Charles K. Hagedon; set d, Henry Grace, Chuck Pierce; animation supervisors, Ben Washam, Hal Ambro, George Nicholas; animation, Irv Spence, Bill Littlejohn, Richard Thompson, Tom Ray, Philip Roman, Alan Zaslove, Edwin Aardal, Ed DeMattia, Xenia, Lloyd Vaughan, Carl Bell; backgrounds, Philip DeGuard, Irving Weiner, Robert McIntosh.

Animated Fantasy   Cas.   (PR:AAA MPAA:G)

PHANTOM VALLEY*½   (1948) 53m COL bw

Charles Starrett (Durango Kid), Smiley Burnette (Smiley), Virginia Hunter (Janice Littlejohn), Joel Friedkin (Sam Littlejohn), Robert W. Filmer (Bob Reynolds), Mikel Conrad (Crag Parker), Zon Murray (Frazer), Sam Flint (Jim Durant), Fred Sears (Ben Theibold), Teddy Infuhr, Jerry Jerome, Ozie Walters and His Colorado Rangers.

A fairly routine Starrett B western until the end when our hero guns down the female villain, Hunter, by shooting her in the back. The action revolves around Starrett's efforts to prevent a nasty range war. In the end Hunter is the one behind all the trouble. The real trouble is that it takes so long for Starrett to uncover this that nobody cares anymore. (See DURANGO KID series, Index.)

p, Colbert Clark; d, Ray Nazarro; w, J. Benton Cheney; ph, George F. Kelley; ed, Paul Borofsky; art d, Charles Clague; set d, David Montrose; m/l, Smiley Burnette.

Western   (PR:A MPAA:NR)

PHARAOH'S CURSE*½   (1957) 66m Bel-Air/UA bw

Mark Dana (Capt. Storm), Ziva Rodann (Simira), Diane Brewster (Sylvia Quentin), George Neise (Robert Quentin), Alvaro Guillot (Numar), Ben Wright (Walter Andrews), Guy Prescott (Dr. Michael Faraday), Terence de Marney (Sgt. Smollett), Richard Peel (Sgt. Gromley), Kurt Katch (Hans Brecht), Robert Fortin (Claude Beauchamp), Ralph Clanton.

Yet another archeological expedition ventures into Egypt and digs up tombs they're not supposed to. A crazed Egyptian follows the members of the expedition and kills them off one by one while getting progressively older and older. A dull film, especially for the fans of the Universal "Mummy" series.

p, Howard W. Koch; d, Lee Sholem; w, Richard Landau; ph, William Margulies; m, Les Baxter; ed, John F. Schreyer, George A. Gittens.

Horror   (PR:A MPAA:NR)

PHARAOH'S WOMAN, THE*   (1961, Ital.) 88m Vic-Faro/UNIV c (LA DONNA DEI FARAOINI)

John Drew Barrymore (Prince Sabaku), Linda Cristal (Akis), Armando Francioli (Prince Ramsis), Pierre Brice (Amosi, Court Physician), Lilly Lembo (Mareth), Guido Celano, Ugo Sasso, Andreina Rossi, Nerio Bernardi, Nando Angelini, Nadia Brivio, Enzo Fiermonte, Fedele Gentile, Nino Marchetti, Anna Placido, Wilma Sempetery, Anita Todesco.

In ancient Egypt, two Egyptian princes, Barrymore and Francioli, go into battle against each other. At stake is the leadership of Egypt and the hand of a beautiful girl played by Cristal. But Cristal is in love with Brice, the court physician, and

when Barrymore is killed in battle, Francioli leaves the pair in the desert to die. A happy ending ensues, however, when the lovers are rescued by a passing caravan.

p, Giorgio Venturini; d, Wenceslav Tourjansky, Giorgio Rivalta; w, Ugo Liberatore, Remigio Del Grosso, Virgilio Tosi, Massimo Vitalo (based on a story by Tosi, Vitalo); ph, Pier Ludovico Pavoni (Techniscope, Eastmancolor); m, Giovanni Fusco; ed, Antoniette Zita; art d, Arrigo Equini; cos, Giancarlo Bartolini Salimbeni; ch, Adriano Vitale.

Adventure   (PR:A MPAA:NR)

PHASE IV**½   (1974) 93m Alced/PAR c

Nigel Davenport (Ernest Hubbs), Michael Murphy (James Lesko), Lynne Frederick (Kendra), Alan Gifford (Eldridge), Robert Henderson (Clete), Helen Horton (Mrs. Eldridge).

Nice idea for a science fiction film, but it just didn't (and probably couldn't) work. Due to pollution and other various vague factors, all the ants in Arizona have banded together to strike a blow against mankind. The ants manage to devour livestock and humans in seconds and have built huge, elaborate tunnels under the earth. Puzzled scientists Davenport, Murphy, and Frederick investigate and set up a complex post in the desert. After a lot of nonsensical scientific mumbo-jumbo and endless close-ups of ants climbing all over the place, the little critters attack the scientist. They kill Davenport and grab Murphy and Frederick for ". . .what purpose, we didn't know." Neither do we. One would think that director Saul Bass, whose credit sequences for such films as Hitchcock's PSYCHO are nearly as interesting as the films themselves, could pump some energy into this potentially interesting premise, but all he comes up with is an overly intellectual bore. This film won the Grand Prix at the 1975 Trieste festival of science fiction films.

p, Paul B. Radin; d, Saul Bass; w, Mayo Simon; ph, Dick Bush, Ken Middleham (Technicolor); m, Brian Gascoigne, Yamashta; ed, Willy Kemplen; art d, John Barry; cos, Verena Coleman; spec eff, John Richardson.

Science Fiction   Cas.   (PR:A MPAA:PG)

PHENIX CITY STORY, THE**½   (1955) 100m AA bw

John McIntire (Albert Patterson), Richard Kiley (John Patterson), Kathryn Grant (Ellie Rhodes), Edward Andrews (Rhett Tanner), James Edwards (Zeke Ward), Lenka Peterson (Mary Jo Patterson), Biff McGuire (Fred Gage), Truman Smith (Ed Gage), Jean Carson (Cassie), Katherine Marlowe (Mamie), John Larch (Clem Wilson), Allen Nourse (Jeb Bassett), Helen Martin (Helen Ward), Otto Hulett (Hugh Bentley), George Mitchell (Hugh Britton), Ma Beachie (Herself), James Ed Seymour (Himself), Meg Myles (Singer), Clete Roberts (Interviewer in Prolog).

Kiley returns from the service to his Alabama home town and finds it even worse than when he left. Lying just across the state line from Columbus, Georgia, and that state's Ft. Benning, the town featured prostitution, drugs, and crooked gambling, all under the control of down-home crime czar Andrews, earning Phenix City the tag "wickedest city in the U.S." Kiley's father is elected attorney general on a reform ticket, and then is brutally murdered. Kiley accepts the job with the help of some angry citizens, and after trouble breaks out later, calls out the Alabama National Guard. Despite warnings such as a murdered black child dumped on his front lawn and the murder of Grant (one of Andrew's casino card dealers who decides to go straight), Kiley finally triumphs. Based on the true events that took place only a year previously, the film opens with a 13-minute prolog in which Roberts interviews some of the actual participants of the events dramatized in the film, including the widow of Albert Patterson, the reformer murdered by the mobsters in the town. This portion of the film, which helped get the extremely violent film past censors by grounding it in actual events, was optional and many exhibitors in the South cut it as too inflammatory. Although not director Karlson's best movie, it is in many ways his most remembered. Significantly, perhaps, he returned to the "Lone Crusader versus Corrupt Southern town" in 1973 with WALKING TALL, likewise based on real-life events.

p, Samuel Bischoff, David Diamond; d, Phil Karlson; w, Crane Wilbur, Daniel Mainwaring; ph, Harry Neumann; m, Harry Sukman; ed, George White; md, Sukman; cos, Chuck Keehne, Ann Peck; m/l, Harold Spina.

Crime Drama   (PR:C MPAA:NR)

PHFFFT!***   (1954) 91m COL bw

Judy Holliday (Nina Tracy), Jack Lemmon (Robert Tracy), Jack Carson (Charlie Nelson), Kim Novak (Janis), Luella Gear (Mrs. Chapman), Donald Randolph (Dr. Van Kessel), Donald Curtis (Rick Vidal), Arny Freeman (Language Teacher), Merry Anders (Marcia), Eddie Searles (Tommy), Wendy Howard (Artist's Model), William Lechner (Boy), Sue Carlton (Girl), Olan Soule (Mr. Duncan), Geraldine Hall (Nina's Secretary), Harry Cheshire (Lawyer), William Newell (Workman), Eugene Borden, Alphonse Martell (Maitre D's), Jerry Hausner (Radio Actor), Charlotte Lawrence (Radio Actress), Patrick Miller, George Hill (Pages), Tom Kingston (Manager), Fay Baker (Serena), Sally Mansfield (Miss Comstock), Vivian Mason, Maxine Marlowe, Shirlee Allard, Joyce Jameson (Secretaries), Hamil Petroff, Mylee Andreason (Dance Teachers), Charles Heard, Virgil Johansen (Doormen), Jimmie Dodd (Taxi Driver), Frank Arnold (Art Teacher), Richard Gordon, Edwana Spence, Joe Karnes (Extras Converted to Bits), Walter Hastings, Gil Warren, Ted Thorpe (Ad Lib Bits).

PHFFFT! was based on an unproduced play (with good reason) that author Axelrod reshaped for the movies. It's basically the story of an estranged couple whose divorce doesn't work out. Lemmon is a bright attorney and Holliday writes TV soap operas. They are married with no children and a gorgeous home in the suburbs. Things aren't going smoothly between them and, since they have no responsibility, she goes to Reno for a quickie divorce and it's all over. But if that were the case, there'd be no movie, right? Now, suddenly single, both buy new wardrobes, take dance lessons (the "Mambo" was the popular step back then), and seek new relationships. Holliday begins going out with Lemmon's pal, Carson, an amiable boor. At the same time, she's learning French from Freeman and mangling it, and having regular psychiatric appointments with Randolph in an attempt to improve her mind and her psyche. Lemmon begins dating Novak but she is more of a problem than a pleasure. Through it all, Lemmon and Holliday keep meeting accidentally and both get involved in a Mambo contest. They soon realize that they miss each other and reconcile after a while and the picture ends happily. It's a whipped-up omelet and seems more substantial than it is. Holliday and Lemmon were in their second film in a row together and proved a solid comedy duo at the box office. They were perfectly suited for each other as he played "exasperation" to her "flightiness." Carson was excellent in his secondary role. He was always an actor who could be counted upon to deliver a top-notch job in comedy or drama.

p, Fred Kohlmar; d, Mark Robson; w, George Axelrod; ph, Charles Lang; m, Frederick Hollander; ed, Charles Nelson; m, Morris Stoloff; art d, William Flannery; set d, William Kiernan; cos, Jean Louis.

Comedy **(PR:A MPAA:NR)**

PHILADELPHIA STORY, THE***** (1940) 112m MGM bw

Cary Grant *(C.K. Dexter Haven)*, Katharine Hepburn *(Tracy Lord)*, James Stewart *(Macauley Connor)*, Ruth Hussey *(Elizabeth Imbrie)*, John Howard *(George Kittredge)*, Roland Young *(Uncle Willie)*, John Halliday *(Seth Lord)*, Mary Nash *(Margaret Lord)*, Virginia Weidler *(Dinah Lord)*, Henry Daniell *(Sidney Kidd)*, Lionel Pape *(Edward)*, Rex Evans *(Thomas)*, Russ Clark *(John)*, Hilda Plowright *(Librarian)*, Lita Chevret *(Manicurist)*, Lee Phelps *(Bartender)*, David Clyde *(Mac)*, Claude King *(Willie's Butler)*, Robert De Bruce *(Dr. Parsons)*, Veda Buckland *(Elsie)*, Dorothy Fay, Florine McKinney, Helen Whitney, Hillary Brooke *(Mainliners)*.

The story is thin but the peformances and Cukor's direction make this film one of the classic comedies of all time. All of the cliched kudos apply here—ebullient, frothy, consistently amusing, and, most of all, great entertainment. Hepburn is the vibrant, attractive daughter of a super wealthy family living outside of Philadelphia. She is slated to marry stuffed-shirt coal company executive Howard but Hepburn's life is turned topsy-turvy when her ex-husband, playboy Grant, shows up to ostensibly attend the nuptials but he's really there to protect the reputation of his ex-inlaws. Grant has learned that newspaper tycoon Daniell plans to publish an expose about Hepburn's stagedoor Johnny father, Halliday, revealing in his *Spy*magazine that Halliday has been carrying on a secret love affair. To mollify the publisher, Grant arranges for the magazine's chief scandal reporter, Stewart, and a photographer, Hussey, to visit Hepburn's family. To impress the visitors, the family puts on a grand display of impeccable etiquette. But Howard resents the intrusion of Stewart and Hussey and says so. Moreover, Hepburn fights incessantly with Grant and finally, on the night before her wedding to Howard, she gets tipsy with Stewart who is smitten with her. Stewart tells her: "There's magnificence in you, Tracy. You're lit from within. You're the golden girl, full of life and warmth and delight." Later he carries Hepburn, who has passed out, to her bedroom, then appears still later on the terrace of the Lord home to be confronted by an incensed bridegroom, Howard. Before Howard can hit Stewart, Grant does the deed himself, knocking the stringy reporter down and unconscious. Howard stomps off, blaming Grant for the whole mess and telling him not to be present at the wedding the next day. When Stewart comes to, he asks Grant why he hit him and Grant tells him he did it to save him his jaw, that Howard hits harder. The next day Hepburn suffers a titantic hangover and can only think of tomato juice and shade. Howard arrives and upbraids her for her conduct the previous evening and he calls off the wedding. But it's too late, the family tells her, all the guests are arriving. Stewart volunteers to stand in for Howard, telling Hepburn that he truly loves her, but she gently rejects him. Then Grant at the last minute dictates to Hepburn the announcement to the guests and the fact that he, Grant, ex-husband, will also be Hepburn's new husband and she accepts with alacrity. As she walks down the aisle to wed again the man she has loved all along, Hepburn tells her father Halliday that she feels "like a human being." Witty, with hilarious scenes, such as rakish uncle Young pinching every bottom in sight and precocious Weidler dancing on tiptoes while singing "Lydia the Tattooed Lady," THE PHILADELPHIA STORY is Cukor's perfect comedy. Not one scene is dull and the effervescence of the actors, particularly Hepburn, Grant, and Stewart, shines through brilliantly. This was a tour de force for Hepburn whose eccentric and entrancing abilities were tailor-made for her role. Playwright Barry actually wrote the part for Hepburn and she appeared in the smash Broadway hit before making the film. She covered 25 percent of the play's cost and took no salary, but did take 45 percent of the profits and these were considerable. Joseph Cotten essayed the role of the playboy ex-husband in the play and Van Heflin portrayed the lovestruck reporter. Hepburn actually controlled the film rights to the play and she shrewdly encouraged Louis B. Mayer to deal with her, engineering him into not only paying her $250,000 for the rights but guaranteeing her the right to select her own director, screenwriter, and costars. She picked her favorite director, Cukor, who played his cameras rightly to Hepburn, and Donald Ogden Stewart as the writer, he being a close friend, besides one of the wittiest writers in Hollywood. Grant accepted his role only on the proviso that he receive top billing, which he did. He then demanded a then- whopping salary of $137,000 for the film and got it. (Grant then donated his entire salary from THE PHILADELPHIA STORY to the British War Relief Fund.) Hepburn particularly wanted James Stewart, who was suddenly one of the most important young actors around since his smash success in MR. SMITH GOES TO WASHINGTON a year earlier, receiving an Oscar nomination for his stunning portrayal of a patriotic young senator. Cukor brought the film in under schedule, shooting the entire picture in eight weeks. MGM felt that the movie would be successful but studio executives never envisioned it becoming an overnight box-office smash. It broke all records at the Radio City Music Hall with a return of almost $600,000 in six weeks. Stewart received an Oscar as Best Actor, and was surprised, stating that he had voted for his dear friend Henry Fonda for his great role in THE GRAPES OF WRATH. Donald Ogden Stewart received an Oscar for his spritely screenplay and when accepting the statuette, proudly stated, "I have no one to thank but myself!" Other nominations went to Best Picture, Hepburn as Best Actress, Hussey as Best Supporting Actress, and Cukor as Best Director. Hepburn, who won the coveted New York Film Critics Award, was defeated by Ginger Rogers for her role in KITTY FOYLE, but most later said she should have won, and rumors persisted that Hedda Hopper and other gadfly but powerful journalists had persuaded many Academy people to switch their votes from Hepburn (since she had already won the New York Critics Award) to Rogers. The film was remade as a charming but less effective musical, HIGH SOCIETY, in 1956, starring Bing Crosby, Frank Sinatra, and Grace Kelly.

p, Joseph L. Mankiewicz; d, George Cukor; w, Donald Ogden Stewart, (uncredited) Waldo Salt (based on the play by Philip Barry); ph, Joseph Ruttenberg; m, Franz Waxman; ed, Frank Sullivan; art d, Cedric Gibbons, Wade B. Rubottom; set d, Edwin B. Willis; cos, Adrian; makeup, Jack Dawn.

Comedy **Cas.** **(PR:A MPAA:NR)**

PHILIP (SEE: RUN WILD, RUN FREE, 1969, Brit.)

PHILO VANCE RETURNS** (1947) 64m PRC bw

William Wright *(Philo Vance)*, Terry Austin *(Lorena Simms)*, Leon Belasco *(Alexis)*, Clara Blandick *(Stella Blendon)*, Ramsey Ames *(Virginia)*, Damian O'Flynn *(Larry Blendon)*, Frank Wilcox *(George Hullman)*, Iris Adrian *(Choo-Choo Divine)*, Ann Staunton *(Helen Sandman)*, Tim Murdock *(Policeman)*, Mary Scott *(Maid)*.

The last of the short-lived Philo Vance films produced by PRC. This one stars Wright as Vance, who is hot on the trail of the murderer of a noted playboy. Wright must catch the killer before he murders the dead playboy's many ex-wives and girl friends, who have all been willed a share of his fortune. As usual, director William "One Shot" Beaudine does a competent hack job. (See PHILO VANCE series, Index).

p, Howard Welsch; d, William Beaudine; w, Robert E. Kent (based on the character created by S.S. Van Dine); ph, Jackson Rose; m, Albert Glasser; ed, Gene Fowler, Jr.; md, Irving Friedman; art d, Perry Smith; set d, Armor Marlow.

Mystery **(PR:A MPAA:NR)**

PHILO VANCE'S GAMBLE** (1947) 62m PRC bw

Alan Curtis *(Philo Vance)*, Terry Austin *(Laurian March)*, Frank Jenks *(Ernie Clark)*, Tala Birell *(Tina Cromwell)*, Gavin Gordon *(Oliver Tennant)*, Cliff Clark *(Inspector Heath)*, Toni Todd *(Geegee Desmond)*, James Burke *(Lt. Burke)*, Francis Pierlot *(Robert Butler)*, Joseph Crehan *(District Attorney Stone)*, Garnett Marks *(Charles O'Mara)*, Grady Sutton *(Mr. Willetts)*, Charles Mitchell *(Guy Harkness)*, Joanne Frank *(Norma Harkness)*, Dan Seymour *(Jeff)*.

The second Philo Vance mystery from PRC features Curtis (his second, and last, stab at the role) as the intrepid detective, who investigates several murders that occur after the theft of a valuable emerald. The body count begins when the thieves' ringleader is bumped off. Dead folks begin popping up everywhere and eventually, after all the other suspects are dead, Curtis figures out who the killer is. (See PHILO VANCE series, Index.)

p, Howard Welsch; d, Basil Wrangell; w, Eugene Conrad, Arthur St. Clair (based on an original story by Lawrence Edmund Taylor, based on characters created by S. S. Van Dine); ph, Jackson Rose; ed, W. Donn Hayes; md, Irving Friedman; art d, Perry Smith; set d, Armor Marlowe, William Kiernan.

Mystery **(PR:A MPAA:NR)**

PHILO VANCE'S SECRET MISSION½** (1947) 58m PRC bw

Alan Curtis *(Philo Vance)*, Sheila Ryan *(Mona Bannister)*, Tala Birell *(Mrs. Phillips)*, Frank Jenks *(Ernie Clark)*, James Bell *(Harry Madison)*, Frank Fenton *(Paul Morgan)*, Paul Maxey *(Martin Jamison)*, Kenneth Farrell *(Joe the Photographer)*, Toni Todd *(Louise Roberts)*, David Leonard *(Carl Wilson)*.

In the late 1940s, PRC bought the rights to S.S. Van Dine's novels and brought the Philo Vance character back to the screen for three films. Unfortunately, there was nothing new added to the material, and the films therefore became routine mysteries. Curtis starred as Vance, who investigates the strange murder of mystery magazine publisher Maxey. The case interests Curtis because Maxey had recently hired him to write a mystery novel for which Maxey would provide the ending. Upon investigation, Curtis learns Maxey may have solved the murder of Birell's spouse, and decides the publisher probably was bumped off so he couldn't tell anyone. To solve Maxey's murder, Curtis determines he must first figure out who killed Birell's husband. (See PHILO VANCE series, Index).

p, Howard Welsch; d, Reginald Le Borg; w, Lawrence Edmund Taylor (based on characters created by S. S. Vine); ph, Jackson Rose; ed, W. Donn Hayes; art d, Perry Smith; set d, Armor Marlowe, Clarence Steenson; spec eff, George Teague.

Mystery **(PR:A MPAA:NR)**

PHOBIA*½ (1980, Can.) 94m Spiegel-Bergman/PAR c

Paul Michael Glaser *(Dr. Peter Ross)*, John Colicos *(Inspector Barnes)*, Susan Hogan *(Jenny)*, Alexandra Stewart *(Barbara)*, Robert O'Ree *(Bubba)*, David Bolt *(Henry)*, David Eisner *(Johnny)*, Lisa Langlois *(Laura)*, Kenneth Welsh *(Sgt. Wheeler)*, Neil Vipond *(Dr. Clegg)*, Patricia Collins *(Dr. Toland)*, Marian Waldman *(Mrs. Casey)*, Gwen Thomas *(Dr. Clemens)*, Paddy Campanero, Gerry Salsberg, Peter Hicks, Joan Fowler, John Stoneham, Terry Martin, Ken Anderson, Janine Cole, Karen Pike, Wendy Jewel, Coleen Embry, Diane Lasko.

A fairly routine horror film from noted director John Huston, featuring television actor Paul Michael Glaser. Glaser essays the role of a controversial psychologist who treats the fears of convicted murderers by making them confess and confront their basic, deep-rooted phobias. Unfortunately, someone is taking things a bit far and killing the patients, using their basic fears as his tool. The whole thing is very contrived, with a solution a simpleton could decipher after the credits sequence. Basically this is an unsavory film with a very weak central performance.

p, Zale Magder; d, John Huston; w, Lew Lehman, Jimmy Sangster, Peter Bellwood (based on a stroy by Gary Sherman, Ronald Shusett); ph, Reginald H. Morris; m, Andre Gagnon; ed, Stan Cole; art d, David Jaquest.

Mystery **(PR:O MPAA:R)**

PHOBIA, 1981 (SEE: THE NESTING, 1981)

PHOENIX CITY STORY (SEE: PHENIX CITY STORY, 1955)

PHONE CALL FROM A STRANGER*** (1952) 96m FOX bw

Shelley Winters *(Binky Gay)*, Gary Merrill *(David Trask)*, Michael Rennie *(Dr. Fortness)*, Keenan Wynn *(Eddie Hoke)*, Evelyn Varden *(Sally Carr)*, Warren Stevens *(Marty Nelson)*, Beatrice Straight *(Mrs. Fortness)*, Ted Donaldson *(Jerry Fortness)*, Craig Stevens *(Mike Carr)*, Helen Wescott *(Jane Trask)*, Bette Davis *(Marie Hoke)*, Sydney Perkins *(Stewardess)*, Hugh Beaumont *(Dr. Brooks)*, Thomas Jackson *(Mr. Sawyer)*, Harry Cheshire *(Dr. Fletcher)*, Tom Powers *(Dr. Fernwood)*, Freeman Lusk *(Thompson)*, George Eldredge *(Doctor)*, Nestor Paiva *(Headwaiter)*, Perdita Chandler *(Mrs. Brooks)*, Genevieve Bell *(Mrs. Fletcher)*, George Nader *(Pilot)*, John Doucette *(Bartender)*, William Neff *(Copilot)*, Ruth Robinson *(Nurse)*.

This is a well-made episodic film that sustains interest by excellent acting on the part of everyone in the cast. Merrill leaves his wife, Westcott, when he learns that she is about to desert him and their children for a lover. He is flying to Los Angeles to think things out. While on the plane he meets Winters, an ex-stripper, who is nervous about the fact that this is her first time on an airplane. She's been in New York for an audition in a new musical and didn't make it. This has caused her to give up her hopes for a career and to devote herself to the husband she loves dearly, Craig Stevens. Her mother-in-law, Varden, runs a Los Angeles night spot and wishes her son would dump Winters, but she is determined to make things work. The plane hits turbulence and must make a forced landing at a small airport in the U.S. heartland. Rennie, another passenger, is a doctor who needs legal advice and when he learns that Merrill is a lawyer, he tells him the problem. Rennie is going to California to face the music over the deaths of three people whom he killed while driving in a drunken state. He's kept that under wraps for five years now and cannot contain himself any longer. He must exorcise this demon so he can establish a better relationship with his son, Donaldson, who dearly loves him but has some doubts about the accident. Wynn, a blustery traveling salesman given to hoary old jokes, joins the other two. He suggests that they all get together in California for a drink sometime to talk about this "adventure" that they've shared. Wynn is a noisy man and neither Merrill nor Rennie really wants to get to know him any better but, for the sake of appearances, they all exchange phone numbers and promise to see each other in L.A. in the future. Wynn talks about his wife, Davis, and brags about what a knockout she is and all of her other attributes but the others think it's just smoke he's blowing. They get aboard their plane and it takes off, then bad weather attacks them and the plane is downed again, this time half-crashing and half-landing. Merrill is knocked senseless and when he recovers, he is shocked to see that Rennie, Winters, and Wynn are all dead and he is one of very few survivors. The airlines people want to inform the families but Merrill asks if he can do it personally, rather than have the airlines do it, as he has come to know the dead trio. He goes to the Rennie home and tells Donaldson what his father intended to do. Donaldson is about to run away to South America but Merrill persuades the youth to stay and comfort his mother, Straight. Next, he visits Winter's husband, Stevens, and his mother, Varden. Knowing that it won't hurt anything if he lies, Merrill tells them both that Winters had won the role in the Broadway show and was coming home to celebrate. This takes the wind out of Varden who had spent much time trying to convince her son that Winters had no musical ability whatsoever. Finally, he goes to see Wynn's widow, Davis, and is shocked to discover that she's not the raving beauty Wynn had bragged about. Rather, she is a crippled woman who is doomed to spend the rest of her life in bed. Davis, in a terrific performance, tells Merrill that she became paralyzed in an accident after having left Wynn for Warren Stevens. When the guy left quickly, Wynn took her back and forgave her. He spent the next years taking care of her and worshipping the ground she could no longer walk upon. Merrill is touched by Davis and tells her his own marital situation. She pleads with him to call his wife, let her know he's alive, and to go back to her. Merrill makes that call and plans to return to Westcott. It was a four-story movie with the one link in the chain being Merrill and yet it was so adroitly done that the episodes blended well into each other.

p, Nunnally Johnson; d, Jean Negulesco; w, Johnson (based on the story by I.A.R. Wylie); ph, Milton Krasner; m, Franz Waxman; ed, Hugh Fowler; art d, Lyle Wheeler, J. Russell Spencer; set d, Thomas Little, Bruce MacDonald; cos, Elois Jenssen; spec eff, Ray Kellogg.

Drama **(PR:A-C MPAA:NR)**

PHONY AMERICAN, THE** (1964, Ger.) 72m Astra-Film Kunst/Signal International bw (TOLLER HECHT AUF KRUMMER TOUR)

Christine Kaufmann *(Inge)*, Michael Hinz *(Helmut)*, William Bendix *(Sgt. Harrigan)*, Ron Randell *(Capt. Smith)*, Walter Gross *(Max)*, Alfred Pongratz *(Rudolf)*, Karl Lieffen *(Moritz)*, Gary Marshall *(McNulty)*, Oskar Paulig *(Hermann)*, Wera Frydtberg *(Mary)*, Gotz Burger, Bob Cunningham, Charles Hickman, Mal Sondock, Holger Hagen, Stefan Schnabel, Fred Durr, William H. Taylor, Inge Benz, Leonardo Putzgruber, Al Hoosman, Burt Bertez, Paula Braend, Cheril Bernard, James Saeger, Frithjof Vierock, Karl Otto Alberty, Axel Scholz.

German comedy-melodrama detailing the efforts of WW II orphan Hinz as he bounces around from one surrogate family to another. He is first adopted by an American pilot who is later killed during the Korean War. As a teenager, Hinz is adopted by a German family and falls in love with his stepsister Kaufmann. Wanting desperately to join the U.S. Air Force, Hinz steals a uniform and gets hold of phony documentation so he can join up. The trick works and he's on his way, with the help of Bendix, a friendly sergeant. But just as he's about to be transported to the states, Hinz's real indentity is discovered and he's booted out of the service. Though Bendix offers to adopt him, Hinz decides to remain in Germany with Kaufmann.

p, Alfred Strauss, Harold N. Even; d, Akos von Rathony; w, Michael Krims, Alexander Badal (based on the story by Heinz Gross, Egon G. Schleinitz); ph, Ernst W. Kalinke; m, Herbert Jarczyk; ed, Annaliese Schoennenbeck, Margot Mohrbutter; art d, Hans Sahnle, Friedrich Tahler.

Drama/Comedy **(PR:A MPAA:NR)**

PHYNX, THE zero (1970) 91m Cinema Organization/WB c

A. Michael Miller, Ray Chippeway, Dennis Larden, Lonny Stevens *(The Phynx)*, Lou Antonio *(Corrigan)*, Mike Kellen *(Bogey)*, Michael Ansara *(Col. Rostinov)*, George Tobias *(Markevitch)*, Joan Blondell *(Ruby)*, Martha Raye *(Foxy)*, Larry Hankin *(Philbaby)*, Teddy Eccles *(Wee Johnny)*, Ultra Violet *(Herself)*, Pat McCormack *(Father O'Hoolihan)*, Joseph Gazal *(Yakov)*, Bob Williams *(No 1)*, Barbara Noonan *(Bogey's Secretary)*, Rich Little *(Voice in Box)*, Sue Bernard, Ann Morrell, Sherry Miles *(Belly Girls)*, Patty Andrews, Busby Berkeley, Xavier Cugat, Fritz Feld, John Hart, Ruby Keeler, Joe Louis, Marilyn Maxwell, Maureen O'Sullivan, Harold "Oddjob" Sakata, Ed Sullivan, Rona Barrett, James Brown, Cass Daley, Leo Gorcey, Louis Hayward, Patsy Kelly, Guy Lombardo, Butterfly McQueen, Richard Pryor, Col. Harland Sanders, Rudy Vallee, Johnny Weissmuller, Edgar Bergen and Charlie McCarthy, Dick Clark, Andy Devine, Huntz Hall, George Jessel, Dorothy Lamour, Trini Lopez, Pat O'Brien, Jay Silverheels, Clint Walker *(Cameos)*, Sally Ann Struthers *(World's No. 1 Fan)*.

A disappointing all-star extravaganza with a silly plot that must have been sold to the assembled cast by one of the greatest con-men of all time. The "plot" concerns a secret American government agency that forms a rock 'n' roll band to infiltrate Communist Albania and rescue the American entertainers who are being held hostage there. A computer advises the agency to gather together a black model, a college radical, an athlete, and an American Indian for a typical, youth-oriented band eventually christened "The Phynx." After some "hilarious comedy episodes," the band eventually makes its way to Albania, collapses the prison walls by churning out unbelievably loud electric guitar chords, and frees the trapped entertainers! The film is supposed to be a ridiculous, light-hearted farce, but the filmmakers and stars are so un-hip and so condescending that the whole thing just comes off as ignorant and infantile. Just take a gander through the cast list to see the unbelievable variety of "stars" that got suckered into this mess. Must be seen to be believed.

p, Bob Booker, George Foster; d, Lee H. Katzin; w, Stan Cornyn (based on a story by Booker, Foster); ph, Michel Hugo (Technicolor); ed, Dann Cahn; prod d, Stan Jolley; set d, Ralph S. Hunt; cos, Donfeld; m/l, Mike Stoller, Jerry Leiber; spec eff, Westheimer Co.

Comedy **(PR:C MPAA:GP)**

PIAF—THE EARLY YEARS*** (1982, U.S./Fr.) 104m Moritz-Weissman/FOX c

Brigitte Ariel *(Edith Piaf)*, Pascale Christophe *(Simone [Momone] Berteaut)*, Guy Trejan *(Lucien Leplee)*, Pierre Vernier *(Raymond Asso)*, Jacques Duby *(Julien)*, Anouk Ferjac *(Madeleine)*, Sylvie Joly *(Lulu)*, Yvan Varco *(Felix)*, Michel Bedetti *(Constantini)*, Francois Dyrek *(Henri)*, Betty Mars *(Vocals for Ariel)*.

A musical biography of France's most beloved singer, Edith Piaf, depicting her rise to fame in the legendary Paris of the 1920s and early 1930s. Beginning with her birth, the picture works its way through her early, temporary, blindness, the street performances with her father, and her relationship with half-sister Simone Berteaut (played by Christophe), who wrote the book on which the film is based. Also included is Piaf's relationship with a Parisian worker and the subsequent birth of a child. While the marriage took a turn for the worst, her career skyrocketed with the release of her first hit, "L'Accordianiste." PIAF—THE EARLY YEARS was originally released in France in 1974 with an English version prepared for U.S. release. The picture didn't see a U.S. release until eight years later in a subtitled version. Another period of Piaf's life made it to the screen in 1984 in Claude Lelouch's EDITH AND MARCEL, detailing her affair with boxer Marcel Cerdan. For diehard Piafophiles, the great chanteuse can be glimpsed in a handful of films including Jean Renoir's FRENCH CAN-CAN (1956) and Sacha Guitry's ROYAL AFFAIRS AT VERSAILLES (1957). (In French; English subtitles.)

p, Cy Feuer, Ernie Martin; d, Guy Casaril; w, Casaril, Francoise Ferley, Marc Behm (based on the book *Piaf* by Simone Berteaut); ph, Edmond Sechan (Eastmancolor); ed, Henri Taverna, Louisette Hautecoeur; art d, Francois DeLamothe; cos, Rosine Delamare; ch, Danny Daniels.

Musical/Biography **(PR:A-C MPAA:PG)**

PICCADILLY*½ (1932, Brit.) 92m BIP/World Wide bw

Gilda Gray *(Mabel Greenfield)*, Jameson Thomas *(Valentine Wilmot)*, Anna May Wong *(Shosho)*, King Ho Chang *(Jim)*, Cyril Ritchard *(Victor Smiles)*, Hannah Jones *(Bessie)*, Charles Laughton *(A Night Club Hawk)*, Ellen Pollock *(Vamp)*, Harry Terry *(Publican)*, Gordon Begg *(Coroner)*, Charles Paton *(Doorman)*, Raymond Milland, Debroy Somers and his Band.

The title of this almost totally silent film refers to the area around Piccadilly Circus, which is the British equivalent of New York's Broadway, the center of nightlife and the theater. It was shot with no sound whatsoever, then a dialog sequence at the top was added in the hopes that it might merit some attention from audiences. Wong and Gray are Americans although it's technically a British picture, having been made there with a mostly English cast. Wong is the dishwasher in a Piccadilly nightclub were Gray dances for a living. Thomas, the owner of the *boite*, spots

Wong dancing in the kitchen for her pals and decides that she might be better suited as a performer than a dishwasher. This is not a happy moment for Gray, who is the featured dancer with Ritchard. Gray likes Thomas and Ritchard likes her but keeps him away when they are not tripping the light fantastic. Thomas gets Ritchard out of the picture and business starts to fade so everyone figures that Ritchard was the reason why the habitues frequented the club. Thomas gets Wong to dance, with accompaniment by her ukulele-playing boy friend, Ho Chang. With more money in her pocket, Wong moves to a better apartment but stays in the Chinatown section known as "Limehouse." When Thomas starts to make a move on Wong, Gray is incensed and goes to visit her one night, after Thomas has taken her home. There's a scuffle and it looks as though Wong pulled a knife as Gray shoots her down. That's a cheat. Later, Ho Chang testifies at the inquest and thinks Wong was killed by Thomas, then Ho Chang kills himself after having confessed that it was he who killed Wong. Gray had already testified that she thought she'd done it. In the end, no one knows what happened and the whole thing ends in a muddle. Gray's famed "shimmy dance" is never seen and Wong more than acquits herself well in the terpsichore department. In all, they shouldn't have added sound to this, as it takes away rather than enhances the story because it is so incongruous and obviously a late addition. In small roles, note Charles Laughton in his first feature film after two shorts, and Ray Milland when he was still using his full first name. Cyril Ritchard will, of course, always be remembered for his work as "Captain Hook" in the TV version of PETER PAN.

p&d, E.A. Dupont; w, Arnold Bennett; ph, Werner Brandes; ed, J.W. McConaughy; art d, Alfred Junge.

Crime/Love Story **(PR:A-C MPAA:NR)**

PICCADILLY INCIDENT** (1948, Brit.) 88m ABF/MGM bw (AKA: THEY MET AT MIDNIGHT)

Anna Neagle *(Diana Fraser)*, Michael Wilding *(Capt. Alan Pearson)*, Michael Laurence *(Bill Weston)*, Frances Mercer *(Joan Draper)*, Coral Browne *(Virginia Pearson)*, A. E. Matthews *(Sir Charles Pearson)*, Edward Rigby *(Judd)*, Brenda Bruce *(Sally Benton)*, Leslie Dwyer *(Sam)*, Maire O'Neill *(Mrs. Milligan)*, Reginald Owen *(The Judge)*, Neville Mapp, Duncan McIntyre, Michael Medwin, Madge Brindley, Roger Moore, Harry Locke.

Soppy British melodrama stars Neagle as a WREN who is listed as missing in action during WW II and presumed dead, only to resurface three years later very much alive and shocked to find that her husband, Wilding, has remarried and fathered a child.

p&d, Herbert Wilcox; w, Nicholas Phipps (based on a story by Florence Tranter); ph, Bryan Langley, Max Greene [Mutz Greenbaum]; ed, Flora Newton; md, Anthony Collis; art d, William C. Andrews.

Drama **(PR:A MPAA:NR)**

PICCADILLY JIM½** (1936) 100m MGM bw

Robert Montgomery *(Jim Crocker)*, Frank Morgan *(Mr. Crocker)*, Madge Evans *(Ann Chester)*, Eric Blore *(Bayliss)*, Billie Burke *(Eugenia)*, Robert Benchley *(Macon)*, Ralph Forbes *(Lord Charles)*, Cora Witherspoon *(Nesta Pett)*, Tommy Bupp *(Ogden Pett)*, Aileen Pringle *(Paducah)*, Grant Mitchell *(Herbert Pett)*, E.E. Clive *(Editor)*, Billy Bevan *(Taxi Driver)*, Grace Hampton *(Mrs. Brede)*, Torben Meyer *(Butler)*, Sidney Miller *(Messenger Boy)*, Dennis Morgan *(Bit)*.

Montgomery plays the title character, a famous London newspaper cartoonist. His father, Morgan, is an actor who is posing as a count so he can be accepted into his latest sweetheart's rich family. After spoiling his father's scheme and losing his job, Montgomery comes up with the idea to draw a strip featuring the members of the family Morgan tried to marry into. It's all very silly, but Morgan is wonderful and the film is fun.

p, Harry Rapf, d, Robert Z. Leonard; w, Charles Brackett, Edwin Knopf (based on the novel by P.G. Wodehouse); ph, Joseph Ruttenberg; m, Dr. William Axt; ed, William S. Gray.

Comedy **(PR:A MPAA:NR)**

PICCADILLY NIGHTS** (1930, Brit.) 90m Kingsway General/Film Booking Office bw

Billie Rutherford *(Billie)*, Elsie Bower *(Elsie)*, Julian Hamilton *(Jackson)*, June Grey *(Dolly)*, Pat Courney *(Eros)*, Maurice Winnick and His Band, Ralph Goldsmith and His Band.

Rutherford is an aspiring singer who gets the inevitable big break when the leading lady of an important production shows up at the theater too drunk to perform. Standard plot is just an excuse to display some pleasant enough musical acts.

p&d, Albert H. Arch; w, Arch, Roger Burford.

Musical **(PR:A MPAA:NR)**

PICCADILLY THIRD STOP** (1960, Brit.) 90m Sydney Box-Ethiro/Rank bw

Terence Morgan *(Dominic Colpoys-Owen)*, Yoko Tani *(Seraphina Yokami)*, John Crawford *(Joe Pready)*, Mai Zetterling *(Christine Pready)*, William Hartnell *(Colonel)*, Dennis Price *(Edward)*, Ann Lynn *(Mouse)*, Charles Kay *(Toddy)*, Douglas Robinson *(Albert)*, Gillian Maude *(Bride's Mother)*, Trevor Reid *(Bride's Father)*, Ronald Leigh Hunt *(Police Sergeant)*.

Another routine caper-gone-bad movie starring Morgan and Crawford as two crooks who latch onto the daughter of a foreign ambassador, Tani, when she unthinkingly reveals her father, away on business, has left $280,000 behind in the embassy safe. Morgan works his charms on the innocent girl, who becomes so enamored with him that she actually helps the crooks with their plan to steal the money by entering the embassy through an old underground subway tunnel. Swedish film actress-turned director Mai Zetterling has a small part.

p, Norman Williams; d, Wolf Rilla; w, Leigh Vance; ph, Ernest Steward; m, Philip Green; ed, Bernard Gribble; cos, Joan Ellacott.

Crime **(PR:A MPAA:NR)**

PICK A STAR** (1937) 76m MGM bw (AKA: MOVIE STRUCK)

Stan Laurel *(Himself)*, Oliver Hardy *(Himself)*, Patsy Kelly *(Nellie Moore)*, Jack Haley *(Joe Jenkins)*, Mischa Auer *(Rinaldo Lopez)*, Lyda Roberti *(Dagmar)*, Rosina Lawrence *(Cecilia Moore)*, Charles Halton *(Malheimer)*, Tom Dugan *(Dimitri Hogan)*, Russell Hicks *(J. Aubrey Stone)*, Spencer Charters *(Judge Pike)*, Sam Adams *(Sheriff)*, Robert Gleckler *(Nightclub Steward)*, Johnny Arthur *(Ernie)*, Joyce Compton *(Ernie's Bride)*, James Finlayson *(Laurel and Hardy's Director)*, Walter Long *(Mexican Tough Guy)*, James C. Morton *(Bartender)*, Ralph Malone, Blair Davies *(Pilots)*, Eddie Kane *(Albert, Headwaiter)*, Charles A. Bachman, Charles McMurphy, Frank O'Connor *(Studio Guards)*, Charlie Hall, Ray Cooke *(Assistants to Finlayson)*, Cully Richards *(Master of Ceremonies)*, Sam Lufkin *(Mexican hit with a chair)*, Wesley Barry *(Assistant Director)*, John Hyams *(Mr. McGregor)*, Leila McIntyre *(Mrs. McGregor)*, Otto Fries, Howard Brooks *(Other Judges)*, Benny Burt *(Tony)*, Margie Roanberg *(Miss Gopher City)*, Alice Moore *(Miss Centerville)*, Mary Blackwell *(Mrs. Apple Valley)*, Arline Abers *(Miss Mill Creek)*, Brooks Benedict *(Eddie)*, May Wallace *(Joe Jenkins' Landlady)*, Jack Norton *(Oscar, the Souse)*, Wilma Cox *(Oscar's Wife)*, Barbara Weeks *(Hostess)*, Edward Clayton *(Bellboy)*, Bob (Mazooka) O'Conor *(Announcer of Bandits' Arrival)*, Syd Saylor *(Street Sweeper)*, Jack Hill *(Dress Extra)*, Jack Egan *(Orchestra Conductor)*, Charley Sullivan *(Juicer)*, Eddie Hart *(Benny, the Chauffeur)*, Si Jenks *(Old-Timer)*, Wilbur Mack *(Door Greeter)*, Murdock MacQuarrie *(Undertaker)*, Mary Gordon *(Undertaker's Wife)*, Al Williams, Jr. *(Cashier)*, Barney Carr *(Grip)*, Felix Knight, Patricia Ka *(Nightclub Singers)*, James Burke *(Detective Nolan)*, Bob McClung *(Off-Camera Harmonica Player for Laurel and Hardy)*.

Although Laurel and Hardy were top-billed on some of the studio publicity, there scenes are totally extraneous to the movie and could have been cut out just as well. However, since they got most of the laughs in this trite story, their loss would have resulted in a huge hole. Lawrence is a sweet young Iowa girl who comes to Hollywood as part of a contest. But it's all publicity and soon no one will pay any attention to her at the studio. She winds up knocking the studio bosses out when Haley, the publicity man, arranges a screen test and she winds up as a full-fledged actress. In the course of events, she meets Auer, an egotistical movie star, makes friends with Patsy Kelly, who chimes in with some nice wisecracks, and gets to see how movies are made as Laurel and Hardy show the studio visitors the intricacies of "breakaway" bottles and furniture in a saloon brawl for a Western they are shooting. Of course, both men manage to knock themselves out when they pick up the wrong merchandise for the demonstration. The other Laurel and Hardy sequence is the old wheeze where Hardy swallows a harmonica and makes a funny noise each time Laurel pushes in Babe's huge stomach. It begins when Laurel is seen with a horn and Hardy tells him to put it down as he doesn't know how to play it. Laurel proves he can and makes the horn sound like a tuba while playing "Old Black Joe" (Stephen Foster). Laurel then picks up a harmonica and plays "Reuben, Reuben" (Traditional). Not to be outdone, Hardy pulls out a teeny harmonica and does "Listen To the Mockingbird" (Traditional), then Laurel retaliates by doing the same tune, only better. Hardy is non-plussed so he puts the harmonica under his tongue and does "Yankee Doodle" then swallows the harmonica. Laurel ends the scene by playing Hardy's stomach in a marvelous rendition of "Pop Goes The Weasel!" (Traditional) and that's the comedy highlight of this otherwise forgettable movie.

p, Hal Roach; d, Edward Sedgwick; w, Richard Flournoy, Arthur Vernon Jones, Thomas J. Dugan; ph, Norbert Brodine, Art Lloyd; m, Arthur Morton, Marvin Hatley; ed, William Terhune; md, Morton, Hatley; art d, Arthur I. Royce; set d, William L. Stevens; cos, Ernest Schrapps; spec eff, Roy Seawright; ch, Edward Court; m/l, Fred Stryker, Johnny Lange, Hatley, "Pick a Star," R. Alexander Anderson (sung by Lawrence); makeup, Jack Dawn.

Comedy **(PR:AAA MPAA:NR)**

PICK-UP*½ (1933) 76m PAR bw

Sylvia Sidney *(Mary Richards)*, George Raft *(Harry Glynn)*, William Harrigan *(Jim Richards)*, Lilian Bond *(Muriel Stevens)*, Clarence Wilson *(Sam Foster)*, George Meeker *(Artie Logan)*, Louise Beavers *(Magnolia)*, Florence Dudley *(Freda)*, Patricia Farley *(Sadie)*, Eddie Clayton *(Don)*, Dorothy Layton *(Peggy)*, Alice Adair *(Sally)*, Robert McWade *(Jerome Turner)*, Purnell Pratt *(Prosecuting Attorney)*, Brooks Benedict *(Tony)*, Charles Middleton *(Mr. Brewster)*, Eleanor Lawson *(Matron)*, Oscar Apfel *(The Warden)*, Al Hill *(Johnson, the Reporter)*, Lona Andre, Gail Patrick *(Pantry Girls)*.

There weren't too many actresses who were better at playing the victim than Sylvia Sidney. In this, one of five films she made under director Gering's aegis, Sidney is Mary Richards (oddly, that was the name Mary Tyler Moore used for her TV show), who had been known as "Baby Face Mary" when she was part of a con game she used to pull with her husband, Harrigan, who is still in the slammer as the picture opens. Sidney is just getting out of prison on a rainy day when she hops into a cab driven by Raft, just to get out of the downpour. She can't afford to take the taxi anywhere but he feels sorry for her and lets her stay at his apartment that night without making any demands, sexual or otherwise. He comes home the following day after working and is happy and surprised to see that this attractive jailbird did not steal a thing from his residence. Some months pass and the two of them fall in love, but they can't cement it permanently because she is still the wife of Harrigan, who is languishing in jail. Sidney, a smart cookie, convinces Raft to give up the cab job and move to the suburbs. Since he has a great knowledge of automobiles and their innards, he opens a garage and is on the way to turning himself into a successful mechanic. Their love flourishes and all seems well until Bond, a local society type with the scruples of an alley cat, comes on the scene and begins to vamp Raft. He starts to run around with Bond and faithful Sidney is distraught over his behavior. But since she has no legal hold on him, she is powerless to get the stars he sees when he looks at Bond out of his eyes. Harrigan breaks out of jail and Sidney learns that he's looking for her. Since she doesn't want to put Raft in jeopardy, she races away. Harrigan is captured and Sidney is brought to trial, falsely charged as an accessory to the jailbreak. She is cleared of any complicity, her marriage to Harrigan is annulled, Raft has come to his senses and realizes that Sidney is the woman for him, and they decide to make it a marriage. In one of his earliest roles, Raft was still unsure of himself, especially in the unaccustomed white hat of the "good guy," and Sidney, who had been in movies for years, acted rings around him.

p, B. P. Schulberg; d, Marion Gering; w, S.K. Lauren, Agnes Brand Leahy (based on a story by Vina Delmar); ph, David Abel.

Crime/Romance **(PR:A MPAA:NR)**

PICKPOCKET**** (1963, Fr.) 75m Lux/New Yorker bw

Martin Lassalle *(Michel)*, Marika Green *(Jeanne)*, Pierre Leymarie *(Jacques)*, Jean Pelegri *(Police Inspector)*, Kassagi *(Master Pickpocket)*, Pierre Etaix *(Accomplice)*, Dolly Scal *(Michel's Mother)*, Cesar Gattegno *(Detective)*.

Using Dostoyevsky's *Crime And Punishment* as a point of departure, director Bresson has created a wonderful study of a criminal on the road to redemption in PICKPOCKET (released in Paris in 1959). Lassalle stars as a lonely young man who resigns himself to the fate of becoming a pickpocket. An initial attempt is unsuccessful and he is easily caught. It is during his arrest that Lassalle's consciousness is raised on the rights and wrongs of theft. When his sickly mother dies, Green and Leymarie, his two closest friends, offer advice and solace. Lassalle, however, chooses to return to crime, taking lessons from master pickpocket Kassagi. The police inspector observes Lassalle's criminal life but fails to arrest him, partly because of flimsy evidence and partly because he is intrigued with Lassalle's ideas. When Lassalle's partners in crime are arrested, the pickpocket flees France, leaving behind Green, who has by now fallen in love with him. When he returns years later he finds Green unmarried and with a child. Again he resorts to stealing and again he is caught. Green visits him in his cell and for the first time he realizes that he loves her. In the memorable final moments, Green and Lassalle embrace through the bars of the cell as he tells her, "What a strange way I have traveled to find you at last." As Bresson has so often done in his films, PICKPOCKET details a man's struggle between his inner feelings and his attempt to survive in society. What separates PICKPOCKET from so many other films is Bresson's use of Lassalle's inner voice (which corresponds to the written words in his diary) as a narrative element. Those familiar with the work of screenwriter-director Paul Schrader will note a few similarities in style and thought, which comes as no surprise since Schrader wrote a book entitled *Transcendental Style On Film: Ozu, Bresson, and Dreyer*. Elements of TAXI DRIVER's narrative (voiceover and diary passages corresponding) are lifted from PICKPOCKET, as in the final line of AMERICAN GIGOLO (1980). While Schrader's transcendental style has failed to achieve the status of a Bresson, or Ozu, or Dreyer (TAXI DRIVER, his finest achievement, comes closest), he has, at least, brought an interesting philosophical element into American film. (In French, English subtitles.)

p, Agnes Delahie; d&w, Robert Bresson (based on the novel *Crime And Punishment* by Fyodor Dostoyevsky); ph, Leonce-Henri Burel; m, Jean-Baptiste Lully; ed, Raymond Lamy; art d, Pierre Charbonnier.

Drama/Crime **(PR:A MPAA:NR)**

PICKUP* (1951) 76m Forum/COL bw

Hugo Haas *(Jan Horak)*, Beverly Michaels *(Betty)*, Allan Nixon *(Steve)*, Howland Chamberlin *(Professor)*, Jo Carroll Dennison *(Irma)*, Mark Lowell *(Waiter)*, Art Lewis *(Driver)*, Jack Daly *(Doctor)*, Bernard Gorcey *(Joe)*.

The first in a long series of low-budget features produced, written, starring and directed by Czechoslovakian character actor Haas, who, for some inexplicable reason, decided to go into business himself at the age of 50. Haas plays a middle-aged widower who picks up floozy Michaels, foolishly brags about the size of his savings account, and soon finds himself married to her. Her obvious dislike of him brings on a fit of deafness (?!), and a hearing-impaired Haas is soon the object of a murder plot formulated by Michaels and her lover. The evil pair decides to run Haas over with the car, but the lily-livered lover loses his nerve at the last second and only knocks the older man down. Haas miraculously regains his hearing and kicks the bums out. It plays as well as it reads.

p&d, Hugo Haas; w, Haas, Arnold Phillips (based on the novel *Watchman 47* by Joseph Kopta); ph, Paul Ivano; m, Harold Byrns; ed, Douglas W. Bagier.

Drama **(PR:A MPAA:NR)**

PICKUP ALLEY** (1957, Brit.) 92m Warwick/COL bw (GB: INTERPOL; AKA: INTERNATIONAL POLICE)

Victor Mature *(Charles Sturgis)*, Anita Ekberg *(Gina Broger)*, Trevor Howard *(Frank McNally)*, Bonar Colleano *(Amalio)*, Dorothy Alison *(Helen)*, Andre Morell *(Breckner)*, Martin Benson *(Jarolli)*, Eric Pohlmann *(Fayala)*, Peter Illing *(Capt. Baris)*, Sydney Tafler *(Curtis)*, Lionel Murton *(Murphy)*, Danny Green *(Bartender)*, Sidney James *(Joe)*, Yana *(Singer)*, Alec Mango *(Salko)*, Marne Maitland *(Guido)*, Betty McDowall *(Drug Addict)*, Gaylord Cavallaro *(Amalio's Brother)*, Harold Kasket *(Kalish)*, Peter Elliott *(Badek)*, Alfredo Rizzo *(Abbata)*, Umberto Fiz *(Monello)*, Kevin Stoney *(Policeman)*, Brian Wilde, Van Boolen, Brian Nissen, Charles Lloyd Pack, Al Mullock, Alfred Burke, Maurice Browning, Cyril Shaps, Paul Stassino, Yvonne Romain, Russell Waters, Richard Molinas, Wolfe Morris.

After his sister is killed, Interpol agent Mature swears vengeance on Howard, the drug kingpin responsible for her death. Fortunately he is assigned to do just that and after a chase through London, Rome, Athens, Paris and New York, Howard falls from a crane. Howard's the only bright spot in this dark alley.

p, Irving Allen, Albert R. Broccoli; d, John Gilling; w, John Paxton (based on a story by A.J. Forrest); ph, Ted Moore (CinemaScope); m, Richard Bennett; ed, Richard Best; md, Muir Mathieson; art d, Paul Sheriff; cos, Elsa Fennell; makeup, Roy Ashton.

Crime **(PR:A MPAA:NR)**

PICKUP IN ROME (SEE: FROM A ROMAN BALCONY, 1961, Fr./Ital.)

PICKUP ON 101½** (1972) 93m AIP c

Jack Albertson *(Obediah Bradley)*, Lesley Warren *(Nickie)*, Martin Sheen *(Les Cavanaugh)*, Michael Ontkean *(Chuck)*, Hal Baylor *(Railroad Cop)*, George Chandler *(Pawnshop Owner)*, Mike Road *(Desk Sergeant)*, Eddie Firestone *(Auto Mechanic)*, William Mims *(Antique Shop Owner)*, Robert Donner *(Jesse, Ist Farmer)*, Kathleen Harper *(Jesse's Wife)*, Harold J. Stone *(2nd Farmer)*, Don Spruance *(Highway Patrolman)*, Buck Young, Peggy Stewart, Grey Young, Cynthia Johnson *(Family in Car)*, William Bryant, William Lally, Fran Ryan, Chuck Dorsett, Earl Brown, Shayna Rockwell, Dorothy Brewer, Shirley Hayward, Serina Rockwell, Sandra Rockwell, Ricky Rockwell.

While hitchhiking through the Southwest, Warren hooks up with lovable hobo Albertson. Soon they are picked up by unemployed rock'n'roll star Sheen. They have a series of unpleasant experiences with the "Establishment" before Albertson suffers a fatal heart attack, asking to be buried on his old farm: Sheen and Warren are denied permission by the current owner, so they have Albertson cremated and scatter his ashes over the farm. Sappy counterculture movie isn't offensive, just stupid. Best reason to see this is for another look at Sheen's apprenticeship before becoming a star. Don Dunn sings "Echos Of The Road" (Stu Phillips, Bob Stone), "Electric Ethel" (Murphy and Castleman), and "Flowers For My Bed" (Nino Candido).

p, Christian Whittaker, Ed Garner; d, John Florea; w, Anthony Blake; ph, Carl F. Marquard (Movielab Color); m, Stu Phillips; ed, The Jamez; md, Igo Kantor; cos, Oscar Rodrigues; makeup, Dan Greenway.

Drama **(PR:C MPAA:PG)**

PICKUP ON SOUTH STREET*½** (1953) 80m FOX bw

Richard Widmark *(Skip McCoy)*, Jean Peters *(Candy)*, Thelma Ritter *(Moe)*, Murvyn Vye *(Capt. Dan Tiger)*, Richard Kiley *(Joey)*, Willis B. Bouchey *(Zara)*, Milburn Stone *(Winoki)*, Henry Slate *(MacGregor)*, Jerry O'Sullivan *(Enyart)*, Harry Carter *(Dietrich)*, George E. Stone *(Police Clerk)*, George Eldredge *(Fenton)*, Stuart Randall *(Police Commissioner)*, Frank Kumagi *(Lum)*, Victor Perry *(Lightning Louie)*, Maurice Samuels *(Peddler)*, Parley Baer *(Stranger)*, Jay Loftin *(Librarian)*, Virginia Carroll *(Nurse)*, Roger Moore *(Mr. Victor)*, Clancy Cooper *(Lean Man)*, John Gallaudet *(Campion)*, Wilson Wood *(Driver)*, Ray Montgomery, Ray Stevens *(F.B.I. Agents)*, Ralph Moody *(Captain)*, George Berkeley *(Customer)*, Emmett Lynn *(Sandwich Man)*.

A rough and brutal melodrama set against a backdrop of New York's seedy underworld which delves into the secret workings of federal agents and Communist spies. Widmark is a petty crook—the proverbial "three-time loser"—whose actions are motivated solely by greed. When he lifts a wallet from the purse of Peters, he finds himself in deeper trouble than he ever imagined. Contained in the wallet is top-secret microfilm that Peters is unwittingly transporting for her lover, Kiley—a Communist spy—whom she mistakenly believes to be a patents lawyer. When Kiley discovers that the microfilm has been stolen, he orders Peters to find Widmark and get it back. Also on Widmark's track are two federal agents who have been shadowing Peters. Both the agents and Peters get information on Widmark's whereabouts from Ritter, an aging ex-pickpocket who supports her scant income from tie peddling by selling information on underworld criminals. Peters appeals to Widmark initially on a sexual level, but fails to get the microfilm. The agents appeal to Widmark's sense of patriotism, but this too fails since Widmark doesn't know or care about the effect of Communism on the American way of life. With all the interest in the microfilm, Widmark knows that it is worth a great deal of money, so he holds out for an offer from Kiley. By now Peters has fallen for Widmark, and has turned against Kiley, whom she sees as un-American. Kiley attempts to buy Widmark's address from Ritter, but she proudly refuses to sell to a Communist—at any price. Enraged, Kiley kills Ritter. Widmark now has a reason to keep the microfilm out of Kiley's hands—not because Kiley is a Communist but because he killed a friend of his. Kiley then returns to Peters (who by now has obtained the film) and mercilessly beats her when he learns of her part in the scheme. Having discovered that some of the microfilm is missing and having obtained Widmark's waterfront address, Kiley pays him a visit. Widmark eludes him and follows him to a subway station where he manages to steal back the microfilm from Kiley. In retaliation for the death of Ritter and the attack on Peters, Widmark pounds Kiley into the pavement and turns him over to the federal agents, who barricade him in an apartment and finally gun him down. Only then is it revealed that his contact is none other than the federal agent who is heading up the search. Having assisted the feds, Widmark is left to finish his romance with Peters and return, free from the law, to his gutter life. A truly provocative film from Fuller, PICKUP ON SOUTH STREET originally was a simple story about drug pushers written by Dwight Taylor and titled "Blaze of Glory." (This original theme was retained in a dubbed version released in France and titled LA PORTE DE LA DROGUE, literally "The Door of the Pusher".) Fox head Darryl Zanuck had planned for Fuller to direct the project with Betty Grable terribly miscast in Peters' role (a more fitting choice was Shelley Winters who was originally slated). Fuller, however, had his own ideas and decided to politicize the film. Unfortunately it has been viewed by some as rabidly anti-Communist, ignoring the subtleties and screenwriting talents of Fuller, who contributes much more depth and complexity to the film than blind anti-Communism would allow. Even more than being a political film in an era of McCarthyism, PICKUP ON SOUTH STREET is the story of a criminal who, like so many of Fuller's heroes, fights to retain his individuality in the midst of expectations and societal pressures. Widmark's "Skip McCoy" character does not foil a Communist scheme because of his devotion to the American ideal but because Kiley, who just happens to be a Communist spy, did him wrong and deserved to be avenged. Both Widmark and Peters are superb in their lead roles, but it is Ritter as the seedy but much-loved Moe that gives the film an emotional punch. One is instantly attracted to Ritter's tough edge and further feels an emotional tie to her as she dies by Kiley's wicked hand while spending her final moments listening to her phonograph. Strangely, though deservedly, Ritter's performance was recognized at Oscar time when she was awarded a Supporting Actress nomination—an oddity for a brutal B movie directed by Fuller.

p, Jules Schermer; d&w, Samuel Fuller (based on the story by Dwight Taylor); ph, Joe MacDonald; m, Leigh Harline; ed, Nick de Maggio; md, Lionel Newman; art d, Lyle R. Wheeler, George Patrick; set d, Al Orenbach; cos, Travilla; spec eff, Ray Kellogg.

Crime/Spy Drama **(PR:C MPAA:NR)**

PICK-UP SUMMER zero (1981) 92m Film Ventures International c (AKA: PINBALL SUMMER, PINBALL PICK-UP)

Michael Zelniker, Carl Marotte, Karen Stephen, Helene Udy.

Yes, it's scantily clad teenagers getting drunk or stoned or both, driving vans and cars, having sex, and playing video games. That's about it. This film had two former titles with the word "pinball" in it. When the trend fizzled, Film Ventures International changed the title again.

p, Jack F. Murphy; d, George Mihalka; w, Richard Zelniker; m, Jay Boivin, Germain Gauthier.

Comedy **(PR:O MPAA:R)**

PICKWICK PAPERS, THE*** (1952, Brit.) 109m REN/Mayer-Kingsley bw

James Hayter *(Samuel Pickwick)*, James Donald *(Mr. Winkle)*, Alexander Gauge *(Mr. Tupman)*, Lionel Murton *(Mr. Snodgrass)*, Nigel Patrick *(Mr. Jingle)*, Kathleen Harrison *(Rachael Wardle)*, Joyce Grenfell *(Mrs. Leo Hunter)*, Hermione Gingold *(Miss Tomkins)*, Donald Wolfit *(Sgt. Buzfuz)*, Hermione Baddeley *(Mrs. Bardell)*, Harry Fowler *(Sam Weller)*, Diane Hart *(Emily Wardle)*, Joan Heal *(Isabel Wardle)*, William Hartnell *(Irate Cabman)*, Athene Seyler *(Miss Witherfield)*, Sam Costa *(Job Trotter)*, George Robey *(Tony Weller)*, Gerald Campion *(Fat Boy)*, Walter Fitzgerald *(Mr. Wardle)*, Mary Merrall *(Grandma Wardle)*, Raymond Lovell *(Surgeon)*, Cecil Trouncer *(Mr. Justice Stareleigh)*, June Thorburn *(Arabella)*, D.A. Clarke-Smith *(Mr. Dodson)*, Alan Wheatley *(Mr. Fogg)*, Felix Fenton *(Dr. Slammer)*, Max Adrian *(Aide)*, Barry MacKay *(Mr. Snubbins)*, Hattie Jacques *(Mrs. Nupkins)*, Noel Purcell *(Roker)*, Gibb McLaughlin *(Foreman)*, Dandy Nichols, Helen Goss, Jack MacNaughton, Noel Willman, Helen Burls, May Hallatt, Raf de la Torre, David Hannaford, Jessie Evans, Linda Gray, Joan Benham, Pamela Deeming, John Vere, John Kelly, William Strange.

If ever a Dickens novel shouted to be filmed, it was *The Pickwick Papers* and they did a jolly good job with this version. In later years, a stage musicalization by Leslie Bricusse was attempted with lesser results, although it did have one hit song, "If I Ruled the World." The Pickwick club is a group of middle-class, middle-aged men chaired by Hayter. Their sole mission in life is studying the English life. To that end, Hayter, Donald, Gauge, and Murton set out on a series of episodic adventures filled with much more humor than the usual Dickens novel or film version. Patrick is a very cavalier Casanova whom they meet and who gets them into several hassles including a duel, a fancy dress breakfast that turns out hilariously funny, a breach of promise suit brought against Hayter, and a sojourn in debtor's prison. In the end, Patrick, who turns phrases mightily but doesn't have a farthing to his name, manages to make enough money to begin his life anew. Baddeley, one of the two Hermiones in the film (the other being Gingold), runs a boarding house for bachelors but they don't notice that the sign announcing rooms for rent also commits the roomers to marriage to her, if they are not already wed. It's a very funny film with some of England's best light comedians and comediennes in attendance including the duet of Hermiones, delicious Joyce Grenfell, rotund Hattie Jacques (so wonderful in MAKE MINE MINK and the "Carry On" series), and Dandy Nichols, who died in early 1986 but will always be recalled for her role as the dingbat wife in "Till Death Us Do Part," the British TV show which inspired "All In the Family." All the period costumes and sets are spot-on and the fun that the actors were having is evident every second.

p, Noel Langley, George Minter; d&w, Langley (based on the novel by Charles Dickens); ph, Wilkie Cooper; m, Antony Hopkins; ed, Anne V. Coates; md, Hopkins; cos, Beatrice Dawson.

Historical Comedy **(PR:AA MPAA:NR)**

PICNIC**** (1955) 115m COL c

William Holden *(Hal Carter)*, Rosalind Russell *(Rosemary Sydney* Kim Novak *(Madge Owens)*, Betty Field *(Flo Owens)*, Susan Strasberg *(Millie Owens)*, Cliff Robertson *(Alan)*, Arthur O'Connell *(Howard Bevans)*, Verna Felton *(Mrs. Helen Potts)*, Reta Shaw *(Linda Sue Breckenridge)*, Nick Adams *(Bomber)*, Raymond Bailey *(Mr. Benson)*, Elizabeth W. Wilson *(Christine Schoenwalder)*, Phyllis Newman *(Juanita Badger)*, Don C. Harvey, Steven Benton *(Policemen)*, Henry P. Watson *(Chamber of Commerce President)*, Floyd Steinbeck, Paul R. Cochran, Harold A. Beyer, Adlai Zeph Fisher, Harry Sherman Schall *(Chamber of Commerce Men)*, Abraham Weinlood *(Trainman)*, Wayne R. Sullivan *(Foreman)*, Warren Frederick Adams *(Stranger)*, Carle E. Baker *(Grain Elevator Worker)*, Henry Pegueo *(Mayor)*, Flomanita Jackson *(Committee Woman)*, George E. Bemis *(Neighbor)*.

Inge's severely critical play about small-town America, which won a Pulitzer Prize, was brought to the screen with faithful application by Logan and offered Holden a marvelous opportunity to render a bravura performance, which he did. Holden, a drifter, enters a small Kansas town just as the community is preparing to celebrate Labor Day. Seeking out an old college friend, Robertson, Holden is asked to attend the festivities. Robertson insists that Holden meet his fiancee, beautiful blonde Novak, attractive but as wooden as a cigar store Indian, and the two fall in love at first sight. Holden's original intention was to get work from Robertson, whose father is the richest man in the county. Holden struts about the town flexing his muscles and most of the local ladies, including Novak's younger, naive sister, Strasberg, and schoolmarm Russell, fall for the handsome stranger. Holden brags about his adventures and Russell gets drunk while admiring him, thrusting aside her reliable date, O'Connell, and losing control, ripping Holden's shirt right off his back in her seizure of lust. Coupled to this humiliation, Holden is forced into a fight with Robertson so that he beats up his old friend and then must run from the law, dragging Novak with him. He finally persuades her to return home, confessing that he's nothing but a bum and a liar. Novak does go home while Holden exits the way he arrived, by hopping a freight. Novak, however, realizes that her love for Holden is stronger than the security of home and she takes a bus heading in the same direction as the train, intending to catch up with the love of her life. The love scenes between Holden and Novak steam up the screen and the sequence showing their dance together is about as sensual as ever sizzled the celluloid. This was Holden's last film for Columbia, one which he initially refused to do since he was 37 years old and his part called for a much younger man. Yet he pulled it off brilliantly. He also told off Columbia chief Harry Cohn and scared director Logan by pumping down countless martinis during a production party and then standing on the window ledge of Logan's fourteenth floor suite. On another occasion he dangled himself from Rosalind Russell's tenth floor suite by only two fingers. The nervous Russell told her guests: "If we don't pay any attention to him, he'll stop this nonsense." She later stated that Holden was "strong as an ox, stubborn as a monkey, and luckier than anything." This was Novak's first leading role and she was terrified of botching the job. She became reclusive, declining all offers for dinner from cast members. Instead she went to church regularly, praying that she would be a success. Snorted Holden when hearing about this, "She'd be better off if she spent more time learning her lines and less time reciting her rosary." But it was Holden who stumbled when it came to the soft, slow dance he had to perform with Novak to the strains of "Moonglow." He exploded, telling choreographer Miriam Nelson: "I can't do it! I'm a lousy dancer." Replied Nelson: "You don't have to be Gene Kelly. It's just a little ad lib dance." Logan, who rubbed every scene in the film to high gloss, took Holden to roadhouses and compelled him to dance with Nelson to jukebox songs until he was confident he could perform with Novak. Yet he almost backed out at the last moment, telling Cohn that he wanted a "stunt" check for $8,000 to do the scene. Rather than delay the film, the mogul paid the fee. Just before doing the scene Holden swigged down several martinis and when Novak objected, he said, "I'm sure as hell not going to do this sober." Cinematographer Howe used his camera to circle the two dancers, showing them mostly from the waist up, their eyes riveted to each other, capturing the love scene in one take. That scene became one of the most famous of the 1950s and it made the light-weight song "Moonglow" a sensational hit as women coast to coast dreamed of dancing with Holden on a clammy night atop a boat landing somewhere in Kansas. The film was shot in Hutchinson, Kansas and in Columbia's Burbank Studio.

p, Fred Kohlmar; d, Joshua Logan; w, Daniel Taradash (based on the play by William Inge); ph, James Wong Howe (CinemaScope, Technicolor); m, George Duning; ed, Charles Nelson, William A. Lyon; md, Morris Stoloff; prod d, Jo Mielzinger; art d, William Flannery; set d, Robert Priestly; cos, Jean Louis; ch, Miriam Nelson; makeup, Clay Campbell.

Drama **(PR:A MPAA:NR)**

PICNIC AT HANGING ROCK*** (1975, Aus.) 110m Atlantic Releasing c

Rachel Roberts *(Mrs. Appleyard)*, Dominic Guard *(Michael Fitzhubert)*, Helen Morse *(Dianne De Poiters)*, Jacki Weaver *(Minnie)*, Vivean Gray *(Miss Greta McGraw)*, Kirsty Child *(Dora Lumley)*, Anne Lambert *(Miranda)*, Karen Robson *(Irma)*, Jane Vallis *(Marion)*, Christine Schuler *(Edith Horton)*, Margaret Nelson *(Sara)*, John Jarratt *(Albert, Chauffeur)*, Ingrid Mason *(Rosamund)*, Martin Vaughan *(Ben Hussey)*, Jack Fegan *(Doc McKenzie)*, Wyn Roberts *(Sgt. Bumpher)*, Garry McDonald *(Jim Jones)*, Frank Gunnell *(Edward Whitehead)*, Tony-Llewelyn Jones *(Tom)*, Kay Taylor *(Mrs. Bumpher)*, Jenny Lovell, Janet Murray, Bridgette Phillips.

The recognition of Australia as having a strong film industry in the late 1970s can, to a large degree, be credited to the works of Peter Weir. After his first feature, THE CARS THAT ATE PARIS, films like PICNIC AT HANGING ROCK and THE LAST WAVE exhibited a peculiar and fascinating mystical quality that proved Weir to be a filmmaker with a very high degree of creativity and the ability to transfer his personal vision to the film medium. Perhaps no other film has been able to capture mysteries that lurk in some unknown realm in such a powerful fashion as does PICNIC AT HANGING ROCK. In one aspect a frightening revelation is created: that some unknown forces exist that have total control over a person's fate. Yet, this remains a subservient theme (to use the word loosely) to the beauty that Weir managed to capture from the Australian backland during the turn of the century, as well as from the young girls who are the film's subject. Particular among these is the young Lambert, a blonde-headed Venus who is compared to the Botticelli angel by one of her teachers. The viewer cannot help but become entranced by such a vision of this girl with the mystical beauty of a Botticelli painting, a beauty that transcends times. It is the mysterious disappearance of Lambert and two of her schoolmates that makes for the plot of PICNIC AT HANGING ROCK. The girls go on a picnic with the rest of their peers on Valentine's Day in the year 1900. While all the others are napping, these three, and one other who tags along, decide to climb to the top of the large rock. As they go higher and higher, they seem to become possessed by a force that keeps pulling at them. The warnings of the tag-along are of no use, so in a near delirium she runs down the rock to warn the teachers supervising the outing. One of these, Gray, takes it upon herself to track down the girls, and is drawn by the mysterious force. None of these women reappears after their journey up the rock, creating a widespread search in which the entire countryside participates. One young aristocrat, who had spotted Lambert climbing the rock and immediately fallen in love with her, takes it upon himself to search. Oddly enough he is able to find one of the girls hovering in the rocks, her clothes torn. Frightened out of her mind, she has no recollection of what happened during her disappearance and can offer no clues in an effort to locate the others. None of these girls or their teacher is ever found again, making the sojourn to Hanging Rock a mystery to baffle the police and community. Needless to say, the girls' disappearance does little to help the school's reputation. Parents begin to withdraw their children, spurring Roberts to devise a scheme to keep her school open. She ultimately fails and takes out her frustrations, in a sadistic and cruel manner, on the orphaned Nelson, whose benefactor has not paid her fees. Nelson, who was prevented from going on the picnic as a form of punishment, was also Lambert's closest friend. Both share intimate moments at the beginning of the film, which enhances the supernatural appearance of the girl who will soon disappear into oblivion. It would be hard not to criticize Weir for leaving the story so open-ended and the audience frustrated at trying to figure what has happened. But it was this form of integrity that gave the film such a powerful effect and is responsible for much of its magic. Weir's adaptation of the novel remains quite close to the original's narrative development and structure. This includes a number of anecdotes used to give an air of realism to the events that occur during the film. However, one hard working researcher did a bit of investigating into the history of the supposed school and discovered such a disappearance at Hanging Rock never took place.

p, Jim McElroy, Hal McElroy; d, Peter Weir; w, Cliff Green (based on the novel by Joan Lindsay); ph, Russell Boyd (Eastmancolor); m, Bruce Smeaton; ed, Max Lemon; art d, David Copping; cos, Judy Dorsman.

Drama/Fantasy   Cas.   (PR:C-O   MPAA:PG)

PICNIC ON THE GRASS*   (1960, Fr.) 91m Compagnie Jean Renoir/
Kingsley International c (LE DEJEUNER SUR L'HERBE; GB: LUNCH ON THE
                                                                    GRASS)

Paul Meurisse (Etienne), Catherine Rouvel (Nenette), Fernand Sardou (Nino), Jacqueline Morane (Titine), Jean-Pierre Granval (Ritou), Robert Chandeau (Laurent), Micheline Gary (Madeleine), Frederic O'Brady (Rudolf), Ghislaine Dumont (Magda), Ingrid Nordine (Marie-Charlotte), Andre Brunot (The Old Curate), Helene Duc (Isabelle), Jacques Dannoville (Mons. Paignant), Marguerite Cassan (Mme. Paignant), Charles Blavette (Gaspard), Jean Claudio (Rousseau), Raymond Jourdan (Eustache), Francis Miege (Barthelemy), Regine Blaess (Claire), Pierre Leproux (Bailly), Michel Herbault (Montet), Jacqueline Fontel (Mlle. Michelet), Paulette Dubost (Mlle. Forestier), M. You (Chapuis), Dupraz, Lucas, Roland Thierry, Michel Pericart (Announcers).

One of director Renoir's oddest films, PICNIC ON THE GRASS is visually influenced by the impressionist paintings of his father, Auguste Renoir and Edouard Manet (who painted a picture called "Le Dejeuner Sur L'Herbe", but has a plot which could almost be considered science fiction. Meurisse plays a scientist who is running for the presidency of the United States of Europe on a platform of artificial insemination. He is engaged to Nordine, a woman he communicates with chiefly via television. To boost his earthy image he decides to have a "picnic on the grass." Before long Meurisse is literally blown into the arms of a perky peasant girl, Rouvel. He is taken by Rouvel's vivaciousness and re-evaluates his scientific approach of love, declaring that the old-fashioned method is superior to the artificial one. Similar in "look" and title to his short A DAY IN THE COUNTRY (1936), PICNIC ON THE GRASS is a homage to his father's work (and in turn influenced Agnes Varda's LE BONHEUR, 1965, which incorporates a clip of the film). Filmed almost exclusively at Auguste Renoir's Les Collettes estate, PICNIC ON THE GRASS held a special place for the director. In his autobiography, My Life and my Films he states, "I had the immense pleasure of filming the olive trees my father had so often painted. That film was like a bath of purity and optimism. We felt, in its making, that we had been transformed into fauns and nymphs." Some critics were less than enthusiastic about Renoir's idyllic tone, thinking it was a trite and infantile choice of subject matter. Many people just refused to accept the fact that Renoir was trying to make a charming, and somewhat silly, picture about love. The 63-year old Renoir was enjoying himself and, perhaps, reveling in a glorious second childhood where he found complexity in simple themes. Nowhere is this more evident than in the superb THE LITTLE THEATER OF JEAN RENOIR (1974), which shows the director at his most carefree and whimsical.

p, Ginette Doynel; d&w, Jean Renoir; ph, Georges Leclerc (Eastmancolor); m, Joseph Kosma; ed, Renee Lichtig, Francoise London; set d, Marcel-Louis Dieulot, Andre Piltant, Pierre Cadiou; cos, Monique Dunan, Josiane Landic; makeup, Yvonne Fortuna, Fernande Ugi.

Drama   (PR:C   MPAA:NR)

PICTURE BRIDES*   (1934) 66m Allied Pictures bw

Dorothy Mackaill (Mame), Regis Toomey (Dave Hart), Dorothy Libaire (Mary Lee), Alan Hale (Van Luden), Will Ahern (Brownie), Fred Malatesta (Castro), Mary Kornman (Mataeo Rogers), Esther Muir (Flo), Gladys Ahern (Laoma), Mae Busch (Gwen), Harvey Clark (Dr. Rogers), Viva Tattersall (Lena), Al Hill (Steve, Detective), Michael Visaroff (Pete), Brooks Benedict (Joe), Franklin Parker (Bill), Larry McGrath (Tom), Jimmy Aubrey (Skipper).

Hale and Toomey are two American fugitives who high-tail down to Brazil to dig for diamonds. The boys get lonely pretty darn quick and send away to the States for mail-order brides. When the good looking one, Mackaill, falls for Toomey, Hale gets a bit nasty and kills a native out of frustration. Eventually he gets his, and Toomey gets the girl. The performances of Mackaill, a silent film star, and Kornman, formerly of "Our Gang," stand out.

p, M.H. Hoffman; d, Phil Rosen; w, Adele Buffington, Will Ahern (based on a play by Charles E. Blaney, Harry Clay Blaney); ph, Harry Neumann, Tom Galligan; ed,

Mildred Johnston; md, Abe Meyer; art d, Harold H. MacArthur; cos, Elizabeth Coleman.

Adventure   (PR:A   MPAA:NR)

PICTURE MOMMY DEAD½   (1966) 88m Berkeley/EM c

Don Ameche (Edward Shelley), Martha Hyer (Francene Shelley), Zsa Zsa Gabor (Jessica), Susan Gordon (Susan Shelley), Maxwell Reed (Anthony, Caretaker), Wendell Corey (Clayborn), Signe Hasso (Sister Rene), Anna Lee (Elsie Kornwald), Paule Clark (1st Woman), Marlene Tracy (2nd Woman), Steffi Henderson (3rd Woman), Robert Sherman (Father), Kelly Corcoran (Boy).

A pretty creepy Bert I. Gordon thriller in which the producer-director cast his daughter Susan in a lead role. Gordon plays a young woman released from the sanitarium after suffering a nervous collapse when her mother, Gabor, is killed in a fire. Her daddy, Ameche, has remarried in the interim and his new bride, Hyer, is really only in it for the large inheritance left to Gordon by her dead momma. Hyer tries to drive Gordon nuts again so the dough will be transferred to Ameche, giving the evil gold digger easy access. Aided by her lover, caretaker Reed, Hyer deludes a distraught Gordon into believing she (Hyer) is her dead mother. Reed chickens out and calls the cops, Hyer plunges a knife into him, and Ameche jumps in and strangles Hyer to death, just as he had done to Gabor. Gordon flips out again and sets the house on fire. In the end a very contented, and crazy, father and daughter watch as the fire consumes the house.

p&d, Bert I. Gordon; w, Robert Sherman; ph, Ellsworth Fredricks (Pathe Color); m, Robert Drasnin; ed, John Bushelman; set d, Ray Moyer, Robert R. Benton; cos, Leah Rhodes; spec eff, Charles Spurgeon; makeup, Dan Striepeke, Hal Lierley.

Horror   (PR:O   MPAA:NR)

PICTURE OF DORIAN GRAY, THE*½   (1945) 110m MGM bw-c

George Sanders (Lord Henry Wotton), Hurd Hatfield (Dorian Gray), Donna Reed (Gladys Hallward), Angela Lansbury (Sybil Vane), Lowell Gilmore (Basil Hallward), Peter Lawford (David Stone), Richard Fraser (James Vane), Reginald Owen (Lord George Farmoor), Lydia Bilbrook (Mrs. Vane), Morton Lowry (Adrian Singleton), Douglas Walton (Alan Campbell), Mary Forbes (Lady Agatha), Robert Greig (Sir Thomas), Lisa Carpenter (Lady Henry Wotton), Moyna Macgill (Duchess), Billy Bevan (Chairman Malvolio Jones), Miles Mander (Sir Robert Bentley), Devi Dja and Her Balinese Dancers (Specialty Act), Sir Cedric Hardwicke (Narrator), William Stack (Mr. Erskine), Natalie Draper (Mrs. Vandelear), Renie Carson (Young French Woman), Lillian Bond (Kate), Alan Edmiston (Cabby), Charles Coleman (Butler), Carol Diane Keppler (Gladys as a Child), Emily Massey (Parker, the Nurse), Jimmy Conlin (Piano Player), James Aubrey (Cabby), Joe Yule (Stage Manager), Rex Evans (Lord Gerald Goodbody), Audrey Manners (Lady Alice Goodbody), Renie Riano (Lady Ruxton), Gibson Gowland (Gibson, David's Driver), Toby Doolan, Major Sam Harris (Club Members), Lee Powell, Will Patton (Loaders), Frank O'Connor (Butler), Mary Benoit, Elyse Brown (Guests At Mayfair Tea).

A subtle and frightening filmization of the classic Oscar Wilde novel which here allows the audience's imagination to do most of the scaring. Hatfield stars as the title character—a young and wealthy 19th-Century London aristocrat whose gentle and angelic appearance is dangerously deceptive. Coaxed by the manipulative and hedonistic Sanders, Hatfield becomes as evil and scandalous as his mentor. The impressionable Hatfield soon becomes a philandering louse who entertains sadistic and perverse thoughts, alluding to (unseen) orgies and unspeakable evils. Early on he meets and falls in love with a virginal dance hall singer, Lansbury (whose singing was reportedly dubbed), who performs numerous renditions of "Little Yellow Bird." He proposes marriage, but before the ceremony is ever carried out, Hatfield (following Sanders' callous ways) leaves her. The jilted Lansbury then commits suicide. Hatfield's increasing vanity results in a portrait painted by his friend, Gilmore. Afterwards, Hatfield makes a mysterious supernatural pact while standing in front of the painting. He trades his soul for eternal youth, which results in the picture aging hideously while his appearance never alters. When Gilmore confronts Hatfield with the grotesque portrait, an angered Hatfield kills the painter. Years after the portrait's completion, Hatfield has a romance with Reed, the painter's niece. She is unaware that Hatfield had killed her uncle and fails to pay heed to the warnings of an admirer of hers, Lawford. Also on Hatfield's trail is Lansbury's brother, Fraser, who is sure of Hatfield's guilt, but confounded by his ageless appearance. Lawford finally discovers the repulsive portrait locked away in Hatfield's attic. Hatfield, now over the brink of madness, plunges a knife into the canvas. By destroying the portrait he has destroyed himself. He falls to the ground and is transformed into the hideous man in the painting, while the youthful Hatfield image is restored on the canvas. In much the same manner as the Val Lewton horror films of the 1940's (CAT PEOPLE, I WALKED WITH A ZOMBIE, and THE LEOPARD MAN), THE PICTURE OF DORIAN GRAY frightens the audience by mere suggestion, without ever resorting to distracting visual representations of the horrible. All that is evil about Hatfield's character is implied. The result for the audience is a building up of evil so horrible that it becomes unspeakable. The only visual shock that the audience is subjected to is the portrait itself (which one never expects to see and pops onto the screen in Technicolor with a violent musical crash), painted in a brilliant, though grotesque, style by Ivan Albright. THE PICTURE OF DORIAN GRAY not only frightened many viewers, it also earned the respect of the Motion Picture Academy which bestowed two Oscar nominations—one to Lansbury for Best Supporting Actress and another to Gibbons and Peters for black-and-white art direction—and one statuette for the deep-focus camerawork of Harry Stradling.

p, Pandro S. Berman; d, Albert Lewin; w, Lewin (based on the novel by Oscar Wilde); ph, Harry Stradling; m, Herbert Stothart; ed, Ferris Webster; art d, Cedric Gibbons, Hans Peters; set d, Edwin B. Willis, Hugh Hunt.

Horror/Drama   Cas.   (PR:C   MPAA:NR)

PICTURE SHOW MAN, THE*** (1980, Aus.) 99m Limelight c (AKA: PICTURE SHOW MAN)

Rod Taylor (*Palmer*), John Meillon (*Pop*), John Ewart (*Freddie*), Harold Hopkins (*Larry*), Patrick Cargill (*Fitzwilliam*), Yelena Zagon (*Mme. Cavalli*), Garry McDonald (*Lou*), Sally Conabere (*Lucy*), Judy Morris (*Miss Lockhart*), Jeannie Drynan (*Mrs. Duncan*).

A charming Australian film about the early days of Australian movie-making in the 1920s. Meillon plays an ambitious mogul who drags his movie equipment into the outback to bring the wonderful magic of motion pictures to amazed citizens. Taylor plays the rather melodramatic villain, Meillon's competitor, who gets his hands on the latest equipment before Meillon can afford to. Filled with well-drawn characters, touching moments, and great humor. A portion of the funding for THE PICTURE SHOW MAN came from a feminist organization, according to the film's closing credits, which some critics believe accounts for the inclusion of several noble, independent-minded female characters.

p, Joan Long; d, John Power; w, Long; ph, Geoff Burton (Panavision, Eastmancolor); m, Peter Best; ed, Nick Beauman; art d, David Copping; cos, Judy Dorsman.

Drama   **(PR:A MPAA:PG)**

PICTURE SNATCHER**½ (1933) 76m WB bw

James Cagney (*Danny Kean*), Ralph Bellamy (*McLean*), Patricia Ellis (*Patricia Nolan*), Alice White (*Allison*), Ralf Harolde (*Jerry*), Robert Emmett O'Connor (*Casey Nolan*), Robert Barrat (*Grover*), George Pat Collins (*Hennessy the Fireman*), Tom Wilson (*Leo*), Barbara Rogers (*Olive*), Renee Whitney (*Connie*), Alice Jans (*Colleen*), Jill Dennett (*Speakeasy Girl*), Billy West (*Reporter*), George Daly (*Machine Gunner*), Arthur Vinton (*Head Keeper*), Stanley Blystone (*Prison Guard*), Don Brodie (*Hood*), George Chandler (*Reporter*), Sterling Holloway (*Journalism Student*), Donald Kerr (*Mike, Colleen's Boy Friend*), Hobart Cavanaugh (*Drunken Reporter*), Phil Tead (*Reporter Strange*), Charles King (*Sick Reporter*), Milton Kibbee (*Reporter Outside Prison*), Dick Elliott, Vaughn Taylor (*Editors*), Bob Perry (*Bartender*), Gino Corrado (*Barber*), Maurice Black (*Speakeasy Proprietor*), Selmer Jackson (*Record Editor*), Jack Grey (*Police Officer*), John Ince (*Captain*), Cora Sue Collins (*Little Girl*).

A routine crime melodrama that is spruced up by Cagney's electric portrayal of a gangster-turned-newspaper-photographer. Upon his release from Sing Sing, he hooks up with a sleazy New York City tabloid and uses his criminal know-how to get a scoop. Before long he's fallen in love with Ellis, whose father, O'Connor, is the police lieutenant who sent Cagney to prison. Cagney quickly becomes hot property as a cameraman, securing a photo of a frenzied fireman standing in front of his burning house while his wife and her lover lie dead inside. Because of the unscrupulous nature of his job, Cagney is accused by Ellis of being a "picture snatcher"—no better than the criminal he used to be. To win her and her father over, Cagney gets a story printed about O'Connor, resulting in a promotion for the policeman. A grateful O'Connor changes his opinion of Cagney and gives him the okay to romance Ellis. Cagney is up to his old tricks, however, when he learns of the execution of a famed murderess. He sneaks into the prison with a camera hidden under his pant leg. Just as the current throws her body back, Cagney snaps the shot. With the picture plastered across the front page of the tabloid, the issue is a sellout (this trick actually happened on January 12, 1928, when an enterprising New York *Daily News* photographer caught the death of Ruth Snyder on film). O'Connor, as the man in charge of security, is demoted when the picture hits the streets. Cagney later finds his way back into good graces when he gets a picture of a famed killer in the act. A fast-paced programmer, PICTURE SNATCHER gave Cagney a chance to harden his already tough image even more—this time by throwing a punch at White, in a wonderfully fresh role as a moll in love with the "picture snatcher." Having carefully rehearsed the punch with White, it came time to actually try it. All White had to do was remain still. Undoubtedly a bit nervous, White mistakenly leaned forward and caught a punch on the chin. As Cagney described it: "There was poor little Alice down there on the floor, crying her heart out. I was mighty sorry to hit that cute little kisser." In a later scene, however, Cagney was on the receiving end. Bellamy, who played the city editor, was to deliver a punch to Cagney's chin. Bellamy, who had never thrown a punch in his life (and subsequently promised never to try again), was dreading the scene, fearing that he would actually connect. After some coaching from Cagney, Bellamy cocked his arm and let his fist fly. Unfortunately for Cagney, Bellamy misjudged his reach and struck him squarely on the jaw. Cagney ended up on the other side of the room, breaking a chair on impact and chipping his tooth. Luckily Cagney was a good sport and a strong friendship between him and Bellamy soon developed.

p, Ray Griffith; d, Lloyd Bacon; w, Allen Rivkin, P.J. Wolfson, Ben Markson (based on a story by Danny Ahearn); ph, Sol Polito; ed, William Holmes; md, Leo F. Forbstein; art d, Robert Haas; cos, Orry-Kelly; makeup, Perc Westmore.

Drama   **(PR:A-C MPAA:NR)**

PICTURES** (1982, New Zealand) 87m Pacific Films-New Zealand Film Commission-New Zealand National Film Unit/Cinegate c

Kevin J. Wilson, Peter Vere-Jones, Helen Moulder, Elizabeth Coulter, Terence Bayler, Matiu Mareikura, Ron Lynn, John Callen, Ken Blackburn, Suzanne Furner, Frank Edwards, Peter Hayden, Louise Petherbridge, Murray Hutchinson, Winiata Tapa, Peter Wiari, Bill Te Hore, Michael Bennett, Honey Thompson, Maria Toho, George Williamson.

New Zealand's colonial history as interpreted through this biographical film about Walter and Alfred Burton, pioneer photographers. High-minded, serious, and unwatchable.

p, John O'Shea; d, Michael Black; w, Robert Lord, O'Shea (based on an idea by

Black); ph, Rory O'Shea (Eastmancolor); m, Jan Preston; ed, John Kiley; art d, Russell Collins.

Biography   **(PR:A-C MPAA:NR)**

PIE IN THE SKY*** (1964) 86m AA bw (AKA: TERROR IN THE CITY)

Lee Grant (*Suzy*), Richard Bray (*Brill*), Michael Higgins (*Carl*), Roberto Marsach (*Paco*), Robert Allen (*Brill's Father*), Sylvia Miles (*Rose*), Ruth Attaway (*Farmer's Wife*), Robert Earl Jones (*Farmer*), Jaime Charlemagne (*Rick*), Charles Jordan (*Artificial Inseminator*), Roscoe Browne (*Preacher*), Rick Colitti (*Pickpocket*), Muriel Franklin, Debby Bliss, Susie Dresser (*Brill's Sisters*), Monroe Arnold (*Pitchman*), Boris Marshalov (*Haberdasher*), Spencer Davis (*Doorman*), Fred Feldt (*Gas Station Attendant*), Bill Da Prato (*Hot Dog Vendor*), Joseph Leberman (*Delicatessen Man*), Milton Luchan (*Bartender*), Danny Dresser (*Brill's Brother*), Mel Brown (*Truck Driver*), Edward Greenberg, Willie Tomlin, Carmelo de la Cruz, Orlando Rosa, John Evans, Johnny Paczynski (*Rick's Gang*).

A fairly moving low-budget independent film starring Bray as a 9-year-old runaway who ventures into Manhattan after running away from his small farmhouse, where he lives with his bitter, widowed father. There he meets up with a mean-spirited teen, Charlemagne, who controls all the shoeshine boys and newspaper sellers in the area and cuts himself in for half their take. Bray hooks up with a friendly Puerto Rican kid, Marsach, and he is soon selling papers. Soon after, Bray is involved in a crap game with Charlemagne, during which he wins most of the punk's money. After a night on the town, Bray is beaten by Charlemagne's toadies and rescued by helpful hooker Grant before much damage is done. Brill stays with her, and the next day she takes him on a shopping spree and buys him new clothes. This relationship is busted up by the cops, who haul Grant into the can for soliciting. Bray then takes the money he has left, buys a bicycle, and heads back to the farm. He has an accident with a truck and his bike is ruined. He finds temporary refuge with an elderly black couple and eventually finds his way home, where all his experiences help him and his father become closer.

p, Merrill Brody, Allen Baron, Dorothy E. Reed; d&w, Baron; ph, Donald Malkames; m, Robert Mersey; ed, Ralph Rosenblum; md, Mersey.

Drama   **(PR:A MPAA:NR)**

PIECE OF THE ACTION, A**½ (1977) 134m First Artists-Verdon/WB c

Sidney Poitier (*Manny Durrell*), Bill Cosby (*Dave Anderson*), James Earl Jones (*Joshua Burke*), Denise Nicholas (*Lila French*), Hope Clarke (*Sarah Thomas*), Tracy Reed (*Nikki McLean*), Titos Vandis (*Bruno*), Frances Foster (*Bea Quitman*), Jason Evers (*Ty Shorter*), Marc Lawrence (*Louie*), Janet DuBois (*Nellie Bond*).

The third Poitier-Cosby UPTOWN SATURDAY NIGHT team-up casts the duo as two well-off crooks who suddenly find themselves blackmailed into community service by retired cop Jones. Jones persuades the pair to help him out with some unruly street kids who have been sentenced to do their time in a community center instead of reform school. While the film does get pretty preachy at times, Cosby and Poitier are able to carry enough humor into the situation to make the socially redeeming sequences tolerable.

p, Melville Tucker; d, Sidney Poitier; w, Charles Blackwell (based on a story by Timothy March); ph, Donald H. Morgan (Metrocolor); m, Curtis Mayfield; ed, Pembroke J. Herring; prod d, Alfred Sweeney; set d, William J. McLaughlin; cos, David Rawley, Marie V. Brown; stunts, Henry Kingi.

Comedy   **Cas.**   **(PR:C MPAA:PG)**

PIECES* (1983, Span./Puerto Rico) 85m FVI-Artists Releasing-Amena and Fort/Spectacular c (MIL GRITOS TIENE LA NOCHE)

Christopher George (*Lt. Bracken*), Lynda Day George (*Mary*), Edmund Purdom (*Dean*), Paul Smith (*Willard*), Frank Brana (*Sgt. Hoden*), Ian Sera (*Kendall*), Jack Taylor (*Prof. Brown*), Gerard Tichy (*Dr. Jennings*).

More mad-slasher action, this time with the cleaver-wielding psycho lurking in the halls of a Boston university. George is the detective baffled by the slayings. The psycho is keeping body parts to construct a jigsaw puzzle woman at home. The end comes when the segmented cadaver comes to life and takes its revenge. The film borders on parody, but just misses being funny.

p, Dick Randall, Steve Manasian; d, Juan Piquer Simon; w, Randall, John Shadow; ph, Juan Marino; m, Cam.

Horror   **Cas.**   **(PR:O MPAA:NR)**

PIECES OF DREAMS** (1970) 99m RFB Enterprises/UA c

Robert Forster (*Father Gregory Lind*), Lauren Hutton (*Pamela Gibson*), Will Geer (*Bishop*), Ivor Francis (*Father Paul Schaeffer*), Richard O'Brien (*Monsignor Francis Hurley*), Edith Atwater (*Mrs. Lind*), Mitzi Hoag (*Anne Lind*), Rudy Diaz (*Police Sgt. Bill Walkingstick*), Sam Javis (*Leo Rose*), Gail Bonney (*Mrs. Tietgens*), Helen Westcott (*Mrs. Straub*), Joanne Moore Jordan (*Bar Girl*), Miriam Martinez (*Mrs. Rios*), Kathy Baca (*Estella Rios*), Eloy Phil Casados (*Charlie the Jailed Boy*), Raimundo Baca (*Gunshot Victim*), Robert McCoy (*Employment Agency Interviewer*).

Young Catholic priest Forster begins to have doubts about the church when he meets social worker Hutton and falls in love. After going through several heavy emotional episodes in their work (treating poor people with gunshot wounds, troubled pregnancies, etc.), the priest and social worker begin an affair. Seeking advice from his mother and his sister, Forster is shocked when they harangue him for even questioning his dedication to the Lord. That night the confused clergyman gets beaten up by a group of punks who accuse him of being gay. Forester eventually decides to leave the church and make a go of it with Hutton. A bit dull and maudlin.

p, Robert F. Blumofe; d, Daniel Haller; w, Roger O. Hirson (based on the novel *The Wine and the Music* by William E. Barrett); ph, Charles F. Wheeler (DeLuxe

Color); m, Michel Legrand; ed, William Chulack; art d, Herman A. Blumenthal; set d, James Payne; cos, Halston, Ray Phelps, Phyllis Garr; m/l, title song, Legrand, Alan Bergman, Marilyn Bergman (sung by Peggy Lee).

Drama   **(PR:C MPAA:GP)**

PIED PIPER, THE*½**   (1942) 86m FOX bw

Monty Woolley (Howard), Roddy McDowall (Ronnie Cavanaugh), Anne Baxter (Nicole Rougeron), Otto Preminger (Maj. Diessen), J. Carrol Naish (Aristide Rougeron), Lester Matthews (Mr. Cavanaugh), Jill Esmond (Mrs. Cavanaugh), Ferike Boros (Madame), Peggy Ann Garner (Sheila Cavanaugh), Merrill Rodin (Willem), Maurice Tauzin (Pierre), Fleurette Zama (Rose), William Edmunds (Frenchman), Marcel Dalio (Foquet), Marcelle Corday (Mme. Bonne), Edward Ashley (Charendon), Morton Lowry (Roger Dickinson), Odette Myrtil (Mme. Rougeron), Jean Del Val (Railroad Official), George Davis (Barman), Robert O. Davis [Rudolph Anders] (Lieutenant), Henry Rowland (Military Policeman), Helmut Dantine (Aide), Otto Reichow, Henry Guttman (German Soldiers), Hans von Morhart, Hans von Twardowski (Sergeants), William Yetter (Officer at Road), Adrienne d'Ambricourt (Servant), Mici Gory (Proprietress), Jean De Briac (Fisherman), Ernst Hausman (Soldier), Julika (Anna), Wilson Benge (Waiter), Brandon Hurst (Major-domo), Thomas Louden (Medford).

An unabashed propaganda picture made at the nadir of WW II, THE PIED PIPER is a warm, loving, heart-tugging story based on a novel by Nevil Shute that was serialized in Collier's magazine. Woolley is fishing in France to forget that his only son was one of the first Englishmen killed in the fracas. While there, the Nazis come by way of Belgium, and Matthews and Esmond, a British couple, asks Woolley if he will squire their two young children to the Brittany coast where they hope the kids will be able to cross the English Channel to safety. The children, Garner and McDowall, are placed in the crusty Woolley's care and he begins the hegira. Along the way, they are joined by several other war waifs and he is amazed that these children, who do not speak each other's languages, are still able to communicate in the way only children can. Naish, a local resident of Brittany, helps them arrange for a boat while Baxter, as a French girl, is what must be deemed the heroine, although there is no real attraction between her and Woolley, the hero. Just before they are to escape, the group is captured by Preminger, a Nazi officer. Now a battle of wits ensues between Woolley and Preminger with Woolley getting all the good lines and zings, something audiences applauded when the picture was shown in the 1940s. At the conclusion, Woolley manages to convince Preminger that these are innocent children and Preminger relents and allows them to evacuate, provided they take his niece along with them. (Why a Nazi officer should be traveling with a pre-teen niece while he's pillaging villages is never adequately explained.) Woolley, a former drama and English instructor at Yale, gave up that life and took to the stage when he was 48 years old. His first film was done at the age of 49, one of the most elderly debuts in film history, though surpassed by John Houseman (62) and Sidney Greenstreet (61) among the major actors. Some actual war footage of Nazi planes strafing villagers might cause youngsters a problem so the caution flag is up for tykes on this one.

p, Nunnally Johnson; d, Irving Pichel; w, Johnson (based on the novel by Nevil Shute); ph, Edward Cronjager; m, Alfred Newman; ed, Allen McNeil; art d, Richard Day, Maurice Ransford; set d, Thomas Little; cos, Dolly Tree.

War Drama   **(PR:C MPAA:NR)**

PIED PIPER, THE, 1968   (SEE: CLOWN AND THE KIDS, 1968,
                                                          U.S./Bulgaria)

PIED PIPER, THE***   (1972, Brit.) 90m Sagittarius-Goodtimes
                                                          Enterprises/PAR c

Jack Wild (Gavin the Crippled Boy, Melius' Apprentice), Donald Pleasence (Baron), John Hurt (Franz, Baron's Son), Donovan (The Piper), Michael Hordern (Melius, Alchemist), Roy Kinnear (Burgermeister), Peter Vaughn (Bishop), Diana Dors (Burgermeister's Wife, Frau Poppendick), Cathryn Harrison (Burgermeister's Daughter, Lisa), Keith Buckley (Mattio, Gypsy Leader), Patsy Puttnam (Gypsy's Wife Helga), Peter Eyre (Foppish Pilgram), Hamilton Dyce (Papal Nuncio), Arthur Hewlett (Otto), Andre Van Gyseghem (Friar), John Falconer, Clive Elliott (Priests), David Netheim (Kulik), Paul Hennen (Karl), David Leland (Officer), Sammie Winmill (Gretel), John Welsh (Chancellor), Gertan Klauber (Town Crier), Mary McLeod (Maidservant), Michael Goldie, Edwin Brown, George Cormack, Roger Hammond (Burgers).

A downright scary telling of the "Pied Piper" legend starring Donovan as the mysterious rat catcher who enters the corrupt, seedy, rat-infested 14th-Century town of Hamelin and offers to remove the plague-carrying beasts, but for a price. When that price isn't met, he takes their children instead. While the legend is left intact, the presentation by director Demy paints a dreary, horribly realistic portrait of life in the Middle Ages which is hard to forget. This is no fairy tale for the kiddies.

p, David Puttnam, Sanford Lieberson; d, Jacques Demy; w, Demy, Andrew Birkin, Mark Peploe (based on the fairy tale by Jakob and Wilhelm Grimm and the poem by Robert Browning); ph, Peter Suschitzky (Eastmancolor); m, Donovan; ed, John Trumper; prod d, Assheton Gorton; md, Kenneth Clayton; art d, George Djurkovic; cos, Vangy Harrison; spec eff, John Stears; m/l, Donovan; makeup, Bob Lawrence; rat trainer, John Holmes.

Drama   **(PR:C MPAA:G)**

PIEGES   (SEE: PERSONAL COLUMN, 1939, Fr.)

PIEL DE VERANO   (SEE: SUMMERSKIN, 1962, Arg.)

PIER 5, HAVANA*½   (1959) 67m Premium/UA bw

Cameron Mitchell (Steve Daggett), Allison Hayes (Monica Gray), Eduardo Noriega (Fernando Ricardo), Michael Granger (Lt. Garcia), Logan Field (Hank Miller), Nestor Paiva (Lopez), Otto Waldis (Schluss), Paul Fierro (Sergeant), Edward Foster (lst Man), Ken Terrell (2nd Man), Donna Dale (Monica's Maid), Vincent Padula (General), Fred Engelberg (Capt. Emilio), Rick Vallin (Pablo), Walter Kray (Radio Operator), Joe Yrigoyan (Burly Man).

Interesting only because it was one of the only films shot in Cuba after Fidel Castro took over, PIER 5, HAVANA is just a routine adventure film with the usual cast of ho-hum talent. Mitchell stars as a Yank who comes to Havana in search of an old friend who disappeared during the Cuban Revolution. While nosing around, Mitchell discovers a group of Fulgencio Batista sympathizers plotting to overthrow Castro. Believe it or not, Mitchell runs to Castro's cops and blows the whistle on the conspirators and saves the glorious people's revolution. Comrade Cameron!

p, Robert E. Kent; d, Edward L. Cahn; w, James B. Gordon, Bernard Schoenfeld (based on a story by Joseph Hoffman); ph, Maury Gertsman; ed, Grant Whytock; art d, William Glasgow.

Adventure   **(PR:A MPAA:NR)**

PIER 13, 1932   (SEE: ME AND MY GAL, 1932)

PIER 13**   (1940) 66m FOX bw

Lynn Bari (Sally Kelly), Lloyd Nolan (Danny Dolan), Joan Valerie (Helen Kelly), Douglas Fowley (Johnnie Hale), Chick Chandler (Nickie), Oscar O'Shea (Skipper Kelly), Michael Morris (Al Higgins), Louis Jean Heydt (Bill Hamilton), Frank Orth (Dead Pan Charlie), Charles D. Brown (Capt. Blake).

Nolan is a cop with an eye for the ladies who falls in love with waitress Bari, who works at a waterfront eatery. While trailing a robber, Fowley, Nolan is surprised to learn that his gal's sister, Valerie, appears to be involved in the crooked activities up to her neck. Upon further investigation, Nolan is relieved to be able to clear Valerie of any wrongdoing, catch Fowley, and weasel an engagement from Bari. Routine in all respects.

p, Sol M. Wurtzel; d, Eugene Forde; w, Stanley Rauh, Clark Andrews (based on a story by Barry Conners, Philip Klein); ph, Virgil Miller; ed, Fred Allen; md, Cyril J. Mockridge; art d, Richard Day, Lewis Creber.

Crime   **(PR:A MPAA:NR)**

PIER 23*½   (1951) 59m Spartan/Lippert bw

Hugh Beaumont (Dennis O'Brien), Ann Savage (Ann Harmon), Edward Brophy (Prof. Shicker), Richard Travis (Lt. Bruger), Margia Dean (Flo Klingle), Mike Mazurki (Ape Danowski), David Bruce (Charles Giffen), Raymond Greenleaf (Father Donovan), Eve Miller (Norma Harmon), Harry Hayden (Doc Tompkins), Joi Lansing (Cigarette Girl), Peter Mamakos (Nick Garrison), Chris Drake (Joe Harmon), Johnny Indrisano (Mushy Cavelli), Bill Varga (Willie Klingle), Richard Monahan (Henry the Bartender), Charles Wagenheim (Insurance Agent).

With the advent of television came a number of goofy schemes dreamed up by movie producers to combat the medium (3-D, CinemaScope, and Smell-O-Vision among the more notable). The message from the producers of PIER 23 seems to be, "If you can't beat 'em, join 'em.". PIER 23 was a nearly hour-long programmer that followed the beat of private detective Beaumont (later the "Beaver's" dad on TV) in two separate half-hour adventures, which basically make the film a television show that could be split and shown on separate nights. The first mystery sees Beaumont in the sweaty world of professional wrestling, where he investigates the strange death of one of the wrestlers who died of a heart attack while in the ring. He goes through the usual snooping, flirting, and head-banging until he comes up with the solution. After a brief break (insert commercial here), Beaumont returns to help a distraught priest talk an escaped convict back into prison. There is a mix-up, a dead man appears, and Beaumont again goes through the snooping, flirting, and head-banging until he comes up with the answers.

p&d, William Berke; w, Julian Harmon, Victor West (based on stories by Louis Morheim, Herbert Margolis); ph, Jack Greenhalgh; m, Bert Shefter; ed, Carl Pierson, Harry Reynolds; art d, F. Paul Sylos.

Mystery   **(PR:A MPAA:NR)**

PIERRE OF THE PLAINS**   (1942) 66m MGM bw

John Carroll (Pierre), Ruth Hussey (Daisy Denton), Bruce Cabot ("Jap" Durkin), Phil Brown (Val Denton), Reginald Owen (Noah Glenkins), Henry Travers (Mr. Wellsby), Evelyn Ankers (Celia Wellsby), Pat McVey (Sgt. Dugan), Frederic Worlock (Inspector Cannody), Charles Stevens (Crying Loon), Sheldon Leonard (Clerou), Lois Ranson (Clara).

A routine outdoor adventure except that it was produced by Edgar Selwyn, who had written and appeared in this very same drama on stage in 1907 and who would eventually join his brother and their friend Samuel Goldfish to form Goldwyn Pictures in 1929 (Goldfish Selwyn . Goldwyn). Despite the fact that he was one of the major partners in a successful movie company, Edgar returned to Broadway and spent many years there cranking out dramas like this on stage until he returned to Hollywood as a producer-director-writer and cranked them out for the movies. By the time PIERRE OF THE PLAINS hit the screen he was 66 years old and running actor Carroll through his paces as a French trapper who gets himself into all sorts of trouble with bad guys (Cabot and Leonard), Indians, and women (Hussey). Carroll sings too, but only "Saskatchewan"—more than once.

p, Edgar Selwyn; d, George B. Seitz; w, Lawrence Kimble, Bertram Millhauser (based on the play by Selwyn); ph, Charles Rosher; m, Lennie Hayton; ed, George White; art d, Cedric Gibbons; m/l, "Saskatchewan," Herbert Stothart, Ralph Freed (sung by John Carroll).

Adventure   **(PR:A MPAA:NR)**

PIERROT LE FOU**   (1968, Fr./Ital.) 110m Rome-Paris-DD-S.N.C./
                                                          Pathe-Corinth c

Jean-Paul Belmondo (Ferdinand Griffon, "Pierrot"), Anna Karina (Marianne

Renoir), Dirk Sanders *(Fred, Marianne's Brother)*, Raymond Devos *(Man on the Pier)*, Graziella Galvani *(Ferdinand's Wife)*, Roger Dutoit, Hans Meyer *(Gangsters)*, Jimmy Karoubi *(Dwarf)*, Christa Nell *(Mme. Staquet)*, Pascal Aubier *(2nd Brother)*, Pierre Hanin *(3rd Brother)*, Princess Aicha Abidir *(Herself)*, Samuel Fuller *(Himself)*, Alexis Poliakoff *(Sailor)*, Laszlo Szabo *(Political Exile from Santo Domingo)*, Jean-Pierre Leaud *(Young Man in Cinema)*.

Belmondo leaves behind his Parisian wife and child during a party and takes off on an adventure with Karina, the family babysitter with whom he'd had an affair five years earlier. The following morning a man is found with a scissors sticking out of his throat in Karina's apartment. They set out for the Riviera (heading South like the characters in Godard's previous film, ALPHAVILLE, hoped to do) in the hope of locating Karina's gunrunner brother. Belmondo spends his time writing a journal, but Karina grows increasingly impatient and gets herself involved once again in more gangster activities. Again the result is a mobster—a dwarf—being found dead with a scissors in the throat, The pair is separated when Belmondo is kidnaped and tortured by gangsters who are interested in finding Karina. Belmondo eventually meets up with Karina and learns that her brother is really her lover. A double-cross follows and Belmondo ends up shooting them both. Having had enough of the adventure, Belmondo phones his wife in Paris but cannot get through to her. He goes to the top of a hill, paints his face blue, ties red and yellow sticks of dynamite to his head, and lights the fuse. He makes an effort to put out the fuse as he changes his mind about the suicide, but from a distance we see a devastating explosion. PIERROT LE FOU was Godard's tenth film in six years (not including four sketches that he contributed to compilation films) and perhaps the first to contain all the elements that have been called "Godardian." He combined everything which came before—the romanticism of BREATHLESS, the inner monologue externalized in LE PETIT SOLDAT, the structural divison of MY LIFE TO LIVE, and the epic odyssey of CONTEMPT—with the linguistic diary format that would overpower some of his later films. It is arguably the one Godard picture which has the desired balance of romance, adventure, violence, and humor on one side, and philosophy, literary, cinematic and artistic allusion, sound-picture juxtaposition, and Brechtian distancing on the other. Like BAND OF OUTSIDERS before it and the incomprehensible MADE IN U.S.A. afterwards, PIERROT LE FOU is based on a pulp detective novel, providing Godard with a simple story that he can hang his personal, artistic, and philosophical beliefs on. Given this outline, Godard was able to go onto the set without a script. Godard said of PIERROT that it "is a completely spontaneous film. I have never been so worried as I was two days before shooting began. I had nothing, nothing at all." Having nothing to work from, Godard was forced to rely on himself perhaps more in this picture than in any other, putting more of himself on the screen than in his previous pictures. PIERROT is a collection of the lives Godard has lived in his other films and is an exception, in that it seems to stand on its own better than most of his pictures. Godard, because of the personal nature of his pictures, is difficult to judge on the basis of one film. His body of work is brilliant, but each of his films serves more as a component of the whole, than as the whole itself. Allusions to art fill PIERROT, from Karina's surname of Renoir to the inclusion of a scene fom Godard's short LE GRAND ESCROC with Jean Seberg, as well as references to Picasso, Velasquez, Laurel and Hardy, van Gogh, Celine, Coca-Cola, Jules Verne, and PEPE LE MOKO, to name only a few. As with Fritz Lang's appearance in CONTEMPT, Godard again cast a favorite director, this time Sam Fuller. Supposedly in Paris to direct a version of Baudelaire's "Fleurs Du Mal" (a bizarre idea which would probably be worth seeing), Fuller tells Belmondo and Karina, Godard, and the audience: "Film is like a battleground. Love. Hate. Action. Violence. Death. In one word. . .emotion." That is what Godard learned in PIERROT and he passed it along to us. PIERROT LE FOU was filmed quickly in May, June, and July of 1965 and then edited even more quickly for a showing at the Venice Film Festival in the end of August. Despite the mixed reaction that inevitably accompanies a new Godard film, PIERROT was soon elevated to the position of runner-up in the prestigous SIGHT AND SOUND poll of 1972.

p, Georges de Beauregard; d&w, Jean-Luc Godard (based on the novel *Obsession* by Lionel White); ph, Raoul Coutard (Techniscope, Eastmancolor); m, Antoine Duhamel, Antonio Vivaldi; ed, Francoise Collin; art d, Pierre Guffroy; m/l, "Jamais Je Ne T'Ai Dit Que Je T'Aimerai Toujours," Boris Bassiak, "Ma Ligne de Chance," Bassiak, Duhamel.

Crime/Romance   (PR:O MPAA:NR)

PIGEON THAT TOOK ROME, THE**   (1962) 101m PAR bw

Charlton Heston *(Capt. Paul MacDougall)*, Elsa Martinelli *(Antonella Massimo)*, Harry Guardino *(Sgt. Joseph Contini)*, Baccaloni *(Ciccio Massimo)*, Marietto *(Livio Massimo)*, Gabriella Pallotta *(Rosalba Massimo)*, Debbie Price *(Luigina)*, Brian Donlevy *(Col. Sherman Harrington)*, Bob Gandett *(The General)*, Authur Shields *(Msgr. O'Toole)*, Rudolph Anders [Robert O. Davis] *(Oberst Wilhelm Krafft)*, Gary Collins *(Maj. Wolff)*, Vadim Wolkonsky *(Conte Danesi)*, Richard Nelson *(The Chief, F.D.R.)*.

Heston felt comfortable in Rome, having been there in another era when he played Ben Hur. That had to have been the reason why they used this title, to plant the Roman/Heston image in audience's mind. Shavelson and Rose had jsut finished their splendid partnership and gone their seperate ways, Shavelson made this his first solo effort but Heston in a comedy just didn't wash. It's 1944, Mussolini has already been killed with mistress Clara Petacci in Milan. Heston and his assistant, Guardino, are smuggled into Rome, a city still occupied by the Fascists. Their job is to investigate and report on troop movements but they are ill-suited for that kind of work, having no training in it whatsoever. They are greeted on the beach by 11 year-old Marietto and his father, Baccaloni (the former operatic basso buffo), who are partisans in the fight against the Nazis. Heston and Guardino are taken to their home against the wishes of Baccaloni's two daughters, Martinelli and Pallotta, the latter pregant due to a sexual liason she'd had some time before the film began. Both women wish the two Americans would go away as they have no interest in

politics and the like. Heston is using carrier pigeons to send the information back and when Guardino falls for Pallotta and announces that he wishes to marry her (despite her burgeoning stomach), a feast is planned for the occasion. However, there is no food to be found, so Martinelli mistakenly roasts all but one of the carrier pigeons for the dinner. Marietto gets some German carrier pigeons to replace the Allied birds and, of course, the pigeons carry Heston's messages right back to Nazi headquarters. The one exception is the Allied bird who carries the important message to the right place and the troops attack at Anzio as Heston is sending false messages to the Nazis to throw them off. The armies attack Rome, liberate it, and Guardino and Pallotta marry at, you guessed, the precise moment the baby appears. Heston marries Martinelli and the pigeon gets the Congressional Medal of Honor, something that he will probably show to all the other birds in the coop for years. A silly picture made even sillier by the wrong lead, THE PIGEON THAT TOOK ROME was a dead duck.

p,d&w, Melville Shavelson (based on the novel *The Easter Dinner* by Donald Downes); ph, Daniel L. Fapp (Panavision); m, Alessandro Cicognini; ed, Frank Bracht; md, Irvin Talbot; art d, Hal Pereira, Roland Anderson; set d, Sam Comer, Frank R. McKelvy; spec eff, John P. Fulton, Farciot Edouart; makeup, Wally Westmore.

War/Comedy   (PR:C MPAA:NR)

PIGEONS   (SEE: SIDELONG GLANCES OF A PIGEON KICKER, 1970, Brit.)

PIGSKIN PARADE***   (1936) 95m FOX bw (GB: HARMONY PARADE)

Stuart Erwin *(Amos Dodd)*, Patsy Kelly *(Bessie Winters)*, Jack Haley *("Slug" Winston Winters)*, Johnny Downs *(Chip Carson)*, Betty Grable *(Laura Watson)*, Arline Judge *(Sally Saxon)*, Dixie Dunbar *(Ginger Jones)*, Judy Garland *(Sairy Dodd)*, Anthony [Tony] Martin *(Tommy Barker)*, Fred Kohler, Jr., *(Biff Bentley)*, Elisha Cook, Jr. *(Herbert Terwilliger Van Dyck)*, Eddie Nugent *(Sparks)*, Grady Sutton *(Mortimer Higgins)*, Julius Tannen *(Dr. Burke)*, Sam Hayes *(Radio Announcer, Himself)*, Robert McClung *(Country Boy)*, George Herbert *(Professor)*, Jack Murphy *(Usher)*, Pat Flaherty *(Referee)*, Dave Sharpe *(Messenger Boy)*, Si Jenks *(Baggage Master)*, John Dilson *(Doctor)*, Jack Stoney *(Policeman)*, George Y. Harvey *(Brakeman)*, Ben Hall *(Boy in Stadium)*, Lynn Bari *(Girl in Stadium)*, Charles Wilson *(Yale Coach)*, George Offerman, Jr. *(Freddy, Yale Reporter)*, Maurice Cass *(Prof. Tutweiler)*, Jack Best *(Prof. McCormick)*, Douglas Wood *(Prof. Dutton)*, Charles Croker King *(Prof. Pillsbury)*, Alan Ladd *(Student)*, Edward Le Saint *(Judge)*, Jed Prouty *(Mr. Van Dyke)*, Emma Dunn *(Mrs. Van Dyke)*, The Yacht Club Boys.

A fun melange of college antics, songs, football and love, PIGSKIN PARADE marked 15-year-old Garland's first feature and the only time she was ever loaned out by MGM. The frail plot had to do with a football team from the mythical Texas State University which is coached by Haley and led by Erwin, a man who can hurl watermelons further than most people can hit a golf ball. By mistake, the team is invited to play Yale in New Haven. Haley's wife is snappy Patsy Kelly and she has as much to do with coaching the team as her husband does. Lots of fun and several actors who went on to become stars later. Ladd does a bit and sings with the Yacht Club Boys, playing undergrads who've been in the freshman class for the past six years. Betty Grable, Lynn Bari and Tony Martin (who had taken to calling himself "Anthony" at the time. Franciosa, Martin and Curtis never could make up their minds whether to be "Tony" or "Anthony" and, at various times in their careers, used both) are there. The plot is forgettable and so are most of the songs but while you're watching PIGSKIN PARADE, you'll enjoy it. Tunes by Lew Pollack and Sidney Mitchell are: "Balboa," "The Texas Tornado," "It's Love I'm After" (sung by Judy Garland), "You're Simply Terrific" (Tony Martin, Dixie Dunbar), "You Do the Darndest Things, Baby" (Jack Haley, Arline Judge) "T.S.U. Alma Mater," "Hold That Bulldog," (sung by the Company). The Yacht Club Boys chimed in with some songs of their own, including: "Down With Everything" (sung by Alan Ladd and the Boys), "We'd Rather Be In College," "Woo! Woo!" Most of these football musicals had songs for their own sake but this one was an exception as most of the tunes really had something to do with the story, one of the first times attempt at integration of music with plot was made for an original film musical. Erwin was so good he received an Oscar nomination.

p, Bogart Rogers; d, David Butler; w, Harry Tugend, Jack Yellen, William Conselman (based on a story by Arthur Sheekman, Nat Perrin, Mark Kelly); ph, Arthur Miller; ed, Irene Morra; md, David Buttolph; cos, Gwen Wakeling.

Musical/Comedy   (PR:A MPAA:NR)

PIKOVAYA DAMA   (SEE: QUEEN OF SPADES, 1961, USSR)

PILGRIM, FAREWELL**   (1980) 102m Post Mills c

Elizabeth Huddle *(Kate)*, Christopher Lloyd *(Paul)*, Laurie Prange *(Ann)*, Lesley Paxton *(Rebecca)*, Shelley Wyant *(Maggie)*, Elizabeth Franz *(Doctor)*, Robert Brown *(Luke)*.

A quiet, tasteful, well-intentioned, but ultimately dull and uninspiring tale of a woman, Huddle, who learns she is dying of cancer. The film focuses on Huddle's fight to adjust to the reality of death and on her attempts to make amends with her family in her time of crisis. There is nothing wrong with any of this; it is just told in a manner typical of made-for-TV movies, which, therefore, renders the whole experience soon forgettable.

p, Stanley Plotnick; d&w, Michael Roemer; ph, Franz Rath; ed, Terry Lewis.

Drama   (PR:C MPAA:NR)

PILGRIM LADY, THE**   (1947) 67m REP bw

Lynne Roberts *(Henrietta Rankin)*, Warren Douglas *(Dennis Carter, Publisher)*, Alan Mowbray *(Clifford Latimer, Radio Commentator)*, Veda Ann Borg *(Eve*

Standish), Clarence Kolb *(Prof. Rankin)*, Helen Freeman *(Aunt Phoebe)*, Doris Merrick *(Millicent Rankin)*, Russell Hicks *(Thackery Gibbs)*, Ray Walker *(Blackie Reynolds)*, Charles Coleman *(Noel)*, Carlyle Blackwell, Jr. *(Wayne Talbot, III)*, Harry V. Cheshire *(Dr. Bekins)*, Dorothy Christy *(Nell Brown)*, Paul E. Burns *(Oscar)*, Tom Dugan *(Workman)*, Jack Rice *(Hotel Clerk)*, William Haade *(Cab Driver)*, William Benedict *(Bellboy)*.

A fitfully amusing comedy about a prim college teacher, Freeman, who writes a steamy sex novel under a pseudonym and sends it off to the New York publishers. Much to her surprise, the novel is published and she is soon faced with having to reveal her true identity. Desperate, Freeman drafts her niece, Roberts, to stand in as the authoress of the book. Of course, the young publisher of the novel falls in love with Roberts, much to the dismay of Freeman. All works out well, however, when Freeman too falls in love with a different man.

p, William J. O'Sullivan; d, Lesley Selander; w, Dane Lussier; ph, Reggie Lanning; ed, Arthur Roberts; md, Richard Cherwin; art d, James Sullivan; set d, John McCarthy, Jr., Charles Thompson; cos, Adele Palmer.

Comedy **(PR:A MPAA:NR)**

PILGRIMAGE*½** (1933) 90m FOX bw

Henrietta Crosman *(Hannah Jessop)*, Heather Angel *(Suzanne)*, Norman Foster *(Jim Jessop)*, Marian Nixon *(Mary Saunders)*, Maurice Murphy *(Gary Worth)*, Lucille La Verne *(Mrs. Hatfield)*, Charley Grapewin *(Dad Saunders)*, Hedda Hopper *(Mrs. Worth)*, Robert Warwick *(Maj. Albertson)*, Betty Blythe *(Janet Prescott)*, Francis Ford *(Mayor)*, Louise Carter *(Mrs. Rogers)*, Jay Ward *(Jim Saunders)*, Francis Rich *(Nurse)*, Adele Watson *(Mrs. Simms)*.

This movie was made only a few years after talkies began and Ford was able to keep the visual beauty of the silent era without making any concessions to the microphones. Crosman is the possesive and domineering mother of Foster who won't allow him to have his own life. Despite that, Foster meets and falls for Nixon. To keep Foster away from his girl friend, Crosman deliberately enlists her own son in the army. As if he doesn't have enough trouble with Crosman, Foster impregnates Nixon, although she won't tell him and he leaves for the service without knowing of her state. While fighting in the war, Foster is the third light on a match in the trenches. Bullets begin to hail and before we can see what has happened, the film cuts to Nixon as she sits up in bed shouting Foster's name. Nixon's father, Grapewin, walks into Crosman's house to ask her to help in the delivery of Nixon's baby, a child that is born at the precise time when the father, it is presumed, dies. The following day, Ford, the mayor, tells Crosman that her son has been killed and she responds by reassembling the torn picture of Foster she had ripped up in anger when he chose Nixon over her. We look at her face and wonder if she has any guilt whatsoever as it was her actions that caused Foster to be drafted and later killed. A decade passes and Crosman is crueler than ever. She denies her own grandson, Ward, the chance to play with her dead son's dog and she is totally immersed in anger, unable to release her pent-up self-hatred for having done what she did. Crosman goes on a "Gold Star Mothers" trip to France with a group of women of all races, creeds, and colors. It is on this journey she meets hillbilly La Verne, who also lost a son. La Verne is a totally different kind of woman, warm and loving, and it is her influence which causes Crosman to have a revelation. She admits to the other mothers that her son's death was, she feels, her doing. In France, she visits Foster's grave, then finds Murphy, a young potential suicide, about to leap off a bridge. She takes Murphy home with her. Next day, Murphy tells her that his mother, Hopper, doesn't approve of his girl friend, Angel, who is carrying his baby. Talking to Hopper, she manages to understand that she did the same thing. Back in the U.S., Crosman goes to Nixon, begs forgiveness and finally accepts her grandson, Ward. In the final scene, everyone is united and the feeling is that this family will never be parted again. Crosman, a *grande dame* of the theatre, didn't make many movies but when she did, she was magnificent. A tough movie with no phony sentiment, PILGRIMAGE concentrates on heart and is quite unlike most of Ford's early action pictures.

d, John Ford; w, Philip Klein, Barry Connors, Dudley Nichols (based on the story "Gold Star Mother" by I. A. R. Wylie); ph, George Schneiderman; m, R. H. Bassett; ed, Louis R. Loeffler; md, Samuel Kaylin; art d, William Darling; cos, Earl Luick.

Drama **(PR:A-C MPAA:NR)**

PILGRIMAGE** (1972) 90m Crimmins-Noumena c

Cliff de Young *(Garry)*, Bennett Hammond *(Father)*, Kay Leperc *(Mother)*, Bob Latourneaux *(Peter)*, Loulou De LaFalaise *(Susie)*, Joan Tysen *(Prostie)*, Idanna Pucci De Montalembert *(Mara)*.

A strange, self-consciously arty film starring de Young as a nihilistic young man from a rich family who wanders through the movie feeding off disturbing experiences and sad people (prostitutes, suicidal individuals, manic depressives). Eventually de Young's father dies (he seems to be the root of some of his son's problems), and de Young goes to the wake and performs a bizarre, ritualistic exorcism by dropping the buffet food on the floor around him, which drives his hypocritical relatives away.

p, William Anthony & Ann Duncan Crimmins; d, Beni Montresor; w, Montresor, James Berry; ph, Tonino Delli Colli.

Drama **(PR:C MPAA:NR)**

PILL, THE (SEE: GIRL, THE BODY, AND THE PILL, THE, 1967)

PILLAR OF FIRE, THE ** (1963, Israel) 75m Geva/Noel Meadow-Hoffberg-Frank Kassler bw

Michael Shillo *(Uri)*, Lawrence Montaigne *(David)*, Nehama Hendel *(Rachel)*, Moshe Yaari *(Moshe)*, Amos Macadi *(Kantrowitz)*, Uri Zohar. *(Yossi)*.

The brave exploits of six Jewish soldiers who battle it out with the evil Arabs during the Israeli War of Independence of 1948. They learn that the Arabs are about to launch a major offensive on a Jewish city, and are picked off one by one as they desperately try to make it back to headquarters to warn the high command. During all of this the two remaining Israeli soldiers, Montaigne and Hendel (she's female), fall in love. Luckily they make it back and warn the troops. A routine war film, just a different war.

p, Izhak Agadati, Mordechali Navon, Larry Frisch; d, Frisch; w, Hugh Nissenson, Frisch; ph, Haim Shreiber; m, Moshe Willensky; ed, Nelly Bogor; md, Willensky.

War **(PR:A MPAA:NR)**

PILLARS OF SOCIETY½** (1936, Ger.) 82m UFA bw (STUETZEN DER GESELLSCHAFT)

Heinrich George *(Consul Bernick)*, Maria Krahn *(Betty, His Wife)*, Horst Teetzmann *(Olaf, His Son)*, Albrecht Schoenhals *(Johann Tonnessen)*, Suse Graf *(Dina Dorf)*, Oskar Sima *(Krapp)*, Hansjoachim Buttner *(Hammer)*, Karl Dannemann *(Aune)*, Walter Sussenguth *(Urbini the Circus Manager)*, Paul Beckers *(Hansen the Clown)*, Franz Weber *(Vigeland)*, S.O. Schoening *(Sandstadt)*, Maria Hofen *(Frau Vigeland)*, Tony Tetzlaff *(Frau Sandstadt)*, Gerti Ober *(Thora Sandstadt, Her Daughter)*.

An average Douglas Sirk melodrama (he was still in Germany under the name Detlef Sierck) produced at a time when his films were at the peak of their popularity in Germany. George plays a powerful shipping magnate who has kept secret the fact that he sired an illegitimate daughter, Graf, many years ago. His past begins to catch up to him when Schoenhals, a circus man, returns to town from the U.S. Schoenhals knows the truth and took responsibility for the indiscretion many years ago, but threatens to spill the beans. Standard story material given a bit of a boost by Sirk. Ibsen's play also came to the screen in a 1916 silent version directed by Raoul Walsh. (In German).

p, Kruger-Ulrich; d, Detlef Sierck [Douglas Sirk]; w, Dr. Georg C. Klaren, Peter Gillman (based on the play by Henrik Ibsen); ph, Carl Drews; m, Franz R. Friedl; ed, Friedel Buckow; set d, O. Gulstorff, H. Minzloff.

Drama **(PR:A MPAA:NR)**

PILLARS OF THE SKY½** (1956) 95m UNIV c (GB: THE TOMAHAWK AND THE CROSS)

Jeff Chandler *(lst Sgt. Emmett Bell)*, Dorothy Malone *(Calla Gaxton)*, Ward Bond *(Dr. Joseph Holden)*, Keith Andes *(Capt. Tom Gaxton)*, Lee Marvin *(Sgt. Lloyd Carracart)*, Sydney Chaplin *(Timothy, Indian Scout)*, Willis Bouchey *(Col. Edson Stedlow)*, Michael Ansara *(Kamiakin, Indian Chief)*, Olive Carey *(Mrs. Anne Avery)*, Charles Horvath *(Sgt. Dutch Williams)*, Orlando Rodriquez *(Malachi)*, Glen Kramer *(Lt. Winston)*, Floyd Simmons *(Lt. Hammond)*, Pat Hogan *(Jacob)*, Felix Noriego *(Lucas)*, Paul Smith *(Morgan)*, Martin Milner *(Waco)*, Robert Ellis *(Albie)*, Ralph J. Votrian *(Music)*, Walter Coy *(Maj. Donahue)*, Alberto Morin *(Sgt. Major Desmonde)*, Richard Hale *(Isaiah)*, Frank de Kova *(Zachariah)*, Terry Wilson *(Capt. Fanning)*, Philip Kieffer *(Maj. Randall)*, Gilbert Conner *(Elijah)*.

A relatively satisfying cowboys and Indians film starring Chandler as a cavalry scout who is literally a voice in the wilderness when he tries to dissuade colonel Bouchey from building a road and a fort on government granted Indian territory. Nobody listens to him, of course, and the usual bloodshed occurs. Good cast. The outdoor location shooting was done in Oregon.

p, Robert Arthur; d, George Marshall; w, Sam Rolfe (based on the novel *Frontier Fury* by Will Henry); ph, Harold Lipstein (CinemaScope, Technicolor); ed, Milton Carruth; md, Joseph Gershenson; art d, Alexander Golitzen, Bill Newberry; cos, Rosemary Odell.

Western **(PR:A MPAA:NR)**

PILLOW OF DEATH** (1945) 55m UNIV bw

Lon Chaney, Jr. *(Wayne Fletcher)*, Brenda Joyce *(Donna Kincaid)*, Clara Blandick *(Belle Kincaid)*, Rosalind Ivan *(Amelia Kincaid)*, J. Edward Bromberg *(Julian Julian (George Cleveland (Sam Kincaid)*, Bernard B. Thomas *(Bruce Malone)*, Wilton Graff *(Detective McCracken)*, Fern Emmett *(Mrs. Williams)*, J. Farrell MacDonald *(Sexton)*, Victoria Horner *(Vivian Fletcher)*.

Another "Inner Sanctum" mystery movie starring Chaney as the highly suspicious main character who, this time out, may or may not be smothering people to death with pillows. After several smotherings, it is revealed that lawyer Chaney is really not entirely to blame. You see, he has a dual personality, one good, one evil and. . .you get the picture. (See INNER SANCTUM series, Index.)

p, Ben Pivar; d, Wallace Fox; w, George Bricker (based on a story by Dwight V. Babcock); ph, Jerome Ash; ed, Edward Curtiss; md, Frank Skinner; art d, John B. Goodman, Abraham Grossman; set d, Russell A. Gausman, Leigh Smith; cos, Vera West; spec eff, John P. Fulton.

Mystery **(PR:A MPAA:NR)**

PILLOW TALK*½** (1959) 105m Arwin/UNIV c

Rock Hudson *(Brad Allen)*, Doris Day *(Jan Morrow)*, Tony Randall *(Jonathan Forbes)*, Thelma Ritter *(Alma)*, Nick Adams *(Tony Walters)*, Julia Meade *(Marie)*, Allen Jenkins *(Harry)*, Marcel Dalio *(Pierot)*, Lee Patrick *(Mrs. Walters)*, Mary McCarty *(Nurse Resnick)*, Alex Gerry *(Dr. Maxwell)*, Hayden Rorke *(Mr. Conrad)*, Valerie Allen *(Eileen)*, Jacqueline Beer *(Yvette)*, Arlen Stuart *(Tilda)*, Don Beddoe *(Mr. Walters)*, Robert B. Williams *(Mr. Graham)*, Perry Blackwell *(Entertainer)*, Muriel Landers *("Moose", Fat Girl)*, William Schallert *(Hotel Clerk)*, Karen Norris *(Miss Dickerson)*, Lois Rayman *(Jonathan's Secretary)*, Harry Tyler *(Hansom Cabby)*, Joe Mell *(Dry Goods Man)*, Boyd "Red" Morgan *(Trucker)*, Dorothy Abbott *(Singer)*.

The first of the witty, well-produced sex comedies featuring Day and Hudson that saved both of their careers from type-cast oblivion (but, on the other hand, began a new form of type-casting for them both). Hudson is a playboy songwriter and Day is a successful, independent interior designer who learn to loathe each other even before they have met. During a Manhattan phone-line shortage, the two are forced to share a party line and begin to form opinions over the phone. Day gets increasingly angry everytime she tries to make a call and hears the very insincere Hudson talking to yet another unsuspecting femme whom he's trying to bed. After listening to his same suave baloney to a different number of women, she begins causing trouble. He thinks she's an uptight old hag, and eventually they agree to take turns using the phone every half an hour. Coincidentally, Hudson's buddy, Randall, is in love with Day and the phone-sharers finally meet when Randall brings her to see the progress of a Broadway show he's funding and in which Hudson is writing the tunes. Surprised and intrigued by Day's looks, Hudson pretends to be a dopey Texan and begins to work his charms on her. Day quickly realizes who Hudson really is and puts an end to the romance. Now hooked, Hudson desperately seeks advice from Day's gravely maid Ritter (who nearly steals the movie) and she suggests letting Day decorate his apartment. This backfires, however, when the not-to-be-fooled Day gets her licks in by doing over Hudson's pad in a hideous manner. Frustrated that he can get her no other way, Hudson does some quick thinking and states that he hopes his apartment will be to her liking when they get married. Day finally gives in and agrees to marry Hudson. Though PILLOW TALK is silly and at times overly "cute", it was the first time Day was allowed to show a more sexually frank side to her character, and Hudson was able to prove he was more than just a good-looking "hunk". The combination clicked, leaving Hudson and Day among the most popular stars of the next five years. PILLOW TALK garnered five Academy Award nominations (Best Actress, Best Supporting Actress [Ritter], Best Original Screenplay, Best Art Direction, and Best Music) and won the award for Best Screenplay. PILLOW TALK was also among the bigger box-office successes of its day, taking in $7.5 million in domestic distribution. Songs include: "Pillow Talk" (Buddy Pepper, Inez James, sung by Doris Day, Rock Hudson), "Possess Me" (Joe Lubin, I. J. Roth, sung by Day), "Inspiration" (Lubin, Roth, sung by Hudson), "I Need No Atmosphere," "You Lied" (Lubin, Roth, sung by Perry Blackwell), "Roly Poly" (Elsa Doran, Sol Lake, sung by Day, Hudson, Blackwell).

p, Ross Hunter, Martin Melcher; d, Michael Gordon; w, Stanley Shapiro, Maurice Richlin (based on a story by Russell Rouse, Clarence Greene); ph, Arthur E. Arling (CinemaScope, Eastmancolor); m, Frank DeVol; ed, Milton Carruth; md, Joseph Gershenson; art d, Alexander Golitzen, Richard Riedel; set d, Russell A. Gausman, Ruby Levitt; cos, Bill Thomas, Jean Louis; makeup, Bud Westmore.

Comedy **Cas.** **(PR:A MPAA:NR)**

PILLOW TO POST½** (1945) 92m WB bw

Ida Lupino *(Jean Howard)*, Sydney Greenstreet *(Col. Michael Otley)*, William Prince *(Lt. Don Mallory)*, Stuart Erwin *(Capt. Jack Ross)*, Johnny Mitchell *(Slim Clark)*, Ruth Donnelly *(Mrs. Wingate)*, Barbara Brown *(Mrs. Kate Otley)*, Frank Orth *(Taxi Driver)*, Regina Wallace *(Mrs. Mallory)*, Willie Best *(Lucille)*, Paul Harvey *(J. R. Howard)*, Carol Hughes *(Loolie Fisher)*, Bobby Blake *(Wilbur)*, Anne O'Neal *(Mrs. Bromley)*, Marie Blake *(Wilbur's Mother)*, Victoria Horne *(Charlotte Mills)*, Lelah Tyler *(Jerry Martin)*, Sue Moore *(Doris Wilson)*, Don McGuire *(Archie, Sailor on Bus)*, Grady Sutton *(Alex)*, Leah Baird *(Sailor's Mother)*, Joyce Compton *(Gertrude Wilson)*, Bob Crosby *(Clarence Wilson)*, Charles Jordan *(Cpl. Corliss)*, Anne Loos *(Pudge Corliss)*, Bunny Sunshine *(Celeste Corliss)*, Ferdinand Munier *(Traveling Salesman)*, Diane Dorsey *(Young Girl)*, Dorothy Dandridge *(Herself)*, Johnny Miles *(Marine)*, Louis Armstrong Orchestra *(Themselves)*.

Goofy comedy starring Lupino as a young saleswoman who wants to stop and rest her weary bones, but to her dismay finds that the only available lodging is a camp that caters exclusively to married servicemen. Desperate for a place to stay, Lupino sets out to find herself a "husband" so that she can check in. She soon spots Prince, a young lieutenant, and decides he will fill the bill. Through a series of circumstances he is forced to go along with the scheme, but, of course, complications arise which lead to a near court-martial for Prince, and loads of disapproving glances for Lupino. Silly, but fast paced and fun for the indiscriminating.

p, Alex Gottlieb; d, Vincent Sherman; w, Charles Hoffman (based on the play "Pillar to Post" by Rose Simon Kohn); ph, Wesley Anderson; m, Frederick Hollander; ed, Alan Crosland, Jr; md, Leo F. Forbstein; art d, Leo Kuter; set d, Walter F. Tilford; cos, Milo Anderson; spec eff, Warren Lynch.

Comedy **(PR:A MPAA:NR)**

PILOT, THE** (1979) 92m New Line/Summit c

Cliff Robertson, Frank Converse, Diane Baker, Gordon MacRae, Dana Andrews, Milo O'Shea, Ed Binns.

Dreary drama involves the story of a once-great pilot who insists on taking to the air despite a severe problem with alcohol. It's sad to see such talents as Robertson, MacRae, and Andrews (among others) reduced to this fare to earn their paychecks. Robertson directed this effort, boosted by some spectacular aerial photography.

p, C. Gregory Earls; d, Cliff Robertson; w, Robertson, Robert P. Davis (based on the novel by Davis); ph, Walter Lassally; m, John Addison; ed, Evan Lottman, Fima Noveck; prod d, Davis; set d, Bonnie De Rahm; cos, Jody Mecurio.

Drama **Cas.** **(PR:C MPAA:PG)**

PILOT NO. 5** (1943) 70m MGM bw

Franchot Tone *(George Braynor Collins)*, Marsha Hunt *(Freddie)*, Gene Kelly *(Vito S. Allesandro)*, Van Johnson *(Everett Arnold)*, Alan Baxter *(Winston Davis)*, Dick Simmons *(Henry Willoughby Clavens)*, Steven Geray *(Maj. Eichel)*, Howard Freeman *(Hank Durbin)*, Frank Ferguson *(Tully)*, William Tannen *(American Soldier)*, Carl Saxe *(Dutch Boy)*, Peter Lawford *(Englishman)*, Jack Gardner *(Mechanic)*, Sara Haden *(Landlady)*, James Davis, Cliff Danielson *(Military Police)*, Hobart Cavanaugh *(Boat Owner)*, William Halligan *(Bartender)*, Kay Medford *(Secretary)*, Billy Wayne, Eddie Acuff *(Cameramen)*, Marie Windsor, Betty Jaynes, Marilyn Maxwell, Jaqueline White *(Party Girls)*, William Bishop, Leigh Sterling *(Cadets)*, John Dilson *(Defense Instructor)*, Harry Semels *(Barber)*, Ava Gardner *(Girl)*, Frank Puglia *(Nikola)*, Edward Fielding *(Dean Barrett)*.

Wartime propaganda starring Tone as a controversial pilot who volunteers for a dangerous mission which will almost certainly lead to his death. After takeoff, his various friends and acquaintances recall the events that brought Tone to this fate. Kelly tells those gathered that Tone used to be a successful lawyer, but he unwittingly became involved with a right-wing, neo-fascist politician who was seeking the governorship of a southern state (a character obviously patterned after Huey Long). When Tone finally learned of the politician's true ambitions, he revealed the disturbing facts to the public, ruining his own career. Having become obsessed with stamping out fascism, Tone joined the Air Corps in the hopes of seeing as much action as possible. Immediately after Kelly relates the tale, Tone establishes radio contact with the base and tells his buddies that he is going to crash his plane into a Japanese aircraft carrier in a kamikaze-like suicide dive. This was Kelly's second film, and he took the role to prove to the studios that he was not just a song and dance man, and could handle dramatic roles as well.

p, B. P. Fineman; d, George Sidney; w, David Hertz; ph, Paul C. Vogel; m, Lennie Hayton; ed, George White; art d, Cedric Gibbons, Howard Campbell; set d, Edwin Willis, Glen Barner; spec eff, Arnold Gillespie, Don Jahraus.

War **(PR:A MPAA:NR)**

PIMPERNEL SMITH*½** (1942, Brit.) 100m BN/UA bw (AKA: MISTER V)

Leslie Howard *(Prof. Horatio Smith)*, Francis L. Sullivan *(Gen. von Graum)*, Mary Morris *(Ludmilla Koslowski)*, Hugh McDermott *(David Maxwell)*, Raymond Huntley *(Marx)*, Manning Whiley *(Bertie Gregson)*, Peter Gawthorne *(Sidimir Koslowski)*, Allan Jeayes *(Dr. Beckendorf)*, Dennis Arundell *(Hoffman)*, Joan Kemp-Welch *(Teacher)*, Philip Friend *(Spencer)*, Lawrence Kitchen *(Clarence Elstead)*, David Tomlinson *(Steve)*, Basil Appleby *(Jock McIntyre)*, Percy Walsh *(Dvorak)*, Roland Pertwee *(Sir George Smith)*, A.E. Matthews *(Earl of Meadowbrook)*, Aubrey Mallalieu *(Dean)*, Ernest Butcher *(Weber)*, Ben Williams *(Graubitz)*, Hector Abbas, Oriel Ross, George Street, Arthur Hambling, Harris Arundel Suzanne Clare, Charles Paton, Ronald Howard, Roddy Hughes.

Leslie Howard more or less reprises his most famous swashbuckling role, that of THE SCARLET PIMPERNEL, moving its tale of disguise and rescue from Paris during the Reign of Terror to Germany under the Nazis. Howard plays an absent-minded professor of archaeology involved in digs for Aryan artifacts near the Swiss border, but secretly involved in running refugees over the border to safety while disguising himself in a bewildering variety of get-ups. Sullivan is the corpulent Gestapo officer who sets out to stop the elusive Pimpernel, munching candy while considering his next move. Eventually Howard's students figure out what their professor is up to and help him smuggle a large group of persecuted scientists across the border. He goes back one more time, all the way to Berlin, to free a young woman, Morris, who is being held by the Gestapo and forced to work as a dupe. The rescue succeeds, Sullivan is foiled again, and Howard lives on for more derring-do. As he makes it across the Swiss border just steps ahead of the Germans, his voice comes back to their ears: "We'll be back. We'll all be back." This was the actor's first directorial chore (although he had codirected PYGMALION earlier) and he does a creditable job, keeping his film moving right along with the right mixture of action and suave, stiff-upper-lip heroism; but it his acting, relaxed and immensely likable, that carries the film. In one especially memorable scene, Howard runs through a field as soldiers shoot at him. They seem to miss and Howard disappears, until the camera zooms in on a scarecrow, blood dripping from his arm.

p&d, Leslie Howard; w, Anatole de Grunwald, Roland Pertwee, Ian Dalrymple (based on a story by A.G. MacDonnell, Wolfgang Wilhelm); ph, Jack Hildyard, Mutz Greenbaum; m, John Greewood; ed, Douglas Myers; md, Muir Mathieson.

Spy Drama **Cas.** **(PR:A MPAA:NR)**

PIMPERNEL SVENSSON*½ (1953, Swed.) 80m A. B. Europa/Scandia bw

Edvard Persson *(Pimpernel Svensson)*, Ivar Wahlgren *(Willy Lundgren)*, Aurore Palmgren *(Willy's Mother)*, Gunnel Wadner *(Willy's Wife)*, *Arne Wiren (Gen. Badajsky)*, Rodja Persidsky *(Maj. Pusjkin)*, Signe Wirff *(Refugee)*, Ove Flodin *(Landowner)*, John Degerberg *(Sacristan)*, Walter Sarmel *(Station Master)*, Maj. Britt Thorn *(Night Butterfly)*.

Swedish-style borrowing from the classic film THE SCARLET PIMPERNEL sees comedian Persson as a bumbling hayseed who, in his secret identity, goes behind the Iron Curtain to rescue his nephew, who is being held captive by the Communists. None of the style, flair, or excitement that made the Leslie Howard version so enjoyable. (In Swedish; English subtitles.)

d, Emil A. Linghelm; w, Ake Ohlmarks, Margit Beckman; ph, Karl-Erik Alberts; m, Knut Edgradt.

Comedy/Adventure **(PR:A MPAA:NR)**

PIN UP GIRL** (1944) 83m FOX c

Betty Grable *(Lorry Jones)*, John Harvey *(Tommy Dooley)*, Martha Raye *(Marian)*, Joe E. Brown *(Eddie)*, Eugene Pallette *(Barney Briggs)*, Skating Vanities *(Themselves)*, Dorothea Kent *(Kay)*, Condos Brothers *(Specialty)*, Dave Willock *(Dud Miller)*, Charlie Spivak and Orchestra *(Themselves)*, Robert E. Homans *(Stage Doorman)*, Marcel Dalio *(Headwaiter)*, Roger Clark *(George)*, Leon Belasco *(Captain of Waiters)*, Irving Bacon *(Window Cleaner)*, Walter Tetley *(Messenger Boy)*, Ruth Warren *(Scrubwoman)*, Max Willenz *(Waiter)*, Mantan Moreland, Charles Moore *(Redcaps)*, Gloria Nord *(Roller-Skating Headliner)*, Hermes Pan, Angela Blue *(Specialty Number)*, J. Farrell MacDonald *(Trainman)*, Lillian Porter *(Cigarette Girl)*.

That famous pinup poster of Grable in a white bathing suit looking over her right shoulder with a come-hither glance had already sold 2 million copies so it seemed like a natural for Fox bosses to make this movie. Too bad it didn't work. PIN UP GIRL is the essential "mindless musical" with just enough plot to hang the many tunes on. Grable is a bespectacled stenographer from Missouri who crashes a party tossed for Navy hero Harvey. Next thing you know, they're in Washington at the USO canteen and she is pretending to be a famous New York musical star. That causes the people who run the canteen to get her on stage to perform for the boys, which she does and she is, of course, a big hit, which transforms her into the star she's been saying she was all along. Most of the action takes place in nightclubs or theaters or in any other venue they can use to justify a production number. As in so many of this type of movie, the little stage soon expands to incredible width and eventually resembles the interior of the Louisiana Superdome. All the ho-hum songs were by Mack Gordon and James Monaco. They include: "Once Too Often" (danced by Betty Grable and Hermes Pan), "Yankee Doodle Dandy" (sung by Martha Raye), "I'll Be Marching to a Love Song" (sung by Grable, company), "You're My Little Pin Up Girl," "Story of the Very Merry Widow," "Time Alone Will Tell," "Don't Carry Tales out of School," "Red Robins, Bob Whites and Blue Birds," and some skating music for the Skating Vanities troupe. A story of how a young woman gets to be a pinup girl would have made more sense. This was a totally escapist film and did okay at the box office during those depressing days just before the Allies invaded Europe in June, 1944. Brown and Raye are around for some low comedy. This duo had the biggest mouths in movies (size, not gossip) and when standing next to each other in a close-up, resembled nothing more than railroad tunnels, side by side.

p, William LeBaron; d, H. Bruce Humberstone; w, Robert Ellis, Helen Logan, Earl Baldwin (based on a story by Libbie Block); ph, Ernest Palmer (Technicolor); ed, Robert Simpson; md, Emil Newman, Charles Henderson; art d, James Basevi, Joseph C. Wright; cos, Rene Hubert; spec eff, Fred Sersen; ch, Hermes Pan.

Musical/Comedy   **(PR:A   MPAA:NR)**

PINBALL PICK-UP   (SEE: PICK-UP SUMMER, 1981, Can.)

PINBALL SUMMER   (SEE: PICK-UP SUMMER, 1981, Can.)

PINK FLOYD—THE WALL**   (1982, Brit.) 99m Tin Blue-Goldcrest/
                                                                   MGM-UA c

Bob Geldof (Pink), Christine Hargreaves (Pink's Mother), James Laurenson (Pink's Father), Eleanor David (Pink's Wife), Kevin McKeon (Young Pink), Bob Hoskins (Rock and Roll Manager), David Bingham (Little Pink), Jenny Wright (American Groupie), Alex McAvoy (Teacher), Ellis Dale (English Doctor), James Hazeldine (Lover), Ray Mort (Playground Father), Marjorie Mason (Teacher's Wife), Robert Bridges (American Doctor), Michael Ensign (Hotel Manager), Marie Passarelli (Spanish Maid), Winston Rose (Security Guard), Joanne Whalley, Nell Campbell, Emma Longfellow, Lorna Barton, Rod Beddall, Peter Jonfield, Philip Davis, Gary Olsen, Eddie Tagoe, Dennis Fletcher, Jonathan Scott.

Overlong, tedious, and self-important rock 'n roll film based on the multimillion-selling record album by the band Pink Floyd. Rock singer Geldof (lead singer and driving force behind the sporadically interesting Irish band known as The Boomtown Rats and the guiding light for Band Aid, the musicians' relief effort for Ethiopian famine victims) stars as a successful, frustrated, narcissistic, and wholly unsympathetic rock star who is on the verge of burning himself out and going insane. Driven to the edge by the news that his lonely wife has left him for another man, Geldof spirals into a conglomeration of flashbacks and fantasies which detail his neurotic, depressing life style. A child of WW II, we see the young Geldof's early years among the horrors and ruins of wartime Britain. Eventually he grows to manhood and becomes a rock star, soon discovering his power to manipulate a crowd for his own satisfaction (much as his own schoolteachers manipulated and dehumanized him and his mates when he was a student). Desensitized to human feelings and emotions, Geldof slowly builds a wall around himself to deflect the pain and suffering of life. While the album may be interesting and effective rock 'n roll (and that's debatable), on film it is repetitious, pretentious, and boring, despite the flair for the flashy visuals that director Parker constantly relies on to advance the narrative. Thematically, the film is simplistic to the point of banality, but even the simple themes of alienation, loneliness, and paranoia are muddled beyond comprehension and sapped of any relevancy by the overblown and bombastic treatment. Geldof, surprisingly, is fairly effective in the lead role, and the animation sequences by political cartoonist Gerald Scarfe are interesting and well executed, though they are on screen too long. None of the above will have any effect on the opinions of rabid Pink Floyd fans, who have supported this film enthusiastically since its inception and look upon it as one of the greatest rock 'n roll films of all times (it isn't).

p, Alan Marshall; d, Alan Parker; w, Roger Waters (based on the album "The Wall" by Pink Floyd); ph, Peter Biziou (Metrocolor); ed, Gerry Hambling; prod d, Brian Morris; art d, Chris Burke, Clinton Cavers; spec eff, Martin Gutheridge, Graham Longhurst; animation, Gerald Scarfe.

Musical   **Cas.**   **(PR:O   MPAA:R)**

PINK JUNGLE, THE**½   (1968) 104m UNIV-Cherokee/UNIV c

James Garner (Ben Morris), Eva Renzi (Alison Duquesne), George Kennedy (Sammy Ryderbeit), Nigel Green (Crowley), Michael Ansara (Raul Ortega), George Rose (Capt. Stopes), Fabrizio Mioni (Col. Celaya), Vincent Beck (Sanchez), Val Avery (Rodriguez), Robert Carricart (Benavides), Natividad Vacio (Figeroa), Nacho Galindo (Hotel Proprietor), Pepito Galindo (Bellboy), Victor Millan (Helicopter Pilot), Than Wyenn (Customs Agent), Pepe Callahan (Hoodlum).

Garner is a fashion photographer on assignment in a South American village, who, along with model Renzi, is stranded when eccentric adventurer Kennedy steals his helicopter. After reporting the theft to the local authorities, Garner and Renzi bump into Kennedy, who has crashed the whirlybird. Kennedy informs them that he is searching for a lost diamond mine, and the photographer and model join him. Soon they meet up with Green, an untrustworthy Australian who intends to take the loot for himself. Seeing his chance, Green leaves the trio stranded in the desert and takes off with the map to the mine and the supplies. Eventually Kennedy catches up to Green and kills him. When the trio finally makes it to the mine, they discover that a rival troupe of treasure seekers led by Ansara has already found the treasure. A fight ensues, Ansara is captured, and the rest of his gang killed or run off. Kennedy grabs the diamonds and steals another helicopter for his getaway. Ansara is discovered to be a revolutionary leader, who was going to use the diamonds to further his political cause, and Garner reveals himself to be a CIA agent. Garner turns Ansara over to the authorities and then goes off in pursuit of Kennedy.

p, Stan Margulies; d, Delbert Mann; w, Charles Williams (based on the novel Snake Water by Alan Williams); ph, Russell Metty (Techniscope, Technicolor); m, Ernie Freeman; ed, William B. Murphy; art d, Alexander Golitzen, Alfred Ybarra; set d, John McCarthy, James S. Redd; cos, Edith Head; stunts, John Daheim; makeup, Bud Westmore.

Adventure   **(PR:A   MPAA:NR)**

PINK MOTEL zero   (1983) 88m New Image c (AKA: MOTEL)

Slim Pickens (Roy), Phyllis Diller (Margaret), John Macchia (Skip), Cathryn Hartt (Charlene), Christopher Nelson (Max), Terri Berland (Marlene), Tony Longo (Mark), Cathy Sawyer-Young (Lola), Brad Cowgill (Larry), Heidi Holicker (Lisa), Squire Fridel (George), Andrea Howard (Tracy).

Rotten sex comedy starring the unlikely duo of Pickens and Diller as owner-managers of a small motel which is a haven for clandestine rendezvous between secretive lovers. The film is mostly talk (there's very little nudity), and the dialog is stiff and uninteresting, as are the characters' lives.

p, M. James Kouf, Jr., Ed Elbert; d, Mike McFarland; w, Kouf, Jr.; ph, Nicholas J. von Sternberg (Movielab Color); m, Larry K. Smith; ed, Earl Watson; art d, Chester Kaczenski; m/l, "Pink Motel," Michael Bunnell (performed by Nile).

Comedy   **Cas.**   **(PR:O   MPAA:R)**

PINK PANTHER, THE**½   (1964) 113m Mirisch-G&E/UA c

David Niven (Sir Charles Lytton), Peter Sellers (Inspector Jacques Clouseau), Robert Wagner (George Lytton), Capucine (Simone Clouseau), Claudia Cardinale (Princess Dala), Brenda De Banzie (Angela Dunning), Fran Jeffries (Greek "Cousin"), Colin Gordon (Tucker), John Le Mesurier (Defense Attorney), James Lanphier (Saloud), Guy Thomajan (Artoff), Michael Trubshawe (The Novelist), Riccardo Billi (Greek Shipowner), Meri Wells (Hollywood Starlet), Martin Miller (Photographer).

This was the first of the long-running series and what most people don't recall is that the "Pink Panther" referred to in the titles of the films was not Sellers, rather it was the name of a legendary jewel. However, when the cartoon "Panther" starred in his own series of shorts, and the Mancini tune caught the ear of the public, Sellers and the title got mixed up in the public's mind and the follow-up movies always used the same cartoon treatment of the titles. Niven, in a role not unlike his RAFFLES character (or the part played by Cary Grant in TO CATCH A THIEF almost a decade before), is a famous jewel thief. He is suave beyond suavity, dripping sophistication from every pore. He is vacationing at the Alpine resort of Cortina D'Ampezzo, where all the skiers are swathed in clothes by famous French designers. One of the guests is Cardinale, an Indian princess who owns the famous "Pink Panther" gem, a bauble whose price cannot be measured. Niven wants the jewel and will stop at nothing to get it. He has been the scourge of Interpol for the past 15 years, as he's pulled off one daring robbery after another. All that time, Niven has been tailed by Sellers, a French inspector, who also wants to nail Niven's female accomplice. The fact that Sellers can never seem to catch up with Niven must have something to do with his wife, Capucine, who is Niven's mistress and is therefore able to alert Niven before Sellers can nab him. Meanwhile, Niven's American-born nephew, Wagner, is being supported by his uncle and pretending to be a college student, although genetics have caused him to be in the same "occupation" as Niven. Niven is moving in on Cardinale and the gem when Wagner arrives, also intent on purloining the "Panther." Cardinale plans to toss a huge costume ball at her Roman villa and all the people at the ski resort are invited. Sellers tells her that he has no doubt a pilfering attempt will be made on the jewel, so she intends to keep it in the library safe. The night of the party, two gorilla-dressed thieves come into the library and crack the safe, only to find that the gem has already been stolen and the only thing in the safe is a single white glove, the trademark of the famed "Phantom." All the lights go out, the gorillas flee, and a chase begins. Cars keep whizzing past some sleepy old Italians in a small town square and finally wind up smashed around the fountain in the center. Sellers arrests Wagner and Niven. Meanwhile, Capucine begs Cardinale to help her get these guys out of jail. A trial is held, with Le Mesurier serving as the counsel for the defense. No one can find the prime bit of evidence, the jewel itself, but that doesn't stop the wheels of justice from turning. Sellers is called to testify and Le Mesurier gets him to admit that he was also present at all of the jewel thefts for which Niven has been accused over the past 15 years. Under the relentless questioning, Sellers begins to perspire and reaches for his handkerchief. The courtroom is stunned when, attached to the hankie, they see the gem! Capucine and Cardinale had arranged this little contretemps and Wagner and Niven are released in the arms of the two women. Meanwhile, Sellers has been accused of being the thief and is suddenly thrust into the limelight, with hundreds of adoring women throwing themselves at him. Instead of protesting his innocence, he revels in this adoration and goes smilingly to jail. Niven will travel to South America with Capucine and, once there, he promises to send a letter to the Italian authorities which will get Sellers off the hook. Although he had less time on screen than most of the other principals, Sellers stole the film and the ensuing pictures proved his staying power. Gorgeous photography and sets, huge guffaws, and lots of fun. Fran Jeffries, in a rare acting role, sings the Johnny Mercer-Henry Mancini-Fran Misliacci tune "Meglio Stasera" ("It Had Better Be Tonight"). It's not easy to sustain a fast-moving comedy for 113 minutes, but they managed to do it quite well and the picture was a hit everywhere it was shown. Sequels included: A SHOT IN THE DARK, INSPECTOR CLOUSEAU (Alan Arkin in the lead), THE RETURN OF THE PINK PANTHER, THE REVENGE OF THE PINK PANTHER, THE PINK PANTHER STRIKES AGAIN. Mancini stuck around to do the PP's music and took an Oscar nomination for this one, his first in the series. (See PINK PANTHER series, Index.)

p, Martin Jurow; d, Blake Edwards; w, Edwards, Maurice Richlin; ph, Philip Lathrop (Technirama, Technicolor); m, Henry Mancini; ed, Ralph Winters, Marshall M. Borden, David Zinnemann; art d, Fernando Carrere; set d, Reginald Allen, Jack Stevens, Arrigo Breschi; cos, Yves St. Laurent; spec eff, Lee Zavitz; ch, Hermes Pan; m/l, Mancini, Johnny Mercer, Franco Misliacci.

Comedy   Cas.   (PR:A MPAA:NR)

PINK PANTHER STRIKES AGAIN, THE***   (1976, Brit.) 103m
Amjo/UA c

Peter Sellers (Inspector Jacques Clouseau), Herbert Lom (Ex-Chief Inspector Dreyfus), Colin Blakely (Alex Drummond), Leonard Rossiter (Quinlan), Lesley-Anne Down (Olga), Burt Kwouk (Kato), Andre Maranne (Francois), Richard Vernon (Dr. Hugo Fassbender), Michael Robbins (Jarvis), Briony McRoberts (Margo Fassbender), Dick Crockett (President Gerald Ford), Byron Kane (Secretary of State Kissinger), Paul Maxwell (CIA Director), Jerry Stovin (Presidential Aide), Phil Brown (Virginia Senator), Bob Sherman (CIA Agent), Robert Beatty (U.S. Admiral), Dudley Sutton (McLaren), Vanda Godsell (Mrs. Leverlilly), Norman Mitchell (Mr. Bullock), Patsy Smart (Mrs. Japonica), Tony Sympson (Mr. Shork), George Leech (Mr. Stutterstut), Murray Kash (Dr. Zelmo Flek), April Walker (Pretty Lady), Hal Galili (Danny Salvo), Dinny Powell (Marty the Mugger), Terry Richards (Bruce the Knife), Bill Cummins (Hindu Harry), Terry York (Cairo Fred), Terry Plummer, Peter Brace (Kidnapers), John Sullivan (Tournier), Cyd Child (Bouncer), Eddie Stacey (West German Assassin), Rocky Taylor [Omar Sharif] (Egyptian Assassin), Fred Haggerty (Taxi Passenger), Joe Powell (Munich Hotel Doorman), Jackie Cooper (Service Repairman), Priceless McCarthy (Stewardess), Fran Fullenwider (Fat Lady).

Director Edwards and co-author Maurice Richlin created the Clouseau character in the first PINK PANTHER picture and it is hoped that they had some sort of financial interest, as the dolls and toys became a huge success. In 1974, THE RETURN OF THE PINK PANTHER took in huge amounts at the theaters, so this one was rushed out to take advantage of the wave and it looks it. That's not to say that there aren't plenty of laughs in the picture, but it lacks a credible story, something that was present in the earlier ones. Lom, the head of the French police, has been driven mad by Sellers' behavior and is now incarcerated, with Sellers in his fourth Clouseau movie, sitting in the chief's seat. Lom escapes, kidnaps scientist Vernon, who has invented a "death ray," and he threatens to use it to end the world unless the authorities see fit to offer Sellers as a scapegoat so Lom can kill him. With the future of the world at stake, the U.S. and the U.S.S.R. are consulted. Kane and Crockett are Henry Kissinger and Gerry Ford (remember him?), while Down plays a Soviet spy who is put on the case but defects, NINOTCHKA-style, because she falls in love with Sellers. There are some marvelous sight gags, but the film goes over the top into mindless farce at times, this removing much of the Chaplinesque believability that Sellers had earlier engendered. Mancini and Don Black teamed on "Come To Me" (sung by Tom Jones) to get an Oscar nomination, the only notice the picture had from the Academy. Nevertheless, it took in almost $20 million, even more than THE RETURN OF THE PINK PANTHER, which was a better film. The titles were again cartoons and including the names of Jackie Cooper, Howard K. Smith, and Marne Maitland, all of whom were cut from the final release print. Omar Sharif does a cameo as an Egyptian killer. (See: PINK PANTHER series, Index.)

p&d, Blake Edwards; w, Edwards, Frank Waldman; ph, Harry Waxman (Panavision, DeLuxe Color); m, Henry Mancini; ed, Alan Jones; prod d, Peter Mullins; art d, John Siddall; spec eff, Kit West; makeup; Harry Frampton; animation, Richard Williams Studio.

Comedy   Cas.   (PR:A MPAA:PG)

PINK STRING AND SEALING WAX**   (1950, Brit.) 75m EAL/
Pentagon bw

Mervyn Johns (Mr. Edward Sutton), Mary Merrall (Mrs. Ellen Sutton), Gordon Jackson (David Sutton), Googie Withers (Pearl Bond), Sally Ann Howes (Peggy Sutton), Catherine Lacey (Miss Porter), Garry Marsh (Joe Bond), John Carol (Dan Powell), Jean Ireland (Victoria Sutton), Maudie Edwards (Mrs. Webster), Valentine Dyall (Police Inspector), Frederick Piper (Dr. Pepper), Pauline Letts (Louise), Margaret Ritchie (Mme. Patti), Don Stannard (John Bevan), Colin Simpson (James Sutton), David Wallbridge (Nicholas Sutton), Charles Carson (Editor), John Owers, Helen Goss, John Ruddock, Ronald Adam, David Keir.

Victorian crime drama which sees Withers, the wife of brutal pub owner Marsh, poison her husband and then blackmail a chemist by involving the man's son in her husband's death. Good period flavor and a few interesting twists. Bit players Lacey, Carol, and Marsh turn in the film's best performances, upstaging the featured actors. Set in the coastal town of Brighton.

p, Michael Balcon; d, Robert Hamer; w, Diana Morgan, Hamer (based on a play by Roland Pertwee); ph, Richard S. Pavey, R. Julius; m, Norman Demuth; ed, Michael Truman; art d, Duncan Sutherland.

Crime   (PR:A MPAA:NR)

PINKY****   (1949) 102m FOX bw

Jeanne Crain (Pinky, Patricia Johnson), Ethel Barrymore (Miss Em), Ethel Waters (Granny Dysey Johnson), William Lundigan (Dr. Thomas Adams), Basil Ruysdael (Judge Walker), Kenny Washington (Dr. Canady), Nina Mae McKinney (Rozelia), Griff Barnett (Dr. Joe McGill), Frederick O'Neal (Jake Walters), Evelyn Varden (Melba Wooley), Raymond Greenleaf (Judge Shoreham), Dan Riss (Stanley), Arthur Hunnicutt (Police Captain), Bert Conway (Loafer), Harry Tenbrook (Townsman), Robert Osterloh (Police Officer), Jean Inness (Saleslady), Shelby Bacon (Boy), Everett Glass (Mr. Wooley), Rene Beard (Teejore), Tonya Overstreet, Juanita Moore (Nurses), William Hansen (Mr. Goolby).

Darryl F. Zanuck was never a man to shrink from a social issue, even when it meant taking a chance with the studio's money. For all his personal peccadilloes, the Wahoo, Nebraska, native was a softie at heart, and when he saw something that needed correcting in the U.S., he took action in the only way he knew: he made a movie about the subject. In 1947, Zanuck, whom everyone mistakenly thought was Jewish, attacked anti-Semitism in GENTLEMAN'S AGREEMENT and this time he went for racial bigotry against the blacks. There had been two prior movies on the subject, HOME OF THE BRAVE and LOST BOUNDARIES, with INTRUDER IN THE DUST to follow, but this one was, perhaps, the best. Crain is Pinky (which is an expression blacks used to designate anyone with light skin who could "pass" into the white community), a bright young woman who has been going to school in New England to study nursing. While there, she's met Lundigan, a handsome physician who would like to marry her, despite the mescegnation. She believes that it could never work, as she is unwilling to give up her black heritage, so she returns to the southern town where she was born. Crain's grandmother, Waters, works for feisty dowager Barrymore, and when the old woman becomes ill, Crain goes to work for her as a nurse and stays until her death. Barrymore's will has an inheritance for Crain but the family decides to contest the document on the grounds that Crain is black and had influenced Barrymore. There's a trial and Crain wins the estate, then turns it into a nursing home and school for blacks. That's a bare synopsis but there is much more in the detailing of the black-white relationships as well as the black-black relationbships. When Zanuck originated the project he picked John Ford to direct. After two weeks of shooting Ford asked to be taken off the picture. His heart wasn't in it and he had not been getting along with actress Waters. Zanuck was relieved. The producer felt that the blacks in Ford's movies were stereotypical "Aunt Jemimas" and that PINKY was going to suffer for it (if Zanuck felt this way from the beginning, one wonders why Ford was picked to direct in the first place). Zanuck immediately called Kazan in New York and eight weeks later the film was completed with Ford's footage totally scrapped. Almost three decades later, PINKY holds up because it goes right to the core and doesn't mince any words or avoid any confrontations. Crain, Waters, and Barrymore all received Oscar nominations for their roles. Crain's attitude toward Lundigan is heartbreaking because she feels he is being racially "tolerant" rather than honestly believing in equality. Perhaps she was wrong, as the screenplay hints, and perhaps they might have made a happy duo. We'll never know. This is a mature film, with great respect for the humanity of people who care about each other. We could not have expected less from Zanuck and director Kazan.

p, Darryl F. Zanuck; d, Elia Kazan; w, Philip Dunne, Dudley Nichols (based on the novel Quality by Cid Ricketts Sumner); ph, Joe MacDonald; m, Alfred Newman; ed, Harmon Jones; art d, Lyle Wheeler, J. Russell Spencer; set d, Thomas Little; cos, Charles Lemaire; m/l, "Blue (With You or Without You)," Newman, Harry Ruby.

Drama   (PR:A MPAA:NR)

PINOCCHIO*****   (1940) 88m Disney/RKO c

Voices: Dickie Jones (Pinocchio), Christian Rub (Geppetto), Cliff Edwards (Jiminy Cricket), Evelyn Venable (The Blue Fairy), Walter Catlett (J. Worthington Foulfellow), Frankie Darro (Lampwick), Charles Judels (Stromboli the Coachman), Don Brodie (Barker).

This was Disney's second full-length animated feature and it remains one of his greatest classics, brilliantly (and, in some scenes, terrifyingly) created, with awesome detail and images so startling that one generation of children after another has been enthralled by its gripping and unforgettable tale. PINOCCHIO is a technical masterpiece far exceeding most of what Disney did earlier or during the remainder of his life. As the main titles come onto the screen, the unusual and memorable voice of Jiminy Cricket (Edwards) sings "When You Wish Upon a Star" and he is shown sitting on a book entitled Pinocchio. The wisecracking little cricket then tells the tale of the wooden puppet who underwent a miraculous transformation into flesh-and-blood with no little danger accompanying his metamorphosis. Jiminy guides the scene to Geppetto's little toy shop, where the old, kindly woodcarver is just finishing painting a smile on his newest marionette, a little boy he calls Pinocchio. The old man goes to bed and sees through the open window the Wishing Star and wishes that Pinocchio could be a real boy, his own son to love and raise. While the old man sleeps and his pets Figaro, a cat, and Cleo, a goldfish, slumber, the Blue Fairy descends from the Wishing Star and enters the shop, turning the marionette Pinocchio into a live being, although he is still made of wood. She tells him that if he will prove himself to be brave, and is unselfish and learns right from wrong, he will change into a flesh and blood little boy. She also makes Jiminy Cricket Pinocchio's conscience and promises the little creature a gold badge if he does well. When Geppetto and his pets awaken they are delirious with joy to find Pinocchio very much alive. Pinocchio is sent off to school with warnings from Geppetto to behave and mind the teacher. But on his way to school, with Jiminy at his side, Pinocchio encounters two sly rascals, J. Worthington Foulfellow, who calls himself "Honest John," a clever, insidious fox, and his cat friend, Gideon. The venal pair soon discover that a living wooden puppet is worth a fortune to them so they quickly convince Pinocchio that going to school is a waste of time, that appearing on the stage offers excitement and fun, and soon, despite Jiminy's protests, are singing "An Actor's Life for Me," and are off to make a name for Pinocchio on the stage. He is taken to sinister stage impresario Stromboli and that night Jiminy watches as Pinocchio appears with lifeless marionettes, singing "I've Got No Strings," fumbling about but endearing himself to the audience. He is so successful that Jiminy is forced to conclude that perhaps the wooden boy belongs on the stage. Going to bid his friend farewell, Jiminy sees to his horror that the evil Stromboli has put Pinocchio in a cage and is holding him prisoner, threatening to reduce him to fire kindling if he does not do as he is told. The obese and terrifying Stromboli tells the wooden boy, "When you grow too old you will make good firewood!" With that he hurls a hatchet into the splintered remains of another marionette which has a weak smile on its dead face. Jiminy tries to pry the lock from the cage but can't budge it. Then the Blue Fairy arrives and asks Pinocchio how he came to be locked up. Pinocchio begins to spin a tale piled high with fabrications until his nose begins to grow longer and longer with each lie, so long and ridiculous that it even sprouts branches. Says the Blue Fairy: "A lie grows and grows until it's as plain as the nose on your face." She restores Pinocchio's face and then, after the wooden boy and his conscience, Jiminy, promise to follow the right path, the Blue Fairy breaks the lock on the cage and Pinocchio escapes. But before the wooden boy can reach the safety of Geppetto's home he is again approached by the smooth-talking "Honest John" who easily convinces him to join a group of happy boys en route to Pleasure Island. In reality, the coachman who carries the boys and the sneaky fox are in league to shanghai these boys to an island from which "they never come back. . .as boys," smirks the coachman. Upon arrival at the island, the cautious cricket still at Pinocchio's side, the coachman ruefully states, "Give a bad boy enough rope and he'll soon make a jackass of himself." Later that night the entire island goes black, except for a pool hall which is shaped like an eight ball and here Pinocchio and his newly made friend Lampwick busy themselves by smoking and drinking beer and shooting pool. Jiminy loudly condemns Pinocchio's conduct but Lampwick makes fun of the cricket and Pinocchio ignores him and the little fellow marches out angrily. Says the arrogant Lampwick: "You'd think something was going to happen!" And with that he suddenly grows donkey's ears. Pinocchio steps back, stunned, staring at Lampwick who now has a donkey's tail shooting out of him. Pinocchio laughs instinctively at the sight but what comes out is a donkey's voice and Lampwick laughs in response but all that comes out of him is a loud hee-haw. Lampwick implores Pinocchio to help him, putting a hand which is now a donkey's hoof on Pinocchio's shoulder. As the background music grows louder and more discordant, the complete transformation of Lampwick to donkey takes place before a horrified Pinocchio, until only one human word—"mama"—escapes Lampwick before he can only make loud, hideous braying sounds. Looking into a mirror, Lampwick sees that he has become a donkey. Pinocchio himself has just sprouted the ears and tail of a donkey but Jiminy, who has seen how the other boys have been transformed into donkeys and are being herded into pens for sale by the unscrupulous owners of Pleasure Island, rushes to save his friend. He and Pinocchio flee, returning to Geppetto's shop only to find that the loving father has gone with Figaro and Cleo. They find a note from the Blue Fairy which tells them that Geppetto, in his search for his lost Pinocchio, has gone to sea and been swallowed by the huge whale, Monstro, but that he is still alive in the whale's stomach. Pinocchio resolves to save his father, though the cricket isn't too enthusiastic about this adventure. He and Pinocchio go to the sea and dive in, walking about at the bottom of the ocean. Whenever they ask schools of fish where they can find the whale Monstro, the fish scatter in a terrified manner. Then they come upon the incredible whale just as Monstro is about to feed. Jiminy taps on the clenched teeth of the slumbering whale with his cane and gurgles an underwater command: "Hey, blubbermouth—open up!" The whale opens his gigantic mouth to trap a school of fish and Pinocchio and Jiminy are swallowed whole. (This is one of the most startling scenes in the film, one where the swallowing is shown from inside of the whale, the mouth opening to an avalanche of fish, with Pinocchio and Jiminy turning over and over in the onrushing cascade of water pouring inside.) Geppetto, who is surviving on his wrecked ship with Cleo and Figaro, is overjoyed to see Pinocchio but the old man tells the wooden boy that it's too late for all of them, that they will perish inside of Monstro's stomach from which there is no escape. Pinocchio thinks hard and then tells Geppetto to make his raft ready because they will build a fire and the smoke will make the whale sneeze and when that happens they will be able to escape. The smoke comes pouring from Monstro's nostrils and the huge sea beast gives a mighty sneeze and blows Geppetto, Pinocchio, and the others right out of his stomach, sending their little raft scudding across the sea. The whale is incensed at being tricked, however, and he goes racing after the little craft. Geppetto and Pinocchio frantically row to escape the on-coming whale but it's hopeless. Monstro charges through the sea, creating a gigantic sea path, roaring, racing forward. But he overswims the little raft and misses swallowing his prey. As he turns, however, his enormous tail rises in the air, so big as to cover the raft with its shadow. Geppetto looks up, terrified, and yells: "Jump!" The tail comes down full force on the raft just as its occupants dive into the sea. Geppetto is in the water, telling Pinocchio to save himself, but the wooden boy ignores his own safety and paddles Geppetto ashore. When the woodcarver comes to, he finds Pinocchio lifeless on the beach. Taking the wooden boy home, Geppetto is in agony; Figaro and Cleo and even the compassionate cricket cannot console him. The voice of the Blue Fairy is then heard, repeating her words to Pinocchio earlier, that if he proved himself unselfish and brave he would become a real, live boy. At that miraculous moment Pinocchio comes to life, a flesh-and-blood boy. He sees Geppetto weeping and says, "Father, whatcha crying for?" Geppetto absent-mindly responds by mournfully stating: "Because you're dead, Pinocchio. . .now lie down." Then Geppetto's eyes bug out and he does a triple take, overcome with joy that he now has a real son whom he clasps to his bosom in an enormous hug. "This is practically where I came in," Jiminy Cricket says to the viewer. He stares skyward to see the twinkling star from which the Blue Fairy has come and thanks her for all she's done. Magically, a badge appears on Jiminy's chest bearing the words: "Official Conscience/18Kt." Jiminy is delighted, twinkling back at the star with his shiny badge and going off with the opening song in reprise, "When You Wish Upon a Star." Everything about this film is wonderful and awesome. Disney and scores of artists labored several years to produce PINOCCHIO and it shows in every frame. The incredible detail of this animated feature (its sharp dimensions achieved by a multiplane camera set-up) is everywhere in evidence. Disney characters, at least in this best of all eras for the company, move not only their heads and mouths, but their eyes, ears, arms, legs, noses, constant movement replete in backgrounds—leaves swaying in the breeze, water rippling—images of constant life so sadly lacking in the flat and uninspired animation of today. The opening shot panning back from the Wishing Star shows an ever-widening panorama of the little European village with Geppetto's shop at the apex, a shot of the rooftops and roadways where the viewer can count every chimney and cobblestone. The voices used in the film were perfect for the parts, Jones having the ideal childlike voice for Pinocchio, where wise-cracking Darro's voice is well-suited to the punky Lampwick. Jiminy Cricket's voice is so special and well-remembered that its owner, Edwards, went on doing the little character in many Disney films, including one other animated feature, FUN AND FANCY FREE (1947) and a host of shorts, particularly the I'M NO FOOL Disney series, until he found a permanent home on the "Mickey Mouse Club" TV show. Edwards, who had scored a smashing success in the 1920s as "Ukelele Ike" (and sang the first sound rendition of "Singing in the Rain") had skidded downward in his career until PINNOCCHIO rebounded his fortunes and made his unique voice, with its pure and sweet high singing range (he does hit C above high C on the last note in "When You Wish Upon a Star") identified by almost every child on earth. With such an identifiable voice, Edwards was used sparingly by Disney but he does sing the outrageously funny "When I Seen an Elephant Fly" along with four others doing the voices of the crows in DUMBO. Rub, who played Geppetto, not only had the perfect voice for the kindly woodcarver but the animated character was heavily created in his likeness. Venable's voice is well-suited as the sweet-throated Blue Fairy and Catlett's wheedling voice is tailor-made for the insidious fox, J. Worthington Foulfellow. Judels, who had a booming stentorian bass, is a magnificent Stromboli. Other songs include: "Little Woodenhead" and "Give a Little Whistle." Although we recommend this film with a AAA rating, very small children might be frightened by certain scenes.

p, Walt Disney; d, Ben Sharpsteen, Hamilton Luske; sequence d, Bill Roberts, Norman Ferguson, Jack Kinney, Wilfred Jackson, T. Hee [Disney]; animation d, Fred Moore, Milton Kahl, Ward Kimball, Eric Larson, Franklin Thomas, Vladimir Tytla, Arthur Babbitt, Woolie Reatherman; w, Ted Sears, Otto Englander, Webb Smith, William Cottrell, Joseph Sabo, Erdman Penner, Aurelius Battaglia (based on the story by Collodi [Carlo Lorenzini]; m, Paul J. Smith; art d, Charles Philippi, Hugh Hennesy, Dick Kelsey, Terrell Stapp, John Hubley, Kenneth Anderson, Kendall O'Connor, Thor Putnam, McLaren Stewart, Al Zinnen; m/l, Leigh Harline, Ned Washington, Smith; character designs, Joe Grant, Albert Hurter, Campbell Grant, John P. Miller, Martin Provenson, John Walbridge; backgrounds, Claude Coats, Ed Starr, Merle Cox, Ray Huffine; animation, Jack Campbell, Berny Wolf, Don Lusk, Norman Tate, Lynn Karp, Oliver M. Johnston, Don Towsley, John Lounsberry, John Bradbury, Charles Nichols, Art Palmer, Don Tobin, George Rowley, Don Patterson, Les Clark, Hugh Fraser, Joshua Meador, Robert Martsch, John McManus, Preston Blair, Marvin Woodward, John Elliotte.

Animated Feature **Cas.** **(PR:AAA MPAA:NR)**

PINOCCHIO** (1969, E. Ger.) 74m DEFA/Childhood Productions c (TURLIS ABENTEUER)

Martin Florchinger *(Papa Geppetto)*, Alfred Muller *(Stromboli)*, Martin Hellberg *(Arturo)*, Vera Oelschlegel *(Mirzilla the Fox)*, Peter Pollatschek *(Eusebius the Cat)*, Marianne Wunscher *(Euphrosina the Good Fairy)*, Detlef Wolf *(Pippifax)*, Herwart Grosse *(Mr. Lehrer, Schoolmaster)*, Helmut Schrieber *(Ringmaster)*, Carola Zschockelt *(Pudel)*, Harald Popig *(Malte)*, Hans Hardt-Hardtloff *(Karsten)*, Jurgen Marten *(A Father)*, Detlef Salzseider *(Thomas)*, Andreas Nehring *(Alfons)*, Lutz Kruger *(Eduard)*, Heinz Muller *(Konrad)*, Uwe Thielisch *(Pinocchio as a Boy)*, Klaus-Dieter Thiedemann *(Young Boy)*, Kerstin Berger *(Young Girl)*, Gerrhard Rosenlocher *(Trumpeter)*, Ellen Prince *(Voice of Pinnochio)*.

A pleasant enough version of the classic children's tale produced behind the Iron Curtain. Actors and puppets are combined to tell the story of old Papa Geppetto and the little boy puppet Pinocchio who wants to become a real boy. Children's films like this one have been staples for the East German state film organization, DEFA.

p, Ron Merk; d, Merk (English version); w, Ellen Prince, Merk (English version), Margot Beichler, Gudrun Rammler, Beck, Wilhelm Pach (German version), (based on the book Le Avventure di Pinocchio by Carlo Collodi); ph, Gunter Haubold; m, Joseph Scott (English version), Gerhard Wohlgemuth (German version); ed, Margrit Brusendorf; set d, Harald Horn; cos, Dorit Grundel; m/l, "A Boy Named Pinocchio," Merk, Scott (sung by Jason Cane); makeup, Bernhard Kalisch, Irmgard Lippman, Liane Wilk.

Fantasy **(PR:AA MPAA:NR)**

PINOCCHIO IN OUTER SPACE** (1965, U.S./Bel.) 71m Swallow-Belvision/UNIV c (PINOCCHIO DANS LE SPACE; AKA: PINOCCHIO'S ADVENTURE IN OUTER SPACE)

Voices: Arnold Stang *(Nurtle the Turtle)*, Peter Lazer *(Pinocchio)*, Conrad Jameson, Cliff Owens, Mavis Mims, Kevin Kennedy, Minerva Pious, Jess Cain, Norman Rose.

Feature length animated film starring Pinocchio, who, at the beginning of the film, is turned back into a puppet by Geppetto as punishment for bad behavior. Later, Pinocchio meets outer-space creature Nurtle the Turtle, whose spaceship has accidentally landed on Earth. Nurtle invites Pinocchio along for a ride and together they go to Mars where they meet the dangerous Astro the Flying Whale, who threatens to invade Earth. Eventually the puppet and turtle defeat the whale, and Pinocchio returns to Earth a hero and is rewarded by being turned back into a real boy. Well animated, but nowhere near the quality of Disney.

p, Norm Prescott, Fred Ladd; d, Ray Goossens; w, Fred Laderman (based on an idea by Prescott from the story by Carlo Collodi); ph, (Pathe Color); m, F. Leonard, H. Dobelaere, E. Schurmann; m/l, Robert Sharp, Arthur Korb.

Fantasy   Cas.   (PR:AA MPAA:NR)

PINOCCHIO'S ADVENTURE IN OUTER SPACE   (SEE:
PINOCCHIO IN OUTER SPACE, 1965, U.S./Bel.)
19147

PINTO BANDIT, THE**   (1944) 56m PRC bw

Dave O'Brien, Jim Newill, Guy Wilkerson, Mady Lawrence, James Martin, Jack Ingram, Edward Cassidy, Budd Buster, Karl Hackett, Robert Kortman, Charles King, Jimmy Aubrey.

There's a horse thief on the loose. Leave it to the erstwhile ways of the Texas Rangers to ride in and put a stop to the nefarious doings. (See TEXAS RANGERS series, Index.)

p, Alfred Stern; d&w, Elmer Clifton; ph, Edward Kull; ed, Charles Henkel, Jr.; md, Lee Zahler.

Western   (PR:A MPAA:NR)

PINTO CANYON**   (1940) 55m Metropolitan bw

Bob Steele, Louise Stanley, Kenne Duncan, Ted Adams, Steve Clark, Budd Buster, Murdock McQuarrie, George Chesebro, Jimmy Aubrey, Carl Matthews.

Some cattle thieves are operating their ring in sheriff Steele's domain. In rides every loyal good guy to save the day. Typical Steele western with his fists riding herd over the bad men until they leave his territory.

p, Harry S. Webb; d, Raymond Johnson; w, Carl Krusada (based on a story by Richard D. Pearsall).

Western   Cas.   (PR:AA MPAA:NR)

PINTO KID, THE*½   (1941) 61m COL bw

Charles Starrett (Jud Calvert), Louise Currie (Betty Ainsley), Bob Nolan (Bob), Paul Sutton (Vic Landreau), Hank Bell (Hank), Francis Walker (Curt Harvey), Ernie Adams (Ed Slade), Jack Rockwell (Marshal), Roger Gray (Dan Foster), Richard Botiller (Cheyenne), Sons of the Pioneers, Pat Brady, Steve Clark, Frank Ellis.

Post-Civil War western which sees evil cattle rustler-bank robber Sutton trying to frame Starrett for his crimes. The Sons of the Pioneers toss off some harmonies in between the barking of Starrett's six guns and the hammering of his flying fists.

p, Jack Fier; d, Lambert Hillyer; w, Fred Myton; ph, George Meehan; ed, Mel Thorsen; m/l, Bob Nolan, Tim Spencer.

Western   (PR:A MPAA:NR)

PINTO RUSTLERS*½   (1937) 60m Reliable-William Steiner bw

Tom Tyler (Tom Dawson), George Walsh (Nick), Al St. John (Mack), Catherine Cotter (Ann Walton), Earl Dwire (Bud Walton), William Gould (Inspector), George Chesebro (Spud), Roger Williams (Lugo), Bud Osborne (Buck), Murdock McQuarrie (Dad), Charles "Slim" Whitaker (Sheriff), Milburn Morante, Sherry Tansey.

Tyler stars as a young cowboy orphaned by a band of rustlers. Seeking revenge, Tyler pretends to be a notorious ex-con and manages to worm his way into the gang in order to get the goods on the bunch. St. John appears in one of his first westerns as Tyler's sidekick. St. John, a Mack Sennett regular, came out of vaudeville with bowlegs, which were formed from his unicycle act, making his stance natural for westerns.

p, Bernard B. Ray; d, Henri Samuels [Harry S. Webb]; w, Robert Tansey; ph, William Hyer; ed, Fred Bain.

Western   Cas.   (PR:A MPAA:NR)

PIONEER BUILDERS   (SEE: CONQUERORS, THE, 1932)

PIONEER DAYS*½   (1940) 54m MON bw

Jack Randall (Dunham), June Wilkins (Mary), Frank Yaconelli (Manuel), Nelson McDowell (Judge), Ted Adams (Slater), Bud Osborne (Saunders), Robert Walker (Trigger), George Chesebro (Roper), Glenn Strange (Sheriff), James Aubrey (Guard), Lafe McKee (Agent), Richard Cramer (Bartender).

Cowboy Randall and his two comedy sidekicks, Yaconelli and McDowell, help out sweet young thing Wilkins, who has inherited half her uncle's interest in a saloon and is now battling for her share with the uncle's shady partner Adams. Randall, brother of "One Rider" series star Bob Livingston, played a number of cowboy crooner leads similar to this one for Monogram before he died on location, falling off a horse.

p&d, Harry S. Webb; w, Bennett Cohen (based on a story by Forrest Sheldon); ph, Edward A. Kull; ed, Robert Golden.

Western   Cas.   (PR:A MPAA:NR)

PIONEER, GO HOME.   (SEE: FOLLOW THAT DREAM, 1962)

PIONEER JUSTICE**½   (1947) 56m PRC bw

"Lash" LaRue (Cheyenne), Al "Fuzzy" St. John (Fuzzy), Jennifer Holt (Betty), William Fawcett (Uncle Bob), Jack Ingram (Bill Judd), Dee Cooper (Criler), Lane Bradford (Joe), Henry Hall (Sheriff), Steve Drake (Al Walters), Bob Woodward (Jackson), Terry Frost, Wally West, Slim Whitaker.

Baddie-cum-hero LaRue (one of the few oater heroes who demonstrated a downright nasty disposition under his heroic facade) snaps his whip in defense of Holt and other settlers who are being run off their land by the maniacal Ingram, who seeks to control the territory like a feudal lord. Fast paced and well directed. One of LaRue's better efforts.

p, Jerry Thomas; d, Ray Taylor; w, Adrian Page; ph, Ernie Miller; ed, Hugh Winn.

Western   (PR:A MPAA:NR)

PIONEER MARSHAL*   (1950) 60m REP bw

Monte Hale (Ted Post), Paul Hurst (Huck Homer), Nan Leslie (Susan Forester), Roy Barcroft (Clip Pearson), Damian O'Flynn (Bruce Burnett), Myron Healey (Larry Forester), Ray Walker (Harvey Masters), John Hamilton (Elliott), Clarence Straight (Bartender), Robert Williams (Rodney).

A good performance by Barcroft as a killer is the only thing of interest in this routine oater starring Hale as a lawman who disguises himself as a criminal in order to pursue embezzler Healy. Healy has taken refuge in a hideout run by O'Flynn, who charges a percentage of the crook's loot as rent. An outraged Hale decides to bring Healey in and close down O'Flynn's operation. Little action and fairly tedious.

p, Melville Tucker; d, Philip Ford; w, Bob Williams; ph, John MacBurnie; m, Stanley Wilson; ed, Robert M. Leeds; md, Wilson; art d, Frank Hotaling.

Western   Cas.   (PR:A MPAA:NR)

PIONEER TRAIL**   (1938) 59m COL bw

Jack Luden (Breezy), Joan Barclay (Alice), Slim Whitaker (Curley), Leon Beaumon (Joe), Hal Taliaferro (Smokey), Marin Sais (Belle), Eva McKenzie (Ma Allen), Hal Price (Baron Waite), Dick Botiller (Pedro), Tom London (Sam Harden), Tuffy (Tuffy, the Dog), Tex Palmer, Art Davis, Fred Burns, Bob McKenzie.

Luden stars as the foreman of a cattle drive who runs afoul of a gang of rustlers and is kidnaped and brought to their leader, Whitaker. Whitaker offers to free Luden if he will go back to his bosses and inform them that the trail is safe, in the hopes that an even bigger herd of cattle will be sent next time. Luden refuses the crook's offer and escapes with the help of Tuffy the wonder dog. He returns to the ranch and puts together a massive herd of cattle and a small army of cowboys with which to do battle. He then drives the troops to the gang's town and stampedes the herd through the main street during a nasty gun battle. The cattle decimate the town and Luden gets his men.

p, Larry Darmour; d, Joseph Levering; w, Nate Gatzert (based on a story by Gatzert); ph, James S. Brown, Jr.; ed, Dwight Caldwell.

Western   (PR:A MPAA:NR)

PIONEERS, THE*½   (1941) 58m MON bw

Tex Ritter (Tex), Arkansas "Slim" Andrews (Slim), Red Foley (Red), Doye O'Dell (Doye), Wanda McKay (Suzanna), George Chesebro (Wilson), Del Lawrence (Ames), Post Park (Benton), Karl Hackett (Carson), Lynton Brent (Jingo), Chick Hannon (Pete), Gene Alsace (Sheriff), Jack C. Smith (Judge), Chief Many Treaties (Warcloud), Chief Soldani (Lonedeer), Art Dillard, Red Foley's Saddle Pals, White Flash the Horse.

Ritter and his mule-riding sidekick Andrews are hired to protect a wagon train in search of the promised land. Unfortunately, Ritter is kept busy by a gang of villains who are stirring up the Indians in an effort to prevent the settlers from taking up residence on valuable land. Inspired (barely) by James Fenimore Cooper's novel.

p, Edward Finney; d, Al Herman; w, Charles Anderson (based on the novel by James Fenimore Cooper); ph, Marcel A. LePicard; ed, Fred Bain.

Western   Cas.   (PR:A MPAA:NR)

PIONEERS OF THE FRONTIER**   (1940) 58m COL bw (AKA: THE ANCHOR)

Bill Elliott (Wild Bill Saunders), Linda Winters [Dorothy Comingore] (Joan Darcey), Dick Curtis (Matt Brawley), Dub Taylor (Cannonball), Stanley Brown (Dave), Richard Fiske (Bart), Carl Stockdale (Jim Darcey), Lafe McKee (Mort Saunders), Ralph McCullough (Lem Watkins), Al Bridge (Marshal Larsen), Edmund Cobb, George Chesebro, Lynton Brent, Jack Kirk, Ralph Peters.

Elliott rides again as Wild Bill Saunders in this routine oater which sees him put an end to the villainous efforts of crook Curtis, who is out to grab as much land as he can. Winters, who plays Kane's puzzle-obsessed second wife in CITIZEN KANE, is the tough-as-nails heroine. Her real name is Dorothy Comingore, but she used the name Winters in a series of "B" westerns and adventure films.

p, Leon Barsha; d, Sam Nelson; w, Fred Myton; ph, George Meehan; ed, James Sweeney.

Western   (PR:A MPAA:NR)

PIONEERS OF THE WEST**   (1940) 56m REP bw

Robert Livingston (Stony Brooke), Raymond Hatton (Rusty Joslin), Duncan Renaldo (Rico), Noah Beery, Sr. (Judge Platt), Beatrice Roberts (Anna), George Cleveland (Dr. Bailey), Lane Chandler (Steve Carson), Hal Taliaferro (Jed Clark), Yakima Canutt (Nolan), John Dilson (Morgan), Joe McGuinn (Sheriff Gorham), Earl Askam (Mac), George Chesebro, Jack Kirk, Herman Hack, Bob Burns, Tex Terry, Chuck Baldra, Hansel Warner, Art Dillard, Ray Jones, Artie Ortego.

The Three Mesquiteers (sans John Wayne) come to the rescue of a group of settlers who are being driven off their land by the evil Beery. Beery runs the town and is able to steal land by taxing the residents until they can no longer afford to live there. Wayne, who had appeared in eight Mesquiteer movies, now had dropped out and, after making STAGECOACH (1939) while four of his Mesquiteer pictures still had not been released, began his successful rise to stardom, complaining that Republic had done him dirt by sending out "those terrible Mesquiteer pictures" after he had become a star. Livingston on the other hand was returning to the B western genre after having been groomed for stardom and not clicking. (See THREE MESQUITEERS series, Index.)

p, Harry Grey; d, Les Orlebeck; w, Jack Natteford, Karen De Wolf, Gerald

Geraghty (based on characters created by William Colt MacDonald); ph, Jack Marta; ed, Tony Martinelli; m, Cy Feuer.

Western   **(PR:A   MPAA:NR)**

PIPE DREAMS**½   (1976) 87m AE c

Gladys Knight (*Maria Wilson*), Barry Hankerson (*Rob Wilson*), Bruce French (*The Duke*), Sherry Bain (*Loretta*), Wayne Tippit (*Mike Thompson*), Altovise Davis (*Lydia*), Sylvia Hayes (*Sally*), Frank McRae (*Moose*), Carol Ita White (*Rosey Rottencrotch*), Bobbi Shaw (*Slimey Sue*), Arnold Johnson (*Johnny Monday*), Robert Corso (*Mini-Guinea*), Sally Kirkland (*Two Street Betty*), Redmond Gleeson (*Hollow Legs*), David Byrd (*Easy Money*), Bruce Kimball (*Dave Anderson*), John Mitchum (*Franklin*), John Leoning (*Palooka*), Kelly Britt (*Dirty Diane*), Lisa Leslie (*Maryalyce*), Ben Bates (*Big Red*), Isabelle Horn (*Burly Woman*), Margaret Wiley (*Old Lady*), Charles Silverman (*Boat Captain*).

Singing star Knight made a respectable acting debut here as a woman who travels to the wilds of Alaska to track down her husband, Hankerson (Knight's husband in real life), who has left her to work on the pipeline. Once in town, she is forced to room with Bain, a prostitute (the frontier-town ratio of men to women is out of proportion, making prostitution a very lucrative venture for women so inclined). Tippit, a pipeline tycoon, finds himself very enamored of Knight and attempts to convince her to become a call-girl. She refuses and eventually finds Hankerson, and the couple are reunited. Director, producer, and writer Verona (THE LORDS OF FLATBUSH) handles the plot with sensitivity and humor. Knight does a fine job and does not sing on screen (though the soundtrack songs are done by Knight and the Pips).

p,d&w, Stephen Verona; ph, Steve Larner (Panavision, CFI Color); m, Dominic Frontiere; ed, Robert L. Estrin; cos, Glenda Ganis; m/l, Michael Masser, Jerry Goffin, Tony Camillo, Ivory Joe Hunter, Rev. James Cleveland, Jerry Spikes, Mildred Spikes, Clyde Otis, Vin Corso, Barry Mann, Cythia Weil, Bobby Arvon (songs sung by Gladys Knight and the Pips).

Drama   **(PR:C   MPAA:PG)**

PIPER, THE   (SEE: CLOWN AND THE KIDS, THE, 1968, US/Bul.)

PIPER'S TUNE, THE**½   (1962, Brit.) 62m ACT/Children's Film Foundation bw

Mavis Ranson (*Anna*), Roberta Tovey (*Suzy*), Angela White (*Maria*), Malcolm Ranson (*Thomas*), Brian Wills (*Paul*), Graham Wills (*Peter*), Christopher Rhodes (*Captain*), Frederick Piper (*Gonzales*).

During the Napoleonic wars, a group of children is forced to flee. Problems arise for the plucky youngsters when a doctor impersonating a spy turns them in. A sort of espionage-adventure tale the younger set probably will enjoy.

p, Robert Dunbar; d, Muriel Box; w, Michael Barnes (based on a story by Frank Wells).

Children's Adventure   **(PR:AA   MPAA:NR)**

PIPPI IN THE SOUTH SEAS**½   (1974, Swed./Ger.) 85m N.W. Russo/G.G. Communications c (PIPPI LANGSTRUMP PA DE SJU HAVEN)

Inger Nilsson (*Pippi Longstocking*), Maria Persson (*Annika*), Par Sundberg (*Tommy*), Beppe Wolgers (*Capt. Longstocking*), Jarl Borssen (*Pirate Boss Blood-Svente*), Martin Ljund (*Pirate Boss Knife-Jocke*), Alfred Schieske (*Innkeeper*), Wolfgang Volz (*Oscar*), Nikolaus Schilling (*Kalle*), Tor Isedal (*Franco*), Hakan Serner (*Pedro*), Ollegard Welton (*Mrs. Zettergren*), Frederik Olsson (*Zettergren*), Staffan Hallerstam (*Marco*).

Okay kiddie film based on Lindgren's novel character. In her second film as Pippi, Nilsson is left to babysit Perrson and Sundberg and she promises their parents never to leave them alone. A dilemma arises, however, when strolling down the beach with the children, Nilsson finds a note in a bottle. The note is from Nilsson's father, Wolgers, a sea-faring man who begs to be rescued from a band of pirates in the South Seas. Not wanting to break her word to Persson and Sundberg's parents, but having to save her father, Nilsson decides to take the kids, along with a pet parrot and monkey, with her. She rigs a balloon to carry them and off they sail to the South Seas. Eventually she finds her father being tortured by the pirates who are trying to learn the location of gold buried by Wolgers when his ship was grounded. Nilsson comes to the rescue, frees her father, and then leads the nasty pirates through a series of adventures that has them left behind on the island, while Nilsson, Wolgers, Persson, and Sundberg sail off in their pirate ship. Technically shaky at times (the editing and English dubbing are poor), but will prove fun for young children, especially the avid readers of the Long Stocking series. (See PIPPI series, Index.)

p, Allan Eckelund, Ernest Liesenhoff; d, Olle Hellbom; w, Astrid Lindgren (based on the books by Lindgren); ph, Kalle Bergholm (Movielab Color); m, Georg Riedel; set d, Leif Nilsson.

Adventure   **Cas.**   **(PR:AAA   MPAA:G)**

PIPPI ON THE RUN**½   (1977) 91m G.G. Communications c

Inger Nilsson, Par Sundberg, Maria Persson.

The further adventures of the popular children's character Pippi Longstocking, follow the plucky red-haired heroine as she takes off after some friends who've run away from home. There's plenty of adventure along the way, until the kids eventually realize that home is where they really belong. At just over 1½hours, this may be a bit long for the youngest of viewers, but fans of the Astrid Lindgren books will enjoy seeing their favorite character on the screen. (See PIPPI series, Index.)

p, N.W. Russo; d, Olle Hellbom; ph, (Movielab Color).

Children's Adventure   **Cas.**   **(PR:AAA   MPAA:G)**

PIRANHA**½   (1978) 92m New Piranha/World c

Bradford Dillman (*Paul Grogan*), Heather Menzies (*Maggie McKeown*), Kevin McCarthy (*Dr. Robert Joak*), Keenan Wynn (*Jack*), Dick Miller (*Buck Gardner*), Barbara Steele (*Dr. Mengers*), Belinda Balaski (*Betsy*), Melody Thomas (*Laura*), Bruce Gordon (*Col. Waxman*), Barry Brown (*Trooper*), Paul Bartel (*Dumont*), Shannon Collins (*Suzie*), Shawn Nelson (*Whitney*), Richard Deacon (*Earl*), Janie Squire (*Barbara*), Roger Richman (*David*), Bill Smillie (*Jailer*), Guich Koock (*Pitch-man*), Jack Pauleson (*In Canoe*), Eric Henshaw (*Father in Canoe*), Robert Vinson (*Soldier*), Virginia Dunnam (*Girl*), Hill Farnsworth, Bruce Barbour, Robyn Ray, Mike Sullivan, Jack Cardwell, Roger Creed, Nick Palmisano, Bobby Sargent.

Early effort from director Dante (THE HOWLING, GREMLINS) in which he successfully combines laughs and chills in a parody of JAWS. Menzies is the female detective out to trace a missing couple who have disappeared somewhere in the backwoods. During her search she meets up with recluse Dillman whom she enlists to help her. Together they trace the couple to a supposedly deserted army base. Menzies decides to drain the pool to see what is on the bottom. After pulling the switch to drain the pool, mad scientist McCarthy appears and the pair learns that they have just released a school of super-bred killer piranha into the river. McCarthy informs them that the army had hired him to develop an indestructible strain of piranha to infest the rivers of Vietnam in an effort to slow down the Viet Cong army. The experiments were a success, but the war was over by the time the fish were ready to be released. Meanwhile, the killer fish have killed a few people (including Wynn in a cameo role) and are heading for a children's summer camp in which Dillman's daughter is enrolled. At the camp all the children have been ordered into the water by Bartel (veteran Corman exploitation director of DEATH RACE 2000, EATING RAOUL) to participate in an inner-tube race. Before the camp can be warned, the piranha attack the children and munch on quite a few of them, but Dillman's daughter escapes. After decimating the summer camp, the vicious fish move on to a new lakeside resort that is celebrating its grand opening, and wreak a lot of havoc before Dillman can lure them into an old smelt fishery and poison them. The silliness of the whole concept is dealt with a sly sense of humor by director Dante and tongue-in-cheek cameo appearance by Wynn, McCarthy, Bartel, Steele, and Miller add to the fun. New World attempted a promotion for PIRANHA in which exhibiting theaters were asked to place a piranha filled aquarium in their lobbies, with a number of old trinkets such as rings and wrist watches placed in the bottom.

p, Jon Davison; d, Joe Dante; w, John Sayles (based on a story by Richard Robinson, Sayles); ph, Jamie Anderson (Metrocolor); m, Pino Donaggio; ed, Mark Goldblatt, Dante; art d, Bill & Kerry Mellin; spec eff, Jon Berg; stunts, Conrad Palmisano.

Horror   **Cas.**   **(PR:O   MPAA:R)**

PIRAHANA II: FLYING KILLERS   (SEE: PIRAHNA II: THE SPAWNING, 1981, Neth.)

PIRANHA II: THE SPAWNING*½   (1981, Neth.) 95m Saturn International/COL c (AKA: PIRANHA II: FLYING KILLERS)

Tricia O'Neil (*Anne*), Steve Marachuk (*Tyler*), Lance Henriksen (*Steve*), Ricky G. Paull (*Chris*), Ted Richert (*Raoul*), Leslie Graves (*Allison*), Carole Davis, Connie Lynn Hadden, Arnie Ross, Tracy Berg, Albert Sanders, Anne Pollack, Hildy Magnasun, Phil Colby, Lee Krug, Sally Ricca, Ward White, Ancil Gloudon, Paul Drummond, Dorothy Cunningham, Aston S. Young, Paul Issa, Gaetano Del Grande, Myra Weisler, Johnny Ralston, Jim Pair, Capt. Kidd Brewer, Jr., Jan Eisner Mannon.

Though the title suggests that this is a sequel to the Joe Dante film PIRANHA, it isn't. Totally unrelated to the earlier film, PIRANHA II takes place at a Caribbean resort that suddenly finds itself besieged by killer piranha that have, through breeding by the government (the only remotely similar connection to the Dante film), learned to fly and survive out of the water. Of course, the little critters gather their forces and attack the resort leaving lots of bloody bodies behind. The special effects are awful (the piranhas are obviously hand-puppets), the script worse, and the only spawning to be seen is that of human couples who fall into bed with each other during the lulls in the action.

p, Chako van Leuwen, Jeff Schectman; d, James Cameron [Ovidio Assonitis]; w, H.A. Milton; ph, Roberto D'Ettore Piazzoli (Technicolor); m, Steve Powder; ed, Robert Silvi; art d, Medusa Paltrinieri; spec eff, G. De Rossi, Corridori, Carbonaro, De Rossi.

Horror   **Cas.**   **(PR:O   MPAA:R)**

PIRATE, THE***½   (1948) 102m MGM c

Judy Garland (*Manuela*), Gene Kelly (*Serafin*), Walter Slezak (*Don Pedro Vargas*), Gladys Cooper (*Aunt Inez*), Reginald Owen (*The Advocate*), George Zucco (*The Viceroy*), The Nicholas Brothers (*Specialty Dancers*), Lester Allen (*Uncle Capucho*), Lola Deem (*Isabella*), Ellen Ross (*Mercedes*), Mary Jo Ellis (*Lizarda*), Jean Dean (*Casilda*), Marion Murray (*Eloise*), Ben Lessy (*Gumbo*), Jerry Bergen (*Bolo*), Val Setz (*Juggler*), The Gaudsmith Brothers (*Themselves*), Cully Richards (*Trillo*).

The story is often wearisome, the acting fever-pitched with exclamation points at every utterance, but the music and dancing of this colorful film are spectacular. The setting is the Caribbean island of San Sebastian in the 1820s and Garland is a native girl who fantasizes about a notorious pirate named Macoco, better known as "Mack the Black." Kelly is a strolling minstrel who falls in love with her and, to impress and win her heart, impersonates the pirate Macoco. Meanwhile, wealthy, girthsome Slezak fulminates against the rascal Kelly, Slezak being Garland's fiance. But Kelly persists in his charade, entering the town and boldly demanding that Garland be turned over to him or he will let loose his fierce pirates. Before that happens Garland discovers Kelly is a fraud and a knock-down, drag-out fight between the fiery lovers takes place while they sing-shout "Love of My Life" (Cole

Porter). Then Kelly learns that portly Slezak is really the dreaded Macoco, though he is ostensibly in retirement. Garland could care less by this time since she's hopelessly in love with the romantic Kelly and she runs away with him to join a troupe of players, ending the film with the rousing "Be a Clown" (Porter) number with Garland and Kelly singing and dancing as clowns, several of their teeth blackened out and with large red noses gleaming. THE PIRATE is an old-fashioned, lavish MGM musical, dripping with lush color and peppered with wonderful song-and-dance numbers with little care given to the script and the dramatics. It's a scenic treat, however, offering magnificent sets and a frenetic pace typical of director Minnelli (Garland's husband). The Behrman stage play, which ran for 177 performances on Broadway in 1942, starring Alfred Lunt and Lynn Fontanne, was purchased by MGM for $225,000. The play was revamped several times before the film went into production and the studio spared no cost. Wardrobe expenses alone soared over $140,000. This was the first film for Garland since TILL THE CLOUDS ROLL BY (1946), the actress having taken out time to have a baby. And it was the second teaming with Kelly, their first appearance together being FOR ME AND MY GAL (1942). The production was slowed down considerably by Garland who was repeatedly ill, suffering nervous fits and always on the verge of a breakdown. Said Minnelli about his wife in *I Remember It Well*: "She began to feel she wasn't functioning and turned again to the pills that had sustained her during past crises. I stood helplessly by, knowing she had started taking them again but unable to determine who was supplying them to her." Half the time Garland was hysterical, screaming on the set that her husband and Kelly were trying to ruin her career and giving Kelly all the major scenes. At times she refused to leave her makeup trailer and collapsed so that she had to be carried to a limousine and driven home with her costume and makeup still on. She became extremely paranoid and told gossip-columnist Hedda Hopper and others that the whole world had turned against her, including her mother. Minnelli and Garland were talking just before the shooting of the "Be a Clown" number and the director got his actress-wife to begin laughing, so that both of them were laughing hysterically just before Minnelli abruptly stopped, placed Garland before the camera and frantically shot the scene. Witnesses later described this off-camera event as bizarre. Garland decided that famed songwriter Porter was her enemy too, and her attitude toward him changed drastically during the 135-day shooting schedule to the point where she would not talk to him at the film's end. The film was met with favorable reviews from critics but the public was less enthusiastic; the film, which cost MGM $3,768,000, earned back only $2,290,000 in its initial release. Among cultists today, THE PIRATE ranks high, chiefly for its extravagant choreography, particularly the sweeping "Nina" and "Mack the Black" (Porter) numbers, danced energetically by Kelly. Of special delight are the marvelous Nicholas Brothers who dance with Kelly and Garland in the "Be a Clown" number; they were edited out of this scene in Southern theaters at the time of release. Other songs include: "You Can Do No Wrong" (Porter), "Sweet Ices, Papayas, Berry Man," "Sea Wall," "Serafin" (Roger Edens), "The Ring," "Judy Awakens," "Not Again," "The Tight Rope" (Lennie Hayton), "Gene Meets Mack the Black," "The Mast" (Conrad Salinger), "Voodoo" (Porter, deleted), "Manuela" (Porter, not used).

p, Arthur Freed; d, Vincente Minnelli; w, Albert Hackett, Frances Goodrich, (uncredited) Joseph L. Mankiewicz, Joseph Than, Lillian Braun, Anita Loos, Wilkie Mahoney (based on a play by S.N. Behrman); ph, Harry Stradling (Technicolor); m, Cole Porter; ed, Blanche Sewell; md, Lennie Hayton; art d, Cedric Gibbons, Jack Martin Smith; set d, Edwin B. Willis, Arthur Krams; cos, Tom Keogh, Barbara Karinska; ch, Robert Alton, Gene Kelly; makeup, Jack Dawn.

Musical   **Cas.**   **(PR:A   MPAA:NR)**

PIRATE AND THE SLAVE GIRL, THE*½   (1961, Fr./Ital.) 87m
Romano-Fortunate Misiano-S.N.C./Crest c (LA VENGEANCE DU SARRASIN; LA SCIMITARRA DEL SARACENO)

Lex Barker *(Dragut)*, Chelo Alonso *(Princess Miriam)*, Massimo Serato *(Capt. Diego)*, Graziella Granata *(Bianca)*, Daniele Vargas *(Gamal)*, Luigi Tosi *(Francisco)*, Bruno Corelli *(Selim)*, Enzo Maggio *(Candela)*, Michele Malaspina, Anna Arena, Franco Fantasia, Ubaldo Lay, Evelina Laudani, Nadia Brivio, Valeria Gramignani, Genevieve Audry, Rina Mascetti, Gianni Rizzo.

Serato plays an imprisoned 15th century adventurer who is released to rescue Granata, the daughter of the governor of Rhodes, from the clutches of pirate Barker. Serato joins the pirates, but is beaten and left for dead after he is caught staring at Granata, whom Barker intends to sell to white slave owner, Alonso. Eventually, Serato manages to rescue Granata from the clutches of Barker and Alonso with the help of some friendly and heroic fishermen.

d, Piero Pierotti; w, Luciano Martino, Bruno Rasia, Pierotti; ph, Augusto Tiezzi (Colorscope, Eastmancolor); m, Michele Cozzoli; ed, Iolanda Benvenuti; art d, Bruno Rasia.

Adventure   **(PR:A   MPAA:NR)**

PIRATE MOVIE, THE zero   (1982, Aus.) 98m Joseph
                                         Hamilton/FOX c

Kristy McNichol *(Mabel)*, Christopher Atkins *(Frederic)*, Ted Hamilton *(Pirate King)*, Bill Kerr *(Maj. General)*, Maggie Kirkpatrick *(Ruth)*, Garry McDonald *(Sgt./Inspector)*, Linda Nagle *(Aphrodite)*, Kate Ferguson *(Edith)*, Rhonda Burchmore *(Kate)*, Catherine Lynch *(Isabel)*, Chuck McKinney *(Samuel)*, Marc Colombani *(Dwarf Pirate)*, John Allansu *(Chinese Captain)*, Paul Graham, Nic Gazzana, Chris Hession, Kjell Nilsson, Tony Deary, Roy Dudley, Gene Del'Mace, George Novak, Kurt Schneider, Bernard Ledger, Richard Boue, Stephen Fyfield, Peter Pantellic, Harry Morris, Roger Ward, Ian Mortimer, George Zakaria, Zev Eletheriou, Edward Brodsky-Schuster, Pamela Jones.

A direct ripoff of Gilbert and Sullivan's "The Pirates of Penzance," this film takes place as the daydream of modern-day girl McNichol who is vacationing in Australia. Features pop music score mixed with some of the original G&S songs in a pirate

period setting that grates on the nerves, along with inane toilet humor that substitutes for any real wit. All the performers, especially McNichol, look as if they can't wait until the film is over, and who can blame them? The producers shot this one in a hurry in an attempt to beat the film version of Joseph Papp's Broadway hit to the theater, and it shows in every frame.

p, David Joseph; d, Ken Annakin; w, Trevor Farrant (based on "The Pirates of Penzance" by Sir William Gilbert and Sir Arthur Sullivan); ph, Robin Copping (Colorfilm); ed, Kenneth W. Zemke; prod d, Tony Woollard; art d, Nic Hepworth; cos, Aphrodite Kondos; ch, David Atkins; m/l, Peter Sullivan, Terry Britten, Kit Hain, Sue Shifrin, Brian Robertson, Gilbert and Sullivan.

Musical/Comedy   **Cas.**   **(PR:C   MPAA:PG)**

PIRATE OF THE BLACK HAWK, THE**   (1961, Fr./Ital.) 75m
Filmgroup c (IL PIRATA DELLO SPARVIERO NERO; LE PIRATE DE L'EPERVIER NOIR)

Mijanou Bardot *(Eleanor)*, Gerard Landry *(Richard)*, Andrea Aureli *(Manfred)*, Ettore Manni *(Johnny)*, Pina Bottin *(Eva)*, Eloisa Cianni *(Stella)*, Germano Longo *(Mark)*, Andrea Miano.

Swashbuckler starring Landry as the heroic pirate who has gathered a band of loyal followers in an effort to defeat the evil Aureli, who has taken the throne by force with his own band of villainous pirates. Once in power, Aureli kidnaps the deposed Duke's daughter, Bardot, and forces her to agree to marry him. On the day of the wedding, Landry and his pirates attack, and a lengthy battle ensues. Bardot and the other women flee to the dungeon, but Aureli orders the rooms flooded. Landry rescues the women and Aureli is impaled on a booby-trap device he had designed for Landry.

p, Giorgio Pescino, Carl Pescino; d, Sergio Grieco; w, Grieco, Enzo Alfonsi, Mario Caiano, Guido Zurli; ph, Vincenzo Seratrice (SuperCinescope, Ferraniacolor); m, Roberto Nicolosi; ed, Enzo Alfonsi; art d, Saverio D'Eugenio; set d, Luigi D'Andria; cos, Giulia Mafai.

Adventure   **(PR:A   MPAA:NR)**

PIRATE SHIP   (SEE: MUTINEERS, THE, 1949)

PIRATES OF BLOOD RIVER, THE**½   (1962, Brit.) 87m Hammer/
                                                            COL c

Kerwin Mathews *(Jonathan Standing)*, Glenn Corbett *(Henry)*, Christopher Lee *(LaRoche)*, Marla Landi *(Bess)*, Oliver Reed *(Brocaire)*, Andrew Keir *(Jason Standing)*, Peter Arne *(Hench)*, Michael Ripper *(Mac)*, Jack Stewart *(Mason)*, David Lodge *(Smith)*, Marie Devereux *(Maggie)*, Diane Aubrey *(Margaret Blackthorne)*, Jerold Wells *(Commandant)*, Dennis Waterman *(Timothy)*, Lorraine Clewes *(Martha Blackthorne)*, John Roden *(2nd Settler)*, Desmond Llewelyn *(Blackthorne)*, Keith Pyott *(Silas)*, Richard Bennett *(Seymour)*, Michael Mulcaster *(Martin)*, Denis Shaw *(Silver)*, Michael Peake *(Kemp)*, John Collin *(Lance)*, Don Levy *(Carlos)*, John Bennett *(Penal Colony Guard)*, Ronald Blackman *(Pugh)*.

Hammer sails the high seas again, with Lee at the helm as an evil pirate with an eye-patch and a useless left arm. Lee enlists the aid of the unjustly imprisoned Mathews who, against his will, leads the pirates to his home on a Caribbean island where Lee believes treasure is buried. After a lengthy battle, Lee takes control of the area and kills many of Mathews' friends and relatives in an effort to make them reveal the location of the treasure. Shocked by the killings, Mathews, his step-sister Landi, and her fiance Corbett manage to escape. When Lee discovers that the statue of Mathews' grandfather is made of pure gold, he has his crew drag it to the beach and load it onto a raft. While on the raft, Lee and company are ambushed by Mathews and his cohorts. The statue falls overboard and sinks, Mathews kills Lee, and they all return home. Good production values and cast help this otherwise ordinary adventure.

p, Anthony Nelson Keys; d, John Gilling; w, John Hunter, Gilling (based on a story by Jimmy Sangster); ph, Arthur Grant (Megascope, Eastmancolor); m, Gary Hughes; ed, Eric Boyd-Perkins; prod d, Bernard Robinson; md, John Hollingsworth; art d, Don Mingaye; cos, Rosemary Burrows; spec eff, Les Bowie; makeup, Roy Ashton.

Adventure   **(PR:A   MPAA:NR)**

PIRATES OF CAPRI, THE**½   (1949) 94m FC bw (GB: THE
                                   MASKED PIRATE; AKA: CAPTAIN SIROCCO)

Louis Hayward *(Capt. Sirocco)*, Binnie Barnes *(Queen Carolina)*, Alan Curtis *(Commodore Van Diel)*, Rudolph Serato *(Von Holstein)*, Mariella Lotti *(Countess Mercedes)*, Mikhail Rasumny *(Pepino)*, Virginia Belmont *(Annette)*, Franca Marzi *(Carla)*, William Tubbs *(Pignatelli)*, Alberto Califano *(1st Officer)*, Mario Auritano *(2nd Officer)*, Eric Culton *(3rd Officer)*, Michel Sorel *(Nicolo)*.

An enjoyable, swashbuckling romp directed by Ulmer who knew how to do much with the little the studio gave him to work with. Hayward stars in this SCARLET PIMPERNEL-like tale as a prim and unassuming character in the Naples court who has a secret identity, and ventures out as a heroic swordsman in defense of a group of rebels seeking to overthrow queen Barnes and her evil police chief Curtis. Great action scenes and clever direction by Ulmer pull this one out of the doldrums. Several scenes that are direct references to the classical theater could easily be viewed as a bit of playfulness on the part of Ulmer, who has his original training in the theater of Germany before turning to film.

p, Victor Pahlen; d, Edgar G. Ulmer; w, Sidney Alexander (based on the story by G.A. Colonna, George Moser, based on an idea by Victor Pahlen); ph, Anchise Brizzi; m, Nino Rota; set d, Guido Fiorina.

Adventure   **Cas.**   **(PR:A   MPAA:NR)**

PIRATES OF MONTEREY*½   (1947) 78m UNIV c

Maria Montez (*Marguerita*), Rod Cameron (*Phillip Kent*), Mikhail Rasumny (*Pio*), Philip Reed (*Lt. Carlos Ortega*), Gilbert Roland (*Maj. De Roja*), Gale Sondergaard (*Senorita de Sola*), Tamara Shayne (*Filomena*), Robert Warwick (*Governor*), Michael Raffetto (*Sgt. Gomara*), Neyle Morrow (*Manuel*), Victor Varconi (*Capt. Cordova*), Charles Wagenheim (*Juan*), Joe Bernard (*Doctor*), George Navarro (*Lieutenant*), Victor Romito (*Don Driggers* (*Thugs*), George Magrill, George J. Lewis (*Pirates*), Lucius Villegas (*Padre*), Chris-Pin Martin (*Caretta Man*), Julia Andre (*Young Woman*), Lilo Yarson, Fred Cordova (*Sentries*), Dick Dickinson (*Jailer*).

With only a beautiful Technicolor look to bolster its sagging screenplay, PIRATES OF MONTEREY stars Cameron as an American soldier-of-fortune who signs on to take a wagon train full of brand-new rifles through the Mexican-controlled area of the California territory and deliver it to an Army outpost beyond. Typical run-ins with outlaws occur with regularity, and eventually Cameron is able to romance Montez.

p, Paul Malvern; d, Alfred Werker; w, Sam Hellman, Margaret Buell Wilder (based on a story by Edward T. Lowe, Bradford Ropes); ph, Hal Mohr (Technicolor), W. Howard Greene, Harry Hallenberg; m, Milton Rosen; ed, Russell Schoengarth; art d, Jack Otterson, Richard H. Reidel; set d, Russell A. Gausman, Leigh Smith; cos, Travis Banton, Vera West.

Western   (PR:A MPAA:NR)

PIRATES OF PENZANCE, THE***   (1983) 112m UNIV c

Kevin Kline (*Pirate King*), Angela Lansbury (*Ruth*), Linda Ronstadt (*Mabel*), George Rose (*Major-General*), Rex Smith (*Frederic*), Tony Azito (*Sergeant*), David Hatton (*Samuel, sung by Stephen Hanan*), Louis Gold (*Edith, sung by Alexandra Korey*), Teresa Codling (*Kate, sung by Marcia Shaw*), Leni Harper, Clare McIntyre, Louise Papillon, Tilly Vosburgh, Nancy Wood (*Other Daughters*), Anthony Arundell, John Asquith, Mohamed Aazzi, Tim Bentinck, Ross Davidson, Mike Grady, Simon Howe, Tony Millan, G.B. Zoot Money, Andrew Paul, Ken Leigh Rogers, Mohamed Serhani, Mike Walling (*Pirates*), Peppi Borza, Nicholas Chagrin, Frankie Cull, David Hampshire, Phillip Harrison, Maurice Lane, Neil McCaul, Jerry Manley, Rhys Nelson, Garry Noakes, Chris Power, Kenny Warwick (*Policemen*), Romolo Bruni (*Pinafore Captain*), John Bett, Lennie Byrne, Jo Cameron-Brown, Zulema Dene, Marta Eitler, Carole Forbes, Jack Honeyborne, Carol Macready, Brian Markham, Valerie Minifie, Linda Spurrier, Ursula Stedman (*Pinafore Company*).

Better than expected, this film version of Broadway producer Joseph Papp's successful stage rendition of the classic Gilbert and Sullivan piece is fun, lively, and fairly entertaining. Broadway cast intact (with the addition of Lansbury as the pirates' den-mother), the story follows young pirate Smith who decides to leave the ship upon his 21st birthday and go straight (he has been raised by the pirates). On shore, he meets a family of eight sisters and becomes very smitten with one of them, Ronstadt. Pirate king Kline, however, will not let Smith go that easily and informs him that since his birthday falls on leap year, he won't be 21 for quite some time. Reluctantly rejoining the gang, Smith soon finds himself involved in an attack on the home of Ronstadt's father (he's a major-general), and the nutty assault ends with the pirates humbled in front of a statue of Queen Victoria and then running off with every one of the major-general's eight daughters. The cast is charming, the sets intentionally stagy, and the musical performances fine. The film stirred up a minor controversy when the producers decided to release it in the theaters and on cable television simultaneously, which led to theater owners claiming they wouldn't show it. They did, though the negative publicity somewhat hurt the film at the box office.

p, Joseph Papp; d&w, Wilford Leach (based on the operetta by Sir William Gilbert, Sir Arthur Sullivan); ph, Douglas Slocombe (Panavision, Technicolor); m, Sullivan; ed, Anne V. Coates; prod d, Elliot Scott; md, William Elliott; art d, Ernest Archer, Alan Cassie; set d, Peter Howitt; cos, Tom Rand; ch, Graciela Daniele; m/l, Gilbert, Sullivan.

Musical   **Cas.**   (PR:A MPAA:G)

PIRATES OF THE PRAIRIE**   (1942) 57m RKO bw

Tim Holt, Cliff "Ukelele Ike" Edwards, Nell O'Day, John H. Elliott, Roy Barcroft, Karl Hackett, Dick Cramer, Edward Cassidy, Eddie Dew, Merrill McCormack, Reed Howes, Charles King, Bud Geary, Lee Shumway, Russell Wade, Ben Corbett, Frank McCarroll, Artie Ortego, George Morrell.

Exciting Holt western has our hero as a clever deputy marshal who poses as a gunsmith in order to infiltrate the vigilantes who are out terrorizing local ranchers and driving them off their lands. With the help of the disgruntled ranchers, Holt manages to put an end to the villains' land snatching. Climax sees a well-choreographed gun battle on Main Street.

p, Bert Gilroy; d, Howard Bretherton; w, Doris Schroeder, J. Benton Cheney (based on a story by Berne Giler); ph, Nicholas Musuraca; ed, John Lockert; md, Paul Sawtell; art d, Albert S. d'Agostino, Walter E. Keller; m/l, "Grandpop," "Where the Mountain Meets the Sunset" Fred Rose, Ray Whitley.

Western   (PR:A MPAA:NR)

PIRATES OF THE SEVEN SEAS**   (1941, Brit.) 62m Film Alliance/
                                     Associated British Pictures bw (GB: QUEER CARGO)

John Lodge (*Capt. Harley*), Judy Kelly (*Ann Warren*), Keneth Kent (*Monty Cabini*), Louis Borell (*Benson*), Bertha Belmore (*Henrietta Travers*), Wylie Watson (*Rev. James Travers*), Geoffrey Toone (*Lt. Stocken*), Jerry Verno (*Slops*), Frank Pettingell (*Dan*), Frank Cochrane (*Ho-Tang*).

Lodge is a sea captain who suddenly finds himself stuck in a doubly sticky situation.

His crew mutinies *and* at the crucial moment his ship is also invaded by pirates, led by Kent. The pirates are searching for some valuable pearls that Lodge has smuggled, but he won't talk. Eventually Lodge's mutinous crew decides they've had enough of the pirates and they attack.

p, Walter c. Mycroft; d, Harold Schuster; w, Patrick Kirwan, Walter Summers (based on a play by Noel Langley); ph, Otto Kanturek.

Adventure   (PR:A MPAA:NR)

PIRATES OF THE SKIES**   (1939) 60m UNIV bw

Kent Taylor (*Nick Conlan*), Rochelle Hudson (*Barbara Conlan*), Lucien Littlefield (*Dr. Pettingill*), Ray Walker (*Hal Weston*), Stanley Andrews (*Maj. Smith*), Marion Martin (*Kitty*), Regis Toomey (*Bill Lambert*), Guy Usher (*Capt. Higgins*), Frank Puglia (*Jerry Petri*), Henry Brandon (*Jake*), Dorothy Arnold (*Waitress*), Samuel S. Hinds (*Commissioner*), Horace MacMahon (*Artie*), Eddy Chandler (*Slug*), John Harmon (*Ralph*), Syd Saylor (*Owner*), Hooper Atchley (*Jeweler*), Gladden James (*Rental Salesman*), Fern Emmett (*Customer*), Philip Trent (*Pilot*), William Royle, Lee Phelps, Ed Peil, Sr. (*Cops*), Harry Harvey (*Concessionaire*), Hugh Huntley (*Bill Melford*), Charles Sherlock (*Man on Street*), Frank O'Connor (*Doorman*), Roy Brent (*Orderly*), Tom O'Grady (*Barker*), Jack Gardner (*Curtis*).

Hudson stars as a waitress who has left her air pilot husband because he was never home. The husband, Taylor, quits his job as a commercial pilot and joins the state police air service to be near his wife. The ploy doesn't work, however, because Taylor becomes embroiled in inter-departmental rivalry between the police motor patrol and the air patrol. (The motor-boys think that the air-boys are hot shots stealing their thunder.) When a sophisticated gang of jewel thieves begins working the area, Taylor and company set to work and capture them. This earns Hudson's respect and the couple are finally reunited.

p, Barney A. Sarecky; d, Joe A. McDonough; w, Ben G. Kohn (based on the story "Sky Police" by Lester Cole); ph, Jerry Ash; ed, Ted Kent.

Drama   (PR:A MPAA:NR)

PIRATES OF TORTUGA**   (1961) 97m Clover/FOX c

Ken Scott (*Bart Paxton*), Leticia Roman (*Meg Graham*), David King (*Pee Wee*), John Richardson (*Percy*), Rafer Johnson (*John Gammel*), Robert Stephens (*Henry Morgan*), Rachel Stephens (*Phoebe*), Stanley Adams (*Capt. Montbars*), Edgar Barrier (*Sir Thomas Modyford*), James Forrest (*Reggie*), Patrick Sexton (*Randolph*), Arthur E. Gould-Porter (*Bonnett*), Hortense Petra (*Lola*), Malcolm Cassell (*Kipper*), Maxwell Reed (*Fielding*), Alan Caillou (*Ringose*), Kendrick Huxham (*Sir Francis Day*).

Scott is hired by King Charles II of England to infiltrate a gang of pirates and capture their leader, the infamous Henry Morgan, played by R. Stephens. When Scott decides to attack the pirates, the wily Stephens proves he's no fool and is prepared to meet him. The two fight hand to hand, but are knocked out and taken to the governor of Tortuga who is about to hang them both as pirates. Scott is saved after his stowaway gypsy, Roman, reveals his true identity, and Morgan goes to his doom.

p, Sam Katzman; d, Robert D. Webb; w, Melvin Levy, Jesse L. Lasky, Jr., Pat Silver (based on a story by Levy); ph, Ellis W. Carter (CinemaScope, DeLuxe Color); m, Paul Sawtell, Bert Shefter; ed, Hugh S. Fowler; md, Max Reese; art d, Jack Martin Smith, George Van Marter; set d, Walter M. Scott, Lou Hafley; ch, Hal Belfer; makeup, Ben Nye.

Adventure   (PR:A MPAA:NR)

PIRATES OF TRIPOLI**   (1955) 72m COL bw

Paul Henreid (*Edri-Al-Gadrian*), Patricia Medina (*Princess Karjan*), Paul Newland (*Hammid Khassan*), John Miljan (*Malek*), Mark Hanna (*Ben Ali*), Jean Del Val (*Abu Tala*), Lillian Bond (*Sono*), Mel Wells (*Tomedi*), Louis G. Mercier (*The Cat*), Karl Davis (*Assassin*), Maralou Gray (*Rhea*), Peter Mamakos (*Keppa*), William Fawcett (*Beggar*), Frank Richards (*Zurtah*), Gene Borden (*Italian Ship's Captain*).

Medina plays a 16th-Century princess whose kingdom is besieged by invaders who conquer her armies with ease. In desperation she goes to pirate captain Henreid for help. He agrees, and using footage lifted from another swashbuckler, THE GOLDEN HAWK, to help relieve the woodenness of the star, Henreid and Medina defeat the ravaging hordes. For fans of the blustering, swaggering fighting man and helpless but beautiful maiden, this is just the ticket to adventure.

p, Sam Katzman; d, Felix Feist; w, Allen March; ph, Henry Freulich (Technicolor); ed, Edwin Bryant; md, Mischa Bakaleinikoff; art d, Paul Palmentola.

Adventure   (PR:A MPAA:NR)

PIRATES ON HORSEBACK*½   (1941) 69m PAR bw

William Boyd (*Hopalong Cassidy*), Russell Hayden (*Lucky Jenkins*), Andy Clyde (*California*), Eleanor Stewart (*Trudy Pendleton*), Morris Ankrum (*Ace Gibson*), William Haade (*Bill Watson*), Dennis Moore (*Jud Carter*), Henry Hall (*Sheriff Blake*), Britt Wood (*Ben Pendleton*).

Boyd, Hayden, and Clyde ride off to find the mine owned by Stewart, who was swindled out of its ownership by gambler Ankrum. The cowboys find the mine and a wild fist fight between Boyd and Ankrum wins the gold back for Stewart. A weak entry in the Hopalong Cassidy series, but with some stunning photography in uncharted filmic territory around the base of Mt. Whitney in California. (See HOPALONG CASSIDY series, Index.)

p, Harry Sherman; d, Lesley Selander; w, J. Benton Cheney, Ethel La Blanche (based on characters created by Clarence E. Mulford); ph, Russell Harlan; ed, Fred Feitshans, Jr.; art d, Lewis J. Rachmil.

Western   (PR:A MPAA:NR)

PISTOL FOR RINGO, A½** (1966, Ital./Span.) 97m P.C.M.-Balcazar/ EM c (UNA PISTOLA PER RINGO; UNA PISTOLA PARA RINGO)

Montgomery Wood [Giuliano Gemma] (*Ringo*), Fernando Sancho (*Sancho*), Hally Hammond [Lorella De Luca] (*Ruby*), Nieves Navarro (*Dolores*), Antonio Casas (*Maj. Clyde*), George Martin [Jorge Martin] (*Sheriff*), Paco Sanz, Jose Holupi, Nazzareno Zamperla, Jose Manuel Martin, Juan Cazalilla, Pajarito, Frank Oliveras.

Better than average spaghetti epic starring Wood/Gemma as a drifter helping a small Texas family whose ranch has been invaded by a gang of Mexican bandits. Posing as one of the gang, Wood/Gemma saves the family and disposes of the bandits. Director Tessari, who cowrote (uncredited) Sergio Leone's A FISTFUL OF DOLLARS, handles the film with a sure style and holds the violence characteristic of the genre to a minimum, while borrowing freely from Howard Hawks and John Ford.

p, Luciano Ercoli, Alberto Pugliese; d&w, Duccio Tessari (based on a story by Tessari, Alfonso Balcazar); ph, Francisco Marin (Techniscope, Technicolor); m, Ennio Morricone; ed, Licia Quaglia; md, Bruno Nicolai; art d, Juan Alberto Soler, Carlo Gentili; cos, Gentili; m/l, "Angel Face," Morricone (sung by Graf Maurizio).

Western **(PR:C MPAA:NR)**

PISTOL HARVEST** (1951) 60m RKO bw

Tim Holt (*Tim*), Joan Dixon (*Felice*), Robert Clarke (*Jack*), Mauritz Hugo (*Norton*), Robert Wilke (*Baylor*), William Griffith (*Prouty*), Guy Edward Hearn (*Terry*), Harper Carter (*Johnny*), Joan Freeman (*Little Felice*), F. Herrick (*Capt. Rand*), Richard Martin (*Chito Rafferty*), Lee Phelps.

Holt and Martin are employed by Hearn to work on his ranch. When Hugo, a shipping magnate, refuses to pay back $30,000 he borrowed from Hearn, he kills the rancher and blames it on two strangers, Clarke and Wilke. After some digging, Holt and Martin decide that the strangers are innocent and conclude that it was indeed Hugo who killed their boss. A neatly done Holt entry by all concerned, in spite of having to hew to a tightly controlled $93,000 budget line.

p, Herman Schlom; d, Lesley Selander; w, Norman Houston; ph, J. Roy Hunt; ed, Douglas Biggs; md, C. Bakaleinikoff; art d, Albert S. D'Agostino, Feild Gray.

Western **(PR:A MPAA:NR)**

PISTOL PACKIN' MAMA½** (1943) 64m REP bw

Ruth Terry (*Vicki Norris/Sally Benson*), Robert Livingston (*Nick Winner*), Wally Vernon (*The Joker*), Jack LaRue (*Johnny Rossi*), Kirk Alyn (*J. Leslie Burton III*), Eddie Parker (*Mike*), Helen Talbot (*Young Wife*), Lydia Bilbrook (*Mrs. Burton*), George Lessey (*Mr. Burton*), The King Cole Trio (*Themselves*).

Not as much fun as its title suggests, PISTOL PACKIN' MAMA is a musical starring Terry as the owner of a Nevada gambling den. Livingston arrives in town after being kicked out of New York by gang leader LaRue, and immediately breaks the bank and makes off with enough money to return to New York and set up his own gambling place. When Terry learns of his cheating, she assumes a new identity, follows Livingston back to New York, and gets a job singing in his club. She cons Livingston into cutting cards for ownership of his club and she wins, but then LaRue and his mob crash the doors in an attempt to take over. Luckily, Terry is as good with a gun as she is with a tune and she soon wipes out LaRue's gang, leaving her and Livingston to clinch at the end. Songs include the title song and "I've Heard that Song Before," "Love is a Corny Thing" (all sung by Terry), and "I'm an Errand Boy for Rhythm" (sung by the King Cole Trio).

p, Eddy White; d, Frank Woodruff; w, Edward Dein, Fred Schiller (based on a story by Arthur Caesar, Dein); ph, Reggie Lanning; ed, Tony Martinelli; md, Morton Scott; art d, Fred Ritter.

Musical **(PR:A MPAA:NR)**

PISTOLERO (SEE: LAST CHALLENGE, THE, 1967)

PIT, THE (SEE: FIVE MILLION YEARS TO EARTH, 1968, Brit.)

PIT AND THE PENDULUM, THE*½** (1961) 85m Alta Vista/AIP c

Vincent Price (*Nicholas Medina*), John Kerr (*Francis Barnard*), Barbara Steele (*Elisabeth Barnard Medina*), Luana Anders (*Catherine Medina*), Anthony Carbone (*Dr. Charles Leon*), Patrick Westwood (*Maximillian, Butler*), Lynne Bernay (*Maria*), Larry Turner (*Nicholas as a Child*), Mary Menzies (*Isabella*), Charles Victor (*Bartolome*).

The second and best of Roger Corman's Edgar Allan Poe series once again stars Price as the owner of a large and spooky castle which houses an elaborate torture chamber built by his father during the Spanish Inquisition. Stricken with grief after the death of his wife, Steele (in her American film debut), Price becomes obsessed with the notion that he accidentally buried her alive. Steele's brother, Kerr, suspects foul play and travels to the castle of his brother-in-law looking for answers. What he finds however, is that Price is slowly going mad and claims he can hear Steele's voice calling to him from throughout the castle. Eventually it is revealed that Steele is not dead at all, but had conspired with her lover, family doctor Carbone, to drive her husband insane. To put the seal of doom on Price, Steele calls for him and he follows her voice to the crypt where she rises from the grave. Price's mind snaps, much to the delight of Steele and Carbone (who can now inherit his fortune), but Price suddenly assumes the identity of his father and becomes a lord high torturer of the Inquisition. In a fight with Price, Carbone falls into the pit to his death. Steele is locked in an iron box, and the innocent Kerr is strapped under the swinging and ever-descending pendulum which has a massive steel blade attached to the end. Just as the blade is about to slice him in two, Kerr is rescued by Prince's sister, Anders, and the butler. While attempting to stop them, Price falls into the pit and Anders declares that she will seal up the torture chamber forever, not realizing that Steele is still alive in the iron box. Corman brought in THE PIT AND THE PENDU-LUM on a 15-day shooting schedule and the result is a very entertaining horror film

with chills, humor, and a bravura performance by Price who was just beginning to fine-hone his wickedly delightful, villainous characters. Shot in a lush and almost garish color by cinematographer Crosby (who had also shot Corman's previous Poe film THE HOUSE OF USHER), the film is filled with some impressive techniques and camera movement for a low-budget, quickly shot feature. Screenwriter Matheson did a fine job of adapting Poe's rather limited (for films) short story by saving the dungeon sequences for the climax and then creating a rather interesting plot line to lead up to it. One of Corman and AIP's best.

p&d, Roger Corman; w, Richard Matheson (based on a story by Edgar Allen Poe); ph, Floyd Crosby (Panavision, Pathe Color); m, Les Baxter; ed, Anthony Carras; prod d&art d, Daniel Haller; set d, Harry Reif; cos, Marjorie Corso; spec eff, Pat Dinga.

Horror **Cas.** **(PR:C MPAA:NR)**

PIT OF DARKNESS½** (1961, Brit.) 76m BUT bw

William Franklyn (*Richard Logan*), Moira Redmond (*Julie Logan*), Bruno Barnabe (*Maxie*), Leonard Sachs (*Conrad*), Nigel Green (*Jonathan*), Bruce Beeby (*Mayhew*), Humphrey Lestocq (*Bill*), Anthony Booth (*Ted Mellis*), Nanette Newman (*Mary*).

After being tricked into helping some jewel thieves into cracking a safe, a safe designer loses his memory. His wife tries to help him retain his memory so that he can clear his name. Decent thriller.

p,d&w, Lance Comfort (based on the novel To Dusty Death by Hugh McCutcheon).

Crime **(PR:A MPAA:NR)**

PIT STOP zero (1969) 92m Goldstone-Crown International bw

Brian Donlevy (*Grant Willard*), Dick Davalos (*Rick Bowman*), Ellen McRae [Burstyn] (*Ellen McLeod*), Sid Haig (*Hawk Sidney*), Beverly Washburn (*Jolene*), George Washburn (*Ed McLeod*).

Bargain-basement drama starring Donlevy as the owner of a successful stock car racing organization who hires ambitious young racer Davalos to compete against local great Haig. During the race, Davalos forces Haig to crash and wins the race. Off the track he steals the injured racer's girl friend. In the next race, Davalos is assigned to work closely with Donlevy's favorite, Washburn, but nevertheless begins an affair with Washburn's wife, McRae (later Burstyn). During the race, Davalos decides that it is he who must win and he forces Washburn into a deadly crash. Shot on a budget of $60,000 in and around Los Angeles with borrowed footage from the Phoenix International stock car race. PIT STOP was two-fisted Donley's last film in a career that started with the 1924 picture DAMAGED HEARTS.

p, Lee Stonsnider; d&w, Jack Hill; ph, Austin McKinney; ed, Hill.

Drama **(PR:O MPAA:R)**

PITFALL*½** (1948) 86m UA bw

Dick Powell (*John Forbes*), Lizabeth Scott (*Mona Stevens*), Jane Wyatt (*Sue Forbes*), Raymond Burr (*Mack MacDonald*), John Litel (*District Attorney*), Byron Barr (*Bill Smiley*), Jimmy Hunt (*Tommy Forbes*), Ann Doran (*Maggie*), Selmer Jackson (*Ed Brawley*), Margaret Wells (*Terry*), Dick Wessel (*Desk Sergeant*).

Grim suburban *film noir* starring Powell as a bored insurance salesman who has become dissatisfied with his perfect wife, Wyatt, his ideal son, Hunt, and his job. During an investigation into the illegally gained goods purchased by bank robber Barr who is now serving time in jail, Powell meets sleazy detective Burr (in a chilling performance) who is to assist him in recovering the items. The trail of merchandise leads to Scott, who uses Barr's loot-bought motor boat for pleasure cruises. Powell informs Scott that all items purchased by Barr are going to be confiscated. Disappointed, Scott decides to seduce Powell, who has obviously become infatuated with her, much to the dismay of Burr who had set his sights on the comely blonde himself. Powell succumbs to Scott's charms and the couple have a brief affair. Guilt-ridden, Powell ends the affair, but not before a jealous Burr warns him to stay away. To ensure that the affair will not resume, Burr arranges for Barr's release and gets him drunk, filling the robber's head with lurid details of his girl friend's fling with Powell. Scott learns of Burr's plan and warns the insurance investigator, who puts his family to bed and awaits the robber's arrival with a gun in his hand. When Barr bursts through the door, Powell shoots him dead. Cornered, Powell reveals the tale of the torrid affair to his wife, who is understandably shocked. Meanwhile, Burr kidnaps Scott and forces her to run off with him, but she resists and kills him. Scott is arrested and Powell freed of a murder charge, but his wife ominously states that their life together will never be the same. A disturbing *film noir* product which sees the disintegration of the noble suburban provider from respectable community member to sordid, impulsive philanderer. Where another drama may have left a bright spot open at the ending, the *film noir* ends with a hopeless declaration of despair.

p, Samuel Bischoff; d, Andre DeToth; w, Karl Kamb (based on the novel by Jay Dratler); ph, Harry Wild; m, Louis Forbes; ed, Walter Thompson; art d, Arthur Lonergan; set d, Robert Priestley; makeup, Robert Cowan.

Crime **(PR:C MPAA:NR)**

PITTSBURGH** (1942) 98m UNIV bw

Marlene Dietrich (*Josie Winters*), Randolph Scott (*Cash Evans*), John Wayne (*Pittsburgh "Pitt" Markham*), Frank Craven (*Doc Powers*), Louise Allbritton (*Shannon Prentiss*), Shemp Howard (*Shorty*), Thomas Gomez (*Joe Malneck*), Ludwig Stossell (*Dr. Grazlich*), Samuel S. Hinds (*Morgan Prentiss*), Paul Fix (*Mine Operator*), William Haade (*Johnny*), Douglas Fowley (*Mort Brawley*), Sammy Stein (*Killer Kane*), Harry Seymour (*Theater Manager*), Charles Coleman (*Butler*), Nestor Paiva (*Barney*), Hobart Cavanaugh (*Derelict*), Virginia Sale (*Mrs. Bercovici*), Wade Boteler (*Mine Superintendent*), Mira McKinney (*Tilda*), Alphonse Martell

(Carlos), Charles Sherlock *(Chauffeur)*, Bess Flowers *(Woman)*, Ray Walker *(Reporter)*, Charles Arnt *(Laborer)*, William Gould *(Burns)*, Harry Cording *(Miner)*.

Following THE SPOILERS (also 1942), PITTSBURGH marked the second teaming of Wayne, Dietrich and Scott—a trio which left the theater audience smiling regardless of the fact that the plot was strictly run-of-the-mill. Wayne and Scott are a pair of rugged, confident coal miners who are content with occupying their rung in the social ladder—until they both fall in love with the same woman. During a boxing match Wayne and Scott take notice of Dietrich. Seated at ringside, Dietrich is dressed in high-priced attire to hide the fact that she is really a "hunky"—a person raised in a coal town. Wayne quickly falls in love with Dietrich and begins calling her "Countess." Scott, too, falls under her spell, but both men are taken aback when she confesses that she will never marry a miner. Hoping to improve his financial and social position, Wayne enters a deal with a steel company which soon turns a profit. Greater success follows for Wayne, who rapidly loses sight of his initial interest—winning Dietrich's affections. Instead, Wayne courts Allbritton, a banker's daughter, seeing her as providing entry into high society. He gradually loses touch with Dietrich and Scott, but on the night he is to wed Allbritton, he chases after Dietrich, explaining, "It got a bit chilly uptown. I thought I'd come down here where it's warmer." It is too late, however, and Dietrich (who has loved Wayne all along) responds by slapping him in the face. Wayne continues his climb to the top, amassing great wealth while at the same time becoming uncharacteristically callous. Long sympathetic to the needs of laborers, Wayne begins to turn his back on his employees, breaking several promises he had made to them. When he refuses to allow company spokesman Gomez access to the firm's books (one of his promises), the workers strike. This is the beginning of Wayne's downhill slide. Before long his company has failed, Allbritton has said farewell, and Scott and Dietrich have turned away. While Wayne was climbing to the top, Scott formed a business partnership with Craven, as well as a romantic one with Dietrich. Paralleling Wayne's decline is the rise of the city which shares his name, Pittsburgh—documented with newsreel footage. Broke and humbled, Wayne uses a false name and takes a job as a laborer with Scott's company. His dedication prompts his supervisor to send him to Scott for an executive postion in the company. What nearly erupts into a violent brawl is turned into a pleasant reunion by Dietrich. In a patriotic finale, Wayne is taken on as a partner and the firm hastens its production of materials for the war effort. PITTSBURGH amounts to little more than a standard love triangle combined with class differences and one man's rise to power (a simple, though perfectly respectable, plot line) not unlike countless other films. What makes this picture work is the superb performances by the three leads (as well as an excellent supporting cast). The casting which proved so effective in THE SPOILERS (and, to a degree, in SEVEN SINNERS, which paired Wayne and Dietrich) again works remarkably well, providing a thoroughly enjoyable film.

p, Charles K. Feldman; d, Lewis Seiler; w, Kenneth Gamet, Tom Reed, John Twist (based on a screen story by George Owen, Reed); ph, Robert De Grasse; m, Frank Skinner, Hans J. Salter; ed, Paul Landres; md, Charles Previn; art d, John B. Goodman; cos, Vera West; spec eff, John P. Fulton.

Drama   (PR:A   MPAA:NR)

PITTSBURGH KID, THE*½   (1941) 76m REP bw

Billy Conn *(Himself)*, Jean Parker *(Patricia Mallory)*, Dick Purcell *(Cliff Halliday)*, Alan Baxter *(Joe Barton)*, Veda Ann Borg *(Barbara Ellison)*, Jonathan Hale *(Max Ellison)*, Ernest Whitman *(Feets Johnson)*, John Kelly *(Knockout Riley)*, Etta McDaniel *(Magenta)*, Dick Elliott *(Garvey)*, John Harmon *(Morrie)*, Robert Barron *(Devlin)*, Arthur Donovan, Henry Armstrong, Freddie Steele, Jack Roper, Sam Balter, Dan Tobey.

Long-time heavyweight boxing contender Billy Conn plays a boxer in this dull drama detailing the battle between sly manager Hale and good-girl Parker, whose father managed the big lug before his death. Seeing that Hale is using his sexy daughter, Borg, to entice Conn to sign up with him, Parker decides to manage the boxer herself. While slowly falling for each other, Parker puts the wheels in motion to get Conn's career to take off. Conn is signed to a championship bout opposite one of Hale's biggest bruisers. Unfortunately, Borg is still trying to seduce Conn, and her boy friend, Baxter, gets jealous and tries to kill the boxer, but he is slain instead. Conn soon finds himself up on murder charges. All works out well when Borg has a sudden case of guilty conscience and gets the boxer out of his jam and back into the waiting arms of Parker. Republic though it had a coup when it signed Conn to star in this picture, inasmuch as the boxer had an upcoming championship fight with Joe Louis to help the turnstiles click. It was not to be, however, as Conn sank out of contention for five years after Louis knocked him out in the 13th round of their battle the year of the film's release. Louis kayoed Conn again in 1946, and that was that for Billy.

p, Armand Schaefer; d, Jack Townley; w, Earl Felton, Houston Branch (based on the story "Kid Tinsel" by Octavus Roy Cohen); ph, Reggie Lanning; ed, Ernest Nims; md, Cy Feuer; art d, John Victor Mackay.

Drama   (PR:A   MPAA:NR)

PIXOTE**   (1981, Braz.) 127m Embrafilm/Palace c

Fernando Ramos da Silva *(Pixote)*, Marilia Pera *(Sueli)*, Jorge Juliao *(Lilica)*, Gilberto Moura *(Dito)*, Jose Nilson dos Santos *(Diego)*, Edilson Lino *(Chico)*, Zenildo Oliveira Santos *(Fumaca)*, Claudio Bernardo *(Garatao)*, Tony Tornado *(Cristal)*, Jardel Filho *(Sapatos Brancos)*, Rubens de Falco *(Juiz)*.

Grim, disturbing, and engrossing Brazilian film about a boy abandoned by his parents who becomes a street-wise pimp and murderer by the age of 10. Da Silva is superb as the boy and Pera is equally powerful as his prostitute. Director Babenco successfully mixes a neorealist style within a somewhat surreal context in a manner reminiscent of Luis Bunuel's masterpiece LOS OLVIDADOS. (In Portuguese; English subtitles.)

p, Paulo Francini; d, Hector Babenco; w, Babenco, Jorge Duran (based on the

novel *Infancia Dos Martos* by Jose Louzeiro); ph, Rodolfo Sanches; m, John Neschling; ed, Luiz Elias; art d, Clovis Bueno.

Drama   Cas.   (PR:O   MPAA:NR)

PIZZA TRIANGLE, THE½** (1970, Ital./Span.) 99m Dean Film-Jupiter Generale Cinematografica-Midega/WB c (DRAMMA DELLA GELOSIA-TUTTI I PARTICOLARI IN CRONACA; AKA: A DRAMA OF JEALOUSY [AND OTHER THINGS]; JEALOUSY ITALIAN STYLE)

Marcello Mastroianni *(Oreste)*, Monica Vitti *(Adelaide)*, Giancarlo Giannini *(Nello)*, Manolo Zarzo *(Uto)*, Marisa Merlini *(Silvana)*, Hercules Cortes *(Ambleto Di Meo)*, Fernando Sanches Polak *(District Head of Communist Party)*, Gioia Desideri *(Adelaide's Friend)*, Juan Diego *(Antonia's Son)*, Bruno Scipioni *(Pizza Maker)*, Josefina Serratosa *(Antonia)*, Corrado Gaipa *(President of Tribunal)*, Giuseppe Maffioli *(Lawyer)*, Paola Natale, Brizio Montinaro.

Despite the fact that Mastroianni won Best Actor at the Cannes Film Festival for his performance, THE PIZZA TRIANGLE is just another dreary Italian sex farce. Vitti plays a beguiling flower vendor who seduces bricklayer Mastroianni into believing she loves him. After a few blissful weeks, Vitti strikes up a torid affair with the bricklayer's friend, Giannini, a pizza baker. When this is discovered the former friends come to blows and Vitti is driven into attempting suicide because she cannot decide between the two men. She fails to kill herself and goes off to live in seclusion with kindly butcher Cortes. When she learns that Giannini has also attempted suicide, she rushes back to tell him that they will marry. Upon leaving the hospital, the couple bumps into Mastroianni, who is now a bum. Another fight breaks out between the men, but this time Vitti is accidentally killed by Mastroianni with her flower shears.

p, Pio Angeletti, Andriano de Micheli; d, Ettore Scola; w, Age, Furio, Scarpelli, Scola (based on the story "Jealousy Italian Style" by Age, Scarpelli); ph, Carlo di Palma (Panavision, Technicolor); m, Armando Trovaioli; ed, Alberto Gallitti; md, Gianfranco Plenizio; art d, Luciano Ricceri; cos, Ezio Altieri.

Comedy/Drama   (PR:O   MPAA:R)

PLACE CALLED GLORY, A½**   (1966, Span./Ger.) 92m Midega-CCC/EM c (DIE HOLLE VON MANITOBA; UN LUGAR LLAMADO "GLORY")

Lex Barker *(Brenner)*, Pierre Brice *(Reece)*, Marianne Koch *(Jade Grande)*, Jorge Rigaud *(Seth Grande)*, Gerard Tichy *(Jack Vallone)*, Angel Del Pozo *(Josh)*, Santiago Ontanon *(Mayor of Glory)*, Hans Nielsen *(Judge of Glory)*, Wolfgang Lukschy *(Barman)*, Victor Israel *(Clerk)*, Antonio Molino Rojo, Aldo Sambrell, Carlos Casaravilla, Roberto Martin.

Fairly interesting Spanish oater that hinges on a barbaric ceremony enacted in the small town of Glory every year to commemorate its founding. On each anniversary the town enlists two of its fastest gunslingers to participate in a showdown on Main Street. This year Barker and a gunman named Deakes are slated to appear. When a drifter, Brice, rides into town and announces that he has killed Deakes, the town's politicians persuade Brice to take the dead man's place, though they keep the change a secret. Before the fight, Brice rides off to another town where he meets and befriends Barker, unaware that he is the other half of the impending showdown. The men find themselves in agreement over the basic lawlessness to be found in Glory, and they vow to go there and clean things up. Upon arrival the men are shocked to discover that they are slated to shoot at each other, so they arrange to fool the townsfolk by faking the ordeal. After the showdown, the men unite and clean Glory of the vile men who insist on the grim tradition.

p, Bruce Balaban, Danilo Sabatini; d, Ralph Gideon [Sheldon Reynolds]; w, Edward Di Lorenzo, Jerold Hayden Boyd, Fernando Lamas (based on a story by Boyd); ph, Federico G. Larraya (Techniscope, Pathe Color); m, Angel Arteaga; ed, Terese Alcocer, Roberto Cinquini; md, Bruno Nicolai; art d, Enrique Alarcon, Heinrich Weidemann; cos, Itala Scandariato.

Western   (PR:C   MPAA:NR)

PLACE FOR LOVERS, A zero   (1969, Ital./Fr.) 88m C.C. Champion-Les Films Concordia/MGM c (AMANTI; LE TEMPS DES AMANTS)

Faye Dunaway *(Julia)*, Marcello Mastroianni *(Valerio)*, Caroline Mortimer *(Maggie)*, Karin Engh *(Griselda)*, Esmeralda Ruspoli, Enrico Simonetti, Mirella Pamphili.

Cock-A-Doodle-Dooooooo is all we can say for this dreadful trash that was foisted upon an unsuspecting public who thought it might be intriguing to see on screen the love affair that Dunaway and Mastroianni were having at the time. What a load of garbage this is. Audiences had to come with gas masks to counter the stench off the screen. The doomed-by-disease story had been done countless times before but never this poorly. Dunaway is an American divorcee who moves into a posh villa near Venice for a short stay. She's a fashion designer (which accounts for her numerous changes of clothes) and a pal has lent her the residence. She looks at her TV set and notes the man being interviewed is Mastroianni, a guy with whom she'd spoken at an airport a while back. Mastroianni had made some mild advances and given her his card. He's an engineer who designs air bags for automobile accidents. She's bored and not terribly interested in watching Italian-dubbed versions of U.S. TV shows, so she calls the number and Mastroianni hurries to the villa. The next several days are spent making love (interminably and boringly). Now a group of friends come by to have a nice old-fashioned orgy, complete with pornographic films and lots of moaning. Mastroianni cannot understand how calmly Dunaway takes this and drives off in a huff (which resembles a Maserati, but only slightly). What he doesn't know is that she's terminally ill (probably from all the heavy pale makeup they've put on her face to convince us she's dying). On the following day, Dunaway happens to go to a local car track where Mastroianni is testing his air bags and she talks him into an Alpine vacation. They are happy again although she shows no interest in his work and doesn't let him know much about herself. Dunaway's friend, Mortimer, finds them in the Alps and tells Mastroianni about the illness. Mortimer suggests Dunaway go to a Paris hospital where she can be given pain-killing drugs to ease her final days. Dunaway runs away and Mastroianni follows her and stops a suicide attempt. Then, in the only exciting moment in the picture, he asks her to drive them back to the chalet, knowing full well that she might just veer off a cliff. The ride is hair-raising and they almost crash. She then gives him the key to the car and they go back to the chalet, with her realizing that he loves her and that to take his life in her suicide would be a terrible deed. They decide to stay together until she dies. De Sica's direction is dismal, his son's music is pukey, the acting is awful, Mastroianni's accent is impenetrable, the five-writer script is pretentious, and the editing is nonexistent. The Alps, however, never looked better. Dunaway's performance in this is bottomed only by her work in MOMMY DEAREST.

p, Carlo Ponti, Arthur Cohn; d, Vittorio De Sica; w, Julian Halevy, Peter Baldwin, Ennio De Concini, Tonino Guerra, Cesare Zavattini, De Sica (based on the play "Amanti" by Brunello Rondi, Renaldo Cabieri); ph, Pasquale De Santis (Metrocolor); m, Manuel De Sica; ed, Adriana Novelli; md, Zeno Vukelich; art d, Piero Poletto; cos, Enrico Sabbatini, Theadora Van Runkle; m/l, "A Place for Lovers," Manuel De Sica, Norman Gimbel (sung by Ella Fitzgerald); makeup, Mario Van Riel, Giuseppe Banchelli.

Romance **(PR:C-O MPAA:R)**

PLACE IN THE SUN, A***** (1951) 122m PAR bw

Montgomery Clift *(George Eastman)*, Elizabeth Taylor *(Angela Vickers)*, Shelly Winters *(Alice Tripp)*, Anne Revere *(Hannah Eastman)*, Keefe Brasselle *(Earl Eastman)*, Fred Clark *(Bellows)*, Raymond Burr *(Marlowe)*, Herbert Heyes *(Charles Eastman)*, Shepperd Strudwick *(Anthony Vickers)*, Frieda Inescort *(Mrs. Vickers)*, Kathryn Givney *(Mrs. Louise Eastman)*, Walter Sande *(Jansen)*, Ted de Corsia *(Judge)*, John Ridgely *(Coroner)*, Lois Chartrand *(Marsha)*, William R. Murphy *(Mr. Whiting)*, Douglas Spencer *(Boatkeeper)*, Charles Dayton *(Kelly)*, Paul Frees *(Morrison)*, Josephine Whittell *(Secretary to Charles Eastman)*, Frank Yaconelli *(Truck Driver)*, Ralph A. Dunn *(Policeman)*, Bob Anderson *(Eagle Scout)*, Mary Kent *(Mrs. Roberts the Landlady)*, Lisa Golm *(Maid)*, Ezelle Poule *(Receptionist)*, Jay Morley *(Executive)*, Kathleen Freeman *(Martha)*, Wallace E. Scott *(Factory Guard)*, Eric Wilton *(Butler)*, Al Ferguson *(Bailiff)*, Gertrude Astor, Lula Mae Bohrman *(Women)*, Major Sam Harris *(Man)*, Harold McNulty *(Jury Foreman)*, Ian Wolfe *(Dr. Wyeland)*, Carmencita Johnson *(Girl)*, Marilyn Dialon *(Frances Brand)*, John Reed *(Joe Parker)*, Laura Elliot *(Miss Harper)*, Maj. Philip Kieffer *(Jailer)*, James W. Horne *(Tom Tipton)*, Mike Mahoney *(Motorcycle Officer)*, Hans Moebus *(Butler at Eastman House)*, Ken Christy *(Warden)*, Pearl Miller *(Miss Newton)*, Robert Malcolm, Len Hendry, Frank Hyers *(Guards)*, Ed O'Neill *(Deputy)*, Frances Driver *(Maid)*, Lee Miller *(Bus Driver)*, Bill Sheehan *(Court Clerk)*, Mike Pat Donovan, Joe Recht, Martin Mason *(Prisoners)*, Louise Lane, Cliff Storey, Harold Miller, Pat Combs, Marion Gray, Ann Fredericks, La Verne "Sonny" Howe, Dolores Hall.

This is a directorial masterpiece by Stevens, one that reaches far beyond the powerful Dreiser novel and offers indelible performances by Clift and Taylor (one of her finest roles, the other being her part in GIANT). The film opens with Clift on a highway trying to hitch a ride. A beautiful brunette, Taylor, drives past him in a shiny sports car, beeps her horn in a flirtatious manner, and keeps going. Clift gapes after her, awed by her stunning beauty. When Clift arrives in the city (never specified by Dreiser), looking for a job in his uncle's bathing-suit factory, he is amazed to discover that Taylor is his cousin. The uncle, Heyes, puts Clift to work in the factory, giving him a menial job but providing the security Clift's doting mother, Revere, has prayed for. Clift looks from afar at the grand life style, the foreign cars, clothes, the estate of Heyes and Taylor and, goaded by unbridled ambition, decides to reach upward into a forbidden caste system for acceptance. Meanwhile, he combats his loneliness by getting emotionally involved with Winters, who works in the factory. As his affair with low-life Winters deepens, so does Clift's association with Heyes and his upper-crust family. Clift is invited to a party at the Heyes mansion and meets and instantly falls in love with the ravishing Taylor and she with him. In a whirlwind of torrid trysts, Clift and Taylor fall so deeply in love that they plan to wed. Clift is about to escape the trap of his low class and elevate himself into the super rich, a poor boy about to make good, as well as marry the unattainable princess. Winters puts a stop to all that by announcing to Clift that she is pregnant and insisting that he marry her. Confused, embittered at being dragged back to the seamy side of his life, Clift takes Winters boating on a lonely lake. There he tries to explain how he really feels about her and how he plans to marry Taylor, but the two begin to argue and Winters falls overboard and drowns. Clift, desperate now, covers up the accident by fleeing, pretending he doesn't even know the victim. But one lie leads to another, bigger lie and he is soon buried in circumstantial evidence that leads to his being charged with murder. A ruthless prosecuting attorney, Burr, graphically demonstrates in court (by having a rowboat placed before the jury and smashing an oar over Winters' imaginary head) how Clift murdered the helpless, pregnant girl. Clift is convicted and sentenced to death. He and Taylor meet once more in death row, she bidding goodbye to the love of her teenage life, he bidding

to kill Winters. This powerful drama and examination of a man's soul was first filmed by Josef von Sternberg in 1931, starkly and realistically told, but Stevens, even in modernizing the tale and stressing the Clift-Taylor love story, lost none of the story's impact. Moreover, through some of the most stunning visuals ever created, Stevens went beyond the story and encompassed a have-not generation in the form of Clift. This is ironically stated at the film's very beginning when Clift, on the bum toward the West Coast and a new life, passes a huge billboard showing the
nd of life in London starring then British pop star
"It's an Eastman, Made in the Heart of America For All of America." The closeup love scenes—enormous blowups of Clift and Taylor kissing passionately—are so imtimate as to languidly drown the viewer's emotions. Stevens does not shrink from the story or any of his characters but pushes up close to them, as close as another can be—in this case his cameras—without getting inside that person, revealing to the viewer the innermost emotions of his characters. Clift is both sensitive and greedy for love to the point of being pitiable. His character is portrayed as less calculating than either Dreiser's fictional anti-hero or the initial filmic characterization by Phillips Holmes in the 1931 version. The cumulative impact of the Stevens film is overwhelming. Mellor's restless cameras fully capture the starkly realistic mood and ambiance of the story and background while Waxman's score superbly complements the overall production. Stevens filmed A PLACE IN THE SUN at Lake Tahoe during the winter months and, to get rid of snow for summer scenes, expensive melting machines were brought in. Though the weather was very cold, Taylor swam in the lake, water skied, and appeared sultry in a skimpy bathing suit. Taylor was only 17 when Stevens cast her in her rich-girl role and she was at first apprehensive of the much more experienced Clift whom she thought to be a "Method Actor," since he had studied acting in New York. The studio tried to promote a romance between the two and did not have to promote very hard. Clift fell in love with his leading lady and helped her through her most difficult scenes. Their performances, especially when on screen together and photographed with almost every pore showing, remain historically memorable. Winters, as the plain woman scorned, was never better before or after this film. When first suggested to Stevens, the director refused to consider her. Then Winters lobbied for the rejected lover role through powerful friends; even writer Norman Mailer sent Stevens a letter asking him to consider the actress. Stevens agreed to meet her at a restaurant and when he walked in, there sat Winters, drab, plainly dressed, no makeup on, so shy and retiring that the director didn't at first recognize the woman who had played brassy blondes for years. He said he would give her the part if she would do a screen test. Winters promised she would do it, but every time the test was to be shot, she found some excuse to be absent. Stevens steamed but gave Winters the part anyway and during the production the director hounded her into playing the distasteful, vulgar, repulsive other woman to the point where Winters refused to talk to him. This role became so indelibly linked to Winters that directors for years to come would have her play no other kind of role. Stevens made the film in his usual painstaking fashion, spending more than $2.5 million and using more than 400,000 feet of film. Yet the film was a huge box-office success and received universal critical acclaim. This was Paramount's prestige film of 1951 and it has since become a classic. Stevens rightly won an Oscar for Best Direction and Oscars also went to Best Screenplay, Best Cinematography, Best Editing, Best Musical Score, and Best Costume Design. Revere, as the coddling but dominating mother to the troubled Clift, made her last screen appearance with A PLACE IN THE SUN. She was branded a Communist by the House Un-American Activities Committee and her career disintegrated. The film—as was Dreiser's unforgettable novel—was based upon the murder of Grace Brown by her social-climbing boy friend Chester Gillette, at Big Moose Lake, New York, in 1906. Dreiser personally sat through Gillette's macabre trial and noted that while the killer awaited execution, he sold photos of himself to admiring young ladies to have catered meals brought to his cell.

p&d, George Stevens; w, Michael Wilson, Harry Brown (based on the novel *An American Tragedy* by Theodore Dreiser and the stage adaptation by Patrick Kearney); ph, William C. Mellor; m, Franz Waxman; ed, William Hornbeck; art d, Hans Dreier, Walter Tyler; set d, Emile Kuri; cos, Edith Head; spec eff, Gordon Jennings; makeup, Wally Westmore.

Drama **Cas.** **(PR:C MPAA:NR)**

PLACE OF ONE'S OWN, A*** (1945, Brit.) 97m Gainsborough/EL bw

Margaret Lockwood *(Annette)*, James Mason *(Mr. Smedhurst)*, Barbara Mullen *(Mrs. Smedhurst)*, Dennis Price *(Dr. Selbie)*, Helen Haye *(Mrs. Manning-Tuthorn)*, Michael Shepley *(Maj. Manning-Tuthorn)*, Dulcie Gray *(Sarah)*, Moore Marriott *(George)*, Gus McNaughton *(Hargreaves)*, Ernest Thesiger *(Dr. Marsham)*, O. B. Clarence *(Perkins)*, John Turnbull *(Sir Roland Jarvis)*, Clarence Wright *(Brighouse)*, Helen Goss *(Barmaid)*, Edie Martin *(Cook)*.

Moody, atmospheric ghost story starring Mason as a retired tradesman who purchases an old mansion that has been vacant for 40 years because it is believed to be haunted by the spirit of a young woman who had died there. Unaware of the mansion's reputation, Mason and his wife Mullen move in and hire a young woman, Lockwood, to keep house. Soon after Lockwood's arrival, strange things begin to happen in the household and it becomes apparent that she is possessed by the spirit of the dead girl, though Mason scoffs at the idea. On death's door and bedridden, Lockwood asks for the same doctor who treated the woman who had died 40 years ago. He arrives and treats her. The next morning Lockwood is cured and it is revealed by the police that the doctor's dead body had been found in his carriage hours before the time Mason claims he arrived to see Lockwood. Convinced that not only the ghost of the girl, but that of the doctor as well entered his home, Mason finally believes in the supernatural.

p, R.J. Minney; d, Bernard Knowles; w, Brock Williams (based on the novel by Sir Osbert Sitwell); ph, Stephen Dade; m, Hubert Bath; ed, Charles Knott; md, Ldmits t

Drama **(PR:A MPAA:NR)**

PLACE TO GO, A** (1964, Brit.) 86m BL bw

Bernard Lee *(Matt Flint)*, Rita Tushingham *(Catherine)*, Michael Sarne *(Ricky Flint)*, Doris Hare *(Lil Flint)*, Barbara Ferris *(Betsy)*, John Slater *(Jack Ellerman)*, David Andrews *(Jim)*, William Marlowe *(Charlie Batey)*, Michael Wynne *(Pug)*, Marjorie Lawrence *(Sally)*, Roy Kinnear *(Bunting)*, Norman Shelley *(Magistrate)*, Jerry Verno *(Nobby Knowles)*.

Sarne in his movie debut as the son of an unemployed dock worker. Frustrated and depressed at his family's economic plight, he turns to crime and steals his brother-in-law's truck to gain membership in a gang that plans to rob a big factory. Predictable and dull.

p, Michael Relph; d, Basil Dearden; w, Relph, Clive Exton (based on the novel *Bethnal Green* by Michael Fisher); ph, Reginald Wyer; m, Charles Blackwell; ed, John D. Guthridge; m/l, Blackwell.

Crime (PR:A MPAA:NR)

PLAGUE* (1978, Can.) 88m Harmony Ridge/Group I c (AKA: PLAGUE-M3: THE GEMINI STRAIN; M3: THE GEMINI STRAIN)

Daniel Pilon, Kate Reid, Celine Lomez, Michael J. Reynolds, Brenda Donohue, Barbara Gordon.

M3, a mutant virus, goes out of control during an experiment and infects the world. Instead of concentrating on gratuitous special effects, PLAGUE has enough sense to devote its attention to developing the scientist character. It's his responsibility to come up with an anti-virus and save humanity from oblivion. Unfortunately there is more in PLAGUE that is laughable than interesting.

p&w, Ed Hunt, Barry Pearson; d, Hunt; m, Eric Robertson; ph, (DeLuxe Color).

Science Fiction (PR:C MPAA:PG)

PLAGUE-M3: THE GEMINI STRAIN (SEE: PLAGUE, 1978, Can.)

PLAGUE OF THE ZOMBIES, THE*** (1966, Brit.) 90m Seven Arts-Hammer/FOX c

Andre Morell *(Sir James Forbes)*, Diane Clare *(Sylvia Forbes)*, John Carson *(Clive Hamilton)*, Alex Davion *(Denver)*, Jacqueline Pearce *(Alice Thompson)*, Brook Williams *(Dr. Peter Thompson)*, Michael Ripper *(Sgt. Swift)*, Marcus Hammond *(Martinus)*, Dennis Chinnery *(P. C. Christian)*, Roy Royston *(Vicar)*, Ben Aris *(John Martinus)*, Tim Condron, Bernard Egan, Norman Mann, Francis Willey *(The Young Bloods)*, Jerry Verno *(Landlord)*, Joylan Booth *(Coachman)*, Louis Mahoney *(Servant)*.

Effective horror film which sees members of a Cornish village dying under mysterious circumstances. When a local doctor gets suspicious, he calls in an expert, Morell, who thinks something strange is going on because the squire, Carson, is refusing to allow autopsies. It is discovered that Carson is having people killed and then brought back to life as zombies, with voodoo rites he has learned in Haiti, to use the living dead to work his tin mine. Morell confronts Carson, battles his way through the zombies, and puts an end to the hideous operation.

p, Anthony Nelson Keys; d, John Gilling; w, Peter Bryan, John Elder [Anthony Hinds]; ph, Arthur Grant (DeLuxe Color); m, James Bernard; ed, Chris Barnes; prod d, Bernard Robinson; art d, Don Mingaye; spec eff, Bowie Films; makeup, Roy Ashton.

Horror (PR:C MPAA:NR)

PLAINSMAN, THE*½** (1937) 115m PAR bw

Gary Cooper *(Wild Bill Hickok)*, Jean Arthur *(Calamity Jane)*, James Ellison *(Buffalo Bill Cody)*, Charles Bickford *(John Latimer)*, Porter Hall *(Jack McCall)*, Helen Burgess *(Louisa Cody)*, John Miljan *(Gen. George Armstrong Custer)*, Victor Varconi *(Painted Horse)*, Paul Harvey *(Chief Yellow Hand)*, Frank McGlynn, Sr. *(Abraham Lincoln)*, Granville Bates *(Van Ellyn)*, Purnell Pratt *(Capt. Wood)*, Pat Moriarty *(Sgt. McGinnis)*, Charles Judels *(Tony the Barber)*, Anthony Quinn *(Cheyenne Warrior)*, George MacQuarrie *(Gen. Merritt)*, George "Gabby"Hayes *(Breezy)*, Fuzzy Knight *(Dave)*, George Ernest *(An Urchin)*, Fred Kohler *(Jack)*, Frank Albertson *(A Young Soldier)*, Harry Woods *(Quartermaster Sergeant)*, Francis McDonald *(Boat Gambler)*, Francis Ford *(Veteran)*, Irving Bacon *(Soldier)*, Edgar Dearing *(Custer's Messenger)*, Edwin Maxwell *(Stanton)*, John Hyams *(Schuyler Colfax)*, Bruce Warren *(Captain of the Lizzie Gill)*, Mark Strong *(Wells Fargo Agent)*, Charlie Stevens *(Injun Charlie)*, Arthur Aylesworth, Douglas Wood, George Cleveland *(Van Ellyn's Assistants)*, Lona Andre *(Southern Belle)*, Leila McIntyre *(Mary Todd Lincoln)*, Harry Stubbs *(John F. Usher)*, Davison Clark *(James Speed)*, Charles W. Herzinger *(William H. Seward)*, William Humphries *(Hugh McCulloch)*, Sidney Jarvis *(Gideon Welles)*, Wadsworth Harris *(William Dennison)*, Bud Flanagan [Dennis O'Keefe], Gail Sheridan, Lane Chandler, Stanhope Wheatcroft, Noble Johnson, Ted Oliver, James Mason, Bud Osborne, Franklyn Farnum, Louise Stuart, Blackjack Ward, Jane Keckley, Cora Shumway, Tex Driscoll, Wilbur Mack, Francis Sayles, Hank Bell.

DeMille sentimentalized his version of the American West but still filled the screen with excitement and high adventure in relating his imaginative story of Calamity Jane and Wild Bill Hickok. Of course, the DeMille story had little to do with the real facts but such incidental details never bothered the great showman who felt it his right to reshape history any way he wished. Cooper is the fast-shooting plainsman, Hickok, and Arthur is the wisecracking, whip-snapping Calamity Jane. Although the real Jane was an odorous drunk and ugly as sin, DeMille does not shrink from glamorizing Arthur, allowing her hair to be coiffed, her eyes made up, and lipstick perfectly fixed to her small mouth. Cooper makes it his business to oppose conniving renegade Bickford, who is selling guns to the Indians. In one confrontation with Bickford, Cooper is prevented from gunning down the cur but risks his friendship with Ellison, playing Buffalo Bill Cody, by breaking the law. Then Arthur, thinking she is helping Cooper, explores Indian territory and is captured. Cooper arrives to save her and is tortured for his efforts. To save him, Arthur tells the savages just where and when the ammunition train will be arriving to supply Miljan (playing Gen. Custer) and his troops. Cooper manages to break free, saves Arthur, then races off to find the ammunition train surrounded by Indians circling their barricaded island in the middle of a river. It looks like the end but Miljan arrives with his troops and drives off the savages. (These fast-moving action scenes were later used as stock footage in GERONIMO.) Later, Cooper goes after Bickford once more but the renegade has three cavalry deserters stand in the gunman's way. Cooper shoots them down when they go for their guns and later kills Bickford. Before the authorities can charge Cooper with the killings, he is shot to death while playing poker by Hall (essaying Black Jack McCall). Arthur runs to Cooper, who dies in her arms, just as old friend Ellison arrives to do nothing more than mourn the loss of the great gunfighter. Cooper is solid and convincing as the legendary Hickok in this, his first film with DeMille. Arthur is a feisty and colorful Calamity Jane but it should be pointed out that most of the period depicting Wild Bill's exploits in the film occurred when the sour-faced Jane was only 15 and living at home with her family. DeMille selected Cooper and Arthur since they had just scored a hugh success together in MR. DEEDS GOES TO TOWN. The flamboyant director selected Burgess for an important part after spotting her in Paramount's commissary, the only inexperienced actress he ever "discovered" and cast in a leading role. Sadly, the 18-year-old Burgess died shortly after the film's completion, succumbing to pneumonia, which also claimed the life of screenwriter Young only weeks after the film was in the can. DeMille employed 2,500 real Sioux and Cheyenne Indians in the film and hired Quinn to do a two-minute chant, celebrating the Custer massacre. Quinn, who would later become the director's son-in-law by marrying Katherine DeMille (the director's adopted daughter), answered a casting call for a real Indian who could do a war chant in native Cheyenne. He made up the words as he went along but so convinced DeMille of his authenticity that the director exclaimed to an assistant: "Now there's a *real*Indian!" DeMille supplied more than 70 pistols from his own gun collection so that the extras would be armed with the correct weapons of the era. Though background footage was shot in remote Montana, most of the scenes for THE PLAINSMAN were shot on six acres of Paramount's backlot where DeMille re-created the Old West. Universal remade this film in 1966 with Don Murray and Abby Dalton, giving it a brief theatrical release before selling it to television; it was a poor imitation of its rousing original.

p&d, Cecil B. DeMille; w, Waldemar Young, Harold Lamb, Lynn Riggs, Jeanie Macpherson (based on the stories "Wild Bill Hickok" by Frank J. Wilstach and "The Prince of the Pistoleers" by Courtney Riley Cooper, Grover Jones); ph, Victor Milner, George Robinson; m, George Antheil; ed, Anne Bauchens; md, Boris Morros; art d, Hans Dreier, Roland Anderson; set d, A. E. Freudeman; cos, Natalie Visart, Dwight Franklin, Joe De Yong; spec eff, Gordon Jennings, Farciot Edouart, Dewey Wrigley.

Western Cas. (PR:C MPAA:NR)

PLAINSMAN, THE 1964 (SEE: RAIDERS, THE, 1964)

PLAINSMAN, THE** (1966) 92m UNIV c

Don Murray *(Wild Bill Hickok)*, Guy Stockwell *(Buffalo Bill Cody)*, Abby Dalton *(Calamity Jane)*, Bradford Dillman *(Lt. Stiles)*, Henry Silva *(Crazy Knife)*, Simon Oakland *(Chief Black Kettle)*, Leslie Nielsen *(Col. George A. Custer)*, Edward Binns *(Lattimer)*, Michael Evans *(Estrick)*, Percy Rodriguez *(Brother John)*, Terry Wilson *(Sgt. Womack)*, Walter Burke *(Abe Ireland)*, Emily Banks *(Louisa Cody)*.

Pointless remake of Cecil B. DeMille's 1937 epic which starred Gary Cooper, Jean Arthur, and James Ellison. This version boasts the much less dynamic talents of Murray, Stockwell, and Dalton as Wild Bill Hickok, Buffalo Bill, and Calamity Jane. The plot revolves around the romance between Murray and Dalton, with several rip-snortin' western type episodes to fill in the frequent gaps.

p, Richard E. Lyons; d, David Lowell Rich; w, Michael Blankfort; ph, Bud Thackery (Eastmancolor); m, Johnny Williams; ed, Danny B. Landres, Bud Small; art d, Alexander Golitzen, William D. DeCinces; set d, John McCarthy, Ralph Sylos; cos, Helen Colvig; makeup, Bud Westmore.

Western (PR:A MPAA:NR)

PLAINSMAN AND THE LADY** (1946) 87m REP bw

William Elliott *(Sam Cotten)*, Vera Ralston *(Ann Arnesen)*, Gail Patrick *(Cathy Arnesen)*, Joseph Schildkraut *(Peter Marquette)*, Donald Barry *(Feisty)*, Andy Clyde *(Dringo)*, Raymond Walburn *(Judge Winters)*, Reinhold Schunzel *(Michael Arnesen)*, Paul Hurst *(Al)*, Russell Hicks *(Sen. Twin)*, William B. Davidson *(Mr. Russell)*, Charles Judels *(Manuel Lopez)*, Eva Puig *(Anita Lopez)*, Jack Lambert *(Sival)*, Stuart Hamblen *(Matt)*, Noble Johnson *(Wassao)*, Hal Taliaferro *(Pete)*, Lola, Fernando *(Specialty Dancers)*, Byron Foulger *(Simmons)*, Pierre Watkin *(Sen. Allen)*, Eddy Waller *(Fred Willats)*, Charles Morton *(Doctor)*, Martin Garralaga *(Alvarades)*, Guy L. Beach *(Bookkeeper)*, Joseph Crehan *(Postmaster General)*, Grady Sutton *(Male Secretary)*, Eddie Parks *(Drunk)*, Norman Willis, Tex Terry, Chuck Roberson *(Deputies)*, Rex Lease *(Croupier)*, Henry Wills *(Indian)*, Daniel Day Tolman *(Young Clerk)*, David Williams *(Clerk)*, Hank Bell *(Yard Master)*, Roy Barcroft *(Cowboy)*, Jack O'Shea *(Bartender)*, Carl Sepulveda *(Big Mex)*, Iron Eyes Cody.

Elliott was so successful as the lead in IN OLD SACRAMENTO that Republic decided to chance him in the lead again. This time Elliott plays a successful cattleman who is determined to bring the Pony Express to his territory. The only hitch is that stagecoach owner Schildkraut would rather commit murder than see his business drop off. He hires dressed-in-black gunman Barry to do his dirty work. Ralston (wife of Republic boss Herbert J. Yates) plays Elliott's wife, and Clyde, usually William Boyd's dopey sidekick, is given the chance to play a character of some intelligence as the hero's friend.

p&d, Joseph Kane; w, Richard Wormser (based on a story by Michael Uris, Ralph Spence); ph, Reggie Lanning; m, George Antheil; ed, Fred Allen; md, Cy Feuer; art d, Gano Chittenden; set d, John McCarthy, Jr., George Milo; spec eff, Howard Lydecker, Theodore Lydecker; cos, Adele Palmer; ch, Fanchon.

Western (PR:A MPAA:NR)

PLAINSONG** (1982) 88m Stabile c

Teresanne Joseph, Jessica Nelson, Lyn Traverse, Steve Geiger, Sandon McCail, Carl Kielblock.

Interesting but unsuccessful effort by a group of independent filmmakers in New Jersey. Shot over the space of a few years on a small western town set in New Jersey, PLAINSONG opens with a sepia-tinted sequence showing the murder of

Joseph. The picture then flashes back to the events that lead up to the murder, with the rest of the film in color. Joseph and a group of widowed women find themselves in Kansas, after becoming involved in a range war that saw the deaths of Nelson and Traverse's husbands, who were shot by Geiger and his partner. When the women again run afoul of the pair, Joseph kills Geiger's partner and the gunman swears revenge. Eventually, Geiger catches up with her and the film comes full circle. Good performances nearly, but not quite, save the weak and contrived script.

p, Tiare Stack; d&w, Ed Stabile; ph, Joe Ritter.

Western   **(PR:C MPAA:NR)**

PLANET OF BLOOD, 1965   (SEE: PLANET OF THE VAMPIRES, 1965, U.S./Ital./Span.)

PLANET OF BLOOD, 1966   (SEE: QUEEN OF BLOOD, 1966)

PLANET OF DINOSAURS**   (1978) Filmpartners/Wells c

James Whitworth (Jim), Louis Lawless (Lee), Pamela Bottaro (Nyla), Charlotte Speer (Charlotte), Harvey Shain, Chuck Pennington, Derna Wylde, Michael Thayer, Mary Appleseth.

An independent production which, as the title implies, has Whitworth battling a planet full of dinosaurs. No more interesting than a Saturday morning kid show, but the stop-motion animation is commendable.

p&d, James K. Shea; w, Ralph Lucas; m, Kelly Lammers, John O'Verlin.

Fantasy/Science Fiction   **(PR:A MPAA:PG)**

PLANET OF HORRORS   (SEE: MINDWARP: AN INFINITY OF TERROR, 1981)

PLANET OF STORMS   (SEE: STORM PLANET, 1962, USSR)

PLAN 9 FROM OUTER SPACE zero   (1959) 79m Distributors
Corporation of America bw (AKA: GRAVE ROBBERS FROM OUTER SPACE)

Gregory Walcott (Jeff Trent), Mona McKinnon (Paula Trent), Duke Moore (Lt. Harper), Tom Keene (Col. Tom Edwards), Vampira [Maila Nurmi] (The Ghoul Woman), Bela Lugosi (The Ghoul Man), Tor Johnson (Police Inspector Clay), Lyle Talbot (Gen. Roberts), Dudley Manlove (Eros), John Breckinridge (The Ruler), Joanna Lee (Tanna), Criswell (Narrator), Paul Marco, Conrad Brooks.

The cult reputation earned by Edward D. Wood, Jr.'s bizarre sci-fi epic has been one of the film industry's strangest success stories. Using a miniscule amount of footage Wood had shot featuring his friend Bela Lugosi that was to be used for a never-realized project (Lugosi died days later), the bargain-basement director, responsible for such other noteworthy oddities as GLEN OR GLENDA? (AKA: I CHANGED MY SEX), BRIDE OF THE MONSTER, and JAIL BAIT, put before the cameras "the sworn testimony of miserable souls who survived the ordeal of. . .graverobbers from outer space!" The above declaration was intoned with all seriousness by the film's host and narrator, famed television psychic (and close personal friend of the director), Criswell, whose impassioned prolog and epilog to PLAN 9 FROM OUTER SPACE frame this fantastic tale. The film opens as we see Lugosi, dressed in his Dracula cape for no apparent reason, mourning at his recently deceased wife's grave. After he leaves, a flash from an alien raygun brings the dead woman (Vampira, a popular L.A. television horror show hostess), back to life and she attacks her gravediggers (or so Criswell tells us because the action takes place off-screen). Seconds later Lugosi is run over by a car (once again off-screen). At Lugosi's funeral, some mourners notice the bodies of the gravediggers and a police inspector, played by ex-wrestler Johnson (another friend of Wood's), arrives to examine the corpses. Soon after, he is killed by Vampira and buried in the same cemetery. Meanwhile, flying saucers invade downtown L.A. (various fans claim that Wood used everything, from his wife's china to hub-caps, to represent his "saucers") and the Army immediately moves to hush things up. This isn't good enough for commercial airline pilot Walcott, who has seen the invaders' craft with his own eyes. Eventually we meet the alien leaders of the invasion, Manlove (perhaps the most consistently unintentionally funny performer in the film) and his female counterpart Lee (now one of the most successful television writers in Hollywood), who declare that they are about to enact "Plan 9" in which they intend to revive all the Earth's dead and take over the planet. Finally, all the various characters meet in the shattering climax which sees Walcott, his wife, McKinnon, and another detective battle for the future of mankind against Manlove, Lee, and their servants Johnson, Vampira, and Lugosi's stand-in, who spends the whole film with his Dracula cape over his face. (By some accounts the man filling in for Bela was Wood's wife's dentist, chiropractor, or homeopathic healer.) In the end, the invaders are defeated, but Criswell warns "God help us in the future!" It is believed by many that Wood used his films as vehicles to spout his political beliefs and fears of the times. He clothed the plots in absurdities in order to escape the watchful censorship eye of the McCarthy era. However, the true entertainment derived from the film lies in the awful production values, combined with the silly script and the lousy performances. A concrete floor, clearly visible under the "grass" in the cemetery (including a few ratty-looking mattresses to cushion the fall of McKinnon when Johnson drops her during a particularly "hair-raising" scene), obviously cardboard tombstones, the sudden shifts from day to night and back again in the same scene, Lugosi's stand-in, the same set of furniture appearing in every room of Walcott's house, and the same three shots of Lugosi repeated over and over again, are consistently amusing throughout the movie. Watching PLAN 9 FROM OUTER SPACE gives one the same feeling that relatives get when subjected to a nephew's first film made with Dad's Super 8 camera; i.e., it's bad, but at least the kid tried.

p,d&w, Edward D. Wood, Jr.; ph, William C. Thompson; m, Gordon Zahler; ed, Wood.

Horror/Science Fiction   Cas.   (PR:A MPAA:NR)

PLANET OF THE APES**   (1968) 112m APJAC/FOX c

Charlton Heston (George Taylor), Roddy McDowall (Cornelius), Kim Hunter (Dr. Zira), Maurice Evans (Dr. Zaius), James Whitmore (President of the Assembly), James Daly (Honorius), Linda Harrison (Nova), Robert Gunner (Landon), Lou Wagner (Lucius), Woodrow Parfrey (Maximus), Jeff Burton (Dodge), Buck Kartalian (Julius), Norman Burton (Hunt Leader), Wright King (Dr. Galen), Paul Lambert (Minister), Diane Stanley (Female Astronaut).

An outstanding science-fiction film that spawned four sequels (BENEATH THE PLANET OF THE APES, 1970, ESCAPE FROM THE PLANET OF THE APES, 1971, CONQUEST OF THE PLANET OF THE APES, 1972, and BATTLE FOR THE PLANET OF THE APES, 1973), an animated cartoon series, a live-action television series, bubble-gum cards, Halloween masks, plastic models, bendable toys, etc. Massive marketing notwithstanding, the original film is still quite an artistic achievement. Heston plays the commander of a lengthy outer space mission that is interrupted when the spaceship crashes on an unknown planet. The three survivors, Heston, Gunner, and Jeff Burton, make their way through an arid wasteland into a lush forest where they observe what appears to be a tribe of human beings in the throes of the stone age. The astronauts join the speechless humans and forage for food. Suddenly a bizarre horn cries and the sound of hoofbeats and gunfire are heard, sending the savage humans running into the woods. The confused astronauts are shocked to see that the armed horsemen are actually gorillas wearing strange looking pseudo-military gear. The apes employ nets to gather up dozens of the humans and lock them in large cages. While attempting to escape, Heston is shot in the throat, rendering him as speechless as the primitive people. Captured, Heston is brought to the ape town along with the rest of the captured humans and thrown into a cage. His comrades have not fared so well. Jeff Burton was killed in the hunt, and Gunner, who could still speak, was given a lobotomy by the orangutan scientist and leader, Evans, to silence him. While in his cage, Heston is befriended by peaceful chimpanzee scientists Hunter and McDowell, who are convinced that the astronaut's frustrated pantomimes are a sure sign of superior intelligence. Evans knows the truth, however, and blocks their efforts to study Heston more closely. At one point, Heston tries to escape and is recaptured, but manages to yell, "Take your stinking paws off me, you damn dirty ape!" This vocal outburst sends shock waves throughout the ape community and soon Evans moves to have Heston destroyed. With the help of Hunter and McDowell, Heston escapes and ventures into the "Forbidden Zone" where McDowell has begun an archeological dig which yields some strange evidence regarding the evolution of "ape-kind." Pursued by Evans and his gorilla soldiers, Heston manages to capture the ape leader and hold him hostage in the dig site. There, Heston forces Evans to reveal that humans once did rule the planet, but their stupid, animalistic tendencies led to a war that destroyed them, leaving the apes to take over. Since then the wiser apes have desperately tried to prevent the violent humans from taking over again. Having extracted the truth from Evans, Heston steals a horse and rides off into the Forbidden Zone alone, despite warnings from Evans that he won't like what he'll find. A few miles up the beach Heston sees something that makes him drop to his knees and pound on the sand in a frustrated rage. "You bastards! You finally did it! You blew it up! Damn you all to hell!" The camera pans up to reveal the battered Statue of Liberty, waist deep in sand. Heston has been on Earth all along. PLANET OF THE APES is a success on all levels of production. The script by Rod Serling is a marvel of twisted logic containing insightful moments of social parody and grim forebodings regarding the future of mankind. The production values are superb. The set design and costumes were something that audiences had never seen before and created a wholly unique, detailed world that helped audiences accept the odd premise of the film. Most praised, and rightly so, was Chambers' special makeup that transformed human actors into living apes. By using a special latex application, Chambers' makeup allowed the actors a full range of facial expressions that aided greatly in creating the illusion of an ape society. Chambers received an Academy Award for his special makeup process, becoming one of the few makeup artists ever honored by the Academy for his craft. These production elements, combined with Shamroy's stunning cinematography, Goldsmith's haunting musical score, and a wonderful cast of performers who rose to the occasion, captured the imaginations of moviegoers throughout the world. Unfortunately, the sequels to PLANET OF THE APES, with few exceptions (BENEATH THE PLANET OF THE APES, and CONQUEST OF THE PLANET OF THE APES being fairly interesting) are pretty lame and lack the spark of imagination that fueled the original. Perhaps because of the unparalleled marketing push, the "Apes" series spiraled into gross self-parody which made even rabid fans of the films a bit sick of the whole thing. But one cannot deny that the original film is a superlative example of fantasy filmmaking. (See PLANET OF THE APES series, Index.)

p, Arthur P. Jacobs; d, Franklin J. Schaffner; w, Michael Wilson, Rod Serling (based on the novel Monkey Planet by Pierre Boulle); ph, Leon Shamroy (Panavision, DeLuxe Color); m, Jerry Goldsmith; ed, Hugh S. Fowler; art d, Jack Martin Smith, William Creber; set d, Walter M. Scott, Norman Rockett; cos, Mortan Haack; spec eff, L. B. Abbott, Art Cruickshank, Emil Kosa, Jr.; makeup, John Chambers, Ben Nye, Dan Striepeke.

Science Fiction   Cas.   (PR:C MPAA:G)

PLANET OF THE VAMPIRES***   (1965, U.S./Ital./Span.) 86m AIP c
(TERRORE NELLO SPAZIO; TERROR EN EL ESPACIO; AKA: PLANET OF BLOOD; DEMON PLANET)

Barry Sullivan (Capt. Mark Markary), Norma Bengell (Sanya), Angel Aranda (Wess), Evi Marandi (Tiona), Fernando Villena (Karan), Stelio Candelli (Mud), Massimo Righi (Nordeg), Mario Morales (Eldon), Franco Andei (Garr), Ivan Rassimov (Kell/Derry), Rico Boido (Keir/Key), Alberto Cevenini (Wan/Toby).

One of Italian cinematographer/horror director Bava's best. Sullivan stars as the captain of a spaceship who sees his companion ship vanish, and then finds that his own ship is being pulled toward the mysterious planet Aura. Once landed on Aura, they find the wreckage of the other ship and discover that the crew members have killed each other. The ship's scientist surmises that the planet is populated with disembodied beings who willed the ships to land and seek to inhabit the bodies. He is proved correct when the dead soon rise and, one by one, Sullivan's surviving crew is killed. Sullivan eventually learns that the aliens plan to leave their planet in search of greener pastures on Earth. Sullivan is able to outwit the aliens and escape the planet, but he suspects that a few of his crew members may be zombies. Wonderfully directed by Bava, with a fluid visual style that makes the most out of the obviously cheap, fog-filled sets.

p, Fulvio Lucisano; d, Mario Bava; w, Alberto Bevilacqua, Callisto Cosulich, Bava, Antonio Roman, Rafael J. Salvia, Ib Melchior, Louis M. Heyward (based on a story by Melchior); ph, Antonio Rinaldi (Colorscope, Pathe Color); m, Gino Marinuzzi, Jr., Antonio Perez Olca; ed, Antonio Gimeno; art d, Giorgio Giovannini; cos, Gabriele Mayer.

Science Fiction (PR:C MPAA:NR)

PLANET ON THE PROWL (SEE: WAR BETWEEN THE PLANETS 1971, Ital.)

PLANETS AGAINST US, THE** (1961, Ital./Fr.) 85m Teleworld/ Vanguard c (I PIANETI CONTRO DI NOI; AKA: THE MAN WITH THE YELLOW EYES; HANDS OF A KILLER; THE MONSTER WITH GREEN EYES)

Michael Lemoine, Maria Pia Luzi, Jany Clair, Marco Guglielmi, Ottello Toso, Peter Dane.

Obscure and interesting science fiction film which sees Lemoine as an escaped humanoid robot from another planet that has managed to make it as far as Earth. Unfortunately, his touch means instant death. Finally he is gunned down by a flying saucer from his home planet, with help from the Italian army. Well-done visually, with some superb special effects.

p, Alberto Chimenz, Vico Pavoni; d, Romano Ferrara; w, Piero Pierotti, Ferrara; ph, Pier Ludovico Pavoni.

Science Fiction (PR:C MPAA:NR)

PLANK, THE**½ (1967, Brit.) 58m Associated London/RFD c

Tommy Cooper (Larger Workman), Eric Sykes (Smaller Workman), Jimmy Edwards (Policeman), Roy Castle (Garbage Man), Graham Stark (Amorous Van Driver), Stratford Johns (Station Sergeant), Jim Dale (House Painter), Jimmy Tarbuck (Barman), Hattie Jacques (Woman with Rose), Dermot Kelly (Concertina Man), Libby Morris, Rex Garner (Tourists), John Junkin (Truck Driver), Dave Freeman (Cement Mixer), Johnny Speight (Chauffeur), Kenny Lynch (Garbage Driver), Howard Douglas (Old Man).

Funny slapstick comedy starring Sykes (who also wrote and directed) and Cooper as two workmen trying desperately to transport a wooden plank through a suburb of London to a building site. All of the gags are of a visual nature and the film is akin to the Mack Sennett comedies of the silent era.

p, Beryl Vertue, Jon Pennington; d&w, Eric Sykes; ph, Arthur Wooster (Technicolor); m, Brian Fahey; ed, John Pomeroy.

Comedy (PR:A MPAA:NR)

PLANTER'S WIFE, THE (SEE: OUTPOST IN MALAYA, 1952, Brit.)

PLANTS ARE WATCHING US, THE (SEE: KIRLIAN WITNESS, THE, 1978)

PLASTIC DOME OF NORMA JEAN, THE*½ (1966) 82m Compton bw

Sharon Henesy (Norma Jean), Robert Gentry (Vance), Marco St. John (Bobo), Samuel Waterston (Andy), Skip Hinnant (Francis), Arthur Hughes (Chris), Henry Oliver (Mayor), Jack Murray (Announcer), Jerry Serempa (Spelunker), Emma Cody (Mrs. Meekas), Gilbert Elmore (Chance Lawson), Stanley Tiffany (Johnny), Carl Wallace (Sheriff), George Jackson (Elmer), Roger Krieger (Finch).

Odd low-budget film shot in the Ozarks and starring Henesy as a 15-year-old girl who possesses the powers of clairvoyance. One day Henesy meets up with rock star St. John who is trying to start an entertainment facility in a large circus-tent structure known as the Plastic Dome. Seeing in Henesy a way to attract large crowds, St. John convinces the youngster to join his act. Soon the money comes pouring in as the tourists come from far and wide to witness Henesy's amazing ESP talents. Henesy, however, becomes increasingly upset when her darker prophecies come true. In the end she quits the act, but the public outcry for her return moves a now-rich (and wants to stay that way) St. John to bring her back by force. Unfortunately, St. John becomes overzealous and accidentally kills Henesy in the attempt.

p, Juleen Compton, Stuart Murphy; d&w, Compton; ph, Roger Barlow; m, Michel Legrand; ed, Murphy; md, Legrand; set d, Sterling Merritt.

Drama (PR:C MPAA:NR)

PLATINUM BLONDE*** (1931) 88m COL bw

Loretta Young (Gallagher), Robert Williams (Stew Smith), Jean Harlow (Anne Schuyler), Louise Closser Hale (Mrs. Schuyler), Donald Dillaway (Michael Schuyler), Reginald Owen (Dexter Grayson), Walter Catlett (Bing Baker), Edmund Breese (Conroy, the Editor), Halliwell Hobbes (Smythe, Butler), Claude Allister (Dawson, the Violinist), Bill Elliott (Dinner Guest), Harry Semels (Waiter), Olaf Hytten (Radcliffe), Tom London, Hal Price, Eddy Chandler, Charles Jordan (Reporters), Dick Cramer (Speakeasy Proprietor), Wilson Benge (Butler), Dick Prichard.

One of the better "newspaper" comedies, PLATINUM BLONDE featured two young players who were not long for this world, Harlow and Williams, Williams having died at the age of 35 with a bright future in front of him. To Capra's credit, this was a fairly authentic glimpse of the real newspaper world and had a number of bright moments. In those days, "breach of promise" suits were all the rage and

when a tawdry chorine threatens to sue Dillaway, a wealthy man-about-town, it's big news. Williams is a newsman working for editor Breese and he gets the letters that Dillaway wrote. He holds them back, not that he cares about the cad but he does like Dillaway's younger sister, Harlow. Williams is loved from afar by reporter Young but she is powerless to keep him from marrying Harlow. It doesn't take long for the action-oriented Williams to yawn in this new life he's leading. He hates the caste system and the hypocrisy of Harlow's family, led by Hale, and he thinks he can get some creative satisfaction if he writes a play. Since he's never done anything of the sort, like most first-timers he seeks a collaborator and finds one in Young. She comes to the Hale mansion to work and brings a horde of other merrymaking, hard-drinking reporters with her. Soon enough, the whole place is rocking and when Harlow comes home, she angrily tells her husband's low-life friends to exit. Williams tells Harlow off and departs with Young and the others. The couple splits and Williams is now free to marry Young, the woman who has understood him from the first reel. Harlow, who was far funnier in other films, does the best with what they've given her, and Young hardly has a thing to do at all. Some good jokes liven matters up, as does the usual fine work by Hobbes, as the snooty family's snootier butler.

p, Harry Cohn; d, Frank Capra; w, Jo Swerling, Dorothy Howell, Robert Riskin (based on the story by Harry E. Chandlee, Douglas W. Chruchill; ph, Joseph Walker; ed, Gene Milford.

Comedy (PR:A MPAA:NR)

PLATINUM HIGH SCHOOL*½ (1960) 95m Zugsmith-Fryman/MGM bw (AKA: RICH, YOUNG AND DEADLY; TROUBLE AT 16)

Mickey Rooney (Steven Conway), Terry Moore (Jennifer Evans), Dan Duryea (Maj. Redfern Kelly), Conway Twitty (Billy Jack Barnes), Warren Berlinger (Crip. Hastings), Yvette Mimeux (Lorina Nibley), Jimmy Boyd (Bud Starkweather), Richard Jaeckel (Hack Marlow), Jack Carr (Joe Nibley), Harold Lloyd, Jr. (Charley Boy Cable), Christopher Dark (Vince Perley), Elisha Cook, Jr. (Harry Nesbitt), Jimmy Murphy (Cadet Phillips), Mason Allan Dinehart (Dingbat Johnston), David Landfield (Drill Instructor).

Rooney stars as the father of a young boy killed accidentally while away at an exclusive military boarding school. Separated by an early divorce, Rooney never really knew his son in life. But when he arrives on the island to claim the body, Rooney begins to suspect that the details surrounding his son's said suicide are being covered up by school commandant Duryea. Upon further investigation, Rooney discovers that the school is the home to terrorizing misfits who have been kicked out of every other school in the country, and that his son was actually killed during a horrible hazing incident. Rooney seems to ruffle everyone's feathers with his persistent questions, and he narrowly escapes death himself before finally fleeing the island to call the police.

p, Red Doff; d, Charles Haas; w, Robert Smith (based on a story by Howard Breslin); ph, Russell Metty; m, Van Alexander; ed, Gene Ruggiero.

Drama (PR:A MPAA:NR)

PLAY DEAD* (1981) 89m Rudine-Wittman and United Construction c

Yvonne De Carlo, Stephanie Dunnam, David Cullinane.

A woman with some definite problems takes her beloved canine and trains the animal to be a vicious killer. De Carlo was long past her heyday as a B movie actress and Lily on TV's much underrated monster sitcom "The Munsters."

d, Peter Wittman; w, Lothrop W. Jordan; ph, Bob Bethard; art d, Robert Burns.

Drama (PR:O MPAA:NR)

PLAY DIRTY*** (1969, Brit.) 117m Lowndes/UA c (AKA: WRITTEN ON THE SAND)

Michael Caine (Capt. Douglas), Nigel Davenport (Cyril Leech), Nigel Green (Col. Masters), Harry Andrews (Brig. Blore), Bernard Archeard (Col. Homerton), Daniel Pilon (Capt. Attwood), Aly Ben Ayed (Sadok), Takis Emmanouel (Kostos Manou), Enrique Avila (Kafkarides), Scott Miller (Boudesh), Mohamed Kouka (Assine), Mohsen Ben Abdullah (Hassan), Patrick Jordan (Maj. Watkins), Vivian Pickles (German Nurse), Mike Stevens (Capt. Johnson), Tony Stamboulieh (Barman in Arab Bar), Martin Burland ("Dead" Officer), Bridget Espeet (Ann, A.T.S. Officer), George McKeenan (Corporal at Quayside), Rafael Albaicin (Chief Arab at Oasis), Jose Halufi (Arab at Oasis), Jeremy Child, Dennis Brennan.

Not nearly as good as Aldrich's THE DIRTY DOZEN, but a fairly entertaining war film nonetheless. Caine plays a novice British Army captain who is assigned the task of leading a band of ex-convicts into the African desert to destroy a Nazi oil depot 650 miles behind Rommel's front lines. Of course the inexperienced captain must earn the respect of his somewhat surly men the hard way, which he eventually does, and the team becomes a crack unit. Unfortunately, the British High Command has also assigned a regular army unit on the same mission, figuring that Caine and his crew will most certainly be killed since they are just being used as a diversion for Rommel's troops. Surprisingly, it is the regular troops that are surrounded and slaughtered by Rommel's forces, with Caine's men breaking through and arriving at their destination. Upon investigation of the site, however, the men are dismayed to learn that the depot is just a decoy. Determined to fulfill their mission, Caine and his troops move on to the real depot. Meanwhile, the British have succeeded in pushing Rommel's forces back and realize that they need the Nazi oil depot open for their own troops. Unable to establish contact with Caine to tell them to abort the mission, the British Command allows their location to slip out to Nazi spies who will be sure to inform Rommel so that the Nazi's can ambush the rag-tag band of mercenaries. Despite the odds, Caine succeeds in blowing up the depot by disguising his men in German uniforms. Left with only three men, Caine leads what is left of his troops back to the British, but they are killed by their own countrymen who fail to realize that the German uniforms are just a disguise.

p, Harry Saltzman; d, Andre De Toth; w, Lotte Colin, Melvyn Bragg (based on a story by George Marton); ph, Edward Scaife (Panavision, Technicolor); m, Michel Legrand; ed, Alan Osbiston, Jack Slade; art d, Tom Morahan; spec eff, Kit West.

War **(PR:C MPAA:M)**

PLAY GIRL* (1932) 60m WB bw

Loretta Young *(Buster)*, Winnie Lightner *(Georgine)*, Norman Foster *(Wallie)*, Guy Kibbee *(Finkelwald)*, James Ellison *(Elmer)*, Edward Van Sloan *(Moffatt)*, Dorothy Burgess *(Ruth, Sarcastic Girl)*, Noel Madison *(Martie)*, Polly Walters *(Ethel)*, Mae Madison *(May)*, Eileen Carlisle *(Rose)*, Rene Whitney *(Arlene)*, Adrienne Dore *(The Reno Girl)*, Harold Waldridge *(Messenger)*, Charles Coleman *(Floor Walker)*, Nat Pendleton *(Dance Hall Plumber)*, Noel Madison, Elizabeth Patterson, Velma Gresham.

Big city melodrama starring Young as a naive young girl who falls in love and marries Foster, a man with a nasty penchant for gambling. The honeymoon ends soon for the couple when Foster's obsession with the horses slowly leads them on the road to ruin, leaving Young to try and scrape by on her own during the Depression. The climax which sees a pregnant Young's distraught face superimposed over footage of a horse race that she bet the family nest-egg on (to insure her child's future) drew laughs from the audience back in 1932. Only point of historical interest is the photography by Gregg Toland, who later shot Orson Welles' CITIZEN KANE.

d, Ray Enright; w, Maurine Watkins, Maude Fulton, Brown Holmes (based on a story "God's Gift to Women" by Frederick Hazlitt Brennan); ph, Gregg Toland; ed, Owen Marks.

Drama **(PR:A MPAA:NR)**

PLAY GIRL½** (1940) 75m RKO bw

Kay Francis *(Grace Herbert)*, James Ellison *(Tom Dice)*, Mildred Coles *(Ellen Daley)*, Nigel Bruce *(Bill Vincent)*, Margaret Hamilton *(Josie, Maid)*, Katharine Alexander *(Mrs. Dice)*, George P. Huntley *(Van Payson)*, Charles Quigley *(Lock)*, Kane Richmond *(Don Shawhan)*, Stanley Andrews *(Joseph Shawhan)*, Selmer Jackson *(Fred Dice)*, Marek Windheim *(Dr. Alonso Corvini, the Orchestra Conductor)*, Dick Hogan *(Bellhop)*, Ralph Byrd *(Doctor)*, Cecil Cunningham *(Dowager)*, Larry Steers *(Cafe Extra)*, Charles Arnt *(Grady, the Private Detective)*, Georgia Carroll *(Alice Sawyer)*.

Francis stars as an aging gold-digger, who, upon realizing her prime earning years are rapidly coming to a close, decides to pass on her manipulative knowledge to a younger gal. After a brief search, Francis settles on ambitious young looker Coles and teaches her the ropes. Coles proves to be a quick study, and soon she is raking in the bucks from hapless, rich romantics. The gravy train comes to a screeching halt, however, when Coles falls in love with young Texan Ellison. Horrified that she's willing to throw her lucrative career out the window for something as trivial as romance, Francis is relieved to discover that Ellison is in fact a multi-millionaire cattle baron, and that Coles has gotten herself the best of both worlds.

p, Cliff Reid; d, Frank Woodruff; w, Jerry Cady; ph, Nicholas Musuraca; ed, Harry Marker; cos, Edward Stevenson.

Drama **(PR:A MPAA:NR)**

PLAY IT AGAIN, SAM*½** (1972) 85m Apjac-Rollins-Joffe/PAR c

Woody Allen *(Allan Felix)*, Diane Keaton *(Linda Christie)*, Tony Roberts *(Dick Christie)*, Jerry Lacy *(Humphrey Bogart)*, Susan Anspach *(Nancy Felix)*, Jennifer Salt *(Sharon)*, Joy Bang *(Julie)*, Viva *(Jennifer)*, Mari Fletcher *(Fantasy Sharon)*, Diana Davila *(Girl In Museum)*, Suzanne Zenor *(Discotheque Girl)*, Michael Greene *(Hood No. 1)*, Ted Markland *(Hood No. 2)*.

A true film buff's film about a film buff, Allen, who has an obsession with the movies, especially CASABLANCA. The impish, neurotic Allen patterns his personality after Humphrey Bogart but has nothing of the actor's "tough guy" image. When Allen's wife, Anspach, leaves him she explains that she wants a new life. "You're one of life's great watchers," she tells him, "I'm not like that, I'm a doer." While the distressed Allen laments over his lack of "cool," he is visited by Bogart, who sits in a dark corner of the room, wearing his usual trenchcoat and smoking a cigarette. Bogart gives him advice—"Dames are simple. I never met one that didn't understand a slap in the mouth or a slug from a forty-five." In order to boost his spirits, Allen's married friends, Roberts and Keaton, try to fix him up with another girl. They first try the genuinely friendly Salt, who is turned off by Allen's excessive machismo; next Allen is paired with nymphomaniac Viva whom he somehow succeeds in turning off; and finally his date with the naive Bang ends with him being beaten by two grizzly bikers who abduct the girl. After striking out with every girl he meets, Allen finds himself becoming more and more desperate. When Roberts goes away on his umpteenth business trip, Keaton is once again left alone and neglected. She agrees to come over to Allen's apartment and cook dinner. Allen, who is now entertaining thoughts of romance with Keaton, sets the mood with candlelight and champagne. When he gets an opportunity to kiss her, however, he loses courage. Again Bogart appears from nowhere to coach the nervous Allen. On Bogart's urging, Allen finally makes his move. Keaton becomes confused, however, and leaves while Allen is professing his love to her. A moment later she returns and they spend the night together in bed. The following morning, a guilt-stricken Keaton struggles with the thought of telling Roberts. Unexpectedly, Roberts returns from a business trip, sensing that Keaton is involved with another man. He tells Allen of his suspicions and confides that he truly loves Keaton. He also threatens to kill her lover if he ever finds out who he is. Keaton comes to the realization that she needs Roberts and chases him to the airport, where he is about to leave on another business trip. Allen also rushes to the airport (driven by Bogart, who coaches him along the way), determined to keep his best friend's marriage together. On a fog-filled runway reminiscent of that in CASABLANCA, all three characters stand dressed in their trenchcoats. Realizing that this is a rare chance to act out the finale of CASABLANCA in real life, Allen paraphrases that film's dialog. He confesses to Roberts that he loves Keaton, but then orders her to get on the plane with her husband. Afterwards Bogart commends Allen on his style. Allen learns to believe in himself without relying on Bogart and the two bid farewell in the fog. As Allen walks away, Bogart delivers his immortal lines, "Here's looking at you, kid." Based on Allen's Broadway play (Allen, Roberts, Keaton, and Jerry Lacy as Bogart all appeared in the stage version, which opened on February 12th 1969 and ran for 453 performances) PLAY IT AGAIN, SAM differs somewhat from his previous pictures TAKE THE MONEY AND RUN (1969) and BANANAS (1971). Having directed those previous films, Allen handed over the helming reins here to Herbert Ross, a director who is a craftsman but has no recognizable style of his own. What Ross brings to Allen's play is a sense of control and drama as opposed to the slapstick vignettes of TAKE THE MONEY AND RUN and BANANAS. While Ross' name is on the credits, PLAY IT AGAIN, SAM is clearly Allen's film. (Atypical, however, for an Allen film is the location. A strike in New York caused filming to move to San Francisco.) Although his character "Allan Felix" is the typical neurotic Allen hero (most clearly seen in ANNIE HALL), he strikes a common chord with film audiences. Like Allan Felix, everyone who watches movies patterns himself (to some extent) after the characters on the screen. What Allen hits on in PLAY IT AGAIN, SAM is a cultural phenomenon unique to the days of movies—audiences living their lives as a movie. However, instead of relying on that crutch, Allan Felix, at the film's end, learns that he has a style of his own and that he doesn't need Bogart to help him anymore. What makes PLAY IT AGAIN, SAM such a success is this universal appeal. While not every audience can relate to the New York intellectual idiosyncracies of ANNIE HALL, they can relate on a gut emotional level to an average man idolizing a movie star. For film buffs, Allen has included countless film references (Erich von Stroheim, Francois Truffaut, Ida Lupino), film posters (ACROSS THE PACIFIC, SAN QUENTIN, THE JUNGLE PRINCESS, ALL THROUGH THE NIGHT, and MARCH OF THE WOODEN SOLDIERS among others) and, of course, clips and music from CASABLANCA. Composer Goldenberg borrows heavily from the themes of Max Steiner, which are heard throughout, as is the unforgettable "As Time Goes By" (Herman Hupfeld, sung by Dooley Wilson) and an Oscar Peterson composition entitled "Blues For Allan Felix." Also deserving special mention is Jerry Lacy's flawless portrayal of Bogart which consistently makes one feel as if Allen somehow managed to get the real Bogart for this film.

p, Arthur P. Jacobs; d, Herbert Ross; w, Woody Allen (based on his play); ph, Owen Roizman (Technicolor); m, Billy Goldenberg, Max Steiner; ed, Marion Rothman; prod d, Ed Wittstein; set d, Doug Von Koss; cos, Anna Hill Johnstone; makeup, Stanley R. Dufford.

Comedy **Cas.** **(PR:C MPAA:PG)**

PLAY IT AS IT LAYS* (1972) 99m UNIV c

Tuesday Weld *(Maria Wyeth)*, Anthony Perkins *(B.Z.)*, Tammy Grimes *(Helene)*, Adam Roarke *(Carter Lang)*, Ruth Ford *(Carlotta)*, Eddie Firestone *(Benny Austin)*, Diana Ewing *(Susannah)*, Paul Lambert *(Larry Kulik)*, Chuck McCann *(Abortionist's Assistant)*, Severn Darden *(Hypnotist)*, Tony Young *(Johnny Waters)*, Richard Anderson *(Les Goodwin)*, Elizabeth Claman *(The Chickie)*, Mitzi Hoag *(Patsy)*, Roger Ewing *(Nelson)*, Richard Ryal *(Apartment Manager)*, Tyne Daly *(Journalist)*, Mike Edwards *(B.Z.'s Lover)*, John Finnegan *(Frank)*, Tracy Morgan *(Jeanelle)*, Darlene Conley *(Kate's Nurse)*, Arthur Knight *(Himself)*, Albert Johnson *(Himself)*, Alan Warnick *(TV Panelist)*.

A depressing look at life with Hollywood as the metaphor for the rotten way things are. Filmed in Malibu, Las Vegas, Hollywood, and the Mojave Desert, this movie could turn an optimist to suicide as it relentlessly examines everything that is wrong, while offering no redeeming happiness. Weld is a 30-year-old actress who is already on the wane. Her career has ended and she is now living at a psychiatric hospital where she recalls the events leading to this situation. Weld was born in a tiny burg in Nevada, fled the confines of small-town life, and became a top model while still not 20 years of age. Roarke, a hot, innovative director, cast her in a unique film where she didn't have to learn lines, just had to tell how she felt about matters (sort of an Andy Warhol-Paul Morrissey picture) and that revelatory role paved the way for her first commercial film vehicle, a sleazy biker epic, also directed by Roarke. Weld and Roarke get married and have a brain-damaged daughter (tended by nurse Conley), but she has to be institutionalized. The marriage is a rocky one, as Roarke becomes an egotistical "auteur" director with little time for her. Consequently, she turns for affection and friendship of a non-sexual sort to Perkins, a gay man who is married, in name only, to Grimes because Perkins's domineering mother, Ford, has paid Grimes to stay with him. Weld is terribly unhappy with her lot and has attempted various means of elevating her depressed state, including a visit to the small Nevada town. She is searching for a meaning to her life and the tragedy of her parents' lives—both of them died unexpectedly. She learns that Thomas Wolfe was correct when she goes home again to see that her natal house has been knocked down to provide space for a rocket facility. She has several loveless affairs, including one with a mobster in Las Vegas and another with Young, a television star. A one-nighter with screenwriter Anderson leads to her pregnancy. Roarke insists she have an abortion through McCann (in an unusual role as the abortionist's assistant). Roarke promptly divorces Weld but she can't let go of him, as he is her first love and a life raft in the sea of trouble. Roarke and Perkins go on location where Perkins is producing the film Roarke is directing. She follows them to the motel and tries to make the marriage work with Roarke but is rejected. Upon visiting Perkins, Weld discovers that he is suicidal because he can't find a reason to live anymore. Weld can't help him on his quest, so he pops a handful of sleeping pills and tosses them down with a beaker filled with vodka. It is his death that brings Weld to where she is at the hospital. When someone asks her why she has chosen to live instead of ending her life the same way Perkins did, she shrugs and replies, "Why not?" Diana Lynn was supposed to play the Grimes role but died unexpectedly at the age of 45 just prior to shooting. Everyone is so pretentious in the movie that it is impossible to care a bit about anyone. Some interesting sidelights in the casting make it worth a look; in that, multi-award winning Daly (from TV's "Cagney and Lacey") does a small role, TV's Anderson (who co-starred in both "Bionic" TV shows simultaneously) has a nice part, film critic-teacher Knight plays himself as only he can, and improvisational comedian Darden also has a neat turn. The apartment house manager was Ryal, a man who came to the U.S. from Holland, worked on his accent and lost the Dutch sound so completely that he became one of the busiest commercial announcers-cartoon voices around. McCann, who is more often seen in comedy roles, lends a winning characterization as the insensitive man who arranges illegal operations for women in trouble. The production manager, Roger Rothstein, later became producer of many Neil Simon films and Roy Lichtenstein, the famed "Pop" artist, was linked as "visual adviser." No question that the picture had a unique look to it, but the lack of any humanity eventually sank the project.

p, Frank Perry, Dominick Dunne; d, Perry; w, Joan Didion, John Gregory Dunne (based on the novel by Didion); ph, Jordan Croneweth (Technicolor); ed, Sidney Katz; prod d, Pato Guzman; cos, Joel Schumacher, Halston, Gustave Tassell; songs, McKendree Spring; makeup, Byron Poindester.

Drama **(PR:O MPAA:R)**

PLAY IT COOL*½ (1963, Brit.) 82m Independent Artists-Coronado-Lynx/ AA bw

Billy Fury *(Billy Universe)*, Michael Anderson, Jr. *(Alvin)*, Dennis Price *(Sir Charles Bryant)*, Richard Wattis *(Nervous Man)*, Anna Palk *(Ann Bryant)*, Keith Hamshere *(Ring-a-Ding)*, Ray Brooks *(Freddy)*, Jeremy Bulloch *(Joey)*, Maurice Kaufmann *(Larry Granger)*, Peter Barkworth *(Skinner)*, Max Bacon *(Lotus Proprietor)*, Felicity Young *(Yvonne)*, Monty Landis *(Beatnik Man)*, Bernie Winters *(Sydney Norman)*, Helen Shapiro, Bobby Vee, Danny Williams, Shane Fenton and the Fentones, Jimmy Crawford, Lionel Blair and His Dancers.

Lame rock 'n' roll movie, worthy of interest only because it provides a glimpse at pre-Beatlemania English pop-rock stars and stardom. Price stars as a stuffy British papa who sends his impressionable daughter Palk off to Europe in order to bust up her romance with worthless rock singer Kaufmann. The plan backfires at the airport, where Palk meets up with sexy rock idol Fury and his band, who are en route to a concert in Brussels. Finding their flight has been cancelled due to fog, Fury and his band take Palk out for a night on the town while searching for Kaufmann. Unfortunately the merry troupe find Kaufmann in the arms of a sleazy nightclub dancer, and Palk realizes her father was right after all. Palk then dumps the bum, bids adieu to Fury and his band, and returns to her daddy. For a youth-oriented film dealing with rock 'n' roll, the ending and moral of this film feels like it was written by somebody's parents. Fury was one of several early English rockers whose images were self-consciously patterned after the tempestuous appeal of Elvis Presley, but who actually conveyed a tamer presence that had more in common with body-next-door pop crooners like Frankie Avalon and Bobby Vee (the latter plays it cool in this film). Director Winner was no stranger to rock 'n' roll, having done a stint as a writer for the British pop music magazine *New Musical Express*. Songs include: "Who Can Say" (sung by Danny Williams), "It's Gonna Take Magic" (sung by Shane Fenton and the Fentones), "Take It Easy" (sung by Jimmy Crawford), "Twist" (performed by Lionel Blair and His Dancers), "Cry My Heart Out," "But I Don't Care" (sung by Helen Shapiro), "Play It Cool" (sung by Billy Fury).

p, David Deutch, Dennis Holt; d, Michael Winner; w, Jack Henry; ph, Reginald Wyer; m, Norrie Paramor; ed, Tristam Cones; md, Paramor; art d, Lionel Couch; set d, Peter Russell; m/l, Paramor, Richard B. Rowe, Bernard Jewry, Norman Newell, Bob Barratt, Ronald Frasere, Larry Parnes.

Drama **(PR:A MPAA:NR)**

PLAY IT COOL½** (1970, Jap.) 93m Daiei c (DENKI KURAGE)

Mari Atsumi *(Yumi)*, Yusuke Kawazu *(Nozawa)*, Akemi Negishi *(Tomi)*, Akira Nishimura *(Kada)*, Ryoichi Tamagawa *(Yoshimura)*, Sanae Nakahara *(Madam)*.

Japanese melodrama which follows the life of geisha-girl Negishi's illegitimate daughter Atsumi. Atsumi grows up to be a beautiful and hardworking young lady who studies to be a dressmaker. Looking upon Atsumi as the only thing she has done right in her life, Negishi allows nothing to spoil her daughter's future. When her latest lover forces himself on Atsumi, Negishi kills the man and is sent to prison. Shattered, Atsumi becomes a hostess in a nightclub and plays cards with the male customers, who can only sleep with her if they win. Being a brilliant card-player, Atsumi manages to stay at the tables longer than on the bed. When the owner of the club expresses his desire to make her his mistress, Atsumi declines and tells of her love for Kawazu. Soon after, the owner dies and Kawazu conceives a child with Atsumi so that she can claim the child is that of the owner, enabling her to inherit his fortune.

d&w, Yasuzo Masumura (based on a story by Masayuki Toyama); ph, Setsuo Kobayashi (Daiei Scope, Fuji Color); m, Hikaru Hayashi; art d, Takesaburo Watanabe.

Drama **(PR:C MPAA:NR)**

PLAY MISTY FOR ME*½** (1971) 102m Malpaso/UNIV c

Clint Eastwood *(Dave Garland)*, Jessica Walter *(Evelyn Draper)*, Donna Mills *(Tobie Williams)*, John Larch *(Sgt. McCallum)*, Jack Ging *(Dr. Frank Dewan)*, Irene Hervey *(Madge Brenner)*, James McEachin *(Al Monte)*, Clarice Taylor *(Birdie)*, Donald Siegel *(Murphy the Bartender)*, Duke Everts *(Jay Jay)*, George Fargo *(Man)*, Mervin W. Frates *(Locksmith)*, Tim Frawley *(Deputy Sheriff)*, Otis Kadani *(Policeman)*, Brit Lind *(Anjelica)*, Paul E. Lippman *(2nd Man)*, Jack Kosslyn *(Cab Driver)*, Ginna Patterson *(Madalyn)*, Malcolm Moran *(Man in Window)*, Walter Spear *(Officer)*, The Johnny Otis Show, The Cannonball Adderley Quintet *(Themselves)*.

Superstar Eastwood was finally given the chance to realize his long-standing ambition—to direct a feature film—and his debut at the helm was auspicious indeed. PLAY MISTY FOR ME is the ultimate nightmare of the uncommitted male for whom no-strings-attached bed-hopping is the preferred way of life. Eastwood plays a popular Carmel, California disk jockey who suddenly finds himself alone when his artist girl friend Mills decides that she needs a break from their relationship. Lonely and looking to satisfy his lust/revenge urges, Eastwood goes to his favorite bar and picks up Walter, an attractive but rather odd woman whom he learns is the caller on his radio show who requests he play Errol Garner's "Misty" every night. The lustful pair adjourn to Walter's apartment where they spend the evening together—with the understanding that it is only a one-night stand. Eastwood is surprised and more than a bit annoyed when Walter shows up unannounced at his house the next night and acts as if she is ready to move in with him. The disk jockey tries to be nice to the poor deluded woman at first, but she never catches on that he couldn't care less about her. Meanwhile, Mills has returned to Carmel and decides to give her relationship with Eastwood another chance. Anxious to patch things up with Mills, Eastwood spends all his free time with her while making feeble excuses to the distressingly persistent Walter who won't stop calling him. Frustrated and fed up, Eastwood finally sets a date with Walter where he gently explains to her that he is in love with another woman and can't possibly continue seeing her. Walter's mind seems to snap when she hears the news and she babbles incoherently about her undying love for Eastwood. No matter—Eastwood stands firm and tells her to leave. Walter retaliates by slashing her wrists. A doctor is called and Walter is told to spend the next few days recuperating in Eastwood's house. The whiny and clinging Walter practically goes into withdrawal every time Eastwood strays from her sight and the disk jockey is forced to sneak out of his own house to make a business luncheon with his station's female owner, Hervey. The meeting goes well until an apparently insane Walter appears at the restaurant and accuses Eastwood of cheating on her. Eastwood tries to humor Walter and hustle her out of the restaurant, but by the time he does so Hervey has had enough embarrassment for one day and the meeting is off. When Eastwood returns home, he is shocked to find that his belongings have been trashed, his clothes ripped to shreds, and most horrible of all, his cleaning lady is near death after being slashed repeatedly by Walter with a razor. The police take Walter away and she is put into a sanitarium. Thinking the nightmare over, Eastwood goes back to work and resumes his romance with Mills. One day Mills informs him that she has found a new roommate by the name of Annabel and that the three of them should get together some time. That night at the radio station, Eastwood gets a request call from a familiar voice asking if he will "Play 'Misty' for me." Walter explains that she has been cured of her emotional problems and is about to go on a trip to Hawaii. Relieved at Walter's apparent lucidity, Eastwood gladly plays the song and says goodbye to her. That night, Eastwood awakens from a sound sleep when he hears "Misty" being played on his stereo. He sits up and discovers Walter, with a knife raised over her head, standing at the foot of his bed. The crazed woman tries to stab Eastwood, but he manages to stay clear of the blade. Before he has a chance to disarm the woman, she runs off into the night. Days later it dawns on Eastwood that Walter must be Mills' new roommate, "Annabel." Hoping that he's not too late, Eastwood calls police detective Larch and asks him to check out Mills' home. When Eastwood arrives, Larch is dead on the floor with a pair of scissors plunged into his chest and Mills is bound and gagged with Walter about to stab her. Eastwood prevents the killing and during his struggle with the deranged Walter he knocks her off balance and she tumbles off the terrace and into the rocks below. PLAY MISTY FOR ME is a gripping suspense thriller and a real surprise from Eastwood. In 1971 Eastwood was associated only with the western genre through his appearances on TV's "Rawhide," and the westerns he made with directors Sergio Leone and Don Siegel. While Siegel's film COOGAN'S BLUFF was a modern-day police drama set in New York City, Eastwood's character was a cowboy sheriff from Arizona—once again strong associations with the western. Eastwood the actor had long wanted to direct and even attempted to do so on an episode of "Rawhide." Unfortunately, CBS wouldn't allow it and Eastwood had to satisfy his directorial urges by working very closely with Leone and Siegel. The script for PLAY MISTY FOR ME was written by a woman-friend of Eastwood's, Heims, who was once the actor's secretary. He optioned the script, but when no studio was interested in Eastwood directing the property, he turned it back over to Heims who then sold it to Universal. Two years later Eastwood talked the studio into letting him direct the film, assuring them he could bring it in on a low budget and take a percentage of the profits instead of a salary. Eastwood annoyed the studio by casting the little-known Walter as the crazed Evelyn, but her stunning performance soon silenced any complaints. In the small role of a cynical bartender, Eastwood cast director and friend Siegel—who had never acted. Telling everyone he cast Siegel because he wanted someone on the set "...more nervous than I was," Eastwood actually managed to get a nice, relaxed performance out of the self-conscious director (Siegel also made a cameo appearance in the remake of his own science-fiction classic INVASION OF THE BODY SNATCHERS (1978)—he played a cab driver). Shooting in and around his home town of Carmel, California, Eastwood's film was budgeted at $1,242,000. Four and a half weeks later, PLAY MISTY FOR ME was completed and only $750,000 of the approved budget had been spent. The film was a big hit at the box office and Roberta Flack's song "The First Time Ever I Saw Your Face," which is played during a love scene in the film, became a chart-buster as well. With the success of PLAY MISTY FOR ME, actor Clint Eastwood established himself as a man who had total control over his career. As an actor-director he demonstrates a keen understanding of his talents as an actor and his public image. Since PLAY MISTY FOR ME Eastwood directed other films in a variety of genres (for the most part big hits at the box office) and has proven himself an intelligent director with a good money sense who can bring films in on time and under budget—indicating that there is still hope for the movie business.

p, Robert Daley; d, Clint Eastwood; w, Jo Heims, Dean Reisner (based on a story by Heims); ph, Bruce Surtees (Technicolor); m, Dee Barton; ed, Carl Pingitore; art d, Alexander Golitzen; set d, Ralph Hurst; cos, Helen Colvig, Brad Whitney; m/l,

"Misty" (Errol Garner), "The First Time Ever I Saw Your Face" (Ewan MacColl, sung by Roberta Flack) "Squeeze Me" (Duke Ellington).

Drama   **Cas.**   **(PR:O MPAA:R)**

PLAY UP THE BAND**   (1935, Brit.) 71m City/ABF bw

Stanley Holloway (Sam Small), Betty Ann Davies (Betty Small), Leslie Bradley (Jack), Frank Atkinson (Alf Ramsbottom), Charles Sewell (Lord Heckdyke), Amy Veness (Lady Heckdyke), Cynthia Stock (Vera), Julie Suedo (Marquise de Vaux), Arthur Gomez (Marquis de Vaux), Hal Gordon (Bandmaster), Louise Selkirk's Ladies Orchestra, London Brass Band, Andrea Malandrinos, Billy Bray, Ian Wilson.

A fairly lively comedy starring Holloway and Atkinson as two members of a brass band from Yorkshire who are framed for the theft of a valuable necklace owned by the band owner's wife. The crime occurs in London, where the band had traveled to play in a competition. It turns out that the necklace was actually stolen by a villain pretending to be a count. Eventually the pair track down the real culprit and is allowed to play with the band at the Crystal Palace.

p, Basil Humphreys; d, Harry Hughes; w, Frank Atkinson.

Comedy   **(PR:A MPAA:NR)**

PLAYBACK**   (1962, Brit.) 62m Merton Park/Anglo-Amalgamated bw

Margit Saad (Lisa Shillack), Barry Foster (Dave Hollis), Victor Platt (Inspector Gorman), Dinsdale Landen (Joe Ross), George Pravda (Simon Shillak), Nigel Green (Ralph Monk), Jerold Wells (Inspector Parkes).

Another DOUBLE INDEMNITY inspired whodunit based on a story by the prolific British mystery writer Edgar Wallace. Evil vamp Saad seduces a foolish cop into murdering her husband by promising him wealth and her undying devotion. Of course, things don't turn out that way.

p, Jack Greenwood; d, Quentin Lawrence; w, Robert Stewart (based on a story by Edgar Wallace).

Crime   **(PR:A MPAA:NR)**

PLAYBOY, THE***   (1942, Brit.) 78m Vogue/GFD bw (GB: KICKING THE MOON AROUND; AKA: MILLIONAIRE MERRY-GO-ROUND)

Ambrose (Himself), Evelyn Dall (Pepper Martin), Harry Richmond (Himself), Florence Desmond (Flo Hadley), Hal Thompson (Bobbie Hawkes), C. Denier Warren (Mark Browd), Julien Vedey (Herbert Stoker), Max Bacon (Gus), Les Carew (Streamline), Dave Burnaby (Magistrate), George Carney (Police Constable Truscott), Edward Rigby (Prof. Scattlebury), Maureen Fitzsimmons [Maureen O'Hara] (Secretary), Edgar Driver, Mike Johnson, Bill Black, Dino Galvani, Frank Atkinson, Frances Day, Ambrose's Orchestra.

Here's a real 1930s rarity: a British-made musical that is equal to, if not better than, some of the American musicals of the time. Dall is a young lady cabaret singer who, with a millionaire's help, is about to hit the big time. Desmond, one of England's strongest comediennes of the time, is the goldigger out to stop the youngster. The script is an absolute delight and high caliber talents Richman and Ambrose are marvelous to watch. The whole thing is nicely put together and great fun for the audience. Musical contributions from Ambrose and His Orchestra.

p, Herbert Wynne; d, Walter Forde; w, Michael Hogan, Angus MacPhail, Roland Pertwee, H. Fowler-Mears (based on a story by Tom Geraghty); ph, Francis Carver; m/l, Michael Carr, Jimmy Kennedy.

Musical/Comedy   **(PR:AA MPAA:NR)**

PLAYBOY OF PARIS**½   (1930) 79m PAR bw (LA PETITE CAFE)

Maurice Chevalier (Albert Loriflan), Frances Dee (Yvonne Phillbert), Dorothy Cristy (Mlle. Berengere), Eugene Pallette (Pierre Bourdin), O. P. Heggie (Phillibert), Cecil Cunningham (Mlle. Hedwige), Stuart Erwin (Paul Michel), Tyler Brooke (Cadeaux), Frank Elliott (Mons. Jabert), William B. Davidson (Mons. Bannack), Charles Giblyn (Gastonet), Erin La Bissoniere (Jacqueline), Frederick Lee (Plouvier), Edmund Breese (General), Olaf Hytten (Doctor), Edward Lynch (Manager), Guy Oliver (Street Cleaner), William O'Brien (Waiter).

Chevalier starred in this his fourth film for Paramount as a goofy young waiter, recently fired by cafe owner Heggie for incompetence, who is unaware that he is about to inherit a large fortune. Upon learning that his former waiter is soon to be a rich man, Heggie hires Chevalier back, signs him to a lengthy contract (which he is sure to want to buy back at any cost), and tries to steer the young man into a romance with his daughter, Dee. When Chevalier finds out about his fortune, he stays on and works as a waiter by day, just to spite his greedy boss. Jealous of his nocturnal wandering revelries throughout Paris accompanied by gold digger Cristy, Dee follows Chevalier and gets involved in a fight with her rival. Chevalier breaks it up, but ends up offending nobleman Davidson who challenges him to a duel. The morning of the duel, Dee tells Davidson that Chevalier is just a waiter and the embarrassed nobleman calls the whole thing off. Chevalier, however, reinsults Davidson and demands the duel to go as planned. Desperate, Dee faints on the battlefield causing Chevalier to drop his gun and rush to her aid. It is then that he realizes that he loves her and he gives up defending his honor. PLAYBOY OF PARIS is no masterpiece and relies on hackneyed situations and contrived plot devices to advance the narrative. A happy exception to the norm for this film is a brilliant comedy scene wherein Chevalier finds himself in a wine cellar taste-testing various barrels of wine as if he was judging a beauty contest. As he gets progressively drunker, his enthusiasm increases with each sip, until he caresses and kisses a cask of Burgundy, which gives him a loving gurgle in response. The moment is classic and in it Chevalier holds his own against Chaplin for a brief shining moment. PLAYBOY OF PARIS was shot in French simultaneously with an all-French cast and by all accounts it is the foreign language version which is superior. That either version was even made was due to Chevalier's enthusiasm for Max Linder's 1920 silent feature LE PETIT CAFE. When the Frenchman was preparing to put his

signature on his first Paramount contract, he suggested that the studio remake the Linden film as his first U.S. project, and to keep Chevalier happy, the studio eventually secured the rights to the picture. Songs include: "My Ideal," "It's a Great Life If You Don't Weaken," "In The Heart Of Old Paree," "Yvonne's Song" (Richard A. Whiting, Newell Chase, Leo Robin).

p&d, Ludwig Berger; w, Percy Heath, Vincent Lawrence (based on the play "La Petite Cafe" by Tristan Bernard); ph, Henry Gerrard; ed, Merrill White; art d, Hans Dreier.

Musical/Comedy   **(PR:A MPAA:NR)**

PLAYBOY OF THE WESTERN WORLD, THE***   (1963, Ireland) 100m Four Provinces/Janus-Lion International c

Siobhan McKenna (Pegeen Mike), Gary Raymond (Christy Mahon), Elspeth March (Widow Quin), Michael O'Briaan (Shawn Keogh), Liam Redmond (Michael James), Brendan Cauldwell (Jimmy Farrell), John Welsh (Philly Cullen), Niall McGinnis (Old Mahon), Eithne Lydon (Susan), Finnuala O'Shannon (Sara), Anne Brogan (Nelly), Katie Fitroy (Honor).

A great Irish-situated comedy starring Raymond as a stranger who arrives in a remote tavern and announces that he has murdered his nasty father by smacking him on the skull with one blow from a shovel. Impressed, the villagers turn Raymond into a hero and he is worshipped by all, including the innkeeper's daughter, McKenna. Raymond's reign as king of the town is brief, however, as his father, McGinnis, shows up very much alive, albeit with a bandage wrapped around his head. Shocked, the villagers shun Raymond, and McKenna refuses to see him. Desperate to regain his status, Raymond once again hits his father over the head with a shovel and presumably kills him. Horrified at witnessing an actual murder, the villagers form a lynch mob and try to hang Raymond. Luckily McGinnis once again recovers from his wounds, reclaims his son, and they return home. A powerful insightful, and witty examination of hero worship and the mentality of a mob adapted from a play by Ireland's greatest playwright.

p, Brendan Smith, Denis O'Dell; d&w, Brian Desmond Hurst (based on the play by John Millington Synge); ph, Geoffrey Unsworth (Eastmancolor).

Comedy   **(PR:C MPAA:NR)**

PLAYERS zero   (1979) 120m PAR c

Ali McGraw (Nicole), Dean-Paul Martin (Chris), Maximillian Schell (Marco), Pancho Gonzalez (Pancho), Steven Guttenberg (Rusty), Melissa Prophet (Ann), Drew Denny (Chris at 10), Ian Altman (Rusty at 10), David Gilruth (Chauffeur), Guillermo Vilas, Ion Tiriac, Dan Maskell, John McEnroe, Ilie Nastase, Tom Gullikson, John Lloyd, Denis Ralston, Vijay Amritraj, Jim McManus, John Alexander, David Pate, Jorge Mendoza (Themselves).

Disappointing soap opera starring McGraw as an older, bored (and boring) woman who begins a complicated affair with young tennis pro Martin (in his film debut). When the couple isn't bedding down with their various partners in this sordid mess, the audience is left to watch unbearably dull tennis scenes that seem to last forever. McGraw, as usual, is awful. Martin is at least competent, but seems more natural swinging a racket and playing clothes-horse for Calvin Klein's fashions (Klein did the costumes) than romancing McGraw. A number of real-life tennis stars swing their rackets before Harvey's cameras, and the glamorous jet-set world of the professional tennis tour is captured with location shots aplenty—Wimbledon, New York, Monte Carlo, Mexico City, Los Angeles, Cuernavaca and Jamaica. Just the same, yech.

p, Robert Evans; d, Anthony Harvey; w, Arnold Schulman; ph, James Crabe (Panavision, Metrocolor); m, Jerry Goldsmith; ed, Randy Roberts; prod d, Richard Sylbert; set d, Robert Gould; cos, Richard Bruno, Calvin Klein.

Romance   **Cas.**   **(PR:O MPAA:PG)**

PLAYERS   1980 (SEE: CLUB, THE, 1980, Aus.)

PLAYGIRL**½   (1954) 85m UNIV bw

Shelley Winters (Fran Davis), Barry Sullivan (Mike Marsh), Colleen Miller (Phyllis Matthews), Richard Long (Barron Courtney), Gregg Palmer (Tom Bradley), Kent Taylor (Ted Andrews), Jacqueline de Wit (Greta Marsh), Dave Barry (Jonathan), Philip Van Zandt (Lew Martel), James McCallion (Paul), Paul Richards (Wilbur), Helen Beverly (Anne), Myrna Hansen (Linda), Mara Corday (Pam), Don Avalier (Pancho), Carl Sklover (Cab Driver).

Miller plays the young innocent from Nebraska who arrives in New York seeking fame and fortune as a model. She soon finds herself in a living situation with Winters, a singer. When Miller is rapidly discovered by magazine publisher Sullivan, who has her face splashed across an issue of his magazine Glitter, Winters reveals she is the man's mistress and tells her roommate to stay away. During a jealous argument with Sullivan, Winters accidentally shoots him, which ruins Miller's career. She soon hits the skids and begins hanging out in nightclubs in the company of gangsters, which eventually leads to her unwitting involvement in a mob murder. Winters, however, comes to Miller's rescue and clears her. Slightly ridiculous, but entertaining in spite of itself.

p, Albert J. Cohen; d, Joseph Pevney; w, Robert Blees (based on a story by Ray Buffum); ph, Carl Guthrie; ed, Virgil Vogel; m/l, "Lie to Me," Ray Gilbert (sung by Shelley Winters), "There'll Be Some Changes Made," Billy Higgins, W. Benton Overstreet, Herbert Edwards.

Drama   **(PR:A MPAA:NR)**

PLAYGIRL, 1968   (SEE: THAT WOMAN, 1968, W. Ger.)

PLAYGIRL AFTER DARK   (SEE: TOO HOT TO HANDLE 1961, Brit.)

PLAYGIRL AND THE WAR MINISTER, THE   (SEE: AMOROUS MR. PRAWN, THE, 1965, Brit.)

PLAYGIRL KILLER (SEE: DECOY FOR TERROR, 1970, Can.)

PLAYGIRLS AND THE BELLBOY, THE zero (1962,Ger.) 94m Rapid/United Producers Releasing bw/c (MIT EVA FING DIE SUNDE AN; AKA: THE BELLBOY AND THE PLAYGIRLS)

June Wilkinson, Gigi Held, Louise Lawson, Lori Shea, Ann Myers, Laura Cummins, Jan Davidson, Don Kenney, Karin Dor, Willy Fritsch, Michael Cramer, Gigi Martine, Merwin Goldsmith, Mady Rahl, Thomas Fabian, Maria Malden-Madsen, Otto Storr, Hanne Weider, Klaus Havenstein, Hans J. Dietrich, Angeles Durand, Max Greger.

A real oddity. This German black-and-white sex comedy about a voyeuristic bellboy who peeps through keyholes at scantily clad showgirls in the hopes of becoming a house detective, has absolutely nothing to recommend it except that a very young Francis Ford Coppola (THE GODFATHER I & II, THE CONVERSATION, APOLCALYPSE NOW) was hired by the American distributor to write and shoot additional color, 3-D nude sequences featuring the likes of buxom June Wilkinson.

p, Wolfgang Hartwig, Harry Ross; d, Fritz Umgelter, Francis Ford Coppola; w, Dieter Hildebrandt, Margh Malina, Coppola; ph, Paul Grupp; m, Klaus Ogermann; art d, Walter Dorfler.

Comedy **(PR:O MPAA:NR)**

PLAYGIRLS AND THE VAMPIRE* (1964, Ital.) 76m Nord Film Italiana/Fanfare bw (L'ULTIMA PREDA DEL VAMPIRO; AKA: CURSE OF THE VAMPIRE)

Lyla Rocco *(Vera)*, Walter Brandi *(Count Gabor Kernassy/Vampire)*, Maria Giovannini *(Katia)*, Alfredo Rizzo *(Lucas)*, Tilde Damiani, Antoine Nicos, Corinne Fontaine, Erika Di Centa, Marisa Quattrini, Leonardo Botta, Ivy Holzer.

More Italian gothic horror. This one takes place in a spooky castle owned by the mysterious Count Brandi and sports a bevy of beautiful showgirls accompanied by their manager and piano player. They have all been forced to take shelter in the castle after being stranded by floods. Soon after their arrival, the creepy Count orders that no one leave their rooms after nightfall. They do, of course, and soon they run into Brandi's ancient ancestor, a vampire (also played by Brandi). Some of the nightgown-clad gals are turned into seductive vampires, and it's up to Brandi (the good guy, not the bloodsucker) to kill his forefather.

p, Tiziano Longo; d&w, Piero Regnoli; ph, Ugo Brunelli; m, Aldo Piga; ed, Mario Arditi; md, Pierluigi Urbini; art d, Giuseppe Ranieri.

Horror **(PR:O MPAA:NR)**

PLAYGROUND, THE zero (1965) 95m General/Jerand bw

Rees Vaughn *(Thomas Smith)*, Inger Stratton *(Eva)*, Edmon Ryan *(Jason Porter)*, Andrea Blayne *(Mrs. Porter)*, Loretta Leversee *(Mary)*, Richard Kilbride *(Father Williams)*, Marian Blake *(Mrs. Williams)*, Carol White *(Virginia Williams)*, Peter MacLean *(Dr. Ronald)*, Conrad Jameson *(Dr. Jacques)*, Roger Talbot *(John)*, Stanley Greene *(Clayton)*, Philip Brown *(Fishback)*, Sol Schwade *(Dr. Zimmerman)*, Ethel Shutta *(Mrs. Cartwright)*, Paul Schmidt *(Duncan Cartwright)*.

Inane "Adults Only" feature starring Vaughn as an athiest drama director who tries to scare his devoutly religious prostitute-date by crawling into an open grave while she's not looking and mouthing obscenities, which include taking the Lord's name in vain. Instead of terrifying the hooker, Vaughn is struck dead by an immediate heart attack, retribution for his blasphemy. The hooker runs from the corpse and falls into the arms of another actor, Schmidt, whom, for some reason, she believes to be the embodiment of Jesus Christ. After falling into a religious rapture, the hooker is taken to her psychiatrist and he too experiences the same religious enlightenment upon seeing Schmidt. The rest of this sick and ridiculous film deals with motorcycle accidents, insanity, and lobotomies, which is what everyone involved in this trash should have been forced to submit to upon its release.

p&d, Richard Hilliard; w, George Garrett (based on ideas from the book *My Brother Death* by Cyrus L. Sulzberger); ph, Urs Furrer; m, Elliot Kaplan.

Comedy **(PR:O MPAA:NR)**

PLAYING AROUND*½ (1930) 64m WB-FN bw

Alice White *(Sheba Miller)*, Chester Morris *(Nicky Solomon)*, William Bakewell *(Jack)*, Richard Carlyle *(Pa Miller)*, Marion Byron *(Maude)*, Maurice Black *(Joe)*, Lionel Belmore *(Morgan)*, Shep Camp *(Master of Ceremonies)*, Ann Brody *(Mrs. Fennerbeck)*, Nellie V. Nichols *(Mrs. Lippincott)*, Helen Werle.

White stars in this strictly formula crime melodrama as a poor slum girl who breaks up with her noble and hardworking boy friend Bakewell in order to latch on to small-time hood Morris. Impressed by his slick talk, fancy car, and money to burn, White ignores the morals of the situation until her new beau is caught murdering her own father during a robbery.

d, Mervyn LeRoy; w, Adele Commandini, Frances Nordstrom, Humphrey Pearson (based on the story "Sheba" by Vina Delmar); ph, Sol Polito; m/l, "That's the Lowdown on the Lowdown," "We Learn About Love Every Day," "You're My Captain Kidd," and "Playing Around" (Sam Stept, Bud Green).

Crime **(PR:A MPAA:NR)**

PLAYING THE GAME (SEE: TOUCHDOWN 1931)

PLAYMATES** (1941) 94m RKO bw

Kay Kyser *(Himself)*, John Barrymore *(Himself)*, Lupe Velez *(Carmen del Torre)*, Ginny Simms *(Ginny)*, May Robson *(Grandma)*, Patsy Kelly *(Lulu Monahan)*, Peter Lind Hayes *(Peter Lindsey)*, George Cleveland *(Mr. Pennypacker)*, Alice Fleming *(Mrs. Pennypacker)*, Kay Kyser's Orchestra, Harry Babbitt, Ish Kabibble, Sully Mason *(Themselves)*, Joe Bernard *(Thomas)*, Ray Cooke *(Bellhop)*, Hobart Cavanaugh *(Tremble)*, Jacques Vanaire *(Alphonse)*, Sally Cairns *(Manicurist)*, Fred Trowbridge *(Hotel Clerk)*, Dorothy Babb *(Autograph Girl)*, Leon Belasco *(Prince Maharoohu)*, Grace Lenard *(Madeline)*, Sally Payne *(Gloria)*, Vinton Haworth *(Commentator)*, William Halligan *(Mr. Loomis)*, Jack Carr *(Pee Wee)*, Bill Cartledge *(Page Boy)*, George McKay *(Taxi Driver)*, Billy Chaney *(Call Boy)*, Dave Willock *(Cameraman)*, Marshall Ruth, Wally Walker *(Comedy Bull Team)*, William Emile *(Fencing Instructor)*, Rube Schaffer *(Masseur)*, The Guardsmen *(Themselves)*.

What a sad bow-out for John Barrymore. It was his final film and did nothing to revere the memory of a man who had once been one of the finest classical stage actors in the U.S. Barrymore plays himself, a has-been, washed-up actor managed by Kelly, who gets him to teach Shakespeare to Kay Kyser on the off chance that this will help Barrymore's flagging career get back in gear. There's to be a Bard Festival on a huge estate on Long Island owned by Fleming and Cleveland. Fleming is taken by the actor and her husband is a well-to-do man who just might sponsor a radio show. Barrymore doesn't want to teach Kyser how to speak the lines and eventually puts some alum in throat spray and hopes Keyser will lose his voice so Barrymore can go on in his stead. But Kyser catches wise, switches the spray and Barrymore winds up unable to speak, thus giving Kyser and his band the opportunity to mutilate "Romeo and Juliet" with a swing music version. Barrymore enlists the aid of Velez, as a female torero, to make Keyser too tired but her vamping only makes the leader of "The College of Musical Knowledge" even stronger. There is nothing to recommend the score, which was written by Jimmy Van Heusen and Johnny Burke and included: "Humpty Dumpty Heart" (sung by Ginny Simms), "How Long Did I Dream?" (sung by Simms, Harry Babbitt), "Que Chica?" (sung by Lupe Velez), "Romeo Smith and Juliet Jones" (performed by Kay Kyser and the orchestra), "Thank Your Lucky Stars And Stripes" (performed by entire cast). Whatever comedy there is comes when watching Barrymore gnaw the sets. His Shakespeare soliloquy still shows that he knew what to do with the right script.

p, Cliff Reid; d, David Butler; w, James V. Kern, Arthur Phillips (based on the story by Butler, Kern, M.M. Musselman); ph, Frank Redman; ed, Irene Morra; ch, Jack Crosby.

Musical/Comedy **(PR:A MPAA:NR)**

PLAYMATES½** (1969, Fr./Ital.) 86m Paris Inter/Goldstone-VIP-Blue Chip c (LE BAL DES VOYOUS; LES FEMMES)

Jean-Claude Bercq *(Henri Verdier)*, Marc Briand *(Robert)*, Donna Michelle *(Karine)*, Michel LeRoyer *(Philippe Leroy)*, Linda Veras *(Sophie Verdier)*, Roland Lesaffre *(Inspector Fougas)*, Jean Distinghin *(Himself, a Photographer)*, Luigi Bellini *(Luigi)*, Georges Bellec *(Paulo)*, Kim Camba *(Jack)*, Katia Chenko *(Ginette)*, Renate Wolfle, Edith Catry, Cathy Reghin *(Playgirls)*.

Meek bank manager Bercq falls in love with fashion model Michelle and is soon persuaded by her shady brother Briand to participate in an embezzling scheme tht will earn them enough money to invest in a uranium deal. When Bercq discovers that Michelle and Briand are not actually related, he tries to back out of the deal, but is forced to continue at gunpoint. During the robbery, they frame Bercq's wife's lover LeRoyer for the crime and he is arrested. Luckily for LeRoyer, a photographer working in the area happened to take pictures of the robbery, and the negatives clearly show Bercq as the guilty party. During the subsequent investigation, Briand is killed by the police while trying to escape, but Bercq manages to get away on a speed boat, taking along Michelle as his hostage. Eventually Bercq is cornered by the cops and killed.

p, Joel Lifschutz; d&w, Jean-Claude Dague, Louis Soulanes; ph, Jacques Robin (Techniscope, DeLuxe Color); m, Norbert Glazberg; ed, Monique Isnardon.

Crime **(PR:O MPAA:R)**

PLAYTHING, THE*½ (1929, Brit.) 78m BIP/Wardour bw

Estelle Brody *(Joyce Bennett)*, Heather Thatcher *(Martyn Bennett)*, Nigel Barrie *(Wallace McKinnel)*, Marguerite Allan *(Madeleine McKinnel)*, John St. John *(Claud)*, Raymond Milland *(Ian)*.

A feeble, part-dialogue romance that stars Barrie as a dull Scotsman who becomes smitten with Brody, a wild, vivacious and sophisticated woman used to the good life. Desperate to start a romance with Brody, Barrie makes a futile attempt at becoming the funny, sparkling and suave man of her dreams, but fails miserably. Realizing that it was just Brody's surface qualities that attracted him anyway, Barrie abandons his romantic notions and decides to be himself. PLAYTHING is one of the films made by Milland in Britain before his arrival in Hollywood in 1930. Milland, who started out with second leads and graduated to roles in which he played the suave, self-assured romantic leading man, would later win an Academy Award in 1945 for his performance as an alcoholic writer in THE LOST WEEKEND.

d, Castleton Knight; w, Violet Powell (based on the play "Life is Pretty Much the Same" by Arthur Black); ph, James Rodgers; prod d, N. Arnold.

Romance **(PR:A MPAA:NR)**

PLAYTIME*** (1963, Fr.) 87m General-Elite/Audubon bw (LA RECREATION; AKA: LOVE PLAY)

Jean Seberg *(Kate Hoover)*, Christian Marquand *(Philippe)*, Francoise Prevost *(Anne de Limeuil)*, Evelyn Ker *(Kate's Friend)*, Paulette Dubost *(Anne's Maid)*.

Fairly engrossing drama starring Seberg as a lonely and bored American student in Versailles who becomes fascinated by the life of a sculptor, Marquand, who lives next-door to her dorm with his patron, an older, rich woman Prevost. Distracted by a loud party being given at the house, Seberg dresses and climbs out her window for a closer look. Too intimidated to enter, she takes a walk and witnesses a fatal hit-and-run accident. Soon after, Seberg finally meets the man she has been voyeuristically fascinated with for so long. The pair soon falls into an affair (encouraged by Prevost, who wants Marquand to get this young girl out of his system as quickly as possible), but one day, while out for a drive, Seberg realizes that Marquand's car is the same one that was involved in the accident she witnessed. After making love to Marquand and feeling nothing in her heart for a man who would coldly take a life, she gives up the affair and returns to school.

p, Herve Messir; d, Francois Moreuil, Fabien Collin; w, Moreuil, Daniel Boulanger (based on a story by Francoise Sagan); ph, Jean Penzer; m, George Delerue; ed, Rene Le Henaff.

Drama **(PR:C MPAA:NR)**

PLAYTIME*½** (1973, Fr.) 108m Specta/Continental c

Jacques Tati *(Mons. Hulot)*, Barbara Dennek *(Young Tourist)*, Jacqueline Lecomte *(Her Friend)*, Valerie Camille *(Mons. Luce's Secretary)*, France Romilly *(Woman Selling Eyeglasses)*, France Delahalle *(Shopper in Department Store)*, Laure Paillette, Colette Proust *(Two Women at the Lamp)*, Erika Dentzler *(Mme. Giffard)*, Yvette Ducreux *(Hat Check Girl)*, Rita Maiden *(Mr. Schultz's Companion)*, Nicole Ray *(Singer)*, Jack Gauthier *(The Guide)*, Henri Piccoli *(An Important Gentleman)*, Leon Doyen *(Doorman)*, Billy Kearns *(Mons. Schultz)*, Francois Viaur *(Reinhart Kolldehoff, Michel Francini.*

Tati's fourth feature was 10 years in the making and he risked everything on it, even going so far as to sell off rights to his previous three films in order to raise the needed money for the immense modernistic set that he required for this. The result was an instant failure when it was released in France at 145 minutes. He soon cut it to 108 minutes, then to 93, but the damage had already been done. As in his other movies, there is no plot to speak of, just a series of incidents that Tati gets into and out of with no comment other than his boundless energy and incurable optimism. One gag after another comes off the screen and we are invited to make what we wish from the melee, which was a mistake on his part and a denial of his position that audiences would understand when to laugh without having to be pointed at the humor. Tati is again "Hulot," the gangly, pipe-smoking innocent who wanders in and out of places, wreaks havoc, and goes on. It's a satire of the glass-and-steel world that was coming to pass in the 1960s, and Tati spent all his money building a set that captured what he thought Paris would come to. In later years, the Pompidou Center, a bizarre slap in the face of the classical Parisian architecture, resembled "TatiVille" (the nickname of the set) by more than a passing likeness. Tati walks into the building to find someone and is soon lost in the maze of corridors. A herd of tourists from the U.S. arrive and Tati gets mixed in the crowd with predictable comic antics. He finds a pal and goes home to an area where people do live in glass houses, then he winds up in a building that is still being erected, a nightclub restaurant that he inadvertently tears down, as mayhem follows him wherever he goes. Since there is no plot, the movie is completely unpredictable and that is both its asset and its liability. A few lines in English are written by Washington columnist-humorist Art Buchwald which are the only verbal gags in an almost totally visual movie. (See MR. HULOT series, Index.)

p, Rene Silvera; d, Jacques Tati; w, Tati, Jacques Lagrange, Art Buchwald; ph, Jean Badal, Andreas Winding (Eastmancolor); m, Francis Lemarque, James Campbell; ed, Gerard Pollicand; prod d, Eugene Roman; m/l, "Take My Band," David Stein.

Comedy **Cas.** **(PR:AAA MPAA:NR)**

PLAZA SUITE**** (1971) 114m PAR c

Walter Matthau *(Sam Nash/Jesse Kiplinger/Roy Hubley)*, Maureen Stapleton *(Karen Nash)*, Jose Ocasio *(Waiter)*, Dan Ferrone *(Bellhop)*, Louise Sorel *(Miss McCormack)*, Barbara Harris *(Muriel Tate)*, Lee Grant *(Norma Hubley)*, Jennie Sullivan *(Mimsey Hubley)*, Tom Carey *(Borden Eisler)*.

To his credit, Neil Simon never stops trying to expand. With several solid successes in the comedy genre behind him, he attempted something here that wasn't merely a pack of one-liners, but had an underlying pathos and humanity. George C. Scott and Maureen Stapleton opened on Broadway in the show that ran more than 1, 000 performances with Mike Nichols directing. Stapleton returns to do one of the three vignettes with Lee Grant, who did the Road Show version, playing another of the parts, and Barbara Harris in the middle segment. Simon's plays are almost always one-set jobs and the task of adapting them for the screen is not an enviable one as movie fans will often carp that they are photographed stage plays of people talking with no cinematic value. Since this picture takes place in one suite at New York's Plaza Hotel, it is all the more evident. The only unifying force in the trio of stories is Matthau, in a tour-de-force job, as three very different men. There were to be four stories in the original and the one that was dropped was used as the basis for Simon's original screenplay of THE OUT-OF-TOWNERS. Director Hiller had just come off LOVE STORY and few people knew if he could direct a comedy but the Canadian had already done several episodes of various TV shows, including "I'm Dickens, He's Fenster." The first segment has Stapleton and Matthau in what she believes is the same suite they'd occupied 24 years before on their honeymoon night. He is a very successful businessman with little time for sentiment and Stapleton senses that this may be the finale to their marriage as he appears to be temporarily out of ardor. She is hoping that a return to the place where they spent their first night together may have some bearing on his attitude. She has room service bring his favorite meal, lean roast beef and champagne. Then, upon his arrival from the office, he tells her that their anniversary is on the following day, that they are in the wrong suite and that they are celebrating their 23rd, not their 24th anniversary. After the roast beef is delivered (far too fatty), Matthau says he will have to get back to his office to work, which destroys Stapleton's plans for a romantic tryst. His secretary, Sorel, arrives to leave some important documents and Stapleton sees right through their charade. Sorel leaves and Stapleton accuses Matthau of having an affair with the attractive Sorel and Matthau doesn't deny it. He's getting older, wonders if he's still got any sex appeal and is doing his best to confirm that with an office affair. She pleads with him to remain but he heads for the door and exits as the waiter brings the champagne. Yet, there is enough indication that, perhaps, Matthau will come to his senses and eventually return to this good woman who loves him more than life itself. One of Simon's best lines in the first sketch is a revelatory speech of Matthau's. He's now quite rich and it's bothering him. When Stapleton asks what it is that will make him happy, Matthau thinks a moment and answers: "I'd like to do it all again." (NOTE: Some years before this film, Sorel was tested with actor-author Stanley Ralph Ross to play in a film called "The Piano Sport" which was to have been directed by Hiller. The movie was never made but Hiller remembered both from the audition and hired Sorel for this and Ross for the role of the "Matinee Idol" in ROMANTIC COMEDY.) This first sketch is almost 50 minutes in length and could have done with a bit of trimming. The surprise is in Stapleton's character, who, while not being a "victim" manages to take the situation without alarm, almost as though it was predestined. In the 33-minute second segment, Matthau is the ultimate Hollywood producer, a man given to gold chains, lots of "babies" and "sweethearts" in his dialogue. He's in New York on business and has two hours to kill so he calls an old girl friend from 15 years before, Harris, who is now a married woman living in Tenafly, New Jersey. Harris, who has followed her high school crush's career over the years, races into town. Matthau pours vodka cocktails down her but Harris resists his advances, insisting all along that she has a terrific marriage. Matthau tries everything to seduce her, even lying about his "loneliness" at the top. Nothing seems to work until Matthau discovers that she is a movie junkie, one of those fans who reads every word about all the stars and who lives vicariously through the pages of the rags one finds at supermarket checkout stands. As he promises to tell her all the dirt about Sinatra and several other names he drops, he leads her into the bedroom and she giggles as she falls onto the bed. (NOTE: Anyone in the movie business who has achieved some sort of celebrity status and gone back to his or her home town will vouch for the validity of this premise.) The 37-minute third and final episode has Matthau and wife Grant in the suite as guests are gathering downstairs for the wedding of their daughter, Sullivan, and her groom, Carey. Sullivan has locked herself in the suite's bathroom and won't come out despite all the pleading by Matthau and Grant. Since the wedding is already paid for and the guests are getting restless, Matthau's frustration hits a peak when he attempts to break down the door and only succeeds in hurting his shoulder and ripping his formal clothing. He crawls out on the window ledge, is attacked by pigeons, drenched in a rainstorm and defeated by Sullivan's refusal to unlock the bathroom window. Carey arrives, walks to the door, yells "Cool It!" and tells Matthau and Grant that everything will be all right now. And it is. Sullivan comes out, the wedding goes off a bit later than expected and the couple ride off on a motorcycle. Matthau's character in the final sketch is similar to the man he played in the first but the wives are quite different. Of the female roles, Harris steals the picture, and that's not easy. Critics were divided in their assessment of PLAZA SUITE but we have to stand in the "Pro" corner. Simon has had some terrible adaptations (STAR SPANGLED GIRL) and even some bummer screenplays of his own, as in THE SLUGGER'S WIFE. This one made us laugh and cry at the same time and those are two emotions that are hard to come by in a single film.

p, Howard W. Koch; d, Arthur Hiller; w, Neil Simon (based on his play); ph, Jack Marta (Technicolor); m, Maurice Jarre; ed, Frank Bracht; md, Jarre; art d, Arthur Lonergan; set d, Reg Allen; cos, Jack Bear; m/l, "Tangerine," Johnny Mercer, Victor Schertzinger; makeup, Gary Morris.

Comedy **Cas.** **(PR:A-C MPAA:GP)**

PLEASANTVILLE** (1976) 85m Visions-KCET-Pleasantville c

Gale Sondergaard *(Ora)*, Suzanne Weber *(Sam)*, Michael Del Viscovo, Jr. *(Matthew)*, John Bottoms *(George)*, Robert Hitt *(Slattery)*, Marcia Jean Kurtz *(Jo)*.

Slow-moving, uneventful film detailing the relationship between a 12-year-old girl, Weber, and her 76-year-old grandmother Sondergaard (who came out of retirement for this film), at whose country home the girl stays for the summer. Eventually the pair grow close, and Sondergaard relates her determination not to be moved off her land by the uncaring contractors who seek to build on it. The girl is instilled with her grandmother's passion, and when the old woman dies, the little girl tries to fight off the workers, but in the end she must relent and let progress have its way. Fairly tedious, with only a few poignant moments to punctuate this otherwise dull tale.

d&w, Kenneth Locker, Vicki Polon; ph, Walter Lassally (TVC Chemtone Color); m, Michael Riesman; ed, Jill Godmillow.

Drama **(PR:A MPAA:NR)**

PLEASE BELIEVE ME½** (1950) 86m MGM bw

Deborah Kerr *(Alison Kirbe)*, Robert Walker *(Terence Keath)*, Mark Stevens *(Matthew Kinston)*, Peter Lawford *(Jeremy Taylor)*, James Whitmore *(Vincent Maran)*, J. Carrol Naish *(Lucky Reilly)*, Spring Byington *(Mrs. Milwright)*, Carol Savage *(Sylvia Rumley)*, Drue Mallory *(Beryl Robinson)*, George Cleveland *(Mr. Cooper)*, Ian Wolfe *(Edward Warrender)*, Bridget Carr *(Lily Milwright)*, Henri Letondal *(Jacques Carnet)*, Gaby Andre *(Mme. Carnet)*, Leon Belasco *(The Croupier)*.

Famed producer Val Lewton's (THE CAT PEOPLE, I WALKED WITH A ZOMBIE) last film, and it happened to be a romantic comedy. Kerr stars as an English girl who has just inherited a valuable 50,000 acre ranch in Texas. As she ventures to the Lone Star state to collect her fortune, opportunist Walker follows and tries to romance Kerr so that she will pay off his massive gambling debts. Also along on the trip are millionaire playboy Lawford, who's out for a good time, and his attorney Stevens, who's out to make sure his boss doesn't have *too* good a time. After all three men try their best to romance Kerr, it is the shy and unassuming Stevens who wins the lady's favor. Good cast of supporting players makes this rather average idea click.

p, Val Lewton; d, Norman Taurog; w, Nathaniel Curtis; ph, Robert Planck; m, Hans J. Salter; ed, Ferris Webster; art d, Cedric Gibbons, Daniel B. Cathcart; set d, Edwin B. Willis, cos, Irene.

Romance/Comedy **(PR:A MPAA:NR)**

PLEASE DON'T EAT THE DAISIES***   (1960) 111m Euterpe/MGM
c

Doris Day (*Kate Mackay*), David Niven (*Lawrence Mackay*), Janis Paige (*Deborah Vaughn*), Spring Byington (*Mrs. Suzie Robinson*), Richard Haydn (*Alfred North, Producer*), Patsy Kelly (*Maggie, Maid*), Jack Weston (*Joe Positano*), John Harding (*Rev. Dr. McQuarry*), Margaret Lindsay (*Mona James*), Charles Herbert (*David Mackay*), Stanley Livingston (*Gabriel Mackay*), Flip Mark (*George Mackay*), Baby Gellert (*Adam Mackay*), Carmen Phillips (*Mary Smith*), Mary Patton (*Mrs. Hunter*), Marina Koshetz (*Jane March*), Geraldine Wall (*Dr. Sprouk*), Kathryn Card (*Miss Yule, Principal*), Donald Foster (*Justin Winters*), Irene Tedrow (*Mrs. Greenfield*), Anatole Winogradoff (*Paul Foster*), Benny Rubin (*Pete*), Madge Blake (*Mrs. Kilkinny*), Peter Leeds (*Larry's Secretary*), Joe Cronin (*Pianist*), Burt Douglas, John Brennan, Guy Stockwell, (*Young Men*), Marianne Gaba (*Girl*), Len Lesser (*Waiter*), Wilson Wood (*Photographer*), Amy Douglass (*Martha*), Gail Bonney (*Woman*), Richard Collier (*Salesman*), Charles Seel (*Upholstery Man*), Frank Wilcox (*Interviewer*), Milton Frome (*Gus the Waiter*), Robert Darin (*Man*), Jhean Burton (*Actress*), Hobo the Dog.

Charming film comedy based on Jean Kerr's popular book which detailed the hectic family life of drama critic Niven, his wife Day, and their four children after they leave New York City and move into a massive, musty old mansion in the country. Admustment to life outside the hustle and bustle of the Big Apple, the hassles of raising four kids, the abuse one gets from being a professional critic, and, of course, new neighbors and in-laws are among the trials and tribulations dealt with by Day and Niven. A very pleasant light comedy that spawned a moderately successful television series featuring Patricia Crowley and Mark Miller in the lead roles. The film marked the return to the big screen for Paige, who had been absent since SILK STOCKINGS (1957), and Kelly, who had been away for 16 years.

p, Joe Pasternak; d, Charles Walters; w, Isobel Lennart (based on the book by Jean Kerr); ph, Robert Bronner (CinemaScope, Metrocolor); m, David Rose; ed, John McSweeney, Jr.; art d, George W. Davis, Hans Peters; set d, Henry Grace, Jerry Wunderlich; cos, Morton Haack; m/l, "Que Sera, Sera," Jay Livingston, Ray Evans, "Please Don't Eat the Daisies," Jay Lubin (sung by Doris Day), "Any Way the Wind Blows," Marilyn and Joe Hooven, by Dunham; (sung by Day); makeup, William Tuttle.

Comedy   **(PR:A MPAA:NR)**

PLEASE! MR. BALZAC*½   (1957, Fr.) 105m EGE-Hoche/Distributors Corp. of America bw (EN EFFEUILLANT LA MARGUERITE; AKA: WHILE PLUCKING THE DAISY; MADEMOISELLE STRIPTEASE)

Brigitte Bardot (*Agnes Dumont*), Daniel Gelin (*Daniel Roy*), Robert Hirsch (*Roger Vital*), Darry Cowl (*Hubert Dumont*), Jacques Dumensil (*Gen. Dumont*), Nadine Tallier (*Magali*), Luciana Paoluzzi (*Sophie*).

Mainly an excuse to show off the physical attributes of the voluptuous Bardot, who plays a young beauty given her first chance to break away from the restrictive reins of her general pappy. She abandons a train bound for school to stay in Paris with her museum custodian brother and drive some of the local males crazy. Pure mayhem which is at least effective in what it set out to do, that is to exploit B.B.

p, Raymond Eger; d, Marc Allegret; w, Allegret, Roger Vadim (based on an idea by William Benjamin); ph, Louis Page; m, Paul Misraki; ed, Suzanne De Troeye.

Comedy   **(PR:C MPAA:NR)**

PLEASE MURDER ME*½   (1956) 78m Distributors Corp. of America bw

Angela Lansbury (*Myra Leeds*), Raymond Burr (*Craig Carlson*), Dick Foran (*Joe Leeds*), John Dehner (*District Attorney*), Lamont Johnson (*Carl Holt*), Robert Griffin (*Lou Kazorian*), Denver Pyle (*Lt. Bradley*), Alex Sharpe (*Sergeant*), Lee Miller (*Policeman*), Madge Blake (*Jenny*), Russ Thorson (*Judge*).

Hopelessly contrived thriller starring Burr as a love sick attorney who learns that his client, Lansbury, (the object of his affections), did indeed kill her husband. Guilt ridden because he has helped her get away with murder, Burr arranges for Lansbury to kill him, so that some semblence of justice will be done. She agrees wholeheartedly to kill the poor sap, because she is involved with a young artist and it would be a load off her mind to do away with the bothersome, fawning attorney. Decent cast *almost* pulls this one into the realm of believability, but not quite.

p, Donald Hyde; d, Peter Godfrey; w, Al C. Ward, Hyde; ph, Allen Stensvold; ed, Kenny Crane; art d, Nick Remisoff.

Crime Drama   **(PR:A MPAA:NR)**

PLEASE, NOT NOW!**   (1963, Fr./Ital.) 74m Francos-Vides/FOX bw
(LA BRIDE SUR LE COU; A BRIGLIA SCIOLTA)

Brigitte Bardot (*Sophie*), Josephine James (*Barbara*), Mireille Darc (*Marie-Jeanne*), Edith Zetling (*Josette*), Michel Subor (*Alain*), Jacques Riberolles (*Philippe*), Claude Brasseur (*Claude*), Serge Marquand (*Prince*), Jean Tissier (*Concierge*), Bernard Fresson (*Serge*), Claude Berri (*Bernard*), Max Montavon (*Waiter*).

Another Bardot-Vadim collaboration, this one stars B.B. as a Parisian model who discovers that her photographer-boyfriend Riberolles has been seeing a young American heiress, James, behind her back. Subor, a man who has worshiped Bardot from afar, suggests she get Riberolles back by making love to him (Subor). She rejects this idea and is determined to settle things the way her Corsican grandmother did—shoot him. Subor warns Ribberolles of his impending fate, and the two-timer grabs James and heads for the Alps. Bardot and Subor follow, with Subor still trying to get Bardot to notice him. After the women have convinced each other that the men in their company are worthless, they team up against the men. Notable only for the controversial "nude" dance scene performed by Bardot, which was cut by the British censors (the scene is in soft-focus and in the production stills it is obvious she wears a body stocking).

p, Jacques Roitfeld; d, Jack Dunn Trop (English version), Roger Vadim; w, Trop

(English version), Claude Brule, Vadim (based on an idea by Jean Aurel); ph, Robert Le Febvre (CinemaScope); m, James Campbell; ed, Albert Jurgenson; art d, Robert Clavel; ch, Michel Renault.

Romance/Comedy   **(PR:C MPAA:NR)**

PLEASE SIR*½   (1971, Brit.) 101m Rank/LWL c

John Alderton, Deryck Guyler, Joan Sanderson, Noel Howlett, Eric Chitty, Richard Davies.

It's that time of year again when the teachers and students of the Fenn Street school head off for a camping trip full of zany, madcap fun which apparently was mistaken by this film's producers as comedy. The film's characters were from a popular British television series but their humor didn't survive the trip to the big screen with much success.

p, Andrew Mitchell; d, Mark Stuart; w, John Esmonde, Bob Larbey; ph, Wilkie Cooper (Eastmancolor); m, Mike Vickers.

Comedy   **(PR:A MPAA:NR)**

PLEASE STAND BY*   (1972) 120m Milton bw

David Peel (*Freemont Zapata*), Wendy Appel (*Marian*), Alex Bennett (*Narrator*), A.J. Weberman (*A.J.*), Roberts Blossom (*Judge Nott*), Charlie (*Cpl. Tuck*), Walter Hadler (*Hugo*).

A misfired low-budget independent shot on 16mm by a husband and wife team of teachers/filmmakers, Jack and Joanne Milton. The film details the activities of a group of New York-based radicals who have stolen some sophisticated electronic equipment and plan to jam the airwaves of the major networks with public service announcements of their own. The group has filmed messages expounding the evils of war, capitalism and other social ills, while pleading for the standard goals of peace, love, and understanding. Though the messages may be less than radical, the FBI will not allow the jamming of the network's airwaves. In an effort to smash the group of broadcast pirates, agents infiltrate the radicals and eventually have enough evidence to throw their leader, Peel, in the clink. After a lengthy trial, Peel is convicted, but his pals break him out of jail and he becomes the stuff of legend among radicals. While the film may have its heart in the right place, the Miltons belittle their efforts by inserting countless movie parodies and unnecessary satire which only tends to weaken the film as a whole.

p,d&w, Jack Milton, Joanna Milton; ph, Paul Goldsmith, Arthur Albert.

Drama/Comedy   **(PR:C MPAA:NR)**

PLEASE TEACHER**   (1937, Brit.) 75m Associated British Pictures/
Wardour bw

Bobby Howes (*Tommy Deacon*), Rene Ray (*Ann Trent*), Wylie Watson (*Oswald Clutterbuck*), Bertha Belmore (*Agatha Pink*), Vera Pearce (*Petunia Trundle*), Lyn Harding (*Wing Foo*), Aubrey Dexter (*Reeves*), Arthur Chesney (*Round*).

Deacon stars as an unemployed rogue who, after sobering up from the previous night's bender in a Turkish bath, receives a telegram informing him that he has inherited a fortune from his deceased aunt and the cash is hidden in a bust of Napoleon in the house that she has left him. He rushes off to the country to collect his windfall, but is shocked to find that it is now a girl's school and he isn't allowed in. This forces Deacon to pose as the brother of one of the girls so that he can gain access to the estate and wander somewhat freely. Of course, a bunch of silly complications ensue.

p, Walter C. Mycroft; d&w, Stafford Dickens (based on the play by K.R.G. Browne, R.P. Weston, Bert Lee); ph, Otto Kanturek.

Comedy   **(PR:A MPAA:NR)**

PLEASE TURN OVER***   (1960, Brit.) 87m Anglo-Amalgamated/COL
bw

Ted Ray (*Edward Halliday*), Jean Kent (*Janet Halliday*), Leslie Phillips (*Dr. Henry Manners*), Joan Sims (*Beryl*), Julia Lockwood (*Jo Halliday*), Tim Seely (*Robert Hughes*), Charles Hawtrey (*Jeweler*), Dilys Laye (*Millicent Jones*), Lionel Jeffries (*Ian Howard*), June Jago (*Gladys Worth*), Colin Gordon (*Maurice*), Joan Hickson (*Saleswoman*), Victor Maddern (*Smithy*), Ronald Adam (*Mr. Appleton*), Cyril Chamberlain (*Mr. Jones*), George Street (*Removal Man*), Marianne Stone (*Mrs. Waring*), Leigh Madison (*Cashier*), Myrtle Reed (*Mrs. Moore*), Anthony Sagar (*Barman*), Celia Hewitt (*Young Woman*), Noel Dyson (*Mrs. Brent*), Paul Cole (*Newspaper Boy*), George Howell (*Butcher's Boy*), Lucy Griffiths, Ursula Hirst, Beryl Hardy, Patrick Durkin, Dominica More O'Ferrall.

Consistently funny British comedy about a precocious, suburban teenage girl, Lockwood, who writes a steamy best-selling novel called *Naked Revolt* based on the scandals to be found in her neighborhood. This causes much craziness when the neighbors all begin treating each other as if they were the actual fictitious characters in the girl's novel. Her father, Ray, is suddenly looked upon as a swindler and philanderer; her aunt a drunk; her uncle and mother as lovers; and the girl herself as a teenage hooker. Done with taste and good humor, PLEASE TURN OVER is a witty and insightful look at suburban paranoia and morals, and at fantasy. This was one of the first major roles for Julia Lockwood, daughter of renowned British actress Margaret Lockwood. A leading lady in her own right, the younger Lockwood first appeared in films at the age of 5.

p, Peter Rogers; d, Gerald Thomas; w, Norman Hudis (based on the play "Book of the Month" by Basil Thomas); ph, Ted Scaife; m, Bruce Montgomery; ed, John Shirley.

Comedy   **(PR:C MPAA:NR)**

PLEASURE zero   (1933) 51m Supreme/Artclass bw

Conway Tearle, Carmel Myers, Francis Dade, Paul Page, Roscoe Karns, Lina Basquette, Harold Goodwin.

Cheap, technically incompetent drama about an author who starts an affair with a model, but doesn't tell her that he's married. Unfortunately his brother happens to be in love with the girl, and when the writer's wife dumps him, and his girl leaves him, he finds his life in ruins.

d, Otto Brower; w, Jo von Ronkel, Thomas Thiteley (based on a story by John Varley); ph, Sidney Hickox; ed, Tom Pearsons.

Drama (PR:A MPAA:NR)

PLEASURE CRAZED*½ (1929) 60m FOX bw

Marguerite Churchill (Nora Westby), Kenneth MacKenna (Capt. Anthony Dean), Dorothy Burgess (Alma Dean), Campbell Gullan (Gilbert Ferguson), Douglas Gilmore (Nigel Blain), Henry Kolker (Col. Farquar), Frederick Graham (Holland), Rex Bell (Peters, Chauffeur), Charlotte Merriam (Maid).

Strictly a programmer, PLEASURE CRAZED had a predictable story with not very good acting. Burgess is married to MacKenna but cheating on him. Meanwhile, Churchill is in love with MacKenna but she won't make a move on the man as he's married. Churchill is involved in a criminal conspiracy, not of her own doing, and would like to get out of it but is so inextricably enmeshed in the scam that she's having a problem pulling out. Donald Gallagher directed the original stage play and received a credit on the film so it must be assumed he staged the actions while Klein took care of the camera moves. Churchill, who would always be remembered for her work in DRACULA'S DAUGHTER, THE WALKING DEAD, LEGION OF TERROR, and several other quickies, manages to convince us of her essential innocence. Bell, born George Beldam, was a cowboy actor in later years. He married Clara Bow, the "It" girl, and moved to Nevada where he may have been the first actor to ever achieve a political office, something that has happened on numerous occasions since.

d, Charles Klein, Donald Gallagher; w, Douglas Z. Doty, Clare Kummer (based on the play "Scent of Sweet Almonds" by Monckton Hoffe); ph, Ernest Palmer, Glen MacWilliams; ed, J. Edwin Robbins; cos, Sophie Wachner.

Drama (PR:A MPAA:NR)

PLEASURE CRUISE*½ (1933) 70m FOX bw

Genevieve Tobin (Shirley Poole), Roland Young (Andrew Poole), Ralph Forbes (Richard Orloff), Una O'Connor (Mrs. Signus), Herbert Mundin (Henry), Minna Gombell (Judy), Theodore Von Eltz (Murchison), Frank Atkinson (Alf), Robert Greig (Crum), Arthur Hoyt (Rollins).

Tobin plays the bored wife of novelist Young, who, after an argument with her spouse, decides to leave for a while and sets out on a pleasure cruise, hoping for romance. She meets suave-but-sly playboy Forbes, and thinks it is he who visits her in her cabin in the dead of night, but it turns out to be her husband, who had used his pull with the owner of the shipping line to get a job as an on-board barber, so that he could keep an eye on his spouse.

d, Frank Tuttle; w, Guy Bolton (based on the play by Austen Allen); ph, Ernest Palmer; ed, Alex Troffey.

Romance (PR:A MPAA:NR)

PLEASURE GIRL (SEE: GIRL WITH A SUITCASE, 1961, Fr./Ital.)

PLEASURE GIRLS, THE*½ (1966, Brit.) 88m Compton-Tekli/Times Film bw

Ian McShane (Keith Dexter), Francesca Annis (Sally Feathers), Klaus Kinski (Nikko), Mark Eden (Prinny), Tony Tanner (Paddy), Rosemary Nicols (Marion), Suzanna Leigh (Dee), Anneke Wills (Angela), Coleen Fitzpatrick (Cobber).

Country girl Annis arrives in London seeking to become a famous model. She soon finds herself rooming in a house with three other girls, Leigh, Nicols, and Fitzpatrick, and Leigh's brother Tanner. While looking to be discovered, Annis meets dashing young photographer McShane and the two are attracted to each other. Meanwhile, Nicols becomes disillusioned with her beau when she discovers that she's pregnant and he encourages her to get an abortion. Leigh finally learns that her lover, Kinski, is a notorious crook and swindler. Even Annis' budding romance comes to an end when the overzealous McShane misreads some body language and tries to seduce her. Upset, she goes home to be confronted by the always understanding Tanner, but she is shocked when she interrupts him while he is in the arms of his homosexual lover. By the next morning, after having had time to think things over, she decides to forgive McShane and is delighted to find him waiting outside the house in his car to drive her to modeling school. An unsuccessful attempt to illustrate young women's problems in the wild and turbulent 1960s.

p, Harry Fine; d&w, Gerry O'Hara; ph, Michael Reed; m, Malcolm Lockyer; ed, Tony Palk; md, Lockyer; art d, Peter James; m/l, "The Pleasure Girls," Bob Barratt (sung by The Three Quarters); makeup, Ken MacKay.

Drama (PR:C MPAA:NR)

PLEASURE LOVER (SEE: PLEASURE LOVERS, THE, 1964, Brit.)

PLEASURE LOVERS, THE** (1964, Brit.) 73m BUT/Joseph Brenner bw (GB: NAKED FURY; AKA: PLEASURE LOVER)

Leigh Madison (Carol), Reed De Rouen (Eddie), Kenneth Cope (Johnny), Arthur Lovegrove (Syd), Thomas Eytle (Steve), Alexander Field (Vic), Arthur Gross (Tom Parker), Ann Lynn (Judy), Marianne Brauns (Joy), Redmond Phillips (Inspector Stevens), Michael Collins (Detective), Eric Woodburn (Frank), Anne Sharpe (Nurse), Petite (The Exotic Dancer).

Routine crime thriller starring De Rouen as an American in England who masterminds a daring bank robbery with the help of three fairly unstable accomplices. Things go wrong when the gang is forced to kill a nightwatchman and kidnap his daughter (Madison). While waiting for two days at a hideout for their getaway boat, Madison's presence causes trouble among the men. De Rouen, who has become

genuinely attracted to the girl, and she to him (inexplicably, after he rapes her), begins to protect her from the others. Alienated by their boss, the other men decide to take the loot for themselves, which leads to a violent struggle. During the fight, the crumbling old building being used for the hideout begins to collapse. De Rouven dies, along with the other crooks, after sacrificing himself to save Madison.

p, Guido Coen; d, Charles Saunders; w, Brock Williams (based on an original story by Coen); ph, James Harvey; ed, Peter Pitt; md, Edwin Astley; art d, Duncan Sutherland.

Crime (PR:C MPAA:NR)

PLEASURE OF HIS COMPANY, THE** (1961) 114m Perlsea-PAR/PAR c

Fred Astaire (Biddeford "Pogo" Poole), Debbie Reynolds (Jessica Poole), Lilli Palmer (Katharine Dougherty), Tab Hunter (Roger Henderson), Gary Merrill (James Dougherty), Charles Ruggles (Mackenzie Savage), Harold Fong (Toy), Elvia Allman (Mrs. Mooney, the Wedding Counselor), Edith Head (Dress Designer).

Fred Astaire did not make very many nonmusical films. This was his second after ON THE BEACH and it felt like a musical without the songs and dances. The original play role was done by Cyril Ritchard and although it was not a hugh success in New York or London, it remains an enduring play that is often seen in little theaters, dinner theaters and, because the content is so squeaky clean, at schools. Astaire is a playboy who returns to San Francisco after not having been there or seen his daughter, Reynolds, for 15 years. She is young and had forgotten how suave her dad was and she is immensely captivated by his charm, which eludes his former wife, Palmer. It's just a few days before Reynolds' wedding and Astaire takes over, altering the plans, changing arrangements, etc. Reynolds is engaged to Hunter, a wealthy but unsophisticated rancher and the difference between the two men is instantly evident. She soon finds Hunter to be rather boorish and arguments erupt. Astaire doesn't think Hunter is worthy of Reynolds and is happy at this turn of events. Palmer is now married to Merrill, a rich man, and Astaire does his best to break that up as well. Merrill begins to be jealous of the way Astaire has insinuated himself into the lives of everyone. The group visits Hunter's spread and Astaire sprains one of his limbs. Reynolds aborts the wedding and tells everyone that she intends spending the next few years traveling with Astaire and helping him through his dotage. Astaire, who had never thought of himself as being old, is not enthused at Reynolds' declaration and bids the wedding go on. It does and Astaire departs taking two souvenirs, a photograph of Reynolds as a child and Merrill's superb house boy, Fong. They are happy and depressed about Astaire. While he was there, he was a disturbing influence but he was so darned interesting that there was no doubt about the pleasure of his company. Ruggles chimes in with some good comedy timing as the remaining grandfather and the picture always seems to be on the verge of song and dance but, aside from the title song, there is none. Edith Head does a cameo as a dress designer.

p, William Perlberg; d, George Seaton; w, Samuel Taylor (based on the play by Taylor, Cornelia Otis Skinner); ph, Robert Burks (Technicolor); m, Alfred Newman; ad, Alma Macrorie; md, Newman; art d, Hal Pereira, Tambi Larsen; set d, Sam Comer, Frank R. McKelvy; cos, Edith Head; spec eff, John P. Fulton; ch, Fred Astaire, Hermes Pan; m/l, "The Pleasure of His Company," Alfred Newman, Sammy Cahn; makeup, Wally Westmore.

Comedy (PR:A MPAA:NR)

PLEASURE PLANTATION zero (1970) 80m Republic Amusements c

William Scope (Jonah Hunt), Gerald Nomes (Jason Hunt), Karil Holmes (Rachel Hunt), Kim Bishop (Lee Hunt), Mike Naylor (Terrence Black), Bob Charles (Cogswell), Linda Boyers (Ruby), Jackie Glenn (Lorna), Sheba Brittan (Prissy), Matt Fortune (Billy Joe), Susan Winters, Jean Parks, Phyllis Randall (Sporting House Girls).

Sick Southern plantation drama set in the 1860s detailing the lives of a bizarre family made up of two brothers, Scope and Nomes, and two sisters, Holmes and Bishop. Scope owns the plantation, Nomes is a drunk, Bishop is a "retarded" nymphomaniac, and Holmes connives to get sole ownership of the homestead. After dozens of revolting episodes involving rape, murder and duels, Holmes realizes her ambitions, only to discover that the Confederate Army has seized the plantation. Upon learning the news, she promptly goes insane and kills herself. This film is definitely one to avoid.

p, Anthony Scaretti; d, Jerry Denby; w, Jon Statkis; ph, Harry August, Joe Mangine (Eastmancolor); m, DAS Associates; ed, Jet Motion Pictures; set d, Dick May.

Drama (PR:O MPAA:NR)

PLEASURE SEEKERS, THE½** (1964) 106m FOX c

Ann-Margret (Fran Hobson), Tony Franciosa (Emilio Lacaye), Carol Lynley (Maggie Williams), Gardner McKay (Pete Stenello), Pamela Tiffin (Susie Higgins), Andre Lawrence (Dr. Andres Briones), Gene Tierney (Jane Barton), Brian Keith (Paul Barton), Vito Scotti (Neighbor Man), Isobel Elsom (Dona Teresa Lacaye), Maurice Marsac (Jose), Shelby Grant (Marian, American Girl), Raoul De Leon (Martinez), Antonio Gades (Flamenco Dancer), Emilio Diego (Guitarist), Ida Romero, Peter Brocco.

Decent enough remake of THREE COINS IN THE FOUNTAIN stars Ann-Margret, Lynley and Tiffin as three American girls who are vacationing in Madrid and looking for romance. The prospective husbands are McKay, an American reporter, Franciosa, a wealthy playboy, and Lawrence, a successful young doctor. While the gals are romancing the guys, the audience is treated to a beautifully photographed travelog of Spain. Negulesco also directed the original film upon which this was based. Songs include "Something to Think About," "Everything Makes Music

When You're in Love," "The Pleasure Seekers," "Next Time" (Sammy Cahn, James Van Heusen; sung by Ann-Margret).

p, David Weisbart; d, Jean Negulesco; w, Edith Sommer (based on the novel by John H. Secondari); ph, Daniel L. Fapp (CinemaScope, DeLuxe Color); m, Lionel Newman; ed, Louis Loeffler; art d, Jack Martin Smith, Edward Carrere; set d, Walter M. Scott, Stuart A. Reiss; cos, Renie; ch, Robert Sidney, Antonio Gades; makeup, Ben Nye.

Romance/Musical   **(PR:A MPAA:NR)**

PLEASURES AND VICES**   (1962, Fr.) 86m Lutetia/William Mishkin c (GUEULE D'ANGE)

Maurice Ronet (Angel Face), Viviane Romance (Loina), Genevieve Kervine (Marie), Simone Paris (Mme. de Fourcroy), Rene Havard ("Caniche"), Dora Doll, France Roche, Elisa Lamothe, Louis Viret, Rosy Varte, Danik Patisson, Roger Normand, Jean-Jacques Lecot, San Juan, Catherine Michard, Robert Seller, Jacques Herrien, Gerard Rolland, Colette Mareuil, Paul Demange.

French romantic melodrama stars Ronet as a dashing gigolo who earns a living by selling the gifts given to him by his lovers. One of his lovers, Kervine, announces she is pregnant, hoping this will encourage him to abandon his lifestyle and settle down. He coldly rejects her, however, and she later has a miscarriage. Meanwhile, Ronet accepts a challenge from a man he meets in a bar to try and seduce Romance, a beautiful woman known to engage in several love affairs at a time. After meeting her and beginning an affair, he slowly starts to feel deep jealousy when she makes love to other men, despite her warnings that she would do so. Eventually she tires of him and moves on, leaving Ronet despondent but aware of the pain that he has inflicted on women.

p, Georges Senamaud, Albert Mazaleyrat; d&w, Marcel Blistene (based on a play by Roger Normand); ph, Jean Isnard; ed, Jacques Mavel; art d, Fred Marpeaux; makeup, Louis Bonnemaison.

Drama   **(PR:C MPAA:NR)**

PLEASURES OF THE FLESH, THE½   (1965) 104m Sozo-sha/ Shochiku c (ETSURAKU)

Katsuo Nakamura (Wakizaka), Mariko Kaga (Shoko), Yumiko Nogawa (Hitomi), Masako Yagi (Shizuko), Toshiko Higuchi (Keiko), Hiroko Shimizu (Mari), Shoji Kobayashi, Mitsuhiro Toura, Akira Hamada, Fumio Watanabe, Naramasa Komatsu, Mamoru Hirata, Daigo Kusano, Kei Sato.

A minor Oshima film, made late in the director's career, details the romantic life of young college graduate Nakamura who is shocked to hear that his long lost love Kaga is about to be married. Years ago, he had saved her from a blackmailer who agreed not to reveal he had raped her. To avenge the rape, Nakamura killed the man, and the police never solved the crime. However, Nakamura is later contacted by a man who had witnessed the murder and kept his silence. The witness, now a powerful, corrupt politician, blackmails Nakamura into holding a fortune he embezzled until he completes a five-year prison sentence. After four years of loneliness and poverty, Nakamura decides to risk death and spend the money, and he soon falls into a series of meaningless affairs with women only out for his money. Eventually he marries a kindly young nurse, but he is plagued by nightmares in which the corrupt official returns for his money. One night he learns that the man has died in prison, and his troubles are over. He later runs into Kaga, who offers to sleep with him if he will make a loan to her bankrupt husband. Nakamura regretfully informs her that he has spent all of the money, and proceeds to tell her about the murder and blackmail. The next day, the police arrive and arrest him, and he is told that it was Kaga who turned him in.

p, Masayuki Nakajima; d&w, Nagisa Oshima (based on the story "Kan No Naka No Etsuraku" by Futaro Yamada); ph, Akira Takada (Shochiku GrandScope, Eastmancolor); m, Joji Yuasa; art d, Yasutaro Kon.

Drama   **(PR:C MPAA:NR)**

PLEDGEMASTERS, THE zero   (1971) 87m Caracal/Signature c

Bruce Gregory, David Knapp (Pledgemasters), Michael Tremor (Pledge No. 1), James Palmer (Pledge No. 2), Trevor Tiffany (Pledge No. 3), Larry Kennedy (Pledge No. 4).

A "dramatization" of an actual college fraternity hazing shot on 16mm with four student volunteers starring as the candidates. Sadistic tortures the students are subjected to are re-created in detail. THE PLEDGEMASTERS is a disgusting, voyeuristic exploitation film, rather than an insightful examination of a serious problem on the nation's campuses.

p&d, David P. Parrish; w, (based on an idea by Bruce Gregory, David Knapp); ph, Parrish (Metrocolor); ed, Paul Brooks.

Drama   **(PR:O MPAA:NR)**

PLEIN SOLEIL   (SEE: PURPLE NOON, 1961, Fr./Ital.)

PLEURE PAS LA BOUCHE PLEINE   (SEE: DON'T CRY WITH YOUR MOUTH FULL, 1974, Fr.)

PLOT THICKENS, THE, 1935   (SEE: HERE COMES COOKIE, 1935)

PLOT THICKENS, THE*½   (1936) 67m RKO bw (GB: THE SWINGING PEARL MYSTERY)

James Gleason (Oscar Piper), ZaSu Pitts (Hildegarde Withers), Owen Davis, Jr. (Robert Wilkins), Louise Latimer (Alice Stevens), Arthur Aylesworth (Kendall), Richard Tucker (John Carter), Paul Fix (Joe), Barbara Barondess (Marie), James Dolan (Jim), Agnes Anderson (Dagmar), Oscar Apfel (Robbins).

The worst of the short-lived series of Stuart Palmer murder mysteries featured the whodunit team of Oscar Piper and Hildegard Withers. While Gleason held his role as the gruff police inspector, a miscast Pitts replaced Helen Broderick (who had previously replaced Edna May Oliver). Pitts' usual flighty antics failed to convince audiences that she could have possibly figured out the convoluted mystery surrounding two seemingly unrelated murders. At length it is revealed that the killings are tied to a scheme by a gang of international art thieves to steal artifacts from a museum.

p, William Sistrom; d, Ben Holmes; w, Clarence Upson Young, Jack Townley (based on a story by Stuart Palmer); ph, Nick Masuraca; ed, John Leckert.

Mystery   **(PR:A MPAA:NR)**

PLOT TO KILL ROOSEVELT, THE   (SEE: CONSPIRACY IN TEHERAN, 1948, Brit.)

PLOUGH AND THE STARS, THE**   (1936) 72m RKO bw

Barbara Stanwyck (Nora Clitheroe), Preston Foster (Jack Clitheroe), Barry Fitzgerald (Fluther Good), Denis O'Dea (The Young Covey), Eileen Crowe (Bessie Burgess), F.J. McCormick (Capt. Brennon), Arthur Shields (Padraic Pearse), Una O'Connor (Maggie Cogan), Moroni Olsen (Gen. Connally), Bonita Granville (Mollser Cogan), J.M. Kerrigan (Peter Flynn), Erin O'Brien-Moore (Rosie Redmond), Neil Fitzgerald (Lt. Kangon), Robert E. Homans (Tommy the Barman), Wesley Barry (Sniper), Brandon Hurst (Sgt. Tinley), Cyril McLaglen (Cpl. Stoddart), D'Arcy Corrigan (Priest), Mary Gordon, Doris Lloyd (Women at Barricades), Mary Quinn (2nd Woman), Lionel Pape (Englishman), Michael Fitzmaurice, Gaylord [Steve]Pendleton (ICA), Frank Hagney, Jack Pennick, Lillian O'Malley, Patricia O'Malley, Francis Ford, Ernie Shields, Ben Hall, Pat Moriarty, Billy Watson, Buck Mack, Margaret Morris, The Irish Abbey Players.

This turbulent tale of the 1916 Easter Rebellion in Ireland was not one of Ford's better efforts, the unwieldy story and RKO's interfering ways having much to do with the classic gone wrong as any other reason. Yet it remains as a stirring if disjointed portrait of the Irish fight for freedom. Stanwyck runs a Dublin boarding house and persuades her patriotic husband Foster to drop his ties with the Irish Citizen Army (loosely termed for the IRA, the Irish Republican Army). Yet when he hears the news that he has been named a commander, Foster rallies to the ranks. Though she tries to protect Foster from his own burning politics, Stanwyck is unsuccessful in having her husband put aside his gun. Foster goes on to command the takeover of the post office during the Dublin uprising which leads to a brief triumph and a bitter failure at the film's end. Stanwyck is excellent as a woman who only wishes to live in peace and hold on to the man she loves. Foster is convincing as the heroic underground leader, a role he had played earlier in Ford's masterpiece, THE INFORMER (1936). The O'Casey play suffered in the film version since RKO demanded that the romance angle take precedence over the historical material dealing with the Irish Rebellion, something that Ford and his erstwhile scenarist Nichols vainly fought against. The battle scenes in the streets are chillingly realistic and this is where Ford shines. Excellent in support are the Abbey Theatre Players, including Fitzgerald, O'Dea, Crowe, McCormick, and Shields. (Arthur Shields was Barry Fitzgerald's brother who had changed his name so as not to tag after his brother's sterling reputation; Shields served as an unofficial assistant director to Ford in keeping the Abbey players in line.) After Ford completed this film, RKO ordered George Nicholls, Jr., to reshoot certain scenes to heighten the romance aspect of the film and when Ford heard about this he exploded, demanding that his name be removed from the credits. His contract with RKO, however, stipulated that he would have to stand still for such tampering and Ford vowed never again to deal with RKO. Years later he would distribute his great U.S. Cavalry trilogy (FORT APACHE, SHE WORE A YELLOW RIBBON, and RIO GRANDE) through this studio under his own production banner of Argosy Pictures. O'Casey's title stems from the flag the IRA flew during the Easter Rebellion, one bearing a plough surrounded by stars.

p, Cliff Reid, Robert Sisk; d, John Ford; w, Dudley Nichols (based on the play by Sean O'Casey); ph, Joseph H. August; m, Roy Webb; ed, George Hively; md, Nathaniel Shilkret; art d, Van Nest Polglase, Carroll Clark; set d, Darrell Silvera; cos, Walter Plunkett; makeup, Bill Cooley.

Drama   **(PR:A MPAA:NR)**

PLUCKED**½   (1969, Fr./Ital.) 90m Summa Cinematografica-Cine Azimut-Les Films Corona/U-M c (LA MORTE HA FATTO L'UOVO, LA MORT A PONDU UN OEUF)

Gina Lollobrigida (Anna), Jean-Louis Trintignant (Marco), Ewa Aulin (Gabri), Jean Sobieski (Mondaini), Renato Romano (Luigi), Giulio Donnini (Motel Manager), Vittorio Andre, Ugo Adinolfi, Cleofe Del Cile, Biagio Pelligra, Conrad Anderson, Livio Ferraro.

The title is worse than the movie. Trintignant stars as the downtrodden husband of domineering wife Lollobrigida, who makes him work the modern chicken factory she owns. The only solace in his miserable existence is the local brothel. A change in his life occurs when his wife's sister, Aulin, arrives to live with them. Trintignant soon has an affair with the girl, and he confides in her his secret plan to kill his wife. Aulin, however, is actually in love with art designer Sobieski, and together they plan to kill Lollobrigida and Trintignant so Aulin will inherit the farm. That night, the evil couple kill Lollobrigida and try to frame Trintignant for the murder. Their plan fails, however, when the now-widowed Trintignant takes his wife's body back to the chicken farm and tries to dump it in the chicken-food machine. Trintignant slips and falls into the machine, killing himself. The police arrive and catch Aulin and Sobieski with both Lollobrigida's body and Trintignant's remains.

p, Franco Marras; d, Guilio Questi, w, Questi, Franco Arcalli; ph, Dario Di Palma (Eastmancolor); m, Bruno Maderna; ed, Arcalli; art d, Sergio Canevasi.

Crime   **(PR:C-O MPAA:NR)**

PLUMBER, THE***½   (1980, Aus.) 76m South Australian Film Corp.-Australian Film Commission-TCN/Cinema Ventures c

Judy Morris (Jill Cowper), Robert Coleby (Brain Cowper), Ivar Kants (Max the Plumber), Candy Raymond (Meg), Henri Szeps (Department Head).

Originally made for Australian television, Weir shows his directorial skill by taking the flimsiest of material and turning it into a taut, tension packed drama, while getting in his jabs at upper-middle class liberalist ideals. The simple premise has Kants as a plumber who invades the home of Morris and Coleby and proceeds to drive Morris into a state of near-hysteria. Though the couple never called for a plumber, Kants appears at the doorstep of their modern flat, gear in hand, and Morris lets him in without a question. But he sticks around for a couple of days, talks about his time in prison and makes an incredible design out of the bathroom pipes. Morris soon becomes a paranoid neurotic, unable to find any sympathy from her husband. But just as quickly as Kants arrived, he finishes the job, packs his gear and leaves, seemingly hurt by the way Morris starts treating him after her initial pleasantries. Tension and suspense continually build, putting THE PLUMBER on a level with Hitchcock's SUSPICION as a treatise in psychological drama.

p, Matt Carroll; d&w, Peter Weir; ph, David Sanderson (Colorfilm Color); m, Gerry Tolland; ed, G. Tunney-Smith; art d, Ken James, Herbert Pinter.

Drama   Cas.   (PR:C-O MPAA:NR)

PLUNDER**   (1931, Brit.) 95m British and Dominions bw

Tom Walls (Freddie Malone), Ralph Lynn (Darcy Tuck), Winifred Shotter (Joan Hewlett), Robertson Hare (Oswald Veal), Doreen Bendix (Prudence Malone), Sydney Lynn (Simon Veal), Ethel Coleridge (Mrs. Orlock), Hubert Waring (Inspector Sibley).

Film adaptation of a British stage farce has all teeth and monocled funnyman Lynn teaming with his old stage pal, Walls, a professional jewel thief, to steal the gems his fiancee, Shotter, is cheated out of by the housekeeper. They pull off the theft, but when Lynn finds out that the old housekeeper committed bigamy to get the gems, he makes a deal with her to split the value. The teaming of Lynn and Walls makes for some witty humor, and bald Hare does his part, but the entire production is photographed as though performed for the stage, and lacks any cinematic emphasis.

p, Herbert Wilcox; d, Tom Walls; w, W.P. Lipscomb (based on the play by Ben Travers); ph, F.A. Young.

Comedy   (PR:A MPAA:NR)

PLUNDER OF THE SUN**½   (1953) 81m WB bw

Glenn Ford (Al Colby), Diana Lynn (Julie Barnes), Patricia Medina (Anna Luz), Francis L. Sullivan (Thomas Berrien), Sean McClory (Jefferson), Eduardo Noriega (Raul Cornejo), Julio Villareal (Ubaldo Navarro), Charles Rooner (Capt. Bergman), Douglas Dumbrille (Carter).

Ford plays an insurance adjuster who joins a group of treasure seekers hunting for long lost gold hidden in the Zapotecan Temples of Oaxaca, Mexico, 350 years earlier by Indians trying to keep the gold from the Spanish invaders. He is joined by his alcoholic girl friend, Lynn, and has things made tough for him by Sullivan and McClory, an archeologist. The use of flashbacks makes for a lack of suspense. Performances are adequate, with the photography of the ruined temples providing the proper atmosphere.

p, Robert Fellows; d, John Farrow; w, Jonathan Latimer (based on the novel by David Dodge); ph, Jack Draper; m, Antonio D. Conde; ed, Harry Marker; art d, Al Ybarra; m/l, "Sin Ella," E. Fabregat.

Adventure   (PR:A MPAA:NR)

PLUNDER ROAD***   (1957) 71m RF/FOX bw

Gene Raymond (Eddie), Jeanne Cooper (Fran), Wayne Morris (Commando), Elisha Cooke, Jr. (Skeets), Stafford Repp (Roly Adams), Steven Ritch (Frankie), Nora Hayden (Hazel), Helene Heigh (Society Woman), Paul Harber (Trooper No. 1), Don Garrett (Policeman), Michael Fox (No. 1 Smog Officer and Narrator), Richard Newton (Guard No. 2), Charles Conrad (Trooper No. 2), Jim Canino (Tibbs), Robin Riley (Guard No. 1 and Narrator), Harry Tyler (Ernie Beach), George Keymas (Officer No. 1), Stacy Graham, Douglas Bank (Narrators).

Taut low budgeter has Raymond masterminding an ingenious scheme to rob a train carrying gold bullion to the San Francisco mint. The holdup is successful, with the booty being divided into three separate trucks. Trucker Repp drives a van with a police radio as a safeguard. He comes to a roadblock, arousing suspicion because his radio is left on. He panics, and is shot. Morris and Cook drive a freight truck supposedly filled with coffee. Stopped at a weight station, they are exposed because their weight is over limit. Only Raymond and Ritch make it to the Los Angeles destination. To disguise the gold, they have it melted down to be cast as bumpers and hubcaps for a Cadillac. On the way to a ship to take them out of the country, the car gets in an accident. The gold is discovered when the chrome scrapes off the bumpers, Raymond and Ritch are killed trying to escape. It is fitting for the film noir universe in which these characters exist that the elaborate safeguards the men create serve as the means by which they are caught. A grade B gem.

p, Leo Chooluck, Laurence Stewart; d, Hubert Cornfield; w, Steven Ritch (based on a story by Ritch, Jack Charney); ph, Ernest Haller (Regalscope); m, Irving Gertz; ed, Warren Adams, Jerry S. Young; md, Gertz.

Crime   (PR:A MPAA:NR)

PLUNDERERS, THE***   (1948) 87m REP c

Rod Cameron (John Druin), Ilona Massey (Lin Conner), Adrian Booth (Julie McCabe), Forrest Tucker (Whit Lacey), George Cleveland (Sam Borden), Grant Withers (Tap Lawrence), Taylor Holmes (Eben Martin), Paul Fix (Calico), Francis Ford (Barnaby), James Flavin (Sergeant Major), Russell Hicks (Cavalry Colonel), Maude Eburne (Old Dame), Mary Ruth Wade (Pioneer Girl), Louis R. Faust (Sentry), Hank Bell, Rex Lease.

A smart plot twist shows Cameron killing a sheriff, thus making him a wanted man, but only as a ploy. The audience does not learn for some time that the killing was a way for him to infiltrate the gang of notorious criminal Tucker. When he finally brings Tucker to justice, an Indian attack has Tucker helping out and dying in the process. Entire cast offers good characterizations, and expert photography helps the scrappy pace.

p&d, Joseph Kane; w, Gerald Geraghty, Gerald Adams (based on the story by James Edward Grant); ph, Jack Marta (TruColor); m, Dale Butts; ed, Arthur Roberts; md, Morton Scott; art d, Frank Arrigo; m/l, "Walking Down Broadway," "I'll Sing A Love Song," lyrics by Jack Elliott, Aaron Gonzales (sung by Ilona Massey).

Western   (PR:A MPAA:NR)

PLUNDERERS, THE***   (1960) 94m AA bw

Jeff Chandler (Sam Christy), John Saxon (Rondo), Marsha Hunt (Kate Miller), Dolores Hart (Ellie Walters), Jay C. Flippen (Sheriff McCauley), Ray Stricklyn (Jeb), James Westerfield (Mike Baron, Saloon Owner), Dee Pollock (Davy), Roger Torrey (Mule), Harvey Stephens (Doc Fuller), Vaughn Taylor (Jess Walters), Joseph Hamilton, (Abilene, Ray Ferrell (Billy Miller), William Challee (1st Citizen), Ken Patterson (2nd Citizen), Ella Ethridge (Mrs. Phelps).

Four young nomadic toughs, led by Saxon and Stricklyn, terrorize a peaceful western town when they realize how easy it is for them to get away with their tricks. But Chandler, a one-armed Civil War hero, with the help of huge but gentle Torrey, puts a stop to the disruptive youths. In the process he regains the courage drained from him with the loss of his arm. Performances tend to be a bit exaggerated, but direction keeps a check on things with some subtle touches. Has been likened to THE WILD ONE (1954), but with a different setting.

p&d, Joseph Pevney; w, Bob Barbash; ph, Eugene Polito; m, Leonard Rosenman; ed, Tom McAdoo; md, Rosenman; art d, David Milton.

Western   (PR:A MPAA:NR)

PLUNDERERS OF PAINTED FLATS**   (1959) 77m REP bw

Corinne Calvet (Kathie), John Carroll (Clint Jones), Skip Homeier (Joe Martin), George Macready (Ed Sampson), Edmund Lowe (Ned East), Bea Benaderet (Ella), Madge Kennedy (Mary), Joe Besser (Andy Heather), Allan Lurie (Cass), Candy Candido (Bartender), Ricky Allen (Timmy Martin), Herb Vigran (Mr. Perry), Bob Kline (Carl), Burt Topper (Bart), William Foster (Bill), Lee Redman (Roy), Roy Gordon (Minister), Wade Lane (Galt Martin), David Waldor (Mark), John Kidd (Glenn).

Republic Studios disappointing last release stars Carroll as a gunfighter with a heart of gold, who helps youngster Homeier track down Macready, a despicable cattle baron who has murdered the boy's father. Aside from the usual handful of sparkling performances from a well-seasoned cast of professionals, the film is sadly routine and uninvolving. Though top-billed, Calvet has only a minor role as a mail-order bride. After this picture, Republic closed its doors and sold off its remaining assets to the highest bidder (the lot itself went to CBS).

p&d, Albert C. Gannaway; w, Phil Shuken, John Greene; ph, John Nickolaus, Jr. (Naturama Color); ed, Asa Clark; md, Alec Compinsky; art d, Dan Haller.

Western   (PR:A MPAA:NR)

PLYMOUTH ADVENTURE**½   (1952) 105m MGM c

Spencer Tracy (Capt. Christopher Jones), Gene Tierney (Dorothy Bradford), Van Johnson (John Alden), Leo Genn (William Bradford), Dawn Addams (Priscilla Mullins), Lloyd Bridges (Coppin), Barry Jones (William Brewster), John Dehner (Gilbert Winslow), Tommy Ivo (William Button), Lowell Gilmore (Edward Winslow), Noel Drayton (Miles Standish), Rhys Williams (Mr. Weston), Kathleen Lockhart (Mary Brewster), Murray Matheson (Christopher Martin), John Dierkes (Greene), Paul Cavanagh (John Carver), Noreen Corcoran (Ellen Moore), Dennis Hoey (Head Constable), Hugh Pryne (Samuel Fuller), Matt Moore (William Mullins), William Self, Loren Brown (Sailors), Elizabeth Flournoy (Rose Standish), Damian O'Flynn, Keith McConnell, Elizabeth Harrower, Owen McGiveney, Iris Goulding, David Sober, Roger Broaddus, Gene Coogan, Kay English, James Logan.

An adventure-filled tale of the voyage of the Mayflower from England to America in 1620 with a cargo of 102 pilgrims. Captained by the stern, disapproving Tracy, the ship departs from the British shores with a list of passengers that includes William Bradford (Genn), who will be the new colony's first governor, John Alden (Johnson), Priscilla Mullins (Addams), Miles Standish (Drayton), and William Brewster (Jones). Their journey is a dangerous one filled with blinding storms, high winds, and choppy seas. The embittered Tracy riles his puritanical passengers by trying to seduce Tierney, who intends to remain loyal to Genn. Tracy finally comes to a point where he understands and respects the pilgrims' plight, but this revelation comes too late. Tierney, having fallen overboard, drowns in the dark and violent sea. The Mayflower eventually reaches its destination. Tracy brings his passengers to shore but in respect for Tierney's memory chooses to keep his ship in the coastal waters to help assure the colonists' survival over their first winter, rather than heading back to England immediately, as planned. Hampered by a mindless script, PLYMOUTH ADVENTURE holds interest only because of Brown's fine ability at directing the action sequences. One can't help but shudder at the sight of the thundering waves against the Mayflower's hull which rock the ship with all their power. Brown, who had been working in films for 37 years and had become best known for his direction of Greta Garbo (FLESH AND THE DEVIL, 1927, and ANNA CHRISTIE, 1930), threw in the directorial towel after PLYMOUTH ADVENTURE.

p, Dore Schary; d, Clarence Brown; w, Helen Deutsch (based on a novel by Ernest Gabler); ph, William Daniels (Technicolor); m, Miklos Rozsa; ed, Robert J. Kern; art d, Cedric Gibbons, Urie McCleary; set d, Edwin B. Willis, Hugh Hunt; cos, Walter Plunkett; spec eff, A. Arnold Gillespie, Warren Newcombe, Irving Ries.

Historical Drama **(PR:AA MPAA:NR)**

POACHER'S DAUGHTER, THE½** (1960, Brit.) 74m Show Corp. of America (GB: SALLY'S IRISH ROGUE)

Julie Harris *(Sally Hamil)*, Harry Brogan *(Rabit Hamil)*, Tim Seely *(Luke Carey)*, Marie Kean *(Ellen Carey)*, Brid Lynch *(Mag Kehoe)*, Eddie Golden *(Ned Shay)*, Philip O'Flynn *("Mad" Henly)*, Finola O'Shannon *(Biddy Henly)*, Noel Magee *(Seamus Doyle)*, Paul Farrell *(Pub Landlord)*, Dermot Kelly *(McKeefry)*, Geoffrey Golden *(Uncle Peter)*, John Hoey *(Postman)*, John Cowley *(Garage Dealer)*.

Not wanting to face up to his future responsibility of the farm he is about to inherit and his coming marriage to Harris, Seely buys a motorcycle and goes for a ride across the Irish countryside. But resourceful Harris, spurred on by her father, Brogan, takes chase, catching up to Seely just before he's forced into a shotgun wedding. Harris joined the Abbey Theater troupe in the making of this pleasant farce.

p, Robert S. Baker, Monty Berman; d, George Pollock; w, Patrick Kirwan, Blanaid Irvine (based on the play "The New Gosson" by George Shiels); ph, Stanley Pavey; m, Ivor Slaney; ed, Gerry Hambling.

Comedy **(PR:A MPAA:NR)**

POCATELLO KID*½ (1932) 60m TIF bw

Ken Maynard, Marceline Day, Dick Cramer, Charles King, Lew Meehan, Jack Rockwell, Bert Lindley, Bob Reeves, Jack Ward, Tarzan the Horse.

Maynard plays a dual role, that of the innocently convicted "Pocatello Kid," and his no-good brother sheriff. It opens with Maynard as the "Kid" breaking jail and gives rise to a manhunt. When the sheriff is killed in a shootout, Maynard switches identity with him. But the sheriff's girl proves to be an honest woman and Maynard can't bring himself to deceive her. So he admits his identity, then goes on the chase for the real culprits. The horse Tarzan takes some acting honors in this likable hoofbeat opera.

p, Phil Goldstone; d, Phil Rosen; w, Scott Darling; ph, Arthur Reed; ed, Roy Luby.

Western **Cas.** **(PR:A MPAA:NR)**

POCKET MONEY** (1972) 102m Coleytown-First Artists/NG c

Paul Newman *(Jim Kane)*, Lee Marvin *(Leonard)*, Strother Martin *(Garrett)*, Christine Belford *(Adelita)*, Kelly Jean Peters *(Wife)*, Fred Graham *(Herb)*, Wayne Rogers *(Stretch Russell)*, Hector Elizondo *(Juan)*, R. Camargo *(Don Tomas)*, Gregg Sierra *(Chavarin)*, Wynn Pearce *(Border Patrolman)*, G. Escandon *(Rustler)*, D. Herrara *(Vasquero)*, John Verros *(Almara)*, Mickey Gilbert, R. Loney *(Stunt Doubles)*, E. Baca *(Nieblas)*, N. Roman *(Filling Station Attendant)*, R. Manning *(Foreman)*, Terry Malick *(Workman)*, Richard Farnsworth, W. Sanders, A. Sandoval, J. Bailey, G. Payne, B. Stout, F. Garcia, P. Johnson, E. Jarvis, J.P. Carranza, P. Avenetti, C. Miranda, R. Westberg, D. Starr, M. Clark, F. Soto, P. Espinosa, B. Cutterr, J. Martinez, L. Armando, Jr., Poupee Bocar, D. Hudkins, R. Gainter, J. Alfasa, P. Regas, R. Montoyo, L. Domingues, R. Romero.

In an attempt to recreate the days of the early United Artists, a company formed by Charlie Chaplin, Mary Pickford, D.W. Griffith, Douglas Fairbanks, et al, Paul Newman, Sidney Poitier, Barbra Streisand, Steve McQueen, and Dustin Hoffman got together to start First Artists and this was their premiere offering. It wasn't as terrible a movie as the first responses to it indicated, but since so much was expected, anything less than brilliance represented a letdown. Newman mugged and grimaced in an attempt at comedy and Marvin's underplaying was lethargic, as though he were a graduate of the Robert Mitchum School of Dramatic Arts. Newman is an easy-going cowboy operating on the Texas-Arizona border. His bad luck follows him around like a black cloud over his head and his current problem is a herd of horses he's brought in from Mexico to Tucson. The animals have been put in quarantine for several weeks and he needs money to pay back alimony and outstanding debts to the bank. While in Tucson, he ambles into a bar and meets Rogers (an old acquaintance he should have forgotten), who tells him that his boss, Martin (a rotten cuss if there ever was one), needs someone to squire 200 steers from Mexico into the U.S. for Martin's rodeo supply business. Newman's uncle, Graham, has been burned by Martin before and alerts his nephew to the fact but Newman is desperate and accepts the assignment. Newman gets pocket money from Martin with the promise that he will later receive his expenses, fee, and a bonus when he makes the delivery. Newman can't do it alone, so he contacts Marvin, a promoter who is flat broke due to the failure of his latest fly-by-night ploy. Marvin is surprised to see that his friend, Newman, is far more slow-witted than he'd thought when Newman overpays for the herd he is to take back from Mexico. Newman's pocket money is depleted and Rogers arrives with a check, post-dated, that Newman will have as good faith. He can cash it once he brings the steers to Chihuahua. Having been through the quarantine problem already, Newman knows that the area is filled with insects and the herd is in danger, but Rogers says it's all been taken care of and that money has changed hands in order to allow the steers to get through unscathed and unstopped by the authorities. Newman and Marvin now learn that their Mexican foreman, Elizondo, has sold the animals' feed and set them out to graze off the land. A few of the cows have since gone off on their own and Newman is livid. Elizondo owns the pens where the cows are staying and his father is a heavyweight in the town but that doesn't stop the angry Newman from going after the man. A fight ensues and Newman is tossed in el clinko. Marvin sells Newman's small truck to raise the needed money for "la mordida" (the bite, which is the Spanish equivalent of a bribe) in order to get Newman out of stir. Needless to say, Martin's check bounces, then the cattle are slammed into quarantine, and when Martin finally does arrive, he won't make good on his check, claiming that by the time the animals are released, he won't have anyone to sell them to. Marvin and Newman threaten Martin with mayhem but he still won't come up with the money. Since neither man is really tough, they don't whack Martin around and eventually walk out of Martin's hotel room after having tossed the motel's TV set through the window. They make their way to the local railroad station and hope to be able to hop a freight and make it back to the U.S. without anything else happening. A couple of good jokes and a superior performance by Martin are all that distinguish this feeble attempt at capturing the same audience who loved Newman in BUTCH CASSIDY AND THE SUNDANCE KID. Rosenberg's direction is pedestrian. For a close analysis of Rosenberg, we refer you to the book by Merle Miller *Only You, Dick Daring*, a devastating account of what happens to a television pilot. POCKET MONEY was filmed mostly on location in Arizona and Mexico.

p, John Foreman; d, Stuart Rosenberg; w, Terry Malick, John Gay (based on the novel *Jim Kane* by J.P.S. Brown); ph, Laszlo Kovacs (Technicolor); m, Alex North; ed, Robert Wyman; art d, Tambi Larsen; set d, Darrell Silvera; cos, Nat Tolmach, Jim Linn; spec eff, Donald Courtney; m/l, "Pocket Money," Carole King (sung by King); makeup, Dick Cobos.

Western **(PR:A-C MPAA:PG)**

POCKETFUL OF MIRACLES*½** (1961) 136m Franton/UA c

Glenn Ford *(Dave the Dude Conway)*, Bette Davis *(Apple Annie, "Mrs. E. Worthington Manville")*, Hope Lange *(Elizabeth "Queenie" Martin)*, Arthur O'Connell *(Count Alfonso Romero)*, Peter Falk *(Joy Boy)*, Thomas Mitchell *(Judge Henry G. Blake)*, Edward Everett Horton *(Hutchins the Butler)*, Mickey Shaughnessy *(Junior)*, David Brian *(Governor)*, Sheldon Leonard *(Steve Darcey)*, Peter Mann *(Carlos Romero)*, Ann-Margret *(Louise)*, Barton MacLane *(Police Commissioner)*, John Litel *(Police Inspector McCrary)*, Jerome Cowan *(Mayor)*, Jay Novello *(Cortega the Spanish Consul)*, Frank Ferguson, Willis Bouchey *(Editors)*, Fritz Feld *(Pierre)*, Ellen Corby *(Soho Sal)*, Gavin Gordon *(Mr. Cole the Hotel Manager)*, Benny Rubin *(Flyaway)*, Jack Elam *(Cheesecake)*, Mike Mazurki *(Big Mike)*, Hayden Rorke *(Capt. Moore)*, Doodles Weaver *(Pool Player)*, Paul E. Burns *(Mallethead)*, Angelo S. Rosito *(Angie)*, Edgar Stehli *(Gloomy)*, George E. Stone *(Shimley)*, William F. Sauls *(Smiley)*, Tom Fadden *(Herbie)*, Snub Pollard *(Knuckles)*, Byron Foulger *(Lloyd, the Assistant Hotel Manager)*, Betty Bronson *(The Mayor's Wife)*, Romo Vincent *(Kidnaped Reporter)*.

This was Frank Capra's swan song as a producer-director and even though it was lashed by critics and didn't make a dent at the box office, it's still a good, if long, movie with some outstanding performances, particularly by Falk, who steals every scene he lurches through. Ford was the associate producer (with Joe Sistrom) and that position may have affected his objectivity to the material and the lack of editing of his scenes. It's far too long, something that Capra was rarely guilty of, and one can only assume the Ford scenes were considered untamperable. Based on the screenplay for 1933's LADY FOR A DAY (which was based on a Damon Runyon tale), the movie travels over familiar and sentimental territory that might have been out of step for the early 1960s. Ford is a New York gangster in a spot of trouble, as he is an independent operator and refuses to go along with the other mobmen. He is a superstitious type and believes that he cannot come to any harm as long as he continues to buy his daily apple from Davis, a drunken fruit salesperson. Davis is a bit of unionist and has united the Broadway mendicants into a little cadre. In essence, Ford's belief is that "an apple a day keeps the Mafia away," and although his bodyguard, Falk, and his chauffeur, Shaughnessy, think it's a lot of hooey, his girl friend, Lange, goes along with whatever Ford wants and encourages his daily intake of pippins. Ford is about to go into business with a Chicago gang thief, Leonard, although Lange wishes he'd quit the rackets and settle down. (A situation not unlike that of Nathan Detroit and his blonde, Adelaide, in GUYS AND DOLLS.) Ford is shocked when Davis is not at her usual Broadway corner, so he searches until she's located, drunk as a skunk, down on the Bowery, where most of the muscatellers go. Davis is thinking about suicide and explains the reasons. Her daughter, Ann-Margret, has been educated abroad since infancy and her tuition has been paid through the fruits of Davis' labors. The daughter believes that her mother is a well-to-do New York dowager and now she is returning to the city with her fiance, Mann, and his wealthy father, O'Connell, to meet the mother and prepare for the uniting of the couple. There is no way she feels she can pull off the deception and she'd rather die than hurt Ann-Margret's feelings. Ford is floored by Davis' devotion to her daughter and the fact that she's been able to keep this charade going for so long, a task which obviously has taken its toll on Davis' own life style. Ford rents an impressive apartment, staffs it with butler Horton, and even gets Davis a rented husband, Mitchell, who is a disbarred alcoholic judge. Next, Lange hires a group of fashion and beauty consultants to transform the old sot into an attractive woman. The trio arrive from Spain and the deception is successful. O'Connell is so impressed by Davis and the way she lives that he will endow the upcoming marriage with a large cash settlement to get the kids on their way in style. Davis is so flushed with success that she promises to toss him a party where he will meet the elite of New York's society. Ford now has become so involved in this that he isn't paying enough attention to his proposed merger with Leonard. He doesn't want to continue but Davis prevails on him, so Ford has a battalion of crooks come to her apartment and pose as the creme de la creme. The gangsters and their molls are all present, but there are several cops outside the building ready to arrest the whole lot of them. Next thing you know, the mayor, the governor, and a horde of real socialites arrive (after they've heard the masquerade story from Ford) and the party is a huge success. Ann-Margret, Mann, and O'Connell return to Spain with the sincere belief that Davis is who she says she is, Mrs. E. Worthington Manville. Ford and Lange decide to get married and he will quit the gangster business and settle down with her in Maryland, and as a final fillip, Davis is about ready to accept a marriage proposal from Mitchell, who has agreed to cease his drinking. . .maybe. At 136 minutes, it took a while to tell this story, a story that would have either benefited from songs or pruning. Both Falk and the title song received Oscar nominations. Cahn and Van Heusen's tune "Pocketful of Miracles" was a large hit and eventually appropriated by the huge Kodak Corporation to advertise its pocket cameras. As with most Damon Runyon stories, the gangsters talked tough but were pussycats underneath. Tugend had written the first screenplay, a lengthy script of nearly 200 pages that included an endless prolog and epilog showing Lange and Ford as apple farmers. Kanter came in and cut the script. Then Cannon, the Broadway sports columnist, was hired to add authentic Runyon-type talk. Helen Hayes had been tapped to play "Apple Annie," but as she was off on a State Department tour in Russia, the dates didn't work out. Ford was hired when Kanter and Capra were having lunch in a restaurant and stopped at Ford's table to say hello. Capra asked, "What are you doing next, Glenn?" and Ford replied, "Your next picture, Frank." When Capra and Kanter returned to their office, they discussed Ford, called his agent, and that's how he came to be the star. Ford was dating Lange at the time and asked for her to co-star, somewhat of a mistake, as she didn't have the brassiness of a Vivian Blaine. Falk had just come off playing Abe Reles in MURDER, INC. and Kanter, after seeing Falk's convincing work in that picture, wondered if Falk had the necessary tools to bring off a comedy role. Capra was sure he could and it was this job that changed Falk's career, taking him out of the realm of hoodlumism and into the exalted ranks of comic actordom. When interviewed, Kanter said, "That kind of decision is why he's Frank Capra and I'm not."

p&d, Frank Capra; w, Hal Kanter, Harry Tugend, Jimmy Cannon (based on the story "Madame La Gimp" by Damon Runyon and the screenplay LADY FOR A DAY by Robert Riskin); ph, Robert Bronner (Panavision, Technicolor); m, Walter Scharf, Petr Ilyich Tchaikovsky; ed, Frank P. Keller; md, Scharf; art d, Hal Pereira, Roland Anderson; set d, Sam Comer, Ray Moyer; cos, Edith Head, Walter Plunkett; spec eff, Farciot Edouart; ch, Nick Castle; m/l, James Van Huesen, Sammy Cahn, Tom Blackburn, George Bruns, "Pocketful of Miracles," Van Heusen, Cahn; makeup, Wally Westmore.

Crime/Comedy **Cas.** **(PR:AA MPAA:NR)**

POCO...LITTLE DOG LOST** (1977) 88m Cinema Shares International c

Chill Wills, Michelle Ashburn, Clint Ritchie, Sherry Bain, John Steadman, Tom Rov Lowe.

A standard "loving dog finds crippled master despite numerous adversities" plot has the title mutt searching for the disabled girl he so dearly loves after they are separated in a car accident. The plucky pup meets the stock amount of zany folks enroute, along with some semi-dangerous exploits (at least in the realm of bad films in the genre) against a desert backdrop. Finally, and to no one's surprise, he and his mistress are reunited in a tearful reunion. Though clearly aimed at children, one might use caution before taking the little ones to this mess. It's little more than a sticky sweet rehash of every dog movie trick in the book.

p&d, Dwight Brooks; w, William E. Carville.

Adventure **(PR:AAA MPAA:G)**

POCOMANIA** (1939) 65m Domino/Lenwal bw (AKA: THE DEVIL'S DAUGHTER; PONCOMANIA)

Nina Mae McKinney *(Isabele Walton)*, Jack Carter *(Philip Ramsay)*, Ida James *(Sylvia Walton)*, Hamtree Harrington *(Percy Jackson)*, Willa Mae Lane *(Elvira)*, Emmett "Babe" Wallace *(John Lowden)*.

Strange, rarely seen all-black film features McKinney as a Jamaican native who inherits her father's rubber plantation when he dies. Her successful sister James arrives from New York in hopes of getting the plantation for herself, but McKinney tries to scare her off with phony voodoo rituals. This fails and the two sisters reconcile and run the plantation together. This was shot on location in Kingston, Jamaica as a remake of OUANGA, a just an obscure effort with a similar story line. McKinney had been one of the stars in HALLELUJAH (1929), and later made a tour of Europe billed as "the black Garbo."

p&d, Arthur Leonard; w, George Terwilliger; ph, Jay Rescher.

Drama **(PR:C MPAA:NR)**

POE'S TALES OF HORROR (SEE: TALES OF TERROR, 1962)

POET'S PUB** (1949, Brit.) 79m Aquila Film-Independent Frame/GFD bw

Derek Bond *(Saturday Keith)*, Rona Anderson *(Joanna Benbow)*, James Robertson Justice *(Prof. Benbow)*, John McLaren *(Van Buren)*, Barbara Murray *(Nelly Bly)*, Peter Croft *(Quentin Cotton)*, Leslie Dwyer *(Holly)*, Joyce Grenfell *(Miss Horsefell-Hughes)*, Fabia Drake *(Lady Mercy Cotton)*, Maurice Denham *(Constable)*, Kay Cavendish *(Jean Forbes)*, Andrew Osborn *(Williams)*, Iris Hoey *(Lady Keith)*, Leslie Weston, Geoffrey Dunn, Roddy Hughes, Philip Stainton, Joan Sterndale-Bennett, Alexander Field, Sam Kydd, Dorothy Green, Ann Codrington, Olwen Brookes, Arthur Lowe, Mona Harris, Anthony Steel.

Struggling poet Bond takes over the management of a country inn and is host to a number of odd characters, including a professor who condemned his early poems, his daughter and a couple of crooks he helps bring to their demise after they kidnap the professor's daughter. Loose structure serves mainly to display caricatures, only these turn out not to be unique. One of handsome British film hero Steel's earliest pictures after graduating from the London stage.

p, Donald B. Wilson; d, Frederick Wilson; w, Diana Morgan (based on the novel by Eric Linklater); ph, Bill Allan, George Stretton, Arthur Ibbetson; cos, Eve Betts, Ltd.

Comedy/Thriller **(PR:A MPAA:NR)**

POI TI SPOSERO (SEE: MALE COMPANION, 1966, Fr./Ital.)

POIL DE CAROTTE**** (1932, Fr.) 80m Films Legrand Majestic bw (AKA: THE RED HEAD)

Harry Baur *(Mons. Lepic)*, Robert Lynen *(Francois, "Poil de Carotte")*, Catherine Fontenay *(Mme. Lepic)*, Louis Gouthier *(Uncle)*, Simone Aubry *(Ernestine Lepic)*, Maxime Fromiot *(Felix Lepic)*, Colette Segall (Mathilde), Marthe Marty *(Honorine)*, Christiane Dor *(Annette)*.

This was Duvivier's second attempt to film the popular stories of Jules Renard, the first being a 1925 silent vehicle. In near lyrical fashion it tells of the unhappy childhood of the pre-adolescent Lynen, a victim of the hatred between his mother, Fonteney, and her husband, Baur; a marriage which exists only for appearances' sake. Lynen is actually his mother's illigitimate child, the result of an affair with a man having the same type of glowing red hair as the boy. The mother treats her son with spite and cruelty, blaming her isolation on the innocent lad. The stepfather, for the most part, treats the boy with indifference, but through the course of the film this changes as the two develop a close friendship based on mutual respect. The events of the film occur during one summer vacation in the country, where Lynen's delight at playing with the animals and his young friend Segall is frequently interrupted by his mother's selfish demands to have him perform heavy tasks. Eventually Baur notes the horrible way in which the wife treats the boy, and he begins to take an interest in his welfare. This new fondness is most poignantly expressed when Lynen meets with a seemingly insurmountable rejection and attempts to hang himself. This news reaches Baur, who has just been elected mayor. He runs to rescue the boy and they have a heart-to-heart talk that solidifies their friendship and finally gives the boy a real father. Though Lynen is a victim of other people's inconsiderations, he is not idealized or treated as a saint. Rather, he is a normal child, at times irrational, at times loving, and often mischievious. The actor assigned this role was encountered by Duvivier walking along a street. The red head was put to use in this film and several other features of the 1930s, providing food for the table of his impoverished family. (Robert Lynen would later be killed by the Nazis for his involvement in the French underground.) Fonteney was quite convincing as the bitchy mother, with Baur proving himself capable of evoking a large amount of information with a simple glance. The camera, in the hands of Armand Thirard who worked in French pictures for more than 40 years, is used to full advantage, drawing emphasis to Lynen's relationship with his family and his environment. Several other attempts to capture this popular story would be done, but none nearly so successful or powerful as Duvivier's version. (In French.)

d&w, Julien Duvivier (based on the novels *Poil de Carotte*and *La Bigote* by Jules Renard); ph, Armand Thirard; m, Alexandre Tansman; ed, Marthe Poncin.

Drama **Cas.** **(PR:A MPAA:NR)**

POINT BLANK 1962 (SEE: PRESSURE POINT, 1962)

POINT BLANK½** (1967) 92m Bernard-Winkler/MGM c

Lee Marvin *(Walker)*, Angie Dickinson *(Chris)*, Keenan Wynn *(Fairfax, "Yost")*, Carroll O'Connor *(Brewster)*, Lloyd Bochner *(Frederick Carter)*, Michael Strong *(Stegman)*, John Vernon *(Mal Reese)*, Sharon Acker *(Lynne)*, James Sikking *(Hired Gun)*, Sandra Warner *(Waitress)*, Roberta Haynes *(Mrs. Carter)*, Kathleen Freeman *(1st Citizen)*, Victor Creatore *(Carter's Man)*, Lawrence Hauben *(Car Salesman)*, Susan Holloway *(Customer)*, Sid Haig, Michael Bell *(Penthouse Lobby Guards)*, Priscilla Boyd *(Receptionist)*, John McMurtry *(Messenger)*, Ron Walters, George Strattan *(Two Young Men in Apartment)*, Nicole Rogell *(Carter's Secretary)*, Rico Cattani, Roland LaStarza *(Reese's Guards)*, Jerry Catron, Joe Mell *(Men)*, Ted White *(Football Player)*, Casey Brandon, Roseann Williams, Bonnie Dewberry, Carey Foster *(Dancers)*, Karen Lee *(Waitress)*, Bill Hickman, Chuck Hicks *(Guards)*, Louis Whitehill *(Policeman)*, Felix Silla *(Bellhop)*, Andrew Orapeza *(Desk Clerk)*.

Style overcomes substance in this Alain Resnais-type violence film that stars the director, rather than the actors. Boorman showed fantastic attention to details and forgot about flesh-and-blood, with a few exceptions, but that didn't seem to hurt the picture which did well in theaters. Marvin has just been involved with a heist of the mob's money, a feat he accomplished with Vernon. They have nailed the cash and are hiding on the deserted island of Alcatraz when Vernon shoots Marvin point-blank. As Marvin begins to go under, he notes that Vernon has his arm around Acker, Marvin's wife, and it dawns on him that he has been gulled in two departments. Acker and Vernon leave Marvin for dead but he is tougher than that and eventually swims to shore (something countless escapees could not manage). Some time later, Marvin meets Wynn while both are taking the city's guided tour of Alcatraz. Wynn says he knows about the robbery and he offers to help Marvin wreak revenge on Vernon and Acker as well as get his hands on his share of the loot, a tidy sum near $100,000. Marvin goes south to Los Angeles, finds Acker's apartment, and shoots the place up but doesn't kill her. She's been deserted by Vernon and is now taking drugs and later commits suicide without revealing Vernon's whereabouts. Marvin, next uses Acker's sister, Dickinson, to get into the heavily guarded residence of Vernon. Dickinson seduces Vernon, Marvin sneaks into the penthouse, but before he can shoot Vernon, the man falls to his death. So where is the money? Wynn appears again and says that it's in the hands of Bochner, who is married to Haynes and is a member of the mob. Bochner and Strong know that Marvin is gunning for them, set a trap, but are hoisted by their own petards and die in the web they've prepared. Marvin gets to the right-hand man of the boss, O'Connor, who wants to take over the top spot, occupied by a man named Fairfax. The plan is to pull another heist of the gang money. O'Connor and Marvin go back to San Francisco to effect the robbery, but O'Connor is shot dead by Wynn, who, it turns out, is not the mob's bookkeeper—he is the top dog. Wynn is happy that Marvin has helped him ferret out the rats in his organization and now offers Marvin a job. Marvin thinks about it, then decides it might be a trap and exits. A blood bath filled with shots, torture, fights, crashes, everything the devoted sadist might enjoy. Flashbacks, flashforwards, instant replays, and gore galore that seem to have been put in only to startle.

p, Judd Bernard, Robert Chartoff; d, John Boorman; w, Alexander Jacobs, David Newhouse, Rafe Newhouse (based on the novel *The Hunter* by Richard Stark [Donald Westlake]); ph, Philip H. Lathrop (Panavision, Metrocolor); m, Johnny Mandel; ed, Henry Berman; art d, George W. Davis, Albert Brenner; set d, Henry Grace, Keogh Gleason; cos, Margo Weintz; spec eff, Virgil Beck, J. McMillan Johnson; m/l, "Mighty Good Times," Stu Gardner (sung by Gardner); makeup, William Tuttle, John Truwe.

Crime   **(PR:O MPAA:NR)**

POINT OF TERROR*   (1971) 88m Jude/Crown International c

Peter Carpenter (*Tony*), Dyanne Thorne (*Andrea*), Lory Hansen (*Helayne*), Paula Mitchell (*Sally*), Leslie Simms (*Fran*), Joel Marston (*Martin*), Roberta Robson (*1st Wife*), Dana Diamond (*Barmaid*), Al Dunlap (*Bartender*), Ernest Charles (*Detective*), Tony Kent (*Priest*).

Through dream sequences, POINT OF TERROR offers some glimpses into the seamier types of characters floating around in our midst. Story has Carpenter dreaming of some grotesque activities with these lurid ones, all involving sex, passion, intrigue, pregnancy, and ending up with his murder. As he falls to his death on the ground he wakes up and sees the voluptuous blonde who was the centerpiece of his dreams approaching him on the beach, as though his dreams are soon to come true. Some stylish touches here and there, but pure B horror otherwise.

p, Chris Marconi, Peter Carpenter; d, Alex Nicol; w, Tony Crechales, Ernest A. Charles (based on a story by Carpenter, Marconi); ph, Robert Maxwell (DeLuxe Color); m, John Caper, Jr.; ed, R.A. Radecki; m/l, "This Is. . .," Bea Verdi, "Lifebeats" Eilene Levenson, Jill Jones, Earl Levenson, "Drifter of the Heart" Jerry Marcellino, Mel Larsen; makeup, Nora Maxwell.

Horror   **Cas.**   **(PR:O MPAA:NR)**

POINTED HEELS½**   (1930) 62m PAR bw-c

William Powell (*Robert Courtland*), Fay Wray (*Lora Nixon*), Helen Kane (*Dot Nixon*), Richard "Skeets" Gallagher (*Dash Nixon*), Phillips Holmes (*Donald Ogden*), Adrienne Dore (*Kay Wilcox*), Eugene Pallette (*Joe Clark*).

Backstage drama has millionaire Powell producing a Broadway show and falling for chorus girl Wray, who is already spoken for by jazz composer Holmes. Wray quits the show upon marrying Holmes, but when his parents cut off his allowance for marrying a showgirl, she goes back to the stage, while Holmes remains at home composing a jazz symphony. Wray's brother and sister-in-law, song and dance man Gallagher and baby-talking Kane, want to try their hand at some serious theater instead of the comedy they have been making. Powell agrees to back a show for them because Wray will be in it. On opening night, Powell gets the stars drunk so that their "serious" play will come out a comedy, thus going over with the audience. His plan works. Holmes decides to leave Wray, because he cannot contend with being supported by a woman, as well as from jealousy of Powell. But Powell gallantly bows out, allowing the young lovers to get back together. Plot suffered from too many subplots, giving a sketchy portrayal of the characters. A poor job in the cutting room did not help. There is one ballet sequence filmed in technicolor; it lasts for three minutes. Future "Thin Man" Powell got star billing for the first time in POINTED HEELS and kept that bill for 25 years.

d, A. Edward Sutherland; w, Florence Ryerson, John V.A. Weaver (based on a story by Charles Brackett); ph, Allen Siegler; ed, Jane Loring; m/l, "I Have to Have You," Richard A. Whiting, Leo Robin, "Ain't Cha," Mack Gordon, Max Rich (sung by Helen [Boopadoop] Kane).

Drama/Musical   **(PR:A MPAA:NR)**

POINTING FINGER, THE**   (1934, Brit.) 68m REA/RKO bw

John Stuart (*Lord Rollestone*), Viola Keats (*Lady Mary Stuart*), Leslie Perrins (*The Honorable James Mallory*), Michael Hogan (*Patrick Lafone*), A. Bromley Davenport (*Lord Edensore*), Henrietta Watson (*Lady Anne Rollestone*), D.J. Williams (*Grimes*), Clare Greet (*Landlady*).

In order to gain the earldom, an aristocrat concocts a plan to do in his royal kin. But as it is with all bad men in simplistic melodramas like this, Perrins gets his comeuppance when his evil plans fall through.

p, Julius Hagen; d, George Pearson; w, H. Fowler Mear (based on the novel by "Rita").

Drama   **(PR:A MPAA:NR)**

POISON PEN***   (1941, Brit.) 66m ABF/REP bw

Flora Robson (*Mary Rider*), Robert Newton (*Sam Hurrin*), Ann Todd (*Ann Rider*), Geoffrey Toone (*David*), Reginald Tate (*Rev. Rider*), Belle Chrystal (*Sucal Hurrin*), Edward Chapman (*Len Griffin*), Edward Rigby (*Badham*), Athole Stewart (*Col. Cashelton*), Mary Hinton (*Mrs. Cashelton*), Cyril Chamberlain (*Peter Cashelton*), Catherine Lacey (*Connie Fateley*), Wally Patch (*Mr. Suggs*), Ella Retford (*Mrs. Suggs*), Jean Clyde (*Mrs. Griffin*), Wilfrid Hyde White (*Postman*), Marjorie Rhodes (*Mrs. Scaife*), Beatrice Varley, Peter Murray Hill, Empsie Bowman, Lawrence Kitchin, Kenneth Connor, Megs Jenkins, Esma Cannon, Eileen Beldon, Merle Tottenham, Charles Mortimer, Roddy Hughes, Roddy McDowall.

An intriguing story of psychological instability, based on a play by the author of *How Green Was My Valley*. It takes place in a small English community that is swept with hysteria when a number of poison pen letters are mailed to villagers, making wild and scandalous accusations. This results in a murder and suicide. Police bring in a handwriting analyst who tracks the letters to the spinster sister of the village vicar, a virtuous figure and town benefactress. Apparently her many years of repression had warped her mind. Robson gives a stunning performance as the aging spinster, at one point a rock of piety, and at another an emotionally overwrought woman.

p, Walter C. Mycroft; d, Paul L. Stein; w, Doreen Montgomery, William Freshman, N.C. Hunter, Esther McCracken (based on the play by Richard Llewellyn); ph, Philip Tannura; ed, Flora Newton.

Drama   **(PR:A MPAA:NR)**

POISONED DIAMOND, THE**   (1934, Brit.) 73m Grafton/COL bw

Anne Grey (*Mary Davidson*), Lester Matthews (*John Reader*), Patric Knowles (*Jack Dane*), Raymond Raikes, Bryan Powley, Lucius Blake, D.J. Williams.

Matthews goes bankrupt and puts the blame on four different people. Later the discovery of a diamond mine makes him a rich man. So the vengeful minded Matthews decides to use his newly acquired fortune to destroy the people who ruined him. He carries out his plan on three but gives in to his sense of mercy on the fourth. Typical British B grade drama of the time.

p, Fred Browett; d&w, W.P. Kellino.

Drama   **(PR:A MPAA:NR)**

POITIN**   (1979, Irish) 65m Cinegael c

Cyril Cusack (*A Poteen Maker*), Niall Toibin (*His Agent*), Donal McCann (*Another Agent*), Mairead Ni Conghaile (*Daughter of the Poteen-Maker*), MacDara O Fatharta (*Garda*), Sean O Coisdealbha (*A Publican*).

An extremely bitter film that focuses on moonshiners in an impoverished area of Ireland, taking the view that the Irish cannot resist the bottle and that they possess limited goals and imagination. Perhaps the only film ever made in Gaelic, its maker, Quinn, says its aim was to rectify some of the "sentimental falsifications" perpetuated by John Ford in THE QUIET MAN. Any so-called rectification of that monumental film is quite an undertaking, and is far from reached in this effort.

p&d, Bob Quinn; w, Colm Bairead; ph, Seamus Deasy; ed, Quinn; art d, Frankie MacDonncha.

Drama   **(PR:A MPAA:NR)**

POLICE BULLETS**   (1942) 61m MON bw

John Archer, Joan Marsh, Milburn Stone, Warren Hymer, Pat Gleason, Tristram Coffin, Ann Eavers, Charles Jordan, Gene O'Donnell, Ben Taggart, Irving Mitchell, Fern Emmett.

A solid crime programmer which details the efforts of the police to wage war against a powerful protection racket that has been terrorizing the city. Director Yarbrough (who began his career as a prop man for Hal Roach in the silent era) helms with a steady, if unremarkable, hand.

p, Lindsley Parsons; d, Jean Yarbrough; w, Edmund Kelso, André Lamb; ph, Mack Stengler; ed, Jack Ogilvie.

Crime   **(PR:A MPAA:NR)**

POLICE CALL*   (1933) 63m Showmen's Pictures bw (GB: WANTED)

Nick Stuart, Merna Kennedy, Roberta Gale, Mary Carr, Warner Richmond, Walter McGrail, Robert Ellis, Eddie Phillips, Harry Myers, Ralph Freud, Charles Stevens.

Amateurish production stars athletic Stuart (one-time husband of actress Sue Carol) as a young fighter trying to make it to the top through honest effort. When hoods send a henchman to talk some sense into the boy, he knocks him cold with a swift punch, and flees, leaving him for dead. He gets away, wins the girl, and leaves a heavy moral question dangling: should a fugitive from the police win all the prizes? Kennedy, a discovery of Charlie Chaplin, retired from the screen after three more films to marry Busby Berkeley, a union that lasted a year.

d, Philip H. Whitman; w, Norman Keene, Jean Hartley (based on a story by Keene); ph, Abe Scholtz; ed, Rose Smith.

Drama   **(PR:A MPAA:NR)**

POLICE CAR 17**   (1933) 58m COL bw

Tim McCoy (*Tim Conlon*), Evalyn Knapp (*Helen Regan*), Wallis Clark (*Dan Regan*), Ward Bond (*Bumps O'Neill*), Harold Huber (*Johnny Davis*), Edwin Maxwell ("*Big Bill*" *Standish*), Charley West (*Harry*), Jack Long (*Ace Boyle*), DeWitt Jennings (*Capt. Hart*).

McCoy, mainly known for his cowboy outings, is given a police story that has all the elements of a classic western except for a difference in settings and dress. He plays an aggressive officer out to help Knapp, and in the process wins her love. Lots of fast-paced action. Auto chases replace McCoy's horse romps and offices replace the wide-open spaces, but he comes through with his fists as of yore.

d&w, Lambert Hillyer; ph, Benjamin Kline; ed, Otto Meyer.

Crime   **(PR:A MPAA:NR)**

POLICE CONNECTION: DETECTIVE GERONIMO   (SEE: MAD BOMBER, THE, 1973)

POLICE COURT   (SEE: FAME STREET, 1932)

POLICE DOG**   (1955, Brit.) 70m Westridge Fairbanks/Eros bw

Joan Rice (*Pat Lewis*), Tim Turner (*Frank Mason*), Sandra Dorne (*Blonde*), Charles Victor (*Sergeant*), Jimmy Gilbert (*Ken Lade*), Nora Gordon (*Mrs. Lewis*), John le Mesurier (*Inspector*), Cecil Brock, Ian Fleming, Norman Mitchell, Michael Scott, Rex the Dog.

Turner is a policeman whose partner has been killed. He is then placed in charge of a stray Alsatian dog now being used for police work. Meanwhile his partner's killer, now working a regular job as a front, decides to break into a safe. After the break-in, Turner and his dog find the man and bring him to the authorities. Average police drama, produced under auspices of Douglas Fairbanks, Jr.'s production company.

p, Harold Huth; d&w, Derek Twist; ph, Cedric Williams.

Crime/Police Drama   **(PR:A MPAA:NR)**

POLICE DOG STORY, THE**   (1961) 62m Zenith/UA bw

James Brown (*Norm Edwards*), Merry Anders (*Terry Dayton*), Barry Kelley (*Bert Dana*), Milton Frome (*Todd Wellman*), Vinton Haworth (*Commissioner*), Francis De Sales (*Capt. Dietrich*), Brad Trumbull (*Bill Frye*), Pat McCaffria (*Keith Early*), Joe Flynn (*Collins*), Charles Waggenheim (*Firebug*), Jack Mann (*Mattson*), Ray D. Barwick (*Royce*), Elvin Frazier (*Adams*), Harry Y. Coul (*Davis*), Lawrence E. Weatherwax (*Fallon*), George Sawaya (*Driver*), Jerry Todd (*Helper*), Rocco (*Wolf the Dog*).

Focusing on the dog corps of a police department, story shows a rookie cop going through training with the dogs, and then the manner in which the dogs help the cops track down an arsonist. Performances are unusually stiff, with the dog hero, a German shepherd, proving a better actor than the stars.

p, Robert E. Kent; d, Edward L. Cahn; w, Orville H. Hampton; ph, Maury Gertsman; ed, Arthur Hilton; art d, Serge Krizman.

Crime   **(PR:A MPAA:NR)**

POLICE NURSE**½   (1963) 64m AP/FOX bw

Ken Scott (*Art Devlin*), Merry Anders (*Joan Olson*), Oscar Beregi (*Dr. Leon Claudel*), Barbara Mansell (*Irene Kersey*), John Holland (*Edward Mayhall*), Byron Morrow (*Capt. Pete Ingersoll*), Ivan Bonar (*Dr. C.F. Sears*), Jerry Murray (*Terry*), Justin Smith (*Pharmacist*), Carol Brewster (*Mrs. Mayhall*), Lorna Thayer, Lee Henry, Glen Marshall.

Anders plays a nurse, newly arrived in Southern California, who finds that her sister has committed suicide. She gets help from police sergeant Devlin, her sister's former husband, and it is soon discovered that the girl had a baby, but the owner of the hospital where she delivered the baby denies she was ever there. Anders gets a job at the hospital, uncovering the proper records. She also discovers that hospital owner Beregi has been operating a black market baby ring to support his heroin addiction, and had sold the dead woman's child to a wealthy childless couple.

p&d, Maury Dexter; w, Harry Spalding; ph, Jack Nickolaus (CinemaScope); m, Richard LaSalle; ed, Richard Einfeld; md, LaSalle; set d, Harry Reif.

Crime/Drama   **(PR:A MPAA:NR)**

POLICE PYTHON 357***   (1976, Fr.) 125m Albina Productions/Les Films La Boetie c

Yves Montand (*Ferrot*), Simone Signoret (*Therese*), Francois Perier (*Ganay*), Stefania Sandrelli (*Sylvia*), Mathieu Carriere (*Menard*).

Montand plays a tough detective, much in the vein of DIRTY HARRY, who falls in love with Sandrelli, evasive because of her affair with Perier, Montand's boss. When Perier kills the girl because she wants to leave him, Montand is assigned the case. The only person all the clues point to is himself, but he eventually puts the pieces together to point his finger on Perier, a man married to the cripple Signoret. A fine cast adds depth to a tightly woven script adorned with psychological undertones.

d, Alain Corneau; w, Corneau, Daniel Boulanger; ph, Etienne Becker (Eastmancolor); m, Georges Delerue; ed, Marie-Joseph Yoyotte.

Crime/Drama   **(PR:C MPAA:NR)**

POLICEMAN OF THE 16TH PRECINCT, THE zero   (1963, Gr.) 84m Greek Motion Pictures bw

Kostas Hadjichristos (*Elias*), Marika Krevata (*Lucy*), Kyveli Theochari (*Alice*), Thanassis Vengos (*Thomas*), Stavros Xenidis (*Angelo*), D. Papagianopoulos (*Lambros*), George Gavrilidis (*Orestis*), Alice Georguli (*Maid*), Thanos Generalis (*Chief of Police*).

Poor ideas for comedies usually make for pointless movies, and this is no exception. The premise has a group of small-time hoodlums hanging out at their favorite cafe and talking about money problems. And that pretty much sums up the film's plot. Short of spending an afternoon with an insurance salesman, it would be hard to find people who talk about money so much. The acting matches the vacuous plot, but with the poor subtitling job that might be considered a fringe benefit. (In Greek; English subtitles.)

d, Alekos Sakellarios; w, Christos Yannakopoulos, Sakellarios.

Comedy   **(PR:A MPAA:NR)**

POLICEWOMAN*   (1974) 99m Saber/Crown International c

Sondra Currie, Tony Young, Elizabeth Stuart, Phil Hoover, Jeannie Bell, Chuck Daniel, Laurie Rose, William Smith, Wes Bishop.

A mindless time-waster with Currie as a martial arts expert-policewoman. Her job is to put a stop to a gang of gold a smugglers and she does so with the usual unrealistic violence.

p, Wes Bishop; d, Lee Frost; w, Frost, Bishop.

Crime   **Cas.**   **(PR:O MPAA:R)**

POLITICAL ASYLUM**   (1975, Mex./Guatemalan) 89m Panamericana Films/IF (DETRAS DE ESA PUERTA)

Rossano Brazzi (*Ambassador Lara*), Cameron Mitchell (*MacPherson*), Emilio Fernandez (*Police Director*), Flor Procuna (*Eloisa*), Richardo Blume (*Barreriro*), Dick Smith (*Secretary of State*), George [Joe] Kelly (*American Ambassador*), Jose Liedra (*Agregado Militar*).

Heavy-handed picture taking place in Guatemala has Blume as the head of a revolutionary movement taking asylum in the Mexican Embassy. The ambassador, Brazzi, though under pressure from the police, refuses to budge on his ideals that an embassy should offer political immunity. He then helps to get a safe exit for the

revolutionary, even though his wife once had an affair with the man. Production values are extremely below par when compared to American standards, with poor sound recordings making dialog hard to hear.

p&d, Manuel Zecena Dieguez; w, Dieguez, S. Federico Inclan (based on the story by Juan Luis de Alarcon); ph, Juan Manuel Herrera (Eastmancolor); ed, Alfredo Rosas Priego.

Drama   **(PR:A MPAA:PG)**

POLITICAL PARTY, A**½   (1933, Brit.) 73m BIP/Pathe bw

Leslie Fuller (*Bill Smithers*), John Mills (*Tony Smithers*), Enid Stamp-Taylor (*Elvira Whitman*), H. F. Maltby (*Sir James Barrington-Oakes*), Viola Lyel (*Mary Smithers*), Hal Gordon (*Alf Jenks*), Marion Dawson (*Sarah Jenks*), Charles Gerrard (*Mr. Whitman*), Daphne Courtenay (*Kathleen Jenks*), Moore Marriott (*Jim Turner*), Rosie Howard, Dorothy Vernon, Fred Watts.

A pleasing comedy casting Fuller as a chimney sweep who finds himself in the middle of a political campaign. Receiving the support of the Labour Party, Fuller challenges Maltby, the uppity incumbent. Fuller's son, Mills, nearly causes irreparable damage when he falls for a backer of Maltby's, but by the finale Fuller is named the winner. Realizing politics isn't for him, however, he decides not to fill his seat in Parliament.

p, Walter C. Mycroft; d, Norman Lee; w, Syd Courtenay, Lola Harvey; ph, Claude Friese-Greene.

Comedy   **(PR:A MPAA:NR)**

POLITICS**   (1931) 73m MGM bw

Marie Dressler (*Hattie*), Polly Moran (*Ivy*), Rosco Ates (*Peter*), Karen Morley (*Myrtle*), William Bakewell (*Benny*), John Miljan (*Curango*), Joan Marsh (*Daisy*), Tom McGuire (*Mayor*), Kane Richmond (*Nifty*), Mary Alden (*Mrs. Evans*), Bob Perry.

Film about crooked politicians has Dressler running for mayor in a town being overrun by gangsters. Her motivation for entering the race is her daughter's involvement with a young hood wrongly framed on a murder charge. With Moran as her campaign manager, she gets all the support of the town's women by having them refuse to serve their husbands unless they vote for Dressler. This strategy winds up working, as Dressler is voted into office. The comedy team of Dressler and Moran gives some life to otherwise weak material.

d, Charles F. Riesner; w, Wells Root, Zelda Sears, Malcom Stuart Boylan (based on a story by Robert E. Hopkins); ph, Clyde De Vinna; ed, William S. Gray.

Comedy   **(PR:A MPAA:NR)**

POLLY FULTON   (SEE: B.F.'S DAUGHTER, 1948)

POLLY OF THE CIRCUS*½   (1932) 72m MGM bw

Marion Davies (*Polly Fisher*), Clark Gable (*Reverend John Hartley*), C. Aubrey Smith (*Reverend James Northcott*), Raymond Hatton (*Downey*), David Landau (*Beef*), Ruth Selwyn (*Mitzi*), Maude Eburne (*Mrs. Jennings*), Little Billy (*Half-Pint*), Guinn "Big Boy" Williams (*Eric*), Clark Marshall (*Don*), Lillian Elliott (*Mrs. McNamara*), Ray Milland (*Rich Young Man*), Phillip Crane.

As in his later picture, PARNELL, Gable was woefully miscast in this one. He's a reverend at a church and they remove any onus of that by showing him boxing in the first reel, just to let us know he's not a namby-pamby. Davies is a trapeze artist working in a circus and when she falls and is hurt, the first place they take her is to the conveniently located home of Gable. Since the movie is only 72 minutes long, Gable and Davies soon fall in love as she recovers from her injuries and they decide to make it legal, albeit quietly so. Gable prevails on Davies to quit the circus as there is too much danger in doing her act. No sooner do they tell everyone they are married when Gable is fired from his job as many of the blue-nose members of his flock begin to make noise about Gable having taken an unsuitable wife. Stripped of his collar, Gable tries to find a job but since being a man of the cloth is so specific, he's hardly been trained for anything else, and encounters problems. Davies pleads with Smith, the bishop of the area, and tries to get Gable back into the fold but Smith is adamantly opposed. Davies thinks that the only way Gable will be taken back is if she leaves, so she goes back to the circus. Smith has some second thoughts about Gable and he was impressed by Davies and her sincerity, so he tells Gable he can have his old position back and the heck with what the believers think. But Davies is gone! Gable and Smith correctly opine that Davies has returned to the Big Top. They race to the location and find her high above the ground, about to do the same "triple twist" that caused her to fall in the first reel. She is nervous about repeating the difficult move but gets her confidence back when she looks down and sees Gable and Smith. She does the trick and is later rewarded by a kiss from the husband she loves so much, as well as the approval of Smith. Gable as a preacher was limited in his ability to be the romantic hero he'd played in so many prior films. Thus, he exhibited great decorum and was boring. Davies was actually better than Gable and showed a dramatic side to her acting that had not been seen before as she'd previously starred in a series of lightweight comedies with her long-time lover, W. R. Hearst, keeping an eye on her career. Based on an old play, this was a sound remake of Goldwyn's silent version in 1917 which starred Mae Marsh.

d, Alfred Santell; w, Carey Wilson, Laurence Johnson (based on the play by Margaret Mayo); ph, George Barnes; ed, George Hively.

Drama   **(PR:A MPAA:NR)**

POLLYANNA****   (1960) 134m BV c

Hayley Mills (*Pollyanna*), Jane Wyman (*Aunt Polly Harrington*), Richard Egan (*Dr. Edmund Chilton*), Karl Malden (*Reverend Paul Ford*), Nancy Olson (*Nancy Furman*), Adolphe Menjou (*Mr. Pendergast*), Donald Crisp (*Mayor Karl Warren*), Agnes Moorehead (*Mrs. Snow*), Kevin Corcoran (*Jimmy Bean*), James Drury (*George Dodds*), Reta Shaw (*Tillie Lagerlof*), Leora Dana (*Mrs. Paul Ford*), Anne

Seymour *(Mrs. Amelia Tarbell)*, Edward Platt *(Ben Tarbell)*, Mary Grace Canfield *(Angelica)*, Jenny Egan *(Mildred Snow)*, Gage Clark *(Mr. Murg)*, Ian Wolfe *(Mr. Neely)*, Nolan Leary *(Mr. Thomas)*, Edgar Dearing *(Mr. Gorman)*, Harry Harvey *(Editor)*, William "Billy" Newell *(Mr. Hooper)*.

Ever since Mary Pickford filmed the silent version of this book in 1920, the name "Pollyanna" has become a part of the English vernacular to mean someone who is an inveterate optimist. It was even used in song lyrics as in "But Not For Me." The title may have been what turned audiences off from coming to see this superior family film, a movie that never once crosses into bathos or banality, but maintains a realistic and loving attitude all through the slightly lengthy running time. Director-screenwriter Swift was making his feature film debut after having had enormous success with his "Mr. Peepers" TV series. He'd worked at Disney before, back in the 1930s, when he began as an office boy and eventually became an animator. Swift's TV experiences were fraught with all sorts of network interference so he was more than pleasantly surprised when Disney stepped aside and gave him total control of the film once the script had been approved. Mills is an orphan who comes to live with her aunt, Wyman, a wealthy woman in a small 1912 town. The village is filled with naysayers and depressing townsfolk and Mills is soon changing matters by always managing to find something good to say in every situation and by seeing the bright side in even the blackest occurrence. Mills makes friends with another orphan, Corcoran, who lives at the local home for parentless children, and they immediately share several experiences. Moorehead is an embittered old hypochondriac invalid who revels in the attention others pay to her health. Mills won't play Moorehead's game, preferring instead to dwell on the other side of Moorehead's life and the woman is soon entranced by Mills. Meanwhile, Wyman is trying her best to be a good, if stern, parent to Mills and she is seen to be a fully rounded person, not the stereotypical wicked stepmother. Menjou is a hermit and when he finds Mills and Corcoran traipsing around on his grounds, he coldly reprimands them until they win him over and he invites them into his home to see his fabulous collection of glass prisms and the way they diffuse light through his house. Malden is a roaring preacher who has little tolerance for anyone and is apparently losing his congregation. When Mills visits him one afternoon, he reads an amulet around her neck which her late missionary-father gave her. It's a quote from Lincoln which reads "If you search for the evil in man expecting to find it, you certainly will." Malden is transformed by the quote and on the following Sunday, he changes the nature of his sermon, eschewing the usual hell and damnation, and preaches about joy, as well as promising to step down from his lofty perch to get to know his parishioners more intimately. Since Wyman is an old maid (and the leading social light of the town), Mills is bound to find her a mate and reunites Wyman with her childhood sweetheart, Egan, after a couple of other plot turns. The town needs money to build a new orphanage so the doctor arranges a "fair" to help raise funds. Malden also chimes in to support the new project. Wyman doesn't want Mills to go to the gala but Corcoran helps Mills climb through her bedroom window and the two of them show up. Mills has a wonderful night and wins a doll, her very first. Later, Mills climbs up a tree to get back into her bedroom surreptitiously, drops the prized doll, reaches for it, and falls to the ground. On the following day, Egan determines that Mills has been severely hurt and needs surgery in Baltimore to correct her paralyzed limbs. The operation may help her walk again but the youngster is now depressed, angry and her state of mind is somewhere in the mental basement. Now, a Capra-type miracle occurs when a raft of people show up at Wyman's home. They are all there to check on Mills' health and to wish her a speedy recovery. Moorehead is now walking, Malden is at one with his flock, Menjou is not only out of his crab-like existence, he even wants to adopt Corcoran as his own son, et al. Wyman comes to the realization that love is the answer. Even though she's donated money and given of her time to the town, it is Mills' unbridled love of humanity that triumphs over all. Mills is escorted to the train station by the entire town and goes off to Baltimore to have her operation and there isn't a dry eye in the house. Along the way, there are several funny moments and jokes in Swift's script, not one of which is out of character or anachronistic to the era. It was filmed in Santa Rosa and the winemaking area of the Napa Valley, California, which doubled quite well for the rural New England setting of the story. The train and all the authentic fire-fighting equipment was from the private collection of Ward Kimball, the long-time Disney animator (who trained Swift 25 years before) who keeps a collection of more than 10,000 toy trains at his San Gabriel Valley museum. When interviewed by your editors, Swift said: "This was truly an ensemble film. Everyone in the cast and crew had a marvelous time and whenever we meet, we remember it lovingly." This was Menjou's final film and his reputation as a curmudgeon preceded him but even the mustachioed millionaire warmed up to the general happiness on the set. Mills had made TIGER BAY with her father, John, and when Disney and production chief Bill Anderson went to England to cast this, they told their wives to have some lunch one day and perhaps see a movie while they worked. Mrs. Disney and Mrs. Anderson went to see TIGER BAY, came back to the hotel and raved about Mills. She was immediately signed and was simply wonderful in this, her first U.S. movie. That quote from Lincoln was so appreciated by Disney that he had buttons made up with the words and sold them at Disneyland. When Swift learned of that, he never did have the heart to tell Disney that the Great Emancipator didn't make that statement at all. It was something Swift wrote into the screenplay, never dreaming it would eventually wind up on buttons worn by millions of Disneyland visitors.

p, Walt Disney; d&w, David Swift (based on the novel by Eleanor H. Porter); ph, Russell Harlan (Technicolor); m, Paul Smith; ed, Frank Gross; art d, Carroll Clark, Robert Clatworthy; set d, Emile Kuri, Fred MacLean; cos, Walter Plunkett, Chuck Keehne, Gertrude Casey; spec eff, Ub Iwerks; makeup, Pat McNalley.

Comedy Cas. (PR:AAA MPAA:NR)

POLO JOE* (1936) 65m WB bw

Joe E. Brown *(Joe Bolton)*, Carol Hughes *(Mary Hilton)*, Richard "Skeets" Gallagher *(Haywood)*, Joseph King *(Col. Hilton)*, Gordon [William] Elliott *(Don Trumbeau)*, Fay Holden *(Aunt Minnie)*, George E. Stone *(1st Loafer)*, Olive Tell *(Mrs. Hilton)*, David Newell *(Jack Hilton)*, Milton Kibbee *(Marker)*, Frank Orth *(Bert)*, John Kelly *(Rusty)*, Charles Foy *(2nd Loafer)*, Sam McDaniel *(Harvey the Waiter)*, Dudley Dickerson *(Porter)*, Stuart Holmes *(Conductor)*, Wayne Morris *(Boy)*, Perc Teeple, Sam Rice *(Men)*, Jacqueline Saunders *(Woman)*, Frank Darien *(Baggage Man)*, Anne Nagel, Majorie Weaver, Shirley Lloyd, Louise Bates, Ed Mortimer, Elsa Peterson, William J. Worthington, Dick French, Bess Flowers *(Guests)*, John Alexander *(William the Waiter)*, Muriel Kearney *(Girl at Polo Field)*, Eddy Chandler, Harry Hollingsworth *(Detectives)*, James P. Burtis, Max Hoffman, Jr. *(Cops)*, Guy Kingsford, Marc Kramer, Leo McCabe, Bruce Warren *(Polo Players)*, Jane Wyman, Victoria Vinton *(Girls at Polo Field)*, Cyril Ring, David Worth, Ted A. Thompson, Maxine Anderson, Thomas Curran, Myrtle Stedman *(Spectators)*.

Brown, who has a strong aversion to horses, pretends to be a star polo player in order to impress Hughes, who will only have an affair with someone who plays the game. But he failed to be very impressive in this role, mainly the fault of the trying material he had to work with.

d, William McGann; w, Peter Milne, Hugh Cummings; ph, L. William O'Connell; ed, Clarence Kolster; cos, Orry-Kelly.

Comedy (PR:A MPAA:NR)

POLTERGEIST** (1982) 114m MGM-UA c

Craig T. Nelson *(Steve)*, Jobeth Williams *(Diane)*, Beatrice Straight *(Dr. Lesh)*, Dominique Dunne, *(Dana)*, Oliver Robins *(Robbie)*, Heather O'Rourke *(Carol Anne)*, Zelda Rubinstein *(Tangina)*, Martin Casella *(Marty)*, Richard Lawson *(Ryan)*, Michael McManus *(Tuthill)*, Virginia Kiser *(Mrs. Tuthill)*, James Karen *(Teague)*, Lou Perry, Clair Leucart, Dirk Blocker, Allan Graf, Joseph R. Walsh, Helen Baron, Noel Conlon, Robert Broyles, Sonny Landham, Jeffrey Bannister, William Vail, Craig Simmons, Phil Stone, Dana Gendian, Jaimi Gendian.

If only director Tobe Hooper had been left alone by producer/writer Spielberg, this might have been a modern masterpiece of suburban family horror (Hooper had done a marvelous, low-budget job of rural family horror in THE TEXAS CHAINSAW MASSACRE). Instead, what we are left with is a vapid, silly horror movie, with occasional moments of promise, but which ultimately fails due to an overdose of Spielberg cuteness. Nelson and Williams play the happy suburban couple who suddenly find that their perfect house, in the perfect neighborhood, has started acting funny and scaring their perfect children. They really sit up and take notice when wide-eyed blonde type O'Rourke becomes possessed by late-night television and then gets sucked into limbo by God-knows-what. Enter clairvoyant Rubenstein who surmises that the subdivision was built on a sacred Indian burial ground and the gods aren't happy. Eventually she saves the day by exorcising the demons (after witnessing seemingly endless special effects; i.e., flashing lights, things whizzing around the room), and the "For Sale" sign soon goes up. POLTERGEIST is frustrating because one gets a hint at what Hooper *really*wanted to do (the face-ripping scene comes to mind), but it is obvious that he was restrained by Spielberg (who would perform similar duty on Joe Dante in GREMLINS) who didn't want to spoil the big box office. The problem is, some of the truly horrifying moments slip through the censorship cracks, scaring little kids (and their parents) who walked in expecting CLOSE ENCOUNTERS OF THE THIRD KIND and not THE TEXAS CHAINSAW MASSACRE, leaving POLTERGEIST a very disjointed, uneven movie.

p, Steven Spielberg, Frank Marshall; d, Tobe Hooper; w, Spielberg, Michael Grais, Mark Victor; ph, Matthew F. Leonetti (Panavision, Metrocolor); m, Jerry Goldsmith; ed, Michael Kahn; prod d, James H. Spencer; cos, L.J. Mower.

Horror Cas. (PR:C-O MPAA:PG)

POLYESTER** (1981) 86m New Line Cinema c

Divine *(Francine Fishpaw)*, Tab Hunter *(Todd Tomorrow)*, Edith Massey *(Cuddles)*, Mink Stole *(Sandra)*, David Samson *(Elmer Fishpaw)*, Joni Ruth White *(LaRue, Mother)*, Mary Garlington *(Lulu Fishpaw)*, Ken King *(Dexter Fishpaw)*, Hans Kramm *(Chauffeur)*, Stiv Bators *(Bo-Bo)*, Rick Breitenfeld, Michael Watson, Derek Neal, Jean Hill, Jim Hill, John Brothers, Mary Vivian Pearce, Sharon Niesp, Cookie Mueller, Susan Lowe, Tom Diventi, George Hulse, Tony Parkham, Alberto Panella, Frank Tamburo, Nancy Morgan, Keats Smith, Gordon Kamka, David Klein, George Stover, Steve Yeager, Mary Egoff, John De La Vega, Chuck Yeaton, George Udell.

Self-proclaimed "King of Schlock" Waters (PINK FLAMINGOS) toned down his usual level of grotesqueness in this parody of a suburban family, while introducing a new format to his repertoire, "Odorama." A scratch-and-sniff card was handed out to customers, with a number on the screen indicating the proper time to indulge in the very unpleasant smells. Cheesy-looking transvestite Divine parades as a housewife in a family of selfish misfits, who do nothing in return for all the attention given them by Divine. Samson, her husband, runs a pornography theater while carrying on an affair with his secretary. Divine's children, King and Garlington, are horrid; the boy always in a haze from sniffing glue, slave to an insane foot fetish. The girl, Garlington, runs around with punk Bators, getting herself pregnant. But Divine's life takes an upward swing when Hunter sweeps her off her feet, posed in *Playboy* style, sports car and all. The films of Waters have always had a large cult following; the biting satire and absurd situations reflect heavily upon how film images affect the viewer's perceptions—Waters' influence coming from underground filmmaker George Kuchar. But POLYESTER is much more cliche-ridden than his other features, making it much less successful as satire. But it still manages some grotesque scenes that will turn the toughest filmgoer's stomach. The cast members, who consist largely of Waters' usual players, are all up to the occasion.

p,d&w, John Waters; ph, David Insley (Cinefax Color); m, Chris Stein, Michael

Kamen; ed, Charles Roggero; prod d, Vincent Pernaio; set d, Peranio; cos, Van Smith; m/l, Stein, Kamen, Deborah Harry.

Drama/Comedy   **Cas.**   **(PR:O MPAA:R)**

POM POM GIRLS, THE*½   (1976) 90m Crown International c

Robert Carradine (Johnny), Jennifer Ashley (Laurie), Lisa Reeves (Sally), Michael Mullins (Jessie), Bill Adler (Duane), James Gammon (Coach), Susan Player (Sue Ann), Rainbeaux Smith (Roxanne), Diane Lee Hart (Judy), Lou Pant (Principal), John Lawrence (Sheriff), Sandra Lowell (Miss Pritchett), Faith Christopher, John Sebastian, Jim Kester, Cooper Huckabee.

This teen exploitation picture centers on the rivalry between two Southern California high schools, with Carradine and Adler having their own individual feud. The picture is realistic in its depiction of youth as a cynical bunch, mistrustful of the adult population or any other type of authority. Incorporated is a fair amount of sex and teen-age antics to attract the younger set, always eager to learn.

p,d&w, Joseph Ruben (based on a story by Ruben and Robert Rosenthal); ph, Stephen M. Katz (DeLuxe Color); m, Michael Lloyd; ed, George Bowers.

Drama/Comedy   **Cas.**   **(PR:O MPAA:R)**

POMOCNIK   (SEE: ASSISTANT, THE, 1982, Czech.)

PONCOMANIA   (SEE: POCOMANIA, 1939)

PONTIUS PILATE**   (1967, Fr./Ital.) 100m Glomer-Lux CCF/U.S. Films c (PONZIO PILATO)

Jean Marais (Pontius Pilate), Jeanne Crain (Claudia Procula), Basil Rathbone (Caiaphas), Leticia Roman (Sarah), Massimo Serato (Nicodemus), Riccardo Garrone (Galba), Livio Lorenzon (Barabbas), Gianni Garko (Jonathan), John Drew Barrymore (Jesus/Judas), Roger Treville, Carlo Giustini, Dante Di Paolo, Paul Miller, Alfredo Varelli, Manoela Ballard, Emma Baron, Raffaella Carra.

The last days of Christ are again put up on the silver screen with an all-star cast. Marais is the emperor's man in Israel, trying to keep the Jews from revolting. Rathbone (turning in the only effective performance in the film) is the nominal leader of the Jews, resentful of Christ's growing influence, and Barrymore, in probably the most bizarre piece of gimmick casting ever seen, plays both Jesus and Judas, both of them badly. Nothing here that Cecil B. DeMille didn't do a hundred times better. Filmed in 1961 in Italy, it was not released in Europe until 1964, and did not reach the U.S. until three years after that.

p, Enzo Merolle; d, Irving Rapper, Gian Paolo Callegari; w, O. Biancolo, Gino DeSanotis, Callegari (based on a story by DeSanotis); ph, Massimo Dallamano (CinemaScope, Technicolor); m, A.F. Lavagnino; md, Pierluigi Urbini.

Historical Drama   **(PR:A MPAA:NR)**

PONY EXPRESS**   (1953) 101m PAR c

Charlton Heston (Buffalo Bill Cody), Rhonda Fleming (Evelyn), Jan Sterling (Denny), Forrest Tucker (Wild Bill Hickok), Michael Moore (Rance Hastings), Porter Hall (Bridger), Richard Shannon (Barrett), Henry Brandon (Cooper), Stuart Randall (Pemberton), Lewis Martin (Sgt. Russell), Pat Hogan (Yellow Hand), James Davies (Cassidy), Eric Alden (Miller), Willard Willingham (Cavalryman), Frank Wilcox (Walstrom), Len Hendry (Maldin), Charles Hamilton (Man), Howard Joslin, LeRoy Johnson, Jimmy H. Burk, Robert J. Miles, Bob Scott, John Mansfield, Jerry James, Bob Templeton, Howard Gardiner, William Hamel.

A fast and furious western actioner which is loosely based on the epic 1925 silent of the same name and directed by the legendary James Cruze. Heston, in the role of the flamboyant Buffalo Bill Cody, travels through the dusty Utah trails and meets up with Fleming and her brother, Moore. Heston, however, is unaware that they are part of a movement to split California from the rest of the Union. Fleming and Moore, though loyal Californians, wrongly believe that state will be better off if it secedes because of its distance from the capitol in Washington, D.C. The actual masterminds behind the secession plot are Brandon, a stagecoach company owner, and Randall, a foreign agent who hopes to profit when California is purchased by a foreign government. Brandon engineers a Sioux Indian war by supplying chief Hogan with an arsenal of weapons. Indian attacks make it difficult for Heston to extend the Pony Express route into California. He meets up with Tucker, portraying Wild Bill Hickok, and the pair engage in a friendly show of sharpshooting before heading to Sacramento to establish the Pony Express station. Along the way Heston is captured by the Sioux and forced into a tomahawk battle with the tribal chief from which he emerges victorious. The climactic battle has Heston surviving an ambush attempt, and ultimately saving both California and the Pony Express. While far from being a factual account of Cody and Hickok, PONY EXPRESS does convey the romance of the era. The plot merely serves as a springboard off of which Heston and Tucker can bounce their clever dialog and their undeniable energy. Instead of understanding why and how the Pony Express evolved, the viewer comes away with an understanding of the myth that surrounds both Cody and Hickok.

p, Nat Holt; d, Jerry Hopper; w, Charles Marquis Warren (based on a story by Frank Gruber); ph, Ray Rennahan (Technicolor); m, Paul Sawtell; ed, Eda Warren; art d, Hal Pereira, Al Nozaki.

Western   **(PR:A MPAA:NR)**

PONY EXPRESS RIDER½**   (1976) 100m Doty-Dayton c

Stewart Petersen (Jimmy), Henry Wilcoxon (Trevor), Buck Taylor (Bovey), Maureen McCormick (Rose), Ken Curtis (Jed), Joan Caulfield (Charlotte), Slim Pickens (Bob), Dub Taylor (Boomer), Ace Reid (Bullfrog), Jack Elam (Crazy), Larry D. Mann (Blackmore), James Almanzar (Puddin), Bea Morris (Marquette), Tom Waters (Button), Cliff Brand (Captain), Bleu McKenzie (Bill), Pamela D'On Thompson (Rebecca), Burtrust T. Wilson (Geech).

Despite the support of such grizzled western veterans as Taylor, Elam, and Pickens,

this weak tale of revenge barely rises above the sagebrush. Petersen stars as a young man out to avenge the murder of his father. To locate the killer, he joins the Pony Express. A bit too innocuous to sustain any real interest.

p, Dan Greer, Hal Harrison, Jr.; d, Harrison; w, Lyman Dayton, Greer, Harrison, Robert Totten; ph, Bernie Abramson (DeLuxe Color); m, Robert O. Ragland; ed, Marsh Hendry; art d, Elayne Cedar; cos, Campbel.

Western   **(PR:A MPAA:G)**

PONY POST*   (1940) 59m UNIV bw

Johnny Mack Brown (Cal Sheridan), Fuzzy Knight (Shorty), Nell O'Day (Norma Reeves), Dorothy Short (Alice), Tom Chatterton (Goodwin), Stanley Blystone (Atkins), Jack Rockwell (Mack Richards), Ray Teal (Claud Richards), Kermit Maynard (Whitmore), Lane Chandler (Fairweather), Eddie Cobb (George Barber), Lloyd Ingraham (Dr. Nesbet), Charles King (Hamilton), Jimmy Wakely and his Rough Riders, Frank McCarroll, Iron Eyes Cody.

Tiresome, unexciting western has Brown running a pony express station, where he must put up with an occasional tiff with weary Indians, or from some villain who wants to get his hands on the mail. Dull.

d, Ray Taylor; w, Sherman Lowe; ph, William Sickner; ed, Paul Landres; md, Charles Previn, H.J. Salter; m/l, Johnny Bond, Milton Rosen, Everett Carter.

Western   **(PR:A MPAA:NR)**

PONY SOLDIER**   (1952) 82m FOX c (GB: MACDONALD OF THE CANADIAN MOUNTIES)

Tyrone Power (Duncan MacDonald), Cameron Mitchell (Konah), Thomas Gomez (Natayo), Penny Edwards (Emerald Neeley), Robert Horton (Jess Calhoun), Anthony Earl Numkena (Comes Running), Adeline DeWalt Reynolds (White Moon), Howard Petrie (Inspector Frazer), Stuart Randall (Standing Bear), Richard Shackleton (Bryan Neeley), James Hayward (Tim Neeley), Muriel Landers (Poks-Ki), Frank De Kova (Gustin), Louis Heminger (Crier), Grady Galloway (Shemawgun), Nipo T. Strongheart (Medicine Man), Carlow Loya (Katatatsi), Anthony Numkena, Sr., John War Eagle, Chief Bright Fire, Richard Thunder-Sky (Indians).

A picturesque and colorful outdoor adventure with Power, in his bright red uniform, starring as a heroic Canadian Mountie. It is 1876 and he is assigned to track down a tribe of of Cree Indians who have wrongly left their reservation and crossed the Montana border. Led by chief Randall, the tribe has been involved with illegally raiding buffalo herds. In addition, the tribe's war chief, Mitchell, storms a wagon train and takes two prisoners—Edwards and ex-convict Horton. Power, with his half-breed guide Gomez, spends two days following the Crees' trail before finally meeting with Randall. Power firmly orders the tribe to return to their reservation, impressing Randall with his assured nature. Mitchell, however, isn't so easily swayed and organizes a faction of Indians who intend to stand their ground. A tribal meeting is called, during which Power and a young Indian boy, Numkena, become friends. Randall agrees to return to Canada in exchange for supplies. Power meets his demands, but before the deal is completed Horton attempts to escape, killing Mitchell's brother in the process. Horton is captured by Mitchell's loyal faction and strung up between two horses, which are ready to pull him in two by running in opposite directions. Power bravely intervenes and makes peace with Randall. Mitchell is still bent on revenge, however, and kidnaps Edwards, taking her high up into the mountains to burn her at the stake. Power comes to her rescue and in a flurry of gunshots and flying arrows the girl is saved while Mitchell is killed. Power then escorts the tribe back across the Canadian border and onto their reservation. Needless to say, Power ends up with the girl at the finale. Not one of Power's finest achievements (Newman's direction is lifeless, to say the least), PONY SOLDIER is still watchable thanks to some solid performances and a well-paced script. By the early 1950s Power, who was at the end of his exclusive contract with Fox, was relegated to second-rate pictures because of his growing devotion to the stage. He still managed, as in PONY SOLDIER, to be a commanding presence on the screen.

p, Samuel G. Engel; d, Joseph M. Newman; w, John C. Higgins (based on a Saturday Evening Post story by Garnett Weston); ph, Harry Jackson (Technicolor); m, Alex North; ed, John McCafferty; md, Alfred Newman; art d, Lyle Wheeler, Chester Gore; set d, Thomas Little, Fred J. Rode; cos, Edward Stevenson; spec eff, Ray Kellogg; tech adv, Chief Nipo T. Strongheart.

Western   **(PR:A MPAA:NR)**

POOKIE   (SEE: STERILE CUCKOO, THE, 1969)

POOL OF LONDON½**   (1951, Brit.) 86m EAL/UNIV bw

Bonar Colleano (Dan MacDonald), Susan Shaw (Pat), Renee Asherson (Sally), Earl Cameron (Johnny), Moira Lister (Maisie), Max Adrian (Vernon), Joan Dowling (Pamela), James Robertson Justice (Trotter), Michael Golden (Andrews), Alfie Bass (Alf), Christopher Hewitt (Mike), Leslie Phillips (Harry), George Benson (George), John Longden (Inspector Williamson), Laurence Naismith (Commissionaire), Beckett Bould (Watchman), Victor Maddern (Tram Conductor), Sam Kydd (2nd Engineer), Michael Corcoran (Sam), Mai Bacon (Barmaid), Mavis Villiers (Drinking Club Blonde), Michael Ward, George Merritt.

Colleano plays a hearty, overly confident sailor who makes a little money on the side through a smuggling operation. He becomes involved with a gang of jewel thieves and the prospect of making some big money. But a murder is committed during the heist, making for a vast manhunt by the police. Inadvertently, Colleano plants the evidence on his closest friend, young black sailor Cameron, who has started a friendship with a white girl. Numerous tangents keep the plot hazy, but evenly paced direction keeps a steady momentum of tension. Both Colleano and Cameron, as the black sailor, are true to the roles they portray. All the action takes place within a two-day period, when a cargo ship is docked at London; the city is used very effectively as a backdrop to the story. The film grew out of a documentary project, which gives it credibility.

p, Michael Relph; d, Basil Dearden; w, Jack Wittingham, John Eldridge; ph, Gordon Dines; m, John Addison; ed, Peter Tanner; art d, Jim Morahan.

Drama/Crime (PR:A MPAA:NR)

POOR ALBERT AND LITTLE ANNIE (SEE: I DISMEMBER MAMA, 1974)

POOR COW*** (1968, Brit.) 101m Vic-Fenchurch/NGP c

Carol White (Joy), Terence Stamp (Dave), John Bindon (Tom), Kate Williams (Beryl), Queenie Watts (Aunt Emm), Geraldine Sherman (Trixie), James Beckett, Billy Murray (Tom's Friends), Simon King (Johnny, Age 1 1/2), Stevie King (Johnny, Age 3), Winnie Holman (Woman in Park), Rose Hillier (Customer in Hairdressers), Ellis Dale (Solicitor), Gerald Young (Judge), Paddy Joyce (Governor in Photo Studio), Gladys Dawson (Bet), Ron Pember (Petal), Malcolm McDowell (Billy), George Tovey, Will Stampe, Bernard Stone, John Halstead (Photographers), Peter Claughton (Driving Examiner), Julie May (Woman in Sheppey), Phillip Rose (Shelley), Martin King (Prison Warden), Muriel Hunte (Woman at Prison), James Thornhill (Prisoner), Mo Dwyer (Prisoner's Wife), Terry Duggan (2nd Prisoner), Ian Christian, Liza Carrol, Tony Selby, Ray Barron, Sian Davis, Mike Negal, George Sewell, Chris Gannon, Philip Newman, Alan Selwyn, Wally Patch, Hilda Barry, Joe Palmer (Customers in Pub).

A complex and poignant look at a woman left to fend for herself and her newborn child after her husband has been jailed, with her attempts to grab survival and even happiness despite her situation. White is married to bullying thief Bindon, who treats her in a gruff and even brutal manner while living in their dingy London flat. When he is sent to jail, White moves in with Stamp, a fellow thief and friend of her husband, but a gentle and caring man who treats her son in an affectionate manner. Her brief happiness with Stamp ends when he is also arrested. Though White promises to be faithful to Stamp, left on her own she makes a living by posing for nude photos and as a barmaid, treating herself to an occasional affair. She begins divorce proceedings against Bindon, but when he is released she attempts to revive their marriage for the benefit of their son. White gives an excellent performance as a woman who finds herself in many squalid situations. The production relies on improvisational techniques to get the proper emotional levels for certain sequences; this works quite effectively.

p, Joseph Janni; d, Kenneth Loach; w, Loach, Nell Dunn (based on a novel by Dunn); ph, Brian Probyn (Eastmancolor); m, Donovan; ed, Roy Watts; md, John Cameron; art d, Bernard Sarron; m/l, "Be Not Too Hard," Donovan, Christopher Logue (sung by Donovan), "Colours," "Poor Love," Donovan (sung by Donovan).

Drama (PR:C MPAA:NR)

POOR LITTLE RICH GIRL** (1936) 72m FOX bw (AKA: THE POOR LITTLE RICH GIRL)

Shirley Temple (Barbara Barry), Alice Faye (Jerry Dolan), Gloria Stuart (Margaret Allen), Jack Haley (Jimmy Dolan), Michael Whalen (Richard Barry), Sara Haden (Collins), Jane Darwell (Woodward), Claude Gillingwater (Simon Peck), Henry Armetta (Tony, Organ Grinder), Arthur Hoyt (Percival Gooch), John Wray (Flagin), Paul Stanton (George Hathaway), Charles Coleman (Stebbins), John Kelly (Ferguson), Tyler Brooke (Dan Ward), Mathilde Comont (Tony's Wife), Leonard Kilbrick (Freckles), Dick Webster (Soloist), Bill Ray, Gayne Whitman (Announcers), Dick Webster [Tony Martin] (Radio Vocalist).

Basically a contrived story to cash in on Fox's greatest box-office attraction of the time, Temple. A much-revised remake of the 1917 vehicle for Mary Pickford, with Temple playing the daughter of widowed wealthy soap manufacturer Whalen. When it's suggested that Temple should go to school in order to be around other kids, nurse Haden packs her off to a train, but is involved in an accident on the way. This gives Temple the chance to imitate her favorite heroine from the stories she has been read, and she takes off on her own. Meeting up with an organ grinder, she tags along to his rooming house, claiming to be an orphan. There she meets upstairs neighbors Faye and Haley, a song-and-dance couple, who incorporate the tot into their routine after seeing her dance. Temple's charm helps the duo get a job on the radio program of soap manufacturer Gillingwater, rival of Temple's father. Father and daughter are reunited when he comes to pay a call on Gillingwater's secretary, Stuart, with whom he has fallen in love. This also makes for a chance for the two companies to merge, using the singing talents of Faye, Dolan, and Temple to do their advertising. Temple added her usual childish charm to this picture, but everything centered on her so much the other performers were put in the background, their talents not utilized or unrecognized. Faye and Haley didn't make their appearance until the film was almost half over; this was Faye's briefest screen appearance, possibly excepting NOW I'LL TELL (1934), of any of her 33 pictures. Following this film, Faye's appearance softened. Her hair was restyled and the much-plucked eyebrows made more natural. A new young singer, unbilled but going by the name of Dick Webster, made quite an impression on audiences in his 80 seconds of screen time singing "When I'm With You"; this was the first of four films Tony Martin was to appear in with throaty singer Faye. All production values are of the highest standards. Songs include: "Oh My Goodness," "Buy a Bar of Barry's," "Wash Your Necks with a Cake of Peck's," "Military Man," "When I'm with You," "But Definitely," and "You've Gotta Eat Your Spinach, Baby" (Mack Gordon, Harry Revel).

p, Darryl F. Zanuck; d, Irving Cummings; w, Sam Hellman, Gladys Lehman, Harry Tugend (based on stories by Eleanor Gates, Ralph Spence); ph, John Seitz; ed, Jack Murray; md, Louis Silvers; art d, William Darling, Rudolph Sternad; cos, Gwen Wakeling; ch, Jack Haskell, Ralph Cooper.

Musical/Comedy (PR:A MPAA:NR)

POOR OLD BILL*½ (1931, Brit.) 52m BIP/Wardour

Leslie Fuller (Bill), Iris Ashley (Emily), Syd Courtenay (Harry), Peter Lawford (Horace), Hal Gordon (Jack), Robert Brooks-Turner (Mick), Dick Francis (Police Constable).

Interesting conception for a farce has Fuller coming home from the war, only to have to put up with an obtrusive guest who won't leave. The man has the idea that since he seemingly saved Fuller's life during the war, Fuller owes him. After several attempts to get the man to leave, including a staged scene where Fuller pretends to save his putative savior's life to repay the debt, the man finally leaves when another war buddy shows up and enlightens them to the fact that this intruder did not save Fuller's life. The second war buddy tosses the first out, then moves in, under the pretension that he was really the hero. Unfortunately, the idea is carried on much too long, stretching what little material there is. This was the first screen appearance of Lawford, who was 8 years old at the time, playing the son of Fuller. The camera lingers long and lovingly on Lawford's much-bathed backside; the creative staff apparently considered bare buttocks to be screamingly funny. An embarrassment, no doubt, to the suave, aristocratic-seeming member of Frank Sinatra's "Rat Pack," but after all, Sinatra had the shame of THE KISSING BANDIT (1948) to bear.

p, Walter C. Mycroft; d, Monty Banks; w, Val Valentine (based on a story by Syd Courtenay, Lola Harvey); ph, Claude Friese-Greene.

Comedy (PR:A MPAA:NR)

POOR OUTLAWS, THE (SEE: ROUND UP, THE, 1969, Hung.)

POOR RICH, THE*½ (1934) 76m UNIV bw

Edward Everett Horton, Edna May Oliver, Thelma Todd, Andy Devine, Leila Hyams, Una O'Connor, E.E. Clive, Grant Mitchell, John Miljan, Edward Brophy, Jack Clifford, Ward Bond, Sidney Bracey, Henry Armetta.

Poorly produced attempt at comedy has two broke cousins, Horton and Oliver, inheriting a British mansion. This sets off a plan by Oliver to get Horton married to wealthy society woman Todd, and Oliver goes about the task of making herself and Horton appear rich in order to attract the woman. But the plan backfires, so they take what little money they have left, hock the furniture, and open a restaurant in the mansion, with the marriage happening anyway. Except for an occasional laugh, the film falls flat. The badly miscast actors can do little with the bungling script.

d, Edward Sedgwick; w, Ebba Havez, Dale Van Every; ph, John J. Mescall; ed, Robert Carlisle.

Comedy (PR:A MPAA:NR)

POOR WHITE TRASH (SEE: BAYOU, 1957)

POOR WHITE TRASH II (SEE: SCUM OF THE EARTH, 1976)

POP ALWAYS PAYS** (1940) 66m RKO bw

Leon Errol (Henry Brewster), Dennis O'Keefe (Jeff Thompson), Adele Pearce (Edna Brewster), Walter Catlett (Tommy Lane), Marjorie Gateson (Mrs. Brewster), Tom Kennedy (Murphy), Robert Middlemass (Mr. Oberton), Effie Anderson (Mary), Erskine Sanford (Hayes), Max Wagner.

Light-hearted fare has Errol allowing his daughter, Pearce, to marry O'Keefe only on the condition that the latter can raise $1,000. If this is done Errol will permit the marriage, plus match the amount that O'Keefe has saved. Never expecting this to take place, Errol finds himself scampering to raise the money when the love-driven O'Keefe almost has the dollars. It is only fitting that Errol's business falls into a slump. Picture moves swiftly, with the action tending toward slapstick, mostly at the hands of Errol.

p, Lee Marcus, Bert Gilroy; d, Leslie Goodwins; w, Charles E. Roberts (based on a story by Arthur J. Beckhard); ph, Jack Mackenzie; ed, Desmond Marquette; md, Paul Sawtell; art d, Van Nest Polglase.

Comedy **Cas.** (PR:A MPAA:NR)

POPDOWN** (1968, Brit.) 54m Fremar c

Diane Keen (Miss 1970), Jane Bates (Aries), Zoot Money (Sagittarius), Carol Rachell (Miss Withit), Debbie Slater (Girl), Bill Aron (Host), Nicole Yarna (Body), Fred Marshall (Boy), Margaret Evans (Nude), Brenton Wood, Treasure Chest, Don Partridge, Tony Hicks, Kevin & Gary, Dantalion's Chariot, Blossom Toes, Hetty Schneider Quartet, Julie Driscoll, The Brian Auger Trinity.

Mainly an excuse to capitalize on the London music scene of the time, the zany plot has a couple of aliens coming to Earth to observe human behavior, but in the process becoming fascinated with rock music. Features appearances from several bands then popular, including Dantalion's Chariot, The Brian Auger Trinity, and Blossom Toes.

p,d&w, Fred Marshall; ph, Oliver Wood (Eastmancolor).

Fantasy (PR:A MPAA:NR)

POPE JOAN* (1972, Brit.) 132m Big City-Command-Triple Eight/COL c (GB: THE DEVIL'S IMPOSTER)

Liv Ullmann (Joan), Olivia De Havilland (Mother Superior), Lesley-Anne Down (Cecilia), Keir Dullea (Dr. Stevens), Trevor Howard (Pope Leo), Jeremy Kemp (Joan's Father), Patrick Magee (Elder Monk), Franco Nero (Louis), Maximilian Schell (Brother Adrian), Robert Beatty (Dr. Corwin), Natasa Nicolescu (Joan's Mother), Sharon Winter (Young Joan), Margareta Pogonat (Village Woman), Richard Bebb (Lord of the Manor), Peter Arne (Richard), George Innes (2nd Monk), Nigel Havers (Young Monk), Susan Macready (Sister Nunciata), Sheelah Wilcocks (Sister Louise), Andre Morell (Emperor Louis), Martin Benson (Lothair), Lorain Bertorelli, Mary Healey (Nuns), Kurt Christian (Prince Charles), Philip Ross (Peasant in Hut), Duncan Lamont, Ion Grafini (Wounded Soldiers), Manning Wilson (Bishop), Katharine Schofield (Alma), Carl Bernard (Ancient Monk), John

Arineri *(Church Official)*, John Shrapnel *(Father James)*, Richard Pearson *(Father Timothy)*, Terrence Hardiman *(Cardinal Anastasius)*, John Byron *(Cardinal Jerome)*, Derek Farr *(Cardinal Brisini)*, Neil Kennedy *(Louis' Emissary)*, Neville Aurelius *(Duty Doctor)*.

Made in England and Romania by several production companies, this picture was picked up by Columbia for distribution but received such scathing notices and did such little business in its few venues that it mercifully sank from sight. There has long been a rumor that a woman held the papal throne between Leo IV and Benedict III. That has been mostly refuted by scholars but since there is a definite gap in the years between those two men, this legend has sprung up and has been in more than one fictional story, including "Top Girls," a British stage play in the 1980s. Ullmann is a small-time Aimee Semple McPherson who takes the stump in little Midwest villages to decry the moral degradation of modern-day humanity. She is the daughter of Kemp, also a traveling shouter a la Billy Sunday (or Graham, depending on how old you are). She has taken to identifying herself with the "mythical" Pope Joan and visits Dullea, a psychiatrist, to work things out. He brings in Beatty and the two men listen to Ullmann as she tries to find out if she may be the reincarnation of Pope Joan, due to the similarities in their lives. Cut back and forth 1000 years and we see Ullmann, raped by three monks who were friends of her dad, finding a haven in a nunnery run by de Havilland, getting hit on by Nero, the prince grandson of Charlemagne, watching her friend, Down, a nun, allow herself to be the object of Nero's sexuality, and more. Ullmann becomes the mistress of Schell, a monk-artist. Violence occurs when Charlemagne dies. Saxons pillage the villages and rape the women, including many of the nuns. Down and de Havilland are cruelly murdered and Ullmann flees by cutting her hair short and masquerading as a man. She goes to Greece with Schell and preaches the Gospel so passionately that she's noticed by Howard (Leo IV) who appoints her his secretary, never knowing that she is not a he. Howard makes Ullmann a Cardinal, then names her as his successor (this was before elections and the puffs of smoke after the ballots). Nero is now the emperor-to-be and protests Ullmann's appointment (not knowing it's the same woman he tried to seduce earlier). They get together and he sees through her new hairdo, makes love to her and leaves with the promise that she'll crown him. Schell thinks she'd better come clean and depart but she won't hear of that. When Nero returns, the Pope is pregnant but wrapping herself tightly to conceal the fact. She walks down the steps of the Lateran Palace to give Nero her blessing then falls from the pain of having been strapped so tightly. The straps are ripped away and the assembled people are astonished at what they see. They turn surly at having been duped, race for the steps and trample Ullmann to death. Cut back to modern-time and Ullmann, the 1970s preacher, is also trying to hide a pregnancy and dies in Dullea's arms. Boring trash, in bad taste, miserable acting from an international cast, lackluster direction. It will appeal only to ardent feminists who might like to believe that Mother Church was once overseen by a mother.

p, Kurt Unger; d, Michael Anderson; w, John Briley; ph, Billy Williams (Panavision, Eastmancolor); m, Maurice Jarre; ed, Bill Lenny; prod d, Elliot Scott; md, Jarre; art d, Norman Dorme; cos, Elizabeth Haffenden, Joan Bridge; makeup, George Partleton; m/l, "Veni Creator Spiritus," "Tu Es Petrus" (sung by the Sistine Chapel Choir under the direction of Domenico Bartolucci).

Drama (PR:C MPAA:PG)

POPE ONDINE STORY, THE (SEE: CHELSEA GIRLS, THE, 1966)

POPEYE** (1980) 114m PAR c

Robin Williams *(Popeye)*, Shelley Duvall *(Olive Oyl)*, Ray Walston *(Poopdeck Pappy)*, Paul L. Smith *(Bluto)*, Paul Dooley *(Wimpy)*, Richard Libertini *(Geezil)*, Roberta Maxwell *(Nana Oyl)*, Donald Moffat *(Taxman)*, MacIntyre Dixon *(Cole Oyl)*, Donovan Scott *(Castor Oyl)*, Allan Nichols *(Rough House)*, Wesley Ivan Hurt *(Swee' Pea)*, Bill Irwin *(Ham Gravy)*, Robert Fortier *(Bill Barnacle, Town Drunk)*, David McCharen *(Harry Hotcash, Gambler)*, Sharon Kinney *(Cherry, His Moll)*, Peter Bray *(Oxblood Oxheart, the Fighter)*, Linda Hunt *(Mrs. Oxheart)*, Susan Kingsley *(LaVerne)*, Paul Zegler *(Mayor Stonefeller)*, Pamela Burrell *(Mrs. Stonefeller)*, Ray Cooper *(Preacher)*, Geoff Hoyle, Wayne Robson, Larry Pisoni, Carlo Pellegrini, Michael Christensen, Noel Parenti, Karen McCormick, John Bristol, Julie Janney, Patty Katz, Diane Shaffer, Nathalie Blossom, Dennis Franz, Carlos Brown, Ned Dowd, Hovey Burgess, Roberto Messina.

E.C. Segar created one of the most enduring comic characters when he first drew "Popeye" and the others in the strip. There had been a series of cartoons in the 1930s and 1940s but never a full-length feature until Altman teamed with Feiffer to make this one. It's yet another good idea gone down the drain under Altman's spotty direction. The first hour is like watching a Ferarri idling. It seems to want to race away with a roar but doesn't until the last 50 minutes when it takes off the way a cartoon does and ultimately manages to achieve some sort of excitement. They built a sensational set on the island of Malta and used it well, as Williams (with fascinating prosthetic arms to simulate the sailor's "muskies") arrives in the little town of Sweethaven to find the father, Walston, who abandoned him years before. Williams meets the skinny girl of his dreams, Duvall, and the two of them find their own abandoned baby, Hurt (who steals every scene he's in and has a huge career in front of him if he doesn't age). Smith is the gargantuan Bluto, scourge of Sweethaven, a man not unlike the role Smith played in MIDNIGHT EXPRESS. Smith loves Duvall and resents Williams for his intrusion and the resultant fight between the two is the comedy-action highlight. The most famous line uttered by "Popeye" in his peregrinations is "I yam what I yam," and we wonder if composer Jerry Herman realized that when he wrote the song for "La Cage Aux Folles" of the same name, with a totally different meaning, as the drag hero (heroine?) states proudly that he (she?) is what he (she?) is and is proud of it. Sound has always played an important part in Altman's work but he goes too far over the edge in having Williams and many of the other characters mutter under their breaths in such a casual fashion that many of the lines are missed, not that they would make a difference. All of the Segar cartoon people are here including "Wimpy" (Paul Dooley), whose name inspired a huge chain of hamburger stands, and the rest of the "Oyl" family, as played by Maxwell ("Nana"), Dixon ("Coal"), and Scott ("Castor"). The star of the film is the magnificent set and little more, and when the backdrop must be cited for its excellence, that tells you something is wrong in front of the furniture. Williams does his best in the lead and even manages to screw up his face and his eye in a credible imitation of the drawings. Dooley, who has appeared time and again in Altman films, wears lots of padding to fill out his medium frame in order to play the corpulent hamburger fanatic. Duvall is perfect as the gangly "Olive Oyl" although her screeching voice sends chills up one's spine, like the scraping of chalk on a blackboard. The two-year-old (or so) Hurt is the most engaging moppet in many years and all eyes go to him whenever he's on the screen. Under the tutelage of veteran dancer-choreographer Lou Wills, Jr., Williams shows that he's not just another scrunched-up face and acquits himself in the dance department very well. Wills and Williams had met originally when the struggling Williams came to Los Angeles and attended Harvey Lembeck's Comedy Class, where Wills was a charter member. When Williams became a star, he never forgot the pals of his early years and used them whenever he could. Harry Nilsson wrote a number of tunes for this and none were memorable.

p, Robert Evans; d, Robert Altman; w, Jules Feiffer (based on comic strip characters created by E.C. Segar); ph, Giuseppe Rotunno (Technovision); m, Harry Nilsson; ed, Tony Lombardo; prod d, Wolf Kroeger; cos, Scott Bushnell; ch, Sharon Kinney, Hovey Burgess, Lou Wills.

Musical/Comedy Cas. (PR:A MPAA:PG)

POPI*** (1969) 115m UA c

Alan Arkin *(Abraham Rodriguez)*, Rita Moreno *(Lupe)*, Miguel Alejandro *(Junior Rodriguez)*, Ruben Figueroa *(Luis Rodriguez)*, John Harkins *(Harmon)*, Joan Tompkins *(Miss Musto)*, Anthony Holland *(Pickett)*, Arny Freeman *(Diaz)*, Barbara Dana *(Receptionist)*, Antonia Rey *(Mrs. Cruz)*, Arnold Soboloff *(Dr. Perle)*, Victor Junquera *(Novitas Man)*, Gladys Velez *(Silvia)*, Anita Dangler *(Nurse)*, Judith Lowry *(Old Lady)*.

Alan Arkin is one of those chameleon actors who can do many different kinds of roles. That works for and against him, as his career has been filled with interesting parts but only the rare successful commercial venture. This time Arkin is a poor Puerto Rican widower living in New York's Spanish Harlem. He's raising his two sons, Figueroa and Alejandro, in a small apartment which has been multiple-locked to protect them against intruders, and whenever someone knocks on the door, Arkin barks to simulate a watchdog. He is devoted to giving his sons a better lot in life than the one he received. Once that's done, he will bestow some pleasure upon himself by marrying his sensuous girl friend, Moreno, and quit Harlem for the relatively safer area of Brooklyn. Arkin works many jobs to support his sons and fears that they might be too influenced by their lives in the area. Soon he learns that the boys have told their schoolyard pals that he is a gangster, the brother of a local underworld hard guy. Arkin is working at a dinner for Cuban refugees and realizes that the U.S. has always been kinder to political refugees than to the average poor guy, so he hits upon a plan. He wants his sons to have the best of everything, so his plot is to set them adrift off the coast of Florida in a boat and let them be picked up by the Coast Guard as two boys fleeing from Castro's tyranny. To that end, he takes his sons to Central Park and instructs them in the art of rowing, then teaches them how to handle a motorboat in the East River. The boys are totally against the idea and even attempt to run away but Arkin prevails, takes them to Florida, robs a small boat, and tells the boys to steer it out to sea, wait until there's no more gas and that they'll be found soon enough. They are frightened but finally agree. Arkin can't get in touch with the Coast Guard and becomes a basket case until he hears the news that two "Cuban" boys have been rescued. They are taken to a hospital to recover from sunburn and lack of water and thousands of messages pour in, including an invitation to meet the President in Washington. When the boys recover, Arkin (disguised) manages to get to them and they tell him that they've received many offers of adoption but that doesn't matter to them. They love Arkin and want to stay with him. There is an argument that alerts the hospital staff. Arkin attempts to escape, the sons run after him, and, in the end, the entire charade is uncovered. Alejandro and Figueroa (a rare name in that it has every vowel in the alphabet) are thrilled to go back home to Harlem, a place they love and never want to leave again. The story and the situation are very "New York" in style and content and many of the jokes are so oriented to the city that they may be lost on anyone who has never visited the Big Mango (which is what Puerto Rican comedienne Liz Torres calls it now that so many of her countrymen have moved there).

p, Herbert B. Leonard; d, Arthur Hiller; w, Tina Pine, Les Pine; ph, Andrew Laszlo (DeLuxe Color); m, Dominic Frontiere; ed, Anthony Ciccolini; art d, Robert Gundlach; cos, Albert Wolsky; m/l, Frontiere, Norman Gimbel; makeup, Mike Maggi.

Comedy (PR:A MPAA:G)

POPIOL Y DIAMENT (SEE: ASHES AND DIAMONDS, 1961, Pol.)

POPPY*** (1936) 75m PAR bw

W.C. Fields *(Prof. Eustace McGargle)*, Rochelle Hudson *(Poppy)*, Richard Cromwell *(Billy Farnsworth)*, Granville Bates *(Mayor Farnsworth)*, Catherine Doucet *(Countess Maggie Tubbs De Puizzi)*, Lynne Overman *(Attorney E.G. Whiffen)*, Maude Eburne *(Sarah Tucker)*, Bill Wolfe *(Egmont)*, Adrian Morris *(Constable Bowman)*, Rosalind Keith *(Frances Parker)*, Ralph M. Remley *(Carnival Manager)*, Wade Boteler *(Bartender)*, Tom Herbert *(Astonished Barfly)*, Cyril Ring, Jack Baxley, Harry Wagner, Frank Sully, Eddie C. Waller, Del Henderson *(Yokels)*, Tammany Young *(Joe)*, Dewey Robinson *(Calliope Driver)*, Tom Kennedy *(Hot Dog Vendor)*, Nora Cecil *(Woman)*, Gertrude Sutton, Grace Goodall *(Gossips)*, Ada May Moore *(Snake Charmer)*, Jerry Bergen *(Gardener)*, Doc Stone, Malcolm Waite, Dick Rush *(Deputy Sheriffs)*, Charles McMurphy *(Constable)*.

A somewhat disappointing sound remake of the Fields-D.W. Griffith silent classic

SALLY OF THE SAWDUST (1925), both based on the hit 1923 stage play that propelled vaudevillian Fields to stardom. While the addition of sound enables the audience to hear Fields' wonderful carny patter and his mumbling asides, the comedian's poor health prevented him from performing his more amazing physical comedy—such as juggling—and kept his scenes in the film to a minimum. The film opens as Fields, a traveling hustler and con man who works small towns with his adopted daughter Hudson, decides to ply his dubious trade at a fair in the town of Green Acres. Fields spots a stray dog, catches the pup, and takes it to the local watering hole. There Fields sets the dog on the bar and asks it what it will have. Using ventriloquism, Fields has the dog answer, "Milk in a saucer." The amazed bartender immediately offers to buy the dog for $20. Fields takes the money and heads for the door. The dog shouts at Fields, "Just for selling me, I'll never talk again." Field's sadly informs the bartender, "He probably means it, too. He's awfully stubborn," and leaves the dog and the bartender locked in stony silence. From there Fields and Hudson set up a booth at the fair and fool customers into giving up their money to the shell game. Fields fleeces the other concession operators as well by fooling a hot dog vendor into giving him two hot dogs for free. During the fair Hudson meets and falls in love with the mayor's son, Cromwell. Meanwhile, Fields learns that the Putnam family, a very rich and well established clan, is being forced to auction off their estate because the legal heir disappeared when she was a baby. Fields has a crooked lawyer friend draw up a document stating that Hudson is the missing heiress. Fields' scheme conflicts with Hudson's plans, however; she and Cromwell become engaged. At a party celebrating the event, Fields wrangles some of the upper-crust crowd into a bizarre game of croquet (which Fields derived in part from his classic golf routine). Eventually Fields' plan to pass off Hudson as the heir to the Putnam fortune is uncovered and the wedding is off. Hudson runs away and is sheltered by a kindly woman, Eburne, who has befriended her. Eburne, who knew the Putnam family intimately, recognizes a resemblance between Hudson and the late Mrs. Putnam. Suspicions are confirmed when a locket is discovered that proves Hudson is actually the missing Putnam heir after all. The good news rights everything: the marriage goes on as planned and Fields can stop running from the police. In what is supposed to be a very moving and emotional scene between father and daughter after Hudson informs Fields she will no longer be his traveling companion, Fields gently tells her, "Let me give you one word of fatherly advice…never give a sucker an even break." While POPPY is frequently very funny and contains some priceless Fields moments like the talking dog scene, it suffers for the very reason that such scenes are few and far between. Fields was working under a myriad of health problems at the time (many brought on by heavy drinking) and during the shooting of POPPY he fell off an old-fashioned bicycle—his police-escape vehicle—and broke a vertebra. The comedian was forced to play the rest of his scenes wearing a restricting back-brace device that was hidden under his costume. His pain was frequent and intense but Fields would play a scene flawlessly—and then pass out when the filming stopped. Because of these problems, Fields' scenes were cut drastically, a double (Johnny Sinclair) was used for the comedian in long shots and over-the-shoulder shots, and needless subplot and musical numbers were used to fill the gaps. It is a pity that neither film version of Fields' 1923 Broadway hit managed to capture the performer in his full glory, but the snatches we are left with are testament enough to the great talent and courage of its star.

p, William LeBaron; d, A. Edward Sutherland; w, Waldemar Young, Virginia Van Upp (based on the play by Dorothy Donnelly); ph, William C. Mellor; ed, Stuart Heisler; md, Boris Morros; art d, Hans Dreier, Bernard Herzbrun; set d, AE Freudeman; cos, Edith Head; m/l, Ralph Rainger, Leo Robin, Sam Coslow, Frederick Hollander.

Comedy   **(PR:A MPAA:NR)**

POPPY IS ALSO A FLOWER, THE***   (1966) 100m Telsun-United
                                                                Nations/Comet c

E.G. Marshall (Jones), Trevor Howard (Lincoln), Gilbert Roland (Marco), Rita Hayworth (Monique), Anthony Quayle (Captain), Angie Dickinson (Linda Benson), Yul Brynner (Col. Salem), Eli Wallach (Locarno), Harold Sakata (Martin), Senta Berger (Nightclub Entertainer), Hugh Griffith (Tribal Chief), Marcello Mastroianni (Inspector Mosca), Georges Geret (Supt. Roche), Howard Vernon (Police Analyst), Stephen Boyd (Benson), Jocelyn Lane (Society Photographer), Amedeo Nazzari (Capt. Dinonno), Jean-Claude Pascal (Leader of Tribesmen), Omar Sharif (Dr. Rad), Nadja Tiller (Dr. Bronovska), Barry Sullivan (Chasen), Jack Hawkins (Gen. Bahar), Trini Lopez (Himself), Gilda Dahlberg (Guest at Marco's Table), Grace Kelly (Introduction), Sylvia Sorrente (Virgia), Bob Cunningham (Fred, Marco's Aide), Luisa Rivelli, Laya Raki, Marilu Tolu, Violette Marceau, Morteza Kazerouni, Ali Oveisi.

Made originally as a 90-minute TV special on ABC and sponsored by Xerox, this all-star vehicle closely resembles the 1947 Dick Powell film, TO THE ENDS OF THE EARTH, although there is no nod to that in the credits. Ian Fleming wrote the story and died before he could do the screenplay and there is more than a little Bondsmanship in it, with the same director who helmed DR. NO handling the chores. After the TV showing in April, 1966, several minutes of footage that were too rough for tube viewing were restored in the theatrical version. Boyd is a drug operative for the U.S. government. He's murdered in the desert wasteland of Iran while attempting an opium buy and Howard and Marshall are sent to solve the crime and put an end to the dealings of the conspiracy that makes and sells the fruit of the poppy. They go to the Iranian capital of Teheran where they meet Dickinson, the "widow" of Boyd. She is missing almost at once and the trail gets cold. Marshall and Howard think they have a way to trace the goods so they hijack a cache of opium, outfit it with tracers that can be followed by Geiger counters and begin to monitor the progress of the narcotics through various places. The Neopolitan cops find the stuff after the agents have lost it and the drugs are known to be in the possession of Roland, apparently a rich ne'er-do-well who lives aboard his yacht in Monaco's harbor. Howard goes to the south of France, gets aboard the

yacht during a party, meets Roland and is surprised to see Dickinson there as well. Howard talks to Roland's wife, Hayworth, and learns that she is addicted to drugs. The next day, Howard is found murdered and Marshall must keep on the job alone. Roland is reached on a train heading for Paris and so is Dickinson, who now admits that she is a special agent for the United Nations. They are almost killed by Roland's minions, then race back to the boat in Monte Carlo to smash the ring. Along the way, there are several cameos: by Quayle as Roland's yacht captain, Wallach as a retired gangster, Griffith as an Iranian sheikh, Hawkins and Brynner as police officers, Sharif as a U.N. scientist, Sullivan as an official with the U.N., Mastroianni as an Italian police inspector, Berger as a nightclub singer hooked on drugs, and, for no apparent reason other than marquee value, the then-hot Trini Lopez as himself. Fast-moving (almost too much so) and colorful, the movie was made in Iran, Monaco, Italy, and the Iranian desert. Nobody made a lot of bucks from the movie as all the actors worked for low wages and even paid some of their own expenses in a sincere desire to put an end to the dope traffic which was then (and still is) killing thousands of people and making billions of dollars.

p, Euan Lloyd; d, Terence Young; w, Jo Eisinger (based on an idea by Ian Fleming); ph, Henri Alekan (Eastmancolor); second unit ph, Tony Brown; m, Georges Auric; ed, Monique Bonnot, Peter Thornton, Henry Richardson; art d, Maurice Colasson, Tony Roman; set d, Freda Pearson; spec eff, Paul Pollard.

Crime   Cas.   (PR:C MPAA:GP)

POPSY POP**   (1971, Fr.) 100m Sofracima/Cannon c (AKA: THE
                                                        BUTTERFLY AFFAIR)

Stanley Baker (Silva), Claudia Cardinale (Popsy), Henri Charriere (Marco), Marc Mazza (Heavy), Georges Aminet (Priest), Ginette Leclerc (Madame).

A return to the 1940s Hollywood film has writer/actor Charriere, a diamond thief, and Baker, a police inspector, tracking down Cardinale across South America after she has cheated them both. Despite some nice photography of the South American jungle, the picture is pretty flat, with Cardinale miscast as the classic femme fatale.

d, Jean Herman; w, Henri Charriere, Herman; ph, Jean-Jacques Tarbes (Eastmancolor); ed, Helene Plemianikoff.

Crime Drama   (PR:A MPAA:NR)

POR MIS PISTOLAS*½**   (1969, Mex.) 123m Posa Films International/
                                                                COL c

Cantinflas [Mario Moreno] (Fidenco), Isela Vega (Lupita), Jorge Rado (Pat O'Connor), Alfonso Mejia (Pablo), Gloria Coral (Winona), Quinton Bulnes (Tom Banana), Manuel Alvarado (Don Serapio), Manver (Indian Chief).

An attempt to capitalize on popular Latin American comedian Cantinflas has him playing a druggist who comes over the border to Arizona to claim an old mine he has inherited. Along the way he is captured by a group of Apaches who plan on burning him at the stake. But the chief of the group has a toothache, which Cantinflas mends, thus getting the help of these Indians to fight a band of villains who are keeping him from the mine. (In Spanish.)

p, Jacques Gelman; d, Miguel Delgado; ph, Jose Ramos (Eastmancolor); m, Sergio Geurrero.

Comedy   (PR:A MPAA:NR)

POR UN PUNADO DE DOLARES   (SEE: FISTFUL OF DOLLARS, A,
                                                        1967, Ital./Span./W. Ger.)

PORGY AND BESS*½**   (1959) 138m Goldwyn/COL c

Sidney Poitier (Porgy), Dorothy Dandridge (Bess), Sammy Davis, Jr. (Sportin' Life), Pearl Bailey (Maria), Brock Peters (Crown), Leslie Scott (Jake), Diahann Carroll (Clara), Ruth Attaway (Serena), Clarence Muse (Peter), Everdinne Wilson (Annie), Joel Fluellen (Robbins), Earl Jackson (Mingo), Moses LaMarr (Nelson), Margaret Hairston (Lily), Ivan Dixon (Jim), Antoine Durousseau (Scipio), Helen Thigpen (Strawberry Woman), Vince Townsend, Jr. (Elderly Man), William Walker (Undertaker), Roy Glenn (Frazier), Maurice Manson (Coroner), Claude Akins (Detective).

Given the talent and the material and the budget of over $6 million, why wasn't this classic American operetta a classic American movie? The fault has to lie in Goldwyn's decision to fire director Mamoulian in favor of Preminger. It was Goldwyn's final film and his abilities may have been impaired by age because if anyone could muddle up a great saga, Preminger was that person. The story of Charleston's "Catfish Row" had first emerged in a 1925 novel by DuBose Heyward. Then the author and his wife fashioned it into a Broadway play in 1927 that ran 217 times. Eight years later, Heyward teamed with the Gershwins for the operetta upon which this picture is based, a success d'estime but not a commercial hit as it only ran 124 performances and did not achieve the status it now merits until after George Gershwin passed away before turning 40. Poitier is the cripple who is towed around on a goat cart. He loves Dandridge, a floozy if there ever was one. She's a heroin-sniffer (supplied to her by Davis who is the local "happy dust" distributor) adored by many men, including Davis, who is always trying to tug her away from the area, and Peters, a tough stevedore. In the course of the play, Peters kills Fluellen in a crap-game argument and the denizens of Catfish Row pass a saucer to raise money for the funeral. Carroll is the wife of a fishing man who is lost at sea in a hurricane. After Peters flees to escape the police, Dandridge settles in with Poitier, then Peters returns and wants his woman back. Poitier, despite his handicap, kills Peters, then hides out and Dandridge finally agrees to follow Davis up to New York. When Poitier comes back to Catfish Row and learns that she's left, he is determined to follow her as the story ends. Not a very complex tale but the music is so glorious that it carries the story into the stratosphere. Mamoulian had directed the 1927 drama and the 1935 musical so he was a logical choice to do this film. He worked closely with Nash on the screenplay for many months and even supervised the pre-recording of the songs. Belafonte was the only well-known black actor at the time and Goldwyn tried to sign him but Belafonte backed away. Poitier had made a little stir with some of his early films and THE DEFIANT ONES was in the can and about to be released. He, too, declined the role of Porgy after having agreed to it for a while. There were various pressure groups who felt that there might be too many stereotypes in the picture and that Poitier would not do his race justice. Goldwyn and Mamoulian tried to find someone else but kept coming back to Poitier and eventually convinced him that the picture would be something of which he could be proud. Dandridge was the first and only choice to co-star and had recently completed CARMEN JONES, the black version of "Carmen" which was also misdirected by Preminger. Poitier had absolutely no musical training and was even embarrassing when he tried to sing on the old Bill Cosby variety show in the 1970s so he was looped by Robert McFerrin. Dandridge was a fine singer but her range was nowhere near the lilting voice needed so she was looped by Adele Addison. Sammy Davis, of course, did his own singing (and was a touch too 1950s in the role of an early 1900s jackanapes) and so did Pearl Bailey, who was kept in check in the role of the cook shop owner. Peters has a magnificent singing voice and was able to do his chores but Carroll, who is a wonderful nightery thrush, had to be looped by Loulie Jean Norman, and Attaway's singing was done for her by Inez Matthews. Everyone else handled their own vocal work. Goldwyn had hoped to get Cab Calloway to play the Davis role but he had other catfish to fry at the time so Davis, who'd campaigned mightily for the job, got the role. Calloway eventually did come into the picture, but only on the cast album in the part of "Sportin' Life" because Davis was signed to a rival record company and therefore not allowed to participate. Shooting was set to commence at the beginning of July, 1958, then the Goldwyn lot was decimated by fire and the set and wardrobe turned to a $2½ million pile of ashes. In the month or so it took to rebuild everything, Goldwyn and Mamoulian began to have that old bugaboo known as "creative differences" and Preminger was called in to replace Mamoulian, something he'd done before on one of his best films, LAURA. Preminger had already worked with Carroll, Dandridge, Bailey, and Peters on CARMEN JONES so a rapport had been established with many of the actors. Since Mamoulian had spent so much time on the project (and was paid his full fee), an arbitration was called for by the Directors Guild. Preminger was awarded sole credit since Mamoulian's labors had all been in pre-production. All the money lavished on the movie was right there for everyone to see and the hurricane sequence, which cost a bundle, was breathtaking. Millions more were spent for advertising and promotion but the movie came nowhere close to recouping costs and stands as a financial disaster. Previn and Darby took Oscars for Best Scoring, Sharaff won one for Best Costume Design, and Gordon Sawyer took home a statuette for his superb Sound Recording but the film was otherwise overlooked. The brilliant score by George and Ira Gershwin and DuBose Heyward will last forever. We've indicated below the actors who perform the songs on screen as we've already named the off-screen voices. The songs include: "Overture" (a three-minute orchestral number before the curtain came up, performed by Andre Previn and the studio orchestra), "Summertime" (Carroll, Chorus), "The Crap Game" (Carroll, Fluellen, Chorus), "A Woman Is a Sometime Thing" (Carroll, Davis, Scott, Jackson, Chorus), "Honey Man's Call" (Muse), "They Pass By Singing" (Poitier), "Yo' Mammy's Gone" (Jackson), "Oh, Little Stars" (Poitier), "Gone, Gone, Gone" (Scott, Chorus), "Porgy's Prayer" (Poitier), "My Man's Gone Now" (Attaway, Chorus), "The Train Is at the Station" (Dandridge, Chorus), "I Got Plenty O' Nuttin" (Poitier, Chorus), "Bess, You Is My Woman Now" (Poitier, Dandridge), "Oh, I Can't Sit Down" (Davis, Bailey, Chorus), "I Ain't Got No Shame" (Chorus), "It Ain't Necessarily So" (Davis, Chorus), "What Do You Want Wid' Bess?" (Peters, Dandridge), "It Takes a Long Pull to Get There" (Scott, Male Chorus), "De Police Put Me In" (Muse), "Time and Time Again" (Attaway), "Strawberry Woman's Call" (Thigpen), "Crab Man's Call" (Townsend, Jr.), "I Loves You, Porgy" (Dandridge, Poitier), "Oh, De Lawd Shake de Heaven" (Chorus), "Dere's Someone Knockin' at de Do" (Jackson, Chorus), "A Red-Headed Woman" (Peters), "Clara, Don't You Be Downhearted" (Chorus), "There's a Boat Dat's Leavin' Soon Fo' New York" (Davis), "Good Mornin', Sistuh" (Chorus), "Bess, Oh, Where's My Bess?" (Poitier), "I'm On My Way" (Poitier, Chorus). You can see by the sheer weight of the songs that there isn't much time for dialog and not much is needed. Ira Gershwin, who was as superb with words as George was with music, is said to have composed an interesting lyrical "dummy" for "It Ain't Necessarily So." (A "dummy" refers to words which adhere to the rhythm of the music and are put in by the lyricist after hearing the tune, just to know where the "beats" are and where to place emphasis on syllables.) Upon hearing the tune, Ira wrote quickly on his yellow pad and when George peeked, he saw that his brother had scribbled "I Used To Eat Bacon And Eggs" to fit the tempo of "It Ain't Necessarily So." Preminger's veteran cameraman, Shamroy, did a wonderful job and the art direction by Krizman and Wright was sensational. Krizman later went on to design the excellent and often-startling sets for the "Batman" TV series. Ken Darby was listed as Associate Music Director and the excellent orchestrations were by Alexander Courage, Conrad Salinger, Robert Franklin, and Al Woodbury. Poitier proved to be a fine selection as "Porgy" and has been quoted as saying, "Other roles may come and go, but I expect the role of Porgy to stay with me for a lifetime." Quite true.

p, Samuel Goldwyn; d, Otto Preminger (pre-production by Rouben Mamoulian); w, N. Richard Nash (based on the operetta by George Gershwin (music), Ira Gershwin (lyrics), DuBose Heyward (libretto and lyrics), on the stage play by DuBose and Dorothy Heyward, and the novel by DuBose Heyward); ph, Leon Shamroy (Todd-AO/Technicolor); m, George Gershwin; ed, Daniel Mandell; md, Andre Previn (with Ken Darby); prod d, Oliver Smith; art d, Serge Krizman, Joseph Wright; set d, Howard Bristol; cos, Irene Sharaff; ch, Hermes Pan; makeup, Frank McCoy, Layne Britton.

Musical (PR:A-C MPAA:NR)

PORK CHOP HILL**** (1959) 97m Melville Productions/UA bw

Gregory Peck (Lt. Clemons), Harry Guardino (Forstman), Rip Torn (Lt. Russell), George Peppard (Fedderson), James Edwards (Cpl. Jurgens), Bob Steele (Kern),

Woody Strode (Franklin), George Shibita (Lt. O'Hashi), Norman Fell (Sgt. Coleman), Robert Blake (Velie), Biff Elliot (Bowen), Barry Atwater (Davis), Michael Garth (S-2 Officer), Ken Lynch (Gen. Trudeau), Paul Comi (Sgt. Kreucheberg), Abel Fernandez (McKinley), Lou Gallo (P.I. Officer), Cliff Ketchum (Cpl. Payne), Martin Landau (Marshall), Bert Remson (Lt. Cummings), Kevin Hagen (Cpl. Kissell), Dean Stanton (MacFarland), Leonard Graves (Lt. Cook), Syl Lamont (Sgt. Kuzmick), Gavin McCloud (Saxon), John Alderman (Lt. Waldorf), John McKee (Olds), Charles Aidman (Harrold), Chuck Hayward (Chalmers), Buzz Martin (Radio Operator), Robert Wiliams (Soldier Runner), Bill Wellman, Jr. (Iron Man), Viraj Amonsin (Chinese Broadcaster), Barry Maguire (Lt. Attridge).

This grim war film, dealing with one battle of the Korean conflict, is a superb offering from Milestone, creator of the stupendous ALL QUIET ON THE WESTERN FRONT. The director expresses all of his weighty cinematic skills here in a technically flawless production with Peck admirably at its head. Moreover, those viewers unfamiliar with the realities of the so-called "police action" in Korea during the early 1950s will learn much about this United Nations military action against Communist North Korea and China. Peck is the commander of a single company of men, ordered to take Pork Chop Ridge, an inconsequential piece of tactical property but one that would become priceless before Peck and his decimated troops staggered down that bloody hill. Further compounding Peck's inexplicable assignment is the fact that the war may be over at any minute. In receiving his orders, his superior tells Peck: "Remember this, you've got a 135 men, all of them thinking of the peace talks at Panmunjom. It's a cinch they won't want to die in what may be the last battle." Peck's company, supported by two others, stealthily begins climbing the hill toward the ridge at night. Halfway up the slope, as they work their way slowly through the barbed wire obstacles, Chinese troops on the ridge switch on loudspeakers and then open a tremendous and withering barrage. Gunfire begins to take a bloody toll of the American troops, but they continue to work their way upward. Adding to the attackers' woes are American floodlights from a nearby position which bathe the U.S. troops in blinding, searing light and allow the Chinese to riddle them. Peck signals the Americans on the distant hilltop to turn off their lights but before they do, many more of his men are dead. By the time Peck and his men take the ridge the next day, his force has been cut in half and the supporting companies have been all but wiped out. Some American troops are found near the summit, barricaded in a bunker, survivors of earlier Chinese attacks. During the mopping up, Peck finds Strode, a black trooper, cowering and lagging behind. He tells him to keep up with the men and when he finds Strode lingering again he tells Edwards, a black corporal, to keep an eye on Strode. (This was quite daring for the time, portraying a black as a deserter and coward, instead of a white, the producers willing to risk criticism over such a sensitive position. Oddly, no criticism was forthcoming.) The Chinese counterattack in force and Peck's men barely manage to keep them off the ridge. By the time reinforcements arrive under the command of Torn, Peck's men are just hanging on. Torn is in shock when he learns that the battle is not over and the so-called American victory is far from being just that. Even more shocking is an order to Torn to withdraw his men and leave Peck and his few soldiers to withstand heavy enemy onslaughts. Peck cannot get support, supplies, or an order to withdraw. At Panmunjom, American high command officers run into a stalemate with their Chinese counterparts who have no intention of calling off their counterattacks on Pork Chop Ridge, testing the Americans to see if they will spend lives for an obviously worthless objective, as they will. Peck is left alone with his few survivors after Torn is ordered down the ridge. The Chinese then attack in force, driving Peck and a handful of Americans to take refuge in a bunker which they quickly barricade with sandbags. The Chinese infiltrate the topmost trenches and begin burning into the bunker with flame throwers, but just at that moment, when it appears hopeless for the Americans, new U.S. troops come storming up the ridge and save Peck and his men. With the enemy driven off Pork Chop, the Chinese now know that America will spend lives to defeat the Communists anywhere and the objective remains in U.S. hands. Peck and his survivors stagger exhausted down the hill, triumphant but forever changed. Peck is outstanding as the calm, resolute, and utterly stalwart commander, and excellent in support is Torn, playing a bewildered brother officer and, incidentally, Peck's brother-in-law. Guardino, a machine-gunner, is a standout, as are Strode, Edwards, and a fumbling but heroic Blake. Milestone employs all of his directorial skills in creating an authentic and sweeping war film, using the long pan shots of the attackers, the boom and truck shots running over and through the trenches atop the ridge, and projecting a grimly realistic film that captures the forlorn atmosphere of that Cold War era. Peck, along with Bartlett, began his own production company to produce this film and they selected Milestone as their director. He was the logical choice, having directed two great earlier war films, ALL QUIET ON THE WESTERN FRONT and A WALK IN THE SUN (which depicted battle during WW I and WW II, so this film really carries forth a third war, making a sort of battle trilogy). Leavitt's photography is topnotch and starkly shows this heroic battle with such detail that the viewer can almost smell the acrid fumes of cordite and taste the dust blown from the dead ridge. Boyler's sets are awesome. The overall effect is almost that of a newsreel quality that further enhances the production. The unpretentious posture of the cast and crew is commendable and adds to the portrait of the American soldier of that day, one of quiet courage and dedication to the then sorely tested cause of freedom.

p, Sy Bartlett; d, Lewis Milestone; w, James R. Webb (based on a story by S.L.A. Marshall); ph, Sam Leavitt; m, Leonard Rosenman; ed, George Boemler; prod d, Nicolai Remisoff; set d, Edward G. Boyler; cos, Eddie Armand; tech adv, Capt. Joseph G. Clemons, Jr.

War Drama (PR:C MPAA:NR)

PORKY'S* (1982) 94m Melvin Simon-Astral Bellevue Pathe/FOX c

Dan Monahan (Pee Wee), Mark Herrier (Billy), Wyatt Knight (Tommy), Roger Wilson (Mickey), Cyril O'Reilly (Tim), Tony Ganios (Meat), Kaki Hunter (Wendy), Kim Cattrall (Honeywell), Nancy Parsons (Balbricker), Scott Colomby (Brian

Schwartz), Boyd Gaines *(Coach Brackett)*, Doug McGrath *(Coach Warren)*, Susan Clark *(Cherry Forever)*, Art Hindle *(Ted Jarvis)*, Wayne Maunder *(Cavanaugh)*, Alex Karras *(Sheriff Wallace)*, Chuck Mitchell *(Porky)*, Eric Christmas *(Mr. Carter)*, Bill Hindman *(Coach Goodenough)*, John Henry Redwood *(Conklin)*, Jack Mulcahy *(Frank)*, Rod Ball *(Steve)*, Julian Bird, Bill Fuller *(Cops)*, Will Knickerbocker *(Bartender)*, Bill Worman *(Ted's Partner)*, Ilse Earl *(Mrs. Morris)*, Jill Whitlow *(Mindy)*, Pat Lee *(Stripper)*, Terry Guthrie *(Miss Walker)*, Joanne Marsic *(Waitress)*, Pete Conrad *(Mule Train Driver)*, Butch Raymond, Gary Maas *(Deputies)*, Cash Baron, Roger Womack, Charles Spadard *(Bouncers)*, Lisa O'Reilly *(Ginny)*, Allene Simmons *(Jackie)*, Cathy Garpershak *(Girl in Shower)*, Jon Cecka *(Highpockets)*, Don Daynard *(Radio Announcer)*.

Made on a comparatively low budget by contemporary standards, this picture became one of the all-time largest grossers, demonstrating the influence a good advertising campaign can have on a worthless picture. Basically just a deluge of locker-room jokes with a thin plot that takes a silly premise one step beyond good taste. A group of Florida high school students are experiencing their first *angst*-ridden frustrations of sexual awareness. They go to all types of extremes to satisfy their new desires, but sometimes come up empty-handed (to use a very mild example of the type of suggestive humor found in the film). One of their sorties is to a local tavern known for the abundance of available women, where the owner kicks them out. But the boys get their vengeance on a return visit in which they tear the place apart. (It's questionable whether or not this supports the thesis that repression of sexual desires leads to violence.) Though the picture has a lot of driving energy, it never makes its way out of the locker room.

p, Don Carmody, Bob Clark; d&w, Clark; ph, Reginald H. Morris; m, Carl Zittrer, Paul Zaza; ed, Stan Cole; prod d, Reuben Freed; set d, Mark Freeborn, Paul Harding; cos, Mary McLeod, Larry Wells.

Comedy **Cas.** **(PR:O MPAA:R)**

PORKY'S II: THE NEXT DAY*½ (1983) 95m Simon-Reeves-Landsburg-Astral Bellevue Pathe/FOX c

Dan Monahan *(Pee Wee)*, Wyatt Knight *(Tommy)*, Mark Herrier *(Billy)*, Roger Wilson *(Mickey)*, Cyril O'Reilly *(Tim)*, Tony Ganios *(Meat)*, Kaki Hunter *(Wendy)*, Scott Colomby *(Brian)*, Nancy Parsons *(Balbricker)*, Joseph Running Fox *(John Henry)*, Eric Christmas *(Carter)*, Bill Wiley *(Rev. Bubba Flavel)*, Edward Winter *(Gebhardt)*, Cisse Cameron *(Sandy Le Tol)*, Else Earl *(Mrs. Morris)*, Art Hindle *(Ted)*, Anthony Penya *(Bill)*, Rod Ball *(Steve)*, Russell Bates *(Mike)*, Jack Mulcahy *(Frank)*, Chuck Wahl *(Stemrick)*, Pete Conrad, Tom Tully, William Fuller, Will Knickerbocker, Mal Jones, Richard Liberty, Fred Buch, Brian Smith, Melanie Grefe, William Hindman, Bill Wohrman, Joe Friedman, Blaine Grose, Baby Jane, Joel Goss, Rooney Kerwin, Robin Paradise, Roger Swaybill, Howard Neu, Daniel Fitzgerald, Tracy Durphy, Carlo Fittanto, Francine Joyce, Wendy Becker, Adrienne Hampton, Madeline Kern, Betty Mae Jumper, Vernon Tiger, Mark Madrid.

The same people who made the original PORKY'S decided to capitalize on their sure-fire financial success one more time, coming up with a sequel that remains true to the tasteless format of the original. The main thrust of this picture is its juvenile humor and adolescent pranks among a group of high school students. This one, however, has done a better job in developing a plot that at least has some sense to it. The high-school students want to stage a Shakespeare festival, but come up against a bigoted reverend, Wiley, who finds the master's works filled with obscene passages. Also against the festival are the local members of the Ku Klux Klan, who don't want to see an Indian in the role of Romeo. In their mindless and grotesque way, the teens manage to get their revenge. The producers added some creative talent to this sequel, including coscripter Alan Ormsby, the Florida-based low-budget horror-comedy writer of such cult classics as CHILDREN SHOULDN'T PLAY WITH DEAD THINGS (1972) and DEATHDREAM (1972).

p, Don Carmody, Bob Clark; d, Clark; w, Clark, Roger E. Swaybill, Alan Ormsby; ph, Reginald H. Morris (DeLuxe Color); m, Carl Zittrer; ed, Stan Cole; art d, Fred Price; set d, Richard Helfritz; cos, Mary E. McLeod.

Comedy **Cas.** **(PR:O MPAA:R)**

PORRIDGE (SEE: DOING TIME, 1979, Brit.)

PORT AFRIQUE*½ (1956, Brit.) 92m COL c

Pier Angeli *(Ynez)*, Phil Carey *(Rip Reardon)*, Dennis Price *(Robert Blackton)*, Eugene Deckers *(Col. Moussac)*, James Hayter *(Nino)*, Rachel Gurney *(Diane Blackton)*, Anthony Newley *(Pedro)*, Guido Lorraine *(Abdul)*, Denis Shaw *(Grila)*, Christopher Lee *(Franz Vermes)*, Guy Du Monceau *(Police Driver)*, Richard Molinas, Jacques Cey, Dorothy White, Maria Hanson, Andre Maranne, Lorenza Colville, Maureen Connell, Eric Connell, Auric Lorand, Larry Taylor, George Leech, Andrea Malandrinos.

Colorful and exotic Morocco acts as the background for a dull and tensionless story in which wounded American pilot Carey returns to his African plantation from WW II to find his wife murdered. The police dismiss the case as suicide, but Carey knows better, and undertakes an investigation on his own. His prime suspects are nightclub owner Hayter who was on the make for the woman, Carey's business partner Price, who wanted them to sell their plantation, and Angeli, a nightclub singer and guest of the dead woman at Carey's home. The final verdict is no surprise to anyone.

p, David E. Rose, John R. Sloan; d, Rudolph Mate; w, Frank Partos, John Cresswell (based on the novel by Bernard Victor Dyer); ph, Wilkie Cooper (Technicolor); m, Malcolm Arnold; ed, Raymond Poulton; md, Muir Mathieson; art d, Wilfred Shingleton; cos, Julia Squire; ch, David Paltenghi; m/l, Oscar Kinleiner, Paddy Roberts, Luis Araque, Jack Fishman, Paul Misraki, Kermit Goell.

Mystery **(PR:A MPAA:NR)**

PORT DES LILAS (SEE: GATES OF PARIS, 1958, Fr./Ital.)

PORT O' DREAMS (SEE: GIRL OUTBOARD, 1929)

PORT OF CALL½** (1963, Swed.) 100m Svensk Filmindustri/Janus bw (HAMNSTAD)

Nine-Christine Jonsson *(Berit)*, Bengt Eklund *(Gosta)*, Berta Hall *(Berit's Mother)*, Erik Hell *(Berit's Father)*, Mimi Nelson *(Gertrud)*, Birgitta Valberg *(Welfare Worker)*, Stig Olin *(Thomas)*, Sif Ruud *(Mrs. Krona)*, Hans Straat *(Engineer Vilander)*, Nils Dahlgren *(Gertrud's Father)*, Nils Hallberg *(Gustav)*, Harry Ahlin *(Skaningen)*, Sven-Eric Gamble.

An early minor work by Bergman, interesting mainly in the light of the great director's career. PORT OF CALL touched upon many themes that would pop up throughout that career, including the oft-treated theme of the problems of breaking away from the tradition inherent in the stoic Lutheran-based Swedish culture. As in nearly all of Bergman's films, a dismal and oppressive atmosphere is created, with a conclusion that does little to instill faith in the future of the characters involved in Bergman's world. In this case the love affair between a young dockhand and a former prostitute is almost brought to a close because of the young man's inability to deal with his girl friend's past life. Deciding that they really need each other, the two get back together, making plans to create a new life for themselves by moving from Goteborg to Stockholm. However, this never takes place; the couple remains in the industrial town of their parents, a place the young man had dreamed of escaping, in the end settling down to a life similar to that of his parents. PORT OF CALL was originally produced in 1948, but was not shown in the U.S. until the early 1960s when interest in Bergman's career made it a film that needed to be seen.

p, Allan Ekelund; d&w, Ingmar Bergman (based on the story by Olle Lansberg); ph, Gunnar Fischer; m, Erland von Koch; ed, Oscar Rosander; art d, Nils Svenwall.

Drama **Cas.** **(PR:C MPAA:NR)**

PORT OF DESIRE*½ (1960, Fr.) 90m Films Univers-Pathe/Kingsley-Union bw (LA FILLE DE HAMBOURG; AKA: THE GIRL FROM HAMBURG)

Hildegarde Neff *(Maria)*, Daniel Gelin *(Pierre)*, Jean Lefebvre *(Georges)*, Daniel Sorano *(Jean-Marie)*, Frederic O'Brady *(Barman)*.

Gelin, a sailor, makes a deliberate pilgrimage to Hamburg in an attempt to locate the girl, Neff, who ten years earlier had befriended him when he was a prisoner of war in Germany. Unexpectedly, he finds her in that city's famed sin section, the Reeperbahn, where she ekes out a precarious existence in the ruins of postwar Deutschland by entertaining minor hoodlums and pimps in a sleazy bistro, mud-wrestling other feckless frauleins. Tired and listless, dreading the demeaning drama she enacts nightly, she welcomes the reappearance of her sailor suitor; though he has married, they fall in love. He promises to return to her that same evening of enlightenment, only to be knifed to death by a robber. When he fails to return to her, the newly hopeful Neff assumes she has been deserted. Despondent over this further denigration, she commits suicide. Director Allegret covered much the same waterfront in his DEDEE (1949). He didn't get it right this time, either. (In French; English subtitles.)

p, Jose Benazeraf; d, Yves Allegret; w, Benazeraf, Frederic Dard, Maurice Auberge; ph, Armand Thirard; m, Jean Ledrut; ed, Claude Nicole.

Drama **(PR:C MPAA:NR)**

PORT OF ESCAPE** (1955, Brit.) 76m Wellington/REN bw

Googie Withers *(Anne Stirling)*, John McCallum *(Mitchell Gillie)*, Bill Kerr *(Dinty Missouri)*, Joan Hickson *(Rosalie Watchett)*, Wendy Danielli *(Daphne Stirling)*, Hugh Pryse *(Skinner)*, Alexander Gauge *(Inspector Levins)*, Ingeborg Wells *(Lucy)*, Ewan Roberts *(Sgt. Rutherford)*, Simon Lack, Carl Jaffe, Gerald Andersen, Basil Dignam, Cameron Hall, Douglas Robinson, Jack Lester, George Rose, Robert Bruce, Norman Pierce, Len Llewellyn.

McCallum and Kerr are a pair of WW II veterans who are forced to dodge the police when, after getting into a fight, McCallum kills a man. Reporter Withers offers them shelter on her boat, but the near-psychotic Kerr is easily panicked and attracts attention. In a battle with police, Kerr is killed and McCallum is left to surrender. A far-from-spectacular British offering. Shortly after this film was released, Withers and husband McCallum moved to Australia, where they continued to do occasional film work including THE NICKEL QUEEN (1970), which starred Withers and was directed by McCallum.

p, Lance Comfort; d, Tony Young; w, Young, Barbara Harper, Abby Mann (based on the story "Safe Harbour" by Harper); ph, Philip Grinrod.

Crime **(PR:A MPAA:NR)**

PORT OF 40 THIEVES, THE*** (1944) 58m REP bw

Stephanie Bachelor *(Muriel/Mrs. Hartford Chaney III)*, Richard Powers *(Scott Barton)*, Lynn Roberts *(Nancy Hubbard)*, Olive Blakeney *(Aunt Caroline)*, Russell Hicks *(Charles Farrington)*, George Meeker *(Frederic St. Clair)*, Mary Field *(Della)*, Ellen Lowe *(Jonesy)*, Patricia Knox *(Gladys)*, John Hamilton *(Mr. Fellows)*, Harry Depp *(Conductor)*.

Suspenseful chiller has Bachelor as a homicidal maniac who murders her rich husband for the inheritance and so she can marry her playboy lover. She then kills her lover for fear he might talk, which then leads to two more murders. The daughter—by a prior marriage—of the first man she killed is on to Bachelor all the way. Smooth scripting helps to fill in the gaps in the story, which takes place almost entirely in a penthouse-apartment set. One of Republic Studio's surprisingly good, cheaply made sleepers, which had no names of any consequence to draw audiences, and was made on the quick with a single inexpensive generic set (which could be used again.) The studio, which teetered on the edge of "Poverty Row," had some talent on its payroll, including cinematographer Marta and director English, who was best known for his work on the studio's serials. With William

Witney, English codirected nearly half the total output of Republic's serials during its "Golden Age of Serials." This was one of English's rare ventures into solo direction of a feature film.

p, Walter H. Goetz; d, John English; w, Dane Lussier; ph, Jack Marta; ed, Richard Van Enger; md, Morton Scott; art d, Russell Kimball.

Crime/Drama (PR:A MPAA:NR)

PORT OF HATE* (1939) 57m Metropolitan-Times Pictures bw

Polly Ann Young (*Jerry Gale*), Kenneth Harlan (*Bob Randall*), Carleton Young (*Don Cameron*), Shia Jung (*Bo Chang*), Monte Blue (*Hammond*), Frank La Rue (*Bartley*), Richard Adams (*Adams*), James Aubrey (*Stone*), Bruce Dane (*Lathrop*), Edward Cecil (*Wing Hi*), John Elliott (*Stevens*), Reed Howes (*Hotel Clerk*).

Shoddy and amateurish production has two adventurers fighting for pearls on a small island. When one is shot, suspicion points to Young, who winds up falling for the other of the two men. Actress Young, Loretta Young's sister, shared her looks but not her talent, and had an undistinguished career.

p&d, Harry S. Webb; w, Joe O'Donnell (based on the story by Forrest Sheldon); ph, Edmund Kull; ed, Bob Johns.

Drama (PR:A MPAA:NR)

PORT OF HELL** (1955) 80m AA bw

Dane Clark (*Pardee*), Carole Mathews (*Julie Povich*), Wayne Morris (*Stanley Povich*), Marshall Thompson (*Marsh Walker*), Harold Peary (*Leo*), Marjorie Lord (*Kay Walker*), Otto Waldis (*Snyder*), Tom Hubbard (*Nick*), Charles Fredericks (*Sparks*), Jim Alexander (*Parker*), Victor Sen Young (*Enemy Radio Operator*), Gene Roth.

Clark plays the tight-fisted head man of Los Angeles Harbor, who proves to have some human qualities when Mathews appears. His strict ways are a godsend when an atomic bomb is discovered planted aboard a freighter by communists. The device is set to go off in twelve hours; Clark keeps the whole thing quiet, calmly towing the freighter out to sea, where the explosion of the bomb will not harm anyone. Producers of the time showed lax research if they thought an explosion of an atomic bomb off the coast wouldn't harm anything. A rather ridiculous iron-curtain-era disaster film which anticipated such opuses as the equally ham-handed AIRPORT (1970).

p, William F. Broidy, Robert Nunes; d, Harold Schuster; w, Tom Hubbard, Gil Doud, Fred Eggers (based on a story by Doud and D.D. Beauchamp); ph, John Martin; m, Edward J. Kay; ed, Ace Herman.

Drama (PR:A MPAA:NR)

PORT OF LOST DREAMS** (1935) 71m IN/CHES bw

Bill [William "Stage"] Boyd (*Lars Christensen*), Lola Lane (*Molly Deshon*), Edward Gargan (*"Porky"*), George Marion (*Morgan Rock*), Harold Huber (*Louis Constolos*), Evelyn Carrington (*Mother McGee*), Robert Elliott (*Lt. Anderson*), John Beck, Charles Wilson, Harold Berquist, Pat Harmon, Lafe McKee, Eddie Phillips, Gordon DeMain, Lew Kelly.

Lane plays a gun moll who stows away on a fishing boat captained by Boyd in order to avoid the police. They fall in love and marry; Lane going straight, with Boyd unaware of her shady past. The police eventually catch up to Lane, but not until she has managed to have a baby. She is taken to prison, prompting Boyd to commit a crime in order to be close to his wife. Able direction and a good cast give some life to this worn and somewhat unbelievable story. The Bill Boyd of this picture was one of the three film actors with that name who did *not* work in westerns. He died prior to the picture's release at the age of 45.

p, Maury M. Cohen; d, Frank Strayer; w, Charles Belden, Norman Maxwell (based on the story by Robert Ellis); ph, M.A. Anderson; ed, Roland Reed.

Drama/Crime (PR:A MPAA:NR)

PORT OF MISSING GIRLS* (1938) 72m MON bw

Judith Allen (*Della*), Milburn Stone (*Jim*), Harry Carey (*Capt. Storm*), Betty Compson (*Chicago*), Matty Fain (*Duke*), Jane Jones (*Minnie*), George Cleveland (*Clinton*), William Costello (*Manoel*), Sandra Karina (*Sonya*), Lyle Moraine (*Granville*).

Haphazardly produced story has Allen stowing away on Carey's freighter in order to avoid a murder rap. After a mishap with pirates outside Shanghai, the police wire the freighter that the real killer has confessed. Supposedly tough guy Carey comes out looking like a wimp. Hero Stone, Allen's love interest, is the ship's wireless operator who, because of his job, wises up early to her predicament. He later won an Emmy award for his 20 years of playing "Doc Adams" on TV's "Gunsmoke."

p, Lon Young; d, Karl Brown; w, Brown; ph, Gilbert Warrenton, W.C. Smith.

Drama (PR:A MPAA:NR)

PORT OF NEW YORK* (1949) 79m EL bw

Scott Brady (*Michael "Mickey" Waters, Customs Agent*), Richard Rober (*Jim Flannery, Customs Agent*), K. T. Stevens (*Toni Cardell, Paul Vicola's Girl Friend*), Yul Brynner (*Paul Vicola*), Arthur Blake (*Dolly Carney*), Lynn Carter (*Lili Long*), John Kellogg (*Lenny, Paul Vicola's Henchman*), William Challee (*Leo Stasser, Boatyard Owner and Front for Paul Vicola*), Raymond Greenleaf (*John J. Meredith, Customs Agent Supervisor*), Henry Rowland (*Sam Harris, Customs Agent*), Tudor Owen (*Apartment Hotel Janitor*), Neville Brand (*Stasser's Henchman*), Fred Graham (*Boatyard Guard*), Stephen Chase (*Police Lieutenant*), Chet Huntley (*Narrator*).

Intriguing, fast-paced story has Brady and Rober as government customs agents trying to break up a narcotics ring run by the notorious Brynner. Their search takes them through the back alleys of New York, where they use common police methods to gather information, winding up on Brynner's yacht. In an attempt to infiltrate the gang, Brady is killed, but Rober continues on his own to bring the crooks to justice. This was a featured-player film debut for Brynner, whose exotic appearance was perfect for the ruthless type of criminal he portrayed; he had a full head of hair at the time.

p, Aubrey Schenck; d, Laslo Benedek; w, Eugene Ling, Leo Townsend (based on a story by Arthur A. Ross, Bert Murray); ph, George E. Diskant; m, Sol Kaplan; ed, Norman Colbert; md, Irving Friedman; art d, Edward Ilou; set d, Armor Marlowe; spec eff, Roy E. Seawright; makeup, Ern Westmore.

Crime **Cas.** (PR:A MPAA:NR)

PORT OF SEVEN SEAS** (1938) 81m MGM bw

Wallace Beery (*Cesar*), Frank Morgan (*Panisse*), Maureen O'Sullivan (*Madelon*), John Beal (*Marius*), Jessie Ralph (*Honorine*), Cora Witherspoon (*Claudine*), Etienne Girardot (*Bruneau*), E. Allyn Warren (*Capt. Escartefigue*), Robert Spindola (*Boy*), Doris Lloyd (*Customer*), Jack Latham (*Man*), Paul Panzer (*Postman*), Jerry Colonna (*Arab Rug Dealer*), Fred Malatesta (*Bird Seller*), George Humbert (*Organ Grinder*), Moy Ming (*Chinese Peddler*).

Adapted from the French classic FANNY by Marcel Pagnol, O'Sullivan and Beal play young lovers in the port town of Marseilles. When Beal takes to the sea, O'Sullivan discovers that she is pregnant by him. She confides her situation to Morgan, lifelong friend to Beal's father Beery and adoring admirer of O'Sullivan. Despite their differences in age and the fact that she does not love him, Morgan and O'Sullivan marry. Beal returns, still very much in love with O'Sullivan, but takes off for the sea again in order to allow the child a stable life. Pagnol had filmed his own play (see FANNY, 1948, Fr.) in 1932; when MGM bought the rights to it, Pagnol's vastly superior production was held up in release for 16 years. The rights had initially been acquired by Carl Laemmle, Jr., for Universal Studios. Laemmle, Jr. assembled the working team of producer Henigson, with William Wyler to direct, and writer—later director—Sturges to do the screenplay. Newcomer Jane Wyatt was slated to play the role of "Fanny" (here changed to "Madelon"). That same year, 1934, the Catholic Legion of Decency had begun a major campaign to rid the movies of immorality. Universal was shaky financially; its mavens felt that they could ill afford to challenge the powerful Legion with a tale of pregnancy out of wedlock, however successfully resolved. Laemmle, Jr. was forced out of Universal, but he took the rights to the film with him, and producer Henigson joined him. They made a deal with MGM. Ernest Vajda (uncredited) wrote the first version of the screenplay, but Henigson got Sturges to do the final rewrite as a personal favor. Sturges was bored by the project by this time; he trimmed the tale to a series of confrontations between the blustering Beery and Morgan. The film finally appeared four years after its initial planning; it was not a success.

p, Henry Henigson; d, James Whale; w, Preston Sturges (based on the play "Fanny" by Marcel Pagnol); ph, Karl Freund; m, Franz Waxman; ed, Frederick Y. Smith.

Drama (PR:A MPAA:NR)

PORT OF SHADOWS** (1938, Fr.) 91m Gregor Rabinovitch/Cine Alliance bw (QUAI DES BRUMES; LE QUAI DES BRUMES)

Jean Gabin (*Jean*), Michele Morgan (*Nelly*), Michel Simon (*Zabel*), Pierre Brasseur (*Lucien Laugardier*), Robert Le Vigan (*Michel Krauss*), Jenny Burnay (*Lucien's Friend*), Marcel Peres (*Chauffeur*), Rene Genin (*Doctor*), Edouard Delmont (*Panama*), Raymond Aimos (*Quart-Vittel*).

The first feature by the directing-writing pair Carne and Prevert (who had collaborated on JENNY, 1936, and BIZARRE, BIZARRE, 1937) to receive critical acclaim (the pair would later collaborate on the much-heralded CHILDREN OF PARADISE) was a fantastic film which mirrored the prevailing mood in prewar France. Gabin plays a war deserter arriving in the port of Le Havre, looking for passage to a distant country. In a local dive he meets and is attracted to Morgan, ward of the owner of a shop that is a front for illicit goods. Morgan waits for her boy friend, who never shows up, then accompanies Gabin on a walk along the docks. Gabin comes to Simon's shop to buy a gift for Morgan, and is importuned by the evil man to kill an enemy of his in exchange for a passport and money, but Gabin refuses. Hope for Gabin's escape comes when prescient poet/painter Le Vigan gifts the doomed deserter with his own passport and clothing, then walks out on the quay and drowns himself; to moody visionary Le Vigan, "a swimmer for me is already a drowned man." After Morgan discovers that her boy friend has been killed, Simon confesses to murdering the man because of his jealousy over Morgan, whom he tries to rape. Gabin smashes Simon's head with a brick but on his way to the ship to gain passage to South America, he is gunned down by mysterious gangster Brasseur. This classic of the French "Poetic Realism" school is unremittingly fatalistic in its statement that humankind is tossed by fate and spurred solely to karma, all of it bad. This theme is carried not only by the simple story line, but also by the superb fog-shrouded sets and the dank, forbidding location shots. The mood of hopelessness expressed by this gray masterpiece perfectly paralleled the prevailing feeling in threatened France; a Vichy-government spokesman was to state, "if we have lost the war, it is. . .the fault of PORT OF SHADOWS." Ironically, the film was first to have been a German production; Carne was introduced to the novel on which the picture is loosely based by Raoul Ploquin, then head of French productions at UFA in Berlin. Nazi propaganda minister Josef Goebbels turned thumbs down on the project, however; he considered this story of a deserter to be decadent. The rights were sold to French producer Rabinovitch, who envisioned a lighter, happier film, and so quarreled constantly with Carne. The latter also had political problems within his own country; the French Minister of War would not permit the word "deserter" to be used and insisted that Gabin's soldier's uniform be treated respectfully. Writer Prevert deviated from Mac Orlan's novel in almost every respect; in the book, Morgan's heroine is no tempest-tossed innocent. She is a prostitute who murders her pimp and ends up wealthy. During the Nazi occupation of France, this remarkable picture was totally banned in that country.

p, Gregor Rabinovitch; d, Marcel Carne; w, Jacques Prevert (based on the novel *Le Quai Des Brumes* by Pierre Mac Orlan [Pierre Dumarchais]); ph, Eugene Schuftan, Louis Page; m, Maurice Jaubert; ed, Rene le Henaff; prod d, Alexandre Trauner.

Drama **(PR:A MPAA:NR)**

PORT OF SHAME (SEE: LOVER'S NET, 1957, Fr.)

PORT SAID** (1948) 69m COL bw

Gloria Henry *(Gila Lingallo/Helena Guistano)*, William Bishop *(Leslie Sears)*, Steven Geray *(Alexis Tacca)*, Edgar Barrier *(The Great Lingallo)*, Richard Hale *(Mario Guistano)*, Ian McDonald *(Jakoll)*, Blanche Zohar *(Thymesia)*, Robin Hughes *(Bunny Beacham)*, Jay Novello *(Taurk)*, Ted Hecht *(Carlo)*, Lester Sharpe *(Lt. Zaki)*, Martin Garralaga *(Hotel Porter)*.

Plodding story has Henry and her father, Barrier, searching through the Egyptian port in order to find the in-laws who killed Barrier's wife during the Fascist regime in Italy. Henry plays a double role as the daughter and the villainous woman they are looking for, making a much better villain.

p, Wallace MacDonald; d, Reginald LeBorg; w, Brenda Weisberg (based on a story by Louis Pollock); ph, Allen Siegler; ed, Richard Fantl; md, Mischa Bakaleinikoff; art d, Rudolph Sternad.

Drama **(PR:A MPAA:NR)**

PORT SINISTER* (1953) 65m RKO bw (AKA: BEAST OF PARADISE ISLAND; BEAST OF PARADISE ISLE)

James Warren *(Tony Ferris)*, Lynne Roberts *(Jean Hunter)*, Paul Cavanagh *(John Kolvac)*, William Schallert *(Collins)*, House Peters, Jr. *(Jim Gerry)*, Marjorie Stapp *(Technician)*, Helen Winston *(Florence)*, Eric Colmar *(Christie)*, Norman Budd *(Akers)*, Anne Kimball *(Nurse)*, Robert Bice *(Burt)*, Merritt Stone *(Nick)*, Ken Terrell *(Hollis)*, Charles Victor *(Coast Guard Lieutenant)*, E. Guy Hearn *(Capt. Crawley)*, Dayton Lummis *(Mr. Lennox)*.

Ridiculous plot has Warren and Roberts going to a sunken South Seas island that Warren believes will surface during an earthquake. His main interest is the pirate booty reportedly on the island. When the captain of the ship, Cavanagh, gets wind of Warren's purpose, he dumps his employer and goes after the treasure himself. Despite some good special effects and a worthy characterization or two, this story should remain submerged.

p, Jack Pollexfen, Aubrey Wisberg; d, Harold Daniels; w, Pollexfen, Wisberg; ph, William Bradford; m, Albert Glasser; ed, Fred R. Feitshans, Jr.

Adventure **(PR:A MPAA:NR)**

PORTIA ON TRIAL½** (1937) 85m REP bw (GB: THE TRIAL OF PORTIA MERRIMAN)

Walter Abel *(Dan Foster)*, Frieda Inescort *(Portia Merriman)*, Neil Hamilton *(Earle Condon)*, Heather Angel *(Elizabeth Manners)*, Ruth Donnelly *(Jane Wilkins)*, Barbara Pepper *(Evelyn)*, Clarence Kolb *(John Condon)*, Anthony Marsh *(Richard Conlan)*, Paul Stanton *(Judge)*, George Cooper *(Efe)*, John Kelly *(Hank)*, Hobart Bosworth *(Governor)*, Ian MacLaren *(Father Caslez)*, Chick Chandler *(Barker)*, Bob Murphy *(Inspector)*, Inez Palange *(Mrs. Gannow)*, Leo Gorcey *(Joe Gannow)*, Huntley Gordon *(Dr. Thorndike)*, Marion Ballou *(Mrs. Manners)*, Hooper Atchley *(Jack Madden)*, Nat Carr *(1st Committeeman)*, Lucie Kaye *(Switchboard Operator)*.

Touching story of a lawyer, Inescort, forced to give up her son after her marriage to Hamilton is annulled. As the son grows up, the secret behind his mother's existence begins to unfold. Inescort gives this picture some sparkle with her realistic portrayal of a professional lawyer and loving mother.

p, Albert E. Levoy; d, George Nicholls, Jr.; w, Samuel Ornitz, E.E. Paramore, Jr. (based on a story by Faith Baldwin); ph, Harry Wild; ed, Howard O'Neill; md, Alberto Colombo.

Drama **(PR:A MPAA:NR)**

PORTLAND EXPOSE½** (1957) 72m AA bw

Edward Binns *(George Madison)*, Carolyn Craig *(Ruth Madison)*, Virginia Gregg *(Clara Madison)*, Russ Conway *(Phillip Jacman)*, Larry Dobkin *(Garnell)*, Frank Gorshin *(Joe)*, Joe Marr *(Larry)*, Rusty Lane *(Tom Carmody)*, Dickie Bellis *(Jimmy Madison)*, Lea Penman *(Mrs. Stoneway)*, Jeanne Carmen *(Iris)*, Stanley Farrar *(Lennox)*, Larry Thor *(Capt. Vincent)*, Francis de Sales *(Alfred Grey)*, Kort Falkenberg *(Speed Bromley)*, Joe Flynn *(Ted Carl)*.

Set in Portland, Oregon, Binns plays an honest saloon keeper forced by the syndicate to let gangsters use his establishment as a hotspot. After they threaten to throw acid in his daughter's face, he becomes an undercover agent for a citizens' organization trying to clean up the city. Story is based upon true events that were actually occurring in Portland at the time, and gave rise to investigations by a Senate committee.

p, Lindsley Parsons; d, Harold Schuster; w, Jack DeWitt; ph, Carl Berger; m, Paul Dunlap; ed, Maurice Wright; md, Dunlap; art d, David Milton.

Crime **(PR:A MPAA:NR)**

PORTNOY'S COMPLAINT* (1972) 101m Chenault/WB c

Richard Benjamin *(Alexander Portnoy)*, Karen Black *(The Monkey)*, Lee Grant *(Sophie Portnoy)*, Jack Somack *(Jack Portnoy)*, Jeannie Berlin *(Bubbles Girardi)*, Jill Clayburgh *(Naomi)*, D.P. Barnes *(Dr. Otto Spielvogel)*, Francesca De Sapio *(Lina)*, Kevin Conway *(Smolka)*, Lewis J. Stadlen *(Mandel)*, Renee Lippin *(Hannah Portnoy)*, Jessica Rains *(Girl in Office)*, Eleanor Zee *(Woman in Hospital Bed)*, William Pabst *(Inn Clerk)*, Tony Brande *(Cab Driver)*, Darryl Seamen *(Alexander, Age 8)*, Mike De Anda *(Mr. Harero)*, Carmen Zapata *(Mrs. Harero)*.

There are some books that are better left unfilmed: THE BIBLE, THE GREATEST STORY EVER TOLD, and this one, to go from the sublime to the ridiculous. It was a very funny book, often shocking for its own sake, and very true to the New York *angst* mentality of a shlemiel. So who better to play the role than Richard Benjamin, who had already established himself in the Shlemiels' Hall of Fame with his work as the ultimate Jewish *kvetch* in GOODBYE, COLUMBUS; DIARY OF A MAD HOUSEWIFE; MARRIAGE OF A YOUNG STOCKBROKER; who would continue that tradition in LOVE AT FIRST BITE and others. If there were a trophy given for whining, Benjamin should have it retired by now. Beckerman, a "packager" rather than a producer at the time, acquired the rights to the book early, so he is listed as being part of the team that dispensed this dismal attempt at a comedy. Lehman, who struck out in three departments (producing, writing, and, for the first time, directing) should have known better. Here was the man who'd written such screenplays as THE SOUND OF MUSIC; THE SWEET SMELL OF SUCCESS; SOMEBODY UP THERE LIKES ME; WEST SIDE STORY; NORTH BY NORTHWEST and many other wonderful pictures. But in all of those movies, Lehman had someone to tell him "no" and push his talents in the right direction. Here, the Emperor of Screenwriting is shown to be totally nude and the movie was an embarrassment for almost everyone concerned. The one notable exception to the carnage was Black, who seemed to be acting in a better movie than everyone else, and who maintained her characterization with depth and grace, while the sound of bombs was being heard in the background. Benjamin spends a great deal of time carping to his analyst, Barnes, who never says a word to the patient. Benjamin works for the city of New York as the Assistant Commissioner of Human Opportunity (whatever that means) and spends his off-hours in marathons of self-abuse. His mother is Grant (miscast badly as she is much too young and attractive to play such a harridan), a shrewish woman who smothers her son like a Hebrew Mildred Pierce. His father is Somack (who was much better in his "Alka-Seltzer" commercial), a man totally involved with his bowels, to no avail. Grant's greatest fear is that she will lose her son to that most dreaded of all creatures, a *shikse* (Gentile woman). Benjamin spends countless hours flogging himself raw in the confines of the bathroom, doing things better left unprinted in a family encyclopedia such as this. Occasionally, he dallies with Berlin, the raunchy Italian daughter of a local hoodlum, but he finds no solace in Berlin and his sexual frustrations continue unbridled as we watch him grow from preteen (played by, can you believe this, Seamen?) to adulthood. We see it all in flashback as Benjamin tells Barnes about having met Black, the girl of his frantic fantasies, an unreconstituted model whose nickname is "Monkey" because she can do all sorts of sexual positions which humans dare not attempt. He is finally happy as he continues his affair with Black but is also somewhat unnerved when she drops hints about a more permanent situation, like, perhaps, marriage. They have a sensational weekend in Dorset, Vermont, and he decides to bring his lover out of the closet and introduce her to his coworkers. There's a large gala at the mayor's mansion on New York's upper East Side and she arrives in a wild outfit, then begins behaving in a fashion that is painful to Benjamin. They squabble and she finally allays his anger by performing an unspeakable act upon his person. Benjamin is becoming sexually uninhibited and takes Black away to Europe where they hire a local Roman streetwalker, De Sapio, to make it a threesome in their hotel room. Benjamin can't handle the evening and winds up tossing his cookies. When Black says she will commit suicide by jumping from a balcony unless he gives her a gold ring, Benjamin does what any chicken-hearted neurotic would do, he leaves. He grabs a flight to Israel and arrives in Tel Aviv, hoping to find his Jewish heritage there. As he strolls the streets, he wonders if Black did in fact jump from the balcony. Now he picks up a gorgeous Israeli, Clayburgh, takes her to his hotel and attempts to force his attentions on her. The result is a swift kick to Benjamin's groin. Back to the present and Benjamin has just completed his session with Barnes, who still shows no response. He exits the psychiatrist's office and goes strolling away, never seeing Black, who is within eyesight and very much alive and kicking. Despite all of the above, it's not as trashy as it sounds, and there are one or two funny moments if you are a devotee of momism or masturbation. Everyone except Black is a slim caricature of real life and the production is done so slickly that it's far better than the script, the actors, or just about anything else.

p, Ernest Lehman, Sidney Beckerman; d&w, Lehman (based on the novel by Philip Roth); ph, Philip Lathrop (Panavision, Technicolor); m, Michel Legrand; ed, Sam O'Steen, Gordon Scott; md, Legrand; prod d, Robert F. Boyle; art d, Harold Michelson; set d, George Nelson; cos, Moss Mabry; makeup, Charles Schram.

Comedy **Cas.** **(PR:O MPAA:NR)**

PORTRAIT FROM LIFE (SEE: GIRL IN THE PAINTING, THE, 1948, Brit.)

PORTRAIT IN BLACK** (1960) 112m UNIV c

Lana Turner *(Sheila Cabot)*, Anthony Quinn *(Dr. David Rivera)*, Sandra Dee *(Catherine Cabot)*, John Saxon *(Blake Richards)*, Richard Basehart *(Howard Mason)*, Lloyd Nolan *(Matthew Cabot)*, Ray Walston *(Cob O'Brien)*, Virginia Grey *(Miss Lee)*, Anna May Wong *(Tani)*, Dennis Kohler *(Peter Cabot)*, Paul Birch *(Detective)*, John Wengraf *(Dr. Kessler)*, Richard Norris *(Mr. Corbin)*, James Nolan, Robert Lieb *(Detectives)*, John McNamara *(Minister)*, Charles Thompson *(Sid)*, George Womack *(Foreman)*, Henry Quan *(Headwaiter)*, Elizabeth Chan *(Chinese Dancer)*, Harold Goodwin, Jack Bryan *(Patrolmen)*.

A glitzy, glossy, murder-suspense picture that was shot like one of Ross Hunter's romantic films. It took 15 years for the 1945 play to reach the screen, after an interesting history. Goff and Roberts' stage production premiered in New Haven with Geraldine Fitzgerald in the lead. There was a two-year hiatus until it went to New York for 61 performances starring Clare Luce, Donald Cook, and Sidney Blackmer. The film rights were bought by Bruce Manning and Jack Skirball who announced Joan Crawford to star and Carol Reed to direct. When that didn't happen, Universal picked up the rights and held them until they needed something for Turner to follow her successful remake of IMITATION OF LIFE. They dressed Turner in some eye-catching Jean Louis gowns and shot the film in beautiful sets, neither of which could conceal the fact that this was essentially a contrived plot. Turner is married to wealthy Nolan, an invalid shipping multimillionaire. She is having an affair with Nolan's doctor, Quinn, and the two of them would like to marry but there is no way to get a divorce. Turner convinces Quinn to murder Nolan in what they believe will be an untraceable way—with the injection of a bubble of air into Nolan's veins. Nolan dies and Turner and Quinn feel safe until she gets an unsigned letter of congratulations on her successful murder. She thinks that the author of the letter may be Basehart, the family's investment advisor, a man who has had his eye on Turner for quite a spell. Quinn and Turner get rid of him and toss his remains in San Francisco Bay. When Basehart's body is found, the police learn that he had argued with Saxon, a boat owner, and the man is mistakenly arrested. The reason they were able to track this lead is that Saxon is engaged to Nolan's daughter, Dee, the stepdaughter of Turner. When Quinn can't mentally handle what he's done, he gives up his medical work and leaves for Switzerland. After a while, Turner calls Quinn and says she has received yet another letter. Quinn rushes back to California. There's an argument between the two and Turner admits that she wrote the second letter in an attempt to get Quinn back to the U.S. Their dialog is heard by Dee and when she confronts them, Quinn tries to murder her but in the fracas, he falls to his death from a high window ledge. Turner must now face the cops alone. Producer Hunter seldom became involved in this type of tawdry story and it is assumed that he rued his association with PORTRAIT IN BLACK although the movie made some money at the box office. In a small role, note Anna May Wong who had starred in an equally silly murder picture in England, PICCADILLY, 30 years before.

p, Ross Hunter; d, Michael Gordon; w, Ivan Goff, Ben Roberts (based on their play); ph, Russell Metty (Eastmancolor); m, Frank Skinner; ed, Milton Carruth; md, Joseph Gershenson; art d, Richard H. Riedel; set d, Julia Heron; m/l, theme, Buddy Pepper, Inez James; makeup, Bud Westmore.

Murder/Mystery **(PR:A-C MPAA:NR)**

PORTRAIT IN SMOKE** (1957, Brit.) 94m COL bw (GB: WICKED AS THEY COME)

Arlene Dahl *(Kathy Allen)*, Phil Carey *(Tim O'Bannion)*, Herbert Marshall *(Stephen Collins)*, Michael Goodliffe *(Larry Buckhan)*, David Kossoff *(Sam Lewis)*, Marvin Kane *(Mike Lewis)*, Sidney James *(Frank Allen)*, Gilbert Winfield *(Chuck)*, Patrick Allen *(Willie)*, Ralph Truman *(John Dowling)*, Faith Brook *(Virginia Collins)*, Jacques Brunius *(Inspector Caron)*, Frederick Valk, Larry Cross, Tom Gill, Alastair Hunter, Raf De La Torre, Pat Clavin, John Salew, Totti Truman Taylor, Paul Sheridan, Frank Atkinson, Guy DuMonceau, Selma Vaz Dias.

Slum-dweller Dahl decides she is destined for a better life. Her two goals are to be a great success and to use men any way she possibly can in order to succeed. A beauty contest is fixed in her favor and from there it's a few short steps up the ladder. After an affair with a wealthy executive, she marries the successful head of a large corporation. When she accidentally shoots him, Dahl ends up in a Paris jail but the truth comes out and she is left to continue on her evil way. This turgid drama is simplistic with its plotting and character motivations but the cast is lively, making this a better drama than it should have been. Dahl is wonderfully icy with some good support by the men in her life. Direction is only average.

p, Maxwell Setton, M.J. Frankovitch; d, Ken Hughes; w, Hughes, Robert Westerby, Sigmund Miller (based on the novel by Bill S. Ballinger); ph, Basil Emmott; m, Malcolm Arnold; ed, Max Benedict; md, Muir Mathieson; art d, Don Ashton; cos, Cynthia Tingey.

Drama **(PR:O MPAA:NR)**

PORTRAIT IN TERROR*½ (1965) 81m AIP bw

Patrick Magee, William Campbell, Anna Pavane.

A bizarre entry which is set in Venice, California, and has Magee as a lunatic hit man and Campbell as an equally demented artist. Their paths cross when they plot to steal a rare Titian painting. Their scheme is foiled, however, by a nightclub stripper who nearly loses her life in the process. The only positive recommendation is the casting of Campbell and Magee, who were both featured in the eerie DEMENTIA 13 (1963).

d, Jack Hill.

Crime **(PR:O MPAA:NR)**

PORTRAIT OF A MOBSTER** (1961) 108m WB bw

Vic Morrow *("Dutch Schultz" [Arthur Flegenheimer])*, Leslie Parrish *(Iris Murphy)*, Peter Breck *(Frank Brennan)*, Ray Danton *(Legs Diamond)*, Norman Alden *(Bo Wetzel)*, Robert McQueeney *(Michael Ferris)*, Ken Lynch *(Lt. D. Corbin)*, Frank de Kova *(Anthony Parazzo)*, Stephen Roberts *(James Guthrie)*, Evan McCord *(Vincent "Mad Dog" Coll)*, Arthur Tenen *(Steve Matryck)*, Frances Morris *(Louise Murphy)*, Larry Blake *(John Murphy)*, Joseph Turkel *(Joe Noe)*, Eddie Hanley *(Matty Krause)*, John Kowal *(Lou Rhodes)*, Harry Holcombe, Jr. *(Capt. Bayridge)*, Anthony Eisley *(Legal Advisor)*, Poncie Ponce *(Master of Ceremonies)*, Gil Perkins *(Joe Murdoch)*, Roy Renard *(Bartender)*, George Werier *(Thompson)*.

This wholly fictitious screen biography of New York gangster "Dutch Schultz" provides little entertainment or insight during its overlong running time. Morrow stars as a small-time punk who, along with his pal, Alden, joins the Legs Diamond gang. Diamond (Danton) sends his new recruits on several missions, but begins to worry when they prove to be somewhat overzealous. The powerful mobster's suspicions are confirmed when Morrow kills a bootlegger without orders to do so. Morrow and Alden break with Danton's mob and begin their own gang. Soon after, Morrow learns that the man he murdered is survived by an attractive daughter, Parrish, and the morally corrupt gangster decides to court her. Though engaged to Breck, a young policeman, Parrish is attracted to Morrow (she is unaware of his involvement in organized crime and her father's death) and agrees to see him. Despite her wanderings, she eventually decides to marry Breck. Outraged, Morrow sets out to destroy the marriage by getting the weak-willed Breck on his payroll. Parrish learns of her husband's corrupt earnings and leaves him in disgust. Her life shattered, Parrish becomes an alcoholic and drifts into Morrow's arms. Meanwhile, Morrow has eliminated the dual problems of Danton and the crazy "Mad Dog" Coll (McCord) from his territory. These brutal moves catapult Morrow to the top of the gangster heap in New York. Eventually Parrish discovers that it was Morrow who killed her father and she leaves him to live in a seedy hotel where she can wash away her troubles with even more booze. A repentant Breck traces her to the hotel and convinces her that they can start over and make a go of their ruined marriage. Meantime, the Italian mobsters have had just about enough of Morrow's strong-arm tactics and they begin to put the screws in. Desperate to maintain his position, Morrow arranges for the Mafia to kill several of his top lieutenants, including Alden. Unknown to Morrow, the Mafia plans to kill him as well. During the bloody gun battle a wounded Morrow manages to escape, but he is gunned down by the mortally wounded Alden who shoots him by mistake. The life of the real Dutch Schultz is more fascinating than this smarmy screen fiction. Despite the portrayal in the film, Schultz never worked for Legs Diamond; Diamond got his start in Schultz' mob. A small war erupted between the two when Diamond branched out on his own and began raiding Schultz' beer deliveries. Diamond *was*eventually eliminated by Schultz, as was Vincent "Mad Dog" Coll. Schultz' friend and aide, Bo Weinberg (named Wetzel in the film), broke from the gang and sought shelter with the likes of Lucky Luciano and Vito Genovese. Schultz had Weinberg stabbed to death. Schultz actually met his end in a small Newark restaurant called the Palace Chophouse. Assassins dispatched by the Mafia gunned down the Dutchman (who was washing his hands in the bathroom) and three of his henchmen. Schultz lingered for several hours and eventually died, ranting and raving, in a Newark hospital. Despite the fanciful nature of the screenplay, PORTRAIT OF A MOBSTER could have been a valuable look at gangsters, but it fails to deliver what its title promises. Though Morrow was a good choice for the role of Schultz, his character is one-dimensional and never really developed. The annoying romantic triangle between Morrow, Parrish, and Breck is terribly melodramatic, uninteresting, and slows the action down to a crawl. The truly fascinating aspects of Schultz' rise to power and his struggle to keep it are glossed over in the traditional movie-gangster fashion, leaving the film devoid of any real insight. Perhaps the most interesting aspect of PORTRAIT OF A MOBSTER is that Ray Danton reprises his memorable portrayal of Legs Diamond from Budd Boetticher's superior THE RISE AND FALL OF LEGS DIAMOND (1960), lending some verisimilitude to the movieland gangster universe.

d, Joseph Pevney; w, Howard Browne (based on the book by Harry Grey); ph, Eugene Polito; m, Max Steiner; ed, Leo H. Shreve; art d, Jack Poplin; set d, George James Hopkins; cos, Howard Shoup; makeup, Gordon Bau.

Crime **(PR:C MPAA:NR)**

PORTRAIT OF A SINNER** (1961, Brit.) 96m REN/AIP bw (GB: THE ROUGH AND THE SMOOTH)

Nadja Tiller *(Ila Hansen)*, Tony Britton *(Mike Thompson)*, William Bendix *(Reg Barker)*, Natasha Parry *(Margaret Goreham)*, Norman Wooland *(David Fraser)*, Donald Wolfit *(Lord Drewell)*, Tony Wright *(Jack)*, Adrienne Corri *(Jane Buller)*, Joyce Carey *(Mrs. Thompson)*, John Welsh *(Dr. Thompson)*, Martin Miller *(Piggy)*, Michael Ward *(Headwaiter)*, Edward Chapman *(Willy Catch)*, Norman Pierce *(Barman)*, Beatrice Varley *(Hotel Manager)*, Myles Eason *(Bobby Montagu-Jones)*, Cyril Smith *(Taxi Driver)*, Geoffrey Bayldon *(Ransom)*.

Britton plays an archaeologist engaged to an heiress, whom he leaves to be with the more down-to-earth and wilder Tiller. She lives with an elderly man, Bendix, in a stricly platonic manner. When another of her lovers, Wright, demands she give him a large sum of money, Tiller turns to Bendix and Britton, but both refuse. She then lets them know that Wright is the only man that can satisfy her sexually. She winds up losing all three men, but is not alone for very long.

p, George Minter; d, Robert Siodmak; w, Audrey Erskine-Lindop, Dudley Leslie (based on the novel *The Rough and the Smooth*by Robin Maugham); ph, Otto Heller; m, Douglas Gamley, Ken Jones; ed, Gordon Pilkington; md, Muir Mathieson; art d, Ken Adam; cos, Julie Harris; makeup, Harold Fletcher.

Drama **(PR:C MPAA:NR)**

PORTRAIT OF A WOMAN*** (1946, Fr.) 80m Mayer-Burstyn bw

Francoise Rosay *(Fanny Helder/Tona/Lucia Delavee/Flora)*, Henry Guisol *(Manager)*, Jean Nohain *(Farmer)*, Ettore Cella *(Barge Captain)*, Claire Gerard *(Barge Captain's Servant)*, Yva Belle *(Farmer's Wife)*, Claude Alain *(Police Inspector)*, Florence Lynn *(School Mistress)*.

Made in Switzerland during the German occupation of France, Rosay plays an opera singer who commits suicide when she no longer captivates her audience. Her body is found without any identification. Police inquiries have four people each believing that the body may belong to a person they know who has been missing. Each then gives their story, with Rosay playing the missing person in each case. One of these is an elderly peasant woman, another a genteel school teacher, and another the wife of a bargekeeper. Rosay showed a good deal of talent in her depiction of the very different women, with the subtle hand of her husband at the time, Feyder, guiding her. (In French; English subtitles.)

p,d&w, Jacques Feyder (based on a novel by Jacques Viot); ph, Jacques Mercanton, Adrien Porchet; ed, John Oser; English subtitles, Herman G. Weinberg.

Drama **(PR:A MPAA:NR)**

PORTRAIT OF ALISON (SEE: POSTMARK FOR DANGER, 1956, Brit.)

PORTRAIT OF CHIEKO* ½**   (1968, Jap.) 125m Shochiku c
                                                    (CHIEKO-SHO)

Tetsuro Tamba *(Kotaro Takamura)*, Shima Iwashita *(Chieko)*, Eiji Okada *(Tsubaki)*, Takamura Sasaki *(Koun Takamura)*, Jin Nakayama *(Hoshu)*, Yoko Minamida *(Kazuko)*.

Based on the real life incidences of Kotaro Takamura, one of Japan's foremost poets and sculptors, concerning wife's [Iwashita] obsession to creatively express herself. When her paintings are criticized, the knowledge that she does not possess the proper talent depresses her. Tamba, as her poet husband, devotes himself to his wife's problems, writing numerous poems for her. But she continues to withdraw, attempts suicide, and eventually goes mad. Slow pacing, and rich color photography combine to create a near poetic effect and the moody atmosphere proper to the film's content. Nominated as Best Foreign Film in the 1968 Academy Awards.

d, Noboru Nakamura; w, Nakamura, Minoru Hirose (based on the novel *Shosetsu Chieko-Sho* by Haruosato); ph, Hiroshi Takamura (Eastmancolor); m, Masaru Sato; art d, Tatsuo Hamada.

Drama   **(PR:A MPAA:NR)**

PORTRAIT OF CLARE**   (1951, Brit.) 100m Associated British/AB-
                                                    Pathe bw

Margaret Johnston *(Clare Hingston)*, Richard Todd *(Robert Hart)*, Robin Bailey *(Dudley Wilburn)*, Ronald Howard *(Ralph Hingston)*, Jeremy Spenser *(Steven Hingston)*, Marjorie Fielding *(Aunt Cathie)*, Molly Urquhart *(Thirza)*, Becket Bould *(Bissell)*, Anthony Nicholls *(Dr. Boyd)*, Lloyd Pearson *(Sir Joseph Hingston)*, Mary Clare *(Lady Hingston)*, S. Griffiths-Moss *(Bates)*, Campbell Copelin *(Inspector Cunningham)*, Bruce Seton *(Lord Steven Wolverbury)*, Yvonne Andre, Hugh Morton, David Keir, Hugh Cort, Robert Adair, Grace Arnold, Ann Codrington, Andrew Leigh, Cameron Miller, Una Venning, Brian Peck, Charles Paton, Anne Gunning, Scott Harrold, Amy Veness.

Slow moving drama centers on a young woman, Johnston, widowed just after the first child is born. She lives alone for 10 years until she marries a local lawyer, which results in an unhappy arrangement. She eventually finds happiness with the lawyer's cousin. Told entirely in flashback form, the pace is a bit slack for the normal audience. Johnston adds a lot of charm and sincerity to her role.

p, Leslie Landau; d, Lance Comfort; w, Landau, Adrian Arlington (from the novel by Francis Brett Young); ph, Gunther Krampf; m, Leighton Lucas; ed, Clifford Boote; md, Louis Levy; art d, Don Ashton.

Drama   **(PR:A MPAA:NR)**

PORTRAIT OF HELL***   (1969, Jap.) 91m Toho c (JIGOKUHEN)

Kinnosuke Nakamura *(Lord Hosokawa)*, Tatsuya Nakadai *(Yoshihide)*, Yoko Naito *(Yoshika)*, Shun Oide.

Set in 10th century Japan, Nakadai plays a stubborn painter who refuses to allow his daughter to see his Korean apprentice, banishing the latter from the house. The girl then flees to the court of the ruler, Nakumura, who tells Nakadai he may only have his daughter if he agrees to paint a mural. Nakadai complies, but only if it is a vision of hell. This ignites a battle of wills between the two headstrong personalities, which ends in both men being driven to suicide.

p, Tomoyuki Tanaka; d, Shiro Toyoda; w, Toshio Yasumi (based on the story "Jigokuhen" by Ryunosuke Akutagawa); ph, Kazuo Yamada (Panavision, Eastmancolor); m, Yasushi Akutagawa; art d, Shinobu Muraki.

Drama   **(PR:A MPAA:NR)**

PORTRAIT OF INNOCENCE**   (1948, Fr.) 90m Pathe/Siritzky
                                                    International bw

Louise Carletti *(Mariette)*, Gilbert Gil *(M. Morin)*, Pierre Larquay *(Le Pere Finot)*, Andre Brunot *(Le Commissaire)*, Emile Genevoix *(Gros Charles)*, Bussieres *(Gaston)*, Coedel *(Pere de Laurent)*, Jean-Pierre Geffroy *(Rozet)*, Georges Reygnier *(Andre)*, Jean Buquet *(Tom Mix)*, Bernard Dayde *(Doudou)*.

Touching story about a group of school children who do odd jobs to raise money to fix the classroom window that one of them broke. When they finally get enough money, the evil Bussieres steals it from them, but the kids manage to see that justice is done. (In French; English subtitles.)

d, Louis Daquin; w, Hilero, Gaston Modot; ph, Bachelet; m, Marius-Francois Gaillard; English subtitles, Charles Clement.

Drama   **(PR:A MPAA:NR)**

PORTRAIT OF JENNIE***   (1949) 86m Vanguard/SELZ bw-c (GB:
                                                    JENNIE; AKA: TIDAL WAVE)

Jennifer Jones *(Jennie Appleton)*, Joseph Cotten *(Eben Adams)*, Ethel Barrymore *(Miss Spinney)*, Cecil Kellaway *(Mr. Matthews)*, David Wayne *(Gus O'Toole)*, Albert Sharpe *(Mr. Moore)*, Florence Bates *(Mrs. Jekes the Landlady)*, Lillian Gish *(Mother Mary of Mercy)*, Henry Hull *(Eke)*, Esther Somers *(Mrs. Bunce)*, Maude Simmons *(Clara Morgan)*, Felix Bressart *(Doorman)*, John Farrell *(Policeman)*, Clem Bevans *(Capt. Caleb Cobb)*, Robert Dudley *(Old Mariner)*, Anne Francis *(Teenager)*.

A tasteful though eerie love story, PORTRAIT OF JENNIE offers a superb performance from Cotten as a struggling painter and a haunting essay from Jones as a girl from another era with whom he falls in love. It is 1932, the nadir of the Depression, and Cotten, a young painter who finds his work lacking depth, sits glumly in New York City's Central Park contemplating his not-so-bright future. A beautiful young girl, Jones, appears and begins to talk to him strangely, speaking in terms that are not of his era, mentioning that she attends a convent school and that her parents are trapeze artists at Hammerstein's Opera House. She then sings Cotten a haunting song with provocative lyrics: "Where I come from nobody knows—and where

I'm going everything goes. The wind blows, the sea flows—and nobody knows." Jones then disappears as abruptly as she arrived. Meanwhile, Cotten struggles on with his art, encouraged by wealthy art dealer Barrymore, who takes a motherly interest in him, buying his water colors while knowing they are inadequate but suggesting he find a new way to express his visions on canvas. Jones reappears throughout that winter while Cotten finds work painting a patriotic mural of Michael Collins and his followers during the Easter Rebellion of 1916 in Ireland on the wall of an Irish saloon, a commisssion arranged for by his good friend Wayne, a cab driver who encourages Cotten's ambitions as an artist. Each time Jones appears she seems older by years, through the following spring and summer, growing up from adolescence to young womanhood. Cotten asks Jones to sit for a portrait and finishes it just as she tells him she's about to graduate from college. The portrait of Jones is viewed by Barrymore and her associate Kellaway and they find it innovative, startling, a new form of expression by Cotten that will certainly establish his artistic reputation. Yet Cotten is haunted by Jones and begins to look into her background, finding that her parents had been killed in a high-wire accident and, through Gish, a mother superior at an all-girl college, learns that Jones was killed during a New England hurricane in the 1920s. Cotten refuses to believe in such supernatural possibilities but, on the eve of the hurricane's anniversary, rushes to New England. Jones comes to him during a raging storm to tell him that their love will live across the barriers of time, then vanishes. Cotten doubts he ever met the beautiful Jones after a while until finding her scarf and believing he will meet his true love in the eternity from which she momentarily escaped. Dieterle's direction is sensitive and wonderfully constructed without any scene bruising the next. He draws forth stellar performances here, especially from Cotten. Jones is seen too briefly but when on screen she projects an ethereal other-world quality. August's photography is stunning and Tiomkin's lyrical score, drawn from Claude Debussy's themes, mostly "The Afternoon of a Faun," is most memorable. The forward of the film, written by Ben Hecht, sums up this touching film: "Out of the shadows of knowledge, and out of a painting that hung on a museum wall, comes our story, the truth of which lies not on our screen but in your heart." (A similar love theme showing the living and departed was at the core of a Ben Hecht romance film of considerable note, MIRACLE IN THE RAIN.)

p, David O. Selznick; d, William Dieterle; w, Paul Osborn, Peter Berneis, Leonardo Bercovici (based on the novel by Robert Nathan); ph, Joseph August (Technicolor sequence); m, Dimitri Tiomkin (based on themes of Claude Debussy); ed, William Morgan; md, Tiomkin; prod d, J. McMillan Johnson; art d, Joseph B. Platt; set d, Claude Carpenter; cos, Lucinda Ballard, Anna Hill Johnstone; spec eff, Clarence Slifer, Paul Eagler, Johnson; m/l, "Jennie's Song," Bernard Herrmann; makeup, Mel Berns.

Romance   **(PR:A MPAA:NR)**

PORTRAIT OF LENIN**   (1967, Pol./USSR) 98m Mosfilm-Studio Film
          Unit-Polski/Artkino-Brandon bw (LENIN V POLSHE; LENIN W POLSCE)

Maksim Shtraukh *(Vladimir Ilich Lenin)*, Anna Lisyanskaya *(Krupskaya, Lenin's Wife)*, Antonina Pavlycheva *(Krupskaya's Mother)*, Ilona Kusmierska *(Ulka)*, Edmund Fetting *(Hanecki)*, Krysztof Kalczynski *(Andrzej)*, Tadeusz Fijewski *(Secretary of the Prison)*, Henryk Hunko, Ludwik Benoit *(Guards)*, Gustaw Lutkiewicz *(Investigator)*, Kazimierz Rudzki *(Priest)*, Zbigniew Skowronski *(Matyszezuk)*, Jarema Stepowski *(Photographer)*, Vladimir Akimov, Nikolay Kashirskiy, Vladimir Monakhov, Andrey Petrov, Gennadiy Yukhtin, J. Gruca, E. Jezewska, W. Jakubinska, A. Jurczak, A. Lodzinski, J. Marchand, B. Michalski, Jerzy Moes, Jozef Nowak, A. Nowak, A. Potapov, W. Rajewski, A. Skupien, R. Zaorski, A. Zulinski.

Biography of the events of the Bolshevik leader prior to the Russian Revolution. Story concentrates mainly on his exile in Poland where he befriends a peasant girl and her boy friend. She is a strong believer in the nationalist cause. Shtraukh, as Lenin, learns that the girl was killed when she withheld information about him.

d, Sergey Yutkevich; w, Yutkevich, Yevgeniy Gabrilovich; ph, Jan Laskowski (Sovscope); m, Adam Walacinski; art d, Jan Grandys; spec eff, Boris Travkin, A. Rudachenko.

Drama   **(PR:A MPAA:NR)**

PORTRAIT OF MARIA**   (1946, Mex.) 96m Films Mundiales/MGM bw
                                                    (AKA: MARIA CANDELARIA; XOCHIMILCO)

Dolores Del Rio *(Maria Candelaria)*, Pedro Armendariz *(Lorenzo Rafael)*, Margarita Cortes *(Lupe)*, Alberto Galan *(El Pintor)*, Beatriz Ramos *(Reporter)*, Manuel Inclan *(Don Damian)*, Rafael Icardo *(Senor Cura)*, Julio Ahuet *(Jose Alfonso)*, Arturo Soto Rangel *(Doctor)*, Irma Torres, Guadalupe Del Castillo.

Del Rio was already 40 years of age when she played a peasant girl far younger in this Mexican-made feature. She'd been around since the days of the silents and managed to preserve her legendary beauty. Del Rio plays the daughter of a woman who had once posed for a painting in the nude by artist Galan and her small town compadres rewarded her efforts by stoning her to death. Now, Del Rio is affianced to Armendariz and when she comes down with malaria, he goes out to steal some quinine (they can't afford to buy any). He is sent to jail and she needs money to get him out, as well as to buy a dress for their wedding. She goes to Galan and agrees to pose for a painting. After he finishes her face, he wants her to take off all her clothes but she refuses. So Galan gets another woman, Cortes, to undress and he adds her body to Del Rio's face. When the painting is exhibited, Del Rio is assumed to have posed for the nude portrait and she suffers the same stoning death as her mother did. (The people in that town are *strict*!) The movie was released in the States without titles and did some business in Spanish-speaking markets as both Del Rio and Armendariz were box office favorites at the time. Later, it was dubbed into English but didn't fare well. Armendariz, director-writer Fernandez and cinematographer Figueroa had far better success with a movie they made a short while later, THE PEARL. Here good small roles were handled by Ramos, as a reporter, and Icardo as the local priest. Inclan plays the heavy like a parody of every Mexican villain ever seen, and if he could have said "I don' have to show you any stinkin' badges," he would have.

p, Agustin J. Fink; d, Emilio Fernandez; w, Fernandez, Mauricio Magdaleno; ph, Gabriel Figueroa; m, Francisco Dominguez; ed, Gloria Schoemann.

Drama **(PR:C MPAA:NR)**

PORTRAIT OF THE ARTIST AS A YOUNG MAN, A**½ (1979, Ireland) 98m Ulysses/Howard Mahler c

Bosco Hogan *(Stephen Dedalus)*, T.P. McKenna *(Simon Dedalus)*, Sir John Gielgud *(Preacher)*, Rosaleen Linhan *(May Dedalus)*, Maureen Potter *(Dante)*, Cecil Sheehan *(Uncle Charles)*, Niall Buggy *(Davin)*, Brian Murray *(Lynch)*, Terence Strick *(Stephen, Age 3)*, Luke Johnson *(Stephen, Age 10.)*.

An attempt at the film adaptation of Joyce's autobiographical novel about an Irish youth's journey into manhood, and his problems in breaking away from his strict Catholic upbringing. The director used a more filmic representation instead of the stream-of-consciousness of the novel. The film still manages to incorporate much of the novel's ideology, but in doing so falls into a trap of long monologues with little action taking place. Actors are all top-notch, and the photography of the Irish countryside is breathtaking.

p, Richard Hallinan, Betty Botley; d, Joseph Strick; w, Judith Rascoe (based on the novel by James Joyce); ph, Stuart Hetherington; m, Stanley Myers; ed, Lesley Walker; cos, Judy Nolan.

Drama **(PR:A MPAA:NR)**

POSEIDON ADVENTURE, THE**½ (1972) 117m FOX c

Gene Hackman *(Rev. Frank Scott)*, Ernest Borgnine *(Mike Rogo)*, Red Buttons *(James Martin)*, Carol Lynley *(Nonnie Parry)*, Roddy McDowall *(Acres)*, Stella Stevens *(Linda Rogo)*, Shelly Winters *(Belle Rosen)*, Jack Albertson *(Manny Rosen)*, Leslie Nielson *(Ship's Captain)*, Pamela Sue Martin *(Susan Shelby)*, Arthur O'Connell *(Ship's Chaplain)*, Eric Shea *(Robin Shelby)*, Fred Sadoff *(Linarcos)*, Sheila Mathews *(Ship's Nurse)*, Jan Arvan *(Dr. Caravello)*, Byron Webster *(Purser)*, John Crawford *(Chief Engineer)*, Bob Hastings *(Master of Ceremonies)*, Erik Nelson *(Tinkham)*, Dave Sharpe *(Passenger)*.

This is the picture that started the disaster film craze of the 1970s, but few proved to be as successful in depicting the incredible situations, or as profitable at the box office, as THE POSEIDON ADVENTURE. Producer Allen had his biggest successes on television where he oversaw the production of classics including THE TIME TUNNEL and LOST IN SPACE. He brought his idea that audiences enjoy seeing dangerous and suspenseful situations and it turned into a financial success. Though many of the situations seem totally implausible to the discerning eye, the majority of audiences were quite taken in. During a New Year's eve celebration aboard a luxury liner, a tidal wave capsizes the ship, killing all but 10 people. Led by Hackman, a priest who believes in action instead of prayer, the 10 make their way through electrical conduits, air shafts, and a blazing engine room before they can reach the bottom of the ship. Along the way Hackman loses his life to allow the others' safety. Cast fits their characters quite effectively, keeping any form of dramatic action down to a minimum. Well thought out script and direction keeps a steady amount of tension and suspense which doesn't let up until the survivors are rescued. The sequel was BEYOND THE POSEIDON ADVENTURE made in 1979 by Warner Bros.

p, Irwin Allen; d, Ronald Neame; w, Stirling Silliphant, Wendell Mayes (based on the novel by Paul Gallico); ph, Harold E. Stine (Panavision, DeLuxe Color); m, John Williams; ed, Harold F. Kress; prod d, William Creber; set d, Raphael Bretton; cos, Paul Zastupnevich; spec eff, L.B. Abbott, A.D. Flowers; m/l, "The Morning After," Al Kasha, Joel Hirschhorn (sung by Carol Lynley); makeup, Ed Butterworth, Del Acevedo, Allan Snyder; stunts, Paul Stader.

Adventure **Cas.** **(PR:A MPAA:PG)**

POSITIONS (SEE: PUT UP OR SHUT UP, 1968, Arg.)

POSITIONS OF LOVE (SEE: PUT UP OR SHUT UP, 1968, Arg.)

POSSE*** (1975) 92m Bryna/PAR c

Kirk Douglas *(Marshal Howard Nightingale)*, Bruce Dern *(Jack Strawhorn)*, Bo Hopkins *(Wesley)*, James Stacy *(Hellman, Editor)*, Luke Askew *(Krag)*, David Canary *(Pensteman)*, Alfonso Arau *(Peppe)*, Katherine Woodville *(Mrs. Cooper)*, Mark Roberts *(Mr. Cooper)*, Beth Brickell *(Mrs. Ross)*, Dick O'Neill *(Wiley)*, Bill Burton *(McCanless)*, Louie Elias *(Rains)*, Gus Greymountain *(Reyno)*, Allan Warwick *(Telegrapher)*, Roger Behrstock *(Sheriff Buwalda)*, Jess Riggle *(Hunsinger)*, Stephanie Steele *(Amie)*, Melody Thomas *(Laurie)*, Dick Armstrong, Larry Finley, Pat Tobin *(Shanty Principals)*.

Douglas produced, directed, and starred in the story of a U.S. Marshal whose political ambitions prove to be his downfall. Douglas heads a posse on the trail of bankrobber Dern, hoping that his efforts will boost his political campaign. But the witty Dern proves too much for Douglas, as he takes the marshal hostage, then demands that the posse return the money they found on him. To get the necessary money they must loot a nearby town, thus making themselves outlaws. Dern allows the men to split the money, making Douglas' followers his new gang. A superb cast, especially Dern, give this picture the needed characterizations. James Stacy had suffered the loss of his arm and leg prior to the film's production, so Douglas had a special part written for the handicapped actor.

p&d, Kirk Douglas; w, William Roberts, Christopher Knopf (based on a story by Knopf); ph, Fred J. Koenekamp (Panavision, Technicolor); m, Maurice Jarre; ed, John W. Wheeler; prod d, Lyle Wheeler; set d, Fred Price, Wheeler.

Western **(PR:C MPAA:PG)**

POSSE FROM HELL*** (1961) 89m UNIV c

Audie Murphy *(Banner Cole)*, John Saxon *(Seymour Kern)*, Zohra Lampert *(Helen Caldwell)*, Vic Morrow *(Crip)*, Robert Keith *(Capt. Brown)*, Ward Ramsey *(Mashal Webb)*, Rudolph Acosta *(Johnny Caddo)*, Frank Overton *(Burt Hogan)*, Royal Dano *(Uncle Billy Caldwell)*, James Bell *(Benson)*, Paul Carr *(Jack Wiley)*, Lee Van Cleef *(Leo)*, Ray Teal *(Larson)*, Forrest Lewis *(Dr. Welles)*, Charles Horvath *(Hash)*, Harry Lauter *(Russell)*, Henry Wills *(Chunk)*, Stuart Randall *(Luke Gorman)*, Allan Lane *(Burl Hogan)*.

Murphy heads a posse in pursuit of four killers recently escaped from prison, who pillaged the small town of Paradise. The men killed several people, robbed a bank, and abducted the town's prettiest lass, Lampert, whom they all rape and leave to die. The original posse starts at seven, but dwindles to three during the pursuit, Murphy, Lampert—who has been picked up on the trail—and Saxon, an easterner newly arrived in the rugged West. They catch up to the crooks, who prove no match for Murphy. Stunning photography, strong characterizations, and well-paced action keep the inconsistencies of the plot in the background. Van Cleef and Morrow offer interesting depictions of two of the murderous villains. This was the directorial debut for Coleman, and western star Lane's last film.

p, Gordon Kay; d, Herbert Coleman; w, Clair Huffaker (based on the novel by Huffaker); ph, Clifford Stine (Eastmancolor); m, Joseph Gershenson; ed, Frederic Knudtson; art d, Alexander Golitzen, Alfred Sweeney; set d, Oliver Emert; makeup, Bud Westmore.

Western **(PR:A MPAA:NR)**

POSSESSED**½ (1931) 72m MGM bw

Joan Crawford *(Marian Martin)*, Clark Gable *(Mark Whitney)*, Wallace Ford *(Al Mannings)*, Skeets Gallagher *(Wally Stuart)*, Frank Conroy *(Travers)*, Marjorie White *(Vernice)*, John Miljan *(John Driscoll)*, Clara Blandick *(Mother)*.

Crawford and Gable were powerful attractions on their own and even more so together. Crawford is a blue-blouse worker at an Erie, Pennsylvania, factory that manufactures boxes. She dreams of a better life and therefore resists the marriage proposal of Ford, a fellow worker who adores her. Ford is a nice enough guy but she doesn't love him and her aspirations are far beyond the constraints of the small town in which she lives and works. When a train breaks down at the local station, Crawford happens to be there and meets Gallagher, a Manhattan sharpie who tells her that she is too beautiful and too hip to stay stuck in this burg. He gives her his card and asks her to look him up if she ever decides to get out of hicksville. She goes to New York on what must be deemed a gold-digging exposition and, through Gallagher, she meets Gable, a wealthy and successful lawyer. Gable is married but separated and he hesitates divorcing his wife because he is thinking about running for office and the resultant publicity might hurt that goal. Gable and Crawford fall in love and she becomes his mistress, living in a posh Park Avenue apartment, wearing gorgeous clothes, bedecked with jewels and now, having shed some of her small-town ways, she is assuming the role of a big-town sophisticate, a seemingly rich divorcee. What began as a matter of convenience has blossomed into love between Crawford and Gable but that's threatened when Ford shows up. He's now a contractor and seeking Gable's okay on a paving contract. Gable is thinking about running for governor and when Ford asks Crawford to marry him, she tells Gable, who thinks that she might actually do it, if only to become an "honest woman." Gable has been kept from marrying Crawford by political ally Conroy, who thinks it would be better if they kept her under wraps. Gable would rather have Crawford than the office of governor and he's willing to pass it by but she insists that he continue his aspirations and that she is going to marry Ford. (That's a ploy, of course, because she won't stand in his way.) There's a huge political rally and someone asks about his relationship with Crawford. Gable is hard-pressed to answer, then Crawford, who is in attendance, stands and makes an impassioned speech on behalf of Gable. She says that she has walked out of his life and that he belongs to the people now and can serve them with no entangling alliances. The audience is impressed by her words and she exits. Gable chases after her, catches her on the street, takes her in his arms, and says that whichever way the election goes, they must always be together. In the original play by Selwyn, the male lead was much older and the ending was teary. For the sake of the movie-going public, an up-beat finale was added and the role was more youthful to accommodate Gable. Crawford sings "How Long Can It Last?" in three languages.

d, Clarence Brown; w, Lenore Coffee (based on the play "The Mirage" by Edgar Selwyn; ph, Oliver T. Marsh; ed, William Levanway; m/l, "How Long Can It Last?" Max Leif, Joseph Meyer.

Drama **(PR:A-C MPAA:NR)**

POSSESSED***½ (1947) 108m WB bw

Joan Crawford *(Louise Howell Graham)*, Van Heflin *(David Sutton)*, Raymond Massey *(Dean Graham)*, Geraldine Brooks *(Carol Graham)*, Stanley Ridges *(Dr. Harvey Williard)*, John Ridgely *(Lt. Harker)*, Nana Bryant *(Pauline Graham)*, Moroni Olsen *(Dr. Ames)*, Erskine Sanford *(Dr. Max Sherman)*, Gerald Perreau *(Wynn Graham)*, Isabel Withers *(Nurse Rosen)*, Lisa Golm *(Elsie)*, Douglas Kennedy *(Assistant District Attorney)*, Monte Blue *(Norris, Caretaker)*, Don McGuire *(Dr. Craig)*, Rory Mallinson *(Coroner's Assistant)*, Clifton Young *(Intern)*, Griff Barnett *(Coroner)*, Ralph Dunn *(Motorman)*, Max Wagner, Dick Bartell *(Men in Cafe)*, Frank Marlowe *(Proprietor)*, Rose Plummer *(Woman in Cafe)*, Jane Harker *(Woman's Voice)*, Robert Lowell, Richard Walsh *(Faces)*, Jack Mower *(Man)*, James Conaty *(Foreman)*, Creighton Hale *(Secretary)*, Jane Harker *(1st College Girl)*, Martha Montgomery *(2nd College Girl)*, Tristram Coffin *(Man at Concert)*, Jacob Gimpel *(Walter Sveldon)*, Nell Craig, Bunty Cutler *(Nurses)*, Henry Sylvester *(Dean's Secretary)*, Sara Padden *(Mrs. Norris, Caretaker's Wife)*, Wheaton Chambers *(Waiter)*, Eddie Hart *(Bartender)*, Philo McCullough *(Edwards, the Butler)*, Paul Bradley, Peggy Leon *(Wedding Guests)*, Jeffrey Sayre *(Dance Extra)*.

A very rare occurrence here in that Crawford had already made a film named

POSSESSED (with Clark Gable) and the two pictures are often, and understandably, confused although this was made 16 years later and secured an Oscar nomination for her. Crawford is found dazed on a street of downtown Los Angeles and taken to a local hospital where they unravel her distraught cries for "David" through the use of drug therapy, and we are flashed back to how she came to be in this state. Sometime before, Crawford had been working as an in-house nurse for invalid Bryant, wife of rich Massey. Crawford is mad about Heflin, an engineer, but he can't take her jealous and possessive attitude toward him. He likes her but doesn't love her nearly as ardently as she loves him and he wants to call it quits. She threatens him but he leaves and takes a job in Canada. Meanwhile, Bryant is as unstable mentally as Crawford and she imagines Massey and Crawford are having an affair. It's all in her mind but that doesn't stop Bryant from drowning herself. Crawford remains in the huge home as governess and general housekeeper for Perreau. Massey's oldest child, Brooks, is away at school but her late mother had written of her suspicions concerning Crawford and Massey and Brooks believes them. Heflin returns to accept a job with Massey and Crawford is hot on his heels again but he fends her off. When Massey asks for Crawford's hand, she accepts but leaves the decision to Brooks and says she won't marry Massey if Brooks doesn't agree. Brooks is won over by that gesture and the wedding takes place. Heflin now goes after Brooks, who has no idea of the way Crawford feels about Heflin. This causes Crawford's already-shaky mind to break and she begins seeing and hearing things and imagining that Bryant is still alive. Crawford attempts to break up Brooks and Heflin and fails, then she goes to Heflin's apartment and shoots him dead. That action puts her over the edge and brings the picture to where it began, in the mental hospital. Psychiatrist Ridges has listened to her tale and determined that she was not mentally responsible for her actions. She'll need lots of therapy and she may eventually recover, a fact that causes Massey to have a shred of happiness in a life that has been filled with tragedy and two mad wives. Bernhardt's direction is moody and atmospheric and the switching between what *is* and what Crawford *thinks* is effective.

p, Jerry Wald; d, Curtis Bernhardt; w, Silvia Richards, Ranald MacDougall (based on the story "One Man's Secret" by Rita Weiman); ph, Joseph Valentine; m, Franz Waxman; ed, Rudi Fehr; md, Leo F. Forbstein; art d, Anton Grot; set d, Fred M. MacLean; cos, Bernard Newman, Adrian; spec eff, William McGann, Robert Burks; makeup, Perc Westmore.

Drama **(PR:A-C MPAA:NR)**

POSSESSION* (1981, Fr./Ger.) 81m Oliane-Soma-Marianne/Limelight International c

Isabelle Adjani (Anna/Helen), Sam Neill (Marc), Heinz Bennent (Heinrich), Margit Carstensen (Margie), Michael Hogben (Bob), Shaun Lawton (Zimmerman), Johanna Hofer (Mother), Carl Duering (Detective), Maximilian Ruethlein, Thomas Frey, Leslie Malton, Gerd Neubart, Kerstin Wohlfahrt, Ilse Bahrs, Karin Mumm, Herbert Chwoika, Barbara Stanek, Ilse Trautschold.

An enormous number of symbols, both sexual and religious, give some meaning to this story of an estranged woman, Adjani, who gives birth to a full-grown man, an exact replica of her husband, after making love to a slimy monster. Neill has been away on a special assignment for a couple of years and comes home to find his wife, Adjani, acting strange. She admits to having a lover, ex-flower child Bennent, so Neill has some private detectives follow her. One detective is killed by Adjani, the other by the tentacled monster. Unaware of this monster, Neill thinks his wife has gone mad and tries to help her, but when he catches her making love to a slimy creature he gains a new view of the situation. The themes, camera angles, and symbolism were handled much more effectively by Roman Polanski in REPULSION (1965) and ROSEMARY'S BABY (1968). POSSESSION is far more extreme than either of these, and because of this is much harder to take seriously. The original European cut ran at 127 minutes.

p, Marie-Laure Reyre; d, Andrzej Zulawski; w, Zulawski, Frederic Tuten; ph, Bruno Nuyteen (Eastmancolor); m, Andrzej Korzynski, Art Phillips; ed, Marie-Sophie Dubus, Suzanne Lang-Willar; art d, Holger Gross.

Horror **Cas.** **(PR:O MPAA:R)**

POSSESSION OF JOEL DELANEY, THE* (1972) 108m ITC-Haworth/PAR c

Shirley MacLaine (Norah Benson), Perry King (Joel Delaney), Michael Hordern (Justin Lorenz), David Elliott (Peter Benson), Lisa Kohane (Carrie Benson), Barbara Trentham (Sherry), Lovelady Powell (Erika Lorenz), Edmundo Rivera Alvarez (Don Pedro), Teodorina Bello (Mrs. Perez), Robert Burr (Ted Benson), Miriam Colon (Veronica, Maid), Ernesto Gonzalez (Young Man at Seance), Aukie Herger (Mr. Perez), Earl Hyman (Charles), Marita Lindholm (Marta Benson), Peter Turgeon (Detective Brady), Paulita Iglesias (Bruja at Seance), Stan Watt (James), Jose Fernandez (Tonio Perez).

A positively horrific story that was part of MacLaine's deal with British TV mogul Sir Lew Grade, this picture has little to recommend it other than MacLaine's job. She'd made a TV series that was cancelled quickly ("Shirley's World"), then DESPERATE CHARACTERS (a better movie than this one), and this was their third attempt together. It was shot for a pittance ($1,300,000) and looked it. Martin Poll had been the producer but when he and MacLaine had squabbles, the real strength emerged and Poll left the production after five weeks. MacLaine is a rich divorcee who lives with her two children, Elliott and Kohane, in a swanky New York residence. Her brother, King, had the opportunity to move in with her but prefers to live downtown in a depressing apartment in the East Village. King goes mad one night and attacks the janitor in his building then can't recall the skirmish. He's put in a mental ward and MacLaine gets him out and moves him into her place, then talks him into seeing Powell, a psychiatrist friend. King is becoming very weird and unable to communicate, except when discussing a Puerto Rican pal named Tonio. MacLaine throws a birthday bash for King but his behavior is maddening as he rails on in Spanish, yells at Colon, the maid and even berates his girl friend, Trentham.

Colon leaves angrily and the next day MacLaine travels to the maid's home in Spanish Harlem to plead for her to return. Colon refuses, and is convinced that King has been "possessed," but MacLaine can't believe that kind of Caribbean voodoo in this day and age (she should have seen ROSEMARY'S BABY). That reluctance continues until MacLaine goes to visit Trentham and finds the young woman's body and her head in distinctly different places. King is taken in by the cops and they want to know more about Tonio, whom they believe may be responsible for this killing as well as several more in the city. When MacLaine goes searching herself for Tonio, she learns that the boy has been dead for quite some time and it might be that his spirit is trying to take over King's body. Since that kind of stuff can only be disposed of with supernatural powers, MacLaine becomes part of a seance that ultimately fails, with MacLaine getting the blame from all the others around the table because she doesn't truly believe in her heart that such things are possible. Powell says the problem may be with King and that MacLaine would be safer if she and her children got out of her apartment right away. The four of them go to the Long Island beach house MacLaine owns and feel safe for the night. The next morning, however, proves to be shattering as MacLaine finds Powell's head and body unattached. King walks in wielding a menacing switchblade and speaking perfect Puerto Rican Spanish. He is now being totally controlled by Tonio and he forces MacLaine and the children into an ordeal. Powell's husband, Hordern, has told the police of his wife's whereabouts and they arrive before King can kill anyone else. He uses Kohane and Elliott as shields and tries to get away but the police shoot him down and he lies bleeding in the sand. MacLaine takes her brother's body in her arms and doesn't realize that as he is dying, the essence of Tonio is moving into her body. King dies, she closes his open eyes, thins her lips at the cop who saved them and reaches for King's knife as the picture ends before she can speak much Spanish. Bad taste, overwrought, and absolute clap-trap. Poll should be happy he left.

p, Martin Poll; d, Waris Hussein; w, Matt Robinson, Grimes Grice (based on the novel by Ramona Stewart); ph, Arthur J. Ornitz (Eastmancolor); m, Joe Raposo; ed, John Victor Smith; prod d, Peter Murton; md, Raposo; art d, Philip Rosenberg; set d, Edward Stewart; cos, Frank Thompson; makeup, Saul Meth.

Horror **(PR:O MPAA:R)**

POST OFFICE INVESTIGATOR** (1949) 60m REP bw

Audrey Long (Clara Kelso), Warren Douglas (Bill Mannerson), Jeff Donnell (April Shaughnessy), Marcel Journet (George Zelger), Tony Cannon (Frank Forenti), Richard Benedict (Louis Reese), Jimmie Dodd (Eddie Waltch), Thomas Browne Henry (Lt. Contreras), Cliff Clark (Inspector Delany), Vera Marshe (Bubbles), Peter Brocco (Bruno Antista), Patricia Knox (Hannah), Holmes Herbert (James Seeley), Jason Robards, Sr. (Henry Hand), Emmett Vogan (Post Office Superintendent).

Long plays a female criminal specializing in rare stamps who harasses mail carrier Douglas to hand over a letter she knows contains some rare stamps. Douglas then helps the postal investigators to recover the stolen property. Long proves to be quite convincing as the tough lass who won't let herself be pushed around. Plot as a whole is weak, but the direction keeps up a suspenseful pace.

p, Sidney Picker; d, George Blair; w, John K. Butler; ph, John MacBurnie; m, Stanley Wilson; ed, Harold Minter, art d, Frank Arrigo; set d, John McCarthy, Jr., James Redd.

Crime **(PR:A MPAA:NR)**

POSTAL INSPECTOR*½ (1936) 60m UNIV bw

Ricardo Cortez (Bill Davis), Patricia Ellis (Connie Larrimore), Bela Lugosi (Benez), Michael Loring (Charlie Davis), Wallis Clark (Pottie), David Oliver (Butch), Arthur Loft (Richards), Guy Usher (Evans), William Hall (Roach), Spencer Charters (Grumpy), Hattie McDaniel (Deborah), Marla Shelton (Stewardess), Robert Davis (Pilot), Henry Hunter (Copilot), Billy Burrud (Boy), Harry Beresford (Ritter), Paul Harvey (Lt. Ordway), Anne Gillis (Little Girl), Russell Wade (Man), Anne O'Neal (Woman with Nose Machine), Gertrude Astor (Woman with Drum Sticks), Flora Finch (Mrs. Armbrister), Margaret McWade (Old Maid), Jerry Mandy (Henchman).

Mundane story has suave Cortez as a government postal inspector trying to pin down nightclub owner Lugosi on the theft of a bag of mail. Lugosi has stolen the mail in a desperate attempt to raise money to pay back a loan shark he fears may kill him. With the usual assortment of letters Lugosi also finds himself possessor of useless contraptions sold through the mail, such as electric hair growers and rheumatism cures. A romance develops between Ellis, a singer for Lugosi, and Loring, Cortez' younger brother, which proves more interesting than the hackneyed plot. Neither Cortez nor Lugosi seemed to exert much energy on this project. In this film, Universal attempted to glamorize another branch of the U.S. government, the postal inspectors, following Warner Bros.' success with its G-man cycle, but the intent was mostly shunted aside by the torrid romance subplot between Ellis and Loring. It did, however, manage to parade before the audience the endless items of worthless junk offered for sale to a gullible public which the postal inspector is eternally on the watch for, and there is a chase sequence through rising flood waters in which, for economy reasons, newsreel flood scenes of devastation in Pennsylvania and New England at the time were used.

p, Robert Presnall; d, Otto Brower; w, Horace McCoy (based on a story by Presnell, McCoy); ph, George Robinson; ed, Phil Cahn; md, Charles Previn.

Crime Drama **(PR:A MPAA:NR)**

POSTMAN ALWAYS RINGS TWICE, THE*** (1946) 113m MGM bw

Lana Turner (Cora Smith), John Garfield (Frank Chambers), Cecil Kellaway (Nick Smith), Hume Cronyn (Arthur Keats), Leon Ames (Kyle Sackett), Audrey Totter (Madge Gorland), Alan Reed (Ezra Liam Kennedy), Jeff York (Blair), Charles Williams (Jimmie White), Cameron Grant (Willie), Wally Cassell (Ben), William

Halligan, Morris Ankrum *(Judges)*, Garry Owen *(Truck Driver)*, Dorothy Phillips *(Nurse)*, Edward Earle *(Doctor)*, Byron Foulger *(Picnic Manager)*, Sondra Morgan *(Matron)*, Jeffrey Sayre, Walter Ridge, Dick Crockett, James Darrell *(Reporters)*, Brick Sullivan, Paul Krueger *(Officers)*, Phillip Ahlm, John Alban, Harold Miller, Reginald Simpson *(Photographers)*, Betty Blythe, Helen McLeod, Hilda Rhodes *(Customers)*, Joel Friedkin *(John X. MacHugh)*, Jack Chefe *(Headwaiter)*, George Noisom *(Telegraph Messenger)*, Frank Mayo, Bud Harrison *(Bailiffs)*, Virginia Randolph *(Snooty Woman)*, Tom Dillon *(Father McConnell)*, Howard Mitchell, John M. Sullivan *(Doctors)*, James Farley *(Warden)*, Edward Sherrod, Dan Quigg, Oliver Cross, Paul Bradley *(Men)*, Paula Ray *(Woman)*.

James M. Cain's hard-hitting, evil romance—not unlike his equally powerful DOUBLE INDEMNITY—comes to startling life under Garnett's shrewd direction. Garfield is a drifter who stops at a California roadside cafe owned by the amiable Kellaway who offers him a job as a handyman. Garfield is disinclined toward such menial work until he catches a glimpse of Turner, Kellaway's young, sexy, blonde wife. He immediately takes the job and then begins making advances to a most receptive lady. The two become lovers and Turner tells Garfield that she married the goodhearted Kellaway to escape a life of poverty but wound up with a life of boredom, living in another trap, having a loveless marriage and a cafe in which she has no financial interest. Kellaway gives no sign of detecting the torrid trysting of his wife with Garfield and goes on his jovial way, treating both of them as if they were his cherished children. Garfield cannot get enough of the voluptuous Turner, telling her at one point, "Give me a kiss or I'll sock ya!" The couple sit guilt-ridden in Kellaway's presence; he seems to be everywhere, smothering them in their claustrophobic romance until, suffocating—as Garnett's careful direction suggests—there is no way for them to breathe except to eliminate Kellaway. The lovers' first plan is to run away together but Turner cannot bear to lose the security of Kellaway's cozy nest egg. She suggests to Garfield that they murder Kellaway, but their initial attempt to kill the kindly cafe owner fails in a clumsy scheme. Next they get the old man drunk and drive him out along a coast road en route to Santa Barbara. While Turner drives and Kellaway sits next to her singing a song, Garfield, in the back seat, smashes a bottle over Kellaway's head, killing him. They then drive the car off a cliff but Garfield cannot get out of the car fast enough and goes over the cliff. He survives but is hospitalized. When he comes to, shrewd prosecuting attorney Ames tells him that Turner has turned him in for killing Kellaway. Garfield believes this lie and signs a complaint against her only to learn that he has been tricked. Weasely attorney Cronyn defends Turner and, in turn, Garfield, getting them off, but Ames and his men continue to watch the conspiring and now estranged lovers for any mistake they might make. Moreover, Cronyn and his goon researcher, Reed, have enough on the venal pair to blackmail them. Though the couple marry, Turner is still seething over Garfield's betrayal of her and she leaves for the East to attend her mother's funeral. Garfield spots Totter in the train station parking lot and immediately makes advances. When Turner returns she tries to patch it up with Garfield. They go swimming together almost as if to cleanse themselves of their guilt and renew their love for each other. But, in an ironic twist, as they drive along the coast road an accident occurs and Turner is killed. Garfield is accused of murdering her and, although innocent, he is convicted and sentenced to death. While awaiting execution, Garfield tells Ames: "You know, there's something about this which is like expecting a letter you're just crazy to get, and you hang around the front door for fear you might not hear 'em ring. You never realize that he always rings twice....The truth is you always hear 'em ring the second time, even if you're way out in the back yard." He turns to a priest and says, "Father, could you send up a prayer for me and Cora and, if you can find it in your heart, make it so we're together... wherever it is." THE POSTMAN ALWAYS RINGS TWICE is narrated by Garfield from his death cell from beginning to end, a technique employed in DOUBLE INDEMNITY where Fred MacMurray narrates his damned relationship with scheming Barbara Stanwyck which also led to murder. Except for two scenes where Turner wears black, one when she contemplates suicide and the other when she goes to her mother's funeral, the alluring platinum blonde actress wears nothing but white in the film, misleadingly suggesting purity. She oozes sex in every scene. Garfield first sees her as the camera does, as he retrieves her lipstick from the floor, looking up to see her white high heels, long naked legs, tight-fitting shorts, and tight blouse. Turner fairly scorched the screen with her essay of the sexy vixen, one of her best performances. Though she is a *femme fatale* here, Turner is a softer, more emotionally vulnerable Lucrezia Borgia than her sisterly counterparts in other Cain stories, such as Stanwyck in DOUBLE INDEMNITY and even Joan Crawford in MILDRED PIERCE. Even at the end she is seeking love, not revenge, telling Garfield after the murder that she wants "kisses that come from life, not death." Cain's narrow, common stories always dealt with sordid love triangles and featured repressed sexuality, but never was this theme better exploited than in this film and no soiled heroine better exemplified his characters than that played by Turner. So impressed was Cain with Turner's performance that he presented her with a leather-bound first edition of the novel, inscribing it, "For my dear Lana, thank you for giving a performance that was even finer than I expected." This film was long in the making. MGM acquired the rights to the novel in 1934 after its sensational release, but there was no way a script could be prepared that would appease the severe restrictions of the Hollywood censors. It was adapted as a play in 1936 and this production, short-lived, starred Mary Philips, Richard Barthelmess, and Joseph Greenwald. In 1939 a French film version, LE DERNIER TOURNANT, starred Michel Simon, Fernand Gravet, and Cortinne Luchaire. Then in 1942 Luchino Visconti ignored the copyright on this property and blatantly and illegally made his own film from the Cain story, OSSESSIONE, starring Clara Calamai, Massimo Girotti, and Elio Marcuzzo, but MGM was quick to retaliate, blocking all prints from American release. (It would not be seen in the U.S. until 1977 and even then only in a brief and limited release in American art houses.) By early 1945, writer-producer Wilson had developed a script that would be acceptable to the censors and the film was cast with Garfield and Turner in the leading roles, an inspired selection as it turned out. The two were electric on screen. "He had terrific magnetism," Turner later said of her costar Garfield. "The lines just bounced back and forth between us....It kept a gal on her toes." Garfield almost missed being in the film, being inducted into the service. Cameron Mitchell was tested for the role and almost got the part, but Garfield was released from service with a bad heart and went into the production. Director Garnett caught the actor playing handball and asked him to stop it. "I've got a tricky ticker, so what?" replied the hard-boiled Garfield. "Don't get me wrong," Garnett said. "I don't want to louse up your fun, but I've got to finish this picture." Garfield promised to stop playing handball until the film was completed. The censor was always looking over Garnett's shoulder during the production and the director later complained: "It was a real chore to do POSTMAN under the Breen Office, but I think I managed to get the sex across. I think I like it better that way. I'm not a voyeur, and I don't like all the body display that you get in pictures nowadays. I think that it's just a crutch for untalented directors and writers." The idea of dressing Turner all in white was Wilson's and it was thought that by adorning her in such clothes her sexy image would be downplayed. Said Garnett: "At that time there was a great problem of getting a story with that much sex past the censors. We figured that dressing Lana in white somehow made everything she did seem less sensuous. It was also attractive as hell. And it somehow took a little of the stigma off everything that she did. They didn't have 'hot pants' then, but you couldn't tell it by looking at hers." THe critical and public response to THE POSTMAN ALWAYS RINGS TWICE was enormous. Turner and Garfield won kudos from the critics, and the supporting players, especially Ames and Cronyn, received plaudits. Cronyn was exceptional as the conniving criminal lawyer and he parleyed his snide lines for all they were worth. After the murder of Kellaway he delivers one of the most caustic quips ever delivered on screen, sneering at Garfield and Turner who have just been married and saying, "I can only think of 15 or 20 reasons why you shouldn't be happy." More than $4 million poured into MGM from the initial box-office receipts. The studio announced in 1972 that it would remake this *film noir*classic but delays in casting and directing stalled the production until 1980 when Bob Rafelson took over the chore of directing Jack Nicholson and Jessica Lange. The remake was an utter disaster, played strictly for sex with such scenes as Nicholson ravishing Lange on the kitchen table in the cafe, a grunting, sweating, animalistic and thoroughly disgusting film with a peep-show script.

p, Carey Wilson; d, Tay Garnett; w, Harry Ruskin, Niven Busch (based on the novel by James M. Cain); ph, Sidney Wagner; m, George Bassman; ed, George White; art d, Cedric Gibbons, Randall Duell; set d, Edwin B. Willis; cos, Irene, Marion Herwood Keyes; m/l, "She's Funny that Way," Neil Moret, Richard Whiting; makeup, Jack Dawn.

Crime Drama Cas. (PR:O MPAA:NR)

POSTMAN ALWAYS RINGS TWICE, THE*½ (1981) 125m Northstar International/PAR c

Jack Nicholson *(Frank Chambers)*, Jessica Lange *(Cora Papadakis)*, John Colicos *(Nick Papadakis)*, Christopher Lloyd *(Salesman)*, Michael Lerner *(Katz)*, John P. Ryan *(Kennedy)*, Anjelica Huston *(Madge)*, William Traylor *(Sackett)*, Tom Hill *(Barlow)*, John Van Ness *(Motorcycle Cop)*, Brian Farrell *(Mortenson)*, Raleigh Bond *(Insurance Salesman)*, William Newman *(Man from Home Town)*, Albert Henderson *(Beeman)*, Ken Magee *(Scoutmaster)*, Eugene Peterson *(Doctor)*, Don Calfa *(Goebel)*, Louis Turenne *(Ringmaster)*, Charles B. Jenkins *(Gas Station Attendant)*, Dick Balduzzi, John Furlong *(Sign Men)*, Sam Edwards *(Ticket Clerk)*, Betty Cole *(Grandmother)*, Joni Palmer *(Granddaughter)*, Ron Flagge *(Shoeshine Man)*, James O'Connell *(Judge)*, William H. McDonald *(Bailiff)*, Elsa Raven *(Matron)*, Lionel Smith, Brion James, Frank Arno, Virgil Frye, Kenneth Cervi *(Crapshooters)*, Chris P. Rellias, Theodoros A. Karavidas, Basil J. Fovos, Nick Hasir, Demetrios Liappas *(Greek Party)*, Kopi Sotiropulos *(Greek Mourner)*, Tom Majer, Glenn Shadix, Tani Guthrie, Carolyn Coates, Jim S. Cash *(Twin Oaks Customers)*.

A sloppy, overlong, and ultimately pointless screen adaptation of James M. Cain's masterfully constructed novel. First filmed in America in 1946 (it had been filmed twice previously as the French LE DERNIER TOURANT in 1939 and the Italian OSSESSIONE in 1942) with John Garfield and Lana Turner as the passionate lovers, Cain's sexually steamy novel fell victim to the restrictions designated by the Hays Code. By 1981, however, director Bob Rafelson felt he could get away with bringing the novel's sex to the screen. Nicholson stars as a Depression era drifter who takes work at a California roadside diner run by a likable but abrasive Greek, Colicos, and his lovely, much younger wife, Lange. In an explosion of uncontrollable passion, Nicholson and Lange are drawn together, secretly carrying on without regard for Colicos. After some heated sexual encounters (including one highly-publicized scene on top of a kitchen table covered with flour and baking goods), Nicholson convinces Lange to pack her bags and leave with him for Chicago. When he gets wrapped up in a crap game at the train station, Lange returns home without telling him. Nicholson, after having won a healthy wad of money, returns to Lange. Their senses dulled by their attraction for each other, they plot to kill Colicos. Their first attempt (killing him while he showers) goes awry during a power outage. Afterwards, Colicos mistakenly thinks that Nicholson saved his life. Having had a brush with death, Colicos takes a renewed interest in life—he looks to Nicholson as a true friend, and falls more deeply in love with Lange with whom he now wants to have a child. This makes murder more difficult for the lovers, but not impossible. After bashing in Colicos' skull, they stage a car wreck, which actually seriously injures Nicholson. Because Lange is named as the sole beneficiary of a $10,000 insurance policy (which neither she nor Nicholson were aware of), they are charged with murdering Colicos. Lawyer Lerner (in a superb performance) defends the couple and manages, through some ingenious finagling, to obtain their freedom, while retaining the $10,000 insurance money for himself. Life gets better for the pair and eventually, after Lange informs Nicholson that she is pregnant, they marry. Afterwards, however, they get involved in an auto accident which sends Lange flying from the car. With his wife and the promise of a good future lying dead on the roadside, Nicholson breaks down in tears. The way Cain has written "The Postman Always Rings Twice" it is seemingly impossible to mess up, but Rafelson has managed to do just that. Where Cain's novel is praised for its lightning pace and economy, Rafelson and screenwriter Mamet should be scolded for stretching the story past its breaking point. THE POSTMAN ALWAYS RINGS TWICE is that rare case where one can read the novel in less time that it takes to watch the film. Although more faithful than the 1946 version, Rafelson has succeeded in making his film utterly confusing to anyone not familiar with the source material. Where Cain fills the reader in on the plotting of Frank and Cora, Rafelson leaves his audience in the dark. Because the times are less restrictive of on-screen sex, Rafelson apparently felt that his film would supply something that was missing from the 1946 version, namely less inhibited eroticism. Reportedly the film was shot for an "X" rating with the intention of toning it down to an "R" for commerciality. Paradoxically, however, there is only the briefest glimpse of nudity, the rest of the "sex" being on the grunt-filled soundtrack. Luckily the film can boast some revealing performances from its leads (though, except for the final scenes, Nicholson tends to rely on his usual Nicholsonisms), as well as the authentic production design by Jenkins and atmospheric photography by Nykvist. The chief fault lies at the feet of Rafelson and Mamet, who don't seem to have the foggiest notion of the economy that makes Cain's novels tick.

p, Charles Mulvehill, Bob Rafelson; d, Rafelson; w, David Mamet (based on the novel by James M. Cain); ph, Sven Nykvist (Metrocolor); m, Michael Small; ed, Graeme Clifford; prod d, George Jenkins; set d, Robert Gould; cos, Dorothy Jeakins; makeup, Dorothy Pearl.

Crime Drama Cas. (PR:O MPAA:R)

POSTMAN DIDN'T RING, THE** (1942) 68m FOX bw

Richard Travis *(Daniel Carter)*, Brenda Joyce *(Julie Martin)*, Spencer Charters *(Judge Ben Holt)*, Stanley Andrews *(Postal Inspector Brennon)*, William Bakewell *(Robert Harwood, Jr.)*, Emma Dunn *(Martha Carter)*, Joseph Cawthorn *(Silas Harwood)*, Oscar O'Shea *(Judge Barrington)*, Erville Alderson *(Robert Harwood, Sr.)*, Jeff Corey *(Harwood Green)*, Frank M. Thomas *(Prosecutor)*, Will Wright *(Mr. Slade)*, Betty Jean Hainey *(Marjorie)*, Ethel Griffies *(Catherine Vandewater)*, Henry Roquemore *(Jason Peters)*, Mary Servoss *(Helen Allen)*.

When a mail sack stolen 50 years previously is recovered, Travis, who is trying to make a living by running a general store in a farming community, finds himself in possession of a stock certificate of his father's, now worth a fortune. The bank which originally issued the certificate attempts to battle Travis, but he wins out in court, making life easier for everyone in his community. Fresh-faced Joyce plays a stamp collector who traces down Travis to obtain possession of the stamp, and winds up falling in love with him. Despite a weak script picture moves along well.

p, Ralph Dietrich; d, Harold Schuster; w, Mortimer Braus (based on a story by Braus, Leon Ware); ph, Joseph MacDonald; ed, Nick DeMaggio; md, Emil Newman; art d, Richard Day, Lewis Creber.

Drama/Comedy (PR:A MPAA:NR)

POSTMAN GOES TO WAR, THE** (1968, Fr.) 95m Les Films J.-J. Vital/Alcinter-Regina/Trans-Lux c (LE FACTEUR S'EN VA-T-EN GUERRE)

Charles Aznavour *(Thibon)*, Daniel Ceccaldi *(Cassagne)*, Jacques Richard *(Klein)*, Maria Minh *(Vang)*, Helmut Schneider *(Maury)*, Jess Hahn *(Jess)*, Franco Fabrizi *(Ritoni)*, Doudou Babet *(Clementine)*, Lucien Barjon.

Aznavour plays a resourceful postman who enlists in the army to fight in the French Indochina war. He soon becomes disillusioned with the war as he is injured and later captured by the Communists. When he is finally free, he returns to France with the Cambodian girl he has grown to love. A stark look at France's folly in Indochina. (In French.)

p, Jean-Jacques Vital, Andre Cotton; d, Claude Bernard-Aubert; w, Rene Hardy, Bernard-Aubert, Claude Accursi, Pascal Jardin; ph, Marcel Grignon (Techniscope, Eastmancolor); m, Georges Garvarentz; ed, Gabriel Rongier.

War Drama (PR:A MPAA:NR)

POSTMAN'S KNOCK** (1962, Brit.) 87m MGM bw

Spike Milligan *(Harold Petts)*, Barbara Shelley *(Jean)*, John Wood *(P.C. Woods)*, Archie Duncan *(Inspector)*, Wilfred Lawson *(Postman)*, Miles Malleson *(Psychiatrist)*, Ronald Adam *(Mr. Fordyce)*, Bob Todd *(District Superintendent)*, Warren Mitchell *(Rupert)*, Arthur Mullard *(Sam)*, John Bennett *(Pete)*, Lance Percival *(Joe)*, Mario Frabizi *(Villager)*.

This is the first film for Milligan, who already had a large following in Britain from his numerous television and radio shows. Here he plays a small town mailman promoted to a position at London's top mail branch. Things do not go as easy for him in the big city as in the country, when he and his girl friend are suspected of masterminding a gang of mail robbers. But Milligan helps catch the real thieves and clears himself. The script does not allow for Milligan to bring any of the type of humor he was popular for, and what is given him is far too little. Next to Milligan none of the cast has a chance to shine, which is a pity for cool, good-looking female lead and former model Shelley, who was trying hard to show British producers that she could act in films other than horror stories.

p, Ronald Kinnoch; d, Robert Lynn; w, John Briley, Jack Trevor Story, Spike Milligan, George Barclay (based on a story by Story); ph, Gerald Moss; m, Ron Goodwin; ed, Geoffrey Foot.

Comedy (PR:A MPAA:NR)

POSTMARK FOR DANGER½** (1956, Brit.) 84m Todon/RKO bw (GB: PORTRAIT OF ALISON)

Terry Moore *(Alison Ford)*, Robert Beatty *(Tim Forrester)*, William Sylvester *(Dave Forrester)*, Josephine Griffin *(Jill Stewart)*, Geoffrey Keen *(Inspector Colby)*, Allan Cuthbertson *(Henry Carmichael)*, Henry Oscar *(John Smith)*, William Lucas *(Reg Dorking)*, Terence Alexander *(Fenby)*.

Complex English thriller in which detectives attempt to break up a diamond smuggling ring operating between the continent and England. Before they can successfully do so a number of mysterious things happen, including six murders. Sexpot Moore plays a girl innocently involved with the gang, who falls for artist Beatty, considered a suspect by the police because his brother is part of the gang. Gifted performances carry the meandering plot through its jigsaw course to a conclusion.

p, Frank Godwin; d, Guy Green; w, Green, Ken Hughes (based on the TV serial "Portrait of Alison" by Francis Durbridge); ph, Wilkie Cooper; m, John Veale; ed, Peter Taylor; md, Philip Martell; art d, Ray Simm.

Crime Cas. (PR:A MPAA:NR)

POSTORONNIM VKHOD VOSPRESHCHEN (SEE: WELCOME KOSTYA!, 1965, USSR)

POT CARRIERS, THE*** (1962, Brit.) 84m ABF/WB-Pathe bw

Ronald Fraser *(Redband)*, Paul Massie *(James Rainbow)*, Carole Lesley *(Wendy)*, Dennis Price *(Smooth Tongue)*, Paul Rogers *(Governor)*, Davy Kaye *(Mouse)*, Eddie Byrne *(Chief Officer Bailey)*, Campbell Singer *(Officer Mott)*, Alfred Burke *(Lang)*, Patrick McAlliney *(Dillon)*, Neil McCarthy *(Bracket)*, Vanda Godsell *(Mrs. Redband)*, David Davies *(Officer Tom)*, David Ensor *(Judge)*, Keith Faulkner *(Young Prisoner)*.

Massie plays a young man sentenced to a year's prison term for slugging a man in a jealous fight over his girl friend. He is assigned kitchen duties and soon fits into the highly structured routines of the prisoners. This includes swiping food from the kitchen to trade with men from other areas. When a cellmate is caught bringing a knife out of the kitchen, Massie takes the blame in order to allow his mate to be set free in a month after a long stay. Script and direction take a personable view of prison life, showing the prisoners as individuals. Though the picture is filled with humorous moments, underneath is the continual feeling of the degradation and humiliation the prisoners must endure.

p, Gordon L.T. Scott; d, Peter Graham Scott; w, Mike Watts, T.J. Morrison (based on the play by Watts); ph, Edwin Hillier; m, Stanley Black; ed, Richard Beat.

Comedy/Drama (PR:A MPAA:NR)

POT LUCK½** (1936, Brit.) 71m Gainsborough/GAU bw

Tom Walls *(Inspector Patrick Fitzpatrick)*, Ralph Lynn *(Reggie Bathbrick)*, Robertson Hare *(Mr. Pye)*, Diana Churchill *(Jane Bathbrick)*, Gordon James *(Cream)*, Martita Hunt *(Mrs. Cream)*, J.A. O'Rourke *(Kelly)*, T. Kirby *(Mackail)*, Sarah Allgood *(Mrs. Kelly)*, Roy Emerton *(Berkley)*, J.H. Roberts *(Bevis)*, H.G. Stoker *(Davey)*, Charles Barrett *(Jacobs)*, Cyril Smith *(Miller)*, Sam Wilkinson *(Lever)*, Louis Bradfield *(Accomplice to Lever)*, Peter Gawthorne *(Chief Constable)*, James Grey *(Country Constable)*.

Another wildly farcical caper with Walls and Lynn. Walls plays a retired Scotland Yard Inspector who undertakes one last job, that of apprehending a gang of thieves who specialize in art treasures, just to make his jealous successor, Lynn, angry. Unfolding of the plot is a bit hard to swallow, but it manages to hold suspense—with the payoff between Walls and Lynn, long-time funnymen associates on the screen, making for plenty of lighter moments.

p, Michael Balcon; d, Tom Walls; w, Ben Travers; ph, Roy Kellino, Arthur Crabtree.

Crime/Comedy (PR:A MPAA:NR)

POT O' GOLD*½ (1941) 86m UA bw (GB: THE GOLDEN HOUR)

James Stewart *(Jimmy Haskell)*, Paulette Goddard *(Molly McCorkle)*, Horace Heidt and His Orchestra *(Themselves)*, Charles Winninger *(C.J. Haskell)*, Mary Gordon *(Ma McCorkle)*, Frank Melton *(Jasper)*, Jed Prouty *(Mr. Louderman)*, Dick Hogan *(Willie McCorkle)*, James Burke *(Lt. Grady)*, Charles Arnt *(Parks)*, Donna Wood *(Donna McCorkle)*, Larry Cotton *(Larry)*, Henry Roquemore *(Samson)*, William Gould *(Chalmers)*, Aldrich Bowker *(Judge Murray)*, Mary Ruth *(Mary Simmons)*, Beverly Andre *(Alice)*, Jay Ward *(Boy Friend)*, James Flavin *(Bud Connolly)*, Master Stan Worth *(Tommy)*, Edgar Dearing *(McGinty)*, Nestor Paiva *(Guide)*, Purnell Pratt *(Thompson)*.

A feeble wheeze of a comedy enlivened somewhat by a few songs and Stewart's ingratiating performance, POT O' GOLD takes the title from a popular radio show of the time. The producer also had a well-known name as he was the son of then President Franklin Delano Roosevelt, who was happy that one of his boys was working. Stewart loves music and plays the harmonica. He finds a poor but excellent band led by Horace Heidt that spends rehearsal hours playing on the roof of a tenement because they can't afford a real studio in which to practice. Stewart thinks they are the cat's pajamas and he's even more interested in the people who own the tenement boarding house. Mary Gordon is the proprietor and her daughter is comely Goddard. The noise from the band's rehearsals gets on the nerves of Winninger, a wealthy man who hates music, so he decides to have them all sued for disturbing the peace in his nearby digs. Stewart signs on with the band, although no one there knows that Winninger is Stewart's uncle. Winninger spends a lot of money advertising his wares on radio and has a show that extols the virtues of his health foods. Stewart works on Winninger and finally convinces the crusty old man to allow the band to perform on the show. Goddard is annoyed at Stewart for not fessing up about his connection to Winninger and she thinks that he means to use the band to his own advantage. Stewart then comes up with the idea of a radio giveaway show and calling it "Pot O' Gold" and letting the band play as money is handed out every week. Songs from a group of writers include: "Do You Believe In Fairy Tales?" (Mack David, Vee Lawnhurst), "When Johnny Toots His Horn" (Hy Heath, Fred Rose), "A Knife, A Fork And A Spoon" (Dave Franklin), "Slap Happy Band," "Hi Cy, What's Cookin'?" "Pete The Piper," "Broadway Caballero" (Henry Sullivan, Lou Forbes). Stewart sings a bit and proves that he is a better actor. His character's name, "Jimmy Haskell," is the real name of a well-known composer/arranger who was responsible for many recording hits including several by Ricky

Nelson, as well as having scored a number of TV movies and features, including LOVE IN A GOLDFISH BOWL. The little boy who played "Tommy" later became a nightclub singer/pianist and backed many stars in their personal appearances.

p, James Roosevelt; d, George Marshall; w, Walter De Leon (based on a story by Monte Brice, Andrew Bennison, Harry Tugend from an idea by Haydn Roth Evans, Robert Brilmayer); ph, Hal Mohr; ed, Lloyd Nosler; md, Lou Forbes; set d, Hans Peters; ch, Larry Ceballos.

Musical Comedy   **Cas.**   **(PR:A MPAA:NR)**

POTIPHAR'S WIFE (SEE: HER STRANGE DESIRE, 1931, Brit.)

POURQUOI PAS!* (1979, Fr.) 93m Dimage/Societe Nouvelle de Doublage/New Line c (AKA: WHY NOT!)

Sami Frey (Fernand), Mario Gonzalez (Louis), Christine Murillo (Alexa), Nicole Jamet (Sylvie), Michel Aumont (Inspector), Mathe Souverbie (Sylvie's Mother), Marie-Therese Saussure (Mme. Picaud), Alain Salomon (Roger), Jacques Rispal (Louis' Father), Bernard Crombe (Roger's Colleague).

A sensitive look at the relationship between three people, Frey, Gonzalez, and Murillo. Frey and Murillo are recent victims of disastrous marriages, finding relief with the bisexual Gonzalez. Frey leaves the setup, creating temporary friction within the lifstyle, but he returns with Jamet, who has conventional values, and who, after some internal conflict, decides to join them for a menage a quatre. Complex theme is given a nice treatment by Serreau in her first feature. Attempting to explain her purpose in making this offbeat film, Serreau says that her characters, who she finds likeable, "have found a way of life convenient for them—not necessarily for everyone. I'm only saying that we must have wider choices in our lives—they might be good choices or they might not." If that explanation of a piece of art that should need no "explaining" pleases, then this is a film to see.

p, Michele Dimitri; d&w, Coline Serreau; ph, Jean-Francois Robin (Eastmancolor); m, Jean-Pierre Mas; ed, Sophie Tatischeff; art d, Denis Martin-Sisteron.

Drama   **(PR:C MPAA:NR)**

P.O.W., THE½ (1973) 82m Dossick c

Howard Jahre (Howie Kaufman), Rudy Hornish (Ruby Craig), Wendy Messier (Wendy Craig), Manuel Sicart (Manuel), Marcia Davis (Marcia), Shelley Kaplan (Shelley Kaufman), Joanna Lee Dossick (Patty).

Jahre is a crippled Vietnam veteran trying to make a life for himself in the States. Enacted by a cast of nonprofessional actors, the film has a documentary feel heightened by the effect of a crew filming Jahre as he tries to get used to his apartment, find a job, and interact with his friends. A very interesting film, one of the first to sympathetically treat the Vietnam veteran.

p, David Mlotok, Jane Dossick; d&w, Philip H. Dossick; ph, Benjamin Gruberg; m, Martin Egan, Neal Goldstein; ed, P. Dossick.

Drama   **(PR:C MPAA:NR)**

POWDER RIVER* (1953) 78m FOX c

Rory Calhoun (Chino Bullock), Corinne Calvet (Frenchie), Cameron Mitchell (Mitch Hardin), Penny Edwards (Debbie), Carl Betz (Loney Hogan), John Dehner (Harvey Logan), Raymond Greenleaf (Prudy), Victor Sutherland (Mayor Lowery), Ethan Laidlaw (Lame Jack Banner), Bob Wilke (Will Horn), Harry Carter (Bo Curry), Robert Adler (Pike Kendreck), Post Park (Stage Coach Driver), Richard Garrick (Ferry Master), Archer MacDonald (Joe), Frank Ferguson (Johnny Slaughter), Henry Kulky (Bartender), Val Setz (Great Balso), Walter Sande (Harris), Zon Murray (Henchman), Ray Bennett (Richards), Harry Hines (Drunk).

Calhoun plays a mine owner who becomes sheriff of a small town in order to track down the man who killed his partner. He befriends Mitchell, a former doctor forced to give up his practice because of a brain tumor. Mitchell is weary of life, flirting with death in hopes that a bullet will put him out of his misery, running from his life with the sweet Edwards to chase after a saloon girl, sexy Calvet. He is also the man who killed Calhoun's friend, and after Calhoun finds out, the two engage in a gun battle. Mitchell outdraws Calhoun, but is suddenly stricken and dies as a result of his tumor. Direction concentrates more upon characterization than upon action, but suspense and tension remain.

p, Andre Hakim; d, Louis King; w, Geoffrey Homes (based on an idea by Sam Hellman, from the novel by Stuart N. Lake); ph, Edward Cronjager (Technicolor); ed, William B. Murphy; md, Lionel Newman, Eliot Daniel; art d, Lyle Wheeler, Chester Gore; ch, Billy Daniel.

Western   **(PR:A MPAA:NR)**

POWDER RIVER RUSTLERS½ (1949) 60m REP bw

Allan "Rocky" Lane (Himself), Eddy Waller (Nugget Clark), Gerry Ganzer (Louise Manning), Roy Barcroft (Bull Macons), Francis McDonald ("Shears" Williams), Cliff Clark (Lucius Statton), Douglas Evans (Devereaux), Bruce Edwards (Bob Manning), Clarence Straight (Telegraph Operator), Ted Jacques (Blacksmith), Tom Monroe (Guard), Stanley Blystone (Rancher), Eddie Parker, Herman Hack, Black Jack the Horse.

Well-produced actioner has Lane wrongly accused of murder after discovering the plot of the town's tailor, a respected citizen, for stealing the $50,000 bond the town has raised to attract the railroad. The tailor plans on having a member of his gang pose as an agent for the railway, and in this way take off with the bond. Expertly staged western has an even pace, with the cast offering good character interpretations.

p, Gordon Kay; d, Philip Ford; w, Richard Wormser; ph, John MacBurnie; m, Stanley Wilson; ed, Robert M. Leeds; art d, Frank Hotaling.

Western   **(PR:A MPAA:NR)**

POWDER TOWN*½ (1942) 79m RKO bw

Victor McLaglen (Jeems O'Shea), Edmond O'Brien (Pennant), June Havoc (Dolly), Dorothy Lovett (Sally), Eddie Foy, Jr. (Meeker), Damian O'Flynn (Oliver Lindsay), Marten Lamont (Chick Parker), Roy Gordon (Dr. Wayne), Marion Martin (Sue), Mary Gordon (Mrs. Douglas), Frances Neal (Carol), Julie Warren (Betty), Jane Woodworth (Helen), George Cleveland (Gus), John Maguire (Harvey Dodge), Frank Mills.

O'Brien plays a loony scientist hired by the Army to continue research on a formula for explosives he has invented. Sent to a powder factory, foreman McLaglen is given the job of watching over the scientist, while numerous spies larded throughout the plant, including its top executive, attempt to get their hands on the formula. O'Brien is miscast as a zany scientist type, with the awkward direction doing little to help him along. The script as a whole is bogged down in a far-fetched theme that never holds together.

p, Cliff Reid; d, Rowland V. Lee; w, David Boehm (based on the novel by Max Brand and an idea by Vicki Baum); ph, Fred Redman; Samuel E. Beetley; md, Roy Webb; art d, Albert S. D'Agostino, Walter Keller; spec eff, Vernon L. Walker.

Spy Drama   **(PR:A MPAA:NR)**

POWDERSMOKE RANGE½ (1935) 71m RKO bw

Harry Carey (Tucson Smith), Hoot Gibson (Stony Brooke), Guinn "Big Boy" Williams (Lullaby Joslin), Tom Tyler ("Sundown" Saunders), William Farnum (Banker Orchan), Bob Steele (Jeff Ferguson/"Guadalupe Kid"), Wally Wales [Hal Taliaferro] (Aloysius "Bud" Taggert), Ethan Laidlaw ("Fin" Sharkey), Adrian Morris (Brose Glascow), William Desmond ("Happy" Hopkins), Frank Rice ("Sourdough" Jenkins), Sam Hardy (Mayor "Big Steve" Ogden), Boots Mallory (Carolyn Sibley), Ray Mayer (Chap Bell), Art Mix (Rube), Buffalo Bill, Jr. (Tex Malcolm), Buddy Roosevelt (Burnett), Irving Bacon (General Storekeeper), Henry Roquemore (Doctor), James Mason (Jordan), Eddie Dunn (Elliott), Buzz Barton (Buck), Barney Furey, Bob McKenzie, Phil Dunham, Silver Tip Baker, Nelson McDowell, Frank Ellis, Franklyn Farnum.

Some of the biggest western stars of the time are brought together in the first of THE THREE MESQUITEER series, which was later to have John Wayne among its ranks of heroes. This one is basically a formula western, with Carey, Gibson, and Williams buying the ranch of a man killed by crooked town official Hardy, who wanted the ranch for himself. Hardy sends a hired gun to take care of the new ranchers, but when Carey outdraws the gunman, Tyler, Tyler joins forces with the threesome to fight off Hardy and restore the town to lawlessness. Shaky direction is glossed over by the many action sequences and the fine cast, much at ease in the roles they had to play. This was the second of two "Three Mesquiteer" stories filmed before Republic took over the series, and the first "Mesquiteer" film to show all three cowboys onscreen. In the first "Mesquiteer" film the year before, LAW OF THE 45s, only two of the characters from the book had been used. (See THREE MESQUITEER series, Index.)

p, Cliff Reid; d, Wallace Fox; w, Adele Buffington (based on the novel by William Colt MacDonald); ph, Harold Wenstrom; ed, James Morley; md, Alberto Colombo; art d, Van Nest Polglase, Feild Gray.

Western   **Cas.**   **(PR:A MPAA:NR)**

POWER½ (1934, Brit.) 105m GAU bw (GB: JEW SUSS)

Conrad Veidt (Joseph "Jew Suss" Oppenheimer), Benita Hume (Marie Auguste), Frank Vosper (Duke Karl Alexander), Cedric Hardwicke (Rabbi Gabriel), Gerald du Maurier (Wessensee), Pamela Ostrer (Naomi Oppenheimer), Joan Maude (Magdalene Sibylle), Paul Graetz (Landauer), Mary Clare (Countess Wurben), Haidee Wright (Michele), Parcy Parsons (Pflug), Eva Moore (Jantje), James Raglan (Lord Suffolk), Sam Livesey (Harprecht), Dennis Hoey (Dieterle), Campbell Gullan (Thurne-Taxis), Gibb McLaughlin (Pancorgo), D. Hay Plumb (Pfaeffle), Francis L. Sullivan (Remchingen), George Merritt (Bilfinger), Percy Walsh, Frank Cellier, Glennis Lorimer, Diana Cotton, Jane Cornell, Robert Nainby, Helen Ferrers, Randle Ayrton, Henry Hallatt, Marcelle Rogez, P. Kynaston Reeves, Grete Hansen, Joseph Markovitch, Lucius Blake, Mickey Brantford, Selma Vaz Dias, Victor Fairley, Vittorio [Robert] Rietti, Henry Hewitt.

Veidt plays a Jewish ghetto dweller in 18th Century Wurtemburg, who, through cunning and ruthlessness, works himself out of the ghetto to a position of some authority and power. One of his tactics is yielding his sweetheart over to an evil duke to be seduced. This also comes back to haunt him, however, as the father of the girl manages to get his revenge on Veidt. When it is discovered that Veidt is really not a Jew, he refuses to believe it, remaining faithful to his religion even as he is brought to be hanged. Production fails to give the atmosphere of the time it is depicting, with the direction hazily dealing with important aspects from the Feuchtwanger novel (titled Power in the U.S. and Jew Suss in Britain). Nevertheless, at the time of its release the film acted as a parallel to the actual situation in Germany (also the original author's intent), and is quite powerful in this respect.

p, Michael Balcon; d, Lothar Mendes; w, Dorothy Farnum, A.R. Rawlinson (based on the novel by Leon Feuchtwanger); ph, Bernard Knowles, Gunther Krampf; ed, Otto Ludwig.

Drama   **Cas.**   **(PR:A MPAA:NR)**

POWER, THE½ (1968) 108m Galaxy/MGM c

George Hamilton (Jim Tanner), Suzanne Pleshette (Margery Lansing), Richard Carlson (N.E. Van Zandt), Yvonne De Carlo (Sally Hallson), Earl Holliman (Talbot Scott), Gary Merrill (Inspector Mark Corlane), Ken Murray (Grover), Barbara Nichols (Flora), Arthur O'Connell (Henry Hallson), Nehemiah Persoff (Carl Melniker), Aldo Ray (Bruce), Michael Rennie (Arthur Nordlund), Miiko Taka (Mrs. Van Zandt), Celia Lovsky (Mrs. Hallson), Vaughn Taylor (Mr. Hallson), Lawrence Montaigne (Briggs), Miss Beverly Hills (Sylvia).

A mysterious possessor of telekinetic powers murders a member of a scientific team researching human endurance. The killer is one of the other members of the group of scientists, with the biochemist Hamilton as the prime suspect. Kicked off the project, Hamilton undertakes an investigation of his own. As the other members of the research team slowly start to perish, Hamilton discovers that Rennie possesses superhuman powers, which he intends to use to take control of the world. His purpose is to give reign to his own twisted conception of good. In a life-saving situation, Hamilton discovers he also possesses a superbrain, which he uses to overpower Rennie. Complex plot falters in some overly stereotyped depictions, but the direction manages to supply a good deal of tension, creating a fairly interesting science fiction yarn.

p, George Pal; d, Byron Haskin; w, John Gay (based on the novel by Frank M. Robinson); ph, Ellsworth Fredricks (Panavision, Metrocolor); m, Miklos Rozsa; ed, Thomas J. McCarthy; md, Rozsa; art d, George W. Davis, Merrill Pye; set d, Henry Grace, Don Greenwood, Jr.; spec eff, Lowell Norman, J. McMillan Johnson, Gene Warren, Wah Chang; makeup, William Tuttle.

Fantasy (PR:A MPAA:NR)

POWER AND GLORY (SEE: POWER AND THE GLORY, THE, 1933)

POWER AND THE GLORY, THE*** (1933) 76m FOX bw (GB: POWER AND GLORY)

Spencer Tracy *(Tom Garner)*, Colleen Moore *(Sally)*, Ralph Morgan *(Henry)*, Helen Vinson *(Eve)*, Clifford Jones *(Tom Garner, Jr.)*, Henry Kolker *(Mr. Borden)*, Sarah Padden *(Henry's Wife)*, Billy O'Brien *(Tom the Boy)*, Cullen Johnston *(Henry the Boy)*, J. Farrell MacDonald *(Mulligan)*, Robert Warwick *(Edward)*.

Spencer Tracy here got his first real opportunity to stretch the acting muscles on which he built his reputation on stage in New York, and Preston Sturges—another Broadway veteran who thought he was just picking up some easy money in California before getting back to the real world—wrote his first screenplay in this once celebrated, but now barely remembered, film. Opening with the funeral of a railway magnate, the film follows Morgan—the former secretary and lifelong friend of the dead tycoon—as first his wife, then an office watchman, revile the dead man's memory. Finally Morgan sits down with his wife and tells her about his former employee, the flashbacks coming in jumbled fashion, skipping from point to point to explain aspects of his character rather than in chronological order. From humble backwoods origins comes Tracy, who marries his schoolteacher, Moore, and with her prodding and guidance first takes a job as trackwalker with the railway and during the following years, through hard work and self-sacrifice, becomes president of the company. While negotiating a merger with another railroad, he becomes infatuated with Vinson—the rival magnate's daughter—and when he tells the ever-faithful Moore that he plans to divorce her and marry the new cookie, Moore, in a daze, steps in front of a bus and is killed. He marries Vinson and when he discovers the younger woman has been having an affair with his own son, Jones, Tracy commits suicide. The picture is more interesting for its unusual nonlinear construction than for its badly dated, moralistic story. The script idea sprang from the stories Sturges used to hear from his second wife, Eleanor Hutton, about her grandfather, C.W. Post, the cereal tycoon of Battle Creek, Michigan. Post built his breakfast cereal company into the conglomerate giant General Foods, then killed himself. Sturges took this basic story, thinking about how he himself came to know about the man—not in one long sequential telling but in a number of small pieces, incidents that revealed facets of character that, added together and sorted out, could explain the character of a man who built himself from nothing, achieved riches and fame, then killed himself at his peak. When he approached Jesse Lasky with the idea, the producer was dubious, especially when Sturges refused to explain the story orally. Instead, he gave him a complete shooting script. Lasky read the script, thinking, as he wrote in his autobiography, "...if it had any merit I could put a team of two or four or a half-dozen skilled writers on it to develop the basic idea in a manner suitable to the film medium." Afterward, Lasky was so impressed that he let it be shot just the way Sturges had written it. The two men cut a revolutionary deal for the property. Sturges asked Lasky for a percentage of the gross, just as he was used to getting on Broadway. Lasky asked him how much he wanted for an outright sale—"$62,475," answered Sturges. Lasky smiled and then they worked out an arrangement where the writer would receive three percent of the first half million dollars grossed, five percent of the second, and seven percent of everything over a million. Word of this unprecedented arrangement rocked Hollywood and B.P. Schulberg, who had just left his post as general manager of Paramount, wrote a long editorial in *The Hollywood Reporter*, attacking Lasky for allowing the deal and for allowing the film to go into production exactly as Sturges had written it. He feared that other writers would follow the reckless example set by Sturges and Lasky and demand similar guarantees of script integrity. Schulberg also took aim at *The Hollywood Reporter* for its editorial supporting the unorthodox deal, suggesting that leaving screenplays alone might be the best thing for films. Sturges was much amused by all the hubbub and wrote a long, sarcastic rebuttal in which he referred to Schulberg as "My Learned Opponent." Sturges also defied Hollywood custom by hanging out on the set during the shooting. Colleen Moore later said, "In my whole career I never saw a writer. They told me they existed, but Preston was the first actually on the set." Tracy also made waves in the movie. Previously cast generally as a hulking convict in films such as UP THE RIVER (1930) and 20,000 YEARS IN SING SING (1932), he was here given his first big dramatic role. Determined to make a success of it, he hid himself away and memorized the script. When director Howard—a polo buddy of Tracy's—saw the amazing performance Tracy was getting into, "I just gulped and said 'Roll'." A great deal was made of the unorthodox structure, which studio publicists dubbed "narratage, " an uneasy bastardization of "narrative" and "montage." The theater in New York where the picture debuted had a bronze plaque placed outside commemorating the historic event, though most critics pointed out it was nothing more than a clumsy use of flashbacks with narration over them. After a fast start at the box office, and generally favorable reviews, the film did disappointing business, perhaps because of the depressing subject matter. Several years later the negative was destroyed in a fire and only after many more years did the American Film Institute put a complete print together. "Narratage" was mostly forgotten until eight years later when, streamlined and adjusted, it was used to tell the story of a man's rise to the heights and the loneliness there—CITIZEN KANE.

p, Jesse L. Lasky; d, William K. Howard; w, Preston Sturges; ph, James Wong Howe; m, J.S. Zamecnik, Peter Brunelli, Louis De Francesco; ed, Paul Weatherwax; md, De Francesco; art d, Max Parker; cos, Rita Kaufman.

Drama (PR:A-C MPAA:NR)

POWER AND THE PRIZE, THE½** (1956) 98m MGM bw

Robert Taylor *(Cliff Barton)*, Elisabeth Mueller *(Miriam Linka)*, Burl Ives *(George Salt)*, Charles Coburn *(Guy Eliot)*, Sir Cedric Hardwicke *(Mr. Carew)*, Mary Astor *(Mrs. George Salt)*, Nicola Michaels *(Joan Salt)*, Cameron Prud'homme *(Rev. John Barton)*, Richard Erdman *(Lester Everett)*, Ben Wright *(Mr. Chutwell)*, Jack Raine *(Mr. Pitt-Semphill)*, Tom Browne Henry *(Paul F. Farragut)*, Richard Deacon *(Howard Carruthers)*.

This is a "big business" indictment and covers much of the same ground as PATTERNS and EXECUTIVE SUITE, which were both superior. Taylor may have been just a bit old to play this part (he was 44) although he always managed to convince audiences that he was what he acted. Ives is the head man of a huge conglomerate who realizes that he's getting close to retirement and he plans to have Taylor take over the reins (which is just about the same relationship between Everett Sloane, as the boss, and Van Heflin as the younger exec in PATTERNS). Ives wants to see if Taylor is sufficiently without ethics to handle the big job so he sends him to England to negotiate an immoral deal that will bring Ives the control over a large British mining company. Taylor bids farewell to his girl friend, Michaels, and goes to England, then finds that he doesn't have the necessary ice water in his veins to bilk Hardwicke, the industrialist who has the mining interests. Meanwhile, he also meets Mueller, an attractive German refugee who is suspected of having a Communist association. She's later vindicated of the accusations. When Ives discovers that Taylor is not following through, he does his best to destroy his hand-picked successor but loses the battle. Mueller was a gorgeous Swiss who made this movie then virtually dropped from sight. Michaels also had a very brief career and both women will hardly be recalled for their work in this picture. It was shot in black and white and CinemaScope, MGM's first attempt at blending the two and the process didn't work as the intimate scenes had no feeling of intimacy on the wide screen. Astor is Ives' wife and Michaels is his daughter so the idea of naming his son-in-law appeals to Ives until he realizes that the boy has far too many ethics to swim in a sea of sharks. Coburn gives his customary dignified performance.

p, Nicholas Nayfack; d, Henry Koster; w, Robert Ardrey (based on the novel by Howard Swiggett); ph, George J. Folsey (CinemaScope); m, Broinslau Kaper; ed, George Boemler; art d, William A. Horning, Hans Peters; cos, Helen Rose.

Drama (PR:A MPAA:NR)

POWER DIVE½** (1941) 71m PAR bw

Richard Arlen *(Brad Farrell)*, Jean Parker *(Carol Blake)*, Helen Mack *(Mrs. Coles)*, Roger Pryor *(Dan McMasters)*, Don Castle *(Doug Farrell)*, Cliff Edwards *(Squid Watkins)*, Billy Lee *(Brad Coles, Jr.)*, Thomas Ross *(Prof. Blake)*, Louis Jean Heydt *(Johnny Coles)*.

Arlen and Castle play brothers—the latter an engineer, the former a test pilot—who are both in love with the same girl, Parker. Parker's father is a blind designer who comes up with a plastic designed plane for the army, which, after surmounting several handicaps, is successfully flown by Arlen. Well-paced action and smooth direction keeps a proper level of suspense up until the film's climactic ending. One of several films (most notably William Wellman's WINGS) in which Arlen—who served as a pilot in the Royal Canadian Flying Corps—found himself at the controls of an airplane.

p, William Pine, William C. Thomas; d, James P. Hogan; w, Maxwell Shane, Edward Churchill (based on the story by Paul Franklin); ph, John Alton; ed, Robert Crandall; art d, F. Paul Sylos.

Aviation Drama Cas. (PR:A MPAA:NR)

POWER OF JUSTICE (SEE: BEYOND THE SACRAMENTO, 1940)

POWER OF POSSESSION (SEE: LAWLESS EMPIRE, 1945)

POWER OF THE PRESS* (1943) 64m COL bw

Guy Kibbee *(Ulysses Bradford)*, Gloria Dickson *(Edwina Stephens)*, Lee Tracy *(Griff Thompson)*, Otto Kruger *(Howard Rankin)*, Victor Jory *(Oscar Trent)*, Larry Parks *(Jerry Purvis)*, Rex Williams *(Chris Barker)*, Frank Sully *(Mack Gibson)*, Don Beddoe *(Pringle)*, Douglas Leavitt *(Whiffle)*, Minor Watson *(John Carter)*.

Kruger plays a villainous big city publisher whose quest for power leads him to killing off anyone who gets in his path, paying off gangsters to act as his henchmen. Tracy plays the honest managing editor (shades of THE FRONT PAGE), supported by his faithful secretary, Dickson, who eventually exposes the evil Kruger. The complicated plot is not given any help through the shaky and off-paced direction; the result is a picture that fails to develop many of the themes it poses. Not to be confused with Frank Capra's silent film of the same name, also a Columbia production, but sharing only the newspaper setting.

p, Leon Barsha; d, Lew Landers; w, Robert D. Andrews (based on the story by Sam Fuller); ph, John Stumar; ed, Mel Thorsen; art d, Lionel Banks; md, M.W. Stoloff.

Crime/Drama (PR:A MPAA:NR)

POWER OF THE WHISTLER, THE** (1945) 66m COL bw

Richard Dix *(William Everest)*, Janis Carter *(Jean Lang)*, Jeff Donnell *(Frances Lang)*, Loren Tindall *(Charles Kent)*, Tala Birell *(Constantina Ivaneska)*, John Abbott *(Kaspar Andropolos)*, Murray Alper *(Joe Blaney)*, Cy Kendall *(Druggist)*.

Chilling suspense story has Dix as a homicidal maniac suffering from amnesia. Carter plays a friendly girl who makes his acquaintance and nearly falls victim to the killer. But her sister, Donnell, figures out Dix's true identity before any harm can be done. Dix is cast in a tough part which he is unable to pull off, though he would be given other chances in similar roles. This was one in the series of "Whistler" films in which he starred in the 1940s. (See WHISTLER series, Index.)

p, Leonard S. Picker; d, Lew Landers; w, Aubrey Wisberg (based on the radio program "The Whistler"); ph, L.W. O'Connell; ed, Reg Browne; art d, John Patu; set d, Sidney Clifford.

Mystery (PR:A MPAA:NR)

POWER PLAY** (1978, Brit./Can.) 109m Magnum International-Cowry/Robert Cooper c

Peter O'Toole (*Col. Zeller*), David Hemmings (*Col. Narriman*), Donald Pleasence (*Blair*), Barry Morse (*Jean Rousseau*), Jon Granik (*Raymond Kasai*), Marcella Saint-Amant (*Mrs. Rousseau*), George Touliatos (*Barrientos*), Chuck Shamata (*Hillsman*), Gary Reineke (*Aramco*), Harvey Atkin (*Anwar*), August Schellenberg (*Minh*), Eli Rill (*Dominique*), Dick Cavett (*Himself*).

Action filled, though somewhat confusing, picture has Hemmings leading a coup d'etat against a corrupt government. O'Toole plays a tank commander who becomes part of the insurrection only to double-cross the conspirators in the end. The picture gives a vivid depiction of violence and brutality in a politically unstable government; the moral ambiguities posed question the validity of revolt, due to the further harshness which can ensue at the hands of the government. The Canadian Army provided the bodies and the hardware (at no small price) necessary to give POWER PLAY a suitable military look. The film's cameras rolled in both Toronto and Germany.

p, Christopher Dalton; d&w, Martyn Burke (based on a novel by Edward N. Luttwak); ph, Ousama Rawi; ed, John Victor-Smith.

War **Cas.** (PR:C MPAA:NR)

POWERFORCE* (1983) 98m Bedford Entertainment c

Bruce Baron, Mandy Moore, James Barnett, Jovy Couldry, Frances Fong, Olivia Jeng, Randy Channel, Seon Blake, Sam Sorono, Bruce Li.

Another dose of martial arts drivel which has a CIA agent kicking, chopping, and punching whomever attempts to obstruct justice. The entire population's safety is on the line, but thankfully the evildoers are overcome. On a par with others of this sort.

p, George Mason; d, Michael King; w, Terry Chalmers, Dennis Thompsett; ph, Bob Huke, Robert Hope; m, Chris Babida.

Martial Arts **Cas.** (PR:O MPAA:R)

POWERS GIRL, THE*½ (1942) 93m UA bw (GB: HELLO BEAUTIFUL)

George Murphy (*Jerry Hendricks*), Anne Shirley (*Ellen Evans*), Carole Landis (*Kay Evans*), Dennis Day (*Himself*), Alan Mowbray (*John Robert Powers*), Jean Ames (*Googie*), Mary Treen (*Nancy*), Raphael Storm (*Vandy Vandergift*), Helen MacKellar (*Mrs. Hendricks*), Harry Shannon (*Mr. Hendricks*), Roseanna Murray (*Edna Lambert*), George Chandler (*Harry*), Willie Best (*Waiter*), Minerva Urecal (*Maggie*), Jack Daley (*Bruised Waiter*), Peggy Lee (*Herself*), Jack Baxley (*Judge*), Benny Goodman and His Orchestra (*Themselves*), Jayne Hazard, Lillian Eggers, Linda Sterling, Evelyn Frey, Eloise Hart, Patricia Mace, Barbara Slater, Rosemary Coleman (*Powers American Beauties*).

Thin plot has Murphy, a cameraman for a model agency, falling in love with Shirley, while her sister Landis, trying to make it as a model, also has claws out for Murphy. This is just an excuse to display some admirable musical performers, including Benny Goodman. Unfortunately the direction does not do a very good job of combining musical pieces with the narrative. Songs include: "Three Dreams," "Out of This World," "The Lady Who Didn't Believe in Love," "Partners," "We're Looking for the Big Bad Wolf" (Jule Styne, Kim Gannon), "A Pretty Girl Is Like a Melody" (Irving Berlin), "I Know That You Know" (Vincent Youmans, Anne Caldwell), "One O'Clock Jump" (Count Basie, Harry James), and "Roll 'Em" (Mary Lou Williams).

p, Charles R. Rogers; d, Norman Z. McLeod; w, E. Edwin Moran, Harry Segall (based on a story by William A. Pierce, Malvin Wald from the book by John R. Powers); ph, Stanley Cortez; ed, George Arthur; md, Louis Silvers.

Musical (PR:A MPAA:NR)

POZEGNANIA (SEE: PARTINGS, 1962, Pol.)

PRACTICALLY YOURS**½ (1944) 90m PAR bw

Claudette Colbert (*Peggy Martin*), Fred MacMurray (*Lt. [S.G.] Daniel Bellamy*), Gil Lamb (*Albert Beagell*), Cecil Kellaway (*Marvin P. Meglin*), Robert Benchley (*Judge Oscar Stimson*), Tom Powers (*Cmdr. Harpe*), Jane Frazee (*Musical Comedy Star*), Rosemary De Camp (*Ellen Macy*), Isabel Randolph (*Mrs. Meglin*), Mikhail Rasumny (*La Crosse*), Arthur Loft (*Uncle Ben Bellamy*), Edgar Norton (*Harvey, the Butler*), Donald MacBride (*Sam*), Donald Kerr (*Meglin's Chauffeur*), Clara Reid (*Meglin's Maid*), Don Barclay (*Himself*), Rommie (*Piggy the Dog*), Charles Irwin (*Patterson*), Will Wright (*Senator Cowling*), Isabel Withers (*Grace Mahoney*), George Carleton (*Mr. Hardy*), Frederic Nay (*Michael*), Stan Johnson (*Pilot*), James Millican (*Co-Pilot*), Byron Barr (*Navigator*), Allen Fox George Turner, Reggie Simpson (*Reporters*), Ralph Lynn, Jerry James, William Meader (*Cameramen*), John Whitney (*Pilot with Bellamy*), Sam Ash, John Wald (*Radio Announcers*), Hugh Beaumont (*Cutter*), Warren Ashe (*Cameraman in News Room*), Roy Brent (*Sound Man*), Gary Bruce (*Camera Operator*), John James (*Usher*), Mike Lally (*Assistant Cameraman*), Jack Rice (*Couturier*), George Melford

(*Senate Vice-President*), Ottola Nesmith (*Hysterical Woman in Senate*), Len Hendry (*Naval Lieutenant in Senate*), Nell Craig (*Meglin's Secretary*), Charles Hamilton (*Prudential Guard*), Yvonne De Carlo, Julie Gibson (*Girl Employees*), Allen Pinson (*Stimson's Chauffeur*), Edward Earle (*Assistant Manager at Hadley's Store*), Mimi Doyle (*Red Cross Worker*), Louise Currie, Dorothy Granger (*Girls*), Helen Dickson (*Woman in Subway*), Gladys Blake (*Brooklyn Girl in Subway*), Jack Clifford (*Subway Conductor*), Thomas Quinn (*Photographer*), Earle Hodgins (*Man with Pen Knfe*), Edwin Maxwell (*Radio Official*), Stanley Andrews (*Shipyards Official*), Charles A. Hughes (*Radio Announcer*), Kitty Kelly (*Wife at Newsreel Theater*), Marjean Neville (*Little Girl at Newsreel Theater*), Tom Kennedy (*Burly Citizen at Newsreel Theater*), Michael Miller, Hugh Binyon, Sonny Boy Williams (*Boys in Park*), Louise La Planche (*Attractive Girl*), Maxine Fife (*Pretty Girl in Park*), Eddie Hall, Stephen Wayne (*Radio Men-PBY*), Larry Thompson (*Right Gunner-PBY*), Tex Taylor (*Mechanic*), Jan Buckingham (*Nursemaid in Park*), Ronnie Rondell (*Left Gunner-PBY*), Anthony Marsh (*Plane Captain-PBY*).

Colbert's last film for Paramount after a 16-year career was a disappointment. She was 40 at the time and MacMurray was 38 and neither felt right playing these roles, which were surely designed for younger thespians. MacMurray is a pilot who goes above and beyond the call of duty by aiming his fighter-bomber directly at a Japanese ship and letting go of the bombs as the plane hits the vessel. While in his crash dive, MacMurray talks about what he'd rather be doing—working at his desk for the typewriter company owned by Kellaway and walking through Central Park with "Peggy." His last words are monitored by Navy radio and then sent out to the Home Front where the citizens can hear the final statement by a true American hero. Somehow, he survives and when the country learns that he is coming home, Colbert (who is thought to be his "Peggy") is crowded by the press, including all manner of radio, newsreel, and newspaper reporters. MacMurray arrives at the airport and is met by Kellaway and Colbert. She also works for Kellaway's typewriter company and everyone assumes that she is the person he was speaking about in his supposed last moments. MacMurray and Colbert go to Kellaway's mansion where he is to be a house guest. It is there that MacMurray admits that the "Peggy" he referred to was his dog. Colbert sighs with relief because she is affianced, unofficially, to Lamb, the 4-F manager of Kellaway's Accounts Receivables. Since there has been so much national publicity, Colbert and MacMurray decide to continue the masquerade until the heat dies down and they agree that Lamb can accompany them on all of their "dates" for the benefit of the press coverage. On one of these evenings, Lamb gets loving toward Colbert (as he has every right to) and MacMurray, half out of jealousy and half out of wanting to keep up the pretense, whacks Lamb on the snoot. Then MacMurray realizes that he loves Colbert and says he would like to marry her as soon as the Axis conspiracy is defeated. Colbert wants vengeance and gets the aid of Kellaway's wife, Randolph, and Randolph's judge brother, Benchley, to help stop their upcoming marriage. But it's a ruse. MacMurray is at a ceremony for the launching of a destroyer and the radio mikes are in place for national news when Benchley makes the announcement that there is another ceremony to take place at this time and he is going to marry Colbert and MacMurray. De Camp does a good job as a "Gold Star" wife, and Frazee plays a musical comedy star as she sings the picture's one song. Lamb was a superb dancer in his early years and continued working into the 1980s, when he did a good job in an ABC-TV movie, "For The Love Of It," as a dotty chauffeur and stole the picture from several ABC stars. In a bit part, note Yvonne De Carlo as one of the Kellaway employees.

p&d, Mitchell Leisen; w, Norman Krasna; ph, Charles Lang, Jr.; m, Victor Young; ed, Doane Harrison; art d, Hans Dreier, Robert Usher; set d, Stephen Seymour; cos, Howard Greer; spec eff, Gordon Jennings, J. Devereaux Jennings, Farciot Edouart; m/l, "I Knew It Would Be This Way," Sam Coslow (sung by Jane Frazee).

Comedy (PR:A MPAA:NR)

PRAIRIE, THE** (1948) 65m Screen Guild bw

Lenore Aubert (*Ellen Wade*), Alan Baxter (*Paul Hover*), Russ Vincent (*Abiram White*), Jack Mitchum (*Asa Bush*), Charles Evans (*Ishmael Bush*), Edna Holland (*Esther Bush*), Chief Thundercloud (*Eagle Feather*), Fred Coby (*Abner Bush*), Bill Murphy (*Jess Bush*), David Gerber (*Gabe Bush*), Don Lynch (*Enoch Bush*), George Morrell (*Luke*), Chief Yowlachie (*Matoreeh*), Jay Silverheels (*Running Deer*), Beth Taylor (*Annie Morris*), Frank Hemingway (*Commentary*).

Adaptation of a novel by James Fenimore Cooper centers on a family that moves into the newly opened Louisiana Territory. The family must fend off starvation and the possibility of attack from Indians in order to survive. They come upon Aubert, whose family has been killed by renegade Indians. The addition of the girl brings strife to the family as the two sons fight for her affection. But she winds up attaching herself to Baxter, an Army cartographer who has more than once helped the family out of some sticky situations. A good cast and decent script could have used higher production values and stronger direction.

p, Edward Finney; d, Frank Wisbar; w, Arthur St. Claire (based on the novel by James Fenimore Cooper); ph, James S. Brown, Jr.; m, Alexander Steinart; ed, Douglas W. Bagler.

Western (PR:A MPAA:NR)

PRAIRIE BADMEN** (1946) 55m PRC bw

Buster Crabbe (*Billy Carson*), Al "Fuzzy" St. John (*Fuzzy Jones*), Patricia Knox (*Linda Lattimar*), Charles King (*Cal*), Ed Cassidy (*Doc Lattimer*), Kermit Maynard (*Lon*), John L. Cason (*Steve*), Steve Clark (*Sheriff*), Frank Ellis (*Thompson*), John L. "Budd" Buster (*Don Lattimer*).

Crabbe and his sidekick St. John help out the owner of a traveling medicine show when a gang of outlaws get wind of the information that he possesses a treasure map. Well-paced direction helps to blend humor into the spots where the plot sags, glossing over the deficiencies in the script. (See BILLY CARSON series, Index.)

p, Sigmund Neufeld; d, Sam Newfield; w, Fred Myton; ph, Robert Cline; ed, Holbrook N. Todd; md, Lee Zahler.

Western   **Cas.**   **(PR:A   MPAA:NR)**

PRAIRIE EXPRESS*½   (1947) 55m MON bw

Johnny Mack Brown (Johnny Hudson), Raymond Hatton (Faro Jenkins), Robert Winkler (Dave Porter), Virginia Belmont (Peggy Porter), William H. Ruhl (Gordon Gregg), Marshall Reed (Burke), Gary Garrett (Kent), Curly Gibson (Langford), Ken Adams (Pete), I. Stanford Jolley (Sheriff), Hank Worden (Deputy), Carl Mathews (Collins), Boyd Stockman (Perry), Bob McElroy (Joe), Jack Hendricks (Blane), Artie Ortego (Torgo), Ted Adams (Lem), Steve Clark (Jarrett), Frank LaRue, Steve Darrell, Jack Gibson.

Western fare has Ruhl, the only person with the knowledge of the coming railroad, trying to scare Winkler and Belmont into selling their ranch. But Brown comes on the scene and spoils Ruhl's plans, in this routinely directed and performed western.

p, Barney A. Sarecky; d, Lambert Hillyer; w, Anthony Coldeway, J. Benton Cheney; ph, William Sickner; ed, Fred Maguire.

Western   **(PR:A   MPAA:NR)**

PRAIRIE JUSTICE**   (1938) 58m Trem Carr/UNIV bw

Bob Baker (Bob), Dorothy Fay (Anita), Hal Taliaferro (Alfalfa), Jack Rockwell (Benson), Forest Taylor (Sheriff), Charleton Young (Dry Gulch), Glenn Strange (Haynes), Jack Kirk (Boots), Tex Palmer, Slim Whitaker, Jimmy Phillips, Murdock McQuarrie.

When his father is murdered, U.S. marshal Baker comes into town under the guise of an easygoing singing cowboy. He spends most of his time sweet-talking Fay and exercising his vocal chords; all the while getting enough information to pin the crime on her uncle. Baker is so overconfident in this role it hurts, but then, this was just one of 10 films he made in 1938. The advent of a loyal and loveable canine in PRAIRIE JUSTICE indicates that Hollywood was at least toying with the idea that a cowboy's best friend didn't necessarily have to be his horse or his six-iron.

p, Paul Malvern; d, George Waggner; w, Joseph West; ph, Gus Peterson; ed, Carl Pierson.

Western   **(PR:A   MPAA:NR)**

PRAIRIE LAW**   (1940) 59m RKO bw

George O'Brien (Brill), Virginia Vale (Priscilla), Dick Hogan (Larry), Slim Whitaker (Silent), J. Farrell MacDonald (Sheriff Austin), Cyrus W. "Cy" Kendall (Pete Gore), Paul Everton (Judge Curry), Henry Hall (Mr. Bramble), Monte Montague, Quen Ramsey, Bud Osborne, Frank Ellis, John Henderson.

When land-shark Everton raises havoc in cattle country by selling land to farmers with the promise that he will build wells for irrigation, a war between cattlemen and settlers develops. O'Brien, as one of the cattlemen, fights off Everton's hired guns to restore order to the land. Good production values and a well-chosen cast are effectively handled in this routine western.

p, Bert Gilroy; d, David Howard; w, Doris Schroder, Arthur V. Jones (based on the story by Bernard McConville); ph, J. Roy Hunt; ed, Frederic Knudson.

Western   **(PR:A   MPAA:NR)**

PRAIRIE MOON**½   (1938) 58m REP bw

Gene Autry (Gene), Smiley Burnette (Frog), Shirley Deane (Peggy), Tommy Ryan (Brains), Walter Tetley (Nails), David Gorcey (Slick), Stanley Andrews (Welch), William Pawley (Banon), Warner Richmond (Mullins), Raphael [Ray] Bennett (Hartley), Tom London (Steve), Bud Osborne (Pete), Jack Rockwell (Sheriff), Peter Potter (Band Leader), Merrill McCormack, Hal Price, Lew Meehan, Jack Kirk, "Champion".

A new twist to the usual western yarn has Autry watching over three tough kids from the streets of Chicago, sent west after their father died and left them a ranch. The kids bring their city ways to the ranch, making life tough for Autry and Burnette, but through Autry's good-heartedness he manages to teach the kids some morals. They, in turn, help Autry round up a gang of cattle rustlers. More of Autry's personality is allowed to shine through in this picture than in many of his others, with him becoming more human around the boys. Direction is well paced, with the changes that the boys go through carried out well. Autry sings three songs: "Hoofbeats of the Prairie," "The Girl in the Middle of My Heart," and "The West, a Nest, and You." Burnette sings "Trigger Joe." (See GENE AUTRY series, Index.)

p, Harry Grey; d, Ralph Staub; w, Betty Burbridge, Stanley Roberts; ph, William Nobles; ed, Lester Orlebeck.

Western   **Cas.**   **(PR:A   MPAA:NR)**

PRAIRIE OUTLAWS**   (1948) 57m EL bw

Eddie Dean, Roscoe Ates, Sarah Padden, Al La Rue, Robert "Buzzy" Henry, Louise Currie, Jean Carlin, Lee Bennett, Terry Frost, Warner Richmond, Lee Roberts, Chief Yowlachie, Bob Duncan, John Bridges, Al Ferguson, Bud Osborne.

Problems arise when a group of bad men try to run a new county. Typical action western.

p&d, Robert Emmett Tansey; w, Frances Kavanaugh.

Western   **Cas.**   **(PR:A   MPAA:NR)**

PRAIRIE PALS*   (1942) 60m PRC bw

Bill "Cowboy Rambler" Boyd, Art Davis, Lee Powell (Themselves), Charles King (Mitchell), Esther Estrella (Betty), John Merton (Ed Blair), J. Merrill Holmes (Wainwright), Kermit Maynard (Crandall), I. Stanford Jolley (Ace Shannon), Karl Hackett (Sheriff), Bob Burns (Deputy), Al St. John (Hank Stoner), Al Taylor (Rancher), Art Dillard (Barfly), Curley Dresden, Frank McCarroll (Henchmen), Bill Patton, Carl Mathews, Frank Ellis, Jack Kinney, Morgan Flowers.

Below-par B western with a farfetched plot about a couple of deputies who go undercover to rescue a kidnaped scientist. Poor production, performances, and story add up to a worthless effort.

p, Sigmund Neufeld; d, Peter Stewart [Sam Newfield]; w, Patricia Harper; ph, Jack Greenhalgh; m, Johnny Lange, Lew Porter; ed, Holbrook N. Todd.

Western   **(PR:A   MPAA:NR)**

PRAIRIE PIONEERS**   (1941) 58m REP bw

Robert Livingston (Stony Brooke), Bob Steele (Tucson Smith), Rufe Davis (Lullaby Joslin), Esther Estrella (Dolores Ortega), Robert Kellard (Roberto Ortega), Guy D'Ennery (Don Miguel), Davison Clark (Carlos Montoya), Jack Ingram (Wade), Kenneth McDonald (Fields), Lee Shumway (Nelson), Mary McLaren (Martha Nelson), Yakima Canutt (Morrison), Jack Kirk (Al), Carleton Young, Wheaton Chambers, Frank Ellis, Cactus Mack, Curley Dresden, Frank McCarroll.

Livingston, Steele, and Davis, play the Three Mesquiteers of the western prairie, as they help prevent a family from selling their ranch in a shady deal and, at the same time, rescue the young son from a framed murder charge. Well-paced action centers on the deeds of the three heroes. This trio was just one combination (albeit not the best known one) of the dozen actors Republic used over an eight-year span to portray the Three Mesquiteers—Alexandre Dumas' dashing triumvirate transformed and transplanted to the Old West via the stories of William Colt MacDonald. (See THREE MESQUITEER series, Index.)

p, Louis Gray; d, Les Orlebeck; w, Barry Shipman (based on an original idea by Karl Brown, based on characters created by William Colt MacDonald); ph, Ernest Miller; m, Cy Feuer; ed, Ray Snider.

Western   **(PR:A   MPAA:NR)**

PRAIRIE ROUNDUP**½   (1951) 53m COL bw

Charles Starrett (Steve Carson/The Durango Kid), Smiley Burnette (Smiley Burnette), Mary Castle (Toni Eaton), Frank Fenton (Buck Prescott), Frank Sully (Sheriff), Paul Campbell (Poke Joe), Forrest Taylor (Dan Kelly), Don Harvey (Hawk Edwards), George Baxter (Jim Eaton), Lane Chandler (Red Dawson), John Cason (Drag Barton), Al Wyatt (Masked Man), Glenn Thompson (Pete), Ace Richmond (Curtis), The Sunshine Boys, Alan Sears.

Starrett stars as both a retired Texas Ranger and his Robin Hood-type double in one of the best efforts of the "Durango Kid" series. In this one Starrett, as the retired ranger, is accused of murdering his alter ego, The Durango Kid. His arrest acts as a ploy, allowing him to uncover a plot by Fenton, who is trying to create a cattle empire by stealing cattle on the Santa Fe trail. Some interesting plot twists, and a variety of camera angles uncommon to westerns of this nature, make this production an intriguing actioner. (See DURANGO KID series, Index.)

p, Colbert Clark; d, Fred F. Sears; w, Joseph O'Donnell; ph, Fayte Browne; ed, Paul Borofsky; md, Mischa Bakaleinikoff; art d, Charles Clague.

Western   **(PR:A   MPAA:NR)**

PRAIRIE RUSTLERS**   (1945) 56m PRC bw

Buster Crabbe (Billy Carson), Al "Fuzzy" St. John (Fuzzy Jones), Evelyn Finley (Helen), Karl Hackett (Dan Foster), I. Stanford Jolley (Matt), Bud Osborne (Bart), Kermit Maynard (Vic), Herman Hack, George Morrell, Tex Cooper, Dorothy Vernon.

Crabbe (of FLASH GORDON fame) is both the good and bad guy in this western tale about a man (Crabbe) accused of committing a murder actually done by his look-alike cousin (also Crabbe). Crabbe manages to catch up with his no-good cousin and brings him to justice. Picture offers a lot of well-paced action, with the dual role setting off confused comedy routines at the expense of St. John. With this picture the "Billy Carson" series, featuring Crabbe and St. John, was winding to a close, and the well-traveled sidekick, St. John, prepared to saddle-pal with Lash LaRue. (See BILLY CARSON series, Index.)

p, Sigmund Neufeld; d, Sam Newfield; w, Fred Myton; ph, Jack Greenhalgh; ed, Holbrook N. Todd.

Western   **(PR:A   MPAA:NR)**

PRAIRIE SCHOONERS*½   (1940) 58m COL bw (GB: THROUGH THE STORM)

"Wild Bill" Elliott (Wild Bill Hickok), Evelyn Young (Virginia Beton), Dub Taylor (Cannonball), Kenneth Harlan (Dalton Stull), Ray Teal (Wolf Tanner), Bob Burns (Jim Gibbs), Netta Packer (Cora Gibbs), Richard Fiske (Adams), Edmund Cobb (Rusty), Jim Thorpe (Chief Sanche), George Morrell, Ned Glass, Sammy Stein, Lucien Maxwell, Merrill McCormack.

Elliott plays the western legend (whose nickname actor Elliott had adopted as his own) in this routine adventure about a group of settlers who leave Kansas for a go at the wilderness of Colorado. But they come up against a band of Indians who don't want any more white settlers on their land. Despite a very good outing by Elliott, incohesive plot details and slack dialog mar any chances this picture had. (See WILD BILL HICKOK series, Index.)

d, Sam Nelson; w, Robert Lee Johnson, Fred Myton (based on a story by George Cory Franklin); ph, George Meehan; ed, Al Clark.

Western   **(PR:A   MPAA:NR)**

PRAIRIE STRANGER*   (1941) 58m COL bw (GB: MARKED BULLET)

Charles Starrett (Steven Monroe), Cliff Edwards (Bones), Patti McCarty (Sue Evans), Forbes Murray (Jud Evans), Frank LaRue (Jim Dawson), Archie Twitchell (Barton), Francis Walker (Craig), Edmond Cobb (Dr. Westridge), James Corey (Undertaker), Russ Powell (Whittling Jones), Lew Preston and His Ranch Hands, George Morrell.

Unexciting outing in the short-lived "Doctor Monroe" series, which ended because

Columbia had legal problems with author Rubel on whose stories the series was based, has Starrett, accompanied by Edwards, trying to be successful as a doctor in a small Nevada town. Because an Eastern doctor has claim to all the patients the pair get jobs as cowhands. Starrett not only cures a disease spreading among the cattle, but also manages to catch the crook responsible for the initial poisoning of the herds. The plot drags on, offering a few moments of adventure near the ending.

p, William Berke; d, Lambert Hillyer; w, Winston Miller (based on the book by James L. Rubel); ph, Benjamin Kline; ed, James Sweeney; m/l, Lew Preston, Lopez Willingham.

Western (PR:A MPAA:NR)

PRAIRIE THUNDER*½ (1937) 54m FN/WB bw

Dick Foran (*Rod Farrell*), Ellen Clancy (*Joan Temple*), Frank Orth (*Wichita*), Wilfred Lucas (*Nate Temple*), Albert J. Smith (*Lynch*), Yakima Canutt (*High Wolf*), George Chesebro (*Matson*), Slim Whitaker (*Blacky*), J.P. McGowan (*Col. Stanton*), John Harron (*Lt. Adams*), Jack Mower (*Foreman*), Henry Otho (*Chris*), Paul Panzer (*Jed*), Frank Ellis, Frank McCarroll, Art Mix, Iron Eyes Cody, Jim Corey, Bob Burns.

Foran rides to his last round-up for Warner Bros. (he'd done 12 films for the studio) in this remake of 1933's THE TELEGRAPH TRAIL. Indians on the rampage have yanked down the all important telegraph wires, and it's up to Foran to get the lines of communication back up. The Indians were stirred up by an evil white wagon-train owner who wants the telegraph down in order to halt the advance of the railroad which will ruin his business. Eventually the cavalry arrives scaring away the Indians and rounding up white villains for the firing squad.

p, Bryan Foy; d, B. Reeves Eason; w, Ed Earl Repp; ph, Warren Lynch; ed, Ted McCord.

Western (PR:A MPAA:NR)

PRAISE MARX AND PASS THE AMMUNITION** (1970, Brit.) 90m Mithras c

John Thaw (*Dom*), Edina Ronay (*Lucy*), Luis Mahoney (*Julius*), Anthony Villaroel (*Arthur*), Helen Fleming (*Clara*), David David (*Lal*), Tanya (*Paraguayan Girl*), Eva Enger (*Swedish Girl*), Tandy Cronyn (*American Girl*), Tina Packer (*Air Hostess*), Jenny Robbins (*Shop Assistant*), John Garvin (*Body*), Carl Davis (*Composer*), Artro Morris (*Union Organizer*), James Mellor (*Shop Steward*), Otto Diamant (*Italian*), Joe Grieg (*Irishman*), Tom Kempinski (*Designer*).

A revolutionary drama starring Thaw as an avowed Marxist who travels around Britain trying to start a revolution, but most of the time he hops into bed with various women willing to listen to his political discourse. Suspected by the party leaders of not being a "true" revolutionary, Thaw is captured and brought before a tribunal located in a warehouse. College-level theoretical political discourse is thrown back and forth until the cops come and break things up. Pretty tedious unless one enjoys pretentious counterculture nostalgia.

p,d&w, Maurice Hatton (based on an idea by Hatton and Michael Wood); ph, Charles Stewart (Eastmancolor); m, Carl Davis; ed, Eduardo Guedes, Tim Lewis; art d, Nick Pollock.

Comedy (PR:A MPAA:NR)

PRATLDWANDI (SEE: ADVERSARY, THE, 1973, Ind.)

PRAYING MANTIS** (1982, Brit.) 119m Portman/Channel Four c

Jonathan Pryce (*Christian Magny*), Cherie Lunghi (*Beatrice Manceau*), Carmen Du Sautoy (*Vera Canova*), Pinkas Braun (*Paul Canova*), Anna Cropper (*Gertrude*), Friedrich Van Thun (*Insurance Director*).

Pryce gets involved in a murder plot to kill his mentor and his wife, but his plans are soon foiled. An attempt which misses the *film noir* mark that it strives for.

p, Ian Warren, Dickie Bamber; d, Jack Gold; w, Philip Mackie; ph, John Coquillon; m, Carl Davis; ed, Keith Palmer; prod d, Robert Cartwright.

Drama (PR:C MPAA:NR)

PREACHERMAN zero (1971) 87m Preacherman/Carolina Film Industries c

Amos Huxley [Albert T. Viola] (*Himself*), Ilene Kristen (*Mary Lou*), Esty F. Davis, Jr. (*Jud Crabtree*), Adam Hesse (*Clyde*), Marian Brown (*Sister Martha*), W. Henry Smith (*Brother Henry*), Bill Simpson (*Sheriff Zero Bull*), Garland Atkins (*Deputy Leon*).

Producer, director and co-writer Viola plays himself (under the pseudonym "Amos Huxley") in this trashy southern exploitation drama which details the illicit wanderings of a bogus preacher out to grab as much sex and cash as he can. After being run out of town because he tried to bilk the sheriff's daughter, Viola hitches a ride with old farmer Davis who brings the stranger home with him. Back at the farm, Davis is shocked to find his daughter, Kristen, engaged in some intense sexual gymnastics with three of the local townsmen. Davis chases the goons off and desperately asks Viola to baptise his daughter. Seeing his opportunity, Viola replies that he cannot perform the religious rite until the girl has been visited by the "Angel Leroy." It seems that this little-known angel visits young girls in the dead of night and spends a few hours with them. After this occurs, the girl is ready to be baptised. That night Viola plays the Angel Leroy. Later the next day, a guilty Davis confesses to Viola that he runs a still. The understanding preacher suggests that Davis use the profits from his still to fund the building of a new church. Having pulled the ultimate con (access to a farmer's daughter, a brand new church, free hooch, etc.), Viola settles down and lives high on the hog for a while. Unfortunately the law catches up with the preacherman once again, and he sneaks out of town. Hope springs eternal for Viola, and before the fade he is picked up by a sexy redhead in a convertible,

and rides off to a sequel, PREACHERMAN MEETS WIDDERWOMAN. Not surprisingly this good 'ol boy garbage grossed $5 million in southern drive-ins alone, a pretty good return on a $65,000 investment.

p&d, Albert T. Viola; w, Harvey Flaxman, Viola; m, W. Henry Smith, Roland Pope.

Comedy/Drama Cas. (PR:O MPAA:R)

PRECIOUS JEWELS* (1969) 77m Art in Motion-Times Ten/Grads Clamil c

Don Auld, Peter Deb, Dee Lockwood, Chet Washington, Bob Ball, Rose M. Howard, Antoinette Maynard, Mary Jane Wallace, Mickey Jines, Marlon Harper, Stuart Lancaster.

Two groups of crooks plot to steal a valuable necklace, one plans to use the money to pay back a gambling debt, the other plans on collecting insurance money. Nothing precious about this one.

d&w, William Stagg; ph, Eastmancolor; ed, Moe Macky.

Crime/Drama (PR:C MPAA:NR)

PREHISTORIC PLANET WOMEN (SEE: WOMEN OF THE PREHISTORIC PLANET, 1966)

PREHISTORIC WOMEN* (1950) 74m Alliance/EL c

Laurette Luez (*Tigri*), Allan Nixon (*Engor*), Joan Shawlee (*Lotee*), Judy Landon (*Eras*), Mara Lynn (*Arva*), Jo Carroll Dennison (*Nika*), Kerry Vaughn (*Tulle*), Tony Devlin (*Ruig*), James Summers (*Adh*), Dennis Dengate (*Kama*), Jeanne Sorel (*Tana*), Johann Peturrson (*Guaddi*), John Merrick (*Tribe Leader*), Janet Scott (*Wise Old Lady*).

A savage clan of women dressed in leopard skins capture men in order to promote their prehistoric race. The dialogue is generally nothing but grunting, but thanks to the help of a narrator some sense of story can be unearthed. Bad film exploiting scantily clad women.

p, Albert J. Cohen, Sam X. Abarbanel; d, Gregg Tallas; w, Tallas, Abarbanel; ph, Lionel Lindon (Cinecolor); m, Raoul Kraushaar; ed, James Graham; art d, Jerome Pycha, Jr.; ch, Bella Lewitsky.

Adventure Cas. (PR:C MPAA:NR)

PREHISTORIC WOMEN* (1967, Brit.) 95m Hammer-Seven Arts/FOX c (GB: SLAVE GIRLS)

Martine Beswick (*Queen Kari*), Edina Ronay (*Saria*), Michael Latimer (*David Marchant*), Stephanie Randall (*Amyak*), Carol White (*Gido*), Alexandra Stevenson (*Luri*), Yvonne Horner (*1st Amazon*), Sydney Bromley (*Ullo*), Frank Hayden (*Arja*), Robert Raglan (*Col. Hammond*), Mary Hignett (*Mrs. Hammond*), Louis Mahoney (*Head Boy*), Bari Johnson (*High Priest*), Danny Daniels (*Jakara*), Steven Berkoff (*John*), Sally Caclough (*Amazon*).

Latimer comes across a tribe of dark-haired, dominant women in animal skins, who worship rhinoceroses, and enslave women with blonde hair. He is imprisoned by the tribal Queen so she can satisfy her sexual appetite. He manages to escape, however, and lead a rebellion along with the other captive males. The ending indicates his whole adventure could have been a dream. Shot on the sets of ONE MILLION YEARS B.C., this film is full of sadistic humor, but is ultimately below average.

p&d, Michael Carreras; w, Henry Younger; ph, Michael Reed (CinemaScope, DeLuxe Color); m, Carlo Martelli; ed, Roy Hyde, James Needs; art d, Robert Jones; cos, Carl Toms; spec eff, George Blackwell; ch, Denys Palmer; makeup, Wally Schneiderman.

Adventure (PR:O MPAA:NR)

PREHISTORIC WORLD (SEE: TEENAGE CAVEMAN, 1958)

PREJUDICE*½ (1949) 58m New World/Motion Picture Sales bw

David Bruce (*Joe Hanson*), Mary Marshall (*Beth Hanson*), Tommy Ivo (*Joey Hanson*), Bruce Edwards (*Al Green*), Barbara Billingsley (*Doris Green*), James Seay (*Minister*), Joseph Crehan (*Mr. Baker*), Billy Kinbley (*Eddie*), Jimmy Conlin (*Young Joe*), Sharon McManus (*Ellen Green*), Ann Nagle, Frank Cady, Mira McKinney, Grace Fields, Ruth Clifford, Kay Christopher, John Dehner, Buddy Swan, Margaret Bert, Belle Mitchell, Clarence Hennecke.

Bruce is paranoid that his Jewish assistant is trying to take over his position as plant manager. His anti-Semitism surfaces in a meeting with the owner and as a result the assistant is transferred. Guilt-ridden, Bruce has a talk with his preacher and realizes his mistake. The intentions are there, but the entertainment isn't. Backed by funds from various civic groups, and produced under the care of the Protestant Film Commission.

p, Edmund I. Dorfman; d, Edward L. Cahn; w, Jarvis Couillard, Ivan Goff, Ben Roberts (based on a story by Couillard); ph, Jackson Rose; m, Irving Gertz; ed, Phil Cahn; art d, Lewis Creber; set d, Harry Reif.

Drama (PR:A MPAA:NR)

PRELUDE TO ECSTASY** (1963, Fin.) 84m Suomen Filmitcollisuus/ Manson bw (KUU ON VAARALLINEN)

Liana Kaarina (*Elsie*), Toivo Makela (*Sten Lehtoja*), Esko Salminen (*Reino*), Eero Roine (*His Father*), Rose-Marie Precht (*Maja*), Ake Lindman (*Sheriff*), Kaarlo Wilska (*Policeman*).

Hitchhiker Kaarina gets a ride from Makela, a middle-aged businessman, who brings her to his summer house. She spends the night and they become lovers, even though he is married. Later that summer, Kaarina also begins an affair with the young Salminen. Makela then agrees to divorce his wife and marry Kaarina. One night, Salminen comes to the bedroom window via a ladder. He falls and breaks his neck, sending Makela into a panic. He hides the body to avoid scandal, but is later arrested when Kaarina feels guilty over the incident and calls the police.

p,d&w, Toivo Sarkka (based on *Besaettelse* by Hans Severinsen); ph, Olavi Tuomi; m, Einar Englund; ed, Elmer Lahti; art d, Aarne Koivisto.

Drama　　　　　　　　　　　　　　　　　　　　**(PR:C MPAA:NR)**

PRELUDE TO FAME*　　　　　　　　(1950, Brit.) 78m TC/UNIV bw

Guy Rolfe (*John Morell*), Kathleen Byron (*Signora Bondini*), Kathleen Ryan (*Catherine Morell*), Jeremy Spenser (*Guido*), Henry Oscar (*Signor Bondini*), Rosalie Crutchley (*Carlotta*), John Slater (*Dr. Lorenzo*), James Robertson Justice (*Sir Arthur Harold*), Ferdy Mayne (*Carlo*), Robert Rietty (*Giuseppe*), Robin Dowell (*Nick*), Hugo Schuster (*Dr. Freihaus*), Michael Balfour (*Lucio*), Christopher Lee (*Newsman*), David McCallum, Sr. (*Orchestra Leader at Albert Hall*), Dora Hyde (*Orchestra Leader in Naples*), Michael Crowdson (*Nick's Friend*), Don Liddel (*Beniamino*), Ben Williams (*Car Driver*), Alex Fields (*Doorkeeper*), Penny Dane (*Maid*), Leonard Trolley.

Spenser is a child prodigy pushed into the classical music world by an ambitious patroness of the arts, who achieves her fame through him. For the child's sake, Rolfe returns the boy, whose talent he originally discovered, to his parents. An engrossing tale topped with a grand selection of classical music. Christopher Lee is featured in a minor role as a newsman.

p, Donald B. Wilson; d, Fergus McDonnell; w, Robert Westerby (from the story "Young Archimedes" by Aldous Huxley); ph, George Stretton; m, Muir Mathieson; ed, Sid Hayers; art d, Fred Pusey; set d, Vernon Dickson.

Drama　　　　　　　　　　　　　　　　　　　　**(PR:A MPAA:NR)**

PREMATURE BURIAL, THE½　　　　　(1962) 81m Santa Clara/AIP c

Ray Milland (*Guy Carrell*), Hazel Court (*Emily Gault*), Richard Ney (*Miles Archer*), Heather Angel (*Kate Carrell*), Alan Napier (*Dr. Gideon Gault*), John Dierkes (*Sweeney*), Richard [Dick] Miller (*Mole*), Brendan Dillon (*Minister*), Clive L. Halliday.

Milland is a 19th-Century victim of catalepsy, a state in which one appears to be dead even though still alive. Obsessed with the idea that he may be buried alive like he believes his father had been, Milland has a burial vault built which is equipped with escape hatches. After seeing his father's contorted skeleton, indicating that he was indeed buried alive, Milland has what appears to be a fatal heart attack and is pronounced dead. He is placed in a casket, but eventually escapes. In an attempt to avenge his near death, he kills his doctor and buries his wife alive. It is then revealed that his wife was plotting to inherit his fortune. A Roger Corman adaptation of an Edgar Allan Poe tale which puts Milland in the role usually reserved for Vincent Price. The ad department of AIP had fun with this one's release, suggesting that theater owners stage an actual burial-alive to boost sales. Another idea was a special midnight screening for gravediggers, which, like the previous brainstorm, did little for the film's box office sales.

p&d, Roger Corman; w, Charles Beaumont, Ray Russell (based on the story by Edgar Allan Poe); ph, Floyd Crosby (Panavision, Eastmancolor); m, Ronald Stein; ed, Ronald Sinclair; art d, Daniel Haller; set d, Harry Reif; cos, Marjorie Corso; spec eff, Pat Dinga; makeup, Louis LaCava.

Horror　　　　　　　　　**Cas.**　　　　　　　**(PR:C MPAA:NR)**

PREMIERE　　　　　　　　　(SEE: ONE NIGHT IN PARIS, 1940, Brit.)

PREMONITION, THE**　　　　　　　　　(1976) 94m Galaxy/AE c

Sharon Farrell (*Sheri Bennett*), Richard Lynch (*Jude, Clown Photographer*), Jeff Corey (*Detective Mark Denver*), Ellen Barber (*Andrea Fletcher*), Edward Bell (*Professor Miles Bennett*), Chitra Neogy (*Dr. Jeena Kingsly*), Danielle Brisebois (*Janie*), Rosemary McNamara (*Lenore*), Thomas Williams (*Todd Fletcher*), Margaret Graham (*Landlady*), Roy White (*Dr. Larabee*), Wilmuth Cooper (*Gypsy Lady*), Robert Harper (*Night Watchman*), Mark Schneider, Stanley W. Winn, Tamara Bergdall, Bonita Chambers, Edward L. Emling, Jr..

Farrell (IT'S ALIVE) is the foster mother of a young girl whose real mother, Barber, is intent on regaining custody. Barber resorts to the use of parapsychology and the aid of an eerie circus mime to achieve her goal. Director Schnitzer is able to achieve a subtlety approaching that of producer Val Lewson's films of the 1940s (CAT PEOPLE, I WALKED WITH A ZOMBIE), but the clouded script never allows him to duplicate Lewton's success. The Mississippi location adds to the atmosphere.

p&d, Robert Allen Schnitzer; w, Schnitzer, Anthony Mahon, Louis Pastore (based on the manuscript "The Adoption"); ph, Victor C. Milt (TVC Color); m, Henry Mollicone, Pril Smiley; ed, Sidney Katz; art d, John Lawless.

Horror　　　　　　　　　**Cas.**　　　　　　　**(PR:C MPAA:PG)**

PRESCOTT KID, THE**　　　　　　　　　(1936) 58m COL bw

Tim McCoy (*Tim Hamlin*), Sheila Mannors (*Dolores*), Joseph Sauers [Joe Sawyer] (*Willoughby*), Alden Chase (*Walton*), Hooper Atchley (*Bonner*), Albert J. Smith (*Frazier*), Harry Todd (*Dr. Haley*), Walter Brennan (*Stage Driver*), Carlos De Valdez (*Ortega*), Ernie Adams (*Red Larson*), Steve Clark (*Crocker*), Slim Whitaker, Charles King, Bud Osborne, Art Mix, Tom London, Edmund Cobb, Lew Meehan, Jack Rockwell.

McCoy turns in a better than average performance in this B-western about the all-too-familiar crime of cattle rustling. His flare with his six guns is more than gang leader Chase can handle.

p&d, David Selman; w, Ford Beebe, Claude Rister; ph, Benjamin Kline; ed, Richard Cahoon.

Western　　　　　　　　　　　　　　　　　　　**(PR:A MPAA:NR)**

PRESCRIPTION FOR ROMANCE**　　　　　　　(1937) 70m UNIV bw

Mischa Auer (*Count Sandor*), Wendy Barrie (*Dr. Valerie Wilson*), Kent Taylor (*Steve Macy*), Dorothea Kent (*Lola Carroll*), Frank Jenks (*Smitty*), Henry Hunter (*Kenneth Barton*), Gregory Gaye (*Dr. Paul Azarny*), Samuel S. Hinds (*Maj. Goddard*), Frank Reicher (*Jozsef*), Hugh S. Sheridan (*Feodor*), William Lundigan (*Officer*), Constance Moore (*Officer's Sweetheart*), Christian Rub (*Conductor*), Greta Meyer (*Marie, the Head Nurse*), Torben Meyer (*Hotel Desk Clerk*), Ralph Sanford (*Hungarian Policeman*), Theodore Osborn (*Corney*), Robert C. Fischer (*Veternarian*), Otto Fries, Bert Roach (*Police Sergeants*), Elsa Janssen (*Elsa*), Paul Weigel (*Peasant*), Joe Cunningham (*Farrell*), Franco Corsaro (*Headwaiter Franz*), Jimmie Lucas (*Waiter*), Alex Palasthy (*Hungarian Roue*), Dorothy Granger (*Cashier*), Dick Wessel (*Sailor*), Michael Mark, George Cleveland, Sidney D'Albrook (*Cab Drivers*), William Gould (*Doorman*), Fred Gehrmann (*Ambulance Driver*), Dan Wolheim (*Policeman*), Paul Newlan (*Bearded Hungarian*).

Detective Taylor and count Auer give chase to embezzler Hunter, who has fled to Budapest. The trail leads to the home of female doctor Barrie, who unknowingly harbors the criminal. Once on the scene, Taylor and Barrie start a romance, with the latter being cleared of any charges. Entertaining continent hopping adds to the fun.

p, Edmund Grainger; d, S. Sylvan Simon; w, James Mulhauser, Robert T. Shannon, Albert R. Perkins (based on a story by John Reinhardt, Robert Neville); ph, Milton Krasner; ed, Paul Landres; md, Charles Previn; art d, Jack Otterson.

Drama　　　　　　　　　　　　　　　　　　　　**(PR:A MPAA:NR)**

PRESENT ARMS　　　　　　　　　　(SEE: LEATHERNECKING, 1930)

PRESENTING LILY MARS*½　　　　　　　　(1943) 104m MGM bw

Judy Garland (*Lily Mars*), Van Heflin (*John Thornway*), Fay Bainter (*Mrs. Thornway*), Richard Carlson (*Owen Vail*), Spring Byington (*Mrs. Mars*), Marta Eggerth (*Isobel Rekay*), Connie Gilchrist (*Frankie*), Leonid Kinskey (*Leo*), Patricia Barker (*Poppy*), Janet Chapman (*Violet*), Annabelle Logan (*Rosie*), Douglas Croft (*Davey*), Ray McDonald (*Charlie Potter*), Marilyn Maxwell (*Chorus Girl*), Tommy Dorsey and His Orchestra, Bob Crosby and His Orchestra.

Garland was 19 when she was pressed into service in this adaptation of Booth Tarkington's novel that had originally been bought by MGM as a dramatic picture for Lana Turner. When the script turned out to be a light-hearted one, Garland was given the role. Garland lives in a tiny Indiana town and when Broadway producer Heflin happens to be there, she chases him around, does the sleepwalking scene from *Macbeth*, and finally convinces him to take her to New York, where he gives her a job in his new show. She falls in love with him, which rankles the star of the show, Eggerth, and the angry woman walks out. Guess who is groomed to replace the star? Well, it isn't Dame May Whitty! Eggerth eventually sees the light and returns to the lead role. But Garland, who has been upped from the chorus, gets the chance to do a few numbers and becomes a huge success, as any tyke of two could have predicted. Pasternak was a master of low-budget films and this was his first picture for MGM after having spent years at Universal. Mayer thought he had something with this movie so he got Pasternak to bring in Charles Walters to stage the finale and put it in a grandiose setting more in keeping with MGM's musicals. The result was that the ending bore little resemblance to the beginning and seemed out of place. Songs for this escapist film came from a raft of cleffers. They include: "When I Look at You" (Paul Francis Webster, Walter Jurmann, sung by Marta Eggerth, Judy Garland), "Three O'Clock in the Morning" (Dorothy Terriss [Theodora Morse], Julian Robledo, sung by Judy Garland), "Kulebiaka," "Is It Love? (Or the Gypsy in Me)" (Webster, Jurmann), "Broadway Rhythm" (Arthur Freed, Nacio Herb Brown), "Sweethearts of America" (Ralph Freed, Burbton Lane), "Where There's Music" (Roger Edens), "Every Little Movement Has a Meaning All Its Own" (Karl Hoschna, Otto Harbach), "Tom, Tom, the Piper's Son" (sung by Judy Garland). E.Y. "Yip" Harburg is also listed in the credits as a songwriter. Look for a very young Marilyn Maxwell as a chorus girl.

p, Joe Pasternak; d, Norman Taurog; w, Richard Connell, Gladys Lehman (based on a novel by Booth Tarkington); ph, Joseph Ruttenberg; ed, Albert Akst; md, Georgie Stoll; art d, Cedric Gibbons; spec eff, Warren Newcombe; ch, Ernst Matray.

Musical/Comedy　　　　　　　　　　　　　　　**(PR:A MPAA:NR)**

PRESIDENT VANISHES, THE**　　　　　(1934) 86m PAR bw (GB: STRANGE CONSPIRACY)

Arthur Byron (*President Stanley Craig*), Janet Beecher (*Mrs. Craig*), Paul Kelly (*Chick Moffat*), Peggy Conklin (*Alma Cronin*), Rosalind Russell (*Sally Voorman*), Sidney Blackmer (*D.L. Voorman*), Douglas Wood (*Roger Grant*), Walter Kingsford (*Drew*), DeWitt Jennings (*Cullen*), Charles Grapewin (*Richard Norton*), Charles Richman (*Corcoran*), Jason Robards, Sr. (*Kilbourne*), Paul Harvey (*Skinner*), Robert McWade (*Vice President Molleson*), Edward Arnold (*Secretary of War Wardell*), Osgood Perkins (*Harris Brownell*), Edward Ellis (*Lincoln Lee*), Andy Devine (*Val Orcott*), Harry Woods (*Kramer*), Irene Franklin (*Mrs. Orcott*), Tommy Dugan (*Nolan*), Clara Blandick (*Mrs. Delling*), Charles K. French, William Worthington, William S. Holmes, Charles Meakin, Art Howard, Ed Lewis, Ed Mortimer, Emmett King, Edgar Sherrod, Henry Herbert (*Senators and Congressmen*).

Byron is cast as the President of the U.S. in this film about a nationwide conspiracy of business tycoons to force a war in Europe to better the economy. The chief executive's assistants decide that it is best for Byron to drop out of the public eye for a period of time, in order to avoid the possibility of being forced into war. A fake kidnaping is staged, diverting the citizens' attentions to the crime and away from the possibility of taking up arms. Interesting mainly for its expression of the anti-intervention policies that many held before our involvement in WW II. Otherwise the premise is weakly constructed. This film was undoubtedly inspired by GABRIEL OVER THE WHITE HOUSE.

p, Walter Wanger; d, William A. Wellman; w, Carey Wilson, Cedric Worth, Lynn Starling (based on an anonymous novel); ph, Barney McGill; ed, Hanson Fritch; md, Hugo Riesenfeld.

Drama **(PR:A MPAA:NR)**

PRESIDENT'S ANALYST, THE*½** (1967) 103m Panpiper/PAR c

James Coburn *(Dr. Sidney Schaefer)*, Godfrey Cambridge *(Don Masters)*, Severn Darden *(Kropotkin)*, Joan Delaney *(Nan Butler)*, Pat Harrington *(Arlington Hewes)*, Barry Maguire *(Old Wrangler)*, Jill Banner *(Snow White)*, Eduard Franz *(Ethan Allan Cocket)*, Walter Burke *(Henry Lux)*, Will Geer *(Dr. Lee Evans)*, William Daniels *(Wynn Quantrill)*, Joan Darling *(Jeff Quantrill)*, Sheldon Collins *(Bing Quantrill)*, Arte Johnson *(Sullivan)*, Martin Horsey, William Beckley *(Puddlians)*, Kathleen Hughes *(Tourist)*.

Coburn is selected to become the President's analyst, a job which makes him hot property for anyone who wants information on the nation's matters. Coburn becomes increasingly suspicious of his surroundings and hitches a ride with the Quantrills (Daniels, Darling, Collins), a gun-toting, karate-kicking family of liberals. Soon the head of the CEA, Franz, the chief of the FBR, Burke, the Canadian Secret Service (disguised as a British rock group), the Russians, and the Chinese are in pursuit of Coburn. The finale has Coburn discovering that the telephone company is the ruling force in this country, with Harrington leading a group of automation midgets bent on domination. A bizarre and daring spoof of spy films, American culture, and our nation's hierarchy. No wonder AT&T was dissolved.

p, Stanley Rubin; d&w, Theodore J. Flicker; ph, William A. Fraker (Panavision, Technicolor); m, Lalo Schifrin; ed, Stuart H. Pappe; prod d, Pato Guzman; art d, Hal Pereira, Al Roelofs; set d, Robert R. Benton, Arthur Krams; cos, Jack Bear; m/l, "Inner Manipulations," Barry McGuire, Paul Potash (sung by McGuire), "She's Ready to Be Free," The Clear Light (sung by The Clear Light), "Hey, Me," Schifrin, Flicker; makeup, Wally Westmore.

Satire **(PR:O MPAA:NR)**

PRESIDENT'S LADY, THE*** (1953) 96m FOX bw

Susan Hayward *(Rachel Donelson Robards)*, Charlton Heston *(Andrew Jackson)*, John McIntire *(Jack Overton)*, Fay Bainter *(Mrs. Donelson)*, Whitfield Connor *(Lewis Robards)*, Carl Betz *(Charles Dickinson)*, Gladys Hurlbut *(Mrs. Phariss)*, Ruth Attaway *(Moll)*, Charles Dingle *(Capt. Irwin)*, Nina Varela *(Mrs. Stark)*, Margaret Wycherly *(Mrs. Robards)*, Ralph Dumke *(Col. Stark)*, Jim Davis *(Jason)*, Robert B. Williams *(William)*, Trudy Marshall *(Jane)*, Howard Negley *(Cruthers)*, Dayton Lummis *(Dr. May)*, Harris Brown *(Clark)*, Zon Murray *(Jacob)*, James Best *(Samuel)*, Selmer Jackson *(Col. Green)*, Juanita Evers *(Mrs. Green)*, George Melford *(Minister)*, George Hamilton *(House Servant)*, Vera Francis *(Slave Girl)*, Leo Curley *(Innkeeper)*, Ann Morrison *(Mary)*, William Walker *(Uncle Alfred)*, Sherman Sanders *(Square Dance Caller)*, Rene Beard *(Black Boy)*, Sam McDaniel *(Henry, Phariss' Driver)*, George Spaulding *(Chief Justice John Marshall)*, Willis Bouchey *(Judge McNairy)*, Mervyn Williams *(Young Senator)*, Ronald Numkena *(Lincoya—Age 8)*.

THE PRESIDENT'S LADY, one of the better biographical films made by Hollywood, adheres closely to the truth, as depicted by Stone in his novelization of the lives of the seventh U.S. President and his wife. Heston is one of the few actors (if not the only) ever to have played the same role in two pictures twice each. He was Marc Antony in JULIUS CAESAR and ANTONY AND CLEOPATRA and played Andrew Jackson in this and THE BUCCANEER. It's 1791 in Nashville, Tennessee. Hayward is married to philandering Connor, a local businessman, when she meets attorney Heston and there is an instant attraction. Hayward is having a tough time with Connor so her mother, Bainter, suggests she go to Natchez, Mississippi, to get some breathing space. Since the area is fraught with danger, Heston will take her to Natchez on the riverboat. While aboard, Indians attack and as Heston and Hayward share excitement they become closer. Heston is all for marrying Hayward and suggests that they have her previous union voided so they can get together. She agrees and will wait at the home of her relative in Natchez. Meanwhile, Heston's law partner, McIntyre, sends a note saying that Connor has sued Hayward for divorce on the grounds of adultery with Heston. Well! The future President is hurt by this accusation (especially since it isn't true) but declares that it will not stop him from marrying her, and so they wed. Back in Nashville, Heston decides that he might like to run for office but those plans are put on hold when he learns that although Connor had filed for divorce, the action wasn't complete until a few days ago, which means that Heston and Hayward have been living in, sigh, sin. They marry once more at Bainter's house and all seems well. But news like that is hard to keep mum in a small town and, at a party later, guest Betz opens his yap and says that Heston may have stolen another man's wife. That's a slap in the face to the couple so cards are exchanged, seconds are called and a duel between Betz and Heston is fought, with Betz coming out the loser and being killed. Heston is wounded but pledges to Hayward that he will place her in such an exalted position someday that nobody can ever touch her with their verbal abuse. Time passes and Heston is nominated by his party to run for the Presidency. The campaign is arduous and Hayward becomes ill. At a campaign rally, Heston is speaking and Hayward is hiding in the crowd, proudly listening to his words, when hecklers begin working him over, bringing up Betz's death and his marriage to Hayward. When one of the hecklers calls Hayward a "woman of ill repute," Hayward faints. By the time Heston learns that he's been elected, Hayward is so ill that she dies in his arms, a "first lady" who never had the chance to live in Washington, because it takes three months from the November election to the January inauguration. Hayward did a good job and special kudos go to Ben Nye for his makeup job which successfully aged the beauteous Hayward from 18 to 61. The real woman used to smoke a pipe and that part of her life is not neglected. The only notice taken by the Academy were nominations for Renie's Costume Design and the Art Direction and Set Direction. It was a colorful story and should have been shot that way. This was the second time Hayward had a run-in (on film) with Connor. The first was in TAP ROOTS when he was engaged to her and ran off with her sister. Whatever liberties were taken by the book and script were kept to a minimum, something not usually the case in biographies. That taste was appreciated by everyone who admired "Old Hickory."

p, Sol C. Siegel; d, Henry Levin; w, John Patrick (based on the novel by Irving Stone); ph, Leo Tover; m, Alfred Newman; ed, William B. Murphy; art d, Lyle Wheeler, Leland Fuller; set d, Paul S. Fox; cos, Renie; spec eff, Ray Kellogg; makeup, Ben Nye.

Biography **(PR:A-C MPAA:NR)**

PRESIDENT'S MYSTERY, THE*½ (1936) 80m REP bw (GB: ONE FOR ALL)

Henry Wilcoxon *(James Blake)*, Betty Furness *(Charlotte)*, Sidney Blackmer *(Sartos)*, Evelyn Brent *(Ilka Blake)*, Barnett Parker *(Roger, Butler)*, Mel Ruick *(Andrew)*, Wade Boteler *(Sheriff)*, John Wray *(Shane)*, Guy Usher *(Police Lieutenant)*, Robert E. Homans *(Sergeant)*, Si Jenks *(Earl)*, Arthur Aylesworth *(Joe Reed)*.

Wilcoxon stars as a lawyer who drops out of society after getting fed up with his environment and way of life. He soon hooks up with Furness, forgetting about his previous marriage to Brent. The story, suggested by President Franklin D. Roosevelt to *Liberty Magazine*, was reportedly better than what wound up on the screen, but it is typical of Republic Studios' commendable record on non-series films, which leaned heavily on action and pacing and were usually quite successful. This is another of the nine identifiable films written by the famous Nathanael West, who loathed his screen work so much that he went on to write the classic pessimistic novel on Hollywood, *The Day of the Locust*.

p, Nat Levine; d, Phil Rosen; w, Lester Cole, Nathanael West (based on the *Liberty Magazine* story suggested by President Franklin D. Roosevelt and written by Rupert Hughes, Samuel Hopkins Adams, Anthony Abbot, Rita Weiman, S.S. Van Dine, John Erskine); ph, Ernest Miller; ed, Murray Selden, Robert Simpson; md, Hugo Riesenfeld.

Mystery **(PR:A MPAA:NR)**

PRESS FOR TIME½** (1966, Brit.) 102m Ivy-Titan/Rank c

Norman Wisdom *(Norman Shields/Wilfred Shields/Sir Wilfred Shields/Emily Shields)*, Derek Bond *(Maj. Bartlett)*, Angela Browne *(Eleanor)*, Tracey Crisp *(Ruby Fairchild)*, Noel Dyson *(Mrs. Corcoran)*, Derek Francis *(Alderman Corcoran)*, Peter Jones *(Willoughby)*, David Lodge *(Ross)*, Frances White *(Liz Corcoran)*, Allan Cuthbertson *(Ballard)*, Tony Selby *(Marsh)*, Michael Balfour *(Sewerman)*, Totti Truman Taylor *(Mrs. Doe Connor)*, Stanley Unwin *(Nottage)*, George Roderick *(Barman)*, Hazel Coppin *(Granny Fork)*.

Wisdom is the grandson of England's Prime Minister, who after embarrassing his grandfather by selling newspapers on a street corner, is sent to a small seaside town as a journalist. There he gets into more scandals than he can handle and soon ends up making a grade-A fool out of himself. His bumbling personality, however, is rather likeable, and makes for a humorous picture.

p, Robert Hartford-Davis, Peter Newbrook; d, Robert Asher; w, Norman Wisdom, Eddie Leslie (based on the novel *Yea Yea Yea*by Angus McGill); ph, Newbrook (Eastmancolor); m, Mike Vickers; ed, Garry Hambling.

Comedy **(PR:A MPAA:NR)**

PRESSURE½** (1976, Brit.) 120m British Film Institute c

Herbert Norville *(Anthony)*, Oscar James *(Colin)*, Frank Singuineau *(Lucas)*, Lucita Lijertwood *(Bopsie)*, Sheila Scott-Wilkinson *(Sister Louise)*, Ed Deveraux *(Police Inspector)*, T-Bone Wilson *(Junion)*, Ramjohn Holder *(Brother John)*, Norman Beaton *(Preacher)*, John Landry *(Mr. Crapson)*, Archie Pool *(Oscar)*, Whitty Vialva Forde *(Reefer)*, Marlene Davis *(Marlene)*.

Norville is a young English black man whose parents are emigrants from the Caribbean. Even though he has no trace of an island accent, speaks "proper" English, and has adopted white ways, he feels the racial pressures of his English environment. His character is contrasted with that of his island parents, his militant brother, and the young blacks he refuses to associate with. Britain's first all-black film, unfortunately, does not deliver what the script promises, due to dated subject matter even at the time this was filmed, stereotyped white and black characters, and a too long running time.

p, Robert Buckler; d, Horace Ove; w, Ove, Samuel Selvon; ph, Mike Davis; ed, Alan J. Cumner-Price.

Drama **(PR:C MPAA:NR)**

PRESSURE OF GUILT*** (1964, Jap.) 113m Toho bw (SHIRO TO KURO)

Keiju Kobayashi *(Ochiai)*, Tatsuya Nakadai *(Hamano)*, Hisashi Igawa *(Wakida)*, Koreya Senda *(Munakata)*, Akira Nishimura *(Hirao)*, Mayumi Ozora *(Muramatsu)*, Chikage Awashima *(Munakata's Wife)*, Nobuko Otoba *(Ochiai's Wife)*.

Nakadai is having an affair with Otoba, the wife of his law partner, Kobayashi. One night during an argument, he kills her. Terrified, he leaves her house before making sure she is really dead. Later, wracked with guilt, Nakadai decides to confess to the strangulation; but before he can, a well-known burglar is arrested for the killing. After days of interrogation, the burglar confesses and is sentenced to death. Afraid that an innocent man will be put to death, Nakadai decides to turn himself in. But before he does so, he is presented with evidence that although he tried to kill his lover, she recovered only to be killed by the burglar. This evidence is made public and the disgraced Nakadai commits suicide. An intriguing study of Japanese honor, and the self-inflicted penalty of losing face in Japanese society.

p, Ichiro Sato, Hideyuki Shiino; d, Hiromichi Horikawa; w, Shinobu Hashimoto; ph, Hiroshi Murai; m, Toru Takemitsu; art d, Hiroshi Muzitani.

Crime Drama **(PR:C MPAA:NR)**

PRESSURE POINT*½** (1962) 87m Larcas/UA bw

Sidney Poitier *(Doctor)*, Bobby Darin *(Patient)*, Peter Falk *(Young Psychiatrist)*, Carl Benton Reid *(Chief Medical Officer)*, Mary Munday *(Bar Hostess)*, Barry Gordon *(Patient as a Boy)*, Howard Caine *(Tavern Owner)*, Anne Barton *(Mother)*, James Anderson *(Father)*, Yvette Vickers *(Drunken Woman)*, Clegg Hoyt *(Pete)*, Richard Bakalyan *(Jimmy)*, Butch Patrick *(Playmate)*, Leonard Geiger, Gilbert Green, Lynn Loring.

This was Bobby Darin's fourth film and perhaps the best in his brief career. He did receive an Oscar nomination for his next picture, CAPTAIN NEWMAN, M.D., but that was due more to studio hype. Psychiatrist Robert Lindner wrote a best-selling book of short case histories, *The Fifty-Minute Hour*, and a few of the pieces were used for films and TV dramas. This was based on "Destiny's Tot." Falk is an analyst who can't break through with his patient and asks for some help from psychiatrist Poitier. This sends Poitier back in time as he recounts some problems he'd had years before. Poitier had been working for the government during WW II and was assigned to work with Darin, an American with Nazi sympathies who had been sent to jail by the Feds because they feared he might be subversive. Darin can't sleep, faints, and when he does finally fall into the arms of Morpheus, his dreams are horrible. Darin distrusts anyone who is not of the "Master Race" but holds that hatred in check and allows Poitier to work closely with him. Sessions reveal that Darin's father, Anderson, was a mean drunk who had always felt it was Darin's conception that forced him to marry the mother, Barton, who has since become bedridden and shrewish. To keep himself from going mad early, Darin's inventive mind created a pal, Patrick, a child he could push around and take advantage of. Later, Darin leaves home, and gets involved with the Nazi party when he's not allowed to date a Jewish girl because her father doesn't feel Darin is a worthy marriage prospect. As Darin discovers why he is the way he is, he can finally get some rest, so he refuses any further sessions with Poitier and remains steadfast in his Nazi beliefs. Poitier won't sign a release for Darin as he feels the man needs more psychiatric help. The powers above Poitier disagree and Darin is released, and Poitier, disappointed in himself, questions his own abilities, wondering if he recommended against Darin's parole out of medical expertise or as a reaction to Darin's racism. Poitier is vindicated in terrible fashion when Darin later murders an innocent old man and is himself executed. Upon hearing the tale, Falk decides that he will continue his attempts to pierce his patient's armor. Darin's childhood image is played by Barry Gordon, who was so sensational in A THOUSAND CLOWNS. His playmate, Patrick, was later seen as the male child on TV's "The Addams Family." Producer Kramer has always made movies with messages. Some have worked, some haven't. This one does. The newsreel clips of a Bund rally at Madison Square Garden are real, and thus all the more frightening than if it had been staged. The entire idea of the flashback was superfluous but, without it, the picture would probably have come in too short for major theaters.

p, Stanley Kramer; d, Hubert Cornfield; w, Cornfield, S. Lee Pogostin (based on a story by Robert Lindner); ph, Ernest Haller; m, Ernest Gold; ed, Frederic Knudtson; prod d, Rudolph Sternad; art d, George C. Webb; set d, George Milo; makeup, George Lane.

Drama **(PR:C MPAA:NR)**

PRESTIGE** (1932) 73m RKO-Pathe bw

Ann Harding *(Therese Du Flos)*, Adolphe Menjou *(Capt. Remy Baudoin)*, Melvyn Douglas *(Lt. Andre Verlaine)*, Ian MacLaren *(Col. Du Flos)*, Guy Bates Post *(Major)*, Carmelita Geraghty *(Felice)*, Rollo Lloyd *(Emil de Fontenac)*, Clarence Muse *(Nham, Verlaine's Servant)*.

Harding ventures into an Indochina penal colony in search of her fiance, Douglas, a young French lieutenant in command of the post. Both brave the rigors of jungle heat and disease, with Douglas combatting alcoholism at the same time. He takes a bullet while quelling a savage uprising, but in the end is still standing, filled with the hope of upholding the prestige of the background he comes from. A fine cast is wasted on a mediocre script.

p, Charles R. Rogers; d, Tay Garnett; w, Francis Edward Faragoh, Rollo Lloyd, Garnett (based on the novel *Lips of Steel* by Harry Hervey); ph, Lucien Andriot; ed, Joe Kane; m/l, "I Don't Know What You Do to Me," Harold Lewis, Bernie Grossman.

Adventure/Romance **(PR:A MPAA:NR)**

PRETENDER, THE*** (1947) 69m W.W./REP bw

Albert Dekker *(Kenneth Holden)*, Catherine Craig *(Claire Worthington)*, Charles Drake *(Dr. Leonard Koster)*, Alan Carney *(Victor Korrin)*, Linda Stirling *(Flo Ronson)*, Tom Kennedy *(Fingers Murdock)*, Selmer Jackson *(Charles Lennox)*, Charles Middleton *(Butler William)*, Ernie Adams *(Butler Thomas)*, Ben Welden *(Mickie)*, John Bagni *(Hank Gordon)*, Stanley Ross *(Stranger)*, Forrest Taylor *(Dr. Stevens)*, Greta Clement *(Margie)*, Peggy Wynne *(Miss Chalmers)*, Eula Guy *(Nurse #1)*, Cay Forrester *(Evelyn Cossett)*, Peter Michael *(Stephen)*, Michael Mark *(Janitor)*, Dorothy Scott *(Miss Michael)*.

A faulted but engrossing example of *film noir* which has Dekker plotting to kill the fiance of Craig, a woman he has been embezzling from and now plans to marry. He tells the hitman that the fiance's picture will appear in the newspaper. Dekker ends up marrying Craig, however, and a picture of the newlyweds is printed instead, causing the hitman to think that Dekker is the intended target. Dekker becomes increasingly paranoid, hiding in his room and eating only canned foods and crackers. Peeking out his window, he notices a shadow under a streetlight and shoots at it. He escapes by car, but is followed by two other autos. He is killed in an accident without realizing that he was being followed by a hired bodyguard and the hitman, who was trying to return the money for the aborted hit. Top-notch lighting and set design make supreme use of Dekker's emotional state, and sets constructed with exaggerated perspective effectively enhance the atmosphere.

p&d, W. Lee Wilder; w, Don Martin, Doris Miller; ph, John Alton; ed, Asa Boyd Clark, John F. Link; md, Paul Dessau; art d, F. Paul Sylos; cos, I.R. Berne; makeup, Don Cash.

Crime Drama **(PR:A MPAA:NR)**

PRETTY BABY** (1950) 92m WB bw

Dennis Morgan *(Sam Morley)*, Betsy Drake *(Patsy Douglas)*, Zachary Scott *(Barry Holmes)*, Edmund Gwenn *(Cyrus Baxter)*, William Frawley *(Corcoran)*, Raymond Roe *(Sidney)*, Ransom Sherman *(Powers)*, Sheila Stephens *(Peggy)*, Eleanor Audley *(Miss Brindel)*, George Chandler *(Henderson)*, Barbara Billingsley *(Receptionist)*.

Drake is a young employee of an advertising agency who takes the subway to work each morning, but never gets a seat. She comes up with the idea of carrying with her a life-sized doll of a baby to insure a seat. The baby, which she names after her firm's biggest client, baby food manufacturer Gwenn, becomes the topic of conversation when Gwenn sits down next to her one morning. Impressed with her creativity, he gets her a promotion at the agency. Later made into a TV movie with Natalie Wood, titled GIRL ON A SUBWAY (1958).

p, Harry Kurnitz; d, Bretaigne Windust; w, Everett Freeman (based on the story "Gay Deception" by Jules Furthman, John Klorer); ph, Peverell Marley; m, David Buttolph; ed, Folmar Blangsted; art d, Charles H. Clarke.

Comedy **(PR:A MPAA:NR)**

PRETTY BABY*½** (1978) 109m PAR c

Keith Carradine *(E.J. Bellocq)*, Susan Sarandon *(Hattie)*, Brooke Shields *(Violet)*, Frances Faye *(Mme. Nell Livingston)*, Antonio Fargas *(Professor, Piano Player)*, Gerrit Graham *(Highpockets)*, Mae Mercer *(Mama Mosebery)*, Diana Scarwid *(Frieda)*, Barbara Steele *(Josephine)*, Matthew Anton *(Red Top)*, Seret Scott *(Flora)*, Cheryl Markowitz *(Gussie)*, Susan Manskey *(Fanny)*, Laura Zimmerman *(Agnes)*, Miz Mary *(Odette)*, Don Hood *(Alfred Fuller)*, Pat Perkins *(Ola Mae)*, Von Eric Perkins *(Nonny)*, Sasha Holliday *(Justine)*, Lisa Shames *(Antonia)*, Harry Braden *(Harry)*, Philip H. Sizeler *(Senator)*, Don K. Lutenbacher *(Violet's 1st Customer)*.

Everyone knows that jazz came up the river from New Orleans but few people know the reason. Many of the musicians worked for brothels in Storyville, that area which seemed to have been built for one reason only: pleasure. When the U.S. secretary of the Navy thought that too many of his men were spending too much time in the neighborhood, he ordered the place shuttered, and since the musicians had no place else to work, they came north to establish their music in the Midwest and, later, New York. Malle's look at life in a Storyville brothel annoyed many people because he refused to take a stand and just presented the facts as he knew them through the original material by Al Rose, the full title of which is: *Storyville, New Orleans: Being an Authentic Account of the Notorious Redlight District*. It's all seen with the eyes and memory of a 12-year-old prostitute (Shields), the daughter of Sarandon. Because there had been such a brouhaha about child pornography and child abuse, the film was banned in a few venues, but the truth is that the picture is mild by comparison to many others. Faye runs a plush brothel and one of her favorites is Sarandon. She gives birth to a son, much to the delight of all the other women and of her daughter, Shields, who has grown up in the house and has no idea who her father is. Sarandon tells the "johns" that Shields is her sister, a virgin, because she wants to get out of the profession and eventually marry. Shields takes everything around her with a sweet naivete. When that's the only life you know, it doesn't seem all that unique. She becomes both friend and surrogate child to all the other women, Scarwid, Steele, Scott, Markowitz, and Zimmerman. She watches Graham do her voodoo and loves to hear Fargas play his barrelhouse piano (in an imitation of Jelly Roll Morton). Shields is not the only child living in the large house and her best pal of the others is Anton. Carradine (playing a real-life character named E.J. Bellocq) is a photographer who uses the women as models for his prints. He loves Shields, thereby causing Sarandon some pain. Carradine is not at all desirous of their wares, just contents himself with taking photographs. (The truth was that Bellocq was barely five feet tall, had a pointed head, and may have been totally asexual.) Since Shields is as yet unsullied, her virginity is a valuable possession, and when the moment arrives for it to end, she is sold for a huge amount, $400, to Lutenbacher. After she has pretended to have fainted from the experience, Lutenbacher leaves hurriedly and Faye keeps selling Shields as a first-timer. Hood is a regular customer of Sarandon and loves her enough to propose marriage. Sarandon leaves with her infant son and Shields stays behind, a gesture Shields resents bitterly. Shields begins to act up, then runs away from the brothel to Carradine's home where they are soon lovers and she becomes the focus for his camera. Soon enough, Shields is making childish demands and Carradine tosses her out. By this time, Storyville has been shuttered and Faye's mind has cracked. Fargas takes his 10 talented fingers to Chicago and Shields has no place to live. Carradine proposes marriage and they tie the knot in the presence of the other women. No sooner is the license signed, when Shields begins her old tricks and her spoiled attitude annoys Carradine. Sarandon and Hood return to New Orleans with the baby and ask Shields to move in with them and make something of herself by attending school. Shields wants to stay with Carradine and is torn by the offer of having her marriage annulled and going into the straight life. In the end, Shields chooses to be with her mother and Carradine is destroyed by her departure. The final shot is a family portrait, taken by Hood, of Sarandon, Shields, and the baby and, looking at it, no one would ever know where they came from and how they spent their lives. The subject matter is shocking, but Malle and his brilliant Swedish cinematographer Nykvist handle it with such taste and such a matter-of-fact fashion that it never goes over the edge. The photography is lush and warm; each shot looks like a painting. The movie is slow in places and takes a bit too long establishing moods, but you'll remember it long after you've forgotten many others. Shields' mother was attacked for allowing her 12-year-old model-daughter to pose in the nude and to be exploited, and they feared that the child would be corrupted. Evidently, none of that came to pass and Shields has grown up to be a well-balanced young woman, albeit an ordinary actress. So far, PRETTY BABY has been her best work.

p&d, Louis Malle; w, Polly Platt (based on a story by Platt, Malle (from the book *Storyville, New Orleans: Being an Authentic Account of the Notorious Redlight District*); ph, Sven Nykvist (Metrocolor); ed, Suzanne Baron, Suzanne Fenn; md, Jerry Wexler; prod d, Trevor Williams; set d, Jim Berkey; cos, Mina Mittelman; spec eff, Maureen Lambray.

Historical Drama **Cas.** **(PR:O MPAA:R)**

PRETTY BOY FLOYD½** (1960) 96m Le-Sac/Continental bw

John Ericson *(Pretty Boy Floyd)*, Barry Newman *(Al Riccardo)*, Joan Harvey *(Lil Courtney)*, Herbert Evers *(Blackie Faulkner)*, Carl York *(Curly)*, Roy Fant *(Jed Watkins)*, Shirley Smith *(Ann Courtney)*, Phil Kenneally *(Baker)*, Norman Burton *(Bill Courtney)*, Charles Bradswell *(Neil Trane)*, Truman Smith *(Mr. Whitney)*, Ted Chapman *(Grindon, Jr.)*, Leo Bloom *(Ed Courtney)*, Casey Peyson *(Gail)*, Effie Afton *(Ma Parks)*, Peter Falk *(Shorty Walters)*, Paul Lipson *(Mike Clouder)*, Jim Dukas *(Big Dutch)*, Dina Paisner *(Lonely Woman)*, Gene O'Donnell *(Oil Field Boss)*, Al Lewis *(Machine Gun Manny)*.

The life and times of infamous Oklahoma murderer and bank robber Charles Arthur "Pretty Boy" Floyd are chronicled in this surprisingly accurate screen biography featuring Ericson as the legendary outlaw. The film begins as Ericson is released from prison after having served time for a stickup. Determined to go straight, he gets a job working on an oil rig. Unfortunately, he takes up with a married woman and her vengeance-seeking husband gets him fired by exposing his prison record. Upon returning home to Oklahoma, Ericson is shocked to learn that his father has been murdered by a farmer who has had a long-standing feud with the family. Vowing vengeance, Ericson tracks the farmer down and murders him. From then on he returns to a life of crime with a vengeance, drifting from one bank robbery to the next, leaving bodies in his wake. Along the way he picks up several different partners (York, Newman, Kenneally) and another girl friend, Harvey, who just happens to be the widow of a stoolie Ericson has murdered. Months of bank robbing and killing soon lead Ericson to the Kansas City Massacre where he participates in the slaughter of two FBI agents and one local lawman (it was actually one FBI agent and three local lawmen) while trying to free a fellow gangster. During the bloody battle the gangster they were trying to free is killed and Ericson becomes the FBI's Public Enemy No. 1 (although Floyd denied to his dying day that he had anything to do with the massacre and there is evidence to support him). After this sensational crime, Ericson is forced to flee to Ohio where he hides out on a farm near East Liverpool. The FBI is right behind him and on October 22, 1934, Ericson is gunned down by the lawmen. Although PRETTY BOY FLOYD was a low-budget effort, director-writer Leder managed to evoke the period with a certain amount of skill. The fast-paced screenplay hums along from one incident to the next, aided by old newsreel footage of the Oklahoma farm community that spawned Floyd. The protection provided by Floyd's friends and neighbors is also documented, as is his delusion that he was some sort of modern-day Robin Hood. While far from a cinematic masterpiece, PRETTY BOY FLOYD is a well-crafted, fairly insightful, low-budget crime film that will please fans of the genre.

p, Monroe Sachson; d&w, Herbert J. Leder; ph, Chuck Austin; m, Del Sirino, William Sanford; ed, Ralph Rosenblum; cos, Bill Walstrom.

Crime/Biography **(PR:C-O MPAA:NR)**

PRETTY BUT WICKED zero (1965, Braz.) 90m Victoria Films-Times Film bw (BONITINHA MAS ORDINARIA)

Jece Valadao *(Edgar)*, Odete Lara *(Rita)*, Lia Rossi *(Maria Cecilia)*, Fregolente *(Hector Wernek)*, Andre Villion *(Perrault)*.

Valadao loves his neighbor (Lara), but a friend tries to bribe him into marrying his daughter (Rossi). The latter's sexual appetite disgusts him, sending him back to his neighbor.

p, Joffre Rodrigues, Jece Valadao; d, J.P. de Carvalho; w, Valadao; ph, Amleto Daisse; m, Carlos Lyra; ed, Rafael Velledde.

Drama **(PR:O MPAA:NR)**

PRETTY MAIDS ALL IN A ROW½** (1971) 92m MGM c

Rock Hudson *(Michael "Tiger" McDrew)*, Angie Dickinson *(Miss Smith)*, Telly Savalas *(Capt. Sam Surcher)*, John David Carson *(Ponce de Leon Harper)*, Roddy McDowall *(Mr. Proffer)*, Keenan Wynn *(Chief John Poldaski)*, James Doohan *(Follo)*, William Campbell *(Grady)*, Susan Tolsky *(Miss Harriet Craymire)*, Barbara Leigh *(Jean McDrew)*, Gretchen Burrell *(Marjorie)*, Amy Eccles *(Hilda Lee)*, JoAnna Cameron *(Yvonne Millick)*, Margaret Markov *(Polly)*, June Fairchild *(Sonya "Sonny" Swingle)*, Joy Bang *(Rita)*, Brenda Sykes *(Pamela Wilcox)*, Diane Sherry *(Sheryl)*, Phillip Brown *(Jim Green)*, Mark Malmborg *(Dink)*, Kyle Johnson *(Dave)*, Warren Seabury *(Harold)*, Gary Tigerman, Tim Ray, Alberto Isaac *(Boys)*, Dawn Roddenberry *(Girl)*, Stephanie Mizrahi *(Tiger's Daughter)*, Larry Marmorstein *(TV Reporter)*, Estrellita Rania *(Hilda's Mother)*, Jomarie Ward *(Gym Teacher)*, Guy Remsen, Joe Quinn *(Board Members)*, Orville Sherman *(Pastor)*, Judy Michie, Adriana Bentley, Joyce Williams, Chris [Allen] Woodley, Fredricka Myers, Linda Morand, Topo Swope, Diane Lambert *(Other Pretty Maids)*, Otis Greene *(Police Doctor)*.

In this attempt at black comedy, Hudson plays a football coach-guidance counselor who spends his time seducing pretty students. One cheerleader threatens to expose him, so he kills her. He seduces another young girl, who threatens to go to the police about the murder if he doesn't divorce his wife and marry her, so he kills her, too. He decides to take Carson under his wing and teach him the art of being a Casanova. But first the sex-shy Carson must be initiated into manhood, so Hudson talks Dickinson into being the initiator. Most of the plot consists of Hudson's rendezvous with girl students, and then their eventual murders. The end of the plot has Hudson driving his car into the sea, his body never found, and Carson returning to high school to pick up on what's left of Hudson's harem. This film was one of many attempts by Hudson to break out of his PILLOW TALK mold.

p, Gene Roddenberry; d, Roger Vadim; w, Roddenberry (based on the novel by Francis Pollini); ph, Charles Rosher (Metrocolor); m, Lalo Schifrin; ed, Bill Brame; art d, George W. Davis, Preston Ames; set d, Robert R. Benton, Charles R. Pierce; cos, William Ware Theiss; m/l, "Chilly Winds" (performed by The Osmonds), Schifrin, Mike Curb; makeup, Allan Snyder.

Comedy **(PR:O MPAA:R)**

PRETTY POISON*½** (1968) 89m Lawrence Turman-Molino/FOX c

Anthony Perkins *(Dennis Pitt)*, Tuesday Weld *(Sue Ann Stepanek)*, Beverly Garland *(Mrs. Stepanek)*, John Randolph *(Azenauer)*, Dick O'Neill *(Bud Munsch)*, Clarice Blackburn *(Mrs. Bronson)*, Joseph Bova *(Pete)*, Ken Kercheval *(Harry Jackson)*, Don Fellows *(Detective)*, Parker Fennelly *(Night Watchman)*, Paul Larson *(Mrs. Stepanek's Boy Friend)*, Tim Callahan *(Plainclothesman)*, George Fisher *(Burly Man)*, William Sorrells *(Cop at Beanery)*, Dan Morgan, Mark Dawson, Gil Rogers *(Men in Police Station)*, John Randolph Jones, Maurice Ottinger *(Highway Policemen)*, Don Fellows, Tom Gorman *(Detectives)*, Bill Fort, Ed Wagner *(Cops)*, George Ryan's Winslow High-Steppers.

It's not easy to seriously take the work of an actress whose first name is "Tuesday" or "Piper" or even "Pippa," but the truth is that Ms. Weld, Ms. Laurie, and Ms. Scott are all superior players who have been saddled with strange monickers. In PRETTY POISON, Tuesday Weld is nothing short of sensational as she portrays a "Bad Seed" who has grown up to be a malevolent flower. Semple, who would later opt for the big money by going to work for Di Laurentiis and writing KING KONG, HURRICANE, and FLASH GORDON, left the "Batman" TV show to strike out in moviedom, and he hit a home run with this tight script based on Stephen Geller's novel. Perkins is again the psychopath. He's being released from custody after several years. His aunt had discovered him playing sex games with a little girl and she beat him. His response was to burn down the house with her in it, although his contention was that he didn't know of her presence in the residence. He's paroled in the care of Randolph, who helps him get a job in a lumber business. Perkins lives modestly in a trailer and his hobby is photography. He has a miniature camera and he loves snapping shots with it. It's a very dull town and there's not much activity of any kind. Perkins meets pert high schooler Weld and regales her with stories about his being an agent for the CIA and that he is investigating the lumber company as part of a hush-hush operation. Weld has grown up watching spy movies and various espionage TV shows and she apparently believes him. Perkins says that the lumber firm may be poisoning the water supply in the town and appeals to her for help, which she agrees to give. Part of her loyalty to him includes making love, an act to which she also cheerfully agrees. Weld's mother is Garland, a stern parent who keeps a tight leash on Weld, and, upon seeing right through Perkins, she forbids Weld to go out with him. Perkins is fired and he and Weld go to the lumber mill. The guard spots them trespassing and Perkins is all for racing out of there but the sweet-faced Weld has other ideas and she kills the guard by smashing in his head with a metal tool; then she puts his body under the bridge over the river. The guard's body is soon found and Perkins is immediately suspected as the killer because of his unstable background. Weld and Perkins prepare to leave for Mexico where they plan on getting married and Garland arrives at the house and attempts to stop them. Weld has stolen the dead guard's weapon and hands it to Perkins to shoot Garland. Perkins can't bring himself to fire, so Weld takes the gun and shoots her mother down, then orders Perkins to dump the body in the river. Perkins takes Garland's body in his car but cannot do the deed, so he drives to police headquarters and gives himself up. But Weld has anticipated that and she is busily telling the cops that Perkins corrupted her, killed Garland and the security guard, and that she was innocent of everything. Perkins listens in bewilderment as she sells him out and his only response is to say that he still loves her. Perkins is in prison for a year and Randolph comes to see him. Randolph is a bright man and never once did he believe Weld's story, but Perkins takes it all with a shrug and says that the truth would never be believed so he didn't even bother. He warns Randolph that Weld is a "pretty poison" who will eventually show her true colors. Weld is now living with foster parents when she meets Kercheval, a new laborer at the lumber mill. She tells him that this family is strict and that she just *has* to get away from them. As she begins convincing Kercheval, she is being watched very closely by Randolph. The picture was made in Great Barrington, Massachusetts, and director Black has not done anything this good since. He was chosen for the project after having made a superior short, SKATER-DATER, and his work was excellent.

p, Marshal Backlar, Noel Black; d, Black; w, Lorenzo Semple, Jr. (based on the novel *She Let Him Continue* by Stephen Geller); ph, David Quaid (DeLuxe Color); m, Johnny Mandel; ed, William Ziegler; art d, Jack Martin Smith, Harold Michelson; set d, John Mortensen; cos, Ann Roth; spec eff, Ralph Winigar, Billy King; makeup, Robert Jiras.

Crime Drama **(PR:C-O MPAA:NR)**

PRETTY POLLY (SEE: MATTER OF INNOCENCE, A, 1968, Brit.)

PREVIEW MURDER MYSTERY½** (1936) 60m PAR bw

Reginald Denny *(Johnny Morgan)*, Frances Drake *(Peggy Madison)*, Gail Patrick *(Claire Woodward)*, Rod LeRocque *(Neil DuBeck)*, Ian Keith *(E. Gordon Smith)*, George Barbier *(Jerome Hewitt)*, Conway Tearle *(Edwin Strange)*, Thomas Jackson *(Lt. McKane)*, Jack Raymond *(Tyson)*, Eddie Dunn *(Tub Wilson)*, Bryant Washburn *(Jennings)*, Lee Shumway *(Chief of Police)*, Chester Conklin *(Himself)*, Jack Mulhall *(Screen Heavy)*, Henry Kleinbach [Brandon] *(Screen Actor)*.

A fine cast is assembled in this routine murder mystery which identifies the killer as a man supposedly dead. Florey's fine direction and a well-handled script adds to the movie set location. Among the satirical elements in this Hollywood mystery was the appearance of Keith, as a director who becomes one of the mysterious victims in a costume that is a derivative of eccentricities of prominent directors of the time, having riding pants like those Cecil B. DeMille wore, a whistle like Rouben Mamoulian, a filter glass like that of King Vidor, and a leather bound stick similar to the one which Josef von Sternberg carried around with him.

p, Harold Hurley; d, Robert Florey; w, Brian Marlow, Robert Yost (based on the story by Garnett Weston); ph, Karl Struss; ed, James Smith; art d, Hans Dreier, Earl Hedrick.

Mystery   **(PR:A MPAA:NR)**

PRICE OF A SONG, THE**   (1935, Brit.) 67m FOX bw

Campbell Gullan (Arnold Grierson), Marjorie Corbett (Margaret Nevern), Eric Maturin (Nevern), Gerald Fielding (Michael Hardwicke), Dora Barton (Letty Grierson), Charles Mortimer (Oliver Bloom), Oriel Ross (Elsie), Henry Cains (Stringer), Sybil Grove (Mrs. Bancroft), Felix Aylmer (Graham), Cynthia Stock (Mrs. Bush), Mavis Clair (Maudie Bancroft).

Intriguing crime drama in which Cullan plays a hard-up bookmaker who persuades his daughter to marry a songwriter (Maturin) in the hopes that the new son-in-law can help him out of a financial bind. Gullan plots to murder Maturin when his daughter opts for divorce, so that he will still have access to the money. Unfortunately, Gullan's plan fails once he talks about a tune the songwriter failed to publish before his death.

p&d, Michael Powell; w, Anthony Gittins; ph, Jimmy Wilson.

Crime   **(PR:A MPAA:NR)**

PRICE OF FEAR, THE**½   (1956) 79m UNIV bw

Merle Oberon (Jessica Warren), Lex Barker (Dave Barrett), Charles Drake (Pete Carroll), Gia Scala (Nina Ferranti), Warren Stevens (Frankie Adair), Phillip Pine (Vince Burton), Mary Field (Ruth McNab), Dan Riss (Lt. Jim Walsh), Konstantin Shayne (Bolasny), Stafford Repp (Johnny McNab), Tim Sullivan (Lou Belden).

Barker is framed for two murders he didn't commit. One of them is a hit-and-run, of which Oberon is guilty and trying to cover up. The other is a murder at a dog-racing track. Fleeing from the gangsters, Barker hops in Oberon's car and is eventually arrested, but the police are able to untangle the events. An interesting idea which the plot doesn't quite pull off.

p, Howard Christie; d, Abner Biberman; w, Robert Tallman (based on the story by Dick Irving Hyland); ph, Irving Glassberg; ed, Ray Snyder; md, Joseph Gershenson; art d, Alexander Golitzen, Robert Clatworthy; cos, Jay A. Morley, Jr.

Crime Drama   **(PR:A MPAA:NR)**

PRICE OF FLESH, THE*   (1962, Fr.) 89m Horizons Cinematographiques/Triad-Audubon bw (DETOURNEMENT DE MINEURES)

Helene Chanel (Christine), Frank Villard (Daniel), Louis Seigner (Max), Michel Roux (Jean), Josette Demay (Gisele), Maria Vincent (Conchita), Nathalie Nattier (Michka), Madeleine Barbulee (Christine's Mother), Robert Burnier (Christine's Father), Jean Payen (Philippe), Yvette Sautereau, Gib Grossac.

Chanel gets mixed up in a crowd which has her posing for nude photos and then sending her into prostitution in Tangiers. Roux, a journalist and fiance of Chanel's sister, hunts her down and returns her to her family.

p, Edgar Roulleau; d, Walter Kapps; w, Pierre Chicherio, Bernard Dimey, Gerard Gohier, Georges Tabet; ph, Jacques Klein; m, Michel Magne; ed, Francoise Diot; art d, Claude Bouxin.

Drama   **(PR:O MPAA:NR)**

PRICE OF FOLLY, THE*   (1937, Brit.) 52m Welwyn/Pathe bw

Leonora Corbett (Christine), Colin Keith-Johnson (Martin), Leslie Perrins (Owen), Judy Kelly (Frances), Andrea Malandrinos (Gomez), Wally Patch, The Trocadero Girls.

Ill-conceived story about a man who becomes the victim of a blackmail scheme. A woman with whom he was having an affair supposedly is murdered, making the man easy prey for a blackmailer. When he gets desperate for money, the man bets and loses his last bit of money at the track. He kills the blackmailer the next time he comes for a payment, and then discovers that the girl never was killed in the first place. This was one of the first screenwriting efforts for Lee-Thompson, who would have a long and illustrious career lasting into the 1970s as both a writer and director. He worked on such films as THE GUNS OF NAVARONE (1961) and THE YELLOW BALLOON (1952). Although the idea for THE PRICE OF FOLLY was good, the hapless manner in which it was brought to the screen did little to foreshadow the future of Lee-Thompson.

p&d, Walter Summers; w, John Lee-Thompson, Summers, Ruth Landon (based on the play "Double Error" by Lee-Thompson).

Crime/Drama   **(PR:A MPAA:NR)**

PRICE OF FREEDOM, THE   (SEE: OPERATION DAYBREAK, 1976)

PRICE OF POWER, THE**   (1969, Ital./Span.) 96m Patry Film/Films Montana bw (IL PREZZO DEL POTERE)

Giuliano Gemma, Van Johnson, Warren Vanders, Fernando Rey, Maria Jesus Cuadra, Ray Saunders.

Gemma puts down a Confederate attempt to restart the Civil War, while trying to avenge his father's death. Mixed in with the rise of the South is the assassination of President Garfield, which here bears a strong resemblance to Kennedy's death, including the murder of the accused while transferring him from one jail to another.

This spaghetti western uses many of the same sets and cast as Sergio Leone's ONCE UPON A TIME IN THE WEST. Originally released at 122 minutes.

p, Bianco Manini; d, Tonino Valerii; w, Massimo Patrizi; ph, Stelvio Massi.

Western   **(PR:C MPAA:NR)**

PRICE OF SILENCE, THE*   (1960, Brit.) 73m Eternal-GN/Exclusive International bw

Gordon Jackson (Roger Fenton), June Thorburn (Audrey Truscott), Maya Koumani (Maria Shipley), Terence Alexander (John Braine), Mary Clare (Mrs. West), Victor Brooks (Superintendent Wilson), Joan Heal (Ethel), Olive Sloane (Landlady), Llewellyn Rees (H. G. Shipley), Annette Kerr (Miss Collins), Norman Shelley (Councilor Forbes), Sam Kydd (Slug), Norman Mitchell.

Jackson plays an ex-con trying to make it in the legitimate world. He changes his name to cover his past as a thief and convict, then obtains a job at a firm that caters to rich clients. Jackson fits in with this new atmosphere quite easily, until his boss' wife (Koumani) begins making passes at him. Wishing to avoid any conflict, he keeps her at a safe distance, only to have his old cellmate Slug (Kydd) show up and threaten to expose him. Kydd blackmails Jackson, and, as a result of his excessive greediness, murders one of the firm's rich clients, making Jackson look like the culprit. When Koumani refuses to inform the police that she was with Jackson during the crime, the ex-con is sent to jail, only to be set free with a contrived ending that allows him to marry the girl of his dreams, Thorburn. Unconvincing script, which lacks cohesiveness and an efficient development of characters.

p, Maurice J. Wilson; d, Montgomery Tully; w, Wilson (based on the novel One Step from Murder by Laurence Meynell); ph, Geoffrey Faithfull.

Crime/Drama   **(PR:A MPAA:NR)**

PRICE OF THINGS, THE*   (1930, Brit.) 84m UA bw

Elissa Landi (Anthea Dane), Stewart Rome (Dick Hammond), Walter Tennyson (John Courtenay Dare), Alfred Tennyson (Courtenay John Dare), Mona Goya (Natasha Boleska), Dino Galvani (Hunya), Marjorie Loring (Daphne), Muriel Minty, David Parr, Vincent Sternroyd.

Royal twin brothers help each other out of women troubles until one day one twin stands in at the other's wedding. The "newlyweds" soon fall in love, while the intended groom has a fatal affair with a shady lady spy. Whatever the price, this one's not worth it.

p&d, Elinor Glyn; w, Lady Rhys Williams (based on the novel by Glyn); ph, Charles Rosher.

Crime Drama   **(PR:A MPAA:NR)**

PRICE OF WISDOM, THE*   (1935, Brit.) 64m British and Dominions/ PAR bw

Mary Jerrold (Mary Temple), Roger Livesey (Peter North), Mary Newland (Jean Temple), Robert Rendel (Alfred Blake), Eric Cowley (Col. Layton), Ann Codrington (Miss Stokes), Ivor Barnard (Bonny), Cicily Oates (Pollitt).

Romantic drama about a country girl, Newland, who finds love and adventure in the big city. She wins the hearts of both a father and his son, the former a successful businessman and the latter an inventor. Newland shows her knack for business when she creates a handbag that sells like hotcakes.

p, Anthony Havelock-Allan; d, Reginald Denham; w, Basil Mason, George Dewhurst (based on the play by Lionel Brown).

Drama   **(PR:A MPAA:NR)**

PRIDE AND PREJUDICE****   (1940) 117m MGM bw

Greer Garson (Elizabeth Bennet), Laurence Olivier (Mr. Darcy), Mary Boland (Mrs. Bennet), Edna May Oliver (Lady Catherine de Bourgh), Maureen O'Sullivan (Jane Bennet), Ann Rutherford (Lydia Bennet), Frieda Inescort (Miss Caroline Bingley), Edmund Gwenn (Mr. Bennet), Karen Morley (Charlotte Lucas), Heather Angel (Kitty Bennet), Marsha Hunt (Mary Bennet), Bruce Lester (Mr. Bingley), Edward Ashley (Mr. Wickham), Melville Cooper (Mr. Collins), Marten Lamont (Mr. Denny), E.E. Clive (Sir William Lucas), May Beatty (Mrs. Phillips), Marjorie Wood (Lady Lucas), Gia Kent (Miss de Bourgh), Gerald Oliver-Smith (Fitz William), Vernon Downing (Capt. Carter), Buster Slaven (Beck's Assistant), Wyndham Standing, Lowden Adams (Committeemen), Clara Reid (Maid in Parsonage), Karen Morley (Mrs. Charlotte Collins), Claude Allister (Yardgoods Clerk).

Making a "classic" into a film is always a ticklish situation because so many people have read the original material that there are bound to be criticisms. That was not the case in this superior adaptation of Jane Austen's comedy/drama of manners and morals in the late 1700s. She'd written her book from 1793 to about 1797, but it was many more years until she found someone willing to publish it in 1813. It then took an additional 122 years for Helen Jerome's play to open in New York. Even though the book was, by then, in the "public domain" (which means that there was no royalty to pay), MGM acquired Jerome's play, which was the basis for the excellent screenplay by noted author Aldous Huxley, and Jane Murfin. Boland and Gwenn are a married couple in the early 1800s who have five daughters and must marry them off before too long or they'll have no money to live on in their dotage. Gwenn is embarrassed by Boland's obvious ploys in securing husbands for Garson, Rutherford, O'Sullivan, Hunt, and Angel. Boland can't stop talking and that works against what she wants for her girls. She's a shopkeeper's daughter and her husband is a gentleman of the old school. They have no son and a modest little sum of money may just go to Cooper, a mean cousin, if no progeny are forthcoming. When two good-looking bachelors move into the town, Olivier and Lester, hearts go fluttering all over the place. Olivier, however, is an arrogant type and not at all interested in the hayseeds of the tiny village. Garson wants to get some revenge on him for his attitude, and when they are at a dance, she won't dance with him. This, of course, intrigues Olivier. At the same time, O'Sullivan and Lester have met and fallen in love. Lester's sister, Inescort, doesn't stop reminding him that there is a great chasm between their classes. When Olivier adds his agreement to Inescort, Lester gives in and leaves for London, with O'Sullivan in tears. Later, Garson meets Olivier once more and he admits that he is fascinated by her, then proposes marriage. At first she is taken by this, but he puts his foot in his mouth and says that he will marry her, despite the disdain he has for her family and her station. This turns her away from him and she rejects the chance to marry. Cooper is toadying up to Olivier, a peeress who happens to be Olivier's aunt, and he comes to visit her as well as to keep an eye on Gwenn's fortunes. When it seems that the old man is in good health, Cooper also proposes marriage to Garson but she'd sooner kiss a frog. Unknown to anyone, Rutherford has been seeing Ashley, a soldier who is thought to be somewhat low in class. The two of them elope (but not necessarily to get married) and there is a scandal in the town. Olivier steps in, finds Ashley, and gives him some money, thus pushing Ashley into making it legal with Rutherford. Olivier and Garson are reunited and will also marry, thus sending the flighty Boland into paroxysms of gaiety, as it seems she is now beginning to get her daughters off her hands. The film is filled with insights, laughter, satire, and an overwhelming feeling of fun. The background of how the picture was made is as follows: Thalberg was running MGM and thought his wife, Norma Shearer, might make a fine Elizabeth. After he passed away, the studio considered Gable as Darcy but he backed off. Melvyn Douglas was considered briefly, as was Robert Donat, with George Cukor to direct. After Donat went back to stage acting in England, Olivier was hired and he wanted his amour, Vivian Leigh, to co-star but Mayer preferred Garson. There was talk of a musical version in 1947 and two scripts were done by Sally Benson, then Sidney Sheldon (yes, *that* Sidney Sheldon), but it never came to pass for the screen, although a stage version was later done. This was the third time Garson worked with Olivier. She'd been in the London production of "Golden Arrow" in 1935 and, in one of the earliest BBC TV transmissions, played Juliet to his Romeo. After Olivier completed his work in this film, he went back to England with Leigh. They'd been in the U.S. for two years and made cinematic history with WUTHERING HEIGHTS, REBECCA, THAT HAMILTON WOMAN, and GONE WITH THE WIND included in their resumes.

p, Hunt Stromberg; d, Robert Z. Leonard; w, Aldous Huxley, Jane Murfin (based on the play by Helen Jerome and the novel by Jane Austen); ph, Karl Freund; m, Herbert Stothart; ed, Robert J. Kern; art d, Cedric Gibbons, Paul Groesse; set d, Edwin B. Willis; cos, Adrian, Gile Steele; ch, Ernst Matray; makeup, Jack Dawn.

Historical Comedy/Drama   Cas.   (PR:A MPAA:NR)

PRIDE AND THE PASSION, THE**½   (1957) 132m UA c

Cary Grant (*Capt. Anthony Trumbull*), Frank Sinatra (*Miguel*), Sophia Loren (*Juana*), Theodore Bikel (*Gen. Jouvet*), John Wengraf (*Sermaine*), Jay Novello (*Ballinger*), Jose Nieto (*Carlos*), Carlos Larranga (*Jose*), Philip Van Zandt (*Vidal*), Paco El Laberinto (*Manolo*), Julian Ugarte (*Enrique*), Felix De Pomes (*Bishop*), Carlos Casaravilla (*Leonardo*), Juan Olaguivel (*Ramon*), Nana De Herrera (*Maria*), Carlos De Mendoza (*Francisco*), Luis Guedes (*French Soldier*).

This splashy, implausible epic was done on a grand scale by producer-director Kramer (one of his rare non-message films) and it reeks of melodrama and unbelievable dialog. But, as spectacles go, THE PRIDE AND THE PASSION is hard to ignore. A huge cannon is abandoned by the retreating Spanish army in 1810 during the Peninsular War and Grant, a British naval officer and artillery expert, is ordered to retrieve it. He enlists the aid of guerrilla leader Sinatra and the cannon is painstakingly lifted from the bottom of a gorge and repaired. But instead of turning over the cannon to Grant, Sinatra insists that it be used to bombard the French occupying the fortress at Avila. Grant reluctantly agrees to accompany Sinatra and his patriotic followers and fire the cannon once it arrives at its destination. Thus begins a marathon trip across Spain as the insurgents drag the cannon around French lines and through cities with the help of the Spanish people, even hiding the monster cannon in a church at one point so that it can be repaired. Grant, during the trip, is attracted to sultry Loren, Sinatra's camp-following paramour, and she to him, but it's a star-crossed romance. She is killed in the assault on Avila as is diehard Sinatra. Grant carries Sinatra's body into the conquered city at the finish to lay the patriot's remains at the base of a fountain in the town square. Grant saunters through his thankless part with a smirk on his face and Sinatra affects the worst Spanish accent on record, while Loren's Italian accent is so thick that it's next to impossible to understand what she is saying. Most of her acting here is done with a low-cut blouse exposing her enormous breasts. The whole thing is a miscast mess into which Kramer pumped $6 million, with Loren receiving $200,000 for lurching across the landscape. But there are thousands upon thousands of extras—count 'em.

p&d, Stanley Kramer; w, Edna Anhalt, Edward Anhalt (based on the novel *The Gun* by C.S. Forester); ph, Franz Planer (VistaVision, Technicolor); m, George Antheil; ed, Frederic Knudtson, Ellsworth Hoagland; prod d, Rudolph Sternad; md, Ernest Gold; art d, Fernando Carrere, Gil Parrondo; cos, Joe King; spec eff, Willis Cook, Maurice Ayers; ch, Paco Reyes; m/l, Peggy Lee; makeup, Bernard Ponedel, John O'Gorman, Jose Ma Sanchez; tech adv, Lt. Col. Luis Cano.

Historical Epic   Cas.   (PR:C MPAA:NR)

PRIDE OF KENTUCKY   (SEE: STORY OF SEABISCUIT, THE, 1949)

PRIDE OF MARYLAND**   (1951) 60m REP bw

Stanley Clements (*Frankie*), Peggy Stewart (*Christine*), Frankie Darro (*Steve*), Joe Sawyer (*Knuckles*), Robert H. Barrat (*Col. Harding*), Harry Shannon (*Walter Shannon*), Duncan Richardson (*Stevie*), Stanley Logan (*Sir Thomas Asbury*), Joseph Crehan (*Mr. Herndon*), Emmett Vogan (*Dr. Paley*), Clyde Cook (*Fred Leach*), Donald Kerr (*Referee*), Guy Bellis (*Lord Blanford*).

Clements is a young jockey whose new style of "crouch" riding brings him fame and fortune, but soon finds that he is barred from the track. The finale has him returning and building up his purse even more.

p, William Lackey; d, Philip Ford; w, John K. Butler; ph, John MacBurnie; m, Stanley Wilson; ed, Harold Minter; art d, Frank Hotaling.

Drama   (PR:A MPAA:NR)

PRIDE OF ST. LOUIS, THE***½   (1952) 93m FOX bw

Dan Dailey (*Dizzy Dean*), Joanne Dru (*Patricia Nash Dean*), Richard Hylton (*Johnny Kendall*), Richard Crenna (*Paul Dean*), Hugh Sanders (*Horst*), James Brown (*Moose*), Leo T. Cleary (*Manager Ed Monroe*), Kenny Williams (*Castleman*), John McKee (*Delaney*), Stuart Randall (*Frankie Frisch*), William Frambes (*Herbie*), Damian O'Flynn (*Johnnie Bishop*), Cliff Clark (*Pittsburgh Coach*), Fred Graham (*Alexander*), Billy Nelson (*Chicago Manager*), Pattee Chapman (*Ella*), Richard Reeves (*Connelly*), Bob Nichols (*Eddie*), John Duncan (*Western Union Boy*), Clyde Trumbull (*Mike*), John Butler (*Waiter*), Freeman Lusk (*Doctor*), Jack Rice (*Voorhees*), Al Green (*Joe*), Phil Van Zandt (*Louis*), Victor Sutherland (*Kendall, Sr.*), Kathryn Carl (*Mrs. Martin*), George MacDonald (*Roscoe*), Joan Sudlow (*Miss Johnson*), Frank Scannell (*Chicago 3rd Base Coach*), Larry Thor, John Wald, Hank Weaver, William Forman, Jack Sherman, Tom Hanlon (*Announcers*), Chet Huntley (*Tom Weaver*), John Doucette (*Benny*), Harris Brown (*Hotel Clerk*).

No one fractured the English language as a sports announcer more than Dizzy Dean, but he was also one of the most wonderful baseball legends in the history of the sport and this film captures the flavor and color of the great pitcher. Dailey is a standout as Dean, the Ozark hillbilly with a lightning delivery who struggled up from poverty to win fame as a great hurler. Dailey is shown being discovered in semipro ball while playing for the Houston Buffalos, more as a lark than as a profession. He goes to work for the St. Louis Cardinals, pitching his heart out and, with his brother Paul (well played by Crenna), leading his team to a World Series championship. A warm and humorous subplot showing Dailey's courtship of Dean's wife, played expertly by Dru, adds depth and feeling to this good-natured story. Director Jones, who does a commendable job of mixing fact and a little fiction, does not fail to include the wonderful Dizzy Dean pranks, like the time he had his team sit down on the playing field while he struck out all three opposing hitters, much to the consternation of his manager. Tover's camerawork is outstanding and the special effects by Sersen cleverly work in newsreel footage with the theatrical side. For baseball lovers, this film is a must.

p, Jules Schermer; d, Harmon Jones; w, Herman J. Mankiewicz (based on a story by Guy Trosper); ph, Leo Tover; m, Arthur Lange; ed, Robert Simpson; md, Lionel Newman; art d, Lyle Wheeler, Addison Hehr; spec eff, Fred Sersen.

Sports Drama/Biography   (PR:AA MPAA:NR)

PRIDE OF THE ARMY**   (1942) 65m MON bw (AKA: WAR DOGS)

Billy Lee (*Billy*), Addison Richards (*Freeman*), Kay Linaker (*Joan*), Bradley Page (*Judge*), Herbert Rawlinson (*Titus*), Bryant Washburn (*Colonel*), John Berkes (*Stoner*), Ace the Dog.

Little Billy Lee gives his dog to the Dogs for Defense, a government organization that recruited and trained dogs for the Army during WW II. The pooch is assigned to protect a defense plant from saboteurs. Also working at the plant is Lee's leathery, hard-drinking father. When an attempt to blow the plant up is made, both dad and dog risk their lives to prevent a disaster.

p, George W. Weeks; d, S. Roy Luby; w, John Vlahos; ph, Robert Kline; ed, Roy Claire.

Drama   (PR:AA MPAA:NR)

PRIDE OF THE BLUE GRASS**   (1954) 71m AA c (GB: PRINCE OF THE BLUE GRASS)

Lloyd Bridges (*Jim*), Vera Miles (*Linda*), Margaret Sheridan (*Helen*), Arthur Shields (*Wilson*), Michael Chapin (*Danny*), Harry Cheshire (*Hunter*), Cecil Weston (*Mrs. Graves*), Emory Parnell (*Mr. Casey*), Joan Shawlee (*Mrs. Casey*), Ray Walker (*Vet*).

Miles talks stable owner Bridges into taking care of her horse. He decides to enter it in a race, but it takes a fall and breaks a leg. Miles, however, won't let the horse be destroyed, insisting on caring for it. Her tactics pay off and the horse is back on its feet, eventually winning the big race.

p, Hayes Goetz; d, William Beaudine; w, Harold Shumate (based on a story by Shumate); ph, Harry Neumann (Color Corp. of America); m, Marlin Skiles; ed, John Fuller.

Drama   (PR:A MPAA:NR)

PRIDE OF THE BLUEGRASS**   (1939) 65m WB bw

Edith Fellows (*Midge Griner*), James McCallion (*Danny Lowman*), Granville Bates (*Col. Bob Griner*), Aldrich Bowker (*Judge*), Arthur Loft (*Dave Miller*), DeWolf [William] Hopper (*Joe*), Frankie Burke (*Willie Hobson*), Fred Tozere (*1st Stranger*), Edgar Edwards (*2nd Stranger*), John Butler (*Mack Lowman*), Sam McDaniel (*Domino Jones*), Bernice Pilot (*Beverly*), Walter Fenner (*Secretary to Stewards*), Raymond Brown (*Sheriff Adams*), Lawrence Grant (*Lord Shropshire*), Sam Butler (*Gantry the Great*).

Fellows persuades her father, Bates, to enter their young colt in the Kentucky Derby. The horse's poor performance is attributed to the discovery that it is blind. With jockey McCallion, the horse is trained and entered into the Grand National. And the horse wins. A pleasant offering.

p, Bryan Foy; d, William McGann; w, Vincent Sherman (based on the story "Gantry the Great" by Sherman); ph, Ted McCord; ed, Frank Dewar.

Drama   (PR:AA MPAA:NR)

PRIDE OF THE BOWERY*½   (1941) 63m Banner/MON bw (GB: HERE WE GO AGAIN)

Leo Gorcey (*Muggs Maloney*), Bobby Jordan (*Danny*), Donald Haines (*Skinny*), Carlton Young (*Norton*), Kenneth Howell (*Al*), David Gorcey (*Peewee*), "Sunshine" Sammy Morrison (*Scruno*), Eugene Francis (*Algy*), Mary Ainsley (*Elaine*), Kenneth Harlan (*Captain Jim White*), Bobby Stone (*Willie*), Nick Stuart (*Ranger*), Lloyd Ingraham (*Doctor*), Steve Clensos (*Man*).

Dead End Kid Gorcey gets himself into a couple of mix-ups when he gets tricked into joining the conservation corps. The government group does its best to reform the two-fisted hooligan, but discovers that much of the wrong-doing in the camp cannot be blamed on Gorcey when it is proved that Stone is the trouble-maker. If this picture was a promotion for President Roosevelt's Civilian Conservation Corps (CCC), and it seems like it was, it did not do much good. It was below par for the series, and the CCC was discontinued a year later. (See BOWERY BOYS series, Index.)

p, Sam Katzman; d, Joseph H. Lewis; w, George Plympton, William Lively (based on the story by Steven Clensos); ph, Robert Cline; ed, Robert Golden; md, Johnny Lange, Lew Porter.

Comedy   **Cas.**   **(PR:A MPAA:NR)**

PRIDE OF THE BOWERY, THE, 1946   (SEE: MR. HEX, 1946)

PRIDE OF THE FORCE, THE**   (1933, Brit.) 75m BIP/Wardour bw

Leslie Fuller (*Bill/Bob Porter*), Faith Bennett (*Peggy Ramsbottom*), Alf Goddard (*Sgt. Brown*), Hal Gordon (*Dick Smith*), Nan Bates (*Sheila*), Ben Welden (*Tony Carlotti*), Frank Perfitt (*Inspector Ramsbottom*), Pat Aherne (*Max Heinrich*), King Curtis (*Steve*), Syd Courtenay, Lola Harvey, Rosie Howard, John Schofield.

Enjoyable farce with Fuller in two roles, one as an efficient police officer and the other as his dimwitted brother. When the policeman joins the circus as a strongman, his brother substitutes for him on the force and, through some miraculous circumstances, becomes a hero. Bates, here playing a minor role, was the real-life wife of star Fuller.

p&d, Norman Lee; w, Lee, Syd Courtenay, Arthur Woods (based on the story by Courtenay, Lola Harvey); ph, Claude Friese-Greene.

Comedy   **(PR:A MPAA:NR)**

PRIDE OF THE LEGION, THE**   (1932) 65m Mascot bw

Barbara Kent, J. Farrell MacDonald, Lucien Littlefield, Sally Blane, Glenn Tryon, Matt Moore, Ralph Ince, Victor Jory, Tommy Dugan, Jason Robards, Sr., Rin Tin Tin, Jr.

A policeman goes through a traumatic experience that sets off psychological reactions detrimental to his work. Can the man once more recover his famed iron will? Director Beebe churned out numerous programmers like this for various B movie companies, as well as doing the FLASH GORDON serials. Surprisingly, he also directed the Beethoven Pastoral Symphony sequence in FANTASIA for Walt Disney.

d, Ford Beebe; w, Peter B. Kyne, Beebe (based on the story "A Film Star's Holiday" by Kyne); ed, Ray Snyder.

Crime Drama   **(PR:A MPAA:NR)**

PRIDE OF THE MARINES**   (1936) 66m COL bw

Charles Bickford (*Steve Riley*), Florence Rice (*Molly Malone*), Billy Burrud (*Ulysses Simpson Smith*), Robert Allen (*Larry Allen*), Thurston Hall (*Col. Gage*), George McKay (*Mac McCabe*), Ward Bond (*Gunner Brady*), Joseph Sawyer (*Tennessee*).

Bickford is heroic and kind-hearted as a Marine who looks after orphan Burrud when the youngster shows up on base. The boy is later adopted by newlywed Rice, and Bickford dutifully goes off to sea. Full of that fight-for-your-country spirit, with an excess of Marine base stock footage making it all look very appealing.

d, D. Ross Lederman; w, Harold Shumate (based on a story by Gerald Beaumont); ph, Benjamin Kline; ed, Richard Cahoon; cos, Samuel Lange.

Drama   **(PR:A MPAA:NR)**

PRIDE OF THE MARINES****   (1945) 119m WB bw (GB: FOREVER IN LOVE)

John Garfield (*Al Schmid*), Eleanor Parker (*Ruth Hartley*), Dane Clark (*Lee Diamond*), John Ridgely (*Jim Merchant*), Rosemary De Camp (*Virginia Pfeiffer*), Ann Doran (*Ella Merchant*), Warren Douglas (*Kebabian*), Don McGuire (*Irish*), Tom D'Andrea (*Tom*), Rory Mallinson (*Doctor*), Stephen Richards (*Ainslee*), Anthony Caruso (*Johnny Rivers*), Moroni Olsen (*Capt. Burroughs*), Dave Willock (*Red*), John Sheridan (*2nd Marine*), John Miles (*Lieutenant*), John Compton (*Corporal*), Lennie Bremen (*Lenny*), Michael Brown (*Corpsman*).

A grand and emotional study in heroism, PRIDE OF THE MARINES is a tour de force for rugged Garfield and a film that allowed director Daves to introduce some startling psychological techniques which made this film exceptional. Based on the true story of Al Schmid, Garfield is shown as a workingman in Philadelphia who falls in love with Parker. They have a rough-and-tumble courtship, then marry on the eve of WW II. Garfield is one of the first to join up, enlisting in the Marines and being sent to Guadalcanal where, in 1942, American troops made their first significant confrontation with invading Japanese troops. Garfield and his small machine gun crew receive orders to be on the alert for a massive Japanese attack one night and, when it comes, the defenders are almost overwhelmed. Machine gunners Caruso and Clark are put out of action and Garfield takes over the gun, literally mowing down hundreds of fanatical Japanese storming his position. One enemy soldier hurls a grenade at the gun and Garfield is blinded. But even blinded, Garfield draws his pistol and fires, sightless, at the enemy. Returned to a San Diego hospital, Garfield undergoes intense medical treatment along with psychological

preparation to face the world without eyesight. But he cannot bring himself to reenter society a cripple and fears rejection by his wife, Parker. (This theme would be intensely developed in THE MEN, starring Marlon Brando.) He not only fights treatment but becomes embittered and insists that he will see again. Some light can be seen by Garfield in one eye but it is only a milky blur and doctors tell him not to hold out too much hope. Finally it is time for him to return to Philadelphia and he is escorted by Clark who encourages him to face the future. Garfield has nightmare visions of himself standing in a train station and Parker, after seeing him in dark glasses, blind, walking away from him. He nevertheless goes home, awkwardly attempting to fit into society. He resents his now clumsy, unsure movements and is embarrassed when bumping into a Christmas tree. Slowly Garfield adjusts and, by the time he is decorated with the Navy Cross for his heroism on Guadalcanal (credited with killing 200 enemy soldiers) the "Pride of the Marines" displays equal courage in facing life with Parker, along with a promise that he might see again out of one eye. Garfield is brilliant in his portrayal of Schmid and Daves' direction is superb, utilizing remarkable techniques such as double printings, negative images, and telescopic shots which all add to the eerie and unnerving experience Garfield is undergoing in his rehabilitation. The battle scenes in this film are some of the most harrowing ever shot. The idea for the film was largely Garfield's. He read an article about Schmid in *Life* magazine and contacted writer Maltz, suggesting a script about the man. Maltz had worked on the film DESTINATION TOKYO, also directed by Daves, and Garfield felt he would be the ideal writer to handle the project. Daves was brought into the project a short time later. This film, along with AIR FORCE and DESTINATION TOKYO, was one of Garfield's favorite films made at Warner Bros. PRIDE OF THE MARINES was a box office smash, released just as WW II came to a close, timed perfectly with the public's curiosity about rehabilitating a generation of wounded American servicemen. Co-author Maltz later became one of the "Hollywood Ten," and some of the dialog in PRIDE OF THE MARINES was later recalled by the House Un-American Activities Committee, those lines dealing with social consciousness and class workingman arguments, mostly expressed by Clark—as an example of communist philosophy insidiously inserted into movies. The film nevertheless remains as a deeply moving, sensitive production, one of the finest war films ever made.

p, Jerry Wald; d, Delmer Daves; w, Albert Maltz, Marvin Borowsky (based on a story by Roger Butterfield); ph, Peverell Marley; m, Franz Waxman; ed, Owen Marks; md, Leo F. Forbstein; art d, Leo Kuter; spec eff, L. Robert Burgs.

War Drama   **(PR:C MPAA:NR)**

PRIDE OF THE NAVY*½   (1939) 63m REP bw

James Dunn (*Speed Brennan*), Rochelle Hudson (*Gloria Tyler*), Gordon Oliver (*Jerry Richards*), Horace MacMahon (*Gloomy Kelly*), Gordon Jones (*Joe Falcon*), Charlotte Wynters (*Mrs. Falcon*), Joseph Crehan (*Brad Foster*), Charles Trowbridge (*Capt. Tyler*).

Dunn is kicked out of Annapolis because of his rowdiness. He becomes a speedboat designer and attracts the navy's attention because they want him to build a small torpedo boat. Dunn's overacting and the dreadful dialog the characters are expected to speak makes this one a less than average programmer.

d, Charles Lamont; w, Ben Markson, Saul Elkins (based on a story by James Webb, Joseph Hoffman); ph, Jack Marta; ed, Edward Mann; md, Cy Feuer; art d, John Victor Mackay; cos, Irene Saltern.

Drama   **(PR:A MPAA:NR)**

PRIDE OF THE PLAINS**   (1944) 55m REP bw

Robert Livingston (*Johnny Revere*), Smiley Burnette (*Fred Milhouse*), Nancy Gay (*Joan Bradford*), Stephen Barclay (*Kenny Revere*), Kenneth MacDonald (*Hurley*), Charles Miller (*Grant Bradford*), Kenne Duncan (*Snyder*), Jack Kirk (*Steve Craig*), Bud Geary (*Gerard*), Yakima Canutt (*Bowman*), Budd Buster, Bud Osborne.

Livingston and Burnette go to work in an attempt to keep the bad guys from repealing a law which prevents them from slaughtering horses for profit. Burnette was Gene Autry's sidekick for a while.

p, Louis Gray; d, Wallace Fox; w, John K. Butler, Bob Williams (based on a story by Oliver Drake); ph, John MacBurnie; m, Mort Glickman; ed, Charles Craft; art d, Fred Ritter.

Western   **(PR:A MPAA:NR)**

PRIDE OF THE WEST**½   (1938) 56m PAR bw

William Boyd (*Hopalong Cassidy*), George Hayes (*Windy Halliday*), Russell Hayden (*Lucky Jenkins*), Charlotte Field (*Mary Martin*), Earle Hodgins (*Sheriff Tom Martin*), Billy King (*Dick Martin*), Kenneth Harlan (*Caldwell*), Glenn Strange (*Saunders*), James Craig (*Nixon*), Bruce Mitchell (*Detective*), Willie Fung (*Sing Loo*), George Morrell (*Townsman*), Earl Askam, Jim Toney, Horace B. Carpenter, Henry Otho.

Top-notch Hopalong Cassidy entry has Boyd on the trail of a stagecoach robber responsible for a string of thefts. Filled from beginning to end with quality gun play and hard-hitting fist fights. (See HOPALONG CASSIDY series, Index.)

p, Harry Sherman; d, Lesley Selander; w, Nate Watt (based on a story by Clarence E. Mulford); ph, Russell Harlan; ed, Robert Warwick.

Western   **(PR:A MPAA:NR)**

PRIDE OF THE YANKEES, THE*****   (1942) 127m RKO bw

Gary Cooper (*Lou Gehrig*), Teresa Wright (*Eleanor Gehrig*), Walter Brennan (*Sam Blake*), Dan Duryea (*Hank Hanneman*), Babe Ruth (*Himself*), Elsa Janssen (*Mom Gehrig*), Ludwig Stossel (*Pop Gehrig*), Virginia Gilmore (*Myra*), Bill Dickey (*Himself*), Ernie Adams (*Miller Huggins*), Pierre Watkin (*Mr. Twitchell*), Harry Harvey (*Joe McCarthy*), Addison Richards (*Coach*), Robert W. Meusel, Mark Koenig, Bill Stern (*Themselves*), Hardie Albright (*Van Tuyl*), Edward Fielding (*Clinic Doctor*), George Lessey (*Mayor of New Rochelle*), Vaughan Glaser (*Doctor in Gehrig*

Home), Douglas Croft *(Lou Gehrig as a Boy)*, Rip Russell *(Laddie)*, Frank Faylen *(Third Base Coach)*, Jack Shea *(Hammond)*, George MacDonald *(Wally Pip)*, Gene Collins *(Billy)*, David Holt *(Billy at 17)*, David Manley *(Mayor Fiorello La Guardia)*, Max Willenz *(Colletti)*, Jimmy Valentine *(Sasha)*, Anita Bolster *(Sasha's Mother)*, Robert Winkler *(Murphy)*, Spencer Charters *(Mr. Larsen)*, Rosina Galli *(Mrs. Fabini)*, Billy Roy *(Joe Fabini)*, Sarah Padden *(Mrs. Robert)*, Janet Chapman *(Tessie)*, Eva Dennison *(Mrs. Worthington)*, Montague Shaw *(Mr. Worthington)*, Jack Stewart *(Ed Burrow)*, Fay Thomas *(Christy Mathewson)*, Lane Chandler *(Player in Locker Room)*, Edgar Barrier *(Hospital Doctor)*, George Offerman, Jr. *(Freshman)*, Dorothy Vaughan *(Landlady)*, Patsy O'Byrne *(Scrubwoman)*, Matt McHugh *(Strength Machine Operator)*, William Chaney *(Newsboy)*, Veloz and Yolanda *(Specialty Dancers)*, Pat Flaherty *(Baseball Player)*, Mary Gordon *(Maid)*, Francis Sales *(Cab Driver)*, Dane Clark, Tom Neal, Jack Arnold [Vinton Haworth], John Kellogg *(Fraternity Boys)*, Lorna Dunn *(Clinic Nurse)*, Ray Noble and His Orchestra.

Eloquently written, stunningly photographed, and directed with sensitivity and care, THE PRIDE OF THE YANKEES was everything the public had come to expect of Sam Goldwyn, a super production. This is a sweet, sentimental, and utterly American story of baseball giant Lou Gehrig, "The Iron Man" first baseman for the indefatigable New York Yankees (in the team's heyday of the 1920s-1930s). Cooper is exceptional as Gehrig and Wright marvelous as his sweetheart and later his wife in this, a romance tale rather than a sports biography. In fact, there is a paucity of baseball footage, oddly enough, in this film, mostly due to the fact that Cooper was inadequate with glove and bat. But the film more than makes up for that deficiency. Cooper is shown as a student at Columbia University in New York where his mother slaves away to pay for his tuition. Cooper plays ball whenever possible and his skills on the diamond are spotted by sportswriter Brennan, who contacts the Yankees. The star athlete is offered a lucrative contract but he refuses, intending to become an engineer to please his mother. But when mother Gehrig (Janssen) requires an operation, Cooper signs with the Yankees to pay for medical expenses. He begins his spectacular career in June, 1925, meeting during his first game in Chicago an attractive Wright who makes fun of his awkward ways as he slips on a row of bats when stepping up to the plate. Although Janssen first disapproves of her son's vocation, she and her husband, meek-mannered Stossel, become enthusiastic baseball fans. Brennan, Cooper's biggest supporter, records the player's triumphs one after another through the years. While helping the Yankees to a World Series championship, Cooper stops off in Chicago and proposes to Wright. She accepts and Cooper takes her home to New York where dominating Janssen has a hard time accepting her daughter-in-law. Janssen tries to organize her son's married life but Cooper puts a stop to that and finally settles down to a long and happy marriage. In 1939 Cooper goes into a bad hitting slump and later learns that he has a lethal neurological disease (amytropic lateral sclerosis, since known as Lou Gehrig's Disease), and only has a short time to live. He resigns from the team and makes a dramatic farewell at Yankee Stadium, standing at home plate and stating heroically, "Some people say I've had a bad break, but I consider myself to be the luckiest man on the face of the earth." As the crowd gives him a tumultuous, ear-deafening ovation, Cooper sadly walks from the field, into the dugout, and up a passageway for an exit into legend. THE PRIDE OF THE YANKEES is the story of simple people and one common man with an uncommon talent and a soaring spirit that made him the idol of every schoolboy in America. Cooper is nothing short of wonderful and Wright sparkles as his devoted wife. Janssen and Stossel, as Gehrig's Old World parents, are quaint and colorful, while Brennan sprinkles a lot of salt to season an already savory story. Duryea, as a sportswriter critical of Gehrig, is properly obnoxious and the film is star-studded with real-life baseball greats, not the least of whom is George Herman "Babe" Ruth, greatest slugger of all time, and Gehrig's erstwhile Yankee teammate, along with such baseball marvels as Dickey, Meusel, and Koenig who bring authenticity to the overall production. Thanks to Gallico's terrific original story upon which the screenplay is faithfully based, the lingo and atmosphere of baseball are held intact and Wood's direction is sure and always stimulating. There is nothing startlingly dynamic about this great film and that is one of its many assets. It is homey, humorous, quaint, down-to-earth, and perfectly natural and this is, in itself, a fine achievement. THE PRIDE OF THE YANKEES is not only believable but its sincerity radiates in every scene. It's a triple-A love story, one that the public has with Gehrig, another Wright has with Cooper. Cooper's portrait of Gehrig is as steady and reliable as the Yankee slugger who played in 2,130 consecutive games without ever missing his time at bat, an incredible record that also included playing in seven World Series. (He was born Henry Louis Gehrig, in New York on June 19, 1903, and died June 2, 1941, age 37.) For his role, Cooper practiced incessantly for weeks with baseball coach Lefty O'Doul who taught him how to bat and field left-handed. This was less needed than originally thought since the film concentrates on the love story between Cooper and Wright. Goldwyn, when deciding to make this film, disregarded most of his potential audience. At the time women were not interested in baseball, baseball enthusiasts did not get much of a glimpse of the sport, and, since the sport is strictly an American pastime, foreign sales would be curtailed. Yet Goldwyn went ahead with this, his only biographical film, and produced a stellar classic. Even though Cooper learned to passably bat and field left-handed, he looked awkward so art director Menzies solved the problem by reversing the print so that when Cooper is really batting right-handed, he appears to be batting lefty to conform to Gehrig's real stance. Adding a memorable touch to the film is the Irving Berlin classic tune "Always," which is employed as the favorite love song of Cooper and Wright (as it was for Lou and Eleanor Gehrig). Berlin was paid a special fee of $15,000 for the use of the song in the film. Spectacular ballroom dancers Veloz and Yolanda perform a great routine in a Chicago nightclub and Ray Noble's band is briefly seen. The film received 10 Academy Award nominations, including Best Picture, Best Actor, Best Actress, Best Original Story, Best Cinematography, Best Scoring of a Dramatic Picture, Best Art/Set Decoration, Best Editing, Best Sound Recording, Best Special Effects. Only Mandell won for editing.

p, Samuel Goldwyn; d, Sam Wood; w, Jo Swerling, Herman J. Mankiewicz (based on a story by Paul Gallico); ph, Rudolph Mate; m, Leigh Harline; ed, Daniel Mandell; prod d, William Cameron Menzies; art d, Perry Ferguson, McClure Capps; set d, Howard Bristol; cos, Rene Hubert; spec eff, Jack Cosgrove; m/l, "Always," Irving Berlin.

Romance/Biography/Sports Drama Cas. (PR:AAA MPAA:NR)

PRIEST OF LOVE**½** (1981, Brit.) 125m Milesian/Filmways c

Ian McKellen *(D.H. Lawrence)*, Janet Suzman *(Frieda Lawrence)*, Ava Gardner *(Mabel Dodge Luhan)*, Penelope Keith *(The Honorable Dorothy Brett)*, Jorge Rivero *(Tony Luhan)*, Maurizio Merli *(Angelo Ravagli)*, [Sir] John Gielgud *(Herbert G. Muskett)*, James Faulkner *(Aldous Huxley)*, Mike Gwilym *(John Middleton Murry)*, Massimo Ranieri *(Piero Pini)*, Marjorie Yates *(Ada Lawrence)*, Jane Booker *(Barbara Weekley)*, Wendy Alnutt *(Maria Huxley)*, Elio Pandolfi *(Orioli)*, Sarah Miles *(Actress)*, Shane Rimmer, Sarah Brackett, Adrienne Burgess, Patrick Holt, Derek Martin, Burnell Tucker, Mary Gifford, John Hudson, Daniel Chatto, Roger Sloman, Gareth Forwood, Frank Marcus, Paco Mauri, La Marimba, Hermanos Lugunas, Adrian Montano, Herminio Carrasco, Mike Morris, Natasha Buchanan, Anne Dyson, Julian Fellowes, Graham Faulkner, Niall Padden, Andrew McCulloch, Andrew Lodge, Sean Mathias, Francesco Carnellitti, Cyrus Elias, Madeleine Todd, Wolf Kahler, Graziana Cappellini, Andrea Occhipinti, John Flint, Brian McDermott, Duccio Dogone, Roberto Bonnanni, Roy Herrick, David Glover, Mellan Mitchell, Indian Dancers from the Taos Pueblo.

The later years in the life of author D.H. Lawrence are brought to the screen. The tale concentrates on his writing of *Lady Chatterley's Lover* at a villa in Florence and his battles against censorship. The film gives too much weight to the trivialities and glosses over the more significant aspects of Lawrence's life. Gielgud turns in a wonderful performance as the censor, but the remaining cast members seem stiff and overly theatrical.

p, Christopher Miles, Andrew Donally; d, Miles; w, Alan Plater (based on a novel by Harry T. Moore and the writings and letters of D.H. Lawrence); ph, Ted Moore; m, Joseph James; ed, Paul Davies; prod d, Ted Tester, David Brockhurst; cos, Anthony Powell.

Biography Cas. (PR:O MPAA:R)

PRIEST OF ST. PAULI, THE**** (1970, Ger.) 103m Allianz and Terra/Constantin c (DER PFARRER VON ST. PAULI)

Curt Jurgens *(Konrad Johannsen, the Priest)*, Heinz Reincke *(Titus Kleinwiche)*, Barbara Lass *(Dagmar)*, Corny Collins *(Ingrid)*, Guenther Stoll *(Heino Docke)*, Dieter Borsche *(Toenning, the Clergyman)*, Horst Naumann *(Willy Krekel)*, Christine Diersch *(Hilde)*, Klaus-Hagen Latwesen *(Holger)*, Ilse Peternell *(Solveig)*.

Veteran German actor Jurgens is cast as a one-time sub commander who devotes himself to God after surviving the sinking of his vessel in WW II. He soon finds his ways are unwelcomed by a disrespectful gang who sees his involvement in community affairs as a threat. Jurgens comes out on top, however, after getting tough with the hoods.

d&w, Rolf Olsen; ph, Franz X. Lederle (Eastmancolor); m, Erwin Halletz; ed, Renate Willeg; set d, Ulrich Schroeder.

Drama (PR:C MPAA:NR)

PRIEST'S WIFE, THE*** (1971, Ital./Fr.) 106m Editions Cinematographiques Francais-Champion/WB c (LA MOGLIE DEL PRETE)

Sophia Loren *(Valeria Billi)*, Marcello Mastroianni *(Don Mario)*, Venantino Venantini *(Maurizio)*, Jacques Stany *(Jimmy Guitar)*, Pippo Starnazza *(Valeria's Father)*, Augusto Mastrantoni *(Monsignor Caldana)*, Giuseppe Maffioli *(Davide Libretti)*, Miranda Campa *(Valeria's Mother)*, Gino Cavalieri *(Don Filippo)*, Gino Lazzari *(Caldana's Secretary)*, Dana Ghia *(Lucia)*, Vittorio Crispo, Nerina Montagnana.

Rancid comedy with a dull edge of anti-church sentiment illustrates once again the mystery that is Sophia Loren's successful, but spectacularly untalented, career. Here she plays a rock 'n' roll singer who learns that her lover of four years has been married all along. She tries to commit suicide by swallowing sleeping pills, and at one point before losing consciousness she calls a crisis hotline and gets priest Mastroianni. When she regains consciousness in the hospital the next day, she asks for the priest to whom she talked, and immediately falls in love with him. His first love is the church, though, although he feels that in the more liberal times of the movie's setting, he might get a special dispensation to violate his vow of celibacy. At night the priest is tortured by thoughts of Loren's ample charms. He asks other priests for advice, some telling him to resign, others to go ahead and have an affair; still others recommend castration as the only final foolproof way to stave off the temptations of the flesh. Meanwhile the case makes the news and Loren's singing career is revived when she performs as "The Priest's Wife." Eventually Mastroianni is summoned to Rome where he is given a cushy Monsignorship and a swell Vatican office to woo him back under the church's spell. Loren learns that she is pregnant (just how and by whom is never explained, at least not in the miserable dubbed version). When she sees Mastroianni during a papal procession, his eyes stay on the pontiff. She realizes that he will never leave the church for her and sadly goes away. There is no doubt that the two stars have a pleasant chemistry for comedy, but the script here is so abysmal and the direction so flaccid, that they come off even worse than they generally do. The film was universally savaged by critics when released and failed miserably at the box office. A nearly concurrent picture, IL PRETE SPOSATO (The Married Priest) with Rosanna Podesta dealt with the same subject in much steamier fashion, but never premiered in the U.S.

p, Carlo Ponti; d, Dino Risi; w, Ruggero Maccari, Bernardino Zapponi (based on a story by Maccari, Risi, Zapponi); ph, Alfio Contini (Technicolor); m, Armando Trovaioli; ed, Alberto Gallitti; art d, Gianni Polidori; set d, Lorenzo Baraldi; cos, Polidori, Mayer of Rome; makeup, Guiseppe Annunziata, Giuseppe Banchelli.

Comedy (PR:O MPAA:GP)

PRIMA DELLA REVOLUTIONA   (SEE: BEFORE THE REVOLUTION, 1964, Ital.)

PRIME CUT*   (1972) 88m Cinema Center/NG c

Lee Marvin (*Nick Devlin*), Gene Hackman (*"Mary Ann"*), Angel Tompkins (*Clarabelle*), Gregory Walcott (*Weenie*), Sissy Spacek (*Poppy*), Janit Baldwin (*Violet*), William Morey (*Shay*), Clint Ellison (*Delaney*), Howard Platt (*Shaughnessy*), Les Lannom (*O'Brien*), Eddie Egan (*Jake*), Therese Reinch (*Jake's Girl*), Bob Wilson (*Reaper Driver*), Gordon Signer (*Brockman*), Gladys Watson (*Milk Lady*), Hugh Gillin, Jr. (*Desk Clerk*), P. Lund (*Mrs. O'Brien*), David Savage (*Ox-Eye*), Craig Chapman (*Farmer Bob*), Jim Taksas (*Big Jim*), Wayne Savagne (*Freckle Face*).

Hackman is a degenerate Kansas City cattleman who sells as many girls as he does cows. Chicago gangster Marvin is sent to teach him a lesson on behalf of a group of factory owners who are fed up with Hackman's insolence. A violent film from director Michael Ritchie which is filled with unlikely settings for a gangster film (a country fair), a wheatfield chase scene (a la NORTH BY NORTHWEST), and a switch in casting (Hackman playing the louse and Marvin playing the relatively good guy). Ritchie breaks tradition by portraying the rural population as far more despicable than the city folk, referring to Chicago as being "as peaceful as anyplace anywhere." Sissy Spacek makes her film debut as one of Hackman's commodities.

p, Joe Wizan; d, Michael Ritchie; w, Robert Dillon; ph, Gene Polito (Panavision, Technicolor); m, Lalo Schifrin; ed, Carl Pingatore; art d, Bill Malley; set d, James Payne; cos, Patricia Norris; spec eff, Logan Frazee; makeup, Ken Chase, Emile La Vigne.

Crime Drama   Cas.   (PR:O   MPAA:R)

PRIME MINISTER, THE**   (1941, Brit.) 94m WB bw

John Gielgud (*Benjamin Disraeli*), Diana Wynyard (*Mary Anne Wyndham-Lewis*), Will Fyffe (*Agitator*), Stephen Murray (*William E. Gladstone*), Owen Nares (*Lord Derby*), Fay Compton (*Queen Victoria*), Lyn Harding (*Bismarck*), Pamela Standish (*Princess Victoria*), Leslie Perrins (*Earl of Salisbury*), Vera Bogetti (*Lady Blessington*), Anthony Ireland (*Capt. d'Orsay*), Irene Browne (*Lady Londonderry*), Frederick Leister (*Lord Melbourne*), Nicolas Hannan (*Sir Robert Peel*), Barbara Everest (*Baroness Lehzen*), Kynaston Reeves (*Lord Stanley*), Gordon McLeod (*John Brown*), Glynis Johns (*Miss Sheridan*), Joss Ambler, Nadine March, Andrea Trowbridge, John Patience, Hugh Beckett, J. Walters.

Benjamin Disraeli was surely one of the most iconoclastic and intriguing leaders of any major country in the world. That they managed to make him dull is a bewilderment. Gielgud doesn't come close to the Oscar-winning Arliss performance in the 1929 version. All of the famed episodes are here as we see Gielgud, a novelist, go into politics when helped along by Wynyard. They marry and he becomes Prime Minister in 1868, then again from 1874 through 1880. Germany, Austria, and Russia have entered into a cabal that threatens the security of England. The Queen, Compton, prevails upon Gielgud to stay on in his position and help beat that alliance, despite Gielgud's desire to quit politics and give it up for a happy retirement. When Gielgud's advisers suggest knuckling under, he goes against their wishes. Parliament attacks him for that position but, in the end, his wisdom prevails and the country is saved from war by his political expertise. Almost nothing is made of his Jewish heritage and his later conversion to Christianity. The screenwriters are so frightened of showing the great man's warts that they fail to show any of his skin at all. Seeing this lackluster version makes one yearn to watch the Arliss version again and, perhaps, to sing aloud; "Disraeli, won't you please come home!"

p, Max Milder; d, Thorold Dickinson; w, Brock Williams, Michael Hogan; ph, Basil Emmott.

Biography   (PR:A   MPAA:NR)

PRIME OF MISS JEAN BRODIE, THE*½   (1969, Brit.) 116m FOX c

Maggie Smith (*Jean Brodie*), Robert Stephens (*Teddy Lloyd*), Pamela Franklin (*Sandy*), Gordon Jackson (*Gordon Lowther*), Celia Johnson (*Miss MacKay*), Diane Grayson (*Jenny*), Jane Carr (*Mary McGregor*), Shirley Steedman (*Monica*), Lavinia Lang (*Emily Carstairs*), Antoinette Biggerstaff (*Helen McPhee*), Margo Cunningham (*Miss Campbell*), Isla Cameron (*Miss McKenzie*), Rona Anderson (*Miss Lockhart*), Ann Way (*Miss Gaunt*), Molly Weir (*Miss Alison Kerr*), Helena Gloag (*Miss Kerr*), John Dunbar (*Mr. Burrage*), Heather Seymour (*Clara*), Lesley Paterson (*Prefect*), Kristen Hatfield, Hilary Berlin, Jennifer Irvine, Gillian Evans, Janette Sattler, Diane Robillard, Helen Wigglesworth, Antonia Moss (*Schoolgirls*).

Maggie Smith won the Oscar for her performance as the slightly mad spinster of the title. The book had been a mild success; then Ms. Jay Presson Allen turned it into a play in 1966 starring Vanessa Redgrave in London and Zoe Caldwell in New York. That made enough noise to warrant its being acquired for a feature production. It's 1932, Edinburgh. Smith teaches in an upscale private school. She inspires her female students with her ideas on art and music but her politics have a darker side, an admiration for fascist dictators. She assembles a small cadre of adoring students, including Carr, Grayson and Franklin, who follow her around. Jackson is a teacher at the school and she occasionally spends time with him at his family home in the country. Not that she likes Jackson all that much, she is just using him to see if that will get Stephens, another teacher, to make a serious commitment to her. But that's impossible as he's a Catholic, a father and not about to break up his marriage. Smith is always at odds with dour Johnson, the woman who runs the school. Franklin is annoyed at how Smith continues to laud Grayson's beauty and she gets even by seducing Stephens away from Smith. Stephens is an aspiring artist and does a picture of Franklin but it looks more like Smith, so Franklin walks out on him. Meanwhile, Smith is a supporter of Franco and Mussolini and when Carr's brother goes to Spain sometime later, Smith encourages Carr to join him and fight for the fascist cause. Carr does so and her train is bombed by the opposing forces,

killing the young woman. More time passes, then Stephens tells Smith that Jackson, who wanted nothing more than to be a spouse to anyone, is about to marry Anderson, a chemistry teacher at the school. Smith goes back to her classroom where she continues to extol the virtues of her heroes until Johnson fires her. Then she learns it was Franklin who ratted on her to Johnson. Franklin goes on to say that she had an affair with Stephens. When the stunned Smith wants to know why she's been dirked in the back, Franklin says it's because of Carr's needless death, which was caused by Smith's prodding. It's Smith's picture all the way as she raves, rants, coos, and runs a gamut of emotions seldom seen outside a Hepburn movie. McKuen's song was nominated for the Oscar and properly lost to "Raindrops Keep Fallin' on My Head." Interiors were shot at London's Pinewood studios and Edinburgh itself served for all location shooting.

p, Robert Fryer, James Gesson; d, Ronald Neame; w, Jay Presson Allen (based on Allen's play from the novel by Muriel Spark); ph, Ted Moore (DeLuxe Color); m, Rod McKuen; ed, Norman Savage; md, Arthur Greenslade; prod d, John Howell; art d, Brian Herbert; set d, Pamela Cornell; cos, Elizabeth Haffenden, Joan Bridge; m/l, "Jean" McKuen (sung by McKuen); makeup, Ernest Gasser.

Drama/Comedy   (PR:C   MPAA:M)

PRIME TIME, THE zero   (1960) 76m Mid-Continent/Essanjay bw

JoAnn LeCompte (*Jean Norton*), Frank Roche (*Detective McKean*), James Brooks (*Tony Jackson*), Ray Gronwold (*The Beard*), Maria Pavelle (*Gloria*), Robert Major (*Shorty*), Karen Black (*Painted Woman*), Betty Senter (*Ruthie*), Joe Greco (*Detective*), Eileen Lindhoff (*Mrs. Norton*), Barry Hopkins (*Norton*), Penny Kunard (*Photographer*), Paul Lamaraux (*Jackson*), Andy Lindhoff (*Bartender*), Bettina Brandt (*Sally*), Ron Siden (*Ray*).

Seventeen-year-old Le Compte leaves the security of her home and is abducted by a freakish beatnik painter who ties her up and forces her to pose naked. Offbeat picture with a largely inexperienced cast was filmed in Chicago on a modest budget, and features some skinny-dipping swim parties and wild, wild music. Black makes her film debut in this horrid hunk of drivel from Herschell Gordon Lewis before he became known as a gore filmmaker under that name.

p&d, Gordon Weisenborn [Herschell Gordon Lewis]; w, Robert Abel; ph, Andrew Costikyan; m, Martin Rubenstein, Buddy Frye; ed, Elsie Kerbinhathorn.

Drama   Cas.   (PR:O   MPAA:NR)

PRIMITIVE LOVE*   (1966, Ital.) 83m Italian International-G.L.M./ American Film Distributing c (L'AMORE PRIMITIVO)

Jayne Mansfield (*Jayne*), Franco Franchi, Ciccio Ingrassia (*Hotel Porters*), Luigi Scattini (*Commentator*), Mickey Hargitay, Lucia Modugno, Carlo Kechler, Alfonso Sarlo, Eugenio Galadini.

Mansfield is an anthropologist who has made a film on the subject of the universal primitiveness of love, but one professor to whom she shows it in Rome is left unconvinced. She performs a striptease for him and a couple of hotel porters who followed her to her room to help change their minds and it does, powerfully. Filmed all over the world, from Paris to Tokyo, from Rome to the South Sea Islands. One of the many low-budget films bosomy Mansfield made in Europe, costarring her second husband, muscle-bound Hargitay, after her career went into a steep decline in the U.S.

p, Dick Randall, Joel Holt, Fulvio Luciano, Pietro Paulo Giordani; d, Luigi Scattini; w, Scattini, Amadeo Sollazzo (based on the story by Scattini, D.M. Pupillo); ph, Claudio Racca (Eastmancolor); m, Lallo Gori; ed, Otello Colangeli; art d, Gastone Carsetti.

Comedy   (PR:O   MPAA:NR)

PRIMITIVES, THE**   (1962, Brit.) 70m Border/RFD bw

Jan Holden (*Cheta*), Bill Edwards (*Peter*), Rio Fanning (*John*), George Mikell (*Claude*), Terence Fallon (*Sgt. Henry*), Derek Ware (*Philip*), Peter Hughes (*Inspector Wills*).

In order to rob some gem dealers, a dancer and her cohorts adopt some disguises. Does the title describe the story just a little too well?

p, O. Negus-Fancey; d, Alfred Travers; w, Travers, Moris Farhi.

Crime   (PR:A   MPAA:NR)

PRIMROSE PATH, THE**   (1934, Brit.) 70m British and Dominions/ PAR British bw

Isobel Elsom (*Brenda Dorland*), Whitmore Humphries (*David Marlow*), Max Adrian (*Julian Leigh*), Virginia Field (*Ianthe Dorland*), Gordon McLeod (*Dr. Dorland*), Helen Ferrers (*Mrs. Hassee*), Ethel Stuart (*Fortune*), Molly Connolly.

While on a cruise with her medico husband, Elsom meets author Humphries and falls in love. Humphries' business partner Adrian in turn falls for Field, Elsom's daughter. In the end Humphries patches up Elsom's marriage, which in turn sweetens the romance for the younger people. Sticky sweet and tedious romance that will probably get more laughs than intended.

p&d, Reginald Denham; w, Basil Mason (based on a story by Joan Temple).

Romance   (PR:A   MPAA:NR)

PRIMROSE PATH*   (1940) 93m RKO bw

Ginger Rogers (*Ellie May Adams*), Joel McCrea (*Ed Wallace*), Marjorie Rambeau (*Mamie Adams*), Henry Travers (*Gramp*), Miles Mander (*Homer Adams*), Queenie Vassar (*Grandma*), Joan Carroll (*Honeybell Adams*), Vivienne Osborne (*Thelma*), Carmen Morales (*Carmelita*), Gene Morgan (*Hawkins*), Lorin Raker, Charles Lane, Mara Alexander, Herbert Corthell, Charles Williams, Larry McGrath, Jack Gardner, Nestor Paiva, Jacqueline Dalya, Lawrence Gleason, Jr., Ray Cooke.

The producers had to make drastic alterations to this play in order to prepare it for the eyes of the Joe Breen Censorship Office. Emphasis was switched from the harridan grandmother to the granddaughter in order to provide a starring vehicle for Rogers, who dyed that gorgeous blonde hair black, for no apparent reason. Rogers is one of two sisters (the other is Carroll) who live with their mother, Rambeau, their father, Mander, and their aged grandmother, Vassar. Rambeau earns her living as an over-the-hill prostitute to support Mander's drinking and the others' eating. McCrea is a fine young man who works at a beachfront hamburger stand, meets Rogers, and the two fall in love. Rogers is thrilled when he proposes because that will get her away from her relatives. When McCrea learns the truth about his in-laws, he is shocked, the couple separate and Rogers is faced with the prospect of going into the same business as Rambeau, who is dying. Providing for the family will now become Rogers' task and she knows of no other way than following in the footsteps of her mother and grandmother. In the end, it all works out, with McCrea and Rogers getting back together. The language was very salty, something not the norm in 1940; and that was after it had been cleaned up as much as possible before filming. Vassar, who was married to character actor Joe Cawthorn, made her debut in this picture after years of working on the stage. The play's locale was Fall River, Massachusetts (where Lizzie Borden attained fame for allegedly hatcheting her parents), but was switched to the West Coast for the movie. Rogers does a good job of acting as a tomboy and Fred Astaire was not missed. It was the first time Rogers and McCrea had worked with each other since CHANCE AT HEAVEN, seven years before. A story about three generations of prostitutes was not the simplest one to make work but they somehow managed to get their points across without ever lapsing into bad taste.

p&d, Gregory LaCava; w, Allan Scott, LaCava (based on the play *The Primrose Path* by Robert L. Buckner, Walter Hart and the novel *February Hill* by Victoria Lincoln); ph, Joseph H. August; m, Werner R. Heymann; ed, William Hamilton; art d, Van Nest Polglase, Carroll Clark; set d, Darrell Silvera; cos, Renie; spec eff, Vernon L. Walker.

Comedy/Drama   **(PR:C MPAA:NR)**

PRINCE AND THE PAUPER, THE***½   (1937) 120m FN-WB bw

Errol Flynn *(Miles Hendon)*, Claude Rains *(Earl of Hertford)*, Henry Stephenson *(Duke of Norfolk)*, Barton MacLane *(John Canty)*, Billy Mauch *(Tom Canty)*, Bobby Mauch *(Prince Edward)*, Alan Hale *(Captain of the Guard)*, Eric Portman *(1st Lord)*, Montagu Love *(Henry VIII)*, Robert Warwick *(Lord Warwick)*, Halliwell Hobbes *(Archbishop)*, Lionel Pape, Leonard Willey *(Lords)*, Elspeth Dudgeon *(Grandmother Canty)*, Fritz Leiber *(Father Andrews)*, Murray Kinnell *(Hugo)*, Ivan F. Simpson *(Clemens)*, Lionel Braham *(Ruffler)*, Helen Valkis *(Jane Seymour)*, Phyllis Barry *(Barmaid)*, Rex Evans *(Rich Man)*, Lester Matthews *(St. John)*, Robert Adair, Harry Cording *(Guards)*, Mary Field *(Tom Canty's Mother)*, Noel Kennedy, Billy Maguire, Clifford Severn *(Urchins)*, Gwendolyn Jones *(Lady Elizabeth)*, Leyland Hodgson *(Watchman)*, Holmes Herbert, Ian MacLaren *(Doctors)*, Forrester Harvey *(Meaty Man)*, Sidney Bracey *(Man in Window)*, Ernie Stanton *(Guard)*, Tom Wilson *(One-Eyed Beggar)*, Lionel Belmore *(Innkeeper)*, Ian Wolfe *(Proprietor)*, Harry Beresford *(The Watch)*, St. Luke's Choristers.

This Mark Twain doppelganger tale of rags and royalty in 16th Century England is sumptuously produced and full of high drama and adventure with Flynn swash-buckling between the precocious Mauch twins. The look-alikes decide that they will switch roles as a lark, one being Prince Edward (later King Edward VI), the other a beggar boy. Despite the fact that the beggar boy acts in an outlandish fashion, the royal court and advisors to the prince accept him as the true monarch to be. The real prince, however, is submerged in the low-life environment of London and, when he decides he's had enough of the game, asserts that he is the real prince. Flynn, a soldier-of-fortune, meets the beggar boy and is amused by his claims to the throne, believing him to be mad. The beggar boy is now about to be crowned king, and Flynn begins to believe the emphatic beggar boy. Enemies at court send Hale, an assassin who knows the beggar boy's real identity, to murder the beggar boy but he is prevented from killing him by Flynn, who saves the real king-to-be at the last moment, dueling with Hale and running him through. Flynn then rushes the prince to the court and here the real prince convinces everyone who he really is by revealing the location of the hidden royal seal, aided by his twin. All ends happily with a fabulous coronation scene, on which Warner Bros. spared no expense. (The release of this film was well-timed with the widely publicized coronation of George VI, following the abdication of Edward VIII, the famous Prince of Wales who abandoned the British throne for commoner Wallis Simpson.) Director Keighley maintains a brisk pace in THE PRINCE AND THE PAUPER and enjoyed his experience with the 12-year-old twins, Billy and Bobby Mauch, later stating: "I worked with the screen's two most unusual actors in that production. It gave me the uncanny feeling of seeing double when I directed them." Keighley's own playful sense of humor comes through in the characterizations of the twins as does the capricious Flynn's who sauntered through the film with a wide grin on his hand-some wolf's face. Flynn had just demanded an enormous salary increase with his CAPTAIN BLOOD being a huge box-office success for Warners but the studio balked and had several other actors, unbeknownst to Flynn, test for the role in THE PRINCE AND THE PAUPER, including Patric Knowles, George Brent, and Ian Hunter. These actors appeared wooden to Keighley and producer Wallis and they finally opted for Flynn, the only man with the dash and color to enhance the lavish epic. Flynn got the part and the raise without ever learning his career had hung in the balance.

p, Hal B. Wallis; d, William Keighley; w, Laird Doyle (based on the novel by Mark Twain and the play by Catherine Chishold Cushing); ph, Sol Polito; ed, Ralph Dawson; m, Erich Wolfgang Korngold; md, Leo F. Forbstein; art d, Robert Haas; cos, Milo Anderson; spec eff, Willard Van Enger, James Gibbons.

Historical Epic/Adventure   Cas.   (PR:AAA MPAA:NR)

PRINCE AND THE PAUPER, THE*½   (1969) 68m Storyland/
Childhood Productions c (AKA: THE ADVENTURES OF THE PRINCE AND THE PAUPER)

Gene Bua, Ken Shaffel.

Mark Twain's classic tale (written in 1883 and dedicated to his two daughters, about a beggar boy who trades places with Edward VI of England a few days before the death of Edward's father, Henry VIII. The prince wanders around in rags, while the urchin suffers the hell of being a prince. The mistake is rectified at the last moment, and the prince is crowned. Filmed in the lush greenery of Ireland.

p, Elliot Geisinger, Ronald Saland; d, Geisinger; w, Geisinger, Alex Tartaglia (based on the novel by Mark Twain); ph, Al Mozell (Eastmancolor); ed, Howard Kuperman; art d, Charles Stockton.

Adventure Drama   **(PR:AA MPAA:NR)**

PRINCE AND THE PAUPER, THE, 1978   (SEE: CROSSED SWORDS, 1978)

PRINCE AND THE SHOWGIRL, THE***½   (1957, Brit.) 117m
Marilyn Monroe-L.O.P. Ltd./WB c

Marilyn Monroe *(Elsie Marina)*, Laurence Olivier *(Charles, Prince Regent)*, Sybil Thorndike *(Queen Dowager)*, Richard Wattis *(Northbrooke)*, Jeremy Spenser *(King Nicholas)*, Esmond Knight *(Hoffman)*, Paul Hardwick *(Major Domo)*, Rosamund Greenwood *(Maud)*, Aubrey Dexter *(The Ambassador)*, Maxine Audley *(Lady Sunningdale)*, Harold Greenwood *(Call Boy)*, Andrea Malandrinos *(Valet with Violin)*, Jean Kent *(Maisie Springfield)*, Daphne Anderson *(Fanny)*, Gillian Owen *(Maggie)*, Vera Day *(Betty)*, Margot Lister *(Lottie)*, Charles Victor *(Theatre Manager)*, David Horne *(The Foreign Officer)*, Dennis Edwards *(Head Valet)*, Gladys Henson *(Dresser)*.

By combining the light comic skills of Monroe and the grandiose acting ability of Olivier, THE PRINCE AND THE SHOWGIRL manages to succeed not only as pleasant entertainment but also as a wonderful mixture of two very different screen personalities. It's 1911 in London and Monroe plays a flighty American showgirl who catches the eye of the Prince Regent of Carpathia, Olivier, who is in town for the Coronation of George V. Traveling with the Prince is his partially deaf mother-in-law, Thorndike, and his son, Spenser. Olivier, who has very little time for courtship, invites Monroe to dinner at his room in the embassy with the hope of seducing her. Monroe rejects Olivier's passes, frustrating the prince to the point of dislike. After drinking an excess of liquor, Monroe falls asleep. When she awakens the next morning she realizes that she is in love with Olivier. He, however, wants nothing more than to see her leave. In between Monroe's attempts to renew Olivier's interest, she becomes a mediator in a feud between the prince and his son. She discovers that Spenser is impatiently awaiting the day, eighteen months away, when he comes of age and inherits the throne of Carpathia. Upset with his father's habit of treating him like a child, Spenser plots to take control as soon as possible. Monroe manages to bring the two together and helps them overcome their differences. Eventually, Olivier is won over by Monroe's beauty and charm, but must return to his country until the end of the eighteen-month period. Olivier travels to Carpathia and promises to return to Monroe, who lovingly agrees to wait. Pro-duced and directed by Olivier and financed by Monroe's newly formed production company (she reportedly was to receive a phenomenal 75 percent of the profits), THE PRINCE AND THE SHOWGIRL shows both actors in fine form. Monroe—in this, her 25th picture—had turned 30 and was as beautiful as ever, delivering a comic performance which is among her very finest. She is thoroughly endearing in her scatterbrained but well-mannered way and ably holds her own opposite her accomplished costar. Olivier had already familiarized himself with the role on the British stage in the Rattigan play "The Sleeping Prince," which costarred his terribly miscast wife Vivien Leigh. Author Rattigan had initially expressed fear in the casting of such a talent as Olivier. The prince's part was written originally as an "unattrac-tive, very conscientious, extremely mundane little man who is dedicated to the routine of his job," but Rattigan envisioned Olivier as turning the character into "Prince Utterly Irresistible." Rattigan's worst fears were overcome when, after much ballyhoo in the press, the play opened to rave reviews. The casting of Monroe in place of Leigh brings to the film a remarkable balance between two of film's most arresting screen personalities.

p&d, Laurence Olivier; w, Terence Rattigan (based on his play "The Sleeping Prince"); ph, Jack Cardiff (Technicolor); m, Richard Addinsell; ed, Jack Harris; md, Muir Mathieson; ch, William Chappell; cos, Beatrice Dawson.

Comedy   Cas.   (PR:A MPAA:NR)

PRINCE OF ARCADIA**½   (1933, Brit.) 80m Nettlefold-Fogwell/Woolf
and Freedman bw

Carl Brisson *(Prince Peter)*, Margot Grahame *(Mirana)*, Ida Lupino *(Princess)*, Annie Esmond *(Queen)*, Peter Gawthorne *(Equerry)*, C. Denier Warren *(Detective)*.

When forced to abdicate from his throne, the exiled prince Brisson heads off to the Riviera to cheer up. There he meets Grahame, an actress, and the two decide to marry. This displeases his royal aunt Esmond, but works out well for princess Lupino who was set to marry Brisson though she had no love for him. Cute and well-produced operetta. London-born Lupino made her screen debut in 1933, and this was one of six films she made in England that year. The following year she went to the U.S. where she would become a film star and director.

p, Archibald Nettlefold, Reginald Fogwell; d, Hans Schwartz; w, Fogwell (based on the play "Der Prinz Von Arkadien" by Walter Reisch); ph, Geoffrey Faithfull; m, Robert Stolz.

Musical   **(PR:AA MPAA:NR)**

PRINCE OF DIAMONDS**   (1930) 67m COL bw

Aileen Pringle *(Eve Marley)*, Ian Keith *(Rupert Endon)*, Fritzi Ridgeway *(Lolah)*, Tyrrell Davis *(Lord Adrian)*, Claude King *(Gilbert Crayle)*, Tom Ricketts *(Williams)*, E. Alyn Warren *(Li Fang)*, Gilbert Emery *(Smith)*, Frederick Sullivan *(Ormsley*

Hatchett), Sybil Grove *(Miss Wren)*, Col. G.L. McDonell *(Betterton)*, Joyzelle *(Dancing Girl)*.

An average tale of romance which has a diamond merchant, 1920s matinee idol Keith, falling for poor girl Pringle, a woman with luxurious tastes. Story takes place mostly in England but then moves to a more exotic jungle sequence later on.

d, Karl Brown, A.H. Van Buren; w, Paul Hervey Fox (based on the story by Gene Markey); ph, Ted Tetzlaff; ed, David Berg; art d, Harrison Wiley.

Romance (PR:A MPAA:NR)

PRINCE OF FOXES**** (1949) 107m FOX bw

Tyrone Power *(Andrea Corsini)*, Orson Welles *(Cesare Borgia)*, Wanda Hendrix *(Camilla Verano)*, Everett Sloane *(Mario Belli)*, Marina Berti *(Angela Borgia)*, Katina Paxinou *(Mona Zeppo Constanza)*, Felix Aylmer *(Count Marc Antonio Verano)*, Leslie Bradley *(Don Esteban)*, Joop van Hulzen *(D'Este)*, James Carney *(Alphonso D'Este)*, Eduardo Ciannelli *(Art Dealer)*, Rena Lennart *(Lady in Waiting)*, Giuseppe Faeti *(Priest)*, Eugene Deckers *(Borgia Henchman)*, Eva Brauer *(Fabio)*, Ves Vanghielova *(Tonia)*, Franco Corsaro *(Mattia)*, Ludmilla Durarowa *(Vittoria)*, Njntsky *(Specialty Dancer)*, Albert Latasha, Adriano Ambrogi *(Townsmen)*, Dave Kurland, Kenneth Lang, Frank Salvi, Alex Serbaroli, Alan Asherman, Clinton Sundeen *(Soldiers)*.

Great adventure, a literate script, and fine performances combine in PRINCE OF FOXES to offer splendid entertainment under King's marvelously brisk direction. Set during the Italian Renaissance, the film opens with Welles, playing the notorious Cesare Borgia, outlining his plans for the domination of Italy to trusted aide Power. He tells Power that he cannot take an Italian city state by storm, its fortress being too well-manned and defended by van Hulzen, a cannon-maker extraordinaire. He assigns Power to persuade the commander of the fortress to marry his sister, the scheming Lucrezia Borgia. This he does with considerable guile and brass and is then ordered by Welles to seduce a young married princess, Hendrix, who is wedded to Aylmer, an elderly city-state count, and then to turn over the mountain fortress to Welles after accomplishing a romantic coup. En route to the duchy controled by Aylmer, Power stops to see his art teacher, Ciannelli (Power is an aspiring painter). He arranges to have one of his works of art available when Hendrix inspects Ciannelli's collection, spotting Power's painting and stating her appreciation of it. He makes it a gift to her and she, in turn, invites him to visit her and her husband. The subtle infiltration has worked but once Power visits Aylmer's court, he realizes that the old man is an honorable, decent human being and that his love for Hendrix is that of a father for a daughter. Power cannot bring himself to betray the trust Hendrix and Aylmer place in him and when Welles can no longer wait for Power to deliver the duchy, he orders his men to march against the mountain fortress. Power offers his sword to Aylmer and Hendrix, betraying his master Welles. A heroic defense is made but Welles' troops eventually overcome the defenders. Aylmer is dead by the time Hendrix and Power surrender the duchy. Sloane, who is Power's friend and advisor, has been prevented from assassinating Aylmer and later reports to Welles how he has seen Power visit his mother, Paxinou, a peasant woman. Realizing that Power, now his prisoner, has not only betrayed him but is not of noble birth, Welles allows Sloane to gouge out Power's eyes before a dinner party at which Hendrix begs for Power's life. Sloane has really crushed two grapes over Power's eyes and offered this gore up as the real thing, whispering to Power to scream in pain. Power is led away but soon organizes a plot to retake Citta del Monte and free Hendrix. He appears magically, slaying his former captors, and, with Sloane's help, and help from the local citizens, routes Welles' overconfident army. The low-born Power is officially elevated to a lordship and weds Hendrix. Beautifully photographed on location in Italy by Shamroy, this Fox production is both tasteful and lavish with Power exceptional in his portrait of an ambitious but noble Renaissance man. The exquisite costuming here loses something in Fox's option to shoot in black and white, despite the fact that King begged for color. Welles, who essays a wholly sinister Cesare Borgia, took the role when desperately in need of cash. In one scene where Florentine royalty gather to pay homage to Welles, the actor complained that the actors weren't bowing and scraping enough to his august presence. "You're getting a damned sight more than you deserve," yelled King from his director's platform. "You just play the part. The people will do what *I* tell them!"

p, Sol C. Siegel; d, Henry King; w, Milton Krims (based on the novel by Samuel Shellabarger); ph, Leon Shamroy; m, Alfred Newman; ed, Barbara McLean; art d, Lyle Wheeler, Mark Lee Kirk; set d, Thomas Little; cos, Vittorio Nino Novarese; spec eff, Fred Sersen.

Adventure/Historical Epic (PR:C MPAA:NR)

PRINCE OF PEACE, THE*½ (1951) 120m Hallmark c

Modern: Ginger Price *(Ginger)*, Forrest Taylor *(Uncle Mark)*, Farris Taylor *(Uncle Jonathan)*, Gwyn Shipman *(Jane)*, Maude Eburne *(Henrietta)*, Willa Pearl *(Willa Pearl Curtis)*, Biblical: Millard Coody *(Jesus Christ)*, Darlene Bridges *(Virgin Mary)*, A.S. Fisher *(Simon Peter)*, Hazel Lee Becker *(Mary Magdalene)*.

An unashamed commercial for a pageant held annually by the Lawton Congregational Church of Lawton, Oklahoma. Every Easter, a re-enactment of Holy Week is held in the foothills of the Wichita Mountains and someone decided that filming this passion play would be a great way to make money. The first portion of the film is a highly fictionalized history of how the pageant began in 1926, poorly put together and stocked with characters who do no justice to the sincerity of the pageant's originators. The second half is a filmed record of the passion play itself, which is infinitely less saccharine than the preceeding portions. While not the greatest portrait of Jesus, the actors do give some credibility and sincerity to their roles. At its New York opening, every last money-making effort possible was used. At intermission, "souvenir programs" were peddled from the stage to eager buyers. Also on the program was ONE TOO MANY, a short dealing with the ever-popular theme of evangelists: demon alcohol.

p, Kroger Babb; d, William Beaudine, Harold Daniels; w, Milton Raison, Mildred A. Horn, Scott Darling (based on a story by Rev. A. Mark Wallock).

Religious Drama (PR:AAA MPAA:NR)

PRINCE OF PIRATES½** (1953) 78m COL c

John Derek *(Prince Roland)*, Barbara Rush *(Nita Orde)*, Carla Balenda *(Princess Maria)*, Whitfield Connor *(Stephan)*, Edgar Barrier *(Count Blanco)*, Robert Shayne *(Treeg)*, Harry Lauter *(Jan)*, Don Harvey *(Koepke)*, Henry Rowland *(Greb)*, Glase Lohman *(Brenner)*, Gene Roth *(Capt. Brock)*, Bob Peoples *(Carl)*, Sandy Sanders *(Meyers)*, Joseph F. McGuinn *(Gen. DuBois)*, Al Cantor *(Lund)*, Edward Colmans *(Spanish Admiral)*.

Derek displays his swashbuckling skills as the native prince of a 16th century mythical island. To free his people from the oppressive hand of his elder brother, Connor, he organizes a group of volunteers to regain control of the island. A great deal of the stock footage is taken from JOAN OF ARC (1948) and adds a noisy, colorful flavor to the whole.

p, Sam Katzman; d, Sidney Salkow; w, John O'Dea, Samuel Newman (based on the story by William Copeland, Herbert Kline); ph, Henry Freulich (Technicolor); m, Mischa Bakaleinikoff; ed, Jerome Thoms; art d, Paul Palmentola.

Adventure (PR:A MPAA:NR)

PRINCE OF PLAYERS*½** (1955) 102m FOX bw

Richard Burton *(Edwin Booth)*, Maggie McNamara *(Mary Devlin)*, John Derek *(John Wilkes Booth)*, Raymond Massey *(Junius Brutus Booth)*, Charles Bickford *(Dave Prescott)*, Elizabeth Sellars *(Asia)*, Eva Le Gallienne *(The Queen)*, Christopher Cook *(Edwin Booth at Age 10)*, Dayton Lummis *(English Doctor)*, Ian Keith *("King" in Hamlet)*, Paul Stader *(Laertes)*, Louis Alexander *(John Booth at Age 12)*, William Walker *(Old Ben)*, Jack Raine *(Theater Manager)*, Charles Cane *(Theater Assistant)*, Betty Flint *(Lady Macbeth)*, Mae Marsh *(Witch in Macbeth)*, Stanley Hall *(Abraham Lincoln)*, Sarah Padden *(Mrs. Abe Lincoln)*, Ruth Clifford *(English Nurse)*, Ivan Hayes *(Bernardo)*, Paul Frees *(Francisco)*, Ben Wright *(Horatio)*, Melinda Markey *(Young Lady)*, Eleanor Audley *(Mrs. Montchesington)*, Percival Vivian *(Polonius)*, George Dunn *(Doorman)*, Ruth Warren *(Nurse)*, Richard Cutting *(Doctor)*, Lane Chandler *(Colonel)*, Steve Darrell *(Maj. Rathbone)*, George Melford *(Stage Doorman)*, Tom Fadden *(Trenchard)*, Henry Kulky *(Bartender)*, Olan Soule *(Catesby)*.

To present high theater to a movie-going audience looking for thrills and adventure is often a mistake, although MGM pulled it off in 1936 with its superb presentation of ROMEO AND JULIET, starring Norma Shearer and Leslie Howard. Here Fox attempts to present the first family of American theater, the so-called "mad Booths of Maryland," as seen through the dramatic perspective of Burton who gives a stellar performance. Burton delivers a terrific interpretation of Edwin Booth, or, at least, his concept of how the greatest American thespian of the 19th Century acted. The story begins with Burton catering to the mad whims of his eccentric father, actor Junius Booth, broadly essayed by Massey, playing manager and nursemaid to a parent obviously talented but demented. (In real life Junius Brutus Booth haunted the New York prison known as The Toombs, paying jailers to let him sleep in cells next to condemned murderers, and dine with the criminally insane.) Watching his father, Burton avoids all his mistakes and adopts all of his actor's tricks and turns actor when Massey dies. He must then contend with hostile audiences, as well as a berserk brother, Derek, who is bent on fame. Derek, playing John Wilkes Booth, assassinates Lincoln and Burton must bear universal hostility after his brother is trapped and killed. He steps onto a stage and begins to perform "Hamlet" and is pelted with garbage. Yet he continues bravely, refusing to retreat from the stage; the audience slowly stops abusing him, catcalls and jeers changing to applause until the endorsement is thunderous and Burton triumphant. Though many liberties are taken with the facts, the film is a solid piece of entertainment that strives for and captures high theatrical artistry, offering excerpts from "Hamlet," "Romeo and Juliet," and "Richard III." Burton is moving and mystical as the famous actor and Derek properly brooding as his mad brother. Massey is the most flamboyant of the lot and his role oozes a bit too much ham. McNamara is wasted in a predictable role as Burton's first wife but Le Gallienne, in her film debut, shines in her brief appearance as Queen Gertrude in "Hamlet." The sets, costumes, and early-day stage lighting by gaslight are authentic and Dunne's direction keeps a steady pace, except for a few lagging scenes. Booth did not, as the film indicates, appear on stage shortly after Lincoln's assassination, but immediately retired and wrote a letter of apology to the world for his brother's actions. When he did appear again on stage it was not until January, 1866, to play in "Hamlet," and he was greeted with a standing ovation from the audience. One report had it that "the sight of that slight, black, seated figure did something to them all. As one man the audience leaped to its feet and cheered ...[Booth] slowly stood up and bowed very deep. His eyes were swimming with tears."

p&d, Philip Dunne; w, Moss Hart (based on the book by Eleanor Ruggles); ph, Charles G. Clarke (CinemaScope, DeLuxe Color); m, Bernard Herrmann; ed, Dorothy Spencer; art d, Lyle Wheeler, Mark-Lee Kirk.

Drama (PR:C MPAA:NR)

PRINCE OF THE BLUE GRASS (SEE: PRIDE OF THE BLUE GRASS, 1954)

PRINCE OF THE CITY*½** (1981) 167m c

Treat Williams *(Daniel Ciello)*, Jerry Orbach *(Gus Levy)*, Richard Foronjy *(Joe Marinaro)*, Don Billett *(Bill Mayo)*, Kenny Marino *(Dom Bando)*, Carmine Caridi *(Gino Mascone)*, Tony Page *(Raf Alvarez)*, Norman Parker *(Rick Cappalino)*, Paul Roebling *(Brooks Paige)*, Bob Balaban *(Santimassino)*, James Tolkan *(D.P. Polito)*, Steve Inwood *(Mario Vincente)*, Lindsay Crouse *(Carla Ciello)*, Matthew Laurance *(Ronnie Ciello)*, Tony Turco *(Socks Ciello)*, Ron Maccone *(Nick Napoli)*, Ron Karabatsos *(Dave DeBennedeto)*, Tony DiBenedetto *(Carl Alagretti)*, Tony

Munafo *(Rocky Gazzo)*, Robert Christian *(The King)*, Lee Richardson *(Sam Heinsdorff)*, Lane Smith *(Tug Barnes)*, Cosmo Allegretti *(Marcel Sardino)*, Bobby Alto *(Mr. Kanter)*, Michael Beckett *(Michael Blomberg)*, Burton Collins *(Young Virginia Guard)*, Henry Ferrantino *(Older Guard)*, Carmine Foresta *(Ernie)*, Conrad Fowkes *(Elroy)*, Peter Friedman *(D.A. Goldman)*, Peter Michael Goetz *(Atty. DeLuth)*, Lance Henricksen *(D.A. Burano)*, Eddie Jones *(Ned)*, Don Leslie *(D.A. Amato)*, Dana Lorge *(Ann)*, Harry Madsen *(Bubba)*, E.D. Miller *(Sgt. Edelman)*, Cynthia Nixon *(Jeannie)*, Lionel Pina *(Sancho)*, Jose Santana *(Jose)*.

As in Friedkin's TO LIVE AND DIE IN L.A., this film examines the thin line between police and crooks, asking one question who is more legitimate. Do the means justify the end when it comes to bringing criminals to justice? The question is never answered in this excellent, albeit overlong, semidocumentary examination of the true story of a policeman who turns informer on his own pals and colleagues. Lumet had already gone over this ground in a better film, SERPICO, so it is questionable why he chose to do it again. Williams, in a performance that should have been acknowledged by the film Academy, is a New York detective recruited by the U.S. Department of Justice to ferret out the enormous abuses in the police department during the 1960s. He is reluctant to inform but he is such a straight arrow that he knows nothing will happen unless someone breaks the code of silence, the cop's version of the Mafia's "Omerta," so he agrees, but with assurances given him. The Feds tell Williams that he won't have to blow the whistle on his close friends but that's never a definite statement and, in the end, they want him to nail everyone. Williams is outfitted with an electronic device that broadcasts his dialog for recording in a nearby sound truck and the investigation begins. As Williams gets deeper into the plot, he learns that the police often supply narcotics to their finks in order to keep them happy, that policemen sometimes use drugs on their own, that bribes are a way of life, and that the minute an officer knows that a bust is coming down, he puts his own money and narcotics in hiding where they can't be traced. PRINCE OF THE CITY is far too long and causes a bit of squirming in the seat. The acting is universally excellent and Lumet's eye for detail is evident throughout. There's no question that someone familiar with police tactics had to have been associated with the film, as so much of it seems totally authentic and it's dubious that director Lumet and writer Allen (who was better known for works like THE PRIME OF MISS JEAN BRODIE and other such non-police films) would have known about such things without benefit of outside aid. There are two New York actors who are almost interchangeable as both are about the same age, both can play comedy, drama or even musicals. They are Orbach and Tony Roberts. In SERPICO, Lumet used Roberts as Pacino's confidante, here he uses Orbach in much the same kind of part opposite Williams. The movie runs nearly three hours, making it perfect for two nights of viewing on television, something that may have been in the back of their minds when it was produced. There's not much of a love story and only a few feminine members of the cast, the main one being Lindsay Crouse, daughter of writer Russel Crouse (LIFE WITH FATHER, etc.) who wrote for many years with partner Howard Lindsay and honored the alliance by naming his child after his associate. One wonders if Lindsay named one of his children "Crouse" as part of the deal. The screenplay was nominated for an Oscar. Gutter language and some gory violence contribute to our "O" rating.

p, Burtt Harris; d, Sidney Lumet; w, Jay Presson Allen, Lumet (based on the book by Robert Daley); ph, Andrzej Bartkowiak (Technicolor); m, Paul Chihara; ed, John J. Fitzstephens; prod d, Tony Walton; art d, Edward Pisoni; cos, Anna Hill Johnstone.

Crime Drama **Cas.** **(PR:O MPAA:R)**

PRINCE OF THE PLAINS** (1949) 60m REP bw

Monte Hale *(Bat Masterson)*, Paul Hurst *(Sheriff Hank Hartley)*, Shirley Davis *(Julie Phillips)*, Roy Barcroft *(Regan)*, Rory Mallinson *(James Taylor)*, Harry Lauter *(Tom Owens)*, Lane Bradford *(Keller)*, George Carleton *(Sam Phillips)*.

A talky Western which stars Hale investigating the death of his father and uncovering a plot to take over the town. It turns out that the man he is looking for is also behind the takeover plot. Pretty uneventful, with Hale delivering the tune "Owensville Jail," a western mourner. One of Republic's typical lower-class westerns, with a seven-day shooting schedule and a $30,000 to $50,000 budget.

p, Melville Tucker; d, Philip Ford; w, Louise Rousseau, Albert DeMond; ph, Bud Thackery; m, Stanley Wilson; ed, Richard L. Van Enger; art d, Fred A. Ritter; set d, John McCarthy, Jr., James A. Ritter.

Western **(PR:A MPAA:NR)**

PRINCE OF THIEVES, THE** (1948) 72m COL c

Jon Hall *(Robin Hood)*, Patricia Morison *(Lady Marian)*, Adele Jergens *(Lady Christabel)*, Alan Mowbray *(The Friar)*, Michael Duane *(Sir Allan Claire)*, H.B. Warner *(Gilbert Head)*, Lowell Gilmore *(Sir Phillip)*, Gavin Muir *(Baron Tristram)*, Robin Raymond *(Maude)*, Lewis L. Russell *(Sir Fitz-Alwin)*, Walter Sande *(Little John)*, Syd Saylor *(Will Scarlet)*, I. Stanford Jolley *(Bowman)*, Fredric Santley *(Lindsay)*, Belle Mitchell *(Margaret Head)*.

Hall, as Robin Hood, helps damsel-in-distress Jergens avoid a marriage to a man she doesn't love, allowing her to marry the man she does, Duane. Of the Merry Men, it is Mowbray as Friar Tuck who steals the show with a performance that borders on slapstick. Mainly a kiddie picture.

p, Sam Katzman; d, Howard Bretherton; w, Maurice Tombragel, Charles H. Schneer (based on the novel by Alexandre Dumas); ph, Fred H. Jackman, Jr. (Cinecolor); ed, James Sweeney; md, Mischa Bakaleinikoff; art d, Paul Palmentola.

Adventure **(PR:A MPAA:NR)**

PRINCE VALIANT**½ (1954) 100m FOX c

James Mason *(Sir Brack)*, Janet Leigh *(Aleta)*, Robert Wagner *(Prince Valiant)*, Debra Paget *(Ilene)*, Sterling Hayden *(Sir Gawain)*, Victor McLaglen *(Boltar)*, Donald Crisp *(King Aguar)*, Brian Aherne *(King Arthur)*, Barry Jones *(King Luke)*, Mary Philips *(Queen)*, Howard Wendell *(Morgan Todd)*, Tom Conway *(Sir Kay)*, Sammy Ogg *(Small Page)*, Neville Brand *(Viking Warrior Chief)*, Ben Wright *(Seneschal)*, Jarma Lewis *(Queen Guinevere)*, Robert Adler *(Sir Brack's Man-at-Arms)*, Ray Spiker *(Gorlock)*, Primo Carnera *(Sligon)*, Basil Ruysdael *(Old Viking)*, Fortune Gordon *(Strangler)*, Percival Vivian *(Doctor)*, Don Megowan *(Sir Launcelot)*, Richard Webb *(Sir Galahad)*, John Dierkes *(Sir Tristram)*, Carleton Young *(Herald)*, Otto Waldis *(Patch Eye)*, John Davidson *(Patriarch)*, Lloyd Aherne, Jr. *(Prince Valiant, Age 12)*, Lou Nova *(Captain of the Guards)*, Hal Baylor, Mickey Simpson *(Prison Guards)*, Eugene Roth *(Viking)*.

Straight from the funny papers to the screen comes PRINCE VALIANT, the heroic King Features Syndicate character, in the form of a young Wagner. Set in the days of King Arthur, this lavishly mounted entry has Wagner playing the son of Crisp, the King of Scandia who is exiled when the evil and powerful Carnera assumes control. Wagner travels to Camelot in hopes of receiving help from King Arthur, played by Aherne. En route, he overhears a plot by the "Black Knight" to capture Crisp and his family, imprison them in Carnera's dungeons, and overthrow Aherne. Wagner hurriedly warns Aherne, who subsequently rewards him by making him a squire to Hayden. Mason, another of Aherne's Knights of the Round Table, also makes a request for Wagner's services. As a pupil of Hayden's, Wagner learns how to handle a sword and quickly becomes a valuable asset to Camelot. Impressed with his derring-do, princess Leigh falls completely in love with "Val," as Wagner soon comes to be known. Wagner receives word from his father, requesting his assistance, and quickly rides off to help. Along the way, however, he is ambushed by the "Black Knight" whom he discovers is Mason in disguise. Wagner and Leigh are carted off to Scandia and reunited with Crisp—in one of Carnera's dungeon cells. Wagner cannot be stopped that easily and soon escapes. He gets help from McLaglen and his loyal Viking followers, who help him storm the castle. Leigh is rescued as Wagner burns the castle to a cinder. On his safe return to Camelot, Wagner exposes Mason as the villain and, after an athletic, exciting sword battle, kills him. Looked upon as a brilliant hero, Wagner is knighted by Aherne and receives the hand of Leigh. One of a handful of medieval knights-in-armor films, PRINCE VALIANT met competition from THE BLACK SHIELD OF FALWORTH (which costarred Leigh with husband Tony Curtis) and KNIGHTS OF THE ROUND TABLE. Originally, PRINCE VALIANT was to star Curtis opposite Leigh, but Wagner, in his first lead role, was chosen instead.

p, Robert L. Jacks; d, Henry Hathaway; w, Dudley Nichols (based on the comic strip *Prince Valiant* by Harold Foster); ph, Lucien Ballard (CinemaScope, Technicolor); m, Franz Waxman; ed, Robert Simpson; art d, Lyle Wheeler, Mark-Lee Kirk; cos, Charles Le Maire; spec eff, Ray Kellogg.

Adventure **(PR:AA MPAA:NR)**

PRINCE WHO WAS A THIEF, THE**½ (1951) 88m UNIV c

Tony Curtis *(Julna)*, Piper Laurie *(Tina)*, Everett Sloane *(Yussef)*, Betty Garde *(Mirna)*, Jeff Corey *(Mokar)*, Peggie Castle *(Princess Yasmin)*, Nita Bieber *(Cahuena)*, Marvin Miller *(Hakar)*, Donald Randolph *(Mustapha)*, Hayden Rorke *(Basra)*, Fred Graff *(Zocco)*, Midge Ware *(Sari)*, Carol Varga *(Beulah)*, Susan Cabot *(Girl)*, Milada Mladova *(Dancer)*, King Donovan *(Merat)*, Robert Rockwell *(Bogo)*, James Vincent *(Babu)*, Richard Morris *(Taif)*, Jack Briggs *(Officer)*, Nolan Leary *(Dignitary)*, Frank Lackteen *(Blind Beggar)*, Buddy Roosevelt *(Merchant)*, George Magrill *(Guard)*.

Curtis is a prince who, as a child, was ordered killed by those who wanted the throne for themselves. Sloane, the thief ordered to kill Curtis, instead decided to raise him, teaching him to live a life of crime. Mixed in with a plot to restore him to his seat as head of the kingdom is a romance with fellow thief Laurie, who has made off with the prized Pearl of Fatima. A typical adventure in the Arabian Nights vein, taken from a story written, surprisingly, by the principal exponent of American naturalism in literature, Theodore Dreiser, who, at the time, was drifting into the mystic strain that characterized his later years.

p, Leonard Goldstein; d, Rudolph Mate; w, Gerald Drayson Adams, Aeneas MacKenzie (based on a story from the book *Chains* by Theodore Dreiser); ph, Irving Glassberg (Technicolor); ed, Edward Curtiss; md, Hans J. Salter; art d, Bernard Herzbrun, Emrich Nicholson.

Adventure **(PR:A MPAA:NR)**

PRINCESS, THE (SEE: TIME IN THE SUN, 1970, Swed.)

PRINCESS AND THE MAGIC FROG, THE** (1965) 80m Fantasy c

David Bailey, Ernest Vaio, Frank Delfino, Clive L. Halliday, Dick Reeves, Nancy DeCarl, Lindsay Workman.

A youngster playing hooky from school captures a frog in a pond and, on his way home, meets a leprechaun in a forest who gives him seven gold coins, each capable of granting him one wish. He travels through an enchanted forest making puppets come to life and a gypsy girl become a princess, and he learns that the frog is actually an enchanted knight, who he sets free. At the end he follows a rainbow to his home, which lies at its base. An enchanting fantasy.

p&d, Austin Green; w, Harold Vaughn Taylor; ph, Donald Gundrey (Eastmancolor); m, Billy Allen, Dave Roberts; ed, Gary Lindsay; makeup, Rod Wilson; song, "At the End of the Rainbow."

Fantasy **(PR:AAA MPAA:NR)**

PRINCESS AND THE PIRATE, THE*** (1944) 94m RKO c

Bob Hope *(Sylvester Crosby/"Sylvester the Great")*, Virginia Mayo *(Princess Margaret/"Margaret Warbrook")*, Walter Brennan *(Featherhead)*, Walter Slezak *(Gov. La Roche)*, Victor McLaglen *(The Hook, Pirate Captain)*, Marc Lawrence *(Pedro)*, Hugh Haas *("Bucket of Blood" Proprietor)*, Maude Eburn *("Boar's Head Inn" Landlady)*, Adia Kuznetzoff *(Don Jose)*, Brandon Hurst *(Mr. Pelly)*, Tom Kennedy *(Alonzo)*, Stanley Andrews *(Captain of the "Mary Ann")*, Robert Warwick *(The*

King), Tom Tyler (*Lieutenant*), Rondo Hatton (*Gorilla Man*), Richard "Dick" Alexander (*Holdup Man*), Ernie Adams, Constantin Romanoff, Robert Hale (*Citizens*), Ralph Dunn (*Murderous Pirate*), Francis Ford (*Drunken Pirate*), Bert Roach (*Drunken Pirate's Companion*), Edwin Stanley (*Captain of the King's Ship*), Jack Carr (*Bartender*), Sammy Stein (*Black Jack Thug*), Colin Kenny (*First Mate "Mary Ann"*), Weldon Heyburn, Edward Peil (*Palace Guards*), Ray Teal (*Guard*), Crane Whitley (*Soldier*), James Flavin (*Naval Officer*), Alan Bridge, Al Hill, Mike Mazurki, Dick Rich (*Pirates*), Frank Moran, Oscar Hendrian (*Hecklers*), Alma Carroll, Ruth Valmy (*Handmaidens*), Bing Crosby (*Himself*), Lillian Molieri, Loretta Daye, Betty Ruth Caldwell, Betty Thurston, Pat Farrell, Kay Morley, Betty Alexander (*The Goldwyn Girls*), Bill Hunter, Stewart Garner, Art Miles, Vic Christy, Helen Thurston, Ted Billings.

In this film set in the mid-1700s, Hope is an actor on board a Jamaica-bound merchant ship. Admittedly a coward, he covers his real personality by staging an act he calls "The Great Sylvester—Man of Seven Faces." When the ship is attacked by a villainous pirate gang led by The Hook (McLaglen), Hope saves the king's daughter (Mayo) and runs from danger. After successfully avoiding the cutthroats it appears that Hope and Mayo will finally go off together. Suddenly, however, Bing Crosby comes into frame and leaves with Mayo. Hope turns to the camera and expresses his anger at that "bit player from Paramount" who takes Hope's catch. He then goes on to tell Sam Goldwyn that he'll never make another picture for him again. A funny movie with a top-ranking cast. Includes the song "How Would You Like to Kiss Me in the Moonlight" (Jimmy McHugh, Harold Adamson). How did Sam Goldwyn lure Paramount's superstar away from the studio to make a picture for him? Easy, according to Goldwyn. He promised Hope a swashbuckling farce, Technicolor, a fresh and beautiful leading lady, and plenty of curvaceous Goldwyn Girls for him to ogle. So, for the second and last time during his 18 years at Paramount, Hope left his home lot and received better production values than Paramount ever gave him. As for his leading lady, Mayo was the only Goldwyn Girl the boss ever made a star, and he did it in this picture. Eyeful Mayo proved herself a charming foil for Hope in THE PRINCESS AND THE PIRATE. Oddly, Goldwyn premiered the picture in the Midwest, and it was three solid months before the Gotham movie bugs saw the sumptuous thing. At year's end it was nominated for Oscars in two categories: Best Scoring of a Dramatic Picture and Best Art-Set Design.

p, Samuel Goldwyn; d, David Butler; w, Don Hartman, Melville Shavelson, Everett Freeman, Allen Boretz, Curtis Kenyon (based on a story by Sy Bartlett); ph, Victor Milner, William Snyder (Technicolor); m, David Rose; ed, Daniel Mandell; art d, Ernst Fegte; set d, Howard Bristol; spec eff, R.O. Binger, Clarence Slifer.

Comedy/Adventure   Cas.   (PR:A MPAA:NR)

PRINCESS AND THE PLUMBER, THE**   (1930) 72m FOX bw

Charles Farrell (*Charlie Peters*), Maureen O'Sullivan (*Princess Louise*), H.B. Warner (*Prince Conrad of Daritzia*), Joseph Cawthorn (*Merkl*), Bert Roach (*Albert Bowers*), Lucien Prival (*Baron von Kemper*), Murray Kinnell (*Worthing*), Louise Closser Hale (*Miss Eden*), Arnold Lucy.

Farrell is the son of the head of a huge plumbing concern, working his way up from the bottom, who is hired to fix the pipes in a European castle which is being rented by an impoverished prince and his daughter, O'Sullivan. The prince wants her to marry someone of his choice, but she's determined to wed Farrell, and ultimately gets things her own way. Farrell and Janet Gaynor usually were paired as lovers ever since SEVENTH HEAVEN in 1927, but Farrell was matched suddenly with O'Sullivan for PRINCESS AND THE PLUMBER. The film closely followed the Farrell-Gaynor bomb HIGH SOCIETY BLUES, a picture which even disgusted Gaynor, who refused to do any more musicals and, in fact, packed up and went to Hawaii with her mother, leaving Farrell to find another partner. While Gaynor was pouting somewhere along Waikiki, Farrell made LILIOM with Rose Hobart, and then THE PRINCESS AND THE PLUMBER, which the critics of the time found undistinguished and conventional.

p, Al Rockett; d, Alexander Korda, John Blystone; w, Howard J. Green (based on the story by Alice Duer Miller); ph, L. William O'Connell, Dave Ragin; ed, Margaret V. Clancy; md, Arthur Kay; set d, Stephen Goosson; cos, Sophie Wachner.

Romance   (PR:A MPAA:NR)

PRINCESS CHARMING**   (1935, Brit.) 74m Gainsborough/GAU bw
          (AKA: THE ESCAPE OF PRINCESS CHARMING)

Evelyn Laye (*Princess Charming*), Henry Wilcoxon (*Capt. Launa*), Yvonne Arnaud (*Countess Annette*), George Grossmith (*King Charles*), Max Miller (*Chuff*), Ivor Barnard (*Ivanoff*), Francis L. Sullivan (*Alakiev*), Dino Galvani (*Louis*), Ivor McLaren (*Ernest*), Finlay Currie (*Seegman*).

Charming Laye is a princess in a revolution-torn country who accepts the proposal of marriage by a neighboring king, Grossmith, though she has never seen him. Naval commander Wilcoxon is sent by the king to escort the girl back, but he is caught in the middle of an uprising. The only way he can get Laye out of the country is to marry her. When the "newlyweds" reach the safety of the king's palace they are told to get the marriage annulled. They refuse and escape the king's grasp. A barely average film with a great many directorial faults, which may be explained by the fact that prolific director Elvey, who started in pictures in 1913, made five movies in the year of PRINCESS CHARMING's release. A tragic note accompanied the release of the picture in the U.S.: Grossmith had died one week before in England.

p, Michael Balcon; d, Maurice Elvey; w, L. du Garde Peach, Lauri Wylie, Robert Edmunds, Arthur Wimperis (based on the play "Alexandra" by F. Martos); ph, Mutz Greenbaum; m/l, Ray Noble, Max Kester; ed, Derek Twist; md, Louis Levy; art d, Erno Metzner.

Musical/Adventure   (PR:A MPAA:NR)

PRINCESS COMES ACROSS, THE***   (1936) 76m PAR bw

Carole Lombard (*Princess Olga*), Fred MacMurray (*King Mantell*), Douglas Dumbrille (*Lorel*), Alison Skipworth (*Lady Gertrude Allwyn*), William Frawley (*Benton*), Porter Hall (*Darcy*), George Barbier (*Capt. Nicholls*), Lumsden Hare (*Inspector Cragg*), Siegfried Rumann (*Steindorf*), Mischa Auer (*Morevitch*), Tetsu Komai (*Kawati*), Bradley Page (*The Stranger*), George Sorel, Jacques Venaire, Keith Daniels, Jack Raymond, Eddie Dunn, Jack Hatfield (*Reporters*), Gaston Glass (*Photographer*), Nenette Lafayette, Andre Cheron (*French Couple*), Gladden James (*Ship's Official*), Charles Fallon, Jean de Briac (*French Baggage Officials*), Phil Tead (*Jones, the American Newsreel Man*), David Clyde (*Assistant Purser*), Milburn Stone (*American Reporter*), Bennie Bartlett (*Ship's Bellhop*), Dick Elliott (*Ship's Surgeon*), Creighton Hale (*Officer*), George Chandler (*Film Man*), Virginia Cabell, Monya Andre, Bess Stafford (*Women*), Isabelle LaMal, Eva Dennison (*Gossips*), Tom Herbert (*Cabin Steward*), Larry Steers (*Assistant Purser*), Pat Flaherty (*Officer*), Paul Kruger (*Assistant Purser*), Harry Hayden (*Master of Ceremonies at Ship Variety Show*), Edward Keane (*Chief Purser*).

A deft blend of satire, comedy, and mystery, THE PRINCESS COMES ACROSS had four writers credited with the screenplay based on material from two other writers. There was uncredited assistance from Claude Binyon and J.B. Priestley as well, and, happy to say, too many scribes did not spoil the script. Lombard is a Brooklyn actress-chorine who thinks she might be able to further her career by shedding her background for a more exotic identity. She goes to Europe and will be coming back on an ocean liner in the masquerade of a Swedish princess (this has to be a poke at Garbo) interested in becoming a movie star. With her is Skipworth, a pal who pretends to be her lady-in-waiting and who helps in the deception. Lombard meets MacMurray, a bandleader, and his manager-associate, Frawley. While on the ship, Lombard's ruse is spotted by Hall, a guy she knows from Flatbush who says he will expose her charade to everyone unless she comes across with some money. When Hall is killed, suspicion falls on Lombard and MacMurray, as they have already fallen for each other and are a shipboard item. Rumann is a German detective on the ship and he begins to investigate the murder as the boat sails toward New York. He is one of several European cops (including Harte as a Scotland Yard man) on their way to a detection convention in the U.S. MacMurray has helped Lombard take Hall's body from her stateroom and put it somewhere else so he is implicated as an accessory after the fact. Rumann gets close to solving the murder but gets rapped on the head before he can divulge the identity of the real killer. MacMurray solves the case, brings the murderer to justice (it's Dumbrille, but his motivation is muddled). Once that's taken care of, MacMurray agrees to help Lombard in her plan to capture the heart of America with her Swedish background. But when they arrive in New York, Lombard is interviewed on the radio and soon blows her cover by lapsing into pure Brooklynese. "My Concertina" was written by Jack Scholl and Phil Boutelje. Several other songwriters are listed but their material must have been cut from the final release print as the Scholl-Boutelje song was the only one heard in its entirety.

p, Arthur Hornblow, Jr.; d, William K. Howard; w, Walter DeLeon, Francis Martin, Frank Butler, Don Hartman (based on the story by Philip MacDonald, from the novel by Louis Lucien Rogger); ph, Ted Tetzlaff; ed, Paul Weatherwax; art d, Hans Dreier, Ernst Fegte; spec eff, Farciot Edouart, Dewey Wrigley; m/l, Phil Boutelje, Jack Scholl, George Marion, Jr., Richard Whiting, Mack Gordon, Harry Revel, Leo Robin, Frederick Hollander.

Comedy/Mystery   (PR:A MPAA:NR)

PRINCESS OF THE NILE**½   (1954) 71m Panoramic/FOX c

Debra Paget (*Princess Shalimar/Taura the Dancer*), Jeffrey Hunter (*Prince Haidi*), Michael Rennie (*Rama Khan*), Dona Drake (*Mirva*), Wally Cassell (*Goghi*), Edgar Barrier (*Shaman*), Michael Ansara (*Capt. Kral*), Jack Elam (*Basra*), Lester Sharpe (*Babu*), Lee Van Cleef (*Hakar*), Billy Curtis (*Tut*), Robert Roark (*Capt. Hussein*), Lisa Daniels, Merry Anders, Suzanne Alexander, Jeanne Vaughn, Kitty London, Phyllis Winger, Honey Harlow, Genice Grayson, Cheryll Clarke, Bobette Bentley (*Handmaidens*).

A lavish girlie-laden costumer set in 13th Century Egypt with Hunter starring as the son of the Caliph of Baghdad. Returning home after winning a decisive battle, he and a traveling companion stop in the city of Halwan only to find that it is being ruled by the villainous Rennie, the head of a Bedouin tribe. Soon afterwards Hunter's friend is murdered. Hunter is determined to uncover the identity of the killer and in the process meets Paget, the daughter of the city's repressed leader. He quickly becomes attracted to Paget in her flowing, colorful clothing. He then learns that Paget is doubling as an exotic dancer at the city's local nightspot. Unfortunately, Rennie also discovers Paget's ruse and flies into a rage, promising to reduce the city to ruins. Trying to calm him, Paget offers herself to him in marriage, but Hunter bravely intervenes and rescues her from an intolerable fate. Paget arms herself with a scimitar, while Hunter recruits the city's thieves to overthrow Rennie. By the finale Halwin rises from under the fist of Rennie, and Paget and Hunter are united in a royal wedding. While PRINCESS OF THE NILE contains very little along the lines of factual information, it does create a wonderfully exotic locale. The costume design by Travilla (who was nominated for an Oscar the same year for his contribution to THERE'S NO BUSINESS LIKE SHOW BUSINESS) is a superb fashion show of colors, designs, and fabrics worn by a vast number of beautiful belly-dancing harem girls who parade across sets previously seen in 1953's THE ROBE. Interestingly, PRINCESS OF THE NILE was one of two Panoramic-Fox pictures that opened in New York on the same day. Opening down the street was GORILLA AT LARGE which shared the same producer (Jacks), and same director (Jones), and much of the same crew.

p, Robert L. Jacks; d, Harmon Jones; w, Gerald Drayson Adams; ph, Lloyd Ahern (Technicolor); m, Lionel Newman; ed, George Gittens; cos, William Travilla.

Adventure   (PR:AA MPAA:NR)

PRINCESS O'HARA**   (1935) 80m UNIV bw

Jean Parker (Princess O'Hara), Chester Morris (Vic Toledo), Leon Errol (Louie), Vince Barnett (Fingers), Henry Armetta (Spidoni), Verna Hillie (Alberta Whitley), Ralph Remley (King O'Hara), Clara Blandick (Miss Van Cortland), Frank Rice (Laramie Pink), Dorothy Gray (Maggie O'Hara), Anne Howard (Hanna O'Hara), Jimmy Fay (Pat O'Hara), Clifford Jones (Tad), Pepi Sinoff (Mrs. Goldberg), Tom Dugan (Deadpan).

Helpless Parker, a princess, gets mixed up with a gang of hoodlums who have a problem delivering the protection they promised in this disappointing and weak bit of Runyonese. She even finds herself in jail, charged with stealing a horse, but by the finale her name is cleared and the horse takes the big race. Based on a story by Damon Runyon, it made it to the screen again in 1943 as the Abbott and Costello vehicle IT AIN'T HAY, but the old difficulty remained: how can Runyon's slang, wild metaphors, and effective use of the present tense be translated to film?

p, Leonard Spigelgass; d, David Burton; w, Doris Malloy, Harry Clork (based on the story by Damon Runyon); ph, Norbert Brodine; ed, Alfred Akst, Maurice Pivar.

Comedy   **(PR:A MPAA:NR)**

PRINCESS O'ROURKE***   (1943) 93m WB bw

Olivia de Havilland (Princess Maria), Robert Cummings (Eddie O'Rourke), Charles Coburn (Uncle), Jack Carson (Dave), Jane Wyman (Jean), Harry Davenport (Supreme Court Judge), Gladys Cooper (Miss Haskell), Minor Watson (Mr. Washburn), Nan Wynn (Singer), Curt Bois (Count Peter de Chandome), Ray Walker (G-Man), David Clyde (Butler), Nana Bryant (Mrs. Mulvaney), Nydia Westman (Mrs. Bower), Ruth Ford (Clare Stillwell), Julie Bishop (Stewardess), Frank Puglia (Greek), Rosina Galli (Greek's Wife), Ferike Boros (Mrs. Pulaski), Dave Willock (Delivery Boy), John Dilson (Elevator Man), Edward Gargan (Stranger), Frank Mayo (Businessman), Jody Gilbert (Truck Driver Woman), Bill Edwards (Switchboard Operator), Christian Rub (Janitor), Vera Lewis, Harry Bradley (Couple), Katherine Price (Housekeeper), Bill Kennedy, Jack Mower, Roland Drew (Dispatchers), Mary Field (Clara Stilwell), Fala the Dog.

Olivia de Havilland was already 27 but Jack Warner still thought of her as a blushing, gushing ingenue, insisting on casting her in frothy material rather than the dramatic roles she yearned to play. Such was the case with this film, which won director-writer Krasna an Oscar for his script. Immediately upon completing his premiere directing effort, Krasna joined the Air Force's motion picture unit and it wasn't until THE BIG HANGOVER (1950) that he took a directing job again. In the interim, two of his plays, "John Loves Mary" and "Dear Ruth," were made as films and he also wrote the stories for BRIDE BY MISTAKE and PRACTICALLY YOURS. Here Coburn is a European diplomat assigned to Washington who brings his niece, de Havilland, to the U.S. to find her a suitable husband. She's a princess and Coburn feels that the European husband-fodder is thin, what with all the intermarriages, and what she needs is a good, strong American to act as her consort. Coburn does his best to help her but she is soon weary of his machinations and decides to vacation at a dude ranch in the West. Cummings and Carson are piloting a small plane and de Havilland climbs aboard for the flight. She doesn't much enjoy flying so she takes a few sleeping pills to keep her drowsy during the trip. But she miscalculates the strength of the pills and goes deeply under. The plane takes off, hits bad weather, and must return to Washington. However, de Havilland is unconscious and cannot be roused. Having no idea who she is, Cummings, Carson, and Carson's fiancee, Wyman, take de Havilland to Cummings' apartment, where they hope to revive her. When she awakens, she is struck by Cummings and his charming ways and hardly any time passes before the two are in love. He asks for her hand and she accepts, but when they tell Coburn, the old man is stunned. He'd hoped for a Rockefeller or a Ford or a Getty and though he has nothing personal against Cummings, he feels that the man is not worthy of marrying a princess. She insists on marrying Cummings, and Coburn gives in, then arranges to have the wedding at the White House, where Coburn is a guest of FDR. Davenport, a justice of the Supreme Court, will perform the service. When Cummings learns that he must give up his U.S. citizenship to make the marriage, he backs out, loving his country as much as he does (one can almost hear the flag waving behind the dialog). But she loves Cummings so much that she gives up her royal standing and the marriage takes place, with FDR lurking in the background with his real dog, Fala. The famed Scottie even plays himself in the picture, acting as a go-between for the lovers. Roosevelt enjoyed the movie and liked being part of it as the picture was witty, joyful, and had an underlying patriotic appeal, so important to the country in the dim days of 1943.

p, Hal B. Wallis; d&w, Norman Krasna; ph, Ernest Haller; m, Frederick Hollander; ed, Warren Low; md, Leo F. Forbstein; art d, Max Parker; set d, George James Hopkins; m/l, "Honorable Man," Ira Gershwin, E.Y. Harburg, Arthur Schwartz.

Comedy   **(PR:A MPAA:NR)**

PRINSESSAN   (SEE: TIME IN THE SUN, A, 1970, Swed.)

PRIORITIES ON PARADE*½   (1942) 79m PAR bw

Ann Miller (Donna D'Arcy), Johnnie Johnston (Johnny Draper), Jerry Colonna (Jeep Jackson), Betty Rhodes (Lee Davis), Vera Vague (Mariposa Ginsbotham), Harry Barris (Harvey Erkimer), Eddie Quillan (Sticks O'Hara), Dave Willock (Push Gasper), Nick Cochrane (Cornetist), Rod Cameron (Stage Manager), Arthur Loft (E.V. Hartley), The Debonaires (Specialty Act), William Forrest (Col. Reeves), Warren Ashe (1st Examiner), Charles Halton (2nd Examiner), Lee Shumway (Jones).

A swing combo led by zestful Ann Miller takes a job at the Eagle Aircraft Company to boost the workers' morale. They are then offered a lucrative Broadway contract, but choose to continue toiling and laboring. Little-remembered tunes in this pathetic outing include "I'd Like to Know You Better," "Here Comes Katrinka," "Co-operate with Your Air-Raid Warden," "Concita, Marquita, Lolita, Pepita, Rosita,

"Juanita Lopez" (Herb Magidson, Jule Styne), "You're in Love with Someone Else but I'm in Love with You" (Frank Loesser, Styne).

p, Sol C. Siegel; d, Albert S. Rogell; w, Art Arthur, Frank Loesser; ph, Daniel L. Fapp; ed, Arthur Schmidt; md, Victor Young; art d, Hans Dreier, Haldane Douglas; ch, Jack Donahue.

Musical   **(PR:A MPAA:NR)**

PRISM**   (1971) 80m Corn King c

Paul Geier (Ben), Dale Soules (Eva), Nancy Volkman (Sally), Ozzie Tortora (Peter), Frank Geraci (Larry), Robert Root (The Heckler).

Geier is a middle-class New York attorney caught between his secure profession and marriage when he'd rather be more radical and leave his wife for his hippie girl friend. All the contemporary issues are taken to task in this dated but well-conceived character study that, thanks to lifeless direction and low-key performances, winds up a yawner.

p, Bob Silverstein, Jay Freund, Anitra Pivnick; d&w, Pivnick; ph, Freund (DuArt Color); m, Tom Manoff; ed, Freund, Pivnick.

Drama   **(PR:C MPAA:NR)**

PRISON BREAK**   (1938) 68m UNIV bw

Barton MacLane (Joaquin Shannon), Glenda Farrell (Jean Fenderson), Paul Hurst (Soapy), Constance Moore (Maria), Ward Bond (Red Kincaid), Edward Pawley (Joe Fenderson), Edmund MacDonald (Chris), John Russell (Jackie), Frank Darien (Cappy), Victor Kilian (Fenderson), Glenn Strange, Edmond O'Brien (Prisoners).

MacLane is a tuna fisherman wrongly jailed for a murder he did not commit. His heroics in prison win him a parole, but he is still a prisoner of an unjust parole system—he cannot travel beyond a specified limit and he cannot marry Farrell. Meantime, he is trying to find out who really committed the crime. A weak script and even worse casting of Farrell, usually a wisecracker, here the loyal sweetheart who waits for her man to be released from prison.

p, Trem Carr; d, Arthur Lubin; w, Norton S. Parker, Dorothy Reid (based on the story "The Walls of San Quentin" by Parker); ph, Harry Neumann; ed, Jack Ogilvie.

Prison Drama   **(PR:A MPAA:NR)**

PRISON BREAKER**   (1936, Brit.) 69m GS Enterprises/COL-Grand bw

James Mason (Bunny Barnes), Andrews Englemann (Stiegelman), Marguerite Allan (Veronica), Ian Fleming (Stephen Shand), George Merritt (Goldring), Wally Patch (Villars), Vincent Holman (Jackman), Andrea Malandrinos (Supello), Tarva Penna (Macallum), Neville Brook (Lord Beldam), Aubrey Mallalieu (Sir Douglas Mergin), Michael Ripper, John Counsell, Clifford Buckton.

Mason is a Secret Service agent assigned to keep Englemann, a known international crook, from stealing a treaty. When Mason accidentally kills one of Englemann's men, he is sent to prison. After a daring escape he apprehends Englemann, but not without the help of the crook's daughter, Allan, whom Mason loves. Mason reportedly said that PRISON BREAKER is one of the few films of his he had not seen. He was scolded by one London critic for his speaking voice, for which he, in turn, blamed his director, Brunel, "who had a distinctly toney speaking voice" and may have influenced him to speak similarly.

p, A. George Smith; d, Adrian Brunel; w, Frank Witty (based on the novel by Edgar Wallace); ph, George Dudgeon Stretton.

Prison Drama   **(PR:A MPAA:NR)**

PRISON CAMP   (SEE: FUGITIVE FROM A PRISON CAMP, 1940)

PRISON FARM**   (1938) 67m PAR bw

Shirley Ross (Jean Forest), Lloyd Nolan (Larry Harrison), John Howard (Dr. Roi Conrad), J. Carrol Naish (Noel Haskins), Porter Hall (Chiston R. Bradby), Esther Dale (Cora Waxley), May Boley ("Shifty" Sue), Marjorie Main (Matron Brand), Anna Q. Nilsson (Matron Ames), John Hart ("Texas" Jack), Diana R. Wood (Dolly), Howard Mitchell, Carl Harbaugh, Jack Hubbard (Guards), Mae Busch (Trixie), Ruth Warren (Josie), Robert Brister (Joe Easy), Virginia Dabney (Maizie), Phillip Warren (Injured Prisoner), Blanche Rose (Woman Trusty), Betty Mack (Meg), Jimmy Conlin (Dave the Clerk), Dick Elliott (Judge), Ethel May Halls, Cecil Weston (Matrons), Bosy Roth (Waitress), Archie Twitchell (Telegraph Operator), Pat West (Station Agent), Edwin J. Carlie (Mailman), Charles C. Wilson (Reardon), Gloria Williams (Woman), William Holden (Inmate).

Nolan comes through with a stellar performance as a man wanted for robbery who runs into trouble when Ross denounces him, sending him up the river. An average prison picture with a fine performance also from Naish as a tough cell guard. It was William Holden's first picture, having signed as an extra straight from Pasadena Junior College. He would have a one-line speaking role in his next film, MILLION DOLLAR LEGS, before crashing into the heavens with GOLDEN BOY, his third movie.

d, Louis King; w, Eddie Welch, Robert Yost, Stuart Anthony (based on the story by Edwin V. Westrate); ph, Harry Fischbeck; ed, Edward Dmytryk; md, Boris Morros; art d, Hans Dreier, Earle Hedrick.

Prison Drama   **(PR:A MPAA:NR)**

PRISON GIRL*½   (1942) 70m PRC bw

Rose Hobart (Rosemary Walsh), Sidney Blackmer (Steve), Claire Rochelle (Nellie), Lynn Starr (Linda), Jane Novak (Lucy Walker), Vince Barnett (Baldy), Jack Baxley (Sheriff Verner), Crane Whitley (Pete Saunders), John Ince (Judge Stevens), Frank Brownley (Luke Walker), Richard Clarke (Nick Morelli), Spec O'Donnell (Ben Walker), Inez Cole (Jane), Pat McKee (Jed Hicks), Ruby Dandridge (Sarah), Henry Hastings (Genesis).

Hobart escapes from prison after doing time for a mercy killing. On the outside, she is harbored by country doctor Blackmer, who is able to clear her name. The performances are up to par, but the technical credits leave something to be desired.

p, Lester Cutler; d, William Beaudine; w, Arthur St. Claire (based on the story "Gallant Lady" by Octavus Roy Cohen); ph, Marcel Le Picard; ed, Fred Bain.

Prison Drama   **(PR:A MPAA:NR)**

PRISON NURSE**   (1938) 65m REP bw

Henry Wilcoxon (Dale), Marian Marsh (Judy), Bernadene Hayes (Pepper Clancy), Ben Welden (Gaffney), Ray Mayer (Jackpot), John Arledge (Mousie), Addison Richards (Warden Benson), Frank Reicher (Dr. Hartman), Minerva Urecal (Sutherland), Selmer Jackson (Parker), Fred Kohler, Jr. (Miller), Norman Willis (Deputy).

Marsh and her nurse friends are called in to assist with an outbreak of typhoid in the midst of a threatening flood that endangers the lives of a prison's inmates. In the meantime, Marsh falls for prisoner Wilcoxon, once a top doctor. The unlikely ending has the pair winding up in each other's arms.

p, Herman Schlom; d, James Cruze; w, Earl Felton, Sidney Salkow (based on the story by Adele S. Buffington, from the novel by Dr. Louis Berg); ph, Ernest Miller; ed, William Morgan; md, Alberto Columbo; cos, Irene Saltern.

Prison Drama   **(PR:A MPAA:NR)**

PRISON SHADOWS*   (1936) 67m Mercury/Puritan bw

Eddie Nugent (Gene Harris), Lucille Lund (Claire Thomas), Joan Barclay (Mary Grant), Forrest Taylor (George Miller), Syd Saylor (Dave Moran), Monte Blue (Bert McNamee), John Elliott (Police Captain), Jack Cowell (Mr. Graham), Willard Kent (Veterinarian), Walter O'Keefe.

This contrived programmer takes place in the boxing ring, despite its title. Nugent plays a boxer who serves three years of a five-year sentence for killing another fighter in the ring. He makes his comeback, but deals another fighter a mortal blow. It turns out that a gambling ring has been murdering the fighters by applying a drug to their backs via their towels. Nugent figures out the scheme when his dog starts chewing on a towel. When the gamblers try it on him, he fakes dead and puts the police on their trail. Everybody involved in this film must have been punch drunk; it's a featherweight loser.

d, Robert Hill; w, Al Martin; ph, William Hyer; ed, Daniel Milner.

Prison Drama   **(PR:A MPAA:NR)**

PRISON SHIP**   (1945) 60m COL bw

Nina Foch (Anne Graham), Robert Lowery (Tom Jeffries), Richard Loo (Capt. Osikawa), Ludwig Donath (Professor), Robert Scott (Maj. Trevor), Barry Bernard (Jim Priestley), Erik Rolf (Jan Van Steen), Moy Ming (Chan Kwan), Louis Mercier (Frenchie), David Hughes (Steve Huntley), Barbara Pepper (Winnie De Voe), Coulter Irwin (Danny), Key Chang (1st Mate).

A Japanese ship full of American prisoners is supposed to be Tokyo-bound, but the POWs on board realize the ship is being used as a decoy for an American submarine. They stage a revolt, which results in the slaughter of 30 women and children. The Americans eventually break into the radio room and signal the U.S. sub that they are on board. Gunfire is exchanged between the two vessels, the crew is overpowered, and the Americans are saved. Another effort reflecting the strong anti-Japanese sentiments that were so prevalent at the end of the war.

p, Alexis Thurn-Taxis; d, Arthur Dreifuss; w, Josef Mischel, Ben Markson; ph, Philip Tannura; ed, Aaron Stell; md, Mischa Bakaleinikoff; art d, Jerome Pycha.

War Drama   **(PR:C MPAA:NR)**

PRISON TRAIN*½   (1938) 66m Malcolm Browne/EPC bw

Fred Keating (Frankie Terris), Linda Winters (Louise Terris), Clarence Muse (George), Faith Bacon (Maxine), Alexander Leftwich (Manny Robbins), James Blakely (Joe Robbins), Sam Bernard (Steward), John Pearson (Red), Nestor Paiva (Sullen), Val Stanton (Morose), Peter Potter (Bill Adams), Kit Guard (Guard), Franklyn Farnum (District Attorney), George Lloyd (Bull), Harry Anderson (Hardface).

Gangster Keating becomes the target of a rival mobster while on his way to Alcatraz on a prison train. Lots of high-speed train action in this somewhat entertaining yarn, which incorporated routine train and gangster film elements.

p, B.F. Zeidman; d, Gordon Wiles; w, Spencer Towne (based on a story by Mathew Borden); ph, Marcel Le Picard; ed, Edward Schroeder; md, David Chudnow; art d, Frank Sylos; spec eff, Howard Anderson.

Crime Drama   **(PR:A MPAA:NR)**

PRISON WARDEN**   (1949) 62m COL bw

Warner Baxter (Victor Burnell), Anna Lee (Elisa Burnell), James Flavin (Pete Butler), Harlan Warde (Al Gardner), Charles Cane (Bill Radford), Reginald Sheffield (English Charlie), Harry Antrim (Dr. Stark), William "Bill" Phillips (Lanning), Frank Richards (Cory), Jack Overman (Henly), Charles Evans (Governor), Harry Hayden (Greene), John R. Hamilton (Webb), Clancy Cooper (McCall), Edgar Dearing (Lt. Davis).

Baxter is a public health official who accepts the job of warden in a prison where reform is badly needed. The reform issue gets pushed aside, however, in favor of a subplot in which Baxter's wife, Lee, helps plan the escape of inmate Warde, her ex-lover.

p, Rudolph C. Flothow; d, Seymour Friedman; w, Eric Taylor; ph, Henry Freulich; m, Mischa Bakaleinikoff; ed, James Sweeney; art d, Carl Anderson.

Prison Drama   **(PR:A MPAA:NR)**

PRISON WITHOUT BARS**   (1939, Brit.) 80m LFP/UA bw

Corinne Luchaire (Suzanne), Edna Best (Yvonne Chanel), Barry K. Barnes (Dr. Georges Marechal), Mary Morris (Renee), Lorraine Clewes (Alice), Sally Wisher (Julie), Martita Hunt (Mme. Appel), Margaret Yarde (Mlle. Artemise), Elsie Shelton (Mme. Remy), Glynis Johns (Nina), Phyllis Morris (Mlle. Pauline), Nancy Roberts (Mlle. Dupont), Enid Lindsey (Mlle. Renard), Joan Ellum, Anne Crawford, Ronald Shiner.

Luchaire is a reform school student in love with the school's doctor, Barnes. She competes for his affection with Best, the superintendent who gives the students the freedom to do as they please. A remake of the French picture PRISON SANS BARREAUX, directed by Leonide Moguy in 1933. The 1939 version was filmed in three languages, with the English version taking pains to tone down the reference to lesbianism.

p, Arnold Pressburger; d, Brian Desmond Hurst; w, Arthur Wimperis, Margaret Kennedy, Hans Wilhelm (based on the play "Prison Sans Barreaux" by Gina Kaus, E. Eis, O. Eis, Hilde Koveloff); ph, Georges Perinal; m, John Greenwood; ed, Charles Crichton; md, Muir Mathieson; art d, Vincent Korda.

Prison Drama   **(PR:A MPAA:NR)**

PRISONER, THE***½   (1955, Brit.) 91m LIP-Facet/COL bw

Alec Guinness (The Prisoner), Jack Hawkins (The Interrogator), Raymond Huntley (The General), Jeannette Sterke (The Girl), Ronald Lewis (The Guard), Kenneth Griffith (The Secretary), Gerard Heinz (The Doctor), Mark Dignam (The Governor), Wilfred Lawson (The Jailer), Richard Leech.

Try as she might, author Boland couldn't convince anyone that she hadn't gotten her inspiration for her play and screenplay from the real-life plight and trial of Hungarian Cardinal Mindszenty, a real hero. In 1944, Mindszenty had been jailed by the Nazis at the age of 52 (then still a bishop) for not allowing his Catholic parishioners to say a mass and sing a Nazi-ordered "Te Deum" in "thanksgiving for the successful liberation of Budapest from the Jews." He was adamantly against such a fraud and served time until Hungary was liberated. Then, in 1948, he rebelled against the Russian domination and was tossed into solitary confinement. It was that sentence that helped spur the Hungarian revolution of 1956. Eventually, Mindszenty was allowed to stay at the U.S. embassy, where he occupied the top floor for the next 15 years, supported by donations from the U.S., although virtually an exile in his own land. In an unnamed East European country, cardinal Guinness is arrested and put under the brilliant interrogation of psychologist Hawkins, now a member of the hierarchy of the police state, although an old friend of Guinness' from their youth. The two men had worked together against the Nazis and Hawkins knows that no amount of physical torture will sway Guinness enough to make the "phony" confession that they want, admissions which will create chaos among the Catholic believers. The picture is a photographed stage play, and although there are a few other actors, it's Hawkins and Guinness most of the time and their mano a mano is a delight to watch. Months pass and Hawkins keeps looking for the crack in Guinness' facade. Eventually, he finds it when he reckons that Guinness did not join the church in a sincere calling from God. Rather, it was because Guinness was attempting to escape his tawdry earlier life with a mother who was a semi-whore. Once Hawkins convinces Guinness that his career in the church is based on a false premise, Guinness begins to crack. There is a "kangaroo court" trial and Guinness, now almost blank-faced, admits to all of the crimes he is alleged to have committed. The sentence is death, but an even graver sentence is carried out when Guinness is commuted and freed to walk among his fellow countrypeople, a broken man. The picture was controversial and the response from each country depended on what kind of government was in power at the time. Ireland called it "pro-communist," while France said it was "anti-communist" and would not allow it to be shown at Cannes. The Italians thought it was "anti-Catholic" and barred it from the Venice Film Festival. Any movie that occasions that kind of stir is worth seeing, and this one is definitely that. It ranks as one of Guinness' best acting jobs and, perhaps, Hawkins' very best. Director Glenville had to use all of his expertise to keep this from being little more than "talking heads" and his touch was sure. The fact that the film only runs just over one and a half hours is also a plus. There were a few chuckles regarding the names of the producers, Cox and Box, as that was the title of an early Gilbert and Sullivan one-act musical about two men who shared the same room but didn't know it, as one worked nights, the other days.

p, Vivian A. Cox; d, Peter Glenville; w, Bridget Boland (based on her play); ph, Reginald Wyer; m, Benjamin Frankel; ed, Freddie Wilson; md, Frankel; art d, John Hawkesworth; cos, Julie Harris; makeup, William Pailleton.

Drama   **(PR:C MPAA:NR)**

PRISONER OF CORBAL**   (1939, Brit.) 75m Capitol/Unity bw (GB: THE MARRIAGE OF CORBAL)

Nils Asther (Varennes), Hugh Sinclair (Marquis of Corbal), Hazel Terry (Cleonie), Noah Beery, Sr. (Sergeant), Ernest Deutsch (Fugutive), Davy Burnaby (Pierre), Clifford McLaglen (Jean), Ralph Truman (Charles), Brian Buchel (Roger), Walter Sondes (Chaplain), Arthur Rigby, Jr. (Major), Moira Lynd (Hostess), Gordon Begg (Shepherd), Vincent Sternroyd (Deaf Peasant), Charles Paton (French Commandant), Percy Walsh (Gamekeeper), Hubert Leslie (General).

This British picture, set in the midst of the French Revolution, casts Terry as the subject of amour of revolutionary Asther and aristocrat Sinclair. It's the latter who emerges with Terry in his arms; Asther eventually commits suicide. Some racy bedroom scenes were clipped for the U.S. release. Performances suffer from miscasting, but Asther gives an outstanding performance. Interesting use of camera angles stands out, as does direction in handling of crowd scenes.

p, Max Schach; d, Karl Grune; w, S. Fullman (based on the novel The Nuptials of

Corbal by Rafael Sabatini); ph, Otto Kanturek, R. Black; m, Allan Gray; ed, E. Stokvis; md, Boyd Neal.

Historical Adventure/Romance **(PR:C MPAA:NR)**

PRISONER OF JAPAN*½ (1942) 54m PRC bw (GB: THE LAST COMMAND)

Alan Baxter *(David Bowman)*, Gertrude Michael *(Toni Chase)*, Ernest Dorian *(Matsuru)*, Corinna Mura *(Loti)*, Tommy Seidel *(Ens. Bailey)*, Billy Boya *(Maui)*, Ray Bennett *(Lt. Morgan)*, Dave O'Brien *(Marine)*, Ann Staunton *(Edie)*, Beal Wong *(Japanese Operator)*, Gilbert Frye *(U.S. Operator)*, Kent Thurber *(Comdr. McDonald)*.

Baxter is an heroic astronomer who discovers that a Japanese spy is operating a Pacific island radio base. One U.S. battleship is sunk by the enemy, but Baxter gets word to the rest of the fleet before the act is repeated. A pretty sorry attempt to cash in on the emotions raised by Pearl Harbor.

p, Leon Fromkess; d, Arthur Ripley; w, Robert Chapin, Ripley (based on the story by Edgar G. Ulmer); ph, Jack Greenhalgh; m, Lee Zahler; ed, Holbrook Todd.

War Drama **(PR:A MPAA:NR)**

PRISONER OF SECOND AVENUE, THE*** (1975) 98m WB c

Jack Lemmon *(Mel)*, Anne Bancroft *(Edna)*, Gene Saks *(Harry)*, Elizabeth Wilson *(Pauline)*, Florence Stanley *(Pearl)*, Maxine Stuart *(Belle)*, Ed Peck *(Man Upstairs)*, Gene Blakely *(Charlie)*, Ivor Francis *(Psychiatrist)*, Stack Pierce *(Detective)*, Sylvester Stallone *(Youth in Park)*.

THE PRISONER OF SECOND AVENUE was not one of Simon's best plays, nor was it one of his better screenplays. Actually, it seemed to have indicated that Simon may have been stealing from himself in his earlier original THE OUT OF TOWNERS. In that one, Lemmon was a man from Ohio to whom every possible problem of being a tourist occurred. This story might just be what happened to Lemmon if he'd accepted the job in the former film and stayed in New York instead of going home to the Midwest. Parallel can also be drawn between this and THE APARTMENT, where Lemmon is a junior executive. This movie takes place 15 years later and Lemmon is now living life near the top. He's married to Bancroft and they dwell in a small, fashionable, expensive, and well-furnished cheese box on the East Side of Manhattan. Lemmon's an ad man who loses his job, has his apartment robbed, then must suffer the embarrassment of his wife going out to win the bread. That brings him to the edge of a nervous collapse. It's not a very funny subject and the picture wavers between comedy and drama. Lemmon's ego is shattered, he feels worthless, and he takes it all out on his wife, Bancroft, who loves him dearly and understands that it's a temporary setback but he must have his brains in order before he goes back into the advertising jungle. In the end, the two of them are united in their defiance of the system which brought him teetering. There are lots of one-liners and just as much pathos to be found. On the stage, the couple was played by Peter Falk and Lee Grant, who may have been better suited to the roles. Simon's favorite stage director, Gene Saks, makes an acting appearance as Lemmon's brother, with Wilson and Stanley doing bits as the concerned sisters. In the play, the "Man Upstairs" was named "Jacoby" and was never seen. They decided to hire deep-voiced Ed Peck (who has made a huge living doing commercials with his booming throat) in the role but neglected to delete one of the play's lines which was then out of place. Lemmon yells to the ceiling, "You think I don't know what you look like but I do." That's wrong because we've just seen Lemmon looking up at Peck when Peck drenches Lemmon. (That scene was shot earlier on the real balcony in New York but the color didn't match so they shot it again on the set at Warner Bros. studios in Burbank.) Director Frank was amazed by Peck's timbre and hired him because of it but someone felt it was just too powerful and Peck was later looped by Joseph Turkel (one of Stanley Kubrick's pets, having appeared in PATHS OF GLORY, THE SHINING, etc.). Turkel, a friend of Peck's, had just a few days before this happened, recommended Peck for a voice job at Fox. Strange but true, and a good indication of what happens in Hollywood. Costumer Schumacher soon gave up sewing and measuring to become a writer-director. Sylvester Stallone does a tiny bit in Central Park.

p&d, Melvin Frank; w, Neil Simon (based on his play); ph, Philip Lathrop (Panavision, Technicolor); m, Marvin Hamlisch; ed, Bob Wyman; art d, Preston Ames; set d, Marvin March; cos, Joel Schumacher.

Comedy **Cas.** **(PR:A-C MPAA:PG)**

PRISONER OF SHARK ISLAND, THE**** (1936) 95m FOX bw

Warner Baxter *(Dr. Samuel A. Mudd)*, Gloria Stuart *(Mrs. Peggy Mudd)*, Joyce Kay *(Marth Mudd)*, Claude Gillingwater *(Col. Jeremiah Dyer)*, Douglas Wood *(Gen. Ewing)*, Fred Kohler, Jr. *(Sgt. Cooper)*, Harry Carey *(Commandant of Fort Jefferson "Shark Island")*, Paul Fix *(David Herold)*, John Carradine *(Sgt. Rankin)*, Francis McDonald *(John Wilkes Booth)*, Arthur Byron *(Mr. Erickson)*, O.P. Heggie *(Dr. McIntire)*, John McGuire *(Lovett)*, Paul McVey *(Hunter)*, Francis Ford *(Cpl. O'Toole)*, Ernest Whitman *(Buck Tilford)*, Frank Shannon *(Judge Advocate Holt)*, Frank McGlynn, Sr. *(Lincoln)*, Arthur Loft *(Carpetbagger)*, Maurice Murphy *(Orderly)*, Paul Stanton *(Orator)*, Ronald "Jack" Pennick *(Signal Man)*, Merrill McCormick *(Commandant's Aide)*, James Marcus *(Blacksmith)*, Jan Duggan *(Actress)*, Lloyd Whitlock *(Maj. Rathbone)*, Leila McIntyre *(Mrs. Lincoln)*, Dick Elliott *(Actor)*, Murdock MacQuarrie *(Spangler)*, Bud Geary, Duke Lee, Robert E. Homans *(Sergeants)*, Robert Dudley *(Druggist)*, Wilfred Lucas *(Colonel)*, Cecil Weston *(Mrs. Surratt)*, Cyril Thornton *(Maurice O'Laughlin)*, Beulah Hall Jones *(Blanche)*, J.M. Kerrigan *(Judge Maiben)*, Etta McDaniel *(Rosabelle Tilford)*, J.P. McGowan *(Ship's Captain)*, Harry Strang *(Mate)*, Whitney Bourne, Robert Parrish, Frank Baker.

Baxter is smashing as an innocent doctor who finds McDonald, playing the fugitive and assassin John Wilkes Booth, and fixes his broken ankle before sending him on his way. He is arrested shortly thereafter and charged with being part of the conspiracy to murder President Abraham Lincoln. Dragged away from his wife, Stuart, and their small child, Baxter is convicted on scant evidence and sent to prison for life at Fort Jefferson on Shark Island in the Dry Tortugas. There he is considered, even by the burly black guards, to be a worthy "southern gentleman" doctor who cares for other prisoners as well as their captors when they fall sick. When a yellow fever epidemic breaks out, Baxter, risking his own life, saves the lives of many. For this heroic act, Baxter's case is reopened and he is exonerated of being part of the Lincoln conspiracy, and returned to his little family. This based-on-fact story about injustice meted out to one man is handled beautifully by Ford, whose cameras, under Glennon's expert guidance, depict the horrors of prison life in starkly shown scenes. Baxter underplays his role superbly and elicits viewer sympathy early on. Ford leaves no doubt as to the man's innocence by stating the facts of the case right at the beginning of the film. The good doctor's sympathies are shown properly when Baxter treats Booth, telling him, "I guess Old Abe's all right after all. He's the only salvation we Southerners can look for—him and God's mercy." He believes that his patient is wrong-headed from the moment he meets McDonald, stating after the stranger leaves that he "smells of snakes." There are some slight similarities between this film and I AM A FUGITIVE FROM A CHAIN GANG and LES MISERABLES but THE PRISONER OF SHARK ISLAND is a distinctive Ford film with his imprint on every frame, offering a taut, believable script by Johnson. Typical of the reverential Ford is the scene depicting the assassination. McGlynn, who played Lincoln many times, is shown seated in his box and when the shot that ends his life rings out, only McGlynn's hand is shown slumping, with a quick full shot of McGlynn dead that dissolves into a magnificent portrait of the President.

p, Darryl F. Zanuck; d, John Ford; w, Nunnally Johnson (based on the life of Dr. Samuel A. Mudd); ph, Bert Glennon; ed, Jack Murray; md, Louis Silvers; art d, William Darling; set d, Thomas Little; cos, Gwen Wakeling.

Prison Drama **(PR:A MPAA:NR)**

PRISONER OF THE IRON MASK** (1962, Fr./Ital.) 80m Cineproduzioni Associate-Mida-Comptoir Francais/AIP c (LA VENGEANCE DU MASQUE DE FER; VENDETTA DELLA MASCHERA DI FERRO)

Michel Lemoine *(Marco)*, Wandisa Guida *(Christina)*, Andrea Bosie, Jany Clair, Giovanni Materassi, Pietro Albano, Tiziana Casetti, Alan Evans, Mimmo Poli, Francesco De Leone, Nando Tamberlani, Marco Tulli, Joe Camel, Silvio Bagolini, Erminio Spalla, Emma Baron, Andrea Fantasia, Piero Pastore.

The umpteenth version of Dumas' tale casts Lemoine as the son of a duke who is placed in an iron mask to prevent him from tattling on a wicked count. Standard costumer without much verve.

p, Francesco Thellung, Salvatore Billitteri (English version); d, Francesco De Feo, Lee Kresel (English version); w, Silvio Amadio, Ruggero Jacobbi, De Feo (based on the novel *Man with the Iron Mask* by Alexandre Dumas); ph, Raffaele Masciocchi (Techniscope, Eastmancolor); m, Carlo Innocenzi; ed, Luciano Cavalieri; art d, Piero Poletto; set d, Ennio Michettoni; cos, Adriana Berselli; makeup, Oscar Pacheli.

Adventure/Drama **(PR:A MPAA:NR)**

PRISONER OF THE VOLGA*½ (1960, Fr./Ital.) 102m Transmonde-Fides/PAR c

John Derek *(Alexis Orloff)*, Elsa Martinelli *(Mascha)*, Dawn Addams *(Tatiana)*, Charles Vanel *(Gorew)*, Gert Froebe *(Professor)*, Rik Battaglia *(Lisekno)*, Wolfgang Preiss *(Ossip)*, Nerio Bernardi *(Elagin)*, Ingmar Zeisberg *(Olga)*, Jacques Caetelot *(Jakowiew)*, Feodor Chaliapin *(Fomitsch)*, Nitza Constantin *(Grisha)*, Nino Marchetti *(Michailow)*, Arturo Bragaglia *(Principe)*.

Derek is a Russian Army captain who gets tough with a general who had impregnated his new wife. The captain is promptly stripped of his rank and placed in a lock-up. His wife, Addams, helps him escape, but is killed in the ensuing battle. Derek then joins a band of gypsies and falls in love with Martinelli. The dubbing (German, Swedish, Italian, and Austrian actors are used), is fairly effective, but does result in a few unintentionally funny moments (Volga boatmen with British accents, for instance).

d, W. Tourjansky; w, Salka Viertel, Al Lyx; ph, Mario Montuori (Totalscope, Eastmancolor); m, Norbert Glanzberg; ed, Robert Cinquini.

Historical Adventure **(PR:C MPAA:NR)**

PRISONER OF WAR** (1954) 80m MGM bw

Ronald Reagan *(Web Sloane)*, Steve Forrest *(Cpl. Joseph Robert Stanton)*, Dewey Martin *(Jesse Treadmun)*, Oscar Homolka *(Col. Nikita I. Biroshilov)*, Robert Horton *(Francis Aloysius Belney)*, Paul Stewart *(Capt. Jack Hodges)*, Henry [Harry] Morgan *(Maj. O.D. Halle)*, Stephen Bekassy *(Lt. Georgi M. Robovnik)*, Leonard Strong *(Col. Kim Doo Yi)*, Darryl Hickman *(Merton Tollivar)*, Ralph Ahn, Weaver Levy *(Red Guards)*, Rollin Moriyama *(Capt. Lang Hyun Choi)*, Ike Jones *(Benjamin Julesberg)*, Clarence Lung *(MVD Officer)*, Jerry Paris *(Axel Horstrom)*, John Lupton *(Lt. Peter Reilly)*, Stuart Whitman *(Captain)*, Bob Ellis *(Alan H. Rolfe)*, Lewis Martin *(General)*, Otis Greene *(David Carey)*, Lalo Rios *(Sachez Rivero)*, Lester C. Hoyle *(Emanuel Hazard)*, Roy Boyle *(Donald C. Jackwood)*, Leon Tyler *(Jacob Allen Lorfield)*, Edo Mita *(Red Doctor)*, Peter Hansen *(Capt. Fred Osborne)*.

This rather immature Korean War drama would have been much less offensive if it wasn't concerned with such a brutal and horrifying topic—the systematic torture and brainwashing of American prisoners of war by the Koreans. Reagan stars as an intelligence officer who volunteers to enter enemy territory to confirm reports that American POWs are being treated brutally by their Communist captors. Reagan is parachuted behind the lines and then makes his way to the nearest POW camp where he infiltrates a fresh group of GIs being led in. Shocked to find that all the rumors about brutal treatment are true, Reagan submits himself to the Communist indoctrination of Russian officer Homolka and pretends to accept their ideology. Another soldier, Martin, also pretends to be brainwashed, but only so that he can smuggle medicine to an ailing GI who won't capitulate. Martin and Reagan's covert method of defying the Communists is directly contrasted with that of tough GI Forrest, who fights against the Russians and Koreans at every turn. Armed with detailed, first-hand knowledge of the Communists' heinous behavior, it is up to Reagan to escape and tell the world. Based on the actual testimony of Korean War prisoners, the events and even parts of the dialog were supposedly based on fact. Unfortunately this very important and serious subject matter is given the classic Hollywood propoganda mill comic-book treatment. Russian and Korean Communists are all portrayed with a one-dimensional, leering, evil quality that is more suitable in the realm of a Saturday afternoon serial. The heartless Reds are easily identifiable because they all maintain unbearably smug expressions and hold their cigarettes in their *left* hands while cackling with glee at the pain of the Americans. Homolka seems to have wandered in from a Warner Bros. cartoon because his performance is so outrageous. These broad, mindless portrayals only work against a film that could have been very engrossing. Homolka and his brood are so ridiculous and distracting that the viewer can never really believe that these men are actually doing anything but pretending to be evil torturers and the joke will be revealed any moment. While the very real crimes committed against the POWs more than warranted a gripping screen treatment, PRISONER OF WAR failed because it was long on sensation and short on insight.

p, Henry Berman; d, Andrew Marton; w, Allen Rivkin; ph, Robert Planck; m, Jeff Alexander; ed, James Newcom; art d, Cedric Gibbons, Malcolm Brown.

War **(PR:C MPAA:NR)**

PRISONER OF ZENDA, THE***** (1937) 101m SELZ/UA bw

Ronald Colman *(Rudolph Rassendyl/King Rudolf V)*, Madeleine Carroll *(Princess Flavia)*, Douglas Fairbanks, Jr. *(Rupert of Hentzau)*, Mary Astor *(Antoinette De Mauban)*, C. Aubrey Smith *(Col. Zapt)*, Raymond Massey *(Black Michael)*, David Niven *(Capt. Fritz von Tarlenheim)*, Eleanor Wesselhoeft *(Cook)*, Byron Foulger *(Johann)*, Montagu Love *(Detchard)*, William Von Brincken *(Kraftstein)*, Phillip Sleeman *(Lauengram)*, Ralph Faulkner *(Bersonin)*, Alexander D'Arcy *(De Gauiet)*, Torben Meyer *(Michael's Butler)*, Ian MacLaren *(Cardinal)*, Lawrence Grant *(Marshal Strakencz)*, Howard Lang *(Josef)*, Ben Webster *(British Ambassador)*, Evelyn Beresford *(British Ambassador's Wife)*, Boyd Irwin *(Master of Ceremonies)*, Emmett King *(Von Haugwitz, Lord High Chamberlain)*, Charles K. French *(Bishop)*, Al Shean *(Orchestra Leader)*, Charles Halton *(Passport Officer)*, Otto Fries *(Luggage Officer)*, Florence Roberts *(Duenna)*, Spencer Charters *(Porter)*, Russ Powell, D'Arcy Corrigan *(Travelers)*, Francis Ford *(Man)*, Henry Roquemore *(Station Master)*, Lillian Harmer *(Station Attendant)*, Pat Somerset, Leslie Sketchley *(Guards at Lodge)*.

This meticulous Selznick production is about as posh as movies come. The viewer, in addition to being dazzled by marvelous sets, costumes, and splendid technical details, is treated to exceptional performances by Colman, Carroll, Fairbanks, Smith, Astor, and Massey. The great Hope adventure is created for the screen with loving loyalty to the story and Cromwell's helmsmanship is decisive and full of affection for the tale. Colman plays the doppelganger roles of Rassendyl and King Rudolf V of the mythical Ruritanian kingdom in Central Europe. (In fact, this film presents *the* Ruritanian tale which all others would emulate.) The film opens by showing Colman arriving in Strelsau (a mythical city). He startles officials and citizens who immediately identify his likeness to the royal prince about to be crowned king; in fact, many believe him to the prince traveling in disguise. He wears a goatee where the prince sports a mustache. Colman goes into the country to fish and is found by Niven and Smith, aides to the prince. The Prince, also played by Colman, also comes upon the English visitor and invites his look-alike, a distant cousin, they discover, to dine with him in the royal hunting lodge. At dawn, Colman is rudely awakened by having a pitcher of water dashed in his face by Smith who asks what he and the prince had been drinking the night before. The prince has been drugged and is in a coma. Smith proposes that Colman substitute for the prince at the coronation by shaving his goatee and, until the prince has recovered, playing his part. They take the prince to a cellar room of the royal hunting lodge while Smith learns that the housekeeper was responsible for giving the prince the drugged wine. He forces the woman to drink the drugged wine, then has Niven tie and gag her at the entrance to the cellar room, entrusting the safety of the prince to a faithful valet. Smith vows to his unconscious prince that he will see him crowned, through the impostor Colman, and that "Black Michael," the prince's evil brother, Massey, will never sit on the throne. In his distant palace Massey sits smugly looking at a message that his brother will not live to be crowned and receives congratulations from his aides who tell him he will be the next king. Yet Massey is cautious, not having heard it confirmed that his brother is dead and he warns his minions that their enthusiasm might be "premature." On a train bound for the capital, Strelsau, Colman sits in regal uniform inside the royal train coach with Niven and Smith, struggling to memorize his coronation speech. As Colman emerges from the coach when arrivng at Strelsau, someone cries, "God save the king!" Says Smith as they emerge from the coach, "God save them *both*!" As Colman arrives, Massey almost goes into shock, ordering his scheming henchman, Fairbanks, to go to the royal lodge and "find out what went wrong." Massey then receives Colman as he marches into the royal court. Dressed in black, squinting through a monocle, Massey looks over his so-called brother and Colman looks apprehensively back at him. Massey then bows obediently, accepting the impostor, and offers his arm, leading Colman to the throne where he is crowned king. Carroll, the beautiful princess betrothed to the prince, arrives and swears her allegiance to him. Colman, unnerved at this beautiful blonde woman kneeling before him, whispers to Smith, "Do I kiss her?" Smith nods and Colman leans forward and kisses Carroll on the cheek, leading her outside to cheering citizens, getting into the royal coach for the grand parade. Both Colman and Carroll nod to the cheering subjects and he learns that the prince has neglected her terribly, sending her "two picture postcards in three years." He tells her she's the loveliest girl in Europe. That night, at the grand ball, Colman falls in love with Carroll and she discovers that the once indifferent prince who has mistreated her is charming, warm, and utterly romantic. He has already slighted Massey by spending his time with Carroll. Colman tells Massey later that his impetuous manner is caused by "the excitement, the first time I've ever been crowned." He then taunts Massey by telling him that he had an excellent wine the night earlier, knowing it was Massey's agents who drugged the real prince. Colman then yawns in Massey's face and Massey withdraws, telling Colman, "I see that I bore your majesty." Carroll later warns Colman against Massey and tells him that his life means much to "your country, your friends, and...your cousin and most loving servant." He begs her to stay but she promises to see him the next day. That night Smith and Colman sneak out of the palace to go to the hunting lodge to reinstate the prince to his true identity. Niven is ordered to stay behind and if Massey insists upon seeing the king, he is to draw his sword: "...and if that door is forced, you're not going to be alive to tell about it." "Do you think I would be, sir?" says the loyal Niven. But Colman and Smith find the lodge empty, the prince gone, and the prince's valet dead. They find a note, ostensibly from Fairbanks, which reads: "One king is enough for any kingdom." Later Smith tells Colman that the kidnapers cannot speak unless they "denounce themselves," and cannot expose Colman the impostor without admitting that they have kidnaped the true prince. He asks that Colman continue his charade, that the kidnapers cannot kill the real prince and leave him on the throne. "Rudolf is my king," Smith says,"I have a feeling for my king." He then tells Colman that if he quits his impersonation, Massey will be crowned king and Carroll will be compelled to marry him. "But you can't let that happen to her," Colman says. "Can you?" replies Smith wisely, knowing Colman is in love with Carroll. Colman goes on with the impersonation, taking Carroll to a great royal ball, marching down an enormous staircase to a huge ballroom where hundreds of distinguished visitors accord him honor. Colman and Carroll begin waltzing but when he stops to talk to her, the hundreds of dancers abruptly stop. Colman stops the dance and refuses to resume dancing, causing all of the others to stop, until Carroll promises to step out on the terrace with him. In a marvelous garden setting, Colman and Carroll stroll past lagoons filled with swans. He tells her, "I love you...I love you more than truth or life or honor." They kiss and Carroll tells him that she loves him. He asks her if she could love him if he were not the king. "In my heart," Carroll tells him, "there is no king, no crown, only you." Colman is about to tell Carroll his true identity but the ever alert Smith interrupts him, telling Colman that he must bid his important guests goodnight. Colman later tells Smith that he is on love with Carroll and is thinking of remaining on the throne to have her. He tells Smith to find the real king "before it's too late." Fairbanks by then has met with Massey, explaining that there are *two* kings, doppelgangers. Massey proposes that they kill Colman and bury him as the real king and then murder the king who is being held by Fairbanks in his castle at Zenda. The way will then be paved for Massey to assume the crown. Fairbanks tries to entice Colman to his death by sending a message to meet Astor, Massey's mistress, with a promise that she will tell him where the real king is being hidden. The two meet in a remote spot and Astor tells Colman that three men are en route to kill him. Next she tells him that the king is a prisoner at Zenda castle. She promises to help him free the king to protect Massey against Fairbanks. Fairbanks arrives with two henchmen and asks for a truce, offering Colman a fortune to depart the country. Colman refuses and escapes the trap, returning to the palace. He tells Carroll that he's going hunting but will come for her soon. Colman then sets off for Zenda with Niven, Smith, and loyal troops to rescue the king. At first they meet Fairbanks who tries to barter with Colman, telling him that Massey will give him 100,000 pounds to leave the country. When he refuses, Fairbanks tells him he will betray Massey if he, Fairbanks, receives Massey's estates. Colman laughs at him and Fairbanks throws a knife in the impostor's direction that barely misses him before escaping into his lair. Meanwhile, the true king languishes in a dank cell at Zenda castle while Astor tends to the sick man. Fairbanks gloats over the stricken king, showing him a trapdoor, and telling him that, if there is any attempt to rescue him, his guards will shove him through the trapdoor to a watery death below. Massey arrives and tries to get the king to sign his abdication. "I will not disgrace a crown I never wore," the king tells Massey, proving his noble spirit. An agent for Astor, Foulger, goes to Colman and Smith, giving them a map of the castle and a promise that he will lower the drawbridge, but one man must enter the castle and prevent the guards from drowning the true king until Smith and his troops enter. Colman insists that he be the one to penetrate the castle and save the king. "I've been an impostor for your sake," he tells Smith. "I won't be one for my own." Colman slips into the castle through a secret entrance. At the same time Fairbanks enters Astor's room but Massey finds the two together and struggles with Fairbanks, who kills him. Fairbanks then finds Foulger trying to lower the drawbridge and crushes his skull with a pike. Colman goes to the king, kills two guards, and is about to take the real king to safety when Fairbanks confronts him with a gun. Colman challenges Fairbanks to a duel, tricking him into swordplay. The pair fight with blades through the castle in a terrific struggle. They thrust and parry back and forth, barbing each other with words. When Fairbanks sees that Colman is trying to work himself toward the rope that holds the drawbridge, attempting to cut it, he says, "I just killed a man for trying that." "An unarmed man, of course," retorts Colman. "Of course," states the arrogant Fairbanks. He then shouts to Colman: "Your golden-haired goddess will look well in black, Rassendyl. I'll console her for you. Kiss away her tears. What, no quotations?" Colman smiles with a swing of his sword: "Yes. 'A barking dog never bites.'" "You'd be a sensation in the circus," sneers Fairbanks. "I can't understand it. Where did you learn such roller-skating?" Replies Colman: "Coldstream Guards, my boy. Come on, when does the fencing lesson begin?" Colman manages to sever the rope holding the drawbridge and Smith and Niven lead their cavalrymen across it, many being shot down by the castle guards who are overwhelmed and hacked to death with sabers wielded by the king's loyal troops. (Here is the symbolism of the old nobility against the modern assassin, men on horseback with swords facing gun-firing thugs in uniform.) Fairbanks, realizing that the game is over, leaps though a window, dives into the moat, and escapes after wounding Colman. The true king thanks his savior and tells him that he "would have been my best and dearest friend," had they known each other earlier and that "you taught me how to be a king." Colman later confronts Carroll who knows the truth. "I love you," he tells her. "In all else I've been an impostor, but never in that." She admits that she loves him but when he begs her to go away with him, Carroll tells him that she is honor-bound to remain loyal to her king and her vows. Colman is escorted to the border by Niven and Smith. "We'll meet again, Fritz," Colman tells Niven. "Fate doesn't always make the right men kings," Niven says. "Goodbye, Colonel," Colman tells Smith, "we've run a good course together." Replies a proud Smith: "Goodbye, Englishman. You're the finest Elphberg of them all!" Colman rides to the crest of a ridge, turns, waves, and then vanishes over the horizon, his adventure ended. Director Cromwell does a marvelous job in extracting great performances from his leading players, as well as carefully developing the Colman-Carroll romance which is touched with gentility and poetic grace, thanks to the elegant appearances of the lovers, as well as their wonderfully modulated voices and deliveries of dialog that only a few screen actors ever possessed. Cromwell was brought in by Selznick because the producer knew that this director would bring out the best from the cast and that he would stay within his budget. Selznick nevertheless hedged his bets and had George Cukor, famed as a "woman's director," helm the final scene between Colman and Carroll and this shows in Carroll's departure from her pose as the soft and gentle Princess Flavia, one where she becomes abruptly assertive and much more expressive, her voice rising to tell Colman that she must do her duty and not run away with him. Action director W.S. Van Dyke was also called in to direct the exciting and dashing duel between Colman and Fairbanks. Selznick was repeatedly warned not to revive this Ruritanian adventure-romance story, his advisors telling him that the production was doomed. The Hope story had been filmed several times before, as early silents in 1912 and 1915, and a major silent in 1922, ornately costumed and directed by Rex Ingram, starring Lewis Stone as the commoner-king, Alice Terry as Flavia, and Ramon Novarro as Rupert. Selznick, however, rightly reasoned that he could capture the public interest in the film, highlighting the coronation scenes, since the public was already keyed to the upcoming coronation of Britain's King Edward VIII. He was right. The film was a smash, enhancing the careers of all involved in the production. Colman was not really a swashbuckling actor, although he retained somewhat that image after appearing in A TALE OF TWO CITIES, CLIVE OF INDIA, LOST HORIZON, and playing the daring French poet Francois Villon in IF I WERE KING. The fabulous duel staged between Fairbanks and Colman in THE PRISONER OF ZENDA suggests more than what really happens. Brilliant cameraman Howe advised Cromwell that Colman, Selznick's all-time favorite actor, who received $200,000 for his work here, had a "bad side," and had to be photographed carefully. When the beautiful but patrician Carroll heard about this she went to Cromwell and said she too had a bad side and wanted special consideration in the camera angles. Her bad side, according to Cromwell, was the same side as Colman's and it would be impossible to shoot the pair by accenting only their best profiles. "I called on Jimmy Howe," Cromwell later said, "and asked if she had a bad side, and he said: 'You couldn't fault her if you stood her on her head!' So I went back to her, pointing out how ridiculous it was, and that we wouldn't be able to shoot the picture if she has the same side as Colman. After that, she would not speak to me for the rest of the picture." Carroll was also upset because Selznick ordered her not to use her usual heavy makeup, desiring a "fresh scrubbed" look to suggest virginity. Yet, years later, Carroll never tired of telling everyone that her role in THE PRISONER OF ZENDA was her favorite. During WW II, Carroll worked as a volunteer Red Cross nurse; the actress recalled how "I was on a hospital train in France wearing khaki trousers and a shirt, my face smudged with dirt, my hair just any way. A wounded soldier on the train stopped me and said, 'You know, it's pretty nice to be waited on by Princess Flavia.'" Beyond the flawless visual elegance provided by Cromwell, the script by Balderston, Root, and Stewart is witty, literate, and lyrical to the point of poetry and Newman's sweeping score encompasses the regal court, the novel adventurer Colman, and the lofty romance, a stirring, memorable score, one of the composer's finest. Fairbanks is superb as the rascally, lethal Rupert and Massey is the perfect scheming Prince Michael, while Astor does commendable work as his ill-fated mistress. Smith is charming, quaint, and heroically stalwart as the king's aide and Niven is superb as his brave protege. Though some critics delivered some fun-poking asides at the film for its grand mannered style, they nevertheless endorsed the film and the public loved it worldwide, making it an enormous box-office success. The venerable C. Aubrey Smith, so memorable as Colonel Zapt, was the dean of the British acting community in Hollywood. He had long developed the habit of sitting regally in a captain's chair off set, waiting to play his part, his hearing aid turned off (he was almost completely deaf during the sound film era) and reading a copy of the London *Times*. Massey, who was having some difficulty with his role of "Black Prince Michael," sought out Smith and found him reading his paper. The knighted Smith turned on his hearing aid and Massey tried to explain his problems with the role. Smith listened with great patience and then said, "Ray, in my time I've played every part in ZENDA except Princess Flavia." He paused and Massey leaned forward, expecting to hear a helpful secret. "And I've always had trouble with Black Michael," concluded Smith. He then switched off his hearing aid and snapped open the paper before his deep-socketed eyes. End of advice. The amazing special effects achieved in this film in showing two Ronald Colmans shaking hands, talking to each other, and drinking together in the royal lodge were achieved through carefully disguised split screen processes. Doubles were used with over-the-shoulder shots and when Colman shook hands with himself one of the hands was that of a stunt man with his arm masked. The remake, produced in 1952, with Stewart Granger as the commoner-king (he is wooden throughout but his duel with Rupert is much more energetic and impressive than the 1937 encounter), Deborah Kerr as Flavia, and James Mason as a much more pensive Rupert, was a lavish picture that fell far short of the Cromwell film. Author Hope, 1863-1933, a barrister by profession, wrote only one blockbuster, *The Prisoner of Zenda*, published in 1894, but it made him world famous and fabulously rich. He wrote a sequel, *Rupert of Hentzau*, published in 1898, which was filmed as a silent, ironically produced in 1923 by Lewis Selznick, David Selznick's father, and starred Lew Cody as villain Rupert. In this sequel Rupert returns to kill the king and is killed by Rudolph Rassendyl. Flavia abdicates and marries Rassendyl, going to England to live in bliss.

p, David O. Selznick; d, John Cromwell, (uncredited) W.S. Van Dyke, George Cukor; w, John Balderston, Wells Root, Donald Ogden Stewart (based on the novel by Anthony J. Hope and the play by Edward Rose); ph, James Wong Howe; m, Alfred Newman; ed, Hal C. Kern, James E. Newcom; art d, Lyle Wheeler; set d, Casey Roberts; cos, Ernest Dryden; spec eff, Jack Cosgrove; tech adv, Prince Sigvard Bernadotte, Col. Ivar Enhorning.

Romance/Adventure **(PR:A MPAA:NR)**

PRISONER OF ZENDA, THE***
(1952) 100m MGM c

Stewart Granger *(Rudolf Rassendyll/King Rudolf V)*, Deborah Kerr *(Princess Flavia)*, James Mason *(Rupert of Hentzau)*, Louis Calhern *(Col. Zapt)*, Jane Greer *(Antoinette de Mauban)*, Lewis Stone *(The Cardinal)*, Robert Douglas *(Michael, Duke of Strelsau)*, Robert Coote *(Fritz von Tarlenheim)*, Peter Brocco *(Johann)*, Francis Pierlot *(Josef)*, Tom Browne Henry *(Detchard)*, Eric Alden *(Krafstein)*, Stephen Roberts *(Lauengram)*, Bud Wolfe *(Bersonin)*, Peter Mamakos *(De Gautet)*, Joe Mell *(R.R. Guard)*, Elizabeth Slifer *(Woman)*, Michael Vallon *(Assistant Passport Official)*, Kathleen Freeman *(Gertrude)*, Bruce Payne *(Court Chamberlain)*, John Goldsworthy *(Archbishop)*, Stanley Logan *(British Ambassador)*, George Lewis, Hugh Prosser *(Uhlan Guards)*, Forbes Murray *(Nobleman with Cardinal)*, Frank Elliott, Gordon Richards *(Dignitaries)*, Mary Carroll *(German Wife)*, Alex Pope *(Husband)*, Jay Adler *(Passport Official)*, Peter Votrian *(Newsboy)*, Doris Lloyd *(Ambassador's Wife)*, Emilie Cabanne *(Lady with Cardinal)*, Paul Marion *(Guard)*, William Hazel, Victor Romito *(Aides)*, George Slocum *(Sandwich Vendor)*, Charles Watts *(Porter)*, Alphonse Martell, Manuel Paris *(Noblemen)*, Guy Bellis *(Lord Chamberlain)*.

The forces of liberal constitutional monarchism are again put to the test by plotting generals in this third film version of the old Anthony Hope novel that introduced the word "Ruritania" to everyone's vocabulary. This time Granger steps into the boots of the profligate monarch and his honorable British doppelganger previously essayed by Lewis Stone in the 1922 silent and Ronald Colman in the fondly remembered 1937 remake. Granger is an Englishman vacationing in the Balkan principality of Ruritania. He meets the King (Granger again) who is about to be coronated and married to princess Kerr. There is a conspiracy in the works, though, as the king's brother (Douglas) plans to usurp the throne by preventing the king from appearing at the appointed hour. The king is drugged and his loyal coterie convince his look-alike, the English tourist, to impersonate him and so foil the plot. Douglas and his followers, led by Mason, are not so easily stopped, though, and they kidnap the real king. The ersatz ruler, although he finds himself falling in love with Kerr, goes to the rescue of the real item. A swordfight erupts among the traitors as tensions between Mason and Douglas come to a head. Mason runs Douglas through as one of the Grangers swims the moat to free the other. One Granger duels with Mason while the other manages to get the drawbridge down so the rescuing cavalrymen can enter. Mason escapes by diving into the moat, paving the way for a sequel that Hope wrote in novel form but which never saw the screen, *Rupert of Hentzau*. This version of the film is an almost shot-for-shot remake of the Colman version without Granger having any of the easy charm of his antecedent. The best performance here comes from Mason, smooth and cunning in his villainous role, although he later said, "I thought the costumes were ghastly." An interesting sidelight is the appearance of Stone, the star of the 1922 version, in the role of the cardinal.

p, Pandro S. Berman; d, Richard Thorpe; w, John Balderstone, Noel Langley (based on the novel by Anthony Hope); ph, Joseph Ruttenberg (Technicolor); m, Alfred Newman; ed, George Boemler; art d, Cedric Gibbons, Hans Peter; set d, Edwin B. Willis, Richard Pefferle; cos, Walter Plunkett; spec eff, Warren Newcombe.

Adventure **Cas.** **(PR:A MPAA:NR)**

PRISONER OF ZENDA, THE**
(1979) 108m UNIV c

Peter Sellers *(Rudolph/Syd)*, Lynne Frederick *(Princess Flavia)*, Lionel Jeffries *(Gen. Sapt)*, Elke Sommer *(The Countess)*, Gregory Sierra *(The Count)*, Jeremy Kemp *(Duke Michael)*, Catherine Schell *(Antoinette)*, Simon Williams *(Fritz)*, Stuart Wilson *(Rupert of Hentzau)*, Norman Rossington *(Bruno)*, John Laurie *(Archbishop)*, Graham Stark *(Erik)*, Michael Balfour *(Luger)*, Arthur Howard *(Deacon)*, Ian Abercrombie *(Johann)*, Michael Segal *(Conductor)*, Eric Cord, Joe Dunne, Dick Geary, Mickey Gilbert, Orwin Harvey, Jaysen Hayes, Larry Holt, John Hudkins, Pete Kellet, John Moio, Victor Paul, Gil Perkins, George Robotham, Joe Yrigoyen.

Following three silent versions (in 1912, 1915, and 1922) and two sound adaptations (1937, 1952) of the Anthony Hope novel, THE PRISONER OF ZENDA was again put before the cameras, this time as a vehicle for the multiple talents of Peter Sellers. The story opens with the death of King Rudolf IV (Sellers) as a champagne cork punctures the hot air balloon he is riding in. After the fatal plunge his son (once more Sellers) becomes the rightful heir to the Ruritanian throne. His brother Kemp also wants the crown. By chance a Cockney cab driver (Sellers again) is found to be an exact double of the future king so he is employed to fill in the heir's shoes until the coronation. Meanwhile, the genuine heir is held prisoner by his jealous brother in a fiendish plot to wrest away the crown from Sellers. The cab driver who would be king begins enjoying his new role and takes up with lovely Frederick, the heir's fiancee whose own country depends on the potatoes Ruritania supplies in order to keep the economy stable. Various complications set in, along with a variety of running gags in a crazy turn of events which leads to an inevitable conclusion. Sellers was master of multiple roles in screen comedy with his pinnacle reached in DR. STRANGELOVE. In THE PRISONER OF ZENDA his dual characters are quite good. As the heir, Sellers suffers from a constant lisp, unable to pronounce his "r's," with some wonderfully zany results. He balances this well with his cab driver role, a more serious characterization that also comes off nicely for good humor. Unfortunately, two Sellers simply aren't enough to carry the entire film. The pacing is surprisingly flat, never capturing the tension or excitement the material demands. In spite of Sellers' funny performances the rest of the picture has a hard time figuring itself out. At times this appears to be an affectionate parody; at other moments it looks like serious drama. The schizophrenic nature never gels, leaving the talents of Sellers and his supporting players to hold it all together. Shot on location in Vienna, Austria, it captures the period well under some fine photography but pretty pictures alone don't make for a successful film. A disappointment but well worth a look for Sellers alone, in what was to be one of his final films.

p, Walter Mirisch; d, Richard Quine; w, Dick Clement, Ian La Frenais (based on the novel by Anthony Hope); ph, Arthur Ibbetson (Technicolor); m, Henry Mancini; ed, Byron "Buzz" Brandt; prod d, John J. Lloyd; art d, Herwig Libowitsky; set d, Joe Chevalier; cos, Susan Yelland; spec eff, Albert Whitlock.

Comedy   **Cas.**   **(PR:A MPAA:PG)**

PRISONERS*½   (1929) 87m FN-WB bw

Corinne Griffith (Riza Riga), James Ford (Kessler), Bela Lugosi (Brottos), Ian Keith (Nicholas Cathy), Julanne Johnston (Lenke), Ann Schaeffer (Aunt Maria), Baron von Hesse (Kore), Otto Matiesen (Sebfi), Harry Northrup (Prosecuting Attorney).

Griffith is an Austrian showgirl in Lugosi's cabaret who makes a living by stealing on the side. She's caught and enlists the aid of Keith to defend her. He isn't much of a lawyer, however, and she is sentenced to a few months in the slammer. He does win her heart and promises to wait for her. Barely a talkie, PRISONERS has a few sound effects and only a minimum of dialog toward the end. Of interest mainly to Lugosi fans.

p, Walter Morosco; d, William A. Seiter; w, Forrest Halsey (based on the story by Ferenc Molnar); ph, Lee Garmes; ed, LeRoy Stone; titles, Paul Perez.

Drama   **(PR:A MPAA:NR)**

PRISONERS IN PETTICOATS*½   (1950) 60m REP bw

Valentine Perkins (Joan Grey), Robert Rockwell (Mark Hampton), Danni Sue Nolan (Francis White), Anthony Caruso (Nickey Bowman), Tony Barrett (Steve London), David Wolfe (Sam Clarke), Alex Gerry (Prof. Grey), Michael Carr (Danny), Queenie Smith (Old Beatrice), Bert Conway (Shack), Rudy Rama (Connie), Marlo Dwyer (Candy Carson), Russ Conway (Detective Blake), Marta Mitrovich (Sadie).

Perkins is a club pianist who inadvertently gets pulled into underworld dealings when a gangster double-crosses her boss by stashing $100,000 with her. She goes to the police and ends up in jail rather than reveal her true identity—the daughter of a respected professor. Shame, shame. An uneventful plot filled with stupid, stereotypical characters.

p, Lou Brock; d, Philip Ford; w, Bradbury Foote (based on the story by Raymond Schrock, George Callahan); ph, Ellis W. Carter; m, Stanley Wilson; ed, Harold Minter; art d, Frank Arrigo.

Crime Drama   **(PR:A MPAA:NR)**

PRISONERS OF THE CASBAH*   (1953) 78m COL c

Gloria Grahame (Princess Nadja), Cesar Romero (Firouz), Turhan Bey (Ahmed), Nestor Paiva (Marouf), Paul E. Newlan, Frank Richards, John Parrish (Thieves), Lucille Barkley (Soura), Philip Van Zandt (Selim), Wade Crosby (Yagoub), Gloria Saunders (Zeida), Mimi Borrel, Willetta Smith (Slave Girls), Eddy Fields (Abdullah), Nelson Leigh (Emir), Ray Singer (Yussem), John Marshall (Ayub), John Mansfield (Mokar).

After Grahame is saved from the evil grasp of Romero by Bey, the pair hides out in the title location. A silly costumer with mediocre performances, even from Grahame, who the same year shone in THE BIG HEAT.

p, Sam Katzman; d, Richard Bare; w, DeVallon Scott (based on a story by William Raynor); ph, Henry Freulich (Technicolor); ed, Charles Nelson; art d, Paul Palmentola.

Adventure/Romance   **(PR:A MPAA:NR)**

PRIVATE AFFAIRS, 1935   (SEE: PUBLIC STENOGRAPHER, 1935)

PRIVATE AFFAIRS**   (1940) 75m UNIV bw

Nancy Kelly (Jane Bullerton), Hugh Herbert (Angus McPherson), Roland Young (Amos Bullerton), Robert Cummings (Jimmy Nolan), Montagu Love (Noble Bullerton), Jonathan Hale (Gilkin), Florence Shirley (Mrs. Gilkin), G.P. Huntley, Jr. (Herbert Stanley), Dick Purcell (Cartwright), Leonard Carey (Butler), Mary Forbes (Mrs. Stanley), Douglas Wood (Mr. Stanley), Granville Bates (Judge), Tim Ryan (Harry).

The humorous antics of the main characters overshadow the contrived plot, which casts Herbert as a cab driver and Young a chalkboard operator on Wall Street. Young manages to straighten out his daughter's romances as well as prevent a gang of crooks from turning the stock market upside-down. Herbert plays a more straight-comedy role and dispenses with most of his usual slapstick antics.

p, Burt Kelly, Glenn Tryon; d, Albert S. Rogell; w, Charles Grayson, Leonard Spigelgass, Peter Milne (based on the story "One of the Boston Bullertons" by Walter Greene); ph, Milton Krasner; ed, Philip Cahn.

Comedy   **(PR:A MPAA:NR)**

PRIVATE AFFAIRS OF BEL AMI, THE**   (1947) 112m UA bw

George Sanders (Georges Duroy), Angela Lansbury (Clottide de Marelle), Ann Dvorak (Madeleine Forestier), Frances Dee (Marie de Varenne), John Carradine

(Charles Forestier), Susan Douglas (Suzanne Walter), Hugh Haas (Mons. Walter), Marie Wilson (Rachel Michot), Albert Basserman (Jacques Rival), Warren William (Laroche-Mathieu), Katherine Emery (Mme. Walter), Richard Fraser (Philippe de Cantel), David Bond (Norbert de Varenne), John Good (Paul de Cazolics), Leonard Mudie (Potin), Wyndham Standing (Count de Vaudrec), Karolyn Grimes (Laurine de Marelle), Judy Cook (Hortense), Lumsden Hare (Mayor of Canteleu), Jean Del Val (Commissioner), Charles Trowbridge (Lawyer), Olaf Hytten (Keeper of the Seals).

Sanders is the "Bel Ami" of the title, using every woman he meets to advance up the social ladder in Paris during the latter half of the 19th Century. Carradine gets him a job on a French newspaper, and Sanders marries his wife after Carradine dies, enabling him to get half the inheritance money. He then dumps her in favor of a chance to acquire a royal title. His womanizing doesn't go over well, however, and he is challenged to a duel, during which he gets killed. Sanders plays his part to the maximum, leering lustfully at the women but never giving in to Lansbury, the only woman he has a chance with. A fine adaptation of Guy de Maupassant's excellent story, beautifully photographed by Metty and powerfully scored by composer Darius Milhaud. The painting "The Temptation of St. Anthony" by Max Ernst is flashed on the screen in Technicolor. The need for compliance with the Motion Picture Production Code required the film's makers to tone down some of the novel's off-color flavor: Prostitutes become dancers of questionable character, and the title character pays for his sins by being killed in a duel, a testimonial that "crime doesn't pay."

p, David L. Loew; d&w, Albert Lewin (based on the novel by Guy de Maupassant); ph, Russell Metty; m, Darius Milhaud; ed, Albrecht Joseph; art d, Frank Sylos; m/l, "My Bel Ami," Jack Lawrence, Irving Drutman.

Drama   **(PR:A MPAA:NR)**

PRIVATE ANGELO½**   (1949, Brit.) 106m Pilgrim/ABF-Pathe bw

Godfrey Tearle (Count Piccologrando), Maria Denis (Lucrezia), Peter Ustinov (Pvt. Angelo), Marjorie Rhodes (Countess), James Robertson Justice (Fest), Moyna McGill (Marchesa Dolce), Robin Bailey (Simon Telfer), Harry Locke (Cpl. Trivet), Bill Shine (Col. Michael), John Harvey (Cpl. McCunn), Diana Graves (Lucia), Norman Watson, Peter Humphries, Peter Jones, Rupert Davies, Arthur Howard, Dervis Ward, Philo Hauser, Ernest Clark, George Bradford, Conrad Tom, John McKnight, John Garson, William C. Tubbs, Brenda Hogan.

Ustinov shines as the title character, a cowardly private in the Italian army who prides himself on being a deserter but accidentally crosses British lines and becomes engaged in battle. His return home makes him appear more heroic than he really is. A better-than-average British import that owes everything to the multi-faceted Ustinov.

p, Peter Ustinov; d, Ustinov, Michael Anderson; w, Ustinov, Anderson (based on the novel by Eric Linklater); ph, Erwin Hillier, Norman Warwick; m, Vittorio Pirone; ed, Charles Hasse; art d, John Howell; cos, Nadia Benois; spec eff, Freddy Ford; makeup, Benny Royston.

Comedy   **(PR:A MPAA:NR)**

PRIVATE BENJAMIN½**   (1980) 109m WB c

Goldie Hawn (Judy Benjamin), Eileen Brennan (Capt. Doreen Lewis), Armand Assante (Henri Tremont), Robert Webber (Col. Clay Thornbush), Sam Wanamaker (Teddy Benjamin), Barbara Barrie (Harriet Benjamin), Mary Kay Place (Pvt. Mary Lou Glass), Harry Dean Stanton (Sgt. Jim Ballard), Albert Brooks (Yale Goodman), Alan Oppenheimer (Rabbi), Gretchen Wyler (Aunt Kissy), Sally Kirkland (Helga), Maxine Stuart (Aunt Betty), Estelle Marlow, Everett Covin, Robert Hanley, Lee Wallace, James Dybas, Lillian Adams, Sandy Weintraub, Tim Haldeman, Kopi Sotiropulos, Stu Nahan, J.P. Bumstead, Hal Williams, Toni Kalem, Damita Jo Freeman, Alston Ahern, P.J. Soles, Craig T. Nelson, James R. Barnett, Ray Oliver, Robin Hoff, Ed Lewis, Carrol Davis Carson, Clayton Wright, Richard Herd, Denise Halma, Lilyan Chauvin, Elie Liardet.

1980 was the year of ORDINARY PEOPLE, TESS, RAGING BULL, and COAL MINER'S DAUGHTER so the U.S. was starved for comedy and this picture did much better business than it deserved and eventually gave birth to a weak TV sitcom. Hawn, Brennan, and the screenplay were nominated for Oscars although the competition that year must be considered when appraising that. Hawn is the ultimate "Jewish princess" with Barrie and Wanamaker as her cartoon Jewish parents. When her husband, Brooks, dies in the middle of making love on their wedding night, she believes the ads for the Women's Army Corps and joins up, fully expecting to have her own room to decorate, fashionable clothes, etc. She's under the thumb of Brennan, a caricature of every top-kick, and Webber as the colonel attached to this unit. There's a brief love interest with Assante, a Jewish French physician, but that's tossed aside when he is discovered to have once been mildly involved with a commie organization. The humor is, unfortunately, predictable and often in bad taste and the movie is not nearly as well done or as funny as STRIPES, another picture about an odd-ball unit in a peacetime army. Hawn has often triumphed over the slim material she chooses and she does it again this time, although any fault for the lack of wit and depth in the screenplay must be laid at her tiny feet as she also served as executive producer. All of the laughs in this movie wind up as less than the number you'll find in half of the first reel of a Howard Hawks or a Billy Wilder comedy of 40 years before. Brooks does a good cameo, proving he's a good comic actor.

p, Nancy Meyers, Charles Shyer, Harvey Miller; d, Howard Zieff; w, Meyers, Shyer, Miller; ph, David M. Walsh; m, Bill Conti; ed, Sheldon Kahn; prod d, Robert Boyle; art d, Jeff Howard; set d, Arthur J. Parker; cos, Betsy Cox; spec eff, Robert Peterson.

Comedy   **Cas.**   **(PR:O MPAA:R)**

PRIVATE BUCKAROO** (1942) 68m UNIV bw

Andrews Sisters (*Themselves*), Dick Foran (*Lon Prentice*), Joe E. Lewis (*Lancelot Pringle McBiff*), Jennifer Holt (*Joyce Mason*), Shemp Howard (*Sgt. "Muggsy" Shavel*), Richard Davies (*Lt. Mason*), Mary Wickes (*Bonnie-Belle Schlopkiss*), Ernest Truex (*Col. Weatherford*), Donald O'Connor (*Donny*), Peggy Ryan (*Peggy*), Huntz Hall (*Cpl. Anemic*), Susan Levine (*Tagalong*), The Jivin' Jacks and Jills (*Themselves*), Harry James and His Music Makers (*Themselves*).

Plot is sacrificed for music as the Andrews Sisters and Harry James exit their nitery and enter a USO theater. The most memorable tune to come out of this one was "Don't Sit Under the Apple Tree with Anyone Else But Me" (Lew Brown, Sammy Stept, Charles Tobias; sung by the Andrews Sisters). Other numbers include: "Three Little Sisters" (Irving Taylor, Vic Mizzy, sung by the Andrews Sisters), "Private Buckaroo" (Charles Newman, Allie Wrubel), "Johnny Get Your Gun Again" (Don Raye, Gene De Paul), "We've Got a Job to Do" (Vickie Knight), "You Made Me Love You" (Joseph McCarthy, James V. Monaco; sung by Helen Forrest), "Six Jerks in a Jeep" (Sid Robin), "That's the Moon My Son" (Art Kassel, Sammy Gallop), "I Love the South," "Nobody Knows the Trouble I've Seen," and "Ma, I Miss Your Apple Pie."

p, Ken Goldsmith; d, Edward F. Cline; w, Edmund Kelso, Edward James (based on the story by Paul Gerard Smith); ph, Woody Bredell; ed, Milton Carruth; md, Harry James; art d, Jack Otterson; ch, John Mattison.

Musical   **Cas.**   **(PR:A MPAA:NR)**

PRIVATE COLLECTION**½ (1972, Aus.) 92m Keisai-Bonza c

Peter Reynolds (*Henry Phillips*), Pamela Stephenson (*Mary Ann Phillips*), Brian Blain (*Joseph Tibbsworth*), Graham Bond (*George Kleptoman*), John Paramor (*The Sailor*), Noel Ferrier (*Police Inspector*).

A surrealistic horror film about a compulsive collector of bizarre objects, Reynolds, and his wife, Stephenson, a former tap-dancer. She resents her husband for pulling her away from her dance lessons years earlier, and obsessively tap dances around the house. She takes a lover, Paramor, from whom she was separated at childhood. Two criminals plot to steal Reynolds' collection, but his elaborate guillotine burglar system is set off, and one of them loses a finger. When he eventually is tripped up and lands head first in the guillotine trap, he is decapitated, causing Reynolds to suffer a fatal heart attack. Stephenson goes off with her childhood sweetheart for the finale. Strange but truly a different horror tale. This film was completed only nine hours before its premiere at the Sydney Film Festival.

p&d, Keith Salvat; w, Salvat, Sandy Sharp; ph, David Gribble (Eastmancolor); m, Mike Perjanik; ed, G. Turney-Smith.

Horror   **(PR:O MPAA:NR)**

PRIVATE DETECTIVE** (1939) 57m FN-WB bw

Jane Wyman (*Myrna Winslow*), Dick Foran (*Jim Rickey*), Gloria Dickson (*Mona Lannon*), Maxie Rosenbloom (*Brody*), John Ridgely (*Donald Norton*), Morgan Conway (*Nat Flavin*), John Eldredge (*Millard Lannon*), Joseph Crehan (*Murphy*), William B. Davidson (*Evans*), Selmer Jackson (*Sanger*), Vera Lewis (*Mrs. Widner*), Julie Stevens (*Mona's Maid*), Jack Mower (*Officer Dolan*), Henry Blair (*Bobby Lannon*), Earl Dwire (*Justice of the Peace*), Willie Best (*Valet*), Creighton Hale (*Coroner*), Leo Gorcey (*Newsboy*), Maris Wrixon (*Telephone Operator*), Sol Gorss (*Taxi Driver*), Lottie Williams (*Mrs. Smith*), Frank Dae (*Judge*).

Private eye Foran gets shown up by Wyman when she solves the murder case they've both been working on. Clues to a millionaire's murder lead her to the dead man's wife and lover, who planned to get their hands on a trust fund. The case brings the private eyes closer than ever, and they decide to wed at the outcome.

p, Bryan Foy; d, Noel Smith; w, Earle Snell, Raymond Schrock (based on the story "Invitation to Murder" by Kay Krausse); ph, Ted McCord; ed, Harold McLernon.

Crime/Romance   **(PR:A MPAA:NR)**

PRIVATE DETECTIVE 62** (1933) 67m FN-WB bw (AKA: MAN KILLER)

William Powell (*Donald Free*), Margaret Lindsay (*Janet Reynolds*), Ruth Donnelly (*Amy Moran*), Gordon Westcott (*Tony Bandor*), James Bell (*Whitey*), Arthur Byron (*Tracey*), Natalie Moorhead (*Helen Burns*), Sheila Terry (*Mrs. Wright*), Arthur Hohl (*Dan Hogan*), Hobart Cavanaugh (*Harcourt S. Burns*), Theresa Harris (*Maid*), Renee Whitney (*Alice*), Ann Hovey (*Rose*), Irving Bacon (*Cab Driver*), Georges Renavent (*Capt. La Farge*), Eddie Phillips (*Lover*), Toby Wing (*Girl Friend*), Pat Wing (*Secretary*), Eddie Dunn (*Doorman*), George Brent (*Club Extra*), Bill Elliott (*Gambling Kibitzer*), Rolfe Sedan (*Casino Man*), Harry Seymour (*Gambler*), Charles Wilson, Heinie Conklin (*Bartenders*), Charles Lane (*Process Server*).

Powell, down on his luck, goes undercover and investigates Lindsay, a gambler hanging out in Paris. He finds her, and doesn't turn her in because he falls in love with her. There are holes in the script that a semi could drive through, but Powell makes it all worthwhile. Typical hack direction from Curtiz.

d, Michael Curtiz; w, Rian James (based on the story by Raoul Whitfield); ph, Tony Gaudio; ed, Harold McLernon; art d, Jack Okey.

Crime Drama   **(PR:A MPAA:NR)**

PRIVATE DUTY NURSES** (1972) 80m Crest/New World c

Kathy Cannon (*Spring*), Joyce Williams (*Lola*), Pegi Boucher (*Lynn*), Joseph Kaufmann (*Dr. Doug Selden*), Dennis Redfield (*Domino*), Herbert Jefferson, Jr. (*Dr. Elton*), Paul Hampton (*Dewey*), Paul Gleason (*Dr. McClintock*), George Sawaya (*Ahmed*), Morris Buchanan (*Kirby*), Cliff Carnell (*Bartender*).

A message drama—of sorts—from the good graces of Roger Corman's New World film factory. The densely packed story line follows the adventures of three nurses who enter a program at a California hospital and find themselves becoming emotionally involved with the people they encounter. Every hot social topic of the early 1970s is touched on: a black nurse (Williams) helps a black doctor overcome racism at the hospital via a sit-in; Cannon meets Redfield, the stereotyped crazed Vietnam veteran who needs a little understanding, in addition to a life-saving operation after a motorcycle accident; Boucher becomes involved with a married doctor and a heroin addict-drug dealer. Despite the soap opera-like handling of the story, the film itself isn't all that bad. The cast handles the material competently under some good direction (by a former director of TV's "Peyton Place"). Water beds were the big phenomenon of the early 1970s and in the sex scenes (with which this film is packed), the new craze is unashamedly exploited. There were five such nurse films from the Corman studios, this being number two.

p,d&w, George Armitage; ph, John McNichol (Metrocolor); m, Sky; ed, Alan Collins; set d, Joe Wertheimer.

Drama   **(PR:O MPAA:R)**

PRIVATE ENTERPRISE, A*½ (1975, Brit.) 75m British Film Institute c

Salmaan Peer, Marc Zuber, Ramon Sinha, Yehye Saeed, Diana Quick, Subhash Luthra, Shukla Bhattercharjee.

A young engineer from Bombay who works in an English factory decides to set up his own business when his company goes on strike. His manufacturing of plastic elephants, however. His frustration mounts as his uncle tries to marry him off to a wealthy businessman's daughter. A well-meaning portrayal of a foreigner's alienation, which fails to say anything new or interesting.

d, Peter K. Smith; w, Smith, Dilip Hiro; ph, Ray Orton; m, Ram Narayan; ed, Smith, Charles Rees; art d, Matthew Knox, Peter Harvey.

Drama   **(PR:A MPAA:NR)**

PRIVATE EYES**½ (1953) 64m AA bw

Leo Gorcey (*Terrence Aloysius "Slip" Mahoney*), Huntz Hall (*Horace Debussy "Sach" Jones*), David Condon (*Chuck*), Bennie Bartlett (*Butch*), Bernard Gorcey (*Louie*), Rudy Lee (*Herbie*), Joyce Holden (*Myra Hagen*), Robert Osterloh (*Prof. Damon*), William Forrest (*John Graham*), William Phillips (*Soapy*), Gil Perkins (*Al*), Peter Mamakos (*Chico*), Lee Van Cleef (*Karl*), Lou Lubin (*Oskar*), Emil Sitka (*Wheelchair Patient*), Chick Chandler (*Eddie the Detective*), Tim Ryan (*Andy the Cop*), Edith Leslie (*Aggie the Nurse*), Myron Healey, Carl Saxe.

Gorcey is punched in the nose and finds that he has acquired the ability to read minds. He opens a detective agency (Eagle Eye Detective Agency) and takes on Holden as his first client. He is given an envelope containing secret mob information that he locks in a vault, for which he forgets the combination. The boys have to disguise themselves to infiltrate the mob hideout and put a lid on their activities. A fast-paced comedy in the tradition of the Three Stooges. Both director Bernds and writer Ullman worked with the Stooges, and the latter also scripted gags for Buster Keaton, Abbott and Costello, and Martin and Lewis. (See BOWERY BOYS Series, Index.)

p, Ben Schwalb; d, Edward Bernds; w, Bernds, Ellwood Ullman; ph, Carl Guthrie; ed, Lester A. Sansom; md, Marlin Skiles; art d, David Milton; set d, Charles Steenson; makeup, Norman Pringle.

Comedy   **(PR:A MPAA:NR)**

PRIVATE EYES, THE**½ (1980) 91m Tri-Star/New World c

Tim Conway (*Dr. Tart*), Don Knotts (*Inspector Winship*), Trisha Noble (*Mistress Phyllis Morley*), Bernard Fox (*Justin*), Grace Zabriskie (*Nanny*), John Fujioka (*Mr. Uwatsum*), Stan Ross (*Tibet*), Irwin Keyes (*Jock*), Suzy Mandel (*Hilda*), Fred Stuthman (*Lord Morley*), Mary Nell Santacroce (*Lady Morley*), Robert V. Barron (*Gas Station Attendant*), Patrick Cranshaw (*Roy*).

Conway and Knotts are a dim-witted pair of Scotland Yard sleuths who visit a mansion to investigate the murders of a millionaire and his wife. They meet a bizarre variety of folks—a samurai cook, a mass-murdering butler, and a well-endowed maid—all of whom get killed off, one at a time. Their antics are embellished with routine haunted house scenarios that include hidden passages and mysterious characters. Funny if you enjoy mindless humor. Set in London in the 1920s, the picture actually was filmed at Biltmore House in Asheville, N.C.

p, Lang Elliott, Wanda Dell; d, Elliott; w, Tim Conway, John Myhers; ph, Jacques Haitkin (DeLuxe Color); m, Peter Matz; ed, Fabien Tordjmann, Patrick M. Crawford; art d, Vincent Peranio; cos, Christine Goulding.

Comedy   **Cas.**   **(PR:A MPAA:PG)**

PRIVATE FILES OF J. EDGAR HOOVER, THE**½ (1978) 112m Larco/AIP c

Broderick Crawford (*J. Edgar Hoover*), Jose Ferrer (*Lionel McCoy*), Michael Parks (*Robert F. Kennedy*), Ronee Blakley (*Carrie DeWitt*), Rip Torn (*Dwight Webb*), Celeste Holm (*Florence Hollister*), Michael Sacks (*Melvin Purvis*), Dan Dailey (*Clyde Tolson*), Raymond St. Jacques (*Martin Luther King, Jr.*), Andrew Duggan (*Lyndon B. Johnson*), John Marley (*Dave Hindley*), Howard Da Silva (*Franklin D. Roosevelt*), June Havoc (*Hoover's Mother*), James Wainwright (*Young Hoover*), Lloyd Nolan (*Atty. Gen. Stone*), Ellen Barber (*FBI Secretary*), Lloyd Gough (*Walter Winchell*), Brad Dexter (*Alvin Karpis*), Jennifer Lee (*Ethel Brunette*), George Plimpton (*Quentin Reynolds*), Jack Cassidy (*Damon Runyon*).

In a chronologically sweeping film that tries to show too much of the half century of Hoover's reign as head of the FBI, writer-producer-director Cohen produces a sometimes fascinating but thoroughly sensational picture. Crawford, who bears some resemblance to the swarthy, corpulent Hoover, fist-thumps his way through his fight with the Kennedy brothers in the 1960s and his persecution of Martin Luther King, Jr. Wainwright plays a laconic, tight-lipped Hoover during the early years of the director's tenure, shown in briefly sketched episodes dealing with the gangsters of the 1930s and the spies of the 1940s. But it's Crawford who occupies most of the footage as the jowly, truculent Hoover in his later years, a Buddha-like tyrant of bureaucracy, intimidation, and outright blackmail, using the FBI files and the threat of his all-powerful office to maintain his awesome authority. Of course, Hoover has since been thoroughly denounced and exposed as a vainglorious despot with serious psychological problems. Hoover is shown to be a shifty-eyed, paranoid, jealous guardian of files which Cohen claims were concentrated on the sex lives of U.S. politicians rather than wanted felons, the files being used as blackmail tools by which Hoover flexed his muscles, fattened the bureau's budget, and made life miserable for any who dared criticize or oppose him. Crawford's always angry posture evokes no sympathy and his demeanor is such as to suggest that he can't wait to deliver his stereotyped, cliche-glutted lines and leave the production. Dailey, as Hoover's associate director sidekick, is rather good but has little to work with. One of the most unintentionally funny scenes of the film occurs when Crawford and Dailey explode when learning that a Washington newshound has suggested they are lovers. Not much of this film is credible, especially Cohen's poorly written script, his inept direction, and an overall production that is best described as sleazy and pandering to bad taste, though it was reportedly made on a "low budget" of $3 million.

p,d&w, Larry Cohen; ph, Paul Glickman (Movielab Color); m, Miklos Rozsa; ed, Christopher Lebenzon; prod d, Cathy Davis; set d, Carolyn Loewenstein; cos, Lewis Friedman; tech adv, John M. Crewdson.

Crime Drama (PR:C MPAA:PG)

PRIVATE HELL 36½** (1954) 81m Filmmakers bw

Ida Lupino *(Lilli Marlowe)*, Steve Cochran *(Detective Sgt. Calvin Brimer)*, Howard Duff *(Jack Farnham)*, Dean Jagger *(Capt. Michaels)*, Dorothy Malone *(Francey Farnham)*, Bridget Duff *(Farnham's Child)*, Jerry Hausner *(Nightclub Boss)*, Dabbs Greer *(Bartender)*, Chris O'Brien *(Coroner)*, Kenneth Patterson *(Superior Officer)*, *George Dockstader (Fugitive)*, Jimmy Hawkins *(Delivery Boy)*, King Donovan *(Burglar)*.

This routine good-cop-gone-bad film is lifted from the doldrums with some stunning direction by Siegel and strong performances by Lupino, Cochran, and Duff. The film opens with a violent robbery in New York City which nets $300,000 and leaves one man dead. The story then picks up in Los Angeles where two detectives, Cochran and Duff, have been assigned to trace a $50 bill that was among those stolen in New York. While close friends and good partners, Cochran and Duff's personalities are practically opposite. Duff is a secure family man married to Malone, while Cochran is a bitter loner always on the make. Both men do share a dissatisfaction with their work, however, resentful of being paid so little to risk so much. Their investigation leads to Lupino, a nightclub singer who was given the $50 bill as a tip. In the hope that she will be able to spot the man again, the detectives take Lupino to the racetrack where she scans the crowd. A romantic relationship develops between Lupino and Cochran, though both know it will not last because the singer is out to marry a rich man. Eventually, the man who passed the hot money is spotted leaving the racetrack and the detectives follow. A high-speed auto chase ends with the criminal being killed when his car cracks up on the side of the road. Cochran and Duff are amazed to find nearly $80,000 blowing around in the ditch. Seeing his chance to get revenge on the police department, Cochran pockets most of the money and gives half to Duff, who accepts it reluctantly. They stash the money in a trailer park (in unit No. 36, hence the title) for safekeeping. The men then report back to the station with their commander, Jagger, apparently none the wiser. Hoping his new-found wealth will convince Lupino to marry him, Cochran pops the question. Lupino, however, deduces where the money came from and wants nothing to do with it. Still in love with Cochran, she decides they would be happier without the money. Meanwhile, the partner of the dead man phones to blackmail the detectives. Cochran arranges to meet the blackmailer at the trailer park and make the payoff. Duff, however, has decided to return all the money and before the blackmailer arrives a fight breaks out between the detectives. During the struggle, Cochran shoots and wounds Duff. Jagger bursts in and kills Cochran, later revealing to Duff that he had suspected them of lifting the money all along and had set them up to find out. Co-authored and co-produced by star Lupino (she and Collier Young owned Filmmakers Productions), PRIVATE HELL 36, though it contains standard plotting, develops some interesting characterizations, especially that of Cochran's bitter and lonely detective. Unable to fall back on the love and support of a family the way his partner can, Cochran hides his desperation behind a facade of cynicism awash in booze. When he meets Lupino, Cochran is too far gone at this point to be salvaged and he sets into motion the events that destroy him. Unromanticized, fast-paced, and gritty, PRIVATE HELL 36 serves as an interesting precursor to director Siegel's subsequent cop films MADIGAN (1968), COOGAN'S BLUFF (1969), and DIRTY HARRY (1971). Good jazz score by Leith Stevens.

p, Collier Young; d, Don Siegel; w, Young, Ida Lupino; ph, Burnett Guffey; m, Leith Stevens; ed, Stanford Tischler; art d, Walter Keller; set d, Edward Boyle; m/l, "Didn't You Know," John Franco (sung by Lupino); makeup, David Newell.

Crime Cas. (PR:C MPAA:NR)

PRIVATE INFORMATION*½ (1952, Brit.) 65m Association of Cinema Technicians/Monarch bw

Jill Esmond *(Charlotte)*, Jack Watling *(Hugh)*, Carol Marsh *(Georgie)*, Gerard Heinz *(Alex)*, Norman Shelley *(Freemantle)*, Mercy Haystead *(Iris)*, Lloyd Pearson *(Mayor)*, Henry Caine *(Forrester)*, Brenda de Banzie *(Dolly)*, Peter Swanwick.

Esmond discovers a secret report written by her architect son, Watling, which indicates that there's corruption within the city government. A typhoid epidemic proves her theory that bribes had been passed to cover defective draining systems, and Esmond's daughter, Marsh, nearly dies of the disease herself. Though the film certainly means well, this is no "Enemy of the People." The acting simply doesn't cut it, with results quickly growing tedious and predictable.

p, Ronald Kinnoch; d, Fergus McDonnel; w, Gordon Glennon, John Baines, Kinnoch (based on the play "Garden City" by Glennon); ph, Eric Cross.

Drama (PR:A MPAA:NR)

PRIVATE JONES** (1933) 86m UNIV bw

Lee Tracy *(Bill Jones)*, Donald Cook *(Lt. Gregg)*, Gloria Stuart *(Mary, Welfare Worker)*, Shirley Grey *(Helen)*, Emma Dunn *(Mrs. Jones)*, Walter Catlett *(Spivey)*, Al Hill *(Howard)*, Berton Churchill *(Winthrop)*, Frank McHugh *(Cook)*, Russell Gleason *(Williams)*, Hans von Twardowski *(Von Bergen)*, Roland Varno *(Lt. Brinkerhoff)*, Richard Carle *(Lecturer)*, Ethel Clayton *(Woman)*, Richard Cramer *(Man)*, Wallis Clark.

Tracy is drafted against his will to fight the Germans. Since he has nothing against them, he spends most of his time doing K.P. duty and romancing Stuart, the commander's wife.

d, Russell Mack; w, Prescott Chaplin, William N. Robson (based on the story by Richard Schayer from the play by Samuel Spewack, Belle Cohn [Spewack], George Jessel); ph, Charles Stumar.

War/Comedy (PR:A MPAA:NR)

PRIVATE LESSONS* (1981) 87m Barry & Enright/Jensen Farley c (AKA: PHILLY)

Sylvia Kristel *(Nicole)*, Howard Hesseman *(Lester)*, Eric Brown *(Philly)*, Patrick Piccininni *(Sherman)*, Ed Begley, Jr. *(Jack Travis)*, Pamela Bryant *(Joyce)*, Meredith Baer *(Miss Phipps)*, Ron Foster *(Philly's Dad)*, Peter Elbling *(Waiter)*, Don Barrows *(Green)*, Marian Gibson *(Florence)*, Dan Greenberg *(Hotel Owner)*.

Yet another of the teen sex fantasies which have hit Hollywood like a plague. This time 15-year-old Brown is initiated into sex by gorgeous maid Kristel, at his father's request. A blackmail subplot with Hesseman serves no purpose except as filler between sexual fantasies. Not surprisingly, audiences flocked to see it, but does anyone still remember it? Kristel appears to bare it all, but "stunt" double Judy Heldon actually does the dirty work. Includes some lethargic tunes by Air Supply, Eric Clapton, and other AM radio stars.

p, R. Ben Efraim; d, Alan Myerson; w, Dan Greenburg (based on the novel *Philly* by Greenburg); ph, Jan de Bont (Metrocolor); ed, Fred Chulack; art d, Linda Pearl; m/l, Air Supply, Rod Stewart, Eric Clapton, Willie Nile, Rudy Van Warner, Earth, Wind and Fire, Earl Klugh, John Cougar, and Crazy Horse.

Comedy Cas. (PR:O MPAA:R)

PRIVATE LIFE (SEE: VERY PRIVATE AFFAIR, A, 1962, Fr.)

PRIVATE LIFE OF DON JUAN, THE** (1934, Brit.) 80m LFP/UA bw (AKA: DON JUAN)

Douglas Fairbanks, Sr. *(Don Juan)*, Merle Oberon *(Antonia)*, Binnie Barnes *(Rosita)*, Joan Gardner *(Carmen)*, Benita Hume *(Dolores)*, Clifford Heatherley *(Pedro)*, Barry Mackay *(Roderigo)*, Melville Cooper *(Leporello)*, Bruce Winston *(Cafe Manager)*, Athene Seyler *(Theresa)*, Hindle Edgar *(Husband)*, Gibson Gowland *(Don Ascanio)*, Lawrence Grossmith *(Guardian)*, Margaretta Scott *(Tonita)*, Edmund Breon *(Author)*, Annie Esmond *(Dolores' Duenna)*, Patricia Hilliard *(One of Don Juan's Loves)*, Natalie Lelong *(Wife)*, Owen Nares *(Actor)*, Gina Malo *(Pepita)*, Heather Thatcher *(Actress)*, Claude Allister *(Duke)*, Diana Napier *(Would-Be Wife)*, Hay Petrie *(Manager of the Golden Pheasant)*, Edmund Willard *(Prisoner)*, Florence Wood *(Cook at the Inn)*, Morland Graham *(Don Juan's Cook)*, William Heughan *(Statue)*, Veronica Brady *(One of Don Juan's Early Loves)*, Betty Hamilton *(Actress)*, Rosita Garcia *(Wife of Tired Business Man)*, Nancy Jones *(Woman)*, Elsa Lanchester *(Maid)*, Abraham Sofaer *(Street Bookseller)*, Toto Koopman *(Actress)*, Spencer Trevor, Virginia Bradford.

In his last film the great Fairbanks plays Don Juan, now middle-aged, as he returns to the site of his earlier conquests, Seville. Soon after his arrival Fairbanks learns that a young impostor has been passing himself off as Don Juan and fulfilling the romantic fantasies of the bored Sevillian housewives. Seeking to reclaim his reputation, Fairbanks engages in an affair with Oberon, a gorgeous dancer. Unfortunately, Fairbanks' doctor advises the lover to stop his overly physical activities lest he lose his health. Fairbanks seriously considers that suggestion since his wife, Hume, has been advising the same. That night the impostor Don Juan is killed by a jealous husband, giving Fairbanks an opportunity to attend his own funeral and retire. Escaping to the country, Fairbanks adopts an alias but finds that after six months of trying, he cannot seduce women unless he tells them he is Don Juan. Desperate to revive his career, Fairbanks returns to Seville and announces that he is the real Don Juan and that an impostor is buried in his grave. The women, of course, refuse to believe this middle-aged man is the world's greatest lover. In an effort to prove his identity, Fairbanks interrupts the opening night of a play based on his life and demands to be recognized as Don Juan. The audience turns to Mrs. Don Juan for confirmation and Hume declares the man an impostor. Finally beaten by his wife, Fairbanks agrees to settle down forever. Seeking to recapture the same audience that attended THE PRIVATE LIFE OF HENRY THE VIII (1933), producer-director Korda employed the aging Fairbanks in a vain attempt to recapture the image of the swashbuckling hero that had once wooed millions. It was wrong for Fairbanks to attempt such a swashbuckling romantic picture, as, by this time, he was all swash and very little buckle. He'd gained weight, lost a great deal of hair, and was showing his age at 51. Fairbanks' age wasn't the only problem with THE PRIVATE LIFE OF DON JUAN; the script suffered from the patchwork typical of Korda's films. The creative team of Arthur Wimperis, Lajos Biro, and Korda came up with a few scenes that they considered to be the crux of the film and then they turned those ideas over to English playwright Lonsdale, who was hired to "fill in" the story between those crucial scenes. Writing by committee nearly always results in an uneven, disjointed product and THE PRIVATE LIFE OF DON JUAN is no exception. The film is confused and repetitive, the dialog frequently ridiculous, and the few well-developed scenes seem almost incongruous when compared to the whole. As a result the film bombed at the box office. Fairbanks was separated from Mary Pickford at the time he went to England to make the film, and they divorced two years later. Two months after the ink on his divorce was dry, Fairbanks married Lady Sylvia Ashley, a former chorus girl, and announced his retirement. He died of a heart attack three years later.

p&d, Alexander Korda; w, Frederick Lonsdale, Lajos Biro, Arthur Wimperis (based on the play by Henri Bataille); ph, Georges Perinal; m, Ernest Toch, Michael [Mischa] Spolianski; ed, Stephen Harrison; prod d, Vincent Korda; md, Muir Mathieson; cos, Oliver Messel; m/l, "Don Juan's Serenade," Spolianski (sung by John Brownlee), Wimperis, Arthur Benjamin.

Adventure/Romance   **Cas.**   **(PR:A MPAA:NR)**

PRIVATE LIFE OF HENRY VIII, THE****   (1933) 97m LFP/UA bw

Charles Laughton (*Henry VIII*), Robert Donat (*Thomas Culpepper*), Lady Tree (*Henry's Old Nurse*), Binnie Barnes (*Katherine Howard*), Elsa Lanchester (*Anne of Cleves*), Merle Oberon (*Anne Boleyn*), Wendy Barrie (*Jane Seymour*), Everley Gregg (*Catherine Parr*), Franklyn Dyall (*Thomas Cromwell*), Miles Mander (*Wriothesley*), Claude Allister (*Cornell*), John Loder (*Thomas Peynell*), Lawrence Hanray (*Archbishop Thomas Cranmer*), William Austin (*Duke of Cleves*), John Turnbull (*Hans Holbein*), Frederick Culley (*Duke of Norfolk*), Gibb McLaughlin (*French Executioner*), Sam Livesey (*English Executioner*), Judy Kelly (*Lady Rochford*), William Heughan (*Kingston*).

The British film industry had not been having much success outside the Empire but all that changed with this film, which was made by Hungarian Korda with cinematography by French Perinal. How the film came to be has been discussed for many years. Some say that Korda was searching for something for Laughton and his wife, Lanchester, and when he saw a statue of the king, he spotted the resemblance and ordered a script written. The other tale states that Korda heard the old British folk song "I'm 'Enery the Eighth, I Am, I Am" (later to become a rock 'n' roll hit by Herman's Hermits) and came up with the idea. There had been many costume epics made in the silent years and some even touched upon the life of the monarch, but this is the one that will be remembered. Laughton's performance was outstanding and won the first Oscar ever for a British-made movie although Jannings and Arliss, two foreigners, had already won Oscars as Best Actors in American films. Alexander Korda called upon his brother Vincent to be set designer and the nepotism was worthwhile, as Vincent managed to make this picture look far more expensive than the 60,000 pounds it cost to produce it in just five weeks. The attitude taken was to dispense with the public utterances and show the intimate side of the monarch, a technique Korda was to use again in the less fulfilling THE PRIVATE LIFE OF DON JUAN. There was a great deal of humor in the picture, which details the life of Henry and five of his six wives. The first, Catherine of Aragon, is dispensed with by a prolog which explains that she was far "too respectable to be included." Oberon is his first spouse pictured (Anne Boleyn, who was to be seen in her own movie, ANNE OF THE THOUSAND DAYS) and is soon beheaded. Barrie is Jane Seymour and dies giving birth. He next marries Lanchester (Anne of Cleves), wearing an odd wig and doing her best to look terrible in order to justify the film's most famous line, uttered with a regal sigh as he enters the bedroom, "The things I've done for England." Lanchester uses a German accent and is the only performer to come close to Laughton in scene-stealing, darned near swiping their sequences entirely. That marriage leads to divorce and next he marries Barnes, who loses her head after losing her heart to Laughton's pal, Donat. At the finale, after raving and roaring and ranting, eating like an animal, ruling his roost like a cock of the walk, Laughton is shown to be a tranquil, almost whipped man at the hands of his last mate, Gregg, a sharp-faced shrew. Laughton was only 33 at the time but already a veteran of nine movies and many stage productions. There are several standout scenes, not the least of which are the "eating" sequences with Laughton chewing on a chop then tossing the remains over his shoulder. Actually, the eating bits are sexier than the bedroom scenes and one wonders if Tony Richardson didn't study them for his directing of TOM JONES. Laughton and Lanchester also have a wonderfully comic interlude as they play cards and she beats him for half his kingdom. Until this movie was released, there had been a mild recession in costume epics but they soon came back with a flurry when the totals were in on the profits, about 10 times the cost. Korda's sets, which were poverty-stricken at best, were photographed so well by Perinal that no one realized how frail they were. Barnes sings a song in the film that was reputedly written by King Henry VIII himself, just another side to this fabulous historical character.

p, Alexander Korda, Ludovico Toeplitz; d, Korda; w, Lajos Biro, Arthur Wimperis; ph, Georges Perinal; m, Kurt Schroeder; ed, Harold Young, Stephen Harrison; art d, Vincent Korda; cos, John Armstrong; ch, Espinosa; m/l, "What Shall I Do for Love?" Henry VIII; historical adviser, Peter Lindsey.

Biography   **Cas.**   **(PR:A-C MPAA:NR)**

PRIVATE LIFE OF LOUIS XIV**   (1936, Ger.) 95m General Foreign bw (FRAUEN UM DEN SONNENKOENIG)

Renate Mueller (*Liselotte*), Eugen Kloepfer (*Karl Ludwig*), Maria Krahn (*His Wife*), Michael Bohnen (*Louis XIV*), Hans Stuewe (*Philipp of Orleans*), Maria Meissner (*Marquise de la Valliere*), Hilde Hildebrand (*Duchesse de Montespan*), Dorothea Wieck (*Mme. de Maintenon*), Ida Wuest (*Duchess of Hannover*), Else Ehser (*Maria Theresia*).

History is bent in favor of the Germans in this Nazi-produced film directed by Carl Froehlich, head of the Reich's film company. Blame is placed on the evil French for all the events which took place during the reign of King Louis XIV. Mueller is conned into a political marriage with a Frenchman at the suggestion of the king, but that changes nothing and the French troops continue pounding on the helpless Germans. The truth is stretched in favor of propaganda and national pride, but the result is fairly entertaining. (In German.)

p&d, Carl Froehlich; w, Froehlich, Dr. Hoffman-Harnisch; ph, Reimar Kuntze; m, Alois Melichar.

Historical Drama   **(PR:A MPAA:NR)**

PRIVATE LIFE OF SHERLOCK HOLMES, THE*½**   (1970, Brit.) 125m Phalanx-Mirisch/UA c

Robert Stephens (*Sherlock Holmes*), Colin Blakely (*Dr. John H. Watson*), Irene Handl (*Mrs. Hudson*), Stanley Holloway (*1st Gravedigger*), Christopher Lee (*Mycroft Holmes*), Genevieve Page (*Gabrielle Valladon*), Clive Revill (*Rogozhin*), Tamara Toumanova (*Petrova*), George Benson (*Inspector Lestrade*), Catherine Lacey (*Old Lady*), Mollie Maureen (*Queen Victoria*), Peter Madden (*Von Tirpitz*), Robert Cawdron (*Hotel Manager*), Michael Elwyn (*Cassidy*), Michael Balfour (*Cabby*), Frank Thornton (*Porter*), James Copeland (*Guide*), Alex McCrindle (*Baggageman*), Kenneth Benda (*Minister*), Graham Armitage (*Wiggins*), Eric Francis (*2nd Gravedigger*), John Garrie, Godfrey James (*Carters*), Ina De La Haye (*Petrova's Maid*), Kynaston Reeves (*Old Man*), Anne Blake (*Madame*), Marilyn Head, Anna Matisse, Wendy Lingham, Penny Brahms, Sheena Hunter (*Girls*), Daphne Riggs (*Lady-in-Waiting*), John Gatrell (*Equerry*), Philip Ross (*McKellar*), Annette Kerr (*Secretary*), Tina Spooner, Judy Spooner (*Twins*), Ismet Hassan, Charlie Young Atom, Teddy Kiss Atom, Willie Shearer (*Submarine Crew*), Phillip Anthony (*Lieutenant Commander*), Martin Carroll, John Scott (*Scientists*), Paul Stassino, Paul Hansard.

The public's expectations of Sherlock Holmes are tossed aside in this surprising and scandalous look at the world's greatest sleuth. Stephens stars as Holmes, a cocaine-addicted, possibly homosexual private detective who is bored with his recent cases. While investigating the disappearance of a family of midgets, Stephens finds Page, who is searching for her husband. He follows the clues to Scotland and is warned by his brother (a thin, balding Christopher Lee) not to take the case. Stephens and Blakely (as Watson) venture onto Loch Ness and have to swim to shore after their boat is overturned by the legendary sea monster. He is informed of a project to launch a submarine piloted by the midgets. Queen Victoria (Maureen) tells Holmes that she is aware of the project and it is halted, but not before he is informed that he was set up by Page, who is actually a German spy. Page is executed and Holmes returns to Baker Street and his cocaine addiction. A satirical, intimate look at the revered character by Billy Wilder, who has always been known for his sexually racy pictures. Wilder's finest film since THE APARTMENT (1960), it bombed at the box office (not surprisingly, since audiences do not like their conventions messed with) and was fiercely cut by United Artists. The sets were designed under the direction of Alexander Trauner, who re-created, in detail, the Victorian atmosphere of Holmes' London residence, including a massive back-lot reproduction of Baker Street. The score by Miklos Rozsa is one of his most impressive, and he can be seen conducting it during the ballet sequence. Only Wilder could get away with this picture (which he called "a personal valentine"), and the allusion that Holmes and Watson were lovers.

p&d, Billy Wilder; w, Wilder, I.A.L. Diamond (based on the characters created by Arthur Conan Doyle); ph, Christopher Challis (Panavision, DeLuxe Color); m, Miklos Rozsa; ed, Ernest Walter; prod d, Alexander Trauner; art d, Tony Inglis; set d, Harry Cordwell; cos, Julie Harris; spec eff, Wally Veevers, Cliff Richardson; ch, David Blair; makeup, Ernest Gasser.

Comedy/Mystery   **Cas.**   **(PR:C MPAA:GP)**

PRIVATE LIVES**   (1931) 92m MGM bw

Norma Shearer (*Amanda Chase Paynne*), Robert Montgomery (*Elyot Chase*), Reginald Denny (*Victor Paynne*), Una Merkel (*Sibyl Chase*), Jean Hersholt (*Oscar*), George Davis (*Bellboy*).

Noel Coward wrote and starred in his play "Private Lives" with Gertrude Lawrence in a 1930 London production, then went to New York in 1931, with Laurence Olivier and Jill Esmond in the secondary roles, and the four enjoyed a run of 248 performances. Producer Irving Thalberg purchased the rights, and had a film made of the stage play (something that's decidedly against the Actors Equity rules these days) as a guideline for his proposed movie. Thalberg's wife, Shearer, and Robert Montgomery had already appeared together in three pictures, THEIR OWN DESIRE, THE DIVORCEE, and STRANGERS MAY KISS, so it was natural for them to do this one together. Their final picture, RIPTIDE, didn't come close to the fun of PRIVATE LIVES. The screenwriters wisely hewed to the stage dialog and situations with the only alteration being the switching of the final locale from an apartment in Paris to a house in Switzerland. The plot is wafer-thin at best but Coward's words crackle with geniality and wit. Montgomery and Shearer were married at one time but have since divorced and married other mates. He's wed to Merkel and she's taken Denny as her lawful wedded spouse. Both Denny and Merkel are conservative sorts with none of the joy and madness that attracted Montgomery and Shearer to each other. By a coincidence, both couples are honeymooning at the same French hotel where Shearer and Montgomery spent their first two weeks of marriage years before. They are struggling to show affection to their new mates but it isn't easy as Merkel is a bland dishrag and Denny is the kind of man who sends out to have his shirts stuffed. Since their suites are next to each other, it isn't long before Shearer and Montgomery meet on their balconies. They are at once delighted and stunned to see each other. In no time, the newlyweds are quarreling and the oldyweds realize that they may have made an error in divorcing each other. They are still in love, so they leave their fresh spouses behind and go to a mountain chalet to have another honeymoon, without benefit of divorce or clergy. Their love is as volcanic as their rages and they are soon arguing viciously in between sexual bouts. The words become blows and Shearer actually knocks Montgomery for a loop, something that director Franklin thought was so funny that he left the "take" in. Merkel and Denny locate their mates at the chalet and the next morning, the two "practical" ones have a spat. Upon seeing that everyone, no matter how placid, argues, Montgomery and Shearer realize that what they have is wonderful and they can settle their disputes as long as they continue to love each other. They slip out, leaving Merkel and Denny together, perhaps even to find something in a new relationship. "Private Lives" is one of those perennials that can't be hurt, even by ordinary actors. In the case of the film, the acting is excellent and the result is charming.

d, Sidney Franklin; w, Hans Kraly, Richard Schayer, Claudine West (based on the play by Noel Coward); ph, Ray Binger; ed, Conrad A. Nervig; art d, Cedric Gibbons; cos, Adrian.

Comedy **(PR:A MPAA:NR)**

PRIVATE LIVES OF ADAM AND EVE, THE*½ (1961) 86m UNIV c-bw

Mickey Rooney *(Nick Lewis/Devil)*, Mamie Van Doren *(Evie Simms/Eve)*, Fay Spain *(Lil Lewis/Lilith)*, Mel Torme *(Hal Sanders)*, [Martin] Marty Milner *(Ad Simms/Adam)*, Tuesday Weld *(Vangie Harper)*, Cecil Kellaway *(Doc Bayles)*, Paul Anka *(Pinkie Parker)*, Ziva Rodann *(Passiona)*, Theona Bryant, June Wilkinson, Phillipa Fallon, Barbara Walden, Toni Covington *(Devil's Familiars)*, Nancy Root, Donna Lynne, Sharon Wiley, Miki Kato, Andrea Smith, Buni Bacon, Stella Garcia *(Satan's Sinners)*.

A flash flood grounds a Reno-bound bus, forcing its travelers to take shelter in a nearby church. The folks on board—Rooney, Van Doren, etc.—all share a dream where they are in the Garden of Eden. And Rooney plays the Devil! (What would Judge Hardy say?) Their harmless fantasies got them in trouble with the Catholic Legion of Decency, whose feathers were easily ruffled. Universal bowed to their demands and quickly pulled their 150 prints from distribution and sent them back to the editing table. A year later (1961) the chaotic and ultimately dumb tale of sacrilege was back in the theaters.

p, Red Doff; d, Albert Zugsmith, Mickey Rooney; w, Robert Hill (based on the story by George Kennett); ph, Phil Lathrop (Spectacolor); m, Van Alexander; ed, Eddie Broussard; art d, Alexander Golitzen, Richard Riedel; cos, Frederick; m/l, "Private Lives of Adam and Eve," Paul Anka (sung by Anka).

Comedy/Satire **(PR:C MPAA:NR)**

PRIVATE LIVES OF ELIZABETH AND ESSEX, THE*½** (1939) 106m WB c (AKA: ELIZABETH THE QUEEN)

Bette Davis *(Queen Elizabeth)*, Errol Flynn *(Robert Devereaux, Earl of Essex)*, Olivia de Havilland *(Lady Penelope Gray)*, Donald Crisp *(Francis Bacon)*, Alan Hale *(Earl of Tyrone)*, Vincent Price *(Sir Walter Raleigh)*, Henry Stephenson *(Lord Burghley)*, Henry Daniell *(Sir Robert Cecil)*, James Stephenson *(Sir Thomas Egerton)*, Margaret Fabares [Nanette Fabray] *(Mistress Margaret Radcliffe)*, Ralph Forbes *(Lord Knollys)*, Guy Bellis *(Lord Charles Howard)*, Robert Warwick *(Lord Mountjoy)*, Leo G. Carroll *(Sir Edward Coke)*, Forrester Harvey, Doris Lloyd, Maris Wrixton, Rosella Towne, John Sutton, I. Stanford Jolley.

This lavish but talky 17th-Century extravaganza proved to be a showy vehicle for Davis. Flynn, much to his chagrin, was used as a handsome prop and his experience with his fiery costar did little to inflate his considerable ego or enhance his reputation. This romantic fantasy, which has little to do with historic fact, begins with Flynn's triumphant entry into London after conquering Cadiz. The public adores him but his queen, fearful of his growing power, treats him disgracefully. Davis upbraids him for not communicating properly with her while he was in the field and humiliates Flynn before the court. He has not brought her the riches of Spain, she states, but allowed the Spanish to sink their treasure ships and deprive England of much-needed funds. Davis then turns to Price, playing the slavish Sir Walter Raleigh, and appoints him to high office, one where he instantly becomes Flynn's superior. (Price and Flynn are long-standing rivals for power and the queen's favors.) Flynn retires to his country estates but not before de Havilland, Davis' lady-in-waiting, who loves him from afar, warns him of Davis' dominating ways and that he must curb his appetite for power. Crisp, Flynn's powerful friend at court, goes to Davis and smooths her ruffled feathers, bringing about a conciliatory meeting between the headstrong Flynn and his queen. They are mismatched lovers nevertheless and quarrel over matters of state, Flynn trying to make inroads into her power base and she easily realizing that he intends to marry her and rule England on equal terms with her, something she cannot tolerate. Then, at a cabinet meeting, Flynn is goaded by Price, Daniell, and Stephenson into taking on the impossible mission of stamping out the rebellion in Ireland under the leadership of the crafty Tyrone (Hale). Davis tries to prevent her favorite from rising to the challenge but Flynn's pride insists that he lead an army into Ireland to quell the rebellion. She knows his courage and military acumen have been challenged and he must respond by taking the field, a prospect which angers her. Still, she gives him his royal marching orders and Flynn leads a disastrous expedition against Hale. The Irish forces peck away at the British, gradually reducing their numbers. Worse, Flynn's letters to Davis asking for supplies and reinforcements are intercepted before reaching the queen, Daniell and Stephenson duping de Havilland into turning the letters over to them. Flynn's command thins out due to starvation and is eventually surrounded by Hale's soldiers. Flynn is compelled to surrender but is allowed to leave Ireland with his forces. He returns to London, still popular but incensed at the thought that Davis has betrayed him and his men by ignoring their plight. He marches to the palace where his soldiers seize control and Flynn announces to an enraged Davis that she is his prisoner. She explains that she never received his pleas for help, that his powerful enemies at court have obviously kept his letters from her. Flynn only wants power now, insisting that Davis share the throne with him. While the lovers jockey for position, de Havilland thinks to tell Davis that her assumptions are correct and that she unwittingly kept Flynn's letters from her. Before she can inform her queen of these shadowy intrigues, Daniell frightens her off by ominously stating: "You have a lovely head and neck, milady. It would be pity to separate them." In charge of the Whitehall Palace, Flynn begins dictating terms to his subtle queen. Davis seems to accept his offer of joint rule and Flynn dismisses his men who are replaced by guards loyal to the queen. Davis then has Flynn arrested and taken to the Tower of London. Flynn is later approached by Davis who offers him the role of consort but he refuses, telling her it's all or nothing at all. Davis, in agony, sends her lover to the headsman's block to end their star-crossed relationship and this somewhat overlong film. Much of this picture is attractive from a physical point of view. The rich color, ornate sets and costuming, the swift and sweeping direction by the schedule-pressing Curtiz, and Korngold's succulent score—one of an appropriate heraldic nature that has pomp and circumstance in every beat—present a feast for the eyes. But the acting, especially between Davis and Flynn, is stiff, unyielding, and often forced. This was mainly due to Davis who hated Flynn and his pranks. She had had to bend to the actor's will in 1938, being billed beneath him in THE SISTERS, and this time around demanded and got top billing. She also demanded that Warners give her Laurence Olivier in the Essex role but got Flynn instead. (Davis would later claim that all during her scenes with Flynn, whom she hated, she fantasized that she was acting across from Olivier and was thus able to deliver her lines in a believable manner.) Flynn resented Davis' high-handed ways and he looks uncomfortable with her in almost every scene they share. When he rants about her domineering ways, his heart is not in words supposed to be passionate: "I love her, I hate her, I adore her, " he says without conviction. It all comes off the script as if being read without enthusiasm. The confrontations between Davis and Flynn are somewhat hollow and certainly naive between such august and learned lovers and competitors for power. Davis says at one point: "You believe you'd rule England better because you are a man." Retorts Flynn boyishly: "I would indeed! And that is why you fail. Because you can't act and think like a man!" Flynn and Davis were, at the time, the reigning king and queen of the Warner Bros. lot, but they disliked each other intensely, although Flynn later stated that Davis was "the greatest thing in the movies." He added that she was "not physically my type; dominating everybody around, and especially me...." He said that she resented the fact that he was then receiving $6,000 a week and she much less, in spite of the accepted fact that she was a greater actress than he an actor. There was a built-in, seething animosity between the two and it came out on camera in one scene where Flynn defies the queen and she slaps him. Davis, in the first take of this scene, swung her arm full, which was laden with heavy bracelets and rings, and slammed it full force into Flynn's face, striking him with painful impact. "My jaw went out," he later wrote in *My Wicked, Wicked Ways*, "I felt a click behind my ear and I saw all these comets, shooting stars, all in one flash. It didn't knock me to the ground. She had given me that little dainty hand, laden with a pound of costume jewelry, right across the ear. I felt as if I were deaf." Director Curtiz called for another take while Flynn boiled in anger. Before the second, Flynn went to Davis' elaborate dressing room, the biggest on the lot. As he was about to open his mouth, Davis spat out: "Oh, I know perfectly well what you are going to say...but if you can't take a little slap, that is just too bad! That's a pity!...I knew you were going to complain. I can't do it any other way! If I have to pull my punches, I can't do this. That's the kind of actress I am—and I *stress* actress!" Flynn retreated and then went back to Davis once more, resolved not to take another haymaker to his handsome jaw. "What's your problem now?" carped the actress, still applying her makeup in front of a mirror and barely glancing up at her costar. Flynn said they should rehearse the scene and Davis wheeled about and screamed: "I am telling you I cannot do it any other way!" Flynn stood his ground and said to her with menace in his voice: "I will give you one more chance to try. Do you get me?" "What the hell are you talking about?" Davis asked. "Just what I said." Flynn stormed out, determined to retaliate should the actress again strike him a powerhouse blow. He intended to flatten her in front of the hundreds of extras, the film crew, and take his chances with the press. As he again marched onto the palace set, he fully expected the tempestuous Davis to lash out fully and he was prepared to "whack her and drop her—and I believed that if I did, after what I had just been through, I might break her jaw." He slowly approached Davis, the queen, who waited for him at the end the immense set serving as the grand throne room while trumpets blared. He stood before her, exchanging his own glare for hers. "I braced myself for this hit," Flynn recalled, "and the counterpunch to it. True, I would be disgraced. Me, a man, hitting the world's favorite on the chin was not going to look pretty, but I had to do it. I didn't care." The hostile lines of dialog were traded and Davis lifted her arm and swung mightily, but her hand only breezed by Flynn's face. "I could feel the wind go by," he said. This was the take used by Curtiz but Flynn would take his revenge in another scene where he and Davis were frisking about the palace. The actor "held my hand out there...and it went sailing right through her Elizabethan dresses, slappo, smack on her Academy Award behind. She went about two feet off the ground." Flynn smiled while Davis spun around in fury. "I'm awfully sorry," he said half-heartedly, "I don't know how to do it any other way." Davis never again spoke to Flynn off camera. Whenever he said hello to her she turned her head away. Whether or not director Curtiz was aware of this battle royal going on before his cameras is not recorded. He did his usual yeoman job of producing an eye-pleasing epic with all the panache and fluidity of camerawork which was his hallmark. The usual Curtiz malapropisms were in full force during the production, along with his fractured English, delivered in a thick Hungarian accent. In one scene Curtiz directed a huge throng of extras, instructing them to cheer for Flynn as he entered London with his troops. The character's name, Essex, suffered mightily here at the tip of Curtiz's tongue. Shouted the director to his extras: "Now when I yell *'Isaacs,'* you yell 'Isaacs!' " The title of this film was long in debate, with Jack Warner wanting to shorten the original Maxwell Anderson play title to ELIZABETH AND ESSEX but then he learned that a novel by Lytton Strachey possessed that title and that agents for the novel wanted $10,000 just to use the title. Warner abandoned it immediately. Flynn, who felt that he was only serving as a prop for Davis, demanded that a title be used in which he would at least take precedence, especially since he was losing out on billing. He proposed THE KNIGHT AND THE LADY. When Davis heard about this, she threatened to walk away from the production and the original Anderson title was adopted. Studio booking agents, however, hated the title THE PRIVATE LIVES OF ELIZABETH AND ESSEX, begging Jack Warner to change it, saying that exhibitors were objecting to it on the grounds that it sounded like another British film produced by Alexander Korda who had made THE PRIVATE LIFE OF HENRY VIII (1933) and THE PRIVATE LIFE OF DON JUAN (1934). Gradwell Sears (as quoted in *Inside Warner Brothers, 1935-1951* by Rudy Behlmer) wrote: "I implore you, Jack [Warner] not to use this title for American consumption, because it will cost us hundreds of thousands of dollars....Any other title which suggests romance and adventure will serve far better than the present title which positively identifies the material as an English historical drama." But Davis held firm and Warner let the title stand. The film was not as successful as it might have been, despite Davis' pyrotechnic exhibition. De Havilland has a thankless role as the lady-in-waiting, but she had promised Jack Warner that if he allowed her to go to Selznick to play Melanie in GONE WITH THE WIND, she would return to her parent studio, Warner Bros., and not make any demands. By giving her a small part in this film, the actress later stated, Warner "was provoking me to break my word to him....It was very hard for me to make ELIZABETH AND ESSEX. I was really miserable, but I did it because I had given him my word." The most incongruous fact about the film was that Essex was only 34 when he was beheaded in 1601 and Elizabeth was 68; the two were never lovers. The age difference is suggested in one scene where de Havilland taunts the red-wigged queen about her age difference with young Flynn in a song, which causes Davis to go berserk and smash every mirror in the chambers, while screeching to de Havilland that she's a "brazen wench, a shameless hedge drab!" The song de Havilland sings is with another lady-in-waiting, Nanette Fabray, who later became a huge television success. Even Davis made fun of her age disparity as an actress playing the ancient but determined monarch. Her friend Charles Laughton, who had broadly essayed another British monarch in THE PRIVATE LIFE OF HENRY VIII, visited the set to See Davis. "Hello , Daddy," she said to Laughton, "I have a nerve trying to play Elizabeth at my age." Replied Laughton: "Never stop trying to hang yourself, Bette." Those words, according to Davis (as quoted in *Mother Goddam*by Whitney Stine) "became a credo of mine—in other words, attempt the impossible in order to improve your work." The blank verse employed by playwright Anderson is often marvelously delivered by the actress (as it was by Lynn Fontanne and her husband Alfred Lunt during the Broadway smash run in 1930), especially her keening and melancholy statement at the finale where she sends her lover to his death, announcing: "I could be young with you, but now I'm old. I know how it will be without you. The sun will be empty and circle around an empty earth—And I will be queen of emptiness and death—Why could you not have loved me enough to give me your love and let me keep as I was?" Davis would play Elizabeth once again, this time closer to the age of the character she so dearly loved, in THE VIRGIN QUEEN (1955), where her younger lover this time was Richard Todd, playing the lickspittle Sir Walter Raleigh.

p, Hal B. Wallis; d, Michael Curtiz; w, Norman Reilly Raine, Aeneas MacKenzie (based on the play "Elizabeth the Queen" by Maxwell Anderson); ph, Sol Polito, W. Howard Green (Technicolor); m, Erich Wolfgang Korngold; ed, Owen Marks; md, Hugo Friedhofer, Milan Roder; art d, Anton Grot; cos, Orry-Kelly; spec eff, Byron Haskin, H.F. Koenekamp; makeup, Perc Westmore; tech adv, Ali Hubert.

Romance/Historical Epic Cas. (PR:A MPAA:NR)

PRIVATE NAVY OF SGT. O'FARRELL, THE* (1968) 92m Naho/UA c

Bob Hope *(Master Sgt. Dan O'Farrell)*, Phyllis Diller *(Nurse Nellie Krause)*, Jeffrey Hunter *(Lt. Lyman P. Jones)*, Gina Lollobrigida *(Maria)*, Mylene Demongeot *(Gaby)*, John Myhers *(Lt. Cmdr. Roger Snavely)*, Mako *(Calvin Coolidge Ishimuna)*, Henry Wilcoxon *(Rear Adm. Arthur L. Stokes)*, Dick Sargent *(Capt. Elwood Prohaska)*, Christopher Dark *(Pvt. George Strongbow)*, Michael Burns *(Pvt. Johnny Bannon)*, William Wellman, Jr. *(Cpl. Kennedy)*, Robert Donner *(Marine Pvt. Ogg)*, Jack Grinnage *(Pvt. Roberts)*, William Christopher *(Pvt. Jack Schultz)*, John Spina *(Cpl. Miller)*.

Hope is a sergeant stationed with his troops in the South Seas. As a morale booster he has a shipload of beer sent to the islands but it is lost in transit and his troops are not satisfied with the substitute, nurse Diller. Hope sets out to locate the lost suds and finds not only the alcohol but a Japanese sub that he captures. It would take a shipload of beer to be able to sit through this picture just once, especially with the obnoxious Diller filling up screen time. One of Hope's worst, ditto for Tashlin. Produced by both NBC (the NA—NAtional Broadcasting of the company name) and Hope (the HO of HOpe), a collaboration which thankfully was not too active.

p, John Beck; d, Frank Tashlin; w, Tashlin (based on a story by John L. Greene, Robert M. Fresco); ph, Alan Stensvold (Technicolor); m, Harry Sukman; ed, Eda Warren; art d, Bob Kinoshita; set d, Fred Price; cos, Oscar Rodriguez; spec eff, Charles Spurgeon; makeup, Mike Moshella.

Comedy (PR:A MPAA:G)

PRIVATE NUMBER** (1936) 80m FOX bw (GB: SECRET INTERLUDE)

Robert Taylor *(Richard Winfield)*, Loretta Young *(Ellen Neal)*, Patsy Kelly *(Gracie)*, Basil Rathbone *(Wroxton)*, Marjorie Gateson *(Mrs. Winfield)*, Paul Harvey *(Perry Winfield)*, Joe Lewis *(Smiley Watson)*, Jane Darwell *(Mrs. Meecham)*, Monroe Owsley *(Coakley)*, George Irving *(Judge)*, Frank Dawson *(Graham)*, May Beatty *(Grandma Gammon)*, John Miljan *(Stapp)*, Jack Pennick *(Gus Rilovitch)*, Prince *(Hamlet, a Dog)*, Paul Stanton *(Rawlings)*, Fred Kelsey *(Detective)*, Kane Richmond *(Chauffeur)*, Billy Bevan.

This is a cliche romantic drama that was so creaky, even at this early date, that it could very easily have been turned into a comedy-satire. The original play, done in 1915, starred Jane Cowl. It then became a silent film with Fannie Ward in the lead and was again made in 1930 with Constance Bennett. The script was altered to fit the talents of the hot new team of Taylor and Young and to erase some of the sexier elements. Young works as a servant in the mansion of Taylor's wealthy family. At a summer retreat in Maine, the two fall in love and wed covertly before he goes back to his Ivy League university. Young remains working as maid to Taylor's mother, Gateson, but she is pregnant. When that fact is discovered by the butler, Rathbone (who had made a pass at her in an earlier scene), he tells Gateson and her husband, Harvey. Rathbone is a scurrilous type who takes kickbacks from the other servants and rules the roost with a vicious hand. Young is tossed out of the house and when she later writes letters to Taylor, they never get to him because Rathbone has purloined them. Taylor has no idea where Young is or the fact that she'd given birth to a son. Gateson, Harvey, and Rathbone keep the couple apart and eventually convince Taylor that she's run out on him, suggesting he seek an annulment. It turns out that Young had a contretemps with the law sometime before and when that is presented to Taylor, he is so under the influence of his parents that he agrees to the annulment proceeding. There's a perfunctory courtroom scene in which the judge and Taylor learn that Young had been framed for the earlier criminal charge. Taylor now says that he loves Young, wants to be with her forever, begs her to forgive him, and the picture ends on a happy note. It could have just as easily been a farce. Kelly and Lewis provide what little comedy there is. This was comedian Lewis' first of only two pictures, the other being PRIVATE BUCKAROO, by which time he took the "E" as his middle initial and had already established himself as a big-time nightclub comedian, eventually having his own life portrayed with Frank Sinatra playing the lead role in THE JOKER IS WILD. One wonders if there's such a thing as an "Alphabet Store" where actors go to change their names?

p, Darryl F. Zanuck, Raymond Griffith; d, Roy Del Ruth; w, Gene Markey, William Conselman (based on the play "Common Clay" by Cleves Kinkead); ph, Peverell Marley; ed, Allen McNeil; md, Louis Silvers.

Drama (PR:A MPAA:NR)

PRIVATE NURSE* (1941) 60m FOX bw

Jane Darwell *(Miss Adams)*, Brenda Joyce *(Mary Malloy)*, Sheldon Leonard *(John Winton)*, Robert Lowery *(Henry Hoyt)*, Ann Todd *(Barbara Winton)*, Kay Linaker *(Helene)*, Frank Sully *(Eddie)*, Ferike Boros *(Mrs. Goldberg)*, Claire Du Brey *(Manager Flower Shop)*, Leonard Carey *(Smitty)*, Clara Blandick *(Miss Phillips)*, Myra Marsh *(Miss Sheaffer)*, George Chandler, Steve O'Brien *(Messenger Boys)*.

Nurses Darwell and Joyce go on cases together, one involving a drunken partier (Lowery), the other 10-year-old Todd and her mobster father, Leonard. There is not much more than that, and even if there was it probably would not be any better —just longer.

p, Sol M. Wurtzel; d, David Burton; w, Samuel G. Engel; ph, Virgil Miller; ed, Al DeGaetano.

Drama (PR:A MPAA:NR)

PRIVATE PARTS* (1972) 87m Penelope/MGM c

Ayn Ruymen *(Cheryl Stratton)*, Lucille Benson *(Aunt Martha Atwood)*, John Ventantonio *(George Atwood)*, Laurie Main *(Rev. Moon)*, Stanley Livingston *(Jeff)*, Charles Woolf *(Jeff's Dad)*, Ann Gibbs *(Judy)*, Len Travis *(Mike)*, Dorothy Neumann *(Mrs. Quigley)*, Gene Simms, John Lupton *(Policemen)*, Patrick Strong *(Artie)*.

A bizarre black comedy from Paul Bartel (EATING RAOUL) about a young runaway who turns her back on a "nice" boy (Livingston—Chip from MY THREE SONS) and instead gets involved with Ventantonio. The latter is a voyeuristic photographer who lives in a hotel owned by the runaway's aunt. The boarders are a wacky collection ranging from a strange fellow named Rev. Moon who has a fondness for muscular men to Ventantonio's affair with a water and blood-filled sex doll. A strange picture which was quietly released by MGM under the guise of Premier Productions. A definite candidate for cult movie status. This was Bartel's first full-length feature.

p, Gene Corman; d, Paul Bartel; w, Philip Kearney, Les Rendelstein; ph, Andrew Davis (Metrocolor); m, Hugo Friedhofer; ed, Morton Tubor; set d, John Retsek; cos, Liz Manny.

Comedy (PR:O MPAA:R)

PRIVATE POOLEY** (1962, Brit./E. Ger.) 70m DEFA/Contemporary bw

Garfield Morgan *(Albert Pooley)*, John Rees *(Bill Carter)*, Cecile Chevreau *(Mme. Creton)*, Ferdy Mayne *(Intelligence Officer)*, Alfred Muller *(Hauptsturmerfuehrer)*, Andrew Ray *(Ginger)*, Jennifer Wilson *(Mrs. Pooley)*, Lindsay Anderson *(Narrator)*, Ronald Leigh-Hunt, Charles Houston.

This realistic portrayal of WW II stars Morgan as an English soldier nearly executed by German officer Muller outside Dunkirk. While the rest of his captured battalion are killed, Morgan manages to escape, vowing that upon the war's end he will seek out Muller and avenge his fellow soldiers' deaths. After convincing the British authorities to let him return to Germany, Morgan searches the POW camps until he finds Muller, bringing him to a long overdue justice. English film director Lindsay Anderson provides a grim narration.

d, Kurt Jung-Alsen; w, Franz Fuchmann, narration by Lindsay Anderson (based on the novel *The Vengeance of Private Pooley* by Cyril Jilly); ph, Rolf Sohre; m, Andre Asriel.

War Drama (PR:C MPAA:NR)

PRIVATE POTTER** (1963, Brit.) 89m MGM bw

Tom Courtenay *(Pvt. Potter)*, Mogens Wieth *(Yannis)*, Ronald Fraser *(Doctor)*, James Maxwell *(Lt. Col. Gunyon)*, Ralph Michael *(Padre)*, Brewster Mason *(Brigadier)*, Eric Thompson *(Capt. Knowles)*, John Graham *(Maj. Sims)*, Frank Finlay *(Capt. Patterson)*, Harry Landis *(Cpl. Lamb)*, Michael Coles *(Pvt. Robertson)*, Jeremy Geidt *(Maj. Reid)*.

Courtenay stars as a young soldier who claims he had a vision of God while on a mission. His apparent religious experience resulted in the death of a fellow soldier and his superiors debate whether to court martial him. After his debut in THE

LONELINESS OF THE LONG DISTANCE RUNNER, Courtenay turns in a bravura performance, but the script is a confusing mishmash of religion, conscience, and Army regulations.

p, Ben Arbeid; d, Casper Wrede; w, Wrede, Ronald Harwood (based on the teleplay by Harwood); ph, Arthur Lavis; m, George Hall; ed, John Pomeroy.

War Drama   **(PR:A-C MPAA:NR)**

PRIVATE PROPERTY***   (1960) 79m Kana/Citations bw

Corey Allen (Duke), Warren Oates (Boots), Kate Manx (Ann Carlyle), Robert Wark (Roger Carlyle), Jerome Cowan (Ed Hogate).

Allen is a young hood who plans the seduction of beautiful housewife Manx, so his homosexual friend, Oates, can have a woman for the first time. The act of seduction takes up the majority of the picture, done in a slow and mannered sense. The last 20 minutes, however, erupts with a powerful confrontation between Allen and Oates, climaxing with the still-virginal Oates being drowned in a pool. Made on a budget of $60,000, Leslie Stevens directed and scripted, as well as placing his wife of the time in the starring role. Stevens previously was the creator of TV's "The Outer Limits" and penned Arthur Penn's THE LEFT HANDED GUN, but his role in the professed American New Wave never came to much. Sharply photographed by veteran cameraman Ted McCord, who would later be nominated for his work on THE SOUND OF MUSIC.

p, Stanley Colbert; d&w, Leslie Stevens; ph, Ted McCord; ed, Jerry Young.

Drama   **(PR:O MPAA:NR)**

PRIVATE RIGHT, THE**   (1967, Brit.) 86m Onyx/LIP bw

Dimitris Andreas (Minos Elias), George Kafkaris (Tassos Phantis), Tamara Hinchco (Girl), Cristos Demetriou (Kypros), Charlotte Selwyn (Waitress), Seraphim Nicola (Rebel), John Brogan (Interrogator).

After being tortured in war, a Greek patriot returns to his home in Cyprus. There he hopes to seek out and confront the man who betrayed him.

p,d&w, Michael Papas.

War Drama   **(PR:A MPAA:NR)**

PRIVATE ROAD*½   (1971, Brit.) 87m Maya Films c

Bruce Robinson (Peter), Susan Panhaligon (Ann), Michael Feast (Friend).

A dated tale of a young writer and his sexually free girl friend. She gets pregnant, has her dad perform an abortion, and has to persuade her boy friend to come back to her. Also mixed in are friends who spout Maoist manifestos or utter hippie jibberish. Far from impressive.

d&w, Barney Platts-Mills; ph, Adam Barker-Mills (Eastmancolor); m, George Fenton, Michael Feast, David Dundas.

Drama   **(PR:O MPAA:NR)**

PRIVATE SCANDAL, A*½   (1932) 67m Headline c

Marian Nixon, Lloyd Hughes, Lucille Powers, Theodore Von Eltz, Walter Hiers, Fletcher Norton, Eddie Phillips, George Wells, Burr McIntosh.

Nixon plays an orphaned girl saved from a reformatory by good-hearted crook Hughes, the head of a gang which makes a living off posh residences. She lands a job with district attorney Von Eltz, unaware that her husband is a thief until he is brought in for questioning. But she uses her position to help her husband by avoiding information which would hurt Von Eltz's chance of becoming governor. He in turn gives Hughes a lighter sentence. Lack of proper development makes this little more than a stereotyped plot with thin characters.

d, Charles Hutchinson; w, John Francis Natteford (based on a story by Natteford); ph, Ernest Miller, B.B. Ray; ed, Richard Calhoun, Robert Hughes.

Crime   **(PR:A MPAA:NR)**

PRIVATE SCANDAL**   (1934) 62m PAR bw

ZaSu Pitts (Miss Coates, Secretary), Phillips Holmes (Cliff Barry), Mary Brian (Fran Somers), Ned Sparks (Riordan), Lew Cody (B.J. Somers), June Brewster (Adele Smith), Harold Waldridge (Jerome), Jed Prouty (H.R. Robbins), Charles Sellon (Mr. Terwilliger), Rollo Lloyd (Insurance Agent), Olive Tell (Deborah Lane).

Predictable mystery has Cody on the verge of suicide when his phony real estate business gets in financial trouble. But before he has a chance to actually commit suicide he is murdered. Holmes, as his right-hand man, is put in a situation where he thinks it is suicide, but says it was murder to collect the insurance to pay off debts. Sparks plays the detective with an endless number of questions. Thin plot acts as a background for some good comedy and strong caricatures.

p, Charles R. Rogers; d, Ralph Murphy; w, Garrett Fort (based on a story by Vera Caspary, Bruce Manning); ph, Milton Krasner.

Mystery/Comedy   **(PR:A MPAA:NR)**

PRIVATE SCHOOL zero   (1983) 97m UNIV c

Phoebe Cates (Christine), Betsy Russell (Jordan), Kathleen Wilhoite (Betsy), Matthew Modine (Jim), Michael Zorek (Bubba), Fran Ryan (Miss Dutchbok), Ray Walston (Chauncey), Sylvia Kristel (Ms. Copuletta), Jonathan Prince (Roy), Kari Lizer (Rita), Richard Stahl (Mr. Flugel), Julie Payne (Coach Whelan), Frank Aletter (Mr. Leigh-Jensen), Frances Bay (Birdie Fallmouth), Bill Wray (Bandleader), Karen Chase (Bambi), Burke Byrnes (Ramsay), Zale Kessler (Desk Clerk), Steve Levitt (Bellboy), Robert Ackerman (Maitre D'), Gayle Goldin (Arcade Voice), Lynda Wiesmeier, Christy Curtis, Nadine Van Der Velde, Lori Plager, Joni Lynn Ward, Chris McDermott, Zetta Whitlow, Vernon Scott, Douglas Warhit, Randy Chance Graham, Robert Parker.

Another crass teen-age sexploitation picture in the vein of PORKY'S has the boys from an academy trying to catch glimpses of the girls in the neighboring school as

they go about their daily activities. Absence of any form of plot, or anything even resembling acting, makes for a thoroughly disgusting venture.

p, R. Ben Efraim, Don Enright; d, Noel Black; w, Dan Greenburg, Suzanne O'Malley; ph, Walter Lasally (Metrocolor); ed, Fred Chulack; prod d, Ivo Cristante; set d, K.C. Scheibel; ch, Paula Abdul.

Comedy   **Cas.**   **(PR:O MPAA:R)**

PRIVATE SECRETARY, THE**   (1935, Brit.) 70m Twickenham bw

Edward Everett Horton (Rev. Robert Spalding), Barry Mackay (Douglas Cattermole), Judy Gunn (Edith Marsland), Oscar Asche (Robert Cattermole), Sydney Fairbrother (Miss Ashford), Michael Shepley (Henry Marsland), Alastair Sim (Mr. Nebulae), Aubrey Dexter (Gibson), O.B. Clarence (Thomas Marsland), Davina Craig (Annie).

Asche is a rich Englishman returning home from a trip to India. He hopes to find his nephew a success, but instead the boy has accumulated numerous debts and is on the run. Before leaving, he had taken up the guise of a mild-mannered minister (Horton), who now faces the wrath of the boy's many creditors, as well as Asche. Based on a famous comic farce of the Victorian era, the comedy didn't translate well into later times. Horton and Sim (in a secondary role) serve as the film's saving graces with some nice comic moments.

p, Julius Hagen; d, Henry Edwards; w, George Broadhurst, Arthur Macrae, H. Fowler Mear (based on the play "Der Bibliotheker" by Van Moser); ph, Sydney Blythe, William Luff.

Comedy   **(PR:A MPAA:NR)**

PRIVATE SNUFFY SMITH   (SEE: SNUFFY SMITH, YARDBIRD, 1942)

PRIVATE WAR OF MAJOR BENSON, THE**½**   (1955) 100m UNIV c

Charlton Heston (Maj. Bernard Benson), Julie Adams (Dr. Kay "Lammy" Lambert), William Demarest (John, Handyman), Tim Considine (Cadet Sgt. Hibler), Sal Mineo (Cadet Col. Dusik), Nana Bryant (Mother Redempta), Kay Stewart (Mrs. Flaherty), Mary Field (Sister Mary Theresa), Tim Hovey (Cadet "Tiger" Flaherty), Donald Keeler (Cadet Cpl. Scawalski), Donald Haggerty (Mr. Hibler), Yvonne Peattie (Mrs. Hibler), Mary Alan Hokanson (Sister Mary Thomasina), Edward C. Platt (Monsignor Collins), Butch Jones (Cadet Capt. Petri), Milburn Stone (Maj. Gen. Ramsey), Mickey Little (Cadet Lt. Hanratty), David Janssen (Young Lieutenant), Richard H. Cutting, Gary Pagett.

Heston is a major in the Army, a stern disciplinarian who is always berating his troops and makes the error of shooting off his mouth to Newsweek, a deed which puts him on the carpet in front of his commanding officer, Stone. The hierarchy in the service demands Heston be relieved of his post so he's given one more chance and sent to Santa Barbara, where he is is to whip up the ROTC program at a military school. Upon arrival, he learns that the school is run by nuns, led by Bryant, and that his cadets range from 6 to 15 years of age. The school is on probation and in danger of losing its ROTC certification. When Heston meets his "men," he is shocked and proceeds to treat them in the same way he handled his soldiers before. Naturally, the kids think he's a creep. The school's doctor, Adams, examines Heston when he is hurt during a drill. He'd like to ask her out but the Army has been his life and his wife and he has no idea of how to deal with a woman. He finally works up enough courage, but their first date is a disaster as she brings 6-year-old Hovey along. The cadets are so fed up with Heston that they write a complaining letter to Washington. Heston goes back to meet with Stone, who happens to be Bryant's brother. Heston wants to come back to the service but Bryant has been writing to Stone about the way Heston has treated the kids and Stone is not convinced Heston is ready to lead men if he can't even lead boys. Heston returns to Santa Barbara where Adams's watch has been stolen. Heston tracks down the culprit and learns that it was Considine, a mechanically-minded cadet who just wanted to take it apart and put it back together to see how it worked. Instead of reading him the riot act and clapping the boy in irons, Heston is patient and lets the boy go. Considine tells the other lads how Heston has changed, but by this time their letter has reached Washington and Heston is called back again, throwing a wrench into his burgeoning love relationship with Adams. Heston goes to the hospital to say goodbye to some of the boys, then learns that they have measles and he's been exposed to them so he has to be thrust into quarantine. The Army brass arrive to see if the school will still qualify and the kids come through with a first-rate drill, impressing the Army men as they shout "Rah for Major Benson." In the end, Heston marries Adams, the school keeps the ROTC program, and Heston is reassigned to Fort Dix. Some very good lines in the script and the kids are wonderful, particularly Hovey and Considine. If you want your heart warmed, try watching this. Even Heston gets off a few quips without murdering them.

p, Howard Pine; d, Jerry Hopper; w, William Roberts, Richard Alan Simmons (based on a story by Joe Connelly, Bob Mosher); ph, Harold Lipstein (Technicolor); ed, Ted J. Kent; md, Joseph Gershenson; art d, Alexander Golitzen, Robert Boyle; cos, Rosemary Odell; m/l, "Toy Tiger," Henry Mancini, Herman Stein.

Comedy   **(PR:A MPAA:NR)**

PRIVATE WORE SKIRTS, THE   (SEE: NEVER WAVE AT A WAC, 1952)

PRIVATE WORLDS***   (1935) 84m PAR bw

Claudette Colbert (Dr. Jane Everest), Charles Boyer (Dr. Charles Monet), Joan Bennett (Sally MacGregor), Joel McCrea (Dr. Alex MacGregor), Helen Vinson

(Claire Monet), Esther Dale (Matron), Samuel S. Hinds (Dr. Arnold), Jean Rouverol (Carrie Flynn), Sam Godfrey (Tom Hirst), Dora Clement (Bertha Hirst), Theodore Von Eltz (Dr. Harding), Stanley Andrews (Dr. Barnes), Guinn "Big Boy" Williams (Jerry), Maurice Murphy (Boy in Car), Irving Bacon (McLean, Male Nurse), Nick Shaid (Arab Patient), Monte Vandergrift (Dawson), Arnold Gray (Clarkson), Julian Madison (Johnson), Harry C. Bradley (Johnson's Father), Eleanore King (Carrie's Nurse).

Based on Phyllis Bottome's best-seller about the new psychiatric system instituted by Austrian Alfred Adler, PRIVATE WORLDS was bold in many ways. It was one of the earliest films to get into psychological matters and stood for 13 years as the only major Hollywood movie on the subject until THE SNAKE PIT came along. Colbert had just come off her Oscar for IT HAPPENED ONE NIGHT and chose to expand her career with a serious role as a psychiatrist who plunges herself into her work to forget her one great love, who was killed in WW I. Boyer comes to the mental hospital to take over the reins and is instantly at odds with Colbert as he is a misogynist who thinks that women are 10 percent intelligence and 90 percent emotion. McCrea is a resident physician who wanted the top spot and is angered that he has been bypassed for Boyer. McCrea, while married to Bennett, who is expecting, soon has an affair with Boyer's sister, Vinson, a mentally unstable woman who may or may not have killed her husband, Boyer's good friend. When Bennett learns of McCrea's dalliance, she goes slightly mad and he has to deal with that. There are several episodes, rather than one thrusting story, and the movie spends most of its time depicting what life is like in a "liberated" mental facility. Colbert received an Oscar nomination for her role but lost to Bette Davis for DANGEROUS. Jean Rouverol, one of the schizophrenic inmates, later took up writing and did several soap operas, including "As the World Turns," "The Guiding Light" and "Search for Tomorrow." Her screenplays include LEGEND OF LYLAH CLARE, THE FIRST TIME, and FACE IN THE RAIN, with her husband, Hugo Butler. The title refers to the "Private Worlds" in which we all live and the movie tackled a formerly taboo subject unknown to the general public and made it consistently interesting.

p, Walter Wanger; d, Gregory La Cava; w, Lynn Starling, La Cava, Gladys Unger (based on the novel by Phyllis Bottome); ph, Leon Shamroy; ed, Aubrey Scotto.

Psychological Drama   **(PR:A-C MPAA:NR)**

PRIVATE'S AFFAIR, A**   (1959) 92m FOX c

Sal Mineo (Luigi Maresi), Christine Carere (Marie), Barry Coe (Jerry Morgan), Barbara Eden (Katey), Gary Crosby (Mike), Terry Moore (Louise Wright), Jim Backus (Jim Gordon), Jessie Royce Landis (Elizabeth T. Chapman), Robert Burton (Gen. Hargrave), Alan Hewitt (Maj. Hanley), Robert [Bob] Denver (MacIntosh), Tige Andrews (Sgt. Pickerell), Ray Montgomery (Capt. Hickman), Rudolph Anders [Robert O. Davis] (Dr. Leyden), Debbie Joyce (Magdalena), Robert Montgomery, Jr. (Young Rookie), Dick Whittinghill, Emerson Treacy, Maida Severn, Carlyle Mitchell.

A cooked-up plot line has Coe, while under sedation in an army hospital, forced to marry Landis, the Assistant Secretary of the Army, so that she can adopt an orphaned girl who would otherwise be shipped back to Holland. But this plot is just an excuse to capitalize on some comic situations and the young untried talents of the cast. And the idea pretty much works, with the cast giving the production a lot of spirit without falling into the trap of taking themselves too seriously. Walsh, not noted for his lighter side, directed this farce. This was actress Eden's first appearance in a feature film.

p, David Weisbart; d, Raoul Walsh; w, Winston Miller (based on a story by Ray Livingston Murphy); ph, Charles G. Clarke (CinemaScope, Deluxe Color); m, Cyril J. Mockridge; ed, Dorothy Spencer; md, Lionel Newman; art d, Lyle R. Wheeler, Walter M. Simonds; set d, Walter M. Scott, Stuart M. Reiss; m/l, "Same Old Army," "36-24-36," "Warm and Willing," Jimmy McHugh, Jay Livingston, Ray Evans.

Comedy   **(PR:A MPAA:NR)**

PRIVATES ON PARADE*½   (1982) 100m HandMade Films c

John Cleese (Maj. Giles Flack), Denis Quilley (Capt. Terri Dennis), Nicola Pagett (Sylvia Morgan), Patrick Pearson (Pvt. Steven Flowers), Bruce Payne, Michael Elphick, Joe Melia, David Bamber, Simon Jones, Patrick Pearson, Phil Tan, Vincent Wong, Neil Pearson, Steve Dixon, Jasper Jacob, Leonard Preston, Peter Hutchinson, Neil Phillips, John Standing, Talat Hussain, John Quayle, Brigitte Kahn, Ishaq Bux, Robin Langford, Tim Barlow, William Parker, Mark Elliot, Tim Sinclair, David Griffin, Julian Sands.

This rather bleak attempt at satire has "queen" Quilley organizing a group of homosexual British army would-be entertainers to perform for the troops stationed in Southeast Asia shortly after WW II. He comes up against Cleese, a strait-laced major who is trying to work up his men against what he expects to be the coming Communist attack. Despite a good effort by Quilley, who poses as Marlene Dietrich, Carmen Miranda, and other past femmes, the characters are nothing but stereotyped figures, with much of the comedy dependent on situations which seem thoroughly outdated. Good photography and production values for the low budget, but the film doesn't quite make it as an allegory about the decline and fall of the British empire.

p, Simon Relph; d, Michael Blakemore; w, Peter Nichols (based on his play); ph, Ian Wilson (Rank Film Labs color); m, Denis King; ed, Jim Clark; prod d, Luciana Arrighi; art d, Michael White, Andrew Sanders; cos, Arrighi; m/l, King, Nichols.

Comedy   **(PR:O MPAA:R)**

PRIVATE'S PROGRESS**   (1956, Brit.) 99m Charter/BL bw

Richard Attenborough (Pvt. Cox), Dennis Price (Brigadier Bertram Tracepurcel), Terry-Thomas (Maj. Hitchcock), Ian Carmichael (Stanley Windrush), Peter Jones (Egan), William Hartnell (Sgt. Sutton), Thorley Walters (Capt. Bootle), Jill Adams

(Prudence Greenslade), Ian Bannen (Pvt. Horrocks), Victor Maddern (Pvt. George Blake), Kenneth Griffith (Pvt. Dai Jones), John Warren (Sgt.-Maj. Gradwick), George Coulouris (Padre), Derrick de Marney (Pat), Miles Malleson (Mr. Windrush), Michael Trubshawe (Col. Panshawe), John le Mesurier (Psychiatrist), Sally Miles (Catherine), Brian Oulton, Nicholas Bruce, David Lodge, David King-Wood, Frank Hawkins, Basil Dignam, Henry Longhurst, Henry Oscar, Theodore Zichy, Michael Ward, Robert Bruce, Ludwig Lawinski, Irlyn Hall, Marianne Stone, Lockwood West, Jack McNaughton, Eynon Evans, Glyn Houston, Ronald Adam, Lloyd Lamble.

British farce on army life has Carmichael a well-meaning university student who enlists in the army, only to become a misfit lost in the strict ways of army existence. He is the prototype upper-class English nerd, who fails to turn out for an army training detail because he's "feeling a bit peckish." He somehow manages to get hooked up with his uncle, Price, who has been looting German art treasures. Plot lacks interest, but the fine cast and witty situations make for some fun.

p, Roy Boulting; d, John Boulting; w, J. Boulting, Frank Harvey (based on the novel by Alan Hackney); ph, Eric Cross; m, John Addison; ed, Anthony Harvey.

Comedy   **(PR:A MPAA:NR)**

PRIVATKLINIK PROF. LUND   (SEE: DAS LETZTE GEHEIMNIS, 1959, Ger.)

PRIVILEGE*½   (1967, Brit.) 103m World Film-Memorial/UNIV c

Paul Jones (Steve Shorter), Jean Shrimpton (Vanessa Ritchie), Mark London (Alvin Kirsch), Max Bacon (Julie Jordan), Jeremy Child (Martin Crossley), William Job (Andrew Butler), James Cossins (Prof. Tatham), Frederick Danner (Marcus Hooper), Victor Henry (Freddie K.), Arthur Pentelow (Leo Stanley), Steve Kirby (Squit), Michael Barrington (Bishop of Essex), John Gill (Bishop of Surrey), Edwin Fink (Bishop of Cornwall (Norman Pitt (Bishop of Hersham), Alba (Bishop of Rutland), Malcolm Rogers (Rev. Jeremy Tate), Doreen Mantle (Miss Crawford), Michael Graham (TV Director), George Bean Group (The Runner Beans), Young People and Adults of Birmingham, England.

Satire set in the future in England has the government and church using the mass appeal of rock music to act as a control on the nation's youth. Jones (one-time singer with the Manfred Mann group) plays the rock idol manipulated by the government and the church undergoing a change from a violent, rebellious public image to that of churchgoing worshipper. After feeling himself pulled apart, Jones revolts—with the urging of artist Shrimpton—against the authorities and his followers, putting them all down. Uncertainty in the director's purpose—whether to take the stance of ironic comedy or social commentary—mars the picture's overall effect. Jones fails to give the type of performance that would make people want to follow him as an idol. The production crew was comprised mostly of people under 30. This was Heyman's first production task. Young director Watkins had created quite a stir with his made-for-TV film THE WAR GAME (1956), which was commissioned by the British Broadcasting Company and then banned by it, but which won an Academy Award for best documentary feature. The film has been compared thematically with Stanley Kubrick's A CLOCKWORK ORANGE (1971). The prospect of a church-state liaison using staged violence—performer Jones is caged, handcuffed, and beaten in performance—to divert the young from rebellion seemed frighteningly close to the truth at the time to some audiences. Similarly, the light show revivalist meeting scenes have credibility in context. Songs include "Free Me" and "Bad, Bad Boy."

p, John Heyman; d, Peter Watkins, Derek Ware; w, Norman Bogner, Watkins (based on a story by Johnny Speight); ph, Peter Suschitzky (Technicolor); m, Mike Leander; ed, John Trumper; art d, William Brodie; cos, Vanessa Clarke; m/l, Leander, Mark London; makeup, Jill Carpenter.

Fantasy   **(PR:A MPAA:NR)**

PRIVILEGED*½   (1982, Brit.) 94m Oxford Film Foundation/New Yorker c

Robert Woolley (Edward), Diana Katis (Anne), Hughie Grant (Lord Adrian), Victoria Studd (Lucy), James Wilby (Jamie), Simon Shackleton (Justin), Imogen Stubbs (Imogen), Mark Williams (Wilf), Jenny Waldman (Waitress), Ted Coleman (Barman), Stefan Bednarcyzk (Pianist), Neville Watchurst (Julian), Michael Hoffman (Alan).

Reportedly the first student feature made at Oxford University, the film centers on the goings-on of a group of undergraduates. Escaping any of the intellectual endeavors of the students, the film concentrates upon antics and student pranks. One student, freshman Woolley, sees himself as an actor. His part in a student play —John Webster's 17th-Century "The Duchess of Malfi"—gives him the chance to try to seduce the leading lady, but she is way ahead of him and his attentions turn toward aristocrat Grant's wife. Life begins to parallel the student play in a sense when (in a sequence supposedly based on a true occurrence) Grant catches Woolley in flagrante delicto with his inamorata and challenges him to a duel with pistols. Rather than shooting his cuckolder, Grant puts a bullet into himself during the ensuing duel. The production has lots of energy and some pretty sharp cuts, but the cast lacks the necessary experience and the direction fails to build tension or give proper emphasis to the several situations. John Schlesinger acted as a consulting director on this project. Filmed in 16mm.

p, Richard Stevenson; d, Michael Hoffman; w, Hoffman, David Woolcombe, Rupert Walters; ph, Fiona Cunningham Reid (Technicolor); m, Rachel Portman; ed, Derek Goldman; prod d, Jason Cooper; art d, Peter Schwabach.

Drama   **(PR:C-O MPAA:NR)**

PRIZE, THE***   (1952, Fr.) 82m Pagnol/Classic Pictures bw (LE ROSIER DE MADAME HUSSON)

Bourvil (Isidore), Baconnet (Mayor), Duvaleix (Priest), Christian Lude (Doctor), Vilbert (Brigadier of the Gendarmerie), Jean Dunot (Polyte), Germaine Dermoz

(Madame Husson), Jacqueline Pagnol *(Young Girl)*, Mireille Perrey *(Countess)*, Pauline Carton *(Virginie)*, Suzanne Dehelly *(Mlle. Cadenat)*, Nina Myral *(Mme. de Gondreville)*, Jeanne Veniat *(Mme. Pitart)*, Yvette Etievant *(Marie)*, Germaine Reuver *(Nicoline)*.

Pleasant French farce has Bourvil being awarded a prize for his virtuousness when a committee of small-town gossipy women cannot find a girl able to fill the bill. But the fun and jokes made on Bourvil's behalf only make the young man depressed, and in a drunken bout he threatens to drown himself. Instead he finds himself wandering down the road when he is picked up by Perrey, who takes the youth to her Paris apartment. When Bourvil comes back to the small town, he has changed from an effeminate youth to a man. Bourvil offers his role a lot of charm, pulling off the change in his character effectively. Script and direction are both smooth, making for an imaginative production. The story was originally filmed with Fernandel in the lead role and released here as HE (1934) in a dubbed version. (In French; English subtitles.)

p, Marcel Pagnol; d, Jean Boyer; w, Pagnol (based on the story "Le Rosier de Madame Husson" by Guy de Maupassant); ph, Charles Suin; m, Paul Misraki.

Comedy (PR:A MPAA:NR)

PRIZE, THE½** (1963) 135m Roxbury/MGM c

Paul Newman *(Andrew Craig)*, Edward G. Robinson *(Dr. Max Stratman)*, Elke Sommer *(Inger Lisa Andersen)*, Diane Baker *(Emily Stratman)*, Micheline Presle *(Dr. Denise Marceau)*, Gerard Oury *(Dr. Claude Marceau)*, Sergio Fantoni *(Dr. Carlo Farelli)*, Kevin McCarthy *(Dr. John Garrett)*, Leo G. Carroll *(Count Bertil Jacobssen)*, Sacha Pitoeff *(Daranyi)*, Jacqueline Beer *(Monique Souvir)*, John Wengraf *(Hans Eckart)*, Don Dubbins *(Ivar Cramer)*, Virginia Christine *(Mrs. Bergh)*, Rudolph Anders *(Mr. Bergh)*, Martine Bartlett *(Saralee Garrett)*, Karl Swenson *(Hilding)*, John Qualen *(Oscar)*, Ned Wever *(Clark Wilson)*, Martin Brandt *(Steen Eckberg)*, Ivan Triesault *(Hotel Porter)*, Grazia Narcisco *(Mrs. Farelli)*, Larry Adare *(David Garrett)*, Robin Adare *(Amy Garrett)*, Lester Mathews *(BBC News Correspondent)*, John Banner *(German Correspondent)*, Teru Shimada *(Tokyo Correspondent)*, Jerry Dunphy *(American TV News Correspondent)*, Michael Panaieff *(French Correspondent)*, Edith Evanson *(Mrs. Ahlquist)*, Carol Byron *(Stewardess)*, Sam Edwards *(Reporter)*, Gregg Palmer *(Swedish Commentator)*, Donald Ein *(Waiter)*, Anna Lena Lund *(Blonde)*, Peter Bourne, Gene Roth, Bjorn Foss *(Swedish Men)*, Queenie Leonard *(Miss Fawley)*, Lyle Sudrow *(Swedish Reporter)*, Anna Lee *(American Reporter)*, Albert Carrier *(French Reporter)*, Gregory Gaye *(Russian Reporter)*, Ben Wright *(British Reporter)*, Erik Holland *(Photographer)*, Sigfried Tor *(Swedish Waiter)*, Gene Roth *(Swedish Man)*, Sven-Hugo Borg *(Oscar Lindbloom)*, Bjorn Foss *(Swedish Man)*, Margareta Lund, Alice Frost, Felda Ein *(Swedish Women)*, Noel Drayton *(Police Constable Strohm)*, Karen Von Unge *(Receptionist)*, Birgitta Engstrom *(Young Woman)*, Carl Carlsson *(Swedish Visitor)*, Ike Ivarsen *(Swedish Speaker)*, Carl Rydin, Ronald Nyman *(Burly Swedes)*, Dr. Harold Dyrenforth, Fred Holliday *(Swedish Officers)*, Raanhild Vidar *(Swedish Bellboy)*, John Holland, Mauritz Hugo *(Speakers)*, Peter Coe *(Officer)*, Otto Reichow *(Seaman)*, Robert Garrett, Paul Busch, Danny Klega, Fred Scheiwiller *(Deck Hands)*, Ellie Ein *(Bellboy)*, Sven Peterson *(Swedish Bellboy)*, Sid Raymond *(Actor)*, Britta Eckman, Maiken Thornberg, Maria Schroeder, Jill Carson, Pam Peterson, Sigrid Petterson, Margarto Sullivan *(Nudists)*.

A lengthy but entertaining picture based on a popular Irving Wallace novel and set against the backdrop of the Nobel Prize ceremony in Sweden. Newman is an alcoholic author who accepts the award only for financial reasons, resenting the publicity that it brings. During a speech he offhandedly makes up a plot for a detective novel which centers on the kidnaping of one of the prize recipients. As it so happens, the Russians have already set such a plot into motion. They have kidnaped physicist Robinson, who is traveling with his niece Baker, and replaced him with his twin brother, Baker's father whom she has long believed to be dead. Newman becomes suspicious and begins asking questions. The Communists make attempts on his life, while the Swedish police and Swedish Foreign Office host Sommer refuse to believe his seemingly farfetched tale. Tracked by two Communists intent on murder, Newman takes refuge in a nudist camp where he must strip down (only partly) in order to go unnoticed. He manages to escape and, still determined to prove that an imposter (played by Robinson in a dual role) has taken Robinson's place, Newman sneaks aboard a ship where he is being held prisoner. He smuggles him off and safely returns him to his hotel room. The excitement, however, is too much and Robinson has a heart attack. With help from McCarthy and Fantoni—the two recipients of the prize for medicine—Robinson is revived. When the phony Robinson shows up at the awards ceremony, he realizes that the real Robinson is also in attendance. He tries to escape but is shot down by Communist agents who are trying to cover up their foiled scheme. It is then revealed that the imposter was not really Robinson's brother but a highy-skilled Russian actor and that the real twin brother did die long ago. Newman, whose negative attitude towards the ceremony has now changed, accepts his prize and professes his love for Sommer. While director Robson obviously displays a certain flair for Hitchcockian suspence and intrigue (in the same vein as the same year's CHARADE), THE PRIZE suffers from an unevenness of tone which cannot balance the political turmoil with the sexual playfulness. Somewhat surprisingly, the Swedish government spoke out against the film, charging that it degraded the meaning of the Nobel Prize.

p, Pandro S. Berman; d, Mark Robson; w, Ernest Lehman (based on the novel by Irving Wallace); ph, William Daniels (Panavision, Metrocolor); m, Jerry Goldsmith; ed, Adrienne Fazan; art d, George W. Davis, Urie McCleary; set d, Henry Grace, Dick Pefferle; spec eff, J. McMillan Johnson, A. Arnold Gillespie, Robert R. Hoag; makeup, William Tuttle.

Espionage/Comedy/Romance (PR:C MPAA:NR)

PRIZE FIGHTER, THE*½ (1979) 99m Tri-Star/New World c

Tim Conway *(Bags)*, Don Knotts *(Shake)*, David Wayne *(Pop Morgan)*, Robin Clark *(Mike)*, Cisse Cameron *(Polly)*, Mary Ellen O'Neill *(Mama)*, Michael LaGuardia *(Butcher)*, George Nutting *(Timmy)*, Irwin Keyes *(Flower)*, John Myhers *(Doyle)*, Alfred E. Covington *(Announcer)*, Dan Fitzgerald *(Big John)*.

This picture, set in the 1930s, has Knotts and Conway teaming up to promote Conway's prizefighting career, which burgeons when villain Clark fixes a bunch of boxing matches so that he can face the champion. Clark's plan is to get kindly old Wayne to bet his entire gymnasium on Conway, then have Conway lose the final bout. But Conway manages to beat the champion, saving the day for all. A predictable script filled with aged slapstick mars any possibilities Knotts and Conway might have for creating some genuine humor.

p, Lang Elliott, Wanda Dell; d, Michael Preece; w, Tim Conway, John Myhers; ph, Jacques Haitkin (Panavision, DeLuxe Color); m, Peter Matz; ed, Fabien Tordjmann; art d, Vincent Peranio; cos, Jane Jones.

Comedy Cas. (PR:C MPAA:PG)

PRIZE OF ARMS, A*** (1962, Brit.) 105m Bryanston/BL bw

Stanley Baker *(Turpin)*, Helmut Schmid *(Swavek)*, Tom Bell *(Fenner)*, David Courtenay *(Lt. Davies)*, Tom Adams *(Cpl. Glenn)*, Anthony Bate *(Sgt. Reeves)*, Rodney Bewes *(Pvt. Maynard)*, Richard Bidlake *(Lt. Waddington)*, Douglas Blackwell *(Day)*, Mark Burns *(Lt. Ellison)*, Frank Coda *(Brodie)*, Michael Collins *(Leigh)*, David Comville *(Capt. James)*, Clifford Cox *(RASC Sergeant Major)*, Barry Keegan *(Supt. Cooper)*, Stephen Lewis *(Col. Bates)*, Fulton Mackay *(Cpl. Henderson)*, Patrick Magee *(R. S. M. Hicks)*, Jack May *(M. O.)*, Roddy McMillan *(Sgt. McVie)*, John Phillips *(Col. Fowler)*, Michael Ripper *(Cpl. Freeman)*, John Westbrook *(Capt. Stafford)*, Kenneth Mackintosh *(Capt. Nicholson)*, Frank Gatliff *(Maj. Palmer)*, John Rees *(Sgt. Jones)*, Lynn Furlong *(Canteen Girl)*.

Baker plays a British ex-captain cashiered for black market activities in Hamburg; in order to get his revenge on the army he thinks up a complicated scheme for heisting the money which will accompany the troops as they take off for North Africa to resolve the Suez crisis. He has enlisted the help of Schmid and Bell in his scheme, which requires that the three pose as soldiers while infiltrating the barracks for twelve hours. The carefully thought-out timetable goes haywire when one of the men gets cookhouse duty and another gets sick from an inoculation. But Baker makes off with the cash through the use of a flamethrower, only to be followed by the military police and eventually sending the money up in flames. Well-paced direction keeps the tension mounting, with the cast lending the proper measure of *machismo* to their roles. A pure caper film, with no romance; barring a bit part, it's an all-male cast.

p, George Maynard; d, Cliff Owen; w, Paul Ryder (based on a story by Nicolas Roeg, Kevin Kavanagh); ph, Gilbert Taylor, Gerald Gibbs; m, Robert Sharples; ed, John Jympson.

Crime (PR:A MPAA:NR)

PRIZE OF GOLD, A*** (1955) 98m Warwick/COL c

Richard Widmark *(Sgt. Joe Lawrence)*, Mai Zetterling *(Maria)*, Nigel Patrick *(Brian Hammell)*, George Cole *(Sgt. Roger Morris)*, Donald Wolfit *(Alfie Stratton)*, Joseph Tomelty *(Uncle Dan)*, Andrew Ray *(Conrad)*, Karel Stepanek *(Dr. Zachmann)*, Robert Ayres *(Tex)*, Eric Pohlmann *(Hans Fischer)*, Olive Sloane *(Mavis)*, Alan Gifford *(Maj. Bracken)*, Ivan Craig *(British Major)*, Harry Towb *(Benny)*, Leslie Linder *(Pole)*, Monika Kossmann *(Lisa)*, Edelweiss Malchin *(Girl on Plane)*, Erich Dunskus *(Canal Foreman)*, Nelly Arno *(German Landlady)*, Arnold Bell *(Police Detective)*, John Witty *(British Officer)*, Joel Riordan, Marvin Kane *(G.I.s)*.

A good action-adventure picture with a fair share of comedy, A PRIZE OF GOLD was shot in Europe and featured some excellent cameos by a trio of British actors, Cole, Wolfit, and Patrick, to complement the performances by Widmark and Zetterling. Widmark is a U.S. Army sergeant stationed in the British sector of Berlin when he meets and falls for Zetterling, a refugee with one goal: she wants to take a group of war orphans she is overseeing from Europe to Brazil to begin a new life. In order to do that, she needs money and Widmark assembles a unit to steal a shipment of gold that's being shipped from England to Germany. Wolfit and Tomelty are part of the British group, while Widmark, Cole, and Patrick handle the actual chore of hijacking the plane and landing it at an abandoned airstrip. After the deed is done, Widmark and Cole have seond thoughts and want to give the money back but Patrick doesn't feel the same way and there is a battle among the conspirators. In the end, Widmark takes the fall for the robbery but still manages to provide Zetterling with the money when he gets Wolfit and Tomelty off the hook and they promise to come up with the needed cash for the orphans. The motivation for Widmark is fuzzy and so is his alteration of attitude but while you're watching the movie, most of that will go out the window as it's so quickly-paced that there's hardly any time to punch holes in the story. The title song is sung by Joan Regan and does nothing for the film.

p, Irving Allen, Albert R. Broccoli, Phil C. Samuel; d, Mark Robson; w, Robert Buckner, John Paxton (based on the novel by Max Catto); ph, Ted Moore (Technicolor); m, Malcolm Arnold; ed, William Lewthwaite; md, Muir Mathieson; m/l, Ned Washington, Lester Lee, Tommie Conner, Gerhardt Bronner, "A Prize of Gold," Washington, Lee (sung by Joan Regan).

Crime/Adventure (PR:A MPAA:NR)

PRIZED AS A MATE! (SEE: SPOILED ROTTEN, 1968, Gr.)

PRIZEFIGHTER AND THE LADY, THE*** (1933) 102m MGM bw (GB: EVERY WOMAN'S MAN)

Myrna Loy *(Belle Morgan)*, Max Baer *(Steve Morgan)*, Primo Carnera *(Himself)*, Jack Dempsey *(Himself, Referee)*, Walter Huston *("Professor" Edwin J. Bennett)*,

Otto Kruger *(Willie Ryan)*, Vince Barnett *(Bugsie)*, Muriel Evans *(Linda)*, Robert McWade *(Adopted Son)*, Jean Howard *(Cabaret Girl)*, Jess Willard *(Himself)*, Jim Jeffries *(Himself)*, Strangler Lewis *(Himself)*, Garry Owen *(Jake)*, Matt McHugh, Harry C. Bradley, Arthur Hoyt, Harry Woods, Morgan Wallace.

Frances Marion, who had already written THE CHAMP, turned in the story for this boxing feature and got an Oscar nomination for her work. It was then turned over to Mahin and Meehan for the script, thus making it a "3 M" project. The original title was "The Sailor And The Lady" and it was to have starred Gable and Loy, but Gable had another commitment so the title and concept were changed and May Baer came in to virtually play himself. Baer was an excellent actor as well as a boxer and was a leading contender for the heavyweight crown, a mantle he was to wear the following year, when he beat the champ, behemoth Primo Carnera, who plays himself in this movie (with his real-life managers playing themselves as well). The script called for Baer to beat Carnera but the huge man would not put up with that so a compromise was made and, in the final sequence, they battle to a draw. In order to get Carnera to agree even to that, the producer had to sweeten his paycheck somewhat. Howard Hawks was to have directed Gable, but when that couldn't be, he declined to direct at all, and Van Dyke stepped in to the job at his usual frantic pace, something that worked well for this film. Hawks hung around to help Baer with his acting technique and the results were excellent as the boxer stole the picture from the veterans who surrounded him. Baer was such a natural that he later earned a fine living as an actor, appearing in several movies including THE HARDER THEY FALL, a *roman a clef* about the life of Carnera. Baer plays, of course, a boxer. When he falls in love with Loy, the girl friend of mobster Kruger, she also goes for him and Kruger says he will let his nighclub star Loy leave him for the pug as long as she's made an honest woman. Baer and Loy marry but he begins flaunting his eye for the ladies in front of her. He's arrogant, conceited, and yet, through it all, likable. They fall out and she returns to Kruger, who had hoped she would do that all along. When Baer gets into the ring with Carnera for the big fight, he gets his head handed to him for a number of rounds. Then, as in the scene when "Rocky" sees "Adrian" in the crowd, Baer spots Loy and she gives him a smile. That's enough to inspire Baer to come back mightily and pound Carnera for the remaining rounds, with the fight winding up a tie—which is, as they say, like kissing your sister. Walter Huston plays Baer's manager and many actual athletes also appear. Jess Willard, Jim Jeffries, and Strangler Lewis are on hand with "The Manassa Mauler," Jack Dempsey, playing the role of the referee. The boxer also gets the opportunity in a scene showing Baer appearing in vaudeville, to sing and show his dancing footwork. The fight scenes were excellent although it's hard to believe that no one was knocked out after seeing the tremendous leather thrown by both pugilists. Max's brother, Buddy, also boxed and later went into movies as an actor, and Max's son, Max Baer, Jr., became a TV star in "The Beverly Hillbillies" and a producer-director with films that included MACON COUNTY LINE and ODE TO BILLY JOE. With such Jewish prizefighters as Benny Leonard, Barney Ross, and "Slapsy Maxie" Rosenbloom becoming stars in the ring, Baer wore the Star Of David on his trunks to indicate that he was also Jewish. But that was only a publicity ploy and not the truth, so far as your editors were able to determine from an interview with Rosenbloom before he died. Although the standard prizefight story had been seen many times before (and even more so since), Baer's winning personality and the sharp script make this a worthwhile look-see for anyone who likes boxing movies.

p, Hunt Stromberg; d, W.S. Van Dyke; w, John Lee Mahin, Jr., John Meehan (based on a story by Frances Marion); ph, Lester White; ed, Robert J. Kern.

Sports Drama **(PR:A MPAA:NR)**

PRO, THE (SEE: NUMBER ONE 1969)

PROBATION** (1932) 60m CHES bw (GB: SECOND CHANCES)

Sally Blane *(Janet Holman)*, J. Farrell MacDonald *(Judge Holman)*, Eddie Phillips *(Alan Wells)*, Clara Kimball Young *(Mrs. Humphreys)*, Betty Grable *(Ruth Jarrett)*, David Rollins *(Alec)*, Mary Jane Irving *(Gwen)*, Matty Kemp *(Bert)*, David Durand *(The Kid)*, John Darrow.

Average second feature for early 1930s double bills has judge MacDonald sentencing a handsome young man to serve as chauffeur for his niece Blane, a society girl. Betty Grable makes an appearance in a secondary role, which, ultimately, is all this film is memorable for.

d, Richard Thorpe; w, Edward T. Lowe (based on the story by Arthur Hoerl, Lowe); ph, M. A. Anderson; ed, Thorpe.

Comedy **(PR:A MPAA:NR)**

PROBLEM GIRLS** (1953) 70m COL bw

Helen Walker *(Miss Dixon)*, Ross Elliott *(John Page)*, Susan Morrow *(Jean Thorpe)*, Anthony Jochim *(Prof. Richards)*, James Seay *(Max Thorpe)*, Marjorie Stapp *(Bella)*, Roy Regnier *(Dr. Manning)*, Eileen Stevens *(Mrs. Kargen)*, Tom Charlesworth *(Mr. Clammerley)*, Beverly Garland *(Nancy Eaton)*, Joyce Jameson *(Peggy Carstairs)*, Nan Leslie *(Claire Harris)*, Joyce Jarvis *(Valerie Creighton)*, Mara Corday *(Dorothy Childers)*, Tandra Quinn *(Judith)*, Norma Eberhardt *(Louise)*, Eric Colmar *(Interne)*, Merritt Stone *(Photographer)*, Walter Bonn *(Mr. Carstairs)*, John Oger *(Henderson)*, Gladys Kingston *(Miss Fanshaw)*, Juney Ellis *(Miss Tippins)*.

The routine plot has Elliott taking a temporary job as a teacher at a school for unstable girls. He discovers that headmistress Walker and athletic director Seay are drugging an innocent girl unnecessarily. The two cohorts become suspicious of Elliott, kicking him off the premises. But Elliott continues his snooping, discovering that they plan on panning the girl off as an oil heiress and collect the inheritance, the actual heiress having already been murdered. Production values and performances are all adequate. The script offers some interesting characterizations of the problem girls who attend the school, stunning starlets all. Director Dupont, who had done important cinematic work in his native Germany, went to Hollywood and disappointment in mid-career. He stopped directing for a time in 1940, becoming an agent during a 10-year directorial hiatus. This was his second feature following his return to directing, his final stint spent entirely—as here—in films of little merit, however competently done.

p, Aubrey Wisberg, Jack Pollexfen; d, E. A. Dupont; w, Wisberg, Pollexfen; ph, John L. Russell, Jr.; m, Albert Glasser; ed, Fred Feitshans, Jr.

Drama **(PR:A MPAA:NR)**

PROCES DE JEANNE D'ARC (SEE: TRIAL OF JOAN OF ARC, 1965, Fr.)

PRODIGAL, THE*½ (1931) 76m MGM bw (AKA: THE SOUTHERNER)

Lawrence Tibbett *(Jeffry Farraday)*, Esther Ralston *(Antonia)*, Roland Young *(Doc, a Tramp)*, Cliff Edwards *(Snipe, a Tramp)*, Purnell B. Pratt *(Rodman Farraday)*, Hedda Hopper *(Christine)*, Emma Dunn *(Mrs. Farraday)*, Stepin Fetchit *(Hokey)*, Louis John Bartels *(George)*, Theodore Von Eltz *(Carter Jerome)*, Wally Albright, Jr. *(Peter)*, Suzanne Ransom *(Elsbeth)*, Gertrude Howard *(Naomi)*, John Larkin *(Jackson)*.

Tibbett plays the scion of a well-to-do southern family of plantation owners who turns happy hobo, riding the rails with English-accented Young and smiling Edwards as sidekicks. After years of carefree vagabonding, Tibbett decides to return to his antebellum origins, where he finds himself falling in love with his brother Pratt's genteel bride, Ralston. The film struck a little too close to home in this Depression year when hundreds of thousands of homeless men were riding the rails; 2,294 banks failed in 1931. Rene Clair's A NOUS LA LIBERTE, released at about the same time, dealt with much the same theme, but carried the master's touch of fantasy blended with irony lacking in this picture; it did not do well at the box office despite a capable cast. Tibbett—familiar with the film industry since childhood, a native of Los Angeles who had made his professional singing debut as "Amonasro" in Giuseppe Verdi's "Aida" in the Hollywood Bowl—had been nominated for an Academy Award as best actor for his film debut work in THE ROGUE SONG (1930). His acting talents were employed here more than his operatic baritone; the film contains only about 10 minutes of songs, backed up by a large unbilled chorus of black plantation singing extras. The English-accented Young, his part written to give him an enormously polysyllabic vocabulary, made an anomalous comic bindlestiff. Edwards, who was best known for his "Ukelele Ike" and "Harmony" roles in a succession of films, including Charles Starrett westerns, was an extremely experienced sidekick who handled his role well. At the time, the bumbling, shiftless black stereotype Fetchit was a top comic draw; he was earning $1,500 weekly when other black featured players were paid only $25 a day. The picture bombed; audiences were more ready, in this perilous time, for releases such as DRACULA, SVENGALI, and FRANKENSTEIN, which premiered the same year. Songs include "Life Is a Dream" (Arthur Freed, Oscar Straus), "Home Sweet Home" (John Howard Payne, Sir Henry Bishop), and "Without a Song" (Vincent Youmans, Edward Eliscu, Billy Rose).

d, Harry Pollard; w, Bess Meredyth, Wells Root (based on their story "The Southerner"); m, Herbert Stothart, Jacques Wolfe, Howard Johnson, Arthur Freed; ph, Harold Rosson; ed, Margaret Booth.

Comedy/Drama **(PR:A MPAA:NR)**

PRODIGAL, THE* (1955) 114m MGM c

Lana Turner *(Samarra, High Priestess of Astarte)*, Edmund Purdom *(Micah)*, Louis Calhern *(Nahreeb, High Priest of Baal)*, Audrey Dalton *(Ruth)*, James Mitchell *(Asham)*, Neville Brand *(Rhakim)*, Walter Hampden *(Eli, Micah's Father)*, Taina Elg *(Elissa)*, Francis L. Sullivan *(Bosra the Moneylender)*, Joseph Wiseman *(Carmish)*, Sandra Descher *(Yasmin)*, John Dehner *(Joram)*, Cecil Kellaway *(Governor)*, Philip Tonge *(Barber/Surgeon)*, Henry Daniell *(Ramadi)*, Paul Cavanagh *(Tobiah)*, Dayton Lummis *(Caleb)*, Tracey Roberts *(Tahra)*, Jarma Lewis *(Uba)*, Jay Novello *(Merchant)*, Dorothy Adams *(Carpenter's Wife)*, Peter DeBear *(Carpenter's Son)*, Phyllis Graffeo *(Miriam)*, Patricia Iannone *(Deborah)*, Eugene Mazzola *(David)*, George Sawaya *(Kavak)*, Richard Devon *(Risafe)*, Ann Cameron *(Lahla)*, Gloria Dea *(Faradine)*, John Rosser *(Lirhan)*, Charles Wagenheim *(Zubeir)*, Gordon Richards *(Scribe)*, Paul Bryar *(Townsman)*, Rex Lease *(Purveyor)*, George Lewis *(Guard)*, Almira Sessions *(Old Lady)*, Chuck Roberson *(Chieftain)*, Tom Steele *(Slave)*, Gloria Stone *(Mouse)*, Linda Danson *(Owl)*, Joanne Dale *(Bunny)*, Lucille Maracini *(Ram)*, Lila Zali *(Monkey)*, Diane Gump *(Fox)*, Patricia Jackson *(Lion)*, John Damler *(Jailer)*, Argentina Brunetti *(Woman)*, Jo Gilbert *(Mother)*, George Robotham *(Martyr)*, David Leonard *(Blind Man)*.

Garbage, even when wrapped in silk and tied with a gold cord, is still garbage. They tried to clothe this film in all manner of finery, frippery, and folderol, but couldn't hide the fact that it was garbage from the start. In the New Testament, Luke tells of "The Prodigal Son" in a bit less than 300 well-chosen words. In an effort to cash in on a mild flurry of interest in biblical films, MGM thought they could take the brief verses and expand them into just under two hours. Although the story had been retold before in the 1926 silent THE WANDERER (directed by Raoul Walsh and starring William Collier, Jr., as the son and Greta Nissen as the woman who tempts him), writer Larsen submitted it to the studio in an expanded treatment. Dore Schary assigned Joe Breen, Jr. to help in the development (his father was the censor) and the script chores were given to Maurice Zimm. This sow's ear was never to become a silk purse but they tried, oh how they tried. Herschel McCoy, who had done the costumes for QUO VADIS, JULIUS CAESAR, and JOAN OF ARC did a good job recreating the authentic garb of the era with over 4000 changes of clothing, nearly 300 for the leading players. Didn't help. Purdom, a walking lox if there ever was one, is a nice Jewish boy, the son of Hampden, a venerable Hebrew. Purdom is affianced to Dalton, a nice Jewish girl, and everything seems kosher. Then Purdom visits the fleshpot known as Damascus and meets Turner, who wears as little as the censors could possibly have allowed and worships Baal, a pagan god. Purdom is struck by her blonde beauty (blondes were a rarity in that neighborhood and this was Turner's first time back in flaxen tresses after having been a brunette in her two previous movies) and soon returns to his town, asks for his inheritance and leaves Dalton waiting at the canopy the night before they are to step on the wine glass. Back in Damascus, Turner is in charge of her religion's rites, one of which includes the taking of human life. Purdom, an innocent, is soon in trouble. Calhern, a villainous cohort of Turner, feels that Purdom has no business cavorting with the woman, and does his best to create a rift. Sullivan is a usurious loan shark who also wants Purdom out of the way and even Turner makes the demand that Purdom secure an expensive pearl to give as a token of his esteem for her faith. Everyone is so rotten and duplicitous that the only shred of humanity is a brief romance between Turner's slave, Elg, and Mitchell, a mute runaway. Purdom falls hard for Turner and is soon out of funds. Unable to make good on his IOUs, he is sold into slavery. His captors offer to free him if he will give up Judaism, but Purdom refuses. When they think he's dead, they throw him into a pit of vultures where he single-handedly defeats the creatures, then frees the other slaves. Next he rallies the poor and hungry Damascans and leads a revolt against the powers that be. The final scenes show Turner being stoned by the furious crowd, then falling into the eternal fires where she has roasted many a disbeliever. Purdom is welcomed home by Hampden (The Prodigal Son Returns) and the picture ends on an up note for the audience, although not for the producers, who failed to recover the more than $5 million they spent on the film. The word "prodigal" means "recklessly wasteful and extravagant"—an apt description of this movie. It's Hollywood at its worst as they fill the screen with spectacle and grandiose sets while totally forgetting the humanity of a man who made a mistake, got mixed up with the wrong kind of woman, paid the price, and came home to his loving family. While the movie was being made, Purdom was having a hot time with Linda Christian, who was then married to Tyrone Power, who earlier had been a "great friend" of Turner's. That kind of undercurrent can only happen in the movie business or in PEYTON PLACE, a much better film that Turner also starred in. In a small role as "Tahra," a young Tracey Roberts is seen. She gave up acting for the most part and is now one of the most respected acting teachers in Hollywood. Charles Schnee, who wrote many screenplays, including THE BAD AND THE BEAUTIFUL, was making his producing debut with this and he, of all people, should have known better.

p, Charles Schnee; d, Richard Thorpe; w, Maurice Zimm, Joe Breen, Jr., Samuel James Larsen (based on the Bible story); ph, Joseph Ruttenberg (CinemaScope, Eastmancolor); m, Bronislau Kaper; ed, Harold F. Kress; art d, Cedric Gibbons, Randall Duell; set d, Edwin B. Willis, Henry Grace; cos, Herschel McCoy; spec eff, A. Arnold Gillespie, Warren Newcombe; makeup, William Tuttle.

Biblical Drama (PR:A-C MPAA:NR)

PRODIGAL GUN (SEE: MINUTE TO PRAY, A SECOND TO DIE, A, 1968, U.S./Ital.)

PRODIGAL SON, THE** (1935) 60m UNIV bw

Luis Trenker, Maria Andergast, Marion Marsh.

Leaving his native Germany, a young immigrant hopes to find fame and fortune brimming for him in the streets of New York. Instead he gathers only disillusionment when none of his dreams come true. This B-grade drama was intended as a filler on double bills, and apparently for good reason. Trenker's film career had begun in the early 1920s when he was working as a mountain guide in the Alps. German director Arnold Fanck cast him in a series of ski adventures, often pairing him with Leni Riefenstahl, who would go on to become the Third Reich's noted documentary director. Trenker began writing and directing in the 1930s and continued to work in the German film industry into the 1960s.

p, Paul Kohner; d&w, Luis Trenker; ph, Albert Benitz.

Drama (PR:A MPAA:NR)

PRODIGAL SON, THE** (1964, Jap.) 99m Toho c (ONNA GOROSHI ABURA JIGOKU)

Senjaku Nakamura *(Yohei)*, Ganjiro Nakamura *(Father)*, Eiko Miyoshi *(Mother)*, Kyoko Kagawa *(Sister)*, Michiyo Aratama *(Okichi)*, Takako Fujino *(Kogiku)*.

Set in 18th-Century Japan, S. Nakamura's desire to win the affection of geisha Fujino leads to family disgrace and the eventual murder of the wife of a shop owner who refuses to give him money to help pay off his debts. Director Horikawa, Akira Kurosawa's sometime assistant director, made a number of films dealing with the pettiness of human aspirations.

p, Shiro Horie, Koji Toita; d, Hiromichi Horikawa; w, Shinobu Hashimoto (based on the play by Monzaemon Chikamatsu); ph, Asaichi Nakai (Eastmancolor); m, Koji Taku; art d, Yasuhide Kato.

Drama (PR:C MPAA:NR)

PRODUCERS, THE**** (1967) 88m Springtime-Crossbow/EM c

Zero Mostel *(Max Bialystock)*, Gene Wilder *(Leo Bloom)*, Dick Shawn *(Lorenzo St. Du Bois)*, Kenneth Mars *(Franz Liebkind)*, Estelle Winwood *(Old Lady)*, Christopher Hewett *(Roger De Bris)*, Andreas Voutsinas *(Carmen Giya)*, Lee Meredith *(Ulla)*, Renee Taylor *(Eva Braun)*, Michael Davis *(Production Tenor)*, John Zoller *(Critic)*, Madlyn Cates *(Woman at Window)*, Frank Campanella *(Bartender)*, Arthur Rubin, Zale Kessler, Bernie Allen, Rusty Blitz, Anthony Gardell *(Auditioning Hitlers)*, Mary Love, Amelie Barleon, Nell Harrison, Elsie Kirk *(Old Ladies)*, Barney Martin *(German Officer in Play)*, Diana Eden *(Showgirl)*, Tucker Smith, David Evans *(Lead Dancers)*, Josip Elic *(Violinist)*, William Hickey *(Drunk in Theater Bar)*.

A hilarious, broad farce that spoofs upper-crust Broadway theater as well as its fickle audiences, THE PRODUCERS has long since become a cult film, one surprisingly better than most of what director-writer Brooks would later create (except, of course, for THE TWELVE CHAIRS, 1970). Mostel is a down-and-out but still pompous theater producer who is desperate to retrieve his former glory as an impresario. His new accountant is meek Wilder who finds Mostel's books an utter disaster. He tells the girthsome titan of the theater that the only way he will ever recover is to produce an enormous hit, or, Wilder whimsically suggests that the only other way to find riches is to collect a lot of money from investors for a play that is guaranteed to fail. That way Mostel could keep most of the investors' money. Of course, Wilder points out, he's only talking in theoretical terms. Mostel's eyes bulge, his greed ratio goes out of control, and he avalanches Wilder with cajoling, threats, and prospects of untold wealth, finally getting the shy accountant to not only doctor the books but go into the production scheme with him. They celebrate their venal union by going to the Lincoln Center fountain that night, with Wilder dancing wildly about the fountain as its spray reaches upward, thoroughly committed to larceny, shouting: "I want...I want...every thing I've ever seen...in the movies!" The pair exhaust themselves soliciting and reading the worst scripts ever penned by man or beast. Finally, they hit upon a play which is a surefire flop, one entitled "Springtime for Hitler," written by Mars, a Nazi fanatic living in Yorkville. They find this loony on top of his tenement building tending to his pigeons (he still wears his German helmet from WW II), and sign him to a contract. Next Mostel woos and wins the backing of every spinster in New York, taking in hundreds of thousands of dollars to back his doomed play. To further assure failure Mostel hires an inept tranvestite director, Hewett—assisted by Voutsinas, as swishy a gay as ever to glide across a screen—to helm Mars' montrosity. The role tryouts are disastrous with the worst talent on Broadway turning out, and Mostel selects for the lead a mindless, drug-bombed hippie, Shawn, who believes he is trying out for another role in another theater. He belches out a song called "Love Power," which aptly captures his idiocy, a tune of his own creation which describes how he has been clubbed on the head by a cop, his girl friend has been stuffed into a garbage can, and his landlord has taken his most cherished flower and flushed it down the toilet (ostensibly for non payment of rent), where it ends up "in the sewer with the yuck runnin' through 'er," and winds up as "the water that we drink." "Perfect!" yells Mostel. The play goes on and to further assure a damning review, Mostel tries to bribe the critic from the *New York Times*. He and Wilder retreat to a bar across the street from the theater to celebrate their failure. Mostel is planning to take the remainder of the investment money and "flaunt it," as he has been doing with lavish offices and a buxom, miniskirt-wearing blonde Amazon, Meredith. Wilder just wants everything. The two culprits slip across to the theater to watch the opening extravaganza number of Nazis parading about the stage in S.S. uniforms with voluptuous blondes dressed as Vikings, singing "Springtime for Hitler and Germany." Mars sits in his seat salivating over this theatrical success. The audience is horrified and begins to leave the theater but Shawn appears as a swinging Hitler and patrons return to their seats, mesmerized by this unintentionally comic genius. While Mars goes berserk listening to Shawn make an idiot of his perverted hero—"Vot is dis 'babee?' Der Fuhrer never said 'babee!'"—Mostel and Wilder panic and realize that, no matter their efforts, they have produced a hit. They first conspire to kill all the actors, especially the wacked-out Shawn, but then opt to blow up the theater. Mars sets the fuses and explosives that night but bungles the job and the trio are half blown up, winding up later in court wearing casts and bandages over most of their bodies. Wilder appears to speak on behalf of Mostel but then turns on his mentor hysterically. All three are sent to prison where they immediately open a prison show, Wilder shown in the final scene overselling the stock in the production to inmates, guards, and even the warden while Mostel rehearses his inmate cast. THE PRODUCERS is utterly preposterous and so outlandish as to provide one belly laugh after another. Nothing is too gauche or crude for Brooks in his merciless burlesque of legitimate theater. This was Brooks' first film and he spares no cliches; in fact he heightens every cliche and expands every pun, allowing Mostel to bug-eye his scenes at will and ham it all the way. Wilder is allowed to get hysterical on whim and the whole thing is a free-for-all. The film was not initially a success but it has since become a cult comedy, especially among the college set. Though it is gross, vulgar, and stereotyped on all levels, it is for these very reasons that it appeals, for this is comedy by reason of planned insanity, a not so fine madness embodied in the bumbling characters of blimpy Mostel, inept father figure to naive, childlike Wilder. It's almost a comedic George and Lennie routine OF MICE AND MEN and, of course, the culpable pair pay for their lunatic scheme and, of course, learn nothing by going on bilking the very people who hold them captive in prison. Mostel and Wilder are *dedicated* lunatics who are harmless and disarming in their oddball perspectives and antics and therefore somehow lovable. At least the very clever Brooks makes them so in his witty, off-the-cuff script. And certainly, it's offensive; in fact, this film should offend every sensibility viewers may have. This is how Brooks makes his living, no less than those who scribbled those offensive burlesque scripts decades ago that amused lowbrow audiences into guffaws, catcalls, and horse laughs. That's what makes this film a near classic of the absurd, almost pure Dada in an American sense. Mostel rose to new heights of zany appeal with this film and it made a star of Wilder (who went on playing his original role too many times). Brooks arrived with THE PRODUCERS and hasn't stopped pulling viewers' legs since. Shot on location in New York City.

p, Sidney Glazier; d&w, Mel Brooks; ph, Joe Coffey (Pathe Color); m, John Morris; ed, Ralph Rosenblum; md, Morris; art d, Charles Rosen; set d, James Dalton; cos, Gene Coffin; ch, Alan Johnson; makeup, Irving Buchman.

Comedy Cas. (PR:O MPAA:NR)

PROFESSIONAL BLONDE (SEE: BLONDE FROM PEKING, 1969, Fr./Ital./W. Ger.)

PROFESSIONAL BRIDE (SEE: HEAD GUY, 1941)

PROFESSIONAL GUN, A (SEE: MERCENARY, THE, 1970, Ital./Span.)

PROFESSIONAL SOLDIER½** (1936) 75m FOX bw

Victor McLaglen *(Michael Donovan)*, Freddie Bartholomew *(King Peter)*, Gloria Stuart *(Countess Sonia, Governess)*, Constance Collier *(Augusta)*, Michael Whalen

(George Foster), C. Henry Gordon (Gino), Pedro De Cordoba (Stefan Bernaldo), Lumsden Hare (Valdis), Walter Kingsford (Ledgard), Lester Matthews (Prince Edric), Dixie Dunbar (Entertainer), Rollo Lloyd (Cabinet Member), Maurice Cass (Mons. Le Noir), General Savitsky (Mischa).

McLaglen and his cohort Whalen are hired by some shady individuals to kidnap the boy prince, Bartholomew, of a mythical European kingdom in order to allow a new political party to take control. They have no problem whisking the boy away; he is tired of the stuffy life style he must lead. The kidnapers are caught and jailed, but when McLaglen discovers the evil intentions of the new government, he escapes and goes about rescuing the boy and returning him to his throne. Direction and script are well conceived, but are severely hampered by production standards which harm the believability of the story. Just the charisma of McLaglen is enough to carry his performance, with Bartholomew a likable boy-king. A memorable scene from the picture is when prisoner Bartholomew is allowed to indulge in craps and baseball.

p, Darryl F. Zanuck; d, Tay Garnett; w, Gene Fowler, Howard Ellis Smith (based on a story by Damon Runyon); ph, Rudolph Mate; m, Louis Silvers; ed, Barbara McLean; m/l, "Joan of Arkansas," John W. Green, Edward Heyman.

Adventure (PR:A MPAA:NR)

PROFESSIONAL SWEETHEART*** (1933) 68m RKO bw (GB: IMAGINARY SWEETHEART)

Ginger Rogers (Glory Eden), Norman Foster (Jim Davey), ZaSu Pitts (Esmeralda de Leon), Frank McHugh (Speed), Allen Jenkins (O'Connor), Gregory Ratoff (Ipswich), Edgar Kennedy (Kelsey), Lucien Littlefield (Announcer), Franklin Pangborn (Childress), Frank Darien (Appleby), Betty Furness (Blonde Reporter), Sterling Holloway (Scribe), Theresa Harris (Maid), Akim Tamiroff (Waiter), Grace Hayle (Plump Reporter).

Ginger Rogers did not use her singing voice in this picture, as Etta Moten dubbed her one song, "My Imaginary Sweetheart" (Edward Eliscu, Harry Akst), which, as it turned out, was the basis for the Great Britain title. Just as TV has been the target for barbed satire in the last half of the century, so it was with radio in the first half and this is an often funny comedy on that subject. Rogers is a radio star known as the "Purity Girl of the Air" on a show sponsored by Ratoff, the "Ippsie-Wippsie Radio Hour." Ratoff makes wash cloths and it's important that Rogers have a pristine image. She, on the other hand, is not that way by nature. She likes to go dancing uptown and to have fun with various men. To keep her from straying, she is flanked by a retinue that includes Pangborn, McHugh, and Jenkins. She'd like to have some fun in her life but she's followed around like a new Miss America. Her fan mail is by the carload, so it's suggested that she find a "professional sweetheart" out of all the letters, someone she can see in public, if not in private, to maintain her facade. Foster, a rube from Kentucky, is chosen to be that man and they do, in fact, fall in love, with the plan being to marry them on the radio. Rogers decides that she likes living in the hinterlands and in order to keep her on the show, Ratoff must arrange a business merger with his hated rival, Kennedy, who runs a dish rag company. Rogers comes back to star in the "Ippsie-Kelsey" show and everything is ipsy-pipsy and hunky-dory at the endy-wendy. In later years, the legend states that Marilyn Chambers, star of many "adult" films, was found to have posed for the Ivory Snow company, a situation that was rectified the moment they found out what her sideline was. Producers Cooper and Swanson surrounded Rogers with some of the best comedy characters in the business with Ratoff, Pangborn, McHugh, Pitts, Holloway, Jenkins, et al. and the result was often hilarious. Swanson later gave up producing to become one of the most respected literary agents in Hollywood. Foster, who had been borrowed from Fox, became a director and specialized in low-budget films of the MR. MOTO genre. Prior to this, Foster and Rogers had appeared together in YOUNG MAN OF MANHATTAN.

p, H.N. Swanson; d, William Seiter; w, Maurine Watkins (based on a story by Watkins); ph, Edward Cronjager; m, Edward Eliscu, Harry Akst; ed, James Morley; md, Max Steiner; art d, Van Nest Polglase, Carroll Clark; makeup, Mel Burns.

Comedy (PR:A MPAA:NR)

PROFESSIONALS, THE*½ (1960, Brit.) 61m Independent Artists/ Anglo-Amalgamated bw

William Lucas (Philip Bowman), Andrew Faulds (Inspector Rankin), Colette Wilde (Ruth), Stratford Johns (Lawson), Vilma Ann Leslie (Mabel), Edward Cast (Clayton), Charles Vince (Holden).

When a top safecracker is freed from prison, a notorious gang plots a daring bank robbery. The gang attempts to gain entrance to the bank via the sewer system, but their plot is foiled and they are returned to jail.

p, Norman Priggen; d, Don Sharp; w, Peter Barnes.

Crime (PR:A MPAA:NR)

PROFESSIONALS, THE***½ (1966) 117m Pax/COL c

Burt Lancaster (Bill Dolworth), Lee Marvin (Henry Rico Farden), Robert Ryan (Hans Ehrengard), Jack Palance (Capt. Jesus Raza), Claudia Cardinale (Maria Grant), Ralph Bellamy (J.W. Grant), Woody Strode (Jacob Sharp), Joe De Santis (Ortega), Rafael Bertrand (Fierro), Jorge Martinez de Hoyos (Padilla), Maria Gomez (Chiquita), Jose Chavez, Carlos Romero (Revolutionaries), Vaughn Taylor (Banker), Robert Contreras, Don Carlos (Bandits), Elizabeth Campbell (Mexican Girl), John Lopez (Mexican Servant), Darwin Lamb (Hooper), Dirk Evans (Man at Door), John McKee (Sheriff), Eddie Little Sky (The Prisoner), Leigh Chapman (Lady), Phil Parslow (Deputy Sheriff), Foster Hood, Henry O'Brien, Dave Cadiente, Vince Cadiente.

A truly adventuresome, action-filled film that is played more for thrills than for conveying a story, THE PROFESSIONALS offers a field day for Lancaster, Ryan, Marvin, and Strode. All four are hired by wealthy cattle baron Bellamy to retrieve his voluptuous young wife, Cardinale, who has been kidnaped by Palance, a

Mexican bandit who has no redeeming virtues whatsoever. Each of the professional volunteers is paid for his particular expertise. Lancaster is a dynamiter with an eye for the women, the more endowed the better. Marvin is a long-range rifle marksman, Strode a silent bowman whose arrows never miss their marks, and Ryan a tough pistoleer and horse trainer who has a fatal flaw in that he cannot bear to see an animal suffer. The fierce foursome rides into Mexico—the last wild frontier at this time of Pancho Villa, the teens of the century—and ride hard 100 miles until finding the camp of Palance, whom Marvin describes as "the bloodiest cutthroat in Mexico." They devastate the Mexican fortress by having Strode use his longbow to shoot sticks of dynamite into the encampment. While this diversion is occurring, Lancaster breaks into Palance's bedroom and yanks a half-naked Cardinale from the clutches of the incensed bandit lover. As the four make their escape with Bellamy's pulchritudinous wife, they learn to their surprise that she does not want to be rescued, that she loves the sleazy Palance and wants only to remain within his oily embrace. It becomes instantly apparent that there has not been an abduction after all, that Bellamy has only been trying to use his enormous wealth to buy back a woman who detests him and has fled his insidious control. Yet, the four professionals are being paid $10,000 apiece for their efforts and a job is a job. Actually, the ransom money Palance has demanded of Bellamy is really a fund-raising opportunity to finance his ongoing revolution. Palance follows the group with his men but Lancaster and Strode dynamite a narrow gorge, blocking it so that only a few of the Mexican bandits can get through at a time. While his compatriots flee, Lancaster stays behind and kills off the Mexicans until only Palance is left, and he wounds him. During this running battle Lancaster finds time to frolic with busty Gomez, who actually bears her breasts for a brief moment. She remembers Lancaster from when he fought with Villa and pretends affection for him, but finally shows her loyalty to Palance by trying to kill Lancaster, and he must kill her in self-defense. Before rejoining his friends, Lancaster kisses his dying victim. When Lancaster does catch up to his friends, he brings along a badly wounded Palance. They are back in the U.S. by then and Bellamy gloats over the capture of his rival, then orders one of his goons to kill Palance. Before this happens, Marvin shoots the goon and lets Palance and Cardinale flee, he and his fellow adventurers holding Bellamy's thugs at bay. They have, by their actions, lost their commission but take immense satisfaction in "doing the right thing." Bellamy calls Marvin as the soldiers-of-fortune are about to ride away: "You bastard!" Marvin nods and retorts: "Yes, an unfortunate accident of birth, but you, sir, are a self-made man!" Of course, it's all western fantasy, since no real mercenary would turn his back on $10,000 in those days or any other. The sex, with Cardinale and Gomez fairly bursting the tops of their skimpy blouses, is almost as gratuitous as the excessive violence. In one scene the four adventurers watch from hiding as Palance and his bandits capture a government train, with Palance ordering the surviving officers hanged. (These scenes are based upon the savage Villa's philosophy of never taking prisoners; the rebel leader believed that by hanging prisoners you would not have to fight them another day.) The action in this film is nevertheless fascinating; Brooks' script is witty and full of irony and his direction is whirlwind fast. Although Lancaster's grin is not as ludicrously broad as it was in VERA CRUZ, he is still a one-man tornado, wreaking havoc upon myriad enemies, while sidekick Marvin is droll and deadly. Strode has few words and flexes his considerable muscles with his drawn longbow and Ryan functions well as the conscience of the lot. Bellamy does a good job as the villain of the piece but his two-sided personality is not well developed enough to make the viewer believe that he's really as miserable as the scenes in the finale would have us believe. Cardinale fractures English with her thick Italian accent, and she vies with Gomez in the mammary department; both of these ladies are seldom seen without sweat coating their olive-skinned bodies. It was only natural for Lancaster to immediately accept his role in this film from Brooks, with whom he had made ELMER GANTRY (1960), which earned him his one and only Oscar. Hall's photography is exceptional, although he dotes on the most sensual poses extravagantly postured by Cardinale. He would go on to shoot BUTCH CASSIDY AND THE SUNDANCE KID. Hall and Brooks scouted just the right locations for months for THE PROFESSIONALS and finally shot, in nine weeks, their exteriors in Death Valley, the Valley of Fire State Park near Lake Mead, Nevada, and along a railway line outside Indio, California. Dust and wind storms hampered the production throughout shooting, and, because of the landscapes, the night scenes were shot during the day. None of the spectacular exteriors could be captured during the night, only closeup shots of the principal actors, so Hall used filters to shade the daytime shots into nighttime images. In creating the hacienda fortress of the bandit Palance, Columbia spent $200,000 alone. All marveled at the 53-year-old Lancaster, who performed his own stunts, and even scaled the side of a cliff by rope. Temperatures often fell below freezing and the cast was also endangered by a flash flood that trapped everyone in a box canyon for a few days. Much of the theme for THE PROFESSIONALS was tapped from THE MAGNIFICENT SEVEN but the viewer will also find traces of HIGH NOON and even SHANE in its traumatic scenes. Ironically, this film, which would earn almost $9 million from its initial release and would be considered one of the best films of 1966, presented an old-fashioned type of hero, not one really popular in the 1960s where failure was not only admired but sought out in projecting anti-heroes. The closing down of the Old West is seen in the aging heroes who live more in nostalgic memory than in the present, a theme ground to fine pepper in THE WILD BUNCH. The film is raucous and often repulsive, but never dull.

p,d&w, Richard Brooks (based on the novel A Mule for the Marquesa by Frank O'Rourke); ph, Conrad Hall (Panavision, Technicolor); m, Maurice Jarre; ed, Peter Zinner; md, Jarre; art d, Edward S. Haworth; set d, Frank Tuttle; cos, Jack Martell; spec eff, Willis Cook; makeup, Robert Schiffer.

Western **Cas.** (PR:O MPAA:NR)

PROFESSOR BEWARE**½ (1938) 90m PAR bw

Harold Lloyd (Prof. Dean Lambert), Phyllis Welch (Jane Van Buren), Raymond Walburn (Judge James G. Parkhouse Marshall), Lionel Stander (Jerry), William Frawley (Snoop Donlan), Thurston Hall (J.J. Van Buren), Cora Witherspoon

(Mrs. Ophelia Pitts), Sterling Holloway (Rupert the Bridegroom), Mary Lou Lender (Bride), Montagu Love (Dr. "Prof." Schmutz), Etienne Girardot (Judge Henry), Christian Rub (Gustave the Museum Attendant), Spencer Charters (Sheriff Henry Sweatt), Guinn "Big Boy" Williams, Ward Bond (Motorcycle Officers), Wright Kramer (Dr. Ellerson, Expedition Director), George Humbert (Restaurant Keeper), Leonid Kinskey (Tableau Director), Charlotte Wynters (Dorothy the Reporter), James Donlan (Reporter in Museum), Charles Lane (Joe the Photographer), Clara Blandick (Mrs. Green the Landlady), Tom Herbert (Hobo), Bruce King ("Neferus" in Tableux), Robert Emmett O'Connor (Cop at Estate), Kenner G. Kemp, Frank Hagney (Sailors), John Ward (Captain of "Jasmine" Yacht), James Farley (Fire Chief), Elaine Shepard (Anebi), Duke York, Bobby Barber (Handshakers-Paint-Brush Gag), Eddie Dew, Theodore Lorch (Railroad Workmen), Dewey Robinson (Wrestler/Lemonade-Stand Man), Brandon Hurst (Charlie the Butler), Buster Slaven (Western Union Boy), Bruce Mitchell (Cop by Fire Truck), Wede Boteler (Officer in Court), Bud Geary (Van Buren's Chauffeur), Guy Wilkerson, Billy Bletcher (Shoeshine Customers), William Wagner (Court Clerk), Irving Bacon (Painter), John Wray (Head Lawyer), Eddy Chandler (Camp Boss), Frances Morris (Miss Perkins, Ellerson's Secretary), Harry Tyler (Editor), Eddie Parker (Detective), Hector V. Sarno (Lawyer), Ray Turner, Charles R. Moore (Bootblacks), Walter James (Man with New Hat), Harry Holman (Man Shaving on Boat), Max Wagner (Chinatown Barker), Kit Guard, Harry Tenbrook, Harry Wilton (Brawlers), Constantine Romanoff (Bearded Man), Roger Gray (Brawler-Hand Gag), Huntley Gordon (Mr. Capell, Film Producer), Heinie Conklin (Billboard Sign Painter), Edward Hearn, Chuck Hamilton (Cops), Matt McHugh (Divorced Man on High-way), Arthur Aylesworth (Desert Gas Station Attendant), Paul Bryar (Harry, Radio Patrolman), Nella Walker (Railroad Information Clerk), Rex Lease (Reporter), Jack Perry, James Dime (Dock Workers), Dave Sharpe (Lloyd's Double).

Fast paced, lighthearted fun from popular silent-screen comedian Lloyd has him making his way from Los Angeles to New York while being pursued by the police. The slim plot line has archeologist Lloyd being arrested when he gives his clothes to a stranger—a case of mistaken identity—with the delay of his trial causing him to nearly miss an expedition to Egypt. So he heads out without waiting for the trial, befriending a couple of hobos, Stander and Walburn, and attracting a young girl, Welch, along the way. Film has no pretentions towards seriousness, but is just good-hearted slapstick in the manner done no better than by Lloyd. This was the great chase-master's next-to-last picture, and his last one for Paramount. His leading lady, the winsome Welch, made her first featured appearance in this film.

p, Harold Lloyd; d, Elliott Nugent; w, Delmer Daves, Jack Cunningham, Clyde Bruckman (based on a story by Crampton Harris, Francis M. Cockrell, Marion B. Cockrell); ph, Archie Stout; ed, Duncan Mansfield; art d, Albert D'Agostino.

Comedy　　　　　　　　　　(PR:A MPAA:NR)

PROFESSOR TIM**½　　(1957, Ireland) 60m Emmett Dalton-Dublin/RKO bw

Ray MacAnally (Hugh O'Cahan), Maire Keane (Mrs. Scally), Philip O'Flynn (John Scally), Maire O'Donnell (Peggy Scally), Geoffrey Golden (James Kilroy), Eileen Furlong (Mrs. Kilroy), Michael O'Brien (Joseph Kilroy), Seamus Kavanagh (Prof. Tim), Brid Lynch (Moll Flanagan), John Hoey (Paddy Kinney), Bill Foley (Mr. Allison), Mike Malone, Jack Howarth (Villagers), Robert Mooney (Mr. Dempsey).

Pleasant drama from Ireland with members of the Abbey Players giving naturalistic and lively performances. Tale revolves around Kavanagh as a man who has been wandering around the world for the last 20 years, and returns to the village where his family resides. He has come upon a large inheritance, which he does not reveal to his greedy family.

p, Robert Baker, Monty Berman; d, Henry Cass; w, Robert S. Baker (based on the play by George Shiels); m, Stanley Black.

Comedy　　　　　　　　　　(PR:A MPAA:NR)

PROFILE*½　　(1954, Brit.) 65m Major/Monarch bw

John Bentley (Peter Armstrong), Kathleen Byron (Margot Holland), Thea Gregory (Susan Holland), Stuart Lindsell (Aubrey Holland), Garard Green (Charlie Pearson), Ivan Craig (Jerry), Lloyd Lamble (Michael), Arnold Bell (Inspector Crawford), Frank Henderson, Bruce Beeby, John Parkes, June Charlier, Derek Prentice, Patrick Jordan, John Blake.

Bentley takes a new job as the editor of a magazine called Profile, and becomes interested in the publisher's daughter, Gregory. Bentley, however, is the object of Byron's affections, and she is the publisher's wife. Bentley soon finds himself accused of embezzling. Trouble multiplies when the publisher dies from a heart attack and Byron is mysteriously murdered. Bentley is then targeted as the guilty one. Not surprisingly, Bentley is proven innocent when the real killer is discovered. The film closes with an exciting chase sequence through the press room, but the end alone can't save this one.

p, John Temple-Smith, Francis Edge; d, Francis Searle; w, John Gilling (based on the story by John Temple-Smith, Maurice Temple-Smith); ph, Brendan Stafford.

Crime　　　　　　　　　　(PR:A MPAA:NR)

PROFILE OF TERROR, THE　　(SEE: SADIST, THE, 1963)

PROJECT: KILL*　　(1976) 90m Stirling Gold c

Leslie Nielsen, Gary Lockwood, Nancy Kwan, Vic Silayan, Vic Diaz, Galen Thompson, Pamela Parsons, Maurice Down, Carlos Salazar.

Nielsen, the head of a secret government agency, mysteriously disappears only to be tracked down by his one-time partner Lockwood. A sub-par espionage picture that probably saw more in one week of video rentals than in its entire theatrical run.

p, David Sheldon; d, William Girdler; w, Donald G. Thompson (based on a story by Sheldon, Thompson); m, Robert O. Ragland.

Spy Drama　　　Cas.　　　(PR:O MPAA:R)

PROJECT MOONBASE*　　(1953) 63m Galaxy/Lippert bw

Donna Martell (Col. Britels), Hayden Rorke (Gen. Greene), Ross Ford (Maj. Moore), Larry Johns (Dr. Wernher), Herb Jacobs (Mr. Roundtree), Barbara Morrison (Polly Prattles), Ernestine Barrier (Mme. President), James Craven (Commodore Carlson), John Hedloe (Adjutant), Peter Adams (Capt. Carmody), Robert Karnes (Sam), John Straub (Chaplain), Charles Keane (Spacom Operator), John Tomecko (Blockhouse Operator), Robert Paltz (Bellboy).

Originally made as the first episodes for the television series RING AROUND THE MOON, this film is the last screen effort by the now famous science-fiction author Robert Heinlein. The end result is a shoddy project that centers on a space station that circles around the earth in the future (1970), and is headed by a woman officer. When asked to explore possible sites on the moon suitable for a base, a communist spy aboard the ship sabotages the project, forcing the ship to land on the moon. The crew members remain on the moon, where a surviving couple marries. Lifelessly directed by Talmadge, a former stuntman, with a plot which is impossible to take seriously.

p, Jack Seaman; d, Richard Talmadge; w, Robert A. Heinlein, Seaman; ph, William Thompson; m, Herschel Burke Gilbert; ed, Roland Gross; prod d, Jerome Pycha, Jr.; spec eff, Jacques Fresco.

Science Fiction　　　　　　(PR:A MPAA:NR)

PROJECT M7***　　(1953, Brit.) 86m TC/UNIV bw (GB: THE NET)

Phyllis Calvert (Lydia Heathley), James Donald (Michael Heathley), Robert Beatty (Sam Seagram), Herbert Lom (Alex Leon), Muriel Pavlow (Caroline Cartier), Noel Willman (Dr. Dennis Bord), Walter Fitzgerald (Sir Charles Cruddock), Patric Doonan (Brian Jackson), Maurice Denham (Carrington), Majorie Fielding (Mama), Cavan Watson (Ferguson), Herbert Lomas (George Jackson), Stanley Maxted (American Professor), Hal Osmond (Lawson), Geoffrey Denton (Fisher), Cyril Chamberlain ((Inspector Carter), Tucker McGuire (Myrna), Hartley Power, Geoffrey Denton, Marianne Stone, Johnnie Schofield, Patricia Glyn, John Warren, Philp Ray, Douglas Bradley-Smith, John Martin, John Lorrell.

A group of scientists is cloaked in a veil of high security as they work on a top secret hydroplane, which will fly at three times the speed of anything else. Donald is the inventor, who wants to take the plane up himself for its first test run. His supervisor discourages Donald, declaring that he is too valuable a man to have his life risked, and the supervisor volunteers to take it up himself. Before he can do so, he is found dead, and secret documents are known to have leaked out of the camp, instigating a search for the possible traitor. Asquith does a fine job in depicting a group of men so caught up in what they are doing that they are oblivious to everything. He keeps the tension mounting as the men are faced with the possibility that their project may fail.

p, Anthony Darnborough; d, Anthony Asquith; w, William Fairchild (based on the novel by John Pudney); ph, Desmond Dickinson; m, Benjamin Frankel; ed, Frederick Wilson; art d, John Howell.

Drama　　　　　　　　　　(PR:A MPAA:NR)

PROJECT X*　　(1949) 60m Trans-Continental/FC bw

Keith Andes (Steve Monahan), Rita Colton (Sandra Russell), Jack Lord (John Bates), Kit Russell (Michael Radik), Joyce Quinlan (Joan), Harry Clark (Jed), Robert Noe (Henderson), Joanne Tree (Gert), Craig Kelly (Martin), Tom Ahearn (Fraser), Dorothy Renard (Secretary Henderson), William Gibberson (Headwaiter), Herbert Holcombe (Emil), Vickie Hayes (Hatcheck Girl), Charles Martin (Special Agent).

Haphazard production of a sketchy story about a former communist who helps American agents outwit a gang of communists trying to steal atomic secrets. Neither the direction nor the script manage to evoke much interest.

p, Edward Leven; d, Edward J. Montagne; w, Gene Hurley, Earl Kennedy, Joyce Selznick, Mitchell Johnson; ph, Don Malkames; m, Hi Fuchs; ed, Theodore Waldeyer; cos, Florence Lustig; makeup, Rudolph Liszt.

Spy Drama　　　　　　　　(PR:A MPAA:NR)

PROJECT X**½　　(1968) 97m PAR c

Christopher George (Hagen Arnold), Greta Baldwin (Karen Summers), Henry Jones (Dr. Crowther), Monte Markham (Gregory Gallea), Harold Gould (Col. Holt), Phillip E. Pine (Lee Craig), Lee Delano (Dr. Tony Verity), Ivan Bonar (Col. Cowen), Robert Cleaves (Dr. George Tarvin), Charles Irving (Maj. Tolley), Sheila Bartold (Sybil Dennis), Patrick Wright (Stover), Maryesther Denver (Overseer), Keye Luke (Sen Chiu), Ed Prentiss (Hicks).

George plays a secret agent in the year 2118, who knows that Sino-Asia will unleash a weapon that will destroy the Western world within two weeks. When he is found unconscious and reveals what he knows, it is discovered that he does not know specifically how the Sinoese plan on making their attack. So Jones places him into a freeze, sending his mind back to the year 1968 in the hopes of getting subconscious messages that will reveal the needed information. The experimentation reveals that George has been infected with bubonic plague, which will take effect in a couple of days. This gives Jones the time to immunize George, bringing him back to the future with a new identity. The imaginative direction by Castle makes the inexpensive production and spotty story into a suspenseful and intricate picture. Hanna-Barbera Studios was responsible for the animated sequence involving George's subconscious.

p&d, William Castle; w, Edmund Morris (based on the novels The Artificial Man and Psychogeist by Leslie P. Davies); ph, Harold Stine (Technicolor); m, Nathan Van Cleave; ed, Edwin H. Bryant; art d, Hal Pereira, Walter Tyler; set d, Robert R. Benton, Joseph J. Stone; spec eff, Paul K. Lerpae, Chet Johns; makeup, Wally Westmore, Marvin Westmore; special sequence producers, William Hanna, Joseph

Barbera; special sequence director, Wally Burr; special sequence prod d, Carl Urbano, Alex Toth.

Science Fiction　　　　　　　　　　　　　　**(PR:A MPAA:NR)**

PROJECTED MAN, THE**　　(1967, Brit.) 77m Protelco-M.L.C./UNIV c

Bryant Halliday (*Prof. Steiner*), Mary Peach (*Dr. Pat Hill*), Norman Wooland (*Dr. Blanchard*), Ronald Allen (*Christopher Mitchell*), Derek Farr (*Inspector Davis*), Tracey Crisp (*Sheila Anderson*), Derrick de Marney (*Latham*), Gerard Heinz (*Prof. Lembach*), Sam Kydd (*Harry*), Terry Scully (*Steve*), Norma West (*Gloria*), Frank Gatliff (*Dr. Wilson*).

Technology gone wrong is the theme of this science-fiction film, which stars Halliday as the inventor of a machine that relays matter, much in the manner of the earlier film THE FLY. Halliday's initial experiments fail after the pig he has sent through the machine turns up electrically charged. After a few minor adjustments, he is ready to show his experiments to his superior and fellow scientists. But the experiment fails again, due to tamperings by Wooland at the insistence of an outside party. Frustrated, Halliday, for fear of having his project dismantled, sends himself through the machine, but comes out as a disfigured monster with an electrical charge. He seeks vengeance on those who have wronged him, only to regain his thoughts and realize what he has done. He then destroys the machine and himself along with it. Characters are better portrayed than is usual in films of this nature, keeping the actors from becoming mere stereotypes. Subtle artistic direction and first quality special effects give this picture a strong visual presence.

p, John Croydon, Maurice Foster; d, Ian Curteis; w, John C. Cooper, Peter Bryan (based on the story by Frank Quattrocchi); ph, Stanley Pavey (Techniscope, Technicolor); m, Kenneth V. Jones; ed, Derek Holding; art d, Peter Mullins; spec eff, Flo Nordhoff, Robert Hedges, Mike Hope.

Horror　　　　　　　　　　　　　　　　**(PR:A MPAA:NR)**

PROJECTIONIST, THE***½　　(1970) 88m Maglan/Maron c

Chuck McCann (*Projectionist/Captain Flash*), Ina Balin (*The Girl*), Rodney Dangerfield (*Renaldi,/The Bat*), Jara Kohout (*Candy Man/Scientist*), Harry Hurwitz (*Friendly Usher*), Robert Staats (*TV Pitchman*), Robert King (*Premiere Announcer*), Stephen Phillips (*Minister*), Clara Rosenthal (*Crazy Lady*), Jacquelyn Glenn (*Nude on Bearskin*), Morocco (*Belly Dancer*), Mike Gentry, Lucky Kargo, Sam Stewart, Robert Lee, Alex Stevens (*Ushers/Henchmen*), David Holiday (*Fat Man/Bat's Henchman*).

Long before THE PURPLE ROSE OF CAIRO and DEAD MEN DON'T WEAR PLAID, there was THE PROJECTIONIST, a film made for the pittance of $160,000 and, in its own way, better than either of the two cited because it was the first to utilize the superimposition technique. McCann had already shown his dramatic side in THE HEART IS A LONELY HUNTER after years of delighting New York TV audiences with his daily melange of old films and new satire. Dangerfield was making his film debut after having doffed his real name of Jack Roy to become a nighclub comic and owner. Hurwitz wrote, produced, directed, edited, and even played a small role in this film which was released erratically but now holds a large cult audience and is part of the permanent collection at the Museum Of Modern Art. Anyone who loves movies (and you must be one of us because you're reading this) will love THE PROJECTIONIST, the story of a man, McCann, who spends his working hours running motion pictures in a sleazy theater then goes home to watch even more films on the all-night movie shows. The line between reality and his fantasy life begins to blur and he imagines himself as part of every movie he's ever seen, including newsreels. McCann is a lovable schlemiel, a man who lives for his fantasy moments when he thinks of himself as a super-hero known as "Captain Flash," defender of the downtrodden, crushing evil wherever it lurks and constantly battling the embodiment of malice known as "the Bat" who is played by his real boss, Dangerfield. When McCann meets Balin, an attractive young woman, she is immediately enfolded into McCann's flights of fancy, becoming a dark-haired "Pauline" (from THE PERILS OF PAULINE), whom McCann must save with regularity from the clutches of Dangerfield. McCann and Dangerfield have a quarrel which sends McCann's mind off to an imaginary trailer for "The Terrible World Of Tomorrow," a film about the end of civilization. When McCann sees a poster for BARBARELLA, his brain takes him to "The Wonderful World Of Tomorrow," where everything is sweet and the good guys always triumph over the black hats. One night, McCann finds himself in "Rick's," Humphrey Bogart's bar in CASABLANCA, where he observes Sidney Greenstreet, Peter Lorre, and Conrad Veidt, listens to what they have to say (and by the magic of cinema, is actually *in* the bar), and hears a remark that takes him to the Thuggee hiding place of Eduardo Ciannelli in GUNGA DIN. After work, McCann is walking down the street and sees an ad for the premiere of STAR! and he is soon part of it as a movie personality surrounded by adoring fans. McCann's constant nemesis, both in his life and in his mind, is Dangerfield as the manager and as "The Bat." In yet another mind movie, Dangerfield is aided by Adolf Hitler (mouthing Kennedy's famous speech "Ask not what your country can do for you"), Mussolini, and others. To countermand that onslaught, McCann gets Sam Jaffe (as "Gunga Din") to blow his bugle and bring on the cavalry, led by John Wayne, Gary Cooper, John Garfield, Errol Flynn, and Buster Crabbe (whom Hurwitz and McCann would work with again in the less-successful THE COMEBACK TRAIL). These vaunted movie heroes marshal their strength and smash Dangerfield and his cohorts—who now include a horde of Nazi soldiers and aliens from outer space—and plant the U.S. flag atop Mount Suribachi. McCann whacks Dangerfield, and Balin adoringly takes his arm and they go into the quiet movie theater where the finale has them flanked by everyone in DAMES, including Ruby Keeler and Dick Powell, with an additional appearance by Fred Astaire and Ginger Rogers. Others in the cast include Marilyn Monroe, Clark Gable, and more and more. At one point, Hurwitz intercuts FORT APACHE with THE BIRTH OF A NATION, so John Wayne seems to be leading a charge against the KKK. There are a few attempts at political agit-prop, as when McCann runs his terrible view of the U.S. and the background music is "The Star Spangled Banner"

(which most people don't realize was only officially adopted as the U.S. national anthem in 1931). The war footage and the atrocity scenes are totally uncalled for and make a painful contrast to what otherwise is a very funny movie. THE PROJECTIONIST was made in four weeks but took 18 months to edit. Whereas DEAD MEN DON'T WEAR PLAID seemed like a too-long TV sketch, this picture, aside from the war scenes and some others of urban violence, sustains its time and doesn't feel long at 88 minutes. Although Igo Kantor wrote some of the themes for the film, most of his work consisted of pulling out "stock music" cues to match the footage in the old films. Kantor's experience in the motion picture industry was so vast that he eventually became a TV producer and gave up the piano. Actor Kohout was a refugee making his first film after years of being known as "the Charlie Chaplin of Czechoslovakia."

p,d,w&ed, Harry Hurwitz; ph, Victor Petrashevic (Technicolor); m, Igo Kantor, Erma E. Levin.

Comedy　　　　　　　　　　　　　　**(PR:A-C MPAA:PG)**

PROLOGUE***　　(1970, Can.) 87m National Film Board of Canada/Vaudeo bw

John Robb (*Jesse*), Elaine Malus (*Karen*), Gary Rader (*David*), Christopher Cordeaux (*Neil*), Peter Cullen (*Allen*), Henry Gamer (*Karen's Father*), Victor Knight (*Judge*), Robert Girolami (*Newscaster*), Frank Edwards (*Janitor*), Abbie Hoffman, Allen Ginsberg, Dick Gregory, Jean Genet, John Kenneth Galbraith, William S. Burroughs (*Themselves*), Magnus Flynn, Caroline Cordeaux, Howard Perry, Daniel Cordeaux, Tanya Mackay, Bruce Mackay, Renee Hebert, John Wildman, Fred Smith, Terrence Ross.

This combination of narrative and *cinema verite* footage reflects the philosophical thoughts at work in the minds of youth during the political upheaval of 1968. Robb is a college dropout selling underground newspapers in Montreal, and living with his girl friend, Malus. American draft dodger Rader takes up residence with the couple. A nonpolitical person, he prefers to pursue mystic qualities through the use of drugs and other stimulants. When Robb takes off for the Democratic Convention in Chicago, Malus goes with Rader to a commune, where the escapist life style leaves her disillusioned. She meets Robb in Chicago, where he has been involved in the protests, interviewing prominent activists such as Abbie Hoffman and Dick Gregory. Director Spry effectively shows the influences upon young people's thoughts and actions at that time, depicting his charactors as complex individuals open to various choices. The nonactors used give very convincing performances.

p, Tom Daly, Robin Spry; d, Spry; w, Sherwood Forest (based on a story by Spry and Forest); ph, Douglas Kiefer; m, Saz Williams; ed, Christopher Cordeaux; m/l, The Ventures.

Drama　　　　　　　　　　　　　　**(PR:C MPAA:NR)**

PROM NIGHT*　　(1980) 91m AE c

Leslie Nielsen (*Hammond*), Jamie Lee Curtis (*Kim*), Casey Stevens (*Nick*), Eddie Benton (*Wendy*), Antoinette Bower (*Mrs. Hammond*), Michael Tough (*Alex*), Robert Silverman (*Sykes*), Pita Oliver (*Vicki*), David Mucci (*Lou*), Jeff Wincott (*Drew*), Marybeth Rubins (*Kelly*), George Touliatos (*McBride*), Melanie Morse MacQuarrie (*Henri-Anne*), David Gardner (*Fairchild*), Joy Thompson (*Jude*), Sheldon Rybowski, Rob Garrison, David Bolt, Beth Amos, Sonia Zimmer, Sylvia Martin, Liz Stalker-Mason, Pam Henry, Ardon Bess, Lee Wildgen, Brock Simpson, Debbie Greenfield, Tammy Bourne.

Sterotypical teen-age shocker has a mysterious figure killing all the teens involved in the death of Curtis' little sister 11 years earlier. All the events take place the night of the high-school prom dance, with the deejay, Curtis' brother, murdering the kids in between disco songs.

p, Peter Simpson; d, Paul Lynch; w, William Gray (based on a story by Robert Guza, Jr.); ph, Robert New; m, Carl Zittrer, Paul Zaza; ed, Brian Ravok; art d, Reuben Freed.

Horror　　　　　　　　　　　Cas.　　　　　　**(PR:O MPAA:R)**

PROMISE, THE*　　(1969, Brit.) 98m Howard & Wyndham/Commonwealth United Entertainment c

John Castle (*Marat Yestigneyev*), Ian McKellen (*Leonidik*), Susan Macready (*Like Vasilyevna*), Mary Jones (*Mother*), David Nettheim (*Stepfather*), David Garfield (*Soldier*), Christopher Banks (*Neighbor*), Donald Bain (*Actor*).

Castle and McKellen play a pair of Soviet soldiers who, in the midst of the siege of Leningrad, befriend the homeless Macready. It's not long before they are caught in a three-sided romance as Macready must decide which of the soldiers to love faithfully. An unimpressive picture made unbelievable by the casting of British actors as Russians.

p, Henry T. Weinstein, Anthony B. Unger; d&w, Michael Hayes (based on the play by Aleksei Arbuzov); ph, (Eastmancolor).

Drama　　　　　　　　　　　　　　**(PR:A MPAA:NR)**

PROMISE, THE*½　　(1979) 97m UNIV c (GB: FACE OF A STRANGER)

Kathleen Quinlan (*Nancy/Marie*), Stephen Collins (*Michael*), Beatrice Straight (*Marion*), Laurence Luckinbill (*Dr. Gregson*), William Prince (*George Calloway*), Michael O'Hare (*Ben Avery*), Bibi Besch (*Dr. Allison*), Robin Gammell (*Dr. Wickfield*), Katherine DeHetre (*Wendy Lester*), Paul Ryan (*Dr. Fenton*), Tom O'Neill (*Painter*), Kirchy Prescott (*Nurse*), John Allen Vick (*1st Cab Driver*), Dan Leegant (*2nd Cab Driver*), Jerry Walter (*Cal*), Bob Hirschfeld (*Dr. Sidney Meisner*), Alan Newman (*Barker*), Carey Loftin, Max Balchowsky, Mickey Gilbert (*Truck Drivers*).

Warner Bros. made this kind of movie in the 1930s and 1940s, then threw the genre aside as being passe. They were right, as the failure of this four-hankie soap proved. Quinlan and Collins are lovers in Massachusetts. They attend a fair, he wins a necklace, and they use that as a symbol of their undying love. They bury the cheap bauble under a rock near the Atlantic Ocean (which looks very much like the Pacific, and, as a matter of fact, the streets of "Boston" resemble Los Angeles by more than a passing nod) and talk about marriage. Collins goes home to tell his domineering mother, Straight, that he is to marry Quinlan, while his girl friend spends the time working on a painting. Straight is against the union because Collins is being groomed to take over the construction empire Straight's father had begun many years before. (Why the acquisition of a wife should interfere with a man's ability to erect buildings is never explained.) Collins rebels, gets Quinlan out of her apartment, and the happy duo races away to make it legal. On the way to the wedding, there's a terrible accident. Collins is hurt but Quinlan is devastatingly injured and her lovely face is ruined. Collins is unconscious when Straight comes to Quinlan in the hospital and makes her an offer; she will pay to have Quinlan's face repaired if the young woman leaves New England and never again contacts her fiance. Quinlan agrees. When Collins regains his senses, Straight tells him that Quinlan was killed in the crash and he believes her. Quinlan goes to San Francisco where handsome Luckinbill performs plastic surgery and she comes out looking a great deal like Quinlan. She thanks Luckinbill by giving him the painting she was doing for Collins, who she thinks abandoned her because he couldn't deal with her temporary ugliness. Time passes and Collins becomes a rich construction magnate while Quinlan changes her name and takes up photography, becoming very adroit and successful at it in a brief time. Collins is in San Francisco erecting a skyscraper and needs a photographer, so he is told about Quinlan, in her new identity with a new name. She won't work for Collins and he goes to see her at her studio. She sits in the dark, they talk, he doesn't recall her voice, and when she turns the light on, he still doesn't recognize her, although it's barely 12 months since the accident. Collins can't understand her antipathy toward him and he presses her. She responds by leaving San Francisco and returning to Boston. Collins eventually meets Luckinbill and sees the painting in his house and a bulb flashes over his head. Cut to the area where the necklace was buried and Quinlan is there, searching, and not finding it. She walks away and Collins steps out of the trees, mumbles a few words about his loss of memory due to the accident, the two fall into each other's arms, and the picture ends, with a swell of music. Boring, contrived, and manipulative.

p, Fred Weintraub, Paul Heller; d, Gilbert Cates; w, Garry Michael White (based on a story by Weintraub, Heller); ph, Ralph Woolsey (Panavision, Technicolor); m, David Shire; ed, Peter E. Berger; art d, William Sandell; set d, Jeff Haley; spec eff, Greg Auer; m/l, "I'll Never Say Goodbye," Shire, Marilyn and Alan Bergman (sung by Melissa Manchester).

Drama/Romance   **(PR:A-C MPAA:PG)**

PROMISE AT DAWN✶✶½ (1970, U.S./Fr.) 101m AE-Nathalie/AE c (LA PROMESSE DE L'AUBE)

Melina Mercouri (Nina Kacew), Assaf Dayan (Romain, Age 25), Didier Haudepin (Romain, Age 15), Francois Raffoul (Romain, Age 9), Despo (Aniela), Jean Martin (Igor Igorevitch), Fernand Gravey (Jean-Michel Serusier, Jeweler), Jacqueline Porel (Mme. Mailler), Elspeth March (Polish Matron), Maria Machado (Nathalia Lissenko), Julie Dassin (Royal Navy Wren), Rene Clermont (Mr. Piekielny), Carol Cole (Louison), Marina Nestora (Mariette), Audrey Berindy (Valentine), Jacqueline Duc (Madame de Rare), Muni (Angelique), Terese Thoreaux (Silent Film Heroine), Perlo Vita [Jules Dassin] (Ivan Mosjoukine), Denis Berry.

Filmed in Paris, Nice, and the Soviet Union, this is the touching story of a woman who devotes her entire life to her son, even ending her own career for his sake. Mercouri is a successful actress of the Soviet silent cinema, who has a son illegitimately by a famous screen idol. She joins a troupe that ends its tour in Krakow, where Mercouri poses as a famous Parisian designer. When her true identity is exposed, she flees to Nice and works at a number of jobs in order to support her son. When the son matures, he fights in WW II for the French Air Force and later the RAF. He receives the Cross of the Liberation from General Charles de Gaulle because he was wounded in action, and plans to give it to his mother to make her proud of him. Upon his return to Nice, he discovers she has been dead for two years, but had written 250 letters in advance so that he could regularly receive correspondence and support from her. Actress Mercouri is actually the wife of director Dassin. Dassin, under the name Perlo Vita, plays real-life Russian silent actor Ivan Mosjoukine, who had been the most popular male movie star during the Czarist era.

p,d&w, Jules Dassin (based on the memoir Promise at Dawn by Romain Gary and the play "First Love" by Samuel Taylor); ph, Jean Badal (DeLuxe Color); m, Georges Delerue; ed, Robert Lawrence; prod d, Alexandre Trauner; set d, Charles Merangel; cos, Theoni V. Aldredge; m/l, Richelle Dassin; makeup, Otello Favia.

Drama   **(PR:A MPAA:PG)**

PROMISE HER ANYTHING, 1963   (SEE: PROMISES! PROMISES!, 1963)

PROMISE HER ANYTHING✶✶   (1966, Brit.) 98m Ray Stark-Seven Arts/PAR c

Warren Beatty (Harley Rummel), Leslie Caron (Michele O'Brien), Bob Cummings (Dr. Peter Brock), Hermione Gingold (Mrs. Luce), Lionel Stander (Sam), Asa Maynor (Rusty), Keenan Wynn (Angelo Carelli), Cathleen Nesbitt (Dr. Brock's Mother), Michael Bradley (John Thomas), Bessie Love (Woman in Pet Shop), Riggs O'Hara (Glue Sniffer), Hal Galili (1st Moving Man), Mavis Villiers (Middle-Aged Woman), Warren Mitchell (Panelist), Ferdy Mayne (Vittorio Fettucini), Sydney Tafler (Panelist), Margaret Nolan (Stripper), Vivienne Ventura (3rd Stripper), Anita Sharp Bolster (Baby Sitter), George Moon (Dancer), Charlotte Holland (Dancer's Wife), Chuck Julian (Grocery Clerk), Michael Chaplin (Beatnik), Michael Kane (Staff Doctor), Libby Morris (Clinic Mother), Jill Adams (Mrs. B.M. von Crispin), Donald Sutherland (Baby's Father).

Beatty attempted comedy in the manner of Cary Grant in this film, but lacked

Grant's versatility for slapstick routines. Caron plays a widow residing in Greenwich Village with an 18-month-old baby. She works for child psychologist Cummings, who actually hates kids. Looking for a new mate, she has her eyes set on Cummings, hiding the fact that she has a young child. Beatty is her upstairs neighbor, a would-be filmmaker who makes his living by producing mail-order burlesque pictures. He adores Caron, but she has her mind made up for Cummings. Beatty is willing to babysit the infant and keep him out of the way of Cummings, but when he decides to use the child in one of his pornographic films, Caron loses her patience. A slapstick ending has the baby crawling onto a crane and setting it in motion, with Beatty risking his life to save the child. This forces Caron to reconsider Beatty's worth as a possible husband. Caron and Beatty are totally out of place in this type of comedy, but director Hiller, by concentrating on the baby and the actors better suited to the situation, managed to mold a well-paced effort. The editing relies on gimmicks that do not always pan out, and, though the setting is Greenwich Village, there is no feel for that locale.

p, Stanley Rubin; d, Arthur Hiller; w, William Peter Blatty (based on the story by Arne Sultan, Marvin Worth); ph, Douglas Slocombe (Technicolor); m, Lynn Murray; ed, John Shirley; prod d, Wilfrid Shingleton; set d, David Ffolkes; cos, Beatrice Dawson; ch, Lionel Blair; m/l, "Promise Her Anything," Hal David, Burt Bacharach (sung by Tom Jones); makeup, Bob Lawrence, Charles Parker.

Comedy   **(PR:A MPAA:NR)**

PROMISE OF A BED, A   (SEE: THIS, THAT AND THE OTHER, 1970, Brit.)

PROMISES IN THE DARK✶✶   (1979) 115m Orion/WB c

Marsha Mason (Dr. Alexandra Kenda), Ned Beatty (Bud Koenig), Susan Clark (Fran Koenig), Michael Brandon (Dr. Jim Sandman), Kathleen Beller (Buffy Koenig), Paul Clemens (Gerry Hulin), Donald Moffat (Dr. Walter McInerny), Philip Sterling (Dr. Frucht), Bonnie Bartlett (Nurse Farber), James Noble (Dr. Blankenship), Arthur Rosenberg (Emergency Room Doctor), Peggy McCay (Mrs. Pritkin), Robert Doran (Alan), Lenora May (Sue), Alexandra Johnson (Ellie), Fran Bennett (Emergency Room Nurse), Eloise Hardt (Woman in Restaurant), Bernie Kuby (Tony in Bud's Office), Karen Anders (Secretary in Bud's Office), Edith Fields (Mrs. Gans), Alice Beardsley (Mrs. Kepos), Frank Robinson, Lidia Kristen, M.E. Lorange, Lynn Farrell, Kim Fowler, Janet Taylor, Jack Anderson, Henry D. Fetter, Dayson Decourcy, Teryn Jenkins, Paul Van, Ellen Shaw.

Mason plays a doctor trying to help a young woman, Beller, cope with her inevitable death from cancer. Paralleled to the emotional tribulations of Beller's family and friends is the courtship of Mason by radiologist Brandon. Realistic depiction of the hospital atmosphere, good performances, and a well-produced effort are hindered by the gloomy subject matter.

p&d, Jerome Hellman; w, Loring Mandel; ph, Adam Holender (Metrocolor); m, Leonard Rosenman; ed, Bob Wyman; prod d, Walter Scott Herndon; cos, Ann Roth.

Drama   **Cas.**   **(PR:C MPAA:PG)**

PROMISES, PROMISES zero   (1963) 75m NTD bw (AKA: PROMISE HER ANYTHING)

Jayne Mansfield (Sandy Brooks), Marie McDonald (Claire Banner), Mickey Hargitay (King Banner), Tommy Noonan (Jeff Brooks), Fritz Feld (Ship's Doctor), Claude Stroud (Steward), T.C. Jones (Babbette), Marjorie Bennett (Mrs. Snavely), Eddie Quillan (Bartender), Vic Lundin (Gigolo), Eileen Barton (Girl in Doctor's Office), Pat O'Moore (Ship's Captain), Imogene Coca (Herself).

Mansfield uncovered her body to the public in this worthless sexual farce, in which she plays the wife of a television script writer (Noonan). Both want to have children, but Mansfield can't seem to get pregnant. They go on a cabin cruise in the hopes that Noonan will relax and thus lose his impotency. McDonald and Hargitay (Mansfield's real-life husband) are their neighbors on board. The two couples engage in numerous drinking bouts and the exchanging of mates, though no one can be sure what really happened because they were too drunk. When both wives turn up pregnant, there is a question as to just who the fathers might be. T.C. Jones, a prominent female impersonator of the era, appears in a small role.

p, Tommy Noonan, Donald F. Taylor; d, King Donovan; w, William Welch, Noonan (based on the play "The Plant" by Edna Sheklow); ph, Joseph Biroc; m, Hal Borne; ed, Edward Dutko; art d, Serge Krizman; set d, Victor Gangelin; cos, Patrick Cummings, Vou Lee Giokaris, Mr. Blackwell, Ceil Chapman; m/l, "Lu-Lu-Lu, I'm in Love," "Promise Her Anything," Hal Borne (sung by Jayne Mansfield), "Fairy Tales," Roberta Day (sung by Marie McDonald); makeup, Sidney Perell.

Comedy   **(PR:O MPAA:NR)**

PROMOTER, THE✶✶✶   (1952, Brit.) 88m British Film Makers/UNIV bw (GB: THE CARD)

Alec Guinness (Edward Henry "Denry" Machin), Glynis Johns (Ruth Earp), Valerie Hobson (Countess of Chell), Petula Clark (Nellie Cotterill), Edward Chapman (Mr. Duncalf), Veronica Turleigh (Mrs. Machin), George Devine (Mr. Calvert), Gibb McLaughlin (Emery), Frank Pettingell (Police Superintendent), Joan Hickson (Mrs. Codleyn), Michael Hordern (Bank Manager), Alison Leggatt (Mrs. Cotterill), Peter Copley (Shillitoe), Deirdre Doyle (Widow Hullins), Harold Goodwin (John), Lyn Evans (The Boatman), Michael Trubshawe (Yeomanry Officer), Paul Hopkins (Denry as a Baby), Matthew Guinness (Denry as a Boy), Wilfrid Hyde-White (Lord), Joey the Mule.

Rags to riches story starring Guinness as a young, poverty-stricken student who alters the grade on his high school entrance exam to ensure his enrollment. He later advances from his position as a lowly law clerk through a series of jobs with increasing responsibility and financial reward, until he finally makes it big in business. He founds a loan company and eventually becomes the mayor of his town. Along the way he succumbs to the charms of several women, including Johns as an impoverished tenant from whom Guinness must collect the rent and Clark, who becomes his wife. Somewhat typical Horatio Alger story made interesting by a cast of outstanding performers.

p, John Bryan; d, Ronald Neame; w, Eric Ambler (based on the novel *The Card* by Arnold Bennett); ph, Oswald Morris; m, William Alwyn; ed, Clive Donner; md, Muir Mathieson; art d, T. Hopewell Ash.

Drama												**(PR:A MPAA:NR)**

PROPER TIME, THE*½			(1959) 75m Business Administration
										Company/Lopert bw

Tom Laughlin (*Mickey Henderson*), Nira Monsour (*Doren*), Norma Quine (*Sue Dawson*), Richard Shannon (*Dr. Polery*), Dennis O'Flaherty (*Doug Fearson*), Kip King (*Jerry Rohn*), Ray Loza (*Bobby Pfarr*), Connie Davis (*Mrs. Henderson*), Al Randall (*Mr. Henderson*), Roger Rollie (*Prof. White*).

This is the first cinematic attempt by writer-director-actor Laughlin (of BILLY JACK fame); he plays a freshman at UCLA who has a speech impediment that goes away when he is in contact with girls. Rejected by a fraternity, he sparks a friendship with Quine, but is soon victimized by her lustful roommate Monsour. The two sleep together and soon become engaged, but Laughlin drops her when he finds out that she's been sleeping around. Laughlin then finds that the sympathetic Quine is still willing to lend him her support. She also convinces him to go to a speech clinic for help. Direction is uneven, with the script a bit cliched. The moral aspect of this picture, that sex is something to be saved until after marriage, seems incredibly naive.

p,d&w, Tom Laughlin; ph, James Crabbe; m, Shelly Manne.

Drama												**(PR:A MPAA:NR)**

PROPERTY**								(1979) 92m West Bank c

Walt Curtis, Lola Desmond, Corky Hubbert, M. G. Horowitz, "Marjorie", Christopher Hershey, Nathaniel [Butch] Haynes, Richard Tyler, Jack Ryan, Karen Irwin.

Everyone has a favorite personal story to tell about past days of glory, which more or less was the basis for the creation of this film. It deals with a group of Portland, Oregon, residents who try to establish a community of their own in the 1960s by purchasing some houses set for demolition. The cast of characters—played by the actual participants of the real-life story—includes a 30-year-old-plus poet, a midget who dreams of becoming a comedian on nationwide television, and an older con man who lives with his younger girl friend and their child. The story is told in a semi-improvisational fashion and has the appearance of being made up right on the spot. In the end PROPERTY is like listening to someone else's bar stories: it's got some moments of interest but is best appreciated by those closer to the actual events.

p,d&w, Penny Allen; ph, Eric Edwards; m, Richard Tyler.

Drama											**(PR:A-C MPAA:NR)**

PROPHECIES OF NOSTRADAMUS**½		(1974, Jap.) 90m Toho c
(NOSTRADAMUS NO DAIYOGEN; AKA: CATASTROPHE 1999; LAST
										DAYS OF PLANET EARTH)

Tetsuro Tamba, Toshio Kurosawa, So Yamamura, Kaoru Yumi, Takashi Shimura, Yoko Tsukasa, Kenju Kobayashi, Hiroshi Fujioka.

Based upon the prophecy by the French mystic Nostradamus that the world would end in the year 1999, this picture shows how disproportionate levels of pollution could lead to such a catastrophe. Tamba plays a scientist who charges that the build-up of pollution in the seas is responsible for giant bloodsucking slugs. Almost overnight all marine life dies, with plant life shriveling up and the development of a high infant mortality rate. Crowds react to this by staging mass riots, with the governments resorting to military means of gaining control. Well-thought-out images and chilling depictions of future life make this picture a mark above the normal disaster film.

p, Tomoyuki Tanaka, Osamu Tanaka; d, Toshio Masuda; w, Toshio Yasumi, Shinobu Hashimoto (based on the story by Yasumi); ph, Rokuro Nishigaki (TohoScope); spec eff, Teruyoshi Nakano.

Horror												**(PR:C MPAA:NR)**

PROPHECY*								(1979) 102m PAR c

Talia Shire (*Maggie*), Robert Foxworth (*Rob*), Armand Assante (*Hawks*), Richard Dysart (*Isley*), Victoria Racimo (*Ramona*), George Clutesi (*M'Rai*), Tom McFadden (*Pilot*), Evans Evans (*Cellist*), Burke Byrnes (*Father*), Mia Bendixsen (*Girl*), Johnny Timko (*Boy*), Everett L. Creach (*Kelso*), Charles H. Gray (*Sheriff*), Lyvingston Holms, Graham Jarvis, James H. Burk, Bob Terhune, Lon Katzman, Steve Shemayme, John A. Shemayme, Jaye Durkus, Renato Moore, Mel Waters, Roosevelt Smith, Eric Mansker.

A return to the monster genre of the 1950s in which creatures such as GODZILLA were a warning of the possible effects of radiation, only this one concentrates on industrial pollution in the backwoods of Maine. Foxworth plays a government agent investigating the wildlife of Maine in order to settle a dispute between the local Indians and the paper mill. He is accompanied by his pregnant wife, Shire, as they set up camp in the woods. They encounter giant fish and a man-eating raccoon, relating the disproportionate size to the presence of mercury in the water. They also come across a cub, which resembles a hideous monster. Accompanied by Indian leader Assante, the couple attempts to take the bear to show to the courts, but the cub's mother is a giant bear who wants her baby back. Shire becomes fearful of what her unborn baby will look like after her own exposure to the mercury poisoning. An attempt at showing the possible dangers of mercury poisoning is thwarted by a cliche-ridden script and stereotyped performances. During production, an ex-CIA agent kept a watchful eye to ensure that this plot would not be ripped off by television. A humorous note, considering this type of story has been seen on TV for years.

p, Robert L. Rosen; d, John Frankenheimer; w, David Seltzer; ph, Harry Stradling, Jr. (Panavision, Movielab Color); m, Leonard Rosenman; ed, Tom Rolf; prod d, William Craig Smith; set d, George Gaines; cos, Ray Summers; spec eff, Robert Dawson; makeup, Thomas R. Burman.

Horror			**Cas.**						**(PR:C-O MPAA:PG)**

PROSPERITY**							(1932) 87m MGM bw

Marie Dressler (*Maggie Warren*), Polly Moran (*Lizzie Praskins*), Anita Page (*Helen Praskins*), Norman Foster (*John Warren*), Jacquie Lyn (*Cissy*), Jerry Tucker (*Buster*), Charles Giblyn (*Mayor*), Frank Darien (*Ezra Higgins*), Henry Armetta (*Barber*), John Miljan, John Roche.

A wealthy banking family faces disaster after a financial problem forces the closing of their bank. Dressler, as the family matriarch, keeps everything together, however, by showing them how to make do with the little they have. Much of this picture had to be remade after its initial showing, holding off its release for an entire year. The Dressler-Moran pair gave their roles the proper amount of life, with fine direction, but the purely escapist plot fails to hold much water.

d, Sam Wood; w, Sylvia Thalberg, Frank Butler, Eve Greene (based on the story by Zelda Sears); ph, Leonard Smith; ed, William LeVanway; art d, Cedric Gibbons.

Comedy												**(PR:A MPAA:NR)**

PROTECTORS, THE				(SEE: COMPANY OF KILLERS, 1970)

PROTECTORS, BOOK 1, THE*			(1981) 93m Studios Pan Imago c
										(AKA: ANGEL OF H.E.A.T)

Marilyn Chambers, Stephen Johnson, Mary Woronov, Milt Kogan, Dan Jesse, Remy O'Neill.

Skin teaser has Chambers (known mainly as a popular pornography star) and Woronov teaming up to keep Jesse from going through with his plans for world domination. Pretty silly stuff, with Chambers gracing the screen in her tedious form of nonacting.

p&d, Myrl A. Schreibman; w, Helen Sanford; ph, Jacques Haitkin.

Comedy												**(PR:O MPAA:R)**

PROSTITUTE**½							(1980, Brit.) 96m Kestrel c

Eleanor Forsythe (*Sandra*), Kate Crutchley (*Louise*), Kim Lockett (*Jean*), Nancy Samuels (*Rose*), Richard Mangan (*David Selby*), Ann Whitaker (*Amanda*), Paul Arlington (*Mr. Hanson*), Carol Palmer (*Carol*), Brigid Mackay (*Mrs. T.*), Colin Hindley (*Griff*), Count Prince Miller (*Winston*), Howard Dickenson (*Martin*), Paul Moriarty (*London Detective*), Mary Waterhouse (*TV Researcher*).

A heavily researched project by director Garnett is an attempt to give a realistic portrayal of the working life of a prostitute. The story centers on Forsythe as an English country girl who naively becomes involved in prostitution, then sets about trying to improve herself by moving up in the world of prostitution to wealthier patrons. A parallel is made to the plight of Crutchley, a sociologist, and friend to Forsythe, who is trying to bring about changes in the prostitution laws. Performances have an air of naturalism, and the atmosphere and directorial style provide the proper setting for the situations.

p,d&w, Tony Garnett; ph, Charles Stewart; m, The Gangsters; ed, Bill Shapter; art d, Martin Johnson; cos, Monica Howe.

Drama												**(PR:O MPAA:NR)**

PROSTITUTION**½				(1965, Fr.) 115m Cocifrance/Stratford bw (LA
										PROSTITUTION)

Etchika Choureau (*Olga*), Evelyne Dassas (*Irene*), Alain Lionel (*Mario*), Jean Werner (*Hans*), Alicia Gutirrez (*Concepcion*), Anne Darden (*Martha*), Rita Cadillac (*Rita*), Gabrielle Robinne (*Honorine*), Victor Guyay (*Pauwels*), Robert Dalban (*Robert*), Carl Eich (*Franck*), Raoul Dantes (*Joaquin*), Hinsing Chow (*Bangchow*), Jacques Devos.

Dassas plays a young woman from the country who turns to prostitution in order to keep her lover, Lionel, from committing a robbery. But she becomes trapped inside an international prostitution ring, which takes her to Holland, Germany, and Mexico, winding up in Hong Kong. While in Hong Kong, Dassas becomes addicted to heroin, and after learning the truth behind her affair with Lionel, the drug becomes her solace. Lionel posed as her lover in order to trick her into prostitution, which Dassas learns through a conversation with an Interpol agent. The film treats the theme of prostitution in a very realistic manner, showing the complex ways a woman can become involved in prostitution. Absent are the usual stereotypes present in so many films dealing with this subject.

p&d, Maurice Boutel; w, Boutel, Marcel Sicot; ph, Quinto Albicocco, Paul Fabian, Enzo Riccioni, Jacques Mercanton (CinemaScope); m, Roger-Roger; ed, Etiennette Muse.

Drama												**(PR:C MPAA:NR)**

PROUD AND THE DAMNED, THE*½			(1972) 94m Media Trend-
						Prestige/COL c (AKA: PROUD, DAMNED AND DEAD)

Chuck Connors (*Will*), Aron Kincaid (*Ike*), Cesar Romero (*Alcalde*), Jose Greco (*Ramon*), Henry Capps (*Hank*), Peter Ford (*Billy*), Smoky Roberds (*Jeb*), Maria Grimm (*Maria*), Nana Lorca (*Dancer*), Anita Quinn (*Mila*), Conrad Parkham (*Juan*), Alvaro Ruiz (*Chico*), Andre Marquis (*Gen. Martinez*), Pacheco (*Lieutenant*), Ignacio Gomez (*Padre*), Ernesto Uribe (*Aide*), Rey Vasquez (*Innkeeper*), Bernardo Herrera (*Rollo*), Los Caballeros de Villa de Leyva.

A hollow adventure drama with Connors and four fellow Civil War veterans hiding out in South America. They got mixed up in a local revolution and, in an effort to insure their safety, hire themselves out as mercenaries. Anything but gripping.

p,d&w, Ferde Grofe, Jr.; ph, Remegio Young; m, Gene Kauer, Douglas Lackey; ed, Phillip Innes; art d, Alvaro Botero.

Adventure **(PR:C-O MPAA:PG)**

PROUD AND THE PROFANE, THE*½ (1956) 111m PAR bw

William Holden *(Lt. Col. Colin Black)*, Deborah Kerr *(Lee Ashley)*, Thelma Ritter *(Kate Connors)*, Dewey Martin *(Eddie Wodcik)*, William Redfield *(Chaplain Holmes)*, Ross Bagdasarian *(Louie)*, Adam Williams *(Eustace Press)*, Marion Ross *(Joan)*, Theodore Newton *(Bob Kilpatrick)*, Richard Shannon *(Major)*, Peter Hansen *(Lt. [J.G.] Hutchins)*, Ward Wood *(Sgt. Peckinpaugh)*, Geraldine Hall *(Helen)*, Evelyn Cotton *(Beth)*, Ann Morriss *(Pat)*, Nancy Stevens *(Evvie)*, Lorayne Brox *(Sissy)*, Don Roberts *(Lt. Fowler)*, Bob Kenaston *(Soldier)*, Taylor Measom, Don House *(Marines)*, George Brenlin, Robert Morse, Ray Stricklyn *(Casualties)*, Frank Gorshin *(Harry)*, Genevieve Aumont *(Lili Carere)*, Claude Akins *(Big Soldier)*, Elizabeth Slifer *(French Woman)*, Joseph Moran *(Marine Saying Goodbye)*, Anthony Moran *(Carl)*, Jack Richardson *(Sailor)*, Freeman Morse *(Paul)*.

THE PROUD AND THE PROFANE was neither. Matter of fact, it should have been called "The Putrid and the Predictable." Kerr and Holden were ballyhooed to have a certain chemistry but it was not in evidence at all. After the success of FROM HERE TO ETERNITY, the producers thought they might get the same audiences to flock to this wartime weeper (which actually made some money), but this picture bears as much resemblance to the former as BAMBI does to PSYCHO. It's the middle of WW II and Kerr, a Red Cross worker, has come to the Pacific to locate the grave of her late husband who died in the battle of Guadalcanal. She wants to find out how he died and some details about his final hours. She's part of a Red Cross group led by Ritter and including Brox, Stevens, Hall, Cotton, and Morriss. Holden is a rough Marine who thinks these women should be home knitting or, at least, packaging Bundles for Britain. This is war and it's no place for these doughnut purveyors. Kerr meets Holden and there is a brief attraction. She wants him to tell her about her late husband and he wants to sleep with her. Soon, Kerr is carrying Holden's child. Then she learns that he has a wife, albeit an alcoholic, back in the U.S. and that news triggers a suicide attempt, which results in a miscarriage. Holden, wearing a mustache and portraying a part-Indian, returns to active combat duty. His wife dies off-screen and when he comes back from the front, wounded, Kerr is there to help him and to presumably be his life's companion. In the interim, Kerr has been approached by Martin, who also finds her sexy, but he is soon killed by the Japanese. In small roles, note Frank Gorshin (the impressionist), Claude Akins, and Ross Bagdasarian, whom you may recall as the pianist-composer in the apartment across the way from James Stewart in REAR WINDOW. Bagdasarian would later create "The Chipmunks" and make so much money from those efforts that he didn't have to appear in acorns like this. The Virgin Islands took the place of the South Pacific, although nothing could take the place of the missing script.

p, William Perlberg; d&w, George Seaton (based on the novel *The Magnificent Bastards* by Lucy Herndon Crockett); ph, John F. Warren (VistaVision); m, Victor Young; ed, Alma Macrorie; art d, Hal Pereira, Earl Hedrick; set d, Sam Comer, Frank R. McKelvy; cos, Edith Head; spec eff, John P. Fulton, Farciot Edouart; makeup, Wally Westmore; technical advisers, Lt. John W. Antonelli, USMC; Margaret Hagan, Louise A. Woods, Mary Louise Dowling (American National Red Cross).

War/Romance **(PR:A-C MPAA:NR)**

PROUD, DAMNED AND DEAD (SEE: PROUD AND THE DAMNED, THE, 1972)

PROUD ONES, THE* ** (1956) 94m FOX c

Robert Ryan *(Marshal Cass Silver)*, Virginia Mayo *(Sally)*, Jeffrey Hunter *(Thad)*, Robert Middleton *(Honest John Barrett)*, Walter Brennan *(Jake, Jailer)*, Arthur O'Connell *(Jim Dexter, Deputy)*, Ken Clark *(Pike)*, Rodolfo Acosta *(Chico)*, George Mathews *(Dillon, Saloon Manager)*, Fay Roope *(Markham)*, Edward Platt *(Dr. Barlow)*, Whit Bissell *(Mr. Bolton)*, Paul E. Burns *(Billy Smith, Town Drunk)*, Richard Deacon *(Barber)*, Frank Gerstle *(Tim the Bartender)*, Charles Tannen *(2nd Foreman)*, Lois Ray *(Belle)*, Jack Low *(Guard)*, Ken Terrell *(The Weasel)*, Harrison Lewis *(Editor)*, Don Brodie *(Hotel Clerk)*, William Fawcett *(Driver)*, Ed Mundy *(Saloon Barker)*, Jackie Coogan *(Man on Make)*, Juanita Close *(Helen)*, Harry Carter *(Houseman)*, Steve Darrell *(Trail Boss)*, Mary Thomas, Jonni Paris *(Waitresses)*, I. Stanford Jolley *(Crooked Card Player)*.

Ryan plays the toughened marshal in a town where all hell is about to break loose, with the coming of the railroad and the cattle drives to shortly follow. His main adversary is Middleton, the local saloon keeper, who sees the opportunity to make a lot of money. Hunter plays the son of a man whom Ryan killed in the course of duty. At first wanting to wreak vengeance against the marshal, the misdirected Hunter learns to respect the ways of Ryan, eventually helping him in his fight against the town's roughnecks. Script and direction are evenly paced to provide a suspenseful and climactic finish, with Ryan giving his role the necessary hardness.

p, Robert L. Jacks; d, Robert D. Webb; w, Edward North, Joseph Petracca (based on the novel by Verne Athanas); ph, Lucien Ballard (CinemaScope, DeLuxe Color); m, Lionel Newman; ed, Hugh S. Fowler; art d, Lyle Wheeler, Leland Fuller; cos, Travilla.

Western **(PR:A MPAA:NR)**

PROUD REBEL, THE*½** (1958) 103m Formosa/BV c

Alan Ladd *(John Chandler)*, Olivia de Havilland *(Linnett Moore)*, Dean Jagger *(Harry Burleigh)*, David Ladd *(David Chandler)*, Cecil Kellaway *(Dr. Enos Davis)*, James Westerfield *(Birm Bates, Sheep Buyer)*, Henry Hull *(Judge Morley)*, [Harry] Dean Stanton *(Jeb Burleigh)*, Thomas Pittman *(Tom Burleigh)*, Eli Mintz *(Gorman)*, John Carradine *(Travelling Salesman)*, King *(Lance The Dog)*.

Warm-hearted story teams Ladd with his 11-year-old son David, playing a boy who has lost his power of speech after witnessing his home destroyed and his mother killed by Union cannons during the battle of Atlanta. Ladd travels throughout the country to find a cure for the boy, always accompanied by their faithful dog. He comes to an Illinois town, where two no-good sheep herder brothers (Pittman and Stanton) attempt to steal the dog. This leads to a fight in which Ladd is knocked unconscious, and later arrested when the brothers make up a story. Hardened widow de Havilland takes compassion upon Ladd and his son by offering to pay his fine in return for labor on the large farm she has been running alone. This makes for a nice situation for all involved, with de Havilland having someone around to fight off the sheep herders who earlier hassled Ladd. When the younger Ladd is made fun of by boys in the town because of his muteness, his father sells the dog in order to raise the necesssary money for an expensive treatment at a Minnesota clinic. But the treatment proves a failure, and the Ladds return to town to find their dog in the hands of Jagger, the sheep-herder father of Stanton and Pittman. Jagger continually beats the dog, who won't work for anyone but Ladd and his son. Ladd demands the dog be returned, triggering a gunfight between him and the sheep herders. At the fight one of the sons is about to sneak up on Ladd, but the younger Ladd manages to regain his voice, shouting a warning to his father. Brilliant performances, especially the surprising one by the younger Ladd and the toughness of the de Havilland character, handled in the usual demanding manner of director Curtiz, makes this somewhat over-sentimental boy-and-his-dog story into a compassionate tale of individual strife. David Ladd learned sign language to add realism to his character, with de Havilland actually learning all the aspects of farming necesssary to portray the tough-loner type of woman she played. An added bonus is the fine color photography of the Utah landscape by veteran McCord. Surprisingly THE PROUD REBEL was only moderately successful at the box office, taking in $2.5 million.

p, Samuel Goldwyn, Jr.; d, Michael Curtiz; w, Joe Petracca, Lillie Hayward (based on the story "Journal of Linnett Moore" by James Edward Grant); ph, Ted McCord (Technicolor); m, Jerome Moross; ed, Aaron Stell; md, Emil Newman; art d, McClure Capps; set d, Victor Gangelin; cos, Mary Wills.

Western **Cas.** **(PR:A MPAA:NR)**

PROUD RIDER, THE* ** (1971, Can.) 85m Lighthouse/Cinepix of Canada c

Jeremy Kane *(Michael)*, Karen Gregory *(Jenny)*, Michael Bell *(Eric)*, members of the Satan's Choice Motorcycle Club.

Effective piece which traces Kane's withdrawal from a structured life style into one of disorder and lawlessness as a member of a motorcycle gang. The use of an actual motorcycle club gives a realistic atmosphere to the situations in which Kane is involved. These non-actors are much more impressive on the screen than the real actors, especially Kane.

p, George Fras; d, Walter Baczynsky, Chester Stocki; w, Stocki; ph, Walter Wasik; m, Sol Sherman, Paul Hoffert; ed, Bruce Sabsay; art d, Raymond Telega.

Drama **(PR:C MPAA:NR)**

PROUD VALLEY, THE** (1941, Brit.) 72m Ealing-Capad/Supreme bw

Paul Robeson *(David Goliath)*, Edward Chapman *(Dick Parry)*, Simon Lack *(Emlyn Parry)*, Rachel Thomas *(Mrs. Parry)*, Dilys Thomas *(Dilys)*, Edward Rigby *(Bert Rigby)*, Janet Johnson *(Gwen Owen)*, Charles Williams *(Evans)*, Jack Jones *(Thomas)*, Dilys Davies *(Mrs. Owen)*, Clifford Evans *(Seth Jones)*, Allan Jeayes *(Mr. Trevor)*, George Merritt *(Mr. Lewis)*, Edward Lexy *(Commissionaire)*, Noel Howlett *(Company Clerk)*, Babette Washington, Grant Sutherland.

Robeson plays a stoker working in a Welsh coal town, where he's gotten the job through the efforts of Chapman, anxious to enlist Robeson's voice in the local choir. When a disaster kills Chapman and leaves the town facing starvation, Robeson risks his own life to save the mine. A gas leak has left remnants inside the mine. Knowing this, Robeson lights a match which clears out the gas, but kills Robeson. Weak direction mars the effective performances. Robeson uses his operatic voice to sing "Deep River" and a portion of the "Elijah" chorus.

p, Michael Balcon; d, Penrose Tennyson; w, Roland Pertwee, Louis Goulding, Jack Jones, Tennyson (based on a story by Herbert Marshall, Alfredda Brilliant); ph, Glen Macwilliams, Roy Kellino; m, Felix Mendelssohn; ed, Ray Pitt; art d, Wilfred Shingleton.

Drama **(PR:A MPAA:NR)**

PROVIDENCE**** (1977, Fr.) 104m Action-SFP/Cinema 5 c

John Gielgud *(Clive Langham)*, Dirk Bogarde *(Claud Langham)*, Ellen Burstyn *(Sonia Langham)*, David Warner *(Kevin Woodford)*, Elaine Stritch *(Helen Weiner/Molly Langham)*, Denis Lawson *(Dave Woodford)*, Cyril Luckham *(Dr. Mark Eddington)*, Kathryn Leigh-Scott *(Miss Boon)*, Milo Sperber *(Mr. Jenner)*, Anna Wing *(Karen)*, Peter Arne *(Nils)*, Tanya Lopert *(Miss Lister)*, Samson Fainsilber *(Old Hairy Man)*, Joseph Pittoors *(Old Man)*.

PROVIDENCE takes place on the eve of the 78th birthday of a dying novelist, Gielgud. He lives alone in his country estate (photographed in Providence, Rhode Island) battling his weakness for alcohol, the memory of his dead wife Molly, and a chronic rectal disorder. During the night he struggles with what will probably be his last novel, basing the characters on his own children. His son, Bogarde, and daughter-in-law, Burstyn, are an unhappily married couple who constantly jab one another with their dry wit. Gielgud's illegitimate son, Warner, is a former soldier on trial for killing an old man who turned into a werewolf. Bogarde is the prosecuting attorney, but the defendant is acquitted and soon falls in love with Burstyn. This, however, does not upset Bogarde as much as it disgusts him. Meanwhile, Gielgud is getting increasingly more drunk and his plot is reflecting his inebriated state. He decides to give Bogarde a mistress. Gielgud's imagination is weak and the character he creates is in the image of his dead wife—an older woman facing a terminal disease. Stritch plays the mistress, but Gielgud continually mistakes her for his wife. As Gielgud downs more liquor and suffers more from his rectal pains, his characters and story fall apart. Warner has a habit of forgetting who he is and mistakenly delivering Bogarde's dialog—confusing everything beyond repair. Bogarde and Burstyn play out a scene once, then repeat it by delivering each other's lines. Even the settings change. In one scene Bogarde's veranda is set against a Mediterranean background, but in another there is a city in the background. There are also characters who worm their way into the story, much to Gielgud's consternation—a doctor, Luckham, who performs a gruesome autopsy, and a soccer player, Lawson, who has a habit of running through scenes. Morning finally comes for Gielgud. His children pay him a visit and they are nothing like the characters which he has imposed on them. Bogarde and Burstyn are a quiet, happily married couple, while Warner is a well-mannered son who cares deeply for his father. They exchange presents (a penknife belonging to Hemingway and a novel called The Scales Of Time which is an in-joke of Resnais' and Mercer's—the picture of the man on the back of the book is Mercer) and sit down to a luxurious outdoor dinner. After they've finished, Gielgud asks them to leave. He is then ready for another painful, drunken night of trying to finish his novel. PROVIDENCE is truly a breakthrough film in its attempt to synthesize literature and film into one work with both halves dependent on each other. Resnais, who has often worked with novelists (Marguerite Duras, HIROSHIMA MON AMOUR, 1960; Alain Robbe-Grillet, LAST YEAR AT MARIENBAD, 1962; and Jorge Semprun, THE WAR IS OVER, 1966, and STAVISKY, 1974) collaborated again with another writer, playwright David Mercer who is best known for his play "A Suitable Case for Treatment" which was filmed by Karel Reisz in 1965 as MORGAN! (hence the werewolf which pops up in PROVIDENCE). While most critics attack Resnais for being pretentious and cold, PROVIDENCE should (but won't) put most of them at ease. Gielgud's performance is a virtuoso portrayal and shows a phenomenal range, especially when compared with his lighter role as the butler in ARTHUR (1981). The film is also filled with brilliant, witty humor that was blindly overlooked by most of the film's loudest detractors. PROVIDENCE is a superb film which offers inventive filmmaking with a comic touch and an intellectual theme. (In English.)

p, Yves Gasser, Yves Peyrot, Klaus Hellwig; d, Alain Resnais; w, David Mercer; ph, Ricardo Aronovich (Panavision, Eastmancolor); m, Miklos Rozsa; ed, Albert Jurgenson; art d, Jacques Saulnier; set d, Claude Serre; cos, Catherine Leterrier, Yves St. Laurent, John Bates.

Drama   **Cas.**   **(PR:O MPAA:R)**

PROWL GIRLS zero   (1968) 70m Barry Mahon/Chancellor bw (AKA: RUNAWAY DAUGHTERS)

Leo Schell (Narrator).

A thoroughly unpleasant film about a teenage girl who rejects her middle-class lifestyle to live with her ex-drug pusher boy friend in an East Village hovel. He concocts a profitable scheme to separate well-to-do businessmen from their cash under the guise of social rehabilitation. When the girl discovers his racket, she runs off with one of the businessmen. She is tracked down by her former boy friend's associates and injected with a lethal dose of heroin. Completely unredeeming and ineptly made.

p, Barry Mahon.

Crime/Drama   **(PR:O MPAA:NR)**

PROWLER, THE***   (1951) 92m Horizon/UA bw

Van Heflin (Webb Garwood), Evelyn Keyes (Susan Gilvray), John Maxwell (Bud Crocker), Katherine Warren (Mrs. Crocker), Emerson Treacy (William Gilvray), Madge Blake (Martha Gilvray), Wheaton Chambers (Dr. James), Robert Osterloh (Coroner), Sherry Hall (John Gilvray), Louise Lorimer (Motel Manager), George Nader (Photographer), Benny Burt (Journalist), Louise Bates (Doctor's Wife), Steve Carruthers (Mr. Talbot), Betty Jane Howarth (Mrs. Talbot), Fred Hoose (Foreman), Alan Harris (Clerk), Tiny Jones.

A scary, fascinating film, THE PROWLER is an all-Heflin vehicle and his moody, unpredictable personality dominates every jittery scene. He is a cop who responds one night to a prowler report in the Los Angeles area. He and his partner, Maxwell, find attractive housewife Keyes fearful of an intruder. The officers look about and find nothing. Later Heflin returns to see if Keyes is all right. He is attracted to her and also to her splendid home, telling her he hopes to buy a small motel outside Las Vegas some day, an enterprise that "will make money for you even while you sleep." He discovers that the lady is often alone in the evening since her husband, Treacy, is an all-night radio disc jockey. He seduces her and learns that if anything happens to Keyes' husband, she will inherit a small fortune, one he plans to make his own. Knowing a night when the husband will be home, Heflin himself pretends to be a prowler and then responds to the call Treacy makes to the police. He finds the husband outside with a gun and pulls his own. Treacy is killed by Heflin, who then shoots himself to make it appear that he acted in self-defense. Keyes later marries Heflin and they buy a little motel in Las Vegas. But when Heflin learns that Keyes is pregnant, he panics. He believes that a child will incriminate him since it is known that Treacy was sterile. Heflin tries to deliver the child himself but Keyes begs him to get a doctor when her labor pains become excruciating. Heflin summons a doctor, Chambers, who delivers the child. During the course of the traumatic event, the exhausted, guilt-ridden Heflin admits killing Treacy. He must now murder the doctor to cover up the confession, Keyes knows. She helps the doctor escape just as Heflin is about to kill him and then calls the police. Cops arrive and Heflin makes a break for it, but is shot after ignoring a warning from the officers, ironically dying in the same fashion as his victim, Treacy. Losey does a fine job helming this film noir entry but the offbeat flavor and Heflin's strange mannerisms throw the viewer off balance and allow for little empathy toward an obvious cad and killer. Like THE HITCHHIKER, this film is bleak and offers little relief from the methodical ways of the scheming murderer. One must wait for Heflin to get his just end a little too long.

p, S.P. Eagle [Sam Spiegel]; d, Joseph Losey; w, Dalton Trumbo, Hugo Butler

(based on an original story by Robert Thoeren, Hans Wilhelm); ph, Arthur Miller; m, Lyn Murray; ed, Paul Weatherwax; md, Irving Friedman; art d, Boris Leven; set d, Jacques Mapes; cos, Maria Donovan; m/l, "Baby," Murray, Dick Mack (sung by Bob Carroll).

Crime Drama   **(PR:C-O MPAA:NR)**

PROWLER, THE*   (1981) 88m Graduation/Sandhurst c (AKA: ROSEMARY'S KILLER)

Vicki Dawson (Pam McDonald), Christopher Goutman (Mark London), Cindy Weintraub (Lisa), Farley Granger (Sheriff George Fraser), John Seitz (Kingsley), Lawrence Tierney, Lisa Dunsheath, David Sederholm, Bill Nunnery, Thom Bray, Diane Rode, Bryan Englund, Donna Davis, Carlton Carpenter, Joy Glaccum, Timothy Wahrer, Bill Hugh Collins, Dan Lownsberry, Douglas Stevenson, Susan Monts, John Christian, Richard Colligan, Steven Bock, Matthew Iddings.

Another shocker borrowing from the immensely successful HALLOWEEN, this time duplicating the plot almost exactly. A WW II soldier comes home from a tour of duty only to find his girl friend carrying on with someone else. He then, in an exercise of Tom Savini's exceptional makeup techniques, murders the couple with a pitchfork. He returns to his hometown 35 years later and begins killing off the teenage population, all the time wearing his army helmet. Seemingly the only motivation for his killing spree is to give Savini more practice with effects and makeup. Unfortunately, for fans of excessive gore, certain scenes (a head blowing up and a bayonet being driven through someone else's head) have been clipped from the release print.

p, Joseph Zito, David Streit; d, Zito; w, Glenn Leopold, Neal F. Barbera; ph, Raoul Lumas; m, Richard Einhorn; ed, Joel Goodman; prod d, Lorenzo Mans; art d, Roberta Neiman; spec eff&makeup, Tom Savini.

Horror   **Cas.**   **(PR:O MPAA:R)**

PRUDENCE AND THE PILL**½   (1968, Brit.) 92m Prudence/FOX c

Deborah Kerr (Prudence Hardcastle), David Niven (Gerald Hardcastle), Robert Coote (Henry Hardcastle), Irina Demick (Elizabeth), Joyce Redman (Grace Hardcastle), Judy Geeson (Geraldine Hardcastle), Keith Michell (Dr. Alan Hewitt), Dame Edith Evans (Lady Roberta Bates), David Dundas (Tony Bates), Vickery Turner (Rose, Maid), Hugh Armstrong (Ted, Chauffeur), Peter Butterworth (Chemist), Moyra Fraser (Woman in Tea Shop), Annette Kerr (Gerald's Secretary), Jonathan Lynn (Chemist's Assistant), Harry Towb (Race Track Official).

The mass production of birth-control pills in the 1960s is the basis for this British farce about marriage and infidelity, with the somewhat hidden moral statement that the pill has been developed to keep married couples from having children, and not for rampant sexual conduct. Kerr and Niven, noted for their pairing in several well-crafted farces, are a married couple who have as little as possible to do with each other, which includes having separate bedrooms. When their niece switches her mother's (Redman) birth control pills for aspirin, and Redman becomes pregnant, Niven decides to try the same thing on Kerr. If his plan works Kerr will become pregnant by her lover, Michell, allowing Niven to sue for divorce. But the pills get mixed up again by the maid, who puts vitamins in the place of the aspirin, though in reality these tablets also turn out to be birth control pills. Because the maid has made this mistake, she winds up pregnant—with Niven realizing the mistake and substituting aspirin again. Niece Geeson has exhausted her supply of birth control pills, and winds up becoming pregnant as well. Eventually Kerr does become pregnant, but because Niven's mistress has run off on him, he decides he doesn't want to go through with the divorce, but it comes to pass anyway. In the end, however, everyone winds up with the proper match. The excellent cast make their characters complex and interesting, providing for some good comic situations. But the entire plot does not hold up. The original director Cook, after being well into the project, developed "differences of opinion" with the producers, resulting in his quitting the picture, which was taken over by Ronald Neame, who maintained the tone and style begun by Cook.

bp, Kenneth Harper, Ronald Kahn; d, Fielder Cook, Ronald Neame; w, Hugh Mills (from the novel by Mills); ph, Ted Moore (DeLuxe Color); m, Bernard Ebbinghouse; ed, Norman Savage; prod d, Wilfrid Shingleton; md, Ebbinghouse; art d, Fred Carter; set d, John Jarvis; cos, Julie Harris, John Marks; m/l, "The Pill," "Too Soon To Tell You" Ebbinghouse.

Comedy   **(PR:O MPAA:R)**

PSYCHE 59*½   (1964, Brit.) 94m Troy-Schenck/COL-Royal bw

Patricia Neal (Allison Crawford), Curt Jurgens (Eric Crawford), Samantha Eggar (Robin), Ian Bannen (Paul), Beatrix Lehmann (Mrs. Crawford), Elspeth March (Mme. Valadier), Sandra Lee (Susan), Shelley Crowhurst (Jean), Peter Porteous, Gladys Spencer, Michael McStay.

Neal plays the blind wife of industrialist Jurgens. Her blindness is a result of an injury she suffered during a fall five years earlier, but really seems to be a psychosomatic response to an affair between Jurgens and her sister, Eggar. When Eggar returns to London, staying with her sister, she and Jurgens start their affair again, despite Jurgens' discomfort with the situation. Neal's eyesight slowly begins to return, and when she catches Jurgens and Eggar embracing, she admits to the initial causes of her blindness. Though the direction is well paced, with the art direction and music providing the necessary atmosphere, the story development is too confusing and the characters too complex to allow for an accurate comprehension of the plot.

p, Phillip Hazelton; d, Alexander Singer; w, Julian Halevy (based on the novel by Francoise des Ligneris); ph, Walter Lassally; m, Kenneth V. Jones; ed, Max Benedict; md, Jones; art d, John Stoll; set d, Josie MacAvin; cos, Julie Harris; makeup, Harold Fletcher.

Drama   **(PR:C MPAA:NR)**

PSYCHIC, THE* (1979, Ital.) 90m Group I c (SEITE NOTE IN NERO)

Jennifer O'Neill, Marc Porel, Evelyn Stewart, Jenny Tamburi, Gabriele Ferzetti, Gianni Garko.

Dull attempt at a murder mystery has O'Neill having strange visions of a murder being committed. She should have kept this vision to herself.

p, Fulvio Frizzi; d, Lucio Fulci; w, Fulci, Roberto Gianuiti, Dardano Sarchetti; ph, Sergio Salvati (Deluxe Color); m, Fabio Frizzi.

Horror/Mystery (PR:O MPAA:R)

PSYCHIC KILLER*½ (1975) 90m AE c

Jim Hutton *(Arnold)*, Julie Adams *(Laura, Psychiatrist)*, Paul Burke *(Detective Morgan)*, Nehemiah Persoff *(Dr. Gubner)*, Aldo Ray *(Anderson, Morgan's Assistant)*, Neville Brand *(Lemonowski, Butcher)*, Della Reese *(Mrs. Gibson)*, Rod Cameron *(Dr. Commanger)*, Joe Della Sorte *(Sanders)*, Harry Holcombe *(Judge)*, Robyn Raymond *(Jury Foreman)*, Jerry James *(Dead Doctor)*, Diane Deininger *(Arnold's Mother)*, John Dennis *(Frank)*, Judith Brown *(Anne)*, Mary Wilcox *(Martha)*, Bill Quinn *(Coroner)*, Marland Proctor *(Motorcycle Cop)*, Bill Bonner *(Ambulance Driver)*, Walter Miles *(Coroner)*, Whit Bissell *(Dr. Taylor)*, Stack Pierce *(Emilio)*, Ed Cross *(Old Man)*, Mello Alexandria *(Cop)*, Sheldon Lee *(Inmate)*, Greydon Clark *(Sowash)*.

Hutton plays a man wrongly placed inside a mental institution. Another inmate teaches him the secrets of astral projection, so that upon Hutton's release, he goes about getting his revenge against those people who had him committed. His psychic powers allow him to gruesomely murder his victims without ever leaving his apartment. Direct references to Alfred Hitchcock are overly blatant, with the lead character, Hutton, having a mother complex similar to that of PSYCHO's Anthony Perkins. Overall this film lacks the psychological depth of Hitchcock, concentrating more on gruesome violence and shock effects.

p, Mardi Rustam; d, Raymond Danton; w, Greydon Clark, Mike Angel, Danton; ph, Herb Pearl (Eastmancolor); m, William Kraft; ed, Mike Brown; art d, Joel Leonard.

Horror (PR:O MPAA:PG)

PSYCHIC LOVER, THE (SEE: SWEET SMELL OF LOVE, 1969, Ital./W. Ger.)

PSYCHO*** ** (1960) 109m PAR bw

Anthony Perkins *(Norman Bates)*, Janet Leigh *(Marion Crane)*, Vera Miles *(Lila Crane)*, John Gavin *(Sam Loomis)*, Martin Balsam *(Milton Arbogast)*, John McIntire *(Sheriff Chambers)*, Lurene Tuttle *(Mrs. Chambers)*, Simon Oakland *(Dr. Richmond)*, Frank Albertson *(Tom Cassidy)*, Patricia Hitchcock *(Caroline)*, Vaughn Taylor *(George Lowery)*, John Anderson *(California Charlie, the Car Salesman)*, Mort Mills *(Policeman)*, Francis De Sales *(District Attorney)*, George Eldridge *(Chief of Police)*, Sam Flint *(Official)*, Helen Wallace *(Woman Customer)*, Ted Knight *(Police Guard)*, Alfred Hitchcock *(Man Outside Office in Cowboy Hat)*, Frank Killmond *(Bob Summerfield)*, Virginia Gregg *(Mother's Voice)*, Ann Dore *(Perkins' Double in Shower Scene)*, Marli Renfro *(Leigh's Double in Shower Scene)*.

Perhaps no other film changed so drastically Hollywood's perception of the horror film as did PSYCHO and broke almost all the existing taboos at the same time. More surprising is the fact that this still unnerving horror classic was directed by Alfred Hitchcock, a stellar director who never played to shock values until this film. Hitchcock indulged in nudity, bloodbaths, theft, necrophilia, transvestism, murder, schizophrenia, and a host of other no-no's and got away with it, simply because he was Hitchcock. He further clouded his intent and motives by later stating that the entire film was nothing more than one huge joke. But no one laughed, only cringed in their seats and waited squinty-eyed for the next assault on their senses which would all come, year after bloodletting year, because of this watershed picture. Hitchcock opens PSYCHO in his traditional manner of involving the viewer immediately with his players and his snaky plot, the camera panning the skyline of Phoenix, Arizona, and then focusing on one building, zeroing down to one hotel window and going through the window to show Leigh in bra and slip, reclining sensuously on a bed, her lover Gavin standing over her. From the onset of their conversation we quickly realize that they are having an adulterous affair, a cheap and tawdry tryst where Gavin is not only married but too poor to get a divorce. (The approach is unorthodox for the director who makes the viewer a little uncomfortable in that the technique of showing the scene as a peep show makes the viewer part voyeur.) The unhappy Leigh returns to her real estate office where Taylor, her boss, agrees to hold a large amount of cash, $40,000, given to him by a rich client, the loud-talking Albertson. In a moment of weakness, Leigh steals the money and decides to make a new life for herself. She pays cash for a new car but her nervous behavior draws the attention of a state traffic cop who follows her and, when catching her asleep in the car, warns her not to sleep along the roadside. Leigh drives and drives through the night until she is exhausted and begins looking for a place to lay her pretty blonde head. She spots a sign reading "Bates Motel" and pulls in, meeting Perkins, a jittery young man who gives her a room next to his office. Perkins makes a sandwich for Leigh and she munches on it while they talk. The sensitive young man makes her realize her error and, after he leaves, she resolves to return the money and set matters straight. Sliding back a picture on the wall when returning to his office, Perkins peeps through a hole to watch Leigh undress (more voyeurism) and slip on a robe. He then nervously recovers the peephole, steps outside, and looks furtively up the hill to a bleakly outlined Victorian house, then goes up the long steps to the house. The camera stays outside and the shrill voice of an elderly woman is heard upbraiding Perkins for renting a room to a young woman. It is clear that the woman's voice belongs to Perkins' mother, and that she is insanely jealous of her son. Hitchcock's camera now explores the bathroom where Leigh is taking a shower, showing her naked (neck up) as the invigorating water dashes against her flesh. Through the shower curtain inside the tub a shadow is seen approaching and suddenly the curtain is swept aside, a dark figure in a granny dress holding high a wicked bread knife. Leigh screams and screams as the knife descends again and again, piercing her flesh, slashing her so that her blood gushes forth. The killer vanishes and Leigh collapses half over the tub, clutching the shower curtain, its clamps breaking off, the curtain falling with Leigh's collapsing body, her head smashing onto the bathroom floor. The camera closes in to the drain down which Leigh's blood swirls, then dissolves in to one of her staring dead eyes. (Hitchcock's inventiveness in the shower is present when he shows the spray coming directly out of the shower nozzle, the jets of water actually encompassing the camera but sweeping all around it, with no water striking the lens, as if Leigh is looking directly into the nozzle. What the director did here was order a huge shower nozzle made, one several feet in circumference, and then move his camera in for a closeup.) This filmic slaying is long, terrifying, and gory. Through lightning editing of Leigh, closeups of the knife striking her body—she is stabbed *at least* a dozen times—and penetrating the flesh, or it seems to pierce the flesh, Hitchcock provides for the first time in film the bloody realities of violent murder, breaking several taboos while doing it. He earlier shows a toilet and Leigh flushing down some scraps of incriminating paper. Toilets were long a taboo in films and were never shown, let alone while in action. Leigh's death is shortly discovered by a horrified Perkins who screams out in agony against what his mother has done. He methodically wraps the body in the shower curtain, drags it to the trunk of Leigh's car, then mops up the bathroom and cleans up the room. Perkins then drives the car to a nearby swamp and sends it gurgling to the quicksand bottom. When Leigh does not show up, her sister, Miles, goes to Gavin and begs him to look for her. He agrees but before he can begin his search, private detective Balsam appears and explains that he, too, has been looking for Leigh, that he has been hired by Taylor to recover the missing $40,000. Balsam follows Leigh's trail to the Bates Motel where his inquiries upset Perkins who disappears into the mansion at the top of the hill. Balsam checks the register in his absence even though Perkins has told him that Leigh has never stopped there. He finds evidence to the contrary and then goes up the hill to the old house. Once inside, he calls out and gets no response. He begins to climb a long, straight stairway and, just as he reaches the top, the camera shows, from a high angle, a lean, old woman racing from the bedroom with a bread knife, stabbing Balsam again and again so that he falls backward down the stairs, the camera seeming to fall with him in a fast zoom. Balsam is dead when he hits the floor below while Perkins' voice screams out in terror at what his mother has done, another murder, and now we realize that it was the old lady who killed Leigh. Not hearing from Balsam, Miles and Gavin drive to the area of the Bates Motel and meet with the local sheriff McIntire who tells them that Mrs. Bates, Perkins' strange mother, has been dead for eight years and has long since been buried. Gavin and Miles next go to the motel and, while Gavin occupies Perkins, Miles sneaks up to the mansion on the hill, enters it, and begins to investigate, going from room to room. She finds Mrs. Bates' bedroom, noting the hollowed-out spot on the bed where she apparently sleeps, and the ornate fixtures and dresser top items, one being a powder jar with weird black ivory hands crossed over its top. She goes downstairs, then runs to the basement when she hears footsteps approaching the house. It's Perkins. He has hit Gavin over the head when becoming suspicious of the stranger and raced to the house. In the basement, Miles enters a room to see a figure in a chair, the gray hair of an old lady piled high on the head, her back turned to her. Miles calls out to the old lady but she does not respond. She steps forward under a low-hanging lamp with a glaring naked light bulb and reaches out, swiveling the chair in which the old lady sits. The chair turns around slowly to reveal not a live woman but a sunken-faced, molding cadaver, years old with two black hollow sockets instead of eyes, and a glaring jawbone and teeth. Miles reels back in horror, shrieking, knocking the lamp so that it swings wildly, casting changing shafts of light upon the seemingly grinning corpse. Behind her in a rush appears another woman, bread knife drawn, quickly approaching Miles for the kill, but Gavin also appears and leaps upon the attacker, pulling away the knife and a wig to reveal Perkins, dressed like his mother, killing in the name and image of his mother. Later, psychiatrist Oakland tries to explain it all to Miles, Gavin, and others, telling them that Perkins had never been the same after his mother and her lover were murdered in front of his eyes and he was turned into a schizoid personality with many people living in him, his mother dominating, killing in revenge for her own fate. Oakland also explains that Perkins dug up the old corpse and kept it near him to maintain the illusion that she was truly still alive and he could therefore transfer his own guilt for his many murders on to her. The homicidal lunatic is shown sitting in a padded cell, wearing a strait jacket, as Hitchcock closes the camera slowly in on him, Perkins talking in voice-over as if speaking his mind, saying that he will do nothing to betray himself, that even the fly buzzing about him is safe, that he will not even harm the fly to prove to his guards that he can be trusted, that he is safe, that he is gentle. A closeup of his face dissolves quickly into the skull of his mother and a shot showing Leigh's car being pulled from the swamp by chains as the credits roll up. PSYCHO, based upon the necrophiliac Wisconsin killer, Ed Gein (drawn from real life by author Bloch), is probably Hitchcock's most gruesome and unrelenting dark film, one which touched off the spate of gore movies that blotch and stain our screens to this day, certainly inspiring such less imaginative directors as Sam Peckinpah to explode myriad blood blisters in every frame of THE WILD BUNCH. Enhancing the sustained fright of this film is not only an excellent cast from which the director draws maximum portrayals, but Herrmann's chilling score (for which the composer received $17, 500), especially the composer's so-called "murder music" which is little more than high-screeching sounds similar to birds wailing in rapid beats that flash as quickly as the killer's deadly knife. Herrmann achieved this with a bevy of violinists sawing frantically the same notes over and over again. (PSYCHO is the only film with a score played by an orchestra employing only strings.) Hitchcock really shocked Paramount when he demanded that he film Bloch's sleazy, sensational novel. The departure was vast from Hitchcock's norm of refined types and sophisticated homicide. But the director kept after the studio's front office until executives relented. He was told, however, that he would have to shoot the film on an extremely limited budget, no more than $800,000. Surprisingly, Hitchcock accepted the budget and went ahead with the film, utilizing TV technical people who were less expensive than Hollywood crews. Moreover, the director realized that Paramount expected this to be his first financial failure and went to the studio bosses, proposing that he finance the film with his own money in return for 60 per cent of the profits. Paramount, the director said, would only be the distributor of the film. The studio, feeling relieved that its own coffers were secure, accepted with alacrity. But even Hitchcock's close associates refused to believe that he was making a wise decision. His long-time associate producer Joan Harrison refused to take points in this film, opting for a direct salary and telling him, "You're on your own on this one, Hitch." Writer James Cavanaugh was brought in to work up a script from the Bloch novel but when he delivered it, Hitchcock read it and condemned it. Next, the director, at the urging of MCA, met briefly with writer Stefano, who had only one screenplay credit, for THE BLACK ORCHID, a less-than-inspiring film with top-heavy Sophia Loren and Perkins. (Stefano would later go on to produce "The Outer Limits" for TV.) Though he had expressed doubts about Stefano, Hitchcock changed his mind after meeting the writer and gave him the green light. It was Stefano, the writer later claimed, who told Hitchcock that he could not work up much sympathy for a peeping Tom killer in his forties as Bloch had portrayed him in the novel. Stefano changed his mind, however, when Hitchcock proposed using a killer who was much younger and even suggested to the writer that Perkins get the lead role. "Now you're talking," Stefano was quoted as telling Hitchcock. (Perkins had portrayed the psychotic, venal lead character across from Sophia Loren's slatternly wife character in THE BLACK ORCHID.) When Hitchcock did go into production he was told that he would have to use the facilities at Revue Studios, the TV division of Universal Studios which Paramount had rented for the making of PSYCHO. He was given mostly TV technicians, even TV cinematographer Russell instead of his long-standing cameraman, Robert Burks. Hitchcock managed to convince Paramount that his special editor, George Tomasini, should be included in the production. The director's penchant for detail was in full force here. He insisted that Stefano and others scout Route 99 and inspect motels, how they operated, who stopped at them, who ran them. He didn't like the idea of a handsome, pleasant cop stopping Leigh at the beginning of the film. Hitchcock insisted that the cop appear menacing so he selected tall and heavyset Mills, covering his eyes with wide, dark sunglasses. (Hitchcock had always had a fear of policemen; when he was a child he was taken to a police station by his stern merchant father who, to show him what might happen to him if he ever got in trouble, had him locked in a cell for several hours. Hitchcock had an abnormal fear of policemen since that time, so much so that he refused to learn how to drive a car in case he might be stopped by the very type of traffic cop he portrayed in PSYCHO.) The motel was put together on the Universal back lot and was definitely on the seedy side, with a scaled-down Victorian mansion built on a little hill behind the motel. The mansion cost only $15,000 to construct and technicians cannibalized several other stock buildings on the lot to keep the costs down, throwing onto the structure a tower which had been part of Elwood P. Dowd's (James Stewart) home in HARVEY, 1948. Perkins, then only 27, was hired without the actor even reading the script. The then rising young actor owed Paramount one film under his contract and was taken aboard because Hitchcock thought him right for the neurotic Norman Bates role, and because he would cost little. The role of the female lead was a problem. Hitchcock screened films of Shirley Jones but she was out of the range of his limited budget. He selected Leigh who was more of a starlet up to that time than a ranking actress, although this part would put her into superstardom status. The original name of the victim in the novel was Mary Crane but since the locale of the film was Phoenix, and Hitchcock's researchers had found a real Mary Crane living there, Hitchcock, to avoid lawsuits, changed Leigh's name to "Marion Crane." Leigh received a copy of the Bloch novel before shooting but the director wrote a note to her pointing out that the female victim, who is almost incidental in the novel, would have much more importance in the film. Actually, Hitchcock was about to break another barrier by having Leigh on screen only 45 minutes until the time she is slashed to pieces. This required the viewer to switch focus to Perkins and, again, Hitchcock was able to achieve a convincing transference of attention by showing Perkins to be sensitive and oddly compelling, having the audience believe that it was the unseen, berserk mother who was the culprit. To protect the idea of the mother being real, the clever Hitchcock announced to the press that he was "considering" Helen Hayes or Judith Anderson to play the role of the mother. This little ploy to sidetrack viewers for the forthcoming surprise ending (and this again is untypically Hitchcock in that he always let the viewer know the plot from the beginning and avoided surprise endings) backfired somewhat when Hitchcock was deluged with wires and letters from actresses asking to be considered for the role of the mother. (Originally, the concept for the horrific cadaver was nothing more than a large plastic doll with glass eyes, but Hitchcock changed that quickly enough with his own design of the sunken-faced ancient and ossified corpse.) Leigh quickly became one of Hitchcock's favorite actresses by taking his off-color jokes and pranks good-naturedly. Some of the director's little jokes would have caused apoplexy in an actress less perky than Leigh. Once the cadaver was created, Hitchcock had it placed first in Leigh's dressing room so that when she entered and turned on the light the corpse sat grinning at her, causing the actress to let out piercing screams louder and more frightening than those she shrieked in her shower scene. Hitchcock let Leigh have her head in the acting department, telling her: "I'm not going to direct every nuance. But if you don't come up with what I need I'll bring it out of you. And if you give too much I'll tone it down. What you do has to fit into my framework and within my camera angle...But as long as your concept of her [Marion's character] doesn't interfere with what I need from her, do whatever you want." The actress would later state that Hitchcock was "very cool," meaning that no problems seemed to bother him. When it came to the famous (or infamous as the case may be) shower scene, Hitchcock not only approved of every little detail in the scene, from toilet to shower nozzle, but enacted every move the killer and victim Leigh were to make. He even enacted for Perkins how he was to wrap the body in the shower curtain, showing him how to fold the plastic over the body, and pick it up. Perkins, ironically enough, was not present when Leigh was murdered in the shower. He later commented: "Not many people know this, but I was in New York rehearsing for a play when the shower scene was filmed in Hollywood. It is rather strange to go through life being identified with this sequence knowing that it was my double. Actually the first time I saw PSYCHO and that shower scene was at the studio. I found it really scary. I was just as frightened as anybody else. Working on the picture, though, was one of the happiest filming experiences of my life. We had fun making it—never realizing the impact it would have." It was Hitchcock who specifically ordered this murder shown as a brutal thing, scribbling in his own hand for shot 116: "The slashing. An impression of a knife slashing, as if tearing at the very screen, ripping the film." The knife wielded by the killer appears to enter Leigh's abdomen and this was achieved by a fast-motion reverse shot, according to one authority. Leigh later claimed that for the shower murder "we used a stand-in for that scene as it happens." But in her autobiography, *There Really Was a Hollywood*, she stated that she indeed did perform the shower scene herself but that a stand-in was used for the corpse wrapped in plastic on the bathroom floor. Leigh was concerned about displaying her amply-endowed bosom, even before a few technicians in a closed set. She and aides researched various transparent garments worn by strippers in burlesque magazines but did not come up with anything that would work. A technician finally had the answer by providing a flesh-colored moleskin. But this backfired under the hot water from the shower. Leigh stated, "I felt something strange happening around my breasts. The steam from the hot water had melted the adhesive on the moleskin and I sensed the napped cotten fabric peeling away from my skin. What to do?...To spoil the so far successful shot and be modest? Or get it over with and be immodest. I opted for immodesty...that was the printed take, and no one noticed my bareness before I could cover it up. I think!" Even though the film was shot in a frenzied schedule of a little over a month, Hitchcock doted on the important scenes, taking a full week to shoot the shower scene. On a tower above the set, Hitchcock stood directing with a single cameraman. He had abandoned the use of Technicolor so as not to make the film more gory than it already was and employed chocolate sauce to wash down the drain as if it was Leigh's blood. A makeup man walked onto the set and looked about and then asked Hitchcock: "Isn't this color?" Replied Hitchcock: "My dear boy, it will have so much more impact in black and white." Gavin, the male lead, has less impact than the film process. Later to become Ambassador to Mexico, Gavin was never Hitchcock's top choice for the impoverished lover turned detective. Gavin was a contract player at Universal and that studio, doing business by renting its lot to Paramount, tried to force Gavin upon Hitchcock. That director wanted anybody but and considered Stuart Whitman, Tom Tryon, Brian Keith, Cliff Robertson, Tom Laughlin, Jack Lord, Robert Loggia (who would have a part in PSYCHO II), and Rod Taylor (who would star in Hitchcock's THE BIRDS.) In the end, Hitchcock gave in to pressure from Universal to take Gavin for a less than pivotal role, saying lamely, "I guess he'll be all right." Unlike any other film he made, Hitchcock, since he owned 60 per cent of the profits, turned promotion-minded, devising the entire publicity campaign for his gruesome masterpiece, insisting that no theatergoer be seated during the showing of the film, only before PSYCHO began, demanding that even the critics see the film with the audiences from the beginning, which alienated many a reviewer who lambasted him with such words as "cruel," "sadistic," and even "pornographic." The director's response was to say that he had fun with the film. In an interview with French director Francois Truffaut, Hitchcock stated that "it was rather exciting to use the camera to deceive the audiences...The game with the audience was fascinating. I was directing the viewers. You might say I was playing them like an organ...I didn't start off to make an important movie. I thought I could have fun with this subject and this situation...My main satisfaction is that the film had an effect on the audience...I feel it's tremendously satisfying for us to be able to use the cinematic art to achieve something of a mass emotion. And with PSYCHO we most definitely achieved this. It wasn't a message that stirred the audiences, nor was it a great performance or their enjoyment of the novel. They were aroused by pure film. That's why I take pride in the fact that PSYCHO, more than any of my other pictures, is a film that belongs to filmmakers." This was no news to Hitchcock adherents. As early as 1947 he had stated in a press conference his philosophy of the mystery-horror genre he was to master and, in the horror department to come with PSYCHO, excel. Said Hitchcock then: "I am to provide the public with beneficial shocks. Civilization has become so protective that we're no longer able to get our goose bumps instinctively. The only way to remove the numbness and revive our moral equilibrium is to use artificial means to bring about the shock. The best way to achieve that, it seems to me, is through a movie." *This*movie provided shocks heard 'round the world and became an instant smash. Certainly the queues of people lining around blocks at most theaters showing PSYCHO, all following Hitchcock's dictates not to allow anyone inside until the beginning of the film, caused so much attention for the film that everyone *had* to see it. In its initial release PSYCHO broke all records, gleaning $16 million, the first quarter alone earning for the director $2.5 million as his share of the profits. He had the horse-laugh on Paramount executives who wanted no part of PSYCHO from the beginning. The film became Paramount's third largest grossing picture and it made Hitchcock not only a master of the modern horror film but fabulously wealthy. He had outwitted everyone—the industry, the audience, and the critics.

p&d, Alfred Hitchcock; w, Joseph Stefano (based on the novel by Robert Bloch); ph, John L. Russell; m, Bernard Herrmann; ed, George Tomasini; prod d, Joseph Hurley, Robert Clatworthy; set d, George Milo; cos, Helen Colvig; spec eff, Clarence Champagne.

Horror **Cas.** **(PR:O MPAA:NR)**

PSYCHO A GO-GO!* (1965) 85m Tal/Hemisphere-American General bw (AKA: BLOOD OF GHASTLY HORROR; THE FIEND WITH THE ELECTRIC BRAIN; MAN WITH THE SYNTHETIC BRAIN)

Roy Morton *(Joe Corey)*, Tacey Robbins *(Linda Clarke)*, Kirk Duncan *(David Clarke)*, John Talbert *(Curtis)*, K.K. Riddle *(Nancy Clarke)*, Tanya Maree *(Vicky)*,

John Armond (*Nicky*), Lyle Felice (*Vito*), Joey Benson (*Lt. Ward*), Shary Richards (*Mrs. Ward*), John Carradine (*Dr. Vanard*), The Vendells.

When a gang of jewel thieves plant their stolen merchandise on Duncan's pickup truck, but can't find it when they come to make their claim, they send crazed Vietnam veteran Morton to harass Duncan. Morton has a device implanted in his brain by Carradine, which accounts for his insanity. He abducts the wife and child of Duncan, and Duncan pursues him. The jewels turn up in the doll of Duncan's daughter, who found them in the truck in the first place. Additional footage was shot the following year with Carradine, and the picture was rereleased as THE FIEND WITH THE ELECTRONIC BRAIN. Unbelievably, more footage and characters were added for a 1971 release under the title BLOOD OF GHASTLY HORROR.

p&d, Al Adamson; w, Chris Martino, Mark Eden (based on a story by Adamson); ph, Vilmos Zsigmund (Techniscope/Technicolor); m/l, Don McGinnis, Billy Storm (performed by The Vendells).

Horror   **(PR:O MPAA:NR)**

PSYCHO-CIRCUS** (1967, Brit.) 65m Circus/AIP bw (GB: CIRCUS OF FEAR)

Christopher Lee (*Gregor, Lion Tamer*), Leo Genn (*Inspector Elliott*), Anthony Newlands (*Barberini*), Heinz Drache (*Carl, Ringmaster*), Eddi Arent (*Eddie*), Klaus Kinski (*Manfred*), Margaret Lee (*Gina*), Suzy Kendall (*Natasha*), Cecil Parker (*Sir John*), Victor Maddern (*Mason*), Maurice Kaufmann (*Mario*), Lawrence James (*Manley*), Tom Bowman (*Jackson*), Skip Martin (*Mr. Big*), Fred Powell (*Red*), Gordon Petrie (*Negro*), Henry Longhurst (*Hotel Porter*), Dennis Blakely (*Armored Van Guard*), George Fisher (*4th Man*), Peter Brace, Roy Scammel (*Speedboat Men*), Geoff Silk, Keith Peacock (*Security Men*).

An armored car is held up and its stolen bank notes turn up at a circus. Genn, a Scotland Yard investigator, is sent out to solve the case. The corpse of one of the robbers turns up and soon a circus performer (Margaret Lee) is dead as well. The chief suspects are Christopher Lee, a lion tamer who wears a hideous black mask to cover his scarred face; Drache, a ringmaster who is convinced his father was killed by Lee's twin brother; Kaufmann, a knife thrower driven crazy with jealousy over the dead Margaret Lee's other suitors; and a dwarf (Martin) known as "Mr. Big" who is blackmailing Lee. Other prospects include Arent, a bookkeeper who is a frustrated would-be circus performer and Kendall, Lee's niece and the daughter of the man Drache wants. Lee is found to have the missing money hidden in a suitcase. He tries to get away but is murdered by a mysterious masked figure. After his death numerous secrets are revealed. It seems that he was actually Kendall's father and that Drache's father died in an accidental fall rather than being murdered. However, Genn still thinks Lee was innocent of the murders despite the loot found on him. He arranges for Arent to assist Kaufmann in the knife throwing act. Kaufmann switches his knives, using ones resembling those used in the murder. This causes the bookkeeper to break down, admitting to the murders. He was driven by his jealousy of circus performers to kill the stars. The plot is fairly confusing, occasionally getting out of control with the different complications. Genn and Lee are good in their roles, but otherwise this is a fairly routine murder mystery without much to offer. It was released in black-and-white prints in the U.S. despite being filmed and released as a color film in Britain. The film was simultaneously shot with a German language version, under the helmsmanship of another director.

p, Harry Alan Towers; d, John Moxey; w, Peter Welbeck [Towers](based on a story by Edgar Wallace); ph, Ernest Steward (Eastmancolor); m, Johnny Douglas; ed, John Trumper; art d, Frank White; makeup, Frank Turner.

Crime   **(PR:O MPAA:NR)**

PSYCHO FROM TEXAS zero (1982) 89m Super-Pix/New American c

John King III (*Wheeler*), Herschell Mays (*William Phillips*), Tommy Lamey (*Slick*), Candy Dee (*Connie Phillips*), Janel King (*Ellen*), Juanne Bruno (*Bertha*), Reed Johnson (*Steve*), Jack Collins (*Sheriff*), Christian Feazell (*Young Wheeler*). This cheapie from Louisiana represents just about everything that's wrong with the low-budget films of the American South. King plays a stranger in town who teams up with Lamey, a local outcast. Together they kidnap a wealthy, retired oilman (Mays) and hold him for ransom. Parallel with this is a flashback story dealing with King's childhood. It shows him as a boy (played by Feazell, the director's son), being beaten by his cruel mother, thus excusing his adult behavior as a knife wielding rapist-kidnaper. The film is crudely shot and the flashbacks are amateurishly grafted onto the story. The whole thing is fairly inane, with little attention paid to continuity or plot development. The acting is as bad as can be, further hampered by southern accents that are thick as molasses. Worst of all are the racist values, as blacks are shown in subservient, 1930s stereotyped positions. The film was shot in 1974 and went through various title changes (including WHEELER, THE MAMA'S BOY, and THE HURTING) before settling on its more exploitable title and finally seeing release some eight years after completion.

p,d&w, Jim Feazell; ph, Paul Hipp (Movielab Color); m, Jaime Mendoza-Nava; ed, Arjay; makeup, Dennis March.

Action   **Cas.**   **(PR:O MPAA:R)**

PSYCHO KILLERS   (SEE: MANIA, 1961, Brit.)

PSYCHO II**½**   (1983) 113m UNIV-Oak/UNIV c

Anthony Perkins (*Norman Bates*), Vera Miles (*Lila Loomis*), Meg Tilly (*Mary*), Robert Loggia (*Dr. Raymond*), Dennis Franz (*Toomey*), Hugh Gillin (*Sheriff Hunt*), Claudia Bryar (*Mrs. Spool*), Robert Alan Browne (*Statler*), Ben Hartigan (*Judge*), Lee Garlington (*Myrna*), Tim Maier (*Josh*), Jill Carroll (*Kim*), Chris Hendrie (*Deputy Pool*), Tom Holland (*Deputy Norris*), Michael Lomazow (*District Attorney*), Robert Destri (*Public Defender*), Osgood Perkins (*Young Norman*), Ben Frommer (*Sexton*), Gene Whittington (*Diver*), Robert Traynor (*Desk Clerk*),

George Dickerson (*County Sheriff*), Thaddeus Smith (*Deputy Sheriff*), Sheila K. Adams (*Deputy Woman*), Victoria Brown (*Deputy Clerk*).

It should come as no surprise that someone should decide to film a sequel to Alfred Hitchcock's classic. What *is* a surprise is that it is as good as it is. The film opens in black and white with the classic shower scene from the original (thereby eliminating any fear that the sequel will try to duplicate that scene), although a mortal sin is committed by tampering with the editing and cutting out the *dissolve* from the bloody drain to Janet Leigh's eye. The film then dissolves into color for Norman Bates' return home. Reprising his familiar role is Perkins who, after 22 years in an asylum, is released and allowed to return home. Loudly objecting to this decision is Miles (reprising her role as Lila Crane, though she has since married and become Lila Loomis), who produces a petition to keep Perkins locked up for killing her sister (Janet Leigh in the original). Miles vows to avenge her sister's death and to get Perkins returned to the asylum. Accompanied by psychiatrist Loggia, Perkins returns home to the Bates Motel and that eerie house where he once lived with "mother." Although Perkins appears frightened when he sees the house, he finally seems to be in control of his other self. Before leaving, Loggia gets Perkins settled and finds him a job at a local diner. During his first day at work, Perkins meets Tilly, a cute but spacy waitress who seems completely ignorant of the horrors that occurred 22 years before. After an argument with her boy friend, Tilly accepts Perkins' invitation to spend the evening in one of the motel's vacant rooms. Perkins is shocked to find that the motel, run by the slimy Franz, has been turned into an "adult" motel. He fires Franz and insists that Tilly stay in the house. Tilly becomes uneasy and confesses to Perkins that she knows about his past. She prepares to leave, but when Perkins expresses his need to have her stay—it is his first night in the house and he is just as scared as she—she agrees. Tilly survives the night without incident and even agrees to stay until she can find somewhere else to move. The following morning at the diner Perkins and Franz have another confrontation as Franz taunts not only Perkins but Tilly as well. Perkins then finds a note, supposedly written by his mother, and snaps. He accuses Franz of playing a sick joke, but resists the temptation of going after him with a nearby cake knife. Later that evening, while cleaning out his office, Franz is stabbed to death by a woman who appears to be Mrs. Bates. Before Perkins can discover the body, the office is cleaned and the body dumped into the swamp. Perkins quits his job at the diner and devotes his energies to fixing up the motel. It's not long before Perkins begins seeing his mother standing in the window of the house. He also begins getting phone calls from "mother" and finding notes signed by her. Thinking that "mother" is somewhere in the house, Perkins ventures into the attic, where he is locked in by some unseen person. While Perkins is captive, a teenage boy and girl sneak into the cellar with sex and drugs on their agenda. A noise frightens the girl, sending her scurrying out the window. Her boy friend, however, is less lucky, falling victim to a knife-wielding old woman. Once again the murder site is cleaned before anyone can discover it. Tilly returns home to find Perkins in the attic, only now the door is unlocked. The town sheriff arrives to question Perkins about the boy's disappearance, but before blame can be placed on Perkins, Tilly rises to his defense with an alibi. Afterwards, Tilly goes into town where she meets with Miles, who turns out to be her mother. Together, Miles and Tilly have been plotting to drive Perkins crazy, but now Tilly has reconsidered. She is sympathetic to Perkins and is convinced that someone else murdered the boy. Miles, driven by blind vengeance, refuses to listen to her daughter. When Tilly refuses to aid her mother any longer, Miles takes over. She drives to the Bates house, followed by Loggia, who has discovered the plot. Miles enters the house via the cellar, intent on dressing in Mrs. Bates' garb and scaring Perkins back into insanity; once Perkins is visibly crazy, he will be recommitted. Before she can dress up, however, she is stabbed to death by an old woman. In the meantime, Tilly confesses the entire plot to Perkins, who by now is teetering on the edge of insanity. He admits that he knows Mrs. Bates is dead, but then goes on to explain that the person making the phone calls is his "real" mother. In order to shock Perkins back into sanity, Tilly dresses up as Mrs. Bates. Loggia, thinking that he has apprehended the culprit, frightens Tilly who accidentally stabs him. Perkins goes after Tilly, accusing her of the murders. Eventually the pair wind up in the cellar where Tilly discovers Miles' horrid corpse. Now convinced that Perkins is the killer, Tilly tries to kill him, but is shot to death by police who think they've killed the real murderer. After the dust has settled, Perkins sits alone in his kitchen. A knock comes at the door. It is an old woman, Bryar, who looks suspiciously like Mrs. Bates. She claims that she is Mrs. Spool, Perkins' real mother, and tells him that Mrs. Bates was her sister. Bryar explains that when she was committed to a mental institution many years ago, she handed Perkins over to her sister. Then, when she was released, she was angered to find all these people trying to drive Perkins crazy, and decided to stop them. In keeping with tradition, Perkins kills his mother by slamming a shovel down upon her head. While PSYCHO II could have resorted to cheap slasher techniques (a la FRIDAY THE 13TH and its offspring), it instead concentrates on developing the character of Norman Bates. He is a sympathetic soul who is fighting with all his might to overcome his past and live as a normal person. In PSYCHO II he is a victim of crazed people—Miles, Tilly initially, Bryar, and Franz—and as a result looks incredibly sane by comparison. Perkins only kills this time when driven to it. Unfortunately the end to PSYCHO II contradicts the entire feel of the film. The audience grows to admire Perkins. He overcomes difficulties and manages to keep calm in the face of those who taunt him. During the 22 years Perkins spent in an asylum, he became stronger and can now face the past. The end of the film, however, negates this and turns Perkins into a leering loon—even crazier than before—simply in preparation for another sequel. Perkins kills again, props "mother" up in her bedroom, and reverts right back to square one. (A sequel did indeed follow in 1986, PSYCHO III, which Perkins directed.) Based on the characters created by Robert Bloch, PSYCHO II doesn't follow the story line of Bloch's sequel (which was published around the time of the movie's release). Where Bloch had Bates murdering a nun and going crazy on the set of a movie about his exploits, Franklin's film takes a route which is much more faithful to the character created by Perkins in the original (which also strayed from Bloch's book). Perkins comments, "As I see him Norman would never kill a nun. Period. He just wouldn't. I think he would be able to tell the difference between a mother and a mother superior. I just don't think he would get the two things confused." Directed by Franklin, a fine Australian filmmaker whose ROAD GAMES (1981) is a superb suspenser, PSYCHO II was not only a labor of love but Franklin's first chance to helm an American movie. Defending Franklin and the inevitable comparisons to the original, Perkins stated, "I think Hitchcock would have enjoyed spending a day on the PSYCHO II set...He would have approved of Richard's on-set demeanor, efficiency, and humor. Richard brings to it a youthfulness and dignity that Hitchcock always brought to his films." Since PSYCHO II could only have been made with Perkins' cooperation, one can assume that this sequel was filmed only because Perkins firmly believed in the script. In addition to Perkins reprising his role, Miles also participated. The only other person to survive the massacre in the original (both Leigh and Martin Balsam were killed) was John Gavin, who declined a role because of his duties as U.S. ambassador to Mexico. Before Tom Holland's script was written, however, there was another PSYCHO sequel floating around Hollywood. Two writers—Gary Travis and Michael January—scripted "The Return of Norman," which was scheduled for production in 1982 by the Picture Striking Company with a $9 million budget. The cast was to have included Perkins (who was offered the directing chore as well), Miles, and Balsam, whose character would have come back from the grave to play Perkins' psychiatrist (an unbelievably stupid mistake which would have ruined the film). Bloch, however, had no involvement with the product, and neither did Universal Studios which owned the rights to the sequel. The legal department took action against the Picture Striking Company and discovered that not only were Travis and January not members of the Writers Guild but had never obtained rights to Bloch's copyrighted characters. Travis and January countered by saying their original script had nothing to do with PSYCHO and was merely about a woman living in a haunted motel. Universal won out, Franklin and Holland brought their version to the screen, and thankfully Balsam's character stayed in the grave. The result, while far inferior to Hitchcock, is still a chilling horror picture. Try to ignore the damning comparisons and be thankful that PSYCHO II shows respect to the Master of Suspense instead of merely cashing in on his legend.

p, Hilton A. Green; d, Richard Franklin; w, Tom Holland (based on characters created by Robert Bloch); ph, Dean Cundey (Technicolor); m, Jerry Goldsmith; ed, Andrew London; prod d, John W. Corso; set d, Jennifer Polito; cos, Robert E. Ellsworth, Brian O'Dowd, Marla Denise Schlom; spec eff, Syd Dutton, Albert Whitlock, Melbourne Arnold; makeup, Michael McCracken, Chuck Crafts.

Horror **Cas.** **(PR:O MPAA:R)**

PSYCHOMANIA*½ (1964) 90m Victoria-Emerson bw (AKA: VIOLENT MIDNIGHT)

Lee Philips *(Elliot Freeman)*, Shepperd Strudwick *(Adrian Benedict)*, Jean Hale *(Carol Bishop)*, Lorraine Rogers *(Alice St. Clair)*, Margot Hartman *(Lynn Freeman)*, Kaye Elhardt *(Dolores Martello)*, James Farentino *(Charlie Perone)*, Richard [Dick] Van Patten *(Palmer)*, Sheila Forbes *(Janet "Lolita" Terhune)*, Sylvia Miles *(Silvia)*, Day Tuttle *(Mr. Melbourne)*, Mike Keene *(Inspector Grey)*, Mike O'Dowd *(Max)*.

This cheap little horror flick, the first directorial effort from the screenwriter of THE HORROR OF PARTY BEACH, isn't bad for what it is. Filmed in Stanford, Connecticut, it tells the story of some murders at a girls' college. Philips is an artist who likes to work with nude models. When one of them is found dead, he's a prime suspect. The direction has its moments of imagination but is more often inept and sluggish. The camera work is better than one would expect. In 1964 this was considered quasi-porn for its nudity, but it is relatively mild by today's standards. Don't miss Farentino as a lawyer and "Richard" Van Patten playing a cop. The latter changed his first name to "Dick" and went on to star in TV's "Eight is Enough." His presence alone makes this worth a look for a good cheap laugh.

p, Del Tenney; d, Richard L. Hilliard; w, Robin Miller, Mann Rubin, Hilliard; ph, Louis McMahon; m, W.L. Holcombe; ed, Robert Q. Lovett.

Horror **(PR:O MPAA:NR)**

PSYCHOMANIA** (1974, Brit.) 91m Scotia International c (AKA: THE DEATH WHEELERS)

George Sanders, Beryl Reid, Nicky Henson, Mary Larkin, Roy Holder, Robert Hardy, Patrick Holt, Denis Gilmore.

Henson is the leader of a motorcycle gang who learns the secret of eternal life. He commits suicide, then rides out of the grave on his motorcycle. When the others see their reincarnated leader, they kill themselves and soon there is a plague of unstoppable bikers from the dead. Total trash but some fun. Sanders committed suicide shortly after performing in his embarrassing part here as a devil worshipper.

p, Andrew Donally; d, Don Sharp; w, Arnaud D'Usseau; ph, Ted Moore (Technicolor); m, David Whitaker.

Horror **Cas.** **(PR:O MPAA:PG)**

PSYCHOPATH, THE*** (1966, Brit.) 83m Amicus/PAR c

Patrick Wymark *(Inspector Holloway)*, Margaret Johnston *(Mrs. Von Sturm)*, John Standing *(Mark Von Sturm)*, Alexander Knox *(Frank Saville)*, Judy Huxtable *(Louise Saville)*, Don Borisenko *(Donald Loftis)*, Colin Gordon *(Dr. Glyn)*, Thorley Walters *(Martin Roth)*, Robert Crewdson *(Victor Ledoux)*, Tim Barrett *(Morgan)*, Frank Forsyth *(Tucker)*, Olive Gregg *(Mary)*, Harold Lang *(Briggs)*, John Harvey *(Reinhardt Klermer)*, Greta Farrer *(Cigarette Girl)*, Gina Gianelli, Peter Diamond.

When four men are found brutally murdered Wymark is assigned to the case. Each murder has an odd quirk: the victims are found with look-alike dolls lying next to the corpses. It is learned the four victims were members of a commission that convicted a German industrialist of using slave labor during WW II. After learning the dolls had been purchased by the man's widow (her husband having committed suicide upon his conviction) Wymark pays her a call. He meets the woman (Johnston), finding her an old lady confined to a wheelchair. Her room is filled with dolls with whom she speaks when her son is at work. The inspector goes to visit the son (Standing) at his job in a boathouse. Standing becomes nervous under questioning and finally turns violent, knocking out Wymark. Huxtable, the daughter of one of the victims, decides to take up the investigation herself. She visits the old lady and finds Standing's body propped up in a chair like a doll. Johnston gets up from her chair and begins walking towards the terrified young girl, but loses her balance, falling down a flight of stairs and killing herself. This is a nifty little shock film, full of surprises and some great production values. The script is by Bloch, author of the novel that inspired Hitchcock's film PSYCHO. That probably accounts for the title here and some of the motifs from Hitchcock's classic (such as the crippled mother and strange son) recur in this film. The direction is well laid out, with some good suspense leading up to the surprise ending. All the loose ends are tied up in the end as well, which is to the film's credit. Performances are a lot better than one might expect, with fine characterizations by the leads. Like PSYCHO's Norman Bates, Johnston's character is one of those people that confuses the audience. Do we fell sorry for her or hate her for her murderous ways? It's all well handled in a good piece of entertainment.

p, Max J. Rosenberg, Milton Subotsky; d, Freddie Francis; w, Robert Bloch, ph, John Wilcox (Techniscope, Technicolor); m, Elizabeth Lutyens, Philip Martell; ed, Oswald Hafenrichter; md, Martell; art d, Bill Constable; spec eff, Ted Samuels; makeup, Jill Carpenter.

Horror/Crime **(PR:O MPAA:NR)**

PSYCHOPATH, THE* (1973) 84m Brentwood c (AKA: AN EYE FOR AN EYE)

Tom Basham, Gene Carlson, Gretchen Kanne, Dave Carlile, Barbara Grover, Lance Larson, Jeff Rice, Pete Renoudet, Jackson Bostwick, John D. Ashton, Mary Rings, Margaret Avery, Sam Javis, Brenda Venus, Carol Ann Daniels, Bruce Kimball.

This strange little film may be the ultimate in kiddie fantasies. Basham plays the host of a children's show. He does the usual kid-vid stuff like puppet shows, riding a bike, and playing with some tykes in the park. But he's got a sideline to boot. When any of his beloved viewers are beaten or maltreated by mom and pop he comes 'round to knock off the naughty parents. His weapons include a baseball bat and lawnmower. Basham's performance is infantile and priceless. This is a classic example of bad filmmaking at its very best. In 1980 the film saw a re-release with all the murders strangely cut out. Even so, "Mister Roger's Neighborhood" was never quite like this.

p&d, Larry Brown; w, Brown, Walter C. Dallenbach; ph, Jack Beckett; m, Country Al Ross; ed, John Williams, Dennis Jakob.

Crime **(PR:O MPAA:PG)**

PSYCHOTRONIC MAN, THE* (1980) 90m International Harmony c

Peter Spelson *(Rocky Foscoe)*, Christopher Carbis *(Lt. Walter O'Brien)*, Curt Colbert *(Sgt. Chuck Jackson)*, Robin Newton *(Kathy)*, Paul Marvel *(Dr. Steinberg)*, Jeff Caliendo *(Officer Maloney)*, Lindsey Novak *(Mrs. Foscoe)*, Irwin Lewin *(Professor)*, Corney Morgan *(SIA Agent Gorman)*, Bob McDonald *(Old Man)*.

This is another entry in that category affectionately tagged by its fans as "so bad it's good." Spelson, who also produced and co-wrote this independently made Chicago feature, stars as a barber with a unique gift, so to speak. By looking at a victim and blinking, Spelson can induce instant death or compel the victim to jump out of windows. "Now Rocky," his psychiatrist tells him, "you've got to lay off the booze." The plot is as thin as can be, with amateur production values. A supposedly climactic high-speed chase along Chicago's Wacker Drive is actually filmed at high speed, giving it the look of a Mack Sennett two-reeler, rather than the dramatic conclusion intended. Spelson, who was an insurance agent when not making films, ultimately ends up with a film that's unintentionally funny. It was shot in just 17 days at a cost of $500,000.

p, Peter Spelson; d, Jack M. Sell; w, Spelson, Sell (based on a story by Spelson); ph, Sell (Astro Color Labs); m, Tommy Irons; ed, Bill Reese; art d, Fred Becht; spec eff, Bob Vanni.

Science Fiction **(PR:O MPAA:PG)**

PSYCH-OUT½** (1968) 88m Dick Clark/AIP c

Susan Strasberg *(Jennie Davis)*, Dean Stockwell *(Dave)*, Jack Nicholson *(Stoney)*, Bruce Dern *(Steve Davis)*, Adam Roarke *(Ben)*, Max Julien *(Elwood)*, Henry Jaglom *(Warren)*, Linda Gaye Scott *(Lynn)*, I. J. Jefferson *(Pandora)*, Tommy Flanders *(Wesley)*, Ken Scott *(Preacher)*, Garry Marshall *(Plainclothesman)*, Geoffrey Stevens *(Greg)*, Susan Bushman *(Little Girl)*, John Cardos *(Thug)*, Madgal Dean *(Mother)*, William Gerrity *(Little Boy)*, Robert Kelljan *(Arthur)*, Gary Kent *(Thugs' Leader)*, Beatriz Monteil *(Landlady)*, David Morick *(Stuntman)*, Barbara London *(Sadie)*, The Strawberry Alarm Clock, The Seeds.

This film is a must see. It's populated with so many names that would go on to far better projects that curiosity alone should attract viewers. In addition, it's not that bad of a film, perhaps indicating things to come from its cast and production staff. Strasberg plays a 17-year-old deaf girl who runs away to San Francisco's Haight-Ashbury district. She's looking for her older brother (Dern), an artist who's tuned in, turned on, and dropped out. In a coffee shop she encounters a failed rock band led by none other than Nicholson. He and his cohorts (Roarke and Julien) convince her to change from the "square" clothing she sports to something infinitely more hip, like a mini-skirt. Together with Nicholson's pal Stockwell, they begin the search for Dern. They have no luck but learn that a group of thugs are also looking for Dern. Nicholson's group plays at a local hangout. It turns out that Nicholson has run into Dern and talked him into showing up for the performance. He does but splits when he sees the thugs who want him. Strasberg goes into hysterics but is taken to Nicholson's flat by Stockwell. He gives her some STP to calm her down, but she leaves to continue the search. Strasberg is unaware she has taken a hallucinogen and ends up wandering around the traffic on the Golden Gate Bridge. Meanwhile, Dern has barricaded himself into a nearby house and set fire to the place. Nicholson and Stockwell come to Strasberg's rescue. However, Stockwell has also taken STP and is killed by a car as he walks about in a haze. Nicholson and Strasberg, thrown together by the circumstances and their contempt for the world of "squares," leave the scene. For the low-budget quickie this was intended as, it's really not bad at all. Direction by Rush (who would later do the highly acclaimed film THE STUNTMAN) gets inside the world of San Francisco's hippie culture, giving a fairly accurate portrait of the place and times. His use of overlap and creations of hallucinations are good without seeming the least bit forced. He shows all sides of the hippie world, the good and the bad. Be-ins, dope, and the foraging of food from garbage cans are all included with directness and a good realistic feel. The fine photography was by Kovacs, who would become one of Hollywood's top lensmen. The perfomances give every indication that Nicholson, Strasberg, and Dern would go on to better work. As "Stoney" Nicholson projects the right amount of humor and anger, something he would be known for in his later work as well. Also featured in the cast is Kelljan, the director of COUNT YORGA films. The single biggest detriment to the film is the "acid rock" played by such underground luminaries as The Seeds and the Strawberry Alarm Clock. Songs Include: "The Pretty Song" The Strawberry Alarm Clock (sung by The Storybook), "Rainy Day Mushroom Pillow" Steven Bartek, George Bunnell, Jr. (sung by The Strawberry Alarm Clock), "Two Fingers Pointing on You" Sky Saxon (sung by The Seeds), "Ashburny Wednesday" Rusty Young, Mitchell Mitchell, Joe E. Neddo, George Grantham, S. Bush (sung by Cryque Boenzee), "The World's on Fire" The Strawberry Alarm Clock (sung by The Strawberry Alarm Clock), "Psych-Out Sanctorum," "The Love Children," "Psych-Out" Ronald Stein (sung by The Storybook), "Beads of Innocence" Harlene Stein, Ronald Stein (sung by The Storybook), "Incense and Peppermints" John S. Carter, Jr., Tim Gilbert (sung by The Strawberry Alarm Clock).

p, Dick Clark; d, Richard Rush; w, E. Hunter Willett, Betty Ulius, Betty Tusher (story by Tusher, Willett); ph, Leslie [Lazlo] Kovacs (Pathecolor); m, Ronald Stein; ed, Ken Reynolds; art d, Leon Ericksen; set d, James Cotton; spec eff, Gary Kent; makeup, Rafaelle Patterson.

Drama   (PR:O MPAA:NR)

PSYCHOUT FOR MURDER   (1971, Arg./Ital.) 88m Chiara-Banco-
Glori Art/Times Film c (SALVARE LA FACCIA)

Adrienne La Russa (Licia), Rossano Brazzi (Brigoli), Nino Castelnuovo (Mario), Paola Pitagora (Giovanna), Alberto De Mendoza (Francesco), Idelma Carlo (Laura), Renzo Petretto (Paterlini), Nestor Garay (Politician).

La Russa is the daughter of Brazzi, a wealthy and prominent industrialist. She is a lover of life, completely free of all inhibition. She falls in love with Castelnuovo, not knowing that he wants to use her to his advantage. La Russa is lured to a brothel where the two proceed to make love. They are surprised by a police vice squad and press photographers. To avoid scandal Brazzi has La Russa confined to a mental institution. He also must pay off Castelnuovo when the young man threatens blackmail. Later La Russa is released and returns home. She tells everyone she is happy but really seeks revenge for her confinement. She has Castelnuovo film her father making love with his mistress. When Brazzi shows some business clients film of his trip to the Holy Land, the sex footage is mixed in as well. La Russa then seduces her brother-in-law, thus driving her sister (Pitagora) to suicide. Finally she has her revenge on Castelnuovo. Learning that her father is going to visit the man, she drugs her former lover's champagne. She props up the unconscious man in bed and fixes a pistol to point directly at his face. The trigger is attached by string to the doorknob. When her father enters the room, the gun goes off killing Castelnuovo. She later confronts Brazzi, telling him she knows he murdered the ex-lover but will not tell the cops. But she promises her father one thing: she intends to make the rest of his life a living nightmare. There is some really interesting photography in the film, with some fine editing patterns. The leads also give good performances and instill the film with life. However the dialog, poorly recorded in English is completely insipid. There's also some completely unnecessary elements such as bad rock music, a masturbation in a bathtub sequence, and unrelated conversations about the nature of power and money. These factors bring down what could have been an interesting and intriguing feature.

p, Oscar Brazzi, d, Edward Ross [Rossano Brazzi], Ted Kneeland; w, Brazzi, Mario Proietti, Diana Crispo (based on a story by Brazzi); ph, Luciano Trasatti (Eastmancolor); m, Benedetto Ghiglia; ed, Amedeo Giomini; art d, Francesco Della Noce, Giovanni Fratalocchi; m/l, "Daddy Said the World Was Lovely," Ghiglia, Jo Anna Kneeland.

Drama   (PR:O MPAA:R)

PSYCOSISSIMO   (1962, Ital.) 88m Variety-Flora/Ellis Trans-Lux bw

Ugo Tognazzi (Ugo), Raimondo Vianello (Raimondo), Edy Vessel (Annalisa), Monique Just (Marcella), Spiros Focas (Arturo), Francesco Mule (The Butler), Franca Marzi (The Widow Scarfoni).

This Italian comedy of errors reads like a macabre episode of "I Love Lucy." Tognazzi, Vianello, and Just are three out-of-work actors. They're rehearsing a crime scene in the bedroom of their boarding house, not realizing that their neighbor across the way (Focas, a local butcher) is watching. He believes the trio is a group of professional killers and offers Tognazzi and Vianello money to kill his unfaithful wife (Vessel). The actors agree, hoping to obtain the much needed cash without having to kill anyone. However, Vessel and her lover are creating some plans of their own. Not knowing what her husband is up to, she independently comes up with an idea to kill him. Along with her lover she plans to induce a heart attack to kill the butcher. Through various mixups the two plots get screwed up and intertwined. When Focas actually does die of a heart attack, Vessel and her lover

decide to kill the actors to cover themselves. The evil pair lure the hapless actors to a sausage factory with plans to throw them into the mincemeat machines. But this is foiled by the police, who arrest Vessel and her lover for murder—a crime they ironically never actually committed. Freed from their burden, Tognazzi and Vianello return once more to their struggling careers as actors. p, Leo Cevenini, Vittorio Martino; d, Steno; w, Vittorio Metz, Roberto Gianviti, Steno; ph, Tino Santoni; m, Carlo Rustichelli; ed, Giuliana Attenni; art d, Ivo Battelli.

Comedy   (PR:O MPAA:NR)

PT 109*   (1963) 140m WB bw

Cliff Robertson (Lt.[j.g.] John F. Kennedy), Ty Hardin (Ens. Leonard J. Thom), James Gregory (Comdr. C.R. Ritchie), Robert Culp (Ens. "Barney" Ross), Grant Williams (Lt. Alvin Cluster), Lew Gallo (Yeoman Rogers), Errol John (Benjamin Kevu), Michael Pate (Lt. Reginald Evans), Robert Blake ("Bucky" Harris), William Douglas (Gerard E. Zinser), Biff Elliott (Edgar E. Mauer), Norman Fell (Edmund Drewitch), Sam Gilman (Raymond Starkey), Clyde Howdy (Leon Drawdy), Buzz Martin (Maurice Kowal), James McCallion (Patrick McMahon), Evan McCord (Harold Marney), Sammy Reese (Andrew Kirksey), Glenn Sipes (William Johnston), John Ward (John Maguire), David Whorf (Raymond Albert).

The war adventures of John F. Kennedy are brought to the screen in this serviceable, if routine, naval drama. Young Robertson is a freshly commissioned naval officer who arrives on a remote Pacific island to take command of a battle-scarred PT boat. After repairs and sea trials, the boat and crew see action as they rescue a Marine patrol from a Japanese-infested island. On the return voyage they run out of gas and are towed back to port. Later, while trying to stop Japanese troop landings under cover of darkness, the flimsy plywood craft is split in two by an enemy destroyer. Some members of the crew are killed and the rest swim for a nearby deserted island, Robertson towing a badly burned crewman with him. They try repeatedly to get word of their predicament back to their base but fail until they write a message on a coconut. A friendly native takes the message, then returns later with a canoe in which he smuggles Robertson to a Japanese-occupied island where an Australian coastwatcher (Pate) is hiding out. Robertson uses the man's radio to summon rescuers and after all are picked up, he refuses an opportunity to return to the U.S., instead taking command of another boat. Robertson does a creditable job of impersonating the president without doing an imitation, but his characterization lacks any of Kennedy's charm, and the action scenes, when they finally do arrive (the film is more than 100 minutes into its running time when the much awaited collision comes) are fairly good, but the film as a whole drags as it establishes what a decent guy its hero is and portrays a crew that could only come from the mind of a Hollywood screenwriter who has seen far too many naval movies, filling the decks of the most famous PT boat of the war with the stock characters so familiar: the young man who turns coward under fire but later redeems himself, the clown, and the wise-cracking cook. Many Democrats were embarrassed by the way this film turned the leader of the country into a matinee idol; an interesting contrast to 20 years later, when a matinee idol was turned into the leader of the country. Lewis Milestone began shooting the film, but was replaced early on by Martinson.

p, Bryan Foy; d, Leslie H. Martinson; w, Richard L. Breen, Howard Sheehan, Vincent X. Flaherty; ph, Robert Surtees (Panavision, Technicolor); m, William Lava, David Buttolph; ed, Folmar Blangsted; art d, Leo K. Kuter; set d, John P. Austin; cos, Alexis Davidoff; spec eff, Ralph Webb.

War/Biography   Cas.   (PR:A MPAA:NR)

PT RAIDERS   (SEE: SHIP THAT DIED OF SHAME, 1959, Brit.)

PUBERTY BLUES**½   (1983, Aus.) 81m Limelight/Universal Classics c

Nell Schofield (Debbie), Jad Capelja (Sue), Geoff Rhoe (Garry), Tony Hughes (Danny), Sandy Paul (Tracy), Leander Brett (Cheryl), Jay Hackett (Bruce), Ned Lander (Strach), Joanne Olsen (Vicki), Julie Medana (Kim), Michael Shearman (Glenn), Dean Dunstone (Seagull), Tina Robinson (Freda), Nerida Clark (Carol), Alan Cassell (Vickers), Kirrily Nolan (Mrs. Vickers), Rowena Wallace (Mrs. Knight), Charles Tingwell (Headmaster), Kate Shiel (Mrs. Yelland), Pamela Gibbons (Teacher), Lyn Murphy (Mrs. Hennessy), Andrew Martin (Berkhoff), Rob Thomas (Salesman), Brian Harrison (Little), Brian Anderson (Drive-in Attendent).

Schofield and Capelja are a pair of Australian teen-agers who want to join a group of male surfers. It's not the sex they are interested in but rather an honest interest in the sport. Slowly they become disillusioned and embittered at the chauvinistic hierarchy that will not allow them a deserved chance. Beresford, who would go on to direct several fine films (including the excellent TENDER MERCIES) shows a good deal of sensitivity in this small film, wisely concentrating on the female point-of-view rather than the hormonally charged male films of America. There is some pandering to that element however with crotch and butt shots of some bikini-clad young women, but otherwise this is not too bad in that respect. The film was based on an Australian bestseller by two retired surfing groupies.

p, Joan Long, Margaret Kelly; d, Bruce Beresford; w, Kelly (based on the novel by Kathy Lette, Gabrielle Carey); ph, Don McAlpine (Panavision, Eastmancolor); m, Les Gock; ed, Jeanine Chialvo, William Anderson; md, Gock; prod d, David Copping; m/l, title song, Tim Finn.

Drama   Cas.   (PR:O MPAA:R)

PUBLIC AFFAIR, A*   (1962) 75m Girard-Lewis/Parade bw

Myron McCormick (Sam Clavell), Edward Binns (Sen. Fred Baines), Judson Pratt (Hal Green), Jacqueline Loughery (Phyllis Baines), Paul Birch (Malcomb Hardy), Harry Carey, Jr. (Bill Martin), Grace Lee Whitney (Tracey Phillips), Peter Brocco (Leonard Lohman), Mack Williams (Sen. Armstrong), Noel Drayton (George Babcock), Tyler McVey (Sen. Hopkins), Lou Kane (Marshall Thor), Armand Alzamora (Gardener), Paul Frees (Narrator).

Binns plays a California state senator who is angered by unscrupulous and illegal methods employed by collection agencies. He introduces legislation that establishes a committee to investigate abuses. He is determined to end the problem by the end of the legislative term, with assistance from Carey and Whitney. But Pratt, a conniving lobbyist, plans an attack on Binns' integrity to destroy his credibility and kill the committee. He fails in his mission and the bill ultimately passes. This is certainly a film with great educational interest for it well portrays the inner-workings of state government. However the political ends often overpower the characters, giving the actors little more to do than go about their business. There is little depth to the characters, despite a uniformly good cast. The pacing is excellent, with a direction and script that clearly explain the complicated business of government. This was filmed on location in the state capitol, Sacramento.

p, Bernard Girard, Robert E. Lewis, Lawrence Hanson, Jr.; d&w, Girard; ph, Howard Schwartz; m, Joe Greene; ed, Robert Seiter; set d, Harry Reif.

Drama **(PR:C MPAA:NR)**

PUBLIC BE HANGED, THE (SEE: WORLD GONE MAD, THE, 1933)

PUBLIC COWBOY NO. 1*** (1937) 60m REP bw

Gene Autry *(Autry)*, Smiley Burnette *(Frog)*, Ann Rutherford *(Helen)*, William Farnum *(Sheriff)*, James C. Morton *(Quackenbush)*, Frank LaRue *(Justice)*, Marston Williams *(Thad Slaughter)*, Arthur Loft *(Jack Shannon)*, Frankie Marvin *(Stubby)*, House Peters, Jr. *(Jim Shannon)*, Milburn Morante *(Ezra)*, King Mojave *(Steve)*, Hal Price *(Bidwell)*, Jack Ingram *(Larry)*, Rafael [Ray] Bennett, George Plumes, Frank Ellis, James Mason, Doug Evans, Bob Burns, Champion the Horse.

This is a modern-day western (by 1937 standards) which features Autry as the hero taking on a group of technologically advanced rustlers. Using airplanes, refrigerated trucks, and shortwave radios, the outlaws (led by Loft and Peters) nab the cattle, slaughter them, and ship the beef off to market for a good profit. Is it any wonder Autry sings "The West Ain't What It Used to Be?" Farnum, a former silent film star, calls in the singing cowpoke and his sidekick Burnette. Together they prove that horses and six-guns can outsmart bad guys any time. This is a good Autry western with plenty of action and good pacing that gets the story told without any lags in the plot. The songs are nicely integrated into the picture without stopping things cold. The title comes from the billing Republic Studios was using for Autry as the time. Other songs include: "I Picked up the Trail When I Found You," "Heebie, Jeebie Blues" (sung by Smiley Burnette), and "Defective Detective from Brooklyn" (sung by Burnette).

p, Sol C. Siegel; d, Joseph Kane; w, Oliver Drake (based on a story by Bernard McConville); ph, Jack Marta; ed, Lester Orlebeck, George Reid.

Western **Cas.** **(PR:A MPAA:NR)**

PUBLIC DEB NO. 1*½ (1940) 105m FOX bw

George Murphy *(Alan Blake)*, Brenda Joyce *(Penny Cooper)*, Elsa Maxwell *(Herself)*, Mischa Auer *(Grisha)*, Charlie Ruggles *(Milburn)*, Ralph Bellamy *(Bruce Fairchild)*, Maxie Rosenbloom *(Eric)*, Berton Churchill *(Magistrate)*, Franklin Pangborn *(Bartender)*, Hobart Cavanaugh *(Mr. Schlitz)*, Lloyd Corrigan *(Hugh Stackett)*, Ivan Lebedeff *(Feodor)*, Charles Judels *(Ivan)*, Elisha Cook, Jr. *(Communist)*, Selmer Jackson *(Lawyer)*, Luis Alberni *(Frontenac)*, Hal K. Dawson *(Layout Man)*, Charles Wilson *(Sergeant)*, Dick Rich, William Pawley *(Legionnaires)*, Mary Gordon *(Landlady)*, Addison Richards *(Sanford)*, Paul Stanton, Joseph Crehan, Douglas Wood *(Directors)*, Ralph Dunn *(Policeman)*, John Dilson *(Clerk)*, Chester Clute *(Car Payment Man)*, Herman Bing *(Dutchman)*.

Joyce plays a young socialite who is constantly a newspaper item because of her glamorous doings. Her youthful zeal gets her involved with a Communist rally. This makes the headlines and brings a public spanking from a waiter (Murphy). The girl's uncle (Ruggles) a soup tycoon, is pleased with this turn of events and offers Murphy a job as company vice-president. Murphy proves to be a company asset and manages to wrest Joyce from her scandalous behavior. The plot is fairly insipid with a script to match. The Communists are portrayed as buffoons which ends up being the only really interesting part of the film. Otherwise it is flat and humorless with a slow pacing that kills any hope of comedy. Joyce's switch from communism to an elopement with Murphy is no surprise at all. Murphy is probably the best thing in the picture. Of course the actor later went on to do his part against communism in his real life role of U.S. senator from California.

p, Gene Markey; d, Gregory Ratoff; w, Karl Tunberg, Darrell Ware (based on a story by Tunberg, Don Ettinger); ph, Ernest Palmer; ed, Robert Simpson; md, Alfred Newman.

Comedy **(PR:C MPAA:NR)**

PUBLIC DEFENDER, THE*** (1931) 70m RKO bw

Richard Dix *(Pike Winslow)*, Shirley Grey *(Barbara Gerry)*, Edmund Breese *(Wells)*, Paul Hurst *(Doctor)*, Purnell Pratt *(John Burns)*, Alan Roscoe *(Inspector O'Neill)*, Boris Karloff *(Professor)*, Ruth Weston *(Rose)*, Nella Walker *(Aunt Matilda)*, William Halligan *(Auctioneer)*, Frank Sheridan *(Charles Harmer)*, Carl Gerrard *(Cyrus Pringle)*.

A bank fails and the depositors lose their money. An innocent vice president takes the blame and is sent to prison. Dix believes the man is innocent after meeting with his daughter (Grey). Along with his aide, Karloff, Dix manages to steal some incriminating documents. He finds the real culprits (Pratt, Sheridan, and Gerrard) and frees the innocent man. This is a nicely paced thriller with some fine acting by the cast. Dix and Grey work well together with excellent (and elegant) support by Karloff in his pre-FRANKENSTEIN days. Ruben's direction keeps a healthy balance between plot development and action in a good first effort by the screenwriter turned director. The bank failure theme was a clever ploy by the studio to tap into a subject that was on the mind of just about every American after Black Tuesday.

p, Louis Sarecky; d, J. Walter Ruben; w, Bernard Schubert (based on the novel *The Splendid Crime* by George Goodchild); ph, Edward Cronjager; ed, Archie Marshek.

Crime **(PR:A MPAA:NR)**

PUBLIC ENEMIES*** (1941) 66m REP bw

Phillip Terry *(Bill Raymond)*, Wendy Barrie *(Bonnie Parker)*, Edgar Kennedy *(Biff)*, William Frawley *(George "Bang" Carson)*, Marc Lawrence *(Mike)*, Nana Bryant *(Emma)*, Willie Fung *(Lee Hong)*, Paul Fix *(Scats)*, Russell Hicks *(Lawrence Tregar)*, Tim Ryan *(Trumbull)*, Duke York *(Holmes)*, Ken Lundy *(Lively)*, Peter Leeds, Cy Ring, Eddie Fetherston *(Reporters)*, Francis Sayles *(Copy Man)*, Guy Usher *(Detective Captain)*, Lee Phelps *(Sergeant Operator)*, Charles McAvoy *(Policeman)*, Rod Bacon *(Tubby, the Reporter)*, Pat Gleason *(Maxie, the Reporter)*, Dick Paxton *(Bellboy)*, Chuck Morrison, Jack Kennedy *(Deliverymen)*, Harry Holman *(Fat Reporter)*, Frank Richards *(Shelby)*, Sammy Stein *(Jake)*, Francis Pierlot *(Priest)*, Jerry Jerome *(Duke)*, Wally Albright *(Tommy, the Newsboy)*, Sam Bernard *(Karmourian)*, Sammy McKim, Robert Winkler, Douglas Deems, Larry Harris *(Newsboys)*, Eddy Waller *(Olaf)*, James C. Morton, Dick Rush *(Detectives)*, Arthur Housman *(Drunk)*.

Terry plays an energetic reporter in this better-than-average programmer from Republic. His enthusiasm causes him to print a false story about society deb (Barrie) and consequently lose his job. He gets involved with a gangster smuggling operation in order to win back his job while Barrie somehow falls for Terry. But he will not marry her as she's a might too rich for his blood. When she is kidnaped by the mobsters he rescues her, gets back his job and ultimately marries the girl. This is a cut above average for its style. The direction pumps some real excitement into the routine story with a fast development and some good suspense. The acting is fine with good performances by Terry and Barrie. Kennedy and Frawley (later to become immortal as Fred Mertz on TV's "I Love Lucy") provide some fun moments as well with their portrayals of a bumbling pair of comedy crooks.

p, Robert North; d, Albert S. Rogell; w, Edward T. Lowe, Lawrence Kimble (based on a story by Michael Burke); ph, Ernest Miller; ed, Edward Mann.

Crime **(PR:A MPAA:NR)**

PUBLIC ENEMY, THE***** (1931) 83m WB bw (GB: ENEMIES OF THE PUBLIC)

James Cagney *(Tom Powers)*, Jean Harlow *(Gwen Allen)*, Edward Woods *(Matt Doyle)*, Joan Blondell *(Mamie)*, Beryl Mercer *(Ma Powers)*, Donald Cook *(Mike Powers)*, Mae Clarke *(Kitty)*, Mia Marvin *(Jane)*, Leslie Fenton *(Nails Nathan)*, Robert Emmett O'Connor *(Paddy Ryan)*, Murray Kinnell *(Putty Nose)*, Ben Hendricks, Jr. *(Bugs Moran)*, Rita Flynn *(Molly Doyle)*, Clark Burroughs *(Dutch)*, Snitz Edwards *(Hack Miller)*, Adele Watson *(Mrs. Doyle)*, Frank Coghlan, Jr. *(Tom as a Boy)*, Frankie Darro *(Matt as a Boy)*, Robert E. Homans *(Officer Pat Burke)*, Dorothy Gee *(Nails' Girl)*, Purnell Pratt *(Officer Powers)*, Lee Phelps *(Steve the Bartender)*, Helen Parrish, Dorothy Gray, Nanci Price *(Little Girls)*, Ben Hendricks III *(Bugs as a Boy)*, George Daly *(Machine Gunner)*, Eddie Kane *(Joe the Headwaiter)*, Charles Sullivan *(Mug)*, Douglas Gerrard *(Assistant Tailor)*, Sam McDaniel *(Black Headwaiter)*, William H. Strauss *(Pawnbroker)*, Landers Stevens *(Doctor)*, Russ Powell *(Bartender)*.

Frightening, obsessively fascinating, THE PUBLIC ENEMY, along with LITTLE CEASAR, set the gangster genre for the 1930s, making a star of its pugnacious, volatile leading man, Cagney, and establishing director Wellman as a major helmsman of talkies (he had already made a name for himself in the silent era with such films as WINGS). Where LITTLE CAESAR had its share of violence, its successor portrayed the underworld in much more seedy terms, not shunning the most gruesome and grim situations, Wellman portraying sex and violence as he thought best since THE PUBLIC ENEMY was made before the Hollywood censors, the Hays Office, established its rigid codes. Two young Irish boys are shown growing up in the shantytown south side of Chicago, circa 1909, hanging around pool halls, beer parlors, and saloons and visiting a so-called boys' club which is run by a sinister Fagin, Kinnell, who fences the stolen goods the boys bring to him. One of them, Coghlan (playing Cagney's role as a youngster), is the son of a tight-lipped Chicago cop, and he not only plays brutal pranks on the girls of his run-down neighborhood and leads Darro (playing Woods as a boy) into theft, but defies his parents, causing him in one scene to be taken into a bedroom by his father, Pratt (who wears his police helmet in the house), to be whipped with a strap. "How do you want 'em?" sneers Coghlan, referring to his pants in preparation for the whipping, "up or down?" (He gets it with the pants up.) The boys soon grow to be young men, Cagney and Woods, earning their livings during the day as delivery men. During the night, they plan robberies with their old mentor Kinnell, who gives both of them guns and outlines their first big heist, a fur warehouse. The thieves enter the warehouse but when Cagney sweeps a rack of furs aside, he is startled to see the huge stuffed head of a bear on the wall snarling down at him and impulsively fires several shots into it. The thieves panic, open a window, and slide down a drain pipe to the street. Police are drawn to the site at the sound of the shots and one of the thieves is killed, with Cagney and Woods shooting a pursuing cop to death before escaping. (Like many a violent scene in this film, Wellman only shows the young men racing down a street and up an alley, the cop following, the camera only showing the mouth of the alley and then shots banging and the sound of the cop dying.) Cagney and Woods run breathlessly back to Kinnell's seedy club to find it locked and a goon telling them through a door panel that Kinnell has left town. Deserted by their underworld guide, the boys go to saloon owner O'Connor, a wheeling-dealing criminal operator who talks out of the side of his mouth when telling the boys that Prohibition is coming into effect soon and that will mean a million-dollar racket for anyone selling illegal booze and beer. He intends to organize a mob to control such an enterprise in his district, stating that he will distribute what the boys steal. They strike a deal. Their first job is robbing a federal warehouse of impounded liquor, siphoning hundreds of barrels of booze through a hose from the storage kegs inside the warehouse, running down a drainpipe and into a gas truck parked next to the warehouse. This clever robbery nets the boys more money than they've ever seen before. They buy fancy tailor-made clothes and a flashy car. Cagney and Woods go to a nightclub, roaring up to the place in their new roadster. When a parking attendant begins to start up the car, making the clutch groan in agony, Cagney shouts out: "Hey, mug, that ain't no Ford! It's got gears!" They enter and spot two floozies, Blondell and Clarke, sitting with two men who have passed out drunk at the table. Cagney tells the headwaiter to "get rid of them two stiffs," and the men are dragged away in their chairs with Cagney and Woods sitting down in their places, immediately picking up the two flappers. Cagney takes Clarke and Woods pairs off with Blondell. The foursome move into an apartment while Cagney goes home to lavish his bootleg dollars on his goodhearted mother, Mercer, who is a widow still taking in washing to make ends meet. She tells him that his older brother, Cook, has ordered her not to take any money. Later, at a family party, Woods and Cagney place a huge keg of beer in the middle of the table but Cook sits glumly without drinking any beer or eating his dinner. He has just returned from Europe, having fought in WW I, and he seethes at the thought of his brother Cagney becoming a gangster. When Woods asks Cook why he isn't drinking any beer, the older brother explodes, smashing the keg against a wall and shouting: "You don't think I know what you two have been up to? That's not just beer in that keg, but blood and beer!" He sinks back into his chair, exhausted. Cagney tells Mercer that his brother is "screwy" and leaves. The next morning Cagney walks sleepily to a breakfast table where his moll Clarke greets him without a smile, asking him what's wrong. She tells him she wishes he would cheer up and he sneers back: "I wish you was a wishing well so I could tie a bucket to you and sink you!" Replies Clarke: "Maybe you found someone you like better." Cagney gives her a squint, then reaches for the grapefruit and smashes it into Clarke's face to end their relationship. Later, Cagney and Woods are driving down Michigan Avenue when Cagney spots a voluptuous blonde, Harlow, and orders Woods to stop the car. He picks her up and before letting her off she asks for *his* phone number which he gives to her (Yard 3771). Later, Cagney, now accompanying Harlow, Woods, Blondell, and their new crime boss, Fenton, enters a nightclub where they spot the long-missing Kinnell. Fenton goads the boys about how it was Kinnell who once set them up and then disappeared. Cagney and Woods excuse themselves and follow Kinnell from the club, trailing him to his apartment. There Kinnell realizes that they are seeking revenge for what he did to them and begs them to let him live. "You taught us how to cheat, steal, and kill, then lammed out on us, " Cagney tells Kinnell. Then Woods adds, oddly and regretfully, "Yeah, if it hadn't been for you we might have been on the level." To which Cagney smirks and says: "Yeah, we might've been ding-dongs on a streetcar." Inside the apartment Cagney learns that Kinnell has again been lying to them, that the woman he said was waiting for him in the apartment doesn't exist. He knocks Kinnell down. The old crook begs the boys to remember their youth and how he used to play dirty songs for them. He sits down at the piano and begins to play an old ditty. Off camera, Cagney shoots his mentor and his body is heard collapsing on discordant piano keys as the camera shows Woods staring mutely. Cagney walks into the scene, heading toward the door, telling his sidekick that he will call Harlow, acting as if he had done nothing more than kick an old can into the gutter. Cagney visits his mother once more, trying to shove thousands of dollars into her hand, but she again refuses, saying Cook will get angry. Cook appears and tells Cagney to never again offer "blood money" to them and to not come back into the house. Cagney tries to take a punch at Cook but Cook slugs him first. The gangster leaves, shoving his mother out of the way. Cagney later complains to Harlow that he's unhappy with their inactive sexual relationship: "How long can a guy wait—I'll go screwy." She stops him as he is about to leave, sitting in his lap, throwing off his hat and pressing his head to her bosom, telling him she's fascinated by him because "you don't give, you take...Tommy, I could love you to death!" A phone call from Woods interrupts the tryst; Cagney learns that their boss, Fenton, has been kicked to death on a bridal path by a spirited horse. Cagney and Woods visit the stable and ask to see the horse, Rajah, giving the trainer a pile of money, going into the stable, and shooting the horse (again the viewer only hears the shots and the horse collapsing with an agonizing neigh as the startled trainer is shown looking toward the stables). With Fenton dead, gang war breaks out, and O'Connor's saloon is bombed. O'Connor, now the nominal leader of the gang, orders Cagney, Woods, and other gang members to go into hiding. He takes their guns and money so they will stay in the apartment he has selected for their hideout, one equipped with women, booze, and cards. Cagney gets drunk in the apartment and wakes up to discover from one of the whores that she had seduced him the night before when he was in a drunken stupor. Angrily, Cagney shoves her aside and leaves the building, Woods running after him. Outside, across the street, a rival gang has set up a machine gun in a second-story window. The gun traces the steps of Cagney and Woods as they leave the building. Woods says to Cagney: "What do you want to run out on me for—we're together aren't we?" "Sure," says Cagney and as the two reach the edge of the building, the machine gun opens up and cuts Woods down. Cagney slips behind the corner of the building and looks at Woods who reaches out for his lifelong friend before flopping over dead on his back. Cagney peeks around the edge of the building's corner and is just missed by a spray of machine gun bullets which tear the wall of the building away. He flees. That night he goes to a pawnshop and asks about buying two pistols. The owner, thinking Cagney a novice, loads some bullets into the chambers and Cagney turns the guns on the pawnbroker who thinks he's joking until Cagney roars: "Stick 'em up!" Later Cagney goes to the Western Chemical Company, headquarters of the rival gangster, Schemer Burns. He stands in the rain until the Schemer and a dozen of his goons arrive and enter the building. Cagney follows with a grim smile on his face, pulls out the two stolen guns, and enters after the gang. A fusillade of shots rings out mixed with screams, as Wellman keeps his camera on the front of the building. Cagney emerges coughing; he has been hit. He hurls the pistols through the bay windows of the headquarters, staggers down the street in the rainstorm, and falls to his knees in the gutter, saying, "I ain't so tough!" He collapses on his face. Cook and Mercer visit Cagney in the hospital where they find him bandaged almost head to toe. He promises to quit the rackets and the family resolves to be happy once more. Cagney tells his brother he's sorry and promises his mother that he will be coming home after he recuperates; the family makes preparation for his homecoming. Mercer is shown plumping pillows preparing Cagney's old room, and then learns from Cook that he will be returning from the hospital soon. O'Connor shows up to tell Cook that the Schemer's mob has kidnaped Cagney from the hospital but that he has his mob out looking for him. O'Connor says that he has promised the Burns mob that he will quit the rackets if they return Cagney. Later, Cook goes to the door of his home, upon hearing the doorbell ring, and there stands Cagney, wrapped in bandages and a blanket encircled with rope, a bullet through his head, dead. Cagney falls forward face first as Cook, in shock, examines the body of his brother, then staggers away out of the camera frame while the victrola in the house is playing "I'm Forever Blowing Bubbles" (the theme music in the film, played during the credits and at the end). THE PUBLIC ENEMY is one of the most realistic gangster films ever produced. Wellman's direction is a frontal attack on the subject; other than showing a number of violent deaths offscreen, he spares no brutality of emotion, no ruthlessness of action or thought in his grim portrayal of a lethal criminal. Cagney is *the* gangster of his day, cocky, seemingly invulnerable, and utterly without conscience, a character who is obviously deep-seated toward evil from childhood. Wellman shows us his philosophy of enviornment creating the man. We only see the criminal world, with police barely in the backround. The one cop shown in detail is a brute walking about his house dressed in a half uniform, a silent hulk who can only reach for a razor strop in talking to his unruly youngster. Photographer Jennings shot this film with sharp contrasts: glaring sunlit exteriors, grainy gray interiors that fade to black alleyways and gutters. Cagney, like a blinding rocket, shot to fame with this international hit and also typecast himself for almost a decade as a ruthless, next-to-impossible-to-kill hoodlum, an image that would carry him through the 1930s in such hell-raising films as THE ROARING TWENTIES, ANGELS WITH DIRTY FACES, EACH DAWN I DIE, and G-MEN, in spite of the fact that in the latter film he played an FBI agent. He was a human wolf with an insatiable appetite for violence in THE PUBLIC ENEMY, displaying original screen mannerisms that captivated the viewing public. The profile enacted with pyrotechnic skill by Cagney is based upon the colorful Chicago gangster Charles Dion "Deanie" O'Bannion, arch rival to Al Capone. Fenton enacts the part of Samuel J. "Nails" Morton, who had earned a fistful of medals during WW I as a lieutenant in command of a machinegun company, later utilizing that deadly weapon with great and devastating effect in the gangland wars of Chicago in the early 1920s. The character "Schemer Burns" is supposed to be drawn from another Chicago gangster, Vincent "The Schemer" Drucci (who was, contrary to the film's plot, an ally of O'Bannion's). The scenes involving Cagney and Woods killing the horse that killed Fenton are, surprisingly, based on actual fact. The character Fenton enacted, Morton, was actually kicked to death on the Lincoln Park bridle path and two of his henchmen (one being ace O'Bannion gunner Louis "Three-Gun" Alterie) went to the stables, put down hundreds of dollars in front of the stable owner, entered the stable, and shot the animal to death. The most remembered scene of this film, of course, is where Cagney smashes the grapefruit in Mae Clarke's face. (The face could have been that of Louise Brooks, who was signed to play the unwanted girl friend role but she was dropped at the last minute, thought to be just too beautiful for anyone to abandon, plus the fact that she insisted that her part be beefed up.) Everyone connected with the grapefruit scene remembered it differently. According to Cagney, the incident was concocted for the film after the writers, Bright and Glasmon, learned that Chicago gangster Earl "Hymie" Weiss sat down at the breakfast table and became incensed with his gun moll's endless talk, taking the omelet she has just made for him and slamming it into her face. Wellman thought the omelet too messy so he opted for a grapefruit half. At one time, Cagney claimed that Wellman and he cooked up a conspiracy (later supported by Clarke) that involved the notorious grapefruit. He was to pick it up and then push it *past* her face, along the profile unseen by the camera, not touching the flesh. But he and Wellman decided to actually slam the grapefruit into Clarke's incredulous countenance without telling her in order to capture genuine shock. This it did, if the story be true. Clarke later stated that no grapefruit at all was to be used, that Cagney did the smashing impulsively instead of shouting at her. Still later, Clarke told interviewer Richard Lamparski that Wellman made one take where Cagney was merely to insult her verbally and then asked to do another "gag" take, one "for a laugh." The "gag" involved Cagney shoving the grapefruit into Clarke's face. "I've always tried to be a good sport," said Clarke. "The idea didn't appeal to me. Nobody likes having anything pushed into their face, but since it was only a gag, I consented." The actress forgot about the "gag" take and was shocked when she saw the film and that the "gag" take was the one Wellman used. Women's groups rose up in protest over such brutal abuse of women on screen and this particular scene, it was later claimed, spawned the continuing abuse of film heroines, although its presence, for only a few seconds, could hardly be said to have initiated the trend. According to Wellman, he dreamed up the whole thing. According to the director, Clarke was being too sensitive and uncooperative and was also suffering from a cold. "We needed something big right there in the picture, " Wellman later reported. "That grapefruit on the table looked inviting and I didn't like the dame [Clarke] much anyhow. So I told Jimmy to try socking her with it—but hard. He did." The blow hurt Clarke physically and she showed all the pain and embarrassment in that memorable if crude scene. Wellman almost didn't make the film until he talked Warner Bros. producer Zanuck into the project. When Wellman first went to Zanuck, the future head of 20th Century-Fox told him: "Look, Bill, the gangster picture's dead. We've had LITTLE CAESAR and DOORWAY TO HELL. What do you think you can bring to this one that will possibly make it any different?" Responded Wellman: "What I'll bring you is the toughest, the most violent, most realistic picture you ever did see." Zanuck agreed to let him try but on a limited budget and a short schedule. Wellman met both challenges, finishing the film in a record 26 days and for only $151,000. The film would yield millons in endless reissues as a classic gangster picture. But Wellman had to fight for Cagney as well as the picture itself. Cagney had appeared in only four films for Warner

Bros. and was thought of only as an engaging young supporting player on a low-paying contract. Woods, ironically enough, had been cast in the lead as the tough Tom Powers. Wellman viewed early rushes of the film and said: "We've got the wrong guy playing the lead; the other guy, Cagney, he's the tough one!" He went back to Zanuck and asked that Cagney be recast as the lead and Woods as the sidekick. Wellman told Zanuck that he had watched Cagney in some scenes from an earlier film, DOORWAY TO HELL, and he was as tough as they come on screen. Zanuck doubted Cagney was star material and he also pointed out that Woods had just become the son-in-law of powerful Hollywood gossip columnist Louella Parsons. Wellman stood his ground and demanded he get Cagney as his lead and finally Zanuck yielded. Zanuck would later claim to have masterminded the entire film, especially the grapefruit scene, as well as unearthing the dynamic Cagney. "My complete discovery," Zanuck later boasted. "I got him off the stage. He was in a play with Joan Blondell. . . . It was my idea, the grapefruit. I think I thought of it in a script conference. When I made PUBLIC ENEMY I was way ahead in thinking. No love story but loaded with sex and violence!" Cagney, of course, would be as forever associated with that grapefruit as would Clarke. Whenever he entered a restaurant for years after the film, some lowbrow customer would send over a half grapefruit to his table. The actor would usually surprise the snide gift-sender by eating the grapefruit before his meal. Cagney proved he was as tough as Wellman thought he was many times over in THE PUBLIC ENEMY. He actually stood only a foot away from the wall of a building as a WW I veteran machinegunner named Bailey, hired by the studio to shoot live bullets, sprayed the wall. Cagney was later to state that "Bailey opened up on the edge of the wall. It crumbled to sawdust, and so would I, had I been there two seconds before." The great Warner Bros. star would go on playing the clay pigeon for gun experts using live bullets (in the days before the minature explosive devices were invented and planted into sets) to achieve a realistic scene, almost being killed by bullets sprayed in his direction in THE ROARING TWENTIES and ANGELS WITH DIRTY FACES, finally telling Michael Curtiz, the director of the later film, that he could get someone else to perform such suicidal scenes and never again risking his own neck for filmic reality. In one scene in THE PUBLIC ENEMY, Cook, playing Cagney's brother, is called upon to hit the apprentice gangster in the face. "I think he had some coaching," Cagney later said of Cook's blow, which was not pulled but landed square on Cagney's famous jutting jaw. "I always suspected that Bill Wellman said to him: 'Go ahead. Let him have it. He can take it,' because when Donald belted me, he didn't pull a thing. Instead of faking it as one always does, he just punched me straight in the mouth, broke a tooth, and knocked me galley west." Just as he would in other films, Cagney brought his indelible mannerisms to THE PUBLIC ENEMY. In several scenes he lightly taps Mercer's jaw affectionately. This gesture, though later claimed to have been invented by Zanuck (of course), was one Cagney's own father used on him, a gentle tap of the fist against the jaw, accompanied by the words: "If I thought you meant that...." Ironically, Cagney had tried out for another brutal gangster role, the lead in Howard Hughes' SCARFACE, but when Hughes viewed Cagney's screen test he eliminated him by telling director Howard Hawks: "Not him—he's a runt!" Cagney became a superstar overnight with THE PUBLIC ENEMY but Jack Warner kept him on his meager contract player's salary, which irked this great actor so that he would later battle Warner to the point of suspension to increase his wages. When Warner viewed the film, he expressed dislike for the grim, bleak tale and at his side was his workhorse director, Michael Curtiz. Warner snorted disgust at the final scene where Cagney appears tied up, dead at his mother's doorstep. Curtiz slavishly agreed with Warner and Zanuck jumped up and slugged Curtiz, jamming the director's cigar half down his throat. Wellman, witnessing this display of fisticuffs, admired the producer for physically defending his own product. "I can love this guy Zanuck," he said. "I don't care what he does from now on." Harlow, the sexy blonde bombshell of the decade, has really a small role in the film, playing the part of a hot call girl whose favors are available for money but who practices her own strange perversions by indulging herself with men of violence. This was Harlow's only film with Cagney and her only lead role at Warner Bros. But then all kinds of perversions were practiced in connection with this film. Monte Brice, brother of Fannie Brice, had recently been divorced from Mae Clarke and he made a habit of attending theaters showing THE PUBLIC ENEMY just to see the scene where his ex-wife received the grapefruit, laughing so hysterically that he often had to be asked to leave the theater. Cagney took his new fame in stride. Just after THE PUBLIC ENEMY exploded he was told in New York that he was now a superstar. "Stars come and go," replied Cagney. "Of course, there's an exception now and then, but you can't count on that. Two more years and I'll be looking for a job on the stage again—maybe hoofing. What's the use of kidding myself?"

p, Darryl F. Zanuck; d, William A. Wellman; w, Kubec Glasmon, John Bright, Harvey Thew (based on the original story *Beer and Blood* by Bright); ph, Dev Jennings; ed, Ed McCormick; md, David Mendoza; art d, Max Parker; cos, Earl Luick, Edward Stevenson; m/l, "I'm Forever Blowing Bubbles," Jean Kenbrovin, John W. Kellette, "I Surrender Dear," Harry Barris, Gordon Clifford; makeup, Perc Westmore.

Crime Drama **Cas.** **(PR:O MPAA:NR)**

PUBLIC ENEMY'S WIFE*** (1936) 65m WB bw (GB: G-MAN'S WIFE)

Pat O'Brien *(Lee Laird)*, Margaret Lindsay *(Judith Maroc)*, Robert Armstrong *(Gene Ferguson)*, Cesar Romero *(Gene Maroc)*, Dick Foran *(Thomas Duncan McKay)*, Joseph King *(Wilcox)*, Richard [Dick] Purcell *(Louie)*, Addison Richards *(Warden Williams)*, Hal K. Dawson *(Daugherty)*, Harry Hayden *(Justice of the Peace)*, Alan Bridge *(Swartzman)*, Kenneth Harlan *(G-Man)*, Selmer Jackson *(Duffield)*, William Pawley *(Correlli)*, Paul Graetz *(Mr. Schultz)*, Mary Green, Isabel Withers *(Operators)*, Kathrin Clare Ward *(Matron)*, Bernice Pilot *(Miranda the Maid)*, Don Downen *(Bellhop)*, Ted Oliver, Jack Mower, Ed Hart, Emmett Vogan *(G-Men)*, Ralph Dunn *(Cop)*, Harry Harvey, William Wayne, Bert Kennedy *(Mail Clerks)*, Stuart Holmes *(Telephone Repair Chief)*, Milton Kibbee *(Charlie, the Repair Man)*.

This nice B film features Lindsay as a woman wrongly convicted of a crime. She spends three years in prison before finally being released. Romero is her husband, a jewel thief and prison "lifer." He's insanely jealous of Lindsay and threatens to kill any man with whom she ever gets involved. Lindsay ignores his threat and proceeds to get involved with Foran, a millionaire of weak character. Romero breaks out of prison and it's a matter of time before he discovers what his ex-wife has been up to. Will he carry out his promise? The climactic chase reveals all. O'Brien plays a G-Man who ultimately ends up with Lindsay, in a nicely fleshed out character. He underplays with great effect. Romero works well as the psychotic criminal, with Lindsay filling out the leads in a nifty performance as well. Only Foran is a dud, coming off even weaker than his character. The script is a dandy, full of little moments that build to the climactic ending. Direction moves the story at a fine pace, wringing out every moment for what it's worth. All in all this was better than most films of such nature. The studio tried to pass this off as a sequel to the successful PUBLIC ENEMY and it was later remade as BULLETS FOR O'HARA in 1942.

p, Sam Bischoff; d, Nick Grinde; w, Abem Finkel; Harold Buckley (based on a story by David O. Selznick, P.J. Wolfson); ph, Ernest Haller; ed, Thomas Pratt; art d, Hugh Reticker.

Crime **(PR:A MPAA:NR)**

PUBLIC EYE, THE*½ (1972, Brit.) 95m UNIV c (GB: FOLLOW ME)

Mia Farrow *(Belinda Sidley)*, Topol *(Julian Cristoforou)*, Michael Jayston *(Charles Sidley, Accountant)*, Margaret Rawlings *(Mrs. Sidley)*, Annette Crosbie *(Miss Framer)*, Dudley Foster *(Mr. Mayhew)*, Michael Aldridge *(Sir Philip Crouch)*, Michael Barrington *(Mr. Scrampton)*, Neil McCarthy *(Parkinson)*, Gabrielle Brune *(Lady Crouch)*, Jack Watling *(Wealthy Client)*, David Battley *(Writer)*, Lucy Griffiths *(Bertha)*, David Hutcheson *(Dinner Guest)*, Joan Henley *(Dinner Guest)*.

This attempt to make a full-fledged film out of a tiny stage anecdote falls flatter than Farrow's frontispiece. That it was expanded by the play's author, award-winning Peter Shaffer (AMADEUS), and produced by the legendary Hal Wallis (CASABLANCA, plus) and directed by one of England's greatest directors, Sir Carol Reed, (ODD MAN OUT) sends the imagination reeling. The play was one of two one-acters, "The Private Ear" and "The Public Eye," which had a respectable run as a double bill in London before opening in New York in 1963 as a three-character sketch starring Geraldine McEwan as the wife, Barry Foster as the private eye, and Moray Watson as the husband. It lasted a bit more than six months on Broadway and "The Private Ear" was purchased and produced as THE PAD, AND HOW TO USE IT, a trifle at best, in 1966 but not nearly as trifling as this. For all its forced attempts at lightness, the picture is as frothy as week-old ale. Farrow and Jayston have been married half a year. They are totally opposite. She's an American flower child and he is a stiff-backed British accountant. She disappears daily in London and Jayston thinks she may just be finding balm and solace in another man's arms, so he hires Topol, a Greek detective (he plays it like a combination of Peter Ustinov and Donald Duck) to tail her. Farrow has been missing some of the stodgy social calendar dates Jayston has planned and she lays the blame on her inability to gauge time while she sightsees around Dr. Johnson's favorite city. Ten days of investigation only prove that Farrow is doing what she says she is doing, plus occasionally visiting movie houses to watch horror films. Jayston won't believe Topol's whitewash and he then says that he was lying and that there *is* another man in Farrow's life. Ahah! Jayston puts it to Farrow, who admits that she's been spending time with a man who seemed to have been following her for a while. They've visited all the tourist spots in the city, smiled at each other, but have still not spoken a single word. Jayston realizes that it's Topol and he races to the Greek's place to scream. Farrow is aghast when she learns that Topol was hired by Jayston and exits. Topol gets an idea, and at Jayston's place, tells the couple that Jayston should follow Farrow for 10 days and she'll fall back in love with him. Jayston thinks that's nonsense, but as Farrow races out of Jayston's office, he grabs Topol's white coat and goes out after her. She smiles in his direction and the phone rings. Topol picks it up and tells the caller that he is Jayston's new partner (he didn't much like detective work anyhow). Farrow is like a woman with neurasthenia, Topol (an Israeli) commits the terrible dietary sin of being hammy, and Jayston seems to be in a Noel Coward play. Three different styles and all work against each other. It was too cute for its own good.

p, Hal B. Wallis; d, Carol Reed; w, Peter Shaffer (based on his play); ph, Christopher Challis (Panavision, Technicolor); m, John Barry; ed, Anne V. Coates; prod d, Terence Marsh; md, Barry; art d, Robert Cartwright; set d, Peter Howitt; cos, Julie Harris; ch, Sally Gilpin; makeup, Hugh Richards.

Comedy **(PR:A MPAA:G)**

PUBLIC HERO NO. 1*½** (1935) 81m MGM bw

Chester Morris *(Jeff Crane)*, Jean Arthur *(Theresa O'Reilly)*, Lionel Barrymore *(Dr. Josiah Glass)*, Paul Kelly *(Duff)*, Lewis Stone *(Warden Alcott)*, Joseph Calleia *(Sonny Black)*, Sam Baker *(Mose)*, Paul Hurst *(Rufe Parker)*, John Kelly *(Truck Driver)*, Selmer Jackson *(Simpson)*, Larry Wheat *(Andrews)*, Cora Sue Collins *(Little Girl)*, Lillian Harmer *(Mrs. Higgins)*, George E. Stone *(Butch)*, Frank McGlynn, Jr., James Flavin, Gladden James, Pat O'Malley *(Federal Agents)*, Frank Moran *(Prison Guard)*, Walter Brennan *(Farmer)*, Zeffie Tilbury *(Deaf Woman)*, Helene Costello *(Girl)*, Carl Stockdale *(Train Conductor)*, Greta Meyer *(Housekeeper)*, Tammany Young *(Bartender)*, Bert Roach *(Masher)*, Jonathan Hale *(Prison Board Member)*.

Topnotch gangster movie finds Morris inside the pen posing as a con so he can be next to Calleia, the rat who heads "The Purple Gang." The intention is to break Calleia out of jail and not let him know that it's all a ruse. Then Morris can locate the rest of the mobsters and put the cuffs on them. Stone is the warden of the slammer and his actions are suspect, as he allows the break to happen (that's all explained later when he admits that he was under orders from government man Paul Kelly). Arthur is Calleia's sister and her flirtation with Morris causes Calleia to get angry (shades of Paul Muni and his sister in SCARFACE). Barrymore is a "crime doctor," a drunken physician who will repair bullet wounds without reporting them if he is plied with enough booze. At one point, Calleia needs blood to live and the only person whose type matches Calleia's is Morris, so he donates the blood, knowing full well that it's only to keep the criminal alive until all the evidence is in. At the conclusion, in a scene borrowed from the alleged death of John Dillinger on July 22, 1934, Calleia is gunned down at a Chicago theater on the near north side. This was a fast-paced, violent, and suspenseful picture that took many of the story points right from the newspaper headlines. It was better than many of the Warner Bros. crime pictures and Calleia, who made his mark on the stage the year before in "Small Miracle," was a sensational killer in this, and his cool, deadly mien was frightening. Calleia was a Maltese actor whose real name was Joseph Spurin-Calleja. He'd done a bit in HIS WOMAN, four years before, but this role was his meat, and at the age of 38, he finally got his big break and began a career that lasted for 30 years. Plenty of humor in the script to counterpoint the machine-gunning. The 1941 remake was THE GET-AWAY with Dan Dailey but, like most remakes, it didn't come close. In that one, they used some of the action footage from this. There really was a Purple Gang in Detroit and quite a bit of the action reflected their doings as well as the exploits of a few of the other 1930s gangsters. The intelligence and creativity in script, casting, and production paid off big dividends at the box office. Toland's photography (he did CITIZEN KANE) was superior, as was Sullivan's editing. Walter Brennan does a bit as a farmer.

p, Lucien Hubbard; d, J. Walter Ruben; w, Wells Root (based on the story by Ruben, Root); ph, Gregg Toland; m, Edward Ward; ed, Frank Sullivan.

Crime   **(PR:A   MPAA:NR)**

PUBLIC LIFE OF HENRY THE NINTH, THE**   (1934, Brit.) 60m Hammer/MGM bw

Leonard Henry (Henry), Betty Frankiss (Maggie), George Mozart (Draughts Player), Wally Patch (Landlord), Aileen Latham (Liz), Mai Bacon (Landlady), Herbert Langley (Police Constable), Dorothy Vernon (Mrs. Fickle), Jean Lester.

Henry and Frankiss are a pair of unappreciated workers at the Henry VIII Pub where Henry soon attracts a following who like to hear him sing. His die-hard fans enthusiastically tag him Henry the Ninth, and Frankiss joins him in his act. The owner, however, prefers laborers to singing stars so Henry and Frankiss leave for a life of fame on the stage.

p, Will Hammer; d&w, Bernard Mainwaring.

Comedy   **(PR:A   MPAA:NR)**

PUBLIC MENACE**½   (1935) 73m COL bw

Jean Arthur (Cassie), George Murphy (Red Foster), Douglas Dumbrille (Tonelli), George McKay (Dildy), Robert Middlemass, Victor Kilian, Charles C. Wilson, Gene Morgan, Murray Alper, Shirley Grey, Bradley Page, Arthur Rankin, Thurston Hall, Fred Kelsey.

Murphy plays an egotistical reporter who's tailing mobster Dumbrille aboard an ocean liner. But he lets the big story slip through his fingers when he meets the ship's manicurist (Arthur) and falls in love. They marry and Murphy is unemployed. He and Arthur fight. He decides to get a divorce but she saves the day when she recalls giving a manicure to a supposedly slain mobster. Murphy reports the story but Dumbrille is once more found alive. Murphy is fired again, sure his wife is a detriment. Despite the seemingly downbeat aura of the plot this is a fairly humourous programmer. Murphy and Arthur have a nice chemistry that make the illogical story work. The climactic ending with Arthur tipping off her husband as to the gangster's whereabouts is both funny and dramatic. The newspaper setting is fake as can be but sort of funny in its own way. The production values, while nothing special, do their job nicely.

d, Erle C. Kenton; w, Ethel Hill, Lionel Houser; ph, Henry Freulich; ed, Gene Milford.

Crime/Newspaper   **(PR:C   MPAA:NR)**

PUBLIC NUISANCE NO. 1*½   (1936, Brit.) 79m Cecil/GFD bw

Frances Day (Frances Travers), Arthur Riscoe (Arthur Rawlings), Muriel Aked (Miss Trumps), Claude Dampier (Feather), Peter Hadden (Richard Trelawney), Sebastian Smith (Mr. Snelling), Robert Nainby (Arthur Rawlings, Sr.), Antony Holles (Headwaiter).

Day plays a shop girl working on the Riviera. Riscoe is a waiter working at her rich uncle's hotel. Together they help save the hotel from financial disaster. This dumb comedy is poorly scripted and a real waste for the talented cast. The jokes are lowbrow with no fresh twist to be found. The only saving grace here is the musical numbers which are nicely staged.

p, Herman Fellner, Max Schach; d, Marcel Varnel; w, Val Guest, Roger Burford, Robert Edmunds (based on a story by Franz Arnold); ph, Claude Friese-Greene; m/l, Vivian Ellis.

Comedy   **(PR:A   MPAA:NR)**

PUBLIC OPINION**   (1935) 66m IN/CHES bw

Lois Wilson (Mona Trevor), Crane Wilbur (Paul Arnold), Shirley Grey (Joan Nash), Luis Alberni (Caparini), Andres De Segurola (Enrico Martinelli), Paul Ellis (Carlos Duran), Ronnie Crosby (Tommy), Florence Roberts, Gertrude Sutton, Erville Alderson, Edward Keane, Mildred Gover, Edward Le Saint, Betty Mack, Lew Kelly, Robert Frazer, Richard Carlisle.

Grey plays a young girl infatuated with a bacteriologist (Wilbur). When his wife Wilson, a temperamental opera star, walks out on him Grey sees her chance for romance. But Wilson comes back and reconciles with her husband and Grey settles

for the more juvenile affections of nice guy Crosby. The tale is simple fluff, but nicely played by Wilson and Wilbur. The rest of the cast is adequate though clearly not ready for A pictures. Ellis plays a foreign opera star whose thick European accent is incomprehensible. Production values are standard programmer work.

p, Maury M. Cohen; d, Frank R. Strayer; w, Karen DeWolf; ph, M. A. Anderson; ed, Roland Reed.

Drama   **(PR:A   MPAA:NR)**

PUBLIC PIGEON NO. 1**½   (1957) 79m Val-Ritchie-RKO/UNIV c

Red Skelton (Rusty Morgan), Vivian Blaine (Rita DeLacey), Janet Blair (Edith Enders), Jay C. Flippen (Lt. Ross Qualen), Allyn Joslyn (Harvey Baker), Benny Baker (Frankie Frannis), Milton Frome (Avery), John Abbott (Dipso Dave Rutherford), Howard McNear (Warden), James Burke (Harrigan), Herb Vigran (Club Manager), The Seven Ashtons.

Skelton plays a simple-minded cafeteria worker who is engaged to Blair. He gets caught up with some swindlers who take his savings in a phony stock scheme. They hire him as their courier and he finds himself in jail. But Skelton escapes with the usual hijinks and gets a $10,000 reward for handing over the bad guys. This was an expansion of a fairly good skit from Skelton's popular TV show. However length does nothing for the story but drain any comic potential, resulting in a dumb and unfunny film. Skelton tries his best but never can muster up the needed energy. The other cast members flounder in their roles, ultimately losing the battle against the inherent stupidity of the screenplay.

p, Harry Tugend; d, Norman Z. McLeod; w, Tugend (based on a teleplay by Devery Freeman from a story by Don Quinn, Larry Berns); ph, Paul C. Vogel (Technicolor); m, David Rose; ed, Otto Ludwig; md, Rose; art d, Albert S. D'Agostino, John B. Mansbridge; cos, Bernice Pontrelli; ch, Miriam Nelson; m/l, "Don't Be Chicken, Chicken," Matty Malneck, Eve Marley (sung by Vivian Blaine), "Pardon Me, Got to Go Mambo," Malneck, Marley (sung by Blaine).

Comedy   **(PR:A   MPAA:NR)**

PUBLIC STENOGRAPHER*   (1935) 64m Screencraft/Marcy bw (GB: PRIVATE AFFAIRS)

Lola Lane (Ann McNair), William Collier, Jr. (Jim Martin), Esther Muir (Lucille Weston), Jason Robards, Sr. (Fred White), Duncan Renaldo (Jerome Eagan), Bryant Washburn (Henricks), Al St. John (Country Hick), Richard Tucker, Al Bridge.

At last! A film that blows the lid off a world of danger and excitement in the life of a public stonographer! If you believe that one than you haven't seen enough bad B movies. Lane plays a hardboiled stenographer (apparently they do exist) and Muir (who's best remembered for being wallpapered by the Marx Brothers in A DAY AT THE RACES) is her loyal companion. The dialog is what you would expect, stupid to the point of unintentional comedy all played earnestly. The co-stars Renaldo and St. John went on to better successes with B westerns.

d, Lew Collins; w, Joe O'Donnell, Collins (based on a story by Ellwood Ullman).

Drama   **(PR:C   MPAA:NR)**

PUBLIC WEDDING**   (1937) 58m WB bw

Jane Wyman (Flip Lane), William Hopper (Tony Burke), Dick Purcell (Joe Taylor), Marie Wilson (Tessie), Berton Churchill (Pop Lane), James Robbins (Nick), Raymond Hatton (The Deacon), Veda Ann Borg (Bernice), Zeni Vatoria (Gus), Jimmy Foxe (Jeremiah Boggs), Curtis Karpe (Pete), Carlyle Moore, Jr., Horace MacMahon (Reporters), George Guhl (Sheriff), Eddie Anderson (Porter), Frank Faylen (Trainman), James Burtis, Eddy Chandler (Detectives), Milton Kibbee (Jailer), Cy Kendall (Police Captain), Sarah Edwards (Mrs. Van Drexel), Frank Hammond (Harrison the Banker).

Five carnies find themselves down on their luck and in desperate need of work. In order to gain publicity for a local side show, they are hired to stage a fake wedding in nothing less than the mouth of a stuffed whale! Wyman is the bride and Hopper is the groom. When the wedding is over, they find someone has made an error for the two are now legally man and wife. The script is flat with no real moments of good business for the ensemble to play with. The direction is routine. Wyman went on to prove she was capable of much better work than this film would indicate.

p, Bryan Foy; d, Nick Grinde; w, Roy Chanslor, Houston Branch (based on the story "The Inside" by Branch); ph, L. William O'Connell; ed, Frank DeWar.

Comedy   **(PR:A   MPAA:NR)**

PUDDIN' HEAD**   (1941) 80m REP bw (GB: JUDY GOES TO TOWN)

Judy Canova (Judy Goober), Francis Lederer (Prince Karl), Raymond Walburn (H. L. Montgomery, Sr.), Slim Summerville (Uncle Lem), Astrid Allwyn (Yvonne), Eddie Foy, Jr. (H.L. Montgomery, Jr.), Alma Kruger (Matilda Montgomery), Hugh O'Connell (Kincaid), Chick Chandler (Herman), Paul Harvey (Mr. Harvey), Nora Lane (Miss Jenkins), Gerald Oliver Smith (Hudson), Wendell Niles (Randall), Vince Barnett (Otis Tarbell), The Sportsmen.

Canova and her uncle (Summerville) live on a farm. Trouble is the farm is located on New York City's Fifth Avenue. Walburn and Foy play a pair of city slickers who try to get the country kin to sell out but its nothing doing. They try to trick the hillybilly girl by pretending to give her a spot on the radio. But through a mistake she goes on the air, sings her heart out and naturally is a big hit. Utter cornball, this suffers not only from a dumb idea but also from poor comic timing. The director has no idea of what is going on and consequently this dies quickly. Canova, who always seemed to get parts like this, is the best of the lot. Canova sings: "Hey Junior," "You're Telling I," "Manhattan Holiday," and "Puddin' Head" (all by Eddie Cherkose, Sol Meyer, Jule Styne).

p, Albert J. Cohen; d, Joseph Santley; w, Jack Townley, Milt Gross, Howard

Snyder, Hugh Wedlocks, Jr. (based on a story by Townley); ph, Jack Marta; ed, Ernest Nims; md, Cy Feuer; art d, John Victor Mackay.

Comedy **(PR:AAA MPAA:NR)**

PUFNSTUF** (1970) 98m Sid & Marty Krofft/UNIV c (AKA: H.R. PUFNSTUF)

Jack Wild *(Jimmy)*, Billie Hayes *(Witchiepoo)*, Martha Raye *(Boss Witch)*, Mama Cass *(Witch Hazel)*, Roberto Gamonet *(H.R. Pufnstuf)*, Sharon Baird *(Shirley Pufnstuf)*, Johnny Silver *(Dr. Blinky/Ludicrous Lion)*, Andrew Ratoucheff *(Alarm Clock)*, Billy Barty *(Googy Gopher)*, Felix Silla *(Polkadotted Horse)*, Joy Campbell *(Orson Vulture/Fireman)*, Jane Dulo, Jan Davis, Princess Livingston, Angelo Rossitto, Van Snowden, Lou Wagner, Hommy Stewart, Pat Lytell, Buddy Douglas, Jon Linton, Bob Howland, Scutter McKay, Roberta Keith, Penny Krompier, Brooks Hunnicutt, Barrie Duffus, Evelyn Dutton, Tony Barro, Ken Creel, Fred Curt, Dennis Edenfield, Allison McKay.

In the late 1960s, television had a completely ridiculous Saturday morning kid show called "H.R. Pufnstuf." It featured live actors coupled with giant puppets and hopelessly insipid jokes. These elements were trademarks for the show's producers, the Krofft brothers. PUFNSTUF is a film version of the show featuring most of the TV cast. The story has Wild, a young boy taking his talking magic flute to a magic land where objects, plants, and animals can speak. There they meet Pufnstuf, a nice dragon, the island's mayor. The simplistic plot has Hayes (in the only good performance—a delightful chunk of ham) stealing the magic flute so she can be named "Witch of the Year" at the annual Witches Convention. Wild and his new friends go to her castle to rescue the flute. Raye and Cass (of the rock group "the Mamas and the Papas") play a pair of fellow witches. This film is aimed directly at the under ten set—and they'll probably enjoy it—but you're better off singing "Puff the Magic Dragon" than watching this ill-written fluff. Songs include "Pufnstuf," "Angel Raid," "Charge," "Fire in the Castle," "Happy Hour," "Leaving Living Island," "Rescue Racer to the Rescue," "Witchiepoo's Lament," and "Different."

p, Si Rose; d, Hollingsworth Morse; w, John Fenton Murray, Rose; ph, Kenneth Peach (Technicolor); m, Charles Fox; ed, David Rawlins; art d, Alexander Golitzen, Walter Scott Herndon, Joe Alves; set d, Arthur Parker; spec eff, Luke Tillman, Roland Chiniquy; ch, Paul Godkin; m/l, Fox, Norman Gimbel; makeup, Ziggy Gieke; puppet creation, Rolf Roediger, Evenda Leeper, Troy Barrett.

Fantasy **(PR:AAA MPAA:G)**

PULGARCITO (SEE: TOM THUMB, 1967, Mex.)

PULP*½** (1972, Brit.) 96m Klinger-Caine-Hodges/UA c

Michael Caine *(Mickey King)*, Mickey Rooney *(Preston Gilbert)*, Lionel Stander *(Ben Dinuccio)*, Lizabeth Scott *(Princess Betty Cippola)*, Nadia Cassini *(Liz Adams)*, Al Lettieri *(Miller)*, Dennis Price *(Mysterious Englishman)*, Amerigo Tot *(Sotgio)*, Leopoldo Trieste *(Marcovic)*, Robert Sacchi *(Jim Norman)*, Joe Zammit Cordina *(Santana)*, Ave Nichi *(Chambermaid)*, Werner Hasselman, Louise Lambert *(American Tourists in Restaurant)*, Luciano Pigozzi *(Del Duce)*, Iver Gilborn, Elaine Olcott *(Tourists in Coach)*, Maria Quasimodo *(Senora Pavone)*, Janet Agren *(Silvana)*, Christina Gaioni *(Blonde Typist)*, Cyrus Elias *(Guide)*, Mary Caruana *(Mae West)*, Jeanne Lass *(Marlene Dietrich)*, Kate Sullivan *(Joan Crawford)*, Anna Pace Donnela *(Jean Harlow)*, Jennifer Gauci *(Shirley Temple)*, Tondi Barr *(Gloria Swanson)*, Giuseppe Mallia *(Cripple Outside Bar)*, Cettina Borg Oliver *(Gilbert's Mother)*, Giulio Donnini *(Office Manager of Typing Pool)*, Roy Marmara *(Mario)*, Louis Caruana *(Toni)*, Victor Mercieca *(Prince Cippola)*.

An underrated crime satire made with obvious love for all the old movies, PULP is filled with cinema "inside jokes" and will surely be more appreciated by someone who has a knowledge of film. Caine is a hack writer who publishes books under various names because no publisher would buy such a prodigious output if he knew the work was coming from one mind. A former funeral director, Caine now lives in Rome, having abandoned his family, and spends every waking hour pounding out cheap detective novels. Stander appears and asks Caine if he would be willing to ghostwrite the autobiography of a mysterious celebrity. Stander is a gangster type, but Caine is a prostitute when it comes to his work, so he agrees to take the job when the offer is for far more than he usually gets. The way Caine is to make contact is equally mysterious and he gets aboard a tourist bus, meets Lettieri, and supposes that he is the man who will take him to the person he is to write about. But Lettieri is drowned in a hotel bathtub and his body suddenly vanishes. Enter Cassini, a sweet-looking babe who takes Caine to a remote island to meet Rooney, who is a one-time movie star noted for playing gangsters and also famed for his real-life friendship with crooks (and if you see a parallel between this character and George Raft's life, that appears to have been intended). When Rooney learns that Lettieri is dead, he sighs happily, as it may have been that Lettieri was tailing Caine in order to find Rooney. It turns out that Rooney has terminal cancer and wants to get his memories down on paper before being claimed by the Grim Reaper. For the next reel or so, Rooney tells Caine the story of his rise to fame, his pals, his loves, etc., as Caine dutifully takes notes. Rooney is getting to the good parts of the story when they decide to take a break and go ashore, where Rooney tosses an annual bash in honor of his late father. Rooney's ex-wife is Scott, who is now married to an Italian prince, Mercieca, a reformer running for office on a conservative platform which decries violence and the coddling of criminals. Caine takes up with Scott at the party and they enjoy talking with each other until gunshots shatter the laughter and tinkling of glasses. Rooney is shot by an assassin wearing the garb of a priest. It would seem that this puts an end to Caine's labors, but he is dogged and wants to finish the story, so he continues his investigation and learns that Rooney, Lettieri, and Mercieca had been friends some years ago, and, while out on a hunting expedition, they met a young woman, raped her, and killed her. All three had this kind of blackmail information on the others and all feared that one of the others would crack. Caine goes out looking for the dead woman's grave on a lonely strip of shore and a rifle bullet smashes into his leg. He's hurt but he manages to get to his vehicle and race after the sniper. The ambusher is run over by the ambushee, and when Caine sees that it's a priest, it doesn't make sense. Upon closer inspection, he notes that it's Lettieri, who had faked his own drowning death (a la DIABOLIQUE) in the bathtub. Caine goes to Scott's house to rest his weary leg and allow the bullet wound to heal and the solution comes to him. It must be that Lettieri and Mercieca conspired to kill Rooney, as the publication of Rooney's memoirs would have put an end to Mercieca's political aspiration. Caine is now determined to write the truth, but a bent secret agent tells Caine that his life will be over if he writes anything that will put Mercieca in jeopardy. Caine sighs, knowing on which side his royalties are buttered, and makes the whole story into a fiction and hopes that, perhaps, this one will put him into the ranks of Robert Ludlum. Lots of laughs; some excellent dialog with sharp observations; superb photography of the Italian and Maltese locations (the only thing missing was The Falcon); outrageous situations (such as when a group of legitimate Italian priests have to line up for identification by the guests); the inspired casting of Stander and Scott (who played the hood and the moll in so many pictures before); and the short, but wonderful performance of Rooney as Edward G. Robinson, James Cagney, Raft, Muni, and himself. This picture was not a hit when it came out but will probably take its place as a cult classic next to BEAT THE DEVIL and other delicious satires. Hodges, Caine, and Klinger (Michaels all) had previously collaborated on GET CARTER, a more straightforward detective picture a while before. Hodges went downhill in his next picture, the all-chrome and no-heart THE TERMINAL MAN.

p, Michael Klinger; d&w, Michael Hodges; ph, Ousama Rawi (DeLuxe Color); m, George Martin; ed, John Glenn; prod d, Patrick Downing; md, Martin; art d, Darrell Lass; set d, Downing; cos, Gitt Magrini; spec eff, Ron Ballanger; makeup, George Partleton, Paul Engelen.

Crime/Comedy **(PR:C MPAA:PG)**

PUMPKIN EATER, THE**** (1964, Brit.) 118m Romulus/Royal-COL bw

Anne Bancroft *(Jo Armitage)*, Peter Finch *(Jake Armitage)*, James Mason *(Bob Conway)*, Janine Gray *(Beth Conway)*, Cedric Hardwicke *(Mr. James, Jo's Father)*, Rosalind Atkinson *(Mrs. James, Jo's Mother)*, Alan Webb *(Mr. Armitage, Jake's Father)*, Richard Johnson *(Giles)*, Maggie Smith *(Philpot)*, Eric Porter *(Psychiatrist)*, Cyril Luckham *(Doctor)*, Anthony Nicholls *(Surgeon)*, John Franklin Robbins *(Parson)*, John Junkin *(Undertaker)*, Yootha Joyce *(Woman in Hairdresser's)*, Leslie Nunnerley *(Waitress at Zoo)*, Gerald Sim *(Man at Party)*, Frank Singuineau *(King of Israel)*, Faith Kent *(Nanny)*, Gregory Phillips, Rupert Osborne *(Pete)*, Michael Ridgeway, Martin Norton *(Jack)*, Frances White, Kate Nicholls *(Dinah)*, Fergus McClelland, Christophr Ellis *(Fergus)*, Elizabeth Dear, Sara Nicholls *(Elizabeth)*, Sharon Maxwell, Mimosa Annis *(Sharon)*, Kash Dewar *(Mark)*, Mark Crader *(Youngest Child)*.

Bancroft, in an Oscar-nominated performance, plays a twice-married mother of six. She divorces her second husband (Johnson) and takes up with Finch, a highly successful screenwriter. The two marry; it seems like a perfect marriage until Bancroft realizes her philandering husband will never buckle down to her notions of marital fidelity. She gives birth to her seventh child and suffers a nervous breakdown. This, along with an encounter with an unbalanced woman at her hairdresser's sends Bancroft to a psychiatrist (Porter). He is not much help. Bancroft's father dies and she discovers a baby is due once more. She refuses to accompany Finch to a film location in Morocco but agrees to his arguments for sterilization. Later she runs into Mason, a man who once made a pass at her. Mason reveals that Finch has been having an affair with his wife (Gray) and a child is expected. Bancroft confronts Finch in an ugly scene and returns to Johnson. After she spends the night with Johnson, he gets a phone call from old friend Finch. Finch's father has just passed away. She goes to the funeral but Finch pretends not to notice her. Bancroft chases him but slips and falls in the mud. Demoralized once more, she goes to their unfinished country house and spends the night alone. In the morning she wakes to the sound of her children as Finch leads them up a hill. Bancroft realizes that this is what her life is meant to be and resigns herself to life with the eclectic man. This is a fine film, encompassing the joys and tragedies of life: birth and death, marriage and divorce, love and hate. The leads give their characters life. These seem real people on the screen, not actors in a drama. Bancroft gives her role real depth, switching her moods with eerie and wonderful believability. Mason, in a small supporting role, is nothing short of excellent. The script by noted playwright Pinter is complex and painful but often employs a good sense of the comic as well. The direction, slow and even-handed, allows the story to develop at its own pace, but gradually builds the speed as the story's intensity grows. This is a fine and sensitive work, a truthful portrait of human foibles and complexities. This was charismatic character actor Hardwicke's final film; he died the year of its release. p, James Woolf; d, Jack Clayton; w, Harold Pinter (based on the novel *The Pumpkin Eater* by Penelope Mortimer); ph, Oswald Morris; m, Georges Delerue; ed, James Clark; art d, Edward Marshall; set d, Peter James; cos, Motley; makeup, George Frost.

Drama **(PR:O MPAA:NR)**

PUNCH AND JUDY MAN, THE** (1963, Brit.) 96m Macconkey/Warner-Pathe bw

Tony Hancock *(Wally Pinner)*, Sylvia Syms *(Delia Pinner)*, Ronald Fraser *(Mayor Palmer)*, Barbara Murray *(Lady Jane Caterham)*, John Le Mesurier *(Charles the Sandman)*, Hugh Lloyd *(Edward Cox)*, Mario Fabrizi *(Nevil Shanks)*, Pauline Jameson *(Mayoress)*, Norman Bird, Peter Vaughan, John Dunbar *(Committee Men)*, Walter Hudd *(Clergyman)*, Brian Bedford *(lst Escort)*, Peter Myers *(2nd Escort)*, Eddie Byrne *(Ice Cream Assistant)*, Russell Waters *(Bobby Bachelor (Keven Brennan (Landlord)*, Gerald Harper *(lst Drunk)*, Laurie Main *(2nd Drunk)*, Michael Ripper *(Waiter)*, Fred Berman *(Master of Ceremonies)*, Hattie Jacques *(Dolly Zarathusa)*.

Popular British TV comedian Hancock is the title character, a children's puppeteer at a seaside resort. His wife (Syms) is a social-climbing snob with whom he's constantly bickering. She wants him to move on to bigger things. The town is celebrating its 60th anniversary, which gives Hancock his chance to prove himself. He fails disastrously but his wife forgives him and all is righted between the two. The script (based on a story idea by Hancock) is too slight to work as a whole. There are, however, some fine moments when Hancock is simply allowed to let loose and be funny. Though popular on British TV, he was never able to find the right film vehicle. Here he has some good moments tackling an ice cream sundae, using his expressive face to best advantage. But the film is ultimately too melancholy to work and far too slight in story to be of any use. The direction is fine though it can only do so much. Audiences in the U.S. may miss observing the parallels between the protagonists' own lives and the traditions of the classical Punch and Judy performance.

p, Gordon L. T. Scott; d, Jeremy Summers; w, Tony Hancock, Phillip Oakes (based on a story by Hancock); ph, Gilbert Taylor; m, Derek Scott, Don Banks; ed, Gordon Pilkington.

Comedy   **(PR:A MPAA:NR)**

PUNISHMENT PARK½   (1971) 88m Francoise Films/Sherpix-
                                                    Chartwell-Francoise c

Jim Bohan (Captain, Sheriff's Dept.), Van Daniels (County Sheriff), Frederick Franklyn (Prof. Daly), Sanford Golden (Sen. Harris), Harlan Green (Sheriff), Radger Greene (Federal Marshal), Joe Hudgins (Chief Tribunal Marshal), Mark Keats (Chairman Hoeger), Lee Marks (FBI Agent Donovan), Sigmund Rich (Prof. Hazlett), Paul Alelyanes, Kerry Cannon, Bob Franklin (Policemen), Carmen Argenziano (Jay Kaufman), Stan Armsted (Charles Robbins), Harold Beaulieu, Cynthia Jenkins, Jack London, Bob Lewine (Desert Militants), Roland Gonzalez, Jack Gozdick, Brian Hart, Linda Mandel, Don Pino, Jason Sunners, Conchita Thornston (Desert Semi-Militants), Danny Conlon (National Guardsman), Sandy Cox (Stenographer), Gladys Golden (Mrs. Jergens), George Gregory (Mr. Keagan), Mitchell Harding, Mike Hodel (Newscasters), Gary Johnson, Michele Johnson, Ted Martin, Harold Schneider (Desert Pacifists), Luke Johnson (Luke Valerio), Tom Kemp (Tribunal Marshal), Mary Ellen Kleinhall (Allison Mitchner), Katherine Quittner (Nancy Smith), Patrick Boland (Defendant), Scott Turner (Janus Kohler), Peter Watkins (Documentarist).

A group of draft resisters is given a choice: a long prison sentence or three days in a "Punishment Park". A British film crew (led by the film's director, Watkins) documents life in one such park. The rules state that members are given three days to reach an American flag 57 miles away. National Guardsmen hunt down the "players," but if they can reach the destination they are to be released. No food is provided, but water will be available at the half-way mark. The film is shown as a sort of live television program with interviews on both sides, jerky camera movements, and general TV show esthetics. The background of the players is never revealed as we simply follow them through their tribunals and through the "game". At times this is a powerful film, serving as a sort of allegory for the American involvement in Vietnam. But often it is muddled and unsure of what direction to take. Still, it's an interesting enough experiment that's well worth a look. Made during the U.S. involvement in the Viet Nam conflagration, the picture postulates the continuing escalation of that war, and escalation of opposition to it. The detention camps actually established in the U.S. under the authority of the McCarron Act of 1950 were projected to be filled with dissenters; the adjacent "Punishment Parks" were designed for a pragmatic purpose: to alleviate the overcrowding of the prison camps. The chilling scenario lends itself well to Watkins' choice of a documentary style. Like Watkins' other quasi-documentaries, THE WAR GAME (1967) and PRIVILEGE (1967), this film was commissioned by the British Broadcasting Corporation; like the others, it was rejected by its sponsor, a result of its controversial content.

p, Susan Martin; d&w, Peter Watkins (additional dialog by cast members); ph, Joan Churchill, Peter Smokler (Technicolor); m, Paul Motian; ed, Watkins, Terry Hodel; art d, David Hancock.

Drama   **(PR:O MPAA:R)**

PUO UNA MORTA RIVIVERE PER AMORE?   (SEE: VENUS IN
                                                    FURS, 1970, Brit./Ital./W. Ger.)

PUPPET ON A CHAIN½   (1971, Brit.) 96m Big City/Cinerama c

Sven-Bertil Taube (Paul Sherman), Barbara Parkins (Maggie), Alexander Knox (Colonel De Graaf), Patrick Allen (Inspector Van Gelder), Vladek Sheybal (Meegeren), Ania Marson (Astrid Leman), Penny Casdagli (Trudi), Peter Hutchins (The Assassin), Drewe Henley (Jimmy Duclos), Henni Orri (Herta), Stewart Lane (George Lemay), Mark Malicz (Morgenstern), Michael Mellinger (Hotel Manager).

Taube is a tough-as-nails narcotics agent who heads off to Amsterdam in order to crack a drug smuggling operation. Along with his assistant Parkins he goes to work and uncovers a trail that leads to a strange puppet-making religious order. Parkins is killed—strangled with a chain—and Taube is knocked out. He manages to escape and heads back for Amsterdam. This leads to a climactic boat chase as he tries to prevent the smugglers from escaping from his sight. The boat chase is an exciting sequence, well filmed and alive with crackling energy. Unfortunately, the same can't be said about the rest of the film. The script (by Maclean, adapted from his own novel) is full of implausibilities and cardboard characters. The actors contribute to that quality with their lifeless performances. Direction remains slow-paced until the film's climactic ending. That's about all that's worth viewing in this otherwise mindless thriller.

p, Kurt Unger; d, Geoffrey Reeve; w, Alistair Maclean, Paul Wheeler, Don Sharp (based on the novel by Maclean); ph, Jack Hildyard, Sheets Kelly (Technicolor); m, Piero Piccioni; ed, Bill Lenny; md, Harry Rabinowitz; prod d, Peter Mullins; art

d, Geoffrey Tozer; cos, Yvonne Blake; ch, Robin Winbow; stunts, Joe Dunne, Wim Wagenaar, John Terhaak.

Thriller   **(PR:O MPAA:PG)**

PUPPETS OF FATE   (SEE: WOLVES OF THE UNDERWORLD, 1936,
                                                    Brit.)

PURCHASE PRICE, THE*   (1932) 70m WB bw

Barbara Stanwyck (Joan Gordon), George Brent (Jim Gilson), Lyle Talbot (Ed Fields), Hardie Albright (Don Deslie), David Landau (Bull McDowell), Murray Kinnel (Spike Forgan), Leila Bennett (Emily), Matt McHugh (Waco), Clarence Wilson (Justice of the Peace), Lucille Ward (Wife of Justice of the Peace), Crauford Kent (Peters), Dawn O'Day [Anne Shirley] (A Farmer's Daughter), Victor Potel (Clyde), Adele Watson (Mrs. Tipton), Snub Pollard (Joe).

Stanwyck is the mail order bride of North Dakota farmer, Brent. She was formerly a torch singer (crooning the prophetic song "Take Me Away" early in the film) before becoming sick of the city. Talbot is her bootlegging boyfriend who sets her up with Brent, and after their initial meeting it's hardly a romance made in heaven. But she soon comes to love the simple farmer and marries him. Financial troubles follow and their neighbor, Landau, offers to bail out Brent in exchange for Stanwyck. Naturally this is repelled and a fight breaks out. Talbot re-enters the picture to cause more trouble and Landau retaliates by burning down Brent's wheat fields. But the couple bears up under these new hardships and the film ends happily. Both Brent and Stanwyck, who had worked well together in NIGHT NURSE and SO BIG, are terribly miscast in roles well beneath their talents. In a plot laden with heavy drama, this film often surprisingly goes for slapstick. The redeeming quality here is the fine photography. The wheat fields make a nice study both in planting and eventual burning. But, unfortunately, that's not enough to make a good film.

d, William A. Wellman; w, Robert Lord (based on the story "The Mud Lark" by Arthur Stringer); ph, Sid Hickox; ed, William Holmes; art d, Jack Okey; m/l, "Take Me Away," Peter Tinturin, Sidney Clare, Charles Tobias.

Drama   **(PR:O MPAA:NR)**

PURE HELL OF ST. TRINIAN'S, THE*   (1961, Brit.) 94m Vale-
                                                    BL/CD bw

Cecil Parker (Prof. Canford), Joyce Grenfell (Sgt. Ruby Gates), George Cole (Flash Harry), Thorley Walters (Butters), Eric Barker (Culpepper-Brown), Irene Handl (Miss Harker-Parker), Sidney James (Alphonse O'Reilly), Dennis Price (Gore-Blackwood), Raymond Huntley (Judge), Lloyd Lamble (Superintendent Kemp-Bird), Liz Fraser (Miss Partridge), Elwyn Brook-Jones (Emir), Nicholas Phipps (Major), Cyril Chamberlain (Army Captain), Harold Berens (British Consul), Julie Alexander (Rosalie), Ann Wain (Lolita Chatterly), Gilda Emmanuelli (Minnie Hen), Sally Bulloch (Maud Birdhanger), Mark Dignam (Prosecuting Counsel), George Benson (Defense Counsel), Michael Ripper (Liftman), John Le Mesurier (Minister), Lisa Lee (Miss Brenner), Wensley Pithey (Chief Constable), Monty Landis (Octavius), Clive Morton (V.I.P.), Maria Lennard (Millicent), Dawn Beret (Jane).

This is another of the successful films based on the popular cartoon drawings of Ronald Searle. This time out the naughty girls of the infamous St. Trinian's school are brought to court for setting their alma mater ablaze. They are freed, however, when Parker, a mysterious professor from the University of Baghdad, claims he can rehabilitate the lot. He is financed by James, unaware that Parker wants these girls as wives for a sheik and his many sons. Parker takes the older girls on a tour of the Greek Islands aboard a luxury yacht. Secretly aboard also is Grenfell, a police sergeant who's been ordered to follow the girls and relay any pertinent information to Lamble, her police inspector and long time fiance. When the ship goes off course, she wires back to Lamble. But before anything can be done about the situation, James finds her and puts her in a lifeboat to drift out to sea, along with Parker and Cole, St. Trinian's unofficial matrimonial agent. The younger students set Walters and Barker adrift as well, mistakenly believing that this will help the older girls. They arrive at the sheik's palace and the sons try to have their pick. But the girls fight back in a madcap free-for-all, utilizing the help of the younger girls. The police arrive as well, and all are saved. The film comes full circle, ending with the girls celebrating by once more burning down the school. This picture is briskly paced, with dialog that is fast, furious, and witty.

p, Sidney Gilliat, Frank Launder; d, Launder; w, Launder, Gilliat, Val Valentine (based on the cartoon characters by Ronald Searle); ph, Gerald Gibbs; m, Malcom Arnold; ed, Thelma Connell; md, Arnold; art d, Wilfred Shingleton, Tony Woollard; spec eff, Wally Veevers, George Samuels.

Comedy   **(PR:C MPAA:NR)**

PURE S*½   (1976, Aus.) 77m Australian Film Institute c

Gary Waddell (Lou), John Laurie (John), Ann Heatherington (Sandy), Carol Porter (Gerry), Helen Garner (Jo), Phil Motherwell (Ed), Max Gillies (Doctor).

This is a no-holds barred look at the underworld of Melbourne's drug scene. Employing actual junkies (two of whom over-dosed after the film's completion), the audience is allowed to witness 48 hours within the lives of the drug users. The story is an improvisational "truthful fiction," created by the director and cast members. The pace is quick and direct with actual heroin injections, junkies nodding out, and a death through overdose. There are some moments of macabre black humor interspersed within the tough, realistic dialog. The film suffers from a poor sound recording, though the characters and situations are fascinating enough in and of themselves.

p, Bob Weis; d, Bert Deling; w, Deling (created with cast members); ph, Tom Cowan; m, Red Symons, Martin Armiger; ed, John Scott.

Drama   **(PR:O MPAA:NR)**

PURLIE VICTORIOUS   (SEE: GONE ARE THE DAYS 1963)

e

PURPLE GANG, THE½** (1960) 85m AA bw

Barry Sullivan *(Detective Bill Harley)*, Robert Blake *("Honeyboy" Willard)*, Elaine Edwards *(Gladys Harley)*, Marc Cavell *(Hank Smith)*, Jody Lawrance *(Miss Mac)*, Susy Marquette *(Daisy)*, Joseph Turkel *(Eddie Olsen)*, Victor Creatore *(Al Olsen)*, Paul Dubov *(Burke)*, Kathleen Lockhart *(Nun)*, Nestor Paiva *(Laurence Orlofsky)*, Lou Krugman *(Dr. Rioden)*, Mauritz Hugo *(Licovetti)*, Norman Nazarr *(Ricco)*, John Indrisano *(Castiglione)*, Dirk London *(Tom Olsen)*, Congressman James Roosevelt *(Narrator, Foreword)*, Severio Lo Medico, Don Haggerty, George Baxter, Michael Vallon, Ella Ethridge, Craig Fox, Allen Windsor, Ralph Sanford, Walter Maslow, Cecil Weston, Paul McGuire, David Tomack, Dan Easton, John Close.

A hard-edged sociological crime thriller which drives home its point with brute force. Sullivan and Blake are antagonists in Prohibition-era Detroit—the former is a police officer who has had enough of juvenile delinquents, while the latter is a hard-as-nails punk with no regard for the law. Their rivalry starts when a young social worker, Lawrance, advocates psychiatric treatment for delinquents. The police don't like Lawrance's suggestion because they are convinced that only a stiff prison sentence will do the trick, while the delinquents don't like the implication that they need a shrink. The result is that Lawrance is raped and murdered by the teens. So much for social reform. Sullivan gets assigned to the case, but finds that his hands are tied by rules and regulations that forbid him from arresting the guilty teens without adequate proof. The main offender is Blake, a mean little runt who not only threatens the social order but the local Mafia as well, tearing up their turf with tommy-gun fire. Gradually Blake moves up in the ranks of the gangster world. To get Sullivan off his back he has the officer's pregnant wife, Edwards, pushed to her death from a window. Instead of backing off, Sullivan strengthens his attack and finally gets Blake behind bars. A brutal expose of criminal life, THE PURPLE GANG is made realistic by Carter's gritty photography and the intercutting of newsreel footage from the Prohibition era. Taking its inspiration from the real-life Purple Gang, which plagued Detroit throughout the Prohibition days and was responsible for hundreds of bootleg-related killings, the film pays little attention to the facts which surrounded the rise of these thugs. Director McDonald is more concerned with stating his opinions on how criminals should be dealt with than in dealing with the criminals themselves. What results is little more than a standard drama about an angry cop determined to topple a gangster. THE PURPLE GANG's main selling point, however, is its semi-documentary atmosphere, setting it apart from the usual glamorous treatments of criminals. Appearing in the film's prolog and vouching for the film's authenticity is Congressman James Roosevelt, son of President Franklin Delano Roosevelt.

p, Lindsley Parsons; d, Frank McDonald; w, Jack DeWitt; ph, Ellis Carter; m, Paul Dunlap; ed, Maurice Wright; art d, David Milton; set d, Frank Lombardo; m/l, "Runnin' Wild," Joe Gray, Leo Wood, A. Harrington Gibbs.

Crime **(PR:O MPAA:NR)**

PURPLE HAZE½** (1982) 97m Triumph c

Peter Nelson *(Matt Caulfield)*, Chuck McQuary *(Jeff Maley)*, Bernard Baldan *(Derek Savage)*, Susanna Lack *(Kitty Armstrong)*, Bob Breuler *(Walter Caulfield)*, Joanne Bauman *(Margaret Caulfield)*, Katy Horsch *(Phoebe Caulfield)*, Heidi Helmen *(Angela)*, Tomy O'Brien *(Marcus)*, Dan Jones *(Snitch)*, Don Bakke, James Craven *(NCO's)*, John Speckhardt *(Oath Officer)*, Jean Ashley *(Mrs. Maley)*, Sara Hennessy *(Lori)*, Michael Bailey *(Ed)*, Peter Thoemke *(Bill)*, Hayden Saunier, Donna Moen *(Waitresses)*, Spare Change *(Country Club Band)*, Don Westling, Steve Gjerde *(Campus Cops)*, Jake Braziel *(Bus Driver)*, Ky Michaelson *(Cop)*, Jane Rogers *(Cara)*, Norie Helm *(Penny)*, Mary Bea Arman *(Stacey)*.

This independent feature attempts to chronicle the social upheavals of the 1960s. Nelson is a young man who must fight off the draft, unfeeling parents, and, of course, "The Establishment." Along with his pal, McQuary, he experiences drugs, riots, and evasion from the police. Unfortunately, the plot involves cliched stereotypes from this turbulent era, with little insight into the raw feelings of the time. The best thing that can be said of this film is the musical score. The music of the 1960s (including the superb title tune by Jimi Hendrix) is used to propel this story, a wise directional choice as the dialog is stiff and overly serious, without an ounce of the humor that marked youth's satirical look at the older generation of that time. It anything, PURPLE HAZE shows the powerful influence music had on young people in regard to politics, sex, and drugs. The actors manage to play their roles with conviction, despite the trugid melodrama of the script. But what could have been an important statement about an era still not fully understood, falls far short in its unveiling of what made the 1960s a powerful, influential decade.

p, Thomas Anthony Fucci; d, David Burton Morris; w, Victoria Wozniak (based on the story by Wozniak, Morris, Tom Kelsey); ph, Richard Gibb; ed, Dusty Dennisson; art d, James Johnson; ch, Peter Thoemke.

Drama **(PR:O MPAA:R)**

PURPLE HEART, THE**** (1944) 99m FOX bw

Dana Andrews *(Capt. Harvey Ross)*, Richard Conte *(Lt. Angelo Canelli)*, Farley Granger *(Sgt. Howard Clinton)*, Kevin O'Shea *(Sgt. Jan Skvoznik)*, Donald Barry *(Lt. Peter Vincent)*, Trudy Marshall *(Mrs. Ross)*, Sam Levene *(Lt. Wayne Greenbaum)*, Charles Russell *(Lt. Kenneth Bayforth)*, John Craven *(Sgt. Martin Stoner)*, Tala Birell *(Johanna Hartwig)*, Richard Loo *(Gen. Mitsubi)*, Peter Chong *(Mitsuru Toyama)*, Gregory Gaye *(Peter Voshenksy)*, Torben Meyer *(Karl Kappel)*, Kurt Katch *(Ludwig Kruger)*, Martin Garralaga *(Manuel Siva)*, Erwin Kalser *(Karl Schleswig)*, Igor Dolgoruki *(Boris Evenik)*, Alex Papana *(Paul Ludovescu)*, H.T. Tsiang *(Yuen Chiu Ling)*, Key Chang *(Adm. Kentara Yamagichi)*, Allen Jung *(Itsubi Sakai)*, Wing Foo *(Police Captain)*, Paul Fung *(Court Clerk)*, Joseph Kim *(Prosecutor)*, Luke Chan *(Court Stenographer)*, Beal Wong *(Toma Nogato)*, Marshall Thompson *(Morrison)*, Lee Tung-Foo *(3rd Judge)*, Spencer Chan, Leon Lontoc, Roque Espiritu, Harold Fong, Bruce Wong, Johnny Dong *(Naval Aides)*, James Leong, Eddie Lee, King Kong, Pete Katchenaro, Angel Cruz *(Army Aides)*, Philip Ahn *(Saburo Goto)*, Clarence Lung *(Japanese Lieutenant)*, Nestor Paiva *(Francisco De Los Santos)*, Benson Fong *(Moy Ling)*.

One of the most harrowing and moving WW II films ever produced, THE PURPLE HEART (given to those U.S. servicemen wounded or killed in combat) is the story of two bomber crews captured by the Japanese after the 1942 Gen. Jimmy Doolittle raid against Tokyo. Andrews is the ranking American officer of the eight bomber crew members who are imprisoned in Japan and brought to trial not as prisoners of war but as war criminals. The false charge is made against them that they and their bombers purposely dropped bombs on schools, hospitals, and other nonmilitary targets. When none of the Americans will admit to such atrocities, they are taken from their cells one by one and tortured, not so much to gain the admission but so that their Japanese interrogators can learn the base from which their bombers flew. All of them, of course, launched their planes from the U.S. carrier *Hornet* while at sea, but none succumbs to the fearful torture inflicted upon them and reveals their at-sea base. (In reality, the launching of bombers from a carrier during WW II was top secret in that enemy intelligence officers believed such a feat could not be accomplished. When President Franklin D. Roosevelt was informed that the Japanese were baffled as to where Doolittle's bombers came from and were desperately trying to learn the location he jocularly told American listeners to one of his famous "fire-side chats" that the bombers came from "Shangri-La, " which, of course, was the mythical land of James Hilton's famous novel turned into the Frank Capra screen gem, LOST HORIZON.) As they await their gruesome fate, the crew members think back to more pleasant scenes in civilian life, these being shown in flashback. Though alive, the eight men appear in court for the last time as hopeless cripples, except for Andrews and Levene who are inexplicably spared. Levene excorciates the prejudiced court with a defiant speech, as does Andrews who ends his statements with, "You started this war, you wanted it, and now you're going to get it and it won't be finished until your dirty little empire is wiped off the face of the earth!" With that, heads held high, the crew members march down a prison corridor, sentenced to death, to the strains of the Air Corps hymm. This film, which shows marvelous restraint by master war film director Milestone, was based on an actual kangaroo trial conducted by the Japanese during the war in which some of Doolittle's pilots were condemned as war criminals and later beheaded. Although propagandistic in nature, the script is extremely literate and sensitive and the acting is outstanding, particularly that of Andrews, Levene, Granger, Conte, and Barry. The most hated Oriental of the day, Loo (Gen. Mitsubi), enacts a vicious, sadistic Japanese officer who commits suicide in court after losing face for failing to learn the base of the attacking war planes. Though shocking then and now, this film portrays the gallantry and patriotic spirit of U.S. servicemen during the darkest days of the war in the Pacific. Producer Zanuck wrote the original story for this film under his most-used pseudonym, Melville Crossman. Newman's score is moving and as patriotic as the national anthem. For those unfamiliar with the posture of the Japanese military caste during WW II, this film is an eye-opener as well as a hair-raiser.

p, Darryl F. Zanuck; d, Lewis Milestone; w, Jerome Cady (based on a story by Melville Crossman [Zanuck]); ph, Arthur Miller; m, Alfred Newman; ed, Douglas Biggs; art d, James Basevi, Lewis Creber; set d, Thomas Little, Walter M. Scott; spec eff, Fred Sersen.

War Drama **Cas.** **(PR:C-O MPAA:NR)**

PURPLE HEART DIARY½** (1951) 73m COL bw (GB: NO TIME FOR TEARS)

Frances Langford *(Herself)*, Judd Holdren *(Lt. Mike McCormick)*, Ben Lessy *(Himself)*, Tony Romano *(Himself)*, Aline Towne *(Lt. Cathy Dietrich)*, Brett King *(Lt. Rocky Castro)*, Warren Mills *(Elmo Slimmer)*, Larry Stewart *(Cpl. Reeder)*, Joel Marston *(Kalick)*, Richard Grant *(Bunch)*, Rory Mallinson *(Capt. Sprock)*, Selmer Jackson *(Col. Tappen)*, Lyle Talbot *(Maj. Green)*, Douglas F. Bank *(Sgt. Innes)*, William Klein *(Lt. Hughes)*, Harry Guardino *(Lt. Roberts)*, Marshall Reed *(Stark)*, Steve Pendleton *(Sgt. Morse)*, George Offerman, Jr. *(Ross)*.

Used as a propoganda film for the United Service Organization (USO), showing a trio of players (Langford, Lessy, and Romano playing themselves) entertaining the troops of the Pacific theater. The thin plot involves the joy they bring troops and the inspiration felt by King, an amputee who's lost his self-respect. The USO somehow inspires the man to go on living and to continue his romance with nurse Towne. It's really minor fluff at best, but the musical numbers are enjoyable. In the end that's all this film is about anyway. Songs include: "Hold Me in Your Arms," "Hi, Fellow Tourists," "Where Are You From?" (Johnny Bradford, Barbara Hayden, Tony Romano), "Bread and Butter Woman" (Allan Roberts, Lester Lee), "Tattle-Tale Eyes" (Bradford, Romano).

p, Sam Katzman; d, Richard Quine; w, William Sackheim (based on the wartime column of Frances Langford); ph, William Whitley; ed, Henry Batista; md, Ross Di Maggio; art d, Paul Palmentola.

Drama/Musical **(PR:A MPAA:NR)**

PURPLE HILLS, THE** (1961) 60m FOX c

Gene Nelson *(Gil Shepard)*, Joanna Barnes *(Amy Carter)*, Kent Taylor *(Johnny Barnes)*, Russ Bender *(Deputy Sheriff)*, Jerry Summers *(Martin Beaumont)*, Danny Zapien *(Chito)*, Jack Carr *(A. J. Beaumont)*, Medford Salway *(Young Brave)*, Jack Riggs.

In 1870's Arizona, Nelson is a cowboy who shoots down a wanted outlaw. But when he rides into town to collect the $8,000 reward money, he is met by the dead man's partner, Taylor, who claims to have done the killing. Things get stickier when Summers, the younger brother of the dead man, vows revenge for his brother's killer. Bender, a local sheriff, decides to settle the argument by having all three ride out to the dead man's grave. En route they meet Barnes, Summers' guardian. She's attracted to Nelson, but can't understand his burning desire for money. They attempt to dig up the outlaw's body, but the grave turns out to be empty. Apaches who worshipped the man have stolen the body. Taylor kills the sheriff and the group rides off. During an Indian raid, Taylor is wounded but covers the others so they can make an escape. Taylor finally dies and Nelson realizes that Barnes' love is worth more than money. Summers has learned some things as well, realizing that his brother was a mean man who deserved death. Considering that this was released in 1961, the short (one hour) running time is a real surprise. Essentially this is a routine western, but differs from its program forebears of the 1940s with a crueler sense of violence and confusion over what good and bad amount to.

p&d, Maury Dexter; w, Edith Cash Pearl, Russ Bender; ph, Floyd Crosby (CinemaScope, DeLuxe Color); m, Richard LaSalle; ed, Jodie Copelan; art d, John Mansbridge; cos, Ray Summers, Paula Giokaris; makeup, Bob Mark.

Western **(PR:O MPAA:NR)**

PURPLE MASK, THE½** (1955) 82m UNIV c

Tony Curtis *(Rene)*, Colleen Miller *(Laurette)*, Dan O'Herlihy *(Brisquet)*, Gene Barry *(Capt. Laverne)*, Angela Lansbury *(Mme. Valentine)*, George Dolenz *(Marcel Cadonal)*, John Hoyt *(Rochet)*, Donald Randolph *(Majolin)*, Robert Cornthwaite *(Napoleon)*, Stephen Bekassy *(Baron De Morleve)*, Paul Cavanagh *(Due de Latour)*, Myrna Hansen *(Constance)*, Allison Hayes *(Irene)*, Betty Jane Howarth *(Yvonne)*, Carl Milletaire *(Edouard)*, Gene Darcy *(De Morsanne)*, Robert Hunter *(De Vivanne)*, Richard Avonde *(Roger)*, Glase Lohman *(Raoul)*, Diane Dubois *(Sabine)*, Jane Easton *(Marie)*, Richard Richonne *(Passerby)*, Everett Glass *(Father Brochard)*, Jean De Briac *(Count De Chauvac)*, Adrienne D'Ambricourt *(Mme. Anais)*, George Bruggeman *(French Officer)*, Albert Godderis *(Old Servant)*.

Curtis plays a young French adventurer who secretly is the mysterious Purple Mask, a fabled hero (at least in this film) who rides about as a sort of Scarlet Pimpernel, saving Royalists from Napoleon's guillotine. Once in Curtis' custody, they are spirited out of France to England. Naturally, Napoleon, played by Cornthwaite, wants to get rid of the pesky Curtis. Though more than occasionally far-fetched as a script, THE PURPLE MASK has some good moments of swashbuckling fun. Nothing compared to a Fairbanks' swashbuckler, but cheap fun in its own way just the same.

p, Howard Christie; d, H. Bruce Humberstone; w, Oscar Brodney, Charles Latour (based on the play "Le Chevalier Au Masques" by Paul Armont, Jean Manoussi); ph, Irving Glassberg (CinemaScope, Technicolor); ed, Ted J. Kent; md, Joseph Gershenson; art d, Alexander Golitzen, Eric Orbom; cos, Bill Thomas.

Adventure **(PR:A MPAA:NR)**

PURPLE NOON*** (1961, Fr./Ital.) 115m Paris-Panitalia-Titanus/Times Film c (PLEIN SOLEIL; IN PIENO SOLE; AKA: LUST FOR EVIL)

Alain Delon *(Tom Ripley)*, Marie Laforet *(Marge)*, Maurice Ronet *(Philippe Greenleaf)*, Elvire Popesco *(Mme. Popova)*, Erno Crisa *(Inspector Riccordi)*, Frank Latimore *(O'Brien)*, Billy Kearns *(Freddy)*, Ave Ninchi *(Signora Gianna)*, Viviane Chantel *(La Belge)*.

Delon and Ronet are a pair of Americans on tour in Italy. Delon is trying to earn $5,000, promised by Ronet's father if he can persuade his companion to return to America. It soon becomes obvious that this is going to be an impossible task. As Delon slowly grows envious of his pal's lavish lifestyle, including a fine wardrobe, boat, and a beautiful mistress (Laforet), he decides that instead of persuading Ronet to go home, Delon will take his place. He stabs Ronet with a fish knife, then wraps the body in a tarpaulin and dumps him over the side of the boat. He assumes Ronet's identity and lifestyle with ease. He tells Laforet that her lover is no longer interested in her. Delon's ruse is discovered by an old pal of Ronet's and once more there is a murder. He realizes that Ronet will be suspected of the killing and stages a phony suicide, including signing a fake suicide note leaving all of Ronet's fortune to Laforet. Becoming himself once more, Delon begins to court Laforet, and slowly she falls in love with him. Everything is going well until Laforet pulls the boat into dry dock. Hanging off the propeller is the body on Ronet.

p, Raymond Hakim, Robert Hakim; d, Rene Clement; w, Clement, Paul Gegauff (based on the novel *The Talented Mr. Ripley* by Patricia Highsmith); ph, Henri Decae (Eastmancolor); m, Nino Rota; ed, Francoise Javet; art d, Paul Bertrand; ch, Jean Guelis.

Drama/Crime **(PR:O MPAA:NR)**

PURPLE PLAIN, THE*** (1954, Brit.) 100m TC/RANK-UA c

Gregory Peck *(Forrester)*, Win Min Than *(Anna)*, Bernard Lee *(Dr. Harris)*, Maurice Denham *(Blore)*, Ram Gopal *(Mr. Phang)*, Brenda de Banzie *(Miss McNab)*, Lyndon Brook *(Carrington)*, Anthony Bushell *(Comdr. Aldridge)*, Jack McNaughton *(Sgt. Brown)*, Harold Siddons *(Navigator Williams)*, Peter Arne *(Flight Lieutenant)*, Mya Mya Spencer *(Dorothy)*, Josephine Griffin *(Mrs. Forrester)*, Lane Meddick *(Radio Operator)*, John Tinn *(Burmese Jeweler)*, Soo Ah Song *(Old Woman)*, Dorothy Alison *(Nurse)*.

In THE PURPLE PLAIN, Peck is back in his rightful milieu: a thin-lipped, firm-jawed man who is having trouble fighting inner turmoil and just as much difficulty with what's happening around him. Peck had been married to Griffin, but when she dies in a London air raid on their wedding night, be blames himself (this is shown in a flashback to the early years of the war). It's now 1945 and Peck is in Burma, where he is a Canadian pilot. (Actually, the picture was shot in Ceylon—now Sri Lanka—but how many people would know the difference other than a few Burmese, Sri Lankans, and Arthur C. Clarke?) Peck is taking fellow officer Denham to a routine destination, accompanied by his navigator, Brook. Their plane crashes in the jungle and Brook is hurt. They are downed in the heart of Japanese-held territory and their situation is, at best, precarious. Peck is all for waiting at the wreckage, but since they have no water and that is a precious commodity in the heat of the jungle, they attempt an escape. Peck is a tough type, not given to betraying his feelings, and fills his performance with meaningful expressions rather than dialog. The trek through the jungle is arduous and Denham, who thinks they will never make it and fears being captured by the Japanese, takes his own life, leaving Peck the task of carrying the immobile Brook on his back. Before getting out, Peck meets Burmese beauty Than and she helps to get him out of his psychological doldrums. The romantic interludes seem to have been inserted only for the distaff members of the audience and bear little weight in the overall style and content of the picture. Novelist Eric Ambler wrote the screenplay in between his labors on such books as *The Mask Of Dimitrios, Journey Into Fear*and many more which were made into movies. In a small role, note Brenda De Banzie, who made her mark in THE 39 STEPS, THE ENTERTAINER, and many more. Editor Donner later took up directing and was responsible for THE CARETAKER and WHAT'S NEW PUSSYCAT? among others.

p, John Bryan; d, Robert Parrish; w, Eric Ambler (based on the novel by H.E. Bates); ph, Geoffrey Unsworth; m, John Veale; ed, Clive Donner; md, Muir Mathieson; art d, Jack Maxsted; set d, Dario Simoni; spec eff, Bill Warrinton, Charles Staffell; makeup, Geoffrey Rodway.

War Drama **(PR:A-C MPAA:NR)**

PURPLE RIDERS, THE (SEE: PURPLE VIGILANTES, THE, 1938)

PURPLE TAXI, THE* (1977, Fr./Ital./Ireland) 107m Sofracima-Rizzoli-TFI-Nation Film Studios of Ireland-Sphinx/Quartet c (UN TAXI MAUVE)

Charlotte Rampling *(Sharon)*, Philippe Noiret *(Philippe)*, Agostina Belli *(Anne Taubelman)*, Peter Ustinov *(Taubelman)*, Fred Astaire *(Dr. Scully)*, Edward Albert, Jr. *(Jerry)*, Mairin O'Sullivan *(Colleen)*, Jack Watson *(Sean)*.

Would you believe an Irish soap opera, starring French, American, and British actors, made in English by a French director? No? You're right. There's little to believe in this well-shot picture that goes far beyond drama into postured playing by almost everyone concerned. When Ireland announced that artists would pay no income taxes, it attracted a great many famous authors and others like Fred Forsythe, John Huston, and even Leslie Bricusse. With that in mind, consider the episodic plot of this. Noiret is a French author living in Ireland who makes friends with American Albert, who has come to Ireland after an incident in his life that killed his girl friend in a fire when both were smoking hash. Astaire is an American physician who has come to Ireland to spend his last years (he should have known better after his Irish flop in FINIAN'S RAINBOW). Ustinov is a hammy rakehell who is in Ireland with his apparently mute daughter Belli, who may actually be his niece and might just be in love with Ustinov. Albert's attentions cause her to be able to speak again, while Noiret takes up with Albert's haughty sister, Rampling, but that turns out to be abortive. In the end, Relli and Albert stay in Ireland to raise horses and everyone goes off in opposite directions, something this picture also does. The novel upon which this is based was a hit in Europe and the horde of producers attached to the project must have thought it could be transformed, en toto, to the screen, but once they put the literary characters into flesh and blood, it didn't work. The list of production companies involved indicates that this must have been one of those coproduction deals where each firm contributing gets exclusive release in their country, hence the various nationalities involved. The language and the sexuality make this a dubious picture for anyone under 18. The entire movie is dubious entertainment for anyone under 98.

p, Peter Rawley, Hugo Lodrini; d, Yves Boisset; w, Michel Deon, Boisset (based on the book by Deon); ph, Tonino Delli Colli (Eastmacolor); m, Philippe Sarde; ed, Albert Jurgensen.

Drama **Cas.** **(PR:O MPAA:R)**

PURPLE V, THE** (1943) 58m REP bw

John Archer *(Joe Thorne)*, Mary McLeod *(Katti Forster)*, Fritz Kortner *(Thomas Forster)*, Rex Williams *(Paul Forster)*, Kurt Katch *(Johann Keller)*, Walter Sande *(Otto Horner)*, William Vaughn *(Oberst von Ritter)*, Peter Lawford *(Roger)*, Kurt Kreuger *(Walter Heyse)*, Eva Hyde *(Marta)*, Irene Seidner *(Mrs. Vogel)*.

This routine thriller programmer was built around a WW II theme to satisfy public demand for such fare. Kortner is a German school teacher who refuses to follow Hitler's madness. He helps a lost American flyer, Archer, back to the Allies when the man crashes. Archer carries with him some secrets about the North African campaign which he safely delivers to the intended destination. Kortner is killed by the Germans, but dies a hero. The picture is slow to start, but once the story gets underway, this film has some good suspense elements. Look for an appearance by a young Lawford.

p&d, George Sherman; w, Bertram Millhauser, Curt Siodmak (based on a story by Robert R. Mill); ph, Ernest Miller; ed, Charles Craft; md, Morton Scott; art d, Russell Kimball; set d, Otto Siegel.

War **(PR:O MPAA:NR)**

PURPLE VIGILANTES, THE*** (1938) 58m REP bw (GB: THE PURPLE RIDERS)

Bob Livingston *(Stoney Brooke)*, Ray Corrigan *(Tuscon Smith)*, Max Terhune *(Lullaby Joslin)*, Joan Barclay *(Jean)*, Earl Dwire *(Ross)*, Earle Hodgins *(McAllister)*, Francis Sayles *(Jones)*, George Chesebro *(Eggers)*, Robert Fiske *(Drake)*, Jack Perrin *(Duncan)*, Ernie Adams *(Blake)*, William Gould *(Jenkins)*, Harry Strang *(Murphy)*, Edward Cassidy *(Sheriff Dyer)*, Frank O'Connor *(Tracy)*.

A group of purple hooded vigilantes clean up a town, then decide to clean up for themselves. Using their disguises, they anonymously start fleecing the citizens for everything they can. Leave it to the Three Mesquiteers (Livingston, Corrigan and Terhune) to ride in and save the day. This was the second of the Three Mesquiteers series to be directed by Sherman who would become the series long running helmsman. It's also one of the better films in the series. Rather than the lowbrow comedy found in the Mesquiteers films, this employs wit and style. The pace is steamlined and keeps a nice balance between plot movement and action sequences. Barclay is Livingston's romantic interest, but this barely exists, giving way to the more important action. Entertaining and enjoyable. (See THREE MESQUITEER SERIES, Index.)

p, Sol C. Siegel; d, George Sherman; w, Betty Burbridge, Oliver Drake (based on characters created by William Colt MacDonald); ph, Ernest Miller; ed, Lester Orlebeck; md, Alberto Columbo.

Western **Cas.** **(PR:A MPAA:NR)**

PURSE STRINGS* (1933, Brit.) 69m British and Dominions/PAR bw

Dorothy Bouchier *(Mary Willmore)*, Gyles Isham *(James Willmore)*, G.H. Mulcaster *(Edward Ashby)*, Allan Jeayes *(Walford)*, Joan Henley *(Ida Bentley)*, Evelyn Roberts *(Beauchamp)*.

An improbable comedy starring Bouchier as the wife of stingy, wealthy Isham. She is forced to resort to shoplifting for a source of money, and is eventually caught and taken advantage of by a store manager. In retaliation the husband sues, but loses his fortune in the battle. The not-so-grand finale has Bouchier making her broke husband pay for his meanness.

p, Herbert Wilcox; d, Henry Edwards; w, Bernard Parry (based on the play by Parry); ph, Henry Harris.

Drama **(PR:A MPAA:NR)**

PURSUED½** (1934) 68m FOX bw

Rosemary Ames *(Mona)*, Victor Jory *(Beauregard)*, Pert Kelton *(Gilda)*, Russell Hardie *(David Landeen)*, George Irving *(Dr. Steiner)*, Torben Meyer *(Hansen)*.

Ames is a nice girl on a South Seas island. She's saving her pennies so she can go to San Francisco and open a tea room. Hardie comes to the island to take over his uncle's plantation, but bad guy Jory wants the place and tries to kill Hardie. Ames nurses the boy back to health (and romance), but Jory tries again. This time he takes no chances, kidnaping Ames and really going after Hardie in a brutal fight. Ames shoots the villain and all ends happily. This is a standard plot, but Ames works hard to make it better than it has a right to be. Production values are otherwise standard.

p, Sol M. Wurtzel; d, Louis King; w, Lester Cole, Stuart Anthony (based on the story by Larry Evans); ph, L.W. O'Connell; md, Samuel Kaylin.

Drama **(PR:A MPAA:NR)**

PURSUED*½** (1947) 101m United States Pictures/WB bw

Teresa Wright *(Thorley Callum)*, Robert Mitchum *(Jeb Rand)*, Judith Anderson *(Medora Callum)*, Dean Jagger *(Grant Callum)*, Alan Hale *(Jake Dingle)*, Harry Carey, Jr. *(Prentice McComber)*, John Rodney *(Adam Callum)*, Clifton Young *(The Sergeant)*, Ernest Severn *(Jeb at Age 8)*, Charles Bates *(Adam at Age 10)*, Peggy Miller *(Thorley at Age 8)*, Norman Jolley, Lane Chandler, Elmer Ellingwood, Jack Montgomery, Ian MacDonald *(The Callums)*, Ray Teal *(Army Captain)*, Ian Wolfe *(Coroner)*, Virginia Brissac *(Woman at Wedding)*, Kathy Jeanne Johnson, Mickey Little, Scotty Hugenberg, Eddy Waller, Russ Clark, Crane Whitley, Lester Dorr, Harry Lamont, Tom Fadden.

In this absorbing if offbeat western, Mitchum spends most of his time being victimized for inexplicable reasons, none of them made clear until the end of a very strange film. The laconic, sleepy-eyed hero is one of two sons, the other being Rodney, living under the stern guidance of parents Anderson and Jagger. Rodney is the favorite and Jagger goes out of his way to compel son Mitchum to superhuman efforts to prove himself. The setting is an abandoned ranch house in New Mexico at the turn of the century. Here Mitchum is hiding from a lynch posse with Jagger at its head. He thinks back upon his childhood and the murder of his father and how he had been adopted by Anderson and Jagger, going to live with them and their children, Rodney and daughter Wright. In a flashback, the viewer sees rugged individualist Jagger demand that American honor be served at the outbreak of the Spanish-American War. One of his two boys must enlist and he tosses a coin. Mitchum loses and joins up. He survives to return a hero and seek the affection of stepsister Wright. Rodney and Mitchum then get into a violent fight over each other's claim to the family ranch and Mitchum again loses out after another unlucky toss of the coin. He is more fortunate at gambling and wins a huge amount of money only to be ambushed by Rodney who hates him for some unexplained reason. Mitchum, forced to defend his life, kills his stepbrother and now both Jagger and Anderson demand that he pay with his life. When he is acquitted, Wright promises her parents that she will execute the scoundrel. She deliberately weds Mitchum while planning to kill him but her shot misses on their wedding night and she later believes Mitchum to be innocent, falling in love with him. Jagger, impatient for revenge, then leads a lynch mob after Mitchum. By then the pursued one has learned that his stepbrother Rodney was unbalanced since childhood when witnessing his mother, Anderson, *flagrante delicto* with Mitchum's father who was killed for his dallying. Jagger finally tracks down Mitchum and is about to hang him when a repentant Anderson shoots her husband, allowing Mitchum and Wright to seek happiness beyond the ruins of their youth. Walsh directs this film with great style and takes his time in explaining the mysterious events surrounding Mitchum. The film was written really for Wright by her husband Busch. She is splendid in the role of the confused daughter but Mitchum gives her little enthusiastic support (in those days viewers did not realize that Mitchum's lack of enthusiasm was his greatest attraction). This was one of the first so-called "adult" westerns that approached its dark tale with psychological script and elaborate technical methods. Cameraman Howe uses his cameras as stethoscopes to the heart of the troubled characters, caught in a web-like biblical plot more fully developed a decade later in Elia Kazan's EAST OF EDEN. This one is not for everyone; PURSUED is sort of a western *film noir* entry that is somber and even depressing in spots, but certainly engrossing. p, Milton Sperling; d, Raoul Walsh; w, Niven Busch; ph, James Wong Howe; m, Max Steiner; ed, Christian Nyby; md, Leo F. Forbstein; art d, Ted Smith; set d, Jack McConaghy; cos, Leah Rhodes; spec eff, William McGann, Willard Van Elger.

Western **(PR:C-O MPAA:NR)**

PURSUERS, THE** (1961, Brit.) 63m Danziger/COL bw

Cyril Shaps *(Karl Luther)*, Francis Matthews *(David Nelson)*, Susan Denny *(Jenny Walmer)*, Sheldon Lawrence *(Rico)*, George Murcell *(Freddy)*, John Gabriel *(Wally)*, Tony Doonan *(Wilmo)*, Steve Plytas *(Petersen)*.

A forgettable film about a private investigator's pursuit of an elusive concentration camp head. After tracking him relentlessly, the investigator finds his man hiding out at a nightclub singer's apartment.

p, Philip Elton, Ralph Goddard; d, Godfrey Grayson; w, Brian Clemens, David Nicholl.

Crime **(PR:A MPAA:NR)**

PURSUIT** (1935) 60m MGM bw

Chester Morris *(Mitchell)*, Sally Eilers *(Maxine)*, Scotty Beckett *(Donald)*, Henry Travers *(Reynolds)*, C. Henry Gordon *(Shawn)*, Dorothy Peterson *(Mrs. McCoy)*, Granville Bates *(Auto Camp Proprietor)*, Minor Watson *(Hale)*, Harold Huber *(Jake)*, Dewey Robinson *(Jo Jo)*, Erville Alderson *(Cop)*.

The title tells it all. Morris and Eilers rescue Beckett (of the "Our Gang" comedies) from would-be kidnappers and return him to his rightful mother in Mexico. The film is really a non-stop chase employing an airplane, a truck, a flivver, and finally a broken down station wagon. Morris (who was reduced to this B-Flick after his first A film PUBLIC HERO NO. 1) and Eilers are given the standard wisecracking sort of dialog, that of course inspires movie romances. But it's directed at a pell-mell pace and the script doesn't give anybody much of a chance to show their talents. Though initially exciting, the film quickly burns out long before it's over.

p, Lucien Hubbard, Ned Marin; d, Edwin L. Marin; w, Wells Root (based on the story "Gallant Highway" by Lawrence G. Blochman); ph, Charles Clarke, Sidney Wagner; m, William Axt; ed, George Boemler.

Drama/Action **(PR:A MPAA:NR)**

PURSUIT*½ (1975) 86m Key International c

Ray Danton, DeWitt Lee, Troy Nabors, Diane Taylor, Eva Kovacs, Jason Clark.

Wet in the desert, PURSUIT is the story of an Army scout being chased by a hungry, unfriendly bear. He succeeds in making it to the safety of his fort, only to be gunned down by an over-cautious guard. Danton, whose slick gangster qualities earned him the lead roles in THE RISE AND FALL OF LEGS DIAMOND (1960) and THE GEORGE RAFT STORY (1961), was unfortunately later reduced to second-rate horrors like this one.

p, Vern Piehl; d, Thomas Quillen; w, DeWitt Lee, Jack Lee, ph (DeLuxe Color).

Adventure/Drama **(PR:O MPAA:R)**

PURSUIT OF D.B. COOPER, THE* (1981) 100m Polygram/UNIV c

Robert Duvall *(Gruen)*, Treat Williams *(Meade)*, Kathryn Harrold *(Hannah)*, Ed Flanders *(Brigadier)*, Paul Gleason *(Remson)*, R.G. Armstrong *(Dempsey)*, Dorothy Fielding *(Denise)*, Nicolas Coster *(Avery)*, Cooper Huckabee *(Homer)*, Howard K. Smith *(Himself)*, Christopher Curry *(Hippie)*, Ramon Chavez *(El Capitan)*, Stacy Newton *(Cowboy)*, Pat Ast *(Horse Lady)*, Jack Dunlap, Brad Sergi, Michael Potter, Charles Benton, Mike Casper, James Lee, Henry Kendrick, James Wiers, Mark Jeffreys, D.G. Smilnak, David Adams, Charles Haigh, Stephen Blood, Tommy Ciulla, Karen Newhouse, Richard Brown, Michael O'Hare, Robert Sola, Tom May, Sanford Gibbons, Synn Radcliffe, Mearl Ross, Patrick Garcia, Gregory Suke, Jessica Garcia, Leigh Webb, Jim Clouse, David Falkosky, John Herold, Bill Townsend, Christine Dolny, Michael Goodsite, Glenda Young, Dave Gilbert, Bill Whitman, Conrad Marshall.

Take a terrific true crime story that is still unsolved, give it to the wrong people, and what do you get? Phew! Universal offered a million bucks as part of the publicity for this movie: If anyone could come up with the whereabouts or information leading to the capture of "D.B. Cooper" they might become rich. No one claimed the money but several attempts at it were made. Whoever the real "Cooper" is and wherever he is, he probably laughed himself silly at this fanciful depiction of his escape. In the early 1970s, a man identifying himself as "D.B. Cooper" parachuted out of the back door of a jet after demanding $200,000 to keep him from blowing the plane up. This movie begins at that point as Williams leaps out, goes back to see his wife, Harrold, and is trailed by Duvall, a one-time Green Beret, who recognizes the description of Williams as being one of his former charges. At the same time, Gleason is also an old pal of Williams and goes after him for a share of the money. A series of mindless chases ensues and nothing much else. John Frankenheimer began directing the movie, was replaced by Buzz Kulik, and the final credit goes to Spottiswoode, but he would have been wise to have used a pseudonym, the same way "D.B. Cooper" did. Although Tennant and Kranze are listed as executive producers, it was Peter Guber who was the *eminence grise* behind the scenes, as he was running the ill-fated Polygram Pictures company that made the film. Tennant was a former agent who was depicted in "Helter Skelter," the TV movie about the Charles Manson case, for it was he who was called to identify the bodies of Sharon Tate, Abigail Folger, hairdresser Jay Sebring, and the others killed in that bloody August night in Benedict Canyon. The truth about "D.B. Cooper" has yet to be told and may never be. The same should have been true of this dumb movie.

p, Daniel Wigutow, Michael Taylor; d, Roger Spottiswoode; w, Jeffrey Alan Fiskin (based on the book *Free Fall* By J.D. Reed); ph, Harry Stradling (Metrocolor); m, James Horner; ed, Robbe Roberts, Allan Jacobs; prod d, Preston Ames; m/1 "Shine," Waylon Jennings, (sung by Jennings).

Crime Drama **Cas.** **(PR:C MPAA:PG)**

PURSUIT OF HAPPINESS, THE***   (1934) 72m PAR bw

Francis Lederer (*Max Christmann*), Joan Bennett (*Prudence Kirkland*), Charlie Ruggles (*Aaron Kirkland*), Mary Boland (*Comfort Kirkland*), Walter Kingsford (*Reverend Lyman Banks*), Minor Watson (*Col. Sherwood*), Adrian Morris (*Thad Jennings*), Barbara Barondess (*Meg Mallory*), Duke York (*Jonathan*), Burr Caruth (*Rev. Myles*), Jules Cowles (*The Drunk*), Irving Bacon (*Bijah*), Spencer Charters (*Sam Evans*), John Marston (*Tall Conspirator*), Edward Peil, Sr. (*Peddler*), Paul Kruger (*Orderly*), Georgie Billings (*Little Boy*), Ricca Allen (*Boy's Mother*), Holmes Herbert (*Gen. Sir Henry Clinton*), Boyd Irwin (*Lord William Pitt*), Henry Mowbray (*King George III*), Winter Hall (*Max's Uncle*), Bert Sprotte (*Col. Hoffer*), Colin Tapley (*Aide to Sir Henry Clinton*), Reginald Pasch (*Col. Hoffer's Aide*), Hans Von Morhart (*Corporal*), Baron Hesse (*Coachman*).

In 1700's New England, young betrothed couples engaged in a parctice known as "bundling." This socially acceptable custom would have the loving pair sleep together on cold winter nights, fully clothed of course, because a center board would separate them. Despite the one joke nature of the story, THE PURSUIT OF HAPPINESS works in a fine, good natured way. Bennett plays a Puritan maiden in 1776 Connecticut. She meets Lederer, a Hessian, and the two fall in love and eventually bed. Though the premise is wide open for some cheap sex gags or a good farce, this film is neither. The humor is based on innocence and is well-played by the believable leads. The result is a film that is quite amusing in its own way.

p, Arthur Hornblow, Jr.; d, Alexander Hall; w, Stephen Morehouse Avery, Jack Cunningham, J.P. McEvoy. Virginia Van Upp (based on the play by Lawrence Langner, Armina Marshall); ph, Karl Struss.

Comedy   **(PR:C MPAA:NR)**

PURSUIT OF HAPPINESS, THE**½   (1971) 93m COL c

Michael Sarrazin (*William Popper*), Barbara Hershey (*Jane Kauffman*), Robert Klein (*Melvin Lasher*), Sada Thompson (*Ruth Lawrence*), Ralph Waite (*Detective Cromie*), Arthur Hill (*John Popper*), E.G. Marshall (*Daniel Lawrence*), Maya Kenin (*Mrs. Conroy*), Rue McClanahan (*Mrs. O'Mara*), Peter White (*Terence Lawrence*), Joseph Attles (*Holmes*), Beulah Garrick (*Josephine*), Ruth White (*Mrs. Popper*), Barnard Hughes (*Judge Vogel*), David Doyle (*James Moran*), Gilbert Lewis (*George Wilson*), Albert Henderson (*McArdle*), Tom Rosqui (*Defense Attorney Keller*), Jack Somack (*Judge Palumbo*), Edward Kovens (*1st Guard*), Charles Durning (*2nd Guard*), Ed Setrakian (*Policeman*), Ted Beniades (*Traffic Cop*), William Devane (*Pilot*), Philip Larson (*Student*).

Sarrazin plays an alienated social drop-out who accidentally runs over a woman in a rain storm. Though he can prove it was an accident, Sarrazin refuses to cooperate with "the establishment," and is sentenced to a year in prison. There he gets involved in a knifing, but manages to escape. He looks up his old girlfriend, Hershey, and the two fly off to Canada. This is a well-played drama with some sincere performances by Sarrazin and Hershey. Klein, a noted stand-up comedian, provides some humor as the hippie buddy. The plot, however, is full of illogical actions, and the dialog used by the "young people" was already dated at the time of this shooting. Sarrazin's indifference to his sentencing is completely unbelievable, especially his escape with only a week left to serve. The direction is good, however, giving the film a nice forward movement without cluttering the story. White, who played Sarrazin's grandmother, died following the film's completion. The producer was noted talk show host, Susskind.

p, David Susskind; d, Robert Mulligan; w, Jon Boothe, George L. Sherman (based on the novel by Thomas Rogers); ph, Dick Kratina (Eastmancolor); m, David Grusin; ed, Folmar Blangsted; art d, George Jenkins; set d, Ben Rutter; cos, Ann Roth; m/l, Randy Newman; makeup, Robert Laden.

Drama   **(PR:O MPAA:GP)**

PURSUIT OF THE GRAF SPEE*½   (1957, Brit.) 106m RANK c(GB: THE BATTLE OF THE RIVER PLATE)

John Gregson (*Capt. F.S. Bell, "Exeter"*), Anthony Quayle (*Commodore Henry Harwood, "Ajax"*), Peter Finch (*Capt. Hans Langsdorff, "Admiral Graf Spee"*), Ian Hunter (*Capt. Woodhouse, "Ajax"*), Jack Gwillim (*Capt. Parry, "Achilles"*), Bernard Lee (*Capt. Patrick Dove, "Africa Shell"*), Lionel Murton (*Mike Fowler, American Radio Commentator*), Anthony Bushell (*Mr. Millington-Drake, British Minister*), Peter Illing (*Dr. Guani, Uruguayan Foreign Minister*), Michael Goodliffe (*Capt. McCall, British Naval Attache*), Patrick MacNee (*Lt. Cmdr. Medley, Commmodore Harwood's Aide*), John Chandos (*Dr. Langmann, German Minister*), Douglas Wilmer (*Mr. Desmoulins, French Minister*), William Squire (*Ray Martin*), Roger Delgado (*Capt. Varela*), Andrew Cruickshank (*Capt. Stubs*), Edward Atienza (*Pop*), Christopher Lee (*Manola, Cantina Manager*), April Olrichs (*Dolores, Cantina Singer*), Nigel Stock (*Murphy, Merchant Officer*), Anthony Newley (*Ralph Merchant Seaman*), John Merivale (*Pilot, "Achilles" Bridge*), John le Mesurier (*Chaplain, "Exeter"*), David Farrar (*Narrator*), Brian Worth, Barry Foster, Judd, Ships: H.M.S. Sheffield (*H.M.S. Ajax*), H.M.S. Delhi (*H.M.S. Achilles*), H.M.S. Jamaica (*H.M.S. Exeter*), H.M.S. Cumberland (*H.M.S. Cumberland*), U.S. Heavy Cruiser Salem (*Admiral Graf Spee*).

"The Graf Spee" is a German battleship during World War II. It's chased by a British force all the way to South America. Though the local natives won't help, the Englishmen continue the chase. Problems arise when South American governments help out the Graf Spee, but at last the British forces catch up with the ship and sink it. The real problem with this film is it's focus. Powell was noted for his wonderful humanistic films (such as THE RED SHOES), but here characters are all but subordinated to the mighty ships. The result is a tedious affair with some glimpses of fine performances, particulary Finch as the German commander. The battle scenes are well-staged and exciting to watch. But they are hampered by some occasional confusion as to which ship is firing at whom.

p,d&w, Michael Powell, Emeric Pressburger; ph, Christopher Challis (VistaVision,

Technicolor); m, Brian Easdale; ed, Reginald Mills; prod d, Arthur Lawson; md, Frederick Lewis; art d, Hein Heckroth.

War   **(PR:A MPAA:NR)**

PURSUIT TO ALGIERS**½   (1945) 65m UNIV bw

Basil Rathbone (*Sherlock Holmes*), Nigel Bruce (*Dr. John H. Watson*), Marjorie Riordan (*Sheila Woodbury, Singer*), Rosalind Ivan (*Agatha Dunham*), Martin Kosleck (*Mirko*), John Abbott (*Jodri*), Frederick Worlock (*Prime Minister*), Morton Lowry (*Sanford, Ship's Steward*), Leslie Vincent (*Nikolas "Watson"*), Gerald Hamer (*Kingston*), Rex Evans (*Gregor*), Tom Dillon (*Restaurant Proprietor*), Sven Hugo Borg (*Johansson, Ship's Purser*), Wee Willie Davis (*Gubec*), Wilson Benge (*Mr. Arnold, Clergyman*), Gregory Gay (*Ravez*), Dorothy Kellogg (*Fuzzy Looking Woman*), Olaf Hytten (*Simpson the Gunsmith*).

This is one of the lesser Rathbone SHERLOCK HOLMES films from his famous series in the 1940s. Rathbone and his eternal sidekick Bruce find themselves hot on the trail of an assassin. Vincent is a prince who must return to his home country from London after his father is killed. Rathbone schedules himself a private flight with the monarch while Bruce takes a Mediterranean ship, the S.S. Friesland (actually the name of a sinister ship from an original Doyle "Holmes" story that was never published.) Bruce makes friends with his fellow passengers including Riordan, a young singer from Brooklyn. Also aboard is Ivan, a sinister old spinster with a pistol in her handbag. Bruce hears of a plane going down in the Pyrenees and becomes sick with worry. The captain asks him to look in on the passenger in the cabin next to his; of course it is Rathbone. With him is Vincent, who must now pose as Bruce's nephew. As the ship becomes fogbound things become dangerous. Riordan behaves peculiarly, particularly when she learns that Rathbone is on ship. Bruce also begins to mistrust a steward (Lowry) who is lurking about. When the ship makes an unscheduled stop at Lisbon, an odd trio boards: Evans, a gregarious man, Davis, a gigantic mute, and Kosleck, a small, lithe man. A murder attempt is made on the prince. Poison is found and Kosleck is stopped from hurling a knife when Rathbone drops a porthole cover on him. It seems the great detective recognized Kosleck from his circus days as a knifethrower and knew what was up. Before reaching Algiers Rathbone discovers Riordan's secret: she is an unwilling courier for an international jewel thief. Rathbone promises to help her and that night attends a party thrown by Ivan. Bruce, in a wonderful moment, recites the tale of the giant rat of Sumatra. Rathbone discovers a bomb concealed in a party favor and throws it out to sea in the nick of time. But on pulling into Algiers the detective is overwhelmed, then bound and gagged. Vincent is kidnaped and all seems lost. But it turns out Rathbone has had the last laugh, for the real prince was Lowry, the unusually ominous steward. Press releases promised that this would be "5000 miles of terror!" but PURSUIT TO ALGIERS is hardly that. In fact, it's an often silly, overplayed piece with far too much predictability to work as an example of Holmes' brilliant logic. Bruce is campy and at one point breaks into song with the little ditty "Loch Lomond." Ivan is even more campy. Rathbone appears bored with the whole proceedings, as well he should. The problem with this film is its utter and complete predictability. The clues are all there and easy for the audience to guess at. The difference between the Holmes' films and the original stories is one of dramatics. The films play up the melodrama whereas the originals stressed mental logic. Unfortunately, the film series never really noticed this and reduced the great detective to an extremely stylish detective. (See: SHERLOCK HOLMES Series: Index).

p&d, Roy William Neill; w, Leonard Lee (based on *The Return of Sherlock Holmes* by Sir Arthur Conan Doyle); ph, Paul Ivano; m, Edgar Fairchild; ed, Saul Goodkind; md, Fairchild; art d, John B. Goodman, Martin Obzine; m/l, Jack Brooks-Milton Rosen, Everett Cutler-Rosen.

Mystery   **Cas.**   **(PR:A MPAA:NR)**

PUSHER, THE**   (1960) 82m UA bw

Kathy Carlyle (*Laura*), Felice Orlandi (*The Pusher*), Douglas F. Rodgers (*Lt. Peter Byrne*), Sloan Simpson (*Harriet Byrne*), Robert Lansing (*Steve Carella*), Sara Aman (*Maria Hernandez*), Jim Boles.

A Puerto Rican teenager is found dead in a tenement basement. Near him lies a broken hypodermic needle. Carlyle is a police-man's daughter, engaged to Lansing. He's leading the investigation, helped by Rogers. Little do they realize that Carlyle is a junkie herself. She's a guilty party but goes cold turkey, and Orlandi is found to be the murderer. This turgid melodrama is routine stuff (substitute "alcohol" for drugs and you'll have a 1940s programmer), though the acting is not bad, particularly Orlandi. The real problem with this film is the racist attitudes it portrays. Puerto Ricans are lowlifes and addicts, and a white girl who's a junkie is to be pitied. The screenplay is by Robbins who went on to write a series of delightfully trashy novels.

p, Gene Milford, Sidney Katz; d, Milford; w, Harold Robbins (based on a novel by Ed McBain [Evan Hunger]); ph, Arthur Ornitz; m, Raymond Scott; ed, Katz.

Drama   **(PR:O MPAA:NR)**

PUSHERS, THE   (SEE: HOOKED GENERATION, THE, 1968)

PUSHOVER***½   (1954) 88m COL bw

Fred MacMurray (*Paul Sheridan*), Kim Novak (*Lona McLane*), Phil Carey (*Rick McAllister*), Dorothy Malone (*Ann*), E.G. Marshall (*Lt. Carl Eckstrom*), Allen Nourse (*Paddy Dolan*), Phil Chambers (*Briggs*), Alan Dexter (*Fine*), Robert Forrest (*Billings*), Don Harvey (*Peters*), Paul Richards (*Harry Wheeler*), Ann Morriss (*Ellen Burnett*), Dick Crockett (*Young Man*), Marion Ross (*Young Woman*), Kenneth L. Smith (*Bank Guard*), Joe Bailey (*Hobbs*), Hal Taggart (*Bank Executive*), John De Simone (*Assistant Bank Manager*), Ann Loos (*Teller Who Screams*), Walter Beaver (*Schaeffer*), Mel Welles, Jack Wilson (*Detectives*), Richard Bryan (*Harris*), Paul Picerni (*Dapper Man*) Tony Barrett (*Man*), Mort Mills, Robert Carson (*Bartenders*), John Tarangelo (*Boy*), James Anderson (*Beery*).

A James M. Cain-style suspenser that stars MacMurray (10 years after his role as Walter Neff in the Cain-based DOUBLE INDEMNITY) as an aging policeman who falls under the spell of a beautiful woman and her money. An honest cop, MacMurray is assigned to track the movements of moll Novak in the hope that she will lead him to her gangster boy friend, Richards, and the $200,000 he has just lifted in a bank robbery. MacMurray, with his partners Carey and Nourse, voyeuristically follow Novak's every move with the aid of binoculars and tape recorders. Unknown to his fellow officers, MacMurray has gotten himself romantically involved with Novak. When she suggests that he kill Richards and that they escape together with the money, he angrily objects and leaves her. After days of trailing her, however, he becomes increasingly obsessed. Meantime, Carey has gotten involved with Novak's neighbor Malone after peering in her window one evening. MacMurray finally returns to Novak and agrees to her plan. She arranges a rendezvous with Richards. When Richards arrives at the apartment MacMurray kills him, but is seen by Nourse. MacMurray then kills Nourse. By now Carey and lieutenant Marshall are trying to track down Richards, who was reportedly seen in the area. MacMurray takes Malone as a hostage, but before he can escape he is gunned down by friend and fellow officer Carey. Sharply directed by Quine with an interesting reprise by MacMurray of his DOUBLE INDEMNITY role, PUSHOVER is a compelling story of a man whose morals become twisted by a dangerous and somewhat naive *femme fatale*. What makes PUSHOVER a success, above the participation of Quine and MacMurray, is the image that newcomer Novak brings to the screen. She had previously appeared only in a bit part in the same year's THE FRENCH LINE and from there she was spotted by a talent agency which then referred her to Columbia producer Harry Cohn. After signing the 21-year-old Novak, Cohn tried to change her name to from Marilyn Novak (her given name) to Kit Marlowe. When the name Kim Novak was finally decided on, Cohn devoted himself to manufacturing her as a rival to Marilyn Monroe, replacing Columbia's previous box office draw, Rita Hayworth. Novak was carefully primped by Cohn, who imposed numerous restraints on her personal life to keep her under his control. Fortunately for her, Cohn, and Quine, PUSHOVER, while doing only moderate box office business, garnered a number of favorable reviews for the starlet. Cohn's efforts paid off as Novak was named "the Best Discovery of 1954" by the New York Journal American, and for the next few years she remained a top box-office draw.

p, Jules Shermer; d, Richard Quine; w, Roy Huggins (based on the story "The Killer Wore A Badge," the novel *The Night Watch* by Thomas Walsh, and the novel *Rafferty* by William S. Ballinger); ph, Lester H. White; m, Arthur Morton; ed, Jerome Thoms; md, M.W. Stoloff; art d, Walter Holscher; set d, James Crowe; cos, Jean Louis; makeup, Clay Campbell.

Crime Drama   **(PR:A MPAA:NR)**

PUSHOVER, THE   (SEE: MYTH, THE, 1965, Ital.)

PUSS AND KRAM   (SEE: HUGS AND KISSES, 1967, Swed.)

PUSS 'N' BOOTS★★ (1964, Mex.) 90m Rodriguez/Murray c (EL GATO CON BOTAS)

Rafael Munoz, Humberto Dupeyron, Antonio Raxell, Luis Manuel Pelayo, Armando Guiterrez, Rocio Rosales, Santanon.

A minor Mexican production recounts the tale of the magical cat who helps out his master with the best con jobs this side of Yellow Kid Weil. Strictly for the kids.

p, Roberto Rodriguez, K. Gordon Murray; d, Manuel San Fernando; w, Rodriguez (based on the adaptation by Sergio Magana from the story by Charles Perrault); ph, Rosalio Solano (Eastmancolor); m, Sergio Guerrero; ed, Jose Bustos; set d, Roberto Silva.

Fantasy   **(PR:AAA MPAA:NR)**

PUSS 'N' BOOTS★★ (1967, Ger.) 68m Forster/Childhood c (DER GESTIEFELTE KATER)

Margitta Sonke (*Puss*), Christa Oenicke (*Princess*), Harry Wustenhagen (*Marquis de Carabas*)Gunter Hertel, Martin Volkmann, Helmut Ziegner, Wilhelm Grothe, F.W. Schroder-Schrom, Brigitte Fredersdorf, Waltraud Forster.

Sonke plays the famed witty feline who by various tricks and marvelous strategems wins a fortune and a royal wife for his master, a poor young miller who uses the name "Marquis de Carabas." An old tale, but never too bewhiskered to see once again.

p, Alfred Forster; d, Herbert B. Fredersdorf; w, Christof Schulz-Gellen (based on the adaptation by Jakob, Wilhelm Grimm of the tale by Charles Perrault); ph, Ted Kornowicz (Agfacolor); m, Richard Stauch; ed, Anneliese Krigar; art d, Alfred Butow.

Fantasy   **(PR:AAA MPAA:NR)**

PUSS OCH KRAM   (SEE: HUGS AND KISSES, 1968, Swed.)

PUSSYCAT ALLEY★★½ (1965, Brit.) 93m Cyclops/Goldstone bw (GB; THE WORLD TEN TIMES OVER)

Sylvia Syms (*Billa*), Edward Judd (*Bob Shelbourne*), June Ritchie (*Ginnie*), William Hartnell (*Dad*), Sarah Lawson (*Elizabeth*), Francis De Wolff (*Shelbourne*), Davy Kaye (*Compere*), Linda Marlowe (*Penny*), Jack Gwillim (*Bolton*), Kevin Brennan (*Brian*), Alan White (*Freddy*).

Syms and Ritchie play two aging nightclub hostesses who share an apartment. Ritchie is an extrovert who's fascinated with and attracted to a variety of men while her companion exudes a cynicism that protects her vulnerable self. The two become quite dependent on one another. Syms, hardened by her own failures with men, becomes angry when her companion gets involved with Judd. He's a wealthy businessman, separated from his wife and controlled by his father. Ritchie insists that Judd prove his love and the man responds by getting her a job in the family

business. His father is angered with Judd's defiance. Syms' father, a simple country schoolteacher, comes for a visit. Relations between the two are strained and she tries to shock him by telling about her sordid life. He leaves and Syms tearfully tells Ritchie that she's somehow gotten pregnant. Ritchie refuses to abandon her friend and cancels a trip to the Bahamas with Judd. Judd finally leaves his wife for good and implores Ritchie to come with him. But she drunkenly taunts him, sending him on his way. Ritchie attempts suicide but realizes that her place is with Syms. This is a somewhat stylized film, but the story is too depressing to make it work in the long run.

p, Michael Luke; d&w, Wolf Rilla; ph, Larry Pizer; m, Edwin Astley; ed, Jack Slade; m&md, Astley; art d, Peggy Gick; makeup, Jim Hydes.

Drama   **(PR:O MPAA:NR)**

PUSSYCAT, PUSSYCAT, I LOVE YOU★ (1970) 100m Three Pictures CKF/UA c

Ian McShane (*Fred Dobbs*), Anna Calder-Marshall (*Millie Dobbs*), Severn Darden (*Dr. Fahrquardt*), Joyce Van Patten (*Anna Fahrquardt*), John Gavin (*Grant Granite*), Beba Loncar (*Ornella*), Samy Pavel (*Ottavio*), Katia Christina (*Angelica*), Veronica Carlson (*Liz*), Gaby Andre (*Flavia*), Marino Mase (*Franco*), Dari Lallou (*Hester*), Ian Trigger (*Dr. Ponti*), Leopoldo Trieste (*Desk Clerk*), Paul Muller (*Amo Amas Amat*), Madeline Smith (*Gwendolyn*), Maurizio Lucidi (*Director*), Linda Morand (*Moira*), Solvi Stubing (*Girl with Door*), John Frederick (*Heavy*), Richard Harrison (*Hero*), Janos Prohaska (*Gorilla*), Josiane Tanzilli (*Girl*), Janeth Aigren, Jean Sobieski.

McShane is an American playwright living in Rome. Fearing both baldness and recurring dreams of a sex-craving gorilla, he consults Darden, a rather odd, bewigged and domestically annoyed shrink. In his sessions McShane discusses his past and present amours. He's got problems with his wife (Calder-Marshall), who is having an affair with famed movie idol Gavin. Gavin is just using her to get McShane's play "When in Rome Do as the Romanians." This leads to a wild slapstick chase through a Roman film studio, where McShane's assorted lovers, his wife, and her lover inadvertently end up in a cheap western. The film ends as McShane finishes telling his story to Darden and suddenly the sex-starved gorilla of his dreams jumps in through the window. The film takes its title from the title song of the more successful WHAT'S NEW PUSSYCAT? This poor remake shows none of the wit or charm of Woody Allen's script, and sorely misses the talents of Peter Sellers and Peter O'Toole as the shrink and patient. Instead, it's all reduced to a sniggering little boy sort of humor that is a spiritual kin to those cheap sex jokes traded in third grade. The final chase sequence had some potential, but is so poorly done that it's hardly worth the effort. The direction shows absolutely no sense at all for comedy, with poorly timed sequences and an altogether unfunny series of gags. The players mug away to their hearts' content in an effort at zany humor, but it's all a waste of time and celluloid.

p, Jerry Bresler; d&w, Rod Amateau (based on the screenplay WHAT'S NEW PUSSCAT? by Woody Allen); ph, Tonino Delli Colli (DeLuxe Color); m, Lalo Schifrin; ed, Larry Heath; md, Schifrin; art d, Toni Sarzi-Braga; set d, Arrigo Breschi; cos, Adriana Berselli; spec eff, Danny Lee; m/l, "Groove Into It," Schifrin, Gene Lees (sung by Henry Shed), "What's New, Pussycat?" Burt Bacharach, Hal David.

Comedy   **(PR:O MPAA:GP)**

PUT ON THE SPOT★★ (1936) 69m Principal-Victory bw

Eddie Nugent (*Bob Andrews*), Maxine Doyle (*Joan Williams*), Fuzzy Knight (*Elmer*),Lucille Lund (*Rose Carter*), Don Alvarado (*Jack Carter*), Nick Stuart (*George Bates*), George Walsh (*Joe Bradley*), Joyce Kay (*Patricia Carter*), George Cleveland (*Sheriff Williams*), Forrest Taylor (*Richard Shelby*).

Walsh is wrongly accused of murder. He's arrested and thrown in the pokey. It's up to G-Man Nugent to prove Walsh's innocence, which he does, of course. This routine programmer holds a few interesting twists, but isn't all that different from any one of hundreds of B films like it. Nugent doesn't have the looks for a G-Man but is passable in the role. Doyle is just pretty baggage. Walsh, brother of director Raoul Walsh, is probably the best of the lot in his role. Somewhat of a star in silent films, he spent the last part of his career in more modest roles like this one. The direction is adequate and production values standard.

p, Sam Katzman; d, Bob Hill; w, Al Martin (based on a story by Peter B. Kyne); ph, Bill Hyer; ed, Dan Milner

Crime   **(PR:A MPAA:NR)**

PUT UP OR SHUT UP★ (1968, Arg.) 84m Cambist bw (SABALEROS; AKA: PUT OUT OR SHUT UP; POSITIONS OF LOVE)

Isabel Sarli (*Angela*), Armando Bo, Alba Mujica, Ernesto Baez, Joaquin Petrosino, Alberto Barcel, Adolfo Lenvell, M. Velich, Celso Vidal, Oscal L. Par, Joe Delk.

Sarli is the daughter of a man who leads one faction of a divided fishing village. She loves the son of the leader of the rival faction. Her father kills her lover and her lover assumes leadership. Sarli's father tries to kill her lover and the man kills the father in self-defense. The two lovers are now separated. Her father's mistress takes control and corrupts the organization. She plots to kill two people who witnessed her abuse of power. Sarli manages to warn her lover of the impending trouble and he helps one of the witnesses to cross the border, free from all trouble. The other witness is killed but the survivor's eventual testimony ends up destroying the crooked faction leaders. A fairly turgid little melodrama of little consequence.

p,d&w, Armando Bo (based on a story by Augusto Roa Bastos); ph, Alfredo Traverso; m, Alberto Gnecco.

Drama   **(PR:O MPAA:NR)**

PUTNEY SWOPE** (1969) 84m Herald/Cinema V Distributing bw/c

Arnold Johnson *(Putney Swope)*, Stan Gottlieb *(Nathan)*, Allen Garfield [Goorwitz] *(Elias, Jr.)*, Archie Russell *(Joker)*, Ramon Gordon *(Bissinger)*, Bert Lawrence *(Hawker)*, Joe Engler *(Mr. Syllables)*,David Kirk *(Elias, Sr.)*, Don George *(Mr. Cards)*, Buddy Butler *(Putney's Bodyguard)*, Vincent Hamill *(Man in White Suit)*, Tom Odachi *(Wing Soney)*,Ching Yeh *(Wing Soney, Jr.)*, Spunky-Funk Johnson *(Mr. Major)*, Joe Fields *(Pittsburgh Willie)*, Norman Schreiber *(Messenger)*, Bob Staats *(Mr. War Toys)*, Alan Abel *(Mr. Lucky)*, Sol Brawerman *(Mr. Dinkleberry)*, Ben Israel *(Mr. Pit Stop)*,Mel Brooks *(Mr. Forget It)*, Louise Heath, Barbara Clarke *(Secretaries)*, Catherine Lojacono 4f2(Lady Beaver), Johnjohn Robinson *(Wayne)*, Charles Buffum *(Director)*, Ron Palombo *(Assistant Director)*, Wendy Appel *(Script Girl)*, Antonio Fargas *(The Arab)*, GeegeeBrown *(Secretary)*, Vance Amaker *(Wall Man)*, Al Green *(1st Cowboy)*, Chuck Ender *(2nd Cowboy)*, Anthony Chisholm *(3rd Cowboy)*, Walter Jones *(Jim Keranga)*, Khaula Bakr *(Mrs. Keranga)*, Melvia Marshall, Annette Marshall, Andrea Marshall *(Little Kerangas)*, Laura Greene *(Mrs. Swope)*, Ed Gordon *(Mr. Victrola Cola)*, Eric Krupnik *(Mark Focus)*, George Morgan *(Mr. Token)*, Abdul Hakeim *(Bouncer)*, Allan Arbus *(Mr. Bad News)*, Jesse McDonald *(Young Militant)*, C. Robert Scott *(Militant No. 1)*, Leopoldo Mandeville *(Militant No. 2)*, Vince Morgan, Jr *(West Indian)*, Al Browne *(Moderate)*, Marie Claire *(Eugenie Ferlinger/Nun)*, Eileen Peterson *(Narrator)*, William H. Boesen *(Bert/Mr. Lunger)*, Carol Farber *(Secretary)*, Cerves McNeil *(Youngblood)*, Carolyn Cardwell *(Borman Six Girl)*, Chuck Green *(Myron X)*, Pepi Hermine *(President of the United States)*, Ruth Hermine *(First Lady)*, Paul Storob *(Secret Service Man)*, Lawrence Wolf *(Mr. Borman Six)*, Jeff Lord *(Mr. Bald)*, Tom Boya *(Mr. O'Dinga)*, Major Cole *(Idea Man No. 1)*, David Butts *(Idea Man No. 2)*, Franklin Scott *(Idea Man No. 3)*, Paul Alladice *(Idea Man No. 4)*, Exit *(Idea Man No. 5)*, Ronald Dyson *(Face Off Boy)*, Shelley Plimpton *(Face-Off Girl)*, Elzbieta Czyzewska *(Putney's Maid)*, Paulette Marron *(Air Conditioner Girl)*, Delilah *(1st Stewardess)*, Carol Hobbs *(2nd Stewardess)* Birgitta *(3rd Stewardess)*, Marco Heiblim *(Lucky Passenger)*, Grania *(Interviewer)*, Peter Maloney *(Putney's Chauffeur)*, Larry Greenfield *(Lead Reporter)*, Lloyd Kagin *(Billy Reilly)*, Perry Gerwitz *(Sonny Williams)*, Herbert Kerr *(Bodyguard No. 2)*,Hal Schochet *(President Mimeo's Chauffeur)*, George Marshall *(Mr. Executive)*, Donald Lev *(Poet)*, Fred Hirshhorn *(Mr. Bourbon)*, Donahl Breitman *(Mr. Ethereal Cereal)*, Peter Benson *(Mr. Jingle)*.

Johnson plays the token black on the executive board of an otherwise all white ad agency. When the company chairman kicks off during a meeting, a successor must be elected. Through a quirk in the voting rules (no one can vote for himself), Johnson becomes the chairman. He fires the white board and hires an all-black crew, leaving one space for a token white. The agency is named Truth and Soul, Inc. They radically change the agency clientele by refusing accounts for liquor, cigarettes, or war toys. Instead they create fairly shocking commercials for such products as Face-Off Acne Cream and Ethereal Cereal. The U.S. President (Hermine, a marijuana smoking midget) sees this new company as a threat. Truth and Soul, Inc. puts all their cash in the basement of the company headquarters while malcontents in the agency express displeasure with Johnson. Johnson has other problems, for the diminutive pothead President threatens him with picketing unless he returns to more established advertising. The President also demands that Johnson's agency push the proven unsafe "Borman Six" roadster. A white messenger boy tries to assassinate Johnson, who decides it's time to split. He dresses up in Castro-like garb and takes a sack of money. But before he can escape, a dissident Arab terrorist bombs Truth and Soul's plexiglass vault. The money—representing all of the company's assets—burns up and the agency goes down in history. This is a strange little independent comedy that works in parts. The humor is occasionally forced, with some cliched comedic devices serving as satire. The commercial parodies, however, are devastatingly funny and right on the money. This is satire at its nastiest. Watch for manic comedy director Brooks in a minor role. However, in these more enlightened times the integration humor has aged badly and the film is probably not nearly as good now as it was upon initial release.

p, Ron Sullivan; d&w, Robert Downey; ph, Gerald Cotts (Eastmancolor); m, Charley Cuva; ed, Bud Smith; art d, Gary Weist; cos, New Breed, Inc.; spec eff, Bill Daley, Tom Daniel, Dan List, Josh Zander.

Comedy **Cas.** **(PR:O MPAA:R)**

PUTTIN' ON THE RITZ** (1930) 88m UA bw/c

Harry Richman *(Harry Raymond)*, Joan Bennett *(Dolores Fenton)*, James Gleason *(James Tierney)*, Aileen Pringle *(Mrs. Teddy Van Rensler)*, Lilyan Tashman *(Goldie DeVere)*, Purnell Pratt *(George Barnes)*, Richard Tucker *(Fenway Brooks)*, Eddie Kane *(Bob Wagner)*, George Irving *(Dr. Blair)*, Sidney Franklin *(Schmidt)*, James Bradbury, Jr. *(Subway Guard)*, Oscar Apfel *(House Manager)*, Budd Fine *(Heckler)*, Lee Phelps *(Listener in Audience)*.

Harry Richman was a huge nightclub star back in the 1920s, and also owned a club. His rough face never did translate to the screen and he made just a few films, although he continued delighting audiences with his songs and stories until well into his sixties. Richman, born Harold Reichman, wrote a fine autobiography entitled *A Hell of a Life*, which would have made a better movie than this. In his talkies debut, Richman plays a poor performer who makes it big, forgets about all the little people, takes up with the hoity-toity types of cafe society, drinks too much, downs some tainted bathtub gin, goes blind, and finally winds up with the woman he began with, Bennett. The switch here is that Richman doesn't recover his sight miraculously at the conclusion, so there is some believability in the story. Gleason and Tashman are the comedy relief. This was an early example of color in films, as there is one reel in that process, a musical version of "Alice in Wonderland." It's jarring to have color in an otherwise black-and-white movie, and since they already had the ability to make films with hues, they should have gone all the way. Songs include "Puttin' on the Ritz," "With You" (Irving Berlin), "There's Danger In Your Eyes, Cherie" (Harry Richman, Pete Wendling, Jack Meskill), "I'll Get By" (Fred Ahlert, Roy Turk), "I'll Travel Along" (Sam Messenheimer, Val Burton, Richman). Don't confuse the Sidney Franklin credit as "Schmidt" with the two other men of the same name. There was a Sidney Franklin who directed THE GOOD EARTH, PRIVATE LIVES, and many more as well as having produced MRS. MINIVER, RANDOM HARVEST, WATERLOO BRIDGE, and others. And there was yet another Sidney Franklin who acted in films, after first having established himself as a matador and being known as "The Bullfighter from Brooklyn."

p, John W. Considine, Jr.; d, Edward H. Sloman; w, Considine, William K. Wells (based on a story by Considine; ph, Ray June; m, Hugo Riesenfeld; ed, Hal Kern; art d, William Cameron Menzies, Park French; cos, Alice O' Neill; ch, Maurice L. Kusell; m/l, Irving Berlin, Harry Richman, Jack Meskill, Pete Wendling, Fred Ahlert, Sam Messenheimer, Val Burton.

Musical **(PR:A MPAA:NR)**

PUTYOVKA V ZHIZN (SEE: ROAD TO LIFE, 1932, USSR)

PUZZLE OF A DOWNFALL CHILD½** (1970) 104m Newman-Foreman-Schatzberg/UNIV c

Faye Dunaway *(Lou Andreas Sand)*, Barry Primus *(Aaron Reinhardt)*, Viveca Lindfors *(Pauline Galba)*, Barry Morse *(Dr. Galba)*, Roy Schieder *(Mark)*, Ruth Jackson *(Barbara Casey)*, John Heffernan *(Dr. Sherman)*, Sydney Walker *(Psychiatrist)*, Clark Burckhalter *(Davy Bright)*, Shirley Rich *(Peggy McCavage)*, Emerick Bronson *(Falco)*, Joe George *(1st Man in Bar)*, John Eames *(1st Doctor)*, Harry Lee *(Mr. Wong)*, Jane Halleran *(Joan)*, Susan Willis *(Neighbor)*, Barbara Carrera *(T.J. Brady)*, Sam Schacht *(George)*.

Dunaway, in a series of flashbacks relates her background to Primus. He's recording her words, as he wants to make a film about the former fashion model. Her story is a series of casual and sometimes brutal sexual escapades, but she disguises this reality with glossy detail: a rape turns into a passionate affair with an older man; her various one night stands become a disinterest in sex and her own failure as a lover. In describing her rise to the top of the fashion industry, Dunaway downplays her mentor Lindfors' lesbian attractions and dominance. She also minimizes Lindfors anger when Dunaway becomes engaged to Schieder. Her encounters with Schieder are deliberately vaguer than the other reminiscences. She fled from the courthouse where the two were to be married and later blames him when an important magazine in Paris uses another model for a layout. Gradually her career deteriorates with her mental state, until she attempts suicide. Submitting herself to a life of booze and pills, Dunaway retires to her small cottage by the sea and the scene returns once more to her and Primus. The two stroll along the beach and she poses a question, wondering why the two didn't ever sleep together. Primus explains that they once did and a smile comes over Dunaway's face. This film is a visually magnificent work with a dreamlike feeling to the mise-en-scene. Dunaway gives a tour-de-force performance, with good support particularly from Schieder. But the film is hampered by Dunaway's confession. She tells so many half-truths that it confuses not only Primus but the audience. Occasionally this picture resorts to cliches as well, which is a shame considering its potential. This was the directoral debut for Schatzberg who had previously worked as a fashion photographer himself.

p, John Foreman; d, Jerry Schatzberg; w, Adrien Joyce [Carol Eastman] (based on a story by Joyce and Schatzberg); ph, Adam Holender (Technicolor); m, Michael Small; ed, Evan Lottman; md, Small; art d, Richard Bianchi; set d, Hubert J. Oates; cos, Terry Leong; makeup, Richard Philippe.

Drama **(PR:O MPAA:R)**

PYGMALION***** (1938, Brit.) 96m MGM bw

Leslie Howard *(Prof. Henry Higgins)*, Wendy Hiller *(Eliza Doolittle)*, Wilfrid Lawson *(Alfred Doolittle)*, Marie Lohr *(Mrs. Higgins)*, Scott Sunderland *(Col. Pickering)*, Jean Cadell *(Mrs. Pearce)*, David Tree *(Freddy Eynsford-Hill)*, Everley Gregg *(Mrs. Eynsford-Hill)*, Leueen MacGrath *(Clara Eynsford-Hill)*, Esme Percy *(Count Aristid Karpathy)*, Violet Vanbrugh *(Ambassadress)*, Iris Hoey *(Ysabel)*, Viola Tree *(Perfide)*, Irene Brown *(Duchess)*, Wally Patch *(Bystander)*, H.F. Maltby *(Bystander)*, Stephen Murray *(Police Constable)*, O.B. Clarence *(Vicar)*, George Mozart, Ivor Barnard *(Bystanders)*, Kate Cutler *(Grand Old Lady)*, Cathleen Nesbitt, Cecil Trouncer, Frank Atkinson, Leo Genn, Eileen Belden *(Guests at Embassy Ball)*, Anthony Quayle *(French Haridresser)*.

Shaw's magnificent comedy, a 1913 smash on the London stage, was never better served than in this flawless Pascal production with Howard and Hiller perfectly matched as thoroughly mismatched lovers. Howard is a wealthy phonetics professor who encounters Cockney flower girl Hiller and bets with his friend Sunderland that he can transform the uncouth, uneducated, and thick-accented girl into a grand lady within three months. Hiller is only too happy to shed her flower basket and move into Howard's elegant home, until she is forced to take a bath by Cadell, Howard's forceful housekeeper. But this indignity is nothing compared to the rigorous routines Howard subjects Hiller to in his relentless education of this "lowly guttersnipe." Not only does Howard intend to make this hopeless lowbrow a lady but he plans to pass her off as a duchess at a gathering of royalty and the social elite. Hiller is put through tortuous elocution exercises by Howard. He has her talk correctly, even though he adds marbles to her mouth one by one so that she faces a terrible struggle just to be understood. He measures her verbal response to her questions with a metronome and records her pronunciation, working on the words still sullied by her Cockney accent. Moreover, Howard teaches Hiller manners and a courtly walk. He refines her gestures and explodes when an occasional "ain't" slips through. Over and over Hiller runs through her vocal rituals, particularly one line: "The rain, they say, stays mainly in the plain." (This would become, with modification, one of the most popular of the many hit tunes emanating from the musical remake of this film, MY FAIR LADY, 1964.) The greatest test for the Covent Garden flower girl comes when the perfectionist Howard presents her at the Ambassador's Ball. Not only is she accepted by the princess but she dances with a prince while guests are agog with her beauty, wit, and grace, never suspecting for a moment that she is the whole product of the vainglorious Howard. The professor wins his bet but he then dismisses Hiller, telling her she can now go back to the gutter where he found her. Actually, he has, by then, become deeply fond of her. Earlier he found himself becoming jealous when Hiller briefly became engaged to Tree, a high-society, penniless playboy, Howard having successfully passed off Hiller to Tree and his family. After the ball Hiller confronts Howard, telling him that he has no compassion, let alone a thought for anyone in the world other than himself. She points out that his meddling with her life has left her with a whole new identity but without a personal history to go with it. "What's to become of me?" she wails. "Now that you've made a lady out of me, I'm not fit for anything *else*!" She throws his slippers at him and prepares to leave him once and for all. But Howard realizes that he is as in love with Hiller as she is with him and they might wind up in each other's arms. The film, which Howard codirected with Asquith, is delightful from beginning to end, packed with Shavian wit—barbed, of course—and Hiller is splendid in her impossible role, making an amazing transformation from illiterate to lady. Although the tall Hiller was no raving beauty she possessed a wistful charm and unlimited energy which radiated in this, her second film (the first being a British B-programmer, LANCASHIRE LUCK, 1937). That film was so little seen that Pascal, at Shaw's insistence, "introduced" Hiller with PYGMALION. Shaw, of course, drew his tale from the Greek legend of the sculptor-king who chiseled a marvelous statue of the goddess Aphrodite and then fell in love with his own creation. The irascible Irish dramatist had no great love for film since his plays had been largely butchered in early-day talkies, HOW HE LIED TO HER HUSBAND (1931) and ARMS AND THE MAN (1932). The Germans had a go at PYGMALION in 1935 and another production in Holland left Shaw irate at what had been done to his acerbic dialog and cleverly crafted scenes. When Pascal approached him with the proposition of doing an English version of PYGMALION, the playwright at first refused out of hand but the producer doggedly pestered Shaw, promising him that not a line of dialog would be touched. The playwright relented but insisted that Hiller, whom he had seen on the stage and loved, play the metamorphosed Eliza Doolittle. Shaw was not enthusiastic about Howard playing his autocratic Professor Higgins, telling Pascal that he would rather have Charles Laughton, but he eventually gave in and agreed that Howard would have a broader appeal in America where he had scored many film successes. Howard went beyond the playwright's dour expectations, however, and delivered one of his most effective roles, becoming the epitome of the intellectual tyrant (undoubtedly studying and emulating Shaw's own personality). Sunderland is excellent as the kindly Col. Pickering, and Lawson, as the dustman whose life is suddenly enriched with the discovery of his uneducated daughter, is stupendous. Lawson's speeches, despite Pascal's promise to Shaw, along with many other philosophical diatribes, were cut. The clever Pascal got around Shaw by having the dramatist write many of the scenes, especially the Ambassador's Ball scene which is not present in the play, thus making Shaw a culpable party to the truncating of his own work. Shaw won an Oscar for the screenplay, while the journeymen scriptwriters who put the film together, Lipscomb, Lewis, and Dalrymple, were given Oscars for adaptation. Asquith, who has the lion's credit for direction, and deservedly so, moves the ethereal tale along at a fast clip and gets marvelous performances from his stunning cast. The director had not had many successes in recent years, and this, the best Shavian film to that time, placed him in the front ranks of directors. The film was an international success, especially in America, but Hiller did not heed the siren call of Hollywood, preferring to stay on the British stage, making only rare film appearances thereafter. Her future in Hollywood was thought questionable at the time in that she resembled too closely another popular and well-entrenched star, Rosalind Russell. Shaw was so delighted with Pascal's production that he eagerly endorsed the producer's plan to film *all* of his plays, a herculean task which went uncompleted, although Pascal did manage to make such worthy Shaw films as MAJOR BARBARA (1944), CAESAR AND CLEOPATRA (1951), and ANDROCLES AND THE LION (1951). In 1964 the film was remade as a splendid musical, MY FAIR LADY, which threatened to eclipse the original in that the 1938 classic was taken out of distribution for almost a decade so the Lerner and Loewe musical adaptation could enjoy a monopoly on the Shaw play. PYGMALION, much to the delight of millions of worldwide viewers, returned in all its glory in the early 1970s and it is a film that can be watched many times over with new pleasures derived at each successive showing.

p, Gabriel Pascal; d, Anthony Asquith, Leslie Howard; w, George Bernard Shaw, W.P. Lipscomb, Cecil Lewis, Ian Dalrymple, Asquith (based on the play by Shaw); ph, Harry Stradling; m, Arthur Honegger; ed, David Lean; art d, Laurence Irving; cos, Prof. Czettell, Worth, Schiaparelli.

Comedy   **(PR:A   MPAA:NR)**

PYGMY ISLAND**   (1950) 69m COL bw

Johnny Weissmuller (*Jungle Jim*), Ann Savage (*Capt. Ann Kingsley*), David Bruce (*Maj. Bolton*), Steven Geray (*Leon Marko*), William Tannen (*Kruger*), Tristram Coffin (*Novak*), Billy Curtis (*Makuba*), Tommy Farrell (*Captain*), Pierce Lyden (*Lucas*), Rusty Wescoatt (*Anders*), Billy Barty (*Tembo*).

This entry in Weissmuller's JUNGLE JIM series finds our hero off in the jungle once more, this time to battle foreign agents. An army captain has disappeared and the trail leads to some enemy spies who want a valuable fiberglass plant for their own nefarious purposes. It's all routine stuff with the standard amounts of wild beasties, cutthroat bad guys, and uncivilized natives. The missing army captain is none other than Savage, which is a handy way to work in the love interest. The "pygmies" of the film's title are actually white midgets, who are ruled by Barty, one of Hollywood's favorite little people. (See JUNGLE JIM series, Index.)

p, Sam Katzman; d, William Berke; w, Carroll Young (based on the cartoon strip "Jungle Jim" by Alex Raymond); ph, Ira H. Morgan; ed, Jerome Thomas; md, Mischa Bakaleinikoff; art d, Paul Palmentola.

Adventure   **(PR:A   MPAA:NR)**

PYRO**   (1964, U.S./Span.) 99m SWP-Esamer/AIP c (FUEGO; AKA: PYRO—MAN WITHOUT A FACE; PYRO—THE THING WITHOUT A FACE)

Barry Sullivan (*Vance Pierson*), Martha Hyer (*Laura Blanco*), Sherry Moreland (*Verna Pierson*), Soledad Miranda (*Liz Frade*), Luis Prendes (*Police Inspector*), Fernando Hilbeck (*Julio*), Carlos Casaravilla (*Frade*), Marisenka (*Isabella Blanco*), Hugo Pimentel, Francisco Moran.

Sullivan is an engineer who invents a generator resembling a ferris wheel. He moves to Spain where the device is to be constructed. While looking for a new home for his wife and daughter he meets Hyer. She's about to set her house ablaze for insurance money, but he convinces her not to. They fall into an affair, but Sullivan decides to end it before it destroys him. Jealous, Hyer sets his home on fire, killing his wife and daughter and leaving her ex-lover horribly disfigured. He vows revenge and later sets fire to Hyer's family home. Her mother, brother, and sister-in-law are killed and she goes into seclusion. Meanwhile, Sullivan eludes capture and ends up with a carnival. He falls in love with Miranda, one of the carnies he works with. But once more he finds Hyer and sets her house on fire. She is killed and the crazed man steals her baby, intending to throw it off the top of the carnival ferris wheel. But the police and Miranda convince him not to and Sullivan takes a suicide plunge after placing the baby carefully on the ferris wheel seat. This film could have been really fine but it's riddled with problems. Too much time is spent on the affair and the script is filled with unnatural dialog. Rather than creating drama it inspires laughter. However, Sullivan's makeup job is terrific. His face is horrible, charred with great effect. The ending which reveals that he wore a mask over this face, is somewhat predictable but nicely handled.

p, Sidney W. Pink, Richard C. Meyer; d, Julio Coll; w, Luis de los Arcos, Pink (based on a story by Pink); ph, Manuel Berenguer (Panacolor); m, Jose Sola; ed, Margarita Ochoa; md, Sola; set d, Antonio Simont; cos, Mitzou of Madrid; spec eff, Tony Molina; makeup, Carmen Martin.

Drama   **(PR:O   MPAA:NR)**
(SEE: PYRO, 1964, U.S./Span.)

PYX, THE***   (1973, Can.) 111m Cinerama c

Karen Black (*Elizabeth Lucy*), Christopher Plummer (*Jim Henderson*), Donald Pilon (*Pierre Paquette*), Jean-Louis Roux (*Keerson*), Yvette Brind'Amour (*Meg*), Jacques Godin (*Superintendent*), Lee Broker (*Herbie Lafram*), Terry Haig (*Jimmy*), Robin Gammell (*Worther*), Louise Rinfret (*Sandra*).

This quickly made Canadian feature is a nifty little horror mystery that is rarely seen. Black plays a hooker who wears an upside-down cross. She's murdered and Plummer must investigate. The dialog is excellent, with a good realistic sound. The supporting cast is marvelous; Haig and Pilon, two Canadians, are standouts. The direction speeds the story along with a good feel of suspense. The climactic ending, revealing cults and Catholic guilt, is well handled and fresh. Black wrote and sang three songs for this film, something she would do once more for Altman's NASHVILLE. THE PYX was filmed in Montreal at a cost of $1 million—$300,000 of which reputedly came from the Canadian Film Development Corporation.

p, Maxine Samuels, Julian Roffman; d, Harvey Hart; w, Robert Schlitt (based on the novel by John Buell); ph, Rene Verzier; m, Harry Freedman; ed, Ron Wisman; prod d, Earl Preston; m/l, Karen Black.

Crime/Horror   **(PR:O   MPAA:R)**

Q

Q*½** (1982) 100m United Film Distribution c (AKA: THE WINGED SERPENT)

Michael Moriarty *(Jimmy Quinn)*, Candy Clark *(Joan)*, David Carradine *(Detective Shepard)*, Richard Roundtree *(Sgt. Powell)*, James Dixon *(Lt. Murray)*, Malachy McCourt *(Police Commissioner)*, Fred J. Scollay *(Capt. Fletcher)*, Peter Hock *(Detective Clifford)*, Ron Cey *(Detective Hoberman)*, Mary Louise Weller *(Mrs. Pauley)*, Bruce Carradine *(Victim)*, John Capodice *(Doyle)*, Tony Page *(Webb)*, Larkin Ford *(Curator)*, Larry Pine *(Professor)*, Eddie Jones *(Watchman)*, Shelly Desai *(Kahea)*, Lee Louis *(Banyon)*, Fred Morsell, Ed Kovens *(Robbers)*, Richard Duggan *(Construction Worker)*, Jennifer Howard *(Newscaster)*, David Shell *(Attorney)*, Larry Silverstri, Gabriel Wohl, Peter Genovese *(Police)*, Nancy Stafford *(Eyewitness)*, Bobbi Burns *(Sunbather)*.

Low-budget director Larry Cohen (IT'S ALIVE, IT LIVES AGAIN) once again proves himself to be among the most creative, original, and intelligent American horror film directors in this bizarre masterwork, which successfully combines a *film noir* crime story with a good old-fashioned "giant monster" movie. Moriarty turns in a brilliant performance as an ex-con, former junkie, small-time hood looking to make one big score. He robs a Manhattan diamond center and makes off with a small fortune in gems. Pursued by the police, he hides out in the tower of the Chrysler building and finds a place to stash his loot. While rummaging around, Moriarty discovers a large hole in the dome of the structure and finds a huge nest with an equally large egg and several partially devoured human corpses. Thinking he's hallucinating, Moriarty leaves the gems and returns to the home of his girl friend (Clark) to hide until the heat dies down. Meanwhile, the New York City police have been plagued by a bizarre string of deaths. Detectives Carradine and Roundtree investigate reports of people being snatched off rooftops, body parts falling to the street, and lately, a number of bodies have washed up in the river that appear to have been ritualistically flayed (the skin painstakingly removed). Upon further investigation, Carradine begins to connect the two separate sets of corpses and (combined with strange reports of a giant bird having been spotted flying above the city) concludes that they are the result of ceremonial sacrifices to an Aztec god known as Quetzalcoatl, a winged serpent. He suspects that the high priest performing the sacrifices is a former college professor and sets out to gather enough evidence to prove his theory. Roundtree, who has been investigating the jewel theft, hauls Moriarty in as his prime suspect. Carradine interupts the interrogation when he receives word that 43 people witnessed a giant bird snatch a man out of a roof-top swimming pool. Moriarty overhears this and sees his chance to become rich and famous. He convinces the cops that he knows where the monster's nest is, but he will only spill the beans in exchange for complete amnesty for his crimes and $1 million in cash. The city agrees and Moriarty goes mad with power, thinking he has finally made it to the big time, much to the dismay of Clark, who is disgusted with her boy friend's change of temperament. The cops invade the Chrysler building, but the monster escapes, leaving only the egg, which is destroyed. The city reneges on its deal (they agreed to pay for the capture of the big bird, not the egg), leaving Moriarty with nothing. Meanwhile, Roundtree has tracked the high priest of the cult to the American Museum of Natural History and follows as the man takes his next (willing) victim to a warehouse to be sacrificed. The cops arrive just as the ceremony is about to get bloody and the priest runs to the rooftop. Roundtree gives chase, but is killed by the Quetzalcoatl, which had been summoned by the priest. Eventually the bird returns to its nest and is machine-gunned by dozens of cops. Mortally wounded, the great bird flies to the Manhattan Banker's Trust building, the top of which greatly resembles the bird-god's temple in Mexico, and dies. His dreams of grandeur gone, Moriarty returns to Clark, and Carradine closes the door on the case, not knowing that another egg has just hatched in the attic of the American Museum of Natural History. Though the premise of Q seems fairly silly (as does KING KONG's), Cohen's handling of the material is superior, and he really convinces the audience that a giant bird living in a nest at the top of the Chrysler building isn't as implausible as it sounds. Cohen packs the film with stunning visuals and makes the most of New York City's architecture, capitalizing on its dozens of facades with birds and bird-like carvings. The use of the Chrysler building was a stroke of genius, and Cohen uses its Art Deco design, the featherlike tower, the birdlike carvings and inlays of the lobby and elevators as a place likely to attract an ancient bird-god looking for a place to roost. Q bombed at the box office because it was nearly impossible to package into a nice, simple ad campaign, but the film is a skillful combination of genres, sporting some fine acting, and a literate, fascinating script with dashes of biting humor that is well worth seeing.

p,d&w, Larry Cohen; ph, Fred Murphy; m, Robert O. Ragland; ed, Armand Lebowitz; spec eff, Steve Neill, David Allen, Randy Cook, Peter Kuran; makeup; Dennis Eger.

Horror **Cas.** **(PR:O MPAA:R)**

Q PLANES (SEE: CLOUDS OVER EUROPE, 1939, Brit.)

Q-SHIPS (SEE: BLOCKADE, 1928, Brit.)

QUACKSER FORTUNE HAS A COUSIN IN THE BRONX** (1970) 90m UMC c (AKA: FUN LOVING)

Gene Wilder *(Quackser Fortune)*, Margot Kidder *(Zazel Pierce)*, Eileen Colgan *(Betsy Bourke)*, Seamus Ford *(Mr. Fortune)*, May Ollis *(Mrs. Fortune)*, Liz Davis *(Kathleen Fortune)*, Caroline Tully *(Vera Fortune)*, Paul Murphy *(Damien)*, David Kelly *(Tom Maguire)*, Tony Doyle *(Mike)*, John Kelly *(Tim)*, Liam Sweeney, Robert Somerset, Danny Cummins *(Men in Pub)*, Julie Hamilton *(Charlady)*, Cecil Sheehan *(Coal Merchant)*, Charles Byrne *(Blacksmith)*, Brendan Mathews *(Attendant)*, Robert Carrickford *(Walter)*, Lillian Rapple *(Woman)*, Jeremy Jones *(Student)*, John Hoey *(Hall Porter)*, Martin Crosbie *(Policeman)*, Marjorie McHenry *(Elaine Boland)*, Patrick Smyth *(Man at Foundry)*, David Hogarty.

This picture was made before Wilder fancied himself an *auteur* and fell into acting habits that bordered on the ludicrous. Consequently, it's a good example of his acting abilities and stands as one of his best, and surely one of his most controlled, roles. An offbeat story with a sharp screenplay and the lovely Dublin location are all plusses. Wilder has chosen to earn his living by following delivery horses through the streets, picking up their droppings and selling them to housewives as fertilizer. He makes a good living at what he does, gets plenty of exercise and fresh air, and enjoys his independence, something that is not shared by his father, Ford, who works long and hard hours in the foundry. The ability to be his own man has serendipitous asides, such as a continuing affair with Colgan, one of his regular fertilizer customers. Enter Kidder, an American woman with apparently wealthy parents, who is studying at Trinity College. She is in love with Dublin and its history, which she knows much more about than most of the residents. Kidder is attracted to Wilder, as she's never met anyone who does what he does. They begin traveling around the city together, and when the Trinity students have a fancy ball, Kidder invites Wilder as her date. She is tiring of him by that time and pays little attention to Wilder at the ball, preferring to be with her wealthy pals. The other students cruelly make fun of Wilder and he retaliates physically. Wilder hastily exits with Kidder, who takes him to bed at a posh hotel. After their lovemaking, Kidder leaves. When Wilder wakes up and finds her gone, he hurries to Trinity College and learns that she's left there, with no forwarding address. To add to his woes, Dublin has enacted a new law stating that horses are to be removed from the streets in favor of trucks and his main source of income is now dried up. When it looks as though the animals will be sent to rendering plants, Wilder sets them all free on the streets where there is no way they can all be rounded up. Next, he drinks himself into near-oblivion and his fortunes change when he learns that his cousin, who lives in the Bronx, has died and left him a small inheritance. With that money, Wilder buys a bus and uses the knowledge imparted to him by Kidder to take tourists around the city he loves so much. Kidder is excellent and succeeds in making us believe that she could actually find something intriguing in Wilder. The humor is much subtler than in most of Wilder's other efforts, something he might well reconsider in the light of his overblown pictures since. There is a brief look at Kidder's body that gives the movie an "R" rating but, other than that, it's quite a family picture.

p, Mel Howard, John H. Cushingham; d, Waris Hussein; w, Gabriel Walsh; ph, Gilbert Taylor (Eastmancolor); m, Michael Dress; ed, Bill Blunden; art d, Herbert Smith.

Comedy/Drama **Cas.** **(PR:A-C MPAA:R)**

QUADROON* (1972) 90m Presidio c

Kathrine McKee *(Coral)*, Tim Kincaid *(Caleb)*, Robert Priest *(Antoine)*, Madelyn Sanders *(Celeste)*, George Lupo *(Dupree)*, Marinda French *(Aunt Nancy)*, Bill McGhee *(Jacques)*, David Snow *(Felix)*.

Kincaid is a Northern white boy who arrives in the decadence of 1835 New Orleans. He earns money by teaching a group of mulatto whores how to read and write. He falls for one of them (McKee), which, of course, leads to trouble. Plenty of flesh is seen in this ridiculous exploitation film. There's some attempt at period costuming, but the film is permeated by its hateful attitudes towards black women. Acting and production values are passable but not much more.

p, R.B. McGowen, Jr; d, Jack Weis; w, Sarah Riggs; ph, Tom Smart (Consolidated Color); m, Jack Brokensha, Don Palmer.

Drama **(PR:O MPAA:R)**

QUADROPHENIA**** (1979, Brit.) 120m Who Films/World Northal c

Phil Daniels *(Jimmy Michael Cooper)*, Mark Wingett *(Dave)*, Philip Davis *(Chalky)*, Leslie Ash *(Steph)*, Garry Cooper *(Pete)*, Toyah Wilcox *(Monkey)*, Sting [Gordon Sumner] *(The Ace Face)*, Trevor Laird *(Ferdy)*, Gary Shail *(Spider)*, Kate Williams *(Mrs. Cooper)*, Michael Elphick *(Mr. Cooper)*, Raymond Winstone *(Kevin)*, Kim Neve *(Yvonne)*.

In 1964 London, Daniels and his pals are Mods, snappy dressers who ride Vespa scooters, dividing their time between dancing to bands like The Who and getting in fights with Rockers, who wear black leather, ride motorcycles, and listen to old Gene Vincent records. Oppressed by working-class parents and a go-nowhere job as a mail boy in an advertising firm, Daniels' only out is his peer group, most of whom live similarly grim lives. A three-day bank holiday is the excuse for swarms of Mods and Rockers to descend on the seaside town of Brighton. There Daniels is at his peak—respected by all his fellow Mods and attractive to beautiful Ash. When the armies of Mods and Rockers meet the next morning, a riot erupts and in the commotion Daniels and Ash duck into a back alley for a quick sexual interlude while leaning against a brick wall. On the street again, Daniels is arrested and thrown into a Black Maria with Sting, the coolest Mod of them all. Back in London, a day overdue, Daniels comes home to find his mother has discovered the amphetamines he has been downing and she boots him out of the house. His boss gives him a dressing down for missing a day of work, saying "There are a lot of young men who would like to have your job." Daniels explodes. "Oh yeah," he sputters, "Well, just find one." At his gang's hangout, Daniels spends most of his severance money on more pills, then discovers that Ash has taken up with Wingett, Daniels' best friend. He picks a fight with Wingett and is ostracized by his peers. The next day, while cruising aimlessly around the streets, his scooter is crushed under the wheels of a mail truck. His last link with his life there gone, Daniels takes a fistful of "speeders" and boards a train for Brighton, site of his finest hour. He roams the streets in a daze, wandering up the alley where he and Ash made love and trying to figure out what happened to it all. Outside a seaside hotel he sees Sting's scooter and for a moment his spirits lift. Then Sting bounds out of the hotel, still looking cool, but dressed in a bellboy's uniform and hard-pressed to maintain his attitude under the weight of three suitcases. His last illusion shattered, Daniels yells "bell-boy" at Sting, then steals the scooter and rides it out to the white cliffs of the coast. After racing for a while back and forth along the edge, he begins a long drive straight for the brink at top speed. At the last second he jumps off and the cycle crashes on the rocks below. Adapted from a double album written by Townshend, performed by The Who (who also acted as executive producers for the film), and released in 1973, QUADROPHENIA is one of the best films about youth ever made, beautifully illustrating the frustrations of being young and bright but still having no future. First-time director Roddam does a fine job with his young cast and his re-creation of period detail is nearly perfect. (By comparison, Roddam's next two features, THE LORDS OF DISCIPLINE [1983] and THE BRIDE [1985], were occasionally interesting but flawed films.) The film makes no concession to a popular audience, refusing to show The Who except as a fuzzy black-and-white image Daniels watches on TV. And everyone speaks with the thick, slang-laden accents of the London working class (although the beginning of the film is very difficult for American audiences to understand, after about 20 minutes viewers become used to the accents and it all becomes intelligible, in much the same way as the Jamaican accents in THE HARDER THEY COME [1973] seem to disappear as the viewer gets the rhythm of it). Daniels gives an amazing performance as the confused youth, looking for an identity and coming literally to the brink of self-destruction—so intense and full of divergent emotions, he seems ready to explode at any moment. The film has a loyal cult following, and at any screening in any large city, troops of latter-day Mods turn out, accoutered like the characters in the film and riding scooters, to cheer the bashing of Rockers and the anthems on the soundtrack, seemingly oblivious to the fact that the film ends with a total rejection of that life style. It is, nevertheless, a fine film that deserves a wider audience than the few who have embraced it as a pattern for their lives. Songs include: "I Am the Sea," "The Real Me," I'm One," "5:15," "Love Reign O'er Me," "Get Out and Stay Out," "Four Faces," "Joker James," "The Punk and the Godfather," "Bell Boy," "I've Had Enough," "Helpless Dancer," "Doctor Jimmy" (performed by The Who), "Zoot Suit" (performed by The Who as The High Numbers), "High Heel Sneakers," "Dimples" (performed by Cross Section), "Blazing Fire" (sung by Derrick Morgan), "Night Train" (sung by James Brown), "Da Doo Ron Ron" (sung by The Ronettes), "Wah-Watusi" (sung by The Orlons), "Baby Love" (sung by The Supremes), "Baby Don't You Do It" (sung by Marvin Gaye), "He's So Fine" (sung by The Chiffons), "5-4-3-2-1" (performed by Manfred Mann), "Green Onions" (performed by Booker T and the MGs), "Wishin' and Hopin'" (performed by The Merseybeats), "Rhythm of the Rain" (performed by The Cascades).

p, Roy Baird, Bill Curbishley; d, Franc Roddam; w, Dave Humphries, Martin Stellman, Roddam, Pete Townshend; ph, Brian Tufano; m, The Who [Pete Townshend, Roger Daltrey, John Entwistle, Keith Moon]; ed, Mike Taylor; md, Entwistle, Townshend; prod d, Simon Holland; ch, Gillian Gregory.

Drama   Cas.   **(PR:O MPAA:R)**

QUAI DE GRENELLE   (SEE: DANGER IS A WOMAN, 1952, Fr.)

QUAI DES BRUMES   (SEE: PORT OF SHADOWS, 1938, Fr.)

QUALITY STREET*½   (1937) 84m RKO bw

Katharine Hepburn (Phoebe Throssel), Franchot Tone (Dr. Valentine Brown), Fay Bainter (Susan Throssel), Eric Blore (Recruiting Sergeant), Cora Witherspoon (Patty the Maid), Estelle Winwood (Mary Willoughby), Florence Lake (Henrietta Turnbull), Helena Grant (Fanny Willoughby), Bonita Granville (Isabella), Clifford Severn (Arthur), Sherwood Bailey (William Smith), Roland Varno (Ens. Blades), Joan Fontaine (Charlotte Parratt), William Bakewell (Lt. Spicer), Yorke Sherwood (Postman), Carmencita Johnson (Student).

While "Quality Street" was a fair hit as a play, written by Sir James Barrie and produced in the U.S. in 1901, it fails to satisfy as a film. Marion Davies made it first as a silent in 1927 and it did well enough at the box office but this one lost almost $250,000 and there was some concern that Hepburn was no longer a force to reckon with. That, of course, was soon disproved and she has been one of the most enduring actresses of all time, though not necessarily the best judge of what scripts to accept. It's the 1790s, in England, and Hepburn is being wooed by Tone, a young physician. Before he can ask for her hand, he goes off to help defeat Napoleon. While Tone is away fighting for king and country, years pass and Hepburn and her sister, Bainter, grow into spinsterhood, transform their large home into a school, and settle into old maid existences. Tone returns after the war has been won and must have been shell-shocked because he doesn't recognize Hepburn. She comes up with the far-fetched idea of masquerading as her own niece (purely fictitious), a flirtatious 16-year-old, and attempts to win herself a husband before the bloom is entirely off the rose. That Tone should think of Hepburn seriously as a teenager is ludicrous and destroys any credibility in his role. Hepburn overacts to a fault, raising eyebrows, wringing hands, strutting and fretting until we can barely watch another second. It may have been this neurotic performance that inspired Sandy Dennis to her acting technique. The play was a gentle, often amusing farce that was lost in the cinematic translation by Hepburn and Stevens, who attempted to direct this like a Woody Van Dyke three-week wonder. Any whimsy was totally lathered by the overwrought playing. Webb's score was nominated for an Oscar and lost to Charles Previn's work on ONE HUNDRED MEN AND A GIRL. Excellent costumes, photography, and a superb rendering of gardens in London are far better than the story or the acting.

p, Pandro S. Berman; d, George Stevens; w, Mortimer Offner, Allan Scott (based on the play by Sir James M. Barrie); ph, Robert De Grasse; m, Roy Webb; ed,

Henry Berman; art d, Van Nest Polglase; set d, Darrell Silvera; cos, Walter Plunkett; makeup, Mel Burns.

Drama/Comedy   **(PR:A MPAA:NR)**

QUANDO EL AMOR RIE*½   (1933) 79m FOX bw

Jose Mojica, Mona Maris, Carlos Villarias, Carmen Rodriguez, Rafael Valverda, Rosita Granada.

More Spanish-language offerings from Fox, as Mojica wins a bet by taming a wild horse and marrying a wild woman. Mojica sings a couple of pleasant songs, as well. The title translates as "when love laughs." (In Spanish.)

d, David Howard.

Western   **(PR:A MPAA:NR)**

QUANTEZ**   (1957) 80m UNIV c

Fred MacMurray (Gentry/John Coventry), Dorothy Malone (Chaney), James Barton (Minstrel), Sydney Chaplin (Gato), John Gavin (Teach), John Larch (Heller), Michael Ansara (Delgadito).

A group of outlaws hold up a bank. They flee but are surrounded by a band of Apaches. The gang holes up in a ghost town where MacMurray eventually sacrifices himself so that Gavin and Malone will live. This is a tedious and routine western, suffering from a repetitiveness in both scene and dialog. There's far too much talking and hardly enough action to hold interest. Barton, in a bit part as the wandering peddler, manages to run away with the film, giving the only really lively performance. Otherwise this picture is a complete waste of time.

p, Gordon Kay; d, Harry Keller; w, R. Wright Campbell (based on a story by Campbell, Anne Edwards); ph, Carl E. Guthrie (CinemaScope, Eastmancolor); m, Herman Stein; ed, Fred MacDowell; md, Joseph Gershenson; art d, Alexander Golitzen, Alfred Ybarra; cos, Rosemary Odell; m/l, "The Lonely One," "The True Love," Frederick Herbert, Arnold Hughes (sung by Dorothy Malone).

Western   **(PR:A MPAA:NR)**

QUANTRILL'S RAIDERS**½   (1958) 68m AA c

Steve Cochran (Capt. Alan Westcott), Diane Brewster (Sue Walters), Leo Gordon (William Quantrill), Gale Robbins (Kate), Will Wright (Judge Wood), Kim Charney (Joel), Myron Healey (Jarrett), Robert Foulk (Hager), Glenn Strange (Todd), Lane Chandler (Sheriff), Guy Prescott (Maj. Mathews), Dan M. White (Fred Thomas), Thomas B. Henry (Griggs).

The famed raid on Lawrence, Kansas wherein over 400 innocent people lost their lives to a group of marauders is heavily fictionalized and cleaned up for this quickie western B film. Gordon plans to raid the town in order to get Union munitions for the Confederacy. Cochran is a Confederate officer who's assigned to help plan the raid but discovers the ammunition has been moved. He tries to call off the raid and attack a wagon train instead but Gordon is too far gone to be swayed. He proceeds with his plan and it's up to Cochran to stop him. Gordon is killed but not before Lawrence is under siege in some well-staged action sequences. The thrilling pace and Gordon's persistent sneer make this film work. Editing is tight and although this is not great filmmaking it does make exciting entertainment.

p, Ben Schwalb; d, Edward Bernds; w, Polly James; ph, William Whitley (CinemaScope, DeLuxe Color); m, Marlin Skiles; ed, William Austin; art d, David Milton.

Western   **(PR:A MPAA:NR)**

QUARE FELLOW, THE***   (1962, Brit.) 85m Anthony Havelock-Allan/Astor-Ajay bw

Patrick McGoohan (Thomas Crimmin), Sylvia Syms (Kathleen), Walter Macken (Regan), Dermot Kelly (Donnelly), Jack Cunningham (Chief Warder), Hilton Edwards (Holy Healy), Philip O'Flynn (Prison Governor), Leo McCabe (Dr. Flyn), Norman Rodway (Lavery), Marie Kean (Mrs. O'Hara), Pauline Delany (Mickser's Wife), Geoffrey Golden, Tom Irwin (Customs Officers), Joe O'Donnell (Poet), Agnes Bernelle (Meg), Iris Lawler (Minna), Dominic Roche (Prison Chaplain), Brian Hewitt-Jones (Jenkinson), Arthur O'Sullivan (Himself), Aubrey Morris (Silvertop), Eamonn Brennan (Flaherty), Robert Bernal (Mickser), John Welsh (Carroll), Harry Brogan (Dunlavin), Frank O'Donovan (Clancy).

McGoohan is a new prison warder in Dublin. He's a firm believer in capital punishment and the senior warder (Macken) believes that the death penalty solves nothing. Two "quares" (slang for condemned prisoners) are on death row. One hangs himself though he was offered a reprieve. McGoohan visits the other man's wife (Syms), and a mutual attraction leads to an affair. She tells the warder that her husband killed his own brother when he found the two of them in bed. He hadn't told this at his trial and McGoohan persuades her to tell the prison governor (O'Flynn). She does but there is no reprieve. McGoohan is forced to help in the hanging, his opinion about the death penalty now altered. When his superior retires, McGoohan knows that he will carry on with the fight against capital punishment. This is a stark and moody film with moments of truly black humor. McGoohan and Syms have an interesting chemistry that smolders. Though their affair is unbelievable considering their respective positions, they play it well. The rest of the film reflects genuineness, helped by its location shooting in a Dublin prison. Not for everyone, but certainly a good drama.

p, Anthony Havelock-Allan; d, Arthur Dreifuss; w, Dreifuss, Jacqueline Sundstrom (based on the play by Brendan Behan); ph, Peter Hennessy; m, Alexander Faris; ed, Gitta Zadek; art d, Ted Marshall.

Drama   **(PR:C-O MPAA:NR)**

QUARTERBACK, THE**   (1940) 74m PAR bw

Wayne Morris (Jimmy Jones/Bill Jones), Virginia Dale (Kay Merrill), Lillian Cornell (Sheila), Edgar Kennedy ("Pops"), Alan Mowbray (Prof. Hobbs), Jerome

Cowan *(Townley)*, Rod Cameron *(Tex)*, William Frawley *(Coach)*, Walter Catlett *(Tom)*, Frank Burke *("Slats" Finney)*.

This minor football comedy features Morris in a dual role. He plays twins: one smart, one dumb. The dumb one is a great football player and the smart one dreams of becoming a college professor. The latter gets a football scholarship using his brother as a ruse. Problems arise when love interest Dale ends up being wooed by both brothers. There's a subplot involving gamblers who try to keep the football-playing brother from the Big Game but of course he makes it back just in the nick of time. Kennedy is the best thing here as the frustrated man who must keep the pair from getting mixed up. Cornell signs "Sentimental Me" and "Out with Your Chest, in with Your Chin." This film is amiable enough, and there are a few amusing gags in the climactic game, but it's not terribly clever or original.

p, Anthony Veiller; d, H. Bruce Humberstone; w, Robert Pirosh; ph, Leo Tovar; m, Jack Lawrence, Paul Mann, Stephen Weiss, Frank Loesser, Matty Malneck; ed, Alma Macrorie.

Comedy **(PR:A MPAA:NR)**

QUATERMASS AND THE PIT (SEE: FIVE MILLION YEARS TO EARTH, 1968, Brit.)

QUATERMASS CONCLUSION½** (1980, Brit.) 105m Euston c

John Mills, Simon MacCorkindale, Barbara Kellerman, Margaret Tyzack, Brewster Mason.

This is the final film of the QUATERMASS series taken from a British television show of the 1950s. Befittingly, QUATERMASS CONCLUSION originally aired on British television before being released theatrically in the U.S. Mills plays the title scientist in the final episode. A death beam is being projected onto Earth from an alien being. It has the power to sap the energy from the world's children like a cosmic straw. Mills and his cohorts save the day by giving the alien an atomic bomb to suck on rather than children. This is a spotty film with mixed direction. It alternates styles, showing its television background. The special effects are equally mixed; fine death ray sequences are poorly balanced with bad outer space footage. The story, however, is compelling and survives these flaws. Some sequences are stunning, such as the zombie-like children converging on Stonehenge. This is not the best QUATERMASS film (that honor goes to FIVE MILLION YEARS TO EARTH) but it works within its limitations and is an acceptable end for the series.

p, Ted Childs; d, Piers Haggard; ph, Ian Wilson; w, Nigel Kneale; m, Marc Wilkinson, Nick Rowley; ed, Keith Palmer.

Science Fiction **Cas.** **(PR:C MPAA:NR)**

QUATERMASS EXPERIMENT, THE (SEE: CREEPING UNKNOWN, THE, 1956, Brit.)

QUATERMASS II (SEE: ENEMY FROM SPACE, 1957, Brit.)

QUARTET**** (1949, Brit.) 120m RANK-Gainsborough/EL bw

"The Facts of Life": Basil Radford *(Henry Garnet)*, Naunton Wayne *(Leslie)*, Ian Fleming *(Ralph)*, Jack Raine *(Thomas)*, Angela Baddeley *(Mrs. Garnet)*, James Robertson Justice *(Branksome)*, Jack Watling *(Nicky)*, Nigel Buchanan *(John)*, Mai Zetterling *(Jeanne)*; "The Alien Corn": Dirk Bogarde *(George Bland)*, Raymond Lovell *(Sir Frederick Bland)*, Irene Browne *(Lady Bland)*, Honor Blackman *(Paula)*, George Thorpe *(Uncle John)*, Mary Hinton *(Aunt Maud)*, Francoise Rosay *(Lea Makart)*; "The Kite": Bernard Lee *(Prison Visitor)*, Frederick Leister *(Governor)*, George Merritt *(Prison Officer)*, George Cole *(Herbert Sunbury)*, David Cole *(Herbert, Boy)*, Hermione Baddeley *(Beatrice Sunbury)*, Mervyn Johns *(Samuel Sunbury)*, Susan Shaw *(Betty)*, Cyril Chamberlain *(Reporter)*; "The Colonel's Lady": Cecil Parker *(Col. Peregrine)*, Nora Swinburne *(Mrs. Peregrine)*, J.H. Roberts *(West)*, Claude Allister *(1st Club Man)*, Wilfrid Hyde-White *(2nd Club Man)*, Ernest Thesiger *(Henry Dashwood)*, Henry Edwards *(Duke of Cleverel)*, Linden Travers *(Daphne)*, Felix Aylmer *(Martin)*, John Salew *(John Coleman)*, Lynn Evans *(Bannock)*, Cyril Raymond *(Railway Passenger)*, Clive Morton *(Henry Blane)*, Margaret Withers *(Gushing Woman)*.

Few segmented films are successful, generally because one or more suffers at the hands of the best of the bunch. Here, however, the Maugham wit and charm are in full force throughout the entire film and each segment, though entirely different, is enjoyable and done with great skill by the actors and the individual directors. In "The Facts of Life" conservative father Radford cautions his apparently naive son Watling that he should not gamble, lend money, or trust women while on his tennis tour of Monte Carlo. Watling seems to be as gullible as they come, although he wins big at roulette, only to be duped by an adventuress, Zetterling. But is he? In the end Watling not only escapes the vamp's clutches and recaptures the money, but goes off with the lady's lifetime savings. Bogarde, in one of his early and most memorable roles, plays the part of an aspiring musician in "The Alien Corn," in love with Blackman but obsessed with becoming a world class musician. After studying for two years in Paris he returns to England and is bluntly and cruelly told by a famous composer that he will never make the grade. In despair, Bogarde commits suicide but his death is ruled an accident, the coroner stating that the young man died while cleaning his hunting rifle, unable to believe that anyone would kill himself over not becoming a famous musician. In "The Kite" Cole is dominated by a shrewish mother, Baddeley, and marries the same kind of woman, Shaw, escaping her when she destroys his prize kite and he refuses to support her, winding up in prison, which is where he wanted to go all along. The final entry, "The Colonel's Lady," sees Swinburne suddenly become a famous author after a collection of her love poems is published. Her husband, Parker, is driven to distraction when realizing that the poems are all about a younger, dashing man and, when he can stand it no longer, he confronts his wife, demanding to know the identity of the young man he suspects she has been seeing. Swinburne confesses that the young man is no one but Parker himself, that she wrote the love sonnets about their early years before the love between them had died. This last entry is devastatingly ironic but all of the tales are excellent, disproving the notion that segmented films cannot sustain interest. This one does all the way.

p, Anthony Darnborough; d, Ken Annakin ("The Colonel's Lady"), Arthur Crabtree ("The Kite"), Harold French ("The Alien Corn"), Ralph Smart ("The Facts of Life"); w, R.C. Sherriff (based on the stories of W. Somerset Maugham); ph, Ray Elton; m, John Greenwood; ed, A. Charles Knott, Jean Baker; md, Muir Mathieson; art d, George Provis.

Drama/Comedy **(PR:C MPAA:NR)**

QUARTET** (1981, Brit./Fr.) 101m Lyric International/New World c

Alan Bates *(H.J. Heidler)*, Maggie Smith *(Lois)*, Isabelle Adjani *(Marya)*, Anthony Higgins *(Stephen)*, Armelia McQueen *(Nell)*, Daniel Chatto *(Guy)*, Pierre Clementi *(Theo)*, Suzanne Flon *(Mme. Hautchamp)*, Sheila Gish *(Anna)*, Daniel Mesguish *(Schlamovitz)*, Virginie Thevenet *(Mlle. Chardin)*, Wiley Wood *(Cairn)*, Bernice Stegers *(Miss Nicholson)*, Pierre Bonnafet *(Guard)*, Romain Bremond *(Adolescent)*, Isabelle Canto de Maya *(Cir-Cri)*, Jean-Pierre Dravei *(Guard)*, Sebastien Floche *(Hatuchamp)*, Pierre Julien *(Impresario)*, Monique Mauclair *(Concierge)*, Michel Such *(Guard)*, Paulita Sedgwick, Francois Viaur, Dino Zanghi, Annie Noel, Maurice Ribot, Humbert Balsan, Serge Marquand, Muriel Montosse, Caroline Loeb, Jeffrey Kime, Shirley Allan, Anne-Marie Brissoniere, Marie-France de Bourges, Brigitte Hermetz, Joceline Comellas, Arlette Spetelbroot.

Do not, under any circumstances, confuse this with the far superior picture of the same name made in 1948. Merchant and Ivory have a deserved reputation for making elegant-looking period pictures that lose money at the box office but, as Billy Crystal said on TV, "look mahvelous!" Among their credits are THE WILD PARTY, THE BOSTONIANS, THE EUROPEANS, etc. American-born Ivory teamed with Indian Merchant and German-born Pole Ruth Prawer Jhabvala (who married an Indian) to make several films, this one included. Jean Rhys wrote a novel which was loosely based on her own life and her alliance with Ford Madox Ford in Paris of the 1920s. Here, Adjani is married to Pole Higgins, who has a tiff with the cops over some illegal things he's up to and is clapped in *le clinque*. With no money and no one to turn to for help, Bates steps in and offers his household as a place to rest her head. Bates is married to painter Smith and she allows him to indulge himself in various peccadilloes as long as he remains discreet and always comes back to her. Adjani takes the offer and Bates is soon after her body. She finally allows herself to be made love to, despite the fact that she still adores Higgins and spends as much time as she can visiting him in jail. It's getting a bit thick and Smith can no longer turn her back on matters, so there's a contretemps and Adjani leaves the house. But Bates can't keep away from her, and as he has a few francs to his name, he gets her a room in a hotel and continues seeing her. Higgins is released and learns about the "arrangement." He is more than miffed and leaves her. Adjani turns to Bates but he has made the decision to stay with the comfortable situation he has with Smith, so Adjani is left out in the cold, but there's no doubt in anyone's mind that she's a survivor and will eventually wind up, if not on top, then somewhere just above the middle. It takes too long to tell and Ivory never gets close to the people, preferring instead to keep his distance, so we are never involved in the lives of any of the people and the result is a flat, almost barren look at a colorful era. It's gamey in spots and not recommended for anyone under 18.

p, Ismail Merchant, Jean Pierre Mahot de la Querantonnais; d, James Ivory; w, Ruth Prawer Jhabvala, Ivory (based on the novel by Jean Rhys); ph, Pierre Lhomme (Eastmancolor); m, Richard Robbins; ed, Humphrey Dixon; art d, Jean Jacques Caziot.

Drama **(PR:C MPAA:R)**

QUE LA BETE MEURE (SEE: THIS MAN MUST DIE, 1970, Fr./Ital.)

QUE LA FETE COMMENCE (SEE: LET JOY REIGN SUPREME, 1977, Fr.)

QUEBEC½** (1951) 85m PAR c

John Barrymore, Jr. *(Mark Douglas)*, Corinne Calvet *(Mme. Stephanie Durossac)*, Barbara Rush *(Madelon)*, Patric Knowles *(Charles Douglas)*, John Hoyt *(Father Antoine)*, Arnold Moss *(Racelle)*, Don Haggerty *(Col. Durossac)*, Patsy Ruth Miller *(Germaine)*, Howard Joslin *(Malbouf)*, Paul Guevrement *(Heliodore)*, Adrian Belanger *(Andre)*, Jacques Champagne *(Capt. Forrest)*, Rene Constantineau *(Baptiste)*, Marcel Sylvain *(Hanson)*, Rolland Joseph Beaudet *(Severac)*, Nikki Duval *(Jeanine)*.

In 1837 a revolt took place between French and English forces in the British controlled Canadian North. Barrymore believes his mother to be dead. Little does he know that she lives and is leading the revolution! Calvet plays the fiery woman known as "Lafleur." This causes some major problems—her son is the British governor of the province. There are some misty-eyed scenes when he discovers her identity and that she sacrificed herself so he wouldn't be taken hostage. Rush and Duval are the two lasses competing for his affections. This was filmed on location in the north Canadian woods and the scenery is used well. Sweeping shots of the rugged terrain are mingled with the story, and the action sequences are nicely staged. The dialog is wordy: these characters speak in paragraphs rather than sentences. The pacing is okay but the film could have stood some editing for a better result. The ensemble isn't bad, and Barrymore shows that he inherited some of the family talent.

p, Alan LeMay; d, George Templeton; w, LeMay; ph, W. Howard Green (Technicolor); m, Van Cleave, Edward Plumb; ed, Jack Ogilvie; art d, Ernst Fegte.

Drama **(PR:A MPAA:NR)**

QUEEN BEE*** (1955) 95m COL bw

Joan Crawford *(Eva Phillips)*, Barry Sullivan *(John Avery Phillips)*, Betsy Palmer *(Carol Lee Phillips)*, John Ireland *(Jusdon Prentiss)*, Lucy Marlow *(Jennifer Stewart)*, William Leslie *(Ty McKinnon)*, Fay Wray *(Sue McKinnon)*, Katherine Anderson *(Miss Breen)*, Tim Hovey *(Ted)*, Linda Bennett *(Trissa)*, Willa Pearl Curtis *(Miss George)*, Bill Walker *(Sam)*, Olan Soule *(Dr. Pearson)*, Bob McCord *(Man)*, Juanita Moore *(Maid)*.

The title makes one think that this might be one of those later Crawford horror movies but it's not that at all. Rather, QUEEN BEE is a fairly interesting character study of a shrike who seeks to dominate everyone around her and manipulate them like a lipsticked marionette-master. Crawford seems to be the embodiment of charm and love but the truth is that she's insidious and rotten. She is married to wealthy Sullivan, a mill owner, and they live in a huge Georgia mansion where Sullivan spends most of his time nipping from the bottle and tippling himself to sleep because he sees right through Crawford and despises her. Marlow, a cousin from New York, comes to stay a while with Crawford and Sullivan and she is taken in by Crawford's apparent lovliness. However, it isn't long before she spots Crawford for what she is. Sullivan's sister, Palmer, is due to be married to the man who manages the estate, Ireland, and Crawford does what she can to stop that union because she and Ireland had once been lovers and she can't bear the thought of him sleeping with anyone else. To that end, she attempts to get Ireland back into her hive again. Palmer finds out that Ireland and Crawford once had an affair and she kills herself over the situation (a bit harsh and not really motivated). Crawford plays mind games with Sullivan, but his disdain is so evident that Crawford is frustrated. Meanwhile, Marlow and Sullivan find a great deal in common and a love grows. Crawford would have to be blind not to see what's happening in her own home and tries her darndest to break up this liason. Ireland has finally had it with Crawford and is still in mourning over the loss of his one true love, Palmer, so he takes matters into his own hands (and feet). He asks Crawford to go for a drive with him and she readily accepts, thinking that they might be able to recapture their one-time passion. It is on this seemingly harmless automobile excursion that Ireland reckons his life is worthless without Palmer and crashes the car, killing himself and Crawford (audiences cheered when this happened) and leaving the path clear for Sullivan and Marlow. In a small role, note Fay Wray, who will always be remembered for . . . but wait! If you don't know why Fay Wray is a part of cinematic history, why are you reading this book? After leaving active duty on the screen, Ireland moved to Santa Barbara and operated a successful restaurant for several years. Lang received an Oscar nomination for his cinematography.

p, Jerry Wald; d, Ranald MacDougall; w, MacDougall (based on the novel by Edna Lee); ph, Charles Lang, Jr.; m, George Duning; ed, Viola Lawrence; md, Morris Stoloff; art d, Ross Bellah; cos, Jean Louis.

Drama **(PR:C MPAA:NR)**

QUEEN BEE SEE: CONJUGAL BED, THE, 1963, Fr./Ital.)

QUEEN CHRISTINA***** (1933) 97m MGM bw

Greta Garbo *(Queen Christina)*, John Gilbert *(Don Antonio De la Prada)*, Ian Keith *(Magnus)*, Lewis Stone *(Chancellor Oxenstierna)*, Elizabeth Young *(Ebba Sparre)*, Sir C. Aubrey Smith *(Aage)*, Reginald Owen *(Prince Charles)*, Georges Renavent *(French Ambassador)*, Gustav von Seyffertitz *(General)*, David Torrence *(Archbishop)*, Ferdinand Munier *(Innkeeper)*, Akim Tamiroff *(Pedro)*, Cora Sue Collins *(Christina as a Child)*, Edward Norris *(Count Jacob)*, Lawrence Grant, Barbara Barondess *(Bits)*, Paul Hurst *(Swedish Soldier)*, Ed Gargan *(Fellow Drinker)*, Wade Boteler *(Rabble Rouser)*, Fred Kohler *(Member of the Court)*, Dick Alexander *(Peasant in Crowd)*, Maj. Sam Harris *(Nobleman)*.

Seldom do the productions in which garbo appears match the star's almost mystical persona and magical presence. QUEEN CHRISTINA does and remains a classic to this day. Moreover, the film mates Garbo to her silent screen lover (on and off screen), Gilbert, and their love scenes together are poignant and powerful. By the time of this film Gilbert was supposedly washed up but, as he mightily proves here, he was far from being finished. Garbo is a decisive queen, ruling Sweden with wisdom and compassion. Her former lover, Keith, attempts to arrange a marriage between Garbo and the popular Owen, a dashing prince, but she will have nothing to do with political unions. At the time Sweden is waging a bloody war of attrition and Garbo, at a cabinet meeting, is disgusted with her ministers who go on planning battles. She finally cries out: "Spoil, glory, flags, trumpets—what is behind those words? Cripples, dead men! I want for my people security and happiness. I want to cultivate the arts of happiness. I want peace, and peace I will have!" She is so overjoyed at her triumph of obtaining a peace treaty that she hugs herself; at dawn the next day, her country at peace, Garbo steps out onto a balcony of her royal palace and, drinking in the tranquility, is moved to scoop up some snow and rub it on her face in exhilaration. (The snow could not be manufactured for this film at the time so Mamoulian did the next best thing, using oatmeal which looked more like snow than snow itself. The director also had the star take a few drags of a cigarette and then, when the cameras were rolling, exhale the smoke so that her breath on the balcony would have a frosty effect.) While riding in the snow, Garbo encounters Gilbert, the newly appointed ambassador from Spain. She is intrigued by the handsome, gallant Spaniard and decides to discover his real nature while disguised as a male youth. This garb, topped off by leather pants, is donned by Garbo while her advisor, elderly Smith, actually enters her bed chamber and reluctantly helps her dress. He chastises her for throwing over Owen, saying, "You cannot die an old maid." She responds, perhaps more as an ironic comment on her manly attire than her future: "I have no intention to. I shall die a bachelor!" Garbo goes to an inn where she knows Gilbert is staying and pretends to be a wealthy youth in search of adventure. He befriends her, advising her to be wary of strangers and to always follow a virtuous path. Then swaggering, bragging men at the inn loudly fall to arguing about the number of lovers their queen has had and she suddenly jumps upon a table, firing a pistol and saying in her throaty voice that is mistaken for that of a young man: "Well, gentlemen, I have the painful duty of telling you that you are both wrong—the sixes and the nines. The truth is that the Queen has had twelve lovers this past year. A round dozen . . . And now, if you will permit me, I shall stand a round of drinks for all of you. Landlard, the punch!" Garbo is invited to spend the night in Gilbert's room, the ambassador still unaware that she is female and of the startling fact that he is keeping company with the queen. She eventually makes herself known to him and the two fall in love; she spends two glorious days and nights with him. Toward the end of their gentle, moving love hiatus, Garbo, in one of the most riveting scenes ever put to screen, begins to glide about the room while Gilbert watches her, perplexed, amused. (Only the upper part of her body is shown, Garbo having long legs and rather large feet.) Her hands, like divining rods, stretch out to caress the walls, a spinning wheel, the ornte furniture; she seems to float onto the bed, embracing the sheets and pillows, drifting along like a slow-moving cloud to the bedpost which she embraces (as phallic a scene as ever created). Gilbert can no longer bear the mystery and asks (more to enlighten the unenlightened and less perceptive in the audience): "What are you doing?" Garbo replies, as she continues to touch, rub, and feel almost every object in the room: "Memorizing this room. In the future, in my memory, I shall live a great deal in this room . . . I have imagined happiness, but happiness you cannot imagine—you must feel it. This is how Lord must have felt like whenhe beheld the finished world with all his creatures, loving, breathing." (If she had made only this scene in her entire film career, Garbo's greatness would have been secure.) Their idyll over, Garbo returns to her dreary court and receives Gilbert officially, pretending she knows him only as an official representative of a foreign power. He is there, he informs her, to ask for her hand in marriage—for the king of Spain, not himself. She does not respond but the couple continue to meet secretly. When the manipulative Keith discovers their secret meetings, he rouses the public against Gilbert, labeling him a trifling interloper. Garbo fears for Gilbert's life and sends him away, but tells him she will abandon the throne and meet him, and they shall sail away from Sweden to end their days together in sunny Spain. Against the protests of her loyal subjects and advisors, chiefly Smith, Garbo abdicates and then journeys to her rendezvous with Gilbert, only to find that he has been killed in a duel with the vindictive Keith. Taking his body aboard ship, Garbo and her dead lover sail for Spain, the last classic scene a slow close-in showing the great actress standing at the prow of the ship, mist closing in about her, staring out to sea and into the loveless, lonely future she earlier envisioned for herself. QUEEN CHRISTINA is probably Garbo's finest film, silent or sound. Her own personality and that of the character she is playing are one, even though this is a highly romanticized conception of the 16th-Century monarch. She dominates the film, rightly so, and gives a performance that has never been equalled, one so rich in movement and speech that it is worthy of a Velazquez or a Goya. She is a ruler with more human passion thatn obsession of power, one who decides to control her own destiny, no matter how tragic, rather than to be controlled by the fate a throne may decree. Watching Garbo in QUEEN CHRISTINA is to watch the idealized woman, sensitive, gentle, loving with the intensity of lava seeping from the earth's core. This is the quintessential Garbo film where the great actress encompasses what seems to be every human passion, relating in searing scenes her strength, sorrow, weaknesses, joy, in an extraordinary performance. Mamoulian should receive a great deal of credit for recognizing the star's vast capabilities and extending them as far as his cameras could reach. In the grand set-piece where Garbo fondles the room in which she has made love to Gilbert, Mamoulian, who had a background in opera and choreography, instructed the actress to "do it to music," and had a barely audible but haunting melody, so softly played as to almost vanish from the sound track. To keep Garbo's timing perfect in this scene, the director had a metronome clicking as she floated about the room. The last unforgettable scene of Garbo peering from the prow of the ship is all Mamoulian, who told the actress before starting his cameras: "I want your face to be a blank piece of paper. I want the writing to be done by every member of the audience. I'd like it if you could avoid blinking your eyes, so that you're nothing but a beautiful mask." Garbo complied. Her costar, Gilbert, is far from the failed actor the world and Louis B. Mayer, who hated him, proclaimed the great silent-screen lover to be. He is dashing and empathic and in his love scenes with Garbo there is a tenderness and quality of manliness few actors of his day could project. Unlike the false publicity (spread by Mayer) that Gilbert's voice was too high-pitched for talking pictures, Gilbert's vocal tone and texture is a healthy baritone, a commanding one at that. If MGM and Mayer had had their way, Gilbert would not have been resurrected from the actor's graveyard to which they had assigned him. But it was Garbo who had her way, utilizing an iron-clad contract which paid her $250,000 a film, gave Garbo her choice of director, cameraman (she chose Daniels, of course, for QUEEN CHRISTINA, he being her favorite cinematographer), her leading man, and, in fact, her entire cast, if she cared to select the extras. No one had the kind of power the actress exercised, at MGM or at any other studio. She selected Keith, Smith, and Stone (the latter playing her chancellor in his seventh film and last with Garbo, Stone appearing with Garbo in more films than any other actor). Garbo did not, as popularly thought, immediately select Gilbert to play opposite her in QUEEN CHRISTINA. She had seen a young British actor, Laurence Olivier, in a tear-jerking melodrama, WESTWARD PASSAGE, and liked him. Olivier, at the time, bore an amazing resemblance to a young John Gilbert of an earlier era. The British actor was signed to play the Spanish ambassador and his passage from England to America was paid, first class, by MGM. When he arrived at the studio, Mamoulian suggested that he do a little rehearsal with Garbo, selecting the all-important love scene in the inn. Garbo normally did not rehearse but Mamoulian persuaded her to sit in with the young man she had selected so she could get used to him. Olivier appeared in full costume while Garbo stepped onto the set wearing lounging pajamas and smoking a cigarette. Olivier tried to chat with the actress but she gave him only cold one-word responses. The novice British actor later stated that "the director said I was to come forward, grasp Garbo's slender body tenderly, look into her eyes and, in the gesture, awaken the passion within her . . . I went into my role, giving it everything I had. But at the touch of my hand, Garbo became frigid. I could feel the sudden tautness of her." Mamoulian told them to take a break and the two had a smoke together while Olivier tried to loosen up the actress. His talk was small talk and hers was smaller. They tried the scene again and, according to Olivier, Garbo "froze up as before." Mamoulian saw a disaster on the horizon, a frozen one of solid ice. He threw down the script in frustration and shouted: "In Heaven's name, is there *any* man this woman *will* warm to?" From the darkness came the voice of an unknown technician: "John Gilbert!" The 26-year-old Olivier was told to get out of his costume and forget about appearing in a Garbo film. Mamoulian, following the suggestion of the technician, immediately called Gilbert at his Tower Road mansion in Beverly Hills where he was living with wife No. two, Metro contract starlet Virginia Bruce. He asked the then seldom employed actor to help out, to warm up the woman he had starred with in the heyday of the silent era. Gilbert happily agreed and within hours was wearing Olivier's costume, standing before Garbo. She immediately relaxed and the effect he had upon her was amazing. The actress began to interact with an outpouring of deep affection. It was as if Olivier had merely been a stand-in for the leading man she had wanted all along. Still, Gilbert was only helping out. The studio had proposed other leading players, *anyone* but Gilbert. Leslie Howard was offered the role but refused it, fearing that he would be overwhelmed by Garbo (which certainly would have been the case). Nils Asther, Bruce Cabot, and Franchot Tone were suggested but Garbo said not to them all. Less than two weeks after shooting had started on QUEEN CHRISTINA, Garbo made the public decision she had made privately. It was Gilbert or it was no one. She wired Louis B. Mayer *her orders*: "This is to confirm the approval heretofore given by me that John Gilbert shall be substituted therein, in lieu and instead of Laurence Olivier." Though Mayer fumed, his chief of production, Irving Thalberg, secretly smiled and assigned Gilbert the role. (The two were friends, Thalberg and his wife-actress, Norma Shearer, having stood up at Gilbert's 1932 wedding to Virginia Bruce.) Much has been said about Garbo's magnanimous insistence that Gilbert, the fallen star, join her in a major film production to rescue his almost lost career. She was reportedly no longer in love with him but was returning the great favor he extended to her at the beginning of *her* career when he demanded she co-star with him in the silen classic FLESH AND THE DEVIL which launched Garbo's fabulous movie reign. But not until Gilbert signed his contract to do QUEEN CHRISTINA did Mayer give up trying to replace him, negotiating with producer Wanger at the last minute for Garbo to take John Barrymore as her leading man. Gilbert, of course, was second-billed to Garbo even though Mayer tried to have Keith's name put before the once great lover of the silent screen. He won less on the contract battlefront, agreeing to perform his role for only $20,000, less than a tenth of what MGM had paid him only a few years earlier in his heyday. Thalberg and Garbo hoped for a comeback for Gilbert but, even though he was outstanding in his role, the public was no longer interested, having bought the myth about the actor's inadequacies in talkies, a myth sponsored by Louis B. Mayer. The MGM chief had loathed Gilbert for years, disapproving of his free-thinking, hair-raising life style, as well as his heavy drinking. Moreover, the once brilliant star of MGM had a million-dollar contract with the studio, handed him during his palmy days when millions of women swooned over his forceful image and steamy love scenes in such silent films as FLESH AND THE DEVIL (1927), LOVE (1927), and A WOMAN OF AFFAIRS (1929). Mayer attempted every trick he could conceive to embarrass Gilbert into breaking his contract, putting him into awful early talkies such as HIS GLORIOUS NIGHT (1929) and WAY FOR A SAILOR (1930), where the sound track dealing with Gilbert's dialog was reportedly distorted on orders from Mayer so that he sounded high-pitched and effeminate, causing audiences to jeer and hoot fun at him. Mayer tried to publicly humiliate the actor, announcing him as the starring lead opposite Garbo in GRAND HOTEL and then replacing him with John Barrymore, again announcing him as the lead in RED DUST opposite Jean Harlow and then replacing him with Clark Gable. One story, apochryphal or not, is appropriate in describing Mayer's vicious technique. Gilbert was reportedly ordered to appear at MGM in full evening dress one evening for a scene in one of the programmers he was doing. He was thrown into a swimming pool over and over again, until dawn, the director, at Mayer's conniving insistence, ordering take after endless take, saying that none of the pool scenes were "Just right". But Gilbert would not quit, knowing, of course, that if he walked off the set, MGM would cancel his lucrative contract. He merely took a shot of booze between pool takes and politely allowed himself to be half drowned until the crew members, not Gilbert, wearied of the charade and walked off. Gilbert, divorced by Bruce, living in the past ("In the future, in my memory, I shall live a great deal in this room."), reportedly still in love with Garbo, even though he was supposedly having an affair with Marlene Dietrich, died from alcohol and a heart attack on January 9, 1936, age 38. Mayer went to the furneral and actually had to turn away so that no one would see him grinning in malicious triumph. Dietrich was also present at the ceremonies, so wobbly-legged that she almost collapsed. QUEEN CHRISTINA received major advertising and publicity from MGM and its premiere at the Astor Theatre in New York featured a three-story-high electric sign showing Garbo's face with only the name GARBO circling it like a halo. But it wasn't enough. The film, shot in 68 days, gleaned only $632,000 in its initial release, costing $1,444,000. Although the film was beautifully acted and directed, and sumptuously mounted with wonderful baroque sets, the public in this Depression year found it a strain to pay the $2 top price to see Garbo even at her finest. Though the critics lauded the film, praised Garbo *and* Gilbert, it would be many years before the film earned back its investment. Perhaps some of the Garbo allure had worn thin with the public. She had not appeared in a film in 18 months and was living in Sweden most of the time. In fact she was residing in Sweden when her good friend Salka Viertel suggested she read up on the mysterious Queen Christina (1626-1689), giving Garbo two books, *The Sybil of the North*by Faith Compton Mackenzie and *Christina of Sweden* by Margaret Goldsmith. Although these two tomes are highly romanticized versions of that monarch's life, they still shed some light on a queen who was not only unorthodox but downright perverse. Just the opposite of the character enacted by Garbo. When the actress told Viertel that she felt whe had an affinity for Queen Christina, he and Margaret P. Levine wrote a screenplay about the monarch, sent it to Garbo, and she liked it enough to wire MGM, telling her studio that it would be her next vehicle (her 21st film). Garbo then booked passage in one of the few staterooms offered on a slow freighter and sailed for America, perhaps practicing that memorable scene to come on the prow of the ship. The real Queen Christina of Sweden worried the Hays Office, the Hollywood censors, who knew her actual background and insisted upon seeing the script before approving of the Garbo production. They breathed a sigh of relief and even allowed the trysting in the inn scenes in preference to reality. Queen Christina was a great lover but one who loved women, not men; she slept with her favorite lady-in-waiting. Further, she was short, fat, and ugly, thrived on smutty stories, and she hated to bathe; few of her courtiers approached her beyond 20 feet, such was her odorous presence. Moreover, the real reason for Christina's abdication was the fact that other royal members of the court and nobles forced her into it; it was either publicly marry her own lady-in-waiting or abdicate. Christina abandoned the throne rather than face public ignominy. (At one point, Christina intended to declare herself *king!*) When Christina did sail away from Sweden it wasn't to Spain but to Italy. There the notorious homosexual ex-monarch lived in forgotten exile under the pseudonym of "Count Dohna," dying with this man's name on her tombstone. Ironically, Garbo's first appearance in a major film in Sweden, GOSTA BERLING, had her playing a character named "Countess Dohna." Then there is the strange fact that Garbo was 28 when she made QUEEN CHRISTINA, the very age of the monarch when she departed her throne. The film itself may have given the actress the idea of abdicating her Hollywood throne for she would disappear from the screen in eight years. QUEEN CHRISTINA would be remade disatrously in 1974 as ABDICATION starring Liv Ullmann, a boring costumer that is even further from the truth than its illustrious original. Publicity representatives touted this nonfilm by pointing out that Ullmann was actually wearing the crown Garbo wore in QUEEN CHRISTINA as a way of giving the picture some much-needed status. The sputtering, groping, near-spastic Ullmann could never even hope to wear Garbo's crown, on of off-screen. It would take a real queen to do that.

p, Walter Wanger; d, Rouben Mamoulian; w, H.M. Harwood, Salka Viertel, S.N. Behrman (based on a story by Viertel, Margaret Levin); ph, William Daniels; m, Herbert Stothart; ed, Blanche Sewell; art d, Alexander Toluboff, Edwin B. Willis; cos, Adrian.

Historical Drama/Romance **(PR:A MPAA:NR)**

QUEEN FOR A DAY½** (1951) 107m UA bw (AKA: HORSIE)

"The Gossamer World": Phyllis Avery *(Marjorie)*, Darrwn McGavin *(Dan)*, Rudy Lee *(Pete)*, Frances E. Williams *(Anna)*, Joan Winfield *(Laura)*, Lonny Burr *(Charles)*, Tristram Coffin *(Doctor)*, Jiggs Wood *(Mr. Beck)*, Casey Folks *(Jim)*, George Sherwood *(Mr. Garmes)*; "High Diver": Adam Williams *(Chuck)*, Kasia Orzazewski *(Mrs. Nalawak)*, Albert Ben-Astar *(Mr. Nalawak)*, Tracey Roberts *(Peggy)*, Larry Johns *(Deacon McAllister)*, Bernard Szold *(Daredevil Rinaldi)*, Joan Sudlow *(Mrs. McAllister)*, Grace Lenard *(Mrs. Rinaldi)*, Leonard Nemoy *(Chief)*, Danny Davenport *(Satchelbutt)*, Madge Blake *(Mrs. Kimpel)*; "Horsie": Edith Meiser *(Miss Wilmarth)*, Dan Tobin *(Owen Cruger)*, Jessie Cavitt *(Camilla Cruger)*, Douglas Evans *(Freddy Forster)*, Don Shelton *(Jack Minot)*, Louise Curry *(Secretary)*, Sheila Watson *(Mary)*, Minna Phillips *(Cook)*, Byron Keith *(Chauffeur)*; "Broadcast Studio": Jack Bailey *(Himself)*, Jim Morgan *(Himself)*, Fort Pearson *(Himself)*, Melanie York *(1st Contestant)*, Cynthia Corley *(2nd Contestant)*, Kay Wiley *(3rd Contestant)*, Helen Mowery *(Jan)*, Dian Fauntelle *(Helena)*.

This film is a series of vignettes linked together with the popular game show of the late 1940s and early 1950s "Queen for a Day." Between the three stories is supposed TV studio footage featuring "Queen" host Bailey and his sidekicks Morgan and Pearson. The first story "The Gossamer World" is a simplistic drama featuring Avery, McGavin, and Lee as the perfect suburban family. They're bound for tragedy which comes in the form of polio for darling son Lee. Next is "High Diver" which stars Williams as the poor son of immigrants eager for a college education. He'll do anything to earn money to get to school and ends up as a carnival high diver. Orzazewski and Ben-Astar are the parents who nervously watch their son plummet from the high dive into a vat of water. Szold, the drunken diver that Williams replaces, is a character of pathos. These two stories are average, though entertaining enough. The final vignette is the best thanks to a story by the wonderful humorist Parker. Meiser is the title character of "Horsie" playing a homely spinster who cares for a new-born infant. The baby belongs to Tobin and Cavitt. Tobin is an important radio executive who, along with his wife, all but ignores the kind-hearted woman. They're glad when she leaves and are surprised to see her later on—you guessed it—"Queen for a Day." They are even more surprised when she wins and asks only for an electric razor for her former employer who has been "so nice to her." The various writers on the vignettes and studio links make this a mixed bag of a film. The Parker story is funny and human but its characters lose some of their charm when in the world of the TV studio. All in all this is a cute film that glows in spots and gets by in others. Its tie-in to the television show was well exploited. It was advertised on the show a year before release with a special contest. The winner would have the film premiere in her home town!

p, Robert Stillman; d, Arthur Lubin; w, Seton I. Miller (based on stories by Faith Baldwin, John Ashworth, Dorothy Parker); ph, Guy Roe; m, Hugo Freidhofer; ed, George Amy.

Comedy/Drama **(PR:A MPAA:NR)**

QUEEN HIGH½** (1930) 85m PAR bw

Charles Ruggles *(T. Boggs Johns)*, Frank Morgan *(Mr. George Nettleton)*, Ginger Rogers *(Polly Rockwell)*, Stanley Smith *(Dick Johns)*, Helen Carrington *(Mrs. Nettleton)*, Rudy Cameron *(Cyrus Vanderholt)*, Betty Garde *(Florence Cole)*, Theresa Maxwell Conover *(Mrs. Rockwell)*, Nina Olivette *(Coddles)*, Tom Brown *(Jimmy)*, Edith Sheldon *(Dancer)*, Theresa Klee, Dorothy Walters.

Ruggles and Morgan are partners in a garter business who disagree over who should be running things ("Why don't you sleep at night instead of during business hours?" one shrieks). They finally decide that the winner of their poker hand will take charge for a year, and the loser will become the winner's butler. Rogers, in her second film (reteaming her with Ruggles, but in a secondary role) is the ingenue who's romantically and musically attached to Smith, Ruggles' son. This is an amusing little programmer, based on a Broadway musical comedy which in turn had been based on a 1917 play. The lead comedians really make this film work. In lesser hands, their bickering would have come off as silly, rather than good-natured fun. The direction (by silent comedian Harold Lloyd's director) is a little sluggish; but keeps the story moving and gives the comedians a free reign. Rogers isn't bad, though she serves as little more than decoration. Advance publicity for QUEEN HIGH had indicated the film would be shot entirely in Technicolor. Songs include: "Everything Will Happen for the Best" (B.G. DeSylva, Lewis Gensler; sung by Rogers, Morgan), "Brother, Just Laugh It Off" (Arthur Schwartz, Ralph Rainger; sung by Rogers, Morgan), "It Seems to Me," "I'm Afraid of You" (Dick Howard, Rainger; sung by Rogers, Smith), "I Love the Girls in My Own Peculiar Way" (E.Y. Harburg, Henry Souvain; sung by Ruggles).

p, Laurence Schwab, Frank Mandel; d, Fred Newmeyer; w, Mandel (based on the play "A Pair of Sixes" by Edward H. Peple); adapted from the musical comedy by Schwab, Lewis Gensler, B.G. DeSylva); ph, William Steiner; ed, Barney Rogan; md, Al Goodman; art d, William Saulter.

Musical/Comedy **(PR:A MPAA:NR)**

QUEEN OF ATLANTIS (SEE: SIREN OF ATLANTIS, 1948)

QUEEN OF BABYLON, THE** (1956, Ital.) 98m Pantheon/FOX c (LA CORTIGIANA DI BABILONIA; SEMIRAMIS)

Rhonda Fleming (Semiramis), Ricardo Montalban (Amak), Roldano Lupi (Assur), Carlo Ninchi (Sibari), Tamara Lees (Lysia).

Steamy, vice-ridden Babylon is the setting for this colorful bibical costumer starring Montalban as a heroic Chaldean rebel leader whose rival is the nefarious Assyrian king, Lupi. Montalban first meets Fleming, a curvaceous peasant girl, when he hides out in her hut to avoid capture by Lupi's forces. Fleming is found by Lupi, who becomes enamored of her beauty and takes her into his royal fold. Later Lupi falls victim to poison and the guilty finger is pointed at Fleming. The real killer turns out to be Ninchi, an unscrupulous advisor to the king who has his own ideas about ruling Assyria. Montalban performs many a heroic act to liberate Fleming and the entire kingdom from the corrupt clutches of its ruling body, winning Fleming's love by the finale. Definitely not subscribing to the postulate "less is more," THE QUEEN OF BABYLON is brimming with lavish costumes, spectacular sets, and vibrant color. While the plot and acting are practically negligible, it is the film's sense of epic dimension that makes it so watchable. Also boosting the film's "size" is the bombastic score by Renzo Rossellini, brother of director Roberto. Dubbed in English.

p, Nat Wachsberger; d, Carlo Ludovico Bragaglia; w, Ennio de Concini, Giuseppe Mangione, Bragaglia (based on a story by Maria Bory); ph, Gabor Pogany (Ferraniacolor); m, Renzo Rossellini.

Biblical Drama **(PR:A MPAA:NR)**

QUEEN OF BLOOD*** (1966) 81m Cinema West/AIP c (AKA: PLANET OF BLOOD)

John Saxon (Allan), Basil Rathbone (Dr. Farraday), Judi Meredith (Laura), Dennis Hopper (Paul), Florence Marly ("Queen of Blood"), Robert Boon, Don Eitner, Virgil Frye, J. Robert Porter, Teri Lee, Forrest J. Ackerman.

This surely ranks as one of American International Pictures' finest efforts in plot construction. Literally. After seeing some excellent spaceship footage purchased by Roger Corman from the 1959 Russian film NIEBO ZOWIET, the producers edited out the clips they wanted and fashioned a story around it. The final product cost only $50,000 (the most expensive items being helmets to match the Russian ones purchased for $1,000!) and was shot in approximately eight days. The story casts Rathbone (in quite a different role from his more famous Sherlock Holmes) as a doctor who flies with a crew to Mars to rescue a downed ship. The only survivor is Marly, who now sports a green complexion and sinister glowing eyes. It is revealed that she is an intergalactic vampire intent on draining crew members of their blood. Saxon and Meredith, the only crew members left, discover that Marly is a hemophiliac! Considering the production background, this is an entertaining science fiction horror piece with an off-the-wall sense of the macabre. The direction nicely matches the footage and presents it in an eerie, atmospheric style with great effect. Rathbone remained at the studio after filming was completed to shoot his part in VOYAGE TO THE PREHISTORIC PLANET, another film that also employed the pirated Russian footage.

p, George Edwards; d&w Curtis Harrington (based on the uncredited story "The Veiled Woman"); ph, Villis Lapenieks (Pathe Color); m, Leonard Morand; ed, Leo Shreve; art d, Albert Locatelli; set d, Leon Smith; cos, Sharon Compton; makeup, William Condos.

Science Fiction/Horror **(PR:O MPAA:NR)**

QUEEN OF BROADWAY*½ (1942) 64m PRC bw

Rochelle Hudson, Buster Crabbe, Paul Bryar, Emmett Lynn, Donald Mayo, Isabel LaMal, Blanche Rose, Henry Hall, John Dilson, Milton Kibbee, Vince Barnett, Jack Mulhall, Fred "Snowflake" Toones.

Lady gambler is foiled in her desire to adopt a lovable orphan because of her occupation. But when she marries sportsman Crabbe, they are able to take the child home.

p, Bert Sternbach; d, Sam Newfield; w, Rusty McCullough, George Warren Sayre (based on a story by Sayre); ph, Jack Greenhalgh; m, Leo Erdody; ed, Holbrook N. Todd; md, David Chudnow.

Drama **(PR:A MPAA:NR)**

QUEEN OF BROADWAY, 1943 (SEE: KID DYNAMITE, 1943)

QUEEN OF BURLESQUE** (1946) 68m PRC bw

Evelyn Ankers (Crystal McCoy), Carleton Young (Steve Hurley), Marian Martin (Lola Cassell), Craig Reynolds (Joe Nolan), Rose La Rose (Blossom Terraine), Emory Parnell (Inspector Crowley), Murray Leonard (Chick Malloy), Nolan Leary (Doorman), Gordon Clark (Straight Man Singer), Alice Fleming (Annie), Jacqueline Dalya (Dolly Devoe), Red Marshall (Johnson), David Frisco (Stage Manager Max), Charles King (Dugan).

Ankers, who works in burlesque, is engaged to Young, a journalist. When a series of murders occur at the club she works at, Ankers becomes a suspect. However, the pair finds the real culprit, and Ankers is off the hook. This is a standard programmer, racier than most of its type thanks to the burlesque setting. Nonetheless, the dialog and mystery are routine. Acting and production values are adequate for the material.

p, Arthur Alexander, Alfred Stern; d, Sam Newfield; w, David A. Lang; ph, Vincent J. Farrar; ed, Jack Ogilvie; md, Karl Hajos; art d, Edward Jewell; ch, Larry Ceballos; m/l, "How Can I Tell You," "Flower Song," Gene Lucas, Al Stewart.

Crime **(PR:C MPAA:NR)**

QUEEN OF CLUBS (SEE: LOVE CYCLES 1969, Gr.)

QUEEN OF CRIME (SEE: KATE PLUS TEN, 1938, Brit.)

QUEEN OF DESTINY (SEE: SIXTY GLORIOUS YEARS, 1938, Brit.)

QUEEN OF HEARTS**½ (1936, Brit.) 80m Associated Talking Pictures/ABF bw

Gracie Fields (Grace Perkins), John Loder (Derek Cooper), Enid Stamp-Taylor (Yvonne), Fred Duprez (Zulenberg), Edward Rigby (Perkins), Julie Suedo (Rita Dow), Jean Lister (Mrs. Perkins), Hal Gordon (Stage Manager), Syd Crossley (PC), Madeleine Seymour (Mrs. Vandeleur), H.F. Maltby (Solicitor), Margaret Yarde (Mrs. Porter), Tom Gill, Edith Fields, Vera Hilliard, Tom Payne, Vera Lennox, Mike Johnson, Pat Williams, Balliol and Merton, Monty Banks.

Fields stars as a mild-mannered seamstress mistaken for a local rich woman who's backing an important show. Fields sees her chance to get ahead in the world and plays along. She wins the handsome actor of the show and, of course, lives happily ever after. This is minor fluff without much new or original. But, Fields makes the film work. Fields experienced her peak in popularity, as comedienne and singer, during the early 1930s, and was one of the highest-paid actresses in Britain during that decade. She collaborated in QUEEN OF HEARTS with second husband Monty Banks, who served as director and played a small role. She joined Banks in America in 1940, after which she made two successful films, HOLY MATRIMONY and MOLLY AND ME. She played a character part in PARIS UNDERGROUND before retiring from the screen.

p, Basil Dean; d, Monty Banks; w, Clifford Grey, H.F. Maltby, Douglas Furber, Anthony Kimmins, Gordon Wellesley; ph, John W. Boyle.

Comedy **(PR:A MPAA:NR)**

QUEEN OF OUTER SPACE** (1958) 80m AA c

Zsa Zsa Gabor (Talleah), Eric Fleming (Capt. Neil Patterson), Laurie Mitchell (Yllana, Queen of Venus), Paul Birch (Prof. Konrad), Barbara Darrow (Kaeel), Dave Willock (Lt. Michael Cruze), Lisa Davis (Motiya), Patrick Waltz (Lt. Larry Turner), Marilyn Buferd (Odeena), Marjorie Durant (Amazon Guard), Lynn Cartwright (Guard Leader), Gerry Gaylor (Friendly Guard), Mary Ford, Colleen Drake, Marya Stevens (Other Guards), Laura Mason, Tania Velia, Kathy Marlowe (Councilors).

This is filmmaking at its campiest. Fleming (the star of T.V.'s "Rawhide") leads an expedition to Venus. Along with crew members Waltz and Willock they discover the planet is inhabited by a group of beautiful women. Va-va-va-voom! Fleming falls for Gabor, garbed in slit skirt and with Hungarian accent intact (apparently her character hailed from the Slavic region of Venus). But problems arise when title character Mitchell raises her ugly head. Literally. It seems she must always wear a mask because her face was scarred during the war with men. In an unintentional Freudian analogy, she decides to destroy Earth using a disintegrator ray. Of course she's stopped, and all ends happily. Though there are some attempts at humor, this film is at its best when it takes itself seriously. That's *really* where the laughs come in. The ray guns and costumes, along with the forest setting, were left over from FORBIDDEN PLANET; other sets, some special effects and a giant spider are reaped from WORLD WITHOUT END; and the happy wanderers' rocketship is from FLIGHT TO MARS. The dialog and plot, of course, are reminiscent of every low-budget science fiction film imaginable. The adequate direction is from the same man who somehow got the Three Stooges through their final pictures. And surprisingly enough, the whole thing is based on a story by Ben Hecht!

p, Ben Schwalb; d, Edward Bernds; w, Charles Beaumont (based on a story by Ben Hecht); ph, William Whitley (CinemaScope, DeLuxe Color); m, Marlin Skiles; ed, William Austin; art d, David Milton; makeup, Emile LaVigne.

Science Fiction **(PR:A MPAA:NR)**

QUEEN OF SHEBA* (1953, Ital.) 114m Oro Films/Lopert bw

Leonora Ruffo (Balkis, Queen of Sheba), Gino Cervi (King Solomon), Gino Leurini (Prince Rehoboam), Marina Berti (Princess Zymira), Franco Silva (Kabael), Mario Ferrari (High Priest), Isa Pola (Tabuy), Nita Dover (Kinnor), Umberta Silvestra (Issachar), Dorian Gray (Abner), Franca Tamantini (False Mother), Fulvia Mammi (True Mother).

Leurini plays the son of King Solomon (Cervi), The budding prince is sent to spy on Sheba (Ruffo) and find out her plan for war on Israel. but Leurini takes a little respite from work when he falls in love with Ruffo. The arranged marriage between Leurini and Berti spurs Ruffo to seek revenge by declaring war. This cheaply dubbed affair looks like bargain basement De Mille. The dialog is stiff and overloaded with words, while the acting features an excess of overly theatrical gestures. Plenty of togas, spears, zinging arrows, and an utterly predictable plot. This film can't even qualify as good camp.

p, Mario Francisci; d, Pietro Francisci; w, Richard Heinz, Bernard Luber; ph, Mario Montuori; m, Nino Rota; art d, Guilio Bongini.

Historical Epic **(PR:C MPAA:NR)**

QUEEN OF SPADES*½** (1948, Brit.) 95m ABF-Pathe/MON bw

Anton Walbrook *(Herman Sovotin)*, Edith Evans *(Countess Ranevskaya)*, Yvonne Mitchell *(Lizavetta Ivanova)*, Ronald Howard *(Andrei)*, Mary Jerrold *(Old Varvarushka)*, Anthony Dawson *(Fyodor)*, Miles Malleson *(Tschybukin)*, Michael Medwin *(Ilovaisky)*, Athene Seyler *(Princess Ivashin)*, Ivor Barnard *(Bookseller)*, Maroussia Dmitravitch *(Gypsy Singer)*, Violetta Elvin *(Gypsy Dancer)*, Pauline Tennant *(Young Countess)*, Jacqueline Clark *(Milliner's Assistant)*, Yusef Ramart *(Countess' Lover)*, Gibb McLaughlin *(Birdseller)*, Valentine Dyall *(St. Germain's Messenger)*, Gordon Begg, Drusilla Wills, Aubrey Mallalieu, George Woodbridge, Pauline Jameson, Hay Petrie, Brown Derby, Ian Colin, Clement McCallin, John Howard, Aubrey Woods, David Paltenghi.

Bizarre and atmospheric supernatural drama based on a classic short story by Russian poet Aleksander Pushkin. Walbrook is a dashing but impoverished captain in the imperial Russian army of the 19th Century. His fellow officers gamble constantly, but his poverty excludes him from joining them. One night he meets an aging countess, Evans, who apparently has the secret of winning at faro, a secret for which, it is rumored, she had sold her soul. Determined to gain the secret for himself, Walbrook seduces the countess' companion, Mitchell, and she tells him about a secret staircase. The captain sneaks into her house at night and the countess is frightened to death when she sees him. Walbrook flees the house, but that night dreams that he has the secret. He goes to the gambling house and takes on his chief rival for the affections of a young lady. Just as he is about to play his winning card, an ace, it changes before his eyes to a queen with the face of the countess grinning at him. The story has been filmed at least a dozen times, including eight silents and a French version as recent as 1965, but this is easily the best, blessed with good performances and a skillful, literary style. Dame Edith Evans began her screen career in earnest after her grotesque and effective performance here (she had earlier appeared only in a pair of forgotten silent films some 35 years before). The period settings and costumes are superb, and the film packs a jolt not easily forgotten.

p, Anatole de Grunwald; d, Thorold Dickinson; w, Rodney Ackland, Arthur Boys (based on the novel by Aleksander Pushkin); ph, Otto Heller; m, Georges Auric; ed, H. Wilkinson; md, Louis Levy; art d, William Kellner; ch, David Paltenghi.

Fantasy **(PR:A-C MPAA:NR)**

QUEEN OF SPADES*** (1961, USSR) 105m Lenfilm/Artkino c (PIKOVAYA DAMA)

Oleg Strizhenov *(Hermann, sung by Zurab Andzhaparidze)*, Olga Krassina, *(Liza, sung by Tamara Milashkina)*, Yelena Polevetskaya *(Countess, sung by Sofya Preobrazhenskaya)*, V. Kulik *(Yeletskiy, sung by Yevgeniy Kibkalo)*, Vadim Medvedev *(Tomskiy, sung by V. Nechipailo)*, I. Gubanova-Gurzo *(Polina, sung by Larisa Avdeyeva)*, A. Gustavson, I. Daryalov, V. Kosarev, A. Olevanov, D. Radlov, Yuriy Solovyov, V. Tsitta; voices, V. Volodin, V. Kirpalov, M. Reshetin, V. Vlasov, G. Shulgin, L. Maslov, N. Yaroslavtsev.

Strizhenov plays a poverty-stricken officer in St. Petersburg. He becomes overwhelmed with the desire to acquire a large fortune. He learns about an old countess who became rich with a secret card hand learned from an old lover. Her success gained her the title "The Queen of Spades." Through the woman's granddaughter (Krassina), with whom Strizhenov falls in love, he gains access to the old woman (Polevetskaya.) If she reveals the secret she will die, but Strizhenov's obsession is too great for him to care. When he approaches her with a pistol and demands the secret, the old woman dies of fright. He later meets Krassina on a canal bank near the Winter Palace. A funeral procession goes by, and Polevetskaya's ghost appears. She reveals the three-card secret to the officer: a three, a seven, and an ace. Krassina tries to stop him from going to the gaming tables but, unable to dissuade him, drowns herself in the canal. While gambling, Strizhenov is challenged by Kulik, a prince once engaged to Krassina. The officer places the three and the seven down. He is shocked, however, when the Queen of Spades appears in place of the ace. He shoots himself and crawls to the canal bank to die. As his life slips away, Krassina's scarf blows past him. This adaptation of the noted Pushkin story and Tchaikovsky opera was also filmed in Russia during the silent era in 1910 and 1916. This version is stark and cold but well played by members of the Bolshoi Theater company. A British version was filmed in 1949.

d, Roman Tikhomirov; w, Georgy Vasiliev, Serge Vasilyev, Pavel Veysbrem, Tikhomirov, Boris Yarutovskiy (based on the opera by Peter Ilich Tchaikovsky, from the prose work by Alexander Pushkin); ph, N. Shifirn (Magicolor); ed, R. Izakson; art d, I. Vuskovich; cos, Ye. Slovtsova; spec eff, M. Krotkin; makeup, V. Goryunov.

Drama **(PR:C MPAA:NR)**

QUEEN OF SPIES (SEE: JOAN OF OZARK, 1942)

QUEEN OF THE AMAZONS** (1947) 61m Screen Guild bw

Robert Lowery, Patricia Morison, J. Edward Bromberg, John Miljan, Almira Moustafa, Bruce Edwards, Jack George, Keith Richards, Wilson Benge, Cay Forester.

When Lowery is captured by a tribe of female warriors, his fiancee must go deep into the forbidding jungle to get him back.

p&d Edward Finney; w, Roger Merton; ph, Robert Pittack; ed, Johnny Link; md, Lee Zahler; art d, James Reimer.

Adventure **Cas.** **(PR:A MPAA:NR)**

QUEEN OF THE CANNIBALS (SEE: DR. BUTCHER M.D., 1982, Ital.)

QUEEN OF THE MOB½** (1940) 61m PAR bw

Ralph Bellamy *(Scott Langham)*, Jack Carson *(Ross Waring)*, Blanche Yurka *(Ma Webster)*, Richard Denning *(Charlie Webster)*, James Seay *(Eddie Webster)*, Paul Kelly *(Tom Webster)*, William Henry *(Bert Webster)*, Jeanne Cagney *(Ethel Webster)*, J. Carrol Naish *(George Frost)*, Hedda Hopper *(Mrs. Emily Sturgis)*, Pierre Watkin *(Stitch Torey)*, Billy Gilbert *(Caterer)*, John Harmon *(Pinky)*, Raymond Hatton *(Auto Camp Proprietor)*, Betty McLaughlin *(Girl)*, Charlotte Wynters *(Mrs. Grimley)*, Neil Hamilton *(Murdock)*, Robert Ryan *(Jim)*, Paul Stanton *(Mrs. Edmonds the Banker)*, Donald Douglas *(FBI Director)*, James Flavin *(FBI Chief)*, Mary Gordon *(Janitress)*, Paul Fix, Brooks Benedict *(Men)*, Ethan Laidlaw *(Court Officer)*, John Miljan *(Pan)*, Tommy Conley *(Billy Webster)*, Charles Moore *(Butler)*, Mary Treen *(Billy's Nurse)*, Frank M. Thomas *(Doctor)*, Edward Gargan *(Policeman in Bank)*, Howard Mitchell *(Santa Claus)*, Leona Roberts *(Mrs. Greenough)*, Lloyd Corrigan *(Jason the Photographer)*, Laura Treadwell *(Matron)*, Roy Gordon *(Mr. Milliken)*, Sonny Bupp *(Newsboy)*, Russell Hicks *(Judge)*, William Duncan *(District Attorney)*, Charles Lane *(Horace Grimley)*, Harry Bradley *(Lawyer)*, May Beatty *(Ellen)*, Selmer Jackson *(Bank Manager)*, William Pawley *(Man with Pan)*, John "Skins" Miller *(Man in Hideout)*, Edgar Dearing *(Motorcycle Cop)*, Charles McMurphy *(Bailiff)*, Alec Craig *(Proprietor)*, Herbert Naish.

A short crime thriller loosely based on the real-life exploits of Ma Barker and her sons which is jam-packed with thugs, G-men, and gunplay. Yurka is cast as the Barker-type mother whose wild brood of three sons—Denning, Seay, and Kelly—accompany her on a spree of bank robberies and a kidnaping. Traveling from state to state, the gang leaves a trail of mayhem behind, killing anyone who crosses its path. One holdup nets a hefty $400,000; unknown to the thugs, the money is "marked." The FBI is soon on their trail, led by super G-man Bellamy. Bellamy, a crafty agent who doesn't miss a trick, quickly locates Yurka's hideout. In the process of tracking her down, two of her sons are killed by the "feds." The final confrontation occurs when G-men surround Yurka's home where she is trimming a Christmas tree for the local kiddies (her last surviving son donning a Santa Claus outfit.) A burst of gunfire fells her son, leaving Yurka with no other choice but to surrender. As she gives herself up the defeated grande-dame gangster informs Bellamy, "All right G-man, you win." The fourth and final crime picture based on J. Edgar Hoover's best seller *Persons in Hiding* (PERSONS IN HIDING, UNDERCOVER DOCTOR [both 1939], and PAROLE FIXER [1940] preceded), QUEEN OF THE MOB clearly was based on Barker and her boys, though oddly no reviews at the time made any reference to this fact. Not surprisingly, QUEEN OF THE MOB tells a tale that is far from the truth. Yurka's portrayal of the cold, murderous Barker (who, incidentally, never served a day in prison) is a much more favorable, and therefore publicly acceptable, one. Instead of displaying crazed ferocity, Yurka comes off as a mother who unconditionally loves her children and all the neighborhood kiddies as well—an ideal mom. After putting Yurka on such a pedestal, the filmmakers could hardly kill her off. In real life, Ma Barker put up quite a fight along with her son Fred during a 45-minute gun battle in Florida. Ma and Fred were found afterward, their bullet-ridden bodies slumped on the ground, still clutching their Tommy guns. A Hollywood film just wasn't the place to show a mother—even if it was Ma Barker—being slain by the FBI, especially for fear that the public's perception of the "feds" would suffer. Super-gangster Jimmy Cagney's sister Jeanne does well in a supporting role, as does Robert Ryan in his screen debut. Like the others in the series, this film—far and away the best of the four—was cranked out in less than three weeks.

d, James Hogan; w, Horace McCoy, William R. Lipman (based on the book *Persons in Hiding* by J. Edgar Hoover); ph, Theodor Sparkuhl; ed, Arthur Schmidt; art d, Hans Dreier, Ernst Fegte.

Crime **(PR:C MPAA:NR)**

QUEEN OF THE NIGHTCLUBS½** (1929) 60m WB bw

Texas Guinan *(Tex Malone)*, John Davidson *(Don Holland)*, Lila Lee *(Bee Walters)*, Arthur Housman *(Andy Quinland)*, Eddie Foy, Jr. *(Eddie Parr)*, Jack Norworth *(Phil Parr)*, George Raft *(Gigolo)*, Jimmie Phillips *(Nick)*, William Davidson *(Assistant District Attorney)*, John Miljan *(Lawyer Grant)*, Lee Shumway *(Crandall)*, Joe Depew *(Roy)*, Agnes Franey *(Flapper)*, Charlotte Merriam *(Girl)*, James T. Mack *(Judge)*.

Little remembered today, this tale of speakeasies and murder is significant for two reasons. First, it introduced George Raft to films, and, second, it immortalized one of the great characters of the whole prohibition era, Texas Guinan, here playing a thinly disguised but heavily fictionalized version of herself. Guinan was born in Texas but as a young woman she drifted first to Chicago, then to New York as a dancer, actress, and occasional rodeo bronc rider. After WW I she began appearing in two-reel westerns, eventually making over 300 silent shorts. By the middle of the 1920s, she was the hostess at New York's swankiest nightspot, greeting each customer with a cheery, "Hello, sucker!" Thanks to the attention of such customers as Walter Winchell and Mark Hellinger, Guinan was soon a household name and in 1929 she returned to Hollywood to star in a movie about her life. The story bears little resemblance to real events, with Guinan a nightclub proprietor who hires Lee to perform in her club. This causes the breakup of an act that Lee had with Foy. Later, Davison, a friend of Guinan's, is murdered by an old business associate of hers, Housman. Evidence points to Foy and he is arrested. Guinan discovers that Foy is in reality her long-lost son, and in court she manages to persuade the jurors to come to the nightclub where they find evidence that proves Foy innocent and sends Housman to prison. Soon thereafter, Norworth, Guinan's equally long-lost husband, comes back to her. Raft has a relatively small part doing the dizzyingly fast Charleston he used to perform at the real Guinan's clubs when he wasn't rolling drunks in the bathroom. Raft took the job and the trip to Hollywood it offered because New York was getting too hot for him and his bootlegging activities and because gangster Owney Madden, who had a business interest in Guinan's club, asked his childhood friend Raft to go to California with her as a sort of bodyguard. All this history aside, the film was a tedious melodrama of little interest except to the curious. Guinan hams it up as herself, and none of the other performances is much better. Guinan spent the next years living off her reputation before dying in 1933 at age 49. Includes Guinan singing "It's Tough to Be a Hostess on Broadway."

d, Bryan Foy; w, Murray Roth, Addison Burkhart; ph, Ed Du Par.

Crime **(PR:A-C MPAA:NR)**

QUEEN OF THE NILE**** (1964, Ital.) 97m Max/Colorama c (NEFERTITE, REGINA DEL NILO)

Jeanne Crain *(Tanit/Nefertiti)*, Vincent Price *(Benakon, High Priest)*, Edmund Purdom *(Tumos, Sculptor)*, Amedeo Nazzari *(Amenophis IV)*, Liana Orfei *(Merith)*, Carlo D'Angelo, Clelia Matania, Alberto Farnese, Piero Palermini, Giulio Marchetti, Umberto Raho, Luigi Marturano, Raffaele Baldassare, Romano Giomini, Adriano Vitale, Gino Talamo.

This is one of those countless inferior-quality Italian biblical epics. What makes this one a little more unusual (though no better) is the importing of Americans Crain and Price to play ancient Egyptians. She's a young, naive woman living near Thebes. She can't elope with her sculptor fiance (Purdom), as per orders from Price. He reveals himself as her father, and tells her she must fulfill her destiny by marrying the mentally ill Nazzari. Purdom is sentenced to death but escapes. It turns out Nazzari is an old friend, and Purdom intends to seek a pardon. Nazzari soon is running the country, and Crain changes her name to "Nefertiti" during a purification ceremony. Purdom has taken comfort with a gypsy girl but is imprisoned again, on Price's orders. Price threatens to kill Purdom unless his daughter marries Nazzari. After the marriage takes place and Purdom is commissioned to do a bust of her, she admits she still loves him. She can't leave her husband, but is concerned about his mental state. Price sees Nazzari's madness as his ticket to power and kills the king's pal, a rival priest. This drives Nazzari to suicide, and Crain takes over. Purdom and the army assist, and everyone ends up happy when the spurned gypsy girl kills Price. It's so poorly played and completely tedious that any interest on the part of budding Egyptologists will quickly be nipped.

p, Ottavio Poggi; d, Fernando Cerchio; w, John Byrne, Poggi, Cerchio (based on a story by Poggi, Emerico Papp); ph, Massimo Dallamano (SuperCinescope, Eastmancolor); m, Carlo Rustichelli; ed, Renato Cinquini; cos, Giancarlo Bartolini Salimbeni; ch, Wilbert Bradley.

Historical Epic **(PR:C MPAA:NR)**

QUEEN OF THE PIRATES**** (1961, Ital./Ger.) 80m Max-Rapid Film/COL c (LA VENERE DEI PIRATI; VENUS DER PIRATEN)

Gianna Maria Canale *(Sandra)*, Massimo Serato *(Cesare, Count of Santa Croce)*, Scilla Gabel *(Isabella)*, Paul Muller *(Duke Zulian)*, Jose Jaspe *(Capt. Mirko)*, Livio Lorenzon *(Pirate Chief)*, Giustino Durano *(Battista)*, Moira Orfei *(Jana)*, Andrea Aureli, Franco Fantasia, Nando Tamberlani, Raffaele Baldassarre, Giulio Battiferri, Luigi Marturano, Gianni Solaro, Anna Maria Mustari.

Muller is the tyrannical ruler of the Duchy of Doruzzo in the 16th Century, aided by daughter Gabel. Jaspe is a sea captain unjustly accused of a wrongful act. He is sentenced to be hanged and Canale, who believes she is his daughter, is to be sold to a harem. The pair is freed by Serato, whom Jaspe hopes will marry his daughter. Jaspe and Canale become pirates, and Serato finds he must capture them. Instead he falls for Canale and helps her plan an assault on Muller's palace. Together they lead the pirate band, along with the oppressed peasantry. Muller is mortally wounded and gives a deathbed confession. It seems Canale is his real daughter and rightful heiress. Many years before he had ordered Jaspe to kill the girl, but the sea captain spared her and raised her as his own. A much chagrined Gabel heads off for a convent, and Canale prepares to marry Serato. Together they will right all of Muller's evil doings. The ending's about as easy to swallow as a tractor in this vivid and turgid spectacle. Canale's acting is deadly dull, ruining the film's few otherwise decent moments. This was followed with a sequel: TIGER OF THE SEVEN SEAS. Though QUEEN OF THE PIRATES was filmed in color, it was initially released in this country in black and white. Its Italian director was Mario Costa, with screenplay by Nino Stresa and the producer Ottavio Poggi.

p, Ottavio Poggi; d, Richard McNamara; w, John Byrne (based on a story by Kurt Nachmann, Rolf Olsen); ph, Raffaele Masciocchi (SupercineScope, Eastmancolor); m, Carlo Rustichelli; ed, Renato Cinquini; art d, Ernesto Kromberg; set d, Amedeo Mellone; cos, Giancarlo Bartolini Salimbeni; makeup, Maurizio Giustini.

Action/Adventure **(PR:C MPAA:NR)**

QUEEN OF THE WEST (SEE: CATTLE QUEEN, 1951)

QUEEN OF THE YUKON**** (1940) 73m MON bw

Charles Bickford *(Ace)*, Irene Rich *(Sadie)*, Melvin Lang *(Thorne)*, George Cleveland *(Grub)*,Guy Usher *(Stake)*, June Carlson *(Helen)*, Dave O'Brien *(Bob)*, Tris Coffin *(Carson)*.

Rich runs a boat in the Yukon so her daughter (Carlson) can attend school. Bickford is Rich's partner, a tough man who can take on the best of them. Rich sells the boat to mining company owner Lang so she can be reunited with her daughter. When the independent miners get frozen out, leave it to Bickford to solve everything. This is a slow-moving programmer that has an action-filled ending and plenty of stereotyped characters along the way. The plot is roughly based on a Jack London story.

p, Scott R. Dunlap, Paul Malvern; d, Phil Rosen; w, Joseph West (based on a story by Jack London); ph, Harry Neumann; ed, Russell Schoengarth.

Drama/Action **(PR:A MPAA:NR)**

QUEENS, THE*½ (1968, Ital./Fr.) 110m Documento-Orsay-COL/Royal c (LE FATE/ LES OGRESSES)

"Queen Sabina":Monica Vitti *(Sabina)*, Enrico Maria Salerno *(Gianni)*, Franco Balducci *(1st Motorist)*, Renzo Giovanpietro *(2nd Motorist)*/ "Queen Armenia": Claudia Cardinale *(Armenia)*, Gastone Moschin *(Dr. Aldini)*/ "Queen Elena": Raquel Welch *(Elena)*, Jean Sorel *(Luigi)*, Pia Lindstrom *(Claudia)*, Massimo Fornari *(Alberto)*, Clothilde Sakharoff, Stelvio Rosi/ "Queen Marta": Capucine *(Marta)*, Alberto Sordi *(Giovanni)*, Anthony Steel *(The Professor)*, Gigi Ballista *(The Priest)*, Olga Villi *(Countess Rattazzi)*, Nino Marchetti *(The Guest)*.

This Italian/French production is a series of four short stories filmed by four different directors. They have no real connecting theme other than the titles, which suggest the lead female is a "queen" of sorts. The first episode, entitled "Queen Sabina" and based on a story by Franco Indovina, features Vitti as a young girl hitchhiking home from the beach. Two cars pick her up and both drivers attempt to rape her. She is picked up a third time by Salerno. In a disgusting suggestion of rape inspiring sexual passion, Vitti feels her hormones acting up and chases Salerno into the woods. Next is "Queen Armenia," a confusing tale featuring Cardinale as a gypsy who takes care of neighbors' children and passes them off as her own to get money and bed partners. Moschin is a doctor who at first repels her advances but finally succumbs. The third story, "Queen Elena," features American star Welch as a young housewife who seduces her neighbor, Sorel, while her husband is away. Sorel, who can't believe his luck, returns home to find his wife (Lindstrom) making love with another man. Finally there is the story of "Queen Marta." Capucine is a housewife who gets drunk and seduces hired butler Sordi. Like the wealthy man in Chaplin's CITY LIGHTS, she completely forgets about the affair the next day and becomes angry when Sordi suggests another night of passion. He decides to play her game (maybe he saw CITY LIGHTS) and patiently waits for his would-be lover to quaff a few more. These stories are really just turgid little melodramas that pretend to have a meaning. As a whole, this film projects a real hatred toward women. They are portrayed as catty yet lusty creatures who will do anything for a good roll in the hay. The production values are adequate, though the subtitles have an annoying way of floating around the screen. This film comes off as a witless and boring anthology that's not worth much. Anthology films usually contain at least one good episode, but there's nothing even mildly outstanding here. The four parts were also known as "The Hitchhiker," "The Room With a Juke Box," "The Digestive Tablet," and "Giovanni."

p, Gianni Hecht Lucari/ d, Luciano Salce, Mario Monicelli, Mauro Bolognini, Antonio Pietrangeli/ w, Ruggero Maccari, Suso Cecchi D' Amico, Tonino Guerra, Giorgio Salvioni, Rodolfo Sonego/ ph, Ennio Guarnieri, Dario Di Palma, Leonida Barboni, Armando Nannuzzi (Eastmancolor)/ ed, Sergio Montanari, Ruggero Mastroianni, Nino Baragli, Franco Fraticelli/ art d, Luigi Sabatelli, Pier Luigi Pizzi, Mario Chiari, Piero Gherardi/ m/1, "Walk Into My Life," Armando Trovajoli (sung by Rick Mantovani)/ animation, M.C.S. Lodolo/ English subtitles, Mai Harris.

Comedy/Drama **(PR:O MPAA:NR)**

QUEEN'S AFFAIR, THE (SEE: RUNAWAY QUEEN, THE, 1935, Brit.)

QUEEN'S GUARDS, THE**** (1963, Brit.) 110m Imperial/FOX c

Daniel Massey *(John Fellowes)*, Raymond Massey *(Capt. Fellowes)*, Robert Stephens *(Henry Wynne-Walton)*, Jack Watson *(Sgt. Johnson)*, Peter Myers *(Gordon Davidson)*, Jess Conrad *(Dankworth)*, Ursula Jeans *(Mrs. Fellowes)*, Ian Hunter *(Dobbie)*, Jack Watling *(Capt. Shergold)*, Andrew Crawford *(Biggs)*, Duncan Lamont *(Maj. Wilkes)*, Laurence Payne *(Farinda)*, Judith Stott *(Ruth)*, Elizabeth Shepherd *(Susan)*, Nigel Green *(Abu Sidbar)*, Rene Cutforth *(Commentator)*, Eileen Peel *(Mrs. Wynne-Walton)*, Frank Lawton *(Cmdr. Hewson)*, Anthony Bushell *(Maj. Cole)*, Cornel Lucas *(Photographer)*, Jack Allen *(Brig. Cummings)*, Patrick Connor *(Brewer)*, William Young *(Williams)*.

Daniel Massey plays a young guard. While on duty he begins reminiscing about his past, which is shown in a series of flashbacks. The film chronicles his relationship with his father (played by his real father, Raymond Massey), various romances and, of course, some exciting battles. At the heart of the film is the younger Massey's belief that his brother was killed in a foolish strategic move that also sacrificed the troops under his command. But, Massey discovers his brother died a hero and is able to resolve his feelings. This is all told in magnificent detail by noted director Powell. Unfortunately there's too much detail, and the film quickly bogs down. The elder Massey gives a good performance despite an overwritten part, while the son gives a fairly good characterization. There's an elegance to this picture, which is wonderful to look at. However, the slow pacing gives the stylization a stiffness, which becomes detrimental in the long-run. Costumes and Technicolor (as well as CinemaScope) are all used to their best advantage. Ultimately, THE QUEEN'S GUARDS was a nice try, but should have been a good deal more.

p&d, Michael Powell/ w, Roger Milner (based on a story by Milner, from an idea by Simon Harcourt-Smith)/ ph, Gerald Turpin (CinemaScope, Technicolor)/ m, Brian Easdale/ ed, Noreen Ackland/ art d, Wilfred Shingleton.

Drama **(PR:C MPAA:NR)**

QUEEN'S HUSBAND, THE (SEE: ROYAL BED, THE, 1931)

QUEEN'S SWORDSMEN, THE½** (1963, Mex.) 86m Trans-International c (LOS ESPADACHINES DE LA REINA)

Elmo Michel, Rafael Munoz, Marina Torres, Antonio Raxell, Ariadne Welter, Miguel Manzano, Javier Loya, Ofelia Guilmain, Quintin Bulnes.

An evil king kidnaps a young and beautiful princess who rules an enchanted land. Stinky the Skunk teams up with a wolf to form a bridge of animal musketeers.

Together they rescue the princess and restore order to the enchanted kingdom. Great fantasy for the kids.

p, K. Gordon Murray; d, Roberto Rodriguez; w, Rodriguez, Manuel R. Ojeda; ph, Alex Phillips; m, Sergio Guerrero; ed, Jose Bustos; art d, Roberto Silva.

Fantasy (PR:AAA MPAA:NR)

QUEER CARGO (SEE: PIRATES OF THE SEVEN SEAS, 1941, Brit.)

QUEI DISPERATI CHE PUZZANO DI SUDORE E DI MORTE (SEE: BULLET FOR SANDOVAL, A, 1970,Ital./Span.)

QUEI TEMERARI SULLE LORO PAZZE, SCATENATE, SCALCINATE CARRIOLE (SEE: THOSE DARING YOUNG MEN IN THEIR JAUNTY JALOPIES, 1969, Fr./Brit./Ital.)

QUEIMADA (SEE: BURN!, 1969, Ital./Fr.)

QUELLI CHE NON MUOIONO (SEE: GUILT IS NOT MINE, 1968, Ital.)

QUEMADA! (SEE: BURN!, 1969, Fr./Ital.)

QUELQUES JOURS PRES (SEE: MATTER OF DAYS, A, 1969, Fr./Czech.)

QUELQU'UN DERRIERE LA PORTE (SEE: SOMEONE BEHIND THE DOOR, 1971,Fr./Brit.)

QUENTIN DURWARD*** (1955) 101m MGM c (AKA: THE ADVENTURES OF QUENTIN DURWARD)

Robert Taylor *(Quentin Durward)*, Kay Kendall *(Isabelle, Countess of Marcroy)*, Robert Morley *(King Louis XI)*, George Cole *(Hayraddin)*, Alec Clunes *(Charles, Duke of Burgundy)*, Duncan Lamont *(Count William De la Marck)*, Laya Raki *(Gypsy Dancer)*, Marius Goring *(Count Philip De Creville)*, Wilfred Hyde White *(Master Oliver)*, Eric Pohlmann *(Gluckmeister)*, Harcourt Williams *(Bishop of Liege)*, Michael Goodliffe *(Count De Dunois)*, John Carson *(Duke of Orleans)*, Nicholas Hannen *(John, Cardinal Balue)*, Moultrie Kelsall *(Lord Malcolm)*, Frank Tickle *(Petit-Andre)*, Bill Shine *(Trois-Eschelles)* Ernest Thesiger *(Lord Crawford)*.

It is 15th Century France and King Louis XI (Morley) is worried that his underling (Clunes) may be trying for more power. Meanwhile, Taylor is sent from Scotland by his uncle (Thesiger) to check on the uncle's bride-to-be (Kendall). Taylor falls for Kendall himself, but remains loyal to his uncle and hides his feelings. Morley wants Kendall kidnaped, as she has had former dealings with Clunes. He has Taylor unknowingly escort her into a trap. Morley's plot involves Taylor taking Kendall to Williams, but en route she is to be kidnaped by Lamont, a count known as "the Wild Boar of Ardennes." But Taylor foils the kidnaping. Williams, an important bishop, is murdered by Lamont. Taylor engages in an exciting battle with "the Wild Boar" as the two swing back and forth on bell ropes in a burning church tower. The bells loudly clang as the pair slash each other with knives. Lamont finally falls to his doom and Taylor flees with the much frightened Kendall. Word comes that Thesiger has passed on leaving Kendall free to marry Taylor. Meanwhile Morley has come up with more plans to win Clunes to his cause. He rides to Clunes' castle courtyard and plays up on the man's loyalty. Any plot to lessen the king's power is quickly squashed and Taylor marries Kendall. The plot is a little confusing towards the end, but otherwise this is a fun adventure. Taylor had done several films of this nature and clearly enjoys himself in a neatly played role. The direction well choreographs the different elements of color, costumes, location, and actors for a fine period look. It was filmed on location in English and French countryside castles, which add to the realistic flavor. Of course, there's the swashbuckling action that's nicely played. The bell tower sequence is a real thrill and the supporting cast isn't bad, with Morley as a wonderful standout in his role. Kendall, alas, is merely passable registering the proper emotions but little else. She was to die in 1959. This is based on a little known novel by famed British author, Sir Walter Scott.

p, Pandro S. Berman; d, Richard Thorpe; w, Robert Ardrey, George Froeschel (based on the novel *Quentin Durward* by Sir Walter Scott); ph, Christopher Challis (CinemaScope, Eastmancolor); m, Bronislau Kaper; ed, Ernest Walter; md, Kaper; art d, Alfred Junge; cos, Elizabeth Haffenden.

Historical Drama/Action (PR:A MPAA:NR)

QUERELLE** (1983, Ger./Fr.) 106m Planet-Albatros/Triumph c

Brad Davis *(Querelle)*, Franco Nero *(Lt. Seblon)*, Jeanne Moreau *(Lysiane)*, Laurent Malet *(Roger)*, Nadja Brunkhorst *(Paulette)*, Hanno Poschl *(Robert/Gil)*, Gunther Kaufmann *(Nono)*, Burkhard Driest *(Mario)*, Dieter Schidor *(Vic)*, Roger Fritz *(Marcellin)*, Michael McLernon *(Matrose)*, Neil Bell *(Theo)*, Harry Baer *(Armenier)*, Volker Sprengler, Isolde Barth, Y Sa Lo, Robert van Ackeren, Wolf Gremm, Frank Ripploh, Rainer Will, Gillis Gavois, Karl Scheydt, Werner Asam, Axel Bauer, Vitus Zepplichal, Karl Heinz von Hassel.

German director Fassbinder had a short but prolific life, producing no less than 43 films and a television series before he came to a self-destructive end. QUERELLE was his last feature, released posthumously. Unfortunately, it shows only touches of the German master's great talents. This is an adaptation of the infamous novel by Genet *Querelle de Brest*, dealing with the passions of a sailor who discovers his own homosexuality. Davis (the star of MIDNIGHT EXPRESS) is the lead, a self-absorbed young man who is trying to find himself. When his ship docks at Brest, France, Davis ends up in a bar-whorehouse run by Moreau. He finds himself caught up in a strange and ruthless world where encounters are ruled by chance. In order to sleep with Moreau one must toss a pair of dice. Lose and one ends up sodomized by her husband, a burly black man. Davis loses the game but does so on purpose. He claims to all he is not homosexual, but merely wants the experience. Moreau is attracted to the young sailor, as is the man she is with, who may or may not be Davis' brother. Davis finds this man attractive as well. Nero is the ship's captain who also falls for Davis, confessing his secret into a tape recorder which Davis later finds. Fassbinder has created a dream world of casual attractions, sex, and murder. It was shot on studio sets in a deliberate stylization. Often the dream turns to nightmare with its brilliant colors, phallic symbols, and sailors bedecked in leather. The casualness of life and death is a theme that permeates the film. Unfortunately, the results are banal and tedious. Despite Davis' intense performance, the film never really moves. The story lurches haphazardly from one event to the next, and the theme is all too obvious.

p, Dieter Schidor; d&w, Rainer Werner Fassbinder (based on the novel *Querelle de Brest* by Jean Genet); ph, Xaver Schwarzenberger, Josef Vavra (CinemaScope/Eastmancolor); m, Peer Raben; ed, Juliane Lorenz, Franz Walsch; prod d, Rolf Zehetbauer; art d, Walter Richard; set d, Zehetbauer; cos, Barbara Baum; m/l, Raben.

Drama Cas. (PR:O MPAA:WR)

QUERY*** (1945, Brit.) 90m BN/Anglo-American Film Corp. bw

Billy Hartnell *(Tom Masterick)*, Jimmy Hanley *(Peter Rogers)*, Chili Bouchier *(Doris Masterick)*, John Slater *(Fred Smith)*, Brefni O'Rourke *(Sullivan)*, Dinah Sheridan *(Jill Masterick)*, Petula Clark *(Jill as a Child)*, Kynaston Reeves *(Crossley, King's Counsel)*, John Salew *(Blake,-King's Counsel)*, Edward Rigby *(Spike)*, Ben Williams *(Docker)*, Ethel Coleridge *(Mrs. Green)*, Maire O'Neill *(Mrs. Moore)*.

A tough and realistic thriller which poses the interesting moral question: is murder ever justified? Hartnell, in a distinguished performance as a young stevedore and then as a prematurely aged ex-convict, is sentenced to prison for a murder he did not commit. On his release, he kills the man who framed him, and then must make plausible the legal right to have done so. The script closely follows a silent Fox film, "It Is the Law" (1924), but clearly holds its own with outstanding acting and direction. One blight that mars the picture was in its authorship. The man credited with writing the story from which it was taken, "Seamark," a well-known newspaperman around Fleet Street before he commited suicide in 1935, was suspected of having lifted it almost bodily, with only slight embellishments, from Elmer Rice and Hayden Talbot's hit stage play of the early 1920s, "It Is the Law," from which Fox made its film with proper credits.

d&w, Montgomery Tully (based on a story by "Seamark"); ph, Ernest Palmer

Thriller (PR:O MPAA:NR)

QUEST FOR FIRE*** (1982, Fr./Can.) 97m ICC-Cine-Trail-Belstar/FOX c

Everett McGill *(Naoh, Ulam Tribe Member)*, Ron Perlman *(Amoukar, Ulam Tribe Member)*, Nameer El-Kadi *(Gaw, Ulam Tribe Member)*, Rae Dawn Chong *(Ika, Ivaka Tribe Member)*, Gary Schwartz, Frank Oliver Bonnet, Jean-Michel Kindt, Kurt Schiegl, Brian Gill, Terry Fitt, Bibi Caspari, Peter Elliott, Michelle Leduc, Robert Lavoie, Matt Birman, Christian Benard, Joy Boushell, Mary Lou Foy, Robert Gondek, Sylvie Guilbault, Steve Ramanuskas, Lydia Chaban, Dena Francis, Helene Gregoire, Lloyd McKinnon, Georgette Rondeau, Rod Bennett, Jacques Demers, Michel Drouet, Michel Francoeur, Charles Gosselin, Bernard Kendall, Benoit Levesque, Joshua Melnick, Jean-Claude Meunier, Alex Quaglia, The Great Antonio, Jacques Caron.

Unlike so many cave man pictures (such as ONE MILLION, B.C., 1940) QUEST FOR FIRE is a fascinating look at what the life of early man may have been. McGill, Perlman, and El-Kadi are members of the Ulams who are sent out to find fire after their only source is accidentally extinguished. They find another tribe, the Ivakas, who are barbarous but to the amazement of the Ulams have the knowledge of fire, actually creating it using flint and sticks. The three rescue Chong from the cruel Ivakas and take her along, with the secret of fire-starting. The film employs humor, grief, happiness, anxiety, and other everyday emotions to create realistic ancestors who have much in common with today's human race. Desmond Morris, author of "The Naked Ape," created a body language for the film based on actual simian gestures, while famed novelist Anthony Burgess created a primitive language used by the characters. Chong is the daughter of nightclub and film comedian Tommy Chong (as in Cheech and. . .). Although bleak in many ways, what is thrilling to see is early man learning to laugh, at others and at himself, jumping up and down in delight and amazement at the sight of fire, and getting hit on the head with objects the size of coconuts, and finding it unusual and almost exciting. So has the human race advanced, out of bleakness and ludicrousness into—ludicrousness and bleakness.

p, John Kemeny, Denis Heroux, Jacques Dorfmann, Vera Belmont; d, Jean-Jacques Annaud; w, Gerard Brach (based on the novel *La Guerre de Feu* by J.H. Rosny, Sr.); ph, Claude Agostini (Panavision, Bellevue-Pathe Color); m, Phillippe Sarde: ed, Yves Langlois; prod d, Brian Morris, Guy Comtois; art d, Clinton Cavers; cos, John Hay, Penny Rose; spec eff, Martin Malivoire; makeup, Christopher Tucker.

Drama Cas. (PR:O MPAA:R)

QUEST FOR LOVE*** (1971, Brit.) 91m RANK c

Joan Collins *(Ottilie)*, Tom Bell *(Colin)*, Denholm Elliott *(Tom Lewis)*, Laurence Naismith *(Sir Henry Larnstein)*, Lyn Ashley *(Jennifer)*, Juliet Harmer *(Geraldine Lambert)*, Neil McCallum *(Jimmy)*, Trudy van Doorn.

An unusual science fiction tale that doesn't completely work but does hold interest. Bell is a physicist who finds himself in an earlier world. John F. Kennedy is still President, the war in Vietnam is unheard of, and Mt. Everest is yet to be climbed. He meets Collins, his real wife in the other world, and she is dying. The blow of her death sends Bell back to the real world where he immediately goes looking for Collins before she dies once more. The story gets complicated but the direction juggles the separate worlds without much trouble. Bell's performance makes this project work. He's believable and earnest and brings it off with a guiding clarity.

p, Peter Eton; d, Ralph Thomas; w, Bert Batt, Terence Feely (based on the short story "Random Quest" by John Wyndham); ph, Ernest Steward (Eastmancolor); m, Eric Rogers; ed, Roy Watts; art d, Robert Jones; cos, Emma Porteous

Science Fiction/Romance/Drama (PR:C MPAA:NR)

QUESTI FANTASMI (SEE: GHOSTS—ITALIAN STYLE, 1969, Fr./Ital.)

QUESTION, THE*½** (1977, Fr.) 112m Z Productions-Rush-Little Bear/Planfilm c (LA QUESTION)

Jacques Denis (*Charlegue*), Nicole Garcia (*Wife*), Jean-Pierre Sentier (*Carbonneau*), Francois Dyrek (*Herbelin*), Christian Rist (*Oudinot*), Francoise Thuries (*Josette*), Francois Lalande (*Michaeli*).

Denis plays the editor of a small leftist underground newspaper trying to help Algerians in their war against the French, but his actions catch up with him and he is picked up by French paratroopers, tortured, and imprisoned. He writes a book about his experiences and smuggles it out of jail. The book is published in France and rouses both public and government into action against the sadistic military torture system. One of the first French productions that looked honestly at the Algerian conflict. The troops are presented as neofascists who still feel the pain from French failures in Indochina (Vietnam). The torture sequences are handled with sensitivity and care, and though the guards are portrayed as sadists, the sequences themselves never focus in on their cruel practices. THE QUESTION, based on a true story, is well-directed and acted.

p, B. Tavernier; d, Laurent Heynemann; w, Heynemann, Claude Veillot (based on the book by Henri Alleg); ph, Alain Levent (Eastmancolor); m, Antoine Duhamel; ed, Armand Psenny, Ariane Boeglin.

Drama (PR:O MPAA:NR)

QUESTION OF ADULTERY, A** (1959, Brit.) 86m Eros bw (AKA: THE CASE OF MRS. LORING)

Julie London (*Mary Loring*), Anthony Steel (*Mark Loring*), Basil Sydney (*Sir John Loring*), Donald Houston (*Mr. Jacobus*), Anton Diffring (*Carl Dieter*), Andrew Cruickshank (*Dr. Cameron*), Frank Thring (*Mr. Stanley*), Conrad Phillips (*Mario*), Kynaston Reeves (*Judge*), Mary Mackenzle (*Nurse Parsons*), Georgina Cookson (*Mrs. Duncan*), John Rae (*Foreman of the Jury*), Michael Logan (*Court Usher*), Trevor Reid (*Reporter*), John Charlesworth (*Cub Reporter*), Trader Faulkner, Vola Van Dere (*Flamenco Dancers*), John Fabian, Rodney Burke (*Barristers*), Michael Anthony (*Newspaperman*), Max Brimmel (*Spanish Photographer*), Van Boolen (*Peasant*).

London and Steel are a married couple, he a race car driver who occasionally flies off the handle in jealousy over his wife, and she hoping that a coming baby will make the marriage work. They are involved in an auto accident that causes her to miscarry and renders Steel sterile. She still wants a child and suggests artificial insemination. Steel begrudgingly agrees, but changes his mind after she goes through with it. His father urges him to seek a divorce and Steel does. The case goes to court, but the jury is hung. It's just as well, for the pair reconcile and go on to a happy marriage. An insipid drama masquerading as an issue film, but the real subject is only briefly touched on and its ethical questions carefully waltzed around. Characterizations are extremely limited by the weak script. At best Steel wears a mean look and quietly glowers. London is better but can only go so far with the part. The direction is slow and never builds tension.

p, Raymond Stross; d, Don Chaffey; w, Anne Edwards, Dennis Freeman (based on the play "A Breach of Marriage" by Dan Sutherland); ph, Stephen Dade; m, Philip Green; ed, Peter Tanner.

Drama (PR:C MPAA:NR)

QUESTION OF SUSPENSE, A** (1961, Brit.) 62m Bill and Michael Luckwell/COL bw

Peter Reynolds (*Tellman Drew*), Noelle Middleton (*Rose Marples*), Yvonne Buckingham (*Jean Forbes*), Norman Rodway (*Frank Brigstock*), James Neylin (*Inspector Hunter*), Pauline Delany (*Mrs. Barlow*), Anne Mulvey (*Sally*).

When a wealthy man kills the lover of a young woman, the girl decides to carry out a plan to even the score. Typical B thriller from England.

p, Bill Luckwell, Jock Macgregor; d, Max Varnel; w, Lawrence Huntington (based on the novel by Roy Vickers).

Crime (PR:C MPAA:NR)

QUESTION 7½** (1961, U.S./Ger.) 107m Lutheran Film Associates-Luther Film/Louis de Rochemont Associates bw (FRAGE 7)

Michael Gwynn (*Friedrich Gottfried*), Margaret Jahnen (*Maria Gottfried*), Christian de Bresson (*Peter Gottfried*), Almut Eggert (*Anneliese Zingler*), Erick Schumann (*Rolf Starke*), Max Buchsbaum (*Police Inspector Hermann*), John Ruddock (*Martin Kraus*), Leo Bieber (*Herr Rettmann*), Fritz Wepper (*Heinz Dehmert*), Eduard Linkers (*Otto Zingler*), Marianne Schubarth (*Marta Zingler*), Philo Hauser (*Barber*), Rolf von Nauckshoff (*Karl Marschall*), Helmo Kindermann (*Luedtke*), Manfred Furst (*Prof. Stefl*), Lutz Altschul (*Herr Durfel*), Sigurd Lohde 4f2(*Herr Kesselmaier*), Erik Jelde 4f2(*A.A. Tritschler*), Ernst Constantin (*Bishop*), Galina Probandt-Frank (*Gerda Laube*), Gunter Meisner (*Schmidt*), Gerd Vespermann, Nora Minor, Richard Handwerk, Stefan Schnabel, Gabriele Mascher, Hans Schumm, Hans Piper, Willy Trenk-Trebitsch, Annemarie Braun, Reginald Pasch.

De Bresson is the 15-year-old son of pastor Gwynn. He lives in East Germany where the Communist Party denies education to those who don't hold "politically correct views," which include an anti-religion stance. Before he can enter the music conservatory, De Bresson must answer seven questions, the last of which asks for a major influence on his life. Knowing that it is religion and that he must deny his beliefs to get into the conservatory, De Bresson asks his friends for advice. His teacher encourages the boy to make the politically correct decision while his girl

friend and father tell him to stick to his principles. The Communist Party gives him a chance to perform in the Berlin Youth Festival, which De Bresson gladly accepts despite Gwynn's protests. But upon arrival he sees that he is merely a pawn in a political game. The party wants him as an example to prove that those with religious beliefs are treated equally under their rule. Disgusted with Communism, De Bresson leaves the festival and escapes to freedom in the West. This is obvious propaganda. The story has enough dramatic content in and of itself, but is reduced to stereotypes and a "good versus evil" mentality. The direction is slow, but gives the film a handsome look. This film was invited to the Berlin Film Festival for its heavy anti-Communist messages, and was filmed on location in that city.

p, Lothar Wolff; d, Stuart Rosenberg; w, Allan Sloane; ph, Gunter Senftleben; m, Hans-Martin Majewski; ed, Georges Klotz; art d, Dieter Bartels.

Drama Cas. (PR:C MPAA:NR)

QUESTIONE DI PELLE (SEE: CHECKERBOARD, 1969, Fr.)

QUICK AND THE DEAD, THE** (1963) 92m Manson/Beckman bw

Larry D. Mann (*Parker*), Victor French (*Riley*), Jon Cedar (*Lt. Rogers*), James Almanzar (*Giorgio*), Louis Massad (*Donatelli*), Majel Barrett (*Teresa*), Sandy Donigan (*Maria*), Joseph Locastro, William Kirschner, Frank D'Agostino, Stuart Nisbet, Ted French.

Cedar is ordered to destroy a hidden Nazi munitions dump in northern Italy during the final months of German occupation in WW II. His platoon suffers casualties en route and is finally captured by the Germans. While being held, the men are joined by Barrett and Donnigan, two Italian women. During an air raid everyone escapes and two of the Americans make their way to the dump. They destroy it, but are killed in the process. Meanwhile, the Italian women try to lead the rest of the Americans to their secret hideout. Once more there are casualties but the women and two Americans reach safety. This straightforward war drama has plenty of action but no depth or insight. Character development is consistently sacrificed for battles and explosions, resulting in a good-looking but ultimately hollow picture. The smartly executed production values are solid, with action scenes first rate for such a low budget ($100,000) picture.

p, Sam Altonian; d, Robert Totten; w, Totten, Sheila Lynch; ph, John Arthur Morrill; m, Jaime Mendoza; ed, Weber Ford; art d, O.R.C. Totten.

War (PR:O MPAA:NR)

QUICK, BEFORE IT MELTS½** (1964) 97m MGM c

George Maharis (*Peter Santelli*), Robert Morse (*Oliver Cromwell Cannon*), Anjanette Comer (*Tiare Marshall*), James Gregory (*Vice Admiral*), Michael Constantine (*Mikhail Drozhensky*), Howard St. John (*Harvey T. Sweigert*), Norman Fell (*George Snell*), Janine Gray (*Diana Grenville-Wells*), Bernard Fox (*Leslie Folliott*), Richard LePore (*Ben Livingston*), Conlan Carter (*Orville Bayleaf*), Yvonne Craig (*Sharon Sweigert*), Hal Baylor (*Prison Guard*), Doodles Weaver (*Ham Operator*), Frank London (*Shaggy Type*), Nelson Olmsted (*Scientist*), Tom Vize, John Dennis, Hugh "Slim" Langtry, Fletcher Allen, Davis Roberts, Dale Malone (*Military Men*), Marjorie Bennett, Karen Scott (*Barmaids*), Philip Benjamin (*Guest at Admiral's Party*), Milton Fox the Penguin.

Morse plays a shy journalist who has to cover "Little America" in Antarctica for his magazine. There he becomes embroiled in a series of mishaps involving the military, a rival journalist (Fell), and a penguin named Milton Fox. The comedy culminates around a planned shipping of some women from New Zealand to the base and defections by Russian scientists. Craig is Morse's hapless fiancee, the daughter of his editor (St. John). A mildly amusing comedy that sometimes gets a little carried away with itself but is otherwise enjoyable. The script by Wasserman (who adapted "One Flew Over the Cuckoo's Nest" for Broadway) has some amusing dialog. Morse is good in the lead and carries the film well with some excellent comic support, and the direction shows a good sense of comic timing.

p, Douglas Laurence, Delbert Mann; d, Mann; w, Dale Wasserman (based on the novel by Philip Benjamin); ph, Russell Harlan (Panavision, Metrocolor); m, David Rose; ed, Fredric Steinkamp; md, Rose; art d, George W. Davis, Preston Ames; set d, Henry Grace, Hugh Hunt; makeup, William Tuttle.

Comedy (PR:A MPAA:NR)

QUICK GUN, THE½** (1964) 89m Admiral/COL c

Audie Murphy (*Clint Cooper*), Merry Anders (*Helen Reed*), James Best (*Scotty Grant*), Ted De Corsia (*Spangler*), Walter Sande (*Tom Morrison*), Rex Holman (*Rick Morrison*), Charles Meredith (*Rev. Staley*), Frank Ferguson (*Dan Evans*), Mort Mills (*Cagle*), Gregg Palmer (*Donovan*), Frank Gerstle (*George Keely*), Stephen Roberts (*Dr. Stevens*), Paul Bryar (*Mitchell*), Raymond Hatton (*Elderly Man*), William Fawcett (*Mike*).

A standard western for Murphy features a plot right out of a 1940s programmer. He plays a man returning to the home he left after killing the son of an evil rancher in a forced duel. Murphy wants to live on his father's ranch and rekindle his romance with Anders. En route to his home he discovers that a gang of outlaws are planning to hold up the bank. Most of the men have gone on a cattle drive, leaving the town defenseless, so Murphy agrees to help his old friend, Best, fend off the bad guys. A bloody battle ensues and Best is killed. Murphy, Hatton, and Meredith are the only survivors, and together they defeat the outlaws. Murphy is allowed to remain and is appointed sheriff. The story is well told and has some good action sequences. However, the second half drags until the final battle. It's all been done before, but Murphy is appealing and does a nice job with his role.

p, Grant Whytock; d, Sidney Salkow; w, Robert E. Kent (based on the story "The Fastest Gun" by Steve Fisher); ph, Lester Schorr (Techniscope, Technicolor); m, Richard LaSalle; ed, Whytock; art d, Robert Purcell; set d, Frank Tuttle; makeup, Ben Lane.

Western (PR:A MPAA:NR)

QUICK, LET'S GET MARRIED zero   (1965) 100m Golden Eagle c
(AKA: THE CONFESSION; SEVEN DIFFERENT WAYS)

Ginger Rogers (Mme. Rinaldi), Ray Milland (Mario Forni), Barbara Eden (Pia Pacelli), Walter Abel (The Thief), Pippa Scott (Gina), Elliott Gould (The Mute), Carl Schell (Beppo), Michael Ansara (Mayor Pablo), Cecil Kellaway (The Bishop), David Hurst (Gustave), Vinton Hayworth (A Guest), Leonardo Cimino, Carol Ann Daniels, Mara Lynn, Julian Upton, Michael Youngman, Charlotte.

This is probably best remembered as Gould's film debut. Otherwise it's a completely forgettable bomb featuring Rogers as a brotherly madame who helps Milland, a successful crook, find some buried treasure. When they find the loot under a religious statue, they take one of the girls of the bordello (Eden) and have her claim that she has seen a miracle. But the plan backfires and the scheming pair must flee in the chaos. Rogers and Milland fled not only from the statue but from the production as well. It was riddled with problems from the beginning until well after release. The original director (Victor Stoloff) was fired and replaced by Dieterle, who had directed Rogers before in I'LL BE SEEING YOU. The script was also by a Rogers vet, Scott, who had penned PRIMROSE PATH. Coproduced by Rogers' husband, Marshall, the film was backed by a St. Louis financier who apparently wanted to get into the movie business. Problems arose when the film was edited in New York rather than in Jamaica, where it had been shot, and where Marshall and Rogers insisted that it be edited. Lawsuits were filed and the film was released to small bookings. It was retitled SEVEN DIFFERENT WAYS and released again in 1965 but still on the minor circuit. Finally the title was changed to QUICK, LET'S GET MARRIED for a 1971 release with advertising that plugged Eden and Gould. This wasn't enough to save it, and the film died the natural death it had long deserved.

p, William Marshall; d, William Dieterle; w, Allan Scott; ph, Robert Bronner (Eastmancolor); m, Michael Colicchio; ed, Carl Lerner; art d, Jim Sullivan, Willis Connor.

Comedy   **(PR:C MPAA:NR)**

QUICK MILLIONS***   (1931) 72m FOX bw

Spencer Tracy ("Bugs" Raymond), Marguerite Churchill (Dorothy Stone), Sally Eilers (Daisy de Lisle), Robert Burns ("Arkansas" Smith), John Wray (Kenneth Stone), Warner Richmond ("Nails" Markey), George Raft (Jimmy Kirk), John Swor (Contractor), Edgar Kennedy (Cop), Leon Ames (Hood), Ward Bond (Cop in Montage), Henry Kolker (D.A.), Lee Phelps (Man in Sound Track), Louis Mercier (Chauffeur).

Tracy is a truck driver, by his own admission "too lazy to work and too nervous to steal." What he can do, though, is organize a racket with himself its head that starts out wrecking cars in the street for a share of the profits of the garage owners the vandalized motorists turn to, then moving into extortion, protection rackets, and eventually taking over the trucking business of the whole town. He falls in love with Churchill, a socialite, and he wants to marry her to give him the class his regular moll, Eilers, can't provide. He forces her brother, Wray, into business with him so he can have access to her, but she constantly turns aside his advances. Meanwhile, Tracy's trusted henchman, Raft, is tricked by rival gang lord Richmond into killing a reformer. Word of this unauthorized hit gets back to Tracy and he has his loyal underling taken out and killed. Churchill plans to marry another man and Tracy plots to kidnap her from the altar, but on the way to the church, his men, tired of their boss' constant quest for "class," take him for a "ride." Undeservedly neglected gangster film is one of the best of the era, ranking with pictures like THE PUBLIC ENEMY (1931) and LITTLE CAESAR (1930). Director-writer Brown made his debut here, and would direct only a few others, including the recently rediscovered gangster classic, BLOOD MONEY (1933), before his star would mysteriously fade. Tracy gives a terrific performance as a decent man who lusts after power and class and only ends up dead, and many of the other performers give lucid, interesting performances. Raft made his second feature appearance here and started his career in earnest. He had come to Hollywood some months earlier with his good friend, gangster Owney Madden. Madden introduced Raft to Brown and suggested that Brown might be able to find a place for Raft in his new movie. The next morning, a limousine came and picked up Raft and took him to the studio, a star treatment that even the film's star, Tracy, wasn't receiving. On the set, an argument broke out between Brown and the casting director over Raft's suitability for the role. The actor was shocked to hear himself talked about "like a piece of meat" so he told the bickering pair: "Look, gentlemen, may I say something? Suppose I come in tomorrow and read for the part. If my work is satisfactory, you hire me. If it isn't, you don't." His screen test was successful and he was impressive enough in his small role to convince Howard Hawks to cast him in the film that would cement him forever in the public mind, SCARFACE.

d, Rowland Brown; w, Courtney Terrett, Brown; ph, Joseph August; ed&art d, Duncan Cramer; cos, Sophie Wachner.

Crime   **(PR:C MPAA:NR)**

QUICK MILLIONS**½   (1939) 61m FOX bw

Jed Prouty (John Jones), Spring Byington (Mrs. John Jones), Ken Howell (Jack Jones), George Ernest (Roger Jones), June Carlson (Lucy Jones), Florence Roberts (Granny Jones), Billy Mahan (Bobby Jones), Eddie Collins (Henry "Beaver" Howard), Robert Shaw (Barry Frazier), Helen Ericson (Daisy Landers), Marvin Stephens (Tommy McGuire), Paul Hurst (Sheriff), John T. Murray (Pete [Professor]), Peter Lynn (Hank Pierson), Horace MacMahon (Floyd "Bat" Douglas).

Another film in Twentieth Century Fox's minor comedy series "The Jones Family" finds Prouty and company returning home after a trip to Hollywood. A telegram arrives explaining that a rich uncle has left them a gold mine near the Grand Canyon. The good-hearted family pack their bags once more and head west. They contract with a guide (Collins) who leads them up a mountain to a lonely old cabin. It's not lonely for long, as it turns out to be the hideout of some robbers. Through a

series of comic mishaps, Prouty and his kin manage to round up the bad guys and collect a fat reward. Collins is the standout here, providing some good laughs. This film is funnier than most B comedies as it employs a number of clever visual gags rather than a string of bad jokes. This shouldn't be a surprise considering that the story was written by the famed silent clown Keaton. This was his first screen credit after an absence of many years. Though bad fortune and alcohol had taken their toll, the Great Stone Face was still capable of clever ideas, as this film proves. (See JONES FAMILY series, Index.)

p, John Stone; d, Malcolm St. Clair; w, Joseph Hoffman, Stanley Rauh (based on a story by Hoffman, Buster Keaton, based on characters created by Katharine Kavanaugh); ph, Lucien Andriot; ed, Harry Reynolds; md, Samuel Kaylin; cos, Sophie Wachner.

Comedy   **(PR:A MPAA:NR)**

QUICK MONEY**   (1938) 59m RKO

Fred Stone (Jonas Tompkins), Gordon Jones (Bill), Dorothy Moore (Alice), Berton Churchill (Blueford Smythe), Paul Guilfoyle (Ambrose), Harlan Briggs (Barnstall), Dorothy Vaughan (Mrs. Tompkins), Sherwood Bailey (Freddie), Frank M. Thomas (Clark), Jack Carson (Football Coach), Kathryn Sheldon (Mrs. Otis), Dick Elliott (Walker), James Farley (Sheriff), William Franey (Clerk), Fuzzy Knight (Peter Potter), Hattie McDaniel.

Stone plays a small town mayor trying to save the town from confidence men. Churchill and Guilfoyle are the pair of crooks who want to turn the place into a resort town and will do anything to get at the city treasury. Stone's opposition to the con men makes him unpopular, and a recall election is held. Things look grim, but with the help of a reporter, the two swindlers are exposed and the election is called off. This is a minor programmer straddling the fence between drama and comedy. It never seems to know which way to go and finally goes nowhere. The direction is slow and performances just average.

d, Edward Killy; w, Arthur T. Horman, Franklin Coen, Bert Granet (based on a story by Horman); ph, Nicholas Musuraca; ed, George Crone; cos, Renie.

Drama   **(PR:A MPAA:NR)**

QUICK ON THE TRIGGER**   (1949) 54m COL bw

Charles Starrett (Steve Warren/The Durango Kid), Smiley Burnette (Himself), Lyle Talbot (Garvey Yager), Helen Parrish (Nora Reed), George Eldredge (Alfred Murdock), Ted Adams (Martin Oaks), Alan Bridge (Judge Kormac), Russell Arms (Fred Reed), The Sunshine Boys, Budd Buster, Tex Cooper, Blackie Whiteford.

Typical Starrett outing which sees our hero once again adopt the guise of the Durango Kid to stamp out evil in the West. Talbot plays the crooked lawyer who frames former sheriff Starrett for the murder of Parrish's brother. Parrish owns a stagecoach line, and Talbot manages to convince a gullible jury that Starrett had designs on the business and bumped off Parrish's brother to get it. Starrett is found guilty and sent to the hoosegow, but he escapes and returns disguised as the Durango Kid to expose Talbot as the actual killer. (See DURANGO KID series, Index.)

p, Colbert Clark; d, Ray Nazarro; w, Elmer Clifton; ph, Rex Wimpy; ed, Paul Borofsky, art d, Charles Clague; set d, Frank Kramer.

Western   **(PR:A MPAA:NR)**

QUICKSAND***   (1950) 79m UA bw

Mickey Rooney (Dan Brady, Auto Mechanic), Jeanne Cagney (Vera Novak, Cafe Cashier), Barbara Bates (Helen), Peter Lorre (Nick Dramoshag, Penny Arcade Owner), Taylor Holmes (Harvey), Art Smith (Mackey, Garage Owner), Wally Cassell (Chuck), John Gallaudet (Moriarity), Minerva Urecal (Landlady), Patsy O'Connor (Millie).

A no-nonsense crime thriller starring Rooney as a poor garage mechanic who falls in love with James Cagney's sister Jeanne. Unfortunately, she is only interested in how much money she can get out of the simple mechanic. To fund his night on the town with Cagney, Rooney lifts $20 from the garage's till, fully intending to pay it back before the accountant comes for his weekly book-balancing. While out on the date, Rooney meets slimy arcade owner Lorre, who, it turns out, is a former boy friend of Cagney. Rooney arrives at work the next day only to find that the accountant has come a few days early. Panic sets in and Rooney runs off to purchase an expensive watch on credit so that he can pawn it for $30. He succeeds in replacing the money before the loss is discovered, but then he finds himself in trouble with his creditors. Desperate, he robs a drunk, but Lorre learns of the crime and blackmails Rooney, demanding a car in return for his silence. Rooney steals a car from the garage, but is discovered by his boss, who demands payment. Rooney and Cagney then decide to rob Lorre's arcade to get the money. Cagney blows half the cash on a new fur coat, and Rooney is left with only $1,800 to try to appease his boss. Smith takes the money, and then pulls a gun on Rooney and calls the cops. Rooney jumps the man and strangles him. Believing he has committed a murder, Rooney flees and is eventually cornered by the police. Not wanting to give up, he starts a shootout, is injured, and is finally captured. On the way to the hospital he is informed by the authorities that his boss is not dead after all, and a sympathetic lawyer offers his services to Rooney, telling him that since he is a first offender he'll be able to get out in a year. QUICKSAND was the only film in a proposed three-picture collaboration between Rooney and Lorre. The films, which were to be produced by Rooney's company, at first were to be directed by Lorre, who would also star in them. Later it was announced that Rooney would produce and direct the three films, which would star Lorre. In the end, only QUICKSAND was ever filmed. Disappointed with the result and plagued with financial problems (his business manager having forced the actor into bankruptcy), Lorre returned to Europe where he visited a post-war Germany and was inspired to man the helm on the only film he would ever direct, THE LOST ONE.

p, Mort Briskin; d, Irving Pichel; w, Robert Smith; ph, Lionel Lindon; m, Louis Gruenberg; ed, Walter Thompson; art d, Emil Newman.

Crime **(PR:C MPAA:NR)**

QUIEN SABE? (SEE: BULLET FOR THE GENERAL, A, 1968, Ital.)

QUIET AMERICAN, THE½** (1958) 120m Figaro/UA bw

Audie Murphy *(The American)*, Michael Redgrave *(Fowler)*, Claude Dauphin *(Inspector Vigot)*, Giorgia Moll *(Phuong)*, Kerima *(Miss Hei)*, Bruce Cabot *(Bill Granger)*, Fred Sadoff *(Dominguez)*, Richard Loo *(Mister Heng)*, Peter Trent *(Eliot Wilkins)*, Clinton Anderson *(Joe Morton)*, Yoko Tani *(Hostess)*, Sonia Moser *(Yvette)*, Phuong Thi Nghiep *(Isabelle)*, Vo Doan Chau *(Cao-Dai Commandant)*, Le Van Le *(Cao-Dai Pope's Deputy)*, Le Quynh *(Masked Man)*, Georges Brehat *(French Colonel)*.

An interesting but fatally flawed look at the situation in Vietnam, actually shot in that country. Loosely based on Graham Greene's novel, the film stars Murphy (in a fairly ironic piece of casting) as a naive American who arrives in Vietnam representing a privately funded aid effort designed to help the South Vietnamese in their battle against the Communists and the French. There he meets cynical British reporter Redgrave, who slowly becomes involved in the conflict and eventually is duped by the Communists and made to participate in the murder of Murphy. The film opens as a French police inspector, Dauphin, investigates the murder of Murphy. The events leading up to the tragedy are detailed in flashback. The flaws in the scenario occur when the screenplay departs from the source material. Greene's book was highly critical of the American political involvement in Vietnam. The film, however, portrays Murphy's character not as an official of the American government (as he is in the novel), but as a private citizen with his own naive plan for solving Vietnam's internal problems, not one officially sanctioned by the U.S. government. This switch removes Greene's point of view, which was critical of American involvement in Vietnam, and thereby removes any power the film might have had. Another problem is the casting of Murphy in the lead role. A genuine American hero in WW II, Murphy was not an actor of great depth. His persona was fine for the numerous westerns and war pictures the studios assigned him, but in a film of this seriousness and complexity he flounders. The audience is left emotionally tied to the Redgrave character (due to his superior performance), though his character is also adversely affected by the tampering with the source material. Despite these problems, THE QUIET AMERICAN has some value for its rare Vietnam location photography, and the historically interesting Hollywood interpretation of the troubles in that country before our military involvement.

p,d&w, Joseph L. Mankiewicz (based on the novel by Graham Greene); ph, Robert Krasker; m, Mario Nascimbene; ed, William Hornbeck; art d, Rino Mondellini, Dario Simoni, spec eff, Rosco Cline; George Schlickin; makeup, George Frost.

Drama **(PR:A MPAA:NR)**

QUIET DAY IN BELFAST, A½** (1974, Can.) 91m Twinbay/Ambassador c

Barry Foster *(John Slattery)*, Margot Kidder *(Bridgit Slattery/Thelma)*, Sean McCann *(Peter O'Lurgan)*, Leo Leyden *(Charlie McLarnon)*, Mel Tuck *(Tim Horgan)*, Joyce Campion *(Mrs. McDuatt)*, Sean Mulcahy *(Mike Mahoney)*.

Fairly interesting film adaptation of a stage play that ran in Canada and detailed the strife in Northern Ireland. The action takes place around a small betting shop in Ireland where the lives of several characters intersect. The main thrust of the story deals with an Irish girl, Kidder, who falls in love with British policeman Foster. Of course tragedy comes out of the relationship in the form of an irate group of Irish radicals who accidentally tar and feather Kidder's twin sister (who has just arrived from Canada), when they had intended to humiliate Kidder herself.

p&d, Milad Bessada; w, Jack Gray (based on the play by Andrew Angus Dalrymple); ph, Harry Makin; m, Greg Adams, Eric Robertson; ed, Simon Christopher Dew; set d, Ed Watkins; cos, Aleida MacDonald.

Drama **(PR:C MPAA:NR)**

QUIET GUN, THE½** (1957) 77m FOX bw

Forrest Tucker *(Carl, Sheriff)*, Mara Corday *(Irene, Indian Girl)*, Jim Davis *(Ralph, Rancher)*, Kathleen Crowley *(Teresa, Rancher's Wife)*, Lee Van Cleef *(Sadler, Killer)*, Tom Brown *(Reilly, Saloonkeeper)*, Lewis Martin *(Hardy)*, Hank Worden *(Sampson, Sheriff's Deputy)*, Gerald Milton *(Lesser)*, Everett Glass *(Judge)*, Edith Evanson *(Mrs. Merric)*, Vince Barnett *(Undertaker)*.

Tucker plays a sheriff who is sent out to investigate a potential scandal involving his friend Davis. It has been reported that Davis has been having an affair with Indian girl Corday while his wife Crowley is out of town. An enraged Davis kills the local attorney, and a lynch mob springs up and hangs him in revenge. Thinking the situation a bit strange, Tucker investigates and discovers that saloon owner Brown and evil gunman Van Cleef started the rumors and incited the mob in order to obtain Davis' land. Tucker forces a showdown and kills both men. Standard plot helped greatly by fine performances from Tucker and Davis.

p, Earle Lyon; d, William Claxton; w, Eric Norden; ph, John Mescall (RegalScope); m, Paul Dunlap; ed, Robert Fritch; art d, Ernst Fegte.

Western **(PR:A MPAA:NR)**

QUIET MAN, THE***** (1952) 129m Argosy/REP c

John Wayne *(Sean Thornton)*, Maureen O'Hara *(Mary Kate Danaher)*, Barry Fitzgerald *(Michaeleen Flynn)*, Ward Bond *(Father Peter Lonergan)*, Victor McLaglen *(Red Will Danaher)*, Mildred Natwick *(Mrs. Sarah Tillane)*, Francis Ford *(Dan Tobin)*, Eileen Crowe *(Mrs. Elizabeth Playfair)*, May Craig *(Woman at Railway Station)*, Arthur Shields *(Rev. Cyril Playfair)*, Charles FitzSimmons *(Forbes)*, James Lilburn *(Father Paul)*, Sean McClory *(Owen Glynn)*, Jack McGowran *(Feeney)*, Ken Curtis *(Dermot Fahy)*, Mae Marsh *(Father Paul's Mother)*, Joseph O'Dea *(Guard Maloney)*, Eric Gorman *(Engine Driver Costello)*, Kevin Lawless *(Fireman)*, Paddy O'Donnell *(Porter)*, Web Overlander *(Station Master)*, Harry Tenbrook *(Policeman)*, Maj. Sam Harris *(General)*, Harry Tyler *(Pat Cohan the Publican)*, Patrick Wayne, Michael Wayne, Melinda Wayne, Antonia Wayne, Elizabeth Jones *(The Children)*, David H. Hughes *(Constable)*, Jack Roper *(Boxer)*, Douglas Evans *(Ring Physician)*, Al Murphy *(Referee)*, Don Hatswell *(Guppy)*, Elizabeth Jones *(Tiny Woman)*, Hank Worden *(Trainer in Flashback)*, Pat O'Malley, Bob Perry, Frank Baker.

In one of his greatest films, Ford presents a two-fisted love story on the Old Sod of Ireland, a vibrant, moving, action-filled picture enriched in every frame by the unerring touch of the greatest director of the talking era. It is really a sentimental journey by Ford to the quaint, brawling, and memorable past of his ancestral home, with Wayne stalking through his memory, for Wayne was Ford in front of the camera. A quiet fellow with a brutal past, ex-fighter Wayne is seen looking over the verdant Irish landscape and clean little villages from a speeding train. It is the 1920s. He arrives in Innisfree to be greeted by elfin, capricious, and witty Fitzgerald, who narrates the story. Without waiting to be asked, Fitzgerald, village cabman, matchmaker, and mentor, grabs Wayne's bags at the station and places them in his pony cart. Wayne hops onto the seat and the two are off to a little cottage—Wayne's birthplace, White O'Mornin'—which Wayne has purchased from Natwick, the rich widow of the district. Wayne is taken to a small bridge and there sees in the distance a beautiful, ripe, red-haired woman, her lovely face and voluptuous body framed by a stand of trees, a soft wind whipping her skirts and hair about. She is a vision of another world, one of the past, and Wayne is so shocked by the scene that he asks Fitzgerald, "Is that real?" Quips the coachman: "Only a mirage brought on by your terrible thirst!" He is asking about the scene itself, not O'Hara, the lovely woman inside it. Then she is gone and Wayne hears the voice of his dead mother, talking to him as a little boy: "Don't you remember it, Seannie, and how it was? The old road led up past the chapel and it wound and wound. And there is the field where Dan Tobin's bullock chased you. It was a lovely little house, Seanin, and the roses, well, your father used to tease me about them, but he was that fond of them too." Fitzgerald follows Wayne's gaze and snorts, "Ah, that's nothing but a wee humble cottage." Wayne defends his own past and replies: "I'm Sean Thornton and I was born in that little cottage. I'm home and home I'm going to stay." It's almost a declaration of war, one against the present for the security and snug predictability of the past. In buying the property Wayne has alienated the richest, toughest man in the area, McLaglen, who is doubly angered over the fact that widow Natwick has sold the property to an American, "a dirty Yank," as he sneeringly puts it, when she is the woman he has been thinking to marry. Wayne moves into a small cottage, a stranger in a land he loves, but one that considers him a foreigner, despite his birthright. He will later plant roses in memory of his mother and O'Hara will tell him that planting some vegetables would be more practical. Though his land appears solid green to the gaze, Wayne turns up nothing but rocks when he tries to plough it for planting. He battles the present for the illusion of the past at every turn and is even upbraided for his noble efforts when he proudly shows off his cottage to a neighbor who inspects its trim thatched roof and immaculately painted walls, off-handedly complimenting him with the words: "It looks the way all Irish cottages should, and seldom do. And only an American would think of painting it emerald green." One day, toward dusk, Wayne enters his cottage to find O'Hara there. She has been cleaning the place for him, a gesture that goes far beyond neighborliness. Just as she is about to flee, Wayne grabs hold of her arm, swings her wide of him, and pulls her back to him to kiss her. She gives him a stiff-armed slap but before escaping the cottage, she encourages Wayne by kissing him lightly. Wayne next meets O'Hara's brutish brother McLaglen in the local pub. McLaglen seethes with hate for him, believing him to be an interloper who has upset his plans with Natwick and "backdealing" him out of his property. When Wayne extends his hand, the powerful Mclaglen squeezes it with all his might and Wayne responds with his own strength, until both men let loose with winces of pain on their faces. Witnessing this first of several confrontations to come between the two giants is a bevy of local men, most of whom hate McLaglen and side with the Yank, Wayne, including members of the IRA and local priests Bond and Lilburn. Wayne has already befriended Bond, the obligatory thing to do in predominantly Catholic Ireland, in a meeting where the priest recalls Wayne's family, including his wayward father who "died in Australia...in a penal colony," and his mother, "brave soul," who struggled along to raise their little boy, now returned a strapping man with a mysterious past. (Ironically, in the pub earlier Curtis plays on his accordion, the traditional song "The Wild Colonial Boy," one about Jack Dugan, freedom fighter who also died in Australia.) Wayne's own past is unknown and he goes out of his way to say nothing of his background. But the local Protestant clergyman, Shields (Fitzgerald's brother in real life), knows Wayne's dark secret and tells him so in a quiet meeting. Shields had been an amateur boxer in his youth and kept a scrapbook all his life about boxers the world over. He shows Wayne clippings concerned with an American boxer named "Trooper Thorn," which was Wayne's assumed name, one which was tainted and which he abandoned after he accidentally killed a man in the ring and retired forever from boxing, coming with his prize money to Ireland to find peace and happiness and recapture his boyhood images of the past. Later, Bond has Wayne promise that he will attend church the following Sunday and the big man shows up, spotting O'Hara and McLaglen entering the church. He steps forward, cups holy water in his hand, and offers this to O'Hara who takes it and quickly makes the sign of the cross with the water, then hurries into the church. After Mass, O'Hara watches Wayne depart and he is soon at her doorstep, asking her bully-boy brother for her hand. McLaglen is aware of Wayne's interest in his auburn-haired sister but hates the idea of having him for a brother-in-law. His first response to matchmaker Fitzgerald is, "If he was the last man on earth and my sister the last woman, I'd still say no!" Wayne is told by Fitzgerald that the courtship is hopeless and the embittered suitor throws away the roses he never offers to O'Hara. Moreover, Fitzgerald is dashed into a drunken stupor when later Wayne refuses to fight the hamhock-fisted McLaglen who has insulted him. His refusal to fight, of course, is due to having killed an opponent in the ring. But the situation is saved when Bond and others join in a conspiracy, intimating that if McLaglen will give his permission for the Wayne-O'Hara marriage, his own wedding to Natwick is assured. The boisterous McLaglen agrees and the banns are published announcing the upcoming wedding. Once the ceremony is over, however, McLaglen learns he has been tricked, Natwick telling him that she has no intention of marrying him. McLaglen explodes, accusing one and all of playing him false. He angrily refuses to pay Wayne his sister's dowry or allow her to take her prized furniture. Wayne tells McLaglen he can keep his money and off he goes to his cottage with his new wife. O'Hara proves truculent and Wayne finds himself sleeping on the floor of the living room on his wedding night until he angrily rejects being rejected and bursts into the bedroom. The next morning Fitzgerald and some of Wayne's IRA pals appear at the cottage with O'Hara's furniture, telling them that they "persuaded" McLaglen to part with the furnishings. When Fitzgerald enters the bedroom he finds the bed, smashed to floor, and he exclaims: "Impetuous!...Homeric!" But all is not right between the couple. O'Hara feels married "in name only" since her rightful dowry was not bestowed upon her and her new husband has refused to keep up the tradition. Wayne cannot understand this Old Country way of thinking, telling her that the money means nothing, that he will never accept it anyway. The rift between them grows until O'Hara comes to believe that her husband is a coward and will not fight her brother over what is justly theirs. She leaves him, going to the train station, intending to live with distant relatives. Enraged when he learns of the desertion, Wayne rides his horse wildly to the station and then marches down the platform, looking into each compartment, slamming the doors on empty coaches until he finds O'Hara cringing in one of them, dragging her out and booting her in the rump as he begins to march her "the whole long way" back to her brother's farm. News of the battle about to explode races through the town until all the villagers, including the train personnel, are following Wayne and O'Hara as he drags, pushes, and shoves her across the meadows and up and down hills. A woman races up to Wayne and hands him a tree branch, saying, "And here's a stick with which to beat the lovely lady." Upon arriving at the farm, McLaglen stares in wonder as Wayne drags O'Hara to him, then hurls her across the open ground to land at his feet, snarling, "No dowry, no marriage!" Shamed before the entire population, McLaglen has no choice but to pay, counting out the sum and hurling the "filthy" money at Wayne. O'Hara, despite being humiliated by her husband, is now beaming with pride over his upholding the ancient tradition. As he picks up the money, she runs to a little outdoor rubbish stove which is burning brightly (a kiln), and opens its gate so that Wayne can toss the money into it, showing that they have both triumphed, but not for the money, just for the tradition. The pernicious McLaglen is incensed at the behavior and the insult to his pride. He stands with fists clenched, gritting his teeth, as O'Hara smiles broadly at Wayne and tells him she's on her way home and that "supper will be waiting for you," after he finishes with the most titanic fight of his life, of course. As she walks off, McLaglen smashes his enormous fist into Wayne's face, sending him down. He jumps up and gives the hulking McLaglen a powerhouse blow that sends him reeling. The battle royal is on as the two men smash and thrash each other along the quiet meadows and glens of the farm, across it and into other fields, fighting their way toward the village. The whole community follows, betting life savings on this legendary contest of muscle and will power. Even the priests, watching from hiding, place wagers on the outcome, as does Shields and his visiting bishop who view the battle through binoculars. So does Natwick, who sees that McLaglen is getting the worst of it and finally displays her true feelings for him, these of deep affection, stating aloud to herself McLaglen's own oft-repeated brag: "The best man in Innisfree! As if I didn't know it!" Not only is every living soul in the village crowding to the scene of the moving fight, now going through the village punch by staggering punch, but others in nearby villages call to state that they are coming to the site by bus, motorcar, and bike to witness the historic battle. Francis Ford (the director's brother) playing a white-bearded patriarch who is dying at that moment, hears the sound of the donnybrook and leaps from his deathbed where he is being given the last rites, struggling into his pants and hobbling excitedly outside and down the road, refusing to pass on until seeing this fight of the century. The now tiring battlers, at the suggestion of Fitzgerald, call a momentary truce outside the local pub and enter for a brief refreshment. Here the two bloodied fighters give each other left-handed compliments until drinks are ordered and Wayne puts down money on the bar to pay for the stout. McLaglen sweeps Wayne's money from the bar, telling him his money is no good, and he puts down his own. Wayne then sweeps this money away and puts more of his own down. McLaglen grabs his huge mug of stout and tosses it into Wayne's face. He asks for a bar towel from the frightened bartender and wipes his face. Wayne then asks for the time and is told that it is three o'clock. Outside the pub the entire village waits anxiously, the silence broken when McLaglen comes flying through the closed doors of the pub, blown through the doors by a terrific blow from Wayne, taking both doors with him into the cobblestoned street. The battle rages on deep into dusk and in the cottage O'Hara waits, looking out across the exquisitely green fields brushed by a red sunset beyond, its light glimmering on the little brook nearby. In the far distance she can hear two men singing "The Wild Colonial Boy" as they make their way toward her. It's the badly beaten but now self-avowed blood brothers, Wayne and McLaglen. They stumble through the brook, hobble toward the house, and enter, Wayne tearing his cap from his head, tossing it wildly, and pulling up two chairs to the kitchen table, having McLaglen sit down with him as he tells wife O'Hara "I've brought the brother to dinner!" She runs for the hot food she has prepared, as if knowing this scene would occur, while Wayne tells her to "hurry it up!" When the food is placed on the table, all sit and silently pray. The pummeled but now penitent McLaglen states in a low voice, "And bless all in this house." Peace has come to Innisfree and Ford ends his salute to his beloved Ireland by reprising his wonderful characters, showing how McLaglen and Natwick begin their long-expected courtship, sitting in Fitzgerald's pony cart and having all the cast members appear in frescos to take bows. This is basically a love story with bloody knuckles and the director does not eschew sex, but shows Wayne and O'Hara together in tasteful scenes; even their most tempestuous encounter takes place when he chases her across the fields, the brook, and into the abandoned ruins of an old church where, wet and wild-eyed, they embrace beneath a purple, angry sky that showers them, soaking them to the bone but not chilling their passion for a second. This film is one of Ford's greatest pictures in that it is so carefully constructed, as if the director were painting a series of integrated murals, lavishing the story with some of the most extraordinary scenes ever put on celluloid. Some of his scenes, such as the idealistic portrait of O'Hara in the glen herding her sheep, are presented in muted, diffused tones so as to suggest an ethereal world into which Wayne has barged. The ebullient author Thomas Wolfe once wrote a poignant novel entitled *You Can't Go Home Again*. Here Ford disproves that notion, allowing his own wistful memories to take shape in the form of living, full-blooded characters, some archetypal, who walk back into his envisioned past, who cross over the hearth Ford yearns to see once more, who step into the home of his heart. Wayne is Ford's youth, O'Hara his great love, and here she is all the women of Ireland, while his magnificent stock company—McLaglen, the bully with sentiment running through his muscled arms; Fitzgerald, the conscience and historian of the village (and the nation); Bond, the priest who would rather fish than pray, although all fishermen know that fishing is a form of prayer; Shields, the patient outsider; Natwick, the waiting spinster (which are legion in Ireland); and all the wonderful supporting players who go to make up this utterly moving and fascinating portrait of rural life in Ireland. In an interview with Ford, directer Peter Bogdanovich asked him why he chose to wrap his plot around the idea of a dowry and, as usual, Ford gave his prosaic reply: "I just thought it was good drama. The only mistake we made was having him throw the money on the fire—he should have tossed it to one of the fellows and said, 'Give it to charity' or something....Well, who would he give it to anyway? Not the parish priest—he has more money than the Lord Mayor of Dublin." The film is loaded with nepotism but charming by virtue of that since this was mostly an Irish clan film. Ford's characters possess his own family names. The Abbey Player, McGowran, plays the part of Feeney, McLaglen's little toady who writes down all the names of those who displease McLaglen in a little black book. "Feeney" is the Anglicized version of Ford's real surname. Wayne's last name in the film, Thornton, was the name of Ford's real-life cousins. Wayne's children traveled with him to Ireland to visit the ancestral home and when they met Ford, they chimed, "Uncle John, why don't you let us become actors in this picture?" Ford laughed and then said, "Why not, everyone else is getting into the act!" O'Hara had persuaded the director to put two of her brothers into the film and Fitzgerald and Shields were brothers. Moreover, Ford's own brother, Francis, was again present in THE QUIET MAN, almost like a good luck charm. A wonderful mime and early silent screen star, Francis Ford plays the old man with the white beard who refuses to die until he sees the herculean fight between Wayne and McLaglen. This marked his 29th appearance in his brother's films. Oddly, the two brothers did not socialize. Something mysterious had occurred during their early days in films when Francis was a top star and John just coming up as a director. Rumors had it that they had had a terrible fight over a woman or that, in their cups, they had gone at each other much the same way Wayne and McLaglen battled. But it was never spoken about after Ford became the preeminent American film director. Francis received his assignment by mail, appeared on the set or at the location promptly, did his wonderful little bits, and then walked off and waited for brother John to call him back. The actor and director hardly spoke to each other, only nodded in each other's direction after a completed scene. They were not friends, but they were blood.

p, Merian C. Cooper, John Ford, (uncredited) Michael Killanin; d, Ford; w, Frank S. Nugent, (uncredited) Richard Llewellyn (based on the story by Maurice Walsh); ph, Winton C. Hoch, Archie Stout (Technicolor); m, Victor Young; ed, Jack Murray; art d, Frank Hotaling; set d, John McCarthy, Jr., Charles Thompson; cos, Adele Palmer; m/l, Richard Farrelly, Dr. Arthur Colahan, Michael Donovan, Richard Hayward, Thomas Moore.

Romance/Adventure/Drama Cas. (PR:A MPAA:NR)

QUIET PLACE IN THE COUNTRY, A½** (1970, Ital./Fr.) 106m PEA/Lopert c (UN TRANQUILLO POSTO DI CAMPAGNA; UN COIN TRANQUILLE A LA CAMPAGNE)

Franco Nero *(Leonardo Ferri)*, Vanessa Redgrave *(Flavia)*, Georges Geret *(Attilio)*, Gabriella Grimaldi *(Wanda)*, Madeleine Damien *(Wanda's Mother)*, Rita Calderoni *(Egle)*, Renato Menegotto *(Egle's Friend)*, John Francis Lane *(Asylum Attendant)*, David Maunsell *(Medium)*, Mirta Simionato, Graziella Simionato, Arnaldo Momo, Sara Momo, Otello Cazzola, Marino Bagiola, Piero De Franceschi, Camillo Besenzon, Costantino De Luca, Giulia Menin *(Villagers)*, Valerio Ruggeri, Umberto Di Grazia, Bruno Simionato, Elena Vicini, Renato Lupi, Giuseppe Bella, Onofrio Fulli.

Creepy Italian gothic horror starring Nero as a popular painter who is plagued by nightmares that he and Redgrave, his lover and sales agent, are engaging in bizarre, ritualistic, sadistic sexual acts. Seeking to escape the city for a while, Nero and Redgrave rent a house in the country. Soon after their arrival, strange things begin happening including Nero's canvases being damaged and Redgrave suffering injuries from an unusual accident. The caretaker informs Nero that the house is haunted by the ghost of the former owner's daughter who died during a WW II air raid. Fascinated by the ghost, Nero hires a medium and holds a seance. While trying to contact the dead, Nero goes insane and kills Redgrave. When the police arrive they find Nero guarding a refrigerator which he claims contains the various body parts of Redgrave. Nero is put in an asylum and continues to paint, but he never really committed the murder (it was all in his mind) and Redgrave makes a tidy sum selling his paintings.

p, Alberto Grimaldi; d, Elio Petri; w, Petri, Luciano Vincenzoni (based on a story by Tonino Guerra, Petri); ph, Luigi Kuveiller Techniscope, Technicolor); m, Ennio Morricone; ed, Ruggero Mastrioanni; art d, Sergio Canevari; cos, Giulio Coltellacci.

Mystery/Horror (PR:O MPAA:R)

QUIET PLEASE**   (1938, Brit.) 69m WB-FN bw

Reginald Purdell (Algy Beresford), Lesley Brook (Margery Meadows), Wally Patch (Bill), Julien Mitchell (Holloway), Ian McLean (Woods), Bruce Lister (Dr. Faversham), Winifred Izard (Lady Winterley), Clem Lawrance (Johnson), Ian Fleming (Dr. Craven), Brenda Harvey, Bobby Lawrence.

Patch and Purdell are a pair of street entertainers who get involved with a woman arrested on jewel theft charges. The buskers (London slang for street actors) adopt the guise of a patient and a valet in order to spring her from jail and turn in Mitchell, the head of the gem-swiping gang. Innocuous comedy, which runs too long for its own good.

p, Irving Asher; d, Roy William Neill; w, Reginald Purdell, Anthony Hankey; ph, Basil Emmott.

Comedy   (PR:A MPAA:NR)

QUIET PLEASE, MURDER**½   (1942) 70m FOX bw

George Sanders (Fleg), Gail Patrick (Myra Blandy), Richard Denning (Hal McByrne), Lynne Roberts (Kay Ryan), Sidney Blackmer (Martin Cleaver), Kurt Katch (Eric Pahsen), Margaret Brayton (Miss Oval), Charles Tannen (Hollis), Byron Foulger (Edmund Walpole), Arthur Space (Vance), George Walcott (Benson), Chick Collins (Webley), Bud [Lon] McCallister (Freddie, the Stack Boy), Bud Geary (Gannett), Harold R. Goodwin (Stover), James Farley (Detective), Jack Cheatham (Policeman), Minerva Urecal (Housewife), Bert Roach (Husband), Paul Porcasi (Rebescu), Theodore von Eltz (Lucas), Frank O'Connor (Guard in Library), W.R. Deming (Mr. Daly), Hooper Atchley, Arthur Thalasso (Air Raid Wardens), Mae Marsh (Miss Hartwig), Monica Bannister (Bit), Fern Emmett (Miss Philbert), Bobby Larsen (Boy), Pat O'Malley (Guard), Jill Warren (Girl), Charles Cane (Inspector Henderson), Matt McHugh (Taxi Driver).

Sanders plays a brilliant criminal who kills a library guard, steals original editions of rare books, copies them, and then sells the copies as valuable first editions. He is aided in his endeavors by Patrick, who arranges most of the bogus book sales, but she soon becomes fearful of Sanders and aids young detective Denning in capturing her former employer. A well done and fairly unusual caper movie.

p, Ralph Dietrich; d&w, John Larkin (based on a story by Lawrence G. Blochman); ph, Joseph MacDonald; m, Emil Newman; ed, Louis Loeffler; art d, Richard Day, Joseph C. Wright.

Crime   (PR:A MPAA:NR)

QUIET WEDDING***   (1941, Brit.) 63m Conqueror/UNIV bw

Margaret Lockwood (Janet Royd), Derek Farr (Dallas Chaytor), Marjorie Fielding (Mildred Royd), A.E. Matthews (Arthur Royd), Athene Seyler (Aunt Mary), Jean Cadell (Aunt Florence), Margaretta Scott (Marcia Royd), David Tomlinson (John Royd), Sidney King (Denys Royd), Peggy Ashcroft (Flower Lisle), Frank Cellier (Mr. Chaytor), Roland Culver (Boofy Ponsonby), Michael Shepley (Marcia's Husband Jim), Muriel Pavlow (Miranda), Margaret Halston (Lady Yeldham), Roddy Hughes (Vicar), O.B. Clarence, Wally Patch, Margaret Rutherford (Magistrates), Martita Hunt (Mme. Mirelle), Charles Carson (Mr. Johnson), Lawrence Hanray (Mr. Williamson), Bernard Miles (PC), Hay Petrie, Muriel George, Esma Cannon, Mike Johnson, Ivor Barnard, Peter Bull, R. Brodis-Turner, Mark Stone, Valentine Dunn, Amy Dalby, Viola Lyel.

Fine British comedy based on a hit play by Esther McCracken and sporting an outstanding cast of players. Lockwood stars as the harried bride whose wedding plans are driving her nuts. Her highly charged emotional state begins to affect her relationship with Farr, her fiance, and it begins to look as if there will be no wedding at all. The arrival of her obnoxious relatives only furthers her dilemma, and eventually the couple decide to flee the night before the wedding in order to spend the evening together. The next day they return to get hitched, to the relief of all concerned.

p, Paul Soskin; d, Anthony Asquith; w, Terence Rattigan, Anatole de Grunwald (based on the play by Esther McCracken); ph, Bernard Knowles; m, Nicholas Brodsky; ed, Reginald Beck; art d, Paul Sheriff.

Comedy   (PR:A MPAA:NR)

QUIET WEEKEND**½   (1948, Brit.) 83m Associated British Pictures/
                                                                    Distinguished bw

Derek Farr (Denys Royd), Frank Cellier (Adrian Barrasford), Marjorie Fielding (Mildred Royd), George Thorpe (Arthur Royd), Barbara White (Miranda Bute), Helen Shingler (Rowena Hyde), Edward Rigby (Sam Pecker), Josephine Wilson (Mary Jarrow), Gwen Whitby (Marcia Brent), Ballard Berkeley (Jim Brent), Judith Furse (Ella Spender), Pat Field (Sally Spender), George Merritt (Police Sergeant), Helen Burls (Bella), Christopher Steele (Vicar), Mary Matthew, Conway Palmer, Brian Weske, Richard George.

Another successful adaptation of a popular Esther McCracken play, once again starring Farr. This time he and his relations decide to spend the weekend hunting at a country cottage. When they arrive they are greeted with a nearly uninhabitable ramshackle hut with derelict plumbing and low doorways. If that isn't bad enough, the family is forced to poach due to the stringent hunting laws in the area. Funny and well performed.

p, Warwick Ward; d, Harold French; w, Ward, Victor Skutezky, Stephen Black, T.J. Morrison, (based on the play by Esther McCracken); ph, Eric Cross; ed, Flora Newton; art d, D.W.L. Daniels.

Comedy   (PR:A MPAA:NR)

QUIET WOMAN, THE**   (1951, Brit.) 71m Tempean/Eros bw

Derek Bond (Duncan McLeod), Jane Hylton (Janie Foster), Dora Bryan (Elsie), Michael Balfour (Lefty), Dianne Foster (Helen), John Horsley (Inspector Bromley), Harry Towb (Jim Cranshaw), Campbell Singer (Willis).

Hylton, the wife of an imprisoned man, runs an inn called "The Quiet Woman" where she becomes attracted to Bond, a smuggler. Later her husband escapes from prison and tries to enlist her help in his getaway. Bond tries to help the man get to France via the sea, but they are caught by customs officials and the escapee ends up dead. Tedious unfolding of events gets a little help from the excellent photography.

p, Robert S. Baker, Monty Berman; d&w, John Gilling (based on the story by Ruth Adam); ph, Berman, E. Besche.

Crime   (PR:A MPAA:NR)

QUILLER MEMORANDUM, THE***   (1966, Brit.) 105m Carthay/
                                                                    FOX c

George Segal (Quiller), Alec Guinness (Pol), Max von Sydow (Oktober), Senta Berger (Inge), George Sanders (Gibbs), Robert Helpmann (Weng), Robert Flemyng (Rushington, Gibb's Associate), Peter Carsten (Hengel), Edith Schneider (Headmistress), Gunter Meisner (Hassler), Robert Stass (Jones), Ernst Walder (Grauber), Philip Madoc, John Rees (Oktober's Men).

Made by the consortium of Ivan Foxwell Films and Carthay Films for the Rank Organization and National General Productions, this was released in the U.S. by Fox to disappointing grosses. Despite the good cast and the often interesting screenplay, it was sent to the public in the middle of a flood of rock 'em-sock 'em spy movies and suffered from being a bit too literary and not having enough action to suit the temper of the times. Segal is a U.S. agent who is taken off his vacation to fill a void left when some British agents are killed. The dead men were on the verge of uncovering a neo-Nazi plot and had infiltrated the organization but were caught and murdered. In a brief but excellent (as always) role, Guinness (doing a Cockney accent) is the Brit spy chief and tells Segal what must be done and how to do it. This all takes place in Berlin, which is well-photographed by Hillier. Segal follows a lead when he reads in the newspaper that a local teacher has hung himself after being accused of having been a war criminal. At the school, he meets Schneider, the headmistress, and one of her teachers, Berger, who has replaced the suicide. Segal accepts an invitation to Berger's apartment and is later kidnaped by Nazis, drugged, and brought to meet the leader of the group, Von Sydow. Despite torture, Segal will not let them know where Guinness is and they toss him into a canal where they believe the cold water will kill him. He gets away (they knew he would because they follow him), and instead of seeking Guinness, he goes to Berger's residence, pleading for her aid. She takes him to Schneider, who turns out to be one of the Nazis and he is again in the clutches of Von Sydow. Segal has until morning to reveal Guinness' whereabouts or he and Berger will be killed. Segal has planted an explosive device in his own car that can be detonated remotely. When he does this, he gets away and the Nazis think that he's dead. He tells Guinness where the Nazis are and they are all arrested, but Segal is surprised when Berger is not among them. So where was she? He goes to the school and finds her and she convinces him that Von Sydow let her go. It's all cock-and-bull and it's obvious that Berger is also part of the conspiracy and has somehow been overlooked. With no proof of that, Segal has to leave and Berger goes on teaching the children. Pinter's screenplay is spare, perhaps too much so, as there are many holes that are never filled. Segal has a few funny lines to say and there are brief appearances by Sanders and Helpmann, neither of which mean much in the story. The fact that Segal doesn't carry a gun, nor does he engage in Bondsmanship daring is welcome to audiences who had grown bored with one fantastic exploit after another and yearned for a more human look at spying, which is, at best, an inhuman business.

p, Ivan Foxwell, Sydney Streeter; d, Michael Anderson; w, Harold Pinter (based on the novel The Berlin Memorandum by Adam Hall [Elleston Trevor]); ph, Edwin Hillier (Panavision, DeLuxe Color); m, John Barry; ed, Frederick Wilson; md, Barry; art d, Maurice Carter; set d, Arthur Taksen; cos, Carl Tom; spec eff, Les Bowie, Arthur Beavis; m/l, "Wednesday's Child," Barry, David Mack (sung by Matt Munro); makeup, W.T. Partelton.

Spy Drama   **Cas.**   (PR:C MPAA:NR)

QUINCANNON, FRONTIER SCOUT*   (1956) 83m Bel-Air/UA c

Tony Martin (Linus Quincannon), Peggie Castle (Maylene Mason), John Bromfield (Lt. Burke), John Smith (Lt. Hostedder), Ron Randell (Capt. Bell), John Doucette (Sgt. Calvin), Morris Ankrum (Col. Conover), Peter Mamakos (Blackfoot Sara), Ed Hashim (Iron Wolf).

Crooner Martin is hopelessly miscast as a rough-and-ready frontier type who quits the Army to protest a needlessly bloody slaughter of redskins led by Gen. George Armstrong Custer. He then decides to become a scout and is sent off on a mission to investigate the disappearance of a top secret shipment of repeating rifles that was sent to a faraway post. Veteran B western thespian Castle joins Martin to find out whether or not her kid brother had been killed at the fort during a vicious Indian attack. Even the usually capable low-budget veteran director Selander couldn't do much with this material. Martin should have stayed in front of a microphone.

p, Howard W. Koch; d, Lesley Selander; w, John C. Higgins, Don Martin; ph, Joseph F. Biroc (DeLuxe Color); m, Les Baxter; ed, John F. Schreyer; m/l, "Frontier Scout," Sammy Cahn, Hal Borne.

Western   (PR:A MPAA:NR)

QUINTET zero   (1979) 100m Lion's Gate/FOX c

Paul Newman (Essex), Vittorio Gassman (St. Christopher), Fernando Rey (Grigor), Bibi Andersson (Ambrosia), Brigitte Fossey (Vivia), Nina Van Pallandt (Deuca), David Langton (Goldstar), Tom Hill (Francha), Monique Mercure (Redstone's Mate), Craig Richard Nelson (Redstone), Maruska Stankova (Jaspera), Anne Gerety (Aeon), Michael Maillot (Obelus), Max Fleck (Wood Supplier), Francoise Berd (Charity House Woman).

QUINTET is an incomprehensible piece of claptrap that starts poorly and ends worse. With a cast of actors from five different countries, it's not easy to understand them as they try to speak the lines given them. Perhaps that's better because the words are small talk, filled with metaphors that go nowhere and the whole picture is an allegory of Altman's bleak look at life, something he must have felt after reading the reviews of his last few films. The nuclear war has taken the lives of most people and the world is facing a new Ice Age when Newman arrives in what appears to be Montreal with his pregnant wife, Fossey, and her brother, Hill. The few remaining residents of the city are playing some sort of game known as "Quintet" and the rules are never explained but the penalties are harsh. Fossey and Hill are killed in an explosion (which turns out to be part of the game) as Rey functions as the referee for the fatal shenaningans. Newman is soon part of the game which includes several other players: Nelson, Langton, Andersson, Van Pallandt, and Gassman. Newman wants revenge for Fossey's death, so he seeks her killer only to find that person has been slain. Still annoyed, he seeks out Gassman, who killed Fossey's murderer, and kills him. Along the way, he dallies with Andersson, then kills her. There are two cut throats, a stabbing, and several other bloody scenes, including the one where Pallandt gets an arrow in her head and sits there dead while the others make banal conversation. What does it all mean? Why did they do this? How can Paul Newman get involved with such nonsense? QUINTET is a dumb movie made by a man who once had it (M*A*S*H, NASHVILLE, MC CABE AND MRS. MILLER) and now seems to have misplaced it. Everyone seems to have overdosed on valium, as they walk around like zombies, though not nearly as animated, or as interesting, as the zombies in George Romero's NIGHT OF THE LIVING DEAD. Co-author of the story, Chetwynd, was leader of the faction that nearly splintered the Writers Guild of America in their 1985 contract dispute with the producers.

p&d, Robert Altman; w, Frank Barhydt, Altman, Patricia Resnick (based on a story by Altman, Lionel Chetwynd, Resnick); ph, Jean Boffety (DeLuxe Color); m, Tom Pierson; ed, Dennis M. Hill; prod d, Leon Ericksen; md, Pierson; art d, Wolf Kroeger; cos, Scott Bushnell; spec eff, Tom Fisher, John Thomas.

Drama Cas. (PR:C-O MPAA:R)

QUITTER, THE (SEE: QUITTERS, THE 1934)

QUITTERS, THE* (1934) 68m Chesterfield/FD bw (AKA: THE QUITTER)

Charles Grapewin *(Ed Tilford)*, Emma Dunn *(Cordelia Tilford)*, William Bakewell *(Russell Tilford)*, Glen Boles *(Eddie Tilford)*, Barbara Weeks *(Diana Winthrop)*, Aggie Herring *(Hannah)*, Lafe McKee *(Zack)*, Hale Hamilton, Mary Kornman, Jane Keckley.

Grapewin is the publisher of a small town newspaper who suddenly gets wanderlust and takes off for parts unknown leaving his wife Dunn to take care of their two kids and the newspaper. She tells the boys that the old man was killed in France during the war and she soon turns the paper into a modest success. When her sons are older they try to take control of the paper, but through a series of misjudgments they lose the business and their home. Luckily, through the magic of hopelessly contrived scripting, Grapewin returns a rich man and buys back the paper and the house, reuniting the family.

d, Richard Thorpe; w, Robert Ellis; ph, M.A. Anderson.

Drama (PR:A MPAA:NR)

QUO VADIS*½** (1951) 171m MGM c

Robert Taylor *(Marcus Vinicius)*, Deborah Kerr *(Lygia)*, Leo Genn *(Petronius)*, Peter Ustinov *(Nero)*, Patricia Laffan *(Poppaea)*, Finlay Currie *(Peter)*, Abraham Sofaer *(Paul)*, Marina Berti *(Eunice)*, Buddy Baer *(Ursus)*, Felix Aylmer *(Plautius)*, Nora Swinburne *(Pomponia)*, Ralph Truman *(Tigellinus)*, Norman Wooland *(Nerva)*, Peter Miles *(Nazarius)*, Geoffrey Dunn *(Terpnos)*, Nicholas Hannen *(Seneca)*, D.A. Clarke Smith *(Phaon)*, Rosalie Crutchley *(Acte)*, John Ruddock *(Chilo)*, Arthur Walge *(Croton)*, Elspeth March *(Miriam)*, Strelsa Brown *(Rufia)*, Alfredo Varelli *(Lucan)*, Roberto Ottaviano *(Flavius)*, William Tubbs *(Anaxander)*, Pietro Tordi *(Galba)*, Lia DeLeo *(Pedicurist)*, Sophia Loren *(Extra)*, Elizabeth Taylor *(Guest)*, Walter Pidgeon *(Narrator)*.

One of MGM's all-time box-office bonanzas and a remarkable epic, QUO VADIS offers as spectacular a cast as it does sets, costumes, and everything else that could rightly be construed as colossal, but over all looms a loony Ustinov, playing a berserk Emperor Nero. He steals the show, despite director LeRoy's best efforts to prevent the scenery from disappearing between his jaws. Robert Taylor is the commander of a victorious Roman army returning to Rome in the 1st Century A.D. Laffan, the empress, welcomes the hero and he soon meets Kerr, the hostage daughter of a defeated king who turns out to be a Christian. Taylor is attracted to Kerr for purely carnal reasons at first but is put off by her protector, the giant Baer, and, because of his pagan beliefs, Kerr turns her back on the handsome soldier. Angered, Taylor has Kerr become his slave, but she still won't yield to his advances. He frees her, then follows her to a secret meeting of Christians listening to a sermon by Currie, playing the Apostle Peter. Currie explains the meaning of the Christian religion and Taylor seems to soften toward Kerr who falls in love with him and, against the advice of friends, decides to marry him. He cannot reconcile himself to her beliefs, however, and leaves her when she adamantly clings to her religion. Meanwhile, Ustinov sinks deeper into his egomania, setting fire to Rome so he can build a new white city of his own design, blaming the Christians for the fire (and he does play his lyre and recite his own inane poems while the city burns and thousands perish). Taylor rushes to Kerr's side when the fires break out and saves her, only to be rounded up with the Christians who are to be punished for burning Rome. Taken to a dungeon with other Christians, Kerr and Taylor are married by Currie and are then selected to die by the mad Ustinov. Currie is released and is later crucified but not like Christ, saying he is unworthy of being executed in a like manner and asks his Roman guards to crucify him upside down, which they maliciously agree to do. At the arena, Kerr is tied to a stake and Taylor, as an example of a Roman officer who has betrayed his emperor by loving a hated Christian, is also tied in the royal box, forced to witness his loved one's end. Ustinov plays a vicious game, however, promising the crowd to free the Christian beauty if her faithful servant, the mammoth Baer, can kill the wild bull he orders sent into the arena. In a titanic struggle, Baer does kill the bull, but Ustinov goes back on his word and orders Kerr and Baer killed. Taylor, in a superhuman effort, breaks free of his bonds and leads the crowd—and the Roman soldiers guarding Ustinov—to turn against the already distrusted and hated tyrant. Ustinov and his empress Laffan are executed. The performances are fine, especially those of Kerr, Taylor, and the gentle advisor to the emperor, Genn, but it's the wild Ustinov who scoops up every scene he's in with one of the most outlandish performances ever filmed. Ustinov was tested for the role of Nero by MGM as early as 1949, and the studio chiefs liked what they saw, but the film was slow to develop. A year later, MGM wired Ustinov that they were still interested in him for the part but they were worried that he might be too young for the role. Ustinov wired back, "If you wait much longer I shall be too old." Ustinov was required to sing some of his poems as he plucked his lyre and watched with gimlet eye the city of Rome burn, according to his mad plan. The actor had no voice at all and went to the Rome Opera House where he begged the maestro to instruct him in voice lessons. He was told it would take six weeks of intensive training before he would be even a passable singer. The actor told his illustrious coach that he had only three days and the maestro shrugged and attempted the impossible. Three brief lessons ended with the following sage advice to Ustinov, "Try to breathe with your forehead, think with your diaphragm," and "whatever you do, do not forget, sing with the eye." Before his most important scene, where Ustinov steps out onto the balcony of his palace to survey the fiery city, LeRoy shouted to Ustinov: "Hey, Pete! Don't forget. You're responsible for all this!" LeRoy inherited the QUO VADIS project, which had long been in the making, and almost wasn't made at all after MGM chieftains fell to squabbling over its commercial viability. The story had been filmed as early as 1902 as a 12-minute one-reeler in France; as an Italian opus in 1912 which ran 12 reels, road-showing as a high-ticket epic in the U.S. the following year; in 1924 as another Italian feature, which would run as a silent in the U.S. the following year and be revamped with sound effects in 1929. MGM's Hunt Stromberg planned to make an all-talkie of the chestnut in the mid-1930s and plans went so far as to schedule director Robert Z. Leonard to travel to Italy to scout locations, but when WW II broke out the production was abandoned, then reinstated in 1949 when John Huston was chosen to direct a mammoth version of the tale. He and producer Arthur Hornblow, with stars Gregory Peck and Elizabeth Taylor, went to Italy and began shooting but the Italian movie industry was in such a chaotic post-WW II state that the film soon bogged down with endless problems and soaring costs that exceeded $2 million. This version was to be a rather modern interpretation of the old tale, sanctioned by Dore Schary, who was then in mortal combat with Louis B. Mayer for control of MGM production. It failed and Mayer was delighted. He had argued all along that his choice of the traditional tale would be more broadly accepted by the viewing public. Mayer launched his own production of QUO VADIS in 1950, naming Zimbalist as its producer and entrusting the direction to LeRoy. But LeRoy soon discovered that haphazard techniques had not improved in Italy. The Italian technicians little realized that four times the light was necessary for color photography and they ruined many of LeRoy's setups with the wrong lighting arrangements. Moreover, the director later remembered: "When the cameras turned over for the first time, they went backwards. They had put the switches in wrong. I never forgot that." His crowd scenes were next-to-impossible to manage but somehow he did. Only the lions were uncooperative. He let loose a dozen of the well-fed beasts into an arena crowded with 8,000 extras, among whom stood liontamers with loaded guns, ordered to shoot any lion that tried to eat an extra. But when the lions were let through the gate from the dark tunnel area where they had been kept, they stepped out cautiously into the huge arena and looked up at the burning sun and then retreated back into the tunnels. The liontamers advised LeRoy to "starve them for two weeks." LeRoy did, but had sleepless nights worrying about how to prevent the hungry beasts from devouring his extras. When he did let the lions loose again, the fierce beasts merely looked up at the glaring sun and then retreated into their tunnels. Now the liontamers had no advice at all, and were as mystified as LeRoy. The director finally conceived the idea of stuffing dummies dressed like the Christians with raw meat and letting the starving animals loose once more. This time the lions tore the dummies to pieces fighting for the food, but LeRoy had to keep his cameras at a distance and little of the footage was used in the finished film since authenticity suffered when the distantly shown dummies appeared to be just that as the savage lions dismembered them. The most colossal of many such scenes was the burning of Rome. Dozens of workmen labored for months to construct a four-block area of ancient-looking buildings and place two miles of iron pipe to hundreds of doorways and windows in the outdoor set, and through the pipe sending thousands of gallons of flammable liquid—gasoline, fuel oil, butane, naphthalene—to feed jets of fire and recreate the infamous conflagration. It took LeRoy and his Italian technicians 24 nights to burn down the Rome presented for his cameras where historically it took Nero six days. Incredibly, LeRoy, a master at handling crowds, moved his 2,000 extras through the fires without a single mishap. The scriptwriters not only coughed up some old scenes from the original silent offerings of this epic but borrowed heavily from Cecil B. DeMille's SIGN OF THE CROSS (1932). Fredric March in that film essays a Roman soldier not unlike the character later played by Taylor, and Charles Laughton's effeminate Nero in that spectacle was not lost on Ustinov. QUO VADIS (the title coming from a line uttered by Currie who sees a vision of the Lord and states: "Quo Vadis, Domine?"/"Whither goest Thou, Lord?") proved Mayer correct. The film shot in six months and costing almost $7 million, was an enormous box-office success, gleaning $25 million in world rentals and becoming the second all-time grosser after GONE WITH THE WIND. It led the way to even greater spectacles, including many mighty MGM epics starring Taylor, such as IVANHOE and KNIGHTS OF THE ROUND TABLE. Its success inspired Columbia to produce SALOME (1953) and 20th Century Fox to make DAVID AND BATHSHEBA (1951), THE ROBE (1953), and DEMETRIUS AND THE GLADIATORS (1954).

William Wyler's BEN-HUR, based on the same era and shot in Italy, would finally top QUO VADIS in box-office receipts. Aiding the enormous and sweeping epic is the fine score by Rozsa who, along with MGM librarian George Schneider, located every known instrument of the period amd studied them, bringing the music from the ancient world to the present. Although no clear record of that era's music remained, Rozsa pieced his score together through slave songs, Christian hymns, marches, and fanfares, using ancient instruments—harps and clarsachs—to conform to the sound of the ancient lyre. "For military music," he commented, "cornets, mixed with trumpets and trombones, gave the roughness of the early brass instuments. Bass flute and English horn replaced the sound of the aulos. Our modern percussion instruments come close to the antique ones and therefore it was safe to use tambourines, jingles, drums of different shapes and sizes, and cymbals. Bowed stringed instruments, however, could not be used...as they would have been completely anachronistic." Experts on statuary, costumes, and military uniforms were all brought in at great expense to duplicate the garb of the day.

There were so many thousands of extras in QUO VADIS that most actors claimed to have been in the crowd scenes and who is to dispute them? Sophia Loren and Elizabeth Taylor are somewhere in that swaying, moving mass of humanity, but who can find them?

p, Sam Zimbalist; d, Mervyn LeRoy; w, John Lee Mahin, S.N. Behrman, Sonya Levien (based on the novel by Henryk Sienkiewicz); ph, Robert Surtees, William V. Skall (Technicolor); m, Miklos Rozsa; ed, Ralph E. Winters; art d, William Horning, Cedric Gibbons, Edward Carfagno; set d, Hugh Hunt; cos, Herschel McCoy; ch, Marta Obolensky, Auriel Millos; spec eff, Thomas Howard, A. Arnold Gillespie, Donald Jahrnaus; historical adviser, Hugh Gray.

Historical Epic   **(PR:C   MPAA:NR)**

QUOI DE NEUF, PUSSYCAT?   (SEE: WHAT'S NEW, PUSSYCAT? 1965, U.S./Fr.)

R

R.P.M. zero   (1970) 92m COL c (AKA: R.P.M. (REVOLUTIONS PER MINUTE))

Anthony Quinn (*Prof. F.W.J. "Paco" Perez*), Ann-Margret (*Rhoda*), Gary Lockwood (*Rossiter*), Paul Winfield (*Steve Dempsey*), Graham Jarvis (*Police Chief Henry Thatcher*), Alan Hewitt (*Hewlett*), Ramon Bieri (*Brown*), John McLiam (*Rev. Blauvelt*), Don Keefer (*Dean Cooper*), Donald Moffat (*Perry Howard*), Norman Burton (*Coach McCurdy*), John Zaremba (*President Tyler*), Inez Pedroza (*Estella*), Teda Bracci, Lindo Meiklejohn, Bruce Fleischer, David Ladd, John David Wilder, Bradjose, Raymond Cavaleri, Henry Brown, Jr., Frank Alesia, Robert Carricart, Jr. (*Students*).

Pathetic attempt by Kramer to explain the difficulties honest, sympathetic, hardworking college administrators had during the 1960s when irrational radicals tried to take over a school. Quinn stars as a well-liked, anti-establishment college professor, who sleeps with graduate student Ann-Margret on the side (boy, he's hip!), and suddenly finds himself thrown into the position of college president when a group of student radicals led by Lockwood and Winfield take over the school, forcing the current president to resign. Quinn is chosen by the administration because of his popularity with the students. He soon wins the students over with his easy, "laid back" style, and the radicals sit down to negotiations. Lockwood and Winfield present a list of twelve demands and Quinn manages to get nine of the list approved by the college board (the rest are deemed non-negotiable). Outraged that all the demands have not been met, Lockwood and his radicals threaten to destroy the college's new $2 million computer. Seeing no way to prevent disaster, Quinn finally gets fed up with these crazy kids (especially since they taunt him about his sexual inadequacy) and sends in the cops. This move totally disillusions the student body which has lost all respect for Quinn; they let him know it in a barrage of insults and jeers as he walks off by himself. The script by Erich Segal is as simple-minded and silly as the title (R.P.M. stands for Revolutions Per Minute, get it?), with Quinn horribly miscast and Ann-Margret downright laughable as the sexy graduate student.

p&d, Stanley Kramer; w, Erich Segal; ph, Michel Hugo (Eastmancolor); m, Barry DeVorzon, Perry Botkin, Jr.; ed, William A. Lyon; prod d, Robert Clatworthy; set d, George James Hopkins; cos, Moss Mabry; spec eff, Geza Gaspar; m/l, DeVorzon, Botkin, Jr., Melanie; makeup, Fred Phillips.

Drama   **(PR:C MPAA:R)**

RABBI AND THE SHIKSE, THE**   (1976, Israel) 90m Rolls Films International c (KUNI LEMEL IN TEL AVIV)

Mike Burstyn (*Kuny, Muni, Grandpa Kuni Lem*), Mandy Rice-Davies (*Marilyn Jones*), Zeev Berlinsky (*Reb Shimshon*), Tuvia Tishler, Zvi Lahat, Itamar Gurevich, Shlomo Rozmarin (*The Rabbi's Boys*), Daliah Gur (*Dvoirale*), Yoseph Bashi (*Ovadia Badiji*), Ronit Port (*Malca*).

Jewish comedy featuring Burstyn in a triple role. He plays the elderly grandfather who proposes to give his fortune to the first grandson who moves to Israel and marries a Jewish girl. The grandsons (also played by Burstyn) are opposites in temperament and personality. The timid one goes to school in Yeshiva and hopes that the local Rabbi will arrange a decent match for him. The other brother is a non-religious musician who is involved in a romance with Rice-Davies, a singer who is not Jewish, but plans to win the fortune anyhow. Aside from the ethnic idiosyncrasies, the material is no different from standard screwball comedies and relies on the usual mistaken identity gags for laughs. Perhaps the most interesting thing about the film is the appearance of featured *shikse* Rice-Davies, who attained fame as a participant in the John Profumo-Christine Keeler spy scandal in Britain in 1963. Profumo, then Britain's Minister of War, resigned after it became known that he had been intimate with Keeler—to whom he had been introduced by society osteopath-*cum*-procurer Stephen Ward, during a nude swimming-pool party—who had also been intimate with Evgeny "Honeybear" Ivanov, a Soviet embassy official and known spy who had asked Keeler to pump Profumo about nuclear warhead deliveries to West Germany. Rice-Davies, an attractive blonde associate of Ward, had shared an apartment with brunette Keeler. Her good looks gained her a good press; she sought a film career, and realized it in Israel. Profumo also had a connection with pictures: his wife is British actress Valerie Hobson.

p, Yair Pradelsky, Israel Ringel; d&w, Yoel Silberg; ph, Nissim Leon; m, Dov Seltzer; m/l, Seltzer, Amos Ettinger, Mike Burstyn.

Comedy   **(PR:A MPAA:NR)**

RABBIT, RUN*   (1970) 94m Solitaire-Worldcross/WB c

James Caan (*Rabbit Angstrom*), Anjanette Comer (*Ruth*), Jack Albertson (*Marty Tothero*), Melodie Johnson (*Lucy Eccles*), Henry Jones (*Mr. Angstrom*), Carmen Mathews (*Mrs. Springer*), Virginia Vincent (*Margaret*), Nydia Westman (*Mrs. Smith*), Marc Antony Van Der Nagel (*Nelson*), Josephine Hutchinson (*Mrs. Angstrom*), Don Keefer (*Mr. Springer*), Margot Stevenson (*Mrs. Tothero*), Sondra Scott (*Miriam Angstrom*), Ken Kercheval (*Barney*), Carrie Snodgress (*Janice Angstrom*), Arthur Hill (*Rev. Jack Eccles*), Joanne Helen Deane.

It took nearly 10 years to get John Updike's novel to the screen and it would have been better had they waited another 10, or maybe even 50. This is such a spotty picture, with scenes that waver from excellent to dismal, that one wonders who will take the responsibility, or the blame. Director Smight was so enraged when producer-writer Kreitsek recut the movie that he sought to have his name removed from the credits but was unsuccessful, so Smight bears the brunt. Caan is married to alcoholic Snodgress, who is carrying a child neither of them wants. Why she drinks is never explained, but being married to Caan is probably reason enough, as he is unskilled, never attended college, and lives in the memory of the day when he scored 28 points in the "Big Game" at Reading, Pennsylvania, High School. (This territory would be mined with greater effectiveness in Jason Miller's THAT CHAMPIONSHIP SEASON.) Caan and Snodgress have a quarrel and he exits to visit with Albertson, his basketball coach, a man now living on the edge of poverty. Albertson's solution to Caan's dissatisfaction is to introduce him to semi-pro hooker Comer. Caan moves in with Comer, then the family Episcopalian minister, Hill, tries to effect a reconciliation between Caan and Snodgress. Caan wants no part of it but Hill thinks a job might change his mind, so he arranges employment with Mathews, as her gardener. Caan eventually leaves Comer and returns to Snodgress when she gives birth. He stops running around and she ceases drinking, but their peace doesn't last long, as she begins to deny him sex. Arguments follow and he leaves. Snodgress reaches for the bottle and "accidentally" drowns their infant in the bath. Caan returns home but he is blamed by everyone for what happened, including his only ally, Albertson, who has since been decimated by a stroke. The baby is buried and Caan shouts that it wasn't his fault when everyone at the funeral fixes him with hatred in their eyes. Caan goes to see Comer, who is carrying yet another child in her womb (his) and she won't talk to him unless he agrees to shed Snodgress and make an honest woman of her. Caan says he will, but the next time he leaves Comer's apartment, ostensibly to go to the grocery, he takes off. Caan's performance is okay, Comer is dandy, and Snodgress (who was to score in DIARY OF A MAD HOUSEWIFE, which was made afterward, but released sooner) is convincing. Foul language, explicit sex, and no point of view make this a loser on most counts. Two songs: "Anything Happening?" (Ray Burton, Brian King, M.K. Gregory) and "Gonna Love Me" (Burton, G.K. Michael, sung by Inner Sense).

p, Howard B. Kreitsek; d, Jack Smight; w, Kreitsek (based on the novel by John Updike); ph, Philip Lathrop (Panavision, Technicolor); m, Ray Burton, Brian King; ed, Archie Marshek; md, Sonny Burke; art d, Alfred Sweeney; set d, Marvin March; makeup, Gordon Bau.

Drama   **(PR:O MPAA:R)**

RABBIT TEST*   (1978) 84m Laugh or Die/AE c

Billy Crystal (*Lionel*), Joan Prather (*Segoynia*), Alex Rocco (*Danny*), Doris Roberts (*Mrs. Carpenter*), Edward Ansara (*Newscaster*), Imogene Coca (*Mme. Marie*), Jane Connell (*Anthropologist*), Keene Curtis (*Dr. Lasse-Braun*), Norman Fell (*Segoynia's Father*), Fannie Flagg (*President's Wife*), Jack Fletcher (*The Pope*), Alice Ghostley (*Nurse Tunn*), George Gobel (*President of U.S.*), Roosevelt Grier (*Taxi Driver*), Paul Lynde (*Dr. Vidal*), Murray Matheson (*Dr. Lowell*), Roddy McDowall (*Gypsy Grandmother/Dr. Fishbind*), Sheree North (*Mystery Lady*), Tom Poston (*Minister*), Charlotte Rae (*Cousin Clare*), Joan Rivers (*2nd Nurse*), Sab Shimono (*Chinese Leader*), Mary Steelsmith (*Melody Carpenter*), Jimmy Walker (*Umbuto*), Larry Gelman.

Before director-writer Joan Rivers began this, she should have realized that the story had been done before and somewhat better by Frenchman Jacques Demy in the 1973 film, A SLIGHTLY PREGNANT MAN (also known as THE SINGLE MOST IMPORTANT EVENT SINCE MAN WALKED ON THE MOON). It's a series of one-liners about Crystal, who is engaged to Prather and becomes pregnant. Not her, *him*. This, of course, makes him a very well-known person in the eyes of the world, to the dismay of his mother, Roberts, who is a parody of every Jewish mother ever seen in movies. Along the way, the film takes shots at Poles, physicians, parenthood, motion pictures, religion (Fletcher portrays the Pope), politics (Gobel is the U.S. President, Flagg is the First Lady; How's that for a parlay?), homosexuals, obesity, and anything else Rivers might have had in her copious joke file. Rocco turns in a good performance as a former Vietnam veteran who is now an agent, and there are a few funny moments by nightclub comic Walker, footballer Grier, and improvisational comic Gelman. McDowall, Lynde, Matheson, Coca, Rae, Poston, and Ghostley are wasted. Despite the scathing reviews and bad word-of-mouth, the picture made lots of money, although Rivers gave up directing to do what she does does best. She has a cameo in the film, her husband produced it, and their teenage daughter, Melissa, gets credit as the associate producer, who, as Fred Allen once said, is "the only person in Hollywood who will associate with the producer."

p, Edgar Rosenberg; d, Joan Rivers; w, Rivers, Jay Redack; ph, Lucien Ballard (CFI Color); m, Mike Post, Peter Carpenter; ed, Stanford C. Allen; art d, Robert Kinoshita.

Comedy   **Cas.**   **(PR:C-O MPAA:PG)**

RABBIT TRAP, THE**   (1959) 72m Canon/UA bw

Ernest Borgnine (*Eddie Colt*), David Brian (*Everett Spellman*), Bethel Leslie (*Abby Colt*), Kevin Corcoran (*Duncan Colt*), June Blair (*Judy*), Christopher Dark (*Gerry*), Jeannette Nolan, Russell Collins, Don Rickles.

A dull tale of a common working man trying to change his oppressive life stars Borgnine as a devoted family man who takes his loving wife Leslie and son Corcoran on a well-deserved vacation after slaving away as a draftsman in bull-headed boss Brian's construction firm. When a special job arises, Borgnine is called back to the job by Brian, and the overworked draftsman reluctantly cuts the trip short. When Corcoran realizes they have not picked up a rabbit trap they had set while in the country, he demands that his father turn back and get it so that any poor rabbits that have been captured can be freed (this is what is known as a *symbol*, for those too dim to see the obvious). Brian, however, thinks Borgnine's request for one more day off to do this ridiculous, and makes him come back to work immediately. This finally spurs Borgnine to stand up for himself; he walks off the job to be true to his family. While the intentions and acting are good, the clumsily written material lacks any depth or subtlety.

p, Harry Kleiner; d, Philip Leacock; w, J.P. Miller; ph, Irving Glassberg; m, Jack Marshall; ed, Ted Kent; art d, Edward Carrere; cos, Bill Thomas.

Drama   (PR:A MPAA:NR)

RABBLE, THE½**   (1965, Jap.) 116m Toho/Frank Lee International c (GARAKUTA)

Somegoro Ichikawa (*Kanzaburo*), Yuriko Hoshi (*Midori*), Mayumi Ozora (*Makie*), Tadao Nakamaru, Ichiro Arishima.

Ichikawa is the son of a poor farmer who must sell himself to a wealthy merchant as a servant because his father's farm has been overrun and pillaged by feudal warlords. He is given the duty of caring for the parrot of one of the merchant's granddaughters. The parrot belongs to Hoshi, a shy and unassuming girl. Her ebullient sister Ozora, however, is being courted by both a samurai and a nobleman, and her grandfather arranges a cruise aboard his new ship with both the suitors as his guests. On board are both granddaughters and a full complement of servants including Ichikawa. At sea, the small troupe encounters a vicious storm and the ship sinks, leaving them stranded on a small island. The nobleman and samurai prove to be cowards, leaving Ishikawa to lead them to safety. Ozora suddenly finds this heretofore worthless servant interesting and she tries to seduce him. Ichikawa realizes that her attentions will wane once they get back to civilization (and besides, he's in love with her sister, Hoshi) so he ignores her advances. When help arrives, Ichikawa is left behind/ the samurai tricks him, forcing the resourceful servant to make his way back to civilization alone, though he knows that Hoshi will be waiting for him when he gets there. If the story sounds familiar, it's because the plot line is very close to that of James Barrie's play "The Admirable Crichton," released in movie form as PARADISE LAGOON (1957, British). Inagaki's film SAMURAI won an academy award as Best Foreign Film in 1955.

p, Tomoyuki Tanaka, Hiroshi Inagaki; d, Inagaki; w, Shintaro Mimura, Masato Ide, Inagaki; ph, Kazuo Yamada (Tohoscope, Eastmancolor); m, Ikuma Dan.

Drama   (PR:A MPAA:NR)

RABID   (1976, Can.) 91m Cinepix-Dibar/New World c (AKA: RAGE)

Marilyn Chambers (*Rose*), Frank Moore (*Hart Read*), Joe Silver (*Murray Cypher*), Howard Ryshpan (*Dr. Dan Keloid*), Patricia Gage (*Dr. Roxanne Keloid*), Susan Roman (*Mindy Kent*), J. Roger Periard (*Lloyd Walsh*), Lynne Deragon (*Nurse Louise*), Terry Schonblum (*Judy Glasberg*), Victor Desy (*Claude LaPointe*), Julie Anna (*Rita*), Gary McKeehan (*Smooth Eddy*), Terrence G. Ross (*Farmer*), Miguel Fernandes (*Man in Cinema*), Robert O'Ree (*Police Sergeant*), Greg Van Riel (*Young Man in Plaza*), Jerome Tiberghien (*Dr. Carl*), Allan Moyle (*Young Man in Lobby*), Richard Farrell (*Camper Man*), Jeannette Casanave (*Camper Woman*), Carl Wasserman (*Camper Child*), John Boylan (*Young Cop in Plaza*), Malcolm Nelthorpe (*Older Cop in Plaza*), Vlasta Vrana (*Cop at Clinic*), Kirk McColl (*Desk Sergeant*), Jack Messinger (*Policeman on Highway*), Yvon LeCompte (*Policeman*), Grant Lowe (*Trucker*), John Gilbert (*Dr. Royce Gentry*), Tony Angelo (*Dispatcher*), Peter McNeill (*Leader*), Una Kay (*Jackie*), Madeline Pageau (*Beatrice Owen*), Mark Walker (*Steve*), Bob Silverman (*Man in Hospital*), Monique Belisle (*Sheila*), Ron Mlodzik (*Man Patient*), Isabelle Lajeunesse (*Waitress*), Terry Donald (*Cook*), Louis Negin (*Maxim*), Bob Girolami (*Newscaster*), Harry Hill (*Stasiuk*), Kathy Keefler, Murray Smith (*Interviewers*), Marcel Fournier (*Cab Driver*), Valda Dalton (*Car Lady*), Riva Spier Cecile), Denis LaCroix (*Drunken Indian*), Sherman Maness (*Indian*), Basil Fitzgibbon *Crazy in Plaza*).

Canadian cult director David Cronenberg has fans as feverish as the title of this film, basically a remake of his THE PARASITE MURDERS (1974), but the actual results of his screenplays are less than brilliant. In this film Cronenberg once again explores sexually transmitted horror (another earlier and better film THEY CAME FROM WITHIN, ran over the same territory), but this time through none other than hardcore porno starlet Chambers, who made her non-porno debut here (she only takes her clothes off every three minutes or so in this one) as a woman seriously injured in a motorcycle accident. A local plastic surgeon uses the opportunity to experiment with some new skin grafts he's been developing, but somehow the surgery goes awry (the *somehow* in Cronenberg's films is always the weakest point), and soon Miss Chambers sports a grotesque, phallus-like organ in her armpit that sucks the blood out of her unsuspecting lovers (the original treatment of the film was entitled "Mosquito"). This soon leads to an epidemic that sweeps Montreal and turns its citizens into rabid, blood-seeking, sex-crazed monsters who drool green slime out of their mouths. Once again, Cronenberg's promising premise suffers from a lack of detail (the scripts get hopelessly muddled for those wanting clearer justification for the horors brought before our eyes) and an obsession with disgusting, visceral impact sequences, including a pointless, overindulgent car crash. His characters are nothing but cardboard cutouts whose reactions to these bizarre situations are laughable at best (Chambers kind of shrugs off her affliction). Cronenberg has been called the first horror film director to deal with *adult* horror (i.e. sex, sexually transmitted disease, etc., as opposed to your basic childhood fears) but his films are pseudo-intellectual exercises that lack any real adult insight or sympathy for the victims.

p, John Dunning; d&w, David Cronenberg; ph, Rene Verzier (Panavision, Eastmancolor); ed, Jean LaFleur; art d, Claude Marchand; cos, Erla Gliserman; spec eff, Al Griswold; makeup, Joe Blasco, Byrd Holland, Mireille Recton.

Horror   Cas.   (PR:O MPAA:R)

RACCONTI D'ESTATE   (SEE: LOVE ON THE RIVIERA, 1964, Fr./ Ital.)

RACE FOR LIFE, A½**   (1955, Brit.) 68m Hammer/Lippert bw (GB: MASK OF DUST)

Richard Conte (*Peter Wells*), Mari Aldon (*Pat Wells*), George Coulouris (*Dallapiccola*), Peter Illing (*Bellario*), Alex Mango (*Guido Rizetti*), Meredith Edwards (*Lawrence*), Jimmy Copeland (*Johnny*), Jeremy Hawk (*Martin*), Richard Marner (*Brecht*), Edwin Richfield (*Gibson*), Tim Turner (*Alverez*), Stirling Moss, Reg Parnell, John Cooper, Alan Brown, Geoffrey Taylor.

Typical story line starring Conte as a former world-class car racer who goes to Europe to make a comeback after the war, despite the protestations of his wife Aldon. He joins an Italian team, and Aldon leaves him when he refuses to give up racing. By the time the Grand Prix rolls around, however, Aldon returns to see him win the race and then retire into her arms. Conte proves his point. A man's gotta do what a man's gotta do.

p, Michael Carreras, Mickey Delamar; d, Terence Fisher; w, Richard Landau, Paul Tabori (based on a novel by Jon Manchip White); ph, Jimmy Harvey; m, Leonard Salzedo; ed, Bill Lenny; art d, Jim Elder Wills.

Drama   (PR:A MPAA:NR)

RACE FOR YOUR LIFE, CHARLIE BROWN½**   (1977) 75m PAR c

Voices: Duncan Watson, Greg Felton, Stuart Brotman, Gail Davis, Liam Martin, Kirk Jue, Jordan Warren, Jimmy Ahrens, Melanie Kohn, Tom Muller, Bill Melendez, Fred Van Amburg.

The third animated feature film starring Charles Schulz's popular "Peanuts" characters sees the gang at a summer camp and details their various misadventures, including a harrowing raft race against "the bullies" down a raging river. The animation is no better than competent, but the film has a nice bluegrass-style musical score by Ed Bogas and should be fine for the kiddies and "Peanuts" fans.

p, Lee Mendelson, Bill Melendez; d, Melendez, Phil Roman; w, Charles M. Schulz (based on the "Peanuts" characters by Schulz); ph, Dickson/Vasu (Metrocolor); m, Ed Bogas; ed, Chuck McCann, Roger Donley, Alice Keillor; m/l, "Race for Your Life, Charley Brown," Bogas (sung by Larry Finlayson), "The Greatest Leader," Bogas, Mendelson, "Charmine," Erno Rapee, Lew Pollack, "She'll Be Comin' Round the Mountain," traditional; animation, Don Lusk, Bob Matz, Hank Smith, Rod Scribner, Ken O'Brien, Al Pabian, Joe Roman, Jeff Hall, Sam Jaimes, Bob Bachman, George Singer, Bill Littlejohn, Bob Carlson, Patricia Joy, Terry Lennon, Larry Leichliter.

Animation   Cas.   (PR:AAA MPAA:G)

RACE GANG   (SEE: GREEN COCKATOO, THE, 1947, Brit.)

RACE STREET½**   (1948) 79m RKO bw

George Raft (*Dan Gannin*), William Bendix (*Runson*), Marilyn Maxwell (*Robbie*), Frank Faylen (*Phil Dickson*), Henry "Harry" Morgan (*Hal Towers*), Gale Robbins (*Elaine Gannin*), Cully Richards (*Mike Hadley*), Mack Gray (*Stringy*), Russell Hicks (*Easy Mason*), Tom Keene (*Al*), William Forrest (*Nick Waters*), Jim Nolan (*Herbie*), George Turner (*Dixie*), Richard Benedict (*Sam*), Dean White (*Big Jack*), Freddie Steele (*Monty*), Mike Lally, Eddie Arden, Franklyn Farnum, George Murray (*Men*), Sam McDaniel (*Garage Attendant*), Hercules Mendes (*Chef*), Carl Saxe (*Detective*), Reg Billado (*Clerk*), Steven Flagg (*Clerk*), Artane Wong (*Gannin's Houseboy*), Mickey Martin (*Elevator Operator*), Edna Ryan (*Receptionist*), Charmienne Harker, Joan Myles (*Cigarette Girls*), George Goodman (*Waiter at Turf Club*), Oliver Cross (*Headwaiter at Turf Club*), Frank Scannell (*Burnside*), June Pickrell (*Woman*), Jane Woland (*Hat Check Girl*), George Chandler (*Herman*), Michael Wallace (*Headwaiter at Billy's*), Jason Robards, Sr. (*Desk Clerk*), Al Rhein (*Johnson*), Robert Dudley (*Pop*), Charles Lane (*Desk Clerk at Robbie's Apartment Building*), Cy Kendall (*Fatty Parker*), James Bush (*Male Nurse*), Mary Kent (*Nurse*), Al Murphy (*Drunk*), Barry Brooks (*Intern*).

San Francisco bookmaker Raft decides to abandon his lucrative life of crime and go straight. His plan includes a marriage proposal to Maxwell, the widow of a WW II hero. Raft's blissful retirement is interrupted, however, when he learns that his pal, Morgan, a fellow bookie, has been murdered by East Coast mobsters trying to start a protection racket. Vowing revenge, Raft decides to smash the gang by himself. Enter Bendix, Raft's boyhood friend who is now a police detective. Bendix tries to convince Raft that joining forces with him would hasten justice. Distrustful of Bendix and still operating on the underworld ethic (i.e., he's no stool pigeon), Raft refuses to work with the cop and sets out on his own. Thinking that Maxwell is the only person he can trust, he is shocked to learn that his girl is actually married to the head of the mob, Faylen, and has been funneling information to him. Realizing now that Bendix was right, Raft agrees to help the police. Together the men manage to expose the hoods, but during a violent fistfight with them, Raft sees Bendix about to be shot by a gangster and sacrifices his life for his friend. Raft dies knowing that his friend Morgan has been avenged. This is an average crime film which sees Raft in a genuinely sympathetic light. Though firmly entrenched in the underworld, albeit a nonviolent area of it, Raft is shown to be an honorable, loyal friend whose heart is in the right place. Though he tries to change his life, he cannot abandon those ties which made him rich. Fate, and Hollywood, insist he die for his crimes in the end, despite the fact he wasn't such a bad guy. RACE STREET came during the decline of Raft's career. In his early 50s, the actor found his popularity with the public and studios waning. Though his name was still a box-office draw, he had fallen from superstar status and was forced to work for low-budget independent producers. Considered by Hollywood and the public as a leftover icon of the 1930s, Raft had trouble moving on to new territory like his contemporaries Edward G. Robinson, Humphrey Bogart, and James Cagney had done. In fact, Raft's costar in RACE STREET, Bendix, got the better notices from critics while Raft's performance was practically dismissed. In the next few years allegations of Raft's involvement with real-life mobsters would throw more water on the smoldering ashes of his movie career.

p, Nat Holt; d, Edwin L. Marin; w, Martin Rackin (suggested by the story "The Twisted Road" by Maurice Davis); ph, J. Roy Hunt; m, Roy Webb; ed, Sam E. Beetley; md, C. Bakaleinikoff; art d, Albert S. D'Agostino, Walter E. Keller; set d, Darrell Silvera, William Stevens; cos, Edward Stevenson; spec eff, Russell A. Cully; ch, Charles O'Curran; m/l, "Love That Boy," Don Ray, Gene DePaul (sung by Gale Robbins, Cully Richards), "I'm in a Jam with Baby" Ray Heindorf, Ted Koehler, M.K. Jerome.

Crime   (PR:C MPAA:NR)

RACE WITH THE DEVIL**½   (1975) 88m FOX c

Peter Fonda (*Roger*), Warren Oates (*Frank*), Loretta Swit (*Alice*), Lara Parker (*Kelly*), R.G. Armstrong (*Sheriff*), Clay Tanner (*Delbert*), Carol Blodgett (*Ethel*), Ricci Ware (*Ricci Ware*), James N. Harrell (*Gun Shop Owner*), Paul A. Partain (*Cal Mathers*), Karen Miller (*Kay*), Arkey Blue (*Arkey Blue*), Jack Starrett (*Gas Station Attendant*), Phil Hoover (*Mechanic*), Wes Bishop (*Deputy Dave*), Bob Jutson, Peggy Kokernot, Carol Cannon, Tommy Splittberger.

Fairly effective action film starring Fonda, Parker, Oates, and Swit as two married couples who go to Texas in a large camper. The first night out they accidentally stumble upon a cult of Devil worshipers, and witness a human sacrifice. When the vacationers try to escape, the Satanists give chase. The rest of the film features an incredible, lengthy action sequence which sees the members of the cult leaping onto the moving camper from pick-up trucks and cars, trying to get inside to kill the two couples. The chase sequence is exceptionally well done and bears a remarkable resemblance to the climactic chase scene in THE ROAD WARRIOR, where the crazed desert rats leap onto Mel Gibson's gasoline tanker in an effort to stop him. The scenes are similar enough in style and execution that THE ROAD WARRIOR's director, George Miller, must have seen RACE WITH THE DEVIL, and been inspired by it.

p, Wes Bishop; d, Jack Starrett; w, Bishop, Lee Frost; ph, Robert Jessup (DeLuxe Color); m, Leonard Rosenman; ed, Allan Jacobs; spec eff, Richard Helmer.

Drama   **Cas.**   (PR:C MPAA:PG)

RACERS, THE***   (1955) 112m FOX c (GB: SUCH MEN ARE DANGEROUS)

Kirk Douglas (*Gino*), Bella Darvi (*Nicole*), Gilbert Roland (*Dell 'Oro*), Cesar Romero (*Carlos*), Lee J. Cobb (*Maglio*), Katy Jurado (*Maria*), Charles Goldner (*Piero*), John Hudson (*Michel Caron*), George Dolenz (*Count Salem*), Agnes Laury (*Toni*), John Wengraf (*Dr. Tabor*), Richard Allan (*Pilar*), Francesco de Scaffa (*Chata*), Norbert Schiller (*Dehlgreen*), Mel Welles (*Fiori*), Gene D'Arcy (*Rousillon*), Mike Dengate (*Dell 'Oro's Mechanic*), Peter Brocco (*Gatti*), Stephen Bekassy (*Race Official*), June McCall (*Red-Haired Girl*), Frank Yaconelli (*Luigi*), Ina Anders (*Janka*), Gladys Holland (*Nurse*), Ben Wright (*Dr. Seger*), James Barrett (*Intern*), Chris Randall (*Teen-Age Mechanic*), Anna Cheselka (*Ballerina*), Joe Vitale (*Dr. Bocci*), Salvador Baguez (*Doorman*), Eddie LeBaron (*Race Official*), Peter Norman (*Cashier*), George Givot (*Baron*), Carleton Young (*Race Announcer*).

Fans of European-style road racing will appreciate this far more than the average viewer because it is an authentic look at the lives of those daredevils who make their way around the tracks of France, Italy, and Germany. Very exciting racing footage almost overcomes the slim story and there is, perhaps, too much of it, as it begins to pall somewhere just after the middle of the movie. Douglas is an ambitious Italian bus driver who yearns to be a champion racer and will stop at nothing to achieve that goal. He meets ballerina Darvi and she is fascinated by him. (In the novel she's a fresh, young graduate of an exclusive school and they get married at the finale. Here, she is a dancer and they just live together. A dubious switch.) In no time, she is his mistress despite his telling her that loving him will only bring her pain and sorrow. With her money to back him, Douglas gets a car and wins a big race. Once he's acknowledged as a major driver, he is soon part of the coterie of top dogs in the business, a group that includes Roland and Romero. Douglas goes on the regular tour and wins some and loses some until he's hurt in a crash in Switzerland, nearly suffering a leg amputation. The next year finds him on crutches but still following the tour. Roland needs a co-driver for Le Mans and Douglas signs on. Roland is burned when gasoline explodes during a pit stop and Douglas takes over the wheel, winning the race. He moves up in class and is now ranked fourth but his ruthlessness soon loses the respect of his fellow drivers. Darvi sees the change in him and leaves to reenter her ballet world. Little by little, Douglas' career goes into eclipse until he learns through a pal that Darvi still loves him. He tracks her down and professes his affection, but she fears his alternating personality and won't come back. Douglas goes to Italy to race, and even though he has a chance to win, he gives up that opportunity to save Roland, who has been injured. In the crowd at the race is Darvi and she now knows that he's a changed man, as he climbs back into his car to complete the competition which, by now, has passed him by. It is hoped that they will get together after the race and reawaken their love. Cobb is perfect as the racing manager and Goldner is a standout as Douglas' mechanic. This was Darvi's final U.S. movie.

p, Julian Blaustein; d, Henry Hathaway; w, Charles Kaufman (based on the novel by Hans Ruesch); ph, Joe MacDonald (CinemaScope, DeLuxe Color); m, Alex North; ed, James B. Clark; md, Lionel Newman; art d, Lyle Wheeler, George Patrick; spec eff, Ray Kellogg; m/l, "I Belong to You," North (sung by Peggy Lee); technical advisors, John Fitch, Phil Hill, E. de Graffenried.

Sports/Drama   (PR:A MPAA:NR)

RACETRACK**   (1933) 79m World Wide bw

Leo Carrillo (*Joe Tomasso*), Junior Coghlan (*Jackie*), Kay Hammond (*Myra Curtis*), Lee Moran ("*Horseface*"), Huntley Gordon (*Attorney*), Wilfred Lucas (*Mr. Ryan*), Joseph Girard (*Judge*), Dick Pritchard.

Fairly maudlin drama starring Carrillo as a somewhat crooked gambler who finds himself turning to the straight-and-narrow after "adopting" youngster Coghlan who was caught hanging around the racing stables. Learning that the boy is an orphan, Carrillo takes the kid's interest in horses and trains him to be a jockey. When the boy's real mom, Hammond, arrives, she falls in love with Carrillo and begs him to stop Coghlan from racing. Seeing that the kid needs his mom more than the ponies, Carrillo arranges for Coghlan to be disqualified before the big race, reuniting him with Hammond and hinting that he'll soon be the boy's real dad.

p&d, James Cruze; w, Walter Lang, Douglas Doty, Gaston Glass, Claire Carvalho, Ernest Pagano (based on a story by J. Walter Ruben, Wells Root); ph, Charles Schoenbaum; ed, Rose E. Loewinger.

Drama   (PR:A MPAA:NR)

RACHEL AND THE STRANGER***   (1948) 93m RKO bw

Loretta Young (*Rachel*), William Holden (*Big Davey Harvey*), Robert Mitchum (*Jim Fairways*), Gary Gray (*Little Davey*), Tom Tully (*Parson Jackson*), Sara Haden (*Mrs. Jackson*), Frank Ferguson (*Mr. Green*), Walter Baldwin (*Callus*), Regina Wallace (*Mrs. Green*), Frank Conlan (*Jabez*).

Mitchum had just been busted on his famous marijuana charge and the studio, wanting to take advantage of the publicity (albeit unfavorable), rushed this movie into the theaters. It did very well, turned a profit, and showed another side of Mitchum as he twanged a guitar and sang a few tunes. Mitchum would never be a singing star but he did make a Calypso record album later that had "Laugh-In" producer George Schlatter's wife, Jolene, on the cover, which was the best thing about the album. Immediately following this movie, RKO production boss Dore Schary left for greener pastures at MGM. It's a pleasant film and unreels a trifle slowly in the first half, then has a smashing action sequence. It's the early 1800s on the frontier of the Great Northwest. Holden is a widower who feels that he can't raise his son, Gray, without the aid of a female around the farm, so he goes to a nearby town and buys Young, a woman who is a servant. For the sake of chatterboxes, he marries the woman but the union is loveless and sexless and she is a combination nanny-maid. Gray resists her, as he misses his dead mother and Young can not be an adequate substitute. The same thing holds true for Holden, who lives in the glow of memory. Mitchum, a happy-go-lucky scout, enters and sees that neither Holden or Gray pays much attention to Young, so he begins to court her, which makes Holden jealous. Holden asks Mitchum to leave and Mitchum counters by offering to buy Young. She learns of this and exits angrily back to the town from whence she came. Mitchum, Holden, and Gray rush off after her and vainly attempt to change her mind. There's an Indian attack and all four race to Holden's cabin where they manage to fight off the tribe until they are saved by rescuers. Watching this, Mitchum realizes that Young's place is with Holden and Gray, so he moseys out and leaves them to remain as a family. There are similarities between this tale and PAINT YOUR WAGON that can't be overlooked. Screenwriter Salt, who would later win an Oscar for adapting MIDNIGHT COWBOY, wrote the tunes with composer Webb. They include "Just Like Me," "Foolish Pride," and "Oh He, Oh Hi, Oh Ho" (sung by Mitchum), "Summer Song," and "Tall, Dark Stranger" (sung by Young and Mitchum as duets). With five tunes, it's darn close to a musical. Lots of comedy, warmth, action, and human interest and deftly directed by former actor Foster, the movie is an amiable western with more than something extra. Mitchum gives one of his rare performances that doesn't appear to be under the influence of torpor.

p, Richard H. Berger; d, Norman Foster; w, Waldo Salt (based on the stories "Rachel" and "Neighbor Sam" by Howard Fast); ph, Maury Gertsman; m, Roy Webb; ed, Les Milbrook; md, Constantin Bakaleinikoff; art d, Albert S. D'Agostino, Walter E. Keller, Jack Okey; set d, Darrell Silvera, John Sturtevant; cos, Edith Head; spec eff, Russell A. Cully; makeup, Gordon Bau.

Western/Comedy   **Cas.**   (PR:A MPAA:NR)

RACHEL CADE   (SEE: SINS OF RACHEL CADE, THE, 1960)

RACHEL, RACHEL***½   (1968) 101m Kayos/WB c

Joanne Woodward (*Rachel Cameron*), James Olson (*Nick Kazlik*), Kate Harrington (*Mrs. Cameron*), Estelle Parsons (*Calla Mackie*), Donald Moffatt (*Niall Cameron*), Terry Kiser (*Preacher*), Frank Corsaro (*Hector Jonas*), Bernard Barrow (*Leighton Siddley*), Geraldine Fitzgerald (*Rev. Wood*), Nell Potts (*Rachel as a Child*), Shawn Campbell (*James*), Violet Dunn (*Verla*), Izzy Singer (*Lee Shabab*), Tod Engle (*Nick as a Child*), Bruno Engle (*Bartender*), Beatrice Pons, Dorothea Duckworth, Simm Landres, Connie Robinson, Sylvia Shipman, Larry Fredericks, Wendell MacNeal.

Woodward, Parsons, Stewart Stern's screenplay, and the picture itself were all nominated for Oscars and Newman and Woodward both won awards from the New York Film Critics. While other directors were impressing with their flash and technique in the 1960s, Newman chose to make a small, understated, and very sensitive film as his directorial debut. It was sometimes halting and quite spare but the overall effect was excellent and business was meritorious, something no one expected. Newman had trouble securing the financing and was saved by then-production chief Ken Hyman (who later moved to England to live in baronial splendor outside London), a man with some foresight who recognized the need for this kind of story. Shot on location at various Connecticut sites, it was a departure for Woodward, who had been made into a glamor girl in her early years and resented that. In her thirties at this point, she began an entirely new career and proved that her Oscar for THE THREE FACES OF EVE was not a fluke. Woodward is a 35-year-old spinster and virgin who lives with her widowed mother, Harrington, in a small apartment above the funeral parlor once owned by her late father and now run by Corsaro. She is a teacher who feels that there is nothing left to live for and is constantly questioning why she was ever born. (This is more covert than overt.) Every day is like the day before. She has to look after Harrington and teach the snot-noses at the school and there is virtually no fun in her life. Woodward's best friend is Parsons, another old maid in much the same circumstance.

Searching for a meaning in life, Parsons asks Woodward to accompany her to a revival meeting run by Fitzgerald. When a visiting evangelist, Kiser, takes the pulpit and pounds it, Woodward is surprised to find herself caught up in the emotionalism of the moment. Later, Parsons makes what has to be termed a "pass" at Woodward, which makes her realize that she had better find out what men are like before she falls into a homosexual pattern. Woodward is sexually naive, frustrated, and willing to learn, so when Olson, a childhood friend, comes back to the small town to visit his parents, she is easy for him to seduce. Woodward doesn't know the difference between lust and love and her brief sexual freedom with Olson causes her to become emotionally involved. Olson is frightened by her intensity and lies, telling her that he's married. When that doesn't matter to Woodward, Olson ends the relationship. Woodward thinks she may be pregnant and is secretly delighted and plans to have the child. When her pregnancy turns out to be a minor ovarian cyst (which is the reason for the book's title, A Jest of God), Woodward is disappointed but she pulls herself together and plans to make a new start. Woodward and Harrington take off for Oregon where Woodward hopes she can get out of her doldrums and begin again. The significance of the film's title is even more intriguing because Newman uses his and Woodward's daughter, Nell Potts, to be the young Rachel, so the image of Woodward is occasionally replaced by Potts to indicate that the child in her still remains. Woodward and Harrington climb on the bus that will take them to Oregon, and Woodward waves farewell to Potts, finally bidding goodbye to the child she's been. In later years, there would be a horde of "women's pictures," but this one was the first in the cycle and one of the best. It could have been a drab, weepy story but Stern and Newman collaborated to make it inspiring and proof that one is never too old to change one's life.

p&d, Paul Newman; w, Stewart Stern (based on the novel A Jest of God by Margaret Laurence); ph, Gayne Rescher (Technicolor); m, Jerome Moross, Erik Satie, Robert Schumann; ed, Dede Allen; md, Moross; art d, Robert Gundlach; set d, Richard Merrell; cos, Domingo Rodriguez; m/l, Moross, Stern; makeup, Bob Philippe.

Drama   **Cas.**   **(PR:A-C MPAA:R)**

RACING BLOOD zero   (1938) 61m Conn bw

Frankie Darro (Frankie Reynolds), Kane Richmond (Clay Harrison), Gladys Blake (Phyllis Reynolds), Arthur Housman (Legs), Jimmie Eagles (Smokey Reynolds), Matthew Betz (Tex O'Donnell), Si Wills (Dopey), Snowflake (Sad Sam), Bob Tansill (Magnus), Jones Quintet (Singers).

A thoroughly unbelievable horse race film that plays like the climactic moments in a serial. Darro stars as a budding young jockey, who rescues a crippled horse from the glue factory and nurses it back to health. He does such a good job that the horse is soon fit enough to compete in a major thoroughbred race. Unfortunately Darro is kidnaped, but manages to escape by beating up his kidnapers. With a gunshot wound in his chest, Darro steals the ambulance which was taking him to the hospital, and speeds off to the track for the big race. He gets to the gate in the nick of time, despite the fact that he has not weighed in, paraded his pony, or received a slot in the starting gate. He simply trots off down the track and wins the race. Not only is the film ridiculous, but unfortunately the technical incompetence is a good match for the screenplay's failures.

p, Maurice A. Conn; d, Rex Hale; w, Stephen Norris (based on a story by Peter B. Kyne); ph, Robert Doran, William Hyer, Jack Greenhalgh; ed, Martin G. Cohn; m/l, "Lucky Shoes," "You're So Appealing," Connie Lee, Tommy Reilly (sung by Snowflake and the Jones Quintet).

Drama   **(PR:A MPA:NR)**

RACING BLOOD*½   (1954) 75m FOX c

Bill Williams (Tex), Jean Porter (Lucille), Jimmy Boyd (David), George Cleveland (Gramps), John Eldredge (Mitch), Sam Flint (Doc Nelson), Fred Kohler, Jr. (Emerson), George Steele (Wee Willie), Bobby Johnson (Mullins), Frankie Darro (Jockey Ben), Fred Kelsey.

Boyd plays a young stable boy who adopts a colt born with a split hoof and about to be destroyed by its owners. While the trainers are busy with the colt's perfect twin brother, Boyd's grandfather, the stable handyman, pretends to shoot the misshapen pony and turns it over to the kid. Boyd nurses the mutant colt back to health and he trains the animal to compete against his healthier brother, on whom the stable pins hopes of big winnings. At the big race, Boyd's pony outruns its brother and wins the cup. In between groomings, Boyd finds time to croon the ever popular race track songs "Fa-La-Link-A-Di-Do" and "Pardners."

p&d, Wesley Barry; w, Sam Roeca (based on a story by Roeca, Barry); ph, John Martin (Super Cinecolor); m, Edward J. Kay; ed, Ace Herman.

Drama   **(PR:A MPAA:NR)**

RACING FEVER zero   (1964) 90m AA c

Joe Morrison (Lee Gunner), Charles G. Martin (Gregg Stevenson), Barbara G. Biggart (Connie Stevenson), Maxine Carroll (Linda Gunner), Dave Blanchard (Pop Gunner), Ruth Nadel (Martha Stevenson), John Vella (Johnny), Martha Coastworth (Dancer), Rose Stone (TV Announcer), Ben Hawkins (Mechanic), Perry Mavrelis (Richard Thompson), Tony Gulliver (Man in Bar), Patty Morrison (Waitress), Gerry Granahan.

Another shot-in-Florida exploitation drama from low-budget producer-director William Grefe. This one details the exciting and dangerous world of hydroplane racing and stars Morrison, who witnesses his father's death when millionaire playboy and reckless boater Martin runs his old man down during the International Gran Prix boat race. Morrison travels to the millionaire's home for a confrontation (he knows where it is because his sister Carroll is Martin's mistress), but falls in love with his enemy's daughter Biggart instead, and they decide to marry. Soon after, Carroll catches her millionaire lover in bed with an exotic dancer and announces that she is pregnant and wants to marry. Martin couldn't care less, which enrages Carroll and she shoots him after her brother saved the scum's life in another hydroplane race. Awful, but amusing.

p,d&w, William Grefe; ph, Julio C. Chavez (Eastmancolor); ed, Oscar Barber; m/l, Al Jacobs, Title song, Jacobs (sung by Gerry Granahan); stunts, Ron Von Klausen; makeup, Carlos Perez, Francisca Perez.

Drama   **(PR:C MPAA:NR)**

RACING LADY*½   (1937) 59m RKO bw

Ann Dvorak (Ruth Martin), Smith Ballew (Steven Wendel), Harry Carey (Tom Martin), Berton Churchill (Judge), Frank M. Thomas (Bradford), Ray Mayer (Warbler), Willie Best (Brass), Hattie McDaniel (Abby), Harry Jans (Lewis), Lew Payton (Joe), Harlan Tucker (Gilbert), Alex Hill.

Pretty weak horse race meller starring Dvorak as a professional horse trainer, hired by cynical millionaire Ballew to train his latest purchase. Dvorak and Ballew nearly strike up a romance, but Dvorak begins to realize that the millionaire has no real sense of honor and cares little about his horse, a mere purchase that will provide more publicity for his auto building business. Dvorak struggles painfully against the histrionic performance of Ballew, who made his film debut here after a successful career in radio. Unfortunately, Ballew performs as if he were still on the radio and was unaware of the visual aspects of the film medium.

p, William Sistrom; d, Wallace Fox; w, Dorothy Yost, Thomas Lennon, Cortland Fitzsimmons (based on the stories "All Scarlet" by Damon Runyon, and "Odds Are Even" by J. Robert Bren, Norman Houston); ph, Harry Wild; ed, James Morley; m/l, "Sweeter All the Time," Andy Iona Long, Lysle Tomerlin.

Drama   **(PR:A MPAA:NR)**

RACING LUCK*½   (1935) 59m REP bw

Bill Boyd (Dan), Barbara Worth (June), George Ernest (Jimmy), Esther Muir (Elaine), Ernest Hilliard (Walter), Onest Conley (Mose), Ben Hall (Knapsack), Henry Roquemore (Tuttle), Dick Curtis (Dynamite), Ted Caskey (Secretary).

Boyd is a horse trainer whose prize horse takes first place in a big race, only to be disqualified when drugs are discovered in its system. Though Boyd is innocent, he is suspended from racing for a year, granting him the time he needs to learn the identity of the real culprit. He's finally able to enter his horse in another race, taking second place to a horse named Carnation. He is given the first place money when he proves Carnation is actually another horse illegally entered in the race.

p, George Herliman; d, Sam Newfield; w, Jack O'Donnell, George Sayre; ph, Edgar Lyons; ed, Charles Hunt.

Drama/Crime   **(PR:A MPAA:NR)**

RACING LUCK, 1935   (SEE: RED HOT TIRES, 1935)

RACING LUCK zero   (1948) 66m COL bw

Gloria Henry (Phyllis Warren), Stanley Clements (Boots Warren), David Bruce (Jeff Stuart), Paula Raymond (Natalie Gunther), Harry Cheshire (Radcliffe Malone), Dooley Wilson (Abe), Jack Ingram (George), Nelson Leigh (Hendricks), Bill Cartledge (Joe), Syd Saylor (Pete).

Wretchedly produced racing film which is nothing but a tedious series of horse races with a bit of human interest thrown in. The cast struggles mightily with the slim material, but the odds were against them the moment they came out of the starting gate.

p, Sam Katzman; d, William Berke; w, Joseph Carole, Al Martin, Harvey Gates; ph, Ira H. Morgan; ed, Henry Batista; md, Mischa Bakaleinikoff; art d, Paul Palmentola; set d, David Montrose; m/l, Dooley Wilson, Elliot Carpenter.

Drama   **(PR:A MPAA:NR)**

RACING ROMANCE**   (1937, Brit.) 63m Greenspan and Seligman/RKO bw

Bruce Seton (Harry Stone), Marjorie Taylor (Peggy Lanstone), Eliot Makeham (George Hanway), Sybil Grove (Mrs. Hanway), Elizabeth Kent (Muriel Hanway), Ian Fleming (Martin Royce), Robert Hobbs (James Archer), Charles Sewell (Mr. Lanstone), Michael Ripper, Jonathan Field.

Seton plays a garage owner who is convinced by his selfish fiancee (Kent) to buy a race horse. He purchases Brownie from Taylor and after she trains the horse it is entered in the Oaks (a distinguished race). The horse finishes second and Kent is so disgusted that she leaves Seton, who promptly marries Taylor. After an official investigation, Brownie is declared to be the winner. Okay performances but nothing new.

p, A. George Smith; d, Maclean Rogers; w, John Hunter; ph, Geoffrey Faithfull.

Comedy   **(PR:A MPAA:NR)**

RACING STRAIN, THE*   (1933) 64m Irving/Maxim bw

Wally Reid, Jr., Dickie Moore, Paul Fix, Eddie Phillips, Otto Yama, J. Frank Glendon, Phyllis Barrington, J. Farrell MacDonald, Ethel Wales, Mae Busch, Lorin Raker, Jimmy Burtis, Kit Guard, Donald Reed.

Reid plays a 16 year old terrified of automobiles after witnessing his father's death in an auto racing crash. Inexplicably, the kid has no problem flying airplanes and proves himself to be a crackerjack stunt pilot. In the end he overcomes his fear of auto racing, enters the big race, and wins, in memory of his father.

p, Willis Kent; d, Jerome Storm; w, Betty Burbridge, Kent (based on a story by Mrs. Wallace Reid); ph, William Nobles; ed, Ethel Davey.

Drama   **(PR:A MPAA:NR)**

RACING YOUTH* (1932) 62m UNIV bw

Frank Albertson *(Teddy Blue)*, June Clyde *(Amelia Cruikshank)*, Louise Fazenda *(Daisy Joy)*, Slim Summerville *(Slim)*, Arthur Stuart Hull *(Brown)*, Forrest Stanley *(Sanford)*, Eddie Phillips *(Van)*, Otis Harlan *(Dave)*.

Albertson is the spunky auto designer of a firm owned by Clyde (her father left her the company). The company is in trouble if it doesn't win the upcoming race, and an unscrupulous manager tries to ruin the firm by disapproving of the car's design. Albertson jumps into action, redesigns the car in time to enter the race, and drives it himself to the finish line, saving the company.

d, Vin Moore; w, Earle Snell; ph, George Robinson.

Drama **(PR:A MPAA:NR)**

RACK, THE½** (1956) 100m MGM bw

Paul Newman *(Capt. Edward W. Hall, Jr.)*, Wendell Corey *(Maj. Sam Moulton)*, Walter Pidgeon *(Col. Edward W. Hall, Sr.)*, Edmond O'Brien *(Lt. Col. Frank Wasnick)*, Anne Francis *(Aggie Hall)*, Lee Marvin *(Capt. John R. Miller)*, Cloris Leachman *(Caroline)*, Robert Burton *(Col. Ira Hansen)*, Robert Simon *(Law Officer)*, Trevor Bardette *(Court President)*, Adam Williams *(Sgt. Otto Pahnke)*, James Best *(Millard Chilson Cassidy)*, Fay Roope *(Col. Dudley Smith)*, Barry Atwater *(Maj. Byron Phillips)*, Charles Evans *(General)*, Mary McAdoo *(Cooking Program Woman)*, Byron Kane, Willard Sage *(Announcers)*, David Blair *(Student)*, Ray Stricklyn *(Ryson)*, Lois Kimbrell *(Army Nurse)*, Rod Taylor *(Al)*, Dean Jones *(Lieutenant)*, Bobby Blake *(Italian Soldier)*, Frank Mills *(Courtroom Spectator)*.

With so many excellent TV plays being written by Paddy Chayefsky, Horton Foote, and Rod Serling, it's no wonder that the studios turned to the tube to make some films. In this case, it's an expanded version of a court-martial teleplay Serling wrote. Stern, who was later to write RACHEL, RACHEL for Newman, did the adaptation and the results were haphazard, although this picture and the almost-simultaneous release of SOMEBODY UP THERE LIKES ME made Newman a full-fledged star, after a disastrous beginning in 1954's THE SILVER CHALICE. It was only a couple of years since the end of the Korean Conflict (the government never admitted it was a war, preferring to call it a "police action," but whatever it was people died for no good reason) and there was a question as to why so many Americans collaborated, something that was nearly unheard of in WW II. Serling's TV play laid the blame on dark psychological reasons in the protagonist's history and the traitor is depicted sympathetically, while the men who withstood the brainwashing and the torture are almost clods. Newman returns from Korea to face trial by his military peers. His father is Pidgeon, a career Army man, and his younger brother was killed in the war. Corey is the military prosecutor who would rather not try the case and O'Brien is Newman's defense attorney. Both are military men and the case is conducted in front of an Army jury. There's no doubt that Newman did what he is accused of, but O'Brien tries to convince the jury that the rack he was put on was every bit as painful (in a psychological fashion) as anything the Inquisition might have put the heretics through. O'Brien makes a good case and it looks as though Newman will get off, but then the picture takes a twist and Newman, after hearing all the evidence, incriminates himself by saying that he should have been able to take it and the jury must now find the defendant guilty. Francis does a small bit as his widowed sister-in-law and Marvin is one of the men who testifies against Newman. If you don't blink, you'll see Robert Blake (then known as Bobby), Dean Jones, and Rod Taylor in small roles. The fact that Newman's mother died when he was a child and that his father was cold and unfeeling is not enough to make the soldier a Benedict Arnold. In the end, Pidgeon finally gives Newman the affection he'd wanted all those years and that adds a slightly upbeat end to the tragedy.

p, Arthur M. Loew, Jr.; d, Arnold Laven; w, Stewart Stern (based on the teleplay by Rod Serling); ph, Paul C. Vogel; m, Adolph Deutsch; ed, Harold F. Kress, Marshall Neilan, Jr.; md, Deutsch; art d, Cedric Gibbons, Merrill Pye; set d, Edwin B. Willis, Fred MacLean; makeup, William Tuttle; tech adv, Col. Charles M. Trammel, Jr.

Drama **(PR:A MPAA:NR)**

RACKET, THE**** (1951) 88m RKO bw

Robert Mitchum *(Capt. McQuigg)*, Lizabeth Scott *(Irene)*, Robert Ryan *(Scanlon)*, William Talman *(Johnson)*, Ray Collins *(Welch)*, Joyce MacKenzie *(Mary McQuigg)*, Robert Hutton *(Ames)*, Virginia Huston *(Lucy Johnson)*, William Conrad *(Turck)*, Walter Sande *(Delaney)*, Les Tremayne *(Chief Craig)*, Don Porter *(Connolly)*, Walter Baldwin *(Sullivan)*, Brett King *(Joe Scanlon)*, Richard Karlan *(Enright)*, Tito Vuolo *(Tony)*, Howland Chamberlin *(Higgins)*, Ralph Peters *(Davis)*, Iris Adrian *(Sadie)*, Jane Hazzard, Claudia Constant *(Girls)*, Jack Shea, Eric Alden, Mike Lally *(Sergeants)*, Howard Joslyn *(Sgt. Werker)*, Bret Hamilton, Joey Ray *(Reporters)*, Duke Taylor, Miles Shepard, Curtis Jarrett, Art Dupuis, Harry Lauter *(Policemen)*, Dulcie Day, Hazel Keener *(Secretaries)*, Steve Roberts *(Schmidt)*, Pat Flaherty *(Clerk)*, Milburn Stone *(Foster)*, Max Wagner *(Durko)*, Richard Reeves *(Leo)*, Johnny Day *(Menig)*, Don Beddoe *(Mitchell)*, Matthew Boulton *(Simpson)*, Don Dillaway *(Harris)*, Barry Brooks *(Cameron)*, George Sherwood *(Douglas)*, Jack Gargan *(Lewis)*, Herb Vigran *(Headwaiter)*, Bud Wolfe *(Detective)*, Ronald Lee *(Elevator Boy)*, Dick Gordon, Allen Matthews, Ralph Montgomery *(Men)*, Al Murphy *(Newsboy)*, Bob Bice, Sally Yarnell, Jane Easton, Kate Belmont *(Operators)*, Harriet Matthews *(Librarian)*, Ed Parker *(Thug)*.

A hard-hitting crime melodrama, THE RACKET was a popular 1920s play first released in 1928 as a Howard Hughes film (his second), but here it receives, again under Hughes' supervision, a more modern approach, tied in strongly with the then-controversial Kefauver crime hearings which captured most of the TV viewing audience of the era. Mitchum, in a switch from his usual film roles, is a tough, honest police captain in a midwestern city who, on the eve of an important election, battles with crime boss Ryan over control of the city's government. His superior, Collins, the town's prosecuting attorney, and police inspector Conrad are in Ryan's hip pocket and Mitchum must not only combat the underworld but these government officials. Ryan owns and operates a plush nightclub where Scott is a torch singer, and this headquarters of corruption becomes the focal point of Mitchum's investigations. Ryan is an archaic criminal, a throwback to the days of gunmen who shot first and reasoned later. He is being pressured to assume a more businesslike posture, abandon violence, and clean his own house of trigger-happy goons. Mitchum finds Ryan's weak spot in his kid brother, King, arresting the punk for carrying an unlicensed gun and putting him in jail, then bringing in Scott to testify against him as a material witness. When Scott agrees to talk, Ryan issues orders to have her killed. This hit is learned of by Mitchum and with the help of honest cop Talman, the killers are dispatched, but at the cost of Talman's life. Mitchum then captures Ryan after a rooftop battle and Ryan is tricked into confessing to an earlier murder. Collins and other bigwigs are content to have Ryan stew in a cell until the elections are over but the crime boss compels them to bail him out. Ryan is told that he can take his choice: run or be killed. Mitchum has set up the whole situation to trap Conrad and Collins. The political grafters are nabbed in the end and Ryan is killed by hit men, thus ridding the city of a lethal menace. Director Cromwell does a fine job of keeping a lightning pace to this film, eliciting a great performance from Ryan, who is ultra-sinister and disturbingly psychotic in his profile of the gang boss striving to change his unchangeable violent character. Mitchum is solid if not enthusiastic in his role of an honest cop and the rest of the cast, particularly Collins and Conrad, is excellent. Scott presents a sultry, attractive image but she is really not much more than a prop for the criminal intrigues of Ryan. Hughes, who had just taken over RKO in 1948, immediately scheduled THE RACKET for production, relying on the success the original 1928 film had. The city profiled, of course, is Chicago and its corrupt political practices in the 1920s, and the remake came closer to the play written by Cormack in which, ironically, Cromwell had appeared as an actor. Cromwell had been directing films on and off at RKO since 1932 and this picture marked his last entry as a helmsman for that studio.

p, Edmund Grainger; d, John Cromwell, Nicholas Ray; w, William Wister Haines, W. R. Burnett (based on the play by Bartlett Cormack); ph, George E. Diskant; m, Paul Sawtell, Roy Webb; ed, Sherman Todd; md, Constantin Bakaleinikoff; art d, Albert S. D'Agostino, Jack Okey; set d, Darrell Silvera, William Stevens; cos, Michael Woulfe; Burns; m/l, "A Lovely Way to Spend an Evening" Jimmy McHugh, Harold Adamson; makeup, Mel Burns.

Crime Drama **Cas.** **(PR:C MPAA:NR)**

RACKET BUSTERS*** (1938) 71m Cosmopolitan/WB bw

George Brent *(Denny Jordan)*, Humphrey Bogart *(John "Czar" Martin)*, Gloria Dickson *(Nora Jordan)*, Allen Jenkins *(Skeets Wilson)*, Walter Abel *(Hugh Allison)*, Penny Singleton *(Gladys Christie)*, Henry O'Neill *(Governor)*, Oscar O'Shea *(Pop)*, Elliott Sullivan *(Charlie Smith)*, Fay Helm *(Mrs. Smith)*, Joe Downing *(Joe)*, Norman Willis *(Gus)*, Don Rowan *(Cliff Kimball)*, Anthony Averill *(Dave Crane)*, Mary Currier *(Mrs. Allison)*, Ferris Taylor *(Man)*, Jack Goodrich *(Clerk)*, James Nolan *(Jim Smith, Allison's Secretary)*, Jim Pierce, Ethan Laidlaw *(Martin's Henchmen)*, Herbert Heywood *(Gas Station Owner)*, Irving Bacon *(Counterman)*, Dale Van Sickel *(Special Officer)*, Jan Holm *(Nurse at Sanitarium)*, Monte Vandergrift *(Detective)*, Charles Trowbridge *(Judge)*, William B. Davidson *(Union Chairman)*, Harry Tenbrook *(Hood)*.

Another in the series of quick, low-budget gangster pictures that Warner Bros. trapped an unhappy Bogart into during the late 1930s, but this one turned out better than most. Set in New York City, Bogart plays a powerful crime kingpin seeking to control all the trucking by forcing the drivers to pay him protection money. The truckers prove to be difficult at first, but after Bogart's goons inflict a few severe beatings, the drivers begin handing over most of their salaries. Brent, a young truck driver whose wife, Dickson, is about to give birth to their first child, isn't so easily intimidated and refuses to capitulate. Together with his partner Jenkins, Brent tries to set an example for the other truckers. Learning of this, Bogart orders Brent's trucks burned. Meanwhile, Abel, a crusading young lawyer, is picked by the district attorney as a special prosecutor whose main duty is to put Bogart and his hoods behind bars. With his trucks gone, Brent is left without an income to support his wife and pay her hospital bills. Jenkins quits the trucking business and begins selling tomatoes. Desperate for cash, Brent breaks into Bogart's trucking office and steals enough money to have Dickson moved safely away. Bogart and his thugs turn up at Brent's apartment and tell him that his wife won't be harmed if he will join the rest of the drivers. Seeing no choice, Brent gives in to Bogart and is shunned by the very drivers he had been trying to help. Now in complete control of the trucking industry, Bogart goes after the produce retailers and sends his goons on a rampage of destruction which affects all shopkeepers, including Jenkins. At the same time, special prosecutor Abel has been given the power to prosecute all truckers withholding information. O'Shea, a beloved old trucker who used to be the secretary of the union, comes forward with information helpful to Abel and his men. For this betrayal, O'Shea is killed by Bogart's goons. The drivers are shocked by the killing and unjustly place the blame on Brent. They even go so far as to prevent the trucker from seeing O'Shea's body at the funeral. Suspecting that Brent knows more about Bogart's operation than he's telling, Abel has the truck driver arrested under the new law. In retaliation, Bogart orders a general strike by the truckers and the movement of foodstuffs in New York City grinds to a halt. Realizing Brent would be more help to him from within Bogart's organization, Abel lets him go. Imbued with a new sense of purpose, Brent tries to organize the truckers against Bogart. Jenkins lends a hand and is shot by one of Bogart's men. Fed up with the hoods, the truckers break the strike and get the trucks rolling. Brent confronts Bogart at the gangster's apartment and beats him up. The police arrive to break up the fight and arrest Bogart. Brent provides the evidence necessary to convict Bogart, and is reunited with his wife and new baby. While Bogart confided to friend and biographer Richard Gehman in the book *Bogart* that the cast of RACKET BUSTERS was better than usual for the pictures he made in those days, he still criticized the effort by stating that, "I made so many pictures like that, I used to get the titles mixed up. People would ask me what I was working in, and I'd have to think about what it was called." Despite Bogart's typically sardonic attitude, RACKET BUSTERS is a solid crime film that runs at a rapid clip and remains quite entertaining.

p, Samuel Bischoff; d, Lloyd Bacon; w, Robert Rossen, Leonardo Bercovici; ph, Arthur Edeson; m, Adolph Deutsch; ed, James Gibbon; md, Hugo Friedhofer; art d, Esdras Hartley; cos, Howard Shoup.

Crime   **(PR:A MPAA:NR)**

RACKET MAN, THE**   (1944) 65m COL bw

Tom Neal, Hugh Beaumont, Jeanne Bates, Larry Parks, Douglas Fowley, Lewis Wilson, Clarence Muse, Mary Gordon, Anthony Caruso, Warren Ashe, Pauline Drake.

Neal, a one-time racketeer, is employed by the Army for undercover work. His involvement in shady dealings causes his friends to assume his guilt, but they realize his real identity before the film's end. Neal, who led a rather shady life himself, turns in another performance in which he mesmerizes with mediocrity. None of his roles, however, would match the B-movie intensity which he contributed to DETOUR (1946).

p, Wallace MacDonald; d, D. Ross Lederman; w, Paul Yawitz, Howard J. Green (based on the story by Casey Robinson); ph, James Van Trees; ed, Paul Borofsky; md, M. W. Stoloff; art d, Lionel Banks, Walter Holscher; set d, George Montgomery.

Crime   **(PR:A MPAA:NR)**

RACKETEER, THE**   (1929) 66m Pathe bw

Robert Armstrong (*Mahlon Keane*), Carole Lombard (*Rhoda Philbrooke*), Roland Drew (*Tony Vaughan*), Jeanette Loff (*Millie Chapman*), John Loder (*Jack Oakhurst*), Paul Hurst (*Mehaffy*), Kit Guard (*Gus*), Al Hill (*Squid*), Hedda Hopper (*Karen Lee*), Winter Hall (*Mr. Simpson*), Winifred Harris (*Mrs. Simpson*), Bobbie Dunn (*The Rat*), Bud Fine (*Bernie Weber*).

A very early gangster talkie which relied so heavily on the new technology that nothing much happens but talk, talk, and more talk. Unfortunately, none of it is worth listening to. Lombard plays an attractive young woman who catches the eye of fast-talking, well-dressed, and cultured gangster Armstrong. To win her over, Armstrong offers to help her alcoholic boy friend, Drew, who is a failed classical violinist. With Armstrong's financial assistance, Drew is able to perform a high visibility concert and get the recognition his talents deserve. In return, Lombard reluctantly agrees to marry the gangster after the performance. Before the concert is over, one of Armstrong's goons kills the leader of a rival gang. Assuming Armstrong ordered the hit, the police invade the concert hall and try to arrest the gangster. Armstrong refuses to be taken in and a gun battle breaks out, leading to the hoodlum's death. With Armstrong dead, Lombard can now marry her true love, Drew. Stodgy in all respects, THE RACKETEER is a routine, melodramatic crime story that may have been better served on the stage. All the action takes place off-screen with the characters returning before the cameras to *talk* about the interesting things they have done. The viewer is given little indication of gangster Armstrong's power or influence in the underworld and must rely on the character's own self-aggrandizing nature. Lombard is competent in a thankless role, and Drew is simply fodder for the plot elements, lending no life to his part. Drew is so ineffectual that one wonders why Lombard doesn't opt for the more vital Armstrong voluntarily. For fans interested in the genesis of the gangster genre only.

p, Ralph Block; d, Howard Higgins; w, Paul Gangelin, A.A. Kline; ph, David Abel; ed, Doane Harrison; md, Josiah Zuro.

Crime   **(PR:A MPAA:NR)**

RACKETEERS IN EXILE*½   (1937) 60m COL bw

George Bancroft (*William Waldo*), Evelyn Venable (*Myrtle Thornton*), Wynne Gibson (*Babe DeVoe*), Marc Lawrence (*Blackie*), John Gallaudet (*Happy*), George McKay (*Horseface*), Garry Owen (*Sy*), Jack Clifford (*Thyrus*), William Burress (*Thornton*), Helen Lowell (*Mrs. Thornton*), Richard Carle (*Porky*), Jonathan Hale (*Parker*).

Offbeat gangster film which sees Bancroft as a big-time mobster, hiding out with his gang in his own home town. There he encounters a religious revival which inspires him to start his own lucrative racket by becoming a "born-again" evangelist, and going out on the road seeking donations from guilt-ridden businessmen. Of course Bancroft pockets the dough for himself, but eventually he sees the error of his ways and puts the money to good use. Interesting premise that sadly does not live up to its potential.

d, Erle C. Kenton; w, Harry Sauber, Robert Shannon (based on a story by Sauber); ph, Lucien Ballard; ed, Otto Meyer; md, Morris Stoloff; cos, Robert Kalloch.

Crime   **(PR:A MPAA:NR)**

RACKETEERS OF THE RANGE**½   (1939) 62m RKO bw

George O'Brien (*Barney O'Dell*), Chill Wills (*Whopper*), Marjorie Reynolds (*Helen*), Gay Seabrook (*Penny*), Robert Fiske (*Whitlock*), John Dilson (*Benson*), Monte Montague (*Larkin*), Bud Osborne (*Hank*), Ben Corbett (*Dutch*), Ray Whitley (*Ray*), Cactus Mack (*Flash*), Frankie Marvin (*Skeeter*), Joe Balch, Dick Hunter, Ed Piel, Sr., Frank O'Connor, Mary Gordon, Stanley Andrews, Wilfred Lucas, Harry Cording, Clint Sharp, Del Maggert.

Modern-day O'Brien oater which sees the star as a rancher determined to lead his fellow ranchers against evil packing-combine owner Fiske, who has been rustling their cattle in a desperate effort to hold down the price of beef. O'Brien uses horses against trucks and trains in the surprisingly exciting climax, which has the brave ranchers punching it out with Fiske's army of goons. Quite enjoyable.

p, Bert Gilroy; d, D. Ross Lederman; w, Oliver Drake (based on a story by Bernard McConville); ph, Harry Wild; ed, Frederic Knudtson; m/l, "Sleepy Wrangler," "Caboose on the Red Ball Train," Ray Whitley, Fred Rose.

Western   **Cas.**   **(PR:A MPAA:NR)**

RACKETY RAX**½   (1932) 70m FOX bw

Victor McLaglen ("*Knucks*" *McGloin*), Greta Nissen (*Voine*), Nell O'Day (*Doris*), Arthur Pierson (*Speed Bennett*), Allan Dinehart (*Counsellor Sultsfeldt*), Allen Jenkins (*Mike Dumphy*), Vincent Barnett (*Dutch*), Esther Howard (*Sister Carrie*), Stanley Fields (*Gilotti*), Marjorie Beebe (*Mrs. McGloin*), Ivan Linow (*Tossilitis*), Ward Bond (*Brick Gilligan*), Eric Mayne (*Dr. Vanderveer*), Joe Brown, John Keyes (*McGloin's Bodyguards*).

Very funny satire on the popularity of college football, starring McLaglen as a big-time gangster, who sees lots of money in exploiting the Ivy League home games. He soon devises a plan and sets up a phony college, populated by hoods and professional wrestlers. When football season arrives, his boys stomp out the legitimate opposition and run up ridiculously lopsided scores. The money comes pouring in, until a rival gang steals McLaglen's idea and sets up its own bogus college. Eventually the two teams meet in a championshp match, but instead of the pigskin, lead is thrown around the field when the two rival gangs pull out their guns to settle the contest. Pretty silly stuff, but wacky enough to be good fun.

d, Alfred Werker; w, Ben Markson, Lou Breslow (based on a story by Joel Sayre); ph, L.W. O'Connell; ed, Robert Bischoff; cos, David Cox.

Comedy/Crime   **(PR:A MPAA:NR)**

RACQUET zero   (1979) 89m Harlequin/Cal-Am c

Bert Convy (*Tommy*), Lynda Day George (*Monica*), Phil Silvers (*Arthur*), Edie Adams (*Leslie*), Susan Tyrell (*Miss Baxter*), Bjorn Borg (*Himself*), Bobby Riggs (*Bernie*), Dorothy Konrad (*Mrs. Kaufman*), Monti Rock III (*Scotty*), Tanya Roberts (*Bambi*), Bruce Kimmel (*Arnold*), Kitty Ruth (*Melissa*).

Tennis pro Convy uses his bedroom skills to raise money from Beverly Hills matrons for his own tennis club. Idiotic rip-off of SHAMPOO fails mostly because Bert Convy is probably the most charmless and oily actor around. Cameos by Bjorn Borg and Bobby Riggs prove they can't act either.

p, David Winters, Alan Roberts; d, Winters; w, Steve Michaels, Earle Doud.

Comedy/Drama   **Cas.**   **(PR:O MPAA:R)**

RADAN   (SEE: RODAN, 1958, Jap.)

RADAR SECRET SERVICE*   (1950) 59m Lippert bw

John Howard (*Bill*), Adele Jergens (*Lila*), Tom Neal (*Moran*), Myrna Dell (*Marge*), Sid Melton (*Pill Box*), Ralph Byrd (*Static*), Pierre Watkin (*Hamilton*), Robert Kent (*Benson*), Tristram Coffin (*Michael*), Riley Hill (*Blacky*), Bob Carson (*Tom*), Marshall Reed (*1st Bruiser*), John McKee (*2nd Bruiser*), Holly Bane (*Truck Operator*), Bob Woodward (*1st Henchman*), Boyd Stockman (*2nd Henchman*), Bill Crespinel (*Helicopter Operator*), Kenne Duncan (*Michael's Henchman*), Bill Hammond (*Michael's 2nd Henchman*), Jan Kayne (*Maid*).

A pretty silly programmer filmed when the intricacies of radar still fascinated and amazed bored Hollywood screenwriters. RADAR SECRET SERVICE details the rough-and-tumble life of agents Howard and Byrd, as they go about smashing a ring of crooks. Led by Coffin and Neal, the gangsters manage to hijack a shipment of uranium ore. How do our intrepid agents capture these hardened criminals? Why, they use their radar, of course.

p, Barney Sarecky; d, Sam Newfield; w, Beryl Sachs; ph, Ernest Miller; m, Russell Garcia, Dick Hazard; ed, Carl Pierson.

Spy Drama   **(PR:A MPAA:NR)**

RADIO CAB MURDER**   (1954, Brit.) 70m Insignia/Eros bw

Jimmy Hanley (*Fred Martin*), Lana Morris (*Myra*), Sonia Holm (*Jean*), Jack Allen (*Parker*), Sam Kydd (*Spencer*), Pat McGrath (*Henry*), Bruce Beeby (*Inspector Rawlings*), Elizabeth Seal (*Gwen*), Rupert Evans, Michael Mellinger, Jack Stewart, Frank Thornton, Ian Wilson.

After serving a term in prison for safecracking, Hanley gets a job as a taxi driver. He is approached by a gang that recruits ex-cons, but wishing to go straight, he goes to the police and they send him undercover to join the gang and expose its leader. The gang, however, discovers his identity and tries to kill him by locking him in a deep-freeze. He is saved by his cab buddies who ride to the rescue and corner the crooks. A good cast is all that saves this weakly scripted effort.

p, George Maynard; d&w, Vernon Sewell (based on a story by Pat McGrath); ph, Geoffrey Faithfull.

Crime   **(PR:A MPAA:NR)**

RADIO CITY REVELS**   (1938) 84m RKO bw

Bob Burns (*Lester Robin*), Jack Oakie (*Harry Miller*), Kenny Baker (*Kenny Baker*), Victor Moore (*Paul Plummer*), Milton Berle (*Teddy Jordan*), Helen Broderick (*Gertie Shaw*), Ann Miller (*Billie Shaw*), Jane Froman (*Jane Froman*), Buster West (*Squenchy*), Melissa Mason (*Lisa*), Richard Lane (*Crane*), Marilyn Vernon (*Delia Robin*), Don Wilson (*Announcer*), Hal Kemp and his Orchestra.

A misfired attempt at an all-star comedy musical, which would show off New York City's Radio City Music Hall. Unfortunately the results were less than toe-tapping and side-splitting. Berle and Oakie play a pair of down-and-out songwriters desperate for new material. They soon discover an out-of-towner, Burns, who sings brilliant, catchy tunes in his sleep. Oakie and Berle, of course, are at the poor slob's bedside jotting down the tunes and making a decent buck off of them. As it turns out, their biggest problem is how to keep Burns asleep most of the time. The lackluster musical numbers staged from these dream tunes had trouble keeping audiences attentive in 1938. Ironically, when the film opened, it played at the

Globe Theater in New York, *not* Radio City Music Hall. Songs include: "Goodnight Angel" (sung by Baker), 'Speak Your Heart" (sung by Froman), "Take a Tip from the Tulip" (sung by Burns), "I'm Taking a Shine to You" (sung by Baker), "There's a New Moon over the Old Mill" (sung by Burns), "Love, Honor and Oh Baby," "Why Must I Love You," "Morning Glories in the Moonlight," "You're the Apple of My Eye," "Swinging in the Corn" (Allie Wrubel, Herb Magidson).

p, Edward Kaufman; d, Ben Stoloff; w, Matt Brooks, Eddie Davis, Anthony Veiller, Mortimer Offner (based on a story by Brooks); ph, J. Roy Hunt, Jack MacKenzie; m, Joseph Santley; ed, Arthur Roberts; md, Victor Baravalle; art d, Van Nest Polglase; cos, Edward Stevenson; spec eff, Vernon L. Walker; ch, Hermes Pan.

Musical/Comedy   **(PR:A MPAA:NR)**

RADIO FOLLIES½**   (1935, Brit.) 87m BIP/Alliance bw-c (GB: RADIO PARADE OF 1935)

Will Hay (*William Garland*), Helen Chandler (*Joan Garland*), Clifford Mollison (*Jimmie Clare*), Davy Burnaby (*Sir Ffrederick Ffotheringhay*), Alfred Drayton (*Carl Graham*), Billy Bennett (*Commissionaire*), Lily Morris, Nellie Wallace (*Charladies*), Western Brothers (*Announcers*), Clapham & Dwyer (*Reporters*), Three Sailors (*Assistants*), Haver & Lee (*Effects Men*), Carlyle Cousins (*Telephonists*), Georgie Harris (*Pageboy*), Gerry Fitzgerald, Arthur Young (*Window Cleaners*), Claude Dampier (*Piano Tuner*), Hugh E. Wright (*Algernon Bird*), Robert Nainby (*Col. Featherstone Haugh-Haugh*), Jimmy Godden (*Vere de V. de Vere*), Basil Foster (*Capt. Esme StJ. Entwhistle*), Ivor McLaren (*Eric Lyttle-Lyttle*), Fay Carroll, Peggy Cochrane, Yvette Darnac, Ronald Frankau, Alberta Hunter, Ted Ray, Joyce Richardson, Buddy Bradley Girls, Beryl Orde, Fred Conyngham, Gillie Potter, Sybil Grove, Stanelli and His Hornchestra, Teddy Joyce and his Band, Eve Becke.

Above-average British musical has Hay running a failing radio station. His complaints manager, Mollison, is in love with Chandler, Hay's daughter. The station is saved when Mollison recruits talent from among the station's staff and stages a big show that is televised all over the country. Good acts keep this one going most of the time. One of the few British musicals to get a release in the U.S.

p, Walter C. Mycroft; d, Arthur Woods; w, Jack Davies, Jr., Paul Perez, James Bunting, Woods (based on a story by Reginald Purdell, John Watt); ph, Cyril Bristow, Philip Grindrod (Dufaycolour); ed, E.B. Jarvis; ch, Buddy Bradley.

Musical   **(PR:A MPAA:NR)**

RADIO LOVER   (1936, Brit.) 64m City/ABF bw

Wylie Watson (*Joe Morrison*), Ann Penn (*Miss Oliphant*), Betty Ann Davies (*Wendy Maradyck*), Jack Melford (*Reggie Clifford*), Cynthia Stock (*Miss Swindon*), Gerald Barry (*Sir Hector*), Max Faber (*Brian Maradyck*).

Watson is a talented singer unfortunately cursed with an unattractive face. He enlists a handsome friend, Melford, to mime while he sings. The fraud is quite successful until they are exposed by Penn, but they are given a major contract anyway. Fairly entertaining comedy keeps its sights low and hits the target.

p, Ernest King; d, Austin Melford, Paul Capon; w, Ian Dalrymple (based on a story by Elma Dangerfield).

Comedy   **(PR:A MPAA:NR)**

RADIO MURDER MYSTERY, THE   (SEE: LOVE IS ON THE AIR, 1937)

RADIO ON½**   (1980, Brit./Ger.) 101m British Film Institute-Road Movies-National Film Finance Corp./Unifilm

David Beames (*Robert*), Lisa Kreuzer (*Ingrid*), Sandy Ratcliff (*Kathy*), Andrew Byatt (*Deserter*), Sue Jones-Davies (*Girl*), Sting (*Just Like Eddie*), Sabina Michael (*Aunt*), Katja Kersten (*German Woman*), Paul Hollywood (*Kid*).

British critic Christopher Petit hooked up with German director Wim Wenders and came up with his first feature film, an allegorical mystery tale which explores the cynical, stifling apathy in modern day England. Though Wenders is only credited as the associate producer, his influence can be felt, albeit only mildly. Beames plays a bored, emotionally dead disk jockey, slowly enticed into investigating the mysterious circumstances of his brother's death. Although he comes close to confronting the issues and problems that he has studiously avoided all his life, he never actually becomes involved. While the premise is interesting and needs to be explored in British films, the pace remains slow and dull. Not even the background music of David Bowie, Kraftwerk, Devo and others generates much interest.

p, Keith Griffiths; d, Christopher Petit; w, Petit, Heidi Adolph; ph, Martin Schafer; m, David Bowie, Sting, Kraftwerk, Eddie Cochran, Wreckless Eric; ed, Anthony Sloman; art d, Susannah Buxton.

Drama   **(PR:C MPAA:NR)**

RADIO PARADE OF 1935   (SEE: RADIO FOLLIES, 1935)

RADIO PATROL*   (1932) 67m UNIV bw

Robert Armstrong (*Bill Kennedy*), Russell Hopton (*Pat Bourke*), Lila Lee (*Sue Kennedy*), June Clyde (*Vern*), Andy Devine (*Pete Wiley*), Onslow Stevens (*Carl Hughes*), John L. Johnson (*Smokey Johnson*), Harry Woods (*Kloskey*), Sidney Toler (*Sgt. Keogh*), Jack La Rue (*Slick*), Joe Girard (*Police Captain*).

Below par cops and robbers film starring Armstrong and Hopton as two big city cops battling it out with a powerful mob seeking to grab the payroll of a packing company. The overly melodramatic conclusion sees Armstrong killed, leaving his wife and sickly newborn baby without a father. Hackneyed material is padded by innumerable shots of police cars and motorcycles roaring off with their lights flashing and sirens blaring.

d, Edward Cahn; w, Tom Reed; ph, Jackson Rose; ed, Henry Lieb.

Crime   **(PR:A MPAA:NR)**

RADIO PIRATES**   (1935, Brit.) 89m Sound City/AP&D bw

Leslie French (*Leslie*), Mary Lawson (*Mary*), Warren Jenkins (*Willie Brooks*), Enid Stamp-Taylor, Kenneth Kove, Edgar Driver, Frederick Lloyd, John Turnbull, Fanny Wright, Hughie Green, Teddy Brown, Roy Fox and His Band, H. Saxon-Snell, Hal Booth, Iva Gay, Arthur Mayne.

French, Lawson, and Jenkins band together and start a pirate radio station in the hope of settling their financial woes. A festive dance is broken up by the police and the trio are chased to Big Ben before they are apprehended. This innocuous musical comedy was reissued 5 years later as a pared down 45-minute featurette called BIG BEN CALLING.

p, Norman Loudon; d, Ivar Campbell; w, Donovan Pedelty.

Musical/Comedy   **(PR:A MPAA:NR)**

RADIO REVELS OF 1942   (SEE: SWING IT SOLDIER, 1941)

RADIO STAR, THE   (SEE: LOUDSPEAKER, THE, 1934)

RADIO STARS ON PARADE*½   (1945) 69m RKO bw

Wally Brown (*Jerry Miles*), Alan Carney (*Mike Strager*), Frances Langford (*Sally Baker*), Don Wilson (*Himself*), Tony Romano (*Romano*), Rufe Davis (*Pinky*), Robert Clarke (*Danny*), Sheldon Leonard (*Maddox*), Max Wagner (*George*), Ralph Peters (*Steve*), Ralph Edwards and Co., Skinnay Ennis Band, Town Criers, Cappy Barra Boys.

Despite the fact that RKO didn't have much original material, they went ahead and produced another one of these low-budget musicals populated with famous radio stars of the day. Brown and Carney star as the managers of a floundering Hollywood talent agency who take their promising new client Langford on the rounds of all the popular radio shows (at least the ones RKO had access to). They wind up in the middle of Ralph Edwards' "Truth or Consequences" show which yields the climactic yucks. Having no budget for original songs, RKO borrowed a few popular standbys from some of their previous musicals including: "Can't Get Out of This Mood" (Jimmy McHugh, Frank Loesser), "That Old Black Magic" (Harold Arlen, Johnny Mercer), "Don't Believe Everything You Dream," and "I Couldn't Sleep a Wink Last Night" (McHugh, Harold Adamson).

p, Ben Stoloff; d, Leslie Goodwins; w, Robert E. Kent, Monty Brice (based on a story by Kent); ph, Harry Walker; ed, Edward W. Williams; md, Constantin Bakaleinikoff; art d, Albert S. D'Agostino, Walter Keller; spec eff, Vernon L. Walker.

Musical/Comedy   **(PR:A MPAA:NR)**

RADIOGRAFIA D'UN COLPO D'ORO   (SEE: THEY CAME TO ROB LAS VEGAS, 1969, Fr./Ital./Span./Ger.)

RADISHES AND CARROTS   (SEE: TWILIGHT PATH, 1965, Jap.)

RADON   (SEE: RODAN, 1958, Jap.)

RADON THE FLYING MONSTER   (SEE: RODAN, 1958, Jap.)

RAFFERTY AND THE GOLD DUST TWINS**   (1975) 91m Venture/WB c (AKA: RAFFERTY AND THE HIGHWAY HUSTLERS)

Alan Arkin (*Rafferty*), Sally Kellerman (*Mac Beachwood*), MacKenzie Phillips (*Frisbee*), Alex Rocco (*Vinnie*), Charlie Martin Smith (*Alan*), Harry Dean Stanton (*Billy Winston*), John McLiam (*John*), Richard Hale (*Jesus Freak*), Louis Prima & Co (*Themselves*), Sam Butera (*Himself*), Earl Smith (*Bandleader*), Ed Peck (*Blackjack Player*), Lilian Randolph (*Student Driver*).

This attempt at a gentle comedy was far too gentle and proved a loser at the box office. Arkin is an excellent actor but he seldom does a film that scores, a strange phenomenon when one considers his abilities. Arkin is a driving instructor, a schlepp who is not terribly bright but good-hearted through his dim wits. He is kidnaped by would-be singer Kellerman and runaway Phillips, who force him to drive them from Los Angeles to points east. There are several incidents including a few scenes in Las Vegas, then Kellerman runs off with Earl Smith, a country and western band leader. On their trip the situation alters to where the three are compadres rather than kidnapers and a kidnapee. They get to Tuscon and Phillips has to go back to her orphanage, a plight that is solved when Arkin convinces the authorities that he is her father and rescues her. There's not much depth in the characters or in the plot and it is only faintly amusing at times. Whereas it could have almost been a family film if handled differently (and would have probably done better), the addition of gratuitous foul language brought this an "R" rating from the MPAA and kept parents from bringing their youngsters. Phillips did well in AMERICAN GRAFFITI and later starred on a TV series, but her bouts with personal dependence habits caused her career to wane, even before she was out of her teens, or thereabouts. Ed Peck, who must have the deepest voice in history, does his usual good work as the blackjack player in the Vegas sequence and Charles Martin Smith, another AMERICAN GRAFFITI alumnus, is effective in a short bit as a soldier whom Phillips rolls for his money. Composer Butler's score is aptly bright and the Nevada star, Prima, is also seen with his band. Prima had been a staple in Vegas, Reno, and Tahoe while married to Keely Smith. After their divorce, he continued working the lounges and she moved up to the big rooms. Butler and composer Charles Fox (FOUL PLAY, etc.) opened their own recording studio in the San Fernando Valley because they were not satisfied with what the other studios had to offer and the result, Evergreen Studios, was a huge success.

p, Michael Gruskoff, Art Linson; d, Dick Richards; w, John Kaye; ph, Ralph Woolsey (Panavision, Technicolor); m, Artie Butler; ed, Walter Thompson; art d, Joel Schiller; set d, Donfeld.

Comedy   Cas.   **(PR:C-O MPAA:R)**

RAFFICA DI COLTELLI (SEE: KNIVES OF THE AVENGER, 1967, Ital.)

RAFFLES*½** (1930) 70m UA bw

Ronald Colman *(A.J. Raffles)*, Kay Francis *(Lady Gwen Manders)*, Bramwell Fletcher *(Bunny Manders)*, Frances Dade *(Ethel Crowley)*, David Torrence *(McKenzie)*, Alison Skipworth *(Lady Kitty Melrose)*, Frederick Kerr *(Lord Harry Melrose)*, John Rogers *(Crawshaw)*, Wilson Benge *(Barraclough)*, Virginia Bruce *(Blonde)*.

The first sound version of the popular Hornung novel (1899) and subsequent stage play (1903) which came to the screen twice in the silent days with John Barrymore (1914) and House Peters (1925) cast as the roguish cricket player-cat burglar A.J. Raffles. In a fine performance, Colman is a famed British cricket player by day who prowls around in the evenings as "The Amateur Cracksman," an equally famous criminal who consistently eludes Scotland Yard. After meeting beautiful socialite Francis, Colman falls in love with her and manages to get himself invited to a weekend bash being thrown by royal couple Kerr and Skipworth. Also in attendance is Scotland Yard investigator Torrence, who has a hunch that Colman is his man. Both Colman and Torrence are aware that Skipworth is the owner of an extremely valuable necklace—one Colman is planning to steal in order to help a suicidal friend, Fletcher, through a financial crisis. Torrence watches Colman like a hawk, but the criminal still manages to sneak into Skipworth's boudoir. However, another criminal, Rogers, has the same idea. Just as Rogers is about to take the necklace for himself, Colman snatches it. Rogers is carted away by Scotland Yard, but when no necklace turns up Torrence decides to use the criminal as bait to locate Colman. As Scotland Yard breathes down Colman's neck he manages to give the necklace to Fletcher who then receives a sizable reward. By escaping through a grandfather clock with a secret panel, Colman sneaks out of his apartment and past a horde of detectives. With his freedom ahead, he makes plans to continue his romance with Francis in Paris. Having established himself in the audience's minds as "Bulldog Drummond," Colman now found himself in another crowd-pleasing role as the lovable Raffles. Opening to almost unanimously favorable reviews, RAFFLES marked a farewell to silent films for Sam Goldwyn's production company. A firm believer in the future of sound films, Goldwyn quickly made the transition, this picture being the last that his company produced in both silent and sound versions. Goldwyn's faith in sound recording resulted in an Oscar nomination for sound recordist Oscar Lagerstrom. The picture was begun by D'Arrast who was fired and struck from the credits by Goldwyn after endless disagreements. His replacement was Fitzmaurice, an able craftsman and the one responsible for bringing D'Arrast to Hollywood from France eight years earlier. Remade, practically scene for scene, nine years later with David Niven and Olivia de Havilland in the leads, and again in 1960 as EL RAFFLES MEXICANO, a Spanish language picture with Rafael Bertrand as the "Amateur Cracksman."

p, Samuel Goldwyn; d, Harry D'Abbadie D'Arrast, George Fitzmaurice; w, Sidney Howard (based on the novel *The Amateur Cracksman* by Ernest William Hornung and the play "Raffles, The Amateur Cracksman" by Hornung, Eugene Wiley Presbrey); ph, George Barnes, Gregg Toland; ed, Stuart Heisler; art d, William Cameron Menzies, Park French.

Crime/Romance **(PR:A MPAA:NR)**

RAFFLES*** (1939) 71m UA bw

David Niven *(A.J. Raffles)*, Olivia de Havilland *(Gwen Manders)*, Dame May Whitty *(Lady Kitty Melrose)*, Dudley Diggs *(McKenzie)*, Douglas Walton *(Bunny Manders)*, Lionel Pape *(Lord Harry Melrose)*, E.E. Clive *(Barraclough)*, Peter Godfrey *(Harry Crawshay)*, Margaret Seddon *(Maud Holden)*, Gilbert Emery *(Bingham)*, Hilda Plowright *(Wilson)*, Vesey O'Davoren *(Butler)*, George Cathrey *(Footman)*, Keith Hitchcock *(Morton)*, Forrester Harvey *(Umpire)*, James Finlayson *(Cabby)*, George Atkinson, Eric Wilton, Frank Baker *(Attendents)*, Gibson Gowland, George Kirby, Herbert Clifton *(Villagers)*, David Thursby *(Passenger)*, Wilfred Lucas, Larry Dodds, John Power, Colin Kenny, Charles Irwin, Leyland Hodgson, *(Bobbies)*, Elspeth Dudgeon *(School Mistress)*, Olaf Hytten, Douglas Gordon, John Graham Spacey, Harry Allen.

Closely following the groundwork set in the 1930 version of Hornung's novel, director Wood turned in an admirable product which substitutes Niven (in his twenty-second picture, but his first with top-billing) for Ronald Colman and de Havilland for Kay Francis. It was the now-familiar story (it had also made it to the screen in 1914 with John Barrymore and in 1925 with House Peters) of a fun-loving, adventurous rogue with a penchant for burglary. Niven, in the lead, is a dashing cricket player with a loyal following in England. He is also the mysterious "Amateur Cracksman," an infamous cat burglar who eludes capture. Stealing more for fun than profit, Niven continuously succeeds in frustrating Scotland Yard whose inspector Digges is always one step behind. The cracksman's favorite trick is to steal something and then, to thoroughly confuse Digges, send it back. Niven's first mistake is to fall in love with the very proper de Havilland, the sister of friend Walton. To win de Havilland's affection, Niven decides to give up his life of crime. This time when he sends back a recent acquisition, Digges gains a valuable clue. Niven is tracked to a social gathering at the home of Whitty and Pape. Since Whitty is the owner of a famed emerald necklace, Digges is especially alert. Niven's plan is to steal the necklace and send it to Walton, who is financially strapped. Walton can then return the necklace and collect the reward. Niven's plan is foiled, however, by a second-rate crook who fingers the necklace for his own profit. By the finale, Nivens has reformed, Walton has gotten himself out of trouble, and de Havilland has fallen in love with her gentleman crook. Essentially the same film as the 1930 version, this one just recasts the roles and then duplicates many of the previous films scenes and shots. Wood, who producer Goldwyn had assigned to this film, reportedly had little energy left after a grueling stint on GONE WITH THE WIND. De Havilland, also just off of GONE WITH THE WIND, showed little enthusiasm for the project. Referring to the British atmosphere of RAFFLES, de Havilland said, "I had little to do with that English scene, I had nothing to do with that style of film and I was nothing to the part the way it was written." Hoping to bring the 1930 version up to date, Goldwyn hired author Van Druten to adapt the original script, and then brought Fitzgerald in to add some finishing touches. More than anything, RAFFLES made it clear that Niven's name held water at the box office. Having a strong desire to star in RAFFLES, Niven used the film as a bargaining tool in his contract renewal talks with Goldwyn. Although Goldwyn made an idle threat to cast the then unknown Dana Andrews in the lead, he gladly signed Niven. In a true show of patriotism, Niven, whose career was beginning to shoot forward, chose to return to England where he re-enlisted in the army and took up arms with the Allies in WW II.

p, Samuel Goldwyn; d, Sam Wood, William Wyler; w, John Van Druten, Sidney Howard, (uncredited) F. Scott Fitzgerald (based on the novel *The Amateur Cracksman* by E.W. Hornung); ph, Gregg Toland; m, Victor Young; ed, Sherman Todd; art d, James Basevi; set d, Julie Heron; cos, Travis Banton.

Crime/Romance **(PR:A MPAA:NR)**

RAFTER ROMANCE** (1934) 72m RKO bw

Ginger Rogers *(Mary Carroll)*, Norman Foster *(Jack Bacon)*, George Sidney *(Max Eckbaum, Landlord)*, Robert Benchley *(Hubbell)*, Laura Hope Crews *(Elise)*, Guinn "Big Boy" Williams *(Fritzie)*, Ferike Boros *(Rosie Eckbaum)*, Sidney Miller *(Julius)*.

Contrived but fairly amusing romantic comedy originally intended for Joel McCrea and Dorothy Wilson, but eventually starring Ginger Rogers and Norman Foster as a pair of working stiffs who share a Greenwich Village apartment, but who never see each other. While she works during the day selling ice boxes, he uses the aprtment. When she comes home at night, he has already left to work as a night watchman. Having never met, the pair envision each other as elderly ogres and develop a mutual loathing for one another based entirely on their living habits. Of course, the couple eventually meet on the street one fine day and fall in love, unaware that they are actually rommmates. When the truth finally comes out, they are a bit embarrassed, but blissful.

p, Alexander McKaig; d, William Seiter; w, Sam Mintz, H.W. Hanemann, Glenn Tryon (based on a novel by John Wells); ph, David Abel; ed, James Morley; md, Max Steiner; art d, Van Nest Polglase, John J. Hughes; cos, Bernard Newman; makeup, Mel Burns.

Romance/Comedy **(PR:A MPAA:NR)**

RAG DOLL (SEE: YOUNG, WILLING AND EAGER, 1962, Brit.)

RAGE, THE zero (1963, U.S./Mex.) 90m Cronos bw (LA RABIA; AKA: THE RAGE WITHIN)

June Wilkinson *(Stripper)*, Armando Silvestre *(Gigolo)*.

A tale about a stripper and her gigolo boy friend who plot to steal $80,000. They make it appear as if the money has been lost in an airplane explosion, but find that their plan isn't so easily executed.

p, Massey Creamer; d, Myron J. Gold.

Crime **(PR:O MPAA:NR)**

RAGE½** (1966, U.S./Mex.) 103m Cinematografica Jalisco-Joseph M. Schenck Enterprises/COL c (EL MAL)

Glenn Ford *(Reuben)*, Stella Stevens *(Perla)*, David Reynoso *(Pancho)*, Armando Silvestre *(Antonio)*, Ariadne Welter *(Blanca)*, Jose Elias Moreno *(Fortunato)*, Dacia Gonzalez *(Maria)*, Pancho Cordova *(Old Man)*, Susana Cabrera *(Wife of Old Man)*, David Silva *(Bus Driver)*, Quintin Bulnes *(Pedro)*, Valentin Trujillo *(Jose)*, Maura Monti, Isala Vega, Jorge Russek, Raul Martinez, Jose Angel Espinosa, Gilda Miros, Stim Segar, Alicia Gutirrez, Anita Morgan.

Ford stars as an American doctor who takes a job on a Mexican construction site after his wife dies while giving birth. A group of prostitutes comes to the site to entertain the men, with Ford refusing the advances of Stevens in favor of the bottle. Upon discovering he has been infected by rabies, the doctor makes a mad dash over desert and mountains to get to a treatment center. He is accompanied by Stevens and Reynoso, the man who made Ford deliver his wife's baby before allowing him to take off. A fairly tense level of suspense is maintained while Ford and company battle various handicaps to get to the hospital. This race against time is used to good advantage, and it is what is needed to keep Ford from being a walking dead man.

p&d, Gilberto Gazcon; w, Teddi Sherman, Gazcon, Fernando Mendez (based on a story by Jesus Velasquez, Guillermano Hernandez, Gazcon); ph, Rosalio Solano (Eastmancolor); m, Gustavo Cesar Carrion; ed, Carlos Savage, Walter Thompson; md, Carrion; art d, Ramon Rodriguez Granada; cos, Mario Huarte.

Drama **(PR:C MPAA:NR)**

RAGE*½ (1972) 99m A.J. Ronald Getty-Leon Fromkess/WB c

George C. Scott*(Dan Logan)*, Richard Basehart *(Dr. Caldwell)*, Martin Sheen *(Maj. Holliford)*, Barnard Hughes *(Dr. Spencer)*, Nicolas Beauvy *(Chris Logan)*, Paul Stevens *(Col. Franklin)*, Stephen Young *(Maj. Reintz)*, Kenneth Tobey *(Col. Nickerson)*, Robert Walden *(Dr. Janeway)*, William Jordan *(Maj. Cooper)*, Dabbs Greer *(Dr. Thompson)*, John Dierkes *(Bill Parker)*, Bette Henritze *(Sarah Parker)*, Lou Frizzell *(Spike Boynton), Ed Lauter (Orderly Simpson)*, Terry Wilson *(Truck Driver)*, Fielding Greaves *(Dr. Steenrod)*, Anna Aries.

After having directed the flop play "General Seeger" on Broadway in 1962, Scott waited eight years until he did the superior TV adaptation of "The Andersonville Trial" for which he was awarded an Emmy. Two years later, he attempted to direct himself in this and it was far from satisfying. What began as a good idea, that is still ongoing, turns out to be a boring, verbose, and pretentious drama that might have been a tight action drama had Scott stepped off his soap box and gotten down to moviemaking. Scott, a widower, and his pre-teen son, Beauvy, live in Wyoming and have a good relationship that takes them camping every so often. On one of their overnight excursions, an Army chopper flies over them and accidentally sprays the area with some deadly nerve gas they have been testing. The next day, Scott awakens to find many of his sheep dead and Beauvy in a coma with a heavy nosebleed. He takes Beauvy to the local hospital where the doctor, Basehart, suggests that Scott, too, should be admitted for diagnosis. Scott agrees, then learns that Basehart has been taken off the case and replaced by Sheen, an Army doctor who has given orders to separate Scott from Beauvy in the hospital. Scott is given drugs to keep him quiet and Beauvy dies, but Sheen lies and says that the boy is recovering well and that he, Scott, will be up and about soon. Nobody in the small ranching area knows what's happened, as the authorities have clamped a lid on any news. The reasons are twofold. First, the realization that deadly gas is in the area might create chaos and even panic on the part of the townspeople and second, they want to keep a close eye on Scott, as he has somehow managed to survive the lethal gas and they intend to use him now as a "control" to see how the gas affects a human. When Scott spies Beauvy's clothing being covertly toted out of the hospital in a sterile plastic container, he wises up to what's happened and takes steps. He flees the hospital where he has been kept under tight security, finds Hughes, another doctor, and forces the man to reveal the truth. Beauvy has died and the doctors have performed an unauthorized autopsy on the lad. Further, there's no question in Hughes' mind that Scott is ticking off his final heartbeats and it's only a matter of hours before he follows his son to the grave. Scott is in a rage, purchases dynamite and all the accouterments to go with it, illegally borrows someone else's motorcycle, rides to the laboratory that mixed the gas, and blows the place to bits. A state trooper and a night watchman are killed in the blast. Now he steals a truck and heads for the Army base that, he has learned, is being used to develop weapons for biological warfare. It's a race against the clock as the fatal gas in his system is taking its toll. Hughes has told the Army about Scott and they are all lying in wait for him as he approaches the base, fully intending to destroy it. There are hundreds of soldiers guarding the base on the ground, and overhead there are armed helicopters. Before Scott can unleash his fury (and we can easily see that the moment he raises one hand, he'll be cut down by thousands of bullets), he falls to the ground in pain, shudders, screams, and dies. The picture is thankfully over. This could have been a smasher but Scott must have thought he had something earth-shaking to state, so he filled the movie with countless slow-motion shots for emphasis but they were out of place and served to bring an already tedious movie down to a pace set by an arthritic snail. It isn't easy for an actor to direct himself. A few giants have managed to do it successfully, such as Laurence Olivier, Woody Allen, and Orson Welles, but more have failed, like Paul Newman (HARRY AND SON) and Marlon Brando (ONE-EYED JACKS) and Cliff Robertson (J.W. COOP; THE PILOT) and, of course, now Scott.

p, Fred Weintraub; d, George C. Scott; w, Philip Friedman, Dan Kleinman; ph, Fred Koenekamp (Panavision, DeLuxe Color); m, Lalo Schifrin; ed, Michael Kahn; art d, Frank Sylos; set d, Leonard A. Mazzola; cos, Donald D. Dawson; spec eff, Joe Lombardi, Paul Lombardi; makeup, Del Acevedo.

Drama **(PR:C MPAA:PG)**

RAGE, 1976 (SEE: RABID, 1976, Can.)

RAGE AT DAWN½** (1955) 87m RKO c (AKA: SEVEN BAD MEN)

Randolph Scott *(James Barlow)*, Forrest Tucker *(Frank Reno)*, Mala Powers *(Laura Reno)*, J. Carrol Naish *(Sim Reno)*, Edgar Buchanan *(Judge Hawkins)*, Myron Healey *(John Reno)*, Howard Petrie *(Lattimore)*, Ray Teal *(Constable Brant)*, William Forrest *(Amos Peterson)*, Denver Pyle *(Clint Reno)*, Trevor Bardette *(Fisher)*, Kenneth Tobey *(Monk Claxton)*, Chubby Johnson *(Hyronemus)*, Richard Garland *(Bill Reno)*, Ralph Moody, Guy Prescott, Mike Ragan, Phil Chambers.

A good cast headed by Scott, and decent direction from veteran helmsman Whelan, save this unevenly scripted western purportedly detailing the pursuit of the infamous gang of cutthroats, the Reno Brothers (Tucker, Naish, and Healey). Scott plays a special agent hired by a Chicago law office to capture the renegade gang. Scott goes undercover and poses as a train robber to win the gang's confidence, but he falls in love with their sister, Powers, which complicates things. Not only is the unplanned romance unsettling, but the fact that the Reno boys have insulated themselves from prosecution through a variety of legal loopholes and payoffs to the right politicians makes Scott's job all the more difficult. Eventually he is forced to entrap the gang in a train robbery *he* has planned, and haul them in for it. When Tucker, Naish, and Healey are brought to town for trial, the populace goes mad with blood lust, forms a mob, and lynches the criminals without benefit of jurisprudence. This gives Scott and the script writers a chance to wax eloquent on the subject of mindless mob violence, a la THE OXBOW INCIDENT.

p, Nat Holt; d, Tim Whelan; w, Horace McCoy (based on a story by Frank Gruber); ph, Ray Rennahan (Technicolor); m, Paul Sawtell; ed, Harry Marker; md, Sawtell; art d, Walter Keller.

Western **Cas.** **(PR:A MPAA:NR)**

RAGE IN HEAVEN** (1941) 82m MGM bw

Robert Montgomery *(Philip Monrell)*, Ingrid Bergman *(Stella Bergen)*, George Sanders *(Ward Andrews)*, Lucile Watson *(Mrs. Monrell)*, Oscar Homolka *(Dr. Rameau)*, Philip Merivale *(Mr. Higgins)*, Matthew Boulton *(Ramsbotham)*, Aubrey Mather *(Clark)*, Frederic Worlock *(Solicitor-General)*, Francis Compton *(Bardsley)*, Gilbert Emergy *(Mr. Black)*, Ludwig Hart *(Durand)*, Lawrence Grant *(British Consul)*, Art Dupuis *(Taxi Driver)*, Victor Kendall *(Dr. Boudin)*, Eldon Gorst *(Page Boy)*, Guy Kingsford *(Clerk)*, Olaf Hytten *(Hotel Clerk)*, Pat Moriarity, Frank Shannon, Harry Cording, David Clyde *(Workers' Delegates)*, Bobby Hale, Leyland Hodgson, Damian O'Flynn, Eric Lonsdale, Dave Thursby, Pat O'Malley *(Workers)*, Lilian Kemble-Cooper *(Nurse)*, Leonard Carey *(Eric the Chauffeur)*, Major McBride *(Bank Clerk)*, Stuart Hall, Clive Morgan *(Traveling Salesmen)*, Wyndham Standing *(Dr. McTernan)*, Arthur Stuart Hull *(Maj. Bedford)*, Holmes Herbert *(Judge)*, John Burton *(Court Clerk)*, Harry Allen *(Jury Foreman)*, Colin Kenny *(Warden)*, Jean Del Val *(Porter)*.

After taking off some time to do a comedy, MR. AND MRS. SMITH, for Alfred Hitchcock, Montgomery returns to the maniac role he played in NIGHT MUST FALL. This time, he's the scion of a huge British fortune but he's been confined to a mental hospital in France because his mind is bent to the point of snapping. His mother, Watson, doesn't know that he was incarcerated, and when he escapes from the hospital and returns to England, he doesn't tell her. (Montgomery's attempts at a British accent are negligible and only bottomed by Robert Redford's complete disregard of the British ancestry of the character he played in 1985's OUT OF AFRICA.) Bergman is working for Watson as a social secretary and Montgomery quickly charms her. They are married soon after and it isn't minutes before Montgomery's weirdness surfaces. Sanders is Montgomery's best friend, and when he attempts to be benignly charming to Bergman, Montgomery's anger rises and his jealousy flares. As he has never actually done anything besides being an heir, Montgomery tries to run the family business but he is so bad at it that the employees riot. Sanders and Bergman rush in and Sanders' cool, calm, and detached assessment of the situation saves the day, but Montgomery is so insane now that he tries to kill Sanders and make it look like an accident. The attempt fails but Sanders finally understands something is deeply wrong with Montgomery, who begins to accuse Bergman of having a love affair with Sanders. Montgomery plans to kill himself and elaborately schemes to have Sanders arrested for his "murder." He provokes a fight with Sanders, then ties a knife to a door and pushes himself against it. (Any good detective would see right through this.) Sanders is convicted for Montgomery's death and sentenced to be executed. Bergman saves Sanders by going to see Homolka, Montgomery's Paris psychiatrist, and secures evidence that saves Sanders' life in the nick of time. The picture was begun by Robert Sinclair, but he was replaced by Mayer's "fix-it" man, Van Dyke, who brought the film in on schedule as expected. Montgomery was so obviously nuts in his characterization that it's hard to believe it took everyone that long to notice.

p, Gottfried Reinhardt; d, W.S. Van Dyke II; w, Christopher Isherwood, Robert Thoeren (based on the novel by James Hilton); ph, Oliver Marsh; m, Bronislau Kaper; ed, Harold F. Kress; cos, Adrian.

Drama **(PR:C MPAA:NR)**

RAGE OF PARIS, THE½** (1938) 75m UNIV bw

Danielle Darrieux *(Nicole de Cortillon)*, Douglas Fairbanks, Jr. *(James Trevor)*, Mischa Auer *(Mike, Hotel Headwaiter)*, Louis Hayward *(Bill Duncan)*, Helen Broderick *(Gloria Patterson)*, Charles Coleman *(Rigley, Trevor's Valet)*, Samuel S. Hinds *(Mr. Duncan)*, Nella Walker *(Mrs. Duncan)*, Harry Davenport *(Hunting Lodge Caretaker)*, Mary Martin *(Drama Teacher)*.

French actress Darrieux made her American movie debut here as, what else, a beautiful young French girl who arrives in New York City seeking work as a model. She learns of a job available as a nude model for a commercial photographer and goes to "audition," but she gets the address confused and winds up in a shocked Fairbanks, Jr.'s office and begins to disrobe for him. Thinking her a gold-digging blackmailer, he kicks the girl out. Later, she hooks up with ex-actress Broderick and her accomplice Auer who both see a way to make a quick buck, as they decide to manage her career by enticing millionaire Hayward with the girl's charms. Luckily, Hayward happens to be a close friend of Fairbanks, Jr., and when the latter learns the girl has resurfaced, he warns his buddy that she's no good. Finally, of course, Fairbanks, Jr. and Darrieux fall in love, which solves everybody's problems. Note Mary Martin in her film debut.

p, B.G. De Sylva; d, Henry Koster; w, Bruce Manning, Felix Jackson (based on their story); ph, Joseph Valentine; ed, Bernard Burton; md, Charles Previn; art d, Jack Otterson; cos, Vera West.

Romance **Cas.** **(PR:A MPAA:NR)**

RAGE OF THE BUCCANEERS* (1963, Ital.) 91m Max/Colorama Features c (GORDON IL PIRATA NERO; AKA: THE BLACK BUCCANEER)

Ricardo Montalban *(Gordon the Black Buccaneer)*, Vincent Price *(Romero)*, Guilia Rubini *(Manuela)*, Liana Orfei *(Luana)*, Mario Feliciani *(Tortuga)*, Gisella Sofio, Guistino Durano, Jose Jaspe, Edoardo Toniolo, Andrea Fantasia, Gino Marturano.

Pointless Italian swashbuckler starring Montalban as a hearty ex-slave who returns to the illegal slave-trading capital of the world, San Salvador, seeking to smash the nasty practice out of existence. Unfortunately, he is captured and thrown in prison by the sympathetic governor's evil and treacherous secretary Price, who also just happens to be the leader of the super-secret slave trade in the country. Luckily, Montalban is able to strike up a romance with the governor's daughter, Rubini, and she helps him escape. Too bad for her that Price finally makes his move, overthrows her old man, and tosses her in the hoosegow. Montalban has taken about enough of this, so he organizes a rebellion and defeats Price. The governor is so thrilled by this development that he even allows his little girl to marry the handsome ex-slave for the fadeout.

p, Ottavio Poggi; d, Mario Costa; w, John Byrne, Poggi; ph, Mario Bellero (Totalscope, Eastmancolor); m, Carlo Rustichelli; ed, Renato Cinquini; art d, Ernesto Kromberg, Amedeo Mellone.

Adventure **(PR:A MPAA:NR)**

RAGE TO LIVE, A*½ (1965) 101m Mirisch/UA bw

Suzanne Pleshette *(Grace Caldwell)*, Bradford Dillman *(Sidney Tale)*, Ben Gazzara *(Roger Bannon)*, Peter Graves *(Jack Hollister)*, Bethel Leslie *(Amy Hollister)*, James Gregory *(Dr. O'Brien)*, Carmen Mathews *(Emily Caldwell)*, Ruth White *(Mrs. Bannon)*, Sarah Marshall *(Connie Schoffstall)*, Virginia Christine *(Emma)*,

Linden Chiles *(Brock Caldwell)*, Mark Goddard *(Charlie Jay)*, George Furth *(Paul Reichelderfer)*, Brett Somers *(Jessie Jay)*, Frank Maxwell *George Jay)*.

Badly executed adaptation of John O'Hara's novel starring Pleshette as a young, wealthy nymphomaniac who has numerous affairs with her mother's country club friends. When mom finds out about her daughter's promiscuity, she takes her on a trip to Nassau, but then suffers a fatal heart attack when Pleshette is caught in the sack with a waiter from the hotel's restaurant. Upon her return to the States, Pleshette meets and falls hard for Dillman, but he is too noble and good to jump in the hay with her. Eventually they marry, and Pleshette confesses her past indiscretions to Dillman, but he is sure that the purity of his love for her will stop her from wandering off to other men. This prediction lasts nearly three years until Pleshette seduces one of the construction workers making improvements on their home. Graves also meets Pleshette and becomes enamored, but she spurns his advances. Not wanting to ruin her marriage, she ends her affair with the construction worker. He retaliates by drinking too much and getting himself killed in a car wreck, the investigation of which brings the affair into the newspapers. Dillman is outraged and tells Pleshette that if she steps out of line once more, he will leave her. She behaves herself, but at a party the jealous wife of Graves announces that Pleshette and her husband have been carrying on (they haven't) and a disgusted Dillman leaves for good. In the transfer from novel to screen, O'Hara's characters have been transformed from vital, living personalities into stiff, unmotivated soap-opera fodder.

p, Lewis J. Rachmil; d, Walter Grauman; w, John T. Kelley (based on the novel by John O'Hara); ph, Charles Lawton (Panavision); m, Nelson Riddle; ed, Stuart Gilmore; md, Gil Grau; art d, James Sullivan; set d, Ray Boltz; cos, Howard Shoup; spec eff, Norman Breedlove; m/l, "Rage to Live," Arthur Ferrante, Louis Teicher, Noel Sherman (performed by Ferrante, Teicher); makeup, Stanley Campbell.

Drama **(PR:C MPAA:NR)**

RAGE WITHIN, THE (SEE: RAGE, THE, 1963, U.S./Mex.)

RAGGED ANGELS (SEE: THEY SHALL HAVE MUSIC, 1939)

RAGGEDY ANN AND ANDY** (1977) 84m Lester Osterman-Bobbs-Merrill/FOX c

Claire Williams *(Marcella)*, Voices: Didi Conn *(Raggedy Ann)*, Mark Baker *(Raggedy Andy)*, Fred Stuthman *(The Camel with the Wrinkled Knees)*, Niki Flacks *(Babette)*, George S. Irving *(Capt. Contagious)*, Arnold Stang *(Queasy)*, Joe Silver *(The Greedy)*, Alan Sues *(The Loony Knight)*, Marty Brill *(King Koo-Koo)*, Paul Dooley *(Gazooks)*, Mason Adams *(Grandpa)*, Allen Swift *(Maxi-Fixit)*, Hetty Galen *(Susie Pincushion)*, Sheldon Harnick *(Barney Beanbag/Socko)*, Ardyth Kaiser *(Topsy)*, Margery Gray, Lynne Stuart *(The Twin Pennies)*.

Well-animated, but overlong and boring children's film based on the popular doll characters. Williams plays a little girl whose dolls come to life after she reads them stories. A nice effort, but the film suffers from tedious musical numbers by Joe Raposo that seem to last forever. Songs: "I Look and What Do I See!" (sung by Didi Conn), "No Girl's Toy" (sung by Mark Baker), "Rag Dolly" (sung by Conn, Baker, Chorus), "Poor Babette" (sung by Niki Flacks), "A Miracle" (sung by George S. Irving), "Ho-Yo" (sung by Irving), "Candy Hearts" (sung by Conn, Baker), "Blue" (sung by Fred Stuthman), "The Mirage" (sung by Stuthman, Chorus), "I Never Get Enough" (sung by Joe Silver), "I Love You" (sung by Alan Sues), "Loony Anthem" (sung by Sues, Chorus), "It's Not Easy Being King" (sung by Marty Brill), "Hooray for Me" (sung by Flacks), "You're My Friend" (sung by Irving), "Home" (sung by Conn, Baker, Chorus).

p, Richard Horner; d, Richard Williams; w, Patricia Thackray, Ray Wilk (based on stories and characters created by Johnny Gruelle); ph, Dick Mingalone, Al Rezek (Panavision, DeLuxe Color); ed, Harry Chang, Lee Kent, Kenneth McIlwaine, Maxwell Seligman; prod d, Cornelius "Corny" Cole; art d, William Mickley; animation, Richard Williams, Grim Natwick, Art Babbitt, Emory Hawkins, Tissa David, Gerald Potterton, Hal Ambro, Gerry Chiniquy, Charlie Downs, John Kimball, Chrystall Rusel, Spencer Peel, John Bruno, Doug Crane, George Bakes, Art Vitello.

Children's Animation **Cas.** **(PR:AAA MPAA:G)**

RAGGEDY MAN*** (1981) 94m UNIV c

Sissy Spacek *(Nita)*, Eric Roberts *(Teddy)*, Sam Shepard *(Bailey)*, William Sanderson *(Calvin)*, Tracey Walker *(Arnold)*, R.G. Armstrong *(Rigby)*, Henry Thomas *(Harry)*, Carey Hollis, Jr. *(Henry)*, Ed Geldart *(Mr. Calloway)*, Bill Thurman *(Sheriff)*, Suzi McLaughlin *(Jean Lester)*, Lupe Juarez *(Crescencio, the Barkeeper)*, Jessie Lee Fulton *(Miss Pud)*, LuBelle Camp *(Miss Beulah)*, James N. Harrell *(Ticket Taker)*, Lee Wackerhagen *(Old Man)*, Dave Davis *(Deputy)*, Archie Donahue, Marvin Gardner *(Pilots)*, Mike Washlake, Joe Finnegan.

A compelling, but oddly empty film starring Spacek as a young divorcee who struggles to raise her two sons in Texas during WW II. Since her divorce, Spacek has become a target for the less-than-honorable men in town, who believe that all divorced women are hot-to-trot. She successfully gives them the cold shoulder, but lowlife locals Sanderson and Walker have yet to give up on her. Also making himself a mysterious menace is Shepard, a down-and-out rag man who haunts the area. One day a young sailor, played by Roberts, enters Spacek's life. He hits it off well with her sons, Thomas and Hollis, Jr., and soon Spacek becomes attracted to him herself. Eventually Roberts moves in with Spacek and her boys, which disturbs the two rednecks. But the war looms on the horizon and Roberts eventually is sent away by Spacek. This gives Sanderson and Walker a chance to force themselves on Spacek, which leads to a fairly disturbing, surprisingly bloody climax that just doesn't seem to fit with what has gone on before. Fine performances by Spacek and Roberts, combined with able direction from Spacek's husband, Fisk (it was his first feature), make this one worth a look.

p, Burt Weissbourd, William D. Wittliff; d, Jack Fisk; w, Wittliff; ph, Ralf Bode (Technicolor); m, Jerry Goldsmith; ed, Edward Warschlika; art d, John Lloyd; cos, Joe. I. Tompkins.

Drama **Cas.** **(PR:C MPAA:PG)**

RAGING BULL**** (1980) 129m UA bw-c

Robert DeNiro *(Jake LaMotta)*, Cathy Moriarty *(Vickie LaMotta)*, Joe Pesci *(Joey)*, Frank Vincent *(Salvy)*, Nicholas Colasanto *(Tommy Como)*, Theresa Saldana *(Lenore)*, Frank Adonis *(Patsy)*, Mario Gallo *(Mario)*, Frank Topham *(Toppy/Handler)*, Lori Anne Flax *(Irma)*, Joseph Bono *(Guido)*, James V. Christy *(Dr. Pinto)*, Bernie Allen *(Comedian)*, Bill Mazer *(Reporter)*, Bill Hanrahan *(Eddie Eagan)*, Rita Bennett *(Emma)*, Mike Miles *(Sparring Partner)*, Floyd Anderson *(Jimmy Reeves)*, Johnny Barnes *(Sugar Ray Robinson)*, Kevin Mahon *(Tony Janiro)*, Ed Gregory *(Billy Fox)*, Louis Raftis *(Marcel Cerdan)*, Johnny Turner *(Laurent Dauthuille)*, Martin Scorsese *(Barbizon Stagehand)*.

In a riveting performance that once more assured viewers that he is the most versatile and probably the greatest film actor of the era, DeNiro essays the brutish, plug-ugly boxer, Jake LaMotta. (The actor, to achieve certain physical dissipations by LaMotta toward the end of his spectacular career, ate and ate until his body bloated another 50 pounds, and then he took the weight off for his next role with the alacrity of a snake shedding its skin.) Of course, RAGING BULL is a study in violence, low-life values (or the lack of them), and the kind of people which most sensitive viewers will find fascinatingly sub-human, a continuing vision of gutter life by Scorsese who began with MEAN STREETS and went on to the ultra-violent TAXI DRIVER. Where in the latter film the violence is almost all gratuitous and perverse, in RAGING BULL it all works. We expect a profile on the long-corrupt boxing world to be violent, crude, Neanderthalistic. Scorsese does not fail to fulfill that expectation. DeNiro is shown as an up-and-coming boxer in 1941, trim and full of ambition, beginning his climb to the middleweight championship, beating one opponent after another. He doesn't just best his antagonists but literally pounds them to a pulp, consumed by a hateful, vengeful violence that necessitates his complete destruction of all adversaries. Big, moonfaced Moriarty attracts the boxer's lustful eye while she is a teenager. Though married, DeNiro begins to date the ice-cold blonde, sleeping with her in his parents' home and, after discarding his first wife, marrying her. Pesci, playing LaMotta's brother and his manager, serves as his daffy philosophical advisor as well as marital consultant. He is just as violent as his brother and attacks a bunch of goons in a nightclub when he discovers one of the Mafia leaders, Vincent, trying to bed Moriarty. He breaks Vincent's arm and later makes a truce with the gangster under the watchful eye of Mafia don Colasanto. He also, it is suggested, inadvertently establishes a relationship with the Mafia which seeks to control LaMotta's career for gambling interests. Eventually, the Mafia does control LaMotta's matches and compels him to take a "dive" in one fight that later makes the boxer physically ill, as well as tainting his otherwise clean reputation. So obvious is the fight thrown that DeNiro is almost kicked out of boxing, but he redeems himself in several hard battles and finally wins the championship from Marcel Cerdan, the French boxer. Barnes, as Sugar Ray Robinson, is the constant nemesis of LaMotta's career, one who finally wrests the title from DeNiro, Scorsese profiling Barnes as a mystical threat to a man who could not be beaten by anyone else. While still on top, DeNiro loses all control and discipline, letting his body go, refusing to train, and becoming insanely jealous of his voluptuous wife, believing she is sleeping with Mafia gangsters and even his own brother. He destroys his family ties by attacking Pesci in his own home, screaming that he has slept with his wife, pounding Pesci to a pulp in front of his own family. He also alienates his wife and, after losing the title, loses her too; he has been sleeping with young girls frequenting his seedy nightclub where DeNiro fancies himself a stand-up comedian and stage floor philosopher. He is briefly jailed for serving liquor to underage girls and later makes a nightclub "comeback" by appearing at a New York hotel lounge. DeNiro is shown struggling to memorize Marlon Brando's lines about his boxing days from ON THE WATERFRONT at the beginning and this is where the film ends, just as he saunters on stage to brag of his disastrous life. Scorsese spares no one in this onslaught of brutality, nor does writer Schrader, who is obviously obsessed with violence, religious guilt, and repressed sex. (Pesci more than once has to remind his brother to sleep with his wife more often to keep himself happy and less violent.) The fight sequences are amazing and subjectively realistic, all seen from DeNiro's point of view, many of these shot in traumatic slow motion where every vicious punch breaks a blood vessel and gore squirts forth. The dialog is essentially humorous for its lack of intelligence and is often overwhelmed with obscene words and gestures. The conduct of most everyone shown here is vulgar, crude, even ghastly. The characters are basically uneducated, stupid people who will make any viewer feel superior. All of the story is built around LaMotta's ring experience and Scorsese obviously borrows heavily from such classic boxing films as CHAMPION, BODY AND SOUL, THE HARDER THEY FALL, THE SET-UP, and even SOMEBODY UP THERE LIKES ME, the latter film being a much more heartwarming story of a much more appealing fighter, Rocky Graziano. No doubt the reason why Scorsese elected to film this picture in black and white was to better capture the bleak reality of the so-called sport, as well as to provide a historic feel for the 1940s era, while identifying his film with the masterful black-and-white films of an earlier time. Only at one point, other than the credits, does Scorsese resort to color, when showing home movies of the LaMotta family, which, in a montage chronicle, quickly dispenses with a long period of family relationships. The director sprinkles the film with images of the Catholic religion—crucifixes, holy pictures—as an oblique method of indicting that religion as the repressive culprit that produced the beast LaMotta, an all too patent villain. For lack of a real introspective reason for LaMotta's existence, Scorsese and Schrader are content to put the blame on hosannas and holy water, this rationale being as intellectually idiotic as the characters they present. But it is DeNiro's incredible performance, a virtuoso essay that will shatter any viewer with stomach enough to take this film all the way, which makes RAGING BULL a masterpiece, a dark one, to be sure, as dark as an execution scene by Goya. Technically, Scorsese's direction is flawless and this film, if not its consistently repugnant subject matter, places him in the first rank of filmmakers. He is the Tod Browning of contemporary film, recording the social misfits, freaks, and backwater creatures who slither through the sewers of today's society. Scorsese and his films are anachronisms where the viewer can sit smugly back and watch Cro-Magnon man emerge from his cave, roll his eyes crazily toward an unfamiliar sun, bash beasts and primitive rivals to death, and then hobble bowlegged back into his dark cavern to savor the day's events. No child should be exposed to RAGING BULL for it will certainly provide it trauma, nightmares, and moral confusion. Listening to the cretinous and bivalvic dialog is similar to wading through a sewage treatment plant. Flesh is pounded and abused. Blood cascades like a waterfall, and everywhere in every scene there is a contemptuous disregard for humanity, a perspective obviously at the core of the director. Still, the most heroic viewers will find it hard to turn away from the sight, for it is truly a glimpse of hell. LaMotta reportedly did not like what he saw in the released film which made of him a wild beast. His ex-wife, Vickie LaMotta, went on to minor celebrityhood by exposing her body in *Playboy* magazine following the release of the film. Moriarty, playing the much-abused wife (and one can only wonder how any person, other than a masochist, could take all that punishment from a thug spouse), is a drawback in the film, staring vacantly as if she had undergone a prefrontal lobotomy before production began and speaking in a monotone that delivers one inanity after another. Pesci is genuinely funny with his fractured philosophies of life. Everyone else is just oily and distasteful, which is what this film is about anyway. DeNiro and editor Schoonmaker won Oscars.

p, Irwin Winkler, Robert Chartoff; d, Martin Scorsese; w, Paul Schrader, Mardik Martin (based on the book by Jake LaMotta with Joseph Carter, Peter Savage); ph, Michael Chapman (Technicolor); ed, Thelma Schoonmaker; prod d, Gene Rudolf; art d, Alan Manser, Kirk Axtell, Sheldon Haber; set d, Fred Weiler, Phil Abramson; stunts, Jim Nickerson; tech adv, Al Silvani.

Sports Drama   **Cas.**   **(PR:O MPAA:R)**

RAGING MOON, THE   (SEE: LONG AGO TOMORROW, 1971, Brit.)

RAGING TIDE, THE**   (1951) 93m UNIV bw

Shelley Winters (*Connie Thatcher*), Richard Conte (*Bruno Felkin*), Stephen McNally (*Detective Lt. Kelsey*), Charles Bickford (*Hamil Linder*), Alex Nicol (*Carl Linder*), John McIntire (*Corky Mullins*), Pepito Perez (*Mr. Fancy*), Tito Vuolo (*Barney Schriona*), John "Skins" Miller (*Houlihan*), Robert O'Neil (*Spade-Face*), Chubby Johnson.

Conte plays a tough San Francisco mobster who takes it on the lam after killing a rival gang member. After failing in his effort to locate his girl friend Winters so that he can establish an alibi, Conte stows away on a small fishing boat owned by Bickford and his young son Nicol. After he is discovered, Conte is surprised to find that he is accepted by the father and son. He soon gets a taste of what it's like to perform honest work for a living, and he finds it to his liking. Meanwhile, a detective, McNally, searches for Conte by using Winters. Eventually, the net draws tight, but Conte sacrifices his life to save Nicol. A bit maudlin, but a good cast performs admirably.

p, Aaron Rosenberg; d, George Sherman; w, Ernest K. Gann (based on his novel *Fiddler's Green*); ph, Russell Metty; m, Frank Skinner; ed, Ted J. Kent; art d, Bernard Herzbrun, Hilyard Brown; cos, Bill Thomas.

Drama   **(PR:A MPAA:NR)**

RAGING WATERS   (SEE: GREEN PROMISE, THE, 1949)

RAGMAN'S DAUGHTER, THE**½   (1974, Brit.) 94m Penelope-Harpoon /Independent c

Simon Rouse (*Tony Bradmore*), Victoria Tennant (*Doris Randall*), Patrick O'Connell (*Tony at Age 35*), Leslie Sands (*Doris' Father*), Rita Howard (*Doris' Mother*), Brenda Peters (*Tony's Mother*), Brian Murphy (*Tony's Father*), Jane Wood (*Older Tony's Wife*).

A well done, low-budget feature, the first from director Harold Becker. The film is an offbeat romance starring Rouse as a clever young thief who meets and subsequently falls in love with Tennant, the beautiful daughter of a rich rag dealer. Outstanding performances by the principals, coupled with an insightful, literate script, make for compelling viewing.

p, Harold Becker, Souter Harris; d, Becker; w, Alan Sillitoe (based on his own story); ph, Michael Seresin (Technicolor); m, Kenny Clayton; ed, Antony Gibbs.

Drama   **(PR:C MPAA:NR)**

RAGS TO RICHES*½   (1941) 57m REP bw

Alan Baxter (*Jimmy Rogers*), Mary Carlisle (*Carol*), Jerome Cowan (*Abbott*), Michael Morris (*Bickford*), Ralf Harolde (*Slip Conlan*), Paul Porcasi (*Prof. Del Rio*), Suzanne Kaaren (*Glenda*), Eddie Acuff (*Ace*), Rosina Galli (*Maria*), Charles Trowbridge (*Prosecutor*), Daisy Lee Mothershed (*Julia*), Joan Blair (*Belle Cassidy*), Francis Sayles (*Bert Cassidy*).

Routine programmer starring Baxter as a cab driver who suddenly finds himself accused of a crime he didn't commit. Standing loyally by his side is Carlisle, Baxter's girl friend, who hopes to be a famous opera singer some day. Little do they know that her agent, Cowan, is the mastermind of a fur-smuggling ring. Baxter is eventually released, and he lands a job as a trucker. Unfortunately, his new firm is also involved in fur smuggling. A gang war breaks out between the two fur-smuggling gangs, leaving Baxter an unwilling participant. In the end Baxter hails the coppers and assists the lawmen in capturing all the bad guys.

p&d, Joseph Kane; w, James Webb; ph, William Nobles; m, Cy Feuer; ed, Ernest Nims; art d, John Victor Mackay; cos, Adele Palmer.

Crime   **(PR:A MPAA:NR)**

RAGTIME***   (1981) 155m Sunley/PAR c

James Cagney (*Police Commissioner Waldo*), Brad Dourif (*Younger Brother*), Moses Gunn (*Booker T. Washington*), Elizabeth McGovern (*Evelyn Nesbit*), Kenneth McMillan (*Willie Conklin*), Pat O'Brien (*Delmas*), Donald O'Connor (*Evelyn's Dance Teacher*), James Olson (*Father*), Mandy Patinkin (*Tateh*), Howard E. Rollins (*Coalhouse Walker, Jr.*), Mary Steenburgen (*Mother*), Debbie Allen (*Sarah*), Jeff DeMunn (*Harry Houdini*), Robert Joy (*Harry K. Thaw*), Norman Mailer (*Stanford White*), Bruce Boa (*Jerome*), Hoolihan Burke (*Brigit*), Norman Chancer (*Agent*), Edwin Cooper (*Grandfather*), Jeff Daniels (*O'Donnell*), Fran Drescher (*Mameh*), Frankie Faison, Hal Galili, Alan Gifford, Richard Griffiths, Samuel L. Jackson, Michael Jeter, Calvin Levels, Bessie Love, Christopher Malcolm, Herman Meckler, Billy J. Mitchell, Jenny Nichols, Max Nichols, Zack Norman, Eloise O'Brien, Don Plumley, Ted Ross, Dorsey Wright, Robert Arden, Robert Boyd, Thomas A. Carlin, John Clarkson, Brian E. Dean, Harry Ditson, Robert Dorning, Geoffrey Greenhill, Ray Hassett, Robert Hitt, Rodney James, George Harris, George J. Manos, Val Pringle, Ron Weyand, Bill Reimbold.

Though more than $32 million was pumped into this kaleidoscopic portrait of American life in 1906, RAGTIME is too long, too splintered in characterizations, and too much of a good thing squeezed dry. The most impressive thing about the film is the return, after a 20-year hiatus, of top-billed Cagney, at age 81, portraying feisty Police Commissioner Waldo of New York City, but he's not on screen enough to make the difference. The Doctorow novel, vastly overrated, attempted to blend fiction with fact and wound up going in opposite directions, confusing its readers as much as the film perplexed viewers attempting to balance two themes and two families, one factual, one fictional, while each unexpectedly popped from scene to scene. The most compelling story is that of the infamous Thaw-White murder case, where Joy, playing the mad millionaire Thaw, shoots and kills Mailer, essaying famed architect White, over the affections of Thaw's showgirl wife, McGovern, playing Evelyn Nesbit. But this story was better—if not more luridly—told in THE GIRL IN THE RED VELVET SWING (1955). The fictional tale, which is far less interesting, shows the disintegration of the typical (or atypical as the case may be) upper class American family after wife Steenburgen runs off, leaving her family, to dally with an emigre Russian film director. Her husband, Olson, somehow winds up being held hostage in the exquisite J.P. Morgan Library by a band of black revolutionaries led by Rollins. The revolutionaries have unclear motives and Rollins is seeking an apology from some white firemen who have defecated on the seat of his new car to show him they hate blacks. Improbable? Certainly, but there has to be a reason why Rollins and his confused followers want to blow up the library and kill firemen. Cagney enters the scene when Rollins and his group take over the library; he conducts a siege of the place which does not end until victimized Rollins is killed. This event takes place at about the same time that Joy is released after his millions free him of a clearcut murder charge. This is no pleasant journey down memory lane, but more of an exercise in historical injustice, another unconvincing indictment of the American way of life. Most of the players give limp performances under Forman's heavy-handed direction, Steenburgen appearing to be the worst amateur actress in the world with the most annoying voice heard on a sound track in the last decade. Her mousy image and whining delivery helped to turn viewers away, and those who hung on to the last hour of this overlong and revisionist film were only slightly rewarded by a very old but intrepid Cagney. Mailer's appearance as White is nothing more than a wave and a smile; he is shot to death early, thankfully. The whole confusing film, without a focal point or one really empathic character, died in its initial release, and produced only $11 million, providing a financial disaster for the De Laurentiis production company.

p, Dino De Laurentiis; d, Milos Forman; w, Michael Weller (based on the novel by E.L. Doctorow); ph, Miroslav Ondricek (Todd-AO, Technicolor); m, Randy Newman; ed, Anne V. Coates, Antony Gibbs, Stanley Warnow; prod d, John Graysmark; art d, Patrizia Von Brandenstein, Anthony Reading; cos, Anna Hill Johnstone; ch, Twyla Tharp; m/l, "One More Hour," Randy Newman (sung by Jennifer Warnes).

Drama   **Cas.**   **(PR:C MPAA:PG)**

RAGTIME COWBOY JOE**   (1940) 58m UNIV bw

Johnny Mack Brown (*Steve*), Fuzzy Knight (*Joe*), Nell O'Day (*Helen*), Dick Curtis (*Bo*), Marilyn [Lynn] Merrick (*Mary*), Walter Soderling (*Virgil*), Roy Barcroft (*Putt*), Harry Tenbrook (*Del*), Viola Vonn (*Cabaret Singer*), Jack Clifford, William Gould, Bud Osborne, The Texas Rangers, Bob O'Connor, Eddie Parker, Frank McCarroll, George Plues, Ed Cassidy, Buck Moulton, Harold Goodwin, Wilfred Lucas, Kermit Maynard.

This time out, Brown rides as an agent for a cattlemen's association whose cattle are being rustled under mysterious circumstances. With the help of tough gal O'Day (her second appearance in a Brown oater), Brown discovers that the cattle are being snatched by Curtis, a local politico and under-the-table land speculator. Routine stuff, but some interest is aroused by the suspense over whether Brown will ride off with strong-willed O'Day or more traditional wimpy frontier girl Merrick.

p, Joseph Sanford; d, Ray Taylor; w, Sherman Lowe; ph, Jerome Ash; ed, Paul Landres; md, H.J. Salter; m/l, "Ooh La La" (sung by Viola Vonn), "Cross-Eyed Kate," "Trail Drivers," Milton Rosen, Everett Carter, Bob Crawford.

Western   **(PR:A MPAA:NR)**

RAID, THE***   (1954) 82m FOX c

Van Heflin (*Maj. Neal Benton*), Anne Bancroft (*Katy Bishop*), Richard Boone (*Capt. Foster*), Lee Marvin (*Lt. Keating*), Tommy Rettig (*Larry Bishop*), Peter Graves (*Capt. Dwyer*), Douglas Spencer (*Rev. Lucas*), Paul Cavanagh (*Col. Tucker*), Will Wright (*Banker Anderson*), James Best (*Lt. Robinson*), John Dierkes (*Cpl. Deane*), Helen Ford (*Delphine Coates*), Harry Hines (*Mr. Danzig*), Simon Scott (*Capt. Henderson*), Claude Akins (*Lt. Ramsey*).

Heflin is a Confederate officer who escapes a Northern prison camp with some of his men. They flee to Canada, where they reorganize and plan to strike the Union from the north, hoping to draw forces away from the main fighting. Heflin disguises himself as a Canadian businessman and goes to the sleepy Vermont town of St. Albans to scout it out, taking up residence at a boarding house run by widow Bancroft, with whom his relations become something more than formal. When the time comes for his plan to swing into action, Heflin is stymied by the unexpected arrival of a column of Union cavalry. Hotheaded rebel officer Marvin wants to fight them, and his recklessness endangers the whole mission until Heflin shoots him down. The raid is delayed 48 hours, then goes off as planned, the bank is robbed, and the town ransacked and set ablaze. Helfin leaves a note for Bancroft, apologizing to her personally and telling her that what he did was for the Confederacy. Interesting action film based on a real incident from 1864. Heflin was at the peak of his popularity and his talent makes a character who is basically the villain of the piece a subtle and effective portrayal of conflicting loyalties and the difficulties of command. A number of other performances hold the viewer as well. Boone scores as a veteran Union soldier who has lost his arm to the war. Marvin's rambunctious rebel and Bancroft's kindly landlady are similarly effective. Direction by Fregonese is tight and strong, much aided by the somber camera work.

p, Robert L. Jacks, Leonard Goldstein; d, Hugo Fregonese; w, Sydney Boehm (based on the story by Francis Cockrell, from the article "Affair at St. Albans" by Herbert Ravenal Sass); ph, Lucien Ballard (Technicolor); m, Roy Webb; ed, Robert Golden.

War Drama   Cas.   (PR:A-C MPAA:NR)

RAID ON ROMMEL*   (1971) 99m UNIV c

Richard Burton (Capt. Alec Foster), John Colicos (Sgt. Maj. Al MacKenzie), Clinton Greyn (Maj. Tarkington, Medical Officer), Wolfgang Preiss (Gen. Erwin Rommel), Danielle De Metz (Vivi), Karl Otto Alberty (Capt. Heinz Schroeder), Christopher Cary (Conscientious Objector), John Orchard (Garth), Brook Williams (Sgt. Joe Reilly), Greg Mullavey (Pvt. Peter Brown), Ben Wright (Admiral), Michael Sevareid (Cpl. Bill Wembley), Chris Anders (Tank Sergeant).

The hopelessly inconsistent Burton once again wanders aimlessly through his role as a British commando stationed in North Africa during WW II in this desert epic that lifted all its exciting footage from the vastly superior TOBRUK (1967). Burton leads a group of commandos whose mission is to get behind the German lines and destroy the Nazis' big guns so that the Brits can attack. To do this, Burton and company allow themselves to be captured so that they will be taken behind the lines by the Nazis. The plan works, and they are interred in a POW camp, making it a fairly simple matter to escape and blow up the artillery.

p, Harry Tatelman; d, Henry Hathaway; w, Richard Bluel; ph, Earl Rath (Technicolor); m, Hal Mooney; ed, Gene Palmer; art d, Alexander Golitzen, Henry Bumstead; set d, Robert C. Bradford; spec eff, Albert J. Whitlock.

War   (PR:C MPAA:GP)

RAIDERS, THE½**   (1952) 80m UNIV c (AKA: RIDERS OF VENGEANCE)

Richard Conte (Jan Morrell), Viveca Lindfors (Elena Ortega), Barbara Britton (Elizabeth Ainsworth), Hugh O'Brian (Hank Purvis), Richard Martin (Felipe Ortega), Palmer Lee [Gregg Palmer](Marty Smith), William Reynolds (Frank Morrell), William Bishop (Marshal Bill Henderson), Morris Ankrum (Thomas Ainsworth), Dennis Weaver (Dick Logan), Margaret Field (Mary Morrell), John Kellogg (Welch), Lane Bradford (Pete Robbins), Riley Hill (Clark Leftus), Neyle Morrow (Juan Castillo), Carlos Rivero (Ramon Castillo), George Lewis (Vicente), Francis MacDonald (John Cummings).

Film noir star Conte turns in his slouch hat and mounts a horse for this change-of-genre piece in his career. Conte is the leader of a group of miners trying to scrape out an existence in the California territory in 1849. Trouble arises when villainous combine leader Ankrum begins snatching the honest miners' land through increasingly brutal methods. With the help of formerly wealthy Mexican landowner Martin, Conte is able to organize a defense unit and strike back at Ankrum.

p, William Alland; d, Lesley Selander; w, Polly James, Lillie Hayward (based on a story by Lyn Crost Kennedy); ph, Carl Guthrie (Technicolor); m, Joseph Gershenson; ed, Paul Weatherwax; art d, Bernard Herzbrun, Richard Riedel; set d, Russell A. Gausman, John Austin; cos, Bill Thomas.

Western   (PR:A MPAA:NR)

RAIDERS, THE½**   (1964) 75m UNIV c (AKA: THE PLAINSMAN)

Robert Culp (James Butler "Wild Bill" Hickok), Brian Keith (John G. McElroy), Judi Meredith (Martha "Calamity Jane" Canary), James McMullan (William F. "Buffalo Bill" Cody), Alfred Ryder (Capt. Benton), Simon Oakland (Sgt. Austin Tremaine), Ben Cooper (Tom King), Trevor Bardette ("Uncle Otto" Strassner), Harry Carey, Jr. (Jellicoe), Richard Cutting (Jack Goodnight), Addison Richards (Huntington Lawford), Cliff Osmond (Duchamps), Paul Birch (Paul King), Richard Deacon (Commissioner Mailer), Michael Burns (Jimmy McElroy).

Keith is the real standout in this western which was originally intended as a pilot for a television series, but instead was released theatrically. He plays a former Confederate Army officer, now a Texas cattle rancher who is forced by Northern carpetbaggers to abandon his herds and wage war against the railroad. The railroad executives hire the likes of Wild Bill Hickok (Culp), Buffalo Bill Cody (McMullan), and Calamity Jane (Meredith) to defend their interests against Keith and his band of railroad marauders. Just when it looks like the army is about to slaughter Keith and his gang, Culp, McMullan, and Meredith intervene and save them. With their help, Keith and his followers are able to convince the railroad executives to build a line down to their ranches in Texas, and all is forgiven. Though the script is a bit trite and the production tends to betray its TV origins (library stock footage is badly overused), the actors seem to have had a good time making the film and their enthusiasm shines through.

p, Howard Christie; d, Herschel Daugherty; w, Gene L. Coon; ph, Bud Thackery (Eastmancolor); m, Morton Stevens; ed, Gene Palmer; art d, Alexander A. Mayer; set d, John McCarthy, Robert C. Bradfield; cos, Vincent Dee; makeup, Jack Barron.

Western   (PR:A MPAA:NR)

RAIDERS FROM BENEATH THE SEA**   (1964) 73m Lippert/FOX bw

Ken Scott (Bill Harper), Merry Anders (Dottie Harper), Russ Bender (Tucker), Booth Colman (Purdy), Garth Benton (Buddy), Bruce Anson, Walter Maslow (Policemen), Stacey Winters (Bank Teller), Ray Dannis (Bowman), Larry Barton (Bank Manager), Roger Creed (Bank Guard).

Average caper film starring Scott as the mastermind in a gang of scuba-diving crooks who rob a bank on Catalina Island, dive into the sea with the loot, and head for their getaway boat. Unfortunately, Scott's right-hand man suffers a heart attack and his own airtank is pierced by a police bullet. Nearly dead from lack of oxygen, Scott almost makes it to the boat, but the strong undertow created by the boat's propellers sucks him in and kills him.

p&d, Maury Dexter; w, Harry Spaulding (based on a story by F. Paul Hall); ph, Floyd Crosby; m, Hank Levine; ed, Carl Pierson; set d, Harry Reif; m/l, "The Raiders Theme," Levine, "Two Lovers Theme," Levine, Jim Economides; makeup, Harry Thomas.

Crime   (PR:A MPAA:NR)

RAIDERS OF LEYTE GULF½**   (1963 U.S./Phil.) 90m Lynro/Hemisphere-Manhattan bw

Jennings Sturgeon (Emmett Wilson), Michael Parsons (Lt. Robert Grimm), Efren Reyes (Capt. Shirai Akira), Eddie Mesa (Angel Zabala), Leopold Salcedo (Col. Lino Sebastian), Liza Moreno (Aida Rivas), Oscar Keesee (Leon Magpayo).

Low-budget WW II film stars Sturgeon as an American POW captured by the Japanese while gathering intelligence around the isle of Leyte in preparation for General MacArthur's upcoming invasion. The Japs torture Sturgeon to try to get the information, but he won't talk, so they devise an insidious plan to execute one innocent Filipino a day until he changes his mind. Meanwhile, another American soldier, Parsons, parachutes into the hills and convinces the Filipino rebels to launch an attack to free Sturgeon. The attack fails, however, and the Japanese continue to execute the locals. Sturgeon finally breaks and decides to talk, but he is killed by angry Filipinos before he can speak. This causes a chaotic uprising and the rebels from the hills launch another attack. As he dies, Sturgeon stabs the Japanese commander to death, and the guerrillas defeat the garrison.

p&d, Eddie Romero; w, Romero, Carl Kuntze; ph, Felipe Sacdalan, Arsenia Dona; m, Tito Arevalo; ed, Romero.

War   (PR:A MPAA:NR)

RAIDERS OF OLD CALIFORNIA½**   (1957) 72m REP bw

Jim Davis, Arleen Whelan, Faron Young, Marty Robbins, Lee Van Cleef, Louis Jean Heydt, Harry Lauter, Douglas Fowley, Larry Dobkin, Bill Coontz, Don Diamond, Ric Vallin, Tom Hubbard.

A western which takes place in a Mexican inhabited section of California. When a vulgar cavalry officer pressures a hacienda owner into signing over his property, a heroic pioneer comes to aid the helpless Mexicans.

p&d, Albert C. Gannaway; w, Sam Roeca, Thomas C. Hubbard; ph, Charles Straummer; ed, Carl Pingitore.

Western   (PR:A MPAA:NR)

RAIDERS OF RED GAP**   (1944) 57m PRC bw

Bob Livingston (Rocky Cameron), Al "Fuzzy" St. John (Fuzzy Jones), Myrna Dell (Jane), Ed Cassidy (Roberts), Charles King (Bennett), Kermit Maynard (Bradley), Roy Brent (Butch), Frank Ellis (Jed), George Chesebro (Sheriff), Bud Osborne, Jimmy Aubrey, Merrill McCormack, George Morrell, Wally West, Reed Howes.

Typical LONE RIDER series oater starring Livingston as the defender of a group of ranchers who are being driven off their land by an evil cattle company which is attempting to gain control of all the grazing land in Arizona in an effort to corner the market and dictate prices to the East Coast meat packers. Livingston, aided by sidekick St. John, is sent by state officials to put an end to this nonsense. Unfortuantely, the ranchers think they're gunfighters working for the cattle company, and the cattle company thinks they're lawmen, which makes it difficult for the pair to infiltrate the gang.

p, Sigmund Neufeld; d, Sam Newfield; w, Joe O'Donnell (based on a story by O'Donnell); ph, Robert Cline; ed, Holbrook N. Todd.

Western   Cas.   (PR:A MPAA:NR)

RAIDERS OF SAN JOAQUIN**   (1943) 59m UNIV bw

Johnny Mack Brown (Rocky Morgan), Tex Ritter (Gil Blake), Fuzzy Knight (Eustace Clairmont), Jennifer Holt (Jane Carter), Henry Hall (Bodine Carter), Joseph Bernard (Jim Blake), George Eldredge (Gus Sloan), Henry Roquemore (Rogers), John Elliott (Morgan), Michael Vallon (Clark), Jack O'Shea (Detective), Jack Ingram (Lear), Robert Thompson (Johnson), Carl Sepulveda (Tanner), Scoop Martin (Tripp), Roy Brent (McQuarry), Budd Buster (Deputy), the Jimmy Wakely Trio, Earle Hodgins, Slim Whitaker.

Brown and Ritter find themselves embroiled in another land battle when they aid a group of ranchers whose land is being stolen by Hall, who claims to be buying right-of-way for the railroad that plans to come through. Brown, however, is related to the vice-president of the railroad and knows that it's a scam.

p, Oliver Drake; d, Lewis D. Collins; w, Elmer Clifton, Morgan Cox (based on a story by Patricia Harper); ph, William Sickner; ed, Russel Schoengarth; m/l, "A

Carefree Cowboy," "I'd Ruther Be Footloose and Free," "The Hatches and the Morgans," Drake.

Western **(PR:A MPAA:NR)**

RAIDERS OF SUNSET PASS** (1943) 57m REP bw

Eddie Dew *(John Paul Revere)*, Smiley Burnette *(Frog Millhouse)*, Jennifer Holt *(Betty Mathews)*, Roy Barcroft *(Lefty Lewis)*, Mozelle Cravens *(Carol)*, Nancy Worth *(Janice Clark)*, Kenne Duncan *(Tex Coburn)*, Jack Kirk *(George Meehan)*, Jack Rockwell *(Sheriff Dale)*, Hank Bell *(Old Cowhand)*, Budd Buster *(Nevada Jones)*, Jack Ingram, Frank McCarroll *(Rustlers)*, Fred Burns *(Deaf Cowhand)*, Al Taylor *(Rustler)*, Charles Miller *(Dad Mathews)*, LeRoy Mason *(Henry Judson)*, Maxine Doyle *(Sally Meehan)*.

A fascinating B western about a group of women who join forces to fend off a gang of rustlers attacking Miller's ranch. Because of WW II, Miller has a shortage of ranch hands, rendering him unable to battle the rustlers. With the rustlers stealing his cattle he is unable to meet a government contract he has agreed to. Miller's daughter, Holt, organizes the local girls into a group called the Women's Army of the Plains (WAPS). They band together at Miller's ranch, partaking in daily military drills and communicating with the cowboys via walkie-talkies. Because they are able to alert the local cowboys of the rustlers' attack, the gang is rounded up and Sunset Pass is again made safe. It is interesting not only that the role of women is so predominant in RAIDERS OF SUNSET PASS, but that there is any place at all for them in the traditionally male-dominated B western. The reason, however, is less a progressive one than one of necessity. Not only were the cowboy characters in the film away at war, but cowboy actors in Hollywood were also becoming scarce. The easiest solution (as opposed to stopping the production of oaters) was to use women in the mens' roles much in the same way our country's factories were using them. The return of the western stars (and soldiers) just a few short years later, however, caused Hollywood to revert back to many of its old ways. (See JOHN PAUL REVERE series, Index.)

p, Louis Gray; d, John English; w, John K. Butler; ph, John MacBurnie; m, Mort Glickman; ed, Harry Keller; art d, Russell Kimball.

Western **(PR:A MPAA:NR)**

RAIDERS OF THE BORDER** (1944) 53m MON bw

Johnny Mack Brown *(Nevada)*, Raymond Hatton *(Sandy)*, Craig Woods *(Joe)*, Ellen Hall *(Bonita)*, Raphael [Ray] Bennett *(Harsh)*, Edmund Cobb *(McGee)*, Ernie Adams *(Whiskey)*, Dick Alexander *(Steve)*, Lynton Brent *9Davis)*, Stanley Price *(Blackie)*, Kermit Maynard.

U.S. marshal Brown and his saddle-tramp buddy Hatton go after a gang of rustlers who are stealing cattle, driving the herds to Mexico, and exchanging the beef for stolen jewels. A lot of fisticuffs enliven this slow-mover.

p, Scott R. Dunlap; d, John P. McCarthy; w, Jess Bowers [Adele Buffington] (based on a story by Johnston McCulley); ph, Harry Neumann; ed, Carl Pierson; md, Edward Kay; m/l, "Meadowland," from the Soviet army song "Cavalry of the Steppes," Lev Knipper, Victor Gussev, English lyrics by Harold Rome.

Western **Cas.** **(PR:A MPAA:NR)**

RAIDERS OF THE DESERT** (1941) 60m UNIV bw

Richard Arlen *(Dick Manning)*, Andy Devine *(Andy McCoy)*, Linda Hayes *(Alice Evans)*, Lewis Howard *(Abdullah Ibn El Azora El Karim)*, George Carleton *(Jones)*, Turhan Bey *(Hassen Mohammed)*, John Harmon *(Ahmed)*, Maria Montez *(Zuleika)*, Ralf Harolde *(Sheik Talifah)*, Neyle Marx *(Moviow/Zeid)*, Jamiel Hasson *(Knife-Throwing Warrior)*, Charles Regan *(Warrior)*, Stanley Price *(Gate Cop)*, Sig Arno *(Suliman)*, Ralph Peters *(Max)*, Harry Cording *(Rawlins)*, Armand "Curly" Wright *(Waiter)*, Pat Gleason *(Sailor)*, Evelyn Selbie *(Flower Woman)*, Sheila Darcy, Suzanne Ridgway, Rose Burich, Mayta Palmera *(Arab Girls)*, Bob Wilbur *(Caravan Leader)*, Nick Shaid *(Patriarch)*, Dave Sharpe *(Double for Turhan Bey)*.

Carleton is a well-intentioned philanthropist whose attempt to bring democracy to an Arabian desert village is met with opposition. A revolution breaks out, but Arlen and Devine manage to quell the warmongers and save Carleton. A second-rate script which is saved only by decent performances from Arlen and Devine.

p, Ben Pivar; d, John Rawlins; w, Maurice Tombragel, Victor I. McLeod; ph, John Boyle; ed, Maurice Wright; md, H.J. Salter.

Adventure **(PR:A MPAA:NR)**

RAIDERS OF THE LOST ARK***** (1981) 115m Lucasfilm Productions/PAR c

Harrison Ford *(Indiana Jones)*, Karen Allen *(Marion Ravenswood)*, Paul Freeman *(Belloq)*, Ronald Lacey *(Toht)*, John Rhys-Davies *(Sallah)*, Denholm Elliott *(Brody)*, Wolf Kahler *(Dietrich)*, Anthony Higgins *(Gobler)*, Alfred Molina *(Satipo)*, Vic Tablian *(Barranca)*, Don Fellows *(Col. Musgrove)*, William Hootkins *(Maj. Eaton)*, Bill Reimbold *(Bureaucrat)*, Fred Sorenson *(Jock)*, Patrick Durkin *(Australian Climber)*, Matthew Scurfield *(2nd Nazi)*, Malcom Weaver *(Ratty Nepalese)*, Sonny Caldinez *(Mean Mongolian)*, Anthony Chinn *(Mohan)*, Pat Roach *(Giant Sherpa)*, Christopher Frederick *(Otto)*, Tutte Lemkow *(Imam)*, Ishaq Bux *(Omar)*, Kiran Shah *(Abu)*, Souad Messaoudi *(Fayah)*, Vic Tablian *(Monkey Man)*, Terry Richards *(Swordsman)*, Steve Hanson *(German Agent)*, Pat Roach *(1st Mechanic)*, Frank Marshall *(Pilot)*, Martin Kreidt *(Young Soldier)*, George Harris *(Katanga)*, Eddie Tagoe *(Messenger Pirate)*, John Rees *(Sergeant)*, Tony Vogel *(Tall Captain)*, Ted Grossman *(Peruvian Porter)*, Jack Dearlove *(Stand-In)*, Terry Leonard, Martin Grace, Vic Armstrong, Wendy Leach, Sergio Mione, Rocky Taylor, Chuck Waters, Bill Weston, Paul Weston, Reg Harding, Billy Horrigan, Peter Brace, Gerry Crampton, Romo Garrara.

The old 1930s action-crammed serial was never better served as a full-length feature than in this spectacular cliffhanger. RAIDERS OF THE LOST ARK is not only fraught with incredible action in almost every frame but it is produced with such polish and elan, not to mention humor, that the film achieves classic status. Ford is the stoic but always on the move hero whom no peril can daunt, no woman can conquer (well, maybe one), and no obstacle can stop. He is the only thing larger than life the screen can emotionally bear—pure fantasy—yet without his wonderful ilk there are no dreams nor the stuff they are made of. It is 1936 and Ford is an archeologist and university professor who is seen entering a South American tomb en route to plunder its priceless artifactual treasures. Once inside the tomb with his self-serving guide, Ford dodges primitive booby traps, including light-sensitive poison darts, impaling spikes, and hordes of deadly tarantulas, to get to a small sack squatting on an altar, exchanging this for one of his own which supposedly is of equal weight. As he turns to go, Ford realizes that he has miscalculated the weight and he and his guide must race ahead of an enormous boulder that is released by the descending altar, a mammoth boulder that rolls wildly after them. Ford uses his whip to make a rope by which to swing across a bottomless chasm and the guide swings across first, telling Ford to throw him the sack containing the golden godhead. He does, and the treacherous guide removes the whip, stranding the hero and leaving him as he runs for the mouth of the cave. Ford leaps across the chasm, clings to the other side by his fingertips, and then manages to pull himself up and run forward, just ahead of the thundering boulder. He spots the guide, his body rent with impaling spikes, and he quickly retrieves the sack and dives out of the cave just ahead of the crushing boulder. But once outside, Ford finds himself a prisoner of Freeman, another archeologist who vies with Ford for the world's hidden treasures. With Freeman is an army of well-armed natives who would just as soon spear Ford as say hello. Freeman takes the godhead and orders his rival killed but Ford makes a break for the river and leaps into it just as the natives reach the banks throwing spears after him. He swims to an amphibious plane where his pilot has already started the motors and is engineering the plane up river. It passes Ford and he reaches out, grabs a pontoon, and climbs aboard, working himself into the empty open cockpit in front of the pilot. There he shrinks back in horror as the pilot's pet snake curls itself about him. "I hate snakes!" yells Ford to the pilot. "Aww, show a little backbone, will you?" the pilot shouts back above the drone of the motors as the plane clears the river and shoots skyward. This is but the opening sequence, wholly unrelated to the main story (a device Spielberg borrowed from the James Bond films), which sets the character but certainly not the plot. Once back in the U.S., Ford is sought out at his university by agents from U.S. Intelligence who ask him to look into a rumor concerning, of all things, the Ark of the Covenant in which the Ten Commandments taken down by Moses repose. The Ark, say the agents, is being sought by agents of Adolf Hitler—"He's a nut on the occult"—so that the Fuhrer can use same to psychologically and mystically assure his ambitions of world domination. Ford's assignment is simple. Get to the Ark before the Nazis and return it to the U.S. for safekeeping. The archeologist concludes that anything is possible, especially when one has a hieroglyphic medallion he knows about, one that can actually tell where the Ark is hidden. He goes to the high mountains of Nepal to retrieve the medallion, entering a mountaintop saloon run by his ex-girl friend Allen. She is a spitfire who stands the hero to hard drinks and is about to give him the medallion, despite the fact that she's still angry with him for deserting her some time earlier, when a bevy of Nazi agents appear, led by Lacey, and shoot the place to pieces, setting it afire and driving Ford and Allen into snowdrifts. The two fly to Cairo, where Rhys-Davies, an old Egyptian friend of Ford's, informs Ford that Nazi agents are busy trying to find something important hidden in the nearby ancient ruins. While in Cairo, Allen, after a hair-raising chase through the streets where Ford dispatches several would-be assassins, is kidnaped and taken into the desert, there to be held hostage by the ubiquitous Freeman who is in league with the Nazis in their desperate search for the Ark. Ford and Rhys-Davies go to the ruins which are swarming with German troops wearing Afrika Corps uniforms (an error since Gen. Erwin Rommel's African army did not arrive in North Africa until 1940-41). The ever-present Lacey, still bearing the scars he received in the Nepal battle, arrives and hovers menacingly about Allen. Ford, using the medallion, pinpoints an area in an excavated tomb and lowers himself inside, only to find that the floor is moving—it is carpeted with thousands of venomous snakes, his greatest fear. He manages to use burning torches to keep the snakes away and bundles up the Ark so that Rhys-Davies and his men can lift it to safety but just at that moment Freeman, Lacey, and Nazi troopers arrive, throw Allen into a tomb, take the Ark, and leave Ford and the screaming Allen to fend for themselves in the snake-infested tomb. With their tapers burning low, Ford desperately tries to find a way out, clambering up the sides of walls while thousands of poisonous snakes slither about, tongues darting. Before the last torch burns out, Ford finds a way out and he and Allen escape the reptilian nightmare. When Ford learns that the Nazis have loaded the Ark onto a truck and are racing away with the prize, he traps the truck and battles the German soldiers off the truck, running accompanying vehicles off the road. He himself is knocked from the speeding truck but (in a stunt originating with western film daredevil Yakima Canutt) falls in front of the truck, which runs over him without touching him. He grabs a rear bumper and is dragged along until he can lift himself up, crawl alongside the truck, and leap back into the driver's cab, kicking the last Nazi out onto the road. He swoops up Allen and the two battle a bevy of Nazis about to take off in a waiting plane. They survive many a desert peril and board a boat headed for the U.S., one carrying the great Ark which starts to radiate strange lights in the hold. The ship is stopped by a Nazi sub and Allen and the Ark are taken aboard, sailing to a mysterious island. There Ford tracks the Nazis but, rather than risk Allen's life once more, surrenders to them. He and Allen are tied to stakes while the Ark is ritualistically opened. Ford tells Allen (as the consummate hero he knows what to say and do at all times of stress) not to look at the blinding light the Ark begins to shoot forth. The Germans to a man, however, stare at the searing rays and are consumed, each of them, by shafts of fire which melt their bodies and reduce every evil minion to ashes, including the sinister Freeman and Lacey. The Ark then sends its great light skyward and reseals itself with the aid of Divine Intervention. With Ford and Allen free to pursue new adventures, the Ark, with only a long inventory number to identify its crate, is sent to an enormous U.S.

warehouse where it is held for safekeeping, a warehouse not unlike that depicted in the final scene of CITIZEN KANE. This film is so outlandish and wild that the viewer is required to not only suspend disbelief but completely submit to the fantasy. That done, the sheer pleasure of the film can be felt, although it is extremely violent and Spielberg does not spare the viewer disintegrating corpses, blood, horrors of all kinds. Ford is properly laconic and tunnel-visioned while his erstwhile girl friend Allen is as feisty as they come. The bad guys here are not merely bad, they are disgustingly repulsive, without a shred of decency or honor. Lacey's Nazi agent is a study in outrageous acting; he imitates a hissing Peter Lorre and a snarling Conrad Veidt, while smiling lasciviously at Allen and adjusting telescopic spectacles. He projects one of the most offensive characters to sully the screen since WW II propaganda films paraded human beasts with swastika armbands. The film's special effects are eye-popping and Spielberg directs with the fury of a serial helmsman with only an hour left to go before his budget sinks into quicksand. It's the greatest adventure nonsense to be produced in a decade and it caught on like wildfire with the public, sweeping the critics into kudosland. Spielberg, who talked with Lucas about his concept for RAIDERS OF THE LOST ARK as early as 1977, shot the film in Hawaii, France, Tunisia, and at Elstree Studios in England in a whirlwind 73 days at a staggering cost of $22.8 million (and it showed in every topflight frame). The film has gone on to make as much as $200 million, according to one estimate, and become one of the 10 top box office champions of all time. For chills and thrills, this film is hard to beat, even by its astounding sequel, INDIANA JONES AND THE TEMPLE OF DOOM.

p, Frank Marshall; d, Steven Spielberg; w, Lawrence Kasdan (based on a story by George Lucas, Philip Kaufman); ph, Douglas Slocombe, Paul Beeson (Panavision, Metrocolor); m, John Williams; ed, Michael Kahn; prod d, Norman Reynolds; art d, Leslie Dilley; set d, Michael Ford; cos, Deborah Nadoolman; spec eff, Richard Edlund, Kit West; stunts, Glenn Randall; makeup, Dickie Mills; animation, John Van Vliet, Kim Knowton, Garry Waller, Lording Doyle, Scott Caple, Judy Elkins, Sylvia Keuler, Scott Marshal.

Adventure/Fantasy   **Cas.**   **(PR:C-O MPAA:NR)**

RAIDERS OF THE RANGE**

(1942) 54m REP bw

Bob Steele (Tucson Smith), Tom Tyler (Stoney Brooke), Rufe Davis (Lullaby Joslin), Lois Collier (Jean Travers), Frank Jacquet (Sam Daggett), Tom Chatterton (Doc Higgins), Charles Miller ("Pop" Travers), Dennis Moore (Ned Foster), Fred Kohler, Jr. (Plummer), Max Walzman (The Coroner), Hal Price (Sheriff), Charles Phillips, Bud Geary, Jack Ingram, Al Taylor, Chuck Morrison, Joel Friedkin, Bob Woodward,3 Tom Steele, Monte Montague, Ken Terrell, Dick Alexander, Cactus Mack, John Cason.

The Three Mesquiteers ride again. This time out they aid an enterprising young oil driller, Chatterton, who plans to sink a well in the hope that he'll strike it rich, which would bring the railroad and prosperity to the town. Unfortunately, one of the town's more dim-witted residents accidentally poisons one man and kills another, setting things up for unscrupulous saloon owner Jaquet (who owns a second option lease on the oil property) to blackmail him into sabotaging the operation. Luckily, Steele, Tyler, and Davis arrive and set things straight. (See THREE MESQUITEERS series, Index.)

p, Louis Gray; d, John English; w, Barry Shipman (based on a story by Albert DeMond, based on characters created by William Colt MacDonald); ph, Ernest Miller, m, Cy Feuer; ed, John Lockert; m/l, "The Whistle of the Five Twenty-seven," Raoul Kraushaar, Sol Meyer (sung by Rufe Davis).

Western   **(PR:A MPAA:NR)**

RAIDERS OF THE SEVEN SEAS**

(1953) 87m UA c

John Payne (Barbarossa), Donna Reed (Alida), Gerald Mohr (Salcedo), Lon Chaney, Jr. (Peg Leg), Anthony Caruso (Renzo), Henry Brandon (Capt. Goiti), Skip Torgerson (Datu), Frank DeKova (Romero), William Tannen (Ramon), Christopher Dark (Pablo), Claire DuBrey (Senora Salcedo), Howard Freeman (Pompano), Anthony Warde (Delgado).

Payne stars as a red-bearded pirate (no, it's not Willie Nelson) who takes it on the lam after getting caught goofing around in the Sultan of Morocco's harem. The feisty swashbuckler grabs a Spanish prison ship, liberates the convicts and drafts them into being his loyal crew members. With his new ship and crew, Payne takes on the Spanish fleet, embarrassing the empire at every turn and romancing Reed, the fiancee of Spanish officer Mohr. An ambitious pirate, played by Caruso, betrays the cause and kills Payne's second-in-command, Chaney. Realizing that Caruso was bribed by Mohr, who seeks the governorship of Cuba, Payne threatens to destroy Havana. In the final moments, however, Payne smells a trap and decides against the invasion, leaving a humiliated Mohr trying to justify his actions to his superiors.

p&d, Sidney Salkow; w, John O'Dea, Salkow (based on a story by O'Dea, Salkow); ph, W. Howard Greene (Technicolor); m, Paul Sawtell; ed, Buddy Small; art d, Edward L. Ilou; cos, Yvonne Wood; ch, Willetta Smith.

Adventure   **(PR:A MPAA:NR)**

RAIDERS OF THE SOUTH*

(1947) 55m MON bw

Johnny Mack Brown, Evelyn Brent, Raymond Hatton, Reno Blair, Marshall Reed, John Hamilton, John Merton, Eddie Parker, Frank LaRue, Ted Adams, Pierce Lyden, Cactus Mack, George Morrell, Ray Jones, Artie Ortego, Billy Dix, Dee Cooper, Curt Barrett and The Trailsman.

Brown and his fellow government men chase down a bunch of rebels in the Southwest. With some tough six-gunning they manage to bring the gang under control.

p, Scott R. Dunlap; d, Lambert Hillyer; w, J. Benton Cheney; ph, Harry Neumann; ed, Fred Maguire; set d, Vin Taylor.

Western   **(PR:A MPAA:NR)**

RAIDERS OF THE WEST*½

(1942) 64m PRC bw

Bill "Cowboy Rambler" Boyd, Art Davis, Lee Powell, Virginia Carroll, Rex Lease, Charles King, Glenn Strange, Slim Whitaker, Milt Kibbee, Lynton Brent, John Elliott, Eddie Dean, Curley Dresden, William Desmond, Dale Sherwood, Kenne Duncan, Bill Cody, Jr., Reed Howes, Hal Price, Fred "Snowflake" Toones, Carl Sepulveda, Frank Ellis, John Cason.

Boyd is a range detective who poses as an entertainer for an outlaw gang leader. He learns of the secret hide-out, but is discovered and captured. He manages to escape and bring the law down on his former captors.

p, Sigmund Neufeld; d, Peter Stewart [Sam Newfield]; w, Oliver Drake; ed, Holbrook N. Todd.

Western   **Cas.**   **(PR:A MPAA:NR)**

RAIDERS OF TOMAHAWK CREEK**½

(1950) 55m COL bw

Charles Starrett (Steve Blake/The Durango Kid), Smiley Burnette (Himself), Edgar Dearing (Randolph Dike), Kay Buckley (Janet Clayton), Billy Kimbley (Billy Calhoun), Paul Marion (Chief Flying Arrow), Paul McGuire (Sheriff), Bill Hale (Jeff), Lee Morgan (Saunders), Ted Mapes.

Action-packed Starrett oater which sees the cowboy as the owner of one in a set of five rings, that when pieced together, will yield a map to hidden treasures. The problem is, evil ex-Indian agent Dearing has been obtaining the other four rings using violent methods. Starrett's sidekick Burnette sings two songs, "I'm Too Smart For That," and the ever-popular western tune "Grasshopper Polka." (See DURANGO KID series, Index.)

p, Colbert Clark; d, Fred F. Sears; w, Barry Shipman (based on a story by Robert Schaefer, Eric Freiwald); ph, Fayte Browne; ed, Paul Borofsky; md, Mischa Bakaleinikoff; art d, Charles Clague.

Western   **(PR:A MPAA:NR)**

RAILROAD MAN, THE**½

(1965, Ital.) 105m Ponti-DD-ENIC/CD bw (IL FERROVIERE; AKA: MAN OF IRON)

Pietro Germi (Andrea Marcocci), Luisa Della Noce (Sara Marocci), Sylva Koscina (Giulia), Saro Urzi (Liverani), Renato Spezali (Renato), Carlo Giuffre (Marcello), Edoardo Nevola (Sandrino), Amedeo Trilli.

Heartfelt story of an easygoing railroad engineer, Germi, whose unruly family starts to take its toll on him. It starts with his daughter, Koscina, becoming pregnant and refusing to marry the father, instead running off with another man. Further trouble erupts when Germi drives a train over a suicide victim; shaken by the event, he messes up on the job and is demoted to driving a freight. The whole world seems to be against Germi, except for the son who remains faithful. His spirit broken by the unhappy turn of events, Germi heads to the pub where he had once enjoyed the company of his many friends, only to suffer a stroke when he receives a warm welcome from his old friends. Simple tale of the ironies of life.

p, Carlo Ponti; d, Pietro Germi; w, Germi, Alfredo Gianetti, Luciano Vincenzoni, Ennio De Concini (based on a story by Gianetti); ph, Leonida Barboni, Aiace Parolin; m, Carlo Rustichelli; ed, Dolores Tamburini; md, Franco Ferrara; art d, Carlo Egidi; cos, Mirella Morelli.

Drama   **(PR:A MPAA:NR)**

RAILROAD WORKERS**½

(1948, Swed.) 108m Svensk bw (RALLARE)

Victor Seastrom [Sjostrom] (Stora Ballong), John Elfstrom (Valfrid), Gunnel Brostrom (Viktoria), Bengt Eklund (Amos), Sven Magnusson (Dynamite), Birger Asander (Fabian Bred), Ake Gronberg (Calle-ville), Axel Hogel (Baptist-Anders), Keve Hjelm (Natan), Inga Landgre (Hildur), Ingrid Borthen (Black Bear), Svea Holst (Stina), Sven Bergvall (Hager), Harry Ahlin (Blom).

Well-made Swedish film detailing the rise of the railroad in that country and starring Swedish director Seastrom who directed the Lon Chaney, Sr., silent classic HE WHO GETS SLAPPED (1927) in Hollywood and also acted quite regularly in other people's films (his best known role is that of the old man in Ingmar Bergman's WILD STRAWBERRIES).

d, Arne Matisson; w, Olle Laensberg, Rune Lindstrom (based on the novel Nordanvind by Lindstrom); ph, Martin Bodin; m, E. Eckert-Lundin.

Drama   **(PR:A MPAA:NR)**

RAILROADED***

(1947) 72m EL bw

John Ireland (Duke Martin), Sheila Ryan (Rosa Ryan), Hugh Beaumont (Mickey Ferguson), Jane Randolph (Clara Calhoun), Ed Kelly (Steve Ryan), Charles D. Brown (Capt. MacTaggart), Clancy Cooper (Chubb), Peggy Converse (Marie), Hermine Sterler (Mrs. Ryan), Keefe Brasselle (Cowie), Roy Gordon (Ainsworth).

Disturbing, grim film noir directed by Anthony Mann and starring Ireland as a psychopathic killer who ritualistically dips his bullets in perfume and lovingly strokes his handgun while cleaning it. The story involves the investigation of the robbery of a beauty shop that was really a front for a gambling den. In the robbery, a policeman is killed and one of the robbers, Brasselle, is apprehended. Badly disfigured in the robbery, Brasselle is taken to a hospital and interrogated. Under pressure from the police to name names, he implicates his friend Kelly, who is innocent of any involvement in the crime. Kelly's sister Ryan begs police detective Beaumont to reinvestigate the case because she is convinced her brother is innocent. Eventually they discover that Ireland, a sadistic killer, had robbed the gambling den for the mob, and then pocketed the money himself. Beaumont and Ryan are frustrated in their attempts to track down witnesses to the crime because Ireland has gotten to them first and murdered them with his scented lead. Finally Beaumont corners the creep in a deserted restaurant and kills him. Though its plot is fairly simple, RAILROADED is notable for Ireland's unrelentingly macabre portrayal of a sick, sexually perverted maniac who gets his thrills from guns, a portrayal that must have just barely made it past the censors in 1947.

p, Charles F. Riesner; d, Anthony Mann; w, John C. Higgins (based on a story by Gertrude Walker); ph, Guy Roe; m, Alvin Levin; ed, Louis Sackin; md, Irving Friedman; art d, Perry Smith; set d, Armor Marlowe, Robert P. Fox; cos, Frances Ehren; makeup, Ern Westmore, Tom Tuttle.

Crime Cas. (PR:C MPAA:NR)

RAILS INTO LARAMIE½** (1954) 80m UNIV c

John Payne *(Jefferson Harder)*, Mari Blanchard *(Lou Carter)*, Dan Duryea *(Jim Shanessy)*, Joyce MacKenzie *(Helen Shanessy)*, Barton MacLane *(Lee Graham)*, Harry Shannon *(Judge Pierce)*, Ralph Dumke *(Mayor Brown)*, Lee Van Cleef *(Ace Winton)*, Myron Healey *(Con Winton)*, James Griffith *(Orrie Sommers)*, Alexander Campbell *(Higby)*, George Chandler *(Grimes)*, Charles Horvath *(Pike Murphy)*, Stephen Chase *(Gen. Auger)*, Douglas Kennedy *(Telegraph Operator)*, George Cleveland.

Payne plays an Army sergeant sent to the town of Laramie to stop crooked bartender Duryea and his gang of thugs who have been waging a war against the new railroad to prevent its completion (Duryea is making too much money off booze and women bought by the railroad workers to let them finish and move on). Once Payne captures the gang, Blanchard organizes an all-female jury to convict the creep because previous male juries had let Duryea go on other charges.

p, Ted Richmond; d, Jesse Hibbs; w, D.D. Beauchamp, Joseph Hoffman; ph, Maury Gertsman (Technicolor); m, Frederick Herbert, Arnold Hughes; ed, Ted J. Kent; md, Joseph Gershenson; m/l, "Laramie," Herbert, Hughes (sung by Rex Allen).

Western (PR:A MPAA:NR)

RAILWAY CHILDREN, THE*** (1971, Brit.) 108m EMI/UNIV c

Dinah Sheridan *(Mother)*, Bernard Cribbins *(Perks, Railway Porter)*, William Mervyn *(Old Gentleman)*, Iain Cuthbertson *(Father)*, Jenny Agutter *(Bobbie)*, Sally Thomsett *(Phyllis)*, Peter Bromilow *(Doctor)*, Ann Lancaster *(Ruth)*, Gary Warren *(Peter)*, Gordon Whiting *(Russian)*, Beatrix Mackey *(Aunt Emma)*, Deddie Davies *(Mrs. Perks)*, Christopher Witty *(Jim)*, Brenda Cowling *(Mrs. Viney)*, Paddy Ward *(Cartman)*, Erik Chitty *(Photographer)*, Sally James *(Maid)*, Dominic Allen *(C.I.D. Man)*, David Lodge *(Bandmaster)*.

Effective children's film set in Britain during the Edwardian period and starring Sheridan as the wife of a British Foreign Office employee who is falsely accused of treason and imprisoned. Forced by disgrace and lack of income to move from their lush surroundings to the Yorkshire moors where Sheridan sells the idea to her children as sort of a game (they "pretend" to be poor). The kids take to their new surroundings quickly and it is only a matter of time until they have made new friends and sunk roots in the area. The village they now live in is located near a railway, and much of their play time is spent among the trains. Among their new friends is a wealthy resident of the area who volunteers to help them clear their father's name. Well acted, nicely scripted and produced with the right amount of heart and sentiment.

p, Robert Lynn; d&w, Lionel Jeffries (based on a novel by E. Nesbit); ph, Arthur Ibbetson (Technicolor); m, Johnny Douglas; ed, Teddy Darvas; art d, John Clark; set d, Geoffrey Leggett; cos, Elsa Fennell; spec eff, Pat Moore, John Richardson; makeup, Jock Alexander.

Drama (PR:A MPAA:G)

RAIN½** (1932) 92m UA bw

Joan Crawford *(Sadie Thompson)*, Walter Huston *(Rev. Alfred Davidson)*, William Gargan *(Sgt. O'Hara)*, Guy Kibbee *(Joe Horn)*, Walter Catlett *(Quartermaster Bates)*, Beulah Bondi *(Mrs. Davidson)*, Matt Moore *(Dr. MacPhail)*, Kendall Lee *(Mrs. MacPhail)*, Ben Hendricks *(Griggs)*, Frederic Howard *(Hodgson)*.

Crawford goes overboard as the jaded Sadie in Maugham's fine novel about sex and religion, with Huston giving one of his best performances as the zealot Davidson. A tramp steamer is forced to dock at remote Pago Pago in the Samoas after a disease breaks out on board. Among the passengers is pavement pounder Crawford, whose curves quickly attract the eyes of women-hungry soldiers on the island, especially good-hearted Gargan, a sergeant who naively believes that Crawford is not what the crooked seams of her stockings should easily tell him. Crawford jokes with and teases the soldiers but it's all in suggestive fun which is how layman religious zealot Huston sees her behavior. He and his wife, Bondi, are both fanatical missionaries who will convert the coconut trees if they'll listen to their diatribes. The severe Huston dedicates himself to the crusade of reforming prostitute Crawford. Her initial response to his blandishments is to answer him with smart talk and wry remarks. But he persists like a grasshopper clinging to a leaf and she soon grows impatient and angry with him. Meanwhile, Gargan learns the truth about his mascaraed dream girl and he, too, wants her to take up a new way of life, surprisingly as his wife. The dogged Huston keeps chipping away at Crawford's tough bark until he compels her to confess her sinful ways. Moreover, he lets it be known that, unless she changes her moral attitude, he will have her deported to any number of ports where she may be imprisoned for past indiscretions. Crawford succumbs to his spiritual demands and embraces Huston's rigid religious philosophy, believing he is sincere in wanting her salvation. The rain, meanwhile, and throughout the film, continues to drum down on this little world, fraying nerves to the breaking point. Huston himself loses his iron control and, while natives beat out drum chants in the forest, he is overcome with a feeling about Crawford he has long suppressed—lust. He attacks and rapes her in her room, shattering her newfound religious inclinations. At dawn Crawford emerges from her room more cynical and jaded than before. She learns that her one-time spiritual mentor Huston has committed suicide but she can find no pity for him. Gargan comes to her as she is about to leave the island, and it appears that even though Crawford is more worldly than ever, she can now accept the love of the soldier and, perhaps, plan a new life. Milestone captures the mood and murk of the rain-drenched island and the strange bedfellows compelled to live with each other until redemption or the sun appears. The play, adapted from Maugham's novel, is faithfully produced and Crawford is convincing if overly made-up, while Huston is excellent as the humorless soul-saver who cannot save himself from his own desires. Crawford was terrified of making RAIN, believing that she would be unfavorably compared with stellar actresses who had essayed the Sadie Thompson role in previous productions, particularly Gloria Swanson who appeared in a silent screen version, and Jeanne Eagels who made the role her own on stage. She was compared later to those ladies and it proved an uphill battle to convince the critics that she had brought anything new to the role. Movie mogul Schenck persuaded the star to leave the friendly confines of MGM to make this film at UA, soothing her apprehensions by getting her favorite cinematographer, Marsh, to shoot the film, but Milestone and Crawford did not get along. The director insisted upon innumerable rehearsals and the star balked at such preparations. Said Crawford later: "We rehearsed interminably. From the first day I knew that the picture would be a failure and that I was dreadful." She did not get along with Huston, a polished stage actor, nor did Crawford appreciate the then-crude accommodations available on Catalina Island where the film was shot on location. Moreover, two other New York stage actors, Gargan, her supposed protector onscreen, and Catlett, a man with an acid tongue who had made his name in the Ziegfeld Follies with sketches that were largely character assassinations, proved cold if not outright antagonistic toward her. Early in the production, Crawford joined Gargan and Catlett—who were sitting off camera—and began talking about her previous films to Gargan, who appeared to listen. The actor, who had just arrived from New York after performing in the smash hit "The Animal Kingdom," remained mutely staring at her as she nervously rattled off her screen credits. When she finished he shocked her by bluntly (and smugly) saying, "Miss Crawford, I've never seen you on the screen in my life!" Catlett was even less kind. When the actress tried to engage him in conversation, the actor—a noted tippler who had been pumping down a great quantity of bootleg booze—leaned close to the actress, blew liquor-tainted breath on her wide-eyed face, and snorted: "Listen, fish-cake, when Jeanne Eagels died, RAIN died with her." Such treatment caused Crawford to retreat to her cabin where—when not shooting scenes—she remained, locked inside and having her meals brought to her, playing and wearing out Bing Crosby records until other members of the cast complained to Milestone, who merely shrugged. The director was more upset when Crawford marched onto the set one day and refused to perform until all the visitors gaping at her were sent away. "Put up the 'niggers,'" she demanded, meaning Milestone had to order large black-cloth screens to shield the outdoor set from public view. To keep the peace, he did, but it didn't improve Crawford's attitude nor that of others in the cast. Following the critical reviews of the film upon its release, Crawford stated: "I did it badly, I know it. I would have given anything to recall it. What was the matter with me? Why had I gone so wrong?" She put the blame on her obsession with Swanson and Eagels and how they had achieved success with the role she felt was beyond her. "The two ghosts of Sadie Thompson rose up to haunt me," she concluded, but her portrayal, upon viewing today, is much better than the critics of the time thought. She is sensitive, raucous, bawdy, and yet, when embracing Huston's fever-pitched religion, genuinely touching. Remade as MISS SADIE THOMPSON, (1953), starring Rita Hayworth as the tramp, Jose Ferrer as the religious crackpot, and Aldo Ray as the fun-loving, gullible sergeant.

p, Joseph M. Schenck; d, Lewis Milestone; w, Maxwell Anderson (based on the play "Rain" by John Colton, Clemence Randolph, and the story *Miss Thompson* by W. Somerset Maugham); ph, Oliver T. Marsh; ed, W. Duncan Mansfield; art d, Richard Day.

Drama Cas. (PR:C-O MPAA:NR)

RAIN FOR A DUSTY SUMMER*½ (1971, U.S./Span.) 91m Do-Bar c

Ernest Borgnine *(Dictator)*, Humberto Almazan *(Miguel Pro)*, Sancho Garcia *(Humberto Pro)*, Vicente Sangiovani *(Luis)*, Aldo Sanbrell *(Marinos)*.

Below-par historical drama set in Mexico in 1917 and starring Borgnine as a ruthless despot who goes on a rampage, killing all the priests in the country. Almazan, a former actor who became a priest and appeared in the film with papal permission, plays the noble cleric who makes it his duty to stop the slaughter. Cheap and uninvolving, dubbed import.

p, G.B. Buscemi; d, Arthur Lubin; w, Julius Evans, Buscemi (based on a story by Franklyn Lacey); ph, Manuel Berenguer (Eastmancolor); m, Wade Denning; ed, Rich Greer; art d&set d, Juan Alberto Soler.

Drama (PR:C MPAA:GP

RAIN OR SHINE½** (1930) 90m COL bw

Joe Cook *(Smiley)*, Louise Fazenda *(Frankie)*, Joan Peers *(Mary)*, William Collier, Jr. *(Bud)*, Tom Howard *(Amos)*, David Chasen *(Dave)*, Alan Roscoe *(Dalton)*, Adolph Milar *(Foltz)*, Clarence Muse *(Nero)*, Edward Martindale *(Mr. Conway)*, Nora Lane *(Grace Conway)*, Tyrrell Davis *(Lord Gwynne)*.

A very early Frank Capra film which was based on Broadway comedian Cook's hit musical. Unfortunately, the studio didn't want to pay extra for the songs, so the film is without the musical numbers. The thin plot sees Peers as the inheritor of her late father's financially floundering circus. With the help of her manager, Cook, Peers tries to salvage the big top and bring in bigger crowds. The main focus of the film is on the comic antics of Cook and his sidekicks Chasen and Howard, whose laughs are derived from some fairly inventive slapstick and pun-filled verbal exchanges. Two spectacular set pieces pop up in the film, one a nasty rainstorm (the special effects crew turned the water on a little high during the shooting and almost washed away the set, allowing an elephant to escape), the other a climactic burning of the big top (Capra actually set fire to the tent and filmed the scenes in one take before the whole thing burned down) giving a realistic, exciting air to an otherwise average film.

d, Frank Capra; w, Jo Swerling, Dorothy Howell (based on the play by James Gleason); ph, Joseph Walker; ed, Maurice Wright; m/l, "Happy Days Are Here Again," "Rain or Shine," Jack Yellen, Milton Ager, "Sitting on a Rainbow," Yellen, Jack Dougherty.

Drama **(PR:A MPAA:NR)**

RAIN PEOPLE, THE*** (1969) 101m WB c

James Caan *(Jimmie "Killer" Kilgannon)*, Shirley Knight *(Natalie Ravenna)*, Robert Duvall *(Gordon)*, Marya Zimmet *(Rosalie)*, Tom Aldredge *(Mr. Alfred)*, Laurie Crewes *(Ellen)*, Andrew Duncan *(Artie)*, Margaret Fairchild *(Marion)*, Sally Gracie *(Beth)*, Alan Manson *(Lou)*, Robert Modica *(Vinny Ravenna)*.

This is one of those "better luck next time" pictures and, of course, next time meant THE GODFATHER for Coppola. He'd already directed four films without much success—TONIGHT FOR SURE, DEMENTIA 13, YOU'RE A BIG BOY NOW, and FINIAN'S RAINBOW—and while studios felt sure of his screenwriting capability (He'd also co-written THIS PROPERTY IS CONDEMNED and collaborated with Gore Vidal on IS PARIS BURNING?), his directorial work was seriously in question. This odd odyssey was not a hit, although over the years, it has been looked upon as one of Coppola's more personal pictures and has attained a mild following. Knight is a childless Long Island housewife married to a decent man, Modica. She learns she's pregnant and can't decide what to do, so she bolts out the door early one rainy morning while Modica snores. Once on the road, she phones him and says that she needs some time to herself away from him and will probably come back. . .eventually. She has no idea where she's going, she just wants to go. During the movie, she calls Modica from time to time to let him know she's all right, to admit that she hasn't been a very good wife, and to let him know she's expecting and not certain that she wants to have the child. Modica, who is seen solely in the first sequence and is then only a voice on the phone, is irate when she talks about an abortion but calms down and says she can do what she wishes as long as she returns to him. Knight is a sexually naive woman and eager to find another partner, so when she picks up Caan on the road, he is elected. Then she learns that he is a brain-damaged football player and wears a plate in his head, the result of a gridiron accident for which the school gave him $1,000 when he signed away any claims. He wants to go to West Virginia where he thinks he has a job promised by Duncan, the father of his former girl friend, Crewes. When they get there, Duncan is shocked to see that Caan is no longer the macho young man he was but is, instead, this side of an artichoke in the brains department. Knight doesn't know what to do with Caan, as he now has no place to stay in West Virginia. She takes him to Tennessee and tries to drop him off but it doesn't work, so they go to Nebraska where she manages to find him work as a handyman at one of those roadside reptile farms that put up colorful signs along the highway. She leaves and is soon stopped for speeding by Duvall, a widowed cop who lives with his 12-year-old daughter, Zimmet, in a small trailer. She is taken to the Justice of the Peace, Aldredge, who rules the town and also owns the reptile farm. He fines her and she stays on to dally with Duvall. Caan feels sorry for the caged creatures and allows them to flee. Aldredge exacts most of Caan's savings for that action and fires him. In Duvall's trailer, the cop is putting a heavy make on Knight and Caan is watching through a window. At first, Knight seems ready to acquiesce, then she has second thoughts and Duvall, sexually aroused, begins to force his attentions on her. Caan breaks in and battles with Duvall, beating him badly. Zimmet, who has also observed the situation, grabs her daddy's gun and shoots Caan. Knight cradles Caan's head in her arms and tearfully says that he won't have to worry anymore; she and husband Modica will take care of him. Her words fall on Caan's lifeless ears as the picture ends. Too many flashbacks spoil the narrative and Knight's character is confused and seldom sympathetic and barely motivated for many of her actions. Caan likes to think of himself as a "jock" and played football players and basketball players in a few films. He is convincingly wooden in this. His next film was RABBIT, RUN where he played an ex-basketball player in a small Pennsylvania town. THE RAIN PEOPLE was shot in Colorado, Tennessee, Nebraska, New York, and West Virginia and was one of the first "road" pictures done. It was also way ahead of its time as a "woman's" movie, predating STAND UP AND BE COUNTED and AN UNMARRIED WOMAN in the 1970s cycle of such films. The title is from a line by Caan that is hardly right for the retarded youth. He says: "The rain people are made of rain, and when they cry, they disappear altogether"—whatever that means. The movie races all over the place in a hurry to make points, to illuminate the "little people" who live in quiet desperation. It's a bit too noisy for that and yet there is enough about it to merit your attention.

p, Bart Patton, Ronald Colby; d&w, Francis Ford Coppola (based on the story "Echoes" by Coppola); ph, Wilmer Butler (Technicolor); m, Ronald Stein; ed, Blackie Malkin; art d, Leon Ericksen.

Drama **Cas.** **(PR:C-O MPAA:R)**

RAINBOW, THE** (1944, USSR) 93m Kiev Studio/Artkino bw

Natasha Uzhvey *(Olena Kostiuk)*, Natalia Alisova *(Pasya)*, Elena Tiapkina *(Fedosia)*, Vera Ivasheva *(Olga)*, Anton Dunaysky *(Okhalko)*, Anna Lisyanskaya *(Malluchikha)*, G. Klering *(Capt. Kurt Werner)*, Nikolai Bratersky *(Gaplik)*, Vitya Vinogradov, Alik Letichevsky, Emma Pearlstein, Vova Ponomarlov *(Malluchikha's Children)*, Anne Seymour *(English Voice)*.

A powerful, but unfortunately technically spotty, film that illustrates the horrors suffered by the Russian people at the hands of the Nazis during WW II. Uzhvey stars as a member of a partisan group who leaves her village and goes off to have her baby. Because of a weakling mayor and the Russian mistress of a German officer, Uzhvey is captured by the Nazis, tortured, and eventually she and her baby are killed. Surprisingly the film does not end with a vicious statement or immediate vengeance on the Nazis, but with a civilized plea from a minor character that the Germans should be brought to justice and face their crimes in a court of law. (In Russian; English subtitles.)

d, Mark Donskoy; w, Wanda Wasilewska (based on the novel by Wasilewska); ph, Boris Monastirsky; m, Lev Schwartz; English subtitles, Charles Clement.

War **(PR:C MPAA:NR)**

RAINBOW BOYS, THE½** (1973, Can.) 92m Potterton/Mutual c

Donald Pleasence *(Logan)*, Kate Reid *(Gladys)*, Don Calfa *(Mazella)*, Leonard George, Stanley James, Greg George, Bernard Edwards, Isaac Paul, Frederick Earl, Yvonne Weisner, David Thomas.

A pleasant little film starring Calfa as a hip young New Yorker who arrives in British Columbia on his three-wheeled motorcycle and rides into the life of aging prospector Pleasence and his friend Reid. The youth persuades Pleasence to continue searching for his father's long-lost gold mine, much to the dismay of Reid who had hoped Pleasence had given up prospecting for good. Reluctantly, she joins the adventurers and eventually they locate the mine and find a treasure in gold. While trying to extract the fortune, an accident sees the loot spill into a raging river, washing their dreams out to sea. The conclusion is not as sad as it seems because the trio have formed a deep friendship that has become more valuable than gold. A bit trite, but the film's real gem is Pleasence who obviously delights in his role and whose performance sparks the film.

p, Anthony Robinow; d&w, Gerald Potterton; ph, Robert Saad; m, Howard Blake; ed, Marlene Fletcher; set d, Reg Tunnicliffe, Bob Gurski; cos, Ilse Richter, Maureen Sweeney.

Adventure **(PR:A MPAA:NR)**

RAINBOW ISLAND½** (1944) 97m PAR c

Dorothy Lamour *(Lona)*, Eddie Bracken *(Toby Smith)*, Gil Lamb *(Pete Jenkins)*, Barry Sullivan *(Ken Masters)*, Forrest Orr *(Doctor Curtis)*, Anne Revere *(Queen Okalana)*, Reed Hadley *(High Priest Kahuna)*, Marc Lawrence *(Alcoa)*, Adia Kuznetzoff *(Executioner)*, Olga San Juan *(Miki)*, Elena Verdugo *(Moana)*, George Urchell *(Executioner's Helper)*, Aggie Auld, Renee DuPuis, Iris Lancaster, Lena Belle, Virginia Lucas, Audrey Young, Louise La Planche *(Native Girls)*, Theodore "Pete" Rand, Santini Puailoa, Robert St. Angelo, Rod Redwing, Baudelio Alva, Rudy Masson, Alex McSweyn, Alex Montoya *(Queen's Guards)*, Robert Martinez *(Executioner's Assistant)*, Pua Kealoha *(Native Man)*, Dan Seymour *(Fat Native Man)*, Hopkins Twins *(Specialty Swimmers)*, Stanley Price *(Tonto)*, Yvonne De Carlo, Noel Neill, Leigh Whitney, Nonny Parsons *(Lona's Companions)*, George T. Lee, Leon Lontoc, Jimmie Lano *(Japanese Pilots)*, Luis Alberni *(Jerry, Native with Laundry)*, Bobby Barber *(Native Banana Man)*, Allen Fox, Frank Marlowe, Bob Stephenson *(Merchant Marines)*, Eddie Acuff *(Sailor)*, Larry Thompson *(Lieutenant)*, Frank Wilcox *(Captain)*, Paul McVey *(U.S. Naval Commander)*, Ralph Linn *(U.S. Naval Lieutenant)*, Mrs. Carveth Wells.

It had all become a bit silly to Lamour in what seemed to be her millionth "sarong" movie, so she keeps a charming, self-effacing profile throughout this South Seas epic. Sailors Bracken, Lamb, and Sullivan find themselves washed up on a desert island, the only survivors of a ship that has been sunk by the Japanese. They capture a Japanese plane and, after a harrowing escape, they crash land on another island populated with beautiful, scantily clad native girls, and equally unclothed native boys who like to roast white men for dinner. Luckily the swabbies are saved by Lamour, a white woman who had been shipwrecked on the island years ago, who shows the natives that Bracken resembles their god. To save their skins, Bracken is forced to go along with the trick, but he can no longer eat, drink, or chase the native girls because gods have no use for such trivialities. Songs include: "Beloved," "What a Day Tomorrow," "We Have So Little Time," and "The Boogie Woogie Man Will Get You if You Don't Watch Out" (Ted Koehler, Burton Lane).

p, E.D. Leshin; d, Ralph Murphy; w, Walter DeLeon, Arthur Phillips (based on a story by Seena Owen); ph, Karl Struss (Technicolor); m, Roy Webb; ed, Arthur Schmidt; art d, Hans Dreier, Haldane Douglas; set d, George Sawley; cos, Edith Head; spec eff, Gordon Jennings; ch, Danny Dare.

Musical/Comedy **(PR:A MPAA:NR)**

RAINBOW JACKET, THE** (1954, Brit.) 99m EAL/GFD c

Robert Morley *(Lord Logan)*, Kay Walsh *(Barbara Crain)*, Edward Underdown *(Geoffrey Tyler)*, Fella Edmonds *(Georgie Crain)*, Bill Owen *(Sam Lilley)*, Charles Victor *(Mr. Ross)*, Honor Blackman *(Monica Tyler)*, Wilfrid Hyde-White *(Lord Stoneleigh)*, Ronald Ward *(Bernie Rudd)*, Howard Marion Crawford *(Travers)*, Sidney James *(Harry)*, Michael Trubshawe *(Gresham)*, Colin Kemball *(Archie Stevens)*, Sam Kydd *(Bruce)*, Herbert C. Walton *(Adams)*, George Thorpe *(Ross)*, Michael Ripper *(Benny Loder)*, Eliot Makeham *(Valet)*, Frederick Piper *(Lukey)*, Brian Roper *(Ron Saunders)*, Gordon Richards *(Jockey)*, Raymond Glendenning *(Commentator)*, Katie Johnson, David Hemmings, Glyn Houston.

British horse racing saga starring Owen as an ex-champion jockey who was banned from the track for an indiscretion. Wishing to return to his former glory vicariously through his young protege Edmonds, Owen vows that the kid will never let his moral code slip. However, Owen couldn't predict that Edmonds' mother would hit hard times, giving the kid a very good reason to throw a race for crooks offering a big price. Predictable outcome hurts this fairly entertaining film.

p, Michael Relph; d, Basil Dearden; w, T.E.B. Clarke; ph, Otto Heller (Technicolor); m, William Alwyn; ed, Jack Harris; art d, Tom Morahan.

Drama **(PR:A MPAA:NR)**

RAINBOW MAN*½ (1929) 96m Sono-Art/PAR bw

Eddie Dowling *(Rainbow Ryan)*, Marian Nixon *(Mary Lane)*, Frankie Darro *(Billy Ryan)*, Sam Hardy *(Doc Hardy)*, Lloyd Ingraham *(Col. Lane)*, George Hayes *(Bill)*, Rounders Quintet.

Basically a retread of Al Jolson's THE SINGING FOOL (1928), Dowling plays a singer who is suddenly saddled with raising his close friend's son Darro (a fairly insufferable little Hollywood "brat" who would go on to be a fairly insufferable adult) after his pal is killed. While struggling with his vocal career and the child, Dowling meets and falls in love with an innkeeper's daughter, Nixon, who turns out to be none other than the sister of the little kid's mom. Contrived beyond belief, the screenplay delivers nearly every cliche known to tear-jerkers in 1929. The badly rendered songs include: "Little Pal," "Rainbow Man" (Dowling, James Hanley), "Sleepy Valley" (Andrew B. Sterling, Hanley).

d, Fred Newmeyer; w, Frances Agnew, Eddie Dowling (based on a story by Dowling); ph, Jack MacKenzie; ed, S.R. Crone.

Drama   **(PR:A MPAA:NR)**

RAINBOW ON THE RIVER**   (1936) 87m RKO bw

Bobby Breen (Philip), May Robson (Mrs. Ainsworth), Charles Butterworth (Barrett, Butler), Louise Beavers (Toinette), Alan Mowbray (Ralph Layton), Benita Hume (Julia Layton), Henry O'Neill (Father Josef), Marilyn Knowlden (Lucille Layton), Lillian Yarbo (Seline), Stymie Beard (Lilybell), Eddie "Rochester" Anderson (Doctor), Betty Blythe (Flower Buyer), Theresa Maxwell Conover (Mrs. Logan), Clarence H. Wilson (Pedestrian), Lew Kelly (Cabman), Lillian Harmer (Superintendent), Hall Johnson Choir, St. Luke's Choristers.

Breen, RKO's answer to Shirley Temple, stars in this soaper as a Southern tyke forced to leave his lovin' mammy, Beavers, and go to New York when it is discovered that he has blood relatives up there. Shipped off against his will, Breen soon makes a bad impression on his grandmother, Robson, who decides the kid's no good. To make matters worse, Breen's nasty aunt, Hume, makes the boy's life miserable and subjects him to her bratty kids who drive him to run away from home. He is caught by kindly butler Butterworth who convinces Breen he has gotten off on the wrong foot with Robson, and together they talk her into getting rid of Hume and her brood. To ensure little Breen's happiness, Robson even sends for Beavers to come and live with them in New York. Songs include: "Rainbow on the River," "You Only Live Once," "A Thousand Dreams of Love" (Paul Francis Webster, Louis Alter), "Waiting for the Sun to Rise" (Arthur Swanstrom, Karl Hajos), "Flower Song" (Hugo Riesenfeld, Selma Hautzik), "Old Folks at Home," "Camptown Races" (Stephen Foster).

p, Sol Lesser; d, Kurt Neumann; w, Earle Snell, Harry Chandlee, William Hurlbut, Clarence Marks (based on the story "Toinnette's Philip" by Mrs. C.V. Jamison); ph, Charles Schoenbaum; ed, Robert Crandall; md, Dr. Hugo Riesenfeld.

Drama   **(PR:A MPAA:NR)**

RAINBOW OVER BROADWAY**   (1933) 72m CHES bw

Joan Marsh (Judy), Frank Albertson (Don), Lucien Littlefield (Timothy), Grace Hayes (Trixie), Gladys Blake (Nellie), Glen Boles (Mickey), Dell Henderson (Bowers), Nat Carr (Sanfield), Harry Meyers (Berwiskey), May Beatty (Queenie), Maxine Lewis, Alice Goodwin.

Hayes plays the hated stepmother of a Kansas City family. Seeking to revive her theatrical career, she drags the whole family off to New York and begins singing again to the outrage of family members Marsh and Henderson. Luckily things turn out okay because the brother/sister duo have written some songs and they meet up with a band leader who goes sweet on Marsh and will do anything for her, including making their tunes a hit. Songs include: "I Must Be in Love with Love," "Dance My Blues Away" (Elizabeth Morgan, Harry Von Tilzer).

d, Richard Thorpe; w, Winifred Dunn (based on a story by Carol Webster); ph, M.A. Anderson; m, Albert Von Tilzer.

Musical   **(PR:A MPAA:NR)**

RAINBOW OVER TEXAS**   (1946) 65m REP bw

Roy Rogers (Roy Rogers), George "Gabby" Hayes (Gabby Whittaker), Dale Evans (Jackie Dalrymple), Sheldon Leonard (Kirby Haynes), Robert Emmett Keane (Wooster Dalrymple), Gerald Oliver Smith (Larkin), Minerva Urecal (Mama Lolita), George J. Lewis (Jim Pollard), Kenne Duncan (Pete McAvoy), Pierce Lyden (Iverson), Dick Elliott (Capt. Monroe), Bob Nolan and the Sons of the Pioneers, JoAnn Dean, Bud Osborne, George Chesebro, Trigger the Horse.

Roy rides again, this time back to his home town on a promotional tour with Bob Nolan and the Sons of the Pioneers. There he gets involved with a town-sponsored Pony Express race which irritates some of the local crooks and they set out to make sure he doesn't win.

p, Edward J. White; d, Frank McDonald; w, Gerald Geraghty (based on a story by Max Brand); ph, Reggie Lanning; md, Morton Scott; art d, Hilyard Brown; m/l, "Little Senorita," Jack Elliott, Glen Spencer, Gordon Forster.

Western   **(PR:A MPAA:NR)**

RAINBOW OVER THE RANGE*½   (1940) 62m MON bw

Tex Ritter (Tex), Slim Andrews (Slim), Dorothy Fay (Mary), Gene Alsace (Bart), Warner Richmond (Gene), Jim Pierce (Jim), Chuck Morrison (Buck), Dennis Moore (Manners), John Merton, Tommy Southworth, Romaine Loudermilk, Steve Lorber, Art Wilcox and the Arizona Rangers, White Flash the Horse.

Ritter rides to the rescue of damsel Fay who is about to lose her government contract to provide horses for the army because some unseen horse thieves have been stealing her ponies. After a bit of digging, Ritter discovers the town powers that be are responsible and he sets out to stop their treachery.

p, Edward Finney; d, Al Herman; w, Robert Emmett, Roland Lynch, Roger Merton; ph, Marcel LePicard; m, Art Wilcox; ed, Fred Bain; md, Frank Sanucci; m/l, "Rainbow Over the Range," Fleming Allen, "Poor Slim," Johnny Lange, Lew Porter, "My Tonto Basin Home," Garland Edmundson.

Western   **(PR:A MPAA:NR)**

RAINBOW OVER THE ROCKIES*½   (1947) 54m MON bw

Jimmy Wakely, Lee "Lasses" White, Dennis Moore, Pat Starling, Wesley Tuttle and His Texas Stars, Carl Sepulveda, Budd Buster, John Baxley, Zon Murray, Billy Dix, Jasper Palmer, Robert L. Gilbert.

Singing oater star Wakely breaks up a feud that has brewed between a pair of ranchers. By exposing a malicious gang of rustlers, he is able to bring peace to their Rocky Mountain ranges.

p&d, Oliver Drake; w, Elmer Clifton (based on a story by Drake); ph, Marcel LePicard; ed, Ralph Dixon; md, Frank Sanucci.

Western   **(PR:A MPAA:NR)**

RAINBOW RANCH*   (1933) 54m MON bw

Rex Bell, Cecilia Parker, Robert Kortman, Henry Hall, George Nash, Gordon DeMain, Phil Dunham, Jerry Storm, Tiny Stanford, Van Calbert, Jockey Haefley.

Bell stars as a navy pug who demonstrates his boxing prowess on board the ship he serves. When he gets out of the navy and returns home to his western ranch, he is dismayed to learn that his uncle has been killed, his water rights grabbed, and his gal stolen away. Of course Bell leaps on the nearest horse and rides off seeking vengeance.

p, Trem Carr; d, Harry Fraser; w, Phil Dunham (based on a story by Harry O. Jones [Fraser]); ph, Archie Stout.

Western   **(PR:A MPAA:NR)**

RAINBOW 'ROUND MY SHOULDER**   (1952) 78m COL c

Frankie Laine (Himself), Billy Daniels (Himself), Charlotte Austin (Cathy Blake), Arthur Franz (Phil Young), Ida Moore (Martha Blake), Lloyd Corrigan (Tobias), Barbara Whiting (Suzy Milligan), Ross Ford (Elliot Livermore), Arthur Space (Joe Brady), Frank Wilcox (Sidney Gordon), Diane Garrett (Lana Lamarr), Chester Marshall (Red), Helen Wallace (Mrs. Toomey), Eleanore Davis (Lucia Evans), Eugene Baxter (Bob), Ken Garcia (Roger Stevens), Mira McKinney (Mrs. Abernathy), Edythe Elliott (Mrs. Gilmore), Jean Andren (Mrs. Riley).

Screenwriters Blake Edwards and Richard Quine (who also directed) didn't provide much to get excited about in this oft told tale of a young gal trying to break into show biz. Austin plays the gal who, despite the protestations of her society-bred aunt Moore, sneaks off and gets a job as a messenger at one of the Hollywood studios, with the hope of being discovered. She is, of course, and soon she is slated to sing in the new Laine picture. Moore finds out and is horrified, so Laine and Daniels offer to provide the entertainment for Moore's upcoming charity ball, to prove that Hollywood types aren't all bad. Highlight of this musical is the rare chance to catch a glance of the once prominent Columbia back lot. Songs include: "There's a Rainbow Round My Shoulder" (Dave Dreyer, Billy Rose, Al Jolson), "Bye Bye Blackbird" (Mort Dixon, Ray Henderson), "She's Funny that Way" (Neil Moret, Richard Whiting), "Wrap Your Troubles in Dreams" (Harry Barris, Ted Koehler, Billy Moll), "The Last Rose of Summer" (Thomas Moore, R.A. Milliken), "Wonderful, Wasn't It?" (Hal David, Don Rodney), "Girl in the Wood" (Neal Stuart, Terry Gilkyson), "Pink Champagne" (Bob Wright, George Forrest).

p, Jonie Taps; d, Richard Quine; w, Blake Edwards, Quine; ph, Ellis W. Carter (Technicolor); ed, Richard Fantl; md, George Duning; art d, George Brooks; set d, James Crowe; ch, Lee Scott.

Musical   **(PR:A MPAA:NR)**

RAINBOW TRAIL**   (1932) 60m FOX bw

George O'Brien (Shefford), Cecilia Parker (Fay Larkin), Minna Gombell (Ruth), Roscoe Ates (Ike Wilkins), J.M. Kerrigan (Paddy), James Kirkwood (Venters), W.L. Thorne (Dyer), Robert Frazer (Lone Eagle), Niles Welch (Willets), Ruth Donnelly (Abigail), Laska Winter (Singing Cloud), Landers Stevens (Presbey), Alice Ward (Jane Withersteen), Edward Hearn (Jim Lassiter).

The third version of this Zane Grey story (the first in 1918 starring William Farnum, the second in 1925 starring Tom Mix) and the sequel to RIDERS OF THE PURPLE SAGE (1931). O'Brien once again stars, but this time as the newphew of the character he played in the 1931 film. He sets out on the trail to find his uncle, Hearn, who is trapped in the lost canyon, but runs into the villainous Thorne, who wears a mask over half of his disfigured face. Along the way he meets up with Parker and strikes up a romance. The plot is virtually impenetrable unless connected to the earlier film. The most bizarre aspect of the films, when looked at back to back, is that O'Brien rides off in search of himself in the second film.

d, David Howard; w, Barry Connors, Philip Klein (based on a story by Zane Grey); ph, Daniel Clark.

Western   **(PR:A MPAA:NR)**

RAINBOW VALLEY**   (1935) 52m Lone Star/MON bw

John Wayne (John Martin), Lucille Browne (Eleanor), LeRoy Mason (Rogers), George Hayes (George Hale), Buffalo Bill, Jr. (Austin "Butch" Galt), Bert Dillard (Spike), Lloyd Ingraham (Powell), Lafe McKee (Storekeeper), Fern Emmett, Henry Rocquemore, Eddie Parker, Herman Hack, Frank Ellis, Art Dillard, Frank Ball.

Early Wayne oater sees the Duke as a government agent who goes undercover and has himself sent to prison. He gathers information to determine why the efforts of a group of concerned citizens, who are trying to build a road into a secluded mining town, are being blown up in their faces (literally). Eventually, it is revealed that a gang of goons controlled by town leader Mason and overseen by gunslinger Bill, Jr., are the bad guys. Wayne sets out to stop them. Surprisingly, the cast is almost the same that appeared in TEXAS TERROR, Wayne's previous picture.

p, Paul Malvern; d, Robert N. Bradbury; w, Lindsley Parsons; ph, William Hyer; ed, Carl Pierson.

Western   **Cas.**   **(PR:A MPAA:NR)**

RAINBOW'S END**   (1935) 54m FD bw

Hoot Gibson (Neil Gibson, Jr.), June Gale (Ann Ware), Oscar Apfel (Neil Gibson, Sr.), Ada Ince (Owen Gibson), Charles Hill (Bert), Warner Richmond (Stark), Stanley Blystone (Dorgan), Buddy Roosevelt, John Elliott, Henry Rocquemore, Fred Gilman.

Gibson must defend Gale, a female rancher whose father is incapacitated. Gale is forced to deal with Stark, the villain who is trying to run her and her old man off their property. Gibson, who has been on the trail awhile, is shocked to learn that Stark works for his (Gibson's) father. In the end, the misunderstandings are ironed out, as are the conflicts between Gibson and his pop. Gale, Gibson's romantic lead in this film, played the same role in real life.

d, Norman Spencer; w, Rollo Ward; ph, Gilbert Warrenton; ed, Ralph Dietrich.

Western   Cas.   (PR:A MPAA:NR)

RAINMAKER, THE***   (1956) 121m PAR c

Burt Lancaster (Starbuck), Katharine Hepburn (Lizzie Curry), Wendell Corey (File), Lloyd Bridges (Noah Curry), Earl Holliman (Jim Curry), Cameron Prud'Homme (H.C. Curry), Wallace Ford (Sheriff Thomas), Yvonne Lime (Snookie), Dottie Bee Baker (Belinda), Dan White (Deputy), Stan Jones John Benson, James Stone, Tony Merrill, Joe Brown (Townsmen), Ken Becker (Phil Mackey), Michael Bachus.

THE MUSIC MAN may have owed something to this story, as both concern confidence men who come to small towns to peddle their scams, then fall for spinsters. Nash wrote it as a TV play, then expanded it to work on the Broadway stage, where it ran 124 performances with Geraldine Page in the Hepburn role and Prud'Homme as her father, under the direction of Anthony, who also did this film and, later, the musical version, "110 in the Shade." Composer North garnered an Oscar nomination, as did Hepburn, her seventh. The main problem was that it was far too talky and the leads were somewhat grizzled for the situation. Hepburn is a hick-town spinster in an arid area of the Southwest. (She never really convinces anyone that she's a country girl because that New England accent and her flighty mannerisms constantly intrude.) Lancaster is a brash, lively con artist who comes to the burg claiming that he can bring rain to the drought-ravaged locale for the sum of $100. He is taken into Prud'Homme's house and allowed to live in one of the outbuildings. Hepburn's brothers are Bridges, who never quite buys Lancaster's spiel, and Holliman, an oafish young man who is wooing town beauty Lime. Once Lancaster is ensconced, he begins to change things around—just as Paul Mazursky's character Jerry (Nick Nolte) did in 1986's DOWN AND OUT IN BEVERLY HILLS. Hepburn is being courted, albeit reluctantly, by the town's lawman, Corey, but he doesn't seem to be able to pop the question and time is a-wasting in her old maid life. Lancaster convinces the plain Hepburn that she is gorgeous, and once she feels that's true, her attitude about herself begins to alter. She's been told for years by everyone, mostly her brother Bridges, that she is, at best, plain, but the intrusion of Lancaster works a minor miracle on her self-confidence and she now has a duo of suitors in Lancaster and Corey, who suddenly awakens to the fact that she is a terrific woman. At the end, there is a coincidental downpour and Lancaster, it should go without saying, takes all the credit before departing for his next conquest. Behind him, he has left a changed woman and his visit has been the most exciting thing to happen to the tiny village in their history. Lancaster does one of his ELMER GANTRY bravura performances and was a perfect selection, although a little timeworn at 43. Hepburn was pushing 50 and Corey was 7 years younger. The difference in all their ages was revealed by the close-ups and worked against the believability of the story. Still, it's a pleasant movie with more than many laughs. It could have been called "The Pitchman and the Prude" which is what ABC-TV might have named it if the network were to make a TV movie of the story.

p, Hal B. Wallis; d, Joseph Anthony; w, N. Richard Nash (based on his play); ph, Charles Lang, Jr. (VistaVision, Technicolor); m, Alex North; ed, Warren Low; art d, Hal Pereira, Walter Tyler; set d, Sam Comer, Arthur Krams; cos, Edith Head; spec eff, John P. Fulton; makeup, Wally Westmore.

Comedy   (PR:A MPAA:NR)

RAINMAKERS, THE*½   (1935) 75m RAD bw

Bert Wheeler (Billy), Robert Woolsey (Roscoe), Dorothy Lee (Margie Spencer), Berton Churchill (Simon Parker), George Meeker (Orville Parker), Frederic Roland (Henry Spencer), Edgar Dearing (Kelly).

Dim-witted comedy from the frequently tedious comics Wheeler and Woolsey. They star as two inventors arriving in California bean-growing territory, with a rainmaking machine that will end the drought that has been crippling the crops. Stupid puns and bad slapstick are all the comedians could come up with since the material that made up the majority of their stage act, sexual innuendoes, wouldn't have made it past the censors.

p, Lee Marcus; d, Fred Guiol; w, Grant Garrett, Leslie Goodwins (based on a story by Guiol, Albert Treynor); ph, Ted McCord; ed, John Lookert; md, Roy Webb; m/l, "Isn't Love the Grandest Thing?," Jack Scholl, Louis Alter.

Comedy   (PR:A MPAA:NR)

RAINS CAME, THE***½   (1939) 104m FOX bw

Myrna Loy (Lady Edwina Esketh), Tyrone Power (Maj. Rama Safti), George Brent (Tom Ransome), Brenda Joyce (Fern Simon), Nigel Bruce (Albert, Lord Esketh), Maria Ouspenskaya (Maharani), Joseph Schildkraut (Mr. Bannerjee), Mary Nash (Miss MacDaid), Jane Darwell (Aunt Phoebe Smiley), Marjorie Rambeau (Mrs. Simon), Henry Travers (Rev. Homer Smiley), H.B. Warner (Maharajah), Laura Hope Crews (Lily Hoggett-Egbury), William Royle (Raschid Ali Khan), Montague Shaw (Gen. Keith), Harry Hayden (Rev. Elmer Simon), Herbert Evans (Bates), Abner Biberman (John the Baptist), Mara Alexander (Mrs. Bannerjee), William Edmunds (Mr. Das), Adele Labanset, Sonie Charsaky (Princesses), Rita Page

(Maid), Connie Leon, Rosina Galli (Nurses), Pedro Regas (Official), Frank Lackteen (Engineer), George Regas (Rajput), Leyland Hodgson (Doctor), Eddie Abdo (Soldier), Fern Emmett (Hindu Woman), Dominie Duval (Girl), Guy D'Ennery (Mr. Durga), Maj. Sam Harris (Officer), Jamiel Hasson (Aide-de-Camp), Lal Chand Mehra (Chant Singer).

An exotic romantic melodrama based on the popular novel by Louis Bromfield which details the trials and tribulations of the mythical Indian province of Ranchipur. Loy stars as a bored English lady trapped in a loveless marriage with wealthy, middle-aged businessman Bruce. To keep herself amused, Loy has entered into numerous love affairs—all of which collapse after a brief period. Accompanying her husband to Ranchipur, Loy is bemused to find that one of her former lovers, Brent, an Englishman, now lives in India where he can live cheaply and drink heavily. Brent, however, has his hands full with Joyce, the young daughter of socially ambitious missionaries who would like to see their child wed to a British aristocrat. Brent attempts to renew his romance with Loy, but she is no longer interested because she has met Power, a handsome young Indian doctor who is the court favorite of the maharajah (Warner) and the maharani (Ouspenskaya) and may inherit the throne some day. Power is intensely committed to helping his people and works tirelessly in the hospital to heal the sick. The dedicated young doctor's compassion affects the bored English socialite and she begins to notice the difficult lives of those around her. When a violent earthquake hits Ranchipur, the huge dam cracks and breaks, sending a wall of water through the center of the city. Thousands are killed, including Loy's husband Bruce and maharajah Warner. Because of the disaster, malaria sweeps through Ranchipur, attacking those who were lucky enough to survive the earthquake and flood. Now deeply in love with Power, Loy pitches in and helps him take care of the thousands of injured and sick, determined to prove that she is a changed woman. Power finally admits to himself that he is in love with her, but their joy is short-lived for Loy accidentally drinks from a glass infected with the deadly virus, falls ill, and dies. Because screenwriters Dunne and Josephson drained Bromfield's novel of all its social insight and political intrigue, THE RAINS CAME is really nothing more than an epic tear-jerker, but the film succeeds due to its casting and production values. Budgeted at an incredible (for 1939) $2.5 million, the film spared no expense at creating an exotic locale for the soap-opera histrionics to be played out in. Power is surprisingly convincing beneath his dark makeup, and Loy turns in a solid performance as well. Joyce, who was an 18-year-old Los Angeles high school student when discovered by the studio and given the big buildup, essays her role with a certain amount of likable spunk. The true star of the film, though, is the spectacular earthquake and flood footage engineered by special effects technician Fred Sersen. Remade in 1955 as THE RAINS OF RANCHIPUR.

p, Darryl F. Zanuck; d, Clarence Brown; w, Philip Dunne, Julien Josephson (based on the novel by Louis Bromfield); ph, Arthur Miller; m, Alfred Newman; ed, Barbara McLean; art d, William Darling, George Dudley; set d, Thomas Little; cos, Gwen Wakeling; spec eff, E.H. Hansen, Fred Sersen; m/l, Mack Gordon, Harry Revel, Lal Chand Mehra.

Drama   (PR:A MPAA:NR)

RAINS OF RANCHIPUR, THE***   (1955) 104m FOX c

Lana Turner (Edwina Esketh), Richard Burton (Dr. Safti), Fred MacMurray (Tom Ransome), Joan Caulfield (Fern Simon), Michael Rennie (Lord Esketh), Eugenie Leontovich (Maharani), Gladys Hurlbut (Mrs. Simon), Madge Kennedy (Mrs. Smiley), Carlo Rizzo (Mr. Adoani), Beatrice Kraft (Oriental Dancer), Paul H. Frees (Sundar), King Calder (Mr. Smiley), Argentina Brunetti (Mrs. Adoani), John Banner (Ranchid), Ivis Goulding (Louise), Ram Singh (Major Domo), Lou Krugman (Courier), Rama Bai (Lachmaania), Naji Gabbay (Wagonlit Porter), Jugat Bhatia (Headhunter), George Brand (Mr. Simon), Phyllis Johannes (Nurse Gupta), Trude Wyler (Guest), Ram Chandra (Satter), Aly Wassil (Another Courier), Elizabeth Prudhomme (Nurse Patel).

This remake of 20th Century Fox's 1939 hit THE RAINS CAME boasted color, CinemaScope and an all-star cast but shared the same script problems as its predecessor. Turner stars as the vampish wife of henpecked British lord Rennie (her nationality was changed from British to American for this version) who delights in seducing any man who catches her fancy. Rennie and Turner venture to the Indian city of Ranchipur on the invitation of the Maharani Leontovich. There Turner meets Burton, a handsome young Indian doctor and heir apparent to the throne. The blonde seductress decides to make Burton her next conquest, but the noble doctor resists her charms at the urging of Leontovich. This makes Turner even more determined and as she desperately tries to win Burton over, she begins to realize that for the first time in her life she is feeling true love for a man. Burton eventually succumbs to her advances and the two share a torrid romance. Their idyll is interrupted, however, when Ranchipur is hit by the season's torrential rains, followed by a violent earthquake which causes the dam to burst and flood the city killing thousands. Burton is shaken by the event and realizes that his true destiny is to help his people. He breaks off his relationship with Turner and leaves to help the injured and homeless. Turner, too, is affected by the disaster and her new-found capacity for love and she returns to her husband determined to salvage their marriage (in the 1939 version, as in the novel, the character dies after contracting malaria). Once again, Fox loosened the purse strings for this production, spending $4,000,000. As in the original film, the special effects are the main attraction, with all the melodrama leading up to the real action. Turner, who, ironically, was considered for the role eventually played by Brenda Joyce in THE RAINS CAME in 1939, offers a sultry, more overtly sexual interpretation of the role of Lady Edwina Esketh, but fails to convincingly convey the deep emotional awakening the part requires. Burton, as was Tyrone Power before him, is surprisingly good in a role that could easily backfire on an Anglo actor. MacMurray, unfortunately, is totally wasted in a underdeveloped subplot and later declared that he, "...was just the town drunk in that picture." All was not well on the set during THE RAINS OF RANCHIPUR however, for Turner detested Burton during the shooting and thought him an arrogant boor. Her attitude toward the actor never wavered and years later it affected her relationship with friend Elizabeth Taylor.

p, Frank Ross; d, Jean Negulesco; w, Merle Miller (based on the novel *The Rains Came* by Louis Bromfield); ph, Milton Krasner (CinemaScope, DeLuxe Color); m, Hugo Friedhofer; ed, Dorothy Spencer; md, Lionel Newman; art d, Lyle R. Wheeler, Addison Hehr; set d, Walter M. Scott, Paul S. Fox; cos, Travilla, Helen Rose; spec eff, Ray Kellogg; ch, Stephen Papich.

Drama (PR:A MPAA:NR)

RAINTREE COUNTY*** (1957) 187m MGM c

Montgomery Clift *(John Wickliff Shawnessy)*, Elizabeth Taylor *(Susanna Drake)*, Eva Marie Saint *(Nell Gaither)*, Nigel Patrick *(Prof. Jerusalem Webster Stiles)*, Lee Marvin *(Orville "Flash" Perkins)*, Rod Taylor *(Garwood B. Jones)*, Agnes Moorehead *(Ellen Shawnessy)*, Walter Abel *(T.D. Shawnessy)*, Jarma Lewis *(Barbara Drake)*, Tom Drake *(Bobby Drake)*, Rhys Williams *(Ezra Gray)*, Russell Collins *(Niles Foster)*, DeForest Kelley *(Southern Officer)*, Myrna Hansen *(Lydia Gray)*, Oliver Blake *(Jake the Bartender)*, John Eldredge *(Cousin Sam)*, Isabelle Cooley *(Soona)*, Ruth Attaway *(Parthenia)*, Eileene Stevens *(Miss Roman)*, Rosalind Hayes *(Bessie)*, Don Burnett *(Tom Conway)*, Michael Dugan *(Nat Franklin)*, Ralph Vitti [Michael Dante] *(Jesse Gardner)*, Phil Chambers *(Starter)*, James Griffith *(Man with Gun)*, Burt Mustin *(Granpa Peters)*, Dorothy Granger *(Mme. Gaubert)*, Owen McGiveney *(Blind Man)*, Charles Watts *(Party Guest)*, Stacy Harris *(Union Lieutenant)*, Donald Losby *(Jim Shawnessy at age 2½)*, Mickey Maga *(Jim Shawnessy at age 4)*, Robert Foulk *(Pantomimist in Blackface)*, Jack Daly *(Photographer)*, Bill Walker *(Old Negro Man)*, Gardner McKay *(Bearded Soldier)*, William Challee *(1st Spectator)*, Frank Kreig *(2nd Spectator)*, Janet Lake *(1st Girl)*, Luana Lee *(2nd Girl)*, Judi Jordan *(3rd Girl)*, Phyllis Douglas *(4th Girl)*, Sue George *(5th Girl)*, Nesdon Booth, Robert Forrest *(Spectators)*, Josephine Cummins *(Woman)*, Mil Patrick.

This Civil War extravaganza, thought by its studio to be a successor to GONE WITH THE WIND, was handsomely mounted and boasted a superb cast but it was dogged by serious problems and a story that didn't want to surrender at Appomattox but go on and on and on, mostly waiting for Taylor to regain her southern belle sanity. Taylor is the beauteous visitor who causes every male to turn his head in her direction when she shows up in Raintree County, Indiana, coming from exotic New Orleans on the eve of the Civil War when President Lincoln has just taken office and his new administration is involved in controversy. Clift, studying to be a teacher and questioning the morality of slavery to which he is opposed, is engaged to practical, down-to-earth Saint. But Taylor, a spoiled lady of southern aristocracy, gets what she wants and she wants Clift. She charms him into a romantic trance, then seduces him and later lies, saying she is pregnant. Clift does the right thing and marries her, leaving Saint to pine alone. Clift becomes a schoolteacher and Taylor finally delivers a boy but the war breaks out and soon Taylor and Clift are at odds, he going to fight for the Union, she having deep sympathies for the South. Clift and his Indiana boyhood friends go through four long years of bloody battle, becoming foragers for the Union Army and, in one skirmish, Marvin, Clift's oldest friend, is belly shot and dies in agony while Clift escapes, carrying his boy with him, having retrieved the child from behind enemy lines where his now demented wife had taken him. Returning with his child to Indiana, Clift manages to have Taylor back with him following the end of the war but he realizes by then that the insanity that afflicted her mother is inherent in his wife. Taylor, while living in the South during the war, had spent time in a mental hospital and she does not improve when returning to Clift. She regresses steadily into her own disturbing childhood, clutching a doll which survived a fire with her—the doll is horribly disfigured by the fire as Taylor was psychologically—and is the symbol of Taylor's own unbalanced family ghosts and the early, violent loss of her parents. In a moment of utter madness, stemming from her belief that she has Negro blood, Taylor grabs her little boy and leads him into a fierce night storm, causing Clift to search frantically for them, finding the boy alive and shivering, lying next to his mother, Taylor, dead beneath the legendary raintree Clift all his life has tried to find in the forest. Taylor is free now of her mental anguish and Clift is free to marry Saint who has patiently waited for him through years and years of aberration. RAINTREE COUNTY was a costly production, sapping MGM of more than $6 million, and much of this is evident in the battle scenes, a grand ball, and vintage towns and villages, but it lacks the sweep and grandeur of GONE WITH THE WIND and an empathetic central character. (GWTW had cost $5 million.) Much of this cost was due to MGM's archaic and lavish way of throwing money away. A fortune was spent on Taylor's wardrobe, not only made up of the finest cloth for her outerwear but expensive petticoats that were never seen. Also, the studio still maintained the practice of full costuming for color tests when, by the time of this film, color was refined to the point of capturing exactly what was worn. Director Dmytryk also did not appreciate studio boss Schary calling a reading rehearsal where all the principals read their lines coldly from the script and Schary, "a closet actor," according to Dmytryk, read all of the lines of the supporting players not present. On the sets, technicians showed up with equipment that had been used in the silent era and some cameras were not even equipped for sound. The director had to gently remind some of his top technicians that technical improvements had been made since 1929. When he demanded changes, Dmytryk alienated most of the crew members. "Needless to say," the director later stated, "I never worked at MGM again." During the production, Clift, suffering from a hangover and little sleep, drove into a telephone pole which demolished his car, the pole falling on it and just missing his head. He nevertheless suffered a broken nose, a cut lip, and his jaw was fractured in three places, requiring wires to be inserted to hold the jaw together. Many seeing the film today claim to identify those scenes shot after the accident and note a physical change in the actor. The physical damage is not really discernable but the scars were inside Clift's head and his attitude and posture are markedly different in these scenes/ he is suddenly no longer handsome and youthful but haggard, his eyes furtive, as if he had made one terrible step through an invisible wall and entered old age. Clift was drinking and, as a later incident proved, was certainly indulging in drugs during the filming. On location, near Natchez, Taylor had to struggle in 75-pound period dresses and, on one particularly sultry day, she collapsed from hyperventilation. The production's doctor could not, under the law, prescribe medication and none could be found. Taylor was struggling desperately to breathe and felt as if she were dying. Clift magically appeared with a full bottle of demerol (according to Dmytryk) and a syringe. The doctor administered the drug and the actress relaxed, regaining her normal breathing, though she was bedridden for a week with a simultaneous attack of tachycardia (fast heartbeat). At one point the director found Clift so dead drunk in his hotel room that a cigarette had burned itself out between his fingers. The director later admitted to conducting an illegal search of Clift's hotel room and finding "a hundred containers" of every kind of drug and "a beautiful leather case fitted with needles and syringes." When the company moved on to Danville, Kentucky, for more on-location shooting, Clift's behavior worsened. He and Taylor, to celebrate their first film together since making the classic A PLACE IN THE SUN, went to the best restaurant in town and the actor ordered a "blue-rare" (hardly cooked at all) steak, smothering this with butter and a whole container of pepper, then ate it with his bare hands, the melted butter dripping through his fingers, which sickened the hundreds of people watching through the plate glass window of the restaurant. Clift was later found running naked through the best part of Danville, the upper-crust residents taking great umbrage at his impulsive manners, so much so that a local cop was assigned to stand guard at Clift's hotel room door, preventing him from leaving at night through the remainder of the production while in Danville. Taylor's own conduct also troubled the director. She was often late for shootings and was being wooed by producer Mike Todd during the production. He rented a commercial airliner to make a special trip to Danville to bring her some expensive presents and Taylor became engaged to the entrepreneurial producer just when the film was finished. This film, which was later cut to 166 minutes, was the last production sponsored by outgoing MGM boss Dore Schary and was not a monumental legacy for Schary to leave behind, rather a disjointed though sometimes brilliant film, but more often than not, disappointing. Most of this is due to the rambling, unedited script by Kaufman, whose dialog is predictable and often awkward, although it follows the Lockridge novel closely. Lockridge, who wrote the novel in 1948, died tragically himself, a suicide. Other locations used were near Port Gibson, Louisiana, and in the swamps outside of Reelfort Lake, Tennessee. The film was photographed with MGM's newly created process, called Camera 65, whereby a 65mm negative is reduced to 35mm for release prints.

p, David Lewis; d, Edward Dmytryk; w, Millard Kaufman (based on the novel by Ross Lockridge, Jr.); ph, Robert Surtees (Panavision, Technicolor); m, Johnny Green; ed, John Dunning; art d, William A. Horning, Urie McCleary; set d, Edwin B. Willis, Hugh Hunt; cos, Walter Plunkett; spec eff, Warren Newcombe; m/l, Paul Francis Webster, Green; makeup, William Tuttle; tech adv, Charles H. Hagedon.

Historical Drama (PR-C MPAA:NR)

RAISE THE ROOF** (1930) 77m BIP/FN-Pathe bw

Maurice Evans *(Rodney Langford)*, Betty Balfour *(Maisie Grey)*, Jack Raine *(Atherley Armitage)*, Sam Livesey *(Mr. Langford)*, Ellis Jeffreys *(Mrs. Langford)*, Arthur Hardy *(Croxley Bellairs)*, Dorothy Minto *(Juanita)*, Charles Garry *(Deighton Duff)*, Mike Johnson *(Fred Frisco)*, Louie Emery *(Mrs. Warburton)*, Josephine Earle, Andrea Malandrinos, Plaza Tiller Girls.

Evans is a likable rich kid who is placed in charge of a floundering musical revue. His father, determined to straighten out the boy's life, hires Raine, the show's star, to sabotage the show. Another of the players, Balfour, helps out Evans and convinces the old man to give the boy a chance.

p,d&w, Walter Summers; m, Tom Helmore.

Musical (PR:A MPAA:NR)

RAISE THE TITANIC* (1980, Brit.) 112m Associated Film Distribution c

Jason Robards *(Adm. James Sandecker)*, Richard Jordan *(Dirk Pitt)*, David Selby *(Dr. Gene Seagram)*, Anne Archer *(Dana Archibald)*, Alec Guinness *(John Bigalow)*, J.D. Cannon *(Capt. Joe Burke)*, Bo Brundin *(Capt. Andre Prelov)*, M. Emmet Walsh *(MCPO Vinnie Giordino)*, Robert Broyles *(Willis)*, Norman Bartold *(Kemper)*, Elya Baskin *(Marganin)*, Dirk Blocker *(Merker)*, Paul Carr *(Nicholson)*, Michael C. Gwynne, Harvey Lewis, Charles Macaulay, Stewart Moss, Michael Pataki, Marvin Silbersher, Mark L. Taylor, Maurice Kowalewski, Nancy Nevinson, Trent Dolan, Paul Tuerpe, Sander Vanocur, Ken Place, Michael Ensing, Craig Shreeve, Brendan Burns, Jonathan Moore, George Whiteman, Hilly Hicks, Mike Kulcsar, David Hammond, Mark Hammer, Ron Evans.

This was a huge waste of money—second only, perhaps, to HEAVEN'S GATE and ENEMY MINE. The book had been a hit, for some reason, and the producers mistakenly thought they could do the same with a movie. But when an author writes "Twenty thousand Berber tribesmen came over the crest of the hill," a reader imagines that. When a moviemaker has to assemble and clothe that many people, it becomes an extraordinary expense. So it was with RAISE THE TITANIC. Some secret weapon, circa 1912, was on the ill-fated Cunard liner when it went down that April night. The reason is never totally explained. Robards is a crooked sea captain (an admiral yet!) who is in back of the salvage idea. Guinness is an ancient mariner who was on the ship when it went down, Archer is a newspaper reporter assigned to learn the truth, Jordan is a high-tech guy, and Selby is the cool intellectual who gets hot under the collar. Most of the film takes place with lousy, though expensive, miniatures of subs and equipment attempting to get the ship off the reef. They eventually do, but by that time, the audience, which has become increasingly sophisticated regarding special effects, will have laughed itself silly over the poor depictions and the worse dialog. Typical of the waste was a 55-foot model of the Titanic which couldn't fit into the studio tank for shooting, so a new tank was built for several million dollars. It would have been easier to construct a new model, which cost less than $400,000, but no one thought of that. The budget for this was around $40 million and it returned less than $10 million, if that. Thus, the picture sank in murkier water than the ship. Glub.

p, William Frye; d, Jerry Jameson; w, Adam Kennedy, Eric Hughes (based on the novel by Clive Cussler); ph, Matthew F. Leonetti (Technivision, DeLuxe Color); m, John Barry; ed, J. Terry Williams, Robert F. Shugrue; prod d, John F. DeCuir; art d, John F. DeCuir, Jr.; set d, Mickey S. Michaels, Raphael Breton, Ian Whittaker; spec eff, Alex Weldon, John Richardson.

Adventure   Cas.   (A-C MPAA:PG)

RAISIN IN THE SUN, A***½   (1961) 127m Paman-Doris/COL bw

Sidney Poitier (*Walter Lee Younger*), Claudia McNeil (*Lena Younger*), Ruby Dee (*Ruth Younger*), Diana Sands (*Beneatha Younger*), Ivan Dixon (*Asagai*), John Fiedler (*Mark Lindner*), Louis Gossett (*George Murchison*), Stephen Perry (*Travis*), Joel Fluellen (*Bobo*), Roy Glenn (*Willie Harris*), Ray Stubbs (*Bartender*), Rudolph Monroe (*Taxi Driver*), George DeNormand (*Employer*), Louis Terkel (*Herman*), Thomas D. Jones (*Chauffeur*).

Hansberry's lovely adaptation of her 1959 Broadway hit unites seven of the original cast in the movie, which, while it concerns a black family, is universal enough in concept to touch the hearts of anyone of any race. McNeil is the matriarch of a family who live in cramped quarters on Chicago's South Side (where all the location shots were done). Her husband has just died and she receives a check for $10,000 from the insurance company, a bonanza back then. McNeil has practical notions for the cash. She wants to get out of the dangerous slum in which they live and buy a decent house, then use the other money to pay for medical school for her daughter, Sands. Poitier, her son, has other ideas. He's a chauffeur and longs for the day when he can have his own business and be his own boss, so he asks if he can have the money to invest in a liquor store, which he feels is a moneymaking machine. McNeil won't hear of Poitier's scheme and she promptly puts $3,500 down on a house in a lily-white neighborhood. Poitier is angered, quarrels with McNeil and his wife, Dee, and leaves the apartment, disappearing for three days from the residence as well as from his employment. McNeil finally finds him in a local tavern (which is what they call bars and saloons in Chicago) and offers him $6,500, with the proviso that $3,500 be held for Sands' education. Fiedler, the only white person in the cast, arrives. He's a member of an "improvement association" and on its behalf offers the family more than what they paid for the house. They can turn a profit without even moving. They thank him but decline. Now it's learned that Poitier took all of the cash, including the college fund, and put it into the liquor store deal, which turns out to be a fraud, and they are out the entire sum. Poitier is crushed and guilty and thinks they'd better accept Fiedler's generous offer. The family is against that and turns Poitier's thinking back to the right path. They are going to have to work two jobs, break their backs, but their dream of a home will not be shattered and they unite, indestructibly, to move to the new house and a new life. McNeil gets all the "wise" lines and is a tower of intelligence among her bickering clan. Gossett, before he added the "Junior" to his name, does a small part as a very WASPy black youth. Since much of action takes place in the tiny apartment, director Petrie had to pull out all the stops to keep it from being stage-bound, and, with the help of cinematographer Lawton, he succeeded. It's a bit long and somewhat verbose but remains a good example of humanity in a lower-class family that just happens to be black.

p, David Susskind, Philip Rose; d, Daniel Petrie; w, Lorraine Hansberry (based on her play); ph, Charles Lawton, Jr.; m, Laurence Rosenthal; ed, William A. Lyon, Paul Weatherwax; md, Arthur Norton; art d, Carl Anderson; set d, Louis Diage; makeup, Ben Lane.

Drama   Cas.   (PR:A MPAA:NR)

RAISING A RIOT**   (1957, Brit.) 90m BL/CD c

Kenneth More (*Tony Kent*), Shelagh Fraser (*Mary Kent*), Mandy Miller (*Anne Kent*), Gary Billings (*Peter Kent*), Fusty Bentine (*Fusty Kent*), Ronald Squire (*Grampy*), Olga Lindo (*Aunt Maud*), Lionel Murton (*Harry*), Mary Laura Wood (*Jacqueline*), Jan Miller (*Sue*), Nora Nicholson (*Miss Pettigrew*), Anita Sharp Bolster (*Mrs. Buttons*), Michael Bentine (*Museum Official*), Dorothy Dewhurst (*Mother*), Robin Brown (*Junior*), Arthur Hill, Erik Chitty, Fred Griffiths, Sam Kydd, Bill Shine, Jessie Evans, Charles Lamb, Cyril Chamberlain, Patricia Cree, Victor Maddern, Donald Pascoe.

Sporadically funny comedy starring More as a befuddled British daddy who finds himself alone to contend with his three children when his wife takes a trip to Canada. Thinking a change of venue might do them all some good, More moves his brood to his father's converted windmill in the country, which of course, the children nearly destroy during the course of the film.

p, Ian Dalrymple, Hugh Perceval; d, Wendy Toye; w, Dalrymple, Perceval, James Matthews (based on the novel by Alfred Toombs); ph, Christopher Challis (Technicolor); m, Bruce Montgomery; ed, Albert Rule; art d, Joseph Bato.

Comedy   (PR:A MPAA:NR)

RAISING THE WIND, 1933   (SEE: BIG RACE, THE, 1933)

RAISING THE WIND, 1962   (SEE: ROOMMATES, 1962, Brit.)

RAKE'S PROGRESS, THE   (SEE: NOTORIOUS GENTLEMAN, 1945, Brit.)

RALLY 'ROUND THE FLAG, BOYS!**   (1958) 106m FOX c

Paul Newman (*Harry Bannerman*), Joanne Woodward (*Grace Bannerman*), Joan Collins (*Angela Hoffa*), Jack Carson (*Capt. Hoxie*), Dwayne Hickman (*Grady Metcalf*), Tuesday Weld (*Comfort Goodpasture*), Gale Gordon (*Col. Thorwald*), Tom Gilson (*Opie*), O.Z. Whitehead (*Isaac Goodpasture*), Ralph Osborn III (*Danny Bannerman*), Stanley Livingston (*Peter*), Jon Lormer (*George Melvin*), Joseph Holland (*Manning Thaw*), Burt Mustin (*Milton Evans*), Percy Helton

(*Waldo Pike*), Nora O'Mahoney (*Betty O'Shiel*), Richard Collier (*Zack Crummitt*), Murvyn Vye (*Oscar Hoffa*).

Max Shulman is a witty author with *Barefoot Boy With Cheek*, *Sleep 'Til Noon*, and many others to his credit. This novel was not quite so hilarious as those, but it deserved a better fate than this heavy-handed, overdone, inane, and farcical film. Meant to be a slap at "The American Way" and several other targets, it lays there like a week-old herring most of the time, mainly due to the overplaying of Newman and the clunky direction by veteran McCarey. It's base when it should be subtle, bombastic when it should be gentle, and any light moments are dimmed by Newman's pathetic attempts to be funny, when he should have played it straight, thereby making it funny. Newman is a Connecticut commuter who travels to New York daily from his suburban home. He's married to Woodward and they have two children, although she's so busy being a local do-gooder that she hardly has time for him. Enter Collins, already a *femme fatale* at the purported age of 25. She is hot to trot with anyone who asks, except for TV executive Vye, whom she is married to. The government wants to use the quiet town for some undercover project, and although nobody knows what it is, they're all sure that it's something that's bad for the neighborhood. Woodward comes out against the scheme and Newman goes to Washington to argue with the powers about it. Woodward then goes to the capitol to pay a surprise visit on Newman and finds him in his hotel room with Collins, who is trying to seduce him and wearing only a sheet. Woodward storms out and Newman follows her back to suburbia. Carson is an Army captain who is annoying everyone in the town and Newman is deputized to be the man between the Army and the people. At length (at a *lot* of length), Woodward has her allies dress up as Indians and lead a 4th of July skirmish against the Army. Carson's boss, Gordon, finally tells all. A missile site is to be built in the town, thereby bringing a lot of employment for all. Newman and Woodward eventually kiss and make up and the passion of that buss causes their bodies to press the lever that launches missiles. Inside the projectile is the much-hated Carson and he goes up in space at the conclusion. Weld does a good turn as a teenage nymphet who is turning on Hickman, a lovelorn oaf. Hammy balderdash is intermixed with whatever sharp lines were left over from Shulman's novel. Newman's first comedy should have been his last. Gratuitous and dubious sexuality makes this a poor bet for youngsters.

p&d, Leo McCarey; w, Claude Binyon, McCarey (based on the novel by Max Shulman); ph, Leon Shamroy (CinemaScope, DeLuxe Color); m, Cyril J. Mockridge; ed, Louis R. Loeffler; md, Lionel Newman; art d, Lyle R. Wheeler, Leland Fuller; set d, Walter M, Scott, Stuart A. Reiss; cos, Charles LeMaire; spec eff, L.B. Abbott; makeup, Ben Nye.

Comedy   (PR:C MPAA:NR)

RAMONA**   (1936) 90m FOX c

Loretta Young (*Ramona*), Don Ameche (*Alessandro*), Kent Taylor (*Felipe Moreno*), Pauline Frederick (*Senora Moreno*), Jane Darwell (*Aunt Ri Hyar*), Katherine DeMille (*Margarita*), Victor Kilian (*Father Gaspare*), John Carradine (*Jim Farrar*), Pedro de Cordoba (*Father Salvierderra*), J. Carrol Naish (*Juan Can*), Charles Waldron (*Dr. Weaver*), Claire DuBrey (*Marda*), Russell Simpson (*Scroggs*), William Benedict (*Joe Hyar*), Chief Thundercloud (*Pablo*), Charles Middleton, Tom London (*American Settlers*), Ruth Robinson (*Patient in Doctor's Office*), Cecil Weston (*Pablo's Wife*), Robert Spindola (*Paquito*).

Notable only as 20th Century Fox's first feature shot entirely in Technicolor, this is the first and only sound version but the umpteenth film version of the classic Helen Hunt Jackson novel. The film features the unlikely casting of Young as the half-breed Indian girl who leaves her fiance, white-man Taylor, for the charms of redskin Ameche (equally miscast). Striking out on their own, Young (raised by kindly whites) is shocked to discover rampant racism in old California. Their marriage ends tragically when Ameche is killed by farmer Carradine, who thinks that the Indian has stolen his horse. In reality, Ameche has only borrowed the horse to ride and get help for his sick daughter. Ameche is nearly laughable in this, his first starring role, and Young is visibly ill (she had to withdraw from the production for health reasons and a double was used in several of her sequences).

p, Sol M. Wurtzel; d, Henry King; w, Lamar Trotti (based on a novel by Helen Hunt Jackson); ph, William Skall, Chester Lyons (Technicolor); ed, Alfred De Gaetano; md, Alfred Newman; art d, Duncan Cramer; m/l, Newman, William Kernell.

Western   (PR:A MPAA:NR)

RAMPAGE**   (1963) 98m Talbot-Seven Arts/WB c

Robert Mitchum (*Harry Stanton*), Elsa Martinelli (*Anna*), Jack Hawkins (*Otto Abbot*), Sabu (*Talib*), Cely Carrillo (*Chep*), Emile Genest (*Schelling*), Stefan Schnabel (*Sakai Chief*), David Cadiente (*Baka*), John Keaka (*Malay Warrior*).

Mitchum is totally wasted in this silly safari film (it has been said that Mitchum appeared in the film to provide a nice South Seas vacation for his family during filming). The film features him as an international big-game trapper hired by a German zoo to capture a rare Malaysian cat, which is half tiger, half leopard. He is joined on his journey by aging big-game hunter Hawkins, who is accompanied by his mistress, Martinelli. In the brush, tension soon develops between the hunters as Hawkins begins to demonstrate a disturbing penchant for paranoid behavior, and he accuses Martinelli and Mitchum of having an affair. Though Mitchum does have designs on Martinelli, he keeps it to himself until they capture their quarry. Back in Germany, Martinelli confesses to Hawkins her love for Mitchum. This snaps Hawkins' already thin mind and he releases the big cat with the hope that it will kill Mitchum. As it turns out, the cat kills practically everybody *but* Mitchum. Meanwhile, Hawkins corners Mitchum and Martinelli and raises his rifle to shoot them, but the cat leaps out of nowhere and kills Hawkins.

p, William Fadiman; d, Phil Karlson; w, Robert I. Holt, Marguerite Roberts (based on the novel by Alan Caillou); ph, Harold Lipstein (Technicolor); m, Elmer Bernstein; ed, Gene Milford; art d, Herman Blumenthal; set d, George James Hopkins; cos, Oleg Cassini; m/l, Mack David, Bernstein; makeup, Gordon Bau

Adventure **(PR:A MPAA:NR)**

RAMPAGE AT APACHE WELLS** (1966, Ger./Yugo.) 91m Rialto-Jadran/COL c (DER OLPRINZ; KRALJ PETROLEJA)

Stewart Granger *(Old Surehand)*, Pierre Brice *(Winnetou)*, Macha Meril *(Lizzy)*, Harald Leipnitz *(The Oil Prince)*, Mario Girotti *(Richard Forsythe)*, Antje Weisgerber *(Frau Ebersbach)*, Walter Barnes *(Campbell)*, Gerd Frickhoffer *(Kovacz)*, Paddy Fox *(Old Wabble)*, Heinz Erhardt *(Kantor Hampel)*, Vladimir Leib *(Duncan)*, Dusan Janicijevic *(Butler)*, Slobodan Dimitrijevic *(Knife)*, Davor Antolic *(Paddy)*, Veljko Maricic *(Bergmann)*, Ilija Ivezic *(Webster)*, Zvonimir Crnko *(Billy Forner)*, Petar Petrovic *(Jimmy)*, Slobodan Vedernjak *(John)*, Branko Supek *(Jack)*, Marinko Cosic *(Tobby)*.

Another in the series of European westerns based on the novels of Karl May and starring Granger as Old Surehand and Brice as his faithful Indian companion Winnetou. This time the pair seek to avenge the death of their friend Crnko, a wagon master who has been killed by a ruthless gang of outlaws. Brice volunteers to take the wagon train through the dangerous territory himself, and he uses his negotiating skills to forge an agreement with the Navajos so that the group may pass unharmed. Unfortunately Leipnitz, a greedy landgrabber intent on bilking the settlers out of their land so that he can obtain the oil rights, kills the Navajo chief's son. The Indians assume the dirty deed was done by Brice and the settlers, so they go on the warpath. Luckily, Granger arrives in time with Leipnitz in town, and the Navajos settle down. Typical material somewhat distinguished by the fine cinematography that was the trademark of this series.

p, Horst Wendlandt; d, Harald Philipp; w, Fred Denger, Philipp (based on the novel *Der Olprinz* by Karl Friedrich May); ph, Heinz Holscher (UltraScope, Eastmancolor); m, Martin Bottcher; ed, Hermann Haller; art d&set d, Dusko Jericevic; cos, Irms Pauli; spec eff, Erwin Lange; makeup, Erich-Lothar Schmekel, Claire Fussbach.

Western **(PR:A MPAA:NR)**

RAMPANT AGE, THE*½ (1930) 60m Continental bw

James Murray *(Sandy Benton)*, Merna Kennedy *(Doris Lawrence)*, Eddie Borden *(Eddie Mason)*, Margaret Quimby *(Estelle)*, Florence Turner *(Mrs. Lawrence)*, John Elliott *(Mr. Benton)*, Gertie Messinger *(Julie)*, Pat Cunning *(De Witt)*.

Based on a sensational (in 1930) novel written by an 18-year-old which exposed the seamy side of suburban youth culture, this film version is about as insightful and well executed as the book, which isn't saying much. Murray stars as the young rich kid who dumps on his gal Kennedy by whooping it up at wild gin parties and going off with other women. Kennedy, not the kind of girl to just stay at home and take this kind of abuse, goes out on her own and begins the same cycle of self-destructive behavior. In the end the couple realize their true love for each other when Murray saves Kennedy's life after they are trapped in an airplane that is about to crash.

p, Trem Carr; d, Phil Rosen; w, H.O. Hoyt (based on a novel by R.S. Carr); ph, Herbert J. Kirkpatrick.

Drama **(PR:A MPAA:NR)**

RAMPARTS WE WATCH, THE** (1940) 90m Time/RKO bw

John Adair *(Dan Meredith)*, John Summers *(Joe Kovacs)*, Julia Kent *(Mrs. Joe Kovacs)*, Ellen Prescott *(Anna Kovacs)*, Andrew Brummer *(John Slavetz)*, Myrtle Paseler *(Mrs. Slavetz)*, Alfred U. Wysse *(Prof. Gustav Bensinger)*, Marguerite Brown *(Mrs. Bensinger)*, Georgette McKee *(Hilda Bensinger)*, Robert Rapelye *(Fred Bensinger)*, Frank McCabe *(Edward Averill)*, Myra Archibald *(Mrs. Averill)*, Edward Wragge *(Walter Averill)*, Harry C. Stopher *(Stuart Gilchrist)*, Jane Stuart *(Mrs. Gilchrist)*, Elliott Reid *(Ralph Gilchrist)*, C.W. Stowell *(Hon. John Lawton)*, Ethel Hudson *(Mrs. John Lawton)*, Augusta Durgeon *(Mrs. Dora Smith)*, Albert Gattiker *(Eddie Reed)*, H.G. Brady *(Capt. John Kellogg)*, Thomas S. Burney, Jr. *(Tommy Burney)*, Roberta Manski *(Mrs. Barbara Davis)*, W.W. Pinkerton *(Chief of Police)*, Richard McCracken *(Hal Fisher)*, David Dean *("Montana")*, Lila Lyman *(Lila Bishop)*, George Jackson *(Karl Von Schleich)*, H.G. Westcott *(George Westcott)*, Westbrook Van Voorhis *(Narrator)*, Lorenzo Gallant, A.A. Nourie, E.C. Lucey, Gordon Hall, Reginald Reynolds, Harry Feltcorn, Rev. Byron Ulric Hatfield, Andrew Bizub, Benjamin Semaskay, W.J. Londregan, Thomas McElarney, Gabriel Kerekes, Louis de Rochemont III.

A very unusual docu-drama wherein Time Inc. used footage from their popular March-Of-Time newsreels and intercut it into a narrative structure using actors (most of them non-professionals from the town of New London, Connecticut) to illustrate how WW I affected the lives of a group of average Americans. With America's inevitable participation in WW II just around the historical corner, the film attempts to remind the viewer of the lesson that should have been learned from WW I, namely, that preparedness should be taken seriously.

p&d, Louis de Rochemont; w, Robert L. Richards, Cedric R. Worth; ph, Charles E. Gilson, John A. Geisel; m, Louis De Francesco; ed, Lothar Wolff.

Drama **(PR:A MPAA:NR)**

RAMROD*** (1947) 94m Enterprise/UA bw

Veronica Lake *(Connie Dickason)*, Joel McCrea *(Dave Nash)*, Ian McDonald *(Walt Shipley)*, Charles Ruggles *(Ben Dickason)*, Preston Foster *(Frank Ivey)*, Arleen Whelan *(Rose)*, Lloyd Bridges *(Red Cates)*, Donald Crisp *(Sheriff Jim Crew)*, Rose Higgins *(Annie)*, Chick York *(Dr. Parks)*, Sarah Padden *(Mrs. Parks)*, Don DeFore *(Bill Schell)*, Nestor Paiva *(Curley)*, Cliff Parkinson *(Tom Peebles)*, Trevor Bardette *(Bailey)*, John Powers *(Pokey)*, Ward Wood *(Link Thomas)*, Hal Taliaferro *(Jess Moore)*, Wally Cassell *(Virg Lee)*, Ray Teal *(Burma)*, Jeff Corey *(Bice)*.

A fine, little-appreciated western starring Lake as the firebrand daughter of spineless and seedy ranchowner Ruggles, who has allowed himself to become the lackey of big shot cattleman Foster. Lake, who is trying to operate a sheepherding ranch, soon becomes enraged by Foster's (with her father's acquiescence) efforts to run her out of business. Seeking vengeance, she organizes her own gang of guerrillas to fight fire with fire, much to the dismay of noble ranch hand McCrea, who attempts to be the voice of reason. That voice, however, is drowned out by the thundering hoofbeats of the two warring factions (Lake and Foster), and after much senseless bloodshed McCrea is forced to settle things himself by killing Foster and riding off in disgust. RAMROD boasts a superb supporting cast, gorgeous black and white photography, and a hard-hitting, grimly realistic screenplay that continues to reveal new facets even after several viewings.

p, Harry Sherman; d, Andre de Toth; w, Jack Mofitt, Graham Baker, Cecile Kramer (based on a story by Luke Short); ph, Russell Harlan, Harry Redmond, Jr.; m, Adolph Deutsch; ed, Sherman A. Rose; md, Rudolph Polk.

Western **(PR:A MPAA:NR)**

RAMRODDER, THE* (1969) 92m E.S.I./Entertainment Ventures c (AKA: RAMRODDERS)

Jim Gentry *(The Ramrodder)*, Julia Blackburn *(Lucy)*, Brave Eagle *(Chief)*, Kathy Williams *(Tuwana)*, David Rosenkranz, Bob Beausoleil, Kathy Share, Kedric Wolfe, Marsha Jordan.

A fairly vile western starring Gentry as the title cowboy who has amassed a small fortune for himself through his good will efforts with the local Indians. Little do the redskins know that Gentry and Indian princess Williams are having an affair. Trouble arises when a wandering cowpoke rapes one of the tribe's squaws and Gentry is blamed. The Indians, seeking revenge, pick an innocent settler's daughter and rape her. Gentry then tracks the white rapist down and turns him over to the Indians who castrate him. Having patched things up with both communities, Gentry is once again accepted by the Indians and he marries Williams to insure that he won't get scalped.

d&w, Van Guylder; ph, Bob Maxwell (Eastmancolor); art d, Bud Costello.

Western **(PR:O MPAA:NR)**

RAMSBOTTOM RIDES AGAIN*½ (1956, Brit.) 92m Jack Hylton/BL bw

Arthur Askey *(Bill Ramsbottom)*, Glenn Melvyn *(Charlie)*, Sidney James *(Black Jake)*, Shani Wallis *(Joan Ramsbottom)*, Frankie Vaughan *(Elmer)*, Betty Marsden *(Florrie Ramsbottom)*, Jerry Desmonde *(Blue Eagle)*, Sabrina *(Girl)*, Danny Ross *(Danny)*, Anthea Askey *(Susie Ramsbottom)*, Billy Percy *(Reuben)*, Gary Wayne *(Tombstone)*, Denis Wyndham *(Dan)*, June Grant, Donald Stewart, Campbell Singer, Marne Maitland, Beckett Bould, Sam Kydd, Deryck Guyler, Edie Martin, Leonard Williams, John Carson.

A barely funny British parody of the American western starring Askey as a tenderfoot Englishman who arrives in Canada to run a ranch that he has inherited from his grandfather, a grizzled old sheriff.

p&d, John Baxter; w, Baxter, Basil Thomas, Arthur Askey, Glenn Melvyn, Geoffrey Orme (based on the play by Harold G. Robert); ph, Arthur Grant.

Comedy/Western **(PR:A MPAA:NR)**

RANCHO DELUXE½** (1975) 93m UA c

Jeff Bridges *(Jack McKee)*, Sam Waterston *(Cecil Colson)*, Elizabeth Ashley *(Cora Brown)*, Charlene Dallas *(Laura Beige)*, Clifton James *(John Brown)*, Slim Pickens *(Henry Beige)*, Harry Dean Stanton *(Curt)*, Richard Bright *(Burt)*, Patti D'Arbanville *(Betty Fargo)*, Maggie Wellman *(Mary Fargo)*, Bert Conway *(Wilbur Fargo)*, Anthony Palmer *(Karl)*, Joseph Sullivan *(Dizzy)*, Helen Craig *(Mrs. Castle)*, Ronda Copland *(Dee)*, John Quade *(Circular Face)*, Sandy Kenyon *(Skinny Face)*, Joseph Spinell *(Colson)*, Wilma Riley *(Mrs. Colson)*, Richard McMurray *(McKee)*, Danna Hansen *(Mrs. McKee)*, Doria Cooke *(Anna)*, John Rodgers *(Clerk)*, Paula Jermunson *(Lady Foreman)*, Patti Jerome *(Madame)*, Pat Noteboom *(Prostitute)*, Bob Wetzel *(Truck Driver)*, Ben Mar, Jr. *(Cook)*, Arnold Huppert *(Policeman)*, Richard Cavanaugh *(Judge)*, Angela Cramer *(Ranch Lady)*, Esther Black *(Grandma)*, Oneida Broderick *(Another Lady)*.

McGuane's script for RANCH DELUXE must have been better than the final picture because, every now and again, there are some terrific lines, good-natured humor, and lovely touches. Overall, however, Perry's attempt at directing a comedy falls short. Bridges and Waterston are best friends who make a living rustling a few head from the ranch of James, who is married to pneumatic Ashley, a woman who is love-starved by her conservative husband. Bridges is divorced from Cooke, and when he goes back to see her and, perhaps, effect a reconciliation, her attitude only sends him right back to being a happy-go-lucky drifter. Waterston is an Indian and returns to his tribe for a brief visit, but the other Indians are so hide-bound and stuffy that he wants no part of them. So the two men decide that these little thefts are not enough; they want a big one. They enlist two of James' workers, Bright and Stanton, into a huge heist. Meanwhile, James has employed a crochety private detective, Pickens, to track down those responsible for these Montana misdemeanors. Stanton takes up with Dallas (who claims she is Pickens' niece, but is, in reality, his daughter) and she is the one who blows the whistle on the plot to steal a herd of cattle. D'Arbanville and Wellman are rustler "groupies" who hang around with Bridges and Waterston and add little to the episodic plot. The best parts of the movie are little details that are shown, with no comment, for the eyes to catch. It's hit and miss, although there's an odd charm about the whole thing that is often enjoyable when not preaching about the fate of the "Old West." Nothing much happens and it just ambles along from set-piece to set-piece with occasional glimpses of enough flesh and harsh language to put it into the category of "don't let the kids see this." One of Kastner's better films.

p, Elliott Kastner; d, Frank Perry; w, Thomas McGuane; ph, William A. Fraker (DeLuxe Color); m, Jummy Buffett; ed, Sid Katz; art d, Michael Haller.

Western/Comedy Cas. (PR:C MPAA:R)

RANCHO GRANDE*½ (1938, Mex.) 85m Atlas bw

Tito Guizar *(Jose Francisco)*, Rene Cardona *(Felipe)*, Esther Fernandez *(Cruz)*, Lorenzo Barcelata *(Martin)*, Carlos Lopez *(Florentino)*, Emma Roldan *(Angela)*, Manuel Norlega *(Don Rosendo)*, Herman Vera *(Venancio)*, A. Sanchez Telio *(Don Nabor)*.

Boring Mexican-made musical oater featuring the ever popular Tito Guizar and his guitar. Here he warbles his way through a silly love story with the lovely Fernandez as the object of his adoration. Traditional Mexican songs include: "Rancho Grande" (sung by Guizar). (Spanish, English Subtitles).

p, Alfonzo Rivas Bostamente; d, Fernando de Fuentes; m, Lorenzo Barcelata.

Musical (PR:A MPAA:NR)

RANCHO GRANDE*½ (1940) 68m REP bw

Gene Autry *(Gene)*, Smiley Burnette *(Frog)*, June Storey *(Kay)*, Mary Lee *(Patricia Fairfield Dodge)*, Dick Hogan *(Tom Dodge)*, Ellen E. Lowe *(Effie Tinker)*, Ferris Taylor *(Emory Benson)*, Joseph De Stefani *(Jose)*, Roscoe Ates *(Tex)*, Rex Lease *(Travis)*, Ann Baldwin *(Susan Putnam)*, Roy Barcroft *(Madden)*, Edna Lawrence *(Rita Ross)*, Jack Ingram, Bud Osborne, Slim Whitaker, Pals of the Golden West, Brewer Kids, Boys' Choir of St. Joseph's School, Champion the Horse.

Poor Gene finds himself saddled (ouch!) with looney East Coast heiress Storey and her siblings when she travels out West to take over the ranch she has inherited from her grandfather. Of course the city gal doesn't quite fathom the intricacies of running the Rancho Grande, despite Autry's best efforts to set her straight. Luckily, a nasty bunch of villains threatens to ruin the new irrigation system vital to the ranch's survival, and this crisis pulls the gang together. This is director Frank McDonald's first feature in the Autry series. Songs include the title song and "Swing of the Range" (sung by Lee).

p, William Berke; d, Frank McDonald; w, Bradford Ropes, Betty Burbridge, Peter Milne (based on a story by Milne, Connie Lee); ph, William Nobles; ed, Tony Martinelli.

Western (PR:A MPAA:NR)

RANCHO NOTORIOUS****** (1952) 89m Fidelity/RKO c

Marlene Dietrich *(Altar Keane)*, Arthur Kennedy *(Vern Haskell)*, Mel Ferrer *(Frenchy Fairmont)*, Lloyd Gough *(Kinch)*, Gloria Henry *(Beth)*, William Frawley *(Baldy Gunder)*, Lisa Ferraday *(Maxine)*, John Raven *(Chuck-a-Luck Dealer)*, Jack Elam *(Geary)*, George Reeves *(Wilson)*, Frank Ferguson *(Preacher)*, Francis McDonald *(Harbin)*, Dan Seymour *(Comanche Paul)*, John Kellogg *(Factor)*, Rodric Redwing *(Rio)*, Stuart Randall *(Starr)*, Roger Anderson *(Red)*, Charles Gonzalez *(Hevia)*, Felipe Turich *(Sanchez)*, Joe Dominguez *(Gonzales)*, I. Stanford Jolley *(Deputy Warren)*, John Doucette *(Whitey)*, Charlita *(Mexican Girl in Bar)*, Ralph Sanford *(Politician)*, Lane Chandler *(Sheriff Hardy)*, Fuzzy Knight *(Barber)*, Fred Graham *(Ace Maguire)*, Dick Wessel *(Deputy)*, Dick Elliott *(Storyteller)*, William Haade *(Sheriff Bullock)*.

The last of Fritz Lang's three westerns, following THE RETURN OF JESSE JAMES (1940) and WESTERN UNION (1941), RANCHO NOTORIOUS is a bizarre, strangely poetic, and highly personal ballad of one man's transformation from an innocent, loving cowhand to a man obsessed with avenging his fiancee's murder. Kennedy plays the cowhand who, at the film's opening, is wooing his sweetheart, Henry. After exchanging hugs and kisses, fantasizing about the children they will have when married, and discussing the name of their new ranch, Kennedy presents her with a brooch and goes off to work, leaving her behind in the general store where she is employed. A couple of outlaws, Gough and Doucette, ride into town soon after and stop at the store to empty out the safe. Gough gets rough with the girl, and from an outside vantage point, a gunshot is heard. The outlaws take off as Gough fires a shot at a young boy who witnessed the crime. When Kennedy returns to the store, he is greeted by a crowd of onlookers and a doctor who, after declaring Henry dead, tells Kennedy that "she wasn't spared anything," clearly implying that she was raped as well. As the camera moves down to reveal her hand clawed in a rigor-mortis death grip, Kennedy, along with a posse, begins his search for the killer. The posse soon backs down and Kennedy sets out alone as a reprise of the title song, "The Legend of Chuck-A-Luck," (Ken Darby, sung by William Lee) is heard: "Listen to the legend of the Chuck-a-Luck, Chuck-a-Luck/listen to the wheel of fate, as round and round with a whispering sound it spins, it spins the old, old story of hate, murder, and revenge." He follows the trail that fate has laid for him through the woods until he comes across the dying Doucette, having been betrayed by Gough and shot in the back. Doucette mutters his last words, "Chuck-a-Luck," supplying Kennedy with his first clue. After asking countless men, Kennedy learns that Chuck-a-Luck is the name of a criminal hideout run by a tough and beautiful barroom singer named Altar Keane, played marvelously by Dietrich. Dietrich, like Kennedy, has a past that revolves around "Chuck-a-Luck"—in her case it was a gambling wheel which—in flashback—netted her a sizable winning thanks to the help of much-feared gunman Ferrer. From there Ferrer and Dietrich become lovers. After hearing the story of Dietrich and Ferrer, Kennedy decides that he must find Ferrer in order to find Chuck-a-Luck. The trail leads to a corrupt town which is in the process of overthrowing its corrupt officials and electing a new law and order party. Sitting behind jail bars in this town is Ferrer. Kennedy, in order to get thrown into jail with Ferrer, causes a ruckus in a saloon, is arrested, and achieves his goal. The two men become friends and break jail. To show his appreciation, Ferrer invites Kennedy to Chuck-a-Luck, an unassuming horse ranch nestled into an obscure valley. Dietrich, the only woman on the ranch, runs a tight ship, wielding an all-powerful hand over the nine or ten outlaws who share her roof. She also has rigid rules that all must abide by, most importantly that no one asks questions. In return for her roof, food, and confidence, Dietrich receives a five percent share of any job the outlaws pull. As Dietrich introduces Kennedy to everyone, he hones in on Reeves, a sleazy lady's man with a hideous scar on his face, which Kennedy assumes to have been made by his fiancee. Although Dietrich is clearly Ferrer's, there is a subtle attraction between her and Kennedy. Dietrich, however, laments that she is too old and, in a song she sings for the boys, "Get Away, Young Man" (Ken Darby), clearly makes her sentiments known. Kennedy, however, is still bent on "hate, murder, and revenge" and continues to make a play for Dietrich in order to get the information he needs. When Kennedy sees Dietrich wearing on her dress the brooch that he earlier gave to his fiancee, he tries to get her to reveal where she got it. Naturally, he assumes it was Ferrer. When the sheriff's men come to the ranch, Dietrich orders her men to escape to a nearby hideout until further notice. Kennedy, however, pretends to have gotten separated from the group and returns to the ranch. When the sheriff's aide becomes suspicious because a number of horses seem to have recently left the ranch, Kennedy saves the day by inventing a story about some strays he has just rounded up. The sheriff leaves, convinced that there has been no foul play. Kennedy makes his play for Dietrich, pulling her into his arms and kissing her. After their kiss Dietrich responds, "That was for trying." She then makes an evil switch and slaps Kennedy twice in the face: "That was for trying too hard." When the gang returns to Chuck-a-Luck, they begin making plans for a big bank robbery, but their enthusiasm is undercut by Dietrich's demand of a 10 percent share. Although she tells them it is because of the high risk of the robbery, it is really to keep Ferrer and Kennedy out of trouble. Dissent begins to brew. Kennedy has finally learned that the brooch was given to Dietrich by Gough, as part of her share. When Kennedy confronts Gough, the gang feels betrayed. Kennedy tries to get Gough to draw on him, but Gough refuses, knowing that his opponent has picked up all of Ferrer's superb gunslinging abilities. When the sheriff arrives, Kennedy gets his chance to expose Gough and have him arrested. The gang, however, is not pleased and breaks Gough from jail. They then head back to Chuck-a-Luck to settle with Dietrich. A blazing battle breaks out and, when the gunsmoke settles, Gough has been killed and Dietrich lies dying, having stepped between Kennedy and a bullet meant for him. Having ridden out the wave of fate and settled his score of "hate, murder, and revenge," Kennedy rides off with Ferrer, implying that Kennedy will not, and cannot, ever be redeemed and returned to his previous hateless life. RANCHO NOTORIOUS has the quintessential Lang theme of a man ruled by fate mixed into the generic elements of the western. Although it is set in the West, has western sets and western costumes, it is not a western in the manner of John Ford. Where Ford, along with other western pioneers, has a sense of American mythmaking, Lang is still absorbed in his German heritage and the outward expression and physical representation of a man's inner turmoil. Like Dave Bannion (played by Glenn Ford) in THE BIG HEAT, RANCHO NOTORIOUS' hero Vern Haskell is a basically good man turned inside out by thoughts of revenge. With Bannion the death of his wife sets him into motion, while with Haskell it is the death of his fiancee. From that point, a trail, dictated by an unwritten Teutonic fate of the gods, leads both men to their dark side which is opened up by a *femme fatale*—Gloria Grahame in THE BIG HEAT and Dietrich in this film—who winds up destroyed in the process. RANCHO NOTORIOUS is, on the surface, a western, but doesn't express western themes and ideals, in much the same way as Nicholas Ray's non-western JOHNNY GUITAR. Originally titled "Chuck-a-Luck," this cognomen fell victim to the blind power of RKO head Howard Hughes, who arbitrarily decided that Lang's title (which referred to the vertical gambling wheel known as a chuck-a-luck wheel) would hold no meaning in Europe, and thereby changed it to the even less meaningful, though more appealing, RANCHO NOTORIOUS. Lang's troubles with RKO were not limited to the film's title, however. Even though it was guaranteed that Lang would be consulted before any re-editing, the film was recut under producer Welsch's orders, which removed much of the ambiance. Lang also had troubles with Dietrich who, for the first time, was cast as an aging woman instead of the glamorous glowing beauty of her youth. Like her Altar Keane character, Dietrich could not accept the effects of mortality, begging cameraman Mohr (who at one point asked to be relieved of his duties, but was refused) to make her look as lovely as he did years earlier in 1939's DESTRY RIDES AGAIN. The tensions between Dietrich and Lang drew close to the breaking point, though they were romantically linked for a brief period in 1934 after Lang had left Germany to film LILIOM in France. The working relationship between director and actress was not helped by Dietrich's suggestion that Lang try certain methods and techniques used by her mentor and charisma-creator Josef von Sternberg. By the film's end Lang and Dietrich were not even speaking. None of those problems, however, come out in the film. Dietrich's mature performance is superb (especially memorable is her first scene—riding a man as if on horseback as part of a drunken barroom contest) and her portrayal of a woman torn between two men and between young and old age is a revelation. Her role as Altar Keane also marks a very different *femme fatale* who, instead of causing a lover's death, brings about her own while saving his. In addition to the Dietrich number "Get Away, Young Man," she also sings another Ken Darby tune, "Gypsy Davey." Missing from the credits on the film was actor Lloyd Gough who, because he refused to testify before the House Un-American Activities Committee, was blacklisted and had his name removed by Hughes.

p, Howard Welsch; d, Fritz Lang; w, Daniel Taradash (based on the story "Gunsight Whitman" by Sylvia Richards); ph, Hal Mohr (Technicolor); m, Emil Newman; ed, Otto Ludwig; prod d, Wiard Ihnen; set d, Robert Priestly; cos, Joe King, Don Loper; m/l, Ken Darby; makeup, Frank Westmore.

Western Cas. (PR:A MPAA:NR)

RANDOLPH FAMILY, THE** (1945, Brit.) 78m Gainsborough/EFI bw (GB: DEAR OCTOPUS)

Margaret Lockwood *(Penny Fenton)*, Michael Wilding *(Nicholas Randolph)*, Celia Johnson *(Cynthia)*, Roland Culver *(Felix Martin)*, Helen Haye *(Dora Randolph)*, Athene Seyler *(Aunt Belle)*, Jean Cadell *(Vicar's Wife)*, Basil Radford *(Kenneth)*, Frederick Leister *(Charles Randolph)*, Nora Swinburne *(Edna)*, Antoinette Cellier

(Hilda), Madge Compton *(Marjorie)*, Kathleen Harrison *(Mrs. Glossop)*, Ann Stephens *(Scrap)*, Derek Lansiaux *(Bill)*, Alistair Stewart *(Joe)*, Evelyn Hall *(Gertrude)*, Muriel George *(Cook)*, Annie Esmond *(Nannie)*, Irene Handl *(Flora)*, Arthur Denton *(Mr. Glossop)*, Pamela Western *(Deidre)*, Artie Ash *(Burton)*, Graham Moffatt *(Fred, the Chauffeur)*, Henry Morrell *(Vicar)*, Jane Gill-Davis, Frank Foster, Thelma Rea, Helen Goss, Noel Dainton, Barbara Douglas, Bobby Bradfield, Virginia Vernon, Jack Vyvyan, Leonard Sharp, James Lomas, Sidney Young, Amy Dalby, Jack Leslie.

Routine English comedy of manners centered around a family reunion organized for the celebration of a Golden Wedding anniversary. Among the various family members, each of whom has certain comedic quirks, are the snobby son, the oversexed daughter and assorted obnoxious grandchildren, who drive the family's poor secretary, Lockwood, to distraction. It has its moments.

p, Edward Black; d, Harold French; w, R.J. Minney, Patrick Kirwan (based on the adaptation by Esther McCracken of the play "Dear Octopus" by Dodie Smith); ph, Arthur Crabtree; ed, Michael Chorlton; md, Louis Levy; art d, John Bryan.

Comedy **(PR:A MPAA:NR)**

RANDOM HARVEST*½** (1942) 125m MGM bw

Ronald Colman *(Charles Ranier)*, Greer Garson *(Paula)*, Philip Dorn *(Dr. Jonathan Benet)*, Susan Peters *(Kitty)*, Reginald Owen *("Biffer")*, Edmund Gwenn *(Prime Minister)*, Henry Travers *(Dr. Sims)*, Margaret Wycherly *(Mrs. Deventer)*, Bramwell Fletcher *(Harrison)*, Arthur Margetson *(Chetwynd)*, Jill Esmond *(Lydia Chetwynd)*, Marta Linden *(Jill, Kitty's Mother)*, Melville Cooper *(George)*, Alan Napier *(Julian)*, Pax Walker *(Sheila)*, David Cavendish *(Henry Chilcotte)*, Clement May *(Beddoes)*, Norma Varden *(Julia)*, Ann Richards *(Bridget)*, Elizabeth Risdon *(Mrs. Lloyd)*, Charles Waldron *(Mr. Lloyd)*, Ivan Simpson *(Vicar)*, Rhys Williams *(Sam)*, Henry Daniell *(Heavy Man)*, Helena Phillips Evans *(Ella the Charwoman)*, Marie de Becker *(Vicar's Wife)*, Montague Shaw *(Julia's Husband)*, Mrs. Gardner Crane *(Mrs. Sims)*, Lumsden Hare *(Sir John)*, Frederick Worlock *(Paula's Lawyer)*, Hilda Plowright *(Nurse)*, Arthur Space *(Trempitt)*, Ian Wolfe *(Registrar)*, Terry Kilburn *(Boy)*, Reginald Sheffield *(Judge)*, Arthur Shields *(Chemist)*, Kay Medford *(Wife)*, Olive Blakeney *(Woman)*, Cyril McLaglen *(Policeman)*, Leonard Mudie *(Old Man)*, Peter Lawford *(Soldier)*, Lowden Adams *(Clerk)*, George Kirby *(Conductor)*, Maj. Sam Harris *(Member of the House of Commons)*, Una O'Connor *(Tobacconist)*, Aubrey Mather *(Sheldon)*.

Amnesia is an old standard in the movies, but it was never used better than in the filmed adaptation of James Hilton's popular 1940 novel *Random Harvest*. The setting is England, where WW I has just ended. Colman, a soldier from a wealthy family, is hospitalized for shell shock, having lost his memory in battle. When the armistice is declared, Colman wanders out of the hospital during a joyous celebration, ending up in the town of Medbury, where he meets Garson, a dancer in a local club. Garson quickly realizes Colman is an amnesiac and takes him to a country village to help him put his life back together. Colman is able to overcome a loss of speech, but cannot regain his memory. As he builds a new identity, Colman discovers a talent for writing. Gradually he and Garson come to fall in love, marry, and have a child. Colman, whose writing abilities are quickly developing, goes to Liverpool to sell one of his stories and while there is hit by a car and his memory is restored. Colman's three years with Garson are completely wiped out, and he returns to his family and work in the family industrial business. Garson, during Colman's absence, loses the child and goes through much hardship. Dorn, a psychiatrist, helps her find her husband and Garson gets herself hired as Colman's secretary. Colman is pleased with her work, but doesn't recognize Garson. Dorn tells Garson not to let on, lest she submit Colman to a severe psychological trauma. Peters, Colman's niece, develops a romantic interest in him and eventually the two become engaged. Peters senses there is a woman from Colman's lost years who means a great deal to him, and decides it would be best to call off the engagement. Colman grows depressed and throws himself into his work, coming to rely more and more on Garson, and he eventually proposes to her. Though this marriage is to be in name only, Garson tries to renew the forgotten spark. Colman, with Garson's help, becomes a powerful political leader. Garson grows depressed though and decides to take a vacation to ease her psychological woes. Before her trip begins, she returns to Medbury where she tarries at the cottage she had shared with Colman. Colman is summoned to Medbury at the same time to settle a labor strike. Upon arriving in Medbury, Colman's mind is jarred by some inexplicably familiar sites. Slowly his lost years come back to him, and he finally returns to the cottage, where he has an emotional reunion with Garson. RANDOM HARVEST is a deeply moving film, marked with strong performances by Garson and Colman. Their scenes together are sensitive and heartfelt, giving depth to a story that easily could have turned into a weepy soap opera in the wrong hands. Colman was nominated for an Oscar, as was Peters for Best Supporting Actress (Garson won Best Actress that year, not for this, but for MRS. MINIVER). The film also got a nomination as Best Picture, and proved to be a popular one with the audiences. Its theme of wartime loss on the most initimate of levels struck a deep chord in the heart of the WW II era Americans, many of whom could identify with the psychological pain Garson so eloquently displayed. Garson also displayed her legs in a dance hall number, a delightful piece that was enjoyed by critics and audiences alike. Made at a cost of $2 million, RANDOM HARVEST brought in $4.5 million at the box office, made record receipts for Radio City Music Hall, and became one of the top 25 moneymaking films of the year. LeRoy's direction was superb, delicately guiding the intricate story through the complicated plot developments. With this film's success, Colman won renewed respect in Hollywood while Garson's future at MGM was solidified.

p, Sidney Franklin; d, Mervyn LeRoy; w, Claudine West, George Froeschel, Arthur Wimperis (based on the novel by James Hilton); ph, Joseph Ruttenberg; m, Herbert Stothart; ed, Harold F. Kress; art d, Cedric Gibbons.

Drama **(PR:A MPAA:NR)**

RANDY RIDES ALONE½** (1934) 54m Lone Star/MON bw

John Wayne *(Randy Bowers)*, Alberta Vaughn *(Sally Rogers)*, George Hayes *(Matt the Mute/Marvin Black)*, Yakima Canutt *(Spike)*, Earl Dwire *(Sheriff)*, Tex Phelps *(Deputy)*, Arthur Ortego *(Henchman)*, Mack V. Wright *(Posse Member)*, Tex Palmer *(Henchman)*, Herman Hack.

A well-made early Wayne oater which sees the Duke investigating the work of a mysterious gang of crooks who have been robbing the express offices and leaving a trail of corpses behind (the opening of this film is surprisingly chilling). Highlight of the film contains one of the very few times (luckily) that Wayne sings on screen.

p, Paul Malvern; d, Harry Fraser; w, Lindsley Parsons (based on his story); ph, Archie Stout; ed, Carl Pierson; md, Abe Meyer.

Western **Cas.** **(PR:A MPAA:NR)**

RANDY STRIKES OIL (SEE: FIGHTING TEXANS, 1933)

RANGE BEYOND THE BLUE*½ (1947) 53m PRC bw

Eddie Dean *(Himself)*, Roscoe Ates *(Soapy)*, Helen Mowery *(Margie Rodgers)*, Bob Duncan *(Lash Taggart)*, Ted Adams *(Henry Rodgers)*, Bill Hammond *(Kyle)*, George Turner *(Bragg)*, Ted French *(Sneezer)*, Brad Slavin *(Kirk)*, Steve Clark *(Sheriff)*, The Sunshine Boys, Flash.

Dean and his sidekick Ates ride their ponies to the rescue of pretty stage owner Mowery when the gold shipments sent on her line come under the frequent attack of villain Duncan and his baddies. Though at first it appears that the gold is what is sought after, Dean and Ates eventually reveal that evil banker Adams is really behind the crimes and he seeks control of Mowrey's stage line.

p, Jerry Thomas; d, Ray Taylor; w, Patricia Harper; ph, Robert Cline; ed, Hugh Winn; md, Walter Greene; m/l, Eddie Dean, Bob Dean, Pete Gates, Hal Blair.

Western **(PR:A MPAA:NR)**

RANGE BUSTERS, THE** (1940) 53m MON bw

Ray Corrigan *(Crash)*, John King *(Dusty)*, Max Terhune *(Alibi)*, Luana Walters *(Carol)*, Earle Hodgins *(Uncle Rolf)*, Frank LaRue *(Doc Stegle)*, LeRoy Mason *(Torrence)*, Kermit Maynard *(Wyoming)*, Bruce King *(Wall)*, Duke [Carl]Mathews, Horace Murphy, Karl Hackett.

A mild rip-off of THE THREE MESQUITEERS series of westerns featuring two of its stars, Corrigan and Terhune (who even has the nerve to bring his ventriloquist dummy along on this ride) as they, along with third partner King, investigate the mysterious "phantom" who has been killing off the locals. After some digging, the three strangers conclude that the "phantom" is none other than kindly (but unbelievably cocky) Doc LaRue, the man who called them for help in the first place. (See RANGE BUSTERS series, Index.)

p, George W. Weeks; d, S. Roy Luby; w, John Rathmell; ph, Edward Linden; ed, Roy Claire.

Western **(PR:A MPAA:NR)**

RANGE DEFENDERS** (1937) 56m REP bw

Bob Livingston *(Stoney Brooke)*, Ray Corrigan *(Tucson Smith)*, Max Terhune *(Lullaby Joslin)*, Eleanor Stewart *(Sylvia Ashton)*, Harry Woods *(Harvey)*, Earle Hodgins *(Sheriff Gray)*, Thomas Carr *(The Kid)*, Yakima Canutt *(Hodge)*, John Merton *(Crag)*, Harrison Greene *(Auctioneer)*, Horace B. Carpenter *(Pete)*, Frank Ellis *(Henchman)*, Fred "Snowflake" Toones *(Cook)*, Jack O'Shea, Ernie Adams, Jack Rockwell, Merrill McCormack, Curley Dresden, Jack Kirk, George Morrell, Donald Kirke, C. L. Sherwood, Milburn Morante, Al Taylor.

The THREE MESQUITEERS ride again, this time concentrating a bit more on the cornball yucks as they help out downtrodden sheep herders who are being driven off their land by evil cattle baron Woods. (See THREE MESQUITEER series, Index.)

p, Sol C. Siegel; d, Mack V. Wright; w, Joseph Poland (based on characters created by William Colt McDonald); ph, Jack Marta; ed, Lester Orlebeck; m/l, Fleming Allan.

Western **Cas.** **(PR:A MPAA:NR)**

RANGE FEUD, THE** (1931) 64m COL bw

Buck Jones *(Sheriff Buck Gordon)*, John Wayne *(Clint Turner)*, Susan Fleming *(Judy Walton)*, Ed LeSaint *(John Walton)*, William Walling *(Dad Turner)*, Wallace MacDonald *(Hank)*, Harry Woods *(Vandall)*, Frank Austin *(Biggers)*, Glenn Strange, Lew Meehan, Jim Corey, Frank Ellis, Bob Reeves, "Silver" the Horse.

Wayne makes a very early appearance in this typical Jones oater as a ranch owner's son falsely accused in the murder of a cattle rustler. Just as the Duke is about to get his neck stretched by an angry mob, Jones rides in and reveals the killer's true identity.

p, Irving Briskin; d, D. Ross Lederman; w, Milton Krims (based on his story); ph, Ben Kline; ed, Maurice Wright.

Western **(PR:A MPAA:NR)**

RANGE JUSTICE** (1949) 57m MON bw

Johnny Mack Brown *(Johnny)*, Max Terhune *(Alibi)*, Felice Ingersoll *(Beth Hadley)*, Sarah Padden *(Ma Curtis)*, Riley Hill *(Glenn Hadley)*, Tristram Coffin *(Dutton)*, Fred Kohler, Jr. *(Stoner)*, Eddie Parker *(Lacey)*, Kenne Duncan *(Kirk)*, Bill Hale *(Bud)*, Myron Healey *(Dade)*, Bill Potter *(Bill)*, Bob Woodward *(Bob)*, Bill Williams *(Chuck)*.

Brown plays a wandering cowpoke who lands a job on Padden's ranch. Because he's the new guy in town, he's the first to be suspected when things start going awry. But with a bit of scrutiny, he undercovers a plot by Kohler to usurp Padden's property. The hero then goes about putting the rightful villains behind bars, but not before some fancy riding and shooting take place.

p, Barney Sarecky; d, Ray Taylor; w, Ronald Davidson; ph, Harry Neumann; ed, John Fuller; md, Edward Kay.

Western (PR:A MPAA:NR)

RANGE LAND**
(1949) 56m MON bw

Whip Wilson (Whip), Andy Clyde (Winks), Reno Browne (Doris), Leonard M. Penn (Bart), John L. Cason (Rocky), Kenne Duncan (Sheriff), Kermit Maynard (Shad), Carol Henry (Joe), Reed Howes (Red), Stanley Blystone (Mosley), Dee Cooper (Pete), Carl Mathews (Spike), Michael Dugan (Guard), William M. Griffith (Professor), Steve Clark (Ben Allen).

Wilson becomes a lawman, after taking it easy for a spell, when he discovers that a gang headed by Penn has been stealing shipments of gold that belong to the mill owner, Clark. Posing as a villain, he infiltrates the gang and easily takes care of the ne'er-do-wells. Taut script keeps the action well paced, and Clyde is good in the humorous role.

p, Eddie Davis; d, Lambert Hillyer; w, Adele Buffington; ph, Harry Neumann; m, Edward Kay; ed, John C. Fuller.

Western (PR:A MPAA:NR)

RANGE LAW**
(1931) 63m TIF bw

Ken Maynard, Frances Dade, Charles King, Frank Mayo, Lafe McKee, Jack Rockwell, Tom London, Aileen Manning, William Duncan, "Tarzan", Blackjack Ward.

Maynard is jailed for a crime he did not commit, suspects a frame-up, then breaks out of jail to clear his name. Further accusations are thrown at the hero when a stage is robbed and the driver killed. With a hunch about who is behind it all, Maynard kidnaps Dade, the bride-to-be of the villain. He clears his name after gun battles and fistfights, and wins Dade in the end.

p, Phil Goldstone; d, Phil Rosen; w, Earle Snell; ph, Arthur Reed; ed, Earl Turner.

Western (PR:A MPAA:NR)

RANGE LAW*
(1944) 57m MON bw

Johnny Mack Brown (Nevada), Raymond Hatton (Sandy), Sarah Padden (Boots Annie), Ellen Hall (Lucille Gray), Lloyd Ingraham (Judge), Marshall Reed (Jim Bowen), Steve Clark (Pop McGee), Jack Ingram (Phil Randall) (Sheriff), Stanley Price (Dawson), Art Fowler (Swede Larson), Harry F. Price (Zeke), Ben Corbett (Joe), Bud Osborne (Davis), Tex Palmer, George Morrell, Horace B. Carpenter, Lynton Brent, Forrest Taylor.

Less than exciting outing about Brown and Hatton, as U.S. Marshals, rounding up a gang of villains who have been terrorizing local ranchers with the hope of getting dibs on their property and thus access to the silver reportedly on their land.

p, Charles J. Bigelow; d, Lambert Hillyer; w, Frank H. Young; ph, Harry Neumann; ed, John C. Fuller; md, Edward Kay.

Western (PR:A MPAA:NR)

RANGE RENEGADES*½
(1948) 54m MON bw

Jimmy Wakely, Dub "Cannonball" Taylor, Dennis Moore, Jennifer Holt, John James, Riley Hill, Steve Clark, Frank LaRue, Cactus Mack, Milburn Morante, Don Weston, Arthur "Fiddlin'" Smith, Bob Woodward, Roy Garrett, Agapito Martinez, Carl Mathews.

An interesting but predictable B western which has Wakely and his pals pitted against a hard-edged gang of renegade girls. Though a minor oater entry, RANGE RENEGADES reflects a developing twist to the western—nasty female characters, which soon developed into full-blown femme fatales in films like JOHNNY GUITAR (1954) and RANCHO NOTORIOUS (1952).

p, Louis Gray; d, Lambert Hillyer; w, Ronald Davidson, William Lively; ph, Harry Neumann; ed, Johnny Fuller; md, Edward J. Kay.

Western (PR:A MPAA:NR)

RANGE WAR*½
(1939) 64m PAR bw

William Boyd (Hopalong Cassidy), Russell Hayden (Lucky Jenkins), Willard Robertson (Buck Collins), Matt Moore (Jim Marlow), Pedro de Cordoba (Padre Jose), Betty Moran (Ellen Marlow), Britt Wood (Speedy MacGinnis), Kenneth Harlan (Charles Higgins), Don Latorre (Felipe), Glenn Strange (Sheriff), Earle Hodgins (Deputy Sheriff), Stanley Price (Agitator), Jason Robards, Sr. (Rancher), Francis McDonald (Dave Morgan), Eddie Dean, George Chesebro, Raphael [Ray] Bennett.

Without his usual sidekick George Hayes to clown for laughs, an inferior Wood gets these honors, and Boyd goes underground to round up a gang of ranchers who are trying to keep the railroad from completing its course. The local baron (Robertson), fearing to lose out on tolls charged for passing herds, heads the gang. There are some interesting characterizations by veteran actors. (See HOPALONG CASSIDY series, Index.)

p, Harry Sherman; d, Lesley Selander; w, Sam Robins (based on a story by Josef Montaigue, and characters created by Clarence E. Mulford); ph, Russell Harlan; ed, Sherman A. Rose.

Western **Cas.** (PR:A MPAA:NR)

RANGER AND THE LADY, THE**
(1940) 59m REP bw

Roy Rogers (Capt. Colt), George "Gabby" Hayes (Sgt. Whittaker), Jacqueline Wells [Julie Bishop] (Jane), Harry Woods (Kincaid), Henry Brandon (General LaRue), Noble Johnson (El Lobo), Si Jenks (Purdy), Ted Mapes (Kramer), Yakima Canutt (McNair), Chuck Baldra, Herman Hack, Chick Hannon, Art Dillard, Trigger.

Rogers plays the Texas Ranger forced to impose a tax on the wagon train of Wells,

much to Wells' consternation. It seems that Brandon, assistant to Sam Houston, who is in Washington trying to get the Texas Republic admitted to the U.S., plans to secure his own power while the boss is away. Rogers goes along to keep tabs on Brandon's plans. When he's not involved in fisticuffs, Rogers belts out a couple of songs, including "As Long as We Are Dancing" (Peter Tinturin).

p&d, Joseph Kane; w, Stuart Anthony, Gerald Geraghty (based on a story by Bernard McConville); ph, Reggie Lanning; ed, Lester Orlebeck; md, Cy Feuer; m/l, Peter Tinturin.

Western **Cas.** (PR:A MPAA:NR)

RANGER COURAGE*½
(1937) 59m COL bw

Bob Allen (Bob), Martha Tibbetts (Alice), Walter Miller (Bull), Robert "Buzz" Henry (Buzzy), Bud Osborne (Steve), Bob Kortman (Toady), Harry Strang (Snaky), William Gould (Harper), Horace Murphy (Doc), Franklyn Farnum, Jay Wilsey, Gene Alsace.

Allen provides some unbelievable heroics (they are just that—unbelievable), as he accompanies a wagon outfit through tough Indian country. The settlers have a large sum of money stashed away which some villains masquerading as Indians want to get their hands on, but Allen does his best to make sure they don't. No one knows where the money came from or what's to be done with it.

p, Larry Darmour; d, Spencer G. Bennett; w, Nate Gatzert; ph, Arthur Reed; ed, Dwight Caldwell.

Western (PR:A MPAA:NR)

RANGER OF CHEROKEE STRIP**
(1949) 60m REP bw

Monte Hale (Steve Howard), Paul Hurst (Jug Mason), Alice Talton (Mary Bluebird), Roy Barcroft (Mark Sanders), George Meeker (Eric Parsons), Douglas Kennedy (Joe Bearclaws), Frank Fenton (Randolph McKinnon), Monte Blue (Chief Hunter), Neyle Morrow (Tokata), Lane Bradford.

Kennedy plays a Cherokee Indian who is framed for murder and breaks out of jail. Hale plays a Ranger who follows him back to the Cherokee reservation. Hale learns of a plot by ranchers to get at the land granted to the Indians, and also discovers that actor Morrow disguised himself as an Indian and committed the murder. Hale and Kennedy team up to fight off Barcroft and company.

p, Melville Tucker; d, Philip Ford; w, Bob Williams (based on a story by Earle Snell); ph, Ellis W. Carter; m, Stanley Wilson; ed, Irving M. Schoenberg; md, Wilson; art d, Frank Hotaling.

Western (PR:A MPAA:NR)

RANGER'S CODE, THE*
(1933) 59m MON bw

Bob Steele, Doris Hill, George Hayes, George Nash, Ernie Adams, Ed Brady, Hal Price, Dick Dickinson, Frank Ball.

Sheriff Steele is caught in a bind when he's forced to arrest the brother of the gal he likes. But he releases him only to go about proving the kid's innocence, thus freeing himself to court his girl with a clean conscience.

p, Trem Carr; d, Robert N. Bradbury; w, Harry O. Jones [Harry Fraser] (based on the story by John T. Neville); ph, Archie Stout.

Western (PR:A MPAA:NR)

RANGERS OF CHEROKEE STRIP
(SEE: RANGER OF CHEROKEE STRIP, 1949)

RANGERS OF FORTUNE**½
(1940) 80 PAR bw

Fred MacMurray (Gil Farra), Albert Dekker (George Bird), Gilbert Roland (Sierra), Patricia Morison (Sharon McCloud), Joseph Schildkraut (Lewis Rebstock), Dick Foran (Johnny Cash), Betty Brewer (Mary Elizabeth "Squib" Clayborn), Arthur Allen (Mr. Prout), Bernard Nedell (Tod Shelby), Brandon Tynan (Homer Granville Clayborn), Minor Watson (Clem Bowdry), Rosa Turich (Caressa), Frank Puglia (Stefan), Frank Milan (Sam Todd), Matt McHugh (Horatio Wells), Erville Alderson (Mr. Ellis), Fern Emmett (Mrs. Ellis), Joseph Eggenton (Tom Bagby), Edward LeSaint (Minister), Rod Cameron (Shelby Henchman), Harry Fleishmann (Whitey), Fred Malatesta (Genoa), Martin Garralaga (Mexican Officer), Jesus Topete (Mexican Corporal), Paul "Tiny" Newlan, Charles Middleton, Charles Irwin, Harry Burslem, Frank Hagney, Dewey Robinson, Earl Seaman, Jack Richardson.

A curious trio has MacMurray, a renegade Army officer, Dekker, a former boxer, and Roland as an easy-going Mexican, banding together after narrowly escaping a firing squad to help out a town beset by a group of villains. Between the fights and chases, director Wood adds some charming touches, especially in the appearance of 12-year-old Brewer.

p, Dale Van Every; d, Sam Wood; w, Frank Butler; ph, Theodor Sparkuhl; m, Frederick Hollander; ed, Eda Warren; art d, Hans Dreier, Robert Usher.

Western (PR:AA MPAA:NR)

RANGERS RIDE, THE*½
(1948) 56m MON bw

Jimmy Wakely, Dub "Cannonball" Taylor, Virginia Belmont, Cactus Mack, Bud Taylor, Bud Osborne, Riley Hill, Marshall Reed, Steve Clark, Pierce Lyden, Boyd Stockman, Bob Woodward, Milburn Morante, Carol Henry, Don Weston, Arthur "Fiddlin'" Smith, James Diehl, Jack Sparks, Louis W. Armstrong.

This familiar oater plot has a former Texas Ranger being wrongly accused of murder. The only hope is that his Ranger buddies can help him clear his name and round up the real culprit.

p, Louis Gray; d, Derwin Abrahams; w, Basil Dickey; ph, Harry Neumann; ed, John Fuller; md, Edward Kay.

Western **Cas.** (PR:A MPAA:NR)

RANGER'S ROUNDUP, THE*½   (1938) 55m Stan Laurel/Spectrum bw

Fred Scott, Al St. John, Christine McIntyre, Earle Hodgins, Steve Ryan, Karl Hackett, Robert Owen, Syd Chatan, Carl Mathews, Richard Cramer, Jimmy Aubrey, Lew Porter, Taylor MacPeters [Cactus Mack], Steve Clark, Sherry Tansey.

This was the first picture to be produced by Stan Laurel outside of those he appeared in with Oliver Hardy. Other than that there is nothing to make this any different from other Scott outings. He plays a Texas Ranger who goes undercover to haul in a gang that's operating with a traveling medicine show as a cover. Scott manages to belt out five tunes as he goes about his business.

p, Jed Buell; d, Sam Newfield; w, George Plympton; ph, William Hyer; ed, Robert Johns; md, Lew Porter; m/l, "Spanish Shawl," Porter.

Western   **(PR:A   MPAA:NR)**

RANGERS STEP IN, THE*   (1937) 58m COL bw

Bob Allen (Bob), Eleanor Stewart (Terry Warren), John Merton (Martin), Hal Taliaferro [Wally Wales] (Brock), Jack Ingram (Fred), Jack Rockwell (Marshal), Jay Wilsey [Buffalo Bill, Jr.] (Ranger Captain), Lafe McKee (Jed), Bob Kortman, Billy Townsend, Ray Jones, Lew Meehan, Tommy Thompson, Joseph Girard, George Plues, Harry Harvey, Jr., Tex Palmer, Francis Walker, Ed Jauregi, Herman Hack, Dick Cramer.

Some unbelievable heroics on the part of Allen make this oater almost laughable, or at least hard to swallow. He's a Texas Ranger who resigns his commission in order to get to the bottom of a feud that has been rekindled between his family and that of the girl he loves. Turns out that a group of rustlers has started all the fuss in hopes of getting their hands on some cheap land before the railroad comes through.

p, Larry Darmour; d, Spencer G. Bennett; w, Nate Gatzert (based on a story by Jesse Duffy, Joseph Levering); ph, James S. Brown, Jr.; ed, Dwight Caldwell.

Western   **(PR:A   MPAA:NR)**

RANGERS TAKE OVER, THE*½   (1942) 60m PRC bw

Dave "Tex" O'Brien (Tex Wyatt), Jim Newill (Jim Steele), Guy Wilkerson (Panhandle Perkins), Iris Meredith (Jean Lorin), Forrest Taylor (Capt. Wyatt), I. Stanford Jolley (Rance Blair), Charles King (Kip Lane), Carl Mathews (Weir Slocum), Harry Harvey (Bill Summers), Lynton Brent (Block Nelson), Bud Osborne (Pete Dawson), Cal Shrum and His Rhythm Rangers.

O'Brien tries to hook up with the Texas Ranger outfit of his dad, Taylor, but when he proves unworthy he takes up with the rustlers. He turns out to be a good kid after all, though, as he tips the Rangers on the rustler's activities, leading to an easy roundup of the outlaws.

p, Alfred Stern, Arthur Alexander; d, Albert Herman; w, Elmer Clifton; ph, Robert Cline; ed, Charles Henkel, Jr.; md, Lee Zahler.

Western   **Cas.**   **(PR:A   MPAA:NR)**

RANGLE RIVER**   (1939, Aus.) 72m COL-N/J.H. Hoffberg bw

Victor Jory (Dick Drake), Margaret Dare (Marion Hastings), Robert Coote (Reginald Mannister), George Bryant (Dan Hastings), Rita Pauncefort (Aunt Abbie), Leo Cracknell (Barbwire), Cecil Perry (Lawton), Georgie Sterling (Mina), Stewart McColl (Black), Phil Smith (Green).

Western plot with an Australian setting has Dare as the daughter of rancher Bryant who is having a hard time keeping his ranch up while his daughter is out having a good time traveling. When Jory takes on a job as foreman at the ranch, he gets in touch with the girl and tells her to come home. She does, but takes Coote along for the ride. And when she does arrive, Dare and Jory can't see eye-to-eye, making for more trouble at the already troubled ranch. To make matters worse, a neighboring rancher decides to build a dam in order to force his rival out. Jory manages to sort things out, though, winning the girl in the end. Jory has all the poise of the usual western hero, but Dare remains unimpressive.

p&d, Clarence G. Badger; w, Zane Grey; ph, Errol Hinds; ed, Frank Coffey, Mona Donaldson.

Western   **(PR:A   MPAA:NR)**

RANGO*   (1931) 66m PAR bw

Claude King (The Man), Douglas Scott (The Boy), Ali (Old Hunter), Bin (Hunter's Son), Tua (Old Ape), Rango (Ape's Sone).

Repetitious picture set in the Sumatra jungle, except for the prolog, which is done in a boy's bedroom. Naive gist of the thing seems to be that the tiger is enemy to both man and ape, and so there's a lot of footage showing tigers being killed. There's also some fascinating shots of monkeys scurrying about the trees. As far as an interesting story goes—you can forget it.

p&d, Ernest B. Schoedsack; ph, Alfred Williams; ed, Julian Johnson, Schoedsack.

Adventure   **(PR:A   MPAA:NR)**

RANI RADOVI   (SEE: EARLY WORKS, 1970, Yugo.)

RANSOM***   (1956) 109m MGM bw

Glenn Ford (David G. Stannard), Donna Reed (Edith Stannard), Leslie Nielsen (Charlie Telfer), Juano Hernandez (Jesse Chapman), Robert Keith (Chief Jim Backett), Richard Gaines (Langly), Mabel Albertson (Mrs. Partridge), Alexander Scourby (Dr. Paul Y. Gorman), Bobby Clark (Andy Stannard), Ainslie Pryor (Al Stannard), Lori March (Elizabeth Stannard), Robert Burton (Sheriff Jake Kessing), Juanita Moore (Shirley Lorraine), Mary Alan Hokanson (Nurse), Robert Forrest (Fred Benson), Dick Rich (Sgt. Wenzel).

Adapted from a made-for-TV movie, with footage added to make it feature length, thus harming the overall suspense. Regardless, it's still a well-spun, taut drama which keeps viewers twisting and turning in frustration. When Ford and Reed's young son is kidnaped, the entire town becomes deeply involved in the ordeal. Ford easily comes up with the needed $500,000 ransom. But before delivery he changes his mind, going on the tube instead to offer the money for the capture of the kidnapers should the boy turn up dead. This doesn't set too well with Reed, who goes into hysterics. Ford's plan seems to work, though, as the boy comes back alive. Ford gives a strong performance, with Reed portraying her usual stoic self.

p, Nicholas Nayfack; d, Alex Segal; w, Cyril Hume, Richard Maibaum; ph, Arthur E. Arling; m, Jeff Alexander; ed, Ferris Webster; art d, Cedric Gibbons, Arthur Lonergan; cos, Helen Rose.

Drama   **(PR:A   MPAA:NR)**

RANSOM, 1975   (SEE: TERRORISTS, THE, 1975 Brit.)

RANSOM, 1977   (SEE: MANIAC!, 1977)

RAPE, THE**½   (1965, Gr.) 86m Finos/Zenith bw (AKA: AMOK)

Lefteris Vournas (Peter), Zoras Tsapelis (Johann), Zetta Apostolou (Fanny), Floretta Zana (Sarah), Anna Veneti (Anna).

Ten women escape from a reformatory and seek refuge on a deserted isle, only to be victimized by seven men led by ex-Nazi Tsapelis and his son Vournas as they search for treasure. The women are beaten, forced to dig for treasure, and then raped. One of them manages to escape through the aid of Vournas, returning to the island with the police—but not before another woman has been beaten to death. As her grave is being dug, the women find the treasure the men have been looking for. However, they make sure not to reveal their find.

d, Dinos Dimopoulos; w, Dimopoulos, Lazaros Montanaris; ph, Nikos Kavoudikis; m&md, Stavros Xarhakos.

Drama   **(PR:O   MPAA:NR)**

RAPE, THE, 1968   (SEE: LE VIOL, 1968 Fr./Swed.)

RAPE OF MALAYA   (SEE: TOWN LIKE ALICE, A, 1956, Brit.)

RAPE OF THE SABINES, THE   (SEE: SHAME OF THE SABINE WOMEN, THE, 1962, Mex.)

RAPE SQUAD   (SEE: ACT OF VENGEANCE, 1974)

RAPTURE**½   (1950, Ital.) 79m Goldridge/FC bw

Glenn Langan (Pietro Leoni), Elsy Albiin (Francesca Hutton), Lorraine Miller (Marisa Hutton), Eduardo Ciannelli (Arnaldo), Douglas Dumbrille (W. C. Hutton), Harriet White (Nurse), Goffredo Alessandrini (Renato).

Tragic story of an artist, who loses his inspiration for creativity in an Italy filled with works of the great masters. However, the vision of a woman diving into a lake in the moonlight gives him new inspiration. He rents a cottage by the lake and eventually meets the girl, whom he learns is an American resting after a mental shock. The two fall in love and plan to marry, but the introduction of the girl's sister reveals an old affair between her and the artist. The girl becomes deranged and commits suicide. Picturesque photography of the Roman sites and the Italian countryside are an added plus.

p, David M. Pelham; d, Goffredo Alessandrini; w, Geza Herczeg, John C. Shepridge, Pelham (based on the novel Invasion on the Lake by Dr.Arpad Herczeg); ph, Rudolf Icsey; m, Giuseppe Rosati; art d, Arrigo Equini.

Drama   **(PR:A   MPAA:NR)**

RAPTURE**½   (1965) 104m Panoramic/FOX bw

Patricia Gozzi (Agnes Larbaud), Melvyn Douglas (Frederick Larbaud), Dean Stockwell (Joseph), Gunnel Lindblom (Karen), Leslie Sands (1st Gendarme), Murray Evans (Young Gendarme), Sylvia Kay (Genevieve Larbaud), Peter Sallis (Armand), Christopher Sandford (Young Man), Ellen Pollock (Landlady).

Poignant story finds the young Gozzi forced into a life of lonely seclusion because her embittered father, ex-judge Douglas, can no longer cope with the strain of his existence. Gozzi's only real companions are her maid, Lindblom, and the scarecrow which the young girl dresses as if it were a man. Escaped fugitive Stockwell comes to the farmhouse seeking aid, which Douglas offers out of his hatred for the law. Gozzi soon grows so deeply attached to Stockwell that when she finds him making love to Lindblom, she threatens to kill the maid. But Lindblom leaves, allowing Stockwell and Gozzi to fall in love, which they do, fleeing to Paris. The hectic city, however, proves too much for the girl. As she makes her way back to her father, Stockwell follows, only to be gunned down by the police. The shaky direction of this film depends too heavily on jarring camera angles and movements, and paces the development of the plot much too slowly, severely marring an unusual love story.

p, Christian Ferry; d, John Guillermin; w, Stanley Mann (based on the novel Rapture in Rags by Phyllis Hastings); ph, Marcel Grignon (CinemaScope); m, Georges Delerue; ed, Max Benedict, Francois Diot; art d, Jean Andre; cos, Jacques Fonteray; spec eff, Rene Albouze; makeup, Janine Jarreau, Jeanine Lankshear.

Drama   **(PR:C   MPAA:NR)**

RAQ LO B'SHABBAT   (SEE: IMPOSSIBLE ON SATURDAY, 1966, Fr./Israel)

RARE BREED, THE***   (1966) 97m UNIV c

James Stewart (Sam Burnett), Maureen O'Hara (Martha Price), Brian Keith (Alexander Bowen), Juliet Mills (Hilary Price), Don Galloway (Jamie Bowen), David Brian (Charles Ellsworth), Jack Elam (Deke Simons), Ben Johnson (Jeff Harter), Harry Carey, Jr. (Ed Mabry), Perry Lopez (Juan), Larry Domasin (Alberto), Alan

Caillou (Taylor), Bob Gravage (Cattle Buyer), Wayne Van Horn, Leroy Johnson, John Harris, Buff Brady, Stephanie Epper, Patty Elder (Stunt People), Tex Armstrong (Barker), Charles Lampkin (Porter), Gregg Palmer (Rodenbush), Barbara Werle (Gert), Joe Ferrante (Esteban), Jim O'Hara (Sagamon), Ted Mapes (Liveryman), Larry Blake (Auctioneer).

Title refers to the attempt to crossbreed English Hereford cattle with traditional longhorns. In this version the initial concept comes from O'Hara, the widow of an English breeder who comes to the St. Louis Exposition to look for a rancher willing to take her up on the deal. The man who does is a fiery Scotsman, Keith, who gives Stewart the job of transporting the bull to Texas. Persistent O'Hara, along with her daughter Mills, demands to go along on the trip. Stewart, a cynical cowpoke, has accepted a bribe to swindle the lady, but as he protects her from stampedes, rustlers, and other hazards of the West, he begins to admire O'Hara and her ideals. The bull safely delivered, Keith questions the ability of the Hereford to survive the Texas winter. O'Hara remains a guest in his house, and gradually her attitude begins to resemble Keith's. Only Stewart, who finally feels he has something to believe in, remains a staunch believer. When the spring thaw comes, the bull is found dead, and the experiment has apparently failed, so O'Hara prepares to marry Keith. But Stewart stubbornly refuses to give up his belief that somewhere out on the range there's a half-Hereford calf, and he searches high and low until he finds it. He brings the calf back to the ranch house, and he and O'Hara decide to marry and start their own cattle-breeding operation. The three leads, Stewart, O'Hara, and Keith, all give effective performances, but the most noteworthy is a bit part by Elam as a colorful rustler who attempts to swindle O'Hara. The main fault of the script is that it tugs at our heartstrings in completely predictable ways, especially in the treatment of Stewart's devoted search for the calf.

p, William Alland; d, Andrew V. McLaglen; w, Ric Hardman; ph, William H. Clothier (Panavision, Technicolor); m, Johnny Williams; ed, Russel F. Schoengarth; art d, Alexander Golitzen, Alfred Ybarra; set d, John McCarthy, Oliver Emert; cos, Rosemary Odell; makeup, Bud Westmore.

Western   **Cas.**   **(PR:A MPAA:NR)**

RASCAL*   (1969) 85m Disney/BV c

Steve Forrest (Willard North), Bill Mumy (Sterling North), Pamela Toll (Theo North), Elsa Lanchester (Mrs. Satterfield), Henry Jones (Garth Shadwick), Bettye Ackerman (Miss Whalen), Jonathon Daly (Rev. Thurman), John Fiedler (Cy Jenkins), Richard Erdman (Walter Dabbitt), Herbert Anderson (Mr. Pringle), Robert Emhardt (Constable Stacey), Steve Carlson (Norman Bradshaw), Maudie Prickett (Miss Pince-nez), Walter Pidgeon (Voice of Sterling North).

Delightful story of a boy, Mumy, and the pet raccoon, appropriately named Rascal, that he saved from the jaws of a lynx. The film is set in the summer of 1918 in Northern Wisconsin, where Mumy lives with his widowed father, who is often away from home on sales trips, leaving Mumy and Rascal to entertain each other. They manage to get into a fair amount of mischief, and at one point Mumy even lets the raccoon go free after it gets into a neighbor's corn patch. At the end of the summer, though, the two must part company; Mumy is comforted in knowing the Rascal will have a female raccoon to watch over him. A very simple depiction of a past era, which manages to be warmhearted without wallowing in sentiment. With the comforting narration of Pidgeon to guide the viewer along.

p, James Algar; d, Norman Tokar; w, Harold Swanton (based on the novel Rascal, Memoir of a Better Era by Sterling North); ph, William Snyder; m, Buddy Baker; ed, Norman R. Palmer; art d, John B. Mansbridge; set d, Emile Kuri, Frank R. McKelvy; cos, Rosemary O'Dell; spec eff, Eustace Lycett; makeup, Otis Malcolm.

Drama   **(PR:AAA MPAA:G)**

RASCALS   (1938) 77m FOX bw

Jane Withers (Gypsy), Rochelle Hudson (Margaret Adams), Robert Wilcox (Tony), Borrah Minevitch (Gino), Minevitch Gang (Themselves), Steffi Duna (Stella), Katherine Alexander (Mrs. Adams), Chester Clute (Mr. Adams), Jose Crespo (Baron Von Brun), Paul Stanton (Dr. Carter), Frank Reicher (Dr. Garvey), Edward Cooper (Butler), Kathleen Burke, Myra Marsh (Nurses), Frank Puglia (Florist), Robert Gieckler (Police Lieutenant), Edward Dunn (Dugan), Howard Hickman (Judge).

Lighthearted fare has Hudson losing her memory, wandering into a gypsy camp, and becoming its star fortuneteller. This enables her to raise enough money to have the surgery that will restore her memory. But the surgery only reveals that she had been a society dame about to marry a greedy baron who was only after her money. She goes back to the gypsies, with a little nudge from Withers, and back to the arms of Wilcox, a Yale man who has joined up with the gypsies to get away from women. Both Wilcox and Withers are sourly miscast, but some charm on the parts of Hudson and Minevitch carry the picture through. Songs include: "Blue Is the Evening," "Take a Tip from a Gypsy," "What a Gay Occasion," and "Song of the Gypsy Band" (Sidney Clare, Harry Akst).

p, John Stone; d, H. Bruce Humberstone; w, Robert Ellis, Helen Logan; ph, Edward Cronjager; ed, Jack Murray; md, Samuel Kaylin; ch, Nick Castle.

Drama/Comedy   **(PR:AA MPAA:NR)**

RASHOMON***   (1951, Jap.) 90m Daiei/RKO bw (AKA: IN THE WOODS)

Toshiro Mifune (Tajomaru), Machiko Kyo (Masago), Masayuki Mori (Takehiro), Takashi Shimura (Firewood Dealer) Minoru Chiaki (Priest), Kichijiro Ueda (Commoner), Fumiko Homma (Medium), Daisuke Kato (Policeman).

Japanese films had not been much admired until this one came along to get the Golden Lion at the Venice Film Festival in 1951, followed by the Oscar. They are either very good, as in RASHOMON, or very bad, as in the raft of monsters that seems to menace Tokyo every Wednesday and Sunday (RODAN, GODZILLA, MOTHRA, et al.). The question Kurosawa asks in this movie is: what is the truth?

A sidebar accompanies it: is it the same for everyone? Oddly, when it was released in Japan, it came nowhere close to the success, both critical and financial, that it had in the rest of the world. It's a complex story done simply, with a small, perfect cast. Kurosawa had more than 400 separate cuts in the film, which was very tight at 90 minutes but managed to cover everything without a wasted frame. 8th Century, medieval Japan. People are starving and the entire country is in chaos, although that's intimated rather than depicted. A woodcutter, Shimura, a priest, Chiaki, and a peasant, Ueda, are caught in a rainstorm and wait under the ruined gate of the city of Kyoto for the deluge to cease. While they rest and attempt to keep dry, Shimura tells the others a story. It seems that he discovered a dead body of a wealthy man in the forest. Now we are treated to four flashbacks of how the man died and came to be there, told from four differing points of view, with each believing that it, alone, is the real way things happened. Mifune is a well-known bandit who has been accused of the murder of the man, Mori, and the rape of his wife, Kyo. Mifune readily admits that he is guilty and cites the circumstances: he'd met the couple in the forest, became passionate at Kyo's beauty, tied up Mori, and then had his way with her. Kyo was so mortified at what happened that she told Mifune she could not live with the embarrassment of having two men alive who had seen her defilement. (The story is told with the witnesses speaking directly to the camera as though it was a magistrate hearing the case.) The policeman, Kato, listens dispassionately as he attempts to sort out the various versions of the tale. Mifune and Mori have a duel and Mifune slays the man. But Kyo's story is very different. She claims that Mifune tied up Mori, raped her, and when she freed her husband, he had nothing but disdain for her now that she'd been sullied. She was inflamed by his lack of sympathy and killed him. A third version is told through the use of a medium, Homma, who recounts the incident through the eyes and voice of the dead man, Mori, saying that his wife, Kyo, pleaded with Mifune to kill him. When Mifune found that idea distasteful, he was about to leave and she begged to go with him. The two exited and when Mori was able to free himself, he was so chagrined that he killed himself with his jeweled dagger, committing hara-kiri. The only objective witness to the murder was Shimura, the woodcutter, and his view of the case was again altered. He claimed that Mori was an abject coward and Kyo forced him into the duel with Mifune wherein Mifune defended himself and had to kill Mori or be killed himself. But even Shimura's words are suspect because it seems that he has stolen the dagger from the corpse. Listening to the story, the priest, Chiaki, becomes depressed about man's inhumanity to man. The rain begins to let up and the men hear the squawling of a child. They forage under a bundle of rags and find a baby that has been abandoned. There are many corpses lying about near the ruined gate and Ueda, the peasant, tries to rob the baby's clothes but Shimura, who already has many children, offers to take the baby, and the priest's faith is renewed as the film ends. It was based on two separate tales by Akutagawa who killed himself in the 1920s because he was depressed at the state of the world. The first story translates as "In The Brushwood (or Forest)" and relates the killing. The second is a novel, "Rasho Mon," which means "Rasho Gate." "Rasho" was the ancient name for Kyoto, just as "Edo" is the old name for Tokyo, a fact that crossword puzzle fans already know. The economy of words and the striking visual images, with virtually no editorializing, are what combine to make RASHOMON a cinema classic. Every performance is flawless, something that cannot be said for the U.S. remake, THE OUTRAGE, which changes the location to the Old West and featured Paul Newman as the bandit, Claire Bloom as the wife, and Laurence Harvey as the dead man. Kurosawa should have sued for reparations on that one! The interesting part of this is that we believe that each party believes the story they are telling and the real occurrence in the forest is never fully shown. Thus, we must realize that the actual crime lies somewhere in between. Kurosawa and co-author Hashimoto have chosen to make the audience think, and for this, we must thank them profusely.

p, Jingo Minoura; d, Akira Kurosawa; w, Shinobu Hashimoto, Kurosawa (based on the short story "Yabu no Naka" and the novel Rasho-Mon by Ryunosuke Akutagawa); ph, Kazuo Miyagawa; m, Fumio Hayasaka; art d, So Matsuyama.

Period Drama   **Cas.**   **(PR:A-C MPAA:NR)**

RASPOUTINE   (1954, Fr.) 105m Radius/WB c

Pierre Brasseur (Raspoutine), Isa Miranda (Czarina), Rene Faure (Vera), Micheline Francey (Attendant), Milly Vitale (Girl), Jacques Berthier (Youry).

Brasseur, in a hammy performance, plays the mad monk as he rises from earthy peasant to member of the court of the royal family. Film develops in a literary fashion, showing Brasseur's growing influence over czarina Miranda because of his reputed ability to heal her hemophiliac son. A few orgies are thrown in to illustrate Brasseur's debauched side. Eventually, Brasseur meets his demise at the hands of an army officer. Brasseur is ham-handed in the role, the direction is jumpy, and the color has a disturbing tendency to change from scene to scene.

d, Georges Combret; w, Claude Boissol, Combret; ph, Pierre Petit (Eastmancolor); ed, Germaine Fouquet.

Historical Drama   **(PR:C MPAA:NR)**

RASPUTIN   (SEE: RASPUTIN AND THE EMPRESS, 1932)

RASPUTIN   (1932, Ger.) 82m Gottschalk Tonfilm/Fundus bw

Conrad Veidt, Paul Otto, Hermine Sterler, Kenny Rieve, Alexandra Sorina, Carl Ludwig Diehl, Ida Perry, Charlotte Ander, Elza Temary, Brigitte Horney, Bernhard Goetzke, Franziska Kinz, Marian Chevalier, Heinrich Heilinger, Edith Meinhardt, Willy Trenk-Trebitsch, Magnus Stifter, Theodor Loos, Ernst Reicher, Werner Hollmann, Theo Schall, Friedrich Gnaas, Paul Henckels, Alexander Murski, Fritz Spira.

Veidt's portrayal of the legendary monk has him more a victim of prejudice than an evil influence over the czarist family. Starting in the small village of Poskrowoskoje, where his miracle healings are noted, he is taken to the court to treat the ailing son Aljoscha. Because of his continual drunken disorderliness and womanizing, Veidt is sent back to his village, but he returns to St. Petersburg when the war breaks out to convince the czar to take over the high command. On this sojourn Veidt meets a man whose fiancee he has seduced and a Duke of the War Party; he is drawn into a palace and shot. Ossip Dymow, a personal acquaintance of Rasputin, had a hand in the script, which may account for its depiction of the monk as a much gentler man than the common conception.

d, Adolf Trotz; w, Ossip Dymow, Adolph Lantz, Conrad Linz; ph, Curt Courant; m, Fritz Wennels, Prof. Metzl.

Biography **(PR:A MPAA:NR)**

RASPUTIN**½ (1939, Fr.) 93m Concord bw

Harry Baur *(Rasputin)*, Marcelle Chantal *(The Czarina)*, Pierre Richard Willm *(Count Igor Kourloff)*, Jean Worms *(Czar Nicholas II)*, Carine Nelson *(Ania Kitina)*, Denis d'Ines *(Bishop Gregorian)*, Gabrielle Robinne *(Empress Mother)*, Jacques Baumer *(Prokoff)*, Alexander Rignault *(Capt. Bloch)*, Palau *(Warnava)*, Martial Rebe *(Monk Cyril)*, Lucien Nat *(Ostrowski)*, Georges Prieur *(Grand Duke Nikolaievich)*, Claudio *(The Czarevitch)*, Jany Holt *(Grousina)*.

French attempt at a portrayal of Rasputin stars Baur as the monk, from his days as a faith healer in the Siberian backwoods to his place in the czarist family circle. He is depicted as a man, neither good nor evil, who possesses human frailties, such as a liking for drink and women. Baur greatly influences the entire royal family, and uses it for his own well-being. Baur vividly portrays Rasputin as a many-sided character who is victim to his own whimsical nature. Unfortunately the picture could use a bit more work in the editing room, and the direction is shaky in some sequences. (In French; English subtitles.)

p, Max Glass; d, Marcel L'Herbier; w, (based on the novel *Tragedie Imperiale* by Alfred Neumann); ph, A. Kelber; m, Darius Milhaud.

Biography **(PR:A MPAA:NR)**

RASPUTIN AND THE EMPRESS**** (1932) 135m MGM bw (GB: RASPUTIN—THE MAD MONK)

John Barrymore *(Prince Paul Chegodieff)*, Ethel Barrymore *(Empress Alexandra)*, Lionel Barrymore *(Rasputin)*, Ralph Morgan *(Emperor Nikolai)*, Diana Wynyard *(Natasha)*, Tad Alexander *(Alexis)*, C. Henry Gordon *(Grand Duke Igor)*, Edward Arnold *(Doctor)*, Gustov von Seyffertitz *(Dr. Wolfe)*, Anne Shirley [Dawn O'Day] *(Anastasia)*, Jean Parker *(Maria)*, Sarah Padden *(Landlady)*, Henry Kolker *(Chief of Secret Police)*, Frank Shannon *(Prof. Propotkin)*, Frank Reicher *(German Language Teacher)*, Hooper Atchley *(Policeman)*, Leo White, Lucien Littlefield *(Revelers)*, Mischa Auer *(Butler)*, Dave O'Brien, Maurice Black *(Soldiers)*, Charlotte Henry *(Princess)*.

This superb historical epic gathers the royal family of the American stage, the only film in which the three dynamic Barrymores appeared together. It was a production feast for the eyes as the last royal court of the Czars, the tragic Romanovs of Russia, made its final glittering bow. A greater treat is to see the magnificent Barrymores vie with each other for every frame of this memorable film. John Barrymore, playing the part of a royal prince, arrives at court to warn the weak Czar Nicholas II, Morgan, and his strong-willed Czarina, Ethel, that peasants and revolutionaries are in the streets, demanding food and freedom. He urges quick reforms before a full-scale revolution breaks out. The royal couple's son, Alexander, later suffers a fall and, being a hemophiliac, begins to bleed to death internally. No doctor can stanch the wound but lady-in-waiting Wynyard tells the desperate Ethel that she knows of a mystical holy man who may save her son. The man, Lionel Barrymore, playing Rasputin, the Mad Monk, arrives at court and insists upon being left alone with Alexander in his room. There Lionel, using a single burning candle and riveting the boy's gaze to his own intense stare, hypnotizes him and causes the bleeding to stop. To the Empress Ethel, the monk is a miracle man and she insists that Lionel remain at court, close to her son in case he is needed. Lionel, a perverse, crude peasant who claims to be embodied with great spiritual powers, agrees, only because he sees his opportunity to seize power. He uses Ethel's dependency on him to assume authority and slowly Lionel begins to take control of one governmental department after another, naming his own graft-paying cronies to high office, stealing a fortune from the public treasury, and casting a covetous eye on the older royal daughters. John Barrymore sees the spreading corruption caused by Lionel and moves to stop his insidious takeover of the throne. He obtains "enough poison to kill five men" from court doctor Seyffertitz, and has this administered to many cakes which are served Lionel during a party at which, it is suggested, one of the court princesses is raped. At the party, however, Lionel grows suspicious when spotting Auer, whom he knows is the butler of his arch enemy, John Barrymore. He finds John hiding nearby and attacks him, dragging him to a cellar where he tries to shoot the prince. John gets the better of the monk when the poison begins to take effect. John and Lionel still continue to battle through the cellar rooms until John drags the dying monk outside and to the nearby icy river Neva, throwing him in and drowning him. Publicly, John is disgraced before the court. He is rebuked by Morgan but privately Morgan tells him of his gratitude in ridding the throne of a madman. He and his beloved Wynyard are sent into exile to live out life happily. John begs the royal couple to abdicate and follow him, telling them that their lives will be claimed by the certain revolution to soon erupt. They smile wisely and tell him that they feel secure; their devoted subjects will never raise a hand against them, and decide to remain in Russia, but they are, of course, doomed to die (in 1917, executed by Bolsheviks under the direct command of Vladimir Illich Lenin and Joseph Stalin). Boleslawsky does an admirable job in moving the story along at a brisk pace, one in which MacArthur (of the writing team of Ben Hecht and Charles MacArthur) displays deep sympathies for the royal couple and their afflicted son, showing the revolutionaries as unthinking brutes, a stance which did not endear the film to the new Communist government headed by Stalin; in fact, the film was banned in the USSR, although the picture is factually accurate, based upon the best known sources regarding Rasputin and his diabolical activities. The story stemmed from an inspiration by MGM production chief Irving Thalberg whose special pet project this film became. It was also his idea to star the three Barrymores in the film. He had no trouble with signing John (at $150,000) and assigning Lionel (who was then an MGM contract player getting $1,500 a week). But Ethel was a different matter. She was now a grand dame of Broadway theater. However, she agreed that for $100, 000 she would play the Empress, but only if production could be completed in Hollywood within an eight-week period during the summer months so she could return to a Broadway commitment in the fall. Thalberg agreed and Ethel traveled to the West Coast to join her brothers in their first effort together since they appeared in "Camille" in Baltimore, circa 1916. She had little use for films, her last having been the silent film, THE DIVORCEE (1919). She loathed films, thinking them uncouth and, on one occasion, personally embarrassing. Ethel was once asked to appear on location in New York during the early silent era. When she learned that the location would be in front of a mansion owned by her friend, millionaire Mrs. Whitelaw Reid, she refused to appear on camera until the director selected a different site. She was later quoted as saying that Hollywood was "a set, a glaring, gaudy, nightmarish set, built up in the desert." Later she was quoted as saying that Hollywood "has not been thought in; there is no sediment of thought there. It looks, it feels, as if it had been invented by a Sixth Avenue peep show man. Come to think of it, it probably was." Her capricious brothers heralded her approach to Western Mecca as the signal of fireworks to come, much of their comment geared to publicize a film that had no script. "The three Barrymores are going to be together in one picture," whined Lionel. "Can you imagine what will happen to the poor director?" John was asked by newsmen what his regal sister might do in the film and he responded with an arched eyebrow: "You need not worry about Mrs. Colt [Ethel's married name]. Our sister will be standing right before the camera—in front of us!" But John also had some telling remarks about Lionel's infamous scene-stealing. Thalberg, in a story conference with John, explained how he would kill Rasputin in the last reel. Replied John, "The way Lionel is going to steal this picture, I ought to shoot him in the *first* reel." When Ethel did arrive by train John was at the station to greet her, embracing her and whispering something that the huge crowd thought was an affectionate hello. Later, in her autobiography, *Memories*, Ethel revealed the nature of his comment: "For God's sake, get Bill Daniels." When Ethel later asked who Daniels was, brother John told her that "he's a cameraman, the best in the world. He takes all those sweetbreads away from under my eyes. Garbo won't make a picture without him." When first meeting Thalberg, Ethel immediately demanded that Daniels be her cinematographer and Thalberg, thinking her very knowledgeable, granted her request. Louis B. Mayer also went out of his way to make Ethel welcome and allowed her to select director Charles Brabin for the film, the actress saying that he was an old friend. Still, there was no story to direct and Thalberg suggested that Charles MacArthur, who had written THE FRONT PAGE with Ben Hecht, be called in to work on the script. But, on second thought, Thalberg told Ethel, MacArthur "won't do it," having just moved into a bungalow at the Garden of Allah with wife Helen Hayes, stating to one and all he was there to rest and not work. Ethel told Thalberg: "I'll make him do it!" She soon visited MacArthur and Hayes and demanded he write the script. She grabbed him by the shoulders and shouted: "You are going to write RASPUTIN!" He broke away and refused, slipping behind diminutive Hayes. Shouted Ethel: "You lazy, incompetent, loafing, good-for-nothing ass!" Still MacArthur rejected the assignment but then Ethel started to throw books around and grabbed a lamp, threatening to send it "through a wall!" MacArthur relented and began furiously to pound out the script. He would write six scripts while the rushed production was underway, sometimes not finishing his scenes until a few minutes before they were to be enacted by the Barrymores who stood impatiently on the set. Often as not, he provided them with lines of dialog, according to Ethel, that were written "on the backs of old envelopes...I would learn a scene and then find that I would have to learn an entirely new one after I was on the set." The set was ready to explode at any moment and Ethel was the first to set off the fireworks. The script being rattled off by MacArthur was being researched by a Russian emigre, Mercedes de Acosta, who knew all the White Russians living in exile. She objected to Thalberg when the producer insisted that she insert in her notes for MacArthur that the princess played by Wynyard was to be raped, or seem to be raped. Since this role was based upon Princess Irina Youssoupoff, the wife of the man who murdered Rasputin and was then living in Paris, de Acosta told the production genius that such a scene was not only fiction but that the Youssoupoffs would probably sue the studio for libel. "I don't need you to tell me a lot of nonsense about what is libelous," Thalberg snapped. "I want this sequence in and that is all there is to it!" The scene went in but, as a precaution, Thalberg changed Youssoupoff's name to Chegodieff. Ethel, however, told director Brabin that not only must the suggested rape scene come out, but hundreds of lines which dealt with her own role had to be eliminated, causing MacArthur to sleeplessly work on the set writing new lines. Whenever Brabin suggested a movement or gesture to Ethel she invariably rejected the mild direction, adding imperiously: "I knew her majesty personally." The production slowed down and Ethel fumed, telling Brabin that he had better hurry since her ironclad contract called for only eight weeks of her time. Feeling that the director was dragging his feet, Ethel finally marched off the set and called Mayer (who rued the day he invited her to call on him any time). She stated to the MGM boss, despite the fact that she had earlier insisted that the director was her old, close friend, "See here, Mayer, let's get rid of this Brahbin or Braybin or what's-his-name." With that, Brabin quit on the spot and left the picture for good. Another friend of Ethel's who had been hanging around MGM and looking for his first job at a studio, a newly arrived immigrant, Boleslawsky, on the strength of Ethel's insistence was named the new director of the film. John and Lionel didn't care who directed since they were mostly directing themselves, frantically vying for every scene in which they appeared together. In one scene Lionel belches at the royal table after dinner and John pops his eyes in mock surprise. In another scene, one of Lionel's most important, he, as the mad monk, says "In less than a year, *I* will be Russia!" John actually turns his back on his brother in this scene, draws forth a sabre, and begins to wildly slice the air with it as he struts about in a great scene-stealing effort. Lionel could bear it no longer and ran off camera to a phone where he called Thalberg and told him that someone should tell his brother John to stop hamming it up "lest, at the close of this scene, I be tempted to lay one on him!" John went absolutely wild with the scene where he assassinated brother Lionel. He had been tippling before the scene, it was reported, and was to drag his struggling brother onto a set where Cedric Gibbons and his men had actually constructed a wide river flowing through snowdrifts. Cackling and laughing like a hysterical madman, John dragged Lionel toward the river, about to throw him in. But he became so carried away with the struggle and was already lightheaded from one too many, that John himself toppled into the river and vanished. At the moment, before Boleslawsky could yell "cut!" dozens of stagehands dashed before the still rolling cameras and dove into the river to save the gasping actor. True to her stubborn word, Ethel marched off the set at the end of her time as stipulated by her contract, leaving Boleslawsky to shoot around her. He wrapped up the film in 104 days at an enormous cost (at that time) of $1 million. The film stands as a fine historical piece which is even more enhanced by the histrionic Barrymores. Also, as prophesied by de Acosta, Prince Felix Youssoupoff filed suit in an English court against MGM for the rape scene, as did his wife, and MGM had to settle with them for about $125,000. John Barrymore didn't help matters by telling the press that, indeed, he was playing the real Prince Youssoupoff, even though the name had been changed to Chegodieff. (Reportedly, another Russian prince named Chegodieff also sued MGM because he had nothing to do with killing Rasputin and the studio also paid off this claim.) The film saw on-and-off success before MGM took it out of distribution so as not to further alienate Youssoupoff, but it remains a minor classic to this day. After completing the film, John Barrymore told newsmen: "They seem to think the three Barrymores are just three damn fools! They say we are jealous of one another, that we won't do what the director tells us, that we want to change the story, each for his selfish glorification...Ethel has been marvelous. Lionel, who loves his sarcasm, has never been in better humor. I have, ladies and gentlemen, conducted myself magnificently." Ethel's parting remarks were more pointed about her two scenery-chewing brothers: "They are nothing more than overpublicized and overpaid factory hands!"

p, Bernard Hyman; d, Richard Boleslawsky, (uncredited) Charles Brabin; w, Charles MacArthur; ph, William Daniels; m, Herbert Stothart; ed, Tom Held; art d, Cedric Gibbons, Alexander Toluboff; cos, Adrian.

Historical Drama   (PR:C MPAA:NR)

RASPUTIN THE MAD MONK, 1932   (SEE: RASPUTIN AND THE EMPRESS, 1932)

RASPUTIN—THE MAD MONK½**   (1966, Brit.) 92m Seven Arts-Hammer/FOX bw

Christopher Lee (Rasputin), Barbara Shelley (Sonia), Richard Pasco (Dr. Zargo), Francis Matthews (Ivan), Suzan Farmer (Vanessa), Nicholas Pennell (Peter), Renee Asherson (Csarina), Derek Francis (Innkeeper), Alan Tilvern (Patron), Joss Ackland (The Bishop), John Welsh (The Abbott), Robert Duncan (Csarvitch), John Bailey (Court Physician).

Hammer studios took a shot at the legendary monk of the last czarist regime, using all their know-how for shock effect, using Lee (COUNT DRACULA in numerous films) in the title role, and coming up with a portrayal of the monk as one of the most diabolical figures of all time. A man of almost supernatural powers, he uses hypnotism to win over two court aides, Shelley and Pasco, thus gaining entry to the court of the czar. When Pasco, after Shelley has committed suicide, sees the evil designs of Lee, he uses every method to try to kill the man, from poisoned food to lethal injections, but Lee won't die. Next to Lee's none of the other performances stands a chance. A mood of tension and dreariness is maintained throughout, as in a vampire picture.

p, Anthony Nelson Keys; d, Don Sharp; w, John Elder [Anthony Hinds]; ph, Michael Reed (CinemaScope, DeLuxe Color); m, Don Banks; ed, Roy Hyde; prod d, Bernard Robinson; art d, Don Mingaye; makeup, Roy Ashton.

Horror/Biography   Cas.   (PR:C MPAA:NR)

RAT, THE*½   (1938, Brit.) 70m Imperator/RKO bw

Ruth Chatterton (Zelia de Chaumont), Anton Walbrook ("The Rat" Jean Boucheron), Rene Ray (Odile Verdier), Beatrix Lehman (Marguerite), Mary Clare (Mere Colline), Felix Aylmer (Attorney General), Hugh Miller (Luis Stets), Gordon McLeod (Caillard), Frederick Culley (Judge), Nadine March (Rose), George Merritt (Pierre Verdier), Leo Genn (Defense), Fanny Wright (Therese), J.H. Roberts (Butler), Geraldine Hislop, Aubrey Mallalieu, Bob Gregory, Paul Sheridan, Walter Schofield, Stanley Lathbury, Beatrice "Betty" Marsden, Ivan Wilmot.

Heavy-handed story has Walbrook as a jewel thief who goes by the name "the rat." He is given charge of the daughter of one of his mates when the latter faces life imprisonment. The girl, Ray, makes a cozy home for Walbrook, but trouble erupts when Chatterton takes a liking to the thief, and tosses out the man who has been taking care of her. Piqued and out for revenge, he heads for Walbrook's place where he encounters Ray, and attempts to abduct her. But the girl fights back, murdering the man. Honorable man that he is, Walbrook takes the blame. But Chatterton appears in court and testifies that Walbrook was with her the night of the murder. The girl gets the rap, but due to circumstances, the sentence is light. Story moves along at a plodding pace, with little by way of direction or performance adding the needed spark.

p, Herbert Wilcox; d, Jack Raymond; w, Hans Rameau, Miles Malleson, Romney Brent, Marjorey Gaffney (based on the play by Ivor Novello, Constance Collier); ph, Frederick A. Young; ed, Peggy Hennessey.

Crime/Drama   (PR:A MPAA:NR)

RAT*   (1960, Yugo.) 84m Jadran Film bw (AKA: WAR)

Anton Vrdoljak, Eva Krzyzewski, Ita Rina, Tana Mascarelli, Janez Vrhovic, Lyubisa Jovanovic, Velimir "Bata" Zivojinovic.

Zavattini, famous for his part in the Italian Neo-Realist movement, scripted this sci-fi picture that takes place after an atom bomb explosion leaves only a handful of survivors. Story centers on a couple who were in the process of marrying when the bomb exploded, leaving their marriage unconsummated. Cinematography and settings have a very realistic tone, giving an almost documentary flavor.

d, Velko Bulajic; w, Cesare Zavattini; ph, Kresko Grcevic.

Fantasy   (PR:A MPAA:NR)

RAT FINK*   (1965) 80m Genesis/Cinema bw (AKA: MY SOUL RUNS NAKED; WILD AND WILLING; THE SWINGING FINK)

Schuyler Hayden (Singer), Hal Bokar (Singer's Manager), Warrene Ott (Wife), Judy Hughes (Teenager), Don Snyder, Eve Brenner, Alice Reinheart, Jack Lester, Sirkka Ottonen, Anna Stephen, Peter Wilkins, The Futuras, David Reed, Ernie Crites, Chuck Harrod, Richard Jeffries, Sharon Sutton, Jill Quinn.

Realistic and hard hitting portrayal of a rock singer who does anything to get to the top. Hayden plays the heartless singer, who sleeps with an older woman, only to raid her purse and split to Hollywood, where he buys the services of a top agent. He immediately becomes involved with the agent's wife as well as with a teenager whom he later takes to a veterinarian to have an abortion, then dumps during his rise to the top. Hayden plays the part in a cold and heartless manner, with a gleaming smile that makes the viewer cringe in his seat. Movement is quick, with no sympathy or sentiment generated, just a cold and brutal look at a very common phenomenon in contemporary culture.

p, Lewis Andrews; d&w, James Landis (Based on a story by Matthew Cheney, Jack Miller); ph, William [Vilmos] Zsigmond; m, Ronald Stein; ed, Tom Boutross; art d, Daniel Toledo; songs, "My Soul Runs Naked," "One on Every Corner," sung by Don Snyder.

Drama   (PR:C MPAA:NR)

RAT PFINK AND BOO BOO   (1966) 72m Morgan/Craddock bw

Carolyn Brandt (Cee Bee Beaumont), Vin Saxon (Lonnie Lord/Rat Pfink), Titus Moede (Titus Twimbly/Boo Boo),George Caldwell (Linc), Mike Kannon (Hammer), James Bowie (Benjie), Keith Wester (Cowboy), Mary Jo Curtis (Irma La Streetwalker), Romeo Barrymore (Ape Trainer), Dean Danger (Narrator), Kogar the Swinging Ape.

Spoof on BATMAN and the like has Saxon and Moede as a rock 'n' roll singer and gardener friend respectively, becoming superheroes, capes and all, when Saxon's girl friend Brandt is abducted. Despite the banal subject, picture offers some insightful manipulation of the cinematic medium.

p&d, Ray Dennis Steckler; w, Ronald Haydock (based on a story by Steckler); ph, Steckler; m, Henry Price; ed, Keith Wester.

Comedy   (PR:A MPAA:NR)

RAT RACE, THE½   (1960) 105m PAR c

Tony Curtis (Peter Hammond, Jr.), Debbie Reynolds (Peggy Brown), Jack Oakie (Mac), Kay Medford (Soda), Don Rickles (Nellie), Joe Bushkin (Frankie), Sam Butera (Carl), Gerry Mulligan (Gerry), Marjorie Bennett (Edie Kerry), Hal K. Dawson (Man), Norman Fell (Phone Repairman), Lisa Drake (Toni).

Enjoyable farce has sax player Curtis arriving in New York ready to set it aflame with his talent, but finding it hard to do. After his first step off the bus he is hosed down by a gang of street urchins, setting the tone for the rest of his expedition. But all is not lost as he meets and falls in love with Reynolds, a girl in a position similar to his own. The struggles they go through strengthen the bond between them. Well-paced script, a perceptive directorial eye, and strong performances from some of the lesser players give this picture a warm and charming tone. Curtis' character is inconsistent, as he sways between hipness and total naivete.

p, William Perlberg, George Seaton; d, Robert Mulligan; w, Garson Kanin (based on his play); ph, Robert Burks (Technicolor); m, Elmer Bernstein; ed, Alma Macrorie; art d, Hal Pereira, Tambi Larsen; set d, Sam Comer, Frank McKelvy; cos, Edith Head; spec eff, John P. Fulton; makeup, Wally Westmore.

Comedy   (PR:A MPAA:NR)

RAT SAVIOUR, THE*   (1977, Yugo.) 87m Croatia Film/Jadran c (IZBAVIT-ELJ; AKA: THE REDEEMER)

Ivica Vidovic, Mirjana Majurec, Relja Basic, Fabijan Sovagovic, Ilija Ivezic.

A science-fiction thriller and political allegory in the vein of INVASION OF THE BODY SNATCHERS (1956) has Vidovic discovering a breed of rats which kill and then impersonate their victims. Scientist Sovagovic invents a spray that takes care of the rats, but Vidovic manages to kill his girl friend, thinking that she is one of them. Picture won the Golden Asteroid award at the 1977 Trieste Festival of Science Fiction Films.

d, Krsto Papic; w, Papic, Ivo Brexan (based on a story by Alexander Greene); ph, Iveco Rajkovic.

Fantasy   (PR:A MPAA:NR)

RATATAPLAN½   (1979, Ital.) 100m Vides Cinematografica c

Maurizio Nichetti, Angelo Finocchiaro, Edy Angelillo, Lidia Biondi, Roland Topor, Giorgio White, Umberto Gallone, Enrico Grazioli.

Hilarious comedy has Italian mime artist Nichetti playing a man whose overactive imagination keeps him from any success in the way of a job or romance. He attempts to solve this by building a robot in his image, dressed like the hipsters of the disco generation. The robot succeeds where Nichetti can't, but winds up blowing a fuse when Finocchiaro attempts to seduce it. This leads to the discovery that Nichetti and Finocchiaro are quite similar in the worlds they have created.

p, Franco Cristaldi, Nicola Carraro; d&w, Maurizio Nichetti; ph, Mario Battistoni.

Comedy **(PR:A MPAA:G)**

RATIONING** (1944) 93m MGM bw

Wallace Beery *(Ben Barton)*, Marjorie Main *(Iris Tuttle)*, Donald Meek *(Wilfred Ball)*, Dorothy Morris *(Dorothy Tuttle)*, Howard Freeman *(Cash Riddle)*, Connie Gilchrist *(Mrs. Porter)*, Tommy Batten *(Lance Barton)*, Gloria Dickson *(Miss McCue)*, Henry O'Neill *(Sen. Edward A. White)*, Richard Hall *(Teddy)*, Charles Halton *(Ezra Weeks)*, Morris Ankrum *(Mr. Morgan)*, Carol Ann Beery *(Herself)*, Douglas Fowley *(Dixie Samson)*, Chester Clute *(Roberts)*, Chill Wills *(Bus Driver)*, Arthur Space *(Leafy)*, Milton Parsons *(Hank)*, Suzanne Kaaren, Kathleen Williams, Natalie Draper, Hazel Brooks, Kay Medford *(Information Girls)*, Robert Emmett O'Connor *(Sheriff McGuiness)*, Ed Kilroy *(Minister)*, Erville Alderson *(Gil)*, Eddy Waller *(Smith)*, Al Hill *(Greenie)*, Milton Kibbee *(Wright)*, Anne O'Neal *(Woman)*.

This comic look at wartime rationing has meatpacker Beery at odds with the local prima donna of ration stamps, Main. Meanwhile, Beery's adopted son Batten is romancing Main's daughter, before he is sent off to war. Unfortunately too much of the humor is dependent upon overused slapstick routines, with all other aspects of production undertaken in routine manner. Beery's real-life daughter Carol Ann appears here in a small role as one of the customers in Beery's store.

p, Orville O. Dull; d, Willis Goldbeck; w, William R. Lipman, Grant Garrett, Harry Ruskin; ph, Sidney Wagner; m, David Snell; ed, Ferris Webster; art d, Cedric Gibbons, Howard Campbell; set d, Edwin B. Willis, Glen Barner.

Comedy **(PR:A MPAA:NR)**

RATON PASS½** (1951) 84m WB bw (GB: CANYON PASS)

Dennis Morgan *(Marc Challon)*, Patricia Neal *(Ann)*, Steve Cochran *(Cy Van Cleave)*, Scott Forbes *(Prentice)*, Dorothy Hart *(Lena Casamajor)*, Basil Ruysdael *(Pierre)*, Louis Jean Heydt *(Jim Ponzer)*, Roland Winters *(Sheriff Perigord)*, James Burke *(Hank)*, Elvira Curci *(Tia)*, Carlos Conde *(Germaine)*, John Crawford *(Sam)*, *Rudolpho Hoyos, Jr. (Ben)*.

Odd twist for a western has Neal battling with her husband, Morgan, over ownership of their large ranch. Instigation for the feud comes when Morgan applies for a loan to build a new watering system, but Neal gets other ideas. She plans to take hold of the entire ranch by leaving Morgan, swinging investor Forbes onto her side, and marrying him. She hires a gunman to keep her husband off the ranch, but Morgan rallies the support of the surrounding homesteaders. This leads to a climactic gun battle between the henchman of Neal and the homesteaders, with the latter coming out victorious and Morgan winning back his ranch. Neal is never quite at home in her rather dubious role. The Tom Blackburn-James Webb screenplay is based on a work by Blackburn, though sources differ on which work: some cite his novel *Raton Pass*, others his story "Whiteface."

p, Saul Elkins; d, Edwin L. Marin; w, Tom W. Blackburn, James R. Webb (based on the novel by Blackburn); ph, Wilfred M. Cline; m, Max Steiner; ed, Thomas Reilly; art d, Edward Carrere.

Western **(PR:A MPAA:NR)**

RATS, THE*** (1955, Ger.) 91m CCC/Herzog bw (DIE RATTEN)

Maria Schell *(Pauline Karka)*, Curt Jurgens *(Bruno Mechelke)*, Heidemarie Hatheyer *(Anna John)*, Gustav Knuth *(Karl John)*, Ilse Steppat *(Frau Knobbe)*, Fritz Remond *(Harro Hassenreuter)*, Barbara Rost *(Selma Knobbe)*.

A very depressing look at postwar Germany has Schell as a pregnant girl from East Germany who has been abandoned by her lover. When the baby is born, she gives it to another woman who has wanted a child for a long time, but has been unable to conceive. This sets the stage for a conflict between the two women over their affection for the baby. Brilliantly acted, mounted, and scripted, giving a very bleak and realistic view of the plight of the German people.

d, Robert Siodmak; w, Jochen Huth (based on the play by Gerhart Hauptmann); ph, Goeran Strindberg; m, Werner Eisbrenner; set d, Rolf Zehetbauer.

Drama **(PR:A MPAA:NR)**

RATS, THE, 1982 (SEE: DEADLY EYES, 1982)

RATS ARE COMING! THE WEREWOLVES ARE HERE!, THE zero (1972) 92m William Mishkin c

Hope Stansbury *(Monica Mooney)*, Jacqueline Skarvellis*(Diana)*, Noel Collins *(Mortimer Mooney*,Joan Ogden *(Phoebe Mooney)*, Douglas Phair *(Pa Mooney)*, Berwick Kaler *(Malcolm Mooney)*,Ian Innes *(Gerald)*.

Stupid horror movie features Skarvellis as the daughter of a strange family who brings her new husband to the family estate. Gradually (and after many boring scenes), it is revealed that the entire family (except Skarvellis) are victims of a family curse that turns them into werewolves when the moon is full. To deal with this unfortunate condition, they take tranquilizers and lock themselves in their rooms. Skarvellis decides it is time to finish the curse, so she has husband Innes' silver crucifix melted down into silver bullets and when the family changes that night, she kills them. When everyone but Skarvellis and Innes is dead, Innes says that they will leave the estate, but Skarvellis refuses, saying that it is her home and she will never leave. Innes orders her and she tells him that she is different from the rest of her family because she can turn into a wolf any time she wants, spinning on Innes and adding him to the body count. The last scene shows her the sole owner of the estate, while the nurse hired to care for her wonders aloud if the murderer will ever be caught. An awful movie, shot in England and on Staten Island, it was originally to be titled CURSE OF THE FULL MOON, but when director Milligan found his finished film ran only 67 minutes, he had to add some scenes to pad it out to a length that he could get distributed. Producer Mishkin, seeing the success of WILLARD, suggested some man-eating rats might be just the thing the film needed. Additional scenes were shot in which Stansbury visits a strange merchant who sells her a cage full of rats, telling her about the time he fell asleep and they chewed off one of his arms before he woke up. She takes them home, planning to loose them on her family, and that night she plays with them, saying at one point: "I'll call you Willard, you look like a Willard." When one of the rodents bites her, though, she gets angry, returning to the shop and releasing them on the proprietor. The most interesting thing about the movie is trying to pick out the fake British accents from the real ones.

p, William Mishkin; d,w&ph, Andy Milligan; set d, Elaine; cos, Rafine; makeup, Lois Marsh.

Horror **Cas.** **(PR:O MPAA:PG)**

RATS OF TOBRUK*½ (1951, Aus.) 85m REN bw

Chips Rafferty *(Milo Trent)*, Grant Taylor *(Bluey Donkin)*, Peter Finch *(Peter Linton)*, Pauline Garrick *(Kate Carmody)*, Mary Gay, George Wallace, George Gentry.

Weakly scripted and poorly directed project has an English author going to the backwoods of Australia where he meets up with a trader and a sheepherder, and takes to traveling about the country, reciting poetry along the way. War breaks out and the three men find themselves fighting together at Tobruk, where all but the sheepherder are killed. A very lame picture.

p, Charles Munro, Charles Chauvel; d, Chauvel; w, Mrs. Chauvel, George Heath; ph, Heath.

War/Drama **(PR:A MPAA:NR)**

RATTLE OF A SIMPLE MAN½** (1964, Brit.) 96m Sydney Box-ABF/CD bw

Harry H. Corbett *(Percy Winthram)*, Diane Cilento *(Cyrenne)*, Thora Hird *(Mrs. Winthram)*, Michael Medwin *(Ginger)*, Charles Dyer *(Chalky)*, Hugh Futcher *(Ozzie)*, Brian Wilde *(Fred)*, Alexander Davion *(Ricardo)*, David Saire *(Mario)*, Barbara Archer *(Iris)*, Michael Robbins *(George)*, George Roderick *(Papa)*, Marie Burke *(Mama)*, Carole Gray *(District Nurse)*, John Ronane *(Willie)*, Ingrid Anthofer *(1st Stripper)*, Karen Kaufman *(2nd Stripper)*.

A lovely, gentle play has been somewhat vulgarized for the screen by its author, who also plays a small role in the film. Corbett, Dyer, Medwin, Wilde, and Futcher are a cadre of Northern England laborers who've come to London to see the big football (soccer) game that their team is playing. They are louts, drunks, noisemakers, and, in general, represent everything bad about the British sports fan (something that was seen in real life when many innocent people were killed at a match between a British team and an Italian team). Corbett, at the age of 39, is, unaccountably, a virgin. He lives for sports and is a fanatic fan. Prior to returning to Manchester, the men get together in a tacky Soho bar to toss a few down. Medwin tries to make time with Cilento, a hostess who doubles as a semi-pro hooker. Corbett thinks that she's attractive and makes a bet with his pals that he can sleep with her. The wager is 50 pounds against his precious motorcycle. Corbett, who is dominated by his mother, Hird, is actually tricked into the bet by his pals, who don't think he has a chance, seeing as how he has virtually no *savoir faire*. But Cilento has heard the conversation, and when Corbett asks her out, she sympathetically agrees and takes him back to her apartment. Cilento, in a controlled performance that shot her career skyward, convinces Corbett that she comes from a wealthy family and is only hanging out in the sleazy bar as a lark. At her place, she gives him every possible opening to sleep with her but he is far too inhibited and they spend the night talking. As they do, he comes out of his shell somewhat and she eventually confesses her sordid background, but it doesn't much matter to Corbett, as he finds many things about Cilento to love. They make plans to take a vacation together, and if they can have a good enough time, perhaps even get married. She falls asleep and Corbett develops cold feet, sneaks out before the sun comes up, and joins his friends on the bus back to Manchester. Then he sees an ad and the face on the poster reminds him of Cilento. He has third thoughts (he's had the second thoughts already), tells his friends that he's staying, and races back to Cilento's apartment as the picture ends. It's quite similar to Paddy Chayefsky's MARTY in many ways. Corbett, who had starred in BBC-TV's "Steptoe And Son" (which was adapted into "Sanford And Son") is similar to Ernest Borgnine in his naivete and his relationship with his pals, who don't seem to be going anywhere in life or love. Even the two mothers tsk-tsk in much the same fashion. And the decisions to forego the approval of the male friends in favor of a possibility of love is the exact choice made in both.

p, William Gell; d, Muriel Box; w, Charles Dyer (based on his play); ph, Reg Wyer; m, Stanley Black; ed, Frederick Wilson; art d, Robert Jones.

Comedy/Drama **Cas.** **(PR:C MPAA:NR)**

RATTLERS* (1976) 82m Boxoffice International c

Sam Chew *(Dr. Sam Parkinson)*, Elisabeth Chauvet *(Ann)*, Dan Priest *(The Colonel)*, Ron Gold *(Dr. Delaney)*, Tony Ballen *(Sheriff)*, Richard Lockmiller *(Deputy)*, Jo Jordan *(Mother)*, Al Dunlap *(The General)*, Ancel Cook *(Janitor)*, Gary Van Ormand, Darwin Jostin *(Soldiers)*, Travis Gold, Alan Dekkar *(Boys)*, Celia Kaye *(Woman in Bathtub)*, Scott McCarter *(Son)*, Matt Knox *(Pilot)*.

An unspectacular killer-rodent film set in the Mojave Desert with rattlesnakes in the starring role. Chew is a zoology professor who must uncover a rash of mysterious murders. He brings a female photographer, Chauvet, along for the adventure and finds that the snakes are attacking in packs. He follows his clues to a nearby Army base and learns of a hidden crate of nerve gas. It seems the rattlers were exposed to the gas and driven to mass murder. As ludicrous as it sounds, somehow it all seems to make sense in the film. The film is far too static and slow-paced (if there's any pace at all) to sit through.

p&d, John McCauley; w, Jerry Golding; ph, Richard Gibb, Irv Goodnoff; ed,

Sandy Glieberman; spec eff, Harry Woolman; makeup, John Landon; animal trainer, Ray Folsum.

Horror/Suspense   Cas.   (PR:C   MPAA:PG)

RAUTHA SKIKKJAN   (SEE: HAGBARD AND SIGNE, 1968, Den./ Iceland/Swed.)

RAVAGER, THE*   (1970) 76m Green Dolphin/Manson c

Pierre Gostin [Gaston] (*Joe Salkow*), Jo Long (*Landlady*), Lynn Hayes, Luana Wilcox, Ann Hollis, Diane Thurman, Darlene Dawes (*The Ravager's Victims*).

An attempt to take some swipes at sexual repression and the Vietnam War has soldier Gostin witnessing the rape of a Vietnamese woman by two Viet Cong, which leaves him in a very disturbed condition requiring that he be hospitalized for six months. By his return stateside, he has gotten into such a state that he becomes enraged whenever he is reminded of sex. Anyone he catches having sex he blows to smithereens with dynamite. Then Gostin takes to raping and dynamiting random women, with little hindrance from anyone. Oddly enough, though, when he comes across two lesbians making love, he lets them go—making some nonsensical allegory, like the rest of this movie.

p, Dave Ackerman; d, Charles Nizet; ph, Carl Johnston (Eastmancolor); set d, Herman Thyson.

Horror/War   (PR:O   MPAA:NR)

RAVAGERS, THE**   (1965, U.S./Phil.) 88m Hemisphere bw

John Saxon (*Capt. Kermit Dowling*), Fernando Poe, Jr. (*Gaudiel*), Bronwyn Fitzsimmons (*Sheila*), Michael Parsons (*Reardon*), Kristina Scott (*Mother Superior*), Robert Arevalo (*Capt. Araullo*), Vic Diaz (*Cruz*), Vic Silayan (*Capt. Mori*), Jose Dagumboy (*Joe*).

War adventure set in the Philippines has Saxon and ex-con Poe leading a group of filipino guerrillas against one of the last remnants of Japanese forces in the islands. The Japanese are after a shipment of gold bullion and have taken over a convent in their search for the hidden gold. Poe manages to sneak inside the convent, where he encounters the American Fitzsimmons (the real-life daughter of Maureen O'Hara), who has been sheltered by the nuns. The two take a quick liking to each other before a battle breaks out between Saxon's army and the Japs inside the convent. Tautly made and well-paced action vehicle.

p, Kane W. Lynn; d, Eddie Romero; w, Romero, Cesar Amigo; m, Tito Arevalo; ed, Joven Calub; makeup, Remy Amazan.

War   (PR:A   MPAA:NR)

RAVAGERS, THE*   (1979) 91m COL c

Richard Harris (*Falk*), Ann Turkel (*Faina*), Art Carney (*Sergeant*), Ernest Borgnine (*Rann*), Anthony James (*Leader*), Woody Strode (*Brown*), Alana Hamilton (*Miriam*), Seymour Cassel (*Blindman*).

Another in the flood of post-nuclear films, in which the survivors are left to fight starvation and fend off unruly bands of violent thugs. In this one, Harris lives in a deserted steel mill with his wife Hamilton, who is raped and killed by a gang of lawless motorcycle hoods led by James. Harris then sets out to find revenge (in a plot vaguely similar to MAD MAX) kills one of them, and then sets off down the road. He comes across Carney at an abandoned missile base stocked with food and machine guns. But the two men leave the cozy base to meet with another group of people who live in a cave. They pick up the sexy Turkel and start off down the road again. This time James' gang attacks them and they fight the hoods off with their machine gun, but Carney is captured. Eventually the remaining two come to a ship that is doing pretty well under the leadership of Borgnine. But James attacks and blows the ship up. Too many situations are left unexplained, and little motivation for Harris' actions is given beyond that he represents some high moral code—but it's all impossible to take seriously. Producers seem to have meant well, but their energies were in vain.

p, John W. Hyde; d, Richard Compton; w, Donald S. Sanford (based on the novel *Path to Savagery* by Robert Edmond Alter); ph, Vincent Saizis (Panavision, Metrocolor); m, Fred Karlin; ed, Maury Winetrobe; prod d, Ronald E. Hobbs; cos, Ron Talsky.

Fantasy   (PR:A   MPAA:PG)

RAVEN, THE**   (1935) 62m UNIV bw

Boris Karloff (*Edmond Bateman*), Bela Lugosi (*Dr. Richard Vollin*), Irene Ware (*Jean Thatcher*), Lester Mathews (*Dr. Jerry Holden*), Samuel S. Hinds (*Judge Thatcher*), Inez Courtney (*Mary Burns*), Ian Wolfe ("*Pinky" Geoffrey*), Spencer Charters (*Col. Bertram Grant*), Maidel Turner (*Harriet Grant*), Arthur Hoyt (*Chapman*), Walter Miller.

In a film inspired by, rather than adapted from, the work of Poe, Lugosi and Karloff were in prime form. This is the tale of a demented doctor whose admiration for Edgar Allan Poe has led him to construct a dungeon filled with devices mentioned in the master's works. Lugosi plays a crafty brain surgeon who is begged by judge Hinds to save the life and face of his beautiful daughter Ware. Having fallen in love with the girl, Lugosi asks her for her hand in marriage, but is only scoffed at by the judge, whose daughter is already engaged to be married to Mathews. To get revenge, Lugosi invites the judge, his daughter, and her fiance to a dinner party, at which he offers to show them his collection of Poe artifacts, his intention being to use them on his guests. But his plans are upset by Karloff, the criminal who has begged for plastic surgery, and is only held in check by Lugosi, who performs an operation that only makes Karloff look more hideous, but promises to correct this after some favors are done for him. Lugosi ties the judge to a pit-and-pendulum-type device, in which a swinging blade moves closer and closer to his chest. For the young newlyweds, Ware and Mathews, Lugosi has designed a bridal suite with walls that close in on its inhabitants. But Karloff has a change of heart, and he

rescues the young couple, only to put Lugosi in their place. Script is a bit shaky, but Lugosi is at his prime as the twisted doctor whose cruelty seems limitless. Any inconsistencies can be easily overlooked.

p, David Diamond; d, Louis Friedlander [Lew Landers]; w, David Boehm (based on the poem by Edgar Allan Poe); ph, Charles Stumar; m, Gilbert Harland; ed, Alfred Akst; art d, Albert S. D'Agostino; ch, Theodore Kosloff; makeup, Jack P. Pierce.

Horror   Cas.   (PR:A   MPAA:NR)

RAVEN, THE**   (1948, Fr.) 90m Continental/Westport International bw (LE CORBEAU)

Pierre Fresnay (*Dr. Germain*), Pierre Larquey (*Dr. Verzet*), Noel Roquevert (*Salliens*), Antoine Belpetre (*Delorme*), Jean Brochard (*Bonnevi*), Louis Seigner (*Bertrand*), Robert Clermont (*DeMaquet*), Palau (*Mail Superintendent*), Marcel Delaitre (*Preacher*), Ginette Leclere (*Denise*), Micheline Francey (*Laura*), Helena Manson (*Marie*), Jeanne Fusier-Gir (*Shopkeeper*), Sylvie (*Mother of "No. 13"*), Liliane Maigne (*Rolande*).

Some of the nastiest characters to cross in front of a camera are gathered in a small French town, where a poison pen writer takes note of all the nastiness and sends the town into near hysterics. Fresnay plays the local doctor whose origins are rather mysterious; originally the major target of the letter writer, he later is suspected of being the writer as everyone becomes suspicious of everyone else. But the real culprit, in predictable fashion, is the person considered to be the least likely candidate, psychiatrist Larquey. Good performances, a fitting atmosphere, and some truly unique characterizations give a lift to an otherwise worn idea. (In French; English subtitles.)

d, Henri-Georges Clouzot; w, Clouzot, Louis Chavance; ph, Nicolas Hayer; m, Tony Aubain; English subtitles, Herman G. Weinberg.

Mystery   (PR:A   MPAA:NR)

RAVEN, THE**½   (1963) 86m Alta Vista/AIP c

Vincent Price (*Dr. Erasmus Craven*), Peter Lorre (*Dr. Adolphus Bedlo*), Boris Karloff (*Dr. Scarabus*), Hazel Court (*Lenore Craven*), Olive Sturgess (*Estelle Craven*), Jack Nicholson (*Rexford Bedlo*), Connie Wallace (*Maidservant*), William Baskin (*Grimes*), Aaron Saxon (*Gort*), Jim Jr. (*The Raven*).

Anyone who likes the Corman "Poe" films, and is a fan of horror greats Karloff, Price, and Lorre will delight in this wonderfully funny send-up of the genre wherein everyone involved looks as if he's having a great time. Price stars as a recently retired wizard who has gone into seclusion after the apparent death of his wife, Court. His gloomy meditations are interrupted by the arrival of an obnoxious talking raven who claims he is also a wizard who was put under a spell by the most powerful magician in the land, Karloff. After some clever banter, Price provides his father's cure for the bird (which includes such items as spider eyes and dead man's hair—Price opens his father's crypt and snips some off), but the first batch is too weak and the raven becomes Lorre, albeit with feathered arms. The pudgy little wizard throws a fit and the ever-calm Price stiffens up the next batch, restoring Lorre to his proper state. Once whole, Lorre relates his battle with Karloff which he almost won, but he had had a bit too much to drink. Lorre also mentions that he saw a woman who greatly resembled Price's dead wife Court as Karloff's mistress. Seeking to investigate this shocking phenomenon, Price agrees to return to Karloff's castle accompanied by his daughter Sturgess and Lorre's son, a very young Nicholson (who is constantly assaulted verbally by his father). Upon arrival at Karloff's abode, Price is horrified to discover that his wife Court is indeed alive, and that she faked her death in order to become the old, rich, and powerful sorcerer's mistress. Karloff had planned the whole charade as an elaborate plot to bait Price to his impenetrable castle so that the aging wizard could steal the young and more skilled sorcerer's powers. Price doesn't give up that easily, and in a stunning battle filled with fireballs and flashing lights, the two magicians battle it out. In the end Price wins, having sapped Karloff of his powers and leaving him to his fate with the now-naggy Court. The charming comedic success of THE RAVEN sprang from a Corman cast and crew that had grown tired of the repetitive Poe series and wanted to have some fun. Most of the laughs on the set (and in the film) came from watching an impish Lorre improvising one-liners that would catch cool professionals Price and Karloff by surprise and test their straight-faced skills. Lorre is a joy in THE RAVEN and he obviously relished the role—his infectious wit infuses the screen. Corman brought the film in under budget and ahead of schedule and since he had Karloff contracted for three more days of work, he decided to make another quickie horror film called THE TERROR. Shot on the same sets as THE RAVEN while one step ahead of the crew that was tearing them down, Corman dragged Nicholson and his old stand-by Dick Miller into the cast and slapped together one of the most mind-boggling, confusing films of all time. THE RAVEN was the fifth AIP film to be based on the stories of Poe, and the most costly at $350,000; the production took three weeks to complete, unusual for speed-demon Corman. This was the first time the three horror-film stars—billed as "The Great Triumvirate of Terror"—had appeared together.

p&d, Roger Corman; w, Richard Matheson (based on the poem by Edgar Allan Poe); ph, Floyd Crosby (Panavision, Pathe Color); m, Les Baxter; ed, Ronald Sinclair; art d, Daniel Haller; set d, Harry Reif; cos, Marjorie Corso; spec eff, Pat Dinga; makup, Ted Coodley.

Comedy/Horror   Cas.   (PR:C   MPAA:NR)

RAVEN'S END**½   (1970, Swed.) 100m Europa/New Yorker bw (KVARTERET KORPEN)

Thommy Berggren (*Anders*), Keve Hjelm (*Father*), Emy Storm (*Mother*), Ingvar Hirdwall (*Sixten*), Christina Framback (*Elsie*), Agneta Prytz (*Neighbor*).

Berggren, a factory laborer with literary pretensions, hopes to escape from Raven's End, a slum district in the Swedish city of Malmo. His meager earnings and those of his beleaguered washerwoman mother Storm go to support the lifestyle of his alcoholic father, Hjelm, who views himself as too cultured to accept employment as a common worker. Berggren's first novel is rejected by a publisher, albeit with some encouraging words. The youth, disconsolate, turns for succor to a young neighbor girl. She becomes pregnant and has every expectation that he will marry her. Fearing entrapment in the Malmo slum, Berggren deserts her, running off to the big city of Stockholm.

d&w, Bo Widerberg; ph, Jan Lindestrom; m, Giuseppe Torelli; ed, Wic Kjellin; art d, Einar Nettelbladt.

Drama   **(PR:A MPAA:NR)**

RAVISHING IDIOT, A**   (1966, Ital./Fr.) 105m Belles Rives-Flora Film/Seven Arts bw (UNE RAVISSANTE IDIOTE; AKA: THE RAVISHING IDIOT; AGENT 38-24-36; THE WARM-BLODDED SPY; ADORABLE IDIOT; BEWITCHING SCATTERBRAIN)

Anthony Perkins (Harry Compton/Nicholas Maukouline), Brigitte Bardot (Penelope Lightfeather), Gregoire Aslan (Bagda), Andre Luguet (Sir Reginald Dumfrey), Charles Millot (Balaniev), Helene Dieudonne (Mamie), Jacques Monod (Surgeon), Jean-Marc Tennberg (Cartwright), Hans Verner (Farrington), Paul Demange (Bank Director), Denise Provence (Lady Barbara Dumfrey), Robert Murzeau.

Perkins, a trig clerk at the Bank of England, complete with tightly-furled umbrella, is actually the son of a Russian. Enraptured by Bardot, who works as a couturier for Provence—the wife of British security chief Luguet—the bumbling Perkins loses his job. Disgruntled, he gives up on capitalism and joins his father's old friend, Soviet agent Aslan, in a plan to steal British Admiralty secrets dealing with the dispositions of NATO troops in Europe. Unknown to him, Luguet has substituted fakes for the real documents and given the fakes to blabbermouth Provence, hoping to use them as bait to snare a Soviet spy ring. Luguet has Provence stage a reception as a lure to bring the spies out. Perkins, using the brainless Bardot, wangles an invitation. In a series of silly sequences, the fake documents pass from agent to agent until, finally, mastermind Aslan and his henchmen are killed in a shootout. Perkins is united with the beauteous Bardot, who proves to have been a British agent all along. This mindless piece of fluff had numerous gaffes; London's police constables were depicted stopping pedestrians and asking to see their papers, in typical Gallic fashion, which caused much hilarity among British audiences. Location scenes were originally scheduled to be filmed in England. At the initial set-up, Bardot was fashionably late. Word spread; crowds gathered. When police stepped in, with truncheons at the ready to control the menacing crowd, director Molinaro cut and ran; Bardot piled into a waiting limousine. Cast and crew members headed back to France, where production resumed. Molinaro had anticipated some such trouble months before, and had made preparations: concealed-camera vans and Bardot look-alikes to decoy admirers to alternative locations. Neither tactic was used; Bardot had protested, saying "The English are much kinder to me than the Italians" (rioting paparazzi had caused a similar problem in Rome a short time previously). She was mistaken.

p, Michel Ardan; d, Edouard Molinaro; w, Molinaro, Andre Tabet, Georges Tabet (based on the novel Une Ravissante Idiote by Charles Exbrayat); ph, Andreas Winding; m, Michel Legrand; ed, Robert Isnardon; art d, Jean Andre, Robert Clavel; cos, Tanine Autre; makeup, Odette Berroyer.

Comedy   **Cas.**   **(PR:A MPAA:NR)**

RAW DEAL***   (1948) 79m EL-Reliance bw

Dennis O'Keefe (Joe Sullivan), Claire Trevor (Pat), Marsha Hunt (Ann Martin), John Ireland (Fantail), Raymond Burr (Rick Coyle), Curt Conway (Spider), Chili Williams (Marcy), Richard Fraser, Whitner Bissell, Cliff Clark (Men).

A hard-hitting gangster film with lots of action, good dialog, and fine performances by all, especially Trevor as a gun moll. O'Keefe is serving time in stir for a crime of which he was innocent. His one-time associates arranged a frame and O'Keefe is determined to get even with them when he breaks out of jail. With the aid of Trevor, his lover and pal, O'Keefe flees prison and is on his way to wreak revenge. While he was inside, he was visited by Hunt, a social worker, and he decides that she might be a very good hostage in case the cops close in, so he kidnaps her and the threesome begin a trip to get Burr and his gang, the men responsible. It isn't long before O'Keefe begins to fall for Hunt, much to the jealous consternation of Trevor, who has risked her life and her freedom for O'Keefe. Hunt, a heretofore legal and solid citizen, finds this all very exciting, and when O'Keefe has a battle with Ireland, one of the thugs, and loses, O'Keefe pleads with Hunt to save him and she does this by shooting Ireland in the back. Now she's a full part of the underworld. Hunt feels as though she is in love with O'Keefe, but he wants her out of this hard life, so he temporarily sends her off while he goes to execute Burr, who is playing a pyromaniacal part in the best Laird Cregar-style. O'Keefe busts into the hideout as Burr is experimenting with some flames and Burr shoots O'Keefe. Then the place goes up in a conflagration and Burr leaps out the window to escape the heat and smoke and falls to his death. O'Keefe is dying from the gunshot wound and Hunt holds him in her arms as Trevor watches, now a lost woman with none to love and no one to love her. A film noir picture in the best tradition, with fast-paced direction by Mann and superior photography by Alton. Whit Bissell, while he was still known as "Whitner" does a small role as a hood.

p, Edward Small; d, Anthony Mann; w, Leopold Atlas, John C. Higgins (based on a story by Arnold B. Armstrong, Audrey Ashley); ph, John Alton; m, Paul Sawtell; ed, Afred De Gaetano; md, Irving Friedman; art d, Edward L. Ilou; set d, Armor Marlowe, Clarence Steensen; spec eff, George J. Teague; makeup, Ern Westmore, Ted Larsen.

Crime   **(PR:A-C MPAA:NR)**

RAW DEAL**½   (1977, Aus.) 90m Homestead/GUO c

Gerard Kennedy (Palmer), Gus Mercurio (Ben), Rod Mullinar (Alex), Christopher Pate (Dick), Hu Pryce (Ned), John Cousins (Sir Charles), Michael Carmen (Sir Frederick), Norman Yemm (O'Neill), Patrick Edgeworth (Lt. Godfrey).

Overused plot line has a shady politician, Cousins, hiring two gunmen, Kennedy and Mercurio, to quiet down an overly noisy religious bunch in the Australian wilds of the 1870s. The two men get their needed help from the local prison, making for some original characterizations. This sets the mark for numerous comic situations, and the action needed to sustain the plot.

p, Russell Hagg, Patrick Edgeworth; d, Hagg; w, Edgeworth; ph, Vincent Monton; m, Ron Edgeworth; art d, John Dowding; cos, Clare Griffin.

Western   **(PR:A MPAA:NR)**

RAW EDGE**   (1956) 76m UNIV c

Rory Calhoun (Tex Kirby), Yvonne De Carlo (Hannah Montgomery), Mara Corday (Paca), Rex Reason (John Randolph), Neville Brand (Tarp Penny), Emile Meyer (Pop Penny), Herbert Rudley (Gerald Montgomery), Robert J. Wilke (Sile Doty), John Gilmore (Dan Kirby), Gregg Barton (McKay), Ed Fury (Whitey), Francis McDonald (Chief Kiyuva), Julia Montoya (Indian Squaw), Paul Fierro (Bull, the Bartender), William Schallert (Missionary), Richard James (Clerk), Robert Hoy (Five Crows).

Set in Oregon, where the frontiersmen live by the insane code that a woman is the property of the first man who stakes a claim on her. This leads the way for Calhoun to clear his name from accusations of trying to move in on De Carlo, property of local frontier baron Rudley. Calhoun is also out to get vengeance for his younger brother's murder. Lots of well-paced action in this glorification of the "macho" image.

p, Albert Zugsmith; d, John Sherwood; w, Harry Essex, Robert Hill (based on the story by William Kozlenka, James Benson Nablo); ph, Maury Gertsman (Technicolor); ed, Russell Schoengarth; md, Joseph Gershenson; art d, Alexander Golitzen, Alfred Sweeney; cos, Bill Thomas; m/l "Raw Edge," Terry Gilkyson (sung by Gilkyson).

Western   **(PR:A MPAA:NR)**

RAW FORCE zero   (1982) 86m Ansor/American Panorama c (AKA: SHOGUN ISLAND)

Cameron Mitchell (Captain), Geoff Binney (Mike), Jillian Kessner (Cookie), John Dresden (John), Jennifer Holmes (Ann), Hope Holiday (Hazel), Rey King (Chin), Vic Diaz (Monk), Robert Dennis, Rolly Tan.

Incredibly souped-up plot is an excuse for martial arts exhibitions, soft-core sex, and other thematic devices. The premise has it that members of the Burbank Karate Club are out on a cruise when their ship is attacked. The reason for the attack is, believe it or not, that a group of ex-hippies led by a German, are protecting their illegal jade market. It seems they kidnap prostitutes to trade for jade with the local monks. The cannibalistic monks use the girls as snacks, enabling them to raise the dead—the dead being martial arts experts. Filmed mostly in Hong Kong and the Philippines, this flesh-and-fantasy film of mixed genres uses quite a bit of footage from the equally campy—but much better—PIRANHA (1978). As weird as they come.

p, Frank Johnson; d&w, Edward Murphy; ph, Johnson (CFI Color); m, Walter Murphy; ed, Eric Lindemann; set d, Rodell Cruz; makeup, Cecile Baun.

Adventure/Horror   **Cas.**   **(PR:O MPAA:NR)**

RAW MEAT   (SEE: DEATHLINE, 1973, Brit.)

RAW TIMBER*   (1937) 63m Crescent bw

Tom Keene [George Duryea/Richard Powers] (Corbin), Peggy Keys (Dale), Budd Buster (Kentucky), Robert Fiske (Williams), Lee Phelps (Bull), John Rutherford (Lane), Rafael [Ray]Bennett (Hanlon), Slim Whitaker.

This dull and plodding story has Keene posing as a forest ranger whose job it is to keep the lumber companies from cutting down too many trees. Buster, as a backwoods mountaineer, makes for a joke or two. The versatile Keene, who had three screen careers using as many names, made a succession of westerns with differing characters, rather than a single heroic figure (as was the case with many stars) during his prolific Keene period.

p, E.B. Derr; d, Ray Taylor; w, Bennett Cohen, John T. Neville (based on a story by Cohen); ph, Arthur Martinelli; ed, Donald Barratt.

Western   **(PR:A MPAA:NR)**

RAW WEEKEND*   (1964) 62m Boxoffice International bw

Toni Warren, Shannon Harris, Tim Robinson, Randi Morrow, Ondine, Ralph Conners, Annette Varsi.

This silly excuse for a film has a small movie crew shooting some scenes in the woods when they spot a semi-nude woman walking through the woods. They follow her, finding her and another friend sunbathing in the nude. They have a picnic, then go for a swim, except for one actress who decides to remain indoors and study her script. Tiring of her chore, she gets undressed and goes out to play with her pals. How nice!

p, J. Willard Evans; d, Sidney Niehoff; w, Michael Locke; ph, Armond Selz, Franklin Holmes.

Drama   **(PR:O MPAA:NR)**

RAW WIND IN EDEN*½   (1958) 89m UNIV c

Esther Williams (Laura), Jeff Chandler (Mark Moore/Scott Moorehouse), Rossana Podesta (Costanza), Carlos Thompson (Wally Tucker), Rik Battaglia (Gavino), Eduardo de Filippo (Urbano).

This dull romantic drama has model Williams and playboy Thompson stranded on the Mediterranean island occupied by mystery-man Chandler and natives Podesta, de Filippo, and Battaglia after their plane crashes. Unable at first to find any way off the island, Thompson finally discovers a damaged yacht which he repairs, then takes off leaving Williams and Chandler, a man with a tragic past, to find comfort in each other's arms. Beautiful CinemaScope photography is wasted in this banal script. Williams swims a bit, or course.

p, William Alland; d, Richard Wilson; w, Elizabeth and Richard Wilson (based on a story by Dan Lundberg, Elizabeth Wilson); ph, Enzo Serafin (CinemaScope, Eastmancolor); m, Hans J. Salter; ed, Russell F. Schoengarth; md, Joseph Gershenson; art d, Alexander Golitzen, Alfred Ybarra; set d, Russell A. Gausman; m/l, Jay Livingston, Ray Evans; makeup, Bud Westmore.

Drama (PR:A MPAA:NR)

RAWHIDE½ (1938) 58m FOX bw

Smith Ballew (*Larry Kimball*), Lou Gehrig (*Himself*), Evalyn Knapp (*Peggy Gehrig*), Arthur Loft (*Ed Saunders*), Carl Stockdale (*Bascomb*), Si Jenks (*Pop Mason*), Cy Kendall (*Sheriff Kale*), Lafe McKee (*McDonnell*), Dick Curtis (*Butch*), Cecil Kellogg (*Gillam*), Slim Whitaker (*Biff*), Tom Foreman (*Rudy*), Cliff Parkinson (*Pete*), Harry Tenbrook (*Rusty*), Lee Shumway (*Johnson*), Ed Cassidy (*Fuller*), Al Hill.

Baseball legend Gehrig had a starring role in this feature, not only proving to have acting talent, but also putting his baseball skills to good use when—during a barroom brawl—he throws billiard balls at the opposition. The yarn centers on Gehrig as he hangs up his mitt forever to take up a peaceful existence on a ranch. But things aren't that easy; a group of racketeers, under the guise of a cattlemen's protective association, are squeezing the local ranchers. With the help of lawyer Ballew, the mess is straightened out. Some reviewers at the time of the film's release thought that Gehrig might just fashion a real career in pictures, citing his appearance, his charisma, and his voice. Alas, it was not to be, nor was a quiet retirement to a ranch, as he was stricken by amyotrophic lateral sclerosis, weakened, and died; the film's plot failed to portend his fate. Ballew sings the following along the way: "When a Cowboy Goes To Town," "Drifting," and "A Cowboy's Life." A back-up group renders "That Old Washboard Band." Taut script offers the usual amount of action.

p, Sol Lesser; d, Ray Taylor; w, Dan Jarrett, Jack Natteford (based on the story by Jarrett); ph, Allen Q. Thompson; ed, Robert Crandall.

Western **Cas.** (PR:A MPAA:NR)

RAWHIDE*** (1951) 86m FOX bw (AKA: DESPERATE SIEGE)

Tyrone Power (*Tom Owens*), Susan Hayward (*Vinnie Holt*), Hugh Marlowe (*Zimmerman*), Dean Jagger (*Yancy*), Edgar Buchanan (*Sam Todd*), Jack Elam (*Tevis*), George Tobias (*Gratz*), Jeff Corey (*Luke Davis*), James Millican (*Tex Squires*), Louis Jean Heydt (*Fickert*), William Haade (*Gil Scott*), Milton Corey, Sr. (*Dr. Tucker*), Ken [Kenneth] Tobey (*Wingate*), Dan White (*Gilchrist*), Max Terhune (*Miner*), Robert Adler (*Billy Dent*), Judy Ann Dunn (*Callie*), Howard Negley (*Chickenring*), Vincent Neptune (*Mr. Hickman*), Edith Evanson (*Mrs. Hickman*), Walter Sande (*Flowers*), Dick Curtis (*Hawley*), Si Jenks (*Old Timer*).

A western suspenser which fits into the western genre only in that it is set in a western locale, otherwise it's straight suspense. Power is an assistant to an aged stagecoach manager, Buchanan, at the Rawhide Relay Station tucked away in a remote section of Arizona. When Hayward, a former riverboat entertainer, passes through with her orphaned niece, Dunn, she is told that stage robbers are terrorizing the area and that she'll have to wait until the following day to leave town. Soon afterwards, outlaw leader Marlowe arrives at the station with his gang—Tobias, Jagger, and the highly volatile Elam—to knock over a coach which is carrying $100,000 in gold. Buchanan is gunned down when he recognizes Zimmerman, leaving Power in charge. When Zimmerman discovers Hayward he assumes her to be Power's wife and locks the two, together with Dunn, in a back room. Knowing that they will be killed in the morning, Power and Hayward plot to escape. With a knife that Power has smuggled in, the two begin digging a hole through the room's adobe wall. The hole is small, but not too small for Dunn to slip through unnoticed. When Hayward realizes that her niece is missing she pounds at the door until Elam opens it. A struggle ensues and Marlowe, assuming that Hayward is being molested, gets tough with the lecherous Elam. Elam, however, shoots Marlowe and Tobias, killing them both. In a panic, Jagger flees. During the turmoil, Power slips into a corral to get a gun he's hidden. Elam forces Power to come out unarmed by taking Dunn hostage. Before any harm can come to the girl, Hayward grabs a rifle and drops Elam to the ground. When the stagecoach comes in, Hayward and Dunn bid farewell to Power, who stays behind to run the station. Written by one of Hollywood's finest screenwriters, Dudley Nichols (THE INFORMER, BRINGING UP BABY, and STAGECOACH to name but a few), RAWHIDE is a rather atypical addition to the western genre. The wide-open spaces are missing, as are the thundering hooves of horses, romance on the range, and a wandering, protective hero. Instead, Power plays his character as an anti-hero—he does not wander the plains, choosing rather to settle down in a managerial job; he kills none of the outlaws, leaving that job for Hayward; and watches "wife" Hayward (with whom he has had no romantic involvement) leave instead of taking her in his arms. Hathaway and Nichols have created a suspenseful, single-location drama which relies more on tension and characterization than gunplay. While not wholly successful, RAWHIDE is definitely of interest, especially for those willing to accept variations on the usual western themes. Star Power's first western since JESSE JAMES 12 years previously and director Hathaway's first western in 20 years bears a close plot resemblance to the same studio's gangster-genre movie, SHOW THEM NO MERCY (1935). For television, RAWHIDE underwent a title change to DESPERATE SIEGE, to avoid confusion with the once-popular network show of the same name.

p, Samuel G. Engel; d, Henry Hathaway; w, Dudley Nichols; ph, Milton Krasner;

m, Sol Kaplan, Lionel Newman; ed, Robert Simpson; md, Newman; art d, Lyle Wheeler, George S. Davis; set d, Thomas Little, Stuart Reiss; cos, Travilla; spec eff, Fred Sersen; m/l, "A Rollin' Stone," Newman, Bob Russell; makeup, Ben Nye.

Western (PR:A MPAA:NR)

RAWHIDE HALO, THE (SEE: SHOOT OUT AT BIG SAC, 1962)

RAWHIDE RANGERS*** (1941) 56m UNIV bw

Johnny Mack Brown (*Brand*), Fuzzy Knight (*Porky*), Kathryn Adams (*Joan*), Nell O'Day (*Patti*), Roy Harris (*Steve*), Harry Cording (*Blackie*), Al Bridge (*Rawlings*), Frank Shannon (*Captain*), Ed Cassidy (*Martin*), Bob Kortman (*Dirk*), Chester Gan (*Sing Lo*), James Farley (*Banker*), Jack Rockwell, Frank Ellis, Fred Burns, Tex Palmer, Tex Terry, The Pickard Family, The Texas Rangers.

An old formula yarn is given a couple of new twists to keep from being wholly mechanical. Brown, with his sidekick Knight, uncovers a crooked businessman who heads a gang of outlaws that takes advantage of unsuspecting ranchers. After his brother is killed by the gang, Brown sheds his Texas Ranger gear to take up the search on his own, running into problems when the man he is after is looked upon with great admiration by the local ranchers. Songs include: "A Cowboy Is Happy" sung by O'Day; "Huckleberry Pie" sung by Knight (both by Milton Rosen, Everett Carter); and The Texas Rangers singing "Its a Ranger's Life" (Gomer Cool).

p, Will Cowan; d, Ray Taylor; w, Ed Earl Repp; ph, Charles Van Enger; ed, Edward Curtis.

Western (PR:A MPAA:NR)

RAWHIDE TRAIL, THE*½ (1958) 67m AA bw

Rex [Rhodes] Reason (*Jess Brady*), Nancy Gates (*Marsha Collins*), Richard Erdman (*Rupe Pardee*), Rusty Lane (*Captain*), Frank Chase (*Corporal*), Ann Doran (*Mrs. Cartwright*), Robert Knapp (*Farley Durand*), Sam Buffington (*James Willard*), Jana Davi (*Keetah*), Richard Warren (*Collier*), William Murphy (*Elbe Rotter*), Al Wyatt (*Stagecoach Driver*), John Dierkes, Richard Geary, Chet Sampson.

Two innocent wagon masters are sentenced to be hanged for driving their wagon train into a Comanche raid. Little hope is held for the pair until they produce the evidence that clears their names. A slow-mover that needs some vitality added to its wagon train.

p, Earle Lyon; d, Robert Gordon; w, Alexander J. Wells; ph, Karl Struss; m, Andre S. Brummer; ed, Paul Borofsky; art d, David Milton; m/l, Brummer, Jack Lloyd (sung by The Guardsmen).

Western (PR:A MPAA:NR)

RAWHIDE YEARS, THE*** (1956) 85m UNIV c

Tony Curtis (*Ben Mathews*), Colleen Miller (*Zoe*), Arthur Kennedy (*Rick Harper*), William Demarest (*Brand Comfort*), William Gargan (*Marshal Sommers*), Peter Van Eyck (*Andre Boucher*), Minor Watson (*Matt Comfort*), Robert Wilke (*Neal*), Donald Randolph (*Carrico*), Trevor Bardette (*Captain*), Chubby Johnson (*Gif Lessing*), James Anderson (*Deputy Wade*), Robert Foulk (*Mate*), Leigh Snowden (*Miss Vanilla Bissell*), Don Beddoe (*Frank Porter*), Malcolm Atterbury (*Paymaster*), Charles Evans (*Col. Swope*), I. Stanford Jolley (*Man*), Rex Lease (*Card Player*), Chuck Roberson (*Johnny*), Marlene Felton (*Miss Dal-Marie Smith*), Clarence Lung (*Chinese Steward*), Lane Bradford (*Pirate*).

Gambler Curtis is wrongly accused of a murder and takes to hiding. After three years of keeping a low profile, he comes back to clear his name as well as make his claim for the girl, Miller, he left behind. Miller has since taken up with Van Eyck, a gambler and head of the gang actually responsible for the killing of which Curtis is accused. With aid from happy-go-lucky Kennedy, Curtis takes care of the gang, winning Miller back in the interim. A good cast, especially Kennedy in a role that was to become his trademark during the 1950s, and fast-paced direction help to gloss over the inconsistencies in the plot. Miller sings "Give Me Your Love", "Happy Go Lucky" (Frederick Herbert, Arnold Hughes); and "The Gypsy with the Fire in His Shoes" (Peggy Lee, Laurindo Almeida).

p, Stanley Rubin; d, Rudolph Mate; w, Earl Felton, Robert Presnell, Jr., D.D. Beauchamp (based on the novel by Norman A. Fox); ph, Irving Glassberg (Technicolor); m, Frank Skinner, Hans J. Salter; ed, Russel Schoengarth; md, Joseph Gershenson; art d, Alexander Golitzen, Richard H. Riedel; cos, Bill Thomas.

Western (PR:A MPAA:NR)

RAYMIE**½ (1960) 72m AA bw

David Ladd (*Raymie*), Julie Adams (*Helen*), John Agar (*Ike*), Charles Winninger (*R. J. Parsons*), Richard Arlen (*Garber*), Frank Ferguson (*Rex*), Ray Kellogg (*Neil*), John Damler (*John*), Jester Hairston (*Ransom*), Vincent Padula (*Veulo*), Ida Smeraldo (*Carmen*), Christy Lynn (*Ellen*), Brent Wolfson (*Brent*), Shirley Garner (*1st Girl*), Marianne Gaba (*2nd Girl*), Leslie Glenn (*Camera Girl*), Vance Skarstedt (*Blake*), Doak Roberts (*Mike*).

Touching story about a boy, Ladd, son of actor Alan Ladd, who sets out to catch a legendary giant barracuda. Setting up on a California pier with a number of seasoned veterans, he eventually hooks the fish. But the boy can't bring himself to keep the majestic barracuda, so he cuts the line and lets it go. Though overly sentimental, the simple idealism is quite refreshing. Jerry Lewis sings the title song.

p, A.C. Lyles; d, Frank McDonald; w, Mark Hanna; ph, Henry Cronjager; m, Ronald Stein; ed, George White; spec eff, Milt Olsen, Max Luttenberg.

Drama (PR:AAA MPAA:NR)

RAZOR'S EDGE, THE**** (1946) 146m FOX bw

Tyrone Power (*Larry Darrell*), Gene Tierney (*Isabel Bradley*), John Payne (*Gray Maturin*), Anne Baxter (*Sophie Nelson*), Clifton Webb (*Elliott Templeton*), Herbert

Marshall *(Somerset Maugham)*, Lucile Watson *(Mrs. Louise Bradley)*, Frank Latimore *(Bob MacDonald)*, Elsa Lanchester *(Miss Keith)*, Fritz Kortner *(Kosti)*, John Wengraf *(Joseph)*, Cecil Humphreys *(Holy Man)*, Harry Pilcer *(Specialty Dancer)*, Cobina Wright, Sr. *(Princess Novemali)*, Albert Petit *(Albert)*, Noel Cravat *(Russian Singer)*, Isabelle Lamore *(Maid)*, Andre Charlot *(Bishop)*, Renee Carson *(Sophie's Friend)*, Jean Del Val *(Police Clerk)*, Walter Bonn *(Butler)*, Robert Laurent *(Singer)*, Marie Rabasse *(Flower Woman)*, Bess Flowers *(Matron)*, Barry Norton *(Escort of Princess)*, Helen Pasquelle *(Proprietress)*, Mayo Newhall *(Kibitzer)*, Stanislas Bielski *(Man at Bar)*, Peggy O'Neill, Betty Lou Volder, Mary Brewer, Blanche Taylor, Dorothy Abbott, Marge Pemberton *(Show Girls)*, Ruth Miles, Edward Kover *(Adagio Team)*, Richard [Shaw] Sisson *(Intern)*, Greta Granstedt *(Hospital Telephone Operator)*, Maj. Fred Farrell, Albert Pollet *(Men)*, Lillian Stanford *(Customer in Sulka's)*, Marcel De La Brosse *(Conductor)*, George Sorel *(French Surete Man)*, Dr. Ross Tompson, Dr. Gerald Echeverria *(Doctors)*, Eddie Das *(Hindu)*, Hassan Khayyam *(Dr. Paul Sing)*, Don Graham, Dolores Graham *(Adagio Dancers)*, Saul Gorss *(Drunk)*, Bud Wolfe *(Corsican)*, Patti Behrs *(Guest)*, Susan Hartmann, Suzanne O'Connor *(Daughters)*, Marek Windheim *(Waiter)*, Roger Valmy *(Coco)*, Forbes Murray *(Mr. Maturin)*, Jean De Briac *(Lawyer)*, Robert Norwood *(Priest)*, Ray De Ravenne *(Bartender)*, Joseph Burlando *(Curea)*, Frances Rey *(Trollop)*, Shushella Shakari *(Arab Girl)*, Henri Letondal *(Police Inspector)*, Laura Stevens *(Specialty Dancer)*, Eugene Borden *(Sea Captain)*, Demetrius Alexis *(Abbe)*, Gale Entrekin *(Sophie's Daughter)*, George Davis *(Concierge)*, Louise Colombet *(Concierge's Wife)*, Frank Arnold, Juan Duval, Louis Bacigolupi *(Miners)*.

This is undoubtedly the most expensive and effective filming of any of Somerset Maugham's fictional works and it is excellent production because of Goulding's careful direction and a mature, restrained performance by superstar Power, his first in many years after having served as a Marine in WW II. Power is an idealistic youth, a pilot who has served in WW II, whose experiences in battle have caused him to question moral values and the very fibre of his society. Returning to Chicago, Power disturbs his childhood sweetheart and fiancee Tierney, a producet of high society, by telling her about the inexplicable urge he has to seek out the real meaning of life. She tells him to come down to earth and take the high-paying job she has arranged for him. But Power balks at this, then embarks on his quest to find intellectual and spiritual freedom. He journeys to Paris and Tierney, along with her mother, Watson, follows, the now-troubled fiancee meeting Power at a party. He proposes to her but his view of the world has not changed; he still insists upon traveling the world to find meaning. Tierney cannot abide such talk, which she considers drivel. Her wealthy dilettante uncle, Webb, a vacuous patron of the arts, persuades her not to go running after misguided Power. Without anything but extremely limited funds, Tierney knows Power cannot support her in the style she demands. She turns him down. Tierney makes one more plea to Power to accept her spoiled way of life and return to America. He refuses and goes off to India, then to Nepal where, high in the Himalayas, he finds an elderly Hindu mystic who brings peace to his troubled mind and spirit. After 10 years, Powers returns to Paris and is told by Maugham, an old family friend played by Marshall (who actually narrates the story, much the same way he did Maugham's THE MOON AND SIXPENCE, 1942), that Tierney is now married to Power's boyhood friend Payne, once rich, now impoverished, the stock market crash of 1929 having depleted Payne's fortunes. The couple has two little girls, Power is told, along with news of another old-time friend, Baxter. After an auto accident which claimed the life of Baxter's husband, Latimore, and their infant, Baxter has utterly vanished. Moreover, the impoverished Tierney, Payne, and their girls have moved to Paris to live with the rich, supercilious Webb. Power is reunited through Maugham with his former sweetheart and her family. Tierney suggests they all celebrate by enjoying an evening of nightclubbing. The group finally makes its way to some of the off-the-beaten track dives; by this time the celebrants are "slumming." In one of these sleazy places they discover Baxter, who has turned into a total alcoholic. A greasy looking character, obviously Baxter's saloon protector, orders her to go into the back room and stay away from Power and his friends. Power forcefully tells her to stay where she is and when the protector starts to get abusive, Power reaches out quickly and yanks the man's earring right out of his ear, causing the torn flesh to spurt blood. Power announces that he will spend his full-time efforts rehabilitating Baxter, which shocks Tierney. Though married, she is still in love with Power, and is incensed that he would spend any time with a "derelict." When Tierney later learns that Baxter has stopped drinking and that she and Power plan to wed, the spoiled society girl insidiously invites Baxter to her uncle's apartment, where she insults her and tricks her into getting drunk. Baxter, in anguish over failing Power, disappears again. When Power learns of Tierney's vicious ploy, he confronts her, telling her he will never forgive her for destroying Baxter. Webb, who has lived an empty, dissolute life, has broken down and Power and Maugham arrange to have the Bishop of Paris, Charlot, visit the incorrigible old roue and administer last rites. Then Power learns that Baxter has been killed in a Toulon dive and goes to Tierney, putting the blame for the tragic woman's death squarely on his old flame. Tierney begs him to take her with him, saying she still loves him, but Power will have no part of this vixen and the next day he ships out as a common seaman, sailing to unknown ports and an uncertain future. THE RAZOR'S EDGE possesses just enough philosophical razzle-dazzle to intrigue viewers and convince some of them that they are witnessing a film that deals seriously with intellectual and spiritual meaning, but, as in his novel, Maugham also sprinkles this long melodrama with alcoholism, accidental death, murder, poverty, romance, and seduction to make it brilliantly appealing to a mass audience. Power and Tierney shine in their roles, but Baxter outdoes both of them as the star-crossed Sophie, so expertly conveying her deep sense of loss—the futility of her life—and yet struggling to regain hope to live for another dawn, that she deservedly won an Oscar for her role. The Trotti script is taut and sophisticated and much of Maugham's intent—if not explicit scenes—is retained. Webb is good as the flightly rich uncle with the jaded point of view and Marshall, with his wonderfully mellifluous voice, perfectly narrates as Maugham (the novelist chose to use himself in the story as the connecting link in this multi-character tale, a devise used more in desperation than by plan, one can easily conclude). Miller's photography is splendid and Newman's score is stirring. The entire production was personally pieced together by Fox chief Zanuck. He had originally thought to have Alice Faye essay the role of the tragic Sophie, but that actress had left the studio and vowed never to return. Zanuck thought to sign Maureen O'Hara, but she wasn't available, and he even gave some thought to Betty Grable—she of the luscious legs—but he knew her acting limitations. By default, Baxter got the role and won her Best Supporting Actress Oscar. Oddly, Zanuck gave some thought to newcomer Gregory Peck as playing the idealist Larry, offering Power the lead role in another new project, GENTLEMAN'S AGREEMENT. Power turned it down, took THE RAZOR'S EDGE, and Peck went on to fame in the powerful study on anti-semitism in GENTLEMAN'S AGREEMENT. Fox made an extravaganza out of THE RAZOR'S EDGE, Zanuck paying Maugham $250,000 for the rights to his novel. Shot in 100 days (a very lengthy period of time for that era), the picture cost more than $4 million, and it was obvious. In one scene so much silver was used for a dinner party that Pinkerton men were stationed on the set to guard the costly cutlery. More than $800,000 worth of props were secured, to be positioned on 89 sets specially constructed for the picture. The publicity department bragged than one love scene alone between Tierney and Power cost $121,000. The very concept of the film and story, a rejection of materialism, was betrayed by the opulence Goulding portrayed in his gargantuan takes, which revealed endless candelabra, chandeliers, ornate fountains, and exquisite furnishings everywhere. The film, despite its shallow attempts to encompass philosophy with sex, is first-rate in every regard, far superior to the ridiculous and posturing remake starring Bill Murray, a comedian obviously out of his element.

p, Darryl F. Zanuck; d, Edmund Goulding; w, Lamar Trotti (based on the novel by W. Somerset Maugham); ph, Arthur Miller; m, Alfred Newman; ed, J. Watson Webb; art d, Richard Day, Nathan Juran; set d, Thomas Little, Paul S. Fox; cos, Charles LeMaire, Oleg Cassini; spec eff, Fred Sersen; ch, Harry Pilcer; m/l, "Mam'selle," Mack Gordon, Edmund Goulding.

Drama Cas. (PR:C MPAA:NR)

RE: LUCKY LUCIANO*** (1974, Fr./Ital.) 113m Vides-Les Films la Boetie/AE c (A PROPOSITO LUCIANO; AKA: LUCKY LUCIANO)

Gian Maria Volonte *(Lucky Luciano)*, Rod Steiger *(Gene Giannini)*, Charles Siragusa *(Himself)*, Edmond O'Brien *(Harry J. Anslinger)*, Vincent Gardenia *(American Colonel)*, Silverio Blasi *(Italian Captain)*, Charles Cioffi *(Vito Genovese)*, Magda Konopka *(The Contessa)*, Larry Gates *(Herlands)*, Jacques Monod *(French Commissioner)*, Dino Curcio *(Don Ciccio)*, Karin Petersen *(Igea)*.

A biographical look at the life of underworld figure Luciano who, after his arrest and subsequent serving of nine years of his 50-year sentence during the 1930s and 1940s, was pardoned and deported to Italy. Doting on possible connections between crime and political powers, Rosi avoids gauging the validity of such a connection. Volonte, as Luciano, retreats to Naples, where narcotics investigator Siragusa, Luciano's real-life nemesis, sets up surveillance. After a 10-year investigation, Siragusa was unable to uncover enough evidence to bring Luciano to justice.

p, Franco Cristaldi; d, Francesco Rosi; w, Rosi, Lano Jannuzzi, Tonino Guerra; ph, Pasqualino De Santis (Technicolor); m, Piero Piccioni; ed, Ruggero Mastroianni; art d, Andrea Crisanti; technical consultant, Charles Siragusa.

Crime (PR:O MPAA:R)

RE-UNION (SEE: IN LOVE WITH LIFE, 1934)

REACH FOR GLORY½** (1963, Brit.) 86m Blazer/COL bw

Harry Andrews *(Capt. Curlew)*, Kay Walsh *(Mrs. Curlew)*, Michael Anderson, Jr. *(Lewis Craig)*, Oliver Grimm *(Mark Stein)*, Martin Tomlinson *(John Curlew)*, Freddy Eldrett *(Willy Aldrich)*, James Luck *(Michael Freen)*, John Coker *(Peter Joy)*, Michael Trubshawe *(Maj. Burton)*, Arthur Hewlett *(Vicar)*, Cameron Hall *(Headmaster)*, Allan Jeayes *(Crabtree)*, Richard Vernon *(Dr. Aldrich)*, Russell Waters *(Mr. Freeman)*, Pat Hayess *(Mrs. Freeman)*, George Pravda *(Mr. Stein)*, John Rae *(Lance Freeman)*, Alexis Kanner *(Steven)*, Peter Furnell *(Arthur Chettle)*, John Pike *(Felix)*, Melvin Baker *(Chettle's Lieutenant)*.

A group of young London rogues is evacuated during WW II to a coastal town, where they form a gang and play war games. Too young to fight in the war and afraid it will be over when they come of age, the gang members initiate a battle with the local teenagers. Tomlinson, a troubled local youth, invites an Austrian Jewish refugee to take part in the shenanigans. At first the Jewish boy, Grimm, is scorned because of his Jewish heritage but later allowed to join. When Grimm runs off during a fight, the youths decide to give him a fake court-martial and execution. Real bullets are used by mistake, however, and Grimm is shot and killed. The picture incorporates many heavy issues, including racism and anti-Semitism, but is unable to firmly grasp main thematic points. Director Leacock, known mainly for his documentary work, seems at ease with the young actors and brings out subtleties in their portrayals. This is not true of the adult performers, however.

p, John Kohn, Jud Kinberg; d, Philip Leacock; w, Kohn, Kinberg, John Rae (based on the novel *The Custard Boys* by Rae); ph, Bob Huke; m, Bob Russell; ed, Frederick Wilson; art d, John Blezard.

Drama (PR:A MPAA:NR)

REACH FOR THE SKY*** (1957, Brit.) 123m Pinnacle/Rank bw

Kenneth More *(Douglas Bader)*, Muriel Pavlow *(Thelma Bader)*, Lyndon Brook *(Johnny Sanderson)*, Lee Patterson *(Stan Turner)*, Alexander Knox *(Mr. Joyce)*, Dorothy Alison *(Nurse Brace)*, Michael Warre *(Harry Day)*, Sydney Tafler *(Robert Desoutter)*, Howard Marion Crawford *("Woody" Woodhall)*, Jack Watling *(Peel)*, Nigel Green *(Streatfield)*, Anne Leon *(Sister Thornhill)*, Ronald Adam *(Air Vice

Marshal Leigh-Mallory), Charles Carson (Air Chief Marshal Sir Hugh Dowding), Basil Appleby (Crowley-Milling), Eddie Byrne (Sgt. Mills), Beverly Brooks (Sally), Michael Ripper (Warrant Officer), Derek Blomfield (Civilian Pilot), Avice Landone (Mrs. Bader), Eric Pohlmann (Adjutant of Prison Camp), Michael Gough (Flying Instructor), Philip Stainton, Harry Locke, Sam Kydd, Anton Diffring, Michel Clement, Clive Revill, Michael Balfour.

Moving account of the true story of a British aviator who, after losing both his legs, rejoins the Royal Air Force and becomes a war hero. More plays the cocky flyer who, through agony and determination, masters a set of artificial limbs and takes to the air again at the outset of WW II. In the midst of the Battle of Britain, he is forced to bail out of a plane and is captured by the Germans. After he makes three escape attempts, his captors imprison him in an impregnable castle. Handled in an effective and subtle manner, with convincing performances all the way around, the picture is a dissertation on the effects of individual determination and courage. Tighter editing could have helped to move the story along.

p, Daniel M. Angel; d, Lewis Gilbert; w, Gilbert, Vernon Harris (based on the book Story of Douglas Bader by Paul Brickhill); ph, Jack Asher; m, John Addison; ed, John Shirley; md, Muir Mathieson; art d, Bernard Robinson.

War/Drama (PR:A MPAA:NR)

REACHING FOR THE MOON** (1931) 90m UA bw

Douglas Fairbanks (Larry Day), Bebe Daniels (Vivan Benton), Edward Everett Horton (Rogers, Valet), Jack Mulhall (Jimmy Carrington), Claude Allister (Sir Horace Partington Chelmsford), June MacCloy (Kitty), Walter Walker (James Benton), Helen Jerome Eddy (Secretary), Bing Crosby.

In this lavish and costly production businessman Fairbanks tosses all matters aside to chase after Daniels on a transatlantic cruise. Despite the presence of her fiance, Allister, and news of the stockmarket crash, the madcap happenings aboard the ship result in Fairbanks' and Daniels' marriage. Both leads give their usual charming performances. Unfortunately, the script is weak, with most of the humor taking the form of overused sight gags. Bright spot of the picture is Crosby, as a member of the "Whiteman Rhythm Boys," crooning "Lower Than Lowdown."

d, Edmund Goulding; w, Goulding, Elsie Janis (based on a story by Goulding, Irving Berlin); ph, Ray June, Robert Planck; m, Irving Berlin; ed, Lloyd Nosler, Hal C. Kern.

Comedy **Cas.** (PR:A MPAA:NR)

REACHING FOR THE SUN**½ (1941) 90m PAR bw

Joel McCrea (Russ Elliott), Ellen Drew (Rita), Eddie Bracken (Benny Morgan), Albert Dekker (Herman), Billy Gilbert (Amos), George Chandler (Jerry), Bodil Ann Rosing (Rita's Mother), James Burke (Norm), Charles D. Brown (Johnson, Plant Foreman), Eily Malyon (Landlady), Regis Toomey (Intern), Nella Walker (Maternity Center Lady), Warren Hymer (Prospective Father), James Flavin (Plant Guard), Charles Williams (Truck Driver), Hobart Cavanaugh.

McCrea plays a backwoodsman who comes to Detroit to earn enough money to buy an outboard motor. He falls for and marries waitress Drew, but problems in their marriage soon emerge. McCrea is the outdoors type, while Drew is a confirmed city dweller. The arrival of a baby makes for further complications and arguments. Drew eventually walks out, only to return to the woodlands after McCrea is seriously injured. Poorly paced script and somewhat shaky direction are saved by subtle injections of humor, which help carry the drawn-out husband-wife battles.

p&d, William A. Wellman; w, W.L. River (based on the novel F.O.B. Detroit by Wessel Smitter); ph, William C. Mellor; ed, Thomas Scott.

Drama (PR:A MPAA:NR)

REACHING OUT*½ (1983) 87m Par Films c

Pat Russell (Pat Stuart), Tony Craig (John Stevens), Frank McCarthy (Frank Mesina), Betty Andrews (Mrs. Stuart), Douglas Stark (Mr. Stuart), Tyre Alls (Florence), Ralph Carlson (Agent), Marketa Kimbrel (Acting Teacher), Victor Truro (Psychiatrist), Ron Max (Drunk), Mary Milne (Girl with Apartment), Ric Wynn (Waiter).

This film was originally shot in 1973 and not released for another 10 years. Russell produced, acted in, directed, wrote, and even edited this movie about a young Ohio woman who breaks out of her shell in an effort to make it as an actress on Broadway. The project seems almost self-defeating in its cliche-ridden plot structure, and Russell shows little promise as an actress. However, she does prove to have a knack for setting and mood, capturing a true-to-life depiction of Greenwich Village.

p,d&w, Pat Russell; ph, David Sperling (TVC Color); m, Elizabeth Mazel; ed, Russell, Sperling, Jim McCreading.

Drama (PR:O MPAA:R)

READY FOR LOVE**½ (1934) 77m PAR bw

Ida Lupino (Marigold Tate), Richard Arlen (Julian Barrow), Marjorie Rambeau (Goldie Tate), Trent [Junior] Durkin (Joey Burke), Beulah Bondi (Mrs. Burke), Esther Howard (Aunt Ida), Ralph Remley (Chester Burke), Charles E. Arnt (Sam Gardner), Henry Travers (Judge Pickett), Charles Sellon (Caleb Hooker), Irving Bacon (Milkman), Oscar Smith (Pullman Porter), Ben Taggart (Pullman Conductor), Franklyn Ardell (Dean), Fredric Santley (Farnum), James C. Burtis (Blaine), David Loring (Skyscraper), Wilbur Mack (Davis), Louise Carter (Mrs. Thompson), Eleanor Wesselhoeft (Mrs. Black), Clara Lou [Ann] Sheridan (Bit), Ralph Lewis (Mr. Thompson), Bernard Suss, Burr Caruth.

This lightweight romance follows a young woman in her battle against small-town bigotry. Lupino has run away from her boarding school to stay with her retired aunt. The aunt, Howard, a former actress, has met with nothing but scorn from the snobbish townspeople. Lupino also is spurned and becomes the victim of a Salem witchcraft trial, complete with ducking stool. Newspaper editor Arlen comes to cover the story, and romance sparks between him and Lupino. The ending has Arlen landing a job at a New York paper, where Lupino has also moved. Ann Sheridan, whose career took off after moving to Warner Brothers in 1936 and becoming the studio's "Oomph Girl," had a bit part in this film.

d, Marion Gering; w, J.P. McEvoy, William Slavens McNutt (based on the novel by Roy Flannagan); ph, Leon Shamroy.

Drama (PR:A MPAA:NR)

READY FOR THE PEOPLE** (1964) 57m WB bw

Simon Oakland (Murray Brock), Everett Sloane (Paul Boyer), Anne Helm (Connie Zelenko), Richard Jordan (Eddie Dickinson), Karl Held (Dave Ryan), Bartlett Robinson (John T. McGrane), Simon Scott (District Attorney), Louis Guss (Joe Damico), Harold Gould (Arnie Tomkins), Don Keefer (Dr. Michaels), William Bramley (Nick Williams), Robert Lieb (Judge), King Calder (Chaplain), Jo Helton (Karen Brock).

Originally a pilot for a TV series that never made it to the air. Oakland plays a New York district attorney who believes that Jordan, accused of killing another man in a fight over Helm, is innocent. Several witnesses testify that Jordan is guilty, but Oakland still supports him. Jordan is sentenced and executed, maintaining his innocence right up until his death. But after the execution, Oakland receives a posthumous letter from Jordan in which he confesses to the crime. Routinely handled in every fashion, from script to the cutting room.

p, Anthony Spinner; d, Buzz Kulik; w, E.M. Parsons, Sy Salkowitz (based on the magazine story "Tiger in the Night" by Eleazar Lipsky); ph, Carl Guthrie; m, Frank Perkins; ed, Robert B. Warwick; art d, Perry Ferguson; set d, Hoyle Barrett; makeup, Gordon Bau.

Drama/Crime (PR:A MPAA:NR)

READY, WILLING AND ABLE*½ (1937) 93m WB bw

Ruby Keeler (Jane Clarke), Lee Dixon (Pinky Blair), Allen Jenkins (Jay Van Courtland), Louise Fazenda (Clara Heineman), Carol Hughes (Angie), Ross Alexander (Barry Granville, sung by James Newill), Winifred Shaw (English Jane Clarke), Teddy Hart (Yip Nolan), Hugh O'Connell (Truman Hardy), Addison Richards (Edward McNeil), Shaw and Lee (Moving Men), E. E. Clive (Sir Samuel Buffington), Jane Wyman (Dot), May Boley (Mrs. Beadle), Charles Halton (Brockman), Adrian Rosley (Angelo the Tailor), Lillian Kemble Cooper (Mrs. Buffington), Barnett Parker (Reginald Fortescue, the British Waiter), May Boley (Mrs. Boadle), Charles Halton (Brockman), Dickie Jones (Kid), Milton Kibbee (Steward), Carlyle Moore, Jr., Dennis Moore (Reporters), Saul Gorss (Cameraman), Gertrude Pedlar, William Worthington (Eldery Couple), Elsa Buchanan (Maid), Cliff Saum (Yip's Assistant).

Very weak story that is delivered in an haphazard manner, and mainly serves to plug some mediocre musical and dance numbers. An exception is "Too Marvelous for Words" (Johnny Mercer, Richard Whiting). Story focuses on two downtrodden Broadway would-bes, Dixon and Alexander, who manage to find a backer for their show on the condition that British actress, Shaw, play the lead. But they mistakenly wind up signing Keeler, a star-struck college girl who shares the same name as Shaw. They still manage to put on the show, after Keeler's wealthy fiance agrees to pick up the tab, and Shaw is still willing to do her part. Alexander, who despite secondary billing had one of the meatiest parts, committed suicide prior to the release of READY, WILLING AND ABLE. Alexander had been groomed for stardom by Warner Bros. in the early 1930s, but his career went downhill, and he was relegated to roles in B pictures. This also was Keeler's last film for the Warner Bros. studio. Songs include: "Just a Quiet Evening," "Sentimental and Melancholy," "Gasoline Gypsies," "The World Is My Apple," "Handy with Your Feet," "There's a Little Old House," "Ready Willing And Able" (Johnny Mercer, Richard Whiting).

p, Sam Bischoff; d, Ray Enright; w, Jerry Wald, Sig Herzig, Warren Duff (based on the story by Richard Macaulay); ph, Sol Polito; ed, Doug Gould; ch, Bobby Connelly.

Musical (PR:A MPAA:NR)

REAL BLOKE, A** (1935, Brit.) 70m Baxter & Barter/UNIV bw

George Carney (Bill), Mary Clare (Kate), Diana Beaumont (Mary), Peggy Novak (Lil), Mark Daly (Scotty), Billy Holland (Joe), Wilson Coleman (Watchman), Roddy Hughes (Taffy), Edgar Driver (Titch), C. Denier Warren (Tailor), Dick Francis, Johnnie Schofield, John Turnbull, Freddie Watts, Fred Wynne.

An effective drama which stars Carney as a worker whose opinions on labor-saving technology get him fired from his job. Ashamed, and hoping to avoid panic, he fails to inform his family until after his daughter's wedding. A tragic accident involving his new son-in-law drives him deeper into depression. He is finally pulled out of his despair by the birth of a grandson, giving him a ray of hope for the future. A genuine slice of life from among the English working classes.

p, John Barter; d, John Baxter; w, Herbert Ayres; ph, Desmond Dickinson.

Drama (PR:A MPAA:NR)

REAL GLORY, THE***½ (1939) 95m UA bw

Gary Cooper (Dr. Bill Canavan), Andrea Leeds (Linda Hartley), David Niven (Lt. McCool), Reginald Owen (Capt. Steve Hartley), Broderick Crawford (Lt. Swede Larson), Kay Johnson (Mabel Manning), Charles Waldron (Padre Rafael), Russell Hicks (Capt. George Manning), Roy Gordon (Col. Hatch), Benny Inocencio (Miguel), Vladimir Sokoloff (Datu), Rudy Robles (Lt. Yabo), Henry Kolker (The General), Tetsu Komai (Alipang), Elvira Rios (Mrs. Yabo), Luke Chan (Top Sergeant), Elmo Lincoln (U.S. Army Captain), John Villasin (Moro Priest), Charles Stevens (Cholera Victim), Karen Sorrell (Young Native Woman), Soledad Jimenez

(Old Native Woman), Lucio Villegas, Nick Shaid *(Old Native Men)*, Kam Tong *(Filipino Soldier)*, Martin Wilkins, Bob Naihe, Satini Puailoa, Kalu Sonkur, Sr., George Kaluna, Caiyu Ambol *(Moro Warriors)*.

In the Philippines shortly after the U.S. capture of the islands in the Spanish-American war, an uprising of Moslem Moro tribesmen terrorizes the occupying powers. Most of the islands are evacuated of Americans, and only a small cadre of Army officers is left to lead Filipino soldiers against the rebels, who attack the soldiers headlong with machetes, seemingly impervious to bullets, until they reach their victims and hack them to pieces. (Incidentally, the resistance of the Moros to the .38-caliber bullets of the Army pistols led to the development of the .45-caliber automatic, a gun designed to stop a man in his tracks.) The commander of the base, Hicks, soon falls victim to one of these attacks, killed in front of his wife and a crowd of others. Owen takes over command although he is gradually going blind, and forbids Cooper to go into the hills with a Moro boy to check out the situation. Cooper sees the rites the Moros perform and gathers some valuable information, but when he returns to the base he is arrested and locked up. The Moros dam the river that provides the base with water and cholera breaks out. Cooper is released to treat the sick and accompanies Owen, now completely blind, as he leads an attack on the dam, leaving Niven in charge of the fort. This is exactly what the Moros have been waiting for, and they mount a furious assault on the outpost, launching themselves over the wall with catapults made from bent-over trees. The dam is breached with dynamite, and as the water rushes down from the hills, Cooper rides on a log to the fort and helps save the day, heaving sticks of dynamite over the walls at the attackers in one of the bloodiest battles ever staged for the camera at that time. An exciting film, filled with amazing action scenes highlighting the seeming invincibility of the Moros. Hathaway, who had also directed the stirring Niven-Cooper vehicle THE LIVES OF A BENGAL LANCER, does a magnificent job here, giving Cooper one of his best action roles (although a doctor, he is not loath to pick up a gun and kill). All the performances are good, particularly Cooper's and Niven's, who has a terrific death scene after the final battle. Reportedly the Philippine government objected to the film on the grounds that it portrayed the native soldiers as cowards, though this certainly doesn't show. Everyone is afraid of men who don't die when you shoot them. The movie year 1939 was one of the best ever, with films like GONE WITH THE WIND, THE WIZARD OF OZ, and STAGECOACH. While THE REAL GLORY isn't in that league, it still holds up well as a classic war-adventure film.

p, Sam Goldwyn; d, Henry Hathaway; w, Jo Swerling, Robert R. Presnell (based on the novel by Charles L. Clifford); ph, Rudolph Mate; ed, Daniel Mandell; md, Alfred Newman; art d, James Basevi; set d, Julia Heron; cos, Jeanne Beakhurst; spec eff, R.O. Binger, Paul Eagler; tech adv, Col. William H. Shutan.

War **(PR:A MPAA:NR)**

REAL GONE GIRLS, THE (SEE: MAN FROM O.R.G.Y., THE, 1970)

REAL LIFE***** (1979) 99m PAR c

Dick Haynes *(Harris)*, Albert Brooks *(Himself)*, Matthew Tobin *(Dr. Howard Hill)*, J. A. Preston *(Dr. Ted Cleary)*, Mort Lindsey *(Himself)*, Joseph Schaffler *(Paul)*, Phyllis Quinn *(Donna)*, James Ritz *(Jack)*, Clifford Einstein, Harold Einstein, Mandy Einstein, Karen Einstein *(Role Reversal Family)*, James L. Brooks *(Evaluator)*, Zeke Manners *(Driver)*, Charles Grodin *(Warren Yeager)*, Francis Lee McCain *(Jeanette Yeager)*, Lisa Urette *(Lisa Yeager)*, Robert Stirrat *(Eric Yeager)*, Dudley DeZonia, Barbara DeZonia, Carolyn Silas, Adam Grant *(The Feltons)*, Belle Richter *(Jeanette's Mother)*, Jerry Jensen *(Jeanette's Father)*, Michele Grace *(Nurse)*, Thelma Bernstein *(Margaret)*, Johnny Haymer *(Dr. Rennert)*, Nudie *(Horse Owner)*, Charles H. Reid *(Surgeon)*, Susan Clark *(Nurse)*, Ward Rodgers *(Minister)*, David Spielberg *(Dr. Jeremy Nolan)*, Julie Payne *(Dr. Kramer)*, Jennings Lang *(Martin Brand)*, Leo McElroy *(Jim)*, Carlos Jurado, S. W. Smith, Fred Wolfson *(Reporters)*, Norman Bartold *(Dr. Isaac Steven)*, Harry Shearer *(Pete)*.

Comedian-filmmaker Albert Brooks established himself as a major force in American film comedy with this devastating look at how the media has dominated and nearly destroyed family life in the United States. Brooks plays himself, an obnoxious documentary filmmaker who sets out to find a "typical American family" and then film their lives for a year. After exhaustive behavioral testing, two families tie for the honor, each being deemed perfectly "typical." One lives in Minnesota, the other in Nevada. With clinical scientific precision, Brooks decides which family would be best suited to spend a year with: "You spend the winter in Minnesota. We're off to Nevada!" Grodin and McCain, the parents, have become decidedly star-struck with their new-found fame, but soon things turn sour. Normal family problems are blown up by filmmaker Brooks into crises of disastrous proportions. McCain's simple trip to her gynecologist becomes an expose on her doctor. Eventually the family members start to unravel at the seams and soon stop talking to each other. Needing an *active* family to film, Brooks desperately tries to manipulate the family members so that they will do *something* in front of the cameras. He decides to bribe the parents and children with gifts and emotional support. Meanwhile, other problems threaten the success of Brooks' project. The psychologists who have been monitoring the validity of the project become disgusted with Brooks and disassociate themselves from him. The head of the studio Brooks works for (who attends meetings via a speaker phone) laments that there are no "stars" in the film: "Albert, perhaps you could include a neighbor and we'll cast a Streisand or a Redford, someone the audience can identify with!" Brooks, pushed to the brink as he watches a year's worth of work going down the drain, begins to crack. The last straw comes when Grodin and McCain decide that to save their marriage they will have to abandon the project. Half-crazed, Brooks decides to pull one last stunt to gain some usable footage—he sets the house on fire. ("What are they gonna do? Put me in movie jail?") REAL LIFE was obviously inspired by the PBS television documentary "American Family," which followed the lives of the Loud family and led to the couple's divorce. At the time of that program's airing, critics and psychologists debated whether the cameras present in the household contributed to the collapse of the family, and questioned whether the documentary merely *recorded* the events, or, in fact, *caused* them. Brooks borrowed the basic premise and took it one step further by having a Hollywood lunatic in charge of the project. Not only is REAL LIFE a biting and insightful look at the influence of media on our lives, but it is also one of the most hysterical looks at filmmaking ever put on screen. Dozens of bits regarding the shooting of Brooks' film hit home. His cameramen wear diving-bell type head gear containing camera and microphone, which transforms the men into bug-eyed robots whose faces no one ever sees. At the beginning of the film, Brooks introduces Grodin's family to nearly 20 members of the film crew (makeup, lighting, grip, Teamsters), all of whom are unnecessary due to advanced technology: ". . .but the union says we have to pay these people anyway, so have a nice vacation. See you guys at the premiere!" With REAL LIFE, Brooks pushed his way into the forefront of American comedy and his two subsequent films, MODERN ROMANCE and LOST IN AMERICA, are each just as insightful and funny as his first.

p, Penelope Spheeris; d, Albert Brooks; w, Brooks, Monica Johnson, Harry Shearer; ph, Eric Saarinen (Panavision); m, Mort Lindsey; ed, David Finfer; art d, Linda Spheeris, Linda Marder.

Comedy **Cas. (PR:C MPAA:PG)**

REAP THE WILD WIND*½** (1942) 124m PAR c

Ray Milland *(Stephen Tolliver)*, John Wayne *(Capt. Jack Stuart)*, Paulette Goddard *(Loxi Claiborne)*, Raymond Massey *(King Cutler)*, Robert Preston *(Dan Cutler)*, Lynne Overman *(Capt. Phillip Philpott)*, Susan Hayward *(Drusilla Alston)*, Charles Bickford *(Mate of the "Tyfib")*, Walter Hampden *(Commodore Devereaux)*, Louise Beavers *(Maum Maria)*, Martha O'Driscoll *(Ivy Devereaux)*, Elisabeth Risdon *(Mrs. Claiborne)*, Hedda Hopper *(Aunt Henrietta)*, Victor Kilian *(Widgeon)*, Oscar Polk *(Salt Meat)*, Janet Beacher *(Mrs. Mottram)*, Ben Carter *(Chinkapin)*, Wee Willie [William] Davis *(The Lamb)*, Lane Chandler *(Sam)*, Davison Clark *(Judge Marvin)*, Frank M. Thomas *(Dr. Jepson)*, Keith Richards *(Capt. Carruthers)*, J. Farrell Macdonald *(Port Captain)*, Victor Varconi *(Lubbock)*, Harry Woods *(Mace)*, Raymond Hatton *(Master Shipwright)*, Milburn Stone *(Lt. Farragut)*, Barbara Britton, Julia Faye *(Charleston Ladies)*, Constantine Romanoff *(Pete of Sponge Boat)*, Nestor Paiva *(Man with Suspenders)*, James Flavin *(Father of Girl)*, Frank Lackteen, Alan Bridge, Al Ferguson *(Cutler Men in Barrel Room)*, Dick Alexander *(Stoker Boss)*, Byron Foulger *(Bixby, Devereaux Courier)*, Dorothy Sebastian *(Woman in Ballroom)*, Jack Luden *(Southern Gentleman at Tea)*, Monte Blue *(Officer at Tea)*, Dale Van Sickel *(Roy, Member of Falcon Crew)*, Leo Sulky, Cap Anderson, Sam Appel, Harry Dean, Billy Elmer *(Jurymen)*, Mildred Harris *(Dancing Lady)*, John Saint Polis *(Devereaux Agent)*, Eugene Jackson *(Dr. Jepson's Boy)*, Stanhope Wheatcroft *(Devereaux Secretary)*, Claire McDowell *(Ettie)*, Fred Graham *(Jake)*, Dave Wengren *("Claiborne" Lookout)*, Tony Patton *(Cadge)*, D'Arcy Miller, Bruce Warren *(Charleston Gentlemen)*, Frank Ferguson *(Snaith, Cutler's Co-Counsel)*, William Haade *(Seaman, 1st Wreck)*, Stanley Andrews *(Jailer)*, Davidson Clarke *(Judge Marvin)*, George Reed *(Servant at Mottram House)*.

Memorable DeMille epic of the high seas which sports a top-notch cast, glorious Technicolor photography, and a giant red squid! Set in the 1840s when tall ships were being replaced by steam engines, the film opens as tough and independent woman salvage-schooner owner Goddard ventures her ship out in a hurricane to try to save Wayne, whose ship has been wrecked on the shoals of Key West, Florida. When Goddard gets near the crippled vessel she finds the exhausted Wayne lashed to the mast with Massey, her vicious competitor in the salvage business, already there. Massey and his younger brother Preston seem to have an uncanny knack for being the first at a wreck and some suspect they are in cahoots with dishonorable captains. Since Massey and his crew have dibs on the sinking ship, Goddard tends to the weakened Wayne and nurses him back to health. During this period of convalescence, the pair grow close and begin to fall in love. Wayne frets that the sinking of his ship will cost him the helm of his company's new steamship, but Goddard promises to travel to the company headquarters in Charleston, South Carolina, and convince the investigators that pirates were responsible for the wreck. In Charleston Goddard meets with the company lawyer, Milland, and relates the story. Though he has Wayne's approved commission papers, Milland is ordered to go to Florida and confirm the story before handing them over. Learning of Milland's arrival, Massey recognizes the threat to his shady operation and tries to shanghai both the lawyer and Wayne and toss them on a whaling boat that won't see shore for three years. The two men fight off Massey's goons in a violent struggle (character actor Kilian lost an eye to Wayne during the scene and later remarked: "It was not his fault, but I don't like him. Not for what he did but for the person he is."), but Wayne's commission papers fall out of Milland's pocket during the scuffle and Wayne thinks the lawyer is trying to sabotage his career and steal the affections of Goddard. Angry and hurt, Wayne makes a deal with Massey to wreck the new steamboat. Through no fault of his own, the ship strikes rocks while shrouded in a dense fog and sinks. Wayne is brought up on charges and at his trial it is revealed that Hayward, Preston's young girl friend, had stowed away on the ship and was drowned. Before murder is added to the list of charges against Wayne, the court adjourns to the wreck site and waits while Wayne and Milland go down in diving suits to find any evidence to indicate that the missing girl was aboard. A scarf is found, but before the men return to the surface, a giant squid attacks Milland and threatens to strangle him. Faced with a moral dilemma—letting Milland die would solve all his problems—Wayne nobly cuts the beast's tentacles and frees his rival, only to be caught in the squid's grip himself and die. Milland returns to the surface and tells of Wayne's brave deed. When he produces the scarf, the grief-stricken Preston accuses his brother of piracy. Massey shoots Preston, and then is himself killed by Milland. As Goddard comforts the dying Preston, it is obvious that she and Milland will never forget the bravery of Wayne. Given a typically lavish production by DeMille on a budget of $2 million, $12,000 of which went to the construction of the bright red mechanical squid which was made of rubber and manipulated with a complex series of hydraulic pistons and steel cables that enabled the creature to move its tentacles in any position. The squid scene was the popular highlight of the movie and was much talked about. Six years later Wayne would do battle with another rubber sea monster, an octopus, in Republic Studio's WAKE OF THE RED WITCH, a film which bears a remarkable resemblance to REAP THE WILD WIND—the big difference being that Wayne survives his battle with the tentacled monster in the 1948 film. REAP THE WILD WIND was a big hit at the box office and garnered Oscar nominations for Art and Set Direction and Cinematography, and was awarded an Oscar for special effects. The film gave Wayne the last nudge to full-fledged stardom and helped Hayworth's career considerably. When the film was re-released in 1954, the poster art and billing were changed to capitalize on the super-star status of both Wayne and Hayward, who had since surpassed Milland and Goddard in popularity. A sad note, character actor Kilian, who suffered under the anti-Communist blacklisting during the McCarthy era although he was never called to testify before the House Un-American Activities Committee, was mysteriously murdered in his home in Los Angeles in 1979 by an unknown assailant who beat the 88-year-old widower to death while he was watching television.

p&d, Cecil B. DeMille; w, Alan LeMay, Charles Bennett, Jesse Lasky, Jr., (uncredited) Jeanie Macpherson (based on a story by Thelma Strabel); ph, Victor Milner, William V. Skall (Technicolor); m, Victor Young; ed, Anne Bauchens; art d, Hans Dreier, Roland Anderson; spec eff, Gordon Jennings, W.L. Pereira, Farciot Edouart, Dewey Wrigley.

Drama **(PR:A MPAA:NR)**

REAR WINDOW***** (1954) 112m PAR c

James Stewart *(L.B. "Jeff" Jeffries)*, Grace Kelly *(Lisa Carol Fremont)*, Wendell Corey *(Detective Thomas J. Doyle)*, Thelma Ritter *(Stella)*, Raymond Burr *(Lars Thorwald)*, Judith Evelyn *(Miss Lonely Hearts)*, Ross Bagdasarian [David Seville] *(Songwriter)*, Georgine Darcy *(Miss Torso)*, Sara Berner *(Woman on Fire Escape)*, Frank Cady *(Fire Escape Man)*, Jesslyn Fax *(Miss Hearing Aid)*, Rand Harper *(Honeymooner)*, Irene Winston *(Mrs. Thorwald)*, Harris Davenport *(Newlywed)*, Marla English, Kathryn Grandstaff [Grant] *(Party Girls)*, Alan Lee *(Landlord)*, Anthony Warde *(Detective)*, Benny Bartlett *(Miss Torso's Friend)*, Edwin Parker, Fred Graham *(Stunt Detectives)*, Barbara Bailey *(Choreographer)*, Bess Flowers *(Woman with Poodle)*, Iphigenie Castiglioni *(Bird Woman)*, Ralph Smiley *(Carl the Waiter)*, Harry Landers *(Young Man)*, Dick Simmons *(Man)*, Alfred Hitchcock *(Butler in Songwriter's Apartment)*, Jerry Antes *(Dancer)*, Mike Mahoney, Len Hendry *(Policemen)*, James A. Cornell *(Man)*.

This taut chiller from Hitchcock is a superb example of how to make a film on one set and still make the viewer feel free of claustrophobia and totally engrossed with a wheelchair-bound victim who is desperately trying to solve a murder no one seems to believe happened. Stewart, one of the director's favorite leading players, is simply terrific as a magazine photographer, a man of action, who has had an accident and broken his left leg and is confined to his Greenwich Village apartment. Now he must passively sit back and be content with the mundane day-to-day activities he views from the rear window of his apartment through field glasses and the telescopic lens of his camera. His window looks out on a back court area showing a small garden and the back areas of other apartment buildings. His neighbors are conspicuously unconscious of their own vulnerability to Stewart's constant gaze. He watches housewives, newlyweds (the only persons who actually draw the shades on *their* rear windows), a composer in a posh apartment, a lonely woman he dubs Miss Lonely Hearts, a Broadway ballerina, and, of particular interest to Stewart, Burr, who lives with a shrewish wife. Visiting Stewart is a beautiful cool blonde, Kelly, who is a high-fashion model desperately in love with him. Stewart is also visited regularly by wise-cracking practical nurse Ritter, who attends to his needs and scolds him for his Peeping Tom ways. This, of all Hitchcock films, is an exercise in grand voyeurism; where the sneaky Peeping Tomism practiced by Tony Perkins in PSYCHO is perverse, Stewart's is innocent in that he doesn't spy on people to seek self-stimulation. It's his job to study and photograph people as well as his total passion. Stewart, to while away the time, takes more and more interest in Burr, who can be seen walking through the length of his apartment—kitchen, living room, bedroom—arguing with his wife, who suspects him of cheating on her. Unable to sleep the following night, Stewart sees Burr leave his apartment at 2 a.m., carrying his salesman's suitcase. The following day he grows even more suspicious when he sees that the blinds to Burr's bedroom are drawn and nowhere can Burr's wife be seen. He alerts Kelly and Ritter to the situation and when he observes Burr wrapping a saw and a large carving knife in a newspaper the following evening, he, Kelly, and Ritter are now convinced that foul play has been enacted. Stewart calls his old friend Corey, a laconic plainclothes cop who visits with him and Kelly, patiently hearing out their story and then pooh-poohing the whole possibility that salesman Burr has murdered and then hacked up his wife. To placate Stewart, Corey promises to look into the man's background and recent activities. He later calls to tell Stewart to mind his own business and leave the solving of crimes to the professionals. Stewart is now convinced, however, that Burr has indeed killed his wife, especially after Kelly boldly gets in and out of Burr's apartment to find some incriminating evidence—his wife's wedding ring and some jewelry, items no woman would merely discard when leaving a husband. Returning to Burr's apartment for more evidence, Kelly, as Stewart can plainly see, is trapped when Burr unexpectedly returns. He calls the police and has them rush to the apartment, where Kelly is arrested for breaking and entering; but she is safe, even though taken off to jail. By then Burr is on to Stewart, seeing him across the backyard space, and he invades Stewart's apartment a short time later, with Stewart helpless in his wheelchair. At first the photographer attempts to blind the myopic Burr by squeezing off flashbulbs from his camera in the apartment that Stewart has purposely kept dark, but the man still fumbles forward and he and Stewart struggle, with the heavyset Burr dragging the invalid photographer to the window where he attempts to throw him out. Stewart clings to the ledge while shouting and the police, led by Corey, arrive, but seconds too late as Stewart plunges downward two floors. Burr is apprehended and Stewart survives to solidify his relationship with Kelly, but not without paying a penalty for his prying curiosity. In the last frames of the film he is shown still bound to a wheelchair, this time with *two* broken legs, the right leg having been fractured in the fall. Stewart is exactly right for the role of the meddling photographer, expressing a rather wordly view of life tinged with the annoyance of being cooped up with a bad leg while Kelly is radiant and restrained but lavishes in little ways—mostly seeing to Stewart's creature comforts—her love for him. She is also wise and witty, something few Hitchcock heroines are ever allowed to be. At one point she realizes that she and Stewart are actually disappointed that Burr may not have killed his wife, given some new evidence they have formulated, and quips: "I'm not much on rear window ethics but we're two of the most frightening ghouls I have ever known." Visually, REAR WINDOW is a treat, with the brilliant Hitchcock using his character's profession to capture slice-of-life views without disturbing the central tension-filled story. Interspersed between the mounting segments of the remote murder investigation the viewer sees the composer, Bagdasarian, have a smash hit, then a failure, and then enjoy a rediscovery. The apprentice ballerina, Darcy—a bit on the voluptuous side, a lady Stewart dubs Miss Torso—runs through a bevy of suitors, rejecting the tuxedoed rich men and opting for the returning serviceman. There is something reminiscent about this scene which suggests the classic magazine image of the returning soldier coming toward the back stairs of the tenement building with his jubilant family and neighbors popping out of windows and doors painted by Norman Rockwell. In fact, many of Rockwell's homey and powerful portraits dealt with the backside of tenements and it is not inconceivable that Hitchcock—if not the creator of the tale, Woolrich—took the overall portrait and applied it to REAR WINDOW. But this does not detract from the masterpiece film Hitchcock produced. As usual, he was concerned with every detail to authenticate his characters, story, and setting. The set itself is full of noises, those of the day and those of the night, mixed with a clever, on-and-off Waxman score. With as little explanation as possible, the director immediately tells the viewer how Stewart came to be confined to his wheelchair, his first shots panning from Stewart's face to his broken leg, then to a broken camera on the table, and then photographs on the wall showing a speeding race car and smash-ups. It is obvious that the hero is an action photographer who has had an accident while at the track. Suspense is captured quickly when Stewart resolves to become an investigator with his camera, turning off lights and shrinking back into the shadows to seriously study Burr with his telephoto lens since his own windows are wide open and he, too, can be seen. The suspense heightens when Kelly is seen by the viewer and Stewart inside Burr's apartment, searching the bedroom, while the culprit is coming through the hallway—also seen through a window—and is about to enter the apartment and discover the snooping Kelly. The first inclination the viewer has is identical to that of Stewart, which is to shout, "Hurry up, get out of there! He's coming, hurry, escape, escape!" This is intense visual tension at the high water mark Hitchcock so consistently hit. Like ROPE, which was all shot in one set with continuous takes that still baffle most filmgoers, REAR WINDOW was a magnificent city scene of back porches and windows and balconies that were made up of a realistic-looking set, the director's kind of structure, all his and all controllable and therefore more easily conforming to his own images and action—like every one of his films—he had in preproduction sketched out with his own slender stick-drawings of every scene. He beat the critics to the punch, knowing he would be accused of shamelessly promoting voyeurism, and had the snappy Ritter condemn Stewart's natural (and in his case healthy) curiousity by stating: "We've become a race of Peeping Toms. People ought to get outside and look in at themselves." She is a woman who has an instinct for impending problems and says so: "I can smell trouble right here in this apartment...Look out the window, see things you shouldn't see." And look out the window the viewer does, having the same single and mounting terrifying perspective as does Stewart. Although confining, the set is nowhere as limiting as the one the director was constrained to use in LIFEBOAT (1944), but it was still a challenge for Hitchcock to come up with a real thriller out of a normal backyard setting. He loved such problems, perferring to "box myself in and then figure a way out." He was also very happy with his stars. Stewart performed superbly for him in the remake of THE MAN WHO KNEW TOO MUCH, ROPE, and, to come, VERTIGO. Kelly was Hitchcock's kind of icy blonde with a voice as soft as pudding but with a truck driver's determination. Kelly appeared in Hitchcock's DIAL M FOR MURDER and he early on grew to like her. At one point during the production of that film, Kelly overheard the director telling some raw stories to Ray Milland, who starred with Bob Cummings. Hitchcock turned to her and said, "Are you shocked, Miss Kelly?" She shook her pretty head and replied: "No, I went to a girl's convent school, Mr. Hitchcock. I heard all those things when I was thirteen." This delighted the director as much as Kelly's deep acting ability. She would go on to be one of his favorite leading ladies and appear in TO CATCH A THIEF where Hitchcock would lose her to a Prince Ranier of Monaco while the film was shooting on location on the French Riviera. For REAR WINDOW—which was Hitchcock's favorite film next to SHADOW OF A DOUBT—the director personally supervised the construction of the 31 full-scale apartments on the biggest set ever constructed at Paramount. "We had 12 of those apartments completely furnished," Hitchcock later commented. "We could never have gotten them properly lit in a real location." Stewart later remarked: "The whole production of REAR WINDOW went so very smoothly. The set and every part of the film were (sic) so well designed, and he [Hitchcock] felt so comfortable with everyone associated with it, that we all felt confident about its success." Hitchcock and Stewart had such a fine relationship that the director indulged himself by showing how genius editing could mold the image of an actor. He showed Stewart one scene of the actor with an expression on his face and then a shot of a half-naked woman, suggesting that Stewart was a leering and lascivious creature. The same expression was then out against a shot of a small baby, which reflected a completely different image of Stewart, one which now revealed tenderness and concern. "It's all in the editing," Hitchcock later told his star. (This trick had earlier been used by Soviet film theorist Lev Kuleshov.) As with most of his female leads, Hitchcock selected every gown worn by Kelly in

REAR WINDOW, telling costumer Head exactly what color would work best in each scene. "He was really putting a dream together in the studio," said Head. Even Kelly's shoes were selected by the director, and he studied her bustline and told Head to put "falsies" into her dress. Head and Kelly retired to the dressing room, where Kelly refused to have her bosom padded. She made some adjustments of her dress "and stood as straight as possible, without falsies," Head later reporter. When Kelly emerged, having done little to enlarge the appearance of her breasts but standing erect and jutting herself forward slightly, Hitchcock beamed and said: "See what a difference they make." This film, as well as ROPE, THE TROUBLE WITH HARRY, and VERTIGO, was taken out of distribution because of Hitchcock's proprietorship and studio squabbling but re-released in 1968 (yet another re-release took place in 1983, three years after the director's death). The ad campaign that accompanied the 1968 re-release of REAR WINDOW was actually written by Hitchcock and reflected his dark humor. One blurb ran, "REAR WINDOW is such a frightening picture that one should never see it unless accompanied by an audience." (This in the days before cassette viewing.) Another read, "If you do not experience delicious terror when you see REAR WINDOW, then pinch yourself—you are most probably dead."

p&d, Alfred Hitchcock; w, John Michael Hayes (based on the story by Cornell Woolrich); ph, Robert Burks (Technicolor); m, Franz Waxman; ed, George Tomasini; art d, Hal Pereira, Joseph McMillan Johnson; set d, Sam Comer, Ray Mayer; cos, Edith Head; spec eff, John P. Fulton.

Suspense/Thriller Cas. (PR:C MPAA:NR)

REASON TO LIVE, A REASON TO DIE, A*½ (1974, Ital./Fr./Ger./Span.) 92m Heritage-Sancropsiap-Terza-Europrodis-Corona-Atlantida/K-Tel c (UNA RAGIONE PER VIVERE E UNA PER MORIRE; AKA: MASSACRE AT FORT HOLMAN)

James Coburn *(Col. Pembroke)*, Telly Savalas *(Maj. Ward)*, Bud Spencer *(Eli Sampson)*, Ralph Goodwin *(Sgt. Brent)*, Joseph Mitchell *(Maj. Ballard)*, William Spofford *(Ted Wendel)*, Guy Ranson *(Will Fernandez)*, Joe Pollini *(Half-breed)*, Allan Leroy *(Confederate Sergeant)*, Robert Burton *(Donald MacIvers)*.

Yankee colonel Coburn turns over his fort to Confederate soldiers for no apparent reason, and (a la THE DIRTY DOZEN and THE MAGNIFICENT SEVEN) organizes a group of soldiers sentenced to death to get the fort back. A blood bath ensues, during which Coburn and company wreak havoc with a couple of Gatling guns. The only survivors are Savalas, a Confederate major, and Coburn and Spencer. Of all places to show a bunch of no-goods taking apart a Confederate army, this picture made its U.S. debut in Atlanta.

p, Michael Billingsley; d, Tonino Valerii; w, Valerii, Ernesto Gastaldi; m, Riz Ortolani.

Western Cas. (PR:A MPAA:PG)

REASONABLE DOUBT*½ (1936, Brit.) 73m Pascal/MGM bw

John Stuart *(Noel Hampton)*, Nancy Burne *(Pat)*, Ivan Brandt *(Tony)*, Marjorie Taylor, Marie Lohr, Clifford Heatherley, H. F. Maltby, Cecil Humphreys, Fred Duprez, Cynthia Stock.

A farfetched melodrama about a lawyer who falls in love with a girl he meets, and agrees to take her fiance's case. It turns out that the fiance is really the lawyer's son, and an embarrassing reunion is had by all.

p, Gabriel Pascal; d, George King; w, Edwart Brooks.

Drama (PR:A MPAA:NR)

REBECCA**** (1940) 130m SELZ/UA bw

Laurence Olivier *(Maxim de Winter)*, Joan Fontaine *(Mrs. de Winter)*, George Sanders *(Jack Favell)*, Judith Anderson *(Mrs. Danvers)*, Nigel Bruce *(Maj. Giles Lacy)*, C. Aubrey Smith *(Col. Julyan)*, Reginald Denny *(Frank Crawley)*, Gladys Cooper *(Beatrice Lacy)*, Philip Winter *(Robert)*, Edward Fielding *(Frith)*, Florence Bates *(Mrs. Van Hopper)*, Melville Cooper *(Coroner)*, Leo G. Carroll *(Dr. Baker)*, Forrester Harvey *(Chalcroft)*, Lumsden Hare *(Tabbs)*, Leonard Carey *(Ben)*, Alfred Hitchcock *(Man Outside Phone Booth)*, Billy Bevan *(Policeman)*, Leyland Hodgson *(Chauffeur)*.

Hitchcock had been making one magnificent suspense film after another in England and was already famous among American filmgoers when Selznick brought him to Hollywood to direct du Maurier's eerie novel, REBECCA. Selznick believed Hitchcock would produce another THE 39 STEPS or THE LADY VANISHES, but REBECCA turned into something altogether different, however no less fascinating, a psychological thriller that established Hitchcock once and for all with American audiences. Fontaine, who narrates her own perilous story, is a shy but attractive young lady who meets urbane and handsome Olivier when both are vacationing on the Riviera. Following thier quick marriage, the couple return to England and Olivier's vast estate, Manderley. Fontaine is introduced to an army of servants who immediately, though subtly, display hostility toward her. Especially ice-cold toward Olivier's second wife is housekeeper Anderson, who lurks about in long dark hallways and suddenly appears before a considerably frightened Fontaine from dark rooms and shadowy archways, always to correct the new mistress of the manor in her failing ways and to remind her of what a splendid woman her predecessor was, the beautiful and mysterious Rebecca, since deceased. There hangs in the great hall an oil portrait of this woman, one that intrigues and then begins to haunt Fontaine. Though she probes for information about Olivier's first wife, the servants and distant neighbors offer little but more mystery and Olivier's attitude toward Fontaine turns frosty whenever she brings up Rebecca. So vexed by the pervasive image of the dead wife is Fontaine that she begins to believe she is being haunted by the woman and is losing her sanity. She also begins to doubt Olivier's love for her. Anderson is always on hand to make Fontaine uneasy, then fearful, the housekeeper then launching a psychological campaign to compel Fontaine to commit suicide and she comes very close to doing it. But drastic revelations occur when Rebecca's boat is disgorged by the ocean after a storm and her body is discovered, along with the fact that the vessel was scuttled intentionally. Sanders, a money-seeking conniver, concludes that Rebecca had been murdered and begins the systematic blackmailing of Olivier who is finally forced to admit to Fontaine the truth. He tells her that Rebecca was anything but the wonderful, beautiful person held so dear by Anderson and others. She was a cruel, vicious, and cuckolding creature who drove him half mad, Olivier states, by insisting that she was pregnant with another man's child. He struck her and she accidentally hit her head and was killed, confesses Olivier, and then, to cover the act, he took Rebecca's body to their boat and sank it, claiming later that his first wife was lost at sea during a storm. Now the whole ugly story is about to explode but Olivier is exonerated when it is learned that Rebecca had known all along that she was soon to die of cancer and provoked her husband to strike her down, trying to destroy him, too. Before any more secrets about the hideous Rebecca can be learned, Anderson sets fire to Manderley and walks through the cavernous mansion as the flames lick at her skirts, dedicated to burning with the memory of a mistress she intends to preserve into eternity. Olivier and Fontaine watch as the great building is completely consumed by fire and Anderson with it, then resolve to make a new and happy life together. Aiding Hitchcock—not that he needed much help—was a great, eerie score by Franz Waxman, a composer Hitchcock would use again and again with great effect, and wonderfully moody cinematography by Barnes. Hitchcock took such careful pains with this film that his mannered pace disturbed producer Selznick. The film cost $1 million and that unsettled the producer, although he had heralded the film as being produced on the same costly level as his immortal GONE WITH THE WIND. (He went out of his way to make sure that the Manderley fire certainly appeared to equal the burning of Atlanta in GWTW, even though most of the blaze was done in miniature.) He also tried to duplicate the talent hunt stunt he had so successfully employed for GWTW, causing a search for the leading lady to be conducted throughout the nation. He wanted Loretta Young to play the haunted second wife but this notion was discarded and then Olivier, who was selected for his role after Ronald Colman refused it, urged the producer to put his wife, Vivien Leigh, in the role. She either refused the part or Selznick thought she would not do as a modest and shy character, depending upon which report one wishes to believe. But it is hard to think that Selznick would turn down his greatest living asset and star after Leigh had become an overnight sensation in GWTW. Other leading ladies were suggested—Margaret Sullavan, Olivia de Havilland, and Anne Baxter—but 22-year-old Fontaine was ultimately selected for the part. Though she had a reputation as the "wooden woman" and had only appeared in a half-dozen programmers, Fontaine was given the role at Selznick's insistence, even though *both* Hitchcock and Olivier did not want her. Hitchcock's script bothered Selznick right from the beginning. He felt the director was indulging himself with scenes not pertinent to the film nor relevant to the original story. In one scene Hitchcock had Olivier smoking a cigar on board ship en route to the Riviera and this causes several passengers to vomit. The director was merely dealing with a personal fixation here with motion sickness. Selznick did not find the exercise amusing, writing to Hitchcock (they mostly communicated through memos throughout the production): "I think the scenes of the seasickness are cheap beyond words, and old-fashioned in the bargain. We bought *Rebecca* and we intend to make *Rebecca*, not a distorted and vulgarized version of a provenly successful work." Hitchcock, who was always skirting the Hollywood censor, altered the original story so that Olivier did not appear an outright murderer (which his character in the novel certainly is), by making the death of Rebecca accidental. Hitchcock was summoned on one occasion to Selznick's home and ordered to work on the script with Sherwood. The famous playwright mostly drank and sailed little boats in the producer's swimming pool during the session which exhausted Hitchcock and produced very little copy. "I had a dim recollection of trying to keep awake at 3 a.m. in the producer's summer house," he later said. Selznick later carped about Hitchcock's imperialistic manner and his sly way of demeaning those working with him in an offhand manner, passing little comments about their lethargy or drinking habits. Said Selznick: "I will not pretend that Mr. Hitchcock always was the most consistently amiable of human creatures, nor will I evade that he delighted in needling those around him. He needled stars, staff, press agents, any and all." His way of handling the novice Fontaine was to keep her always on edge and unsure of her position. He would take her aside before she would do an important scene and, according to the actress, whisper in her ear: "Now kid, you go in there and you do this and that...Do you know what so-and-so said about you today? Do you know that Olivier doesn't want you in this role? Well, never you mind, you just listen to me." That Hitchcock and Selznick were bound to clash was a certainty, though the director was on a salary. Each man was a determined and creative genius who wanted the film to project *his* interpretation and *his* stamp of identity. Selznick, as usual, won. Oddly, both producer and director argued politely with each other about Olivier whom Selznick disliked as an actor and Hitchcock admired. In one memo Selznick wrote to the director: "His pauses and spacing in the scene with the girl in which she tells him about the ball are the most ungodly, slow, and deliberate reactions I have ever seen. It is played as though he were deciding whether or not to run for President instead of whether or not to give a ball." Despite Selznick's misgivings, REBECCA was a smash hit and established Hitchcock as a premiere director of American-produced film. He would only go upward from here.

p, David O. Selznick; d, Alfred Hitchcock; w, Robert E. Sherwood, Joan Harrison (based on the novel by Daphne du Maurier, adapted by Philip MacDonald, Michael Hogan); ph, George Barnes; m, Franz Waxman; ed, James Newdom, Hal Kern; art d, Lyle Wheeler.

Suspense Cas. (PR:C MPAA:NR)

REBECCA OF SUNNYBROOK FARM** (1932) 75m FOX bw

Marian Nixon *(Rebecca)*, Ralph Bellamy *(Dr. Ladd)*, Mae Marsh *(Aunt Jane)*, Louise Closser Hale *(Aunt Miranda)*, Alphonz Ethier *(Mr. Cobb)*, Sarah Padden *(Mrs. Cobb)*, Alan Hale *(Mr. Simpson)*, Eula Guy *(Mrs. Simpson)*, Charlotte Henry *(Emma Jane)*, Claire McDowell *(Mrs. Randall)*, Ronald Harris *(Jack-O-Lantern)*,

Willis Marks (*Jacob*), Lucille Ward (*Pig Woman*), Tommy Conlon (*John Randall*), Wally Albright (*Billy Randall*).

Film adaptation of the famous story that Mary Pickford took a shot at in a silent effort back in 1917. This one casts Nixon as the girl who goes to stay on her aunt's farm, and succeeds in entering and changing the lives of several people in the community. Produced and performed in a routine fashion, with only Hale showing anything beyond the typically mundane. Janet Gaynor originally had been selected to play the title character, and Bellamy substituted for Charles Farrell, initially picked for the role of Dr. Ladd.

d, Alfred Santell; w, S.N. Behrman, Sonya Levien (based on the novel by Kate Douglas Wiggin, and the play "Rebecca of Sunnybrook Farm, a State O'Maine Play in Four Acts" by Wiggin, Charlotte Thompson); ph, Glenn MacWilliams; ed, Ralph Dietrich; art d, Duncan Cramer.

Drama   **(PR:A MPAA:NR)**

REBECCA OF SUNNYBROOK FARM**   (1938) 80m FOX bw

Shirley Temple (*Rebecca Winstead*), Randolph Scott (*Anthony Kent*), Jack Haley (*Orville Smithers*), Gloria Stuart (*Gwen Warren*), Phyllis Brooks (*Lola Lee*), Helen Westley (*Aunt Miranda Wilkins*), Slim Summerville (*Homer Busby*), Bill Robinson (*Aloysius*), J. Edward Bromberg (*Dr. Hill*), Alan Dinehart (*Purvis*), Raymond Scott Quartet (*Themselves*), Dixie Dunbar (*Receptionist*), Paul Hurst (*Mug*), William Demarest (*Henry Kipper*), Ruth Gillette (*Melba*), Paul Harvey (*Cyrus Bartlett*), Clarence Hummel Wilson (*Jake Singer*), Sam Hayes, Gary Breckner Carroll Nye (*Radio Announcers*), Franklin Pangborn (*Hamilton Montmarcy*), William Wagner (*Rev. Turner*), Eily Malyon (*Mrs. Turner*), Mary McCarty (*Florabelle*).

Basically a vehicle for Temple, the original story was twisted around to best display her talents. The young star was 10 years old at this point and her singing voice, never better, is aptly showcased in this highly contrived picture. Story has Temple staying at her aunt's farm after her uncle, Demarest, gives up on trying to get the child a radio contract. Although the aunt doesn't want anything to do with show business, who should next door neighbor Scott turn out to be but a talent scout. All Temple and nothing but, with the little star even going so far as performing a medley of her earlier hit tunes including, "On the Good Ship Lollipop," "When I'm with You," and "Animal Crackers." Other songs include: "Crackly Corn Flakes," "Alone with You," "Happy Ending," "Au Revoir" (Sidney Mitchell, Lew Pollack); "An Old Straw Hat" (Mack Gordon, Harry Revel) and "Come and Get Your Happiness" (Jack Yellen, Samuel Pokrass). Temple and Robinson also dance to "Parade of the Wooden Soldiers" (Mitchell, Pollack, Raymond Scott).

p, Raymond Griffith; d, Allan Dwan; w, Karl Tunberg, Don Ettlinger (based on the novel by Kate Douglas Wiggin, and the play "Rebecca of Sunnybrook Farm, a State O'Maine Play in Four Acts," by Wiggin, Charlotte Thompson); ph, Arthur Miller; ed, Allen McNeil, md, Arthur Lange; art d, Bernard Herzbrun, Hans Peters; set d, Thomas Little.

Musical   Cas.   **(PR:AAA MPAA:NR)**

REBEL, THE**   (1933, Ger.) 73m UNIV bw

Luis Trenker (*Severin Anderlan*), Vilma Banky (*Erika Riederer*), Victor Varconi (*Capt. Leroy*), Paul Bildt (*Magistrate Riederer*), Olga Engl (*Anderlan's Mother*), Erika Dannhoff (*Anderlan's Sister*), Arthur Grosse (*Gen. Elliott*), Reinhold Bernt (*George Bird*), Emmerich Albert (*John Haskell*), Luis Gerold (*Samuel Fields*), Hans Jannig (*Louis Klein*).

In the early 1930s Universal planned to produce a series of features in Germany. This was the first of the undertakings and, because of the political situation, the last. Directed, written, and performed by the prolific Trenker, it's a pretty shaky story about the advancement of Napoleon through the Tyrol region of Germany. Trenker gathers up his countrymen to fight the approaching army, only to meet a heroic but certain death. Script offers far too much dialog, with little action. The movie also features the use of silent film technique. The photography is quite good, and Trenker proves himself a highly talented actor.

d&w, Luis Trenker, Edwin H. Knopf; ph, Sepp Algier, Albert Behnitz, Willi Goldberger; m, Dr. Giuseppe Becce; ed, Andrew Marton.

War/Drama   **(PR:A MPAA:NR)**

REBEL, THE   (SEE: CALL ME GENIUS, 1961, Brit.)

REBEL ANGEL*½   (1962) 96m Greyhawk Studios/Hoffman c

Patricia Manning, Richard Flynn, Tom Falk, Denny Ross.

High school student Manning has a problem on her hands—which boy to choose. She must decide whether to stick it out with her regular beau, who seems to take her for granted, or go for the mature college man. But before she can make up her mind, her boy friend murders the child Manning has been babysitting for. The college boy decides he's had enough, and splits.

p, James J. Gannon; d, Lamont Douglas; w, Denny Ross, Elliott Tyne; ph, E.H. Witt (DeLuxe Color); m, The Stardusters.

Drama   **(PR:C MPAA:NR)**

REBEL CITY*½   (1953) 62m Silvermine/AA bw

Wild Bill Elliott (*Frank Graham*), Marjorie Lord (*Jane Dudley*) Robert Kent (*Capt. Ramsey*), Keith Richards (*Temple*), I. Stanford Jolley (*Perry*), Denver Pyle (*Greeley*), Henry Rowland (*Hardy*), John Crawford (*Spencer*), Otto Waldis (*Spain*), Stanley Price (*Herb*), Ray Walker (*Col. Barnes*), Michael Vallon (*Sam*), Bill Walker (*William*).

Weak story set during the Civil War casts Elliott as a gambler who returns home to seek revenge against his father's killers. He attempts to seek aid through the local Union Army, but is rebuffed due to increased attention to activities of Confederate sympathizers. Elliott undertakes his own search, only to discover the sympathizers

are responsible for his father's murder. Elliott's performance is unconvincing, and direction and other facets of production are far below par.

p, Vincent M. Fennelly; d, Thomas Carr; w, Sidney Theil; ph, Ernest Miller (Sepiatone); m, Raoul Kraushaar; ed, Sam Fields; art d, David Milton.

Western   **(PR:A MPAA:NR)**

REBEL GLADIATORS, THE**   (1963, Ital.) 98m Splendor Film/Medallion c (URSUS GLADIATORE RIBELLE; URSUS, IL GLADIATORE RIBELLE)

Dan Vadis (*Ursus*), Jose Greci (*Commodus*), Gloria Milland (*Arminia*), Alan Steel [Sergio Ciani], Andrea Aureli, Gianni Santuccio, Carlo Delmi, Tullio Altamura, Pietro Ceccarelli, Consalvo Dell'Arti, Marco Mariani, Claudio Marzulli, Bruno Sc1poni.

After the death of the Emperor Marcus Aurelius, Greci takes the throne of Rome. A cruel man who wrongly oppresses innocent barbarians, he abducts the gladiator Vadis' mistress. Greci and Vadis battle in the arena, and Greci is badly beaten. Vadis then joins a rebel army that seeks to overthrow the evil ruler.

p, Ignazio Luceri; d, Domenico Paolella; w, Sergio Sollima, Alessandro Ferrau, Paolella; ph, Carlo Bellero (Techniscope, Eastmancolor); m, Carlo Savina; art d, Alfredo Montori.

War/Drama   **(PR:A MPAA:NR)**

REBEL IN TOWN***   (1956) 78m Bel-Air/UA bw

John Payne (*John Willoughby*), Ruth Roman (*Nora Willoughby*), J. Carrol Naish (*Bedloe Mason*), Ben Cooper (*Gray Mason*), John Smith (*Wesley Mason*), James Griffith (*Adam Russell*), Mary Adams (*Grandmaw Anstadt*), Bobby Clark (*Petey Willoughby*), Mimi Gibson (*Lisbeth Anstadt*), Sterling Franck (*Cain Mason*), Joel Ashley (*Doctor*), Ben Johnson (*Frank Mason*).

Suspenseful drama set in the West has Naish and his four sons as Confederate soldiers making a break for it shortly after the Civil War. When they stop to get water from a well, a young boy with a toy pistol points it at one of the sons, who shoots and kills the child. The boy's parents, Payne and Roman, seek revenge for the slaying of their son, and work up the town against the Confederate family. This leads to several violent interludes before peace is finally made. Finely scripted, produced and acted, the level of tension and frustration at the hopeless situation continually mounts to a climactic solution.

p, Howard W. Koch; d, Alfred Werker; w, Danny Arnold; ph, Gordon Avil; m, Les Baxter; ed, John F. Schreyer; m/l, Baxter, Lenny Adelson.

Western   **(PR:A MPAA:NR)**

REBEL ROUSERS½**   (1970) 78m Paragon International/Four Star Excelsior c (AKA: LIMBO)

Cameron Mitchell (*Mr. Collier*), Jack Nicholson ("*Bunny*"), Bruce Dern ("*J.J.*"), Diane Ladd (*Karen*), [Harry] Dean Stanton, Neil Burstyn, Lou Procopio, Earl Finn, Philip Carey (*The Rebels*), Robert Dix, Jim Logan, Sid Lawrence, Johnny Cardas.

A motorcycle gang, led by Dern, wreaks havoc on a small Arizona town, only to have the sheriff chase them away to the local beach. Visiting architect Mitchell, in town to meet with pregnant girl friend Ladd, takes her to the beach to discuss their problems. They meet up with the motorcyclists, who beat up Mitchell and attempt to abduct his girl friend. Dern, a former high school buddy of Mitchell, stalls the gang by suggesting a bike race be held to see who wins the girl. In the meantime, Mitchell makes his way to a local farm, where he enlists a group of Mexicans, armed with pitchforks, to come to his aid. Though REBEL ROUSERS was filmed in 1967, it wasn't released until 1970, a year after Nicholson appeared in EASY RIDER. The film marked his last outlaw biker role, and soon after he was to achieve international fame, after many years of relative obscurity as an actor in Hollywood B pictures. Also appearing as a gang member in REBEL ROUSERS was Dean Stanton, later known as Harry Dean Stanton (PARIS, TEXAS).

p&d, Martin B. Cohen; w, Abe Polsky, Michael Kars, Cohen; ph, Laszlo [Leslie] Kovacs, Glen Smith (Eastmancolor); ed, Thor Brooks.

Drama   Cas.   **(PR:O MPAA:R)**

REBEL SET, THE½**   (1959) 72m E. and L./AA bw (AKA: BEATSVILLE)

Gregg Palmer (*John Mapes*), Kathleen Crowley (*Jeanne Mapes*), Edward Platt (*Mr. Tucker*), John Lupton (*Ray Miller*), Ned Glass (*Sidney Horner*), Don Sullivan (*George Leland*), Vikki Dougan (*Karen*), I. Stanford Jolley (*King Invader*), Robert Shayne (*Lt. Cassidy*), Gloria Moreland (*Bali Dancer*), Colette Lyons (*Rita Leland*), Joe [Tiger]Marsh (*Policeman*).

With an attempt to capture the atmosphere of the "Beat Generation" of the late 1950s, yarn is just a basic crime caper, and a pretty well put together one at that. Platt is the owner of a coffeehouse who comes up with a scheme to rob an armored truck. He enlists the aid of three cohorts, Palmer, a struggling actor, Lupton, an unknown writer, and Sullivan, the son of a once famous film star. They pull the heist off, but they are captured and killed by the police. Only Palmer survives, and he turns himself in. Well acted and highly suspenseful picture, which shows a degree of inventiveness in the editing room.

p, Earle Lyon; d, Gene Fowler, Jr.; w, Lou Vittes, Bernard Girard; ph, Karl Struss; m, Paul Dunlap; ed, William Austin; art d, David Milton.

Crime   **(PR:A MPAA:NR)**

REBEL SON, THE½   (1939, Brit.) 80m Omnia-LFP/UA bw

Harry Baur (*Tarass Boulba*), Anthony Bushell (*Andrew Boulba*), Roger Livesey (*Peter Boulba*), Patricia Roc (*Marina*), Joan Gardner (*Galka*), Frederick Culley (*Prince Zammitsky*), Joseph Cunningham (*Sachka*), Stafford Hilliard (*Stutterer*), Bernard Miles (*Polish Prisoner*), Charles Farrell (*Toukatch*), Ann Wemyss (*Selima*).

A father-and-son rivalry set in the 16th Century is the premise for this failed spectacle. Baur is a Cossack leader whose attack on Poland causes his son to come to that victimized country's aid. The war wages and both Baur and his rebel son, Bushell, rank among the casualties. An English-language version of the 1936 French picture TARASS BOULBA.

p, E.C. Molinier, Charles David; d, Alexis Granowsky, Adrian Brunel, Albert de Courville; w, Brunel (based on a story by Nicolai Gogol); ph, Franz Planer, Bernard Browne; ed, William Hornbeck, Pat Wooley, Lionel Hoare.

Historical/War **(PR:A MPAA:NR)**

REBEL WITH A CAUSE (SEE: LONELINESS OF THE LONG DISTANCE RUNNER, THE, 1962, Brit.)

REBEL WITHOUT A CAUSE**** (1955) 111m WB c

James Dean *(Jim)*, Natalie Wood *(Judy)*, Sal Mineo *(Plato)*, Jim Backus *(Jim's Father)*, Ann Doran *(Jim's Mother)*, Corey Allen *(Buzz)*, William Hopper *(Judy's Father)*, Rochelle Hudson *(Judy's Mother)*, Virginia Brissac *(Jim's Grandma)*, Nick Adams *(Moose)*, Jack Simmons *(Cookie)*, Dennis Hopper *(Goon)*, Marietta Canty *(Plato's Maid)*, Jack Grinnage *(Chick)*, Beverly Long *(Helen)*, Steffi Sidney *(Mil)*, Frank Mazzola *(Crunch)*, Tom Bernard *(Harry)*, Clifford Morris *(Cliff)*, Ian Wolfe *(Lecturer)*, Edward Platt *(Ray)*, Robert Foulk *(Gene)*, Jimmy Baird *(Beau)*, Dick Wessel *(Guide)*, Nelson Leigh *(Sergeant)*, Dorothy Abbott *(Nurse)*, Louise Lane *(Woman Officer)*, House Peters *(Officer)*, Gus Schilling *(Attendant)*, Bruce Noonan *(Monitor)*, Almira Sessions *(Old Lady Teacher)*, Peter Miller *(Hoodlum)*, Paul Bryar *(Desk Sergeant)*, Paul Birch *(Police Chief)*, Robert B. Williams *(Moose's Father, Ed)*, David McMahon *(Crunch's Father)*.

In this pensive, powerful study of juvenile violence, Dean gives a riveting performance as a teenager groping for identity and love from parents, peers, and an adult society he believes to be alien and oppressive. This is the film that umbilically linked Dean to the image of the restless 1950s generation. Dean is a troublemaker when the viewer sees him for the first time, having caused his parents to move from one town to another until they settle in Los Angeles. He is soon picked up by police for being drunk and disorderly, but a patient cop, Platt, learns from him that he is smothered at home by superficial love from his parents, Backus and Doran, but neither ever listens to him or gives him advice. Moreover, he appears to hate his mother since she so thoroughly dominates his weak-willed father. Before Dean is retrieved by his parents who must break off a dinner date at their swanky country club to bail him out, Dean spots Wood, a lonely girl who was walking the streets after curfew, and Mineo, a disturbed rich kid whose family is never living at home with him and who has been brought in for killing a litter of puppies. Upon entering his new high school for the first time the next day, Dean spots Wood and asks her for a date but she rejects him flatly and gets into a car driven by her hot-rodding, leather-jacketed boy friend, Allen, who is surrounded by a group of lemming-like followers, all sporting the zippered, black-leather jackets of the day. The gang makes fun of Dean and speeds off. Later, when the class attends a lecture at the planetarium, Allen confronts Dean, picking a fight. Knives are drawn and Dean bests Allen, but the fight isn't over. Dean accepts Allen's challenge of a "chickie run," wherein both boys are to drive beatup cars at breakneck speed to the edge of a coastal cliff and dive out before the cars carry them over the edge and to their certain deaths. Whoever jumps from the car first is, of course, a chicken, a coward, not worthy of human recognition nor participation in any kind of life on this earth or any other planet. (It's not supposed to be logical.) That night the teenagers gather at the lonely cliffside area and Dean and Allen go roaring off in their junkheap hotrods toward the cliff. Dean jumps out at the last minute but a strap on Allen's leather jacket gets caught on the door handle of his car and he cannot escape the auto which plunges over the cliff and takes him to his death. (There is a message here about those leather jackets that Ray was obviously trying to send.) Dean takes his prize, Wood, who is in shock, back to her house and discovers that she's as confused about her relationship with her parents as he is with his. Dean later tries to tell Backus and Doran about the death of Allen but they only panic, Doran insisting that they move again, her only answer to any crisis. Backus will not stand up to her and because of his willowy backbone, Dean attacks him, knocking his father down and fleeing. He picks up Wood and Mineo and the three go to a deserted mansion. There they are sought by Allen's thug friends, Mazzola, Hopper, and others. Mazzola is shot and wounded by Mineo who has been terrorized by the gang. By that time Mineo has sort of become the adopted child of Wood and Dean, the pathetic little trio forming a strange family. But there's little time to analyze this weird situation. A policeman investigating the break-in enters the mansion and Mineo shoots him and then flees, taking refuge in the planetarium. Dean, Wood, and their parents, plus the weeping housekeeper of Mineo's mansion, arrive at the site with an army of police. Dean persuades Mineo to let him inside and he calms the frenetic youth down, telling him all will be settled if he will only surrender. As a precaution, Dean removes the bullets from Mineo's gun and he steps outside with the younger boy. When Mineo spots the platoons of police outside he panics and begins to run, one officer shooting him dead when he believes Mineo is about to fire at him with his empty gun. Dean weeps for the misguided boy dead in his arms as Backus suddenly finds the courage to stand up to Doran, and tells his son that they will work things out. Dean and Wood embrace, having found new meaning in life through their relationship. This zig-zag plot and less than empathic characterization is somehow made forceful and completely compelling by Ray in a directorial gem. Ray, always a perfectionist, spent endless hours researching hundreds of teenage police cases before doing this film. He shot this CinemaScope movie in black and white for a few weeks during preproduction to get the mood and feel for the muted color patterns he would later use for the final color print. Of course, REBEL WITHOUT A CAUSE is nothing more than a teenage exploitation film without the presence of the intense and fascinating Dean whose appearance here electrified audiences, especially teenagers who went on to identify with him as a powerful symbol of their alienated generation. There is much of Marlon Brando's character from THE WILD ONE (1953) in Dean's supercharged performance, but he remains distinctly his own personality, although he has all of Brando's early hesitancies, gropings, and marble-mouthed delivery. Critics at the time accused Dean of mimicking Brando but he later came to be seen as an actor of singular stature, particularly after completing EAST OF EDEN and GIANT. Here is the disturbed Romeo playing to the equally disturbed Juliet in a modern day interpretation of the Shakespeare romance-tragedy. Adult viewers at the time were genuinely disturbed by this film which has now become a cult picture, stating that it advocated violence, madness, and death, with no other purpose than to dwell on the morose, the dire, and indict parents for sins against their spoiled offspring. And there is some justification for this assumption in that Ray imbues his characters with false sophistication and therefore importance worthy of attention, having no background other than a living teenager to work with, youngsters without notable pasts to discover, only their own embryonic growth. To enhance that sapling state Ray had to introduce trauma as the conflict that would compel viewership. Wood and Mineo, along with the rest of the high-voiced cast, serve only as interesting props to Dean's exploration of self. Ray used Dean as a tool to bring yesterday's clean-cut juveniles into the adult world of *film noir*. He did not anticipate the youth cycle of films by a decade, he began it, and most of what followed in his footsteps was utter trash. THE BLACKBOARD JUNGLE, released the same year, was an exception. When Ray first suggested this film to Warner Bros., executives enthusiastically supported the idea but proposed that, of all people, the stars be Tab Hunter and Jayne Mansfield. Ray rejected this suggestion and said he would only make the film if he could have Dean and Wood. After a struggle, he got them. He had been particularly impressed by Dean after seeing him perform in EAST OF EDEN. He labored long with Dean to produce the scenes he wanted, driving the actor into a frenzy before some scenes, talking endlessly with him before others to bring him down from his always burning high. The tragedy of this film was relived in real life. All three of the principals met sad, premature fates. Mineo was murdered in West Hollywood. He could not cope with becoming an overnight star, a situation created by REBEL WITHOUT A CAUSE. He spent money crazily on clothes, fast cars, and even a $250,000 estate for his parents in Long Island, New York. Buying a handsome place in Hollywood, Mineo gave one expensive party after another and became one of the stars of the chic homosexual set. On the eve of the Academy Awards, he was so convinced that he would win an Oscar for his role in REBEL that he gave an enormous and costly party with a huge banner strung across the facade of his home which read: "Congratulations, Sal!" He did not win and the banner was yanked down and burned before dawn the next day. When Mineo was murdered in West Hollywood, a then known gathering place for homosexuals, few was left of his fortune. His fairly expensive apartment had little furnishings, Mineo having sold most of his furniture, but on the wall, in an expensive frame, was a prized possession he could not part with in life. It was a poster advertising REBEL WITHOUT A CAUSE with the ironic line on it reading: "Teenage terror torn from today's headlines." Wood drowned in a still mysterious accident while boating off Catalina Island with her husband Robert Wagner and Christopher Walken, and Dean himself was killed just as his career began to expand toward greatness. He died much the same way Allen perished in REBEL WITHOUT A CAUSE, speeding at more than 100 miles per hour in a racing car on a public highway in California. He killed himself and seriously injured two other people. Only two hours before his death Dean was stopped by a traffic cop and given a ticket for driving 75 mph in a 45 mph zone. He took the ticket with a smirk and stated a "so what?" before gunning his sports car down the road toward doom. REBEL WITHOUT A CAUSE is still a powerful film today but its indictment of parents seems a little anachronistic.

p, David Weisbart; d, Nicholas Ray; w, Stewart Stern (based on an adaptation by Irving Shulman of a story line by Ray inspired from the story *The Blind Run* by Dr. Robert M. Lindner); ph, Ernest Haller (CinemaScope, Warner Color); m, Leonard Rosenman; ed, William Ziegler; prod d, William Wallace; art d, Malcolm Bert; cos, Moss Mabry.

Drama **Cas.** **(PR:C-O MPAA:NR)**

REBELLION** (1938) 60m Crescent bw

Tom Keene *(Capt. John Carroll)*, Rita Cansino [Hayworth] *(Paula Castillo)*, Duncan Renaldo *(Ricardo Castillo)*, William Royle *(Harris)*, Gino Corrado *(Pablo)*, Roger Gray *(Honeycutt)*, Robert McKenzie *(Judge Moore)*, Allan Cavan *(President Zachary Taylor)*, Jack Ingram *(Hank)*, Lita Cortez *(Marquita)*, Theodore Lorch *(Gen. Vallejo)*, W.M. McCormick *(Dr. Semple)*.

Cansino plays a Mexican lass trying to reside peacefully in the territory of California, only to have a group of land-grabbing outlaws kill her father and make her own existence trying. She makes a plea to Washington for help, and receives the President's own aide, Keene, who arrives in California to set everything straight, winning the hand of Cansino and enough popularity to be elected the first governor of the State. This film is from the period when Rita Hayworth was still performing under her given name, still something of an unknown, acting mostly in action-oriented programmers.

p, E.B. Derr; d, Lynn Shores; w, John T. Neville; ph, Arthur Martinelli; m, Abe Meyer; ed, Donald Barrat; art d, Edward C. Jewell; cos, Lou Brown; makeup, Steve Corso.

Western **(PR:A MPAA:NR)**

REBELLION*** (1967, Jap.) 120m Toho-Mifune/Toho bw (JOI-UCHI)

Toshiro Mifune *(Isaburo Sasahara)*, Takeshi Kato *(Yogoro)*, Yoko Tsukasa *(Ichi)*, Tatsuya Nakadai *(Tatewaki Asano)*, Tatsuyoshi Ebara *(Bunzo)*, Michiko Otsuka *(Suga)*, Tatsuo Matsumura *(Lord Matsudaira)*, Shigeru Koyama *(Steward Takahashi)*, Masao Mishima *(Chamberlain Yanase)*, Isao Yamagata *(Kotani)*, Etsuko Ichihara, Go Kato.

In this film set in 18th-Century Japan, Mifune is forced to question the feudal system he is part of when the local ruling family demands that Mifune's son, Kato, return his wife, an expelled member of that family, to her kindred. The edict comes because the son she bore the ruler will become the ruler. But Kato and his wife have fallen deeply in love, she bears a child that Mifune loves as if it were his own. Not wishing to destroy the bond between his son and wife, he refuses to bring the woman back. The order is then given for Mifune and Kato to commit Hara-kiri, but they refuse. Instead they take on the armies of the ruling forces, thus meeting with their end. An extremely dim view of a life that comes in conflict with tradition, given the appropriate treatment in both atmosphere and direction.

p, Tomoyuki Tanaka; d, Masaki Kobayashi; w, Shinobu Hashimoto (based on the novel *Haiyo Zuma Shimatsu Yori* by Yasuhiko Takiguchi); ph, Kazuo Yamada; m, Toru Takemitsu; art d, Yoshiro Muraki.

Drama   **(PR:C   MPAA:NR)**

REBELLION IN CUBA*   (1961) 79m International bw (AKA: CHIUATO; BETRAYER)

Bill Fletcher, Jake LaMotta, Lon Chaney, Jr., Sonia Marrero, Dan Gould, George Rodriguez, Barbara Lea.

A group of Americans attempts to help an anti-Castro group revolt against the Communist regime in Cuba. Though released a scant few months after the disastrous Bay of Pigs invasion, this film bears little resemblance to that event or to reality. Still, it is intriguing that such an idea would even have occurred to the filmmakers prior to the actual "covert" invasion. Reportedly shot on the Isle of Pines, the film also features a performance by boxer Jake LaMotta, who acted in some minor films long before his own story came to the screen as RAGING BULL.

p&d, Albert C. Gannaway; w, Frank Graves, Mark Hanna.

War   **(PR:A   MPAA:NR)**

REBELLION OF THE HANGED, THE**½**   (1954, Mex.) 90m UA bw (LA REBELION DE LOS COLGADOS)

Pedro Armendariz *(Candido)*, Adriana *(Modesto)*, Carlos Moctezuma *(Felix)*, Victor Junco *(Calso)*, Alvaro Matute *(Picaro)*, Jaime Fernandez *(Urbano)*, Miguel Ferris *(Severo)*, Tito Junco *(Gabriel)*.

Extremely violent look at the mistreatment of workers at a mahogany camp in the Mexican jungle. The story follows Armendariz as he signs up for work at the camp, and then takes his children and beautiful sister into the jungle. There the workers are treated as little more than animals, as they are hung up by their feet and constantly beaten. Some of the punishments are too awful to mention. Overall the message is thoroughly drilled in, but less of the gory visuals and a bit more plot development are in order.

p, Jose Kohn; d, Alfredo Crevenna; w, H. Wlen (based on the book by B. Traven); ph, Gabriel Figueroa; ed, Anton Conde.

Drama   **(PR:C   MPAA:NR)**

REBELLIOUS DAUGHTERS*   (1938) 63m Progressive/Times bw

Marjorie Reynolds *(Claire)*, Verna Hillie *(Babe)*, Sheila Bromley *(Flo)*, George Douglas *(Gilman)*, Dennis Moore *(Jimmie)*, Oscar O'Shea *(Mr. Elliott)*, Irene Franklin *(Ma Delacy)*, Nick Lukats *(Girard)*, Monte Blue *(Huston)*, Lita Chevret *(Rita)*, Dell Henderson *(Stanley)*, Vivian Oakland *(Mrs. Webster)*.

Dreadful depiction of mistreated daughters leaving the family hearth because of an inability to get needed attention. As happens with such stereotypes they end up in the big city, like lambs in front of wolves, unless they have dedicated men to watch over them. A poor production accompanies this worthless script.

p, B.N. Judell; d, Jean Yarbrough; w, John W. Krafft.

Drama   **(PR:A   MPAA:NR)**

REBELLIOUS ONE, THE   (SEE: WILD SEED, 1965)

REBELS AGAINST THE LIGHT**½**   (1964) 93m David bw (AKA: SANDS OF BEERSHEBA)

Diane Baker *(Susan)*, David Opatoshu *(Daoud)*, Tom Bell *(Dan)*, Paul Stassino *(Salim)*, Didi Ramati *(Naima)*, Theodore Marcuse *(Nuri)*, Wolfe Barzell *(Ayub)*.

Shot entirely in Israel, concentrating on the Jewish-Arab skirmishes during 1949, this picture injects several other themes which tend to dull the overall effect. Stassino plays a dedicated, though fanatic, Arab terrorist who assists in the harassment of Jewish outposts. He makes a trek back to his home village in order to stock up on supplies, and winds up killing the police officer he thinks has turned traitor. There is also the story of a romance between a U.S. Jewish boy and a Christian girl, which ends with the girl coming to visit the grave of the young man, killed in his fight for Israel. Though the plot jumbles together too many themes, the direction keeps it moving fairly well, treating all the characters in an individualistic light. The scenic photography is a plus.

p,d&w, Alexander Ramati (based on his book); ph, Wolfgang Shushitsky; m, Mel Keller; ed, Helga Cranston; m/l, Naomi Shemer (sung by Soshana Damari).

Drama/War   **(PR:A   MPAA:NR)**

REBELS DIE YOUNG   (SEE: TOO YOUNG, TOO IMMORAL!, 1962)

REBOUND**½**   (1931) 67m RKO-Pathe bw

Ina Claire *(Sara Jaffrey)*, Robert Ames *(Bill Truesdale)*, Myrna Loy *(Evie Lawrence)*, Hedda Hopper *(Liz Crawford)*, Robert Williams *(Johnnie Coles)*, Hale Hamilton *(Lyman Patterson)*, Walter Walker *(Mr. Henry Jaffrey)*, Louise Closser Hale *(Mrs. Jaffrey)*, Leigh Allen *(Les Crawford)*.

Newly married Ames meets up with old flame Loy, the girl who threw him over for somebody else, and almost destroys his marriage as he goes chasing after her. But he manages to catch his senses in time to keep his wife (Claire) from becoming too involved in an affair of her own. Capable performances and witty dialog, injected with sufficient humor, help save a script that tends to take a moralistic tone. Apparently a strong rivalry existed between Loy, 26 at the time, and stage star Claire, who was 40. After seeing Loy's screen test, Claire is reputed to have

claimed that Loy could never steal a man away from her, as the script demanded. Director Griffith disagreed and used the tension created to the film's advantage, though in the end the picture lost $215,000.

p, Charles Rogers; d, Edward H. Griffith; w, Horace Jackson, Donald Ogden Stewart (based on the play by Stewart); ph, Norbert Brodine; ed, Dan Mandell.

Drama/Comedy   **(PR:A   MPAA:NR)**

RECAPTURED LOVE**   (1930) 77m WB bw

Belle Bennett *(Helen Parr)*, John Halliday *(Brentwood Parr)*, Dorothy Burgess *(Peggy Price)*, Richard Tucker *(Rawlings)*, Junior Durkin *(Henry Parr)*, George Bickel *(Crofts)*, Brooks Benedict *(Pat)*, Sisters "G" *(Specialty Dancers)*, Bernard Durkin, Earle Wallace.

Bennett and Halliday are a happily married couple, until Bennett is taken in by pretty chorus girl Burgess. He divorces his wife to marry the girl, only to be wound around her fingertips while she nonchalantly cheats on him. Almost to the point of tears, Bennett goes back to his first wife, who lovingly takes him back in. Strong performances help save an overly stereotyped script.

d, John G. Adolfi; w, Charles Kenyon (based on the play "Misdeal" by Basil Woon); ph, John Stumar; ed, Jimmy Gibbons.

Drama   **(PR:A   MPAA:NR)**

RECESS**½**   (1967) 90m Edwin c

Charles Brummit, Jean Fowler, Heather MacRae, Drout Miller, Gwenn Mitchell, Aimee Oliver, Michael Patton, Cleve Roller, Christopher Wines.

Based on an off-Broadway play, this picture uses the idea of children's recess at school for a microcosmic look at almost everything that affects an individual during his lifetime, including love, hate, religion, politics, etc... .Starting with a background of only white, the film's set takes on various colors and shapes, mirroring the changes taking place for the individual characters during the recess period. By the end of the film the players are still unable to touch each other—except for a touch to the forehead—perhaps signifying the means by which individual perspectives serve to separate people. Well acted by nonprofessionals, with production values of a high caliber. RECESS won top honors at the 1969 Atlantic Film Festival. It was the first solo production project by Barnes, who had worked for several years with Otto Preminger as casting director and story editor.

p, William E. Barnes; d, Rule Royce Johnson; w, Dolores Walker, Andrew Piotrowski (based on their play); ph, George Silano (DeLuxe Color); m, Luther Henderson; ed, Morty Schwartz; art d, Bill Bell; cos, Prue Hooper.

Drama   **(PR:A   MPAA:NR)**

RECKLESS**½**   (1935) 96m MGM bw

Jean Harlow *(Mona Leslie)*, William Powell *(Ned Riley)*, Franchot Tone *(Bob Harrison)*, May Robson *(Granny)*, Ted Healy *(Smiley)*, Nat Pendleton *(Blossom)*, Robert Light *(Paul Mercer)*, Rosalind Russell *(Josephine)*, Henry Stephenson *(Harrison)*, Louise Henry *(Louise)*, James Ellison *(Dale Every)*, Leon Waycoff [Leon Ames]*(Ralph Watson)*, Man Mountain Dean *(Himself)*, Farina [Allen Hoskins] *(Gold Dust)*, Allan Jones *(Allan)*, Carl Randall *("Trocadero" Dance Partner)*, Nina Mae McKinney *(Herself)*, Hans Steinke, Ernie Haynes *(Wrestlers)*, Robert Andrews *(Mona's Baby)*, Jeanie Gunn *(Little Girl Singer)*, Mickey Rooney, Dick Elliott, Kay Sutton, Mae Madison, Rafael Storm, Wade Boteler, Don Brodie, Sam Ash, Joe Sawyer, Henry Kolker, Hooper Atchley, Libby Taylor, Charles R. Moore, Paul Fix, Sam Flint, Akim Tamiroff, Lee Phelps, Jack Mulhall, Larry Steers, Charles Middleton, Theodore Lorch, Edward Le Saint, Charles C. Wilson, John Davidson, Ed Peil, Claudia Coleman, Margaret Dumont, Harold Huber, Irene Thompson, Lorna Lowe, Donna Roberts, Marian Ladd, Edna Waldron, Lynn Carleton, Earlene Heath, Billie Lee.

A spotty effort which was Selznick's attempt (he produced and wrote the original story) to turn Harlow's gangster moll persona into that of a singing and dancing showgirl. She stars as a Broadway actress who is introduced to wealthy industrialist Tone when he comes to see her in a play. Obsessed with Harlow, Tone purchases all the seats in the theater and watches the performance by himself. Tone's interest in Harlow grows, causing her agent, Powell, to become jealous. Powell has all along loved Harlow but has never had the courage to tell her so. Tone and Harlow grow more intense. Tone throws off his previous fiancee, Russell, and marries Harlow. Instead of becoming angry, Russell strikes up a friendship with Harlow. Unfortunately for the newlyweds, Tone's father, Stephenson, is less accepting of his son's blonde bombshell of a wife. Later, at Russell's wedding (she has quickly bounced back from Tone's rebuff), an inebriated Tone informs Russell that his marriage to Harlow is empty and that she dragged him into it. Harlow, learning of Tone's true feelings, turns to Powell for comfort—a gesture Tone reads as rejection. Now fully depressed, Tone commits suicide. The easily swayed public believes rumors that Harlow killed Tone in order to run off with Powell. Scandal brews and Harlow's career takes a nose dive. To further complicate matters Harlow learns that she is pregnant with Tone's child. Stephenson puts up a battle to gain custody and forces Harlow to surrender her inheritance in exchange for keeping the child. Powell remains by her side throughout, determined to put her back in the footlights. He puts together a new show for her to star in, but the public is still out to get her. A rowdy opening-night audience screams insults at Harlow. In self-defense Harlow answers the crowd's verbal assault with the truth—honestly explaining her side of the story. The crowd is won over by her warmth and sincerity and, instead of booing, begins to cheer. Harlow, never the strongest of actresses, was completely out of her league in RECKLESS. Unable to carry a note, her voice was dubbed by Virginia Verrill, while her dancing was so wretched it had to be spruced up with some creative editing and the use of a more accomplished double. Reportedly based on the life of Broadway actress Libby Holman who was accused of killing her husband in a real-life scandal, RECKLESS was to have starred Joan Crawford. Hoping to capitalize on the headlines which romantically linked Harlow and Powell, Selznick decided to recast. The script, however, is morbidly close to Harlow's tragic career. Her second husband, Paul Bern put a gun to his head, tormented by his impotence. After a third marriage (to cameraman Hal Rosson) Harlow fell in love with Powell. In 1936 they eloped but, unlike the characters they played in RECKLESS, marriage never came. Harlow died the following year at age 26 of cerebral edema (dropsy). Songs include: "Reckless" (Jerome Kern, Oscar Hammerstein II), "Ev'rything's Been Done Before" (Harold Adamson, Edwin H. Knopf, Jack King), "Trocadero," "Hear What My Heart Is Saying" (Adamson, Burton Lane), "Cyclone" (Gus Kahn, Walter Donaldson). Two other songs are billed but were cut from the final print: "Hi-Diddle-Dee-Dum" and "I'm Going Down to Dance at Clancy's" (Con Conrad, Herb Magidson).

p, David O. Selznick; d, Victor Fleming; w, P.J. Wolfson (based on the story "A Woman Called Cheap" by Oliver Jeffries [David O. Selznick]), uncredited, Victor Fleming); ph, George Golsey; ed, Margaret Booth; md, Victor Baravalle; art d, Cedric Gibbons; cos, Adrian; ch, Carl Randall, Chester Hale; makeup, Jack Dawn.

Musical/Romance **(PR:A MPAA:NR)**

RECKLESS AGE**½ (1944) 63m UNIV bw

Gloria Jean *(Linda Wadsworth)*, Henry Stephenson *(J. H. Wadsworth)*, Kathleen Howard *(Sarah Wadsworth)*, Franklin Pangborn *(Mr. Thurtle)*, Andrew Tombes *(Mr. Cook)*, Marshall Thompson *(Roy Connors)*, Jane Darwell *(Mrs. Connors)*, Lloyd Corrigan *(Mr. Connors)*, Judy Clark (Sandra Sibelius), Jack Gilford *(Joey Bagle)*, *Chester Clute (Jerkins)*, Marie Harmon *(Salesgirl O'Toole)*, Ida Moore *(Customer)*, Ian Wolfe *(Prof. Mellasagus)*, David Holt *(Horace Farnsworth)*, Don Hayden *(Huntington Turner)*, Gladys Blake *(Waitress)*, Anita Sparrow *(Wac)*, Beatrice Roberts *(Wave)*, Alice Fleming *(Irish Woman)*, Karen Knoght *(Salesgirl)*, Linda Reed (Salesgirl Turpps), Delta Rhythm Boys, Harold Nicholas.

Thin plot has Jean as a rich girl who finds it hard to live under the strict household of her well-meaning grandfather, Stephenson. She manages to get a job as a clerk in one of the many dime stores owned by her grandfather, belting out three songs along the way: "Il Bacio" (Luigi Arditi), "The Cradle Song" (Irving Bilbo), and "Santa Lucia" (Teodoro Cottrau). Some fine characterizations along with the musical numbers give this picture its needed spark. Other songs include: "Get On Board Little Children" (Don Raye, Gene De Paul); "Very Often On My Face" (Bill Grage, Grace Shannon); and "Mama Yo Quiero" (Al Stillmann, Jaraca and Vincente Paiva).

p&d, Felix E. Feist; w, Gertrude Purcell, Henry Blankfort (based on the story "Make Way for Love" by Al Martin); ph, Jerome Ash; ed, Ray Curtiss; md, Sam Freed, Jr.; art d, John B. Goodman, Harold H. MacArthur.

Musical **(PR:A MPAA:NR)**

RECKLESS AGE, THE, 1958 (SEE: DRAGSTRIP RIOT, 1958)

RECKLESS HOUR, THE** (1931) 70m FN-WB bw

Dorothy Mackaill *(Margaret Nichols)*, Conrad Nagel *(Edward Adams)*, Joan Blondell *(Myrtle Nichols)*, H. B. Warner *(Walter Nichols)*, Helen Ware *(Harriett Nichols)*, Walter Byron *(Allan Crane)*, Joe Donahue *(Harry Gleason)*, William House *(Jennison)*, Dorothy Peterson *(Mrs. Jennison)*, Ivan Simpson *(Stevens)*, *Claude King (Howard Crane)*, Mae Madison *(Rita)*, Robert Allen *(Friend)*.

Mackaill plays a hardworking Fifth Avenue model closely tied to her family back in Jersey City, but her world is turned around when she is taken in by the suave Byron. The latter offers her everything, but delivers nothing, leaving her only a baby and an embittered attitude against all men. However, the sensitive artist Nagel is able to break through to the hurt and hardened girl, keeping her life from becoming totally disastrous. Mackaill is effective in her performance, but is upstaged by Blondell in her role as the snappy sister.

d, John Francis Dillon; w, Florence Ryerson, Robert Lord (based on the play "Ambush" by Arthur Richman); ph, James Van Trees; ed, Harold Young.

Drama **(PR:A MPAA:NR)**

RECKLESS LIVING** (1931) 69m UNIV bw

Ricardo Cortez *(Curly)*, Mae Clarke *(Bee)*, Norman Foster *(Doggie)*, Marie Prevost *(Alice)*, *Slim Summerville (The Drunk)*, Robert Emmett O'Connor *(Ryan)*, Thomas Jackson *(McManus)*, Louis Natheaux *(Block)*, Murray Kinnell *(Alf)*, Russell Hopton *(Kid Regan)*, Perry Ivins *(Spike)*, Brooks Benedict *(Jerry)*, Frank Hagney *(Man)*.

Clarke and Foster are the married owners of a small speakeasy whose main desire is to go straight and open a gas station. But Foster's yen for the track leaves the couple broke, allowing operator Cortez, who has has eye on Clarke, to set up the couple as a front for his crooked organization. But through enough dilligent work, Foster manages to save the needed money to take his wife to their hoped-for gas station. Director Gardner obtained the proper type of underworld atmosphere, but failed to provoke much of the same on the part of his actors.

p, Cyril Gardner; w, Courtenay Terrett, Tom Reed, Gardner (based on the story "Twenty Grand" by Eve K. Flint [Eva Finllestein], Martha Madison [Martha O'Dwyer] from the play "The Up and Up" by Flint); ph, Jackson Rose; ed, Harry W. Lieb.

Crime/Drama **(PR:A MPAA:NR)**

RECKLESS LIVING*½ (1938) 65m UNIV bw

Robert Wilcox *(Danny Farrell)*, Nan Grey *(Laurie Andrews)*, Jimmie Savo *(Stuffy)*, William Lundigan *(Stanley Shaw)*, Frank Jenks *(Freddie)*, Harry Davenport *("General" Jeff)*, May Boley *(Mother Ryan)*, Charles Judels *(Harry Myron)*, Harlan Briggs *("Colonel" Harris)*, Eddie Anderson *(Dreamboat)*, Eleanor Hansen, Mary Brodel, Marilyn Stuart, Constance Moore, *(Girl Singers)*, Lucien Littlefield *(Lucius Carr)*, George Meeker *(Man at Race Track)*, Chester Clute *(Sucker)*, Harry Allen *(Wilkins)*, Ralph Sanford *(Brownie)*, Ferris Taylor *(Pawnbroker)*, Alexander Leftwich *(Tout)*, Bill Marceau *(Counter Man)*, Sidney Miller *(Jockey)*, Drew Demarest *(Croupier)*, Charlie Sullivan, Jack Gardner *(Ticket Sellers)*, George Billings, Jerry Tucker *(Boys on Street)*, Duke York, Marion "Bud" Wolfe, Jack Kenney *(Poker Players)*, Ted Billings *(Harry)*.

Dreary picture has Wilcox horribly addicted to the idea of making it rich at the track, which only leads to conflict with his new-found love Grey. A few laughs and songs are thrown in to try to move the picture along.

p, Val Paul; d, Frank McDonald; w, Charles Grayson (based on the story "Winner's Circle" by Gerald Beaumont); ph, Elwood Bredell; ed, Frank Gross; art d, Jack Otterson; m/l, "You're a Sweetheart," Jimmy McHugh, Harold Adamson (sung by Jimmy Savo), "When the Stars Go By," McHugh, Adamson (sung by Nan Grey).

Drama **(PR:A MPAA:NR)**

RECKLESS MOMENT, THE*** (1949) 82m COL bw

James Mason *(Martin Donnelly)*, Joan Bennett *(Lucia Harper)*, Geraldine Brooks *(Beatrice Harper)*, Henry O'Neill *(Mr. Harper)*, Shepperd Strudwick *(Ted Darby)*, David Bair *(David Harper)*, Roy Roberts *(Nagle)*, Frances Williams *(Sybil)*, Paul E. Burns *(Desk Clerk)*, Danny Jackson *(Drummer)*, Claire Carleton *(Blonde)*, Billy Snyder *(Gambler)*, Peter Brocco *(Bartender)*, Karl "Killer" Davis *(Wrestler)*, Virginia Hunter *(Girl)*, Joseph Palma *(Card Player)*, Penny O'Connor *(Liza)*, Bruce Gilbert Norman *(Dennis)*, Sharon Monaghan *(Bridget)*, Bobby Hyatt *(Mud)*, Ann Shoemaker *(Mrs. Feller)*, Everett Glass *(Drug Clerk)*, Buddy Gorman *(Magazine Clerk)*, Louis Mason *(Mike)*, Charles Marsh *(Newsman)*, Harry Harvey, Norman Leavitt *(Post Office Clerks)*, Boyd Davis *(Tall Man)*, Pat Barton *(Receptionist)*, John Butler *(Pawnbroker)*, Kathryn Card *(Mrs. Loring)*, Pat O'Malley *(Bank Guard)*, Charles Evans *(Bank Official)*, Jessie Arnold *(Old Lady)*, Sue Moore, Dorothy Phillips, Gail Bonney *(Women)*, Charles Jordan *(Man)*, Celeste Savoi *(Waitress)*, Joe Rechts *(Newsboy)*, Mike Mahoney, Glenn Thompson, John Monaghan *(Policemen)*, William Schallert *(Lieutenant)*, Cosmo Sardo, Holger Bendixen, Evelyn Moriarity, Al bayne, Robert Gordon, Ed Pine, Jack Baker, John Roy, Kenneth Kendall, Richard Mickelson, David Levitt, Barbara Hatton, George Dockstader, Barry Regan, Byron Poindexter.

The question asked by this picture is: "How far is a mother willing to go to save her child?" And the answer is . . . beyond what the law allows. This was Max Ophul's last American movie. He'd only directed a few after having come to the U.S. from France where he made his reputation when he was forced to flee his native Germany as Hitler came to power. This very European director was able to capture the American milieu in LETTER FROM AN UNKNOWN WOMAN and CAUGHT with his almost sensuous camera work. comprised of a dazzling assortment of crane shots, tilted angles, fluid tracking shots, and more. Despite the technique, he never lost sight of his narrative and the result was usually a better movie than the script promised. So it was with this, a predictable melodrama that could have been forgettable but remains a fine example of his work. Tense from beginning to end, THE RECKLESS MOMENT is the story of a family torn apart and united by circumstance. Bennett is happily married and living in upper-middle-class luxury on Balboa Island in southern California. Her two children, Brooks and Blair, her father-in-law, O'Neill, and her maid, Williams, also live in the house. At the opening, Bennett's husband is away on business. Bennett learns that Brooks has been having an affair with Strudwick, a much older man, and she has written him a packet of letters that he intends to make public if the family doesn't come across with some money. Strudwick makes that clear to Bennett, who advises Brooks to attempt to get the letters back. That night, Brooks and Strudwick meet for a palaver in the family's small boathouse. When Strudwick won't change his mind, Brooks whacks him with a flashlight as they struggle, then she runs out. Strudwick is stunned by the force of the blow and tries to follow her, but he trips and falls over a rail into the dark water where he drowns. When Bennett finds the body on the sand in front of the family house, she realizes that this will have to be explained to the authorities, something she doesn't want to do, so she puts the body in a boat and hides it there. Meanwhile, we discover that Strudwick no longer had the letters. The gigolo was in trouble with a loan shark and gave the letters to the man as collateral to cover the debt. The shark, Roberts, upon hearing that Strudwick's dead body has been found, suspects that he was murdered and intends using that information to his advantage. The police have been called in to get to the bottom of matters and are not progressing. Roberts is in cahoots with Mason, who is sent to see Bennett to demand $5,000 for the return of the letters that will link Brooks to Strudwick. Bennett tries to get a loan, to pawn her jewels, to do anything to raise the money, and Mason becomes sympathetic to her maternal efforts to save her daughter. As Bennett continues her fruitless fund-raising, she only manages to amass a small part of the money but Mason assures her that Brooks is in the clear, as someone else has been arrested for the murder. This places a burden of guilt on Bennett who can't bear the thought that an innocent man may be executed for a crime he did not commit. Roberts is increasingly fidgety about Mason's inability to secure the maney and decides he'd better take care of this himself. He travels to Balboa to await Bennett and there meets Mason. They battle and Mason chokes Roberts to death but is severely injured in the fight. Bennett comes home, finds the two men, and wants to tend Mason's wounds but he thinks it might be better if he disposed of Roberts before anything else happens. He climbs into his car with the dead man and Bennett follows behind with Williams. On the trip, she explains the entire story to the maid, who now becomes an accessory by having heard the incidents. Mason crashes his car and is dying when the cops arrive. While keeping an eye on the distraught Bennett, Mason tells the cops that *he* killed Strudwick and Roberts, thus taking Bennett and Brooks off the hook. Mason dies and Bennett and Williams return to their peaceful house at Balboa to wait for the imminent appearance of her husband. Brooks, Blair, and O'Neill have no idea what the woman of the house has just gone through to keep their family together. First-class direction of a second-class script makes this an excellent film for anyone interested in middle-cut Hitchcock, which are those stories about "an innocent person being accused of a crime he or she didn't commit." The preview of this film was a disaster, as they took the print to a suburban theater where everything went wrong. The picture broke and several minutes were taken to splice it. Then, when the movie began to unreel, the sound track and the picture were out of synchronization and the words didn't match the lip movements. By the time they re-synched the movie, half the audience had left andy any suspense that might have been generated was lost. It was Mason's third U.S. picture, having appeared for Ophuls in CAUGHT, then MADAME BOVARY before this.

p, Walter Wanger; d, Max Ophul; w, Henry Garson, Robert W. Soderberg, Mel Dinelli, Robert E. Kent (based on the story "The Blank Wall" by Elisabeth S. Holding); ph, Burnett Guffey; m, Hans Salter; ed, Gene Havlick; md, Morris Stoloff; art d, Cary Odell; set d, Frank Tuttle; cos, Jean Louis; makeup, Newt Jones.

Crime (PR:A-C MPAA:NR)

RECKLESS RANGER★★ (1937) 56m COL bw

Bob Allen (Bob), Louise Small (Mildred), Mary MacLaren (Mary), Harry Woods (Barlow), Jack Perrin (Chet), Buddy Cox (Jimmie), Jack Rockwell (Mort), Roger Williams (Snagger), Jay Wilsey, Slim Whitaker, Bud Osborne, Jim Corey, Tom London, Hal Price, Al Taylor, Tex Cooper, Bob McKenzie, Lane Chandler, Frank Ball, George Plues, Lafe McKee, Tex Palmer, Victor Cox, Chick Hannon.

Unusual for the western genre, this picture shows sympathy with the sheepherders over the cattle ranchers. Allen plays a Texas Ranger who undertakes the investigation of his twin brother's murder, a sheepman hung by Woods, the villainous rancher who is trying to grab off sections of the free range for himself. Woods gives one of the more venomous performances to fill the screen in the early westerns.

p, Larry Darmour; d, Spencer G. Bennett; w, Nate Gatzert (based on a story by Joseph Levering, Jesse Duffy); ph, Bert Longenecker; d, Dwight Caldwell.

Western **Cas.** (PR:A MPAA:NR)

RECKLESS ROADS★ (1935) 60m Majestic bw

Judith Allen (Edith Adams), Regis Toomey (Speed Demming), Lloyd Hughes (Fred Truslow), Ben Alexander (Wade Adams), Louise Carter (Mrs. Adams), Gilbert Emery (Amos Truslow), Matthew Betz, Dorothy Wolbert, Kit Guard.

Unbelievable and haphazard production has Toomey masquerading as a reporter, and trying to keep up with the unruly Allen, but the real challenge comes when the audience tries to keep up with this story, if it really wants to.

p, Larry Darmour; d, Burt P. Lynwood; w, Betty Burbridge (based on a story by L. S. Heifetz; H. A. Carlisle); ph, James S. Brown; ed, Dwight Caldwell; md, Lee Zahler.

Drama (PR:A MPAA:NR)

RECKONING, THE★★ (1932) 63m Olympic/Peerless bw

Sally Blane, James Murray, Edmund Breese, Bryant Washburn, Tom Jackson, Pat O'Malley, Mildred Golden, Douglas Scott.

Despite his attempts to go straight, a young juvenile delinquent is forced into a temporary life of crime by an evil doctor. A shrewd detective figures someone is behind the boy's crimes and releases him after the kid has been busted. The detective is led to the mastermind, but the kid shoots the lowlife first. Uninspired in both direction and performances.

d, Dwight Cummings; w, Harry Frazer, Leon Lee.

Crime (PR:A MPAA:NR)

RECKONING, THE★★★ (1971, Brit.) 111m Col c

Nicol Williamson (Michael Marler), Ann Bell (Rosemary Marler), Lilita De Barros (Maria), Tom Kempinski (Brunzy), Kenneth Hendel (Davidson), Douglas Wilmer (Moyle), Barbara Ewing (Joan), Zena Walker (Hilda Greening), Paul Rogers (John Hazlitt), Gwen Nelson (Marler's Mother), Christine Hargreaves (Kath), Ernest Jennings (Dad John Joe), Rachel Roberts (Joyce Eglington), Godfrey Quigley (Dr. Carolan), Desmond Perry (Father Madden), Patricia Gratton (Singer), The Spectrum (Pop Group), J. G. Devlin (Cocky Burke), Joe Gladwin (Drunk), Edward Hardwicke (Mitchell), John Normington (Benham), Joan Henley (Mrs. Reynolds), John Hussey (Sir Miles Bishton), Donald Douglas (Garner), Sheila Gish (Mrs. Garner), Clare Kelly (Mrs. Davies), Joby Blanshard (Bottomly), Catherine Finn (Aunt Tess), Jean Campbell (Aunt Nellie), Marjorie Hogan (Aunt Christina), Christian Rodska (Jones), John Malcolm (Philip), Peter Sallis (Keresley), Kenneth Hendel (Davidson), Don Steadman, Spencer Churchill, Jackie Pallo, Tony Charles (Wrestlers), Wendy Gifford, Sarah Hater (Women at Party), Abby King.

A brutal, violent picture of a lower-class Irishman from Liverpool who has clawed his way to the top, then must revert to his slum background when called upon to avenge the death of his father. Williamson's performance is towering in its intensity, so much so that he often almost breaks out of the film and comes to life. He's a heel, not even a charming one, a man so obsessed with success that he has made it in the tough world of London, although he has little personal satisfaction from his business profits or his life with wife, Bell, a wealthy woman with whom he has little in common. Their entire life is punctuated by harsh lovemaking in between long silences. Williamson has not been back to Liverpool for many years when he learns that his father is dying, the result of having been beaten up by a "Teddy Boy" in a pub (The "Teddy Boys" were a vicious group who dressed in Edwardian suit-coats while exercising their violent ways on anyone who crossed them). Williamson hurries to Liverpool, too late to say goodbye to his father. He decides to spend a few hours in his old neighborhood before returning to London and takes in the wrestling matches, where he picks up Roberts, a married woman who works as a medical receptionist. They spend a sexual, though loveless, evening together and he returns to London. While there, he uses his business acumen to help his employer, Rogers, out of a ticklish situation. For this he is congratulated but it's hollow, as he has a gnawing feeling about what happened to his father. Little by little, the anger wells up in him and he lashes out at whoever is close by. There's a

dinner party thrown by Rogers, and Williamson takes needless umbrage at something said by one of the company's directors and tosses a drunken punch at the man. Rogers considers firing Williamson, Bell walks out on him, and Williamson is drawn to avenge his father's death. He drives back to Liverpool, searches and locates the boy who killed the old man, and pounds the youth with an iron pipe. We're never sure if the boy lives or dies, but Williamson is now satisfied that he has performed "Irish Justice" and can now sleep again. He is soon back in London and takes up with Rogers' secretary, Walker. They have an affair and he uses her passion for him as a wedge to obtain information on Rogers that is damaging to the man. Armed with that, it's not long before Rogers is out of the top spot and Williamson is in. He reconciles with Bell and is now back on top, with a better job and the death of his father avenged. One can neither like nor admire Williamson's character in THE RECKONING. He is 10 times the rat that Laurence Harvey was in ROOM AT THE TOP, although the fact that he is not given his comeuppance comes as a bit of a shock. Prior to this film, villian-protagonists were always made to pay the price, either by a coincidence or by being brought to justice. Not so in THE RECKONING, as Williamson is allowed to continue his terrible ways and, it is presumed, probably winds up in Parliament or wherever it is bad boys go in England. There's something Shakespearean about the theme and about the way Williamson plays it, like "Hamlet" in a Douggie Hayward suit. Sex and violence should keep younster's eyes away.

p, Ronald Shedlo; d, Jack Gold; w, John McGrath (based on the novel The Harp That Once by Patrick Hall); ph, Geoffrey Unsworth (Technicolor); m, Malcolm Arnold; ed, Peter Weatherley; md, Arnold; art d, Ray Simm; set d, Peter James; Cos, Bridget Sellers, Douglas Hayward; makeup, Bob Lawrence.

Drama (PR:C-O MPAA:R)

RECOIL★★ (1953) 79m Tempean/Eros bw

Kieron Moore (Nicholas Conway), Elizabeth Sellars (Jean Talbot), Edward Underdown (Michael Conway), John Horsley (Inspector Tunbridge), Robert Raglen (Sgt. Perkins), Ethel O'Shea (Mrs. Conway), Martin Benson (Farnborough), Michael Kelly (Crouch), Ian Fleming (Talbot), Bill Lowe (Walters), Tony Pelly, Derek Blomfield, Louise Grainger, Michael Balfour, Daphne Newton, Marguerite Brennan.

Sellars is determined to bring justice to the gang that beat and robbed her jeweler father, posing as a crook to do so. She hooks up with the gang and manages to get the police included in an ambush on the culprits in another taut thriller directed by low-budget veteran Gilling.

p, Robert Baker, Monty Berman; d&w, John Gilling; ph, Berman.

Crime (PR:A MPAA:NR)

RECOMMENDATION FOR MERCY★★★ (1975, Can.) 94m Paradise/Cinema Shares International c

Andrew Skidd, Robb Judd, Mike Upmalis, Karen Martin, Michele Fansett, Michael Lewis, Jim Millington, Carl Gall, Ruth Peckham, Rod Rekofski, Howard Wilson, Lawrence Elion, Terry Doyle, Bill Koski, Jack Zimmerman, Arnold Wild, David Wideman, David Murray, Tom Brennan, George Cunnigmfee, Henry Cohen, Berry Belchamber, Michael Lambert, Billey Anderson, Tom Story.

Based on a true event, 14-year-old Skidd is found guilty of raping and murdering a young girl, after he has been grilled, knocked about, injected with sodium pentothal, in an effort to get him to confess to the crime. But the evidence is all circumstantial, gathered from three of his friends and one of the girl's friends—who hung around together and were onto the girls because of easy sex. The material is effectively handled by director Markowitz, who uses a lot of cutting room techniques to push the story forward in a fast-moving manner. Skidd handled his part as the harassed kid well, always keeping the tide of sympathy with him.

p, James P. Lewis, Murray Markowitz; d, Markowitz; w, Fabian Jennings, Joel Weisenfield, Markowitz; ph, Richard Leiterman; m, Don Gillis; ed, George Appleby; art d, Tony Hall.

Drama (PR:O MPAA:R)

RECONSTRUCTION OF A CRIME★★★½ (1970, Ger.) George Samintis 100m c (ANAPARASTASSIS)

Thanos Grammenos (The Husband), Inuta Stathopoulou (The Wife), Yennis Totsicas (The Lover), Petros Hoedas (Investigator), Nicos Alevras (Policeman).

Poignant look at the effects of emigration upon a small village in Greece. By concentrating on one individual situation, the sociological implication is made that rural life in northern Greece is quickly becoming nonexistent, with devastating effects on those villagers who remain behind. Stathopoulou has fallen in love with another man while her husband has been away seeking work in Germany. Upon his return she and the lover kill the husband, then try to leave the country, but are forced to return to the village where an investigation of the man's disappearance has been undertaken. Told in flashbacks, a realistic tone is maintained through the use of nonprofessional actors and the barren photography of the countryside. A nice little gem that won prizes for Best Picture, Best Actress, and Best Photography at the Salonica Film Festival.

d, Theodore Aguelopoulos; w, Stralis Karras, Thanassis Valtinos, Aguelopoulus; ph, George Arvanitis.

Drama (PR:A MPAA:NR)

RECORD CITY★ (1978) 90m AIP c

Leonard Barr (Sickly Man), Ed Begley, Jr. (Pokey), Sorrell Booke (Coznowski), Dennis Bowen (Danny), Ruth Buzzi (Olga), Michael Callan (Eddie), Jack Carter (Manny), Rick Dees (Gordon), Kinky Friedman (Himself), Stuart Getz (Rupert), Alice Ghostley (Worried Wife), Frank Gorshin (Chameleon), Maria Grimm (Rita), Joe Higgins (Doyle), Ted Lange (The Wiz), Alan Oppenheimer (Blind Man), Isaac Ruiz (Macho), Harold Sakata (Gucci), Wendy Schall (Lorraine), Larry Storch (Deaf

Man), Elliott Street *(Hitch)*, Timothy Thomerson *(Marty)*, Susan Tolsky *(Goldie)*, Deborah White *(Vivian)*.

The hopes, dreams, and ambitions of a group of record store employees are given center stage in this humorous musical romp. A host of well-known television stars fill the bill, including Buzzi ("Laugh-In"), Ghostley ("Bewitched"), Lange ("Love Boat"), and Storch ("F-Troop"). Definitely not for discriminating audiences.

p, James T. Aubrey, Joe Byrne; d, Dennis Steinmetz; w, Ron Friedman; ph, William M. Klages (Movielab Color); m, Freddie Perren; ed, Bill Breashears; art d, Gene MacAvoy.

Comedy **(PR:A-C MPAA:PG)**

RECORD 413*½ (1936, Fr.) 83m Franco-London/Eclair bw (GB: DISQUE 413)

Gitta Alpar *(La Salvini)*, Jules Berry *(Capt. Richard Maury)*, Jean Galland *(Count Illeano/British Intelligence Agent)*, Larquey *(Belinsky)*, Constant Remy *(Colonel)*, Gaby Basset *(Cecile)*, Maximilienne *(Princess)*.

Basically a vehicle to display the operatic talents of Alpar, this is a less than routine spy caper. When Alpar is in an auto accident, she meets and falls for Berry, an agent for the British Secret Service. But her supposedly dead husband reappears—a villainous spy who forces his wife to make a recording that will act as a coded message. Agents get hold of the recording, and lock Alpar up for being a spy, with Berry's boss, thinking he has something to do with it. But Berry unravels the mystery so that he can be with his singing sweetheart, who never stops exercising her vocal chords, even while in the pen. (In French.)

d, Richard Pottier; w, Andre Paul-Antoine; ph, Claude Heyman; m, Brodsky.

Spy/Drama **(PR:A MPAA:NR)**

RECORD OF A LIVING BEING (SEE: I LIVE IN FEAR, 1967, Jap.)

RED*** (1970, Can.) 101m Onyx/Cinepix c

Daniel Pilon *(Red)*, Genevieve Deloir *(Georgette)*, Gratien Gelinas *(Frederic)*, Fernande Giroux *(Elisabeth)*, Paul Gauthier *(Amedee)*, Claude Michaud *(Jerome)*, Donald Pilon, Yvon Dufour, Sylvie Heppel, Raymond Cloutier, Katherine Mousseau, Aurie Dion, Michel Leblond, Jean-Pierre Cartier, Beaudion Roussea, Serge Deyglun.

Pilon plays a young man living in Canada who is half Indian, half Quebecois. His inability to adapt to life either in the city or on the pastoral reservation leads him to numerous escapades with fast cars and women, gangsters and a weird initiation rite with a girl he meets, culminating in his death. Very fast-paced picture, with excellent visual footage of the Canadian countryside. (In French.)

d, Gilles Carle; w, Carle, Ennio Flaiano; ph, Bernard Chentrier (Eastmancolor); m, Pierre Brault; ed, Yves Langlois.

Drama **(PR:C MPAA:NR)**

RED AND THE BLACK, THE½** (1954, Fr./Ital.) 145m Franco-London-Documento/GAU c (LE ROUGE ET LE NOIR)

Gerard Philipe *(Julian Sorel)*, Danielle Darrieux *(Mme. Louise de Renal)*, Antonella Lualdi *(Mathilde de la Mole)*, Jean Mercure *(Marquis de la Mole)*, Jean Martinelli *(Mons. de Renal)*, Antoine Balpêtre *(Abbe Pirard)*, Anna Maria Sandri *(Elisa the Maid)*, Andre Brunot *(Abbe Chelan)*, Mirko Ellis *(Norbert de la Mole)*, Suzette Nivette *(Marquise de la Mole)*, Pierre Jourdan *(L'Abbe Frilair)*, Jacques Varennes *(President of the Court)*, Robert Berri *(Palefrenier de Croisenoix)*.

Philipe plays a 19th-Century opportunist whose social position has left him with an overall cynical attitude. This, however, takes on a change when he meets and falls in love with a charming maiden. This picture was the third attempt at an adaptation of the French classic by Stendhal, perhaps remaining closest to the original narrative. (In French; English subtitles.)

d, Claude Autant-Lara; w, Jean Aurenche, Pierre Bost (based on the novel by Stendhal [Marie Henri Beyle]; ph, Michel Kelber (Eastmancolor); m, Paul Cloerec; ed, Madeleine Gug, Bosis Lewin; art d, Max Douy; cos, Rosine Delamere; English titles, Geoffrey Jones.

Drama **(PR:A MPAA:NR)**

RED AND THE WHITE, THE½** (1969, Hung./USSR) 92m Mafilm Studios-Mosfilm/Brandon bw (CSILLAGOSOK, KATONAK; ZVYOZDY I SOLDATY)

Jozsef Madaras *(Hungarian Commander)*, Tibor Molnar *(Andras)*, Andras Kozak *(Laszlo)*, Jacint Juhasz *(Istvan)*, Anatoliy Yabbarov *(Capt. Chelpanov)*, Sergey Nikonenko *(Cossack Officer)*, Mikhail Kozakov *(Nestor)*, Bolot Beyshenaliyev *(Chingiz)*, Tatyana Konyukhova *(Yelizaveta, the Matron)*, Krystyna Mikolajewska *(Olga)*, Viktor Avdyushko *(Sailor)*, Gleb Strizhenov *(Colonel)*, Nikita Mikhalkov *(White Officer)*, Vladimar Prokofyev, Valentin Bryleyev, Vera Bykova, Ye. Yermolayeva, Vitaliy Konyayev, Valeriy Glebov, K. Karyolskikh, Pyotr Savin, Nikolay Sergeyev, Sandor Szili, Roman Khomyatov, Karoly Eizler, Mika Ardova, Vera Berezutskaya, Gabi Daniel, Yelena Kazelkova, Nikolay Parfyonov, Nina Sorina, Natalya Zheromskaya, Julia Coglin.

Filmed depiction of the 1918 Russian revolution as it took place in Hungary, with Hungarian forces siding with the Red armies against the overpowering White forces. The climactic finish has the broken ranks of a Red outfit marching to certain death against the Whites, singing the "Marseillaise" as they march, while reinforcements start their fight to crush the White army. Basically Soviet propaganda, centering on the devotion and gallantry of the revolutionaries.

d, Miklos Jancso; w, Georgiy Mdivani, Gyula Hernadi, Jancso; ph, Tamas Somlo (Agfascope); ed, Zoltan Farkas; art d, Boris Chebotaryov; cos, Mayya Abar-Baranovskaya, Gyula Vardai.

War **(PR:A MPAA:NR)**

RED BADGE OF COURAGE, THE***** (1951) 69m MGM bw

Audie Murphy *(Henry Fleming the Youth)*, Bill Mauldin *(Tom Wilson the Loud Soldier)*, Douglas Dick *(Lieutenant)*, Royal Dano *(Tattered Man)*, John Dierkes *(Jim Conlin the Tall Soldier)*, Arthur Hunnicutt *(Bill Porter)*, Andy Devine *(Fat Soldier)*, Robert Easton Burke *(Thompson)*, Smith Ballew *(Captain)*, Glenn Strange *(Colonel)*, Dan White *(Sergeant)*, Frank McGraw *(Captain)*, Tim Durant *(General)*, Emmett Lynn, Stanford Jolley, William "Bill" Phillips, House Peters, Jr., Frank Sully *(Veterans)*, George Offerman, Jr., Joel Marston, Robert Nichols *(Union Soldiers)*, Lou Nova, Fred Kohler, Jr., Dick Curtis, Guy Wilkerson, Buddy Roosevelt *(Veterans)*, Jim Hayward *(Soldier)*, Gloria Eaton *(Southern Girl)*, Robert Cherry *(Soldier Who Sings)*, Whit Bissel *(Wounded Officer)*, William Phipps *(Officer)*, Ed Hinton *(Corporal)*, Lynn Farr *(Confederate)*, James Whitmore *(Voice)*.

Huston to the time of this writing insists that this film *could have been* his greatest and the claim is supportable to a good degree when viewing this Civil War battle picture which examines the fine line between cowardice and bravery. Like the Crane novel, Huston leaned heavily upon the stark and telling images captured in the early photography of Mathew Brady. (The 21-year-old Crane had never been to war and wrote his novel by studying the Brady photographs.) Murphy, the most decorated hero of WW II, is the youth who joins the Union Army and spends nervous time training and listening to rumors of war bandied about by his fellow soldiers, especially tales spun by his gregarious friend Mauldin (later a Pulitzer Prize winning cartoonist). He grows restless waiting for orders that will take him into battle and later, when news does arrive that his unit will be moving to join other units for an impending battle, he turns braggart. He and his company are positioned in line just as a Confederate charge is mounting against them. Murphy and the others wait anxiously as the fierce Southern troops advance resolutely, waving their banners and screaming like banshees. The company fires its withering volley against the Southerners, which thins their ranks, but to Murphy's horror the Confederates still keep coming. He sees out of the corner of his eyes Union soldiers panicking and fleeing from their position. The Southerners press forward and men around Murphy begin to drop dead, bullets in their heads. Wide-eyed and gripped with terror, he bolts for the rear, running through the smoke and mist of battle as if seized by an invisible hand, dragging him away from the "field of honor" and into disgrace. Murphy runs through forests and over streams, fleeing past officers who brandish sabers and call him and other deserters cowards, telling them that they will be shot for their insidious flight. Later, hiding in a river bed, Murphy hears officers talk about the panicking Union troops and he moves on, dazed. Then a stream of more Union troops races by him and he asks where they are going, but none stop to tell him anything. He grabs one frightened soldier on the run who answers his questions with a gun butt which knocks Murphy to the ground unconscious. Regaining consciousness, Murphy wanders down a road that suddenly fills up with wounded soldiers streaming back from the battle. Among them he finds his friend Dierkes, a tall, introspective soldier who tells him he has been shot and is in shock, talking of nothing but the battle—"Lordy, what a fight! And I got shot!" until he is seized by a compulsion to climb a nearby hill. Murphy and Dano, a ragged soldier who keeps trying to talk to Murphy, race after Dierkes to find him standing atop the hill breathing heavily and telling Murphy to "leave me be...leave me be!" He sways back and forth, towering over Murphy, then, like a huge tree, topples to earth, dead. Dano approaches and shakes his head, telling Murphy: "I ain't never seen no fella do like that afore. He were a dandy, weren't he?" Murphy can only move down to the road in a daze as Dano cries out after him: "Where ya hit? Where ya hit?" At nightfall a kindly quartermaster sergeant, Devine, discovers him wandering about and jovially escorts him to his company, garrulously recounting the day's battle as if describing a horserace, bandaging his head for him. Murphy, embarrassed at his cowardice, makes up a story about being struck by a mine ball which grazed his head and how he then got separated from his company, a tall tale he hesitantly repeats to Mauldin and others when he rejoins his company. When his old friend Mauldin—who believes he has been wounded, as Murphy claims—inspects the wound, he tells him it appears as if he had been bashed in the head. That night, Murphy sleeps with the survivors of the battle, accepted back in their midst as one of them, his secret safe, his identity as a coward unknown. The following day, his unit is once more marched into line and again he and his fellow soldiers await another Confedearte charge. This time anger at the sight of the enemy rises up in Murphy and when the attacking Southern troops waver under the first volley of Union fire, the youth leaves the embankment and inches *toward* the enemy, a few of his friends following, firing and advancing a few steps. The movement groundswells into a charge with Murphy grabbing the flag from a wounded Union soldier and sweeping forward with it, leading the charge, running and firing at the fast-retreating enemy. On and on the Union line swells and rushes until it slips over a low stone wall and engulfs the wounded and demoralized Confederate troops. Murphy sees a Confederate soldier trying to crawl away over a hill, carrying the Southern flag and, approaching the dying man, he grabs the flag just as the soldier dies, holding both banners in the breeze, a symbolic image of two causes held in the hands of one American youth who is unsure now of the causes of warfare, even though he is more aware of his own ability to face its fury. He marches away with his company as Whitmore, who has narrated Crane's poetic lines throughout the film, utters the last lines: "So it came to pass that as he trudged from the place of blood and wrath his soul changed. He had been to touch the Great Death and found that, after all, it was but the Great Death. Scars faded as flowers and the youth saw that the world was a world for him. He had rid himself of the red sickness of battle and the sultry nightmare was in the past. He turned now with a lover's thirst to images of tranquil skies, fresh meadows, cool brooks, an existence of soft and eternal peace." Huston's direction is spare and decisive in every telling scene, extracting great performances from newcomers Murphy and Mauldin and experienced veterans Dano, Dierkes, Hunnicutt, and Devine. The director uses every device to make his cameras move along with the smoky sweep of battle, following the charging men with truck shots, panning shots, and dolly shots, so that the film is alive and full of action. In more pensive moments, the film is a great and moving study of Americans fighting Americans, unsure about their dedication to the death of each other. The dialog is all Huston and is lovingly faithful to Crane's masterpiece, capturing not only the author's poetic descriptions as dynamically related by Whitmore but the quaint dialog and interchanges of the soldiers in this almost all-male cast. "I got holes in my pants, holes in my shoes but there ain't no holes in me other than the ones God intended," says Hunnicutt after the battle, in gratitude for being alive. Much of the credit for the overall visual effect of THE RED BADGE OF COURAGE goes to cameraman Rosson who gives a gritty hardscrabble feel to the film, marvelously capturing the period and a nation then educating itself in the ways of warfare. This film became, along with BATTLE-GROUND, the *cause celebre* which brought about the head-to-head confrontation between MGM studio boss Louis B. Mayer and his chief of production, Dore Schary. Mayer had not liked the script for THE RED BADGE OF COURAGE and Schary did, both men appealing to Nicholas Schenck, head of Loew's Inc., and financial chief of the studio. Schenck sided with Schary but Mayer still tried to talk Huston and producer Reinhardt out of doing the film when Schary was out of the studio for a few weeks with a bad back. "How can you make a picture of boys with funny caps and pop guns, and make people think the war they are fighting is terrible?" he questioned both men. He then went into exaggerated postures of shooting and charging around his office. Later Huston said to him, "L.B., if you feel this strongly against the picture, why, let's forget the whole thing." Surprisingly, Mayer became angered over his quick surrendering of the project, shouting at him: "John Huston, I'm ashamed of you! Do you believe in this picture? Have you any reason for wanting to make it other than the fact that you believe in it?...Stick by your guns! Never let me hear you talk like this again! I don't like this picture. I don't think it will make money. I don't want to make it and I will continue to do everything in my power to keep you from making it. But you—you should do everything in you power to make it!" Such contradictions from the most decisive man in Hollywood only indicated that Mayer was on his way out and he was soon succeeded by Schary, whose productions had brought in more capital than those Mayer had spearheaded. This was not the case with THE RED BADGE OF COURAGE, which was a critical success but a commerical failure. The death scenes were too much for audiences, and many of these were later cut, particularly that of Dano, who marches down the road after Murphy and then realizes that he, like Dierkes, is mortally wounded, and dies in the road. The theme is seen briefly in the charge at the end of the film where a bespectacled soldier is hit and drops to the ground, fumbles about for his spectacles, finds them, and puts them on, only to roll over dead. Huston left the production immediately after completion to fly to a new location across the world to make THE AFRICAN QUEEN and Reinhardt, Schary, and others then cut THE RED BADGE OF COURAGE as they saw fit, reducing it to 69 minutes. It did not play well with premiere audiences and MGM wound up sending the film out without fanfare, playing it as second feature on double bills, hardly a way in which to recoup the film's $1.6 million price tag. Mostly audiences did not identify with the grim realism of the film nor with its unknown cast members; the well-known Crane story was not enough to encourage good box office receipts. Huston himself never knew how long his final print was, although it was reported to be originally 78 minutes, and did not hold onto a copy with the original running time so the truncated version is all there is left, but it is enough. It is still a classic, even if some of the fingers are missing.

p, Gottfried Reinhardt; d&w, John Huston (based on the novel by Stephen Crane, adapted by Albert Band); ph, Harold Rosson; m, Bronislau Kaper; ed, Ben Lewis; art d, Cedric Gibbons, Hans Peters.

Historical War Drama　　　**Cas.**　　　**(PR:C　MPAA:NR)**

RED BALL EXPRESS**½　　　　　(1952) 83m UNIV bw

Jeff Chandler (*Lt. Chick Campbell*), Alex Nicol (*Sgt. Ernest Kalleck*), Charles Drake (*Pvt. Ronald Partridge*), Judith Braun (*Joyce McClellan*), Hugh O'Brian (*Pvt. Wilson*), Jacqueline Duval (*Antoinette DuBois*), Jack Kelly (*Pvt. John Heyman*), Cindy Garner (*Kitty Walsh*), Sidney Poitier (*Cpl. Andrew Robertson*), Howard Petrie (*Gen. Gordon*), Bubber Johnson (*Pvt. Taffy Smith*), Robert Davis (*Pvt. Dave McCord*), John Hudson (*Sgt. Max*), Frank Chase (*Higgins*), John Pickard (*Major*), Palmer Lee [Gregg Palmer] (*Tank Lieutenant*), Jack Warden, Richard Garland.

Chandler plays the officer in charge of bringing fuel to Gen. George Patton's tanks as they make their rush towards Paris in WW II. Along with the demands of the 24-hour-a-day job, Chandler must also contend with a spiteful and mistrusting sergeant, Nicol, as well as a black soldier, Poitier, who feels he is the victim of racial prejudice. But Chandler proves worthy of the task, as he convinces both the men that he is only doing his job, thus warranting a deep-felt respect. Cliched script is astutely handled by director Boetticher, who combines action, drama, and even some comic situations into a well-paced blend.

p, Aaron Rosenberg; d, Budd Boetticher; w, John Michael Hayes (based on the story by Marcel Klauber, Billy Grady, Jr.); ph, Maury Gertsman; ed, Edward Curtiss; art d, Bernard Herzbrun, Richard H. Riedel.

War　　　　　　　　　　　　**(PR:A　MPAA:NR)**

RED BEARD***　　　(1966, Jap.) 185m Kurosawa-Toho bw (AKAHIGE)

Toshiro Mifune (*Dr. Niide, Red Beard*), Yuzo Kayama (*Dr. Noboru Yasumoto*), Yoshio Tsuchiya (*Dr. Mori*), Terumi Niki (*Otoyo*), Tsutomu Yamazaki (*Sahachi*), Yoko Naito (*Masae*), Reiko Dan (*Osuki*), Akemi Negishi (*Okumi*), Kyoko Kagawa (*Mental Patient*), Kamatari Fujiwara (*Rokusuke*), Miyuki Kuwano (*Onaka*), Takashi Shimura (*Tokubei Izumiya*), Eijiro Tono (*Goheiji*), Tatsuyoshi Ehara (*Genzo Tsugawa*), Haruko Sugimura (*Kin*), Ken Mitsuda (*Masae's Father*), Kinuyo Tanaka (*Yasumoto's Mother*), Chishu Ryu (*Yasumoto's Father*), Yoshitaka Zushi (*Choiji*), Reiko Nanao, Koji Mitsui.

This long venture details the events which help a young intern to overcome his greed and romantic ideals about being a doctor. In early 19th Century Japan, Mifune is the head doctor in a poverty stricken public health clinic, whose latest intern, Kayama, has his own ideas about caring for the sick. Despite initial signs of revolt, which include excessive drinking and dressing in clothes other than what doctors usually wear, this young doctor eventually learns that being a good doctor takes quite a bit of sacrifice. The dedicated patience of the elderly Mifune is most instrumental in making Kayama understand the role of a doctor. Kayama's involvement with a 12-year-old girl warped by her stay in a brothel also plays a role in his awakening. All technical and acting credits are excellent, but the adventures of the story are not enough to sustain interest for the full three hours.

p, Tomoyuki Tanaka, Ryuzo Kikushima; d, Akira Kurosawa; w, Masato Ide, Hideo Oguni, Kikushima, Kurosawa (based on the novel *Akahige Shinryo Tan* by Shugoro Yamamoto); ph, Asaichi Nakai, Takao Saito (Tohoscope); m, Masaru Sato; art d, Yoshiro Muraki.

Drama　　　　　　　　　　　　**(PR:C-O　MPAA:NR)**

RED BERET, THE　　　　　　　(SEE: PARATROOPER, 1954)

RED BLOOD OF COURAGE**　　　(1935) 55m Ambassador bw

Kermit Maynard (*Jim Sullivan/James Anderson*), Ann Sheridan (*Beth Henry*), Reginald Barlow (*Mark Henry/Pete Drago*), Ben Hendricks, Jr. (*Bart Slager*), George Regas (*Frenchy*), Nat Carr (*Meyer*), Charles King (*Joe*), "Rocky" (*The Horse*), Carl Mathews (*Indian in Store/Mountie*), Milt Morante (*Gunman*), Art Dillard (*Henchman*).

Maynard plays a Mountie on the trek of his murdered partner, when he stumbles upon a peculiar situation on the ranch of Barlow, whose niece, Sheridan, is visiting from the city. His snooping leads him to discover that the man posing as Sheridan's uncle is really the leader of a notorious gang responsible for the death of his partner, and that the gang is after the oil deposits on her uncle's farm. A bit of snooping, the revealing of the real uncle, and the aid of the Mounties, help to uncover the gang, putting them where they belong. Script offers a large dose of action, which the players deliver in routine fashion.

p, Maurice Cohn, Sigmund Neufield; d, Jack English; w, Barry Barringer (based on the novel by James Oliver Curwood); ph, Arthur Reed; ed, Richard G. Wray.

Western　　　　　**Cas.**　　　　　**(PR:A　MPAA:NR)**

RED CANYON**½　　　　　　　(1949) 82m UNIV c

Ann Blyth (*Lucy Bostel*), Howard Duff (*Lin Slone/Cordt*), George Brent (*Mathew Boatel*), Edgar Buchanan (*Jonah Johnson*), John McIntire (*Floyd Cordt*), Chill Wills (*Brackton*), Jane Darwell (*Aunt Jane*), Lloyd Bridges (*Virgil Cordt*), James Seay (*Joel Creech*), Edmund MacDonald (*Farlane*), Denver Pyle (*Hutch*), Willard Willingham (*Van*), Hank Patterson (*Osborne*), Ray Bennett (*Pronto*), Hank Worden (*Charley*), Sonny Choree (*Indian*), David Clarke (*Sears*), Edmund Cobb, John Carpenter (*Men*).

Duff plays a drifter in the old west, trying to catch a wild stallion when he comes across Blyth, daughter to the territory's top horse breeder. Duff wants the wild stallion to race in an event that Brent, as Blyth's father, has all intentions of winning, thus setting up a confrontation between Brent and the man who is wooing his daughter. Greater conflict is added when it is realized that Duff comes from a family of notorious horse thieves. But Duff clears his name and gets Blyth when he shoots up his pa and brother in a climactic shootout. The color photography of the Utah scenery, along with footage of wild horses, adds a spark to the story of human conflict, giving it credence beyond that of a formula western. Both Duff and Blyth give acceptable performances.

p, Leonard Goldstein; d, George Sherman; w, Maurice Geraghty (based on the novel *Wildfire* by Zane Grey); ph, Irving Glassberg (Technicolor); m, Walter Scharf; ed, Otto Ludwig; art d, Bernard Herzbrun, Frank A. Richards; set d, Russell A. Gausman, Joseph Kish; cos. Rosemary Odell; makeup, Bud Westmore, John Holden.

Western　　　　　　　　　　　**(PR:A　MPAA:NR)**

RED CLOAK, THE**　　　(1961, Ital./Fr.) 95m Franca-Centra-Trio/Sefo International-AA c (IL MANTELLO ROSSO; LES REVOLTES; LE MANTEAU ROUGE)

Patricia Medina (*Laura Lanfranchi*), Bruce Cabot (*Raniero d'Anversa*), Fausto Tozzi (*Luca de Bardi*), Guy Mairesse (*Guercio*), Domenico Modugno (*Saro*), Lyla Rocco (*Stella*), Jean Murat (*Cosimo*), Nyta Dover, Jean Francois Calve, Jeanne Fusier-Gil.

In 16th-Century Pisa, an evil magistrate imposes unjust taxes upon the people, having a strong military force to make sure that the taxes are paid. Tozzi, whose father had been murdered by military captain Cabot, dons a red cloak at night, attacking Cabot's men one-by-one in order to get his revenge. Story culminates in a duel that leaves Cabot dead and Tozzi the victor.

p, Elios Vercelloni; d, Giuseppe Maria Scotese; w, Scotese, Riccardo Pazzaglia, Albino Principe, Jacopo Corsi, France Roche, Pierre Kast (based on a story by Principe); ph, Adalberto Albertini, (Eastmancolor); m, Gino Marinuzzi; art d, Umberto Giovagnoli; m/l, Domenico Modugno.

Historical Drama　　　　　　　**(PR:A　MPAA:NR)**

RED DANUBE, THE**　　　　　(1949) 119m MGM bw

Walter Pidgeon (*Col. Michael "Jokey" Nicobar*), Ethel Barrymore (*The Mother Superior*), Peter Lawford (*Maj. John "Twingo" McPhimister*), Angela Lansbury (*Audrey Quail*), Janet Leigh (*Maria Buhlen*), Louis Calhern (*Col. Piniev*), Francis L. Sullivan (*Col. Humphrey "Blinker" Omicron*), Melville Cooper (*Pvt. David Moonlight*), Robert Coote (*Brig. C.M.V. Catlock*), Alan Napier (*The General*), Roman Toporow (*2nd Lt. Maxim Omansky*), Kasia Orzazewski (*Sister Kasmira*), Tamara Shayne (*Helena Nagard*), Konstantin Shayne (*Prof. Serge Bruloff*), Janine Perreau ("*Mickey" Mouse*), David Hydes (*Lt. Guedalia-Wood*), Audrey Long

(Countess Cressanti), Margo Von Leu *(Lani Hansel)*, Tito Vuolo *(Italian Billposter)*, Argentina Brunetti *(Italian Woman)*, Lotus Thompson *(Woman Private)*, John Royce *(Sergeant)*, Henry Kulky *(Lieutenant)*, Doris Lloyd *(Mrs. Omicron)*, Kenneth Hunter *(Brigadier General)*, Richard Fraser *(Pilot)*, Geoffrey Alah *(Major)*, Sigmund Halperon *(German)*.

Pidgeon and Lawford play two British officers in Allied occupied Vienna shortly after WW II, where the Soviets are rounding up their refugees to take back to Russia for an unmentionable fate. The other Allied forces agree to aid the Soviets. Ballerina Leigh is a problem as the sweetheart of Lawford, yet a major figure wanted by the Soviets. Since Pidgeon agreed to follow all regulations, he delivers the girl only on the promise that she will be treated well. Also included in this anti-communist picture is Barrymore as the Mother Superior trying to convince Pidgeon of the necessity of organized religion. A weighty script appears to be too much for the players to handle, bogging down the film and making the plot unconvincing.

p, Carey Wilson; d, George Sidney; w, Gina Kaus, Arthur Wimperis (based on the novel *Vespers in Vienna* by Bruce Marshall); ph, Charles Rosher; m, Miklos Rozsa; ed, James E. Newcom; art d, Cedric Gibbons, Hans Peters; cos, Helen Rose.

War/Drama **(PR:A MPAA:NR)**

RED DESERT½** (1949) 59m Lippert bw

Don Barry *(Pecos Kid)*, Tom Neal *(John Williams)*, Jack Holt *(Deacon Smith)*, Margia Dean *(Hazel Carter)*, Byron Foulger *(Sparky Johnson)*, Joseph Crehan *(President U.S. Grant)*, John Cason *(Horn)*, Tom London *(Col. McMasters)*, Holly Bane *(Barton)*, Hank Bell *(Stage Driver)*, George Slocum *(Bartender)*.

Barry plays an agent assigned by President Grant (Crehan) to track down the theft of a shipment of gold bullion. His chase leads him to the Red Desert, where men are at the mercy of the blazing sun. He captures the villain there, only to discover that the culprit is merely a tool in the hands of another figure. Expertly directed for a low budget western, with a script that builds to a climactic, suspenseful ending.

p, Ron Ormond; d, Ford Beebe; w, Daniel B. Ullman, Ormond (based on the story by Ullman); ph, Ernest Miller; m, Walter Greene; ed, Hugh Winn.

Western **(PR:A MPAA:NR)**

RED DESERT*½** (1965, Fr./Ital.) 116m Film Duemila-Federiz-Francoriz/Rizzoli Film c (IL DESERTO ROSSO; LE DESERT ROUGE)

Monica Vitti *(Giuliana)*, Richard Harris *(Corrado Zeller)*, Carlo Chionetti *(Ugo)*, Xenia Valderi *(Linda)*, Rita Renoir *(Emilia)*, Aldo Grotti *(Max)*, Valerio Baroleschi *(Valerio)*, Giuliano Missirini *(Workman)*, Lili Rheims *(Workman's Wife)*, Emanuela Pala Carboni *(Girl in Fable)*, Bruno Borghi, Beppe Conti, Giuli Cotignoli, Hiram Mino Madonia, Arturo Parmiani, Carla Ravasi, Ivo Scherpiani, Bruno Scipioni, Giovanni Lolli.

A masterpiece of color cinematography, RED DESERT combines subtle hues to heighten the emotional effect of the total cinematic image, which includes a frightening isolating electronic soundtrack. The purpose was to portray the effects of a modernized culture, one in which the individual withdraws more and more into himself, losing the ability to make contact with others. Vitti plays a depressed woman trapped in an unloving marriage. She is stricken with a form of neurosis that everyone seems to be aware of, yet treats in a totally nonchalant manner without ever questioning what factors are affecting her mental state. Only Harris, as a visiting engineer, seems to have an understanding of what it is that Vitti is going through. In a last desperate attempt to grasp onto her basic emotions, Vitti has two casual sexual encounters, first seducing Harris, then picking up a docked sailor. As the film ends, her son asks her why birds don't fly through the poisonous yellow smoke of Harris' factory, and she responds, "Because they have learned to fly around it," illustrating her realization that she must adapt to the pain and problems of her existence. An extremely disturbing film, yet, RED DESERT manages to capture a rare beauty that pushes the boundaries of the cinema a step forward.

p, Antonio Cervi; d, Michelangelo Antonioni; w, Antonioni, Tonino Guerra; ph, Carlo Di Palma (Eastmancolor); m, Giovanni Fusco, Vittorio Gelmetti; ed, Eraldo Da Roma; md, Carlo Savina; art d, Piero Poletto; cos, Gitt Magrini; spec eff, Franco Freda.

Drama **(PR:O MPAA:NR)**

RED DRAGON, THE*½ (1946) 64m MON bw

Sidney Toler *(Charlie Chan)*, Fortunio Bonanova *(Inspector Luis Carvero)*, Benson Fong *(Tommy Chan)*, Robert E. Keane *(Alfred Wyans)*, Willie Best *(Chattanooga Brown)*, Carol Hughes *(Marguerite Fontan)*, Marjorie Hoshelle *(Countess Irena)*, Barton Yarborough *(Joseph Bradish)*, George Meeker *(Edmond Slade)*, Don Costello *(Charles Masack)*, Charles Trowbridge *(Prentiss)*, Mildred Boyd *(Josephine)*, Jean Wong *(Iris)*, Donald Dexter Taylor *(Walter Dorn, Wyans' Secretary)*.

Toler plays the noble sleuth as he ventures to Mexico City where a number of shady figures are trying to get their hands on the formula for an atomic bomb. When people start dropping like flies, Toler uncovers a gun firing via remote control. He nabs the killer, making the plans for the bomb safe again. Produced and enacted in a strictly mechanical manner. (See CHARLIE CHAN series, Index.)

p, James B. Burkett; d, Phil Rosen; w, George Callahan (based on the story by Callahan); ph, Vincent Farrar; ed, Ace Herman; art d, Dave Milton.

Mystery **(PR:A MPAA:NR)**

RED-DRAGON½** (1967, Ital./Ger./US) 89m Arca-P.E.A./Woolner Bros. c (A-009 MISSIONE HONG KONG; DAS GEHEIMNIS DER DREI DSCHUNKEN)

Stewart Granger *(Michael Scott)*, Rosanna Schiaffino *(Carol)*, Harald Juhnke *(Smoky)*, Paul Klinger *(Norman)*, Margit Sand *(Blanche)*, Sieghardt Rupp *(Pierre Milot)*, Paul Dahlke *(Harris)*, Hilda Somers [Helga Sommerfield], Frank Fontana [Franco Fantasia], Horst Frank, Chitra Ratana, Suzanne Roquette.

Granger and Schiaffino are FBI agents in Hong Kong trying to uncover who controls a smuggling operation that has been selling electrical supplies to the communists. An unimaginative conclusion has Klinger, the FBI man in Hong Kong, as "Mr. Big." Some interesting situations and the exotic atmosphere of Hong Kong give an otherwise predictable story a spark of excitement.

p, Gero Wecker; d, Ernest Hofbauer; w, Hans-Karl Kubiak, W.P. Zibaso, George Higgins, III (based on the story "La Riviere des Trois Jonques" by Georges Godefroy); ph, Werner M. Lenz (Techniscope, Technicolor); m, Riz Ortolani; ed, Lenz, Hella Faust, Eugenio Alabiso; md, Ortolani; art d, Max Mellin; cos, Margarete Simon; spec eff, Richard Richtsfeld; makeup, Werner Schroder.

Spy **(PR:A MPAA:NR)**

RED DRESS, THE** (1954, Brit.) 76m Douglas Fairbanks, Jr./BL bw

Renee Asherson, Joan Tetzel, James Kenney, Clifford Evans, John Warwick, Meredith Edwards, Paul Carpenter, Deborah Turnbull, Warren Stanhope, John Salew, Peter Jones, Bartlett Mullins.

A trilogy of suspense tales, the first casting Asherson as the unhappy wife of a trapped mine worker. Pleased that he is dead, she finds herself a new man, only to have her husband emerge from the mine alive. The second story has Tetzel saving her sister from a planned marriage by locking up the groom-to-be. She is mistaken, however, and locks up the wrong man. The final episode casts Kenney as a saboteur who plants a bomb in a factory. He must struggle to get away from the plant before the explosion, eventually putting a safe distance between himself and the bomb. His time expires, however, when a thoughtful coworker brings him the lunchbox he left behind—a ticking lunchbox. Although the stories have a TV-ish quality, they do rivet the attention.

p, Douglas Fairbanks, Jr.; d, Lawrence Huntington, Charles Saunders; w, Guy Morgan, Selwyn Jepson, Larry Marcus, Peter Quinn; ph, Ken Telbot, Brendan J. Stafford, Jimmy Wilson.

Suspense **(PR:A MPAA:NR)**

RED DUST*½** (1932) 83m MGM bw

Clark Gable *(Dennis Carson)*, Jean Harlow *(Vantine)*, Gene Raymond *(Gary Willis)*, Mary Astor *(Barbara Willis)*, Donald Crisp *(Guidon)*, Tully Marshall *(McQuarg)*, Forrester Harvey *(Limey)*, Willie Fung *(Hoy)*.

The second pairing of Gable and Harlow is a steamy drama of infidelity, set against an exotic background and peppered with dialog and situations that pushed the boundaries of Hollywood self-censorship as far as they would go. Gable plays the head of a rubber plantation located in the Far East, where he is assisted by Marshall and Crisp. Crisp is returning from a trip to Saigon, arriving on a boat on which Harlow, a prostitute running from the law, is also a passenger. She fends off Crisp's drunken wooing, then Gable and Marshall arrive to help out. Gable agrees to let her stay at the plantation until the next boat leaves in a week. Gable gives Harlow a cold shoulder at first, put off by her profession and what it represents. Gradually he sees that her vocation belies her interior, and warms up to her beguiling manner. They have an affair, then Harlow bids adieu. Arriving on the boat on which Harlow will depart are newlyweds Raymond, an engineer, and Astor. Raymond is all set to begin working for Gable when he is suddenly struck down by jungle fever. Gable takes care of the ill man, then is surprised by the return of Harlow. She has been forced to come back when the ship she was aboard became disabled. She wants to renew the affair with Gable, but he has turned his attentions toward Astor. After Raymond recovers, Gable sends him, along with Marshall and Crisp, on a bridge construction project. With Raymond out of the way, Gable and Astor now consummate their affair. Raymond returns, showing nothing but admiration for Gable. This shames the plantation owner, and Gable decides to end his dalliance with Astor. To be rid of her, Gable once more takes up with Harlow, which sends Astor into a rage. When Gable finally tells her it's quits, Astor shoots him in the side. Gable collapses, and Raymond enters after hearing the shot. Harlow explains to him that Astor was forced to shoot Gable to stop his unrelenting sexual advances. Raymond decides to quit his job, and, along with his unfaithful wife, leaves the plantation. Harlow remains behind, helping Gable recover from the wound, and Gable realizes this is the woman he has been looking for. Harlow is at her brazen best here, tossing off lines that brim with sexual insinuations. While jokingly reading a children's story to Gable, Harlow exclaims: "A chipmunk and a rabbit...hey, I wonder how *this* comes out!" She shows a darker side to the character as well, and is a good counterpart to Gable's performance. His rugged personality, with a clear disdain for women, is pushed to the limits by her and forced into a moral turnabout. Harlow and Gable have a terrific chemistry that reflected their abilities as actors. Though reportedly they had little rapport during the filming of their previous effort, THE SECRET SIX, Gable and Harlow enjoyed working together on this, pushing each other to add some realistic spice to their love scenes. Gable was unhappy with the story, finding the subject matter distasteful, but because of his contract he was obliged to make the film. Professional that he was, Gable gave his all, turning in a fine performance. Barechested, with a beard-stubbled chin, his presence was electrifying on screen. Though the film had passionate overtones, the actual shooting was anything but. In the steamy kiss between Gable and Astor, the two actors had to put up with a myriad of set problems while waiting to perform the simple act. There were complaints about the hot lights which were causing the actors to sweat profusely. "So what?" exclaimed director Fleming. "Everybody sweats in the tropics. Let it show, that's the way it is!" After a perspiration-soaked rehearsal, the actors lounged in bathtubs to cool off. The heat was so unbearable that water was literally vaporizing off Gable's and Astor's clothing right before the camera. This was finally resolved by heating up water in tea kettles, then pouring the warm water on the two stars in order to keep them moist for the cameras. Despite these problems, the sequence came off without a hitch. "The scene was shot," Astor recalled in the book *A Life on Film*, "according to the script: 'He kisses her, gently at first and then fiercely.' And it was a print....The weird part of it all is that it never occurred to anyone, including Clark and me, that all this might have had a bad effect on the mood, or on our ability to play a love scene convincingly." Howard Hawks claimed to have contributed to RED DUST's screenplay, though screenwriter Mahin, who had often worked with Fleming, disputed this claim. The production was rocked by a terrible scandal when Harlow's husband, Paul Bern, committed suicide. Bern, who had been an assistant to MGM's *wunderkind* Irving Thalberg, had doused himself with Harlow's perfume, then put a bullet in his head after a night of sexual frustration on Labor Day weekend 1932. Harlow found the body, and the studio made intense efforts to cover up the nature of Bern's death. Gable had spent the weekend on a hunting trip with Harlow's stepfather, and steps were taken to make sure no link would be made between the costars. Louis B. Mayer, the notorious studio chief, was infuriated that the specter of scandal had finally crossed MGM's gates, and decided it would be best to replace Harlow in the picture. Mayer interviewed several actresses for the part, including Tallulah Bankhead, who at that time was still struggling to crack Hollywood stardom. After being informed what he wanted her to do, Bankhead grew furious with Mayer. "To damn the radiant Jean for the misfortune of another would be one of the shabbiest acts of all time," Bankhead recalled in her autobiography. "I told Mr. Mayer as much. I tossed in a survey of the background of some of his box-office pets. He blanched." When Mayer, in his stately office, tried acting out the circumstances of Bern's death for Bankhead, the actress deliberately misinterpreted what he was doing, accusing the powerful man of stepping beyond his boundaries. "It would be 12 years before I'd face a motion picture camera again," Bankhead wrote. "It gave me considerable satisfaction to deflate this Nero in my final gesture." Eventually it was decided to continue shooting with Harlow. Still in shock and mourning, Harlow came to the set in a depressed state of mind. The director took a look at the star, then callously remarked: "How are we going to get a sexy performance with *that* look in her eyes?" However, a poll of theater managers and film exhibitors proved that audiences were eager to see Harlow on screen. Mayer, in a complete turnabout, demanded the film's production be hurried to capitalize on the public sympathy generated for Harlow in the wake of the scandal. Harlow went on a successful publicity tour for the film, and the worst appeared to be over. She would wed Rosson, RED DUST's cinematographer, the next year, though this marriage was short-lived. RED DUST, based on a play that closed after eight performances, was remade twice: first as a programmer for Ann Sothern's MAISIE series, entitled CONGO MAISIE (1940); then in 1953, as MOGAMBO with Gable reprising his role, costarring with Ava Gardner and Grace Kelly, under the direction of John Ford.

p&d, Victor Fleming; sup, Hunt Stromberg; w, John Mahin (based on the play by Wilson Collison); ph, Harold G. Rosson; ed, Blanche Sewell; art d, Cedric Gibbons; cos, Adrian.

Drama **Cas.** **(PR:C MPAA:NR)**

RED ENSIGN (SEE: STRIKE!, 1934, Brit.)

RED FORK RANGE* (1931) 59m National Players/Big Four bw

Wally Wales [Hal Taliaferro] *(Wally Hamilton)*, Ruth Mix *(Ruth Farrel)*, Al Ferguson *(Black Bard)*, Cliff Lyons *("Skeet" Beldon)*, Bud Osborne *("Whip" Reden)*, Lafe McKee *(Charles Farrell)*, Will Armstrong *(Sgt. O'Flaherty)*, George Gerwin *(Steve Alden)*, Jim Corey *("Apache" Joe)*, Chief Big Tree *(Chief Barking Fox)*.

All action, and nothing but, has Wales as the hero who chases after Osborne and Lyons, two crooks masquerading as Indians, in order to save his sweetheart, Mix. A few laughs are injected between fistfights and chase scenes, but there's not too much in the way of "meaningful" dialog. Wales later changed his name to Hal Taliaferro, when he became a noted character actor in the 1930s.

p, John R. Freuler; d, Alvin J. Neitz [Alan James]; w, Neitz, Henry Taylor (based on the story by Taylor); ph, William Nobles; ed, Ethel Dabey.

Western **(PR:A MPAA:NR)**

RED GARTERS½** (1954) 91m PAR c

Rosemary Clooney *(Calaveras Kate)*, Jack Carson *(Jason Carberry)*, Guy Mitchell *(Reb Randall)*, Pat Crowley *(Susana Martinez De La Cruz)*, Joanne Gilbert *(Sheila Winthrop)*, Gene Barry *(Rafael Moreno)*, Cass Daley *(Minnie Redwing)*, Frank Faylen *(Billy Buckett)*, Reginald Owen *(Judge Winthrop)*, Buddy Ebsen *(Ginger Pete)*, Richard Hale *(Dr. J. Pott Troy)*.

RED GARTERS is a very good idea that goes flat near the end. They intended it as a western spoof and, to that end, had special stage-like sets that more resembled a musical play than a movie. To really appreciate the good humor, one must be a fan of the genre so the satire can shine. The cavalry does *not* arrive on time, the hero does *not* win the gunfights at the finale, etc. Audiences stayed away in posses from this movie, while a straight musical oater, SEVEN BRIDES FOR SEVEN BROTHERS, cleaned up at the box office the same year. The place is "Paradise Lost," a little town in "Limbo County," California. Mitchell is an amiable cowpoke who comes to town to avenge the death of his brother, who is being buried at that moment in a gala barbecue funeral. A few people are suspected of having done the deed and Mitchell investigates them all. At the same time, Clooney, a saloon owner-singer, has been seeing Carson, the local lawyer, and she uses Mitchell's presence to get Carson jealous. Mitchell has his eye on Crowley while Barry, a gunslinger-hero, falls for Gilbert, an easterner who has also come to town. There's a triple wedding at the end with all the aforementioned mating. That's about the size of the story, but it's the details that make it worth seeing. The stylistic use of flat set with all props and costumes in garish colors serves to make it look like a regular version of a film that was made in 3-D (which it wasn't). Satire doesn't work unless the subject being satirized is well known to the audience. In this case, it flopped more than it soared. Jay Livingston and Ray Evans had written "Buttons and Bows" a few years before and hoped that one of the songs they wrote for this would do as well. None did. They include: "A Dime and a Dollar," "Meet a Happy Guy," "Vaquero" (sung by Mitchell), "Lady Killer," "Good Intentions," "Bad News," "Brave Man," "Red Garters" (sung by Clooney), "Man and Woman" (sung by Mitchell and Clooney), "This Is Greater Than I Thought" (sung by Gilbert), plus "Big Doin's," "Specialty Dance."

p, Pat Duggan; d, George Marshall; w, Michael Fessier; ph, Arthur Arling (Technicolor); ed, Arthur Schmidt; md, Joseph J. Lilley; art d, Hal Pereira, Roland Anderson; set d, Sam Comer, Ray Moyer; spec eff, John P. Fulton; ch, Nick Castle; m/l, Jay Livingston, Ray Evans.

Western/Musical Comedy **(PR:A MPAA:NR)**

RED-HAIRED ALIBI, THE** (1932) 72m Tower bw

Merna Kennedy *(Lynn Monith)*, Theodore Von Eltz *(Trent Travers)*, Grant Withers *(Rob Shelton)*, Parnell Pratt *(Regan)*, Huntley Gordon *(Kente)*, Fred Kelsey *(Corcoran)*, John Vosburgh *(Morgan)*, Marion Lessing *(Bee Lee)*, Shirley Temple *(Gloria)*, Paul Porcasi *(Margoli)*, Arthur Hoyt *(Henri)*.

This was the first screen appearance in a feature of the curly-haired girl who would soon become a household name and steal the hearts of millions of Americans. Temple had appeared in a few Educational Films Corp. shorts in 1932, but this movie was her first big film. In THE RED-HAIRED ALIBI, Temple stole the heart of Kennedy long enough to help keep her daddy, Von Eltz, out of jail. But Kennedy discovers that despite his daughter, Von Eltz is up to no good.

d, Christy Cabanne; w, Edward T. Lowe (based on the novel by Wilson Collison); ph, Harry Forbes; ed, Irving Birnbaum.

Drama/Crime **(PR:A MPAA:NR)**

RED HANGMAN, THE (SEE: BLOODY PIT OF HORROR, 1967, U.S./Ital.)

RED HEAD, THE (SEE: POIL DE CAROTTE, 1932, Fr.)

RED HEAD** (1934) 76m MON bw

Bruce Cabot *(Ted Brown)*, Grace Bradley *(Dale Carter)*, Regis Toomey *(Scoop)*, Berton Churchill *(Mr. Brown)*, George Humbert, Rita Campagna, LeRoy Mason, Monte Carter, Jack Mack, Ed Brady, Bess Stafford, Addison Page.

Bradley plays an artist model innocently brought into an accidental death because of her looks. Well-meaning playboy Cabot, recently cut off from his parents, takes sympathy and marries the girl in the hopes that his father will be offended and buy Bradley off. But the old man remains stiff, instead making a deal with Bradley to get Cabot working in exchange for a hefty sum. She stands behind Cabot as he runs a lunch wagon and invents a safety device. Everything goes smoothly until Bradley tells of the pact with the old man, at which point Cabot takes off, only to return when he discovers that Bradley did not accept the money. Touching story is handled in mechanical fashion, hampering much of its emotional impact and believability.

p, Dorothy Reid; d, Melville Brown; w, Betty Burbridge, Jesse Lasky, Jr. (based on the novel by Vera Brown); ph, Ira Morgan.

Drama **(PR:A MPAA:NR)**

RED HEADED WOMAN*** (1932) 74m MGM bw

Jean Harlow *(Lil Andrews)*, Chester Morris *(Bill Legendre, Jr.)*, Lewis Stone *(William Legendre, Sr.)*, Leila Hyams *(Irene Legendre)*, Una Merkel *(Sally)*, Henry Stephenson *(Gaerste)*, May Robson *(Aunt Jane)*, Charles Boyer *(Albert)*, Harvey Clark *(Uncle Fred)*.

A saucy and candid tale of sinful redhead, Harlow, who manages to hold down her stenographer's job by appealing to the company's wealthy boss, Morris. He becomes so obsessed with her sensuality that he obtains a divorce from his wife, Hyams, and jumps into a marriage with Harlow. Before long, however, Harlow's true persona begins to surface. She is looked down upon by the high-society crowd and must resort to pressuring the prominent Stephenson into inviting his friend to a party she is throwing. When the guests decide to drop in on Hyams, Harlow becomes vindictive and causes a scene. Morris then learns from his father, Stone, that Harlow is intimately involved with both Stephenson and her chauffeur, Boyer. When Morris learns that Stephenson has offered to marry Harlow, he steps in and tells him that she has been vamping around with Boyer. Morris barely escapes with his life when Harlow, after failing to bring about a reconciliation and losing Stephenson, fires a gun at Boyer. Realizing that he stepped out of his league with Harlow, Morris returns to Hyams and settles down to a simpler life. Some time later, while Morris and Hyams are vacationing, they see Harlow accepting a horseracing trophy at the Grand Prix. Harlow, still accompanied by Boyer, has found herself a new victim by playing mistress to a nobleman. Garnering countless favorable reviews, Harlow proved with RED HEADED WOMAN that she was a sure-fire box office hit, even when she covered her famed platinum hair with a red wig. For Boyer this was only his third American film and although the role was a small one it was pivotal to the plot and added a certain complexity to Harlow's character. After appearing in two Paramount films, Boyer finally got his chance to appear in an MGM production. Larry Swindell's biography of Boyer quotes the star as saying "I liked all the people involved, but the reason I agreed to play the chauffeur was simply that it was an MGM picture. In France and everywhere else, MGM pictures seem more important than those of any other company." The final product (which was originally planned as a Joan Crawford vehicle) titilated many an audience, but also drew strong criticism from the excessively moralistic Hays Office, chiefly because Harlow's wicked ways go unpunished. London censors reacted even stronger by refusing to allow the film a British release.

p, Paul Bern; d, Jack Conway; w, Anita Loos (based on a novel by Katharine Brush); ph, Harold G. Rosson; ed, Blanche Sewell.

Romance **(PR:A MPAA:NR)**

RED, HOT AND BLUE½** (1949) 84m PAR bw

Betty Hutton *(Eleanor Collier)*, Victor Mature *(Denny James)*, William Demarest *(Charlie Baxter)*, June Havoc *(Sandra)*, Jane Nigh *(No-No)*, Frank Loesser *(Hair-*

Do Lempke), William Talman (*Bunny Harris*), Art Smith (*Laddie Corwin*), Raymond Walburn (*Mr. Creek*), Onslow Stevens (*Capt. Allen*), Joseph Vitale (*Garr*), Barry Kelley (*Lt. Gorham*), Robert Watson (*Barney Stratum*), Jack Kruschen (*Steve*), Percy Helton (*Stage Manager*), Philip Van Zandt (*Head Waiter*), Don Shelton (*Hamlet*), Herschel Daugherty (*Laertes*), Dorothy Abbott (*Queen*), Julia Faye (*Housekeeper*), James Davies, Douglas Spencer, Noel Neill, Paul Lees, James Cornell, Joey Ray (*Members of Theater Group*), Julie Adams (*Starlet*), Lester Dorr (*Drug Store Manager*), Billy Daniel, Rita Lupino (*Dance Team*), Harland Tucker (*Saunders*), Bess Flowers (*Woman*), Tim Ryan (*Stranger*), Roscoe Behan (*Bartender, Perrina Club*), Cy Ring (*Photographer*), Lee Phelps (*Policeman*), Jimmie Dundee (*Gangster*), Al Ferguson, Billy Engle, Ed Peil, Sr., Douglas Carter (*Piano Tuners*), Robert Kellard (*Police Switchboard Operator*), Marie Thomas, Jacqueline Park (*Showgirls*), John Marchak (*Guard*), Henry Guttman (*Frankie*), Erno Verebes (*Waiter*), Arlene Jenkins (*Newspaper Woman*), Frank Alten (*Karl Mueller*), James Burke (*Doorman*).

In 1936, Cole Porter wrote a musical with the same name. This has nothing whatsoever in any way, shape, or form to do with that. Instead, we are treated to a musical comedy-crime picture with some funny moments and an enthusiastic (as always) performance by the blonde bombshell, Betty Hutton. She's an aspiring Broadway actress who is dating stage director Mature. When Mature's Broadway "angel" is killed (he's a gangster who has decided to put some money into shows, not unlike some real gangsters who did the same thing in the 1930s) while she's visiting his apartment, Hutton is suspected of the crime. Mature wonders why she was there, and the members of the slain man's gang are eager to get to the bottom of things so they kidnap her. There's a dumb chase at the wind-up that doesn't work at all. But until then, Hutton gets a chance to belt out some songs, Demarest does a nice bit as the show's press agent, Havoc shows her comic ability as Hutton's roomie, and, in a very rare—perhaps his only—on-screen appearance, composer Frank Loesser plays a gangster. His acting was not nearly as meritorious as his writing. All the tunes were penned by Loesser and include: "That's Loyalty," "Where Are You Now That I Need You?" "Hamlet" (sung by Hutton), and "I Wake Up in the Morning Feeling Fine." The "Hamlet" parody is hysterically funny with Shelton as the Melancholy Dane, Daugherty as Laertes, and Abbott as the queen. The picture made money as it rode the crest of Hutton's brief rise and fall. It was Julie Adams' second job in movies (as the starlet) and good comedy was contributed by Helton, Walburn and Talman, who went on to national fame as the always-losing D.A. on the "Perry Mason" TV show.

p, Robert Fellows; d, John Farrow; w, Farrow, Hagar Wilde (based on a story by Charles Lederer); ph, Daniel L. Fapp; ed, Eda Warren; md, Joseph J. Lilley; art d, Hans Dreier, Franz Bachelin; set d, Sam Comer, Ross Dowd; cos, Edith Head; ch, Billy Daniel; makeup, Wally Westmore, Bill Bood, Charles Boerner.

Musical Comedy/Crime   **(PR:A   MPAA:NR)**

RED HOT RHYTHM*1/2   (1930) 75m Pathe bw-c

Alan Hale, Kathryn Crawford, Josephine Dunn, Walter O'Keefe, Anita Garvin, Ilka Chase, Ernest Hilliard, Harry Bowen, James Clemmons.

Hale plays a songwriter in this musical-dance comedy, who makes his living by stealing other people's compositions and then publishing them under his own name. Two color sequences were added, with little or no effect on the weak plot. Songs include: "At Last I'm in Love," "The Night Elmer Died," "Red Hot Rhythm" (Robert Emmet Dolan, Walter O'Keefe).

d, Leo McCarey; w, Earl Baldwin, Walter DeLeon (based on the story by William Counselman, McCarey); ph, John Mescal; cos, Gwen Wakeling.

Musical/Comedy   **(PR:A   MPAA:NR)**

RED HOT SPEED1/2   (1929) 60m UNIV bw

Reginald Denny, Alice Day, Charles Byer, Fritzi Ridgeway, Thomas Ricketts, DeWitt Jennings, Hector V. Sarno.

Weak plot involves Day as the daughter of a publisher who has a campaign out against speeding. Of course, Day is arrested for the very thing her father is adamantly against, and Denny is the parole officer she is assigned to. He attempts to keep her crime a secret from both the public and her father, and, in the process, Denny and Day fell in love. Marked by sporadic dialog, this film attempted to cross over from the silent era to talkies.

d, Joseph E. Henaberry; w, Gladys Lehman, Albert De Mond, Faith Thomas, Matt Taylor (based on a story by Lehman); ph, Arthur Todd; ed, Ray Curtiss, Jack English.

Comedy   **(PR:A   MPAA:NR)**

RED HOT TIRES**   (1935) 61m WB bw (GB: RACING LUCK)

Lyle Talbot (*Wallace Storm*), Mary Astor (*Patricia Sanford*), Roscoe Karns (*Bud Keene*), Frankie Darro (*Johnny*), Gavin Gordon (*Robert Griffin*), Lyle Talbot (*Wallace Storm*), Mary Astor (*Patricia Sanford*), Roscoe Karns (*Bud Keene*), Frankie Darro (*Johnny*), Gavin Gordon (*Robert Griffin*), Mary Treen (*Maggie*), Henry Kolker (*Martin Sanford*), Bradley Page (*Curley Taylor*), John Elliott (*Governor*), Eddie Sturgis (*Old Convict*), Arthur Aylesworth, Howard Hickman, Clarence Muse.

Stock car library footage was used in this film to add to a routine script. It's a predictable yarn in which Talbot plays a race car driver who is wrongly accused of killing his partner, Gordon, in an accident during a race. He is found guilty of murder and is sent to prison. While there, his girl friend, Astor, is aided by Darro as they dig up the evidence needed to clear Talbot's name. But before they can prove his innocence, Talbot escapes from jail and takes off for South America. There he achieves great success under an assumed name, and returns to the States when Astor's father needs a capable driver for his new car. The story concludes with Talbot winning the race, whereupon he learns that his murder conviction has been overturned.

p, Sam Bischoff; d, D. Ross Lederman; w, Tristram Tupper, Dore Schary (based on a story by Tupper); ph, Arthur Todd, Warren Lynch; ed, Frank McGee; art d, Anton Grot, Hugh Reticker.

Drama   **(PR:A   MPAA:NR)**

RED HOUSE, THE***   (1947) 100m UA bw

Edward G. Robinson (*Pete Morgan*), Lon McCallister (*Nath Storm*), Judith Anderson (*Ellen Morgan*), Allene Roberts (*Meg Morgan*), Julie London (*Tibby*), Rory Calhoun (*Teller*), Ona Munson (*Mrs. Storm*), Harry Shannon (*Dr. Byrne*), Arthur Space (*Officer*), Walter Sande (*Don Brent*), Pat Flaherty (*Cop*).

In this taut chiller, Robinson plays a crippled farmer living a secluded life with his sister, Anderson, and his adopted daughter, Roberts. Robinson has strict orders that no one is to visit a red house located in the woods surrounding his property, and he enforces this rule by hiring Calhoun to keep people from trespassing. Because of his need for an extra hand, Robinson also hires McCallister, a backwoodsman. McCallister, along with Roberts, is curious to discover why Robinson is so adamant about people visiting the little red house and so the pair decide to discover for themselves whatever secrets may lie behind its door. As they near the house, however, they are shot at by Calhoun, under Robinson's orders. Realizing that the house poses a mental threat to Robinson, Anderson attempts to burn it down and with it, its secrets, only she is first shot and killed by Calhoun. As she lies dying, she reveals to McCallister and Roberts that 15 years earlier Roberts' parents owned the red house, where they were murdered by Robinson as a result of his unrequited love for Roberts' mother. With the death of his sister, Robinson loses all mental control and attempts to lure Roberts to the house so that she can receive the same fate as her parents. But before he is able to kill her, McCallister and the now-alerted police arrive in time to save her. The story ends with Robinson committing suicide by driving his truck into the marshy swamp where he had dumped the bodies of Roberts' parents 15 years earlier.

p, Sol Lesser; d&w, Delmar Daves (based on the novel by George Agnew Chamberlain); ph, Bert Glennon; m, Miklos Rozsa; ed, Merrill White; art d, McClure Capps.

Horror/Drama   **Cas.**   **(PR:A   MPAA:NR)**

RED, INN, THE***   (1954, Fr.) 95m Memnon bw (L'AUBERGE ROUGE)

Fernandel (*The Monk*), Francoise Rosay (*Marie Martin*), Julien Carette (*Mons. Martin*), Marie-Claire Olivia (*Mathilde*), Jean-Roger Caussimon (*Darwin*), Nane Germon (*Elisa*), Jacques Charron (*Rodolphe*), Didier d'Yd (*Janou*), Lud Germain (*Fetiche*), Gregoire Aslan (*Barbeuf*), A. Vialla (*Marchioness*), Andre Cheff (*The Dandy*), Dalibert (*Woodcutter*), Yves Montand (*Singing Commentator*).

Religious satire has a group of travelers fleeing a snowstorm by taking refuge in a remote inn, where the husband and wife who own the hotel routinely kill their guests and steal their riches. Fernandel hears the confession of these crimes when Rosay comes to confess her sins. But because of his vow of silence, he cannot tell the guests of their preplanned murders. He goes about trying to save their lives through a number of ridiculous situations and tricks. Fernandel added a lot of his comic charm to this "black comedy," which was banned in England.

d, Claude Autant-Lara; w, Pierre Bost, Jean Aurenche, Autant-Lara (based on the story "L'Auberge Sanglante de Peyrebelle"); ph, Andre Bac; m, Rene Cloerec; ed, Madeleine Gug; art d, Max Douy.

Comedy   **(PR:A   MPAA:NR)**

RED LANTERNS***   (1965, Gr.) 85m Times bw (KOKKINA PHANARIA)

Jenny Karezi (*Helen/Princess*), George Foundas (*Mike*), Mary Chronopoulou (*Mary*), Katerina Helmi (*Marina*), Despo Diamantidou (*The Madam*), Dimitris Papamichael (*Peter*), Kostas Kourtis (*Doris*), Phaedon Georgitsis (*Angelo*), Ero Kyriakaki (*Katerina*), Alexander Ladikou (*Anna*), Manos Katrakis (*Capt. Nicholas*), Eleni Anousaki (*Myrsini*), Notis Peryalis.

A poignant look at the lives of five prostitutes, all working for the same madam in the Greek port of Piraeus. Taking an almost sociological perspective, the film explores the personal story behind each woman's situation, forcing them to take to prostitution for various reasons. The emphasis is not upon preachy morals, but rather upon the social phenomena and how personal lives are intertwined.

p, Theophanis A. Damaskinos, Viktor G. Michaelides; d, Vassilis Georgiades; w, Alekos Galanos (based on the play by Galanos); ph, Nikos Gardelis; m, Stavros Xarhakos; art d, Petros Kapoularis; m/l, Grigori Bithikotsis, Georges Zambetas.

Drama   **(PR:C   MPAA:NR)**

RED LIGHT**   (1949) 83m UA bw

George Raft (*John Torno*), Virginia Mayo (*Carla North*), Raymond Burr (*Nick Cherney*), Gene Lockhart (*Warni Hazard*), Barton MacLane (*Strecker*), Bill Phillips (*Ryan*), Arthur Franz (*Jess Torno*), Henry (*Harvey*) Morgan (*Rocky*), Phillip Pine (*Pablo*), Movita Castenada (*Trina*), Arthur Shields (*Father Redmond*), Paul Frees (*Bellhop*), Edwin Max (*Ben Appleton*), Claire Carleton (*Waitress*), Frank Orth (*Stoner*), Robert Espinosa (*Miguel*), Soledad Jiminez (*Pablo's Mother*), Ed Gargan (*Truck Driver*), Polly Moran (*Chambermaid*).

A feeble attempt at combining crime with religious overtones, RED LIGHT suffers from Raft's stone-like performance and a script that attempts to preach. Raft is the successful owner of a trucking company. His brother is Franz, a priest who has been serving in the WW II as a chaplain. Now that the conflict is over, Franz returns and Raft is delighted to see him. Burr, a former employee who had been kicked out and sentenced to jail for embezzling, is now on the streets and he wants to get even with Raft. Killing is too good for Raft so Burr decides to exact revenge by murdering Franz. When Raft goes to Franz's hotel room, he finds his brother in a pool of blood and rapidly giving up the ghost. Raft asks the identity of the killer and Franz's last words are "Look in the Bible," then he dies. Since the ubiquitous Gideon Bible that's in every hotel room is not there, Raft reckons that the killer's name must be in it so he begins his investigation, over and above the disagreement of his girl friend, Mayo, his priest, Shields, and the police, who would rather not have an amateur on the case. Raft leaves Lockhart to take care of the company while he and Mayo search. Burr comes to the company's offices and chases Lockhart around the building. Lockhart is frightened, runs through the garage, and winds up hiding under a truck trailer which is held up by jacks. Burr kicks one supporting jack out and the trailer crushes Lockhart. Raft finds the missing Bible and the only passage that stands out is "Thou Shalt Not Kill," which was underlined by Franz. Raft catches up with Burr atop the freight company building. Raft fully intends to shoot Burr but when he recalls what his brother had underlined, he drops his gun with a sigh. Meanwhile, the neon sign atop the building is blazing with electricity. Burr breaks it and is electrocuted accidentally, thereby allowing vengeance to be exacted, an eye to be collected for an eye, but without Raft having to perform the illegal deed. Some neat character turns by Morgan (who was still known as "Henry Morgan" at the time), MacLane, and, in a small bit, Paul Frees, who later became one of the most successful voices in commercials. Visitors to Disneyland can hear his mellifluous tones on many of the rides as he narrates the words behind the activity.

p&d, Roy Del Ruth; w, George Callahan; ph, Bert Glennon; m, Dimitri Tiomkin; ed, Richard Heermance; art d, F. Paul Sylos.

Crime **(PR:A-C MPAA:NR)**

RED LIGHTS AHEAD* (1937) 70m CHES bw

Andy Clyde, Lucille Gleason, Paula Stone, Roger Imhof, Frank Coughlan, Jr., Ben Alexander, Ann Doran, Matty Kemp, Sam Flint, Addison Randall.

When a fellow gets a chance at investing in a gold mine, he does so without hesitation and reaps sizable profits. Business takes a turn for the worst, but he is saved by his wise old grandfather.

d, Roland D. Reed; ph, M.A. Anderson; ed, Dan Milner.

Comedy **(PR:A MPAA:NR)**

RED LINE 7000½** (1965) 110m PAR c

James Caan (Mike Marsh), Laura Devon (Julie Kazarian), Gail Hire (Holly Mac-Gregor), Charlene Holt (Lindy Bonaparte), John Robert Crawford (Ned Arp), Marianna Hill (Gabrielle Queneau), James Ward (Dan McCall), Norman Alden (Pat Kazarian), George Takei (Kato), Carol Connors (Singer), Idell James (Server), Robert Donner (LeRoy), Diane Strom, Anthony Rogers, Cissy Wellman, Dee Hartford, John Gabriel, Ann Morell, Beryl Hammond, Leslie Summers, Forrest Lewis, Edy Williams, Robert Osterloh.

Not one of Hawks' better pictures, this followed another turkey, MAN'S FAVORITE SPORT? and studios wondered if the master had lost his touch as he approached 70 years of age. Alden runs a car-racing team and one of his drivers is killed in an accident. The following day the dead driver's fiancee, Hire, arrives in Daytona, Florida. Hire is stunned and the other drivers attempt to make her feel welcome and to assuage any guilt she might have (totally uncalled-for). She and Holt, who has also lost a loved one to the race wars, unite to manage Holt's eating establishment. Crawford is a new driver who has been tapped to replace the dead man and Alden's younger sister, Devon, falls in love with him over Alden's objections. Crawford is a sensational driver, wins a race, and feels stifled by Alden so he decides to strike out on his own. He is then replaced by Ward, who comes in from France with his female companion, Hill. It's not long before Ward begins to overlook Hill and pay attention to Hire. Simultaneously, Caan, another driver under Alden, begins showing an interest in Hill although he is jealous that she once loved Ward and he suspects that they might still be having an affair. Caan attempts to ride Ward off the track and cause a fatal accident. Ward crashes but survives and, once he knows why Caan did it, the two men patch up their differences and Caan continues with Hill. Hire accepts Ward's proposal of marriage and Devon winds up with Crawford. It's strictly from sudsville and wouldn't be worth watching except for the superb racing footage (shot by Bruce Kessler) at Daytona, Riverside, California, Charlotte, North Carolina, Darlington, Texas, and Ascot in England. All of the characters sort of blend into each other and there is hardly any differentiation in their roles. Whereas BOBBY DEERFIELD and other films of this ilk concentrated on one or, perhaps, two drivers, this has three stories going at the same time and gets confusing. The title refers to 7,000 RPMs on the tachometer. Driving at a higher revolutions-per-minute can blow the engine. Wellman, the daughter of William Wellman, and Donner were married at the time of the film. Two songs: "Wildcat Jones," (Carol Connors, Buzz Cason) and "Let Me Find Someone New" (Nelson Riddle, Connors) are less than adequate.

p&d, Howard Hawks; w, George Kirgo (based on a story by Hawks); ph, Milton Krasner, Haskell Boggs (Technicolor); m, Nelson Riddle; ed, Stuart Gilmore, Bill Brame; art d, Hal Pereira, Arthur Lonergan; set d, Sam Comer, Claude Carpenter; cos, Edith Head; spec eff, Paul K. Lerpaie, Farciot Edouart.

Sports Drama **(PR:C MPAA:NR)**

RED LION** (1971, Jap.) 116m Toho International c (AKAGE)

Toshiro Mifune (Gonzo), Etsushi Takahashi (Hanzo), Shigeru Koyama (Staff Chief Aragaki), No Terada (Sanji), Shima Iwashita (Tomi), Yunosuke Ito (Magistrate), Tokue Hanazawa (Komatora), Takahiro Tamura (Sozo Sagara), Kaai Okada, Nobuko Otowa, Jitsuko Yoshimura, Yuko Mochizuki.

Samurai saga has Mifune as a representative of the newly restored emperor, assigned to announce to his home village that there has been a cut in taxes, a ploy used by the new government to ensure political control. But Mifune finds the village under the strict authority of an evil magistrate, Ito, who imposes his rule through heavy tax laws. Members loyal to the previous regime try to band together and hire a swordsman to kill Mifune. But before this takes place, the newly victorious army rescinds its tax cuts, then rides into the village attacking its opponents. This only

leaves Mifune in a state of confusion, as he attempts to lay siege upon the entire army single-handedly.

p, Toshiro Mifune, Yoshio Nishikawa; d, Kihachi Okamoto; w, Okamoto, Sakae Hirosawa; ph, Takao Saito (Eastmancolor); m, Masaru Sato; art d, Hiroshi Ueda.

War/Drama **(PR:A MPAA:NR)**

RED LIPS*½ (1964, Fr./Ital.) 90m Rotor-Gray-Orsay/Royal Films International bw (LABBRA ROSSE/ FAUSSES INGENUES)

Gabriele Ferzetti (Paolo Martini), Giorgio Albertazzi (Carrei), Jeanne Valerie (Irene), Christine Kaufmann (Baby), Marina Bonfigli (Signora Martini), Laura Betti (The Painter), Elvy Lissiak (Baby's Sister), Gabriella Serafini, Tullio Altamura, Carla Bizzari, Fabrizio Capucci, Giuseppe Colizzi, Elena Forte, Jacqueline Julien.

Ferzetti plays a lawyer searching for his lost teenage daughter. He discovers that she has run off with an older man with whom she's been having an affair. Accompanied by Valerie, his daughter's friend, he goes after the two. Along the way, Valerie succeeds in seducing Ferzetti. When they finally catch up with Albertazzi, the man who is having an affair with his daughter, they learn that the girl has left the older man for a boy her own age. Ferzetti finds his daughter in bed with the boy and drags her home, only to realize that his younger daughter is following in her older sister's footsteps.

p, Carmine Bologna; d, Giuseppe Bennati; w, Paolo Levi, Federico Zardi, Bennati (based on the story by Bennati, Levi); ph, Tino Santoni; m, Piero Umiliani; ed, Franco Fraticelli; art d, Amedeo Mellone.

Drama **(PR:O MPAA:NR)**

RED MANTLE, THE (SEE: HAGBARD AND SIGNE, 1968, Den./Iceland/Swed.)

RED MENACE, THE* (1949) 81m REP bw

Robert Rockwell (Bill Jones), Hanne Axman (Nina Petrovka), Shepard Menken (Henry Solomon), Barbara Fuller (Mollie O'Flaherty), Betty Lou Gerson (Yvonne Kraus), James Harrington (Martin Vejac), Lester Luther (Earl Partridge), William J. Lally (Jack Tyler), William Martel (Riggs), Duke Williams (Sam), Kay Reihl (Mrs. O'Flaherty), Royal Raymond (Benson), Gregg Martell (Schultz), Mary DeGolyer (Proprietress), Leo Cleary (Father O'Leary), Norman Budd (Reachi), Lloyd G. Davies (O'Toole), Napoleon Simpson (Tom Wright), Robert Purcell (Sheriff).

Pure anti-Communist propaganda, done in documentary style, has Rockwell and Axman fleeing across the country to escape the threat of communism. The film tries to show how Communists take advantage of innocent Americans by offering them sex and money to lure them into the Communist grasp. Except for the extreme naivete behind such a project, the picture is put together quite well, with the performances of an acceptable quality.

p, Herbert J. Yates; d, R.G. Springsteen; w, Albert DeMond, Gerald Geraghty (based on a story by DeMond); ph, John MacBurnie; m, Nathan Scott; ed, Harry Keller; art d, Fran Arrigo; set d, John McCarthy, Jr., James Redd; spec eff, Howard Lydecker, Theodore Lydecker; makeup, Howard Smit.

Drama **(PR:A MPAA:NR)**

RED MONARCH*½ (1983, Brit.) 101m Engima/Goldcrest Films and TV Ltd. c

Colin Blakely (Joseph Stalin), David Suchet (Laurenti P. Beria), Carroll Baker (Brown), Ian Hogg (Shaposhnikov), Nigel Stock (Vyacheslav M. Molotov), Lee Montague (Lee), Glynn Edwards (Vlasek), David Kelly (Sergo).

An interesting attempt at satirizing the political regime of Joseph Stalin by portraying him as an eccentric buffoon, features Blakely playing the Russian premier in a number of incidents. These include a meeting with Mao Tse-tung that ends in an arm wrestling match, and the Soviet political leaders discussing basketball. Though some clever ancedotes are included, the entire project fails because of a lack of a coherent plot or a firm handling of Stalin's psychological makeup.

p, Graham Benson; d, Jack Gold; w, Charles Wood (based on short stories by Yuri Krotkov); ph, Mike Fash; ed, Laurence Mery-Clark; prod d, Norman Garwood.

Comedy **(PR:C MPAA:NR)**

RED MORNING* (1935) 66m RKO Radio bw

Steffi Duna, Regis Toomey, Lionel Belmore, Raymond Hatton, Mitchell Lewis, Charles B. Middleton, George Lewis, Francis McDonald, Willie Fung, Arthur "Cap" West, Brandon Hurst, Olaf Hytten, Alphonz Ethier, James Marcus.

An unseaworthy offering with Duna as a seaman's daughter who barely survives the mutiny of her father's ship. When she finally drifts ashore she encounters angry islanders. Toomey, her brave fiance, manages to save her from an untimely demise and together they sail off into romance. A laugh a minute from this pail of sludge, and not one from the belly. RED MORNING actually began as a Merian C. Cooper (KING KONG) picture with some of its exotic New Guinea footage put to use here instead.

p, Cliff Reid; d, Wallace Fox; w, John Twist, Fox (based on the story by Gouverneur Morris); ph, Harold Wenstrom; ed, Ted Cheesman.

Drama **(PR:A MPAA:NR)**

RED MOUNTAIN** (1951) 84m PAR c

Alan Ladd (Capt. Brett Sherwood), Lizabeth Scott (Chris), Arthur Kennedy (Lane Waldron), John Ireland (Quantrell), Jeff Corey (Skee), James Bell (Dr. Terry), Bert Freed (Randall), Walter Sande (Benjie), Neville Brand (Dixon), Carleton Young (Morgan), Whit Bissell (Miles), Jay Silver Heels (Little Crow), Francis McDonald (Marshal Roberts), Iron Eyes Cody (Indian), Herbert Belles (Indian Guard), Dan White (Braden), Ralph Moody (Meredyth), Crane Whitley (Cavalry Major), Dan White (Quantrell Man).

Ladd and Scott might have made a heck of a team in a big-city gangster tale as they were both such urban types, but their only assignment together was this sprawling western set in Colorado but actually shot in New Mexico. William Quantrell has been portrayed on screen many times by many actors. Walter Pigeon, writer-actor Leo Gordon; and Brian Donlevy did it on two separate occasions. The producers toyed with history in this film by substituting an "e" for the "i" in his name. That's not all they did, though, and anyone familiar with the era will be rankled by the alterations. Be those as they may, this is still a good film, with lots of rootin'-tootin' action. Ladd is a Rebel captain who has come to Colorado to join Ireland (Quantrell) near the end of the War Between The States hoping to join with the "Raiders" and snatch a victory from the jaws of defeat. Before he gets to Ireland, Ladd stops in a pro-North village to exact revenge on White, who stole Ladd's land before the war began. After killing the crook, Kennedy is accused of the murder because the revolver shell found next to White's body is recognized as a Confederate one and Kennedy is known to have fought on the South's side before coming to the town. Kennedy is about to be strung up for the killing but Ladd knows the man is innocent so he rescues Kennedy and the two men get out of town together, now compatriots. They hide out at Kennedy's cabin where Ladd meets Scott, who is soon to marry Kennedy. It isn't long before the couple realize that it was Ladd who murdered White and that he must be turned in if Kennedy is ever to clear his name. Despite the fact that Ladd saved Kennedy's life, the deed must be done. There's a battle between the two men and Kennedy breaks his leg. The three are now in the forest and Ladd would like to dump the couple but he feels responsible for them and his guilt overwhelms his sense of self-preservation. Ladd puts them both in a dank cave and Kennedy is soon ill with fever, the result of not having his leg treated. As he shivers and goes in and out of consciousness, Ladd and Scott find much to like about each other and although they know it's wrong, they are soon in love. Looking down at the valley, Ladd sees Ireland and his band arriving, all wearing Union uniforms taken from a Blue group they've ambushed. When Ladd finally gets to Ireland, he sees that the one-time schoolteacher doesn't really care about "The Cause." Ireland has become a two-bit marauder who is assembling his own small army of mercenaries and renegade Indians. With this elite force, Ireland plans to watch and wait as the North and the South kill each other off; then he can move in as a modern-day emperor and rape the land, amassing a fortune and making the peaceful inhabitants pay him homage and money. Ladd becomes painfully aware that the South won't rise again, not with Ireland leading them anyhow, so he goes into the small town to gather up a squad of Union soldiers to come back and defeat Ireland before things get out of hand. Kennedy and Scott are up in the cave on the side of the hill and keep Ireland's men pinned down with gunfire until Ladd can return. In the melee, Kennedy is killed, then Ladd arrives with the troops and there's a huge gunfight with flags waving, Injuns biting the dust and not one hold barred from showing every single Western fight cliche that you've ever seen before, plus a few that Dieterle tossed in. Ireland and his men are wiped out and news of Lee's surrender ends Ladd's enmity to the North. With Kennedy gone, Scott and Ladd can now go off and find happiness together. Western fans will love this movie. It's not in the class of RED RIVER or SHANE as far as character development goes, but there is enough gunplay and horseplay to keep matters galloping along for the brief 84-minute length.

p, Hal B. Wallis; d, William Dieterle; w, John Meredyth Lucas, George Slavin, George W. George (based on a story by Slavin, George); ph, Charles B. Lang, Jr. (Technicolor); m, Franz Waxman; ed, Warren Low; art d, Hal Pereira, Franz Bachelin.

Western **(PR:A-C MPAA:NR)**

RED OVER RED (SEE: COME SPY WITH ME, 1967)

RED PLANET MARS* (1952) 87m UA bw

Peter Graves *(Chris Cronyn)*, Andrea King *(Linda Cronyn)*, Orley Lindgren *(Steward Cronyn)*, Bayard Vellier *(Roger Cronyn)*, Walter Sande *(Adm. Carey)*, Marvin Miller *(Arjenian)*, Herbert Berghof *(Franz Calder)*, Willis Bouchey *(President)*, Richard Powers *(Gen. Burdette)*, Morris Ankrum *(Secretary Sparks)*, Lewis Martin *(Dr. Mitchell)*, House Peters, Jr. *(Dr. Boulting)*, Claude Dunkin *(Peter Lewis)*, Gene Roth *(UMW President)*, John Topa *(Borodin)*, Bill Kennedy *(Commentator)*, Grace Leonard *(Woman)*, Vince Barnett *(Man)*.

An imaginative effort, although missing an adept knowledge of the language of film, as this McCarthy era anti-communist, pro-Christianity picture overburdens itself with messages about politics, religion, science, and just about anything else. The result is an incoherent, though fairly interesting, jumble of a picture. Scientist Graves locates an instrument that receives transmissions from Mars, setting off widespread pandemonium on Earth. This includes a revolution staged by elderly Russian peasants, who overthrow the Soviet government and replace it with a religious monarchy. Then ex-Nazi Berghof admits to sending the messages himself under the pretense of aiding the communists in ridding the world of capitalism. While Berghof and Graves argue, more messages are received through the transmitor, this time the Martian says that God himself is the ruler of Mars. Technical credits are all standard, with performances the proper caliber of stereotypes. The priest who becomes ruler of the U.S.S.R. bears a striking resemblance to the Ayatollah Khomeini who became ruler of Iran. And Bouchey bears a resemblance to Dwight D. Eisenhower, the former military man who became president of the U.S. Could the filmmakers have been psychic? Author Balderston's claim to fame was that he had worked on BRIDE OF FRANKENSTEIN. Director Horner had worked as a designer and would return to design work in his contribution to the award-winning film THE HUSTLER. And Graves went on to work as an ensemble member of TV's "Mission Impossible."

p, Donald Hyde, Anthony Veiller; d, Harry Horner; w, Veiller, John L. Balderson (based on the play "Red Planet" by Balderson, John Hoare); ph, Joseph Biroc; m, Mahlon Merrick, David Chudnow; ed, Francis D. Lyon; prod d, Charles D. Hall; art d, Hall.

Fantasy **(PR:A MPAA:NR)**

RED PONY, THE½** (1949) 89m REP c

Myrna Loy *(Alice Tiflin)*, Robert Mitchum *(Billy Buck)*, Louis Calhern *(Grandpa)*, Shepperd Strudwick *(Fred Tiflin)*, Peter Miles *(Tom Tiflin)*, Margaret Hamilton *(Teacher)*, Patty King *(Jinx Ingals)*, Jackie Jackson *(Jackie)*, Beau Bridges *(Beau)*, Nino Tempo *(Nino)*, Tommy Sheridan *(Dale)*, Little Brown Jug *(Himself)*, Wee Willie Davis *(Truck Driver)*, George Tyne *(Charlie)*, Poodles Hanneford *(Clown)*, Grace Hanneford, Eddie Borden *(Circus Performers)*, Max Wagner *(Bartender)*, Alvin Hammer *(Telegrapher)*, Dolores Castle *(Gert)*, William Quinlan *(Ben)*.

Stories about "a boy and his pet" have always been marvelous fodder for Hollywood's cannons. From THE YEARLING to THE RED STALLION to BLACK BEAUTY to THE BLACK STALLION to LASSIE, the specter of a young child and his love for his animal has usually rung the cash register. So it was with THE RED PONY, which did well enough at the box office to be re-released in 1957 and inspire a TV movie in 1972 which starred Henry Fonda and Maureen O'Hara. The story was written by Steinbeck (who also wrote the script) and it was a compressing of three tales, "The Gift," "The Leader of the People," and "The Promise." Mitchum's character only appeared in the final story but is used as the protagonist, a la SHANE, throughout. Mitchum was signed to Howard Hughes who lent him to Feldman and Milestone for this picture and their choice was a good one as Mitchum handled the laconic, man-of-few-words role laconically, and with few words. Mitchum is a ranch hand on the spread owned by Strudwick and Loy. Miles is their son and he idolizes Mitchum the way De Wilde idolized Ladd. Miles has a small red pony and spends most of his time training it with Mitchum's help. Strudwick is out of his milieu here. He's a one-time schoolteacher not accustomed to life in the slow lane and he is angry that Miles looks up to Mitchum with such adoration. Calhern is Loy's father, an old man who lives in memory and tells tall tales of how he brought people to the West years ago. Strudwick gives the old man as hard a time as he can without alienating Loy. Strudwick takes a short trip and the pony gets out of its pen when frightened by a storm. Miles thinks it's all Mitchum's fault when the horse gets very sick and dies. Loy, sensing that there's a huge problem with the boy, sends for Strudwick, who is happy to be asked to help in the crisis and feels a lot better about ranching, now that he's gotten closer to his son. Mitchum has a mare that's about to foal and when the colt is born, Mitchum gives the spindly-legged animal to Miles, who again loves Mitchum for having done that. The two men are happy that the boy is happy and the picture ends. A gentle story, more for the kids than anyone else, well-shot by Gaudio, although slowly directed by Milestone. Aaron Copland wrote the score, one of very few he did for films, and it is stirring.

p&d, Lewis Milestone; w, John Steinbeck (based on his novel); ph, Tony Gaudio (Technicolor); m, Aaron Copland; ed, Harry Keller; art d, Victor Greene; spec eff, Howard Lydecker, Theodore Lydecker.

Drama **Cas.** **(PR:AA MPAA:NR)**

RED RIVER***** (1948) 125m UA bw

John Wayne *(Tom Dunson)*, Montgomery Clift *(Matthew Garth)*, Joanne Dru *(Tess Millay)*, Walter Brennan *(Groot Nadine)*, Coleen Gray *(Fen)*, John Ireland *(Cherry Valance)*, Noah Beery, Jr. *(Buster McGee)*, Harry Carey, Sr. *(Mr. Millville)*, Harry Carey, Jr. *(Dan Latimer)*, Paul Fix *(Teeler Yacy)*, Mickey Kuhn *(Matt as a Boy)*, Chief Yowlachie *(Quo)*, Ivan Parry *(Bunk Kenneally)*, Ray Hyke *(Walt Jergens)*, Hank Worden *(Simms)*, Dan White *(Laredo)*, Paul Fiero *(Fernandez)*, William Self *(Wounded Wrangler)*, Hal Taliaferro *(Old Leather)*, Tom Tyler *(A Quitter)*, Lane Chandler *(Colonel)*, Glenn Strange *(Naylor)*, Shelley Winters *(Dance-Hall Girl)*, Lee Phelps, George Lloyd *(Gamblers)*.

There have been many classic westerns but this Hawks masterpiece certainly ranks among the 10 top of the genre. It is a relentless tale of hard men as rugged as the range they rode. It has unforgettable sweeping spectacle and the kind of grandeur few westerns ever achieved. Wayne is shown as a young but determined man at the opening of RED RIVER, taking his wagon out of the line of a train heading west. He and his companion, Brennan, intend to head south, toward Texas and the Red River. The head of the wagon train objects to Wayne's leaving but Wayne, early on showing that his word is his bond, replies: "I signed nothing. If I had, I'd stay." Wayne rides south and Brennan tells the wagonmaster: "He's a mighty set man. When his mind's made up, even you can't change it." Pretty young Gray, Wayne's sweetheart, tries to persuade him to go with her but even the love of his life cannot turn him back from the course he has chosen. He gives her a snake bracelet, kisses her, and heads south with Brennan after telling Gray that he'll send for her later. Only hours later Wayne and Brennan turn around to see in the far distance black smoke curling skyward and they know that Indians have attacked the wagon train. Brennan suggests that they turn back but Wayne tells him it's useless. Later that night a band of Indians attacks Wayne and Brennan but they're ready for them, killing them all. Wayne takes on the last one, the leader, and kills him in a knife fight in the river, finding the snake bracelet on the Indian's arm. "That's too bad," Brennan states when he sees the bracelet in Wayne's hand, and it's clear that Gray has been killed by the savages. The next day Wayne and Brennan find a survivor from the massacre, Kuhn, wandering in a daze, leading a cow. Wayne approaches him and Kuhn babbles about the Indian attack until Wayne slaps him and brings him around. Quick as lightning, the boy draws a pistol and Wayne, in a ruse, takes it away from him. He tells Kuhn that he can go along with them and the youth agrees but he tells Wayne never to try and take his gun away from him again. The pioneers keep heading south and cross the Red River and beyond to find sweeping horizonless plains thick with grazing grass. Wayne unties his bull and Kuhn's cow and lets them free. "They'll get away," Kuhn says. "Wherever they go they'll be on my land," Wayne says, declaring his ranch to be as far as the eye can see and beyond. At that moment two Mexican wranglers approach on horseback and one of them tells Wayne that he's trespassing on the grand ranch of a Mexican land baron who lives hundreds of miles distant. He's welcome to camp there but must eventually move on, the wrangler tells him. Wayne tells him he's there to stay and challenges the wrangler. The Mexican goes for his gun and Wayne is faster pulling his own, shooting the wrangler out of his saddle. He tells the other wrangler to tell the land baron that he, Wayne, is now owner of all the land from the Red River to the Brazos. As the wrangler rides away Wayne kneels in the dirt and draws his Red River brand, two lines to indicate the river and a large D to indicate his last name, Dunson. "I don't see my name on that brand," Kuhn tells him, reminding Wayne that he is contributing his cow to Wayne's empire. Wayne tells him he'll add the youth's name to the brand only "when you've earned it." Years pass and Wayne's cattle empire is exactly that; he has more cattle than anyone in Texas and his ranch is so wide and deep that it takes his many cowhands weeks to cross it. His stepson, Clift (played by Kuhn as a boy) is grown and returned from the Civil War, a quick-on-the-draw rawhider who many think is as tough now as Wayne. The cattle baron is white-haired but still hard as the bark on an oak. He calls his hands together and tells them that he's rich in land and cattle but has no cash and cannot hold onto his enormous empire unless he leads a great cattle drive northward and sells his herd. He rounds up thousands of cows and then pushes the entire herd northward, taking Clift with him as second-in-command. Clift takes along his newfound friend and fellow gunman Ireland. Brennan hasn't changed his position since the beginning; he's still driving the chuck wagon, though now he's toothless, although he has new "store bought" teeth. These he promptly loses to Chief Yowlachie in a poker game and can only have them on loan at mealtime until he pays the dollar he owes the Indian cowpuncher. (The scene depicting the beginning of the drive at dawn on the ranch is jarring as Hawks shows a series of lightning cuts to depict the cowhands all turning in their saddles and letting out yells to get the herd moving.) The herd heads north, Wayne uncertain where he might be able to reach the railhead, knowing that he faces storms, Indians, and marauding bands of cattle-rustling renegades. He intends to follow the old trail to Missouri but en route he is told by Ireland and others that there's a shorter route, to Kansas, where the railhead has already extended its line. But this is mere speculation to Wayne and he won't hear of heading for a state that might not have a railroad to ship his cattle. It's Missouri and that's it. Meanwhile, Parry, a cowhand with a sweet tooth, reaches into the supplies on the chuck wagon to get some sugar and causes Brennan's hanging pots and pans to come crashing down, spooking the herd and causing a stampede which all but destroys the campsite and compels Wayne and his men to ride hell-for-leather to stop them, driving them into a box canyon. Many of the hands are injured in the wild ride and Carey, Jr., a young married cowboy who wanted to go on the drive to buy his wife some red shoes, is found trampled to death. Wayne tells his men that he will "read over him" after they quickly bury the body. Later Wayne corners Parry and tells him that he was responsible for the stampede and Carey's death. Parry expresses his sorrow at the tragedy but Wayne doesn't want to hear an apology. He intends to whip Parry for his negligence and stupidity. Parry tells Wayne that he won't allow himself to be whipped and backs away, his hand hovering near his holstered pistol. Just before Wayne can gun Parry down, Clift goes for his own pistol and wounds Parry. He knows Wayne would have aimed to kill and tells the cattle baron so. Parry is sent on his way back to Texas and the drive pushes on through sandstorms and rainstorms, heading for Missouri. But the trek is long and hard, and food grows short. The men grumble and grow to dislike Wayne who shows them no mercy when it comes to work, driving them relentlessly without sleep and who is still uncertain as to their destination. Three of the men finally have a showdown with Wayne, telling him they are quitting. They reach for their guns but Wayne, with Brennan's and Clift's help, shoots them down. "Bury 'em and I'll read over 'em later," he tells his men and then goes off to his own bedroll, yanks up his pants leg, and pours liquor on a flesh wound he has received from one of the dead cowboys who got off a lucky shot. The gunplay stuns the rest of the cowboys. Ireland sits with Clift and convinces him that by taking the Chisholm Trail, they could shortcut the disastrous Missouri trip and take the herd to Kansas where good reports have it a railhead awaits in Abilene. Wayne does not relax but, half-crazy with lack of sleep and worry, drives his men even harder. Three of his best men desert and he sends Ireland after them. The gunman returns with two of them, and Wayne announces that he will hang them for desertion. Clift, who can take no more of Wayne's tyrannical ways, steps forward, hand on his pistol. "No," says Clift, "you're not going to hang them." With that Wayne goes for his gun and Ireland, not Clift, shoots it out of his hand. Wayne reaches down to pick it up and Beery shoots it away from him. Wounded, Wayne looks up at faithful Brennan who says to him: "You was wrong, Mr. Dunson." Wayne tells Brennan that he can join the other turncoats. The next day Clift leaves the wounded Wayne a horse and supplies and tells him *he's* taking the herd to Kansas, to the railhead in Abilene, and that he, Wayne, will see the fruits of the effort. Clift and the other ranch hands are not stealing the herd, merely delivering it by the fastest route. Wayne stares cold eyes at the young man he has raised. He vows revenge and tells Clift chillingly: "Some day you'll turn around and I'll be there...I'm gonna kill ya, Matt." Clift and the others ride away, driving the herd before them. The men push the herd as hard as did Wayne, hurrying to Abilene and seemingly every hour turning to look back from their saddles, expecting fearfully to see Wayne behind them. He's the true goad of their journey. Days later the advance riders hear gunfire, Clift among them. They ride to a ridge to see a gambler's wagon train being attacked by a large band of Indians. Clift sends one rider back for all the men while he dashes in with the few he has with him. Once inside the circled wagons, Clift begins shooting at the attacking Indians, noticing a beautiful, raven-haired young woman, Dru, firing next to him. He tells her she's aiming too high and then looks up to see that she has been hit in the shoulder by an arrow. He breaks off the back of the arrow pinioning her to a wagon, then cuts off the front. Then, with a swift yank, withdraws the remainder of the shaft. Dru gives him some smart talk before passing out. She is carried off to heal as the rest of Clift's men arrive and drive off the Indians. (Of all the scenes in this mighty movie, Dru's wounding by an arrow and Clift's pulling it out which causes her not to scream out in pain but merely give him a look of defiance is the most fabricated; any normal person would have screamed at the excruciating pain.) Dru and Clift later meet and they fall in love. He gives her the snake bracelet he has worn since boyhood, the very bracelet Wayne had given him. They make love and Dru learns all about Wayne and what Clift expects from the hard, resolute cattle baron when he catches up with the men who took his herd. And Wayne is in pursuit, he and a dozen gunmen he has hired. The cattle baron and his men overtake the gambler's wagon train to find Clift gone but Dru invites Wayne into her wagon and there tries to persuade him to call off his hunt for Clift, whom she loves. "Nothing you can say or do—-" says Wayne, an oft-repeated line of his. He looks over the attractive young woman and discusses the possibility of using her as a breeding cow, thinking of having a new son to replace the one, Clift, he is about to kill. She agrees to fornicate with him and get pregnant with his child but only under one condition—he must call off his pursuit of Clift. This Wayne cannot do and tells her so. Meanwhile, Clift and his men reach the almost mythical railway and the engineer of a speeding train brings his engine to a halt so the mighty herd can cross the tracks, encouraging the cowboys to delay the train all they want; the sight of the great herd brings joy to the eyes of all on the train, such is the scarcity of beef. The small town of Abilene is ecstatic at the sight of the cattle and buyers flock to Clift to buy his beef, chief broker being Carey (real-life father to the young actor "killed" earlier in the stampede). The cattle buyer not only gives Clift the top dollar for all his cattle but learns of the young man's plight with Wayne, telling Beery and other hands to watch out for Clift and guard him well. "I like that young man," he tells them. The next day, Beery comes riding wildly through the massive herd milling around the small town, hooting. He tells Clift that Wayne is approaching with a band of gunmen. Clift and his men march out to the edge of town to meet the challenge. Wayne crosses the railroad tracks and then dismounts, telling his followers to stay where they are. Carey, meanwhile, approaches Ireland and tells the gunmen: "You know that boy won't use his gun [on Wayne]." Ireland stares at Wayne, who is now marching on foot through the giant herd, literally shoving and punching the steers out of his thunderous path. "Yes, I Know," Ireland answers Carey, "but I haven't any such notions." He fills the chambers of his pistol and slips it into his holster, readying to gun down Wayne as soon as he gets clear of the steers. Ireland steps out to meet Wayne, who appears not to look at him, moving directly ahead toward Clift. "Mr. Dunson," Ireland calls out, but Wayne keeps marching forward, past him and toward Clift and the others. "I'm only gonna say it one more time," Ireland says, "Mr. Dunson—" He pulls his pistol and Wayne, almost as an afterthought, turns and fires off a shot with lightning speed, just as Ireland fires. Ireland topples to the dust, dead, and Wayne keeps moving, holding his side where Ireland's bullet has grazed him. Clift stands stoically waiting for the cattle baron who marches up to him, firing as he comes, not shooting him down, but sending his bullets all around the young man who has been his adopted son. Clift does not draw as Wayne keeps coming, despite the fact that Wayne shouts: "Draw!" Wayne shoots away Clift's hat and grazes his cheek with a bullet but the young man only stares at him a thin smile on his lips. Standing before Clift, Wayne shouts: "You once told me never to take your gun away from you." He grabs Clift's pistol from its holster and throws it away. "Isn't anything gonna make a man out of you?" snarls Wayne and punches Clift in the face. Clift takes the punch without fighting back, though Brennan and the others encourage him to do so. Wayne hits Clift again and again, calling him a "yellow, chicken-livered—" and just as he knocks Clift to the ground, Clift shoots back up with a powerful blow that sends Wayne flying into the dirt, surprising him and causing him to spit dust from his mouth. Clift bangs away at the cattle baron, hitting him right and left and Brennan says, almost to himself: "It's gonna be all right...all these years and it's gonna be all right." Wayne and Clift battle right into the wall of a chuck wagon but before they can smash each other to pieces a shot rings out, twanging into a kettle. Dru stands before them with a smoking pistol in her hand. She upbraids them for trying to destroy each other, "when everyone knows that you love each other!" She throws the gun to Beery and marches off, disgusted. Amazed and in shock, Wayne's whole demeanor changes and he grins sheepishly at Clift, saying: "Matt, you'd better marry that girl." Clift returns his smile and says: "When are you going to stop telling people what to do?" Wayne nods and then gives his last order, to change the Red River brand of his cattle empire. He draws a river in the dust which the camera shows in closeup, with a large D at the top and he adds an M (for Matthew) at the bottom. "You've earned it," he says, referring to the promise he made Clift as a boy. RED RIVER appropriately ends with the brand filling the screen, symbolic of the men and struggle it has portrayed. Hawks fills every frame of the movie with action and drama, high drama for the western plains, pitting two strong men against each other to provide necessary conflict and suspense to keep viewers watching anxiously. The film is flawless and is a treat for the eye as well as providing unparalleled adventure. Around his sturdy plot, Hawks builds his gritty characters, constructing them carefully so that there is no doubt in the mind of any viewer as to how they will react, except at the end where the director saved both of them from themselves, liking both men so much he could not bear to see either die. (In the original story by Chase, Dunson is mortally wounded in the fight with Matthews but is taken back by wagon to Texas so he can die on the other side of the Red River and be buried in the empire he created. The author was always resentful of Hawks for changing that ending.) Wayne, next to his roles in STAGECOACH, TRUE GRIT, and a few other films, gives the performance of his long career. No one has ever been as tough in the Old West as John Wayne in RED RIVER. Clift, too, given his opportunity to make his first major film here, is equally magnificent, a perfect counterpoint to Wayne's ruthlessness in his gentle but determined manner. Brennan is his old reliable self and provides more humor than was most probably intended, much at the expense of his toothless face and gummy articulation. It was Hawks who insisted that Brennan remove his false teeth for the running gag with Chief Yowlachie. At first the 42-year-old balked at the idea but he quickly remembered that it was Hawks who expanded his role in COME AND GET IT (1936), which earned Brennan an Oscar for Best Supporting Actor. He played mostly without his teeth and was excellent. All of the supporting players, especially Ireland, Beery, the Careys, and Fix, are excellent in their saddlesore parts. Ireland ran afoul of director Hawks during the film by fooling around with actress Dru, a lady Hawks had fancied for his own (even though the director was then married), according to writer Chase. When Ireland kept corralling Dru, Hawks ordered his part cut to the bone. The director later stated this was done because Ireland was unprepared when it came time to shoot his scenes and was constantly drinking and smoking pot. Wayne told Chase that the real reason was because Ireland was "fooling around with Howard's girl." (Ireland and Dru were married following the completion of RED RIVER.) Dru is the only drawback, overacting in her rather small role, but her part is so insignificant that she cannot detract from the overwhelming epic. Harlan's photography is stunning as it sweeps through the horizonless plains and covers the vast territory the cowboys must travel in their odyssey, storms, rivers, canyons, distant buttes all encompassed beautifully. Matching the elegance of the cinematography is Tiomkin's stirring score, undoubtedly the best musical score ever to grace the soundtrack of any western. It is dynamic and poignant, presenting a sweeping overall theme mixed with plaintive cowboy tunes. The visuals and the sound, the action and dialog, all of it masculine and hearty and as real as Brennan's tin plates heaped with beans and beef. The whole film thunders from beginning to end, like drums muttering in Valhalla, and it validates the opening of the Chisholm Trail, also serving as a historic document. Shockingly impressive is the fact that this film came into the director's repertoire out of the blue; up to the time of RED RIVER, Hawks had never before directed a western, proving the versatility of one of the world's great directors. (Hawks could direct splendid comedy such as BRINGING UP BABY or HIS GIRL FRIDAY, helm *film noir* masterpieces such as SCARFACE, 1932, or heady adventure-drama such as ONLY ANGELS HAVE WINGS, and even create one of the most stirring war films ever made, SERGEANT YORK.) He had originally wanted Gary Cooper to play the hard-knuckled cattle baron but Cooper declined the part, saying he thought the character was a little too ruthless for his tastes. Also turning down Hawks was Cary Grant; the director offered Grant the small "but important" role of gunman Cherry Valance, which was later essayed by Ireland to great effect. Wayne was ready for the part of the single-minded cattle baron, wanting to change his good-guy image with a tougher portrait. Clift was Hawks' first choice as the adopted son, the director having seen Clift on Broadway in a sensitive role in Lillian Hellman's "The Searching Wind." Clift knew how to ride a horse but his kind of riding had been learned at a military school in Munich, Germany, where his parents had vacationed. He threw himself into the part with great vigor, asking Beery, an experienced cowboy star, to teach him the ropes. In weeks he was walking with the rolling gait of a saddle hand and he could jump into a stirrup and mount his horse with one foot and a quick lift of the saddle horn. Said Beery later: "The thing he enjoyed most was becoming a helluva good cowboy and horseman." Clift was splendid in his role but he never liked the film and disliked himself in it. In an interview years later he commented: "Just before it all happened, I was in Hollywood with Kevin McCarthy, and we watched a rough-cut version of RED RIVER. I decided I was awful, and that was it—back to Broadway and never go back to Hollywood again. But then, of course, I made it." Clift received a flat $60, 000 for his role in RED RIVER, a part that made him nervous from the start. He stood 5 foot 10 inches and seemed like a pipsqueak when standing next to 6 foot 5 Wayne, but Hawks told him to play his scenes with Wayne like "David and Goliath." Moreover, he tipped Clift on how to underplay Wayne. When challenging him for the first time and preventing him from hanging Fix and the others, Clift thought to speak his lines very resolutely. Hawks shook his head. "No—don't try to get hard because you'll just be nothing compared to Wayne. Start by taking a cup of coffee and just watching him all over." When Clift did do the scene he underplayed his lines but his quiet intensity offset Wayne's flinty disposition beautifully. Wayne had had great doubts about Clift's ability to perform but, following this scene, he went to Hawks and said: "Any doubts I had about that fella are gone. He's going to be okay." But Wayne had some of his own surprises up his veteran cowboy's sleeve. In the scene where Clift comes to him, after usurping him, to tell him "I'll get your herd to Abilene," Wayne was waiting for him, not even looking at him, turning his back on Clift and saying in a low voice that seemed to crawl under the sod and ripple beneath Clift's feet: "I'm gonna kill you, Matt." Just as Hawks had told Clift how to dominate the previous scene, he had cued Wayne on the last. "Well," said the director later, "Duke didn't even look at him when he said that and Monty didn't know what to do. I let him stand there looking dumfounded just as long as I wanted and then I said: 'Get the hell out of there, Monty!' and he turned and walked away. I knew my voice could be cut out." Later Clift went to Hawks and said: "My big scene didn't amount to much, did it?...I didn't have a chance. He was just marvelous." For Wayne, RED RIVER appeared to be the ending of his career; he considered his role a "character part," and that he was on the way out as an actor, telling newsmen that he would probably be forced into retirement within five years. Twenty years later he would still be going strong as a superstar, and would earn an Oscar as "an old fat man" in TRUE GRIT. The actor was paid $150, 000, plus 10 percent of the profits for his role and he gave Hawks a great deal of advice, some of it taken. Wayne insisted that the director hire mostly experienced cowhands and Hawks concurred, putting more than 70 experienced riders to work on the film that was originally scheduled to have a $1.5 million budget (but it doubled before Hawks was through). The fiery 22-year-old Dru was not Hawks' first choice to play the gambling lady who falls in love with Clift. He had originally planned to star an unknown, Margaret Sheridan, one of his discoveries, but Sheridan informed Hawks just before shooting began that she was five months pregnant and could not undertake the role, so Hawks cast Dru. Since Sheridan could do the card tricks called for in the role of the female sharper and Dru could not, some of the script had to be rewritten for Dru. The location sites for the film were selected by Hawks after he and his technical people scouted more than 15,000 miles of territory, including the states of Texas, New Mexico, Arizona, Oklahoma, and northern Mexico. He finally chose as the site of the great cattle ranch an area near Elgin, Arizona, close to the Mexican border. The area had to look enormous with great vistas and far horizons to suggest the vastness of the King Ranch upon which writer Chase had based his tale. (This was the biggest cattle ranch in the West and still is.) The high plain near Elgin was 5,000 feet high and Hawks shot on location at this site for more than two months, spending $1 million to capture the grandeur of the countryside. Other sites included the Whetstone Mountains and the expansive range running beyond them. The San Pedro River was the site of the Red River through which Wayne and his men drive their steers, more than 9,000 of them, which required 25,000 gallons of water to settle the dust kicked up by their movement so that Hawks could photograph the drive. The San Pedro was located in the quaintly entitled Rain Valley, ironic in that it seldom rained there and Hawks had to order five dams built so that the level of the San Pedro would rise to the appropriate hazard level. Since the company, more than 500 actors and an equal number of technicians, was on location, and all were roughing it two sets of costumes were required to cover the rips, tears, and general abuse. Wardrobe costs soared, along with everything else connected with the production. Each actor had two to four pair of boots costing $150 per pair and $150,000 was spent outfitting the male actors. Dru's costumes cost more than $20,000. To coordinate the massive cast movements and the driving of the steers, Hawks used walkie-talkies and short-wave radios that put him in contact with his assistant directors in the radius of three to ten miles. he controlled the entire film like a general in the field but one thing he could not control was the weather. Rain and dust storms played havoc with the production and at one point Wayne was briefly bedridden with a severe cold and Dru, at another, caught influenza. In the middle of one scene, a centipede bit Hawks and he had to be hospitalized for a few days so that the poison could be drained off. The personal strain and agonies aside, Hawks finally had RED RIVER completed only to face a lawsuit by Howard Hughes, who claimed that the final climactic fight was a lift from the climax of his film THE OUTLAW, which Hawks had worked on. It looked bleak for RED RIVER. Hughes had all the money in the world to carry on a lengthy lawsuit, as well as block the release of Hawks' film. The director had had a long relationship with Hughes but it was, by the time of RED RIVER, a shaky one and he felt he could not make a personal appeal to Hughes. Wayne, however, was a good friend of the eccentric RKO chieftain and went to Hughes and explained that the film needed a roaring finish, and admitted that there was a similarity between some scenes of RED RIVER and THE OUTLAW. Hughes listened patiently and then told Wayne that he would drop his suit and allow the film to be released. It was promoted across the land with the majestic claim summed up in its advertisements: "THE COVERED WAGON, CIMARRON, and now RED RIVER." The film deserved such company. It was just as great as the best of the genre that had gone before. RED RIVER, which would gross almost $5 million in its initial release, was seen by the public and critics alike as a classic and it remains so today.

p&d, Howard Hawks; w, Borden Chase, Charles Schnee (based on the novel *The Chisholm Trail* by Chase); ph, Russell Harlan; m, Dimitri Tiomkin; ed, Christian Nyby; md, Tiomkin; art d, John Datu Arensma; spec eff, Don Steward.

Western **Cas.** **(PR:A MPAA:NR)**

RED RIVER RANGE** (1938) 55m REP bw

John Wayne *(Stony Brooke)*, Ray Corrigan *(Tucson Smith)*, Max Terhune *(Lullaby Joslin)*, Polly Moran *(Mrs. Maxwell)*, Lorna Gray [Adrian Booth] *(Jane Mason)*, Kirby Grant *(Tex Reilly)*, Sammy McKim *(Tommy)*, William Royle *(Payne)*, Perry Ivins *(Hartley)*, Stanley Blystone *(Randall)*, Lenore Bushman *(Evelyn Maxwell)*, Burr Caruth *(Pop Mason)*, Roger Williams *(Sheriff)*, Earl Askam *(Morton)*, Olin Francis *(Kenton)*, Edward Cassidy, Fred Toones, Bob McKenzie, Jack Montgomery, Al Taylor, Theodore Lorch.

A well-organized gang has been rustling cattle in a neat, orderly fashion, leaving no trace. The cattlemen's organization and the beef retailers hire agents Wayne, Corrigan, and Terhune to investigate. Wayne infiltrates the gang by posing as a wanted killer. The plan works and the "Duke" gets his men and the girl. This western concentrates more upon humor than the usual western, keeping the action at a lower key. (See THREE MESQUITEERS series, Index.)

p, William Berke; d, George Sherman; w, Luci Ward, Stanley Roberts, Betty Burbridge (based on characters created by William Colt MacDonald and a story by Ward); ph, Jack Marta; m, William Lava; ed, Tony Martinelli.

Western **(PR:A MPAA:NR)**

RED RIVER RENEGADES*½ (1946) 55m REP bw

Sunset Carson, Peggy Stewart, Bruce Langley, Tom London, LeRoy Mason, Kenne Duncan, Ted Adams, Edmund Cobb, Jack Rockwell, Tex Terry.

Carson goes undercover with London to solve the mysterious disappearance of a number of stagecoaches. They are pitted against Steward, thinking she is an outlaw when, in fact, she is also working under cover. They follow clues to a nearby lake, drain it, and find a missing coach. Finally, the finger of guilt is pointed at the owner of the stagecoach line. Carson manages to save the day, rescuing a captured London in the process and putting the sly owner behind bars.

p, Bennett Cohen; d, Thomas Carr; w, Norman S. Hall; ph, William Bradford; ed, William P, Thompson; md, Mort Glickman; art d, Fred A. Ritter; set d, John McCarthy, Jr., Earl Wooden.

Western **Cas.** **(PR:A MPAA:NR)**

RED RIVER ROBIN HOOD** (1943) 57m RKO bw

Tim Holt, Cliff "Ukulele Ike" Edwards, Barbara Moffett, Eddie Dew, Otto Hoffman, Russell Wade, Tom London, Earle Hodgins, Bud McTaggart, Reed Howes, Kenne Duncan, David Sharpe, Bob McKenzie, Jack Rockwell, Jack Montgomery.

This picture owes more to the legend of ZORRO than to that of ROBIN HOOD, as Holt and Edwards disguise themselves in hoods and black cloaks to thwart a plot by a phony land-grabber. A fake Spanish land-grant lets him evict the local ranchers and claim all the land for himself. But the two hooded figures manage to save the day.

p, Bert Gilroy; d, Lesley Selander; w, Bennett R. Cohen (based on a story by

Whitney J. Stanton); m/l, "Twilight on the Prairie," Fred Rose, Ray Whitley (sung by Cliff Edwards).

Western   **(PR:A   MPAA:NR)**

RED RIVER SHORE*½   (1953) 54m REP bw

Rex Allen (*Himself*), Slim Pickens (*Slim*), Lyn Thomas (*Peggy Taylor*), Bill Phipps (*Ned Barlow*), Douglas Fowley (*Case Lockwood*), Trevor Bardette (*Frank Barlow*), William Haade (*Link Howard*), Emmett Vogan (*Benjamin Willoughby*), John Cason (*Joe*), Rayford Barnes, Koko the Horse.

Dull and stereotyped western formula features Allen keeping out the townspeople from being hoodwinked by local villain Fowley. The citizens have put their money together to pursue an oil interest, and have already endured mishaps. Luckily the oil pans out, making everyone happy except for those who must sit through this plodding picture.

p, Rudy Ralston; d, Harry Keller; w, Arthur Orloff, Gerald Geraghty; ph, Bud Thackery; m, R. Dale Butts; ed, Harold Minter; art d, Frank Hotaling.

Western   **(PR:A   MPAA:NR)**

RED RIVER VALLEY   (1936) 60m REP bw

Gene Autry (*Himself*), Smiley Burnette (*Frog Millhouse*), Frances Grant (*Mary Baxter*), Boothe Howard (*Steve Howard*), Jack Kennedy (*Mike*), Sam Flint (*George Baxter*), George Chesebro (*Butt*), Charles King (*Sam*), Eugene Jackson (*Iodine*), Edward Hearn (*Sheriff*), Frank LaRue (*Hartley Moore*), Ken Cooper (*Long*), Frank Marvin (*Becker*), Cap Anderson [C.E. Anderson], Monty Cass, John Wilson, Lloyd Ingraham, Hank Bell, Earl Dwire, George Morrell, Champion the Horse.

The title is derived from a popular western ballad that is recited throughout by Burnette. The story has Autry and Burnette, though just around to provide the laughs, posing as ditch-diggers to uncover the people responsible for causing numerous mishaps at the construction sight of a new dam. (See: GENE AUTRY Series, Index.)

p&d, B. Reeves Eason; w, Dorrell and Stuart McGowan; ph, William Nobles; m, Harry Gray; ed, Carl Pierson; m/l, "Where a Water Wheel Keeps Turnin' On," Sam Stept, Gene Autry, Smiley Burnette.

Western   **(PR:A   MPAA:NR)**

RED RIVER VALLEY½**   (1941) 62m REP bw

Roy Rogers, George "Gabby" Hayes, Sally Payne, Trevor Bardette, Bob Nolan, Gale Storm, Robert E. Homans, Hal Taliaferro, Lynton Brent, Pat Brady, Edward Piel, Sr., Dick Wessel, Jack Rockwell, Ted Mapes The Sons of the Pioneers, Trigger the Horse.

When ranchers are threatened by a severe water shortage, Rogers comes to the rescue by getting them to donate a total of $182,000 to build a new reservoir. But gambler Bardette cons the people into believing he's helping them and walks off with the money. Rogers lays down his guitar and picks up his gun in pursuit. This picture reunited Rogers with the singers he helped to form before turning to acting: The Sons of the Pioneers. The combination provides for some well interwoven musical numbers in this western that has laughs to go with the action. (See: ROY ROGERS series, Index.)

p&d, Joseph Kane; w, Malcolm Stuart Boylan; ph, Jack Marta; m, Cy Feuer; ed, William Thompson.

Western   **Cas.**   **(PR:A   MPAA:NR)**

RED ROCK OUTLAW*   (1950) 56m Friedgen c

Bob Gilbert, Lee "Lasses" White, Ione Nixon, Forrest Matthews, Virginia Jackson, Wanda Cantlon.

A passable oater which has a murderous outlaw returning to his honest brother's ranch. His plot to kill the rancher brother and pose as a respected frontiersman is luckily foiled, saving Red Rock from dirty dealings.

d&w, Elmer S. Pond [Elmer Clifton].

Western   **(PR:A   MPAA:NR)**

RED ROPE, THE**   (1937) 56m REP bw

Bob Steele (*Tom Shaw*), Lois January (*Betty Duncan*), Forrest Taylor (*Parson Pete*), Charles King (*Red Mike*), Karl Hackett (*Grant Brade*), Bobby Nelson (*Jimmy Duncan*), Ed Cassidy (*Logan*), Lew Meehan (*Rattler Hayne*), Frank Ball (*Pop Duncan*), Jack Rockwell (*Dotkins*), Horace Murphy (*Horner*).

Steele plays the hero who interrupts his honeymoon with January to pursue a group of villains terrorizing the local ranchers. The bad guys use a signature bullet and red-stained rope to indicate who will be their next victim. This picture offers enough fast-paced action and plot twists to be of casual interest.

p, A.W. Hackel; d, S. Roy Luby; w, George Plympton (based on a story by Johnston McCulley); ph, Bert Longenecker; ed, Roy Claire.

Western   **(PR:A   MPAA:NR)**

RED RUNS THE RIVER*1½   (1963) 90m Bob Jones University/Unusual Films c

Bob Jones, Jr. (*Gen. Richard Stoddert Ewell*), Bob Jones III (*Gen. Jeb Stuart*), Jack Buttram (*Gen. "Stonewall" Jackson*), Lonnie Iglesias (*Apache*), Stephen Green (*Charlie*), Jon Jones (*Maj. G. Campbell Brown*), Truman Conley (*Sam Sweeney*), Mike Greene (*Capt. Crossman*), Laura Pratt (*Lizinka Brown Ewell*), Gwen Rees (*Mrs. Thomas J. Jackson*), Charles Applegate (*Photographer*), Nancy Astinger (*Martha Fairfield*), Eddie Beck (*Pvt. Williams*), Miriam Bonner, Donnella Smith (*Winchester Ladies*), Brad Boynton (*Winchester Rebel*), David Bryan (*Pvt. Maxwell*), Tom Butts (*Dr. Hunter McGuire*), Eva Carrier (*Winchester Hostess*), Jim Carter (*Yankee Corporal*), Philip Courter (*Yankee Sentry*), Ray Hansel (*Lt. Gen.*

A.P. Hill), Doris Harris (*Mrs. Cy Fairfield*), Joseph Henson (*Artillery Captain*), Ronald Hill (*Cpl. Woods*), Donald Hudgins (*Pvt. Hall*), Eva P. Kelley (*Mrs. Jackson's Maid*), Leland Klinetop (*Farm Boy*), Billy Lanier (*Pvt. Downs*), Charles Luttrell (*Pvt. Jacobs*), Phillip Luttrell (*Pvt. Russell*), William Moose (*Maj. "Sandie" Pendleton*), Paul Morris (*Federal Private*), Robert Sizelove (*Pvt. Jordan*), Peter Skelly (*Sgt. McDaniel*), Beryl Smith (*Capt. Robinson*), Mel Stratton (*Pvt. Roberts*), Arend J. Ten Pas (*Col. John S. Mosby*), William G. Williams (*Sentry*), Zeb Wolfe (*Cy Fairchild*), Robert Woodward (*Gen. Ewell's Aide*), David Yearick (*Gen. Robert E. Lee*), Marshall Neal, Jr. (*Drummer Boy*), Robert Pratt (*Brig. Gen. Richard B. Garnett*), Tim Rogers (*Brighampton Yankee*), Philip Russell (*Federal Flag Bearer*).

Shot in 16mm, this Christian production takes its shot at the high command of the Civil War. Jones plays a general who loves the excitement of war and battle, but undergoes a change to humility via the guide of his fellow general Buttram. Too much.

d, Katherine Stenholm; w, Charles Applegate (based on a story by Eva Carrier); ph, Wade K. Ramsey; m, Dwight L. Gustafson; ed, George Jensen; md, Gustafson; art d, Tim Morris; cos, Alice Cromley, Jane Morris; makeup, Applegate.

War/Drama   **(PR:A   MPAA:NR)**

RED SALUTE** (1935) 78m UA bw (GB: ARMS AND THE GIRL; AKA: RUNAWAY DAUGHTER; HER ENLISTED MAN)

Barbara Stanwyck (*Drue Van Allen*), Robert Young (*Jeff*), Hardie Albright (*Arner*), Cliff Edwards (*Rooney*), Ruth Donnelly (*Mrs. Rooney*), Gordon Jones (*Lefty*), Paul Stanton (*Louis Martin*), Purnell Pratt (*Maj. Gen. Van Allen*), Nella Walker (*Aunt Betty*), Arthur Vinton (*Joe Beal*), Edward McWade (*Baldy*), Henry Kolker (*Dean*), Henry Otho (*Border Patrolman*), Ben Hall (*Student*), Julian Rivero (*Pedro, Mexican Telegrapher*), Joe Domingues (*Rubio, Chauffeur*), Chris-Pin Martin (*Men's Room Attendant*), Edward Hearn, Jack Cheatham (*Border Patrolmen*), Tom London (*Navy Officer*), Garry Owen (*Gas Station Attendant*), Harry Bowen, Tom Dugan (*Prisoners*), George Reed (*Butler*), Eddy Chandler (*Jailer*), Lester Dorr (*League Speaker*), Jack Mower (*Immigration Officer*), William Moore [Peter Potter], Fred, Kohler, Jr., Dave O'Brien (*Students at Rally*), Alan Cavan, Selmer Jackson, David Newell, Ferdinand Gottschalk.

RED SALUTE is an anti-Communist picture that was so notorious it occasioned a riot by leftist students when it opened at New York's Rivoli Theatre. More then 150 students demonstrated with many being arrested. Constance Cummings was to have played the Stanwyck role but was replaced just before shooting this comedic attempt at another version of "It Happened One Night." Stanwyck, in an unaccustomed part as a happy college girl, is the offspring of patriot Pratt, a general in the U.S. Army. She gets romantically involved with Albright, another young student who has been seduced by Communist propaganda. Pratt wants to put an end to their affair so he sends Stanwyck down to Mexico for a vacation. While there, she meets Taylor, a soldier, and they have a few adventures that include stealing Edwards' trailer, with him in it. Taylor is AWOL and in trouble already but that's compounded when the two steal a car to get back into the U.S. where Taylor is arrested for having departed the service without leave. Stanwyck still plans to marry Albright but Pratt senses that he might drive a wedge into that by using Taylor so he has the soldier released from jail. Albright is speaking at a student rally on behalf of the Communists and Taylor, leading with his right, gets into a battle royal with Albright, whacks him heavily about the head and shoulders, and Stanwyck decides she would be better off with Taylor, to no one's surprise. Without the anti-red preaching, it might have been a good comedy. Later, they did excise some of that and re-released the picture as RUNAWAY DAUGHTER. On TV, it might also be seen as HER ENLISTED MAN.

p, Edward Small; d, Sidney Lanfield; w, Humphrey Pearson, Manuel Seff, Elmer Harris (uncredited) (based on a story by Pearson); ph, Robert Planck; ed, Grant Whytock; art d, John Ducasse Schulze.

Comedy   **(PR:A   MPAA:NR)**

RED SHEIK, THE** (1963, Ital.) 90m Explorer/Medallion c (LO SCEICCO ROSSO)

Channing Pollock (*Ruiz/The Red Sheik*), Luciana Gilli (*Amina*), Mel Welles (*Hassan*), Mary Welles, Ettore Manni, Pietro De Vico, Rosalba Neri, Glauco Onorato, Giulio Battiferri, Alberto Archetti, Ahmed Amer.

Set in 19th-Century Morocco where a mysterious figure known only as the "Red Sheik" aids rebel forces as they attempt to overcome an evil sultan. Uncovered, the noble fighter proves to be a Spanish architect avenging the murder of his father by the sultan.

d, Fernando Cerchio; w, Gino De Santis, Luigi Capuano, Vittoriano Petrilli, Remigio Del Grosso, Montanari; ph, Gianni Narzisi, Angelo Lotti (Euroscope, Eastmancolor); m, Giovanni Fusco.

Adventure   **(PR:A   MPAA:NR)**

RED SHOES, THE*** (1948, Brit.) 133m Archers/EL-RANK c

Anton Walbrook (*Boris Lermontov*), Moira Shearer (*Victoria Page*), Marius Goring (*Julian Craster*), Leonide Massine (*Grischa Ljubov*), Robert Helpmann (*Ivan Boleslawsky*), Albert Basserman (*Sergei Ratov*), Esmond Knight (*Livy*), Ludmilla Tcherina (*Irina Boronskaja*), Jean Short (*Terry*), Gordon Littman (*Ike*), Julia Lang (*A Balletomane*), Bill Shine (*Her Mate*), Austin Trevor (*Prof. Palmer*), Eric Berry (*Dimitri*), Irene Browne (*Lady Neston*), Jerry Verno (*Stage-door Keeper*), Derek Elphinstone (*Lord Oldham*), Mme. Rambert (*Herself*), Joy Rawlins (*Gwladys, Vicky's Friend*), Marcel Poncin (*Mons. Boudin*), Michel Bazalgette (*Mons. Rideaut*), Yvonee Andre (*Vicky's Dresser*), Hay Petrie (*Boisson*), Irene Browne, Joan Harris.

You don't have to be a balletomane to enjoy THE RED SHOES, although ballet is so integral a part of the film that it might help. THE TURNING POINT was a much more realistic look at pirhouettes and plies, but this is the one that will stand out in your memory as the ultimate ballet picture, until a better one comes along, if ever. It's a backstage love story that is, in many ways, similar to any of several Warner Bros. musicals of the 1930s but the dancing is so glorious and the acting so excellent that the resemblance ends quickly. When it was finished, everyone suspected a disaster. It had gone well over budget and the makers and distributors wondered if there would be a market for such a specific kind of film. The receipts in England were not terrific and it was only after it opened in the U.S. and other countries that it began to take off and played to full houses, grossing many more millions than anyone had imagined it might. Walbrook is a ballet impresario on the order of Serge Diaghilev, the Russian who masterminded the Ballet Russe. His company has just completed a performance of "Heart of Fire"—a ballet written by Trevor. Walbrook goes to a party and meets Shearer, a young ballerina. He abhors amateurs but is soon taken by her apparent sincerity in wanting to dance and arranges an audition for her at his company. Meanwhile, Goring, a fledgling composer, sends the stern and reclusive Walbrook a letter claiming that it was he who wrote "Heart Of Fire" and that the music had been "appropriated" by his teacher, Trevor. Walbrook meets Goring, listens to him play, and sees that the lad is telling the truth, so he offers him a job with the company in a minor musical position. Walbrook goes to observe Shearer dance and realizes that she is still raw but has unmistakable talent so he signs her on with his organization. At the same time, Walbrook notes that Goring is a gifted musician and rewards him by allowing Goring to do the company's musical arrangements. The lead dancer, Tcherina, decides that she would rather be married than dance, and Walbrook is stunned that anyone would give up the chance to perform in favor of a marriage. They are now on the road and need a new piece, so Goring gets the job of adapting Hans Christian Andersen's fairy tale, "The Red Shoes," as a ballet. (The original story is not a pretty one, as an impoverished young woman dons a pair of magical shoes and almost dies when her feet won't stop dancing. She is saved when her feet are cut off by an axe-wielding executioner and the shoes and her feet dance on. She has wooden feet attached, finds peace in religion, and manages to live, albeit hobbling for the rest of her life). Shearer, who has continued to impress Walbrook with her work (and whom he secretly loves) is given the prima ballerina role in Goring's ballet. Shearer and Goring discuss the ballet as he writes it. They fight, laugh, and fall in love. The ballet is done. (The 20-minute sequence in the middle of the film that is breathtaking: Shearer, wearing white and blue that perfectly complemented her rich, red hair, is surrounded by enormous, intricate sets and the stage opens up like one of those Busby Berkeley sets of yore.) It is a critical and popular hit and Walbrook is thrilled, promising Shearer more leading roles to play. Then his mood turns dark when he learns that she and Goring are passionately in love with each other, an emotion that is forbidden by Walbrook in his company because he feels it can only detract from dedication to ballet. Walbrook begins to exact vengeance on the union. Goring turns in a new score and Walbrook unfairly criticizes it, while everyone else in the company thinks it is superb. Goring can only react by resigning and Shearer, faithful to her lover, also resigns. Shearer and Goring marry and Walbrook feigns indifference to their wedding and to their defection. He tells his associates that her career is over and she will never achieve prominence as long as she remains with Goring. Since Walbrook controls all rights to Goring's most popular work, "The Red Shoes," he refuses to allow it to be danced by anyone outside his company and Shearer soon finds that she cannot find employment unless she can dance it. Some time later, Goring and Shearer are still happily married. He's in London to present a new musical piece at Covent Garden and she has come to Paris where Walbrook finds her at the train station and asks if she will agree to do one performance of "The Red Shoes" in Monaco. She chews on it a bit, then agrees, but there is a domestic price to pay, as she can't be in two places at once and will not be at Goring's London recital. She plans to go on with the show and is in her dressing room donning her shoes and costume when Goring arrives, irate at what's happened. He'd given the job of conducting the orchestra to someone else in order to get to Monte Carlo and convince Shearer that she's making a mistake by dancing for Walbrook, who soon adds his own voice to the disagreement. Meanwhile, a strange phenomenon has occurred. The shoes have taken on a life of their own. Shearer cannot stop herself as the shoes carry her out of the theater and onto a high balcony overlooking a set of railway tracks. Unable to stop herself, she leaps off the balcony and is hit by a train, the Nice Express. Goring rushes to her side, removes the ballet shoes, and she dies in his arms. Later, Walbrook tells the audience that Shearer is dead but the performance will go off on schedule. It begins, and a solo spotlight follows the moves as though Shearer were dancing, but all one sees is the empty space on the stage. THE RED SHOES won three Oscars for Best Art Direction, Best Set Decoration, and Best Scoring. The melodramatic aspects of the plot can't be overlooked when it comes to evaluating the entire film. A happy ending would have been far more satisfying but the authors were steadfastly against that. The history of the film began when Alexander Korda hired Hungarian Pressburger to write a script for Korda's wife, Merle Oberon, that would call for her to act and a dancer to double for her in the ballet scenes. They got busy with other things and the picture was scrubbed. Years later, Pressburger joined with Powell to become a powerful team and they bought the script back from Korda and rewrote it for Shearer, a Sadler's Wells ballerina who proved to be a much better actress than anyone had dreamed. Matter of fact, all of the ballet people, Massine, Helpmann (who also did the "Red Shoes" choreography), Tcherina, et al, were excellent in their acting roles, and Goring, who had already made many movies, was weak by comparison. Walbrook was brilliant as the impresario and it would be hard to picture anyone else in the role, with the exception of, perhaps, Basil Rathbone. The movie was colorfully photographed by Jack Cardiff and had the added benefit of some picturesque locations in Paris, Monaco, and London. Although it is one of the most popular "women's pictures" ever made, that's an improper designation, as it will be appreciated for years to come by anyone with taste. Easdale's music goes well with excerpts from "Giselle," "Swan Lake," "les Sylphides," and "Coppelia." For years, the female members of dance companies have been known as "ballet nuns" because their devotion to their work borders on religion. In order to succeed at ballet, one must totally dedicate oneself to perfection, something that the makers of this film also did, and the movie is a classic. In the 1980s, Broadway producer David Merrick toyed with the notion of bringing the story to the stage as a musical-drama-ballet (with no songs), but his plans were put on hold when he suffered a stroke. The picture was also Oscar-nominated as Best Picture and for Best Screenplay.

p&d, Michael Powell, Emeric Pressburger; w, Powell, Pressburger, Keith Winter; ph, Jack Cardiff (Technicolor); m, Brian Easdale; ed, Reginald Mills; md, Sir Thomas Beecham; art d, Hein Heckroth, Arthur Lawson; ch, Robert Helpmann; cos, Heckroth.

Drama **Cas.** **(PR:A MPAA:NR)**

RED SKIES OF MONTANA**½ (1952) 89m FOX c (AKA: SMOKE JUMPERS)

Richard Widmark *(Cliff Mason)*, Constance Smith *(Peg)*, Jeffrey Hunter *(Ed Miller)*, Richard Boone *(Dryer)*, Warren Stevens *(Steve)*, James Griffith *(Boise)*, Joe Sawyer *(Pop Miller)*, Gregory Wolcott *(Randy)*, Richard Crenna *(Noxon)*, Bob Nichols *(Felton)*, Ralph Reed *(Piney)*, William Murphy *(Winkler)*, Charles Buchinsky [Bronson] *(Neff)*, Larry Dobkin *(Spotter)*, Robert Adler *(McMullen)*, Mike Mahoney *(Kenner)*, John Close *(Lewisohn)*, Grady Galloway *(Sabinson)*, Henry Kulky *(Dawson)*, Harry Carter *(Philippe)*, Charles Tannen *(Pilot)*, Ron Hargrave *(Grayson)*, Robert Osterloh *(Dispatcher)*, Ted Ryan *(Foreman)*, John Kennedy *(Telegraph Operator)*, Parley Baer *(Doctor)*, Barbara Woodell *(Nurse)*, Ray Hyke, Wilson Hood *(Inspectors)*, Ann Morrison *(Mrs. Miller)*.

Raging forest fires in spectacular Technicolor are the main attraction here. Widmark stars as a veteran firefighter of the U.S. Forestry Service who takes his men paratrooping into the heart of yet another inferno. This fire proves disastrous, however, and it consumes all the the brave firefighters except Widmark, who somehow survives. Upon his recovery, Widmark is confronted by Hunter, the son of one of the men who perished. Hunter accuses Widmark of cowardly fleeing the flames, leaving his men to die. Since Widmark blacked out during the incident and has no clear recollection of what actually did happen, Hunter's accusations shake him deeply. Apparently Hunter's claims are heard by the forestry service, for Widmark is given the safe task of training new recruits. Hunter, however, follows in his father's footsteps and joins the ranks of the firefighters. Eventually, Widmark is given the chance to redeem himself when another forest fire erupts. Accompanied by his rookies, Widmark goes into battle. During the fire, Hunter continues his belligerent attitude towards Widmark until the older man risks his life to save him. Shamed by this heroic deed, Hunter admits he was wrong about Widmark. Though the plot is fairly standard stuff, the scenes of men battling the raging forest fires are well crafted, vivid, and exciting. The cast is filled with good supporting characters including Boone, Crenna, and a young Charles Bronson (still named Buchinsky at this point). Just before the film's release, the studio panicked and thought the public might assume the title RED SKIES OF MONTANA meant that the film was a western. The title was changed to SMOKE JUMPERS in New York and other test areas, but prints released to television retained the original title.

p, Samuel G. Engel; d, Joseph M. Newman; w, Harry Kleiner (based on a story by Art Cohn); ph, Charles G. Clarke (Technicolor); m, Sol Kaplan; ed, William Reynolds; md, Lionel Newman; art d, Lyle Wheeler, Chester Gore; set d, Thomas Little.

Drama **(PR:A MPAA:NR)**

RED SKY AT MORNING*½ (1971) 112m UNIV c

Richard Thomas *(Josh Arnold)*, Catherine Burns *(Marcia Davidson)*, Desi Arnaz, Jr. *(Steenie Moreno)*, Richard Crenna *(Frank Arnold)*, Claire Bloom *(Ann Arnold)*, John Colicos *(Jimbob Buel)*, Harry Guardino *(Romeo Bonino)*, Strother Martin *(John Cloyd)*, Nehemiah Persoff *(Amadeo Montoya)*, Pepe Serna *(Chango Lopez)*, Mario Aniov *(Lindo Velarde)*, Victoria Racimo *(Viola Lopez)*, Gregory Sierra *(Chamaco)*, Lynne Marta *(Vebenay Ann Cloyd)*, Christina Hart *(Velva Mae Cloyd)*, Elizabeth Knowles *(Shirley)*, Linda Burton *(Gwendolyn)*, Alma Beltran *(Excilda Montoya)*, Jerome Guardino *(Paolo Bertucci)*, Joy Bang *(Corky)*, Claudio Miranda *(Native)*, Joaquim Garay *(Ratoncito)*, Karen Klett *(Miss Rudd)*.

Murky tale of a boy who is forced to come to terms with his manhood when his father is killed during WW II. Thomas is a teenage boy who is sent with his mother, Bloom, to live in New Mexico when his father is sent to war. He comes to terms with making new friends in an area where whites are the minority, falls in love for the first time with Burns, and adapts to an alienated mother. His final test of manhood comes with the news that his father has died and he must fight Colicos, Bloom's lover, to be the man of the house. Any possibilities from the original story are lost in the slack and uninspired direction of a cast consisting of little more than stereotypes.

p, Hal B. Wallis; d, James Goldstone; w, Marguerite Roberts (based on the novel by Richard Bradford); ph, Vilmos Zsigmond (Technicolor); m, Billy Goldenberg; ed, Edward A. Biery, Richard M. Sprague; art d, Alexander Golitzen, Walter Tyler; set d, John Austin; cos, Edith Head; m/l, "Don't Sit Under the Apple Tree with Anyone Else but Me" (sung by the Andrews Sisters); makeup, Bud Westmore.

Drama **(PR:C MPAA:GP)**

RED SNOW** (1952) 75m COL bw

Guy Madison *(Lt. Johnson)*, Ray Mala *(Sgt. Koovuk)*, Carole Mathews *(Lt. Jane)*, Gloria Saunders *(Alak)*, Robert Peyton *(Maj. Bennett)*, John Bryant *(Alex)*, Richard Vath *(Elia)*, Philip Ahn *(Tuglu)*, Tony Benroy *(Cpl. Savick)*, Gordon Barnes *(Capt. MacLoflin)*, John Bleifer *(Commissar Volgan)*, Gene Roth *(Maj. Duboff)*, Muriel Maddox *(Ruth)*, Robert Bice *(Chief Nanu)*, Renny McEvoy *(Sgt. Koops)*, Bert Arnold *(Riggs)*, Richard Emory *(Stone)*, Richard Pinner *(Long)*, George Pembroke *(Maj. Slavin)*, Robert Carson *(General)*, William Fletcher *(Kresnick)*, Richard Barton *(Russian Officer)*.

Old stock footage of Eskimo life was put to fairly good use here in this story about

Eskimo soldiers sent back to their Northern tribes to investigate possible Soviet shenanigans on the other side of the Bering Strait. Their search uncovers the Russians' development of a new secret weapon. A Soviet pilot rebels and lands his plane, with the weapon, on the U.S. side. Performances are as frozen as the landscape.

p, Boris L. Petroff; d, Petroff, Harry S. Franklin, Ewing Scott; w, Tom Hubbard, Orville H. Hampton (based on a story by Robert Peters); ph, Paul Ivano; m, Alex Alexander, June Starr; ed, Merrill White, Albert Shaff; md, Michael Terr; art d, Daniel Hall; cos, Edith Head.

Adventure/Spy   **(PR:A MPAA:NR)**

RED STALLION, THE**   (1947) 81m EL bw

Robert Paige (*Andy McBride*), Noreen Nash (*Ellen Reynolds*), Ted Donaldson (*Joel Curtis*), Jane Darwell (*Mrs. Curtis*), Ray Collins (*Barton*), Guy Kibbee (*Dr. Thompson*), Willie Best (*Jackson*), Robert Bice (*Ho-Na*), Pierre Watkin (*Richard Moresby*), Bill Cartledge (*Johnny Stevens*), Big Red the Horse, Daisy the Dog.

Animal lovers' story features Donaldson raising a foal to become a racehorse. The horse saves Donaldson and his grandmother's (Darwell) ranch from foreclosure when it wins the big race. The horse also protects Donaldson from a bear that was destined to attack the boy. Nice outdoor photography and some exciting animal sequences help to save an off-paced picture that falters when it comes to human dimensions.

p, Ben Stoloff; d, Lesley Selander; w, Robert E. Kent, Crane Wilbur; ph, Virgil Miller (Cinecolor); m, Frederick Hollander; ed, Fred Allen; md, Irving Friedman; art d, Perry Smith.

Adventure/Drama   **(PR:A MPAA:NR)**

RED STALLION IN THE ROCKIES**½   (1949) 85m EL bw

Arthur Franz (*Thad Avery*), Wallace Ford (*Talky Carson*), Ray Collins (*Matthew Simpson*), Jean Heather (*Cindy Smith*), James Davis (*Dave Ryder*), Leatrice Joy (*Martha Simpson*), Dynamite (*Red Stallion*).

When a wild stallion starts stealing mares from the local ranchers for his own harem, the ranchers band together to hunt him. But a couple of circus workers recognize the horse as a trick circus animal and protect him from the angry ranchers. The horse is forgiven when he saves the life of a rancher's wife when she is attacked by a wild elk. With all this going on, a subtle romance develops between Heather, a rancher's daughter, and circusman Franz. The color photography of the majestic Colorado Rockies serves as an alluring backdrop to this nicely staged animal story.

p, Aubrey Schenk; d, Ralph Murphy; w, Tom Reed (based on the story by Francis Rosenwald); ph, John Alton (Cinecolor); m, Lucien Callient; ed, Norman Colbert; md, Irving Friedman; art d, Walter Koessler; set d, Armor Marlowe; spec eff, Roy W. Seawright; m/l, C. Harold Lewis, Ralph Murphy; makeup, Ern Westmore, Dave Grayson.

Adventure   **(PR:AA MPAA:NR)**

RED SUN**   (1972, Fr./Ital./Span.) 112m Corona-Oceania-Balcazar/NG c
(SOLEIL ROUGE)

Charles Bronson (*Link*), Ursula Andress (*Cristina*), Toshiro Mifune (*Kuroda, Samurai Bodyguard*), Alain Delon (*Gauche*), Capucine (*Pepita*), Satoshi Nakamoura (*Ambassador*), Bart Barry (*Sheriff*), Lee Burton, Anthony Dawson, John Hamilton, George W. Lycan, Luke Merenda, Jose Nieto, Julio Pena, Monica Randall, Hiroshi Tanaka, John Vermont.

An international cast provided a sure-fire success in Europe and the Far East, but failed to evoke much excitement in the U.S. Based on a true story, Mifune plays the samurai who accompanies a Japanese ambassador bringing a jewelled, and symbolic, sword to be presented to the president. However during the train ride, Bronson and Delon attack and steal the sword. But Delon double-crosses Bronson and then leaves. This motivates the teaming, amidst an air of cultural confusion, of Mifune and Bronson as they stalk Delon. Their search takes them to a brothel where the two men enjoy the favors of Andress and Capucine before catching up with Delon. A Comanche raid forces the three men to band together to fight the Indians, the sole survivor being Bronson, who returns the sword to the Japanese ambassador. Both Mifune and Bronson give the stoical types of performances that have made them actors of such great standing. Delon is horribly miscast as the villain, with Andress only having to look nice. The levels of tension and excitement provided by the story are never fully met under Young's direction.

p, Ted Richmond; d, Terence Young; w, Laird Koenig, D.B. Petitclerc, W. Roberts, L. Roman (based on a story by Koenig); ph, Henri Alekan (Technicolor); m, Maurice Jarre; ed, Johnny Dwyre; md, Jarre; art d, Enrique [Henry] Alarcon; set d, Rafael Salazar; cos, Tony Pulo; spec eff, Karl Baumgartner; makeup, Alberto De Rossi.

Western   **(PR:A MPAA:PG)**

RED SUNDOWN**   (1956) 81m UNIV c

Rory Calhoun (*Alec Longmire*), Martha Hyer (*Caroline Murphy*), Dean Jagger (*Sheriff Jade Murphy*), Robert Middleton (*Rufus Henshaw*), Grant Williams (*Chet Swann*), Lita Baron (*Maria*), James Millican (*Purvis*), Trevor Bardette (*Sam Baldwin*), Leo Gordon (*Rod Zellman*), David Kasday (*Hughie Clore*), Stevie Wooton (*Chuck*), Steve Darrell (*Bert Flynn*), John Carpenter (*Zellman*), Henry Wills, Alex Sharp.

Briskly paced depiction of a familiar and well-used tale has Calhoun playing the former gunslinger who has turned to life on the ranch after the death of a good buddy. When a cattle baron, Middleton, threatens a range war to extend his empire, Calhoun, at Hyer's insistence, puts on his gunbelt again. He also puts a star on his chest, because he becomes deputy to Hyer's father. And he must prove

himself against the gunman Middleton hired. Proper treatment is given this conventional story.

p, Alfred Zugsmith; d, Jack Arnold; w, Martin Berkeley (based on the novel *Black Trail* by Lewis B. Patten); ph, William Snyder (Technicolor); m, Hans J. Salter; ed, Edward Curtiss; art d, Alexander Golitzen, Eric Orbom; cos, Jay Morley, Jr.; m/l, "Red Sundown," Terry Gilkyson (sung by Gilkyson).

Western   **(PR:A MPAA:NR)**

RED TENT, THE***   (1971, Ital./USSR) 121m Vides Cinematografica-Mosfilm/PAR c (KRASNAYA PALATKA; LA TENDA ROSSA)

Sean Connery (*Roald Amundsen*), Claudia Cardinale (*Nurse Valeria*), Hardy Kruger (*Aviator Lundborg*), Peter Finch (*Gen. Umberto Nobile*), Massimo Girotti (*Romagna, Rescue Coordinator*), Luigi Vannuchi (*Capt. Zappi*), Mario Adorf (*Biagi, Radio Operator*), Edward Marzevic (*Finn Malmgren, Meteorologist*), Grigori Gaj (*Samoilovich, Captain of Krassin, Russian Icebreaker*), Nikita Mikhalkov (*Chuknousky, Icebreaker Pilot*), Nicolai Ivanov (*Kolka, Amateur Radioman*), Boris Kmelnizki (*Viglieri*), Juri Solomin (*Troiani*), Juri Vizbor (*Behounek*), Donatas Banionis (*Mariano*), Otar Koberidze (*Cecioni*).

Gripping adventure tale has Finch as an Italian explorer who has been rescued at the expense of his men. Years later, his guilt catches up with him as he begins recalling the events that led to his rescue. Connery plays Amundsen, who dies in his attempt to rescue the downed dirigible based on a real event. The northern climate provides the existential atmosphere appropriate to the material, with a score by Morricone that underlines these conditions. This costly Italian-Russian coproduction proved a box office failure.

p, Franco Cristaldi; d, Mikhail K. Kalatozov; w, Ennio De Concini, Richard Adams; ph, Leonid Kalashnikov (Technicolor); m, Ennio Morricone; ed, Peter Zinner; art d, Giancarlo Bartolini Salimbeni, David Vinitsky; set d, Juri Ekonomzev, Franco D'Andria; cos, Natalia Meshkova; makeup, Max Alautdinov, Antonio Mecacci.

Adventure   **(PR:A MPAA:G)**

RED TOMAHAWK**   (1967) 82m PAR c

Howard Keel (*Capt. Tom York*), Joan Caulfield (*Dakota Lil*), Broderick Crawford (*Columbus Smith*), Scott Brady (*Ep Wyatt*), Wendell Corey (*Elkins*), Richard Arlen (*Telegrapher*), Tom Drake (*Bill Kane*), Tracy Olsen (*Sal*), Ben Cooper (*Lt. Drake*), Donald Barry (*Bly*), Reg Parton, Roy Jenson (*Prospectors*), Gerald Jann (*Wu Sing*), Dan White (*Ned Crone*), Henry Wills (*Samuels*), Saul Gorss (*Townsman*).

A highly economical and tightly woven, though horribly cliche-ridden, depiction of the aftermath of the battle of Little Big Horn. Keel plays a cavalry captain who comes to warn the small town of Deadwood about the possibility of a Sioux attack. At first treated with mistrust as being a deserter, the townspeople fail to heed his warnings. But Brady, as the local gunfighter, persuades the people of Keel's validity. The two men prepare for the blockade of the city. This includes the use of two Gatling guns, whose whereabouts are known only by Caulfield, who refuses to disclose the information because she doesn't want to see any more killings. But Keel talks her into helping out. He then takes the guns to the aid of a cavalry division under Sioux attack. Acting is uninspired, with the action sequences looking awfully staged.

p, A.C. Lyles; d, R.G. Springsteen; w, Steve Fisher (based on a stroy by Fisher, Andrew Craddock); ph, W. Wallace Kelley (Panavision, Pathe Color); m, Jimmie Haskell; ed, John F. Schreyer; art d, Hal Pereira, Al Roelofs; set d, Robert R. Benton, Ray Moyer.

Western   **(PR:A MPAA:NR)**

RED WAGON**   (1936) 97m Alliance/FD bw

Charles Bickford (*Joe Price*), Raquel Torres (*Sheba Price/Starlina*), Greta Nissen (*Zara*), Don Alvarado (*Davey Heron*), Anthony Bushnell (*Toby Griffiths*), Paul Graetz (*Max Schultze*), Amy Veness (*Petal Schultze*), Jimmy Hanley (*Young Joe*), Frank Pettingell (*McGinty*), Alexander Fields (*Harry Crank*), Francis L. Sullivan (*Cranley*), Stella Bonheur (*Ella*), Sybil Grove (*Mrs. Crank*), Percy Parsons (*Cowboy Charlie*), Arthur Goullet (*Plato*), Nancy Brown (*Lamentina*), Aubrey Mather (*Blewett*), Helen Ferrers, Hay Petrie, Charles Farrell, Torin Thatcher.

Bickford plays a young man who runs away to join the circus. The owner, who had taken Bickford under his wing, dies and leaves the circus to him. Bickford then becomes the object of desire for animal trainer Nissen and gypsy Torres. A misunderstanding with Nissen, who Bickford really loves, forces him to marry Torres. But she is only after his money. When Torres eventually leaves to be with her own people, Bickford and Nissen are reunited. Bickford fails to bring the needed romanticism required to his part.

p, Walter C. Mycroft; d, Paul L. Stein; w, Roger Burford, Arthur Woods, Edward Knoblock (based on the novel by Lady Eleanor Smith); ph, Jack Cox; ed, Leslie Norman; cos, Paula Newman.

Drama   **(PR:A MPAA:NR)**

RED, WHITE AND BLACK, THE**½   (1970) 103m Hirschman-Northern c (AKA: SOUL SOLDIERS; SOUL SOLDIER; MEN OF THE TENTH)

Robert DoQui (*Trooper Eli Brown*), Janee Michelle (*Julie*), Lincoln Kilpatrick (*Sgt. Hatch*), Issac Fields (*1st Sgt. Robertson*), Rafer Johnson (*Pvt. Armstrong*), Cesar Romero (*Col. Grierson*), Barbara Hale (*Mrs. Grierson*), Isabel Sanford (*Isabel*), Steve Drexel (*Capt. Carpenter*), Russ Nannarello, Jr. (*Lt. Bitelow*), Robert Dix (*Walking Horse*), Otis Taylor (*Pvt. Adams*), Bill Collins (*Pvt. Washington*), John Fox (*The Sigifier*), Byrd Holland (*The Sutler*), Bobby Clark (*Kayitah*), Bernard Brown, Clarence Comas, Donald Diggs, Jeff Everett, Cal Fields, Perry Fluker, Noah Hobson, Earl Humphrey, DeVaughn LaBon, Rod Law, Jim Pace, John Nettles, Eric Richmond (*Troopers of the 10th Cavalry*), Jon-Jon, Rava Malmuth, John Ramsey, Charles Wells, George Wells, Paul Wheaton, David White, Barbara Brown, Edith Hazley, Lee James, Hank Lowery, Barry Noble, Maurishka, Steve

Paullada, Wanda Roberts, Marchita Stanton, Mollie Stevenson, Leah Weed, Stuart Z. Hirschman.

DoQui plays a recruit in the all-black 10th U.S. Cavalry regiment stationed in Texas shortly after the Civil War. The commander and only white man at the fort is Romero, who forces his men to do things for the benefits of whites. One is to attack an Indian tribe, led by Dix, for stealing horses. Dix is a close friend of trooper Johnson, who is sent to attack the Indians after the death of his friend. Several members of the cavalry are killed in the attack. The survivors question their reasons for risking their lives for the white man. Several intertwining stories provide an interesting depiction of the overall picture, with novice director Cardos proving capable at staging action scenes. The film's success in re-release gave rise to THE LEGEND OF NIGGER CHARLEY in 1972.

p, James M. Northern, Stuart Z. Hirschman; d, John Cardos; w, Marlene Weed; ph, Lewis J. Guinn (Eastmancolor); m, Stu Phillips; ed, Guinn, Mort Tubor, Russ Mannarelli, Dick Dixon; art d&set d, Phedon Papamichael; cos, Frances Dennis; spec eff, Harry Woolman; m/l, "Ordinary Huckleberry," Phillips, Bob Stone (sung by Don Reed); makeup, Barry Noble.

Western   **(PR:C MPAA:GP)**

REDEEMER, THE**   (1965, Span.) 93m Cruzada del Rosario en Familia/Empire c (LOS MISTERIOS DEL ROSARIO)

Luis Alvarez (*Jesus Christ*), Maruchi Fresno (*Virgin Mary*), Manuel Monroy (*Judas Iscariot*), Felix Acaso (*Joseph Caiaphas*), Antonio Vilar (*Pontius Pilate/Saint Peter*), Sebastian Cabot (*Narrator*), Virgilio Teixeira, Jose Marco Davo, Carlos Casaravilla, Hebe Donay, Jacinto San Emeterio, Felix de Pomes, Antonio Casas, Carlota Bilbao, Francisco Arenzana.

Alvarez plays Christ in this depiction of the last three days of his life, beginning with his arrest and ending with a group of disciples visiting the tomb to find it empty.

p, Patrick Peyton; d, Joseph Breen; w, Tom Blackburn, Robert Hugh O'Sullivan, John T. Kelley, James O'Hanlon; ph, Edwin Du Par (Todd-AO, Eastmancolor); m, David Raksins; art d, Enrique Alarcon.

Religion   **(PR:A MPAA:NR)**

REDEEMER, THE   (SEE: RAT SAVIOUR, THE, 1977, Yugo.)

REDEEMER, THE zero   (1978) 84m Dimension c

Jeannetta Arnette, T.G. Finkbinder, Damien Knight, Nick Carter, Gyr Patterson, Nikki Barthen, Christopher Flint.

Six former students return to their school for a reunion organized, unknown to them, by a psychotic fellow student. It seems the psycho is displeased with his classmates' immorality and he mutilates and kills them. Among his murder weapons are a flame thrower and a wash basin. Pretty sticky going in this inept, unpleasant picture which cloaks itself in supposed religious themes.

p, Sheldon Tromberg; d, Constantine S. Gochis; w, William Vernick.

Horror   **Cas.**   **(PR:O MPAA:R)**

REDEEMING SIN, THE*½   (1929) 75m WB bw

Dolores Costello (*Joan Villaire*), Conrad Nagel (*Dr. Raoul Deboise*), George Stone (*A Sewer Rat*), Philippe de Lacy (*Petit*), Lionel Belmore (*Father Colomb*), Warner Richmond (*Jetteur Lupine*), Nina Quartero (*Mitzi*).

Costello plays a dancer whose brother is wounded during a church robbery. Nagel, the local doctor, is called upon to help the boy. Not only does he inform on the boy and his partner, Richmond, but he fails to save the boy's life. Costello and Nagel become lovers, sending Richmond into a jealous fury. Richmond attacks the doctor, leaving him for dead, and blackmails Costello into marrying him. Nagel, however, turns up alive and alerts the police to Richmond's whereabouts. A tedious part-talkie that didn't thrill them then and won't thrill us now.

d, Howard Bretherton; w, Harvey Gates, Joseph Jackson. (based on the story by L.V. Jefferson); ph, Byron Haskin; ed, Tommy Pratt. m, Louis Silvers.

Romance/Drama   **(PR:A MPAA:NR)**

REDEMPTION*   (1930) 75 MGM bw

John Gilbert, conrad Nagel, Eleanor Boardman, Renee Adoree, Claire McDowell, Augustino Borgato, Charles Quartermaine, George Spelvin, Mack Swain, Tully Marshall, Nigel de Brulier.

Irving Thalberg did not leave anything out in this expensive adaptation of Leo Tolstoy's "The Live Corpse", which was to be billed as Gilbert's first talkie. But the result was so bad and in such desperate need of repair that the film spent a year in the cutting room, allowing HIS GLORIOUS NIGHT to earn the billing as Gilbert's first talking picture. This heavy-handed story has Gilbert mistaken as dead, which gives his wife and best friend, Boardman and Nagel respectively, the chance to marry. When it is discovered that Gilbert is indeed alive, a trial and arrest leads to Gilbert's suicide so the two lovers may carry on their lives. The script has little of the moral ironies found in Tolstoy's play, therefore coming out as an unrealistic and overly dramatic mess.

d, Fred Niblo; w, Dorothy Farnum, Edwin Justus Mayer (based on the play "The Live Corpse" by Leo Tolstoy); ph, Percy Hilburn; ed, Margaret Booth; cos, Adrian.

Drama   **(PR:A MPAA:NR)**

REDHEAD   (SEE: RED HEAD, 1934)

REDHEAD*   (1941) 64m MON bw

June Lang (*Dale Carter*), Johnny Downs (*Ted Brown*), Eric Blore (*Digby*), Frank Jaquet (*T.H. Brown*), Weldon Heyburn (*Winston*), Anna Chandler (*Peppy*), Harry Burns (*Nick*), Baron Emerson (*Tramp*), Ralina Zarova (*Entertainer*).

Remake of 1934 Monogram production that starred Bruce Cabot and Grace Bradley. This version has Downs as the spoiled rich kid whose father pays Lang $10,000 to take the kid off his hands and put him to good use. She takes up the assignment, falling in love with Downs at a roadside hamburger joint. Dull and predictable.

p, I.E. Chadwick; d, Edward Cahn; w, Dorothy Reid, Conrad Seiler (based on the novel by Vera Brown); ph, Andre Barlatier; ed, Carl Pierson.

Drama/Comedy   **(PR:A MPAA:NR)**

REDHEAD AND THE COWBOY, THE**½   (1950) 82m PAR bw

Glenn Ford (*Gil Kyle*), Edmund O'Brien (*Dunn Jeffers*), Rhonda Fleming (*Candace Bronson*), Alan Reed (*Lamartine*), Morris Ankrum (*Sheriff*), Edith Evanson (*Mrs. Barrett*), Perry Ivins (*Mr. Barrett*), Janine Perreau (*Mary Barrett*), Douglas Spencer (*Perry*), Ray Teal (*Brock*), Ralph Byrd (*Capt. Andrews*), King Donovan (*Munroe*), Tom Moore (*Gus*).

A light-hearted tone creates the atmosphere for this spy caper set during the closing days of the Civil War. Fleming plays a Confederate sympathizer carrying a message to irregular Grays who are seeking a shipment of Union gold. Ford plays a cowpoke who follows her because he needs her as a witness to clear him of a murder charge. Tailing along is O'Brien, a Union undercover agent, who hopes Fleming will lead him to the brains behind the operation, Reed, a swindler intent on keeping the gold for himself. Ford, Fleming, and O'Brien give performances which offset the incongruities in the direction by Fenton in his last assignment as a director before retiring after 30 years in the motion picture industry as both actor and director. It was also the last movie in a long career for one-time romantic lead in the silents, Tom Moore.

p, Irving Asher; d, Leslie Fenton; w, Jonathan Latimer, Liam O'Brien (based on the story by Charles Marquis Warren); ph, Daniel L. Fapp, m, David Buttolph; ed, Arthur Schmidt; art d, Hal Pereira, Henry Bumstead.

Western/Spy   **(PR:A MPAA:NR)**

REDHEAD FROM MANHATTAN*½   (1954) 63m COL bw

Lupe Velez (*Rita/Elaine Manners*), Michael Duane (*Jimmy Randall*), Tim Ryan (*Mike Glendon*), Gerald Mohr (*Chick Andrews*), Lillian Yarbo (*Polly*), Arthur Loft (*Sig Hammersmith*), Lewis Wilson (*Paul*), Douglas Leavitt (*Joe*), Clancy Cooper (*Policeman*), Douglass Drake (*Marty Britt*), Ben Carter (*Boy*), Al Herman (*Bartender*), Alma Carroll, Shirley Patterson (*Telephone Operators*), Ben Gerien, Peter Gunn (*Henchmen*), Stanley Brown (*Clarinet Player*), Jack Gardner (*Booker*), Lynton Brent (*Musician*), Donald Kerr (*Orchestra Leader*), Edythe Elliott (*Nurse*), Robert Hill (*Counterman*), Larry Parks (*Man Flirt*), Adele Mara (*Check Girl*), Pat O'Malley (*Cop*), Dewey Robinson (*Truck Driver*), Roger Gray, Frank Richards, Richard Talmadge (*Fishermen*), Jerry Franke, Gertrude Messinger, John Estes, Mickey Rentschler, Frank Sully, Connie Evans, Ezelle Poule.

A dual role for Velez has her the star of a Broadway show, who quickly substitutes her twin sister when she becomes pregnant. The latter is just back from a sojourn on a beach with a sax player after the ship on which she was a stowaway was torpedoed, and she turns up as part of the orchestra for the show. A confusing yarn about mistaken identities, which the performances do little to remedy. Songs include: "Why Be Down-hearted?" "An Ounce of Bounce," "The Fiestango," "Let's Fall in Line," "I'm Undecided" (Walter G. Samuels, Saul Chaplin); and "Twiddlin My Thumbs" (Sammy Cahn, Chaplin).

p, Wallace MacDonald; d, Lew Landers; w, Joseph Hoffman (based on a story by Rex Taylor); ph, Philip Tanura; ed, James Sweeney; art d, Lionel Banks; md, M.W. Stoloff; art d, Lionel Banks.

Musical   **(PR:A MPAA:NR)**

REDHEAD FROM WYOMING, THE**½   (1953) 81m UNIV c

Maureen O'Hara (*Kate Maxwell*), Alex Nicol (*Stan Blaine*), Robert Strauss ("*Knuckles*" *Hogan*), William Bishop (*Jim Averell*), Alexander Scourby (*Reece Duncan*), Jack Kelly (*Sandy*), Jeanne Cooper (*Myra*), Stacy Harris (*Chet Jones*), Dennis Weaver (*Matt Jessup*), Claudette Thornton (*Girl*), Palmer Lee [Gregg Palmer](*Hal Jessup*), Ray Bennett (*Wade Burrows*), Joe Bailey (*Jack*), Russ Williams (*Ned*), David Alpert (*Wally Beggs*), Betty Allen (*French Heels*), Joe Bassett, Buddy Roosevelt, Larry Hudson (*Men*), Edmund Cobb (*Sprague*), Philo McCullough (*Aldrich*), Keith Kerrigan (*Girl in Katie's Place*), Bob Merrick (*Professor*), Sid Saylor (*Drunken Settler*), George Taylor (*Doctor*), Harold Goodwin (*Henchman*), Jack Hyde (*Chuck*).

A stunningly adorned O'Hara takes the rap for sinister Bishop, who has aims at political office, when he sets her up in a saloon as the easy register for the blame if his rustling activities attract too much notice. Then Bishop instigates a ranch war between ranchers and settlers, and O'Hara catches on and tries to put an end to the fighting by organizing an association of the settlers. Her efforts land her in jail on phony rustling and murder charges, but sheriff Nicol realizes what's up and sets everything straight, winning O'Hara in the process. A sorely miscast Nicol is out of place against the brilliance of O'Hara and Bishop.

p, Leonard Goldstein; d, Lee Sholem; w, Polly James, Herb Meadow (based on a story by James); ph, Winton C. Hoch (Technicolor); ed, Milton Carruth; md, Joseph Gershenson; art d, Bernard Herzbrun, Hilyard Brown; set d, Russell A. Gausman, Joseph Kish.

Western   **(PR:A MPAA:NR)**

RED-HEADED WOMAN***   (1932) 74m MGM bw

Jean Harlow (*Lil Andrews*), Chester Morris (*Bill Legendre, Jr.*), Lewis Stone (*William Legendre, Sr.*), Leila Hyams (*Irene Legendre*), Una Merkel (*Sally*), Henry Stephenson (*Gaersate*), May Robson (*Aunt Jane*), Charles Boyer (*Albert*), Harvey Clark (*Uncle Fred*).

This was Harlow's first production on her new MGM contract, in which she played a woman who climbs her way to success from poverty through the seduction of numerous men. Its original release met with a lot of opposition from the Hays office (an oddity for the usually over-moralizing Louis B. Mayer), because it allowed a sinning girl to make out all right. The British public never had a chance to see the sexy platinum blonde as a redhead, as the London censors never let it pass. This was the last of three films made by Boyer in America in attempting to work his way from the French stage into Hollywood, before he gave up the effort and returned to Europe. Three years later the Paris-style matinee idol tried it again, and this time he clicked and became one of the screen's "great lovers."

p, Paul Bern; d, Jack Conway; w, Anita Loos (based on the novel by Katherine Brush); ph, Harold G. Rosson; ed, Blanche Sewell.

Drama **(PR:A MPAA:NR)**

REDHEADS ON PARADE*½ (1935) 78m FOX bw

John Boles *(John Bruce)*, Dixie Lee *(Ginger Blair)*, Jack Haley *(Peter Mathews)*, Raymond Walburn *(Augustus Twill)*, Alan Dinehart *(George Magnus)*, Patsy O'Connor *(Patsy Blair)*, Herman Bing *(Lionel Kunkel)*, William Austin *(Trelawney Redfern)*, Wilbur Mack *(Johnson)*.

Another picture dealing with the problems of getting a show off the ground. This time Lee is a beautician and girl friend of producer Boles, who goes about getting the backing for the show when the original money man walks out. Her intentions are to give Boles another chance in his failing career, and her methods are sly as she nearly seduces the owner of a dye company, Bing, into lending his support. This puts Lee in the precarious position of having to please two men, without getting either jealous. Musical numbers include: "I Found a Dream," "Good Night Kiss," "I Like Myself for Liking You," "Redheads on Parade," "I've Got Your Future All Planned," "Tinsel Town," and "You Beautiful Thing" (Don Hartman, Jay Gorney), none of which are outstanding.

p, Jesse L. Lasky; d, Norman Z. McLeod; w, Don Hartman, Rian James (based on the story by Gertrude Purcell, Jay Gorney, Hartman); ph, John Seitz, Barney McGill; m, Jay Gorney; ch, Larry Ceballos.

Musical **(PR:A MPAA:NR)**

REDNECK zero (1975, Ital./Span.) 89m International Amusements c

Telly Savalas, Franco Nero, Mark Lester, Ely Galleani, Duilio Del Prete, Maria Michi.

A lunatic from Memphis and his mindless partner are on the run from the law. Along the way they accidentally kidnap a young boy and then decide to use him as a hostage. The vile and sadistic acts by the fugitives thankfully come to a violent end by the finale. Aside from a wholly unbelievable script, the cast is of international origin—Savalas is a Greek, Nero is Italian, Lester is British—and they're rednecks?

d, Silvio Narizzano; w, Win Wells.

Crime **Cas.** **(PR:O MPAA:NR)**

REDS*½** (1981) 200m PAR c

Warren Beatty *(John Reed)*, Diane Keaton *(Louise Bryant)*, Edward Herrmann *(Max Eastman)*, Jerzy Kosinski *(Grigory Zinoviev)*, Jack Nicholson *(Eugene O'Neill)*, Paul Sorvino *(Louis Fraina)*, Maureen Stapleton *(Emma Goldman)*, Nicolas Coster *(Paul Trullinger)*, M. Emmet Walsh *(Speaker at the Liberal Club)*, Ian Wolfe *(Mr. Partlow)*, Bessie Love *(Mrs. Partlow)*, MacIntyre Dixon *(Carl Walters)*, Pat Starr *(Helen Walters)*, Eleanor D. Wilson *(Mrs. Reed)*, Max Wright *(Floyd Dell)*, George Plimpton *(Horace Whigham)*, Harry Ditson *(Maurice Becker)*, Leigh Curran *(Ida Rauh)*, Kathryn Grody *(Crystal Eastman)*, Brenda Currin *(Marjorie Jones)*, Nancy Duiguid *(Jane Heap)*, Norman Chancer *(Barney)*, Dolph Sweet *(Big Bill Haywood)*, Ramon Bieri *(Police Chief)*, Jack O'Leary *(Pinkerton Guard)*, Gene Hackman *(Pete Van Wherry)*, Gerald Hiken *(Dr. Lorber)*, William Daniels *(Julius Gerber)*, Dave King *(Allan Benson)*, Joseph Buloff *(Joe Volski)*, Stefan Gryff *(Gomberg)*, Denis Pekarev *(Interpreter)*, Roger Sloman *(Vladimir Lenin)*, Stuart Richman *(Leon Trotsky)*, Oleg Kerensky *(Alexsandr/Witness Kerensky)*, Nikko Seppala *(Young Bolshevik)*, John J. Hooker *(Sen. Overman)*, *Shane Rimmer (MacAlpine)*, Jerry Hardin *(Harry)*, Jack Kehoe *(Eddie)*, Christopher Malcolm, Tony Sibbald *(CLP Members)*, R.G. Armstrong *(Agent)*, Josef Sommer *(Official)*, Jan Triska *(Radek)*, Ake Lindman *(Escort)*, Pertti Weckstrom *Finnish Doctor)*, Nina Macarova *(Russian Nurse)*, Jose DeFillippo *(Russian Doctor)*, Andres LeCasa *(Boy)*, Roger Baldwin, Henry Miller, Adela Rogers St. Johns, Dora Russell, Scott Nearing, Tess Davis, Heaton Vorse, Hamilton Fish, Issac Don Levine, Rebecca West, Will Durant, Will Weinstone, Emmanuel Herbert, Arne Swabeck, Adele Nathan, George Seldes, Kenneth Chamberlain, Blanch Hays Fagen, Galina Von Meck, Art Shields, Andrew Dasburg, Hugo Gellert, Dorothy Frooks, George Jessel, Jacob Bailin, John Ballato, Lucita Williams, Bernadine Szold-Fritz, Jessica Smith, Harry Carlisle, Arthur Mayer *(Witnesses)*.

REDS is a sprawling yet highly personal epic, representing a great artistic achievement for writer-producer-director-star Beatty. That he would be drawn to the life of John Reed, author of *Ten Days That Shook the World*, seems quite natural. Like Beatty, Reed led a colorful life populated with famous names, both political and artistic. His affair with noted socialite patron Mabel Dodge was one of the many reasons for Upton Sinclair to dub Reed "a playboy revolutionary." Yet unlike Reed, Beatty is not a champion of people's causes, but instead a talented, well-respected Hollywood playboy. In controlling the creative end of Reed's biography, Beatty achieved long-deserved prominance as a filmmaker of serious ambitions. He accomplishes a monumental task with great skill: creating a wide-scoped epic which never fails to realize that history's sweep is comprised of the small, personal moments of its participants. The film is framed in truth by "witnesses," the voices and faces of Reed's intimates and contemporaries, simply photographed against a plain black background. Their stories are woven throughout the film, giving events an historical and personal perspective. Henry Miller, one of the witnesses (all of whom remained unidentified as Beatty thought super-imposition of names would be too similar to documentary), says in the film's introduction "a guy who is interested in the condition of the world has no problems of his own, or refuses to face them." This characterizes Beatty's Reed well, a haunting statement that follows the man throughout the film. The story opens in Portland, Oregon, in 1915. Keaton, Beatty's then off-screen romance, is Louise Bryant, Reed's great love after politics, a woman of passion whose life would become forever intertwined with Reed's. After interviewing Beatty for a small magazine, she eventually leaves her prosaic dentist husband to follow her new love to New York. Through a series of montages, Keaton's introduction to the Bohemian community of Greenwich Village is explored. She meets Beatty's friends: Emma Goldman (Stapleton, in a fine and historically honest representation of that great woman), radical Max Eastman (Herrmann), and Nicholson in a tightly controlled, powerful portrayal of the playwright Eugene O'Neill. Keaton doesn't fit into this world of passion and politics, feeling ignored whenever she's with Beatty. To save their relationship, Beatty and Keaton join some friends in Provincetown to create a radical artist's cell, writing and producing experimental plays, poetry, and music. As fever for the war in Europe grows, Beatty goes to Chicago to cover the Democratic convention, much to Keaton's displeasure. She falls into an affair with Nicholson, which ends abruptly with Beatty's return. The two proponents of free love surprise themselves by getting married, then settle in a house in Massachusetts. When Beatty discovers a note left to his love from Nicholson, the two argue. Beatty accidentally and callously reveals he's been less than faithful himself. Tired of his consistent absences and excuses, Keaton takes off to Europe to become a war correspondent. Beatty is hospitalized when an old kidney problem flares up, resulting in removal of the organ. Though warned to slow down, Beatty cannot and heads to Europe himself. He meets up with Keaton, asking her to come to Russia with him. After rejecting his offer, Keaton later joins with Beatty on a train to Petrograd. Her only provisions are that there will be no shared byline or bed. In Russia, the pair chronicle events and interview principal characters involved in the Bolshevik revolution. (Among those interviewed is Kerensky, leader of the provisional government, who was played by Kerensky's real life grandson.) At one worker's meeting, Beatty becomes enraged when a speaker suggests American workers are not behind their Russian counterparts. Beatty crosses the line from viewer to active participant as he fires up the crowd (via interpreter) with a proclamation of American support for the Bolsheviks. This leads to the denouemont of the film's first half, an emotionally charged, finely constructed montage portraying the Bolshevik's eventual victory and rekindled romance of the lovers. The second half opens as the pair returns to New York. Beatty's notes are confiscated but he writes his account, *Ten Days That Shook The World*. (Lenin was impressed with Reed's book, proclaiming that this definitive account should be translated into all languages and spread around the world.) Inspired by Soviet comrades, Beatty becomes more involved with radical politics, forsaking both his writing and Keaton. She is embittered at being ignored once more. She sees "the cause" as merely mental exercises for its participants, knowing a worker's revolution is impossible in America. Beatty continues, despite his wife's objections, and splits his faction of the American Socialist Party from the main branch. He is elected to go to the Soviet Union for official acknowledgement and blessings. This must be done through secret channels, as travel to the Communist state is now restricted. Keaton, at her wit's end with her husband, tells Beatty she may not be waiting for him when he returns. Beatty leaves, promising to be home by Christmas. Keaton visits her former lover, Nicholson, who verbally tears apart her relationship with Beatty. Unknown to Keaton, she is followed home by government agents who want to arrest Beatty for sedition. Meanwhile, Beatty has troubles of his own in a rapidly changing Moscow. No longer is the energy of hope and idealism in the air. It has been replaced by a cold bureaucracy with Kosinski (the noted Polish writer, impressive in his acting debut) as Zinoviev, a party leader and Beatty's nemesis. He will not acknowledge Beatty's party nor allow him to leave the country. Beatty tries to escape but is arrested at the Finnish border. He is denied food, water, and outside communication, never learning that a telegram has arrived from Keaton. Soon he develops typhus, but is released when Lenin trades three Finnish professors for his freedom. Word of the arrest reaches Keaton, and with Nicholson's help she steals away to Finland in hopes of releasing Beatty. After a perilous journey, Keaton arrives at the jail, only to find her love gone and no word of his whereabouts left behind (in reality Reed had sent for Bryant from Russia, meeting her on arrival, though the voyage did go through underground channels). In Moscow Beatty meets with Stapleton, who had been deported from America for her radical activities. However, she has grown disillusioned with the Soviet system. (Goldman eventually left the USSR for Canada, where she spent the remainder of her life. Her book on the Soviet government *My Disillusionment With Red Russia* remains a classic and prophetic document of the Communist rule). Beatty remains idealistic in spite of her warnings, returning to Kosinski to volunteer for the propaganda bureau. He realizes that this is a moment in history that will not be repeated, and he must be a part of it. Beatty is sent to a conference in Baku to help convince Arab populations of the Soviet government's grandeur. Keaton arrives in Moscow, where she runs into Stapleton. At the conference, Beatty is stunned by the anti-American sentiments expressed, and becomes enraged when he learns some words had been changed in the translation of his speech. As he argues with Kosinski on the train ride home, the White Army, determined to restore the old Russian government, attacks. The well-equiped train lets loose a mini-army of it's own. Beatty, disillusioned, ill, and spiritually defeated, runs after a cannon hoping to be taken to the battle scene. He cannot reach the cart, and for once is left behind from the action. The train finally returns to Moscow where Keaton, not knowing whether Beatty is alive or dead, anxiously awaits its arrival. The two lovers grasp one another in an overwhelming emotional embrace. "Don't leave me," whispers the sick, broken man. (Another moment of fiction for drama's sake. In reality Bryant and Reed had been in contact, arranging to meet on his return from the conference.) Beatty is taken to a Soviet hospital, where he sinks into delirium and passes away. "Grand things are worth dying for. He himself said that," says one witness over the closing credits. Beatty's opus is a work of great artistic magnitude, yet falters on occasion to a point of unashamed cuteness. The film's strengths and weaknesses ironically walk hand in hand. Beatty's ability to maintain the small moments against the enormous swirl of history is excellent. Repeated motifs and phrases within the film define character and relationships with subtlety. "There's a taxi waiting," an oft-repeated sentence by Keaton to Beatty, shows first her excitement at being with the man, before gradually becoming a statement of anger and resentment at his constant absences. Yet it is also within moments like this where REDS falters. The relationship between the two lovers never jells as strongly as needed. Keaton in particular is too much like her autobiographical character in ANNIE HALL, a charming yet nervous woman who is more of a companion to Beatty rather than the important influence Bryant was to Reed. Though introduced as a serious, vibrant woman, Keaton is quickly reduced to a frivolous love interest, making one wonder how she accomplishes all her work before the film ends. Beatty is also mixed in his dealing with history. The witnesses are a fine frame for the story, helping to project historical perspective. Reed's and Bryant's correspondence and writings are also blended well into the screenplay, but Beatty occasionally gets caught up with his characters' politics to the point of confusion. Anyone unfamiliar with the history of the Bolshevik revolution or radical American politics undoubtedly will find this a confusing work at times. REDS has the unusual distinction of being an anticapitalist film produced by the decidingly capitalist system of Hollywood. Beatty spent four years on the project, amassing everything he could about Reed. After cowriting the script with British playwright Griffiths, he hired Elaine May, in an uncredited role, to punch up the finished product with jokes. Her work unfortunately sticks out, inserting cute lines when they're far from necessary. May had been Beatty's cowriter on his previous film, the light romantic comedy HEAVEN CAN WAIT. Also contributing an uncredited polishing to the final script was Robert Towne, Beatty's cowriter on SHAMPOO. Paramount sunk an initial $34 million into the production, but came close to cancelling REDS several times as costs ballooned to an estimated $45 million. One unusual production cost surely would have made Reed himself a proud man. Explaining to extras for the Baku conference sequences how Reed was a champion for the worker, fighting for better salaries and working conditions, the director found himself undermined by his hero. Taking Reed's principles to heart, the extras went on strike for higher wages—which they got! Though a critical success, which saw Oscars for Beatty's direction, Stapleton's performance, and Storaro's beautiful cinematography, REDS was not a box office success. Perhaps it was the times, which discouraged patrons. A year into Reagan's first term as president, America was being swept by a conservative tide, making a film about left wing radicals an unpopular subject for many filmgoers. REDS inspired pickets by some conservative groups who felt it was little more than Communist propaganda. Perhaps these protestors should have ventured into the theaters. Beatty's position is clearly against the Communist government, certainly the type of message that would appeal to anyone who finds the USSR to be an evil empire. In retrospect, REDS is an important American film, which gives audiences a portrait of a genuine hero: a man who was willing to live—and ultimately die—for his principles.

p&d, Warren Beatty; w, Beatty, Trevor Griffiths; ph, Vittorio Storaro (Technicolor); m, Stephen Sondheim, Dave Grusin; ed, Dede Allen, Craig McKay; prod d, Richard Sylbert; art d, Simon Holland; cos, Shirley Russell.

Historical Drama/Biography Cas. (PR:C-O MPAA:PG)

REDUCING** (1931) 77m MGM bw

Marie Dressler *(Marie Truffle)*, Polly Moran *(Polly Rochay)*, Anita Page *(Vivian Truffle)*, Buster Collier, Jr. *(Johnnie Beasley)*, Lucien Littlefield *(Elmer Truffle)*, Sally Eilers *(Joyce Rochay)*, William Bakewell *(Tommy Haverly)*, Billy Naylor *(Jerry Truffle)*, Jay Ward *(Marty Truffle)*.

The teaming of Moran and Dressler makes for a non-ending supply of some creative slapstick routines. This time the setting is a ritzy beauty parlor run by Moran, who calls her sister, Dressler, away from her meager existence as the wife of a letter carrier. Problems erupt when Collier, the man Moran's daughter, Page, intended to marry, winds up going for Dressler's offspring, Eilers. But everything turns out for the better when it is discovered that Collier's designs on both girls are not very honorable. It takes a shotgun-toting Dressler, speaking on behalf of her niece, to sort out the troubles and put them right.

d, Charles F. Reisner; w, Willard Mack, Beatrice Banyard, Robert E. Hopkins, Zelda Sears (based on a story by Mack, Banyard); ph, Leonard Smith; ed, William Levanway.

Comedy (PR:A MPAA:NR)

REDWOOD FOREST TRAIL** (1950) 67m REP bw

Rex Allen *(Himself)*, Jeff Donnell *(Julie Westcott)*, Carl "Alfalfa" Switzer *("Alfalfa" Donahue)*, Jane Darwell *(Hattie Hickory)*, Marten Lamont *(Craig Denvers)*, Pierre Watkin *(Arthur Cameron)*, Jimmy Ogg *(Two Bits)*, Dick Jones *(Mighty Mite)*, John Cason *(Curley)*, Jimmy Frasher *(Wyomin')*, Bob Larson *(Chips)*, Robert W. Wood *(Luna Mason)*, Jack Larson *(Dusty)*, Ted Fries *(Hawk)*, Joseph Granby *(Bart Bryant)*, Robert E. Burns *(Wescott)*, Koko the Horse.

A camp for underprivileged city boys is the object of some good deeds by Allen and his sidekick, Switzer (THE LITTLE RASCALS). The boys of the camp are blamed for the death of the landowner whose daughter then refuses to renew the camp's mortgage. Allen sets her straight by proving the men of the local sawmill are actually the guilty party, because of their greedy desires to get at the valuable timber on the property. During this process Smokey the Bear makes a few points against careless forest fires and the need to preserve the woods.

p, Franklin Adreon; d, Philip Ford; w, Bradford Ropes; ph, John MacBurnie; m Stanley Wilson; ed, Harold Minter; art d, Frank Arrigo; m/l, "Old Smokey," "Sourwood Mountain," "America the Beautiful" (sung by Rex Allen).

Western (PR:A MPAA:NR)

REEFER MADNESS* (1936) 67m G&H/Motion Picture Ventures-New Line bw (AKA: TELL YOUR CHILDREN; THE BURNING QUESTION; DOPE ADDICT; DOPED YOUTH; LOVE MADNESS)

Dorothy Short *(Mary)*, Kenneth Craig *(Bill)*, Lillian Miles *(Blanche)*, Dave O'Brien *(Ralph)*, Thelma White *(Mae)*, Carleton Young *(Jimmy)*, Pat Royale *(Agnes)*, Josef Forte *(Dr. Carroll)*, Warren McCollum.

One of the most notorious exploitation films of the 1930s, largely because youth audiences in the 1960s and 1970s made a cult film out of it, giggling at the lurid picture of marijuana and its effects. The film opens with a high school principal, Forte, lecturing parents on the evils of the weed. He relates the story of two youngsters from his own school, Craig and Short, who become entangled with dope dealers, with tragic results. White and her male cohort have an apartment where high school students go to get high. One day Young, Short's brother, goes there with a friend, O'Brien. After one puff he is hopelessly addicted and he soon brings his friend Craig, who equally quickly becomes a reefer-head. Young drives the sinister supplier over to his connection to buy some more pot, but the stoned boy runs over a pedestrian on the return trip. Concerned about her brother's newly lackadaisical behavior, Short trails him to the apartment. He isn't there, but O'Brien is. He gives the innocent girl a joint, telling her it is a regular cigarette, and when she's stoned he tries to rape her. Craig stumbles out of a bedroom where he's just spent the night with O'Brien's girl friend, Miles. In his drugged-out state, he hallucinates that Short is willingly succumbing to O'Brien's advances. A fight ensues in which a gun goes off, killing Short. Craig proceeds to lapse into unconsciousness and when he wakes, White and the others convince the poor boy that he killed Short. O'Brien is nearly killed to keep him quiet, but his supplier ends up dead himself. The police break in and O'Brien, found to be hopelessly addicted to marijuana, is committed to a home for the criminally insane "for the rest of his natural life." White goes off to jail; Miles is so overwhelmed by her guilt that she jumps out the high window of the courthouse. The truth about the shooting comes out and Craig is let off with a reprimand. Crude technique, bad acting, and a ridiculous script are generally considered liabilities for a film, but here they're the very reason for its popularity. Some of the dialog is hilarious, like O'Brien (usually a star of B westerns, whose presence here is very curious) demanding that Miles play the piano "Faster, faster!" as he becomes more and more agitated. When the principal, Forte, is called to testify at Craig's trial about the boy's sanity or lack thereof, he gives damning evidence: "In the middle of a perfectly serious discussion of 'Romeo and Juliet' he suddenly broke into an hysterical fit of laughter." All the performers either overact laughably or underact to the point of just standing in place speaking lines in a monotone. Whether the film ever stopped anyone from smoking marijuana is doubtful, but it is certainly a greater success than its producers ever dreamed.

p, George A. Hirliman; d, Louis Gasnier; w, Arthur Hoerl, Paul Franklin (based on an original story by Lawrence Meade); ph, Jack Greenhalgh; ed, Carl Pierson; md, Abe Meyer.

Crime Cas. (PR:C-O MPAA:NR)

REFLECTION OF FEAR, A** (1973) 89m COL c (AKA: LABYRINTH)

Robert Shaw *(Michael)*, Sally Kellerman *(Anne)*, Mary Ure *(Katherine)*, Sondra Locke *(Marguerite)*, Signe Hasso *(Julia)*, Mitchell Ryan *(Inspector McKenna)*, Gordon DeVol *(Hector)*, Gordon Anderson *(Voice of Aaron)*, Victoria Risk *(Peggy)*, Leonard John Crofoot *(Aaron)*, Michael St. Clair *(Kevin)*, Liam Dunn *(Coroner)*, Michelle Marvin *(Nurse)*, Michele Montau *(Mme. Caraquet)*.

Psycho-drama much in the vein of PSYCHO stars Locke as a young girl secluded from the world in the gloomy mansion of her grandmother, Hasso, and mother, Ure. She creates a world all her own, making her prime companion her doll, Aaron, who she believes can kill people. When her long-absent father, Shaw, shows up with Kellerman, Locke loses the little control she maintains over herself and goes on a killing rampage, doing away with everyone but Shaw and Kellerman. An atmosphere of sexual confusion is maintained throughout which reaches a climax with the revelation that Locke was originally a male as a baby. Locke is very effective in her psychotic role, giving the story a needed eerie quality that is lacking in other areas.

p, Howard B. Jaffe; d, William A. Fraker; w, Edward Hume, Lewis John Carlino (based on the novel *Go to Thy Deathbed* by Stanton Forbes); ph, Laszlo Kovacs; m, Fred Myrow; ed, Richard Brockway; md, Myrow; art d, Joel Schiller; set d, Phillip Abramson; cos, Patti Norris; makeup, Emile Lavigne.

Horror (PR:C MPAA:PG)

REFLECTIONS IN A GOLDEN EYE* (1967) 109m WB c

Elizabeth Taylor *(Leonora Penderton)*, Marlon Brando *(Maj. Weldon Penderton)*, Brian Keith *(Lt. Col. Morris Langdon)*, Julie Harris *(Alison Langdon)*, Zorro David *(Anacleto)*, Gordon Mitchell *(Stables Sergeant)*, Irvin Dugan *(Capt. Weincheck)*, Fay Sparks *(Susie)*, Robert Forster *(Pvt. Williams)*, Douglas Stark *(Dr. Burgess)*, Al Mulock *(Old Soldier)*, Ted Beniades *(Sergeant)*, John Callaghan *(Soldier)*.

A weird picture based on a slim novel (or novella) by Carson McCullers, this movie fails to engender any sympathy or interest due to several miscalculations. Brando plays his Southern soldier role as though he has a mouthful of corn pone, Taylor tries to recreate the screaming shrillness of "Martha" in WHO'S AFRAID OF VIRGINIA WOOLF? and the picture is shot in muted color so it almost seems sepia or black and white, something Huston insisted upon. Later prints were made in full color but it didn't make much difference as this story had little to recommend it. Although ostensibly about the South, Taylor insisted it be shot in Rome, and so it was, at Dino Di Laurentiis' studios. Lest you think that's odd, remember that Taylor demanded that THE ONLY GAME IN TOWN, a Las Vegas story, be made in Paris. She'd intended to make it with Montgomery Clift as her costar but he died a couple of months before the picture was to begin. Burton and Lee Marvin were approached to play the repressed homosexual and both refused so she got Brando and their predicted box office dynamite wound up fizzling. Brando is a major in the Army married to Taylor. They are at a remote base somewhere in the South in 1948 and, while she is a lustful woman bordering on nymphomania, he pays no sexual attention to her as he is impotent and a latent homosexual who masks his effeminate tendencies with a stern martinet attitude toward his underlings. Despite it being such a confined area, Taylor makes no bones about the affair she is carrying on with neighbor Keith, a bird colonel, who is married to Harris, a woman on the edge of total psychosis When Harris gave birth to a deformed child, her response was to snip off her nipples with a heavy pair of scissors. She has stopped trying to win her husband away and spends most of her time in the companionship of her houseboy, David, an apparently gay young man. (David was a New York City hairdresser making his film debut.) Forster is a young private who has been assigned to tend Taylor's favorite horse. He is also somewhat unique and given to naked bareback riding, peeking into windows, and playing with female underwear. (Forster had scored in the Broadway show "Mrs. Daily Has A Lover" and was making his first appearance in movies.) Forster enjoys sneaking around the Brando-Taylor home in the early morning hours, gazing at Taylor as she sleeps and playing with her underthings. Brando spies Forster riding nude and can't hide his sexual interest, following him on the sly and watching him sunbathe with no clothes on. Harris sees Forster slip into the next door home one night, watches him looking at Taylor asleep and toying with her "Teddies," then goes slightly mad and tells Keith she wants a divorce. She intends to leave the post with the only man she has any relationship with, David. Keith has her slapped into a mental hospital where she dies of a heart attack. Forster comes back to the Brando-Taylor home in a rain storm and Brando spots him and happily believes that Forster has come to have a homosexual experience. When Forster bypasses Brando's room and walks into Taylor's, Brando walks into the bedchamber and shoots Forster dead. Taylor wakes up and begins screaming, the camera whips from Taylor to Brando to Forster until one's head spins, and the picture ends. Definitely not a plot for a musical, this movie is second-rate Tennessee Williams as adapted by the scripters. Even the score is heavy-handed as it tips off every movement by the actors. When John Huston is good, he is great. When he isn't good, he can make some of the most boring and pretentious movies ever, such as this, THE BARBARIAN AND THE GEISHA, and A WALK WITH LOVE AND DEATH. Taylor is sometimes convincing as the pneumatic wife, a slightly older version of her "Maggie the Cat" in CAT ON A HOT TIN ROOF. Keith is better than the lines he gets and Harris is always believable. Forster doesn't have much to do and is the most enigmatic member of an all-enigma award winner. The South will never rise again as long as people like this live there.

p, Ray Stark; d, John Huston; w, Chapman Mortimer, Gladys Hill (based on the novel by Carson McCullers); ph, Aldo Tonti (Panavision, Technicolor); m, Toshiro Mayuzumi; ed, Russell Lloyd; prod d, Stephen Grimes; md, Marcus Dods; art d, Bruno Avesani; set d, William Kiernan, Joe Chevalier; cos, Dorothy Jeakins; spec eff, Augie Lohman; makeup, Frank Larue, Phil Rhodes, Amato Garbini; Horsemaster, Friedrich von Ledebur.

Drama Cas. (PR:O MPAA:NR)

REFORM GIRL*½ (1933) 70m Tower bw

Noel Johnson *(Lydia Johnson)*, Skeets Gallagher *(Joe Burke)*, Hale Hamilton *(Santor Putnam)*, Robert Ellis *(Kellar)*, Dorothy Peterson *(Mrs. Putnam)*, Stanley Smith *(David Carter)*, Ben Hendricks, Jr. *(Rafferty)*, De Witt Jennings *(Capt. Balfour)*.

Overly contrived dramatics finds Johnson getting out of jail to continue in the manner she did before she went in; namely, helping to frame an honest politician. Her reformation comes when she falls for the campaign manager of the person she's trying to frame, but this man gets killed . Farfetched twist at the end has the politician turning out to be Johnson's father.

d, Sam Neufeld; w, George Wallace Sayre; ph, Harry Forbes, ed, Lou Sackin.

Crime/Drama (PR:A MPAA:NR)

REFORM SCHOOL** (1939) 58m Million Dollar Production bw

Louise Beavers *(Mother Barton)*, Reginald Fenderson *(Freddie Gordon)*, Monte Hawley *(Jackson)*, Freddie Jackson *(Eddie)*, Eugene Jackson *(Pete)*, Eddie Lynn *(Joe)*, De Forrest Covan *(Bill)*, Bob Simmons *(Johnny)*, Maceo Sheffield *(Mr. Stone)*, Edward Thompson, Vernon McCalla *(Reform School Officials)*, Alfred Grant *(Jones the Guard)*, Milton Hall *(Jackie Rogers)*, Clifford Holland *(Slim)*, Edward Patrick *(Mr. Gordon)*, Charles Andrews *(Gas Station Attendant)*, Harold Garrison *(Guard)*, Edward Tony *(Tony)*.

An all-black cast adorns this routine yarn about a reform school that switches from a strict form of enforcing its rules to the honor system when Beavers takes over. Although her intentions are laughed at, she is proved right when the kids rally to catch a thief. Fenderson and other kids pave the way for the comedy routines.

p, Harry M. Popkin; d, Leo C. Popkin; w, Zelda Young, Hazel Jamieson, Joe O'Donnell (based on the story by Jamieson, O'Donnell); ph, William Hyers; ed, Bart M. Rauw.

Drama (PR:A MPAA:NR)

REFORM SCHOOL GIRL½** (1957) 71m Carmel/AIP bw

Gloria Castillo *(Donna Price)*, Ross Ford *(David Lindsay)*, Edward Byrnes *(Vince)*, Ralph Reed *(Jackie)*, Jan England *(Ruth)*, Yvette Vickers *(Roxy)*, Helen Wallace *(Mrs. Trimble)*, Donna Jo Gribble *(Cathy)*, Luana Anders *(Josie)*, Diana Darrin *(Mona)*, Nesdon Booth *(Deetz)*, Wayne Taylor *(Gary)*, Sharon Lee *(Blonde)*, Jack Kruschen *(Mr. Horvath)*, Linda Rivera *(Elena)*, Elaine Sinclair *(Midge)*, Dorothy Crehan *(Matron)*, Claire Carleton *(Mrs. Horvath)*, Lillian Powell *(Mrs. Patton)*, Sally Kellerman *(A Girl)*.

Joy-riding Castillo is the victim of the madcap antics of Byrnes, when he steals a car and then mows down a pedestrian. Castillo is caught and put into a reformatory for refusing to squeal. Byrnes' original girl friend, who he is trying to get rid of, winds up in the same school as Castillo after being framed by Byrnes, making for some lively violence between the two girls before Castillo realizes that Byrnes is the one who should really be behind bars. Fine display of young talent, with a bit part by a young Sally Kellerman, then 19 years old, in her first screen appearance.

p, Robert J. Gurney, Jr., Samuel Z. Arkoff; d&w, Edward Bernds; ph, Floyd Crosby; m, Ronald Stein; ed, Richard C. Meyer; art d, Don Ament.

Drama (PR:A MPAA:NR)

REFORMATORY*½ (1938) 59m COL bw

Jack Holt *(Robert Dean)*, Bobby Jordan *(Pinkey Leonard)*, Charlotte Wynters *(Adele Webster)*, Grant Mitchell *(Arnold Frayne)*, Tommy Bupp *(Fibber Regan)*, Frankie Darro *(Louie Miller)*, Ward Bond *(Mac Grady)*, Sheila Bromley *(Mrs. Regan)*, Paul Everton *(Gov. Spaulding)*, Lloyd Ingraham *(Dr. Blakely)*, Joe Caits *(Jim Leonard)*.

Holt is given the job of warden at a boy's reformatory as long as he can keep the place out of the papers. He tries to treat the inmates fairly, which is hard for one of the guards to do. But the guard is quickly fired when Holt catches him beating a boy, with Holt landing a few punches of his own. Everything shapes up nicely when toughie Jordan (of DEAD END KIDS fame) takes to the new system in an exemplary manner. Last bit of trouble occurs when Darro stages an escape, which brings Holt before the governor. But it turns out all right in a predictable fashion, like the rest of the film.

p, Larry Darmour; d, Lewis D. Collins; w, Gordon Rigby; ph, James S. Brown, Jr., ed, Dwight Caldwell.

Crime/Drama (PR:A MPAA:NR)

REFORMER AND THE REDHEAD, THE*** (1950) 90m MGM bw

June Allyson *(Kathleen Maguire)*, Dick Powell *(Andrew Rockton Hale)*, David Wayne *(Arthur Colner Maxwell)*, Cecil Kellaway *(Dr. Kevin G. Maguire)*, Ray Collins *(Commodore John Baldwin Parker)*, Robert Keith *(Tim Harveigh)*, Marvin Kaplan *(Leon)*, Kathleen Freeman *(Lily Rayton Parker)*, Wally Maher *(Jerry Nolard Boyle)*, Alex Gerry *(James I. Michell)*, Charles Evans *(Mr. Eberle)*, Paul Maxey *(Thompson)*, Herman the Lion.

Zesty piece of entertainment has Powell playing an ambitious lawyer seeking to become mayor and using as a political ploy the shady dealings of the present mayor. When Allyson, daughter of the local zookeeper, supports him because her father has been kicked out of his job for political reasons, Powell is faced with a problem regarding ethics. A romance develops in which forthright and spunky Allyson takes an old-fashioned view of courtship, but a setback occurs when she discovers Powell's conniving to get himself elected. The two get back together, with Powell making friends with an affectionate lion, Herman, at the zoo. This was the first film to feature the husband and wife team of Powell and Allyson, who rose to the occasion with splendid performances. The rest of the cast handle their assignments appropriately, with credit going to the scripters for snappy dialog and wit. THE REFORMER AND THE REDHEAD was the first of two films Powell and Allyson made together while Powell was at MGM (the other was RIGHT CROSS, 1950), in his continuing attempts that lasted through the 1940s to escape the early singing assignments, especially with Ruby Keeler, which he felt limited him professionally. But by 1952 and THE BAD AND THE BEAUTIFUL, he was washed up in the movies, later finding great success as a producer and director in TV.

p,d&w, Norman Panama, Melvin Frank (based on the story by Robert Carson); ph, Ray June; m, David Raksin; ed, George White; art d, Cedric Gibbons, William Ferrari.

Comedy (PR:A MPAA:NR)

REFUGE* (1981) 90m Separate Dreams c

Anne Twomey, James Congdon, Alexandra O'Karma, Will Jeffries.

The gathering of four people—a Boston painter and his social worker wife, an aspiring woman novelist, and the ex-headmaster of a private school—on a small deserted island off the coast of Maine makes for an extremely bad film. Overly talky script is totally unrealistic, with the characters bearing no resemblance to real people.

p, Charlotte McKim, Huck Fairman; d, Fairman; w, Fairman, Luther Sperberg; ph, Robert M. Baldwin; m, Rich Look.

Drama (PR:O MPAA:NR)

REFUGEE, THE (SEE: THREE FACES WEST, 1940)

REGAL CAVALCADE½** (1935, Brit.) 100m BIP/Alliance bw (GB: ROYAL CAVALCADE)

Marie Lohr *(Mother)*, Hermione Baddeley *(Barmaid)*, Robert Hale, J.H. Roberts *(Drinkers)*, Charles Paton *(Taxi Driver)*, C.V. France *(Father)*, John Singer *(Boy)*, Esme Percy *(Lloyd George)*, Frederick Lloyd *(Neighbor)*, C. Denier Warren *(Smith)*, Pearl Argyle *(Anna Pavlova)*, Frank Vosper *(Capt. Robert Falcon Scott)*, Austin Trevor *(Capt. Oates)*, John Stuart *(Explorer)*, Jane Baxter *(Girl)*, John Mills *(Boy)*, Jimmy Hanley *(Newsboy)*, Wally Bosco *(MP)*, Alice Lloyd *(Marie Lloyd)*, Amy Veness *(Suffragette)*, Antoinette Cellier *(Marjorie Wilkinson)*, Jimmy Godden *(Harry)*, Chili Bouchier, Renee Macready *(Landgirls)*, Annie Esmond *(Lady)*, Bertha Belmore *(Schoolmistress)*, C.M. Hallard *(Winston Churchill)*, H. Saxon-Snell *(Sir Edward Grey)*, Fred Groves *(Soldier)*, George Graves *(Old Bill)*, Ronald Shiner *(Soldier)*, Rene Ray, Iris Ashley, Judy Kelly, Constance Shotter, Hilda Mundy (Girls), Patric Knowles *(Officer)*, Billy Caryll *(Agent)*, Gus McNaughton *(Workman)*, W.H. Berry *(Bob)*, Clifford Mollison *(Customer)*, Gene Gerrard *(Passenger)*, Vera Pearce, Ellen Pollock *(Wives)*, Diana Napier *(Actress)*, Syd Walker *(Doorman)*, Elaine Benson *(Child)*, Leonora Corbett *(Nurse)*, Olga Lindo *(Tourist)*, Mary Glynne *(Waitress)*, Sam Livesey, Robert Nainby *(Drinkers)*, Seymour Hicks,

Owen Nares (Gentlemen), Ellaline Terriss (Wife), Aileen Marson (Lady), Gyles Isham, Arthur Margetson (Officers), Basil Gill (Bishop), Jerry Verno (Taxpayer), Craighall Sherry (Chancellor), Ivan Samson (Man), Carol Goodner, James Carew (Tourists), Ben Welden (Businessman), Matheson Lang (Henry V), Athene Seyler (Queen Elizabeth), Reginald Gardiner (Conductor), Reginald Purdell (Listener), Roy Russell, Edward Chapman, D.A. Clarke-Smith (Narrators), Florrie Forde, George Robey, Arthur Prince, Harry Tate, Bert Feldman, Norman Long, Stanton Jefferies, Stuart Hibberd, Leonard Henry, Debroy Somers and His Band, Sydney Baines and His Band, Band of HM Scots Guards, Roy Russell, Edward Chapman, D.A. Clarke-Smith (Narrators), Lady Astor, Jack Judge, Arthur Wontner, Henry Mollison, Iris Hoey, Margaret Bannerman.

A penny passed from hand to hand is witness to the reign of King George V from 1910 to 1935. It buys a program at his coronation, is in the pocket of a soldier killed in Flanders Field, serves as fare on a bus during the general strike of 1926, and more. Also seen are the deaths of captains Scott, Oates, and the rest of the British Antarctic team in 1912. Some scenes were lifted from ATLANTIC, DRAKE OF ENGLAND, and various newsreels. Overblown and rather self-congratulatory, the film is still well-made entertainment featuring almost every British actor and actress in its monstrous cast.

p, Walter C. Mycroft, Frank Mills, Roy Goddard, Jack Martin, David Horne, John Sloan; d, Thomas Bentley, Herbert Brenon, Norman Lee, Walter Summers, Will Kellino, Marcel Varnel; w, Marjorie Deans (based on a story by Val Gielgud, Holt Marvell, Eric Maschwitz); ph, Jack Cox, H. Wheddon, Bryan Langley, Leslie Rowson, Philip Grindrod.

Historical (PR:A MPAA:NR)

REGISTERED NURSE* (1934) 62m FN-WB bw

Bebe Daniels (Sylvia Benton), Lyle Talbot (Dr. Connolly), John Halliday (Dr. Hedwig), Irene Franklin (Sadie), Sidney Toler (Sylvestrie), Gordon Westcott (Jim), Minna Gombell (Schloss), Beulah Bondi (McKenna), Vince Barnett (Jerry), Phillip Reed, Mayo Methot, Renee Whitney, Virginia Sale, Ronnie Cosbey, Ed Gargan, Gordon Elliott, George Humbert.

An early version of GENERAL HOSPITAL has Daniels portraying a nurse involved in a love triangle when her husband goes insane and must be operated on. She finds herself pursued by two surgeons, Talbot, who is just out for kicks, and Halliday, a sincere admirer. Daniels is most taken by Talbot, but when her husband commits suicide by jumping out of a window at the suggestion of another wacky patient, she turns to Halliday. Ridiculous script doesn't give the players much of a chance.

p, Sam Bischoff; d, Robert Florey; w, Lillie Hayward, Peter Milne (based on the play by Florence Johns, Wilton Lackaye, Jr.); ph, Sid Hickox; ed, Jack Killifer; art d, Robert Haas; cos, Orry-Kelly.

Drama (PR:A MPAA:NR)

REG'LAR FELLERS*½ (1941) 60m Arthur Dreifuss/PRC bw

Sarah Padden (Hetty Carter), Roscoe Ates (Emory McQuade), Maren Mayo (Caroline Carter), Netta Packer (Martha), Jack C. Smith (Officer Flynn), Margueritte de la Motte (Mrs. Dugan), Pat O'Malley (Mr. Dugan, Sr.), Anna Ruth Hughes (Molly Dugan), Don Stowell (Ferrel), Lew Lauria (Lubec), Daisy Ford (Mrs. Duffy), Herbert Vigran (Radio Announcer), Billy Lee (Pinhead), Carl "Alfalfa" Switzer (Bump Hudson), Buddy Boles (Jimmie Dugan), Janey Dempsey (Aggie Reilly), Jerry Wilson (Skeeter), Malcolm Hutton (Pudd'n-head), Danna Callahan (Jane Watson), Diana Ware (Hazel Barry), Leonard Grassi (Warren Hamilton), Sharon Lynne (Baby Carter), Billy Lee's Band with Meglin Glee Club.

This sloppily produced farce that carries a simple idea for far too long, has Padden developing a strong hatred for children when her son marries despite Padden's discouragement. She becomes a mean old girl who kicks her grandchildren around and is a general fright to the entire community. But the son has been sent to prison via a frameup by a couple of thugs. When the thugs turn up in town to stage a robbery, Padden's grandchildren and friends gather their resources together and thwart the criminals. Padden begins to grow fond of the kids for the first time and decides to become part of the community again.

p, Joe Eudemiller; d, Arthur Dreifuss; w, Arthur Hoerl, William C. Kent, Dreifuss (based on the story by Hoerl, after the cartoon strip by Gene Byrnes); ph, Mack Stengler; m, Ross DiMaggio; ed, Carl Pierson; art d, Frank Dexter; m/l, Ethel Meglin, Dean Marmon.

Comedy **Cas.** (PR:A MPAA:NR)

REHEARSAL FOR A CRIME (SEE: CRIMINAL LIFE OF ARCHIBALDO DE LA CRUZ, THE, 1962, Mex.)

REIGN OF TERROR (SEE: BLACK BOOK, THE, 1949, Brit.)

REINCARNATE, THE*½ (1971, Can.) 122m Meridian/International Film Distributor c

Jack Creley (Everet Julian), Jay Reynolds (David Payne), Trudy Young (Ruthie), Terry Tweed (Ann), Gene Tyburn (Stedley), Rex Hagon (Gene), Hugh Webster (Berryman), Colin Fox (Ormsby), Ron Hartmann (Danton), Alan Clowes (Llewelyn).

An interesting theme has a dying lawyer, Creley, as a member of an ancient cult. In order to ensure the continued existence of his eons-old spirit and mind he must go through a ritual that involves the sacrifice of a virgin. First he must find someone willing to accept his spirit, which he does in struggling sculptor Reynolds. Unfortunately, most of the movie centers around Creley trying to talk Reynolds into being a part of the ritual, making the long-awaited finale overly predictable. The sacrificed maiden returns as the child of the sculptor. A few good touches, such as the score by Kymlicka, and a black cat that keeps popping up—making for an eerie effect—are displayed; otherwise, the story just plods along.

p, Seelig Lester; d, Don Haldane; w, Lester; ph, Norman Allin; m, Milan Kymlicka; art d, Harry Maxfield; cos, Web Catherfield; spec eff, Wally Gentleman.

Horror (PR:C MPAA:GP)

REINCARNATION OF PETER PROUD, THE**½ (1975) 104m BCP/AIP c

Michael Sarrazin (Peter Proud), Jennifer O'Neill (Ann Curtis), Margot Kidder (Marcia Curtis), Cornelia Sharpe (Nora Hayes), Paul Hecht (Dr. Samuel Goodman), Tony Stephano (Jeff Curtis), Normann Burton (Dr. Frederick Spear), Anne Ives (Ellen Curtis), Debralee Scott (Suzy).

This picture is, in some ways, similar to another reincarnation film made three years before, THE POSSESSION OF JOEL DELANEY. Max Ehrlich's best-seller was adapted by the author for the screen and manages to spend more time on character development than most of these occult stories, a plus. Sarrazin is a bright young professor who realizes that he harbors a ghost inside him when his dreams take a strange, bizarre turn. In order to track down the source of these nightmares, he goes to a small New England town where he learns that Kidder (who is wonderful in the role and plays it in two time frames, then and now) murdered her cheating husband, Stephano, whose spirit now haunts Sarrazin. Kidder is frustrated, drunk, filled with remorse, and both loves and hates the memory of the man she killed. (In one explicit sequence, she recalls their passion as she plays with herself in the bathtub.) When she meets Sarrazin, she realizes that he is the reincarnation of Stephano but another complication arises as Kidder's daughter, O'Neill, falls in love with Sarrazin, although she is, after a fashion, his own daughter. Sarrazin's girl friend, Sharpe, can only stand and watch as matters begin to entangle. Through this, Hecht, a parapsychologist, is monitoring Sarrazin to see where it leads. The denouement is a cheat but we feel it's best to allow you to see the film rather than explain it. The plot gets mired in its own complications at times and you'll have to concentrate on what's happening or lose the thread. Ehrlich, the writer, was about as mild-mannered a man as ever sat at a Smith-Corona and yet he wrote several superior sci-fi and terror pieces as well as First Train to Babylon which became THE NAKED EDGE. The bathtub scene and some of the eerier sequences make this a poor picture for anyone under the age of consent.

p, Frank P. Rosenberg; d, J. Lee Thompson; w, Max Ehrlich; ph, Victor J. Kemper (Technicolor); m, Jerry Goldsmith; ed, Michael Anderson; art d, Jack Martin Smith.

Thriller **Cas.** (PR:C-O MPAA:R)

REIVERS, THE*½ (1969) 111m Duo-Solar/NG c

Steve McQueen (Boon Hoggenbeck), Sharon Farrell (Corrie), Will Geer (Boss McCaslin), Michael Constantine (Mr. Binford), Rupert Crosse (Ned McCaslin), Mitch Vogel (Lucius McCaslin), Lonny Chapman (Maury McCaslin), Juano Hernandez (Uncle Possum), Clifton James (Butch Lovemaiden), Ruth White (Miss Reba), Dub Taylor (Dr. Peabody), Allyn Ann McLerie (Alison McCaslin), Diane Shalet (Hannah), Diane Ladd (Phoebe), Ellen Geer (Sally), Pat Randall (May Ellen), Charles Tyner (Edmonds), Vinnette Carroll (Aunt Callie), Gloria Calomee (Minnie), Sara Taft (Sarah), Lindy Davis (Otis), Raymond Guth (Uncle Ike), Shug Fisher (Cousin Zack), Logan Ramsey (Walter Clapp), Jon Shank (Joe Poleymus), Ella Mae Brown (Mrs. Possum), Florence St. Peter (Mary Possum), John McLiam (Van Tosch), Lou Frizzell (Doyle), Roy Barcroft (Ed), Burgess Meredith (Narrator).

Whenever a picture makes no sense, add a narration. This film, based on Faulkner's final novel (which was close to being unreadable), needs Meredith's voice to tie up all the loose ends in order to make it palatable. The word in the title doesn't refer to a family name. It's an archaic designation for "thieves" and aptly describes the protagonists. THE REIVERS looks as though it was produced by Robert Radnitz from a tale by Tennessee Williams. It was neither. The time is 1905 in rural Mississippi (it was actually filmed in Carrolton, Mississippi) and the Geer family awaits the delivery of their new Winton, a big, gaudy car that represented adventure and excitement. Geer's young grandson, the preteen Vogel, is more excited about it than anyone else and he's delighted when McQueen, a hired hand, gets the job of being the car's chauffeur. Geer and his son, Chapman, more or less run the town, and they learn that they must attend a funeral in St. Louis so they entrust Vogel's care to Carroll, the black woman who has been with the family for many years. Once Chapman and Geer have departed, McQueen gets Vogel to lie to Carroll so they can take the car on a spin to Memphis. They ride off and in the back seat, up pops Crosse, a black man who is related to the family by dint of a mating between Geer's ancestor and a slave woman on the property. The trio travel to Memphis and the 80-mile jaunt takes them almost two turns around the clock until they get there. Crosse was found as a child in the family's yard but since he is related, they don't treat him poorly. Once in Memphis, Crosse leaves to seek his own pleasure and McQueen squires Vogel to a bordello run by White. McQueen favors Farrell, a veteran of the whorehouse, and she lets him know that she is no longer interested in plying this trade; she'd like to give it all up for the love of a good man (the same motivation as Susan Sarandon's in PRETTY BABY). Vogel has to spend the night with Farrell's nephew, Davis, and when the youth insults his aunt, Vogel jumps to her defense and Davis cuts him with a knife. It's not a bad wound but Vogel backs off after that. Next day, Crosse shows up with some startling news; he's traded the Winton for a racehorse! McQueen is seething and Crosse explains that they will get the car back because their horse is due to race against another one and the Winton is the prize for the winner. They test the animal and he's a definite prospect for the glue factory until Crosse takes out a sandwich made of sardines and the horse responds to the smell by running like Man O' War. James is a typical redneck lawman and he has several racial insults to say in Crosse's presence so McQueen hits the sheriff in the snoot and all concerned are clapped in the clink. Farrell comes to the jail, uses her well-worn wiles on James, and gets them out. But McQueen is annoyed that she did that and hits her in the face. Vogel can't stand seeing his idol with fists of clay so he plans to go home without jockeying their horse in the race. Then the prized Winton arrives at the track and Vogel realizes it was he who arranged for this trip so he'd better make every effort to win the car back or his behind will be in a sling. The race takes place and the other horse wins when it jumps a rail. Since that's illegal, they run the race a second time and their horse takes the prize. Geer arrives in town and will help them bring their car and their horse back to the small town. Once home, Chapman is about to take a switch to Vogel but Geer stays his hand and tells the grandson that they'll forgive him this time, but that he'll have to do a lot of truth-telling before they ever believe him again. Vogel is relieved that his backside hasn't been reddened and then he's even more elated when Farrell and McQueen announce that they are to tie the knot and that they'll name their first child after him (since his first name is "Lucius" that's a bad bet if the premiere baby is a girl). Crosse steals the picture with his characterization. He died a few years later after having been on "The Partners," a TV comedy show, and after having been in one of the best "Monkees" episodes ever in a satire of Robinson Crusoe as his man "Thursday." Crosse could make any line sing and when he turned to the camera in that TV show and said, upon three occasions, "Can you believe someone actually *writes* this stuff?" you could fall off your chair with laughter. Meredith's narrative tried to keep the proceedings together but could not circumvent Rydell's ordinary direction and the silly script. McQueen could do a lot of things well but comedy wasn't one of them. Crosse and composer Williams were nominated for Oscars.

p, Irving Ravetch; exec p, Robert E. Relyea; d, Mark Rydell; w, Ravetch, Harriet Frank (based on the novel by William Faulkner); ph, Richard Moore (Panavision, Technicolor); m, Johnny Williams; ed, Thomas Stanford; art d, Charles Bailey, Joel Schiller; set d, Philip Abramson; cos, Theadora Van Runkle, Allen Levine, Joanne Haas; spec eff, A. Paul Pollard; makeup, Emile LaVigne.

Comedy/Drama **Cas.** **(PR:C MPAA:M)**

REKOPIS ZNALEZIONY W SARAGOSSIE (SEE: SARAGOSSA MANUSCRIPT, THE, 1966, Pol.)

RELAZIONI PERICOLOSE (SEE: LES LIAISONS DANGEREUSES, 1961, Fr./Ital.)

RELENTLESS*** (1948) 91m Cavalier/COL c

Robert Young *(Nick Buckley)*, Marguerite Chapman *(Luella Purdy)*, Willard Parker *(Jeff Moyer)*, Akim Tamiroff *(Joe Faringo)*, Barton MacLane *(Tex Brandow)*, Mike Mazurki *(Jake)*, Robert Barrat *(Ed Simpson)*, Clem Bevans *(Dad)*, Frank Fenton *(Jim Rupple)*, Hank Patterson *(Bob Pliny)*, Paul E. Burns *(Len Briggs)*, Emmett Lynn *(Nester)*, Will Wright *(Horse Dealer)*, John Carpenter, Bob Cason *(Posse Men)*, Byron Foulger *(Assayer)*, Nacho Galindo *(Peon)*, Ethan Laidlaw *(Miner)*.

A western setting provides the background for the story of a man wrongly accused of a murder, Young, who while trying to escape the continual pursuit of the law (in the form of Parker) searches out the man who can clear him of the charges. During his search he meets up with Chapman, owner of a covered-wagon store, finding a place to hide for a while. He eventually traps the man he has been looking for, MacLane, in the desert, where MacLane faces drying up underneath the hot sun unless he gives in to Young. Poignant story is a character study that concentrates on the themes of the hunted and the hunter, handled by direction that heightens seemingly simple moments. The color photography makes good use of the various locations.

p, Eugene B. Rodney; d, George Sherman; w, Winston Miller (based on the story "Three Were Thoroughbreds" by Kenneth Perkins); ph, Edward Cronjager (Technicolor); m, Martin Skiles; ed, Gene Havlick; md, Morris Stoloff; art d, Stephen Goosson, Walter Holscher.

Western **(PR:A MPAA:NR)**

RELIGIOUS RACKETEERS (SEE: MYSTIC CIRCLE MURDERS, 1939)

RELUCTANT ASTRONAUT, THE½** (1967) 101m UNIV c

Don Knotts *(Roy Fleming)*, Leslie Nielsen *(Maj. Fred Gifford)*, Joan Freeman *(Ellie Jackson)*, Jesse White *(Donelli)*, Jeanette Nolan *(Mrs. Fleming)*, Frank McGrath *(Plank)*, Arthur O'Connell *(Buck Fleming)*, Joan Shawlee *(Blonde in Bar)*, Guy Raymond *(Bert)*, Nydia Westman *(Aunt Zana)*, Paul Hartman *(Rush)*, Robert F. Simon *(Cervantes)*, Robert Pickering *(Moran)*, Burt Mustin *(Ned)*, Ceil Cabot *(Waitress)*, Fay De Witt *(Secretary)*, Fabian Dean *(Bus Driver)*.

Knotts plays a man with an exaggerated fear of heights who, through a weird series of events, finds himself an astronaut. It all starts when his rather pushy father enlists his son in an astronaut training program, with graduate Knotts being assigned the job of janitor's assistant. He loses this job, however, when he tries to show off to his father and friends by donning a space suit and showing them around the base. But when there is a search for the least-qualified candidate to go on a mission, Knotts is called up for duty. His exploits in space make him a hero, winning him the hand of Freeman. A little joke is carried a bit too far, with fall-guy Knotts stereotyped into the role of the total nincompoop, incapable of doing much of anything. The possibility for some sharp satire, in the vein of Charlie Chaplin, is somewhere beneath this characterization of Knotts', but it's never explored, making Knotts little more than an idiot who winningly gets himself into absurd situations. Other roles in this picture are basically caricatures, but they are very good ones.

p&d, Edward J. Montagne; w, Jim Fritzell, Everett Greenbaum (based on an idea by Don Knotts); ph, Rexford Wimpy (Technicolor); m, Vic Mizzy; ed, Sam E. Waxman; md, Joseph Gershenson; art d, Alexander Golitzen, William D. DeCinces; set d, John McCarthy, John Austin; cos, Rosemary Odell; spec eff, Dave Lee, George Brown; makeup, Bud Westmore, Hank Edds.

Comedy **(PR:A MPAA:NR)**

RELUCTANT BRIDE (SEE: TWO GROOMS FOR A BRIDE, 1957)

RELUCTANT DEBUTANTE, THE*½** (1958) 94m MGM c

Rex Harrison *(Jimmy Broadbent)*, Kay Kendall *(Sheila Broadbent)*, John Saxon *(David Parkson)*, Sandra Dee *(Jane Broadbent)*, Angela Lansbury *(Mabel Claremont)*, Peter Myers *(David Fenner)*, Diane Clare *(Clarissa Claremont)*, Sheila Raynor *(Maid)*, Ambrosine Phillpotts *(Secretary)*, Charles Cullum *(English Colonel)*.

Let's all say a prayer for the immortal soul of Kay Kendall, who died a year after this film was released, and whose few performances captured on screen continue to be a delight for anyone who sees them. Kendall and Harrison were married in real life and a problem with Inland Revenue (which is what the British call their I.R.S.) caused this most-English picture to have to be shot in most-French Paris. Based on a play by Home, it's a trifle at best but done with such elan and verve that the fact that it's thinner than a slice of pastrami on a two-dollar sandwich doesn't stop the enjoyment. A sophisticated comedy in the best sense of the word, THE RELUCTANT DEBUTANTE tells all with the title. Harrison and Kendall are husband and wife and he would like his daughter by a former marriage, Dee, to make her society debut in London, where she can meet all the right boys and, perhaps, find herself a husband in the no-jawed set. She finds the British boys as interesting as a nun's memoirs and is soon crazy over Saxon, an American musician with a bad reputation. All of the gossip about Saxon is false but that's not learned until later, when Saxon is suddenly the recipient of a large bequest and a title from an aged Italian relative who picked the right time to die (Act III). This was Harrison's first film since his triumph in MY FAIR LADY and he is properly suave and urbane as the concerned father. Dee exhibits a greater acting skill than she'd ever shown before and Saxon indicates that he's not just another pretty face with a rapidly receding hairline. Lansbury chimes in with a few good scenes but it's Kendall's film from start to end as she is charming, lovable, bubbly, and funny in what was to be her penultimate motion picture. If there is such a thing as reincarnation, let Kendall come back soon.

p, Pandro S. Berman; d, Vincente Minnelli; w, William Douglas Home (based on his play); ph, Joseph Ruttenberg (CinemaScope, Metrocolor); m, Eddie Warner; ed, Adrienne Fazan; art d, A.J. d'Eaubonne; set d, Robert Christides; cos, Helen Rose, Pierre Balmain; makeup, Jean-Paul Ulysse.

Comedy **(PR:A MPAA:NR)**

RELUCTANT DRAGON, THE½** (1941) 72m Disney/RKO c/bw

Robert Benchley *(Himself)*, Nana Bryant *(Mrs. Benchley)*, Buddy Pepper *(Guide)*, Frances Gifford *(Doris, Studio Artist)*, Barnett Parker *(Dragon's Voice)*, Claude Allister *(Sir Giles' Voice)*, Billy Lee *(Little Boy's Voice)*, The Rhythmaires, Clarence Nash *(Donald Duck's Voice/Animator)*, Pinto Colvig *(Goofy's Voice)*, Gerald Mohr *(Baby Weems Narrator/Guard)*, Florence Gill *(Voice of Clara Cluck/Animator)*, John Dehner, Alan Ladd, Truman Woodworth, Hamilton McFadden, Maurice Murphy, Jeff Corey *(Animators)*, Henry Hall *(Studio Cop)*, Frank Faylen *(Orchestra Leader)*, Walt Disney *(Himself)*, Lester Dorr *(Slim)*, Ward Kimball, Norman Ferguson, Jimmy Luske, Members of the Staff at Walt Disney Studios.

Disney's first excursion into live action cinema, though the action is extremely limited and consists mainly of Benchley walking through the studios, giving the audience a chance to see what is responsible for those fantastic cartoons like PINOCCHIO and FANTASIA. But there is really very little indication of what actually is taking place behind the scenes in such masterpieces, and much of the information is not quite correct. The aim is more for the juvenile population which was sure to get quite a kick from seeing the voices behind such characters as Donald Duck and Clara Cluck. The premise that keeps the whole thing together is the attempt of Benchley to sell the idea of the fairy tale "The Reluctant Dragon" to Disney. He arrives at the studio and a guide attempts to take him directly to the boss. Only Benchley's reluctance to really face Disney with the idea—it was his wife's pushing that brought him there—forces him to wander off through the various parts of the studio. In one sequence he walks into the color department and the picture changes from black-and-white to color. In another he witnesses the storyboarding of the BABY WEEMS cartoon, a really great little piece about a baby born a genius and thus lost to its loving parents. Eventually the guide grabs hold of Benchley again, delivering him directly to the big cheese in the projection room. Disney wants to show Benchley the new cartoon he has just made, entitled, of course, THE RELUCTANT DRAGON. This short was later released by itself, and is now known as one of the studio's biggest successes, as it concerns a friendly dragon who doesn't like having to live up to the image of a ferocious beast. Portions of the live-action parts were put together later in a short entitled BEHIND THE SCENES OF WALT DISNEY STUDIO. Oddly enough, this picture tries hard to stress how the Disney studios work in an atmosphere of togetherness, when just weeks before its release hundreds of the studio's employees went on strike. It's always a pleasure to see Benchley up to his fumbling antics, but his performance here is much more tame than in many of his how-to shorts. Disney had used the storyboard technique—single-frame drawings depicting scenes and sequences of a production—for his animated films for years. This was the first time the storyboarding technique had been used for a live-action film by the studio; the method was so successful that it was incorporated in all the Disney live-action films to come. The picture has one song, "The Reluctant Dragon" (T. Hee, Charles Wolcott, Ed Penner).

d, Alfred Werker; cartoon d, Hamilton Luske, Jim Handley, Ford Beebe, Erwin Verity, Jasper Blystone; w, Ted Sears, Al Perkins, Larry Clemmons, Bill Cottrell; ph, Bert Glennon, Winton C. Hoch (Technicolor); ed, Paul Weatherwax, Earl Rettig; art d, Gordon Wiles; cartoon art d, Ken Anderson, Hugh Hennesy, Charles Philippi; anim, Ward Kimball, Fred Moore, Milt Neil, Wolfgang Reitherman, Bud Swift, Walt Kelly, Jack Campbell, Claude Smith, Harvey Toombs; spec eff, Ub Iwerks, Josua L. Meador.

Animation/Live action **(PR:AAA MPAA:NR)**

RELUCTANT HEROES** (1951, Brit.) 80m Byron/ABF bw

Ronald Shiner *(Sgt. Bell)*, Derek Farr *(Michael Tone)*, Christine Norden *(Gloria Dennis)*, Brian Rix *(Horace Gregory)*, Larry Noble *(Trooper Morgan)*, Betty Impey *(Pat Thompson)*, Angela Whitehead *(Penny Roberts)*, Anthony Baird *(Sgt. McKenzie)*, Colin Morris *(Capt. Percy)*, Elspet Gray *(Lt. Virginia)*, Joan Henley, George Radford.

Bell, a drill sergeant at a boot camp, has his patience sorely tested by a new group of recruits. The usual stereotyped characters pull the same stunts seen in a score of other service comedies, but for some reason this one hit the jackpot with British audiences.

p, Henry Halstead; d, Jack Raymond; w, Colin Morris (based on a play by Morris); ph, James Wilson.

Comedy (PR:A MPAA:NR)

RELUCTANT SAINT, THE** (1962, U.S./Ital.) 105m Dmytryk-Weiler/Davis-Royal bw (CRONACHE DI UN CONVENTO) (AKA: JOSEPH DESA)

Maximilian Schell *(Giuseppe Desa)*, Ricardo Montalban *(Father Raspi)*, Lea Padovani *(Francesca Desa)*, Akim Tamiroff *(Bishop Durso)*, Harold Goldblatt *(Father Giovanni)*, Arnoldo Foa *(Felixa Desa)*, Mark Damon *(Aldo)*, Luciana Paluzzi *(Carlotta)*, Carlo Croccolo *(Gobbo)*, Giulio Bosetti *(Brother Orlando)*, Elisa Cegani *(Sister Nunziata)*.

Semi-farcical story about the village idiot who becomes a saint has Schell playing a happy-go-lucky youth who can't manage a job because of his ineptitude. To get rid of him, his mother packs him off to a monastery. Schell proves a further menace there as he breaks a statue of the Madonna, and is then confined to the stables. Passing bishop Tamiroff takes a liking to the lad when he notices his strong affection for the animals. He is sent through training as a priest, but when Schell is spotted floating while praying, everyone thinks he's possessed by the devil. An exorcism is called for, but the boy continues floating, and is promptly declared a saint. A light-hearted tone is kept throughout, but the stereotyped performances, unbelievable settings, and lifeless direction hurt whatever promises are inherent in the material.

p&d, Edward Dmytryk; w, John Fante, Joseph Petracca; ph, C.M. Pennington-Richards; m, Nino Rota; ed, Manuel Del Campo; art d, Mario Chiari, Pasquale Romano; cos, Maria De Matteis; makeup, Otello Fava.

Drama/Comedy (PR:A MPAA:NR)

RELUCTANT WIDOW, THE*½ (1951, Brit.) 86m TC/FA bw

Jean Kent *(Elinor)*, Guy Rolfe *(Lord Carlyon)*, Paul Dupuis *(Lord Nivelle)*, Lana Morris *(Becky)*, Kathleen Byron *(Mme. de Chevreaux)*, Julian Dallas [Scott Forbes]*(Francois Cheviot)*,Anthony Tancred *(Nicky)*, Peter Hammond *(Eustace Cheviot)*, Jean Cadell *(Mrs. Barrows)*, Andrew Cruickshank *(Lord Bedlington)*, George Thorpe *(Col. Strong)*, Ralph Truman *(Scowler)*, James Carney *(Maj. Forbes)*, Allan Jeayes *(Colonel)*, Hector MacGregor *(Sir Malcolm Torrens)*, Noel Howlett, Roddy Hughes, Cecil Bevan, Peter Bull, Johnnie Schofield, Ernest Jay, Maxwell Foster, John Warren, Jack Vyvyan, H.G. Stoker, Barry Denville, Janet Kaye, Peter Dunlop, John Bell.

Choppy yarn set in Napoleonic times has Kent, a simple governess, marrying a wealthy Lord, thus inheriting his estate upon his untimely death. She soon finds her residence filled with some nasty people who are working for Napoleon and trying to get their hands on some papers concerning the plans of Wellington's army. But Kent saves the day by getting to the papers first, making sure they reach the proper place. The script weakens itself in attempting to make a complex thriller out of this simple tale, thus losing any impact it may have had.

p, Gordon Wellesley; d, Bernard Knowles; w, Wellesley, J.B. Boothroyd (based on the novel by Georgette Heyer); ph, Jack Hildyard; m, Allan Gray; md, Norman Del Mar; art d, Carmen Dillon.

Drama (PR:A MPAA:NR)

REMAINS TO BE SEEN** (1953) 89m MGM bw

June Allyson *(Jody Revere)*, Van Johnson *(Waldo Williams)*, Louis Calhern *(Benjamin Goodwin)*, Angela Lansbury *(Valeska Chauvel)*, John Beal *(Dr. Glenson)*, Dorothy Dandridge *(Herself)*, Barry Kelley *(Lt. O'Flair)*, Sammy White *(Ben)*, Kathryn Card *(Mrs. West)*, Paul Harvey *(Mr. Bennett)*, Helene Millard *(Mrs. Bennett)*, Peter Chong *(Ling Tan)*, Charles Lane *(Examiner Delapp)*, Larry Blake *(Detective Minetti)*, Morgan Farley *(Kyle Manning)*, Howard Freeman *(Clark)*, Frank Nelson *(Fleming)*, Robert Fouik *(Officer Miller)*, Dabbs Greer *(Julius)*, Emmett Smith *(Buck)*, Thomas P. Dillon *(Frank)*, Dave Willock *(Driver)*, Don Anderson *(Attendant)*, Gregory Gay *(Head Waiter)*, Lawrence Dobkin *(Captain)*, Frank Scannell, Erno Verebes *(Waiters)*, Shep Menken *(Man)*, Veronika Pataky, Fernanda Eliscuo *(Women)*, Dick Simmons *(M.C.)*, Fred Welsh *(Taxi Driver)*, Stuart Holmes.

Johnson plays the manager of a Park Avenue apartment building who finds a dead tenant. He immediately phones the dead man's lawyer, who contacts the deceased's niece, Allyson (a singer in a jazz band), and requests that she come and take care of things. Allyson has never liked her millionaire uncle, but she comes anyway. This sets the scene for a boring mystery in which Lansbury tries to get hold of the deceased man's money. She has problems with Allyson, who decides to accept the inheritance so Lansbury won't get her hands on it. Lansbury attempts to hypnotize Allyson into jumping off the balcony, but Johnson saves the day by blaring the radio. Johnson manages to uncover the plot by Lansbury and crooked doctor Beal, and through his efforts hitches up with Allyson and with her band. (In addition to managing the apartment building, Johnson plays the drums.) Neither Allyson or Johnson are very convincing in their roles, with the rest of the cast overplaying their parts terribly. The setting of the dead man's apartment is supposedly exotic and eerie, but it looks anything but that. A few songs act as a relief to the story: "Too Marvelous For Words," "Toot, Toot, Tootsie" (sung by June Allyson, Van Johnson), and "Taking A Chance On Love" (sung by Dorothy Dandridge). This film was to be Allyson's last as a contract player for MGM. She was anxious to be move beyond the girl-next-door parts with which she made her name, but which no longer seemed believable from an actress of her age. MGM appeared unwilling or unable to come up with the parts she needed to make this transition.

p, Arthur Hornblow, Jr.; d, Don Weis; w, Sidney Sheldon (based on the play by Howard Lindsay, Russel Crouse); ph, Robert Planck; ed, Cotton Warburton; md, Jeff Alexander; art d, Cedric Gibbons, Hans Peters; m/l, Gus Kahn, Ernie Erdman, Dan Russo, John Latouche, Ted Fetter, Vernon Duke, Johnny Mercer, Richard A. Whiting.

Comedy/Mystery (PR:A MPAA:NR)

REMARKABLE ANDREW, THE** (1942) 80m PAR bw

William Holden *(Andrew Long)*, Ellen Drew *(Peggy Tobin)*, Brian Donlevy *(Gen. Andrew Jackson)*, Rod Cameron *(Jesse James)*, Richard Webb *(Randall Stevens)*, Porter Hall *(Art Slocumb)*, Frances Gifford *(Halsey)*, Nydia Westman *(Miss Van Buren)*, Montagu Love *(George Washington)*, George Watts *(Benjamin Franklin)*, Brandon Hurst *(Justice Marshall)*, Gilbert Emery *(Thomas Jefferson)*, Jimmy Conlin *(Henry Smith)*, Spencer Charters *(Dr. Upjohn)*, Wallis Clark *(R.R. McCall)*, Tom Fadden *(Jake Pearl)*, Minor Watson *(Orville Beamish)*, Milton Parsons *(Sam Savage)*, Thomas W. Ross *(Judge Krebbs)*, Clyde Filmore *(Mayor Ollie Lancaster)*, Martha O'Driscoll *(Secretary)*, James Millican *(Onlooker)*, Ben Taggart *(Bailiff)*, Emory Parnell, Monte Blue *(Policemen)*, Harlan Briggs *(Clem Watkins)*, Helene Phillips *(Mrs. Grundes)*.

After the failure of THE DEVIL AND DANIEL WEBSTER (AKA: ALL THAT MONEY CAN BUY), it's interesting that Paramount thought they could make a light-hearted fantasy work during the first dark days of WW II. It didn't. Trumbo, who always had a reputation for doing offbeat and/or powerful scripts, submitted the idea to producer Arthur Hornblow, Jr., who suggested that it might make a good book. Since novels adapted for films usually command a good price, Trumbo was able to be paid twice for his work—first for the book's rights and second for the screenplay. Holden is a virtuous civil servant whose avocation is acting as secretary to the local "Andrew Jackson" society and who lives in the memory of "Old Hickory" having also been named for him. When bookkeeper Holden is framed for misappropriating city funds, he seems to have no way to prove himself innocent, until the ghosts of Jackson (Donlevy), Washington (Love), Jefferson (Emery), Franklin (Watts), and Supreme Court Justice Marshall (Hurst) all arrive to help him clear his name. Even Jesse James (Cameron) comes to life, so to speak, to aid Holden and bring the culprits to light. Of course, no one sees the spirits but Holden and he stands aside and watches and listens as the group argues politics and makes comments on how the U.S. has changed. Watts, the discoverer of electricity, is thrilled how the power has been harnessed, Donlevy thinks that the radio is a shocking discovery, etc. Cameron arranges a jail break for Holden as the others forage through the records to learn who is really responsible for the deed. Once Holden is cleared and about to marry his fiancee, Drew, Holden expects the ghosts to depart. However, Donlevy is having such a good time that he wants to stay and live with Drew and Holden but they talk him out of it and Drew finally sees Donlevy's ghost. Under the guise of fantasy, Trumbo was able to get in some satiric digs at what was bothering him, although it got too cute for its own sake after a while and the historical jokes required that the viewer have a knowledge of who these spirits were and what they did. It was the kind of plot that might serve well today as a 30-minute situation comedy, though it was stretched to 80 minutes for the film and audiences found it wanting.

p, Richard Blumenthal; d, Stuart Heisler; w, Dalton Trumbo (based on his novel); ph, Theodor Sparkuhl; ed, Archie Marshek.

Comedy/Fantasy (PR:A MPAA:NR)

REMARKABLE MR. KIPPS** (1942, Brit.) 86m FOX bw (GB:KIPPS)

Phillip Frost *(Arthur Kipps as a boy)*, Michael Redgrave *(Arthur Kipps)*, Diana Wynyard *(Helen Walshingham)*, Diana Calderwood *(Ann Pornick as a girl)*, Phyllis Calvert *(Ann Pornick as a woman)*, Arthur Riscoe *(Chitterlow)*, Max Adrian *(Chester Coote)*, Helen Haye *(Mrs. Walshingham)*, Michael Wilding *(Ronnie Walshingham)*, Lloyd Pearson *(Shalford)*, Edward Rigby *(Buggins)*, Mackenzie Ward *(Pearce)*, Hermione Baddeley *(Miss Mergle)*, Betty Ann Davies *(Flo Bates)*, Arthur Denton *(Carshot)*, Betty Jardine *(Doris)*, Frank Pettingell *(Old Kipps)*, Beatrice Varley *(Mrs. Kipps)*, George Carney *(Old Pornick)*, Irene Browne *(Mrs. Bindon-Botting)*, Peter Garves *(Sidney Revel)*, Viscount Castlerosse *(Man in Bath Chair)*, Robert McCarthy, Felix Aylmer, Marda Shannon, Carol Gardiner, Kathleen Harrison, Muriel Aked.

A very good cast; an able director, Carol Reed (better known for THE THIRD MAN); a slick production; and an H.G. Wells story should add up to a fairly good movie. But something went wrong in this story about shop clerk Redgrave who remains a virtual nonentity until he becomes the heir to a vast fortune. He becomes hoodwinked by society girl Wynwyard into almost marrying her. But at the last minute he backs out and runs off with his childhood sweetheart, Calvert. The two marry, but their marriage is marred when Calvert demands a simple existence, while Redgrave is still flirting with the rich ways he's acquired. However, Redgrave loses all his money, which causes him and Calvert to lead a humble life ever after. The story takes place in a rural English community at the turn of the century, which may be the problem with the picture: the characters are all so smug, it's hard to generate any form of feeling for them.

p, Edward Black; d, Carol Reed; w, Frank Launder, Sidney Gilliat (based on the novel by H.G. Wells); ph, Arthur Crabtree; ed, R.E. Dearing; md, Lois Levy.

Comedy (PR:A MPAA:NR)

REMARKABLE MR. PENNYPACKER, THE**½   (1959) 87m FOX c

Clifton Webb (*Pa Pennypacker*), Dorothy McGuire (*Ma Pennypacker*), Charles Coburn (*Grampa*), Jill St. John (*Kate Pennypacker*), Ron Ely (*Wilbur Fielding*), Ray Stricklyn (*Horace Pennypacker III*), David Nelson (*Henry Pennypacker*), Dorothy Stickney (*Aunt Jane*), Larry Gates (*Rev. Dr. Fielding*), Richard Deacon (*Sheriff*), Mary Jayne Saunders (*Laurie Pennypacker*), Mimi Gibson (*Elizabeth Pennypacker*), Donald Losby (*Benny*), Chris Van Scoyk (*David*), Jon Van Scoyk (*Edward*), Terry Rangno (*Teddy*), Nora O'Mahoney (*Mrs. McNair*), Doro Merande (*Miss Haskins*), Harvey B. Dunn (*The Verger*), Ralph Sanford (*The Fire Chief*), Joan Freeman (*Mary Pennypacker*), David Harrison, Donald Harrison (*Twins*), Pamela Baird (*Nancy*), Nancy Ann DeCarl (*Ann*), Anna Marie Nanasi (*Babs*), Diane Mountford (*Trudy*), Ray Ferrell (*Charlie*).

Clifton Webb had become a major movie star after his "Mr. Belvedere" character scored in two films. He'd spent many years on the stage and done several smaller roles that always delighted, but the prissy genius established himself in the public's mind as a charming, albeit stiff, person, making him the perfect candidate to play the title role of an 1890s bigamist who blithely went through life siring 17 children in two separate households. Coburn is the patriarch of a sausage-making family with facilities in two Pennsylvania cities, Harrisburg and Philadelphia. His son, Webb, must spend alternate months in each city and has been doing that for two decades. His Harrisburg spouse, McGuire, is a feminist and a free-thinker and Webb shares those views. Since Philadelphia can be a lonely town for a man alone, Webb took the tack of starting a second life there, with all the attendant accoutrements, such as a wife and children. His Philadelphia wife died eight years before but he remains an excellent father to his brood. When his double life is discovered, chaos erupts. With 17 children, there are almost that many complications once Webb's true existence is uncovered, but, since the Philadelphia wife is dead, it all works out in the end. Webb takes the discovery with a shrug. He and McGuire had always spoken of such things and he merely assumed that she would understand what he did. Given the strict morality of the 1890s U.S., there were many chances for humor, most of which were missed by Reisch's adaptation of O'Brien's stage hit. The sets and costumes are authentic and attractive and Webb's suavity is always appreciated but there are so many people rushing about the screen that it gets overpopulated and confusing at times, although never unbelievable. Due to the obvious immorality of a man with two wives, there was some objection by Catholics at the time, yet the treatment of the theme was most benign and could be appreciated by anyone of any age without corrupting them.

p, Charles Brackett; d, Henry Levin; w, Walter Reisch (based on the play by Liam O'Brien); ph, Milton Krasner (CinemaScope, DeLuxe Color); m, Leigh Harline; ed, William Mace; md, Lionel Newman; art d, Lyle R. Wheeler, Mark-Lee Kirk; cos, Charles LeMaire, Mary Wills.

Comedy   Cas.   (PR:A MPAA:NR)

REMBRANDT****   (1936, Brit.) 84m LFP/UA bw

Charles Laughton (*Rembrandt van Rijn*), Gertrude Lawrence (*Geertje Dirx*), Elsa Lanchester (*Hendrickje Stoffels*), Edward Chapman (*Fabrizius*), Walter Hudd (*Banning Cocq*), Roger Livesey (*Beggar Saul*), John Bryning (*Titus van Rijn*), Allan Jeayes (*Dr. Tulp*), John Clements (*Gavaert Flink*), Raymond Huntley (*Ludvig*), (Abraham Sofaer (*Dr. Menasseh*), Lawrence Hanray (*Hertsbeeke*), Austin Trevor (*Marquis*), Henry Hewitt (*Jan Six*), Gertrude Musgrove (*Agelintje*), Basil Gill (*Adriaen*), Edmund Willard (*Van Zeeland*), Marius Goring (*Baron Leivens*), Richard Gofe (*Titus, as Child*), Meinhart Maur (*Ornia*), George Merritt (*Church Warden*), John Turnbull (*Minister*), Sam Livesey (*Auctioneer*), William Fagan (*Burgomaster*), Lewis Broughton, Frederick Burtwell (*Saskia's Brothers*), Baroness Barany (*Waitress*), Barry Livesey (*Peasant*), Herbert Lomas (*Miller Harmen van Rijn*), J, Baroness Barany (*Waitress*), Barry Livesey (*Peasant*), Herbert Lomas (*Miller Harmen van Rijn*), Jack Livesey (*Journeyman*), Quintin McPherson (*Official*), James Carney (*Peasant*), Roger Wellesley (*Burgomaster's Secretary*), Byron Webber, Bellenden Powell (*Court Members*), Charles Paton, Hector Abbas, Leonard Sharpe (*Burghers at Auction*), George Pughe, Jerrold Robert Shaw (*Museum Directors*), Evelyn Ankers, James Carney.

In later years, LUST FOR LIFE and MOULIN ROUGE would come along to commercially succeed in limning artist's lives but this box-office failure far outstrips either of those in delineating the creative process and presenting an unromanticized look at one of art's geniuses. Laughton had already won an Oscar for his part as Henry VIII and producer-director Korda thought he had a good idea doing the private lives of famous men. Laughton dominated the film in the title role, as he'd done when playing Henry, Nero, Javert, and Bligh before. He was in every scene save one and gave such a restrained performance that people who were expecting his thespian fireworks were somewhat disappointed. It's about the final 27 years of the Dutchman's life and had Korda named it "The Private Life of Rembrandt" it might have had a larger return. When covering that long a period, it's not easy to sustain a single, driving story so what we see are several vignettes, each a gem, and the maturing of a man who goes from being the most successful painter in a Europe filled with great artists, to a poor, wretched man at the time of his death, living on charity handouts. Korda and Laughton spent a great deal of time looking for their next project after THE PRIVATE LIFE OF HENRY VIII and tried, for a while, to make a script work for "Cyrano"—something that Ferrer eventually did to unanimous approval. Korda was an art collector and used his appreciation for paints to team with his brother in designing a marvelous "look" to the movie. Every scene is an artwork and looks as though it were taken from one of Rembrandt's own paintings. The picture begins as Laughton's beloved first wife has passed away and he is busily at work on "The Night Watch." It turns out that the men who appear in the famous painting were annoyed at having been depicted that way by Rembrandt. Since all of them had paid a fee for the privilege of sitting for the master, some were angry because their faces retreated into the background and they felt cheated. Laughton, however, remains true to his vision and will not allow anyone

to criticize his work. With his first wife buried, he feels the need to have a woman of his own and turns to the female closest to him, Lawrence, his housekeeper. She is also his sometime model and he is able to overlook the fact that she is a vulgar woman whom he might never have noticed if still happily married. The moment he begins his alliance with Lawrence, things go rotten. He owes a great deal of money and must sell his regal house and most of his assets in order to satisfy his outstanding bills. When he turns his attentions on the maid, Lanchester, Lawrence leaves him. Lanchester is soon pregnant (something that didn't happen in their real wedded life) and they are married after she gives birth. When Lanchester dies, Laughton becomes almost instantly old, a doddering old fool on the brink of total senility. The synopsis doesn't sound like much but the picture is far more than the sum of the aforementioned parts. Laughton is a marvel to watch. He did his research by traveling to Holland, studying the art and whatever biographical material he could lay hands on, then steeped himself in the information and became the painter, offering a superb, complex characterization that must rank among his best ever, and, perhaps, one of the very best biographical roles in film history. That the movie was not a hit does not detract from the achievements of the Kordas, Laughton and everyone associated with this tasteful, mostly accurate, and satisfying motion picture. What a shame that it was not done in color, a process that screamed to be used in this multi-hued story.

p&d, Alexander Korda; w, Carl Zuckmayer, Lajos Biro, June Head, Arthur Wimperis; ph, Georges Perinal, Richard Angst; m, Geoffrey Toye; ed, William Hornbeck, Francis Lyon; md, Muir Mathieson; prod d, Vincent Korda; cos, John Armstrong; spec eff, Ned Mann.

Biography   Cas.   (PR:A MPAA:NR)

REMEDY FOR RICHES**½   (1941) 60m RKO bw

Jean Hersholt (*Dr. Paul Christian*), Dorothy Lovett (*Judy Price*), Edgar Kennedy (*George Browning*), Jed Prouty (*D.B. "Emerson" Vanderveer*), Walter Catlett (*Clem*), Robert Baldwin (*Roy Davis*), Warren Hull (*Tom Stewart*), Maude Eburne (*Mrs. Hastings*), Margaret McWade (*Gertrude Purdy*), Halline Hill (*Abby Purdy*), Renie Riano (*Mrs. Gattle*), Barry Macollum (*Harvey Manning*), Lester Scharff (*Eddie*), Prudence Benny (*Herself*).

Hersholt is at it again as the small town American doctor Christian whose experience and wisdom help save River's End from folding because of a phony oil scheme. Hull comes to town presumably to build a hotel and resort. During initial spading, oil is discovered, and the town goes wild in an effort to get at it. Hersholt calls in a geologist friend for verification of the oil find, but Hull manages to frame him and the geologist is locked up, leaving Hersholt to rescue the town before it is too late. There are a few scenes which could use reediting, but as a whole the story is one of the best in the series. (See DR. CHRISTIAN series, Index.)

p, William Stephens; d, Erle C. Kenton; w, Lee Loeb; ph, John Alton; ed, Paul Weatherwax; md, C. Bakaleinikoff; art d, Bernard Herzbrun.

Drama/Comedy   (PR:A MPAA:NR)

REMEMBER?*   (1939) 83m MGM bw

Robert Taylor (*Jeff Holland*), Greer Garson (*Linda Bronson*), Lew Ayres (*Sky Ames*), Billie Burke (*Mrs. Bronson*), Reginald Owen (*Mr. Bronson*), George Barbier (*Mr. McIntyre*), Henry Travers (*Judge Milliken*), Richard Carle (*Mr. Piper*), Laura Hope Crews (*Mrs. Carruthers*), Sara Haden (*Miss Wilson*), Sig Ruman (*Dr. Schmidt*), Halliwell Hobbes (*Butler*), Paul Hurst (*Policeman*).

Garson's U.S. debut was not an auspicious one. She'd just come off GOODBYE, MR. CHIPS and the studio teamed her with Taylor for this weak attempt at a romantic comedy. It was Taylor's third flop in a row (the other two were LUCKY NIGHT and LADY OF THE TROPICS), and caused some concern at the studio about his drawing power. That was assuaged when he made WATERLOO BRIDGE the following year to critical and financial success. It should have also proved to the bosses at MGM that no star can triumph over a clunky script and that the play is the thing. Still, even in the 1980s, producers give untold millions to personalities and too little to the screenwriters who must sit alone in their offices with nothing but blank paper and imagination and wait until, as Gene Fowler once said, "little beads of blood break out on the forehead." Garson is a rich young woman engaged to Ayres. She meets Taylor, finds him adorable, and bids ta-ta to Ayres, who is a brick about the whole thing, sighs once, then offers the happy couple his congratulations. Taylor is a workaholic and can't find time in his packed schedule to marry Garson until the couple is stopped by patrolman Hurst for speeding and he takes them to a justice of the peace to be married. Burke is Garson's society mother, fluttering and tripping over her tongue as always, and Owen is her stiff father. The marriage is short-lived because Taylor spends too much time on his career and not enough on his domestic situation, so Garson seeks a divorce. So far, so light, right? Now comes the totally bogus twist. Ayres feels that Garson and Taylor are truly made for each other. He has a drug that will cause them both to have amnesia as he figures that if they can only forget what's gone before, they might fall in love again. He slips this miracle potion into their drinks, they quaff the brew and forget about each other, totally. Now Ayres arranges for them to meet again and, of course, they fall in love once more and marry for the second time. It's just after this wedding that Garson gleefully announces that she's about to have a baby and the picture ends and we wonder if her mind is gone or if it's a joke or is she really expecting? Since they repeat the same "falling in love" sequence, it's a bore to watch, despite a few amusing moments and some crackling dialog. Silly stuff made better than it seems by lighthearted acting from the principals and solid secondary work from the supporting cast. REMEMBER? is a picture that is easily forgotten.

p, Milton Bren; d, Norman Z. McLeod; w, Corey Ford, McLeod; ph, George Folsey; m, Edward Ward; ed, Harold F. Kress, art d, Cedric Gibbons.

Comedy   (PR:A MPAA:NR)

REMEMBER LAST NIGHT*½ (1935) 81m UNIV bw

Edward Arnold *(Danny Harrison)*, Constance Cummings *(Carlotta Milburn)*, Sally Eilers *(Bette Huling)*, Robert Young *(Tony Milburn)*, Robert Armstrong *(Fred Flannagan)*, Reginald Denny *(Jack Whitridge)*, Monroe Owsley *(Billy Arliss)*, George Meeker *(Vic Huling)*, Edward Brophy *(Maxie)*, Jack LaRue *(Baptiste Bouclier)*, Louise Henry *(Penny Whitridge)*, Gregory Ratoff *(Faronea)*, Arthur Treacher *(Clarence Phelps)*, Rafaela Ottiano *(Mme. Bouclier)*, Gustav von Seyffertitz *(Professor Carl Herman Eckhart Jones)*, Louise Henry *(Penny Whitridge)*, Monte Montague *(Mechanic)*, Ted Billings *(Sailor)*, Tiny Sandord *(Truck Driver)*, E.E. Clive *(Photographer)*, Kate Price *(Cook)*, Wade Boteler, James Flavin *(Cops)*, Frank Reicher, Alice Ardell.

Supposedly a sophisticated comedy—at least, that's what the original billing advertised—and it's pretty hard to understand what is meant by sophisticated here; for that matter, it's really hard to figure what's going on with this rather inane plot. A group of wealthy socialities, including Cummings and Young, go out for a night of drinking rounds. During their excursion they pick up a pretty large group, all of whom put away quite a few drinks, when it is discovered that a murder has occurred. Arnold, a good-natured detective, goes about solving the case, but before he comes up with the criminal a total of four murders and two suicides occur. Not such good sleuthing. His reasonable excuse is that all of his society friends were drunk out of their minds, so no one can recall the events of the evening. A hypnotist, von Seyffertitz, is brought in to jar the memories of the misguided witnesses, but he quickly becomes a murder victim just at the point of disclosure. Bright spot among all this mish-mash is the appearance of Arthur Treacher in the role of butler; he supplies the much-needed laughs in a very witty manner.

p, Carl Laemmle, Jr.; d, James Whale; w, Doris Malloy, Harry Clork, Louise Henry, Dan Totheroh (based on the novel *Hangover Murders* by Adam Hobhouse); ph, Joseph A. Valentine; ed, Ted J. Kent.

Comedy/Mystery **(PR:A MPAA:NR)**

REMEMBER MY NAME½** (1978) 95m Lion's Gate/COL c

Geraldine Chaplin *(Emily)*, Anthony Perkins *(Neil Curry)*, Berry Berenson *(Barbara Curry)*, Moses Gunn *(Pike)*, Jeff Goldblum *(Mr. Nudd)*, Timothy Thomerson *(Jeff)*, Alfre Woodard *(Rita)*, Marilyn Coleman *(Teresa)*, Jeffrey S. Perry *(Harry)*, Carlos Brown *(Rusty)*, Dennis Franz *(Franks)*.

Perkins is a construction worker, happily married to Berenson and leading a quiet, modest lifestyle. After becoming the victim of some of vandalism, Perkins discovers his ex-wife (Chaplin) is out on the streets after serving a long jail sentence for murder. She, in her zombie-ish, pathetic manner, tries to win back Perkins. She also terrorizes Berenson (in the film's best scene) by creeping around the house with a butcher knife while Berenson goes about her daily routine. Chaplin overstays her welcome and soon gets tossed back in the slammer, where an obligatory exposition scene takes place. Produced by Robert Altman (who hasn't done a film anywhere near the quality of this one in quite some time) and directed by Alan Rudolph (CHOOSE ME, a more recent picture that has since achieved near-cult status), REMEMBER MY NAME attempts to be both a thriller and a character study. It isn't very suspenseful (there is rarely any sense of danger) and cannot decide whether Perkins or Chaplin is the main character. What is most disturbing are the constant, insulting messages blaring on television sets that are always in the background—apparently telling us the problems in Perkins and Chaplin's lives are minor compared with the disasters that occur throughout the world. This picture is nothing more than an average thriller, along the lines of studio programmers, which is blessed with some captivating performances. Giving credit where credit is due, Rudolph did attempt to elevate this picture above the norm by making what he called a "contemporary blues drama." An interesting film for what it could have been, not for what it is.

p, Robert Altman; d&w, Alan Rudolph; ph, Tak Fujimoto (DeLuxe Color); m, Alberta Hunter; ed, Thomas Walls; William A. Sawyer; cos, J. Allen Highfill.

Drama **(PR:O MPAA:R)**

REMEMBER PEARL HARBOR** (1942) 75m REP bw

Donald M. Barry *(Steve "Lucky" Smith)*, Alan Curtis *(Bruce Gordon)*, Fay McKenzie *(Marcia Porter)*, Sig Rumann *(Van Hoorten)*, Ian Keith *(Capt. Hudson)*, Rhys Williams *(Senor Anderson)*, Maynard Holmes *(Portly Porter)*, Diana Del Rio *(Doralda)*, Robert Emmett Keane *(Mr. Littlefield)*, Sammy Stein *(Sgt. Adams)*, Paul Fung *(Japanese Bartender)*, James B. Leong *(Japanese Major)*.

This film's played strictly for the action, as a group of young soldiers stationed in the Phillipines after the Japanese invasion of Pearl Harbor get ready to fight for their country. Soldier Barry, in his first non-western role, goes so far as to drive his plane into a Japanese troop transport, in a hara-kiri-like sacrifice. What this film lacks in logic it makes up for in heroic feats.

p, Albert J. Cohen; d, Joseph Santley; w, Malcolm Stuart Boylan, Isabel Dawn; ph, Ernest Miller; ed, Charles Craft; md, Cy Feuer; art d, Russell Kimball; spec eff, Howard Lydecker; technical advisor, Col. Robert C. Cotton.

War **(PR:A MPAA:NR)**

REMEMBER THAT FACE (SEE: MOB, THE, 1951)

REMEMBER THE DAY*** (1941) 85m FOX bw

Claudette Colbert *(Nora Trinell)*, John Payne *(Dan Hopkins)*, John Shepperd [Shepperd Strudwick] *(Dewey Roberts)*, Ann Todd *(Kate Hill)*, Douglas Croft *(Dewey, as a Boy)*, Jane Seymour *(Mrs. Roberts)*, Anne Revere *(Miss Price)*, Frieda Inescort *(Mrs. Dewey Roberts)*, Harry Hayden *(Mr. Roberts)*, Francis Pierlot *(Mr. Steele)*, William Henderson *(Peter)*, Chick Chandler *(Mr. Mason)*, George Ernest *(Bill Tower)*, Harry Tyler *(Mr. Avery)*, Jody Gilbert *(Mrs. Avery)*, Paul Harvey *(Mr. Phillips)*, Billy Dawson *(Steve)*, Geraldine Wall *(Beulah)*, Marie Blake *(Miss Cartwright)*, John Hiestand *(Announcer)*, Selmer Jackson *(Graham)*, William Halligan *(Tom Hanlon)*, Irving Bacon *(Cecil)*, Kay Linaker *(Society Reporter)*, Thurston Hall *(Gov. Teller)*, George Chandler *(Telegraph Operator)*, Mae Marsh, Lillian West, Cecil Weston, Vera Lewis, Maxine Tucker *(Teachers)*, Paul Stanton, William B. Davidson *(Committee Men)*, Ed Dearing *(Detective)*, Harry Harvey, Jr. *(3rd Baseman)*, David Holt *(Pitcher)*, Virginia Brissac *(Mrs. Hill)*, Byron Foulger *(Photographer)*, Ruth Robinson *(Mrs. Pettit)*, Paul McVey *(Jeweler)*, James Blaine *(Doorman)*, Allen Wood *(Bell Boy)*, Mel Ruick *(Hotel Clerk)*, Roseanne Murray *(Flower Girl)*, Charles Tannen *(Slicker)*, Ethel Griffies.

Heartwarming story that gets to the root of American idealism casts Colbert as an aging school teacher about to meet with Presidential candidate Shepperd, who was her pupil 25 years earlier. Her mind quickly drifts back to the time when the young boy, who had a crush on her, becomes jealous upon discovering she is secretly married to another teacher. Colbert gives the boy special attention, encouraging him to pursue his hobbies and other interests. Colbert's husband joins up with the Canadian forces at the onset of WW I, and is killed in battle. This tear-jerker, which plays on memories of adolescent puppy love, is handled smoothly in both script and direction. Colbert musters all her charms for her role, which takes her from young school teacher to aging woman.

p, William Perlberg; d, Henry King; w, Tess Slesinger, Frank Davis, Allan Scott (based on the play by Philo Higley, Philip Dunning); ph, George Barnes; m, Alfred Newman; ed, Barbara McLean; art d, Richard Day.

Drama **(PR:A MPAA:NR)**

REMEMBER THE NIGHT*½** (1940) 86m PAR bw

Barbara Stanwyck *(Lee Leander)*, Fred MacMurray *(John Sargent)*, Beulah Bondi *(Mrs. Sargent)*, Elizabeth Patterson *(Aunt Emma)*, Willard Robertson *(Francis X. O'Leary)*, Sterling Holloway *(Willie)*, Charles Waldron *(Judge—New York)*, Paul Guilfoyle *(District Attorney)*, Charlie Arnt *(Tom)*, John Wray *(Hank)*, Thomas W. Ross *(Mr. Emory)*, Fred "Snowflake" Toones *(Rufus)*, Tom Kennedy *(Fat Mike)*, Georgia Caine *(Lee's Mother)*, Virginia Brissac *(Mrs. Emory)*, Spencer Charters *(Judge at Rummage Sale)*, Chester Clute *(Jewelry Salesman)*, George Melford *(Brian)*, James Flavin *(Tough Attendant)*, George Guhl *(Prison Guard)*, Kate Drain Lawson *(Jail Matron)*, Fuzzy Knight *(Band Leader)*, John Beck *(Lee's Stepfather)*, Bernard Suss, Frank Conklin, Julius Tannen, Galan Galt, Milton Kibbee, Walter Soderling, Pat O'Malley, Harry Depp, Julia Faye, Avril Cameron, Joan Acker, Beth Hartman *(Jury Members)*, Ambrose Barker *(Customs Official)*, Brooks Benedict *(Court Spectator)*, Ruth Warren, Roy Crane, Martha Mears.

You'd have to be a grump not to like this funny, sentimental blend of pathos, drama and zaniness that borders on being Capra-corn but never goes over the edge. It may have been former art director Leisen's best directorial effort, mainly due to the superior Sturges script. Sturges had a way with designing a picture so it could get right to the brink of syrup, then pull back with an hysterical comedy sequence. Conversely, just as the humor was about to disintegrate into chaotic slapstick, Sturges would throw a curve that put the story back onto a firm, dramatic footing. Stanwyck is a tough cookie with a shoplifting habit. Christmas is approaching and she decides to give herself a present, a bracelet of diamonds. She's caught by the security people and sent to jail to await trial. She's been in twice before for the same sort of crime and the judge decides to wait until after the Christmas holidays. MacMurray is to prosecute her in his job as assistant district attorney. He's going home to Indiana for the winter vacation and when he learns that Stanwyck is also from the same state, he gets her out of jail in his custody and will drop her off at her home, on the promise that she will return to face the charges. She goes to her residence but her mother, Caine, has no use for her and Stanwyck is hurt. MacMurray takes her to his home to meet his mother, Bondi, his aunt, Patterson, and their handyman, Holloway. Stanwyck has never been part of such a loving family and is struck by the closeness. She and MacMurray are soon in love but she holds back, fearing that it could never be permanent. She considers fleeing, then changes her mind and returns to New York for the trial. Her defense attorney, Robertson (who usually played the stern judge or vicious no-nonsense prosecutor) makes an impassioned and funny plea on Stanwyck's behalf, but that all goes out the window when she pleads guilty and accepts the brief jail term. It goes without saying that MacMurray will be waiting for her when she is released. It could have been maudlin and dreary in many other hands but Leisen and Sturges have made this a wonderful Yuletide movie that's good watching any time of year. Three songs: "Easy Living" (Ralph Rainger, Leo Robin, sung by Martha Mears in a nightclub sequence), "Back Home in Indiana" (James F. Hanely, Ballard MacDonald, performed by Mears and the King's Men), and "End of a Perfect Day" (Carrie Jacobs Band, sung by Holloway as Stanwyck plays the piano).

p&d, Mitchell Leisen; w, Preston Sturges; ph, Ted Tetzlaff; m, Frederick Hollander; ed, Doane Harrison; md, Irvin Talbot; art d, Hans Dreier, Roland Anderson; set d, A.E. Freudeman; cos, Edith Head; makeup, Wally Westmore.

Comedy/Drama/Romance **(PR:A MPAA:NR)**

REMEMBER WHEN (SEE: RIDING HIGH, 1937, Brit.)

REMEMBRANCE½** (1982, Brit.) 117m Channel 4/Mainline c

John Altman *(Steve)*, Al Ashton *(John)*, Martin Barrass *(Malcolm)*, Nick Dunning *(Chris)*, Sally Jane Jackson *(Sue)*, David John *(Mark)*, Peter Lee-Wilson *(Vincent)*, Gary Oldman *(Daniel)*, Ewan Stewart *(Sean)*, Timothy Spall *(Douglas)*, Kim Taylforth *(Christine)*, Michele Winstanley *(Gail)*, Kenneth Griffith *(Joe)*, Roger Adamson, Dawn Archibald, Sean Arnold, Dicken Ashworth, Sheila Ballantine, John Barrett, Derek Benfield, Jesse Birdsall, Mark Drewry, Roger Booth, Jon Croft, Alison Dowling, Nicola Wright, Nick Ellesworth, Peter Ellis, Myra Frances, Michael Godley, Dave Hill, Peter Jonfield, Wolf Kahler, Marjie Lawrence, Doel Luscombe, Tony Mathews, Lisa Maxwell, Anna Rees, Don Munday, Eileen Page, Robert Pitman, John Price, Lawrie Quayle, John Rutland, Flip Webster.

The last 24 hours spent by a group of sailors in England before setting sail frames an unrelentingly grim depiction of the down side of empire. Drinking, violence and discos are the only attractions in an ugly landscape. Not the sort of film to show prospective tourists.

p&d, Colin Gregg; w, Hugh Stoddart; ph, John Metcalfe (Eastmancolor); ed, Peter Delfgou; art d, Jamie Leonard.

Drama   **(PR:C-O MPAA:NR)**

REMORQUES   (SEE: STORMY WATERS, 1946, Fr.)

REMOTE CONTROL**   (1930) 62m MGM bw

William Haines (*William J. Brennan*), Charles King (*Sam Ferguson*), Mary Doran (*Marion Ferguson*), John Miljan (*Prof. Kruger*), Polly Moran (*Polly*), J.C. Nugent (*Smedley*), Edward Nugent (*Radio Engineer*), Wilbur Mack (*Chief of Police*), James Donlan (*Blodgett*), Edward Brophy (*Al*), Warner P. Richmond (*Max*), Russell Hopton (*Frank*).

Script tailored to fit the Haines personality, which could become grating at times. In this film, he's a radio announcer at a station where Miljan, posing as a clairvoyant answering fan letters, codes messages to his mob about bank robberies. Miljan, a real smoothie, quickly gets the girl, Doran, who Haines has been trying to get at all along. To get Haines out of the way, Miljan has him kidnaped. Through his ingenuity, he breaks loose and foils the plans of Miljan and company. Well-tuned script and snappy direction keep the rather tired material from getting too bogged down.

d, Malcolm St. Clair, Nick Grinde; w, Clyde North, Albert C. Fuller, Jack Nelson (based on their play).

Comedy   **(PR:A MPAA:NR)**

REMOVALISTS, THE**½   (1975, Aus.) 88m Seven Keys c

John Hargreaves (*Constable Ross*), Peter Cummins (*Sgt. Simmonds*), Kate Fitzpatrick (*Kate Mason*), Jacki Weaver (*Marilyn Carter*), Martin Harris (*Kenny Carter*), Chris Hayward (*The Removalist*).

Adaptation of a popular Australian play focuses on a police officer, Cummins, who claims he's never had to use his gun in 23 years on the force. When he gets a new recruit, Hargreaves, the two men don't have a heck of a lot to do except watch TV and do crossword puzzles. One day a woman, accompanied by her sister, comes to the station to complain that her husband is beating her. She wants to leave her husband, Harris, but he won't allow her to take her furniture. Cummins goes to the apartment and ties up Harris while the furniture is removed. Harris is beaten by the two police officers until they fear he may be dead. He lives, and the two cops make a deal with him so he will keep quiet. He agrees and, after a night of drinking with the two cops, he falls over dead. Statements about the relationship between sex and power and the misuse of power were handled more effectively in the stage version.

p, Margaret Fink; d, Tom Jeffrey; w, David Williamson (based on his play); ph, Graham Lind (Eastmancolor); m, The Galapagos Duck; ed, Anthony Buckley; md, Nathan Waks.

Drama   **(PR:C MPAA:NR)**

**RENALDO AND CLARA*½   (1978) 232m Lombard Street/Circuit c

Bob Dylan (*Renaldo*), Sara Dylan (*Clara*), Joan Baez (*Woman in White*), Ronnie Hawkins (*Bob Dylan*), Ronee Blakely (*Mrs. Dylan*), Jack Elliott, Harry Dean Stanton, Bob Neuwirth, Helena Kalloaniotes, Allen Ginsberg, David Blue, Roger McGuinn, Sam Shepard, Arlo Guthrie, Roberta Flack, Joni Mitchell.

Dylan in all his pretentiousness made this overly long concert film of his 1975/76 Rolling Thunder Revue. Between numbers the tried to make some philosophical points by having himself, his wife Sara, Joan Baez, Allen Ginsberg and other figures of the once popular counterculture perform some improvisational pieces. Dylan doesn't even play himself, but leaves that honor to Hawkins. Dylan plays a character named Renaldo, an intentionally ambiguous character representative of some form of humility. It all looks pretty silly. The concert footage is all right, but the in-between stuff just has to go. Dylan later cut the film down to 122 minutes, leaving mostly concert footage. Some of the songs include: "Isis I Want You," "It Ain't Me Babe," "Knockin' On Heaven's Door," "Hurricane," "Romance In Durango," "One Too Many Mornings," "One More Cup of Coffee," "Sara," "Patty's Gone to Laredo," "Just Like a Woman," "A Hard Rain's Gonna Fall," "Sad-Eyed Lady Of The Lowland," "When I Paint My Masterpiece" (Bob Dylan); "Chestnut Mare" (Roger McGuinn); "Diamonds And Rust" (Joan Baez); "Suzanne" (Leonard Cohen); "Need A New Sun Rising" (Ronee Blakely); "Salt Pork West Virginia" (Jack Elliott); "Kaddish" (Allen Ginsberg); "Cucurrucucu Paloma" (Thomas Mendez); and "Time Of The Preacher" (Willie Nelson).

p, Mel Howard; d, Bob Dylan; w, Dylan, Sam Shepard; ph, David Myers, Paul Goldsmith, Howard Alk, Michael Levine; ed, Dylan, Alk.

Concert Film   **(PR:O MPAA:R)**

RENDEZ-VOUS*½   (1932, Ger.) 81m Harmonie/Henry Kaufman bw

Ralph Arthur Roberts (*Leon*), Alexandra von Engstroen (*Antoinette*), Walter Rilla (*Armand*), Fritz Schulz (*Claude*), Szoeke Szakall [S. Z. "Cuddles" Sakall] (*Crepin*), Lucie Englisch (*Yvonne*), Trude Lieske, Paul Morgan, Margrete Kupfer.

Farce in which a society matron hires a music teacher just to make her husband jealous. The lad hired as a teacher doesn't know a thing about music, which doesn't seem to matter much to the husband, who then asks him to give his mistress some lessons. Excellent cast does a very good job handling the comedy routines, making for lighthearted fun. Includes the song, "Kennst Du Schon das Neuste Spiel: Sex Appeal, Sex Appeal?"

d, Carl Boese; w, Walter Hasenclever (based on the play by Jacques Bousquet, Henry Falk); m, Fritz Grothe, Eduard Kuenecke.

Musical/Comedy   **(PR:A MPAA:NR)**

RENDEZVOUS*   (1935) 91m MGM bw

William Powell (*Lt. Bill Gordon/Anson Meridan*), Rosalind Russell (*Joel Carter*), Binnie Barnes (*Olivia Karloff*), Lionel Atwill (*Maj. Charles Brennan*), Cesar Romero (*Capt. Nikki Nikolajeff*), Samuel S. Hinds (*John Carter, Assistant Secretary of War*), Henry Stephenson (*Russian Ambassador Gregory*), Frank Reicher (*Dr. Jackson*), Charles Grapewin (*Prof. Martin*), Leonard Mudie (*Roberts*), Howard Hickman (*G-Man*), Charles Trowbridge (*Secretary of War Baker*), Margaret Dumont (*Mrs. Hendricks*), Sid Silvers (*Recruiter*), Eileen O'Malley (*Red Cross Nurse*), Murray Kinnell (*de Segroff*), William Stack (*Headwaiter*), Bob Perry (*G-Man*), Richard Powell (*Taxi Driver*), Samuel R. McDaniel (*Porter*), James P. Burtis (*Private*), James Flavin, Edgar Dearing (*M.P.s*), Arno Frey (*Army Officer*), Al Bridge (*Sergeant*), John Harmon (*Telegrapher*), Lee Phelps (*Cop*), Harry "Zoup" Welsh (*Barber*), Morgan Wallace (*Gardner, Decoding Expert*), Monte Vandergrift (*Sailor*), Rudolph Anders (*Radio Operator*), Sam Ash (*Mexican*), Sidney Bracy (*Doctor's Assistant*), Frank Lackteen (*Customs Officer in Mexico*), Charles Coleman (*Doorman*), Wally Maher (*Reporter*), Harry C. Bradley (*Cashier*), Lee Kohlmar (*Tailor*), Tom Dugan (*Agent Patrick O'Reilly*), Guy Usher (*Ship's Captain*), Milburn Stone (*Carter's Aide*), Theodore Von Eltz (*Desk Clerk-Assistant*), William V. Mong (*Desk Clerk*), Edward Earle (*Man in Code Room*), Gino Corrado (*Code Room Clerk*), Belle Mitchell (*Mexican Peasant*), Lynton Brent (*Decoder*), Larry Steers (*Extra in Church*), David Burns (*Bellhop who Speaks German*), Frank O'Connor (*Officer*), Sterling Holloway.

This fictional spies-and-laughs movie was based on a non-fiction book about cipher-breakers during WW I. Myrna Loy was on strike at MGM so this role was given to Russell and she did very well with it. Powell is the puzzle editor at a Washington newspaper. He quits to join the army during the Great War. He's about to go off when he meets Russell, a bright young woman who is well connected to the government as her uncle is a mucky-muck in the War Department. They fall in love in a day and promise to meet when the war is over. He gets on a troop train but she has already pulled strings and has him taken off and brought back to the capitol to use his puzzle-brain to decode German messages which are being sent out of the Russian embassy, where the Kaiser's men have taken refuge. Powell meets Barnes, a Russian spy, and that almost knocks his romance out with Russell. Powell eventually breaks the code and the German plot and is on his way to the front when Russell does it again and he is taken from his task to come back to Washington. Witty, urbane and with some real menace, this movie has a lot going for it. The truth is that they did use puzzle-types to help in deciphering codes and that process is shown. Margaret Dumont is seen here without the Marx Brothers but is hardly noticed. Powell and Russell are a good team and play off each other well.

p, Lawrence Weingarten; d, William K. Howard; w, Bella Spewack, Samuel Spewack, P.J. Wolfson, George Oppenheimer (based on the book *American Black Chamber* by Herbert O. Yardley); ph, William Daniels; m, Dr. William Axt; ed, Hugh Wynn.

Comedy/Spy   **(PR:A MPAA:NR)**

RENDEZVOUS, 1951   (SEE: DARLING, HOW COULD YOU?, 1951)

**RENDEZVOUS AT MIDNIGHT*½   (1935) 60m UNIV bw

Ralph Bellamy (*Bob Edmonds*), Valerie Hobson (*Sandra Rogers*), Catharine Doucet (*Fernande*), Irene Ware (*Myra*), Helen Jerome Eddy (*Emmy*), Kathlyn Williams (*Angela*), Vivian Oakland (*Lillian Haskins*), Purnell Pratt (*Mayor*), W.P. Carleton (*Judge*), Edgar Kennedy (*Mahoney*), William Arnold (*Ryan*), Gail Arnold (*Carlotta*), Katherine Williams (*Annette*), Katherine Hall (*Style Thief*), William Ruel (*Schultz*), James Bush (*George*), Arthur Vinton (*Myles Crawford*).

Plodding drama has police commisioner Bellamy trying to figure out who was responsible for the murder of his predecessor. He spends alot of time in dress shops, giving the viewers a chance to cast their eyes on fashions of the time. Horribly miscast, with dreadful direction.

p, L.L. Ostrow; d, Christy Cabanne; w, Gladys Unger, Ferdinand Reyher (based on the play "The Silver Fox" by Gaetano Sazio); ph, Robert Planck; ed, Harry Markey.

Crime/Drama   **(PR:A MPAA:NR)**

RENDEZVOUS 24**   (1946) 70m FOX bw

William Gargan (*Larry*), Pat O'Moore (*Timothy*), David Leonard (*Kleinheldt*), Maria Palmer (*Greta*), John Bleifer (*Becker*), Kurt Katch (*Heligmann*), Henry Rowland (*Mannfred*), Paul Kruger (*Leopold*), Herman Bing (*Herr Schultz*), Ilka Gruning (*Frau Schmidt*), Boyd Irwin (*Carstairs*), Evan Thomas (*Sinclair*), Leslie Denison (*Clark*), Douglas Fowley, Jon Gilbreath, Drew Allen, Lorraine Miller, Kay Connors, Leyland Hodgson, Jack Norton, Eilene Janssen, Marin Sais, John Banner, Otto Reichow, Arno Frey, Claude Wisberg, Betty Fairfax, Bert Roach, Frieda Stoll, Charles Knight, Clifford Moore, Jimmy Aubrey, Arthur Gilmore, Emmett Vogan, Bernard Berg, Hans Tanzler, Angela DeWitt, Ann Harper, Gary Gray, Castle McCall, Frederic Brunn, John Dehner, Ferris Taylor, George Carleton, Charles Miller.

Shortly after WW II, a group of Nazi scientists hides out in the Hartz mountains of Germany, where it plans to develop an atom bomb. The bomb is to be used on the large cities of the Allied nations and thus restore Germany to power. Agents Gargan and O'Moore fend off pretty German spies and armed killers and manage to prevent the bombing of Paris in the nick of time. Acting, script, and direction are done in a routine, synthetic fashion. At the time of its original release, the Federation of American Scientists disapproved of using the bomb as the theme of this low-budget picture.

p, Sol M. Wurtzel; d, James Tinling; w, Aubrey Wisberg (based on his story); ph, Penjamin Kline; ed, William F. Claxton; md, Emil Newman; art d, Jerome Pycha.

Spy (PR:A MPAA:NR)

RENDEZVOUS WITH ANNIE**½ (1946) 89m REP bw

Eddie Albert, Faye Marlowe, Gail Patrick, Philip Reed, Sir C. Aubrey Smith, Raymond Walburn, William Frawley, James Millican, Wallace Ford, Will Wright, Lucien Littlefield, Edwin Rand, Mary Field, Richard Sale, Bob Foy.

Albert, a lonely soldier stationed in Britain during WW II, goes AWOL and travels to New York City to visit his wife. His abrupt departure from the military sets into motion a bizarre series of amusing complications that must be sorted out before the happy ending. An innocuous little comedy directed by the amazingly prolific Allan Dwan, who from 1911 to 1961 directed *at least* 400 films (many of his silent masterworks are lost) while producing and writing hundreds more.

p&d, Allan Dwan; w, Richard Sale, Mary Loos; ph, Reggie Lanning; m, Joseph Dubin; ed, Arthur Roberts; md, Cy Feuer; art d, Hilyard Brown; set d, John McCarthy, Jr., George Milo; spec eff, Howard Lydecker, Theodore Lydecker; ch, Fanchon.

Comedy (PR:A MPAA:NR)

RENEGADE GIRL** (1946) 65m Affiliated/Screen Guild bw

Alan Curtis, Ann Savage, Edward Brophy, Russell Wade, Jack Holt, Ray Corrigan, John King, Chief Thunder Cloud, Edmund Cobb, Claudia Drake, Dick Curtis, Nick Thompson, James Martin, Harry Cording.

Curtis is a special agent sent out West to catch Savage, the vixenish leader of a gang of outlaws. Of little interest except to the tiny cult of Ann Savage fans.

p&d, William Berke; w, Edwin K. Westrate; ph, James Brown, Jr.; m, Darrell Calker; ed, Arthur A. Brooks; md, David Chudnow.

Western (PR:A MPAA:NR)

RENEGADE GIRLS*½ (1974) 83m New World c (AKA:CAGED HEAT)

Juanita Brown (*Maggie*), Erica Gavin (*Jackie Wilson*), Roberta Collins (*Belle*), Barbara Steele (*McQueen*), Ella Reid (*Pandora*), Rainbeaux Smith (*Lavelle*), Warren Miller (*Randolph*), Lynda Gold (*Crazy*), Mickey Fox, Desiree Cousteau, Joe Viola, George Armitage, Tobi Carr Rafelson, Ann Stockdale, Irene Stokes, Cynthia Songey, Carmen Argenziano, John Aprea, Leslie Otis, Mike Shack, Patrick Wright, Gary Littlejohn, Hal Marshall, Carol Miller, Cindy Cale, Essie Hayes, Layla Gallaway, Dorothy Love, Bob Reese, Valley Hoffman, Amy Randall, Keisha.

Gavin (formerly of Russ Meyer's VIXEN fame) is sent to a brutal women's prison run by sadistic, wheelchair-bound Steele. Unjustifiably accused of assisting a failed escape attempt, she is subjected to horrible shock treatments by the prison doctor. During a work assignment she and Brown steal a car and escape. They learn that the doctor is planning to lobotomize a fellow inmate, so they decide to go back and rescue her. The pair goes to rob a bank but find a gang of male robbers ahead of them. They rob the robbers and, after stealing a prison van, drive back through the gates. They stop the operation just in the nick of time and take the doctor and Steele hostage. Guards fire on the van and the hostages are killed, but the women escape. Director Demme's auspicious debut transcends the sleazy dictates of its genre and stands along with Stephanie Rothman's TERMINAL ISLAND as a genuine feminist political statement in a milieu lifted straight out of the most misogynistic fantasies of men (RENEGADE GIRLS is all the more notable for having been written and directed by a man). These women aren't passively suffering the indignities heaped on them by men; they take guns and rebel. Even the nudity, obligatory in New World's exploitation mill, is kept to a minimum and deglamorized whenever possible. Steele, a cult favorite for a number of Italian horror films by Mario Bava, does a wonderful turn as the crippled, demented warden. In one superb, spooky scene she fantasizes while dancing with top hat and cane in a bathroom. The viola and harmonica score by ex-Velvet Underground member John Cale is excellent. An exciting film, and one that proves that even the most exploitative of films can make a relevant statement.

p, Evelyn Purcell; d&w, Jonathan Demme; ph, Tak Fujimoto (DeLuxe Color); m, John Cale; ed, Johanna Demetrakis, Carolyn Hicks; art d, Eric Thiermann.

Prison Drama (PR:O MPAA:R)

RENEGADE POSSE (SEE: BULLET FOR A BADMAN, 1964)

RENEGADE RANGER**½ (1938) 60m RKO bw

George O'Brien (*Capt. Jack Steele*), Rita Hayworth (*Judith Alvarez*), Tim Holt (*Larry Corwin*), Ray Whitley (*Happy*), Lucio Villegas (*Juan Capillo*), William Royle (*Ben Sanderson*), Cecilia Callejo (*Tonia Capillo*), Neal Hart (*Sheriff Joe Rawlings*), Monte Montague (*Monte*), Bob Kortman (*Idaho*), Charles Stevens (*Manuel*), James Mason (*Hank*), Tom London (*Red*), Guy Usher (*Maj. Jameson*), Chris-Pin Martin (*Felipe*), Hank Bell (*Barfly*), Jack O'Shea (*Henchman*), Tom Steele, Ken Card.

O'Brien plays the Texas Ranger assigned to bring Hayworth to justice for the murder of a tax collector. But when he catches up to her he finds a fiery lass capable of riding a horse and handling a six-gun better than most men. He also discovers that the local ranchers are all on her side and are feuding with local politico Royle, who is trying to make off with some land. O'Brien teams with Hayworth and Holt to bring the real culprits to justice. This was probably the best of the two dozen oaters O'Brien made for director Howard. Hayworth also exhibited some of the qualities that would make her one of Hollywood's biggest stars. Songs

include "Move Over, Little Doggie" (Willie Phelps), "Senorita" (Albert Hag Malotte; sung by Ray Whitley).

p, Bert Gilroy; d, David Howard; w, Oliver Drake (based on a story by Bennett Cohen); ph, Harry Wild; ed, Frederic Knudtson; md, Roy Webb; art d, Van Nest Polglase, Lucien Croxton.

Western **Cas.** (PR:A MPAA:NR)

RENEGADE TRAIL** (1939) 61m PAR bw

William Boyd (*Hopalong Cassidy*), George "Gabby" Hayes (*Marshal "Windy" Halliday*), Russell Hayden (*Lucky Jenkins*), Charlotte Wynters (*Mary Joyce*), Russell Hopton ("*Smoky" Joslin*), Sonny Bupp (*Joey Joyce*), Jack Rockwell (*Slim*), Roy Barcroft ("*Stiff Hat" Bailey*), John Merton (*Traynor*), Bob Kortman (*Haskins*), Ken Darby, Rad Robinson, Jon Dobson, Bud Linn [The King's Men](*Riders*), Eddie Dean.

Boyd wanders into town to help out his buddy Hayes, a town marshal who has problems with rustlers. But the real heroics start when Boyd tries to impress widow Wynters, who asks him to capture a couple of con artists who are trying to steal her herd. The King's Men handle the musical chores in the 26th "Hopalong Cassidy" film without upsetting the pace of the action; some of their songs include: "Hi Thar Stranger", and "Lazy Rolls the Rio Grande." (See HOPALONG CASSIDY series, Index.)

p, Harry Sherman; d, Lesley Selander; w, John Rathmell, Harrison Jacobs (based on characters created by Clarence E. Mulford); ph, Russell Harlan.

Western (PR:A MPAA:NR)

RENEGADES** (1930) 90m FOX bw

Warner Baxter (*Deucalion*), Myrna Loy (*Eleanore*), Noah Berry, Sr. (*Machwurth*), Gregory Gaye (*Vologuine*), George Cooper (*Biloxi*), C. Henry Gordon (*Capt. Mordiconi*), Colin Chase (*Sgt. Maj. Olson*), Bela Lugosi (*The Marabout*), Victor Jory (*Young Officer*), Noah Beery, Jr., Fred Kohler, Jr. (*Young Legionnaires*).

A confusing plot hurts the good efforts by the cast in this tale of the French Foreign Legion. Baxter heads a small group that includes Beery, Sr., Gordon, and Cooper against desert heathens. Loy, a spy, wanders into camp and turns everything topsy-turvy. A bit more work in the cutting room would have helped. Certain aspects of the plot also were unclear. RENEGADES utilized Movietone, the first sound system to employ sound directly on film.

p, William Fox; d, Victor Fleming; w, Jules Furthman (based on the novel *Le Renegat* by Andre Armandy), ph, L. William O'Connell; ed, Harold Schuster; set d, William Darling; cos, Sophie Wachner; m/l, "I Got What I Wanted" Cliff Friend, Jimmy Monaco; technical advisor, Louis Van Den Ecker.

War/Drama (PR:A MPAA:NR)

RENEGADES**½ (1946) 88m COL c

Evelyn Keyes (*Hannah Brockway*), Willard Parker (*Dr. Sam Martin*), Larry Parks (*Ben "Taylor" Dembrow*), Edgar Buchanan (*Kirk Dembrow*), Jim Bannon (*Cash Dembrow*), Forrest Tucker (*Frank Dembrow*), Ludwig Donath (*Jackorski*), Frank Sully (*Link*), Willard Robertson (*Nathan Brockway*), Paul E. Burns (*Alkali Kid*), Eddy Waller (*Davy Lane*), Vernon Dent (*Caleb Smart*), Francis Ford (*Eph*), Hermine Sterler (*Mrs. Jackorski*), Eileen Janssen (*Janina Jackorski*), Virginia Brissac (*Sarah Dembrow*), Addison Richards (*Sheriff*).

Unusual western plot centers on a woman, Keyes, who finds life with doctor Parker rather dull. She splits with Parks, a member of an outlaw family that includes patriarch Buchanan, Tucker, and Bannon. But, life ouside the law proves too much for Keyes and, despite Parks' attempts to go straight, she winds up back with her doctor in the end. The color photography and all other aspects of production make this a far cry above the normal B western.

p, Michael Kraike; d, George Sherman; w, Melvin Levy, Francis Edwards Faragoh (based on the story by Harold Shumate); ph, William Snyder (Technicolor); m, Paul Sawtell; ed, Charles Nelson; md, M.W. Stoloff; art d, Stephen Goosson, Walter Holscher, Perry Smith; set d, Albert Richerd.

Western (PR:A MPAA:NR)

RENEGADES OF SONORA** (1948) 60m REP bw

Allan "Rocky" Lane, Eddy Waller, William Henry, Douglas Fowley, Roy Barcroft, Frank Fenton, Mauritz Hugo, George J. Lewis, Holly Bane, Dale Van Sickel, Marshall Reed, House Peters, Jr., Art Dillard, Black Jack the Horse.

While on a trip to Wyoming to purchase a ranch, Lane finds himself the victim of a frameup when he is accused of a murder actually done by Barcroft who is after a sacred Indian belt. Lane returns the belt to the tribe proving his innocence & brings Barcroft to justice.

p, Gordon Kay; d, R.G. Springsteen; w, M. Coates Webster; ph, John MacBurnie; m, Stanley Wilson; ed, Tony Martinelli; art d, Frank Arrigo; set d, George Milo; makeup, Howard Smit.

Western (PR:A MPAA:NR)

RENEGADES OF THE RIO GRANDE** (1945) 57m UNIV bw (GB: BANK ROBBERY)

Rod Cameron (*Buck Emerson*), Eddie Dew (*Cal Benedict*), Jennifer Holt (*Dolores Salezar*), Fuzzy Knight (*Trigger Bidwell*), Ray Whitley (*Tex Henry*), Glenn Strange (*Bart Drummond*), Edmund Cobb (*Karl Holbrook*), Dick Alexander (*Pete Jackson*), Iris Clive (*Maria*), John James (*Johnny Emerson*), Dick Bottiler (*Clem*), Jack Casey (*Hank*), Virgil Drake (*Villager*), Hal Hart (*Juan*), Larry McGrath (*Villager*), Roy Butler (*Sheriff*), Ethan Laidlaw, Percy Carson, Ray Whitley's Bar-6 Cowboys.

Seeking vengeance for the murder of his father, Cameron goes undercover as an outlaw to trap the gang of bank robbers responsible. Solid cast of veterans keeps this one on the trail.

p, Oliver Drake; d, Howard Bretherton; w, Ande Lamb; ph, Maury Gertsman; ed, Edward Curtiss; md, Paul Sawtell; art d, John B. Goodman; set d, Russell A. Gausman, Ray L. Jeffers.

Western　　　　　　　　　　　　　**(PR:A　MPAA:NR)**

RENEGADES OF THE SAGE**　　　　　(1949) 56m COL bw

Charles Starrett (Steve Duncan/The Durango Kid), Smiley Burnette (Himself), Leslie Banning (Ellen Miller), Trevor Bardette (Miller), Douglas Fowley (Sloper), Jock O'Mahoney (Lt. Hunter), Fred Sears (Lt. Jones), Jerry Hunter (Johnny), George Chesebro (Worker), Frank McCarroll (Drew), Selmer Jackson (Brown).

Better-than-average series western has government agent Starrett tracking down a gang that has been tearing down telegraph lines. Taking place right at the end of the Civil War, the finger points toward Bardette, a one-time a guerilla band leader. But, the allegation is unfounded, and the real culprits eventually are caught. Action is almost nonstop, with Burnette around for some comic relief. In 1949, the year RENEGADES OF THE SAGE was released, Magazine Enterprises began publishing a Durango Kid comic book. Durango's sidekick looked just like Smiley Burnette but, because the comics could not use the name, the character was renamed Muley Pike. (See DURANGO KID series, Index.)

p, Colbert Clark; d, Ray Nazarro; w, Earle Snell; ph, Fayte Browne; ed, Paul Borofsky; art d, Charles Clague.

Western　　　　　　　　　　　　　**(PR:A　MPAA:NR)**

RENEGADES OF THE WEST*　　　　　(1932) 55m RKO bw

Tom Keene, Betty Furness, Rosco [Roscoe] Ates, Rockcliffe Fellowes, Jack Pennick, Max Wagner, James Mason, Joseph Girard, Joseph Ramos, Billy Franey, Roland Southern, Carl Miller, Josephine Ramous, Jules Cowles.

A remake of THE MIRACLE BABY (1923), which starred Harry Carey, this was to be one of Keene's worst efforts as a western hero. He went through his role without an ounce of enthusiasm. His job in this one was to pursue the cattle thieves who also were responsible for murdering his father. Keene goes undercover and winds up in jail to get the lowdown. A baby adoption story line allowed Keene to display a softer side, but the whole thing comes off as pretty silly.

d, Casey Robinson; w, Albert Shelby LeVino (based on the story by Frank Richardson Pierce); ph, Al Seiger.

Western　　　　　　　　　　　　　**(PR:A　MPAA:NR)**

RENFREW OF THE ROYAL MOUNTED*½　(1937) 57m GN bw

James Newill (Renfrew), Carol Hughes (Virginia Bronson), William Royle (George Hollis), Donald Reed (McDonald), Chief Thundercloud (Pierre), David Barclay [Dave O'Brien](Nolan), William Austin (Constable), Dickie Jones (Tommy), Herbert Corthell (Bronson), Robert Terry (Duke), Kenneth Harlan (Carroll), William Gould (Inspector Newcomb), Lightning the Dog.

In 1937, then-struggling Grand National started production of RENFREW OF THE ROYAL MOUNTED, in the footsteps of a Mountie B feature released by 20th Century Fox in 1936. When the film was made, Grand National characterized its audience largely as small-town theater and neighborhood house goers, who looked to these places as their only source of entertainment during the days of the Depression. This was the first in the short-lived series about the Canadian Mountie hero. Adapted from a radio series, the film's hero was Newill, known for his work as a singer on the Burns and Allen radio show. The action-packed plot is very simple: Newill pursues a group of counterfeiters. Hughes provides the romance angle and a chance for Newill to display his singing talent. Songs include: "Little Son," "Mounted Men," "Barbecue Bill." (See RENFREW series, Index.)

p&d, Al Herman; w, Charles Logue (based on the books by Laurie York Erskine); ph, Francis Corley; ed, Holbrook N. Todd; md, Arthur Kaye.

Western　　　　　　**Cas.**　　　　　**(PR:A　MPAA:NR)**

RENFREW OF THE ROYAL MOUNTED ON THE GREAT WHITE TRAIL　　　(SEE: ON THE GREAT WHITE TRAIL, 1938)

RENFREW ON THE GREAT WHITE TRAIL　　(SEE: ON THE GREAT WHITE TRAIL, 1938)

RENO*　　　　　　　　　　　(1930) 65m Sono-Art-World Wide/WB bw

Ruth Roland (Felicia Brett), Montagu Love (Alexander W. Brett), Kenneth Thompson (Richard Belden), Sam Hardy (J.B. Berkley), Alyce McCormick (Ann Hodge), Edward Hearn (Tom Hodge), Doris Lloyd (Lola Fealy), Judith Vosselli (Rita Rogers), Virginia Ainsworth (Marie), Beulah Monroe (Mrs. Martin), Douglas Scott (Bobby Brett), Emmett King (Judge Cooper), Henry Hall (Prosecuting Attorney), Gayne Whitman (Defending Attorney).

Dull picture has Love and Roland going to Reno to get a divorce, with some of the reasons for divorce revealed during the proceedings The courtroom scenes are the most interesting aspect, and they read like a law book. There is little in this picture to be recommended; even the cast of seasoned pros perform as if this were a high school play. The novel on which the film is based was written by journalist-turned-novelist Cornelius Vanderbilt Jr., son of the wealthy financier.

d, George W. Crone; w, Douglas Churchill, Harry E. Chandlee (based on the novel by Cornelius Vanderbilt, Jr.); ph, Harry Jackson.

Drama　　　　　　　　　　　　　**(PR:A　MPAA:NR)**

RENO**½　　　　　　　　　　(1939) 73m RKO bw

Richard Dix (Bill Shear), Gail Patrick (Jessie Gibbs), Anita Louise (Mrs. Ryder), Paul Cavanagh (John Banton), Laura Hope Crews (Mrs. Gardner), Louis Jean Heydt (Judge Howard), Hobart Cavanaugh (Abe Compass), Charles Halton (Welch), Astrid Allwyn (Flora McKenzie), Joyce Compton (Bonnie), Frank Faylen (Hezzy Briggs), William Haade (George Fields), Carole Landis (Bit).

This epic yarn concentrates on the development of the title city from a small silver-mining town to a divorce and gambling center. Dix plays a young lawyer who seizes upon the lenient divorce laws to build up a solid practice while ignoring wife Patrick. As irony would have it she leaves him, with Dix receiving flack when the city's elite go into some hokum about maintaining virtue. This leads to Dix's disbarment and his opening a gambling casino. Years later the daughter he never knew, Louise, comes to Reno to get a divorce. Although their relationship is unknown to her, Dix talks her out of a divorce; she then realizes their tie, and both leave the city behind. A story that could easily fall into undue sentiment, but keeps out of that trap, with Dix lending a solid air of conviction to his portrayal. This was the third of three pictures with the same title; all had very different plots. Landis, who had had a featured role in FOUR'S A CROWD the year before, played a bit part in this film. A year later, the shapely blonde hit it big as a cavegirl in ONE MILLION B. C.

p, Robert Sisk; d, John Farrow; w, John Twist (based on the story by Ellis St. Joseph); ph, J. Roy Hunt; ed, Harry Marker; md, Roy Webb; art d, Van Nest Polglase.

Drama　　　　　　　　　　　　　**(PR:A　MPAA:NR)**

"RENT-A-GIRL"*　　　　(1965) 77m Corsair/Cambist-Lambs bw (AKA: RENTED)

Barbara Wood, Frank Spencer, Inge Christopher, David Ransom, Teresa Morgano, Elizabeth Walker, Gary Takata, Darlene Bennett, Paul Dare, June Roberts, Margareta Lindblom, Gigi Darlene.

This silly sadism story has a woman getting a job at a New York modeling agency only to discover it specializes in offering more than just models; the firm is a front for prostitution with wealthy, kinky clients. When the new girl is asked to come to a party, she discovers an orgy going on in which she is the main attraction. She goes into hysterics and winds up being beaten and branded by the host. But the rest of the girls revolt, and the operation is ended.

p,d&w, William L. Rose; ph, Maximillian Strasser, Bernie Smith; set d, Eda Buschatzky.

Drama　　　　　　　　　　　　　**(PR:O　MPAA:NR)**

RENT CONTROL***　　　　　　　(1981) 95m Group S c

Brent Spiner (Leonard), Elizabeth Stack (Anne), Leonard Melfi (Milton), Jeanne Ruskin (Margaret), Annie Korzen (Nancy), Leslie Cifarelli (Barbara), Charles Lalken (Jim), Roy Brocksmith (Stan), Anita Bosic (Mrs. Spovic), Robin Pogrebin (Shelley), Abigail Pogrebin (Sharon), Kimberly Stern (Jeanne).

Witty comedy features Spiner as an aspiring writer whose wife has run off with a cosmetician. Spiner is living with relatives and sets out on a near-impossible quest for a rent-controlled apartment in Manhattan, believing $300-a-month, two-bedroom living quarters will help him put his life and his marriage back together. His search is fraught with complications as he gets embroiled in a newspaper's efforts to reveal a senator's involvement in murder. Despite its obvious low-budget origins, RENT CONTROL is an amusing satire with solid performances from its cast of relative unknowns. Elizabeth Stack, who plays a newspaper editor, is the daughter of actor Robert Stack.

p, Benni Korzen; d, Gian L. Polidoro; w, John Menegold, Sherill Tippins; ph, Benito Frattari; m, Oscar De Mejo, Ian North; ed, Ed Orshan, Jim Cookman.

Comedy　　　　　　　　　　　　　**(PR:C　MPAA:NR)**

RENTADICK**　　　　(1972, Brit.) 94m Rank-Paradine/Virgin c

James Booth, Richard Briers, Julie Ege, Donald Sinden, Roy Kinnear, Michael Bentine, Ronald Fraser, Spike Milligan.

A secret gas which paralyzes its victims from the waist down is stolen. It's up to the incompetent detectives of Rentadick, Inc. to track down the criminals and stop their evil plans. At times this comedy, penned by Cleese and Chapman of television's "Monty Python's Flying Circus", has some wonderful moments, but overall it is a hit-and-mostly-miss spoof. Rather than stick with a central theme, the humor meanders off onto tangents which kill it. That sort of formula worked well with the Python's half-hour television show, but it's not enough to sustain a feature-length film.

p, Ned Sherrin; d, Jim Clark; w, John Cleese, Graham Chapman; ph, John Coquillon (Eastmancolor); m, Carl Davis.

Comedy　　　　　　　　　　　　　**(PR:O　MPAA:NR)**

RENTED　　　　　　　　(SEE: "RENT-A-GIRL", 1965)

REPEAT PERFORMANCE**½　　　(1947) 91m Bryan Foy/EL bw

Louis Hayward (Barney Page), Joan Leslie (Sheila Page), Richard Basehart (William Williams), Virginia Field (Paula Costello), Tom Conway (John Friday), Natalie Schafer (Eloise Shaw), Benay Venuta (Bess Nichols), Ilka Gruning (Mattie).

Legitimate theater star Leslie is on her way to seek advice from a friend after having just murdered her alcoholic husband on New Year's Eve. She wishes she had the entire year to live over again to prevent her from performing her evil deed. Lo and behold, her wish is granted, but things don't change at all as she finds her husband being shot once again. But she also discovers she wasn't the person to do the shooting; a friend who had just gone over the edge is the real killer. This was the screen debut of Basehart (VOYAGE TO THE BOTTOM OF THE SEA, MOBY DICK) after he won the New York Drama Critics' award; he plays the poet friend who goes crazy and shoots husband Hayward. Why he goes crazy is never fully explained, which is one of the problems with this script; it is slack in areas of motivation. All other aspects are up to par in what could have been a nice little shot at man's ability to control his fate. This was Eagle Lion's first try at a big-budget, all-star-cast feature; it was a notable failure due to the overacting of Hayward and the totally unsympathetic performance of Leslie, in her first film since a bitter, litigious altercation with Warner Bros. The film also marked the movie debut of musical-comedy star Venuta in a non-singing, non-dancing straight dramatic role.

p, Aubrey Schenck; d, Alfred Werker; w, Walter Bullock (based on the novel by William O'Farrell); ph, Lew O'Connell; m, George Antheil; ed, Alfred DeGaetano, Louis H. Sackin; md, Irving Friedman; art d, Edward C. Jewell; set d, Armor Marlowe.

Drama   (PR:A MPAA:NR)

REPENT AT LEISURE*½   (1941) 66m RKO bw

Kent Taylor (Richard Hughes), Wendy Barrie (Emily Baldwin), George Barbier (R.C. Baldwin), Thurston Hall (Buckingham), Charles Lane (Morgan), Nella Walker (Mrs. Baldwin), Rafael Storm (Prince Paul), Ruth Dietrich (Miss Flynn), Cecil Cunningham (Mrs. Morgan), Fred "Snowflake" Toones (Rufe), George Chandler (Conductor), Charles Coleman (Butler), Hooper Atchley (Floorwalker), Jane Patten (Richard's Secretary), Jack Briggs (Stockboy), Virginia Vale (Elevator Girl), Michael Dunaway (Baby Richard), Eddie Arden (Messenger), Dorothy Lee (Flip Salesgirl), Wanda Cantlon (Salesgirl), Paul Lepere, Barbara Burke (Clerks), Georgia Backus (Nurse), Norman Mayes (Porter).

A scatter-shot ending does in this light love story. Impetuous Barrie wants a good American man for marriage who is not just in it for her money, instead of her current husband, a greedy foreigner. She takes up with and marries a tie salesman in her father's store without telling him who she is, and he thereupon gets one promotion after another. Learning at last who his wife is related to, in anger he joins forces with the competition. The muddled ending has the two trying to make up with one wild scene that involves the child the pair had adopted and a merger of the two stores. A big enough turkey to feed several families.

p, Cliff Reid; d, Frank Woodruff; w, Jerry Cady (based on a story by James Gow, Arnaud D'Usseau); ph, Nicholas Musuraca; ed, Harry Marker; spec eff, Vernon L. Walker.

Drama   (PR:A MPAA:NR)

REPLICA OF A CRIME   (SEE: MANIAC MANSION, 1978, Ital.)

REPORT ON THE PARTY AND THE GUESTS, A**   (1968,
Czech.) 70m Barrandov Film Studio-Ceskoslovensky/Sigma III bw (O
                                                    SLAVNOSTI A HOSTECH)

Ivan Vyskocil (Host), Jan Klusak (Rudolf), Jiri Nemec (Josef), Zdena Skvorecka (Eva), Pavel Bosek (Frantisek), Helena Pejskova (Marta), Karel Mares (Karel), Jana Pracharova (Wife), Evald Schorm (Husband).

Seven people decide to picnic in the woods and come across a group with Klusak as their leader. Klusak takes them to a clearing and starts brutally interrogating them as a game. His authority is challenged by one of the picnickers and Klusak promptly abuses him. Another stranger arrives, apologizes for Klusak's behavior, and takes the group to a banquet. Not seated properly, they are ordered to change seats, when it is discovered that one of the guests has departed because he is still angry at Klusak. Saying that the man's behavior is ruining the banquet, the host gets up a party with dogs and guns to search for the missing man. A bizarre ending to what started out as a beautiful day. Another Czechoslovakian "new wave" entry by talented director Nemec, whose fascination with the themes of persecution and oppression provide fuel for his controversial experimental style.

d, Jan Nemec; w, Ester Krumbachova, Nemec (based on a story by Krumbachova); ph, Jaromir Sofr; m, Karel Mares; ed, Miroslav Hajek; art d, Oldrich Bosak; cos, Krumbachova.

Drama   (PR:A MPAA:NR)

REPORT TO THE COMMISSIONER**½   (1975) 112m UA c (GB:
                                                    OPERATION UNDERCOVER)

Michael Moriarty (Beauregard "Bo" Lockley), Yaphet Kotto (Richard "Crunch" Blackstone), Susan Blakely (Patty Butler), Hector Elizondo (Capt. d'Angelo), Tony King (Thomas "Stock" Henderson), Michael McGuire (Lt. Hanson), Edward Grover (Capt. Strichter), Dana Elcar (Chief Perna), Robert Balaban (Joey Egan), William Devane (Assistant District Attorney Jackson), Stephen Elliott (Police Commissioner), Richard Gere (Billy), Vic Tayback (Lt. Seidensticker), Albert Seedman (Detective Schulman), Noelle North (Samantha), Bebe Drake Hooks (Dorothy), Sonny Grosso, Lee Delano, Vincent Van Lynn, Bob Golden (Detectives).

The sedentary title works against this police film in the SERPICO and PRINCE OF THE CITY vein. Police commissioner Elliott gives underling Grover the assignment of finding out why Blakely, an undercover police officer, was killed when the apartment she shared with narcotics czar King was raided. In a flashback, we learn that Moriarty, a young detective, was on the case and didn't know Blakely was working for the cops. The investigation is bogged down in a series of bureaucratic maneuvers and it becomes more a character study of the men behind the badges as we meet Elizondo and McGuire, two dedicated cops whose only knowledge of the Miranda Act is when they saw Carmen sing and dance. Elcar leads the undercover narcotics squad and Devane is one of those barracuda prosecutors who will stop at nothing to get a conviction. Moriarty has been teamed with Kotto, his senior in the department, and the two men try their best to do their jobs but are detoured at every crossroads by the politics of the department. There are only two action sequences of any note with the major one being a confrontation in a department store elevator between Moriarty and King as they draw their guns on each other and wait to see who fires first. Mann and Tidyman attempted to mix social commentary with the gritty realism but Katselas directed everyone at such a breakneck pace that many of the actors sounded like tobacco auctioneers hawking their bright leaf. Good work from Balaban as a street person to whom Moriarty has shown some sympathy and Tayback, as Moriarty's immediate boss. In a small role, note Richard Gere as a sleazy pimp. A couple of songs are heard for no apparent reason.

p, M.J. Frankovich; d, Milton Katselas; w, Abby Mann, Ernest Tidyman (based on the novel by James Mills); ph, Mario Tosi (Metrocolor); m, Elmer Bernstein; ed, David Blewitt; prod d, Robert Clatworthy; set d, John Kuri; cos, Anna Hill Johnstone; m/l, Vernon Burch, Spencer Proffer, Jeffrey Marmelzat (sung by Burch); stunts, Paul Baxley.

Crime Drama   **Cas. (PR:C MPAA:PG)**

REPORTED MISSING*½   (1937) 64m UNIV bw

William Gargan (Steve Browning), Jean Rogers (Jean Clayton), Dick Purcell (Paul Wayne), Hobart Cavanaugh (Al Steele), Michael Fitzmaurice (Jack Clayton), Joseph Sawyer (Brad Martin), Billy Wayne (Duffy), Robert Spencer (Bill Evans), Jack Carson.

The old ogre story with an up-to-date twist, resembling that of the seafaring ship salvors who darken the lighthouse to cause ships to founder on a rocky coastline, this thriller has enough turns to keep the audience interested. Gargan is a former pilot who invents a navigating device. The test-run plane crashes, as do a couple of others; all the crashes are followed by robberies of the corpses of rich passengers. Gargan sets out to discover the bad guy and is on the edge of catching him every time. But the audience doesn't discover who the villain is until the end, with the story line winding it up in a nice, neat package.

p, E.M. Asher; d, Milton Carruth; w, Jerome Chodorov, Joseph Fields (based on the story "Channel Crossing" by Verne Whitehead); ph, George Robinson; ed, Paul Landres.

Thriller   (PR:A MPAA:NR)

REPRIEVE   (SEE: CONVICTS FOUR, 1962)

REPRIEVED   (SEE: SING SING NIGHTS, 1935)

REPRISAL**   (1956) 74m COL c

Guy Madison (Frank Madden), Felicia Farr (Catherine Cantrell), Kathryn Grant (Taini), Michael Pate (Bert Shipley), Edward Platt (Neil Shipley), Otto Hulett (Sheriff Jim Dixon), Wayne Mallory (Tom Shipley), Robert Burton (Jeb Cantrell), Ralph Moody (Matara), Frank de Kova (Charlie Washackle), Paul McGuire (Whitey), Don Rhodes (Buck), Phillip Breedlove (Takola), Malcolm Atterbury (Luther Creel), Eve McVeagh (Nora Shipley), Victor Zamudio (Keleni), Pete Kellett (Foreman), Jack Lomas (Bartender), Addison Richards (Judge), John Zaremba (Mister Willard).

Indian gets revenge on the white man is the theme here. Madison is the part-Indian who buys some land to raise beef in an anti-Indian area of Oklahoma. His newly purchased land happens to be adjacent to that of three Indian-hating brothers who were recently found innocent of killing two Indians for being on their property. While the white Farr sets her sights on Madison, he does battle with the brothers, finally killing two of them to end his troubles. One of the brothers had been killed earlier by another Indian. Madison doesn't say much in the film, letting his actions and Farr and Grant do most of the talking. Grant, often stereotyped in Indian-maiden roles, is the sympathetic squaw who claims she has bedded Madison in order to give him an alibi and save him from a lynch mob.

p, Lewis J. Rachmil; d, George Sherman; w, David P. Harmon, Raphael Hayes, David Dortort (based on the novel by Arthur Gordon); ph, Henry Freulich (Technicolor); m, Mischa Bakaleinikoff; ed, Jerome Thoms; md, Bakaleinikoff; art d, Walter Holscher.

Western   (PR:A MPAA:NR)

REPTILE, THE*½   (1966, Brit.) 90m Seven Arts-Hammer/FOX c

Noel Willman (Dr. Franklyn), Jennifer Daniel (Valerie), Ray Barrett (Harry), Jacqueline Pearce (Anna), Michael Ripper (Tom Bailey), John Laurie (Mad Peter), Marne Maitland (Malay), David Baron (Charles Spalding), Charles Lloyd Pack (Vicar), Harold Goldblatt (Solicitor), George Woodbridge (Old Garnsey).

People in a Cornish village start turning up black and dead, sending the villagers into hysterics. Barrett comes into town with his wife to investigate his brother's death and is met with hostility and silence. After snooping around, he finds out his brother died from a snakebite and finds out Pearce is the victim of a Malayan curse that turns her into a snake when she contacts heat. Barrett is bitten by the snake/human and when his wife Daniel comes to the rescue, a fire starts, turning Pearce into an enormous reptile. The reptile attacks her own father before dying in the flames while Daniel and Barrett escape. A mild thriller where the monster has human characteristics.

p, Anthony Nelson Keys; d, John Gilling; w, John Elder [Anthony Hinds]; ph, Arthur Grant; m, Don Banks; ed, James Needs, Roy Hyde; md, Philip Martell; prod d, Bernard Robinson; art d, Don Mingaye; spec eff, Bowie Films; makeup, Roy Ashton.

Horror   (PR:C MPAA:NR)

REPTILICUS*   (1962, U.S./Den.) 81m Saga Film-Cinemagic-Alta Vista/
                                                                        AIP c

Carl Ottosen (Mark Grayson), Ann Smyrner (Lise Martens), Mimi Heinrich (Karen Martens), Asbjorn Andersen (Prof. Martens), Marla Behrens (Connie Miller), Bent Mejding (Svend Viltofft), Poul Wildaker (Dr. Dalby), Dirk Passer (Dirk Mikkelsen), Ole Wisborg (Capt. Brandt), Bodil Miller, Mogens Brandt, Kjeld Petersen, Alex Suhr, Alfred Wilken, Bent Vejlby, Knud Hallest, Benny Juhlin, Martin Stander, Borge Moller Grimstrup, Hardy Jensen, Poul Thomsen, Svend Johansen, Jorgen Blaksted, Birthe Wilke, Claus Toksvig.

A fair-to-poor monster film has a group of oil drillers coming up with the mangled tail of some prehistoric beast (the film's most gruesome and best scene). Sent to a famous professor for study, a door is accidentally left open and the tail starts to regenerate. It grows into a fierce beast that wreaks havoc on Copenhagen. American troops can't stop the beast but are able to force it into the water. A depth charge severs its feet but it still keeps up the devastation of Copenhagen. Finally, a deadly drug is shot into the monster, and it seems to perish. But those feet are still around and growing by the minute.

p&d, Sidney Pink; w, Ib Melchior, Pink (based on a story by Pink); ph, Aage Wiltrup (Pathecolor); m, Sven Gyldmark; ed, Svend Mehling, Edith Nisted Nielsen; md, Gyldmark; set d, Otto Lund, Helge Hansen, Kai Koed.

Horror **(PR:A MPAA:NR)**

REPULSION***** (1965, Brit.) 104m Compton-Tekli/Royal bw

Catherine Deneuve *(Carol Ledoux)*, Ian Hendry *(Michael)*, John Fraser *(Colin)*, Patrick Wymark *(Landlord)*, Yvonne Furneaux *(Helen Ledoux)*, Renee Houston *(Miss Balch)*, Helen Fraser *(Bridget)*, Valerie Taylor *(Mme. Denise)*, James Villiers *(John)*, Hugh Futcher *(Reggie)*, Mike Pratt *(Workman)*, Monica Merlin *(Mrs. Rendlesham)*, Imogen Graham *(Manicurist)*, Roman Polanski *(Spoons Player)*.

Quite simply, REPULSION is one of the most frightening pictures ever made. It has in many instances been compared to Hitchcock's PSYCHO (1960) (which Polanski won't deny), but instead of presenting a portrait of a psychotic killer, REPULSION pulls the audience into the mind of the individual, in this case Catherine Deneuve. She plays a Belgian manicurist working in Paris and living in an apartment with her sister. She slowly becomes unhinged from reality due to her feelings on sex, a simultaneous repulsion and attraction. She innocently walks into her bathroom one day to find her sister's lover, Hendry, shaving—an act she finds too intimate and thereby disturbing. That evening she lays quietly in her bed listening to the sound of her sister's lovemaking from the next room, hiding her head under her pillow. With her sister taking a holiday in Italy, Deneuve is left to fend for herself, becoming more and more detached from the outside world. She takes little interest in her surroundings (a potato begins to mold, as does a skinned rabbit ready for cooking) or appearance, wandering around in a zombie-like trance. Her coworkers notice her state and a friend tries to cheer her up by telling her the plot of Chaplin's THE GOLD RUSH, but realizes that she is getting nowhere with Deneuve. She then notices that in Deneuve's purse is the head of the rabbit, rotting from the heat. After absent-mindedly injuring a woman during a manicure, Deneuve is sent home for some rest. Once home she locks herself in, pulls the phone from the wall after an obscene phone call (meant for her sister from the wife of Hendry), and begins to hallucinate. The most frightening shot in the picture lasts for just a fraction of a second. As Deneuve is opening a wardrobe she glimpses the reflection of a man standing in her room. She turns and he is gone. These hallucinations become more intense as her grasp on sanity loosens: the walls crack with a blistering crispness; lights turn on and off; a man (who previously whistled at her on the street) appears in her room and rapes her. Meanwhile the potato continues to rot and flies buzz around the decapitated rabbit carcass. Fraser, a male admirer/boy friend, pays a visit and expresses concern for Deneuve. He begs for her to let him in, but she refuses, speaking to him only through her frontdoor peephole (which grotesquely distorts his face). Frustrated by her obstinancy, he smashes through the door, and Deneuve bludgeons him to death with a candlestick. She then half-heartedly wipes up the blood and places the corpse in the bathtub. Her hallucinations have become more intense by now—the hallway becomes a deathtrap as arms burst through the plaster (two of them belonging to screenwriter Brach) and grab at her. Eventually the landlord calls on her, concerned about the month's rent. He struggles through the barricaded door, appalled at the condition of the flat. When he sees Deneuve barely clad in her nightgown, he assumes it to be an advance. Armed with Hendry's razor, Deneuve slashes out at the shocked old man, again and again, striking in both fear and anger, releasing all her pent up sexual inhibitions. When her sister returns with her lover from Italy, she finds the two blood-spattered bodies and Deneuve burrowed under the living room couch. They call the police and an ambulance and try to comfort the traumatized girl. Curious and frightened neighbors (like those in THE TENANT and ROSEMARY'S BABY) peer at her and the scene she's created. The final shot is a remarkable feat. After panning the living room, the camera zooms into a family portrait on a mantel, into a close-up on Deneuve, and then into an extreme, full screen close-up of her eye. In an interview with Ivan Butler, Alastair McIntyre comments on that amazingly difficult final shot: "It was made in three shots. First the camera zoomed in as close as possible to the photograph, but we couldn't get anywhere like near enough to the eye. So we had an enormous blow-up made of the picture, much bigger than the wall of an ordinary room. We tracked in again as far as we could, but even this wasn't enough, so we continued with a miniature camera right into the girl's eye, and the three shots were joined together by 'invisible' dissolves." Essentially REPULSION tells a simple story, but it is Polanski's direction which makes it so undeniably brilliant. He took great pains in creating the proper composition for the shot of the razor blade, for getting the plaster to crack just right, and for constructing a hallway which not only seemed to expand and elongate throughout the picture, but actually did with the help of wall panels. A powerfully engrossing film, which owes much to the realistic, nearly silent performance of Deneuve.

p, Gene Gutowski; d, Roman Polanski; w, Polanski, Gerard Brach, David Stone; ph, Gilbert Taylor; m, Chico Hamilton; ed, Alastair McIntyre; md, Hamilton; art d, Seamus Flannery.

Drama **Cas.** **(PR:O MPAA:NR)**

REPUTATION (SEE: LADY WITH A PAST, 1932)

REQUIEM FOR A GUNFIGHTER½** (1965) 91m Premiere Productions/EM c

Rod Cameron *(Dave McCloud)*, Stephen McNally *(Red Zimmer)*, Chet Douglas *(Larry Young)*, Mike Mazurki *(Ivy Bliss)*, Tim McCoy *(Judge Irving Short)*, Johnny Mack Brown *(Enkoff)*, Chris Hughes *(Billy Parker)*, Olive Sturgess *(Bonnie Young)*, Lane Chandler *(Bryan Comer)*, Bob Steele *(Max)*, Raymond Hatton *(Hoops)*, Dick Jones *(Fletcher)*, Rand Brooks *(Gentry)*, Dale Van Sickel *(Kelly)*, Doris Spiegel, Zon Murray, Frank Lackteen, Ronn Delanor, Edmund Cobb, Margo Williams, Dick Alexander, Fred Carson, Red Morgan.

A better-than-average shoot 'em-up-western has professional gunfighter Cameron mistaken for a judge in a small town plagued by McNally and his henchmen. Only a local couple knows his true identity and they talk him into keeping the peace and staging the trial for one of the bad guys. But outlaw Jones recognizes Cameron and reveals his true identity in the middle of the trial. A duel is staged and in a classic scene, Cameron shoots the gun out of Jones' hand, throws down his own gun and rides off into the sunset, never to fight again. The gang members are arrested and the local citizens talk Cameron into taking up residence in their town. Brown, who had made numerous westerns and B movies throughout the 1930s and 1940s, returned to the screen after an 11-year absence in REQUIEM FOR A GUNFIGHTER. He also appeared in THE BOUNTY HUNTER that year and in APACHE UPRISING the following year. The former University of Alabama All-American football player then retired to his Woodland Hills, California home where he died in 1974 at the age of 70.

p, Alex Gordon; d, Spencer G. Bennett; w, R. Alexander (based on a story by Evans W. Cornell, Guy J. Tedesco); ph, Frederick E. West (Techniscope, Technicolor); m, Ronald Stein; ed, Charles H. Powell; art d, Don Ament.

Western **(PR:A MPAA:NR)**

REQUIEM FOR A HEAVYWEIGHT*½** (1962) 85m COL bw

Anthony Quinn *(Mountain Rivera)*, Jackie Gleason *(Maish Rennick)*, Mickey Rooney *(Army)*, Julie Harris *(Grace Miller)*, Stanley Adams *(Perelli)*, Mme. Spivey *(Ma Greeny)*, Herbie Faye *(Bartender)*, Jack Dempsey *(Himself)*, Cassius Clay [Muhammad Ali] *(Ring Opponent)*, Steve Belloise *(Hotel Desk Clerk)*, Lou Gilbert *(Ring Doctor)*, Arthur Mercante *(Referee)*, Val Avery, Rory Calhoun, Barney Ross, Alex Miteff, Willie Pep, J.J. Balargeon, Michael Conrad, Gus Lesnevich, Paoli Rossi, Abe Simon, Stan Ross.

Rod Serling's classic teleplay that won him an Emmy and showed Jack Palance to be an actor of some power came to the big screen some six years later, with Anthony Quinn giving an even better performance in the title role. As Mountain Rivera, Quinn is a veteran of 17 years in the ring, and the victor of 111 fights, but as the film begins he is beaten senseless by a younger and faster opponent (Cassius Clay, soon to be known as heavyweight champion Muhammad Ali), and is finally knocked out in the seventh round. After the fight a doctor tells him that if he fights again he will probably be blinded, so Quinn retires from the ring and tries to find another job. Gleason, Quinn's manager, is upset by this turn of events, particularly with Quinn lasting past the fourth round when he had placed a large bet with Spivey that he would not do so, a bet Gleason is now unable to pay off. Quinn goes to employment counselor Harris and she tries to get him several jobs, but when he goes to interview for a job as athletic director at a summer camp, Gleason gets him drunk and prevents him from getting the job. He tries to persuade Quinn to turn to the fake world of professional wrestling using his American Indian heritage as a gimmick to help him get the money. At first Quinn refuses to strip himself of his dignity in that way and he is shocked that his old friend would have bet against him in, but when he sees that Gleason's life is really in danger if he doesn't come up with $3,000, he relents and enters the ring in a war bonnet, waving a tomahawk and doing a dance, the last of his self-respect gone. An unforgettable film, with one of Quinn's very best performances, and excellent support from Gleason and Rooney, but the whole thing misses the mark just slightly. Director Nelson also helmed the "Playhouse 90" production in 1956 and wanted to do the film version with the same script. This was found to be too short for feature consumption so scenes originally dropped from the teleplay were reinserted over Nelson's objections. He asked that his name be removed from the credits, but it wasn't. Quinn and Gleason reportedly argued frequently on the set over details of their respective acting styles. Technically, the film is less impressive than the TV version, in which the very limitations of live studio shooting called for greater ingenuity in moving the camera and making scene transitions. Instead of the freedom of the movie camera liberating the film, it simply allows it to be done in the standard way. Gleason, who is either superb or embarrassing, is the former here, conveying desperation and fear so convincingly that we can see why Quinn humiliates himself for the benefit of his old friend. Rooney also is impressive and, in one card-playing scene, he steals the show from Gleason. Most of the faults of the film can be attributed to the very thing that Nelson objected to. The scenes cut from the teleplay were cut for very good reasons; they slow the story down with needless repetition of points already strongly made. Quinn, as a man whose whole life has been boxing and who now must leave it behind, along with what dignity he acquired through his noble suffering, and who in the end debases himself for the benefit of a friend who really isn't, to show that he has real honor, is truly outstanding.

p, David Susskind; d, Ralph Nelson; w, Rod Serling (based on his TV play); ph, Arthur J. Ornitz; m, Laurence Rosenthal; ed, Carl Lerner; art d, Burr Smidt; set d, Francis J. Brady; cos, John Boxer.

Drama **Cas.** **(PR:C MPAA:NR)**

REQUIEM FOR A SECRET AGENT* (1966, Ital.) 94m Intercontinental-Metheus c

Stewart Granger *(John "Bingo" Merrill)*, Daniela Bianchi *(Edith)*, Peter Van Eyck *(Oscar Gregory)*, Guilio Borsetti *(Eric)*, Georgia Moll *(Mrs. Bressart)*, Gianni Rizzo *(Alexei)*, Maria Granada *(Betty Lou)*, France Andrei *(O'Brien)*, Wolf Hillinger, Benny Deus.

One of the many James Bond clones made in the 1960s, this one had Granger as a veteran of the spy world who is hired to put a stop to the covert activities of an evil secret organization. Bianchi provides the love interest as a woman whose parents were murdered by the head of the organization. Shot in Tangiers, the scenery is lovely, but the plot empty.

d, Sergio Sollima; w, Sollima, Sergio Donati; ph, Carlo Carlini; m, Antonio Perez Olea.

Action/Adventure   **(PR:A MPAA:NR)**

RESCUE SQUAD*   (1935) 61m Empire bw

Ralph Forbes, Verna Hillie, Leon Waycoff [Ames], Kate Pentzer, Sheila Terry, Beth Bartman, Frank Leigh, Catherine Cotter, Jimmy Aubrey.

The never-ending battle against arson, explosions, oily rags and smoking in bed are chronicled here with a squadron of brave firemen putting their lives on the line daily. Naturally, the work-related stress puts a strain on the personal lives of the firefighters, and their efforts to cope are detailed as well.

d, Spencer Gordon Bennett; w, George Morgan, Betty Burbridge (based on a story by Charlotte Arthur, Margel Gluck); ph, Gilbert Warrenton.

Drama   **(PR:A MPAA:NR)**

RESCUE SQUAD, THE**   (1963, Brit.) 54m World Wide/Childrens Film
Foundation bw

Christopher Brett (Bill), Shirley Joy (Ann), Malcolm Knight (Tom), Gareth Tandy (Charlie), Linda Leo (Carol), Danny Grove (Joe), Renee Houston (Mrs. Manse), Leslie French (Mr. Manse), Michael Balfour (Barrow-Boy), Peter Butterworth (Mr. Maggs).

Mildly interesting children's film about a group of kids who become trapped in a decrepit old tower after venturing in to retrieve a toy airplane that had flown inside.

p, Hindle Edgar; d, Colin Bell; w, Mary Cathcart Borer (based on a story by Frank Wells).

Drama   **(PR:A MPAA:NR)**

THE RESCUERS***   (1977) 76m Disney c

The voices of: Bob Newhart (Bernard), Eva Gabor (Miss Bianca), Geraldine Page (Mme. Medusa), Joe Flynn (Mr. Snoops), Jeanette Nolan (Ellie Mae), Pat Buttram (Luke), Jim Jordan (Orville), John McIntire (Rufus), Michelle Stacy (Penny), Bernard Fox (Chairman), Larry Clemmons (Gramps), James MacDonald (Evinrude), George Lindsey (Rabbit), Bill McMillan (TV Announcer), Dub Taylor (Digger), John Fiedler (Owl).

Four years in the making and costing nearly $8 million, THE RESCUERS was a beautifully animated film which showed that the Disney studio still knew a lot about making quality children's fare. The story concerns two mice, with voices provided by Newhart and Gabor, who set out to rescue a girl (Stacy) from the evil Mme. Medusa (Page). The girl is held captive in a swamp, which offers the setting for some genuinely frightening action. Comic relief is provided by a bird named Orville, who transports the mice as they search for the girl. The voices are all well-suited to the characters, and the film is a delight for children, as well as adults who appreciate good animation and brisk storytelling. The music nicely complements the story and includes: "The Journey," "Rescue Aid Society," and "Tomorrow Is Another Day" (Carol Conners, Ayn Robbins); "Someone's Waiting For You" (Connors, Robbins, Sammy Fain, sung by Shelby Flint); and "The U.S. Air Force Song" (Robert Crawford).

p, Wolfgang Reitherman; d, Reitherman, John Lounsbery, Art Stevens; w, Ken Anderson, Vance Gerry, Larry Clemmons, David Michener, Burny Mattinson, Frank Thomas, Fred Lucky, Ted Berman, Dick Sebast (based on the stories "The Rescuers" and "Miss Bianca" by Margery Sharp); ph, (Technicolor); m, Artie Butler; ed, James Melton, Jim Koford; anim d, Ollie Johnston, Frank Thomas, Milt Kahl, Don Bluth; art d, Don Griffith.

Animation/Fantasy   **(PR:AAA MPAA:G)**

RESERVED FOR LADIES***   (1932, Brit.) 71m PAR bw (GB: SERVICE FOR LADIES)

Leslie Howard (Max Tracey), George Grossmith (Mr. Westlake), Benita Hume (Countess Ricardi), Elizabeth Allan (Sylvia Robertson), Morton Selten (Mr. Robertson), Cyril Ritchard (Sir William Carter), Ben Field (Breslmeyer), Annie Esmond (Duchess), Martita Hunt (Aline the French Maid), Gilbert Davis (Chef), Merle Oberon.

This wonderfully witty comedy features Howard as the headwaiter in a posh London hotel restaurant. One fine day Allan and her father, Selten, in from South Africa, come to dine and, of course, it's love at first sight for Howard. Realizing that his social standing is well below Allan's, the clever man concocts a scheme to fool his would-be love. Howard follows Allan when she goes off on a trip to the Austrian Tyrol, but his plans are nearly foiled when he is recognized as a favorite waiter of king Grossmith. The quick-thinking servitor explains his dilemma to the monarch, who promises to keep Howard's true identity secret. He invites Howard to take a seat at the royal table during a dinner, which leads Allan to believe the charming and handsome gentleman is actually a prince. Eventually the two must return to the hotel, where Howard's identity is revealed to Allan. She is angered by this revelation and vows to humiliate the spurious prince. Try though she may, Howard is able to overcome her attempts, and he finally wins her favors when Selten tells his daughter that his own rise to power began with the simple position of dishwasher. There is no disgrace in loving someone of another social class, he tells her, particularly someone as charming and ambitious as Howard. Originally filmed in 1927 as SERVICE FOR LADIES with Adolphe Menjou, this version holds up nicely, though dated by technique. The lighter-than-air story is well told, keeping things moving at a fine clip. Though the dialog is a touch overwritten, the ensemble is a tight one, all delivering their lines with smart comic timing. Howard was already a success in Hollywood at this point in his career but he came back to his native England for this picture. This marked the first British directorial effort for Korda and, despite the programmer status of the production, he did a fine job. Howard, a product of Hungarian parents, upon being told his director was the Hungarian Korda, responded, "I have heard of Maria Corda, the actress. Any relation?"

Paramount's British studios usually pumped more money into their quota productions than other British film companies, and executives were highly impressed by what Korda had turned out. Though budgets were small by comparison with Hollywood productions, Korda was given enough money to come up with a fine example of light comedy at its best. In her book *Alexander Korda: The Man Who Could Work Miracles*, author Karol Kulik recounted a story where the talented director was confronted by a studio executive visiting from California. Surprised by what he saw from a modest production cost, the executive exclaimed to an undoubtedly surprised Korda "...it isn't your job over here to compete with us in Hollywood!" Seen as an extra is Merle Oberon, who would become Korda's second wife and have her own career guided by him in the early 1930s.

p&d, Alexander Korda; w, Eliot Crawshay-Williams, Lajos Biro (based on the novel *The Head Waiter* by Ernst Vajda); m, Percival Mackey; ed, Harold Young; prod d, Alfred Junge.

Comedy   **(PR:AA MPAA:NR)**

REST IS SILENCE, THE½   (1960, Ger.) 106m Freie/Films Around
The World c (DER REST IST SCHWEIGEN)

Hardy Kruger (John H. Claudius), Peter Van Eyck (Paul Claudius), Ingrid Andree (Fee von Pohl), Adelheid Seeck (Gertrud Claudius), Rudolf Forster (Dr. von Pohl), Boy Gobert (Mike R. Krantz), Rainer Penkert (Maj. Horace), Heinz Drache (Herbert von Pohl), Charles Regnier (Inspector Fortner), Richard Allan (Stanley Goulden), Robert Meyr (Dr. Voltmann).

A German version of Shakespeare's "Hamlet" takes the story of the melancholy Dane and changes him into a disenchanted Harvard boy. "Hamlet" (Kruger) is the son of a wealthy German who was killed in the war. The ghost of his father returns to him in the form of mysterious phone calls, Ophelia is turned into a schizophrenic, the tell-tale play within the play becomes a visiting American ballet company, and the Polonius character dies falling off a balcony when caught eavesdropping. Other than that, coupled with some Freudian references tossed in for good measure, this film is really just an intellectual exercise with little insight. There's nothing original added to the "Hamlet" legacy with this version, for, aside from the modernizations, it's essentially just an average production of the story. Shakespeare aficionados might be interested, but ultimately this is little more than a curio. (In German; English subtitles.)

p,d&w, Helmut Kautner (based on the play "Hamlet" by William Shakespeare).

Drama   **(PR:C MPAA:NR)**

RESTLESS   (SEE: MAN-TRAP, 1961)

RESTLESS BREED, THE**   (1957) 81m FOX c

Scott Brady (Mitch Baker), Anne Bancroft (Angelita), Jay C. Flippen (Marshal Steve Evans), Rhys Williams (Ed Newton), Jim Davis (Rev. Simmons), Leo Gordon (Cherokee), Scott Marlowe (Allan), Eddy Waller (Caesar), Harry Cheshire (Mayor Johnson), Myron Healey (Sheriff William), Gerald Milton (Bartender), Dennis King, Jr. (Hotel Clerk), James Flavin (Secret Service Chief), Clegg Hoyt, Marilyn Winston, Billy Miller, Evelyn Rudie, Marty Cariosa.

A tightly made western with vengeance as the overriding theme. Set at the Texas border, a Secret Service agent is murdered by gun runners. His young son, Brady, shows up in town to seek out his father's killers. The leader, Davis, hightails it over the border and sends his men to kill Brady. Brady foils their attempts, and Davis and Brady meet in a showdown in which Brady gains the final act of revenge. Bancroft, always making her presence known, is the half-breed love interest for Brady.

p, Edward L. Alperson; d, Allan Dwan; w, Steven Fisher; ph, John W. Boyle (Eastmancolor); m, Edward L. Alperson, Jr.; ed, Merrill G. White; md, Raoul Kraushaar; art d, Ernst Fegte; m/l, "Angelita," "Never Alone," Alperson, Jr., Dick Hughes, Richard Stapley.

Western   **(PR:A MPAA:NR)**

RESTLESS NIGHT, THE**   (1964, Ger.) 102m Carlton-Filmaufbau-
Real/Casino bw (UNRUHIGE NACHT)

Bernhard Wicki (Pastor), Ulla Jacobsson (Melanie), Hansjorg Felmy (Fedor), Ann Savo (Ljuba), Erik Schuman (Ernst), Werner Hinz (Arnim), Richard Munch, Werner Peters, Paul Esser, Joseph Offenbach, Emmerich Schrenk, Albert Bessler, Werner Folger, Karlheinz Kreienbaum, Erik von Loewis, Hans Krull, Peter A. Lehmbrock.

As the Germans retreat from Stalingrad, deserter Felmy is sentenced to be executed. While getting him ready for the execution, the pastor (Wicki) discovers why Felmy did what he did—he wanted to protect a Russian widow from both sides. But an order is an order, and, despite his good intentions, he is executed in the morning.

p, Gunther Stapenhorst; d, Falk Harnack; w, Horst Budjuhn (based on the story "Unruhige Nacht" by Albrecht Goes); ph, Friedl Behn-Grund; m, Hans-Martin Majewski; ed, Eva Kroll, Georg Jaun; set d, Franz Bi, Bruno Monden.

Drama   **(PR:C MPAA:NR)**

RESTLESS ONES, THE**   (1965) 103m World Wide bw

Georgia Lee (Mrs. Winton), Robert Sampson (Mr. Winton), Johnny Crawford (David Winton), Kim Darby (April), Jean Engstrom (April's Mother), Billy Graham (Himself), Jerome Courtland, Lurene Tuttle, Don O'Rourke, Rick Murray, Bob Random, Patrick Moore, Joe Eilers, Timothy Sims, I. Stanford Jolley, Burt Douglas, Kay Cousins, Robert Clarke, Pam McMyler, Marlene Ludwig, Rick Kelman, Paula Baird, David Wright.

Lee and Sampson are a husband-and-wife television writing team who are writing a script on restless teenagers. During their research, they become born-again Christians, while their son Crawford runs away with Darby. Darby is pregnant and hopes to find the man who's responsible, but when she doesn't she attempts suicide. Crawford then attends a Billy Graham Crusade meeting with his father and he, too, finds religion.

p&d, Dick Ross; w, James F. Collier; ph, Ernest Haller; m, Ralph Carmichael; ed, Eugene Pendleton; art d, Stan Jolley; set d, William Calvert; m/l, "The Restless Ones," "Sing, Sing, Sing a Song of Strength," "He's Everything to Me," Carmichael.

Drama   **(PR:A MPAA:NR)**

RESTLESS YEARS, THE*½   (1958) 86m UNIV bw (GB: THE
                                            WONDERFUL YEARS)

John Saxon (Will Henderson), Sandra Dee (Melinda Grant), Luana Patten (Polly Fisher), Margaret Lindsay (Dorothy Henderson), Virginia Grey (Miss Robson), Jody McCrea (Bruce), Alan Baxter (Alex Fisher), Hayden Rorke (Mr. Booth), Dorothy Green (Laura), Teresa Wright (Elizabeth Grant), James Whitmore (Ed Henderson).

Tuned for the younger generation, the plot has too much an old-fashioned feel to carry it off. Dee suffers the stigma of being an illegitimate child, even though her mother told her that her father died when she was young. However, everyone else in this small close-minded town knows otherwise. Saxon, who has come into town with his luckless father, falls in love with Dee. With her mother on the brink of insanity and his father trying for one last grasp at success, the pair have an uphill fight to grow into normal adults.

p, Ross Hunter; d, Helmut Kautner; w, Edward Anhalt (based on the play "Teach Me How to Cry" by Patricia Joudry); ph, Ernest Laszlo (CinemaScope); m, Joseph Gershenson; ed, Al Joseph; art d, Alexander Golitzen, Philip Barber.

Drama   **(PR:A MPAA:NR)**

RESURRECTION**   (1931) 81m UNIV bw

John Boles (Prince Dmitri Nekhludoff), Lupe Velez (Katusha Maslova), Nance O'Neil (Princess Marya), William Keighley (Maj. Schoenblock), Rose Tapley (Princess Sophya), Michael Mark (Simon Kartkinkin), Sylva Nadina (Eupremia Botchkova), George Irving (1st Judge), Edward Cecil (Merchant), Mary Forman (Beautiful Exile), Grace Cunard (Olga), Dorothy Flood (Princess Hasan).

A plodding film that does no justice to Leo Tolstoy's Resurrection. Nice sets and scenic shots help this period piece about the upper crust of 1876 Russia. Story is about a Russian prince and peasant girl falling in love and the troubles they encounter. Plenty to look at, not much to digest. This is the eighth time RESURRECTION had come to the screen. There was also a remake called WE LIVE AGAIN by United Artists in 1934, a Russian version appearing in 1963, and a Spanish version shot at the same time as this one, starring Gilbert Roland.

p&d, Edwin Carewe; w, Finis Fox (based on the novel by Leo Tolstoy); ph, Robert B. Kurrie, Al Green; m, Dimitri Tiomkin; ed, Edward L. Kahn, Maurice Pivar; m/l, Tiomkin, Bernard Grossman.

Drama   **(PR:A MPAA:NR)**

RESURRECTION***   (1963, USSR) 152m Mosfilm/Artkino bw
                                            (VOSKRESENIYE)

Tamara Syomina (Katyusha Maslova), Yevgeniy Matveyev (Prince Nekhlyudov), Pavel Massalskiy (Presiding Judge), V. Kulakov, V. Bokaryov (Members of the Court),Lenoid Zolotukhin (Prosecutor), V. Sez (Court Secretary), V. Sushkevich (Prison Warden), N. Svobodin (Retired Colonel), Aleksandr Khvylya (Merchant), A. Smirnov (Nikiforov), V. Vanyshev (Teacher), Sergey Kalinin (Member of Workers' Collective), A. Kasapov (Shopkeeper), Nina Samsonova (Bochkova), V. Boriskin (Kartinkin), Nikolay Sergeyev (Supervisor of Prisons), A. Zuyeva (Matryona Kharina), V. Gusev (Simonson), K. Rumyanova (Bogodukhovskaya), V. Lanovaya (Shchetinina), Vasiliy Livanov (Kryltsov), V. Belokurov (Maslennikov), N. Pazhitnov (Maslova's Lawyer), Valentina Telegina (Korablyova), L. Ivanova (Red-Headed Woman), M. Vinogradova (Khoroshavka), L. Arkhipova (Fenichka), M. Sidorkin (Lawyer Fonarin), G. Konskiy (Korchagin), L. Zhukovskaya (Missi Korchagina), Ye. Yelina (Sofya Ivanovna), S. Garel (Marya Ivanovna), A. Panova (Agrafena Petrovna), N. Bogoyavlenskaya (Matryona Pavlovna), A. Konsovskiy (Commentator), A. Georgiyevskaya, Boris Smirnov, V. Makhov, N. Ofitserov, S. Tikhonravov, P. Voloshin, P. Mikhaylov, Ye. Volskaya, Ye. Sokolova, V. Vladimirova, Larisa Kadochnikova, A. Zarzhitskaya, V. Burlakova, V. Marenkov, G. Nechayev, N. Agapova, P. Vinnik, N. Grabbe, V. Dukhina, I. Zhevago, V. Kostina, S. Krylov, B. Lyaush, M. Novikova, A. Plavan, M. Semenikhin, Lena Sugrobova, V. Chayeva, G. Shapovalov, Gennadiy Yukhtin.

Russian version of Leo Tolstoy's story and much better than the American version made in 1931. A young woman is on trial for murder, and on the jury is a young prince who recognizes her from a joyous summer he spent with her 10 years before. After getting her pregnant, he had gone back to his career and left her in care of his aunts who shipped her away because she was pregnant. The child does not live long and the girl enters the hard, cold world of prostitution. The jury at the trial sentences her to four years of hard labor, but the prince uses his powers to appeal the decision. He proposes marriage but she turns him away, blaming him for her troubled past. Prison solitude gets to her and she becomes nicer toward him. He does get her sentence lightened, but she takes a liking toward prison politics and decides to stay in exile rather than compromise her new ideals. This was originally a five hour movie made in two parts.

d, Mikhail Shveytser; w, Yevgeniy Gabrilovich, Shveytser (based on the novel by Leo Tolstoy); ph, Era Savelyeva, Sergey Poluyanov; m, Georgiy Sviridov; ed, K. Aleyeva; md, A. Roytman; art d, David Vinitskiy, A. Freydin; set d, O. Alikin; cos, G. Ganevskaya; spec eff, A. Vinokurov, G. Ayzenberg; makeup, A. Patenovskaya.

Drama   **(PR:A MPAA:NR)**

RESURRECTION**   (1980) 103m UNIV c

Ellen Burstyn (Edna McCauley), Sam Shepard (Cal Carpenter), Richard Farnsworth (Esco), Roberts Blossom (John Harper), Clifford David (George), Pamela Payton-Wright (Margaret), Jeffrey DeMunn (Joe McCauley), Eva LeGallienne (Grandma Pearl), Lois Smith (Kathy), Madeleine Thornton-Sherwood (Ruth), Richard Hamilton (Earl Carpenter), Carlin Glynn (Suzy Kroll), Lane Smith (Don), Penelope Allen (Ellie), Ebbe Roe Smith (Hank Peterson), John Tillinger (Dr. Herron), Trazana Beverley (Dr. Ellen Baxter), Ralph Roberts (Buck), George Sperdakos (Dr. Hankins), Bernard Behrens (Dr. Fisher), James Blendick, Vernon Weddle, David Calkins, Harvey Christiansen, Therese East, Lou Fant, Jessie Lee Fulton, David Haney, Claudette Harrell, James N. Harrell, Jennifer McAllister, Don Michaelson, A.G. Mills, Edith Mills, Tom Taylor, Sylvia Walden, Carol Williard, Tracy Wilson.

Burstyn and LeGallienne both received Oscar nominations for their work in a losing cause. Occult movies usually dwell on the evil side of matters and this one is the exception, which also made it a box-office dud. Burstyn is a well-to-do woman who gives a sports car to her husband as his birthday present. The two go out for a spin around Los Angeles which results in a crash that kills spouse DeMunn and causes Burstyn to be crippled. She goes home to Kansas to recover after catching a brief look at what life after death is when she is temporarily in that limbo world before being brought back by the doctors. Once in Kansas (which was shot in Texas and is so blatantly Lone Star that it's almost an insult to anyone who ever donned a 10-gallon hat), she discovers that she has the power to heal people by laying her hands on them. This is refuted by her stern father, Blossom, but it does work and she is soon joined by Farnsworth who believes she has been touched by God. Burstyn meets Shepard, the young son of a preacher, and they have a sexual relationship. Burstyn won't acknowledge that this power is Divine and continues being an earthbound woman with normal desires and wants. Shepard is a hick, and the fact that he and Burstyn have a fling is not totally believable, despite his sincerity and doting on her. She is far too hip to go for that kind of yokel. Shepard begins to believe that Burstyn is the embodiment of Christ. When he can no longer perform sexually for fear of affecting The Second Coming, he is convinced that Burstyn is Jesus and, to prove the point that she is who he thinks she is, he shoots her. It's a weeper and an attempt to show the good side of the occult, and though Petrie's direction is sturdy and all the performances are good, the movie never catches fire. Even the Fundamentalists were not thrilled. LeGallienne, a noted stage actress, makes one of her infrequent appearances on film, having appeared in PRINCE OF PLAYERS and THE DEVIL'S DISCIPLE.

p, Renee Missel, Howard Rosenman; d, Daniel Petrie; w, Lewis John Carlino; ph, Mario Tosi (Technicolor); m, Maurice Jarre; ed, Rita Roland; prod d, Paul Sylbert; art d, Edwin O'Donovan; set d, Bruce Weintraub.

Drama   **(PR:C MPAA:PG)**

RESURRECTION OF ZACHARY WHEELER, THE**½   (1971)
                                            100m GOLD KEY/VIDTRONICS c

Leslie Nielsen (Harry Walsh), Bradford Dillman (Senator Zachary Wheeler), James Daly (Dr. Redding), Angie Dickinson (Dr. Johnson), Robert J. Wilke (Hugh Fielding), Jack Carter (Dwight Childs), Don Haggerty (Jake), Jim Healy, Lou Brown, Pat O'Moore, Richard Schuyler, Richard Simmons, Ruben Moreno, Peter Mamakos, Jill Jaress, Jim Healey, Lee Giroux.

Two stories are told in this compelling drama about a secret medical station in the U.S. Nielsen is a television reporter who comes across the car accident of a U.S. senator. Near death, the senator is rushed off by ambulance to the hospital. Even though Nielsen has film footage of the accident, hospital personnel tell him no one has been brought in. Nielsen gets even more suspicious when someone from the senator's office calls and reports that the senator is out fishing and was not in an accident. Nielsen's findings take him to the medical station where he uncovers Daly's scheme of using transplants to bring back the dead and change the course of the world. Tightly woven story, with just a few unravelings, that moves at a good pace.

p, Robert Stabler; d, Robert Wynn; w, Jay Simms, Tom Rolf; ph, Bob Boatman (Technicolor); m, Marlin Skiles; ed, Fred Berger.

Science Fiction   **Cas.**   **(PR:A MPAA:G)**

RESURRECTION SYNDICATE   (SEE: NOTHING BUT THE NIGHT,
                                            1972, Brit.)

RETURN, THE*   (1980) GREYDON CLARK bw

Cybill Shepherd (Daughter), Raymond Burr (Industrialist), Jan-Michael Vincent (Deputy), Martin Landau (Marshal), Vinnie Schiavelli (Prospector), Zachary Vincent (Boy), Farah Bunch (Girl), Neville Brand, Susan Kiger.

Never released to theaters and for good reason. A UFO zapped Shepherd, Vincent, and Schiavelli, all from Earth, and the story picks up 20 years later. Schiavelli is a hermit prospector, taken to mutilating cattle and people he comes across. His cave is a direct line to the UFO creatures. Shepherd, a scientific genius (!), and Vincent are drawn to the prospector and the cave but think the UFO is an evil thing until the end. Sitting through this is the only evil part.

p&d, Greydon Clark; w, Jim Wheat, Ken Wheat, Curtis Burch; ph, Daniel Pearl; m, Dan Wyman; ed, Richard Brummer; art d, Chester Kaczenski; spec eff, Dana Rheaume; makeup, Ken Horn, Tom Schwartz.

Science Fiction   **Cas.**   **(PR:C MPAA:NR)**

RETURN FROM THE ASHES**   (1965, U.S./Brit.) 107m Mirisch-
                                            Orchard/UA bw

Maximilian Schell (Stanislaus Pilgrin), Samantha Eggar (Fabienne), Ingrid Thulin (Dr. Michele Wolf), Herbert Lom (Dr. Charles Bovard), Talitha Pol (Claudine), Vladek Sheybal (Manager), Jacques Brunius (1st Detective), Andre Maranne (2nd

Detective), Yvonne Andre (Woman on Train), John Serret (Man in Train), Pamela Stirling (Mother in Train), Jacques Cey (Hotel Desk Clerk), Andre Charise (Restaurant Captain), Daniele Noel (Nurse), Arnold Diamond (Neighbor), Franco DeRosa (Boy in Nightclub), Doreen Moore, Harriet Harper (Girls in Nightclub), Engene Keeley (Boy in Train), Jean Driant (Train Conductor), Mischa De La Motte (Mr. Friedheim), Rica Fox (Mrs. Friedheim), Viviane Ventura (Receptionist).

Tense but unfulfilling film about an attempt at the perfect murder. Schell is living with his stepdaughter, Eggar, during this post-WW II Paris setting. His wife, Thulin, was tortured at Dachau, one of the Jewish prison camps, and finds Schell in the arms of and setting up house with her stepdaughter. Schell is driven by unrelenting greed as he kills Eggar and then tries to murder his wife to fulfill his passion for money. But he doesn't and Thulin and Lom, the doctor who reconstructed Thulin's face, end up together.

p, J. Lee Thompson, Lewis J. Rachmil; d, Thompson; w, Julius J. Epstein, Charles Blair (based on the novel Le Retour des Cendres by Hubert Monteilhet); ph, Chris Challis (Panavision); m, John Dankworth; ed, Russell Lloyd; prod d, Michael Stringer; set d, Terence Morgan II; cos, Margaret Furse; makeup, John O'Gorman, Tom Smith.

Drama **(PR:A MPAA:NR)**

RETURN FROM THE PAST (SEE: DR. TERROR'S GALLERY OF HORRORS, 1967)

RETURN FROM THE SEA**½ (1954) 79m AA bw

Jan Sterling (Frieda, Waitress), Neville Brand (Maclish), John Doucette (Jimmy, Taxi Driver), Paul Langton (Lt. Manley), John Pickard (Spike), Don Haggerty (Tompkins), Alvy Moore (Smitty), Robert Arthur (Porter), Lloyd Corrigan (Pinky), Lee Roberts (Doctor), Robert Wood (Clarke), Robert Patten (Welch), James Best (Barr), John Tarangelo (Doyle), Bill Gentry (Harris), Walter Reed (Captain).

A little romance, a little war puts this in the pleasing middle-of-the-road category. Brand plays a sailor who likes his liquor while on leave. He meets Sterling in San Diego and they fall in love and start mapping out the future. Everything is put on hold when he gets badly hurt in Korea. But just when things look bleak, the writers make everything better, and Brand and Sterling close it with a wonderful wedding and promising future ahead.

p, Scott R. Dunlap; d, Lesley Selander; w, George Waggner (based on a story by Jacland Marmur); ph, Harry Neumann; m, Marlin Skiles; ed, John C. Fuller.

War Drama **(PR:A MPAA:NR)**

RETURN FROM WITCH MOUNTAIN**¼ (1978) 93m Walt Disney/ BV c

Bette Davis (Letha), Christopher Lee (Victor), Kim Richards (Tia), Ike Eisenmann (Tony), Jack Soo (Mr. Yokomoto), Anthony James (Sickle), Dick Bakalyan (Eddie), Ward Costello (Mr. Clearcole), Christian Juttner (Dazzler), Poindexter (Crusher), Brad Savage (Muscles), Jeffrey Jacquet (Rocky).

Sequel to the successful Disney film, ESCAPE TO WITCH MOUNTAIN that was released in 1975. Richards and Eisenmann return in their roles as the sister and brother with special powers. On Earth for a little vacation, they encounter Lee, who is the typical mad scientist bent on taking control of the world. After witnessing Eisenmann's mental powers, the chase is on as Lee and his aide Davis go after the pair. There are plenty of visual gags to please the kids. It's kids versus adults for the rest of the film. After being separated, the young pair battle Lee and Davis, having to use all their special powers, giving the special effects people much to do in this pleasing lightweight Disney film.

p, Ron Miller, Jerome Courtland; d, John Hough; w, Malcolm Marmorstein (based on the characters by Alexander Key); ph, Frank Phillips (Technicolor); m, Lalo Schifrin; ed, Bob Bring; art d, John B. Mansbridge, Jack Senter; set d, Frank R. McKelvy; cos, Chuck Kechne; spec eff, Eustace Lycett, Art Cruickshank, Danny Lee.

Adventure **Cas.** **(PR:AA MPAA:G)**

RETURN OF A MAN CALLED HORSE, THE** (1976) 125m UA c

Richard Harris (John Morgan), Gale Sondergaard (Elk Woman), Geoffrey Lewis (Zenas Morro), Bill Lucking (Tom Gryce), Jorge Luke (Running Bull), Claudio Brook (Chemin d'Fer), Enrique Lucero (Raven), Jorge Russek (Blacksmith), Ana De Sade (Moonstar), Pedro Damien (Standing Bear), Humberto Lopez-Pineda (Thin Dog), Patricia Reyes (Grey Thorn), Regino Herrerra (Lame Wolf), Rigobert Rico (Owl), Alberto Mariscal (Red Cloud).

Breathtaking visuals carry this sequel to A MAN CALLED HORSE. Harris returns as the aristocratic Englishman who returns to the American West to save the Indian tribe that adopted him. After seeing his tribe's land taken away and the Indians forced into slavery, Harris enters their midst and rallies them to take back their land. The movie includes another long-drawn out torture scene to please those sadists in the audience. Another sequel, TRIUMPHS OF A MAN CALLED HORSE, came in 1983.

p, Terry Morse, Jr.; d, Irvin Kershner; w, Jack DeWitt (based on characters by Dorothy M. Johnson); ph, Owen Roizman (Panavision, DeLuxe Color); m, Laurence Rosenthal; ed, Michael Kahn; prod d, Stewart Campbell, set d, Ernesto Carrasco; cos, Dick La Motte; spec eff, Joe Azomar, Frederico Farfan; stunts, Mickey Gilbert.

Western **Cas.** **(PR:C MPAA:PG)**

RETURN OF A STRANGER, 1940 (SEE: FACE BEHIND THE SCAR, 1940, Brit.)

RETURN OF A STRANGER**½ (1962, Brit.) 63m Danziger/WPD bw

John Ireland (Ray Reed), Susan Stephen (Pam Reed), Cyril Shaps (Homer Trent), Timothy Beaton (Tommy Reed), Patrick McAlinney (Whittaker), Kevin Stoney (Wayne), Ian Fleming (Meecham), Raymond Rollett (Somerset), Frederick Piper (Fred).

Creepy, very suspenseful thriller starring Ireland and Stephen as a young couple terrorized by recently released mental patient Shaps, who has returned for revenge. Shaps, who had attacked Stephen when she was still in school (which landed him in custody), plans to make her pay by killing Ireland. Taut direction by Varnel and good performances from the principals make this one memorable.

p, Brian Taylor; d, Max Varnel; w, Brian Clemens.

Crime/Suspense **(PR:C MPAA:NR)**

RETURN OF BULLDOG DRUMMOND, THE** (1934, Brit.) 73m ABF/British International bw

Ralph Richardson (Hugh Drummond), Ann Todd (Phyllis Drummond), Joyce Kennedy (Irma Peterson), Francis L. Sullivan (Carl Peterson), Claud Allister (Algy Longworth), H. Saxon-Snell (Zadowa), Spencer Trevor (Sir Bryan Johnstone), Charles Mortimer (Inspector McIver), Wallace Geoffrey (Charles Latter), Pat Aherne (Jerry Seymour).

After living the married life in relative seclusion, Capt. Drummond (Richardson) gets back into the fray when his wife is kidnaped by old arch-enemy Sullivan and gang. Film suffers from up-and-down pacing, and the climactic battle between the good and bad guys is more like a bunch of brawling women. (See BULLDOG DRUMMOND series, Index.)

p, Walter C. Mycroft; d&w, Walter Summers (based on the novel Sapper by H.C. McNeile); ph, Jack Parker; cos, Norman Hartnell.

Mystery **(PR:A MPAA:NR)**

RETURN OF CAPTAIN INVINCIBLE, THE** (1983, Aus./U.S.) 90m 7 Keys c (AKA: LEGEND IN LEOTARDS)

Alan Arkin (Capt. Invincible), Christopher Lee (Mr. Midnight), Kate Fitzpatrick (Patty), Bill Hunter (Tupper), Graham Kennedy (Prime Minister), Michael Pate (President), Hayes Gordon (Kirby), Max Phipps (Admiral), Noel Ferrier (General).

Ex-superhero Arkin is called out of retirement to set things right and defeat the minions of the evil Lee. Attempt at parody fails utterly, leaving a talented cast to embarrass themselves.

p, Andrew Gaty; d, Philippe Mora; w, Steve de Souza, Gaty; ph, Mike Molloy; m, William Motzing; ed, John Scott; prod d, David Copping; art d, Owen Patterson.

Comedy **(PR:C MPAA:PG)**

RETURN OF CAROL DEANE, THE** (1938, Brit.) 77m WB-FN Teddington bw

Bebe Daniels (Carol Deane), Arthur Margetson (Mark Poynton), Zena Dare (Lady Brenning), Chili Bouchier (Anne Dempster), Michael Drake (Lord Robert Brenning), Wyndham Goldie (Francis Scott-Vaughan), Peter Coke (Lord David Brenning), Lesley Brook (Diana), David Burns (Nick Wellington), Ian Maclean (Prosecution), Aubrey Mallalieu (Lamont), Ian Fleming.

A story of a mother's sacrifice for the love of her son. Daniels is a model who works with an artist who has cashed in on her beauty. While keeping house with the leeching artist, she falls for someone more her own age, gets married, and gives him a son. Her real love dies in the war and the conniving artist tries to get her back. He cons her into coming up to the studio, draws a gun, and she accidentally kills him. After 15 years in prison, she flees to America to make sure her son never discovers her dramatic history. She takes up with a gambler but soon comes back to England where she sees her son being taken by gamblers. She saves him from losing everything and then slowly disappears from view as he focuses all his attentions on his fiancee. A mother's love is never joyful.

p, Jerome Jackson; d, Arthur Woods; w, John Meehan, Jr., Paul Gangelin, Tom Phipps (based on a story "The House on 56th Street" by Joseph Santley); ph, Basil Emmott.

Crime Drama **(PR:A MPAA:NR)**

RETURN OF CASEY JONES** (1933) 67m CHAD/MON bw (GB: TRAIN 2419)

Charles Starrett, Ruth Hall, Robert Elliott, George "Gabby" Hayes, Jackie Searl, George Walsh, Margaret Seddon, G. D. Wood [Gordon DeMain], George Nash, Anne Howard.

Only a train crash could have helped this weak railroad tale. Casey Jones gives advice to a young engineer and acts as role model. That's it, plus some shots of fast-moving trains careening across the country. Missing this train won't hurt anyone.

p, Trem Carr; d, J.P. McCarthy; w, McCarthy, Harry O. Jones (based on a story by John P. Johns); ph, John Mescall.

Drama **(PR:A MPAA:NR)**

RETURN OF COUNT YORGA, THE** (1971) 96m AIP c

Robert Quarry (Count Yorga), Mariette Hartley (Cynthia Nelson), Roger Perry (Dr. David Baldwin), Yvonne Wilder (Jennifer), Tom Toner (Rev. Thomas), Rudy DeLuca (Lt. Madden), Philip Frame (Tommy), George Macready (Prof. Rightstat), Walter Brooke (Bill Nelson), Edward Walsh (Brudah), Craig Nelson (Sgt. O'Connor), David Lampson (Jason), Karen Houston (Ellen), Helen Baron (Mrs. Nelson), Jesse Wells (Mitzi Carthay), Mike Pataki (Joe), Corrine Conley (Witch), Allen Joseph (Michael Farmer), Peg Shirley (Claret Farmer), Liz Rogers (Laurie Greggs), Paul Hansen (Jonathan Greggs).

A send-up with a dramatic flair as the vampire Count Yorga comes back once again to haunt. Yorga (Quarry) and his gang of vampires take residence in a decrepit mansion that houses an orphanage. Quarry sets his sights and fangs on Hartley but to no avail. Perry is her love interest who tries to find out why people keep disappearing from the mansion. Perry does discover the solution to the mystery, and Hartley gets a surprise at the end.

p, Michael Macready; d, Bob Kelljan; w, Kelljan, Yvonne Wilder; ph, Bill Butler (Movielab Color); m, Bill Marx; ed, Fabien Tordjman, Laurette Odney; art d, Vince Cresceman; spec eff, Roger George; m/l, "This Song," Marilynn Lovell, Wilder, Kelljan, Marx (sung by The Vocal Arts Studio members), "Think it Over," Lovell (sung by Lovell); makeup, Mark Busson.

Horror   **(PR:C MPAA:GP)**

RETURN OF DANIEL BOONE, THE**   (1941) 60m COL bw (GB: THE MAYOR'S NEST)

Bill Elliott (*Dan Boone*), Betty Miles (*Ellen Brandon*), Dub Taylor (*Cannonball*), Ray Bennett (*Leach Kilgrain*), Walter Soderling (*Mayor Elwell*), Carl Stockdale (*Jeb Brandon*), Bud Osborne (*Red*), Francis Walker (*Bowers*), Lee Powell (*Tax Collector Fuller*), Tom Carter (*Wagner*), Edmund Cobb (*Henderson*), Melinda Rodik, Matilda Rodik, Steve Clark, Hank Bell, Roy Butler, Art Miles, Edwin Bryant, Murdock MacQuarrie, Tex Cooper.

A dishrag western in which Elliott portrays the grandson of the more-famous Boone. The young Boone foils a land deal by two money-grubbers. Most of the laughs come from Taylor who gets involved in a different kind of love triangle: he falls for a pair of twins. Quadruplets couldn't have saved this.

p, Leon Barsha; d, Lambert Hillyer; w, Paul Franklin, Joseph Hoffman (based on a story by Franklin); ph, Philip Tannura; ed, Mel Thorsen.

Western   **(PR:A MPAA:NR)**

RETURN OF DR. FU MANCHU, THE**   (1930) 71m PAR bw (AKA: THE NEW ADVENTURES OF DR. FU MANCHU)

Warner Oland (*Dr. Fu Manchu*), Neil Hamilton (*Dr. Jack Petrie*), Jean Arthur (*Lila Eltham*), O.P. Heggie (*Nayland Smith*), William Austin (*Sylvester*), Evelyn Hall (*Lady Agatha*), Margaret Fealy (*Lady Helen*), Evelyn Selbie (*Fat Lu*), Shayle Gardner (*Inspector Harding*), David Dunbar (*Lawrence*), Tetsu Komai (*Chang*), Toyo Fujita (*Ah Ling*), Ambrose Barker (*Reporter*).

The sequel to THE MYSTERIOUS FU MANCHU (1929) begins with an elaborate funeral ceremony for the evil Chinese criminal (played once again by Oland) who had committed suicide in the first movie. Of course, the insidious doctor didn't die at all, but injected himself with a potion of his own design that would only make him appear dead. During the funeral, Oland slips out of his coffin through a trap door and ventures to England in pursuit of his archenemies, Hamilton and Heggie. An elaborate game of cat-and-mouse soon develops between the Britishers and Oland with the villainous genius leaving cleverly murdered corpses in his wake. Eventually Oland is cornered by his enemies and escapes by jumping into the Thames with a bomb of his own making, which explodes, apparently killing him. Sure. Oland would make a cinematic apology to the people of the Far East for his portrayal of the treacherous Oriental by starring as an honest and honorable Chinese in the lengthy CHARLIE CHAN series of films. (See FU MANCHU series, Index.)

d, Rowland V. Lee; w, Florence Ryerson, Lloyd Corrigan (based on characters created by Sax Rohmer); ph, A.J. Stout.

Crime   **(PR:A MPAA:NR)**

RETURN OF DR. MABUSE, THE**½   (1961, Ger./Fr./Ital.) 88m CCC Filmkunst-Criterion-SPA Cinematografica/Ajay bw (IM STAHLNETZ DES DR. MABUSE; LE RETOUR DU DOCTEUR MABUSE; FBI CONTRO DR. MABUSE; AKA: PHANTOM FIEND)

Gert Frobe (*Inspector Lohmann*), Lex Barker (*Joe Como*), Daliah Lavi (*Maria Sabrehm*), Wolfgang Preiss (*Dr. Mabuse*), Fausto Tozzi (*Prison Governor*), Joachim Mock (*Voss*), Rudolf Forster (*Prof. Sabrehm*), Rudolf Fernau (*Parson Brietenstein*), Werner Peters (*Bohmler*), Laura Solari (*Mme. Pizarro*), Lou Seitz (*Mrs. Lohmann*), Albert Bessler (*Trodler*), Adi Berber (*Sandro*), Henri Coubet (*Blind Man*), Jean-Roger Caussimon, Alexander Engel, Zeev Berlinski.

Super-detective Frobe returns after a handful of gruesome murders. He concludes that the evil Dr. Mabuse (Preiss) is at it again. Frobe gets help from FBI man Barker and reporter Lavi and finds that Preiss has zombie-like slaves committing his crimes for him. Barker goes undercover as Preiss plans to attack a nuclear reactor. He is found out and he and Lavi are taken prisoners. They escape and help Frobe track down Preiss. Frobe and Preiss struggle and Preiss is engulfed by fire; however, his body is never found. Does that mean he will return? (See DR. MABUSE series, Index.)

p, Arthur Brauner; d, Harald Reinl; w, Ladislas Foder, Marc Behm; ph, Karl Lob; m, Peter Sandloff; ed, Hermann Haller; art d, Otto Erdmann, Hans-Jurgen Kiebach; cos, Gisela Nixdorf; makeup, Willi Nixdorf, Charlotte Schmidt-Kersten.

Crime   **(PR:C MPAA:NR)**

RETURN OF DR. X, THE**½   (1939) 62m WB bw

Humphrey Bogart (*Marshall Quesne*), Rosemary Lane (*Joan Vance*), Wayne Morris (*Walter Barnett*), Dennis Morgan (*Michael Rhodes*), John Litel (*Dr. Francis Flegg*), Lya Lys (*Angela Merrova*), Huntz Hall (*Pinky*), Charles Wilson (*Detective Ray Kincaid*), Vera Lewis (*Miss Sweetman*), Howard Hickman (*Chairman*), Olin Howland (*Undertaker*), Arthur Aylesworth (*Guide*), Jack Mower (*Detective Sgt. Moran*), Creighton Hale (*Hotel Manager*), John Ridgely (*Rodgers*), Joe Crehan (*Editor*), Glenn Langan, DeWolf Hopper (*Interns*), Ian Wolfe, Virginia Brissac, George Reeves, John Harmon, Howard Hickman, Ed Chandler.

Not really a sequel to the 1932 two-strip Technicolor classic DR. X, this strange

Bogart film was merely an attempt by Warner Bros. to cash in on the second talkie horror boom. While rival studio Universal was making a fortune resurrecting the Frankenstein monster in SON OF FRANKENSTEIN (and later Dracula, the Mummy, and the Wolfman), Warners found itself without any resident monster to revive. The studio had practically ignored the horror genre in the early 1930s, but did manage to produce two classics starring Lionel Atwill and Fay Wray, DR. X and THE MYSTERY OF THE MUSEUM (1933). In an attempt to emulate Universal's formula for success, Warners decided to revive the "Dr. X" character for its new horror film. Morris stars as a scoop-hungry reporter who discovers the dead body of famous actress Lys. As the story breaks in the papers, however, Lys turns up very much alive although her skin has taken on an ashen pallor. The actress, whose face is hidden behind a black veil, sues Morris' newspaper for its irresponsible journalistic practices. Morris soon finds himself out of a job, but remains convinced that Lys was really dead. While digging for clues, Morris discovers that Lys has given up acting and spends much of her time at the office of Litel, an eccentric but brilliant blood specialist. Morris begins to suspect that the recent series of murders in New York (where all the victims were drained of their blood) can be traced to Litel. Further investigation reveals that all the victims had donated blood at Litel's hospital, and that they all shared the same rare blood type. Luckily, one of Morris' best pals is Morgan, a young medical intern who happens to study under Litel. Together they decide to crack the mysterious case. While nosing around Litel's laboratory, Morris and Morgan are discovered by Litel's lab assistant, Bogart, an odd-looking man with a pale complexion and short-cropped hair streaked with white down the middle (Bogart's makeup, especially the hair, is remarkably similar to that of Boris Karloff in Warner Bros.' 1936 shocker, THE WALKING DEAD—both were done by Perc Westmore). Litel reveals that he has been experimenting with a synthetic blood mixture that has brought small animals back to life. The next step is to test it on human beings. Morris and Morgan soon learn that Litel has already pumped his synthetic blood into humans and Bogart is the result. In reality Bogart is the infamous Dr. Maurice Xavier who was electrocuted years earlier for murdering a patient during an experiment. Litel confesses that Bogart, actress Lys, and others he has brought back to life have turned into monsters searching for fresh blood. Soon after this revelation, Litel is murdered. Meanwhile, Bogart has learned that Morgan's girl friend, Lane, possesses the proper blood type he needs to stay alive. Bogart traps Lane in the marshes of New Jersey, but Morgan, Morris, and the police arrive in time to save her. Bogart is once again killed by the law. Although rather silly at times and inferior when compared to the horror films produced by Universal, THE RETURN OF DR. X does have some effectively chilling moments. The chance to see tough-guy gangster Bogart play a ghoul is worth the price of admission, and it is the only time the actor ever appeared in a horror movie. As to his participation in the film, Bogart simply stated, "This was one of the pictures that made me march in to Jack Warner and ask for more money again....You can't believe what this one was like. I had a part that somebody like Bela Lugosi or Boris Karloff should have played. I was this doctor, brought back to life, and the only thing that nourished this poor bastard was blood. If it had been Jack Warner's blood, or Harry's or Pop's, maybe I wouldn't have minded as much. The trouble was, they were drinking mine and I was making this stinking movie."

p, Bryan Foy; d, Vincent Sherman; w, Lee Katz (based on the story "The Doctor's Secret" by William J. Makin); ph, Sid Hickox; m, Bernhard Kaun; ed, Thomas Pratt; art d, Esdras Hartley; cos, Milo Anderson; makeup, Perc Westmore; tech adv, Dr. Leo Schulman.

Horror   **(PR:C MPAA:NR)**

RETURN OF DRACULA, THE**   (1958) 77m UA bw (GB: THE FANTASTIC DISAPPEARING MAN)

Francis Lederer (*Bellac*), Norma Eberhardt (*Rachel*), Ray Stricklyn (*Tim*), Jimmie Baird (*Mickey*), Greta Granstedt (*Cora*), Virginia Vincent (*Jennie*), John Wengraf (*Merriman*), Gage Clark (*Reverend*), John McNamara (*Sheriff Bicknell*), Harry Harvey, Sr. (*Station Master*), Mel Allen (*Porter*), Hope Summers (*Cornelia*), Dan Gachman (*County Clerk*), Robert Lynn (*Doctor*).

Cute yes, horror, no. Lederer is the main guy, a zombie-style Dracula, who heads to Southern California. On the way he kills a man and assumes his identity. Eberhardt sets Lederer's mouth watering but he first takes care of Vincent before getting to her. Eberhardt is saved by her teenage boy friend Stricklyn. But they don't take care of Lederer—U.S. Immigration does when they come to check his passport. Although filmed in black and white, the one bit of color does not add to the movie: a splash of blood does not make a horror film.

p, Jules V. Levy, Arthur Gardner; d, Paul Landres; w, Pat Fielder; ph, Jack MacKenzie; m, Gerald Fried; ed, Sherman Rose; art d, James Vance.

Horror   **(PR:C MPAA:GP)**

RETURN OF FRANK JAMES, THE***½   (1940) 92m FOX c

Henry Fonda (*Frank James/Ben Woodson*), Gene Tierney (*Eleanor Stone*), Jackie Cooper (*Clem/Tom Grayson*), Henry Hull (*Maj. Rufus Cobb*), John Carradine (*Bob Ford*), J. Edward Bromberg (*Runyon*), Donald Meek (*McCoy*), Eddie Collins (*Station Agent at Eldora*), George Barbier (*Ferris the Judge*), Ernest Whitman (*Pinky Washington*), Charles Tannen (*Charles Ford*), Lloyd Corrigan (*Randolph Stone*), Russell Hicks (*Prosecutor*), Victor Kilian (*Preacher*), Edward McWade (*Col. Fentridge Jackson*), George Chandler (*Boy*), Bud Fine (*Deputy*), Irving Bacon (*Man at Wagon Sale*), Frank Shannon (*Sheriff Daniels*), Barbara Pepper (*Nellie Blane*), Louis Mason (*Wilson the Watchman*), Stymie Beard (*Mose the Bellboy*), William Pawley ("*Jesse James" Actor*), Frank Sully (*Pappy the Old Actor*), Davison Clark (*Officer*), Edmund Elton (*Jury Foreman*), Sherry Hall (*Court Clerk*), A.S. Byron (*Engineer*), Lee Phelps, James Morton (*Bartenders*), Lillian Yarbo (*Maid*), Bob McKenzie (*Old Man on Rocker*), Hattie Noel (*Chambermaid*), Adrian Morris (*Detective*), Almeda Fowler (*Mrs. Edna Stone*), Bob Battier ("*Frank James" Actor*), Milton Kibbee, Dale Van Sickel, Frank Melton, Lester Dorr (*Reporters*), Kermit Maynard (*Courtroom Extra*), Lew Meehan (*Bailiff*), Kernan

Cripps (Deputy), Russ Powell (Juror), Nelson McDowell (Confederate Veteran/Juror).

Producer Zanuck shocked the Hollywood community when he chose German director Lang to helm the sequel to the studio's extremely popular western JESSE JAMES (1939). When asked how he expected a German to make a film about America's Old West Zanuck replied, "Because he'll see things we won't." The film opens with a reprise of the assassination of Jesse James at the hands of the Ford brothers (Carradine and Tannen) from the first film. Jesse's brother Frank (Fonda) resolves to let the law handle the Ford brothers and goes back to farming under an assumed name. When Carradine and Tannen are pardoned by the governor, however, Fonda vows revenge and, accompanied by his ward, Cooper, he sets out to find the Fords. To finance his search, Fonda robs an express office and a clerk is accidentally killed by his own friends. The murder is pinned on Fonda. Meanwhile, the town of Liberty's major and newspaper publisher, Hull, sends his pretty young female reporter Tierney out to get the true story from Fonda himself. Fonda isn't interested in the press, but he is in Tierney. Eventually Cooper and Fonda catch up with Carradine and Tannen. There is a dramatic chase into the mountains and Tannen is killed when he falls off his horse. Carradine escapes. Soon after, Fonda learns from Tierney that his servant, Whitman, has been accused of the express office killing and is about to stand trial. Fonda returns to Liberty and gives himself up. Carradine has enough nerve to show up during the trial and watch—confident that Fonda will soon be hung. The villainous murderer is wrong, however, because Fonda is acquitted. After the trial Carradine finds himself trapped in a gun duel with young Cooper and both men are killed. His quarry dead, Fonda returns to his farm to start a new life. THE RETURN OF FRANK JAMES marked several firsts in Lang's career. It was the director's first film shot in color and it was his first foray into a distinctly American genre—the western. Having spent time living with Navajo Indians to prepare for a failed project which would have been called "Americana," and making several car trips throughout the Southwest, Lang eagerly accepted the assignment and looked forward to using the knowledge he had acquired about the American West. One not so eager to be in the picture was Fonda. Fonda had found Lang extremely unpleasant during the shooting of YOU ONLY LIVE ONCE and wasn't keen on repeating the experience. When Lang heard of the actor's worries, he confronted Fonda with tears in his eyes—Fonda later called them "crocodile tears"—and promised that he would treat the performers with more respect. Fonda agreed to give Lang a second chance, but the same problems started all over and Fonda never worked under the director again. Personal problems aside, THE RETURN OF FRANK JAMES is a beautifully photographed western which de-emphasizes action in favor of mood, atmosphere, and character detail. Fonda, Cooper, and Carradine turn in fine performances here, while Hull's usual hammy histrionics are used to good advantage by Lang. Tierney, in her film debut, is pretty and does well in a role that really isn't necessary. Perhaps the only problem with THE RETURN OF FRANK JAMES is the veritable whitewashing of Fonda's character. Because the Hays code decreed that a bad man could not be the hero of a film, Fonda's character is shown in an almost saintly light and his past is practically ignored. This is a tale of revenge, but cirumstances are manipulated in such a way as to keep Fonda from having to do anything remotely brutal. The deaths of both the express clerk and Tannen are accidents and Carradine is finally gunned down by a third party—Cooper. Poor Cooper pays for Fonda's sins and enables the former bandit to ride off into the sunset. Though Lang tries to put the sharp edge back on the material through subtle moments of character study, the script stays far away from any real portrayal of the destructive consequences of revenge. Because Fonda is the hero, he must not be tainted too badly by his drive for revenge. This soft approach to the subject of revenge in westerns would change drastically by the 1950s, especially in the films of directors Budd Boetticher and Anthony Mann, whose obsessive heros—usually played by Randolph Scott and James Stewart—border on the psychotic.

p, Darryl F. Zanuck; d, Fritz Lang; w, Sam Hellman; ph, George Barnes, William V. Skall (Technicolor); m, David Buttolph; ed, Walter Thompson; art d, Richard Day, Wiard B. Ihnen; set d, Thomas Little; cos, Travis Banton.

Western   Cas.   (PR:A MPAA:NR)

RETURN OF JACK SLADE, THE*½   (1955) 79m AA bw (GB: TEXAS ROSE)

John Ericson (Jack Slade), Mari Blanchard (Texas Rose), Neville Brand (Harry Sutton), Casey Adams [Max Showalter](Billy Wilcox), John Shepodd (Johnny Turner), Howard Petrie (Ryan), John Dennis (Kid Stanley), Angie Dickinson (Polly Logan), Donna Drew (Laughing Sam), Mike Ross (Little Blue), Lyla Graham (Abilene), Alan Wells (George Hagen), Raymond Bailey (Professor).

Jack Slade returns, but actually as Jack Slade, Jr. since the original was killed in the first movie. Ericson is a Pinkerton agent in this gun blazer who has to chase down a gang of bad guys in Wyoming. He infiltrates the gang, knocks off the outlaws, and romances Blanchard, who was at first part of the bad-guy entourage. Good guy wins everything in the end.

p, Lindsley Parsons; d, Harold Schuster; w, Warren Douglas; ph, William Sickner (SuperScope); m, Paul Dunlap; ed, Maurice Wright; art d, A. Leslie Thomas; m/l, "Yellow Rose of Texas," Don George.

Western   (PR:A MPAA:NR)

RETURN OF JESSE JAMES, THE**½   (1950) 75m Lippert bw

John Ireland (Johnny), Ann Dvorak (Sue Younger), Henry Hull (Hank Younger), Hugh O'Brien (Lem), Reed Hadley (Frank James), Victor Kilian (Rigby), Byron Foulger (Bakin), Tom Noonan (Charlie Ford), Clifton Young (Bob Ford), Margia Dean, Sid Melton, Paul Maxey, Sam Flint, Robin Short, Barbara Woodell.

Ireland is a petty crook who falls in with some of the former James gang in his first top-name role. He resembles Jesse James so much that the locals are all abuzz about Jess being alive again. That forces Frank James, now an upstanding citizen,

to bring Ireland to justice and stop all the hullabaloo over his brother. Hadley as Frank James tracks down gang leader Hull and Ireland and leaves no doubts about Jesse's death.

p, Carl K. Hittleman; d, Arthur David Hilton; w, Jack Natteford (based on a story by Hittleman); ph, Karl Struss; m, Albert Glasser; ed, Harry Coswick; art d, F. Paul Sylos.

Western   (PR:A MPAA:NR)

RETURN OF JIMMY VALENTINE, THE**½   (1936) 67m REP bw (AKA: JIMMY VALENTINE)

Roger Pryor (Gary Howard), Charlotte Henry ("Midge" Davis), Robert Warwick ("Jimmy"Davis), James Burtis (Mac), Edgar Kennedy (Callahan), J. Carroll Naish (Tony Scapelli), Lois Wilson (Mary Davis), Wade Boteler ("Red" Dolan), Gayne Whitman (Radio Actor), Dewey Robinson (Augie Miller), Hooper Atchley (Rocco), William P. Carlton (Warden Keeley), Frank Melton (Dixon), Jeanie Roberts (Kitty), George Lloyd (Louie), George Chesebro (Nick), Charles Wilson (Kelley), Franklin Parker (Grogan), Harry Bowen (Price), Lane Chandler (Finney), Jack Mack (Clerk), Gertrude Messinger (Blonde), Lucille Ward.

An updating of the "Jimmy Valentine" stories previously filmed in 1920 and 1928. A newspaper, in an effort to boost circulation and combat the rising popularity of radio, offers a reward to anyone who can find the aging safecracker. Pryor is their ace reporter who wants the reward himself and gets on the trail of the former thief. Henry is the crook's daughter, whom Pryor meets and falls in love with. Together they meet some of her father's old enemies and combat their crooked schemes. The film starts off slowly but gradually builds to a fairly exciting conclusion. Warwick, who played the safecracker in the 1920 film, returns to play the character in retirement. Armstrong, Jr., who contributed to the story, is the son of "Jimmy Valentine's" creator. Though an average gangster film, this one is helped by using the romance within the story rather than just grafting it on, as love stories usually were in the genre. Kennedy, as usual, is fine in comic relief.

p, Victor Zobel; d, Lewis D. Collins; w, Jack Natteford, Olive Cooper (based on a story by Scott Darling, Wallace Sullivan, Paul Armstrong, Jr.); ph, William Nobles; ed, Dan Milner.

Crime   (PR:A MPAA:NR)

RETURN OF MARTIN GUERRE, THE***½   (1983, Fr.) 111m La Societe Francaise Production Cinematographique-France Region 3-La Societe de Production des Films Marcel Dassault-Roissi-Palace/European International c

Gerard Depardieu (Martin Guerre), Bernard Pierre Donnadieu (Martin Guerre), Nathalie Baye (Bertrande de Rols), Roger Planchon (Jean de Coras), Maurice Jacquemont (Judge Rieux), Isabelle Sadoyan (Catherine Boere), Rose Thiery (Raimonde de Rols), Maurice Barrier (Pierre Guerre), Stephane Peau (Young Martin), Sylvie Meda (Young Bertrande), Chantal Deruaz (Jeanne), Valerie Chassigneux (Guillemette), Tcheky Karyo (Augustin), Dominique Pinon (Antoine), Adrien Duquesne (Sanxi), Andre Chaumeau (The Cure), Philippe Babin (Jacques), Francis Arnaud, Axel Bogousslavsky, Neige Dolsky, Gilbert Gilles, Jean-Claude Perrin, Alain Recoing, Rene Bouloc, Alain Frerot, Andre Delon, Daniele Loo, Marcel Champel, Yvette, Petit, Jean Julliac, Guy Bertrand, Jean-Paul Barathieu, Bruno Bentegeac, Pierre Bouchet, Francis Chevillon, Andre D'Avant-Cour, Christian Fiter, Daniel Giraud, Guy Jacquet Roger Payrot.

The engrossing period piece, set in 16th Century France, is based on an actual case which took place in a small peasant village. Depardieu and Baye marry but cause rumors to spread when they do not produce any children. Depardieu remains strangely distant and one day disappears. When he returns, nine years later, he receives a warm and cordial welcome from the townsfolk as well as Baye, who has remained faithful to him. Occasional lapses of memory, faces he does not recognize, and accusations that he is an imposter divide the town: there are those who believe that he is Martin Guerre, while others are convinced that Guerre lost a leg during a war and never returned home. Baye grows increasingly confused, at times defending her husband and on other occasions condemning him with her silence. The matter is brought before a magistrate (the inquiry has been intercut throughout the entire picture) and he sentences Depardieu to hang, convicting him of impersonating the real Martin Guerre. One of the most successful art-house films in recent years, MARTIN GUERRE relies on two powerful performances—Depardieu, France's top actor of late and the one most in view of American audiences (GET OUT YOUR HANDKERCHIEFS, THE LAST METRO, 1900) is perfectly cast as the baffling peasant and Baye (equally as accomplished as Depardieu and quite familiar to Truffaut fans) is superb in a role that asks for quiet reservation. Director Vigne attempts nothing more than an elaborately costumed courthouse romance and accomplishes nothing more, but tells a compelling tale all the same. (In French; English subtitles.)

p&d, Daniel Vigne; w, Vigne, Jean-Claude Carriere; ph, Andre Neau (Fujicolor); m, Michel Portal; ed, Denise de Casabianca; art d, Alain Negre; cos, Anne-Marie Marchand; makeup, Jacky Bouban, Didier Lavergne, Francoise Embry Kernevez.

Historical Drama   Cas.   (PR:C MPAA:NR)

RETURN OF MAXWELL SMART, THE   (SEE: NUDE BOMB, THE, 1980)

RETURN OF MR. H, THE   (SEE: THEY SAVED HITLER'S BRAIN, 1964)

RETURN OF MR. MOTO, THE**½   (1965, Brit.) 71m Lippert/FOX bw

Henry Silva (Mr. Moto), Martin Wyldeck (Dargo), Terence Longdon (Jonathan Westering), Suzanne Lloyd (Maxine Powell), Marne Maitland (Wasir Hussein), Harold Kasket (Shahrdar of Wadi), Henry Gilbert (David Lennox), Brian Coburn (Magda), Stanley Morgan (Inspector Halliday), Peter Zander (Ginelli), Anthony

Booth (*Hovath*), Gordon Tanner (*McAllister*), Richard Evans (*Chief Inspector Marlow*), Dennis Holmes (*Chapel*), Ian Fleming (*Rogers*), Tracy Connell (*Arab*), Sonyia Benjamin (*The Belly Dancer*), Alister Williamson (*Maitre d'Hotel*).

Mr. Moto is back (Silva) but not in his usual surroundings of Hawaii. This time the famous Interpol agent is working in London. The evil Dargo, an ex-Nazi, thinks he has killed Silva when he tosses him into the river. But the scrutable Mr. Moto returns and gets involved in foiling a sabotage involving Middle East oil production. In disguise, Mr. Moto learns that Dargo is pressuring the Middle East people to give in along with Beta Oil Company of Britain. An executive's secretary is kidnaped for company secrets and Mr. Moto must rescue her. He kills Dargo, arrests his henchmen, who had been working against but with the Middle East people, and the world's oil supply is safe once more.

p, Robert L. Lippert, Jack Parsons; d, Ernest Morris; w, Fred Eggers (based on a character created by John P. Marquand); ph, Basil Emmott; m, Douglas Gamley; ed, Robert Winter; art d, Harry White; makeup, Harold Fletcher.

Mystery (PR:A MPAA:NR)

RETURN OF MONTE CRISTO, THE½** (1946) 91m COL bw (GB: MONTE CRISTO'S REVENGE)

Louis Hayward (*Edmond Dantes*), Barbara Britton (*Angele Picard*), George Macready (*Henri De La Roche*), Una O'Connor (*Miss Beedle*), Henry Stephenson (*Prof. Duval*), Steven Geray (*Bombelles*), Ray Collins (*Emil Blanchard*), Ludwig Donath (*Judge Lafitte*), Ivan Triesault (*Maj. Chavet*), Jean Del Val (*Pinot*), Eugene Borden (*Jacques*), Crane Whitley (*Durce*), John Cory (*Guard*).

This tightly woven film, complete with twisting plots and counter strategies, follows Hayward as he works his way through the movie in a variety of disguises. Hayward plays the count's grandson, who is trying to get back the family fortune. He has to go up against Britton, who has naively become controlled by a group of villains. To get back at his foes, he escapes from Devil's Island and makes his way back to France. He battles his foes and one by one they fall by the wayside. The final climactic battle occurs in a dark theater with Hayward emerging victorious. He and Britton finish the job by becoming lovers.

p, Grant Whytock; d, Henry Levin; w, George Bruce, Alfred Neumann (based on a story by Curt Siodmak, Arnold Phillips); ph, Charles Lawton, Jr.; m, Lucien Morawek; ed, Richard Fantl; md, Lud Gluskin; art d, Stephen Goosson, Carl Anderson; set d, Fay Babcock.

Adventure (PR:A MPAA:NR)

RETURN OF OCTOBER, THE* (1948) 89m COL c

Glenn Ford (*Prof. Bassett*), Terry Moore (*Terry Ramsey*), Albert Sharpe (*Vince, the Tout*), James Gleason (*Uncle Willie*), Dame May Whitty (*Aunt Martha*), Henry O'Neill (*President Hotchkiss*), Frederic Tozere (*Mitchell*), Samuel S. Hinds (*Judge Northridge*), Nana Bryant (*Therese*), Lloyd Corrigan (*Dutton*), Roland Winters (*Col. Wood*), Stephen Dunne (*Prof. Stewart*), Gus Schilling (*Benny*), Murray Alper (*Little Max*), Horace MacMahon (*Big Louie*), Victoria Horne (*Margaret*), Byron Foulger (*Jonathan*), Bill Pearson (*Tommy*), Russell Hicks (*Taylor*), Robert Malcolm (*Detective*), Ray Walker (*Reporter*).

A giggly comedy, lightweight enough that even the worst gags can be dismissed as fun. Moore is the girl who remembers her uncle's vow that if he ever came back to life, it would be as a horse to win the Kentucky Derby. That memory sets Moore off as she spots October, a horse, and thinks it is her uncle. Her relatives quickly try to have her put away to gain control of her estate. But October *does* win the Derby and a psychology professor starts having some second thoughts on the whole matter. Ford is the professor who uses all the goings on to publish a best-seller. A whimsical story that pleases all ages.

p, Rudolph Mate; d, Joseph H. Lewis; w, Melvin Frank, Norman Panama (based on a story by Connie Lee, Karen DeWolf); ph, William Snyder (Technicolor); m, George Duning; ed, Gene Havlick; md, M.W. Stoloff; art d, Stephen Goosson, Rudolph Sternad; set d, Wilbur Menefee, William Kiernan; cos, Jean Louis; makeup, Clay Campbell.

Fantasy (PR:A MPAA:NR)

RETURN OF OLD MOTHER RILEY, THE (SEE: OLD MOTHER RILEY, 1937, Brit.)

RETURN OF PETER GRIMM, THE** (1935) 83m RKO bw

Lionel Barrymore (*Peter Grimm*), Helen Mack (*Catherine*), Edward Ellis (*Dr. Andrew Macpherson*), Donald Meek (*Mayor Batholomew*), George Breakston (*William Van Dam*), Allen Vincent (*Frederik*), James Bush (*James*), Ethel Griffies (*Mrs. Batholomew*), Lucien Littlefield (*Col. Lawton*), Greta Meyer (*Marta*), Ray Mayer.

After making a shambles of his life, a dead man (Barrymore) returns to set things straight. Instead he makes more of a mess, trying to push his adopted daughter (Mack) into an engagement with his insipid nephew (Vincent). She, however, loves another man (Bush). Lacking direction, this film rambles around to nowhere. Director Nicholls seemed unable to decide whether he wanted to play the story straight or for laughs, and the film suffers for it. A play written and produced by David Belasco in 1911 served as the inspiration for this film, as well as for a silent released by Fox in 1926. This was the last film produced for RKO by Macgowan, who moved on to Fox.

p, Kenneth Macgowan; d, George Nicholls, Jr.; w, Francis Edwards Faragoh (based on the play by David Belasco); ph, Lucien Andriot; ed, Arthur Schmidt.

Fantasy (PR:A MPAA:NR)

RETURN OF RAFFLES, THE* (1932, Brit.) 71m Markham/Williams and Pritchard bw

George Barraud (*A.J. Raffles*), Camilla Horn (*Elga*), Claude Allister (*Bunny*), A.

Bromley Davenport (*Sir John Truwode*), Sydney Fairbrother (*Lady Truwode*), H. Saxon-Snell (*Von Spechen*), Philip Strange.

Gentleman jewel thief Barraud is foiled in his scheme to lift some gems when someone beats him to the safe. When he learns that the victim was an old flame, he pursues and catches the crook, and returns the emeralds.

p&d, Mansfield Markham; w, W.J. Balef (based on stories by E.W. Hornung); ph, Geoffrey Faithfull, Emil Schunemann.

Crime (PR:A MPAA:NR)

RETURN OF RIN TIN TIN, THE½** (1947) 65m EL c

Donald Woods (*Father Matthew*), Bobby [Robert] Blake (*Paul, the Refugee Lad*), Claudia Drake (*Mrs. Graham*), Gaylord Pendleton (*Melrose*), Earle Hodgins (*Joe*), Rin Tin Tin III.

Strictly for the kids, this film features then child star Blake as a refugee boy, a psychological casualty of the war in Europe who is spending the summer at a California mission. The kid looks to be a lost cause, but Rin Tin Tin shows up after escaping from a Santa Barbara kennel. From there on the two are inseparable as they fight off Rin Tin Tin's owners and the dog returns the favor by saving the kid from a pack of rabid dogs. After getting out of that scrape, they are paired forever.

p, William Stephens; d, Max Nosseck; w, Jack De Witt (based on a story by Stephens); ph, Carl Berger (Vitacolor); m, Leo Erdody; ed, Eddie Mann; art d, F. Paul Sylos.

Adventure (PR:AA MPAA:MR)

RETURN OF RINGO, THE*½ (1966, Ital./Span.) 96m Mediterranee-Balcazar/Rizzoli bw (IL RITORNO DI RINGO)

Giuliano Gemma, Fernando Sancho, Hally Hammond, Nieves Navarro, Antonio Casas, Pajarito.

In the "spaghetti western" mode, but passable, this picture centers on Gemma, a man supposed to be dead, who returns to his village and finds his family held by Sancho and his gang. Gemma doesn't come off as a super hero, which makes this movie believable and realistic. He is just someone who is scared and has to do battle to free his family using everything in his power to do so. Tessari's first "Ringo" film was A PISTOL FOR RINGO (1966).

p, Alberto Pugliese, Tuciano Ercoli; d, Duccio Tesssari; w, Tessari, Fernando Di Leo; ph, Francisco Marin.

Western (PR:A MPAA:NR)

RETURN OF SABATA zero (1972, Ital./Fr./Ger.) 106m Produzioni Europee Associate-Les Productions Artistes Associes-Artemis/UA c (E'TORNATO SABATA; HAI CHIUSO UN'ALTRA VOLTA)

Lee Van Cleef (*Sabata*), Reiner Schone (*Clyde*), Annabella Incontrera (*Maggie*), Gianni Rizzo (*Jeremy Sweeney*), Gianpiero Albertini (*McIntock*), Jacqueline Alexandre (*Jackie*), Pedro Sanchez [Ignazio Spalla] (*Bronco*), Nick Jordan [Aldo Canti] (*Angel*), Karis Vassili (*Acrobat*), Annibal Venturi (*McIntock's Henchman*), Benito Vasconi (*Bouncer*), Sylvia Alba (*Saloon Girl*), Hershel Kerrona, Miguel Vascez, Ernesto Hayes, Steffen Zacharias, Maria Pia Giancaro, Janos Bartha, Gunther Stoll, Carmelo Reade, Vittorio Fanfoni.

This is the third in the "Sabata" films, although the second one starred Yul Brynner and was originally named INDIO BLACK but was later retitled ADIOS, SABATA and his name changed in the English looping. Van Cleef's career was a rollercoaster until he got the chance to star in one of the early "spaghetti westerns" and soon became a huge star in Europe, where Westerns had always been popular. His face is like one of those on Mount Rushmore although not nearly that animated. This Italian-made movie is about an Irish family that resembles the Corleones in the way they operate. It's just after the Civil War and Van Cleef, an unreconstituted Johnny Reb, is now working as a trick-shot artist in a small circus. The group arrives in a tiny Texas town where Van Cleef accidentally meets Schone, a former friend who owes Van Cleef a tidy sum. Schone promises to pay the debt and Van Cleef decides to stick around the town, which is run by Albertini, a domineering red-haired Irishman who consults his Bible as often as he counts his money, which is a good deal more than somewhat. Albertini levies huge taxes on the populace on the promise that the money will be used to fund various civic projects. Van Cleef's unmoving nostrils smell a rat and when he looks deeper into Albertini's affairs, the redhead is resentful of the intrusion and gives Schone the order for Van Cleef to be killed. Since this would also effectively erase Schone's debt to Van Cleef, the man agrees to set a snare, then reckons that the moment Van Cleef is dead, he'll be next. So he tells Van Cleef and the two men join forces against Albertini. They recruit two of Van Cleef's circus pals plus a local hired gun and rob Albertini's bank, only to find that all the paper money is counterfeit and that the cash has been turned into gold and is now secreted on Albertini's property. They find the money in an abandoned mine, kill Albertini and his gang, and it all ends happily. Director-cowriter Parolini uses an alias and well he might. Lots of acrobatics and odd weapons that range from mini-guns to a cigar that shoots darts to a pistol shaped like brass knuckles and on and on. A stinkeroo that needed production companies from three countries to back it, RETURN OF SABATA was financed by P.E.A. (Rome), Artemis Films (Berlin), and Les Productions Artistes (Paris). After a beautiful opening sequence, the picture collapses into a mindless shoot-em-up that is a travesty of that most American of all film genres, the western. With a few more intended laughs, it could have been a funny satire. Unfortunately, everyone here was dead serious.

p, Alberto Grimaldi; d, Frank Kramer [Gianfranco Parolini]; w, Renato Izzo, Parolini; ph, Sandro Mancori (Techniscope, Technicolor); m, Marcello Giombini; ed, Parolini, Salvatore Aventario; art d, Luciano Puccini; set d, Claudio De Santis; cos, De Santis.

Western (PR:C MPAA:PG)

RETURN OF SHERLOCK HOLMES, THE½** (1929) 71m PAR bw

Clive Brook *(Sherlock Holmes)*, H. Reeves-Smith *(Dr. Watson)*, Betty Lawford *(Mary Watson)*, Charles Hay *(Capt. Longmore)*, Phillips Holmes *(Roger Longmore)*, Donald Crisp *(Col. Moran)*, Harry T. Morey *(Prof. Moriarty)*, Hubert Druce *(Sgt. Gripper)*, Arthur Mack.

Sir Arthur Conan Doyle's famous detective made his first speaking appearance in this otherwise unmemorable effort. Morey is the sleuth's old nemesis, now the head of a "radio-tapping" ring, who kills one of his underlings with a poisoned needle hidden in a cigarette case by evil cohort and surgeon Crisp. Later the captain of the ship Crisp works on as ship's doctor is murdered by the gang, which plans to set up headquarters on board. When the captain's son, Holmes, comes to investigate he is kidnaped and held aboard the ship, bound for America. His sudden disappearance in the wake of his father's murder leads the police to suspect him. Lawford, Holmes' girl friend—and loyal sidekick Reeves-Smith's daughter—asks Brook to come out of his bee-keeping retirement to help Holmes. Together Brook, Reeves-Smith, and Lawford manage to catch the ship in France. Brook disguises himself as an Austrian violinist with the ship's orchestra, and after one musical performance he puts on an impromptu magic show during which he manages to slip an incriminating document from Crisp's pocket. Next, in another disguise, the master detective coats the soles of Crisp's shoes with phosphorescent paint, then follows the glowing trail to the cabin where Holmes is held. Morey, also on board, figures out the identity of the hero and the pair sit down for dinner and a chat. Morey offers Brook a cigarette from the poisoned case. The detective uses his sleight-of-hand to make Morey think he has been pricked with the needle and is dying from its effects. Morey is arrested when he disembarks in New York and kills himself with the cigarette case. When Reeves-Smith compliments Brook on his sleuthing, movie fans heard for the first time the familiar litany that never appears in any of the original stories, "Elementary, my dear Watson, elementary." Shot indoors at the Astoria New York studios because of the primitive sound recording equipment used, the film does have one shot on the deck of the ship with the Manhattan skyline (such as it was in 1929) visible in the background. More significant than good, the film does sport decent performances by Brook and Morey, but these are lost in the claustrophobic settings and awkward line readings of Reeves-Smith, Lawford, and others.

d, Basil Dean; w, Dean, Garrett Fort (based on "The Dying Detective" and "His Final Bow" by Sir Arthur Conan Doyle); ph, William Steiner, Jr.; ed, Helene Turner.

Mystery (PR:A MPAA:NR)

RETURN OF SOPHIE LANG, THE** (1936) 65m PAR bw

Gertrude Michael *(Sophie Lang)*, Sir Guy Standing *(Max Bernard)*, Ray Milland *(Jimmy Lawson)*, Elizabeth Patterson *(Araminta Sedley)*, Colin Tapley *(Purser)*, Paul Harvey *(Inspector Parr)*, Garry Owen *(Nosey Schwartz)*, Don Rowan *(Buttons McDermott)*, Purnell Pratt *(Mr. Chadwick)*, Ted Oliver, James Blaine *(Detectives)*, Charles Coleman *(Dining Steward)*, Keith Daniels, Don Roberts, Jack Chapin, Jay Owens, Ralph McCullough, Eddie Fetherston, Arthur Rowland, Frank MacCready *(Reporters)*, Jack Raymond *(Cameraman)*, Anderson Lawler *(Jennings)*, Forrester Harvey, David Thursby *(Deck Stewards)*, Guy Usher *(Dr. Dutton)*, Herbert Evans *(Butler)*, Monte Vandergrift, Budd Fine, Hal Price *(Cops)*, Paddy O'Flynn *(Man)*, Oscar Rudolph *(Bellboy)*, Edward Earle *(Hotel Clerk)*, Arthur S. "Pop" Byron *(Porter)*, Tom Kennedy *(Cop on Switchboard)*, Joseph R. Tozer *(Ship's Captain)*, Frank Benson *(Taxi Driver)*, Harry Allen *(Caretaker at Graveyard)*, James Aubrey *(Steward)*, Lee Phelps *(Police Announcer)*, Harry Owen *(McOwen)*.

Jewel thief Sophie Lang was successful enough in her screen debut in THE NOTORIOUS SOPHIE LANG (1934) that Paramount brought her back two years later. Michael still had the title role, but now her character was attempting to go straight as the companion to wealthy English matron Patterson, who has a fondness for expensive jewelry. Much of the story takes place on board a U.S.-bound ship which carries not only Michael and her employer, but master thief Standing and newsman Milland. Romance begins between Milland and Michael, while Standing tries to enlist the ex-criminal's aid in stealing Patterson's prize possession, the Krueger diamond. Michael refuses, but Standing gets the gem anyway, leaving Michael as the number one suspect. It all gets sorted out in the end, well enough for Michael to reprise her character once more in SOPHIE LANG GOES WEST (1937). An appealing cast and some good technical work make up for some rather bland plotting.

p, A.M. Botsford; d, George Archainbaud; w, Brian Marlow, Patterson McNutt (based on a story by Frederick Irving Anderson); ph, George Clemens.

Crime (PR:A MPAA:NR)

RETURN OF THE APE MAN*½ (1944) 60m MON bw

Bela Lugosi *(Prof. Dexter)*, John Carradine *(Prof. Gilmore)*, Frank Moran *(Ape Monster)*, Judith Gibson *(Anne)*, Michael Ames [Tod Andrews] *(Steve Rogers)*, Mary Currier *(Mrs. Gilmore)*, Ed Chandler *(Sergeant)*, Mike Donovan *(Policeman)*, George Eldridge *(Patrolman)*, Horace Carpenter *(Watchman)*, Ernie Adams *(Bum)*, Frank Leigh.

This was Lugosi's last film for Monogram and he trotted out his usual mad scientist routine for a horror film with more laughs than screams. Lugosi and colleague Carradine find a prehistoric man frozen in ice (actually wrapped in cellophane) and they bring him back to the laboratory to thaw him out. The ape man (played by former boxer Moran) recovers from the deep freeze nicely, though he proves to be more than a little on the stupid side. Lugosi wants to help the creature out by giving him a new brain and, when Carradine objects, he kills the scientist and snatches his brain for Moran. Lugosi then attempts to civilize his creation, and does succeed in teaching him to play the piano, but then Moran goes ape and embarks on a trail of murder and mayhem, until he is finally destroyed. Good, inane fun, especially for Lugosi fans.

p, Jack Dietz, Sam Katzman; d, Phil Rosen; w, Robert Charles; ph, Marcel Picard; ed, Carl Pierson.

Horror (PR:A MPAA:NR)

RETURN OF THE BADMEN*** (1948) 90m RKO bw (AKA: RETURN OF THE BAD MEN)

Randolph Scott *(Vance)*, Robert Ryan *(Sundance Kid)*, Anne Jeffreys *(Cheyenne)*, George "Gabby" Hayes *(John Pettit)*, Jacqueline White *(Madge Allen)*, Steve Brodie (Cole Younger), Richard Powers [Tom Keene] *(Jim Younger)*, Robert Bray *(John Younger)*, Lex Barker *(Emmett Dalton)*, Walter Reed *(Bob Dalton)*, [Michael Harvey] *(Grat Dalton)*, Dean White *(Billy the Kid)*, Robert Armstrong *(Wild Bill Doolin)*, Tom Tyler *(Wild Bill Yeager)*, Lew Harvey *(Arkansas Kid)*, Gary Gray *(Johnny)*, Walter Baldwin *(Muley Wilson*, Minna Gombell *(Emily)*, Warren Jackson *(George Mason)*, Robert Clarke *(Dave)*, Jason Robards, Sr. *(Judge Harper)*, Harry Shannon *(Wade Templeton)*, Charles McAvoy *(Elmer)*, Larry McGrath *(Scout)*, Ernie Adams *(Leslie the Townsman)*, Billy Vincent, Howard McCrorey *(Deputies)*, George Nokes *(Donald Webster)*, Ronnie Ralph *(Tim Webster)*, Polly Bailey *(Mrs. Webster)*, Forrest Taylor *(Farmer)*, Lane Chandler *(Ed the Posse Leader)*, Bud Osborne *(Steve the Stagecoach Driver)*, Brandon Beach *(Conductor)*, Charles Stevens *(Grey Eagle)*, Kenneth McDonald *(Col Markham)*, Ida Moore *(Mrs. Moore)*, Dan Foster *(Outlaws)*, Richard Thorne *(Soldier)*, John Hamilton *(Doc Peters)*, Cyril Ring *(Bank Clerk)*, Earl Hodgins *(Auctioneer)*.

This sequel to the 1946 film BADMAN'S TERRITORY takes the same premise as it's precursor, presenting numerous figures of the old West and throwing historical accuracy to the winds. Through he plays a different character this time, Scott's role is essentially the same. Scott is a marshal who has put down his guns for a peaceful retirement. Meanwhile, in the Oklahoma territory, Ryan is busy assembling what amounts to a "Who's Who" gang of outlaws including Brodie, Powers, and Bray as the Younger brothers; Barker, Reed, and Harvey as the Daltons; White as Billy the Kid; Armstrong as Bill Doolin; and Tyler and Harvey as Bill Yeager and the Arkansas Kid. This supergang begins a reign of terror that includes stage hold ups and train robberies. Scott faces up to the gang and ends up standing as the victor when the haze of gunsmoke has cleared by the film's end. Considering the large cast of outlaws this easily could have degenerated into an action-packed mess with the name bandits popping for periodic color. However, Enright has orchestrated the action with a fine feel for the material, never losing sight of the central conflict between Ryan and Scott amid the mayhem. The two men play well off one another, creating some realistic tension that carries through to the very end. The supporting players fill out the picture as well, with not a role wasted. Brodie and Armstrong are standouts among the gang members with their lively and colorful performances. Jeffreys, as a reformed lady gunslinger, gives some good support as one of Scott's love interests, while perennial B western sidekick Hayes provides some comic relief as a banker. A good compendium of many western elements.

p, Jack J. Gross, Nat Holt; d, Ray Enright; w, Jack Natteford, Luci Ward, Charles O'Neal (based on a story by Natteford, Ward); ph, J. Roy Hunt; m, Paul Sawtell; ed, Samuel E. Beetley; md, C. Bakaleinikoff; art d, Albert S. D'Agostino, Ralph Berger; set d, Darrell Silvera, James Altwies; cos, Renie; spec eff, Russell A. Cully; m/l, "Remember the Girl You Left Behind," Mort Greene, Harry Revel; makeup, Gordon Bau.

Western Cas. (PR:C MPAA:NR)

RETURN OF THE BLACK EAGLE½** (1949, Ital.) 112m Lux bw

Rossano Brazzi *(Vladimir Dubrowski)*, Irasema Dilian *(Masha)*, Gino Cervi *(Kirila)*, Harry Feist *(Prince Serge)*, Angelo Calabrese *(Judge)*, Paolo Stoppa *(Bandit)*, Rina Morelli *(Irina)*.

Set in Russia, this film stars Brazzi as a Russian soldier who returns home after his discharge to find his family has been severely mistreated by local landowner Cervi. Brazzi assumes the identity of the masked Black Eagle and wreaks havoc in Cervi's domain, looting and stealing at will. Then he meets Cervi's daughter, Dilian, and falls in love with her. He poses as a French tutor to gain access to Cervi's castle and to pursue Dilian. Eventually, he is exposed, but escapes as his men enter the castle for a spectacular battle. Cervi is killed and Brazzi wins the hand of Dilian. This elaborate production featured some impressive interiors and well-staged action scenes, along with good performances, especially by Brazzi as the swashbuckling hero. Though it was filmed in Italy in 1946, RETURN OF THE BLACK EAGLE wasn't released in the U.S. until three years later, the same year Brazzi made his American film debut in LITTLE WOMEN. (In Italian; English subtitles.)

d, Riccardo Freda; w, Mario Monicelli, Braccio Agnoletti (based on a novel by Alexander Pushkin); ph, Rodolfo Lombardi.

Action-Adventure (PR:A MPAA:NR)

RETURN OF THE CISCO KID*½ (1939) 70m FOX bw

Warner Baxter *(Cisco Kid)*, Lynn Bari *(Ann Carver)*, Cesar Romero *(Lopez)*, Henry Hull *(Colonel Jonathan Bixby)*, Kane Richmond *(Alan Davis)*, C. Henry Gordon *(Mexican Captain)*, Robert Barrat *(Sheriff McNally)*, Chris-Pin Martin *(Gordito)*, Adrian Morris *(Deputy Johnson)*, Soledad Jimenez *(Mama Soledad)*, Harry Strang *(Deputy)*, Arthur Aylesworth *(Stage Coach Driver)*, Paul E. Burns *(Hotel Clerk)*, Victor Kilian *(Bartender)*, Eddie Waller *(Guard)*, Ruth Gillette *(Blonde)*, Ward Bond *(Tough)*.

Hey Cisco! After an eight-year hiatus—THE CISCO KID (1931)—Baxter returned as the Mexican version of Robin Hood, riding again, this time after escaping from a firing squad in the nick of time. He meets Bari and has romance in his heart. But first he has to help Bari and her father retrieve the money they were cheated out of. Her boy friend shows up and when it appears Bari wants him more than Baxter, Cisco sends him on a suicide mission. But Baxter has a change of heart, takes care of the crooks, saves the guy, and romps to Mexico to save more poor souls.

p, Kenneth Macgowan; d, Herbert I. Leeds; w, Milton Sperling (based on the character created by O. Henry); ph, Charles Clarke; ed, James B. Clark; md, Cyril K. Mockridge; art d, Richard Wiard, B. Ihnen; cos, Gwen Wakeling.

Western   **(PR:A MPAA:NR)**

RETURN OF THE CORSICAN BROTHERS   (SEE: BANDITS OF CORSICA, THE, 1953)

RETURN OF THE DRAGON½**   (1974, Chin.) 90m Golden Harvest/ Bryanston c

Bruce Lee (Tang Lung), Chuck Norris (Kuda), Nora Miao (Chen Ching Hua), Huang Chung Hsun (Uncle Wang), Chin Ti (Ah K'ung), Jon T. Benn (Boss), Robert Wall (Robert), Liu Yun, Chu'eng Li, Little Unicorn, Ch'eng Pin Chih, Ho Pieh, Wel P'ing Au, Huang Jen Chih, Mali Sha.

A year after the extraordinarily popular Bruce Lee died, this film was released in the U.S. and was an immediate box office sensation. Filmed in Rome and Hong Kong, the movie followed the ENTER THE DRAGON (1973) formula for kung fu movies—not much plot and lots of action. It does contain a classic confrontation at its climax in which Lee battles Norris—the world karate champ who would soon be a martial arts movie star himself. It would be one of the few times Norris came out the loser. Though numerous following films would include footage of Lee, this was the last film he was actually involved in (he also wrote and directed the project), and it's a favorite of martial arts devotees and action fans.

p, Raymond Chow; d&w, Bruce Lee; ph, Ho Lang Shang (Technicolor); m, KuChia Hui; ed, Chang Yao Chang; art d, Ch'ieng Hsin; cos, Chu Sheng Hsi.

Martial Arts   **Cas.**   **(PR:O MPAA:R)**

RETURN OF THE FLY*½**   (1959) 80m FOX bw

Vincent Price (Francois Delambre), Brett Halsey (Philippe Delambre), David Frankham (Alan Hinds, Scientist), John Sutton (Inspector Charas), Dan Seymour (Max Berthold, Underworld Fixer), Danielle De Metz (Cecile Bonnard), Janine Graudel (Mme. Bonnard), Richard Flato (Sgt. Dubois), Florence Storm (Nun), Pat O'Hara (Detective Evans), Barry Bernard (Lt. Maclish), Jack Daly (Granville), Michael Mark (Gaston), Francisco Villalobos (Priest), Joan Cotton (Nurse).

A sequel to the very successful 1958 film, THE FLY, has Halsey as the son of the scientist who met his demise in the first film after his experiments left him part-man, part-fly. Halsey decides to renew his father's experiments, though his uncle, Price (reprising his role from the original), warns him not to. Halsey recreates the matter transformation mechanisms, then meets the same fate as his dad when his assistant, Frankham, forces him into the device. Frankham is an agent for a foreign power who is intent on getting the secret of the invention. Halsey, now sporting a fly's head and legs, kills Frankham and seems likely to end up just like Dad. But Price finds a way to reverse the procedure, and Halsey ends up his old self again. Bernds, who directed many of The Three Stooges films, provided rather plodding direction to this movie, which was far less entertaining than the original. Still, it was successful enough to inspire Fox to bring back the Fly again in THE CURSE OF THE FLY (1965).

p, Bernard Glasser; d&w, Edward Bernds (based on a story by George Langelaan); ph, Brydon Baker (CinemaScope); m, Paul Sawtell, Bert Shefter; ed, Richard C. Meyer; art d, Lyle R. Wheeler, John Mansbridge; set d, Walter M. Scott, Joseph Kish; makeup, Hal Lierley.

Horror   **Cas.**   **(PR:A MPAA:NR)**

RETURN OF THE FROG, THE*   (1938, Brit.) 73m Imperator/Select Attractions bw

Gordon Harker (Inspector Elk), Una O'Connor (Mum Oaks), Hartley Power (Sandford), Rene Ray (Lila), Cyril Smith (Maggies), Charles Lefeaux (Golly Oaks), Charles Carson (Chief Commissioner), George Hayes (Lane), Meinhart Maur (Alkman), Alexander Field (Sniffy Offer), Aubrey Mallalieu (Banker), Dennis Cowles, Patrick Parsons.

There's a frog on the loose, and Scotland Yard assigns an Elk to the case. Harker is Inspector Elk and it's up to him to track down a gang of thieves who leave a drawing of a frog at the scene of all their crimes. Harker has numerous scrapes with death before he finally captures the villains. A sequel to THE FROG (1937), the film offers an enjoyable mix of comedy and drama and Harker is likable in a role he had filled before in the movies and on stage.

p, Herbert Wilcox; d, Maurice Elvey; w, Ian Hay, Gerald Elliott (based on the story "The India Rubber Men" by Edgar Wallace); ph, George Stretton; ed, Peggy Hanneasey, A. Jeggs.

Crime-Mystery   **(PR:A MPAA:NR)**

RETURN OF THE FRONTIERSMAN**   (1950) 74m WB c

Gordon MacRae (Logan Barrett), Julie London (Janie Martin), Rory Calhoun (Larrabee), Jack Holt (Sam Barrett), Fred Clark (Ryan), Edwin Rand (Kearney), Raymond Bond (Dr. Martin), Matt McHugh (Harvey), Britt Wood (Barney).

Crooner MacRae is a sheriff's son who gets sent to the pokey for allegedly committing a series of bank holdups and a murder. But MacRae sings his innocence and breaks out of jail to find the man who framed him. With London at his side, he gathers the clues that point to Calhoun and the two fight it out at the end. Even MacRae's singing can't overcome the dull action. MacRae sings "The Cowboy" and "Underneath a Western Sky."

p, Saul Elkins; d, Richard Bare; w, Edna Anhalt; ph, Peverell Marley (Technicolor); m, David Buttolph; ed, Frank Magee; art d, Charles M. Clarke.

Western   **(PR:A MPAA:NR)**

RETURN OF THE JEDI**½**   (1983) 133m Lucasfilm/FOX c

Mark Hamill (Luke Skywalker), Harrison Ford (Han Solo), Carrie Fisher (Princess Leia), Billy Dee Williams (Lando Calrissian), Anthony Daniels (See Threepio [C-3PO]), Peter Mayhew (Chewbacca), Sebastian Shaw (Anakin Skywalker), Ian McDiarmid (Emperor Palpatine), Frank Oz (Yoda), David Prowse (Darth Vader), James Earl Jones (Voice of Darth Vader), Alec Guinness (Ben Obi-Wan Kenobi), Kenny Baker (Artoo-Detoo [R2-D2]), Michael Pennington (Moff Jerjerrod), Kenneth Colley (Adm. Piett), Michael Carter (Bib Fortuna), Denis Lawson (Wedge), Tim Rose (Adm. Ackbar), Dermot Crowley (Gen. Madine), Caroline Blakiston (Mon Mothma), Warwick Davis (Wicket), Kenny Baker (Paploo), Jeremy Bulloch (Boba Fett), Femi Taylor (Oola), Annie Arbogast (Sy Snootles), Claire Davenport (Fat Dancer), Jack Purvis (Teebo), Mike Edmonds (Logray), Jane Busby (Chief Chirpa), Malcom Dixon, Mike Cottrell (Ewok Warriors), Nicki Reade (Nicki), Adam Bareham (1st Stardestroyer Controller), Jonathan Oliver (2nd Stardestroyer Controller), Pip Miller (1st Stardestroyer Captain), Tom Mannion (2nd Stardestroyer Captain), Margo Apostocos, Ray Armstrong, Eileen Baker, Michael H. Balham, Bobbie Bell, Patty Bell, Alan Bennett, Sarah Bennett, Pamela Betts, Dan Blackner, Linda Bowley, Peter Burroughs, Debbie Carrington, Maureen Charlton, William Coppen, Sadie Corrie, Tony Cox, John Cummings, Jean D'Agostino, Luis De Jesus, Debbie Dixon, Margarita Fernandez, Phil Fondacaro, Sal Fondacaro, Tony Friel, Dan Frishman, John Gavam, Michael Gilden, Paul Grant, Lydia Green, Lars Green, Pam Grizz, Andrew Herd, J.J. Jackson, Richard Jones, Trevor Jones, Glynn Jones, Karen Lay, John Lummiss, Nancy MacLean, Peter Mandell, Carole Morris, Stacy Nichols, Chris Nunn, Barbara O'Laughlin, Brian Orenstein, Harrell Parker, Jr., John Pedrick, April Perkins, Ronnie Phillips, Katie Purvis, Carol Read, Nicholas Read, Diana Reynolds, Daniel Rodgers, Chris Romano, Dean Shakenford, Kiran Shah, Felix Silla, Linda Spriggs, Gerald Staddon, Josephine Staddon, Kevin Thompson, Kendra Wall, Brian Wheeler, Butch Wilhelm (Ewoks), Toby Philpott, David Barclay, Mike Edmonds (Jabba Puppeteers), Michael McCormick, Deep Roy, Simon Williamson, Hugh Spirit, Swim Lee, Michael Quinn, Richard Robinson (Puppeteers).

This was the final segment of the trilogy that included STAR WARS and THE EMPIRE STRIKES BACK. It was also the most spectacular of the trio as, by that time, George Lucas and his cohorts at the Industrial Light and Magic Company had perfected their special effects craft and this film is a tribute to their unique talents. But effects do not an engaging picture make and that's proven here as they eschew humanity in favor of chrome and steel and hardware, thus giving us a fabulous picture to look at but seldom involving. What is galling is that several new characters have been introduced for what appears to be the sole purpose of selling toys to breathless youngsters who adored the first two films. So it's all spectacle without much heart and the actors take second position to the creatures and the action. Darth Vader (Prowse, with a breathy voice by James Earl Jones) is up to no good again. He's building a new Death Star vehicle, one that cannot be destroyed with the ease seen in the other films. Ford has been placed in carbonite as a trophy by the heinous Jabba, a toad with elephantiasis, who is a combination of the space GODFATHER and something you'd dissect in your biology class. Hamill has sent his pals, Daniels and Baker (as the robot and the whatever-it-is) to try and get Ford out of the place. Fisher arrives, masquerading as a bounty hunter, and brings Mayhew (The Wookie) as a prize for Jabba. While there, the group manages to free Ford but his freedom is short-lived and the entire set of good guys is snared and Jabba is about to make them a dinner for his pet, a huge and disgusting creature that will eat almost anything (except of course, turnips). Williams has been pretending to be one of the palace guards and he aids the others in escaping. Then Fisher slays Jabba and they get away to join the Alliance, a group of rebels who will never give up the good fight. Hamill talks to Yoda (played by Frank Oz, the long-time associate of "Muppets" man Jim Henson and the voice of "Miss Piggy" in falsetto). Through the little creature he learns that Fisher is his twin sister and that the evil Prowse is, shock upon shock, his father! Well! Since Fisher is his sister, that means she also has the potential ability to be a Jedi, if she can ever call upon "The Force." They go to the planet of Endor and high above the heavily wooded place, Prowse is just about ready to put his new Death Star into action. It's protected by a seemingly impenetrable shield that will fend off anything (we'll soon see about that) and the task now is to get rid of that protection so Williams and the others can smash the miles-long space ship out of the skies. In order to do that, Hamill allows himself to be captured. Once aboard the Death Star, Hamill is amazed to learn that the bad guys know all about the plot and that the Rebels are going to their doom. McDiarmid is the supreme boss of all bosses and attempts to recruit Hamill into his group and promises him Prowse's position as second in command, if Hamill is willing to duel Prowse for the job. A duel commences between father and son as the Death Star begins firing everything in its arsenal at the attacking Rebels. Hamill almost kills Prowse, then holds back. Meanwhile, there's a cute group of beings on Endor called the Ewoks and, with their help, the Death Star is destroyed. Hamill escapes before it blows up and Ford and Fisher are united in love at the fade out. Sensational effects include floating barges, incredible creatures, airborne cycles, death ray machines, light-swords and more and more. Prowse, in a sudden change of heart, kills McDiarmid and sacrifices his own life for the sake of his son, Hamill, and we who have been taught to believe that Prowse is the most heinous man in space don't believe it for a second. The space battles are overwhelming photographically and every technical credit is first rate. The amount of dialog and characterization in the script could be printed on the back of a matchbook and there'd still be room left over to put every truthful statement any agent ever said. It won the 1983 Oscar for Special Visual Effects and will be best appreciated by the hearing-impaired, especially those who cannot read lips. A technical triumph but a disappointing and unfulfilling end to Lucas' dream, although the box office returns could have fed Ethiopa for a century.

p, Howard Kazanjian, Robert Watts, Jim Bloom; exec p, George Lucas; d, Richard Marquand; w, Lawrence Kasdan, Lucas (based on a story by Lucas); ph, Alan Hume, Jack Lowin, Jim Glennon (Panavision, Rank Color); m, John Williams; ed, Sean Barton, Marcia Lucas, Duwayne Dunham, Arthur Repola; prod d, Norman Reynolds; art d, Fred Hole, James Schoppe, Joe Johnston; set d, Michael Ford, Harry Lange; cos, Aggie Guerard Rodgers, Nilo Rodis-Jamero; spec eff, Roy Arbogast, Kit West, Richard Edlund, Dennis Muren, Ken Ralston; m/l, Joseph

Williams, Annie Arbogast, Ben Butt; stunts, Glenn Randall, Peter Diamond; ch, Gillian Gregory; makeup, Tom Smith, Graham Freeborn; creature design, Phil Tippett, Stuart Freeborn; animation, James Keefer.

Science Fiction   Cas.   (PR:A-C MPAA:PG)

RETURN OF THE LASH zero   (1947) 61m PRC/EL bw

"Lash" LaRue (Cheyenne), Al "Fuzzy" St. John ("Fuzzy"), Mary Maynard (Kay), Brad Slaven (Grant), George Chesebro (Kirby), Lee Morgan (Clark), Lane Bradford (Dave), John Gibson (Pete), Dee Cooper (Hank), Carl Mathews, Bud Osborne, Slim Whitaker, Kermit Maynard, Frank Ellis, Bob Woodward.

LaRue and his whip return, this time to aid Slaven and his fellow ranchers who are being victimized by Chesebro's villainous scheme to acquire all the land in the area. The ranchers need cash, so LaRue and St. John set out after outlaws whose capture will net them reward money. After they round up a sufficient number of criminals, St. John goes off to get the reward money, but gets hit on the head while returning with the booty and suffers amnesia. He can't remember what happened to the money until the movie's climactic battle with Chesebro's gang in which another blow to the head restores his memory. As always, LaRue's expertise with the whip is entertaining, but the film has nothing else to offer.

p, Jerry Thomas; d, Ray Taylor; w, Joseph O'Donnell; ph, Ernest Miller; m, Walter Greene; ed, Hugh Winn; md, Dick Carruth; art d, Jack Mills.

Western   (PR:A MPAA:NR)

RETURN OF THE LIVING DEAD   (SEE: DEAD PEOPLE, 1974)

RETURN OF THE PINK PANTHER, THE***½   (1975, Brit.) 115m
UA c

Peter Sellers (Inspector Jacques Clouseau), Christopher Plummer (Sir Charles Litton), Catherine Schell (Claudine Litton), Herbert Lom (Chief Inspector Dreyfus), Peter Arne (Col. Sharki), Burt Kwouk (Cato), Andre Maranne (Francois), Gregoire Aslan (Chief of Police), Peter Jeffrey (Gen. Wadafi), David Lodge (Jean Duval), Eric Pohlmann (The Fat Man), John Bluthal (Beggar), Victor Spinetti (Concierge), Mike Grady (Bellboy), Carol Cleveland (Sari Lady), Jeremy Hawk (Jealous Escort), Graham Stark (Pepi), Claire Davenport (Masseuse), Milton Reid (Restaurant Owner).

This was the third in the "Pink Panther" series which starred Sellers. Arkin and director Bud Yorkin had attempted their version with INSPECTOR CLOUSEAU but it couldn't compare to the comedy engendered by Sellers under Edwards' direction. This sequel took in better than $30 million and earned every cent. The famous diamond which is named in the title has been stolen from the museum where it had been residing for the past several years. Blame is laid at the feet of retired jewel thief Plummer (doing the Niven role established in THE PINK PANTHER) although he is innocent. Plummer is married to Schell and is in danger of being arrested for a crime he didn't commit so he has to find out who the real crook is. Lom is again Sellers' boss and he reluctantly gives Sellers the task of solving the crime. There follows a series of sight gags and misplaced-word jokes with Sellers playing off Aslan and Arne, two Middle Eastern cops, Spinetti and Grady, employees at a Gstaad resort, and all of the villains, led by Pohlmann in an imitation of Sydney Greenstreet. The picture comes to life only when Sellers is on screen and the rest of the time it's just vamping. The locations were visually satisfying with scenes being shot at Gstaad, Switzerland, the French Riviera, Marrakesh, and Casablanca. The picture races along like a "Road Runner" cartoon with occasional stops to catch its breath. Try to see it on TV in a room alone because the laughter in a full-theater audience will be overpowering. Julie Andrews, who is Mrs. Edwards, did a small cameo as a chambermaid but was cut out in the final print. Edwards comes from directorial genes as his grandfather, J. Gordon Edwards, was in charge of the lensing of many films, including several by Theda Bara. (See PINK PANTHER series, Index.)

p&d, Blake Edwards; w, Frank Waldman, Edwards; ph, Geoffrey Unsworth (Panavision, DeLuxe Color); m, Henry Mancini; ed, Tom Priestly; prod d, Peter Mullins; art d, Mullins; cos, Bridget Sellers; spec eff, John Gant; m/l, Mancini, Hal David; makeup, Harry Frampton; animation, Richard Williams Studio.

Comedy   Cas.   (PR:A-C MPAA:PG)

RETURN OF THE RANGERS, THE*   (1943) 60m PRC bw

Dave O'Brien, Jim Newill, Guy Wilkerson, Nell O'Day, Glenn Strange, Emmett Lynn, I. Stanford Jolley, Robert Barron, Henry Hall, Harry Harvey, Dick Alexander, Charles King.

The Texas Rangers don disguises to catch a band of cattle rustlers. While incognito, one of their number is charged with murder, so another ranger bends the law a little bit and pretends he's a judge to free his compatriot. Everything turns out well when the Rangers find the guilty party and bring him to justice. (See TEXAS RANGERS series, Index.)

p, Arthur Alexander; d&w, Elmer Clifton; ph, Robert Cline; ed, Charles Hankel, Jr.; md, Lee Zahler.

Western   (PR:A MPAA:NR)

RETURN OF THE RAT, THE**½   (1929, Brit.) 84m Gainsborough/
Woolf and Freedman bw

Ivor Novello (Pierre "The Rat" Boucheron), Isabel Jeans (Zelia de Chaumet), Mabel Poulton (Lisette), Bernard Nedell (Henri), Marie Ault (Mere Colline), Gordon Harker (Morell), Scotch Kelly (Bill), Harry Terry (Alf), Gladys Frazin.

The third and final installment in the series of "Rat" films starring Novello. Filmed silent with sound added later, the plot sees Novello giving up his life of crime to marry the woman he loves, Jeans. Unfortunately, the relationship soon crumbles and Novello leaves her to return to the life he knows best. Back in the underworld, Novello falls in love with a young barmaid, Poulton, but the ghost of his failed

marriage comes back to haunt him when his former wife's lover arrives and demands a duel.

p, Michael Balcon; d, Graham Cutts; w, Edgar C. Middleton, A. Neil Lyons, Angus McPhail (based on characters created by Ivor Novello, Constance Collier); ph, Roy Overbaugh.

Crime/Romance   (PR:A MPAA:NR)

RETURN OF THE SCARLET PIMPERNEL**   (1938, Brit.) 80m
LFP/UA bw

Barry K. Barnes (Sir Percy Blakeney/The Scarlet Pimpernel), Sophie Stewart (Marguerite Blakeney), Margareta Scott (Theresa Cabarrus), James Mason (Jean Tallien), Francis Lister (Chauvelin), Anthony Bushell (Sir Andrew Ffoulkes), Patrick Barr (Lord Hastings), David Tree (Lord Harry Denning), Henry Oscar (Maximilien de Robespierre), Hugh Miller (De Calmet, Robespierre's Secretary), Allen Jeayes (Judge of the Tribunal), O.B. Clarence (de Marre), George Merritt (Chief of Police), Evelyn Roberts (Prince of Wales), Esme Percy (Richard Brinsley Sheridan, Playwright), Edmund Breon (Col. Winterbottom), Frank Allenby (Professor Wilkins), John Counsell (Sir John Selton), Torin Thatcher.

A sequel to THE SCARLET PIMPERNEL (1935) has Barnes playing the heroic nobleman portrayed by Leslie Howard in the original. In this film, the Frenchman Robespierre (Oscar) is anxious to get even with the Scarlet Pimpernel for helping members of the French aristocracy to escape from the guillotine. He has Lister kidnap Barnes' wife (Stewart) and bring her to France in an effort to trap Barnes. Barnes foils the plan and gains freedom for his wife so they may happily return to England. The setting and costumes are handsomely mounted, but the story is thoroughly uninspired, and the project wasn't helped by a lackluster cast.

p, Alexander Korda, Arnold Pressburger; d, Hans Schwartz; w, Lajos Biro, Arthur Wimperis, Adrian Brunel (based on a novel by Baroness Orczy); ph, Mutz Greenbaum; m, Arthur Benjamin; ed, Philip Charlot; md, Muir Mathieson; cos, Rene Hubert.

Historical Drama   (PR:A MPAA:NR)

RETURN OF THE SECAUCUS SEVEN***½   (1980) 110m
Salsipuedes/Libra c

Mark Arnott (Jeff), Gordon Clapp (Chip), Maggie Cousineau (Frances), Brian Johnston (Norman Gaddis), Adam LeFevre (J.T.), Bruce MacDonald (Mike), Jean Passanante (Irene), Maggie Renzi (Kate), John Sayles (Howie), David Strathairn (Ron), Karen Trott (Maura), Marisa Smith, Carolyn Brooks, Steven Zaitz, Ernie Bashaw, Jessica MacDonald, Jeffrey Nelson, Amy Schewel, Eric Forsythe, Betsy Julia Robinson, John Medillo, Jack LaValle, Benjamin Zaitz, Nancy Mette, Cora Bennett.

After scripting low-budget horror films such as PIRANHA (1978) and ALLIGATOR (1980), John Sayles made a rather auspicious directorial debut with this film. Working with a tiny budget (reportedly $60,000) and using inexperienced actors, Sayles succeeded in creating an intelligent and sometimes compelling study of former 1960s political activists coming to grips with their lives 10 years after graduation from college. In the late 1960s, the seven friends were arrested in Secaucus, New Jersey, on their way to a march on the Pentagon. The film opens with the Secaucus Seven, and a few new companions, getting together on the New Hampshire farm of Renzi and MacDonald for a reunion. Over the course of the few days, much is revealed about the past and present lives and romances of the friends. While that's about all there is to the movie, it is nevertheless an honest examination of the characters and their relationships. The movie is virtually all dialog, much of it fresh and witty, and the rather unspectacular characters are engaging enough to sustain interest. Sayles brought a lot of energy to the film and it shows, overcoming the technical deficiencies which are inherent in projects with such meager funding. Overall, it's a very worthwhile movie, especially for those who are weary of films dominated by action and high technology and short on character development.

p, William Aydelott, Jeffrey Nelson; d&w, John Sayles; ph, Austin de Besche (DuArt Color); m, K. Mason Daring; ed, Sayles.

Drama   Cas.   (PR:O MPAA:R)

RETURN OF THE SEVEN*½   (1966, Span.) 95m Mirisch/UA c

Yul Brynner (Chris), Robert Fuller (Vin), Julian Mateos (Chico), Warren Oates (Colbee), Jordan Christopher (Manuel), Claude Akins (Frank), Virgilio Texeira (Luis), Emilio Fernandez (Lorca), Rudy Acosta (Lopez), Elisa Montes (Petra), Fernando Rey (Priest), Gracita Sacromonte, Carlos Casaravilla, Ricardo Palacios, Felisa Jiminez, Pedro Bermudez, Francisco Anton, Moises Menedez, Hector Quiroga, Jose Telavera.

A weak sequel to THE MAGNIFICENT SEVEN (1960) having only Brynner as a throwback to the original, and with a lot of added violence. The same small Mexican village is harassed, and this time crazy rancher Fernandez sends 50 gunmen to roundup the inhabitants of the village to construct a church as a memorial to his dead son. Mateos, original member of the seven, is one of these farmers; his wife sets about contacting Brynner, who then enlists the aid of other gunslingers, some from prison and others from the local watering hole. They ride in to save the villagers and restore peace. Oates, as a skirt-chasing gunslinger, remains behind to teach the villagers how to defend themselves. Project is marred by an implausible script, slack direction, and a cast that lacks any enthusiasm. Another sequel, GUNS OF THE MAGNIFICENT SEVEN, followed.

p, Ted Richmond; d, Burt Kennedy; w, Larry Cohen; ph, Paul C. Vogel (Panavision, DeLuxe Color); m, Elmer Bernstein; ed, Bert Bates; art d, Jose Alguero; set d, Antonio Mateos; spec eff, Dick Parker; makeup, Jose Maria Sanchez.

Western   Cas.   (PR:A MPAA:NR)

RETURN OF THE SOLDIER, THE*** (1983, Brit.) 102m Brent Walker-Barry R. Cooper-Skreba/FOX c

Julie Christie (Kitty), Glenda Jackson (Margaret), Ann-Margret (Jenny), Alan Bates (Chris), Ian Holm (Ernest), Frank Finlay (William), Jeremy Kemp (Frank), Hilary Mason (Ward), John Sharp (Pearson), Elizabeth Edmunds (Emery), Valerie Whittington (Beatrice), Patsy Byrne (Mrs. Plummer), Robert Keegan (Chauffeur), Amanda Grinling (Alexandra), Edward De Souza (Edward), Michael Cochrane (Stephen), Vickery Turner (Jessica), Sheila Keith (Sister), Shirley Caine (Ward Sister), Emily Irvin (Young Jenny), William Booker (Young Chris), Valerie Aitken (Ballerina), Nicholas Frankau (Young Civilian Gentleman), Llewellyn Rees (Lord Lieutenant), Jeremy Arnold (Ballerina's Boy Friend), Allan Corduner (Pianist at Party), John Lonsdale (Groom), Pauline Quirke (Girl Searching in Hospital), Cathy Finlay (Downstairs Nurse), Charles Morgan (Weeping Man), Gerry Cowper (Ward Nurse), Patrick Gordon (Wounded Officer), Stephen Whittaker (Hostile Soldier), Kevin Whately (Hostile Soldier's Mate), Larry Gordon (Delivery Man), Jack May (Brigadier General), Dorothy Alison (Brigadier's Wife), Martin Ransley, Jane Laurie (Young Couple in Boat), Robin Langford, Stephen Finlay (Young Officers).

Bates is a shell-shocked WW II vet who returns home with no memory of his marriage to Christie, a snobbish woman who comes to represent his dissatisfaction with life. Seeing the opportunity to finally attract Bates after years of yearning, old-maid Ann-Margret tries to fulfill her unrequited love, but soon finds herself competing for his affections with Jackson, his childhood flame. Bates, however, finds all of these emotional entanglements difficult to deal with, so he retreats into the past. A rather slow-moving film, but one filled with touching, genuine performances from a fine cast.

p, Ann Skinner, Simon Relph; d, Alan Bridges; w, Hugh Whitemore (based on the novel by Rebecca West); ph, Stephen Goldblatt (Technicolor); m, Richard Rodney Bennett; ed, Laurence Mery Clark; prod d, Luciana Arrighi; art d, Ian Whittaker; cos, Shirley Russell.

Drama (PR:C MPAA:NR)

RETURN OF THE TERROR* (1934) 65m FN-WB bw

Mary Astor (Olga Morgan), Lyle Talbot (Dr. Goodman), John Halliday (Dr. Redmayne), Frank McHugh (Joe the Reporter), Irving Pichel (Burke), Frank Reicher (Reinhardt), J. Carrol Naish (Steve Scola), Renee Whitney (Virginia Mayo), Robert Barrat (Pudge), George E. Stone (Soapy), Robert Emmet O'Connor (Bradley the Detective), Etienne Girardot (Mr. Tuttle), George Cooper, Charles Grapewin, George Humbert, Maude Eburne, Cecil Cunningham, Frank Conroy, Edmund Breese, Howard Hickman.

A murder mystery in which Halliday stars as a scientist who has been institutionalized after claiming insanity to avoid prosecution for a series of brutal murders he didn't commit. He escapes from the asylum and the murders begin anew, while the audience tries to guess which one of the many suspects is the real murderer. Eventually, Halliday is cleared as the actual killer is caught. A remake of THE TERROR (1928), which was the first sound horror film, this movie features some competent performances, but suffers from too many complications thrown in to keep the viewers from easily identifying the madman.

p, Sam Bischoff; d, Howard Bretherton; w, Eugene Solow, Peter Milne (based on the story "The Terror" by Edgar Wallace); ph, Arthur Todd; ed, Owen Marks; art d, John Hughes; cos, Orry-Kelly.

Horror/Mystery (PR:C MPAA:NR)

RETURN OF THE TEXAN*** (1952) 88m FOX bw

Dale Robertson (Sam Crockett), Joanne Dru (Ann Marshall), Walter Brennan (Firth Crockett), Richard Boone (Rod), Tom Tully (Stud Spiller), Robert Horton (Dr. Harris), Helen Westcott (Averill), Lonnie Thomas (Yo-Yo), Dennis Ross (Steve), Robert Adler (Foreman), Kathryn Sheldon (Housekeeper), Aileen Carlyle (Cordy Spiller), Linda Green (Spiller Girl), Brad Mora (Spiller Boy).

A back-to-the-soil theme highlights this story of a man, Robertson, who returns to his Texas ranch after his wife dies in the big city. Along with his father, Brennan, and two sons, he goes about rebuilding the broken down ranch which is surrounded by wealthy landowners. One rancher, Boone, is not very receptive to Robertson's return, and especially doesn't take kindly to Brennan's poaching on his land. Although obsessed with the past and the memory of his dead wife, Robertson manages to find love again in Boone's sister-in-law, Dru, and is able to build himself a happy family once again. Cast and direction are superb in creating an honest and warm atmosphere.

p, Frank P. Rosenberg; d, Delmer Daves; w, Dudley Nichols (based on the novel The Home Place by Fred Gipson); ph, Lucien Ballard; m, Sol Kaplan; ed, Louis Loeffler; md, Lionel Newman; art d, Lyle Wheeler, Albert Hoysett; cos, Renie.

Western (PR:A MPAA:NR)

RETURN OF THE VAMPIRE, THE**½ (1944) 69m COL bw

Bela Lugosi (Armand Tesla), Frieda Inescort (Lady Jane Ainsley), Nina Foch (Nicki Saunders), Roland Varno (John Ainsley), Miles Mander (Sir Frederick Fleet), Matt Willis (Andreas Obry), Ottola Nesmith (Elsa), Gilbert Emery (Professor Saunders), Leslie Denison (Lynch), William C.P. Austin (Gannett), Jeanne Bates, Sherlee Collier, Donald Dewar, Billy Bevan, George McKay.

Lugosi played a vampire again for the first time since DRACULA (1931), though the "Dracula" name couldn't be used in the film because Universal owned the rights to it. The film is set in London during WW II where bombings have released Lugosi from his grave. He then goes out in search of young ladies to supply him with blood, this time with the aid of a werewolf, Willis. Inescort, who operates an asylum, is Lugosi's nemesis, seeking to destroy the vampire. Lugosi's undoing is at the hands of Willis, however, who in the end decides to go straight and finishes off the vampire with a dreaded crucifix. For the final scene, a wax mask was made of

Lugosi and placed over a skull. The vampire's deterioration was then depicted as the wax melted, exposing the skull, a scene that proved to be too graphic for British audiences and so was edited out of the English release. Lugosi is wonderfully menacing as the vampire, and Landers' direction makes this a properly chilling horror venture. Surprisingly, though he is most often identified with his vampire roles, Lugosi only played the infamous blood-sucker three times—in this film, DRACULA, and ABBOTT AND COSTELLO MEET FRANKENSTEIN (1948).

p, Sam White; d, Lew Landers; w, Griffin Jay, Randall Faye (based on an idea by Kurt Neumann); ph, John Stumar, L.W. O'Connell; ed, Paul Borofsky; md, M.W. Stoloff; art d, Lionel Banks; makeup, Clay Campbell.

Horror Cas. (PR:A MPAA:NR)

RETURN OF THE VIGILANTES, THE (SEE: VIGILANTES RETURN, THE, 1947)

RETURN OF THE WHISTLER, THE** (1948) 63m COL bw

Michael Duane (Ted Nichols), Lenore Aubert (Alice Bradley), Richard Lane (Gaylord Travers), James Cardwell (John), Ann Shoemaker (Mrs. Bradley), Wilton Graff (Dr. Grantland), Olin Howlin (Jeff Anderson), Eddy Waller (Sam), Trevor Bardette (Arnold), Ann Doran (Sybil), Robert Emmett Keane (Hart), Edgar Dearing (Capt. Griggs), Sarah Padden (Mrs. Huiskamp).

Loosely based on the CBS radio program "The Whistler," Duane is faced with a problem when the girl he is about to marry, Aubert, is missing. He knows almost nothing about her past (hard to believe when he is set on marrying her), but through clues provided by some of her belongings, and the aid of private detective Lane, the girl turns up. Shoddy script has a hard time holding any level of suspense. (See WHISTLER series, Index.)

p, Rudolph C. Flethow; d, D. Ross Lederman; w, Edward Bock, Maurice Tombragel (based on the story by Cornell Woolrich, suggested by the CBS radio program "The Whistler"); ph, Philip Tannura; ed, Dwight Caldwell; md, Mischa Bakaleinikoff; art d, George Brooks.

Mystery (PR:A MPAA:NR)

RETURN OF WILD BILL, THE** (1940) 60m COL bw

Bill Elliott (Wild Bill Saunders), Iris Meredith (Sammy Lou Griffin), George Lloyd (Matt Kilgore), Luana Walters (Kate Kilgore), Edward J. LeSaint (Lige Saunders), Frank LaRue (Ole Mitch), Francis Walker (Jake Kilgore), Chuck Morrison (Bart), Dub Taylor (Cannonball), Buel Bryant (Mike), William Kellogg (Hep), Jack Rockwell, Jim Corey, John Merton, Donald Haines, John Ince.

Elliott is in for a surprise when he comes home to find his father dying from the hands of a ruthless gang that has been terrorizing the land. The pace is set for Elliott to seek his revenge, sidelined only for occasional interludes of romanticizing Meredith. There's an interesting twist in Walters as the do-gooder sister of the gang's leader, who winds up dead despite her honest efforts.

p, Leon Barsha; d, Joseph H. Lewis; w, Robert Lee Johnson, Fred K. Myton (based on the story by Walt Coburn); ph, George Meehan; ed, Richard Fantl.

Western (PR:A MPAA:NR)

RETURN OF WILDFIRE, THE*** (1948) 80m Lippert/Screen Guild bw (GB: BLACK STALLION)

Richard Arlen (Dobe), Patricia Morison (Pat Marlowe), Mary Beth Hughes (Judy Marlowe), James Millican (Frank Keller), Chris-Pin Martin (Pancho), Stanley Andrews ("Pop" Marlowe), Holly Bane (Dirk), Highland Dale (Wildfire), Reed Hadley (Marty Quinn).

Considered to be one of the best westerns in its time to feature wild horses, this tale centers around Hadley as the villain who is pressuring horse ranchers to sell their land in an attempt to get the corner on the horse market. One of the ranchers refuses to budge and he winds up dead, leaving his two sisters, Morison and Hughes, to fend for the ranch themselves. Arlen plays a drifter who wanders into town and tries to help the sisters defend their property. He winds up falling in love with Morison in the process, with a finale that includes a showdown gunfight between Arlen and Hadley. This picture features an incredible fight scene between two wild stallions, with Highland Dale as the stallion leader of the herd. Includes the song "Just an Old Sombrero," sung by Morison.

p, Carl K. Hittleman; d, Ray Taylor; w, Hittleman, Betty Burbridge; ph, Ernest Miller (Sepiatone); m, Albert Glasser; ed, Paul Landres; md, Glasser; set d, Dave Milton.

Western (PR:A MPAA:NR)

RETURN TO BOGGY CREEK*½ (1977) 87m 777 Distributors c

Dawn Wells, Dana Plato.

A sequel of sorts to THE LEGEND OF BOGGY CREEK (1972), which is more like a children's film than the docudrama/horror film that preceded it. A group of young tykes becomes disoriented during a storm and gets lost. A bigfoot-type creature shows up and helps the kids out. A fairly harmless kiddie outing. Dana Plato would later go on to television fame in "Different Strokes."

p, Bob Gates; d, Tom Moore; w, Dave Woody; ph, (Technicolor).

Fantasy Cas. (PR:AA MPAA:G)

RETURN TO CAMPUS*½ (1975) 100m Cinepix c

Earl Keyes (Hal Norman), Ray Troha (Bruce Norman), Al Raymond (Rupp Brubaker), Paul Jacobs (Pighead Smith), Paul Jacobs (Esco Schmidt), Helen Killinger (Joyce Kutner), Norma Joseph (Barbara Lewis), Arnold Palmer (Spike Belfry), John Barner (Dean of Men), Connie O'Connell (Night Club Singer), Tom Harmon, Jesse White (Sports Announcers).

Filmed in and around Cleveland, this production takes off on some of producer, writer, and director Cornsweet's daydreams, and is an extremely saccharine depiction of a former football punter who never had the chance to finish his college career before being called off to WW II. Keyes is now a middle-aged retired widower, who is asked by the neighborhood coach to help out with the high school's football team. He does so, and develops a yearning to return to his days of college. He does just that, returning to his alma mater with a specially designed shoe that allows him to kick very long field goals. He wins all the games for the ailing team, falls for the professor of his dreams, and helps to solve many of the problems rampant on the campus.

p,d&w, Harold Cornsweet; ph, Steve Shuttack, Pierre Janet (DeLuxe Color); m, Gordon Zahler, Harry Fields, OSU Band.

Drama   **(PR:C MPAA:PG)**

RETURN TO MACON COUNTY*   (1975) 89m AIP c

Nick Nolte (Bo Hollinger), Don Johnson (Harley McKay), Robin Mattson (Junell), Robert Viharo (Sgt. Whittaker), Eugene Daniels (Tom), Matt Greene (Peter), Devon Ericson (Betty), Ron Prather (Steve), Philip Crews (Larry), Laura Sayer (Libby), Walt Guthrie (Big Man in Coffee Shop), Mary Ann Hearn (Pat), Sam Kilman (Cook), Bill Moses (Sheriff Jackson), Pat O'Connor (Officer Harris), Maurice Hunt (Motel Owner), Kim Graham (Girl in Car), Don Higdon (Boy in Car).

A sorry exploitation film that sought to capitalize on the success of MACON COUNTY LINE, this sort-of sequel uses the area's name in the title but there's little else as most of the cast was slain in the first film. Nolte and Johnson, who have both gone on to be major stars in their own media, are best friends in 1958, like the two guys in "Route 66" except that they don't drive a Corvette. If they did, they wouldn't have room to pick up Mattson, a nutty young woman who has a beguiling smile but a sadistic streak. The two men get into a "chicken" race with Daniels and Greene, a pair of tough teenagers, and are pursued by them as well as by red-neck cop Viharo. Greene and Daniels are killed mistakenly and Viharo winds up under arrest by his officers. Johnson and Sayer share a brief romantic fling while Mattson and Nolte have a go at it in the next room at their motel. It's mindless, stupid and altogether too much time is spent in travelog shots. It resembles many of the AIPictures of earlier days but it's not as good. Some blue language and badly shot love scenes that might have been more apropos in a Santa Monica Boulevard "Grind House" than a real movie theater. Johnson and Nolte are good actors hampered by an inane script whose only reason for being was to make use of the "Macon County" name. At best, it might have made a fair 30-minute segment for a TV anthology show. At 90 minutes, it's thick with padding. It was Nolte's first picture after making his name in the TV mini-series "Rich Man, Poor Man." After Arkoff sold his American International Pictures to Filmways, it promptly folded. Arkoff became an independent and called his firm Arkoff International, thereby gaining back the same acronym he'd used before.

p, Elliot Schick; ex p, Samuel Z. Arkoff; d&w, Richard Compton; ph, Jacques Marquette (Movielab Color); m, Robert O. Ragland, Roger Christian; ed, Corky Ehlers; stunts, Terry Leonard, Jesse Wayne.

Period Action   **Cas.**   **(PR:C-O MPAA:PG)**

RETURN TO PARADISE**   (1953) 100m UA c

Gary Cooper (Mr. Morgan), Roberta Haynes (Maeva), Barry Jones (Pastor Corbett), Moira MacDonald (Turia), John Hudson (Harry Faber), Va'a (Rori, Age 9), Hans Kruse (Rori, Age 21), Mamea Mataumua (Tonga), Herbert Ah Sue (Kura), Henrietta Godinet (Povana), La'ili (Kim Ling), Ezra Williams (Interpreter), George Miedeske (Hawkins), Donald Ashford (Cutler), Terry Dunleavy (Mac), Howard Poulson (Russ), Malia (Maeva's Aunt), Webb Overlander (Will Talbot), Frances Gow (Mrs. Talbot), Brian McEwen (Hank Elliott), Kathleen Newick (Mrs. Elliott), Kalapu (Tomare).

A yawnable South Seas love story that's only fair, despite yeoman work by Cooper. Haynes made her debut in the film and her acting career was soon bypassed for behind-the-scenes work as she became a network TV executive, then a TV producer. It's the late 1920s and Cooper is a soldier of fortune meandering through the Polynesian islands. He lands on a small island which is run by Jones, a fire-and-brimstone missionary not unlike Walter Huston in RAIN. Jones has gone crazy from the heat and humidity and rules the natives with an iron fist and a Bible. He has several underlings who make sure that the natives obey his rules, which include full attendance and no dozing while he preaches. Cooper's appearance gives the natives hope as he refuses to knuckle under Jones' dictates. Meanwhile, Cooper falls in love with Haynes, a local beauty, over the objections of Jones, who wants to keep the island as his own territory. The natives eventually rise up against Jones and he grumbles but allows them to return to the easygoing life that late they led. Haynes has a child and dies as Cooper has sailed off in search of more adventure. Years pass, WW II is raging and Cooper returns to Paradise to find that he has a full-grown daughter, MacDonald, who wants him to stay on and fight the Japanese. Cooper's performance was pro but the production was lackluster and spent more time developing the greenery than the characters. Many Samoans were recruited to play roles, the largest of which was given to MacDonald, a part-Polynesian. The title song was written by Tiomkin and sung by Kitty White and it became a hit. Several native dances are seen but only serve as time-wasters to fill out the script. The situations are cliches that have been seen often since the first film was made about the subject.

p, Theron Warth, Robert Wise, Mark Robson; d, Robson; w, Charles Kaufman (based on "Mr. Morgan," a short story in the book Return to Paradise by James A. Michener); ph, Winton Hoch (Technicolor); m, Dimitri Tiomkin; ed, Daniel Mandell.

Romance   **(PR:A MPAA:NR)**

RETURN TO PEYTON PLACE**½   (1961) 123m FOX c

Carol Lynley (Allison MacKenzie), Jeff Chandler (Lewis Jackman), Eleanor Parker (Connie Rossi), Mary Astor (Roberta Carter), Robert Sterling (Mike Rossi), Luciana Paluzzi (Raffaella Carter), Tuesday Weld (Selena Cross), Brett Halsey (Ted Carter), Gunnar Hellstrom (Lars Hedlom), Kenneth MacDonald (Dexter), Joan Banks (Mrs. Humphries), Bob Crane (Peter White), Bill Bradley (Mark Steele), Tim Durant (John Smith), Casey Adams (Nick Parker), Pitt Herbert (Mr. Wadley), Warren Parker (Lupus Wolf), Arthur Peterson (Selectman), Jennifer Howard (Mrs. Jackman), Emerson Treacy (Bud Humphries), Wilton Graff (Dr. Fowlkes), Laura McCann (Miss Wentworth), Hari [Harry] Rhodes (Arthur), Leonard Stone (Steve Swanson), Alex Dunand (Pierre Galante), Jack Carr (Postman), Reedy Talton (Frank O'Roark), Tony Miller (Photographer), Max Mellinger (Nevins), Collette Lyons (Mrs. Bingham), Charles Seel (Counterman), Carol Veazie, Helen Bennett (Interviewers).

Sequel to the very popular PEYTON PLACE, the film that inspired the long-running soap opera, follows its predecessor closely as a story that exposes a small New England town's bigotry and backstabbing. Lynley plays a young author about to have her first book published. The book is a realistic depiction of the people in her small town and holds nothing back in relating to the world the gossip and goings-on of the people who live there. When the book is published, the whole town is outraged, and Lynley's father, Sterling, loses his job as principal when he refuses to remove the book from the library shelves. Weld plays a young woman who was raped by her stepfather and has problems holding onto her current love. Astor is the self-righteous mother-in-law who tries to destroy her son's marriage because he is married to an Italian. A town meeting is called, and Sterling has the chance to defend the novel, making points about freedom of speech and its importance in society. Lynley grows through the experience, realizing that she cannot go through with her affair with her publisher, Chandler, a married man. Astor's son stands up to her in the end and points out how her bigotry will destroy their relationship, and Weld is reunited with her boy friend. Given the best of glossy Hollywood treatment, with none of the original's authentic New England countryside scenes, themes tend to have a predictable ending. Astor, however, is marvelous in her role as the overbearing mother, and Weld, virtually unknown at the time, starred in a role that displayed her natural sex appeal. An interesting note to the story is that writer Grace Metalious really was rejected by her home town when her novel Peyton Place was first published. She was, in fact, never welcomed back as her book hit too close to the homes of most of the residents.

p, Jerry Wald; d, Jose Ferrer; w, Ronald Alexander (based on the novel by Grace Metalious); ph, Charles G. Clarke (CinemaScope, DeLuxe Color); m, Franz Waxman; ed, David Bretherton; md, Leonid Raab; art d, Jack Martin Smith, Hans Peters; set d, Walter M. Scott, Fred Maclean; cos, Don Feld; m/l, "The Wonderful Season of Love," Paul Francis Webster, Waxman (sung by Rosemary Clooney); makeup, Ben Nye.

Drama   **Cas.**   **(PR:A MPAA:NR)**

RETURN TO SENDER**   (1963, Brit.) 61m Merton Park/Anglo-
Amalgamated bw

Nigel Davenport (Dino Steffano), Yvonne Romain (Lisa), Geoffrey Keen (Robert Lindley), William Russell (Mike Cochrane), Jennifer Daniel (Beth Lindley), Paul Williamson (Tony Shaw), John Horsley (Superintendent Gilchrist), Richard Bird (Fox).

When an evil businessman is caught making shady deals by the district attorney, he hires a goon to ruin the prosecutor's life. Competent thriller based on a story from the ever-ready pen of Edgar Wallace.

p, Jack Greenwood; d, Gordon Hales; w, John Roddick (based on a story by Edgar Wallace).

Crime   **(PR:A MPAA:NR)**

RETURN TO THE HORRORS OF BLOOD ISLAND   (SEE:
BEAST OF BLOOD, 1970, U.S./Phil.)

RETURN TO TREASURE ISLAND**   (1954) 75m UA c

Tab Hunter (Clive Stone), Dawn Addams (Jamesina Hawkins), Porter Hall (Maximillian Harris), James Seay (Felix Newman), Harry Lauter (Parker), William Cottrell (Cookie), Henry Rowland (Williams), Lane Chandler (Cardigan), Dayton Lummis (Capt. Flint), Robert Long (Long John Silver), Ken Terrell (Thompson).

This return excursion has Addams in possession of a pirate map that leads to some buried treasure on a South Sea island. Accompanied by archaeology professor Hall, Addams is abandoned when rival money hunters led by Seay and Hall steal the map and go on their own search. But Hunter turns up on the island, having been previously taken for dead by Seay. He and Addams team up to outwit the gang, and finally retrieve their rightful treasure.

p, Aubrey Wisberg, Jack Pollexfen; d, E.A. Dupont; w, Wisberg, Pollexfen (based on the story by Wisberg, Pollexfen); ph, William Bradford (Pathecolor); m, Paul Sawtell; ed, Fred Feitshans, Jr.

Adventure   **(PR:A MPAA:NR)**

RETURN TO WARBOW*½   (1958) 67m COL c

Phil Carey (Clay Hollister), Catherine McLeod (Kathleen Fallam), Andrew Duggan (Murray Fallam), William Leslie (Johnny), Robert J. Wilke (Red), James Griffith (Frank Hollister), Jay Silverheels (Indian Joe), Chris Olsen (David Fallam), Francis de Sales (Sheriff), Harry Lauter (1st Deputy), Paul Picerni (2nd Deputy), Joe Forte (Doc Appleby).

Unexciting western fare has Carey escaping from prison to make claim to the $30,000 stolen from a stagecoach 11 years earlier, and left in the hands of his drunken brother Griffith. The plan is to split the take with Leslie and Wilke, who have some plans of their own, which include doing away with Carey once the money is in eyesight. But everything falls through when it is discovered that downtrodden Griffith has gambled all the money away.

p, Wallace MacDonald; d, Ray Nazarro; w, Les Savage, Jr. (based on the novel by Savage); ph, Henry Freulich (Technicolor); m, Mischa Bakaleinikoff; ed, Charles Nelson; art d, Carl Anderson.

Western   **(PR:A MPAA:NR)**

RETURN TO YESTERDAY**   (1940, Brit.) 65m Capad-Ealing/ABF bw

Clive Brook (Robert Maine), Anna Lee (Carol Sands), Dame May Whitty (Mrs. Truscott), Hartley Power (Regan), Milton Rosmer (Sambourne), David Tree (Peter Thropp, Playwright), Olga Lindo (Grace Sambourne), Garry Marsh (Charlie Miller), Arthur Margetson (Osbert), Elliot Mason (Mrs. Priskin, Landlady), O.B. Clarence (Mr. Truscott), David Horne (Morrison), Frank Pettingell (Prendergast), Ludwig Stossel (Capt. Angst), Wally Patch (Watchman), H.F. Maltby (Inspector), Mary Jerrold, Alf Goddard, John Turnbull, Patric Curwen, Molly Rankin, Peter Glenville.

Script concerns the efforts of a Hollywood star, Brook, to recapture some of the freedom he had before he started making it big. He joins a small acting company, gets them to make money and attract some interest. But the leading lady of the play decides that she has fallen in love with Brook, which poses a problem because Brook is married and she is spoken for by the writer of the group. Brook decides that it's best not to go through with possible romance, proving that he really can't recapture those days gone by. A bad recording, unfortunately, makes the English accents barely audible. Stevenson, who directed and co-wrote the script, was a pacifist at the time of this filming, who bitterly attacked British filmmakers who were leaving their country in droves for Hollywood.

p, S.C. Balcon; d, Robert Stevenson; w, Stevenson, Margaret Kennedy, Roland Pertwee, Angus MacPhail (based on the play "Goodness How Sad!" by Robert Morley); ph, Ronald Neame; m, Ernest Irving; ed, Charles Saunders; art d, Wilfred Shingleton.

Drama   **(PR:A MPAA:NR)**

RETURNING, THE zero   (1983) 80m Shapiro/Willow c

Susan Strasberg, Gabriel Walsh, Ruth Warrick, Victor Arnold, Brian Foleman.

A fairly disgusting possession picture about two men who wander into a sacred (and haunted) Indian burial ground. The Indian spirits get a bit angry and enter the bodies of the intruders, leading to the usual supernatural happenings enhanced by a bit of gore. Shot in the Mojave Desert.

d, Joel Bender; w, Patrick Nash; ph, Oliver Wood; m, Harry Manfredini.

Horror   **(PR:O MPAA:NR)**

REUBEN, REUBEN**   (1983) 101m Saltair-Taft Entertainment/FOX c

Tom Conti (Gowan McGland), Kelly McGillis (Geneva Spofford), Roberts Blossom (Frank Spofford), Cynthia Harris (Bobby Springer), E. Katherine Kerr (Lucille Haxby), Joel Fabiani (Dr. Haxby), Kara Wilson (Edith McGland), Lois Smith (Mare Spofford), Ed Grady (Dr. Ormsby), Damon Douglas (Tad Springer), Rex Robbins (C.B. Springer), Jack Davidson (George Spofford), Robert Nichols (Harry Pycraft), Tom McGowan (TV Interviewer), Dan Doby (Alvin), Barry Bell (Man at Bar), Rene Copeland (Girl at Bar), Roger Black (Bartender), Angus MacLahlan (Waiter), Gladys Levitan (Woman at Party), Mac McGuire (Conductor), Paul Austin (N.Y. Bartender), Mary-Fran Lyman, Claudia Geraghty, Joanna Morgan (Club Women).

A thankless role for Conti has him as a poet who spends very little of his time writing. Instead, he gets drunk and makes a fool out of himself in a small New England community. He sponges from older women until he meets McGillis, who decides that there is still something left in the old boy worth saving. She then goes about trying to set him straight. A rather dated and somewhat forced comedy that depends on obvious conflicts between Conti's rudeness and the conservatism of the New England town.

p, Walter Shenson; d, Robert Ellis Miller; w, Julius J. Epstein (based on the novel by Peter DeVries, and the play "Spofford" by Herman Shumlin); ph, Peter Stein (CFI Color); m, Billy Goldenberg; ed, Skip Lusk; prod d, Peter Larkin; set d, Jeff Ginn; cos, John Boxer.

Comedy   **Cas.**   **(PR:O MPAA:R)**

REUNION***½   (1932, Brit.) 60m Sound City/MGM bw

Stewart Rome (Maj. Tancred), Antony Holles (Padre), Fred Schwartz (Pawnbroker), Robert Dudley (Sgt. Dudley), Eric Pavitt (Boy), George Bishop (Jews-Harpist), Kit Keen (Bones), Roddy Hughes, Philip Ritti, Bob Wilkins, Harry Terry, James Prior, Leonard Morris, Randolph McLeod, Bernard Dudley, Gerald Steyn, Colin Wark, Lohn Lalette, Terry Irvine, Harry Blue, Fred Watts, James Stadden, Noel Dainton, Robert Newton, Japp the Dog.

Rome is a down-on-his-luck officer invited to speak at a regimental dinner. Pawning the last of his valuables, he travels to London and, after making a speech about hope and self-sufficiency, gives his last pound note to a collection to help a corporal. Of higher quality than other British films of the time, this movie is an excellent character drama with Rome, a former star of British silents, very good in an underplayed role.

p, Norman Loudon; d, Ivar Campbell; w, Herbert Ayres (based on an article by Reginald Hargreaves).

Drama   **(PR:A MPAA:NR)**

REUNION**½   (1936) 80m FOX bw (GB: HEARTS IN REUNION)

Jean Hersholt (Dr. John Luke), Rochelle Hudson (Mary MacKenzie), Helen Vinson (Gloria Sheridan), Slim Summerville (Constable Jim Ogden), Robert Kent (Tony Luke), Dorothy Peterson (Nurse Katherine Kennedy), John Qualen (Asa Wyatt), Alan Dinehart (Gov. Phillip Crandell), J. Edward Bromberg (Charles Renard), Sara Haden (Ellie), Montagu Love (Sir Basil Crawford), Tom Moore (Dr. Richard Sheridan), George Ernest (Rusty), Katherine Alexander (Mrs. Martha Crandall), Esther Ralston (Janet Fair), Julius Tannen (Sam Fisher), George Chandler (Jake), Edward McWade (Editor), Maude Eburne (Mrs. Barton), Grace Hayle (Mrs. Williams), Joen Howard (Baby Williams), Claudia Coleman (Mrs. Simms), Hattie McDonald (Sadie), Dionne Quintuplets.

The likable doctor, Hersholt, in a follow-up to THE COUNTRY DOCTOR, is about to retire after having delivered his 3,000th baby. The townspeople decide to honor Hersholt by staging a reunion of as many of the people he's brought into the world as can be mustered. This includes quite a few characters, including a governor, a pickpocket, an actress, and the Dionne Quintuplets, a group of babies which fascinated everybody in the 1930s. There is not much of a plot to this picture, rather a concentration upon characterization and the good deeds of the doctor.

p, Darryl Zanuck, Bogart Rogers; d, Norman Taurog; w, Sam Hellman, Gladys Lehman, Sonya Levien (based on a story by Bruce Gould); ph, Daniel B. Clark; ed, Jack Murray; md, Emil Newman; cos, Royer.

Drama   **(PR:A MPAA:NR)**

REUNION IN FRANCE**½   (1942) 104m MGM bw (GB: MADEMOISELLE FRANCE; AKA: REUNION)

Joan Crawford (Michele de la Becque), John Wayne (Pat Talbot), Philip Dorn (Robert Cortot), Reginald Owen (Schultz), Albert Basserman (Gen. Hugo Schroeder), John Carradine (Ulrich Windler), Ann Ayars (Juliette), J. Edward Bromberg (Durand), Moroni Olsen (Paul Grebeau), Henry Daniell (Emile Fleuron), Arthur Space (Henker), Howard da Silva (Anton Stregel), Charles Arnt (Honore), Morris Ankrum (Martin), Edith Evanson (Genevieve), Ernest Dorian (Captain), Margaret Laurence (Clothilde), Odette Myrtil (Mme. Montanot), Peter Whitney (Soldier with Candy), Ann Codee (Rosalie), Oliver B. Blake (Hypolite), Natalie Schafer (Frau Schroder), George Travell (Jeannot), Michael Visaroff (Vigouroux), Felix Basch (Pawnbroker), Paul Weigel (Old Man), John Considine, Jr. (Little Boy), Claudia Drake (Girl), Peter Leeds (Boy), Barbara Bedford (Mme. Vigouroux), Basil Bockasta (Delivery Boy), Henry Kolker (Gen. Bartholomae), George Calliga (Mons. Bertheil), Harry Adams (Mons. Clemens), Larry Grenier (Mons. de Brun), Ed Rickard (Chauffeur), Philip Van Zandt (Customer), Louis Mercier (Conductor), Jean Del Val (Porter), Lester Sharpe (Warden), Adolph Milar (Gestapo Agent), Carl Ekberg, Hans Furberg (Soldiers), William Edmunds (Driver), Arno Frey (Guide), Joel Friedkin (Frenchman), Wilda Bieber (Little Girl), Rodney Bieber (Little Boy), Greta Keller (Baroness von Steinkamp), Walter O. Stahl (Baron von Steinkamp), Doris Borodin (Saleslady), Jody Gilbert (Brunhilde), Jack Zeller (Young Man), Edgar Licho (Hawker), Jacqueline White (Danielle), Bob Stevenson (Emile), Gayne Whitman (Maitre d'Hotel), George Aldwin (Pilot), Ray de Ravenne (Bartender), Eddie Lee, Tommy Lee (Japs), Muriel Barr, Norma Thelan (Girls In Cafe), Ava Gardner (Girl).

A glitzy MGM WW II drama set in Paris against the backdrop of the German occupation. Crawford plays a wealthy, career-minded Frenchwoman who lives in luxurious comfort with her fiance, industrial designer Dorn. However, when the German troops march into the City of Light, Crawford finds her lifestyle taking a turn for the worse. Her mansion is taken over by the Nazis and turned into a coal allotment bureau, while she is pushed into cramped living quarters. Her suspicions are raised when she finds that Dorn has managed to keep his possessions. Believing that he is a Nazi collaborator, she confronts him. When he does not deny the charge, she leaves him and finds within herself a sense of patriotism that she never before felt. While walking home she meets a desperate American RAF pilot, Wayne, who has been shot down and is now being hunted by the Gestapo. She offers to shelter him and they soon fall in love. After an escape attempt by Wayne fails, Crawford turns to Dorn for help. He arranges safe passage to the South of France. After complications and a Nazi chase, Wayne reaches safety. It is then that Crawford learns that Dorn is actually working for the Resistance—secretly sabotaging Nazi weapons and arranging the escape of hundreds of pilots. Wayne returns to London and the RAF, while Crawford heads back to Dorn to continue the fight for freedom. Essentially a Crawford vehicle with Wayne in a thankless supporting role, REUNION IN FRANCE suffers from MGM's desire to turn a serious and volatile subject into a mindless backlot entertainment. Nowhere is this more evident than in the decision to pay more attention to Crawford's dazzling wardrobe (if the Nazis commandeered her possessions, why does she continue to dress so well?) than to historical accuracy. REUNION IN FRANCE will suffice as entertainment if you're prepared to shut your mind off for 104 minutes, but don't expect much more than fluff. Filmed and tradeshown as REUNION, this film's title was lengthened to REUNION IN FRANCE for theatrical release. For a more pointed Hollywood view of the period, spend your time watching the following year's THIS LAND IS MINE.

p, Joseph L. Mankiewicz; d, Jules Dassin; w, Jan Lustig, Marvin Borowsky, Marc Connelly, (uncredited) Charles Hoffman, (based on a story by Ladislas Bus-Fekete); ph, Robert Planck; m, Franz Waxman; ed, Elmo Veron; art d, Cedric Gibbons; cos, Irene; spec eff, Warren Newcombe.

War Drama/Romance   **(PR:A MPAA:NR)**

REUNION IN RENO**½   (1951) 79m UNIV bw

Mark Stevens (Norman), Peggy Dow (Laura), Gigi Perreau (Maggie), Frances Dee (Mrs. Linaker), Leif Erickson (Mr. Linaker), Ray Collins (Judge Kneeland), Fay Baker (Miss Pearson), Myrna Dell (Mrs. Mason), Dick Wessel (Taxi Driver).

Lighthearted story has nine-year-old Perreau traveling to Reno to apply for a divorce from her parents, Erickson and Dee. Stevens plays the lawyer who is willing to take up the case, with the intention of getting to the bottom of the matter as to why the girl wants a divorce from her parents. The parents are contacted and make their way to Reno where Erickson, Dee, and a sympathetic judge, Collins, stage a fake divorce proceeding to find out what problems the little girl has that make her want to rid herself of her parents. It turns out that Dee is expecting a child, and Perreau, an adoptee, fears she'll now be in the way. All are reconciled in the end.

p, Leonard Goldstein; d, Kurt Neumann; w, Hans Jacoby, Shirley White, Lou Breslow (based on the story by Brenda Weisberg, William Sackheim); ph, Maury Gertsman; ed, Virgil Vogel; md, Joseph Gershenson; art d, Bernard Herzbrun, Nathan Juran; cos, Rosemary Odell.

Comedy   **(PR:A MPAA:NR)**

REUNION IN VIENNA**   (1933) 100m MGM bw

John Barrymore (Rudolf), Diana Wynyard (Elena), Frank Morgan (Anton), Henry Travers (Father Krug), May Robson (Frau Lucher), Eduardo Ciannelli (Poffy), Una Merkel (Isle), Bodil Rosing (Kathie), Bela Loblov (Musician), Morris Nussbaum (Musician), Nella Walker (Countess von Stainz), Herbert Evans (Count von Stainz), Ferdinand Gottschalk (Tour Guide).

Robert Sherwood's fluffy stage comedy starred Alfred Lunt and Lynne Fontanne and was far more adult than this adaptation which had to rinse out a few of the innuendoes to avoid the censor's shears. Barrymore and Wynyard had once been lovers when Barrymore held the title of archduke. All that is over now and he's been reduced to driving a taxi in Vienna although she still often thinks about her one-time amour. Wynyard is now married to Morgan, a psychiatrist, and he realizes that Wynyard retains a fixation on Barrymore so he decides to allow things to occur naturally. Barrymore goes to a party and Wynyard is there. They spend the night together but we're never sure if anything transpired. In the play, there was no doubt that the couple made love, but in the film, Barrymore takes the tack that since Morgan put them both in such a position, there was no way he would sully her honor (and his) by taking advantage of the situation. Barrymore overplays but he's fun to watch. Travers and Ciannelli repeat the roles they played in the stage version. Good sets include the Morgan home, a modernistic type of place totally out of keeping with what we think of as Vienna, and the hotel where the party occurs, a once-proud hostelry that has fallen upon bad times. The play was dated when it ran on the stage and the movie is even more so. Barrymore tries a bit too hard to be funny and whenever that happens, It's forced and frantic where it should be light and bubbly.

d, Sidney Franklin; w, Ernest Vajda, Claudine West (based on the play by Robert E. Sherwood); ph, George Folsey; ed, Blanche Sewell.

Comedy   **(PR:A-C MPAA:NR)**

REVEILLE WITH BEVERLY**   (1943) 78m COL bw

Ann Miller (Beverly Ross), William Wright (Barry Lang), Dick Purcell (Andy Adams), Franklin Pangborn (Vernon Lewis), Tim Ryan (Mr. Kennedy), Larry Parks (Eddie Ross), Adele Mara (Evelyn Ross), Walter Sande (Canvassback), Wally Vernon (Stomp McCoy), Barbara Brown (Mrs. Ross), Andrew Tombes (Mr. Smith), Eddie Kane (Medical Officer), Boyd Davis (Gen. Humphrey), Eddy Chandler (Top Sergeant), Doodles Weaver (Elmer), Eugene Jackson (Jackson), Harry Anderson (Sgt. Anderson), Si Janks (Jenks), David Newell (Sentry), Jack Rice (Davis), Irene Ryan (Elsie), John T. Murray (Director), Virginia Sale (Mrs. Browning), Herbert Rawlinson (Announcer), Ernest Hilliard (Mr. Oliver), Jean Inness (Mrs. Oliver), Shirley Mills (Laura Jean), Maude Eburne (Maggie), Bobby Barber (Collins), Lee Wilde, Lyn Wilde (Singing Twins), Bob Crosby and His Orchestra, Freddie Slack and His Orchestra, Ella Mae Morse, Duke Ellington and His Orchestra, Count Basie and His Orchestra, Frank Sinatra, the Mills Brothers, The Radio Rogues.

Made for a meager $40,000, this wartime entertainment movie made millions for Columbia, and looking at its slim plot, its unexceptional mounting, and poorly performed musical numbers, it's hard to understand why. One explanation could be the appearance of Sinatra as he belts out just one tune, a rendition of Cole Porter's "Night and Day." This was just his third appearance in a film, but he was rapidly becoming a major attraction to teenage girls. Thin plot has Miller working her way into a job as a disc jockey on a show that caters to the soldiers at a nearby camp. While she spins the records, a visualized depiction of the performers is given. Miller's talents were wasted in this effort, as she dances only one quickie. But wartime America ate it all up. Other musical numbers include, "Big Noise from Winnetka" (Gil Rodin, Bob Crosby, Ray Bauduc, Bob Haggart), "One O'Clock Jump" (Count Basie, Harry James), "Take the A Train" (Billy Strayhorn), "Cow-Cow Boogie" (Don Raye, Gene De Paul, Benny Carter), "Thumbs Up and V for Victory," "Cielito Lindo," "Sweet Lucy Brown."

p, Sam White; d, Charles Barton; w, Howard J. Green, Jack Henley, Albert Duffy; ph, Philip Tannura; ed, James Sweeney; md, Morris W. Stoloff; art d, Lionel Banks; set d, Joseph Kish.

Musical   **(PR:A MPAA:NR)**

REVEILLE-TOI ET MEURS   (SEE: WAKE UP AND DIE, 1967, Fr./Ital.)

REVENGE, 1936   (SEE: END OF THE TRAIL, 1936)

REVENGE, 1971   (SEE: TERROR FROM UNDER THE HOUSE, 1971, Brit.)

REVENGE, 1979   (SEE: BLOOD FEUD, 1979, Ital.)

REVENGE AT EL PASO**   (1968, Ital.) 103m Crono Cinematografica/IT c (IL QUATTRO DELL' AVE MARIA)

Terence Hill [Mario Girotti], Bud Spencer [Carlo Pedersoli], Eli Wallach, Brock Peters, Kevin McCarthy, Livio Lorenzon.

This was the first teaming of Hill and Spencer, who were later to gain notoriety in the TRINITY series. Meaty actioner has Wallach as a condemned killer, saved from hanging when a bank president hires him to track down the men who have robbed

his bank. Hill and Spencer are the two culprits, and they have some fun playing tricks with Wallach, who later must face McCarthy's gang in a showdown.

p, Bino Cicogna, Giuseppe Colizzi; d&w, Colizzi; ph, Marcello Masciocchi.

Western   **(PR:A MPAA:NR)**

REVENGE AT MONTE CARLO*½   (1933) 63m Mayfair bw (GB: MYSTERY AT MONTE CARLO)

June Collyer, Jose Crespo, Wheeler Oakman, Dorothy Gulliver, Edward Earle, Lloyd Ingraham, Clarence Geldert, Lloyd Whitlock.

Overly talky script mars any potential that exists in the capable acting, direction, and presentation. Story centers on a document that has extreme bearing on the future of several important figures, landing in the hands of an international criminal. The efforts by several parties to get their hands on the paper, and thus clear their names from any possible damage, take up the rest of the footage. Bright spot comes when the suave criminal makes friends with a New York thug.

p, Fanchon Royer; d, Brezzy Eason; w, Frank E. Fenton, John T. Neville; ph, Ernest Miller.

Crime   **(PR:A MPAA:NR)**

REVENGE OF DRACULA   (SEE: DRACULA—PRINCE OF DARKNESS, 1966, Brit.)

REVENGE OF FRANKENSTEIN, THE**½   (1958, Brit.) 91m COL c

Peter Cushing (Dr. Victor Stein), Francis Matthews (Dr. Hans Kleve), Eunice Gayson (Margaret), Michael Gwynn (Karl), John Welsh (Bergman), Lionel Jeffries (Fritz), Oscar Quitak (Karl, Dwarf), Richard Wordsworth (Up Patient), Charles Lloyd Pack (President), John Stuart (Inspector), Margery Cresley (Countess Barscynska), Arnold Diamond (Molke), Anna Walmsley (Vera Barscynska), George Woodbridge (Janitor), Michael Ripper (Kurt), Ian Whittaker (Boy), Avril Leslie (Girl).

Cushing is at it again as the doctor set on creating a man. But something goes amiss as the monster turns into a cannibal and is forced to be destroyed. This was director Fisher's second attempt at the Frankenstein myth, and like the first, THE CURSE OF FRANKENSTEIN, he concentrates upon the figure of Cushing as basically a well-meaning doctor who runs a charity hospital, and is the victim of undue prejudice. The gory effects, however, come out the same, with the mounting of this one surpassed in its shocking effects perhaps only by Warhol's version. (See FRANKENSTEIN series, Index.)

p, Anthony Hinds; d, Terence Fisher; w, Jimmy Sangster, H. Hurford Janes (based on the characters created by Mary Shelley); ph, Jack Asher (Technicolor); m, Leonard Salzedo; ed, Alfred Cox; prod d, Bernard Robinson; makeup, Phil Leakey.

Horror   **(PR:C MPAA:NR)**

REVENGE OF GENERAL LING   (SEE: WIFE OF GENERAL LING, THE, 1937, Brit.)

REVENGE OF KING KONG   (SEE: KING KONG ESCAPES, 1968, Jap.)

REVENGE OF MILADY, THE   (SEE: FOUR MUSKETEERS, THE, 1975)

REVENGE OF THE BLOOD BEAST, THE   (SEE: SHE BEAST, THE, 1966, Brit./Ital.)

REVENGE OF THE CHEERLEADERS zero   (1976) 88m Cheerful/Monarch c

Jeril Woods (Gail), Rainbeaux Smith (Heather), Helen Lang (Leslie), Patrice Rohmer (Sesame), Susie Elene (Tishi), Eddra Gale (Nurse Celia Beam), William Bramley (Walter Hartlander), Norman Thomas Marshall (Hal Walker), Regina Gleason (Mrs. Watson), Carl Ballantine (Dr. Ivory), Fred Gray (School Clown), Carrie Dietrich (Joanne Hartlander), Sheri Myers (Barb), Lillian McBride, Bert Conroy, Gary Walberg (State Inspectors), David Hasselhoff (Boner), Mike Steele (Dunn), David Robinson (Jordan), Patrick Wright (Cop), Ivanna Moore (Lincoln Teacher).

In this comedy that never really panned out, Walker plays the principal of Aloha High School, and he's in charge of cleaning up the sexually permissive atmosphere of the school. The Board of Education is giving the school one more chance to straighten up or else the alternative is a merger with rigid Lincoln Vocational. The cheerleaders want to protect their domain, however, so when the Board comes to inspect, they spike the cafeteria's food with drugs and an all-out orgy occurs. After they've come down off their high, the Board decides to merge the schools and kick out the present cheerleaders. But when the girls cheer their basketball team on to victory, the merger is cancelled. This is much to the dismay of land developer Hartlander, who was counting on the merger as a chance to buy up Aloha's land. He concocts a plan with the school nurse, to blow up the school and make it look like Walker did it. The cheerleaders thwart their plan, however, and join in the celebration of Aloha's independence in the end.

p, Richard Lerner, Nathaniel Dorsky; d, Lerner; w, Ted Greenwald, Ace Baandage, Dorsky (based on a story by Lerner, Dorsky); ph, Dorsky (Movielab Color); m, John Sterling; ed, Richard S. Brummer, Joseph Ancore, Jr.; ch, Xavier Chapman; m/l, "I Feel Good" (sung by Cathy Carlson), "Come to the Party" (sung by Jimmy Whitney), Sterling.

Comedy   **Cas.**   **(PR:O MPAA:R)**

REVENGE OF THE CREATURE**   (1955) 82m UNIV bw

John Agar (Clete Ferguson), Lori Nelson (Helen Dobson), John Bromfield (Joe Hayes), Robert B. Williams (George Johnson), Nestor Paiva (Lucas), Grandon

Rhodes (Foster), Dave Willock (Gibson), Charles Cane (Captain of Police), Ricou Browing (The Gill Man), Clint Eastwood (Lab Technician).

Follow up to THE CREATURE FROM THE BLACK LAGOON didn't have quite the wallop of the original, even though it had the advantage of 3-D photography. In this one the half-man, half-beast is captured in his Amazon surroundings and brought to be studied at Florida's Marine Land Aquarium. Nelson and Agar are the scientists in charge and they try to teach the creature how to talk, but to no avail. Concentration is placed on the sexual interest of the beast in Nelson, as he watches the girl swim and fondle with her boyfriend Agar. When the creature begins to get restless in his captive surroundings, he easily escapes and makes for the ocean, causing a lot of fright in his path. Clint Eastwood had a brief part in his first screen appearance; he plays a lab technician who has problems holding onto a little white mouse. Picture had the dubious honor of being the first 3-D film to be aired on television.

p, William Alland; d, Jack Arnold; w, Martin Berkeley (based on a story by Alland); ph, Charles S. Welbourne; m, Herman Stein; ed, Paul Weathermax; md, Joseph Gershenson; art d, Alexander Golitzen, Alfred Sweeney; makeup, Bud Westmore.

Horror (PR:A MPAA:NR)

REVENGE OF THE DEAD (SEE: NIGHT OF THE GHOULS, 1960)

REVENGE OF THE GLADIATORS*½ (1965, Ital.) 100m Leone/PAR c (LA VENDETTA DI SPARTACUS)

Roger Browne (Valerius), Scilla Gabel (Cynthia), Giacomo Rossi Stuart (Fulvius), Daniele Vargas (Lucius Transone), Gordon Mitchell (Arminius), Germano Longo (Marcellus), Gianni Solaro.

Dirty politics among members of the Roman Senate set the stage for Browne to gather together a small band of gladiators to avenge the death of his brother, Longo. Vargas wants to be named dictator of Rome, so he plants the rumor that Longo has rebelled against the Empire. When Browne finds his family brutally murdered, he sets out to get the culprits, joining with a legion led by Mitchell. But Mitchell turns out to be working for Vargas, which leads to an ingenious plan on the part of Browne to play dead, and then rise to attack the unsuspecting culprits. Action sequences are remarkably staged, but the plot is filled with so many inequities that it's hard to take seriously. Sequel to SPARTICUS.

p, Elio Scardamaglia; d, Michele Lupo; w, Lionello De Felice, Ernesto Guida (based on the story by Felice); ph, Guglielmo Mancori (Techniscope, Technicolor); m, Francesco De Masi; ed, Alberto Gallitti; art d, Pier Vittorio Marchi.

Adventure (PR:A MPAA:NR)

REVENGE OF THE LIVING DEAD (SEE: MURDER CLINIC, THE, 1967, Ital./Fr.)

REVENGE OF THE NINJA* (1983) 88m MGM-UA-Cannon c

Sho Kosugi (Cho), Keith Vitali (Dave), Virgil Frye (Lt. Dime), Arthur Roberts (Braden), Mario Gallo (Caifano), Grace Oshita (Grandmother), Ashley Ferrare (Cathy), Kane Kosugi (Kane), John LaMotta (Joe), Melvin C. Hampton (Det. Rios), Oscar Rowland (One-eyed Informant), Toru Tanaka (Sumo Servant), Dan Shanks (Chief), Joe Pagliuso (Alberto), Ladd Anderson (Thief), Cyrus Theibeault (Thief), Steve Ketcher (Big Thug), Don ReSimpson (Shooting Thug), Steven Lambert (Cowboy Thug), Jogi Holland (Thug), Al Lai (Tatooed Torturer), Alan Amiel (Red Ninja Leader), Eddie Tse (Masked Ninja), David Barth (Donny), George Sullivan, Tim Eisenhart, Dan Rogers, Jerry North, Jack North, Jack Turner, Ken McConnell, Jody Asbury, Frank Bare.

Take out the weak acting and what's left in this film is a fairly good display of martial arts. The story starts out with Kosugi witnessing his entire family wiped out by Ninja warriors. Then the film quickly switches to an unknown city in the U.S. six years later. Kosugi is now selling Japanese dolls with his grandmother and only surviving child. Unknown to him the store is a front for heroin smuggling, run by his friend Roberts. But when Roberts goes on a rampage and kills Kosugi's grandmother and best friend, Vitali, and then kidnaps his child, Kosugi dons the black guard of the Ninja and goes out to seek his revenge. Sequel to ENTER THE NINJA.

p, Menahem Golan, Yoram Globus; d, Sam Firstenberg; w, James R. Silke; ph, David Gurfinkel (TVC Lab Color); m, Rob Walsh, W. Michael Lewis, Laurin Rinder; ed, Mark Helfrich, Michael J. Duthie; art d, Paul Staheli; set d, Diane Perryman; spec eff, Joe Quinlivan; ch, Sho Kosugi.

Martial Arts Cas. (PR:A MPAA:R)

REVENGE OF THE PINK PANTHER** (1978) 98m UA c

Peter Sellers (Chief Inspector Jacques Clouseau), Herbert Lom (Former Chief Inspector Charles Dreyfus), Dyan Cannon (Simone Legree), Robert Webber (Philippe Douvier), Burk Kwouk (Cato Fong), Paul Stewart (Julio Scallini), Robert Loggia (Marchione), Graham Stark (Dr. Auguste Balls), Tony Beckley (Guy Algo), Valerie Leon (Tanya), Adrienne Corri (Therese Douvier), Andre Maranne (Francois), Sue Lloyd (Claude Russo/Claudine Russo), Alfie Bass (Fernet), Danny Schiller (Cunny), Douglas Wilmer (Police Commissioner), Elisabeth Welch (Madame Wu), Ferdy Mayne (Dr. Laprone), Charles Augins (Vic Vancouver), Anthony Chinn (Doorman), Maureen Tann, Me Me Lai, Jacqui Simm, Fiesta Mei Ling (Chinese Women), John Newbury (President), John Clive (Aide to President), Margaret Anderson (Police Chief's Wife), Andrew Lodge (Police Sergeant), Henry McGee (Officer Bardot), Christine Shaw (Nurse), Julian Orchard (Hospital Clerk), Michael Ward (Realtor), John Bluthal (Cemetery Guard), John A. Tinn (Mr. Chow), Kien Jing (Assistant Manager), Bernie R. Hickban (Hotel Employee), John Wyman (Toledo), Irvin Allen, Christine Labassiere (Haig & Haig), Lon Satton, Rosita Yarboy, Pepsi Maycock, Keith Hodiak (Sam Spade and The Private Eyes).

The 5th picture of the "Pink Panther" series, this wasn't as good as most of the others but Sellers and Edwards, even when they are merely adequate, are still

better than almost anyone else at making this kind of movie. It's a bit too unfocused and jumps all over the world, looking for many scenes like a comic version of a "James Bond" movie, which is, of course, a comic parody of itself. Lom is again Sellers' boss and he assigns the bumbling Inspector to break a narcotics ring run by Webber, who has dumped his mistress, Cannon, who then becomes the aide to Sellers in clearing up the case. Cannon's character is "Simone Legree"—which should give you an inkling of the level of humor in this. A few other in-jokes will be found in the cast list that includes characters named "Mr. Chow" and "Madame Wu" which are two high-line Chinese restaurants in southern California frequented by the movie set. Playing the role of a swarthy villain is the always reliable Paul Stewart, who died in Los Angeles in February, 1986. Stewart, who was fairly well-known by the public, was a beloved man to his peers. He spearheaded both AFTRA and SAG in his union efforts and was proud to carry card number 39 in the former. His funeral was attended by John Houseman (with whom he worked in "The Mercury Theater of the Air"), Burt Lancaster, Lee Van Cleef, Norman Lloyd, Ed Asner, Patty Duke, and 200 more. After 25 paid their homage to Stewart, Bert Freed, actor and SAG executive, suggested the audience give Stewart the sendoff every actor wants. Then, as one, the crowd at the Directors Guild Auditorium rose and gave Stewart his final standing ovation. It lasted four minutes and there was hardly an eye that didn't have some moisture in it. (See PINK PANTHER series, Index.)

p, Blake Edwards; exec p, Tony Adams; d, Edwards; w, Frank Waldman, Ron Clark, Edwards (based on a story by Edwards); ph, Ernie Day (Panavision, Technicolor); m, Henry Mancini; ed, Alan Jones; prod d, Peter Mullins; art d, John Siddall; set d, Jack Stephens; cos, Tiny Nichols; spec eff, Brian Johnson, Dennis Lowe; m/l, "Move 'Em Out," Mancini, Leslie Bricusse (sung by Lon Satton); makeup, Harry Frampton; stunts, Joe Dunne, Dick Crockett.

Comedy Cas. (PR:A-C MPAA:PG)

REVENGE OF THE SCREAMING DEAD (SEE: DEAD PEOPLE, 1974)

REVENGE OF THE SHOGUN WOMEN zero (1982, Taiwan) 98m Eastern Media International/21st Century c (AKA: 13 NUNS)

Shisuen Leong, Shirley Han, Pai-Ying.

Made in 3-D with poor English dubbing, the entire plot consists of 13 women who are raped by bandits. Set in the late 1700s, we find the women three years later, studying to become nuns. At the convent they learn the skills of martial arts and are thus able to seek their revenge. Introduction takes advantage of 3-D perspective, concentrating on an explicit sexual scene of the women being raped.

p, Frank Wong; d, Mei Chung Chang; w, Lin Huang Kun, Terry Chambers; ph, Zon Su Chang, Lorenz Somma (Technicolor); m, Rob Walsh; ed, Niels Rasmussen.

Martial Arts (PR:O MPAA:R)

REVENGE OF THE ZOMBIES*½ (1943) 61m MON bw

John Carradine (Von Altermann), Robert Lowery (Larry), Gale Storm (Jen), Veda Ann Borg (Lila), Mantan Moreland (Jeff), Mauritz Hugo (Scott), Barry Macollum (Kesting), Bob Steele (Agent), James Baskett (Lazarus), Mme. Sul-Te-Wan (Beulah), Robert Cherry (Pete), Sybil Lewis (Rosella).

Mad scientist Carradine is at it again; this time he's trying to help out Hitler by developing a group of zombies to do some nasty dealings in the States. But he is thwarted when his trusted servant turns out to be an FBI agent. His wife, Borg, a zombie herself, also pitches in to do away with her husband's plot. Moves much too slow to generate any form of suspense, with Carradine in a part he should be right at home with, but isn't given the material with which to do much of anything. Sequel to I WALKED WITH A ZOMBIE.

p, Lindsley Parsons; d, Steve Sekely [Istvan Szekely]; w, Edmund Kelso, Van Norcross; ph, Mack Stengler; ed, Richard Currier; art d, David Milton.

Horror (PR:A MPAA:NR)

REVENGE OF UKENO-JO, THE (SEE: ACTOR'S REVENGE, AN, 1963, Jap.)

REVENGE RIDER, THE* (1935) 60m COL bw

Tim McCoy, Robert Allen, Billie Seward, Edward Earle, Frank Sheridan, Jack Clifford, Jack Mower, George Pierce, Alan Sears, Harry Semels, Joseph Sauers [Joe Sawyer], Lafe McKee.

McCoy takes up the trail of the bad guys who killed his parents. Average second feature western has typically good performance by McCoy.

p, Harry Decker; d, David Selman; w, Ford Beebe; ph, Benjamin Cline; ed, Al Clark.

Western (PR:A MPAA:NR)

REVENGERS, THE*½ (1972, U.S./Mex.) 110m NG c

William Holden (John Benedict), Susan Hayward (Elizabeth), Ernest Borgnine (Hoop), Woody Strode (Job), Roger Hanin (Quiberon), Rene Koldehoff (Zweig), Jorge Luke (Chamaco), Jorge Martinez De Hoyos (Cholo), Arthur Hunnicutt (Free State), Warren Vanders (Tarp), Larry Pennell (Arny), John Kelly (Whitcomb), Scott Holden (Lieutenant), James Daughton (Morgan), Lorraine Chanel (Mrs. Benedict), Raul Prieto (Warden).

Just when the public thought they didn't need to see another standard western, THE REVENGERS came along, a standard western. Some big stars were inexplicably attracted to the script, a routine melange of the usual stuff, although with lots of money lavished on the big scenes. Two of the original stars were replaced; Mary Ure couldn't wait for Holden to recover from a temporary ailment and went off to do something else, so she was replaced with Hayward; and Van Heflin was to have played the Borgnine role but he died of a heart attack while swimming in the pool of his hotel in West Hollywood. It was almost 30 years since Hayward and Holden had been together in YOUNG AND WILLING and here they were again, with Holden's son, Scott, now in his middle twenties, playing the role of a lieutenant. Borgnine had also appeared with Hayward in DEMETRIUS AND THE GLADIATORS but that was before he played MARTY and catapulted to star status. Holden is a Colorado rancher and a veteran of the Civil War who's been out in the wilds on a hunting expedition. He comes back to his spread to find his wife and four children dead at the hands of Comanches, who are led by Vanders, a renegade white man. With his family slain and all of his stock stolen, Holden decides that his next course of action is to exact revenge. Vanders is holing up in a small Mexican town, a village almost totally populated by thieves, brigands and murderers. Holden masquerades as a mine owner looking for laborers and makes a deal with a Mexican warden, Prieto, to hire six convicts: De Hoyos, Hanin, Strode, Luke, Koldehoff and Borgnine, desperate men all. Of course, the sextet are of different cultural backgrounds so what we have is a grimy (not dirty) half-dozen. Holden and the convicts pretend to be innocent trappers and make their way to the den of thieves where they attack Vanders' hideout but he gets away before they can catch him. Holden, who is used to leading men, finds that handling six convicts is not as easy as handling soldiers in the Army and there is friction between them that erupts into violence when Luke shoots Holden. The men think that Holden is a goner, so they shake hands and go off in various directions. Hayward enters, an Irish woman who has come to the area to carve out a new life. She finds Holden, helps him recover his health and, in the natural course of movie events, they fall in love. When Holden admits why he is so far from home, Hayward does her best to dissuade him from his quest but Holden is adamant. He gains some of his strength back, bids her farewell with a promise to return, then sets out and is almost immediately captured by Prieto, who was fired from his warden's job for allowing the convicts to leave. Luke learns about this and that Holden is still alive (a surprise) and feels guilty, so he gathers the others and they break Holden out of Prieto's clutches. Meanwhile, Vanders has been captured by the Army and is being held at a small post by Scott Holden and his soldiers. The Comanches attack the post in an attempt to free their leader. Holden and his crew arrive, use some explosives from the Army's ammo dump and toss some dynamite, thus causing the Indians to retreat. Luke is wounded in the fracas and soon dies. Finally, Holden seeks out Vanders who is being held in a small shed. He walks in expecting to find the hard-bitten Vanders ready to fight back and he sees that Vanders is now a broken man, a coward pleading not to be hurt by Holden. This causes Holden to realize that his thirst for revenge has caused him to be almost as bad an animal as the quarry, so he leaves Vanders to face due process for his crimes. Holden gets on his horse and rides toward Colorado to put his life back together. The lighting was poor, the photography was ordinary, the dialog was dull and the plot turns were predictable by several minutes. The title, however, was a winner and the picture did some business until word of mouth began to dampen enthusiasm.

p, Martin Rackin; d, Daniel Mann; w, Wendell Mayes (based on a story by Steven W. Carabatsos); ph, Gabriel Torres (Panavision, DeLuxe Color); m, Pino Calvi; ed, Walter Hannemann, Juan Jose Marino; art d, Jorge Fernandez; set d, Carlos Grandjean; cos, Carlos Chavez; spec eff, Frank Brendell, Jesus Doran, Laurencio Bordero; makeup, Felisa L. Guevara, Elvira Oropeza.

Western   (PR:A-C   MPAA:PG)

REVENUE AGENT*   (1950) 72m COL bw

Douglas Kennedy (Steve Adams), Jean Willes (Marge King), Onslow Stevens (Sam Bellows), William "Bill" Phillips (Harry Reardon), Ray Walker (Lt. Bob Ullman), David Bruce (Cliff Gage), Archie Twitchell (Ernie Medford), Lyle Talbot (Augustus King), Rick Vallin (Al Chaloopka).

Fast-paced and hard-hitting yarn that centers on the work of the Internal Revenue Service in uncovering a plot by Stevens to sneak $1 million in gold dust out of the country, and thus avoid having to pay taxes. Kennedy is the agent who goes undercover to join forces with the hoods, whom he eventually brings to justice via a shootout in a small Mexican border village. Told in a documentary style, the tension is kept boiling throughout.

p, Sam Katzman; d, Lew Landers; w, William Sackheim, Arthur A. Ross (based on a story by Sackheim, Ross); ph, Ira H. Morgan; ed, Edwin Bryant; m, Mischa Bakaleinikoff; art d, Paul Palmentola.

Crime   (PR:A   MPAA:NR)

REVERSE BE MY LOT, THE*   (1938, Brit.) 68m Rock/COL bw

Ian Fleming (Dr. Murray), Marjorie Corbett (Margaret), Mickey Brantford (Ralph), Georgie Harris (George), Jackie Heller (Jackie), Helen Goss (Helen), Audrene Brier (Bubbles), Aubrey Mallalieu (Dr. Davidson), Joan Ponsford.

Doctor Fleming, working on an influenza cure, hires starving actress Corbett to be a guinea pig. Both Fleming and his son, who has lost his fiancee to the disease, fall in love with Corbett. He refuses to inject her, fearing his drug might not work. She injects herself, however, and the doctor is forced to trust his vaccine. Of course, the serum works, and Corbett realizes she is in love with the son. Dumb melodrama with an awful title. A film to miss.

p, Nat Ross; d, Raymond Stross; w, Syd Courtenay (based on a novel by Margaret Morrison); ph, John Silver.

Drama   (PR:A   MPAA:NR)

REVOLT AT FORT LARAMIE½   (1957) 73m Bel-Air/UA c

John Dehner (Maj. Seth Bradner), Gregg Palmer (Capt. James Tenslip), Frances Helm (Melissa Bradner), Don Gordon (Jean Salignac), Robert Keys (Sgt. Darrach), William [Bill]Phillips (Serrell), Cain Mason (Ezra), Robert Knapp (Lt. Waller), Eddie Little (Red Cloud), [Harry] Dean Stanton (Rinty), Bill Barker (Hendrey), Clay Randolph (Caswell), Kenne Duncan (Capt. Foley), Frederick Ford.

Set at the outbreak of the Civil War, film concerns a cavalry fort divided according to the loyalties of its troops. Dehner as the Virginian commander promptly hands over leadership to Palmer, then leaves with those who side with the Confederacy. This leaves Palmer the problem of coping with a group of Indians who demand $50,000 to sign a treaty. When Dehner's forces are attacked by the Indians, Palmer joins him to fight them off. Performed and presented in routine fashion, with enough action and colorful photography to carry the story through.

p, Howard W. Koch; d, Lesley Selander; w, Robert C. Dennis; ph, William Margulies (DeLuxe Color); m, Les Baxter; ed, John F. Schreyer.

Western   (PR:A   MPAA:NR)

REVOLT IN THE BIG HOUSE*   (1958) 79m AA bw

Gene Evans (Gannon), Robert Blake (Rudy), Timothy Carey (Kyle), John Qualen (Doc), Sam Edwards (Al), John Dennis (Red), Walter Barnes (Starkey), Frank Richards (Jake), Emile Meyer (Warden), Arlene Hunter (Girl), Francis De Sales, Ed Gelb.

Low-budget but captivating prison yarn has kingpin racketeer Evans imprisoned after years of narrowly escaping the law. He gets a fiery young Mexican, Blake ("Baretta") as a cellmate, and finds he can easily manipulate the young man. The first thing Evans sets out to do is to plan an escape, for which he enlists the aid of several other inmates, including Blake. The plan is to stage a riot that will allow Evans to slip over the back wall. At the last minute Blake has a change of heart when he realizes that several of his friends will be machine gunned in order to allow Evans to escape in a different direction. He attempts to warn his fellow prisoners not to riot, and is knifed by Evans. Evans escapes, only to meet his well-deserved end when he is stabbed in the subway. Director Springsteen makes the most of his meager budget and sets, giving a tautly woven depiction of prison life, with Blake superb in a touching performance as the boy caught up in the underworld happenings.

p, David Diamond; d, R.G. Springsteen; w, Daniel Hyatt, Eugene Lourie; ph, William Margulies; ed, William Austin; art d, David Milton.

Crime/Drama   (PR:A   MPAA:NR)

REVOLT OF MAMIE STOVER, THE½   (1956) 92m FOX c

Jane Russell (Mamie Stover), Richard Egan (Jim), Joan Leslie (Annalea), Agnes Moorehead (Bertha Parchman), Jorja Curtright (Jackie), Michael Pate (Harry Adkins), Richard Coogan (Eldon Sumac), Alan Reed (Gorecki), Eddie Firestone (Tarzan), Jean Willes (Gladys), Leon Lontoc (Aki), Kathy Marlowe (Zelda), Margia Dean (Peaches), Jack Mather (Bartender), John Halloran (Henry), Boyd "Red" Morgan (Hackett), Naidi Lani, Anita Dano (Hula Dancers), Dorothy Gordon, Irene Bolton, Merry Townsend, Claire James, Sally Jo Todd, Margarita Camacho (Dance Hall Girls), Richard Collier (Photographer), Max Reed (Hawaiian Cop), Janan Hart (Hostess), Johnny Caler (Soldier), Sherwood Price (Sailor), Frank Griffin (M.P.), Charles Keane (Detective), Jay Jostyn (Doctor), Arthur Grady (Young Soldier), Kayoka Wakita (Japanese Girl).

A watered-down portrayal of a real-life prostitute, played by Russell, who gets kicked out of San Francisco and takes refuge in Honolulu in the early 1940s. On board a Hawaii-bound ship, Russell meets a science fiction writer, Egan, who treats her with more respect than any man she's ever met. Although Egan tries to steer her away from a career in a dance hall, Russell pays no heed and takes work at Moorehead's Bungalow Club. With WW II heating up, Egan is sent off to the service, leaving behind Russell and a pretty socialite, Leslie, who loves him. While Egan is away, Russell becomes hot property at the dance hall where American sailors line up around the block just to get a few minutes with the curvacious hooker. After the attack on Pearl Harbor, Russell invests wisely in real estate that is unloaded at low prices by their panicked owners. Egan returns to find Russell not only the star attraction at the Bungalow Club, but an extremely wealthy woman. However, Russell's fortune is amassed at the expense of her reputation—a reputation Egan cannot live with. Instead, he returns to the respectable Leslie. Having learned her lesson, Russell leaves her fortune and reputation behind, starting off for a new and respectable life in her Mississippi home town. Although THE REVOLT OF MAMIE STOVER promised to be a daring and compelling story, Fox's production heads refused to allow Walsh and Russell to take the film in the direction they wanted. Hoping to portray Mamie Stover honestly as the enterprising prostitute that she was, Walsh was disheartened by the constraints of turning her into a one-dimensional, cliched hooker-with-a-heart-of-gold. Fox had initially planned to put Marilyn Monroe in the lead, but when that idea fell through, Russell, who had worked previously with Walsh in THE TALL MEN (1955), was called upon. Adding to the dance hall atmosphere are a pair of tunes delivered by Russell, "Keep Your Eyes on the Hands" (Tony Todaro, Mary Johnston) and "If You Wanna See Mamie Tonight" (Paul Francis Webster, Sammy Fain).

p, Buddy Adler; d, Raoul Walsh; w, Sydney Boehm (based on the novel by William Bradford Huie); ph, Leo Tover (CinemaScope, DeLuxe Color); m, Hugo Friedhofer; ed, Louis Loeffler; md, Lionel Newman; art d, Lyle R. Wheeler, Mark Lee Kirk; cos, Travilla.

Drama   (PR:C   MPAA:NR)

REVOLT OF THE BOYARS, THE   (SEE: IVAN THE TERRIBLE, PART II, 1958, USSR)

REVOLT OF THE MERCENARIES½   (1964, Ital./Span.) 102m
Prodas-Chapalo/WB c (LA RIVOLTA DEI MERCENARI; LOS MERCENARIOS)

Virginia Mayo (Lady Patrizia), Conrado Sanmartin (Lucio di Rialto), Susana Canales (Katia), Livio Lorenzon (Keller), Carla Calo (Miriam), Tomas Blanco, Franco Fantasia, Alfredo Mayo, John Kitzmiller, Luciano Benetti, Marco Tulli, Alberto Tedecco.

Mayo plays a widowed duchess who takes a liking to the leader of a band of mercenary soldiers, Sanmartin, who offers his services to protect the lady from greedy neighbor Lorenzon. But Sanmartin pulls a quick one and accepts a better offer by Lorenzon. An infuriated Mayo is taken aback by this change, but Sanmartin proves loyal in the end when he rescues Mayo's wedding party from an attack by Lorenzon.

p, Antonio Canelli; d, Piero Costa; w, Luciano Vincenzoni, Carlo Musso, E. Falletti, Antonio Boccacci, Costa; ph, Godofredo Pacheco (Totalscope, Eastmancolor).

Drama   **(PR:A MPAA:NR)**

REVOLT OF THE SLAVES, THE**   (1961, Ital./Span./Ger.) 102m
Ambrosiana-C.B.-Ultra/UA c (DIE SKLAVEN ROMS; LA RIVOLTI DEGLI
SCHIAVI; LA REBELION DE LOS ESCLAVOS)

Rhonda Fleming (Fabiola), Lang Jeffries (Vibio), Gino Cervi (Fabio), Ettore Manni (Sebastian), Wandisa Guida (Agnese), Rafael Rivelles (Rutilio), Dario Moreno (Massimiano), Fernando Rey (Valerio), Serge Gainsbourg (Corvino), Jose Nieto (Sesto), Julio Pena (Torquato), Dolores Francine (Liubala), Van Aikens (Iface), Burt Nelson (Catulo), Benno Hoffman (Pretoriano), Rainer Penkert (Massimo), Antonio Casas (Tertulio).

Fleming was used in a role typical of her numerous Hollywood outings, where she played the nasty girl with a heart of gold underneath her tough exterior. In this tale of the persecution of the Christians during the later years of the Roman Empire, she plays the daughter of a wealthy patrician. Her father buys a Christian slave who refuses to take to the ring and wrestle. An infuriated Fleming whips the poor man, but turns around and falls in love with him when it seems that the Christians are in for some hard times at the hands of the Empire. She also discovers that some people whom she never suspected, including her cousin, are turning out to be Christians. Some interesting facts about the beginnings of Christianity are revealed in this costume drama.

p, Paolo Moffa; d,Nunzio Malasomma; w, Duccio Tessari, Stefano Strucchi; ph, Cecilio Paniagua (Totalscope, Eastmancolor); m, Angelo Francesco Lavagnino; ed, Eraldo Da Roma; art d, Ramiro Gomez Garcia, Francisco R. Asensio; cos, Vittorio Rossi; makeup, Carmen Martin, Mario Bonotti; English dialog, Daniel Mainwaring.

History/Drama   **(PR:C MPAA:NR)**

REVOLT OF THE ZOMBIES*   (1936) 65m Academy bw

Dorothy Stone (Claire Duval), Dean Jagger (Armand Louque), Roy D'Arcy (Col. Mazovia), Robert Noland (Clifford Grayson), George Cleveland (Gen. Duval), Fred Warren (Dr. Trevissant), Carl Stockdale (Ignacio McDonald), Teru Shimada (Buna), William Crowell (Hsiang), Selmer Jackson (Officer), Hans Schumm (German Soldier).

A pretty good idea is turned into a cornball story, with a bunch of zombies running around that look as menacing as a baby in a carriage. Yarn has it that the French have developed a secret regiment of zombie fighters, through secrets kept by a mysterious priest in Cambodia. When WW I ends, the government orders that all remaining zombies be destroyed. Cleveland is in charge of the mission, but Jagger creates a problem when he discovers the secret to raising the dead. When Cleveland's daughter spurns him, he decides to use his new powers to get even—which he does, but in the most unconvincing manner, and he winds up the prey of the zombies himself. Slack production techniques, direction with no feel for suspense, and performances which make it hard to distinguish who are the zombies keep the possibilities in the original idea from being realized.

p, Edward Halperin; d, Victor Halperin; w, Howard Higgin, Rollo Lloyd, V. Halperin; ph, Arthur Martinelli, J. Arthur Feindel; ed, Douglas Biggs; md, Abe Meyer; art d, Leigh Smith; spec eff, Ray Mercer.

Horror   **(PR:C MPAA:NR)**

REVOLUTIONARY, THE***½   (1970, Brit.) 101m Pressman-Williams/
UA c

Jon Voight (A), Jennifer Salt (Helen Peret), Seymour Cassel (Leonard), Robert Duvall (Despard), Collin Wilcox-Horne (Anne), Lionel Murton (Professor), Reed De Rouen (Mayor), Warren Stanhope (A's Father), Mary Barclay (A's Mother), Richard Pendry (N.C.O.), Alexandra Berlin (Nurse), Julie Garfield (Girl), Libby Glenn (Mrs. Peret), Tucker McGuire (Lady Guest), Tom Duggan (Man Guest), Alan Tilvern (Sid), Kenneth J. Warren (Sergeant), Reginald Cornish (Judge), Bill Nagy (Gansard), Earl Cameron (Speaker), James Dyrenforth, Bruce Boa (Guests at Party), Julian Close, Henry Gilbert.

Well-made Kafkaesque story with overtones of 1984. Although shot in London, the locale is never specified though most of the lead actors are from the U.S. It's "somewhere in the free world" and Voight is a radical student who feels that he has been betrayed by the college association to which he belongs because they are establishing a policy of cooperation while he thinks more violent actions must be taken in order to alter the existing system. Voight and his lover, Wilcox-Horne, quit the university group and join forces with Duvall, a tough factory worker who leads what must be the neighborhood communist cell, although they never identify it that way. In his new liaison, Voight becomes part of a general strike but the authorities seek to quell it and once Voight is known to be a leader, he must seek a hiding place to avoid being arrested for his activities. He gets a draft notice and goes into the service, then learns that his first assignment is to squash a strike, the very action he was behind. Rather than battle against his political beliefs, Voight goes A.W.O.L. and stays with Salt, an attractive woman he'd met earlier who is somewhat sympathetic to him, if not his cause. With Duvall's group under surveillance and soft-peddling themselves to avoid arrest, Voight decides that he must move on and now associate himself with Cassel, an even more radical revolutionary who wants to kill Cornish, a judge, in protest for some of the man's anti-labor decisions. Cassel plans to place a bomb in the courtroom and Voight's job is to have a second

explosive, just in case the first one is a dud. Cornish sentences some of the workers to jail for their activities but Cassel's bomb doesn't go off, thus leaving Voight holding the second bomb as he stands in front of Cornish. What is so intriguing here is that it's a film of ideas, although it doesn't stop to cram them down our throats. The movie moves at a quick clip and Voight's persona is carefully written and acted to give an audience insight into what makes this kind of fanatic tick. So it is at once a character study and a story film and that kind of blend is seldom seen. Whether or not one agrees or disagrees with the political rhetoric espoused won't detract from the experience of seeing the movie.

p, Edward Pressman; d, Paul Williams; w, Hans Koningsberger (based on his novel); ph, Brian Probyn (DeLuxe Color); m, Michael Small; ed, Henry Richardson; prod d, Disley Jones; md, Small.

Fantasy/Drama   **(PR:A-C MPAA:GP)**

REVOLUTIONS PER MINUTE   (SEE: R.P.M., 1970)

REWARD, THE**½   (1965) 92m Arcola/FOX c

Max von Sydow (Scott Swanson), Yvette Mimieux (Sylvia), Efrem Zimbalist, Jr. (Frank Bryant), Gilbert Roland (Capt. Carbajal), Emilio Fernandez (Sargento Lopez), Henry Silva (Joaquin), Nino Castelnuovo (Luis), Rodolfo Acosta (Patron), Julian Rivero (El Viejo), Rafael Lopez (Indian Boy), Carmen Rivero, Roque Ybarra.

A reward offered for a man who was framed for a murder sets the action for a tale of greed in a desert in Mexico. The fugitive, Zimbalist, is spotted driving through Mexico by crop-duster pilot von Sydow, who has just flown his plane into a water tower. As compensation, von Sydow makes an arrangement with the local police chief to split the reward for Zimbalist. A posse sets out to trap the fugitive, who is accompanied by Mimieux. This proves to be no problem; what does is getting him back to collect the reward. The police captain, Roland, hasn't told his men about the reward, but one of them, Fernandez, finds out and starts to make demands of his own, and everyone but von Sydow and Mimieux wind up dead. Plot takes a long time to start developing, with the cast showing little interest in the project except for Fernandez, who is quite frightening as the crazed police sergeant. Von Sydow, on the other hand, barely impresses at all, slogging through his lines as if they didn't impinge on his consciousness. The photography of Death Valley is used effectively, showing a keen visual sense on director Bourguignon's part, in his first American production.

p, Aaron Rosenberg; d, Serge Bourguignon; w, Bourguignon, Oscar Milland (based on the novel by Michael Barrett); ph, Joseph MacDonald (CinemaScope, DeLuxe Color); m, Elmer Bernstein; ed, Robert Simpson; art d, Jack Martin Smith, Robert Boyle; set d, Walter M. Scott, Lucien Hafley; cos, Moss Mabry; spec eff, L.B. Abbott, Emil Kosa, Jr.; makeup, Ben Nye.

Drama   **(PR:A MPAA:NR)**

REY DE AFRICA   (SEE: ONE STEP TO HELL, 1969, US/Ital./Span.)

RHAPSODIE IN BLEI   (SEE: HOT MONEY GIRL, 1962, Brit./Ger.)

RHAPSODY***   (1954) 115m MGM c

Elizabeth Taylor (Louise Durant), Vittorio Gassman (Paul Bronte), John Ericson (James Guest), Louis Calhern (Nicholas Durant), Michael Chekhov (Prof. Schuman), Barbara Bates (Effie Cahill), Richard Hageman (Bruno Furst), Richard Lupino (Otto Krafft), Celia Lovsky (Frau Sigerlist), Stuart Whitman (Dove), Madge Blake (Mrs. Cahill), Jack Raine (Edmund Streller), Brigit Nielsen (Madeleine), Jacqueline Duval (Yvonne), Norma Nevens (Student Pianist).

Essentially a saccharine soap opera, RHAPSODY is saved by some fabulous European locations, lushly romantic concertos, and above all else, a superb performance by a 21-year-old Taylor. She stars as a rich girl with an insatiable desire to be needed by men, namely young violinist Gassman. He loves Taylor but not as much as he loves his music. Unable to compete with his devotion and strict discipline, she leaves him and becomes involved with pianist Ericson. In the meantime Gassman rises to fame, a goal Ericson is also trying to achieve. Taylor marries Ericson but soon realizes that it is Gassman that she loves. Ericson, who needs Taylor as much as she needs Gassman, takes refuge in an alcohol-induced stupor as his wife runs off to Paris with her violinist. Gassman, however, is angered at her treatment of a fellow musician and turns her away. Determined to disprove Gassman's theories about her, Taylor returns to Ericson in Zurich and forces him to continue practicing. Then comes Ericson's big concert—a performance of Rachmaninoff's "Second Piano Concerto in C Minor" (played by Claudio Arrau). Gassman is in attendance with the notion of taking Taylor back—a notion that she is pleased with and that Ericson is aware of. After Ericson's virtuoso performance, however, she decides that she belongs with the pianist, not the violinist. Based on a considerably more grave 1908 novel written by Richardson (an Australian woman) which ends in suicide for the pianist, RHAPSODY had been kicked around Hollywood for a few years. In 1948 Hal Wallis bought the rights and sold them to Paramount three years later. The Goetzes' script was given to Vidor to direct but a year later Paramount sold the script and Vidor's services to MGM, where it was rewritten by the Kanins. Besides Rachmaninoff, RHAPSODY includes Tchaikovsky's "Violin Concerto in D Major"(played by Michael Rabin) and Liszt's "Hungarian Rhapsody."

p, Lawrence Weingarten; d, Charles Vidor; w, Michael Kanin, Fay Kanin, Ruth Goetz, Augustus Goetz (based on the adaptation of the Henry Handel Richardson novel Maurice Guest); ph, Robert Planck (CinemaScope, Technicolor); m, Bronislau Kaper, Peter Ilich Tchaikovsky, Sergei Rachmaninoff, Franz Liszt; ed, John Dunning; md, Johnny Green; art d, Cedric Gibbons, Paul Groesse; set d, Edwin B. Willis, Hugh Hunt; cos, Helen Rose; spec eff, A. Arnold Gillespie, Warren Newcombe, Peter Ballbusch; makeup, William Tuttle.

Musical Romance   **Cas.**   **(PR:A MPAA:NR)**

RHAPSODY IN BLUE***½

(1945) 139m WB bw

Robert Alda (*George Gershwin*), Joan Leslie (*Julie Adams*), Alexis Smith (*Christine Gilbert*), Charles Coburn (*May Dreyfus*), Julie Bishop (*Lee Gershwin*), Albert Basserman (*Prof. Frank*), Morris Carnovsky (*Poppa Gershwin*), Rosemary De Camp (*Momma Gershwin*), Anne Brown (*Bess*), Herbert Rudley (*Ira Gershwin*), John B. Hughes (*Commentator*), Mickey Roth (*George Gershwin as a Boy*), Darryl Hickman (*Ira Gershwin as a Boy*), Charles Halton (*Mr. Kast*), Andrew Tombes (*Mr. Milton*), Gregory Goluhoff (*Mr. Katzman*), Walter Soderling (*Mr. Muscatel*), Eddie Marr (*Buddy De Sylva*), Theodore Von Eltz (*Foley*), Bill Kennedy (*Herbert Stone*), Robert Shayne (*Christine's Escort*), Oscar Loraine (*Ravel*), Johnny Downs (*Dancer*), Ernest Golm (*Otto Kahn*), Martin Noble (*Jascha Heifetz*), Hugo Kirchhoffer (*Walter Damrosch*), Will Wright (*Rachmaninoff*), Ivan Lebedeff (*Guest in Nightclub*), George Riley (*Comic*), Virginia Sale (*Cashier*), Yola d'Avril (*Prima Donna*), Claire DuBrey (*Receptionist*), Christian Rub (*Swedish Janitor*), Odette Myrtil (*Mme. De Breteuil*), Jay Novello (*Orchestra Leader*), Robert Johnson (*Sport*), William Gillespie (*Porgy*), Mark Stevens (*Singer*), Al Jolson, Paul Whiteman and His Orchestra, Oscar Levant, George White, Hazel Scott, Tom Patricola (*Themselves*).

After only hearing a couple of bars, most people recognize a George Gershwin tune. He died before he was 40 but his music continues to be a source of delight and inspiration to everyone. Woody Allen used Gershwin to score MANHATTAN and the songs were timeless and wonderful. When motion picture companies decide to do a biography, why is it that they often tamper with the truth? NIGHT AND DAY, the life of Cole Porter; WORDS AND MUSIC, the story of Rodgers and Hart; and this film bear little resemblance to what actually happened, but all three managed to make money despite that, as the glorious songs of the authors were prominently featured. Porter and Hart were both men whose heterosexuality was suspect and there is some talk that Gershwin was similar. He never married and, to the best of anyone's recollection, had only "friendly" dates with various women. It could have been that he was so involved in creating that he had no time for anything else. The script for RHAPSODY IN BLUE invents a character, Leslie, who never existed and alters a few others to the point of laughability for anyone who knew the originals. It's not a good script and all the sharp lines go to Levant, a great friend of Gershwin's who plays himself in the movie and who was an acknowledged wit, so we think that Levant must have written his own dialog, as it is so superior to the corny words put in the other actors' mouths. The story of the film is a "rags-to-riches" tale of two young men from the lower East Side of Manhattan who rise to fame. The usual scenes of song-plugging, struggles, a few failures, rehearsals, backstage life, episodes in New York, London, and Paris, etc., are all there, but they are no reason to see the movie. Alda, in his second film, is an Italian playing a Jew, and while he isn't Laurence Olivier, he manages to convince us of his ethnic background. Rudley, as Ira Gershwin, looks very much like the master wordsmith did at that age and carries off his part well. Coburn plays Gershwin's publisher, Dreyfus, who was in real life about the size of a jockey. There are many celebrity impersonations as well as several stars who play themselves, as only they can. It would be possible to remove all the talk scenes, leave the music in, and still have a good movie. We get the chance to hear Gershwin's immortal "Rhapsody in Blue" played in its entirety by Levant (although it had been heard before in KING OF JAZZ, a 1929 color pastiche of music and sketches which starred Paul Whiteman), "Concerto in F," "The Cuban Overture," "Fascinatin' Rhythm," "The Man I Love" (George Gershwin, Ira Gershwin), "Yankee Doodle Blues" (George Gershwin, Buddy DeSylva, Irving Caesar, played by Hazel Scott), "Somebody Loves Me" (George Gershwin, De Sylva, Ballard MacDonald, sung by Tom Patricola), "Swanee" (George Gershwin, Caesar, sung by Al Jolson). Other songs by the Gershwin brothers include: "The Man I Love," "Mine," "Lady Be Good," "Clap Yo' Hands," "Bidin' My Time," "Love Walked In," "Someone To Watch Over Me," "'S Wonderful," "I Got Rhythm," "My One And Only," "Delicious," "Embraceable You." Other instrumentals by George Gershwin include: "Variations on 'I Got Rhythm'," "An American in Paris." There were a number of other lyricists who collaborated with George besides Ira. Their contributions include: "Summertime" (George and Ira Gershwin, DuBose Heyward), "I Got Plenty O' Nuttin'," (George and Ira Gershwin, Heyward), "Liza" (George and Ira Gershwin, Gus Kahn), "Do It Again" (George Gershwin, De Sylva), "I'll Build A Stairway To Paradise" (George Gershwin, De Sylva, Ira (writing under the name of Arthur Frances), "Blue Monday Blues" (George Gershwin, De Sylva). Piano solos by Levant and Ray Turner, Leslie's vocals looped by Louanne Hogan. Max Steiner did the musical adaptation with orchestrations by Ray Heindorf and Ferde Grofe, composer of "Grand Canyon Suite." The actors did as well as the script they were handed allowed. All the cliches and the lack of truth aside, see this movie and revel in the Gershwin music that will never perish.

p, Jesse L. Lasky; d, Irving Rapper; w, Howard Koch, Elliott Paul (based on a story by Sonya Levien); ph, Sol Polito; m, George Gershwin; ed, Folmer Blangsted; md, Leo F. Forbstein; art d, John Hughes, Anton Grot; spec eff, Ray Davidson, Willard Vanenger; ch, LeRoy Prinz; m/l, Gershwin, Ira Gershwin, Arthur Frances, B.G. DeSylva, Ballard MacDonald, DuBose Heyward, Gus Kahn, Irving Caesar.

Musical/Biography   **(PR:AA MPAA:NR)**

RHINO***

(1964) 92m MGM c

Harry Guardino (*Alec Burnett*), Shirley Eaton (*Edith Arleigh*), Robert Culp (*Dr. Jim Hanlon*), Harry Mekela (*Jopo*), George Lane (*Haragay*).

The Dark Continent serves as the setting for this adventure yarn about an idealistic doctor who wants to use a tranquilizer gun to capture a pair of rare white rhinos. He enlists the aid of big game hunter Guardino, who has made an underhanded deal on the black market to deliver the animals. When Guardino takes off with Culp's equipment, his irate girl friend, Eaton, gives Culp a hand in tracking down the culprit. A fight ensues, cleverly cut with shots of questioning looks on the faces of the animals, as if to ask which species is more advanced. Guardino is bitten by a snake and goes through an extreme change of heart when Culp saves his life. The two men become friends and devote themselves to animal research. A rather spotty script is given a lift by able direction which takes full advantage of its players and the African background, and the naturalistic photography of the wild animals almost makes them seem part of the cast. Photography as a whole is a plus.

p, Ben Chapman; d, Ivan Tors; w, Art Arthur, Arthur Weiss (based on a story by Arthur); ph, Sven Persson, Lamar Boren (Metrocolor); m, Lalo Schifrin; ed, Warren Adams; md, Schifrin.

Adventure/Drama   **(PR:A MPAA:NR)**

RHINOCEROS**

(1974) 101m American Film Theatre c

Zero Mostel (*John*), Gene Wilder (*Stanley*), Karen Black (*Daisy*), Robert Weil (*Carl*), Joe Silver (*Norman*), Marilyn Chris (*Mrs. Bingham*), Robert Fields (*Logician*), Melody Santangelo (*Young Woman*), Lou Cutell (*Cashier*), Don Calfa (*Waiter*), Kathryn Harkin (*Lady with Cat*), Lorna Thayer (*Restaurant Owner*), Howard Morton (*Doctor*), Percy Rodrigues (*Mr. Nicholson*).

When Joseph Anthony directed this as a play in 1961, it was hailed as a good example of "theatre of the absurd," so who better than Julian Barry, the head of the *avant garde* Living Theatre, to write the adaptation? Before his death in 1985, Barry had squired his charges through many weird plays and will also be recalled for his portrayal as the knife-thin, pasty-faced killer in THE COTTON CLUB. Mostel starred on Broadway and repeats his role here as one of a coterie of people who are turning into rhinoceroses (rhinoceri?). It's a farce with metaphors and symbolism tossed in for bad measure. A bunch of people sit around and talk about their plight while our ears hear the pounding hooves of hundreds of the huge animals going past. Just as Kafka's character became a cockroach, these people are on the verge of metamorphosing into the beasts and are trying to decide if they should allow that to happen or should they fight it? Wilder is the one person who is not a caricature, while the others overplay their roles like high schoolers. Black is a good actress, as long as she doesn't look directly at the camera, as her crossed eyes can be disconcerting. O'Horgan, who directed flashy stage productions of "Jesus Christ, Superstar," "Hair," and "Lenny," tries a bit too hard to infuse cinematic techniques into the movie to offset the long dialog passages. Mostel, without benefit of anything except his ability, turns into a human rhino on the screen and it's a treat to see. Otherwise, the picture is missable. Ionesco fans, and there are not all that many, may find something in this minestrone to like, but it's hard locating it behind the allegory. It was one of several plays to be brought to the screen by Landau in an attempt to adapt stage productions almost en toto at a low enough price to make them worth shooting.

p, Ely A. Landau; d, Tom O'Horgan; w, Julian Barry (based on a play by Eugene Ionesco); ph, Jim Crabe; m, Galt MacDermot; ed, Bud Smith; prod d, Jack Martin Smith; cos, Noel Taylor.

Fantasy/Comedy   **Cas.**   **(PR:A-C MPAA:PG)**

RHODES***½

(1936, Brit.) 94m GAU bw (GB: RHODES OF AFRICA)

Walter Huston (*Cecil Rhodes*), Oscar Homolka (*Paul Kruger*), Basil Sydney (*Dr. Jamison*), Peggy Ashcroft (*Ann Carpenter*), Frank Cellier (*Barney Barnato*), Renee De Vaux (*Mrs. Kruger*), Bernard Lee (*Cartwright*), Lewis Casson (*Helm*), Ndaniso Kumala (*King Lobengula*), Glennis Lorimer (*Cartwright's Fiancee*).

Cecil Rhodes was an empire builder who became so important in Africa that they named an entire country after him. Now you don't get to do that by being "Mr. Nice Guy," although some of his deeds are softened in this semi-truthful film about his life. Rhodes' personal life is barely explored and there is virtually no woman to whom he was close, with the exception of Ashcroft, as a novelist who argues his decisions with him. Several scenes were shot in Africa and are magnificently done. (The South African location work was directed by Geoffrey Barkas and photographed by S.R. Bennett.) One can see that the terrain has not changed much since the dawn of creation and there is no substitute for location shooting to enhance a story. It begins about 1870 as fortune hunters are flocking to Africa to seek their destinies. In this way, it's not unlike an American western with miners in wagons, crowd scenes of frantic prospectors attempting to make their claims, etc. Huston finds a huge trove of diamonds and establishes the Kimberley Mines Company, Ltd. But it's not enough to be filthy rich, now Huston wants to control the continent and he sees an opportunity to unite the warring factions (and there are thousands of tribes with hundreds of languages in Africa to this day) in the southern half as one country. But he is not as dictatorial as he is benevolent and his dream is to improve the lot of these poor natives. The Boer War takes place and Huston has to give up his plans; then fate takes a hand and he dies and is buried high on a hill in the country which bore his name. He was not yet 50. Rhodes began at the age of 27 with Alfred Beit, another 27-year-old. They started the DeBeers company, then bought out Barnato Diamond Mining in 1888 to establish a monopoly. The following year, his British South Africa Company was empowered to take over everything north of the Transvaal and west of Mozambique. He became prime minister of the Cape Colony in 1890, then pioneered the copper mining industry in 1891. His men successfully withstood a revolt by a king (they killed him) and he continued coining money. Rhodes resigned his prime minister's post when word got out that he was behind the raid that took the life of the king. He died March 26, 1902, and left a fortune for public service as well as having established the famed Rhodes Scholarships with $10 million for deserving youths from Great Britain, the U.S., and Germany. One of the beneficiaries of this largesse was Kris Kristofferson. Not that any of this has anything to do with the movie, we just thought you might like to know more about the real man behind the name.

p, Geoffrey Barkas; d, Berthold Viertel; w, Michael Barringer, Miles Malleson, Leslie Arliss (based on the book by Sarah Millin); ph, Bernard Knowles; ed, D. N. Twist; cos, Joe Strassner.

Biography   **(PR:A MPAA:NR)**

RHODES OF AFRICA

(SEE: RHODES, 1936, Brit.)

RHUBARB**½ (1951) 95m PAR bw

Ray Milland (Eric Yeager), Jan Sterling (Polly Sickles), Gene Lockhart (Thaddeus J. Banner), William Frawley (Len Sickles), Elsie Holmes (Myra Banner), Taylor Holmes (P. Duncan Munk), Willard Waterman (Orlando Dill), Henry Slate (Dud Logan), James J. Griffith (Oggie Meadows), Jim Hayward (Doom), Donald Mac-Bride (Phenny), Hal K. Dawson (Mr. Fisher), Strother Martin (Shortly McGirk), Hilda Plowright (Katie), Adda Gleason (Maid), Richard Karlan (Pencil Louie), Edwin Max (Fish Eye), Anthony Radecki, Leonard Nimoy, Bill Thorpe, Frank Fiumara, Lee Miller (Ball Players), Roy Gordon, Stuart Holmes, Eric Wilton, Wilbur Mack (Golfers), Harry Cheshire (Mr. Seegle), John Breen (Western Union Boy), Tristram Coffin (Dr. Stillman), Donald Kerr (Taxi Driver), Mack Gray (Detective), Oliver Blake (Cadaver Jones), Paul Douglas (Man in Park), Stanley Orr (Newspaper Reporter), Roberta Richards (Reporter).

Crazy satire has millionaire Lockhart being taken by the antics of tough alley cat Rhubarb, and deciding to take the cat home with him. His admiration for the cat grows to the point where he makes it the principal heir to his vast fortune, which includes a major league ball club, of which Rhubarb has become mascot. Milland is the man responsible for the cat, but this causes problems with his girl friend Sterling, who is allergic to furry animals. However the allergy turns out to be a godsend when the cat is kidnaped by gamblers who want the ball club to lose. Sterling uses her allergy to sniff out the whereabouts of the cat. Plot offers the chance for a number of lively gags and zany situations. Unfortunately, when these fail the result is failed slapstick. There's also room for one song: "It's a Privilege To Live In Brooklyn" (Jay Livingston, Ray Evans).

p, William Perlberg, George Seaton; d, Arthur Lubin; w, Dorothy Reid, Francis Cockrell, David Stern (based on the novel by H. Allen Smith); ph, Lionel Lindon; m, Van Cleave; ed, Alma Macrorie; art d, Hal Pereira, Henry Bumstead.

Comedy (PR:A MPAA:NR)

RHYTHM HITS THE ICE (SEE: ICE-CAPADES REVUE, 1942)

RHYTHM IN THE AIR** (1936, Brit.) 72m FOX bw

Jack Donohue (Jack Donovan), Tutta Rolf (Mary), Vic Oliver (Tremayne), Leslie Perrins (Director), Kitty Kelly (Celia), Tony Sympson (Alf).

Donohue, a riveter who works on tall buildings, falls and breaks both ankles when he is distracted by tap dancer Rolf. She visits him in the hospital and persuades him to learn tap dancing as a way of strengthening the broken joints. When he recovers, he tries to go back to his job, but discovers he's afraid of heights. He then decides to become a professional dancer and marry Rolf. Adequate British musical.

p, John Findlay; d, Arthur Woods; w, Jack Donohue, Vina de Vesci; ph, Roy Kellino.

Musical (PR:A MPAA:NR)

RHYTHM IN THE CLOUDS** (1937) 64m REP bw

Patricia Ellis (Judy), Warren Hull (McKay), William [Billy] Newell (Clyde), Richard Carle (Boswell), Zeffie Tilbury (Duchess), Charles Judels (Luigi), David Carlyle [Robert Paige] (Hale), Joyce Compton (Amy), Suzanne Kaaren (Dorothy), Esther Howard, Ed Parker, James C. Morton, Rolfe Sedan.

Zesty little picture that was billed as a musical even though it has only three songs. Down-and-out aspiring songwriter Ellis forges a letter that gives her an admittance to the apartment of a wealthy songwriter. This works out just fine for a bit, as the successful songwriter is out of town, Ellis is long past due on her rent, and her stomach is starting to make noises. But Carlyle, the owner of the apartment, returns and things turn topsy-turvy. The three songs are: "Don't Ever Change," "Hawaiian Hospitality," and "Two Hearts are Dancing" (Lou Handman, Walter Hirsch, Harry Owens, Ray Kinney).

d, John H. Auer; w, Olive Cooper (based on a story by George Mence and Ray Bond); ph, Murray Selden, Ernest Miller; ed, Edward Mann.

Musical/Comedy (PR:A MPAA:NR)

RHYTHM INN*½ (1951) 73m MON bw

Jane Frazee (Carol Denton), Kirby Grant (Dusty Rhodes), Charles Smith (Eddie Thompson), Lois Collier (Betty Parker), Fritz Feld (Prof. Rinaldo), Ralph Sanford (Pete Harris), Armida (Specialty Dancer), Anson Weeks and Orchestra (Joe Riggan Orchestra), Jean Ritchie (Specialty Skater), Amos & Arno (Comedy Dance Team), Ramon Ros (Specialty Dancer).

Hard-up Dixieland band led by Grant is forced to smuggle its instruments out of a pawn shop each night in order to play at the local nightclub. Smith, the air-headed clerk of the shop, goes along with the plot when he is promised that the songs he's been writing will be used. This causes problems with his gal, Collier, a would-be singer, who sees sexy Frazee cajoling him and assumes the worst. The ending has Smith's songs being sung over the air by Collier. Musical numbers include: "It's A Big Wide Wonderful World" (John Rox); "Chi Chi" (Armida); "Love" (Bill Raynor, Edward J. Kay); "B Flat Blues," "Return Trip," "What Does it Matter" (Kay); and "With A Twist Of The Wrist" (Irvin Graham).

p, Lindsley Parsons; d, Paul Landres; w, Bill Raynor; ph, William Sickner; ed, Ace Herman; art d, David Milton; md, Edward J. Kay.

Musical (PR:A MPAA:NR)

RHYTHM OF THE ISLANDS** (1943) 59m UNIV bw

Allan Jones (Tommy), Jane Frazee (Joan Holton), Andy Devine (Eddie Dolan), Ernest Truex (Mr. Holton), Marjorie Gateson (Mrs. Holton), Mary Wickes (Susie Dugan), Burnu Acquanetta (Luani), Nestor Paiva (Chief Nataro), John Maxwell (Marco), Maceo Anderson (Abercrombie), The Step Brothers (Abercrombie's Assistants), The Leslie Horton Dancers (Themselves), Ruth Lee (Miss Widdicomb), Francis McDonald (Native Leader), Mira McKinney (Miss Priddy), William Ruhl

(Guide), Dan Seymour (Native Guard), Kate Lawson (Fat Woman), Dick Botiller (Tuira), Rico de Montez (Hotel Clerk).

There was not a single serious intention when the plot for this flimsy film was penned. It seems to have been conceived as a way to get from one song to the next, and it succeeds in doing just that. Two inhabitants of a small South Sea island, Jones, the tribal chief, and Devine, a beachcomber, try to sell their little paradise to millionaire Truex. The rich man's daughter, Frazee, is busy trying to grab hold of Jones. Devine is along for laughs, while Frazee and Jones take care of the songs, which include: "Savage Serenade," "Tropic Lullaby," "Blue Mist," "Chant Of The Tom Tom," "Manhattan Isle," "Isle Of Romance," and "I've Set My Mind On You" (Inez James, Buddy Pepper).

p, Bernard W. Burton; d, Roy William Neill; w, Oscar Brodney, M.M. Musselman (based on a story by Brodney); ph, George Robinson; ed, Paul Landres; md, Charles Previn; art d, John B. Goodman; cos, Vera West; m/l, Dave Franklin, Louis Herscher, Andy Iona, Inez James, Buddy Pepper, Frank Skinner.

Musical/Comedy (PR:A MPAA:NR)

RHYTHM OF THE RIO GRANDE** (1940) 54m MON bw

Tex Ritter (Tex), Suzan Dale (Ruth), Warner Richmond (Buck), Martin Garralaga (Pablo), Frank Mitchell (Shorty), Mike J. Rodriguez (Lopez), Juan Duval (Rego), Tristram Coffin (Banister), Chick Hannon (Pete), Earl Douglas (Blackie), Forrest Taylor (Crane), Glenn Strange (Hayes), James McNally (Ransom), Wally West, Lloyd "Arkansas Slim" Andrews, White Flash the Horse.

Singing cowboy Ritter sets out to avenge the murder of his pal and winds up helping a young Mexican, Garralaga, clear his name from every murder that's occurred north of the border. The real culprits are a band of crooks who've thought out a complicated plan to rid the valley of ranchers, and thus get their hands on the gold deposits. Ritter manages a few songs en route to his good deed, which include: "Mexicali Moon," "Rhythm Of The Rio Grande," and "Pablo, The Mexican Bandit."

p, Edward Finney; d, Al Herman; w, Robert Emmett; ph, Marcel A. LePicard; m, Frank Sanucci; m/l, Frank Harford, Johnny Lange, Lew Porter.

Western (PR:A MPAA:NR)

RHYTHM OF THE SADDLE*½ (1938) 57m REP bw

Gene Autry (Gene), Smiley Burnette (Frog), Pert Kelton (Aunt Hattie), Peggy Moran (Maureen), LeRoy Mason (Pomeroy), Arthur Loft (Chase), Ethan Laidlaw (Tex Robinson), Walter de Palma (Leach), Archie Hall (Rusty), Eddie Hart (Alec), Eddie Acuff (Dixie Erwin), Tom London, William Norton Bailey, Roger Williams, Curley Dresden, Rudy Sooter, Douglas Wright, Kelsey Sheldon, Lola Monte, Alan Gregg, James Mason, Jack Kirk, Emmett Vogan, Champion the Horse.

Autry plays the foreman on the ranch of wealthy rodeo-owner Moran, who will lose her rodeo contract unless she manages the best sales ever. Autry comes to the rescue of this damsel in distress (why she needs help at all is beyond comprehension. If she can own both a ranch and a rodeo, she must be doing pretty well for herself) and must battle with Mason to overcome a number of obstacles, including a burning barn, fixed rodeo events, and a murder rap. The problem with this one is that there's no explanation for the action that takes place.

p, Harry Grey; d, George Sherman; w, Paul Franklin (based on a story by Franklin); ph, Jack Marta; ed, Lester Orlebeck.

Western (PR:A MPAA:NR)

RHYTHM ON THE RANGE*** (1936) 85m PAR bw

Bing Crosby (Jeff Larrabee), Frances Farmer (Doris Halliday), Bob Burns (Buck Burns), Martha Raye (Emma), Samuel S. Hinds (Robert Halliday), Lucille Webster Gleason (Penelope Ryland), Warren Hymer (Big Brain), George E. Stone (Shorty), James Burke (Wabash), Martha Sleeper (Constance), Clem Bevans (Gila Bend), Leonid Kinskey (Mischa), Charles Williams (Gopher), Beau Baldwin (Cuddles), Emmett Vogan (Clerk), Dennis O'Keefe (Heckler), Duke York (Officer), James Blaine (Conductor), Herbert Ashley (Brakeman), James "Slim" Thompson (Porter), Jim Toney (Oil Station Proprietor), Syd Saylor (Gus), Sam McDaniel (Porter), Harry C. Bradley (Minister), Charles E. Arnt (Steward), Oscar Smith (Waiter), Bob McKenzie (Farmer), Heinie Conklin (Driver), Frank Dawson (Butler), Otto Yamaoka (Chinese Houseboy), Irving Bacon (Announcer), Eddy Waller (Field Judge), Sons of the Pioneers [Roy Rogers, Bob Nolan, Tim Spencer, Hugh Farr, Carl Farr], Louis Prima.

One of only two westerns made by Crosby (the other was the 1966 remake of STAGECOACH in which the Old Groaner didn't sing), this amiable musical was also the debut of Martha Raye, who was only 27 and had already established herself as a nightclub and vaudeville star. She was spectacular and stole every scene she was in. Further, she was so good that while she wasn't on screen, you waited and wondered when she'd return. Crosby is a singing cowboy who manages a dude ranch in California with drawling Burns, his slow-witted partner. (When you think that one is a singer and the other is comedy relief, that makes it sound like a perfect film for Dean Martin and Jerry Lewis. So thay remade it as PARDNERS in 1956.) Burns and Crosby are in New York at Madison Square Garden (the long-shots were actually shot there) where they've won a prize bull for their efforts at the rodeo. Crosby will squire the steer home on a freight train and tells Burns to go by himself on a passenger train. Once Crosby and the animal are aboard the car, he discovers befurred and bejeweled Farmer as a stowaway and wonders what she's up to. She admits that she's fleeing a boy friend in New York whom her parents wish she'd marry, but whom she finds a bore. She's on her way to California because that's as far as a train can go. Farmer doesn't know a soul and has no place to stay, so Crosby asks if she'd like to pass a little time at the dude ranch and she agrees. When they get to California, Burns is there to greet them with his new sweetie, Raye. She's a society lady and loves Burns madly and it's just a matter of time until they marry. Raye is willing to bypass her social status in order to be close to Burns and to find happiness as a cowgirl. Weeks go by and a large party is tossed to celebrate Burns and Raye's upcoming union. It's then that Farmer admits to Crosby that she loves him and the way he lives, indicating that if he popped the question, she would not give him a negative answer. Crosby asks for her hand, she agrees, and he announces to all assembled that there will be a double wedding. Gleason does well as the ranch owner and there's a brief complication with some villains trying to kidnap Farmer but it's extraneous. Lots of fine songs from various sources plus good comedy from Burns and, especially, Raye. Tunes include: "I'm An Old Cowhand" (Johnny Mercer, sung by Crosby and Raye), "Empty Saddles" (Billy Hill, J. Keirn Brennan, sung by Crosby), "I Can't Escape From You" (Leo Robin, Richard Whiting, sung by Crosby), "The House that Jack Built for Jill" (Frederick Hollander, Robin, sung by Crosby), "If You Can't Sing It You'll Have To Swing It (Mr. Paganini)," (Sam Coslow, sung by Raye and Crosby). Other songs include: "Roundup Lullaby" (Bager Clark, Gertrude Ross), "Drink It Down" (Ralph Rainger, Robin), "Memories" (Whiting, Hollander), "Hang Up My Saddle," "Rhythm On The Range" (Walter Bullock, Whiting). The Sons of the Pioneers are in evidence, and see if you don't recognize one of the singers as Leonard Slye, the Cincinnati cowboy. What? You don't recognize that name? Try the name he changed it to. . .Dick Weston. That doesn't mean anything to you either? Well, how about the final *nom de chanson* he took: Roy Rogers. It may be a misnomer to call this a western, as much of the picture takes place in New York, on the train, and in various interiors. Audiences didn't mind and it proved to be one of the studio's most profitable pictures for that year.

p, Benjamin Glazer; d, Norman Taurog; w, John C. Moffett, Sidney Salkow, Walter DeLeon, Francis Martin (based on a story by Mervin J. Houser); ph, Karl Struss; ed, Ellsworth Hoagland; md, Boris Morros; art d, Hans Dreier, Robert Usher; set d, A.E. Fruedeman; cos, Edith Head; m/l, Leo Robin, Richard Whiting, Johnny Mercer, Frederick Hollander, Ralph Rainger, Walter Bullock, Richard Whiting, Bager Clark, Gertrude Ross, Billy Hill, J. Keirn Brennan.

Western/Musical Comedy **(PR:A MPAA:NR)**

RHYTHM ON THE RANGE, 1932 (SEE: ROOTIN' TOOTIN' RHYTHM, 1937)

RHYTHM ON THE RIVER (SEE: FRESHMAN LOVE, 1936)

RHYTHM ON THE RIVER*½** (1940) 92m PAR bw

Bing Crosby *(Bob Summer)*, Mary Martin *(Cherry Lane)*, Basil Rathbone *(Oliver Courtney)*, Oscar Levant *(Billy Starbuck)*, Oscar Shaw *(Charlie Goodrich)*, Charlie Grapewin *(Uncle Caleb)*, Lillian Cornell *(Millie Starling)*, William Frawley *(Mr. Westlake)*, Jean Cagney *(Country Cousin)*, Charles Lane *(Mr. Bernard Schwartz)*, John Scott Trotter *(Himself)*, Phyllis Kennedy *(Patsy Flick)*, Wingy Manone *(Woody)*, Brandon Hurst *(Bates)*, Pierre Watkin *(Uncle)*, Billy Benedict *(Elevator Boy)*, Helen Bertram *(Aunt Della)*, Ken Carpenter *(Announcer)*, Harry Barris *(Bass Player)*.

After the success Crosby had with RHYTHM ON THE RANGE, it was a few years until they could come up with another "Rhythm" title to capitalize. The "river" referred to in this is the Hudson, as it's a backstage show-business story about Broadway and some of the chicanery involved with writing songs for the stage. Rathbone is a famous tunesmith who seems to have lost his talent to compose but not the demand for his work. To that end, he's employed Crosby, an able songwriter with no ambition. Crosby's abilities could probably earn him lots of money but he doesn't much care about that. Rathbone's assistant is Levant, who is also his conscience. Rathbone's dry period began when his wife left him for an Italian restaurateur, a fact Rathbone won't acknowledge and he continues to refer to her as dead. Rathbone has also tapped Martin to write lyrics to Crosby's melodies, but neither knows that the other has been hired. Martin goes to a quiet resort owned by Grapewin to have some solitude and meets Crosby, who is Grapewin's nephew. They fall in love, discover that both are working for Rathbone, and decide to join forces and write with each other. They announce this to Rathbone, who laughs at them and says it will be impossible for the two to get anywhere without his name. They attempt to get their songs published and are spurned by a few companies, then meet Frawley, a big-time music man, who says that they are obviously copying Rathbone's unique style and that they'll never have a hit as long as they continue that. It's a bottleneck and they can't get a thing done, so Martin takes a job singing in a nightclub and Crosby goes back to Grapewin's to think things out. Rathbone has an assignment for a new show and, of course, can't come up with a tune, so he pulls out one Crosby and Martin wrote and puts it into the show, knowing full well it was a love song Martin and Crosby wrote to each other with the proviso that Rathbone never use it. Crosby hears what's happened and is about to take legal action when Rathbone relents and tells the world that he's taken on a pair of collaborators to help with his new project. Lots of very funny Dwight Taylor lines and a good story that was co-written by Billy Wilder. Rathbone is marvelous in a comedic role as an arrogant egomaniac who is more insecure than Woody Allen. Many "in-jokes" in the story, including one where Levant picks up a copy of his own book *A Smattering of Ignorance*," looks at it, and says, "It stinks!" All songs save one were written by Johnny Burke and James V. Monaco. They were: "Rhythm on the River" (sung by Crosby), "When the Moon Comes Over Madison Square," "Ain't It a Shame About Mame?" "What Would Shakespeare Have Said?" "Only Forever," and "That's for Me." The lone exception was written by director Schertzinger, who was a good songwriter as well as an excellent director. His hits include: "Tangerine," "I Remember You," and he even wrote the score for the silent film CIVILIZATION. For this film, he penned "I Don't Want to Cry Anymore." "Only Forever" was Oscar-nominated.

p, William Le Baron; d, Victor Schertzinger; w, Dwight Taylor (based on a story by Billy Wilder, Jacques Thery); ph, Ted Tetzlaff; m, Victor Young; ed, Hugh Bennett; art d, Hans Dreier, Ernst Fegte; cos, Edith Head.

Musical/Comedy **(PR:A MPAA:NR)**

RHYTHM PARADE** (1943) 68m MON bw

Nils T. Granlund [N.T.G.]*(Granny)*, Gale Storm *(Sally)*, Robert Lowery *(Jimmy)*, Margaret Dumont *(Ophelia)*, Chick Chandler *(Speed)*, Cliff Nazarro *(Rocks)*, Jan Wiley *(Connie)*, Candy Candido *(Candy)*, Julie Milton *(Sparkie)*, Sugar Geise *(Patsy)*, Jean Foreman *(Dancer)*, Florentine Gardens Revue, Mills Bros., Ted Fio Rito's Orchestra, Yvonne De Carlo.

The Los Angeles nightclub of Nils T. Granlund served as the setting for a rather meager story about a singer, Storm, who is left to care for an 8-month-old baby when its mother takes off for Hawaii. This gives a jealous competitor, Wiley, the chance to cause some problems for Storm. The rest was just a display of musical talent and the girls of the nightclub. Songs include: "Tootin' My Own Horn" (Edward Kay, Eddie Cherkose), "Petticoat Army," "Mimi from Tahiti," "You're Drafted," (Dave Oppenheim, Roy Ingraham), "Wait Till the Sun Shines Nellie," (Andrew B. Sterling, Harry von Tilzer), "Sweet Sue," (Will J. Harris, Victor Young), and "'Neath the Yellow Moon In Old Tahiti" (Kay, Cherkose).

p, Sydney M. Williams; d, Howard Bretherton, Dave Gould; w, Carl Foreman, Charles Marion (based on a story by Foreman, Marion); ph, Mack Stengler; ed, Carl Pierson; md, Edward Kay.

Musical **(PR:A MPAA:NR)**

RHYTHM RACKETEER* (1937, Brit.) 84m Rock/BIFD bw

Harry Roy *(Harry Grand/Nap Connors)*, Princess Pearl [Pearl Vyner Brooke]*(Karen Vosper)*, James Carew *(Clinton Vosper)*, Norma Varden *(Della Nash)*, Johnny Hines *(Nifty)*, Johnny Schofield *(Spike)*, Judith Wood *(Lola)*, Georgie Harris *(The Rat)*, Pamela Randall, Harry Roy's Band, James Pirrie.

Chicago gangster Roy, while on a transatlantic liner to London, finds that a bandleader on board is his exact double (both men are played by Roy). Seizing the opportunity to commit a crime and have an easy fall guy, Roy (the gangster) steals some valuable jewels and pins the deed on the bandleader. The bandleader makes a narrow escape and finds that he must avoid the police and the gangster while trying to clear his name.

p, Joe Rock; d, James Seymour; w, John Byrd (based on a story by Betty Laidlaw, Robert Lively); ph, Ernest Palmer.

Crime/Musical **(PR:A MPAA:NR)**

RHYTHM ROMANCE (SEE: SOME LIKE IT HOT, 1939)

RHYTHM SERENADE** (1943, Brit.) 87m COL bw

Vera Lynn *(Ann Martin)*, Peter Murray Hill *(John Drover)*, Julien Mitchell *(Mr. Jimson)*, Charles Victor *(Mr. Martin)*, Jimmy Jewel *(Jimmy Martin)*, Ben Warriss *(Ben Martin)*, Joss Ambler *(Mr. Preston)*, Rosalyn Boulter *(Monica Jimson)*, Betty Jardine *(Helen)*, Irene Handl *(Mrs. Crumbling)*, Lloyd Pearson *(Mr. Simkins)*, Jimmy Clitheroe *(Joey)*, Joan Kemp-Welch, Aubrey Mallalieu, Maurice Rhodes, Peter Madden.

A bit of wartime propaganda masquerading as a romantic musical comedy starring Lynn as a young teacher who accepts an offer to run a day school for the employees of a munitions factory. She arranges for the school to be located in the empty house next to the building where she lives and by the end of the film she falls in love with the owner of the property, Hill. A likable enough diversion, but nothing special.

p, Ben Henry, George Formby; d, Gordon Wellesley; w, Marjorie Deans, Basil Woon, Margaret Kennedy, Edward Dryhurst (based on a story by Deans); ph, Bert Mason, Erwin Hillier, Geoffrey Faithfull.

Romance/Musical **(PR:A MPAA:NR)**

RICE GIRL*** (1963, Fr./Ital.) 90m EX-Ponti/Ultra c (LA FILLE DE LA RIZIERE; LA RISAIA)

Elsa Martinelli *(Elena)*, Folco Lulli *(Pietro)*, Michael Auclair *(Mario)*, Rik Battaglia *(Gianni)*, Vivi Gioi *(Elena's Mother)*, Lilla Brignone *(Pietro's Wife)*, Gianni Santuccio *(Lawyer)*, Susanne Levesy *(Carmen)*, Lillian Gerace *(Little Boy's Mother)*, Edith Jost *(Field Crew Captain)*, Emilia Ristori, Bianca Maria Fabbri.

Poignant story of an Italian rice farmer, Lulli, whose life is made miserable through an unhappy marriage. Among the migrant workers on the farm, he notices a young girl who looks oddly familiar. He follows the girl to discover that she is his illegitimate daughter. He now showers the girl with special favors without disclosing their real relationship. The girl, Martinelli, falls in love with auto mechanic Battaglia, who becomes jealous when he see Lulli's attentions to his girl. A reunion is facilitated by Lulli when he tells Battaglia of the true relationship. The latter then rescues Martinelli from an attempted rape at the hands of Lulli's worthless nephew Auclair.

p, Carlo Ponti; d, Raffaello Matarazzo; w, Aldo De Benedetti, Ennio De Concini, Carlo Mussi; ph, Luciano Trasatti (CinemaScope, Eastmancolor); m, Angelo Francesco Lavagnino; ed, Mario Serandrei; art d, Enrico Cerrelli.

Drama **(PR:C-O MPAA:NR)**

RICH AND FAMOUS* (1981) 117m Jacquet-William Allyn/MGM-UA c

Jacqueline Bisset *(Liz Hamilton)*, Candice Bergen *(Merry Noel Blake)*, David Selby *(Doug Blake)*, Hart Bochner *(Chris Adams)*, Steven Hill *(Jules Levi)*, Meg Ryan *(Debby at Age 18)*, Matt Lattanzi *(The Boy Jim)*, Daniel Faraldo *(Ginger Trinidad)*, Nicole Eggert *(Debby at Age 8)*, Joe Maross *(Martin Fornam)*, Kres Mersky *(Judy Heller)*, Cloyce Morrow *(Martha Antilles)*, Cheryl Robinson *(Voice, UCLA)*, Allan Warnick *(Desk Clerk)*, Ann Risley *(Max's Wife)*, Damion Sheller *(Max's Son)*, Haley Fox *(Max's Daughter)*, Fay Kanin *(Prof. Fields)*, Tara Simpson *(Stewardess)*, Herb Graham *(Waiter)*, Charlotte Moore *(Clerk in Cartier)*, William Schilling *(Waldorf Doorman)*, John Perkins *(Limo Driver)*, Herb Bress *(Waiter in Hallway)*, Alan Berliner *(Photographer)*, Don Bachardy, Ruth Conte, Marsha Hunt, Christopher Isherwood, Pola Miller, Paul Morrissey, Jennifer Nairn-Smith, Karen Somerville, Roger Vadim, Sandra Smith Allyn, Frances Bergen, Ray Bradbury, Ellen Brill,

Gwen Davis, Frank De Felitta, Michael Dewell, Nina Foch, Elizabeth Forsythe-Hailey, Oliver Hailey, Randal Kleiser, Gavin Lambert, Michael Brandon.

This could have been a very funny picture. As it was, there were many laughs, although hardly any of them were intended. Van Druten's play "Old Acquaintance" had been made once as a film with Bette Davis and Miriam Hopkins. That one had some real emotion going for it and a pair of superb actresses. Here, the plot has been made sexier, the language more explicit, and the entire affair so pretentious that it fails to satisfy on many levels. Robert Mulligan was to have directed the movie, but when the Actors Strike occurred, everything was put in abeyance after four days of shooting. By the time the strike was over, Mulligan had other things to do, so Cukor was pulled from retirement at the age of 82 to finish this essentially "woman's picture." Bisset and Bergen meet in 1959 at Smith College, then we dissolve to a decade later. Bergen is now living in Malibu with husband Selby, and Bisset is a well-known but poor novelist who agonizes over every word and has only turned out one book that excited the critics but not the public. The two women get together for a rap session and Bergen, who fancies herself a writer as well, reads Bisset a trashy novel she's written about the lives and loves of the people who reside around her in Malibu (something that was actually done later and made into a TV mini-series). Although Bisset sees the essential shallowness in the piece, she gets the book placed with her publisher and the result is a runaway best seller, like a Jackie Collins or Jackie Susann work. Six more years go by and Bergen now lives in Beverly Hills and has written a number of equally silly books, all of which have climbed to the top of the list. Now Bergen wants to achieve some respectability and she's written a novel that is being considered for a national book award. Bisset is one of the judges on the panel and takes some time away from reading Bergen's opus to dally with Bochner, a much younger man who proposes marriage. Bochner is a reporter from *Rolling Stone* and his character as a newsman is totally unbelievable, as he takes no notes, uses no tape recorder, and trusts his memory for their interview session. Selby leaves Bergen and makes a pass at Bisset, but that's extraneous. Many arguments occur between the two women, but in the end, their bond of friendship transcends any petty spats, any jealousy, and any drama. It's a glossy soap opera that suffers from an impoverishment of ideas and Cukor's failure to control his actors. The costumes are atrocious and the entire movie has none of the sophisticated style that made Cukor famous. He'd worked for many years in the "studio system" which allowed for huge sets to be erected. Whereas Mulligan actually did some lensing in New York's Central Park, Cukor had a phony one built and also called for a mock version of New York's Algonquin Hotel to be constructed. Note the cast list to see that many rich and famous literary and movie people were included—authors like Isherwood, Bradbury, De Felitta, Hailey, and Lambert. Would that one of them might have written this script. Joe Maross does a parody of Norman Mailer in this and had his hair curled for the part. Maross and producer Allyn were both Yale drama students way back when, and when Maross had a problem memorizing one speech in his scene, he jotted the words down on a book lying on the table. Look at the scene and note his cribbing of the speech.

p, William Allyn; d, George Cukor; w, Gerald Ayres (based on the play "Old Acquaintance" by John Van Druten); ph, Don Peterman (Metrocolor); m, Georges Delerue; ed, John F. Burnett; prod d, Jan Scott; art d, Fred Harpman; James A. Taylor; set d, Alan Hicks, Dan Robert; cos, Theoni V. Aldredge.

Drama **Cas.** **(PR:O MPAA:R)**

RICH AND STRANGE*** (1932, Brit.) 83m BIP/Power Pictures bw (AKA: EAST OF SHANGHAI)

Henry Kendall *(Fred Hill)*, Joan Barry *(Emily Hill)*, Percy Marmont *(Comdr. Gordon)*, Betty Amann *(Princess)*, Elsie Randolph *(Miss Imery)*, Hannah Jones *(Mrs. Porter), Aubrey Dexter (Colonel)*.

Though this is lightweight fare from Hitchcock, and has nothing to do with the mystery-suspense genre he later became the master of, RICH AND STRANGE is both entertaining and well-crafted. Kendall and Barry are a small town pair who inherit some money and suddenly decide to take a world cruise. Thrust into a foreign atmosphere of sophistication and wealth, the two change drastically, Barry becoming involved with a middle-aged man and the rather oafish Kendall falling for a phony princess who winds up bilking him of most of his funds. Down-and-out, the couple book passage on a freighter which sinks at sea and they are rescued by Chinese fishermen and taken aboard a junk. The rest of the voyage, before they find more conventional means of transportation back to England, is weird. In one scene Kendall and Barry watch as one of the Chinese fishermen chops up a cat and uses it to make chop suey. This was a pet project of Hitchcock's, based on one of his original stories and taken from his experience of a cruise in the Mediterranean with newly married spouse Alma Reville. It's primitive by talkie standards in 1932 with only one fifth of the film offering dialog. The rest tells the story visually. RICH AND STRANGE was originally released in the U.S. under the title of EAST OF SHANGHAI, but American showings over the years reverted to the British title under which the film is best known today. The original running time when released in Britain was 92 minutes but this was cut down to 83 minutes for release in the U.S. Hitchcock did not like either of his leading players in this film. Barry had a problem in talking, frightened by microphones, and sometimes froze before uttering her lines, which caused Hitchcock no end of frustration. He would have to beg and cajole her to finally spit out her lines and often as not order many takes to get them right. Kendall, a comic character actor from London's West End musical halls, was blatantly homosexual in his manner and Hitchcock had a hard time getting him to tone down the swish.

p, John Maxwell; d, Alfred Hitchcock; w, Val Valentine, Alma Reville, Hitchcock (based on a novel by Dale Collins); ph, Charles Martin, John Cox; m, Hal Dolphe; ed, Rene Marrison, Winifred Cooper; md, John Reynders; art d, Frank Mills; set d, C. Wilfred Arnold.

Drama **(PR:C MPAA:NR)**

RICH ARE ALWAYS WITH US, THE½** (1932) 73m FN-WB bw

Ruth Chatterton *(Caroline Grannard)*, George Brent *(Julian Tierney)*, Adrienne Dore *(Allison Adair)*, Bette Davis *(Malbro)*, John Miljan *(Greg Grannard)*, Mae Madison *(3rd Girl)*, John Wray *(Davis)*, Robert Warwick *(The Doctor)*, Walter Walker *(Dante)*, Eula Guy *(Mrs. Drake)*, Edith Allen *(1st Girl)*, Ethel Kenyon *(2nd Girl)*, Ruth Lee *(4th Girl)*, Berton Churchill *(The Judge)*, Virginia Hammond *(Flo)*, Ruth Hall *(Gossip in 1930)*, Georges Renavent *(Headwaiter)*, Bill Elliott *(Gambling Extra)*, Sam McDonald *(Max the Butler)*, Cecil Cunningham *(Admirer)*, Lee Phelps *(Messenger)*.

An attempt to take a behind-the-scenes look at the love affairs of the rich and famous has produced such television soap operas as "Dallas" and "Dynasty," to name but a few. This 1930s version is no different from those of the 1980s; it is glossed over with fancy settings and expensive costumes, and it never really lives up to our expectations. The one saving grace of RICH is the appearance of Chatterton in the lead. She added all the charm she could muster, impressing even the hard-to-please Bette Davis. Chatterton's marriage to Miljan heads for divorce when he admits his love for Dore. Chatterton takes off for Paris with her admirer and confidant Brent, who is somewhat taken aback by the attention Chatterton pays to her no-good husband. Through contacts with powerful friends, she helps Miljan's ailing business, and when he is seriously injured in a car crash that kills Dore, she rushes to be at his side. In the meantime, Brent has become frustrated at contending with Chatterton and has taken up with flapper Davis, who is madly in love with him. But everything is straightened out when Brent is assigned a job in China, and asks Chatterton to accompany him as his wife. Incidentally, Brent and Chatterton fell in love in real life during the filming of this project, marrying soon after. Photography is top-notch with effective direction, but it all has the effect of some pretty shallow personalities being exposed.

p, Samuel Bischoff; d, Alfred E. Green; w, Austin Parker (based on the novel by E. Petit [Mrs. Arthur Somers Roche]); ph, Ernest Haller; m, W. Franke Harling; ed, George Markes; cos, Orry-Kelly.

Drama **(PR:A MPAA:NR)**

RICH BRIDE, THE (SEE: COUNTRY BRIDE, 1938, USSR)

RICH, FULL LIFE, THE (SEE: CYNTHIA, 1947)

RICH KIDS*** (1979) 96m Lion's Gate/UA c

Trini Alvarado *(Franny Phillips)*, Jeremy Levy *(Jamie Harris)*, Kathryn Walker *(Madeleine Philips)*, John Lithgow *(Paul Philips)*, Terry Kiser *(Ralph Harris)*, David Selby *(Steve Sloan)*, Roberta Maxwell *(Barbara Peterfreund)*, Paul Dooley *(Simon Peterfreund)*, Diane Stilwell *(Stewardess)*, Dianne Kirksey *(Ralph's Secretary)*, Irene Worth *(Madeleine's Mother)*, Olympia Dukakis *(Lawyer)*, Jill Eikenberry *(Juilliard Student)*, Kathryn Grody *(Gym Teacher)*, Bea Winde *(Corine)*, Stacy Peppell *(Susan)*, Jack Hausman *(Jamie's Grandfather)*, Lacey Neuhaus *(Receptionist)*, Patti Hansen *(Beverly)*, Michael Miller *(Boy on Bus)*, Shag Starbird *(Shag)*.

A clever story presented through Robert Altman's Lions Gate Films is a look through the eyes of a child at a divorce in an upper-class New York family. Alvarado plays the 12-year-old daughter of Walker and Lithgow, whose marriage is on its last legs. Alvarado knows that the blow is coming, and can only wait for the final showdown. Levy plays the brainy friend whose family has already gone through a breakup. He's an old hand at this stuff, and coaches Alvarado as she copes with the emotional trauma, emphasizing the freedom he has achieved as a result of his parents' split. Never losing a sense of humor toward a touchy subject, the film is a refreshing look at those people—the children—who are the real victims of divorce, but who are seldom given a voice in the matter. The young actors give convincing performances, with Levy perhaps a bit overly smug, and are handled effectively through the well-paced direction of Young.

p, George W. George, Michael Hausman; d, Robert M. Young; w, Judith Ross; ph, Ralph D. Bode (Panavision, Technicolor); m, Craig Doerge; ed, Edward Beyer; art d, David Mitchell; cos, Hilary M. Rosenfeld; m/l, Doerge, Allan Nichols.

Drama/Comedy **Cas.** **(PR:C MPAA:PG)**

RICH MAN, POOR GIRL½** (1938) 65m MGM bw

Robert Young *(Bill Harrison)*, Ruth Hussey *(Joan Thayer)*, Lew Ayres *(Henry Thayer)*, Guy Kibbee *(Phillip Thayer)*, Lana Turner *(Helen Thayer)*, Rita Johnson *(Sally Harrison)*, Don Castle *(Frank Thayer)*, Sarah Padden *(Mrs. Thayer)*, Gordon Jones *(Tom Grogan)*, Virginia Grey *(Selma Willis)*, Marie Blake *(Mrs. Gussler)*, Dorothy Tennant *(Woman in Shoe Store)*, Edwin Maxwell *(Manager of Shoe Store)*, Barbara Bedford *(Kate)*, Mitchell Lewis *(Man Who Yells)*, Jules Cowles *(Man with Radio)*, Francisco Maran *(Maitre d'Hotel)*.

All you have to know about this movie is contained in the title. Young is a wealthy young businessman who falls for Hussey, his executive secretary. She is part of a YOU CAN'T TAKE IT WITH YOU family that includes Kibbee and Padden as her parents and Turner as her jitterbugging sister. Young is in love with Hussey, but she doesn't want to marry him until he sees the kind of family from whence she's sprung (which is very close to the plot in the George S. Kaufman-Moss Hart play). Young decides that the only way to get Hussey is to prove his love and his ability to understand her background, so he moves in with the large family. Ayres does a neat bit as a middle-class young man and proves he is as adroit at comedy as he is at drama, something he'd already shown glimpses of in HOLIDAY. The picture concludes with Hussey and Young getting together and the wealthy man learning a great deal about how the other, poorer, half lives. This was a remake of a 1929 movie that had been directed by William DeMille, brother of Cecil. That one starred Conrad Nagel, Bessie Love, and Leila Hyams and was called THE IDLE RICH. The original title of this four-week wonder was "It's Now Or Never" but that was tossed aside in favor of the more on-the-nose name they gave it. It was Turner's best part after several bits, including the one she did as the "Kissing Bug" in LOVE FINDS ANDY HARDY. The legend about Turner being discovered at the world-famous Schwab's Drug Store (now closed) is untrue. It was *Hollywood Reporter* owner Billy Wilkerson who found her at Currie's ice cream parlor across from Hollywood High School at Sunset Boulevard and Highland Avenue. Hussey was appearing in her third movie and would go on to get an Oscar nomination for her role as the hard-boiled photographer in THE PHILADELPHIA STORY two years later. Five years after that, she triumphed on Broadway in "State of the Union" but lost the movie role to Katharine Hepburn.

p, Edward Chodorov; d, Reinhold Schunzel; w, Joseph A. Fields; Jerome Chodorov (based on the play "White Collars" by Edith Ellis from the story by Edgar Franklin); ph, Ray June; m, Dr. William Axt; ed, Frank E. Hull; art d, Cedric Gibbons, Gabriel Scognamillo; set d, Edwin B. Willis; cos, Dolly Tree.

Comedy   **(PR:A MPAA:NR)**

RICH MAN'S FOLLY*** (1931) 80m PAR bw

George Bancroft (*Brock Trumbull*), Frances Dee (*Ann Trumbull*), Robert Ames (*Joe Warren*), Juliette Compton (*Paula Norcross*), David Durand (*Brock Trumbull, Jr.*), Dorothy Peterson (*Katherine Trumbull*), Harry Allen (*McWylie*), Gilbert Emery (*Kincaid*), Guy Oliver (*Dayton*), Dawn O'Day [Anne Shirley] (*Anne, Age 8*), George McFarlane (*Marston*), William Arnold (*Johnson*).

The Dickens' novel *Dombey and Son* is updated and transplanted from late 1800s England to 1931 America for this somewhat interesting feature. Bancroft is the egotistical owner of a family shipbuilding firm. He becomes overwhelmed by ambition and forgets the needs of his family. He ignores his daughter (Dee,) for he feels that a woman cannot continue the family business. Bancroft's son, Durand, is a frail youth, but his father is determined that one day the boy will take over the business. Bancroft's wife dies, and the man refuses to allow anyone to baby his son. Consequently, Durand weakens even further, and eventually dies. Seemingly unmoved, Bancroft remarries, ever determined to produce an heir. Dee is completely ignored and ends up marrying her father's rival. Bancroft's new wife, unable to live with a man who is so obsessed, walks out on him. In the end Bancroft destroys a new ship that was to bring him great wealth. He has learned that there is more to life than power and money. This is a well-produced and handsomely mounted film. Portions were shot on location in shipyards for a realistic touch. The leads are well played, particularly the parts of Bancroft and the children. Durand is surprisingly good, a natural actor rather than a "movie kid," while Dee is soft-spoken and eloquent. The direction, particularly during Durand's death scene, is sensitive and well handled. It shows a compendium of character emotions from Bancroft's attempt at self-control to Dee's loneliness and overwrought grief. Through the use of close-ups and intelligent *mise-en-scene*, the moment's pure, raw emotion is made to shine through.

d, John Cromwell; w, Grover Jones, Edward Paramore, Jr. (based on the novel *Dombey and Son* by Charles Dickens); ph, David Abel.

Drama   **(PR:A MPAA:NR)**

RICH PEOPLE**½ (1929) 75m Pathe bw

Constance Bennett (*Connie Hayden*), Regis Toomey (*Jeff MacLean*), Robert Ames (*Noel Nevins*), Mahlon Hamilton (*Beverly Hayden*), Ilka Chase (*Margery Mears*), John Loder (*Capt. Danforth*), Polly Ann Young (*Sally Vanderwater*).

Rich, young, and bored heiress Bennett rebels against her class and decides she does not want to marry her fiance, Ames, who is quite wealthy himself. She soon meets no-nonsense insurance salesman Toomey and falls in love with him. While she dreads having to marry Ames, Toomey will not marry her because he wants no part of her wealthy family. Eventually Bennett and Toomey make up, but she cannot get out of her engagement to Ames. On the day of the wedding, Toomey's dog arrives with a note in its mouth informing Bennett that Toomey is leaving town. Knowing that she is about to make a drastic mistake, Bennett leaves Ames at the altar and rushes to Toomey in her wedding gown professing her love for him. A well-made melodrama that was quite a hit for Bennett in the early talkie days.

p, Ralph Block; d, Edward H. Griffith; w, A. A. Kline (based on the story by Jay Gelzer); ph, Norbert Brodine; ed, Charles Craft; art d, Edward Jewell; set d, Ted Dickson; cos, Gwen Wakeling.

Romance   **(PR:A MPAA:NR)**

RICH, YOUNG AND DEADLY (SEE: PLATINUM HIGH SCHOOL, 1960)

RICH, YOUNG AND PRETTY*** (1951) 95m MGM c

Jane Powell (*Elizabeth Rogers*), Danielle Darrieux (*Marie Devarone*), Wendell Corey (*Jim Stauton Rogers*), Vic Damone (*Andre Milan*), Fernando Lamas (*Paul Sarnac*), Marcel Dalio (*Claude Duval*), Una Merkel (*Glynnie*), Richard Anderson (*Bob Lennart*), Jean Murat (*Mons. Henri Milan*), Duci de Kerekjarto (*Gypsy Leader*), Hans Conried (*Jean the Maitre D'*), George and Katrin Tatar (*Hungarian Dancers*), Monique Chantal (*Maid*), Four Freshmen Quartet (*Four Musicians*).

MGM spun out musicals like cotton candy: sweet, enjoyable, and completely forgettable when finished. This one features Powell as a young girl from Texas visiting Paris with her rancher father Corey. Of course what's a visit to gay Paree without amour? This comes in the form of Damone, who naturally turns out to be the man Powell has been dreaming of. Also encountered is Darrieux, the independent woman who ran off to Europe after giving birth to Powell. Powell doesn't know that this woman is her mother and also her father's ex-wife. Lamas plays Darrieux's heartthrob. As is the custom with these musicals, there's a variety of solos and duets, penned here by the talented team of Sammy Cahn and Nicholas Brodszky, including "Dark is the Night," "L'Amour Toujours, Tonight For Sure" (sung by Darrieux), "Wonder Why," "I Can See You" (sung by Damone, Powell), "Paris" (sung by Powell, reprised by Lamas), "We Never Talk Much" (sung by Darrieux, Lamas, reprised by Damone, Powell), "How Do You Like Your Eggs in the Morning?" (sung by Damone, Powell, The Four Freshmen). Other songs include "There's Danger in Your Eyes, Cherie" (Jack Meskill, Pete Wendling, sung

by Darrieux), "The Old Piano Roll Blues" (Cy Coben, sung by Powell, Damone, Lamas), and "Deep in the Heart of Texas" (June Hershey, Don Swander). Damone and Powell's enjoyable number "Wonder Why" received an Acadamy Award nomination for best song. The script was co-written by Sidney Sheldon, who later produced a number of television sitcoms (such as "I Dream of Jeannie") in addition to writing some delightfully trashy novels.

p, Joe Pasternak; d, Norman Taurog; w, Sidney Sheldon, Dorothy Cooper (based on a story by Cooper); ph, Robert Planck (Technicolor); ed, Gene Ruggiero; md, David Rose; art d, Cedric Gibbons, Arthur Lonergan; ch, Nick Castle.

Musical   **(PR:A-C MPAA:NR)**

RICHARD*** (1972) 83m Aurora City Group c-bw

Richard M. Dixon (*Richard*), Dan Resin (*Young Richard*), Lynn Lipton (*Young Pat*), Hazen Glifford, Hank Garrett, Paul Forrest (*Advisors*), Mickey Rooney (*Guardian Angel*), John Carradine (*Plastic Surgeon*), Paul Ford, Kevin McCarthy, Vivian Blaine (*Washington Doctors*), Marvin Braverman (*Hardhat*), Imogene Bliss (*Mother*), Tyrus Cheeney (*Father*), Richard M. Nixon (*Himself*).

This pre-Watergate satire, like the 1972 Philip Roth novel *Our Gang*, points out what America would soon be learning: Our President was indeed a crook. Resin plays the young Richard Nixon, an "aw-shucks" boy-next-door type. He answers an advertisement for a Congressional candidate and becomes subject to Glifford, Garrett, and Forrest, a trio of unholy advisors. After some political failures, they advise the hopeful to submit to some plastic surgery under the knife of facial reconstruction whiz Carradine (the same job he held in MYRA BRECKENRIDGE). The result is Richard M. Dixon, a popular Nixon look-alike who had steady work from 1968 to 1974. This incarnation still can't cut the political mustard, so the Powers Up Above send down a guardian angel for the future President (played here by Rooney in a parody of his boyhood role of "Puck" in A MIDSUMMER NIGHT'S DREAM). Dixon is forced to undergo a filmic brainwashing not unlike that of A CLOCKWORK ORANGE. Ford, McCarthy, and Blaine subject him to newsreel footage of the actual Nixon (which is funny stuff in and of itself—the infamous "Checkers" speech, a classic in unintentional self-parody). Dixon learns his lessons well and goes on to political fame and fortune. This is a clever comedy that pokes fun not only at the subject but at itself as well. Often hilarious, it is a frighteningly honest film, and the newsreel footage proves that comedy and reality were a lot closer than anyone liked to think. Considering what happened over the next few years, RICHARD is weirdly prophetic as well.

p, Lorees Yerby, Bertrand Castelli; d, Yerby, Harry Hurwitz; w, Castelli, Yerby, Hurwitz; ph, Victor Petrashevic; ed, Emil Haviv; set d, Raymond Maynard; m/l, title song, Castelli, Galt MacDermot.

Comedy   **(PR:C MPAA:G)**

RICHARD TAUBER STORY, THE (SEE: YOU ARE THE WORLD FOR ME, 1964, Aust.)

RICHARD III***** (1956, Brit.) 158m LFP-Big Ben/Lopert c

Laurence Olivier (*King Richard III*), Ralph Richardson (*Buckingham*), Claire Bloom (*Lady Anne*), John Gielgud (*Clarence*), Cedric Hardwicke (*King Edward IV*), Mary Kerridge (*Queen Elizabeth*), Pamela Brown (*Jane Shore*), Alec Clunes (*Hastings*), Stanley Baker (*Henry Tudor*), Michael Gough (*Dighton*), Laurence Naismith (*Stanley*), Norman Wooland (*Catesby*), Helen Haye (*Duchess of York*), John Laurie (*Lovel*), Esmond Knight (*Ratcliffe*), Andrew Cruickshank (*Brankenbury*), Clive Morton (*Rivers*), Nicholas Hannen (*Archbishop of Canterbury*), Russell Thorndike (*Priest*), Paul Huson (*Prince of Wales*), Douglas Wilmer (*Dorset*), Dan Cunningham (*Grey*), Michael Ripper (*2nd Murderer*), Stewart Allen (*Page*), Wally Bascoe, Norman Fisher (*Monks*), Terence Greenridge (*Scrivener*), Andy Shine (*Young Duke of York*), Roy Russell (*Abbot*), George Woodbridge (*Lord Mayor of London*), Willoughby Gray (*2nd Priest*), Peter Williams (*Messenger to Hastings*), Timothy Bateson (*Ostler*), Anne Wilton (*Scrubwoman*), Bill Shine (*Beadle*), Derek Prentice (*1st Clergyman*), Deering Wells (*2nd Clergyman*), Richard Bennett (*George Stanley*), Patrick Troughton (*Tyrell*), John Phillips (*Norfolk*), Bernard Hepton (*Knight*), John Greenwood (*Knight*), Brian Nissen, Alexander Davion, Lane Meddick, Robert Bishop (*Messengers*).

Laurence Olivier had a lot of things going for him during his heyday. Taste, talent, a sonorous voice, and a magnificently "neutral" body. Being of average height and weight was a plus, as he could totally submerge himself in so many roles and seem to be tall when the occasion arose (Rochester) or to be woefully small (Archie Rice in THE ENTERTAINER). Here, he becomes the crippled Richard and we are never in doubt that he is who he says he is. Acting is lying; it's convincing an audience that you are another person. If that's the case, put Olivier down for the Baron Munchhausen Award as one of the greatest liars who ever lived. This was his third attempt at bringing Shakespeare to the masses. The first two were HENRY V and HAMLET, for which he won an Oscar. RICHARD III is as good or better than both of the others. The rise and fall of the cunning hunchback was first essayed by Olivier on the stage in the 1940s, but it took this long to raise the money for the film. It's wise that they waited, as Olivier had the benefit of color film, a fairly decent 17-week shooting schedule, and a cast of actors who were otherwise engaged fighting Nazis 11 years before. Author Dent, a screenwriter and a Shakespearean expert, had Olivier to help him with this superb adaptation that made a few cuts, added some characters, but never left the inspiration of The Bard of Avon. The picture begins with the coronation of Hardwicke (Edward IV) in a scene borrowed from the final sequence of "Henry IV, Part III" with Olivier watching jealously in the background. Hardwicke is soon murdered by drowning in a vat of wine and Olivier is the king, engaging in a series of back-stabbings and duplicities that eventually bring him to the Battle of Bosworth where he is unseated from his steed, screams "A Horse, A Horse! My kingdom for a horse!" and is then set upon by the minions of Baker (Henry Tudor) who kill him. This battle was the first scene shot (in Spain) and the picture began dangerously as Olivier was accidentally pierced by a bolt shot from the film's stunt archer which was supposed to hit the protected horse, an animal that had been trained to fall and play dead on command. Olivier continued the scene until a natural break in the action was called for, then he asked for medical aid. Olivier was to have played the role with an acquired limp, but the limp he used in the rest of the film was real and caused by the accident. Shakespeare never meant for us to "like" Richard, but he does his best to help us understand why he came to be the most villainous and unscrupulous monarch that ever reigned over England. Olivier plays the man in a mincing walk, a raspy, almost effeminate voice, and a persona that drips evil from every pore. It took three hours a day to put on the complex makeup (the same prosthetics he wore in the play) that included a false nose, the hunched back, a false hand, and a black pageboy wig that made him look a bit like Sid Ceasar in the famous "Clock Tower" sketch on TV's "Your Show of Shows." Olivier and Dent added two monks, Fisher and Bascoe, who act as a silent Greek Chorus as they view the intrigues. This was not as spectacular a film as HENRY V and the battle scenes might have benefitted by another director who knew how to stage that kind of action. In HAMLET and HENRY V, Olivier did not speak the soliloquies; he stared off in space with closed lips and the words were heard off-camera. This time, he looks directly at the lens and the effect is startling. Directors have always avoided that kind of move (except for the comedic moments when Oliver Hardy glanced at the camera to offer his consternation at another fine mess that Stan Laurel had gotten them into) because it stops the flow of action and breaks the "fourth wall" between audience and performer. But the use of the technique is effective here and seems right for the material. HAMLET took twice as long to shoot and HENRY V's schedule was two-thirds longer, although the rapidity of the schedule for this in no way harmed the outcome. It was not a hit when it came out in England, so the producers made a unique deal for the U.S. and premiered it on NBC television for the sum of $500,000. In later years, after the word of mouth began, it was re-released to resounding success and has been, perhaps, the most financially rewarding of the three. Olivier and Alexander Korda had hoped to film their version of "Macbeth" with Vivian Leigh as Lady MacBeth, but Korda died a year after this and the lack of interest in the project caused it to be tabled. The U.S. TV version had three scenes cut that were deemed too violent for the tube audiences. All they had to do was look at the Saturday morning cartoons to see what real violence was and realize that the brutality in RICHARD III was lemonade by comparison. The British Film Acadamy gave it awards as Best British Film, Best Film, and Best Actor, totally overlooking the superior photography by Czech-born Heller and the sets by Furse and Dillon. Olivier was nominated as Best Actor by the Academy of Motion Picture Arts and Sciences and lost to Yul Brynner for the THE KING AND I. Jeremy Taylor and Jack Curran were in charge of the horses (and there were many) while John Greenwood and Bernard Hepton handled all the sword play. Shakespearean scholars may be slightly irked by the inclusion of the early scene and the exclusion of some others. In addition to Dent and Olivier, script work was done by David Garrick and Colley Cibber, who made their contributions many years before. Although Richardson, Hardwicke, Baker, and everyone else is excellent, the play is a one-man vehicle and so is the movie. That Richard III was a heinous creature is a matter of record. That Olivier was able to engender sympathy for him by his magnificent performance and direction is a tribute to his genius.

p, Laurence Olivier; d, Olivier, Anthony Bushell; w, Alan Dent, Olivier, Colley Cibber, David Garrick (based on the play by William Shakespeare); ph, Otto Heller (VistaVision, Technicolor); m, Sir William Walton; ed, Helga Cranston; prod d, Roger Furse; md, Muir Mathieson; art d, Carmen Dillon; cos, L&H Nathan, Ltd.; spec eff, Wally Veevers; makeup, Tony Sfronzini.

Historical/Drama   Cas.   (PR:A-C MPAA:NR)

RICHARD'S THINGS   (1981, Brit.) 104m Southern/New World c

Liv Ullmann (Kate), Amanda Redman (Josie), Tim Pigot-Smith (Peter), Elizabeth Spriggs (Mrs. Sells), David Markham (Morris), Mark Eden (Richard), Gwen Taylor (Margaret), John Vine (Dr. Mace), Michael Maloney (Bill), Tracy Childs (Joanna), Peter Burton (Colonel), Margaret Lacey (Miss Beale), Ian McDiarmid (Burglar), Lucinda Curtis, Stella Kemball (Receptionists), Athar Malik (Dr. Mustag), Zelah Clarke (Nurse), Dawn Hope (Jamaican Nurse), Amanda Walker (Sister), Willie Holman (Cleaner), Sally Watkins (Brenda), Franco Derosa (Ricci), Alec Linstead (Desk Clerk), Philip York (Man in Train), Glyn Grimstead (Boy), Lesley West (Girl Student), Michael Kingsbury (Boy Student), Oscar Narciso (Porter), Rose Power (Mrs. Jenkins), James Galloway (Josh).

A Bergmanesque tale without any of the master's keen insights into human foibles. Ullman, in an often catatonic performance, is the wife of a man who dies of a heart attack while making love with his mistress. Ullman goes through her late husband's belongings and traces a book of poetry to a secretary (Redman) at his office. The two meet and grow close, eventually developing a lesbian relationship. This film is troubled by a talky script. Characters are constantly speaking in long, drawn-out speeches that cause the film to drag on endlessly. Redman is wrong for her part, coming off as a fragile personality rather than the implied charmer that can seduce both a man and his wife. The film never finds the proper balance between the direct and the implied, thus creating a drama of serious pretenses and poor follow-through.

p, Mark Shivas; d, Anthony Harvey; w, Frederic Raphael (based on the novel by Raphael); ph, Freddie Young; m, Georges Delerue; ed, Lesley Walker; art d, Ian Whittaker.

Drama   Cas.   (PR:O MPAA:NR)

RICHELIEU   (SEE: CARDINAL RICHELIEU, 1935)

RICHES AND ROMANCE   (SEE: ROMANCE AND RICHES, 1937, Brit.)

RICHEST GIRL IN THE WORLD, THE*½**   (1934) 76m RKO bw

Miriam Hopkins (Dorothy Hunter), Joel McCrea (Tony Travis), Fay Wray (Sylvia Vernon), Henry Stephenson (Jonathan Connors), Reginald Denny (Philip Vernon), Beryl Mercer (Marie the Maid), George Meeker (Donald), Wade Boteler (Orsatti), Herbert Bunston (Cavendish), Burr McIntosh (David Preston), Edgar Norton (Butler), Fred Howard (Haley), William Gould (Executive), Selmer Jackson (Dr. Harvey), Olaf Hytten (Valet), Dale Van Sickel (Dance Extra).

Hopkins plays a poor little rich girl. She wants to be sure that men love her for herself and not for money so she talks secretary Wray into switching places for a while. McCrea is the man of Hopkins' dreams who comes through and proves his genuine love. This fresh and clever twist on old themes works well thanks to the strong script by Krasna. The dialog is wonderful and natural with some clever (and believable) plot twists all imaginatively handled. At the time Krasna was being blackballed by MGM head Louis B. Mayer (who was notorious for his cruel treatment of the studio's stars, writers, and directors). Producer Berman saw the script and bought it with his own money for RKO. Mayer's conduct proved to be a creatively costly mistake as Krasna received an Oscar nomination for his script and went on to a highly successful career. Hopkins, a fine comedienne loaned from Paramount for this film, is wonderful in the lead giving a funny and honest performance. Wray (loaned from 20th Century-Fox) is fine in the supporting role, as is McCrea as the earnest young lover. The directon is smart and snappy, bringing out the best performers and script. RKO advertised this as "the season's most electrifying comedy drama, lavish with humor, romance and glamour." It was not quite that but came pretty close. This was later remade as BRIDE BY MISTAKE.

p, Pandro S. Berman; d, William A. Seiter; w, Norman Krasna (based on the story by Krasna); ph, Nick Musuraca; ed, George Crone; md, Max Steiner.

Comedy   (PR:A MPAA:NR)

RICHEST MAN IN THE WORLD, THE   (SEE: SINS OF THE CHILDREN, 1930)

RICHEST MAN IN TOWN*½   (1941) 70m COL bw

Frank Craven (Abb Crothers), Edgar Buchanan (Pete Martin), Eileen O'Hearn (Mary Martin), Roger Pryor (Tom Manning), Tom Dugan (Jack Leslie), George McKay (Jerry Ross), Jimmy Dodd (Bill), Jan Duggan (Penelope Kidwell), John Tyrrell (Ozzie Williams), Harry Tyler (Cliff Smithers), Will Wright (Frederick Johnson), Joel Friedkin (Ed Gunther), Edward Earle (Berton), Erville Alderson (Frank Jaquet the Barber), Thomas W. Ross (Dr. Dickinson), Ferris Taylor (W. Hawkins the Grocer), George Guhl (Sheriff), Netta Packer (Miss Andrews), William Gould (Thorpe), Kathryn Sheldon (Martha), Lee Prather (Game Warden), Edythe Elliott (Elderly Woman), Harry Depp, Ralph Peters (Townsmen), James Farley (Elderly Man), Glenn Turnbull (Dancer), Billy Benedict (Young Man), Harry Johnson (Juggler), Ned Glass, Milburn Morante (Men), Dorothy Vernon, Jessie Arnold (Women), Ernie Adams (Porter), Abe Reynolds (Lounger), Murdock MacQuarrie (Postman), Harry Bailey (Teller), Edward McWade (Old Timer), Richard Fiske (Son).

Buchanan is a small-town newspaper publisher, Craven, the local banker. Though bound by a strong friendship, the two constantly fight. When Buchanan publishes an obituary he's written for his pal, predictable complications ensue. This is a simplistic one-joke comedy tediously stretched out well beyond its natural length. The story moves at a snail's pace, resulting in some pretty unfunny and flat situations. A love story between traveling showman Pryor and Buchanan's daughter, O'Hearn, is needlessly grafted in. Buchanan, a former dentist from Pasadena, does a creditable job despite the odds he's up against.

p, Jack Fier; d, Charles Barton; w, Fanya Foss, Jerry Sackheim (based on a story by Sackheim); ph, Phillip Tannura; m, M.W. Stoloff; ed, Al Clark; art d, Lionel Banks.

Comedy   (PR:A MPAA:NR)

RICKSHAW MAN, THE*½**   (1960, Jap.) 98m Toho/Cory c (MUHOMATSU NO ISSHO)

Toshiro Mifune (Muhomatsu), Hideko Takamine (Mrs. Yoshioka), Hiroshi Akutagawa (Capt. Yoshioka), Chishu Ryu (Mr. Yuki), Choko Iida (Innkeeper), Haruo Tanaka (Kumakichi), Jun Tatara (Theater Employee), Kenji Kasahara (Toshio as a Boy), Kaoru Matsumoto (Toshio as a Youth).

A simple drama of great power. Mifune is a Japanese rickshaw driver in early 20th-Century Japan. He becomes friendly with a shy young boy, the son of a military officer. When the boy's father dies, Mifune becomes a sort of surrogate father. He helps the boy learn how to run a race and in a wonderfully funny and touching moment ignores a rickshaw customer in order to help the lad untangle a kite string. But slowly Mifune falls in love with the boy's widowed mother (Takamine). He confesses his love for her, but their social classes are too different to allow such a love. The boy has grown beyond his need for Mifune as well, leaving the man desolate and alone. With nothing left to live for, Mifune ends up drinking himself to death. This is a story of great drama told with care and sensitivity under a sure-handed direction. The visuals are often overwhelming yet graceful, and they never intrude on the actors or the story. Mifune handles his role with a quiet eloquence, showing all of the man's moods, from anger to unbridled joy. There's also a skillful use of flashback to portray Mifune's own unhappy childhood and its contrast with his adult life.

d, Hiroshi Inagaki; w, Inagaki, Mansaku Itami; ph, Kazuo Yamada (CinemaScope, Agfacolor); m, Ikuma Dan.

Drama   (PR:C-O MPAA:NR)

RICOCHET½** (1966, Brit.) 64m Merton Park/Schoenfeld bw

Maxine Audley *(Yvonne Phipps)*, Richard Leech *(Alan Phipps)*, Alex Scott *(John Brodie)*, Dudley Foster *(Peter Dexter)*, Patrick Magee *(Inspector Cummins)*, Frederick Piper *(Siddall)*, June Murphy *(Judy)*, Virginia Wetherell *(Brenda)*, Alex Bregonzi *(Max)*, Keith Smith *(Porter)*, Peter Torquill *(Sgt. Walters)*, Nancy Nevinson *(Elsie Siddall)*, William Dysart *(1st Skater)*, Barbara Roscoe *(Pretty Girl Skater)*, Anne Godley *(Wardress)*.

After Audley has an affair with Scott, her husband, Leech, a solicitor, decides to blackmail her. At the same time he hopes to get his revenge on Scott. He tells Scott to demand payments from Audley to keep the affair hushed up. Leech tells Scott that the two of them will split the blackmail payments between them. He then gives his wife a loaded gun, falsely telling her it contains merely blanks. Scott comes to collect his money and Audley shoots him dead. She's arrested on murder charges and Leech seemingly has his revenge. But unknown to him Scott had discussed the blackmail with his pal Foster, who in turn starts to blackmail Leech. Leech, driven to desperate measures, tries to kill Foster but is stopped in the nick of time by the sudden arrival of the police.

p, Jack Greenwood; d, John Moxey; w, Roger Marshall (based on the novel *The Angel of Terror* by Edgar Wallace); ph, James Wilson; m, Bernard Ebbinghouse; ed, Derek Holding; art d, Peter Mullins; makeup, Michael Morris.

Crime **(PR:C MPAA:NR)**

RICOCHET ROMANCE½** (1954) 80m UNIV bw

Marjorie Main *(Pansy Jones)*, Chill Wills *(Tom Williams)*, Pedro Gonzales-Gonzales *(Manuel Gonzales)*, Alfonso Bedoya *(Alfredo Gonzales)*, Rudy Vallee *(Worthington Higgenmacher)*, Ruth Hampton *(Angela Ann Mansfield)*, Benay Venuta *(Claire Renard)*, Judith Ames *(Betsy Williams)*, Lee Aaker *(Timmy Williams)*, Irene Ryan *(Miss Clay)*, Darryl Hickman *(Dave King)*, Phillip Tonge *(Mr. Webster)*, Phillip Chambers *(Mr. Daniels)*, Charles Watts *(Mr. Harvey)*, Marjorie Bennett *(Mrs. Harvey)*.

MA AND PA KETTLE was a popular homespun series that brought Main much success. When Percy Kilbride left the series, Ma Kettle was forced to go solo. Here Main plays a clone of her old role, a well-meaning woman of simple ways. She arrives at a dude ranch owned by Wills to become the replacement cook for the mostly unhappy guests. Wills prefers playing magic tricks to running his ranch. Gonzales-Gonzales and Bedoya are a pair of comical Mexican employees (in what plays as a racist portrayal by today's standards) and Vallee is a rich guest who becomes enamoured of Main's good cooking. The plot is ultra-thin, merely a frame to hang some mild slapstick routines on. This film is no different than any other film of Main's, though it is amusing in an amiable sort of way. Songs include "Ricochet Romance" (Larry Coleman, Jr., Joe Darion, sung by Bedoya), "Las Altenitas," "Para Vigo Me Voy," and "Un Tequila" (Ernesto Lecuona, Arturo G. Gonzales, sung by The Guadalajara Trio).

p, Robert Arthur, Richard Wilson; d, Charles Lamont; w, Kay Lennard (based on a story by Lennard); ph, George Robinson; ed, Russell Schoengarth; md, Joseph Gershenson; art d, Alexander Golitzen, Alfred Sweeney; m/l, Larry Coleman, Jr., Joe Darion, Norman Gimbel, J.J. Espinosa, Ernesto Lecuona, Arturo G. Gonzales.

Comedy **(PR:AAA MPAA:NR)**

RIDE A CROOKED MILE*½** (1938) 70m PAR bw

Akim Tamiroff *(Mike Balan)*, Leif Erickson *(Johnny Simpkins)*, Frances Farmer *(Trina)*, Lynne Overman *(Oklahoma)*, John Miljan *(Lt. Col. Stuart)*, J.M. Kerrigan *(Sgt. Flynn)*, Vladimir Sokoloff *(Glinka)*, Genia Nikola *(Marie Simpkins)*, Wade Crosby *(George Rotz)*, Robert Gleckler *(Warden)*, Nestor Paiva *(Leroyd)*, Archie Twitchell *(Byrd)*, Gaylord Pendleton *(Bilks)*, Fred Kohler, Jr. *(Cpl. Bresline)*, Dewey Robinson, William Newell, John Bleifer, Alex Woloshin, James Flavin.

Raised to be a hard-fighting Cossack, Tamiroff is the wealthy head of a gang of outlaws. They take to hijacking cattle en route to market. Tamiroff is joined by his 21-year-old son Erickson, sent to him by his divorced wife. "Like father, like son," goes the old saying, and this certainly applies to Erickson, for he is just as aggressive and manly as his father. The two try to outdo each other in various feats and a mutual admiration and respect soon blossoms. But the law catches up with Tamiroff and he is sent off to Leavenworth. Erickson joins a cavalry unit and plots to help his father escape. The escape works, but a moral crisis arises for the son when his unit must search for the escapees. He leads the search party and finally catches up with his father. Explaining that his loyalty to the troops must come first, Erickson attempts to arrest his still-loved father. But Tamiroff tries to escape and ends up running off the edge of a cliff. RIDE A CROOKED MILE, despite its B western sounding title, is an exciting, well-made action film. Tamiroff and Erickson give vigorous performances seething with machismo. There's not a wasted moment in this film, with each scene adding information rather than simply filling time. The prison sequences are comprised of scenes showing the would-be escapees making plans. These scenes are filmed in tight close-ups and two-shots. There are no extraneous scenes depicting day-to-day prison life. Perhaps the only glaring fault in the film is Farmer's bit role as Erickson's girl friend. It's not that she's bad; she does a good job in this limited part. However, Farmer, a veteran of the Group Theater and a talented, accomplished actress, clearly deserved better roles than a small throwaway part like this. Eventually her rebellious attitude towards her castings and the entire studio system would do her in, a downfall well chronicled in the harrowing version of her life story FRANCES (1983).

p, Jeff Lazarus; d, Alfred E. Green; w, Ferdinand Reyher, John C. Moffitt (based on a story by Reyher, Moffitt); ph, William C. Mellor; ed, James Smith; spec eff, Farciot Edouart.

Action/Adventure **(PR:C MPAA:NR)**

RIDE A CROOKED TRAIL** (1958) 87m UNIV c

Audie Murphy *(Joe Maybe)*, Gia Scala *(Tessa Milotte)*, Walter Matthau *(Judge Kyle)*, Henry Silva *(Sam Teeler)*, Joanna Moore *(Little Brandy)*, Eddie Little *(Jimmy)*, Mary Field *(Mrs. Curtis)*, Leo Gordon *(Sam Mason)*, Mort Mills *(Pecos)*, Frank Chase *(Ben the Deputy)*, Bill Walker *(Jackson)*, Ned Wever *(Attorney Clark)*, Richard Cutting *(Mr. Curtis)*.

A runaway bank robber (Murphy) enters the western town of Little Rock. There a local judge (Matthau) mistakes the newcomer for the marshal whom the town is awaiting. Of course Murphy plays along and finds that his new role wins him admiration and respect. Scala is a Creole who serves as the love interest. This has all been done before, and much more refreshingly. Matthau has a few good comic moments in his drunken caricature. Otherwise this is a slow-moving affair with only a few moments of interest. The color photography manages to make some use of the gorgeous scenery.

p, Howard Pine; d, Jesse Hibbs; w, Borden Chase (based on a story by George Bruce); ph, Harold Lipstein (CinemaScope, Eastmancolor); m, Joseph Gershenson; ed, Edward Curtiss; md, Gershenson; art d, Alexander Golitzen, Bill Newberry; cos, Bill Thomas.

Western **(PR:A-C MPAA:NR)**

RIDE A NORTHBOUND HORSE** (1969) 79m Disney c

Carroll O'Connor, Michael Shea, Ben Johnson, Andy Devine, Edith Atwater, Jack Elam.

A Disney western for the younger set features Shea as another of the studio's plucky film orphans. He heads off for Texas determined to become a cattleman. Once there the hardy 15-year-old finds himself involved with a confidence man and a pair of racehorses. The film starts off well, but once the subplots start to pile up it turns into a confusing mess that will probably bore its intended child audience.

p, Ron Miller; d, Robert Totten; w, Herman Groves; ph, Robert Hoffman.

Western **(PR:AA MPAA:NR)**

RIDE A VIOLENT MILE* (1957) 80m Emirau/FOX bw

John Agar *(Jeff)*, Penny Edwards *(Susan)*, John Pickard *(Marshal Thorne)*, Richard Shannon *(Sam)*, Charles Gray *(Dory)*, Bing Russell *(Norman)*, Helen Wallace *(Mrs. Bartold)*, Richard Gilden *(Gomez)*, Sheb Wooley *(Jonathan Long)*, Patrick O'Moore *(Bartender)*, Rush Williams *(Edwards)*, Roberto Contreras *(Abruzo)*, Eve Novak *(Townswoman)*, Mary Townsend, Dorothy Schuyler *(Dance Hall Girls)*, Rocky Shahan, Norman Cram, Karl MacDonald.

In order to infiltrate a group of Confederates plotting to exchange cattle for help from Mexico, Union spy Edwards poses as a dance hall girl. Agar is the stranger who falls for the pretty agent and finds himself involved in her mission as he rescues Edwards from Confederate agents Shannon and Gray (a name appropriate enough for a Confederate!). In the end the two lovebirds cause a cattle stampede that defeats the Rebel plan. Even THE WIZARD OF OZ had a more realistic story line and characters. RIDE A VIOLENT MILE seems to have more holes than Swiss cheese. The basic premise is unbelievable, so the plot suffers all the way through. The acting is passable, but not much more.

p, Robert Stabler; d, Charles Marquis Warren; w, Eric Norden (based on a story by Warren); ph, Brydon Baker (RegalScope); m, Raoul Kraushaar; ed, Fred W. Berger; md, Kraushaar; art d, James W. Sullivan.

Western **(PR:C MPAA:NR)**

RIDE A WILD PONY½** (1976, U.S./Aus.) 90m Disney/BV c

Michael Craig *(James Ellison)*, John Meillon *(Charles E. Quayle)*, Robert Bettles *(Scotty Pirie)*, Eva Griffith *(Josie Ellison)*, Graham Rouse *(Bluey Waters)*, Alfred Bell *(Angus Pirie)*, Peter Gwynne *(Sgt. Collins)*, John Meillon, Jr. *(Kit Quayle)*, Roy Haddrick *(J.C.)*, Melissa Jaffer *(Angus' Wife)*, Lorraine Bayly *(James' Wife)*, Wendy Playfair.

Typical Disney affair with beautiful location work in the Australian outback. A wild pony causes two children—one (Bettles) the son of a poor farmer, the other a disabled rich girl (Griffith)—to fight over its ownership. Though Griffith is introduced in the most maudlin fashion possible (the old Disney standard of "Let's All Feel Sorry for the Cripple"), she makes the role much more than that, giving the best performance in the film. The story culminates with Bettles as the rightful owner of the pony, but along the way he and Griffith have learned a few things about love, selfishness, and sharing. The message is presented in a refeshingly non-preachy fashion that encourages the intended child audience to actively involve itself in moral judgments. Unfortunately, after Griffith's wonderful, stereotype-breaking role (a marvelous debut for a child as well), the rest of the performances are quite standard and often seem as flat as cardboard cutouts. However this is a good film for the younger set. Unlike many children's films, it gives the audience something to think about.

p, Jerome Courtland; d, Don Chaffey; w, Rosemary Anne Sisson (based on the novel *A Sporting Proposition* by James Aldridge); ph, Jack Cardiff (Technicolor); m, John Addison; ed, Mike Campbell; md, Marcus Dods; art d, Robert Hilditch; cos, Judith Dorsman.

Children's Drama **(PR:AAA MPAA:G)**

RIDE BACK, THE*½** (1957) 79m The Associates-Aldrich/UA bw

Anthony Quinn *(Kallen)*, William Conrad *(Hamish)*, George Trevino *(Guard)*, Lita Milan *(Elena)*, Victor Millan *(Padre)*, Ellen Hope Monroe *(Child)*, Joe Dominguez *(Luis)*, Louis Towers *(Boy)*.

Lawman Conrad (who normally worked as a producer for westerns) is a loner who decides to take captured outlaw Quinn across the Mexican border back to Texas. The trip will require four days through desert and hostile territory. Despite protests from his girlfriend Milan, Conrad is determined to make the trip. The trek becomes a psychological cat-and-mouse game, and Quinn constantly challenges Conrad's authority, causing doubts in the lawman's mind about his position and life. In their travels they happen onto the site of an Indian massacre. The only survivor is a little girl whom they must take along. During another Apache attack Conrad is wounded and Quinn sees an opportunity for escape. But guilt catches up with him for the first time in his life, and Quinn returns to the wounded man and little girl. He leads them to safety although he knows that if he goes back he will stand trial for murder. The intensity of the two leads make this a cut above most westerns. Each man carries his own set of attitudes, performing according to the role society has thrust upon him. But along the trail a friendship of necessity emerges in an unspoken and tentative manner. This was the feature debut for director Miner, who had previously made the fine documentary THE NAKED SEA. The direction allows the story to unfold slowly with a building intensity that works well. Unfortunately, this film was virtually ignored upon release and sank into obscurity. THE RIDE BACK was old hat for Quinn. In the earlier made-for-television feature THE LONG TRAIL he had to bring an extradited murderer from Texas to Oregon. And in a later feature, LAST TRAIN FROM GUN HILL, Kirk Douglas played a sheriff determined to bring Quinn's son along another lonesome trail to justice. This film had noted director Robert Aldrich as executive producer.

p, William Conrad; d, Allen H. Miner; w, Antony Ellis; ph, Joseph Biroc (Sepiatone); m, Frank de Vol; ed, Michael Luciano; md, de Vol; art d, William Glasgow; cos, Oscar Rodriguez; title song sung by Eddie Albert.

Western   (PR:C MPAA:NR)

RIDE BEYOND VENGEANCE zero   (1966) 100m Tiger-Sentinal-
                                    Fenady/COL c (AKA: NIGHT OF THE TIGER)

Prologue cast: James MacArthur (Delahay, the Census Taker), Arthur O'Connell (Narrator), Ruth Warrick (Aunt Gussie), Buddy Baer (Mr. Kratz), Frank Gorshin (Tod Wisdom), Robert Q. Lewis (Hotel Clerk). Main cast: Chuck Connors (Jonas Trapp), Michael Rennie (Brooks Durham), Kathryn Hays (Jessie), Joan Blondell (Mrs. Lavender), Gloria Grahame (Bonnie Shelley), Gary Merrill (Dub Stokes), Bill Bixby (Johnsy Boy Hood), Claude Akins (Elwood Coates), Paul Fix (Hanley), Marissa Mathes (Maria), Harry Harvey, Sr. (Vogan), William Bryant (Bartender), Jamie Farr (Pete), Larry Domasin (Mexican Boy), Bill Catching (A Drunk).

A census taker (MacArthur) wanders into a bar in a small Texas town. There the bartender (O'Connell) tells him a story which becomes the body of the film. Connors plays a man of the 1880s. He marries Hays but it soon becomes apparent that this is not a marriage of love. Rather Connors has married Hays in order to get at her sick aunt's money. Connors runs off from the town but returns 11 years later only to discover that Thomas Wolfe was right when he said you can't go home again. He's met outside the town by Rennie, a banker, and his two henchmen, Bixby and Merrill. Despite the $17,000 Connors has earned from buffalo hunting, the trio think he's a rustler. In an absolutely disgusting scene Connors is held down and sadistically branded with a "T." Connors passes out and wakes up in the care of Fix, the real rustler, who's in cahoots with Rennie. Connors' money has been taken and Hays is now engaged to Rennie. Connors vows revenge and heads off into an orgy of killings and suicides. The violence in this film is brutal and almost gleefully sadistic. It was made in the same period that many of the ultra-violent Italian "Spaghetti" westerns were coming to the U.S. RIDE BEYOND VENGEANCE seems to be saying "Look, we can be just as depraved." It has the look of a made-for-television film (it was produced by the same team that was making Connors' TV series "Branded"), which suggests that this may have originally been slated for the airwaves. As it is, RIDE BEYOND VENGEANCE is little more than a violence-riddled film with lots of story padding that fitfully gives the impression that something is going on. The acting is pretty awful and the story line gets muddled by the film's various uses of flashbacks. This was produced by Mark Goodson and Bill Todman, the same company that gave us such insipid game shows as "Let's Make a Deal."

p, Andrew J. Fenady; d, Bernard McEveety; w, Fenady (based on the novel The Night of the Tiger by Al Dewlin); ph, Lester Shorr (PatheColor); m, Richard Markowitz; ed, Otho Lovering; art d, Stan Jolley; set d, William Calvert; cos, Gordon Dawson, Frances Hamilton; spec eff, Lee Vasque; m/l, "You Can't Ever Go Home Again," Markowitz, Fenady (sung by Glenn Yarbrough); makeup, Fred B. Phillips.

Western   (PR:O MPAA:NR)

RIDE CLEAR OF DIABLO*   (1954) 80m UNIV c

Audie Murphy (Clay O'Mara), Dan Duryea (Whitey Kincade), Susan Cabot (Laurie), Abbe Lane (Kate), Russell Johnson (Ringer), Paul Birch (Sheriff Kenyon), William Pullen (Meredith), Jack Elam (Tim), Lane Bradford (Harry), Mike Regan (Jim), Denver Pyle (Rev. Moorehead).

Birch, the local sheriff, along with lawyer Pullen, murders a man and one of his sons. The surviving son (Murphy) vows revenge and goes after the pair with the help of gunfighter Duryea. Johnson ("Professor" of TV's "Gilligan's Island") is a henchman of Birch and Pullen with Cabot as the sheriff's niece engaged to marry Pullen. After the climactic shootout she's had the usual change of heart, ending up with Murphy. Though the film is routine fare, its direction and camera work improve the formula material noticeably. There are some unusual plot twists as well, which add to the film's interest. The ensemble, led by the macho Murphy, do a fine job. All of these elements, along with the fine use of Technicolor, make RIDE CLEAR OF DIABLO a better-than-average B western.

p, John W. Rogers; d, Jesse Hibbs; w, George Zuckerman, D.D. Beauchamp (based on a story by Ellis Marcus); ph, Irving Glassberg (Technicolor); ed, Edward Curtiss; cos, Rosemary Odell; m/l, "Wanted," Frederick Herbert, Arnold Hughes, "Noche De Ronda," Maria Teresa Lara (both sung by Abbe Lane).

Western   (PR:C MPAA:NR)

RIDE 'EM COWBOY½**   (1936) 59m UNIV bw (AKA: COWBOY
                                    ROUNDUP)

Buck Jones (Jess Burns), George Cooper (Chuck Morse), William Lawrence (Sandy Adams), Luana Walters (Lillian Howard), J. P. McGowan (Jim Howard), Joseph Girard (Sam Parker), Donald Kirke (Sam Parker, Jr.), Charles Lemoyne (Sheriff Stanton), Edmund Cobb, Lester Dorr, Silver the Horse.

With this film Jones began producing his own westerns, which he had been scripting and starring in for some time. This innocuous feature plays havoc with suspension of disbelief but it is an enjoyable little romp nonetheless. Jones plays a modern cowpoke who's mystified by automobiles. He gives up his beloved horse Silver for a racing car. Walters is the daughter of a racing promoter who will be forced to marry the evil Kirke if her father loses the race. Kirke does all the bad guy tricks you've ever seen: paying off the other driver, sabotage, and other dirty tricks. Of course, Jones comes to the comical climactic rescue, winning both the race and Walters' heart. It's all fairly silly, but directed with a lively style and some surprisingly creative camera work.

p, Buck Jones; d, Les Selander; w, Francis Guihan (based on a story by Jones); ph, Allen Thompson, Herbert Kirkpatrick.

Western   **Cas.**   (PR:A MPAA:NR)

RIDE 'EM COWBOY*   (1942) 86m UNIV bw

Bud Abbott (Duke), Lou Costello (Willoughby), Anne Gwynne (Anne Shaw), Samuel S. Hinds (Sam Shaw), Dick Foran (Robert "Bronco Bob" Mitchell), Richard Lane (Peter Conway), Judd McMichael (Tom), Ted McMichael (Dick), Joe McMichael (Harry), Mary Lou Cook (Dotty Davis), Johnny Mack Brown (Alabam), Ella Fitzgerald (Ruby), Douglas Dumbrille (Jake Rainwater), Jody Gilbert (Moonbeam), Morris Ankrum (Ace Anderson), Charles Lane (Martin Manning), Russell Hicks, Tom Hanlon (Announcers), Wade Boteler (Rodeo Manager), James Flavin (Railroad Detective), Boyd Davis (Doctor), Eddie Dunn (2nd Detective), Isabel Randolph (Lady), James Seay (Ranger Captain), Harold Daniels (Reporter), Ralph Peters (1st Henchman), Linda Brent (Sunbeam), Lee Sunrise (2nd Indian Girl), Chief Yowlachie (Chief Tomahawk), Harry Monty (Midget), Sherman E. Sanders (Square Dance Caller), Carmela Cansino (1st Indian Girl), The Hi-Hatters, The Buckaroos Band, The Ranger Chorus of Forty, The Congoroos.

Abbott and Costello play a pair of peanut and hotdog vendors who end up on a dude ranch as cowhands. Foran as a western novelist and Gwynne as the ranch owner's daughter are the love interests. It's typical A & C fare, with the pair going through their usual antics. What separates this from their other films is the unusual quality of the musical talents. Fitzgerald of all people is a featured singer doing some marvelous numbers, including a rousing version of "A Tisket, A Tasket," which she adapted with Al Feldman. There are also some good Raye and De Paul numbers, including what was to become a classic, "I'll Remember April." The Merry Macs (replacing the Andrews Sisters) do a few numbers as well, including "Wake Up Jacob," "Beside the Rio Tonto" and "Rock 'n' Reelin," (with Fitzgerald). Other songs include "Give Me My Saddle" and "Cow Boggie." If you look sharply, you will also see Dorothy Dandridge doing the jitterbug as one of the Congoroos. (See ABBOTT AND COSTELLO series, Index.)

p, Alex Gottlieb; d, Arthur Lubin; w, True Boardman, John Grant, Harold Shumate (based on a story by Edmund L. Hartmann); ph, John W. Boyle; ed, Phillip Cahn; md, Charles Previn; art d, Jack Otterson; ch, Nick Castle; m/l, Don Raye and Gene De Paul, Patricia Johnston.

Musical/Comedy   (PR:AAA MPAA:NR)

RIDE 'EM COWGIRL**   (1939) 52m Coronado/GN bw

Dorothy Page (Helen Rickson), Milton Frome (Oliver Shea), Vince Barnett (Dan Haggerty), Lynn Mayberry (Belle), Frank Ellis (Sheriff Larson), Harrington Reynolds (Boyle), Stanley Price (Robert Weylan), Warner Richmond (Wiley), Lloyd Ingraham (Judge), Merrill McCormack, Fred Berhle, Pat Henning, Edward Gordon, Fred Cordova, Lester Dorr, Walter Patterson, Snowey the Horse.

This was Grand National's attempt to bring a singing cowgirl to the forefront of B westerns in what amounted to the only series of films (three) to feature a woman in the principal role. Page plays the daughter of a man cheated out of $5,000. She steals back the money but is branded an outlaw. Page enters a horse race and wins, exposing Girard as the true bad guy. Frome is an undercover G man and love interest as well. The idea of putting a woman in the lead for a B western is interesting but unfortunately does not work. Page can do little more than ride and toss a lariat in addition to her vocalizing. Page cannot overcome this series restraint for the script and direction are clearly meant for the typical male hero. The result is a poorly made western that plays as high camp. Still it is worth a look for what it attempted to do.

p, Arthur Dreifuss; d, Samuel Diege; w, Arthur Hoerl; ph, Mack Stengler; ed, Guy B. Thayer; m/l, Al Sherman and Walter Kent.

Western   **Cas.**   (PR:A MPAA:NR)

RIDE HIM, COWBOY*   (1932) 55m VIT/WB bw (GB: THE HAWK)

John Wayne (John Drury), Ruth Hall (Ruth Gaunt), Henry B. Walthall (John Gaunt), Harry Gribbon (Clout), Otis Harlan (Judge Jones), Charles Sellon (Judge Bartlett), Frank Hagney (The Hawk), Duke the Devil Horse.

A horse named Duke is charged with murdering a rancher and sentenced to death. In comes Wayne who saves the horse and together man and beast discover that Hagney, the bank robber, is the real killer who tried to frame the horse. Believe it or not! This was the first of six series films Wayne was to make for Warner's, all of which costarred Duke. It's entertaining enough with better direction than most films of this nature. RIDE HIM, COWBOY is a remake of the 1926 Ken Maynard silent film THE UNKNOWN CAVALIER.

p, Leon Schlesinger; d, Fred Allen; w, Scott Mason (based on the story by Kenneth Perkins); ph, Ted McCord; ed, William Clemens.

Western   **(PR:A MPAA:NR)**

RIDE IN A PINK CAR*½   (1974, Can.) 83m Clarion/Ambassador c
Glenn Corbett, Morgan Woodward, Ivy Jones, Big John Hamilton, Ed Faulkner.
A Vietnam vet, thought to have been killed in action, returns to his rural home town only to find hate and animosity toward him. He fights against their terrorist tactics and eventually is able to find a place for himself back in "the world."
d, Robert J. Emery.

Drama   **Cas.**   **(PR:C-O MPAA:PG)**

RIDE IN THE WHIRLWIND*   (1966) 82m Favorite-Jack H. Harris c
Cameron Mitchell (Vern), Jack Nicholson (Wes), Tom Filer (Otis), Millie Perkins (Abby), Katherine Squire (Catherine), George Mitchell (Evan), Brandon Carroll (Sheriff), Rupert Crosse (Indian Joe), [Harry] Dean Stanton (Blind Dick), Peter Cannon (Hagerman), John Hackett (Sheriff's Aide), B.J. Herholz (Outlaw).

Nicholson wrote, coproduced, and costarred in this low-budget western which was purportedly written after Nicholson had pored over various frontier diaries which he found at The Los Angeles Public Library. He would have been better off reading a few good western scripts at the Motion Picture Acadamy. Hellman's direction is flat and the acting is mostly a lot of talk with hardly any point in it. Nicholson, Mitchell, and Filer are itinerant cowpokes who have employment as part of a cattle roundup. On their trip to the job, they note the result of a vigilante lynching swaying in the wind and shake their heads at the fate of the hanged. They decide to rest a spell at a mountain cabin, walk in and meet Stanton (who now uses the name Harry Dean Stanton), the one-eyed leader of a gang of murderers who've just killed a stage-coach driver. Stanton is pleasant to the trio, offers them a place to rest their heads as well as some booze and some food. Sheriff Carroll's posse is soon surrounding the cabin. Stanton and his men are captured and hanged by the posse. Filer is killed, and Mitchell and Nicholson, who are totally innocent (but go to tell that to the bloodthirsty posse), have to run for their lives. They arrive at the cabin of George Mitchell, a homesteader, and take a breather. Now Nicholson thinks Perkins, the rancher's daughter, might be a good hostage. When Cameron Mitchell tries to steal George Mitchell's horses, he is shot down by the latter, thus motivating Nicholson to have to kill the old man and then run off, now a full-fledged killer who will, no doubt, eventually wind up swinging for it. It's an endless chase across the desolate Utah landscape with good photography from Sandor but not much else. The film had trouble getting a distributor and was finally picked up by a small company, Favorite Films, and Jack H. Harris, the schlockmeister who gave us THE BLOB and PUSSYCAT A GO-GO.

p, Jack Nicholson, Monte Hellman; d, Hellman; w, Nicholson; ph, Gregory Sandor (Eastmancolor); m, Robert Drasnin; ed, Monte Hellman.

Western   **Cas.**   **(PR:C MPAA:G)**

RIDE, KELLY, RIDE*½   (1941) 59m FOX bw
Eugene Pallette (Duke Martin), Marvin Stephens (Corn Cob Kelly), Rita Quigley (Ellen Martin), Mary Healy (Entertainer), Richard Lane (Dan Thomas), Charles D. Brown (Bob Martin), Chick Chandler (Knuckles), Dorothy Peterson (Mrs. Martin), Lee Murray (Tuffy Graves), Frankie Burke (Skeeziks O'Day), Cy Kendall (Louis Becker), Hamilton MacFadden (Steward), Walter "Spec" O'Donnell (Kalinski), Ernie Adams (Sandy), Edwin Stanley, Edward Keane, Edward Earle (Stewards).

Stephens is an eager young jockey who accidentally gets in with some gamblers. They want him to throw a race but it's nothing doing for the honest young man. They replace him with a seasoned rider but thanks to Pallette, the stable trainer who took Stephens off a ranch and onto the race track, the ambitious lad enters the big race and wins, much to the gambler's chagrin. Stephens also wins the heart of Quigley, Pallette's daughter. Standard formula stuff using every cliche of the genre. Both script and direction are hackneyed, going for easy (and amateurish) payoffs. Acting is standard.

p, Sol M. Wurtzel; d, Norman Foster; w, William Conselman, Jr., Irving Cummings, Jr. (based on a story by Peter B. Kyne); ph, Virgil Miller; ed, Louis Loeffler; md, Emil Newman.

Drama   **(PR:A MPAA:NR)**

RIDE LONESOME***   (1959) Ranown/COL c
Randolph Scott (Ben Brigade), Karen Steele (Carrie Lane), Pernell Roberts (Sam Boone), James Best (Billy John), Lee Van Cleef (Frank), James Coburn (Wid), Dyke Johnson (Charlie), Boyd Stockman (Indian Chief), Roy Jenson, Boyd "Red" Morgan, Bennie Dobbins (Outlaws), Lee Marvin, Donna Reed.

Using all the elements of B westerns (as well as Eastmancolor and CinemaScope) RIDE LONESOME is an intelligent western making good use of old formulas. Eternal hero Scott (who served as executive producer) is a bounty hunter looking for the murderer Best. At first it seems that Scott merely wants the money but eventually it is revealed that the bounty hunter hopes Best will lead him to his brother, Van Cleef, who murdered Scott's wife. Along the way Scott picks up Steele, a young widow and a pair of outlaws also looking for Best. They are Coburn (in a fine film debut) and Roberts who hope Best's capture will lead to a pardon. In the end Scott revenges Van Cleef's deed and allows Roberts to turn in Best, thus collecting their pardon. Scott rides off with Steele to begin a new life. This is a film full of intelligent dialog and a variety of good performances ranging from Scott's sternness to the comedy of Best as a giggling killer. Using turns both serious and humorous, a real slice of life is built up within the small group. Full of ironies in the script as well as gorgeous scenery, RIDE LONESOME is an intelligent and thoughtful western, refreshing with its clever reworkings of old stereotypes and themes.

p&d, Budd Boetticher; w, Burt Kennedy; ph, Charles Lawton, Jr. (CinemaScope,

Eastmancolor); m, Heinz Roemheld; ed, Jerome Thoms; md, Roemheld; art d, Robert Peterson; set d, Frank A. Tuttle.

Western   **(PR:C MPAA:NR)**

RIDE ON VAQUERO***   (1941) 64m FOX bw
Cesar Romero (Cisco Kid), Mary Beth Hughes (Sally), Lynne Roberts (Marguer-ita), Chris-Pin Martin (Gordito), Robert Lowery (Carlos), Ben Carter (Watchman), William Demarest (Barney), Robert Shaw (Cavalry Officer), Edwin Maxwell (Clark), Paul Sutton (Sleepy), Don Costello (Redge), Arthur Hohl (Sheriff), Irving Bacon (Baldy), Dick Rich (Curly), Paul Harvey (Colonel), Joan Woodbury (Dolores).

Romero rides for the last time in the CISCO KID series he did for 20th Century-Fox. Here the Kid is after some kidnapers who are using his name in their nefarious deeds. In between the action, gun play and eventual rounding up of the baddies, Romero finds a moment for two for romance with Hughes, a lusty vibrant dancehall girl. RIDE ON VAQUERO is an exciting programmer with plenty of action and a well-paced direction. Though the high standards were maintained throughout Romero's entries in the series, this version of the CISCO KID never really caught on with the public. The series came to an abrupt ending when Romero was drafted into the Army. Fox heads looked for a suitable replacement but finding none, decided to kill the series altogether. However the kid made a triumphant return when Monogram revived him for their own series beginning with THE CISCO KID RETURNS in 1945. (See CISCO KID series, Index.)

p, Sol M. Wurtzel; d, Herbert I. Leeds; w, Samuel G. Engel (based on characters created by O. Henry); ph, Lucien Andriot; ed, Louis Loeffler; md, Emil Newman.

Western   **(PR:A MPAA:NR)**

RIDE OUT FOR REVENGE**   (1957) 79m Bryna/UA bw
Rory Calhoun (Tate), Gloria Grahame (Amy Porter), Lloyd Bridges (Capt. George), Joanne Gilbert (Pretty Willow), Frank DeKova (Yellow Wolf), Vince Edwards (Little Wolf), Michael Winkelman (Billy), Richard Shannon (Garvin), Cyril Delevanti (Preacher), John Merrick (Lieutenant).

By the late 1950s, the popular formula B westerns were going through many changes to keep up with the increasingly sophisticated audiences. Gone were the days of handsome hero and villainous bad guys. The new cliches were drunken, cowardly anti-heros and Indians who finally were treated like human beings. RIDE OUT FOR REVENGE is a classic example of the new formula. Bridges plays a corrupt cavalry officer who is put in charge of the Cheyenne migration from ancestral grounds to a reservation. When gold is discovered on the new property, the whites change their mind about where the Indians should be placed. Calhoun is a cavalry scout who sympathizes with the displaced Indians and tries to get them some fair treatment, of course to no avail. This is a film full of good intentions, almost an apology for the countless number of films where the Indians were sadistic and mindless. However, the action here is too melodramatic and overwrought with the new cliches. Direction is never sure which way to go, resulting in a film of mixed quality. Still it is an honest effort at changing some past Hollywood (as well as historical) misdeeds and worth a look.

p, Norman Retchin; d, Bernard Girard; w, Retchin; ph, Floyd Crosby; m, Leith Stevens; ed, Leon Barsha; md, Stevens, art d, McClure Capps.

Western   **(PR:C MPAA:NR)**

RIDE, RANGER, RIDE***   (1936) 63m REP bw
Gene Autry (Gene), Smiley Burnette (Frog), Kay Hughes (Dixie), Monte Blue (Tavibo/Duval), George J. Lewis (Lt. Cameron), Max Terhune (Rufe), Robert E. Homans (Col. Summerall), Lloyd Whitlock (Maj. Crosby), Chief Thundercloud (Little Wolf), Tennessee Ramblers, Frankie Marvin, Iron Eyes Cody, Sunny Chorre, Bud Pope, Nelson McDowell, Shooting Star, Arthur Singley, Greg Whitespear, Robert Thomas, Champion the Horse.

Undercover Texas Ranger Autry is assigned to be a scout for the Army. He is out to stop a group of Commanches from raiding a wagon train loaded with ammunition and supplies. Of course the Army refuses to believe Autry but do a quick change of mind when the Indians come a-ridin'. Full of action, suspense, comedy, song, and even a little romance (with Hughes as an officer's daughter) this programmer balances its elements well, resulting in a better than average series flick that is good fun to watch.

p, Nat Levine; d, Joseph Kane; w, Dorrell and Stuart McGowan (based on a story by Bernard McConville, Karen DeWolf); ph, William Nobles.

Western   **Cas.**   **(PR:A MPAA:NR)**

RIDE, RYDER, RIDE!**   (1949) 58m Equity/EL c
Jim Bannon (Red Ryder), Don Kay "Little Brown Jug" Reynolds (Little Beaver), Emmett Lynn (Buckskin), Peggy Stewart (Libby Brooks), Gaylord [Steve] Pendleton (Gerry), Jack O'Shea (Keno), Jean Budinger (Marge), Marin Sais (Duchess), Stanley Blystone (Sheriff), Bill Fawcett (Judge), Billy Hammond (Pinto), Edwin Max (Frenchy), Steve Clark.

This is the first RED RYDER film, based on the famous comic strip. Eagle Lion introduced this series as a replacement for their retired set of films featuring Eddie Dean. Here Bannon is the title character who stops a stagecoach robbery early on, then joins Stewart, a newspaper publisher. She is out to clean up her town from its crime waves which is accomplished thanks to Bannon and his Indian sidekick Reynolds (later to be replaced with Bobby Blake of "Our Gang" comedies, who was cast as one of the IN COLD BLOOD killers). Simplistic in script, direction, and thespian qualities, RIDE, RYDER, RIDE! was made with a juvenile audience clearly in mind. (See RED RYDER series, Index.)

p, Jerry Thomas; d, Lewis D. Collins; w, Paul Franklin (based on the "Red

Ryder"comic strip created by Fred Harman); ph, Gilbert Warrenton (Cinecolor); ed, Joe Gluck.

Western   **(PR:A MPAA:NR)**

RIDE, TENDERFOOT, RIDE***   (1940) 65m REP bw

Gene Autry (Gene), Smiley Burnette (Frog), June Storey (Ann Randolph), Mary Lee (Patsy Randolph), Warren Hull (Donald Gregory), Forbes Murray (Henry Walker), Joe McGuinn (Martin), Joe Frisco (The Haberdasher), Isobel Randolph (Miss Spencer), Herbert Clifton (The Butler), Mildred Shay (Stewardess), Si Jenks (The Sheriff), Cindy Walker (Singer), Patty Saks, Jack Krik, Slim Whitaker, Fred Burns, Robert Burns, Fred "Snowflake" Toones, Chuck Morrison, Frank O'Connors, Curley Dresden, The Pacemakers, Champion the Horse.

Quintessential Autry with every one of his famed trademarks firmly in place. He is a shy cowpoke who becomes the heir to a meat-packing plant. Storey is the snotty owner of a rival plant whose executives are determined to put Autry out of business. But Storey has an early run-in with Autry and comes out looking like the fool she is. To complicate matters, her younger sister (Lee) has a thing for the singing cowboy and undermines her sister's plans. Autry, of course, does not want the precocious youngster but with her, and Burnette manages to save the business and oddly enough ends up with Storey. She has obviously come to a change of heart in this silly and highly enjoyable Autry feature. The clever dialog made the story a lot better than it had a right to be and Autry is a good deal of fun. Audiences apparently agreed, for the film was quite successful at the box office.

p, William Berke; d, Frank McDonald; w, Winston Miller (based on a story by Betty Burbridge, Connie Lee); ph, Jack Marta; ed, Lester Orlebeck; md, Raoul Kraushaar; m/l, Johnny Mercer, Richard Whiting, E. Di Lazzaro, Harold Adamson, Nick Kenny, Charles Kenny, Johnny Marvin, Gene Autry, Smiley Burnette, Arthur Fields, Fred Hall, "Woodpecker Song," "Ride, Tenderfoot, Ride" (sung by Gene Autry, Mary Lee).

Western   **(PR:A MPAA:NR)**

RIDE THE HIGH COUNTRY*****   (1962) 94m MGM c (GB: GUNS
                                                IN THE AFTERNOON)

Randolph Scott (Gil Westrum), Joel McCrea (Steve Judd), Mariette Hartley (Elsa Knudsen), Ronald Starr (Heck Longtree), R.G. Armstrong (Joshua Knudsen), Edgar Buchanan (Judge Tolliver), John Anderson (Elder Hammond), L.Q. Jones (Sylvus Hammond), Warren Oates (Henry Hammond), James Drury (Billy Hammond), John Davis Chandler (Jimmy Hammond), Jenie Jackson (Kate), Carmen Phillips (Saloon Girl), Percy Helton.

One of the best loved and most fondly remembered westerns of all time, director Sam Peckinpah's second feature film, RIDE THE HIGH COUNTRY, proved to be a bittersweet swan song for the Old West and a classy farewell to the screen for actors Scott and—for some years—McCrea. Set at the turn of the century, the film opens in the town of Hornitos, which is in the midst of a celebration. Down the crowded main street rides McCrea, an aging, somewhat haggard former lawman who has fallen on hard times but still manages to maintain an undeniable air of dignity. He hears the cheers of the crowd and, pleasantly surprised at being recognized, tips his hat to the people. His reverie is interrupted by a policeman who tells him to get out of the way because he is blocking the path of a race being run down the street. Embarrassed, McCrea realizes that the cheers from the crowd were actually jeers for him to clear the road. The race turns out to be a vulgar display of a horse against a camel. Slightly befuddled by the whole thing, McCrea is then nearly run over by an automobile as he tries to cross the street (the automobile is a recurring image in Peckinpah's westerns and also plays significant roles in THE WILD BUNCH and THE BALLAD OF CABLE HOGUE). McCrea enters the local bank and announces that he is the man the owner had hired to escort a shipment of gold from the mountainous mining town of Coarse Gold back to the bank. The banker is a bit taken aback by McCrea's age and expresses doubt that he can do the job. McCrea tries to hide his frayed cuffs from the man, and then goes to the bathroom with the contract so that he can read it without the banker having to see him use his spectacles. The old lawman is finally given the job, and McCrea sets out to hire a second man to help him on the trip. In town he runs into Scott, an old friend and fellow former lawman. Scott has learned to survive by selling out his heroic image, dressing up as the "Oregon Kid," a ridiculous looking "Wild West" sharpshooter with a carnival patter. Almost unrecognizable in his huge cowboy hat, long-haired wig, phony beard, and frilly outfit, Scott agrees to have dinner with McCrea after the show. At a Chinese restaurant McCrea offers the job to Scott and his young sidekick Starr. The two accept the offer, with Scott planning to steal the gold at the first opportunity. The men begin their ascent into the high country, with McCrea and Scott trading stories about the good old days. It is obvious that McCrea has clung to his strict code of honor during hard times, while Scott has proved to be more pragmatic and prone to stray from the straight and narrow. Acknowledging that bad times can drive men to do bad things, McCrea sticks to his code of self-respect and later states, "All I want is to enter my house justified." That evening the men stop at the farmhouse of Armstrong, a widower and religious fanatic whose repression of his daughter, Hartley, borders on the deranged. Armstrong has buried his wife on the property and her tombstone bears the ominous inscription: "Wherefore, O Harlot, hear the word of the Lord. I will judge thee as women that break the wedlock and shed blood are judged." Obviously the woman was driven from her home by her husband's insane obsessions and sought refuge in the arms of another man. At dinner, Armstrong and McCrea swap interpretations of the Bible backed by chapter and verse, with Scott lightheartedly ending the discussion by stating, "You cook a lovely hamock, Miss Knudsen, just lovely. Appetite, Chapter One." Later that night Hartley reveals to the trio that she has accepted a marriage proposal from Drury, a miner in Coarse Gold, and begs the lawmen to let her ride with them. Sympathetic to her plight, they agree. The next day McCrea, Scott, Starr, and Hartley arrive in Coarse Gold. The beautiful snowy landscape of

the mountainous terrain is contrasted sharply to the filthy looking tents and run-down shacks that pepper the area. The travelers find the encampment where Drury lives and are shocked to discover that the reasonably attractive miner has four slimy, vulgar brothers, Oates, Jones, Anderson, and Chandler. The men are extremely wild and openly slobber over the thought of having Hartley a member of the family. Taken aback, but determined to make the best of it, Hartley agrees to go through with the wedding. The ceremony is performed by Buchanan, a broken-down alcoholic judge, at the local bordello which is run by a grotesquely obese madam, Jackson. As seen through the eyes of Hartley, the wedding is a nightmarish experience. After the ceremony, fights break out among the drunken brothers to decide who will be next in line for Hartley after Drury consummates the marriage. McCrea, Scott, and especially Starr, who has developed a crush on Hartley, are disgusted by the spectacle, but the decision was hers to make and they do not interfere. Despite her protests, Hartley is dragged upstairs in the bordello by Drury to consummate their marriage. In the room, the extremely blotto Drury slips off a chair while trying to close the window and is knocked unconscious. Seizing on the fact that Drury is unable to protest, brothers Jones and Oates decide to fill in for him. With the help of McCrea and Starr, Hartley is able to escape her new "family" and begs McCrea to take her with them when they leave with the gold. McCrea, however, sees no legal way to help her since she had married Drury of her own free will; he tells her that the miner's court will have to decide. Scott holds no respect for a law that will keep a young, innocent girl a captive of sleazy varmints like Drury and his brothers, so he sets out to free Hartley on his own. Confronting Buchanan, Scott takes the judge's license at gunpoint and threatens to kill him unless he testifies that he was never legally licensed to perform weddings. The trick works and the court allows Hartley to leave with Scott, McCrea, and Starr after they pick up the gold shipment. Back on the trail, Scott tries to convince his old partner that the gold would make a nice retirement sum for them and a handsome start in life for Starr. Scott figures that they are owed the money because they have been treated poorly by this new society after repeatedly risking their lives to tame the West. McCrea disagrees and states that all a man can expect from life is that which he had contracted to receive. Still feeling tied to Scott, Starr reluctantly agrees to help steal the money, but he has gained respect for McCrea and no longer wants the gold. That night Scott and Starr make an attempt at the gold but are caught by McCrea who emotionally states: "It all pointed this way...ungrateful citizens, what we had coming but never got paid. I knew in my bones what you were aiming for but I wouldn't believe it. I kept telling myself you were a good man, you were my friend." Scott angrily responds, "This is bank money, not yours." Bitterly McCrea answers, "And what they don't know won't hurt them. Not them, only me!" McCrea slaps Scott across the face and tries to force a showdown. When Scott refuses and drops his gun belt, McCrea binds both Scott and Starr. This leads to trouble, however, because Drury and his brothers refuse to give up so easily and ambush the party the next day. During the attack, McCrea unties Starr, but leaves Scott bound. The attack fails and two of the brothers are killed. That night, a totally demoralized Scott asks to be untied because, "I don't sleep so good any more." A somewhat embarrassed McCrea agrees and in the middle of the night, Scott escapes. The next day McCrea, Starr, and Hartley return to Hartley's farm. McCrea notices Armstrong hunched over his wife's grave praying, but what his weakened eyes fail to see is the bullet hole planted right between the religious zealot's eyes. Drury and his brothers have invaded and occupied the farmhouse. Before McCrea has time to react, the brothers open fire and wound Starr. Pinned down in a nearby ditch, the trio appears doomed. McCrea is determined to make a good stand of it, but he knows that they are hopelessly outnumbered. To everyone's surprise, Scott rides through a hail of bullets and returns to the group in an effort to regain his self-respect. Together again, Scott and McCrea goad the brothers from their hiding places and have it out in a face-to-face showdown. When the smoke clears all the brothers are dead and McCrea is mortally wounded. Dying, McCrea asks that the youngsters leave him to die alone. Scott assures McCrea he will deliver the gold. "Don't worry about anything. I'll take care of it—just like you would have." "Hell, I know that," McCrea responds, "I always did. You just forgot it for a while, that's all...So long, partner." "I'll see ya later," says Scott. As Scott walks off to join Starr and Hartley, McCrea takes one last look at the gorgeous mountains of the high country, gently leans back and dies. In RIDE THE HIGH COUNTRY, director Peckinpah began what was to be an obsession with men who have lived past their era in history and find it difficult to adapt to changing times (THE WILD BUNCH, THE BALLAD OF CABLE HOGUE, and PAT GARRETT AND BILLY THE KID all share the same themes). Integral to this theme are the emotional and moral dilemmas Peckinpah's main characters undergo. McCrea and Scott in RIDE THE HIGH COUNTRY, Charlton Heston and Richard Harris in MAJOR DUNDEE, William Holden and Robert Ryan in THE WILD BUNCH, and James Coburn and Kris Kristofferson in PAT GARRETT AND BILLY THE KID are all men struggling with their identities. Each protagonist serves as a mirror image of the other, showing what their lives would have been like if they had made different choices. These men also believe in upholding a personal code of honor which separates them from the vermin whom they invariably encounter. Peckinpah's heroes are very human. To some extent they are failures who have lived past their usefulness. These are men wracked with guilt, for they have made bad decisions, misjudgments, and failed to live up to the standards they have set for themselves. Eventually, these tortured souls attain a sort of grace because in the end, they do what it takes to regain their self-respect (with the exception of Coburn, who sells out in PAT GARRETT AND BILLY THE KID, Peckinpah's bleakest western). Peckinpah's feuding with producers to bring his films out intact has become legendary, but his experience with producer Lyons on RIDE THE HIGH COUNTRY proved remarkably amicable. Lyons had acquired a screenplay about two aging lawmen written by N.B. Stone, Jr. called "Guns in the Afternoon" which had subsequently been rewritten by William S. Roberts (who was never credited). The producer eventually persuaded McCrea (who was a friend) and Scott to star in his movie. Soon after, McCrea—who had originally agreed to play the part of Gil Westrum, the lawman gone bad—felt uncomfortable with the role (he had never played a villain before, albeit, here, a sympathetic one) and asked Lyons if he could see how Scott felt about switching parts. Later that same afternoon, Lyons received a call from Scott who confessed that he was feeling insecure about his role and wondered if McCrea would mind a swap. Much to the actor's relief, the roles were switched, with McCrea playing Steve Judd and Scott playing Gil Westrum. Searching for a director, Lyons was told of Peckinpah, a young television writer-director who had written for "Gunsmoke" (13 episodes) and created "The Rifleman" and "The Westerner." Lyons viewed several episodes of "The Westerner" and was duly impressed. Conscious of MGM's negative attitude toward television people, Lyons had the episodes screened for the studio's head of production, Sol Siegal. Siegel was also impressed with the shows (he asked to see all of them) and gave Lyons the go-ahead to hire Peckinpah. Peckinpah accepted the project with the provision that he be allowed to rewrite the script—which was granted. The director then improved the dialog and brought much of his own personal experience into the story. The Peckinpah family were true westerners (there is a Peckinpah mountain in California near the real Coarse Gold, which was bought by the director's grandfather in 1883) and as a child the director was taken by his father, who was a judge, to a mining town much like the one in the film. Garner Simmons, in his book on the director entitled *Peckinpah*, quotes Peckinpah's sister Fern Lea. "We went to see RIDE THE HIGH COUNTRY at a sneak preview, and when it was over, I went to the ladies room and cried and cried because the character played by Joel McCrea reminded me so much of my father who had just died the year before." The famous line "All I want is to enter my house justified" was a phrase often echoed by Peckinpah's father. The director also changed the ending of the script. The original draft had Scott's character dying in the end, thus receiving salvation for his wicked ways, but Peckinpah thought it more effective to have Scott's character survive and let McCrea "enter his house justified." Both Scott and McCrea thought Peckinpah's improvements brilliant. Now armed with a good script, enthusiastic stars, and an eager director, the only problem was to decide who would receive top billing. Scott and McCrea agreed to a public coin toss at the Brown Derby restaurant and Scott won. Shooting was planned on location at Mammoth Lake in the High Sierras, but after four days the weather turned foul (snow) and cost-conscious MGM insisted the production be moved to a more workable area. Peckinpah was upset, but the film continued shooting at Bronson Canyon in Hollywood and soap suds were used to simulate snow. Other money-saving efforts saw art director Davis stealing sails from the *Bounty* used in the remake of MUTINY ON THE BOUNTY from which to make the miners' tents, and cast and crew sneaking onto the set of HOW THE WEST WAS WON at night to shoot the confrontation scene between McCrea and Scott. Shooting was completed in an astounding 26 days, and that's when things turned for the worst. After making a well-received rough cut of the film, a shakeup at MGM saw production head Siegel ousted (he supported Peckinpah) and replaced by Joseph R Vogel. Peckinpah was barred from the studio, leaving his editor and sound mixers to finish the film without him. To keep Peckinpah involved, the technicians took to playing the director the daily sound mixes over the phone for his approval. At the screening of the final cut, Vogel promptly fell asleep and when it was over awoke and called it the worst film he had ever seen. This, of course, did not endear Peckinpah to Vogel or vice versa. Despite the director and producer's protests, RIDE THE HIGH COUNTRY was dumped on the market on the lower half of ludicrous double bills with films like BOYS' NIGHT OUT, a comedy starring Kim Novak and James Garner, and THE TARTARS, a medieval drama produced in Italy starring Victor Mature and Orson Welles. The film was a commercial disaster in America, despite favorable reviews, but abroad it became a major hit. RIDE THE HIGH COUNTRY won First Prize at the Cannes Film Festival, the Grand Prize at the Brussels Film Festival—beating out Federico Fellini's 8½—and the Silver Goddess from the Mexican Film Festival for Best Foreign Film. The film went on to become one of MGM's biggest grossing films in Europe. Over the years European and American critics have kept the praise for RIDE THE HIGH COUNTRY flowing, enabling the public to discover the film through revival screenings and television showings. Peckinpah's attention to detail, realistic settings, and total understanding of character makes this film a multifaceted jewel to be studied and enjoyed again and again. The honest, subtle, and consummately skillful performances by Scott and McCrea continue to amaze and endear. Scott never made another film and while McCrea has made a few screen appearances since, most consider RIDE THE HIGH COUNTRY his finest effort. Peckinpah went on to gain an infamous reputation among Hollywood studios, producers, and some critics for his strong-willed, violent, and highly personal brand of filmmaking, but he proved himself to be one of the most interesting modern American directors, although certainly one of the most inconsistent. Not only did producer Lyons and director Peckinpah create one of the greatest westerns ever made in RIDE THE HIGH COUNTRY, they also made it possible for two of America's most popular and beloved actors to bid a moving, passionate, and memorable farewell to the silver screen.

p, Richard E. Lyons; d, Sam Peckinpah; w, N.B. Stone, Jr.; ph, Lucien Ballard (CinemaScope, Metrocolor); m, George Bassman; ed, Frank Santillo; art d, George W. Davis, Leroy Coleman; set d, Henry Grace, Otto Siegel; makeup, William Tuttle.

Western   Cas.   (PR:C MPAA:NR)

RIDE THE HIGH IRON**   (1956) 74m COL bw

Don Taylor *(Hugo Danielchik)*, Sally Forrest *(Elsie Vanders)*, Raymond Burr *(Ziggy Moline)*, Lisa Golm *(Mrs. Danielchik)*, Otto Waldis *(Yanusz Danielchik)*, Nestor Paiva *(Yardboss)*, Mae Clarke *(Mrs. Vanders)*, Maurice Marsac *(Maurice)*, Robert Johnson *(Porter)*.

Standard soaper features Burr as a powerful and influential public relations man. It is his job to keep snooty VIPs' scandals out of print. The job embitters him because none of his clients will accept him as a peer. Taylor is a Korean War veteran Burr hires, a man whose father was a poverty-stricken railroad worker. Taylor conceals his past because he wants to rise above it all. He is assigned to take care of Forrest,

a poor little rich girl who is constantly getting into trouble. Taylor falls in love and admits his past to her, which Forrest accepts. This turgid melodrama was originally conceived as a television film but was withheld from broadcast and released theatrically. The translation from small to big screen does not work well as the restricted camera movements and simplistic, stagey action comes off poorly. As a TV film, it is nothing out of the ordinary with standard performances and production values.

p, William Self; d, Don Weis; w, Milton Gelman; ph, Joe Novak; m, Melvyn Lenard; ed, Joseph Gluck; art d, Serge Krizman; cos, Gerry Bos.

Drama   (PR:A MPAA:NR)

RIDE THE HIGH WIND**½   (1967, South Africa) 77m Killarney/
                                                          Feature Film c

Darren McGavin *(Mike Gregory)*, Maria Perschy *(Helena Hansen)*, Albert Lieven *(Karl Du Val)*, Alison Seebohm *(Maria Du Val)*, Michael McGovern *(Jack Dillon)*, John Hayter *(Maj. Dillon)*, Brian O'Shaughnessy, Michael Todd, Eric Egan, Fiona Fraser, Valerie Miller, Jan Fenn, Geoffrey Morris.

A plane crashes in the desert of Southwest Africa and the pilot (McGavin) ends up near the remains of a dilapidated wagon. He meets Lieven and Seebohm, a husband and wife, who help him regain his strength and mention the mysterious wagon. Seebohm tries to seduce McGavin but it is unsuccessful and the pilot returns to Johannesburg. There he learns the wagon was lost in the Boer War and is loaded with gold bullion. Hayter, along with his son and his son's girl friend (McGovern and Perschy), go back with McGavin to retrieve the gold. They fly out in a small plane but are attacked by a mysterious party. The plane crashes and burns with Hayter hurt and McGovern killed. It turns out that Lieven and Seebohm are behind the crash, taking the survivors prisoner. Seebohm once more tries to seduce McGavin but is repelled. She feels guilty about the situation and helps her hostage escape. But her husband has gone mad and shoots her. McGavin and Perschy trace the gold to a nearby cave, guarded by a skeleton holding a machine gun. Lieven arrives but McGavin tells him the bullion is really lead. Enraged, Lieven lunges at the pair. The skeleton's machine gun is knocked loose and goes off killing Lieven. Filmed on location in the Namib Desert of Southwest Africa.

p, Hyman Kerstein; d, David Millin; w, (based on the story "North of Bushman's Rock" by George Harding); m/l, "Ride the High Wind," Joe Kentridge, Bob Adams (sung by Michael McGovern).

Drama   (PR:A MPAA:NR)

RIDE THE MAN DOWN**   (1952) 90m REP c

Brian Donlevy *(Bide Marriner)*, Rod Cameron *(Will Ballard)*, Ella Raines *(Celia Evarts)*, Forrest Tucker *(Sam Danfelser)*, Barbara Britton *(Lottie Priest)*, Chill Wills *(Ike Adams)*, J. Carrol Naish *(Joe Kneen)*, Jim Davis *(Red Courteen)*, Taylor Holmes *(Lowell Priest)*, James Bell *(John Evarts)*, Paul Fix *(Ray Cavanaugh)*, Al Caudebec *(Mel Young)*, Roydon Clark *(Jim Young)*, Roy Barcroft *(Russ Schultz)*, Douglas Kennedy *(Harve Garrison)*, Chris Pin-Martin *(Chris)*, Jack LaRue *(Kennedy)*, Claire Carleton *(Amelia)*.

When the owner of a ranch passes away, his foreman (Cameron) must fight to maintain the land. Neighboring ranchers want to take the empire and divide it among themselves. Adding to the complications is Tucker, the fiancee of Raines the ranches' heiress. Donlevy is leader of the opposition ranchers. They converge on Cameron and have a shoot-out. Tucker and Donlevy die and the ranch is saved. The performances are appropriately tough and forthright but severely hampered by an overabundance of dialog. The direction does not quite have the flair that this material requires, though a nice use of scenery (with the rapidly improving Trucolor process) helps the overall production.

p&d, Joseph Kane; w, Mary McCall, Jr. (based on a story by Luke Short); ph, Jack Marta (Trucolor); m, Ned Freeman; ed, Fred Allen; art d, Frank Arrigo; set d, John McCarthy, Jr., Theodore F. Offenbecker.

Western   Cas.   (PR:C MPAA:NR)

RIDE THE PINK HORSE***½   (1947) 101m UNIV bw

Robert Montgomery *(Blackie Gagin)*, Thomas Gomez *(Pancho)*, Wanda Hendrix *(Pila)*, Andrea King *(Marjorie)*, Fred Clark *(Hugo)*, Art Smith *(Bill Retz)*, Richard Gaines *(Jonathan)*, Martin Garralaga *(Barkeeper)*, Rita Conde *(Carla)*, Iris Flores *(Maria)*, Edward Earle *(Locke)*, Harold Goodwin *(Red)*, Grandon Rhodes *(Mr. Edison)*, Tito Renaldo *(Bellboy)*, Maria Cortez *(Elevator Girl)*, Paul Maxey *(Portly Man)*, Howard Negley, Jimmy Ames, John Doucette, Jack Worth *(Thugs)*, Leon Lenoir *(Mexican Workman)*, Beatrice Roberts *(Manageress)*, Julian Rivero, Jerry De Castro *(Mexican Men)*, Paul Bryar, Lyle Latell *(State Troopers)*, Harry J. Vejar *(Barber)*, Charles Stevens *(Drunken Mexican)*, William Ruhl *(Mr. Blaine)*, Ernest Hilliard *(Elderly Man)*, Virginia Wave *(Waitress)*, Ralph Montgomery *(Waiter)*, Amadita Garcia, Connie Asins, Rose Marie Lopez, Martha Brenes, Olga Perez, Carmen Pallais *(Mexican Girls)*, Miguel Tapia, Roque Ybarra, Jr., Jose Alvarado, Harry Garcia *(Mexican Boys)*, Robert Espinosa *(Mexican Boy Crying)*, Enrique Valades, Robert Cabal *(Muchachos)*, Donald Kerr *(Headwaiter)*, Kenneth Rose MacKenzie *(Man)*.

An oddball title tops a tough crime melodrama with Montgomery outstanding as a rather moral blackmailer seeking revenge for the death of a friend. Montgomery arrives in a small New Mexico town during fiesta time looking for crime boss Clark. Smith, an FBI agent who has been tracking shady Montgomery, confronts him, telling him he has suspicions that Montgomery has evidence that will incriminate Clark—a mobster he has long been trying to nail—and asks Montgomery to cooperate. Montgomery tells Smith he doesn't know what he's talking about but he *does* have the evidence, a cancelled check that links Clark to vast illegal profits Clark has pocketed. At first Montgomery goes to Clark and offers to sell the check to him but his blackmail scheme backfires and he is beaten senseless by Clark's goons. Now he is out for revenge, especially when he discovers that Clark was responsible for the death of one of his friends. Montgomery has earlier befriended Gomez, who operates a small carousel, and Hendrix, a naive but affectionate Mexican girl. After the beating, he retreats to the carousel to recuperate (ergo the title of the film), and to be nursed by Gomez and Hendrix. The girl tries to talk Montgomery out of confronting mobster Clark again but he is set on revenge. He does face Clark once more and tricks him into exposing his rackets. Hendrix, who has contacted Smith, actually saves Montgomery's life as Clark's goons close in for the kill, with Smith arriving just in time to shoot Clark. The plot of this offbeat *film noir* entry is convoluted and sometimes confusing but the acting is above par and Montgomery's direction is intriguing and introspective. He was then determined to change his profession from actor to director, having recently done a bang-up job helming the Raymond Chandler tale LADY IN THE LAKE. This entry, however, was so far off the beaten track that the film failed to make much impact upon audiences or critics.

p, Joan Harrison; d, Robert Montgomery; w, Ben Hecht, Charles Lederer (based on the novel by Dorothy B. Hughes); ph, Russell Metty; m, Frank Skinner; ed, Ralph Dawson; art d, Bernard Herzbrun, Robert Boyle; set d, Russell A. Gausman, Oliver Emert; cos, Yvonne Wood; makeup, Bud Westmore.

Crime Drama   **(PR:C MPAA:NR)**

RIDE THE WILD SURF**½   (1964) 101m Jana/COL c

Fabian *(Jody Wallis)*, Shelley Fabares *(Brie Matthews)*, Tab Hunter *(Steamer Lane)*, Barbara Eden *(Augie Poole)*, Peter Brown *(Chase Colton)*, Susan Hart *(Lily Kilua)*, James Mitchum *(Eskimo)*, Anthony Hayes *(Frank Decker)*, Roger Davis *(Charlie)*, Catherine McLeod *(Mrs. Kilua)*, Murray Rose *(Swag)*, Robert Kenneally *(Russ)*, David Cadiente *(Ally)*, Alan LeBuse *(Phil)*, Paul Tremaine *(Vic)*, John Kennell *(TV Commentator)*, Yanqui Chang *(Mr. Chin)*.

The wave action at Oahu Island, Hawaii, is where it's at so surfers Fabian, Hunter, and Brown head out to where the sun is hot, the sand is white, and the girls are out-of-sight! Hunter falls for Hart but her mother disapproves of the romance since he is little more than "a beach bum." Fabian also has a romance of his own, falling for Fabares. She persuades him that there is more to life than surfing. Brown, the stodgiest member of the trio meets Eden who persuades him to have more fun with life (if he is so stuffy how did he get involved with surfing in the first place?). Fabian is nearly killed in an accident but continues to surf despite a growing fear of the sport. There is an old Hawaiian legend (films like this always have old Hawaiian legends) that claims a surfer leaping 80 feet into a rocky pool will bring big waves. Brown, who has learned his lessons too well takes the plunge and nearly kills himself. Fabian risks his own life to save his buddy. Hunter is dropped from competition when his board breaks but is more than compensated when his beau's mom relents to his romantic intentions. In the final climactic competition it's Fabian against last year's champ, Mitchum. Who will win? You need ask? Mitchum drops out of competition and the exhausted but happy Fabian rides a 40-foot wave to glory and the waiting arms of Fabares. This is no great shakes but a lot of fun in its own way. The surfing footage is well done and the cast is so earnest it is hard not to enjoy this. There's also a great theme song by those beach kings Jan and Dean. Originally producer Art Napoleon was to direct the film but dropped out shortly after the project began with Taylor taking over.

p, Jo Napoleon, Art Napoleon; d, Don Taylor; w, Jo Napoleon, Art Napoleons; ph, Joseph Biroc (PatheColor); m, Stu Phillips; ed, Eda Warren, Howard A. Smith; art d, Edward S. Haworth; m/l "Ride the Wild Surf," Jan Berry, Brian Wilson, Roger Christian (sung by Jan and Dean); makeup, Ben Lane.

Comedy/Drama   **(PR:A MPAA:NR)**

RIDE TO HANGMAN'S TREE, THE**½   (1967) 90m UNIV c

Jack Lord *(Guy Russell)*, James Farentino *(Matt Stone)*, Don Galloway *(Nevada Jones)*, Melodie Johnson *(Lillie Malone)*, Richard Anderson *(Steve Carlson)*, Robert Yuro *(Jeff Scott)*, Ed Peck *(Sheriff Stewart)*, Paul Reed *(Corbett)*, Richard Cutting *(Ed Mason)*, Bing Russell *(Keller)*, Virginia Capers *(Teressa Moreno)*, Robert Sorrells *(Blake)*, Robert Cornthwaite *(T.L. Harper)*, Fabian Dean *(Indian)*.

Lord and Farentino are on the verge of being hung for their thievery but are rescued at the last minute by Galloway, an old pal. They rob a stagecoach for some needed funds and Farentino heads off for California, presumably to retire. But once arriving in Sacramento he teams with Yuro, a lawyer friend with connection to Wells Fargo shipments. He supplies Farentino with information about incoming shipments. The outlaw comes out of his retirement, dons a mask (calling himself "The Black Bandit"), and holds up stagecoaches. On one coach Johnson, a singer, manages to catch the Bandit's eye. Also on this coach are his old partners, Lord and Galloway, who foil the robbery. Wells Fargo rewards the pair by hiring them as drivers and they later run into their old friend in Sacramento. They suspect he is the Black Bandit but cannot prove it. Lord tries to win the heart of Johnson but she belongs to Farentino. Word reaches them that a $30,000 shipment is being made and Farentino and Lord cannot resist making one more robbery together. Little do they know that this is a dummy plot with a top Wells Fargo agent riding along to capture the thieves. But Galloway rides in to save them once more and the trio escapes. Realizing that they have nowhere to turn, the three bandits decide to turn themselves in. Before he goes Farentino decides to spend one last night with Johnson who reveals she knew he was the bandit all along. This low-budget western is fairly amusing in its own way. The opening stagecoach robbery is nicely put together and the film just rolls along from there. It is all routine but enjoyable enough. Lord, Farentino, and Galloway have a good three-way chemistry that makes the material work. An unnecessary nude scene featuring Johnson skinny-dipping is painfully gratuitous. This film resembles its low-budget ancestors from the 1930s and 1940s programmers with its stereotypes and stock situations, though the heroes are bad guys. Director Rafkin went from movies to TV, directing such shows as "One Day at a Time" and "Alice."

p, Howard Christie; d, Alan Rafkin; w, Luci Ward, Jack Natteford, William Bowers (based on a story by Ward, Natteford); ph, Gene Polito (Technicolor); m, Frank Skinner; ed, Gene Palmer; art d, Alexander Golitzen, John T. McCormack; set d,

John McCarthy, Ralph Sylos; cos, Rosemary Odell; ch, Hal Belfer; makeup, Bud Westmore.

Western   **(PR:A MPAA:NR)**

RIDE, VAQUERO!**   (1953) 90m MGM c

Robert Taylor *(Rio)*, Ava Gardner *(Cordelia Cameron)*, Howard Keel *(King Cameron)*, Anthony Quinn *(Jose Esqueda)*, Kurt Kasznar *(Father Antonio)*, Ted DeCorsia *(Sheriff Parker)*, Charlita *(Singer)*, Jack Elam *(Barton)*, Walter Baldwin *(Adam Smith)*, Joe Dominguez *(Vicente)*, Frank McGrath *(Pete)*, Charles Stevens *(Vaquero)*, Rex Lease, Tom Greenway *(Deputies)*, Paul Fierro *(Valero)*, Percy Helton *(Storekeeper)*, Norman Leavitt *(Dentist)*, Movita Castenda *(Hussy)*, Almira Sessions *(Woman)*, Monte Blue *(Bartender)*, Philip Van Zandt *(Dealer)*, Stanley Andrews *(Gen. Sheridan)*, Italia De Nubila *(Specialty Dancer)*, Kay English *(Woman in Park)*, Joey Ray *(Croupier)*.

The Civil War has ended and the Western frontier is faced with a horde of new ranchers. This threatens outlaw Quinn's control of the territory and he decides to retaliate. With his sidekick, Taylor (who is also Quinn's foster brother), newly planted rancher, Keel, and his bride, Gardner, are attacked, their ranch burned to the ground. Rather than frighten him off, this move gives Keel renewed strength and the will to rebuild his ranch. DeCorsia, the local sheriff, refuses to help Keel or attempt to stop Quinn and his band of outlaws. Keel calls a meeting of the local ranchers but this is broken up by Quinn and company. With no choice left, Keel decides to go after the bad man himself and stocks his home with ammunition, turning it into a mini-fortress. Quinn orders another attack on the Keel ranch but is surprised that the man (along with help from Kasznar, the local priest) is able to fight back. Taylor is captured in the confrontation and Keel persuades the man to work as a ranch-hand. Taylor agrees and soon finds he shares a mutual attraction with Gardner. Quinn, furious at his brother's seeming change of loyalties, convinces himself that Taylor will soon return. Meanwhile, Gardner persuades Taylor to take her to the outlaw's hideout where she hopes to persuade Quinn to leave her and Keel alone. But Quinn merely laughs at this, instigating an argument between Taylor and Gardner. Quinn decides that Taylor has let him down by weakening and raids the town. There he kills the sheriff and takes over, setting up headquarters in the local saloon. He waits for Taylor and has his men kill locals on a whim. Keel enters the saloon and is challenged by the outlaw to a gunfight. Quinn easily wounds the rancher, shooting him over and over. But the gunfire is interrupted by Taylor who faces off against his foster brother. The two shoot and kill one another just as the cavalry rides in to save the day. Despite its well known and talented leads RIDE, VAQUERO! is a poorly made and unintentionally funny film. Keel and Gardner are completely wasted with trite dialog unworthy of their acting skills. Only Quinn looks good, giving a performance far better than the film deserved. He manages to rise above the one-dimensional characterization with an interesting performance bordering on the psychotic. This was his second western with director Farrow in what was MGM's first wide-screen production.

p, Stephen Ames; d, John Farrow; w, Frank Fenton; ph, Robert Surtees (Ansco Color); m, Bronislau Kaper; ed, Harold F. Kress; art d, Cedric Gibbons, Arthur Lonergan; cos, Walter Plunkett.

Western   **(PR:A MPAA:NR)**

RIDER FROM NOWHERE   (SEE: RIDERS FROM NOWHERE, 1940)

RIDER FROM TUCSON***   (1950) 60m RKO bw

Tim Holt *(Dave)*, Elaine Riley *(Jane)*, Douglas Fowley *(Rankin)*, Veda Ann Borg *(Gypsy)*, Robert Shayne *(Avery)*, William Phipps *(Tug/Caldwell)*, Harry Tyler *(Hardrock Jones)*, Luther Crockett *(Sheriff)*, Dorothy Vaughan *(Mrs. O'Reilly)*, Stuart Randall *(Slim)*, Marshall Reed *(Jackson)*, Richard Martin *(Chito Rafferty)*.

From the word go this is an exciting, action-filled Western that gives Holt fans everything they want and expect from their hero. He and Martin are a pair of rodeo riders who ride off to Colorado for old pal Phipps' wedding. Upon arrival they discover he is under siege from a group of outlaws. The baddies have jumped his rich gold strike and kidnaped the bride to be (Riley). After plenty of rootin', tootin' action all is righted. The pace is well maintained in this 60 minute feature with action fierce and steady. The same things found in any B western are given a fresh and lively treatment with excellent results.

p, Herman Schlom; d, Lesley Selander; w, Ed Earl Repp; ph, Nicholas Musuraca; ed, Robert Swink; md, C. Bakaleinikoff; art d, Albert S. D'Agostino, Walter E. Keller.

Western   **Cas.**   **(PR:A MPAA:NR)**

RIDER IN THE NIGHT, THE*   (1968, South Africa) 78m
Suidafrikaanse Rolprentproduksies-Killarney/Barney Pitkin Associates c (DIE RUITER IN DIE NAG)

Annette De Villiers, Johan Van Heerdan, Brian O'Shaughnessy, Emsie Botha, Gert Van den Bergh, Willie Van Rensburg.

It is the Boer War and the fighting is furious. The Boers use a secret courier to supply their armies with information, thus preventing an important squad from being surrounded by British troops. This is more of a flag-waving pageant piece than a film about war. Everyone is oh-so-polite and there is nary a scratch incurred or sweat raised upon any fighting man's brow. Sequences are dragged out to unreasonable lengths with a too-much-talk (and over-acted) dialog. An interesting note and about the only point of interest here: The British soldiers spoke English for the film in their own unique accent but the Boers spoke Afrikaan, a derivative of the Dutch language. For the American release English accents were kept but the Boers were dubbed with American voices to distinguish the difference. Being a South African production, THE RIDER IN THE NIGHT reflects that country's apartheid politics. No black member is to be found in the cast.

d, Jan Perold; w, (based on the novel *Die Ruiter in de Nag* by Mikro [C.H. Kalin]);

ph, John Brown (CinemaScope, Eastmancolor); ed, Peter Grosset; art d, George Canes, Sydney Mendoza.

Drama   **(PR:C MPAA:NR)**

RIDER OF DEATH VALLEY***½   (1932) 76m UNIV bw

Tom Mix *(Tom Rigby)*, Lois Wilson *(Helen Joyce)*, Fred Kohler, Sr. *(Lew Grant)*, Forrest Stanley *(Doc Larribe)*, Willard Robertson *(Bill Joyce)*, Edith Fellowes *(Betty Joyce)*, Mae Busch *(Dance Hall Girl)*, Otis Harlan, Max Ascher, Pete Morrison, Edmund Cobb *(Citizens)*, Iron Eyes Cody, Tony the Horse.

When her brother is murdered Wilson heads West to take over his gold mine. It's hidden at an isolated location in the desert and she must contend with Kohler and Stanley, two bad men also after the mine. Finally with the help of Mix and his faithful steed Tony, Wilson is able to reclaim the mine. Considering that this was a period of simplistic and often wretched western fare, Mix's film is a fine and well-done outing. This is probably the movie cowboy's best sound film greatly enhanced by its superior production quality. Mix, who made his reputation in silent film oversaw the entire production, making sure that accuracy to detail was maintained. The results are terrific. A stampede of runaway horses looks like the real thing and a harrowing desert sequence where the cast seems doomed without any water is brutally honest. The cinematography reflects the bleak feelings of the film's drama with a fine use of the Death Valley location work. Mix and Kohler are excellent as the respective good and bad men. The real hero of the film is Tony, Mix's beloved horse. He saves Mix from circling buzzards and other denizens of the desert wasteland with surprisingly realistic effect. One would swear the horse was really acting rather than doing something for which he'd been trained.

p, Carl Laemmle, Jr.; d, Albert Rogell; w, Jack Cunningham, Al Martin (based on a story by Cunningham, Stanley Bergerman); ph, Dan Clark.

Western   **(PR:A MPAA:NR)**

RIDER OF THE LAW, THE**   (1935) 59m Supreme/William Steiner bw

Bob Steele, Gertrude Messinger, Si Jenks, Earl Dwire, Forrest Taylor, Lloyd Ingraham, John Elliott, Sherry Tansey, Tex Palmer, Chuck Baldra.

Steele, a government agent, goes undercover and disguises himself as an eastern tenderfoot in order to trap a band of outlaw bank robbers. An early film in Steele's series for Supreme, most of which were directed by his father, Robert N. Bradbury.

p, A.W. Hackel; d, Robert N. Bradbury; w, Jack Natteford; ph, Gus Peterson; ed, Roy Luby.

Western   **(PR:A MPAA:NR)**

RIDER OF THE PLAINS**   (1931) 57m SYN bw (GB: THE GREATER LOVE)

Tom Tyler, Andy Shuford, Lillian Bond, Alan Bridge, Gordon DeMain, Jack Perrin, Ted Adams, Fern Emmett, Slim Whitaker.

Bad guy Tyler, accompanied by a child sidekick, rides into town. The sheriff finds out Tyler's history and lets the man know he is being watched. Tyler discovers that an old partner in crime is now the town clergyman and this inspires the outlaw to reform his habits. A dull western, hampered by implausibilities and little, if any, action.

d, J.P. McCarthy; w, Wellyn Totman (based on a story by Totman); ph, Archie Stout.

Western   **(PR:A MPAA:NR)**

RIDER ON A DEAD HORSE**   (1962) 72m Phoenix/AA bw

John Vivyan *(Hayden)*, Bruce Gordon *(Barney Senn)*, Kevin Hagen *(Jake Fry)*, Lisa Lu *(Ming)*, Charles Lampkin *(Taylor)*.

Vivyan, Gordon, and Lampkin are prospectors who bury their gold so warring Apaches will not be able to get to it. As Lampkin rides off he is shot in the back by Gordon who permits the third man to live since Vivyan knows how to get back to the gold. The Apaches attack and the two men are forced to abandon their horses. Lampkin's riderless horse runs by and Gordon finally shoots Vivyan, riding off on his victim's horse. Vivyan is not dead though and is healed by Lu, a young Chinese girl who hopes the white man will take her to San Francisco. Meanwhile, Gordon rides into a nearby town and meets Hagen, a bounty hunter. He tells Hagen that he saw Vivyan shoot Lampkin and the pair agree to split the $1,000 reward money. Hagen tracks down Vivyan and finds him with Lu while Gordon goes back for the gold. Vivyan gets locked up and Lu is forced to take Hagen to the secret spot where the gold is buried. But Vivyan escapes, rescuing Lu. Hagen accidentally sets off a dynamite charge which reduces the gold to dust. This causes Gordon to go mad. He attacks Lu but is gunned down by Vivyan who rides off with the girl. Fairly seedy western melodrama, typical for its period. Some nice location shooting helps but not much.

p, Kenneth Altose; d, Herbert L. Strock; w, Stephen Longstreet (based on a story by James Edmiston); ph, Frank Phillips; m, Fairlane; ed, Melvin Shapiro; cos, Joseph Dimmitt; m/l, "Rider on a Dead Horse," Joseph Hooven, Edward Alperson, Jr., Jerry Winn (sung by Millard Woods); makeup, Ernie Park.

Western   **(PR:C MPAA:NR)**

RIDER ON THE RAIN***½   (1970, Fr./Ital.) 119m Greenwich Film-Medusa Distribuzione/AE c (LEPASSAGER DE LA PLUIE)

Marlene Jobert *(Melancolie "Mellie" Mau)*, Charles Bronson *(Col. Harry Dobbs)*, Annie Cordy *(Juliette)*, Jill Ireland *(Nicole)*, Gabriele Tinti *(Tony)*, Jean Gaven *(Toussaint)*, Marc Mazza *(The Stranger [Bruno Sakki, alias McGuffin])*, Corinne Marchand *(Tania)*, Jean Piat *(M. Armand)*, Marika Green *(Hostess at Tania's)*, Ellen Bahl *(Madeline Legauff)*, Marcel Peres *(Station Master)*.

A young woman (Jobert) who lives in a small seaside resort in France happens to see a stranger exit from a bus. While trying on a dress the next day at Ireland's boutique, she sees the stranger watching her. That evening the man breaks into Jobert's home after her husband (Tinti), a jealous airline pilot has left. The stranger rapes Jobert and knocks her unconscious. Upon waking she hears the man in the basement. The frightened woman grabs a shotgun and kills the man in two blasts as he tries to attack her once more. She throws the body into the sea, fearful of what could happen should she report the incident to the authorities. After a few days the stranger's body washes up on the beach, and this makes newspaper headlines. Jobert goes to a wedding reception and there is confronted by another stranger (Bronson). Bronson, an American, accuses her of murdering a sex fiend who escaped from prison and stole $60,000 from the U.S. Army. He demands she return the airline bag that held the money, but Jobert ignores his threats. Bronson continues to harass her, and this sparks childhood memories of how Jobert discovered her mother had a lover, and how her father badgered a confession out of the confused girl. Once he learned the truth, Jobert's father ran out on the family. Eventually Jobert finds the bag in question and goes to Bronson's hotel to return it. She gets into his room and, upon searching Bronson's luggage, learns he is a colonel in the U.S. Army. Suddenly Bronson bursts into the room, and informs Jobert that another woman has been arrested for the stranger's murder. She goes to Paris and meets with the woman's sister, the operator of a brothel. Jobert is attacked by a trio of crooks who think she knows more than she should about the crime. Bronson rescues her, and the two return to the resort town where they are informed by the police that the body washed ashore is not the man Bronson wants. The stranger's corpse eventually turns up with a button from Jobert's dress clutched in the hand. Bronson, satisfied to get back the money, decides against causing Jobert any further strife. RIDER ON THE RAIN is a tautly made, well executed thriller. Plot twists are unexpected and well handled, and Bronson handles his character's ambivalent nature with great skill. For once his stock three expressions are put to good use. The location work on the French coast (as well as Paris) is used with effective results. The scenery adds to the tension in a careful cinematography. This stylish, Hitchcock-like thriller was filmed in French and dubbed into English for American distribution. Unlike most other films, the dubbing for RIDER ON THE RAIN was almost unnoticeable. Bronson, who had starred in several American television series, never caught on with film audiences at home in the 1960s. It wasn't until he hit Europe that he achieved his enormous popularity with a string of hits. In just one year he scored quite well with ONCE UPON A TIME IN THE WEST; FAREWELL, FRIEND; and this film. These three films, along with the French gangster film BORSALINO, broke all previous box-office records in France, a remarkable achievement that gave Bronson some real clout. Ireland, Bronson's wife, had a minor role in this film and played her husband's leading lady in the majority of his films in the 1970s.

p, Serge Silberman; d, Rene Clement; w, Sebastian Japrisot, Lorenzo Ventavoli; ph, Andreas Winding (Eastmancolor); m, Francis Lai; ed, Francoise Javet; art d, Pierre Guffroy; cos, Rosine Delamare.

Crime/Suspense   **(PR:C MPAA:GP)**

RIDERS FROM NOWHERE**   (1940) 47m MON bw

Jack Randall *(Jack Rankin)*, Ernie Adams *(Manny)*, Margaret Roach *(Marian Adams)*, Tom London *(Mason)*, Charles King *(Trigger)*, Nelson McDowell *(Undertaker)*, Dorothy Vernon *(Mrs. Gregory)*, George Chesebro *(Bart)*, Ted Adams, Carl Mathews, Jack Evans, Herman Hack, Archie Ricks, Ray Henderson.

The body of a sheriff is found by Randall, a stranger in town. Along with his sidekick, Adams, he discovers a plot by some bad guys to rob a gold mine. Naturally the outlaws are rounded up after some two-fisted action and gun play. Randall gets the late sheriff's sister to boot. Another standard horse opera from Monogram with an ample number of formula cliches and stereotypes.

p, Harry S. Webb; d, Raymond K. Johnson; w, Carl Krusada (based on a story by Richard Piersall); ph, Edward A. Kull, William Hyer; ed, Robert Golden; md, Lange and Porter.

Western   **(PR:A MPAA:NR)**

RIDERS FROM THE DUSK   (SEE: RIDERS OF THE DUSK, 1950)

RIDERS IN THE SKY**½   (1949) 69m COL bw

Gene Autry *(Himself)*, Gloria Henry *(Ann Lawson)*, Pat Buttram *(Chuckwalla Jones)*, Mary Beth Hughes *(Julie Steward)*, Robert Livingston *(Rock McCleary)*, Steve Darrell *(Ralph Lawson)*, Alan Hale, Jr. *(Marshal Riggs)*, Tom London *(Old Man Roberts)*, Hank Patterson *(Luke)*, Ben Welden *(Dave)*, Dennis Moore *(Bud Dwyer)*, Joe Forte *(Willard Agnew)*, Kenne Duncan *(Travis)*, Frank Jaquet *(Coroner)*, Roy Gordon *(J.B. Balloway)*, Loie Bridge *(Widow Cathart)*, Boyd Stockman, Vernon Johns, Pat O'Malley, John Parrish, Kermit Maynard, Bud Osborne, Lynton Brent, Isobel Withers, Sandy Sanders, Denver Dixon, Robert Walker, Champion, Jr. the Horse.

Autry's pal Darrell has been framed for murder and thrown in jail. The town is run by the evil Livingston, a gambler with a choke hold on all the citizens. Leave it to Autry to ride in and save the day, as well as win the heart of Henry, Darrell's daughter. This film got its title from a song by Jones, which Autry sang over the title credits and was used in the scene where London is killed at a trail side. A ghostly rendition of the song, along with thundering hoofbeats, is used with good effect, unusual for westerns. This western is also noted for its toning down of Autry's usually outlandish costumes and its introduction of more action than usual for the singing cowpoke. Livingston, formerly the head of the good guy THREE MESQUITEERS for Republic, did an about face and became the baddie in this film. The film's writer (Geraghty) was upholding a family tradition by working in B westerns. His brother Maurice was a producer-director, and sister Carmelita had appeared in several Buck Jones series westerns.

p, Armand Schaefer; d, John English; w, Gerald Geraghty (based on a story by

Herbert A. Woodbury); ph, William Bradford; ed, Henry Batista; md, Mischa Bakaleinikoff; art d, Harold MacArthur; m/l, Stan Jones, Jimmie Davis.

Western (PR:A MPAA:NR)

RIDERS OF BLACK HILLS (SEE: RIDERS OF THE BLACK HILLS, 1938)

RIDERS OF BLACK MOUNTAIN* (1941) 58m PRC bw

Tim McCoy (Tim), Pauline Hadden (Betty), Rex Lease (Clay), Ralph Peters (Tombstone), Julian Rivero (Jose), Edward Piel, Sr. (Harris), Ted Adams (Pete), Frank LaRue (Judge), Jack Rutherford (Biff), Alden Claire (Emmett), George Chesbro (Burt), Dirk Thane, Carl Mathews.

A group of outlaws commits a series of stagecoach robberies that costs an insurance company a large chunk of cash. McCoy and sidekick Peters are sent out to get to the bottom of things. They pose as card sharks and end up meeting the gang members. After a fight, the bad guys are rounded up and handed to the authorities. This is a poorly done B flick with production standards well below the average western. The film's pacing is much too slow, and it is further hampered by poorly staged fight scenes and occasionally blurry photography. The acting itself is a joke, with McCoy rolling his eyes on cue and Hadden giving us a nice view of her back and not much more. Director Newfield, who used the pseudonum Stewart here, was the brother of producer Neufeld. RIDERS OF BLACK MOUNTAIN was one of the hundreds of low-budget films Newfeld made for small production companies such as PRC. He often used the name Stewart, or sometimes Sherman Scott, to avoid having so many low-budget programmers attributed to his own name.

p, Sigmund Neufeld; d, Peter Stewart [Sam Newfield]; w, Joseph O'Donnell; ph, Jack Greenhalgh; ed, Holbrook Todd.

Western (PR:A MPAA:NR)

RIDERS OF BLACK RIVER** (1939) 59m COL bw

Charles Starrett (Wade Patterson), Iris Meredith (Linda Holden), Dick Curtis (Blaze Carewe), Stanley Brown (Terry Holden), Bob Nolan (Bob), Francis Sayles (Doc Greene), Edmund Cobb (Colt Foster), Forrest Taylor (Sheriff Dave Patterson), George Chesebro (Ranch Hand), Carl Olin Francis (Whit Kane), Lew Meehan (Rustler), Maston Williams (Ed Gills), Carl Sepulveda, Ethan Allen, Clem Horton, The Sons of the Pioneers.

Starrett's an ex-Texas Ranger whose girl friend, Meredith, is in trouble with rustlers. He fights off the bad guys and croons some tunes in this lesser outing from Columbia. Starrett usually was given better material than this to work with. Production values are so-so. A remake of THE REVENGE RIDER (1935) with Tim McCoy.

d, Norman Deming; w, Bennett Cohen (based on the story "The Revenge Rider" by Ford Beebe); ph, George Meehan; ed, William Lyon.

Western (PR:A MPAA:NR)

RIDERS OF DESTINY*** (1933) 56m Lone Star/MGM bw

John Wayne (Singin' Sandy Saunders), Cecilia Parker (Fay Denton), George "Gabby" Hayes (Sheriff Denton), Forrest Taylor (Kincaid), Al "Fuzzy" St. John (Bert), Heinie Conklin (Stage Driver), Earl Dwire (Slip Morman), Lafe McKee (Sheriff), Fern Emmett (Farm Woman), Yakima Canutt, Hal Price, S. Jenks, Duke the Devil Horse.

In the first of Wayne's films for Monogram, he actually plays a singing cowboy! He's an undercover government agent who is trying to find out if Taylor and sidekick Canutt are stealing water from farmers. Wayne fools Taylor into blowing up a well, thus releasing water into a dry creek bed and providing water for the valley. Wayne, whose singing possibly was dubbed by Smith Ballew, was asked to croon while shooting down the bad guys. The Duke, of course, refused this foolishness. The film's writer-director was the father of Wayne's old boyhood pal and fellow movie cowboy Bob Steele. This film was better than many formula westerns of the day thanks to the direction, which kept it lively and well paced. Best of all, through some interesting camera angles and clever editing, Wayne and stuntman Canutt were able to create a fight scene that looked surprisingly realistic. This was a giant step forward for B westerns, whose fights usually suffered from a stagy flatness. Despite a small budget of $10,000, RIDERS OF DESTINY looks like a high-quality production. Canutt was referred to on the set as the film's "dog heavy," a studio term for any bad guy whose evil character is established upon kicking a dog!

p, Paul Malvern; d&w, Robert North Bradbury; ph, Archie Stout; ed, Carl L. Pierson; stunts, Yakima Canutt.

Western Cas. (PR:A MPAA:NR)

RIDERS OF PASCO BASIN** (1940) 56m UNIV bw

Johnny Mack Brown (Leo Jameson), Bob Baker (Bruce Moore), Fuzzy Knight (Luther), Frances Robinson (Jean Madison), Arthur Loft (Matt Kirby), Frank La Rue (Joel Madison), James Guilfoyle (Evans), Lafe McKee, Chuck Morrison, Edward Cassidy, Robert Winkler, William Gould, Ted Adams, Kermit Maynard, David Sharpe, Hank Bell, Edward Piel, John Judd, Gordon Hart, Rudy Sooter and His Californians.

A group of outlaws is tricking ranchers out of money with a phony promise to build a dam. In rides Brown, leading a group of vigilantes to save the day. Routine fare with competent acting and production credits. The opening, a rodeo sequence, is poorly shot and smacks of stock footage.

d, Ray Taylor; w, Ford Beebe; ph, William Sickner; ed, Louis Sackin; m/l, "Tying Up My Bridle to the Door of Your Heart," "Song of the Prairie" (Milton Rosen, Everett Carter, sung by Bob Baker, Rudy Sooter and His Californians).

Western (PR:A MPAA:NR)

RIDERS OF THE BADLANDS**½ (1941) 58m COL bw

Charles Starrett (Mac Collins/Steve Langdon), Russell Hayden (Lucky Barton), Cliff "Ukelele Ike" Edwards (Bones Malloy), Ilene Brewer (Flo), Kay Hughes (Celia), Roy Bancroft (Capt. Martin), Rick Anderson (Sheriff Taylor), Edith Leach (Ellen), Ethan Laidlaw (Bill), Harry Cording (Higgins), Hal Price (Warden James), Ted Mapes, George J. Lewis, John Cason, Edmund Cobb, Francis Walker.

Starrett has a dual role of both ranger and outlaw. Of course there's the usual case of mistaken identity, with Starrett's men arresting their boss and nearly hanging him before he can prove his innocence. Eventually the ranger's evil look-alike is caught, and all ends happily. Right amounts of gun play and action sequences make this an entertaining albeit average cowboy film. This was one of the movies in the eight-film series to co-star Starrett and Hayden. Hayden retained his "Lucky" nickname from the "Lucky Jenkins" role in the "Hopalong Cassidy" series for Paramount. He would take the same nickname to a later series with Jimmy Ellison, another "Hopalong Cassidy" alumnus.

p, William Berke; d, Howard Bretherton; w, Betty Burbridge; ph, Benjamin Kline; ed, Charles Nelson.

Western (PR:A MPAA:NR)

RIDERS OF THE BLACK HILLS**½ (1938) 61m REP bw

Bob Livingston (Stony Brooke), Ray Corrigan (Tucson Smith), Max Terhune (Lullaby Joslin), Ann Evers (Joyce Garth), Roscoe Ates (Sheriff Brown), Maude Eburne (Mrs. Garth), Frank Melton (Don Weston), Johnny Lang Fitzgerald (Buck), Jack Ingram (Lefty), Edward Earle (Steward), Monte Montague (Sam), Ben Hall (Ethelbert), Frank O'Connor (Doctor), Tom London (Rod), Snowflake [Fred Toones] (Himself), Milburn Morante, Jack O'Shea, Art Dillard.

The Three Mesquiteers (Livingston, Corrigan and Terhune) never seem to leave their horses in this routine entry from their popular series. A famous racehorse is stolen en route to the track. The Mesquiteers are horse dealers who own a stallion that resembles the stolen nag. The trio is tossed into the pokey, but the owner of the purloined pony gets them out, and off they go to look for the real thieves. Using a horsy double, they fool the real kidnapers and recover the prize animal. The film has its amusing moments and standard action scenes. Terhune's ventriloquism doesn't really fit, but doesn't detract from the main story. While not one of the cowboy trio's better efforts, it was acceptable western fare. Republic generally is credited with developing the concept of teaming a trio of stars to perform in B western series. (See THREE MESQUITEERS series, Index.)

p, William Berke; d, George Sherman; w, Betty Burbridge (based on a story by Burbridge, Bernard McConville, from characters created by William Colot MacDonald); ph, William Nobles; ed, Lester Orlebeck.

Western (PR:A MPAA:NR)

RIDERS OF THE CACTUS* (1931) 56m Big Four bw

Wally Wales, Buzz Barton, Lorraine LaVal, Fred Church, Ed Cartwright, Don Wilson, Joe Lawliss, Tete Brady, Etta Delmas, Gus Anderson.

Some bad guys are after a map showing the site of a buried treasure. This document falls into the hands of a luckless lass who finds herself being chased by the bad guys. Lucky for her that the good guy rides in to save the day, with help from the border patrol. This independent B western suffers from confusing plot development and a too cute "aw-shucks" grin that seems permanently plastered on Wales' face.

p, David Kirkland, Charles Connell; d&w, Kirkland (based on a story by Connell); ph, R.B. Hooper.

Western (PR:A MPAA:NR)

RIDERS OF THE DAWN** (1937) 55m MON bw

Jack Randall, Peggy Keyes, Warner Richmond, George Cooper, James Sheridan, Earl Dwire, Lloyd Ingraham, Ed Brady, Yakima Canutt, Steve Clark, Frank Hagney, Ella McKenzie, Ed Coxen, Chick Hannon, Tim Davis, Jim Corey, Oscar Gahan, Forrest Taylor, Tex Cooper, Chief Dark Hawk.

Richmond is the bad guy who runs a small western town, and Marshal Randall is out to stop him. The film climaxes with an exciting fight between Randall and Richmond on a runaway stagecoach. The fight ends with an improbable act of God, when Richmond is killed by a bolt of lightning. This film had some novel ideas and good action sequences, but ultimately ended up an inept production. Plot is sacrificed for speed, making for an often confusing story line. Worst of all was the unconvincing synching of Randall's songs; his voice and lip movements never match and his guitar obviously is being played by someone else. Randall was the older brother of Monogram's cowboy star Bob Livingston and the studio hoped he would follow in his sibling's successful footsteps. Despite the studio's big plans for Randall, he never caught on with the public, and consequently faded away. His stint at Republic was equally short-lived.

p&d, R.N. Bradbury; w, Robert Emmett [Tansey]; ph, Bert Longenecker; m/l, "White Clouds in the Moonlight," Bradbury.

Western (PR:A MPAA:NR)

RIDERS OF THE DAWN*½ (1945) 57m MON bw

Jimmy Wakely (Himself), Lee "Lasses" White (Lasses), John James (Dusty), Sarah Padden (Melinda), Horace Murphy (Sheriff), Phyllis Adair (Penny), Jack Baxley (Doc), Bob Shelton (Bob), Dad Picard (Himself), Arthur "Fiddlin" Smith (Arthur), Eddie Taylor, Brooks Temple, Bill Hammond, Michael Joseph Ward, Wesley Tuttle and His Texas Stars.

Wakely's a member of a traveling show in the old West. The troupe finds a baby whose parents were brutally murdered by outlaws. Wakely goes after the bad guys, who killed the couple to get valuable oil deposits on their land. Lots of hard riding and shooting and an overabundance of cowboy tunes in this routine, unexciting programmer. Wakely can sing but is barely passable as a cowpoke.

p&d, Oliver Drake; w, Louise Rousseau; ph, William Sickner; ed, William Austin.

Western   **(PR:A MPAA:NR)**

RIDERS OF THE DEADLINE**½   (1943) 70m UA bw

William Boyd (*Hopalong Cassidy*), Andy Clyde (*California Carlson*), Jimmy Rogers (*Jimmy*), Richard Crane (*Tim Mason*), Frances Woodward (*Sue*), William Halligan (*Crandall*), Tony Ward [Anthony Warde] (*Madigan*), Bob [Robert] Mitchum (*Drago*), Jim Bannon (*Tex*), Hugh Prosser (*Martin*), Herbert Rawlinson (*Capt. Jennings*), Montie Montana (*Calhoun*), Earle Hodgins (*Sourdough*), Bill Beckford (*Kilroy*), Pierce Lyden (*Sanders*), Herman Hack (*Tom*), Art Felix, Roy Bucko, Cliff Parkinson.

Boyd's young pal Crane is in trouble with some gamblers. He gets the local lawmen to let the kid hide out at his Bar 20 ranch to trap the real crooks, whose leader turns out to be local banker Halligan. This marked the 50th film of the Hopalong Cassidy series, of which critics apparently were rapidly tiring. Boyd's earlier films had received good reviews. However, at this point critics unofficially began lowering them to B status and giving them short, inconsequential reviews. This also marks Mitchum's last B western villain role. RIDERS OF THE DEADLINE apparently proved the critics right with its standard production credits and story line. (See HOPALONG CASSIDY series, Index.)

p, Harry Sherman; d, Lesley Selander; w, Bennett Cohen (based on characters created by Clarence E. Mulford); ph, Russell Harlan; ed, Fred Berger; md, Irvin Talbot; art d, Ralph Berger.

Western   **(PR:A MPAA:NR)**

RIDERS OF THE DESERT**   (1932) 63m Sono Art-World Wide bw

Bob Steele, Gertrude Messinger, George Hayes, Al St. John, Greg Whitespear, Horace B. Carpenter, Louise Carver, Joe Dominguez, John Elliott, Tex O'Neill.

Steele comes home from college on a vacation just in time for some real action. A stagecoach is held up, and the Arizona Rangers, which had disbanded, but regroup to go after the bad guys and get the loot. Steele goes back to school and returns a year later to find the money hadn't been returned to its rightful owners, and a recently released outlaw is after it. Plot and story development are constantly sacrificed for action, which grows a little tiresome after awhile. The final sequence is worth waiting for, however: a well staged shoot-out and subsequent brawl in an area surrounded by cliffs. Steele's dad Bradbury directs with a good sense of excitement but not much else, which is typical of most of his pictures.

p, Trem Carr; d, Robert N. Bradbury; w, Wellyn Totman; ph, Archie Stout; ed, Carl Pierson.

Western   **Cas.**   **(PR:A MPAA:NR)**

RIDERS OF THE DUSK**   (1949) 57m MON bw

Whip Wilson (*Whip*), Andy Clyde (*Winks*), Reno Browne (*Nora*), Lee Roberts (*Barney*), Myron Healey (*Sheriff*), Tris Coffin (*Hall*), Marshall Reed (*Bradshaw*), Holly Bane (*Gus*), John Merton (*Art*), Dee Cooper (*Tom*), Thorton Edwards, Ray Jones.

Wilson is a U.S. marshal after some cattle rustlers, aided by Clyde and love interest Browne. Using both gun and whip, Wilson manages to round up the gang almost single-handedly. By the time of this film's release the formula B western was just about gone, having made way for TV westerns. Consequently, this was a tired entry to a genre that was past its prime.

p, Eddie Davis; d, Lambert Hillyer; w, Jess Bowers [Adele Buffington], Robert [Emmett] Tansey; ph, Harry Neumann.

Western   **Cas.**   **(PR:A MPAA:NR)**

RIDERS OF THE FRONTIER*½   (1939) 58m MON bw

Tex Ritter (*Tex*), Jack Rutherford (*Lane*), Hal Taliaferro [Wally Wales](*Buck*), Glen Francis (*Sam*), Nolan Willis (*Gus*), Roy Barcroft (*Carter*), Bill McCormick (*Boney*), Mantan Moreland (*Cookie*), Edward Cecil (*Doctor*), Bruce Mitchell (*Marshal*), Jean Joyce (*Martha*), Marin Sais (*Sarah*), Maxine Leslie (*Goldie*), Nelson McDowell, Charles King, Forrest Taylor, Robert Frazer, White Flash the Horse.

A crooked ranch foreman (Barcroft) is cheating pretty ranch owner Sais and stealing her cattle. Ritter poses as an outlaw, infiltrates the badman's scheme and saves the day. This routine programmer is a poor entry for Ritter's popular series. Production values are stretched beyond budget limitations, and it shows. Ritter's series didn't get much better after this.

p, Edward Finney; d, Spencer Bennett; w, Jesse Duffy, Joseph Levering; ph, Marcel LePicard; ed, Fred Bain; md, Frank Sanucci; m/l, Frank Harford.

Western   **(PR:A MPAA:NR)**

RIDERS OF THE GOLDEN GULCH**   (1932) 51m West Coast Studios/State Rights bw

Buffalo Bill, Jr., Mary Dunn, Yakima Canutt, Pete Morrison, Edmund Cobb, Jack Harvey.

A cowboy helps a lass with her runaway horses but then is accused of trying to rob her father's bank. It takes him the rest of the film to prove his innocence and catch the bad guys. The son of the famous western showman is featured in this minor independent western. Lots of riding, shooting and other standards, but nothing new here. Canutt, who plays the sidekick, also wrote the original story.

d, Clifford Smith; w, Harry Sauber (based on a story by Yakima Canutt); ph, William Thompson.

Western   **(PR:A MPAA:NR)**

RIDERS OF THE NORTH**   (1931) 59m SYN bw

Bob Custer [Raymond Glenn], Blanche Mehaffey, Frank Rice, Eddie Dunn, George Rigas, Buddy Shaw, William Walling.

Two men are murdered and it's up to the Mounties to find out what's going on. Every cliche is snugly fit into place in this routine western. Custer, who made his film debut in 1924, gained popularity as a cowboy star in silent and early sound westerns, several of which were produced by Joseph Kennedy, the father of the former president. He appeared in several non-westerns under his real name, Raymond Glenn, and also shared top billing with animal stars Rex, "King of the Wild Horses," and Rin-Tin-Tin Jr. in LAW OF THE WILD (1934).

p, G.A. Durlam; d, J.P. McGowan; w, Durlam; ph, Carl Himm; ed, Charles Hunt.

Western   **(PR:A MPAA:NR)**

RIDERS OF THE NORTHLAND**½   (1942) 58m COL bw (GB: NEXT IN LINE)

Charles Starrett (*Steve Bowie*), Russell Hayden (*Lucky Laidlaw*), Shirley Patterson (*Sheila Taylor*), Cliff Edwards (*Harmony Bumpas*), Bobby Larson (*Buddy Taylor*), Lloyd Bridges (*Alex*), Kenneth MacDonald (*Matt Taylor*), Paul Sutton (*Chris Larsen*), Robert O. Davis (*Nazi Agent*), Joe McGuinn (*Stacy*), Francis Walker (*Dobie*), George Piltz (*Luke*), Blackjack Ward (*Henchman*), Dick Jensen.

This series entry for Starrett has the unique distinction of being one of the first B westerns to acknowledge America was at war. A variety of films with war themes were being cranked out by the studios, and it was only a matter of time before western producers caught on to the patriotic fervor. Here Starrett and pals Hayden and Edwards are three Texas Rangers anxious to join the Army and do their part for the war effort. Before being allowed to join up, the trio is sent to Alaska to stop a secret Nazi operation. The Germans are running a submarine refueling station up north, behind seemingly inpenetrable barbed wire fences. With the help of Patterson, MacDonald and youngster Larson, the Rangers discover that Sutton is a traitorous spy. Starrett runs a cattle stampede through the barbed wire and stops the operation cold. Other than the war-based twists, this is routine Western material, competently acted and directed, with good production values all around. Edward, noted for his performing under the name of "Ukelele Ike," doesn't sing in this film, but yodels a few tunes, including "We'll Carry the Torch for Miss Liberty" and "Silver Sage in the Twilight."

p, Jack Fier; d, William Berke; w, Paul Franklin; ph, Benjamin Kline; ed, Burton Kramer.

Western   **(PR:A MPAA:NR)**

RIDERS OF THE NORTHWEST MOUNTED*½   (1943) 57m COL bw

Russell Hayden, Dub Taylor, Adele Mara, Bob Wills and the Texas Playboys, Dick Curtis, Richard Bailey, Jack Ingram, Leon McAuliffe, Vernon Steele.

A standard Northwest Mountie adventure tale has Hayden and Taylor trudging through the woods in search of an elusive outlaw. This one's bright spot is the musical contribution of Bob Wills and the Texas Playboys, the finest of the country-western swing bands.

p, Leon Barsha; d, William Berke; w, Fred Myton; ph, Benjamin Kline; ed, James Sweeney; art d, Lionel Banks.

Western   **(PR:A MPAA:NR)**

RIDERS OF THE PURPLE SAGE**½   (1931) 58m FOX bw

George O'Brien (*Jim Lassiter*), Marguerite Churchill (*Jane Withersteen*), Noah Beery (*Judge Dyer*), Yvonne Pelletier (*Bess*), James Todd (*Venters*), Stanley Fields (*Oldring*), Shirley Nails (*Fay Larkin*), Lester Dorr (*Judkins*), Frank McGlynn (*Jeff Tull*).

O'Brien plays a cowboy out to rescue his kidnaped sister (Nails) in this adaptation of the noted Grey novel. Though a bit creaky as far as dialog goes, there are several sequences that feature topnotch action. A wide-angle lens was used in the photography with great effect. O'Brien is fine as the hero and fits the characterization of the strong, silent type. This first sound version was followed by a sequel, THE RAINBOW TRAIL, in 1932. Two silent versions were also filmed, the first in 1918 with William Farnum and the second in 1925 with silent legend Tom Mix. Mix also made a sequel to his version. A second sound version, starring George Montgomery, was produecd by Fox in 1941. *Riders of the Purple Sage* was the first really successful novel by noted western writer Grey, who formerly caught fish for a living.

d, Hamilton MacFadden; w, John F. Goodrich, Philip Klein, Barry Connors (based on the novel by Zane Grey); ph, George Schneiderman.

Western   **(PR:A MPAA:NR)**

RIDERS OF THE PURPLE SAGE**   (1941) 56m FOX bw

George Montgomery (*Jim Lassiter*), Mary Howard (*Jane Withersteen*), Robert Barrat (*Judge Dyer*), Lynne Roberts (*Bess*), Kane Richmond (*Adam Dyer*), Patsy Patterson (*Fay Larkin*), Richard Lane (*Oldring*), Oscar O'Shea (*Judkins*), James Gillette (*Venters*), Frank McGrath (*Pete*), LeRoy Mason (*Jerry Card*).

This fourth film version of the popular Grey novel is probably the weakest. Montgomery is the cowboy who discovers judge Barrat is cheating his niece out of a rightful inheritance. What's more, Barrat is the secret leader of a gang of outlaws who pose as vigilantes so they can control the territory via thievery and murder. With the help of love interest Howard, Montgomery stops the mayhem and puts the wrongdoers behind bars. This story, first filmed in 1918, had become somewhat dated 23 years later. The overly melodramatic action and plot implausibilities overlooked earlier just didn't work any longer. The script differs from the novel slightly, in an effort to cover some plot holes. But this remake twice-removed bears little difference from any programmer western of the time. Montgomery, a standout as the hero, would soon jump to A pictures and make a second Zane Grey feature, LAST OF THE DUANES.

p, Sol M. Wurtzel; d, James Tinling; w, William Bruckner, Robert Metzler (based on the novel by Zane Grey); ph, Lucien Andriot; ed, Nick De Maggio.

Western (PR:A MPAA:NR)

RIDERS OF THE RANGE*** (1949) 60m RKO bw

Tim Holt (*Kansas*), Richard Martin (*Chito*), Jacqueline White (*Dusty*), Reed Hadley (*Burrows*), Robert Barrat (*Sheriff*), Robert Clarke (*Harry*), Tom Tyler (*Kid Ringo*), William Tannen (*Trump*).

Rancher White hires Holt and pal Martin as ranch hands. When her ne'er-do-well brother Clarke gets himself into hot water with gambler Hadley, Clarke is forced to take up rustling to pay off his debts. Holt and Martin foil this scehem, and White gives her brother money to pay the debt. When someone knocks off Hadley, the two heroes are blamed. They prove their innocence and bring in the real killer, Tyler. Exciting and well-paced, this was a good feature in Holt's popular series. However, by 1949, television was beginning to take its toll on series westerns, evidenced by the fact that RIDERS OF THE RANGE lost $50,000. The 1940s, which proved to be the westerns' most popular era, also saw their downfall at decade's end.

p, Herman Schlom; d, Lesley Selander; w, Norman Houston; ph, J. Roy Hunt; m, Paul Sawtell; ed, Robert Swink; art d, Albert S. D'Agostino, Feild Gray.

Western Cas. (PR:A MPAA:NR)

RIDERS OF THE RIO GRANDE**½ (1943) 55m REP bw

Bob Steele (*Tucson Smith*), Tom Tyler (*Stony Brooke*), Jimmie Dodd (*Lullaby Joslin*), Lorraine Miller (*Janet Owens*), Edward Van Sloan (*Pop Owens*), Rick Vallin (*Tom Owens*), Harry Worth (*Sam Skelly*), Roy Barcroft (*Sarsaparilla*), Charles King (*Thumbe*), Jack Ingram (*Berger*), John James, Jack O'Shea, Henry Hall, Bud Osborne.

A banker (Van Sloan), ashamed when his son robs a bank, arranges to have himself killed to make up for the misdeed. He has three killers come after him, but, as luck (and script) would have it, Van Sloan confuses the Three Mesquiteers (Steele, Tyler and Dodd) for the hired gunmen. Some amusing moments in this slightly imaginative Western, though it's not one of the best in the Mesquiteers series.

p, Louis Gray; d, Howard Bretherton; w, Albert DeMond (based on characters created by William Colt MacDonald); ph, Ernest Miller; ed, Charles Craft.

Western (PR:A MPAA:NR)

RIDERS OF THE ROCKIES*** (1937) 56m GN bw

Tex Ritter (*Tex Rand*), Louise Stanley (*Louise Rogers*), Charles King (*Regan*), Yakima Canutt (*Sgt. Beef*), Earl Dwire (*Jeffries*), Snub Pollard (*Pee Wee*), Horace Murphy (*Doc*), Martin Garralaga (*Mendoza*), Jack Rockwell (*Capt. Hayes*), Paul Lopez (*Pete*), Heber Snow (*Hank Worden*)(*Henchman*), Tex Palmer, Clyde McClary, The Texas Tornados, White Flash the Horse.

Ritter is the leader of a trio of ranchers. Constantly getting themselves into trouble, they unwittingly help a gang of rustlers led by King. With his buddies jailed, it's up to Ritter to right all the wrongdoing. Some fairly routine action in this standard western, improved by Ritter's performance and some realistic (for B westerns) blood letting. Pollard, who plays Ritter's sidekick for the first time here, had been the cowboy's favorite silent clown in the 1920s. King by now had become a staple as Ritter's nemesis. This was Ritter's seventh starring role and featured his 11th fight with King!

p, Edward F. Finney; d, Robert North Bradbury; w, Robert Emmett [Tansey] (based on a story by Lindsley Parsons); ph, Gus Peterson; m/l, Tex Ritter, Frank Sanucci

Western Cas. (PR:A MPAA:NR)

RIDERS OF THE SANTA FE*½ (1944) 60m UNIV bw (GB: MILE A MINUTE)

Rod Cameron (*Matt Conway*), Jennifer Holt (*Carla/Paula Anderson*), Eddie Dew (*Larry*), Fuzzy Knight (*Bullseye*), Ray Whitley (*Hank*), Lane Chandler (*Earl Duncan*), Earle Hodgins (*Ed Milton*), George Douglas (*Tom Benner*), Dick Alexander (*Biff Macauley*), Budd Buster (*Otis Wade*), Ida Moore (*Luella Tucker*), Al Ferguson (*Bartender*), Ray Whitley's Bar-6 Cowboys, Ray Jones, Henry Wills.

Cameron heads an outlaw round-up in the Santa Fe Territory, saving a group of trail drivers from losing their water rights. The round-up is complete only when Cameron captures the townsman who organized the illegal doings.

p, Oliver Drake; d, Wallace Fox; w, Ande Lamb; ph, Maury Gertsman; ed, Ray Snyder; md, Paul Sawtell; art d, John B. Goodman, Abraham Grossman.

Western (PR:A MPAA:NR)

RIDERS OF THE TIMBERLINE*** (1941) 59m PAR bw

William Boyd (*Hopalong Cassidy*), Brad King (*Johnny Nelson*), Andy Clyde (*California*), J. Farrel McDonald (*Kerrigan*), Eleanor Stewart (*Elaine*), Anna Q. Nilsson (*Donna*), Edward Keene (*Yatos*), Hal Talliaferro (*Petrie*), Tom Tyler (*Slade*), Victor Jory (*Baptiste*), Mickey Eissa (*Larry*), Hank Bell, The Guardsman Quartet.

Boyd is sent out to timber country with the assignment of thwarting some Easterners who want to take over a tract of valuable land and will stop at nothing to get it. Boyd manages to quelch their evil plans and stop them from blowing up a dam just in the nick of time. This is a refreshing change from most westerns as it has Boyd's famous cowboy character in a much different setting than normally found in this (or any other) series. Some good action sequences, and Clyde is great as the comic support. (See HOPALONG CASSIDY series, Index.)

p, Harry Sherman; d, Lesley Selander; w, J. Benton Cheney (based on characters created by Clarence E. Mulford); ph, Russell Harlan; m, John Leopold; ed, Fred

Feitshans, Jr.; md, Irvin Talbot; art d, Ralph Berger; m/l, Grace Hamilton, Jack Stern.

Western (PR:A MPAA:NR)

RIDERS OF THE WEST* (1942) 58m MON bw

Buck Jones (*Buck Roberts*), Tim McCoy (*Tim*), Raymond Hatton (*Sandy*), Sarah Padden (*Ma Turner*), Harry Woods (*Duke Mason*), Walter McGrail (*Miller*), Walter Frazer (*Holt*), Dennis Moore (*Steve*), Christine MacIntyre (*Hope*), Bud Osborne (*Red*), Charles King, Lee Phelps, Kermit Maynard, Milburn Morante, Edward Piel, Sr., Lynton Brent, J. Merrill Holmes, George Morrell, Tom London, Silver the Horse.

A surprisingly dull entry in Monogram's *Rough Rider* series finds Jones fighting some cattle rustlers. Woods is the leader of the gang, rustling beef and trying to swindle farmers out of their land. Naturally Jones puts a stop to it all. The direction takes this film nowhere fast in an aimless slow-paced style. There's far too much dialog and the cinematography is unusually bad, all adding up to a real waste of time and effort. (See ROUGH RIDERS series, Index.)

p, Scott R. Dunlap; d, Howard Bretherton; w, Jess Bowers [Adele Buffington]; ph, Harry Neumann; ed, Carl Pierson.

Western Cas. (PR:A MPAA:NR)

RIDERS OF THE WHISTLING PINES*½ (1949) 70m COL bw

Gene Autry (*Himself*), Patricia White (*Helen Carter*), Jimmy Lloyd (*Joe Lucas*), Douglas Dumbrille (*Henry Mitchell*), Damian O'Flynn (*Bill Wright*), Clayton Moore (*Pete*), Harry Cheshire (*Dr. Daniel Chadwick*), Leon Weaver (*Abner Weaver*), Loie Bridge (*Loie Weaver*), Jerry Scoggins (*Jerry*), Fred S. Martin (*Freddie*), Bert Dodson (*Bert*), Roy Gordon (*Hoagland*), Jason Robards (*Charlie Carter*), Britt Wood (*Smith*), Len Torrey (*Marshall*), Lane Chandler, Lynn Farr, Al Thompson, Emmett Vogan, Virginia Carroll, Nolan Leary, Steve Benton, The Pinafores, Champion the Horse.

A gang of outlaws led by Dumbrille, O'Flynn, and Moore are destroying the timberlands. Autry tries to save the day but the baddies frame him on a charge of poisoning cattle and then lay a murder rap on him. But Autry proves his innocence and saves the day in this simple-minded, subpar outing. Unlike Autry's usual film work, this is a slow-moving picture with a notable lack of suspense and excitement. Moore would soon be switching from bad guy to good guy for the popular television series "The Lone Ranger." (See GENE AUTRY series, Index.)

p, Armand Schaefer; d, John English; w, Jack Townley; ph, William Bradford; ed, Aaron Stell; md, Mischa Bakaleinikoff; art d, Harold MacArthur.

Western Cas. (PR:A MPAA:NR)

RIDERS OF THE WHISTLING SKULL*** (1937) 58m REP bw (GB: THE GOLDEN TRAIL)

Bob Livingston (*Stony Brooke*), Ray Corrigan (*Tuscon Smith*), Max Terhune (*Lullaby Joslin*), Mary Russell (*Betty Marsh*), Roger Williams (*Rutledge*), Fern Emmett (*Henrietta*), C. Montague Shaw (*Faxon*), Yakima Canutt (*Otah*), John Ward (*Brewster*), George Godfrey (*Fronc*), Earle Ross (*Prof. Cleary*), Frank Ellis (*Coggins*), Chief Thunder Cloud (*High Priest*), John Van Pelt (*Prof. Marsh*), Edward Piel (*Sheriff*), Jack Kirk (*Deputy*), Iron Eyes Cody (*Indian*), Tracy Layne (*Henchman*), Eddie Boland, Ken Cooper, Tom Steele, Wally West.

One of the THREE MESQUITEERS films and one of the series' best outings. Livingston, Corrigan, and Terhune are off in the Southwest guiding an archeological expedition to an ancient Indian city. The lost city is surrounded by an unusual rock formation that causes a strange whistling whenever the wind blows. Williams leads a gang of outlaws who've been raiding the city (known as Lukachakai) of its golden treasures. They're holding a professor captive, and his daughter (Russell) hires the Mesquiteers to rescue him. The use of unusual lighting achieved some interesting effects in this entry in a normally straightforward B western series. Indians are hidden carefully among the shadows and the action is nicely staged. There are some honestly exciting suspense sequences, and the eerie whistling is used with great effect. Terhune is the comic relief to Livingston and Corrigan's (relatively) straight performances. His use of a ventriloquist's dummy and his constant battles with man-hungry spinster Emmett provide the needed relief from the spooky goings-on. This unusual film proved to be enormously popular at the box office, a well-deserved honor. (See THREE MESQUITEERS series, Index.)

p, Nat Levine; d, Mack V. Wright; w, Oliver Drake, John Rathmell (based on a story by Bernard McConville), Drake, from the novels *Riders of the Whistling Skull* and *The Singing Scorpion* by William Colt MacDonald); ph, Jack Marta; m, Hugo Riesenfeld, Karl Hajos, Arthur Kay, Leon Rosebrook, J. S. Zamecnik, Jacques Aubran, Sidney Cutner; ed, Murray Seldeen, Tony Martinelli; md, Harry Grey.

Western (PR:A-C MPAA:NR)

RIDERS OF VENGEANCE (SEE: RAIDERS, THE, 1952)

RIDERS TO THE STARS** (1954) 80m A-Men/UA c

William Lundigan (*Richard Stanton*), Herbert Marshall (*Dr. Donald Stanton*), Richard Carlson (*Jerry Lockwood*), Martha Hyer (*Jane Flynn*), Dawn Addams (*Susan Manners*), Robert Karnes (*Walter Gordon*), Lawrence Dobkin (*Dr. Delmar*), George Eldredge (*Dr. Drayden*), Dan Riss (*Dr. Warner*), Michael Fox (*Dr. Klinger*), King Donovan (*Mr. O'Herll*), Ken Dibbs (*Kenneth Wells*), James K. Best (*Sidney Fuller*), John Hedloe (*Archibald Guiness*).

Marshall leads a group of scientists who are studying meteors. The scientists don't understand how meteors avoid being burned up by the cosmic rays of outer space. A rocket is developed that can fly slightly faster than meteors. The scientists plan to use the rocket to capture a meteor for study so that they will be able to design and build rockets impervious to cosmic rays. Lundigan, Karnes, and Carlson (the latter being the film's director as well) are trained for the mission. In 1954 Americans were terrified of the Russians getting ahead in the space race and quickly became fascinated with all things scientific. The films of the period reflect this interest in roughly two science categories: films which presented monsters and evil creatures from outer space or films which sought to explain scientific processes. RIDERS TO THE STARS falls in the latter category. It shows a step-by-step progression, taking great care to explain each plot point and scientific fact with detail. Though released as a science fiction film, it played more like science fact with its painstaking documentary style. Tors was well known as a producer of such films, and they were considered to be quite informative in their era. But several moonwalks and space shuttle flights later, films like RIDERS TO THE STARS seem outdated and boring with little factual material that can inform modern-day audiences, a far more sophisticated group than their 1950s counterparts. Still, this is an interesting historical curio that may be of some interest to students of the era.

p, Ivan Tors; d, Richard Carlson; w, Curt Siodmak; ph, Stanley Cortez (Color Corporation of America); m, Harry Sukman; ed, Herbert L. Strock; art d, Jerome Pycha, Jr.; spec eff, Harry Redmond, Jr., Jack R. Glass; makeup, Louis Phillippi; m/l "Riders to the Stars," Sukman, Leon Pober (sung by Kitty White).

Science Fiction   **Cas.**   **(PR:A MPAA:NR)**

RIDIN' DOWN THE CANYON½   (1942) 54m REP bw

Roy Rogers (Roy), George "Gabby" Hayes (Gabby), Dee "Buzzy" Henry (Bobbie Blake), Linda Hayes (Alice Blake), Addison Richards (Jordan), Lorna Gray (Barbara Joyce), Olin Howlin (Jailer), James Seay (Burt Wooster), Hal Taliaferro (Pete), Forrest Taylor (Jim Fellowes), Roy Barcroft (Lafe Collins), Art Mix, Art Dillard, Bob Nolan and the Sons of the Pioneers, Trigger the Horse.

The U.S. government is in need of horses for the war, and patriotic ranchers try to do their part. But their efforts are hampered by a group of outlaws (led by Richards) who want to rustle the ponies and get the cash for themselves. Leave it to Rogers and company to save the day. This twist on the common B western cattle-rustling plot is fairly standard but a good entry in Rogers' popular series. In between the action, Rogers, along with the Sons of the Pioneers, manages to croon a few tunes, including "Sagebrush Symphony," "Blue Prairie," "Who Am I?" and "Curley Joe" (Tim Spencer, Bob Nolan).

p, Harry Gray; d, Joseph Kane; w, Albert De Mond (based on a story by Robert Williams, Norman Houston); ph, Jack Marta; ed, Edward Mann; md, Morton Scott; art d, Russell Kimball.

Western   **Cas.**   **(PR:A MPAA:NR)**

RIDIN' DOWN THE TRAIL½   (1947) 53m MON bw

Jimmy Wakely, Dub "Cannonball" Taylor, Beverly Jons, Douglas Fowley, John James, Doug Aylesworth, Charles King, Matthew B. Slaven [Brad Slaven], Kermit Maynard, Harry Carr, Milburn Morante, Ted French, Post Park, Dick Reinhart, Don Weston, Jesse Ashlock, Stanley Ellison, Wayne Burson, Doug Farnsworth.

Singing cowboy star Wakely has a tough time with an outlaw gang who pose as Rangers. He manages to uncover their rustling plot and clean up the trail for his fellow riders. Routine fare from veteran B western director Bretherton.

p, Bennett Cohen; d, Howard Bretherton; w, Cohen; ph, James S. Brown; ed, John C. Fuller; md, Edward Kay.

Western   **(PR:A MPAA:NR)**

RIDIN' FOR JUSTICE½   (1932) 61m COL bw

Charles "Buck" Jones, Mary Doran, Russell Simpson, Walter Miller, Bob McKenzie, William Walling, Billy Engle, Hank Mann, Lafe McKee, Silver the Horse.

An early effort for Jones. He plays a broncho buster who's popular with all the gals in town, from saloon girls to the marshal's wife. Naturally the marshal isn't too pleased with this, which causes Jones some problems. But he and the marshal (Doran) get caught up in a murder mystery and Jones eventually proves that Doran's the killer. A good enough entry for Jones. At the time he preferred "Charles 'Buck' Jones" for a billing, but he soon dropped the first name for a more cowboy-sounding moniker.

p, Irving Briskin; d, D. Ross Lederman; w, Harold Shumate (based on a story by Shumate); ph, Benjamin Kline; ed, Maurice Wright.

Western   **(PR:A MPAA:NR)**

RIDIN' LAW zero   (1930) 54m Biltmore/Big Four bw

Jack Perrin, Yakima Canutt, Rene Borden, Jack Mower, Ben Corbett, Pete Morrison, Fern Emmett, Olive Young, Robert Walker, Starlight the Horse.

Perrin's father is murdered by Canutt, and the boy is out for revenge. Naturally he gets it in this early and amateurish Western. The soundtrack is poorly recorded and what dialog is intelligible is unintentionally hysterial. Borden is supposed to be a Mexican lass but keeps going in and out of her accent before finally dumping it altogether. This film was made by a minor independent studio, the likes of which were beginning to specialize in westerns. Big studios rarely touched westerns at this point, leaving the field wide open for smaller production houses. Canutt went on to become the ubiquitous villain in B westerns featuring John Wayne.

p, Harry S. Webb, F. E. Douglas; d, Webb; w, Carl Krusada (based on a story by Krusada); ph, William Nobles; ed, Fred Bain.

Western   **(PR:A MPAA:NR)**

RIDIN' ON A RAINBOW**   (1941) 79m REP bw

Gene Autry (Gene), Smiley Burnette (Frog), Mary Lee (Patsy), Carol Adams (Sally), Ferris Taylor (Capt. Bartlett), Georgia Caine (Maria Bartlett), Byron Foulger (Matt Evans), Ralf Harolde (Binke), Jimmy Conlin (Frisco), Guy Usher (Sheriff), Anthony Warde (Morrison), Forrest Taylor (Jeff Billings), Burr Caruth (Eben Carter), Ed Cassidy, Ben Hall, Tom London, William Mong, Champion the Horse.

A local bank is robbed and Autry investigates. The case takes him to a showboat where teenaged singer Lee croons her heart out. It soon becomes obvious that Lee's pop (Foulger) has been in cahoots with the robbers. Seems he was worried about how to provide for Lee's future and turned to bank robbery for needed funds. Autry and sidekick Burnette catch up with the outlaws and engage in a standard shoot-'em-up before resolving everything. Actually this film is less Autry's and more Lee's. She is seen more in the footage than the singing cowboy and gets more songs as well. Unfortunately she's not all that talented, and the result is a below-par entry for Autry's popular series.

p, Harry Grey; d, Lew Landers; w, Bradford Ropes, Doris Malloy (based on a story by Ropes); ph, William Nobles; ed, Tony Martinelli; md, Raoul Kraushaar; m/l, "What's Your Favorite Holiday?" Jule Styne, Sol Meyer (sung by Lee), "Ridin' on a Rainbow," Don George, Jean Herbert, Teddy Hall (sung by Autry).

Western   **Cas.**   **(PR:A MPAA:NR)**

RIDIN' THE LONE TRAIL zero   (1937) 56m REP bw

Bob Steele (Bob McArthur), Claire Rochelle (Joan Randall), Charles King (Dusty Williams), Ernie Adams (Peters), Lew Meehan (Sparks), Julian Rivero (Pedro), Steve Clark (Sheriff), Hal Price (Furman), Frank Ball (Randall), Jack Kirk.

A poorly made outing from Republic. It involves problems along a stagecoach line, and features a relatively unknown Steele. He was to go on to better films than this. RIDIN' THE LONE TRAIL is plagued with poorly dubbed sound, numerous unexplained anachronisms (such as steel windmills and the drone of airplanes!) and poorly produced effects. A film with such inferior production values was a rare disappointment, falling far below the quality of Republic westerns.

p, A.W. Hackel; d, Sam Newfield; w, Charles Francis Royal (based on a story by E.B. Mann); ph, Robert Cline; ed, S. Roy Luby.

Western   **Cas.**   **(PR:A MPAA:NR)**

RIDIN' THE OUTLAW TRAIL***   (1951) 56m COL bw

Charles Starrett (Steve Forsythe), Smiley Burnette (Himself), Sunny Vickers (Betsy Willard), Edgar Dearing (Pop Willard), Peter Thompson (Tom Chapman), Jim Bannon (Ace Conley), Lee Morgan (Sam Barton), Chuck Roberson (Reno), Ethan Laidlaw, Pee Wee King and His Golden West Cowboys.

$20,000 worth of newly minted $20 gold pieces are stolen and it's up to Starrett to recover the swag from outlaw Morgan. Morgan is killed by Bannon, who wants to melt down the coins and pass them off as gold nuggets. Dearing is an old prospector in cahoots with Bannon who swipes Burnette's blacksmith forge for the project. But Starrett, the Tex Ranger-cum-masked avenger stops them before they can have time to carry out the plan. This is a well-paced, exciting entry in the popular DURANGO KID series. (See DURANGO KID series, Index.)

p, Colbert Clark; d, Fred F. Sears; w, Victor Arthur; ph, Fayte Browne; ed, Paul Borofsky; md, Mischa Bakaleinikoff; art d, Charles Clague.

Western   **(PR:A MPAA:NR)**

RIDING AVENGER, THE**   (1936) 58m Diversion bw

Hoot Gibson (Buck Conners), Ruth Mix (Chita), Buzz Barton (Tony), June Gale (Jessie McCoy), Stanley Blystone (Mort Ringer), Roger Williams (The Marshal), Francis Walker (Welch), Charles Whitaker (Slim), Bud Buster (Bud), Blackie Whiteford.

Typical Western fare has Gibson going undercover to get at some rustlers. Lots of action and gunplay, though gunshots aren't as well synched on the soundtrack as possible. The dialog also leaves a little to be desired with its simplistic "oh yeahs" dotting characters' speech.

p, Walter Futter; d, Harry Fraser; w, Norman Houston (based on the story "Big Bend Buckaroo" by Walton West); ph, Paul Ivano; ed, Carl Himm.

Western   **Cas.**   **(PR:A MPAA:NR)**

RIDING HIGH**   (1937, Brit.) 68m EM/BL bw (AKA: REMEMBER WHEN)

Claude Dampier (Septimus Earwicker), John Garrick (Tom Blake), Kathleen Gibson (Grace Meadows), Helen Haye (Miss Broadbent), John Warwick (George Davenport), Billy Merson (Popping), Mai Bacon (Mrs. Winterbottom), Peter Gawthorne (Sir Joseph Wilmot), Billy Holland (Jack Adamson), Billy Bray (Ted Rance), Bertie Kendrick, The Georgian Singers, Mansell & Ling.

Garrick is a village blacksmith who invents a newfangled bicycle in his spare time. With the help of Dampier, the inventor enters the bike in a race and to everyone's surprise takes first place. A well-done comedy set against a convincing 1879 backdrop.

p, George King; d, David Macdonald; w, H. Fowler Mear; ph, Hone Glendinning.

Comedy   **(PR:A MPAA:NR)**

RIDING HIGH*½   (1943) 89m PAR c (GB: MELODY INN)

Dorothy Lamour (Ann Castle), Dick Powell (Steve Baird), Victor Moore (Mortimer J. Slocum), Gil Lamb (Bob "Foggy" Day), Cass Daley (Tess Connors), Bill Goodwin (Chuck Stuart), Rod Cameron (Sam Welch), Glenn Langan (Jack Holbrook), Milt Britton and His Band (Themselves), George Carleton (Dad Castle), Andrew Tombes (P. D. Smith), Douglas Fowley (Brown), Tim Ryan (Jones), Pierre Watkin (Masters), James Burke (Pete Brown), Roscoe Karns (Shorty), Patricia Mace (Jean Holbrook), Gwen Kenyon (Ginger), Lorraine Miller (Blanche), Stanley Andrews (Reynolds), Wade Boteler (Mailman), Fred A. Kelsey (Honest John Kelsey), Russell Simpson (Frenchy McQuire), Matt McHugh (Murphy), Tom Kennedy (Wilson), Cy Landry (Specialty Dancer), Stanley Price (Train Conductor), Dwight Butcher, Lane Chandler, William Edwards (Cowboys), Bruce Cameron (Head of Cameron Troupe), Leonard St. Leo, Ray Spiker, Walter Pietila, Bonnadene Wolfe, Flash Gordon, Paul Unger, Ramon Schaller, Richard Gottlieb (Members of the Cameron

Troupe), Charles Soldani *(Indian Chief)*, John Heistand *(Commentator)*, Napoleon Whiting *(Red Cap)*, Hal K. Dawson *(Master of Ceremonies)*, Louise La Planche, Marie McDonald, James Flavin, Charles R. Moore.

Lamour is an ex-burlesque star who heads out west for a visit to poppa Moore. He's a silver miner, but things haven't been going so well for him. Powell is a mining engineer and a convenient love interest for Lamour. She puts on a show for a local dude ranch to raise everyone's spirits and helps Powell run in a band of counterfeiters. The film is full of energy and spirit, but unfortunately the script is short on wit and long on stupidity. The songs are unmemorable, well beneath the talents of Powell and Lamour. The numbers include "You're the Rainbow," "Get Your Man," "Whistling in the Dark" (Ralph Rainger, Leo Robin), "I'm the Secretary to the Sultan" (Robin), "Injun Gal Heap Hep" (Rainger, Robin, Joseph Lilley), "Willie the Wolf of the West" (Johnny Mercer, Lilley), and "He Loved Me Till the All-Clear Came" (Mercer, Harold Arlen). How's that for song titles? The color photography is used well but is really wasted on this empty musical. An early outing for then 20-year-old Marie "The Body" McDonald.

p, Fred Kohlmar; d, George Marshall; w, Walter De Leon, Arthur Phillips, Art Arthur (based on the play "Ready Money" by James Montgomery); ph, Karl Struss, Barry Hallenberger (Technicolor); m, Victor Young; ed, LeRoy Stone; md, Young; art d, Hans Dreier, Ernst Fegte; ch, Danny Dare.

Musical/Western **(PR:A MPAA:NR)**

RIDING HIGH*½** (1950) 112m PAR bw

Bing Crosby *(Dan Brooks)*, Coleen Gray *(Alice Higgins)*, Charles Bickford *(J. L. Higgins)*, William Demarest *(Happy McGuire)*, Frances Gifford *(Margaret Higgins)*, Raymond Walburn *(Prof. Pettigrew)*, James Gleason *(Racing Secretary)*, Ward Bond *(Lee)*, Clarence Muse *(Whitey)*, Percy Kilbride *(Pop Jones)*, Harry Davenport *(Johnson)*, Irving Bacon *(Hamburger Man)*, Margaret Hamilton *(Edna)*, Douglas Dumbrille *(Eddie Morgan)*, Gene Lockhart *(J. P. Chase)*, Charles Lane *(Erickson)*, Frankie Darro *(Jockey Williams)*, Paul Harvey *(Whitehall)*, Marjorie Lord *(Mathilda Winslow)*, Marjorie Hoshelle *(Mary Early)*, Rand Brooks *(Henry Early)*, Willard Waterman *(Arthur Winslow)*, Dub Taylor *(Joe)*, Max Baer, Ish Kabibble, Oliver Hardy, Joe Frisco, Paul Harvey.

RIDING HIGH is one of the rare remakes that's on a par with the original. There's good reason for that, as Capra also did the fist version, BROADWAY BILL, and Robert Riskin's screenplay for that adaptation of a Mark Hellinger story has been kept as the basis for this one, with additional dialog by Rose and Shavelson. The first one starred Warner Baxter and Myrna Loy, who have been replaced here by Crosby and Gray, so you can expect some crooning to punctuate the jokes. Crosby is a horse trainer who is devoted to his steed. He falls for wealthy Gray but she's jealous of his affection for the animals and he is forced to choose between the two. Like a latter-day Gene Autry, he chooses the horse, who repays his love by winning the big race, making Crosby rich, and then dying in the process. She runs off with Max Baer and Crosby supervises the touching funeral for the horse. Many excellent set pieces in the picture, including a funny scene at a posh private club where Crosby is trying to con Walburn and Demarest out of some money, thinking that they're rich. The truth is that both men are trying to do the same to Crosby. Oliver Hardy does a brief bit as a harassed gambler and Joe Frisco, the stuttering comedian who lost it all to the swaybacks and made it back joking about it, also has a moment on screen. Songs by Jimmy Van Heusen and Johnny Burke include: "Someplace on Anywhere Road," "Sunshine Cake," "We've Got a Sure Thing," and "The Horse Told Me." Also included are two chestnuts: "The Whiffenpoof Song" (Tod B. Galloway, George S. Pomeroy, Meade Minnigerode) and "De Camptown Races" (Stephen Foster). It was getting near the end of the line for long-time actor Dumbrille, who was 60 at the time. His energy was boundless, though, and he proved it 10 years later when, at the age of 70, he married pal Alan Mowbray's 28-year-old daughter, Patricia.

p&d, Frank Capra; w, Robert Riskin, Nelville Shavelson, Jack Rose (based on the story "Broadway Bill" by Mark Hellinger); ph, George Barnes, Ernest Laszlo; ed, William Hornbeck; md, Victor Young; art d, Hans Dreier, Walter Tyler; set d, Emile Kuri; cos, Edith Head; spec eff, Farciot Edouart; makeup, Wally Westmore.

Musical Comedy **(PR:A MPAA:NR)**

RIDING ON*½ (1937) 59m Reliable bw

Tom Tyler *(Tom Roarke)*, Germaine Greer *(Gloria O'Neill)*, Rex Lease *(Danny)*, John Elliott *(Jess Roarke)*, Earl Dwire *(Buck O'Neill)*, Robert McKenzie *(Onderdonk)*, Roger Williams *(Bolton)*, Charles Whitaker *(Mike Gonzado)*.

Tyler returns home to find his father (Elliott) warring with rival Dwire over a cattle ford. Problems arise when Tyler falls in love with Greer, Dwire's daughter. Four gunfights later, all the troubles are over. It didn't even take an hour! Routine western with some pretty unbelievable action and so-so production qualities.

p, Bernard B. Ray; d, Harry S. Webb; w, Jack Neville (based on a story by Arthur H. Carhart); ph, Pliny Goodfriend; ed, Fred Bain.

Western **(PR:A MPAA:NR)**

RIDING ON AIR½** (1937) 70m RKO bw

Joe E. Brown *(Elmer Lane)*, Guy Kibbee *(Doc Waddington)*, Florence Rice *(Betty Harrison)*, Vinton Haworth *(Harvey Schumann)*, Anthony Nace *(Bill Hilton)*, Harlan Briggs *(Mr. Harrison)*, Andrew Tombes *(Mr. Byrd)*, Clem Bevans *(The Sheriff)*.

Complicated plot features Brown as the editor of a small town newspaper. He's in love with Rice, a local storekeeper's daughter, but her father (Briggs) doesn't approve of him. Brown is involved in a correspondence with a rival editor (Haworth), and the pair get mixed up with some smugglers and the invention of a radio beam. There's an aerial chase in small planes, one armed with a machine gun and Brown parachutes to safety. Kibbee is featured as a stock swindler in one of the film's sub-plots. There's a lot going on in this film, which sometimes makes it confusing for the audience. The fast-paced direction glosses over this, though, and Brown carries the comedy well. RIDING ON AIR was based on a series of short stories from the "Saturday Evening Post."

p, David L. Loew; d, Edward Sedgwick; w, Richard Flournoy, Richard Macaulay (based on stories by Macaulay); ph, Al Gilks; m, Arthur Morton; ed, Jack Ogilvie; art d, John Dycasse Schultze; spec eff, Fred Jackman.

Comedy **Cas.** **(PR:AA MPAA:NR)**

RIDING SHOTGUN** (1954) 74m WB c

Randolph Scott *(Larry Delong)*, Wayne Morris *(Tub Murphy)*, Joan Weldon *(Orissa Flynn)*, Joe Sawyer *(Tom Biggert)*, James Millican *(Dan Marady)*, Charles Buchinsky [Charles Bronson]*(Pinto)*, James Bell *(Doc Winkler)*, Fritz Feld *(Fritz)*, Richard Garrick *(Walters)*, Victor Perrin *(Bar-M Rider)*, John Baer *(Hughes)*, William Johnstone *(Col. Flynn)*, Kem Dibbs *(Ben)*, Alvin Freeman *(Johnny)*, Ned Young *(Manning)*, Paul Picerni *(Bob Purdee)*, Jay Lawrence *(Lewellyn)*, Jack Woody *(Hardpan)*, Richard Benjamin *(Blackie)*, Boyd Red Morgan *(Red)*, Mary Lou Holloway *(Cynthia Biggert)*, Lonnie Pierce *(Ellie)*, Dub Taylor *(Eddie)*, Evan Lowe, Holly Brooke *(Dance Hall Girls)*, Allegra Varron *(Mrs. Fritz)*, Edward Coch, Jr., Eva Lewis, Frosty Royse, Jimmy Mohley, Ruth Whitney, Bud Osborne, Budd Buster, Buddy Roosevelt, Joe Brockman, Harry Hines, Clem Fuller, Opan Evard, Morgan Brown, Bob Stephenson.

Scott's shotgun rider for a stagecoach. When some outlaws led by Morris discredit him, Scott has to convince the whole town that he's honest. It ends with a terrific gun battle in which Scott takes on the gang singlehandedly. For anyone else, this outing would have been considered routine, but it was well beneath the talents of an actor like Scott. By now he was a cowboy star of some stature, and a simplistic film like RIDING SHOTGUN was unworthy of him. Production credits are okay and instill some life into the film, but often it's an unintentionally funny piece. Buchinsky, who here made his first appearance in a western, later changed his name to Bronson, and the rest is history.

p, Ted Sherdeman; d, Andre de Toth; w, Tom Blackburn (based on the story "Riding Solo" by Kenneth Perkens); ph, Bert Glennon (Warner Color); m, David Buttolph; ed, Rudi Fehr; art d, Edward Carrere; set d, Benjamin S. Bone.

Western **(PR:A MPAA:NR)**

RIDING SPEED* (1934) 50m Superior bw

Buffalo Bill, Jr., Joile Benet, Bud Osborne, Lafe McKee, Clyde McClary, Allen Holbrook, Ernest Scott.

Buffalo Bill, Jr. stars in this forgettable western set along the Mexican border. A smuggling racket makes life dangerous for the locals but the film's heroic star clears the path for justice. Buffalo Bill, Jr., who also directed this programmer under his real name, Wilsey, had been a popular cowboy actor during the silent era, but, by the time this film was made his star had begun to fade rapidly. RIDING SPEED represents one of his last starring roles.

p, Victor Adamson [Denver Dixon]; d, Jay Wilsey [Buffalo Bill, Jr.]; w, Dolores Booth (based on the story by Ella May Cook).

Western **(PR:A MPAA:NR)**

RIDING TALL (SEE: SQUARES, 1972)

RIDING THE CHEROKEE TRAIL** (1941) 61m MON bw

Tex Ritter *(Tex)*, Slim Andrews *(Slim)*, Forrest Taylor *(Craven)*, Betty Miles *(Ruth)*, Jack Roper *(Squint)*, Fred Burns *(Wyatt)*, Bruce Nolan *(Dirk)*, Gene Alsace *(Bat)*, Bob Card, Ed Cassidy, Hal Price, The Tennessee Ramblers: Gillette Blair, Happy Tex Martin, Cecil Campbell, Kid Clark, Chuck Baldra, White Flash the Horse.

With some vacation time coming, Ritter takes off from the Texas Rangers with mule-riding buddy Andrews and heads for Idaho to go fishing. But trouble arises and the vacation ends abruptly as the pair find themselves entangled in a murder. Taylor's the culprit, but Ritter saves the day. He fools Taylor and his gang into heading to Texas where the rangers can put the cuffs on them. A weak outing for Ritter, more predictable than usual.

p, Edward Finney; d, Spencer G. Bennett; w, Edmond Kelso; ph, Marcel LePicard; ed, Robert Golden; m/l, Jack Gillette, Harry Blair.

Western **(PR:A MPAA:NR)**

RIDING THE SUNSET TRAIL*** (1941) 56m MON bw

Tom Keene *(Tom Sterling)*, Betty Miles *(Betty Dawson)*, Frank Yaconelli *(Lopez Mendoza)*, Sugar Dawn *(Sugar Dawn)*, Slim Andrews *(Jasper Raines)*, Ken Duncan *(Jay Lynch)*, Fred Hoose *(Judge Little)*, Gene Alsace [Rocky Camron]*(Pecos Dean)*, Tom Seidel *(Bronco West)*, Earle Douglas *(Drifter Smith)*, Tom London *(Sheriff Hays)*, James Sheridan [Sherry Tansey] *(Rip Carson)*, Jimmy Aubrey *(Jim Dawson)*, Rusty the Horse.

Good effort from Keene features the movie cowboy chasing down a mystery. Aubrey has been shot dead by Seidel and Douglas who are working for Aubrey's half brother Duncan. Duncan's got a fake will that will allow him to get his hands on Aubrey's fortune. He forces Miles and Dawn (a Shirley Temple type) off their late father's property and takes their cattle. In rides Keene with sidekick Yaconelli to solve the crime and save the day. Some good production values and a rousing performance by Keene give this routine programmer some good moments. It was the best Keene film in a while after a string of turkeys.

p&d, Robert Tansey;w, Robert Emmett, Francis Kavanaugh; ph, Marcel LePicard; m, Frank Sanucci; ed, Fred Bain.

Western **(PR:A MPAA:NR)**

RIDING THE WIND½** (1942) 60m RKO bw

Tim Holt *(Clay Stewart)*, Ray Whitley *(Smokey)*, Mary Douglas *(Joan)*, Lee "Lasses" White *(Whopper)*, Eddie Dew *(Henry Dodge)*, Earle Hodgins *(Burt MacLeod)*, Kate Harrington *(Martha)*, Charles Phipps *(Ezra Westfall)*, Ernie Adams *(Jones)*, Larry Steers *(Jackson)*, Bud Osborne *(Chuck Brown)*, Karl Hackett, Hank Worden, Larry Steers, Frank McCarroll, Bob Burns.

A group of ranchers are forced to pay dearly for water rights when Dew builds a dam that cuts their land off from the river. Holt is a rancher who tries to stop the nefarious goings-on, which causes Dew to nearly blow up the dam and flood all of the cattle country. Of course, Holt puts a stop to any such plans. Production values are okay, though the script could have been better. It's all formula, with Holt playing his part nicely. Dew sports a Scottish accent, a real rarity for villains (or good guys for that matter) in B westerns.

p, Bert Gilroy; d, Edward Killy; w, Earl Snell, Morton Grant (based on a story by Bernard McConville); ph, Harry Wild; ed, Fred Knudtson; md, Paul Sawtell; m/l, "Ridin' the Wind," "I'll Live Until I Die," "Goin' on a Hayride Tonight,"Fred Rose, Ray Whitley.

Western **(PR:A MPAA:NR)**

RIDING TORNADO, THE½** (1932) 64m COL bw

Tim McCoy, Shirley Grey, Wallace MacDonald, Russell Simpson, Montague Love, Wheeler Oakman, Vernon Dent, Lafe McKee, Bud Osborne, Hank Bell, Art Mix [George Kesterson], Silver Tip Baker, Tex Palmer, Artie Ortego.

Famed bronc rider McCoy takes a job on Grey's ranch. He falls for her, which annoys the ranch foreman no end. The foreman (Oakman) is really the leader of a gang of rustlers, and he quits his job to concentrate more on thievery. He takes Grey with him and McCoy goes a-chasing after them. This routine horse opera is vastly improved by McCoy's better-than-required performance. He maintains a certain intensity throughout the place. Facial close-ups in a poker game are used to great effect, something quite rare in Western programmers.

p, Irving Briskin; d, D. Ross Lederman; w, Kurt Kempler (based on a story by William Colt MacDonald); ph, Benjamin Kline); ed, Otto Mayer.

Western **Cas.** **(PR:A MPAA:NR)**

RIDING WEST½** (1944) 58m COL

Charles Starrett *(Steve Jordan)*, Arthur Hunnicutt *(Prof. Arkansas Higgins)*, Shirley Patterson *(Alice Morton)*, Ernest Tubb *(Ernie)*, Steve Clark *(Alexander Morton)*, Wheeler Oakman *(Capt. Amos Karnes)*, J. P. "Blackie" Whiteford *(Sgt. Dobbs)*, Clancy Cooper *(Blackburn)*, Bill Wilkerson *(Red Eagle)*, Johnny Bond.

Starrett is trying to start a Pony Express run, but he is hampered by some nasty gamblers who want a piece of the action. Routine western with some fairly exciting action. Patterson is the romantic interest, though her role is virtually nonexistent.

p, Jack Fier; d, William Berke; w, Luci Ward; ph, Benjamin Kline; ed, Jerome Thomas; art d, Lionel Banks.

Western **(PR:A MPAA:NR)**

RIFF RAFF GIRLS½** (1962, Fr./Ital.) 97m l'Etoile-Dismage-Transalpina-Techno Stampa/CD bw (DU RIFIFI CHEZ LES FEMMES; RIFIFI FRA LE DONNE; AKA: RIFIFI FOR GIRLS)

Nadja Tiller *(Vicky)*, Robert Hossein *(Marcel)*, Silvia Monfort *(Yoko)*, Roger Hanin *(The Bug)*, Pierre Blanchar *(The Pirate)*, Francoise Rosay *(Berthe)*, Eddie Constantine *(Williams)*, Jean Gaven *(James)*, Georges Rigaud *(The Marquis)*, Andre Cellier *(Bank Guard)*, Carlo Campanini, Tiberio Murgia.

Some major repairs are being made on the Bank of Belgium's roof while the Brussels Exposition is going on. A group of thieves, masterminded by Rigaud, a Parisian crook, decide that this would be the perfect time to help themselves to Exposition receipts held by the bank. Tiller, the money-mad operator of a river barge-cum-nightclub, is a member of the gang. She's been scarred by childhood memories of wartime France. Other robbers include Gaven as her assistant and Hossein. He's the inside man, posing as a construction worker in the bank's rehabbing. But problems arise when Tiller won't sell her nightclub to a deported gangster called "The Bug" (Hanin). Hanin gets angry and has his mistress Monfort lead a group of lady gangsters in wrecking the club. Hossein realizes that this could destroy all the plans and arranges a meeting between Rigaud and Hanin. A third party (Blanchar) arranges a truce and Tiller agrees to sell her club within the week. But Hanin is faced with deportation once more unless he blows the lid on an important waterfront drug-smuggling operation. He mistakenly assumes that Tiller's club is the headquarters and rats on her. He kidnaps Gaven and tries to work his way into the robbery scheme. A ferocious gun battle follows in which the rival gangs kill each other off.

p, Jacques Mage; d, Alex Joffe; w, Auguste Le Breton, Joffe, Mage, Jose Giovanni, Gabriel Arout (based on Le Breton's novel *Du Riffi Chez Les Femmes*; adaptation by Le Breton, Joffe, Mage, Jose Giovanni, Gaberiel Arout); ph, Pierre Montazel; m, Louiguy; ed, Leonide Azar; art d, Rino Mondellini; m/l, Louiguy, Charles Aznavour.

Crime **(PR:O MPAA:NR)**

RIFF-RAFF*** (1936) 89m MGM bw (AKA: RIFFRAFF)

Jean Harlow *(Hattie)*, Spencer Tracy *(Dutch Miller)*, Joseph Calleia *(Nick Appopolis)*, Una Merkel *(Lil)*, Mickey Rooney *(Jimmy)*, Victor Kilian *(Flytrap)*, J. Farrell MacDonald *(Brains)*, Roger Imhof *(Pops)*, Baby Jane "Juanita" Quigley *(Rosie)*, Paul Hurst *(Red Belcher)*, Vince Barnett *(Lew)*, Dorothy Appleby *(Gertie)*, Judith Wood *(Mabel)*, Arthur Housman *(Ratsy)*, Wade Boteler *(Bert)*, Joe Phillips *(Al)*, William Newell *(Pete)*, Al Hill *(Speed)*, Helen Flint *(Sadie)*, Lillian Harmer *(Mrs. McCall)*, Robert Perry *(Lefty)*, George Givot *(Markis)*, Helene Costello *(Maisie)*, Rafaela Ottiano *(Head Matron)*, King Mojavea, Al Herman, Philo McCullough, Sherry Hall, Jack Byron, Stanley Price, Herman Marx, Eddie Sturgis, John George *(Fishermen)*, Ivor McFadden *(Moving Man)*, Mary Wallace *(Fisherman's Wife)*, Wally Maher *(Newsreel Cameraman)*, Marshall Ruth *(Agitator)*.

A tragic romance with Harlow donning a brown wig in place of her platinum blonde trademark and being cast as a fisherman's daughter who works in a tuna cannery. She falls in love with Tracy, a big-headed fisherman who leads his fellow workers to a strike at the urging of Hurst, a strike-maker who is hired by cannery owner Calleia. Calleia benefits from the strike, while the fishermen lose out. Tracy is kicked out of the union and, distressed, leaves his waterfront home and his newlywed wife Harlow. Later Harlow receives word that Tracy is penniless and sickly. She begs Calleia for money and when he refuses she decides to steal it. Tracy is too proud to accept her offering, so she gives the money to Hurst, who promises to deliver it to her husband. Hurst keeps the money for himself, and Harlow winds up in prison. When Tracy discovers what she's done he roughs up Hurst and rushes to the prison. Unknown to Tracy, Harlow has given birth to a child while behind bars. Having returned to the waterfront, Tracy gets back into good graces with Calleia by preventing Hurst from carrying out a plot to sabotage the tuna ships. Hearing of the sabotage attempt, Harlow mistakenly assumes that Tracy has been injured, and escapes from prison to be at his side. After finding him healthy, she agrees to finish her jail term. Tracy, in return, promises to await her release and the family life that will follow. While not Tracy's or Harlow's most-remembered film, RIFF-RAFF provides a fine waterfront locale as well as some snappy, hard-boiled dialog penned by two of Hollywood's top female writers, Marion and Loos, with help from Hanemann. Although saddled with a basically unlikable character, Tracy skillfully tackles his role and manages to keep the audience in sympathy throughout.

p, Irving Thalberg; d, J. Walter Ruben; w, Frances Marion, H.W. Hanemann, Anita Loos (based on a story by Marion); ph, Ray June; m, Edward Ward; ed, Frank Sullivan; art d, Cedric Gibbons, Stanwood Rogers; cos, Dolly Tree.

Drama **(PR:A MPAA:NR)**

RIFFRAFF½** (1947) 80m RKO bw

Pat O'Brien *(Dan)*, Walter Slezak *(Molinar)*, Anne Jeffreys *(Maxine)*, Percy Kilbride *(Pop)*, Jerome Cowan *(Walter Gredson)*, George Givot *(Rues)*, Jason Robards *(Dominquez)*, Marc Krah *(Hasso)*, Bonnie Blair *(Girl at Airport)*, Drew Miller *(Pilot)*, Julian Rivero *(Passenger Agent)*, Bob O'Connor *(Taxi Driver)*, Tom Noonan *(Drunk)*, Betty Hill, Virginia Owen *(Singers)*, Carmen Lopez *(Hula Dancer)*, Lou Lubin *(Rabbit)*, Eduardo Noriega *(Felice)*, Eddie Borden *(Man)*.

O'Brien's after a map that will lead him to some rich oil deposits in Panama. Also after the prized piece of paper is Slezak, the leader of some baddies. Jeffreys plays a nightclub singer who provides O'Brien with some relief now and then. Generally this is a well acted piece, though the script isn't very interesting. Jeffreys had previously served as a B film actress, and this was her first crack at a bigger picture. The direction is by Tetzlaff, a first effort for the man who had photographed Hitchcock's NOTORIOUS the previous year. The influence of the master director is obvious in the interesting use of camera angles and shadowing to achieve effect.

p, Nat Holt; d, Ted Tetzlaff; w, Martin Rackin; ph, George E. Diskant; m, Roy Webb; ed, Philip Martin; md, C. Bakaleinikoff; art d, Albert S. D'Agostino, Walter E. Keller; set d, Darrell Silvera, Michael Orenbach; spec eff, Russell A. Cully; m/l, "Money Is the Root of All Evil," Joan Whitney, Alex Kramer; cos, Renie.

Comedy/Drama **(PR:A MPAA:NR)**

RIFIFFI A TOKYO (SEE: RIFIFI IN TOKYO, 1963, Fr.)

RIFIFI***** (1956, Fr.) 117m Indus-Pathe-Prima/United Motion Pictures bw (AKA: DU RIFIFI CHEZ DES HOMMES)

Jean Servais *(Tony le Stephanois)*, Carl Mohner *(Jo Le Suedois)*, Robert Manuel *(Mario)*, Perlo Vita [Jules Dassin] *(Cesar)*, Magali Noel *(Viviane)*, Marie Sabouret *(Mado)*, Janine Darcy *(Louise)*, Pierre Grasset *(Louis Grutter)*, Robert Hossein *(Remi Grutter)*, Marcel Lupovici *(Pierre Grutter)*, Dominique Maurin *(Tonio)*, Claude Sylvain *(Ida)*.

RIFIFI is the grandfather of all the caper movies that followed. Not that there hadn't been any prior to this, but few of them came close to the detail seen here. Dassin, an American, had been in trouble with the House Un-American Activities Committee and when that hassle with HUAC made it impossible for him to ply his trade as a writer-director-actor, he went to Europe and reestablished himself. His direction of BRUTE FORCE, THE NAKED CITY, and THIEVES HIGHWAY made him a powerful man in movies while still in his thirties. RIFIFI, which is French slang for "brawl" or "trouble," was his second movie overseas. It began a cycle of caper films which included TOPKAPI, BANK SHOT, THE KILLING, and many more. Four crooks get together to rob an expensive jewelry salon on the Rue Rivoli in Paris. Servais is the leader of the quartet (Mohner, Manuel, Vita) who execute the robbery. The sequence takes about a half-hour, has not one word of dialog, no music, and the only sound heard are the actual ones made as they go into the apartment above the store, drill a hole in the floor of the apartment, then slip an umbrella through and open it so the debris does not hit the floor and trip the alarm. The fire extinguisher's contents are used to dull the alarm bell to only a mild purr where it would otherwise be a loud clang. They peel away the safe's door like the top of a can and make the grab. Then, of course, things begin to happen. A rival gang led by Hussein and Lupovici learns of the robbery and wants to cut themselves in, so the child of one of the conspirators is kidnaped and held. One of the crooks gives a stolen piece of jewelry to a girl and dies for his passion. The other gang is killed, the child is saved, and the lone remaining member of the gang finally dies in his car of gunshot wounds. It's the usual "stroke of Fate" ending that the French often tacked on to the finales of their gangster movies, but this time it's right. There are a few comic moments to relieve the tension and the editing is superlative. Dassin's directorial styles make the viewer feel as though a co-crook in the proceedings. Dassin shared a Best Director award at Cannes for his work and can be seen under his acting pseudonym here as Perlo Vita. So many movies owe their inspiration to RIFIFI that it would take page after page to name them. There were funny versions, BIG DEAL ON MADONNA STREET and CRACKERS, tongue-in-cheek versions like GAMBIT, and direct lifts like THIEF. Further, life did imitate art, as many criminals used some of the techniques in the film to perpetrate actual thefts. There are some similarities to THE ASPHALT JUNGLE, but this is so very French (despite the American director, co-writer) that it seems to be a fresh look at the subject. A cinematic achievement. (In French; English subtitles).

p, Rene G. Vuattoux; d, Jules Dassin; w, Dassin, Rene Wheeler, Auguste Le Breton (based on the novel by Le Breton); ph, Philippe Agostini; m, Georges Auric; ed, Roger Dwyre; art d, Auguste Capelier; m/l, "Rififi," Phillipe Gerard, Jacques Laure.

Crime   Cas.   (PR:A-C MPAA:NR)

RIFIFI FOR GIRLS (SEE: RIFF RAFF GIRLS, 1962, Fr./Ital.)

RIFIFI FRA LE DONNE (SEE: RIFF RAFF GIRLS, 1962, Fr./Ital.)

RIFIFI IN PARIS (SEE: UPPER HAND, THE, 1967, Fr./Ital./Ger.)

RIFIFI IN TOKYO½ (1963, Fr./Ital.) 89m C.C.M.-CIPRA/MGM bw (RIFIFI A TOKYO)

Karl Boehm (Carl Mersen), Michel Vitold (Merigne), Charles Vanel (Van Hekken), Eric Okada (Danny Riquet), Keiko Kishi (Asami), Barbara Lass (Francoise Merigne), Eijiro Yanagi (Ishimoto), Hideaki Suzuki, Dante Maggio, Masao Oda.

This is one of several pictures that attempted to cash in on the success of RIFIFI. Another caper plot with not enough time taken to let us know who the people are. RIFIFI IN TOKYO has Vanel coming to the Japanese capital to steal a huge jewel that is protected by an impregnable security system in the largest bank vault in town. But Vanel, like all the crooks one sees in this kind of movie, has a plan. Vanel's assistant is Okada (an Oriental with an occidental name) and he's killed by a local crime boss who also wants the diamond. Upon hearing of Okada's murder, Boehm joins Vanel. Okada and Boehm had been service buddies and now Boehm wants to exact revenge. Boehm falls for Merigne, who is married to Vitold, the electrical whiz who will knock out the security system. The crime is committed and Vanel gets the gem. Just as Vanel is about to follow Boehm and the others out, a barred door slides down and traps Vanel inside with no hope of escape. Vanel knows that it's all over for him, as the cops are probably on their way by now, so he puts his hand through the bars to give the gem to Boehm. But Boehm, knowing that he might be caught and that if he's caught with the jewel, that's evidence, says "no" and races out just before the authorities descend. As he's fleeing, Boehm hears the unmistakable sound of a gunshot. Vanel has killed himself rather than face arrest. Nice location photography in and around the wrong side of the Ginza in Tokyo and some good acting, but it was 8 years after the original and many others had been made since, so we are left with the uncomfortable feeling of deja vuupon seeing this.

p, Jacques Bar; d, Jacques Deray; w, Jose Giovanni, Deray, Rodolphe M. Arloud (based on the story by Auguste Le Breton); ph, Tadashi Arakami; m, Georges Delerue; art d, Hirataka; ed, Albert Jurgenson.

Crime   (PR:A-C MPAA:NR)

RIFIFI INTERNAZIONALE (SEE: UPPER HAND, THE, 1967, Fr./Ital./Ger.)

RIGHT AGE TO MARRY, THE** (1935, Brit.) 69m GS Enterprises/RKO bw

Frank Pettingell (Lomas), Joyce Bland (Ellen), Tom Helmore (Stephen), Ruby Miller (Mrs. Carlisle), Moira Lind (Carol), Hal Walters (Crowther), H. F. Maltby (Tetley), Gerald Barry (Maj. Locke), Isobel Scaife (Clara), Vincent Holman, Reginald Bates.

Pettingell retires from the mill he has built up, leaving it in the hands of nephew Helmore. A widow looking for a rich new husband brings him into high society, but the socialites make fun of him and his Yorkshire manners. All his new friends desert him when the uninsured mill burns down, so he marries his likable housekeeper and goes back to work rebuilding the mill. Good performance by Pettingell helps this otherwise standard comedy.

p, A. George Smith; d, Maclean Rogers; w, H. F. Maltby, Kathleen Butler (based on the play by Maltby); ph, Geoffrey Faithfull.

Comedy   (PR:A MPAA:NR)

RIGHT APPROACH, THE** (1961) 92m FOX bw

Frankie Vaughan (Leo Mack), Martha Hyer (Anne Perry), Juliet Prowse (Ursula Poe), Gary Crosby (Rip Hulett), David McLean (Bill Sikulovic), Jesse White (Brian Freer), Jane Withers (Liz), Rachel Stephens (Helen), Steve Harris (Mitch Mack), Paul Von Schreiber (Granny), Robert Casper (Horace).

After being discharged from the Army, five buddies take an empty Pasadena restaurant and turn it into an apartmant complex for themselves. Harris convinces the other four to take in his brother Vaughan, who turns out out be an unethical, self-centered would-be actor. He soon talked the other guys out of their cash and their clothing. In addition he cozies up to Prowse, a money-hungry car hop who's after one of the residents. (It seems the guy's mother is a millionaire.) While helping Prowse, Vaughan manages to have an affair with her as well, and he expects a share of the money if she succeeds. Vaughn then takes up with Hyer, a photographer for Life magazine. He talks her into doing a story on the complex, taking most of the credit as well as finagling his picture on the cover of the magazine. This gets him just what he wants, fame and an agent. But at a party Hyer finally sees him for what he is and Prowse turns up pregnant. He's forced to marry her, and the other guys throw him out of the complex. He is on the verge of

fame but has paid a high price for it. THE RIGHT APPROACH is a film that never lives up to its title. Vaughan's character has not a single redeeming quality, which makes this a difficult film to watch. He's just too unsavory to be believed. Direction is lackluster with a naive attitude toward what could have been sophisticated material. This was supposed to be the film that would catapult Vaughan to Hollywood stardom, but of course, it missed that mark by a long way. The script is an adaptation of a play by Garson Kanin done by his brother Michael and sister-in-law Fay Kanin.

p, Oscar Brodney; d, David Butler; w, Fay and Michael Kanin (based on the play "The Live Wire" by Garson Kanin); ph, Sam Leavitt (CinemaScope); m, Dominic Frontiere; ed, Tom McAdoo; art d, Duncan Cramer, Herman A. Blumenthal; set d, Walter M. Scott, Fred MacLean; ch, Josephine Earl; makeup, Ben Nye; m/l, title song, Marilyn Keith, Alan Berhman, Lew Spence, "When You Least Expect It, " Sammy Stept, "Lady, Love Me," Kirby Stone (sung by the Kirby Stone Four, Frankie Vaughan).

Drama   (PR:A MPAA:NR)

RIGHT CROSS*** (1950) 90m MGM bw

June Allyson (Pat O'Malley), Dick Powell (Rick Gavery), Ricardo Montalban (Johnny Monterez), Lionel Barrymore (Sean O'Malley), Teresa Celli (Marian Monterez), Barry Kelley (Allan Goff), Tom Powers (Robert Balford), Mimi Aguglia (Mom Monterez), Marianne Stewart (Audrey), John Gallaudet (Phil Tripp), David Fresco (Gump), Smoki Whitfield (Nassau), Harry Shannon (Haggerty), Frank Ferguson (Dr. George Lamond), David Wolfe (Totem), Marilyn Monroe (Blonde), Dewey Robinson (Hanger-On), Jim Pierce (Moe), Ed Dearing (Ring Announcer), Tom Hanlon (Sports Announcer), Larry Keating, King Donavan, Wally Maher, Bert Davison, Ken Tobey (Reporters).

Fairly good fight story with the extra attraction of some humor, good boxing footage, and an overtone of social studies. Montalban is a prizefighter at the top of his form. He's the champ in his weight class but still unhappy, as he feels that there is prejudice against him because he's a Mexican. It's all in his head, though. No one much cares where a boxer is from as long as he can feint, spar, and deliver the old one-two when he has to. Montalban is handled by Barrymore, a wheelchair-rider who used to be one of the top dogs in the business but now only manages the fortunes of Montalban. Kelley is a successful promoter-manager and wants Montalban's contract, but the champ won't hear of it because Barrymore's daughter is Allyson and he loves her. Their relationship is sparked by excellent dialog as he is, at once, being bugged by her (in her role as the dutiful daughter) and enamored of her. Montalban is a loner, suspicious of everyone and almost paranoid about his heritage. He lets few people into his confidence. One of them is Powell, a newspaper-man who specializes in the fights. It's questionable if Powell hangs around Montalban because he likes him or because he's sweet on Allyson (his real life sweetie). Powell isn't blind and sees she loves Montalban, so he finds solace in booze and blondes, (one of them being Marilyn Monroe in her eighth film, an unbilled role). Montalban's powerful right cross is fading and his fear is that he doesn't have much more time wearing the crown. He loves Allyson and Barrymore so much that he decides to go with Kelley on the chance that the old-timer can promote some lucrative bouts and he can retire with enough dinero to marry Allyson and support Barrymore. No sooner does Barrymore hear of Montalban's decision to leave, than he keels over with coronary arrest. Allyson is hurt, angry, frustrated, and now hates Montalban for what he did, although she doesn't know the real reason. Montalban risks his crown in one last fight and loses, but collects a huge purse for his efforts. Afterward, in his dressing room, he gets in a fight with Powell, throws a punch, and breaks his already-weakened right hand, thus effectively putting an end to his career. In the final scenes, Montalban is at his training camp and Powell and Allyson follow him, convincing him that all is well and that they now understand what he did. Allyson and Montalban will be together and Powell is just happy to be the best friend. No underworld characters, no fixing of fights, and, in a refreshing turn of events, the boxer loses the big fight. For that alone, this picture forgets cliches and has a few good reasons to see it. Barrymore's wheelchair was real. He had a combination of arthritis and an old leg injury that put him in the chair since the late 1930s. He was 72 when he made this and was still going strong as an actor and a painter until he died four years later.

p, Armand Deutsch; d, John Sturges; w, Charles Schnee; ph, Norbert Brodine; m, David Raksin; ed, James E. Newcom; art d, Cedric Gibbons, James Scognamillo.

Boxing Drama   (PR:A-C MPAA:NR)

RIGHT HAND OF THE DEVIL, THE* (1963) 75m Aram Katcher/Cinema Video International bw

Aram Katcher (Pepe Lusara), Lisa McDonald (Miss Sutherland), Brad Trumbull (Williams), James V. Christy (Sammy), Chris Randall (Spooky), Monte Lee (Carter), Luigi Gardneri (Dino's Bartender), Georgia Holden (The Dancer), Jack Elton (Dino's Pianist).

Upon arriving in Los Angeles, gangster Katcher leases a deserted Laurel Canyon mansion as his base of operations. He plans to rob the Hollywood Sports Arena and hires some local thugs as his crew. McDonald is the lonely cashier at the Arena whom Katcher proceeds to court, soon he has her involved as well. The robbery is successful and Katcher manages to elude the police who try to nab him in a wild chase. Katcher steals some acid from a chemical warehouse and puts it in a bathtub. This he uses to destroy the bodies of the accomplices whom he has already done away with. Assuming that everyone who had helped him is dead, Katcher heads for Rio. But after his money's gone he returns to Hollywood, only to be killed by McDonald. Katcher is a one-man show here, serving as producer, director, writer, and star. The result is a sort of strange ego-fest in which he mugs it up like a bad Peter Lorre. As a writer/director he lacks any sense of style or comprehension of how to build suspense. The result is either a bad crime picture or an unintentional laugh-fest. Take your pick.

p&d, Aram Katcher; w, Ralph Brooke (based on a story by Katcher); ph, Fouad Said; m, John Bath; ed, Katcher; makeup, Katcher.

Crime Drama **(PR:C MPAA:NR)**

RIGHT MAN, THE (SEE: HER FIRST ROMANCE, 1940)

RIGHT OF WAY, THE* (1931) 65m WB-FN

Conrad Nagel *(Charles "Beauty" Steele)*, Loretta Young *(Rosalie Evantural)*, Fred Kohler *(Joseph Portugais)*, William Janney *(Billy Wantage)*, Snitz Edwards *(Luis Trudel)*, George Pierce *(The Cure)*, Halliwell Hobbes *(The Seigneur)*, Olive Teil *(Katherene Steele)*, Brandon Hurst *(Crown Attorney)*, Yola d'Avril *(Suzette)*.

Nagel is a dapper Quebec attorney. He has an unhappy marriage and is constantly harrassed for money by his brother-in-law. When the punk steals some money from Nagel, the lawyer goes searching for him and ends up in a waterfront saloon. There Nagel gets knocked around by some thugs and ends up losing his memory. Not knowing who he is or what he does, Nagel becomes a tailor and falls for a young post office clerk; but eventually his memory returns and he has no choice but to go back to his wife. Luckily for him the woman has believed him to be dead and has consequently remarried. This is the third version of the story after two silent filmings, one in 1915 and the other in 1920. Sound doesn't do much for the story, an overly dramatic cliche-ridden soaper. The dialog is simplistic and over-written. The cast tries awfully hard and ends up being awfully trying. Nagel is miscast with the worst results.

d, Frank Lloyd; w, Francis E. Faragoh (based on the novel by Sir Gilbert Parker); ph, John Seitz; ed, Terrill Morse.

Drama **(PR:A MPAA:NR)**

RIGHT STUFF, THE***** (1983) 192m Ladd/WB c

Sam Shepard *(Chuck Yeager)*, Scott Glenn *(Alan Shepard)*, Ed Harris *(John Glenn)*, Dennis Quaid *(Gordon Cooper)*, Fred Ward *(Gus Grissom)*, Barbara Hershey *(Glennis Yeager)*, Kim Stanley *(Bancho Barnes)*, Veronica Cartwright *(Betty Grissom)*, Pamela Reed *(Trudy Cooper)*, Scott Paulin *(Deke Slayton)*, Charles Frank *(Scott Carpenter)*, Lance Henriksen *(Wally Schirra)*, Donald Moffat *(Lyndon B. Johnson)*, Levon Helm *(Jack Ridley)*, Mary Jo Deschanel *(Annie Glenn)*, Scott Wilson *(Scott Crossfield)*, Kathy Baker *(Louise Shepard)*, Mickey Crocker *(Marge Slayton)*, Susan Kase *(Rene Carpenter)*, Mittie Smith *(Jo Schirra)*, Royal Dano *(Minister)*, David Clennon *(Liaison Man)*, Jim Haynie *(Air Force Major)*, Jeff Goldblum, Harry Shearer *(Recruiters)*, Scott Beach *(Chief Scientist)*, Jane Dornacker *(Nurse Murch)*, Anthony Munoz *(Gonzales)*, John P. Ryan *(Head of Program)*, Darryl Henriques *(Life Reporter)*, Eric Sevareid *(Himself)*, William Russ *(Slick Goodin)*, Edward Anhalt *(Grand Designer)*, Mary Apick *(Woman Reporter)*, Robert Beer *(Dwight D. Eisenhower)*, Erik Bergmann *(Eddie Hodges)*, Maureen Coyne *(Waitress)*, Peggy David *(Sally Rand)*, John Denner *(Henry Luce)*, Robert Elross *(Review Board President)*, Robert J. Geary *(Game Show M.C.)*, David Gulpilil *(Aborigine)*, Anthony Wallace *(Australian Driver)*, Kaaren Lee *(Young Widow)*, Gen. Chuck Yeager *(Fred)*.

The fact that this $25 million, three-years-in-the-making picture crashed at the box office in no way detracts from its being one of the best ever about what its like to be an astronaut. In the light of the 1986 tragedy that took the lives of other brave adventurers into space, seeing this movie now makes it all the more powerful when one realizes that so many months of training go into what they do and that life in a six-story skyscraper with a solid rocket fuel fuse attached can be precarious. William Goldman (MAGIC, BUTCH CASSIDY AND THE SUNDANCE KID, etc.) wrote a first draft that eliminated the Chuck Yeager role and was to have been directed by Michael Ritchie (THE CANDIDATE, etc.), but when Ritchie's picture THE ISLAND sunk faster than Krakatoa, that was aborted. Kaufman came aboard as helmsman and he and Goldman did not see eye to eye. Goldman stepped aside after having finished his adaptation of Wolfe's factual book, then Kaufman took a totally different tack, included Yeager's story, and was quite right to do that. What is "THE RIGHT STUFF"? Yeager, who was technical advisor on the film and played a small part, said: "We were doing a job. If you had the experience and the training and a little luck, you were successful." Yeager was modest. It's having the courage and the intelligence and the desire to be the best and is not limited to astronauts by any means. The movie spans about 15 years in time, beginning with Shepard (as Yeager) breaking mach 1 and concluding with the huge barbecue at the Astrodome at which President Johnson (Moffat) hosted the astronauts. In between, it's more than three hours of excitement. The actors are similar in looks to their real-life counterparts and Ed Harris as John Glenn is downright eerie. So much so that there was a bit of a problem because Glenn was running for the presidential nomination and his opponents felt there was unfair advantage in seeing him in such a heroic fashion. The movie takes few liberties with the truth because it didn't have to, as the real stories were fascinating. Yeager was not considered as having "The Right Stuff" because he didn't have a college degree, so Kaufman intercuts Shepard with the others and we see the differences between them as well as the similarities. The training is, to say the least, arduous and not a beat of it is omitted. Also not omitted is the home life of the men and their wives, limned with economy and sympathy, although their stories are not the focus of the film. Despite the seriousness of the space race (which came to the fore after the Russians launched their Sputnik and the U.S. was determined to stay out of second place), there is a great deal of humor in the intertwining of the lives. Some of the laughs were criticized at the time of the picture's release, but they never get in the way and are a welcome respite from the tension. All of the individual incidents are handled wonderfully. Ward (as Gus Grissom) has his capsule sink upon splashing into the sea and barely makes it out alive; Shepard (Yeager) crashes his plane in the desert in an attempt to set a new high-altitude record; Harris (as Glenn) has his heat shield almost disintegrate as he makes his way back into the Earth's atmosphere; the men have to provide the scientists with sperm samples; Deschanel (as Glenn's wife, Annie) won't go on TV with Moffat because she fears her stuttering will set people laughing and Harris backs her up all the way; Quaid (as Cooper) shows himself to have an ego every bit as tall as a rocket booster, and so on. There is even a bit of the occult as Quaid travels to the forsaken Austalian outback to oversee a tracking station. While there, he encounters an ancient aborigine (Gulpilil) who is said to be on familiar terms with what happens "Up There." Harris' flight is becoming a difficulty and the natives start to brew a special concoction to help. This sends up a shower of sparks and we cut to the sky and see Harris' capsule surrounded by sparks. Although the film doesn't say that Gulpilil's magic did the trick, there is no mistaking that's what they meant. These first men are celebrated, whereas the bureaucrats are scorned. That the group has "The Right Stuff" is never in doubt. That very few of anyone else in the film can come close is also hammered home. The wives should be cited for their work as well; particularly Hershey as Shepard's spouse. The film garnered three Academy Award nominations: Best Picture, Shepard for Best Supporting Actor, Caleb Deschanel for Best Cinematography. The only glaring omission is the lightly treated lives of Slayton, Carpenter, and Schirra. On January 27, 1967, Grissom, Edward Higgins White and Roger Chaffee all died on the launch pad as they were about to go up as part of the Apollo program. They were the first casualties. In 1986, it was suggested that the newly discovered moons of our solar system be named for the seven who died in the Space Shuttle. Let that be the case and add the names of the other three so we'll always remember these people who had "The Right Stuff."

p, Irwin Winkler, Robert Chartoff; d&w, Philip Kaufman (based on the book by Tom Wolfe); ph, Caleb Deschanel (Technicolor); m, Bill Conti; ed, Glen Farr, Lisa Fruchtman, Stephen A. Rotter, Tom Rolf, Douglas Stewart; prod d, Geoffrey Kirkland; art d, Richard J. Lawrence, W. Stewart Campbell, Peter Romero; set d, Craig Edgar, Joel David Lawrence, Nicanor Navarro; spec eff, Gary Gutierrez, Jordan Belson.

Biography **Cas.** **(PR:A-C MPAA:PG)**

RIGHT TO LIVE, THE* (1933, Brit.) 72m FOX bw

Dave Burnaby *(Sir George Kessler)*, Pat Paterson *(June Kessler)*, Richard Bird *(Richard Fulton)*, Francis L. Sullivan *(Roger Stoneham)*, Lawrence Anderson *(Hugh Latimer)*, Frank Atkinson *(Harry Woods)*.

When a secret formula that will neutralize poison gas is stolen from scientist Burnaby, his daughter's suitor, Fulton, is framed. Eventually he clears himself and saves Burnaby's life in the bargain. A rare noncomic role for British comedian Burnaby in this otherwise uninteresting crime programmer.

p, Ernest Garside; d, Albert Parker; w, Gordon Wong Wellesley, R. J. Davis, Frank Atkinson (based on a story by Michael Barringer).

Crime **(PR:A MPAA:NR)**

RIGHT TO LIVE, THE** (1935) 75m WB bw (GB: THE SACRED FLAME)

Josephine Hutchinson *(Stella Houghton)*, George Brent *(Colin Trent)*, Colin Clive *(Maurice Trent)*, Peggy Wood *(Nurse Wayland)*, Henrietta Crosman *(Mrs. Trent)*, C. Aubrey Smith *(Maj. Liconda)*, Leo G. Carroll *(Dr. Harvester)*, Claude King *(Mr. Pride)*, Nella Walker *(Mrs. Pride)*, Halliwell Hobbes *(Sir Stephen Barr)*, Phyllis Coghlan *(Maid)*, Gunnis Davis *(Gardner)*, Jack H. Richardson *(Chauffeur)*, Vesey O'Davoren *(Waiter)*, Forrester Harvey *(English Bobbie)*.

Clive and Brent are brothers. The former has been injured and now lies in bed, a hopeless invalid. His wife, Hutchinson, can't live with this and has an affair with Brent. Finally Clive dies but his nurse (Wood), who secretly loved Clive, suspects that this was a mercy killing. Clive overacts outrageously in this version of the play by Maugham. The direction gets the story across without much trouble, but adds no insight to a weighty subject. This is a remake of the 1929 film THE SACRED FLAME.

d, William Keighley; w, Ralph Block (based on the play "The Sacred Flame" by W. Somerset Maugham); ph, Sid Hickox; ed, Jack Killifer; art d, Esdras Hartley.

Drama **(PR:A MPAA:NR)**

RIGHT TO LIVE, THE, 1945 (SEE: FOREVER YOURS, 1945)

RIGHT TO LOVE, THE*** (1931) 79m PAR

Ruth Chatterton *(Naomi Kellogg/Brook Evans)*, Paul Lukas *(Eric)*, David Manners *(Joe Copeland)*, George Baxter *(Tony)*, Irving Pichel *(Caleb Evans)*, Veda Buckland *(Mrs. Kellogg)*, Oscar Apfel *(William Kellogg)*.

A young boy and girl fall in love but their marriage is opposed. The couple can't fight their urges, though, and the girl ends up pregnant. The boy is killed soon after, leaving the girl alone in the world. When an older man begins to show interest in her, the family encourages the romance, and she reluctantly agrees to marry the man. She gives birth to a daughter and determines that this child shall have all the romance that she missed out on. Her fanatically religious husband won't allow this, though, so the girl is sent to China to become a missionary. There she meets a young man and falls in love but is unsure about what to do. Meanwhile her mother lies dying and somehow sends a telepathic message that influences her daughter to indulge in the romance. This is a well-handled drama with some fine perfomances that are never too mushy. Chatterton played both mother and father in the film debut of the Dunning process, a new technique which allowed for a more realistic look when an actor played two characters required in the same shot. It looked good and made this soaper better than most of its ilk.

d, Richard Wallace; w, Zoe Akins (based on the novel *Brook Evans* by Susan Glaspell); ph, Charles Lang.

Drama **(PR:C MPAA:NR)**

RIGHT TO ROMANCE** (1933) 67m RKO bw

Ann Harding *(Dr. Margaret Simmons)*, Robert Young *(Bob Preble)*, Nils Asther *(Dr. Heppling)*, Sari Maritza *(Lee Joyce)*, Irving Pichel *(Dr. Beck)*, Helen Freeman

(Mrs. Preble), Alden "Stephen" Chase *(Bunny)*, Delmar Watson *(Bill)*, Louise Carter, Bramwell Fletcher, Patricia O'Brien, Howard Hickman, Thelma Hardwick.

Harding plays a plastic surgeon who's so devoted to her career that she's never had time for fun and romance. Giving in to an impulse, she decides to leave her practice in New York one day, and take a vacation in California. There she meets Young, a daredevil aviator, and she's attracted to his sense of spirited fun. After a short courtship the two marry, but their differences soon drive them apart. He takes up with a girl more suited to his carefree personality, but in a freak plane accident, his new flame suffers numerous facial injuries that require the touch of a skilled plastic surgeon. Although hurt by Young's infidelity, Harding agrees to perform the operaton. In the end, she decides to give romance a go with a quiet doctor who has worshipped her from afar for quite some time.

p, Merian C. Cooper; d, Alfred Santell; w, Sidney Buchman, Henry McCarty (based on a story by Myles Connolly); ph, Lucien Andriot; ed, Ralph Dieterle.

Drama **(PR:A-C MPAA:NR)**

RIGHT TO THE HEART½** (1942) 74m FOX bw

Brenda Joyce *(Jenny Killian)*, Joseph Allen, Jr. *(John T. Bromley III)*, Cobina Wright, Jr. *(Barbara Paxton)*, Stanley Clements *(Stash)*, Don De Fore *(Tommy Sands)*, Hugh Beaumont *(Willie Donovan)*, Charles D. Brown *(Jim Killian)*, Ethel Griffies *(Minerva Bromley)*, Frank Orth *(Pete)*, Phil Tead *(McAllister)*, William Haade *(Morgan)*, Spencer Charters *(Jonah)*.

After too much goofing around, wealthy young New Yorker, Allen, is disinherited by his wealthy aunt, Griffies. His girl friend, Wright, dumps him as well and he goes to a bar to drown his sorrows. There he's knocked flat by a former boxer and this sends the humiliated young man to a training camp for would-be fighters. Upon arrival he meets the camp director's daughter, Joyce, with whom he falls head over heels in love. But Clements, her foster brother, doesn't care for the rich kid and gives him a hard time. Gradually Allen learns a few things about humility, gets the girl, and ends up once more in the good graces of his aunt. This programmer comedy is a bit slow to start, but once it gets rolling RIGHT TO THE HEART is an amusing bit of nonsense.

p, Sol M. Wurtzel; d, Eugene Forde; w, Walter Bullock (based on a story "You Can't Always Tell" by Harold McGrath); ph, Virgil Miller; ed, Louis Loeffler; md, Emil Newman.

Comedy **(PR:A MPAA:NR)**

RIGOLETTO½** (1949) 105m Minerva/Superfilm bw

Tito Gobbi *(Rigoletto)*, Mario Filippeschi *(Duke of Mantua)*, Lina Pagliughi/Marcella Govoni *(Gilda)*, Anna Maria Canali *(Maddalena)*, Giulio Neri *(Sparafucile)*, Marcello Giorda *(Monterone)*, Giuseppe Varni *(Conte Di Ceprano)*, Gentilumini Alabardiera.

Filmed presentation of the famous Guiseppi Verdi opera is a good effort in capturing the music and the story in a visual manner. Though it tends to lag in pace, there is enough energy behind the production to pull it through. Story centers on the court jester, Gobbi, whose daughter, Gonovi, sacrifices her life to save that of the amorous Duke played by Filippeschi. Though Gonovi acts the part of Gilda, Pagliughi dubs the singing, but the synchronization between voice and lips aften doesn't match.

p, Giulio Fiaschi; d, Carmine Gallone; m, Giuseppe Verdi; ph, Anchise Brizzi; md, Tullio Serafin.

Opera **(PR:A MPAA:NR)**

RIM OF THE CANYON½** (1949) 70m COL bw

Gene Autry *(Gene Autry/Gene Autry the Elder)*, Nan Leslie *(Ruth Lambert)*, Thurston Hall *(Big Tim Hanlon)*, Clem Bevans *(Loco John)*, Walter Sande *(Jake Fargo)*, Jock O'Mahoney *(Pete Reagan)*, Francis McDonald *(Charlie Lewis)*, Alan Hale, Jr. *(Matt Kimbrough)*, Amelita Ward *(Lily Shannon)*, John R. McKee *(Tex Rawlins)*, Denver Pyle, Bobby Clark, Boyd Stockman, Sandy Sanders, Lynn Farr, Rory Mallison, Frankie Marvin, Champion, Jr. the Horse.

Autry plays a double role in this oater, first as his father in a sequence occurring twenty years earlier, toting only a mustache to portray the different characters. Yarn has it that Autry Senior jailed crooks Sande and Mahoney for stealing $30, 000 from mine owner Hall. The money was hidden and never found by the authorities. Twenty years later the crooks escape from prison, and return to the ghost town where the money was hidden. Autry Junior follows in his father's footsteps by bringing the thugs to justice once again. Photography adds the proper atmosphere of the ghost town location.

p, Armand Schaefer; d, John English; w, John K. Butler (based on the story "Phantom .45s Talk Loud" by Joseph Chadwick); ph, William Bradford; ed, Aaron Stell; md, Mischa Bakaleinikoff; art d, Harold MacArthur; m/l, Hy Heath, Johnny Lange, Gene Autry.

Western **Cas.** **(PR:A MPAA:NR)**

RIMFIRE** (1949) 63m Lippert/Screen Guild bw

James Millican *(Capt. Tom Harvey)*, Mary Beth Hughes *(Polly)*, Reed Hadley *(The Abilene Kid)*, Henry Hull *(Editor Greeley)*, Fuzzy Knight *(Porky)*, Victor Kilian *(Sheriff Jordan)*, Chris-Pin Martin *(Chico)*, Margia Dean *(Lolita)*, Jason Robards, Sr. *(Banker Elkins)*, John Cason *(Blazer)*, George Cleveland *(Judge Gardner)*, Ray Bennett *(Barney)*, Glenn Strange *(Stagecoach Driver)*, I. Stanford Jolley *(Toad)*, Ben Erway *(Deputy Sheriff Wilson)*, Stanley Price *(Lamson)*, Lee Roberts *(Norton)*, Don Harvey *(Rainbow Raymond)*, Cliff Taylor *(Bartender)*, Dick Alexander *(Weber)*, Marjorie Stapp *(Dancehall Girl)*.

Millican plays an undercover agent in the old west trying to find the whereabouts of some stolen U.S. Army gold. The hanging of an innocent gambler framed for cheating sparks a number of killings by what the townspeople believe is the dead man's ghost. But investigation by Millican uncovers the real culprits and the gold at the same time. Well paced action and a good job of staging is marred only by a plot that has too many tangents.

p, Ron Ormond; d, B. Reeves Eason; w, Arthur St. Clair, Frank Wisbar, Ormand; ph, Ernest Miller; ed, Hugh Winn; m, Walter Greene; art d, Fred Ritter.

Western **(PR:A MPAA:NR)**

RING, THE*** (1952) 79m UA bw

Gerald Mohr *(Pete)*, Rita Moreno *(Lucy)*, Lalo Rios *(Tommy)*, Robert Arthur *(Billy Smith)*, Robert Osterloh *(Freddy)*, Martin Garralaga *(Vidal)*, Jack Elam *(Harry Jackson)*, Peter Brosco *(Barney Williams)*, Julia Montoya *(Rosa)*, Lillian Molieri *(Helen)*, Pepe Hern *(Rick)*, Victor Millan *(Pablo)*, Tony Martinez *(Go-Go)*, Ernie Chavez *(Joe)*, Edward Sieg *(Benny)*, Robert Altuna *(Pepe)*, Art Aragon *(Art Aragon)*.

Early boxing tale explores prejudice against Mexican Americans on the West Coast. Mohr plays a promising fighter who has a hard time getting a decent job. This brings him to the ring, only to be thwarted when his aspirations to make a name for himself and gain respect in the world lead him to fight in matches for which he is unprepared. He temporarily quits the ring, but decides to return after an embarrassing scene in a restaurant where the waitress refuses to serve him because he is Mexican American. He believes that the ring is the only way to overcome racial prejudice and achieve a better life for himself and his girl friend, Moreno, but a shot at the championship leaves him severely beaten. He quits the ring forever and is depressed at what he visualizes as failure, until Moreno convinces him that there are other ways to fight for what he believes in. Poignant story is carried by the excellent performances of the entire cast, effectively handled through the keen direction of Neumann.

p, Maurice King, Frank King, Herman King; d, Kurt Neumann; w, Irving Shulman (based on the novel by Shulman); ph, Russell Harlan; m, Herschel Burke Gilbert; ed, Bruce B. Pierce; art d, Theobold Holsopple; set d, Ray Boltz.

Drama **(PR:A MPAA:NR)**

RING-A-DING RHYTHM½** (1962, Brit. 73m Amicus/COL bw (G.B: IT'S TRAD, DAD!)

Helen Shapiro *(Helen)*, Craig Douglas *(Craig)*, Felix Felton *(Mayor)*, Arthur Mullard *(Police Chief)*, Timothy Bateson *(Coffeeshop Owner)*, Hugh Lloyd *(Usher)*, Ronnie Stevens, Frank Thornton *(TV Directors)*, Derek Nimmo *(Head Waiter)*, Mario Fabrizi *(Spaghetti Eater)*, Arnold Diamond *(TV Panelist)*, Bruce Lacey *(Gardner)*, Deryck Guyler *(Narrator)*, John Leyton, The Brook Brothers, Chubby Checker, Del Shannon, Gary "U.S." Bonds, Gene Vincent, Gene McDaniels, The Paris Sisters, The Dukes of Dixieland, Chris Barber's Jazz Band, Ottilie Patterson, Mr. Acker Bilk and His Paramount Jazz Band, Kenny Ball and His Jazzmen, Bob Wallis and His Storyville Jazzmen, Terry Lightfoot and His New Orleans Jazz Band, The Temperance Seven, Sounds Incorporated, David Jacobs, Pete Murray, Alan Freeman.

This was Lester's first feature effort, and in this respect acted as the springboard for his highly stylized direction that relied heavily on fancy editing techniques and a variety of camera angles. These same techniques would later be used in the classics THE KNACK and A HARD DAY'S NIGHT. Other than that, the plot is a direct successor to the 1950s teen pics where the town's prominent citizens react negatively to the wildness depicted in rock music, so the kids go about finding a way to remedy the situation. In this case, it's the town mayor who goes so far as to take away one coffeeshop's license for having a jukebox. Crafty teens Shapiro and Douglas then get the idea to stage a festival, overcoming the hardest of tasks to see their plan through. And in the tradition of the surfer flicks, no picture is complete without the culprit repenting, and the mayor does just that by trying to twist his hips to a few songs. Among the featured musicians is a rare screen appearance by Gene Vincent recording "Space Ship to Mars" (Norrie Paramor, Milton Subotsky). Other songs include "Tavern in the Town" (Paramor, Subotsky, sung by Terry Lightfoot), "Nineteen-Nineteen March" (Paramor, Subotsky, sung by Kenny Ball), "Double Trouble" (Geoff Brook, Ricky Brook, sung by The Brooks Brothers), "Everybody Loves My Baby" (Jack Palmer, Spencer Williams, sung by the Temperance Seven), "Dream Away Romance" (Paul McDowell, Clifford Beven, sung by the Temperance Seven), "Bellissima" (Subotsky, performed by Bob Wallis and His Storyville Jazzmen), "In a Persian Market" (Albert Ketelbey, Mack David, performed by Mr. Acker Bilk and His Paramount Jazz Band), "Lonely City" (Geoffrey Goddard, sung by John Leyton), "High Society" (Clarence Williams, A.J. Piron, performed by the Bilk Jazz Band), "Frankie and Johnny" (Subotsky, performed by the Bilk Jazz Band), "Aunt Flo" (Bob Wallis, performed by Wallis and His Jazzmen), "Rainbows" (Paramor, Bunny Lewis, sung by Craig Douglas), "Let's Talk About Love" (Paramor, Lewis, sung by Helen Shapiro), "Sometime Yesterday" (Clive Westlake, sung by Shapiro), "My Maryland" (arranged by Lightfoot, sung by Lightfoot), "Beale Street Blues" (W.C. Handy, sung by Kenny Ball), "Yellow Dog Blues" (Handy, performed by Chris Barber's Jazz Band), "Down by the Riverside" (Chris Barber, sung by Ottilie Patterson), "When the Saints Go Marching In" (arranged by Barber, performed by Barber's Jazz Band), "Ring-a-Ding" (Paramor, Lewis, sung by Shapiro), "Seven Day Weekend" (Doc Pomus, Mort Shuman, sung by Gary "U.S." Bonds), "What Am I to Do?" (Pomus, Shuman, sung by the Paris Sisters), "Another Tear Falls" (Hal David, Burt Bacharach, sung by Gene McDaniels), "Lose Your Inhibition Twist" (Kal Mann, Dave Appell, performed by Chubby Checker), "By and By" (performed by the Dukes of Dixieland), "You Never Talk About Me" (Pomus, Shuman, sung by Del Shannon).

p&d, Richard Lester; w, Milton Subotsky; ph, Gilbert Taylor; m, Ken Thorne; ed, Bill Lenny; md, Norrie Paramor; prod d, Al Marcus; art d, Maurice Carter; cos, Gamp Ferris; Maude Churchill; makeup, Freddie Williamson.

Musical/Comedy **(PR:A MPAA:NR)**

RING AROUND THE CLOCK½** (1953, Ital.) 88m International Film Associates c bw

Patrizia Mangano (*Luisa*), Nando Burno (*Parboni*), Lauro Gazzolo (*Guerrieri*), Pepino Spadaro (*Don Paolo*), Arturo Brogaglia (*Mayor*), Mario Mazza (*De Mori*), Paolo Stoppa (*Rocchetti*), Renato Micali (*Sub-Chief*), Alfred De Leo (*Gino Maruchelli*), Mario Nicotra (*Police Chief*), Carlo Della Piane (*Vincenzo*), John Pasetti (*Alfred*), Leda Gloria (*Rosa*).

Political farce has a small village in Italy going up for grabs when the square clock is broken, and the various political factions argue over a way to get it fixed. This includes a mayor who believes in a democratic settlement, a communist who tries to get advice from higher officials in Rome only to be butted around while spouting off a bunch of empty slogans, and a priest who runs a lottery to get the needed money. Clever story, that makes for a nifty satire with the smallest of material, is hampered by characterizations that never live up to their possibilities (In Italian; English subtitles.)

p, Paolo W. Tamburella, Sonio Coletti; d, Tamburella; w, G. Collegare, J. Corsi, B. Costa, G. Leoni (based on a *Time Magazine* story by William Rospigliosi); m, G. Icini, A. Ciaognini; ed, Walter Klee; titles, A.J. Liebling.

Comedy   (PR:A MPAA:NR)

RING AROUND THE MOON* (1936) 65m CHES bw

Donald Cook (*Ross Graham*), Erin O'Brien Moore (*Gloria Endicott*), Ann Doran (*Kay Duncan*), Alan Edwards (*Pete Maitland*), Douglas Fowley (*Ted Curlew*), John Qualen (*Bill Harvey*), Barbara Bedford (*Carla Anderson*), Richard Tucker (*Baxter*), John Miltern (*Mr. Endicott*), Carl Stockdale (*Brenton*), Dicky Dewar (*The Baby*), Mildred Gover (*Emma*), Dot Farley (*Bella*), Eddie Phillips (*Charlie*), Vera Steadman (*Mayme*).

Poorly made adaptation of Hobart's story about two love affairs, with a plot so twisted no one will recognize the novel. Story is about a working class girl's romance contrasted against the affair of a beautiful society deb.

p, George R. Batcheller; d, Charles Lamont; w, Paul Perez (based on the novel by Vera Hobart); ph, M.A. Anderson; ed, Roland Reed.

Drama   (PR:A MPAA:NR)

RING OF BRIGHT WATER* (1969, Brit.) 107m Brightwater-Palomar Pictures International/Cinema-RANK c

Bill Travers (*Graham Merrill*), Virginia McKenna (*Mary MacKenzie*), Peter Jeffrey (*Colin Wilcox/Colin Clifford*), Jameson Clark (*Storekeeper*), Helena Gloag (*Mrs. Flora Elrich*), W.H.D. Joss (*Lighthouse Keeper*), Roddy McMillan (*Bus Driver*), Jean Taylor-Smith (*Mrs. Sarah Chambers*), Archie Duncan (*Road Mender*), Kevin Collins (*Fisherman*), John Young (*Guard*), James Gibson (*Sleeping Car Attendant*), Michael O'Halloran (*Herman*), Philip McCall (*Frank*), Christopher Benjamin (*Fishmonger*), Philippa Gail (*Pet Stall Girl*), June Ellis (*Barmaid*), Tommy Godfrey (*Ticket Seller*), Walter Hall, Bill Horsley, Philip Morant.

Filmed depiction of the autobiography by Gavin Maxwell about his adventures with a playful otter, was given a semi-documentary flavor and the presence of Travers and McKenna (then recently of BORN FREE fame, another animal story). Travers plays an increasingly distraught London clerk who decides to purchase the otter he sees in the pet shop he passes everyday on his way to work. When the otter's antics get him evicted from his apartment, Travers takes to the Scottish highlands, intending to devote himself to writing about Arabia. But the otter, whom he named Mij, takes up much of Travers' attention, and he's unable to spend much time writing. When Travers leaves Mij in the local veterinarian's care while he returns to London for a business trip, Mij is killed in a road accident. Depressed to hear of the bad news, a happy ending is provided when a female otter and her three cubs are spotted near Mij and Travers' favorite hangout, and Travers decides that they must be Mij's family. He then decides to write about his experiences with his otter. The lush photography of the Scottish Highlands makes for a pleasant background to this delightful and moving tale.

p, Joseph Strick; d, Jack Couffer; w, Couffer, Bill Travers (based on the book by Gavin Maxwell); ph, Wolfgang Suschitzky (Technicolor); m, Frank Cordell; ed, Reginald Mills; md, Cordell; prod d, Terry Lens; art d, Ken Ryan; cos, Ernie Farrer; m/l, title song, Cordell, Betty Botley (sung by Val Doonican); makeup, Catherine Shirley; wild life consultants, Hubert Wells, Tom Beecham, Mabel Beecham.

Comedy/Drama   **Cas.**   (PR:A MPAA:G)

RING OF FEAR** (1954) 92m Wayne-Fellows/WB c

Clyde Beatty (*Clyde Beatty*), Pat O'Brien (*Frank Wallace*), Mickey Spillane (*Mickey Spillane*), Sean McClory (*Dublin O'Malley*), Marian Carr (*Valerie St. Denis*), John Bromfield (*Armond St. Denis*), Emmett Lynn (*Twitchy*), Pedro Gonzales-Gonzales (*Gonzales*), Jack Strang (*Paul Martin*), Kenneth Tobey (*Shreveport*), Kathy Cline (*Suzette*), Clyde Beatty Circus.

Despite some very good footage of circus stunts and the inclusion of Spillane playing himself as the detective, this story of a maniacal ringmaster out to destroy the circus is pretty flat. McClory is the ringmaster whose jealousy of Beatty makes him want to destroy Beatty's circus. He uses a drunken clown as the device to carry through his plans. He's also jealous because the girl he fancies is getting ready to marry someone else. Spillane and cop Strang are called in to uncover the strange happenings underneath the circus tent. McClory gives a stunning performance as the half-crazed man, making himself likable despite his ruthlessness.

p, Robert M. Fellows; d, James Edward Grant, William A. Wellman; w, Paul Fix, Philip MacDonald, Grant (based on a story by Fix, MacDonald, Grant); ph, Edwin B. DuPar (CinemaScope, WarnerColor); m, Emil Newman, Arthur Lange; ed, Fred MacDowell.

Crime/Drama   (PR:A MPAA:NR)

RING OF FIRE* (1961) 91m MGM c

David Janssen (*Sgt. Steve Walsh*), Joyce Taylor (*Bobbie Adams*), Frank Gorshin (*Frank Henderson*), Joel Marston (*Deputy Pringle*), James Johnson (*Roy Anderson*), Ron Myron (*Sheriff Niles*), Marshall Kent (*Deputy*), Doodles Weaver (*Mr. Hobart*).

A good, old-fashioned, rip-snorting adventure picture that grabs the audience immediately and doesn't let go until the exciting conclusion, when the heroes have to fight a huge forest fire. The footage of the fires was shot during two real conflagrations that took place in Oregon and California, then ingeniously cut into the picture and, with matching shots, no one was the wiser. Taylor, Gorshin, and Anderson are three delinquents who are captured by Sheriff Janssen for having robbed a gasoline station in Oregon, near a large wooded area. He's squiring them to the hoosegow when Taylor, the female member, brings out a gun. Janssen hadn't patted her down, preferring to wait until they got to the jail where a female matron would do that. The more fool he. Janssen goes from captor to captive in a twinkling. They dump Janssen's car and use him as a kidnap victim-guide to take them through the forbidding forest to what they think will be safety. Night descends, and by this time, Janssen is beginning to find Taylor interesting, so she tries to seduce him but he resists, never forgetting that he's a lawman and they are criminals. The next day, Johnson gets drunk and wants to push Janssen off a cliff. The two men battle and Johnson goes over the edge to his death. Since Janssen has not checked in by radio for many hours, a search-and-rescue group has been formed. When Janssen and his two remaining kidnapers come out of the woods, the other police are waiting and nab them. Gorshin tells the cops that Janssen had his way with Adams, who is underage. Janssen denies this vociferously, and as the verbal fireworks continue, Gorshin tosses a cigarette aside and the area goes up in flame almost immediately. The small town is threatened and soon decimated (It was Veronia, Oregon). Before that happens, Janssen gets the frightened townspeople into a pair of railroad cars and, with Adams to help, they drive the cars over a precarious trestle that sways a couple of hundred feet above a ravine. The train stalls and the people have to get out of the cars and make their way across the trestle by gingerly walking along the railroad ties, some of which are now beginning to smolder and break into flame. Gorshin uses this panicky moment to make an escape attempt by climbing down the wooden structure. Just as the townspeople reach the other side, the trestle erupts in flame and the weight of the cars causes it to collapse, with Gorshin going to his death. Some holes in the story mar the believability, but the action is fast and furious, in the Stone tradition (they did THE LAST VOYAGE) and well-edited by the director's wife. A nail-biter from the start, so bring some extra fingers.

p, Virginia and Andrew L. Stone; d&w, Andrew L. Stone; ph, William H. Clothier (CinemaScope, Metrocolor); ed, Virginia Stone; spec eff, Herman Townsely; m/l, "Ring of Fire," Duane Eddy (performed by Eddy).

Adventure/Crime   (PR:A-C MPAA:NR)

RING OF SPIES (SEE; RING OF TREASON, 1964, Brit.)

RING OF TERROR½** (1962) 71m Playstar/Ronnie Ashcroft bw

George Mather (*College Student*), Esther Furst (*His Girl Friend*), Austin Green, Joseph Conway, Jerry Zinneman, June Smavey.

Based on allegedly true incidents of fraternity hazing on college campuses, Mather plays a seemingly courageous pre-med who doesn't lose his gumption to those things that normal students cringe at in horror. But when his one fear is discovered he's petrified of corpses, the frat that he needs to get into poses an initiation in which Mather must remove a ring from the finger of a corpse. He makes it to the tomb, only to open the coffin and die of shock.

p, Alfreo Bocchicchio; d, Clark Paylow; w, Lewis Simeon, G.J. Zinnerman; ph, Brydon Baker; m, James Cairncross; makeup, Roland Ray.

Drama/Horror   (PR:A MPAA:NR)

RING OF SPIES½** (1964, Brit.) 90m BL (G.B. RING OF TREASON) bw

Bernard Lee (*Henry Houghton*), William Sylvester (*Gordon Lonsdale*), Margaret Tyzack (*Elizabeth Gee*), David Kossoff (*Peter Kroger*), Nancy Nevinson (*Helen Kroger*), Thorley Walters (*Cmdr. Winters*), Gillian Lewis (*Marjorie Shaw*), Brian Nissen (*Lt. Downes*), Newton Blick (*P.O. Meadows*), Philip Latham (*Capt. Ray*), Cyril Chamberlain (*Anderson*), Justine Lord (*Christina*), Patrick Barr (*Capt. Warner*), Derek Francis (*Chief Supt. Croft*), Hector Ross (*Supt. Woods*), Richard Marner (*Col. Monat*), Norma Foster (*Ella*), Anita West (*Tilly*), Edwin Apps (*Blake*), Garry Marsh (*1st Member at Lord's*), Basil Dignam (*2nd Member at Lord's*), Hector Ross (*Supt. Woods*), Margaret Ward (*Supt. Muriel*).

A film depicting the uncovering of a British spy ring caught revealing information to the Soviets concentrates on factual evidence leading up to the crack in the case. There is an introduction in which the actual spies are displayed. Lee plays the man fired from his position at the British Embassy in Warsaw because of security reasons, making easy prey for a blackmail scheme by Soviet agents. He befriends aging spinster Tyzack in order to take advantage of the safe keys in her possession. Getting hold of the proper documents, contact Sylvester has them photographed, then sent through a middle-aged suburban couple via short-wave to Moscow. The new-found wealth of Lee raises some suspicion among the authorities, who go to extreme pains to get the evidence to uncover the ring, including agents masquerading as nuns. Despite the documentary flavor, there are a few witty touches by the hand of Tronson.

p, Leslie Gilliat; d, Robert Tronson; w, Frank Launder, Peter Barnes; ph, Arthur Lavis; ed, Thelma Connell; art d, Norman Arnold.

Spy   (PR:A MPAA:NR)

RING UP THE CURTAIN (SEE: BROADWAY TO HOLLYWOOD, 1933)

RINGER, THE*½   (1932, Brit.) 60m Gainsborough/BL bw (AKA: THE GAUNT STRANGER)

Patric Curwen (*Dr. Lomond*), Franklin Dyall (*Maurice Meister*), Carol Goodner (*Cora Ann Milton*), Gordon Harker (*Samuel Hackett*), Esmond Knight (*John Lenley*), Arthur Stratton (*Sgt. Carter*), Henry Hallett (*Inspector Bliss*), Dorothy Bartlam (*Mary Lenley*), Kathleen Joyce (*Gwenda Milton*), John Longden (*Inspector Wembury*), Eric Stanley (*Commissioner*).

In this plot, Curwen plays a criminal who's a master of disguises. No one is quite sure what the "ringer" really looks like. He further baffles police when he poses as a physician and kills his partner, whom the cops have had under police protection in the hope that he'll lead them to Curwen. It seems that his partner has killed Curwen's sister, and the ringer is out for revenge.

p, Michael Balcon; d, Walter Forde; w, Angus MacPhail, Robert Stevenson, Edgar Wallace (based on the novel *The Gaunt Stranger*, and the play by Wallace); ph, Leslie Howson, Alec Spryce.

Crime   **(PR:A MPAA:NR)**

RINGER, THE**   (1953, Brit.) 78m London/Regent bw

Herbert Lom (*Maurice Meister*), Donald Wolfit (*Dr. Lomond*), Mai Zetterling (*Lisa*), Greta Gynt (*Cora Ann Milton*), William Hartnell (*Sam Hackett*), Norman Wooland (*Inspector Bliss*), Denholm Elliott (*John Lenley*), Dora Bryan (*Mrs. Hackett*), Charles Victor (*Inspector Wembury*), Walter Fitzgerald (*Commissioner*), John Stuart (*Gardener*), John Slater (*Bell*), Campbell Singer (*Station Sgt. Carter*).

Crooked lawyer Lom is being pursued by the ringer, a master of disguise who holds Lom, his former partner, responsible for the suicide of his sister. While the police try to protect the terrified Lom, the ringer appears before Lom and reveals himself to be police doctor Wolfit. He strangles Lom with a wire from the burglar alarm, then escapes. Old-fashioned melodrama with an excellent cast.

p, Hugh Perceval; d, Guy Hamilton; w, Val Valentine, Lesley Storm (based on the novel *The Gaunt Stranger* and the play by Edgar Wallace); ph, Ted Scaife; m, Malcolm Arnold; ed, Bert Bates; md, Muir Mathieson; prod d, Joseph Bato, W.E. Hutchinson.

Crime   **(PR:A MPAA:NR)**

RINGO AND HIS GOLDEN PISTOL**   (1966, Ital.) 88m Sanson (AKA: JOHNNY ORO)

Mark Damon, Valeria Fabrizi, Ettore Manni, Giulia Rubini, Franco De Rosa, Andrea Aureli.

Unusual for a spaghetti western in that it takes it easy on the violence, while Damon resorts to dynamite to defend himself against a ruthless bunch of bandits. The original title for the lead character, Johnny Oro, was dubbed to Ringo in foreign versions in order to take advantage of the popular series by Duccio Tessari.

p, Joseph Fryd; d, Sergio Corbucci; w, Adriano Bolzoni, Franco Rossetti; ph, Riccardo Pallotini.

Western   **(PR:A MPAA:NR)**

RINGS ON HER FINGERS**   (1942) 85m FOX bw

Henry Fonda (*John Wheeler*), Gene Tierney (*Susan Miller [Linda Worthington]*), Laird Cregar (*Warren*), John Shepperd (*Tod Fenwick*), Spring Byington (*Mrs. Maybelle Worthington*), Frank Orth (*Kellogg*), Henry Stephenson (*Col. Prentice*), Marjorie Gateson (*Mrs. Fenwick*), George Lessey (*Fenwick, Sr.*), Iris Adrian (*Peggy*), Thurston Hall (*Mr. Beasley*), Clara Blandick (*Mrs. Beasley*), Harry Hayden (*Train Conductor*), Gwendolyn Logan (*Mrs. Callahan*), Billy Benedict (*Newsboy*), Sarah Edwards (*Mrs. Clancy*), Charles Wilson (*Capt. Hurley*), Edgar Norton (*Paul*), George Lloyd (*Chick*), Kathryn Sheldon (*Landlady*), Frank Sully (*Cab Driver*), Mel Ruick (*Roulette Dealer*), Frank Coghlan, Jr. (*Page Boy*), Clive Morgan (*Charles*), Herb Ashley (*Policeman*), Brooks Benedict (*Crap Dealer*), David Newell, Russell Huestis (*Players*), Tom O'Grady (*Bystander*), Wilbur Mack (*Onlooker*), Hooper Atchley (*Onlooker*), Constance Purdy (*Party Giver*), Evelyn Mulhall (*Miss Alderney*), Charles Moore (*Porter*), Bob Ryan (*Attendant*), James Adamson (*Redcap*), Gen. Samuel Savitsky (*Barney*), Phil Tead (*Ticket Agent*), Eric Wilton (*Butler*), Mary Treen.

An ordinary comedy that blatantly took much from THE LADY EVE, but obviously not enough, as it was a disappointment when one considers all the excellent talent recruited for the film. Mamoulian had a three-picture agreement with Zanuck at Fox that included his stellar work on THE MARK OF ZORRO, followed by BLOOD AND SAND. This was the final film on that deal and suffered by comparison. Byington and Cregar are two con artists in search of a millionaire to bilk. They enlist the aid of Tierney, an attractive sales clerk, and plan to use her to ensnare their prey. Fonda is a poor accountant on vacation in Southern California. He's saved up a bundle to buy a sailboat, and when Byington and Cregar hear him talking about boats, they think they have a dupe. Tierney's job is to get Fonda to fall in love with her so she can gull him out of his supposed wealth. But she's far too honest for this kind of work and decides that she can't be part of the plan. Add that to her growing love for Fonda and it's easy to see the best laid plans go out the window. The two leads confess the truth to each other and get married, but Cregar and Byington are not done yet and try to split the couple by finding Tierney a real millionaire. One funny scene in which Fonda goes into a specially rigged casino where every slot machine pays off and every roulette table has been tampered with. A couple of other mildly amusing interludes, though most of the plot points are hard to swallow. A trivial picture that looks better than it actually is because of Fonda's comic timing and Tierney's radiant presence.

p, Milton Sperling; d, Rouben Mamoulian; w, Ken Englund (based on a story by Robert Pirosh, Joseph Schrank); ph, George Barnes; ed, Barbara McLean; md,

Cyril J. Mockridge; art d, Richard Day, Albert Hogsett; set d, Thomas Little; cos, Gwen Wakeling; m/l, "The Moon Looked the Other Way," Alfred Newman.

Comedy   **Cas.**   **(PR:A MPAA:NR)**

RINGSIDE**½   (1949) 68m Lippert/Screen Guild bw

Don Barry (*Mike*), Tom Brown (*Joe*), Sheila Ryan (*Janet*), Margie Dean (*Joy*), Joe Adams (*Duke*), Tony Canzoneri (*Swinger*), Mark Plant (*Gangster*), Joseph Crehan (*Oscar*), Lyle Talbot (*Radio Announcer*), William Edmunds (*Prof. Berger*), Edit Angold (*Mama Berger*), John Cason (*Tiger Johnson*), Harry Brown (*Manager*), Frankie Van (*Referee*), Dan Toby (*Fight Announcer*), Chester Clute (*Timid Man*), Jimmie Martin (*Second*), Ned Roberts (*Fighter*).

Tightly paced low-budgeter has concert pianist Barry turning to the ring to avenge his brother, Brown, who was blinded in a fight. Along the way he also picks up on his brother's girl friend, Ryan, making for a triangle complication that is settled when Brown takes a liking to his nurse. Actual ring footage is put to good use, contrasting with the staged bouts.

p, Ron Ormond; d, Frank McDonald; w, Daniel B. Ullman, Ormond; ph, Ernest Miller; ed, Hugh Winn.

Drama   **(PR:A MPAA:NR)**

RINGSIDE MAISIE**   (1941) 96m MGM bw

Ann Sothern (*Maisie Ravier*), George Murphy (*Skeets Maguire*), Robert Sterling (*Terry Dolan*), Natalie Thompson (*Cecelia Reardon*), Maxie Rosenbloom (*Chotsie*), Margaret Moffat (*Mrs. Dolan*), John Indrisano (*Peaches*), Virginia O'Brien (*Virginia O'Brien*), Eddie Simms (*Billy-Boy Duffy*), Jack LaRue (*Ricky DuPrez*), Purnell Pratt (*Dr. Taylor*), May McAvoy (*Day Nurse*), Tom Dugan (*Checker*), Jonathan Hale (*Dr. Kramer*), Roy Lester (*Jitterbug*), Oscar O'Shea (*Conductor*), "Rags" Ragland (*Vic*), Oscar O'Shea.

Cliche-ridden boxing yarn has Sothern wandering into the boxing camp of up-and-coming Sterling, who has a manager overly anxious to get the lad to the top and cash in on some big bucks. Sothern's role carries enough charm to move the picture along with a few other bits in for laughs. (See MAISIE series, Index.)

p, J. Walter Ruben; d, Edwin L. Marin; w, Mary C. McCall, Jr.; ph, Charles Lawton; m, David Snell; ed, Frederick Y. Smith; cos, Robert Kalloch.

Comedy/Drama   **(PR:A MPAA:NR)**

RIO**½   (1939) 75m UNIV bw

Basil Rathbone (*Paul Reynard*), Victor McLaglen (*Dirk*), Sigrid Gurie (*Irene Reynard*), Robert Cummings (*Bill Gregory*), Leo Carrillo (*Roberto*), Irving Bacon (*Mushy*), Maurice Moscovitz (*Old Convict*), Henry Armetta (*Head Waiter*), Billy Gilbert (*Manuello*), Samuel S. Hinds (*Lamartine*), Irving Pichel (*Rocco*), Ferike Boros (*Maria*).

Rathbone plays a ruthless financier sent to prison for his part in several swindles. His wife, Gurie, and faithful servant, McLaglen, help him escape from prison, only to find that his wife has fallen in love with Cummings. When Rathbone attempts to kill Cummings, McLaglen fights for Gurie's happiness and does away with Rathbone. Even though Rathbone has an unsympathetic role, he plays it in a manner which evokes feeling on the audience's part, and McLaglen is also effective as the faithful stooge. A stylish piece of direction under the eye of Brahm. Gurie delivers two numbers, "Love Opened My Eyes" and "Heart of Mine."

d, John Brahm; w, Stephen Morehouse Avery, Frank Partos, Edwin Justus Mayer, Aben Kandel (based on a story by Jean Negulesco); ph, Hal Mohr; ed, Phil Cahn; md, Charles Previn; m/l, Jimmie McHugh, Frank Skinner, Ralph Freed.

Drama   **(PR:A MPAA:NR)**

RIO BRAVO****   (1959) 141m Armada/WB c

John Wayne (*John T. Chance*), Dean Martin (*Dude*), Ricky Nelson (*Colorado Ryan*), Angie Dickinson (*Feathers*), Walter Brennan (*Stumpy*), Ward Bond (*Pat Wheeler*), John Russell (*Nathan Burdette*), Pedro Gonzalez-Gonzales (*Carlos*), Estelita Rodriguez (*Consuela*), Claude Akins (*Joe Burdette*), Harry Carey, Jr. (*Harold*), Malcolm Atterbury (*Jake*), Bob Steele (*Matt Harris*), Bing Russell (*Cowboy Murdered in Saloon*), Myron Healey (*Burdette Henchman in Saloon*), Eugene Iglesias (*1st Burdette Man in Shootout*), Fred Graham (*2nd Burdette Man in Shootout*), Tom Monroe (*Henchman*), Riley Hill (*Messenger*), Bob Terhune (*Charlie, the Bartender*), Ted White (*Bart*), Nesdon Booth (*Clark*), George Bruggerman (*Clem*), Jose Cuchillo (*Pedro*), Joseph Shimada (*Burt the Funeral Director*).

Annoyed that the critically acclaimed and immensely popular western HIGH NOON portrayed a sheriff so afraid of the bad men coming to get him that he spends most of the movie asking the townsfolk for help, director Howard Hawks—whose first western, RED RIVER, stands as a masterpiece of the genre—decided to make a filmed response and its title was RIO BRAVO. Hawks and star Wayne both felt that a frontier professional would never seek help from those he has been assigned to protect, and that a sheriff should face danger only with those skilled enough to do the job and take care of themselves—amateurs would get in the way. A lengthy, leisurely paced film, RIO BRAVO is set in a small Texas border town under the grip of evil cattle baron Russell and his dim-witted brother Akins. The film begins as Martin, a former deputy who has become a pathetic alcoholic because of a tragic love affair, enters the back door of the local saloon and begs for a drink. Akins, who is enjoying a drink and a card game with his men, tosses a coin in Martin's direction, but it lands in a full spittoon—which is what he was really aiming for. Desperate for alcohol, Martin gets on his hands and knees and is about to reach into the gruel of saliva for the coin when the spittoon is violently kicked away. Martin looks up and sees the sheriff, Wayne, staring down at him. Angered, Martin conks Wayne on the head and then goes after Akins. Akins and his men restrain Martin and then begin beating on the sheriff. When a bystander tries to stop them, Akins calmly draws his pistol and kills the man at point-blank range. Wayne gathers himself up and arrests Akins for murder. The sheriff throws Akins into a cell and tells him he'll sit there until the U.S. marshal comes to get him. Akins brags that Wayne won't be able to keep him in the cell long because his brother, Russell, will come with their men and bust him out. Wayne concedes that that may be true, but Akins will be the first to die. Fully aware that he's outnumbered 40 to 1, Wayne wonders if his former deputy can be relied upon to do his share. Wayne's only other help is a toothless, cranky old cripple named "Stumpy" (Brennan), and all he's good for is standing at the cell door with a shotgun. Enter wagonmaster Bond, an old friend of Wayne's who's come through town with his crew. At the saloon Bond offers to help, but Wayne tells him that he's not "good enough" to take on Russell's men, but thanks anyway. Wayne does notice that Bond has hired a new hand, a young, confident gunslinger of few words, Nelson. Wayne would like to enlist the youngster because "he's so good he doesn't feel like he's got to prove it." Bond asks Nelson if he wants to help out, but Nelson declines, saying that he doesn't want to stick his nose into other people's business. This reponse confirms Wayne's opinion of the gunslinger: "He made sense. I'd like to have him." During this discussion Wayne has been keeping his eye on a beautiful young stranger who has been playing cards, Dickinson. He suspects she's been cheating and he takes her upstairs for a confrontation. She catches the shy Wayne off guard by demanding that he search her if he's so smart. Wayne is taken aback by her aggressiveness —but also intrigued. At the same time, Nelson has come to suspect another man at the poker table of cheating and proves it. With Dickinson cleared, Wayne retracts his demand that she "get outa town." That night, Bond is shot in the back and killed by one of Russell's men. Martin manages to wound the culprit and sees him run off into the saloon. Wayne and Martin enter the bar—which is filled with Russell's men—and Martin makes them drop their gunbelts to the floor and show him their boots (the killer had stepped in a muddy puddle during his escape). None of the men is the killer and the villainous group's taunts of Martin's drunkenness begin to wear on him. While standing at the bar, Martin notices blood dripping into a beer glass. He walks to the far end of the bar and orders a drink (he has been on the wagon for a few days now). As he brings the drink to his lips, he suddenly whirls around and shoots into the rafters. The killer falls to the floor—dead. "You were good in there," Wayne tells Martin and with renewed confidence in himself, Martin buys a new set of clothes and once again proudly wears his deputy's badge. The next day, the battle stations are assigned. Martin stands at the entrance to town and collects guns from Russell and his men before they go to the jail to visit Akins. Brennan stays by the cell with his shotgun—thus allowing Wayne freedom of movement. Nelson, who has stayed in town to avenge Bond despite Wayne's orders to leave, stays in the backround and keeps a watchful eye. While Russell goes to the jail to visit Akins, Martin keeps an eye on his men. Unfortunately, they get the drop on him and knock him cold. One of the men dons Martin's clothes and gun and they go to confront Wayne, who is standing in front of the hotel—his rifle leaning against a post on the porch. Thinking the villains are accompanied by Martin, Wayne drops his guard and the men draw on him. Nelson, who is in the hotel, tells Dickinson to throw a flower pot through the window after he wanders out to the porch. Pretending to be a stranger, Nelson innocently walks outside and asks what's going on. At that moment the flower pot comes crashing through the window and Nelson uses the diversion to toss Wayne his rifle and draw his own pistol. Russell's men are gunned down in short order. Wayne finally lets Nelson stay and help as his deputy. Once again, however, Russell's men get the drop on Wayne and Martin and both are held hostage. While Martin is kept under wraps, two of Russell's men take Wayne to the jail and force him to tell Brennan to release Akins. Despite the danger, Brennan answers with a blast from his shotgun and kills both men. Wayne is freed but is forced to arrange a swap of Akins for Martin. When morning comes, Wayne and Nelson prepare to make the swap at the building where Martin is being held at the far side of town. Brennan readies himself to come with them, but Wayne flatly tells him no, because he is crippled and will only get in the way. Wayne and Nelson arrive at the location and send Akins toward the house while Russell sends Martin toward them. As the hostages pass each other, Martin tackles Akins and drags him behind the ruins of an adobe hut. There is a vicious fistfight and Martin manages to subdue Akins. A full-scale gun battle ensues, and at one point three of Russell's men manage to escape the house and come around behind Nelson, Wayne, and Martin. Because of their position, there is nothing the lawmen can do to stop the outlaws from getting the drop on them. Suddenly there is gunfire and the three men fall back dead. Brennan has disobeyed Wayne's orders and tagged along. Nelson sees that the old man is standing next to one of Bond's wagons filled with dynamite. A stray bullet could blow Brennan to kingdom come. Wayne runs over and tells Brennan of the danger, but Brennan goes back and pulls a case of dynamite off the truck and throws a stick at the house while Wayne shoots it in the air to make it explode. The trick works, and after several huge explosions rock the hideout, Russell's men give up. Peace returns to the town of Rio Bravo and Wayne goes to the hotel to visit Dickinson. She is dressed in a skimpy dance-hall girl outfit and Wayne is shocked. She tells him that if she's to sing in the saloon for a living she needs all the help she can get. Wayne's indifferent response infuriates Dickinson and she admits that she put on the outfit to make Wayne jealous so that he'd tell her not to wear it. He responds by saying that he'll arrest her if she wears it in public. Dickinson beams at the threat—which is as close as Wayne is going to get to saying "I Love You" to her —changes her clothes, and kisses him. Wayne tosses her sexy tights out the window and they land next to Martin and Brennan, who happen to be walking by. Brennan picks up the tights, looks up to the window, and both men laugh as they walk off. With its simple plot line, familiar characters, songs, and frequent humor RIO BRAVO is outstanding entertainment. The film has been overrated by some zealous critics who either ignore its weak points or incorporate them into their thesis as praiseworthy achievements. As enjoyable as the film is, there are some nagging flaws that prevent it from reaching the immortal status of RED RIVER—particularly in the casting. Pop star Nelson was cast on the basis of his vast popularity with teenagers—with little regard for his acting talent—thus ensuring additional box office from young girls who wouldn't normally think of going to see a western (in interviews Hawks even bragged that Nelson meant "a million dollars more" at the box office). Despite his moneymaking potential, Nelson simply couldn't act—and Hawks must have known it. The singer is given the fewest lines possible for an actor billed third under Wayne and Martin and his physical presence is restricted to the background or shared with the other leads. He is never given center stage alone—the boy is no Montgomery Clift. Also somewhat weak is Dickinson. While she is given all the right Hawksian dialog and demonstrates herself as the quintessential Hawks female who is tough enough to stand up to any man who comes her way, she doesn't possess the spunkiness of a Jean Arthur or the sultry sensuality of a Lauren Bacall. Wayne, however, turns in a fine performance (though not as good as in RED RIVER or any John Ford film) and Brennan is superb as the grouchy, nasty old man who is undyingly loyal to his friends. The real revelation is Martin. His role as the drunken deputy who redeems himself is crucial to the film and the singer-actor handles his part with skill. Hawks enjoyed working with Martin and found him eager and willing to take direction. Martin was so eager to please Hawks that on the first day of shooting he showed up on the set, as the director described in an interview: "...dressed like a musical-comedy cowboy. I said, 'Dean, look, you know a little about drinking. You've seen a lot of drunks. I want a *drunk*. I want a guy with an old dirty sweatshirt and an old hat.' He went over, and he came back with the outfit he wore in the picture. He must of have been successful because Jack Warner said to me, 'We hired Dean Martin. When's he going to be in this picture?' I said, 'He's the funny-looking guy in the old hat.' 'Holy smoke, is that Dean Martin?'" Hawks' response to HIGH NOON was very successful at the box office, and the director made two slim variations of the story (same character types, similar situations, sometimes even the same sets) as his last two westerns—EL DORADO (1967) and RIO LOBO (1970). The films were all cowritten by female screenwriter Brackett and form a sort of informal trilogy (unfortunately, each film was weaker than the last). Though Hawks was inspired to make RIO BRAVO as a rebuttal to HIGH NOON (3:10 TO YUMA also annoyed the director for the same reasons), his daughter Barbara Hawks McCampbell—who wanted to be a writer—came up with the basic plot line that later became the climax of the movie (outlaws holed up in a house with the heroes exploding sticks of dynamite by shooting them like clay targets) and was paid for her work and given screen credit for the story. Despite its flaws, RIO BRAVO is an excellent film that presents strong, proud, but very human characters who fight against their various handicaps and pull together to do a job and do it right. The characters in RIO BRAVO have the same kind of deep affection and understanding of one another as do members of a close family who are not afraid to speak truthfully for fear of hurting each other's feelings, and it is that aspect of the film that is so appealing. Young director John Carpenter's second feature, ASSAULT ON PRECINCT 13 (1976), is an updated remake of RIO BRAVO.

p&d, Howard Hawks; w, Jules Furthman, Leigh Brackett (based on a story by Barbara Hawks McCampbell); ph, Russell Harlan (Technicolor); m, Dimitri Tiomkin; ed, Folmar Blangsted; md, Tiomkin; art d, Leo K. Kuter; set d, Ralph S. Hurst; cos, Marjorie Best; m/l, "My Rifle, My Pony and Me," "Cindy," "Deguello," Tiomkin, Paul Francis Webster; makeup, Gordon Bau.

Western **Cas.** **(PR:A MPAA:NR)**

RIO CONCHOS*** (1964) 105m FOX c

Richard Boone *(Lassiter)*, Stuart Whitman *(Capt. Haven)*, Tony Franciosa *(Rodriguez)*, Wende Wagner *(Sally)*, Warner Anderson *(Col. Wagner)*, Jim Brown *(Sgt. Ben Franklyn)*, Rodolfo Acosta *(Bloodshirt)*, Barry Kelley *(Croupier)*, Vito Scotti *(Mexican Bandit)*, House Peters, Jr. *(Pardee Officer)*, Kevin Hagen *(Blondebeard)*, Edmond O'Brien *(Col. Theron Pardee)*, Timothy Carey *(Barman)*.

The search for a shipment of stolen rifles leads to the home of Boone, a sadistic Indian-hater who is arrested by officer Whitman because he won't disclose where he obtained his rifle. After a brief stay in the Union prison with Mexican bandit Franciosa, Boone agrees to help Whitman uncover the stolen rifles. As it turns out, the rifles were stolen by a Confederate officer, O'Brien, who wants to rekindle the Civil War by selling the guns to Apaches and thus lay siege to the Union soldiers. Four men, Whitman, Boone, Franciosa, and Brown in his first screen appearance, go after O'Brien, and find him in a camp about to turn the rifles over to the Indians. An heroic effort by Brown blows the camp and just about everything else apart. Superb characterizations, especially by Boone, who is as venomous and bitter as they come, make this a western with power. The Monument Valley locations are nice background.

p, David Weisbart; d, Gordon Douglas; w, Joseph Landon, Clair Huffaker (based on the novel *Guns of the Rio Conchos* by Huffaker); ph, Joe MacDonald (CinemaScope, DeLuxe Color); m, Jerry Goldsmith; ed, Joseph Silver; art d, Jack Martin Smith, William Creber; set d, Walter M. Scott, Lucien Hafley; makeup, Ben Nye.

Western **(PR:A MPAA:NR)**

RIO GRANDE** (1939) 58m COL bw

Charles Starrett *(Houston)*, Ann Doran *(Jean)*, Bob Nolan *(Bob)*, Dick Curtis *(Barker)*, George Chesebro *(Kruger)*, Hank Bell *(Hank)*, Pat Brady *(Pat)*, Art Mix *(Durkin)*, Lee Prather *(Goulding)*, Hal Taliaferro [Wally Wales], Edward J. LeSaint, Ed Piel, Sr., Ted Mapes, Harry Strang, Fred Burns, Forrest Taylor, Stanley Brown, George Morrell, Sons of the Pioneers, John Tyrell, Fred Evans.

Routine western fare is about Starrett rescuing Doran when Curtis tries to run her off her land. A bit of new life is given by inducting Doran in a role usually reserved for Iris Meredith. Special notice should be taken of the photography by the great cinematographer Lucien Ballard. The Sons of The Pioneers are along to help Starrett, as well as to provide a few tunes, including: "Tumblin Tumbleweeds," "West is in My Soul," "Slumbertime on the Range," and "Old Bronco Pal" (Bob Nolan).

p, Harry Decker; d, Sam Nelson; w, Charles Francis Royal; ph, Lucien Ballard; ed, William Lyon; cos, Adele Palmer.

Western **(PR:A MPAA:NR)**

RIO GRANDE**** (1950) 105m Argosy Pictures/REP bw

John Wayne *(Lt. Col. Kirby Yorke)*, Maureen O'Hara *(Mrs. Kathleen Yorke)*, Ben Johnson *(Trooper Tyree)*, Claude Jarman, Jr. *(Trooper Jeff Yorke)*, Harry Carey, Jr. *(Trooper Daniel "Sandy" Boone)*, Chill Wills *(Dr. Wilkins)*, J. Carrol Naish *(Gen. Philip Sheridan)*, Victor McLaglen *(Sgt. Maj. Quincannon)*, Grant Withers *(Deputy Marshal)*, Peter Ortiz *(Capt. St. Jacques)*, Steve Pendleton *(Capt. Prescott)*, Karolyn Grimes *(Margaret Mary)*, Alberto Morin *(Lieutenant)*, Stan Jones *(Sergeant)*, Fred Kennedy *(Heinze)*, Chuck Roberson *(Officer)*, Ken Curtis, Hugh Farr, Karl Farr, Lloyd Perryman, Shug Fisher, Tommy Doss [The Sons of the Pioneers]*(Regimental Singers)*, Jack Pennick *(Sergeant)*, Cliff Lyons *(Soldier)*, Pat Wayne.

This fine portrait of the U.S. Cavalry was the third in Ford's magnificent trilogy about the troopers of the Old West. The earlier entries are FORT APACHE (1948) and SHE WORE A YELLOW RIBBON (1949). Actually, in the chronology of these three films, RIO GRANDE is the true sequel to FORT APACHE, with Wayne shown to be a middle-aged commanding officer of a remote cavalry outpost. He is rough but his bark is worse than his proverbial bite. To Wayne's post comes his only son, Jarman. He is cool toward the boy, who rebuffs his initial welcome, and later tells the recruit what Army life is really about: "Put out of your mind any romantic ideas that it's a way of glory. It's a life of suffering and hardship, an uncompromising devotion to your oath and your duty." Jarman is quickly adopted by Johnson, Carey, and other seasoned veterans while Wayne is disturbed to find that his estranged wife O'Hara has arrived at the post to look after her son. He treats her with cordiality, allows her to move into his quarters, and he movies out into a tent. The two have been separated for 15 years, ever since Wayne, following orders of General Sheridan (Naish) burned down the southern plantation belonging to O'Hara's family, loyal Confederates. Wayne finds her very attractive and is soon courting her all over again while Jarman adjusts to military service. O'Hara finds it hard to adjust to Wayne's top sergeant, McLaglen, for it was he who carried out Wayne's orders and burned the mansion in the southland. O'Hara calls McLaglen "that arsonist," and later, in his cups, McLaglen tells the fort doctor, Wills, how he burned the house down around O'Hara while "silent as death she was, with her babe in her arms." Weepy and full of remorse, McLaglen holds out his enormous paw of a hand and says: "And there's the dirty hand that did it!" He notices Wills whittling a large piece of wood, and adds: "I wish you'd knock it off with that stick!" Wills spins about and gives McLaglen's hand such a mighty whack that the stick breaks in two and McLaglen, wincing in great pain, looks at Wills with shock, as if to say, "I didn't really mean for you to knock off my hand!" O'Hara and Wayne, meanwhile, argue over their son. Though Wayne is disappointed that Jarman has dropped out of West Point, he feels that a tour of duty with rough-and-ready cavalrymen will make a man out of him. O'Hara doesn't, telling Wayne that their son enlisted out of shame and sorrow. She is there to buy back his enlistment, a custom accepted during that era. But she requires the cooperation of the commanding officer, Wayne, and he refuses to let her buy Jarman out of what he considers the boy's duty. Indians then attack the fort, breaking loose some of the Apache captives Wayne has taken in his last skirmish with a renegade tribe. Naish visits the post and during a dinner party O'Hara stands to deliver a potent toast: "To my only rival, the United States Cavalry." (This toast, of course, summarizes the theme of this film, career over home and the struggle between O'Hara and Wayne to reconcile their life styles.) As with many of Ford's films, a group of soldiers arrives and they sing "I'll Take You Home Again, Kathleen," honoring O'Hara. "This music...is not of my choosing," Wayne tells O'Hara apologetically. "I wish it had been," she replies softly. After the Indian attack it is decided that the poorly defended fort cannot withstand a full-scale attack by the Apaches and Wayne decides to send the women and children to a safer military post, telling O'Hara that he is assigning Jarman as one of the wagon train's escorts. "He'll hate you for it," O'Hara tells him, "but I'll love you for it." Before O'Hara joins the women and children leaving the post, she turns to Wayne and says, "Aren't you going to kiss me goodbye?" Wayne takes her in his arms and kisses her, delivering a line that only he could master: "I never want to kiss you goodbye, Kathy." The wagon train with the women and children is attacked by Indians who make off with one wagon loaded with children. Jarman breaks through the Indian lines and rides for help, running into Johnson who has fled the post ahead of a marshal, Withers, looking for him to answer a charge of murder in Texas. Indians behind Jarman are fast approaching and Johnson holds them off as Jarman continues his frantic ride for help. O'Hara and the other women and troopers hold off Indian attacks from behind their overturned wagons; they later see Wayne and his troopers arrive, having been brought to the scene by Jarman. Wayne then leads an expedition to regain the stolen children, violating international law by crossing into Mexico to chase the Apache band. He finds the Indian encampment and sends Jarman, Johnson, and Carey into the camp to secure the children. The three young troopers find the children alive and well, held hostage in an abandoned church. They bolt the doors and prepare to defend the children while waiting for Wayne to lead his men against the encampment. Wayne comes charging in with his full regiment just as the Indians, having concluded their drunken ritual dances, head for the church to dispose of the children. The troopers ride through the camp, battling the Apaches, while Johnson, Jarman, and Carey drive off the savages trying to enter the church. Wagons are brought up to the church steps and the children are bundled safely inside with McLaglen and other troopers driving the wagons pell-mell to safety while Jarman, Carey, and Johnson join the other troopers and Wayne who conduct a rear-guard action. Just as the soldiers ride through the encampment one more time, Wayne receives an arrow in his chest and is knocked from his horse. Jarman and others rush to him and Wayne tells his son to "pull it out, Jeff!" Jarman yanks the arrow from his father's chest and Wayne is taken away. The regiment returns to the fort where O'Hara is waiting, she and the other women having returned earlier. O'Hara sees Wayne being dragged into the fort on a litter and goes to him holding his hand. "Our boy did well," he tells her with pride. Later, Wayne recovers and he and O'Hara join Naish on a reviewing stand where medals are given out to Jarman, Carey, Johnson, and others. Withers shows up and demands that Johnson be turned over to him but Wayne shouts to Johnson that he is on an extended furlough and Johnson jumps on Naish's horse and rides off. (Wayne by then has learned from O'Hara that the murder charge in Texas is a case of self-defense by Johnson and that the young man had gunned down a man who had despoiled his sister.) The troopers then parade in review with a band blaring out cavalry marches. This changes in the last scene to the tune of "Dixie," in honor of Southern belle O'Hara. Naish points to himself to indicate that he has ordered the southern song played. O'Hara twirls her parasol and smiles winningly at Wayne and it is obvious that the two will reconcile their differences and live happily together. As with FORT APACHE and SHE WORE A YELLOW RIBBON, Ford projects a powerful portrait of the wild and far Southwest during the Indian wars, showing the traditions and exploits of the old cavalry in very realistic terms. In his scenes showing the cavalry in action Ford presents no glory but tired, dirty, wounded men moving to their assignments in pain and discomfort, emphasizing the real glory of these men, typified by their leader Wayne. The director's camera angles, those where he broadly encompasses whole lines of riding cavalrymen, accentuate the prosaic nobility of these men and their dedication to taming a frontier that would run with blood without their presence. Much of the musical score supports the story here, outlining the Irish background of the cavalrymen and properly presenting their sentimentality. (In the 19th Century when the great Irish migration to the U.S. took place, men from Ireland invariably joined either police forces in cities or joined the Army, preferably the cavalry, to serve on the frontier.) Wayne is larger than life in his role of fort commander and he did his own riding and stunts as usual. Debuting in the film as a trooper is Patrick Wayne, his father having secured a small bit part for him from director Ford. Oddly, Ford had not intended to make this film, but wanted to appease Republic Studios which asked for it, believing it would be more commercial than THE QUIET MAN, Ford's next film and one Republic had doubts about. Yet RIO GRANDE proved to be an excellent western with some unforgettable scenes and it marked the first appearance of Wayne and O'Hara together. They would make five films together and all would prove their chemistry just right, both of them being proud, determined, and aggressive personalities who complemented each other. Wayne wears a small goatee in RIO GRANDE much the same way Henry Fonda wore one in FORT APACHE, the predecessor to this film. This would be the only film where he wore anything approximating a beard, although he appeared heavily unshaven in two films, BACK TO BATAAN and TEXAS TERROR. Songs include: "My Gal Is Purple," "Footsore Cavalry," "Yellow Stripes" (Stan Jones), "Aha, San Antone" (Dale Evans), "Cattle Call" (Tex Owens), "Erie Canal," "I'll Take You Home Again, Kathleen," "Down by the Glen Side," "You're in the Army Now" (sung by the Sons of the Pioneers).

p, John Ford, Merian C. Cooper; d, Ford; w, James Kevin McGuinness (based on the story "Mission with No Record" by James Warner Bellah); ph, Bert Glennon; m, Victor Young; ed, Jack Murray; art d, Frank Hotaling; set d, John McCarthy, Jr., Charles Thompson; cos, Adele Palmer; spec eff, Howard and Theodore Lydecker; m/l, Stan Jones, Dale Evans, Tex Owens.

Western **Cas.** **(PR:A MPAA:NR)**

RIO GRANDE PATROL*½ (1950) 60m RKO bw

Tim Holt *(Nebraska)*, Jane Nigh *(Sherry)*, Douglas Fowley *(Bragg)*, Cleo Moore *(Peppie)*, Rick Vallin *(Trevino)*, John Holland *(Fowler)*, Tom Tyler *(Vance)*, Larry Johns *(Doctor)*, Harry Harvey *(Station Master)*, Richard Martin *(Chito Rafferty)*, Forrest Burns.

Holt with his sidekick Martin, present solely for laughs and very few at that, play patrol guards along the Mexican border who discover that a gang of outlaws, led by a dastardly Vallin, are trying to smuggle machine guns to insurrectionists. The rest of the spotty script is about the hero trying to uncover the guns and get the crooks in jail, and taking care of nasty hired killer Tyler.

p, Herman Schlom; d, Lesley Selander; w, Norman Houston; ph, J. Roy Hunt; ed, Desmond Marquette.

Western **(PR:A MPAA:NR)**

RIO GRANDE RAIDERS½** (1946) 56m REP bw

Sunset Carson, Linda Stirling, Bob Steele, Tom London, Tristram Coffin, Edmund Cobb, Jack O'Shea, Tex Terry, Kenne Duncan, Al Taylor, Fred Burns, Roy Bucko, Blackie Whiteford.

Carson's last film in his long-running series of B westerns for Republic involves the cowboy's kid brother, Steele, being released from prison to the custody of Coffin, an evil stagecoach operator locked in a fierce competition with rival operator Cobb (whom Carson works for). Coffin soon has Steele behind a mask and robbing Cobb's coaches. Carson learns of his brother's activities, and though he could go to the sheriff with his information, he decides to remain silent in the hope that he will be able to turn his brother around. Steele does have a change of heart when, during a stagecoach race between the brothers, he learns that Coffin has planted one of his henchmen in the coach to sabotage Carson. Seeing his brother struggle with the evil cowboy, Steele slows down his coach until Carson is able to rid himself of the intruder and continue the race. Carson wins and Steele marches off to confront his boss. Before he can face Coffin, Steele is gunned down in the street by one of the stage boss's henchmen. Steele dies in Carson's arms. Carson then eliminates Coffin and his triggerman. After RIO GRANDE RAIDERS, Carson disappeared from the screen for two years until he returned in a vastly inferior series of B westerns for Yucca Productions.

p, Bennett Cohen; d, Thomas Carr; w, Norton S. Parker (based on a story by

Norman S. Hall); ph, Alfred Keller; ed, William P. Thompson; md, Mort Glickman; art d, Gano Chittenden; spec eff, Howard Lydecker, Theodore Lydecker.

Western Cas. (PR:A MPAA:NR)

RIO GRANDE RANGER* (1937) 54m COL bw

Bob Allen *(Bob)*, Iris Meredith *(Sandra)*, Paul Sutton *(Jim)*, Hal Taliaferro [Wally Wales] *(Hal)*, Robert Henry *(Buzzy)*, John Elliot *(Allen)*, Tom London *(Smeed)*, Slim Whitaker *(Jack)*, Jack Rockwell *(Capt. Walter)*, Dick Botiller, Art Mix, Frank Ellis, Jack Ingram, Al Taylor, Jim Corey, Henry Hall, Jack C. Smith, Edward Cassidy, Ray Jones.

Once again Allen illustrates that a western hero he ain't, though in this one exhibiting a bit of his trickster nature as he tries to round up a gang of outlaws who use the convenience of the state line to make their getaway. Temporarily taking the badge from his chest, he crosses the state line to join up with the crooks, then lets them know his true identity so they'll chase him across the line and fall into a trap of lawmen.

p, Larry Darmour; d, Spencer G. Bennett; w, Nate Gatzert (based on a story by Jacques Jaccard, Ceila Jaccard); ph, James S. Brown, Jr.; ed, Dwight Caldwell.

Western (PR:A MPAA:NR)

RIO GRANDE ROMANCE*½ (1936) 60m Victory bw

Eddie Nugent *(Bob Andrews)*, Maxine Doyle *(Joan Williams)*, Fuzzy Knight *(Elmer)*, Lucille Lund *(Rose Carter)*, Don Alvarado *(Jack Carter)*, Nick Stuart *(Bates)*, George Walsh *(Bradley)*, Joyce Kay *(Patricia)*, George Cleveland *(Sheriff)*, Forrest Taylor *(Shelby)*, Ernie Adams *(Lampson)*, Ed Cassidy *(Lewis)*.

Dull picture is about FBI agent, Nugent, who is vacationing and chasing Taylor, a knave posing as a straight lawyer, at the same time. Sour job of casting doesn't do much to help the weak story.

p, Sam Katzman; d, Robert Hill; w, Al Martin (based on a story by Peter B. Kyne); ph, William Hyer; ed, Dan Milner.

Crime (PR:A MPAA:NR)

RIO LOBO*½ (1970) 114m Malabar-Cinema Center/NG c

John Wayne *(Col. Cord McNally)*, Jorge Rivero *(Capt. Pierre Cordona)*, Jennifer O'Neill *(Shasta Delaney)*, Jack Elam *(Phillips)*, Victor French *(Ketcham)*, Susana Dosamantes *(Maria Carmen)*, Chris Mitchum *(Tuscarora)*, Mike Henry *(Sheriff Tom Hendricks)*, David Huddleston *(Dr. Jones)*, Bill Williams *(Sheriff Pat Cronin)*, Edward Faulkner *(Lt. Harris)*, Sherry Lansing *(Amelita)*, Dean Smith *(Bitey)*, Robert Donner *(Whiter Carter)*, Jim Davis *(Riley)*, Peter Jason *(Lt. Forsythe)*, Robert Rothwell, Chuck Courtney, George Plimpton *(Whitey's Henchman)*, Bob Steele *(Deputy Sheriff)*, Boy "Red" Morgan *(Train Engineer)*, Hank Worden *(Hank)*, Chuck Roberson *(Corporal/Guard)*, William Byrne *(Machinist)*, Don "Red" Barry, Jose Angel Espinosa, Anthony Sparrow Hawk, Charlie Longfoot, Frank Kennedy, John McKee, Stanley Corson, Chuck Hayward, Sandra Curie, Jim Preiean, Danny Sands, Harold Cops.

This is probably the hardest film to watch that either Howard Hawks or John Wayne ever took part in, surpassing even Wayne's early days in Republic's THREE MESQUITEER series for forced acting and situations. The 1930s pictures are more forgivable because the budgets were limiting and the outings were approached routinely. But for such a refined director as Hawks to end his career on a note like this, having made some of the finest, if not *the best*, films in the history of American cinema is an atrocity not worth the silver used in the negative. The story isn't so bad, taking place soon following the Civil War, in which Union captain Wayne teams up with two Confederate soldiers to track down the man responsible for stealing a shipment of gold. Their efforts land them in the middle of a town being terrorized by a crooked sheriff, to which Wayne and company put an end by rallying the townspeople to stand up for their rights. Witty lines are injected that would normally provide a chuckle, but are delivered here in a manner that only makes one want to sigh. The common Hawksian theme of male comradeship can be felt in the relationship between Wayne and his Confederate cohorts as fighting men of honor. But the way Wayne and his supporting cast walk through their lines is ridiculous. Rivero and O'Neill face the Duke like beginning stars in the shadow of a great master, something Wayne is aware of and can't seem to shake. Only the performance of Elam remains lively, but it is the type of characterization he has done dozens of times. A sad finale to a magnificent career.

p&d, Howard Hawks; w, Leigh Brackett, Burton Wohl (based on a story by Wohl); ph, William Clothier (Technicolor); m, Jerry Goldsmith; ed, John Woodcock; prod d, Robert Smith; set d, William Keirnan; cos, Luster Bayless, Ted Parvin; spec eff, A.D. Flowers, Clifford Wenger; makeup, Monte Westmore, David Grayson, Dick Cobos.

Western Cas. (PR:A MPAA:G)

RIO RITA*½** (1929) 135m RKO bw-c

Bert Wheeler *(Chick Bean)*, Robert Woolsey *(Lovett)*, Bebe Daniels *(Rita Ferguson)*, John Boles *(Capt. Jim Stewart)*, Dorothy Lee *(Dolly)*, Don Alvarado *(Roberto Ferguson)*, Georges Renavent *(Gen. Ravenoff/"Kinkajou")*, Eva Rosita *(Carmen)*, Sam Nelson *(McGinn)*, Fred Burns *(Wilkins)*, Sam Blum *(Cafe Owner)*, Nick De Ruiz *(Padrone)*, Tiny Sandford *(Davalos)*, Helen Kaiser *(Mrs. Bean)*, Benny Corbett, Fred Scott *(Rangers)*.

Wheeler and Woolsey made their film debut in this adaptation of Florenz Ziegfeld's 1927 stage hit that ran well over a year. The comedy team had starred in the play and repeated their success in this half color-half black-and-white movie that grossed a fortune at the box office and was one of the first musical spectaculars ever done. Daniels was also making her sound film debut after having played in several Harold Lloyd comedies while still a teenager. Boles, who had a wonderful singing voice, was on his way to becoming a matinee idol. Shot in only 24 days, RIO RITA's plot was the least of its assets. Boles is a Texas Ranger in pursuit of a bandit known as El Kinkajou. The writers must have found that word in the dictionary and thought it sounded vaguely Hispanic. It is, of course, the name for the Australian marsupial one sees in all the Qantas TV commercials. In the process, Boles meets Daniels. They fall for each other but Boles is worried, as the crook he is tailing may be Daniels' brother, Alvarado. The affair is not smooth and they separate when Boles begins to suspect Alvarado. Daniels is soon being courted by Renavent, a rat if there ever was one. Meanwhile, Wheeler wants out of his marriage and seeks the counsel of shyster lawyer Woolsey. In the end, Renavent is unmasked as the criminal, thereby paving the way for Daniels and Boles to be united. Admittedly not much of a story, but the comedy was good, the acting excellent, and the dances sensational. The well-integrated musical numbers included: "Rio Rita," "The Ranger Song," "Sweetheart, We Need Each Other," "If You're in Love, You'll Waltz," "You're Always in My Arms (But Only in My Dreams)," "The Kinkajou," "Following the Sun Around" (Joseph McCarthy, Harry Tierney), and "Long Before You Came Along" (E.Y. Harburg, Harold Arlen). Wheeler and Woolsey provided the funny stuff for this unusually long (135 minutes) film. It was transferred almost totally from stage to screen with very little alteration, and audiences loved it. Shooting the film in two processes was an error, and since they already had color, they should have made it entirely that way. Lee, who had made her name as one of Fred Waring's Pennsylvanians, does well in a small second lead. This was remade in 1942 with Kathryn Grayson as Rita, John Carroll as the Ranger, and Abbott and Costello adding comic relief. That one had Nazis and intrigue to fill out the plot and was quite different, retaining only the title and a few other bits.

p, William LeBaron; d, Luther Reed; w, Reed, Russell Mack (based on the musical by Guy Bolton, Fred Thompson), ph, Robert Kurrle, Lloyd Knetchel; m, Harry Tierney; ed, William Hamilton; md, Victor Baravalle; art d&cos, Max Ree; ch, Pearl Eaton.

Musical Comedy (PR:A MPAA:NR)

RIO RITA½** (1942) 91m MGM bw

Bud Abbott *(Doc)*, Lou Costello *(Wishy)*, Kathryn Grayson *(Rita Winslow)*, John Carroll *(Ricardo Montera)*, Patricia Dane *(Lucille Brunswick)*, Tom Conway *(Maurice Craindall)*, Peter Whitney *(Jake)*, Arthur Space *(Trask)*, Joan Valerie *(Dotty)*, Dick Rich *(Gus)*, Barry Nelson *(Harry Gantley)*, Eva Puig *(Marianna)*, Mitchell Lewis *(Julio)*, Eros Volusia *(Dancer)*, Julian Rivero *(Mexican Gent)*, Douglass Newland *(Control Man)*, Lee Murray *(Little Mexican)*, Inez Cooper *(Pulque)*, Frank Perry *(Chef)*.

MGM decided to do a remake of the 1929 RKO film, and borrowed Abbott and Costello from Universal, fixed up the plot to fit in with war happenings, and hired a writer to think up some new gags for the boys. The sole intention was a sure-fire box-office hit. Excepting the presence of Abbott and Costello, the story is a routine outing in which Conway plays a Nazi spy while in the employ of hotel owner Grayson. Abbott and Costello aid, or hinder, depending upon one's perspective, Carroll in abating the criminal and provide a few original gags along the way, but mostly get by with old faithfuls. Credit director Simon with maintaining a fair level of suspense and injecting humor and music at just the right spots to move the picture along. Songs include: "Ranger's Song," "Rio Rita" (Joseph McCarthy, Harry Tierney), "Long Before You Came Along" (E.Y. Harburg, Harold Arlen), "Brazilian Dance" (Nilo Barnet), "Ora O Conga" (Lacerdo). (See ABBOTT AND COSTELLO series, Index.)

p, Pandro S. Berman; d, S. Sylvan Simon; w, Richard Connell, Gladys Lehman, John Grant; ph, George Folsey; ed, Ben Lewis; md, Herbert Stothart; cos, Robert Kalloch, Gile Steele; spec eff, Warren Newcombe.

Comedy (PR:AAA MPAA:NR)

RIO 70* (1970, U.S./Ger./Span.) 79m Ada/Terra/Udastex c (DIE SIBEN MANNER DER SU-MARU; SUMURU; AKA: RIVER 70; FUTURE WOMEN; THE SEVEN SECRETS OF SU-MARU)

Shirley Eaton *(Sumuru)*, Richard Wyler, George Sanders, Herbert Fleischman, Maria Rohm, Marta Reves, Elisa Montes.

The equally ridiculous sequel to THE MILLION EYES OF SUMURU (1967), which marks the return of Eaton, a sadistic savage whose all-girl tribe is trying to conquer the world. While this one's predecessor offered both Frankie Avalon and Klaus Kinski in supporting roles, RIO 70 can only boast the presence of professional cad Sanders.

p, Harry Allan Towers; d, Jesus Franco; w, Towers, Franz Eicchorn (based on characters created by Sam Rohmer); ph, Manuel Merino; m, Daniel White; ed, Angel Serrano; art d, Peter Manhardt.

Science Fiction/Adventure (PR:C MPAA:NR)

RIO VENGENCE (SEE: MOTOR PSYCHO, 1965)

RIOT½** (1969) 97m PAR c

Jim Brown *(Culley Briston)*, Gene Hackman *(Red Fletcher)*, Ben Carruthers *(Joe Surefoot)*, Mike Kellin *(Bugsy)*, Gerald S. O'Louglin *(Grossman)*, Clifford David *("Big Mary" Sheldon)*, Bill Walker *(Jake)*, Ricky Summers *("Gertie")*, Michael Byron *(Murray)*, Jerry Thomson *(Deputy Warden Fisk)*, M. Gerri, John Neiderhauser *(Homosexuals)*, Frank A. Eyman *(The Warden)*.

RIOT is a better-than-average exploitation picture with a script by Academy Award winner James Poe that takes it out of the ordinary status. If the warden and the 600 convicts smack of authenticity, that's because they were real people who lived at the Arizona State Prison, although this was based on something that happened at a jail in Minnesota, as detailed by ex-con Frank Elli's book. The warden, Eyman, is on holiday when Brown gets into a disagreement with a guard and is tossed into the isolation block for his efforts. Hackman is already there and planning a jailbreak and Brown becomes involved, albeit reluctantly. The prisoners take a few guards as hostages and are now in control of a small section of the facility. Although Hackman tells the press that the riot is due to poor treatment of the inmates, he is using this riot to cover the fact that there's a tunnel under the place which he intends using as his route to freedom. With TV and radio and newspapers watching, Hackman assumes leadership of the group and tells them of the alleged abuses. While negotiations are being attempted, the men get out of hand, as they have no one to stop them in their small section. Whiskey is manufactured and the drinking begins. That leads to the gay prisoners holding an all-out dress-in-drag party. This is now a chance to get even for old grievances and a prisoner's court is set up to mete punishment for finks who have cooperated with the authorities in the past. Carruthers is an insane Indian who has to be restrained from killing the hostages by Brown. Eyman hurries back from his vacation and will tolerate none of the prisoners' demands because he knows they are all a ruse. He is about to order the militia to go into the area and take no prisoners. Hackman intuits that Eyman won't put up with the negotiations, so he leads a group of desperate men into the tunnel, then closes the entrance behind them so it won't be discovered by any of the other cons or the guards. The moment they come up out of the tunnel, they are fired upon by the soldiers as well as subjected to tear gas. Brown, Hackman, and Carruthers have gas masks and manage to make their way to a guard tower through a large steam pipe. Carruthers, who thirsts for blood, kills the guard and tries to do the same to Brown, but Hackman stops him just as he is about to plunge the knife into Brown. Hackman and Carruthers fight to the finish and Brown gets away. Nonstop sadism, gore, action, and foul language, but Poe's script makes a few points not usually seen in this type movie. Righteous Brother Bill Medley sings the title tune several times in bits and pieces and the old standard "Rag Mop" is also heard, so it almost breaks into being a prison musical. Since every criminal inside seems to be armed with something, what RIOT mainly does is convince anyone on the edge of criminality that it's better to be on the outside looking in.

p, William Castle; d, Buzz Kulik; w, James Poe (based on the novel The Riot by Frank Elli); ph, Robert Hauser (Technicolor); m, Christopher Komeda; ed, Edwin H. Bryant; prod d &art d, Paul Sylbert; m/l, "100 Years," Komeda, Robert Wells (sung by Bill Medley), "Rag Mop," Johnnie Lee Willis, Deacon Anderson; Charles Blackman.

Drama   **(PR:O MPAA:R)**

RIOT AT LAUDERDALE   (SEE: HELL'S PLAYGROUND, 1967)

RIOT IN CELL BLOCK 11***½   (1954) 80m AA bw

Neville Brand (Dunn), Emile Meyer (The Warden), Frank Faylen (Haskell), Leo Gordon (Carnie), Robert Osterloh (The Colonel), Paul Frees (Monroe), Don Keefer (Reporter), Alvy Moore (Gator), Dabbs Greer (Schuyler), Whit Bissell (Snader), James Anderson (Acton), Carleton Young (Capt. Barrett), Harold J. Kennedy (Reporter), William Schallert (Reporter), Jonathan Hale (Russell), Robert Patton (Frank), William Phipps (Mickey), Joel Fluellen (Al), Roy Glenn (Delmar), Joe Kerr (Mac), John Tarangelo (Manuel), Robert Burton (Ambrose), Frank Hagney (Roberts).

This is a stunning, powerful, and intelligent prison film which sees the inmates of Folsom Prison rise up under the leadership of convict Brand, not to escape incarceration, but to improve the horrendous conditions under which they live. Aided by his psychotic lieutenant,Gordon, Brand overpowers a guard and their takeover of the cell block begins. While holding a handful of other guard hostages, Brand contacts the warden, Meyer, and, with the help of fellow inmate Osterloh, lists his demands. The prisoners are fed up with their pointless activities, sadistic guards, bad food, shoddy recreation, dilapidated cells, and the fact that the truly dangerous inmates (like Gordon) are thrown in with the mainstream population. Meyer, who has been fighting the politicians for more money to make such reforms, is sympathetic to the prisoners' demands but his pleas have fallen on deaf ears. As news of the uprising sweeps throughout the prison, other cellblocks take up the revolt. Worried that the whole prison might explode into an orgy of violence, Meyer is forced to call the local militia for assistance, though he knows this may provoke further bloodshed. Meanwhile, Brand struggles to keep Gordon under control and the violence to a minimum. The homicidal maniac cares nothing about Brand's reform demands and has participated in the riot to serve his own selfish ends. The revolt threatens to collapse because of Gordon. Meyer in the meantime has his hands full trying to convince Faylen, a senator, that the requests are reasonable. Though the governor has agreed to the demands and to let the prisoners continue their sentences with no reprisals, the legislature rejects his proposal and demands that Brand be given an additional 30 years for instigating the riot. During the negotiations, Gordon has whipped the other inmates into a frenzy, and even goes so far as to stab senator Faylen in the arm. When the tense situation finally concludes, the inmates, the politicians, and the public have gained little from the experience. Directed with a sure hand by Siegel, RIOT IN CELL BLOCK 11 is one of his best films and one of the best of the prison genre. Veteran producer Wanger, whose impressive lists of credits include YOU ONLY LIVE ONCE (1937), ALGIERS (1938), FOREIGN CORRESPONDENT (1940), and later Siegel's science-fiction classic INVASION OF THE BODY SNATCHERS (1956), had a special interest in the project because he had served time in prison during the early 1950's for shooting and wounding his wife's (Joan Bennett) agent, Jennings Lang. Convinced his wife's relationship with Lang was destroying his home, Wanger confronted the pair with a gun in Lang's office parking lot across the street from a Beverly Hills police station. Wanger shot at Lang's car and then at the ground, but the bullet ricocheted and hit Lang in the groin. Wanger turned himself in and was sentenced to serve four months at the Wayside Honor Farm in Castiac, California. While not exactly Folsom State Prison, Wagner's time at Wayside obviously affected his perceptions of the American prison system. The script of RIOT IN CELL BLOCK 11 was written by Richard Collins and deals clearly and intelligently with the realtionship between prisoners, guards, politicians, and society. None of the groups portrayed are crammed into categories of "good" or "bad." There are rational, irrational, honorable, dishonorable, caring, and uncaring individuals

among each group involved with the uprising. Siegel keeps the violence to a minimum because his main character, Brand, tries to prevent bloodshed. The filmmakers never make excuses or apologies for the prisoners. They are all in jail because they deserve to be in jail, a fact the inmates freely admit. Their only concern is that their incarceration serve some beneficial purpose for themselves and society. Shot on location in Folsom Prison, the film has a gritty, documentary appearance that enhances the overall effect. Siegel would again venture into a real-life prison, this time Alcatraz, to shoot another superior entry in the genre, ESCAPE FROM ALCATRAZ (1979).

p, Walter Wanger; d, Don Siegel; w, Richard Collins; ph, Russell Harlan; m, Herschell Burke Gilbert; ed, Bruce Pierce; art d, David Milton; set d, Robert Priestly.

Prison Drama   **Cas.**   **(PR:C MPAA:NR)**

RIOT IN JUVENILE PRISON**   (1959) 71m Vogue/UA bw

Jerome Thor (Dr. Paul Furman), Marcia Henderson (Grace Hartwell), Scott Marlowe (Eddie Bassett), John Hoyt (Col. Walton), Dick Tyler (Stu Killion), Virginia Aldridge (Kitty), Dorothy Provine (Babe), Jack Grinnage (Dink), George Brenlin (Matches), Ann Doran (Bess Monahan), Richard Reeves (Andy Quillan), Al McGranary (Governor), Paul Jasmin (Bobby).

When shootings of two juvenile inmates brings public protest, psychologist Thor is brought in to see if he can do anything to control problems peacefully, while sadistic warden Hoyt looks on with indignation. Thor works by the principle of loving kindness, and his first act is the introduction of coed facilities. Trouble soon erupts when trouble makers Marlowe and Tyler fight over a girl and Tyler attempts to rape one of the female inmates. This only causes more brutal treatment of the young prisoners, which incites a riot. So Thor is given another chance, and this time is successful when the prisoners start acting a bit nicer. Able direction and a decent cast do what they can to a script that is filled with implausable characterizations and situations. One such instance is that we never see the prisoners change, but are given the knowledge that they have changed by word of mouth, probably because its visual depiction was beyond the scripter's capabilities.

p, Robert E. Kent; d, Edward L. Cahn; w, Orville H. Hampton; ph, Maury Gertsman; m, Emil Newman; ed, Eddie Mann; art d, William Glasgow.

Drama   **(PR:C MPAA:NR)**

RIOT ON PIER 6   (SEE: NEW ORLEANS UNCENSORED, 1955)

RIOT ON SUNSET STRIP***   (1967) 87m AIP c

Aldo Ray (Lt. Walt Lorimer), Mimsy Farmer (Andy), Michael Evans (Sgt. Tweedy), Laurie Mock (Liz-Ann), Tim Rooney (Grady), Gene Kirkwood (Flip), Hortense Petra (Marge), Anna Mizrahi (Helen Tweedy), Schuyler Hayden (Herby), Dick Winslow, Bill Baldwin, Sr., Tony Benson, Jim LeFevre, Al Ferrara, Pat Renella, The Standells, Forrest Lewis, Frank Alesia George E. Carey, The Enemies, Deborah Travis, John Hart, The Longhairs, The Chocolate Watch Band.

Inspired by the actual police riots on Hollywood's Sunset Strip, at one time a hangout for hippie youths bearing protest signs. Story focuses on Ray as a police captain caught between businesses operating on the Strip who don't like the punks hanging out, and his belief in allowing the kids their rights. But when his daughter, Farmer, gets involved with an unruly bunch, his attitude starts to change. The daughter, whom he hadn't seen for four years because his alcoholic wife took her away, has returned to Los Angeles, and to avoid her mother's dreary household, she hooks up with Rooney and friends. One night when the kids are bored with the happenings at Pandora's Box, they break into an abandoned mansion. They do some wild partying and eventually take LSD, the unsuspecting Farmer getting some in her drink. The boys can't control themselves, and take Farmer, unable to control herself, into the bedroom for a gang rape. The girl is brutalized and must be taken to the hospital emergency room. An enraged Ray goes after the boys individually, using only his bare hands to get revenge. Realism is achieved through the injection of footage from police cars cruising the streets during the actual riots and music from the cult bands, The Chocolate Watch Band and the Standells, is added for the proper flavor.

p, Sam Katzman; d, Arthur Dreifuss; w, Orville H. Hampton; ph, Paul C. Vogel (Pathe Color); m, Fred Karger; ed, Ben Lewis; art d, George W. Davis, Merrill Pye; set d, Don Greenwood; ch, Hal Belfer; makeup, William Tuttle.

Drama   **(PR:C MPAA:NR)**

RIOT SQUAD**   (1941) 55m MON bw

Richard Cromwell (Dr. Tom), Rita Quigley (Mary), John Miljan (Grusso), Mary Ruth (Betty), Herbert Rawlinson (Police Chief), Mary Gordon (Mrs. McGonigle) Donald Kerr (Herbert), Jack C. Smith (Dan O'Conner), Richard Clarke (Lenny), Noel Cravat (Frankie), Arthur Space (Butch), Sparky.

Cromwell plays an intern who goes undercover as a doctor for the mob to pin down those responsible for a police captain's slaying. The anticipated riot squad appears at the end to save the day. Includes one song: "Endearing Young Charms" sung by eight-year-old Ruth, who plucks away at the piano at the same time.

p&d, Edward Finney; w, C.C. Coons; ph, Marcel Le Picard; ed, Fred Bain; md, Frank Sanucci.

Crime   **(PR:A MPAA:NR)**

RIOTOUS BRUIN, THE   (SEE: RUINED BRUIN, THE, 1961)

RIP-OFF***   (1971, Can.) 94m Phoenix/Alliance c

Don Scardino (Michael), Ralph Endersby (Steve), Michale Kukulewich (Cooley), Peter Gross (Richie), Sue Helen Petrie (Sue), Hugh Webster (Mr. Dunken), Maxine Miller (Mrs. Dunken), Teddy Moore (Nancy).

A look at the disoriented youths of the early 1970s, this film focuses on a group of high school students who indulge in activities for the immediate satisfaction they bring. They try to make films, form a rock band, and start a commune only to discover that they can't stand the taste of organic food. A good understanding of teenagers' problems is displayed: their search to find something with which to identify and the dissatisfaction of discovering they're really not so special. A sense of humor is maintained throughout, making this an effective exposure of the media at work on the minds of the young.

p, Bennet Fode; d, Donald Shebib; w, William Fruet; ph, Richard Leiterman; m, Murray McLaughlan, Gene Martynec; ed, Shebib, Tony Lower.

Drama **(PR:O MPAA:R)**

RIP ROARIN' BUCKAROO*½ (1936) 58m Victory bw

Tom Tyler, Beth Marion, Sammy Cohen, Charles King, Forrest Taylor, Dick Cramer, John Elliott.

Tyler is a fighter who gets caught up in dishonest dealings and sets out to clear his name, taking vengeance on those who oppose him. Tyler turns in a convincing performance, helped along by his real-life experience as a prizefighter.

p, Sam Katzman; d, Robert Hill; w, William Buchanan.

Western **Cas.** **(PR:A MPAA:NR)**

RIP ROARING RILEY*½ (1935) 57m Puritan bw (GB: THE MYSTERY OF DIAMOND ISLAND)

Lloyd Hughes *(Rip Roaring Riley)*, Grant Withers *(Maj. Grey)*, John Cowell *(Prof. Baker)*, Marion Burns *(Ann Baker)*, Eddie Gribbon *(Sparky)*, Kit Guard *(Bruno)*, Paul Ellis, Joe Hiakawa.

There's not much to roar about in this story about agent Hughes who goes to an island to uncover a couple of spies (Withers and Ellis) trying to get the secret formula of a poison gas from a professor, Cowell. An ending that shows the Marines coming to the rescue leaves one wondering what should have been rescued instead.

p, C.C. Barr; d, Elmer Clifton; w, Homer King Gordon.

Crime **(PR:A MPAA:NR)**

RIPPED-OFF** (1971, Ital.) 83m White Mountain/Cinema Shares c (UN UOMO DALLA PELLE DURA; AKA: THE BOXER)

Robert Blake, Ernest Borgnine, Catherine Spaak, Gabriel Ferzetti, Tomas Milian.

Blake is as good as this second-rate Italian import will let him be, starring as a boxer framed for the murder of his manager. He convinces Spaak, the manager's daughter, of his innocence and sets out to nab the real killer.

d, Franco Prosperi; ph, (Eastmancolor).

Crime Drama **(PR:C-O MPAA:R)**

RIP TIDE*** (1934) 90m MGM bw

Norma Shearer *(Lady Mary Rexford)*, Robert Montgomery *(Tommy Trent)*, Herbert Marshall *(Lord Philip Rexford)*, Mrs. Patrick Campbell *(Lady Hetty Riversleigh)*, Richard "Skeets" Gallagher *(Erskine)* Ralph Forbes *(David Fenwick)*, Lilyan Tashman *(Sylvia)*, Arthur Jarrett *(Percy)*, Earl Oxford *(Freddie)*, Helen Jerome Eddy *(Celeste)*, George K. Arthur *(Bertie Davis)*, Halliwell Hobbes *(Bollard)*, Cora Sue Collins *(Child)*, Arthur Treacher, George Cowl, Victor Gammon, Donald Stuart *(Reporters)*, Robert A'Dair *(Bartender)*, Charles Requa *(Maj. Mills)*, E.E. Clive *(Sleigh Driver)*, Conrad Seidemann *(German Porter)*, Otto H. Fries *(Doorman)*, Nola Luxford *(English Girl)*, Anderson Lawler *(Henry)*, Walter Brennan, Stanley Mann *(Chauffeurs)*, Adrian Rosely *(Hotel Manager)*, Andre Cheron *(Surete Officer)*, Paul Porcasi *(House Detective)*, Leo White *(Assistant Manager)*, Fred W. Malatesta *(Headwaiter)*, Lillian Rich *(Girl)*, Yvonne Parker, Erin La Bissoniere *(French Women)*, Louis Mercier *(Concierge)*, Barlowe Borland *(Nightingale the Butler)*, Horace Cooper *(General)*, Harry Allen *(Fire Chief)*, Constant Franke *(Waiter)*, Desmond Roberts *(Hotel Manager)*, Ferdinand Gottschalk *(Orchestra Leader)*, T. Roy Barnes *(Clogg)*, Emile Chautard *(Doctor)*, Herbert Bunston *(Maj. Bagdall)*, Clarissa Selwynne *(Mrs. Bagdall)*, Elsa Buchanan *(Daphne)*, Bruce Bennett *(Brix)*, Francisco Maran *(French Butler)*, Montague Shaw *(Tring)*, Ramsey Hill *(Sir Geoffrey Mapel)*, Bobbie Bolder, Herbert Evans, Cosmo Kyrle Bellew *(Bits at Aunt Hetty's)*, *Lawrence Grant (Farrington)*.

Shearer plays a carefree American who has a child after an affair with Marshall, an English lord. The two marry and their future seems blissful. Marshall goes off on a business trip to America, leaving his wife behind with nothing to do. Shearer is soon bored and attends a swanky party where she bumps into an old flame, Montgomery. At one time Montgomery's playboy personality had quelled any hopes of marriage between the two but their reunion fires up some old passions. He makes an unsuccessful pass at Shearer, then follows her home in a drunken stupor. Montgomery climbs up Shearer's terrace in his efforts to renew his love and ends up taking a bad fall. He is taken to the hospital which results in some scandalous press for both Montgomery and Shearer. When Marshall returns home he is incensed at the accounts of his wife's would-be affair. Though Shearer tries to explain what really happened, Marshall refuses to listen. Convinced his wife has been dallying with Montgomery behind his back, Marshall decides to separate from Shearer. This leaves her free to pursue other men and she quickly finds herself in Montgomery's arms. Marshall comes to his senses and tries to win back his wife but upon discovering she has been secretly carrying on with Montgomery, he goes ahead with the divorce proceedings. Before the legal work is completed, however, Marshall and Shearer realize how much they really do love each other and decide to remain together after all. Yet another story of infidelity among the wealthy, this soap opera works well thanks to the sincerity of its cast. This was Shearer's first film in a year and a half and was produced by her husband, Thalberg. The famed producer had recently recovered from the ill health that had plagued him since childhood and was eager to work again with his wife. This had all the earmarks of a good Thalberg production with its entertaining qualities and intelligent approach to the material. RIP TIDE also marked the Hollywood debut for English actress Campbell, whose eccentricity had put off a number of important people. Studio executives did the best they could in weeding out what they considered a grave hiring mistake by giving Campbell small cameo roles starting with this film. Eventually Campbell caught on but was reassured by director Goulding in a telegram which read "...you are being put on the screen with all the charm and technique that made you... Relax, trust, don't worry, sleep well, feel well and give me your confidence." The actress more or less sealed her own coffin later while dining with Thalberg and Shearer to discuss future parts. In her book *An Unfinished Woman* Campbell's friend Lillian Hellman recounted Campbell's compliment to Thalberg on Shearer's eyes. "Your wife has the most beautiful little eyes I've ever seen," gushed the actress, not realizing that both husband and wife were highly sensitive about Shearer's unfortunate squint.

p, Irving Thalberg; d&w, Edmund Goulding; ph, Ray June; ed, Margaret Booth; art d, Alexander Toluboff, Fredric Hope; set d, Edwin B. Willis; cos, Adrian.

Drama **(PR:A MPAA:NR)**

RISATE DI GIOLA (SEE: PASSIONATE THIEF, THE, 1961, Fr.)

RISE AGAINST THE SWORD½** (1966, Jap.) 101m Toho bw (ABARE GOEMON)

Toshiro Mifune *(Abare Goeman)*, Makoto Sato, Ryo Tamura, Yuriko Hoshi, Mayumi Ozora, Nobuko Otowa, Daisuke Kato.

This film portrays conflict from Japan's Muromachi era. Mifune plays the head of one of the groups of Kaga, which refuses to aid the head Lord, a samurai, when he asks for assistance in fighting a battle. To try and enlist Mifune's help, the Lord sends his daughter to seduce Mifune's younger brother. When this fails the brother is slain and all the Kaga rise against the Lord.

p, Tomoyuki Tanaka; d, Hiroshi Inagaki; w, Masato Ide, Inagaki; ph, Kazuo Yamada (Tohoscope).

Martial Arts **(PR:A MPAA:NR)**

RISE AND FALL OF LEGS DIAMOND, THE*½** (1960) 101m United States/WB bw

Ray Danton *(Jack "Legs" Diamond)*, Karen Steele *(Alice Shiffer)*, Elaine Stewart *(Monica Drake)*, Jesse White *(Leo Bremer)*, Simon Oakland *(Lt. Moody)*, Robert Lowery *(Arnold Rothstein)*, Judson Pratt *(Fats Walsh)*, Warren Oates *(Eddie Diamond)*, Frank De Kova *(Chairman)*, Gordon Jones *(Sgt. Cassidy)*, Joseph Ruskin *(Matt Moran)*, Dyan Cannon *(Dixie)*, Richard Gardner *(Vince Coll)*, Sid Melton *(Little Augie)*, Nesdon Booth *(Fence)*, Buzz Henry, Dyke Johnson, Roy Jenson *(Bodyguards)*, Joe Marr, Jim Drum *(Officers)*, Dorothy Neumann, Frances Mercer *(Women)*, Judd Holdren *(Haberdashery Clerk)*, George Taylor *(Switchboard Operator)*, Robert Herron, Carey Loftin *(Thugs)*, Norman Dupont *(Maitre d'Louis)*.

While not exactly a documentary presentation of the historical facts behind the man, this film does manage to convey the proper mood and feel for the flamboyant New York gangster known as Legs Diamond. Played with the proper amount of verve, self-absorption, and cunning by Danton, the film shows the future mobster as something of a smooth confidence man even in his young days. While working at the Hotsy Totsy Club as a dancer, Danton constantly looks for ways to make a buck. Accompanmied by his alcoholic and consumptive brother Oates, Danton robs a jewelry store to steal diamonds for his girl friend. Together, the brothers continue their petty life of crime, with the ambitious Danton determined to weasel his way into the Arnold Rothstein (Lowery) gang through the mobster's bored girl friend, Stewart. His affair with Stewart works and he eventually becomes one of Lowery's bodyguards. Danton's new job proves risky, however, when he and the chief bodyguard are shot by rival gang members. The chief is killed, but Danton recovers and murders the men responsible. For this he is made head bodyguard. Capitalizing on his new position, Danton learns the details behind Lowery's rackets and begins to consolidate his power. He even finds time to marry his childhood sweetheart, Steele, though he continues to have affairs. One day Lowery is killed under mysterious circumstances, and though some suspect Danton set it up, the gang members split the holdings among themselves. Having gotten what he wanted from her, Danton dumps Stewart. To celebrate his newfound power and money, Danton buys the Hotsy Totsy Club and makes it his headquarters. Soon wars break out among the new gangs and the cold-hearted Danton sends Oates, his increasingly drunken and ill brother, off to Denver to minimize the risk to his position. In Denver, Oates' tuberculosis becomes worse and Danton ignores him, refusing to pay his medical bills. Oates dies alone. During the gang wars, Danton manages to take over most of the bootlegging rackets. His top-dog status is brief, however, for while on a trip to Europe, prohibition is repealed and the Mafia moves in on his territory. Upon his return to New York, Danton desperately tries to hang on to his business, but the challenge proves to be too much. Finally fed up with him and his rancid business, Steele leaves Danton. His career collapsing around him, Danton turns to the bottle and is set up by his former flame, Stewart, who seeks revenge for Lowery's murder. Alone, ruined, and drunk, Danton is shot to death in his hotel room bed by the Mafia. Though in reality Diamond was killed under very similar circumstances, the killers were probably members of the Dutch Schultz mob, a gang with whom Diamond had been feuding for some time. While some of the characters and incidents are amalgamations of the truth (Diamond rose through the ranks as Little Augie Orgen's bodyguard, not Rothstein's, and he earned his nickname for his ability to quickly elude police, not for his dancing), the basic flavor of the film is accurate. Having completed his outstanding series of westerns for Renown starring Randolph Scott (SEVEN MEN FROM NOW, THE TALL T, DECISION AT SUNDOWN, BUCHANAN RIDES ALONE, RIDE LONSOME, and COMANCHE STATION), director Boetticher experimented with a different genre. Continuing his view of the hero as an intelligent though self-absorbed anachronism, Boetticher and screenwriter Landon warp the truth somewhat to fit the story into this thesis. Instead of being a casualty of a long-running gang war, Danton is forced out and killed by the faceless Syndicate that operates as a corporation and shuns individuality. Danton embodies the archaic notion that gangsters should be highly visible, flashy, and flamboyant, and therefore he must be eliminated. THE RISE AND FALL OF LEGS DIAMOND presents the mobster as a strangely tragic character whose inability to see past his own wants and desires ensures his loneliness and death. Because he cannot return affection, share power, or adapt to change, Danton must die a pathetic, drunken loner who is killed in bed and not in a blaze of glory. In a somewhat unusual occurrence, Danton reprised his role as Legs Diamond in a film about Dutch Schultz entitled PORTRAIT OF A MOBSTER (1961).

p, Milton Sperling; d, Budd Boetticher; w, Joseph Landon; ph, Lucien Ballard; m, Leonard Rosenman; ed, Folmar Blangsted; art d, Jack Poplin; set d, Clarence I. Steensen; cos, Howard Shoup; makeup, Gordon Bau.

Crime   **(PR:C MPAA:NR)**

RISE AND RISE OF MICHAEL RIMMER, THE½**   (1970, Brit.)
                                                    94m David Paradine/WB Seven Arts/WB c

Peter Cook (Michael Rimmer), Denholm Elliott 4f2(Peter Niss), Ronald Fraser (Tom Hutchinson), Arthur Lowe (Ferret), Vanessa Howard (Patricia Cartwright), George A. Cooper (Blackett), Graham Crowden (Bishop of Cowley), Harold Pinter (Steven Hench), James Cossins (Crodder), Richard Pearson (Wilting), Ronnie Corbett (Interviewer), Dennis Price (Fairburn), Dudley Foster (Federman), John Cleese (Plumer), Roland Culver (Sir Eric Bentley), Julian Glover (Col. Moffat), Michael Barrington (Maj. Scott), Ann Beach (Receptionist), Jonathan Cecil ("Spot"), Diana Coupland (Mrs. Spimm), Percy Edwards (Bird Impersonator), Arthur Lovegrove (Doorman), Nicholas Phipps (Snaggott), Frank Thornton 4f2(Stoddart), Desmond Walter-Ellis (Buffery), Michael Bates (Mr. Spimm), Norman Bird 4f2(Alderman Poot), Graham Chapman (Fromage), William Job (Waring), Elspeth March (Mrs. Ferret), Norman Rossington (Guide), Michael Trubshawe (Mandeville).

Clever satire on political power and the importance of the advertising image (with some added humor by Monty Python's John Cleese and Graham Chapman in the script department) has Cook as a young opportunist who will stop at nothing to get to the top. He gets a job in a crumbling ad agency and quickly shapes everything up to the point where he's awfully chummy with the owner. He uses his newfound prestige to launch a political campaign for himself. He gets himself elected to Parliament; then, through enough backstabbing—all exaggerated to the utmost—he makes it to President of England, a position created just for Cook because nothing else will suffice. There is nothing heavy beneath the script, it's just a big mishmash of farcical humor, with the main philosophical intentions being a bit obvious. But that's the fun of it, with a long list of cameo performances going along whole-heartedly. This was a first feature film for executive producer David Frost, best known heretofore as a TV personality (he used his middle name, Paradine, for his film production company). The long-established English cast handle their cameo roles brilliantly in this "what-if" farce which has a number of elements in common with Berthold Brecht's play "The Resistible Rise of Arturo Ui". Look for famed playwright Harold Pinter in a cameo role as a TV commentator.

p, Harry Fine; d, Kevin Billington; w, Peter Cook, John Cleese, Graham Chapman, Billington; ph, Alex Thompson (Technicolor); m, John Cameron; ed, Stan Hawkes; art d, Carmen Dillon; cos, Ken Lewington.

Comedy   **(PR:C MPAA:R)**

RISE AND SHINE½**   (1941) 93m FOX bw

Jack Oakie (Boley), George Murphy (Jimmy M'Gonigle), Linda Darnell (Louise Murray), Walter Brennan (Grandpa), Milton Berle (Seabiscuit), Sheldon Leonard (Menace), Donald Meek (Prof. Murray), Ruth Donnelly (Mame), Raymond Walburn (Col. Bacon), Donald MacBride (Coach Graham), Emma Dunn (Mrs. Murray), Charles Waldron (President), Mildred Gover (Mrs. Robertson), William Haade (Butch), Dick Rich (Gogo), John Hiestand (Announcer), Claire Dubrey (Miss Pinkham), Francis Pierlot (Prof. Schnauzer), Paul Harvey (Orville Turner), Edward Arnold, Jr. (Student), Robert Shaw (Assistant Manager), Tim Ryan (Doorman), Nestor Paiva (Captain), Billy Wayne (Cab Driver).

Zesty little comedy has Oakie as the star football player who is carrying his team to the Big Ten championship. Gangster Leonard decides to bet heavily on the team and sends down Murphy to watch over Oakie. But Murphy is so taken by Darnell, daughter of professor Meek, he decides to make the college town his permanent residence. At the last moment Leonard changes his mind about the championship game, betting against Oakie's team. Oakie is kidnaped, only to be rescued just in time to save the game. Although the plot is not something to be taken in the least seriously, the fine caricatures and the slapstick antics are blended in a brisk pace that never lets up for a moment and that make for a lot of fun. Producer Hellinger, a celebrated writer and journalist in his own right, had been an associate producer at Warner Bros. He moved to 20th Century-Fox in 1941 with a better contractual deal; this was his first film as a full-rank producer. Songs include: "I'm Making a Play for You," "Central Two Two Oh Oh," "I Want to Be the Guy," "Hail to Bolenciecwez," "Get Thee Behind Me Clayton," and "Men of Clayton" (Ralph Rainger, Leo Robin).

p, Mark Hellinger; d, Allan Dwan; w, Herman J. Mankiewicz (based on the book My Life and Hard Times by James Thurber); ph, Edward Cronjager; ed, Allen McNeil; md, Emil Newman; cos, Gwen Wakelin; ch, Hermes Pan; m/l, Leo Robin, Ralph Rainger.

Musical/Comedy   **(PR:A MPAA:NR)**

RISE OF CATHERINE THE GREAT   (SEE: CATHERINE THE
                                         GREAT, 1934, Brit.)

RISE OF HELGA, THE   (SEE: SUSAN LENOX: HER FALL AND RISE,
                                1931)

RISE OF LOUIS XIV, THE***   (1970, Fr.) 100m O.R.T.F./Brandon c
                                         (LA PRISE DE POUVOIR PAR LOUIS XIV)

Jean-Marie Patte (Louis XIV), Raymond Jourdan (Colbert), Silvagni (Mazarin), Katherina Renn (Anne of Austria), Dominique Vincent (Mme. du Plessis), Pierre Barrat (Fouquet), Fernand Fabre (Le Tellier), Francoise Ponty (Louise de la Valliere), Joelle Langeois (Marie-Therese), Jacqueline Corot (Mme. Henrietta), Maurice Barrier (D'Artagnan), Andre Dumas (Father Joly), Francois Mirante (Mons. de Brienne), Pierre Spadoni (Noni), Roger Guillo (Pharmacist), Louis Raymond (1st Physician), Maurice Bourdon (2nd Physician), Michel Ferre (Mons. de Gesvres), Raymond Pelissier (Pomponne), Guy Pintat (Master Chef), Michele Marquais (Mme. de Motteville), Jean-Jacques Daubin (Mons. de Vardes), Georges Goubert (Mons. de Soyecourt), Pierre Pernet (Monsieur), Claude Rio (Vardes), Daniel Dubois (Lionne), Ginette Barbier (Pierrette Dufour), Jean Obe (Le Vau), Jacques Charby (Le Vau's Assistant), Micheline Muc (Mlle. de Pons), Michel Debranne (Tailor), Rene Rabault (Mons. De Gramont), Francois Bernard (Archbishop), Georges Spannelly (Seguir), Jean Soustre (Mons. de Guiche), Axel Ganz (Ambassador), Jean-Jacques Lecomte (1st Chamberlain), Violette Marceau (Mlle. de Chemerault), Paula Dehelly (Mme. d'Elboeuf), Jacques Preboist, Robert Cransac (Musketeers), Andre Daguenet (Master Bargeman), Marc Fraiseau, Pierre Frag, Jean Coste (Bargemen), Rita Maiden (Peasant), Francoise Deville (Woman), Mons. le Marquis de Brissac, Mons. le Vicomte de Chabot (Leaders of the Hunt), Helene Manesse (The Naiad), Jean-Claude Charnay (Messenger), Le Rallye Boissiere.

Rossellini's sparse, brief near-documentary on the young Sun King, and how he codified an empire by an exercise in choreography, framing fashions to ensure absolute obedience. Picture OPEN CITY (1946) in the costumes of the French courtiers of the mid-17th Century and you get the idea. No detail of the artful young king's set designs and graces—which culminated in the structured elegance of the court at Versailles—is too small to be captured by the camera; the big events, the executions and rebellions are, quite properly, trivialized. What won obeisance for Louis was fashion, fashion carefully crafted for conquest. Rossellini's pans and zooms follow these strategies of manners and mores intimately: Louis' dying mentor Mazarin (Silvagni) rouges his pallid cheeks prior to his audience with the young king; Louis demands more height to his wigs to enhance his stature; the king choreographs the rituals attendant on funerals, cabinet meetings, banquets. The complexities of Louis' life-structurings consolidate his previously shaky power; all eyes are on the young king, hoping to spot each new nuance, each fad-to-be. Intrigues and plots are forgotten in this atmosphere of utter attendance: the Sun King is all-powerful. This is a historian's view of history; a history not of battles and bravado, but rather one of guile, manipulation, and role-playing charisma. Originally made for French TV, this is an impressive piece of work from a master. An exciting film, albeit wanting in blood and bombast, and as historically accurate as any picture one is ever likely to see.

d, Roberto Rossellini; w, Philippe Erlanger, Jean Gruault; ph, Georges Leclerc (Eastmancolor); ed, Armand Ridel; art d, Maurice Valay; cos, Christiane Coste.

History/Drama   **(PR:A MPAA:G)**

RISING DAMP***   (1980, Brit.) 96m Cinema Arts International-Black
                              Lion/ITC c

Leonard Rossiter (Rigsby), Frances de la Tour (Miss Jones), Don Warrington (Philip), Christopher Strauli (John), Denholm Elliott (Seymour), Carrie Jones (Sandra), Glynn Edwards (Cooper), John Cater (Bert), Derek Griffiths (Alec).

Witty farce focuses on the happenings at a boarding house run by Rossiter. Devoid of much plot line, the picture is basically a bunch of sketches blended together to create a snappy little story. The main thrust is Rossiter's attempt to catch the girl of his dreams, de la Tour, who is hot for Warrington, whom everyone believes is the son of an African chief. But in the end de la Tour and confidence man Elliott wind up together. Beneath all the well-paced laughs are a few cuts at racial prejudice.

p, Roy Skeggs; d, Joe McGrath; w, Eric Chappell; ph, Frank Watts; m, David Lindup; ed, Peter Weatherley.

Comedy   **(PR:C MPAA:NR)**

RISING OF THE MOON, THE***   (1957, Ireland) 81m Four
                                          Provinces/WB bw

Tyrone Power (Introduction); "The Majesty of the Law": Cyril Cusack (Inspector Michael Dillon), Noel Purcell (Dan O'Flaherty the Old Man), Jack MacGowran (Mickey J. the Poteen Maker), Eric Gorman, Paul Farrell (Neighbors), John Cowley (The Gombeen Man); "A Minute's Wait": Jimmy O'Dea (Porter), Tony Quinn (Station Master), Paul Farrell (Engine Driver), Maureen Potter (Barmaid), Michael Trubshawe (Col. Frobisher), Anita Sharp Bolster (His Wife), Harold Goldblatt (Matchmaking Father), Godfrey Quigley (Christy, His Boy), May Craig (Matchmaking Aunt), Maureen O'Connell (May Ann McMahon, Her Niece), Michael O'Duffy (The Singer), J.G. Devlin (The Guard), Ann D'Alton (Fisherwoman); "1921": Denis O'Dea (The Police Sergeant), Eileen Crowe (His Wife), Frank Lawton (British Major), Dennis Brennan, David Marlowe, Dennis Franks (Black and Tan Officers), Joseph O'Dea (Warder), Doreen Madden, Maureen Cusack (False Nuns), Donal Donnelly (Sean Curran), Maurice Good (Constable O'Grady), Maureen Delaney (Old Woman), Martin Thornton (Sergeant), John Horan (Billposter), Joe Hone, John Comeford, Mafra McDonagh (IRA Men), Edward Lexy (R.Q.M.S.), Players from the Abbey Theatre Company.

This little-seen Ford film was a personal project for the director—"I made it just for fun and enjoyed it very much," he would later state—and another in his series of films steeped in the mores of Irish culture. THE RISING OF THE MOON is an anthology film made up of three parts with an introduction by Tyrone Power. The first, entitled "The Majesty of the Law," sees a modern-day Irish policeman, Cusack, going to serve a warrant on Purcell, an old-world Irishman who struck his neighbor for selling him inferior moonshine. Fully aware that Purcell is a proud man who disdains the "new" Ireland, Cusack walks to the old man's cabin instead of taking an automobile. Purcell welcomes the officer into his home and the men chat awhile before Cusack hesitantly brings up the matter of the assault. Purcell can go free if he pays a fine, but the man refuses. The old man bemoans the fact that the Irish have lost the wonderful "secrets" that make things special. The moonshiner no longer knows the secrets of making good Irish whiskey, and, worst of all, children no longer know the beloved folk songs because "...the films, and the radio, and that other new thing along with it..." have stolen their heritage. To prove he's going to go to jail on principle, Purcell kneels painfully before the hearth (the man suffers from arthritis) and pulls out a stone revealing his hidden savings, more than enough money to pay the fine. Cusack understands Purcell's position and leads him off to jail. Suddenly the man whom Purcell assaulted comes running up, money clutched in hand, and offers to pay the fine for him. Purcell refuses the offer. Before leaving his property, Purcell bends down and picks up a stone, kisses it, and puts it in his pocket as a memento of his home during his stay in jail. As Cusack accompanies the man out of town, all the neighbors come out and pay tribute. The second episode, "A Minute's Wait," is a broadly comic scene in which a passenger train stops at a depot for "just a minute" to wait for some fresh lobsters to be delivered for the Bishop's Jubilee Dinner. Of course, the minute's wait turns into a two-hour stay with a variety of situations detaining the train, including the engineer who is determined to finish telling the barmaid a ghost story despite the interruptions. Among all the Irish characters is a British couple on holiday who get kicked out of their first-class berth to make room for a prize goat that is being delivered to its new owner. The last episode, entitled "1921," is more serious and sees the players of the Abbey Theatre Company stage an escape attempt to free imprisoned Irish patriot Donnelly before he is to be executed. Two of the actresses dress as nuns and visit Donnelly in his cell. When the guards aren't looking, Donnelly slips into a nun's habit while one of the women dresses in his clothes. O'Dea, an Irish police sergeant who resents the British Black and Tans, has a vague idea that Donnelly—now dressed as a folk singer—is the escaped man. O'Dea's wife works desperately on the deep Irish emotions of her husband and eventually persuades him to let Donnelly escape. While THE RISING OF THE MOON offers some touching and amusing moments, it is minor Ford. Because of the restricted length of each segment, the characters and situations seem sketched instead of painted and the emotion seems surface instead of deep. Of course, the director felt passionately about the Irish and Ireland, but the film seems more melancholy musing than a fully developed tribute. To promote filmmaking in Ireland, Ford formed a production company with Lord Michael Killanin, Michael Scott, Brian Desmond Hurst, Roger Greene, and Tyrone Power and called it Four Provinces. The men had great hopes for the company, but most of their dreams went unrealized. THE RISING OF THE MOON failed at the box office, probably due to its lack of American stars, and only grossed a little over $100,000 worldwide. The film had cost over $500,000 to make and distribute. Ford had initially hoped to star Tyrone Power in the longest of the episodes—he had worked with Power recently, in THE LONG GRAY LINE (1955)—and also to utilize the talents of two other favored Ford players, Maureen O'Hara and Barry Fitzgerald. Other commitments prevented these marquee names from being in the picture, but Power was recruited as narrator in post-production filming that was not supervised by the director. The film is interesting for its thinly veiled references to previous Ford directorial efforts such as THE QUIET MAN (1952) and THE INFORMER (1935).

p, Michael Killanin; d, John Ford; w, Frank S. Nugent (based on the short story "The Majesty of the Law" by Frank O'Connor and the plays "A Minute's Wait" by Martin J. McHugh and "The Rising of the Moon" by Lady Gregory); ph, Robert Krasker; m, Eamonn O'Gallagher; ed, Michael Gordon; art d, Raymond Simm; cos, Jimmy Bourke.

Drama   **(PR:A MPAA:NR)**

RISING TO FAME   (SEE: SUSAN LENOX: HER FALL AND RISE, 1931)

RISK, THE**½   (1961, Brit.) 81m Charter/Kingsley International bw (GB: SUSPECT)

Tony Britton (*Bob Marriott*), Virginia Maskell (*Lucy Byrne*), Peter Cushing (*Prof. Sewall*), Ian Bannen (*Alan Andrews*), Raymond Huntley (*Sir George Gatling*), Thorley Walters (*Mr. Prince*), Donald Pleasence (*Brown*), Spike Milligan (*Arthur*), Kenneth Griffith (*Dr. Shole*), Robert Bruce (*Levers*), Anthony Booth (*Parkin*), Basil Dignam (*Dr. Childs*), Brian Oulton (*Director*), Sam Kydd (*Slater*), John Payne (*Iverson*), Murray Melvin (*Teddy Boy*), Andre Charisse (*Heller*), Geoffrey Bayldon (*Rosson*), Margaret Lacey (*Prince's Wife*), Bruce Wightman (*Phil*), Ian Wilson (*Pin Table Man*).

Cushing heads a group of scientists who discover a serum that could bring an end to typhus and bubonic plague, but the government won't let them release their discovery because of the chance of the information getting into enemy hands and leading to germ warfare. But assistant Britton's frustration leads him to attempt publication through Pleasence, a rather shady underground figure. Cushing intercepts Britton's plot in the nick of time, persuading the young scientist to help police investigators uncover Pleasence. This film was shot in just 17 days on a deliberately low budget. The result isn't bad. At times it is highly crafted and the careful planning behind the production comes through well. However, the rapid shoot and low budget occasionally give this the look of a made-for-television film and despite the tautness of the direction, the story is merely a routine thriller. The acting isn't bad at all and gives the drama an added edge.

p&d, Roy and John Boulting; w, Nigel Balchin, Jeffrey Dell, Roy Boulting (based on the novel *A Sort of Traitors* by Balchin); ph, Max Greene; m, Frederic Francois Chopin, Aleksander Nikolaevich Scriabin; ed, John Jympson; md, John Wilkes; art d, Albert Witherick; set d, Peter James; makeup, Freddie Williamson.

Crime/Drama   **(PR:A MPAA:NR)**

RISKY BUSINESS**½   (1939) 67m UNIV bw

George Murphy (*Dan Clifford*), Dorothea Kent (*Mary Dexter*), Eduardo Ciannelli (*De Carne*), Leon Ames (*Hinge Jackson*), El Brendel (*Lucius*), Richard Tucker (*District Attorney*), Frances Robinson (*Norma Jackson*), John Wray (*Silas*), Arthur Loft (*Capt. Wallace*), Pierre Watkin (*Abernathy*), Grant Richards (*Norman*), Charles Trowbridge (*Jameson*), Mary Forbes (*Mrs. Jameson*).

Decent crime drama has Murphy as a radio gossip columnist who meets a bit of excitement when he decides to take on the mob in filmland. His efforts lead to the rescue of a producer's kidnaped daughter. Heroic Murphy kills Ciannelli, only to get himself killed when two mobsters sneak into the radio booth just when the radio man is about to tell the public of his latest explorations. A remake of the 1932 Universal release OKAY AMERICA.

p, Burt Kelly; d, Arthur Lubin; w, Charles Grayson (based on the story "Okay America" by William Anthony McGuire); ph, Stanley Cortez.

Crime   **(PR:A MPAA:NR)**

RISKY BUSINESS***   (1983) 98m Geffen/WB c

Tom Cruise (*Joel*), Rebecca De Mornay (*Lana*), Joe Pantoliano (*Guido*), Richard Masur (*Rutherford*), Bronson Pinchot (*Barry*), Curtis Armstrong (*Miles*), Nicholas Pryor (*Joel's Father*), Janet Carroll (*Joel's Mother*), Shera Danese (*Vicki*), Raphael Sbarge (*Glenn*), Bruce A. Young (*Jackie*), Kevin C. Anderson (*Chuck*), Sarah Partridge (*Kessler*), Nathan Davis (*Business Teacher*), Scott Harlan (*Stan Licata*), Sheila Keenan (*Nurse Bolik*), Lucy Harrington (*Glenn's Girl Friend*), Jerry Tullos (*Derelict*), Jerome Landfield (*Kessler's Father*), Ron Dean (*Detective*), Bruno Aclin (*Mechanic*), Robert Kurcz (*Service Manager*), Fern Persons (*Lab Teacher*), Cynthia Baker (*Test Teacher*), Wayne C. Kneeland (*Russell Bitterman*), Jade Gold (*Evonne Williams*), Karen Grossman (*Hall Marshal*), Brett Baer (*Howie Rifkin*).

Several smarmy teenage comedies came out about the same time with nothing to recommend them. They showed lots of skin, had sniggering juvenile humor, and virtually no characterization. This was a cut above the others and had some genuinely funny moments. It begins as a sit-com when Pryor and Carroll, an upscale couple, leave their Chicago-area home on a short trip. Their model son, Cruise, is entrusted with watching the house and making certain nothing goes awry. Since he's a high schooler with a good grade average and an application to Princeton, he appears to be right out of "The Donna Reed Show." Not so. The moment his folks depart, Cruise becomes a teenage version of "Mr. Hyde" in that, he has the chance to exercise all of his baser instincts. Out comes the blaring stereo, the cigars, the whiskey, the all-night poker sessions, etc. De Mornay is a local whore who is "managed" by Pantoliano and would like to flee his clutches. Cruise takes her in and the suburban home becomes a house of ill repute serving tea and strumpets. Cruise wrecks Pryor's prized Porsche by allowing it to find its way into Lake Michigan; several other complications arise, and it looks as though Cruise is in big trouble. Then, miraculously, everything straightens out and his parents return home to find nothing in disarray, the Porsche totally repaired so there is no way of knowing what it went through, and the acceptance from Princeton in the mail. Cruise has taken some big chances and succeeded. Brickman does well in his first directing assignment and what could have been a sleazy PORKY'S film winds up as good fun. Made for a pittance, the picture grossed well from the young moviegoers, and Brickman, when he gets a better script, will be heard from. The music was by the European group "Tangerine Dream" who also did another Chicago-based picture, THIEF. Tough language and some sexual scenes take this out of the "Saturday Matinee" classification.

p, Jon Avnet, Steve Tisch; d&w, Paul Brickman; ph, Reynaldo Villalobos (Technicolor); m, Tangerine Dream; ed, Richard Chew; prod d, William J. Cassidy; cos, Robert de Mora.

Comedy   **Cas.**   **(PR:O MPAA:R)**

RITA**   (1963, Fr./Ital.) 93m Les Films Modernes-Agiman-Euro International/Parallel-49-Colorama Features bw (LETTERE DI UNA NOVIZIA; LA NOVICE; AKA: LETTER FROM A NOVICE)

Pascale Petit (*Margherita "Rita" Passi*), Jean-Paul Belmondo (*Giuliano Verdi*), Massimo Girotti (*Don Paolo Conti*), Lilla Brignone (*Sister Giulietta*), Hella Petri, Elsa Vazzoler, Emilio Cigoli.

Petit plays a woman about to take the vows to become a nun when her guilt-ridden past is revealed through a letter of denouncement. She confesses to priest Girotti she had a lover, Belmondo, whom she killed when she found out he was intimate with her own mother. Her mother then gave her the choice of prison or the convent. She chose the convent, only to be rejected and prosecuted when her own guilt led her to write the letter of denouncement. (In French; English subtitles.)

p, Carlo Ponti; d, Alberto Lattuada; w, Roger Vailland, Lattuada (based on the novel *Lettere di Una Novizia* by Guido Piovene); ph, Roberto Gerardi; m, Robert Nicolosi; ed, Leo Catozzo; English subtitles, Herman G. Weinberg.

Drama   **(PR:C MPAA:NR)**

RITEN   (SEE: RITUAL, THE, 1970, Swed.)

RITUAL, THE**   (1970, Swed.) 75m Svensk Filmindustrie-Sveriges TV-Cinematograph/Janus bw (RITEN)

Ingrid Thulin (*Thea Winkelmann*), Anders Ek (*Albert Emanuel Sebastian Fischer*), Gunnar Bjornstrand (*Hans Winkelmann*), Erik Hell (*Judge Abramson*), Ingmar Bergman (*Clergyman*).

A theatrical troupe, Les Riens—The Nothings—comprising Thulin, Ek, and Bjornstrand—is refused permission to perform a happening, "The Ritual," which has been called obscene. The local judge, Hell, attempts to extract from the three a description of the performance; they all aver that it must be seen rather than described. To discredit the troupe and lay the grounds for his assured censorship, Hell explores the actors' backgrounds, discovering their hedonistic personal life styles: the trio form a *maison a trois*, with hot-blooded Ek desperately trying to evoke a sensual response from the beautiful, enigmatic Thulin, wife of icy, phlegmatic Bjornstrand, from whom—ironically—he seeks romantic advice. Physically enraptured by Thulin himself, the hypocritical Hell interviews her privately. She tells him of herself: she is, she reports, merely a restructured creature, a product of plastic surgery and corrective dentistry, hardly an object of desire. Moreover, she is neurotic and epileptic. Hell's desire grows during Thulin's monotonous litany of self-abnegation; as she is taken with a seizure, he throws himself upon her and attempts—unsuccessfully—to rape her. Later, the troupe performs the dreaded "Ritual" privately for the licentious judge. It proves to be a virtually classical Grecian masque, a stilted set piece with masked actors and enormous wooden phalluses. At the end of the brief performance, the judge is discovered to have died of a heart attack. Bergman's often entertaining allegory deals rather brutally with the location of beauty—it's in the eye of the beholder—and the artist's answer to the query, "What does it mean?" It means what you think it means. Definitely not a film for everyone, this was made for Swedish TV. Its explicit sexuality would have ruled out its TV exposure in the U.S., where it was released theatrically.

d&w, Ingmar Bergman; ph, Sven Nykvist; ed, Siv Kanalv; art d, Lennart Blomkvist; cos, Mago.

Drama (PR:O MPAA:NR)

RITUALS (SEE: CREEPER, 1978, Can.)

RITZ, THE*½ (1976) 90m Courtyard/WB c

Jack Weston (*Gaetano Proclo*), Rita Moreno (*Googie Gomez*), Jerry Stiller (*Carmine Vespucci*), Kaye Ballard (*Vivian Proclo*), F. Murray Abraham (*Chris*), Paul B. Price (*Claude*), Treat Williams (*Michael Brick*), John Everson (*Tiger*), Christopher J. Brown (*Duff*), Dave King (*Abe*), Bessie Love (*Maurine*), Tony DeSantis (*Sheldon Farenthold*), Ben Aris (*Patron with Bicycle*), Peter Butterworth (*Patron in Chaps*), Ronnie Brody (*Small Patron*), Hal Gallili (*Patron With Cigar*), John Ratzneberger, Chris Harris (*Patrons*), George Coulouris (*Old Man Vespucci*), Leon Greene (*Musclebound Patron*), Freddie Earle (*Disgruntled Patron*), Hugh Fraser (*Disc Jockey*), Bart Allison (*Old Priest*), Samantha Weysom (*Gilda Proclo*), Richard Holmes (*Pianist*).

A gay comedy (in the *new* sense of the word) about a steam bath not unlike the Continental Baths in New York (where Bette Midler used to entertain before she became BETTE MIDLER!!!) that is very funny in spots and features F. Murray Abraham, who later won an Oscar for AMADEUS. This very New York film was made in England at Twickenham Studios where they re-created the bathhouse seen in the successful stage play by McNally, who also originally wrote the screenplay. The homosexuality aspect is so muted that the picture initially received a "PG" rating from the MPAA, although it's an iffy prospect for anyone under 18. The play starred Weston, Moreno, Stiller, Everson, Brown, and three others who also appear here. It's the classic French farce that could have been written by Feydeau. Weston is trying to get away from his gangster brother-in-law Stiller and takes refuge in a gay bathhouse, but he doesn't know that's what it is. His father-in-law is Coulouris, a Godfather who is dying, and Stiller has been assigned the job of erasing Weston. Once inside the bathhouse, Weston gets involved on several levels. Moreno is a terrible singer waiting for her big break and performing for the homosexuals. She thinks Weston is a big-time producer. Price is a gay man who is a "chubby chaser," and since Weston is rotund, he becomes the apple of Price's eye. Williams, speaking in a high falsetto, is a private detective searching for Weston in the bathhouse which, Weston discovers, is owned by the "family." Doors slam, people hide under beds, actors race in and out of the various rooms, a swimming pool is filled with bodies, etc. In order to disguise himself, Weston gets into drag and sings, with Abraham and Price, a take-off of "The Three Caballeros" (Manuel Esperton, Ray Gilbert) in an Andrews Sisters parody. Moreno vainly attempts to sing the Stephen Sondheim-Jule Styne classic "Everything's Coming Up Roses" and the worse she does it, the funnier she is. Made in 25 days, it has boundless energy under Lester's direction, and if a joke or a set-up misfires, wait a few seconds and there'll be another laugh soon enough. Very funny and, considering the milieu, surprisingly tasteful.

p, Denis O'Dell; d, Richard Lester; w, Terrence McNally (based on his play); ph, Paul Wilson (Technicolor); m, Ken Thorne; ed, John Bloom; prod d, Phillip Harrison; cos, Vangie Harrison.

Comedy Cas. (PR:C-O MPAA:R)

RIVALEN DER MANEGE (SEE: BIMBO THE GREAT, 1961, Ger.)

RIVALS, THE* (1963, Brit.) 56m Merton Park/AA bw

Jack Gwillim (*Rolf Neilson*), Erica Rogers (*Kim Harris*), Brian Smith (*Steve Houston*), Tony Garnett (*Jimmy Vosier*), Barry Linehan (*Paul Kenyon*), Murray Hayne (*Alex Nichols*), Howard Greene (*Eddy McQuire*), Philip Latham (*Lawrence*).

An appealing entry based on an Edgar Wallace novel about a couple of car thieves who disrupt a kidnaping scheme by stealing a car containing the ransom money. They are then targeted by both the kidnapers and the Swedish millionaire whose daughter's life is at stake. The film's quick pace and unique premise make it a fun way to pass an hour.

p, Jack Greenwood; d, Max Varnel; w, John Roddick (based on the novel *Elegant Edward* by Edgar Wallace).

Crime (PR:A MPAA:NR)

RIVALS* (1972) 101m AE c

Joan Hackett (*Christine Sutton*), Robert Klein (*Peter Simon*), Scott Jacoby (*Jaimie Sutton*), Jeanne Tanzy (*Mary*), Gene Hayes (*Douglas*), Phoebe Dorin (*Madge*), James Karen (*Child Psychiatrist*), Randy Digeronimo (*Tony*), Frank Fiore (*Phil*), Bill Herndon (*Bob*), William Shust (*Calloux*), Leib Lensky (*Rabbi*), Viola Swayne

(*Mrs. Sturgess*), Noel Craig (*Salesman*), Iris Whitney (*Matron*), Ann Miles (*Stunt Girl*), Ben Wikson, Robert Kya-Hill (*Policemen*).

Trapped by her motherly role to her 10-year-old son Jacoby, Hackett faces new difficulties when she takes on lover Klein. Frustrated with trying to hide her lover from her son, and her son from her lover, she marries Klein. But Jacoby fails to give, showing fits of jealousy which would make any mother cringe with embarrassment. The attempt to give some substance to this exploration of some pretty complex problems lacks performances which dwell beneath the surface, expressing exactly what the characters are feeling. The New York settings, which could be manipulated to add to the tension of the characters, only limit the already slim portrayals.

p, Williard W. Goodman; d&w, Krishna Shah; ph, Harvey Goodman (Eastmancolor); m, Peter Matz; ed, Arline Garson; prod d, Warren Clymer; md, Matz; art d, Clymer; cos, Charles Tomlinson.

Drama (PR:O MPAA:R)

RIVER, THE*½ (1928) 84m FOX bw

Charles Farrell (*Allen John Pender*), Mary Duncan (*Rosalee*), Ivan Linow (*Sam Thompson*), Afredo Sabato (*Marsdon*), Margaret Mann (*Widow Thompson*), Bert Woodruff (*The Miller*).

A slim plot line serves the purpose of depicting the torrid love affair between burly outdoorsman Farrell and society woman Duncan, which culminates in an outrageous attempt by the giant to express his life through a song. The song falls flat, but director Borzage was pretty good at handling romantic sentimentality such as this, managing to give substance to the material, while keeping a struggling tension beneath the surface. The attempts at creating an allegory between the flowing waters of the river and the purity of love does not stay afloat.

d, Frank Borzage; w, Philip Klein, Dwight Cummins (based on the novel by Tristram Tupper); ph, Ernest Palmer; m, Maurice Baron; ed, Barney Wolf.

Romance (PR:A MPAA:NR)

RIVER, THE*½ (1951) 99m UA c

Nora Swinburne (*The Mother*), Esmond Knight (*The Father*), Arthur Shields (*Mr. John*), Thomas E. Breen (*Capt. John*), Suprova Mukerjee (*Nan*), Patricia Walters (*Harriet*), Radha (*Melanie*), Adrienne Corri (*Valerie*), Richard Foster (*Bogey*), Penelope Wilkinson (*Elizabeth*), Jane Harris (*Muffie*), Jennifer Harris (*Mouse*), Cecelia Wood (*Victoria*), Ram Singh (*Sajjan Singh*), Nimai Barik (*Kanu*), Trilak Jetley (*Anil*), June Hillman (*Narrator*).

Before returning to France after his stay in Hollywood, Renoir stopped over in India, where he had the creative freedom to explore his fascination with nature. The colorful life along the Ganges River proved the perfect setting, resulting in a lively, yet subtle, depiction of the picturesque environment, which is wholly romanticized, but nonetheless captivating. Simple story centers on a British family whose routine life is interrupted by Breen, a visiting war veteran who has come to claim his cousin's daughter. The teenage daughters of the family fall deeply in love with the soldier, the eldest believing that her "Prince Charming" has come to take her away. Renoir brings out the best from his child actors, presenting their complex emotions in a fair and mature manner.

p, Kenneth McEldownery; d, Jean Renoir; w, Renoir, Rumer Godden (based on the novel by Godden); ph, Claude Renoir, Ramananda Sen Gupta (Technicolor); m, M.A. Partha Sarathy; ed, George Gale; set d, Bansi Chandragupta.

Drama (PR:A MPAA:NR)

RIVER, THE½ (1961, India) 105m Cine Art. bw (GANGA)

Niranjan Ray (*Bilas*), Janash Muknerii (*Panchu*), Sandhya Ray (*Himi*), Ruma Gangaly (*Damini*).

Visualized account of a simple fisherman who longs to follow the river to the sea in order to find work, but is unable to overcome the fear that keeps him put.

w&d, Rajen Tarafder; ph, Dinen Gupta; ed, A. Rajan.

Drama (PR:A MPAA:NR)

RIVER BEAT (1954) 70m Insignia/Lippert bw

Phyllis Kirk (*Judy Roberts*), John Bentley (*Inspector Dan Barker*), Robert Ayres (*Capt. Watford*), Leonard White (*Sgt. McLeod*), Ewan Roberts (*Blake*), Glyn Houston (*Charlie Williamson*), Charles Lloyd Pack (*Hendrick*), David Hurst (*Paddy Maclure*), Margaret Anderson (*Nell*), Michael Balfour (*Adams*), Isabel George (*Anna*), Harold Ayer, Patrick Jordan.

Contrived action film has Kirk as the radio operator aboard an American freighter. She is being used as a diamond smuggler while the ship is docked in London. It does not look good for Anglo-American relations when the girl is caught, so police inspector Bentley does his best in capturing the real crooks. Despite some neat plot twists, the story fails to offer anything of interest, including the performances.

p, Victor Hanbury, Herman Cohen; d, Guy Green; w, Rex Rienits; ph, Geoffrey Faithfull; m, Hubert Clifford; ed, Peter Graham Scott.

Crime (PR:A MPAA:NR)

RIVER CHANGES, THE* (1956) 91m WB bw

Rossana Rory, Harald Maresch, Renate Mannhardt, Henry Fisher, Jasper von Oertzen, Nick Solomatin, Otto Friebel, Rene Magron, Bert Brandt, Ilse Ruth Roskam, H. Freuschtenicht, Helge Lehmann, H.C. Clemmstein, Rolf Menke.

Moving story of how the changing course of a river affects the borders of a Communist-dominated country, making the inhabitants of a small village part of the Communist country with their lives undergoing extreme changes as they adapt to their new rulers. Shot in Germany as a piece of anti-Communist propaganda, the film still manages a pretty powerful punch.

p,d&w, Owen Crump; m, Roy Webb; ph, Ellis W. Carter; ed, James Moore

Drama **(PR:A MPAA:NR)**

RIVER GANG*½ (1945) 64m UNIV bw

Gloria Jean *(Wendy)*, John Qualen *(Uncle Bill)*, Bill Goodwin *(Mike)*, Keefe Brasselle *(Johnny)*, Sheldon Leonard *(Peg Leg)*, Gus Schilling *(Dopey Charley)*, Vince Barnett *(Organ Grinder)*, Bob Homans *(Police Captain)*, Jack Grimes *(Goofy)*, Mendy Koenig *(Butch)*, Rocco Lanzo *(Fatso)*, Douglas Croft *(Slug)*.

Flimsy story has Jean as the secluded assistant at her uncle's (Qualen), pawn shop, where her uncle attempts to keep her sheltered from the nasty world while he is involved in a racket of his own. But when a composer is murdered and his valuable violin is found in the shop, things get a bit too tense for Qualen, and Jean realizes who her uncle really is. Jean and Qualen are bland in the leads, with the rest of the cast totally unbelievable. Blame it all on the script, which offers nothing.

p&d, Charles David; w, Dwight V. Babcock, Leslie Charteris (based on the story "Fairy Tale Murder" by Hugh Gray, David); ph, Jerome Asch; ed, Saul A. Goodkind; md, H.J. Salter; art d, John B. Goodman, Abraham Grossman; cos, Vera West.

Crime/Drama **(PR:A MPAA:NR)**

RIVER HOUSE GHOST, THE*½ (1932, Brit.) 52m WB/FN bw

Florence Desmond *(Flo)*, Hal Walters *(Walter)*, Joan Marion *(Sally)*, Mike Johnson *(Johnson)*, Shayle Gardner *(Skeleton)*, Erle Stanley *(Black Mask)*, Helen Ferrers *(Martha Usher)*.

An all-too-familiar haunted house tale about an innocent cockney girl, Desmond, who discovers that the spooks in her river house are actually sly gangsters. They want the house for a hideout and are trying to scare her off, but she proves to be tougher than they ever imagined. Occasionally humorous, but the film quickly gets bogged down in predictability.

p, Irving Asher; d, Frank Richardson; w, W. Scott Darling.

Comedy/Horror **(PR:A MPAA:NR)**

RIVER HOUSE MYSTERY, THE* (1935, Brit.) 56m Imeson-Foulsham/UNIV bw

G.H. Mulcaster *(Sir John Harpenden)*, Ena Moon *(Anna)*, Bernard Lee *(Wade Belloc)*, A.B. Imeson *(Drang)*, Roddy Hughes *(Higgins)*, Boris Ranevsky *(Krilloff)*, Clifford Evans *(Ivan)*, W.E. Holloway, Davy Hayward, Percy Walsh, Frank Snell.

Mulcaster, a crime novel devotee, enthusiastically becomes entangled in a mystery about a young lady, Moon, and her efforts to dodge her pursuers. She is trying to keep a gang of crooks and a group of Russians from stealing her jewels, and receives help from Mulcaster in doing so. When Mulcaster thinks he has killed a man, he is informed that the whole thing was a ruse engineered by his friends.

p, A.B. Imseon; d, Fraser Foulsham; w, F.G. Robertson; ph, Alex Bryce.

Crime **(PR:A MPAA:NR)**

RIVER LADY½** (1948) 78m UNIV c

Yvonne De Carlo *(Sequin)*, Dan Duryea *(Beauvais)*, Rod Cameron *(Dan Corrigan)*, Helena Carter *(Stephanie)*, Lloyd Gough *(Mike)*, Florence Bates *(Ma Dunnigan)*, John McIntire *(Mr. Morrison)*, Jack Lambert *(Swede)*, Esther Somers *(Mrs. Morrison)*, Anita Turner *(Esther)*, Edmund Cobb *(Rider)*, Dewey Robinson *(Bouncer)*, Eddy C. Waller *(Hewitt)*, Milton Kibbee *(Limpy)*, Billy Wayne *(Dealer)*, Jimmy Ames *(Logger)*, Edward Earle *(Executive)*, Paul Maxey *(Mr. Miller)*, Dick Wessel, Charles Sullivan, Mickey Simpson, Reed Howes, George Magrill, Ray Spiker, Jack Van Zandt, Charles Morton, Don MacCracken, Carl Sepulveda *(Lodgers)*, John McGuire *(Collins)*, Howard Negley *(McKenzie)*, Jack G. Lee, Charles Wagenheim, Bob Wilke, Perc Launders, Kenneth Ross-MacKenzie *(Men)*, Al Hill *(Lumberjack)*, Harold Goodwin *(Larson)*, Paul Fierro *(Man on Deck)*, Beverly Warren *(Girl)*, Jack Shutta *(McGee)*, Jerry Jerome *(Croupier)*, Frank Hagney *(Sands)*.

A logging-camp serves as the setting for rich gambler De Carlo to win Cameron. Her methods are to set him up in business, hoping to get some romance in the bargain. But Cameron does not take to being a gigolo, so he leaves De Carlo and marries Carter. An upset De Carlo decides to get even by ruining Cameron's career; she has the power to do it, but Cameron's integrity wins out. Slim story is given a boost through some well-staged fistfights and the activities of the lumberjacks, the latter providing the tension the story lacks.

p, Leonard Goldstein; d, George Sherman; w, D.D. Beauchamp, William Bowers (based on the novel by Houston Branch, Frank Waters); ph, Irving Glassberg (Technicolor); m, Paul Sawtell; ed, Otto Ludwig; art d, Bernard Herzbrun, Emrich Nicholson; m/l, Walter Schumann, Jack Brooks.

Western **(PR:A MPAA:NR)**

RIVER NIGER, THE** (1976) 105m Cine Artists c

Cicely Tyson *(Mattie Williams)*, James Earl Jones *(Johnny Williams)*, Lou Gossett *(Dr. Dudley Stanton)*, Glynn Turner *(Jeff Williams)*, Roger E. Mosley *(Big Moe Hayes)*, Jonelle Allen *(Ann Vanderguild)*, Hilda Haynes *(Wilhemina Geneva Brown)*, Theodore Wilson *(Chips)*, Charles Weldon *(Skeeter)*, Ralph Wilcox *(Al)*, Shirley Joe Finney *(Gail)*, Ed Crick *(White Police Lieutenant)*, Tony Burton *(Black Policeman)*.

This attempt to give a film presentation of the Tony Award winning play missed the mark through Shah's clumsy direction. The story takes place in the black ghetto, with a concentration upon the individual ideological goals which are tearing the black community apart. Various levels of the community are explored, with the brunt of the focus on cancer victim Tyson and her husband Jones, an aspiring poet who pays the bills by painting houses. Tyson's character is one-dimensional, but she does what she can with her meager lines. Jones' part is just the opposite, he is bursting with energy in a manner that displays his wide range of talent, but it comes off a bit overdone. The setting of the grisly ghetto, with its gang members who are close to going over the edge, is unrealistic, hampering whatever genuine performances are delivered.

p, Sidney Beckerman, Isaac L. Jones; d, Krishna Shah; w, Joseph A. Walker (based on the play by Walker); ph, Michael Marguiles (Movielab Color); m, War; ed, Irving Lerner; prod d, Seymour Klate; set d, Frank Lombardo; cos, Nedra Watt; spec eff, Richard Helmer; m/1, "The River Niger," War, Jerry Goldstein (performed by War); stunts, Marvin Walters; makeup, Ray Brooks.

Drama **(PR:O MPAA:R)**

RIVER OF FOREVER* (1967, Jap.) 102m Tokyo Eiga/Toho bw (CHIKUMAGAWA ZESSHO)

Kinya Kitaoji, Yuriko Hoshi, Mikijiro Hira, Ayumi Ishida, Kunie Tanaka.

A young Japanese truck driver avoids hospitals and doctors until during a visit to a sick friend he meets a nurse. After an auto accident, he submits to a checkup which reveals he has incurable leukemia. The nurse takes him to her home in the country where they idyllically spend the last months of his life. Tedious Japanese melodrama that does not travel well. (In Japanese; English subtitles.)

p, Ichiro Sato, Hideyuki Shiino, d, Shiro Toyoda; w, Zenzo Matsuyama; ph, Kozo Okazaki; (Tohoscope); m, Masaru Sato.

Drama **(PR:A-C MPAA:NR)**

RIVER OF MISSING MEN (SEE: TRAPPED BY G-MEN, 1937)

RIVER OF NO RETURN*½** (1954) 90m FOX c

Robert Mitchum *(Matt Calder)*, Marilyn Monroe *(Kay Weston)*, Rory Calhoun *(Harry Weston)*, Tommy Rettig *(Mark Calder)*, Murvyn Vye *(Dave Colby)*, Douglas Spencer *(Sam Benson)*, Ed Hinton *(A Gambler)*, Don Beddoe *(Ben)*, Claire Andre *(Surrey Driver)*, Jack Mather *(Croupier)*, Edmund Cobb *(Barber)*, Will Wright *(Merchant)*, Jarma Lewis *(Dancer)*, Hal Baylor *(Drunken Cowboy)*, Arthur Shields *(The Minister)*, John Doucette *(Spectator in the Black Nugget)*, Barbara Nichols *(Blonde Dancer)*, Paul Newlan *(Prospector)*, Ralph Sanford *(Bartender)*, Mitchell Lawrence, John Veich, Larry Chance, Fay Morley, Harry Seymour, Jerome Schaeffer, Ann McCrea, Geneva Gray, John Cliff, Mitchell Kowal.

The only western ever directed by Preminger, RIVER OF NO RETURN is a simple, frequently charming, and beautifully photographed film blessed with fine performances from Mitchum and Monroe who make a great team. Set during the gold rush days in northwest Canada, the film opens as Mitchum returns to town to pick up his young son, Rettig, after having served a prison sentence for shooting a man in the back. The details of Mitchum's conviction have been kept from the boy, though Mitchum was forced to shoot the man to stop him from murdering a friend. When Mitchum shows up to claim his son, he is introduced to Monroe, a saloon singer who has befriended the boy. Mitchum thanks the woman for keeping an eye on his child, but looks with suspicion on Monroe's boy friend Calhoun, who is a shifty gambler. Mitchum and Rettig return to their farm on the banks of a large river. Father and son are busy about the farm when one day they spot Monroe and Calhoun adrift on a raft that is about to fall apart. Mitchum rescues the pair and Calhoun explains that he is in a hurry to register a gold claim he won in a game of poker. Mitchum advises caution, but the impatient Calhoun knocks Mitchum over the head and steals the farmer's horse and rifle, leaving a shocked Monroe behind. Monroe tends to Mitchum's wounds and tries to make amends. Mitchum is angry about losing his horse and rifle because the Indians are on the warpath and he has been left defenseless. The farmer decides that all will be safer if they go to town until the uprising blows over, so the trio board the raft and head downriver. During their voyage, Mitchum lets it slip that he intends on getting revenge on Calhoun. Angered, Monroe blurts out how Mitchum killed a man by shooting him in the back. Deeply shocked by the revelation, Rettig, who now idolizes his father, refuses to believe Mitchum's explanation of the incident. As the trio fend off Indian attacks, outlaws, and the rapids, Monroe and Mitchum begin to fall in love. Eventually they arrive in town and Monroe finds Calhoun and begs him to apologize for his behavior. Calhoun agrees, but when he sees Mitchum he produces a pistol and tries to kill him. Rettig sees the commotion from a general store across the street and impulsively uses the rifle he was examining to save his father's life. The boy is forced to shoot Calhoun in the back, only then realizing that his father must have felt the same emotions when he pulled the trigger. Still angry with Monroe, Mitchum takes Rettig and leaves her to go back to singing at the saloon. After some serious brooding, Mitchum returns to the saloon. The big man walks up to the stage, grabs Monroe, throws her over his shoulder and takes her back to live on the farm with him and Rettig. Filled with action, adventure, music, and romance, RIVER OF NO RETURN is an enjoyable, engaging little western that never fails to entertain. Mitchum and Monroe are superb together and it is a shame that the pair never worked together again. Eleven-year-old Rettig turns in a mature, detailed performance and Calhoun is perfect as the evil gambler. Director Preminger relished the chance to use a CinemaScope lens on the lovely Canadian Rockies, and managed to balance breathtaking scenery with human drama quite successfully. Mitchum and Monroe got along well during filming, but in one scene where he had to kiss her, the deadpan actor suddenly pulled away and protested, "How in hell can I take aim when she's undulating like that?" Preminger also liked Monroe, but he could not abide her pretentious acting coach Natasha Lytess—a German woman who, for some reason known only to herself, pretended to be Russian. Her phony accent didn't fool Preminger, and neither did her lousy coaching. Preminger liked Monroe's naturally breathy delivery and was dismayed to discover that Lytess was advising the actress to enunciate every syllable precisely. When Monroe followed Lytess' instructions, her beautiful face contorted horribly from the effort. Luckily Mitchum would not stand for such nonsense and, as Preminger relates in his autobiography, the actor would "...slap her sharply on the bottom and snap, 'Now stop that nonsense! Let's play it like human beings. Come on!" Because

Monroe was the studio's biggest star and felt she had to rely on people like Lytess, Preminger couldn't kick the annoying woman off the set—even though she was tampering with the performance of child actor Rettig as well. Eventually the entire crew learned to despise the woman and she was ignored by everyone but Monroe for the duration of the filming.

p, Stanley Rubin; d, Otto Preminger; w, Frank Fenton (based on a story by Louis Lantz); ph, Joseph La Shelle (CinemaScope, Technicolor); m, Cyril J. Mockridge; ed, Louis Loeffler; md, Lionel Newman; art d, Lyle Wheeler, Addison Hehr; set d, Walter M. Scott, Chester Bayhi; cos, Charles Le Maire, Travilla; spec eff, Ray Kellogg; ch, Jack Cole; m/l, "The River of No Return," "I'm Gonna File My Claim, " "One Silver Dollar," "Down in the Meadow," Newman, Ken Darby (sung by Monroe).

Cas. **(PR:A MPAA:NR)**

RIVER OF POISON (SEE: SOUTH OF DEATH VALLEY, 1950)

RIVER OF ROMANCE★★ (1929) 78m PAR bw

Charles "Buddy" Rogers (Tom Rumford/Col. Blake), Mary Brian (Lucy Jeffers), June Collyer (Elvira Jeffers), Henry B. Walthall (Gen. Jeff Rumford), Wallace Beery (Gen. Orlando Jackson), Fred Kohler, Sr. (Capt. Blackie), Natalie Kingston (Mexico), Walter McGrail (Maj. Patterson), Anderson Lawler (Joe Patterson), Mrs. George Fawcett (Mme. Rumford), George Reed (Rumbo).

Rogers, the son of a southern plantation owner, returns to his father's home upon completing his education in Philadelphia. He soon becomes enamored of Collyer, a young southern belle, and they are engaged, though her younger sister, Brian, is also in love with Rogers. Unfortunately, Collyer's former beau, McGrail, recently released from jail, arrives on the scene and challenges Rogers to a duel. Finding this archaic test of manhood silly, Rogers declines McGrail's challenge but soon finds that the rest of his family takes the duel quite seriously. Shamed that his son has dishonored the family name, Rogers' father banishes the boy from his plantation. Faced with nowhere to go, Rogers heads down the Mississippi, drifting wherever fate will take him. During his wanderings he meets up with Beery, an infamous scoundrel who takes the youngster under his wing. Unwittingly, Rogers soon becomes a legend after he knocks out a local villain who insulted him. Now armed with the alias "Col. Blake," Rogers returns to his father's plantation to exact revenge on McGrail and marry Brian. A bit too melodramatic to be taken seriously, RIVER OF ROMANCE was remade five years later as a musical comedy entitled MISSISSIPPI, starring Bing Crosby, W.C. Fields, and Joan Bennett, this time with better results.

d, Richard Wallace; w, Ethel Doherty, Dan Totheroh, John V.A. Weaver (based on the play "Magnolia" by Booth Tarkington); ph, Victor Milner; ed, Allyson Shaffer; m/l, "My Lady Love," (Leo Robin, Sam Coslow).

Drama/Comedy **(PR:A MPAA:NR)**

RIVER OF UNREST★★½ (1937, Brit.) 70m BIP/GAU bw (GB: OURSELVES ALONE)

John Lodge (County Inspector Hannay), John Loder (Capt. Wiltshire), Antoinette Cellier (Maureen Elliott), Niall MacGinnis (Terence Elliott), Clifford Evans (Com. Connolly), Jerry Verno (Pvt. Parsley), Maire O'Neill (Nanny), Tony Quinn (Maloney), Paul Farrell (Hogan), Pat Noonan (Sgt. Halloran), Bruce Lister (2nd Lt. Lingard), E.J. Kennedy (District Inspector Sullivan), Harry Hutchinson (Henessy), Fred O'Donovan (Publican), Cavan O'Connor (Singer).

A hard-edged drama centering on the battles between the British and the Irish. Cellier is an Irish lass in love with Britisher Loder. He shoots and kills her brother when he tries to escape, but is unaware of the murdered boy's identity. Her loyalty to her country takes over and she lures him to his seemingly inevitable demise.

p&d, Brian Desmond-Hurst; w, Dudley Leslie, Marjorie Jeans, Dennis Johnston, Philip MacDonald (based on the play "The Trouble" by Dudley Sturrock, Noel Scott); ph, Walter Harvey, Bryan Langley; ed, J. Corbett.

Drama **Cas.** **(PR:A MPAA:NR)**

RIVER WOLVES, THE★ (1934, Brit.) 56m REAL/RAD bw

Helga Moray (Moira Clare), Michael Hogan (Capt. Guest), John Mills (Peter Farrell), Ben Welden (Flash Lawson), Hope Davy (Heather Patton), Martin Walker (Trevor Rowe), Norman Shelley (Jim Spiller), D.J. Williams (Tod), Mark Daly (Jock Brodie), Edgar Driver (George), Barbara Everest.

Sea captain Hogan is researching a novel in a waterfront town. He meets Mills, another writer, and both men fall in love with Davy, the daughter of the landlady. Blackmailers threaten Mills, but Hogan rescues him, before leaving Davy to him. Okay thriller, nicely shot.

p, Julius Hagen; d, George Pearson; w, Terence Egan (based on the play "The Lion and the Lamb" by Edward Dignon, Geoffrey Swaffer); ph, Ernest Palmer.

Crime **(PR:A MPAA:NR)**

RIVER WOMAN, THE★★ (1928) 73m Gotham/Lumas bw

Lionel Barrymore (Bill Lefty), Jacqueline Logan (The Duchess), Charles Delaney (Jim Henderson), Sheldon Lewis (Mulatto Mike), Harry Todd (The Scrub), Mary Doran (Sally).

Mississippi melodrama starring Barrymore as a tough saloon owner in love with Logan. He proposes to her, but she is in love with Barrymore's rival, Delaney. One night the bar is invaded by Lewis and his gang of cutthroats and a fight breaks out. Together, Barrymore and Delaney fend off the roughnecks, gaining new respect for each other. Soon afterwards the river overflows and threatens the community. Seeing that Logan really loves Delaney, Barrymore allows them to escape the flood in a small boat while he drowns trying to save his saloon. An unremarkable early talkie with only Barrymore's performance to recommend it.

p, Harold Shumate; d, Joseph E. Henabery; w, Adele Buffington, Shumate; ph, Ray June; ed, Donn Hayes.

Drama **(PR:A MPAA:NR)**

RIVERBOAT RHYTHM★½ (1946) 65m RKO bw

Leon Errol (Matt Lindsey), Glenn Vernon (John Beeler), Walter Catlett (Mr. Witherspoon), Marc Cramer (Lionel Beeler), Jonathan Hale (Edward Beeler), Joan Newton (Midge), Dorothy Vaughan (Belle Vrowley), [Ben]Carter and [Mantan] Moreland, Frankie Carle and His Orchestra.

Errol is a riverboat captain in financial straits who is operating his Mississippi showboat without a license. When he docks on the grounds of a resort hotel, he gets mixed up in a feud between a pair of southern families, and becomes the target of a local sheriff. Frankie Carle provides the riverboat with his rhythmic "Carle Boogey."

p, Nat Holt; d, Leslie Goodwins; w, Charles E. Roberts (based on a story by Robert Faber); ph, Robert de Grasse; ed, Marvin Coil; md, C. Bakaleinikoff; art d, Albert S. D'Agostino, Lucius Croxton.

Drama/Comedy **(PR:A MPAA:NR)**

RIVERRUN★★ (1968) 95m Korty/COL c

Louise Ober (Sarah), John McLiam (Jeffries), Mark Jenkins (Dan), Josephine Nichols (Sarah's Mother), Joseph Miksak (Bartender), Stefanie Priest (Waitress), George Hellyer, Jr. (Doctor), Esther Sutherland (Madame), Laura Kwong, Orion De Winter (Prostitutes), Paula Preston, Wilhelm Joerres (Hippie Couple), Sheila Emmett (Sarah as a Child), Roy Parks (Farmer), Robert Bertrand (Sheriff's Deputy).

A couple of Berkeley students, Ober and Jenkins, leave their campus town for life on a sheep farm, where they are visited by Ober's hard-drinking, sailor father. Ober's subsequent pregnancy leads to the usual generation gap tensions, climaxing in a bloody natural childbirth. Turning in a fine performance is McLiam, as the father. He can also be seen assuming a paternal role in IN COLD BLOOD, as the victimized Mr. Clutter.

p, Stephen Schmidt; d, John Korty; w, Korty, Bill Brammer; ph, Korty (Eastmancolor); m, Richard Greene, Peter Berg, Johannes Brahms; ed, Paddy Monk; cos, Arleen Sterling.

Drama **(PR:O MPAA:R)**

RIVER'S EDGE, THE★★½ (1957) 87m FOX c

Ray Milland (Nardo Denning), Anthony Quinn (Ben Cameron), Debra Paget (Meg Cameron), Harry Carey, Jr. (Chet), Chubby Johnson (Whiskers), Byron Foulger (Barry), Tom McKee (U.S. Border Patrol Captain), Frank Gerstle (U.S. Border Patrolman Harry Castleton).

An outdoor crime drama that was the final big film directed by Dwan (who made about 400 of them), THE RIVER'S EDGE was shot in Mexico on a generous budget and the actors made more of the script than was there. In a very rare hyphenated job, the co-author was also the editor of the film, so he had a chance to write it down, then cut it out. Milland is a thief who has just stolen a million dollars and is trying to get out of the U.S. and down to Mexico where he can spend his ill-gotten gains. In order to do that, he wants to get Quinn, an outdoorsman, to guide him across the border. Quinn is married to Milland's former sweetheart, Paget. As Milland arrives at their mountain ranch, Paget is ready to walk out on Quinn after a huge disagreement. Milland agrees to take her to the nearby town where she can find transportation back to whence she came. They drive off and are halted by Gerstle, a border cop. Milland panics, runs the officer down, and Paget attempts to flee, now realizing that Milland is a desperate man. Milland chases after her on foot. Meanwhile, Quinn is in the local sheriff's office when he learns what's happened as Gerstle tells them in his dying last words. Quinn returns to his ranch, finds Milland and Paget, and Milland pulls a gun on him and forces the innocent Quinn to show him the way to Mexico. Milland is carrying a small suitcase filled with money, and as they are climbing the side of a mountain, he drops the case and the money flies out. Johnson is a grizzled prospector who is in the wrong place at the wrong time. When he picks up the money, Milland kills him, which makes the point to Quinn and Paget that Milland will stop at nothing and that their lives are in danger. Paget intimates that she would rather be with Milland anyhow (a ploy to take Quinn out of harm's way) and the two exit. Quinn gets a rifle from an Indian village and catches them in the dark, cold woods. They take a respite in a cave as Quinn holds the rifle on Milland. They will freeze if there's no fire, and since the only flammable material they have is the money, Quinn tries to persuade Milland to set some of it afire. The two men battle; a rattler comes out and is just about ready to bite when Paget kills the serpent. Next day Quinn is hurt in another fight and Milland goes off alone. Then, with a dumb turn of events, Milland is hit by a truck on a dark mountain road and sent off a high precipice. In the morning, Quinn and Paget are about to go home united and the camera spies some young campers finding the wet money in the river. Milland is dead, and the couple have become closer for their struggle and will eventually tell the cops what happened. Excellent cinematography and good locations but little else.

p, Benedict Bogeaus; d, Allan Dwan; w, Harold Jacob Smith, James Leicester (based on the story "The Highest Mountain" by Smith); ph, Harold Lipstein (CinemaScope, DeLuxe Color); m, Louis Forbes; ed, Leicester; art d, Van Nest Polglase; cos, Gwen Wakeling; m/l, "The River's Edge," Forbes, Bobby Troup (sung by Bob Winn)

Crime/Adventure **(PR:C MPAA:NR)**

RIVER'S END★★½ (1931) 75m WB bw

Charles Bickford (John Keith/ Sgt. Conniston), Evelyn Knapp (Miriam), J. Farrell McDonald (O'Toole), David Torrence (Col. McDowell), ZaSu Pitts (Louise), Junior Coghlan [Frank Coghlan, Jr.] (Mickey), Walter McGrail (Martin), Tom Santschi.

Bickford takes on a dual role as a Canadian Mountie and the convict he is chasing. When the former dies, the latter assumes his identity. He then falls in love with Knapp and the truth comes out, but the fugitive turns out to be innocent. First filmed as a silent in 1920 by First National, then again in 1940 by Warner Bros.

d, Michael Curtiz; w, Charles Kenyon (based on the story by James Oliver Curwood); ph, Robert Kurrle; ed, Ralph Holt.

Western (PR:A MPAA:NR)

RIVER'S END**½   (1940) 69m WB bw

Dennis Morgan (*John Keith/ Sgt. Conniston*), George Tobias (*Andy Dijon*), Elizabeth Earl (*Linda Conniston*), Victor Jory (*Norman Talbot*), James Stephenson (*Inspector McDowell*), Steffi Duna (*Cheets*), Edward Pawley (*Frank Crandall*), John Ridgely (*Constable Jeffers*), Frank Wilcox (*Constable Kentish*), David Bruce, Gilbert Emery, Stuart Robinson.

The third version of this interesting tale about a Canadian mounted policeman tracking down a wanted criminal, both played by Morgan. After the Mountie gets killed, the fugitive takes on the dead man's role in an attempt to prove that he was framed.

p, William Jacobs; d, Ray Enright; w, Barry Trivers, Bertram Millhauser (based on the story by James Oliver Curwood); ph, Arthur L. Todd (Sepiatone); ed, Clarence Kolster.

Western (PR:A MPAA:NR)

RIVERSIDE MURDER, THE**   (1935, Brit.) 64m FOX British bw

Basil Sydney (*Inspector Winton*), Judy Gunn (*Claire Harris*), Alastair Sim (*Sgt. McKay*), Tom Helmore (*Jerome*), Ian Fleming (*Sanders*), Reginald Tate (*Perrin*), Martin Lewis (*Gregg*), Aubrey Mallalieu (*Norman*), Zoe Davis (*Mrs. Harris*).

When three wealthy financiers are murdered before a big meeting, reporter Gunn helps inspector Sydney track down the killer. Average crime programmer, interesting chiefly for Sim's film debut.

d, Albert Parker; w, Selwyn Jepson, Leslie Landau (based on the novel *Six Dead Men* by Andre Steedman).

Crime (PR:A MPAA:NR)

ROAD, THE   (SEE: LA STRADA, 1956, Ital.)

ROAD AGENT**   (1941) 60m UNIV bw (AKA: TEXAS ROAD AGENT)

Dick Foran (*Duke Masters*), Leo Carrillo (*Pancho*), Andy Devine (*Andy*), Anne Gwynne (*Patricia Leavitt*), Samuel S. Hinds (*Sam Leavitt*), Anne Nagel (*Lola*), Richard Davies (*Martin*), Morris Ankrum (*Big John Morgan*), John Gallaudet (*Steve*), Reed Hadley (*Shayne*), Eddy Adams (*Lewis*), Ernie Adams (*Jake*), Lew Kelly (*Luke*), Emmett Lynn, Luane Walters (*Teresa*).

Foran and pals Carrillo and Devine are released from jail and appointed marshals. They then set out to locate the real culprits and prove their innocence. Foran, who had previously cowpoked and crooned for Warners and Fox, sings two songs in this film. ROAD AGENT departs little from formula, but is worth sitting through just the same.

p, Ben Pivar; d, Charles Lamont; w, Morgan Cox, Arthur Strawn, Maurice Tombragel (based on a story by Sherman Lowe, Arthur St. Claire); ed, Frank Gross; md, H.J. Salter; art d, Jack Otterson; m/l, "Cielito Lindo," C. Fernandez (sung by Dick Foran), "Ridin' Home," Jimmy McHugh, Harold Adamson (sung by Foran).

Western (PR:A MPAA:NR)

ROAD AGENT**   (1952) 60m RKO bw

Tim Holt (*Tim*), Noreen Nash (*Cora Drew*), Mauritz Hugo (*Milo Brand*), Dorothy Patrick (*Sally Clayton*), Bob Wilke (*Slab*), Tom Tyler (*Larkin*), Guy Edward Hearn (*Sheriff*), William Tannen (*Bill Collins*), Sam Flint (*George Drew*), Forbes Murray (*Adams*), Stanley Blystone (*Barton*), Richard Martin (*Chito Rafferty*), Tom Kennedy.

A nonviolent oater which has Holt and Martin shocked to learn that they are expected to pay a $20 toll fee to ride a certain trail. They then uncover a plot by area cheats who hope to bankrupt the ranchers by charging such high tolls. The heroic duo don handkerchiefs and disguised as thieves, break into the safe containing the toll profits. The money is returned to the ranchers, who can then easily pay the fee and begin their cattle drive. A neat idea, but lamely executed with a zero in the action column.

p, Herman Schlom; d, Lesley Selander; w, Norman Houston; ph, J. Roy Hunt; ed, Paul Weatherwax, art d, Albert S. D'Agostino, Feild Gray.

Western **Cas.** (PR:A MPAA:NR)

ROAD BACK,THE***   (1937) 103m UNIV bw

John King (*Ernst*), Richard Cromwell (*Ludwig*), Slim Summerville (*Tjaden*), Andy Devine (*Willy*), Barbara Read (*Lucy*), Louise Fazenda (*Angelina*), Noah Beery, Jr. (*Wessling*), Maurice Murphy (*Albert*), John Emery (*Capt. Von Hagen*), Etienne Girardot (*Mayor*), Lionel Atwill (*Prosecutor*), Henry Hunter (*Bethke*), Larry Blake (*Weil*), Gene Garrick (*Giesicke*), Jean Rouverel (*Elsa*), Greta Gynte (*Maria*), Spring Byington (*Ernst's Mother*), Frank Reicher (*Ernst's Father*), Laura Hope Crews (*Ernst's Aunt*), Charles Halton (*Uncle Rudolph*), Arthur Hohl (*Heinrich*), William B. Davidson (*Bartscher*), Al Shean (*Mr. Markheim*), Edwin Maxwell (*Principal*), Samuel S. Hinds (*Defense Attorney*), Robert Warwick (*Judge*), Clara Blandick (*Woman*), Reginald Barlow (*Manager*), E.E. Clive (*General*), Edward Van Sloan (*President*), Dwight Frye (*Small Man*), Francis Ford (*Street Cleaner*), Dorothy Granger (*French Girl*), Tempe Pigott (*Woman*), Tiny Sandford (*Door Keeper*).

Mostly forgotten sequel to the all-time classic ALL QUIET ON THE WESTERN

FRONT suffered from a checkered production history replete with Nazis trying to stop the production and a series of bad decisions by the top brass at Universal. The film concerns the survivors of the company that set out so merrily to war in the first film, now only a few remaining. After a last battle, the Armistice is signed and the men are sent home. Their commander, Emery, assembles them for one last roll call. Only a dozen or so appear, but scores of their dead comrades are seen like ghosts behind them. Then they go home, where each man has difficulties in adjusting to life in defeated Germany after four years in the trenches trying only to survive. When Devine returns to the school where their heads had been filled with patriotic nonsense, his teacher gives him a toy gun that only a few years before had been taken away from him. In the runaway inflation and shortages that plague the country, a mob forms that tries to storm the shop owned by the mayor. Summerville manages to stave off the mob and out of gratitude the mayor allows the ex-soldier to marry his daughter. Another mob forms and another of the former warriors, young Blake, now turned revolutionary, steps in front of it to present their demands. Under the orders of his former commander, Emery, Blake is shot by soldiers. Murphy returns to his old sweetheart only to find that she has been sleeping with an unsavory war profiteer. Murphy kills the man and is put on trial for murder. He tries to defend himself by telling the court that for four years he was trained to kill men just because he was told to, men who had never done anything to him. Why could he not now kill a man who had taken away his love? The film ends with a new batch of schoolchildren out on the playground being drilled in goose stepping by an malignant-looking dwarf. Universal studios had just been wrested from the control of Carl Laemmle and the new owners, a syndicate headed by Charles R. Rogers, wanted to get their concern off to a good start, so they got their best director, Whale, and put him in what they felt to be a sure-fire hit, a sequel to one of the studio's biggest hits ever. The studio had purchased the rights to Remarque's sequel years before, but they had never gotten around to filming it. They realized that the film would probably be banned in Germany, as ALL QUIET had eventually been, and because of certain agreements between nations along the lines of "I'll ban this film you don't like if you ban that film I don't like," the studio heads knew that other nations would probably not see the film, but they counted on the publicity that such measures would garner the film to make a big hit in the U.S. and Britain. The Germans weren't content, though, to simply keep the film from most of Europe; they actually tried to stop the production by such measures as sending letters to all the actors threatening that any film they appeared in would henceforth be banned in Germany if they stayed with the film. Protests were filed with the State Department, and the press took notice. When the film was finally finished, it was the strong statement Whale had hoped to make, and when *Life* magazine reviewed the first cut, they called the opening battle sequence "...the most cruel war scenes ever filmed by Hollywood." Suddenly, though, Universal backed down from its original "Damn the European Market" attitude and decided to reshoot some scenes and recut the film to blunt its punch, turning it into little more than a sad comedy in which the Germans could find nothing objectionable. The studio tried to get the German ambassador to view the film, but he refused, and the film never received the sought-after approval of the Nazis. It was, however, permanently ruined. Some of Whale's film does show through, though. The battle scenes are still powerful, and a special traveling crane was developed to shoot them, a gadget the director was so enamored of that he used it throughout the film. Whale, for the most part, found the whole experience very disheartening and it marked the beginning of the end of his career.

p, Charles R. Rogers; d, James Whale; w, R.C. Sherriff, Charles Kenyon (based on the novel by Erich Maria Remarque); ph, John J. Mescall (George Robinson, uncredited); m, Dimitri Tiomkin; ed, Ted Kent (Charles Maynard, uncredited); md, Charles Previn; art d, Charles D. Hall; spec eff, John P. Fulton; makeup, Jack Pierce.

Drama (PR:A MPAA:NR)

ROAD DEMON**   (1938) 65m FOX bw

Henry Arthur (*Blake*), Joan Valerie (*Joan*), Henry Armetta (*Gambini*), Thomas Beck (*Rogers*), Bill Robinson (*Zephyr*), Jonathan Hale (*Connors*), Thomas MacMahon (*Speed*), Murray Alper, Edward Marr, Lon Chaney, Jr. Eleanor Virzie, Betty Greco, Inez Palange, Johnny Pironne, Jr..

Truck driver Arthur lends a hand to the efforts of Beck, an Indianapolis 500 racer, who is trying to follow in the footsteps of his dad, killed on the track years before. Arthur does some fancy driving and is able to overpower the hoods that killed Beck's dad, and tried to do the same to Beck. Some standard stock footage of race crashes isn't nearly as much fun as seeing Bill "Bojangles" Robinson do a tap dance routine in his junk yard.

p, Jerry Hoffman; d, Otto Brower; w, Robert Ellis, Helen Logan; ph, Edward Snyder; ed, Jack Murray; md, Samuel Kaylin; art d, Bernard Herzbrun, Boris Leven; cos, Herschel.

Action Drama (PR:A MPAA:NR)

ROAD GAMES**½   (1981, Aus.) 101m Quest/AE c

Stacy Keach (*Pat Quid*), Jamie Lee Curtis (*Hitch/Pamela*), Marion Edward (*Frita Frugal*), Grant Page (*Smith or Jones*), Thaddeus Smith (*Abbott*), Bill Stacey (*Capt. Careful*), Stephen Millichamp (*Costello*), Alan Hopgood (*Lester*), John Murphy, Robert Thompson, Angie La Bozzetta, Colin Vancao.

Keach is a truck driver who takes up the search for a killer of hitchhikers when the police fail to come up with any answers. He finds the maniacal Aussie after befriending hitchhiker Curtis, who then takes a ride from the killer. Some suspenseful moments, but on the whole it delivers only a fraction of its potential.

p, Barbi Taylor, Richard Franklin; d, Franklin; w, Everett DeRoche; ph, Vincent Monton (Panavision, Eastmancolor); m, Brian May; ed, Edward McQuinn-Mason; prod d, art d, Jon Dowding; cos, Aphrodite Kondos.

Suspense **Cas.** (PR:O MPAA:PG)

ROAD GANG★★   (1936) 65m FN-WB bw (GB: INJUSTICE)

Donald Woods (*James Larrabee*), Carlyle Moore, Jr. (*Bob Gordon*), Kay Linaker (*Barbara*), Harry Cording (*Sam Dawson*), Ed Chandler (*1st Guard*), Marc Lawrence (*Pete*), Olin Howland (*Doctor*), Joe King (*Winston*), Henry O'Neill (*Metcalfe*), Addison Richards (*Warden*), Charles Middleton (*Mine Warden*), Edward Van Sloan (*Dudley*), Eddie Schubert (*Buck Draper*), William B. Davidson (*Marsden*), Herbert Heywood (*Convict*), Joseph Crehan (*Shields*), John Irwin (*Old Convict*), Ben Hendricks, Tom Manning, Edward Le Saint, George Lloyd, Tom Wilson, Constantine Romanoff.

A harsh portrayal of the South's penal system and the injustices it breeds. After the inmates of a prison camp are unmercifully beaten, a local newspaper reports their unlawful treatment. A Chicago newsman is sent to right their wrongs, and does so in only one afternoon. ROAD GANG covers the same well-traveled route taken by a number of earlier and better prison-oriented films.

d, Louis King; w, Dalton Trumbo (based on a story by Abem Finkel, Harold Buckley); ph, L. William O'Connell; ed, Jack Killifer; art d, Hugh Reticke, Jr.

Prison Drama   **(PR:C MPAA:NR)**

ROAD GANGS, ADVENTURES IN THE CREEP ZONE   (SEE: SPACEHUNTER: ADVENTURES IN THE FORBIDDEN ZONE, 1983)

ROAD HOME, THE★★   (1947, USSR) 89m Leningrad-Riga/Artkino bw

Oleg Zhakov (*Yanis*), Anna Smirnova (*Ilga, His Wife*), Nikolai Chibbius (*Voldemar, His Brother*), Vassili Vanin (*The Miller*), Anna Petukhova (*Milda, Miller's Daughter*), Victor Merkuriev (*Karlis, the Mechanic*), Ludmilla Sukharevskaya (*Christina*), Gregory Michurin (*Partisan Leader*), Vassili Politselmako (*Col. Grabbe*), Georgi Spiegel (*Lt. Brenner*).

Zhakov and his fellow peasants battle the Nazi's in defense of the small Latvian village, after escaping from a concentration camp-bound train. Some exceptional camera work and lighting add to a number of fine performances. (In Russian; English subtitles.)

d. Alexander Ivanov; w, Fedor Knorre; ph, Ivan Goldberg, Alexander Zavialov.

War Drama   **(PR:A MPAA:NR)**

ROAD HOUSE★★   (1934, Brit.) 76m GAU bw

Violet Loraine (*Bell Trout*), Gordon Harker (*Sam Pritchard*), Emlyn Williams (*Chester*), Aileen Marson (*Kitty*), Hartley Power (*Darcy*), Anne Grey (*Lady Chetwynde*), Stanley Holloway (*Donovan*), Marie Lohr (*Lady Hamble*), Edwin Styles (*Archie Hamble*), Romilly Lunge (*Romily*), Horace Kenney, Geraldo and His Band, Wylie Watson, Frank Atkinson.

Loraine is a young mother widowed by war and left to find a means of supporting herself. She takes a job as a music hall singer and sends her baby off to a boarding school. Years later, her "orphaned" daughter is up to her neck in trouble, but her now-famous mother steps in to straighten things out. A well-done mother-and-child reunion scene momentarily lifts the film above its mediocrity.

p, Michael Balcon; d, Maurice Elvey; w, Austin Melford, Leslie Arliss (based on the play by Walter Hackett)

Drama   **(PR:A MPAA:NR)**

ROAD HOUSE★★★   (1948) 95m FOX bw

Ida Lupino (*Lily Stevens*), Cornel Wilde (*Pete Morgan*), Celeste Holm (*Susie Smith*), Richard Widmark (*Jefty Robbins*), O.Z. Whitehead (*Arthur*), Robert Karnes (*Mike*), George Beranger (*Lefty*), Ian MacDonald (*Police Captain*), Grandon Rhodes (*Judge*), Jack G. Lee (*Sam*), Marion Marshall (*Millie*), Jack Edwards, Jr., Don Kohler, Lee MacGregor, Edgar Caldwell (*Men*), Kathleen O'Malley, Blanche Taylor (*Girls*), Charles Flynn, Ray Teal, Robert Foulk (*Policemen*), Clancy Cooper (*Policeman at Club*), Harry Seymour (*Desk Clerk*), Heinie Conklin (*Court Clerk*), Geraldine Jordan (*Woman*), Douglas Gerrard (*Waiter*), Robert Cherry (*Pinboy*), Tom Moore (*Foreman*), Cecil Weston.

A stylish and perverse *film noir* which stars Widmark as the owner of a roadhouse near the Canadian border and Wilde as his best friend and manager. When they hire Lupino as the joint's singer and piano player, the friendship takes a strange turn. Widmark becomes obsessed with Lupino, who in turn finds herself attracted to Wilde. Wilde, however, also the object of cashier Holm's desires, remains aloof. When Widmark goes away on a hunting trip, Wilde finally gives in to Lupino and the two become lovers. When Widmark returns and is told by Wilde of the new situation, the owner's dark side come to light. He stages a robbery which points to Wilde as the guilty party. Rather than watch the framed Wilde go to jail, however, he persuades the judge to release the "criminal" into his custody. Widmark's form of imprisonment is a psychological one—forcing Wilde to stay on at the roadhouse but keeping him from Lupino and, ultimately, his freedom. To further torment him, Widmark arranges for a trip to a lodge nestled in the woods, placing Wilde even closer to the border than before. Widmark hopes that his "prisoner" will make an attempt to escape across the border, thereby giving him the chance to shoot him. Meantime, Holm, who has come along to the lodge, is still silently in love with Wilde. A chance finally comes to escape and Wilde and Lupino run off into the woods. Holm tries to warn them that Widmark is on their trail, hunting them with a psychotic vengeance, but in the process she is wounded by the crazed hunter. A battle follows between Widmark and Wilde. Lupino, determined to fight for her man, intervenes and guns down Widmark like the animal he is. A strong movie scattered with land mines of psychotic characters, ROAD HOUSE has a disturbing quality of psychological torture to it—a quality magnified by the claustrophobic atmosphere of the stylized diner and the false outdoors of the studio's sound stage. Wilde does fine as the victimized lover, Widmark plays his archetypal villain with his usual intensity, and Lupino is remarkable in her raw toughness. Holm, however, is the one who keeps ROAD HOUSE from going over the edge by playing a normal girl with a foothold on reality. Adding to the film's atmosphere is Lupino's delivery

of a few bluesy numbers including "Again," (Dorcas Cochran, Lionel Newman), "One for My Baby" (Johnny Mercer, Harold Arlen), "and "The Right Time."

p, Edward Chodorov; d, Jean Negulesco; w, Chodorov (based on a story by Margaret Gruen, Oscar Saul); ph, Joseph La Shelle; m, Cyril Mockridge; ed, James B. Clark; md, Lionel Newman; art d, Lyle Wheeler, Maurice Ransford; set d, Thomas Little; cos, Kay Nelson; spec eff, Fred Sersen; makeup, Ben Nye, Tom Tuttle, Bill Riddle.

Crime/Drama   **(PR:C MPAA:NR)**

ROAD HUSTLERS, THE★½   (1968) 95m Saturn/AIP c

Jim Davis (*Noah Reedy*), Scott Brady (*Earl Veasey*), Bruce Yarnell (*Matt Reedy*), Robert Dix (*Mark Reedy*), Victoria Carroll (*Nadine*), Andy Devine (*Sheriff Estep*), Sue Raney (*Helen*), Christian Anderson (*Luke Reedy*), Ted Lehmann (*Hagar*), John Cardos (*Chandler*), Bill McKinney (*Hays*), Bill MacDowell (*Bassett*), Jack Lester (*Eskie*), Sid Lawrence (*Deke*), Monica David (*Martha Lu*), Derek Hughes (*Ted*), Marshall Lockhart (*Nelly*), Jim Quick (*Imhoff*), Jack Morey (*Harrison*).

Davis and his three sons try to protect their million-dollar moonshine operation from a local sheriff, federal agents, and the mob. After some near disastrous confrontations and a hair-raising boat chase, the moonshiners come out on top. The mountains of the Carolinas provided the settings and locations for this film.

p, Robert M. Newsom; d, Larry E. Jackson; w, Robert Barron; ph, Gerhard Maser; m&md, Michael Colicchio.

Action   **(PR:C MPAA:NR)**

ROAD IS FINE, THE★★   (1930, Fr.) 75m Braunberger bw (LA ROUTE EST BELLE)

Andre Bauge (*Tony Landrin*), Leon Bary (*Comte Armand Hubert*), Saturnin Fabre (*Mons. Pique*), Serge Freddy Karl (*Jacquot*), Tonia Navar (*Mme. Delaccarrier*), Dorothy Dickson (*Dancer Guest*), Leon Bellieres (*Samuel Ginsberg*), Nady Berry (*Mme. Landrin*), Laurette Fleury (*Huguette Bouquet*).

After directing COCOANUTS, the first Marx Brothers feature, Robert Florey went back across the Atlantic to film this French musical, shot in England's Elstree studio. Bauge plays a poor boy whose vocal talents send him to the top of the entertainment world. He has a great voice, but, unfortunately, none of the tunes is worthy of a second listening. (In French.)

p, Pierre Braunberger; d, Robert Florey; w, Pierre Wolff; ph, Charles Rosher.

Musical   **(PR:A MPAA:NR)**

ROAD MOVIE★★★   (1974) 88m Grove Press c

Robert Drivas (*Gil*), Regina Baff (*Janice*), Barry Bostwick (*Hank*), David Bauer (*Harry*).

Depressing highway character drama has Drivas and Bostwick as a pair of independent truckers trying to stay in business despite the economy, the cops, and the conglomerates. They pick up prostitute Baff who offers herself to the pair in return for a ride to New York. When they cynically take up her offer, then later reject her, she begins to make their lives a living hell, reciting long monologs about how bad her life has been. Inexorably, she drags the unprotesting pair to their destruction. One of the bleakest American pictures of the 1970s, ROAD MOVIE barely got a release before disappearing into obscure cult status. Excellent performances, particularly by Baff as the beaten and furious hooker clawing at everyone around her. Well worth seeking out, if you don't mind being depressed for a while.

p&d, Joseph Strick; w, Judith Rascoe; ph, Don Lenzer; m, Stanley Meyers; ed, Sylvia Sarner.

Drama   **(PR:O MPAA:R)**

ROAD SHOW★★½   (1941) 87m UA bw

Adolphe Menjou (*Col. Carleton Carraway*), Carole Landis (*Penguin Moore*), John Hubbard (*Drogo Gaines*), Charles Butterworth (*Harry Whitman*), Patsy Kelly (*Jinx*), George E. Stone (*Indian*), Margaret Roach (*Priscilla*), Polly Ann Young (*Helen Newton*), Edward Norris (*Ed Newton*), Marjorie Woodworth (*Alice*), Florence Bates (*Mrs. Newton*), Willie Best (*Willie*), Paul Stanton (*Dr. Thorndyke*), Ted Stanhope (*Stanhope*), Clarence Wilson (*Sheriff*), Lane Chandler (*State Trooper*), Jack Norton (*Drunk*), The Charioteers (*Themselves*).

Menjou and millionaire Hubbard escape from a mental hospital and hook up with bankrupt carnival owner Landis. Some completely zany moments add a nice touch to this otherwise standard picture. Some sources include Gordon Douglas and Hal Roach, Jr. in the directing credits with Hal Roach, Sr. The younger Roach added a helping hand on a number of his father's projects, and at the time of this film he would have been a mere 20 years old. Note also that silent star Harry Langdon contributed to the screenplay for ROAD SHOW. Langdon fell on hard times with the advent of sound, but Roach enlisted the silent comic's talents after his star had faded. Songs include: "I Should Have Known Years Ago" (Hoagy Carmichael, sung by Carole Landis), "Slav Annie," "Yum, Yum," "Calliope Jane" (Carmichael, Stanley Adams).

p, Hal Roach; d, Hal Roach, Hal Roach, Jr., Gordon Douglas; w, Arnold Belgard, Harry Langdon, Mickell Noval (based on a novel by Eric Hatch); ph, Norbert Brodine; m, George Stoll; ed, Bert Jordan; art d, Charles D. Hall; spec eff, Roy Seawright.

Comedy   **(PR:A MPAA:NR)**

ROAD TO ALCATRAZ★★   (1945) 60m REP bw

Robert Lowery (*John Norton*), June Storey (*Kit Norton*), Grant Withers (*Inspector Craven*), Clarence Kolb (*Philip Angreet*), Charles Gordon (*Gary Payne*), William Forrest (*Charles Cantrell*), Iris Adrian (*Louise Rogers*), Lillian Bronson (*Dorothy Stone*), Harry Depp (*House Manager*), Kenne Duncan (*Servant*).

An economical crime drama about a young lawyer who is suspected of murdering his law partner. He's sure that he's innocent, but since the real killer drugged him during the crime he can't remember anything. He then discovers it was his best friend that did the deed.

p, Sidney Picker; d, Nick Grinde; w, Dwight V. Babcock, Jerry Sackheim (based on the short story "Murder Stole My Missing Hours" by Francis K. Arlen); ph, Ernest Miller; ed, Richard Van Enger; md, Richard Cherwin; art d, Lucius Croxton; spec eff, Howard and Theodore Lydecker.

Crime (PR:A MPAA:NR)

ROAD TO BALI½** (1952) 90m PAR c

Bob Hope *(Harold Gridley)*, Bing Crosby *(George Cochran)*, Dorothy Lamour *(Lalah)*, Murvyn Vye *(Ken Arok)*, Peter Coe *(Gung)*, Ralph Moody *(Bhoma Da)*, Leon Askin *(Ramayana)*, Jane Russell, Dean Martin, Jerry Lewis, Bob Crosby *(Themselves)*, Jack Claus *(Specialty Dancer)*, Bernie Gozier *(Bo Kassar)*, Herman Cantor *(Priest)*, Shela Fritz, Ethel K. Reiman, Irene K. Silva *(Chief's Wives)*, Kuka L. Tuitama, Charles Mauu, Al Kikume, Satini Puailoa *(Warriors)*, Mylee Haulani *(Beautiful Girl in Basket)*, Kukhie Kuhns *(Fat Woman in Basket)*, Michael Ansara *(Guard)*, Larry Chance *(Attendant)*, Bunny Lewbel *(Lalah at Age 7)*, Pat Dane, Sue Casey, Patty McKaye, Judith Landon, Leslie Charles, Jean Corbett, Betty Onge *(Handmaidens)*, Roy Gordon *(Eunice's Father)*, Harry Cording *(Verna's Father)*, Carolyn Jones *(Eunice)*, Jan Kayne *(Verna)*, Allan Nixon *(Eunice's Brother)*, Douglas Yorke *(Verna's Brother)*, Mary Kanae *(Old Crone)*, Raymond Lee, Luukia Luana *(Boys)*, Bismark Auelua, Bhogwan Singh, Chanan Singh Sohi, Jerry Groves *(Lesser Priests)*, Richard Keene *(Conductor)*, Donald Lawton *(Employment Agency Clerk)*, Katharine Hepburn, Humphrey Bogart.

Hope and Crosby had been making "Road" films for 12 years when they did this, their sixth and the only one in color. It was getting tiresome by that time, although they managed some fun out of the slim plot. Hope and Crosby are a pair of vaudevillians working in Sydney, Australia, when they are run out of town by the fathers of some wenches whom they'd made off-handed promises to. With no other employment, they take jobs as divers for Vye, a South Seas type who sails them to an island where they meet Lamour, in her customary sarong. She's rich and Vye wants to steal her treasure, but that's circumvented and Crosby winds up with Lamour as well as Jane Russell, in a cameo. Several good jokes, some strong physical comedy, and a number of cameo appearances, including an unbilled duet by Bogart and Hepburn as he hauls the "African Queen" through a swamp. Along the way, Hope and Crosby fight cannibals, a giant squid, crazed animals, and predatory women. The loose, easy air of the prior films seemed to have been lost in this and the humor feels much more studied, with little of the apparently improvised camaraderie audiences loved before. Martin and Lewis are seen as themselves and brother Bob Crosby also gets a few seconds on screen. The Johnny Burke, Jimmy Van Heusen score included: "Moonflowers" (sung by Lamour), "Chicago Style" (sung by Hope, Crosby), "Hoots Mon" (sung by Hope, Crosby), "To See You" (sung by Crosby), "The Merry-Go-Runaround" (sung by Hope). Stan Kenton and Pete Rugolo added the instrumental "Chorale For Brass, Piano And Bongo." It was 10 more years until the boys reached the end of the "Road" with ROAD TO HONG KONG.

p, Harry Tugend; d, Hal Walker; w, Frank Butler, Hal Kanter, William Morrow (based on a story by Butler, Tugend); ph, George Barnes (Technicolor); ed, Archie Marshek; md, Joseph J. Lilley; art d, Hal Pereira, Joseph McMillan Johnson; set d, Sam Comer, Russ Dowd; cos, Edith Head; ch, Charles O'Curran

Comedy/Musical Cas. (PR:AA MPAA:NR)

ROAD TO DENVER, THE½** (1955) 90m REP c

John Payne *(Bill Mayhew)*, Mona Freeman *(Elizabeth Sutton)*, Lee J. Cobb *(Jim Donovan)*, Skip Homeier *(Sam Mayhew)*, Andy Clyde *(Whipsaw)*, Lee Van Cleef *(Pecos Larry)*, Karl Davis *(Hunsaker)*, Glenn Strange *(Big George)*, Buzz Henry *(Pete)*, Daniel White *(Joslyn)*, Robert Burton *(Kraft)*, Anne Carroll *(Miss Honeywell)*, Tex Terry *(Passenger)*, Ray Middleton *(John Sutton)*.

A feud between brothers is at the center of this action-packed western with Payne as the responsible elder sibling and Homeier the young hood. Payne, tired of bailing Homeier out of trouble, heads for Colorado, where he gets work setting up a stagecoach line. It's not long before Homeier ends up in the same town, but on the side of Cobb, the nasty head of a local outlaw gang. Not only does Payne win the battle, but he also gets the girl, Freeman. Bill Gulick's novel "Man From Texas," which was serialized in *The Saturday Evening Post*, provided the basis for this satisfying ride through the Old West. Though set in Colorado, the location shooting for the film was done in Utah.

p, Herbert J. Yates; d, Joseph Kane; w, Horace McCoy, Allen Rivkin (based on the novel *Man From Texas* by Bill Gullick); ph, Reggie Lanning (Trucolor); m, R. Dale Butts; ed, Richard Van Enger; art d, Walter Keller; cos, Adele Palmer.

Western (PR:A MPAA:NR)

ROAD TO ETERNITY*** (1962, Jap.) 181m Shochiku/Shochiku-Beverly bw (ZOKU NINGEN NO JOKEN; NINGEN NO JOKEN II)

Tatsuya Nakadai *(Kaji)*, Michiyo Aratama *(Michiko)*, Keiji Sada *(Kageyama)*, Michio Minami *(Yoshida)*, Hideo Kisho *(Kudo)*, Kei Sato *(Shinjo)*, Taketoshi Naito *(Tange)*, Kunie Tanaka *(Obara)*, Kokinjo Katsura *(Sasa)*, Kaneko Iwasaki *(Tokunaga)*, Jun Tatara *(Hino)*, Yusuke Kawazu, Hideo Kidokoro.

Nakadai is a young Japanese man sent to Manchuria for training near the end of WW II. He finds that the soldiers are living in constant fear of the drill sergeants who treat them very badly. When he protests, he is accused of being a Communist sympathizer. After escapes and beatings, Nakadai nearly kills an officer, and out of frustration kills a fellow soldier. When the Japanese troops are defeated, Nakadai is left alone on the battlefield. This is the second episode in Kobayashi's trilogy entitled "The Human Condition," which severely criticised Japan's treatment of its troops and the entire social system. It was preceded by THE HUMAN CONDITION (1959) and followed by A SOLDIER'S PRAYER (1970). (In Japanese; English subtitles.)

p, Tatsuo Hasoya; d, Masaki Kobayashi; w, Kobayashi, Zenzo Matsuyama (based on the third and fourth volumes of Jumpei Gomigawa's six-volume novel *The Human Condition*); ph, Yoshio Miyajima (Shochiku Grand Scope);m, Chuji Kinoshita; ed, Keiichi Uraoka; art d, Kazue Hirataka.

War Drama (PR:O MPAA:NR)

ROAD TO FORT ALAMO, THE*½ (1966, Fr./Ital.) 82m Protor-Piazzi-Comptoir Francais/World Entertainment c (ARIZONA BILL; LA STRADA PER FORT ALAMO)

Ken Clark, Jany Clair, Michel Lemoine, Andreina Paul, Kirk Bert, Antonio Gradoli, Dean Ardow.

A disliked outlaw is abandoned by his gang, rescued by a wagon train, and makes good after the gang robs a bank and everyone is attacked by Indians. The outcast kills the gang leader, returns the stolen money, and starts anew with his gal and buddy. A stale spaghetti western, directed by Mario Bava under a pseudonym.

d, John M. Old [Mario Bava]; w, Vincent Thomas, Charles Price, Jane Brisbane (based on a story by Thomas); ph, Bud Third (Totalscope, Eastmancolor).

Western (PR:C MPAA:NR)

ROAD TO FRISCO (SEE: THEY DRIVE BY NIGHT, 1940)

ROAD TO GLORY, THE½** (1936) 95m FOX bw (AKA: WOODEN CROSSES; ZERO HOUR)

Fredric March *(Lt. Michel Denet)*, Warner Baxter *(Capt. Paul LaRoche)*, Lionel Barrymore *(Papa LaRoche)*, June Lang *(Monique)*, Gregory Ratoff *(Bouffiou)*, Victor Kilian *(Regnier)*, Paul Stanton *(Relief Captain)*, John Qualen *(Duflous)*, Julius Tannen *(Lt. Tannen)*, Theodore von Eltz *(Major)*, Paul Fix *(Rigaud)*, Leonid Kinskey *(Ledoux)*, Jacques Lory *(Courier)*, Jacques Vanaire *(Doctor)*, Edythe Raynore *(Nurse)*, George Warrington *(Old Soldier)*, Louis Mercier *(Soldier)*.

Baxter is a French regimental commander during WW I who is constantly being sent replacements to whom he gives a standardized speech about the proud traditions of the regiment. He then sends them into the line to be slaughtered before the German trenches for a gain of a few yards that will only be lost the next day. He lives almost exclusively on a diet of cognac and aspirin. Into the unit comes idealistic and carefree junior officer March, who is soon disillusioned by the waste of life all around him. The two men fall in love with pretty nurse Lang, although she prefers March. Into the regiment comes Barrymore (in one of his last walking parts), the oldest private in the French army, a veteran of the Battle of Sedan in the Franco-Prussian War in 1870, and Baxter's father. Baxter is not happy about having his own father under his command and his drinking becomes heavier. In another senseless assault, Baxter is blinded and brought back to the field hospital. Barrymore offers to be his eyes and leads him back to the front, where both are killed while directing French artillery fire. March is left with Lang and command of the regiment, and we last see him giving the same speech about tradition to another batch of replacements. The film is certainly one of Hawks' weaker efforts, but it is interesting for a number of reasons. Fox had purchased a French film entitled LES CROIX DES BOIS, which had done big business throughout the world (except for the U.S., where it was never released) and was much praised for its realistic battle scenes. Fox wanted to cannibalize the film for those scenes, then construct a new film around them. Faulkner, with whom Hawks had already established a working relationship, was called in and together with Sayre they came up with the script, although Nunnally Johnson later claimed to have rewritten the whole thing himself. The story is just another stale wartime romantic triangle, but it does have a few moments of undeniable power, such as when a squad of French *poilus* sit in terror in their trench as they listen to the Germans dig a tunnel below their feet and pack it with explosives. The men are relieved just in time (unlike the Italian unit on whom the incident was based; they held their positions until they were blown up by the charges they had heard being prepared for days). Another unforgettable moment comes at the end as Barrymore, knowing death is imminent for him and his blinded son, begins to blow the bugle he had carried at Sedan. Faulkner was at the peak of his ability to write for the screen at this time, and he turned out an average of 35 densely handwritten pages per day. When he finished, he went on a one-week drinking binge that ended up with him in the hospital.

p, Darryl F. Zanuck; d, Howard Hawks; w, Joel Sayre, William Faulkner (based on the film LES CROIX DES BOIS directed by Raymond Bernard and the novel by Roland Dorgeles); ph, Gregg Toland; ed, Edward Curtiss; md, Louis Silvers; art d, Hans Peters; set d, Thomas Little; cos, Gwen Wakeling.

War Drama (PR:A-C MPAA:NR)

ROAD TO HAPPINESS* (1942) 84m MON bw

John Boles *(Jeff Carter)*, Mona Barrie *(Millie Rankin)*, Billy Lee *(Danny Carter)*, Roscoe Karns *(Charley Grady)*, Lillian Elliott *(Mrs. Price)*, Paul Porcasi *(Pacelli)*, Selmer Jackson *(Sam Rankin)*, Brandon Hurst *(Swayne)*, Sam Flint *(Col. Gregory)*, Antonio Filauri *(Almonti)*, Harlan Tucker *(Foster)*, Byron Foulger.

Boles returned to the screen after an absence of several years in this sticky melodrama about a divorced father trying to make a home for his son despite the obstacles put in his way.

p, Scott R. Dunlap; d, Phil Rosen; w, Robert D. Andrews (based on a story by Matt Taylor); ph, Harry Neuman; ed, Carl Pierson; md, Edward Kay.

Drama (PR:A MPAA:NR)

ROAD TO HONG KONG, THE** (1962, U.S./Brit.) 91m Melnor/UA bw

Bing Crosby *(Harry Turner)*, Bob Hope *(Chester Babcock)*, Joan Collins *(Diane)*, Dorothy Lamour *(Herself)*, Robert Morley *(The Leader)*, Walter Gotell *(Dr. Zorbb)*,

Roger Delgardo *(Jhinnah)*, Felix Aylmer *(Grand Lama)*, Peter Madden *(Lama)*, Alan Gifford, Robert Ayres, Robin Hughes *(American Officials)*, *Julian Sherrier (Doctor)*, Bill Nagy *(Agent)f1, Guy Standeven (Photographer)*, John McCarthy *(Messenger)*, Simon Levy *(Servant)*, Mei Ling *(Chinese Girl)*, Jacqueline Jones *(Lady at Airport)*, Katya Douglas *(Receptionist)*, Harry Baird, Irving Allen *(Nubians)*, Victor Brooks, Roy Patrick, John Dearth, David Randall, Michael Wynne *(Leader's Men)*, Peter Sellers, Frank Sinatra, Dean Martin, David Niven, Zsa Zsa Gabor, Dave King, Jerry Colonna *(Guest Stars)*, Yvonne Shima, Camilla Brockman, Lena Margot, Sheree Winton, Edwina Carroll, Diane Valentine, April Ashley, Jacqueline Leigh, Sein Short, Lier Hwang, Michele Mok, Zoe Zephyr *(Girls)*.

The final "Road" picture, an awkward attempt at recreating the fun of the previous sextet, this one has a few funny moments, but it's so filled with inside jokes that a lot of it will be lost on anyone who hasn't seen the other movies in the series. It was made in England and that was a plus, as there were a number of good British actors involved, including a brilliant cameo by Sellers as an Indian doctor. As usual, Hope and Crosby are a duo of vaudevillians. As the picture opens, they've given up the stage in favor of confidence work and are in India, attempting to sell their "Fly-It-Yourself" space kit for interplanetary travel. The cops get onto them, and in the attempt at arrest, Hope falls and is taken to the local hospital where Sellers examines him and determines that amnesia has set in. Crosby doesn't believe it until Hope admits that he doesn't remember what women are. That convinces Crosby. They learn of a potion that can cure Hope, but it can only be found in the Tibetan lamasery where Aylmer is the head lama. The drug is a success and now Hope has total recall. They go to the local airport to return to the U.S. and meet Collins, a spy for a group of intellectuals who plan to conquer the world by taking over space. She thinks Hope is also an agent and shows him a stolen Russian formula for a secret rocket fuel. Hope glances at the equation and it is immediately committed to memory. The scientists, led by Morley, capture Hope and Crosby and put them aboard a rocket in place of monkeys. The rocket takes off, goes around the moon, then comes down, and the boys are not harmed. Morley makes plans for their deaths, but decides to give them one last taste of happiness and places them in a harem. They escape into the back alleys of Hong Kong, lurch into a nightclub where Lamour is singing (as herself), and she helps them get away from Morley's gang. The bad guys are captured but Hope, Crosby, and Collins (who has now joined them, as she realized Morley was nuts) stumble into a rocket which goes up (in a very long sequence) and they land on a remote planet. Once there, they are met by Sinatra and Martin as two space travelers who came via another route. Silly, inane script saved only by the choreography by Baker and Meyers (who were married at the time but used different names) and the songs by Sammy Cahn and Jimmy Van Heusen that included: "Teamwork" (sung by Hope, Crosby, Collins), "Let's Not Be Sensible" (sung by Crosby), "It's the Only Way To Travel" (sung by Hope, Crosby), "We're on the Road To Hong Kong" (sung by Hope, Crosby, Collins), "Warmer Than a Whisper" (sung by Lamour). Panama's direction lacked pace and you know you're in trouble when the funniest sequence is due to a guest star (Sellers).

p, Melvin Frank; d, Norman Panama; w, Panama, Frank; ph, Jack Hildyard; m, Robert Farnon; ed, Alan Osbiston, John Smith; prod d, Roger Furse; md, Farnon: art d, Sydney Cain, Bill Hutchinson; set d, Maurice Fowler; cos, Anthony Mendleson; spec eff, Wally Veevers, Ted Samuels; ch, Jack Baker, Sheila Meyers; makeup, Dave Aylott, Eric Allwright.

Comedy/Musical **(PR:AA MPAA:NR)**

ROAD TO LIFE*½** (1932, USSR) 101m Mejrabpom/Amkino bw(PUTYOVKA V ZHIZN)

Mikhail Zharov *(Fomka Zhigan)*, Maria Gonta *(Lelka Mazikha)*, Tzyvan Kyrla *("Dandy" Mustapha)*, Mikhail Djagafarov *(Kolka)*, Vladimir Veshnovsky *(Kolka's Father)*, Regina Yanushkevich *(Kolka's Mother)*, Nikolai Batalov *(Nikolai Sergeyev)*, M. Antropova.

One of the finest Soviet films to come along with the advent of sound. It tells the tale of a group of street urchins in Moscow who are brought before a board of inquiry with the hope of setting them straight. The board allows the homeless youngsters to form their own commune to teach them the fundamentals of hard work. The gang, led by Kyrla, begins work on a railway line, but as it is completed Kyrla is killed by Zharov, a member who tries to break away and form his own gang. The dead leader's body is transported on the front of the locomotive. A fine essay on problems of poverty and rehabilitation, which director Ekk never again came close to equalling. A year later William Wellman, in WILD BOYS OF THE ROAD, dealt with identical themes. Originally released at 121m, and re-released in 1957 with a new soundtrack and re-edited by Ekk at 98m. (In Russian; English subtitles.)

d, Nikolai Ekk; w, Ekk, Alexander Stolper, R. Yanushkevitch; ph, Vasili Pronin; m, E. Nesterov; art d, I. Stepanov, A. Yevemnenko; English subtitles, Mike Gold.

Drama **(PR:A MPAA:NR)**

ROAD TO FORTUNE, THE* (1930, Brit.) 60m Starcraft/PAR bw

Guy Newall *(Guy Seaton)*, Doria March *(June Eastman)*, Florence Desmond *(Toots Willoughby)*, Stanley Cooke *(Prof. Kingsbury)*, J.H. Wakefield *(Willard)*, Jean Lester *(Miss Lurcher)*, George Vollaire *(Dr. Killick)*, Anne Kelagh.

The beautifully photographed Cornish landscape makes this quota quickie easier to take. Tediously told, the story is about a willful woman whose disregarded lover saves her from the seamy life her wild nature is hurtling her into. Dialog is ho-hum and acting is nothing to remember.

p&d, Arthur Varney; w, Hugh Broadbridge (based on the novel *Moorland Terror* by Broadbridge).

Crime Drama **(PR:A MPAA:NR)**

ROAD TO MOROCCO**** (1942) 83m PAR bw

Bing Crosby *(Jeff Peters)*, Bob Hope *(Turkey Jackson)*, Dorothy Lamour *(Princess Shalmar)*, Anthony Quinn *(Mullay Kasim)*, Dona Drake *(Mihirmah)*, Mikhail Rasumny *(Ahmed Fey)*, Vladimir Sokoloff *(Hyder Khan)*, George Givot *(Neb Jolla)*, Andrew Tombes *(Oso Bucco)*, Leon Belasco *(Yusef)*, Monte Blue, Jamiel Hanson *(Aides to Mullay Kasim)*, Louise La Planche, Theo de Voe, Brooke Evans, Suzanne Ridgeway, Yvonne De Carlo, Patsy Mace, Poppy Wilde *(Handmaidens)*, George Lloyd, Sammy Stein *(Guards)*, Ralph Penney *(Arabian Waiter)*, Dan Seymour *(Arabian Buyer)*, Pete G. Katchenaro *(Philippine Announcer)*, Brandon Hurst *(English Announcer)*, Richard Loo *(Chinese Announcer)*, Leo Mostovoy *(Russian Announcer)*, Vic Groves, Joe Jewett *(Knife Dancers)*, Michael Mark *(Arab Pottery Vendor)*, Nestor Paiva *(Arab Sausage Vendor)*, Stanley Price *(Idiot)*, Rita Christiana *(Specialty Dancer)*, Robert Barron *(Gigantic Bearded Arab)*, Cy Kendall *(Fruit Stand Proprietor)*, Sara Berner *(Voice for Female Camel)*, Kent Rogers *(Voice for Male Camel)*, Edward Emerson *(Bystander)*, Sylvia Opert *(Dancer)*, Blue Washington *(Nubian Slave)*, Harry Cording, Dick Botiller *(Warriors)*.

The third in the "Road" series and the best. This one had everything going for it. It was still early in the game and Hope and Crosby had not yet tired of the formula so their breezy acting wafted the picture along in a melange of gags, songs, excitement, and calculated absurdities. They had already taken shots at adventure movies in ROAD TO SINGAPORE and jungle films in ROAD TO ZANZIBAR so the next logical target was the Arabian Nights genre and they put that away, but good. Don't look for rhyme or reason here as they are in short supply. Just let yourself be regaled by the machine-gun wit and the well-staged slapstick. It's an irreverent send-up of every Middle East movie ever made and was the first original screenplay for the series, after Hartman and Butler had adapted some tossed-away stories for the first two. (Butler was educated at Oxford and tried his hand at acting before striking it rich as a writer.) Crosby and Hope are seen as the lone survivors of a ship wrecked in the Mediterranean. They land on a beach, board a passing camel who is unusually receptive, and go off toward Morocco where they learn that things aren't swell. The area is parched, the people are poor, and aliens are looked upon with scorn. They are penniless and hungry when Seymour, a chubby local, offers Crosby some money if Hope can be sold into slavery and taken to be the personal plaything of the princess, Lamour. Crosby makes the deal, pockets the cash, and Hope is forcibly removed to the palace. Later, Crosby has a vision of Hope's aunt (Hope in drag) who berates him for selling her nephew the way he did. Crosby gets an attack of guilt and goes to the palace to see if he can rescue his partner. Upon arriving at the fabulous residence (the art direction was sensational and what everyone imagined to be authentic), Crosby sees that Hope has wound up on his feet and in the arms of Lamour, who intends to take him as her husband. Crosby can't believe Hope's good fortune. He stays at the palace and begins to charm Lamour but she remains true to Hope as she believes her marriage to him has been divined by the heavens above. She'd been consulting with the palace astrologer, Sokoloff, and since the stars tell her that Hope is her true love, she must adhere to the wishes of the celestial beings. Then Sokoloff informs Lamour that he miscalculated his charts because the telescope lens had been blurred by a horde of insects. She needn't marry Hope. Lamour sighs with relief and now plans to take Crosby as her lawful wedded pasha. But there's trouble in store when Quinn, an Arab nogoodnik, hears that she no longer must marry Hope. Quinn, in a parody of the role he would play many years later in LAWRENCE OF ARABIA, wants Lamour and will stop at nothing to get her. He captures Crosby and Hope, ties them up and sends them out on the cruel desert with no food and no water. Lamour thinks she's been abandoned and consents to marry Quinn. Hope and Crosby wander in the desert until they can break free, then rush to Quinn's camp a short while before the marriage is to occur. With the help of a rival desert tribe, they break up the wedding, rescue Lamour, and get away. Dissolve and Hope and Crosby are now on their way home aboard a ship with Lamour and harem girl Drake, Hope's new sweetheart, when Hope mistakenly walks into the ship's arsenal with a cigarette. The whole ship blows up and the foursome are on a raft floating at sea when next we find them. Days pass and Hope begins to go mad, screams: "No food! No water! I can't take it! etc. Crosby waits until Hope has finished emoting, then calmly informs him that they are a few minutes outside New York and will be rescued very soon. Hope is angry at that and says: "You spoiled the only good scene I had in the movie! If you'd have kept your mouth shut, I might have won an Academy Award!" (which he still hasn't won for his acting). The camel seen earlier caps the madness by remarking "This is the screwiest picture I've ever been in!" (in the voice of Kent Rogers). The screenplay and Loren Ryder's sound recording took Oscar nominations but that was it from the Academy. The movie was a huge success and is still delightful, almost 50 years later. Johnny Burke and Jimmy Van Heusen wrote the songs, including: "Constantly" (sung by Lamour), "Moonlight Becomes You" (sung by Crosby), "Ain't Got a Dime To My Name" (sung by Crosby), and "Road To Morocco" (sung by Crosby, Hope), which contains the memorable line "Like Webster's Dictionary, we're Morocco-bound." Many of the jokes are of the period, such as the one where Hope, as his late aunt who has come down from heaven to tell Crosby off, hears approaching footsteps and says "I can't talk now. Here comes Mr. Jordan"—a direct reference to the Claude Rains-Robert Montgomery film. When Hope and Crosby try their "patty-cake" routine on Quinn (the one where they play "patty-cake," then turn and sock the person they want to avoid), Quinn backs off and the men whack their heads together causing Crosby to shake the cobwebs out of his brain and remark; "Hmmm. That gag sure got around." In Quinn's "nodding room," there are a series of heads on columns which nod whenever Quinn wants assurance (a takeoff on the Hollywood "yes-men" who can still be found nodding at every studio), and Hope and Crosby join the nodders as they try to elude capture. It would be hard to picture anyone else in these "Road" pictures, although the very first one had been offered to, and refused by, Burns and Allen, then Fred MacMurray and Jack Oakie. Thank heaven no one did this one but Hope and Crosby. In a small role, look for Yvonne De Carlo, who later went on to make these kinds of movies for real. "Moonlight Becomes You" became a standard as sung by Crosby. Hope tries it once in the movie with hilarious results although the truth is that Hope came from the musical stage and had a very pleasant voice, though nowhere in Crosby's class. Quinn played it straight, which made it funnier. He'd already been in ROAD TO SINGAPORE and thoroughly enjoyed the experience, as did everyone who saw this crackling-good comedy. It's hysterical and it's clean. Would that they could make this kind of film today when humor often depends on sniggering and scatology.

p, Paul Jones; d, David Butler; w, Frank Butler, Don Hartman; ph, William Mellor; ed, Irene Morra; md, Victor Young; art d, Hans Dreier, Robert Usher; cos, Edith Head; ch, Paul Oscard.

Comedy/Musical **(PR:AA MPAA:NR)**

ROAD TO PARADISE** (1930) 76m FN bw

Loretta Young *(Margaret Waring/Mary Brennan)*, Jack Mulhall *(George Wells)*, Raymond Hatton *(Nick)*, George Barraud *(Jerry "The Gent")*, Kathlyn Williams (Mrs. Wells), Fred Kelsey *(Casey)*, Purnell Pratt *(Updike)*, Ben Hendricks, Jr. *(Flanagan)*, Dot Farley *(Lola)*, Winter Hall *(Brewster)*, Georgette Rhodes *(Yvonne)*.

Young is a society gal who takes up with a couple of crooks and breaks into the house of her long-lost twin sister. Far-fetched, but enjoyable if the implausibilities are put to the side.

d, William Beaudine; w, F. Hugh Herbert (based on the play "Cornered" by Dodson Mitchell, Zelda Sears); ph, John Seitz; ed, Edward Schroeder.

Drama **(PR:A MPAA:NR)**

ROAD TO RENO** (1931) 74m PAR bw

Lilyan Tashman *(Mrs. Jackie Millet)*, Charles "Buddy" Rogers *(Tom Wood)*, Peggy Shannon *(Lee Millet)*, William Boyd *(Jerry Kenton)*, Irving Pichel *(Robert Millet)*, Wynne Gibson *(Mrs. It-Ritch)*, Skeets Gallagher *(Hoppie)*, Tom Douglas *(Jeff Millet)*, Judith Wood *(Elsie Kenton)*, Leni Stengel *(Mrs. Stafford-Howes)*, Emil Chautard *(Andre)*.

This cheap and quick picture follows a "relationship gone wrong" theme as Tashman goes through a pair of husbands before settling on a third. Her daughter Shannon is just as flighty when it comes to finding a fella. Tashman's son Douglas takes matters into his own hands and kills husband number three during the wedding ceremony, then turns the gun on himself. Stunned by the goings-on, Shannon shapes up and settles down with a nice young man. It's just as funny as it is serious, but no matter how it is taken, ROAD TO RENO is easily forgotten.

d, Richard Wallace; w, Josephine Lovett, Brian Marlow (based on a story by Virginia Kellogg); ph, Karl Struss.

Comedy/Drama **(PR:A MPAA:NR)**

ROAD TO RENO, THE½** (1938) 72m UNIV bw

Randolph Scott *(Steve Fortness)*, Hope Hampton *(Linda Halliday)*, Glenda Farrell *(Sylvia Shane)*, Helen Broderick *(Aunt Minerva)*, Alan Marshall *(Walter Crawford)*, David Oliver *(Salty)*, Ted Osborne *(Linda's Attorney)*, Charles Murphy *(Mike)*, Spencer Charters *(The Judge)*, Dorothy Farley *(Mrs. Brumleigh)*, Mira McKinney *(Hannah)*, Renie Riano *(Woman Bailiff)*, Samuel S. Hinds *(Sylvia's Attorney)*.

Hampton is cast as cowboy Scott's wife, who wants to take that well-trodden path to Reno and get a divorce. Scott then discovers that he is competing with Easterner Marshall for his wife's hand. Marshall proves that he can do the cowboy routine as well as Scott, embarrassing him in a bronco-riding exhibition, but Hampton ends up back in the arms of her husband. Hampton performs a bit of "La Boheme" as part of her opera performance and delivers a few other tunes: "I Gave My Heart Away, " "Ridin' Home," and "Tonight Is The Night" (Jimmy McHugh, Harold Adamson). This was one of a handful of pleasant little pictures in which Hampton appeared, thanks in large part to her husband, multi-millionaire Kodak executive Jules Brulator. Reportedly, he would get roles for his wife by offering studios film stock at low prices. "The Duchess of Park Avenue," as Hampton was known, didn't disappoint her supportive husband (30 years her senior), nor did she let down her audiences with her distinctive voice.

p, Edmund Grainger; d, S. Sylvan Simon; w, Roy Chanslor, Adele Commandini, Brian Marlowe, F. Hugh Herbert, Charles Kenyon (based on the novel *Puritan at Large* by I.A.R. Wylie); ph, George Robinson; ed, Maurice Wright, Paul Landres; md, Charles Previn; art d, Jack Otterson, Charles H. Clarke; cos, Vera West; m/l, Jimmy McHugh, Harold Adamson.

Comedy/Romance **(PR:A MPAA:NR)**

ROAD TO RIO*½** (1947) 100m PAR bw

Bing Crosby *(Scat Sweeney)*, Bob Hope *(Hot Lips Barton)*, Dorothy Lamour *(Lucia Maria De Andrade)*, Gale Sondergaard *(Catherine Vail)*, Frank Faylen *(Trigger)*, Joseph Vitale *(Tony)*, Frank Puglia *(Rodrigues)*, Nestor Paiva *(Cardoso)*, Robert Barrat *(Johnson)*, Jerry Colonna *(Cavalry Captain)*, Wiere Brothers *(Musicians)*, Andrews Sisters, Carioca Boys, Stone-Baron Puppeteers *(Themselves)*, George Meeker *(Sherman Malley)*, Stanley Andrews *(Capt. Harmon)*, Harry Woods *(Ship's Purser)*, Tor Johnson *(Samson)*, Donald Kerr *(Steward)*, Stanley Blystone *(Assistant Purser)*, George Sorel *(Prefeito)*, John "Skins" Miller *(Dancer)*, Alan Bridge *(Ship's Officer)*, Arthur Q. Bryan *(Mr. Stanton)*, Babe London *(Woman)*, Gino Corrado *(Barber)*, George Chandler *(Valet)*, Paul Newlan, George Lloyd *(Butchers)*, Fred Zendar *(Stevedore)*, Ralph Gomez, Duke York, Frank Hagney *(Roustabouts)*, Ralph Dunn *(Foreman)*, Pepito Perez *(Dignified Gentleman)*, Ray Teal *(Buck)*, Brandon Hurst *(Barker)*, Barbara Pratt *(Airline Hostess)*, Tad Van Brunt *(Pilot)*, Patsy O'Bryne *(Charwoman)*, Raul Roulien *(Calvary Officer)*, Charles Middleton *(Farmer)*, Albert Ruiz, Laura Corbay *(Specialty Dancers)*.

The fifth "road" picture was a far more standard comedy than most of the others and paid off at the box office as it was the top-grossing film of the year. Gone were the talking animals and some of the zany humor of the others. In their place was a more conventional story sans Hollywood in-jokes and, in some ways, a more rewarding film because it could stand on its own without the viewer needing to have seen any of the four that went before. Insanity was replaced by logic in the plot and the verbal jokes were on a higher plane than most pictures of the time. Hope and Crosby are musicians who accidentaly cause a fire at the carnival where they are working. Rather than be arrested on an arson charge, they jump aboard an ocean liner headed for Rio and stow away. Once on the ship, they meet Lamour, a woman who runs hot and cold toward them. She is friendly then chilly, smiling then frowning, and the boys can't figure out if she's nuts or just an average Gemini. Lamour is on the ship with her tall, dark aunt, Sondergaard. (Now if Hope and Crosby had ever seen a Sondergaard film before, that would have been enough of a clue that this was a woman with evil lurking behind her eyes.) Unable to determine why Lamour is subject to such wide mood swings, Hope and Crosby investigate and discover that Lamour has been hypnotized by Sondergaard and is to marry a man she doesn't love once they reach Rio. The boat arrives and Hope and Crosby need work to support themselves so they haunt the local nightlife and meet the Wiere Brothers, a trio of manic performers. Through them, they encounter Paiva, a nightclub boniface, and the quintet is hired to play in Paiva's club. Paiva thought he was employing five Americans and if he ever learns that the Wieres are unable to speak English, the job goes out the window, so Hope and Crosby hold a frantic class and teach the Wieres one expression per brother that they can use for every occasion. Dutifully, the Wieres practice their single line of English each; "You're in the groove, Jackson," "This is murder," and "You're telling me"—hardly the right phrases for certain situations. It isn't long before they are discovered and all are out of work. Shortly thereafter, Hope and Crosby hear that Lamour is due to be married so they crash the wedding party dressed as a pirate (Crosby) and a Latin American bombshell (Hope in drag). They perform a song and everyone at the wedding thinks they are entertainers who have been hired to work the affair. But Sondergaard's men, Vitale and Faylen, see right through the masquerade and go after them. Hope and Crosby are chased until they uncover some secret information that frees Lamour and gets Sondergaard and her minions arrested. The information is never revealed to the audience (probably because no one writing the script could figure out what in the world it could be) and when Hope asks Crosby what it is (the way everyone in the theater must have been wondering), Crosby replies: "The world must never know." Lamour, now free to marry the man of her choice, says that she will wed Hope, a surprising turn of events since it was Crosby who usually got her. Hope and Lamour honeymoon at Niagara Falls and Crosby, still scratching his head over what's happened, cannot understand how he lost Lamour to Hope. After he leaves, he squints through the hotel suite's keyhole and gets his answer; Hope is busily reinforcing the hypnotic spell he's put on Lamour to cause her to fall in love with him. Several good songs by Johnny Burke and Jimmy Van Heusen include: "But Beautiful" (sung by Crosby), "You Don't Have to Know the Language" (sung by Crosby, The Andrews Sisters) "For What?" (sung by The Andrews Sisters), "Experience" (sung by Lamour), "Apalachicola, Florida" (sung by Hope, Crosby), "Cavaquinho," as well as a host of other Latin ditties including "Brazil" by Ary Barroso with English lyrics by Bob Russell, long-time partner of Duke Ellington. Russell was one of the rare songwriters who could adapt himself to any era and wrote such diverse lyrics as "Crazy He Calls Me," "You Came A Long Way From St. Louis," "Babalu," and "He Ain't Heavy, He's My Brother." The Wiere Brothers were a delightful comedy trio who were the European version of the Ritz Brothers but never had great success in films, although they continued to earn well in Las Vegas and other resorts well into their dotage. Dolan was nominated for an Oscar.

p, Daniel Dare; d, Norman Z. McLeod; w, Edmund Beloin, Jack Rose; ph, Ernest Laszlo; ed, Ellsworth Hoagland; md, Robert Emmett Dolan; art d, Hans Dreier, Earl Hedrick; cos, Edith Head; spec eff, Gordon Jennings, Paul Lerpal; ch, Bernard Pearce, Billy Daniels; m/l, Johnny Burke, Jimmy Van Heusen, Ary Barroso, Bob Russell; makeup, Wally Westmore.

Comedy/Musical **(PR:AA MPAA:NR)**

ROAD TO RUIN*½ (1934) 62m FD bw

Nell O'Day, Glen Boles, Paul Page, Virginia True Boardman, Richard Tucker, Mae Busch, Bobby Quirk.

A stark portrait of a young school girl who first has a romance with a school chum and then gets involved in a more serious affair, resulting in her pregnancy. She goes under the knife of an abortionist and dies after complications. Made as a silent in 1928 by Kent, who must have felt he had a good thing when he reshot the picture with sound. The film was released with the self-imposed restriction of keeping children under age 18 out of the theater, because of nudity and the subject matter.

p, Willis Kent; d, Mrs. Wallace Reid, Melville Shyer; ph, James Diamond; ed, S. Roy Luby.

Drama **(PR:O MPAA:NR)**

ROAD TO SALINA½** (1971, Fr./Ital.) 96m Corona-Transinter-Fono/AE c (SUR LA ROUTE DE SALINA)

Mimsy Farmer *(Billie)*, Robert Walker [Jr.] *(Jonas)*, Rita Hayworth *(Mara)*, Ed Begley *(Warren)*, Bruce Pecheur *(Charlie)*, David Sachs *(Sheriff)*, Sophie Hardy *(Linda)*, Marc Porel *(Rocky)*, Ivano Staccioli, Albane Navizet.

Rita Hayworth makes one of her later appearances in this better-than-average drama about a young wanderer who happens upon a desert cafe and gas station. The proprietor (Hayworth) insists that he is her long-lost son and, although he is disbelieving, he accepts her offer of room and board. An incestuous relationship develops between the wanderer and his "sister," Hayworth's daughter. In an attempt to resolve his mounting confusion, the young man digs into the family history and learns the shocking truth about the nature of his "sister's" behavior. A bizarre, hardly-seen picture in which Hayworth turns in a gleaming performance.

ROAD TO SALINA was Begley's last film; he was attending a Hollywood party at the time of his death in April of 1970.

p, Robert Dorfmann, Yvon Guezel; d, George Lautner; w, Lautner, Pascal Jardin, Jack Miller (based on the novel *Sur la Route de Salina* by Maurice Cury); ph, Maurice Fellous (Panavision, DeLuxe Color); m, Bernard Gerard, Christophe and Ian Anderson; ed, Michelle David, Elizabeth Guido; md, Gerard; art d, Jean D'Eaubonne; m/l, "Clinic," "Bouree," Gerard, Christophe and Ian Anderson.

Drama **(PR:O MPAA:R)**

ROAD TO SHAME, THE** (1962, Fr.) 85m Sirius-Jacques Roitfeld/ Atlantic bw (DES FEMMES DISPARAISSENT)

Robert Hossein *(Pierre Rossi)*, Magali Noel *(Coraline)*, Estella Blain *(Beatrice)*, Philippe Clay *(Tom)*, Pierre Collet *(Nasol)*, Jacques Dacqmine *(Quaglio)*, Monique Vita *(Nina)*, Liliane David *(Madeleine)*, Anita Treyens *(Brigitte)*, Claudie Laurence *(Jacqueline)*, Jane Marken *(Madame Cassini)*, Robert Lombard *(Merlin)*, Francois Darbon, Jean Juillard, Jean Degrave, Dominique Boschero, Yvon Sarray, Olivier Mathot, William Sabatier.

Hossein gets knocked around by members of a female slave ring that nabs young women and forces them into prostitution. When his fiancee mistakenly ends up with the gang, Hossein puts all his effort into freeing her. The police eventually surround the criminals, emerging victorious after an exchange of gunfire, and Hossein and his fiancee are safely reunited.

p, Jean Mottet; d, Edouard Molinaro; w, Albert Simonin (based on the story "Des Femmes Disparaisset," by Gilles-Maurice Morris-Dumoulin); ph, Robert Juillard; m, Art Blakely, The Jazz Messengers; ed, Laurence Mery; art d, Georges Levy.

Crime Drama **(PR:C-O MPAA:NR)**

ROAD TO SINGAPORE½** (1931) 70m WB bw

William Powell *(Hugh Daltrey)*, Doris Kenyon *(Philippa March)*, Marian Marsh *(Rene March)*, Louis Calhern *(Dr. George March)*, Alison Skipworth *(Mrs. Wey-Smith)*, Lumsden Hare *(Wey-Smith)*, Tyrell Davis *(Nikki)*, A.E. Anson *(Dr. Muir)*, Ethel Griffies *(Mrs. Everard)*, Arthur Clayton *(Mr. Everard)*, Douglas Gerrard *(Simpson)*, H. Reynolds *(Duckworth)*, Colin Campbell *(Reginald)*, Amar N. Sharma *(Khan)*, Huspin Ansari *(Ali)*, Margaret Martin *(Ayah)*.

Kenyon is the wife of a doctor newly stationed in Singapore who is tired of competing with her husband's profession. She winds up in the arms of Powell, who is reluctant to begin an affair. The doctor, however, jumps to conclusions, sending Kenyon into a greater fit of anger. She threatens to leave both men when the next boat arrives, but instead Powell gets on the boat, calmly walking away from the doctor and his loaded gun. Powell turns in a top-notch debonair performance, and Kenyon a seductively charged one. Tunes include: "African Lament," "Hand in Hand," "Yes or No," "Singapore Tango," and "I'm Just a Fool in Love with You."

d, Alfred E. Green; w, J. Grubb Alexander (based on the story by Denise Robins and the play "Heat Wave" by Roland Pertwee); ph, Robert Kurrle; ed, William Holmes.

Drama **(PR:A MPAA:NR)**

ROAD TO SINGAPORE½** (1940) 84m PAR bw

Bing Crosby *(Josh Mallon)*, Dorothy Lamour *(Mima)*, Bob Hope *(Ace Lannigan)*, Charles Coburn *(Joshua Mallon IV)*, Judith Barrett *(Gloria Wycott)*, Anthony Quinn *(Caesar)*, Jerry Colonna *(Achilles Bombanassa)*, Johnny Arthur *(Timothy Willow)*, Pierre Watkin *(Morgan Wycott)*, Gaylord [Steve] Pendleton *(Gordon Wycott)*, Miles Mander *(Sir Malcolm Drake)*, Pedro Regas *(Zato)*, Greta Granstedt *(Babe)*, Edward Gargan *(Bill)*, Don Brodie *(Fred)*, John Kelly *(Sailor)*, Kitty Kelly *(Sailor's Wife)*, Roger Gray *(Father)*, Harry C. Bradley *(Secretary)*, Richard Keene *(Cameraman)*, Gloria Franklin *(Ninky Poo)*, Carmen D'Antonio *(Dancing Girl)*, Monte Blue *(High Priest)*, Cyril Ring *(Ship's Officer)*, Helen Lynd *(Society Girl)*, Paula DeCardo *(Native Dancing Girl)*, Benny Inocencio *(Native Boy)*, Jack Pepper *(Columnist)*, Arthur Q. Bryan *(Bartender)*, Robert Emmett O'Connor *(Immigration Officer)*, Belle Mitchell *(Shopkeeper)*, Fred Malatesta, Bob St. Angelo *(Native Policemen)*, Marguerita Padula *(Proprietress)*, Bobby Barber *(Dumb-Looking Little Man)*, Claire James *(Girl at Party)*, Grace Hayle *(Chaperone)*, Richard Tucker *(Ship's Officer)*, Elvia Allman *(Homely Girl)*.

This is the one that started it all and it is also one of the weakest of the "Road" pictures. There are two stories as to how it came to be. The studio bought a Harry Hervey original entitled "The Road to Mandalay" which was an adventure story. It was then tailored into a comedy and rejected by George Burns and Gracie Allen, as well as Fred MacMurray and Jack Oakie before being seen by Hope and Crosby. The other tale is that producer Thompson and director-songwriter Schertzinger played golf one afternoon with Hope and Crosby and such a good time was had by all that they decided to work together. This movie, although never intended to be more than a one-shot, did such huge business when released that everyone was happily amazed. It was Paramount's biggest grosser of the year and it came at the right time as the studio had turned out a series of less-than-rewarding pictures in the previous months. Crosby is an affable young man, the son of hard-driving Coburn, a millionaire shipping mogul. Coburn wants Crosby to give up his life of playboy ease and take his place as the head of the company, but Crosby hates the thought of sitting behind a desk and walks out on the job as well as his fiancee, Barrett. Crosby would rather spend his life bumming around the world with his best friend, Hope. The two take off for the furthest point they can find on the map, Singapore. Once there, they rent a tiny house and begin pub-crawling. At one of the clubs, they see Lamour as part of a dangerous vaudeville act. She puts a cigarette in her mouth and it is snatched out by Quinn, a South American who snaps a bullwhip. They can't bear the thought of that lovely face being marred by a whip so they take her back to their place where she sincerely appreciates what they've done and agrees to become their housekeeper in return for room and board. The *menage* begins to get complicated as both men are falling for Lamour who admits that she likes one of them over the other but won't reveal her preference until she is certain that she is right about her emotions. Time passes and Coburn and Barrett are applying pressure on Crosby to return to the U.S. and marry, as well as take over the company. Crosby puts it to Lamour and says he will go back if she chooses Hope. Lamour's answer is that she does prefer Hope. Crosby is shattered, but being a gentleman, congratulates the couple and goes back. Dissolve and we then learn that Lamour was only saying that because she couldn't bear to come between Crosby and a woman he'd known before. Once Crosby discovers the truth, he books passage to Singapore and returns to the woman he's wanted from the first reel, thereby leaving Hope out in the cold for the first of many times in the ensuing movies. While there were a few zippy moments, Hope and Crosby had yet to develop their style when this was made. As the years passed, Hope's quick lines began to blend well with Crosby's more relaxed manner and the contrast proved to be pleasing to millions of happy theater-goers. Songs by Johnny Burke and James V. Monaco included: "Too Romantic" (sung by Crosby, Lamour), "Sweet Potato Piper" (sung by Crosby), "Kaigoon," and then Burke teamed with director Schertzinger to write "Captain Custard" (sung by Hope, Crosby) and "The Moon And The Willow Tree" (sung by Lamour). ROAD TO SINGAPORE confounded all the pundits with the money it brought in and proved to be a refreshing start to a series of seven, almost all of which were better than the original.

p, Harlan Thompson; d, Victor Schertzinger; w, Don Hartman, Frank Butler (based on a story by Harry Hervey); ph, William C. Mellor; ed, Paul Weatherwax; md, Victor Young; art d, Hans Dreier, Robert Odell; spec eff, Farciot Edouart; ch, LeRoy Prinz.

Comedy **(PR:AA MPAA:NR)**

ROAD TO THE BIG HOUSE*½ (1947) 74m Somerset/Screen Guild bw

John Shelton *(Eddie)*, Ann Doran *(Agnes)*, Guinn Williams *(Butch)*, Dick Bailey *(Sutter)*, Joe Allen, Jr. *(Bates)*, Rory Mallinson *(Fred)*, Eddy Fields *(Kelvin)*, Walden Boyle *(Prosecutor)*, Keith Richards *(Harvey)*, Jack Conrad *(Collins)*, Charles Jordan *(Benson)*, C. Montague Shaw *(Judge)*, John Doucette *(Danny)*, Mickey Simpson *(Case)*.

Shelton is a distraught bank clerk who decides to amend his financial status by ripping off a bank to the tune of $200,000. He gets caught, but not until after he has stashed the cash. He figures he will do his time, then get out and enjoy the money, but another gang has different ideas. They engineer a prison break, but Shelton is caught trying to get out. The picture ends with Shelton finishing his jail term and learning that his wife located and returned the money to the bank. A charming picture which is not especially well handled.

p, Selwyn Levinson, Walter Colmes; d, Colmes; w, Aubrey Wisberg; ph, Walter Strenge; ed, Jason Bernie.

Prison Drama **(PR:A MPAA:NR)**

ROAD TO UTOPIA*½** (1945) 90m PAR bw

Bing Crosby *(Duke Johnson/Junior Hooton)*, Bob Hope *(Chester Hooton)*, Dorothy Lamour *(Sal Van Hoyden)*, Hillary Brooke *(Kate)*, Douglas Dumbrille *(Ace Larson)*, Jack LaRue *(LeBec)*, Robert Barrat *(Sperry)*, Nestor Paiva *(McGurk)*, Robert Benchley *(Narrator)*, Will Wright *(Mr. Latimer)*, Jimmy Dundee *(Ringleader of Henchmen)*, Jim Thorpe *(Passenger)*, William Benedict *(Newsboy)*, Art Foster *(Husky Sailor)*, Arthur Loft *(Purser)*, Stanley Andrews *(Official at Boat)*, Alan Bridge *(Boat Captain)*, Lee Shumway, Al Ferguson *(Policemen)*, Romaine Callender *(Top Hat)*, George Anderson *(Townsman)*, Edgar Dearing, Charles C. Wilson *(Official Cops)*, Brandon Hurst, Don Gallaher, Bud Harrisons *(Men at Zambini's)*, Edward Emerson *(Master of Ceremonies)*, Ronnie Rondell *(Hotel Manager)*, Allen Pomeroy, Jack Stoney *(Henchmen)*, Frank Moran, Bobby Barber, Pat West *(Bartenders)*, Larry Daniels *(Ring-leader)*, Ferdinand Munier *(Santa Claus)*, Ethan Laidlaw *(Saloon Extra)*, Jimmy Lono *(Eskimo)*, Charles Gemora *(Bear)*, Paul Newlan *(Tough Ship's Purser)*, Claire James, Maxine Fife *(Girls)*, Jack Rutherford *(1st Man)*, Al Hill *(2nd Man)*, George McKay *(Waiter)*.

There are those who feel that this, the fourth in the "Road" series, was the funniest one of the bunch. Coming on the heels of ROAD TO MOROCCO would have been too fast so even though they finished shooting in March, 1944, it was held back until December, 1945, in order to give the preceding picture a chance to play out all the dates. The script was rightly nominated for an Oscar although nobody ever knows who wrote what in a picture involving Hope. The usual case was for a screenplay to be written, then punched up by all the gag writers who worked on Hope's radio and TV shows. Panama and Frank had come from Hope's personal stable of jokesters and it showed as they stopped at nothing to get laughs in this hilarious script. The film is told in flashback as Hope and Lamour are a wealthy couple recalling the way they came to be living in their huge mansion. They'd gained control of a Klondike gold mine but lost their best friend, Crosby, in the process. As they are reminiscing, they suddenly hear a familiar croon of "Sunday, Monday and Always" (from an earlier Crosby film, DIXIE), and he pops in, very much alive. They begin to talk about the old days and we go back in time to see Hope and Crosby, a couple of failed vaudevillians, who have attempted a shady deal in San Francisco and now must flee that city. They climb on a ship headed north and purloin the deed to a gold mine in Alaska from Paiva and Barrat, a duo of vicious murderers. With that in hand, plus the fact that they are on the run from authorities, Hope and Crosby pretend to be the tough guys and when they arive in Skagway, Dumbrille, a local hoodlum, hires them to guard his body. Lamour is working at the local saloon as a singer-dancer and puts the make on both Hope and Crosby in an attempt to extract the deed to the mine (it had been the property of Lamour's late father). She tries to seduce Hope by claiming how thrilled she is to be the amour of such a well-known killer. Since Crosby is holding the deed, she quickly abandons old Ski Snoot and turns to Der Bingle but that doesn't work out because she falls in love with Crosby, despite the fact that he confesses their true identities. Hope and Crosby add Lamour to their association and agree to a three-way split. They then run into Paiva and Barrat, still smarting over having lost the deed. The criminals are about to kill the heroes who quickly get away by grabbing a dog sled and racing across the frozen tundra. Paiva and Barrat are after them as well as Dumbrille and his men. The chase continues and the quarry is almost nailed a few times until the ice melts and breaks apart and Hope and Lamour are on one side with Crosby on the other. It looks as though Crosby will be killed by the villains as Hope and Lamour get to safety where she agrees to marry him. Flash forward to the present and Crosby is about to leave when Lamour and Hope ask him to stay a moment and meet their son, Junior. In walks the lad, a spitting image of Crosby! Hope turns to the camera to quip: "We adopted him!" as the picture ends. Robert Benchley adds a dry and funny narration to keep things going. Since the picture was released several months after Benchley's death, one could assume it was his last movie, but it wasn't. Two more movies came out with Benchley, THE BRIDE WORE BOOTS and JANIE GETS MARRIED. Lots of excellent gags punctuate the story including the one where Hope and Crosby are in the boiler room of the steamer taking them to Alaska when a formally dressed Callender walks in looking for a match. Hope and Crosby want to know if he's supposed to be in this movie and the man replies with a shrug: "Nope, I'm taking a shortcut to stage 10." The good score was by Johnny Burke and Jimmy Van Heusen and included: "Put it There, Pal" (sung by Hope, Crosby), "Welcome to My Dreams" (sung by Crosby), "Good-Time Charley" (sung by Hope, Crosby), "It's Anybody's Spring" (sung by Crosby), "Would You?" (sung by Lamour), and the hit tune "Personality," (sung by Lamour). Once again, animals talk, sight gags abound and the complementing demeanors of Hope and Crosby are mined for great advantage. Terrific secondary performances by Dumbrille (the ultimate screen villain) and Jack LaRue, who elevated the accomplice role to a high art. Even Hillary Brooke, who was usually seen in melodramas, does a good turn in a Barbara Nichols/Iris Adrian-type role as a dance hall moll.

p, Paul Jones; d, Hal Walker; w, Norman Panama, Melvin Frank; ph, Lionel Lindon; m, Leigh Harline; ed, Stuart Gilmore; md, Robert Emmett Dolan; art d, Hans Dreier, Roland Anderson; set d, George Sawley; cos, Edith Head; spec eff, Farciot Edouart; ch, Danny Dare; m/l, Johnny Burke, James Van Heusen; animation, Jerry Fairbanks.

Comedy/Musical (PR:AA MPAA:NR)

ROAD TO ZANZIBAR*½** (1941) 92m PAR bw

Bing Crosby *(Chuck Reardon)*, Bob Hope *(Fearless [Hubert] Frazier)*, Dorothy Lamour *(Donna Latour)*, Una Merkel *(Julia Quimby)*, Eric Blore *(Charles Kimble)*, Iris Adrian *(French Soubrette in Cafe)*, Lionel Royce *(Mons. Lebec)*, Buck Woods *(Thonga)*, Leigh Whipper *(Scarface)*, Ernest Whitman *(Whiteface)*, Noble Johnson *(Chief)*, Leo Gorcey *(Boy)*, Joan Marsh *(Dimples)*, Luis Alberni *(Proprietor of Native Booth)*, Robert Middlemass *(Police Inspector)*, Norma Varden *(Clara Kimble)*, Paul Porcasi *(Turk at Slave Mart)*, Ethel Loreen Greer *(Fat Lady)*, Georges Renavent *(Saunders)*, Jules Strongbow *(Solomon)*, Priscilla White, LaVerne Vess *(Curzon Sisters)*, Harry C. Johnson, Harry C. Johnson, Jr. *(Acrobats)*, Alan Bridge *(Policeman)*, Henry Roquemore *(Cafe Proprietor)*, James B. Carson *(Waiter)*, Eddy Conrad *(Barber)*, Charlie Gemora *(Aqua the Gorilla)*, Ken Carpenter *(Commentator)*, Richard Keene *(Clerk)*, Douglas Dumbrille *(Slave Trader)*.

TARZAN movies had been a staple for years and ROAD TO ZANZIBAR, the second in the series of "Road" pictures, took the opportunity to satirize every jungle picture that had ever been lensed to that time. The script was funny, although much of the humor allegedly derived from improvisations on the set, so much so that the director felt matters were getting out of hand. Hope and Crosby are connivers again and must get out of town because they sold a bogus diamond mine to Royce, a criminal type who does not take well to being fleeced. When Royce learns he's been bilked, Hope and Crosby light out for Zanzibar where they meet Brooklynites Lamour and Merkel, two entertainers who are in Africa to find Lamour's brother. Merkel and Lamour convince Hope and Crosby to put up the money for a safari into the interior, but the boys soon realize that they've been duped. It isn't Lamour's brother they're tailing, it's a British millionaire Lamour hopes to marry. Since Hope and Crosby have used up their return fare money on this wild goose-that-lays-the-golden-egg chase, they must continue in the belief that they can recover their money somewhere down the line. After running into several dangerous situations, Hope and Crosby think it's best that they leave and attempt to get back to Zanzibar. Before they can go, they are chagrined to discover that Merkel and Lamour have already gone. Hope and Crosby are humiliated at having been conned but a more clear and present danger faces them as they find they've been surrounded by a horde of cannibals who haven't eaten a decent human being in months. As they are preparing to be dinners, Hope and Crosby are pleasantly surprised when the cannibal chief, Johnson, is convinced by the witch doctor, Whipper, that Hope and Crosby, while tender enough to make a fine meal, are nothing less than gods and therefore to be revered, not dined upon. Johnson is not so sure that these men are divine so, to put them to the test, he arranges a wrestling match between Hope and a pint-size King Kong (Gemora in a gorilla suit) which is hilarious. The battle wages across the compound and Hope winds up on the short end. It looks mighty bad for the boys as the natives close in with hunger in their eyes and salt shakers in their hands. Just before they become entrees, Hope and Crosby use their patented "patty-cake" routine to escape, race into the jungle, meet Lamour and Merkel and wind up as a foursome at Zanzibar where they are working a sideshow in order to raise money to get back to the U.S. It was a good change of pace for Lamour as she wasn't playing one of her saronged heroines. The Johnny Burke/Jimmy VanHeusen score was serviceable although not up to some of the tunes they wrote for the other films. Songs included: "It's Always You" (sung by Crosby), "You're Dangerous" (sung by Lamour), "On the Road to Zanzibar" (sung by Hope, Crosby), "You Lucky People," "Birds of a Feather," "African Etude." The lyrics in "On the Road to Zanzibar" were banal compared to Cahn's words for "Road to Morocco" but it was a funny routine as the cannibals chanted a nonsense background. Woody Allen owes a great deal to these movies because he uses one-liners as part of the screenplay in much the same fashion. Allen has always looked up to Hope for his timing and wrote of his influence in an early book. Hope employed so many writers in his career that when the Writers' Guild of America had their annual party a few years ago, anyone who had ever toiled for Hope was asked to come on stage and more than 40 of Hollywood's best assembled for a group shot. The list of Hope alumni reads like a roster of the finest joke men around and even when Hope did not have a regular weekly show, he kept a staff employed to pen one-liners for concerts, TV guest shots and movie re-writes. Some comedians hate to admit that they have writers, such as Red Skelton, who used to have the scripts slipped under his door so he wouldn't have to meet the men and women who made him funny. Not so with Hope, who understands that he owes it all to the people at the typewriters. This generosity has paid off many times as Hope is one of the richest men in show business and is the single largest landowner in the San Fernando Valley, where he continues to live in the same house he's always maintained in Toluca Lake, a wealthy section of Burbank, which is also the home of the immensely gifted Jonathan Winters.

p, Paul Jones; d, Victor Schertzinger; w, Frank Butler, Don Hartman (based on the story "Find Colonel Fawcett" by Hartman, Sy Bartlett); ph, Ted Tetzlaff; m, Victor Young; ed, Alma Macrorie; art d, Hans Dreier, Robert Usher; cos, Edith Head; ch, LeRoy Prinz.

Comedy/Musical (PR:AA MPAA:NR)

ROAD WARRIOR, THE*½** (1982, Aus.) 94m WB c (AKA: MAD MAX II)

Mel Gibson *(Max)*, Bruce Spence *(Gyro Captain)*, Vernon Wells *(Wez)*, Emil Minty *(Feral Kid)*, Mike Preston *(Pappagallo)*, Kjell Nilsson *(Humungus)*, Virginia Hey *(Warrior Woman)*, Syd Heylen *(Curmudgeon)*, Moria Claux *(Big Rebecca)*, David Slingsby *(Quiet Man)*, Arkie Whiteley *(Lusty Girl)*, Steve J. Spears *(Mechanic)*, Max Phipps *(Toadie)*, William Zappa *(Farmer)*, Jimmy Brown *(Golden Youth)*, David Downer *(Wounded Man)*, Tyler Coppin *(Defiant Victim)*, Max Farchild *(Broken Victim)*, Kristoffer Greaves *(Mechanic's Assistant)*, Guy Norris *(Mohawk Biker with Bearclaw)*, Tony Deary *(Mohawk Biker)*, Anne Jones, James McCaedell *(Tent Lovers)*, Kathleen McKay *(Young Woman)*.

Director George Miller, whose film MAD MAX set new standards of kinetic, visceral excitement, surpassed himself with that film's sequel, THE ROAD WARRIOR. The second film begins with a brilliantly executed montage of scenes from the first film, intercut with stock newsreel footage that explains the events leading to the apocalypse and subsequent society that has established itself—a cruel, savage world devoted solely to the pursuit of gasoline and oil with which to fuel the vehicles. The death of Gibson's wife and child and his eventual revenge are all detailed in a matter of minutes, bringing us to the present, which comes screaming at us in Dolby sound and wide-screen color. In THE ROAD WARRIOR, Gibson has become an alienated, detached drifter whose only purpose is to survive in this hostile new world. After a breathtaking opening chase scene where we meet the bizarre arch-villain Wez played with manic, savage intensity by Vernon Wells, Gibson meets up with an oddity known only as the Gyro Captain (Spence) a scrawny, disheveled man who flies a small gyro-copter. After Gibson establishes himself as the stronger of the two, Spence leads him to a small oil refinery populated by the "good" people led by Preston. Their precious encampment is constantly attacked by an army of grotesque, nomadic desert rats decked out in pseudo-punk wardrobes and armed to the teeth with a variety of strange weapons. This ragtag force is led by a massive body builder who wears a metal hockey mask (which hides his nasty facial scars probably incurred in some unnamed skirmish) known as the Humungus (Nilsson), and he wants their gasoline. Eventually Gibson ends up in the middle of the fray, playing one side off the other to get as much gas as he can carry. Of course, the basically noble wanderer becomes attached to Preston and his clan, especially to a speechless savage child played by Minty, and willingly aids them in their flight from the refinery. The good people load an old semi-tanker to the brim with gasoline and then join a caravan of buses in which they hope to make a dash for the shore and resettle. Gibson volunteers to drive the tanker, thus distracting the Humungus and his forces from the civilians. In one of the most spectacular chase scenes ever put on film, Gibson and his comrades fight off a series of vicious, high-speed attacks until a massive head-on collision overturns the semi and ends the battle. Gibson barely survives the crash and looks to the tanker, realizing that the people he was trying to help have filled it with sand (the real gas tanks were hidden in the buses). Having served his purpose, Gibson stands among the wreckage and watches as the buses drive off to the promised land, leaving him alone once again. While the plot line is that of a simple B western, director Miller brings every visual trick in the book to play, creating a stunningly detailed, vibrant new world that never ceases to amaze. In THE ROAD WARRIOR, Miller pulled all the fresh and original elements of MAD MAX together and ironed out his somewhat muddled narrative style into a strict line that zooms from Point A to Point B without stopping to catch its breath. Unfortunately, the third film in the series, MAD MAX, BEYOND THUNDERDOME, returns to the haphazard pacing of the first film and falls far short of the impact felt in THE ROAD WARRIOR.

p, Byron Kennedy; d, George Miller; w, Terry Hayes, Miller, Brian Hannat; ph, Dean Semler (Panavision, Technicolor); m, Brian May; ed, David Stiven, Tim Wellburn, Michael Chirgwin; art d, Graham Walker; cos, Norma Moriceau; spec eff, Jeffrey Clifford, Kim Priest; makeup, Bob McCarron; stunts, Max Aspin.

Fantasy Cas. (PR:O MPAA:R)

ROADBLOCK*** (1951) 73m RKO bw

Charles McGraw *(Joe Peters)*, Joan Dixon *(Diane)*, Lowell Gilmore *(Kendall Webb)*, Louis Jean Heydt *(Harry Miller)*, Milburn Stone *(Egan)*, Joseph Crehan *(Thompson)*, Joe Forte *(Brissard)*, Barry Brooks, Frank Marlowe *(Policemen)*, Ben Cameron, Joey Ray *(Hoods)*, Harold Landon *(Bartender at Larry's Club)*, Martha Mears *(Singer at Larry's Club)*, John Butler *(Hotel Clerk)*, Peter Brocco *(Bank*

Heist Man), Dewey Robinson *(Mike the Bartender)*, Harry Lauter *(Saunders)*, Howard Negley *(Police Captain)*, Dave McMahon *(Radio Operator)*, Phyllis Planchard *(Bobbie Webb)*, Steve Roberts *(De Vita)*, Richard Irving *(Partos)*, Taylor Reid *(Green)*, Clarence Straight *(Talbot)*, Jean Dean *(Airline Hostess)*, Janet Scott *(Mrs. MacDonald)*, Dave Willock *(Airport Clerk)*.

McGraw, a content insurance investigator, meets and falls in love with Dixon, an easy-living woman with a penchant for money and the pleasures it can buy. She tells McGraw that she is falling for him, but is afraid that his income will not be able to support her tastes. They decide to marry anyway, but not before McGraw gets involved in a scheme to steal more than $1 million in bills which are about to be destroyed. Complications arise when a postal worker is killed and McGraw is framed. He and Dixon leave their mountain hideaway, but are detoured by a number of roadblocks. Panicked, McGraw drives through the concreted Los Angeles riverbeds. A police pursuit follows and McGraw is gunned down. A classic film noir example of a man being brought down by his desire for sex and money, keenly photographed by Nicholas Musuraca.

p, Lewis J. Rachmil; d, Harold Daniels; w, Steve Fisher, George Bricker (based on a story by Richard Landau, Geoffrey Holmes); ph, Nicholas Musuraca; m, Paul Sawtell; ed, Robert Golden; md, Constantin Bakaleinikoff; art d, Albert S. D'Agostino, Walter E. Keller; set d, Darrell Silvera, Jack Mills; cos, Michael Woulfe; m/l, "So Swell of You," Leona Davidson.

Crime **(PR:A MPAA:NR)**

ROADHOUSE GIRL (SEE: MARILYN, 1953, Brit.)

ROADHOUSE MURDER, THE½** (1932) 77m RKO bw

Eric Linden *(Chick Brian)*, Dorothy Jordan *(Mary Agnew)*, Bruce Cabot *(Fred Dykes)*, Phyllis Clare *(Louise Rand)*, Roscoe Ates *(Joyce)*, Purnell Pratt *(Inspector Agnew)*, Gustav von Seyffertitz *(Porter)*, David Landau *(Kraft)*, Roscoe Karns *(Dale)*, William Morris.

Linden is a rookie reporter who hits on the idea of incriminating himself as a murderer and then writing a special series for his paper. The problem is that he is soon convicted, and attempts to free him are not seen as genuine until the real murderer is apprehended. A neat idea which takes journalistic fervor to the extreme.

p, Willis Goldbeck; d, J. Walter Ruben; w, Ruben, Gene Fowler (based on the play "Lame Dog Inn" by Laszoo Bus Fekets and the novel by Maurice Level); ph, J. Roy Hunt; ed, Jack Kitchin.

Drama **(PR:A MPAA:NR)**

ROADHOUSE NIGHTS½** (1930) 68m PAR bw

Helen Morgan *(Lola Fagan)*, Charles Ruggles *(Willie Bindbugel)*, Fred Kohler *(Sam Horner)*, Jimmy Durante *(Daffy)*, Fuller Mellish, Jr. *(Hogan)*, Leo Donnelly *(City Editor)*, Tammany Young *(Jerry)*, Joe King *(Hanson)*, Lou Clayton *(Joe)*, Eddie Jackson *(Moe)*.

Morgan, the great torch singer of the 1920s, was nearly at the end of her career here, sliding into alcoholism and obscurity which would kill her from cirrhosis of the liver in 1941 at the age of 41. Here she plays a nightclub singer not too far removed from her own life, but the film is overloaded with awkward dialog and songs not really suited for Morgan's talent. King is a reporter sent by his editor to the town of Moran, controlled by bootlegger Kohler, to get some dirt on the corruption there. Kohler finds out and has him killed. The paper immediately dispatches another reporter, Ruggles, to the scene and he is surprised to find Morgan, his old flame, is the singer at the roadhouse run by Kohler. She knows what happened to the first reporter so she tries to protect Ruggles, convincing him that he has been fired and they should elope. As they are leaving town, Kohler's men catch up to them and they are taken back to the roadhouse. Ruggles pretends to be drunk and manages to get a message back to his newspaper by tapping it out in Morse code on the phone. Kohler finds out about the message and is about to shoot Ruggles when Durante, a comedian working at the club, thwarts him. Just then the Coast Guard inexplicably comes to the rescue and puts an end to Kohler's gang. Not terribly interesting and a disappointing film for Morgan fans (who are really the only audience for this film today) after her fine, sad performances in SHOW BOAT (1929) and APPLAUSE (1929). Durante made a good impression in his film debut here, although his partnership with Clayton and Jackson was soon to end as he became a star. Includes the songs "Everything Is on the Up and Up," "Hello, Everybody, Folks," and "Everybody Wants My Girl" (written and performed by Lou Clayton, Eddie Jackson, and Jimmy Durante), and "It Can't Go on Like This" (E.Y. Harburg, Jay Gorney, sung by Helen Morgan).

d, Hobart Henley; w, Garrett Fort (based on a story by Ben Hecht); ph, William Steiner; ed, Helene Turner.

Crime **(PR:A MPAA:NR)**

ROADIE* (1980) 105m Alive Enterprises Vivant/UA c

Meatloaf *(Travis W. Redfish)*, Kaki Hunter *(Lola Bouilliabase)*, Art Carney *(Corpus C. Redfish)*, Gailard Sartain *(B.B. Muldoon)*, Don Cornelius *(Mohammed Johnson)*, Rhonda Bates *(Alice Poo)*, Richard Marion *(George)*, Sonny Davis *(Bird)*, Joe Spano *(Ace)*, Alice Cooper, Roy Orbison, Hank Williams, Jr., Merle Kilgore, Ramblin' Jack Elliot, Ray Benson, Sheryl Cooper, Alvin Crow, Larry Marshall, Hector Britt, Larry Lindsey, Hamilton Camp, Ginger Varney, Cindy Wills, Allan Graf, Deborah Harry, Chris Stein, Clem Burke, Jimmy Destri, Nigel Harrison, Frank Infante.

Appropriately named and quickly forgotten rock star Meatloaf stars as a roadie for a rock band who travels with Hunter in the hopes of meeting Alice Cooper. Director Alan Rudolph (REMEMBER MY NAME, CHOOSE ME) attempts to paint a portrait of the backstage world of rock 'n' roll, but instead just proves that he cannot handle comedy; at least, not intentional comedy. The character names provide the necessary insight into ROADIE's brand of humor. Besides the aforementioned Mr. Meatloaf, the picture also boasts the appearance of faded punk band Blondie, Roy "Pretty Woman" Orbison, Hank Williams, Jr., and Don "Soul Train" Cornelius.

p, Carolyn Pfeiffer; d, Alan Rudolph; w, Big Boy Medlin, Michael Ventura (based on a story by Medlin, Ventura, Rudolph, Zalman King); ph, David Myers (Technicolor); m, Craig Hundley; ed, Carol Littleton, Tom Walls; prod d, Paul Peters; set d, Richard Friedman; cos, Jered Edd Grenn, Gail Bixby.

Comedy **(PR:A-C MPAA:PG)**

ROADRACERS, THE* (1959) 73m AIP bw

Joel Lawrence *(Rob)*, Marian Collier *(Liz)*, Skip Ward *(Greg)*, Sally Fraser *(Joanie)*, Mason Alan Dinehart, Jr. *(Kit)*, Irene Windust *(Alice)*, John Shay *(Harry)*, Michael Gibson *(Bartender)*, Richard G. Pharo *(Wilkins)*, Sumner Williams *(Mechanic)*, Haile Chane, Gloria Marshall.

Lawrence is yanked from competing on the auto-racing circuit after being involved in a crash that killed another driver. He spends some time in Europe proving his worth as a driver, then makes his comeback in the States. Filled to the brim with stock footage. Actress Sally Fraser's claim to fame is appearing as an extra in the U.N. sequence of NORTH BY NORTHWEST; fortunately, almost no one saw her, or anyone else, in this dumb picture.

p, Stanley Kallis; d, Arthur Swerdloff; w, Kallis, Ed Lasko (based on the story by Kallis); m, Richard Markowitz; m/l, "Here You Are" Haru Yanai, Markowitz, "Leadfoot," "Liz," Lasko.

Action **(PR:A MPAA:NR)**

ROAMING COWBOY, THE** (1937) 56m Spectrum/Advance bw

Fred Scott *(Cal Brent)*, Al [Fuzzy] St. John *(Fuzzy)*, Lois January *(Jeanie)*, Forrest Taylor *(Evans)*, Roger Williams *(Walton)*, Dick Cramer *(Morgan)*, Buddy Cox *(Buddy)*, Oscar Gahan *(Tom)*, Art Miles *(Red)*, George Chesebro, Rudy Sooter.

Scott and St. John are a pair of drifters who happen to blow into a town where the local ranch owners are receiving threats to clear out. After some standard gunplay, Scott brings the bad guys to justice, wins the girl, and secures a job on her dad's ranch. Not bad for a day's work.

p, Jed Buell; d, Robert Hill; w, Fred Myton; ph, Bill Hyer; m/l, Stephen Foster, Rudy Sooter.

Western **Cas.** **(PR:A MPAA:NR)**

ROAMING LADY½** (1936) 68m COL bw

Fay Wray *(Joyce)*, Ralph Bellamy *(Dan)*, Thurston Hall *(E.J. Reid)*, Edward Gargan *(Andy)*, Roger Imhof *(Capt. Murchison)*, Paul Guilfoyle *(Wong)*, Tetsu Komai *(Fang)*, Arthur Rankin *(Blaney)*.

Wray is a wealthy young lass who is compelled by love to stow away on Bellamy's China-bound plane when he is sent on a mission by her father. It's not long, however, before the two are captured by Chinese revolutionaries. Bellamy has to agree to do some flying for the rebels in order to gain freedom, which he does, resulting in a skilled show of aerial adventures. He also does a credible anticipation of the work later assigned to John Wayne, wiping out a whole army of Oriental bandits with a hand-held machine gun. Gargan's mechanic sidekick is terrific.

p, Sig Rogell; d, Albert S. Rogell; w, Fred Niblo, Jr., Earle Snell (based on a story by Diana Bourbon, Bruce Manning); ph, Allen G. Seigler; ed, Otto Meyer.

Adventure/Romance **(PR:A MPAA:NR)**

ROAR*½ (1981) 102m Alpha-Filmways c

Tippi Hedren *(Madeline)*, Noel Marshall *(Hank)*, John Marshall *(John)*, Melanie Griffith *(Melanie)*, Jerry Marshall *(Jerry)*, Kyalo Mativo *(Mativo)*, Frank Tom, Steve Miller, Rick Glassey.

Hedren and her real-life children venture to Africa (really sunny Soledad Canyon, California) to meet Noel Marshall, her real-life husband, playing a scientist living among, and studying, a collection of wild beasts. They arrive, but thanks to a mix-up in plans, are not greeted by Marshall. Instead, they find a number of hungry cats with big teeth. When Marshall realizes what has happened he rushes back before his visitors become the cats' dinner snack. A baffling failure which was financed by Hedren and Marshall at a cost of $17 million. Instead of putting together a blockbuster adventure tale, they ended up with a big-budgeted nightmare which combines THE BIRDS and BORN FREE. The filmmakers' intentions were no doubt good, and their persistence in finishing the project should serve as a role model—they spent 11 years, mortgaged their belongings, suffered fire, flood, and a disease which wiped out a number of cats, and were plagued with cat-inflicted maimings. All this for only $2 million worldwide gross. Yawn.

p,d&w, Noel Marshall; ph, Jan De Bont (Panavision, Technicolor); m, Dominic Frontiere, Terrence P. Minogue; prod d, Joel Marshall.

Adventure **(PR:A MPAA:NR)**

ROAR OF THE CROWD*½ (1953) 71m AA c

Howard Duff *(Johnny Tracy)*, Helene Stanley *(Marcy Parker)*, Dave Willock *(Ruster)*, Louise Arthur *(Rose Adams)*, Harry Shannon *(Pop Tracy)*, Minor Watson *(Mackey)*, Don Haggerty *(Chuck Baylor)*, Edna Holland *(Mrs. Atkinson)*, Ray Walker *(Tuffy Adams)*, Paul Bryar *(Max Bromski)*, Duke Nalon, Johnnie Parsons, Henry Banks, Manuel Ayulo, Lucien Littlefield.

Duff is a racer following in his father's footsteps, who has to contend with his new wife, Stanley, and her wishes that he stop racing. He agrees, but not until he tries his hand at the Indianapolis 500. Before he makes it to the big race, he's in a wreck and injures his leg. With his wife's support, however, he makes it to Hoosierville for the race of races, finishing a disappointing ninth. He is discouraged, but his wife hands him the "wait 'til next year" line. The acting is weak, as in the inclusion of stock footage; where the picture differs is in its non-spectacular, realistic ending.

p, Richard Heermance; d, William Beaudine; w, Charles R. Marion (based on the the story by Marion, Robert Abel); ph, Harry Neumann (Cinecolor); m, Marlin Skiles; ed, William Austin; art d, David Milton.

Action   **(PR:A MPAA:NR)**

ROAR OF THE DRAGON**   (1932) 68m RKO bw

Richard Dix (Carson), Gwili Andre (Natascha), Edward Everett Horton (Busby), Arline Judge (Helen), ZaSu Pitts (Gabby Tourist), C. Henry Gordon (Voronsky), Dudley Digges (Johnson), Arthur Stone (Sholen), William Orlamond (Dr. Prausnitz), Toshi Mori, Jimmy Wang, Will Stanton.

Dix and his fellow Americans are stranded in war-torn Manchuria awaiting the repair of their boat. In the meantime they have to fight off the advancing rebels with a single machine gun. But, not to worry, the able hand of the screenwriter is behind them and they get away in the nick of time. Norwegian newcomer Gwili Andre does her best Garbo/Dietrich in a commendable performance, but why not take the time and see the real thing instead of wasting your time on second-rate Gwili (whose studio build-up didn't take; she graduated to B pictures). Based on a story co-penned by Merian C. Cooper.

p, William Le Baron [uncredited]; d, Wesley Ruggles; w, Howard Estabrook (based on the story by Merian C. Cooper, Jane Bigelow, and from the novel A Passage to Hong Kong by George Kibbe Turner); ph, Edward Cronjager; ed, William Hamilton.

Action/Drama   **(PR:A MPAA:NR)**

ROAR OF THE PRESS*½   (1941) 72m MON bw

Wallace Ford (Wally Williams), Jean Parker (Alice Williams), Jed Prouty (Gordon MacEwen), Suzanne Kaaren (Angela Brooks), Robert Frazer (Louis Detmar), Harland Tucker (Harry Brooks), John Holland (Robert Mallon), Paul Fix (Sparrow McGraun), Eddie Foster (Fingers), Matty Fain (Nick Paul), Betty Compson (Thelma Tate), Dorothy Lee (Frances), Donald Kerr (Red Keane), Evalyn Knapp (Evelyn), Maxine Leslie, Eddie Foster, Charles King, Frank O'Connor, Dennis Moore, Robert Pittard.

Ford turns in a tired performance as a newspaperman who is on the trail of a pair of murderers, ignoring the fact that he has just, on the same day, been married. The newlyweds are finally united when both are kidnaped by the murderers, who turn out to be WW II fifth columnists. The two are rescued, and the villains captured, with the assistance of police reporter Ford's gangster acquaintances in a wind-up reminiscent of Fritz Lang's M (1931). Familiar territory is poorly trod upon with some weak and miscast roles.

p, Scott R. Dunlap; d, Phil Rosen; w, Albert Duffy (based on a story by Alfred Block); ph, Harry Neumann; ed, Jack Ogilvie; md, Edward Kay.

Drama   **(PR:A MPAA:NR)**

ROARIN' GUNS*½   (1936) 59m Puritan bw

Tim McCoy (Tim Corwin), Rosalinda Price (May Carter), Wheeler Oakman (Walton), Earl Hackett (Evans), John Elliott (Bob Morgan), Tommy Bupp (Buddy), Jack Rockwell (Barry), Lou Meehan (Sanderson), Rex Lease (Kerry), Frank Ellis, Edward Cassidy, Dick Alexander, Artie Ortego, Tex Phelps, Al Taylor, Jack Evans.

McCoy is sent by a cattleman's association to put an end to a range war. He does so with the help of little Tommy Bupp, who saves McCoy on a couple of occasions. Technical shabbiness draws one demerit for this oater. From the prolific Neufeld/Newfield brother team.

p, Sig Neufeld, Leslie Simmonds; d, Sam Newfield; w, Joseph O'Donnell; ph, Jack Greenhalgh.

Western   **Cas.**   **(PR:A MPAA:NR)**

ROARIN' LEAD**   (1937) 57m REP bw

Robert Livingston (Stony Brooke), Ray Corrigan (Tucson Smith), Max Terhune (Lullaby Joslin), Christine Maple (Doris), Hooper Atchley (Hackett), Yakima Canutt (Canary), George Chesebro (Gardner), Tommy Bupp (Bobby), Mary Russell (Blondie), Tamara Lynn Kauffman (Baby Mary), Beverly Luff (Prima Donna), Theodore Frye, Katherine Frye (Apache Dancers), The Meglin Kiddies (Dancers), Baby Jane Keckley, Harry Tenbrook, Pascale Perry, Georges Plues, Grace Kern, Newt Kirby.

Livingston, Corrigan and Terhune continue their fight against injustice when they are named trustees of an estate that funds an orphanage, as well as supports a cattlemen's association. When they discover mishandling of cattlemen's monies, they put a lid on the wrongdoings. (See THREE MESQUITEERS series, Index.)

p, Nat Levine; d, Mack V. Wright, Sam Newfield; w, Oliver Drake, Jack Natteford (based on characters created by William Colt McDonald); ph, William Nobles; ed, William Thompson.

Western   **(PR:A MPAA:NR)**

ROARING CITY*   (1951) 60m Lippert bw

Hugh Beaumont, Edward Brophy, Richard Travis, Joan Valerie, Wanda McKay, Rebel Randall, William Tannen, Greg McClure, Anthony Warde, Abner Biberman, Stanley Price, Paul Brooks, A.J. Roth.

Beaumont is a hard-edged city detective who pounds the pavement in search of the person behind a series of unsolved murders. Prize fighters and small time gangsters keep showing up dead until he finally unmasks the guilty party. Beaumont turns in an okay, if not calculated, performance as he proves his own innocence amid the deception and dirty dealing of the city streets.

p&d, William Berke; w, Julian Harmon, Victor West (based on stories by Louis

Morheim, Herbert Margolis); ph, Jack Greenhalgh; m, Bert Shefter; ed, Carl Pierson, Harry Reynolds; art d, F. Paul Sylos.

Crime   **(PR:A MPAA:NR)**

ROARING RANCH*½   (1930) 65m UNIV bw

Hoot Gibson (Jim Dailey), Sally Eilers (June Marlin), Wheeler Oakman (Ramsey Kane), Bobby Nelson (Teddie), Frank Clark (Tom Marlin), Leo White (Reginald Sobuski).

Gibson is expected to take care of an infant child while, at the same time, protecting his oil-soaked ranch from the malevolent Oakman. A weak oater entry. This was the first of two films Gibson made with Eilers for Universal. Gibson and Eilers were later married and divorced.

p, Hoot Gibson; d&w, B. Reeves Eason (based on the story "Howdy Cowboy" by Eason; ph, Harry Neumann; ed, Gilmore Walker.

Western   **Cas.**   **(PR:A MPAA:NR)**

ROARING ROADS*   (1935) 58m Marcy bw

David Sharpe, Gertrude Messinger, Mickey Daniels, Mary Kornman, Jack Mulhall.

An insignificant picture about a young fellow who inherits a fortune and decides to devote himself to car racing. His interest in the roar of speeding cars doesn't translate to much more than a whimper on screen.

p, William Berke; w, David Sharpe.

Drama   **(PR:A MPAA:NR)**

ROARING SIX GUNS*½   (1937) 57m Ambassador bw

Kermit Maynard (Buck Sinclair), Mary Hayes (Beth), Sam Flint (Ringold), John Merton (Mileaway), Budd Buster (Wildcat), Robert Fiske (Harmon), Ed Cassidy (Commissioner), Curley Dresden (Slug), Dick Morehead (Bill), Charles "Slim" Whitaker (Skeeter), Earl Hodges (Sundown), Rene Stone (Rene).

Maynard is pitted against his fiancee's father and his louse of a partner, both of whom want to get their hands on Maynard's property. A run-of-the-mill B western.

p, Maurice Conn; d, J.P. McGowan; w, Arthur Everett (based on a story by James Oliver Curwood); ph, Jack Greenhalgh; ed, Richard G. Wray.

Western   **Cas.**   **(PR:A MPAA:NR)**

ROARING TIMBER**   (1937) 65m COL bw

Jack Holt (Jim Sherwood), Grace Bradley (Kay MacKinley), Ruth Donnelly (Aunt Mary), Raymond Hatton (Tennessee), Willard Robertson (Harrigan), J. Farrell MacDonald (Andrew MacKinley), Charles Wilson (Sam Garvin), Ernest Wood (Slim Bagnell), Philip Ahn (Crooner), Fred Kohler, Jr. (Curley), Ben Hendricks (Stumpy), Tom London (Duke).

Bradley inherits her father's lumber business and tries to run it even though she doesn't know a thing about logging. She ends up firing all the worthwhile workers and hiring a group of thugs who try to swindle her. The day is saved by Holt, his axe raised and his fists clenched. The logging scenes, as expected, are undeniably phony.

p, Larry Darmour; d, Phil Rosen; w, Paul Franklin, Robert James Cosgriff (based on the story by Cosgriff); ph, James S. Brown, Jr.; ed, Dwight Caldwell.

Action/Drama   **(PR:A MPAA:NR)**

ROARING TIMBERS   (SEE: COME AND GET IT, 1936)

ROARING TWENTIES, THE****   (1939) 104m WB bw

James Cagney (Eddie Bartlett), Priscilla Lane (Jean Sherman), Humphrey Bogart (George Hally), Jeffrey Lynn (Lloyd Hart), Gladys George (Panama Smith), Frank McHugh (Danny Green), Paul Kelly (Nick Brown), Elisabeth Risdon (Mrs. Sherman), Ed Keane (Pete Henderson), Joseph Sawyer (Sgt. Pete Jones), Abner Biberman (Lefty), George Humbert (Luigi, Proprietor), Clay Clement (Bramfield, Broker), Don Thaddeus Kerr (Bobby Hart), Ray Cooke (Orderly), Vera Lewis (Mrs. Gray), Murray Alper (1st Mechanic), Dick Wessel (2nd Mechanic), Joseph Crehan (Fletcher, Foreman), Norman Willis (Bootlegger), Robert Elliot (1st Officer), Eddy Chandler (2nd Officer), John Hamilton (Judge), Elliott Sullivan (Man in Jail), Pat O'Malley (Jailer), Arthur Loft (Proprietor of Still), Al Hill, Raymond Bailey, Lew Harvey (Ex-Cons), Joe Devlin, Jeffrey Sayre (Order Takers), Paul Phillips (Mike), George Meeker (Masters), Bert Hanlon (Piano Player), Jack Norton (Drunk), Alan Bridge (Captain), Fred Graham (Henchman), James Blaine (Doorman), Henry C. Bradley, Lottie Williams (Couple), Milton Kibbee (Taxi Driver), Creighton Hale (Customer), Cyril Ring (Charlie the Clerk), Maj. Sam Harris (Man in Club), John Deering (Commentator), John Harron (Soldier), Robert Dobson (Lieutenant), Stuart Holmes (Man for Turkish Bath).

This slick, whirlwind-paced crime melodrama is another tour de force for Cagney, oozing nostalgia and providing a companion piece to ANGELS WITH DIRTY FACES. It was the brainchild of journalist-turned-producer Hellinger who assured audiences in voice-over of the opening credits that what they were about to see was based upon real characters and events he covered as a newsman during the 1920s when the gangster was king and Prohibition was nothing more than a bad law that elevated the gangster to his dangerous throne. The film is also the story of three men, Cagney, Bogart, and Lynn, all of them doughboys. In fact the picture opens with Bogart in a bomb crater during a battle in France. As a barrage sends up smoke and dirt, another soldier, Cagney, comes tumbling into the crater, landing right on Bogart's head. "You always come into a hole like that?" carps Bogart. "What did you want me to do, knock?" replies Cagney. Later, Cagney is with Lynn and Bogart in a trench, talking about what they will do when the war is over. Cagney calls to Bogart who is peering through his gunsight at the parapet, smiling as he spots an enemy soldier and then squeezing off a round. "You should've seen 'm," he says, relishing his kill, "he jumped up like a board!" Cagney learns that Lynn intends to be a lawyer when he is mustered out and he tells the others that he will go back to repairing cabs, a job he enjoys. Not Bogart. He holds up his rifle and tells the others that "they spent a lot of money training me how to use this and I'm gonna put it to good use when I get out." It's clear that Bogart is the real criminal of the lot. When the war ends Cagney goes back to his old garage but the owner tells him he's hired mechanics to replace him. So insulting are two of the mechanics who now hold his old job that Cagney punches one of them who falls backward, taking the other mechanic to the floor with him and causing Cagney to yell out: "Two for one!" He goes to his old friend, taxi driver McHugh, who advances him money and puts him up in his little room. Cagney lives like thousands of returning veterans in those days, hand to mouth, getting and losing menial jobs. He finally gets a job driving a cab and one of his fares asks him to deliver a package to a store. Cagney enters the store, asks for George as he has been told, and is sent through a secret door and into a speakeasy, where George takes the package (which is bonded whiskey). She asks Cagney to stay a few minutes and he does, ordering a glass of milk. She tells him that there is golden opportunity for him in distributing booze. Sure it's breaking the law, she says, but Prohibition is a bad law and everyone ignores it, except Temperance fanatics and do-gooder cops. As if emphasizing her point, a policeman enters the secret saloon and asks who has a car parked outside. When a man nervously admits to the car being his, the cop tells him to move it or get a ticket for illegal parking. Cagney watches, surprised, as the cop steps up to the bar and is served a free shot of booze. Cagney accepts George's proposition and begins distributing booze but he is arrested and thrown into jail. George bails him out and Cagney goes into the bootlegging business in a big way, first making his own bathtub gin with McHugh, then producing his synthetic gin on an assembly-line basis, becoming rich and powerful. He meanwhile meets pert blonde Lane, who had written him when he was overseas, a girl he has never met. She is only a teenager and Cagney tells her to look him up when she grows up. He later sees her very grown up and trying to get a singing job which he arranges for her to have. He meets her and escorts her home via train, as she lives in a small town outside New York City. She doesn't have time for him, she says, since she's too busy trying to establish a singing career. He nevertheless takes her to her front door, still getting rejected. "Is it okay if I honk my horn when I drive by?" cracks Cagney before leaving her. Standing in his expansionist way is rival bootlegger Kelly, who operates his large gangster enterprises from his Italian restaurant. Cagney learns that Kelly is obtaining imported whiskey and then he learns that he has ocean-going ships bringing the booze into the U.S. Pretending to be Coast Guard men, Cagney and his men stop a freighter at sea, boarding it, and confiscating its cargo of liquor. The boss of the ship, Cagney learns, is Bogart and the two of them strike a bargain. Bogart doesn't like working for Kelly and agrees to be Cagney's junior partner. When visiting George, who is now a hostess at a swanky nightclub (essaying the famous Texas Guinan, who greeted all patrons with a brassy "hello, sucker!"), Cagney spots his old flame Lane in the chorus. When the proprietor complains about the girl, Cagney buys the place and makes Lane the star singing attraction, much to the chagrin of George who is and will always be in love with him. He has also taken good care of his Army buddy Lynn, now a lawyer, turning over all his legal work to him, giving him tens of thousands of dollars to buy fleets of taxicabs, his first love, and obviously as a way of holding on to a legitimate pursuit. Bootlegger Kelly sees his empire eroding and Cagney becoming more and more powerful. Cagney realizes that gang war between him and Kelly is about to break out and tries to effect a truce. He meets with Kelly in the gangster's Italian restaurant, but Kelly ignores him as he gulps down large heaps of spaghetti. "Take that mile of rope out of your mouth and listen to me!" Cagney tells him, but Kelly won't make peace. He kidnaps Cagney's friend, McHugh, and then delivers McHugh's body in front of Cagney's club with a note pinned to the corpse reading: "Leave me alone and I'll leave you alone." Cagney explodes and rounds up his men, telling Bogart that he's going to have a showdown with Kelly. Bogart, who is seething by this time at having to play second fiddle to Cagney, refuses to participate in the gun battle to come and even warns Kelly that Cagney and his boys are coming. Bogart's disaffection with his pal Cagney is expressed by the lisping, snarling gangster in a humorous line: "First you ask me, then you tell me, then you don't tell me anything at all. My feeling's is hoit." Kelly clears out his restaurant, except for a few people, hiding his men and waiting. (Kelly is essaying a real-life turn-of-the-century mob boss whose name was also Kelly, having been changed from an Italian name. When he walks through his restaurant ordering people out in preparation for the forthcoming gun battle, Kelly shouts: "Go on, get outta here...spaghetti's no good for ya, makes ya fat!" This remark caused members of the Italian-American League to later complain to Warner Bros. about defaming Italians, but nothing was done about the reaching claim.) When Cagney enters Kelly's restaurant the gun battle is on, with Kelly's men shot to pieces and Cagney himself dispatching Kelly. This marks the end of Cagney's reign as crime boss. Lynn—who has been in love with Lane all along and she with him—and Lane are found kissing by Cagney and he slugs Lynn, who does not retaliate. He sees that he's wrong in insisting upon Lane's love and apologizes to Lynn and then walks away. Slowly, Cagney's rackets are smashed by the law and he loses his money, millions, in the stock market crash, even selling off his fleets of cabs to Bogart, who leaves him just one taxi. At the end of the wild decade Cagney is reduced to driving that cab and spending most of his time drinking, hanging out in a dive where George sings. Lynn by then has become one of the city's top prosecuting attorneys. He has been going after big-shot Bogart, now the town's top crime kingpin. Bogart sends his men to warn Lane that if her husband doesn't stop he will be killed. Lane finds Cagney in an alcoholic state in George's club and begs him to stop Bogart. "What can I do?" says Cagney. "Same old thing," he comments to George, "whenever she wants something, she comes to me." He refuses to lift a finger to save Lynn, but when a broken-hearted Lane leaves, Cagney thinks it over and, still hopelessly in love with Lane, decides he'll talk to Bogart. He goes to Bogart's mansion and there Bogart's army of killers makes fun of the shabby Cagney before he is allowed to see the big shot. Cagney tries to persuade Bogart to lay off Lynn but Bogart tells him he intends to kill their one-time army buddy, just as ruthlessly as Bogart earlier killed Sawyer, a sergeant he hated during the war and later shot when robbing a booze warehouse. He then decides that he must also kill Cagney because he knows too much about his operation and might help Lynn destroy his empire. He motions for a goon, Biberman, to take Cagney "for a ride" home. Cagney realizes he has received a death sentence and, while being ushered out, grabs Biberman's gun and knocks him down, turning to Bogart who twitches in fear, shakes his hands like an old man with palsy, and begs for mercy. But Cagney shows him no mercy, no more than he was going to show to Lynn and his family, and shoots the mobster to death. Then, using Biberman as a shield, he steps from Bogart's second-floor rooms, kicking a goon who rushes up to him over the balcony, hustling downstairs with Biberman as his shield. Bogart's gang, massed in the living room of the mansion (all wearing tuxedoes, as it is New Year's Eve and the gang intended to celebrate with their boss), fires at Cagney as he moves toward the front door, killing Biberman. Cagney returns fire and shoots several gangsters, then flees. Outside, as the snow falls, Cagney makes his dash for life. Several gangsters step outside firing after him. He is hit in mid-flight but keeps running, turning to fire and killing another mobster. He is shot again by yet another gangster while police, answering a call to the gang battle, close in on the mansion, shooting the gangsters at the entrance. George, who had been waiting for Cagney in his cab, runs after Cagney, who is now mortally wounded and attempting to climb the steps of a church but his wobbly legs will not carry him upward. He slips sideways, head down, tumbling, falling, rolling downward on the steps until lying upon them, dying. George runs up to him, embracing him, weeping as she holds the now dead gangster's head. A cop runs forward and looks down. "Who was he?" the cop asks. George looks up tearfully and says: "His name is Eddie Bartlett." "What did he do?" the cop grills, writing down George's words. As the camera pulls back slowly, George is heard to reply: "He used to be a big shot." The camera pulls back and back to show George cradling Cagney's head, the cop leaning over them, the huge and sweeping steps and the snow falling, falling like a blanket covering not only a dead gangster, but his reckless era. Walsh's direction of this third and last film in which Cagney and Bogart appeared together is awesomely swift, encompassing an entire decade in slick episodes, interspersed with a semi-documentary approach showing newsreels of gangsters, rum-running, and booze being made on an assembly line. Cagney is shown to be a good man ruined by the excesses of the times, a forgotten man of the day, like so many millions of returning servicemen who were forgotten, their jobs forfeited by their devotion to country and duty. Though Cagney is a good man gone bad, he has strains of decency as shown in his relationship with Lynn and Lane and his final self-sacrificing gesture to save them both and their child from the violence of Bogart, a truly bad man bent on the destruction of society as shown in the early WW II scenes. The film wholly and poignantly depicts how Cagney's innocence is corrupted, even though he remains at heart a basically decent person. Cagney is a dynamo whose performance is akin to an electrical storm and he is marvelous in every frame, particularly when down and out and enacting the role of a drunk in a stupor. He was a teetotaler of sorts, his father having been an alcoholic, and he looked back upon the boyhood image of his father to dredge up his shocking performance as a man in an alcoholic daze, eyes glazed and droopy, head unsteady, hair messed, a man lurching between sobriety and drunkenness. Bogart is all ice, a sinister creature without human kindness or human affection, where George is terrific as the loyal saloon gal who will go to the Devil for her man, Cagney. Lane and Lynn are almost too good and pure to be spending so much time with Cagney but the point is well made here that it was the good people who went along with the gangsters and allowed them to flourish. Much of the film is tied to the era by clever use of 1920s music, sung by Lane and others, as well as played, particularly jazz numbers that set the mood and pace. Hellinger had long planned to make this film, and its initial title was "The World Moves On." The film was originally set to be directed by Anatole Litvak but Walsh was assigned to the film at the last minute and it was his first with Cagney. He and the supercharged star of the Warner Bros. lot got along famously, especially when Walsh encouraged Cagney to drop his own little bits and pieces of business and dialog into the film (such as the line about "can I honk my horn as I drive by," a line Cagney had overheard when a grip was trying to get a date over the phone and was having no luck). Though the tragic hero of this stellar film dies broke, Cagney himself was doing splendidly, closing out the year with a salary of $368,333, and ranking second to Gary Cooper at the box office. This would be the last gangster film Cagney would make for almost a decade until taking on the psychotic gangster role in WHITE HEAT, again made with his good friend Walsh. Cagney's role in THE ROARING TWENTIES is based upon the spectacular rise and fall of New York gangster Larry Fay, a colorful and enigmatic underworld character who promoted the career of Texas Guinan and who was also used as the inspiration for *The Great Gatsby* by F. Scott Fitzgerald. The role of the Guinan-type hostess was all-important since it set the whole temper of the film. At first Ann Sheridan was selected to play this role but she was replaced by Lee Patrick and she was replaced by Glenda Farrell, all salty character types, but, at the last minute, Gladys George was given the part and she was perfect as the brassy blonde who mistreated customers right and left and was loved for it.

p, Hal B. Wallis; d, Raoul Walsh, Anatole Litvak; w, Jerry Wald, Richard Macaulay, Robert Rossen (based on a story by Mark Hellinger); ph, Ernest Haller; m, Heinz Roemheld, Ray Heindorf; ed, Jack Killifer; md, Leo F. Forbstein; art d, Max Parker; cos, Milo Anderson; spec eff, Byron Haskin, Edwin B. DuPar; m/l, "My Melancholy Baby," Ernie Burnett, George A. Norton, "I'm Just Wild About Harry," Eubie Blake, Noble Sissle, "It Had to Be You," Isham Jones, Gus Kahn, "In a Shanty in Old Shanty Town," Jack Little, Joseph Young, John Siras; makeup, Perc Westmore.

Crime Drama **Cas.** **(PR:C MPAA:NR)**

ROARING WESTWARD* (1949) 55m MON bw (AKA: BOOM TOWN BADMEN)

Jimmy Wakely *(Jimmy)*, Dub "Cannonball" Taylor *(Cannonball)*, Lois Hall *(Susan)*, Jack Ingram *(Marshal Braden)*, Claire Whitney *(Aunt Jessica)*, Kenne Duncan *(Morgan)*, Buddy Swan *(Perry)*, Dennis Moore *(Sanders)*, Holly Bane

(Bart), Marshall Reed (Jorgen), Nolan Leary (Mossy), Ted French (Burns), Bud Osborne (Deputy Blake), Bob Woodward (Bob), Al Haskell, Tom Smith, Denver Dixon, Art Mix, Rudy Bowman.

Singing cowboy star Wakely comes to the aid of a faltering Sheriff's School when an outlaw gang begins to interfere. Justice and the sheriff's badge prevail as Wakely and his pals rid the West of a couple more badmen.

p, Louis Gray; d, Oliver Drake; w, Ronald Davidson; ph, Marcel Le Picard; ed, Carl Pierson; md, Edward Kay.

Western **(PR:A MPAA:NR)**

ROB ROY (SEE: ROB ROY, THE HIGHLAND ROGUE, 1954, Brit.)

ROB ROY, THE HIGHLAND ROGUE* (1954, Brit.) 81m Disney/ RKO c (AKA: ROB ROY)

Richard Todd (Rob Roy MacGregor), Glynis Johns (Helen Mary MacGregor), James Robertson Justice (Duke of Argyll), Michael Gough (Duke of Montrose), Jean Taylor Smith (Lady Glengyll), Geoffrey Keen (Killearn), Finlay Currie (Hamish MacPherson), Archie Duncan (Dougal MacGregor), Russell Waters (Hugh MacGregor), Marjorie Fielding (Maggie MacPherson), Eric Pohlmann (King George I), Ina de la Haye (Countess Von Pahlen), Michael Goodliffe (Robert Walpole), Martin Boddy (Gen. Cadogan), Ewen Solon (Maj. Gen. Wightman), James Sutherland (Torcal), Malcolm Keen (Duke of Marlborough), Kitty McLeod, Marietta McLeod (Mouth Music Singers), Max Gardner, John McEvoy, Ian McNaughton, Stevenson Lang, Charles Hubbard, Campbell Godley, Howard Douglas, May Hallatt, Hamilton Keene, Henry Hewitt, David Keir, Hal Osmond, Middleton Woods, Andrew Laurence, Rupert Evans, Paddy Ryan.

Todd leads the Scottish people in revolt against England's stodgy King George I, while trying to gain the support of the Scot Secretary of State. When the latter is replaced by a spiteful louse who wants to undermine Todd's mission, Todd has to fight battles on both fronts. Heavy-handed plot from Disney might have been better had it been directed by the intended Ken Annakin (ROBIN HOOD, THE SWORD AND THE ROSE). Instead, at the blunt request of J. Arthur Rank, Annakin was told he could no longer work for Disney and was replaced by French. This fiasco, as well as the picture's failure (though it oddly received some good press and a Royal Command performance), caused Disney to split from RKO after 21 pictures and he decided to return to the States for his live-action films. Far too confusing a film to recommend as a kid picture, though they'll be drawn to the constant stream of action.

p, Perce Pearce; d, Harold French; w, Lawrence E. Watkin; ph, Guy Green (Technicolor); m, Cedric Thorpe Davie; ed, Geoffrey Foot; md, Muir Mathieson; prod d, Carmen Dillon; cos, Phyllis Dalton.

Adventure **(PR:A MPAA:NR)**

ROBBER SYMPHONY, THE* (1937, Brit.) 136m Concordia/Al Friedlander-Fortune bw

George Graves (The Grandfather), Magda Sonja (The Mother), Hans Feher (Giannino), Michael Martin Harvey (Man With Straw Hat), Tela-Tchai (The Waitress), Webster Booth (The Singer), Al Marshall (The Clarinet Player), Jack Tracy (The Bassoon Player), Oscar Asche (The Chief Gendarme), Ivor Wilmot (Magistrate), Vinette (Fortune Teller), Jim Gerald (Charcoal-Burner), Georges Andre Martin (Mayor), Alexandre Rignault (Black Devil).

One of the most bizarre movies in the history of cinema, THE ROBBER SYMPHONY stars Feher as a young piano player who gets involved with a gang of burglars after they stash stolen money in the piano-organ. Feher's mother (played by Feher's wife Sonja) is arrested when she is mistakenly believed to be a gang member. Feher flees across the snowy mountains with the burglar's cash, but after a long pursuit, the gang is arrested. All of this, however, is conveyed with a minimum of dialog. Instead, Feher (who also wrote and directed) relies on music, establishing a comic pace which is based in his rhythmic approach to editing. Billed as "The First Surrealistic Picture" (America was obviously behind the times and had missed UN CHIEN ANDALOU and L'AGE D'OR), THE ROBBER SYMPHONY most definitely is rooted in surrealism, with the film's musicians playing in the background. Produced by Weine and directed by Feher, this interesting picture does recall THE CABINET OF DR. CALIGARI, in which both had appeared some 16 years earlier. Feher made this picture after being forced from his native Germany because of his Jewish descent. He later ventured to the U.S., where he soon faded from the public eye, dying in Hollywood in 1945. (Bilingual versions.)

p, Robert Weine; d, Friedrich Feher; w, Feher, Anton Kuh, Jack Trendall; ph, Eugene Schufftan; m, Feher; art d, Erno Metzner.

Musical/Fantasy **(PR:A MPAA:NR)**

ROBBERS OF THE RANGE½ (1941) 61m RKO bw

Tim Holt (Drummond), Virginia Vale (Alice), Ray Whitley (Smokey), Emmett Lynn (Whopper), LeRoy Mason (Rankin), Howard Hickman (Tremaine), Ernie Adams (Greeley), Frank LaRue (Higgins), Ray Bennett (Daggett), Tom London (Monk), Ed Cassidy (Sheriff), Bud Osborne (Blackie), George Melford (Col. Lodge), Malcolm McTaggart (Curly), Harry Harvey (Brady), Lloyd Ingraham.

Holt is a landowner who gets framed by a scheming railroad company when he refuses to sell his land. Before coming to trial, Holt is able to prove his innocence and place the murder rap where it belonged. Handsome Holt replaced George O'Brien in the series of westerns produced by Gilroy and directed by Killy; this was his third. Vale had played the menaced feminine lead in six of the O'Brien westerns and easily segued into the Holt series. Holt followed this role with a featured part in THE MAGNIFICENT AMBERSONS (1942). One song, "The Railroad's Comin' to Town" (Fred Rose, Ray Whitley, sung by Whitley).

p, Bert Gilroy; d, Edward Killy; w, Morton Grant, Arthur V. Jones (based on a

story by Oliver Drake); ph, Harry Wild; m, Fred Rose, Ray Whitley; ed, Frederick Knudtson.

Western **(PR:A MPAA:NR)**

ROBBERS' ROOST* (1933) 60m FOX bw

George O'Brien (Jim Wall), Maureen O'Sullivan (Helen), Walter McGrail (Brad), Maude Eburne (Aunt Ellen), Reginald Owen (Herrick), Ted Oliver, Doris Lloyd, Frank Rice, William Pawley, Bill Nestall, Clifford Santley, Gilbert Holmes, Vinegar Roan, Robert Greig.

O'Brien is wrongly accused of cattle rustling. With the lovely O'Sullivan at his side he struggles to clear his name. Scripted by the brilliant Dudley Nichols from a story by Zane Grey.

p, Sol Lesser; d, Louis King; w, Dudley Nichols (based on a novel by Zane Grey); ph, George Schneiderman.

Western **(PR:A MPAA:NR)**

ROBBERS' ROOST½ (1955) 83m UA bw

George Montgomery (Tex), Richard Boone (Hays), Sylvia Findley (Helen), Bruce Bennett (Herrick), Peter Graves (Heesman), Warren Stevens (Smokey), Tony Romano (Happy Jack), William Hopper (Robert Bell), Leo Gordon (Jeff), Stanley Clements (Chuck), Joe Bassett (Stud), Leonard Geer (Sparrow), Al Wyatt (Slocum), Boyd "Red" Morgan (Brad).

Bennett plays a wheelchair-confined rancher who hires both Boone's gang and Graves' gang to watch each other and his cattle. His theory is that they will be too busy watching each other to rustle his cattle. Montgomery joins Graves because he is seeking revenge against Boone for the murder of his wife. Barely better than routine.

p, Robert Goldstein, Leonard Goldstein; d, Sidney Salkow; w, John O'Dea, Maurice Geraghty, Salkow (based on a novel by Zane Grey); ph, Jack Draper (Eastmancolor); m, Paul Dunlap; ed, George Gittens; m/l, Tony Romano, John Bradford, Barbara Hayden (sung by Romano).

Western **(PR:A MPAA:NR)**

ROBBERY* (1967, Brit.) 114 m Oakhurst/EM c

Stanley Baker (Paul Clifton), Joanna Pettet (Kate Clifton), James Booth (Inspector Langdon), Frank Finlay (Robinson), Barry Foster (Frank), William Marlowe (Dave), Clinton Greyn (Jack), George Sewell (Ben), Michael McStay (Don), Patrick Jordan (Freddy), Ken Farrington (Robber), Glyn Edwards (Squad Chief), Anthony Sweeney (Detective Inspector), David Pinner (Constable, Information Room), Rachel Herbert (School Teacher), Martin Wyldeck (Chief Constable), Roger Booth (Detective), Malcolm Taylor (Delta 1 Observer), Linda Marlowe (Debutante at Nightclub), Frank Williams (Prison Contact), Barry Stanton (Car Lot Owner), Michael David (C.I.D. Chief), Roger Booth (Detective).

The title gives away the plot in this fast-moving British caper film that has a bit of a thank-you to give to RIFIFI. Instead of ending with a chase, this begins with one. Baker is the brains behind the scheme and first engineers a jewelry theft in order to raise the needed money to embark on his ultimate robbery, the heisting of 3 million pounds from a mail train going south to London from Glasgow. As is always the case in this genre, Baker has to gather a group of experts in their fields to help with the crime. The first 20 minutes of the film has almost no dialog as Baker steals a car, robs the jewels, then eludes the cops. Whereas the theft sequence in RIFIFI had no words and no music, this one benefits from Keating's rock 'em score that keeps pace with the tight cutting. Baker needs one more man to complete his crew so he breaks Finlay, a money expert, out of the slammer. Baker is on the outs with his wife, Pettet, and they have one brief romantic scene (out of place and it doesn't work at all as it's edited more like a suspense scene than a loving one) before getting back to the business of thievery. The train is successfully held up, the money removed and the gang members assemble at an airfield that's grown over with weeds where they will divvy up the swag. Robinson calls his wife but Scotland Yard man Booth is already on to the case and has the house phone tapped. The coppers get the information, rush to the gang's hideout and grab them all, save one. Baker escapes to the U.S. with the money. There's a bare minimum of dialog as director Yates allows the faces and the actions to deliver the story. It's based on the real train robbery that took place in England for which many were captured. The leader of that band is, at this writing, happily living in Brazil with a new wife and children. Baker not only starred, he also coproduced and arranged the financing for the film. After leading a most interesting life and being knighted, Baker died while still in his 40's. He was the kind of man who loved taking chances and once challenged an American dart thrower to a game at "Dave's Dive," a British pub in the heart of Rome owned by a former British boxer. The American said "One thousand." Baker replied with a sneer: "Lira?" (about $5 at the time). The American said: "Pounds" (about $2400). When Baker's pal, who had already lost lots of money to the American shook his head, Baker suggested they lighten the bet to "drinks for everyone." The American won the "301" game before Baker got on the board. Baker happily bought drinks.

p, Michael Deeley, Stanley Baker; d, Peter Yates; w, Edward Boyd, Yates, George Markstein (based on a story by Gerald Wilson); ph, Douglas Slocombe (Eastmancolor); m, Johnny Keating; ed, Reginald Beck; art d, Michael Seymour; cos, Brian Owen-Smith; makeup, Wally Schneiderman.

Caper **Cas.** **(PR:A-C MPAA:NR)**

ROBBERY UNDER ARMS (1958, Brit.) 83m Rank c

Peter Finch (Capt. Starlight), Ronald Lewis (Dick Marston), Maureen Swanson (Kate Morrison), David McCallum (Jim Marston), Vincent Ball (George Storefield), Jill Ireland (Jean), Dudy Nimmo (Eileen), Jean Anderson (Ma), Ursula Finlay (Grace Storefield), Johnny Cadell (Warrigal), Larry Taylor (Burke), Russell Napier

(*Mr. Green*), Laurence Naismith (*Ben Marston*), Yvonne Buckingham (*Saloon Girl*), George Cormack (*Minister*), Doris Goddard (*Madam Franciana*).

Set in Australia during the mid-1800's this tale centers on Finch's outlaw gang and its escapades through the open landscape down under. Lewis and McCallum join the gang, but soon wish they were living a decent life. They blow their chance at freedom, and in the end the entire gang is put out of commission. Nothing more than a British western set in Australia. At the time, the J. Arthur Rank Organization took an extreme interest in Australia and other commonwealth countries, with a distributing deal for English-made films through Australia's Greater Union Theatres; reciprocally, the Rank Organization felt compelled to make pictures dealing with Australia, and to distribute them widely.

p, Joseph Janni; d, Jack Lee; w, W.P. Lipscomb, Alexander Baron (based on the novel by Rolf Boldrewood); ph, Harry Waxman (Eastmancolor); m, Matyas Seiber; ed, Manuel Del Campo; md, Seiber; art d, Alex Vetchinsky; cos, Olga Lehmann.

Western/Adventure (PR:A MPAA:NR)

ROBBERY WITH VIOLENCE* (1958, Brit.) 67m GIB/RF bw

Ivan Craig (*Peter Frayne*), Sally Day (*Brenda Bailey*), Michael Golden (*Inspector Wilson*), John Martin Lewis (*Derek Bailey*), John Trevor-Davis (*Inspector Greenway*).

A worthless crime melodrama about a bank robber, Craig, who skips town with his partners' money and hides out with former love Day. The louse then kills Day's husband, is railroaded by his former partners, nearly caught by the police, and finally (and thankfully) gunned down. ROBBERY WITH VIOLENCE just proves that if a film's lead character is hated, then the film itself will be.

p&d, George Ivan Barnett; w, David Cumming (based on a story by Edith M. Barnett); ph, George Ivan Barnett.

Crime (PR:A MPAA:NR)

ROBBO (SEE: ROBIN AND THE 7 HOODS, 1964)

ROBBY*½ (1968) 90m Bluewood c

Warren Raum (*Robby*), Ryp Siani (*Friday*), John Garces (*Horton Crandall/Lloyd Woodruff*), Rita Elliot (*Janet Woodruff*), John Woodbridge (*Simmons*), Ralph C. Bluemke (*Chauffeur*), Norvin Baskerville (*Vocalist*).

A young boy is shipwrecked and floats ashore on a tiny tropical island. He is saved from drowning by a small black boy, and together they experience a series of adventures. A writer then arrives on the island and, recognizing the boy, decides to take him back to the estate of his wealthy relatives, who have offered a reward for the missing boy. The boys are assured that they will be allowed to remain together, but when they reach their destination the black boy is taken to an orphanage. An attempt to address friendship across racial lines that goes drastically downhill when it leaves the island. At least it looks great.

p, Stacey Enyeart, Ralph C. Bluemke; d&w, Bluemke; ph, Al Mozell (Eastmancolor); m, John Randolph Eaton; ed, Bill Buckley; md, Eaton.

Adventure/Drama (PR:AA MPAA:NR)

ROBE, THE***½ (1953) 135m FOX c

Richard Burton (*Marcellus Gallio*), Jean Simmons (*Diana*), Victor Mature (*Demetrius*), Michael Rennie (*Peter*), Jay Robinson (*Caligula*), Dean Jagger (*Justus*), Torin Thatcher (*Sen. Gallio*), Richard Boone (*Pilate*), Betta St. John (*Miriam*), Jeff Morrow (*Paulus*), Ernest Thesiger (*Emperor Tiberius*), Dawn Addams (*Junia*), Leon Askin (*Abidor*), Frank Pulaski (*Quintus*), David Leonard (*Marcipor*), Michael Ansara (*Judas*), Helen Beverly (*Rebecca*), Nicholas Koster (*Jonathan*), Francis Pierlot (*Dodinius*), Thomas Browne Henry (*Marius*), Anthony Eustrel (*Sarpedon*), Pamela Robinson (*Lucia*), Jay Novello (*Tiro*), Emmett Lynn (*Nathan*), Sally Corner (*Cornelia*), Rosalind Ivan (*Julia*), George E. Stone (*Gracchus*), Marc Snow (*Auctioneer*), Mae Marsh (*Woman*), George Keymas (*Slave*), John Doucette (*Ship's Mate*), Ford Rainey, Sam Gilman (*Ship's Captains*), Cameron Mitchell (*Voice of Christ*), Harry Shearer (*David*), Virginia Lee (*Specialty Dancer*), Leo Curley (*Shalum*), Jean Corbett, Joan Corbett, Gloria Saunders (*Slave Girls*), Percy Helton (*Caleb*), Roy Gordon (*Chamberlain*), Ben Astar (*Cleander*), Frank De Kova, George Melford, Eleanor Moore, Irene Demetrion, Dan Ferniel, George Robotham, Alex Pope, Ed Mundy, Anthony Jochim, Van Des Autels, Hayden Rorke.

It's majestic, it's huge, it's stirring, and, for Catholic viewers, THE ROBE was utterly inspirational. Tens of thousands of Catholic students were taken en masse by their teachers to see this film as Fox studios knew they would. This was the film with which Fox answered the upstart, TV, employing its heavy gun, CinemaScope, a wide, thought to be overpowering, image that could project films on an enormous screen (68 by 24 feet). Unlike Cinerama, which literally wrapped itself around audiences, CinemaScope gave a panoramic view that assured the viewer that he was not being sucked into the screen. THE ROBE was the first to use the new technique and had a tremendous impact on audiences which deserted TV briefly to see another version of the oft-told morality play which Cecil B. DeMille had been rehashing for decades. Burton is the young Roman officer ordered to crucify Christ and he goes about his chore with indifference, even rolling dice with his fellow soldiers for the rich red robe worn by the victim on the cross. A storm comes up just as Christ dies (He is shown at a distance hanging on the cross) and Burton, who has won his robe, is suddenly startled and perplexed by strange emotions. His Greek slave, Mature, swoops up the robe and presses it to his tearful face, then vanishes, only to meet Rennie, playing Peter the Apostle, who converts Mature to Christianity. The earthy Burton goes on with his pagan life, participating in military campaigns and, when not lopping off the heads of Rome's enemies, indulging himself in various orgies and revels where good wine flows faster than the Tiber River. He woos his childhood sweetheart, Simmons, who by then is infected with Christianity. Mad emperor Caligula (Robinson), who cannot abide Christians, hears

that the robe possesses magical powers and he demands that Burton secure it for him. But the emperor, played with sustained hysteria and queenly gestures by Robinson, is not able to use the robe for his own evil ends and explodes in wrath. He learns that Burton, one of his favorite tribunes, is sympathetic to the Christians through his lover, Simmons, now a devout convert to Christianity, and demands that both of them renounce Christ. Burton defies Robinson, who condemns his tribune and Simmons, ordering them both executed. "Go!" he screams at them, "To your God!" Both walk blissfully to their doom, but not before Burton hands the all-powerful robe to Mature on his way to the executioner. This last gesture, of course, assured Fox of a sequel starring Mature who would go on more adventures with the robe in DEMETRIUS AND THE GLADIATORS. THE ROBE was already under production when Fox mogul Zanuck saw a demonstration of what CinemaScope could do with its anamorphic lens created by Prof. Henri Chretien. The problem was that there was only one lens. Zanuck, always a risk-taker, stopped production of THE ROBE and ordered another lens made so that this film would be the first to use the new process. So protective was Zanuck about his new process that he had detectives guard the lens night and day, as if it were the Norden Bombsight. Zanuck had little trouble convincing Fox money man Spyros Skouras that CinemaScope would be the answer to the threat of TV. "This will save the movies!" exclaimed Skouras, and he went about cajoling, begging, threatening almost every theater owner in the U.S. to tear down his old screen and put up the new wide screens necessary for CinemaScope. Announced the confident Skouras: "We're hoping to establish a hallmark of the highest in entertainment. We want the public to say there never was a bad CinemaScope film, just like there never was a bad Cadillac." To make sure that the theater owners converted to the wide screens, Zanuck called a meeting of all the studio heads—MGM, Warner Bros., Paramount—to see a spectacular short with the CinemaScope process, hoping to lease the new lens to the other studios. All of the other moguls were astounded at the process and signed up, except Paramount, which later developed its own wide-screen process, Panavision. CinemaScope became the only process used at Fox, which was an expensive proposition, and to meet its costs the studio cut its film output in half, figuring it would make up the difference in overall box office receipts by charging a higher ticket price for its CinemaScope offerings. The concept worked for a while, until CinemaScope became commonplace. Zanuck was later to admit: "CinemaScope was all wrong mechanically. We cut too low and too circular. Visual experts told us—not then—but later, that the correct proportion is Panavision. Panavision is the perfect proportion to fit the eyes." But when THE ROBE premiered it was similar to the electric shock that petrified the industry and audiences alike when THE JAZZ SINGER burst forth with dialog. In its first week at the Roxy Theater in New York, THE ROBE grossed a whopping $264,000 and within a few months the film had more than made up its price tag of a reported $8 million and was on its way to establishing box office records. The story of the robe was purchased by Fox for $100,000 when author Douglas had only finished half of his manuscript. Burton, then an accomplished Shakespearean actor, had really no film experience to speak of but gambler Zanuck took a chance on him and he did a fine job with a difficult role. appearing in 96 percent of all the scenes in the movie and delivering 313 speeches out of the 700-some in the picture. Burton threw himself wholeheartedly into the film and hardly slept throughout the entire production, wearing his togas and tribune uniforms home and often sleeping in them. He proclaimed to friends that this was the opportunity of his lifetime and he would not fail Fox, Zanuck, or CinemaScope. "After what I am and what I've come from," said the future superstar, "where can I go but to the top?" He did. THE ROBE made Richard Burton an international star and one of Fox's hottest film properties. Though critics hailed Burton's performance as stunning, the actor privately told friends that he considered his part in THE ROBE "a prissy role." It mattered not. Burton was part of history now and had helped to make THE ROBE a watershed picture best summed up by one reviewer who stated, "All roads should lead to THE ROBE—and Fort Knox—for a long time to come."

p, Frank Ross; d, Henry Koster; w, Philip Dunne (based on the novel by Lloyd C. Douglas, adaptation, Gina Kaus); ph, Leon Shamroy (CinemaScope, Technicolor); m, Alfred Newman; ed, Barbara McLean; md, Edward Powell; art d, Lyle Wheeler, George W. Davis; spec eff, Ray Kellogg.

Historical Epic/Religious Drama Cas. (PR:A MPAA:NR)

ROBERTA**** (1935) 105m RKO bw

Irene Dunne (*Stephanie*), Fred Astaire (*Huck Haines*), Ginger Rogers (*Countess Scharwenka/Lizzie Gatz*), Randolph Scott (*John Kent*), Helen Westley (*Roberta/Aunt Minnie*), Victor Varconi (*Ladislaw*), Claire Dodd (*Sophie*), Luis Alberni (*Voyda*), Ferdinand Munier (*Lord Delves*), Torben Meyer (*Albert*), Adrian Rosley (*Professor*), Bodil Rosing (*Fernando*), Lucille Ball, Jane Hamilton, Margaret McChrystal, Kay Sutton, Maxine Jennings, Virginia Reid, Lorna Low, Lorraine DeSart, Wanda Perry, Diane Cook, Virginia Carroll, Betty Dumbries, Donna Roberts (*Mannequins*), Mike Tellegen, Sam Savitsky (*Cossacks*), Zena Savine (*Woman*), Johnny "Candy" Candido, Muzzy Marcellino, Gene Sheldon, Howard Lally, William Carey, Paul McLarind, Hal Bown, Charles Sharpe, Ivan Dow, Phil Cuthbert, Delmon Davis, William Dunn (*Orchestra*), Mary Forbes (*Mrs. Teal*), William B. Davidson (*Purser*), Grace Hayle (*Reporter*), Dale Van Sickel (*Dance Extra*), Judith Vosselli, Rita Gould (*Bits*).

RKO had been in trouble until the returns from THE GAY DIVORCEE began pouring in. They had relinquished bidding for high-ticket items because they couldn't afford them but Berman saw the play "Roberta" on Broadway and insisted the studio acquire it. They did and the result was a wonderful turn for Astaire and Rogers that brought scads of money into the studio and served to up the reputations of everyone involved, with the possible exception of Scott, in a non-singing role, who was a stick with a Southern accent. The play starred Bob Hope, George Murphy, and Lyda Roberti. In the film, the Hope and Murphy roles were combined for Astaire while Rogers did the Roberti part. Although Dunne and Scott were the romantic leads, it was ho-hum at best when they were on screen and just marking time for Fred and Ginger to return. Scott and Astaire have a jazz band called "The Wabash Indianans." Scott is actually a football player who travels with the group on a lark. They are in Paris where Scott's aunt, Westley, is a famed dress designer. While there, Scott meets Dunne, a White Russian princess who has had to earn a living for herself since the Revolution and has become a well-known couturier. Astaire takes up again with his former sweetheart, Rogers, who is posing as a Polish countess (and very funny at it). The final scene of the movie is an endless fashion show (with Lucille Ball as one of the models—she was making her first film for RKO and would, 20 years or so later, buy the entire studio for her Desilu Productions Company), so you can see there's not much of a plot. But what is hung on that bare skeleton is some of Jerome Kern's most beautiful music and a set of dances that caused audiences to spontaneously applaud in the theaters. ROBERTA may be the most overlooked of the Astaire-Rogers films as they played second leads, rather than starring roles. It's not been on TV so one has to be of an age to recall the film's release in theaters or have been privy to one of the many revivals in art houses. Berman had also produced THE GAY DIVORCEE and replaced many of Cole Porter's tunes. This time, he's much kinder to the Kern music and kept four of the original songs in the film written by Kern and Otto Harbach. They were: "Let's Begin" (performed by Astaire and the band, with interpolated bits by Candido and banjoist Gene Sheldon), "Yesterdays," "Smoke Gets In Your Eyes" (sung by Dunne), and "I'll Be Hard To Handle" with new lyrics by Bernard Dougall (Rogers, Astaire dance and sing). Kern and Oscar Hammerstein II had written "I Won't Dance" for a show called "Three Sisters" and it was lyrically altered by Dorothy Fields and Jimmy McHugh (Astaire, Rogers). "Lovely To Look At" was also written by Kern, Fields, and McHugh (Dunne) for this movie and was Oscar-nominated. The old chestnut "Back Home Again In Indiana" by James Hanley and Ballard MacDonald is also heard and three Kern tunes are used as background music: "The Touch Of Your Hand," "You're Devastating," and "Don't Ask Me Not To Sing." The reason for altering "I Won't Dance" was to include a line that referred to "The Continental," which was the dance done by Astaire and Rogers in their previous film. The remake, LOVELY TO LOOK AT, starred Kathryn Grayson, Howard Keel, Red Skelton, Marge and Gower Champion, and was pale. The song "Yesterdays" has nothing to do with the tune of the same name by the Beatles which became a classic. This one is as well. Kern's best song in many minds is "All The Things You Are" and it was chosen in a poll of songwriters as one of the 10 greatest songs ever written.

p, Pandro S. Berman; d, William A. Seiter; w, Jane Murfin, Sam Mintz, Allan Scott, Glenn Tryon (from the musical play "Roberta" by Jerome Kern and Otto Harbach based on the novel *Gowns By Roberta* by Alice Duer Miller); ph, Edward Cronjager; m, Jerome Kern; ed, William Hamilton; md, Max Steiner; art d, Van Nest Polglase, Carroll Clark; set d, Thomas K. Little; cos, Bernard Newman; ch, Fred Astaire, Hermes Pan.

Musical/Comedy **(PR:A MPAA:NR)**

ROBIN AND MARIAN*** (1976, Brit.) 106m COL c

Sean Connery *(Robin Hood)*, Audrey Hepburn *(Maid Marian)*, Robert Shaw *(Sheriff of Nottingham)*, Richard Harris *(King Richard)*, Nicol Williamson *(Little John)*, Denholm Elliott *(Will Scarlett)*, Kenneth Haigh *(Sir Ranulf de Pudsey)*, Ronnie Barker *(Friar Tuck)*, Ian Holm *(King John)*, Bill Maynard *(Mercadier)*, Esmond Knight *(Old Defender)*, Veronica Quilligan *(Sister Mary)*, Peter Butterworth *(Surgeon)*, John Barrett *(Jack)*, Kenneth Cranhan *(Jack's Apprentice)*, Victoria Merida Roja *(Queen Isabella)*, Montserrat Julio *(1st Sister)*, Victoria Hernandez Sanguino *(2nd Sister)*, Margarita Minguillon *(3rd Sister)*.

What might have been a wonderful movie is only so-so due to Lester's unnecessarily frantic direction and a ponderous script by James Goldman, who had so much success with THE LION IN WINTER that some of his lines for this seem like bon mots he may have cut from that screenplay. It's ROMEO AND JULIET for the gray-haired set. Twenty years have passed since the bandit who robbed from the rich to give to the poor ran off to fight in the Crusades with his beloved King. He's now back, in the form of wizened Connery and in the two decades since he left, much has transpired. His love, Hepburn, is now a nun; his King, Harris, has become a mad man dedicated to amassing a fortune, etc. The one thing remaining constant in Connery's life is that the sheriff of Nottingham, Shaw, is still eager to see him hang. Connery is traveling in France with Harris and they pass an old seedy castle occupied by a crazed ancient man, Knight, as well as several women and children. Harris thinks there might be something of value inside the ramshackle structure so he orders Connery to go in and take it. Connery refuses and the two men get into an argument. Knight sends an arrow into Harris, who is mortally wounded. Before dying, Harris has his loyal men destroy the castle but his death stops his chastisement of Connery. Williamson (a slight "Little John" if there ever was one) and Connery are now free to leave Europe and finally go home to England. They immediately return to Sherwood Forest and look with nostalgia at the old landmarks. Two of their old friends, Elliott and Barker, appear and smiles are in order. The two gang members tell Connery that he is now a hero, celebrated in song by men like their late friend, Alan-A-Dale, who used to sing folk tunes. Harris's heinous brother, Holm, now rules the area with Shaw, while Hepburn is now running a nearby nunnery. Connery goes off to see her and notes that she is no longer the twittering maid of so many years ago. Rather, she is one tough cookie who is risking her life by staying in England because Holm has decreed that anyone loyal to Rome must be exiled. Hepburn steadfastly remains, true to her faith and willing to go to jail or even death to uphold it. Connery thinks that's foolish so he knocks her unconscious and carts her off. Williamson and Connery masquerade as sellers of goods, fight the soldiers inside Nottingham Castle, and save the nuns who have already been incarcerated—Julio, Sanguino, and Minguillon. (If the presence of so many Hispanic names in the cast is surprising, that's because much of the movie was shot in Spain.) Later, Hepburn admits that she tried killing herself when he departed twenty years before and she wishes he would finally sheath his sword as she could not bear his death at this point. Meanwhile, Haigh, one of Holm's nobles, thinks it would be quite a feather in his cap if he captured Connery so he sets a trap in Sherwood Forest. The battle commences and all of Haigh's men are killed by Connery's band, with Haigh barely escaping with his life. Haigh goes to Holm and gets a battalion of two hundred to come back and finish off Connery. Meanwhile, Hepburn and Connery are spending a peaceful few days in the quiet woods. Soon enough, the story about Connery returning has been shouted around the countryside and he is beset with many who want to join him. Unfortunately, the prospective Merry Men are mostly underage lads and overage grandfathers. Nevertheless, Connery thinks he can forge a fighting force out of them. Shaw's men and Haigh's small army are already descending on Sherwood Forest and it looks as though a bloody battle will ensue. Hepburn pleads with Connery to back off and tries to get Williamson to intervene. Connery has an idea. Why kill so many when this dispute is really between two men, himself and Shaw? He suggests that they fight each other, with a promise that no matter who wins, no other blood will be shed. Shaw agrees and the two men have a go at it with axes and swords. It's a long, cruel fight and Connery eventually vanquishes Shaw but is badly wounded in the fray. Hepburn kneels beside the dying Connery and Haigh orders his men to attack. The fight they tried to avoid takes place and many are slain. Williamson kills Haigh, and Connery, who doesn't have much time, is taken to the abbey where they will attempt to stanch the flow of blood. Hepburn is well aware that Connery doesn't have much time left. She puts some poison in a wine glass and drinks it, then hands it to him. Connery sips, then asks why she's done what she's done and Hepburn replies that she could not live without him and loves him more than God. Williamson walks in and Connery, with his last bit of strength, shoots an arrow out the window and instructs Williamson to bury them both where the arrow has landed. A touching conclusion to a spotty picture that was satirical, sometimes pretentious, often slow and occasionally exciting. If they'd decided to shoot an all-out comedy that showed Connery creakily trying to recapture his old derring-do, it might have made more sense. Hepburn came back to movies after a nine-year absence to accept this role and had nothing but praise for Lester's quick direction. Her only reservation was about the love scenes with Connery where she would have liked more time. Connery and Hepburn personally raised the stature of the movie above the script. At 47, she was still radiant, but it never came close to what might have been. Ray Stark presented the film and it is presumed that it was his personal appeal to all that got this movie made. Since the memory recalls Flynn and a few other, much younger actors as Robin Hood, perhaps it would have been better to allow sleeping legends to lie where they fell, instead of pounding their chests with cinematic CPR.

p, Denis O'Dell; d, Richard Lester; w, James Goldman; ph, David Watkin (Technicolor); m, John Barry; ed, John Victor Smith; prod d, Michael Stringer; art d, Gil Parrondo; cos, Yvonne Blake; spec eff, Eddie Fowlie; makeup, Jose Antonio Sanchez; stunts, Joaquin Parra, Miguel Pedregosa (fights by Ian McKay, William Hobbs).

Adventure **Cas.** **(PR:A-C MPAA:PG)**

ROBIN AND THE SEVEN HOODS*** (1964) 123m P-C/WB c

Frank Sinatra *(Robbo)*, Dean Martin *(Little John)*, Sammy Davis, Jr. *(Will)*, Bing Crosby *(Allen A. Dale)*, Peter Falk *(Guy Gisborne)*, Barbara Rush *(Marian)*, Edward G. Robinson *(Big Jim)*, Victor Buono *(Sheriff Potts)*, Barry Kelley *(Police Chief)*, Hank Henry *(Six Seconds)*, Robert Carricart *(Blue Jaw)*, Allen Jenkins *(Vermin)*, Jack LaRue *(Tomatoes)*, Hans Conried *(Mr. Ricks)*, Sig Rumann *(Hammacher)*, Robert Foulk *(Sheriff Glick)*, Sonny King, Phil Crosby, Richard Bakalyan *(Robbo's Hoods)*, Phil Arnold *(Hatrack)*, Harry Swoger *(Soup Meat)*, Joseph Ruskin *(Tick)*, Bernard Fein *(Charlie Bananas)*, Carol Hill *(Cocktail Waitress)*, Diane Sayer *("Booze" Witness)*, William Zuckert, Richard Simmons *(Prosecutors)*, Milton Rudin *(Judge)*, Maurice Manson *(Dignitary)*, Chris Hughes *(Jud)*, Harry Wilson, Joe Brooks, Richard Sinatra, Roger Creed *(Gisborne's Hoods)*, Carolyn Morin *(House Guard)*, Aldo Silvani *(Guard)*, Joe Gray, John Delgado, Boyd "Red" Morgan, John Pedrini, Al Wyatt, Tony Randall *(Hoods)*, Eddie Ness, Frank Scannell *(Lawyers)*, Thom Conroy, Joey Jackson *(Butlers)*, Linda Brent *(Woman Derelict)*, Jerry Davis, Manuel Padilla, Mark Sherwood *(Boys)*, Ron Dayton *(Man)*, Larry Mann *(Workman)*.

The title indicates exactly what this is: a parody of the famed archer and his Merry Men set in Chicago, just before the crash, when Prohibition was the road to riches for hoodlums. It was another summit meeting of "the Clan," with Joey Bishop and Peter Lawford being the only members missing from the cast. It owes much to the Damon Runyon-derived GUYS AND DOLLS in style and content and even includes one Crosby number that resembles "Sit Down You're Rockin' The Boat"—the Stubby Kaye number in the aforementioned film. Robinson is the undisputed boss of all bosses. It's his birthday party and all the mobsters sing their praise to him. Then, less than three minutes into the film, Robinson is shot to death. Falk immediately announces himself as the chief and Sinatra and Henry accept that, but make sure he realizes that the North Side of Chicago is theirs. Martin, a small-timer from the sticks, arrives in Chi and joins Sinatra's band. Several battles break out, Sinatra's and Falk's nightclubs are destroyed. Sinatra decides to build again and arranges the edifice so that it can become a revival hall at the press of a button. Falk doesn't know this, tips the cops off through his personal flunky, Buono (a sheriff), and when the officers raid the place, all they find is a group of singers shouting lots of "hallelujahs." Robinson's daughter, Rush, wants to avenge her father's death so she presses $50,000 on Sinatra to kill whoever it was that took Robinson's life. Sinatra doesn't want the money or the assignment, so he gives the scratch to Davis with orders to get rid of it as he sees fit. Davis thinks it can be put to good use, so he hands it over to Crosby, who runs an orphanage (like the role he played in GOING MY WAY without the clerical collar). When Crosby finds it's a donation from Sinatra, he alerts the press and the criminal is soon plastered all over the papers as being Chicago's own Robin Hood. So pleased is Sinatra with his publicity that he employs Crosby to run his personal charitable donations. Sinatra gets to know Rush and thinks she's a dan-dan-dandy. Being Robinson's daughter has provided her with an elegant education and Sinatra wonders if he can live up to such a classy dame. Then he's chagrined to learn that for all her uppity airs, she's a thief and is using the charitable foundation to front for a counterfeiting ring run by her and Martin. Sinatra throws Martin out of his group and tells Rush this town isn't big enough for both of them and he's not about to leave, so she'd better. Rush approaches Falk, stating that she is willing to pay him to kill both Sinatra and Martin. Falk would be happy to do that for nothing, and now he has an even better reason. Falk doesn't quite make it and winds up encased in cement. Rush is still smarting at what's happened, so she becomes a reformer and organizes a women's crime-fighting club to put these criminals out of business. This time it works and Sinatra, Martin, and Davis are soon ruined and forced to be hoboes, cadging quarters in the street. In the final sequence, the trio of beggars move up to a limousine and are shocked when the two occupants of the car are Rush and Crosby, who blithely toss the men a few coins, then walk into Rush's Reform headquarters. Some funny lines, a few good songs, and a feeling that the actors were having a wonderful time all help to make this a pleasant way to pass two hours. When Robinson tells the crooks "I never asked my boys to work on holidays, except maybe once. On St. Valentine's Day," he gets a huge laugh from anyone who knows from whence the joke sprung. They were shooting the Robinson funeral scene at a local cemetery on November 22, 1963. There was a gravestone for a man named John Kennedy who died 80 years before, and since the President was a pal of Sinatra's, there was some laughter about the stone. Then, near lunchtime, the word was flashed around the location set that Kennedy had been shot in Dallas. In December, they were still making the movie and had planned a kidnaping sequence. While rehearsing that, Sinatra learned that his son, Frank Jr., had been kidnaped in Nevada. There is no kidnap scene in ROBIN AND THE SEVEN HOODS. Falk was excellent as the crook and showed he had a great capacity for comedy as well as drama, something that had already been glimpsed in POCKETFUL OF MIRACLES. Victor Buono was, as always, a delight to watch and all the supporting crooks had been previously seen in serious versions of the roles they played in this: Jenkins, La Rue, Carricart, et al. Sammy Cahn and Jimmy Van Heusen's score included the Oscar-nominated "My Kind of Town (Chicago Is)" (sung by Sinatra), "Don't Be A Do-Badder" (sung by Crosby), "All For One" (sung by Falk), "Mr. Booze" (sung by Crosby, Martin, Sinatra, Davis), "Style" (sung by Sinatra, Martin, Crosby), "Any Man Who Loves His Mother" (sung by Martin), "Bang Bang" (sung by Davis) "Charlotte Couldn't Charleston," "Give Praise" (sung by Chorus). Richard Bakalyan, who earns a fine living playing crooks or cops (CHINATOWN) is briefly seen and Bernard Fein quit acting to co-create "Hogan's Heroes" for TV and retire a rich man. Hank Henry was a longtime pal of Sinatra's and earned his living as a burlesque comic in Las Vegas when he wasn't making movies. Gordon Douglas was Sinatra's kind of director, a one-take man who was always ready when Sinatra was. That kind of speedy work endeared him to Old Blue Eyes who doesn't like directors that spend forever lining up shots. That's why Douglas directed several Sinatra pictures including TONY ROME, THE DETECTIVE, and LADY IN CEMENT.

p, Frank Sinatra; d, Gordon Douglas; w, David R. Schwartz; ph, William H. Daniels (Panavision, Technicolor); m, Nelson Riddle; ed, Sam O'Steen; md, Riddle; art d, LeRoy Deane; set d, Raphael Bretton; cos, Don Feld; ch, Jack Baker; makeup, Gordon Bau.

Crime/Comedy   **Cas.**   **(PR:A-C MPAA:NR)**

ROBIN HOOD, 1938   (SEE: ADVENTURES OF ROBIN HOOD, THE, 1938)

ROBIN HOOD, 1952   (SEE: STORY OF ROBIN HOOD, THE, 1952)

ROBIN HOOD***   (1973) 83m Disney-BV c

Voices of: Roger Miller (*Allan-A-Dale*), Brian Bedford (*Robin Hood*), Monica Evans (*Maid Marian*), Phil Harris (*Little John*), Andy Devine (*Friar Tuck*), Carole Shelley (*Lady Kluck*), Peter Ustinov (*Prince John*), Terry-Thomas (*Sir Hiss*), Pat Buttram (*Sheriff*), George Lindsay (*Trigger*), Ken Curtis (*Nutsy*).

An enjoyable animated feature from the people at Disney. This time they took the Robin Hood fable and transposed its characters to animals; hence Robin Hood became a fox, Allan-A-Dale a rooster, Friar Tuck a badger, Little John a bear, and the sheriff a wolf. Maid Marian remains a compatible fox for her loving hero. An inventive, well-animated, appropriately cast film.

p&d, Wolfgang Reitherman; w, Larry Clemmons (based on characters and story by Ken Anderson); m, George Bruns; ed, Tom Acosta, Jim Meltor; art d, Don Griffith; m/l, "Whistle Stop," "Oo-de-Lolly," "Not in Nottingham," Roger Miller (sung by Miller), "Love," Floyd Huddleston, George Bruns (sung by Nancy Adams), "The Phoney King of England," Johnny Mercer (sung by Phil Harris); directing animators, Milt Kahl, Frank Thomas, Ollie Johnston, John Lounsberry; character anim, Hal King, Art Stevens, Cliff Norberg, Burny Mattinson, Eric Larson, Don Bluth, Dale Baer, Fred Hellmich.

Animated Feature   **Cas.**   **(PR:AAA MPAA:G)**

ROBIN HOOD OF EL DORADO**½   (1936) 86m MGM bw

Warner Baxter (*Joaquin Murrieta*), Ann Loring (*Juanita de la Cuesta*), Bruce Cabot (*Bill Warren*), Margo (*Rosita Murrieta*), J. Carrol Naish (*Three-Fingered Jack*), Soledad Jimenez (*Madre Murrieta*), Eric Linden (*Johnnie Warren*), Edgar Kennedy (*Sheriff Judd*), Charles Trowbridge (*Ramon de la Cuesta*), Harvey Stephens (*Capt. Osborne*), Ralph Remley (*Judge Perkins*), George Regas (*Tomas*), Francis McDonald (*Pedro, the Spy*), Kay Hughes (*Louise*), Paul Hurst (*Wilson*), Boothe Howard (*Tabbard*), Harry Woods (*Pete*).

Baxter is an honest Mexican farmer who turns into the vicious leader of a band of marauders. His rampage is sparked by the murder of his wife (Margo) after he refuses to leave his land when ordered to do so by four desperados. A bitter portrayal of a Pancho Villa/Zorro type who doesn't have the appeal that the more familiar Robin Hood carries.

p, John W. Considine, Jr.; d, William A. Wellman; w, Wellman, Joseph Calleia, Melvin Levy (based on the novel by Walter Noble Burns); ph, Chester Lyons; m, Herbert Stothart; ed, Robert H. Kern; cos, Dolly Tree.

Action   **(PR:C MPAA:NR)**

ROBIN OF TEXAS***   (1947) 71m REP bw

Gene Autry (*Himself*), Lynne Roberts (*Virginia*), Sterling Holloway (*Droopy*), Adele Mara (*Julie Reeves*), James Cardwell (*Duke Mantel*), John Kellogg (*Nick Castillo*), Ray Walker (*Lacey*), Michael Branden (*Jim Preston*), Paul Bryar (*Ace Foley*), James Flavin (*Capt. Danforth*), Dorothy Vaughan (*Mrs. O'Brien*), Stanley Andrews (*Mr. Hamby*), Alan Bridge (*Sheriff*), Cass County Boys (*Themselves*), Hank Patterson, Edmund Cobb, Lester Dorr, William Norton Bailey, Irene Mack, Opal Taylor, Eve Novak, Norma Brown, Frankie Marvin, Billy Wilkerson, Duke Greene, Ken Terrell, Joe Yrigoyen, Champion Jr. the Horse.

This top-line Autry western has his placid ranch disturbed by the arrival of a gang of bank robbers. He inadvertently gets involved in their activities, but in the finale chases them and their $100,000 purse through the dusty West. A fine combination of genres and Autry's commanding performance make this one special. Includes the tunes "Goin' Back To Texas," "Merry-Go-Round-Up," "You're the Moment of a Lifetime," all sung by Autry with instrumentals by the Cass County Boys. This was to be the last of Gene's Republic pictures after a long and tiring battle with the studio.

p, Sidney Picker; d, Lesley Selander; w, John K. Butler, Earle Snell; ph, William Bradford; ed, Harry Keller; md, Morton Scott; art d, Paul Youngblood; cos, Adele Palmer; m/l, Gene Autry, Carson, J. Robison, Sergio DeKarlo, Kay Charles.

Western   **Cas.**   **(PR:A MPAA:NR)**

ROBIN HOOD OF THE PECOS**   (1941) 59m REP bw

Roy Rogers (*Vance Corgin*), George "Gabby" Hayes ("*Gabby*" *Hornaday*), Marjorie Reynolds [Peg Riley] (*Jeanie Grayson*), Cy Kendall (*Ballard*), Leigh Whipper (*Kezeye*), Sally Payne (*Belle Starr*), Eddie Acuff (*Sam Starr*), Robert Strange (*Cravens*), William Haade (*Capt. Morgan*), Jay Novello (*Stacy*), Roscoe Ates (*Guffy*), Jim Corey, Chick Hannon, Trigger the Horse.

Roles are reversed in this Roy Rogers oater with Roy taking a back seat to Hayes. The latter is a night-rider who bands together his fellow Texans during post-Civil War times. His main objective is to protect the Lone Star State from unscrupulous northerners. Rogers sings and strums to Reynolds between gun fights.

p&d, Joseph Kane; w, Olive Cooper (based on a story by Hal Long); ph, Jack Marta; ed, Charles Craft; md, Cy Feuer; m/l, Peter Tinturin, Eddie Cherkose.

Western   **Cas.**   **(PR:A MPAA:NR)**

ROBIN HOOD OF THE RANGE**   (1943) 57m COL bw

Charles Starrett (*Steve Marlowe*), Arthur Hunnicutt (*Arkansas*), Kay Harris (*Julie Marlowe*), Kenneth MacDonald (*Henry Marlowe*), Douglass Drake (*Ned Harding*), Hal Price (*Sheriff*), Edward Piel, Sr. (*Grady*), Frank LaRue (*Carter*), Bud Osborne (*Thompson*), Stanley Brown (*Santana*), Frank McCarroll, Ray Jones, Johnny Bond, Merrill McCormack, The Jimmy Wakely Trio.

Starrett performs the Robin Hood gig out West as a foster son of the railroad manager who comes to the aid of homesteaders in their battle against the greedy railway company.

p, Jack Fier; d, William Berke; w, Betty Burbridge; ph, Benjamin Kline; ed, Jerome Thoms; art d, Lionel Banks; m/l, Gene Autry, Jimmy Wakely, Dick Heinhart, Johnny Bond.

Western   **(PR:A MPAA:NR)**

ROBINSON CRUSOE   (SEE: ADVENTURES OF ROBINSON CRUSOE, THE, 1952, Mex.)

ROBINSON CRUSOE ON MARS***   (1964) 109m Devonshire-PAR/PAR c

Paul Mantee (*Comdr. Christopher "Kit" Draper*), Vic Lundin (*Friday*), Adam West (*Col. Dan McReady*), Mona the Woolly Monkey.

Loosely based on Daniel Defoe's classic tale, this surprisingly fresh science-fiction tale surpasses its moronic title. Mantee and West (who was soon to become Batman) are astronauts who are nearly smashed to smithereens by a passing meteor. Mantee is able to abandon ship, but West is killed. He lands on the dusty, desolate surface of Mars with Mona, the test monkey. Mantee eventually learns how to breathe their oxygen, eat their food, and drink their water. He befriends Lundin, an escaped slave, and teaches him English. Lundin's wicked captors begin bombing the surface of the red planet, but in the path of impending doom, the trio is rescued by a U.S. spacecraft. Shot in Death Valley (the surface was matted in the lab to appear reddish), this picture's chief attribute is the realistic atmosphere that makes the characters' chances of survival seem entirely hopeless. The 109-minute running time was unmercifully cut by nearly one-half hour for its British release.

p, Aubrey Schenck; d, Byron Haskin; w, Ib Melchior, John C. Higgins (based on the novel *Robinson Crusoe* by Daniel Defoe); ph, Winton C. Hoch (Techniscope, Technicolor); m, Nathan Van Cleave; ed, Terry O. Morse; art d, Hal Pereira, Arthur Lonergan; spec eff, Lawrence W. Butler; makeup, Wally Westmore, Bud Bashaw.

Science-Fiction   **Cas.**   **(PR:A MPAA:NR)**

ROBINSON CRUSOELAND   (SEE: UTOPIA, 1950)

ROBINSON SOLL NICHT STERBEN   (SEE: GIRL AND THE LEGEND, THE, 1969, Ger.)

ROBO DE DIAMANTES   (SEE: RUN LIKE A THIEF, 1968, Span.)

ROBO NO ISHI   (SEE: WAYSIDE PEBBLE, THE, 1960, Jap.)

ROBOT MONSTER zero   (1953) 62m Three Dimensional Pictures bw/3-d (AKA: MONSTERS FROM THE MOON)

George Nader (*Roy*), Claudia Barrett (*Alice*), Selena Royle (*Mother*), Gregory Moffett (*Johnny*), John Mylong (*Professor*), Pamela Paulson (*Carla*), George Barrows (*Ro-Man*), John Brown (*Voice*).

The press release called it brilliant, thrill-packed, overwhelming, vivid, and suspenseful. But ROBOT MONSTER (in 3-D) is one of the most hackneyed, and lowest-budgeted science fiction films ever made. It concerns the attempt by Ro-Man Barrows to obliterate the last six Hu-Mans on Earth. Dressed in a gorilla suit with a diver's helmet, Barrows flails his arms and acts generally scary, while receiving television-transmitted messages from "The Great One." After killing two survivors, Barrows begins to feel human emotions. He finds himself in a dilemma—he knows he must kill but feels that he cannot. Oh, such a confused monster was Ro-Man. However, the whole thing is just a dream—or nightmare—depending on your tastes. Budgeted at only $16,000 (though filmmakers announced the budget at "under $50,000" so people wouldn't dismiss it too quickly), the picture grossed over $1 million. Producer-director Tucker didn't see a cent of the profits, however, and, after becoming despondent over his partners' scheming and terrible reviews, attempted suicide. He recovered and moved up through the motion picture ranks to become a top post-production supervisor. Includes stock footage from ONE MILLION B.C. (1940) and FLIGHT TO MARS (1951), as well as an early score from Oscar-winning composer Bernstein (THOROUGHLY MODERN MILLIE, 1967). Another one of those "so-bad-it's-good" pictures.

p&d, Phil Tucker; w, Wyott Ordung; ph, Jack Greenhalgh (Tru-Stereo); m, Elmer Bernstein; ed, Bruce Schoengarth; spec eff, Jack Rabin, David Commons.

Science-Fiction   Cas.   (PR:A MPAA:NR)

ROBOT VS. THE AZTEC MUMMY, THE zero   (1965, Mex.) 65m Cinematografica Calderon/K. Gordon Murray bw (EL ROBOT HUMANO; LA MOMIA AZTECA CONTRA EL ROBOT HUMANO)

Ramon Gay, Rosita Arenas, Crox Alvarado, Luis Aceves Castaneda, Emma Roldan, Angel d'Esteffani, Arturo Martinez, Jaime Gonzalez Quinones, Julian de Meriche, Alberto Yanez, Enrique Yanez, Guillermo Hernandez, Jesus Velazquez, Alejandro Cruz, Francisco Segura.

Director Portillo continues his insult to the intelligence in this addition to his mummy series. This time the mad scientist creates a pathetic robot with light bulbs for ears to assist him in his quest for a treasure buried deep in a mummy's tomb. Most people would rather watch water freeze than sit through anything with Portillo's name on it. Released in Mexico in 1959.

p, William C. Stell [Guillermo Calderon]; d, Rafael Portillo; w, Stell, Alfredo Salazar (based on a story by Salazar); ph, Enrique Wallace; m, Antonio Diaz Conde; ed, Jorge Bustos, Jose Li-Ho; art d, Javier Torres Torija.

Horror   Cas.   (PR:O MPAA:NR)

ROCCO AND HIS BROTHERS*½**   (1961, Fr./Ital.) 175m Titanus-Les Films Marceau/Astor bw (ROCCO ET SES FRERES; ROCCO E I SUOI FRATELLI)

Alain Delon (*Rocco Parondi*), Renato Salvatori (*Simone Parondi*), Annie Girardot (*Nadia*), Katina Paxinou (*Rosaria Parondi*), Roger Hanin (*Morini*), Paolo Stoppa (*Boxing Impresario*), Suzy Delair (*Luisa*), Claudia Cardinale (*Ginetta*), Spiros Focas (*Vincenzo Parondi*), Max Cartier (*Ciro Parondi*), Rocco Vidolazzi (*Luca Parondi*), Corrado Pani (*Ivo*), Alessandra Panaro (*Ciro's Fiancee*), Claudia Mori, Adriana Asti (*Laundry Workers*), Franca Valeri (*Vedova*), Enzo Fiermonte.

Luchino Visconti's episodic prize-winning study of five brothers and their widowed mother, transplanted from rural Sicily to industrial Milan in northern Italy, is violent, sometimes hard to believe, and makes ambiguous social statements. The characters' relationships are explored over a period of 12 years, concentrating chiefly on Delon and Salvatori as they alternately enjoy and abuse the affections of Girardot, a prostitute who yearns to be free. She loves Delon, but he sacrifices her to the brutal Salvatori, because the latter seems to have greater need of her love. Unable to return Salvatori's affection or to put up with his possessiveness, she returns to her former profession. Enraged, he stabs her to death (the 13 on-screen stabbings in European versions are cut to three for American audiences). ROCCO exists in a variety of running times. The American premiere audience found the 175-minute version overlong and began walking out before the film's final scene ended, but the raped 95-minute version should be avoided.

p, Giuseppe Bordogni; d, Luchino Visconti; w, Visconti, Suso Cecchi d'Amico, Pasquale Festa Campanile, Massimo Franciosa, Enrico Medioli (based on the novel *The Bridge Of Ghisolfa* by Giovanni Testori); ph, Giuseppe Rotunno; m, Nino Rota; ed, Mario Serandrei; art d, Mario Garbuglia; cos, Piero Tosi; makeup, Giuseppe Banchelli.

Drama   (PR:C MPAA:NR)

ROCCO E I SUOI FRATELLI   (SEE: ROCCO AND HIS BROTHERS, 1961, Fr./Ital.)

ROCCO PAPALEO**   (1974, Ital./Fr.) 120m Dean-Rizzoli-Francoriz Paris/Rumson c (PERMETTE? ROCCO PAPALEO; AKA: EXCUSE ME, MY NAME IS ROCCO PAPALEO)

Marcello Mastroianni (*Rocco*), Lauren Hutton (*Jenny*).

Sicilian ex-boxer Mastroianni comes to Chicago to see a bout with some friends, but after some battering in the big city, he becomes a hardened cynic with anarchist leanings. This you-can-take-the-boy-out-of-the-country-but film, nominally set in Chicago, was—oddly—originally scheduled to be shot in New York City. More permissive labor conditions ultimately mandated Europe for the production, which

was released there in 1971. It was top model Hutton's first international starring venture. Vaguely intriguing, but no more.

p, Pio Angeletti, Adriano De Micheli; d, Ettore Scola; w, Ruggero Maccari, Scola; ph, Claudio Cirillo (Eastmancolor); m, Armando Trovaioli; ed, Ruggero Mastroianni; art d, Luciano Ricceri.

Comedy/Drama   (PR:O MPAA:NR)

ROCK-A-BYE BABY**   (1958) 103m PAR c

Jerry Lewis (*Clayton Poole*), Marilyn Maxwell (*Carla Naples*), Connie Stevens (*Sandy Naples*), Salvatore Baccaloni (*Salvatore Naples*), Reginald Gardiner (*Henry Herman*), Hans Conried (*Mr. Wright*), Ida Moore (*Bessie Polk*), Gary Lewis (*Young Clayton*), Judy Franklin (*Young Carla*), Isobel Elsom (*Mrs. Van Cleve*), Alex Geary (*Judge Jenkins*), James Gleason (*Dr. Simkins*), George Sanders (*M.C.*), Snub Pollard, Hank Mann, Chester Conklin, Franklyn Farnum, Danny Lewis.

Lewis stars in this Frank Tashlin directed film as a gawky TV repairman who falls in love with actress Maxwell. She couldn't care less about Lewis, and instead weds a Mexican bullfighter who dies the next day. She is pregnant, however, and due to star in a religious epic entitled "The White Virgin On The Nile." Lewis comes to the rescue by agreeing to watch after her newborn. His hands are full when she unexpectedly delivers triplets. He ends up marrying the actress' sister, Stevens, who gives birth to quintuplets. Lewis got Sammy Cahn and Harry Warren to pen a few tunes for the occasion, including "In the Land of La La La" (sung by Lewis and son Gary Lewis), "Dormi, Dormi, Dormi" (sung by Lewis and Baccaloni), "The White Virgin of the Nile" (sung by Maxwell), "Love is a Lonely Thing," and "Why Can't He Care for Me?"

p, Jerry Lewis; d, Frank Tashlin; w, Tashlin (based on the screenplay "The Miracle of Morgan's Creek" by Preston Sturges); ph, Haskell Boggs (VistaVision, Technicolor); m, Walter Scharf; ed, Alma Macrorie; art d, Hal Pereira, Tambi Larsen; set d, Sam Comer, Robert Benton; cos, Edith Head; ch, Nick Castle; makeup, Wally Westmore.

Comedy   (PR:A MPAA:NR)

ROCK ALL NIGHT**   (1957) 62m SUN/AIP bw

Dick Miller (*Shorty*), Abby Dalton (*Julie*), Robin Morse (*Al*), Richard Cutting (*Steve*), Bruno VeSota (*Charley*), Chris Alcaide (*Angie*), Mel Welles (*Sir Bop*), Barboura Morris (*Syl*), Clegg Hoyt (*Marty*), Russell Johnson (*Jigger*), Jonathan Haze (*Joey*), Richard Karlan (*Jerry*), Jack DeWitt (*Philippe*), Bert Nelson (*Bartender*), Beech Dickerson (*The Kid*), Ed Nelson (*Pete*), The Platters, The Blockbusters.

Spend a wild night at the Cloud Nine, a rockin' rollin' nightspot where all the kids hang out and listen to the Platters. Dick Miller plays Shorty, a hip fellow who stands only 5 foot 1 inch and hates guys taller than himself. Enter a couple of murderers who take refuge in the bar and watch Shorty tell them who is boss. Mediocre fun which Roger Corman cranked out in just five days, on only one set. Most memorable, however, is the ad, "Some gotta dance, some gotta kill!" Singing by The Platters and The Blockbusters opens the film but is unrelated to the story.

p&d, Roger Corman; w, Charles B. Griffith (based on the story by David P. Harmon); ph, Floyd Crosby; ed, Frank Sullivan.

Crime Drama   (PR:A MPAA:NR)

ROCK AROUND THE CLOCK**   (1956) 77m COL bw

Bill Haley and the Comets (*Themselves*), The Platters (*Themselves*), Tony Martinez and His Band (*Themselves*), Frankie Bell and His Bellboys (*Themselves*), Alan Freed (*Himself*), Johnny Johnston (*Steve Hollis*), Alix Talton (*Corinne Talbot*), Lisa Gaye (*Lisa Johns*), John Archer (*Mike Dennis*), Henry Slate (*Corny LaSalle*), Earl Barton (*Jimmy Johns*), Johnny Johnstone (*Manager*).

The rock 'n' roll movie. Producer Sam Katzman and director Fred Sears again pooled their exploitative talents to deliver a film not so much *about* rock'n'roll, but a film that *was* rock 'n' roll. The story is barely evident—legendary rock deejay Alan Freed discovers Bill Haley and the Comets in a mountain village and brings them back to New York, where they quickly become a musical phenomenon. Katzman was correct in assuming that if rock concerts could cause youth riots, so could a movie. In England, soon after a couple of screenings, young rockers were tearing up the seats and dancing up a storm. Of course all their moms and dads were bowled over with shock and banned the film from the theaters. Even now it can still make the feet move to the beat. Haley's tunes include "Razzle Dazzle," "Happy Baby," "See You Later, Alligator," "Rudy's Rock," and the greatest rocker of them all "Rock Around The Clock." And then there's "The Great Pretender," "Only You," (The Platters), "Codfish And Potatoes," "Sad And Lonely," "Cuero," "Mambo Capri" (Tony Martinez), and "Giddy Up, Ding Dong," "We're Gonna Teach You To Rock" (Freddie Bell).

p, Sam Katzman; d, Fred F. Sears; w, Robert E. Kent, James B. Gordon; ph, Benjamin H. Kline; ed, Saul A. Goodkind, Jack W. Ogilvie; md, Fred Karger; art d, Paul Palmentola; ch, Earl Barton.

Musical   Cas.   (PR:A MPAA:NR)

ROCK AROUND THE WORLD*½   (1957, Brit.) 71m Anglo-Amalgamated/AIP bw (GB: THE TOMMY STEELE STORY)

Tommy Steele (*Himself*), Patrick Westwood (*Brushes*), Hilda Fenemore (*Mrs. Steele*), Charles Lamb (*Mr. Steele*), Peter Lewiston (*John Kennedy*), John Boxer (*Paul Lincoln*), Mark Daly (*Junkshop Man*), Lisa Daniely (*Hospital Nurse*), Bryan Coleman (*Hospital Doctor*), Cyril Chamberlain (*Chief Steward*), Bernard Hunter (*Busker, The Guitarist*), Alan Weighell (*Steelmen's Bass*), Dennis Price (*Steelmen's Pianist*), Leo Pollini (*Steelmen's Drummer*), Alan Stuart (*Steelmen's Saxophonist*), Tom Littlewood (*Judo Instructor*), Chris O'Brien's Caribbeans, Tommy Eytle's

Calypso Band, Humphrey Lyttelton's Band, Charles McDevitt's Skiffle Group, Hunter Hancock, Nancy Whiskey.

An unmemorable film biography of unmemorable British rocker Tommy Steele whose meager claim to fame is his hit single (in England) of "Singin' the Blues." Steele was a poor boy from South London whose appealing voice and personality enabled him to break into the entertainment world. The story of his beginnings is faintly interesting but as a post-Elvis, pre-Beatles hysteria picture, there's nothing special about the movie or the music. Steele's performance of the ballad "A Handful of Songs" is his best in the film. Other hits in the movie are "Freight Train" (Paul James, Fred William, performed by Nancy Whiskey and the Charles McDevitt Skiffle Group) "Butterfingers," "Bermondsey Bounce" (Humphrey Lyttelton), "It's Fun Finding Out About London" (Roger Paul), and "Narrative Calypso" (Russell Henderson). Many other musical numbers, most of them written by Steele, Lionel Bart, Michael Pratt.

p, Herbert Smith; d, Gerard Bryant; w, Norman Hudis; ph, Peter Hennessy; ed, Ann Chegwidden; art d, Eric Saw.

Musical/Biography   (PR:A MPAA:NR)

ROCK BABY, ROCK IT zero   (1957) 84m Freebar bw

Johnny Carroll, Johnny Dobbs, Don Coats, Linda Wheeler, Kay Wheeler, Joan Arnold, Cell Block Seven, Bill Brookshire, Five Stars, Gayla Graves, Rosco Gordon, Mike Biggs, Belew Twins, Kay Moore, Preacher Smith's Deacons, Lee Young, Bon Aires, Dave Miller.

A mindless rock 'n' roll crime drama that gives both rock 'n' roll and crime dramas a bad name. Carroll and his pals occupy a building that some bookies want as their own. They try to drive the kids out, but when the young rabble-rousers stage a musical benefit the building is saved. ROCK BABY, ROCK IT has achieved minor cult status, but you'll be better off if you skip it baby, skip it.

p, J. G. Tiger; d, Murray Douglas Sporup; w, Herbert Margolis, William Raynor.

Musical Drama/Crime   (PR:A MPAA:NR)

ROCK ISLAND TRAIL½**   (1950) 90m REP c (GB: TRANSCONTINENT EXPRESS)

Forrest Tucker (Reed Loomis), Adele Mara (Constance Strong), Adrian Booth (Aleeta), Bruce Cabot (Kirby Morrow), Chill Wills (Hogger), Barbara Fuller (Annabelle), Grant Withers (David Strong), Jeff Corey (Abe Lincoln), Roy Barcroft (Barnes), Pierre Watkin (Major), Valentine Perkins (Annette), Jimmy Hunt (Stinky), Olin Howlin (Saloon Keeper), Sam Flint (Mayor), John Holland (Maj. Porter), Kate Drain Lawson (Mrs. McCoy), Dick Elliott (Conductor), Emory Parnell (Sen. Wells), Billy Wilkerson (Lakin).

Tucker is trying to extend his railway line further west from Illinois but runs into Cabot's villainous tactics, which he takes care of with clenched fists. He also runs out of cash, but with some help from Mara, a banker's daughter, Tucker and his men continue to drive spikes. A unique battle between Tucker and Cabot is fought with mops soaked in boiling hot soup. Otherwise average.

p, Paul Malvern; d, Joseph Kane; w, James Edward Grant (based on the novel A Yankee Dared by Frank J. Nevins); ph, Jack Marta (Trucolor); m, R. Dale Butts; ed, Arthur Roberts; art d, Frank Arrigo; m/l, "Rock Island Trail," William Roy, sung by Adele Mara.

Western   (PR:A MPAA:NR)

ROCK 'N' ROLL HIGH SCHOOL**   (1979) 93m New World c

P. J. Soles (Riff Randell), Vincent Van Patten (Tom Roberts), Clint Howard (Eaglebauer), Dey Young (Kate Rambeau), Mary Woronov (Evelyn Togar), Dick Miller (Police Chief Klein), Paul Bartel (Mr. McGree), Alix Elias (Coach Steroid), Don Steele (Screamin' Steve Stevens), Loren Lester (Fritz Hansel), Daniel Davies (Fritz Gretel), Lynn Farrell (Angel Dust), Herbie Braha (Manager), Grady Sutton (School Board President), Chris Somma (Shawn), Marla Rosenfield (Cheryl), Barbara Ann Walters (Cafeteria Lady), Terry Soda (Norma), Joe Van Sickle (Cop), Ann Chatterton, Debbie Evans, Jack Gill, John Hately, Kay Kimler, The Ramones.

Soles is a rock 'n' roll teenager and aspiring songwriter who lives for the rock band The Ramones. The band is coming to play at a local theater and she has to be the first in line. Problem is her high school principal, Woronov, and her henchmen Fritz Hansel (Lester) and Fritz Gretel (Davies) despise rock 'n' roll. Every time Soles tries to play rock on campus, Fritz and Fritz come running. To keep the principal from learning that Soles is ditching school to wait in line for tickets, Soles' best friend, Young, brings in phony notes. First, Soles' mother died, then her father, and then her goldfish, according to the notes. Woronov begins to suspect something and the Fritzes bring in Soles' live goldfish to confirm the principal's suspicions. At the same time, football jock Patten wants to go out with Soles, but he's too much of a nerd for her. Patten goes to Howard, the kid who can get anything for a price. Howard has an office in the boys' room that looks like a sleazy talent agent's place in L.A. He gives Patten lessons on how to make it with Soles, using Young as a model. Howard's scheme is actually to match the jock with Young who is in love with him. Soles buys tickets for the whole school, but the principal takes them away as punishment for ditching. Now it looks as though Soles won't be able to give the song she's written to the Ramones, but luckily she wins tickets from a local radio station. Soles and Young go to the show, Patten arrives, Farrell steals Soles' song, and during the chase Patten falls in love with Young as Soles gets her song to the Ramones. The next day, the students find to their horror that Woronov has organized a record-burning. The Ramones arrive, help take over the school, and Soles and friends blow it up as the Ramones play her song. A wacky film in the spirit of the rock musicals of the 1950s and early 1960s, its humor warps reality with sequences like the mice that explode when exposed to the Ramones music, and Patten's lessons in picking up women. In many ways, we are seeing the twisted memories of high school of the screenwriters and director Arkush along with their

parody of all high school films. nothing is taken seriously and nothing should be—it's only rock 'n' roll. Using the Ramones as the band adds greatly to the quirky quality of this film. They are not good-looking boys and their music is rock 'n' roll at its core (hard and fast). Cheap Trick was the band that was chosen first, but they backed out because they thought the movie would flop. The film wasn't a box-office smash because New World released it as a cult film, showing it only at midnight screenings. The film has built a large cult following, but it's a shame it didn't get wider distribution when released. There would be a lot more Ramones fans if it had. During their big concert scene, the extras, the real-life Ramones fans playing the audience, got so excited that actress Soles was reportedly terrified throughout. Also, the film is rated PG and it's really refreshing to find a teenage film that doesn't base all of its jokes on the female anatomy. Music includes "Did We Meet Somewhere Before?" (Paul McCartney), "Albatross," "Jigsaw Puzzle" (Fleetwood Mac), "School's Out (Alice Cooper), "School Days" (Chuck Berry), "A Dream Goes On Forever" (Todd Rundgren), "High School" (MC5), "Teenage Depression" (Eddie and the Hot Rods), "C'mon Let's Go," "You're The Best" (Paley Brothers), "Alley Cat" (Bent Fabric), "Come Back Jonee" (Devo), "So It Goes" (Nick Lowe), "Spirits Drifting," "Alternative 3," "M386," "Energy Fools the Magician" (Brian Eno), "Rock 'n 'Roll" (Velvet Underground), "Smoking in the Boy's Room" (Brownsville Station), "Blitzkrieg Bop," "Teenage Lobotomy," "Pinhead," "Sheena Is a Punk Rocker," "I Want You," and "Rock 'n 'Roll High School" (The Ramones).

p, Michael Finnell; d, Allan Arkush; w, Richard Whitley, Russ Dvonch, Joseph McBride (based on a story by Arkush, Joe Dante); ph, Dean Cundey (Metrocolor); m, The Ramones; ed, Larry Bock, Gail Werbin; art d, Marie Kordus; set d, Linda Perl; cos, Jack Buehler; ch, Siana Lee Hall.

Comedy   **Cas.**   (PR:C MPAA:PG)

ROCK, PRETTY BABY*   (1956) 89m UNIV bw

Sal Mineo (Angelo Barrato), John Saxon (Jimmy Daley), Luana Patten (Joan Wright), Edward C. Platt (Thomas Daley, Sr.), Fay Wray (Beth Daley), Rod McKuen ("Ox" Bentley), John Wilder ("Fingers" Porter), Alan Reed, Jr. ("Sax" Lewis), Douglas Fowley ("Pop" Wright), Bob Courtney ("Half-Note" Harris), Shelley Fabares (Twinkey Daley), Susan Volkmann (Carol Saunders), Carol Volkmann (Claire Saunders), April Kent (Kay Norton), Sue George (Lori Parker), Walter Reed (Mr. Reid), Glen Kramer (Bruce Carter), Johnny Grant (Himself), George "Foghorn" Winslow (Thomas Daley, Jr.), Geri Wilder (Girl).

A flimsy rock'n'roll picture about aspiring guitarist Saxon who scrapes up enough cash to buy a six-string and join Sal Mineo's band. The combo plays, but their show results in a riot and Saxon has to hock his guitar to pay for the damages. The pseudo-rock rhythms provided by Mancini, McKuen, and Troup are without much spark. The only authentic youngster in the film is Mineo and Fay Wray makes a token appearance as Saxon's mom. Songs include "Rock, Pretty Baby,"and "What's It Gonna Be," "Rockabye Lullaby Blues," "Picnic By the Sea" (Bobby Troup), and Jimmy Daley and His Ding-a-lings provide more music. SUMMER LOVE (1958) was a sequel.

p, Edmond Chevie; d, Richard H. Bartlett; w, Herbert Margolis, William Raynor; ph, George Robinson; m, Henry Mancini; ed, Frederick Y. Smith; md, Joseph Gershenson; art d, Alexander Golitzen, Philip Barber; cos, Rosemary Odell; m/l, Sonny Burke, Bill Carey, Bobby Troup, Rod McKuen, Phil Tuminello.

Musical   (PR:A MPAA:NR)

ROCK RIVER RENEGADES*½   (1942) 56m MON bw

Ray Corrigan, John King, Max Terhune, Christine McIntyre, John Elliott, Weldon Heyburn, Kermit Maynard, Frank Ellis, Carl Mathews, Dick Cramer, Tex Palmer, Hank Bell, Budd Buster, Steve Clark.

Another entry in the RANGE BUSTERS series which has Corrigan, King, and Terhune rounding up a renegade gang and making the once quiet Rock River a pleasant place to live again. (See RANGE BUSTERS series, Index.)

p, George W. Weeks; d, S. Roy Luby; w, John Vlahos, Earle Snell (based on a story by Faith Thomas); ph, Robert Cline; ed, Roy Claire; md, Frank Sanucci.

Western   (PR:A MPAA:NR)

ROCK, ROCK, ROCK!½**   (1956) 85m Vanguard/Distributor Corp. of America bw

Tuesday Weld (Dori), Jacqueline Kerr (Gloria), Ivy Schulman (Baby), Fran Manfred (Arabella), Jack Collins (Father), Carol Moss (Mother), Eleanor Swayne (Miss Silky), Lester Mack (Mr. Bimble), Bert Conway (Mr. Barker), David Winters (Melville), Alan Freed, Teddy Randazzo, Chuck Berry, The Moonglows, Frankie Lymon and The Teenagers, The Flamingos, Jimmy Cavallo House Rockers, Johnny Burnette Trio, Cirino and The Bowties, The Coney Island Kids, LaVern Baker.

The film debut of Tuesday Weld has the barely pubescent teenie-bopper trying to raise enough money to buy a strapless gown for the prom after her father has closed her charge account. The story is weak from start to finish, but the music is a triumph. Frankie Lymon's Teenagers doing "I'm Not a Juvenile Delinquent" is worth the price of 10 admissions. Chuck Berry is almost as impressive belting out "You Can't Catch Me." Another highlight is LaVern Baker's rendition of "Tra La La." Connie Francis serves well as the singing voice behind young Weld.

p, Milton Subotsky, Max J. Rosenberg; d, Will Price; w, Subotsky (based on a story by Subotsky, Phyllis Coe); ph, Morris Hartzband; ed, Blandine Hafela; md, Subotsky; m/l, Subotsky, Glen Moore, Al Weisman, Ben Weisman, Aaron Schroeder, Buddy Dufault, George Goldner, Johnny Parker, Al Sears, Charles F. Calhoun, Freddie Mitchell, Leroy Kirkland, Chuck Berry.

Musical   **Cas.**   (PR:A MPAA:NR)

ROCK YOU SINNERS*   (1957, Brit.) 59m Small bw

Philip Gilbert (Johnny), Adrienne Scott (Carol), Colin Croft (Pete), Jackie Collins (Jackie), Michael Duffield (Selway), Beckett Bould (McIver), Tony Hall, Dickie Bennett, Joan Small, Diana Chesney, Martin Lyder, Red Montgomery, Tony Crombie and His Rockets, Rory Blackwell and The Blackjacks, Don Sollash and His Rockin' Horses, Art Baxter and His Rockin' Sinners, George "Calypso" Browne, Curly Pat Barry.

A lame-brained story about a super-devoted disc jockey, Gilbert, who broadcasts a rock 'n' roll show that catapults him to stardom. He becomes so wrapped up in his work that his girl friend leaves him. When his show is turned into a television series, both his career and his love life are a smashing success. The songs are bad and the acting is worse.

p, Jeffrey Kruger, B.C. Fancey; d, Denis Kavanaugh; w, Beatrice Scott; ph, Hal Morey; m, Kruger.

Musical   **Cas.**   **(PR:A   MPAA:NR)**

ROCKABILLY BABY**   (1957) 81m FOX bw

Virginia Field (Eleanor Carter), Douglas Kennedy (Tom Griffith), Les Brown (Himself), Irene Ryan (Eunice), Ellen Corby (Mrs. Wellington), Lewis Martin (Mr. Hoffman), Norman Leavitt (Mr. Rogers), Gene Roth (Mr. Johnson), June Jocelyn (Mrs. Rogers), Mary Benoit (Mrs. Hoffman), Hazel Shermet (Mrs. Hill), Renny McEvoy (Charles Leonard), Tony Marshall (Chuck Hoffman), James Goodwin (Tex), Ken Miller (Ray Hill), Jimmy Murphy (Bill Haney), Barry Truex (Pete Rudd), Sandy Wirth (Jackie), Cindy Robbins (Nancy, Vougette No. 1), Susan Easter (Vougette No. 2), Barbara Gayle (Vougette No. 3), Susan Volkmann (Vougette No. 4), Caryl Volkmann (Vougette No. 5), Judy Busch (Cathy Carter), Marlene Willis (Linda), Gary Vinson (Jimmy Carter), Phil Tead (Coach Stone), Watson Downs (Butler), Frank Marlowe (Drunk), Frank Sully (Bum), Ronald Foster (Carnival Barker), Fred Darian (Singer).

Field stars as a former fan dancer who settles down in a small town with her two teenage children. She becomes a pillar of the community and falls for the school principal, but soon her past is dredged up. She's gained too much respect, however, for it to count against her. Includes the songs, "We're On Our Way," "Why Can't I?" "Is It Love?" "I'd Rather Be," and "My Calypso Baby" (Paul Dunlap), "Teenage Cutie" (Dick Kallman, sung by Luis Amando).

p&d, William F. Claxton; w, Will George, William Driskill; ph, Walter Strenge (Regalscope); m, Paul Dunlap; ed, Robert Pritch, md, Dunlap; prod d, Ernst Fegte.

Musical/Drama   **(PR:A   MPAA:NR)**

ROCKABYE**   (1932) 71m RKO bw

Constance Bennett (Judy Carroll), Joel McCrea (Jacob "Jake" Van Riker Pell), Paul Lukas (Anthony De Sola), Walter Pidgeon (Commissioner Al Howard), Jobyna Howland (Snooks Carroll), Virginia Hammond (Mrs. Van Riker Pell), Walter Catlett (Jimmy Dunn), June Filmer (Lilybet), J. M. Kerrigan (Dugan), Clara Blandick (Brida), Edgar Kennedy (Driver), Sterling Holloway (Speakeasy Customer), Edwin Stanley (Defense Attorney), Richard Carle (Doc), Charles Middleton (District Attorney), Lita Chevret (Party Guest).

Bennett plays a Broadway performer whose career topples when news leaks out that she is the mistress of a corrupt politician. She loses her child, but then regains her stature on the stage. She falls in love with her playwright, McCrea, though this romance is cut short when his wife gives birth. RKO exec David O. Selznick took the heat for this box-office flop. After the finished film was shown the response was so venomous that director George Fitzmaurice was replaced, as was lead Phillips Holmes. George Cukor and McCrea were then called in for two weeks of retakes. It didn't help much.

p, David O. Selznick; d, George Cukor; w, Jane Murfin, Kubec Glasmon (based on the play by Lucia Bronder); ph, Charles Rosher; ed, George Hively; md, Max Steiner; art d, Carroll Clark; m/l, "Till the Real Thing Comes Along" (Edward Eliscu, Harry Akst), "Sleep, My Sweet" (Jeanne Borlini, Nacio Herb Brown).

Drama   **(PR:A   MPAA:NR)**

ROCKERS**   (1980) 100m Rockers/New Yorker c

Leroy Wallace (Horsemouth), Richard Hall (Dirty Harry), Monica Craig (Madgie), Marjorie Norman (Sunshine), Jacob Miller (Jakes), Gregory Isaacs (Jah Tooth), Winston Rodney (Burning Spear), Frank Dowding (Kiddus I), Robert Shakespeare (Robbie), Manley Buchanan (Big Youth), Lester Bullocks (Dillinger), The Mighty Diamonds (Themselves), Ashley Harris (Higher), Leroy Smart (Himself), Peter Honiball (Honeyball), L. Lindo (Jack Ruby), Trevor Douglas (Leggo Beast), Herman Davis (Bongo Herman), Raymond Hall (Jeep Man), Junior Wilby (Natty Majesty), Errol Brown (Natty Garfield), Robert Van Campbell (Jah Wise), Berris Simpson (Prince Hammer), Theophilus Beckford (Easy Snapping), Phylip Richards (John Dread), Peter Tosh (Himself), Bynn Wailer (Bunny).

Reggae music galore in this comedy-drama about a rasta drummer who puts down his sticks and becomes a record distributor. This endeavor is soon soured by the intrusion of criminals who want a cut. Wallace and the gang resort to stealing back their profits from the crooks and distributing the money among the island people. Marijuana and island funk abound as this entertaining picture features everyone who's anyone (except Bob Marley) in the reggae music scene. Seeing ROCKERS is like spending $5 to go to Jamaica without the sun.

p, Patrick Hulsey; d&w, Theodoros Bafaloukos; ph, Peter Sova; ed, Susan Steinberg; art d, Lilly Kilvert; cos, Eugenie Bafaloukos.

Musical/Crime/Comedy   **(PR:O   MPAA:NR)**

ROCKET ATTACK, U.S.A. zero   (1961) 71m Exploit bw

John McKay (John Manston), Monica Davis (Tannah), Daniel Kern, Edward Czerniuk, Philip St. George.

Less-than-classic garbage about American spies in Moscow who push the Russians just one step too far. The commies retaliate by attacking Manhattan with nuclear bombs and blowing it into the heavens. Inept photography filled with stock footage teams with inane dialog, substandard effects, and a terrible cast.

p&d, Barry Mahon; ph, Mike Tabb; ed, Alan Smiler.

Science Fiction   **(PR:A   MPAA:NR)**

ROCKET FROM CALABUCH, THE   (SEE: CALABUCH, 1956, Span./Ital.)

ROCKET MAN, THE*½   (1954) 79m Panoramic/FOX c

Charles Coburn (Mayor Ed Johnson), Spring Byington (Justice Ameilia Brown), George Winslow (Timmy), Anne Francis (June Brown), John Agar (Tom Baxter), Emory Parnell (Big Bill Watkins), Stanley Clements (Bob), Beverly Garland (Ludine), June Clayworth (Miss Snedley), Don Haggerty (Officer O'Brien), Lawrence Ryle.

George "Foghorn" Winslow stars as a young orphan who is given a magic space ray gun which makes people tell the truth. He uses it to stop Parnell from taking over the orphanage, and to help out mayor Coburn in his political career. Although the script was co-penned by Lenny Bruce, it is really a children's or "family" movie, not written for most Bruce fans!

p, Leonard Goldstein; d, Oscar Rudolph; w, Lenny Bruce, Jack Henley (based on a story by George W. George, George F. Slavin); ph, John Seitz; m, Lionel Newman; ed, Paul Weatherwax.

Science Fiction   **(PR:A   MPAA:NR)**

ROCKETSHIP X-M**   (1950) 77m Lippert bw (AKA: EXPEDITION MOON)

Lloyd Bridges (Floyd Oldham), Osa Massen (Lisa Van Horn), John Emery (Karl Eckstrom), Noah Beery, Jr. (William Corrigan), Hugh O'Brian (Harry Chamberlin), Morris Ankrum (Dr. Fleming), Patrick Ahern, John Dutra, Katherine Marlowe (Reporters), Sherry Moreland (Martian Girl), Judd Holdren.

Bridges, Massen, Emery, Beery, and O'Brian are the crew of a spaceship bound for the moon. A meteor storm knocks them far off course and they end up landing on Mars. Exploring the planet, they find the ruins of a great civilization that was destroyed by nuclear war. Soon blind, mutated survivors of this civilization appear and attack our intrepid quintet of explorers and by the time they get back to their ship they've been reduced to a trio. The rocketship blasts off and heads back to Earth, but—not being intended for such a long journey—it runs out of fuel short of home and, after radioing a message back to base about the dangers of nuclear war, it crashes to Earth, killing the rest of the crew. One of the first of the post-WW II generation of American science-fiction films, this production was made to directly compete with George Pal's DESTINATION MOON (also 1950). Director Neumann heard about Pal's work-in-progress and approached Robert Lippert with the idea of shooting a low-budget space movie to beat Pal into the theaters. To save the cost of building a moon set, they placed the action on Mars and shot on location at Red Rock Canyon, tinting the scenes red. The film did beat Pal's detailed, expensive, and rather dull film into the theaters by several months and did excellent business. Today the film in many ways seems better than DESTINATION MOON, less pretentious and a lot more exciting. In 1978, Wade Williams shot some new special effects sequences and long shots of actors dressed in the original costumes and added them to a restored print of the film that can be seen on videocassette.

p,d&w, Kurt Neumann; ph, Karl Struss; m, Ferde Grofe; ed, Harry Gerstad; art d, Theobold Holsopple; spec eff, Jack Rabin, Irving A. Block.

Science Fiction   **Cas.**   **(PR:A   MPAA:NR)**

ROCKET TO NOWHERE½**   (1962, Czech.) 73m Studio Barrandov bw (KLAUN FERDINAND A RAKETA; AKA: CLOWN FERDINAND AND THE ROCKET

Jiri Vrstala, Eva Hrabetova, Hanus Bor, Vladimir Horka, Vaclav Stekl, Jaroslav Valek, Ludek Kindermann, Jan Kurcik, Karel Smrz.

A fine children's science-fiction tale about a robot-controlled spaceship that saves a group of kids and a clown from their city, which lies in ruin. A well-conceived and dreamy atmosphere contributes to this film's magical appeal.

d, Jindrich Polak; w, Polak, Ota Hofman; ph, Jan Kallis; spec eff, Kallis, Milan Nejedly, Jiri Hlupy, Pavel Necesal, Karel Cisarovsky, Frantisek Zerslicka.

Children's Film/Science-Fiction   **(PR:AAA   MPAA:NR)**

ROCKET TO THE MOON   (SEE: CAT WOMEN OF THE MOON, 1954)

ROCKETS GALORE   (SEE: MAD LITTLE ISLAND, 1958, Brit.)

ROCKETS IN THE DUNES*½   (1960, Brit.) 65m Anvil/Children's Film Foundation bw

Gena Yates (Sandra), Heather Lyons (Celia), Gordon Adam (Bruce), James Luck (Ned), Peter Wood (Andy), Christopher Witty (Joey), Fiona Davie (Betty), Hilary Mason (Mrs. Allen), John Lawrence (Mr. Allen).

A harmless kiddie film about a group of youngsters who are upset with the army's plans to hold military maneuvers on a nearby beach. The kids' sneaky tactics and undying persistence eventually pay off and the beach is left to the children.

p, Ralph May; d, William C. Hammond; w, Gerard Bryant (based on the novel by Louis Lamplugh).

Children's Film   **(PR:AA   MPAA:NR)**

ROCKIN' IN THE ROCKIES* (1945) 63m COL bw (GB: PARTNERS IN FORTUNE)

Moe Howard, Jerry "Curly" Howard, Larry Fine *(The Three Stooges)*, Mary Beth Hughes *(June McGuire)*, Jay Kirby *(Rusty)*, Gladys Blake *(Betty)*, Tim Ryan *(Tom Trove)*, Jack Clifford *(Sheriff Zeke)*, Forrest Taylor *(Sam Clemens)*, Vernon Dent *(Stanton)*, The Hoosier Hotshots, The Cappy Barra Boys, Spade Cooley.

Described as a "western action musical," ROCKIN' IN THE ROCKIES has no action and bears little resemblance to a western or a musical. The Stooges go through the picture trying to land work in a Broadway show and en route get mixed up in wild west rustling and prospecting.

p, Colbert Clark; d, Vernon Keays; w, J. Benton Cheney, John Gray (based on a story by Louise Rousseau, Gail Davenport).

Comedy **(PR:A MPAA:NR)**

ROCKING HORSE WINNER, THE*½** (1950, Brit.) 91m Rank-Two Cities/GFD bw

Valerie Hobson *(Hester Grahame)*, John Howard Davies *(Paul Grahame)*, Ronald Squire *(Oscar Cresswell)*, John Mills *(Bassett)*, Hugh Sinclair *(Richard Grahame)*, Charles Goldner *(Mr. Tsaldouris)*, Susan Richards *(Nannie)*, Cyril Smith *(The Bailiff)*, Antony Holles *("Bowler Hat")*, Melanie McKenzie *(Matilda)*, Caroline Steer *(Joan)*.

This faithful adaptation of the Lawrence story is both moving and disturbing as Davies, who was a superb "Oliver Twist" under David Lean's direction, turns in a stunning performance as a boy in the grip of a deadly fantasy. Davies is a little boy whose greedy mother Hobson upsets his tender sensibilities; she is always complaining about her straitened finances, although the family is fairly well-to-do. Davies receives a new and strange-looking hobby horse for Christmas and handyman Mills teaches him how to ride like a jockey. The boy discovers that when he rides the wooden horse at a furious pace he can somehow pick the winners of real horse races that have yet to be run. Bets are placed and the family starts to enjoy enormous riches, but Hobson, a profligate spender, squanders the money faster than bets can be placed, causing Davies to ride faster and faster, driving himself into a frenetic and traumatic state which produces more and more money. Still he cannot appease his mother's insatiable appetite for money and rides the horse one more time, driving himself into a delirious state to obtain the name of just one more winner, the house itself crying out to him: "We need more money!" He picks a winner but dies in the effort. After Davies is buried, handyman Mills, the only real friend the child ever had, takes the money won on the derby and gives it to Hobson who draws back from it, telling him to take the "blood money" away and burn it, her lesson in greed learned too late to save her selfless child. This offbeat story isn't for everyone, certainly not for children, but it conveys a powerful message in a beautifully crafted film with excellent performances by Mills, Hobson, and Squire supporting the brilliant Davies.

p, John Mills; d&w, Anthony Pelissier (based on the story by D.H. Lawrence); ph, Desmond Dickinson; m, William Alwyn; ed, John Seabourne; md, Muir Mathieson; art d, Carmen Dillon.

Drama **Cas.** **(PR:C-O MPAA:NR)**

ROCKS OF VALPRE, THE (SEE: HIGH TREASON, 1937, Brit.)

ROCKY* (1948) 76m MON bw

Roddy McDowall, Edgar Barrier, Nita Hunter, Gale Sherwood, Jonathan Hale, William Ruhl, Claire Whitney, Irving Bacon, John Alvin.

An over-emotional tale about a teenage boy, McDowall, who wanders through the West with his canine companion. ROCKY was only one of many pictures that had McDowall paired with an animal. He had a small role in SCRUFFY (1938) and a lead in LASSIE COME HOME (1943), both pictures with loveable dogs. He also appeared in three horse movies, MY FRIEND FLICKA (1943), THUNDERHEAD—SON OF FLICKA (1945), BLACK MIDNIGHT (1949); two cat films, THAT DARN CAT (1965) and THE CAT FROM OUTER SPACE (1978); and a shark movie, KILLER SHARK (1950). These roles so influenced his career that McDowall went on to play an ape in all five "Planet of the Apes" pictures and on the subsequent television series.

p, Lindsley Parsons; d, Wesley Barry; w, Jack DeWitt (based on a story by George W. Sayre); ph, William Sickner; ed, Robert Warwick, Jr.; md, Edward J. Kay; art d, Dave Milton

Drama **(PR:A MPAA:NR)**

ROCKY****** (1976) 119m UA c

Sylvester Stallone *(Rocky Balboa)*, Talia Shire *(Adrian)*, Burt Young *(Paulie)*, Carl Weathers *(Apollo Creed)*, Burgess Meredith *(Mickey)*, Thayer David *(Miles Jergens)*, Joe Spinell *(Tom Gazzo)*, Jimmy Gambina *(Mike)*, Bill Baldwin *(Fight Announcer)*, Al Silvani *(Cut Man)*, George Memmoli *(Ice Rink Attendant)*, Jodi Letizia *(Marie)*, Diana Lewis, George O'Hanlon *(TV Commentators)*, Larry Carroll *(TV Interviewer)*, Stan Shaw *(Dipper)*, Don Sherman *(Bartender)*, Billy Sands *(Club Fight Announcer)*, Pedro Lovell *(Spider Ricco)*, DeForest Covan *(Apollo's Corner)*, Simmy Bow *(Club Cornerman)*, Tony Burton *(Apollo's Trainer)*, Hank Rolike *(Apollo Cornerman)*, Shirley O'Hara *(Jergens' Secretary)*, Kathleen Parker *(Paulie's Date)*, Frank Stallone *(Timekeeper)*, Lloyd Kaufman *(Drunk)*, Jane Marla Robbins *(Gloria, Pet Shop Owner)*, Jack Hollander *(Fats)*, Joe Sorbello *(Buddy, Bodyguard)*, Christopher Avildsen *(Chiptooth)*, Frankie Van *(Club Fight Referee)*, Lou Fillipo *(Championship Fight Announcer)*, Frank Stallone, Jr., Robert L. Tangrea, Peter Glassberg, William E. Ring, Joseph C. Giambelluca *(Street Corner Singers)*, Butkus Stallone *(Butkus the Dog)*, Joe Frazier *(Paris Eagle)*.

The story of ROCKY closely parallels the story of the man who wrote and starred in it. Stallone was a bit player with just a few credits as an actor and one featured role in THE LORDS OF FLATBUSH. He took the money he'd earned in that film, packed up wife, child, and dog (seen in the movie as his dog) and moved west where he tried his fingers at screenwriting with no success for nearly two years. While living in a small West Hollywood apartment, he pounded out script after script to the dismay of the neighbors as they had to listen to the incessant clacking. While watching a TV bout between Muhammad Ali and underdog Chuck Wepner, Stallone and everyone else was surprised to see the New Jersey club fighter go all the way and lose on a decision. He was an inspiration to anyone who had ever felt like a loser, the kind of guy Terry Malloy might have been if he hadn't got mixed up in labor problems in ON THE WATERFRONT. Wepner "could have been a contender" and he proved it with his courageous match against Ali, who was at the top of his form. Stallone sat down and banged out the screenplay for ROCKY in what was reputed to be only three days. It was shown to Gene Kirkwood, who brought it to Winkler and Chartoff. They agreed to pay the near-starving Stallone $75,000 for it and make a small movie (under a million) with a star. Stallone knew instinctively that this was his chance to get out of being just another screenwriter and refused to sell the picture at any price. The offers went higher, until they were over a quarter of a million dollars! Stallone could barely afford to take his family to MacDonald's, but remained steadfast in his insistence that he play the lead. Chartoff and Winkler saw how passionate Stallone was and went to the bosses at UA with their recommendation that he star. The deal was set and the movie was made for less than a million. To date it has grossed more than 60 times the cost and each TV viewing adds to that. Stallone plays a bum, a club fighter on his way to Palookaville. He lives in a cramped Philadelphia apartment surrounded by relics of a career that never got off the canvas. He earns his living collecting debts for loan shark Spinell, but he doesn't have the viciousness to beat up the deadbeats, something that rankles Spinell. He boxes every once in a while to keep his skills sharp but his time has obviously come and gone. His ex-trainer, Meredith, needles Stallone for being lazy. He might have risen to the top if he was willing to work. Stallone goes to a local pet shop where Shire works. She is shy, almost retarded, a spinster with no ability to talk to men. Stallone finds her interesting and makes friends with her. Her brother, Young, is an employee in a local meat-packing firm and thrilled that someone has taken an interest in his sister. They share a Thanksgiving dinner and Stallone works up enough courage to ask Shire for a date. He takes her to the local ice rink, which is about to close, and gives the attendant, Memmoli, $10 to allow them to use the ice for 10 minutes. She puts on skates and he walks next to her as they talk and break down the barriers of a first date. Later, he takes her to his ratty flat and she admits that she's never been to a man's apartment. Stallone is tender, never pushes the situation, and they become lovers. Meanwhile, Weathers, an Ali-type given to flamboyance, is the heavyweight champion. He has a thought. Why not give some poor unknown the chance to fight for the title? What could be a better public relations ploy? He'll carry the bum for a few rounds, flick his lightning punches at his opponent for the crowd's laughter, then put the guy out of his misery before the 11 o'clock News. It's the 1976 Bi-Centennial and what typifies the American Dream more than giving some guy the opportunity to be Cinderella in Everlast trunks? Weathers looks through the local Philadelphia boxing book, sees Stallone and says, "That's the man!" Fight promoter David (who was so good in Avildsen's triumph SAVE THE TIGER) sets the machinery in gear. Stallone contacts Meredith and begins training in earnest. It is grueling, painful, and arduous. Stallone runs, spars, punches hanging meat in Young's packing plant, runs some more, and gets better and better. Soon enough, he's no longer huffing, and when he is able to run up a flight of stairs on his dawn run, the moment is thrilling. (Although if one watches it without Conti's stirring music underscoring the scene, it's just a guy running.) He reaches the top of the long staircase to the Museum of Art and raises his arms in victory. At that moment, after having seen his dedication, do we think that there just might be a chance he could win? The fight begins. Local boy Stallone has his coterie of admirers and acknowledges his mild applause. Weathers, in an Uncle Sam outfit, enters to a fanfare and huge cheers. The fight begins and Stallone looks bad, slow, and unable to keep up with the classy Weathers. Stallone is a southpaw and that spells trouble for anyone not accustomed to fighting someone with a right-hand lead. After fooling around with Stallone, Weathers has his bell rung when hit by a thunderous left. The fight waxes and wanes for round after round. Stallone looks like he's been beaten up by 12 people and Weathers can barely stand. Wham! Pow! Crunch! The blows rain on both men and it looks like they will both collapse, but they slam each other with everything they have. Meanwhile, Shire could not at first bring herself to come to the arena but she gets there in the middle of the fight. In a scene that recalls many other fight movies, Stallone draws a second wind at seeing her. The fight ends with both men barely standing and Weather's ribs cracked. The decision comes down from the judges and the ref and it's a split, with two men voting for the champ and one for Stallone. Weathers says he won't give Stallone a rematch and Stallone says he doesn't want one. All he wanted to prove was that he could go the distance. The bloody Stallone grabs Shire and lumps appear in everyone's throat as the picture ends in a freeze-frame of his face. ROCKY was a stunning picture that combined sentiment with action and won the Best Movie Oscar as well as the Best Director Award for Avildsen. Stallone, Shire, Young, and Meredith took nominations for their acting, Stallone's screenplay was nominated, and so was the song "Gonna Fly Now." Halsey and Conrad justly won Oscars for their editing, but this was the year for NETWORK and ALL THE PRESIDENT'S MEN, two prestigious pictures that copped the other Oscars. It's a little bit of MARTY, THE SECRET LIFE OF WALTER MITTY, BODY AND SOUL, CHAMPION, and GOLDEN BOY, but the fact that it's a derivative story doesn't detract from the impact. Whether Stallone realized it or not, he had stumbled on the essential formula for drama (that also works in comedy) stated by William Faulkner when he wrote, and we must paraphrase here, "An appealing protagonist. . .struggles against overwhelming odds. . .in search of a worthwhile goal." There's no question that we have to find Stallone appealing. He's sweet, simple, and good-hearted. The odds are definitely stacked against him from the outset and his goal is not a selfish one. He doesn't much care about becoming the champion. All he wants is self-respect. It adds up to a movie that made nothing but money for the producers and catapulted a near-unknown to superstar status. Even though Avildsen did a superb job, he was bypassed for the directorial assignments in the sequels, as Stallone felt that nobody knew the character better than he did. In small roles, comedians Don Sherman and Simmy Bow stand out. Be careful with little children as the boxing violence is very graphic.

p, Irwin Winkler, Robert Chartoff; d, John G. Avildsen; w, Sylvester Stallone; ph, James Crabe (Technicolor); m, Bill Conti; ed, Richard Halsey, Scott Conrad; prod d, Bill Cassidy; art d, James H. Spencer; set d, Raymond Molyneaux; cos, Robert Cambel, Joanne Hutchinson; spec eff, Garrett Brown; m/l, "Rocky's Theme (Gonna Fly Now)," Conti, Carol Connors, Ayn Robbins, "Take Me Back," Frank Stallone, Jr. (performed by Valentine); makeup, Mike Westmore; stunts, Jim Nickerson; ch, Sylvester Stalone; technical adviser, Jimmy Gambina.

Sports Drama   Cas.   (PR:A-C MPAA:PG)

ROCKY II***½   (1979) 119m UA c

Sylvester Stallone (*Rocky Balboa*), Talia Shire (*Adrian*), Burt Young (*Paulie*), Carl Weathers (*Apollo Creed*), Burgess Meredith (*Mickey*), Tony Burton (*Apollo's Trainer*), Joe Spinell (*Gazzo*), Leonard Gaines (*Agent*), Sylvia Meals (*Mary Anne Creed*), Frank McRae (*Meat Foreman*), Al Silvani (*Cutman*), John Pleshette (*Director*), Stu Nahan (*Announcer*), Bill Baldwin (*Commentator*), Jerry Ziesmer (*Salesman*), Paul J. Micale (*Father Carmine*), Earl Montgomery, Herb Nanas, Stuart Robinson, Frank Stallone, Charles Coles, Doug Flor, Robert Kondyra, James Zazzarino, Eddie Lopez, Taurean Blacque, James Casino, Samuel Davis, Ruth Ann Flynn, Linda Grey.

After the success of ROCKY, Stallone took three years off to make F.I.S.T (directed by Norman Jewison) and PARADISE ALLEY, which he directed, wrote, and starred in. Neither was a success and Stallone knew what the public wanted, so he wrote, directed, choreographed, and again starred in this sequel. (All of his ROCKY films have been hits, as have been his "Rambo" movies. Perhaps he should limit himself to movies that begin with "R"—although that didn't mean much when he co-starred with Dolly Parton in the horrific RHINESTONE COW-BOY.) This begins with several minutes out of the original closing fight, so the audience is on the edge of their seats immediately. Then Stallone goes to the hospital where he hears that Weathers thought he did a hell of a job. It takes a long time for him to heal. He marries Shire, buys a sports car, and is a star in the old neighborhood. The medical men tell him to lay off boxing forever, as Weathers had hurt his eye and he could be permanently blind if he fights again. Stallone tries to get a job, is besieged by sycophants, ad men wanting him to endorse their products, etc. Since he is unable to hold any other kind of job, Stallone decides to make some TV commercials, but is soon disillusioned by the inanity and stupidity of the people involved and walks off the set, feeling that the copy he's been asked to read is insulting. With no money coming in and a wife to support, Stallone is in financial trouble. He sells his beloved car to his brother-in-law, Young, and seeks work. Meanwhile, Weathers has been twitted for allowing such a bum to go the distance with him, so he agrees to a rematch to prove to the world that he still has the talent and that Stallone's showing was a fluke. Stallone thinks a lot about the offer and then, against Shire's wishes, decides to fight one more time. She's now pregnant and he is a man who needs money. He calls upon Meredith again to help him get into condition. Shire is livid and won't talk to him while Meredith sleeks the fat off and gets him ready. Stallone can't take Shire's shunning and he loses interest in the training. Shire is still employed in the pet shop, and when she collapses from overwork and must go to the hospital, he is crestfallen. She gives birth to a son, a perfectly-formed miniature of Stallone, but she doesn't awaken from her unconsciousness. Stallone stops his workouts and remains at her side until she finally opens her eyes. He is so thrilled to have his beloved wife back that he swears he'll call off the fight if she wants him to. She and their child are the most important people in his life and he won't do anything that she doesn't want. Shire changes her mind and gives Stallone the okay to fight. And suddenly the movie comes to life, as though it had been vamping until ready. Stallone goes back to training with a vengeance and the rematch takes place. If possible, it's even bloodier and more violent than the first fight. The battle ends with Stallone holding the championship belt aloft and shouting "I did it!" and he must have been the only person surprised at the outcome, as it was tipped off from the start. To have had the character lose twice in a row would have put an effective end to the series, so it was only natural that he win, thereby leaving room for yet another sequel. Some repeaters from the first film, plus several new faces, including Stallone's manager (at the time), Herb Nanas, in a small role. Conti again did the music and Stallone's brother, Frank, wrote two less-than-memorable songs. Not as good as the original but pleasing nonetheless and the recipient of almost $50 million at the wickets. Not for the squeamish.

p, Irwin Winkler, Robert Chartoff; d&w, Sylvester Stallone; ph, Bill Butler (Panavision, Technicolor); m, Bill Conti; ed, Danford B. Greene, Stanford C. Allen, Janice Hampton, James Symons; art d, Richard Berger; set d, Ed Baer; cos, Thomas Bronson, Sandra Berke; m/l, "Two Kinds of Love," "Street Seat," Frank Stallone; makeup, Michael Westmore; ch, Sylvester Stallone; technical adviser, Al Silvani.

Sports Drama   Cas.   (PR:A-C MPAA:PG)

ROCKY III***   (1982) 99m MGM-UA c

Sylvester Stallone (*Rocky Balboa*), Carl Weathers (*Apollo Creed*), Mr. T. (*Clubber Lang*), Talia Shire (*Adrian Balboa*), Burt Young (*Paulie*), Burgess Meredith (*Mickey*), Ian Fried (*Rocky, Jr.*), Hulk Hogan (*Thunderlips*), Al Silvani (*Al*), Wally Taylor (*Clubber's Manager*), Tony Burton (*Duke*), Jim Hill, Don Sherman, Leslie Morris, Dennis James, Jim Healy, Ray Gideon, Leroy Neiman, Frank Stallone, Russell Forte, Stu Nahan, Bill Baldwin, Marty Denkin, John David Morris, Mario Machado, Lou Filippo, Jeff Temkin, Bill Medley, Jeff Bannister, Tony Hernandez, Fred Roggin, Chad Cooperman.

Herb Nanas, seen briefly in a bit role in ROCKY II, suddenly sprang to the role of

executive producer in this, the third of the series that threatens to go on until the boxer is in his eighties and still winning bouts in a special division for seniors. Either that, or the ultimate fight when Rocky meets Rambo for Championship of the Universe. With two hits behind him, Stallone had to come up with a twist to bring in the customers. It's three years after Stallone took the crown from Weathers. He's beaten all comers, 10 of them, and is getting a bit complacent. He's been lionized by the world, is happily married to Shire, and his son, Fried, is a healthy youngster. All's right in Rocky's world. Then, like the new shooter in town looking to knock off the veteran gunslinger, along comes Mr. T., a vicious boxer with blood in his eyes. Mr. T. is the perfect villain, a loudmouth with the fists to back up his claims. Meredith takes a look at the challenger and determines that Stallone would be better off to avoid him, as there is no way he can beat this behemoth. Meanwhile, Stallone is doing his best to be a good brother-in-law to Young, who feels as though he's been neglected by the family. That mild domestic crisis is just in there as a filler and means nothing to the plot. Stallone ignores Meredith's advice, meets Mr. T., and loses the bout under the pounding of the hungry challenger. Meredith, who hasn't been well, dies (which is like killing Knobby Walsh, Joe Palooka's manager) and Stallone turns to ex-champ Weathers to develop a new style for the rematch. Weathers teaches Stallone how to box like a black man in order to battle Mr. T. Stallone does everything but put on burnt cork as Weathers works on Stallone's footwork and transforms him from a heavy-footed puncher into a fast-moving and quicker ringmaster. Along the way, Stallone has a battle royal with wrestler Hogan that's just a comic interlude. (It was this appearance and a host of carefully devised moves that made Hogan into a national figure with his own Saturday morning cartoon show.) The training is, again, the focal point, as Stallone has to whip himself into shape under Weathers until it's time for the finale, the rematch. Stallone regains his "Eye of the Tiger" (which is the ROCKY version of Muhammad Ali's "Float Like a Butterfly, Sting Like a Bee" theory). The battle that ends the picture, staged by Stallone as usual, is a bit shorter than the climax attached to the other ROCKY movies but it's still satisfying as Stallone regains his title by making Mr. T. into mincemeat. Mr. T. was terrific as the bad guy and used his persona to good advantage when hired to play in the successful TV series "The A Team." In 1985, Mr. T. also became a professional wrestler and appeared in many matches, thereby earning enough money to add to the ton of gold he wears around his neck. Several actual sports commentators appear in the film, including KNBC's Stu Nahan, Fred Roggin (also from Los Angeles' NBC station), radio's Jim Healey, and more. Righteous Brother Bill Medley does a cameo, comedian Don Sherman returns to reprise his role as the local bartender and artist LeRoy Neiman chimes in with a neat turn. All of the ROCKY films have simplistic themes, black versus white (figuratively), and there is never any doubt who's good and who is bad. This one is even more basic than the others. It mattered not to the public who continued to flock to the theaters. This version is 20 minutes shorter than the others but feels longer because there are not enough surprises to maintain interest. Stallone knows how to direct himself in action, but his attempts at anything outside the ring or the training sequences seem to be more like a student film from an undergraduate. As in the others, it's advised to keep smaller children away from this, as there is more blood shed here (in a very realistic fashion) than the average Red Cross plasma drive.

p, Irwin Winkler, Robert Chartoff; d&w, Sylvester Stallone; ph, Bill Butler (Technicolor); m, Bill Conti; ed, Don Zimmerman, Mark Warner; prod d, William J. Cassidy; art d, Ronald Kent Foreman; song, "Eye of the Tiger" (performed by Survivor).

Sports Drama   Cas.   (PR:A-C MPAA:PG)

ROCKY HORROR PICTURE SHOW, THE*   (1975, Brit.) 100m
                                                                  Adler-White FOX c

Tim Curry (*Dr. Frank N. Furter*), Susan Sarandon (*Janet Weiss*), Barry Bostwick (*Brad Majors*), Richard O'Brien (*Riff Raff*), Jonathan Adams (*Dr. Everett Scott*), Nell Campbell (*Columbia*), Peter Hinwood (*Rocky Horror*), Patricia Quinn (*Magenta*), Meatloaf (*Eddie*), Charles Gray (*Criminologist*), Jeremy Newson (*Ralph Hapschatt*), Hilary Labow (*Betty Munroe*), Frank Lester (*Wedding Dad*), Mark Johnson (*Wedding Guest*), Koo Stark, Petra Leah, Gina Barrie (*Bridesmaids*), John Marquand (*Father*).

This film has become the official definition of a cult movie—so much so that the audience watching (or more accurately, participating in) the picture is the most interesting element. Depending on the quality of the audience's performance ROCKY HORROR can be a fantastic viewing experience or just a really fun experience. But the movie alone—blah, what a waste! The audiences around the country that line up every Friday and Saturday at midnight are *the* show. What happens on the screen is secondary. Audience members dress up like their favorite character and carry with them an arsenal of props. Based on a British musical stage play by O'Brien (who also appears in the film and wrote all the music), RHPS eventually made it to the screen with the help of Lou Adler and Michael White. After a short run in New York it closed, but soon was revived on the midnight circuit. It is the story of Brad and Janet (Bostwick and Sarandon) whose car breaks down during a rainstorm in Ohio. They look for shelter in a mansion, which turns out to be the residence of Dr. Frank N. Furter, wildly played by Curry. They soon find themselves in the middle of a convention of alien transsexuals from the planet Transsexual in the galaxy Transylvania. Curry is ready to reveal his Frankenstein-esque creation—a monster named Rocky who is to be the ultimate sexual male. What follows, in a nutshell, is sex, cannibalism (Meatloaf is appropriately eaten), murder, seduction, more sex; people are turned into statues, RKO Radio Pictures is spoofed, and Brad and Janet (dammit!) escape before everything is blown up. The film itself is trash—its script and direction poor, its music mediocre—but audience participation has taken Bertolt Brecht into the twilight zone. Weird to the maximum. Songs: "The Time Warp," "Science Fiction Double Feature," "Wedding Song," "Sweet Transvestite," "The Sword Of Damocles," "Charles Atlas Song," "What Ever Happened To Saturday Night," "Touch-a Touch-a Touch-a Touch

Me," "Eddie's Teddy," "Planet Schmanet," "Over at the Frankenstein Place," "It Was Great When It All Began," "I'm Going Home," and "Super-Heroes." SHOCK TREATMENT was a sequel of sorts.

p, Michael White, John Goldstone; d, Jim Sharman; w, Sharman, Richard O'Brien (based on the stage musical by O'Brien); ph, Peter Suschitzky (Eastmancolor); m, O'Brien; ed, Graeme Clifford; md, Richard Hartley; prod d, Brian Thomson; art d, Terry Ackland Snow; cos, Sue Blane, Richard Pointing, Gillian Dods; spec eff, Wally Veevers; ch, David Toguri; m/l, O'Brien.

Musical Comedy/Horror   **(PR:O MPAA:R)**

ROCKY MOUNTAIN*   (1950) 83m WB bw

Errol Flynn (Lafe Barstow), Patrice Wymore (Johanna Carter), Scott Forbes (Lt. Rickey), Guinn "Big Boy" Williams (Pap Dennison), Dick Jones (Jim Wheat), Howard Petrie (Cole Smith), Slim Pickens (Plank), Chubby Johnson (Gil Craigie), Buzz Henry (Kip Waterson), Sheb Wooley (Kay Rawlins), Peter Coe (Pierre Duchesne), Rush Williams (Jonas Weatherby), Steve Dunhill (Ash), Alex Sharp (Barnes), Yakima Canutt (Ryan), Nakai Snez (Man Dog).

Flynn's last western sees him as a Confederate officer sent with a small group of soldiers to California where they are supposed to meet with a powerful group of outlaws and persuade them to take the territory in the name of the Confederacy. The two groups are to meet at a hot, arid plateau in the desert that is fraught with danger and has been the site of many skirmishes between warring Indians and Union soldiers. As Flynn and his men wait for their party, a stagecoach being attacked by Indians roars by. The Confederate soldiers repel the Indians and inside the stagecoach is a beautiful young woman, Wymore, who was on her way to meet her fiance, Forbes, a Union Army officer. Though Flynn is quite taken with the girl, he uses her as bait to lure her fiance and his patrol into the desert in search of her. The Confederates manage to capture the Yankees, but then the Indians launch a massive attack. Now in love with Wymore, Flynn lets her and the Union soldiers escape while he and his men engage the Indians as a diversion. Wymore does escape, but the heroic Confederates are hopelessly outnumbered and all are massacred. Aside from the outstanding action set-pieces (the attack on the stagecoach and the final massacre), ROCKY MOUNTAIN is thin entertainment. The plot and situations are all too familiar and the performances uninspired. Western fans should note that this was the acting debut of beloved character actor Slim Pickens (formerly Louis Lindley) who would become an icon of sorts in westerns of the 1950s and 1960s. Perhaps the most notable aspect of ROCKY MOUNTAIN is that star Flynn fell head-over-heels in love with his costar Wymore (she was 24, he 41). Intrigued by her unpretentious manner, Flynn paid close attention to the young actress and even arranged for her to share part of his large dressing room trailer (she was given a small tent by the studio). To demonstrate his affection, practical joker Flynn had her arrested for fishing in a nearby lake without a license—the whole thing was a hoax. The pair discarded both their prospective spouses and ran off to Paris soon after the shooting was over to be married. Wymore became Mrs. Errol Flynn No. 3, and in his autobiography (written in 1959) Flynn reminisced about their romance: "I was deeply impressed to see her pick up some instrument and dig a hole in the ground, place corn and potatoes in aluminum foil, and bake them in a fire under the bright Arizona stars. The Kansas home-baked food tasted fantastic and I looked at Pat with wonder. What she was doing around the theater when she could cook like that—in the ground itself? I still don't know what that dinner of baked corn and potatoes is going to cost me. Patrice and I have been separated for about two years."

p, William Jacobs; d, William Keighley; w, Alan LeMay, Winston Miller (based on the story Ghost Mountain by LeMay); ph, Ted McCord; m, Max Steiner; ed, Rudi Fehr; art d, Stanley Fleischer; set d, L.S. Edwards; cos, Marjorie Best.

Western   **(PR:A MPAA:NR)**

ROCKY MOUNTAIN MYSTERY½** (1935) 63m PAR bw (AKA: THE FIGHTING WESTERNER)

Randolph Scott (Larry Sutton), Charles "Chic" Sale (Tex Murdock), Mrs. Leslie Carter (Mrs. Borg), Kathleen Burke (Flora), George Marion, Sr. (Ballard), Ann Sheridan (Rita Ballard), James C. Eagles (John Borg), Howard Wilson (Fritz), Willie Fung (Ling Yat), Florence Roberts (Mrs. Ballard).

Sale is a hare-brained deputy trying to solve a series of murders occurring in a radium mine. He enlists the aid of Scott who knows where to point the finger. A solid piece of mystery more than anything else, but it has its share of western elements and comic bits. Twenty-year-old "Search for Beauty" contest winner Sheridan, now on her way to becoming the "Oomph Girl," finally graduated out of more than a year and a half of bit parts to take a leading role in this film, and won the attention of critics for her solid support of Scott. For Scott, who had been the lead in a series of romantic stories, it was a return to westerns where he would make his mark later in the decade.

p, Harold Hurley; d, Charles Barton; w, Edward E. Paramore, Jr., Ethel Doherty (based on the Zane Grey novel Golden Dreams); ph, Archie Stout; ed, Jack Dennis.

Western/Mystery/Comedy   **(PR:A MPAA:NR)**

ROCKY MOUNTAIN RANGERS**   (1940) 58m REP bw

Robert Livingston (Stony Brooke), Raymond Hatton (Rusty Joslin), Duncan Renaldo (Rico), Rosella Towne (Doris Manners), Sammy McKim (Daniel Burke), LeRoy Mason (King Barton), Pat O'Malley (Capt. Taylor), Dennis Moore (Jim Barton), John St. Polis (Manners), Robert Blair (Sgt. Bush), Burr Caruth (John), Jack Kirk (Harris), Budd Buster, Hank Bell.

Dashing "Mesquiteer" Stony Brooke (Livingston) takes on a dual role this time out, first as a law-abiding panhandler trying to bring peace to the community, and then as "The Laredo Kid," a blackhat who gets killed early on, but is impersonated by Livingston in order to defeat the gang.(See THREE MESQUITEERS series, Index.)

p, Harry Grey; d, George Sherman; w, Barry Shipman, Earle Snell (based on a story by J. Benton Cheney, from the characters created by William Colt MacDonald); ph, Jack Marta; m, Cy Feuer; ed, Lester Orlebeck.

Western   **(PR:A MPAA:NR)**

ROCKY RHODES**   (1934) 64m UNIV bw

Charles "Buck" Jones (Rocky Rhodes), Sheila Terry (Nan), Stanley Fields (Harp), Walter Miller (Murtch), Alf P. James (Street), Paul Fix (Hilton), Lydia Knott (Mrs. Rhodes), Lee Shumway, Jack Rockwell, Carl Stockdale, Monte Montague, Bud Osborne, Harry Semels, Silver the Horse.

Starting out with newsreel footage of the Chicago Stockyards fire, this standard Buck Jones picture moved the character quickly to Arizona where he gets involved in a land battle, aided by gruffly humorous Fields, a sometimes criminal. Miller played the money-grabbing outlaw to Terry's young and innocent landowner. This was the first of 22 films Jones made, along with four serials, for Universal, in a reign as top cowboy around the Hollywood lots until the singing gunslingers (Gene Autry and Roy Rodgers, especially) came on the scene. In ROCKY RHODES, it is curious that Jones still bills himself Charles "Buck" Jones, a label the kids never bought.

p, Buck Jones; d, Al Raboch; w, Edward Churchill (based on a story by W.C. Tuttle); ph, Ted McCord.

Western   **(PR:A MPAA:NR)**

RODAN*½ (1958, Jap.) 70m Toho/DCA bw (AKA: RADON; RADON THE FLYING MONSTER)

Kenji Sawara, Yumi Shirakawa, Akihiko Hirata, Akio Kobori, Yasuko Nakata, Minosuke Yamada, Yoshibumi Tajima, Kiyoharu Ohnaka.

A humungous flying reptile is hatched in a coal mine, eats a swarm of oversized dragonflies, and wreaks havoc on the unsuspecting citizens of Japan. The big bird belts out blistering screeches as it careens at supersonic speeds through the skies, sending the characters into fits of terror which cause them to speak out of synchronization with the sound track. One of the cornerstones in Japanese monster movies and called the first monster movie in Eastmancolor, RODAN was released there in 1956. Only a voiceover was added to the U.S. version, with obnoxious commentary by David Duncan.

p, Tomoyuki Tanaka; d, Inoshiro Honda; w, Takeshi Kimura, Takeo Murata (based on story by Takashi Kuronuma); ph, Isamu Ashida (Eastmancolor); m, Akira Ifukube; art d, Tatsuo Kita; spec eff, Eiji Tsuburaya.

Science Fiction   **(PR:A MPAA:NR)**

RODEO**   (1952) 71m MON c

Jane Nigh (Nancy Cartwright), John Archer (Slim Martin), Wallace Ford (Barbecue Jones), Gary Gray (Joey Cartwright), Frances Rafferty (Dixie Benson), Sara Haden (Agatha Cartwright), Frank Ferguson (Harry Cartwright), Myron Healey (Richard Durston), Fuzzy Knight (Jazbo Davis), Robert Karner (Charles Olenick), Jim Bannon (Bat Gorman), I. Stanford Jolley (Pete Adkins), Ann Doran, Dave Willock, Milton Kibbee.

Nigh takes over the reins of a mismanaged rodeo and turns it into a success. Gabby old rider Ford becomes part of the show and overhears Nigh make fun of him. Trying to prove he is still a top rider he has an accident and seriously injures himself. The rest of the performers, angry with Nigh, stage a walkout, but when they learn that she is taking care of Ford's doctor bills, they return. Decent family entertainment which includes some impressive rodeo scenes in color.

p, Walter Mirisch; d, William Beaudine; w, Charles R. Marion; ph, Harry Neumann (Cinecolor); m, Marlin Skiles; ed, William Austin; art d, Martin Obzina.

Western   **(PR:A MPAA:NR)**

RODEO KING AND THE SENORITA**   (1951) 67m REP bw

Rex Allen (Himself), Mary Ellen Kay (Janet Wells), Buddy Ebsen (Muscles Benton), Roy Barcroft (Steve Lacey), Tristam Coffin (Jack Foster), Bonnie DeSimone (Juanita Morales), Don Beddoe (Bill Richards), Jonathan Hale (Dr. Sands), Harry Harvey (Jed Bailey), Rory Mallinson (Sheriff), Joe Forte (Dr. Teal), Buff Brady (Pablo Morales), Koko the Horse.

Allen and his horse Koko uncover an illegitimate business partner who is behind a plot to bankrupt a Wild West show, as well as an unsolved murder. DeSimone is the woman who tries to keep the show on the road after the death of her dad. A remake of Roy Rogers' 1946 picture MY PAL TRIGGER. Full of Allen's fisticuffs and balladeering. Another neat outing from Republic's efficient B western corral.

p, Melville Tucker; d, Philip Ford; w, John K. Butler; ph, Walter Strenge; ed, Robert M. Leeds; art d, Fred A. Ritter; cos, Adele Palmer; m/l, "Strawberry Roan," "Juanita," Fred Howard, Nat Vincent, Curley Fletcher, Caroline Norton.

Western   **(PR:A MPAA:NR)**

RODEO RHYTHM*½   (1941) 75m PRC bw

Fred Scott (Buck Knapp), Loie Bridge (Aunt Tillie), Pat Dunn (Jim Corey), Patricia Redpath (Ellen Knapp), Jack Cooper (Joe Stegge), John Frank (Grandpa Twitchell), H. "Doc" Hartley (Sheriff Bates), Landon Laird (Lawyer), Gloria Morris (Gloria), Roylene Smith (Small Fry), Vernon Brown (Slow Burn), Donna Jean Meinke (Juanita), Roy Knapp's Rough Riders, Dopey the Dog.

A group of 30 pony-riding kids help miserly landlord Frank after a car crash, making him more sympathetic to the needs of their orphanage. Instead of shutting it down, he decides to give them enough money to put on a rodeo. An overabundance of cute, wide-eyed youngsters. Logistically, the specially trained children, aged 3 to 13, could not easily be transported to Hollywood, so the picture was filmed in Kansas City, home of Roy Knapp, who trained the little trick riders. Part of the movie's lack of interest is that everyone in the cast was an amateur except

Scott and Bridge, and the story was simply a framework on which to hang the unique children's ensemble.

p, Leo J. McCarthy; d, Fred Newmeyer; w, Eugene Allen, Gene Tuttle (based on a story by McCarthy); ph, Eddie Kull; ed, George Halligan; m/l, Morrill Moore, Eugene Moore, Dave Oppenheim.

Western/Drama (PR:AA MPAA:NR)

ROGER TOUHY, GANGSTER!** (1944) 65m FOX bw (GB: THE LAST GANGSTER)

Preston Foster *(Roger Touhy)*, Victor McLaglen *(Owl Banghart)*, Lois Andrews *(Daisy)*, Kent Taylor *(Steve Warren)*, Anthony Quinn *(George Carroll)*, William Post, Jr. *(Joe Sutton)*, Henry "Harry" Morgan *(Smoke Reardon)*, Matt Briggs *(Cameron)*, Moroni Olsen *(Riley)*, Trudy Marshall *(Gloria)*, Frank Jenks *(Troubles Connors)*, George E. Stone *(Ice Box Hamilton)*, Charles Lang, Reed Hadley, John Archer *(FBI Agents)*, Kane Richmond *(Mason)*, Frank Orth *(Comic in Theater)*, George Holmes *(McNair)*, Horace MacMahon *(Max Sharkey)*, Edmund MacDonald *(Barnes)*, Murray Alper *(Ralph Burke)*, Byron Foulger *(Court Clerk)*, Joseph Crehan *(Warden)*, Addison Richards *(Priest)*, Jim Farley *(Bailiff)*, Charles Wilson *(Police Captain)*, Ralph Peters *(Clanahan)*, Roy Roberts *(Frank Williams)*, John Harmon *(Lefty Rowden)*, Cy Kendall *(Edward Latham)*, William Pawley *(Prison Guard Briggs)*, Selmer Jackson *(Principal Keeper)*, George Lessey *(Judge)*, Ralph Dunn *(Patrolman)*, Arthur Aylesworth *(Farmer)*, Dick Rich, Joey Ray, Ferris Taylor, William Haade, William Ruhl, Thomas Jackson, Stanley Blystone, Charles Wilson, Ralf Harolde, Herbert Ashley, Ivan Miller, Grant Withers.

A loose-fitting crime melodrama which claims to be a factual record of Chicago gangster Roger Touhy, but is nothing more than a weak B picture. Foster's story begins in the Prohibition era with a highly profitable bootlegging enterprise that rivals that of the city's toughest mobster (an unnamed Al Capone). To put a lid on the competition, Foster is framed for kidnaping and sent to Stateville with a 199-year sentence. With cohort McLaglen (cast as Basil "The Owl" Banghart, the only other named personality in the film), Foster engineers a prison break only to be captured by the FBI soon afterward. The film's grand finale has Stateville's warden sternly warning the audience that crime doesn't pay. Grossly straying from the facts, ROGER TOUHY, GANGSTER! makes the mistake of not paying more attention to Touhy's real-life and vastly more interesting career. Touhy, who started as a wheeler-dealer in the Chicago suburb of Des Plaines, made his fortune by supplying tavern owners (and city officials) with top quality beer. He quickly drew the attention of Capone, a virtual stranger to the suburbs, who had no idea of Touhy's power—or lack thereof. As it turns out, Touhy wasn't nearly as "terrible" as his moniker threatened—or as ROGER TOUHY, GANGSTER! claims. Instead of being the hardened criminal Foster portrayed, Touhy was more of a profitable bootlegger with a keen business sense. Framed by Capone (who wanted his territory) on a phony kidnaping charge, Touhy was put behind bars. Upon his escape, amidst a flurry of news headlines, Fox decided to film his story, originally casting Lloyd Nolan in the lead and Foster as the chief detective. Before shooting began, however, Nolan dropped out and Taylor was chosen to play Touhy. A last-minute decision switched Taylor and Foster. Meanwhile Touhy and his lawyers tried to prevent the film from being released because it wrongly portrayed him as "a vicious law violator and gangster." The first version of the film, shown to an audience at Stateville (where some scenes were shot), drew loud and angry protests from the FBI which insisted that the investigative work was wrongly credited to local police. After reshooting and additional cutting, a final version was released. What ROGER TOUHY, GANGSTER! doesn't tell is what occurred after the film's release. Touhy was recaptured and given another stiff sentence for "aiding and abetting" in the prison escape. He was finally released in 1959. Three weeks later he was gunned down by a vengeful unknown who literally blew away Touhy's legs with several shotgun blasts.

p, Lee Marcus; d, Robert Florey; w, Crane Wilbur, Jerry Cady (based on a story by Wilbur); ph, Glen MacWilliams; m, Hugo W. Friedhofer; ed, Harry Reynolds; md, Emil Newman; art d, James Basevi, Lewis Creber; set d, Thomas Little, Al Orenbach; spec eff, Fred Sersen.

Crime (PR:A MPAA:NR)

ROGUE COP*** (1954) 92m MGM bw

Robert Taylor *(Christopher Kelvaney)*, Janet Leigh *(Karen Stephanson)*, George Raft *(Dan Beaumonte)*, Steve Forrest *(Eddie Kelvaney)*, Anne Francis *(Nancy Corlane)*, Robert Ellenstein *(Sidney Y. Myers)*, Robert F. Simon *(Ackerman)*, Anthony Ross *(Father Ahern)*, Alan Hale, Jr. *(Johnny Stark)*, Peter Brocco *(Wrinkles Fallon)*, Vince Edwards *(Langley)*, Olive Carey *(Selma)*, Roy Barcroft *(Lt. Vince D. Bardeman)*, Dale Van Sickel *(Manny)*, Ray Teal *(Patrolman Mullins)*, Guy Prescott *(Detective Ferrari)*, Dick Simmons *(Detective Ralston)*, Phil Chambers *(Detective Dirksen)*, Herbert Ellis *(Barkeep)*, Lillian Buyeff *(Gertrude)*, Jimmy Ames *(News Dealer)*, Joe Waring *(Rivers)*, Paul Brinegar, Paul Hoffman *(Clerks)*, Nesdon Booth *(Detective Garrett)*, Connie Marshall *(Frances)*, Nicky Blair *(Marsh)*, Richard Deacon *(Stacy)*, Gilda Oliva *(Italian Girl)*, Dick Ryan *(Elevator Man)*, Dallas Boyd *(Patrolman Higgins)*, George Taylor *(Dr. Leonard)*, Paul Bryar *(Policeman Marx)*, Russell Johnson *(Patrolman Carland)*, Michael Fox *(Rudy)*, Milton Parsons *(Tucker)*, Robert Burton *(Inspector Cassidy)*, Carleton Young *(District Attorney Powell)*, George Selk *(Parker)*, Benny Burt *(Proprietor)*, Gene Coogan *(Truck Driver)*, Mitchell Kowall *(Guard)*, Jarl Victor *(Orderly)*.

A biting look at the involvement of a veteran police officer, played by Taylor, with an underworld gang led by Raft. With payoffs from Raft, Taylor is able to live luxuriously—far more than would be the case on his meager police salary. Taylor's kid brother, Forrest, is a rookie on the force who is determined to infuse his position with integrity. When he witnesses a mob hit he refuses to appease Raft by covering it up. Raft calls upon Taylor to persuade Forrest to stay quiet by offering him a $15,000 bribe. Forrest still upholds his morals. Taylor tries to reach Forrest through his girl friend, Leigh, but that also proves unsuccessful. Impatient with Forrest's obstinacy, Raft hires an out-of-town hit man, Edwards, to permanently silence Forrest. Upon hearing the news of his brother's murder, Taylor becomes enraged and vows to seek revenge. Enlisting the aid of fellow officer Ellenstein (a Jew, castigated by his anti-Semitic co-workers), Tayor hunts down Edwards and, finally, Raft. In a frenzy of gunshots Raft is killed and Taylor seriously injured. Taylor is loaded into an ambulance, having restored his integrity but still facing the possibility of a jail term. One of only a handful of *films noir* to emerge from MGM, ROGUE COP works chiefly because of Taylor's fine performance. While the "blood is thicker than money" philosophy is rather commonplace and predictable, Taylor manages to pull it off convincingly. As compelling as ROGUE COP is, it is simply a variation on the previous year's THE BIG HEAT—both derived from novels written by McGivern. In both cases a cop (where Taylor is easily corrupted, THE BIG HEAT's Glenn Ford is solidly incorruptible) is driven to vengeance after the murder of a loved one (for Taylor it's a brother, and for Ford a wife), busting open a corrupt organization (Taylor cracks the mob, Ford shakes up the police department) in the process. Unlike THE BIG HEAT, ROGUE COP didn't have Fritz Lang's brilliant directorial hand to make it all click.

p, Nicholas Nayfack; d, Roy Rowland; w, Sydney Boehm (based on the novel by William P. McGivern); ph, John Seitz; m, Jeff Alexander; ed, James E. Newcom; art d, Cedric Gibbons, Hans Peters; set d, Edwin B. Willis, Keogh Gleason; cos, Helen Rose; spec eff, A. Arnold Gillespie; makeup, William Tuttle.

Crime (PR:C MPAA:NR)

ROGUE OF THE RANGE*½ (1937) 58m Principal/Supreme bw

Johnny Mack Brown *(Dan Doran)*, Lois January *(Stella)*, Alden Chase *(Branscomb)*, Phyllis Hume *(Tess)*, Jack Rockwell *(Stone)*, Horace Murphy *(Sheriff)*, Frank Ball *(Express Agent)*, George Ball *(Mitchell)*, Lloyd Ingraham *(Doctor)*, Fred Hoose, Forrest Taylor, George Morrell, Blackie Whiteford, Slim Whitaker, Tex Palmer, Horace B. Carpenter, Max Davidson, Art Dillard.

Brown poses as an outlaw but is really a lawman in this below-par programmer. While fighting the bad guy, he is also concerned with which girl he wants—the preacher or the singer—and he chooses the latter, January.

p, A.W. Hackel; d, S. Roy Luby; w, Earle Snell (based on a story by Snell); ph, Jack Greenhalgh; ed, Roy Claire.

Western (PR:A MPAA:NR)

ROGUE OF THE RIO GRANDE** (1930) 65m Sono-Art/World Wide bw

Jose Bohr *(El Malo)*, Raymond Hatton *(Pedro)*, Myrna Loy *(Carmita)*, Carmelita Geraghty *(Dolores)*, Walter Miller *(Sheriff Rankin)*, Gene Morgan *(Seth Landport)*, William P. Burt *(Tango Dancer)*, Florence Dudley *(Big Bertha)*.

Fun-loving trickster Bohr makes his money by working as a Mexican bandit. He gets away with a heist in the small town of Sierra Blanca, but since there is no description of him, he stays on and enjoys the dancing and drinking at the local saloon, spending his time with the slender, gay Loy. The bandit soon catches the town sheriff involved in a robbery and pins the original heist on the lawman. He and Loy calmly and indifferently leave town for the Mexican border. Overall, the film has an amateurish quality although there are quite a few pleasant moments, and songs, in it. Loy was on loan from Warner Bros. for this so-called "musical western," and, for Bohr, it was one of his very few American pictures. Thereafter he devoted himself almost exclusively, as both actor and director, to Mexican films. Loy fans will be delighted to see her dance in her role as a saloon girl of shady morals. Songs include: "Argentine Moon," "Carmita," "Song of the Bandoleros" Herbert Meyers, Oliver Drake.

p, George W. Weeks; d, Spencer Gordon Bennett; w, Oliver Drake (based on a story by Drake); m/l, Drake, Herbert Meyers.

Musical Western (PR:A MPAA:NR)

ROGUE RIVER½** (1951) 81m Ventura/EL c

Rory Calhoun *(Ownie Rogers)*, Peter Graves *(Pete Dandridge)*, Frank Fenton *(Joe Dandridge)*, Ralph Sanford *(Max Bonner)*, George Stern *(H.P. Jackson)*, Ellye Marshall *(Judy Haven)*, Roy Engel *(Ed Colby)*, Jane Liddell *(Eileen Reid)*, Robert Rose *(Carter Laney)*, Stephen Roberts *(Mayor Arthur Judson)*, Duke York *(Bowers)*.

An intriguing plot lifts this western above the average plateau. Fenton is a local cop who is willed $70,000 in gold by an old prospector whom the cop once framed. The catch is that Fenton must prove the old feller innocent of a bank heist, which is how most folks think he acquired the gold. Calhoun, as Fenton's nephew, is responsible for bringing the whole thing into the light.

p, Frank Melford; d, John Rawlins; w, Louis Lantz; ph, John H. Greenhalgh, Jr. (Cinecolor); m, Paul Sawtell.

Western/Crime (PR:A MPAA:NR)

ROGUE SONG, THE*** (1930) 115m MGM c

Lawrence Tibbett *(Yegor)*, Catharine Dale Owen *(Princess Vera)*, Judith Voselli *(Countess Tatiana)*, Nance O'Neil *(Princess Alexandra)*, Stan Laurel *(Ali-Bek)*, Oliver Hardy *(Murza-Bek)*, Florence Lake *(Nadja)*, Lionel Belmore *(Ossman)*, Ullrich Haupt *(Prince Serge)*, Kate Price *(Petrovna)*, Wallace McDonald *(Hassan)*, Burr McIntosh *(Count Peter)*, James Bradbury, Jr. *(Azamat)*, H.A. Morgan *(Frolov)*, Elsa Alsen *(Yegor's Mother)*, Harry Bernard *(Guard)*, The Albertina Rasch Ballet *(Dancers)*.

Lawrence Tibbett, in his debut performance, was nominated for Best Actor as a Russian bandit leader who falls in love with princess Owen, whose brother wronged Tibbett's sister. He kills the brother, then kidnaps the princess, but she is less than responsive. He is captured and flogged, though as the whip is being brought down, Owen realizes that she loves him. Weakly received upon its release, THE ROGUE

SONG was acclaimed only for Tibbett's (a Metropolitan Opera baritone) vocalizing, and not at all for its comedy. The film, in fact, was ready for release when MGM decided to shoot a few scenes with Laurel and Hardy. Unfortunately we can no longer judge the quality of Tibbett's voice, or L&H's humor, or Barrymore's direction, or especially the Technicolor process of THE ROGUE SONG—as far as is known, no existing prints are to be had. If one shows up it could be a pleasant surprise.

p&d, Lionel Barrymore (Laurel and Hardy scenes directed by Hal Roach); w, Frances Marion, John Colton (based on the operetta "Gypsy Love" by Franz Lehar, A.M. Willner, Robert Bodansky); ph, Percy Hilburn, C. Edgar Schoenbaum (Technicolor); m, Dimitri Tiomkin; ed, Margaret Booth; art d, Cedric Gibbons; cos, Adrian; m/l, "When I'm Looking at You," "Song of the Shirt," "Rogue's Song," Herbert Stothart, Clifford Grey, "The White Dove," Franz Lehar, Grey.

Musical/Comedy   **(PR:A MPAA:NR)**

ROGUE'S GALLERY, 1942   (SEE: DEVIL'S TRAIL, THE, 1942)

ROGUES GALLERY**   (1945) 60m PRC bw

Frank Jenks (Eddie), Robin Raymond (Patsy), H.B. Warner (Reynolds), Ray Walker (Jimmy), Davison Clark (Foster), Robert E. Homans (O'Day), Frank McGlynn (Blake), Pat Gleason (Red), Edward Keane (Gentry), Earl Dewey (Griffith), Milton Kibbee (Wheeler), Gene Stutenroth [Roth] (Joyce), George Kirby (Duckworth), Norval Mitchell (Seawell), John Valentine (Board Member), Jack Raymond (Mike), Parker Gee (Detective).

News photographer Jenks and femme reporter Raymond interview inventor Warner about his new device but are soon tangled up in a murder mystery. Eventually it turns out that Walker, a rival of Warner who wants to steal his plans, is the guilty party.

p, Donald C. McKean, Albert Herman; d, Herman; w, John T. Neville; ph, Ira Morgan; ed, Fred Bain; md, Lee Zahler; art d, Paul Palmentola.

Mystery   **(PR:A MPAA:NR)**

ROGUE'S MARCH**   (1952) 84m MGM bw

Peter Lawford (Capt. Dion Lenbridge), Richard Greene (Capt. Thomas Garron), Janice Rule (Jane Wensley), Leo G. Carroll (Col. Lenbridge), John Abbott (Herbert Bielensen), Patrick Aherne (Maj. Wensley), John Dodsworth (Maj. Mac Street), Herbert Deans (Prosecutor), John Lupton (Lt. Jersey), Hayden Rorke (Maj. Fallow), Barry Bernard (Sergeant), Charles Davis (Cpl. Biggs), Jack Raine (Gen. Woodbury), Richard Hale (Emissary), Michael Pate (Crane), Skelton Knaggs (Fish), Sean McClory (McGinty), Otto Waldis (Alex), Hugh French (Capt. Foster), Leslie Denison (Lt. Col. Harvill), Lester Matthews (Brigadier General), Arthur Gould-Porter, Ramsey Hill, Robin Hughes, Francis Bethancourt, Bruce Lester, Elaine Stewart.

Disgraced son Lawford takes off for India and fights bravely, but is still seen in the eyes of his father as a traitor. He returns to England, where his father Carroll finally accepts the fact that his son fought heroically and is not a traitor after all. Lots of stock footage of India's exotic locale, but everything else is rather familiar.

p, Leon Gordon; d, Allan Davis; w, Gordon; ph, Paul C. Vogel; m, Alberto Colombo; ed, Gene Ruggiero; art d, Cedric Gibbons, William Ferrari; set d, Edwin B. Willis, Arthur Krams.

Action/War   **(PR:A MPAA:NR)**

ROGUES OF SHERWOOD FOREST**   (1950) 80m COL c

John Derek (Robin, Earl of Huntington), Diana Lynn (Lady Marianne), George Macready (King John), Alan Hale (Little John), Paul Cavanagh (Sir Giles), Lowell Gilmore (Count Of Flanders), Billy House (Friar Tuck), Lester Matthews (Alan-A-Dale), William [Billy] Bevan (Will Scarlett), Wilton Graff (Baron Fitzwalter), Donald Randolph (Archbishop Stephen Langton), John Dehner (Sir Baldric), Gavin Muir (Baron Alfred), Tim Huntley (Baron Chandos), Paul Collins (Arthur), Campbell Copelin, James Logan (Officers), Valentine Perkins (Milk Maid), Gilliam Blake (Lady In Waiting), Pat Aherne (Trooper), Olaf Hytten (Charcoal Burner), Symona Boniface (Charcoal Burner's Wife), Paul Bradley (Court Official), Matthew Boulton (Abbot), Nelson Leigh (Merton), Colin Keith Johnson (Munster), Byron Poindexter (Man).

John Derek adds little to this familiar tale in which he is cast as Robin Hood's son. Macready as King John raises the taxes for the poor peasants, so Derek rounds up his dad's merry band to steal from the rich, etc. Eventually Derek's methods force the king to pay attention and sign the Magna Carta.

p, Fred M. Packard; d, Gordon Douglas; w, George Bruce (based on a story by Ralph Bettinson); ph, Charles Lawton, Jr. (Technicolor); m, Heinz Roemheld, Arthur Morton; ed, Gene Havlick; md, Morris Stoloff; art d, Harold MacArthur.

Adventure   **(PR:A MPAA:NR)**

ROGUES' REGIMENT**   (1948) 85m UNIV bw

Dick Powell (Whit Corbett), Marta Toren (Lili Maubert), Vincent Price (Mark Van Ratten), Stephan McNally (Carl Reicher), Edgar Barrier (Col. Mauclaire), Henry Rowland (Erich Heindorf), Carol Thurston (Li-Ho-Kay), James Millican (Cobb), Richard Loo (Kao Pang), Philip Ahn (Tran Duy Gian), Richard Fraser (Rycroft), Otto Reichow (Stein), Kenny Washington (Sam Latch), Dennis Dengate (O'Hara), Frank Conroy (Col. Lemercier), Martin Garralaga (Hazarat), James F. Nolan (American Colonel), Paul Bryar (Chief of Police), Gordon Clark (Lt. Verdier), Harry Meller, Robert Verdaine, Kell Nordenshield, Willy Wickerhauser, John Royce (Legionnaires), Lester Sharpe (Kavenko), Eugene Borden (Doctor), Maurice Marsac (Lieutenant), Victor Sen Yung (Rickshaw Boy), Charles J. Flynn (Dispatch Rider), John Doucette (German), Artarne Wong (Chinese Vendor), Leo Schlesinger (Soldier), Kei Thing Chung (Viet Guard), Paul Coze (Commander),

John Peters (Lutheran Minister), Albert Pollett (Frenchman), Jerry Mills (Soldier on Train).

Powell is a U.S. Intelligence officer who enlists in the French Foreign Legion as part of a plan to track down Nazi war criminal McNally (a character who clearly represents Martin Bormann, the number-three man on the Nazi totem pole). Enroute to McNally, Powell gathers clues and has a run-in with gun dealer/antique collector Vincent Price, who sounds ludicrous with his German accent. This one even includes a couple of tunes to make that nasty Nazi taste go down better: "Just For A While" and "Who Can Tell" (Serge Walter, Jack Brooks, sung by Marta Toren).

p, Robert Buckner; d, Robert Florey; w, Buckner (based on a story by Buckner, Florey); ph, Maury Gertsman; m, Daniele Amfitheatrof; ed, Ralph Dawson; md, Milton Schwarzwald; cos, Orry Kelly; ch, Billy Daniels; makeup, Bud Westmore.

Adventure   **(PR:A MPAA:NR)**

ROGUES' TAVERN, THE**   (1936) 67m Mercury/Puritan bw

Wallace Ford (Jimmy Flavin), Barbara Pepper (Marjorie Burns), Joan Woodbury (Gloria), Clara Kimball Young (Mrs. Jamison), Jack Mulhall (Bill), John Elliott (Mr. Jamison), John Cowell (Hughes), Vincent Dennis (Bert), Arthur Loft (Wentworth), Ivo Henderson (Harrison), Ed Cassidy (Mason), Silver Wolf the Dog.

Ford and Pepper are a couple about to be married who are sidetracked by a series of grisly murders which appear to be the doings of a wolf-dog. Closer investigation on Ford's part uncovers proof that the guilt is on a murderer's hands, not paws.

p, Edward W. Rote; d, Bob Hill; w, Al Martin; ph, Bill Hyer; ed, Dan Milner; md, Abe Meyer; set d, Fred Preble.

Mystery   **Cas.**   **(PR:A MPAA:NR)**

ROGUE'S YARN**   (1956, Brit.) 80m Cresswell/Eros bw

Nicole Maurey (Michele Cartier), Derek Bond (John Marsden), Elwyn Brook-Jones (Inspector Walker), Hugh Latimer (Sgt. Adams), John Serret (Inspector Lefarge), John Salew (Sam Youles), Joan Carol (Nurse), Nigel Fitzgerald, Madoline Thomas, Agatha Carroll, Barbara Christie, Hugh Morton, John Helier, Eric Corrie, Vernon Sewell.

A gripping crime drama starring Brook-Jones as a suspicious investigator who has trouble believing that Bond's rich invalid wife died in a yachting accident. He probes the clues until he is able to prove that Bond and his mistress Maurey plotted the woman's murder. Sewell, who, in the course of his career, performed in a number of filmmaking capacities, directed and acted in this movie.

p, George Maynard; d, Vernon Sewell; w, Ernie Bradford, Sewell; ph, Hal Morey.

Crime   **(PR:A MPAA:NR)**

ROLL ALONG, COWBOY*   (1938) 57m FOX bw

Smith Ballew (Randy), Cecilia Parker (Janet Blake), Stanley Fields (Barry), Wally Albright, Jr. (Danny Blake), Ruth Robinson (Mrs. Blake), Gordon [Bill] Elliott (Fenton), Frank Milan (Arthur Hathaway), Monte Montague (Bixby), Bud Osborne (Burgen), Harry Bernard (Shep), Budd Buster (Shorty), Buster Fite and His Six Saddle Tramps, Sheik the Horse.

A bottom-rung oater which has crooning cowboy Ballew assist Robinson in her fight against a crooked lawyer, while falling in love with her daughter Parker. Ballew delivers the tunes: "On the Sunny Side of the Rockies" (Roy Ingram, Harry Tobias); "Roll Along, Ride 'Em Cowboy" (Lyle Womack, Lew Porter). Band leader Ballew was Fox's attempt to cash in on the singing cowboy bonanza that Gene Autry had struck in 1935. It was an unfortunate decision for Ballew, who sang quite well but was not suited to the Stetson and boot crowd, and he soon vanished from the sagebrush scene.

p, Sol Lesser; d, Gus Meins; w, Dan Jarrett (based on a story by Zane Grey); ph, Harry Neumann; ed, Arthur Hilton, Albert Jordan.

Western   **(PR:A MPAA:NR)**

ROLL ON   (SEE: LAWLESS PLAINSMEN, 1942)

ROLL ON TEXAS MOON**½   (1946) 68m REP bw

Roy Rogers (Himself), George "Gabby" Hayes (Gabby Whittaker), Dale Evans (Jill Delaney), Dennis Hoey (Cole Gregory), Elizabeth Risdon (Cactus Kate Taylor), Francis McDonald (Steve Anders), Edward Keane (Frank B. Wilson), Kenne Duncan (Brunnigan), Tom London (Bert Morris), Harry Strang (Don Williams), Edward Cassidy (Tom Prescott), Lee Shumway (Ned Barnes), Steve Darrell (Joe Cummings), Pierce Lyden (Stuhler), Bob Nolan and The Sons of the Pioneers, Trigger the Horse.

Rogers is a peaceable man who is hired as a troubleshooter to prevent a range war between the ever-feuding sheepmen and ranchers. It turns out that the feuding was instigated by the villainous Hoey and his gang as a way of getting their grubby hands on Evans' property. Not with Roy around, they won't. Tunes include: "Roll on Texas Moon" (Jack Elliott; sung by Rogers), "Wontcha Be a Friend of Mine?" (Jack Elliott) and "The Jumpin' Bean" (Tim Spencer; sung by the Sons of the Pioneers). The first of 27 Rogers pictures to be helmed by William Witney, notorious for the violence in the serials he had directed in the 1930s and 1940s. Just returned from the war, as a Marine, Witney said he was tired of bloodshed, but his experience as an action director came to the forefront and changed the format of the Rogers series from costumers and musical extravaganzas to rapidly paced action stories, often with themes that bordered on the brutal.

p, Edward J. White; d, William Witney; w, Paul Gangelin, Mauri Grashin (based on a story by Jean Murray); ph, William Bradford; m, Dale Butts; ed, Les Orlebeck; md, Morton Scott; art d, Paul Youngblood.

Western   **Cas.**   **(PR:A MPAA:NR)**

ROLL, THUNDER, ROLL*½ (1949) 60m EPC/EL c

Jim Bannon *(Red Ryder)*, Don Kay "Little Brown Jug" Reynolds *(Little Beaver)*, Emmett Lynn *(Buckskin)*, Marin Sais *(Duchess)*, I. Stanford Jolley *(El Conejo)*, Nancy Gates *(Carol Loomis)*, Glenn Strange *(Ace Hanlon)*, Lee Morgan *("Happy" Loomis)*, Lane Bradford *(Wolf)*, Steve [Gaylord] Pendleton *(Marshal Bill Faugh)*, Charles Stevens *(Felipe)*, William Fawcett *(Josh Culvert)*, Joe Green *(Pat)*, Dorothy Latta *(Dorothy Culvert)*, Rocky Shahan *(Red's Double)*, Carol Henry *(Henchman)*, George Chesebro *(Garson)*, Jack O'Shea *(Bartender)*.

Bannon tries to stop a series of outlaw raids which result in dynamitings and fires in his third outing as Red Ryder. The culprits are trying to blame Jolley, a Mexican Robin Hood, but Bannon knows better. Audiences knew better, too, and after one more installment, the short-lived series was given the deep six by Equity Pictures. (See RED RYDER Series, Index.)

p, Jerry Thomas; d, Lewis D. Collins; w, Paul Franklin (based on Fred Harmon's comic strip character "Red Ryder"); ph, Gilbert Warrenton (Cinecolor); m, Ralph Stanley; ed, Frank Baldridge.

Western (PR:A MPAA:NR)

ROLL, WAGONS, ROLL½** (1939) 52m MON bw

Tex Ritter *(Tex Masters)*, Nelson McDowell *(Lucky)*, Muriel Evans *(Ruth)*, Nolan Willis *(Slade)*, Steve Clark *(Trigger)*, Tom London *(Grimes)*, Reed Howes *(Coleman)*, Frank Ellis *(Doc)*, Kenneth [Kenne]Duncan *(Clay)*, Frank LaRue *(Benson)*, Chick Hannen *(Pioneer Rider)*, Charles King, White Flash the Horse.

Ritter fills this horse opry with all the necessary action as he leads a wagon train to Oregon. He sings, pops off his six-gun, and kills Indians dead, all in the name of Westward expansion. Includes the songs "Oh, Suzannah" (Stephen Foster, new words by Ritter; sung by Ritter), "Roll Wagon Wheels" (Dorcas Cochran, Charles Rosoff; sung by Ritter).

p, Edward Finney; d, Al Herman; w, Victor Adamson, Roger Merton, Edmond Kelso (based on a story by Adamson, Merton, Kelso); ph, Marcel LePicard; m, Frank Sanucci; ed, Fred Bain; md, Sanucci.

Western Cas. (PR:A MPAA:NR)

ROLLER BOOGIE zero (1979) 103m UA c

Linda Blair *(Terry Barkley)*, Jim Bray *(Bobby James)*, Beverly Garland *(Lillian Barkley)*, Roger Perry *(Roger Barkley)*, Jimmy Van Patten *(Hoppy)*, Kimberly Beck *(Lana)*, Rick Sciacca *(Complete Control Conway)*, Sean McClory *(Jammer)*, Mark Goddard *(Thatcher)*, Albert Insinnia *(Gordo)*, Stoney Jackson *(Phones)*, M.G. Kelly *(J.D.)*, Chris Nelson *(Franklin)*, Patrick Wright *(Sgt. Danner)*, Dorothy Meyer *(Ada)*, Shelley Golden *(Mrs. Potter)*, Bill Ross *(Nick)*, Carey Fox *(Sonny)*, Nina Axelrod *(Bobby's Friend)*.

Rich youngster Blair runs away from her shallow parents to roller skate with some kids in the beach skating scene in Venice, California. A totally inane script designed to cash in on the roller-boogie craze. Watching CAN'T STOP THE MUSIC and THE WIZ every day for a year would be better than this.

p, Bruce Cohn Curtis; d, Mark L. Lester; w, Barry Schneider (based on a story by Irwin Yablans); ph, Dean Cundey (Technicolor); m, Bob Esty; ed, Howard Kunin, Byron "Buzz" Brandt, Ediberto Cruz, Edward Salier; art d, Keith Michl; ch, David Winters; m/l, Esty, Michele Aller, Michael Brooks.

Drama/Musical Cas. (PR:C MPAA:PG)

ROLLERBALL*** (1975) 129m UA c

James Caan *(Jonathan E.)*, John Houseman *(Bartholomew)*, Maud Adams *(Ella)*, John Beck *(Moonpie)*, Moses Gunn *(Cletus)*, Pamela Hensley *(Mackie)*, Barbara Trentham *(Daphne)*, Ralph Richardson *(Librarian)*, Shane Rimmer *(Team Executive)*, Alfred Thomas *(Team Trainer)*, Burnell Tucker *(Jonathan's Captain of Guard)*, Angus MacInnes *(Jonathan's Guard No. 1)*, Rick Le Parmentier *(Bartholomew's Aide)*, Burt Kwouk *(Oriental Doctor)*, Robert Ito *(Oriental Instructor)*, Nancy Blair *(Girl In Library)*, Loftus Burton, Abi Gouhad *(Black Reporters)*, Stephen Boyum, Alan Hamane, Danny Wong, Bob Leon *(Bikers)*, Craig Baxley, Tony Brunaker, Gary Epper, Bob Minor, Jim Nickerson, Chuck Parkinson, Jr., Dar Robinson, Roy Scammell, Walter Scott, Dick Warlock, Jerry Wills *(Stuntmen)*.

James Caan turns in his expected excellent performance as the star player of the title sport. It is the year 2018 and society has been rid of war, poverty, and violence—except for the political corporation-controlled rollerball teams, who fight to the bloody finish with spikes and motorcycles in a sport which combines roller derby and basketball. When Caan is asked to retire, he fights the move, and soon the corporate executives are interfering with his love life. They then decide to slacken the rules, resulting in more deaths as well as the maiming of Caan's buddy, Beck. As with many of Caan's characters (notably the role he played in THIEF), emotions build up until an explosive climax when Caan expresses all the anger the audience is feeling toward the villains. Caan's performance and the action sequences are this film's saving grace. The direction by Norman Jewison limps along, burdened with attempted philosophizing and pseudo-intellectualizing. Perhaps if ROLLERBALL had been directed by Paul Bartel, who the same year directed the similar DEATH RACE 2000, a better picture would have emerged.

p&d, Norman Jewison; w, William Harrison (based on his story "Rollerball Murders"); ph, Douglas Slocombe (Technicolor); m, Andre Previn; ed, Anthony Gibbs; md, Previn (excerpts from Johann Sebastian Bach, Petr Illich Tchaikovsky, Dmitri Shostakovich, Tomaso Giovanni Albinoni); prod d, John Box; art d, Robert Laing; cos, Julie Harris; spec eff, Sass Bedig, John Richardson, Joe Fitt; makeup, Wally Schneiderman.

Science Fiction Cas. (PR:O MPAA:R)

ROLLERCOASTER*** (1977) 119m UNIV c

George Segal *(Harry Calder)*, Richard Widmark *(Agent Hoyt)*, Timothy Bottoms *(Young Man)*, Henry Fonda *(Simon Davenport)*, Harry Guardino *(Lt. Keefer)*, Susan Strasberg *(Fran)*, Helen Hunt *(Tracy Calder)*, Dorothy Tristan *(Helen)*, Harry Davis *(Benny)*, Stephen Pearlman *(Park Manager Lyons)*, Gerald Rowe *(Wayne Moore)*, Wayne Tippit *(Police Captain Christie)*, Michael Bell *(Demerest)*, Charlie Tuna *(Rock Concert M.C.)*, Lonny Stevens, Tom Baker *(Federal Agents)*, Ava Readdy, Craig Wasson *(Hippies)*, William Prince *(Quinlan)*, Dick McGarvin, Quinn Redeker, Harry Basch, Arthur Peterson *(Owners)*, Richard Altman *(Mandell)*, Gloria Calomee *(Jackie)*, Robert Quarry *(Mayor)*, Jean Rasey *(Girl in Line)*, Greg Elliot *(Boy in Line)*, Bruce Kimbell, Bruce French, Stephen Mendillo, Charles W. Bennett, Jr., Larry Holt, Gene Tyburn *(Bomb Squad)*, Bill Sorrells *(Selby)*, Monica Lewis *(Tourist Mother)*, Dick Wesson *(Tourist Father)*, Joe George *(Guard)*, Gary Franklin *(Radio Reporter)*, Dave Milton *(Man in Robe)*, David Byrd *(Pet Store Owner)*, Henry Olek *(Smoking Technician)*, Dennis Speigel *(Pierce)*, Bill Saito, Takayo Doran *(Orientals)*, Roger Steffens *(Radio Technician)*, Dianne T. Murray *(Pregnant Agent)*, Mark Hulcher *(Delivery Boy)*, John F. Swanson *(Lansing)*, Denice Harlow *(Hertz Girl)*, Mark Thomas *(Agent)*, J. Michael Hunter *(Shooting Gallery Attendant)*, Tara Buckman, Louis Weisberg *(Coaster Attendants)*.

What begins as a crackling-good high adventure peters out at the end, the result of management's decision to hold back on a spectacular closing sequence, not the idea of the authors. The original idea was from child star Tommy Cook, then scripted by the two men who created TV's "Columbo" and wrote the teleplays for some excellent made-for-TV movies, including MY SWEET CHARLIE and THAT CERTAIN SUMMER. Levinson and Link have been writing together since high school, more than 30 years ago, and this was their first full screenplay after having supplied the adaptation for THE HINDENBURG. The picture opens at a seaside resort, an upscale version of Coney Island, where Bottoms is surreptitiously placing a small bomb under the tracks of the rollercoaster that is the park's No. 1 attraction. Dissolve to evening and the place is packed to capacity with revelers. Bottoms watches as the cars go through their paces, then he electronically sets off the bomb, and the result is a terrible crash with innocent victims being sent to their deaths and falling on the crowds below. Fonda is the local chief of the city's Standards and Safety Department and he sends an underling, Segal, to see if this accident was caused by a dereliction of the park's duty to keep the rides in good condition. Segal, in a role not unlike the one he played in NO WAY TO TREAT A LADY, is a nervous type, trying to quit smoking and also attempting to keep his emotions in check after having been shed by his wife, Tristan. The preliminary investigation seems to indicate that this was an accident. A short while later, another amusement facility is burned down in Pennsylvania. Segal begins to snoop around and discovers that the proprietors of both parks have traveled to Chicago at the same time. Segal goes to the hotel where they are staying and learns that five parks have been the recipients of cassette tapes from an extortionist who wants $1 million from them to cease and desist. The owners, McGarvin, Redecker, Basch, and Peterson, discuss the matter as they are being eavesdropped upon by Bottoms as well as Segal. Segal tells the owners that they have a formidable opponent in this nut-case. Widmark, the head of a government department, arrives and takes Segal off the project. Segal goes home to California, but Bottoms, who heard every word Segal said in the room (by using an electronic listening device), likes Segal and thinks that he is the only one attached to this crime who has a scintilla of brains. Bottoms communicates with the owners and says he'll accept the million only if Segal delivers it. The exchange is to take place at a Virginia amusement park and Segal is tapped for the assignment, over Widmark's carping. Segal is given a two-way radio and told to tune it to a certain frequency and await further instructions. Bottoms begins giving Segal orders as the man with the money is sent all around the Virginia park, going on ride after ride, purchasing food, etc. Bottoms is watching Segal every inch of the way, and despite the many operatives in the park, Bottoms gets away with the money on a daring snatch. When Bottoms sees that the money is all marked, he is enraged and phones Segal to tell him that he is now about to unleash his explosive equipment in a spectacular display. But he won't say where this will happen. More deducing from Segal (which is an unlikely leap of faith) determines that the park where Bottoms will strike next must be Magic Mountain in the Los Angeles suburb of Valencia. It could have been Coney Island's "Cyclone" or any of several other parks or rollercoasters, but Segal manages to convince Widmark that MM is the location because the approaching Fourth of July weekend will see the initiation of "Revolution," a spectacular new ride. ("Revolution" has a total loop in it and is, in fact, among the very best coasters ever built.) The park is filled with agents dressed in janitorial clothes. Sure enough, Segal was right. The bomb is found and rendered harmless. Bottoms watches this and decides that it isn't over until it's over, so he builds another bomb, gets on the coaster for it's very first ride, and puts the new bomb under his seat. Segal is there waiting when the inaugural riders disembark and are questioned by reporters. He recognizes Bottoms' voice and they are about to close in when Bottoms holds up his electronic detonator for all to see. The ride has taken off again and is filled with many innocent people, all of whom will be killed if Bottoms presses the button that will kaboom the bomb under the seat. Bottoms wants a gun given to him and safe passage out of the park where he is now surrounded. A radio expert (Steffens) jams the frequency and Bottoms, knowing the game is over, tries to run away. Segal wounds him with a shot, Bottoms runs for the coaster and climbs it, then is killed when hit by the cars as they race along the track. Widmark, who has been a grim-faced cynic the entire time, wants to finally thank Segal, but Segal, who has developed a respect for Bottoms during the picture, feels awful and walks away. The movie used Universal's "Sensurround" sound technique, which was so well-done in the studio's EARTHQUAKE and MIDWAY and here is expertly utilized to excellent advantage. The script is more than unusually intelligent for this type of picture and owes more to the suspense films of Hitchcock than the blatant disaster epics by Irwin Allen. When director Goldstone is good, he can be superior, as in this picture. When he is bad, as in SWASHBUCKLER and THE GANG THAT COULDN'T SHOOT

STRAIGHT, he is just miserable. The "Sensurround" equipment is expensive, about $2000 each, and many theaters did not have it, so the sound effects were lost on many ears. Producer Lang cast his wife, singer Monica Lewis, in a small role. Other cameos worth mentioning are Henry Olek, who later became a writer and has a credit on Steve Martin's ALL OF ME; Michael Bell, who is seldom seen in films, and is a hugely successful voice-over actor who made a fortune saying "butter" in the Parkay margarine commercials; and Charlie Tuna, a local L.A. radio disk jockey with an enormous following. Location shooting took place at Magic Mountain, King's Dominion in Richmond, Virginia, and Ocean View in Norfolk. Fonda had very little to do in the movie and one wonders why he took the job. One of the picture's problems is that Bottoms' character is never truly developed. His motivation is money, not mania, and the fact that he served in Vietnam is tossed in as an attempt to motivate his actions. Lost in all the action is Strasberg, as Segal's girl friend, and Hunt, as his daughter. With a little more attention paid to Bottoms and a bit more of a finale, this would have done far better business than the $12 million or so that it garnered.

p, Jennings Lang; d, James Goldstone; w, Richard Levinson, William Link (based on a story by Sanford Sheldon, Levinson, Link, from a story by Tommy Cook); ph, David M. Walsh, William Birch (Panavision, Technicolor); m, Lalo Schifrin; ed, Edward A. Biery, Richard Sprague; prod d, Henry Bumstead; md, Schifrin; set d, James W. Payne; cos, Burton; song, "Big Boy" (performed by Sparks); makeup, Emile La Vigne, Rich Sharpe; stunts, John Danheim.

Crime/Thriller   Cas.   (PR:C-O MPAA:PG)

ROLLIN' PLAINS*½   (1938) 61m GN bw

Tex Ritter (Tex Lawrence), Horace Murphy (Ananias), Snub Pollard (Pee Wee), Harriet Bennet (Ruth Moody), Hobart Bosworth (Gospel Moody), Edward Cassidy (Sheriff Tomlin), Karl Hackett (Dan Barrow), Charles King (Trigger Gargan), Ernest Adams (Cain Moody), Lynton Brent (Lope), Hank Carpenter (Hank Tomlin), Hank Worden (Squint), Augie Gomes (Weevil), Oscar Gaghan (Telegraph Clerk), The Beverly Hillbillies.

Ritter is a Texas Ranger who arrives in town on his horse White Flash to settle a water rights war and solve a murder. The sheepherders and cattlemen are feuding over who owns the water, and the singing cowboy plays diplomat and brings about a peaceful solution after the two factions have shot at each other enough. Ritter also solves a murder by tricking the killer into confessing, 'a la Sherlock Holmes. Not one of the better Ritter westerns. Grand National was teetering on the brink of bankruptcy, and the last reel of the film is footage from an earlier Ritter western (SING COWBOY SING, 1937).

p, Edward Finney; d, Al Herman; w, Lindsley Parsons, Edmund Kelso (based on a story by Jacques and Ciela Jacquard); ph, Francis Corby; m/l, Walt Samuels, Leonard Whiteup, Teddy Powell, Frank Harford.

Western   Cas.   (PR:A MPAA:NR)

ROLLIN' WESTWARD*½   (1939) 55m MON bw

Tex Ritter (Tex), Horace Murphy (Missouri), Dorothy Fay (Betty), Slim Whitaker (Bart), Herbert Corthell (Lawson), Harry Harvey (Watkins), Charles King (Haines), Hank Worden (Slim), Dave O'Brien (Red), Tom London (Sheriff), Estrelita Novarro (Dancer), White Flash the Horse.

A typical singing cowboy western using a formula that's almost worn threadbare. All the trite characters and plot elements are here—a greedy land-hungry gang controls all the water and forces the cattlemen out of business one by one. Ritter rides in, sings a few songs, and saves the town with the help of his faithful sidekick (Murphy). Fay provides the mild love interest.

p, Edward Finney; d, Al Herman; w, Fred Myton; ph, Marcel LePicard; ed, Fred Bain.

Western   (PR:A MPAA:NR)

ROLLING CARAVANS*½   (1938) 55m COL bw

John Luden (Breezy), Eleanor Stewart (Alice), Harry Woods (Dalton), Lafe McKee (Rankin), Buzz Barton (Jim), Slim Whitaker (Boots), Bud Osborne (Groucher), Cactus Mack, Richard Cramer, Tex Palmer, Sherry Tansey, Oscar Gahan, Curley Dresden, Jack Rockwell, Horace Murphy, Francis Walker, Franklyn Farnum, Tuffy the Dog.

In between singing and playing ventriloquist, Luden finds time to jail a gang of outlaws who want the "treasure" which they've heard lies on a newly claimed piece of land. They are shocked to find out that the only treasure there is rich soil that's fit for crops. Luden, and therefore the picture, doesn't have much appeal.

p, Larry Darmour; d, Joseph Levering; w, Nate Gatzert; ph, James S. Brown; ed, Dwight Caldwell.

Western   (PR:A MPAA:NR)

ROLLING DOWN THE GREAT DIVIDE**   (1942) 59m PRC bw

Bill "Cowboy Rambler" Boyd (Himself), Art Davis (Himself), Lee Powell (Himself), Wanda McKay (Rita), Glenn Strange (Joe), Karl Hackett (Pete), J. Merrill Holmes (Sheriff), Ted Adams (Martin), Jack Ingram (Dale), John Elliott (Lem), George Chesebro (Henchman), Horace B. Carpenter (Townsman), Jack Roper (Henchman), Curley Dresden, Dennis Moore, Tex Palmer.

"High tech" cattle rustlers use shortwave radios to track down lost steers. Boyd and Davis get help from the government, but it's not until they find the transmitter and send its location over the air (cryptically hidden in a cowboy song) that the gang is finally broken. Average B-Western fare with some okay singing.

p, Sigmund Neufeld; d, Peter Stewart [Sam Newfield]; w, George Milton [George W. Sayre, Milton Raison]; ph, Jack Greenhalgh; m, Johnny Lange, Lew Porter; ed, Holbrook N. Todd.

Western   Cas.   (PR:A MPAA:NR)

ROLLING HOME*   (1935, Brit.) 68m Sound City/AP&D bw

Will Fyffe (John McGregor), Ralph Ince (Wally), Molly Lamont (Ann), James Raglan (Capt. Pengelly), Ruth Maitland (Mrs. Murray), Mrs. Graham Moffatt (Mrs. McGregor), H. Saxon-Snell (Callaghan), Jock McKay (Jock), Charles Castella, Douglas Stewart, Herbert Cameron.

Fyffe is a ship's engineer who is fired when he takes the blame for a collision which is actually the captain's fault. A friend stows him away on a freighter, and when a mutiny breaks out on the ship, Fyffe and his pal prevent the mutineers from taking over the ship. Not very good, but a major box office success.

p, Norman Loudon; d, Ralph Ince; w, Frank Launder; ph, George Dudgeon Stretton, Hone Glendinning.

Comedy   (PR:A MPAA:NR)

ROLLIN' HOME TO TEXAS**   (1941) 63 MON bw

Tex Ritter (Tex), Cal Shrum (Cal), Slim Anderson (Slim), Eddie Dean (Sheriff), Virginia Carpenter (Mary), I. Stanford Jolley (Red), Harry Harvey (Lockwood), Cal Shrum's Rhythm Rangers, Gene Alsace, Jack Rutherford, Minta Durfee, Walt Shrum, Charles Phillips, Olin Francis, Harold Landon, Bob Battier, Donald Kerr, Rusty Cline, Gene Haas, Tony Flores, Mack Williams, Robert Hoag, Hal Blaire, White Flash the Horse.

Singing cowboy Ritter is a U.S. Marshal on the trail of a gang using convicts to rob banks. The gang sets up the con to hold up a bank, and then kills the unsuspecting man and collects the bounty money. Ritter puts a stop to this after a fair amount of action. Comic relief is provided by Anderson, and Shrum and his Rhythm Rangers help provide the saddle music.

p, Edward Finney; d, Al Herman; w, Robert Emmett [Tansey]; ph, Marcel A. LePicard; ed, Fred Bain; md, Frank Sanucci; m/l, Cal Shrum, Pappy Hoak, Hal Blair.

Western   (PR:A MPAA:NR)

ROLLING IN MONEY*   (1934, Brit.) 85m FOX British bw

Isabel Jeans (Duchess of Braceborough), Leslie Sarony (Mr. Hopkinson), Horace Hodges (Earl of Addleton), John Loder (Lord Gawthorpe), Lawrence Grossmith (Duke of Braceborough), Garry Marsh (Dursingham), Anna Lee (Lady Eggleby), Rene Ray (Eliza Dibbs), C.M. Hallard (Carter), Frank Atkinson (Wiggins), Arnold Lucy, Elaine Inescort.

Sarony is a cockney barber who suddenly finds himself the inheritor of a large fortune. Impoverished duchess Jeans and daughter Lee decide that he is the most likely candidate to marry Lee and bring money back to the family. Too much talk, evidence of stage origins, ruin this farce.

p, John Barrow; d, Al Parker; w, R.J. Davis, Sewell Stokes, Frank Atkinson (based on the play "Mr. Hopkinson" by R.C. Carton).

Comedy   (PR:A MPAA:NR)

ROLLING THUNDER***   (1977) 99m AIP c

William Devane (Maj. Charles Rane), Tommy Lee Jones (Johnny Vohden), Linda Haynes (Linda Forchet), Lisa Richards (Janet), Dabney Coleman (Maxwell), James Best (Texan), Cassie Yates (Candy), Lawrason Driscoll (Clif), Jordan Gerler (Mark), Luke Askew (Slim), James Victor (Lopez), Jane Abbott (Sister).

Hot on the heels of the success of TAXI DRIVER came a new film penned by prolific screenwriter (soon to turn director) Paul Schrader and shot on a shoestring in Texas. ROLLING THUNDER stars Devane (in a superb performance) as a Vietnam POW who after years of captivity is returned home along with cellmate Jones. Devane, a major, is given a hero's welcome by his small Texas town and presented with a small fortune in silver dollars—one for each day he was in captivity. While all this attention is heart-warming, Devane has actually come home to a wife who no longer loves him, a son who doesn't remember him, and a society that doesn't understand him. Emotionally deadened by his experiences in Vietnam ("You learn to love the pain," Devane tells his wife's lover), Devane only comes alive when he seeks vengeance for the death of his wife and son, who are killed by thieves who invade their home to steal the silver coins. The crooks try to torture the information out of Devane by shoving his hand down a garbage disposal, but he refuses to break—a display of macho that leads to his family's murder. Fitted with a hook to replace his mangled hand, Devane goes to Mexico in search of the killers. He eventually catches up with them and, seeing that there are too many to face alone, he returns to Texas to enlist the aid of his former comrade, Jones, who is rotting away in the bosom of his stiflingly polite family, who refuse to discuss the war with their son (the short scene in Jones' home is the best part of the film). After dinner, Devane simply tells Jones "I've found the men who killed my son." Jones replies "I'll get my gear." Together the men leave Texas behind and return to Mexico where a lengthy bloodbath in a brothel leaves all the killers dead and Devane and Jones alive, though one gets the distinct feeling they both wish they had been killed as well. While the film suffers from what has become Schrader's predictable obsession with ritual and gun-play, Devane and Jones overpower the material with their detailed and sensitive portrayals of men who lost their souls and emotions in another land.

p, Norman T. Herman; d, John Flynn; w, Paul Schrader, Heywood Gould; ph, Jordon Croneweth (Deluxe Color); m, Barry DeVorzon; ed, Frank P. Keller; art d, Steve Berger; spec eff, Richard Helmer.

Drama   Cas.   (PR:O MPAA:R)

ROLLOVER**   (1981) 118m IPC-Orion/WB c

Jane Fonda (Lee Winters), Kris Kristofferson (Hub Smith), Hume Cronyn (Maxwell Emery), Josef Sommer (Roy Lefcourt), Bob Gunton (Sal Naftari), Macon McCalman (Mr. Fewster), Ron Frazier (Gil Hovey), Jodi Long (Betsy Okamoto), Crocker Nevin (Warner Ackerman), Marvin Chatinover (Mr. Lipscomb), Ira B.

Wheeler *(Mr. Whitelaw)*, Paul Hecht *(Khalid)*, Norman Snow *(Hishan)*, Nelly Hoyos *(Lee Winter's Maid)*, Lansdale Chatfield *(Mrs. Emery)*, Sally Sockwell *(Mrs. Fewster)*, Martha Plimpton *(Fewster's Older Daughter)*, Gaby Glatzer *(Fewster's Younger Daughter)*, Howard Erskine *(Dodds)*, Michael Fiorillo *(Winterchem Limo Driver)*, Marilyn Berger *(Newscaster)*, Alex Wipf *(Mystery Man)*, Ahmed Yacoubi *(Older Arab Father)*, Charlie Laiken *(Faculty Member)*, Stanley Simmonds *(Sam, Nightwatchman)*, E. Brian Dean *(Nightwatchman)*, James Sutton *(Vice-President)*, Joel Stedman *(Asst. Vice-President)*, Garrison Lane *(Winters)*, Nina Reeves *(Secretary)*, Michael Prince, Carolyn Larsen, Ron Vaad, Rebecca Brooks, Richard Barbour, Danny Redmon, Eric Bethancourt, Steve Bullard, Neela Eriksen, Lawrence Sellars, Ernie Garrett, Art Hansen, Ira Lewis, Sharon Casey, Bernie Rachelle, Keith Eager, Dave Ellsworth, Bill Anagnos, Art Lambert, Jerry Hewitt, Mark Sutton, Debbie Watkins.

Fonda and Kristofferson are involved in the high-finance world of banking deals which teeters on the brink of disaster when Arab countries threaten to pull their money from U.S. banks instead of letting it "roll over." Director Alan J. Pakula continues his 1970s style of intrigue and conspiracy in cinema. Here, as in ALL THE PRESIDENT'S MEN with Redford and Hoffman and PARALLAX VIEW with Beatty, Pakula uses America's favorite superstars to deliver a sociopolitical message. Unfortunately, with ROLLOVER he has less success.

p, Bruce Gilbert; d, Alan J. Pakula; w, David Shaber (based on a story by Shaber, Howard Kohn, David Weir); ph, Giuseppe Rotunno, William Garroni (Panavision, Technicolor); m, Michael Small; ed, Evan Lottman; prod d, George Jenkins, Jay Moore; cos, Ann Roth.

Drama **Cas.** **(PR:O MPAA:R)**

ROMA*½** (1972, Ital./Fr.) 119m Ultra-Les Productions Artistes Associates/UA c (AKA: FELLINI'S ROMA)

Federico Fellini *(Himself)*, Peter Gonzales *(Fellini at age 18)*, Stefano Majore *(Fellini as a child)*, Pia De Doses *(The Princess)*, Renato Giovanneli *(Cardinal Ottaviani)*, Fiona Florence *(Young Prostitute)*, Marne Maitland *(Underground Guide)*, Galliano Sbarra *(Music Hall Compere)*, Alvaro Vitali *(Tap Dancer Imitating Fred Astaire)*, Britta Barnes, Angela De Leo, Elisa Mainardi, Stefano Mayore, Mario Del Vago, John Francis Lane, Libero Frissi, Sbarra Adami, Bireno, Anna Magnani, Gore Vidal, Paule Rout, Paola Natale, Marcelle Ginette Bron, Alfredo Adami, Gudrun Mardou Khiess, Giovanni Serboli, Libero Frissi, Dante Cleri, Mimmo Poli, Norma Giacchero, Alberto Sordi, Marcello Mastroianni.

ROMA is a confounding picture that is as much a documentary as it is a story. It was Fellini's intention to blend reality, fantasy, dreams, and pain and he succeeded but divided audiences and critics with the result. To Fellini, Rome is more than bricks and stone and mortar. It's a living, breathing being that has several million components. The story begins in Rimini, where Fellini was born, and Majore is seen as the young child from the resort who learns early that this seaside village on the Adriatic is not where he wants to be. He takes a trip with his classmates to the Eternal City in 1931, then finally moves there in 1938, just before war breaks out. Majore gives way to Gonzales as Fellini and the youth is treated to a panorama of Roman customs as he moves in with a family in a tenement and watches as the gregarious citizens live out their rich, noisy lives. Jump to the early 1970s and Fellini, as himself, is now a renowned director making a picture. They shoot a scene in a lengthy traffic jam during a heavy rain and Fellini's memory is jogged back to his early days in the city when he attended a vaudeville show during the war. The show features dreadful entertainment punctuated by various projectiles thrown at the stage, including a dead cat. Back to the present as Fellini is shooting the construction of the subway that has been in the process of being built for decades. Every time they dig in the streets, another archaelogical find is made and the area becomes off-limits to the builders and necessitates another diversion. They find an ancient villa under the city, and when an attempt is made to bring out the priceless frescoes they fall apart upon hitting Rome's fetid air. Fellini sees a young couple in love and goes back in reverie to a visit to a bordello where the girls walked up and down shamelessly in front of their ogling prospects. Then another, more upscale whorehouse is seen and the young Fellini thinks he is truly in love with Florence, one of the hookers. Back to today and an hysterical scene of a clerical fashion show set in the home of De Doses, an elderly peeress who is entertaining a cardinal, Giovanelli. Priests on roller skates and nuns in neon habits parade for the assemblage. There's a street festival in Trastevere (a section of Rome that means "across the Tiber") where the local hippies are besieged by the cops. Fellini begins interviewing people on camera. Magnani, Vidal, Sordi, and Mastroianni among others. (The latter two were cut from the U.S. print.) Darkness descends, the city begins to snore, and the silence is overwhelmed by a horde of motorcyclists careening through the city past the relics of what once was, winding up at the Colosseum as they appear to be just one of the many groups who have sacked Rome since time began. What does it all mean? Who knows? Fellini made two movies about blocked people in LA DOLCE VITA, where Mastroianni is a journalist who can't write, and 8½, where he is a director with no ideas. Here, Fellini has too many ideas and uses several that he's used before in other films, so it appears to be a remake of those pictures, albeit with several other actors and more scenes added. It's episodic and enigmatic and almost a grotesque parody of Fellini's other movies, as though the master was making fun of his own work. Two versions were released, in English and with subtitles. The dubbed version is excellent and loses nothing unless one is an Italian scholar. Rome has never looked so inviting and depressing as seen in this $3 million paean to the city Fellini loves and hates so much. Many laughs and just as many winces.

p, Turi Vasile; d, Federico Fellini; w, Fellini, Bernardino Zapponi; ph, Giuseppe Rotummo (Technicolor); m, Nino Rota; ed, Ruggero Mastroianni; prod d, Danilo Donati; md, Carlo Savina; set d, Andrea Fantacci; cos, Danilo Donati; spec eff, Adriano Pischiutta; ch, Gino Landi; makeup, Rino Carboni.

Drama **(PR:O MPAA:R)**

ROMA, CITTA APERTA (SEE: ROME, OPEN CITY, 1946, Ital.)

ROMA CONTRO ROMA (SEE: WAR OF THE ZOMBIES, THE, 1970, US/Jap.)

ROMA RIVUOLE CESARE (SEE: ROME WANTS ANOTHER CAESAR, 1974, Ital.)

ROMAN HOLIDAY**** (1953) 119m PAR bw

Gregory Peck *(Joe Bradley)*, Audrey Hepburn *(Princess Anne)*, Eddie Albert *(Irving Radovich)*, Hartley Power *(Mr. Hennessy)*, Laura Solari *(Hennessy's Secretary)*, Harcourt Williams *(Ambassador)*, Margaret Rawlings *(Countess Vereberg)*, Tullio Carminati *(Gen. Provno)*, Paolo Carlini *(Mario Delani)*, Claudio Ermelli *(Giovanni)*, Paolo Borboni *(Charwoman)*, Heinz Hindrich *(Dr. Bonnachoven)*, Gorella Gori *(Shoe Seller)*, Alfredo Rizzo *(Taxi Driver)*, John Horne *(Master of Ceremonies)*, Count Andre Eszterhazy, Col. Ugo Ballerini, Ugo De Pascale, Bruno Baschiera *(Embassy Aides)*, Princess Alma Cattaneo, Diane Lante *(Ladies-in-Waiting)*, Giacomo Penza *(H.E. the Papal Nuncio, Monsignor Altomonto)*, Eric Oulton *(Sir Hugo Macy de Farmington)*, Rapindranath Mitter, Princess Lilamani *(H. R.R. The Maharajah and The Raikuuari of Khanipur)*, Cesare Viori *(Prince Istvan Barossy Nagyavaros)*, Col. Nichola Kohopleff, Baroness Teresa Gauthier *(Ihre Hoheit der Furst und die Furstin von und zu Luchtenstichenholz)*, Hari Singh, Kmark Singh *(Themselves)*, Luigi Bocchi, Helen Fondra *(Count and Countess Von Marstrand)*, Mario Lucinni, Gherdo Fehrer *(Senor y Senora Joaquin de Capoes)*, Luis Marino *(Hasaan El Din Pasha)*, Armando Annuale *(Admiral Dancing with Princess)*, Luigi Moneta *(Old Man Dancing with Princess)*, Marco Tulli *(Pallid Young Man Dancing with Princess)*, Maurizio Arena *(Young Boy with Motorcar)*, John Fostini, George Higgins, Alfred Browne, John Cortay, Richard McNamara, Sidney Gordon *(Correspondents at Poker Game)*, Richard Neuhaus *(Embassy Guard Reporting)*, Alcide Tico *(Sculptor)*, Tania Weber *(Irving's Model)*, Armando Ambrogi *(Man at the Telephone)*, Patricia Varner *(Schoolmarm at Fontana de Trevi)*, Gildo Bocci *(Flower Seller)*, Giustino Olivieri *(Cafe Waiter)*, Dianora Veiga, Dominique Rika *(Girls at Cafe)*, Gianna Segale *(Girl With Irving)*, Carlo Rizzo *(Police Official)*, Mimmo Poli *(Workman Hugging Three outside Police Station)*, Octave Senoret, Pietro Pastore *(Faceless Men on Barge)*, Giuliano Raffaelli *(Faceless Man on Gangplank)*, Hank Werbe, Adam Jennette, Jan Dijkgraaf *(Correspondents)*, Piero Scanziani, Kurt Klinger, Maurice Montabre, Sytske Galema, Jacques Ferrier, Otto Gross, J. Cortes Cavanillas, Friedrich Lampe, Julio Moriones, Stephen House, Ferdinando De Aldisio *(Themselves)*, Edward Hitchcock *(Head of Foreign Correspondents)*, Desiderio Nobile *(Embassy Official at Press Conference)*.

What might have been an ordinary romantic comedy turned out to be one of the most charming films of the decade under the hand of Wyler, who had eschewed comedies for about 18 years before returning to the genre for this. A total of 10 nominations were given to ROMAN HOLIDAY, with Oscars awarded to Hepburn, Head, and Hunter. It was charming, wistful, frothy, and touched many hearts, resulting in strong receipts at the box office. Hepburn had made six appearances in European movies, then came to the U.S. and scored on Broadway in "Gigi" before winning international acclaim in this, her first Hollywood movie (although it was made entirely in Rome at Cinecitta Studios and on location). Hepburn had been filming MONTE CARLO BABY in the south of France when she met novelist Colette who was immediately struck by Hepburn's fragile beauty and told the New York producers that she wanted her to play the lead in "Gigi." The rest was a *fait accompli*, as Hepburn took advantage of her opportunity and was an overnight sensation. Here, she is the princess of a small country who arrives in Rome on a visit, surrounded by her coterie, which includes Rawlings as her chaperone and Carminati as her aide. She's always been protected and hasn't the vaguest idea of what life is like outside the environs of the castle in which she lives. She's only in her teens and beginning to rebel against the formality of the official rites she must endure and feels that here is her chance to see how the other half lives, so she bolts. While the frantic search for her goes on, she falls asleep on a park bench and meets one of the very reporters who has been trying to interview her, Peck. Since she is such a fairy-tale character, the entire world's press seeks to have her answer some questions (the way it was with Lady Diana before she became princess Di), so meeting her is a coup for Peck. Albert is a news photog who secretly snaps shots of her as she plays hookey from her life for 24 hours. Peck knows full well who she is but feigns ignorance and takes Hepburn on a sightseeing tour of Rome that includes all of the well-known places plus some not so famous as the police of her country and of Italy are desperately searching for her. Peck takes her on a motorcycle, they go dancing, they are briefly arrested, etc. As the incidents happen, Peck's hard-boiled reporter's outlook begins to soften and he falls in love with the innocent Hepburn, who is as guileless as a toddler. The long day comes to a close with the two of them desperately in love, but both know full well that it would never work on a permanent basis, as he is a commoner and she is royalty. (Don't forget, this was before Britain's royal family began to marry ordinary people.) At the finale, Hepburn returns to her cloistered regal world and Peck rightly decides that he will not violate her privacy by writing the exclusive story he sought so eagerly at the start. It's bubbly, carefree, has enough adventure and excitement to satisfy anyone, and the unrequited love story leaves an audience faintly bittersweet but knowing that it was the right move for both of them. ROMAN HOLIDAY set the stage for several other films of the genre, although none came close to the carefree insouciance of the original.

p&d, William Wyler; w, Ian McLellan Hunter, John Dighton (based on a story by Hunter); ph, Frank F. Planer, Henri Alekan; m, Georges Auric; ed, Robert Swink; art d, Hal Pereira, Walter Tyler; cos, Edith Head; makeup, Wally Westmore.

Romance/Comedy **Cas.** **(PR:A MPAA:NR)**

ROMAN SCANDALS*½** (1933) 85m UA bw

Eddie Cantor *(Eddie)*, Ruth Etting *(Olga)*, Gloria Stuart *(Princess Sylvia)*, David Manners *(Josephus)*, Verree Teasdale *(Empress Agrippa)*, Edward Arnold

(Emperor Valerius), Alan Mowbray *(Major-domo)*, Jack Rutherford *(Manius)*, Grace Poggi *(Slave Dancer)*, Willard Robertson *(Warren F. Cooper)*, Harry Holman *(Mayor of West Rome)*, Lee Kohlmar *(Storekeeper)*, Stanley Fields *(Slave Auctioneer)*, Charles C. Wilson *(Police Chief Pratt)*, Clarence Wilson *(Buggs the Museum Keeper)*, Stanley Andrews *(Official)*, Stanley Blystone *(Cop/Roman Jailer)*, Harry Cording, Lane Chandler, Duke York *(Soldiers)*, William Wagner *(Slave Buyer)*, Louise Carver *(Lady Slave Bidder)*, Francis Ford *(Citizen)*, Charles Arnt *(Caius the Food Tester)*, Leo Willis *(Torturer)*, Frank Hagney *(Lucius, Aide)*, Michael Mark *(Assistant Cook)*, Dick Alexander *(Guard)*, Paul Porcasi *(Chef)*, John Ince *(Senator)*, Jane Darwell *(Beauty Salon Manager)*, Billy Barty *(Little Eddie)*, Iris Shunn [Meredith] *(Girl)*, Aileen Riggin *(Slave Dancer)*, Katharine Mauk, Rosalie Fromson, Mary Lange, Vivian Keefer, Barbara Pepper, Theo Plane, Lucille Ball *(Slave Girls)*, The Abbottiers [Florence Wilson, Rose Kirsner, Genevieve Irwin, Dolly Bell], Jane Hamilton, Gigi Parrish, Bonnie Bannon, Dolores Casey.

Cantor made six films for Goldwyn. This was his fourth and second only to THE KID FROM SPAIN in popularity. In later years, Goldwyn's next discovery was Danny Kaye and the similarity of the themes of both actors' movies is clearly evident. It had been Goldwyn's thought to adapt George Bernard Shaw's "Androcles And The Lion" as a vehicle for Cantor, but when that proved a difficult deal, the producer hired Robert Sherwood and George S. Kaufman to fashion a story that would take Cantor to Rome at the time of the Caesars. He was displeased with their draft and they had to sue him to recover the promised fee. Perrin, Oppenheimer, and Sheekman were brought in to add jokes and McGuire was then hired to whip the whole thing into suitable shooting shape. Too many cooks did not spoil this broth, and it was one of the best Cantor-Goldwyn associations. Funny, musical, and with more than a little female flesh, ROMAN SCANDALS is a sort-of WIZARD OF OZ, in that, Cantor is a wacky delivery boy in West Rome, Oklahoma, who goes into a dream sequence and imagines himself to be a slave in old Rome. His major job is to be official food-taster to the evil Arnold, emperor of the city-state. The slim plot includes Cantor proving that Arnold is a fraud, a love story between Stuart and Manners, the usual chase (this time around it's a chariot chase, a direct satirical shot at BEN HUR, satirically shot by the sequence's director Ralph Cedar). In the end, he wakes up and is back in the present. Making it all a dream was a mistake and the opening prolog and closing epilog were not needed. Berkeley, in his last choreographic job before going on to Warner Brothers and film history, does one scene where The Goldwyn Girls are totally nude except for long blonde wigs. It was shot on a strictly closed set late at night and one of the naked women was Lucille Ball, whom Berkeley hired despite Goldwyn's protests. Slapstick nonsense from the moment the picture goes to Rome, it's verbally funny as well, and every penny of the then-huge million dollar budget is on screen. Harry Warren and Al Dubin, who would later join Berkeley at Warner Bros. for a host of hits, wrote several tunes including: "No More Love" (sung by Ruth Etting, the Goldwyn Girls, danced by Grace Poggi), "Build a Little Home" (sung by Cantor, Goldwyn Girls), "Keep Young And Beautiful" (sung by Cantor, Goldwyn Girls, Billy Barty), "Rome Wasn't Built in a Day." Warren and L. Wolfe "Wolfie" Gilbert teamed to write "Put a Tax on Love" (sung by Cantor). Ruth Etting was a popular blues singer of the era and even had a movie made about her life, LOVE ME OR LEAVE ME, that starred Doris Day and James Cagney. Her appeal as a singer is not realized in this, as she only does one song and doesn't act very well. Little Billy Barty's career continues into the 1980s and his work on behalf of "little people" is famous all over the world. In a totally anachronistic move, they managed to put Cantor into "black face" in one scene and it sticks out.

p, Samuel Goldwyn; d, Frank Tuttle; w, William Anthony McGuire, George Oppenheimer, Arthur Sheekman, Nat Perrin (based on a story by George S. Kaufman, Robert E. Sherwood); ph, Gregg Toland; ed, Stuart Heisler; md, Alfred Newman; art d, Richard Day; cos, John Harkrider; ch, Busby Berkeley.

Musical Comedy **(PR:A-C MPAA:NR)**

ROMAN SPRING OF MRS. STONE, THE*½** (1961, U.S./Brit.) Anglo-Amalgamated-Seven Arts/WB c (AKA: THE WIDOW AND THE GIGOLO)

Vivien Leigh *(Karen Stone)*, Warren Beatty *(Pablo di Leo)*, Coral Browne *(Meg)*, Jill St. John *(Bingham)*, Lotte Lenya *(Contessa Magda Terribili-Gonzales)*, Jeremy Spenser *(Young Man)*, Stella Bonheur *(Mrs. Jamison-Walker)*, Josephine Brown *(Lucia)*, Peter Dyneley *(L. Greener)*, Carl Jaffe *(Baron)*, Harold Kasket *(Tailor)*, Viola Keats *(Julia)*, Cleo Laine *(Singer)*, Bessie Love *(Bunny)*, Elspeth March *(Mrs. Barrow)*, Henry McCarthy *(Kennedy)*, Warren Mitchell *(Giorgio)*, John Phillips *(Tom Stone)*, Paul Stassino *(Barber)* Ernest Thesiger *(Stefano)*, Mavis Villiers *(Mrs. Coogan)*, Thelma D'Aguir *(Mita)*.

This picture, like some French wines, grows better with age and is a good example of Beatty's acting ability, a talent that was really there, before he became a matinee idol. Leigh was 48, her husband, Olivier, had just left her for a younger woman. Beatty was 23, eager, ambitious, and sincerely wanting to change his image after SPLENDOR IN THE GRASS. Based on Williams' only novel (he'd written many books of short stories, some of which became plays and others, films), the screenplay by Lambert became far more explicit in many ways than the subtlety of the short book. Leigh was making her first appearance in six years and would only do one more film, SHIP OF FOOLS, before her death. Williams loved Leigh's work in the film but never said a thing about Beatty, perhaps because he was, at first, against the man in the role, then changed his mind when Beatty arrived in Puerto Rico masquerading as an Italian and totally fooled Williams. After Beatty admitted it was only an accent he acquired for the role, Williams shrugged and gave his blessing. Beatty's Italian accent was occasionally spotty, but it was actually fairly good when one considers Beatty's Virginia heritage. The film is filled with Williams' bon mots, many of which are quotable and most of which went right over the heads of the people who decried the movie. Leigh is a fading actress who has just failed in a role tailored for her but which should have gone to a younger actress. She decides that it's time for a vacation in Europe with husband Phillips, a wealthy man in poor health who adores her. Phillips dies on their way to Italy and she continues to Rome where she makes an attempt to enjoy herself. Browne is Leigh's friend and confidante. When the widow admits that she misses being with a man, journalist Browne arranges for her to meet Lenya, a pimp who specializes in romance for anyone who has the money to buy. Lenya's newest find is Beatty, an Italian youth who takes Lenya's orders. It's not long before Beatty is making love to this woman more than twice his age and Leigh rewards him with expensive gifts and folderol which annoys Lenya. She would prefer that Leigh pay Beatty real money so a percentage could be cut from the cash. Lenya decides that it's time to break this up, so she introduces Beatty to rich movie star St. John. When Leigh learns of this, there is a bitchy confrontation between her and the younger actress. While all of this is going on, Spenser, a mysterious young man, has been tailing Leigh from the minute she arrived in Rome. Leigh pleads with Beatty to return to her arms, but he shows her contempt and sneers that she is now the object of all Rome's derision because she has thrown herself so completely at him. She follows Beatty to St. John's hotel, and when there is no longer any question that the two of them are having an affair, Leigh sadly returns to her home, still followed by Spenser. Once there, she removes Beatty's photo from its frame, wraps her keys in a handkerchief, goes to the open window, and tosses them to the furtive Spenser, still not knowing who he is or what he wants. The few glimpses we've had of Spenser are enough to know that he is homicidal. Leigh sits in a chair, lights a cigarette, sighs, and looks up as Spenser enters the room and walks toward her, his coat filling the frame like the Angel of Death who has come to claim his latest victim as the movie ends. The lines are purely Williams. When Lenya has a complaint, Leighs states: "The beautiful make their own laws." Beatty mentions a middle-aged woman he knows of who died in bed with her throat cut. Leigh, who has been concentrating on her card hand, looks up and says, "After three more years of this, assassination would be a convenience." Lenya was superb and received an Oscar nomination but lost to Rita Moreno in WEST SIDE STORY. The great German actress never had much success in U.S. movies, although she will always be remembered as the villainess in FROM RUSSIA WITH LOVE. Married for years to Kurt Weill (who wrote "The Threepenny Opera" among other things), her name probably sounds familiar because it appears in the song her husband penned with Bertolt Brecht, "Mack, The Knife." The assistant director, who went on to great fame, was Peter Yates.

p, Louis de Rochemont; d, Jose Quintero; w, Gavin Lambert, Jan Read (based on the novel by Tennessee Williams); ph, Harry Waxman (Technicolor), m, Richard Addinsell; ed, Ralph Kamplen; md, Douglas Gamley; prod d, Roger Furse; art d, Herbert Smith; set d, John Jarvis; cos, Pierre Balmain, Bumble Dawson; m/l, "Che Noia L'Amour," Addinsell, Paddy Roberts; makeup, Bob Lawrence.

Drama **Cas.** **(PR:C MPAA:NR)**

ROMANCE*** (1930) 76m MGM bw

Greta Garbo *(Rita Cavallini)*, Lewis Stone *(Cornelius Van Tuyl)*, Gavin Gordon *(Tom Armstrong)*, Elliott Nugent *(Harry)*, Florence Lake *(Susan Van Tuyl)*, Clara Blandick *(Miss Armstrong)*, Henry Armetta *(Beppo)*, Mathilde Comont *(Vannucci)*, Countess de Liguoro *(Nina)*.

This was Garbo's second talkie and it tried to capture the fiery seductions of her silent-era films such as FLESH AND THE DEVIL but her leading man, Gordon, was no John Gilbert. Garbo is an Italian opera diva (supposedly a soprano but really a contralto) who is attracted to a young curate, Gordon, and seduces him. We see these lovers in a flashback related by Gordon when Gordon, as an elderly bishop, is trying to dissuade his grandson, Nugent, from marrying an actress. Garbo is shown falling in love with the younger Gordon and confessing that she has been the kept woman of wealthy Stone. Garbo gives a final performance and then goes to Stone, telling him that she is leaving him for her one true love, Gordon. But Gordon discovers that Garbo has seen the elderly man once again and believes she has been unfaithful to him, denouncing her. He then apologizes and begs that she spend the night with him. Garbo is stunned, believing Gordon to be different, and asks that he not treat her as other men have. When she begins to pray, Gordon realizes that he has been controlled by lust and leaves Garbo forever, bringing the story in flash-forward to Gordon's discussion with Nugent. The grandson cannot be put off from marrying his actress and does. Gordon then reads of Garbo's death in a newspaper account and sinks into sorrow. This film does not quite come off, though Garbo is fascinating to watch. The story line and Gordon are just too weak for Garbo to drag the film into greatness, try as she might. Her skill with dialog is evident and just watching this magnificent actress is reward enough to sit through a less-than-spectacular film. The Garbo portion of the film is set in 1850 and Gordon is looking back half a century, yet the surroundings of his old age are more in the style of the 1930s than 1900, where the last setting should be.

d, Clarence Brown; w, Bess Meredyth, Edwin Justus Mayer (based on the play "Signora Cavallini" by Edward Sheldon); ph, William Daniels; ed, Hugh Wynn, Leslie F. Wilder.

Romance **(PR:A MPAA:NR)**

ROMANCE A LA CARTE* (1938, Brit.) 72m GS Enterprises/RKO bw

Leslie Perrins *(Louis)*, Dorothy Boyd *(Anne)*, Antony Holles *(Rudolph)*, Charles Sewell *(Roberto)*, Michael Bazalgette *(Tony)*, Paul Sheridan *(Strelini)*, Betty Shale *(Lady Eleanor Clure)*, Michael Ripper.

Maitre d' Holles is always fighting with head chef Perrins, but when the recalcitrant cook gives a broke diner (Boyd) a job, Holles fires them both. By the fade out, though, they are all together again, opening a restaurant of their own. Boring comedy.

p, George Smith; d, Maclean Rogers; w, Vera Allinson (based on a story by Paul Hervey Fox); ph, Geoffrey Faithfull.

Comedy **(PR:A MPAA:NR)**

ROMANCE AND RHYTHM   (SEE: COWBOY FROM BROOKLYN, 1938)

ROMANCE AND RICHES½**   (1937, Brit.) 70m Garrett Klement/GN bw (GB: THE AMAZING QUEST OF ERNEST BLISS; AKA: RICHES AND ROMANCE; AMAZING ADVENTURE)

Cary Grant (Ernest Bliss), Mary Brian (Frances Clayton), Peter Gawthorne (Sir James Aldroyd), Henry Kendall (Lord Ronnie Honiton), Leon M. Lion (Dorrington), John Turnbull (Masters), Arthur Hardy (Crawley), Iris Ashley (Clare Winters), Garry Marsh (The Buyer), Andrea Malandrinos (Giuseppe), Alfred Wellesley (Montague), Marie Wright (Mrs. Heath), Buena Bent (Mrs. Mott), Charles Farrell (Scales), Hal Gordon (Bill Bronson), Quinton MacPherson (Clowes), Frank Stanmore (Mr. Mott), Alf Goddard (Butcher Bill), Moore Marriott (Edwards), Ralph Richardson (Waiter).

An entertaining comedy about a man with a problem everyone wishes they might have. Grant is a multi-millionaire by inheritance in England and he continues to be morose and unhappy. He goes to Harley Street in London (where all the expensive doctors have their offices) and consults with Gawthorne, who charges him 25 guineas and tells him that his problem is "underwork." Since Grant has never had to toil a moment in his wastrel existence, he takes stock of what Gawthorne has said and bets a bundle that he can earn his own way for one year and never touch the cash that has been willed to him. He takes a room in a rundown boarding house and is soon unable to pay his rent. Then he gets a job as an oven salesman, meets Brian, who works as the secretary at the company, and is soon successful at the firm when he comes up with an idea of offering free meals to anyone who buys. The company offers him a partnership if he buys in but he won't do it. While maintaining his love relationship with Brian, he has a few jobs, including work as a porter (that goes out the window when his female employer's husband comes home and suspects hanky-panky) and as a chauffeur, getting involved with some thieves in the latter capacity. Just before the year is up, Grant learns that Brian is set to marry her boss at the oven company because she has a financial problem, as she is supporting her sister who is ill. Grant calls off the bet he made and rushes to Brian and proposes. When they are married, the guests are not his hoity-toity friends. Rather, they are the poor and downtrodden (but with hearts of gold) people he met while living in the tenement district. This Oppenheim story was previously made as a silent. A note about Harley Street. . .when a British doctor becomes a surgeon, they no longer refer to him as "Doctor" and he becomes "Mister." A few unbelievable plot complications get in the way, but it's fairly good fun most of the time. The picture has also been released under the titles: ROMANCE AND RICHES, THE AMAZING QUEST OF ERNEST BLISS and AMAZING ADVENTURE. There was nothing amazing about a person having to earn his own living. Grant's career was already booming in the U.S. when he took some time out to go to England for this. A "guinea" is a pound plus a shilling and represents what professionals in England always ask for. At one time, it was an actual coin but has since been dropped from the British treasury, although the custom lingers.

p, Robert Garrett, Otto Klement; d, Alfred Zeisler; w, John C. Balderston (based on the novel The Amazing Quest of Ernest Bliss by E. Phillips Oppenheim); ph, Otto Heller; m, Werner Bachman; ed, Merrill White; art d, David Rawnsley.

Comedy   **(PR:A MPAA:NR)**

ROMANCE FOR THREE   (SEE: PARADISE FOR THREE, 1938)

ROMANCE IN FLANDERS, A, 1937, Brit.   (SEE: LOST ON THE WESTERN FRONT, 1937, Brit.)

ROMANCE IN MANHATTAN**   (1935) 79m RKO bw

Francis Lederer (Karel Novak), Ginger Rogers (Sylvia Dennis), Arthur Hohl (Attorney Pander), Jimmy Butler (Frank Dennis), J. Farrell MacDonald (Officer Murphy), Helen Ware (Miss Anthrop), Eily Malyon (Miss Evans), Oscar Apfel (The Judge), Lillian Harmer (Landlady), Reginald Barlow (Customs Inspector), Donald Meek (Minister), Sidney Toler (Sergeant), Harold Goodwin (Doctor), Christian Rub (Immigrant), Frank Sheridan (Customs Inspector), Irving Bacon (Counterman), Andy Clyde (Scots Liquor Store Owner).

Rogers left her dancing shoes in the closet for this romantic drama about a Czech immigrant (Lederer) who makes a go for it in the States. He becomes a taxi driver and meets all sorts of people, mostly unfriendly. Rogers, however, is just the opposite, and the pair fall in love by the finale.

p, Pandro S. Berman; d, Stephen Roberts; w, Jane Murfin, Edward Kaufman (based on a story by Norman Krasna, Don Hartman); ph, Nick Musuraca; ed, Jack Hively; md, Al Colombo; art d, Van Nest Polglase, Charles Kirk; spec eff, Vernon Walker; makeup, Mel Burns.

Drama/Romance   **(PR:A MPAA:NR)**

ROMANCE IN RHYTHM**   (1934, Brit.) 73m Allied/MGM bw (AKA: NIGHT CLUB MURDER)

Phyllis Clare (Ruth Lee), David Hutcheson (Bob Mervyn), David Burns (Mollari), Queenie Leonard, Paul Tillett, Geoffrey Goodheart, Philip Strange, Julian Vedey, Carroll Gibbons and His Savoy Orpheans.

After nightclub chorus girl Clare breaks up with boy friend Hutcheson, a musician, her new fiance is found murdered. Of course Hutcheson is the immediate suspect, but eventually Burns, the nightclub manager who secretly wanted Clare for himself, is proven to be the killer. Typical of the many nightclub-based crime pictures English studios were producing at the time.

p,d&w, Lawrence Huntingdon.

Crime   **(PR:C MPAA:NR)**

ROMANCE IN THE DARK*½   (1938) 80m PAR bw

Gladys Swarthout (Ilona Boros), John Boles (Antal Kovach), John Barrymore (Zolton Jason), Claire Dodd (Countess Monica Foldessy), Fritz Feld (Fritz), Curt Bois (Von Hemisch), Carlos de Valdez (Baliot), Torben Meyer (Prof. Jacobsen), Ferdinand Gottschalk (Pianist), Margaret Randall (Kovach's Maid), Fortunio Bonanova (Tenor), Esther Muir (Prima Donna), Eddy Conrad (Barber), Lois Verner (Fat Girl Singer), Janet Elsie Clark (Girl Singer), Alexander Schonberg (Doorman), Otto Hoffman (Stage Doorman), Otto Fries, George B. Hickman.

Swarthout stars as a Hungarian peasant girl who is stuck in the middle of a rivalry between tenor Boles and his manager Barrymore. Both men are trying to prove their manliness to countess Dodd. Boles' plan is to turn Swarthout into a star ("the Persian Nightingale") so that Barrymore will be attracted to her. Boles will then be free to move in on Dodds, the girl he is really after. Swarthout, with her mediocre N.Y. Metropolitan voice, warbled the following with her co-stars: "Bewitched By The Night" (Jay Gorney), "Tonight We Love" (Ralph Rainger, Leo Robin), "Blue Dawn" (Ned Washington, Phil Boutelje), "The Nearness Of You" (Washington, Hoagy Carmichael), "Romance In The Dark" (Sam Coslow, Gertrude Niesen).

p, Harlan Thompson; d, H.C. Potter; w, Frank Partos, Ann Morrison Chapin (based on the play "The Yellow Nightingale" by Hermann Bahr); ph, William Mellor; ed, Jimmy Smith; md, Boris Morros; cos, Travis Banton.

Musical   **(PR:A MPAA:NR)**

ROMANCE IN THE RAIN**   (1934) 76m UNIV bw

Roger Pryor (Charlie Denton), Heather Angel (Cynthia), Victor Moore (J. Franklyn Blank), Esther Ralston (Gwen), Ruth Donnelly (Sparks), Paul Kaye (Rex), Christian Rub (Slotnick), Guinn "Big Boy" Williams (Panya), David Worth (Hedgwick), Yellow Horse (Eskimo), Henry Armetta, Clara Kimball Young, King Baggott.

Moore is the publisher of a lurid book entitled Livid Love Tales. One of his writers, Pryor, concocts a publicity scheme that has the magazine sponsoring a national contest to pick a Prince Charming and a Cinderella, then have them marry in front of a huge audience. At the last moment the scheme fails and Moore is forced to marry his own girl friend (Ralston). Basically a star vehicle for Moore, whose personality carries this generally weak comedy.

d, Stuart Walker; w, Barry Trivers, Gladys Unger, John V. A. Weaver (based on a story by Sid Herzig, Jay Gorney); ph, Charles Stumar; m/l, Gorney, Don Hartmen.

Comedy   **(PR:A MPAA:NR)**

ROMANCE IS SACRED   (SEE: KING AND THE CHORUS GIRL, THE, 1937)

ROMANCE OF A HORSE THIEF**   (1971) 101m AA c

Yul Brynner (Stoloff), Eli Wallach (Kifke), Jane Birkin (Naomi), Oliver Tobias (Zanvill Kradnik), Lainie Kazan (Estusha), David Opatoshu (Schloime Kradnik), Serge Gainsbourg (Sigmund), Henri Sera (Mendel), Linda Veras (Countess Grabowsky), Branko Plesa (Lt. Vishinsky), Vladimir Bacic (Gruber), Alenka Rancic (Sura), Branko Spoljar (Strugatch), Dina Rutic (Cheitche), Marilu Tolo (Manka), Marla Mizar (Schoolteacher), Mile Sosa (Grisha), Aljosa Vuckovic (Tailor), Mort Shuman (Piano Player), Vida Jerman, Vera Stanojevic, Mira Blaskovic, Nada Cibic (Girls), Eugen Werber.

Brynner is the Cossack captain who rules a village of Jewish peasants in Poland, none of whom is especially fond of the way they are ruled. Birkin returns from a school in France where she learned the politics of revolution, and soon persuades her people to stand up to Brynner's oppressive tactics. Polonsky's slow-moving direction and Brynner's lack of screen time hamper this well-intentioned picture.

p, Gene Gutowski; d, Abraham Polonsky; w, David Opatoshu (based on a story by Joseph Opatoshu); ph, Piero Portalupi (Technicolor); m, Mort Shuman; ed, Kevin Connor; art d, Otto Pischinger; cos, Ruth Myers.

Drama   **Cas.**   **(PR:A MPAA:GP)**

ROMANCE OF RIO GRANDE   (SEE: ROMANCE OF THE RIO GRANDE, 1929)

ROMANCE OF ROSY RIDGE, THE**   (1947) 105m MGM bw

Van Johnson (Henry Carson), Thomas Mitchell (Gill MacBean), Janet Leigh (Lissy Anne MacBean), Marshall Thompson (Ben MacBean), Selena Royle (Sairy MacBean), Charles Dingle (John Dessark), Dean Stockwell (Andrew MacBean), Guy Kibbee (Cal Baggett), Elizabeth Risdon (Emily Baggett), Jim Davis (Badge Dessark), Russell Simpson (Dan Yeary), O. Z. Whitehead (Ninny Nat), James Bell (John Willhart), Joyce Arling (Mrs. Willhart), William Bishop (Ad Buchanan), Paul Langton (Tom Yeary).

Johnson is a veteran of the Civil War who finds work on the farm of bitter Missourian Mitchell. Although a treaty has been signed, feuding is still going on between those who fought on opposing sides. Johnson proves himself after romancing Mitchell's daughter (Leigh in her film debut) and battling barn-burning night raiders. Enough charm and action to overcome the schmaltzy title.

p, Jack Cummings; d, Roy Rowland; w, Lester Cole (based on a story by MacKinlay Kantor); ph, Sidney Wagner; m, George Bassman; ed, Ralph E. Winters; art d, Cedric Gibbons, Eddie Imazu, Richard Duce; set d, Edwin B. Willis, Elliot Morgan; ch, Jack Donohue; m/l, Earl Robinson, Lewis Allan.

Drama   **(PR:A MPAA:NR)**

ROMANCE OF SEVILLE, A*½   (1929, Brit.) 62m BIP/FN-Pathe c

Alexandre D'Arcy (Ramon), Marguerite Allan (Pepita), Randle Ayrton (Estavian), Cecil Barry (Estaban), Hugh Eden (Juan), Eugenie Anami (Dolores), Koblenzova.

The dapper D'Arcy plays a romantic jewel thief in danger of losing his mistress to an artist who's obsessed with her beauty. A unique example of pre-1930's color photography, A ROMANCE IN SEVILLE was shot silent in Spain's beautiful Andalusia. It wasn't until one year later that sound was added. Alma Reville, a contributor to the screenplay, was on her way to achieving a place in cinema history as Alfred Hitchcock's wife and co-writer.

d, Norman Walker; w, Garnett Weston, Alma Reville (based on the story "The Majo" by Arline Lord); ph, Claude Friese-Greene.

Romance (PR:A MPAA:NR)

ROMANCE OF THE LIMBERLOST**   (1938) 75m MON bw

Jean Parker (Laurie), Eric Linden (Wayne), Marjorie Main (Nora), Edward Pawley (Corson), Betty Blythe (Mrs. Parker), Sarah Padden (Sarah), George Cleveland (Nathan), Hollis Jewell (Chris), Guy Usher (Judge), Jean O'Neill (Ruth), Jack Kennedy (Abner), Harry Harvey (Jones).

Parker is a girl from the swamp who meets and falls in love with an aspiring lawyer from the better part of town. She is about to be married to a wealthy widower by her greedy aunt (Main) when the groom-to-be is knocked off. Linden defends the accused, Jewell, in his first case, clearing everyone's name, winning Parker, and reuniting her with Main. Slow-moving but rewarding remake of GIRL OF THE LIMBERLOST (1934).

d, William Nigh; w, Marion Orth (based on the novel Girl Of The Limberlost by Gene Stratton Porter); ph, Gilbert Warrenton; ed, Russell Schoengarth.

Romance (PR:A MPAA:NR)

ROMANCE OF THE REDWOODS*½   (1939) 61m COL bw

Charles Bickford (Steve), Jean Parker (June), Alan Bridge (Whittaker), Gordon Oliver (Malone), Ann Shoemaker (Mother), Lloyd Hughes (Carter), Pat O'Malley (Yerkes), Marc Lawrence (Joe), Earl Gunn (Socko), Don Beddoe (Forbes), Erville Alderson (Jackson), Lee Prather (Judge Handley).

Bickford runs into trouble in a lumberjack town when co-worker Oliver is fatally mangled by a logger's saw. Everyone suspects foul play since Bickford lost the affection of Parker to Oliver, who flaunted his city superiority. Bickford tries to clear himself, and his bravery in the face of a devastating forest fire helps his cause. Tiredly directed by Vidor.

d, Charles Vidor; w, Michael L. Simmons (based on a story by Jack London); ph, Allen G. Siegler; ed, Byron Robinson.

Drama (PR:A MPAA:NR)

ROMANCE OF THE RIO GRANDE**½   (1929) 95m FOX bw

Warner Baxter (Pablo Wharton Cameron), Mary Duncan (Carlotta), Antonio Moreno (Juan), Mona Maris (Manuelita), Robert Edeson (Don Fernando), Agostino Borgato (Vincente), Albert Roccardi (Padre Miguel), Soledad Jiminez (Catalina), Major Coleman (Dorry Wayne), Charles Byers (Dick Rivers), Merrill McCormick (Luca).

Baxter plays a man who, after a long absence, returns to his grandfather's hacienda, much to the pleasure of the older man. Gramps is afraid that his less-than-desirable nephew, Moreno, will be his heir, but Baxter eases the old fellow's mind. . .and wins the hand of Maris. Crisply photographed by Arthur Edeson, who the same year was nominated for an Academy Award for his work on IN OLD ARIZONA, and the following year for ALL QUIET ON THE WESTERN FRONT.

d, Alfred Santell; w, Marion Orth (based on the novel Conquistador by Katherine Fullerton Gerould); ph, Arthur Edeson; cos, Sophie Wachner.

Western (PR:A MPAA:NR)

ROMANCE OF THE RIO GRANDE**   (1941) 73m FOX bw

Cesar Romero (Cisco Kid), Patricia Morison (Rosita), Lynne Roberts (Maria), Ricardo Cortez (Ricardo), Chris-Pin Martin (Gordito), Aldrich Bowker (Padre), Joseph McDonald (Carlos Hernandez), Pedro De Cordoba (Don Fernando), Inez Palange (Mama Lopez), Raphael [Ray]Bennett (Carver), Trevor Bardette (Manuel), Tom London (Marshal), Eva Puig (Marta), Richard Lane.

An inferior remake of the 1929 version which puts the Cisco Kid (Romero) in the lead role. He is given the job of locating elderly cattleman De Cordoba's missing grandson, in order to keep a malevolent nephew from getting his fortune. (See CISCO KID series, Index.)

p, Sol M. Wurtzel; d, Herbert I. Leeds; w, Harold Buchman, Samuel G. Engel (based on the novel Conquistador by Katherine Fullerton Gerould and on a character created by O. Henry); ph, Charles Clarke; ed, Fred Allen; md, Emil Newman; cos, Herschel.

Western (PR:A MPAA:NR)

ROMANCE OF THE ROCKIES**   (1938) 53m MON bw

Tom Keene (Tom), Beryl Wallace (Betty), Don Orlando (Mike), Bill Cody, Jr. (Jimmy), Franklyn Farnum (Stone), Earl Dwire (Joe), Charles Murphy (Sheriff), Steve Clark (Trigger), Russell Paul, Jim Corey, Tex Palmer, Jack C. Smith, Blackie Whiteford, Frank Ellis.

Keene is a small-town doctor who settles a water-rights battle by dynamiting the underground stream to the surface. His blast topples the plans of Farnum and Dwire to control the area's ranchers.

p&d, R. N. Bradbury; w, Robert Emmett [Tansey]; ph, Bert Longenecker.

Western (PR:A MPAA:NR)

ROMANCE ON THE BEACH   (SEE: SIN ON THE BEACH, 1964, FR.)

ROMANCE ON THE HIGH SEAS***   (1948) 99m WB c (GB: IT'S MAGIC)

Jack Carson (Peter Virgil), Janice Paige (Elvira Kent), Don DeFore (Michael Kent), Doris Day (Georgia Garrett), Oscar Levant (Oscar Farrar), S. Z. Sakall (Uncle Lazlo), Fortunio Bonanova (Plinio), Eric Blore (Ship's Doctor), Franklin Pangborn (Rio Hotel Clerk), Leslie Brooks (Miss Medwick), William Bakewell (Travel Agent), Johnny Berkes (The Drunk), Kenneth Britton (Bartender), Frank Dae (Minister), John Holland (Best Man), Janet Warren (Organist), John Alvin (Travel Agent), Douglas Kennedy (Car Salesman), Mary Field (Elvira's Maid), Tristram Coffin (Headwaiter on Ship), Grady Sutton (Radio Operator), Barbara Bates (Stewardess), Sandra Gould (Telephone Operator), Avon Long, Sir Lancelot, The Samba Kings, Page Cavanaugh Trio.

Paige, thinking that her husband (DeFore) is cheating on her, decides to skip her ocean cruise and stay home to spy on him. DeFore, thinking that his wife is cheating on him, wonders why she is taking a cruise without him and hires a private eye to go along. Day is sent by Paige to take her place on the cruise and, naturally, is mistaken by the detective as Paige. What follows is the obligatory romance between the pair. A great premise which doesn't quite deliver what it promises but it's fun anyway. This was the film debut for Miss Day, who got the part through a couple of strokes of luck. The one-time singer in Les Brown's band, Doris Von Kappelhoff (as she was then known), was performing at a Hollywood party where composer Jule Styne heard her rendition of "Embraceable You." Judy Garland was intended to take the role in Curtiz's new picture, but was replaced by a soon-to-be pregnant Betty Hutton. A worried Curtiz then took a look at and listen to Doris, upon Styne's request. She was on her way to a busy career in pictures. Songs include: "It's Magic," "It's You or No One," "The Tourist Trade," "Put 'Em in a Box, Tie 'Em with a Ribbon, and Throw 'Em in the Deep Blue Sea," "Two Lovers Met in the Night," "Run, Run, Run," "I'm in Love" (Sammy Cahn, Jule Styne), "Cuban Rhapsody" (Ray Heindorf, Oscar Levant).

p, Alex Gottlieb; d, Michael Curtiz; w, Julius J. Epstein, Philip G. Epstein, I. A. L. Diamond (based on a story "Romance in High C" by S. Pondal Rios, Carlos A. Olivari); ph, Elwood Bredell (Technicolor); ed, Rudi Fehr; md, Leo F. Forbstein; art d, Anton Grot; set d, Howard Winterbottom; cos, Milo Anderson; spec eff, David Curtiz, Wilfred M. Cline, Robert Burks; ch, Busby Berkeley.

Musical/Comedy (PR:A MPAA:NR)

ROMANCE ON THE RANGE**   (1942) 63m REP bw

Roy Rogers (Roy), George "Gabby" Hayes (Gabby), Sally Payne (Sally), Linda Hayes (Joan Stuart), Edward Pawley (Banning), Harry L. Woods (Steve), Hal Taliaferro (Sheriff Wilson), Glenn Strange (Stokes), Roy Barcroft (Pete), Jack Kirk, Pat Brady, Jack O'Shea, Dick Wessel, Dick Alexander, Bob Nolan and The Sons of the Pioneers, Trigger the Horse.

Linda Hayes is the owner of a trading post who lives in the East, but has hired Pawley to manage the business out West. Concerned with his honesty, Hayes pays a visit incognito. She learns that Pawley is part of an outlaw gang stealing furs through the post. With the help of Rogers and his maid (Payne), she gets her post running right again. Tunes include: "When Romance Rides The Range," "Coyote Serenade," "Sing as You Work," "Oh, Wonderful World," "Rocky Mountain Lullaby" (Tim Spencer, Glen Spencer, Sam Allen, Bob Nolan, sung by Rogers and The Sons of the Pioneers).

p&d, Joseph P. Kane; w, J. Benton Cheney; ph, William Nobles; ed, Lester Orlebeck; md, Cy Feuer; art d, Russell Kimball.

Western Cas. (PR:A MPAA:NR)

ROMANCE ON THE RUN*½   (1938) 68m REP bw

Donald Woods (Barry Drake), Patricia Ellis (Dale), Grace Bradley (Lily Lamont), Edward Brophy (Whitey), William Demarest (Eckhart), Craig Reynolds (Cooper), Andrew Tombes (Ridgeway), Bert Roach (Happy Drunk), Leon Weaver (Pappy Hatfield), Edwin Maxwell (Mondoon), Granville Bates (Phelps), Jean Joyce (Dolly), Georgia Simmons (Ma Hatfield).

Woods is a private eye hired by an insurance company to locate some stolen jewels. With Ellis tagging along, the detective chases the crooks from the city to the back roads of the South before emerging as the victor. Well below par.

p, Herman Schlom; d, Gus Meins; w, Jack Townley (based on a story by Eric Taylor); ph, Ernest Miller; ed, Ernest Sims; md, Alberto Colombo; cos, Irene Saltern; m/l, Jack Lawrence, Peter Tinturim.

Comedy (PR:A MPAA:NR)

ROMANCE RIDES THE RANGE*   (1936) 59m Spectrum bw

Fred Scott, Cliff Nazarro, Marion Shilling, Buzz Barton, Bob Kortman, Ted [Theodore]Lorch, Frank Yaconelli, Phil Dunham, Jack Evans, William Steele, Allen Greer, White King the Horse.

Scott is cast as a one-time opera singer who goes West to prevent an outlaw gang from acquiring land which supposedly contains a buried treasure. Pretty dumb.

p, Jed Buell, George H. Callaghan; d, Harry Fraser; w, Tom Gibson; ph, Robert Cline; ed, Helen Curley.

Western (PR:A MPAA:NR)

ROMANOFF AND JULIET***½   (1961) 103m Pavla/UNIV c

Peter Ustinov (The General), Sandra Dee (Juliet Moulsworth), John Gavin (Igor Romanoff), Akim Tamiroff (Vadim Romanoff), Alix Talton (Beulah Moulsworth), Rik Von Nutter (Freddie van der Stuyt), John Phillips (Hooper Moulsworth), Peter Jones (Otto), Tamara Shayne (Evdokia Romanoff), Suzanne Cloutier (Marfa Zlotochienka), Edward Atienza (Patriarch), John Alderson (Randle Wix), Thomas Chalmers (Chief Executive), Carl Don (Spy), Tonio Selwart (President of U. N.), Ernato Chiantoni (Joseph the Pilot), Booth Colman (Customs Officer), Moura Budberg (Cook), Gianpaolo Maffei, Strelsa Brown.

Peter Ustinov wrote, produced, directed, and starred in this adaptation of his play and, for once, here was a person who could wear all the hats without becoming a fool. The play opened in London in 1956, then went to New York with Ustinov in the lead. He took some time off from writing to act in SPARTACUS (winning an Oscar as Best Supporting Actor) and also helped shape the script. The studio agreed to film this one in return, but only if he took Gavin and Dee, two Universal Studios contract players, as part of the deal. He agreed, but was not thrilled with either of them, although Dee came off well. Gavin eventually quit acting to go into politics and wound up Ambassador to Mexico in the Reagan administration. Ustinov is the leader of the small country of Concordia (not unlike the Grand Duchy of Fenwick in THE MOUSE THAT ROARED, etc.), a country so small that everyone in the government must double in their jobs. The ambassador to the U.S. is also Ustinov's chauffeur, the Minister of Communications runs the switchboard at the castle, et al. Ustinov's country doesn't even get a spot on the map, but it does belong to the UN, and when Ustinov abstains from a deadlocked vote and goes home, the structure of the United Nations is threatened. Both the Russians and the Americans go after his deciding vote and try to bribe him with aid to the tiny country whose army numbers fewer than a dozen, most of whom are napping on duty. Tamiroff is the Russian ambassador to Concordia and his handsome son is Gavin. Phillips is the U.S. ambassador and his daughter is Dee. Ustinov fears offending either super-power and wants to be Swiss-like in his neutrality. He makes sure that Gavin and Dee meet and lets nature take its course. Gavin's Russian sweetheart, Cloutier, tries to break up the affair but fails. She's a staunch Red but comes to see that life in the decadent West is not as horrifying as she'd thought. Both powers are lampooned as they embark on a pattern of wiretapping, espionage, distributing money, etc., but Ustinov reigns supreme and sees to it that Dee and Gavin get married, much to the annoyance of Tamiroff and Phillips. In the end, happiness through love prevails. It's a total farce and the scene for slapstick is set early in the opening sequence when Ustinov does all the voices of the delegates at the UN voting "Yes" and "No" in the many dialects he commands in his throat. By playing cupid for the young couple, Ustinov hopes that an example will be set for Russia and the U.S. to settle their differences in peace and harmony. Would that it were that easy. The interiors were made at Cinecitta Studios in Rome and the little town of Todi doubled as Concordia. Todi is about 800 years old, sits 100 miles north of Rome, and was once an Etruscan city. What happened to this tiny town when a large movie company descended on it to knock the economy into the stratosphere might make a movie on its own. Cloutier is Ustinov's wife, although this is the only movie of his in which she has appeared. She was a Canadian debutante who became a model, then an actress in Hollywood. After spending some time in Charles Laughton's acting troupe in California, she went to France, joined the Comedie Francaise, then met Orson Welles, who cast her as Desdemona in his OTHELLO. In 1951, she met Ustinov and they began courting. He cast her in his play "No Sign Of The Dove" in 1953 and they were married the following year. She should act more often.

p,d&w, Peter Ustinov (based on his play); ph, Robert Krasker (Technicolor); m, Mario Nascimbene; ed, Renzo Lucidi; md, Nascimbene; art d, Alexander Trauner; set d, Maurice Barnathan; cos, Orietta Nasalli-Rocca, Annalisa Nasalli-Rocca, Bill Thomas; makeup, Jack Freeman, Giuseppe Annunziata.

Comedy   **(PR:A MPAA:NR)**

ROMANTIC AGE, THE, 1934   (SEE: SISTERS UNDER THE SKIN, 1934)

ROMANTIC AGE, THE, 1949, Brit.   (SEE: NAUGHTY ARLETTE, 1949, Brit.)

ROMANTIC COMEDY½**   (1983) 103m MGM-UA c

Dudley Moore (Jason), Mary Steenburgen (Phoebe), Frances Sternhagen (Blanche), Janet Eilber (Allison), Robyn Douglass (Kate), Ron Leibman (Leo), Roziska Halmos (Maid), Alexander Lockwood (Minister), Erica Hiller (Young Woman), Sean Patrick Guerin (Timmy), Dick Wieand (TV Reporter), Brass Adams (Bartender), Stephen Roberts (Maitre d'), Santos Morales (Bus Boy), Tom Kubjak (Passerby), Fran Bennett, George Tyne (Doctors), Karen Raskind, Allan Kilman, Carole Hemingway, Stanley Ralph Ross, June Sanders, Darrah Meley, Rochelle Robertson (Actors).

Bernard Slade's adaptation of his own play was not romantic, nor very comedic. The stage presentation starred Mia Farrow and Tony Perkins and was produced by Morton Gottlieb, a savvy Broadway guy who specializes in small-cast shows like this, "Same Time, Next Year," and "Sleuth." Moore had come off two bombs, SIX WEEKS and LOVESICK, and this made three in a row. Moore is a writer who meets Steenburgen, another writer. They team up to do plays together, have some success in their work, some failure, and can't seem to get their romantic lives together. She marries Liebman; he's wed to Eilber and their work relationship continues. (It would appear to be what Betty Comden and Adolph Green go through. Each is married to someone else but their writing partnership has flourished, despite some dreadful flops like "A Doll's Life.") A very New York piece that is as weighty as a sackful of feathers, ROMANTIC COMEDY came and went so quickly that it was barely noticed. In one scene shot in an old theater in downtown Los Angeles (to simulate a Boston tryout of the new Moore-Steenburgen play), note Hemingway, a radio personality in Los Angeles, and Meley as the wife and girl friend of matinee idol Ross. The play that they were supposedly doing was so lame that the actors had to ask director Hiller if it was a hit or a flop in the script, as the scene itself was not funny. Needless to say, they added the sound of uproarious laughter to the sequence so the nervous Moore and Steenburgen could react happily as they paced in the lobby. Years before, when Hiller was casting "The Piano Sport," a picture that never was made, Ross and Louise Sorel read for him and he never forgot either, casting Ross in this and Sorel as Matthau's office romance in PLAZA SUITE. Author Slade, who also fancies himself an actor, often went out on the road in his own shows and did "Same Time, Next Year" in his native Canada.

p, Walter Mirisch, Morton Gottlieb; d, Arthur Hiller; w, Bernard Slade (based on

his play); ph, David M. Walsh (Metrocolor); m, Marvin Hamlisch; ed, John C. Howard; prod d, Alfred Sweeney; cos, Joe I. Tompkins.

Comedy   Cas.   **(PR:A-C MPAA:PG)**

ROMANTIC ENGLISHWOMAN, THE*½   (1975, Brit./Fr.) 115m Dial-Meric-Matalon/New World c

Glenda Jackson (Elizabeth Fielding), Michael Caine (Lewis Fielding), Helmut Berger (Thomas), Marcus Richardson (David Fielding), Kate Nelligan (Isabel), Rene Kolldehof (Herman), Michel Lonsdale (Swan), Beatrice Romand (Catherine), Anna Steele (Annie), Nathalie Delon (Miranda), Bill Wallis (Hendrik), Julie Peasgood (New Nanny), David De Keyser (George), Phil Brown (Mr. Wilson), Marcella Markham (Mrs. Wilson), Lillias Walker (1st Meal-ticket Lady), Doris Nolan (2nd Meal-ticket Lady), Norman Scace (Headwaiter), Tom Chatto (Neighbor), Frankie Jordan (Supermarket Cashier), Frances Tomelty (Airport Shop Assistant).

Caine is a successful writer whose imagination becomes increasingly vivid when his wife (Jackson) takes a trip to Europe. Separated by hundreds of miles and angry emotions, Jackson forgets about her husband and becomes attracted to German drug-smuggler Berger. She returns home to Caine in Britain and the pair invite Berger to stay with them. Caine is intent on having the fellow help do some writing, but instead finds him fondling his wife. Jackson runs away with Berger, but Caine pursues and retrieves his wife. An intelligent comedy (of sorts) from Joseph Losey which explores Luigi Pirandello's concept of characters being under control of the author.

p, Daniel M. Angel; d, Joseph Losey; w, Tom Stoppard, Thomas Wiseman (based on the novel by Wiseman); ph, Gerry Fisher (Eastmancolor); m, Richard Hartley; ed, Reginald Beck; art d, Richard MacDonald; cos, Ruth Myers.

Comedy/Drama   Cas.   **(PR:O MPAA:R)**

ROMANY LOVE*   (1931, Brit.) 58m Patrick K. Heale/MGM bw

Esmond Knight (Davy Summers), Florence McHugh (Taraline), Roy Travers (Joe Cayson), Jack Barnes, Rita Cave.

An uninteresting musical tale of gypsy life which has Knight battling a malicious rival who wants to steal away his girl. Knight proves to be the better man and wins the girl at the end.

p, Patrick K. Heale; d, Fred Paul; w, Heale.

Musical/Romance   **(PR:A MPAA:NR)**

ROME ADVENTURE**   (1962) 118m WB c (GB: LOVERS MUST LEARN)

Troy Donahue (Don Porter), Angie Dickinson (Lyda), Rossano Brazzi (Roberto Orlandi), Suzanne Pleshette (Prudence Bell), Constance Ford (Daisy), Al Hirt (Al), Hampton Fancher (Albert Stillwell), Iphigenie Castiglioni (Contessa), Chad Everett (Young Man), Gertrude Flynn (Mrs. Riggs), Pamela Austin (Agnes), Lili Valenty (Angelina), Mary Patton (Mrs. Bell), Maurice Wells (Mr. Bell).

Producer, director, writer Delmer Daves needs work on all three fronts in this cliched tale of librarian Pleshette who vacations in Rome with the hope of experiencing love. She is soon working in a bookstore. Donahue goes out with her when his rich girl friend Dickinson returns to the U.S. Pleshette falls in love with him, and when Dickinson returns to Rome to reclaim him, Pleshette goes home discouraged. She is surprised to find Donahue waiting for her to arrive. The only thing that hits the mark here is Max Steiner's score.

p,d&w, Delmer Daves (based on a novel by Irving Fineman); ph, Charles Lawton (Technicolor); m, Max Steiner; ed, William Ziegler; art d, Leo K. Kuter; set d, John P. Austin; cos, Howard Shoup; makeup, Gordon Bau; m/l, "Rome Adventure," Steiner, Hugo Peretti, Luigi Creatore, George David Weiss, "Al-di-La," C. Donida, Mogol (sung by Emilio Pericoli).

Drama/Romance   **(PR:A MPAA:NR)**

ROME EXPRESS**   (1933, Brit.) 90m GAU/UNIV bw

Esther Ralston (Asta Marvelle), Conrad Veidt (Zurta), Hugh Williams (Tony), Donald Calthrop (Poole), Joan Barry (Mrs. Maxted), Harold Huth (Grant), Gordon Harker (Tom Bishop), Eliot Makeham (Mills), Cedric Hardwick (Alistair McBane), Frank Vosper (Mons. Jolif), Muriel Aked (Spinster), Finlay Currie (Publicist).

One of a number of "Express" pictures of the early 1930s (China, Orient, Shanghai, and Silk), the ROME EXPRESS is a crime picture which takes place on board a Paris-to-Rome train. A murder occurs and the entire cast is suspect, from Calthrop, a crook who is wanted for double-crossing Veidt and Williams, to Ralston, a movie star, and Barry and Huth—married, but not to each other. The cast is large but is never lost sight of, thanks to Forde's adroit directing hand. The first picture to come out of Britain's Gaumont Studios, and not half bad either.

p, Michael Balcon; d, Walter Forde; w, Clifford Grey, Sidney Gilliat, Frank Vosper, Ralph Stock (based on a story by Grey); ph, Gunther Krampf; cos, Gordon Conway.

Crime/Mystery   **(PR:A MPAA:NR)**

ROME, OPEN CITY   (SEE: OPEN CITY, 1946, Ital.)

ROME WANTS ANOTHER CAESAR**   (1974, Ital.) 100m RAI-SPA c (ROMA RIVUOLE CESARE)

Daniel Olbrychsky (Claudius), Hiram Keller (Ottavius), Lino Troisi (Proconsul), Gino Lavagetto (1st Republican), Luigi Montini (2nd Republican), Guido Lollobrigida (Blue Tunic), Jose De Vega (Oxyntas), Renato Baldini (Old Senator).

Rome during the final days of Julius Caesar is brought to the screen by Hungarian director Jancso with brilliant Polish actor Olbrychsky taking the starring role of rebel leader Claudius. The title is a variation on the line spoken by Olbrychsky after being deposed: "I dream of a world without Caesars." This is one of a number of pictures

Jancso made in Italy, this one for television. Shot in the Tunisian desert, the awesome visual style—the vast landscape, rolling hills, and sweeping horizons—are only enhanced by their transfer to the big screen.

d, Miklos Jancso; w, Jancso, Giovanna Gagliardo; ph, Janos Kende (Eastmancolor); m, Uberta Bertacca; ed, Guilano Mattioli; cos, Bertacca.

Historical Drama (PR:A MPAA:NR)

ROMEO AND JULIET**** (1936) 127m MGM bw

Norma Shearer *(Juliet)*, Leslie Howard *(Romeo)*, Edna May Oliver *(Nurse to Juliet)*, John Barrymore *(Mercutio)*, C. Aubrey Smith *(Lord Capulet)*, Basil Rathbone *(Tybalt)*, Andy Devine *(Peter)*, Henry Kolker *(Friar Lawrence)*, Violet Kemble-Cooper *(Lady Capulet)*, Ralph Forbes *(Paris)*, Reginald Denny *(Benvolio)*, Maurice Murphy *(Balthasar)*, Conway Tearle *(Prince of Verona)*, Virginia Hammond *(Lady Montague)*, Robert Warwick *(Lord Montague)*, Vernon Downing *(Samson Capulet)*, Ian Wolfe *(Apothecary)*, Anthony Kemble-Cooper *(Gregory Capulet)*, Anthony March *(Mercutio's Page)*, Howard Wilson *(Abraham Montague)*, Carlyle Blackwell, Jr. *(Tybalt's Page)*, John Bryan *(Friar John)*, Katherine De Mille *(Rosalind)*, Wallis Clark *(Town Watch)*, Dean Richmond Bentor, Lita Chevret, Jeanne Hart, Dorothy Granger *(Bits)*, Harold Entwistle, Charles Bancroft, Jose Rubio *(Noblemen)*.

MGM production chief and lover of the classics, Thalberg spared no expense in this superb filming of Shakespeare's famous tragedy-romance, starring the queen of the MGM lot Shearer (Thalberg's wife) and the sensitive Howard. In historic Verona Howard meets Shearer and they quickly fall in love, despite the fact that their families, the Montagues and the Capulets, are mortal enemies in a feud that trails back for decades. But their bliss is brief, shattered when Rathbone, a truculent sort, who is Shearer's cousin, duels with and kills the ebullient Barrymore, Howard's close friend. The incensed Howard then battles Rathbone and kills him and is punished by being banished from Verona. Shearer's family, not knowing she is secretly wed to Howard, arranges for a marriage between her and Forbes. Desperate and alone, Shearer consults with her confessor, Kolker, who devises a plan by which she can escape her marriage to Forbes. He gives her a sleeping potion that will make her appear dead. Kolker than states that while she is in this death sleep, he will have Shearer's body placed in the family vault. She will sleep her sleep of the dead until Howard returns and, when she awakens, she and Howard will flee to Mantua and live happily. But the plan goes awry. Shearer ostensibly dies and is placed in the vault but the message from Kolker to Howard that tells the lover that she is only in a deep sleep is waylaid. Howard arrives and discovers his beloved, thinking her really dead. He takes poison to join her in eternity and when Shearer awakens and finds to her horror that Howard is dead, she drives a dagger into her heart. Finding the young lovers dead, the warring families sorrowfully settle their feud. The eternal Romeo and Juliet story has never been brought to the screen with such verve and lavish production values as in this picture. Although Howard and Shearer are technically too old for their parts (the characters were teenagers) they perform splendidly, rendering their parts with great sensitivity. Cukor was the perfect director for this romance, a man of genuine emotions who was able to imbue his cast members with his own passion toward the characters, and it shows in every frame of ROMEO AND JULIET. This was Thalberg's pet project for years and he had to battle MGM boss Louis B. Mayer all the way to get the film in the can, along with some members of the cast, including a wild Barrymore, who was drunk more often as not during the filming. Thalberg banked on his wife, Shearer, saying to doubting executives that "I believe Norma can play anything and do it better than anyone else. Marie Antoinette and Juliet mark the end of Norma Shearer's acting career. Too many stars stay on camera too long. I want her to bow out at her highest point." Thus Thalberg had decreed his wife's swan song, although she would go on appearing before the cameras several years after Thalberg's premature death. Shearer was 31 when she did ROMEO AND JULIET. Howard was 49 and at first refused the part by saying that he was too old. Thalberg's first choice for Romeo was Fredric March who turned down the part immediately when it was offered to him. Clark Gable, of all actors, was then approached and asked to do the role. He did a double take and then exclaimed: "I don't look Shakespeare. I don't talk Shakespeare. I don't like Shakespeare, and I won't do Shakespeare." A half dozen more film Lotharios were approached, including Errol Flynn and Robert Donat, and all turned the role down. Thalberg went back to work on Howard and finally argued the British actor into undertaking the role. He didn't have to argue Barrymore into his spritely role of Mercutio, which he delivered with a slight Irish brogue and with enough flighty gestures as to border on the homosexual, but it is a stunning performance nevertheless, one of the most flamboyant ever attached to a Shakespearean character. The actor needed funds desperately, having begun a new affair with starlet Elaine Barrie, and he accepted a flat $20,000 fee for his role when only a few years earlier he was receiving $150,000 per film from MGM. To keep him from drinking during the production Thalberg placed Barrymore in a sanitarium near the studio and had armed guards watch him night and day, escorting him to and from the studio, lest he slip into a bar and drink himself into a stupor. Barrymore got around this imprisonment by having his friend, writer Gene Fowler, stand outside his sanitarium window and tie bottles of booze to the ends of bedsheets Barrymore lowered to him. When on the set Barrymore vexed the gentle Cukor no end by inserting foul words into the beautiful Shakespearean lines. "Jack, please," begged Cukor. "Strange how me heritage encumbereth me speech," Barrymore told him. He carried on, made fun of the duel he was supposed to perform with Rathbone, and finally Cukor could bear it no more, calling Thalberg and begging the producer to calm Barrymore down. The producer talked patiently to the great actor, asking him to deliver the lines correctly. "Very well," sighed Barrymore. "I shall say it that thou mayest see how it stinketh." His performance was nonetheless superb and when Barrymore delivered the Queen Mab speech the entire company stopped everything and applauded. "F—- the applause," Barrymore shouted. "Who's got a drink?" To do the film, Thalberg had to promise Mayer that he would bring it in for $800,000, not

the the $1.5 million as originally planned. Thalberg supervised the costumes and sets down to the last balcony. These were beautifully constructed under the supervision of Gibbons, the studio's workhorse designer. "I've never had a picture closer to my heart," Thalberg told Mayer, and the boss believed him, as Thalberg exhausted himself to reach perfection in this film. He instructed Shakespeare experts William Strunk, Jr., and James Tucker Murray to supervise the script-which was not to have one line in it that was not Shakespeare's-and added: "Your job is to protect Shakespeare from *us!*" Thalberg met endlessly with director Cukor, urging him to complete the film with taste and speed at the same time. Cukor would later state: "It was unfamiliar territory for me....It's one picture that if I had to do over again, I'd know how. I'd get the garlic and Mediterranean into it." Thanks to production delays, of which the illustrious Barrymore was no small part, ROMEO AND JULIET went over $2 million, and when released the film barely recouped its investment. Shearer was lauded for her role but Howard was criticized for lacking passion as the boy lover. Mayer sat through a private screening of the film with Thalberg and, overwhelmed by Thalberg's passion for the film, stated his enthusiasm that it might do well at the box office. It didn't and Mayer stayed away from the classics for the next decade.

p, Irving Thalberg; d, George Cukor; w, Talbot Jennings (based on the play by William Shakespeare); ph, William Daniels; m, Herbert Stothart; ed, Margaret Booth; art d, Cedric Gibbons; set d, Gibbons, Oliver Messel; cos, Messel, Adrian; ch, Agnes De Mille; liberary adv, Prof. William Strunk, Jr.

Romance/Drama (PR:C MPAA:NR)

ROMEO AND JULIET**** (1954, Brit.) 138m Verona/UA c

Laurence Harvey *(Romeo)*, Susan Shentall *(Juliet)*, Flora Robson *(Nurse)*, Mervyn Johns *(Friar Laurence)*, Bill Travers *(Benvolio)*, Enzo Fiermonte *(Tybalt)*, Aldo Zollo *(Mercutio)*, Giovanni Rota *(Prince of Verona)*, Sebastian Cabot *(Capulet)*, Lydia Sherwood *(Lady Capulet)*, Norman Wooland *(Paris)*, Guilio Garbinetti *(Montague)*, Nietta Zocchi *(Lady Montague)*, Dagmar Josipovich *(Rosaline)*, Luciano Bodi *(Abraham)*, Thomas Nicholls *(Friar John)*, John Gielgud *(Chorus)*.

For years, people have wondered why Shakespeare, that most British of all writers, set so many of his plays in Italy. One theory is that he took a few years off from Stratford to travel the Boot. Otherwise, how would he have known what he did about the country? His decriptions of various Veronese buildings were accurate and even some of the local Italian jargon was correctly translated. The story of the star-crossed lovers Romeo and Juliet was not originated by Shakespeare. It was first told by a writer from Vicenza, Luigi da Porto, who said he heard the tale while relaxing at the Calderan baths. In 1535, the version saw the press. Almost 20 years later, Bandello wrote and published it at Lucca. Subsequent versions were written and presented in other languages, then Shakespeare added his genius and his version is the one that has survived time. Castellani's script, which took him almost two years to adapt, sets the time in the early years of the 15th Century, which is slightly different from the Leslie Howard-Norma Shearer film made 18 years before. Shot entirely on location in various cities around Italy, the film proves Castellani is a painter as well as a director. By that we mean to say that he uses his camera and his actors in such a way that each scene looks like a work done by a master. In order to achieve that effect, Castellani spent months in museums, had the costumes based upon the paintings of Piero della Francesca, Filippino Lippi, Fiorenzo di Lorenzo, Antonio Pisanello, Sandro Boticelli, Vittore Carpaccio, and many others. As Romeo, he chose the 26-year-old Laurence Harvey, a Yugoslavian-born actor who mastered English in South Africa, and 20-year-old Susan Shentall, who made her only appearance in film here as Juliet. Shentall had been discovered dining in a restaurant by the director. She gave up acting immediately after the film in favor of a marriage. Castellani's unerring eye for detail allowed him to shoot in widely varying geographical locations that had been untouched by time. He blended the moves so seamlessly that it's impossible to tell that he'd shot in Venice, Siena, Montagna, Verona, and several other locations. In an attempt to make it feel authentic as well as look that way, actors were chosen who were not all that familiar to the public and several others who were not actors at all. Thus, Friar John was played by a member of the crew (Nicholls), a local architect named Zollo was chosen to be Mercutio, Montague was played by a Venetian canal worker, and more than 200 extras were culled from the immediate population. The resulting film was a delight to see and listen to, but it never found large favor among audiences. Castellani's adaptation deleted much but it never felt as though it had been truncated. Scenes were shifted and so was emphasis. To Castellani's credit, his writing maintained the literacy of the Bard and his direction, though a trifle slow at times, looked like paintings set in motion. It was Shakespeare as he might have liked to see it done. Although the movie did not even get a mention at the Oscars, it won the Venice Film Festival's Grand Prix Award, nosing out classics like LA STRADA and ON THE WATERFRONT. Castellani's version is so gorgeous that the words could be dialed out on the sound board and it would still stand above most movies.

p, Sandro Ghenzi, Joseph Janni; d&w, Renato Castellani (based on the play by William Shakespeare); ph, Robert Krasker (Technicolor); m, Roman Vlad; ed, Sydney Hayers; cos, Leonor Fini; ch, Medy Oboiensky.

Tragedy Cas. (PR:A MPAA:NR)

ROMEO AND JULIET** (1955, USSR) 90m Mosfilm c

Oulanova *(Juliet)*, Jdanov *(Romeo)*, Koren *(Mercutio)*, Lutchiline *(Lorenzo)*, Erminislaiev *(Tybett)*, Lapouri *(Paris)*.

A filmed ballet version of the classic tale of love from Shakespeare. Of little cinematic interest, but beautifully danced to Prokofiev's score.

d&w, L. Arachtam, L. Lavosky (based on the play by William Shakespeare); ph, A. Chelenov, Tehen-You-Lin (Sovcolor); m, Sergei Prokofiev; ed, Lichorshin.

Tragedy (PR:A MPAA:NR)

ROMEO AND JULIET*** (1966, Brit.) 124m Poetic/EM c

Margot Fonteyn *(Juliet)*, Rudolf Nureyev *(Romeo)*, David Blair *(Mercutio)*, Desmond Doyle *(Tybalt)*, Julia Farron *(Lady Capulet)*, Michael Somes *(Lord Capulet)*, Anthony Dowell *(Benvolio)*, Derek Rencher *(Paris)*, Leslie Edwards *(Escalus)*, Georgina Parkinson *(Rosaline)*, Gerd Larsen *(Nurse)*, Ronald Hynd *(Friar Laurence)*, Christopher Newton *(Lord Montague)*, Betty Kavanagh *(Lady Montague)*, Ann Jenner, Ann Howard, Carol Hill, Margaret Lyons, Jennifer Penney, Dianne Horsham *(Juliet's Friends)*, Keith Rosson, Robert Mead, Lambert Cox, Ian Hamilton, Kenneth Mason, Laurence Ruffel *(Mandolin Dancers)*, Deanne Bergsma, Monica Mason, Carole Needham *(Three Harlots)*, Royal Ballet *(Ballroom Guests, Townspeople)*.

Producer-director Czinner made "Der Rosenkavalier" a few years before as a film and it played to moderate houses. He tried the same thing here as he set up eight cameras at Pinewood Studios and photographed the Prokofiev ballet that played at London's Royal Opera House in 1965. With spotty choreography by Kenneth MacMillan and a Juliet who was old enough to be the real Juliet's mother (Fonteyn was 46 when she made this) plus a Romeo who wore more makeup than his lover, it was little more than a lensed ballet. The picture is in three acts, with a brief intermission after the first. To help the audience know what's happening, there is a prolog before each act to set the scene and what's about to transpire. The more intimate moments are danced well but the ensemble pieces leave much to be desired and the post-production dubbing of sound effects is shoddy. The glorious score is wonderfully conducted by Lanchbery, and if you don't like ballet, just turn down the picture on your TV set and listen to the music. The dancing is uniformly well done but one had wished George Balanchine could have done the choreography instead of MacMillan. The film was "presented" by Joseph E. Levine.

p&d, Paul Czinner; w, (based on the ballet by Sergei Prokofiev, Kenneth MacMillan, from the play by William Shakespeare); ph, S.D. Onions (Eastmancolor); m, Prokofiev; ed, Philip Barnikel; md, John Lanchbery; set d&cos, Nicholas Georgiadis; ch, MacMillan; makeup, George Claff.

Tragedy **Cas.** **(PR:A MPAA:NR)**

ROMEO AND JULIET*½** (1968, Brit./Ital.) 138m British Home Entertainments-Verona-DD/PAR c

Olivia Hussey *(Juliet)*, Leonard Whiting *(Romeo)*, Milo O'Shea *(Friar Laurence)*, Murray Head *(The Chorus)*, Michael York *(Tybalt)*, John McEnery *(Mercutio)*, Pat Heywood *(The Nurse)*, Natasha Parry *(Lady Capulet)*, Robert Stephens *(Prince of Verona)*, Keith Skinner *(Balthazar)*, Richard Warwick *(Gregory)*, Dyson Lovell *(Sampson)*, Ugo Barbone *(Abraham)*, Bruce Robinson *(Benvolio)*, Paul Hardwick *(Lord Capulet)*, Antonio Pierfederici *(Lord Montague)*, Esmeralda Ruspoli *(Lady Montague)*, Roberto Bisacco *(Count Paris)*, Roy Holder *(Peter)*, Aldo Miranda *(Friar John)*, Dario Tanzini *(Page to Tybalt)*, Laurence Olivier *(Prolog Narrator)*, Maria Fracci, Roberto Antonelli, Carlo Palmucci.

Produced by the consortium of British Home Entertainments, Verona Productions, and Dino Di Laurentiis, this version of the Veronese love story was by far the most successful at the box office, although Zeffirelli took a huge chance casting two unknowns in the leads. Whiting was 17 and Hussey was 15, the closest any actors have actually come to the ages of the characters. It's a visually stunning adaptation with more action, more broad humor, and surely more sexiness than had ever been seen for the tale. The Italian director had made THE TAMING OF THE SHREW the year before with two stars, Elizabeth Taylor and Richard Burton, and although it was not a big hit, his backers felt that his assured direction merited another attempt at Shakespeare. Filmed in Tuscany at Pienza, Gubbio, Artena, and in the palace once owned by the Borgias, it was Oscar-chosen for Best Photography (De Santis), with nominations also going to it for Best Picture and Best Director. In order to take the onus off the relatively inexperienced leads, Zeffirelli trimmed some of the longer speeches, used reaction shots to break matters up, and gave them bits of business to do so it wouldn't seem like talking heads. That technique was successful although both leads did betray their youth on several occasions. Laurence Olivier was around to lend his mellifluous voice as a narrator, a definite plus, but the director is the true star here as he gives us the most rousing crowd scenes, the most vicious fights, and a heretofore unseen look at Romeo's nudity and the partial nakedness of Juliet. It was that flesh which caused the British to not allow teenagers under 16 to see the film without an adult. The sets were magnificent, the supporting actors excellent, and the costumes attractive enough to warrant an Oscar for Donati, beating out another period piece that year, OLIVER! Young people have been turned off by some Shakespearean films because they could not identify with them. By casting these teenagers in the starring roles, Zeffirelli brought millions of youngsters into the theater who had been born and bred on a diet of BEACH PARTY pictures.

p, Anthony Havelock-Allan, John Brabourne; d, Franco Zeffirelli; w, Zeffirelli, Masolino D'Amico, Franco Brusati (based on the play by William Shakespeare); ph, Pasquale [Pasqualino] De Santis (Technicolor); m, Nino Rota; ed, Reginald Mills; prod d, Renzo Mongiardino; art d, Luciano Puccini, Emilio Carcano; set d, Christine Edzard; cos, Danilo Donati; m/l, "What Is Youth," Rota, Eugene Walter (sung by Bruno Filippini); makeup, Mauro Gavazzi.

Drama **Cas.** **(PR:C MPAA:PG)**

ROMEO AND JULIET*½** (1968, Ital./Span.) 90m Imprecine-Hispamer/World Entertainment c (GIULIETTA E ROMEO; LOS AMANTES DE VERONA)

Gerald Meynier *(Romeo)*, Rosemarie Dexter *(Juliet)*, Carlos Estrada *(Mercutio)*, Umberto Raho *(Friar Lawrence)*, Toni Soler *(Nurse)*, Andrea Bosic *(Capulet)*, Antonella Della Porta *(Lady Capulet)*, Jose Marco *(Paris)*, German Grech *(Tybalt)*, Mario de Simone *(Peter)*, Bruno Scipioni *(Balthasar)*, Franco Balducci *(Benvolio)*, Elsa Vazzoler *(Lady Montague)*, Antonio Gradoli *(Montague)*.

This very different version of the Shakespearean story was shot in 1964 but unreleased until 1968, when Franco Zeffirelli's successful and more opulent rendition came out. It was made in Italian and looped into English and suffered for that. Some pictures are more easily loopable, but when one must deal in the long phrases of Shakespeare, the loss of synchronization between the lips of the on-screen actors and the voice of the off-screen actors is shabby. Compressed to 90 minutes, huge chunks were removed from the script which was both an asset and a liability. By paring the play, it moves very quickly and easily and almost seems like a new version, rather than a truncated one. But the loss of the language and the poor looping does not serve it well. Made as a co-production between Hispamer (Spain) and Imprecine (Italy), they tried mightily to make this Shakespeare for the masses. The acting is not easy to determine because, while the faces reflect the situations, the choice of voices was questionable, and regional U.S. accents are heard in the mouths of these mainly Italian performers. Picture Laurence Olivier as "Hamlet" but with Sylvester Stallone's voice reading the lines and you'll have a small idea of what this sounded like. Everything about the film seems slightly sped-up to keep the pace moving. Meynier and Dexter look right for their leads but the revelation is Raho as Friar John. He is not the usual rotund comedy relief. Instead, the role has been altered to make the priest more youthful and ascetic, more like Francis of Assisi than Friar Tuck. The battles are scaled-down and the Capulet ball, which was so ornate in the Zeffirelli picture, has been made to look more like a small family party. There was a flurry of legal action between Paramount and World Entertainment because the two films were coming out at the same time, but the only person who deserved to make a few bucks from this bonanza was long dead...the playwright.

d&w, Ricardo Freda (based on the play by William Shakespeare); ph, Gabor Pogany (Chromoscope, Eastmancolor); m, Peter Ilyich Tchaikovsky, Sergei Rachmaninoff; ed, Anna Amidei; art d, Teddy Villalba.

Drama **(PR:A-C MPAA:NR)**

ROMEO IN PYJAMAS (SEE: PARLOR, BEDROOM & BATH, 1931)

ROMEO, JULIET AND DARKNESS (SEE: SWEET LIGHT IN A DARK ROOM, 1966, Czech.)

ROMANCE OF THE WEST*½ (1946) 58m PRC c

Eddie Dean *(Himself)*, Joan Barton *(Melodie)*, Emmett Lynn *(Ezra)*, Forrest Taylor *(Father Sullivan)*, Robert McKenzie *(Matthews)*, Jerry Jerome *(Marks)*, Stanley Price *(Rockwood)*, Chief Thundercloud *(Chief Eagle Feather)*, Don Reynolds *(Little Brown Jug)*, Rocky Camron *(Chico)*, Lee Roberts *(Hadley)*, Lottie Harrison *(Miss Twitchell)*, Don Williams *(Brent)*, Jack Richardson *(Smithers)*, Matty Roubert *(Wildhorse)*, Forbes Murray *(Commissioner Wright)*, Jack O'Shea *(Marshall)*, Tex Cooper, Grace Christy, Jerry Riggio.

Writer Kavanaugh dug into the barrel of Western script ideas an pulled out the familiar tale of an agent (Dean) who prevents the bad guys from starting an Indian disturbance in order to get control of their silver-laden lands. Emmett (again using his pseudonym) fails to inject any life into this bloodless script. Dean finds time to croon the following: "Indian Dawn," "Ridin' the Trail to Dreamland," and "Love Song of the Waterfall."

p&d, Robert Emmett [Tansey]; w, Frances Kavanaugh; ph, Marcel LePicard (Cinecolor); ed, Hugh Winn; md, Carl Hoefle; art d, Edward C. Jewell; m/l, Bob Nolan, Sam Franklin, Bernard Barnes, Carl Wiage.

Western **(PR:A MPAA:NR)**

ROMMEL-DESERT FOX (SEE: DESERT FOX, 1951)

ROMMEL'S TREASURE*½ (1962, Ital.) 85m Imperial/Medallion c (IL TESORO DI ROMMEL)

Dawn Addams *(Sofia)*, Paul Christian *(von Brunner)*, Bruce Cabot *(Wells)*, Isa Miranda *(Mrs. Fischer)*, Vittorio Massimo *(Krikorian)*, Luigi Visconti, Andrea Checchi, Wolfgang Lukschy, John Stacy.

The recovery of a secret treasure buried by Field Marshal Rommel during WW II is the passion of a small group of people, each with different plans for the fortune. Christian plans to aid families of war veterans; Cabot wants the scoop for a news story; and Miranda wants to make a sale to foreign powers. None of them has a smile on his, or her, face, however, when the treasure is blown up as the result of a mine explosion. Nothing to write home about in this tired adventure picture.

p, Luigi Rovere; d, Romolo Marcellini; w, Marcellini, Gino De Santis, Ugo Guerra, Frank Gervasi, Duncan Elliott; ph, Renato Del Frate, Hans Haas, Raimondo Bucher (CinemaScope, Technicolor); m, Carlo Rustichelli.

Adventure **(PR:A MPAA:NR)**

ROMOLO E REMO (SEE: DUEL OF THE TITANS, 1963, Ital.)

ROOF, THE** (1933, Brit.) 58m REA/RKO bw

Leslie Perrins *(Inspector Darrow)*, Judy Gunn *(Carol Foster)*, Russell Thorndike *(Clive Bristow)*, Michael Hogan *(Samuel Morton)*, Ivor Barnard *(Arthur Stannard)*, Eliot Makeham *(John Rutherford)*, Barbara Everest *(Mrs. Foster)*, George Zucco *(James Renton)*, Leo Britt *(Tony Freyne)*, D.J. Williams, Hector Abbas, Cyril Smith.

When a millionaire is found dead, detective Perrins, who is sent to investigate, discovers that some jewels belonging to the dead man are missing. Perrins uncovers proof that the dead man's lawyer, Makeham, was entrusted with the missing jewels and is responsible for the murder. A well-crafted murder mystery.

p, Julius Hagen; d, George A. Cooper; w, H. Fowler Mear (based on the novel by David Whitelaw).

Crime **(PR:A MPAA:NR)**

ROOGIE'S BUMP*   (1954) 71m REP bw (GB: THE KID COLOSSUS)

Robert Marriot *("Roogie" Rigsby)*, Ruth Warrick *(Mrs. Rigsby, His Mother)*, Olive Blakeney *(Mrs. Andrews)*, Robert Simon *(Boxi)*, William Harrigan *(Red O'Malley)*, David Winters *(Andy)*, Michael Mann *(Benji)*, Archie Robbins *(P.A. Riker)*, Louise Troy *(Kate)*, Guy Rennie *(Danny Doowinkle)*, Tedd Lawrence *(Sports Announcer, Narrator)*, Michael Keene *(Barney Davis)*, The Brooklyn Dodgers, Roy Campanella, Billy Loes, Carl Erskine, Russ Meyer, Robbie the Dog.

Marriot is an aspiring baseball player who never gets to play with the neighborhood kids. One day, however, the ghost of a one-time Brooklyn Dodger great (Harrigan) gives Marriot's ball skills a boost. He soon is hitting, throwing, and catching on par with the major leaguers. Naturally, he lands a position with the team, giving a reason to put real-life Dodgers Campanella, Loes, Erskine, and Meyer on the silver screen. Uninspired.

p, John Bash, Elizabeth Dickenson; d, Harold Young; w, Jack Hanley, Dan Totheroh (based on a story by Frank Warren, Joyce Selznick); ph, Durgi J. Contner; m, Lehman Engels.

Fantasy   (PR:A MPAA:NR)

ROOK, THE   (SEE: SOMETHING FOR EVERYONE, 1970)

ROOKERY NOOK   (SEE: ONE EMBARRASSING NIGHT, 1930, Brit.)

ROOKIE, THE*   (1959) 86m FOX bw

Tommy Noonan *(Himself)*, Pete Marshall *(Master Sgt. Marshall)*, Julie Newmar *(Lili Marlene)*, Jerry Lester *(Jerry Mann)*, Joe Besser *(Medic)*, Vince Barnett *(1st Janitor)*, Claude Stroud *(Col. Taylor)*, Richard Reeves *(1st MP)*, Herb Armstrong *(Lt. Sumner)*, Norman Leavitt *(Maj. Evers)*, Peter Leeds *(Man at Bar)*, Patrick O'Moore *(Ship's Captain)*, Rodney Bell *(2nd Janitor)*, Don Corey *(Cook)*, George Eldredge *(Gen. Bechtel)*.

Eager draftee Noonan insists upon being inducted into the Army on V-J Day. The government is forced to keep one base open and staffed just to train the soldier. He eventually finds himself on board a carrier to Japan with his sergeant (Marshall) and the sergeant's movie-star girl friend Newmar. They fall overboard and are washed up onto a deserted island. Unfortunately they are rescued—a fate never seen by this lost, water-logged picture.

p, Tommy Noonan; d, George O'Hanlon; w, Noonan, O'Hanlon; ph, Floyd Crosby (CinemaScope); m, Paul Dunlap; ed, Harry Gerstad; art d, Lyle Wheeler, John Mansbridge; m/l, O'Hanlon, Noonan, Dunlap.

Comedy   (PR:A MPAA:NR)

ROOKIE COP, THE*   (1939) 60m RKO bw (GB: SWIFT VENGEANCE)

Tim Holt *(Clem)*, Virginia Weidler *(Nicey)*, Janet Shaw *(Gerry)*, Frank M. Thomas *(Lane)*, Robert Emmett Keane *(Commissioner)*, Monte Montague *(Tom)*, Don Brodie *(Frankie)*, Ralf Harolde *(Joey)*, Muriel Evans *(Fern)*, Ace the Wonder Dog.

Holt tries to convince his police captain that the force should use canine patrols to solve criminal cases, but isn't taken seriously. With "wonder dog" Ace, however, they put the lid on a crime ring and assure the pup a place on the force. Produced on a budget which couldn't cover the cost of a bag of dog bones.

p, Bert Gilroy; d, David Howard; w, Morton Grant, Jo Pagano (based on the story by Guy K. Austin, Earl Johnson); ph, Harry Wild; ed, Frederick Knudson; cos, Renie.

Drama   (PR:A MPAA:NR)

ROOKIE FIREMAN*   (1950) 63m COL bw

Bill Williams *(Joe Blake)*, Barton MacLane *(Capt. Jess Henshaw)*, Marjorie Reynolds *(Margie Williams)*, Gloria Henry *(Peggy Walters)*, Richard Quine *(Johnny Truitt)*, John Ridgely *(Harry Williams)*, Richard Benedict *(Al Greco)*, Cliff Clark *(Capt. Mack Connors)*, Barry Brooks *(Harris)*, George Eldredge *(Floyd)*, Gaylord Pendleton *(Potts)*, Frank Sully *(Charlie)*, Ted Jordan *(Hanover)*.

Williams is a hard-edged dock worker who tries a stint with the fire department after a dock strike. He soon takes a liking to fighting fires, running into buildings when even the cockroaches are running out. A trite picture which smouldered for a while before being (almost) completely forgotten.

p, Milton Feldman; d, Seymour Friedman; w, Jerry Sackheim (based on the story by Harry Field); ph, Vincent Farrar; m, Mischa Bakaleinikoff; ed, Aaron Stell; art d, Victor Greene.

Drama   (PR:A MPAA:NR)

ROOKIES   (SEE: BUCK PRIVATES, 1941)

ROOKIES COME HOME   (SEE: BUCK PRIVATES COME HOME, 1947)

ROOKIES IN BURMA*   (1943) 62m RKO bw

Wally Brown *(Jerry Miles)*, Alan Carney *(Mike Strager)*, Erford Gage *(Sgt. Burke)*, Claire Carleton *(Janie)*, Joan Barclay *(Connie)*, Ted Hecht *(Capt. Tomura)*.

The comedy team of Brown and Carney romp through unsuspecting Burma after escaping from a Japanese concentration camp. They hook up with sergeant Gage and a pair of showgirls trying to avoid the enemy, eventually making it to safety. Producer Gilroy was on less than sure ground with RKO, however, and received his pink slip after 11 years of cranking out B pictures.

p, Bert Gilroy; d, Leslie Goodwins; w, Edward James; ph, Harry J. Wild; ed, Harry Marker; md, C. Bakaleinikoff; art d, Albert S. D'Agostino, Al Herman.

Comedy/War   (PR:A MPAA:NR)

ROOKIES ON PARADE*   (1941) 69m REP bw (GB: JAMBOREE)

Bob Crosby *(Duke Wilson)*, Ruth Terry *(Lois Rogers)*, Gertrude Niesen *(Marilyn Fenton)*, Eddie Foy, Jr. *(Cliff Dugan)*, Marie Wilson *(Kitty Mulloy)*, Cliff Nazarro *(Joe Martin)*, William Demarest *(Mike Brady)*, Sidney Blackmer *(Augustus Moody)*, Horace MacMahon *(Tiger Brannigan)*, William Wright *(Bob Madison)*, Jimmy Alexander *(Tommy)*, Louis DaPron *(Harry Haxom)*, Bill Shirley *(Bill)*.

A pair of privates make use of their songwriting skills by putting on a show for their fellow soldiers. The British title of JAMBOREE serves the picture far better than its American tag, since the story is minimal and the songs predominate. Tunes include: "The Army Builds Men," "I Love You More," "Mother Never Told Me Why," "My Kinda Love," "You'll Never Get Rich," "What More Do You Want" (Sammy Cahn, Saul Chaplin), "Rookies on Parade" (Eddie Cherkose, Jule Styne).

p, Albert J. Cohen; d, Joseph Santley; w, Karl Brown, Jack Townley, Milt Gross (based on a story by Sammy Cahn, Saul Chaplin); ph, Ernest Miller; ed, Charles Craft; md, Cy Feuer; ch, Nick Castle; cos, Adele Palmer.

Musical   (PR:A MPAA:NR)

ROOM AT THE TOP***   (1959, Brit.) 115m Romulus bw

Laurence Harvey *(Joe Lampton)*, Simone Signoret *(Alice Aisgill)*, Heather Sears *(Susan Brown)*, Donald Wolfit *(Mr. Brown)*, Ambrosine Philpotts *(Mrs. Brown)*, Donald Houston *(Charles Soames)*, Raymond Huntley *(Mr. Hoylake)*, John Westbrook *(Jack Wales)*, Allan Cuthbertson *(George Aisgill)*, Mary Peach *(June Samson)*, Hermione Baddeley *(Elspeth)*, Thelma Ruby *(Miss Breith)*, Anne Leon *(Janet)*, Wendy Craig *(Joan)*, Stephen Jack *(Darnley)*, Avril Elgar *(Miss Gilchrist)*, Beatrice Varley *(Aunt)*, Miriam Karlin *(Gertrude)*, Richard Pasco *(Teddy)*, April Olrich *(Mavis)*, John Welsh *(Mayor)*, Everley Gregg *(Mayoress)*, Delena Kidd *(Eva)*, Ian Hendry *(Cyril)*, Basil Dignam *(Priest)*, Paul Whitson-Jones *(Man at Bar)*, Wilfrid Lawson *(Uncle Nat)*, Yvonne Buckingham *(Girl at Window)*, Doreen Dawn *(High Stepping Girl)*, Harry Moore, Joan Leake, Honoria Burke, Allan Bracewell, Brian Worth, Ann Gunning, Linda Leon, Mandy Priestly, Bob Palmer, Bill Morgan, Eric Louro, Pamela Manson, Ruth Kettlewell, Derek Benfield, Isla Cameron, Sandra Thompson, Kendrick Owen, Bonita Bridgeman, Kathleen Fox, Angela Culbert, Prunella Scales, Katherine Page, Anthony Elgar, Kenneth Waller, Anthony Newlands, Andrew Irvine, Derry [Derren] Nesbitt, May Hallatt, Sheila Raynor, Gilda Emmanueli, Jane Eccles, Denis Linford, Edward Palmer, Michael Atkinson, Julian Somers, Richard Caldicot, Pat Lanski.

A ruthless indictment of the British "class system" which is every bit as vicious as the Indian "caste system" but much more subtle. ROOM AT THE TOP broke new ground in the realism genre of films and triggered several movies that followed within the next few years, such as SATURDAY NIGHT AND SUNDAY MORNING, A TASTE OF HONEY, and other "kitchen sink" pictures. Harvey has spent several years as a P.O.W. and is now ambitiously involved in finding himself some room at the top. The little town in which he operates is Warnley, a bleak, gray, soot-filled Yorkshire village. He secures a poor-paying job as an accountant for the government and soon realizes that all the ability in the world will stand him in bad stead. There has to be another way to rise. The richest man in the town is Wolfit, a millionaire industrialist who lords his power over the town as though it were his own feudal fiefdom. Wolfit's daughter is the naive Sears and Harvey sets his cap for her, knowing that an advantageous marriage is the answer. Wolfit recognizes a bit of himself in the calculating, cold Harvey and attempts to break up the relationship by shipping Sears off to Europe until her passion for Harvey cools. At no time is Harvey apparently in love with Sears. She is the means to an end, nothing more. When Sears is sent to the Continent, Harvey meets Signoret, a woman 10 years older than he is and the star of the local theater group. She is married to Cuthbertson but it's not a happy union. Harvey and Signoret become lovers, and, for the first time, there appears to be a spark of warmth in Harvey, but he soon douses that in his quest for elevating himself. Signoret would like to get a divorce but Cuthbertson won't hear of it. Sears returns home and Harvey hits upon a plan to bring his dreams to fruition. He impregnates her. Wolfit has tried everything to get Harvey away from his daughter, but bribery, threats, and the like will not stay Harvey from his goal. When Signoret learns that the man she loves is to marry Sears, she drinks herself into a near-coma, gets into her car, and drives to her death. Just before the marriage is to take place, Harvey is set upon by some "teddy boys"—the hoodlums who used to bash heads in England's streets while dressing fashionably. Harvey allows himself to be beaten, almost as penance for what he's done. He is found in time for the wedding and suddenly realizes that, even though he will be a rich man, his life is now all determined for him, the one woman he loved is dead, and he must now spend his days with a woman he has only married to get to the top. Paterson's incisive screenplay won the Oscar and Signoret's brief, telling performance was a revelation and also gained her the coveted Academy Award as Best Actress. Director Clayton had only made a short before garnering this assignment. That film was "The Bespoke Overcoat," which won the Best Short Feature Award at the Venice Film Festival. Author Braine was one of the early "Angry Young Man" who came upon the British literary scene and his novel was one of the rare ones to get a fine screen treatment. For 1959, this was a breakthrough picture, in that the dialog was much more realistic and the sexual scenes far more explicit than any that had ever come out of England. That caused a furor in Great Britain and it was given an "X" rating there. One problem for U.S. ears was the heavy "North Country" accent used by most of the actors. It was so thick and regional that many Londoners had trouble understanding what was said and the effect on Midwest ears was even more difficult. The hero, Harvey, is a villain and, in the end, is given his comeuppance as we realize he is trapped forever in a web of his own making and will never have the kind of happiness he'd experienced in the arms of Signoret. The British Film Academy called it the Best Picture of the Year out of England as well as the Best Picture from anywhere. Signoret won Best Foreign Actress from the BFA and also took the Best Actress award at Cannes. The Motion Picture Academy nominated Harvey, Clayton, Baddeley (in a cameo), and the movie. Harvey does well enough in the lead but there is an underlying weakness in his character that makes some of his devious moves seem a bit out of place. Wolfit and his wife, Philpotts, are smashing as the wealthy parents who want nothing but the best for their daughter and must settle for one of the worst. Without taking a position, the film exposes the snobbism, the poverty, the desperation, and the politics of living in a small town and therefore almost resembles the British version of a Sinclair Lewis story, with overtones of Theodore Dreiser. Mary Peach, an actress who would later marry well, does a small role and is, as always, outstanding. The sexual scenes and the raw language compel any parent to leave the kids at home while watching ROOM AT THE TOP. The sequel, LIFE AT THE TOP (1965), was far less rewarding on every level and the TV series "Man at the Top" brought forth yet another sequel of the same name. Neither came close to the original for style, intensity and drama.

p, John and James Woolf; d, Jack Clayton; w, Neil Paterson (based on the novel by John Braine); ph, Freddie Francis; m, Mario Nascimbene; ed, Ralph Kemplen; art d, Ralph Brinton.

Drama   Cas.   (PR:O MPAA:NR)

ROOM FOR ONE MORE*½   (1952) 98m WB bw (AKA: THE EASY WAY)

Cary Grant ("Poppy" Rose), Betsy Drake (Anna Rose), Lurene Tuttle (Miss Kenyon), Randy Stuart (Mrs. Foreman), John Ridgely (Harry Foreman), Irving Bacon (The Mayor), Mary Lou Treen (Mrs. Roberts), Hayden Rorke (The Doctor), Iris Mann (Jane), George "Foghorn" Winslow (Teensie), Clifford Tatum, Jr. (Jimmy-John), Gay Gordon (Trot), Malcolm Cassell (Tim), Larry Olsen (Ben), Mary Newton, Ezelle Poule, Dorothy Kennedy, Marcorita Hellman, Karen Hale, Doris Kemper, Mary Alan Hokanson Felice Richmond (Women), Ray Page (Gas Station Attendent), Charles Meredith (Mr. Thatcher), Oliver Blake (Mr. Doran), Frank Ferguson (Steve), Don Beddoe (School Principal), Lilliam Bronson (Teacher), William Bakewell (Milkman), Douglas Fowley (Ice Man), John McGovern (Senior Patrol Leader), Gretchen Hartman (Chairwoman), Tony Taylor (Joey), Dabbs Greer (Scoutmaster), Stevie Wooten (Little Brother).

A warmhearted domestic comedy which stars Grant and Drake as husband and wife living in their middle-class home with three children—Cassell, Gordon, and Winslow. Drake's generosity gets the best of her when she agrees to house Mann—a withdrawn 13-year-old girl—for two weeks. Although Grant balks at the idea, he consents at Drake's insistence. At the end of the two weeks, Mann has become a permanent member of the household. Drake then hears of Tatum, an emotionally scarred crippled boy who has received nothing but abuse from previous foster parents. Through love and sincerity, Drake gains Tatum's confidence. Drake not only wins the trust of the children, but also wins over Grant, whose initial resistance to the new additions is overcome. Truly a domestic tale, ROOM FOR ONE MORE was based on an actual Lynwood, New Jersey, couple—Poppy and Anna Perrot Rose—whose good samaritan acts were published in book form. Also adding to the authenticity was the real-life marriage between Grant and Drake, resulting in a screen relationship which rang true. Grant not only found a part for his wife in ROOM FOR ONE MORE, but also for 5-year-old George "Foghorn" Winslow. Having spotted Winslow on Art Linkletter's "People Are Funny" show (where Winslow had become a familiar name), Grant quickly signed the boy. At the tender age of 5, Winslow gained fame as the boy with the basso profundo voice, hence the nickname "Foghorn." At the age of 12, after appearing in such classics as MONKEY BUSINESS (1952), GENTLEMEN PREFER BLONDES (1953), and ARTISTS AND MODELS (1955), Winslow permanently left show business. The film's favorable and honest attitude toward children won it a special mention from the Venice Film Festival's "Films for Children Fete."

p, Henry Blanke; d, Norman Taurog; w, Jack Rose, Melville Shavelson (based on the book by Anna Perrott Rose); ph, Robert Burks; m, Max Steiner; ed, Alan Crosland, Jr.; art d, Douglas Bacon; set d, William L. Kuehl; cos, Leah Rhodes, Marjorie Best; makeup, Gordon Bau.

Comedy   (PR:AA MPAA:NR)

ROOM FOR TWO*   (1940, Brit.) 77m Hurley/GN bw

Frances Day (Clare Spencer), Vic Oliver (Michael Brent), Basil Radford (Robert Spencer), Greta Gynt (Hilda Westby), Hilda Bayley (Dressmaker), Leo de [von] Porkony (Manager), Magda Kun (Mimi), Victor Rietti (Gaston), Andrea Malandrinos (Gondolier), Rosamund Greenwood, Charles Goldner, Glenys Mortimer.

A tedious comedy set in Venice, starring Oliver as a philandering Englishman who falls in love with the married Day. In order to be closer to her, he gets himself hired as her maid (under the moniker Sophie). The charade ends, however, when Day's husband becomes disillusioned with his mistress and returns to his wife.

p, Victor Katona; d, Maurice Elvey; w, (based on a play by Gilbert Wakefield); ph, Bernard Browne, Bryan Langley.

Comedy   (PR:A MPAA:NR)

ROOM 43*   (1959, Brit.) 88m United Co-Productions/Cory bw (GB: PASSPORT TO SHAME)

Eddie Constantine (Johnny), Diana Dors (Vicki), Odile Versois (Malou), Herbert Lom (Nick), Brenda De Banzie (Madame), Robert Brown (Mike), Elwyn Brook-Jones (Heath), Cyril Shaps (Willie), Dennis Shaw (Mac), Joan Sims (Miriam), Lana Morris (Girl), Robert Fabian (Himself), Percy Cartwright, James Ottaway, Jackie Collins, Margaret Tyzack, Pat Pleasence, Steve Plytas, Charles Price, Michael Caine.

Constantine is a taxi driver who agrees to marry Versois, a French national, so that she can get British papers. He falls in love with her and with the help of his fellow cabbies rescues her from the gang that runs the marriage racket-white slave business so that he can really marry her. This was the first English-speaking film made with Constantine, who was already very popular in France and Germany in gangster parodies.

p, John Clein; d, Alvin Rakoff; w, Patrick Alexander; ph, Jack Asher; m, Ken Jones, Jeff Davis; ed, Lee Doig.

Drama   (PR:A MPAA:NR)

ROOM IN THE HOUSE**   (1955, Brit.) 74m ACT/Monarch bw

Patrick Barr (Jack Richards), Hubert Gregg (Hugh Richards), Marjorie Rhodes (Betsy Richards), Leslie Dwyer (Benji Pugh), Rachel Gurney (Mary), Margaret Anderson (Christine), Josephine Griffin (Julia), Helen Shingler (Ethel), Anthony Marlowe (David Richards), Billie Whitelaw, Oliver Johnston, Julian d'Albie, Barbara Cavan, Douglas Ives, Hilda Fenemore, Barry Steele, John Watson, Brian Carleton, Edie Martin, Bert Sim.

A weak comedy about a widowed woman, Rhodes, who moves in with each of her three sons for a short period of time. When her favorite son, Gregg, leaves for the U.S. she becomes distressed and disappointed. The film ends on a positive note, however, when her sons buy her a village cottage that she can call her own.

p, Alfred Shaughnessy; d, Maurice Elvey; w, Shaughnessy (based on the play "Bless This House" by E. Eynon Evans); ph, Gerald Gibbs.

Comedy   (PR:A MPAA:NR)

ROOM SERVICE**   (1938) 78m RKO bw

Groucho Marx (Gordon Miller), Chico Marx (Harry Binelli), Harpo Marx (Faker Englund), Lucille Ball (Christine), Ann Miller (Hilda Manney), Frank Albertson (Leo Davis), Donald MacBride (Gregory Wagner), Cliff Dunstan (Joseph Gribble), Philip Loeb (Timothy Hogarth), Philip Wood (Simon Jenkins), Alexander Asro (Sasha), Charles Halton (Dr. Glass).

The hit Broadway comedy by Allen Boretz and John Murray was not given a great treatment by the Marx Brothers and the production team. Harpo didn't play the harp, Chico didn't play the piano, Groucho didn't have Margaret Dumont to play off, and there were no songs other than "Swing Low, Sweet Chariot" and all of that was missed by fans of the trio. It cost more than a quarter of a million for the stage rights, and despite the fact that the budget was low, the movie still lost almost $400,000 the first time around. Scenarist Ryskind did what he could to adapt the farce for the unique talents of the Marxes but it was apples and oranges and the result was just another comedy, with little of the anarchistic madness which had endeared the brothers to millions. Groucho and Chico are living at a Broadway hotel. They are planning a new stage show and are waiting for the financing to come through. Their room is packed with members of the cast and the hotel bill is now well over $1000, which rankles MacBride, an executive of the hotel, and Dunstan, the inn's manager. Since this debt is outstanding and results in the hotel's books being on the debit side, MacBride tells Dunstan that the time has come to evict the guests in room 920. Ball is Groucho's secretary and she thinks she has a live one as a potential backer, so the Marxes have to come up with a way to stay in the room until the next day, when Mr. Moneybags will arrive. Albertson, the play's author, arrives. He hasn't a dime and moves into the already-crowded room. Miller, a secretary, has come to see Groucho to set up a reading for Asro, a Russian waiter who wants to be in the show. The moment Miller and Albertson set eyes on each other, bells clang. The following morning, Ball enters the room to announce that she has a potential angel who is willing to sink some money into the show, if they can just hold out for one more day in the room. Albertson is tapped to fake a case of measles so they have to be quarantined and no one can be tossed out. However, his passion for Miller causes him to slip out of the room and go to the lobby to see her. Dunstan and MacBride spot him. Meanwhile, Harpo fakes being ill and Ball pretends to be his nurse. When Halton, an outside doctor, is called in to determine the illness of Harpo, he spots the fraud and, rather than have him tell the management, they tie him up and put him in the bathroom. Wood enters with the check from his client but changes his mind about the deal. They think that they have talked him into it, Wood signs the check, and Groucho gives it to MacBride to pay for the bills run up by the cast and crew. Albertson learns that Wood only signed the check so he could get out of the room and will stop payment on it as soon as he can call his bank. Groucho realizes he must work fast, so he sets up the show to open in the hotel's theater right away. MacBride tries to cash the check and learns that there is a stop payment on it. While the play is being presented on stage, MacBride has the hotel cops keep the Marxes and Albertson in the room. Albertson pretends to commit suicide and Miller, seing that it's a fake, goes downstairs to see the show so she can report back to him. Albertson "expires" and MacBride is desperately attempting to get the body out of the hotel because the resultant publicity might cost him his job. Harpo now fakes having been assaulted with a knife and he is taken down the back way to an alley. Albertson has slipped inside the theater with Miller and the show is getting laughs in all the right places. MacBride walks into the theater, sees the "dead" Albertson, and responds by fainting dead away. The play's script calls for a dead man and Harpo is carried on in that capacity. The show is a smash and the picture ends on a high note. In 1944, it was turned into the musical STEP LIVELY, with Frank Sinatra in the lead. Holdovers from the Broadway show include Wood, Asro, Dunstan, MacBride, and Loeb. The play was, and still is, an excellent vehicle for stock companies, and, when directed with pace, as funny as it was in the 1930s. The picture, however, is not that good.

p, Pandro S. Berman; d, William A. Seiter; w, Morrie Ryskind (based on the play by John Murray, Allen Boretz); ph, J. Roy Hunt; ed, George Crone; md, Roy Webb; art d, Van Nest Polglase, Al Herman; set d, Darrell Silvera; cos, Renie.

Comedy   Cas.   (PR:A MPAA:NR)

ROOM TO LET**   (1949, Brit.) 68m Hammer/Exclusive bw

Jimmy Hanley (Curley Minter), Valentine Dyall (Dr. Fell), Christine Silver (Mrs. Musgrave), Merle Tottenham (Alice), Charles Hawtrey (Mike Atkinson), Constance Smith (Molly Musgrave), J. Anthony la Penna (J.J.), Reginald Dyson (Sgt. Cranbourne), Laurence Naismith, Aubrey Dexter, John Clifford, Stuart Sanders,

Cyril Conway, Charles Houston, Harriet Petworth, Charles Mander, H. Hamilton Earle, F.A. Williams, Archie Callum.

A crime thriller set in turn-of-the-century England amidst the Jack-the-Ripper scare. Silver is a crippled widow who, with her daughter Smith, rents rooms to boarders. Dyall shows up one day claiming to be a doctor. He takes a room and before long has practically imprisoned the women in their own home. They fear for their lives, thinking that Dyall is Jack-the-Ripper. Reporter Hanley investigates and learns that Dyall is not the Ripper, but an escaped mental patient. A fairly disturbing programmer which remains suspenseful to the end.

p, Anthony Hinds; d, Godfrey Grayson; w, John Gilling, Grayson (based on the radio play by Margery Allingham); ph, Cedric Williams.

Crime   **(PR:A   MPAA:NR)**

ROOM UPSTAIRS, THE½**   (1948, Fr.) 88m Alcina/Lopert bw (MARTIN ROUMAGNAC)

Marlene Dietrich (Blanche Ferrand), Jean Gabin (Martin Roumagnac) Margo Lion (Martin's Sister), Marcel Herrand (Consul), Jean D'Yd (Blanche's Uncle), Daniel Gelin (The Lover), Jean Darcante (The Lawyer), Henri Poupon (Gargame), Marcel Andre (Judge), Paulot (Perez), Charles Lemontier (Bonnemain), Michel Ardan, Paul Faivre, Marcelle Genait, Lucien Nat.

Made just after the war, it took a couple of years to get to the U.S. and then had to have more than 20 minutes cut in order to get past the Catholic Legion of Decency who objected strenuously to the casual way in which prostitution was depicted. Dietrich and Gabin had been great friends in Hollywood when he went there after France fell, and this pairing was thought to be box office dynamite but it turned out to be a dud. Gabin, a construction engineer, is hired to build a home for Dietrich in a small town. She has spent many years in Austria, where she found the men dull, and so when she meets the handsome Gabin, she is more than passingly interested. As the work continues, the two of them find much about each other to love, and their scenes together indicate that each may have found a lifetime partner. Gabin is an old-fashioned man with old-fashioned virtues and he cannot put them aside when he learns that Dietrich is paying for the house construction with her earnings as a prostitute. It causes him to kill Dietrich and he is immediately brought to trial. Evidence at the proceedings indicates that she really loved him and he is morose, then elated when he is acquitted, because all that exists is circumstantial evidence. Free to live his life (and suffer his guilt), Gabin does not last too long because he is later slain by Gelin, Dietrich's one-time lover who will not rest until he sees justice done. It was around this time that Dietrich was spending many hours entertaining the Allied troops in various locations around the world. The leader of the orchestra who backed her show in Greenland, Charles Cox, states that Dietrich had a most unusual act in those years. She sang, danced, told funny stories, then put those famous legs together and wowed the troops as she expertly played the musical saw. Is there no end to her talents? The picture ran 115 minutes in France and just 88 minutes in the United States so we never got much of a chance to see the details of what happened in THE ROOM UPSTAIRS.

p, Marc Le Pelletier; d, Georges Lacombe; w, Pierre Very (based on the novel by Pierre-Rene Wolf); ph, Roger Hubert; m, Marcel Mirouze; art d, George Wakhevitch.

Crime Drama   **(PR:C   MPAA:NR)**

ROOMMATES**   (1962, Brit.) 91m G.H.W. Production/Herts-Lion International c (GB: RAISING THE WIND)

James Robertson Justice (Sir Benjamin), Leslie Phillips (Mervyn), Sidney James (Sid), Paul Massie (Malcolm), Kenneth Williams (Harold), Eric Barker (Morgan Rutherford), Liz Fraser (Miranda), Jennifer Jayne (Jill), Esma Cannon (Mrs. Deevens), Geoffrey Keen (Sir John), Jill Ireland (Janet), Jimmy Thompson (Alex), David Lodge (Taxi Driver), Lance Percival (Harry), Ambrosine Phillpotts (Mrs. Featherstone), Joan Hickson (Mrs. Bostwick), Michael Nightingale (Invigilator), Oliver Johnston (Prof. Parkin), Cyril Chamberlain (L.A.M.A. Porter), Dorinda Stevens (Doris), Brian Oulton (Concert Agent), George Woodbridge (Yorkshire Orchestra Leader), Peter Howell (Prof. Lumb), Frank Forsyth (Prof. Abrahams), Michael Miller (Barman), Henry Davies (Carpenter), Horace Seguira (Old Professor), Victor Maddern, Charles Stanley (Removal Men), Erik Chitty (Elderly Man), Douglas Ives, Ian Wilson, Tom Clegg, John Antrobus, Kenneth Cove (Street Musicians), Bernard Hunter (1st Flute), Peter Berton (1st Viola), Terence Holland (1st Trombone), Jim Dale (Bass Trombone), Nigel Arkwright (4th Cellist), Peter Byrne (1st Horn).

A collection of young musicians shares a house after meeting at the London Academy of Music, where they are all in competition for a prestigious scholarship. Tension rises between the five students, with Fraser finally taking the coveted prize and the rest of the group pairing off, romantically, as couples.

p, Peter Rogers; d, Gerald Thomas; w, Bruce Montgomery; ph, Alan Hume; m, Montgomery; ed, John Shirley; art d, Carmen Dillon.

Comedy   **(PR:AA   MPAA:NR)**

ROOMATES, 1969   (SEE: MARCH OF THE SPRING HARE, 1969)

ROOMMATES zero   (1971) 97m Gulliver/Clayton Pantages c

Dan Mason (Henry), Harvey Marks (Solly), Barbara Press (Sandy), Theon Banos (Rhoda), Allen Garfield (Martin Axborough), Rick Wessler (Bookmaster), Stanley Brock (Madison).

A meandering group of youngsters plays pessimist, always talking about how rotten the older generation is or how bleak their own lives are thus far. They try to remember where they came from and they preach about where they're going. The script is pathetically pretentious and the acting is wretched, despite decent editing work and fair music.

p, Harvey Bernstein, Leo Baran; d&w, Jack Baran; ph, Bruce Sparks; m, Earth Opera; ed, David Wilson.

Drama   **(PR:O   MPAA:R)**

ROOMMATES, THE*   (1973) 87m A.G.&S./General Film Corp. c

Pat Woodell (Heather), Roberta Collins (Beth), Marki Bey (Carla), Laurie Rose (Brea), Christina Hart (Paula), Connie Strickland (Alice), Barbara Fuller (Sylvia), David Moses (Mike), Ken Scott (Marty), Gary Mascaro (Arnie), Ben Pfeiffer (Lee), Kipp Whitman (Don), Greg Mabrey (Harold), Darl Severns (Nick), David Ankrum (Andy), John Morgan Evans (Warren), Peter Oliphant (Aaron), John Durren (Socks), Richard Mansfield (Mickey), Charles Stroud (The Drunk), James V. Christy (The Professor), Paula Shaw, Pam Stroud.

A fun-filled vacation of sun and sex ends up in tragedy for five voluptuous girls—Woodell, Collins, Bey, Rose, and Hart—when one of their lovers turns out to be a demented murderer. Woodell finds herself a personable camper; Collins falls for a divorced architect; Bey has a meaningful romance with a local black policeman, and Rose and Hart both become involved with the shy, virginal Mascaro. The vacation takes a sour twist when a female figure is seen stabbing someone to death. A second murder follows—a young girl shot while water skiing. In attendance at a party, the girls find that they and the other guests are being shot at. Bey's policeman boy friend chases down the assailant and kills him. The dead "female" killer is stripped of her wig and dress, and identified as the castigated and sexually maladjusted Mascaro. Just one of many PSYCHO-influenced pictures, this one having a "Norman Bates Goes To Malibu" appeal.

p, Chuck Stroud; d, Arthur Marks; w, Marks, John Durren; ph, Harry May (Eastmancolor); m, Post Production Associates; ed, Richard Greer; cos, Alan Hoffman; makeup, Chuck House, Mitchell Clay.

Crime/Drama   **(PR:O   MPAA:R)**

ROONEY*   (1958, Brit.) 88m RANK bw

John Gregson (James Ignatius Rooney), Muriel Pavlow (Maire Hogan), Barry Fitzgerald (Grandfather), June Thorburn (Doreen O'Flynn), Noel Purcell (Tim Hennessy), Marie Kean (Mrs. O'Flynn), Liam Redmond (Mr. Doolan), Jack MacGowran (Joe O'Connor), Eddie Byrne (Micky Hart), Philip O'Flynn (Paddy Ryan), Harold Goldblatt (Police Inspector), Pauline Delaney (Mrs. Wall), Godfrey Quigley (Tom Reilly), Irene Browne (Mrs. Manning French), Joan Phillips (Sheila O'Flynn), Maureen Toal (Kathleen O'Flynn).

Gregson is cast as the title character, an Irish garbageman who is much admired for his athletic ability on the hurley field. Before long, he is boarding with an uppity widow who disapproves of his handling trash for a living but is well aware of the respect others have for his athletic skills. Gregson is attracted to the widow's niece (Pavlow), a plain, hard-working lass whose merits are thus far recognized only by her grandfather. Gregson surprises all (except the audience) when he takes the colleen's hand in marriage. 'Tis a fine picture, it 'tis.

p, George H. Brown; d, George Pollock; w, Patrick Kirwan (based on the novel Rooney by Catherine Cookson); ph, Christopher Challis; m, Philip Green; ed, Peter Bezencenet; md, Muir Mathieson; art d, Jack Maxsted; m/l, Tommie Connor (sung by Michael Holliday).

Comedy   **(PR:A   MPAA:NR)**

ROOSTER COGBURN*½**   (1975) 107m UNIV c

John Wayne (Rooster Cogburn), Katharine Hepburn (Eula Goodnight), Anthony Zerbe (Breed), Richard Jordan (Hawk), John McIntire (Judge Parker), Strother Martin (McCoy), Richard Romancito (Wolf), Warren Vanders (Bagby), Tommy Lee (Chen Lee), Jon Lormer (Rev. Goodnight), Paul Koslo (Luke), Lane Smith (Leroy), Jack Colvin (Red), Jerry Gatlin (Nose), Mickey Gilbert, Chuck Hayward, Gary McLarty (Hawk's Gang).

Ample proof that even an excellent cast can't save a faulty script, especially if it's a sequel to an Oscar-winner. John Wayne again plays the part of Rooster Cogburn, for which he took Best Actor accolades in TRUE GRIT six years earlier. The story picks up with Wayne having the chance to get his badge back, after another of his trigger-happy incidents. He must capture a gang of bandits, led by Jordan, who have hijacked a shipment of nitroglycerin. Making things tougher, albeit more colorful, is bible-toting Hepburn's insistence on joining him. She's upset because her preacher father was offed by the gang—a plot device and characterization that are more than reminiscent of THE AFRICAN QUEEN. A bitter disappointment, chiefly because director Millar didn't seem to have the slightest idea of how to direct such awe-inspiring stars.

p, Hal B. Wallis; d, Stuart Millar; w, Martin Julien (based on the character created by Charles Portis in his novel True Grit); ph, Harry Stradling, Jr. (Panavision, Technicolor); m, Laurence Rosenthal; ed, Robert Swink; art d, Preston Ames; set d, George Robert Nelson; cos, Edith Head; spec eff, Jack McMasters.

Western   Cas   **(PR:A   MPAA:PG)**

ROOT OF ALL EVIL, THE*   (1947, Brit.) 110m Gainsborough/GFD bw

Phyllis Calvert (Jackie Farnish), John McCallum (Joe Bartle), Michael Rennie (Charles Mortimer), Brefni O'Rourke (Farnish), Arthur Young (George Grice), Hubert Gregg (Albert Grice), Pat Hicks (Lucy Grice), Hazel Court (Rushie Farnish), George Carney (Bowser), Reginald Purdell (Perkins), Moore Marriott (Scholes), Diana Decker (Pam), Rory MacDermot (Overthwaite), Brian Herbert (Stubley).

Calvert makes a fortune in oil by stepping on a few peoples' backs and eventually hooks up with mining engineer Rennie. They make more than their share of cash but, to Calvert's dismay, romance doesn't play a part. An act of revenge by a disgruntled farmer helps Calvert come to her senses. Some fine performances can't put a sheen on this dull script.

p, Harold Huth; d&w, Brock Williams (based on the novel by J.S. Fletcher); ph, Stephen Dade; ed, Charles Knott; prod d, Albert Fennell; md, Louis Levy; art d,

Maurice Carter; set d, John Bryan; cos, Dorothy Broomham; makeup, William Partleton.

Drama   **(PR:A MPAA:NR)**

ROOTIN' TOOTIN' RHYTHM*** (1937) 60m REP bw (GB: RHYTHM ON THE RANCH)

Gene Autry (Gene), Smiley Burnette (Frog), Armida (Rosa), Monte Blue (Stafford), Al Clauser and The Outlaws (Band), Hal Taliaferro (Buffalo), Ann Pendleton (Mary), Max Hoffman, Jr. (Kid), Charles King (Jim), Frankie Marvin (Hank), Nina Campana (Ynez), Charles Mayer, Karl Hackett, Jack Rutherford, Henry Hall, Curley Dresden, Art Davis, Champion The Horse.

Autry and Burnette assume the identities of what they think are dead bandits, but they soon find themselves in quite a mix-up. Their plan is to stop a ring of cattle rustlers, and in the end their disguises work for the better. As always, Gene gets a chance to do some strummin' and some croonin'. One of the better Autry serials. (See GENE AUTRY Series, Index)

p, Armand Schaefer; d, Mark V. Wright; w, Jack Natteford (based on the story by Johnston McCulley); ph, William Nobles; ed, Tony Martinelli.

Western   **Cas.**   **(PR:A MPAA:NR)**

ROOTS OF HEAVEN, THE*** (1958) 131m FOX c

Errol Flynn (Maj. Forsythe), Juliette Greco (Minna), Trevor Howard (Morel), Eddie Albert (Abe Fields), Orson Welles (Cy Sedgewick), Paul Lukas (Saint Denis), Herbert Lom (Orsini), Gregoire Aslan (Habib), Andre Luguet (Governor), Friedrich Ledebur (Peer Qvist), Edric Connor (Waitari), Olivier Hussenot (The Baron), Pierre Dudan (Maj. Scholscher), Marc Doelnitz (De Vries), Dan Jackson (Madjumba), Maurice Cannon (Haas), Jacques Marin (Cerisot), Habib Benglia (Korotoro), Bachir Toure (Yussef), Alain Saury (A.D.C.), Roscoe Stallworth (N'Dolo), Assane Fall (Inguele), Francis de Wolff (Father Fargue).

A misfired film through which the potential still shows, THE ROOTS OF HEAVEN deals with the misguided attempts of zealot Howard to save the elephant herds of French Equatorial Africa from the depredations of both hungry natives and big-game hunters. He portrays a man who has spent years in a Nazi POW camp, only thinking about the elephants and their freedom. When he comes to Africa after the war he tries to drum up support for his crusade, but everyone around him in the pestilential community is either unconcerned or actively engaged in profiting from the continued slaughter. The only support he can muster is from Greco, a prostitute who was also a victim of the Nazis, and Flynn, a drunken former officer in the British army who is accused of betraying his men to the Germans. When Howard is stymied at every turn by official indifference, he takes his campaign into the bush, sabotaging hunting parties. When American radio personality Welles shows up for a little hunting, Howard fills his backside with rock salt from a shotgun, but instead of being furious, Welles goes back to the States and begins boosting Howard over the airwaves. In time Howard is joined in the bush by Greco and Flynn, as well as photojournalist Albert, Danish scientist Ledebur, and German nobleman Hussenot, who has refused to speak any more as a protest against humanity. The campaign is also joined by a Pan-African liberation group that hopes to co-opt it for its own ends, though these two factions soon split and the liberation group, headed by Connor, throws in its lot with the ivory poachers under Lom. The poachers set out in force to wipe out a herd and Howard gets wind of it. A gun battle breaks out in which Flynn and some of the others are killed. As the film ends, Howard, Greco, and Albert head off into the bush to continue their crusade. The story suffers frequently from bloated speeches and badly drawn characters, and director Huston seems uninterested in the proceedings. In fact, Greco complained later that Huston's direction of the actors consisted of little more than telling them to "show me what you're feeling. Do what you want to do." (This was Huston's habit on many of his efforts.) Huston later said that the films that are the hardest to make are usually the worst, and this film must have set some kind of record for suffering by the crew. The location was one of the worst places in the world, where the daytime temperatures sometimes reached 130 degrees and the nighttime temperatures never dropped below 90. Shooting could only go on until noon, when the heat would stop everything. Actors were constantly sweating off their makeup. At one time or another nearly everyone got sick with malaria or dysentery or some other tropical disease. One member of the cast caught something that even the Pasteur Institute in Paris couldn't identify. Flynn recalled that one Italian in the cast forgot to take his malaria pills and caught "the most virulent type of African malaria, the mortality rate of which is so tremendously high, and he died." Greco had to be flown out when she contracted the disease as well. Only Flynn and Huston stayed reasonably healthy, probably because they avoided the local water and drank vodka continually. Welles recalled that Flynn was in constant need of heroin, which the nursing order of nuns at the local hospital refused to give him until Zanuck promised to build them a new wing on the building. Eddie Albert was stricken with a fever and spent three weeks shaking naked on the concrete floor of his hut. Zanuck would have to have him tied to a pole and carried to the latrine, though when Albert recovered he refused to believe any of it. William Holden was originally cast in the Howard part, but he turned it down, a decision he was probably happy with. Most of the performances are indifferent, in keeping with Huston's indifferent manner of directing, but Flynn, in the last real movie of his life (after this there was only CUBAN REBEL GIRLS and death within a year) manages to show a bemused nobility through the alcohol that audiences had almost forgotten he had. The second-unit photography of African fauna and flora by Skeets Kelly, Henri Persin, and Gilles Bonneau is fine, but the cast members hardly melded with the location backgrounds, and might have been deployed in a Hollywood sound stage, saving themselves a lot of physical agony. Author Gary might then more readily have gotten personally involved in the production; at the time, he was French consul general in Los Angeles.

p, Darryl F. Zanuck; d, John Huston; w, Romain Gary, Patrick Leigh-Fermor (based on the novel by Gary); ph, Oswald Morris (CinemaScope, DeLuxe Color);

m, Malcolm Arnold, Henri Patterson; ed, Russell Lloyd; art d, Stephen Grimes, Raymond Gabutti; set d, Bruno Avesani; cos, Rosine Delamare; spec eff, Fred Etcheverry, L.B. Abbott; makeup, George Frost.

Drama   **Cas.**   **(PR:C MPAA:NR)**

ROPE*** (1948) 80m Transatlantic/WB c

James Stewart (Rupert Caldell), John Dall (Shaw Brandon), Farley Granger (Philip), Joan Chandler (Janet Walker), Sir Cedric Hardwicke (Mr. Kentley, David's Father), Constance Collier (Mrs. Atwater), Edith Evanson (Mrs. Wilson the Governess), Douglas Dick (Kenneth Lawrence), Dick Hogan (David Kentley).

A phenomenal mastery of technique from cinema's greatest craftsman, Alfred Hitchcock, ROPE is famous for being the first, and thus far only, film which appears as one continuous shot for the duration of its 80 minutes. Based on a 1929 stage play, which in turn was drawn from the infamous Leopold and Loeb murder case of 1924, ROPE tells the story of two young, intelligent, collegiate homosexuals—Dall and Granger—who murder a weak-willed friend, Hogan, simply for the intellectual thrill of it. In their New York penthouse apartment, safely hidden behind the darkness of the drawn window shades, Dall and Granger strangle the life out of Hodges with a section of rope, and then stuff his corpse into an antique chest. After hiding the rope in an kitchen drawer, the pair celebrate their gruesome feat with champagne. The apartment is then prepared for the evening's cocktail party, including among its guests Hardwicke, the murdered boy's father, Chandler, the boy's fiancee, and Stewart, a college professor whose philosophical discussions of Friedrich Nietzsche's "superman" theory have inspired the murderers. Dall, the more cocksure of the killers, enjoys toying with the crime he just committed—insisting that dinner be served off of the chest-coffin, playing with the danger of getting caught, and dropping verbal hints of the crime to his unsuspecting guests like "I could kill you" or "Knock 'em dead." Granger, on the other hand, appears not to enjoy the game, reacting nervously to such purposely ironic Dall comments as "these hands will bring you great fame" when the nervous Granger sits at the piano to play a portion of Francis-Jean-Marcel Poulenc's "Perpetual Movement No. 1" (a title which is itself indicative of the camera's nonstop movement). As the night wears on, everyone becomes concerned with Hogan's absence, fearing that something may have happened to him. The dinner party begins to take on an even more morbid tone when Dall pulls Stewart into a conversation about murder. Stewart, on an abstract level, speaks of man's right and moral duty to rid the world of the weak. This philosophy, which disgusts most of the guests, excites Dall who tries to bring the conversation into more concrete, realistic terms. By this point, Granger has gotten himself quite drunk and becomes carelessly emotional, raising Stewart's suspicions. Dall pushes the proceedings too far when he gives Hardwicke some books which he ties together with the piece of rope used in the murder. An hour after the party began, with Hogan still unaccounted for, the guests clear out and it looks as if Dall and Granger have succeeded. Stewart, however, returns and presses the issue of their earlier conversation about murder. When he puts the facts together and finds the body, he calls the police. As the three wait for their arrival, Stewart realizes that he taught his pupils too well, assuming guilt for the murder—the guilt that Dall shrugs off and that is deservedly Stewart's for his irresponsibility of thought and teaching. Although the story of the murder and the suspense of awaiting Stewart's discovery is intriguing, it is not what people remember ROPE for, nor is it top-drawer Hitchcock in terms of storytelling, complexity, and structure. ROPE is, like LIFEBOAT (1944) before it, an experiment in overcoming technical barriers and restrictions—a chore which always thrilled Hitchcock. Known for his deliberate and meticulous preproduction planning of a film, Hitchcock was widely known to have thought of his actors in a secondary light. Here this is most clear since all of his energies go into technique. (Paradoxically, though not intentionally on Hitchcock's part, ROPE, with its long takes, can be seen as favorable to the actors since their performances are closer to theater than film.) The construction of ROPE is simple—eight 10-minute takes cut together to appear as one continuous shot. Where most films have an average of 600 shots (Hitchcock's THE BIRDS had over 1,300, while the shower scene alone in PSYCHO had dozens more shots than the entirety of ROPE), ROPE would appear as just one (this appearance is deceptive, however—there is a separate shot which opens the film and a couple of direct reverse angle cuts within the film, which are often forgotten). Since the maximum length for a reel of 35mm film is around 10 minutes, these reels were joined inconspicuously by stopping the camera movement behind a character so his back would fill the entire frame. The cameraman would then reload a new reel of film, pick up the shot on the actor's back, and film for another 10 minutes. By cutting the scenes together at the spot where the actor's back fills the frame, the illusion of one continuous take is achieved. Not surprisingly, there were many other hurdles for Hitchcock and his crew to overcome. Together with cameraman Valentine, art director Ferguson, set designers Kuri and Bristol, and editor Ziegler, Hitchcock outlined specific plans for the production. Ziegler's job was to choreograph the actor's movements (he did this with a small scale model of the set and miniatures as his actors) in relation to the camera movements of Valentine. To complicate things further, the camera needed the freedom to travel through the set without crashing into lights, walls, furniture, and technicians. Breakaway walls were built, which were suspended from ceiling beams and rolled along by technicians to allow camera passage. The furniture and the chest which hid the corpse were also on rollers. Because dialog was being recorded, the movement of the walls and the crew members had to be done almost silently with the walls moving on tracks coated with petroleum jelly. The floors of the sound stage were specially built with one-inch tongue-and-groove lumber, soundproofing, and felt-lined carpeting to prevent any creaking that might occur. Even a special camera dolly was invented (by head grip Morris Rosen) to allow for greater freedom of movement. Countless lights were hung overhead, as were microphones. On some occasions there were as many as five boom operators recording sound at the same time, adding to the already crowded sound stage. Because of the number of people and number of things that could go wrong, many takes were needed for each scene. One perfectly good take was ruined when, after nearly winding out the 10-minute reel, an electrician was spotted in the background. Valentine, in a 1948 interview with *American Cinematographer* magazine, said: "My biggest problem was the lighting, especially the job of eliminating mike and camera shadows. In the reel in which we had 10 mikes in operation we had to have electricians operating five dimmer panels." Special care was also taken on the New York City skyline which is seen outside the penthouse window. Since the film took place in real time, night had to fall over the city. A set was built which encompassed 35 square miles of skyline—landmarks such as the Empire State Building and the Chrysler Building, complete with 6,000 flashing miniature lights, 200 miniature neon signs, 26,000 feet of wire, 150 transformers, and 126,000 watts of electricity, all of which were controlled by an electrician operating 47 different switches. (This skyline also included a neon sign for a product called Reduco, which features a before and after silhouette of Hitchcock—a gag also seen in a newspaper ad in LIFEBOAT.) All of which was constructed in diminishing perspective and in a semicircle outside the window to keep the constantly mobile camera from accidentally photographing part of a bare set. Even precise and technically correct cloud formations were constructed from spun glass and chickenwire, under the expert instructions of a specially hired advisor and meteorologist Dr. Dinsmore Alter. Budgeted at $1.5 million, with $300,000 paying off Stewart's star value, ROPE was scripted first by Hitchcock's friend, actor Hume Cronyn, from Hamilton's play. Playwright Laurents was then brought in to improve on Cronyn. Even Ben Hecht (who previously scripted SPELLBOUND and NOTORIOUS) added some lines, uncredited, however, to the final climactic scene. Rehearsals began on January 12, 1948, to perfect the interplay between camera, cast, and crew. Numbers were placed on the floor marking everyone's specific spots, each of which corresponded with the actors' dialog cues. Filming commenced on January 22 and, after 21 days in production—for only eight shots—shooting finished on February 21. Besides being a great technical achievement, this was also Hitchcock's first film in color, thereby paving the way for even more problems. Valentine, who was experienced only with black-and-white photography, was unable to capture the color Hitchcock needed during sundown. Technicolor advisor Skall was brought in and, after Valentine left the production due to illness, reshot the final five reels (over half of the film). According to Hitchcock, "I undertook ROPE as a stunt; that's the only way I know how to describe it." As a result, ROPE is chiefly of interest to filmmakers curious to learn how things were achieved; it lacks much of the flair and audience manipulation that Hitchcock has become famous for. Stewart's performance is competent, but never reaches the level of disturbance or authority that it should have. Dall and Granger (whom Hitchcock spotted after screening Nicholas Ray's first picture THEY LIVE BY NIGHT) are both superb, especially Granger as the pathetically disturbed victim of Dall's plot. Their characters, and their thinly shrouded homosexuality, were based on the murderous exploits of Richard A. Leopold, the 18-year-old son of a multi-millionaire shipping magnate, and Nathan F. Loeb, the 17-year-old son of a wealthy Sears, Roebuck and Company vice president. Together, in 1924, they kidnaped and killed 14-year-old Bobbie Franks of Chicago just for the intellectual and phlosopical thrill of trying to get away with murder. Pampered, bored, and sexually deviant rich kids, they were both extraordinary youngsters—Leopold, with an IQ of 200, graduated from the University of Chicago at age 18 (the youngest graduate up to that time) with a strong interest in Nietzsche's "superman" theory, and Loeb with his passion for criminology and detective work and his desire to commit the elusive "perfect crime." After carefully investigating the crime, police put together clues and won a conviction for murder. Superstar defender Clarence Darrow was hired to save the killers from the death penalty, which he did. Loeb was murdered in prison 12 years after the crime, while Leopold received parole in 1958, started life anew in Puerto Rico, and died in 1971. Because of the underlying homosexuality in ROPE, the film was initially banned in Chicago (perhaps as a reaction to the raking up of the memory of the real murder case), Spokane, Memphis, Seattle, and morally condemned in many other towns. Only after an "adults only" policy was enacted in Chicago, and the opening murder scene deleted in Sioux City, Iowa, could the film be shown in those cities. ROPE was one of five Hitchcock films—REAR WINDOW, THE TROUBLE WITH HARRY, VERTIGO, and the 1956 version of THE MAN WHO KNEW TOO MUCH were the others—held from distribution for many years until their re-release in 1983.

p, Sidney Bernstein, Alfred Hitchcock; d, Hitchcock; w, Arthur Laurents, Hume Cronyn, (uncredited) Ben Hecht (based on the play "Rope's End" by Patrick Hamilton); ph, Joseph Valentine, William V. Skall (Technicolor); m, Leo F. Forbstein, (uncredited) David Buttolph (adapted from "Perpetual Movement No. 1" by Francis Poulenc); ed, William H. Ziegler; art d, Perry Ferguson; set d, Emile Kuri, Howard Bristol; makeup, Perc Westmore; cos, Adrian; cloud tech adv, Dr. Dinsmore Alter.

Crime Drama Cas. (PR:C-O MPAA:NR)

ROPE, 1965 (SEE: ROPE OF FLESH, 1965)

ROPE OF FLESH*½ (1965) 92m Delta/Eve bw (AKA: MUD HONEY; MUDHONEY!; ROPE)

Hal Hopper *(Sidney Brenshaw)*, Lorna Maitland *(Clara Belle)*, Antoinette Cristiani *(Hannah Brenshaw)*, John Furlong *(Calif McKinney)*, Stu Lancaster *(Lute Wade)*, Rena Horten *(Eula)*, Princess Livingston *(Maggie Marie)*, Sam Hanna *(Injoys)*, Nick Wolcuff *(Sheriff)*, Frank Bolger *(Brother Hanson)*, Lee Ballard *(Sister Hanson)*, Mickey Foxx *(Thurmond Pate)*, F. Rufus Owens *(Milton)*.

Furlong is an ex-con who finds work on a Missouri farm owned by Lancaster. He becomes involved with the farmer's niece, Cristiani, and soon has to answer to her sadistic husband, Hopper. Furlong is pushed into several situations where violence could occur but he backs down, leaves Cristiani, and turns to prostitutes. A lynch mob's plans go wrong, resulting in a barn-burning and murder after Hopper learns that Lancaster willed his farm to Furlong. An early Russ Meyer rural sexploitation picture.

p, Russ Meyer, George Costello; d, Meyer; w, Raymond Friday Locke, William E. Sprague; ph, Walter Schenk; ed, Charles Schelling; md, Henri Price.

Drama (PR:O MPAA:NR)

ROPE OF SAND*** (1949) 104m PAR bw

Burt Lancaster *(Mike Davis)*, Paul Henreid *(Commandant Paul Vogel)*, Claude Rains *(Arthur Martingale)*, Peter Lorre *(Toady)*, Corinne Calvet *(Suzanne Renaud)*, Sam Jaffe *(Dr. Francis Hunter)*, John Bromfield *(Thompson)*, Mike Mazurki *(Pierson)*, Kenny Washington *(John)*, Josef Marais,Miranda *(South African Veldt Singers)*, Edmond Breon *(Chairman)*, Hayden Rorke *(Ingram)*, David Hoffman *(Waiter)*, Carl Harbord *(Operator of Perseus Club)*, Georges Renavent *(Jacques the Headwaiter)*, Ida Moore *(Woman)*, David Thursby *(Henry the Bartender)*, Trevor Ward *(Switchboard Operator)*, Martin Wilkins, Everett G. Brown, Darby Jones *(Batsuma Chiefs)*, Byron Ellis *(Callboy)*, James R. Scott *(Clerk)*, Blackie Whiteford, Harry Cording, Art Foster *(Guards)*, Nestor Paiva *(Ship's Captain)*.

In the dusty South African mining town of Diamondstad, a hunter makes off with some diamonds from a forbidden zone but while crossing the desert he dies. Lancaster, the guide who had taken the hunter out, is arrested by Henreid, the chief of security for the mining company, who tries to beat the location of the still-missing diamonds out of him. Lancaster holds his tongue, and Henreid unwillingly lets him go. Rains, the head of the mining company, uses his influence to make Lancaster's life difficult and force him to return for the diamonds he has hidden. Eventually the strategy succeeds and Lancaster returns to Diamondstad. Henreid asks permission from Rains to try more torture, but instead Rains enlists prostitute Calvet to entice the information out of Lancaster. Lancaster resists her blandishments, but Henreid falls in love with her while she falls in love with Lancaster. Lancaster confronts Henreid and forces him to take them both into the forbidden area to retrieve the diamonds. Lancaster gets away and Henreid murders one of Lancaster's friends, the company doctor, Jaffe, and leaves evidence that Calvet has committed the crime. Lorre, a barfly and local character known appropriately as "Toady," lets Lancaster know that Calvet is about to be executed. Lancaster returns and approaches Rains with a proposition, the diamonds in exchange for the girl. Rains agrees and calls for Henreid, forcing him to sign an exonerating document. Then he slips Henreid a gun, but calls out a warning to Lancaster, who shoots the hated commandant dead. Together again, Lancaster and Calvet leave as Rains rehearses the speech he will tell the police when they arrive. Entertaining, though hardly classic, attempt to recapture some of the CASABLANCA magic by reuniting three of its stars, Rains, Lorre, and Henreid. The first two play their roles from the earlier movie with only slight variations, but Henreid does a 180-degree turn, becoming the sadistic villain and doing it quite effectively. Of course, Lancaster doesn't approach Bogart, but he does provide for a lot of exciting action, particularly in the climactic fight between him and Henreid during a furious sandstorm. Above average adventure film that fans of CASABLANCA won't find too disappointing.

p, Hal B. Wallis; d, William Dieterle; w, Walter Doniger, John Paxton; ph, Charles B. Lang, Jr.; m, Franz Waxman; ed, Warren Low; art d, Hans Dreier, Franz Bachelin; set d, Sam Comer, Grace Gregory; spec eff, Gordon Jannings; m/l, "The Zulu Warrior," "The Crickets," Josef Marais; makeup, C. Silvera.

Adventure (PR:A MPAA:NR)

ROSALIE*** (1937) 123m MGM bw

Nelson Eddy *(Dick Thorpe)*, Eleanor Powell *(Rosalie Romanikoff)*, Ray Bolger *(Bill Delroy)*, Frank Morgan *(King Frederic Romanikoff)*, Ilona Massey *(Brenda)*, Edna May Oliver *(Queen)*, Billy Gilbert *(1st Officer Oloff)*, Reginald Owen *(Chancellor)*, George Zucco *(Gen. Maroff)*, Virginia Grey *(Mary Callahan)*, Tom Rutherford *(Prince Paul)*, Janet Beecher *(Miss Baker)*, Clay Clement *(Capt. Banner)*, Oscar O'Shea *(Mr. Callahan)*, William Demarest *(Army's Coach)*, Rush Hughes *(Announcer)*, Wallis Clark *(Maj. Prentice)*, Richard Tucker *(Col. Brandon)*, Jerry Colonna *(2nd Officer Joseph)*, Wilson Benge *(Steward)*, Pierre Watkin *(Supt. of Academy)*, Tommy Bond *(Mickey)*, Purnell Pratt *(Ship Captain)*, Ricca Allen *(Schoolteacher)*, Al Shean *(Herman Schmidt)*, Frank Du Frane *(Superintendent's Aide)*, Ocean Claypool, Katharine Aldridge *(Ladies in Waiting)*, Edward Earle *(Navy Officer)*, George Magrill *(Assistant Army Coach)*, Lane Chandler *(Army Coach)*, Phillip Terry, William Tannen *(Cadets)*, George Humbert *(Carlo)*, Max Davidson *(Chamberlain)*, Harry Semels, Roy Barcroft, John Picorri, Sidney Bracy *(Conspirators)*, The Albertina Rasch Dancers.

Produced on the stage by Ziegfeld in 1928, the play ran more than a year at the New Amsterdam Theatre in New York with Marilyn Miller in the title role, Oliver McLennan as the male star and Frank Morgan as the king of the small land whence his daughter hails. To reproduce this film today would cost the receipts of the entire Kuwait oil industry for a year. It came in at more than 2 million dollars and every penny was on the screen with thousands of extras, all dressed in expensive costumes, and a host of musical numbers that made this seem like a cross between an operetta and a campus musical. The score for the play was done by Sigmund Romberg and George Gershwin but it was all tossed out, including Gershwin's "How Long Has This Been Going On?" in favor of a new score by Porter and several others. Marion Davies had made another version of "Rosalie" but the film was never released and some of the footage was used in this. Director Van Dyke, who was so well-known as being fast and the master of the well paced comedy, seemed lost in the awesome size of this, a movie whose set pieces far outweighed any story. Producer McGuire also wrote the screenplay based on the musical book he wrote earlier with Guy Bolton. Considering the flimsy plot, it was overproduced, with more than 20 cameras used in some scenes and scores of acres of the MGM back lot put to work. Eddy, who was 36 at the time, is playing football for West Point in the big game against Navy which ends in a tie with Eddy the hero. Powell, a Vassar student who tells no one that she is the princess of a small country, thinks Eddy is conceited but makes plans to meet him later in the year in Europe. Eddy flies his own plane overseas to see her. Meanwhile, Powell has been promised to chancellor Owen's son, Rutherford, in an arranged marriage. Eddy is flying in and the airport radio is run by Colonna and Gilbert (who does his famous sneezing bit with Colonna doing a double talk stint). He finally lands and learns that the country is in chaos. Eddy doesn't know that Powell is a princess and thinks she's just a peasant. Morgan greets the Lindbergh-type pilot and agrees to help him find the woman he loves. It takes forever until the couple is united, with a skinny subplot between Bolger and Grey to spice matters up. The countrypeople revolt, the royal family flees and that's where the picture should end, but no, it goes on. The two meet again in the U.S., have a few love problems at West Point, work things out and sing of their love to each other in a huge finale. It's a heavy, heavy treatment of a lightweight subject with enough music to satisfy everyone. Besides using medleys of marches and of classical operas and operettas, the movie offers a full complement of original songs with music and lyrics by Cole Porter, and more. Cole Porter tunes include: "I've Got a Strange New Rhythm in My Heart" (sung by Powell), "Why Should I Care?" (sung by Morgan), "Spring Love Is in the Air" (sung by Massey), "Rosalie," "It's All Over but the Shouting," "Who Knows?" "In the Still of the Night," "To Love or not To Love" (sung by Eddy), and "Close" (instrumental). In the beginning of the movie, Eddy and the male chorus perform medleys and snatches of "The Caissons Go Rolling Along" (Edmund L. Gruber), "On, Brave Old Army Team," (Philip Egner), "Anchors Aweigh" (Alfred Miles, Royal Lovell, Charles A. Zimmerman). As the plot thickens, Eddy sings "M'Appari" ("Ah, So Pure," an aria from the opera "Martha" by Friedrich von Flotow) and some of those Porter melodies. As romance blossoms further, the Albertina Rasch dancers perform to the music of the "Polovetsian Dances" from "Prince Igor" by Aleksandr Borodin and of "Swan Lake," Act II, by Peter Ilich Tchaikovsky, and Eddy sings "Goodbye Forever" ("Addio") by Paolo Tosti. A rousing medley of marches to which Powell dances includes John Philip Sousa's "Washington Post March," "Stars and Stripes Forever," "Semper Fidelis," and "El Capitan," as well as one more march, "Parade," by long-time arranger Herbert Stothart. And finally, if that's not enough, the "Wedding March" from Felix Mendelsohn's "A Midsummer Night's Dream" is followed with Eddy's renditions of the traditional "Gaudeamus Igitur" and "Oh, Promise Me" (Reginald DeKoven, Scott Clement) at the conclusion. With all the music and the incredible sets and dances, it's still an empty exercise. Massey made her film debut here after having been discovered by Louis Mayer on a trip to Europe. He also signed Hedy Lamarr, Greer Garson, and a few others on that sojourn, including Rose Stradner, who decided that she didn't like acting and chose to marry Joe Mankiewicz instead. ROSALIE had too much music and not enough comedy to make it anything more than a huge but essentially unsatisfying movie. Katherine Aldridge, a lady in waiting, and Roy Barcroft, a conspirator, both went on to minor fame at Republic Studios.

p, William Anthony McGuire; d, W.S. Van Dyke; w, McGuire (based on the play by McGuire, Guy Bolton); ph, Oliver T. Marsh; ed, Blanche Sewell; md, Herbert Stothart; art d, Cedric Gibbons; set d, Edwin B. Willis; cos, Dolly Tree; ch, Albertina Rasch.

Musical/Comedy **(PR:A MPAA:NR)**

ROSARY, THE*½ (1931, Brit.) 70m Twickenham/Williams and Pritchard bw

Margot Grahame *(Mary Edwards)*, Elizabeth Allan *(Vera Mannering)*, Walter Piers *(Capt. Mannering)*, Leslie Perrins *(Ronald Overton)*, Robert Holmes *(Dalmayne)*, Charles Groves *(Hornett)*, Irene Rooke *(Mother Superior)*, Les Allen *(The Singer)*.

A pair of half-sisters find themselves at odds after learning they are both involved with the same man. One of the girls gets pregnant and is talked into marriage by the other girl, who then decides to enter the convent. A combination of forgery, blackmail, and murder add a criminal atmosphere to this religious-based romance.

p, Julius Hagen; d, Guy Newall; w, John McNally

Drama **(PR:O MPAA:NR)**

ROSE, THE*** (1979) 134m FOX c

Bette Midler *(Rose)*, Alan Bates *(Rudge)*, Frederic Forrest *(Dyer)*, Harry Dean Stanton *(Billy Ray)*, Barry Primus *(Dennis)*, David Keith *(Mal)*, Sandra McCabe *(Sarah)*, Will Hare *(Mr. Leonard)*, Rudy Bond *(Monty)*, Don Calfa *(Don Frank)*, James Keane *(Dealer)*, Doris Roberts *(Rose's Mother)*, Sandy Ward *(Rose's Father)*, Michael Greer *(Emcee)*, Claude Sacha, Michael St. Laurent, Sylvester, Pearl Heart *(Female Impersonators)*, Butch Ellis *(Waiter)*, Richard Dioguardi *(Trucker)*, John Dennis Johnston *(Milledge)*, Jonathan Banks *(TV Promoter)*, Jack O'Leary *(Short Order Cook)*, Luke Andreas, Harry Northup, Cherie Latimer, Seamon Glass, Pat Corley, Dennis Erdman, Hugh Gillin, Joyce Roth, Frank Speiser, Constance Cawlfield, Annie McGuire, Hildy Brooks, Jack Starrett, David Garfield, Jack Hollander, Sandra Seacat, Chip Zien.

Bette Midler turns in an energetic performance in this story of a down-and-out rock singer a la Janis Joplin. Exhausted from the pressures of touring, Bette tells her manager/mentor that she wants a year off to rest. He resists her wishes and sends the singer into a tailspin. One night she picks up a chauffeur (Forrest) and embarks on the most fulfilling romance of her life. Forrest cannot deal with the penalties of fame that come with Midler's success; however, and he leaves. She turns back to music and prepares for a hometown performance. On stage she wows the audience with her most dazzling performance, but this performance turns out to be her last as the troubled singer resorts to a fatal combination of booze and drugs. Midler successfully brings her charged stage persona to the screen, allowing the audience to get a good dose of the backstage life of a rock and roll performer. Forrest as the chauffeur and Stanton in a cameo as a country singer add an earthy contrast to the glamorous aspects. Only Bates is wasted in a relatively minor role as the manager whose desire for success is greater than Midler can handle. A number of hard-hitting tunes are featured: "Fire Down Below" (Bob Seger), "I've Written A Letter To Daddy" (Larry Vincent, Harry Tobias, Mo Jaffe), "Let Me Call You Sweetheart" (Leo Friedman, Beth Slater Whitson), "The Rose" (Amanda McBroom), "Stay With Me" (Jerry Ragavoy, George Weiss), "Camellia" (Stephen Hunter), "Sold My Soul To Rock'n'Roll" (Gene Pistilli), "Keep On Rockin'" (Sammy Hagar, John Carter), "When A Man Loves A Woman" (C. Lewis, A. Wright), "Whose Side Are You On?" (Kenny Hopkins, Charley Williams), "Midnight In Memphis" (Tony Johnson), "The Night We Said Good-bye" (Bill Elliott), and "Evil Lies" (Greg Prestopino, Carol Locatell).

p, Marvin Worth, Aaron Russo; d, Mark Rydell; w, Bo Goldman, William Kerby, Michael Cimino (from the story by William Kerby); ph, Vilmos Zsigmond (DeLuxe Color); m, Paul A. Rothchild; ed, Robert L. Wolfe; prod d, Richard MacDonald; art d, Jim Schoppe; cos, Theoni V. Aldredge; ch, Toni Basil.

Musical Drama **Cas** **(PR:O MPAA:R)**

ROSE BOWL* (1936) 75m PAR bw (GB: O'RILEY'S LUCK)

Eleanor Whitney *(Cheers Reynolds)*, Tom Brown *(Paddy O'Riley)*, Larry "Buster" Crabbe *(Ossie Merrill)*, William Frawley *(Coach Soapy Moreland)*, Benny Baker *(Dutch Schultz)*, Nydia Westman *(Susie Reynolds)*, Priscilla Lawson *(Florence Taylor)*, Adrian Morris *(Doc)*, James Conlin *(Browning Hills)*, Nick Lukats *(Donavan)*, Terry Ray [Ellen Drew] *(Mary Arnold)*, Bud Flanagan [Dennis O'Keefe] *(Jones)*, William Moore *(Peter Potter/Holt)*, Lon Chaney, Jr., Ray Wehba, Donald McNeil, Gil Kuhn, Phil J. Duboski, Gene Hibbs, Joe Preninger, Charles Williams, Owen Hansen, Jim Henderson, Boyd "Red" Morgan, Nick Pappas, Angelo Peccianti, James Jones, Leavitt Thurlow, Jr., Miles Norton, Lyman H. Russell, Edward Shuey, Glen Galvin, Tod Goodwin, David Newell, David Horsley *(football players)*, Louis Mason *(Thornton)*, John Sheehan *(Orville Jensen)*, Joe Ploski *(Swenski)*, Hugh McArthur *(Russell)*, Charles Judels *(Mr. Schultz)*, Sid Saylor, George Ovey, Milburn Stone, Henry Roquemore, Jerry Fletcher *(Rubber Band)*, Billy Lee *(Little Boy)*, Bodil Ann Rosing *(Mrs. Schultz)*, Bert Moorhouse, Hal Price, Earl Jamison, Arthur Rowlands, Buck Mack *(Reporters)*, Pat O'Malley, Hooper Atchley, Charles Sherlock *(Photographers)*, Herbert Ashley *(Pitt Fan)*, Bernard Suss *(Spectator)*, Thomas Pogue *(Rooter)*, Anthony Pawley, Donald Kerr *(Reporters)*, Edward Peil, Jr. *(Undergraduate)*, Dick Winslow *(Boy)*, Gertrude Messinger, June Johnson *(Girls)*, Joseph Sawyer, Garry Owen *(Announcers)*, Ray Hanford *(Football Fan)*, Jack Murphy *(Player)*, Spec O'Donnell *(Underclassman)*, Paul Perry *(Manager)*, Paul Kruger *(Team Manager)*, Harry Depp *(King)*, William Jeffrey *(Hay)*, Wheaton Chambers *(Wallace)*, Antrim Short *(Assistant Director)*, Frances Morris *(Assistant Publicist)*, Richard Kipling *(Barber)*, Charles C. Wilson *(Burke)*.

Brown and Baker are school chums who become big names on the college football roster, but they still can't seem to get the girls, especially with the undesirable Crabbe (desirable only to the girls) in the way. They get their way at the end by showing up Crabbe in the title gridiron game.

p, A.M. Botsford; d, Charles Barton; w, Marguerite Roberts (based on the novel *O'Reilly of Notre Dame* by Francis Wallace); ph, Henry Sharp; ed, William Shea; md, Borris Morros; m/l, Charlie Rosco, Leo Robin.

Romance/Sports Comedy **(PR:A MPAA:NR)**

ROSE BOWL STORY, THE** (1952) 73m MON c

Marshall Thompson *(Steve Davis)*, Vera Miles *(Denny Burke)*, Richard Rober *(Coach Hadley)*, Natalie Wood *(Sally Burke)*, Keith Larsen *(Bronc Buttram)*, Tom Harmon *(Himself)*, Ann Doran *(Mrs. Burke)*, James Dobson *(Allie Bassler)*, Jim Backus *(Mike Burke)*, Clarence Kolb *(Gramps)*, Barbara Woodell *(Mrs. Hadley)*, Bill Welsh *(Himself)*, William Forrest, Paul Byrar, Parc Launders, Herb Vigran, Nancy Thorne, Sharon Ann Kelley, Anne Cottingham, Diana Dial, Carolyn Graves, Barbara Fisher, Marcia Long.

Few trick plays are used in this standard football tale of a star quarterback who falls in love with the fur-coated Miles. He tries extra hard initially to impress her, believing that she is an heiress when she is just putting on in a borrowed coat. After his coach's wife takes ill and star Thompson has a falling out with Miles, the QB begins to straighten up. Instead of putting his star image before the team, he concentrates on impressing his coach and girlfriend with sportsmanship. Natalie Wood is cast as Miles' laugh-getting little sister. Includes an abundance of Rose Bowl stock footage and the 1952 Rose Queen, Nancy Thorne.

p, Richard Heermance; d, William Beaudine; w, Charles R. Marion; ph, Harry Neumann (Cinecolor); m, Marlin Skiles; ed, Walter Hannemann; art d, David Hilton.

Sports/Romance **(PR:A MPAA:NR)**

ROSE FOR EVERYONE, A½** (1967, Ital.) 107m Vides/Royal c (UNA ROSA PER TUTTI; AKA: EVERY MAN'S WOMAN; EVERYMAN'S WOMAN)

Claudia Cardinale *(Rosa)*, Nino Manfredi *(The Doctor)*, Mario Adorf *(Paolo)*, Akim Tamiroff *(Basilio)*, Lando Buzzanca *(Lino)*, Luis Pellegrini *(Silvano)*, Milton Rodriguez *(Sergio)*, Oswaldo Loureiro *(Nino)*, Jose Lewgoy *(Floreal)*, Grande Othelo *(Ze Amoro)*, Celia Bilar *(Nilse)*, Laura Soares *(Donna Natalia)*.

An inspired comedy which casts Cardinale as Rosa, a beautiful woman living in Rio de Janeiro who offers her love to everyone. This keeps her and her lovers content for some time, but a jealous Lino becomes violent and Cardinale lands in a hospital. Her doctor prescribes fidelity, hoping to convince Cardinale to love only one man. She tries, but unsatisfied, returns to her many loves.

p, Franco Cristaldi; d, Franco Rossi; w, Eduardo Borras, Ennio De Concini, Rossi, Nino Manfredi (based on the play "Procura-se Uma Rosa" by Glaucio Gill); ph, Alfio Contini (Technicolor); m, Luis Enriquez Bacalov; ed, Giorgio Serralonga; prod d, Roberto Machado; art d, Gianni Polidori; cos, Gaia Romanini; m/l, "Rosamor," Bacalov, Juca Chaves (sung by Chaves); makeup, Giannetto De Rossi.

Comedy **(PR:O MPAA:NR)**

ROSE MARIE**** (1936) 110m MGM bw (AKA: INDIAN LOVE CALL)

Jeanette MacDonald *(Marie de Flor)*, Nelson Eddy *(Sgt. Bruce)*, James Stewart *(John Flower)*, Reginald Owen *(Myerson)*, George Regas *(Boniface)*, Robert Greig *(Cafe Manager)*, Una O'Connor *(Anna)*, James Conlin *(Joe the Piano Player)*, Lucien Littlefield *(Storekeeper)*, Dorothy Gray *(Edith)*, Alan Mowbray *(Premier)*, Mary Anita Loos *(Corn Queen)*, Aileen Carlyle *(Susan)*, Halliwell Hobbes *(Mr. Gordon)*, Paul Porcasi *(Emil the Chef)*, David Nivens [Niven]*(Teddy)*, Herman Bing *(Mr. Danielle)*, Gilda Gray *(Belle)*, Allan Jones *(Romeo/Mario Cavaradossi)*, Bert Lindley *(Pop)*, Ed Dearing *(Mounted Policeman)*, Pat West *(Traveling Salesman)*, Milton Owen *(Stage Manager)*, David Clyde *(Doorman)*, Russell Hicks *(Commandant)*, Rolfe Sedan, Louis Mercier *(Admirers in Hall)*, Jack Pennick *(Brawler)*, Leonard Carey *(Louis)*, David Robel, Rinaldo Alacorn *(Dancer)*, Matty Roubert *(Newsboy)*, Major Sam Harris *(Guest)*, Ernie Alexander *(Elevator Operator)*, James Mason *(Trapper)*, John George, Lee Phelps *(Barflies)*, Fred Graham *(Corporal)*, Agostino Borgato, Adrian Rosley *(Opera Fans)*, Delos Jewkes *(Butcher at Hotel)*.

Of all the MacDonald and Eddy films, ROSE MARIE is the one that made the most money and will be best recalled. It began as a stage play by Friml, Stothart, Harbach, and Hammerstein in 1924, with Mary Ellis in the lead, Dennis King as the outlaw, and Arthur Deagon as the Mountie. In 1928, it was done as a silent, ROSE-MARIE (note the hyphen), starring Joan Crawford, House Peters, and James Murray. Grace Moore was to play the lead in this talkie version but schedules conflicted and MacDonald replaced her, which was just as well as Eddy and MacDonald had just come off the smash hit NAUGHTY MARIETTA. The play's plot was altered to suit MacDonald's abilities and the result was a superior blend of music and story starring "the Iron Butterfly" and "the Singing Capon" (as they were known behind their backs). Three newish faces made appearances in the film. James Stewart, in his second movie, played MacDonald's outlaw brother, Allan Jones was her operatic co-star (more about that later), and David Nivens (with an "s" at the end) was MacDonald's rejected and dejected boy friend. MacDonald is an opera star on tour across Canada (which is always what she wanted to do in real life). Her brother, Stewart, is in jail for robbing a bank and MacDonald uses her visit to Montreal to plead with the Premier, Mowbray, to get Stewart out of the slammer. While that's being considered, Stewart escapes from incarceration and kills a Mountie. He goes into the deep woods to hide and MacDonald is determined to find him. She leaves the opera (where they had somehow managed to compress five acts of Charles Gounod's "Romeo et Juliette" into about six minutes), employs a guide, Regas, and sets out for the wilderness. Regas is a half-breed Indian and not to be trusted. It is he who told MacDonald about Stewart's escape, and the man is obviously in this for a large payoff. MacDonald takes her maid's coat and a thin cardboard suitcase, as time is of the essence and she doesn't have the right kind of clothes for foraging in the forest. MacDonald and Regas make it to the final outpost store before heading for "The Great Out There" (as Jack London called it). Regas steals MacDonald's purse and she is out of money. Littlefield, the shopkeeper (a veteran of the Keystone Kops) advises her to tell the Mounties but she decides not to and goes to the local saloon. There, she meets Gray (the famed "shimmy" dancer) who helps her learn how to sing songs that these grizzled miners and prospectors will like. Eddy, a sergeant with the Royal Mounted Police, arrives looking for Stewart, and spots MacDonald. She exits the dance hall and Eddy tails her, then catches up and says that her purloined suitcase is at the Mountie headquarters. Later, Eddy takes MacDonald to see where the local Indians hold their tribal dances. She spots Regas and he embarrassedly returns her money and says that he will now help her go deeper into the backwoods to help locate Stewart. Eddy, who thinks that MacDonald's name is "de Flor" now realizes that's the Spanish word for "flower," and since Stewart's name is "John Flower" she must be related to him. Alas! He is torn between his attraction to MacDonald and his occupation. Since "The Mounties Always Get Their Man," he follows MacDonald and Regas as they slip out of town. It isn't long before Regas spots the trailing Eddy, so he bolts and leaves MacDonald in the woods alone. Eddy joins her and hopes that she will lead him to Stewart. She does this and Stewart is captured. Back in civilization, MacDonald has a mental breakdown and no one can figure why. She was doing "Tosca" when she suddenly stopped and hasn't sung a word since. Her manager, Owen, knows the reason and he contacts Eddy who arrives to be reunited with MacDonald in a loving finale. The movie was shot near Lake Tahoe over a summer (it was evidently too cold to shoot in the Canadian Rockies) and the exteriors make it almost a musical western. The advertising campaign said this was about "A Pampered Pet of the Opera Who Meets a Rugged Canadian Mountie!" and there was more truth to that than anyone knew, as MacDonald was, by that time, feeling her popularity and making difficult demands of the studio. Further, when Jones was allowed too much time on screen in his operatic scenes, Eddy let the studio know he was not pleased and Jones's role was trimmed, although he came back a while later to be MacDonald's co-star in THE FIREFLY. Director Van Dyke, who was easy to get along with, and, as has been stated, worked very fast, said that he was able to make just about anyone, including animals, act, but he felt that he failed with the wooden Eddy. He was self-conscious and did not have a large ego when it came to acting (only singing), so MacDonald was able to manipulate him to her advantage and even arranged some of the camera shots so she was featured in what would ordinarily be a two-shot. She stole just about every scene, a fact Eddy never realized until he saw the movie. MacDonald, when she was making MAYTIME with John Barrymore, was such a scene-stealer that Barrymore said he would jam the kerchief she played with down her throat if she ever touched it while he was speaking. MacDonald must have enjoyed working with the speedy Van Dyke, as they teamed with Clark Gable to make the extraordinarily popular SAN FRANCISCO later that year. Even though composer Rudolf Friml is always remembered for this, it was actually MGM musical director Herbert Stothart who wrote many of the tunes. "Indian Love Call" (Friml, Otto Harbach, Oscar Hammerstein II) is sung several times by almost everyone in the cast. Other musical numbers include: "Pardon Me, Madame" (Stothart, Gus Kahn, sung by MacDonald, chorus), "The Mounties" (Friml, Stothart, Harbach, Hammerstein II, sung by Eddy, chorus), "Rose Marie" (Friml, Harbach, Hammerstein II, sung by Eddy), "Totem Tom Tom" (Friml, Stothart, Harbach, Hammerstein II, sung by chorus), "Just for You" (Friml, Stothart, Kahn, sung by Eddy), "Tex Yeux" (Rene Alphonse Rabey, sung by MacDonald), "St. Louis Blues" (W.C. Handy, sung by Gilda Gray), "Dinah" (Harry Akst, Sam Lewis, Joe Young, sung by MacDonald, James Conlin), "Three Blind Mice" (traditional, sung by MacDonald, chorus). Arias from Gounod's "Romeo et Juliette" and Giacomo Puccini's "Tosca" are sung by MacDonald and Jones. "Some of These Days" (sung by MacDonald, Gilda Gray) was written by Shelton Brooks and served for many years as Sophie Tucker's theme. A few laughs, some excellent singing, and wonderful photography. There's a story that a British singer, when handed the sheet music for "Indian Love Call" was not certain of the way the lines should be sung. The words said "When I'm calling you-oo-oo-oo-oo-oo-oo-oo," and the British singer sang, "When I'm calling you, double-'Oh,' double-'Oh.'" It may not be true but it's fun to imagine. Under no circumstances confuse this offering with the remake in 1954. Retitled INDIAN LOVE CALL for TV showings, the remake is inferior, despite its wide-screen, color treatment.

p, Hunt Stromberg; d, W.S. Van Dyke II; w, Frances Goodrich, Albert Hackett, Alice Duer Miller (based on the operetta by Otto A. Harbach, Oscar Hammerstein II, Rudolf Friml, Herbert Stothart); ph, William Daniels; m, Friml, Stothart; ed, Blanche Sewell; md, Stothart; art d, Cedric Gibbons, Joseph Wright, Edwin B. Willis; cos, Adrian; ch, Chester Hale, William von Wymetal.

Musical Comedy Cas. (PR:AA MPAA:NR)

ROSE MARIE*** (1954) 115m MGM c

Ann Blyth *(Rose Marie Lemaitre)*, Howard Keel *(Mike Malone)*, Fernando Lamas *(James Severn Duval)*, Bert Lahr *(Barney McGorkle)*, Marjorie Main *(Lady Jane Dunstock)*, Joan Taylor *(Wanda)*, Roy Collins *(Inspector Appleby)*, Chief Yowlachie *(Black Eagle)*, James Logan *(Clerk)*, Thurl Ravenscroft *(Indian Medicine Man)*, Abel Fernandez *(Indian Warrior)*, Billy Dix *(Mess Waiter)*, Al Ferguson, Frank Ragney *(Woodsmen)*, Marshall Reed *(Mountie)*, Sheb Wooley *(Corporal)*, Dabbs Greer *(Committeeman)*, John Pickard, John Damler *(Orderlies)*, Sally Yarnell *(Hostess)*, Gordon Richards *(Attorney)*, Lumsden Hare *(Judge)*, Mickey Simpson *(Trapper)*, Pepi Lanzi *(Johnny Lang)*.

Although this was technically a remake, it had very little to do with either the play or the two films that preceded it. This was the first musical to be shot in color and CinemaScope (though not the first released) and the added dimension of the screen helped the picture look better than it actually was. Four songs from the original were kept and the Canadian Rockies location was glorious to gaze upon, but when an audience's eyes go to the mountains and not the people standing in front of them, the picture is in trouble. Blyth is a French-Canadian backwoods woman who loves Lamas, a mean trapper (but not the killer played by James Stewart in the Nelson Eddy-Jeanette MacDonald version). Lamas is being trailed by Mountie Keel, who is beloved by Indian maid Taylor, daughter of Chief Yowlachie. Lahr, who doesn't get nearly enough time on screen, is a comedy Mountie and Main owns the saloon-dance hall-hotel in the small town. Busby Berkeley came in to stage the dances and his touch is instantly evident, but not nearly enough to save the dreary reworking of the script. Blyth is no MacDonald, although Keel does project more sex appeal than Eddy, and Lamas is believable as the trapper. Tunes from the original score include: "Rose Marie" (Rudolf Friml, Otto Harbach, Oscar Hammerstein II, sung by Keel), "Indian Love Call" (Friml, Harbach, Hammerstein II, sung by Keel, Blyth), "Totem Tom Tom" (Friml, Harbach, Hammerstein II, Herbert Stothart, sung by chorus), "The Mounties" (Friml, Harbach, Hammerstein II, Stothart, sung by Keel, chorus). Friml teamed with Paul Francis Webster to add three more songs: "I Have The Love," "The Right Place For A Girl," and "Free To Be Free." George Stoll and the brilliant Herbert Baker wrote a special material tune for Lahr called "The Mountie Who Never Got His Man." In the end, Lamas gets the girl—a definite surprise—and they both walk off into the sunset together. In small roles, note Sheb Wooley, who later had a million-seller record as a singer; Dabbs Greer, who later became a TV sit-com star; and Thurl Ravenscroft, who is best known for his mellifluous voice on various radio and TV commercials and who, for many years, was the narrator at the Laguna Beach Art Festival, where "living paintings" are presented on stage with real Laguna Beach residents holding in a frozen position for a minute to simulate old masters and various sculptures. It may have been this spectacular and long-running summer show that inspired Stephen Sondheim and James Lapine in some of their staging for their Broadway musical about art, "Sunday In The Park With George," which received critical approval from Frank Rich at the *New York Times* and lost a great deal of money. Yes, the above is a digression, but we just thought you'd like to know.

p&d, Mervyn LeRoy; w, Ronald Miller, George Froeschel (based on the operetta by Otto A. Harbach, Oscar Hammerstein II, Rudolf Friml, Herbert Stothart; ph, Paul Vogel (CinemaScope, Eastmancolor); m, Friml, Stothart; ed, Harold F. Kress; md, Georgie Stoll; art d, Cedric Gibbons, Merrill Pye; cos, Helen Rose; spec eff, A. Arnold Gillespie, Warren Newcombe; ch, Busby Berkeley.

Musical Comedy (PR:AA MPAA:G)

ROSE OF CIMARRON½** (1952) 72m FOX c

Jack Buetel *(Marshal Hollister)*, Mala Powers *(Rose of Cimarron)*, Bill Williams *(George Newcomb)*, Jim Davis *(Willie Whitewater)*, Dick Curtis *(Clem Dawley)*, Tom Monroe *(Mike Finch)*, William Phipps *(Jeb Dawley)*, Bob Steele *(Rio)*, Alex Gerry *(Judge Kirby)*, Lillian Bronson *(Emmy Anders)*, Irving Bacon *(Sheriff)*, Art Smith *(Deacon)*, Monte Blue *(Lone Eagle)*, Argentina Brunetti, Lane Bradford.

Powers is the girl of the title who, after her parents were killed, is raised by Cherokees. When her Indian parents are also killed, she vows to avenge their deaths. She enlists the help of Buetel, who guns down two of the three killers. The third, unknown to Powers, has become her lover. Buetel makes sure, however, that the killer pays for his deed and in the meantime, Buetel gets Powers' hand.

p, Edward L. Alperson; d, Harry Keller; w, Maurice Geraghty; ph, Karl Struss

(Natural-Color): m, Raoul Kraushaar; ed, Arthur Roberts; art d, Boris Levin; cos, Norma Koch.

Western (PR:A MPAA:NR)

ROSE OF THE RANCHO*½ (1936) 85m PAR bw

John Boles *(Jim Kearney)*, Gladys Swarthout *(Rosita Castro, Don Carlos)*, Charles Bickford *(Joe Kincaid)*, Willie Howard *(Pancho Spiegelgass)*, Herb Williams *(Phineas P. Jones)*, Grace Bradley *(Flossie)*, H.B. Warner *(Don Pascual Castro)*, Charlotte Granville *(Dona Petrona)*, Don Alvarado *(Don Luis)*, Minor Watson *(Jonathon Hill)*, Louise Carter *(Guadalupe)*, Pedro de Cordoba *(Gomez)*, Paul Harvey *(Boss Martin)*, Arthur Aylesworth *(Sheriff James)*, Russell Hopton *(Frisco)*, Bennie Baker, Harry Woods.

Boles is a government agent hired to capture a villainous fellow by the name of "Don Carlos," the leader of a Spanish gang who repeatedly attacks U.S. landowners. Boles' search is fruitless until he learns that the wanted "man" is really Swarthout, a shady senorita. A very proper lady during the day, by night Swarthout is a vicious vigilante. She proves no match, however, for Boles' law-abiding ways. This picture was Swarthout's film debut, and although she was an opera singer at the Met, she didn't open her mouth on any of the following tunes: "If I Should Lose You," "Thunder Over Paradise," "Little Rose Of Rancho," "Got A Girl In Cal-i-for-ni-ay," "There's Gold in Monterey," "Where Is My Love," and "The Padre And The Bride" (Ralph Rainger, Leo Robin).

p, William LeBaron; d, Marion Gering; w, Frank Partos, Charles Brackett, Arthur Sheekman, Nat Perrin, Harlan Thompson, Brian Hooker (based on the play by Richard Walton Tully, David Belasco); ph, Leo Tover; ed, Hugh Bennett; cos, Travis Banton; m/l, Ralph Rainger, Leo Robin.

Western/Musical (PR:A MPAA:NR)

ROSE OF THE RIO GRANDE (SEE: GOD'S COUNTRY AND THE MAN, 1931)

ROSE OF THE RIO GRANDE* (1938) 61m MON bw

Movita *(Rosita)*, John Carroll *(El Gato)*, Antonio Moreno *(Lugo)*, Lina Basquette *(Anita)*, Don Alvarado *(Don Jose)*, George Cleveland *(Pedro)*, Duncan Renaldo *(Sebastian)*, Gino Corrado *(Castro)*, Martin Garralga *(Luis)*, Rose Turich *(Maria)*.

A poor oater about a rebel gang from Mexico's upper class that avenges its own class by killing those who offend them. Why this one carries the Rio Grande title is a mystery, since the entire picture runs without even a glimpse of a body of water.

p, George E. Kann; d, William Nigh; w, Ralph Bettinson (based on the story by Johnston McCulley); ph, Gilbert Warrenton; m, Charlie Rosoff; md, Hugo Reisenfeld; m/l, Rossoff, Eddie Cherkose.

Western (PR:A MPAA:NR)

ROSE OF THE YUKON** (1949) 69m REP bw

Steve Brodie *(Maj. Geoffrey Barnett)*, Myrna Dell *(Rose Flambeau)*, William Wright *(Tom Clark)*, Emory Parnell *(Tim MacNab)*, Jonathan Hale *(Gen. Butler)*, Benny Baker *(Jack Wells)*, Gene Gary *(Frenchy Frenay)*, Dick Elliot *(Doc Read)*, Francis McDonald, Wade Crosby *(Alaskan Men)*, Lotus Long *(Eskimo Girl)*, Eugene Signaloff *(Capt. Rossoff)*.

Brodie is a U.S. Army major who is sent to Alaska to investigate the mysterious resurfacing of a supposedly dead Army captain (Wright). The captain is identified at a gambling den and tagged with a murder charge. After a fast-paced dog sled race, Brodie gets his man. Dell, as a barroom singer, delivers the film's sole tune "It's Not The First Love" (Eddie Maxwell, Nathan Scott).

p, Stephen Auer; d, George Blair; w, Norman S. Hall; ph, John MacBurnie; m, Stanley Wilson; ed, Harry Keller; art d, Frank Hotaling.

Adventure (PR:A MPAA:NR)

ROSE OF TRALEE* (1938, Ireland) 78m But/Dublin bw

Binkie Stuart *(Rose O'Malley)*, Kathleen O'Regan *(Mary O'Malley)*, Fred Conyngham *(Paddy O'Malley)*, Danny Malone *(Singer)*, Dorothy Dare *(Jean Hale)*, Sydney Fairbrother *(Mrs. Thompson)*, Talbot O'Farrell *(Tim Kelly)*, C. Denier Warren *(Henry Collett)*, Patrick Ludlow *(Frank)*, Scott Harold *(Gleeson)*, Dorothy Vernon, Paul Hanson, Jack Lester, Hamilton Keene, Henry Adnes, Harvey Brinton.

The young daughter of Irish parents reunites her divided family after Dad, a tenor, returns from America, where he sought the dream of fame. Mom, meanwhile, was left in London with the little one, working on a theatrical career to put bread on the table. Pretty poor script includes the tunes "Believe Me If All Those Endearing," "Come Back To Ireland," and "Did Your Mother Come From Ireland?"

p, Norman Hope-Bell; d&w, Oswald Mitchell (based on the story by Mitchell, Ian Walker, Kathleen Tyrone); m, W. Debroy Somers.

Musical (PR:A MPAA:NR)

ROSE OF TRALEE*½ (1942, Brit.) 77m But bw

John Longden *(Paddy O'Brien)*, Lesley Brook *(Mary O'Brien)*, Angela Glynne *(Rose O'Brien)*, Mabel Constanduros *(Mrs. Thompson)*, Talbot O'Farrell *(Tim Kelly)*, Gus McNaughton *(Gleeson)*, George Carney *(Collett)*, Virginia Keily *(Jean Hale)*, Iris Vandeleur *(Mrs. Crawley)*, *Morris Harvey (McIsaac)*.

A slowly paced programmer about an Irish singer who leaves his wife and child behind in England to become a success in the U.S. When he earns enough money in the States, he returns to England but finds that his family has gone—their lives disrupted by the onset of WW II. He joins the RAF and after some time is reunited with his loved ones.

p, F.W. Baker; d, Germain Burger; w, Kathleen Butler, H.F. Maltby (based on a story by Oswald Mitchell, Ian Walker); ph, Jack Parker, Robert Krasker.

Musical Drama (PR:A MPAA:NR)

ROSE OF WASHINGTON SQUARE*** (1939) 86m FOX bw

Tyrone Power *(Bart Clinton)*, Alice Faye *(Rose Sargent)*, Al Jolson *(Ted Cotter)*, William Frawley *(Harry Long)*, Joyce Compton *(Peggy)*, Hobart Cavanaugh *(Whitey Boone)*, Moroni Olsen *(Buck Russell)*, E.E. Clive *(Barouche Driver)*, Louis Prima *(Himself)*, Charles Wilson *(Mike Cavanaugh)*, Hal K. Dawson, Paul Burns *(Chumps)*, Ben Welden *(Toby)*, Horace MacMahon *(Irving)*, Paul Stanton *(District Attorney)*, Harry Hayden *(Dexter)*, Charles Lane *(Kress, Booking Agent)*, Igor and Tanya *(Specialty Performers)*, Chick Chandler *(Master of Ceremonies)*, Murray Alper *(Candy Butcher)*, Ralph Dunn *(Officer)*, Edgar Dearing *(Lieutenant)*, Robert Shaw *(Reporter)*, James Flavin *(Guard)*, Leonard Kibrick *(Newsboy)*, Irene Wilsen *(Miss Lust)*, Bert Roach *(Mr. Paunch)*, Charles Lane *(Sam Kress)*, Adrian Morris *(Jim)*, John Hamilton *(Judge)*, Winifred Harris *(Mrs. Russell)*, Maurice Cass *(Mr. Mork, Furniture Buyer)*.

Faye is a singer in the 1920s who can only get bookings at various amateur night contests. She grows disgusted with her lot and heads off with her pal Compton for a vacation on Long Island. There she meets Power, a handsome rogue involved in a variety of get-rich-quick schemes. After Power takes Faye to a fancy party, he leaves without a word when the law closes in on him. Back in New York Faye's former partner Jolson gets the opportunity he's been waiting for when he performs his act for some important showmen. Things don't go as planned when Cavanaugh, a drunk in the balcony, heckles from above. Jolson is able to use this to his advantage and is signed up with Cavanaugh by the producers. Faye has returned to the city where she obtains a job singing in a speakeasy. Power arrives with some of his cronies, then smuggles Faye out when the place is raided. The couple renew their affections and later attend a party in Jolson's honor. Faye sings a song that catches the attention of Frawley, an important agent. Power tries to foist himself off as Faye's agent but Jolson distrusts the man. Power sells off some furniture belonging to some people traveling abroad while he uses their apartment. With this money he marries Faye and it's off to Cuba for their honeymoon. While in Havana Faye gets word that she has been selected to be the newest member of the famed Ziegfeld's Follies. Faye becomes an overnight sensation but Power finds himself getting deeper into trouble as his various plots catch up with him. He joins a gang in a desperate effort to make money but the crooks botch their intended crime. Jolson graciously posts Power's bail but the resulting scandal proves embarrassing to Faye's career. Power leaves town but eventually sneaks back in to hear his wife in her moment of glory. As he listens to her belt out "My Man" (Channing Pollock, Maurice Yvain) Power realizes what he must do. After turning himself in Power is sentenced to five years at Sing Sing. Faye takes her husband to Grand Central Station in a sob-ridden farewell and promises to wait for him on the outside. This was the third and last teaming of Faye and Power but the show clearly belonged to Jolson. Though his film career was coming to a quick close Jolson had a field day singing some of his greatest numbers. His songs included: "California, Here I Come" (B.G. De Sylva, Joseph Meyer, Jolson), "My Mammy" (Joe Young, Sam Lewis, Walter Donaldson), "Pretty Baby" (Gus Kahn, Tony Jackson, Egbert Van Alstyne), "Toot Toot Tootsie Goodbye" (Kahn, Ernie Erdman, Dan Russo), and "Rock-A-Bye Your Baby With a Dixie Melody" (Jean Schwartz, Young, Lewis). Faye gave the part a good deal of zest, belting out her songs with real energy. Her role was a not-too-thinly disguised portrait of Fanny Brice, whose own romance with gambler Nicky Arnstein had some strikingly similar turns as those Faye experienced in the story, including using Brice's signature tune "My Man". It was all a little too coincidental for Brice who took the studio to court for defamation of character, invasion of privacy, and using events from her life without permission. Brice's initial damage claim was $750,000 but she eventually settled out of court for $25,000. Other songs included: "I'm Just Wild About Harry" (Noble Sissle, Eubie Blake), "I Never Knew Heaven Could Speak" (Mack Gordon, Harry Revel), "Rose of Washington Square" (James Hanley, Ballard MacDonald, Joseph McCarthy), "The Curse of an Aching Heart" (Al Piantadosi, Henry Fink), "I'm Sorry I Made You Cry" (N.J. Clesi), "The Vamp" (Byron Gay), "Ja-da" (Bob Carleton). Cinematographer Karl Freund had previously worked on such classic German silents as THE LAST LAUGH, VARIETY, and METROPOLIS.

p, Darryl F. Zanuck; d, Gregory Ratoff; w, Nunnally Johnson (based on a story by John Larkin, Jerry Horwin); ph, Karl Freund; ed, Louis Loeffler; md, Louis Silvers; art d, Richard Day, Rudolph Sternad; set d, Thomas Little; cos, Royer; ch, Seymour Felix.

Musical/Crime (PR:A MPAA:NR)

ROSE TATTOO, THE**** (1955) 117m PAR bw

Anna Magnani *(Serafina Delle Rose)*, Burt Lancaster *(Alvaro Mangiacavallo)*, Marisa Pavan *(Rosa Delle Rose)*, Ben Cooper *(Jack Hunter)*, Virginia Grey *(Estelle Hohengarten)*, Jo Van Fleet *(Bessie)*, Sandro Giglio *(Father De Leo)*, Mimi Aguglia *(Assunta)*, Florence Sundstrom *(Flora)*, Dorrit Kelton *(Schoolteacher)*, Rossana San Marco *(Peppina)*, Augusta Merighi *(Guiseppina)*, Rosa Rey *(Mariella)*, Georgia Simmons *(The Strega)*, Zolya Talma *(Miss Mangiacavallo)*, George Humbert *(Pop Mangiacavallo)*, Margherita Pasquero *(Grandma Mangiacavallo)*, May Lee *(Mamma Shigura)*, Lewis Charles, Virgil Osborne *(Taxi Drivers)*, Larry Chance *(Rosario Delle Rose)*, Jean Hart *(Violetta)*, Roger Gunderson *(Doctor)*, Roland Vildo *(Salvatore)*, Fred Taylor *(Cashier)*, Albert Atkins *(Mario)*.

Tennessee Williams wrote "The Rose Tattoo" as a play vehicle for Anna Magnani several years before but she was still struggling with English and declined the role. Five years later, after a fairly successful run, Williams did the screenplay and Mann, the director of the stage production, handled the lensing chores. Magnani, by this time, had enough confidence in her command of the language (plus the added convenience of being able to shoot again and again until she got it right) to take the role, her first U.S. job. The result was a hit. Oscars were given to Magnani, cinematographer Howe, Pereira and Larsen for their art direction (black-and-white), Comer and Krans for their black-and-white set decoration, and nominations went to the picture, Pavan, and composer North. Magnani is a Sicilian-born widow with a 15-year-old daughter, Pavan. She cremates her dear husband, whom she'd always felt was totally faithful to her, so she can keep his ashes—a violation of the Catholic religion in which she was raised. Cooper, a young sailor, makes eyes at Pavan in the little Louisiana town and Magnani forces him to promise not to lay a hand on her until they are married. Lancaster enters, a banana hauler like her late husband. He also has a rose tattoo on his chest, just as the late mister did. The tattoo is a superstitious indication of great sexual virility and she is drawn to Lancaster but reveres her husband's memory so much that she holds her emotions in check. It's only when Magnani learns that the dead mate was trifling with Grey that she realizes she is free to accept Lancaster as her lover at the conclusion. Magnani is not an attractive woman to look at. She's earthy, robust, and doesn't mind being harshly photographed. Lancaster is grossly miscast, as he was opposite Shirley Booth in COME BACK, LITTLE SHEBA. Magnani later appeared opposite Marlon Brando in THE FUGITIVE KIND, another Williams piece, but never came close in any of her other U.S. pictures to the dynamic performance she gave in THE ROSE TATTOO. North's excellent music helped the mood enormously. North was honored at the 1985 Oscars (in March, 1986) and came on television to accept his award with an impassioned plea to put good taste back in films, something he's always shown. Pavan, the sister of the tragic Pier Angeli, later married Jean-Pierre Aumont.

p, Hal B. Wallis; d, Daniel Mann; w, Tennessee Williams, Hal Kanter (based on the play by Williams); ph, James Wong Howe (VistaVision); m, Alex North; ed, Warren Low; md, North; art d, Hal Pereira, Tambi Larsen; cos, Edith Head.

Drama (PR:C-O MPAA:NR)

ROSEANNA McCOY***
(1949) 100m RKO bw

Farley Granger (Johnse Hatfield), Joan Evans (Roseanna McCoy), Charles Bickford (Devil Anse Hatfield), Raymond Massey (Old Randall McCoy), Richard Basehart (Mounts Hatfield), Gigi Perreau (Allifair McCoy), Aline MacMahon (Sarie McCoy), Marshall Thompson (Tolbert McCoy), Lloyd Gough (Phamer McCoy), Peter Miles (Young Randall McCoy), Arthur Franz (Thad Wilkins), Frank Ferguson (Ellison Hatfield), Elisabeth Fraser (Bess McCoy), Hope Emerson (Levisa Hatfield), Dan White (Abel Hatfield), Mabel Paige (Grandma Sykes), Almira Sessions (Cousin Zinny), William Mauch (Cap Hatfield), Alan Bridge (Medicine Seller), Sherman Saunders (Dance Caller), Bert Goodrich (Strong Man), Pat Flaherty (Joe McCoy), Ray Hyke, Ethan Laidlaw, Jerry Anderson, Donald Gordon, Cliff Clark, Hank Mann, John "Skins" Miller, Lester Dorr, Dawn Hudson, Corinne Van Lissel, Ida Moore, Myra Marsh, Ruth Sanderson, Guy Wilkerson, Gertrude V. Hoffman, Al Kunde, Chuck Hamilton, James Kirkwood, Robert O'Neill, Rory Mallinson, Pat Walshe.

A quality production from Goldwyn who departed from Hollywood expectations and delivered a love story set against a Blue Ridge Mountain hillbilly backdrop without resorting to one-dimensional "L'il Abner" stereotypes. Taking liberties with the infamous feud between the Hatfields and the McCoys, the story concentrates on a romance between two young members of the clans. While at a country fair Granger, a Hatfield, spots the lovely teenage Evans, a McCoy. Although Evans tries to put him out of her mind, she cannot prevent herself from falling in love. Granger comes to her house one evening and carries her off. They end up back at the Hatfields' house, where the rest of the clan greet her with mixed reactions. Bickford, the Hatfield patriarch, opposes a marriage and, in a move to keep the peace between the two families, sends Evans back home. Basehart, the most unstable member of the Hatfield clan, doesn't want peace, however. He attacks Evans and then, in a senseless rage, refuels the feud by gunning down a McCoy youngster, Mills. Warfare is once again waged between the two sides. In the meantime, Granger and Evans have been reunited and make plans to run off together. The path they choose takes them right through the middle of the gunfire, forcing both sides to cease their warring, presumably for good. Although ROSEANNA McCOY, with its "Romeo and Juliet" stylings, made very little impact at the box office, it is obvious that Goldwyn was more concerned with rendering an honest sketch of hillbilly life. Great attention is paid to detail and atmosphere (Kudos for Garmes' superb lensing), capturing better than most Hollywood pictures a sense of locale and history. Another plus is Goldwyn's insistence on using two youthfully innocent actors—Granger and Evans—to portray the destined lovers. Granger had previously appeared in one other Goldwyn-Reis film, ENCHANTMENT, (1948), which costarred Teresa Wright, who had been slated for Evans' part before being discharged by Goldwyn for being "uncooperative." For ROSEANNA McCOY, Goldwyn simply went out and discovered Evans, the 14-year-old daughter of New York playwright Dale Eunson, whose collaboration with wife Katherine Albert resulted in HOW TO MARRY A MILLIONAIRE (1953) and GIDGET GOES TO ROME (1963). Evans, with her natural quality before the cameras, received numerous favorable reviews but never lived up to Goldwyn's expectations and appeared in only a handful of other films, two of which reunited her with Granger.

p, Samuel Goldwyn; d, Irving Reis; w, John Collier (based on the novel by Alberta Hannum); ph, Lee Garmes; m, David Buttolph; ed, Daniel Mandell; md, Emil Newman; art d, George Jenkins; m/l, "Roseanna McCoy," Frank Loesser.

Drama/Romance (PR:AA MPAA:NR)

ROSEBUD*
(1975) 126m UA c

Peter O'Toole (Larry Martin), Richard Attenborough (Sloat), Cliff Gorman (Hamlekh), Claude Dauphin (Fargeau), John V. Lindsay (U.S. Sen. Donovan), Peter Lawford (Lord Carter), Raf Vallone (George Nikolaos), Adrienne Corri (Lady Carter), Amidou (Kirkbane), Yosef Shiloa (Hacam), Brigitte Ariel (Sabine), Isabelle Huppert (Helene), Lalla Ward (Margaret), Kim Cattrall (Joyce), Debra Berger (Gertrude), Hans Verner (Freyer), Georges Beller (Patrice), Francoise Brion (Melina Nikolaos), Julian Pettifer, Edward Behr (Themselves), Mark Burns (Shute), Klaus Lowitsch (Schloss), Maria Machado (Else), Ori Levy (Avivi).

Otto Preminger hired his son (by Gypsy Rose Lee) to adapt the novel upon which this boring film is based. Shot in France, Corsica, Israel, and Germany, it's a dull thriller about a group of PLO terrorists that includes Shiloa and Amidou who kidnap some wealthy young women (Cattrall, Ariel, Huppert, Ward, Berger) from the yacht upon which they are vacationing. O'Toole (who replaced Robert Mitchum) works at Newsweek but that's only a cover job, as he is a CIA agent. Attenborough does a cameo as a fanatic devoted to the Arabs, Gorman is inept as the Israeli secret-agent liaison, and former New York mayor John Lindsay proves he should have stayed in politics. The picture darts back and forth from the plight of the women to the anguish of their fathers (Lindsay, Vallone, Lawford, Verner, Dauphin), the various attempts to save them, and whatever else the Premingers can conjure up. What seems like an exciting idea bogs down in excess verbiage where action was called for. The title has nothing to do with Charles Foster Kane's sled. Rather, it is the name of the yacht. The final prolog is an unnecessary wrap to an unnecessary movie. The troubles in the Middle East have never been so yawnable.

p&d, Otto Preminger; w, Eric Lee Preminger, Marjorie Kellogg (based on the novel by Joan Hemingway, Paul Bonnecarrere); ph, Denys Coop (Eastmancolor); m, Laurent Petitgirard; ed, Peter Thornton, Thom Noble; prod d, Michael Seymour; art d, Simon Holland.

Action/Adventure (PR:C MPAA:PG)

ROSELAND***
(1977) 103m Merchant-Ivory/Cinema Shares International c

Teresa Wright (May), Lou Jacobi (Stan), Don de Natale (Master of Ceremonies), Louise Kirtland (Ruby), Geraldine Chaplin (Marilyn), Helen Gallagher (Cleo), Joan Copeland (Pauline), Christopher Walken (Russel), Conrad Janis (George), Lilia Skala (Rosa), David Thomas (Arthur), Edward Kogan (Bartender), Madeline Lee (Camille), Stan Rubin (Bert), Annette Rivera, Floyd Chisholm (Hustle Couple).

The setting serves as the central character in this threefold tale of dancers who spend their time at New York's Roseland ballroom. The three main characters are Wright, a widow whose memories flow when on the dance floor with Jacobi; Walken, a gigolo involved with the dying Copeland and the pesty Chaplin; and Skala, the film's one treasure as an elderly German lady who works as a cleaning woman in order to pay for her night out. Technically careless and below par, but this is due unfortunately to a meager three-week shooting schedule. The stories that surface from the technical problems, however, are filled with liveliness and charm. Some of the dance classics on the soundtrack are: "Baubles, Bangles and Beads," "Stranger in Paradise" (George Forrest, Robert Wright), "Moon of Manakoora" (Alfred Newman, Frank Loesser), "On a Slow Boat to China" (Loesser), "Rockin' Chair" (Hoagy Carmichael), and "Super Cool."

p, Ismail Merchant; d, James Ivory; w, Ruth Prawer Jhabvala; ph, Ernest Vincze; m, Michael Gibson; ed, Humphrey Dixon, Richard Schmiechen; ch, Patricia Birch; cos, Dianne Finn Chapman.

Drama Cas. (PR:C MPAA:PG)

ROSEMARY***½
(1960, Ger.) 105m Roxy/Films-Around-the-World bw (ROSEMARIE)

Nadja Tiller (Rosemary), Peter Van Eyck (Fribert), Carl Raddatz (Hartog), Gert Frobe (Bruster), Mario Adorf (Horst), Horst Frank (Student), Hanna Wieder (Marga), Jo Herbst (Walter), Werner Peters (Nakonski), Karin Baal (Das Madchen Do), Erich von Loewis (von Killenschiff), Arno Paulsen (Schmidt), Hubert von Meyerinck (Kleie), Helen Vita (Eveline), Tilo von Berlepsch (Oelsen), Ruth Hausmeister (Frau Hartog).

This was based on the true life and death of one of Germany's most famous strumpets, Rosemarie Nitribitt. In 1957, after several years of plying her trade, she was found strangled and the killers have not, to the best of our knowledge, ever been brought to justice. It was big news in Europe and a fictional account was instantly written and shot to take advantage of the headlines (the film was released in Europe in 1958). Tiller is first seen as a street singer. When she learns that music doth not have enough charms to make her rich, she soon segues into prostitution and is given a posh flat in a good neighborhood. But her aim is to take more than a fee for her services, so she hides a tape recorder and lets her wealthy, influential customers talk about what's troubling them in their lives, their businesses, etc. When one of them gives details of an important matter in his company, Van Eyck steps in to get the tape and use it to his advantage. Frobe and Raddatz are two of Tiller's regulars and she has all of their innermost secrets on tape, so at the end, when she is killed, there are so many who have motives for her death that we never know the identity of the murderer. The strangulation scene is not shown, but the feeling is that all of the men who used her services have combined to end her life, because a fleet of expensive Mercedes-Benzes is seen driving away from the death scene. Since it has been established that her Johns (or is it "Jans" in German?) all drive this kind of car, we can only surmise that they, like the many killers in Agatha Christie's MURDER ON THE ORIENT EXPRESS, all teamed up to snuff her out. Several songs are heard but no credits were given for them. (In German; English subtitles.)

p, Luggi Waldleitner; d, Rolf Thiele; w, Erich Kuby, Thiele, Klaus von Rautenfeld; m, Norbert Schultze.

Mystery/Drama (PR:C MPAA:NR)

ROSEMARY'S BABY****
(1968) 136m PAR c

Mia Farrow (Rosemary Woodhouse), John Cassavetes (Guy Woodhouse)f1, Ruth Gordon (Minnie Castevet), Sidney Blackmer (Roman Castevet), Maurice Evans (Hutch), Ralph Bellamy (Dr. Sapirstein), Angela Dorian (Terry Fionoffrio), Patsy Kelly (Laura-Louise), Elisha Cook, Jr. (Mr. Nicklas), Charles Grodin (Dr. Hill), Emmaline Henry (Elise Dunstan), Marianne Gordon (Joan Jellico), Phil Leeds (Dr. Shand), Hope Summers (Mrs. Gilmore), Wendy Wagner (Tiger), Hanna Landy (Grace Cardiff), Gordon Connell (Guy's Agent), Janet Garland (Nurse), Joan T. Reilly (Pregnant Woman), Tony Curtis (Voice of Donald Baumgart), Patricia Ann

Conway *(Mrs. John F. Kennedy)*, William Castle *(Man at Telephone Booth)*, Walter Baldwin *(Mr. Wees)*, Charlotte Boerner *(Mrs. Fountain)*, Sebastian Brooks, *(Argyron Stavropoulos)*, Ernest Kazuyoshi Harada *(Young Japanese Man)*, Natalie Park Masters *(Young Woman)*, Elmer Modlin *(Young Man)*, Patricia O'Neal *(Mrs. Wees)*, Robert Osterloh *(Mr. Fountain)*, Almira Sessions *(Mrs. Sabatini)*, Bruno [Bronislaw]Sidar *(Mr. Gilmore)*, Roy Barcroft *(Sun-Browned Man)*, D'Urville Martin *(Diego)*, Bill Baldwin *(Salesman)*, George Savalas *(Workman)*, Viki Vigen *(Lisa)*, Marilyn Harvey *(Dr. Sapirstein's Receptionist)*, Paul A. Denton *(Skipper)*, Gail Bonney *(Voice of Babysitter)*, Frank White, *(Hugh Dunstan)*, Mary Louise Lawson *(Portia Haynes)*, Gale Peters *(Rain Morgan)*, George Ross Robertson *(Lou Comfort)*, Carol Brewster *(Claudia Comfort)*, Clay Tanner *(Devil)*, Michael Shillo *(Pope)*, Jean Inness *(Sister Agnes)*, Lynn Brinker *(Sister Veronica)*, Michel Gomez *(Pedro)*, Linda Brewerton *(Farrow's Double)*, Mona Knox *(Mrs. Byron)*, Joyce Davis *(Smith) (Dee Bertillon)*, Floyd Mutrux, Josh Peine *(Men at Party)*, Duke Fishman *(Man)*, Al Szathmary *(Taxi Driver)*, John Halloran *(Mechanic)*.

Ira Levin is one of America's most versatile and successful authors. He writes stories, books, plays, and runs the gamut from comedy (NO TIME FOR SERGEANTS), Nazism (THE BOYS FROM BRAZIL), and mystery (DEATHTRAP) to horror, with this one. Polanski adapted the novel (getting an Oscar nomination for his writing) and then directed a first-class horror story that went beyond the usual screaming meemie tale, elevating it somewhat into the Henry James classification. It's a shocker, but not like the various HALLOWEEN movies and their ilk which followed. Instead, Polanski is patient and builds the story suspensefully with small shocks along the way, each of which contributes to the gooseflesh on the audience's arms. Cassavetes and Farrow are newly married when they move into a huge, old apartment house on 72nd street and Central Park West in New York. (It's called the Bramford, but it is, in reality, the famed Dakota, where John Lennon met his death that tragic December 8th. The Dakota was also the locale for Jack Finney's novel *Time and Again* and was named that because when it was built, in the 1880s, it was so far uptown and away from the center of action in Manhattan that someone said, "It might as well be in Dakota." That quip caused the builder to name it that.) Cassavetes is a struggling actor and a pal, Evans, tells the couple that this building has a very bizarre history and advises them to move out. But the price is right, the apartment is large, and they don't believe in superstition. Farrow meets a young woman in the laundry room and casually mentions that she looks a great deal like an actress named Victoria Vetri. It's a gag that's strictly for the film's makers, as the young woman, Dorian, used to be known by that name when she posed as a *Playboy* centerfold the year before. Dorian is the ward of Gordon and Blackmer, who live next door to Farrow and Cassavetes. Gordon is a very nosey type but she masquerades as a "good neighbor" who just wants to help the young couple adjust. Dorian, with no warning, commits suicide by jumping from the high apartment. Farrow thinks there is something weird about Blackmer and Gordon but her husband pooh-poohs the idea. He's entranced by the old couple and enjoys the fact that Blackmer recalls some of Cassavetes' television acting roles. Good things begin to happen for the couple. Cassavetes, who had been passed over and came in second in an audition for a Broadway show, has another chance at it when the man who got the role goes blind, for no earthly reason. Cassavetes, with a job in front of him, suggests that they can now have a child to celebrate. Gordon and Blackmer stop by and Gordon has prepared a strange dessert. Farrow hates the taste of it but eats some anyhow, just to be neighborly. There's something in the dessert that doesn't agree with Farrow and she gets sick to her stomach and slightly woozy. Gordon and Blackmer exit, and Cassavetes puts Farrow in bed. When she awakens the next morning, she remembers a strange dream of having been made love to by a huge creature and the entire affair having been witnessed by several strange people. Cassavetes laughs it off and says it must have been due to the food the night before. She isn't so sure, as there are scratch marks and bruises on her body. Cassavetes says that he'd gotten a bit too drunk last evening and wasn't as tender as he usually is when they made love. Farrow discovers she's pregnant and is recommended to Bellamy, a kindly old obstetrician. She expects to be given vitamins to help build her frail body during this important time, but Bellamy suggests she take a concoction made by Gordon, who has helped nurse many young women through pregnancy. Farrow dutifully heeds Bellamy but she feels awful. Her already-meager weight lessens, she is subject to heavy cramps, and she understands that she is supposed to feel *good* at a time like this. When she details her symptoms to Evans, he asks to look at Gordon's "tonic." Evans has the stuff analyzed and sees that it is not what Gordon claims it is. Before he can reveal this to Farrow, Evans mysteriously dies. Evans has left Farrow something in his will, a book entitled *All of Them Witches*. Farrow reads the book and learns of a famous warlock named Steven Marcato. A few minutes of anagramming show Farrow that if the letters were toyed with, they would be the same as Blackmer's name in the film, Roman Castevet. Farrow, who had been thinking she was paranoid, now realizes that her fears are real and that Cassavetes, Gordon, Bellamy, and Blackmer are all in this together but she still can't understand why. She calls upon Grodin, her former gynecologist, and asks him to help. She hides in his office and rests while the young doctor says he will contact the right parties and put a stop to this. But Grodin has instead called Cassavetes and Bellamy, thinking that Farrow is going through some sort of mental breakdown. They take her back to the apartment where she gives birth. When she awakens, Cassavetes regretfully tells her that her child was dead at delivery. She stays in bed and thinks she hears a crying baby in the Gordon-Blackmer apartment. Struggling to her feet, she grabs a huge knife from the kitchen and makes her way next door to find a party in progress. It's a coven of witches and they are all celebrating the birth of the Antichrist, the son Farrow had when she mated with the devil nine months before. She looks at the child in the bassinet (someone remarks "He has his father's eyes") and a mother's love overcomes her horror. She drops the knife and begins to sing a lullaby to the child as the picture ends. Robert Redford and Jane Fonda were the first choices for the film but didn't make it. Gordon won the Oscar as Best Supporting Actress and it was well-deserved. Putting a devil-worship story in the heart of New York was a stroke of genius because everything that surrounded the central tale is so innocuous and normal. One year later, Polanski was to experience real-life horror when his wife, Sharon Tate, along with hairdresser Jay Sebring, coffee heiress Abigail Folger, and several others were massacred by the Charles Manson gang, a group of cultists who thought that their leader was divine. Komeda, a Polish emigre who often works with Polanski, did the excellent score and Bill Castle, the veteran producer of many lower-class horror films, makes a cameo appearance. Four-letter words and very scary scenes should preclude any youngsters from seeing this. A much inferior made-for-television sequel, "Look What's Happened to Rosemary's Baby" followed in 1976.

p, William Castle; d&w, Roman Polanski (based on the novel by Ira Levin); ph, William A. Fraker (Technicolor); m, Krzysztof Komeda; ed, Sam O'Steen, Robert Wyman; prod d, Richard Sylbert; art d, Joel Schiller; set d, Robert Nelson; cos, Anthea Sylbert; spec eff, Farciot Edouart; makeup, Allan Snyder.

Horror **Cas.** **(PR:O MPAA:R)**

ROSEMARY'S KILLER (SEE: THE PROWLER, 1981)

ROSEN FUR DEN STAATSANWALT (SEE: ROSES FOR THE PROSECUTOR, 1961, Ger.)

ROSES ARE RED** (1947) 67m FOX bw

Don Castle *(Thorne/Carney)*, Peggy Knudsen *(Martha)*, Patricia Knight *(Jill)*, Joe Sawyer *(Wall)*, Edward Keane *(Locke)*, Jeff Chandler *(Knuckle)*, Charles McGraw *(Duke)*, Charles Lane *(Lipton)*, Paul Guilfoyle *(Cooley)*, Doug Fowley *(Oliver)*, James Arness *(Ray)*.

Castle is a good-hearted district attorney whose honesty gets him kidnaped by the mob. An exact duplicate (again played by Castle) is put in his place to undermine the city's operations. The kidnaped Castle escapes, however, and eventually blows the whole crime ring out of the water. Implausible, but Castle's fine performance makes it watchable.

p, Sol M. Wurtzel; d, James Tinling; w, Irving Elman; ph, Benjamin Kline; m, Rudy Schrager; ed, Frank Baldridge; art d, Walter Koessler.

Crime **(PR:A MPAA:NR)**

ROSES FOR THE PROSECUTOR*** (1961, Ger.) 92m American Metropolitan Enterprises-Altura Films International bw (ROSEN FUR DEN STAARSANWALT)

Walter Giller *(Rudi Kleinschmidt)*, Martin Held *(Dr. Wilhelm Schramm)*, Ingrid van Bergen *(Lissy)*, Camilla Spira *(Hildegard Schramm)*, Roland Kaiser *(Werner Schramm)*, Werner Peters *(Otto Kugler)*, Wolfgang Wahl *(Defense Counsel)*, Werner Finck *(Haase)*, Ralf Wolter *(Hessel)*, Paul Hartmann *(Diefenbach)*, Burkhard Orthgies, Inge Meysel, Wolfgang Neuss, Wolfgang Muller, Wolfgang Preiss, Ingrid Andree.

A gripping postwar tale which has Giller, years after his near-execution in a concentration camp, recognizing his town's public prosecutor as a Nazi. Although Giller was nearly put to death (for stealing two chocolate bars) by the Nazi (Held), he holds no bad feelings, trying hard to forget the atrocity. Held, however, believes Giller to be plotting something and tries to have him removed from the town. The citizens offer no support so Giller, in an attempt to be brought to trial, steals some chocolate from a shop window. Haunted by his past, Held goes into a rage during the prosecution. He flees the courtroom, leaving Giller a free man. (In German, English subtitles.)

p, Kurt Ulrich; d, Wolfgang Staudte; w, George Hurdalek (based on the story by Staudte); ph, Erich Claunigk; m, Raimund Rosenberger; art d, Walter Haag, Hans Kutzner.

Drama **(PR:A MPAA:NR)**

ROSIE!*½ (1967) 98m Ross Hunter/UNIV c

Rosalind Russell *(Rosie Lord)*, Sandra Dee *(Daphne Shaw)*, Brian Aherne *(Oliver Stevenson)*, Audrey Meadows *(Mildred Deever)*, James Farentino *(David Wheelwright)*, Vanessa Brown *(Edith Shaw)*, Leslie Nielsen *(Cabot Shaw)*, Margaret Hamilton *(Mae)*, Reginald Owen *(Patrick)*, Juanita Moore *(Nurse)*, Virginia Grey *(Mrs. Peters)*, Dean Harens *(Willetts)*, Richard Derr *(Lawyer)*, Harry Hickox, Eddie Ness *(Detectives)*, Hal Lynch *(Telephone Man)*, Ann Doran *(Old Lady)*, Than Wyenn *(Psychiatrist)*, Walter Woolf King *(Judge)*, Ronald Chisholm *(Pianist)*, Doris Lloyd *(Sedalia)*, Ron Stokes *(Taxi Driver)*, Eugene Roth *(Joseph)*, Kathleen O'Malley *(Secretary)*, Doodles Weaver *(Florist)*.

Russell is superb in this cliched, stereotyped look at an elderly millionairess whose daughters have her put in a rest home and declared her senile. The daughters are solely interested in getting their grubby hands on her money. Granddaughter Dee, however, is concerned only with Russell's well-being. Dee enlists the aid of attorney Aherne, an old flame of Russell's. Adapted by Ruth Gordon from a play staged by husband Garson Kanin, it has all the characteristics (though the play was written by neither of them) that are identified with their later work—cute, honest and tough old folks who are well aware that they can lay on the charm.

p, Jacques Mapes; d, David Lowell Rich; w, Samuel Taylor (adapted by Ruth Gordon as "A Very Rich Woman" from the play "Les Joies De La Famille" by Philippe Heriat); ph, Clifford Stine (Technicolor, Techniscope); m, Lyn Murray; md, Joseph Gershenson; ed, Stuart Gilmore; art d, Alexander Golitzen, George C. Webb; set d, Howard Bristol; m/l, Johnny Mercer, Harry Warren (sung by The Boyfriends); makeup, Bud Westmore.

Drama/Comedy **(PR:A MPAA:NR)**

ROSIE THE RIVETER** (1944) 75m REP bw (GB: IN ROSIE'S ROOM)

Jane Frazee *(Rosie Warren)*, Frank Albertson *(Charlie Doran)*, Vera Vague *(Vera Watson)*, Frank Jenks *(Kelly Kennedy)*, Maude Eburne *(Grandma Quill)*, Lloyd Corrigan *(Clem Prouty)*, Frank Fenton *(Wayne Calhoun)*, Carl "Alfalfa" Switzer

(*Buzz*), Louise Erickson (*Mabel*), Ellen Lowe (*Stella Prouty*), Arthur Loft (*Sgt. Mulvaney*), Tom Kennedy (*Piano Mover*).

A wartime comedy which has four femme factory workers sharing a boarding house with four male counterparts, each sex trying to dictate who gets to use the house at which time. Pretty silly, but harmless. With Alfalfa from the Our Gang comedies.

p, Armand Schaefer; d, Joseph Santley; w, Jack Townley, Aleen Leslie (based on the story "Room for Two" by Dorothy Curnow Handley); ph, Reggie Lanning; ed, Ralph Dixon; md, Morton Scott; art d, Russell Kimball; ch, Dave Gould; m/l, "Rosie the Riveter," Redd Evans, John Jacob Loeb, "Why Can't I Sing a Love Song?," Harry Akst, Sol Meyer.

Comedy (PR:A MPAA:NR)

ROSMUNDA E ALBOINO (SEE: SWORD OF THE CONQUEROR, 1962, Ital.)

ROSSINI** (1948, Ital.) 90m Lux/Best bw

Nino Besozzi (*Gioacchino Rossini*), Paola Barbara (*Isabella Colbran*), Camillo Pilotto (*Impresario*), Armando Falconi (*Ferdinando I*), Greta Gonda (*Teresa Coralli*), Paolo Stoppa (*Tottola*), Memo Benassi (*Beethoven*), Lamberto Picasso (*Col. Negri*), Gianna Pedersini (*Rosina*), Tancredi Pasero (*Don Basilio*), Gabriella Gatti (*Desdemona*), Mariano Stabile (*Figaro*), Enzo De Muro Lomanto (*Almaviva*), Vito De Taranto (*Don Bartolo*), Piero Panli (*Otello*).

A lifeless biography of the Italian composer Rossini which fails to capture any sense of spontaneity. The picture begins in 1815 and covers a twelve-year period which includes his travels to Paris, Rome (where he writes "Otello"), and Vienna (where he and Beethoven chat). Originally released in 1942. (In Italian; English subtitles).

d, Mario Bonnard; w, Bonnard, Parsifal Bassi, Vittorio Novrese; ph, Mario Albertelli; m, Vittorio Gui (and selections from Rossini's "Barber of Seville" and "Otello.")

Biography/Musical (PR:A MPAA:NR)

ROSSITER CASE, THE*½ (1950, Brit.) 75m Hammer/Exclusive bw

Helen Shingler (*Liz Rossiter*), Clement McCallin (*Peter Rossiter*), Sheila Burrell (*Honor*), Frederick Leister (*Sir James Ferguson*), Henry Edwards (*Dr. Bendix*), Ann Codrington (*Marty*), Dorothy Batley (*Nurse West*), Gabrielle Blunt (*Alice*), Stanley Baker (*Joe*), Ewen Solon, Eleanore Bryan, Robert Percival, Dennis Castle, Frederic Steger, Anthony Allen.

An improbable story about an unfaithful husband, McCallin, who has an affair with his wife's sister, Burrell. The jealous wife, Shingler, who is also paralyzed, confronts her sister. A gun is produced and Burrell is killed. Because of Shingler's supposed paralysis, McCallin is blamed for the killing. His life is spared, however, when Shingler confesses that she was miraculously cured. The ending speaks for itself in this ridiculous programmer.

p, Anthony Hinds; d, Francis Searle; w, Kenneth Hyde, John Gilling, Searle (based on Hyde's play "The Rossiters"); ph, Jimmy Harvey.

Crime (PR:A MPAA:NR)

ROTHSCHILD** (1938, Fr.) 78m Escalmel/RF bw

Harry Baur (*Rothschild*), Pasquali (*Flip*), Pauley (*Barsac*), Casadessus (*Marcel*), Claudie Cleaves (*Madeleine*), Germaine Michel (*Mlle. Fallot*), Germaine Auger (*Gaby*), Philippe Heriat (*Diegot*), Georges Paulais (*Marty*), Jean d'Yd (*Professor*).

Baur is a traveling French hobo with a name that implies grandeur. He is soon capitalizing on that name and familiarizing himself in the social circle, thanks to a scheme of Pasquali's. Truly convincing performances from both Baur and his sidekick Pasquali. (In French; English subtitles).

d, Marco De Gastyne; w, Jean Guitton, E.R. Escalmel (based on the novel by Paul Lafitte); ph, Gaston Nrun; m, Guido Curto; English titles, Mark A. Brum, Charles Jahrblum.

Comedy (PR:A MPAA:NR)

ROTTEN APPLE, THE* (1963) 85m Headliner-Studio 10,001 bw (AKA: 5 MINUTES TO LOVE, IT ONLY TAKES 5 MINUTES)

Paul Leder (*Harry*), King Moody (*Blowhard*), Will Gregory (*Ben*), Rue McClanahan (*Sally "Poochie"*), Gail Gordon (*Edna*), Geraldine Leder (*Ben and Edna's Daughter*).

A husband and wife (Gregory and Gordon) en route to San Diego pay a visit to a junkyard when their car breaks down. The husband becomes a scapegoat for the yard owner (Leder), a dealer in stolen cars who is about to be arrested. To distract attention from himself, Leder pins a charge of auto theft on Gregory. Gregory is beaten and nearly arrested by a police sergeant on the take who decides to arrest Leder's mechanic, Moody, instead. In the finale the cops kill Moody and Gregory kills Leder. Set in a junkyard, which is where it belongs.

d, John Hayes; w, William Norton (based on a story by Norton, Paul Leder).

Drama (PR:O MPAA:NR)

ROTTEN TO THE CORE**½ (1956, Brit.) 89m Tudor-BL/Cinema V bw

Eric Sykes (*Hunt*), Ian Bannen (*Vine*), Dudley Setton (*Jelly*), Kenneth Griffith (*Lenny*), James Beckett (*Scapa*), Avis Bunnage (*Countess*), Anton Rodgers (*Duke*), Charlotte Rampling (*Sara*), Victor Maddern (*Anxious*), Thorley Walters (*Preston*), Peter Vaughan (*Sir Henry*), Raymond Huntley (*Prison Governor*), Ian Wilson (*Chopper Parsons*), Richard Coleman (*Inspector Hewlett*), Barbara Everest (*Mrs. Dick*), Cameron Hall (*The Admiral*), Basil Dignam (*The General*), Robert Bruce (*War Office Major*), Neil Hallet (*Guard Commander*), Kenneth Dight (*Dirty*)

Bertie), John Baker (*Drainpipe Fred*), Frank Jarvis (*Moby*), Arthur Skinner (*Nick the Bible*), Margaret Lacey (*Miss Rossiter*).

A trio of petty criminals fresh out of the slammer search for their boss, Rodgers, who has been holding onto their cut of the robbery they were doing time for. They are first told that he is dead, but discover that he is hiding out in a health clinic, plotting to undertake a major robbery. The trio soon become part of the operation, which results in Rodgers being reduced to a petty criminal, while the others get off scot-free, but without the loot. Charlotte Rampling made her film debut in a sizeable role as Rodgers' girlfriend.

p, Roy Boulting; d, John Boulting; w, John Warren, Len Heath, Jeffrey Dell, Roy Boulting (based on a story by Warren, Heath, Dell, R. Boulting; based on an idea by Warren, Heath); ph, Freddie Young (Panavision); m, Michael Dress; ed, Teddy Darvas; art d, Alex Vetchinsky; spec eff, Wally Veevers; m/l, title song, Dress (sung by Pamela Michaels).

Crime Comedy (PR:C MPAA:NR)

ROUGH AND THE SMOOTH, THE (SEE: PORTRAIT OF A SINNER, 1961, Brit.)

ROUGH COMPANY (SEE: VIOLENT MEN, THE 1954)

ROUGH CUT**½ (1980, Brit.) 112m PAR c

Burt Reynolds (*Jack Rhodes*), Lesley-Anne Down (*Gillian Bromley*), David Niven (*Chief Inspector Cyril Willis*), Timothy West (*Nigel Lawton*), Patrick Magee (*Ernst Mueller*), Al Matthews (*Ferguson*), Susan Littler (*Sheila*), Joss Ackland (*Inspector Vanderveld*), Isobel Dean (*Mrs. Willis*), Wolf Kahler (*DeGooyer*), Andrew Ray (*Pilbrow*), Julian Holloway (*Ronnie Taylor*), Douglas Wilmer (*Maxwell Levy*), Geoffrey Russell (*Tobin*), Ronald Hines (*Capt. Small*), David Howey (*1st Officer Palmer*), Alan Webb (*Sir Samuel Sacks*), Frank Mills (*Passport Clerk*), Roland Culver (*Mr. Palmer*), Cassandra Harris (*Mrs. Palmer*), Sue Lloyd, Hugh Thomas, Paul McDowell, Stephen Reynolds, David Eccles, Stephen Moore, Peter Schofield, Jonathan Elsom, Ron Pember, Cyril Appleton, John Slavid, Brian Tipping, Carol Rydall.

Reynolds is a diamond thief who has continually eluded Scotland Yard inspector Niven. Niven, approaching retirement, is determined to nab Reynolds and blackmails Down, a kleptomaniac society lady, into helping. Together they set Reynolds up for a $30,000,000 heist which is to occur in mid-air as the characters fly from Antwerp to Amsterdam. Reynolds should be given credit for trying to break away from his redneck SMOKEY AND THE BANDIT image, as he did successfully in THE MAN WHO LOVED WOMEN, but he just doesn't have what it takes to pull it off. Here he resorts to doing Cary Grant (or, as he quips in the film, "doing Tony Curtis doing Cary Grant"), but doesn't have the range. Entertaining in spots, especially those with Niven, the picture suffers from directorial problems. First conceived in 1977, ROUGH CUT (which looks more like a rough cut than a final product) was to be directed by Blake Edwards and scripted by Larry Gelbart. Siegel was then signed on, fired, rehired, and then after production ended, replaced by Robert Ellis Miller, who reshot the ending. Gelbart, meanwhile, went undercover with the pseudonym Francis Burns. The musical score comprises sanitized versions of such classics as "Sophisticated Lady" (Duke Ellington, Irving Mills, Mitchell Parrish), "In a Sentimental Mood" (Ellington, Mills, Manny Kurtz), "Mood Indigo" (Ellington, Mills, Barney Bigard), "Caravan" (Ellington, Mills, Juan Tizol), "Prelude to a Kiss" (Ellington, Mills, Irving Gordon), "Satin Doll" (Ellington, Johnny Mercer, Billy Strayhorn), "I Got it Bad and That Ain't Good" (Ellington, Paul Webster), "Don't Get Around Much Anymore" (Ellington, Bob Russell), and "C Jam Blues" (Ellington).

p, David Merrick; d, Don Siegel; w, Francis Burns [Larry Gelbart](based on the novel *Touch the Lion's Paw* by Derek Lambert); ph, Freddie Young (Movielab Color); m, Nelson Riddle (adapted from the music of Duke Ellington and collaborators); ed, Doug Stewart; prod d, Ted Haworth; art d, Tim Hutchinson; set d, Peter James; cos, Anthony Mendelson; spec eff, Ted Grumbt.

Romantic Comedy Cas. (PR:C MPAA:PG)

ROUGH NIGHT IN JERICHO*½ (1967) 102m UNIV c

Dean Martin (*Alex Flood*), George Peppard (*Dolan*), Jean Simmons (*Molly Lang*), John McIntire (*Ben Hickman*), Slim Pickens (*Yarbrough*), Don Galloway (*Jace*), Brad Weston (*Torrey*), Richard O'Brien (*Ryan*), Carol Anderson (*Claire*), Steve Sandor (*Simms*), Warren Vanders (*Harvey*), John Napier (*McGivern*), Dean Martin, Jr. [Dean Paul Martin] (*Cowboy*).

Martin is oddly cast as a rotten ex-lawman intent on taking over the stagecoach line which serves the town of Jericho. Owners Simmons and McIntire work together with ex-marshal-turned-gambler Peppard to stop Martin's evil doing. It appears hopeless, but a final bloody gun battle leaves Martin dead and Peppard wounded, with the coach line ready to roll. An excess of violence, a failed attempt at casting, and a predictable plot sink this western.

p, Martin Rackin; d, Arnold Laven; w, Sidney Boehm, Marvin H. Albert (based on the novel *The Man in Black* by Albert); ph, Russell Metty (Techniscope, Technicolor); m, Don Costa; ed, Ted J. Kent; md, Joseph Gershenson; art d, Alexander Golitzen, Frank Arrigo; set d, John McCarthy, James S. Redd; cos, Rosemary Odell, Helen Colvig; m/l, "The Devil Rides in Jericho," "Hold Me Now and Forever," Costa, Phil Zeller (sung by The Kids Next Door); makeup, Bud Westmore.

Western (PR:O MPAA:NR)

ROUGH RIDERS OF CHEYENNE** (1945) 56m REP bw

Sunset Carson, Peggy Stewart, Mira McKinney, Monte Hale, Wade Crosby, Kenne Duncan, Michael Sloane, Tom London, Eddy Waller, Jack O'Shea, Bob Wilke, Tex Terry, Jack Rockwell, Jack Luden, Rex Lease, Hank Bell, Henry Wills, Cactus Mack, Artie Ortego.

Mediocre B-western action has Carson finally putting an end to the feud that has separated his family from one another for years. Carson's best friend, Hale, sings "The Old Chisholm Trail" before catching a bullet meant for Sunset. Hale would later make his own series of western programmers for Republic.

p, Bennett Cohen; d, Thomas Carr; w, Elizabeth Beecher; ph, William Bradford; md, Richard Cherwin; art d, Frank Hotaling.

Western **Cas.** **(PR:A MPAA:NR)**

ROUGH RIDERS OF DURANGO** (1951) 60m REP bw

Allan "Rocky" Lane (Himself), Walter Baldwin (Cricket Adams), Aline Towne (Janis), Steve Darrell (John Blake), Ross Ford (Sheriff Walters), Denver Pyle (Lacey), Stuart Randall (Jed), Hal Price (Johnson), Tom London (Evans), Russ Whiteman, Dale Van Sickel, Bob Burns, Black Jack the Horse.

An outlaw devises a plot to bankrupt landowners and ranchers, thereby allowing him to purchase their properties for next to nothing. He steals incoming wheat shipments and then, when the ranchers take out a loan to cover their losses, he has his gang steal that too. Rocky Lane sees to it that the low-life's plot is squashed before too much damage is done. Fast-paced oater.

p, Gordon Kay; d, Fred C. Brannon; w, M. Coates Webster; ph, John MacBurnie; m, Stanley Wilson; ed, Irving M. Schoenberg; art d, Frank Hotaling.

Western **(PR:A MPAA:NR)**

ROUGH RIDERS' ROUNDUP**½ (1939) 55m REP bw

Roy Rogers (Roy), Mary Hart [Lynne Roberts] (Dorothy), Raymond Hatton (Rusty), Eddie Acuff (Tommy), William Pawley (Arizona), Dorothy Sebastian (Rose), George Meeker (Lanning), Jack Rockwell (Harrison), Guy Usher (Blair), George Chesebro (Mosby), Glenn Strange (Boggs), Duncan Renaldo (Alcalde), Jack Kirk, Hank Bell, Dorothy Christy, Fred Kelsey, Eddy Waller, John Merton, George Letz [George Montgomery], Al Haskell, Frank Ellis, Augie Gomez, Frank McCarroll, Dan White, Trigger the Horse.

Rogers teams up with the Rough Riders again to rid a mining town of crooked mine manager Meeker and his dishonorable methods. An average Rogers pic set just after the end of the Spanish-American War. Made in 1939 before Republic began billing Rogers as "King of the Cowboys," the film shows how vapid Rogers really was when he wasn't dressed up in a glittery outfit. (See ROY ROGERS series, Index.)

p&d, Joseph Kane; w, Jack Natteford; ph, Jack Marta; m, Cy Feuer; ed, Lester Orlebeck.

Western **Cas.** **(PR:A MPAA:NR)**

ROUGH RIDIN' RHYTHM*½ (1937) 57m Ambassador bw

Kermit Maynard (Jim Langley), Ralph Peters (Scrubby), Beryl Wallace (Helen Hobart), Olin Francis (Jake Horne), Betty Mack (Ethyle Horne), Curley Dresden (Soapy), Cliff Parkinson (Hank), David O'Brien (Detective Waters), Newt Kirby (Detective Thomas), J.P. McGowan (Hobart).

Wallace is kidnaped from her ranch to take care of the orphaned child of a bandit's sister. Maynard is accused of being the murderer and has to fight the gang to clear his name.

p, Maurice Conn; d, J.P. McGowan; w, Arthur Everett (based on the story "Getting a Start in Life" by James Oliver Curwood); ph, Jack Greenhalgh; m, Connie Lee; ed, Richard G. Wray.

Western **Cas.** **(PR:A MPAA:NR)**

ROUGH RIDING RANGER* (1935) 56m Merrick/Superior bw (GB: THE SECRET STRANGER)

Rex Lease, Bobby Nelson, Janet Chandler, Yakima Canutt, Mable Strickland, David Horsley, George Chesebro, Robert Walker, Carl Mathews, Artie Ortego, William Desmond, Allen Greer, Johnny Luther's Cowboy Band, George Morell, Milburn Morante, "Sunday".

Lease rides to the rescue of a ranching family that has been receiving threatening letters from an unknown person. Below-average heroics, but some good stunts from Canutt.

p, George M. Merrick, Louis Weiss; d, Elmer Clifton; w, Clifton, Merrick.

Western **(PR:A MPAA:NR)**

ROUGH RIDING ROMEO (SEE: FLAMING GUNS, 1932)

ROUGH ROMANCE*½ (1930) 55m FOX bw

George O'Brien (Billy West), Helen Chandler (Marna Reynolds), Antonio Moreno (Loup LaTour), Noel Francis (Flossie), Eddie Borden (Laramie), Harry Cording (Chick Carson), Roy Stewart (Sheriff Milt Powers), David Hartford (Dad Reynolds), Frank Lanning (Pop Nichols), John Wayne.

O'Brien plays a lumberjack in the great Northwest who has to fight to maintain law in the logging town and to win the affections of Chandler. John Wayne played a bit part in this, his fifth picture.

d, A.F. Erickson; w, Donald Davis, Elliott Lester (based on the story "The Girl Who Wasn't Wanted" by Kenneth B. Clarke); ph, Daniel B. Clark; ed, Paul Weatherwax; m/l, George A. Little, John Burke.

Western **(PR:A MPAA:NR)**

ROUGH SHOOT (SEE: SHOOT FIRST, 1953, Brit.)

ROUGH, TOUGH AND READY** (1945) 66m COL bw (GB: MEN OF THE DEEP)

Chester Morris (Brad Crowder), Victor McLaglen (Owen McCarey), Jean Rogers (Jo Matheson), Veda Ann Borg (Lorine Gray), Amelita Ward (Kitty Duval), Robert

Williams (Paul), John Tyrrell (Herbie), Fred Graff (Tony), Addison Richards (Capt. Murray), William Forrest (Lt. Freitas), Tex Harding (Brille), Loren Tindall (Peterson), Bob Meredith (Sparks), Ida Moore (Nana), Blackie Whiteford (O'Toole).

Morris and McLaglen are great buddies until the former starts moving in on the latter's girl. They are soon off to war, which gives Morris a chance to save McLaglen's life and renew their friendship. Standard.

p, Alexis Thurn-Taxis; d, Del Lord; w, Edward T. Lowe; ph, George Meehan; ed, Richard Fantl; art d, Walter Holscher.

War Comedy **(PR:A MPAA:NR)**

ROUGH, TOUGH WEST, THE** (1952) 54m COL bw

Charles Starrett (Steve Holden), Smiley Burnette (Himself), Jack [Jock] Mahoney (Big Jack Mahoney), Carolina Cotton (Carolina), Marshall Reed (Fulton), Fred Sears (Peter Walker), Bert Arnold (Jordan MacCrea), Tommy Ivo (Buzz Barett), Valeria Fisher (Matty Barett), Boyd "Red" Morgan (Bill), Pee Wee King and His Band.

Starrett helps out a group of miners who are being forced to pay the greedy Mahoney to travel across his land, which he acquired illegally. Starrett enlists the aid of his alter ego, "The Durango Kid," and ends Mahoney's evil reign. (See DURANGO KID series, Index.)

p, Colbert Clark; d, Ray Nazarro; w, Barry Shipman; ph, Fayte Browne; ed, Paul Borofsky; m/l, "Cause I'm in Love," Stan Jones (sung by Carolina Cotton).

Western **(PR:A MPAA:NR)**

ROUGH WATERS**½ (1930) 53m WB bw

Rin-Tin-Tin (Rinty), Lane Chandler (Cal Morton), Jobyna Ralston (Mary), Edmund Breese (Capt. Thomas), Walter Miller (Morris), William Irving (Bill), George Rigon (Fred), Richard Alexander (Little), Skeets Noyes (Davis).

When robbers Alexander and Little take crippled sea dog Breese and his daughter, Ralston, hostage to cover their escape, it's wonder dog Rin-Tin-Tin who saves the pair and keeps the bad guys from escaping, even after they wound him and master Chandler. Good entertainment as Rinty proves himself one of the most exciting performers of the era.

d, John Daumery; w, James A. Starr; ph, William Rees.

Adventure **(PR:AA MPAA:NR)**

ROUGHLY SPEAKING** (1945) 117m WB bw

Ray Collins (Mr. Randall), Kathleen Lockhart (Mrs. Randall), Cora Sue Collins (Elinor Randall), Ann Todd (Louise Randall), Andy Clyde (Matt), Arthur Shields (Minister), Helene Thimig (Olga the Maid), Greta Grandstedt (Anna the Maid), Rosalind Russell (Louise Randall), Ann Doran (Alice Abbott), Hobart Cavanaugh (The Teacher), Eily Malyon (The Dean), Alan Hale (Mr. Norton), Donald Woods (Rodney Crane), Craig Stevens (Jack Leslie), John Alvin (Lawton Meckall), Mary Servoss (Rose), Francis Pierlot (Dr. Lewis), Manart Kippen (Dr. Bowditch), George Carleton (The Judge), Jack Carson (Harold Pierson), Frank Puglia (Tony), John Qualen (Ole Olsen), Chester Clute (The Proprietor), Irving Bacon (Customer in Music Shop), Barbara Brown (Relief Worker), Sig Arno (George), Ann Lawrence (Barbara, Age 9-11), Mona Freeman (Barbara, Age 15-20), Andrea King (Barbara, Age 21-29), Mickey Kuhn (John, Age 7-10), Johnny Treul (John, Age 14-19), Robert Hutton (John, Age 20-28), John Calkins (Rodney, Age 6-9), Richard Winer (Rodney, Age 13-18), John Sheridan (Rodney, Age 19-27), Jo Ann Marlowe (Louise Jr., Age 5-6), Patsy Lee Parsons (Louise Jr., Age 12-17), Jean Sullivan (Louise Jr., Age 18-26), Gregory Muradian (Frankie, Age 3-4), John Sheffield (Frankie, Age 9), Robert Arthur (Frankie, Age 17), Joyce Compton (Prissy Girl), Marie Blake, Claire Meade (Nurses), Harry Harvey, Jr. (Billy Winters), Emmett Vogan (Auctioneer), Pierre Watkin, Charles Anthony Hughes (Financiers), Jody Gilbert (Woman in Store), Bill Moss (Sergeant), George Meader.

A long-winded, dull movie written by the woman who lived it, Louise Randall Pierson. It begins in 1902, long before the dawn of the ERA, and immediately shows Todd, a 12-year-old, to be a determined young girl who will never take no for an answer. When her father, Collins, dies, he leaves a small amount of money to take care of his wife, Lockhart, and their daughters, Todd and Cora Sue Collins. Quick cut from turn-of-the-century New England to about 1908. Todd has been replaced by Russell. She's going to a New Haven business school and plans a career for herself. She meets Woods, a Yale student who is very conservative and hide-bound. They marry, quickly have many children, and Woods, who can't take her vitality and her domineering ways, soon opts for the arms of another, more traditional woman, and a divorce occurs. Russell then meets amiable Carson at a party. Carson is a happy-go-lucky type who has a history of gambling, but once he encounters Russell, he decides to bypass his old and wicked ways and make a new life for himself and the woman he loves. More children arrive and this marriage is successful and warm. They have their elevator ride from the heights to the depths and each must take whatever employment comes along in order to support their increasing brood, but the closeness of the family and the love between all conquers whatever difficulties arise in their financial status. WW II begins and they must send three of their sons off to fight. They have finally achieved a bit of prosperity as the picture concludes. It goes on and on for more than two hours, a time frame that is far too long for the slim and episodic material presented. Curtiz, who had just come off MILDRED PIERCE, did what he could to put some humor and life into the script but someone else would have been better to adapt the book into screenplay form, as authors are notorious for not wanting to cut out anything of their original works. Russell's character is not far away from Auntie Mame and there are slight inklings of that in her portrayal. The movie took four months to shoot, a longer period than most of the Warner Brothers films of the era. In small roles as the children, note Andrea King, Robert Hutton, and Mona Freeman. Arthur Shields, Barry Fitzgerald's brother, plays a minister for the umpteenth time. He's been a man of the cloth so often he's just about eligible for sainthood.

p, Henry Blanke; d, Michael Curtiz; w, Louise Randall Pierson (based on her book); ph, Joseph Walker; m, Max Steiner; ed, David Weisbart; md, Leo F. Forbstein; art d, Robert Haas; set d, George James Hopkins; cos, Leah Rhodes, Travis Banton; spec eff, Roy Davidson, Hans Koenekamp.

Biography **(PR:A MPAA:NR)**

ROUGHSHOD*** (1949) 88m RKO bw

Robert Sterling *(Clay)*, Gloria Grahame *(Mary)*, Claude Jarman, Jr. *(Steve)*, John Ireland *(Lednov)*, Jeff Donnell *(Elaine)*, Myrna Dell *(Helen)*, Martha Hyer *(Marcia)*, George Cooper *(Jim Clayton)*, Jeff Corey *(Jed Graham)*, Sara Haden *(Ma Wyatt)*, James Bell *(Pa Wyatt)*, Shawn McGlory *(Fowler)*, Robert B. Williams *(McCall)*, Steve Savage *(Peters)*, Edward Cassidy *(Sheriff)*.

Sterling and Jarman are brothers traveling from Nevada to California with a herd of horses. On the way they unwillingly pick up a group of dancehall girls whose wagon is out of commission. They soon discover that they are being pursued by the ruthless Ireland, who wants to settle a score with Sterling. They continue on their trail, but eventually the showdown occurs. Ireland is killed, of course, and Sterling survives, with every indication that he'll wed Grahame, the dancehall operator. A well-written screenplay which could have used a more heroic cast.

p, Richard H. Berger; d, Mark Robson; w, Geoffrey Homes, Hugo Butler (based on a story by Peter Viertel); ph, Joseph F. Biroc; ed, Marston Fay; md, Constantin Bakaleinikoff; art d, Albert D'Agostino, Lucius O. Croxton; cos, Renie.

Western **(PR:A MPAA:NR)**

ROUND TRIP* (1967) 86m Chablis/Continental c (AKA:ROUNDTRIP)

Venantino Venantini *(Marc Daumel)*, Ellen Faison *(Ellen Tracy)*, Larry Rivers *(Himself)*, Joan Thornton *(Diana Evremont)*, Clarice Rivers *(Clarice)*, Jacques Kaplan *(Jacques)*, Sheila Clarke *(Sheila)*, Melinda Lasson *(Drama Coach)*, Henri Abehsera *(Travis, the Playwright)*, Silverstein the Loft King *(Silverstein)*, Boscoe Holder *(Boscoe)*.

Venantini is a Frenchman who leaves behind a failed marriage and a child and voyages to New York, where he falls in love with a gorgeous black model. The relationship falters when he becomes intrigued by the black culture of Harlem which she is trying to escape, and she prefers the high-society parties which he now detests. When his child is injured in an accident, he decides to return to France, dissolving the relationship. An overwrought attempt at social relevance. Artist Larry Rivers appears as his avant-garde self.

p, Mitchell R. Leiser; d, Pierre Dominique Gaisseau; w, William Duffy; ph, Victor Petroshevic (Movielab Color); ed, Sidney Katz.

Drama **(PR:C MPAA:NR)**

ROUNDUP TIME IN TEXAS½** (1937) 63m REP bw

Gene Autry *(Gene)*, Smiley Burnette *(Frog)*, Maxine Doyle *(Gwen)*, The Cabin Kids *(Themselves)*, LeRoy Mason *(Cardigan)*, Earle Hodgins *(Barkey)*, Dick Wessel *(Johnson)*, Buddy Williams *(Bosuto)*, Elmer Fain *(Chief's Son)*, Cornie Anderson *(Namba)*, Frankie Marvin *(Second Cape Cop)*, Ken Cooper *(Tex)*, Al Ferguson, Slim Whitaker, Al Knight, Carleton Young, Jack C. Smith, Jim Corey, Jack Kirk, George Morrell, Champion the Horse.

The roundup occurs in Texas, but most of the picture is set in Africa, where Autry and Burnette deliver a herd of horses to Autry's diamond prospector brother. There's a gang of baddies with their eyes on the gems, however, who cause hassles for the Texas bunch. After encounters with wild animals, South African officials, drumming voodoo men, and left-over footage from Tarzan films, Autry and the boys round up the bandits. They also have enough energy left to deliver "The Rose That Grows on the Prairie" and "Moon of Desire" (Autry, et. al.).

p, Nat Levine; d, Joseph Kane; w, Oliver Drake; ph, William Nobles; ed, Lester Orlebeck.

Western/Adventure **Cas.** **(PR:A MPAA:NR)**

ROUNDERS, THE*½** (1965) 85m MGM c

Glenn Ford *(Ben Jones)*, Henry Fonda *(Howdy Lewis)*, Sue Ann Langdon *(Mary)*, Hope Holiday *(Sister)*, Chill Wills *(Jim Ed Love)*, Edgar Buchanan *(Vince Moore)*, Kathleen Freeman *(Agatha Moore)*, Joan Freeman *(Meg Moore)*, Denver Pyle *(Bull)*, Barton MacLane *(Tanner)*, Doodles Weaver *(Arlee)*, Allegra Varron *(Mrs. Norson)*, Casey Tibbs *(Rafe)*.

Richard Lyons had some bad luck with MGM. He produced two first-rate Westerns and the studio had no idea what to do with them. The first was cult movie RIDE THE HIGH COUNTRY and the second was this contemporary cowboy comedy that should have had much greater success than it did. Unfortunately, nobody at MGM thought much about the tale of two grizzled cowboys trying to eke their way through life and it was tacked on to the bottom of a double bill with the memorable GET YOURSELF A COLLEGE GIRL as the top half of the entry. That picture starred Mary Ann Mobley, Nancy Sinatra, and Chad Everett and almost destroyed several careers. Under Kennedy's expert hand (working from his own adaptation of the book by Max Evans), this is a charmer all the way. Fonda and Ford are a pair of ancient cowhands who travel the area around Sedona, Arizona. They have a dream to make enough money busting broncos to retire, open a bar in some exotic location like Tahiti and watch the rest of the world go by. It'll never happen because they are also given to blowing all their money on fast women, slow horses, and good booze when they're done working. Right now, they are in the employ of skinflint Wills, who gives them seven dollars for every horse they can break. They live in a drafty cabin and are to spend the winter rounding up the strays. Wills has a roan named "Ol' Fooler" that no one has been able to break. They have to teach that recalcitrant beast how to be a kind animal and spend the cold months vainly attempting that. Buchanan is a local moonshiner with two daughters, Freeman and Freeman. They sell the horse in exchange for whiskey but when Buchanan discovers that the horse is a drunk who loves to eat the corn mash that makes the liquor, Buchanan returns him. Fonda and Ford accept the horse as partial payment from Wills and think they can enter him in a rodeo as an unbreakable steed. Before the rodeo, Fonda and Ford meet Vegas strippers Holiday and Langdon and go for a nude swim in the state fish hatchery. At the rodeo, the horse throws everyone and the boys make a bundle on bets. Then the animal is hurt and the local vet says it will have to be destroyed. Neither one can bring himself to shoot the animal, who suddenly wakes up when he sees the gun. He wasn't hurt, just drunk from the corn mash. The horse begins to wreck the stable by bucking. It's soon a shambles and Fonda and Ford have to cough up all their winnings to pay the damage. With no money, and only this mean horse as an asset, it's back to work for Wills again and another winter of discontent. Filmed in the Coconino Forest of Arizona, it's funny, fast-moving, has plenty of action, a little sex and deserved a far better treatment from the distributors. Real-life rodeo star Casey Tibbs makes an appearance.

p, Richard E. Lyons; d, Burt Kennedy; w, Kennedy (based on the novel by Max Evans); ph, Paul C. Vogel (Panavision, Metrocolor); m, Jeff Alexander; ed, John McSweeney; art d, George W. Davis, Urie McCleary; set d, Henry Grace, Jack Mills; stunts, Buzz Henry; makeup, William Tuttle.

Western **(PR:A-C MPAA:NR)**

ROUNDTRIP (SEE: ROUND TRIP, 1967)

ROUNDUP, THE* (1941) 90m PAR bw

Richard Dix *(Steve)*, Patricia Morison *(Janet)*, Preston Foster *(Greg)*, Don Wilson *(Slim)*, Ruth Donnelly *(Polly)*, Betty Brewer *(Mary)*, Douglas Dumbrille *(Capt. Lane)*, Jerome Cowan *(Wade McGee)*, Dick Curtis *(Ed Crandall)*, William Haade *(Frane Battles)*, Morris Ankrum *(Parenthesis)*, Clara Kimball Young *(Mrs. Wilson)*, Douglas Kennedy *(Trooper)*, Weldon Heyburn, Lane Chandler, Lee "Lasses" White, The King's Men.

The wedding day of Dix and Morison is interrupted when Morison's past love (Foster), whom she had believed to be dead, returns. He makes a pest of himself, trying to ruin the couple's happiness, but in the end he gets polished off. A remake of a 1920 silent which starred Wallace Beery and Fatty Arbuckle. Unusually weak direction from Selander.

p, Harry Sherman; d, Lesley Selander; w, Harold Shumate (based on a story by Edmund Day); ph, Russell Harlan; ed, Carrol Lewis.

Western **(PR:A MPAA:NR)**

ROUSTABOUT½** (1964) 101m PAR c

Elvis Presley *(Charlie Rogers)*, Barbara Stanwyck *(Maggie Morgan)*, Joan Freeman *(Cathy Lean)*, Leif Erickson *(Joe Lean)*, Sue Ann Langdon *(Mme. Mijanou)*, Pat Buttram *(Harry Carver)*, Joan Staley *(Marge)*, Dabbs Greer *(Arthur Nielsen)*, Steve Brodie *(Fred)*, Norman Grabowski *(Sam, the College Student)*, Jack Albertson *(Lou)*, Jane Dulo *(Hazel)*, Arthur Levy *(Gus)*, Joel Fluellen *(Cody Marsh)*, Toby Reed *(Dick)*, Kenneth M. Becker *(Gregg)*, Ray Kellogg *(Ernie)*, Marianna Hill *(Viola)*, Lester Miller *(B.J.)*, Beverly Adams *(Cora)*, Glenn R. Wilder *(Craig)*, Wilda Taylor, Mercedes G. Ford *(Dancers)*, Eddie Marr, Bob Matthews, Buddy Lewis, Jack Whalen, Lance LeGault *(Barkers)*, K.L. Smith *(Sheriff)*, Mike Mahoney, Roger V. Creed *(Deputies)*, Billy Barty *(Billy the Midget)*, Jerry James *(Stage Manager)*, Barbara Hemingway *(Fat Lady)*, Richard Kiel *(Strong Man)*, Max Manning *(Juggler)*, Dianne Simpson *(Elephant Girl)*, John Turk *(Volcano Man)*, Chester Hayes *(Clown)*, Joe Forte, Howard Joslin, Lynn Borden, Linda Foster, Teri Hope, Raquel Welch, Steve Condit, Dean Moray, Dianne Libby, Owen Bush, Jimmy Gaines, Richard DiPaolo, Theodore F. Lehmann, Maugene H. Gannon, Katie Sweet, Linda Rand, Carey Foster, Connie Ducharme.

Presley is hired to work as a handyman at Stanwyck's carnival and falls in love with fellow worker Freeman. The carnival is in dire financial straits until Presley opens his mouth and gyrates his hips. The crowds are soon overflowing and it's all due to the "King of Rock and Roll." Stanwyck adds some status to the cast, usually awful in Presley pictures. This time there are fine actors all the way to the end of the credits—Jack Albertson, Raquel Welch (in her film debut), Richard Kiel, and Billy Barty, as well as *Playboy*'s Miss November of 1958, Joan Staley. Elvis' barrage of 11 tunes includes: "Roustabout," "Poison Ivy League," "One Track Heart" (Bill Giant, Bernie Baum, Florence Kaye), "Little Egypt" (Jerry Leiber, Mike Stoller), "Wheels on My Heels," "It's a Wonderful World" (Sid Tepper, Roy C. Bennett), "It's Carnival Time" (Ben Weisman, Sid Wayne), "Carny Town" (Fred Wise, Randy Starr), "Hard Knocks," "There's a Brand New Day on the Horizon" (Joy Byers), "Big Love, Big Heartache" (Dolores Fuller, Lee Morris, Sonny Hendrix).

p, Hal B. Wallis; d, John Rich; w, Paul Nathan, Anthony Lawrence, Allan Weiss (based on a story by Weiss); ph, Lucien Ballard (Techniscope, Technicolor); process ph, Farciot Edouart; m, Joseph L. Lilley; ed, Warren Low; art d, Hal Pereira, Walter Tyler; set d, Sam Comer, Robert R. Benton; ch, Earl Barton; cos, Edith Head; spec eff, Paul K. Lerpae.

Musical/Drama **Cas.** **(PR:A MPAA:NR)**

ROVER, THE* (1967, Ital.) 103m Arco-Selmur/Cinerama c (L'AVVENTURIERO; AKA: THE ADVENTURER)

Anthony Quinn *(Peyrol)*, Rosanna Schiaffino *(Arlette)*, Rita Hayworth *(Aunt Caterina)*, Richard Johnson *(Real)*, Ivo Garrani *(Scevola)*, Mino Doro *(Dussard)*, Luciano Rossi *(Michel)*, Mirko Valentin *(Jacot)*, Gianni Di Benedetto *(Lt. Bolt)*, Anthony Dawson *(Capt. Vincent)*, Franco Giornelli *(Simmons)*, Franco Fantasia *(Admiral)*, Fabrizio Jovine *(Archives Officer)*, John Lane *(Captain of the Port)*, Vittorio Venturoli *(French Officer)*, Gustavo Gionno *(Sans-Culotte)*, Lucio De Santis *(Fisherman)*, Raffaela Miceli *(Arlette as a Child)*, Ruggero Salvadori *(Hoodlum)*, Paola Bossalino, Rita Klein, Cathy Alexander *(Girls)*.

Involved with counterrevolutionary forces during the Napoleonic War, Quinn breaks through a British naval blockade in order to get a message to another rebel. He barely escapes, taking refuge with Schiaffino in the home of her aunt, Hayworth. Quinn grows attached to the mentally unstable girl, and grows jealous when he learns that she is interested in Johnson, a French naval officer who also boards at Hayworth's. Johnson discovers that Quinn is a fugitive rebel, causing Quinn to flee. He then resumes his counterrevolutionary mission and is killed. Yet another illustration of how difficult it is to film Joseph Conrad, whose conflicts are philosophical and moral rather than physical. An obscure, dull adaptation of a minor Conrad novel, the film wasn't released in the U.S. until four years after it first appeared on the festival circuit. It came and went and no one noticed, which isn't surprising at all.

p, Alfredo Bini; d, Terence Young; w, Luciano Vincenzoni, Jo Eisinger (based on the novel *The Rover* by Joseph Conrad); ph, Leonida Barboni (Eastmancolor); m, Ennio Morricone; ed, Peter Thornton; md, Bruno Nicolai; art d, Gianni Polidori; set d, Dario Micheli, Luciano Spadoni; cos, Veniero Colasanti; makeup, Otello Fava; fight director, Franco Fantasia.

War Drama **(PR:C MPAA:NR)**

ROVIN' TUMBLEWEEDS* (1939) 62m REP bw (AKA: WASHINGTON COWBOY)

Gene Autry *(Gene)*, Smiley Burnette *(Frog)*, Mary Carlisle *(Mary)*, Douglas Dumbrille *(Holloway)*, William Farnum *(Nolan)*, Lee "Lasses" White *(Storekeeper)*, Ralph Peters *(Satchel)*, Gordon Hart *(Fuller)*, Vic Potel *(Zeke)*, Jack Ingram *(Blake)*, Sammy McKim *(Eddie)*, Reginald Barlow *(Higgins)*, Eddie Kane *(Congressman)*, Guy Usher *(Craig)*, Horace Murphy, David Sharpe, Jack Kirk, Rose Plummer, Robert Burns, Art Mix, Horace B. Carpenter, Fred "Snowflake" Toones, Frank Ellis, Fred Burns, Edward Cassidy, Forrest Taylor, Tom Chatterton, Crauford Kent, Maurice Costello, Charles K. French, Lee Shumway, Bud Osborne, Harry Semels, Chuck Morrison, Nora Lou Martin and the Pals of the Golden West, Champion the Horse.

An interesting Frank Capra-influenced (MR. SMITH GOES TO WASHINGTON) oater which has Autry cast as a congressman exposing a politician who is holding up a flood control bill. The Washington politico plans to buy up large quantities of land and then sell them for a big profit after the bill is passed. Republic took a chance with this one and failed...but at least they tried. Songs include: "Paradise in the Moonlight" (Gene Autry, Fred Rose) and "Ole Peaceful River" (Johnny Marvin).

p, William Berke; d, George Sherman; w, Betty Burbridge, Dorrell McGowan, Stuart McGowan; ph, William Nobles; ed, Tony Martinelli; md, Raoul Kraushaar.

Western **(PR:A MPAA:NR)**

ROVING ROGUE, A (SEE: OUTLAWS OF THE ROCKIES, 1945)

ROWDYMAN, THE½** (1973, Can.) 95m Agincourt-Film Associates-Canadian Film Development/Crowley c

Gordon Pinsent *(Will Cole)*, Frank Converse *(Andrew Scott)*, Will Geer *(Stan)*, Linda Gorenson *(Ruth Lowe)*, Ted Henley *(Constable Williams)*, Estelle Wall *(Mary Cole)*, Stuart Gillard *(Constable Bill)*, Austin Davis *(Walt)*, Dawn Greenhalgh *(Women on Train)*.

Pinsent (who also scripted) stars as the title fellow, a drunken carouser and woman-chaser, whose live-fast-leave-a-good-looking-corpse way of life takes a turn when he accidentally causes the death of a childhood friend. A sometimes gripping character study which never fully develops and ultimately falls by the wayside.

p, Lawrence Z. Dane; d, Peter Carter; w, Gordon Pinsent; ph, Edmund Long; m, Ben McPeak; ed, Michael Manne; set d, Barry Lavendar.

Drama **(PR:C MPAA:NR)**

ROXIE HART*** (1942) 75m FOX bw

Ginger Rogers *(Roxie Hart)*, Adolphe Menjou *(Billy Flynn)*, George Montgomery *(Homer Howard)*, Lynne Overman *(Jake Callahan)*, Nigel Bruce *(E. Clay Benham)*, Phil Silvers *(Babe)*, Sara Allgood *(Mrs. Morton)*, William Frawley *(O'Malley)*, Spring Byington *(Mary Sunshine)*, Michael "Ted" North *(Stuart Chapman)*, Helene Reynolds *(Velma Wall)*, George Chandler *(Amos Hart)*, Charles D. Brown *(Charles E. Murdock)*, Morris Ankrum *(Martin S. Harrison)*, George Lessey *(Judge)*, Iris Adrian *(Two-Gun Gertie)*, Milton Parsons *(Announcer)*, Billy Wayne *(Court Clerk)*, Charles Williams *(Photographer)*, Leon Belasco *(Waiter)*, Lee Shumway, Jim Pierce, Phillip Morris, Pat O'Malley, Stanley Blystone *(Policemen)*, Frank Orth, Alec Craig, Edward Clark *(Idlers)*, Larry Lawson, Harry Carter *(Reporters)*, Jack Norton *(Producer)*, Arthur Aylesworth *(Mr. Wadsworth)*, Margaret Seddon *(Mrs. Wadsworth)*, Frank Darien *(Finnegan)*, Bob Perry *(Prisoner's Bailiff)*, Jeff Corey *(Orderly)*, Leonard Kibrick *(Newsboy)*, Mary Treen *(Secretary)*.

This was a departure for director Wellman, and he handles it in good order, giving ROXIE HART a loud and brash nature that only occasionaly stretches the burlesque comedy beyond its boundaries. Rogers is a sassy, gum-snapping dance hall girl in 1920s Chicago. When her husband, Chandler, murders a man, Rogers takes the fall, figuring the trial publicity will give her career a boost. She hires Menjou as her lawyer, and the crafty attorney schools her in how to sway a jury. Menjou's out to make a name as well, so getting Rogers to play the part is of the utmost importance. His trial strategy depends, among other things, on Rogers' shapely legs, which she flashes to the jury without mercy. After a trial worthy of any burlesque review, Rogers is not too surprisingly found innocent. She quickly jettisons Chandler for the favors of Montgomery, a reporter who has fallen in love with her while covering the trial. ROXIE HART is a wonderful farce, with Rogers delivering a nice-sized chunk of ham with her performance. It's a role that the actress clearly enjoys, giving the film an energetic center that just doesn't stop as she chews the scenery along with her gum. Menjou and the supporting cast rally around her in good style, an enjoyable ensemble that electrifies the farce. Wellman directs at a fevered pitch, firing this along at a delirious pace that occasionally overwhelms itself. Rather than let some subtle humor sneak in, Wellman goes for the broad every time. Wellman was impressed by Chandler's performance, and promised him a part in his next picture, A GREAT MAN'S LADY. The two developed a symbiotic actor-director relationship and would work together often in the future. This was based on a play by Maurine Watkins, and had hit the screens once before, in 1928, under the title CHICAGO. In 1975, stage and film director Bob Fosse resurrected the material for a new Broadway musical, once again using the title "Chicago."

p, Nunnally Johnson; d, William A. Wellman; w, Johnson (based on the play "Chicago" by Maurine Watkins); ph, Leon Shamroy; m, Alfred Newman; ed, James B. Clark; art d, Richard Day, Wiard B. Ihnen; set d, Thomas Little; cos, Gwen Wakeling; ch, Hermes Pan; makeup, Guy Pearce.

Comedy/Crime **(PR:A MPAA:NR)**

ROYAL AFFAIR, A*** (1950) 100m Discina International bw (LE ROI; AKA: THE KING)

Maurice Chevalier *(The King)*, Annie Ducaux *(Therese Marnix)*, Sophie Desmarets *(Mme. Beaudrier)*, Alfred Adam *(Beaudrier)*, Jean Wall *(LeLorrain)*, Robert Murzeau *(Blond)*, Robert Vattier *(Marquis de Chamarande)*, Felix Paquet *(Postmaster General)*, Henry Charrett *(Minister of Commerce)*, Francois Joux *(Marcel Rivelot)*, Delaitre *(Count Martin)*.

Chevalier turns on the charm as a king arriving in Paris to sign a treaty. He is quickly initiated into the ways of the French when he is hit in the face with a creampuff thrown by Desmarets, the wife of senator Adam. The senator is soon shocked to discover that his visitor is quite interested in both Desmarets and Ducaux, his mistress. In a scheme to get Chevalier to sign the treaty, the senator makes it painfully easy for the king to seduce the two women. The treaty is signed and the king returns to his homeland, forever convinced of his charm. Chevalier doesn't disappoint in his delivery of "C'est Fini" and "Danser La Cachucha," both of which are delivered with the maximum of grace. As THE KING (LE ROI), with Victor Francen and Raimu, a film based on the same play was made in France in 1936 (released in the U.S. in 1941).

p, Michael Safra, Andre Paulve; d&w, Marc-Gilbert Sauvajon (based on the play "Le Roi" by R. De Flers, G.A. Caillavet, E. Arene); ph, Robert LeFebvre; m, Jean Marion; ed, Roger Dwyre; prod d, Guy de Gastyne; set d, Andre Boutie.

Comedy **(PR:A MPAA:NR)**

ROYAL AFFAIRS IN VERSAILLES*** (1957, Fr.) 152m C.L.M.-Cocinor/Times c (SI VERSAILLES M'ETAIT CONTE; AKA: AFFAIRS IN VERSAILLES)

Sacha Guitry *(Louis XIV)*, Claudette Colbert *(Mme. de Montespan)*, Orson Welles *(Benjamin Franklin)*, Jean-Pierre Aumont *(Cardinal de Rohan)*, Edith Piaf *(Woman of the People)*, Gerard Philippe *(D'Artagnan)*, Micheline Presle *(Mme. du Pompadour)*, Jean Marais *(Louis XV)*, Daniel Gelin *(Jean Collinet)*, Daniele Delorme *(Louison Chabray)*, George Marchal *(Louis XIV as a Young Man)*, Gaby Morlay *(Countess de la Motte)*, Gilbert Boka *(Louis XVI)*, Lana Marconi *(Marie Antoinette)*, Marie Marquet *(Mme. de Maintenon)*, Michel Auclair *(Jacques Damien)*, Jean-Louis Barrault *(Francois Fenelon)*, Jeanne Boitel *(Mme. de Sevigne)*, Pauline Carton *(The Neighbor)*, Gino Cervi *(Alessandro de Cagliostro)*, Jean Chevrier *(Marshal Turenne)*, Aime Clariond *(Rivarol)*, Nicole Courcel *(Mme. de Chalis)*, Yves Deniaud *(A Peasant)*, Jean Desailly *(Marivaux)*, Renee Devillers *(Mme. Campan)*, Fernand Gravey [Gravet] *(Jean Moliere)*, Claude Nollier *(Countess de Soissons)*, Gisele Pascal *(Axel de Fersen)*, Jean Richard *(Du Croisy)*, Tino Rossi *(Gondolier)*, Louis Seigner *(Antoine Lavoisier)*, Raymond Souplex *(Auctioneer)*, Maurice Reynac *(Mons. de Montespan)*, Bourvil, Jean Tissier, Pierre Larquey *(Museum Guards)*, Charles Vanel *(M. de Vergennes)*, Louis Arbessier *(Louis XIII)*, Jacques Berthier *(Maximillien de Robespierre)*, Georges Chamarat *(La Fontaine)*, Paul Colline *(Visitor)*, Anny Cordy *(Mme. Langlois)*, Jean-Jacques Delbo *(Mons. de La Motte)*, Duvaleix *(A Buyer)*, Samson Fainsilber *(Cardinal Mazarin)*, Tania Fedor *(Marie Leczinska)*, Jacques Francois *(Saint-Simon)*, Jeanne Fusier-Gir *(A Revolutionary)*, Gilbert Gil *(Jean-Jacques Rousseau)*, Marie Mansart *(Mme. de Kerlor)*, Nicole Maurey *(Mlle. de Fontanges)*, Jacques Morel *(Boehmer)*, Jean Murat *(Louvois)*, Constant Remy *(Mons. de La Reynie)*, Germaine Rouer *(Mlle. Moliere)*, Jacques Varennes *(Jean Baptiste Colbert)*, Howard Vernon *(The English Buyer)*, Martine Alexis *(Mme. de Nouchy)*, Jean-Louis Allibert *(Le Vau)*, Paul Azais *(A Revolutionary)*, Brigitte Bardot *(Mlle. de Rosille)*, Lily Baron *(Mme. de Balto)*, Liliane Bert *(Armande Bejart)*, Roland Bourdin *(Jean Fragonard)*, Jany Castel *(Marie-Therese of Spain)*, Andre Chanu *(Duke de Noailles)*, Anne Carriere *(Mme. de Chamarat)*, Claudie Chapland *(Louis XIII as a Child)*, Rene Charles *(A Lord)*, France Delahalle *(A Woman of the Court)*, Jacques Derives *(A Lord)*, Bernard Dheran *(Pierre Beaumarchais)*, Emile Drain *(Emperor Napoleon I)*, Alain Durtal *(Bontemps)*, Cecile Eddy *(Mme. de Frepons)*, Robert Favart *(Mons. de Carlene)*, Jacques de Feraudy *(Voltaire)*, Roger Gaillard *(d'Alembert)*, Lucienne Granier *(Mme. de Sentis)*, Robert Hommet *(Count de Langeais)*, Journet *(Mons. de Beytz)*, Pierre Lord *(J.H. Mansart)*, Jacques Mafioly *(Mons. de Puiset)*, Olivier Mathot *(Boileau)*, Gilbert Moryn *(Bossuet)*, Lucien Nat *(Montesquieu)*, Gilles Queant *(Jean Racine)*, Fernand Rene *(Citizen Poet)*, Gaston Rey *(Henri IV)*, Philippe Richard *(King Louis-Phillippe)*, Rene Worms *(Bassenge)*, Pierre Would *(Vaupan)*.

An impressive historical document which stars not Welles, Colbert, Aumont, or writer-director Guitry but the Palace of Versailles itself. The magnificent decor, which is both amazing and repulsive at the same time, appears precisely as it did in the late 1700s before the peasants took it upon themselves to revolt. Guitry, France's most historically minded filmmaker, was the first to receive permission to film at Versailles (THE THREE MUSKETEERS was also shot there in 1973). The idea of the film is to trace the history of the great palace beginning with its construction by Louis le Vau and J.H. Mansart (played by Jean-Louis Allibert and Pierre Lord) through its occupation by the young Louis XIV (Marchal), the older Louis XIV (Guitry), and the revolution of Louis XVI (Boka). We also see visits made by Welles' Ben Franklin, Gravet's Moliere, Queant's Racine, as well as countless other French historical figures. However, instead of a strict historical lecture, ROYAL AFFAIRS AT VERSAILLES underlines the ambiguities of the word "affair." Guitry has admitted that he is less concerned with accuracy than with the period's atmosphere or, using his word, its "heart." It is of no importance to Guitry that Robespierre and Marie Antoinette never met, though they do in the film. The joy Guitry finds is in imagining what would have occurred had they met. This rather scandalous approach to history was not met with approval by the committee in charge of Versailles. Whether or not the film stays faithful to documents and calendars is unimportant; what makes ROYAL AFFAIRS AT VERSAILLES so interesting is that the audience gets the feeling they visited Versailles during the 1700's. Originally released in France in 1953 at 165 minutes. (In French, English subtitles.)

p,d&w, Sacha Guitry; ph, Pierre Montazel (Eastmancolor); m, Jean Francaix; ed, Raymond Lamy; set d, Rene Renoux; cos, Monique Dumas; song, "Ca Ira" (sung by Edith Piaf).

Historical Drama (PR:A MPAA:NR)

ROUND UP, THE*½** (1969, Hung.) 94m Mafilm/Altura bw
(SZEGENYLEGENYEK NEHEZELETUCK; AKA: THE HOPELESS ONES;
THE POOR OUTLAWS)

Janos Gorbe (Janos Gajdor), Tibor Molnar (Kabai), Andras Kozak (Kabai's Son), Gabor Agardy (Torma), Zoltan Latinovits (Veszelka), Istvan Avar (1st Interrogator), Lajos Oze (2nd Interrogator), Bela Barsi, Janos Koltai, Attila Nagy, Jozsef Madaras, Rudolf Somogyvari, Zoltan Basilides, Gyorgy Bardi, Zsigmond Fulop, Laszlo Csurka, Ida Simenfalvy, Sandor Simenfalvy, Laszlo Gyorgy, Jozsef Horvath, Lorinc G. Szabo, Laszlo Horvath, Gyula Szersen, Jacint Juhasz, Tibor Szilagyi, Jozsef Kautzky, Endre Tallos, Jozsef Konrad, Geza Tordy, Istvan Velenczei.

Gorbe is one of hundreds of outlaws and peasants rounded up by the Austrian army after an unsuccessful revolt during the mid-1800s. He is told that he will be freed if he gives the names of outlaws who have killed more than he. The first he identifies escapes, but is caught and hanged. The second, upon seeing his wife tortured, leaps to his death, along with his two comrades. The Austrian guards, satisfied with the information he has given them (and, therefore, no longer needing him), let the other prisoners kill Gorbe. The guards continue their reign of terror, this time choosing as their pawns a father and son who must betray murderer Agardy in order to save each other from death. Agardy is then allowed to pick a calvary squadron as a reward for defeating his betrayers in a match of horsemanship. When he boasts that the men he has picked belonged to the band of a famous revolutionary, the Austrians overhear and seize the entire group, which they have been trying to identify. A superb film from Hungarian director Jancso which brought him (and the entire Hungarian cinema) worldwide attention. It is (as are all Jancso's pictures) a fine example of the creation of mood through the use of expansive landscapes and austere horizons. It is also a poignant, stark look at the insensitivity and fear that fester when people are imprisoned. Released in Hungary in 1966.

d, Miklos Jancso; w, Gyula Hernadi; ph, Tamas Somlo (Agascope); ed, Zoltan Farkas; art d, Tamas Banovich; cos, Zsuzsa Vicze.

Historical Drama (PR:O MPAA:NR)

ROYAL AFRICAN RIFLES, THE** (1953) 75m AA c (GB: STORM OVER AFRICA)

Louis Hayward (Denham), Veronica Hurst (Jennifer), Michael Pate (Cunningham), Angela Greene (Karen Van Stede), Steven Geray (Van Stede), Roy Glenn (Cpl. John), Bruce Lester (Saxon), Barry Bernard (Eakins), Robert Osterloh (Carney), John Warburton (Col. Burke), Pat Aherne (Capt. Curtis).

Hayward is a British officer sent to East Africa to supply the Royal African Rifles with the necessary machine guns. The picture suffers from a sacrifice of action to dialog, despite Selander's apt direction.

p, Richard Heermance; d, Lesley Selander; w, Dan Ullman; ph, Ellis Carter (Cinecolor); m, Paul Dunlap; ed, Walter Hanneman; art d, David Milton.

Adventure (PR:A MPAA:NR)

ROYAL BED, THE** (1931) 75m RKO bw (GB: THE QUEEN'S HUSBAND)

Lowell Sherman (The King), Nance O'Neil (The Queen), Mary Astor (Princess Anne), Anthony Bushell (Granton), Robert Warwick (Premier Northrup), Alan Roscoe (Birten), Hugh Trevor (Crown Prince), Gilbert Emery (Phipps), J. Carrol Naish (Laker), Frederick Burton (Fellman), Desmond Roberts (Maj. Blent), Lita Chevret, Nancy Lee Blaine (Ladies in Waiting).

Sherman is king of a small island in the North Sea who finds he has a lot on his hands when his wife, the queen, makes a trip to America. He must decide how to respond when a revolution erupts, as well as when his daughter announces that she will not marry the crown prince, but a commoner. For the first time, Sherman acts without the queen's approval, with the result that the rebellion is crushed and the daughter allowed to marry the man she loves.

d, Lowell Sherman; w, J. Walter Ruben (based on the play "The Queen's Husband" by Robert E. Sherwood); ph, Leo Tover; ed, Arthur Roberts.

Comedy **Cas.** (PR:A MPAA:NR)

ROYAL BOX, THE* (1930) 76m WB bw

Alexander Moissi (Edmund Kean), Camilla Horn (Alice Doren), Lew Hearn (Solomon), Elsa Ersi (Countess Toeroek), Egon Brecher (Count Toeroek), William F. Schoeller (H.R.H. Prince of Wales), Leni Stengel (Lady Robert), Carlos Zizold (Lord Melville), Greta Meyer (Mrs. Barker), William Gade (Tommy Widgetts), Siegfried [Sig] Rumann (The Bailiff).

An over-talky talkie which was filmed entirely in the German language, but in the U.S. It is the biography of a British stage actor in the early 1800s, Edmund Kean,

centering mainly on his illustrious relationship with a countess. The first U.S.-made foreign-language talking picture.

d, Bryan Foy; w, Murray Roth, Edmund Joseph, Arthur Hurley, Dr. Harry Rundt (based on Charles Coughlan's adaptation of the play "Kean" by Alexandre Dumas); ph, E.B. DuPax, Ray Foster; m, Harold Levy.

Biography (PR:A MPAA:NR)

ROYAL CAVALCADE (SEE: REGAL CAVALCADE, 1935, Brit.)

ROYAL DEMAND, A* (1933, Brit.) 62m Moorland/PAR bw

Cyril McLaglen (Lord Forrest), Marjorie Hume (Lady Forrest), Fred Rains (Walters), Vi Kaley (Nana), Powell Edwards (Gen. Orring), Howard Fry (Lord Wentover), Tich Hunter (Robin), Gisela Leif Robinson (Lady Ann), Cynthia Clifford.

Atrocious historical drama has McLaglen, an aristocrat with Royalist sympathies during the English Civil War, disguising himself as a member of Cromwell's Roundheads and managing to save his family from capture. Only good for laughs.

p, Mrs. C.P. Wiliams; d, Gustave Minzenty; w, Jane Moorland [Mrs. Williams].

Historical Drama (PR:A MPAA:NR)

ROYAL DIVORCE, A* (1938, Brit.) 85m Imperator/PAR bw

Ruth Chatterton (Josephine), Pierre Blanchar (Napoleon), Frank Cellier (Talleyrand), Carol Goodner (Mme. Tallien), Auriol Lee (Napoleon's Mother), George Curzon (Barras), Lawrence Hanray (Klemens von Metternich), John Laurie (Joseph), Jack Hawkins (Capt. Charles), Rosalyn Boulter (Hortense), Allan Jeayes (Murat), Moran Caplat (Eugene), Romilly Lunge (Junot), Hubert Harben (De Tracy), David Farrar (Louis), Sonia Carol, Maureen Glynne, Ivy Shannon, Julien Somers, Stephen Jack, Tamara d'Etter, Daisy Thomas.

The story of Napoleon and Josephine—one of the most celebrated romances in history—is brought to the screen in this mediocre adaptation. Chatterton is Josephine to Blanchar's Napoleon, and their relationship is seen developing as the French emperor rises to power, building up to their marriage, and culminating in divorce. Fails to capture the vigor which most certainly surrounded the bizarre personalities of this couple.

p, Herbert Wilcox; d, Jack Raymond; w, Miles Malleson (based on the novel Josephine by Jacques Thery); ph, Frederick A. Young.

Historical Biography (PR:A MPAA:NR)

ROYAL EAGLE* (1936, Brit.) 69m Quality/COL bw

John Garrick (Jim Hornby), Nancy Burne (Sally Marshall), Edmund Willard (Burnock), Lawrence Anderson (Vale), Hugh E. Wright (Albert Marshall), Muriel Aked (Miss Mimm), Fred Groves (Sam Waldock), Felix Aylmer (Windridge), Betty Shale (Mrs. Marshall), Ian Fleming, Clare Greet.

Garrick is a warehouse worker falsely accused of robbery and killing a policeman. While traveling on the title boat between London and Margate, he unmasks one of the real culprits and proves his innocence. Average crime drama features a good performance by Garrick.

p, Clive Loehnis; d, George A. Cooper, Arnold Ridley; w, Ridley; ph, Bryan Langley.

Crime (PR:A MPAA:NR)

ROYAL FAMILY OF BROADWAY, THE** (1930) 68m PAR bw (GB: THEATRE ROYAL)

Ina Claire (Julia Cavendish), Fredric March (Tony Cavendish), Mary Brian (Gwen Cavendish), Henrietta Crosman (Fanny Cavendish), Charles Starrett (Perry Stewart), Arnold Korff (Oscar Wolff), Frank Conroy (Gilbert Marshall), Royal G. Stout (Joe), Elsie Edmond (Della), Murray Alper (McDermott), Wesley Stack (Hall Boy), Herschel Mayall (Doctor).

There were more plays opening the last week of 1927 (17) than appear in an entire season these days. One of the most successful was "The Royal Family" by George S. Kaufman and Edna Ferber (yes, that Edna Ferber). It starred Otto Kruger in a thinly veiled parody of the Barrymores. When the play opened in Los Angeles, a young Fredric March took the road show role. It was seen by the Paramount bosses and March was offered the job in the movie, thus gaining an Oscar nomination and a huge following. The title was changed to THE ROYAL FAMILY OF BROADWAY so people in the sticks wouldn't think it had something to do with kings and queens. Adaptors Mankiewicz and Purcell wisely jettisoned some extraneous subplots and hammered it into a tight script that Cukor snappily directed, with assistance from Cyril Gardner. Crosman is the mother of the lot. She lives in a fabulous apartment and talks of her ancient theatrical triumphs. When son March arrives, with the press and various process servers snapping at his trousers, he is not welcomed. By leaving the stage and going to California to become a cinematic matinee idol, he incurred the wrath of the purists in the family. Now a Polish actress is trying to get a couple of hundred thousand out of March as she claims he'd promised to marry her but reneged. March is also being sought by a film director he'd decked in a fit of pique. As the biggest star in pictures, he is the target of many eager young women who would seek to snatch his hand in marriage and the family apartment is the only place he can hide and rest. March is stopping in New York for a brief visit before he goes to the Continent. His sister, Claire (in a part that enraged Ethel Barrymore), has been dating wealthy Conroy but has managed to keep from marrying him and would prefer to keep the relationship friendly, rather than passionate. Conroy is willing to bide his time. Claire's daughter by a previous marriage is Brian. The family realizes that she's an immensely gifted actress and wish for her to follow in their footsteps but she is totally against it, hates the idea of the theater, and intends to marry Starrett, a vapid society type, a gesture that puts the family up in arms. With March in the movies, Claire semi-retired, and Brian unwilling to carry on the family tradition, Crosman decides that she must do it herself and accepts an offer to go on tour with a rep company, despite the fact that she is old and not feeling well. March goes to Europe, returns, and learns that Crosman has had a heart attack while performing. The family gather around the old woman and she dies, the result of being once again thrilled and touched by the waves of applause. Still, for an actress, it's the only way she would have wanted to have a curtain. The family is comfortable, though not rich, and Claire has to make an important decision. Conroy presses marriage on her again but she opts to substitute for her late mother and continue the tour. Brian comes to the realization that Starrett is a twit and that her only real happiness will be gleaned on the stage, so she tosses the nerd aside and returns to the fold. Conroy sadly goes back to his South American mineral holdings and Starrett will return to his stock market dealings, the only topic of conversation he has managed throughout the story. Even though March is on screen for the least amount of time, his presence is powerful as he has, by far, the flashiest role. He must have studied John Barrymore for months to get every gesture, every raised eyebrow, every sneer so perfectly. The funny lines are tempered by the drama of Crosman's death but even then, the authors have managed to make the scene tug the heart while up-turning the mouth. The only character missing was Lionel Barrymore. A must-see for anyone who loves the theatre despite some technical motion picture boo-boos. Film editor Dmytryk went on to become a successful director of such films as THE JUGGLER, RAINTREE COUNTY, WALK ON THE WILD SIDE, and many more.

d, George Cukor, Cyril Gardner; w, Herman Mankiewicz, Gertrude Purcell (based on the play "The Royal Family" by George S. Kaufman, Edna Ferber); ph, George Folsey; ed, Edward Dmytryk.

Comedy   **(PR:A   MPAA:NR)**

ROYAL FLASH*   (1975, Brit.) 98m FOX c

Malcolm McDowell (Harry Flashman), Alan Bates (Rudi von Sternberg), Florinda Bolkan (Lola Montez), Oliver Reed (Otto von Bismarck), Britt Ekland (Duchess Irma), Lionel Jeffries (Kraftstein), Tom Bell (de Gautet), Joss Ackland (Sapten), Christopher Cazenove (Hansen), Roy Kinnear (Old Roue), Alastair Sim (Mr. Greig), Michael Hordern (Headmaster), Henry Cooper (John Gully).

Richard Lester's patented brand of comedy is again put to good use in this satirical adventure picture. McDowell is a cowardly swashbuckler who worms his way into European high society, where he meets Reed and Bates. They use McDowell for a plan to advance their political cause, by which he must pose as a Prussian nobleman and wed a duchess, Eckland. Its twisting plot is pushed along by Lester's energetic direction. One of the best of author Fraser's series of novels featuring the grown-up braggart-bully of Thomas Hughes' novel Tom Brown's School Days, with smatterings of history and real period characters such as Bismarck and Lola Montez, ROYAL FLASH is loosely based on Anthony Hope Hawkins' novel The Prisoner of Zenda. The latter was made into one of the all-time great action films, THE PRISONER OF ZENDA (1937), a remake of a 1922 silent (it was remade again in 1952) starring Ronald Colman, with Douglas Fairbanks, Jr. a terrific Rudi.

p, David V. Picker, Denis O'Dell; d, Richard Lester; w, George MacDonald Fraser (based on his novel); ph, Geoffrey Unsworth (DeLuxe Color); m, Ken Thorne; ed, John Victor Smith; prod d, Terence Marsh; art d, Alan Tomkins.

Comedy/Adventure   Cas.   (PR:A-C   MPAA:PG)

ROYAL FLUSH   (SEE: TWO GUYS FROM MILWAUKEE, 1946)

ROYAL GAME, THE   (SEE: BRAINWASHED, 1961, Ger.)

ROYAL HUNT OF THE SUN, THE½   (1969, Brit.) 121m Royal-
                                                        Benmar-Security-Rank/NG c

Robert Shaw (Francisco Pizarro), Christopher Plummer (Atahualpa), Nigel Davenport (Hernando De Soto), Michael Craig (Estete), Leonard Whiting (Young Martin), Andrew Keir (Valverde), James Donald (King Carlos V), William Marlowe (Candia), Percy Herbert (Diego), Alexander Davion (De Nizza), Sam Krauss (Felipillo), David Bauer, Danny Yordan, Alfredo Porras, Joaquin Parra Jose Panzio, Oscar Alvarez, Lisarao de la Inglesia.

Shaw plays the role of Spanish explorer Francisco Pizarro who, with a small expeditionary force, travels to South America in search of Incan treasure. He builds a relationship with the Inca king, Plummer, which is both suspicious and trusting, rooted in their mutual respect for each other. Shaw deifies himself, angering Plummer's people, and eventually Shaw's rebellious minions sentence the Inca ruler to death, above the loud protests of Shaw. It is only after Plummer is killed that Shaw realizes the troubles he has caused the Peruvians. Talky and philosophical, and not to be regarded as historically accurate.

p, Eugene Frenke, Philip Yordan; d, Irving Lerner; w, Yordan (based on the play by Peter Shaffer); ph, Roger Barlow, Francisco Sempere (Technicolor); m, Marc Wilkinson; ed, Peter Parasheles; art d, Eugene Lourie; cos, Anthony Powell; spec eff, Manuel Baquero; makeup, Julian Ruiz.

Historical Drama   **(PR:A   MPAA:G)**

ROYAL MOUNTED PATROL, THE*   (1941) 59m COL bw (GB:
                                                              GIANTS A'FIRE)

Charles Starrett (Tom Jeffries), Russell Hayden ("Lucky" Lawrence), Lloyd Bridges (Hap Andrews), Wanda McKay (Betty Duvalle), Evan Thomas (Commander), Donald Curtis (Frenchy Duvalle), Ted Adams (Pete), Harrison Greene (Office Manager), Kermit Maynard (Sgt. Coburn), Ted Mapes, George Morrell.

Starrett, Hayden and Bridges are young mounties assigned to bring the law down on lumberjack Curtis, whose disregard for safety results in a blazing forest. The rascal also causes the death of Bridges before the mounties can bring Curtis in. Well-crafted on all accounts. This is one of eight pictures made by the studio featuring cowboy heroes Starrett and Hayden as a team. Hayden, who had played "Lucky Jenkins" in 26 "Hopalong Cassidy" films, continued to use the role name "Lucky" in all eight, though with differing surnames. The young Bridges had made

his mark in legitimate theater and had just been signed to a contract by Columbia. Young model (and sweater girl, in this film) McKay had entered pictures in the previous year; this was her first female-lead role.

p, William Berke; d, Lambert Hillyer; w, Winston Miller; ph, George Meehan; ed, James Sweeney

Western   **(PR:A   MPAA:NR)**

ROYAL ROMANCE, A*½   (1930) 66M COL bw

William Collier, Jr., Pauline Starke, Clarence Muse.

Collier is an empty-pocketed writer living in a boarding house who inherits a fortune. He gets enough cash to come to the aid of Starke, who is living in a castle with her unfaithful husband. He buys the castle and succeeds in winning her over. Black actor Clarence Muse, in one of the early films of his long picture career, steals every scene he's in, even though his is merely a secondary supporting role.

d, Erle C. Kenton; w, George Barr McCutcheon, Norman Houston (based on the story "Private Property" by Houston); ph, Ted Tezlaff.

Romance   **(PR:A   MPAA:NR)**

ROYAL SCANDAL, A*   (1945) 94m FOX bw (GB: CZARINA)

Tallulah Bankhead (Czarina Catherine the Great), Charles Coburn (Chancellor Nicolai Ilyitch), Anne Baxter (Countess Anna Jaschikoff), William Eythe (Lt. Alexei Chernoff), Vincent Price (Marquis de Fleury), Mischa Auer (Capt. Sukov), Sig Ruman (Gen. Ronsky), Vladimir Sokoloff (Malakoff), Mikhail Rasumny (Drunken General), Grady Sutton (Boris), Don Douglas (Variatinsky), Egon Brecher (Wassilikow), Eva Gabor (Countess Demidow), Frederick Ledebur, Paul Baratoff, George A. Gleboff, Fred Nurney, Leonid Snegoff, Henry Victor, Wilton Graff, Michael Visaroff, Gen. Sam Savitsky, Eugene Beday, Nestor Eristoff, Richard Ryan, Eugene Sigaloff (Russian Generals), Virginia Walker Renee Carson, Sandra Foloway Roxanne Hiltron, Dina Smirnova, Martha Jewett, Ann Hunter (Ladies in Waiting), John Russell (Guard), Fred Essler, Marek Windheim, Torben Meyer, Victor Delinsky (Stooges), Arno Frey (Captain), Harry Carter (Footman), Feodor Chaliapin, Mario Gang, George Shdanoff (Lackeys).

Catherine The Great had been portrayed by Mae West, Elizabeth Bergner, Marlene Dietrich, and Pola Negri. She lived to be 67 years old. Amazing, if we are to believe her amorous ways. Lubitsch was to have directed this but he became ill and the reins were handed to Preminger, with Ernst looking over his shoulder and making sure that Otto's customary heavy hand was somewhat lightened. The ancient Biro/Lengyel play "Czarina"—which had been used before as the basis for other movies about the Russian queen, was adapted this time by Mayer and Frank, veteran screenwriters who knew what they were doing. To Bankhead's St. Petersburg castle comes Eythe, a young cavalry officer who has ridden days and nights to tell her of a coup planned by two generals. Eythe admits that he has plenty of energy left despite the travel and Bankhead requests that he return later that night for a "private" interview. Eythe is handsome, albeit a bit sappy, but he must have some smarts in the lovemaking department because his rise in the hierarchy is quick and he shoots through the lower ranks to become a general. Eythe is soon in love with Baxter, a virginal woman who is a lady in waiting. Bankhead falls hard for Eythe and when she learns that he is affianced to Baxter, the young woman is sent away. Eythe is heartbroken but still owes allegiance to his queen so he helps overcome the plot to dethrone her. Bankhead is so happy at what he's done, she allows Eythe and Baxter to reunite while she finds new thrills in the arms of Price, the French ambassador. With all of the sleeping around Bankhead does, it's a wonder any state business ever got done in the years when Catherine was Great. A few laughs, but Bankhead chews up the scenery and the pacing is a beat off. Lubitsch had filmed this before as FORBIDDEN PARADISE in 1924.

p, Ernst Lubitsch; d, Otto Preminger; w, Edwin Justis Mayer, Bruno Frank (based on the play "The Czarina" by Lajos Biro, Melchior Lengyel); ph, Arthur Miller; m, Alfred Newman; ed, Dorothy Spencer; md, Edward Powell; art d, Lyle R. Wheeler, Mark Lee Kirk; set d, Thomas Little, Paul S. Fox; cos, Rene Hubert; spec eff, Fred Sersen.

Comedy   **(PR:C-O   MPAA:NR)**

ROYAL TRACK, THE   (SEE: OBSESSION, 1968, Swed.)

ROYAL WALTZ, THE**   (1936) 80m UFA bw

Paul Hoerbiger (King Max II of Bavaria), Kurt Juergens [Curt Jurgens] (Emperor Franz Joseph of Austria), Carola Hoehn (Duchess Elisabeth of Bavaria), Anton Pointer (Count Tettenbach), Willi Forst (Ferdinand), Kurt Von Ruffin (Count Otto Preising), Hans Leibelt (Minister Doenniges), Theodore Danegger (Ludwig Tomasoni), Heli Finkenzeller (Theres), Ellen Schwanneke (Anna), Hugo Schrader (Franz).

When a count falls in love with a peasant girl the townsfolk call for them to marry, but this notion is complicated by the marriage of the Bavarian king's daughter. Songs include "Like a Miracle Love Came Overnight." A standard costumed operetta. Look for this early film appearance of the young Curt Jurgens who, at the age of 23, played the equally youthful Franz Josef. (In German; English subtitles).

d, Herbert Maisch; w, E. Burri, W. Forster; m, Franz Doelle.

Romance   **(PR:A   MPAA:NR)**

ROYAL WEDDING**   (1951) 93m MGM c (GB: WEDDING BELLS)

Fred Astaire (Tom Bowen), Jane Powell (Ellen Bowen), Peter Lawford (Lord John Brindale), Sarah Churchill (Anne Ashmond), Keenan Wynn (Irving Klinger/Edgar Klinger), Albert Sharpe (James Ashmond), Viola Roache (Sarah Ashmond), Henri Letondal (Purser), James Finlayson (Cabby), Alex Frazer (Chester), Jack Reilly (Pete Cumberly), William Cabanne (Dick), John Hedloe (Billy), Francis Bethancourt (Charles Gordon), Dee Turnell, Judy Lenson, Doreen Hayward, Shirley Rickert, Marian Horosko, Carmes Clifford, Italia De Nubelo, Betty Hannon,

Charlotte Hunter, Janet Lavis, Sheila Meyers, Pat Simms, Dorothea Ward, Joan Vohs, Marietta Elliott, Svetlana McLe, Doris Wolcott, Bee Allen, Joane Dale, Shirley Glickman, Jean Harrison, Lucille Lamarr, Virginia Lee, Jetsy Parker, Dorothy Tuttle *("Haiti" Number)*, Andre Charisse *(Steward)*, Bess Flowers *(Woman Guest)*, Mae Clarke.

Princess Elizabeth was about to marry Philip so the timing on this could not have been better although there was some difficulty at the start. The original female lead was June Allyson, then she learned she was pregnant and bowed out. They searched high and low for a replacement and by the time they got Judy Garland, the first director, Charles Walters, was committed to another film. Garland was already into her difficult period and when she began showing up late for rehearsals and acting strangely, she was let go, a move that effectively ended her tenure at MGM after many years. Powell was paged and did a smashing job. Thirty five years later, when she appeared on the Oscar telecast in March of 1986, she hardly looked much older than she did in this, perhaps her best film. Powell and Astaire are a brother-sister vaudeville act in London getting ready to open their show. While there, he falls in love with Churchill, a music hall dancer. (Originally, MGM tried to get Moira Shearer for the role but she was otherwise engaged). At the same time, Powell finds Lawford attractive. He's an English lord but not one of the weak-chinned supercilious types. Rather, he is good fun and Powell sees much in his character. Wynn plays twin brothers, both agents for Astaire and Powell, and adds what comedy there is. The picture ends as the couple have been united, after the usual misunderstandings and rocky love plot twists. That's about it for the story but what shines here is the singing, dancing and two of the most spectacular Astaire routines ever devised. In the first, he dances with a hat rack and the darn thing nearly comes alive as his partner. In the second and most celebrated, Astaire seems to be dancing on the walls and ceiling of a room. This was accomplished by building the room so it could be rotated at the exact same speed as the camera. The camera operator was strapped in his chair and when Astaire seems to be dancing on the ceiling it's actually the floor, but the camera man and his camera are upside down. Although Nick Castle is listed as choreographer, one has to believe that it was Astaire's genius that inspired the aforementioned routines. A lovely score by Alan Jay Lerner and Burton Lane with orchestrations by Conrad Salinger and Skip Martin that include: "Too Late Now" (sung by Powell), "Sunday Jumps" (danced by Astaire with the hat rack), "How Could You Believe Me When I Said I Love You When You Know I've Been a Liar All My Life?" (Astaire, Powell), "You're All the World to Me" (Astaire, in the rotating room), "The Happiest Day of My Life" (Powell), "Open Your Eyes" (Powell, Astaire), "Ev'ry Night at Seven" (Powell, Astaire), "I Left My Hat in Haiti" (Powell, Astaire), "What a Lovely Day for a Wedding" (Powell, Astaire, Lawford, Churchill, Wynn), plus "How About You?" (Burton Lane, Ralph Freed, used only in background), and "The Devonshire Regiment," (arranged by Paul Marquardt). The melody for "You're All The World To Me" was originally heard in KID MILLIONS as sung by Eddie Cantor in 1934 when it was titled "I Wanna Be A Minstrel Man." Sarah Churchill, the daughter of Sir Winston Spencer Churchill, makes her only U.S. appearance here and acquits herself well enough. When Sir Winston began writing, he used his middle initial in his credit because one of the most popular writers of novels in the early part of this century had the same name. ROYAL WEDDING is a lovely bit of frou-frou and served as Donen's first solo directorial assignment after having worked with Gene Kelly. Lane and Lerner got an Oscar nomination for "Too Late Now."

p, Arthur Freed; d, Stanley Donen; w, Alan Jay Lerner; ph, Robert Planck (Technicolor); ed, Albert Akst; md, Johnny Green; art d, Cedric Gibbons, Jack Martin Smith; set d, Edwin B. Willis, Alfred E. Spencer; spec eff, Warren Newcombe; ch, Nick Castle; makeup, William J. Tuttle.

Musical/Comedy **Cas.** **(PR:A MPAA:NR)**

ROZMARNE LETO (SEE: CAPRICIOUS SUMMER, 1968, Czech.)

RUBA AL PROSSIMO TUO (SEE: FINE PAIR, A, 1969, Ital.)

RUBBER GUN, THE** (1977, Can.) 86m St. Lawrence/Schuman-Katzka c

Steve Lack *(Steve)*, Pierre Robert *(Pierre)*, Peter Brawley *(Peter)*, Alain Moyle *(Bozo)*, Pam Holmes *(Pam)*.

A group of sub-culture bohemians struggle between being artists and pushing drugs when they must decide whether or not to recover a cache of dope from a railway baggage locker. Even though the cops are watching the checkroom, they opt to try for it, but wind up getting nabbed. The performances are all commendable but that isn't enough to keep the pretensions from sinking the picture.

d, Allan Moyle; w, Steve Lack; ph, Frank Vitale, Jim Lawrence; m, Lewis Furey; ed, John Laing.

Drama **(PR:C MPAA:NR)**

RUBBER RACKETEERS*½ (1942) 67m King Bros./MON bw

Ricardo Cortez *(Gilin)*, Rochelle Hudson *(Nikki)*, Bill Henry *(Bill Barry)*, Barbara Read *(Mary Dale)* Milburn Stone *(Angel)*, Dewey Robinson *(Larkin)*, John Abbott *(Dumbo)*, Pat Gleason *(Curley)*, Dick Rich *(Mule)*, Alan Hale, Jr. *(Red)*, Sam Edwards *(Freddy Dale)*, Kam Tong *(Tom)*, Dick Hogan *(Bert)*, Marjorie Manners *(Lila)*, Alex Callam *(Butch)*.

A bootleg tire blows out and Henry's buddy is killed in the accident. He rallies his defense plant workers to stop this illegal activity and sets out to stop Cortez and his gang. The climactic scene shows Henry's forces battling the bad guys at the gang's headquarters. When the movie was released, rubber bootlegging was a real activity, and a warning at the end of the movie tells people to be leery of low-handed dealers.

p, Maurice King; d, Harold Young; w, Henry Blankfort; ph, L. William O'Connell; ed, Jack Dennis; md, David Chudnow; art d, Frank Dexter.

Crime Drama **(PR:A MPAA:NR)**

RUBY½** (1971) 90m Bartlett c

Ruth Hurd *(Ruby)*, Phillip Webber *(Clifford)*, Joanie Andrews *(Mother)*, George Bartlett *(Father)*, Danny Kosow *(Singer)*, Susan Peters *(Girl)*.

An amusing low-budget black comedy which chronicles the dull lives of a Midwestern community. Filmmaker Bartlett cast a group of nonprofessional actors to play his characters and they rise to the occasion admirably, breathing life and compassion into roles that could have been quite unsympathetic with viewers.

p&d, Dick Bartlett; w, Ray Loring, Bartlett; ph, Bartlett; m, Loring; ed, Bartlett.

Comedy **(PR:C MPAA:NR)**

RUBY* (1977) 84m Steve Krantz/Dimension c

Piper Laurie *(Ruby Claire)*, Stuart Whitman *(Vince Kemper)*, Roger Davis *(Dr. Keller)*, Janit Baldwin *(Leslie Claire)*, Crystin Sinclaire *(Lila June)*, Paul Kent *(Louie)*, Len Lesser *(Barney)*, Jack Perkin *(Avery)*, Edward Donno *(Jess)*, Sal Vecchio *(Nicki)*, Fred Kohler *(Jake Miller)*, Rory Stevens *(Donny)*, Raymond Kark *(1st Man)*, Jan Burrell *(1st Woman)*, Kip Gillespie *(Herbie)*, Tamar Cooper *("A"Woman)*, Patricia Allison *(Pickup Man's Wife)*, Stu Olson *("A" Man)*, Mary Robinson *(Sheriff's Wife)*, Michael Alldredge *(Sheriff's Wife's Date)*, Allison Hayes *(The Fifty-Foot Woman)*.

Laurie stars as the owner of a drive-in who had an affair with a gangster who was gunned down 16 years earlier. His spirit returns through their deaf-mute daughter and he sets out to get revenge. Plenty of revenge is gotten, but the suspense and thrills just aren't there.

p, George Edwards; d, Curtis Harrington, Stephanie Rothman; w, Edwards, Barry Schneider (based on a story by Steve Krantz); ph, William Mendenhall; m, Don Ellis; ed, Bill McGee; art d, Tom Rasmussen; set d, Charles D. Tomlinson; cos, Rasmussen; m/l, "Ruby," Ellis, Don Dunn (sung by Dunn), "Love's So Easy," Ellis, Sally Stevens; makeup, Jeffery B. Angell, Cid Urrutia.

Horror **Cas.** **(PR:O MPAA:R)**

RUBY GENTRY** (1952) 82m Fox bw

Jennifer Jones *(Ruby Gentry)*, Charlton Heston *(Boake Tackman)*, Karl Malden *(Jim Gentry)*, Tom Tully *(Jud Corey)*, Bernard Phillips *(Dr. Saul Manfred)*, James Anderson *(Jewel Corey)*, Josephine Hutchinson *(Letitia Gentry)*, Phyllis Avery *(Tracy McAuliffe)*, Herbert Heyes *(Judge Tackman)*, Myra Marsh *(Ma Corey)*, Charles Cane *(Cullen McAuliffe)*, Sam Flint *(Neil Fallgren)*, Frank Wilcox *(Clyde Pratt)*.

The best thing about this sordid melodrama is Roemheld's subtle score; nothing else about the movie is subtle . There are so many story "conveniences" that it's soon unbelievable, as though written by Tennessee Williams but edited by Irwin Allen. Jones is the daughter of Tully, a North Carolina manager of a hunting lodge next to a swamp. She meets Heston, the poor scion of a once-rich local family. They fall in love but when Heston's pleas for financing his new ventures fall on the deaf ears of Malden, a wealthy man who controls the area, and the other business people, Heston decides that a marriage of convenience might be just the ticket (same thing as in ROOM AT THE TOP). Heston marries Avery, the rich daughter of Cane. Jones is miffed at being rejected and she weds Malden when his crippled wife, Hutchinson, dies. The local snobs won't accept Jones into their society because she's from dirtpoor people. Malden knows that Jones and Heston once had an affair and he is jealous. Malden dies in a boating accident but Jones is suspected of having done him in and is shunned by everyone. She is now the heiress to all of Malden's wealth and exacts revenge by calling in loans, foreclosing properties, etc. Heston's lands are flooded and he rapes her. This suddenly brings the two of them together again, much to the consternation of Jones' brother, a religious zealot, Anderson. He wants to save her soul and thinks she can find salvation only if she stays away from Heston. Anderson, in his fervor, kills Heston, then is himself killed by Jones and she is left alone, a rich woman who will probably be able to buy her way out of all this. A muddy, steamy picture that owes much to Larry Adler's harmonica version of the song, which became a hit, and probably boosted the box office take, even though it wasn't deserved.

p, Joseph Bernhard, King Vidor; d, Vidor; w, Silvia Richards (based on a story by Arthur Fitz-Richard); ph, Russell Harlan; m, Heinz Roemheld; ed, Terry Morse; md, David Chudnow; art d, Dan Hall; set d, Ed Boyle; m/l, "Ruby," Mitchell Parish, Roenheld.

Drama **Cas.** **(PR:C-O MPAA:NR)**

RUBY VIRGIN, THE (SEE: HELL'S ISLAND, 1955)

RUCKUS½** (1981) 91m New World c (AKA: THE LONER)

Dirk Benedict, Linda Blair, Richard Farnsworth, Matt Clark, Jon Van Ness, Ben Johnson, Taylor Lacher.

For those rabid RAMBO fans out there, here is news: hero Stallone wasn't the first one to come up with the troubled-Vietnam-vet-vs.-narrow-minded-small-town concept used in FIRST BLOOD. Good ol' Roger Corman and his crew at New World were a full year ahead of him. Benedict stars as a reticent vet wandering through Alabama minding his own business who runs afoul of local town boss Johnson and his goons. Refusing to stop and talk to a rowdy group of rednecks looking for trouble, Benedict is forced to perform some karate moves on the boys, an act which does not endear him to kindly sheriff Farnsworth who must then track him down. While not as expensive and slick as FIRST BLOOD, it's not as violent, mindless, or pretentious either.

p, Paul Maslansky; d&w, Max Kleven; m/l, Willie Nelson, Hank Cochran.

Drama **Cas.** **(PR:C MPAA:PG)**

RUDE BOY*** (1980, Brit.) 120m Buzzy Enterprises/Atlantic c

Ray Gange *(Ray)*, The Clash [Joe Strummer, Mick Jones, Paul Simonon, Nicky "Topper" Headon] *(Themselves)*, John Green *(Road Manager)*, Barry Baker

(*Roadie*), Terry McQuade (*Terry*), Caroline Coon (*Clash Girl Friend*), Elizabeth Young, Sarah Hall (*Ray's Girl Friends*), Colin Bucksey (*CID Officer*), Colin Richards (*Sex Shop Customer*), Lizard Brown (*Byron*), Hicky Etienne (*Drum*), Inch Gordon (*Inch*), Lee Parker (*Eel*), Kenny Joseph (*Solicitor's Clerk*), Jimmy Pursey (*Guest Singer*).

Often annoying, but ultimately fascinating feature has Gange a young man in bleak modern London with no job, no prospects, and no hope. As he drifts through the decline of empire, he gets a job as a roadie with the punk rock group, The Clash (playing themselves), gets fired in short order, drinks a lot, and ends up not far from where he started, nowhere. An intriguing mixture of documentary, improvisation, and fiction, the film's aimless structure reflects the apathy gripping Gange. The highlights of the film are several actual concert performances by The Clash, easily the best of the groups to come out of the punk rock movement of the late 1970s. A surprisingly well-made film, RUDE BOY is hardly for all audiences, but a provocative experience for those willing to put up with it. The British version runs 133 minutes.

p&d, Jack Hazan, David Mingay; w, Hazan, Mingay, Ray Gange; ph, Hazan; m, Joe Strummer, Mick Jones; ed, Mingay, Peter Goddard.

Drama   Cas.   (PR:O MPAA:R)

RUDYARD KIPLING'S JUNGLE BOOK   (SEE: JUNGLE BOOK, 1942)

RUGGED O'RIORDANS, THE**   (1949, Aus.) 76m UNIV bw (AKA: SONS OF MATTHEW)

Michael Pate (*Shane*), Wendy Gibb (*Cathy*), John O'Malley (*Matthew*), Thelma Scott (*Jane*), Ken Wayne (*Barney*), John Unicombe (*Terry*), John Ewart (*Mickey*), Tommy Burns (*Luke*), Jimmy White (*The Boy Mickey*).

Irish immigrants try to make a go of it on the rugged outland terrain of Australia. After raising the family, the sons make their own marks in the untamed wilderness. One thing two of them try to tame is love for the same girl. The Australian footage is spectacular and adds a great deal to the story that enjoys a good balance of romance and heroism.

p&d, Charles Chauvel; w, Chauvel, Elsa Chauvel, Maxwell Dunn; ph, Bert Nicholas, Carl Kayser; m, Henry Cripps; ed, Terry Banks.

Drama   (PR:A MPAA:NR)

RUGGLES OF RED GAP**   (1935) 76m PAR bw

Charles Laughton (*Marmaduke Ruggles*), Mary Boland (*Effie Floud*), Charlie Ruggles (*Egbert Floud*), ZaSu Pitts (*Mrs. Judson*), Roland Young (*George Van Bassingwell*), Leila Hyams (*Nell Kenner*), Maude Eburne (*Ma Pettingill*), Lucien Littlefield (*Charles Belknap-Jackson*), Leota Lorraine (*Mrs. Belknap-Jackson*), James Burke (*Jeff Tuttle*), Dell Henderson (*Sam*), Baby Ricardo Lord Cezon (*Baby Judson*), Brenda Fowler (*Judy Ballard*), Augusta Anderson (*Mrs. Wallaby*), Sarah Edwards (*Mrs. Myron Carey*), Clarence Hummel Wilson (*Jake Henshaw*), Rafael Storm (*Clothing Salesman*), Frank Rice (*Hank*), Victor Potel (*Curly*), George Burton (*Buck Squires*), William J. Welsh (*Eddie*), Lee Kohlmar (*Red Gap Jailer*), Harry Bernard (*Bartender*), Alice Ardell (*Lisette*), Rolfe Sedan (*Barber*), Jack Norton (*Barfly*), Jim Welch (*Bit in Saloon*), Willie Fung (*Chinese Servant*), Libby Taylor (*Servant*), Armand Kaliz (*Clothing Salesman*), Harry Bowen (*Photographer*), Henry Roquemore (*Frank, Patron*), Heinie Conklin (*Waiter*), Edward LeSaint (*Patron*), Charles Fallon (*Waiter in Paris Cafe*), Genaro Spagnoli (*Frank the Cabman*), Albert Petit (*Waiter at Carousel*), Carrie Daumery, Isabelle La Mal (*Effie's Guests in Paris*), Ernest S. [Ernie] Adams (*Dishwasher*), Frank O'Connor (*Station Agent*).

The 1915 novel by Wilson was first done by Essanay as a silent starring Taylor Holmes in 1918. Paramount acquired the rights and made it again in 1923 with a youthful Edward Everett Horton in the lead. Casting Laughton in this version was inspired. Another of his films, MUTINY ON THE BOUNTY, won the Best Picture Award (this was also nominated) from the Academy and audiences had the chance to see, in one season, the breadth of Laughton's talents. He'd already proved himself as HENRY VIII but few knew that he could be funny as well as pompous, underplay as well as emote, and show a subtle comedic side to match the sinister characters he'd essayed in a few other films. This is a movie filled with "character" actors. Nobody sleek or svelte or jut of jaw or even with a well-turned ankle. In other words, they all look like real human beings and that's what makes it such a pleasure. Laughton is a Jeeves character, the ultimate valet. He works for Roland Young, an impoverished Bertie Wooster type with a penchant for poker. Ruggles, a rough U.S. rancher is in Europe with his wife, Boland, who would like to be a lady, but her husband is given to boots, outlandish clothes, and huge cowboy hats. Ruggles and Young get into a poker game, and when Young loses everything, he bets his butler, Laughton, against the pot and loses again. Laughton, Ruggles, and another crude pal of Ruggles', Burke, have a night on the town in Paris that is hysterically funny before Laughton packs up everything and goes to Red Gap, a brawling frontier town in the West. Once there, the locals think that Laughton is a member of British aristocracy and he decides that since he is here in the land of the free, there is no need to be an indentured servant. Laughton meets and falls for Pitts and leaves Ruggles and Boland to open his restaurant with his new mate. Eventually, Young comes to visit the small town, meets Eburne, falls in love with her, and decides to stay in Red Gap. Ninety fast-moving minutes directed with an eye toward huge laughs, RUGGLES OF RED GAP ends with a startling scene where the slightly tipsy Laughton stands and recites Lincoln's "Gettysburg Address, " and although it's seemingly out of place at first, Laughton's masterful reading and his sincerity soon win over the listeners and everyone in the audience. The picture was remade as FANCY PANTS, starring Bob Hope in 1950, but it was a tepid imitation. This isn't satire and it never disintegrates into farce. Rather, RUGGLES OF RED GAP stands as comedy with heart and probably could not be remade

again, as the kind of character actors who appeared in it just don't seem to be around any longer. More's the pity. One of McCarey's best.

p, Arthur Hornblow, Jr.; d, Leo McCarey; w, Walter DeLeon, Harlan Thompson, Humphrey Pearson (based on the play and novel by Harry Leon Wilson); ph, Alfred Gilks; m, Ralph Rainger, Sam Coslow; ed, Edward Dmytryk; art d, Hans Dreier, Robert Odell; cos, Travis Banton.

Comedy   (PR:A MPAA:NR)

RULER OF THE WORLD   (SEE: MASTER OF THE WORLD, 1935, Ger.)

RULERS OF THE SEA**   (1939) 96m PAR bw

Douglas Fairbanks, Jr. (*David Gillespie*), Margaret Lockwood (*Mary Shaw*), Will Fyffe (*John Shaw*), George Bancroft (*Capt. Oliver*), Montagu Love (*Malcolm Grant*), Vaughan Glaser (*Junius Smith*), David Torrence (*Donald Fenton*), Lester Matthews (*Lt. Comdr. Roberts*), Alan Ladd (*Colin Farrell*), David Clyde (*Second Mate Evans*), Mike Driscoll (*Helmsman*), Mary Gordon (*Mrs. Ogilvie*), Lionel Pape (*1st Secretary*), Ivan Simpson (*2nd Secretary*), Olaf Hytten (*3rd Secretary*), Denis D'Auburn (*First Officer Lewis*), David Dunbar (*Boatswain*), Barry Macollum (*Miller*), George Melford (*Landlord*), Wilson Benge, Dave Thrusby, John Power, Earl Askam, Charles McAvoy, Napier Rakes, Lawrence Grant, Jane Dewey, Clare Verdera, Neil Fitzgerald, Alec Craig.

A colorful story set when the steamboat was just being introduced as means to travel the colorful seas. Fyffe is the inventor trying to drum up interest in his machine. Fairbanks, a mate on a windjammer, wants to be the man to make it go and gets financial backing in London. The film gains speed when the ship moves out to sea as the crew stages a near-mutiny, the ship breaks down, and the storms buffet the ship night after night. The story is partly narrated, and is appealing throughout in both its historical and adventure aspects.

p&d, Frank Lloyd; w, Talbot Jennings, Frank Cavett, Richard Collins; ph, Theodor Sparkuhl, Archie Stout; m, Richard Hageman; ed, Paul Weatherwax; art d, Hans Dreier, John Goodman; spec eff, Gordon Jennings.

Drama   (PR:A MPAA:NR)

RULES OF THE GAME, THE***   (1939, Fr.) 110m N.E.F./Janus bw (LA REGLE DU JEU)

Marcel Dalio (*Robert de la Chesnaye*), Nora Gregor (*Christine de la Chesnaye*), Roland Toutain (*Andre Jurieu*), Jean Renoir (*Octave*), Mila Parely (*Genevieve de Marrast*), Paulette Dubost (*Lisette*), Gaston Modot (*Schumacher*), Julien Carette (*Marceau*), Odette Talazac (*Charlotte de la Plante*), Pierre Magnier (*The General*), Pierre Nay (*M. de Saint-Aubin*), Richard Francoeur (*M. La Bruyere*), Claire Gerard (*Mme. La Bruyere*), Anne Mayen (*Jackie*), Roger Forster (*Effeminate Guest*), Nicolas Amato (*The South American*), Tony Corteggiani (*Berthelin*), Eddy Debray (*Corneille*), Leon Larive (*The Cook*), Jenny Helia (*The Servant*), Celestin (*Kitchen Servant*), Lise Elina (*The Radio Reporter*), Andre Zwoboda (*The Engineer from Caudron's*), Camille Francois (*The Announcer*), Henri Cartier-Bresson (*The English Domestic*).

One of cinema's most monumental achievements, THE RULES OF THE GAME has become as important to the history of film as it's subject matter—the French bourgeoisie—has to history itself. Renoir passionately tackles the overwhelming pre-WW II class system, and succeeds in bringing forth the human complexities and frailties that accompany it. The catalyst that sets the social game in motion is a heroic aviator, Toutain, whose record-setting trans-Atlantic flight puts him on a plateau with Lindbergh. He is met by his trusted, rotund friend Renoir and a horde of ecstatic reporters. Toutain's elation turns to misery as he tells the listening radio audience that he made the flight for the sake of a woman—a woman who failed to greet him at the airport. Unsatisfied with Toutain's emotional burst, the reporter proceeds to interview the plane's engineer about the engine and gas tanks—a topic which is much more suited to the emotionally paralyzed upper class. Gregor, the one Toutain loves, is in the meantime being readied by her maid, the bubbly Dubost, for an evening out with her husband, a mechanical toy enthusiast played with a cool air by Dalio. Dalio's acceptance of his wife's relationship with Toutain leads him to break off with his mistress, the alluring Parely, but he chooses instead to continue the affair for fear of causing her pain. While this web of romance is escalating under Dalio's roof (Dubost has also boasted of her "open" relationship with her husband, Modot, extending the charade to the servile class), Renoir and Toutain are on their way home from the airport. A depressed Toutain veers off the road and steers the car into a ditch. (Years earlier, at the same location, Renoir was a passenger in a near-fatal auto wreck.) An irate Renoir insists on walking, angrily replying to Toutain's inquiry, "Are you hurt?" with a witty "I don't know if I'm alive. Your dashboard sneaked up and slugged me." Renoir, the film's centerpiece and the character with the clearest understanding of his environment, admits that he too loves Gregor (though he calls it friendship, and like the others, has difficulty distinguishing it from love) and proceeds to tell Toutain that he will never have her because he doesn't care about "the rules" that govern society. Renoir does, however, manage to get Toutain invited to a weekend shooting party at Dalio's country estate, La Coliniere, a remarkably beautiful location which pays respect to the impressionist works of Auguste Renoir (the director's father) and is greatly enhanced by the crystal clear deep-focus photography. The guests begin to file in, each bringing with them their own little drama—Dalio, who has invited his mistress, and is afraid of losing his wife to Toutain; Gregor, who is surprised that her friendship with Toutain has been perceived as love; Toutain, who can't live without Gregor; Parely, who can't live without Dalio; and Renoir, who is friend to everyone, lover to no one, and expected (though unable) to sort out the entire mess. The bourgeoisie aren't the only ones playing the game. On a parallel level, the servants also have their dramas, centering around maid Dubost; her seemingly stolid groundskeeper husband Modot; and Carette, a rather pathetic but loveable poacher who makes a play for Dubost. The shooting party becomes the central point of the film—a brutal game which comes complete with its rigid set of rules. If one fails to heed to them, death is the only alternative. Everyone partakes in the festive slaughter of the rabbits and pheasant except for Toutain and Renoir who are correct in fearing that they could be mistaken for the animals. After bagging their hits, the guests head inside for another round of entertainment. This time, however, it is of a less grizzly sort as Dalio holds a stage show in honor of Toutain's heroics. A song and dance number with Renoir dressed in a bear suit; a "danse macabre" with a performer dressed in a skeleton outfit; and Dalio's proud presentation of his most prized mechanical toy are meant to be the highlights. The guests become much more enthralled in a real-life drama that has a jealous Modot engaged in a slapstick chase of Carette, who scampers like a rabbit through La Coliniere as his pursuer chases him with a pistol. The chase continues and bullets are fired as onlookers roar with laughter. Each character's personal drama reaches its climax ("Stop this farce," demands Dalio of his major-domo, Debray, only to be asked, "Which one?"), but with little help from Renoir, who is engaged in an intense struggle to shed his stubborn bear suit. In the process of it all, Dalio has come to love his wife again and is willing to fight Toutaine to keep her. She, however, slips off with Renoir, who instead of preventing disaster inadvertantly causes it. They decide to take a walk outside with Gregor dressed in Dubost's coat. While inside, Modot has been disarmed and fired by Dalio. Dubost ignores her husband's wishes and chooses to stay on as Gregor's maid. In the name of fairness Dalio also fires Carette, realizing that it would be against the rules to let him continue his relationship with Dubost. In the most French of manners, Carette and Modot becomes friends as they leave the chateau, noticing on their way out Renoir walking to a secluded greenhouse with whom they believe to be Dubost, but is really Gregor. Driven to jealous insanity and goaded by Carette, Modot gets his shotgun and plans to kill both his wife and Renoir. Renoir and Gregor (whose back is to Modot and Carette, thereby making it impossible to see her face) exchange vows of love and a kiss. Upon deciding to leave on the next train together, Renoir runs back in the house to get his own jacket. A sudden wave of guilt and the realization that he is not the man for Gregor causes him to tell Toutaine that Gregor is awaiting him in the greenhouse. Toutaine runs to his love dressed in Renoir's coat and in a case of mistaken identity (actually a dual case) is shot down like a rabbit by Modot. Retaining his dignified air and heeding to his class' rules, Dalio reports to his guests that Toutaine's murder is simply an "unfortunate accident." A labor of love and passion, THE RULES OF THE GAME was born out of Renoir's discontent with the attitudes of his contemporaries in France—a country facing the impending Nazi occupation. "My awareness to the danger we were in," Renoir stated in an interview, "enabled me to find the right situations, gave me the right words, and my friends thought the same way as I did. How worried we were! I think the film is good. But it is not very difficult to work well when your anxiety acts as a compass, pointing you in the right direction." The film's production was not without its difficulties, however. Renoir had hoped to secure Simone Simon for the role of Christine, but a rising career in Hollywood taught her how to demand too large a salary. He decided instead to cast Gregor, a rather gawky Austrian princess and aspiring actress with whom he had fallen in love. Upon leaving the film's premiere, film critic and friend of Renoir's, Andre Bazin expressed his overwhelming support of the picture, but questioned why he cast such an "ugly woman" (a rather harsh description) in Christine's role. Bazin, unaware of Renoir's feelings for Gregor, received no answer from the surprised Renoir. When Renoir became aware of her limited acting range, however, he minimized her role and allowed the other characters (who were originally minor, such as Carette) to grow. The result is Renoir's most improvised film. As is always the case with improvisation, the production ran over-schedule and over-budget, but eventually, with the advancing Nazi troops approaching, THE RULES OF THE GAME made it to the screen. The drama did not stop with the film's premiere; however, instead, with all the excitement, adventure, and heartache of a wartime melodrama, the situation surrounding the film worsened. Booed unrelentlessly at its 1939 Paris premiere and banned both by the French government (who called it "demoralizing") and the Vichy government, THE RULES OF THE GAME is a classic example of how audiences react when confronted with a truthful portrayal of the world around them. Renoir set out to make a film which would be "an exact description of the bourgeoisie of our time." Judging from the film's violent reaction (Renoir saw one theater patron trying to start a fire in order to prevent the picture from being shown), the public does not want to see themselves on the screen. Renoir tried to appease his audience by recutting the picture. A 113-minute film soon became a 100 minutes long; then 90 minutes, then 85. The masterwork of French cinema was quickly being whittled away to nothing. After being pulled from distribution by the Nazis, THE RULES OF THE GAME was stored away in a warehouse which was subsequently bombed, making the dream of a complete version of the film seem unrealistic. It wasn't until 1959 that the film was restored to its nearly original form, thanks to the work of two enthusiasts, Jean Gaborit and Jacques Durand, who gathered up hundreds of cans of original footage and pieced the film together again with the help of Renoir. The Venice Film Festival premier of the restored version quickly put the film onto nearly every "top 10" list imaginable, eventually seating at the right hand of CITIZEN KANE in the 1972 "Sight and Sound" poll.

d, Jean Renoir; w, Renoir (in collaboration with Carl Koch, Camille Francois, and the cast); ph, Jean Bachelet; m, Saint-Saens ("Danse Macabre"), Salabert ("Nous Avons L've L'pied"), E. Rose ("Tout Le Long DeLa Tamise"), Vincent Scotto ("A Barbizon"), Mozart ("Danse Allemande"), Johann Strauss ("La Chauve-Souris"), Chopin ("Valse"), Monsigny ("Le Deserteur"), G. Claret, Camille Francois ("C'est La Guinguette"), Desormes, Delonnel-Garnier ("En Revenant D'la Revue"); ed, Marguerite Renoir; md, Roger Desormieres, Joseph Kosma; set d, Eugene Lourie, Max Douy; cos, Coco Chanel.

Drama Cas. (PR:C MPAA:NR)

RULING CLASS, THE*½** (1972, Brit.) 148m Keep/AE c

Peter O'Toole *(Jack, 14th Earl of Gurney)*, Alastair Sim *(Bishop Lampton)*, Arthur Lowe *(Tucker)*, Harry Andrews *(13th Earl of Gurney)*, Coral Browne *(Lady Claire Gurney)*, Michael Bryant *(Dr. Herder)*, Nigel Green *(McKyle)*, William Mervyn *(Sir Charles Gurney)*, Carolyn Seymour *(Grace Shelley)*, James Villiers *(Dinsdale Gurney)*, Hugh Burden *(Matthew Peake)*, Graham Crowden *(Truscott)*, Kay Walsh *(Mrs. Piggot-Jones)*, Patsy Byrne *(Mrs. Treadwell)*, Joan Cooper *(Nurse Brice)*, James Grout *(Inspector)*, Margaret Lacey *(Midwife)*, James Hazeldine *(Detective Sgt. Fraser)*, Hugh Owens *(Toastmaster)*, Griffith Davies, Oliver MacGreevy, Henry Woolf *(Inmates)*, Neil Kennedy *(Dr. Herder's Assistant)*, Julian D'Albie, Llewellyn Rees, Ronald Adam, Kenneth Benda *(Lords)*, Declan Mulholland, Cyril Appleton, Leslie Schofield.

A controversial comedy with plenty of tragedy mixed in, this was adapted by the playwright for the screen and would have been better with a crueler set of fingers at the typewriter to remove some of the indulgences. It's too lengthy but has many wonderful moments and mixes satire with farce and pain to create a movie with many faults, though it remains unforgettable. Andrews is a member of the House of Lords. He comes back to the family manse after having delivered a scathing speech to Parliament, and his alcoholic butler, Lowe, helps him prepare for what is apparently his nightly ritual. He dons long underwear, a tutu, a Napoleonic hat, puts a silken noose around his neck, and will swing a few times before landing on the ladder top that gives him safety and his life. This night, he inadvertently kicks the ladder over and dies of strangulation, thus leaving his membership in the House of Lords and his estate to his insane son, O'Toole. The sum of 30,000 pounds has been bequeathed to Lowe, but the rest of the family, Mervyn (Andrews' brother), Browne (Merwyn's wife), and Villiers (their dotty son) are shocked upon hearing the will read by Sim, their local bishop. Lowe chooses to stay in service, but now that he is rich, his attitude changes. He begins spouting communist slogans, drinking in public, and telling everyone in the family exactly what he thinks of them. O'Toole has been in a mental hospital for the last several years and he returns dressed as Jesus, a role he insists he is playing for real. He admits that when he prays to God, he finds that he's talking to himself. O'Toole spends many of his hours on a huge cross in the large living room and prates about distributing the family's wealth to the meek and downtrodden, something that frightens the others in the family who would never stand for that. There is only one way to rectify matters: have O'Toole sire a child, then toss him back in the looney bin and the family can assume control of the money by becoming the unborn child's guardians. Mervyn has been keeping a woman on the side, Seymour, and his plan is to get O'Toole and her wed as soon as possible. O'Toole, however, keeps telling everyone that he's already married to The Lady of the Camellias. Seymour arrives, dressed as Camille, sings a snatch from "La Traviata," and O'Toole is convinced that she is who she says she is. They get married and Seymour falls in love with O'Toole and admits that this is all Mervyn's plan. O'Toole sighs, understands, and, in his Jesus fashion, forgives them as they know not what they do. He totally accepts Seymour, they sing a duet of "My Blue Heaven," and he rides her into the bedroom on his tricycle. She's instantly pregnant. O'Toole's doctor, Bryant, wants to help and works on the crazed peer through the months of the pregnancy. Seymour is about to deliver their child when Bryant shows O'Toole the folly of his ways by introducing him to Green, another nut-case who thinks that he, too, is Jesus. O'Toole is shattered by meeting Green and must admit that he isn't Jesus at all; he's Jack. Everyone in the family is thrilled that he's come to his senses and ceases preaching the gospel of love and truth. What they don't know is that the "Jack" he refers to is, in fact, "Jack the Ripper," which they learn the hard way when O'Toole kills his aunt, Browne, then tosses the blame for it on Lowe's drunken shoulders. O'Toole takes his seat in the House of Lords and makes a stinging speech that endorses bigotry and revenge and sets the sleeping peers on their feet, madly applauding the nonsense he's espoused. By this time, Mervyn, Bryant, and Sim have all gone bonkers themselves and so the castle is almost empty. O'Toole returns home and Seymour runs to put her arms around him. O'Toole responds by stabbing her. She screams her last and in the background, their child repeats, "I am Jack!" so there's no question that the genetic strain of madness has been passed through O'Toole's loins to his young son. There's hardly a segment of British society that comes out of this unscathed: the public school system, the Houses of Parliament, snobbism, the Church, Jesus, homosexuality, servants, the upper classes, and just about everything else it's fashionable to decry. It's caustic, funny, often goes too far and stays too long to make the points. O'Toole was oscar-nominated as the mad earl and bites off Barnes' speeches with Shavian diction. Lowe steals every scene he is in and the creators of the TV show "Benson" may have looked long and hard at Lowe's irrascible butler before they turned him into a black man. There is more than just a passing similarity in the two. Sim's role as the aged bishop is one of his best in a long career. A lot of money was spent on this movie, making it one of the best produced British films of the year. Barnes' play was produced in England in 1969, then had a short run in Washington, D.C., in 1971, but it has yet to find anyone in the Broadway area to mount it. Joseph E. Levine, who made his fortune making sandals-and-swords Italian films was the presenter here, a far cry from his Steve Reeves epics. Interiors were done at Twickenham with locations shot in Buckinghamshire, Lincolnshire, Surrey, Hampshire, and London.

p, Jules Buck, Jack Hawkins; d, Peter Medak; w, Peter Barnes (based on his play); ph, Ken Hodges (DeLuxe Color); m, John Cameron; ed, Ray Lovejoy; prod d, Peter Murton; md, Cameron; cos, Ruth Myers; spec eff, Roy Whybrow; ch, Eleanor Fazan; makeup, Charles Parker.

Comedy Cas. (PR:O MPAA:R)

RULING VOICE, THE*½ (1931) 76m FN-WB bw (AKA: UPPER UNDERWORLD)

Walter Huston *(Jack Bannister)*, Loretta Young *(Gloria Bannister)*, Doris Kenyon *(Mary Stanton)*, David Manners *(Dick Cheney)*, John Halliday *(Burroughs)*, Dudley Digges *(Snead)*, Gilbert Emery *(Gregory)*, Willard Robertson *(Bailey)*, Douglas Scott *(Malcolm Stanton)*, Al Hill, Francis McDonald *(Hoods)*, Robert Elliott *(A

Reformer), Sidney Bracey *(Butler)*, Nora Cecil *(Nurse)*, Nat Pendelton, Carl Stockdale *(Board Members)*.

A lifeless gangster film starring Huston as the boss of an extortion racket. Huston and his thugs come down on produce merchants with what they call "The System." At the peak of his underworld power Huston begins to have second thoughts about his life of crime, spurred by his daughter Young's repudiation of him. Just as Huston decides to go straight, he is betrayed by his trusted henchman, Digges, and is killed. An early gangster film, but produced without the skill, insight, or passion of genre masterpieces LITTLE CAESAR (1930), SCARFACE (filmed in 1930 but not released until 1932) or PUBLIC ENEMY (1931).

d, Roland V. Lee; d, Byron Morgan, Robert Lord (based on a story by Roland V. Lee, Donald W. Lee); ph, Sol Polito; ed, George Amy.

Crime **(PR:A MPAA:NR)**

RUMBA** (1935) 77m PAR bw

George Raft *(Joe Martin)*, Carole Lombard *(Diane Harrison)*, Margo *(Carmelita)*, Lynne Overman *(Flash)*, Monroe Owsley *(Hobart Fletcher)*, Iris Adrian *(Goldie Allen)*, Gail Patrick *(Patsy Fletcher)*, Samuel S. Hinds *(Henry B. Harrison)*, Virginia Hammond *(Mrs. Harrison)*, Jameson Thomas *(Jack Solanger)*, Soledad Jimenez *(Maria)*, Paul Porcasi *(Carlos)*, Raymond McKee *(Dance Director)*, Akim Tamiroff *(Tony)*, Mack Gray *(Assistant Dance Instructor)*, Dennis O'Keefe *(Man in Diane's Party at Theater)*, Eldred Tidbury *(Watkins)*, Bruce Warren *(Dean)*, Hugh Enfield *(Bromley)*, Rafael Corio *(Alfredo)*, Rafael Storm *(Cashier)*, James Burke, Eddie Dunn, James P. Burtis *(Reporters)*, Dick Rush *(Policeman)*, Bud Shaw *(Ticket Taker)*, E.H. Calvert *(Police Captain)*, Hooper Atchley *(Doctor)*, Dick Alexander *(Cop)*, Don Brodie, Charlie Sullivan, Jack Raymond *(Gangsters)*, Frank Mills *(Bouncer)*, Ann Sheridan *(Dance Girl)*, Zora *(Specialty Dancer)*, Olga Barrancos, Luis Barrancos, Lara Puente, The Pimento Twins *(Rumba Dancers)*, Brooks Benedict *(Extra in Audience)*, Jane Wyman *(Chorus Girl)*.

Three "hos" and a "hum" to this blatant attempt to cash in on the success of BOLERO, another Raft starrer. This time he's a half-Cuban dancer working in Havana with Adrian. They do a dance act and he has plans to move up in the world before his strong legs are overtaken by varicose veins. Lombard is an heiress slumming in Cuba and she comes to the club one night with some of her society pals. He thinks Lombard is a knockout and when he discovers that she has her own posh yacht, she becomes even more attractive. She stops to pay him a compliment on his dancing, which annoys Lombard's escort, Owsley. The two men fight and Raft loses his job. He goes into the Cuban jungle and meets Margo, who teaches him the latest dance, the rumba. Raft gets a flash in his head and thinks that this will be the next big craze. He soon opens his own Havana night spot, and his dancing with Margo packs the joint every night. Lombard returns and offers to back Raft in a New York opening. Then Raft gets a message saying that he'll be killed if he goes back to New York because he allegedly once finked on an old gangster pal. Thomas owns the club where Raft will introduce his rumba with Margo but the press is agog with the story that he'll be risking his life for his art if he shows up. Tossing caution to the wind, Raft and Margo go on stage in the jam-packed club. Margo buckles under all the pressure and faints and Raft plans to do a solo when Lombard steps in and volunteers to be his new partner. The dance, which was staged by terps Veloz and Yolando, is a hit and Lombard and Raft fall in love. Then it's learned that the whole thing was a publicity stunt devised by Raft's manager, Overman, and Raft and Margo never knew it. Pheh! Veloz and Yolanda may be the only dance team ever to have two streets named after them. There is a corner in the San Fernando Valley of Veloz and Yolanda Streets where they lived for many years. Their daughter, Yolanda Veloz, didn't follow in their dance steps. She married Bernie Kopell of TV's "Love Boat" instead. In small roles as dancers, note Ann Sheridan and Jane Wyman. Wyman would marry a young Warner Brothers actor five years later, a man who made his name as "The Gipper' in KNUTE ROCKNE, ALL AMERICAN, and then gave up after playing the villain in the remake of THE KILLERS in order to do public service. And if you still haven't figured out who that is, we're not about to tell. Songs include: "I'm Yours for Tonight," "The Magic of You," "The Rhythm of the Rumba," "Your Eyes Have Said," "If I Knew" (Ralph Rainger, Leo Robin).

p, William LeBaron; d, Marion Gering; w, Howard J. Green, Harry Ruskin, Frank Partos (based on a story by Guy Endore, Seena Owen); ph, Ted Tetzlaff; ed, Hugh Bennett; art d, Hans Dreier, Robert Usher; cos, Travis Banton; ch, LeRoy Prinz, Raft-Lombard specialty by Veloz and Yolanda; m/l, Francois B. de Valdes.

Drama **(PR:A MPAA:NR)**

RUMBLE FISH**** (1983) 105m Zoetrope UNIV c

Matt Dillon *(Rusty-James)*, Mickey Rourke *(Motorcycle Boy)*, Diane Lane *(Patty)*, Dennis Hopper *(Father)*, Diana Scarwid *(Cassandra)*, Vincent Spano *(Steve)*, Nicholas Cage *(Smokey)*, Christopher Penn *(B.J.)*, Larry Fishburne *(Midget)*, William Smith *(Patterson)*, Michael Higgins *(Harrigan)*, Glenn Withrow *(Biff)*, Tom Waits *(Benny)*, Herb Rice, Maybelle Wallace, Nona Manning, Domino, Gio, S.E. Hinton, Emmett Brown, Tracey Walter, Lance Guecia, Bob Maras, J.T. Turner, Keeva Clayton, Kirsten Hayden, Karen Parker, Sussannah Darcy, Kristi Somers.

Director Francis Ford Coppola is a risk-taker and sometimes it pans out (APOCALYPSE NOW) and sometimes it doesn't (ONE FROM THE HEART). RUMBLE FISH pays off in a big way. An art film for kids: that is what Coppola set out to create, and he did just that, but not just for kids. A highly stylized film that moves at the pace of a teenager remembering his summer vacation. Dillon is that teenager who strives to be like his hero-worshiped brother, Rourke, and bring back the days of the gangs. Rourke returns from a trip from California and disapproves of his brother's fighting. Dillon sees his brother's return as the catalyst to start the gangs up again. The film follows the two brothers as each tries to find his place in the world. Rourke finds that his reputation has his brother trying to live up to it and a lone police officer wanting him gone. Dillon wants to be like his brother and Rourke, knowing that the path he has taken has gone nowhere, must lead his brother in a different direction. In the end, Rourke is shot dead by the police officer when he breaks into a pet store and tries to set fish free into the river. Dillon finishes the deed and rides off to California. There are a couple of sub-plots that don't move the story but fill out Dillon's character. He has a relationship with Lane and loses her when his friend Cage sets him up with another girl at a party. Dillon learns later that Cage did so in order that he could go out with Lane. It becomes more and more obvious as Dillon interacts with people and handles situations that he will never be like his brother no matter how hard he tries. But this is only apparent to everyone else. Rourke is too much of a hero for Dillon; he will never measure up to his brother. This is a multi-layered film and it is to Coppola's credit that he kept things in vague terms and didn't become preachy as in so many teenage dramas. Burum's filming is fresh and surreal using deep focus and time-lapse photography. Steward Copeland's (drummer for the rock group The Police) haunting score blends well with Coppola's art-house elements making this film a real treat for all the senses. Rourke's mystic performance works well in Coppola's structured world and Dillon shows promising depth. The most underrated performance is Vincent Spano's, who plays Dillon's nerdy friend. With bleached hair and glasses, Spano shows great range as he plays a character totally opposite from those he has played in previous films. A brave and invigorating film from a filmmaker who stands above the mega-hit, mindless movies that have dominated Hollywood.

p, Fred Roos, Doug Claybourne; d, Francis Ford Coppola; w, S.E. Hinton, Coppola (based on a novel by Hinton); ph, Stephen H. Burum (Technicolor); m, Stewart Copeland; ed, Barry Malkin; prod d, Dean Tavoularis; cos, Marge Bowers; ch, Michael Smuin.

Drama **Cas.** **(PR:O MPAA:R)**

RUMBLE ON THE DOCKS** (1956) 82m COL bw

James Darren *(Jimmy Smigelski)*, Laurie Carroll *(Della)*, Michael Granger *(Joe Brindo)*, Jerry Janger *(Rocky)*, Robert Blake *(Chuck)*, Edgar Barrier *(Pete Smigelski)*, Celia Lovsky *(Anna Smigelski)*, David Bond *(Dan Kevlin)*, Timothy Carey *(Frank Mangus)*, Dan Terranova *(Tony Lightning)*, Barry Froner *(Poochie)*, Don Devlin *(Wimpie)*, Stephen H. Sears *(Cliffie)*, Joseph Vitale *(Ferdinand Marchesi)*, David Orrick *(Gotham)*, Larry Blake *(Fitz)*, Robert C. Ross *(Gil Danco)*, Steve Warren *(Sully)*, Don Garrett *(Bo-Bo)*, Joel Ashley *(Fuller)*, Salvatore Anthony *(14-year-old)*, Freddy Bell and his Bellboys.

Darren is the leader of a New York street gang who gets involved with mobster Granger who runs the local longshoremens' union. The youth's father, Barrier, was crippled by Granger and his thugs in a union riot and throws his son out of the house when he learns of Darren's new friend. Barrier and a few friends are trying to set up a rival union, and, when one of the men is killed by the gangsters, Darren decides to go to the police. Granger and his men try to stop him, but the youth handles them, and right prevails once again. RUMBLE ON THE DOCKS ran as the second bill with DON'T KNOCK THE ROCK starring Bill Haley and The Comets.

p, Sam Katzman; d, Fred F. Sears; w, Lou Morheim, Jack Dewitt (based on a novel by Frank Paley); ph, Benjamin H. Kline; ed, Jerome Thoms; art d, Paul Palmentola; m/l Jimmy DeKnight, Mildred Phillips, Freddie Bell, Pep Latanzi.

Crime Drama **(PR:A MPAA:NR)**

RUMPELSTILTSKIN** (1965, Ger.) 79m Forster /Trans-International c (RUMPELSTILZCHEN)

Werner Kruger *(Rumpelstiltskin)*, Liane Croon *(Miller's Daughter)*, Wilhelm Grothe, Gunter Hertel, F.W. Schroder-Schrom, Harry Wustenhagen, Helmut Ziegner.

A German version of the Grimm Brothers' written version of the old folk tale about the miller's daughter who mortgages her first-born to a deformed dwarf in return for the secret of the ability to spin straw into gold, a trick which gains her a king's hand in marriage. Strictly for children. Released in West Germany in 1955.

p, K. Gordon Murray; d, Herbert B. Fredersdorf; w, Christof Schulz-Gellen (based on the folk tale recounted by Jakob and Wilhelm Grimm), ph, Ted Kornowicz (Agfacolor); m, Richard Stauch; ed, Lisa Thiemann; art d, Alfred Butow.

Fantasy **(PR:A MPAA:NR)**

RUMPELSTILZCHEN (SEE: RUMPELSTILTSKIN, 1965, Ger.)

RUN ACROSS THE RIVER* (1961) 74m Cameo/Citation-Sutton-Pathe bw

William Lazarus *(Artist)*, Joan Calistri *(Artist's Sister)*, Curt Conway *(Engineer)*, Gordon Peters *(Gang Leader)*, George Cathery *(Gang Leader's Partner)*, Shirley Grayson, Robert Carricart.

A predictable crime film with Lazarus witnessing the kidnaping and ultimate murder of his girl friend's engineer brother, Conway. The engineer is abducted by a group of thugs led by businessman Peters, who believes Conway knows of uranium mines in South Africa. Conway is killed, Lazarus goes to the police, Peters is captured, and Lazarus gets the girl. The story line is so old and worn out that you'll enjoy it more with your eyes closed and with a comfortable pillow.

p, Everett Chambers, Charles Weiss, David J. Cogen; d, Chambers; w, Lee Gillen.

Crime Drama **(PR:A MPAA:NR)**

RUN, ANGEL, RUN** (1969) 95m Fanfare c

William Smith *(Angel)*, Valerie Starrett *(Laurie)*, Gene Shane *(Ron)*, Lee De Broux *(Pappy)*, Eugene Cornelius *(Space)*, Paul Harper *(Chic)*, Earl Finn *(Turk)*, William Bonner *(Duke)*, Dan Kemp *(Dan Felton)*, Ann Fry *(Flo Felton)*, Margaret Markov *(Meg Felton)*, Brian Rapp, Jennifer Starrett, Jeb Adams *(The Felton Children)*, Lou Robb *(Roger)*, Homer Thurman *(Elmo)*, Austin Roberts *(Harry)*, Stafford Morgan *(Stan)*, Rachel Romen *(Maggy)*, Joy Wilkerson *(Estelle)*, Wally Berns *(Doctor)*.

Smith, a member of the Devil's Advocates motorcycle gang, writes an expose on a motorcycle gang and sells it to a magazine for $10,000. Before long, his fellow bikers come after him. With his girl friend, Starrett, he hightails it out of San Francisco and ends up at a sheep ranch in northern California. The ranch owner, Kemp, a former biker, gives Smith and his woman a job and a place to stay. In their search for Smith, meanwhile, the bikers run into Kemp's teenage daughter, Markov. Innocently, she tells them that Smith is staying with her family and, as her reward, she is gang raped by the group. After their fun with Markov, the bikers pursue Smith. Kemp arrives in time to send the bikers fleeing with a few shots from his gun. Starrett also helped write the screenplay under the alias "V.A. Furlong."

p, Joe Solomon; d, Jack Starrett; w, Jerry Wish, V.A. Furlong (based on a story by Richard Compton); ph, John Stephens; m, Stu Phillips; ed, Renn Reynolds; prod d, Peter Fain, Madeleine Oolie; art d, Paul Sylos; set d, Ray Boltz; m/l, "Run, Angel, Run," Billy Sherrill, Phillips (sung by Tammy Wynette), other songs, Byron Cole, James East, Phillips (sung by The Windows); makeup, Harry Thomas; stunts, Bill Catching.

Drama   **Cas.**   **(PR:O MPAA:R)**

RUN FOR COVER*½   (1955) 93m PAR c

James Cagney (Mat Dow), Viveca Lindfors (Helga Swenson), John Derek (Davey Bishop), Jean Hersholt (Mr. Swenson), Grant Withers (Gentry), Jack Lambert (Larsen), Ernest Borgnine (Morgan), Ray Teal (Sheriff), Irving Bacon (Scotty), Trevor Bardette (Paulsen), John Miljan (Mayor Walsh), Gus Schilling (Doc Ridgeway), Emerson Treacy (Bank Manager), Denver Pyle (Harvey), Henry Wills (Townsman), Phil Chambers, Harold Kennedy, Joe Haworth, Rocky Shahan, Bob Folkerson, Jack Montgomery, Frank Cordell, Fred Bailes, Howard Joslin.

Cagney was about 56 when he made this interesting western. A bit long in the tooth but his vitality showed through his wrinkles and the result was a pleasing picture with more time spent on characterization than is usual in horse operas. He's just done six years in prison for a crime he didn't commit, the result of a mistaken identity. His son died years before, and when he meets Derek, who reminds him of the late youth, the two team up. They're riding along, minding their own business, when a train robbery takes place and they are suspected of it. A posse comes after them and Derek is crippled in the fracas. Cagney takes Derek to the farm of Hersholt, where his daughter, Lindfors, helps nurse Derek. Meanwhile, Cagney and Lindfors fall in love. To rectify matters, the people of the nearby town appoint Cagney as their local sheriff with Derek as his deputy. Cagney has to go off on assignment, and while he does, Derek allows the mob to lynch a prisoner. Next, Derek makes a deal with another prisoner (Withers) to allow him to escape in return for a cut of the crook's money from a robbery. Cagney returns and goes after the escaped crook with Derek alongside. It's then that Cagney realizes Derek's double-dealing. Derek joins up with Withers and attempts to kill Cagney a couple of times; then, in the end, recovers his senses and saves his surrogate father before dying himself. Cagney didn't make many westerns and this was his first since THE OKLAHOMA KID. In Cagney's first film, SINNER'S HOLIDAY, he played under Withers, and he did the same thing in his third movie, OTHER MEN'S WOMEN. The times changed and Withers was now supporting Cagney. This picture also marked the end of the 40-year career of beloved Jean Hersholt, a man who had a special Academy Award named after him. The Danish actor was known for his humanitarian works and the Oscar is annually given to someone who best represents Hersholt's memory. In 1985, it was awarded to Buddy Rogers, who has helped more causes with time and money than just about anyone.

p, William H. Pine, William C. Thomas; d, Nicholas Ray; w, Winston Miller (based on a story by Harriet Frank, Jr., Irving Ravetch); ph, Daniel Fapp (VistaVision, Technicolor); m, Howard Jackson; ed, Howard Smith; md, Jackson; art d, Hal Pereira, Henry Bumstead; set d, Sam Comer, Frank McKelvy; cos, Edith Head; spec eff, John P. Fulton, Farciot Edouart; m/l, "Run For Cover," Jackson, Jack Brooks; makeup, Wally Westmore.

Western   **(PR:A-C MPAA:NR)**

RUN FOR THE HILLS zero   (1953) 72m Kinego-Rand bw

Sonny Tufts (Johnson), Barbara Payton (Jane Johnson), John Harmon (Jed), Mauritz Hugo (Hudson), Vici Raaf (Mrs. Cornish), Jack Wrightson (George), Paul Maxey (Sheriff), Harry Lewis (Mr. Carew), John Hamilton (Mr. Harvester), Byron Folger (Mr. Simpson), Sid Slate (Wagstaff), Charles Victor (Craig), Bill Fawcett (Orin Hadley), Deeann Johnson (Malinda), George Sanders (Tele Commentator), Rosemary Colligan (Cave Girl), Jack McElroy (Radio Announcer), Ray Parsons (Hermit), Michael Fox (Paleontologist), Jean Wills (Prancer Veach), Richard Benedict (Happy Day).

An interesting and almost daring comical story line is ruined by unintelligent writing and directing. Tufts is an insurance salesman who is so paranoid about atomic war, that he moves his family into a cave. Every opportunity for satire and social comment is missed; instead, the viewer is subjected to lame slapstick and predictable situations. Just as their money runs out, an earthquake moves a rock and Tufts and his wife find a gold mine. To call this film a bomb doesn't do it justice.

p, Mark O. Rice; R.D. Ervin; d, Lew Landers; w, Richard Straubb (based on a story by Leonard Neubauer); ph, Paul Ivanechevitch; ed, Irving Berlin.

Drama   **(PR:A MPAA:NR)**

RUN FOR THE ROSES*½   (1978) 93m Pan-American/Kodiak c (AKA: THOROUGHBRED)

Vera Miles (Clarissa), Stuart Whitman (Charlie), Sam Groom (Jim), Panchito Gomez (Juanito), Theodore Wilson (Flash), Lisa Eilbacher (Carol).

Gomez is the stepson of Whitman, the manager of a thoroughbred horse farm. More than anything, Gomez wants a horse of his own. His wish comes true when one of the horses gives birth to a colt with a deformed knee. The owner of the farm, Miles, doesn't want the bother of raising a hopeless horse, so she gives it to Gomez. Of course, the boy raises the horse to become a racer and, to the surprise of everyone but the audience, the horse wins the Kentucky Derby.

p, Mario Crespo, Jr., Wolf Schmidt; d, Henry Levin; w, Joseph G. Prieto, Mimi Avins; ph, Raul Dominguez (Metrocolor); m, Raul Lavista; ed, Alfredo Rosas Priego; stunts, Tom Sutton.

Drama   **(PR:C MPAA:PG)**

RUN FOR THE SUN   (1956) 99m Russ-Field/UA c

Richard Widmark (Mike Latimer), Trevor Howard (Browne), Jane Greer (Katy Connors), Peter Van Eyck (Van Anders), Carlos Henning (Jan), Juan Garcia (Fernandez), Margarito Luna (Hotel Proprietor), Jose Chavez Trowe (Pedro), Guillermo Talles (Paco), Guillermo Bravo Sosa (Waiter), Enedina Diaz de Leon (Paco's Wife).

Widmark is an adventurer and writer who is sought out by reporter Greer. She goes to Mexico hoping to do a story on why Widmark stopped writing, and when she does find him they fall in love. They hop on a plane which crashes in the Mexican jungles. The couple meet up with two strange men, Howard and Van Eyck, and Widmark discovers that Van Eyck is a wanted Nazi war criminal and Howard a British traitor. With their true identities known, the two subject Greer and Widmark to a deadly game of cat-and-mouse. Widmark uses his knowledge of the jungle and survival to turn the tables on the two men. This was an initial effort for the Russ-Field production company, and the first film in three years for the lovely Greer. The film includes two songs, "Taco" and "Triste Ranchero" (Frederick Steiner, Nestor Amaral).

p, Harry Tatelman; d, Roy Boulting; w, Dudley Nichols, Boulting (based on the story "The Most Dangerous Game" by Richard Connell); ph, Joseph La Shelle (SuperScope, Eastmancolor); ed, Fred Knudtsen; m, Frederick Steiner; art d, Al Y'Barra.

Adventure   **(PR:A MPAA:NR)**

RUN FOR YOUR MONEY, A*   (1950, Brit.) 83m Ealing Studios-Michael Balcon/UNIV bw

Donald Houston (Dai Jones), Moira Lister (Jo), Alec Guinness (Whimple), Meredith Edwards (Twm Jones), Hugh Griffith (Huw Price), Clive Morton (Editor), Leslie Perrins (Barney), Joyce Grenfell (Mrs. Pargiter), Edward Rigby (Beefeater), Julie Milton (Bronwen), Peter Edwards (Davies), Dorothy Bramhall (Jane Benson), Desmond Walter-Ellis (Announcer), Mackenzie Ward (Photographer), Patric Doonan (Conductor), Andrew Leigh (Pawnbroker), Gabrielle Brune (Crooner), R. Meadows White, Charles Cullum, Ronnie Haines, Diana Hope, Dudley Jones, David Davies, Tom Jones, Richard Littledale.

Two Welsh coal-mining brothers win a contest and earn an all-day trip to London in a light-hearted comedy that puts them in one predicament after another. The two brothers win a contest for the most coal output sponsored by a local newspaper. But when they arrive in London, they miss their newspaper escort—Guinness—and become separated. One has a gold-digger after him who wants nothing more than to separate him from his wallet. As the other searches for his brother, he meets a friend from the village who is now residing in the local gutters. All this time, the newspaper escort has been feverish in attempting to find the two and ends up in jail. The brothers finally do find each other again—on the train back home.

p, Leslie Norman; d, Charles Frend; w, Frend, Norman, Richard Hughes, Diana Morgan (based on a story by Clifford Evans); ph, Douglas Slocombe; m, Ernest Irving; ed, Michael Truman; art d, William Kellner; cos, Anthony Mendleson.

Comedy   **(PR:A MPAA:NR)**

RUN FOR YOUR WIFE½   (1966, Fr./Ital.) 97m Sancro-Films Borderie/AA c (MES FEMMES AMERICAINES UNA MOGLIE AMERICANA)

Ugo Tognazzi (Riccardo Vanzi), Marina Vlady (Nicole), Rhonda Fleming (Nita), Juliet Prowse (Jenny), Graziella Granata (Louise), Carlo Mazzone (Carlo), Ruth Laney (Teenager), Sharon Obeck (Mary), Cherie Latimer, Louisette Rousseau (Call Girls), Robert Hulsh, Gigette Reiner, George Clow, Deanna Lund, Alex Johnson, Soni Compagna, Raniero Di Giovanbattista, Jamie Wyatt, Nancy McCarter, Michele Weigand, Carol Landrie, Marisa Malachini, Egidio Casolari, Michael Briggs.

Tognazzi is an Italian businessman who, while on business in the U.S., decides he's going to marry an American woman. He has an encounter with a woman in Miami, Prowse, but she's married; with Fleming, a rich Texan who has had too many husbands for Tognazzi. Every woman he meets either doesn't want to marry him or something about them scares him off. A stewardess, Granata, says no to his marriage proposal; his budding relationship with a teenager frightens the bachelor, and his relationship with a divorcee falls apart when her ex-husband comes back because of Tognazzi's praise of her. Things come to a halt when his marriage proposal to a whore is turned down. Dejected, Tognazzi goes back to his unexciting, but stable, relationship with his fiancee of 13 years.

p, Henry Chroscicki, Alfonso Sansone; d, Gian Luigi Polidoro; w, Rafael Azcona, Ennio Flajano, Polidoro (based on a story by Rodolfo Sonego); ph, Benito Frattari, Marcello Gatti, Enzo Serafin (Techniscope, Technicolor); m, Nino Oliviero; ed, Eraldo Da Roma; art d, Maurizio Chiari.

Comedy   **(PR:C MPAA:NR)**

RUN HERO RUN   (SEE: HELL WITH HEROS, THE, 1968)

RUN HOME SLOW**   (1965) 75m Joshua/Emerson bw

Mercedes McCambridge, Linda Gaye Scott, Allen Richards, Gary Kent.

Another bizarre performance for McCambridge has her leading her two brothers and sister-in-law on a rampage of bank robberies as a form of vengeance against the banker who refused her father the loan for necessary medical treatment. The father dies, sending McCambridge and her siblings on their road of revolt. McCambridge's role as the fiery gang head fits right in with the other odd characters she's portrayed throughout her career, most notably the gun-toting ranch owner in

JOHNNY GUITAR and the Mexican girl who aids in the ravishment of Janet Leigh with drugs during the motel sequence from TOUCH OF EVIL. This curious film is highlighted by a soundtrack by the outrageous Frank Zappa, done a year or two before he hooked up with the Mothers of Invention.

p&d, Tim Sullivan; m, Frank Zappa.

Western **(PR:C MPAA:NR)**

RUN LIKE A THIEF (SEE: MAKE LIKE A THIEF, 1966, Fin.)

RUN LIKE A THIEF*½ (1968, Span.) 92m Twincraft-Coral/Feature Film c (ROBO DE DIAMANTES)

Kieron Moore *(Johnny Dent)*, Ina Balin *(Mona Shannon)*, Keenan Wynn *(Willy Gore)*, Fernando Rey *(Col. Romero)*, Charles Regnier *(Piet De Jonge)*, Victor Maddern *(Abel Baker)*, Sancho Gracia, Bobby Hall, Luis Rivera, Vicente Roca, Scott Miller, Mike Brendel, Roman Ariznavaretta, Xan Das Bolas.

Moore is the only witness to an armored car robbery on a road in the Mexican jungle. All but one of the robbers are killed and Moore kills the survivor for the diamonds he had taken from the armored car. American mobster Wynn captures Moore, but Moore won't reveal where he hid the blue diamonds. Balin, Wynn's girl friend, aids in Moore's escape and the two try to get to the American border. Wynn and his men take chase and so does Rey, a colonel in the Diamond Syndicate Police. Rey kills Wynn and his hoods and Moore realizes that it was Rey who was behind the armored car heist. The corrupt police officer is killed in a glass factory when he tries to take the diamonds from Moore and falls into a furnace.

p&d, Bernard Glasser; w, Myron J. Gold; ph, Jack Willoughby, Federico Gutierrez Larraya; m, Johnny Douglas; ed, Peter Parasheles, Nicholas Wentworth; art d, Juan Estelrich, Santiago Ontanon; stunts, Joe Zboran.

Crime Drama **(PR:C MPAA:NR)**

RUN OF THE ARROW*** (1957) 86m Globe-RKO/UNIV c

Rod Steiger *(O'Meara)*, Sarita Montiel *(Yellow Moccasin)*, Brian Keith *(Capt. Clark)*, Ralph Meeker *(Lt. Driscoll)*, Jay C. Flippen *(Walking Coyote)*, Charles Bronson *(Blue Buffalo)*, Olive Carey *(Mrs. O'Meara)*, H.M. Wynant *(Crazy Wolf)*, Neyle Morrow *(Lt. Stockwell)*, Frank de Kova *(Red Cloud)*, Col. Tim McCoy *(Gen. Allan)*, Stuart Randall *(Col. Taylor)*, Frank Warner *(Ballad Singer)*, Billy Miller *(Silent Tongue)*, Chuck Hayward *(Corporal)*, Chuck Roberson *(Sergeant)*, Carleton Young *(Doctor)*, Don Orlando *(Vinci)*, Bill White, Jr. *(Sgt. Moore)*, Frank Baker *(Gen. Lee)*, Emile Avery *(Gen. Grant)*, Angie Dickinson *(Dubbed Voice of Yellow Moccasin)*.

A violent western drama about a man's search for his identity, starring Steiger as a Confederate soldier who hates the North with a bloodthirsty vengeance. On April 9, 1865, the last day of the Civil War, Steiger fires the war's last bullet. The victim is a Union lieutenant, Meeker, who eventually recovers from his wound. As a souvenir, Steiger gets the bullet back with an inscription that reads: "To Private O'Meara, Virginia 6th Volunteers, who shot this last bullet of the war and missed." Although Generals Lee and Grant sign the treaty at Appomattox, the war does not end for Steiger. He refuses to accept the "death" of the South, choosing instead to escape to the West. Once there, he joins a Sioux Indian tribe and, after proving himself in a ritual endurance test—"the Run of the Arrow"—he is taught their language and customs. He falls in love with Indian girl Montiel (whose voice was dubbed by RKO contract player Angie Dickinson because of Montiel's thick accent), who earlier defied Sioux tradition and risked being skinned alive by aiding Steiger during the Run. Tension grows between the Sioux and the cavalry when the latter announces plans to build a new fort—Fort Abraham Lincoln—on Indian hunting grounds. The fort is completed outside Sioux boundaries, although one rebellious Sioux, Wynant, refuses to trust the cavalry's peacekeeping gesture. When honorable U.S. captain Keith is killed by Wynant, Meeker (having fully recovered from his wound) is provided with an excuse to wage an all-out attack on the Sioux. Steiger travels to the fort in an attempt to quell the anger, but is promptly knocked unconscious by the vile and untrustworthy Meeker. The Sioux retaliate and, in a gruesome, painfully graphic battle, burn the fort to the ground. Meeker is taken prisoner and readied for skinning. Steiger, who is neither fully Sioux nor fully American, cannot stand to see such savagery or hear the victim's tortured screams and puts Meeker out of his misery with a gunshot—firing the same bullet into him as before. This time, however, he doesn't miss. Having made peace with himself and ending his own personal Civil War with the U.S., Steiger leaves the reservation, taking with him Montiel and their adopted son Miller. Carrying the Union flag, Steiger leads Meeker's wounded and fatigued troops to the safety of a nearby fort. Originally titled "The Last Bullet," RUN OF THE ARROW concerns itself with the obsessive and self-destructive frustration of Steiger's personal war. Instead of accepting the end of he Civil War as the "birth of the United States," Steiger's character prefers to see it as a death—an ending he will not accept. Steiger is the ultimate Fuller hero, filled with contradictions, but made richer and more complex because of them. By the film's finale, part of Steiger has rejected the Sioux by interrupting their ritual killing of Meeker. On the other hand, however, he cannot rid himself of the part which loves the Sioux ways—choosing to remain with Montiel and Miller. He doesn't fully accept the Sioux, nor does he fully accept the U.S. He kills Meeker at the end both out of hatred for him and his army and out of sympathy for the phyical torture he is experiencing. Far from the standard Hollywood B picture—this one makes you think—RUN OF THE ARROW is an exemplary entry which shows Fuller in top form. Completed during the last of RKO's production-distribution days, RUN OF THE ARROW was picked up by Universal-International for release.

p,d&w, Samuel Fuller; ph, Joseph Biroc (RKO-Scope, Technicolor); m, Victor Young; ed, Gene Fowler, Jr.; art d, Albert S. D'Agostino, Jack Okey; set d, Betty Granger.

Western **Cas.** **(PR:C-O MPAA:NR)**

RUN ON GOLD, A (SEE: MIDAS RUN 1969)

RUN SHADOW RUN (SEE: COVER ME BABE, 1970)

RUN SILENT, RUN DEEP*** (1958) 93m Hecht-Hill-Lancaster/UA bw

Clark Gable *(Comdr. Richardson)*, Burt Lancaster *(Lt. Jim Bledsoe)*, Jack Warden *(Mueller)*, Brad Dexter *(Cartwright)*, Don Rickles *(Ruby)*, Nick Cravat *(Russo)*, Joe Maross *(Kohler)*, Mary LaRoche *(Laura)*, Eddie Foy III *(Larto)*, Rudy Bond *(Cullen)*, H.M. Wynant *(Hendrix)*, John Bryant *(Beckman)*, Ken Lynch *(Frank)*, Joel Fluellen *(Bragg)*, Jimmie Bates *(Jessie)*, John Gibson *(Capt. Blunt)*.

After the lucrative teaming of Lancaster with Gary Cooper in VERA CRUZ (1954), Lancaster and his partners, Harold Hecht and James Hill, decided to pair their rising young star with a fading (but still box office) star, Clark Gable. Gable is a submarine commander in WW II whose sub is sunk by a Japanese destroyer dubbed "Bongo Pete" by Navy men, leaving Gable the only survivor. Back at Pearl Harbor, he is given command of another sub, the *Nerka*. Lancaster, the sub's executive officer, is upset because he expected to get the command, and the crew is upset because they don't trust a commander whose last ship went down with all hands save himself. Gable verbally battles with Lancaster, who is just short of mutinous, and drills the crew over and over in a tricky maneuver designed to torpedo "Bongo Pete" head on, an operation Gable calls the "down the throat shot." Ordered to stay well clear of Japan's dangerous Bongo Straits, the obsessed Gable disobeys. In short order the Japanese destroyer appears, barreling down on the sub. The long hours of drill pay off and the *Nerka*'s torpedoes go down "Bongo Pete's" throat. There's no time to celebrate, though, because a Japanese submarine was working in tandem with the sunken ship. The two subs stalk each other until Gable puts a couple of torpedoes into the enemy craft. But the perils aren't over yet. Surfacing, they find Japanese planes buzzing around like angry hornets. The sub manages to get below the surface, but Gable is killed, though he has earned the respect of Lancaster and the crew. Gable, two years and three films away from death, is plainly too old for his role, but he makes the most of it with a very good performance. The entire film, in fact, is one of the better submarine dramas ever made, tense and claustrophobic, and—in defiance of the Hollywood dictum that no movie without a love interest can succeed—a minimum of dalliances back at the base. On the set, things were rather tense, with Lancaster and his two partners arguing over the script. Gable was becoming worried about what was going to happen with his character when the dust settled. Although reasonably successful at the box office, it was ultimately overshadowed by another film that put an old star and a new star in a submarine, Cary Grant and Tony Curtis in OPERATION PETTICOAT (1959).

p, Harold Hecht; d, Robert Wise; w, John Gay (based on a novel by Comdr. Edward L. Beach); m, Franz Waxman; ed, George Boemler; art d, Edward Carrere; spec eff, Arnold Gillespie.

War Drama **Cas.** **(PR:A-C MPAA:NR)**

RUN, STRANGER, RUN (SEE: HAPPY MOTHER'S DAY. . .LOVE, GEORGE, 1973)

RUN WILD, RUN FREE½** (1969, Brit.) 100m Irving Allen/COL c

John Mills *(The Moorman)*, Gordon Jackson *(Mr. Ransome)*, Sylvia Syms *(Mrs. Ransome)*, Mark Lester *(Philip Ransome)*, Bernard Miles *(Reg)*, Fiona Fullerton *(Diana)*.

Lester (OLIVER! 1968) plays a 10-year-old boy who is psychosomatically mute. He becomes friendly with an ex-army colonel, Mills. The boy's parents, Jackson and Syms, have had no luck curing the boy, but Mills finds that the boy responds easily to a wild white colt. When the pony disappears from the moors Mills has young Fullerton give her kestrel to Lester to befriend for a while. Lester almost kills the bird when he spots his horse and chases after it with the falcon tied to his arm. Mills retrieves the horse and when Lester and Fullerton go riding the horse in a fog, the animal gets caught in a bog. Neither Mills nor Lester's parents can save the horse; it's only when the young boy speaks that the horse pulls itself out. An entertaining family film that is intelligently written and doesn't patronize its audience.

p, John Danischewsky; d, Richard C. Sarafian; w, David Rook (based on the novel *The White Colt* by Rook); ph, Wilkie Cooper, m, David Whitaker; ed, Geoffrey Foot; md, Whitaker; art d, Ted Tester; spec eff, Bill Warrington; m/l, "Run Wild, Run Free" Whitaker, Don Black.

Drama **(PR:A MPAA:G)**

RUN WITH THE DEVIL*½ (1963, Fr./Ital.) 93m Documento-Le Louvre/Jillo bw (VIA MARGUTTA; LA RUE DES AMOURS FACILES)

Antonella Lualdi *(Donata)*, Gerard Blain *(Stefano)*, Franco Fabrizi *(Giosue)*, Yvonne Furneaux *(Marta)*, Cristina Gajoni *(Marisa Maccesi)*, Spiros Focas *(Marco Belli)*, Claudio Gora *(Pippo Cantigliani)*, Corrado Pani *(Youth)*, Alex Nicol *(Bill Rogers)*, Marion Marshall *(Grace)*, Wera Dekormos *(Greta)*, Walter Brofferio.

A superficial recounting of a group of struggling artists in Rome and how each sells out, gives up, or commits suicide. The film is episodic, going from one poor artist to another with all the old cliches. Blain commits suicide when he finds out that the only person buying his paintings is his homosexual sponsor. Furneaux, a singer, does nothing but sleep with men and Fabrizi gives up his art and marries a German woman 20 years older than himself. As the colony's numbers diminish through suicide and departure, fresh young faces—filled with hope—turn up in the quarter to take their place. Expatriate American actor Nicol plays a would-be sculptor who stays in the environs only because he enjoys the life style in this lowbrow nonmusical rehash of Giacomo Puccini's opera "La Boheme".

p, Gianni Hecht Lucari; d, Mario Camerini; w, Franco Brusati, Camerini, Ennio De Concini, Uga Guerra (based on the novel *Gente al Babuino* by Ugo Moretti); ph, Leonida Barboni; m, Piero Piccioni; ed, Giuliana Attenni; art d, Dario Cecchi, Massimiliano Capriccioli.

Comedy/Drama **(PR:A MPAA:NR)**

RUN WITH THE WIND* 					(1966, Brit.) 95m GEFD bw

Francesca Annis (*Jean Parker*), Sean Caffrey (*Frank Hiller*), Shawn Phillips (*Paul Walton*), Jack Smethurst (*Bernie*), George Pastell (*Lennie*), Sheena Campbell (*Sue*), Mark York (*Tony*), Leslie Lawton (*Steve*).

Overly sentimental tear-jerker in which Annis leaves her boxer lover when blond-haired folk singer Phillips tickles her imagination with promises of a different life style. Annis tires of Phillips and heads back to her old beau, but by this time he wants no part of her. Songwriter-singer Phillips was best known for his obnoxiously long, blond hair; his ballads and folk songs were easily forgettable, all belonging to an era that is long dead.

p, James Ward; d, Lindsay Shonteff; w, Jeremy Craig Dryden.

**Drama					(PR:O MPAA:NR)**

RUNAROUND, THE* 					(1931) 82m RKO c (GB: WAITING FOR THE BRIDE; AKA: LOVABLE AND SWEET; WAITING AT THE CHURCH)

Geoffrey Kerr (*Fred*), Mary Brian (*Evelyn*), Johnny Hines (*Howard*), Marie Prevost (*Margy*), Joseph Cawthorne (*Lou*).

Brian is a chorus girl being pushed into marrying a wealthy man by her friend Prevost. Brian can't go along with the scheme and the expensive bracelet that has the man's apartment key attached to it. Her good behavior is rewarded by marriage to Kerr. A dud of a film that lost $160,000 at the box office. One reason for this was that the cast members were not big draws; another was that the entire film was shot in the expensive two-color Technicolor process, which was unusual for the time (most of its contemporaries which used the process had only brief sequences in color). The color process had been refined by this time; this was the first picture to use the reduced-grain Technicolor system. Critics of the time thought that the leading players looked better in black and white; Kerr had a blemish on one cheek which the process reproduced too perfectly.

p, Louis Sarecky; d, William J. Craft; w, Alfred Jackson, Barney Sarecky (based on a story by Zandah Owen); ph, Ray Ranahan; ed, Ann McKnight, George Marsh.

**Comedy Drama					(PR:A MPAA:NR)**

RUNAROUND, THE** 					(1946) 86m UNIV bw

Rod Cameron (*Eddie Kildane*), Ella Raines (*Penelope Hampton*), Broderick Crawford (*Louis Prentice*), Frank McHugh (*Wally Quayle*), Samuel S. Hinds (*Norman Hampton*), Joan Fulton (*Baby*), George Cleveland (*Feenan*), Joe Sawyer (*Hutchins*), Nana Bryant (*Mrs. Hampton*), Dave Willock (*Billy*), Charles Coleman (*Butler*), Jack Overman (*Cusack*), Dorothy Granger (*Desk Clerk*), Jack Rice (*Information Clerk*), Jane Adams.

Cameron and Crawford are competing private detectives who are hired by industrialist Hinds to find his presumed daughter, Raines. Father doesn't want daughter to marry a ship's deck hand and the first detective to bring her back will get $15,000. The two detectives battle with each other as they chase Raines down from San Francisco to New York and back. Turns out that Raines isn't the industrialist's daughter but his secretary, with whom he's madly in love. Highly derivative of Frank Capra's 1934 classic IT HAPPENED ONE NIGHT. One song, "My Blue Heaven," is sung by Cameron and Raines.

p, Joe Gershenson; d, Charles Lamont; w, Arthur T. Horman, Sam Hellman (based on a story by Horman, Walter Wise); ph, George Robinson; m, Frank Skinner; ed, Ted J. Kent; art d, Jack Otterson, Robert Clatworthy.

**Comedy					(PR:A MPAA:NR)**

RUNAWAY, THE*½ 					(1964, Brit.) 62m Luckwell/COL bw

Greta Gynt (*Anita Peshkin*), Alex Gallier (*Andrian Peshkin*), Paul Williamson (*Thomas*), Michael Trubshawe (*Sir Roger Clements*), Tony Quinn (*Prof. Hawkley*), Wendy Varnals (*Tania*), Denis Shaw (*Agent*), Howard Lang (*Norring*), Ross Hutchinson (*Leopold Cleaver*), Stuart Sanders (*Conway Brockfield*), John Watson (*Hazleton*), John Dearth (*Sgt. Hardwick*), Leonard Dixon (*Constable*), Ian Wilson (*Caretaker*), Arnold Bell, Anthony Pendrell (*Staff Officers*).

Gallier plays a chemist working as a spy for the Soviet Union in Paris shortly before the German takeover of France. With the imminent coming of the Nazis, Gallier and his wife steal money from their government and attempt to flee to South America. On their trip they are forced to stop at Trinidad, where Williamson does not allow the duo to pass without giving up their money. The action leaps 24 years into the future. Williamson is still working as a British agent, now involved in the investigation of a formula which has leaked through security. Once again he is brought in contact with Gallier, this time helping him to escape the ruthless clutches of Soviet agents. Despite a slight effort to add human qualities to the characters, this reads like nothing other than a stereotypical spy story.

p, Bill Luckwell, David Vigo; d, Tony Young; w, John Perceval, John Gerrard Sharp (based on the story by Perceval); ph, Jimmy Harvey; m, Wilfred Burns; ed, Norman Cohen; art d, Don Mingaye.

**Spy/Drama					(PR:A MPAA:NR)**

RUNAWAY BRIDE* 					(1930) 69m RKO bw

Mary Astor (*Mary*), Lloyd Hughes (*Blaine*), David Newell (*Heavy*), Natalie Moorehead (*Clara*), Maurice Black (*Dugan*), Paul Hurst (*Daly*), Edgar Norton (*Williams*), Esther Morton, Francis McDonald, Harry Tenbrook, Phil Brady, Theodore Lorch.

An idiotic comedy that is bogged in irrational situations and poorly timed jokes. Astor has jewels hidden in her purse by a thief who broke into her and her husband-to-be's pre-honeymoon hotel room. The crook is killed by the police and Astor is pursued by the dead man's cronies. Characters zip in and out like flies and the story line blurs into an undistinguishable garbage pile. Astor falls in love with

wealthy Hughes, cops chase crooks, crooks chase Astor, and everything falls into a predictable ending.

p, William Sistrom; d, Donald Crisp; w, Jane Murfin (based on the story "Cooking Her Goose" by H.H. Van Loan, Lolita Ann Westman); ph, Leo Tover; ed, Archie Marshek.

**Comedy					(PR:A MPAA:NR)**

RUNAWAY BUS, THE½** 					(1954, Brit.) 80m Conquest-Guest/Eros Films bw

Frankie Howard (*Percy Lamb*), Margaret Rutherford (*Cynthia Beeston*), Petula Clark (*Lee Nichols*), George Coulouris (*Edward Schroeder*), Belinda Lee (*Janie Grey*), Reginald Beckwith (*Collector*), Toke Townley (*Henry Waterman*), Terence Alexander (*Peter Jones*), John Horsley (*Inspector Henley*), Anthony Oliver (*Duty Officer*), Stringer Davis (*Administrative Officer*), Lisa Gastone (*Receptionist*), Frank Phillips (*Newsreader*), Sam Kydd, Michael Gwynne, Marianne Stone, Lionel Murton, Jimmy Young, Tedwell Chapman, Richard Beynon, Cyril Conway, Arthur Lovegrove, James Brown, Alistair Hunter.

British comic Howard—in his screen debut—is a bus driver who finds himself inadvertently involved in a gold heist. Howard is driving a bus load of passengers and a stolen cargo of gold from one airport to another in a blinding fog. The mixed nuts of passengers and the bumbling Howard make this light comedy an enjoyable, but soon forgotten, ride. Rutherford is superb as the feisty, umbrella-wielding old virago who turns out to be the criminal mastermind.

p, d&w, Val Guest; ph, Stan Pavey; m, Ronald Binge; ed, Doug Myers.

**Comedy					(PR:A MPAA:NR)**

RUNAWAY DAUGHTER 					(SEE: RED SALUTE, 1935)

RUNAWAY DAUGHTERS** 					(1957) 90m AIP bw

Marla English (*Audrey Barton*), Anna Sten (*Ruth Barton*), John Litel (*George Barton*), Lance Fuller (*Tony Forrest*), Adele Jergens (*Dixie*), Mary Ellen Kaye (*Mary Rubeck*), Gloria Castillo (*Angela Forrest*), Jay Adler (*Rubeck*), Steven Terrell (*Bob Harris*), Nicky Blair (*Joe*), Frank J. Gorshin (*Tommy*), Maureen Cassidy (*Maureen*), Reed Howes (*Henry*), Anne O'Neal (*Miss Petrie*), Edmund Cobb (*Detective*).

Three teenage girls leave their parents and head for the bright lights of Hollywood. The three girls all have problems at home, which is the cause of their trip west. Things in the sun don't go much better for the girls. One is killed when she drives a car over a cliff, another is forced into marriage when she becomes pregnant, and the third goes back to her family and finds that her parents have turned over a new leaf. The film was double-billed with SHAKE, RATTLE AND ROLL.

p, Alex Gordon; d, Edward L. Cahn; w, Lou Rusoff; ph, Frederick E. West; m, Ronald Stein; ed, Ronald Sinclair.

**Drama					(PR:A MPAA:NR)**

RUNAWAY DAUGHTERS, 1968 					(SEE: PROWL GIRLS, 1968)

RUNAWAY GIRL** 					(1966) 62m Caren/United Screen Arts bw

Lili St. Cyr (*Edella*), Jock Mahoney (*Randy Marelli*), Ron Hagerthy (*Mario Marelli*), Laurie Mitchell (*Winnie Bernay*), Booth Colman (*Angelo Guglietta*), Robert Shayne (*Walter Quillen*), June Jocelyn (*Louise*), Lisa Pons (*Tina*), Shary Layne (*Betsy*), Suzi Carnell (*Ruth*), Dusty Enders (*Jeanette*), Sandra Phelps (*Cleo*), Anne Graves (*Ginger*).

St. Cyr is a stripper who becomes a grape picker at a vineyard in California. The workers are suspicious of her, and the vineyard manager and his brother begin to compete for her affection. St. Cyr tells the women she works with who she really is and gives them her jewelry and perfumes. The dancer's manager shows up to take her back to the night clubs and strip joints, but St. Cyr decides to marry the manager and stay on at the vineyard.

p&d, Hamil Petroff; w, Stewart Cohn; ph, Ed Fitzgerald; m, Richard LaSalle.

**Drama					(PR:C MPAA:NR)**

RUNAWAY LADIES** 					(1935, Brit.) 56m International Players/Exclusive bw

Betty Stockfield (*Betty*), Hugh Wakefield (*Lord Ramsden*), Edna Searle (*Lady Ramsden*), Roger Treville (*Georges*), Raymond Cordy.

Inane farce centers on a lost dancing shoe which disappears from its owner, Searle, and threatens her marriage. Stockfield is the well meaning, but dumb, girl who attempts to return the slipper before any complications arise, but her efforts get Searle arrested as a jewel thief. Laughs are very few, with performers yielding their talent to the absurdity of the material. This film appears to have been shot simultaneously with a French version which was released in the U.S. in 1938 with the title THE SLIPPER EPISODE.

p, M. Haworth Booth; d, Jean de Limur; w, Tristram Bernard (based on the novel *Le Voyage Imprevu* by Bernard).

**Comedy					(PR:A MPAA:NR)**

RUNAWAY QUEEN, THE** 					(1935, Brit.) 69m British and Dominions/UA bw (GB:THE QUEEN'S AFFAIR)

Anna Neagle (*Queen Nadina*), Fernand Graavey (*Carl*), Muriel Aked (*Marie Soubrekoff*), Michael Hogan (*The Leader*), Gibb McLaughlin (*Gen. Korensky*), Miles Malleson (*The Chancellor*), Stuart Robertson Hay Petrie (*Revolutionaries*), Edward Chapman, Reginald Purdell (*Soldiers*), Clifford Heatherley (*A Diplomat*), David Burns (*Manager*), Trefor Jones (*Singer*), Tarva Penna, Herbert Langley, Helen Mar, Dino Galvani, Arthur Chesney.

When Neagle inherits a Ruritanian throne, revolutionaries led by Graavey force her into exile before her coronation. The revolution soon fails and Neagle is rethroned.

She falls in love with Graavey and they marry, forming a constitutional monarchy supported by all the people. This average musical features a good star turn by Neagle, but the whole film looks awfully dated.

p&d, Herbert Wilcox; w, Samson Raphaelson, Monckton Hoffe, Miles Malleson (based on the play "Die Konigin" by Ernst Marischa, Bruno Granichstaedten, Oscar Strauss; ph, F.A. Young; m, Strauss.

Musical (PR:A MPAA:NR)

RUNAWAY RAILWAY** (1965, Brit.) 55m Fanfare/Children's Film Fund bw

John Moulder-Brown (Charlie), Kevin Bennett (Arthur), Leonard Brockwell (John), Roberta Tovey (Carole), Sydney Tafler (Mr. Jones), Ronnie Barker (Mr. Galore), Graham Stark (Grample), Hugh Lloyd (Disposals Man).

When the local rail line threatens to shut down, a group of children rally to save it, capturing a gang of robbers in the bargain. Kids will like this average offering from the Children's Film Fund; adults beware. It features an infrequent film appearance by Barker, best known as one-half of the British TV comedy team, the Two Ronnies.

p, George H. Brown; d, Jan Danley-Smith; w, Michael Barnes (based on a story by Henry Geddes).

Children (PR:AA MPAA:NR)

THE RUNNER STUMBLES** (1979) 99m FOX c

Dick Van Dyke (Father Rivard), Kathleen Quinlan (Sister Rita), Maureen Stapleton (Mrs. Shandig), Ray Bolger (Monsignor Nicholson), Tammy Grimes (Erna), Beau Bridges (Toby), Allen Nause (Prosecutor), John Procaccino (Amos), Billy J. Jacoby (James), Sister Marguerite Morrissey (Sister Immaculata), Zoaunne LeRoy (Sister Martha), Don Riley (Maurice), Ted D'Arms (Sheriff), Kendall Kay Munsey (Louise), Casey Kramer (Marie), Jim Doyle (Matt Webber), Katharine Kramer (Sophie), Bill Dore (Judge), Jock Dove (Dr. McNabb), Larry Buck (Fire Chief).

This film casts Van Dyke as a Catholic priest accused of murdering a young nun with whom he was in love. In this film adaptation of the Broadway play, told in flashbacks, Quinlan plays the murdered nun, who taught at the parish school. Stapleton, who gives the movie's best performance, is Van Dyke's housekeeper, who knows exactly what happened and why. Director Kramer develops three stories at once: the accused priest's stay in jail, his relationship with the nun, and the trial. This device works well, allowing all three stories to be developed evenly, without becoming confusing or trite. The main problem with the film is a problem inherent to most play adaptations: too talky. This is a very static film, with most of the responsibility for story development left to explanatory dialog. The play and film are based on a 1927 murder case.

p&d, Stanley Kramer; w, Milan Stitt (based on his Broadway play); ph, Laszlo Kovacs (CFI Color); m, Ernest Gold; ed, Pembroke J. Herring; prod d, Alfred Sweeney, Jr.

Drama (PR:C MPAA:PG)

RUNNERS* (1983, Brit.) 110m Hanstall c

James Fox (Tom), Jane Asher (Helen), Kate Hardie (Rachel), Robert Lang (Wilkins), Eileen O'Brien (Gillian), Ruti Simon (Lucy), Max Hafler, Peter Turner, Bridget Turner, Lisa Howard, Deborah Hawley, Hazel Berry, Charla Haughton, Nicola Glew, Robert Lang, Shay Gorman, Anna Wing, Ursula Camm, Laurin Kaski, Paul Angelis, Julian Firth, Patrick O'Connell, Sarah London, Bridget Meade, John Holmes, Norman Lumsden, Ashley Harvey, Johnny Shannon, Holli Hoffman, Tim Faulkner, Ian West, Sidney Johnson.

Fox searches through the streets of London for his runaway daughter in this film, which is unable to reach its lofty goals. The film tries to tackle several issues but doesn't develop any theme well enough to make any serious statement. The story line follows Fox in his search for his daughter after everyone else has given up. On the way, he meets a woman searching for her son. Finally, father finds daughter working at a car rental firm, but she has no desire to return home. The reasons for her leaving home are as cliched as the themes the film tries to develop.

p, Barry Hanson; d, Charles Sturridge; w, Stephen Poliakoff; ph, Howard Atherton; m, George Fenton; ed, Peter Coulson; prod d, Arnold Chapkis; art d, Mark Nerin.

Drama (PR:A MPAA:NR)

RUNNING*½ (1979, Can.) 102m UNIV c

Michael Douglas (Michael Andropolis), Susan Anspach (Janet Andropolis), Lawrence Dane (Coach Walker), Eugene Levy (Richard Rosenberg), Charles Shamata (Howard Grant), Philip Akin (Chuck), Trudy Young (Pregnant Woman), Murray Westgate (Mr. Finlay), Jennifer McKinney (Susan Andropolis), Lesleh Donaldson (Andrea Andropolis), Jim McKay (Himself), Lutz Brode (Boston Race Winner), Deborah Templeton Burgess (Debbie Rosenberg), Gordon Clapp (Kenny), Marvin Goldhar (Maloney), David Laurence (Commentator), Robert Hannah (Stuntman), Donny Cooper (Black Teenager), Joel Bergman (Italian Teenager), Giancarlo Esposito (Puerto Rican Teenager).

A trite film about a man who trains to run in the Olympic marathon in Montreal. In this lifeless ripoff of ROCKY, Douglas (ROMANCING THE STONE, CHINA SYNDROME) is at the same time trying to patch up his marriage to Anspach. Douglas wants to make the U.S. team in an effort to redeem himself for failing to show up for the Pan-American games 10 years before. He makes the team, finishes last in the race, but is cheered on by the other runners as he makes it into the stadium.

p, Robert Cooper, Ronald Cohen; d&w, Steven Hilliard Stern; ph, Laszlo George; m, Andre Gagnon; ed, Kurt Hirschler; prod d, Roy Forge Smith; art d, Susan Longmire; cos, Lynda Kemp.

Drama **Cas.** (PR:C MPAA:PG)

RUNNING BRAVE*½ (1983, Can.) 105m Englander/BV c

Robby Benson (Billy Mills), Pat Hingle (Coach Easton), Claudia Cron (Pat Mills), Jeff McCraken (Dennis), August Schellenberg (Billy's Father), Denis Lacroix (Frank), Graham Greene (Eddie), Margo Kane (Catherin), Kendall Smith, George Clutesi, Derek Campbell, Maurice Wolfe, Albert Angus, Barbara Blackhorse, Carmen Wolfe, William Berry, Kaye Corbett, John Littlechild, Tantoo Martin, Gail Omeasoo, Billy Runsabove, Seymour Eaglespeaker, Merrill Dendoff, Michael J. Reynolds, Chris Judge, Paul Hubbard, Jack Ackroyd.

The film version of the life of Olympic runner Billy Mills trips over a number of cliches. Benson is cast as Mills, a Sioux Indian who finds it hard to adjust to life outside the reservation. He attends the University of Kansas, where he finds some success as a runner. He then joins the Marines, gets married, and prepares for the 1964 Olympics in Tokyo. The film handles the issue of prejudice against Indians superficially, and the stereotyped characterizations are offensive. Benson's portrayal of the winner of the 10,000-meter run just doesn't jell. There is something very irritating about Benson's performance; it's obvious he's acting, and he's trying hard to hide it. Benson's performance and the cliche-ridden script turn this biographical film into a quickly forgotten bore. Director Donald Shebib took his name off the film's credits.

p, Ira Englander; d, D.S. Everett [Donald Shebib]; w, Henry Bean, Shirl Hendryx; ph, Francois Protat (Medallion Color); m, Mike Post; ed, Tony Lower, Earl Herdan; prod d, Carol Spier; art d, Barbara Danphy; set d, Rose Marie McSherry.

Drama **Cas.** (PR:C MPAA:PG)

RUNNING MAN, THE** (1963, Brit.) 103m Peet/COL c

Laurence Harvey (Rex Black), Lee Remick (Stella Black), Alan Bates (Stephen Maddox), Felix Aylmer (Parson), Eleanor Summerfield (Hilda Tanner), Allan Cuthbertson (Jenkins), Harold Goldblatt (Tom Webster), Noel Purcell (Miles Bleeker), Ramsay Ames (Madge Penderby), Fernando Rey (Police Official), Juan Jose Menendez (Roberto), Eddie Byrne (Sam Crewdson), Colin Gordon (Solicitor), John Meillon (Jim Jerome), Roger Delgado (Spanish Doctor), Fortunio Bonanova (Bank Manager), Shirley Gale (Florence), Jose Calvo, Joe Lynch, Freddy Roberts, Adriano Dominguez, James Neylin, Pamela Mant, Herbert Curiel, Antonio Padilla Ruiz, Lockwood West, Bob Cunningham.

The story of someone who fakes his (or her) own death to collect insurance is not new and a similar plot was used in the Tony Perkins-Sophia Loren picture FIVE MILES TO MIDNIGHT a year or so before this. The difference between the movies was the director. This one had Sir Carol Reed and that one was handled by Anatole Litvak, no slouch but not in Reed's class. Shot in Spain, with interiors at Ardmore Studios in Ireland, THE RUNNING MAN tells the tale of Harvey, an owner-operator of a small air-transport company. He's enraged when he can't collect on a glider crash because he missed renewing the policy by one day. He then does what so many people would like to: he devises a plan to defraud the monolith insurance company. By crashing a plane that he is supposed to be in, he plans to cash a huge death benefits policy. He alters his looks, changes his name, and goes to wait in Spain for his wife, Remick, who stays in England awaiting the payment. Bates is an insurance man who meets Remick, approves the claim, and puts it through, with Remick getting the cash. She immediately goes to Spain and is perturbed to find Harvey has assumed the identity of Meillon, a millionaire from down under. Harvey found Meillon's lost passport and now plans to kill Meillon and collect his insurance. Bates turns up in Spain on what appears to be a holiday. He meets Harvey and seemingly accepts the new identity and the trio begin palling around together. Harvey thinks that Bates is on to them and insists Remick and he flee right away, never knowing that Bates was telling the truth about being on vacation and that he has left his company. Bates has fallen in love with Remick, and since he believes that she is a widow, he makes no bones about it. Harvey believes that Bates is coming close to uncovering the truth and tries to kill him by forcing his car off a cliff. Remick is in the car with Harvey and can't stop him. When Harvey decides that he has to escape from Spain and will steal a plane at a local airport to do that, Remick jumps out of her car. Later, Harvey climbs into the plane, takes off and doesn't notice that the gas gauges are on empty, so he crashes to his death in the sea. Style counts more than substance here and Reed extracts the most from the least. Not that Mortimer's script isn't witty and well-written; it's merely that there is just not enough to sustain the 103 minutes it takes to tell a story that could have just as well been a 24-minute segment on the old "ALFRED HITCHCOCK" TV show.

p&d, Carol Reed; w, John Mortimer (based on the novel The Ballad of The Running Man by Shelley Smith); ph, Robert Krasker (Panavision, Eastmancolor); m, William Alwyn; ed, Bert Bates; md, Muir Mathieson; art d, John Stoll; makeup, George Frost.

Drama (PR:A-C MPAA:NR)

RUNNING SCARED (SEE: GHOST AND MR. CHICKEN, THE, 1966)

RUNNING SCARED½** (1972, Brit.) 98m Wigan-Hemmings-O'Toole/PAR c

Robert Powell, Gayle Hunnicutt, Barry Morse, Stephanie Bidmead, Edward Underdown, Maxine Audley, Georgia Brown.

Downbeat drama about a college student driven to suicide by his friends after he stood by and allowed a friend to kill himself. Bleak and unrelenting, RUNNING SCARED shows youth as a world of little hope toward life or love. This film was the directorial debut of famed British actor Hemmings.

p, Gareth Wigan; d, David Hemmings; w, Clive Exton, Hemmings (based on the novel by Gregory MacDonald); ph, Ernest Day (Panavision, Technicolor); m, Michael J. Lewis.

Drama (PR:C-O MPAA:NR)

RUNNING TARGET*** (1956) 83m Canyon/UA c

Doris Dowling (Smitty), Arthur Franz (Scott), Richard Reeves (Jaynes), Myron Healy (Kaygo), James Parnell (Pryor), Charles Delaney (Barker), James Anderson (Strothers), Gene Roth (Holesworth), Frank Richards (Castagna), Nicholas Rutgers (Weyerhauser).

Franz is a sheriff who leads a posse through the mountains of Colorado after four escaped convicts. The sheriff has his hands full with hunting down the men as well as controlling the members of his posse. Reeves is a bar owner who wants blood to spill. Dowling, the only female of the posse, is there because the cons had robbed her gas station. Franz soon discovers, however, that Dowling is in love with one of the criminals. An exciting film that builds the characters and the tension between the members of the posse with a skillful hand.

p, Jack C. Couffer; d, Marvin R. Weinstein; w, Weinstein, Couffer, Conrad Hall (based on the story, "My Brother Down There" by Steve Frazee); ph, Lester Shorr (DeLuxe Color); m, Ernest Gold; ed, Carlo Lodato; cos, George Herrington; m/l, Gold, Fred Jordan.

Thriller (PR:A MPAA:NR)

RUNNING WILD*½ (1955) 81m UNIV bw

William Campbell (Ralph Barclay), Mamie Van Doren (Irma Bean), Keenan Wynn (Ken Osanger), Kathleen Case (Leta Novak), Jan Merlin (Scotty Cluett), John Saxon (Vince Pomeroy), Walter Coy (Lt. Ed Newpole), Grace Mills (Osanger's Mother), Chris Randall (Arkie Nodecker), Michael Fox (Delmar Graves), Will J. White (State Trooper), Richard Castle (Herbie), Otto Waldis (Leta's Father), Sumner Williams (Monty).

Teenagers get involved with a slimy Wynn and his car theft racket. Rookie cop Campbell goes undercover and joins the delinquents at Wynn's gas-station front. Case is forced into becoming Wynn's girl friend after the hood threatens to expose that her father entered the country illegally. Campbell shuts down the operation after he's gathered enough evidence and wins Van Doren, previously the girl friend of car thief Merlin.

p, Howard Pine; d, Abner Biberman; w, Leo Townsend (based on the novel by Ben Benson); ph, Ellis W. Carter; ed, Edward Curtiss, Ray Snyder; md, Joseph Gershenson; art d, Alexander Golitzen, Robert Boyle; cos, Bill Thomas.

Crime Drama (PR:A MPAA:NR)

RUNNING WILD**½ (1973) 104m Golden Circle c

Lloyd Bridges, Dina Merrill, Pat Hingle, Morgan Woodward, Gilbert Roland, Fred Betts, Slavio Martinez.

Reporter Merrill visits the high country and gets involved with saving a herd of wild horses from dog food canners. Okay family entertainment with some good supporting players (anything with Gilbert Roland is worth a look).

p,d&w, Robert McCahon.

Western **Cas.** (PR:AA MPAA:G)

RUSSIAN ROULETTE** (1975) 93m AE c

George Segal (Cpl. Timothy Shaver), Cristina Raines (Bogna Kirchoff), Bo Brudnin (Col. Sergei Vostik), Denholm Elliott (Comdr. Petapiece), Gordon Jackson (Detective Sgt. Brian Hardison), Peter Donat (Inspector McDermott), Richard Romanus (Raymond "Rags" Ragulia), Val Avery (Rudolph Henke), Nigel Stock (Ferguson), Louise Fletcher (Midge), Jacques Sandulescu (Gorki), Graham Jarvis (Benson), Constantin de Goguel (Samuel), Wally Marsh (Taggart), Hagan Beggs (Kavinsky), Douglas McGrath (Lars).

Mildly entertaining thriller based on the Russian Premiere's visit to Canada in 1970. Based on Ardies' novel Kosygin Is Coming, it's the story of a plot formed by angry members of the Russian KGB who want to assassinate their own leader, whom they feel is too soft on capitalism. They want to put the blame on the West, stir up trouble, and cause a war. Kosygin is due to arrive in Vancouver, British Columbia, and Segal, an atypical Mountie, has the job of making certain that the chief of the U.S.S.R. has enough security. There's a bit of the feeling of DAY OF THE JACKAL in the intent but not in the execution. Everyone knows that Kosygin was not killed on his visit, so the ending is pretty well determined from the start. Lots of stunts, some action, and good performances by Romanus (the loan shark in MEAN STREETS) and Elliott as a boozy agent. Producer Bick was married to Fletcher at the time and she makes her second film appearance. In the 1950s and 1960s she'd done many TV shows before moving to England with Bick, but her height, 5' 10", made it tough for her to get much work, as she towered above many of the TV actors she played opposite. This was not the first fictional picture about the attempted assassination of a real person. There was, of course, DAY OF THE JACKAL, and HENNESSY a film which dealt with the attempt on the life of the Queen of England and caused a huge furor when actual newsreel footage was mixed into the film to heighten the suspense. RUSSIAN ROULETTE might have been a better movie if more attention had been paid to detail and if Segal had even tried to do something other than his patented and, by this time, stereotyped role. Film editor Lombardo made his directoral debut with this.

p, Jerry Bick; d, Lou Lombardo; w, Tom Ardies, Stanley Mann, Arnold Margolin (based on the novel Kosygin is Coming by Ardies); ph, Brian West (Eastmancolor); m, Michael J. Lewis; ed, Richard Marden; art d, Roy Walker; stunts, Bill Couch, Alf Joint.

Thriller (PR:C MPAA:PG)

RUSSIANS ARE COMING, THE RUSSIANS ARE COMING, THE***½ (1966) 126m Mirisch/UA c

Carl Reiner (Walt Whittaker), Eva Marie Saint (Elspeth Whittaker), Alan Arkin (Rozanov), Brian Keith (Link Mattocks), Jonathan Winters (Norman Jonas), Theodore Bikel (Russian Captain), Paul Ford (Fendall Hawkins), Tessie O'Shea (Alice Foss), John Phillip Law (Alexei Kolchin), Andrea Dromm (Alison Palmer), Ben Blue (Luther Grilk), Sheldon Golomb (Pete Whittaker), Cindy Putnam (Annie Whittaker), Guy Raymond (Lester Tilly), Cliff Norton (Charlie Hinkson), Richard Schaal (Oscar Maxwell), Philip Coolidge (Isaac Porter), Don Keefer (Irving Christiansen), Parker Fennelly (Mr. Everett), Doro Merande (Muriel Everett), Vaughn Taylor (Mr. Bell), Johnnie Whitaker (Jerry Maxwell), Danny Klega (Polsky), Ray Baxter (Brodsky), Paul Verdier (Maliavin), Nikita Knatz (Gromolsky), Constantine Baksheef (Vasilov), Alex Hassilev (Hrushevsky), Milos Milos (Lysenko), Gino Gottarelli (Kregitkin), Michael J. Pollard (Stanley, Airport Worker), Peter Brocco (Rev. Hawthorne).

Hysterically funny parody of cold war tensions which sees a Russian submarine get stuck in a sandbar off the coast of New England after its commander, Bikel, ventures too close to shore in order to get a good look at America. Bikel dispatches his second-in-command, Arkin, and a small crew to find a power boat to tow the sub off the sandbar before they are discovered and cause an international incident. Arkin and his men descend upon the summer home of Reiner, a Manhattan television writer who can't wait to get off the damp island and back to the city. When Arkin fails to convince Reiner and his family that he and his men are Norwegian sailors (they are all dressed in black), he pulls a pistol and marches Reiner off in search of a motorboat, leaving young Russian Law in charge of Reiner's wife, Saint, his children, Golomb and Putnam, and the 18-year-old neighbor girl, Dromm. After the Russians—with Reiner in tow—steal postmistress Merande's sedan, the rumor mill on the little island begins spinning and soon the whole town is up in arms. Ford, the local patriotic zealot, dons his American Legion hat and grabs a saber in an effort to mobilize the town's civil defense forces. The sheriff, Keith, and his bumbling assistant Winters have their hands full just trying to keep Ford from throwing the entire town into a panic. Ford tosses the town drunk, Blue, onto a horse and tells him to warn the countryside that "The Russians Are Coming! The Russians Are Coming!" Unfortunately the inebriated Paul Revere has trouble steering the horse and spends much of the film just trying to stay on the bucking animal. Meanwhile, Reiner and Arkin, who have come to respect each other, find a speedboat and pull the sub off the reef. The Russian landing crew dashes for the sub, but Arkin realizes that he has forgotten about Law and goes back to retrieve the young sailor. Law and Dromm have fallen in love, of course, and Arkin has a hard time persuading Law to return to the submarine. While waiting for Arkin and Law to return, commander Bikel watches from the conning tower as the whole town gathers around him. Keith, ever calm and efficient, issues the Russian sub a parking ticket. Eventually Bikel tires of this silliness and threatens to blow up the town unless his men are returned posthaste. The tension between the Russians and the Americans is suddenly broken when a young boy who was sitting on the steep roof of a house watching the proceedings slips and falls. The boy's pants catch on the gutter and he hangs precariously over the edge. The Russians and Americans immediately forget their rivalry and unite in an effort to save the child. Bikel sends his sailors to help form a human pyramid which reaches the child and carries him to safety. Meanwhile, the drunken Blue has finally managed to get his horse headed in the right direction and has gone to warn the armed forces. The heroic action brings together the rival peoples and the New Englanders take to the sea in their small boats and escort the Russian submarine out of the area so that the American jet planes will not bomb it. THE RUSSIANS ARE COMING, THE RUSSIANS ARE COMING pokes fun at nearly everything from small-town life to xenophobia. Though the film is more than two hours long, the pace is always quick thanks to the fine editing done by Williams and future director Ashby (THE LAST DETAIL, COMING HOME). Arkin, in a film debut that earned him an Oscar nomination, is great as the alternately polite and menacing Soviet sailor trying to get his men back to safety. Reiner, Keith, Bikel, Ford, Saint, O'Shea, Winters, and child actor Golomb are consistently funny throughout. Though set on the East Coast, the film was shot in Mendocino County in Northern California, an area which greatly resembles New England. The film was a surprise hit at the box office and one of the most fondly remembered comedies of the 1960s.

p&d, Norman Jewison; w, William Rose (based on the novel The Off-Islanders by Nathaniel Benchley); ph, Joseph Biroc (Panavision, DeLuxe Color); m, Johnny Mandel; ed, Hal Ashby, J. Terry Williams; art d, Robert Boyle; set d, Darrell Silvera; spec eff, Daniel W. Hays; m/l, "The Shining Sea," Mandel, Peggy Lee; makeup, Del Armstrong.

Comedy (PR:A MPAA:NR)

RUSTLERS** (1949) 61m RKO bw

Tim Holt (Dick), Richard Martin (Chilo), Martha Hyer (Ruth), Steve Brodie (Wheeler), Lois Andrews (Trixie), Harry Shannon (Sheriff), Addison Richards (Abbott), Frank Fenton (Carew), Robert Bray (Hank), Don Haggerty (Drake), Monte Montague (Hawkins), Stanley Blystone (Cook), Pat Patterson, Mike Jeffers, Tom Lloyd, George Ross, Art Souvern, Bob Robinson, Francis McDonald.

Cowboy Holt and his partner Martin get entangled in a cattle-rustling scheme after they win marked bills in a roulette game. The marked bills were planted in an effort to track down the rustlers, who steal the cattle and ransom them back to the owners. The mastermind behind this scam, Brodie, has the two innocent men arrested by sheriff Shannon so he can continue rustling. Holt and his buddy break out of jail and catch the crooks. Andrews, who plays a saloon singer, performs "Anabella" and "My Darling Nellie Gray."

p, Herman Schlom; d, Lesley Selander; w, Jack Natteford, Luci Ward; ph, J. Roy Hunt; ed, Frank Doyle; md, C. Bakaleinikoff; art d, Albert S. D'Agostino, Feild Gray.

Western (PR:A MPAA:NR)

RUSTLER'S HIDEOUT* (1944) 60m PRC bw

Buster Crabbe (Billy Carson), Al "Fuzzy" St. John (Fuzzy James), Patti McCarty (Barbara), Charles King (Buck Shaw), John Merton (Harry Stanton), Terry Frost

(*Jack Crockett*), Hal Price (*Dave Crockett*), Lane Chandler (*Hammond*), Al Ferguson (*Steve*), Frank McCarroll (*Squint*), Ed Cassidy (*Sheriff*), Bud Osborne.

A feeble western in which Crabbe breaks up a cattle-rustling ring with the help of the ever faithful "Fuzzy" St. John. Crabbe also exposes card cheat Chandler and prevents a scheme to swindle Frost and Price out of their meat-packing company. Everything is so familiar and poorly done that even hard core western fans will have a difficult time sitting through this one. Producer Neufeld, known for his ability to trim production costs, arrived at PRC at the start of its operations in 1939. With his brother, Sam Newfield, he was responsible for turning out several low-budget westerns, among them the Billy the Kid series (in which Crabbe replaced Bob Steele). (See BILLY CARSON series, Index.)

p, Sigmund Neufeld; d, Sam Newfield; w, Joe O'Donnell; ph, Jack Greenhaigh; ed, Holbrook N. Todd.

Western   (PR:A   MPAA:NR)

RUSTLERS OF DEVIL'S CANYON**½   (1947) 58m REP bw

Allan Lane (*Red Ryder*), Bobby Blake (*Little Beaver*), Martha Wentworth (*The Duchess*), Peggy Stewart (*Bess*), Arthur Space (*The Doctor*), Emmett Lynn (*Blizzard*), Roy Barcroft (*Clark*), Tom London (*The Sheriff*), Harry Carr (*Tad*), Pierce Lyden (*Matt*), Forrest Taylor (*Doc Glover*), Bob Burns.

Lane, after fighting in the Spanish-American War returns to his ranch and his little Indian buddy Blake. He also finds a range war going on between homesteaders, ranchers, and rustlers. Plenty of action in this RED RYDER entry, as Lane exposes Space as the rustlers' leader and puts an end to their evil deeds. He also finds enough time to make peace between the ranchers and the homesteaders around the fisticuffs and gunfights. Bobby Blake, who had his start in the Our Gang shorts during the late 1930s and early 1940s, later appeared as a Mexican boy in THE TREASURE OF THE SIERRA MADRE. After a stint in the military, he returned to the screen as Robert Blake and made his mark as a young murderer in IN COLD BLOOD and in the title role in TELL THEM WILLY BOY IS HERE. He also went on to become the star of the television series "Baretta." (See RED RYDER series, Index.)

p, Sidney Picker; d, R.G. Springsteen; w, Earle Snell; ph, William Bradford; ed, Harry Keller; md, Mort Glickman; art d, Frank Arrigo.

Western   (PR:A   MPAA:NR)

RUSTLERS ON HORSEBACK**   (1950) 60m REP bw

Allan Lane (*Rocky Lane*), Eddy Waller (*Nugget Clark*), Roy Barcroft (*Leo Straykin*), Claudia Barrett (*Carol Reynolds*), John Eldredge (*George Parradine*), George Nader (*Jack Reynolds*), Forrest Taylor (*Josh Taylor*), John Cason (*Murray*), Stuart Randall (*Clune*), Douglas Evans (*Jordan*), Tom Monroe (*Guard*), Black Jack the Horse.

Lane and sidekick Waller infiltrate a bunch of rustlers to prevent them from stealing a ranch and selling it to an unknowing party. Story is as stale as roadside apples, but the action will keep some entertained. Of course, Lane stops the thieves and returns the ranch to its rightful owner. Lane, who appeared in more than 100 features and serials, later was the voice of "Mr. Ed," the talking horse, in the television series.

p, Gordon Kay; d, Fred C. Brannon; w, Richard Wormser; ph, John MacBurnie; m, Stanley Wilson; ed, Robert M. Leeds; art d, Frank Arrigo.

Western   (PR:A   MPAA:NR)

RUSTLER'S PARADISE**   (1935) 61m Ajax bw

Harry Carey (*Cheyenne Kincaid*), Gertrude Messinger (*His Daughter*), Edmund Cobb (*El Diablo*), Carmen Bailey (*Ranch Owner*), Theodore Lorch, Roger Williams, Chuck Morrison, Allen Greer, Charles "Slim" Whitaker, Chief Thunder Cloud.

Carey is seeking revenge on the man who stole his wife and daughter years ago in this western, which is saved only by Carey's performance. Carey locates the man, Cobb, and discovers that Cobb's child (Messinger) is really his own daughter. With his long search finally over, the tired cowboy takes his revenge, saves Bailey from losing her ranch and begins to enjoy life with his long-lost daughter.

p, William Berke; d, Harry Fraser; w, Weston Edwards (based on a story by Monroe Talbot); ph, Robert Cline; ed, Arthur A. Brook.

Western   (PR:A   MPAA:NR)

RUSTLERS' ROUNDUP**   (1933) 60m UNIV bw

Tom Mix, Diane Sinclair, Noah Beery, Jr., William Desmond, Roy Stewart, Douglas Dumbrille, Gilbert "Pee Wee" Holmes, Bud Osborne, Frank Lackteen, William Wagner, Nelson McDowell, Walter Brennan, Tony, Jr..

Mix rides to the rescue of Sinclair, whose father has been murdered by villains out to steal his ranch. The hero makes short work of the criminals, then woos Sinclair. It adds up to a good Mix western with above-average production values.

d, Henry McRae; w, Frank Howard Clark, Jack Cunningham (based on a story by Ella O'Neill); ph, Dan Clark.

Western   Cas.   (PR:A   MPAA:NR)

RUSTLER'S ROUNDUP*½   (1946) 57m UNIV bw (AKA: RUSTLER'S HIDEOUT)

Kirby Grant (*Bob Ryan*), Jane Adams (*Jo Fremont*), Fuzzy Knight (*Pinky*), Edmund Cobb (*Vic Todd*), Ethan Laidlaw (*Louie Todd*), Earle Hodgins (*Sheriff Fin Elder*), Charles Miller (*Judge Wayne*), Mauritz Hugo (*Faro King*), Eddy Waller (*Tom Fremont*), Roy Brent (*Chuck*), Frank Marlo (*Jules Todd*), Hank Bell (*Rancher*), Rex Lease (*Saloon Proprietor*), Budd Buster (*Gunsmith*), Steve Clark (*Cal Dixon*), Bud Osborne (*Jury Foreman*), Alfred Wagstaff (*Todd's Friend*), Jack

Curtis (*Wrangler*), Ray Spiker (*Andy*), George Morrell (*Doc Davitt*), Artie Ortego, Kermit Maynard.

Grant is a tune-carrying cowboy who becomes the sheriff of the town of Rawhide. The singing cowboy finds himself responsible for ridding the town of problems caused by three brothers, which he does in quick fashion. Producer-director Fox started as an entertainer in minstrel shows, and after performing briefly in vaudeville became a film prop man in 1919. He debuted as a director in 1927, turning out low-budget westerns and action pictures for various studios. He directed many East Side Kids (later known as the Bowery Boys) comedies in the 1940s, and went on to direct television works in the 1950s.

p&d, Wallace Fox; w, Jack Natteford (based on a story by Sherman Lowe, Victor McLeod); ph, Maury Gertsman; ed, Sol Goodkind; art d, Jack Otterson, Frank A. Richards.

Western   (PR:A   MPAA:NR)

RUSTLER'S VALLEY*   (1937) 58m PAR bw

William Boyd (*Hopalong Cassidy*), George "Gabby" Hayes (*Windy Halliday*), Russell Hayden (*Lucky Jenkins*), Agnes Glenn (*Muriel Evans*), Stephen Morris [Morris Ankrum] (*Randall Glenn*), John Beach (*Sheriff Boulton*), Lee J. Cobb (*Cal Howard*), Oscar Apfel (*Clem Crawford*), Ted Adams (*Taggart*), Horace B. Carpenter (*Party Guest*), John Powers (*Stuttering Man*), Al Ferguson (*Joe*), Bernadine Hayes, John St. Polis.

This film, the 12th and probably the dullest of the Hopalong Cassidy series, has a story that can't sustain 58 minutes. Boyd is the foreman on Morris' ranch who prevents corrupt lawyer Cobb from pressuring the old man into mortgaging his property. With guns blasting, Boyd sends the bad guys running and wins the heart of Morris' daughter, Evans. (See HOPALONG CASSIDY series, Index.)

p, Harry Sherman; d, Nate Watt; w, Harry O. Hoyt; ph, Russell Harlan; ed, Robert Warwick; art d, Lewis Rachmil.

Western   Cas.   (PR:A   MPAA:NR)

RUSTY LEADS THE WAY*½   (1948) 59m COL bw

Ted Donaldson (*Danny Mitchell*), Sharyn Moffett (*Penny Waters*), John Litel (*Hugh Mitchell*), Ann Doran (*Ethel Mitchell*), Paula Raymond (*Louise Adams*), Peggy Converse (*Mrs. Waters*), Harry Hayden (*Harry Ainesworth*), Ida Moore (*Mrs. Mungy*), Mary Currier (*Miss Davis*), Fred Sears (*Jack Coleman*), Mickey McGuire (*Gerald*), Teddy Infuhr (*Squeaky*), Dwayne Hickman (*Nip*), David Ackles (*Tuck*), Flame the Dog (*Rusty*).

Columbia's boy-and-his-dog series casts Donaldson as the kind, young kid who's always helping someone or performing good deeds with the help of his canine buddy, Flame. The pair helps blind girl Moffett cope with her handicap. Only the very little might buy this trite material. (See RUSTY series, Index.)

p, Robert Cohn; d, Will Jason; w, Arthur Ross (based on a story by Nedrick Young, from characters by Al Martin); ph, Vincent Farrar; ed, James Sweeney; md, Mischa Bakaleinikoff; art d, George Brooks.

Drama   (PR:A   MPAA:NR)

RUSTY RIDES ALONE*½   (1933) 59m COL bw

Tim McCoy (*Tim Burke*), Barbara Weeks (*Mollie Martin*), Rockliffe Fellowes (*Bart Quillan*), Dorothy Burgess (*Mona Quillan*), Clarence Geldert (*Tom Martin*), Wheeler Oakman (*Poe Powers*), Edmund Cobb, Edmund Burns, Silver King the Dog.

McCoy rides into town and does what every cowboy hero must do: take care of the bad guy. This time around it's Oakman and after he's taken care of, the hero marries Weeks. But, there's still one problem: Who is Rusty, and why does he ride alone?

d, D. Ross Lederman; w, Robert Quigley (based on a story by Walt Coburn); ph, Al Siegler; ed, Otto Meyer.

Western   (PR:A   MPAA:NR)

RUSTY SAVES A LIFE*½   (1949) 68m COL bw

Ted Donaldson (*Danny Mitchell*), Stephen Dunne (*Fred Gibson*), Gloria Henry (*Lyddy Hazard*), John Litel (*Hugh Mitchell*), Ann Doran (*Mrs. Mitchell*), Thurston Hall (*Counselor Gibson*), Harlan Briggs (*Dr. McNamara*), Dwayne Hickman (*Nip*), David Ackles (*Tuck*), Ronnie Ralph (*Gerald*), Robert E. Scott (*Squeaky*), Ellen Corby (*Miss Simmons*), Harry Harvey (*Mr. Hebble*), Emmett Vogan (*Mr. Foley*), Rudy Robles, Flame the Dog (*Rusty*).

Donaldson and his dog Rusty, along with a bunch of kids, are told they will inherit a wealthy man's property. When the man dies before the will is made, his nephew takes over, and the kids give him one headache after another. The kids' pranks catch up with them, but in the end everything is squared away with the nephew when Rusty saves him from drowning. (See RUSTY series, Index.)

p, Wallace MacDonald; d, Seymour Friedman; w, Brenda Weisberg (based on characters by Al Martin); ph, Henry Freulich; ed, Gene Havlick; md, Mischa Bakaleinikoff; art d, Sturges Carne.

Drama   (PR:A   MPAA:NR)

RUSTY'S BIRTHDAY*½   (1949) 60m COL bw

Ted Donaldson (*Danny Mitchell*), John Litel (*Hugh Mitchell*), Ann Doran (*Mrs. Mitchell*), Jimmy Hunt (*Jeff Neeley*), Mark Dennis (*Bill Neeley*), Ray Teal (*Virgil Neeley*), Lillian Bronson) (*Carrie Simmons*), Ronnie Ralph (*Gerald*), Teddy Infuhr (*Squeaky*), Dwayne Hickman (*Nip Worden*), David Ackles (*Tucky Worden*), Robert B. Williams (*Vagrant*), Myron Healey (*Jack Wiggins*), Raymond Largay (*Amos Wembley*), Lelah Tyler (*Mrs. Wembley*), Flame the Dog (*Rusty*).

Rusty is taken by tourists who mistakenly believe they bought him from Donaldson's father, Litel. Little Donaldson searches high and low for his pet, who soon